Leslie Halliwell was born in Bolton in 1929, and saw his first film in 1933. The silver screen caught his fancy very early: at school, in the army and at university he ran film societies. Turned out into the world at large, he was a journalist on *Picturegoer* and the manager/booker of a specialized cinema in Cambridge, before coming to Granada TV in 1958 as a film researcher. Since 1968 he has been programme buyer for the entire TV network, and more recently for Channel 4, where his nostalgic seasons of films from the golden age have won wide approval.

He travels to Hollywood twice a year in search of material, but finds the film city now wanting in glamour. He has however become an *aficionado* of the California desert; and back at home country driving has always been a principal interest, along with second-hand books and snooker.

His published works include *Halliwell's Filmgoer's Companion* and *Halliwell's Hundred* (both available in Paladin), *The Filmgoer's Book of Quotes*, *The Clapperboard Book of the Cinema* (co-author) and *Mountain of Dreams*.

LESLIE HALLIWELL

HALLIWELL'S FILM GUIDE

FIFTH EDITION

PALADIN
GRAFTON BOOKS
A Division of the Collins Publishing Group

LONDON GLASGOW
TORONTO SYDNEY AUCKLAND

Paladin
Grafton Books
A Division of the Collins Publishing Group
8 Grafton Street, London W1X 3LA

Published in Paladin Books 1979
Reprinted 1980 (twice)
Second Edition 1982, 1983
Third Edition 1984
Fourth Edition 1985
Fifth Edition 1986

First published in Great Britain by
Granada Publishing 1977

ISBN 0-586-08649-8

Printed and bound in Great Britain by
Collins, Glasgow

Set in Times

CONTENTS

Preface to the Fifth Edition

The fourth edition was such a rapid sell-out that a revision is offered two years later. The films and awards of the intervening period are of course fully represented, but the opportunity has been taken to improve the work in a number of ways, in addition to the obvious corrections which have come to hand.

The three-column setting has reduced the number of pages, which means that there is still room for expansion, and so I have decided to bring the past into sharper focus than at one time seemed possible. My plan is to explore one decade per edition, and to bring in many more titles of moderate interest, which were previously omitted for reasons of space. In the current edition, the period chosen for this thickening of texture is the thirties, and approximately one thousand new entries have resulted. If many of them are unimportant historically, most do involve well-known actors, writers and directors and so have a strong claim to be recorded.

I have aimed to increase the number of critical quotes, especially those given at the time of release by the American trade paper *Variety*, whose reviews were often a key to commercial success and whose pithy comments give a significant edge to changing film fashions. Other opinions, however, have not been neglected.

Another means of judging a film is the way in which it is promoted. I have therefore collected a thousand or more original publicity taglines, which apart from being amusing in themselves tell us much about the audiences of their time. These, in the manner of trailers, precede their entries, and I shall be grateful to hear of others for future editions.

Films made for television – including those commissioned by Channel Four – will continue to be consigned to my *Television Companion*, a bulkier edition of which is due for publication at the end of 1986. In this present volume, however, I have done my best to indicate what films readers may hope to enjoy again on their television screens by means of video cassettes. Alas, this information may date rather quickly. Video distributors tend to take on films for shortish periods, and titles which prove uncommercial may be quickly withdrawn; but the information has been asked for and I am pleased to make it as complete as I can. Bear in mind only that I have concentrated on major films of all countries which are available in Great Britain at the end of 1984. American distributors differ in the main, in their title selection; to my American friends I apologize for being unable to cover their country in the same way, but at least the information I give may be a useful guide, for I find that fans have much the same interests in both countries. All video users should note that I am neither willing nor able to comment on the plethora of independently made, low-budget productions which fill video shop shelves. If they have not been good enough to warrant a cinema release, I assume that I may overlook them too. Even the most casual enquirer will know that the vast majority of available videos harp on horror and sex themes, a nauseous flood of celluloid with which no commentator could hope to keep up, even if he wanted to.

Once again I am grateful for unsolicited advice from correspondents, especially E. A. Layzell and Richard Chatten. Please note, however, that I cannot agree to insert every piece of information submitted, for too much emphasis on small-part players or silent films would upset the balance of the book, which as ever aims to be convenient and amiable but is not intended to replace the detailed research which must be undertaken by specialists. A review of the last edition dismissed my comments as 'increasingly weary and blimpish'! I feel myself to be neither, but I remain suspicious of the films of the last fifteen years or so, which have followed fashion to the exclusion of permanent value. Just as poetry was once said to be emotion recollected in tranquillity, my evaluations are intended to set films in their historical context, which is impossible until they have some years on them; and I reserve the right in each edition to add or subtract from the number of stars previously given.

The illustrations as usual are mainly nostalgic; but bear in mind that they are reminders of films which many viewers are seeing for the first time through the courtesy of Channel Four.

Leslie Halliwell
January 1985

Alphabetical Index of Alternative Titles

If the film you seek does not appear in the main section of the book and you suspect it to have more than one title, check it here. (NB: Foreign-language films are listed here only if they have more than one foreign- or English-language title. See the following lists for original titles or English-language versions.)

Abandon Ship *see* Seven Waves Away
Abbott and Costello Meet the Ghosts *see* Abbott and Costello Meet Frankenstein
Abdulla's Harem *see* Abdulla the Great
Absinthe *see* Madame X (1929)
Adamson of Africa *see* The Killers of Kilimanjaro
Adventure for Two *see* The Demi-Paradise
Adventures of a Young Man *see* Hemingway's Adventures of a Young Man
The Adventures of Huckleberry Finn *see* Huckleberry Finn (1960)
The Adventures of Quentin Durward *see* Quentin Durward
The Adventuress *see* I See a Dark Stranger
Affair at the Villa Fiorita *see* The Battle of the Villa Fiorita
Affair in Monte Carlo *see* Twenty-Four Hours of a Woman's Life
Affairs of a Rogue *see* The First Gentleman
Affairs of Sally *see* The Fuller Brush Girl
African Fury *see* Cry the Beloved Country
After Eight Hours *see* Society Doctor
After Midnight *see* Captain Carey USA
Agent 8¾ *see* Hot Enough for June
Ah! Les Belles Bacchantes *see* Femmes de Paris
Airport '80: The Concorde *see* The Concorde: Airport '79
Alias Bulldog Drummond *see* Bulldog Jack
All at Sea *see* Barnacle Bill
All These Women *see* Now About All These Women. . .
All This and Glamour Too *see* Vogues of 1938
All This and Money Too *see* Love is a Ball
Along Came Sally *see* Aunt Sally
Almost a Bride *see* A Kiss for Corliss
The Amazing Mr Beecham *see* The Chiltern Hundreds
The Amazing Mr Forrest *see* The Gang's All Here (1939)
The Anatolian Smile *see* America, America
And Woman . . . Was Created *see* And God Created Woman
Angel Street *see* Gaslight (1939)
Angels and the Pirates *see* Angels in the Outfield
April Romance *see* Blossom Time
Armored Attack *see* North Star
Arms and the Girl *see* Red Salute
Arms and the Woman *see* Mr Winkle Goes to War
Arouse and Beware *see* The Man from Dakota
Arrivederci Baby *see* Drop Dead Darling
The Assassin (1947) *see* Gunfighters
The Assassin (1952) *see* Venetian Bird
At Dawn We Die *see* Tomorrow We Live
Atlantic Episode *see* Catch As Catch Can
Atoll K *see* Robinson Crusoeland
The Avengers *see* The Day Will Dawn

Baby Be Good *see* Brother Rat and a Baby
The Baby Vanishes *see* Broadway Limited

Bachelor Bait *see* Adventure in Baltimore
Bachelor Girl Apartment *see* Any Wednesday
Bachelor Girls *see* The Bachelor's Daughter
Bachelor Knight *see* The Bachelor and the Bobbysoxer
Bad Man of Wyoming *see* Wyoming (1940)
Bad Sister *see* The White Unicorn
The Baited Trap *see* The Trap
The Ballad of Tam-Lin *see* Tam-Lin
The Bank Breaker *see* Kaleidoscope
The Bank Detective *see* The Bank Dick
The Battle for Anzio *see* Anzio
Battle Hell *see* Yangtse Incident
The Battle of City Hall *see* Angels Wash Their Faces
The Battle of Gallipoli *see* Tell England
The Battle of Midway *see* Midway
Battle of Powder River *see* Tomahawk
Battle on the Beach *see* The Battle at Bloody Beach
Battle Stripe *see* The Men
Battling Bellhop *see* Kid Galahad (1937)
The Beachcomber *see* Vessel of Wrath
Beau Chumps *see* Beau Hunks
Beautiful but Dangerous *see* She Couldn't Say No
The Beautiful Cheat *see* What a Woman
The Beautiful Rebel *see* Janice Meredith
Behemoth the Sea Monster *see* The Giant Behemoth
Behind the Door *see* The Man with Nine Lives
Bengal Rifles *see* Bengal Brigade
Betrayed *see* When Strangers Marry
Beyond the Limit *see* The Honorary Consul
Beyond the River *see* The Bottom of the Bottle
The Big Bankroll *see* King of the Roaring Twenties
The Big Carnival *see* Ace in the Hole
Big Deal at Dodge City *see* A Big Hand for the Little Lady
Big Deal on Madonna Street *see* Persons Unknown
The Big Heart *see* Miracle on 34th Street
The Big Story *see* Appointment with a Shadow
Big Time Operators *see* The Smallest Show on Earth
Billy Rose's Diamond Horseshoe *see* Diamond Horseshoe
Billy Rose's Jumbo *see* Jumbo
The Birds and the Bees *see* Three Daring Daughters
The Bishop's Misadventures *see* The Bishop Misbehaves
The Black Arrow Strikes *see* The Black Arrow
Black Bart, Highwayman *see* Black Bart
Black Flowers for the Bride *see* Something for Everyone
Blackout *see* Contraband
Blonde Bombsell *see* Bombshell
A Blonde in Love *see* Loves of a Blonde
Blonde Sinner *see* Yield to the Night
Blood Money *see* Requiem for a Heavyweight

Desert Patrol *see* Sea of Sand
Desperate Siege *see* Rawhide
The Destructors *see* The Marseilles Contract
The Detective *see* Father Brown
The Devil and Daniel Webster *see* All That Money Can Buy
The Devil Never Sleeps *see* Satan Never Sleeps
The Devil Takes the Count *see* The Devil is a Sissy
The Devil Within Her *see* I Don't Want to be Born
The Devil's Bride *see* The Devil Rides Out
The Devil's Brother *see* Fra Diavolo
The Devil's Impostor *see* Pope Joan
The Devil's Own *see* The Witches
The Devil's Widow *see* Tam-Lin
Diabolique *see* Les Diaboliques
The Diamond Wizard *see* The Diamond
Diary of a Bride *see* I, Jane Doe
Dick Turpin's Ride *see* The Lady and the Bandit
Die! Die! My Darling *see* Fanatic
The Dividing Line *see* The Lawless
The Doctor and the Debutante *see* Dr Kildare's Victory
Doctor from Seven Dials *see* Corridors of Blood
Dog Soldiers *see* Who'll Stop the Rain?
The Domino Killings *see* The Domino Principle
Doomed Cargo *see* Seven Sinners
Doppelganger *see* Journey to the Far Side of the Sun
The Dover Road *see* Where Sinners Meet
Down Went McGinty *see* The Great McGinty
Dracula Is Alive and Well and Living in London *see* The Satanic
  Rites of Dracula
Dragonfly *see* One Summer Love
Drake the Pirate *see* Drake of England
A Dream of Life *see* Life Begins
The Dream of Olwen *see* While I Live
Drum Crazy *see* The Gene Krupa Story
Drums *see* The Drum
Drums Along the Amazon *see* Angel on the Amazon
Du Rififi chez les Hommes *see* Rififi
Duck, You Sucker *see* A Fistful of Dynamite
Dulcimer Street *see* London Belongs to Me
Dynamite Man from Glory Jail *see* Fools Parade

East End Chant *see* Limehouse Blues
East of Java *see* South Sea Sinner
East of Shanghai *see* Rich and Strange
East of the Rising Sun *see* Malaya
Edge of Divorce *see* Background
Eight on the Run *see* Eight on the Lam
The Electric Man *see* Man Made Monster
Elephant Gun *see* Nor the Moon By Night
Elephants Never Forget *see* Zenobia
Elizabeth of England *see* Drake of England
Elizabeth the Queen *see* The Private Lives of Elizabeth and
  Essex
Ellen *see* The Second Woman
Emergency! *see* Emergency Call
Emperor of the North *see* Emperor of the North Pole
L'Empire des Sens *see* Ai No Corrida
End as a Man *see* The Strange One
End of the Rainbow *see* Northwest Outpost
Enemies of the Public *see* The Public Enemy
Enemy Agent *see* British Intelligence
Enemy from Space *see* Quatermass II
Entebbe: Operation Thunderbolt *see* Operation Thunderbolt
Escapade *see* Robinson Crusoeland
Escape If You Can *see* St Benny the Dip
Escape of the Amethyst *see* Yangtse Incident
Escape to Happiness *see* Intermezzo
Escape to Victory *see* Victory
Every Minute Counts *see* Count the Hours
Every Other Inch a Lady *see* Dancing Co-Ed
Every Woman's Man *see* The Prizefighter and the Lady
Everybody's Cheering *see* Take Me Out to the Ball Game

Everything Happens to Us *see* Hi Ya Chum
Evils of Chinatown *see* Confessions of an Opium Eater
Eye Witness (1950 *see* Your Witness

Face of a Stranger *see* The Promise
The Fall of the House of Usher *see* House of Usher
False Faces *see* Let 'Em Have It
False Witness *see* Zigzag
Falstaff *see* Chimes at Midnight
Family Doctor *see* RX Murder
The Fantastic Disappearing Man *see* The Return of Dracula
Fear o'God *see* The Mountain Eagle
Fellini Satyricon *see* Satyricon
Fellini's Casanova *see* Casanova
ffoulkes *see* North Sea Hijack
The Fifth Chair *see* It's in the Bag
The Fighting Pimpernel *see* Pimpernel Smith
The Fighting Seventh *see* Little Big Horn
The Fighting Sullivans *see* The Sullivans
Fine and Dandy *see* West Point Story
Finger of Guilt *see* The Intimate Stranger
Fire Over Africa *see* Malaga
The First and the Last *see* Twenty-One Days
The First Rebel *see* Allegheny Uprising
Fitzwilly Strikes Back *see* Fitzwilly
Five Angles on Murder *see* The Woman in Question
Five Million Years to Earth *see* Quatermass and the Pit
Flame over India *see* Northwest Frontier
The Flaming Torch *see* The Bob Mathias Story
The Flight of the White Stallions *see* The Miracle of the White
  Stallions
The Flying Circus *see* Flying Devils
Fontane Effi Briest *see* Effi Briest
For Love of a Queen *see* The Dictator
For You Alone *see* When You're in Love
Forbidden Alliance *see* The Barretts of Wimpole Street
Forbidden Music *see* Land without Music
The Forbidden Street *see* Britannia Mews
Forever England *see* Brown on Resolution
Forever in Love *see* Pride of the Marines
Forever Yours *see* Forget Me Not
The Forsyte Saga *see* That Forsyte Woman
Forty Eight Hours *see* Went the Day Well?
Four Against Fate *see* Derby Day
Four Dark Hours *see* The Green Cockatoo
Four Desperate Men *see* The Siege of Pinchgut
Forward March *see* Doughboys
Fox and His Friends *see* Fox
Fraternally Yours *see* Sons of the Desert
Free to Live *see* Holiday (1938)
The French They Are a Funny Race *see* The Diary of Major
  Thompson
Frenzy *see* Latin Quarter
The Frightened Bride *see* The Tall Headlines
Frightened City *see* The Killer That Stalked New York
Frou Frou *see* The Toy Wife
The Fugitive (1939) *see* On the Night of the Fire
Full House *see* O. Henry's Full House
Funny Face (GB) *see* Bright Lights
Fuss over Feathers *see* Conflict of Wings

G Man's Wife *see* Public Enemy's Wife
Gaiety Girls *see* Paradise for Two
Gang War *see* Odd Man Out
The Gay Divorce *see* The Gay Divorcee
The Gay Duellist *see* Meet Me at Dawn
The Gay Imposters *see* Gold Diggers in Paris
The Gay Lady *see* Trottie True
The Gay Mrs Trexel *see* Susan and God
The Gay Nineties *see* The Floradora Girl
A Genius in the Family *see* So Goes My Love
The Gentle Sergeant *see* Three Stripes in the Sun

The Mean Machine *see* The Longest Yard
Medals *see* Seven Days Leave (1929)
Meet Whiplash Willie *see* The Fortune Cookie
Melody Inn *see* Riding High
Melody of Life *see* Symphony of Six Million
Melody of Youth *see* They Shall Have Music
The Memory Expert *see* The Man on the Flying Trapeze
Men Behind Bars *see* Duffy of San Quentin
Men of the Sea *see* Midshipman Easy
Men on Her Mind *see* The Girl from Tenth Avenue
The Message *see* Mohammed, Messenger of God
MGM's Big Parade of Comedy *see* The Big Parade of Comedy
Michael Strogoff *see* The Soldier and the Lady
Middle of Nowhere *see* The Webster Boy
Midnight Melody *see* Murder in the Music Hall
Military Policemen *see* Off Limits
Millionaire Merry Go Round *see* Kicking the Moon Around
A Minute to Pray, a Second to Die *see* Dead or Alive
A Miracle Can Happen *see* On Our Merry Way
The Miracle of Fatima *see* The Miracle of our Lady of Fatima
Missiles from Hell *see* The Battle of the V1
Missing Ten Days *see* Ten Days in Paris
Mr Arkadin *see* Confidential Report
Mr Ashton Was Indiscreet *see* The Senator Was Indiscreet
Mr Griggs Returns *see* The Cockeyed Miracle
Mr Hobo *see* The Guvnor
Mr Lord Says No *see* The Happy Family
Mr Mum *see* Mr Mom
Mr Potts Goes to Moscow *see* Top Secret
Mister V *see* Pimpernel Smith
Mrs Loring's Secret *see* The Imperfect Lady
The Model Murder Case *see* The Girl in the Headlines
A Modern Hero *see* Knute Rockne, All American
The Modern Miracle *see* The Story of Alexander Graham Bell
Money for Jam *see* It Ain't Hay
Monsieur Ripois et Son Nemesis *see* Knave of Hearts
Monster *see* Humanoids of the Deep
Monte Carlo or Bust *see* Those Daring Young Men in Their Jaunty Jalopies
Morituri: The Saboteur *see* The Saboteur, Code Name Morituri
Mother Joan of the Angels *see* The Devil and the Nun
Mother Knows Best *see* Mother Is a Freshman
Mother, Sir! *see* Navy Wife
Movietone Follies of 1929 *see* Fox Follies of 1929
The Moving Target *see* Harper
La Mura de Malapaga *see* Au dela des Grilles
Murder at the Baskervilles *see* Silver Blaze
The Murder in Thornton Square *see* Gaslight (1944)
Murder Inc *see* The Enforcer
Murder Is News *see* The Delavine Affair
Murder My Sweet *see* Farewell My Lovely (1944)
Murder on Diamond Row *see* The Squeaker
Murder on Monday *see* Home at Seven
Murder Will Out *see* The Voice of Merrill
My Heart Goes Crazy *see* London Town
My Hero *see* A Southern Yankee
My Old Man's a Fireman *see* The Chief
My Son Alone *see* American Empire
My Son the Vampire *see* Mother Riley meets the Vampire
My Two Husbands *see* Too Many Husbands
My World Dies Screaming *see* Terror in the Haunted House
Mysterious Invader *see* The Astounding She-Monster
The Mystery of the Wentworth Castle *see* Doomed to Die

The Naked Night *see* Sawdust and Tinsel
Naked Under Leather *see* Girl on a Motorcycle
A Natural Born Salesman *see* Earthworm Tractors
Naughty Arlette *see* The Romantic Age
The Navy Steps Out *see* A Girl a Guy and a Gob
The Nelson Affair *see* Bequest to the Nation
The Nelson Touch *see* Corvette K 225

The Neptune Disaster *see* The Neptune Factor
Never Give an Inch *see* Sometimes a Great Notion
Never to Love *see* A Bill of Divorcement (1940)
The New Adventures of Don Juan *see* The Adventures of Don Juan
New Face in Hell *see* P.J.
Next Time We Live *see* Next Time We Love
Nick's Movie *see* Lightning Over Water
Night Ambush *see* Ill Met by Moonlight
Night Club Hostess *see* Unmarried
Night Creatures *see* Captain Clegg
Night Fighters *see* A Terrible Beauty
A Night in Cairo *see* The Barbarian
A Night in Havana *see* The Big Boodle
The Night Is Ending *see* Paris After Dark
The Night They Invented Striptease *see* The Night They Raided Minsky's
Night Train *see* Night Train to Munich
Nine Days a Queen *see* Tudor Rose
No Highway in the Sky *see* No Highway
No Sleep Till Dawn *see* Bombers B52
None But the Brave *see* For the Love of Mike (1960)
Notorious Gentleman *see* The Rake's Progress
A Novel Affair *see* The Passionate Stranger
Now Barabbas Was a Robber *see* Now Barabbas . . .

Obsessed *see* The Late Edwina Black
Off the Beaten Track *see* Behind the Eight Ball
Oh! For a Man! *see* Will Success Spoil Rock Hunter?
OK Connery *see* Operation Kid Brother
Old and New *see* The General Line
The Old Curiosity Shop *see* Mister Quilp
Old Dracula *see* Vampira
On My Way to the Crusades I Met a Girl Who . . . *see* The Chastity Belt
On the Carpet *see* Little Giant
On Wings of Song *see* Love Me Forever
Once Upon A Thursday *see* The Affairs Of Martha
One Against Seven *see* Counterattack
One Born Every Minute *see* The Flim Flam Man
One for the Book *see* The Voice of the Turtle
One Hour with You *see* The Marriage Circle
One Hundred Per cent Pure *see* The Girl from Missouri
One Man Mutiny *see* The Court Martial of Billy Mitchell
The One Piece Bathing Suit *see* Million Dollar Mermaid
One Woman's Story *see* The Passionate Friends
Only the Best *see* I Can Get It for You Wholesale
Operation Disaster *see* Morning Departure
Operation Snafu *see* On the Fiddle
Operation Undercover *see* Report to the Commissioner
Operation X *see* My Daughter Joy
Oriental Dream *see* Kismet (1944)
O'Rourke of the Royal Mounted *see* Saskatchewan
The Outcast *see* Man in the Saddle
Outpost in Malaya *see* The Planter's Wife
The Outsider (US 1948) *see* The Guinea Pig
Over the River *see* One More River

Palm Springs Affair *see* Palm Springs
Panic in the Parlor *see* Sailor Beware (1956)
Panther's Moon *see* Spy Hunt
Paradise Lagoon *see* The Admirable Crichton
Paratrooper *see* The Red Beret
Paris Express *see* The Man Who Watched Trains Go By
Paris Love Song *see* Paris in Spring
Passing Clouds *see* Spellbound (GB)
Passion *see* Madame Dubarry
The Passionate Sentry *see* Who Goes There?
Passport to Fame *see* The Whole Town's Talking
The Patient Vanishes *see* This Man Is Dangerous
Patterns of Power *see* Patterns

Vacation from Marriage *see* Perfect Strangers (GB)
Valley of Fury *see* Chief Crazy Horse
Vaudeville *see* Variety
The Violent Hour *see* Dial 1119
Violent Streets *see* Thief
Viva Las Vegas! (1956) *see* Meet Me in Las Vegas
A Voice in the Night *see* Freedom Radio

Wages of Fear *see* Sorcerer
Walking Down Broadway *see* Hello Sister
War Correspondent *see* The Story of GI Joe
War Gods of the Deep *see* City under the Sea
The Warriors *see* The Dark Avenger
Waterfront Women *see* Waterfront
We Humans *see* Young America
Web of Evidence *see* Beyond This Place
Wedding Bells *see* Royal Wedding
Wedding Breakfast *see* The Catered Affair
Wee Geordie *see* Geordie
Welcome Home *see* SNAFU
We're in the Army Now *see* Pack Up Your Troubles
West of Montana *see* Mail Order Bride
What a Man *see* Never Give a Sucker an Even Break
What Lola Wants *see* Damn Yankees
What Shall It Profit *see* Hard Steel
When Boys Leave Home *see* Downhill
When New York Sleeps *see* Now I'll Tell
When the Door Opened *see* Escape (1940)
When Thief Meets Thief *see* Jump for Glory
Where the River Bends *see* Bend of the River
White Blood *see* The Planter's Wife
White Captive *see* White Savage
The White Man *see* The Squaw Man
White Savage *see* South of Tahiti
Whoever Slew Auntie Roo? *see* Who Slew Auntie Roo?
Why Bother to Knock *see* Don't Bother to Knock
The Wicked Wife *see* Grand National Night
The Wild Heart *see* Gone to Earth
Wild Seed *see* Fargo
Wildcat *see* The Great Scout and Cathouse Thursday
Will Tomorrow Ever Come? *see* That's My Man
A Window to the Sky *see* The Other Side of the Mountain
Wings and the Woman *see* They Flew Alone
The Winning Way *see* The All American

Witch Doctor *see* Men of Two Worlds
Within the Law *see* Paid
A Woman Alone *see* Sabotage
The Woman Between *see* The Woman I Love
A Woman Destroyed *see* Smash-Up, The Story of a Woman
A Woman in Her Thirties *see* Side Streets
The Woman in His House *see* The Animal Kingdom
Woman of Dolwyn *see* The Last Days of Dolwyn
Woman of Summer *see* The Stripper
A Woman of the World *see* Outcast Lady
Woman without a Face *see* Mister Buddwing
Wonderful to Be Young *see* The Young Ones
Wooden Soldiers *see* Babes in Toyland (1934)
The World and His Wife *see* State of the Union
The World in My Pocket *see* On Friday at Eleven
The Wrong Kind of Girl *see* Bus Stop
The Wyoming Kid *see* Cheyenne

X, Y and Zee *see* Zee and Co

A Yank in Dutch *see* The Wife Takes a Flyer
A Yank in London *see* I Live in Grosvenor Square
A Yankee in King Arthur's Court *see* A Connecticut Yankee in
   King Arthur's Court
Years without Days *see* Castle on the Hudson
The Yellow Passport *see* The Yellow Ticket
You Belong to My Heart *see* Mr Imperium
You Can't Do That to Me *see* Maisie (Maisie Goes to Reno)
You Can't Sleep Here *see* I Was a Male War Bride
You Can't Take Money *see* Internes Can't Take Money
You Don't Need Pajamas at Rosie's *see* The First Time
You Never Know *see* You Never Can Tell
Young and Eager *see* Claudelle Inglish
Young and Willing *see* The Wild and the Willing
The Young Invaders *see* Darby's Rangers
Young Man of Music *see* Young Man with a Horn
Young Scarface *see* Brighton Rock
Your Past is Showing *see* The Naked Truth
You're in the Army Now *see* O.H.M.S.

Zoltan, Hound of Dracula *see* Dracula's Dog
Zombies *see* Dawn of the Dead

English-Language Titles of Foreign Films

The American Beauty *see* La Belle Américaine
Are We All Murderers? *see* Nous Sommes Tous Les Assassins
An Artist with Ladies *see* Coiffeur pour Dames

The Baker's Wife *see* La Femme du Boulanger
The Ballad of Berlin *see* Berliner Ballade
The Battle of Austerlitz *see* Austerlitz
Bay of Angels *see* La Baie des Anges
Beyond the Gates *see* Au dela des Grilles
Birds of a Feather *see* La Cage aux Folles
Bizarre, Bizarre *see* Drôle de Drame
Bluebeard *see* Landru
Boudu Saved from Drowning *see* Boudu Sauvé des Eaux
Breathless *see* A Bout de Souffle
The Butcher *see* Le Boucher

Carnival in Flanders *see* La Kermesse Héroïque
Children of Paradise *see* Les Enfants du Paradis
Clean Slate *see* Coup de Torchon
Cold Cuts *see* Buffet Froid
Comradeship *see* Kameradschaft
The Crazy Ray *see* Paris Qui Dort
The Cry *see* Il Grido

A Day in the Country *see* Une Partie de Campagne
Daybreak *see* Le Jour Se Lève
Days of Hope *see* Espoir
Devil in the Flesh *see* Le Diable au Corps
The Devil's Envoys *see* Les Visiteurs du Soir
Dirty Hands *see* Les Mains Sales
The Does *see* Les Biches
A Dog's Life *see* Mondo Cane
Doomed *see* Ikiru
The Double *see* Kagemusha

The Earrings of Madame de *see* Madame de
Ecstasy *see* Extase
Empire of the Passions *see* Ai No Corrida
Empire of the Senses *see* Ai No Corrida
Every Second Counts *see* Les Assassins du Dimanche

Father and Master *see* Padre Padrone
The Fiends *see* Les Diaboliques
Film without Title *see* Film ohne Titel
Forbidden Games *see* Les Jeux Interdits
Françoise Steps Out *see* Rue de l'Estrapade
Frontier *see* Aerograd

Gate of Lilacs *see* Porte des Lilas
Gates of Night *see* Les Portes de la Nuit
The Girl Friends *see* Le Amiche
Girls in Uniform *see* Maedchen in Uniform
God Needs Men *see* Dieu a Besoin des Hommes
The Goddess *see* Devi
Golden Marie *see* Casque d'Or
A Good Marriage *see* Le Beau Mariage

Hands off the Loot *see* Touchez pas au Grisbi
Handsome Antonio *see* Il Bell'Antonio
Hanged Man's Farm *see* La Ferme du Pendu
Heroism *see* Eroica
The Hole *see* Onibaba
Holiday for Henrietta *see* La Fête à Henriette
Honour Among Thieves *see* Touchez pas au Grisbi
The Human Beast *see* La Bête Humaine
Hungry for Love *see* Adua e le Compagne

I Have a New Master *see* L'Ecole Buissonière
In the Woods *see* Rashomon
The Inquisitor *see* Garde a Vue
Isle of Sinners *see* Dieu a Besoin des Hommes
It Happened at the Inn *see* Goupi Mains Rouges
It's in the Bag *see* L'Affaire est dans le Sac

Judas Was a Woman *see* La Bête Humaine

Keep an Eye on Amelia *see* Occupe-Toi d'Amélie

Life Dances on *see* Un Carnet de Bal
Living *see* Ikiru
The Long Absence *see* Une Aussi Longue Absence
Love Is My Profession *see* En Cas de Malheur
Love Story *see* Une Histoire d'Amour
The Lovers *see* Les Amants
The Lovers of Verona *see* Les Amants de Vérone
The Lower Depths *see* Les Bas-fonds

Madame *see* Madame Sans-Gène (1962)
Man's Hope *see* Espoir
Moscow Distrusts Tears *see* Moskva Slezam Ne Verit
My Night at Maud's *see* Ma Nuit chez Maud

Nights of Cabiria *see* Cabiria

The Outsiders *see* Bande à Part

The Phantom Baron *see* Le Baron Fantôme
Port of Shadows *see* Quai des Brumes

The Raven *see* Le Corbeau
The Road *see* La Strada
The Road to Hope *see* Il Cammino della Speranza
The Rules of the Game *see* La Règle du Jeu

The Saga of Anatahan *see* Anatahan
Savage Princess *see* Aan
Scarlet and Black *see* Le Rouge et le Noir
The Secret Game *see* Les Jeux Interdits
Secret Meeting *see* Marie Octobre
Shadow Warrior *see* Kagemusha
The Spies *see* Les Espions
Spivs *see* I Vitelloni
Stormy Waters *see* Remorques

Original Titles of Foreign-Language Films Listed in English

Aimez-Vous les Femmes? *see* Do You Like Women?
Akahige *see* Redbeard
Akasen Chitai *see* Street of Shame
Alskande Par *see* Loving Couples
Les Amants du Tage *see* The Lovers of Lisbon
Un Amour de Swann *see* Swann in Love
Les Amours de la Reine Elisabeth *see* Queen Elizabeth
El Angel Exterminador *see* The Exterminating Angel
Ansiktet *see* The Face
L'Argent de Poche *see* Small Change
Ascenseur pour l'Echafaud *see* Lift to the Scaffold
Attilo Flagello di Dio *see* Attila the Hun
Au Hasard, Balthazar *see* Balthazar
L'Auberge Rouge *see* The Red Inn
Un Autre Homme, une Autre Chance *see* Another Man, Another Chance
L'Aveu *see* The Confession

Babette S'en Va-t-en Guerre *see* Babette Goes to War
Baisers Volés *see* Stolen Kisses
Ballada o Soldate *see* Ballad of a Soldier
Banditi a Orgoloso *see* Bandits of Orgoloso
Baron Prasil *see* Baron Münchhausen
La Battaglia di Algeri *see* The Battle of Algiers
Berlin, die Symphonie einer Grosstadt *see* Berlin, Symphony of a Great City
Betrogen bis zum Jungsten Tag *see* Duped Till Doomsday
Bezhin Lug *see* Bezhin Meadow
Bij de Beesten Af *see* Ape and Super Ape
Les Bijoutiers du Clair de Lune *see* Heaven Fell That Night
Biruma no Tategoto *see* The Burmese Harp
Die Blechtrommel *see* The Tin Drum
Die Bleierne Zeit *see* The German Sisters
Den Blodiga Tiden *see* Mein Kampf
La Bonne Année *see* Happy New Year
Das Boot *see* The Boat
Bronenosets Potemkin *see* Battleship Potemkin
El Bruto *see* The Brute
Die Büchse der Pandora *see* Pandora's Box
Il Buono, il Bruto, il Cattivo *see* The Good, the Bad and the Ugly

Cadaveri Eccellenti *see* Illustrious Corpses
La Caida *see* The Fall
O'Cangaceiro *see* The Bandit
Le Caporal Epinglé *see* The Vanishing Corporal
Les Carnets de Major Thompson *see* The Diary of Major Thompson
Le Carrosse d'Or *see* The Golden Coach
La Casa del Angel *see* The House of the Angel
La Casse *see* The Burglars
Celui Qui Doit Mourir *see* He Who Must Die
Un Chapeau de Paille d'Italic *see* An Italian Straw Hat
Le Charme Discret de la Bourgeoisie *see* The Discreet Charm of the Bourgeoisie
Chelovek s Kinoapparatom *see* The Man with the Movie Camera
La Ciociara *see* Two Women
La Città delle Donne *see* City of Women

Compartiment Tueurs *see* The Sleeping Car Murders
Il Conformista *see* The Conformist
Cybèle ou les Dimanches de Ville d'Avray *see* Sundays and Cybèle

Dama s Sobachkoi *see* The Lady with the Little Dog
Déjeuner sur l'Herbe *see* Lunch on the Grass
Les Demoiselles de Rochefort *see* The Young Girls of Rochefort
La Dentellière *see* The Lacemaker
Il Deserto Rosso *see* The Red Desert
Destinées *see* Love, Soldiers and Women
Le Diable, Probablement *see* The Devil, Probably
La Diga sul Pacifico *see* This Angry Age
Un Dimanche à la Campagne *see* Sunday in the Country
Ditte Menneskebarn *see* Ditte, Child of Man
Divorzio all'Italiana *see* Divorce Italian Style
En Djungelsaga *see* The Flute and the Arrow
Doktor Mabuse, der Spieler *see* Doctor Mabuse
Don Camillo e l'Onorevole Peppone *see* Don Camillo's Last Round
Dorp aan de Rivier *see* Doctor in the Village
Dyrygent *see* The Conductor

L'Eclisse *see* The Eclipse
E la Nave Va *see* And the Ship Sails On
En Compagnie de Max Linder *see* Laugh with Max Linder
Eine Reise ins Licht *see* Despair
Ensayo de un Crimen *see* The Criminal Life of Archibaldo de la Cruz
Ercolé e la Regina di Lidia *see* Hercules Unchained
Es Geschah am 20 Juli *see* Jackboot Mutiny
L'Espion *see* The Defector
L'Eté Meurtrier *see* One Deadly Summer
Et Dieu Créa la Femme *see* And God Created Woman
Et Mourir de Plaisir *see* Blood and Roses
L'Eternel Retour *see* Love Eternal

Die Fälschung *see* Circle of Deceit
Fängelse *see* The Devil's Wanton
Le Fatiche di Ercole *see* Hercules
Faustrecht der Freiheit *see* Fox
La Femme de l'Aviateur *see* The Aviator's Wife
Une Femme Mariée *see* A Married Woman
La Fin du Monde *see* End of the World
Frau im Mond *see* The Woman in the Moon
Die Freudlose Gasse *see* Joyless Street
Le Fruit Défendu *see* Forbidden Fruit

Il Gattopardo *see* The Leopard
Giulietta degli Spiriti *see* Juliet of the Spirits
Gosta Berlings Saga *see* The Atonement of Gosta Berling
Götterdämmerung *see* The Damned (1969)
La Grande Vadrouille *see* Don't Look Now . . . We're Being Shot At!
Gruppo di Famiglia in un Interno *see* Conversation Piece
Gycklarnas Afton *see* Sawdust and Tinsel

Explanatory Notes
Please stop here and read!

Alternative titles

Three lists are given at the front of the book, immediately preceding this section. Readers are recommended to consult them before wading in exasperation through the book for films which are in fact listed under apparently unfamiliar titles, i.e. those used in their country of origin at the time of release. Any subsequently-used titles (unless they are at least as well known as the original) will be found only in the alternative title lists. British readers in particular should consult these lists with care: *Lady Hamilton*, for instance, is to be found in the main section under 'T', for *That Hamilton Woman*, the correct and original American title of this film which was made in America. Please note also that in all cases the complete title is given as billed, though the definite and indefinite articles are not counted in the alphabetical arrangement. The spelling of the country of origin is invariably used, e.g. *My Favorite Blonde* and not *My Favourite Blonde*.

Alphabetical order

This too has caused occasional problems. Some books in formulating the sequence take the complete title into account, as though there were no gaps between words. We have always persevered with the old-fashioned word-at-a-time arrangement: for instance, all the titles starting with *In*, including *In Which We Serve*, are used up before one goes on to titles beginning *Incredible*, *Inspector*, *Intolerance*. Hyphenated or apostrophized words are counted as one word. Compressions such as *Dr* and *St* are treated as though they had been spelled out, as *Doctor* and *Saint*. *Mac* and *Mc* are regarded as interchangeable under *Mac*.

The remaining explanatory notes are only slightly changed from previous editions and are set out below in the order in which they will be encountered in the fuller entry format. (There are also compressed entries for the less outstanding films.)

Publicity tags   These were used in the original promotion for the film and, in the manner of trailers, precede the entry.

Ratings   It would be absurd to classify films selected from a period of eighty years as to which are the best or the worst. Techniques improve, standards change, and personal preferences have to be accounted for. I have tried, however, to give credit for what seemed excellent or innovative at the time, even though it may have been overtaken by imitators; I have tried to judge each film by its own standards (how could one sensibly compare *Frankenstein Meets the Wolf Man* with *Gone with the Wind*?), and I have rescrutinized it now to see what historical or artistic interest it retains. Mere entertainment value has not been derided, nor have films which may seem naive but give an accurate picture of the standards of their own time. To sum up in one word, the ratings indicate how much *interest* a film is thought to have for the modern viewer, whether he be a student or a reasonably alert seeker of entertainment.

Four stars, then, indicate a film outstanding in many ways, a milestone in cinema history, remarkable for acting, direction, writing, photography or some other aspect of technique. Three stars indicate a very high standard of professional excellence or high historical interest: or if you like, three strong reasons for admiring it. Two stars indicate a good level of competence and a generally entertaining film. One star draws attention to minor points of merit, usually in a film not very satisfactory as a whole; it could be a failed giant or a second feature with a few interesting ideas among the dross. No stars at all indicates a totally routine production or worse; such films may be watchable but are at least equally missable.

It will be seen that my judgements are fairly harsh, but I hope they are consistent. For further elucidation of my personal prejudices see the essay, 'The Decline and Fall of the Movie', at the end of the book.

Country of origin   First item on second line.

Year of release   Comes after country of origin, and is intended to be the year in which the film was first shown. If it was made earlier and held back, I have tried to indicate the fact. Dating is sometimes an onerous task, and the result debatable; please be sympathetic.

Running time   In minutes, signified by 'm'. So far as possible this is the original release time. Very many films are cut when they cross the water, sometimes by twenty minutes or more, but I have not tried to indicate this, as when the film appears on television a new print is usually taken from the original negative (but may be cut again). Remember, however, that an engineering function of British television results in an imperceptible speeding-up of projection and a consequent loss of one minute in every twenty-five. A hundred-minute film, therefore, will run only ninety-six minutes on the box, so check your facts before complaining.

Black and white or colour   I have given the colour process where known (it is not always stated these days) and have coined the single word Eastmancolor to equate with Technicolor.

Other notable points   are given at the end of the second line: whether the film is in some special process (3-D, Vistavision, etc). See separate essay on screen shape.

Production credit   The central credit on the third line is the production company. To the left, however, comes the distributor if different from the production company, in brackets if his rights subsequently lapsed. To the right is the actual producer, except for early thirties films in which he was seldom credited. He is also in brackets unless he has a stake in the production, in which case he follows an oblique.

Alternative title   This is given on a separate line, usually with a note of the country in which it was used. If no such fine line exists, I have used the formula *aka* (also known as). Indexes of alternative titles will be found at the beginning of the book, and should be consulted if any film for which the reader is looking cannot at first be found.

Synopsis   Self-explanatory, with brevity and accuracy the keynote.

Assessment   Again very brief, so flippancy will inevitably be suspected. Not so, but for more considered judgements look for books which have more space.

Writer credit   (*w*)   It seems to me that this is, at least sometimes, more important than the director credit, and as script in any case precedes direction, it comes first in this book. The author of the screenplay is always given; if this derives from a novel, play or story, this is given next, together with the original author.

Director credit   *d*.

Photography credit   *ph*.

Music credit   (*m*)   This means the composer of the background music score. Sometimes there is only a music director (*md*) who orchestrates library or classical music.

Other credits   Production designer (*pd*), music and lyrics (*m / ly*), art director (*ad*), special effects (*sp*), editor (*ed*), etc, are given when they seem important and can be found. In some cases it has not been possible to track down all the credits one would wish.

Cast   The principal actors are given, where possible, roughly in order of importance. I have stopped before the bit parts, and given fewer names in the case of foreign films, where the actors tend to be less well known.

Italics   These denote a contribution of a particularly high standard. Arguments are expected and additions welcomed.

Comments from critics   To approximately half the items I have appended brief quotes from well-known professional critics, sometimes because they wittily confirm my own findings, and sometimes because they disagree with me entirely. I hope these will be enjoyable and illuminating; the absence of a quote casts no reflection whatever on the film, only on my own ability as a researcher.

Additional notes   Any other significant remarks about the film are given after the symbol †.

Academy Awards   Awards (AA) and also nominations (AAN) are listed for all principal categories, including acting, direction, photography, music score, songs and best picture.

Video   Where major films are available in Britain on video I have indicated which company distributes them. Titles which prove uncommercial are quickly withdrawn, but I have tried to make the information as complete and up-to-date as I can. Unfortunately it has not been possible to include information about video films in the USA.

Dedication

This edition is dedicated to those optimistic producers who launched their films upon the waters with the following unprepossessing titles – and still expected them to take money:

CHU CHU AND THE PHILLY FLASH
THOSE DARING YOUNG MEN IN THEIR JAUNTY JALOPIES
PHFFFT
W.W. AND THE DIXIE DANCE KINGS
LOLLY MADONNA XXX
OLLY OLLY OXEN FREE
–30–
ATTACK OF THE KILLER TOMATOES
THE EFFECT OF GAMMA RAYS ON MAN-IN-THE-MOON MARIGOLDS
SANTA CLAUS CONQUERS THE MARTIANS
COME BACK TO THE FIVE AND DIME, JIMMY DEAN, JIMMY DEAN
FROM THE MIXED UP FILES OF MRS BASIL E. FRANKWEILER
I SAILED TO TAHITI WITH AN ALL-GIRL CREW
WHAT CHANGED CHARLEY FARTHING?
I AM THE CHEESE
WHO IS HARRY KELLERMAN AND WHY IS HE SAYING THESE TERRIBLE THINGS ABOUT ME?
FIRE MAIDENS FROM OUTER SPACE
WRESTLING WOMEN vs THE AZTEC MUMMY
QUACKSER FORTUNE HAS A COUSIN IN THE BRONX
THE LIVING DEAD AT THE MANCHESTER MORGUE
JESSE JAMES MEETS FRANKENSTEIN'S DAUGHTER
OH DAD, POOR DAD, MUMMY'S HUNG YOU IN THE CLOSET AND I'M FEELING SO SAD
LET US BE GAY
VALIANT IS THE WORD FOR CARRIE
I DISMEMBER MAMA
THE INCREDIBLY STRANGE CREATURES WHO SUDDENLY STOPPED LIVING AND BECAME CRAZY MIXED-UP ZOMBIES
BELA LUGOSI MEETS A BROOKLYN GORILLA
ZOTZ
SHANKS
PULP
CAN HIERONYMUS MERKIN EVER FORGET MERCY HUMPPE AND FIND TRUE HAPPINESS?

NB: Not all of these have been felt to deserve an item to themselves between these covers.

À Bout de Souffle**
France 1959 90m bw
SNC (Georges de Beauregard)
aka: *Breathless*

A young car thief kills a policeman and goes on the run with his American girl friend.
Casual, influential, New Wave reminiscence of both *Quai des Brumes* and innumerable American gangster thrillers. (The film is dedicated to Monogram.)

w François Truffaut *d* Jean-Luc Godard *ph* Raoul Coutard *m* Martial Solal

Jean-Paul Belmondo, Jean Seberg, Daniel Boulanger, Jean-Pierre Melville

'A film all dressed up for rebellion but with no real tangible territory on which to stand and fight.'—*Peter John Dyer*
† See also *Breathless*, American remake.

À Double Tour
France / Italy 1959 110m Eastmancolor
Paris / Panitalia (Robert and Raymond Hakim)
aka: *Web of Passion*

A wealthy wine grower has trouble with his wife, his children, his best friend, and his mistress across the way, who is murdered.
Talented but irritating mixture of Hitchcock and *Les Parents Terribles*; rather an undergraduatish romp.

w Paul Gégauff, *novel* La Clé de la Rue Saint-Nicolas *d* Claude Chabrol *ph* Henri Decaë *m* Paul Misraki

Jacques Dacqmine, Madeleine Robinson, Jean-Paul Belmondo, Bernadette Lafont, Antonella Lualdi, André Jocelyn

A-Haunting We Will Go*
US 1942 68m bw
TCF (Sol M. Wurtzel)

Gangsters dupe Laurel and Hardy into escorting a coffin, which is accidentally switched with one used in a magic act.
Nothing whatever to do with haunting: a poor comedy with no typical material for the stars, but interesting as a record of the touring show of Dante the Magician.

w Lou Breslow *d* Alfred Werker *ph* Glen MacWilliams *m* Glen MacWilliams

Stan Laurel, Oliver Hardy, *Dante*, Sheila Ryan, John Shelton, Elisha Cook Jnr

'The comedians' lack of enthusiasm for their material is rather evident.'—*William K. Everson, 1967*

À Nous la Liberté****
France 1931 95m bw
Tobis
US title: *Freedom for Us*

A factory owner is blackmailed about his past, and helped by an old prison friend, with whom he finally takes to the road.
Operetta-style satirical comedy with leftish attitudes and several famous sequences later borrowed by Chaplin for *Modern Times*. In terms of sheer film flair, a revelation, though the plot has its tedious turns.

wd René Clair *ph* Georges Périnal *m* Georges Auric *pd* Lazare Meerson

Raymond Cordy, Henri Marchand, Rolla France, Paul Olivier

'Different from the usual run . . . easily understandable even to those who do not know French.'—*Variety*
'He demonstrates that sound pictures can be as fluid as silents were, and the picture is rightly considered a classic.'—*Pauline Kael, 1970s*

À Propos de Nice**
France 1930 30m bw

A satirical documentary on the millionaire's paradise of the French Riviera.
Cheaply made and rather naive-looking after fifty years, this amusingly belligerent lampoon still has its striking moments.

wd Jean Vigo *ph* Boris Kaufman

Aan*
India 1952 190m approx (English version 130m) Technicolor
All India Film Corporation / Mehboob Productions
aka: *Savage Princess*

A usurping young prince and his sister are tamed by an athletic peasant and his girl friend.
One of the few examples to reach the west of Indian costume melodrama with music, spectacle and swashbuckling. Distinctly intriguing, if overpowering.

w Chaudary, Ali Raza *d* Mehboob *ph* Faredoon A. Irani *m* Naushad Dilip Kumar, Nimmi, Premnath, Nadira

'Disarmingly enthusiastic . . . exotic and yet charmingly naive.'—*MFB*

Aaron Slick from Punkin Crick*
US 1952 95m Technicolor
Paramount (William Perlberg, George Seaton)
GB title: *Marshmallow Moon*

A small-town girl is tricked into selling her farm and moving to the city, but eventually marries the simple farmer who rescues her.
Homespun entertainment based on a staple success of the American provincial theatre, with pleasant songs added.

wd Claude Binyon, *play* Walter Benjamin Hare *ph* Charles B. Lang Jnr *m / ly* Jay Livingston, Ray Evans *ch* Charles O'Curran

Alan Young, Dinah Shore, Robert Merrill, Adele Jergens, Minerva Urecal

Abandoned
US 1949 79m bw

Reporter breaks baby-farming racket.
Competent action thriller for double billing. Dennis O'Keefe, Gale Storm, Raymond Burr (and young Jeff Chandler). Written by Irwin Gielgud; directed by Joseph Newman; for Universal-International.

'They're too wild for one world!'
Abbott and Costello Go to Mars
US 1953 76m bw
U-I (Howard Christie)

Two incompetents accidentally launch a space ship and land first in Louisiana, then on Venus.
Dismal knockabout, badly made.

w John Grant, D. D. Beauchamp *d* Charles Lamont *ph* Clifford Stine *m* Joseph Gershenson •

Bud Abbott, Lou Costello, Mari Blanchard, Robert Paige, Martha Hyer

Abbott and Costello in Hollywood*
US 1945 85m bw
MGM (Martin Gosch)

Two agents have hectic adventures in a film studio.
Tolerable star romp on one of their biggest budgets, climaxing in a roller coaster ride.

w Nat Perrin, Lou Breslow *d* S. Sylvan Simon *ph* Charles Schoenbaum *m* George Bassman

Bud Abbott, Lou Costello, Francis Rafferty, Warner Anderson, Robert Z. Leonard

Abbott and Costello in the Foreign Legion

US 1950 80m bw
U-I (Robert Arthur)

Incompetent legionnaires become heroes to
the fury of their sergeant.
Dull star vehicle on ramshackle sets, with no
memorable routines.

w John Grant, Leonard Stern, Martin
Ragaway *d* Charles Lamont *ph* George
Robinson *m* Joseph Gershenson

Bud Abbott, Lou Costello, Patricia Medina,
Walter Slezak, Douglass Dumbrille

Abbott and Costello Lost in Alaska

US 1952 76m bw
U-I (Howard Christie)

Two San Francisco firemen take a melancholy
prospector back to Alaska to find a gold mine.
Sub-standard comedy vehicle with poor
production.

w Martin Ragaway, Leonard Stern *d* Jean
Yarbrough
ph George Robinson *m* Joseph Gershenson

Bud Abbott, Lou Costello, *Tom Ewell*, Mitzi
Green, Bruce Cabot

Abbott and Costello Meet Captain Kidd*

US 1952 70m Supercinecolor
Warner / Woodley (Alex Gottlieb)

Two servants have a treasure map, and a
fearsome pirate wants it.
Crude knockabout: the stars are way below
their best, and a famous actor is embarrassed.

w Howard Dimsdale, John Grant *d* Charles
Lamont
ph Stanley Cortez *m* Raoul Kraushaar

Bud Abbott, Lou Costello, Charles Laughton,
Hillary Brooke, Leif Erickson

● *Video: Kingston*

Abbott and Costello Meet Dr Jekyll and Mr Hyde*

US 1953 77m bw
U-I (Howard Christie)

In Victorian London, two rookie policemen
catch a monster.
Quite a lively spoof with some well-paced
comedy sequences.

w John Grant, Lee Loeb *d* Charles Lamont
ph George Robinson *m* Joseph Gershenson

Bud Abbott, Lou Costello, Boris Karloff,
Reginald Denny, Craig Stevens, Helen
Westcott, John Dierkes

'Gracious Boris Karloff is superior to his
surroundings.'—*MFB*. (Though it is doubtful
whether he ever got behind the Hyde make-
up.)
† In Britain, the film was given an 'X'
certificate, though it later played on children's
television.

Abbott and Costello Meet Frankenstein**

US 1948 83m bw
U-I (Robert Arthur)
GB title: *Abbott and Costello Meet the
Ghosts*

ABBOTT AND COSTELLO MEET FRANKENSTEIN. 'He's behind you!' the audience is
shouting as Lou Costello is menaced by Lon Chaney Jnr, who as Lawrence Talbot has
been metamorphosed by the full moon into the Wolf Man.

Two railway porters deliver crates containing
the Frankenstein monster, Dracula, and the
Wolf Man.
Fairly lively spoof which put an end to
Universal's monsters for a while. Good typical
sequences for the stars, a few thrills, and some
good lines. Dracula to Costello, lovingly:
'What we need is young blood . . . and
brains . . .'

w Robert Lees, Frederic I. Rinaldo, John
Grant *d* Charles Barton *ph* Charles van
Enger *m* Frank Skinner

*Bud Abbott, Lou Costello, Bela Lugosi, Lon
Chaney Jnr, Glenn Strange, Lenore Aubert,
Jane Randolph*

WOLF MAN: 'You don't understand. Every
night when the moon is full, I turn into a
wolf.'
COSTELLO: 'You and fifty million other
guys!'
† Probably the Abbott and Costello film which
survives best.

Abbott and Costello Meet the Invisible Man*

US 1951 82m bw
U-I (Howard Christie)

A boxer accused of murder makes himself
invisible while two detectives clear him.
Quite a bright comedy with good trick effects.

w Robert Lees, Frederic I. Rinaldo, John
Grant *d* Charles Lamont *ph* George
Robinson *m* Joseph Gershenson

Bud Abbott, Lou Costello, Arthur Franz,
Nancy Guild, Adele Jergens, Sheldon Leonard

'When every face wore a custard pie, and
vamps broke hearts with a winking eye!'

Abbott and Costello Meet the Keystone Kops*

US 1954 79m bw
U-I (Howard Christie)

In pioneer film days, two incompetents are
sold a dud studio by a con man, but succeed as
stunt men.
Flabby comedy which never seems to get going
until the chase finale; notable chiefly for a
guest appearance by Mack Sennett.

w John Grant *d* Charles Lamont *ph* Reggie
Lanning *m* Joseph Gershenson

Bud Abbott, Lou Costello, Lynn Bari, Fred
Clark, Frank Wilcox, Maxie Rosenbloom

'More ghoulish glee than when they met
Frankenstein!'

Abbott and Costello Meet the Killer, Boris Karloff*

US 1948 84m bw
U-I (Robert Arthur)

Two bellboys help to solve mysterious murders in a remote hotel.
This clumsily titled comedy really does not work until the last sequence in a cavern. Boris Karloff is not the killer and appears very little.

w Hugh Wedlock Jnr, Howard Snyder, John Grant d Charles Barton ph Charles van Enger md Milton Schwarzwald

Bud Abbott, Lou Costello, Boris Karloff, Gar Moore, Lenore Aubert, Alan Mowbray

Abbott and Costello Meet the Mummy*
US 1955 77m bw
U-I (Howard Christie)

A missing medallion leads to a lost tomb and a living mummy.
The comedians show their age in this one, but there is some typical if predictable humour and a thrill or two.

w John Grant d Charles Lamont ph George Robinson m Joseph Gershenson

Bud Abbott, Lou Costello, Kurt Katch, Marie Windsor, Michael Ansara, Dan Seymour

The Abdication
GB 1974 102m Technicolor
Warner (Robert Fryer, James Cresson)

17th-century Queen Christina of Sweden journeys to Rome to embrace the Catholic church and falls in love with a cardinal.
Sombre historical fantasia, more irritating than interesting.

w Ruth Wolff, from her play d Anthony Harvey ph Geoffrey Unsworth m Nino Rota

Liv Ullmann, Peter Finch, Cyril Cusack, Paul Rogers, Graham Crowden, Michael Dunn, Lewis Fiander, Harold Goldblatt
  'Dainty debauchery and titillating tease straight from twenties women's pulp magazines.'—*Variety*
  'Embalmed in such reverence for its own cultural elevation that it loses all contact with the audience.'—*Pauline Kael*

The Abductors*
US 1957 80m bw Regalscope
TCF / Regal (Ray Wander)

Around 1870, criminals steal Lincoln's body as ransom to effect a convict's release.
Interesting minor melodrama, but not sufficiently well made.

w Ray Wander d Andrew V. McLaglen ph Joseph La Shelle

Victor McLaglen, Gavin Muir, George Macready

Abdul the Damned**
GB 1935 111m bw
BIP / Capitol (Max Schach)

In 1900 Turkey, an opera star gives herself to a villainous sultan to protect her fiancé.
Thoroughgoing hokum, well produced, which pleased a lot of people at the time.

w Ashley Dukes, Warren Chetham Strode, Robert Burford d Karl Grune ph Otto Kanturek

Fritz Kortner, Adrienne Ames, Nils Asther, John Stuart, Esme Percy, Walter Rilla, Patric Knowles, Eric Portman

Abdulla the Great
GB / Egypt 1954 103m Technicolor
(Gregory Ratoff)
aka: *Abdulla's Harem*

A pleasure-loving Egyptian potentate sets his sights on an English girl.
Feeble satire on King Farouk, inept and relentlessly boring.

w George St George, Boris Ingster d Gregory Ratoff ph Lee Garmes

Gregory Ratoff, Kay Kendall, Sydney Chaplin

Abe Lincoln in Illinois**
US 1940 110m bw
RKO (Max Gordon)
GB title: *Spirit of the People*

Episodes in the political and domestic life of Abraham Lincoln.
Pleasant, muted, careful film based on a Broadway success: generally informative and interesting.

w Grover Jones, *play* Robert E. Sherwood d John Cromwell ph *James Wong Howe* m Roy Webb

Raymond Massey, Ruth Gordon, Gene Lockhart, Mary Howard, Dorothy Tree, Minor Watson, Howard da Silva
  'If you want attitudes, a five gallon hat, famous incidents, and One Nation Indivisible, they're all here. As a picture and as a whole, it just doesn't stick.'—*Otis Ferguson*
AAN: Raymond Massey, James Wong Howe

Abie's Irish Rose
US 1946 96m bw
(UA) Bing Crosby Productions (Edward A. Sutherland)

Flat filming of the twenties Broadway play about Irish girl marrying Jewish boy, leading to a clash of families.

w Anne Nichols, from her play d Edward A. Sutherland ph William Mellor m John Scott Trotter

Joanne Dru, Richard Norris, Michael Chekhov, Eric Blore, Art Baker
† There had been a silent version in 1928, and the plot was borrowed, to say the least, for the 1972 TV series *Bridget Loves Bernie*.

Abilene Town
US 1946 89m bw

An upright marshal routs crooked cattlemen. Vigorous, enjoyable Western programmer with Randolph Scott and Ann Dvorak on the side of the law. Written by Harold Shumate; directed by Edwin L. Marin; for Jules Levey / UA.
● *Video: VCL*

'Love means never having to say you're ugly!'

The Abominable Dr Phibes**
GB 1971 94m Movielab
AIP (Louis M. Heyward, Ron Dunas)

A disfigured musical genius devises a series of horrible murders, based on the ten curses of Pharaoh, for the surgeons who failed to save his wife.
Brisk but uninspired treatment of a promising theme, with more unintended nastiness than intended laughs. Some good moments and interesting low-budget thirties sets.

w James Whiton, William Goldstein d Robert Fuest ph Norman Warwick m Basil Kirchen, Jack Nathan pd Brian Eatwell

Vincent Price, Joseph Cotten, Hugh Griffith, Terry-Thomas, Peter Jeffrey, Virginia North, Aubrey Woods
† Sequel: *Dr Phibes Rises Again* (1973).

The Abominable Snowman*
GB 1957 91m bw Hammerscope
Hammer / Clarion (Aubrey Baring)

Himalayan explorers are attacked one by one by the Yeti and their own fear.
A thin horror film with intelligent scripting: more philosophizing and characterization than suspense. The briefly glimpsed Yeti are disappointing creations.

w Nigel Kneale, from his TV play d Val Guest ph Arthur Grant m Humphrey Searle

Peter Cushing, Forrest Tucker, Maureen Connell, Richard Wattis, Robert Brown, *Arnold Marle*

About Face
US 1952 96m Technicolor
Warner (William Jacobs)

Moronic remake of *Brother Rat* (qv), shorn of all wit, pace and style.

w Peter Milne d Roy del Ruth ph Bert Glennon songs Charles Tobias, Peter de Rose

Eddie Bracken, Gordon Macrae, Dick Wesson, Virginia Gibson, Phyllis Kirk, Joel Grey

About Mrs Leslie*
US 1954 104m bw
Paramount (Hal B. Wallis)

An ageing nightclub singer has a platonic affair with a mysterious wealthy man, who leaves her enough money to buy a boarding house.
Odd, likeable romantic drama tailored for an unusual star; but its plot is too thin and its direction too drab for real success.

w Ketti Frings, Hal Kanter d Daniel Mann ph Ernest Laszlo m Victor Young

Shirley Booth, Robert Ryan, Alex Nicol, Marjie Miller, Eilene Janssen
  'This quiet and curious film has an unexpectedly gentle, civilized flavour.'—*Gavin Lambert*
  'It's all sunny disposition and sweet sadness for Miss Booth.'—*Judith Crist*
  'One is reminded alternately of Chekhov and of *Back Street*.'—*Sight and Sound*

Above and Beyond*
US 1952 122m bw
MGM (Melvin Frank, Norman Panama)

The training of Colonel Paul Tibbetts, who dropped the first atomic bomb on Japan.

Overstretched flagwaver with laborious domestic interludes. Of little real interest then or now.

w Melvin Frank, Norman Panama, story Beirne Lay Jnr d Melvin Frank, Norman Panama ph Ray June m Hugo Friedhofer

Robert Taylor, Eleanor Parker, James Whitmore, Larry Keating, Larry Gates

AAN: Beirne Lay Jnr, Hugo Friedhofer

Above Suspicion*
US 1943 91m bw
MGM (Victor Saville)

Just before World War II, an Oxford professor on a continental honeymoon is asked to track down a missing agent.
Patchy, studio-bound spy comedy-drama with a couple of good sequences. Notable also for Mr MacMurray's impersonation of a professor who hails a Nazi as 'Hiya, dope!'

w Keith Winter, Melville Baker, Patricia Coleman, novel Helen MacInnes d Richard Thorpe ph Robert Planck m Bronislau Kaper

Fred MacMurray, Joan Crawford, Conrad Veidt, Basil Rathbone, Reginald Owen, Felix Bressart, Richard Ainley

'A story of impudent gallantry!'
Above Us the Waves*
GB 1955 99m bw
(Rank) London Independent Producers (William Macquitty)

In World War II, midget submarines attack a German battleship in a Norwegian fjord.
Archetypal stiff-upper-lip war drama with good action sequences.

w Robin Estridge d Ralph Thomas ph Ernest Steward m Arthur Benjamin

John Mills, John Gregson, Donald Sinden, James Robertson Justice, Michael Medwin, Lee Patterson, Lyndon Brook

● Video: Rank

'The wonder film of the century, about the most romantic figure who ever lived!'
Abraham Lincoln**
US 1930 97m bw
UA / D. W. Griffith

An account of Lincoln's entry into politics and his years of power.
Rather boring even at the time, this straightforward biopic has the virtues of sincerity and comparative fidelity to the facts.

w Stephen Vincent Benet, Gerrit Lord d D. W. Griffith m Karl Struss m Hugo Riesenfeld pd William Cameron Menzies

Walter Huston, Una Merkel, Edgar Dearing, Russell Simpson, Henry B. Walthall

'A startlingly superlative accomplishment, one rejuvenating a greatest Griffith . . . one smooth roll of literally pulsating passion, pathos, laughter . . . it should be his greatest contribution to the exhibitor.'—Variety

'It brings to us—with a curious finality of disappointment, a sentimental sense of the closing of a chapter—the impression of a

director who has nowhere made a valid contact with the condition of the screen today.'—C. A. Lejeune
'A treasure trove of magnificent moments.'—MFB, 1973
'Dull, episodic, overlong . . . it is difficult to understand why contemporary critics were so impressed.'—Anthony Slide, 70s

Abroad with Two Yanks*
US 1944 80m bw
Edward Small

Adventures around the Pacific with two woman-chasing sailors.
This simple-minded farce with its punny title was a great success in its day, and still generates a laugh or two.

w Charles Rogers, Wilkie Maholey, Fred Redsills d Allan Dwan ph Charles Lawton m Lud Gluskin

Dennis O'Keefe, William Bendix, Helen Walker, John Abbott, John Loder

Abschied von Gestern*
West Germany 1966 90m bw
Kairos Film / Alexander Kluge / Independent
aka: Yesterday Girl

A Jewish girl escapes from East to West Germany but is disillusioned and gives herself up.
Witty and remarkably light-hearted satirical comedy which can be fully understood only by those living in Germany in the sixties.

wd Alexander Kluge ph Edgar Reitz, Thomas Mauch

Alexandra Kluge, Gunther Mack, Hans Korte, Eva Marie Meinecke

Absence of Malice*
US 1981 116m De Luxe
Columbia / Mirage (Sydney Pollack)

When a longshoremen's union leader disappears, a lady journalist throws an unfair spotlight on an innocent suspect.
Well-meaning but overwritten attack on journalistic abuses, hampered by unsuitable leading performances.

w Kurt Luedtke d Sydney Pollack ph Owen Roizman m Dave Grusin pd Terence Marsh

Paul Newman, Sally Field, Bob Balaban, Melinda Dillon, Luther Adler, Barry Primus

'Pollack seems to be carving out a new niche for himself as an updater of Hollywood's most tried and true methods of sugaring a message.'—Richard Combs, MFB
'A thoroughly craftsmanlike movie that never quite delivers on the commercial or the artistic front.'—Guardian

AAN: screenplay; Paul Newman; Melinda Dillon

● Video: RCA / Columbia

The Absent-Minded Professor*
US 1960 97m bw
Walt Disney (Bill Walsh)

A lighter-than-air substance called flubber enables its inventor to drive his Model-T through the sky and catch some spies.

Foolishly engaging fantasy comedy with goodish trick effects.

w Bill Walsh d Robert Stevenson ph Edward Colman m George Bruns sp Robert A. Mattey, Peter Ellenshaw, Eustace Lycett

Fred MacMurray, Tommy Kirk, Keenan Wynn, Nancy Olson, Leon Ames, Ed Wynn, Edward Andrews

† Sequel: Son of Flubber (1964).

AAN: Edward Colman

Absolute Quiet
US 1936 71m bw

Interestingly-cast programmer about a murder plot after a planeload of strangers is forced down on a financier's ranch. Lionel Atwill, Louis Hayward, Raymond Walburn, Stuart Erwin, Wallace Ford, J. Carrol Naish. Written by Harry Clark; directed by Edwin L. Marin; for MGM.

Absolution*
GB 1978 95m Technicolor
Bulldog (Danny O'Donovan, Elliott Kastner)
TV title: Murder by Confession

A schoolmaster priest at a Roman Catholic boarding school is taunted by a malicious pupil into committing murder.
Interesting and suspenseful, though finally too complicated compromise between a thriller of the Sleuth type and a downbeat character study.

w Anthony Shaffer d Anthony Page ph John Coquillon m Stanley Myers

Richard Burton, Dominic Guard, Dai Bradley, Billy Connolly, Andrew Keir

'A dire slice of clever-clever narrative trickery.'—Paul Taylor, MFB
'You can't make real bricks from this kind of straw, since a potentially interesting study of character and environment is gradually weakened by the constraints of a second-rate murder mystery.'—Guardian

● Video: Home Video

Accattone*
Italy 1961 120m bw
Cino del Duca / Arco (Alfredo Bini)

A Roman pimp and thief is beset by troubles, and is finally killed escaping from the police.
Sordid and rough-edged but vividly realistic melodrama.

wd Pier Paolo Pasolini ph Tonino delli Colli md Carlo Rustichelli

Franco Citti, Franca Pasut, Roberto Scaringella, Adele Cambria

Accent on Love
US 1941 61m bw

A real estate executive walks out to become spokesman for his former underprivileged tenants. Thin Capraesque romantic comedy. George Montgomery, Osa Massen, J. Carrol Naish, Cobina Wright Jnr, Stanley Clements, Thurston Hall, Minerva Urecal. Written by John Larkin, from a story by Dalton Trumbo; directed by Ray McCarey; for TCF.

Accent on Youth*
US 1935 77m bw
Paramount (Douglas Maclean)

A secretary falls in love with her middle-aged playwright employer.
Reasonably sparkling comedy from a popular play, later remade as *Mr Music* and *But Not for Me*.
w Herbert Fields, Claude Binyon, *play* Samson Raphaelson d Wesley Ruggles ph Leon Shamroy

Herbert Marshall, Sylvia Sidney, Philip Reed, Astrid Allwyn, Holmes Herbert

Accident**
GB 1967 105m Eastmancolor
London Independent Producers (Joseph Losey, Norman Priggen)

An Oxford undergraduate is killed in a car crash; his tutor looks back over the tangle of personal relationships that contributed to his death.
Ascetic drama in which the audience is too often left to observe at length and draw its own conclusions; good characterizations nevertheless.
w Harold Pinter, *novel* Nicholas Mosley d Joseph Losey ph Gerry Fisher m Johnny Dankworth

Dirk Bogarde, Stanley Baker, Jacqueline Sassard, Vivien Merchant, Michael York
'The whole thing is such a teapot tempest, and it is so assiduously underplayed that it is neither strong drama nor stinging satire. It is just a sad little story of a wistful don.'—*Bosley Crowther*
'Everything is calm, unruffled, lacquered in a veneer of civilization, yet underneath it all, one gradually begins to realize, the characters are tearing each other emotionally to shreds.'—*MFB*
'Uneven, unsatisfying, but with virtuoso passages of calculated meanness.'—*New Yorker, 1977*
● Video: Thorn EMI

Accidents Will Happen
US 1938 62m bw

An insurance claims adjuster takes to crime.
Slack little programmer. Ronald Reagan, Dick Purcell, Gloria Blondell, Addison Richards, Hugh O'Connell. Written by George Bricker and Anthony Coldeway; directed by William Clemens; for Bryan Foy / Warner.

According to Mrs Hoyle
US 1951 60m bw

A retired schoolteacher lives in a hotel run by criminals, and becomes involved. Uninspired sentimental comedy providing a rare star part for a well-liked character actress. Spring Byington, Anthony Caruso, Brett King, Tanis Chandler. Written by W. Scott Darling and Barney Gerard; directed by Jean Yarbrough; for Monogram.

Account Rendered
GB 1957 59m bw

A man is suspected of the murder of his unfaithful wife. Adequate lower-billed suspenser. Griffith Jones, Ursula Howells, Honor Blackman, Ewen Solon, John Van Eyssen. Written by Barbara S. Harper, from a novel by Pamela Barrington; directed by Peter Graham Scott; for Major / RFD.

Accused
GB 1936 85m bw

In Paris, a dancer is stabbed and his wife is thought guilty. Overwrought melodrama, chiefly interesting for cast: Douglas Fairbanks Jnr, Dolores del Rio, Googie Withers, Florence Desmond, Basil Sydney. Written by Zoe Akins, George Barraud and Harold French; directed by Thornton Freeland; for Criterion / UA.

'The standout suspense triumph of the year!'
The Accused*
US 1948 101m bw
Paramount (Hal B. Wallis)

In self-defence a lady professor kills a student who has sexually attacked her.
Dullish suspenser with the outcome never in doubt, though the production values are beyond reproach.
w Ketti Frings d William Dieterle ph Milton Krasner m Victor Young

Loretta Young, Robert Cummings, Wendell Corey, Sam Jaffe, Douglas Dick

Accused of Murder
US 1956 76m bw

When a crooked lawyer is murdered, his mistress is suspected. Flat little mystery with unappetizing characters. Vera Ralston, David Brian, Sidney Blackmer, Virginia Grey, Warren Stevens, Lee Van Cleef. Written by Bob Williams and W. R. Burnett, from the novel *Vanity Row* by W. R. Burnett; directed by Joe Kane; for Republic.

Ace Eli and Roger of the Skies
US 1973 92m De Luxe Panavision
TCF (Robert Fryer, James Cresson)

Adventures of a father-and-son aerial barnstorming act after World War I.
Poorly written melodrama, very tame apart from the flying shots.
w Claudia Salter, *story* Steven Spielberg d John Erman ph David M. Walsh, Bill Birch, Don Morgan m Jerry Goldsmith

Cliff Robertson, Pamela Franklin, Eric Shea, Rosemary Murphy, Bernadette Peters, Alice Ghostley
'A tediously inane flop. Nostalgia isn't what it used to be.'—*Variety*

Ace High
Italy 1969 120m Techniscope

A condemned outlaw is offered an opportunity to save his neck. Violent spaghetti western

with vestiges of a sense of humour. Eli Wallach, Brock Peters, Terence Hill, Bud Spencer, Kevin McCarthy. Written and directed by Giuseppe Colizzi; for Paramount.

Ace in the Hole***
US 1951 111m bw
Paramount (Billy Wilder)
aka: *The Big Carnival*

In order to prolong the sensation and boost newspaper sales, a self-seeking journalist delays the rescue of a man trapped in a cave.
An incisive, compelling melodrama taking a sour look at the American scene; one of its director's masterworks.
w Billy Wilder, Lesser Samuels, Walter Newman d Billy Wilder ph Charles B. Lang Jnr m Hugo Friedhofer

Kirk Douglas (Chuck Tatum), Jan Sterling (Lorraine), *Porter Hall* (Boot), Bob Arthur (Herbie), Richard Benedict (Leo), Ray Teal (Sheriff), Frank Cady (Federber)

LORRAINE to Tatum: 'I've met some hard-boiled eggs, but you—you're twenty minutes!'
LORRAINE: 'I don't go to church. Kneeling bags my nylons.'
TATUM to editor: 'I've done a lot of lying in my time. I've lied to men who wear belts. I've lied to men who wear suspenders. But I'd never be so stupid as to lie to a man who wears both belt and suspenders.'
TATUM, dying, to editor: 'How'd you like to make a thousand dollars a day, Mr Boot? I'm a thousand-dollar-a-day newspaperman. You can have me for nothing.'
'Few of the opportunities for irony, cruelty and horror are missed.'—*Gavin Lambert*
'Style and purpose achieve for the most part a fusion even more remarkable than in *Sunset Boulevard*.'—*Penelope Houston*
'As stimulating as black coffee.'—*Richard Mallett, Punch*
'Americans expected a cocktail and felt I was giving them a shot of vinegar instead.'—*Billy Wilder*
'Some people have tried to claim some sort of satirical brilliance for it, but it's really rather nasty, in a sociologically pushy way.'—*New Yorker, 1980*
'A brilliant arrangement of cause and effect . . . unique as a mirror of the morbid psychology of crowds . . . revolting but incontrovertibly true.'—*New York Times*
AAN: script

Ace of Aces*
US 1933 76m bw

On the outbreak of World War I an American sculptor is branded a coward when he does not immediately enlist; but he disappears and turns up in France a hero, though with a sour taste in his mouth. Melodrama of disillusion, dated in many respects but interesting to compare with *The Dawn Patrol* and *The Last Flight*. Richard Dix, Elizabeth Allan, Theodore Newton, Ralph Bellamy, Joseph Sawyer, Frank Conroy, William Cagney. Written by John Monk Saunders and H. W

Hannemann from the story 'Bird of Prey' by John Monk Saunders; directed by J. Walter Ruben; for RKO.

'It's the fine photography and crashes that provide the thrills.'—*Variety*

Aces High°

GB 1976 114m Technicolor
EMI / S. Benjamin Fisz / Jacques Roitfeld

In the air force during World War I, young pilots are needlessly sacrificed.

Spirited if rather unnecessary remake of *Journey's End* transposed to the air war, which makes it almost identical to *The Dawn Patrol*.

w Howard Barker d Jack Gold ph Gerry Fisher, Peter Allwork m Richard Hartley

Malcolm McDowell, Christopher Plummer, Simon Ward, Peter Firth, John Gielgud, Trevor Howard, Richard Johnson, Ray Milland

● *Video: Thorn EMI*

Across 110th Street°

US 1972 102m De Luxe
UA / Film Guarantors (Fouad Said, Ralph Serpe)

A tough New York cop loses his own life tracking down three Harlem criminals who have robbed the Mafia.

Brutish, noisy, incoherent police melodrama, with fashionable sadism and predictable performances. Good location work, though.

w Luther Davis, *novel* Wally Ferris d Barry Shear ph Jack Priestley m J. J. Johnson

Anthony Quinn, Anthony Franciosa, Yaphet Kotto, Paul Benjamin, Ed Bernard

'Not for the squeamish . . . a virtual blood bath, leaving no relief from depression and oppression.'—*Variety*

Across the Bridge°

GB 1957 103m bw
Rank / IPF (John Stafford)

A fugitive financier kills his pursuer, finds he was a murderer, and tries to hide out across the Mexican border.

This star *tour de force* is unconvincing in detail and rather unattractive to watch (British films never could cope with American settings), but the early sequences have suspense.

w Guy Elmes, Denis Freeman, *novel* Graham Greene d Ken Annakin ph Reg Wyer m James Bernard

Rod Steiger, David Knight, Marla Landi, Noel Willman, Bernard Lee

Across the Pacific°°°

US 1942 99m bw
Warner (Hal B. Wallis)

Just before Pearl Harbor, an army officer is cashiered by arrangement in order to contact pro-Japanese sympathizers.

Hasty, easy-going and very enjoyable hokum, partly ship-set and successfully reteaming three stars of *The Maltese Falcon*.

w Richard Macauley, *serial* Aloha Means Goodbye by Robert Carson d John Huston ph Arthur Edeson m Adolph Deutsch

Humphrey Bogart (Rick Leland), *Mary Astor* (Alberta Marlow), *Sydney Greenstreet* (Dr Lorenz), *Sen Yung* (Joe Totsuiko); and Charles Halton, Monte Blue, Richard Loo, Chester Gan, Kam Tong

'A spy picture which tingles with fearful uncertainties and glints with the sheen of blue steel.'—*Bosley Crowther*

† Huston was called up before the film was completed, and allegedly reshaped the script before leaving in order to put the hero in an impossible situation. Direction was eventually completed by Vincent Sherman.

Across the Wide Missouri°

US 1951 77m Technicolor
MGM (Robert Sisk)

In the 1820s, a trapper marries an Indian girl and lives with her people.

Promising credits produce an unsatisfactory western: despite honest efforts, the elements do not jell into a convincing whole.

w Talbot Jennings d William Wellman ph William C. Mellor m David Raksin

Clark Gable, Ricardo Montalban, John Hodiak, Adolphe Menjou, Maria Elena Marques, J. Carrol Naish, Jack Holt, Alan Napier

Act of Love °

US 1954 104m bw
UA / Benagoss (Anatole Litvak)

In Paris in 1944, an American with the liberation army falls in love with a French girl, who commits suicide when he is posted and cannot make their rendezvous.

Cheerless romantic drama, rather thin and unmemorable despite the efforts of all concerned.

w Irwin Shaw, *novel* The Girl on the Via Flaminia by Alfred Hayes d Anatole Litvak ph Armand Thirard m Michael Emer, Joe Hajos pd Alexander Trauner

Kirk Douglas, Dany Robin, Barbara Laage, Robert Strauss, Gabrielle Dorziat, Gregoire Aslan, Fernand Ledoux, Serge Reggiani, Brigitte Bardot

† Made in France, an early Hollywood foreign location film.

An Act of Murder°°

US 1948 90m bw
U-I (Jerry Bresler)
aka: *Live Today for Tomorrow*

A judge insists on being tried for the mercy killing of his incurably ill wife.

Earnest social drama which despite excellent acting can only reach an inconclusive ending.

w Michael Blankfort, Robert Thoeren, *novel* The Mills of God by Ernst Lothar d Michael Gordon ph Hal Mohr m Daniele Amfitheatrof

Fredric March, Florence Eldridge, Edmond O'Brien, Geraldine Brooks

Act of Murder°°

GB 1964 62m bw
Merton Park (Jack Greenwood)

A couple arrange a holiday by swapping houses with strangers, and a complex plot ensues.

Slick, superior example of the Edgar Wallace second feature series.

w Lewis Davidson d Alan Bridges ph James Wilson m Bernard Ebbinghouse

John Carson, Anthony Bate, Justine Lord, Duncan Lewis, Dandy Nichols

'This uncommonly intelligent little thriller is just the sort of film which is likely to arouse critical sneers for reaching too high on a low budget.'—*Tom Milne*

Act of Violence°°

US 1948 82m bw
MGM (William Wright)

After the war, an ex-GI tracks down a prison camp informer.

Moody, glossy melodrama with tension well sustained, though the sentimental ending is a cop-out.

w Robert I. Richards, *story* Collier Young d Fred Zinnemann ph Robert Surtees m Bronislau Kaper

Van Heflin, Robert Ryan, Janet Leigh, Mary Astor

'Strong characterization, fine direction and good photography combine to put this film high among its kind.'—*MFB*

'An effortless narrative control and a real power to maintain tension.'—*Richard Winnington*

Act One°

US 1963 110m bw
Warner (Dore Schary)

Poor Brooklyn boy Moss Hart rises to Broadway eminence via his writing partnership with George S. Kaufman.

Incredibly stilted film version of an excellent autobiography, notable only for fragments of acting and the fact that a film so totally uncommercial was made at all.

wd Dore Schary ph Arthur J. Ornitz m Skitch Henderson

George Hamilton (Hart), Jason Robards Jnr (Kaufman), Jack Klugman, Sam Levene, George Segal, Ruth Ford, Eli Wallach

'From the moment young Hart takes pencil in hand, we have nowhere to go except to that happy ending; and despite all the painstaking detail, we don't believe a word of it.'—*Judith Crist*

Action for Slander°

GB 1937 83m bw
London Films / Saville (Victor Saville)

A bankrupt officer, accused of cheating at cards, defends his honour with a writ.

Lively melodrama of the old school.

w Ian Dalrymple, Miles Malleson, *novel* Mary Borden d Tim Whelan ph Harry Stradling md Muir Mathieson

Clive Brook, Ann Todd, Margaretta Scott, Arthur Margetson, Ronald Squire, Athole Stewart, Percy Marmont, Frank Cellier, Morton Selten

Action in the North Atlantic
US 1943 127m bw
Warner (Jerry Wald)

An American convoy bound for Russia comes
under U-boat attack.
Efficient propaganda potboiler; studio bound,
but still works as a war actioner.

w John Howard Lawson, *story* Guy Gilpatric
d Lloyd Bacon ph Ted McCord m Adolph
Deutsch

Humphrey Bogart, Raymond Massey, Alan
Hale, Julie Bishop, Ruth Gordon, Sam
Levene, Dane Clark

'The production has interludes of
tremendous power. What is lacking is dramatic
cohesion.'—*Howard Barnes*
'Directly in line of descent from *The Perils
of Pauline.*'—*Time*
'The American equivalent of our war
documentaries . . . tough, exciting, with no
concession to flim flam.'—*New Statesman*
'I cannot think I have ever seen such
realistic battles, or lived so intimately with the
characters who comprise the crew.'—*Evening
Standard*

AAN: Guy Gilpatric

Action of the Tiger
GB 1957 93m Technicolor
   Cinemascope
MGM / Claridge (Kenneth Harper)

An adventurer helps a French girl to rescue
her brother from political imprisonment in
Albania.
Dull and poorly constructed action
melodrama.

w Robert Carson, *novel* James Wellard
d Terence Young ph Desmond Dickinson
m Humphrey Searle

Van Johnson, Martine Carol, Herbert Lom,
Gustavo Rocco, Anthony Dawson, Helen
Haye, Sean Connery

Actors and Sin
US 1952 91m bw
(UA) Sid Kuller (Ben Hecht)

Two short stories. When an unsuccessful
actress commits suicide, her father makes it
look like murder so that for once she shall get
attention.
The authoress of a romantic script bought by
Hollywood is discovered to be a horrid little
9-year-old.
Interesting but incompetent compendium
which descends almost to the home movie
level and leaves the actors struggling.

wd Ben Hecht ph Lee Garmes m George
Antheil

Edward G. Robinson, Marsha Hunt, Dan
O'Herlihy, Rudolph Anders, Eddie Albert,
Alan Reed, Jenny Hecht
'A depressing double bill.'—*Lindsay
Anderson*

An Actor's Revenge
Japan 1963 113m Daieicolor
   Daieiscope
Daiei (Masaichi Nagata)
original title: *Yukinojo Henge*

In the early 19th century, a touring actor
comes upon the rich merchant who had ruined
his parents, and his revenge involves several
deaths.
Complex, fascinating period melodrama, both
rich and strange, with strong echoes of
Jacobean melodrama.

w Daisuke Ito, Teinosuke Kinugasa, Natto
Wada, *novel* Otokichi Mikami d Kon
Ichikawa ph Setsuo Kobayashi m Yasushi
Akutagawa

Kazuo Hasegawa, Fujiko Yamamoto, Ayako
Wakao, Ganjiro Nakamura

The Actress
US 1928 90m approx (24 fps) bw
   silent
MGM
GB title: *Trelawny of the Wells*

A young Victorian actress marries a rich
admirer.
Pleasing, well-cast version of a celebrated
play.

w Albert Lewin, Richard Schayer, *play* Sir
Arthur Wing Pinero d Sidney Franklin
ph William Daniels

Norma Shearer, Ralph Forbes, O. P. Heggie,
Owen Moore, Roy D'Arcy
† Opening attraction at London's Empire
Theatre, Leicester Square.

The Actress
US 1953 91m bw
MGM (Lawrence Weingarten)

Ruth Jones becomes an actress against the
wishes of her stubborn seafaring father.
Episodes from Ruth Gordon's early life, based
on her Broadway play *Years Ago*, make a
pleasant though scarcely engrossing film: it is
all a shade too discreet and wanly winning,
and the few key events take place offscreen.

w Ruth Gordon d George Cukor ph Harold
Rosson m Bronislau Kaper ad Cedric
Gibbons, Arthur Lonergan

Jean Simmons, Spencer Tracy, Teresa Wright,
Anthony Perkins, Ian Wolfe, Mary Wickes

Ada
US 1961 109m Metrocolor
   Cinemascope
MGM / Avon / Chalmar (Lawrence
Weingarten)

A political candidate marries a call girl who
becomes his strong right arm and weathers a
threat to reveal her past.
Indecisive romantic drama which pulls too
many punches but has interesting background
detail.

w Arthur Sheekman, William Driskill, *novel*
Ada Dallas by Wirt Williams d Daniel Mann
ph Joseph Ruttenberg m Bronislau Kaper

Susan Hayward, Dean Martin, Wilfrid Hyde
White, Ralph Meeker, Martin Balsam
'A bonanza for connoisseurs of perfectly
awful movies.'—*Judith Crist*
'Its characterizations are sketchy, its
political setting routine and symbolic.'—*New
York Herald Tribune*

Adalen 31
Sweden 1969 115m Technicolor
   Techniscope
Svensk Filmindustri

A prolonged strike at a small-town paper mill
ends in tragedy when the troops move in.
Effective period piece which emphasizes the
idyllic qualities of the backgrounds rather than
the foreground terrors.

wd Bo Widerberg ph Jorgen Persson

Peter Schildt, Kerstin Tidelius, Roland
Hedlund, Stefan Feierbach, Anita Bjork

Adam and Evelyne
GB 1949 92m bw
Rank / Two Cities (Harold French)

A society playboy adopts his dead friend's
daughter, and falls in love with her:
Undernourished romantic drama, a mild
variation on *Daddy Longlegs.*

w Noel Langley, Lesley Storm, George
Barraud, Nicholas Phipps d Harold French
ph Guy Green m Mischa Spoliansky

Stewart Granger, Jean Simmons, Helen
Cherry, Edwin Styles, Beatrice Varley, Wilfrid
Hyde White

Adam Had Four Sons
US 1941 81m bw
Columbia (Robert Sherwood)

A widower's family is cared for by a
governess.
Modest magazine fiction which established
Ingrid Bergman as an American star.

w Michael Blankfort, William Hurlbut, *novel*
Legacy by Charles Bonner d Gregory Ratoff
ph Peverell Marley m W. Franke Harling

Warner Baxter, *Ingrid Bergman*, Susan
Hayward, Richard Denning, Fay Wray

Adam's Rib
US 1949 101m bw
MGM (Lawrence Weingarten)

Husband and wife lawyers are on opposite
sides of an attempted murder case.
A superior star vehicle which also managed to
introduce four promising personalities; slangily
written and smartly directed, but perhaps a
shade less funny than it once seemed.

w Ruth Gordon, Garson Kanin d George
Cukor ph George J. Folsey m Miklos Rozsa

Spencer Tracy, Katharine Hepburn, David
Wayne, Tom Ewell, Judy Holliday, Jean
Hagen, Hope Emerson, Clarence Kolb

'Hepburn and Tracy are again presented as
the ideal US Mr and Mrs of upper-middle
income. This time, as well as being wittily
urbane, both are lawyers.'—*Time*
'It isn't solid food but it certainly is meaty
and juicy and comically nourishing.'—*Bosley
Crowther*
† A 1972 TV series of the same title provided
a boring imitation, with Ken Howard and
Blythe Danner.

Adam's Woman
Australia 1970 115m colour
Panavision

In the 1840s an American finds himself a prisoner in an antipodean penal colony, and schemes to get out. Oddball period drama, unreleased in Britain. Beau Bridges, Jane Merrow, James Booth, John Mills. Written by Richard Fielder; directed by Philip Leacock; for Warner / EMI.

The Adding Machine*
GB 1968 99m Technicolor
Universal / Associated London (Jerome Epstein)

Downtrodden clerk Mr Zero rebels against society by murdering his boss. Tried and executed, he spends thirty years in heaven before being 'laundered' and sent back to start again as another nonentity.
Elmer Rice's satirical fantasy of the twenties is here robbed of its expressionist staging and presented naturalistically, a fatal error from which the film never for one moment recovers.

wd Jerome Epstein *ph* Walter Lassally *m* Mike Leander, Lambert Williamson

Phyllis Diller, Milo O'Shea, Billie Whitelaw, Sydney Chaplin, Julian Glover, Raymond Huntley, Phil Brown, Libby Morris

Address Unknown*
US 1944 72m bw
Columbia (William Cameron Menzies)

A German-American becomes a Nazi and is incriminated by false letters from his one-time friend.
Reasonably engrossing, cheaply-made adaptation of a slim little thriller which was widely read during World War II.

w Kressman Taylor, Herbert Dalmass, *novel* Kressman Taylor *d* William Cameron Menzies *ph* Rudolph Maté *m* Ernst Toch

Paul Lukas, Peter Van Eyck, Mady Christians, Emory Parnell

AAN: Ernst Toch

Adieu Philippine*
France / Italy 1962 106m bw
Unitec / Alpha / Rome-Paris (Georges de Beauregard)

A young TV cameraman is torn between two girls.
Flimsy but attractive romantic comedy, slightly marred by New Wave improvisation with consequent rough edges.

w Michèle O'Glor, Jacques Rozier *d* Jacques Rozier *ph* René Mathelin *m* various

Jean-Claude Aimini, Yveline Céry, Stefania Sabatini, Vittorio Caprioli

The Admirable Crichton*
GB 1957 93m Technicolor Vistavision
Columbia / Modern Screenplays (Ian Dalrymple)
US title: *Paradise Lagoon*

Lord Loam and his family are shipwrecked on a desert island, where his manservant proves the undisputed leader.
Few laughs are to be had from this blunt,

sentimental version of a famous play, but the photography and decor are excellent.

w Vernon Harris, *play* J. M. Barrie *d* Lewis Gilbert *ph* Wilkie Cooper *m* Douglas Gamley *ad* William Kellner
costumes Bernard Nevill *devices* Emmett

Kenneth More, Cecil Parker, Sally Ann Howes, Diane Cilento, Martita Hunt, Jack Watling, Peter Graves, Gerald Harper
'Barrie's play now seems more remote than Gammer Gurton.'—*David Robinson*

The Admiral Was a Lady
US 1950 87m bw

Four ex-airmen and an ex-Wac try to live on their wits. Unappealing comedy which gives the impression that it has tried to find a new style, and failed. Edmond O'Brien, Wanda Hendrix, Rudy Vallee, Johnny Sands, Steve Brodie, Richard Erdman, Hillary Brooke, Richard Lane. Written by Sidney Salkow and John O'Dea; directed and produced by Albert S. Rogell; photographed by Stanley Cortez; for Roxbury (Albert S. Rogell / Jack M. Warner).

Adolf Hitler—My Part in His Downfall*
GB 1972 102m Technicolor
UA / Norcon (Gregory Smith, Norman Cohen)

Episodes in the life of a conscript at the beginning of World War II.
Lumbering anarchic comedy based on Spike Milligan's own sidesplitting memoirs; an enfeebled British *M*A*S*H*.

w Johnny Byrne *d* Norman Cohen *ph* Terry Maher *m* Wilfred Burns

Jim Dale, Spike Milligan (as his own father), Arthur Lowe, Bill Maynard, Windsor Davies, Pat Coombs, Tony Selby, Geoffrey Hughes
'A convincing period shabbiness and sleaziness which are endearing when they're not being overstated.'—*MFB*

Adorable*
US 1933 85m bw
Fox

A Ruritanian princess falls in love with a naval officer.
Charming, lightweight romance of the old school.

w George Marion Jr, Jane Storm, *story* Paul Frank, Billy Wilder *d* William Dieterle *ph* John Seitz

Janet Gaynor, Henri Garat, C. Aubrey Smith, Herbert Mundin, Blanche Friderici, Hans von Twardowski
'Not strong b.o. . . . even the neighbourhood fans have caught up with the musical comedy kingdom idea.'—*Variety*
† The film was remade from German–French originals under a title which translated as *Her Majesty Commands*. The German version starred Kaethe von Nagy and Willy Fritsch, the French Lillian Harvey and Henri Garat.

Adorable Creatures
France 1952 105m bw
Jacques Roitfeld / Sirius

A Paris fashion executive recalls his love affairs.
A collection of four short sex comedies which did well on the heels of *La Ronde*.

w Charles Spaak, Jacques Companeez *d* Christian-Jaque *ph* Christian Matras *m* Georges Van Parys

Daniel Gélin, *Danielle Darrieux*, Edwige Feuillère, Antonella Lualdi, Martine Carol, Marilyn Buferd

Adorable Julia
Austria / France 1962 97m bw

A middle-aged actress takes on a lover.
Moderately pleasing sex comedy, rather more heavily directed than Maugham would have liked. Lilli Palmer, Charles Boyer, Jean Sorel, Jeanne Valerie. Written by Johanna Sibelius and Eberhard Keindorff from the novel Theatre by Somerset Maugham; directed by Alfred Weidenmann; for Wiener Mundus / Etoile. (GB title: *The Seduction of Julia*.)

Adua e le Compagne
Italy 1960 150m bw

When brothels in Italy are officially closed, four of the old girls open a restaurant.
Immensely overlong comedy drama whose rewards come entirely from the actors. Simone Signoret, Marcello Mastroianni, Sanda Milo, Emmanuelle Riva, Gina Rovere. Written by Ruggero Maccari, Ettore Scola, Antonio Pietrangeli, Tullio Pinelli; directed by Antonio Pietrangeli; for Zebra Film. 'The script becomes increasingly episodic, and clichés abound.'—*MFB*. (GB title: *Hungry for Love*.)

Advance to the Rear*
US 1964 97m bw Panavision
MGM / Ted Richmond
GB title: *Company of Cowards?*

After the Civil War, a troop of misfits is sent west out of harm's way, but manages to capture a rebel spy and save a gold shipment.
Semi-satirical western action comedy with a farcical climax; quite sharply made.

w Samuel A. Peeples, William Bowers *d* George Marshall *ph* Milton Krasner *m* Randy Sparks

Glenn Ford, *Melvyn Douglas,* Stella Stevens, Jim Backus, Joan Blondell, Andrew Prine, Alan Hale, James Griffith, Preston Foster

'Gable's back and Garson's got him!'
Adventure*
US 1945 126m bw
MGM (Sam Zimbalist)

A roughneck sailor marries a librarian, but only settles down to love her when their child is born.
Uniquely embarrassing (and fascinating) mishmash of pretentious dialogue and cardboard characters.

w Frederick Hazlitt Brennan, Vincent Lawrence, *novel* Clyde Brion Davis *d* Victor Fleming *ph* Joseph Ruttenberg *m* Herbert Stothart

Clark Gable, Greer Garson, Thomas Mitchell, Joan Blondell, John Qualen, Richard Haydn
  'MGM proudly announce *Adventure* as the meeting of a red-blooded man with a blue-blooded woman. Its impact on the bloodstream of your critic was a chilling one. Fifty years of the cinema, he thought, and this is where we've landed.'—*Richard Winnington*

Adventure in Baltimore
US 1949 89m bw
RKO (Richard H. Berger)
GB title: *Bachelor Bait*

In 1905, a young society girl becomes a suffragette.
Inconsequential period comedy which did nothing for its young star's fading career.
w Lionel Houser, *story* Christopher Isherwood, Lesser Samuels *d* Richard Wallace *ph* Robert de Grasse *m* Frederick Hollander

Shirley Temple, Robert Young, John Agar, Albert Sharpe, Josephine Hutchinson, Johnny Sands, John Miljan, Norma Varden

Adventure in Diamonds
US 1940 76m bw
Paramount (George Fitzmaurice)

A British adventurer in South Africa falls in love with a lady diamond thief.
Acceptable romantic comedy-drama.
w Leonard Lee, Franz Schultz *d* George Fitzmaurice *ph* Charles Lang

George Brent, Isa Miranda, John Loder, Nigel Bruce, Elizabeth Patterson, Matthew Boulton, Cecil Kellaway, Ernest Truex, E. E. Clive

Adventure in Iraq
US 1943 65m bw

Wartime second feature about Americans who fall into Nazi–Arab hands. Interesting only as a remake of *The Green Goddess*, with Paul Cavanagh in the George Arliss role. Also featuring John Loder, Ruth Ford. Written by George Bilson and Robert E. Kent; directed by D. Ross Lederman; for Warner.

Adventure in Manhattan
US 1936 73m bw
Columbia
GB title: *Manhattan Madness*

An actress helps an ace reporter to foil a bank robbery by a master criminal.
Flat romantic mystery comedy which wastes a good cast.
w Sidney Buchman, Harry Sauber, Jack Kirkland *d* Edward Ludwig *ph* Henry Freulich

Jean Arthur, Joel McCrea, Thomas Mitchell, Reginald Owen, Herman Bing

Adventure Island
US 1947 67m bw

Seafarers chance on an uncharted island, ruled by a deadly fanatic. Hokum rehash of Stevenson's *Ebb Tide*, with Paul Kelly as the madman; also featuring Rory Calhoun, Rhonda Fleming. Written by Maxwell Shane; directed by Peter Stewart; for Paramount.

The Adventure of Sherlock Holmes' Smarter Brother
GB 1975 91m De Luxe
TCF / Jouer (Richard A. Roth)

More by good luck than good management, Sherlock's younger brother solves one of his cases.
Infuriating parody with little sense of the original and a hit-or-miss style all of its own. Amusing moments fail to atone for the general waste of opportunity.
wd Gene Wilder *ph* Gerry Fisher *m* John Morris *pd* Terry Marsh

Gene Wilder, Marty Feldman, Madeleine Kahn, Leo McKern, Dom De Luise, Roy Kinnear, John Le Mesurier, Douglas Wilmer, Thorley Walters
  'Like a compilation of the kind of numbers actors like to do at parties.'—*Howard Kissel*
  'He has bitten off more than he can chew or I can swallow.'—*John Simon*
  'A few stray chuckles but nothing more.'—*Sight and Sound*
  'There's no mystery, and since you can't have a parody of a mystery without a mystery, there's no comic suspense.'—*New Yorker, 1980*
● *Video: CBS / Fox*

The Adventurer***
US 1917 21m approx (24 fps) bw silent
Mutual

An escaped convict rescues two wealthy women from drowning and is invited to their home.
Hilarious early Chaplin knockabout, with his physical gags at their most streamlined.
wd Charles Chaplin *ph* William C. Foster, Rollie Totheroh

Charles Chaplin, Edna Purviance, Eric Campbell, Henry Bergman

The Adventurers
GB 1950 86m bw
Rank / Mayflower (Maxwell Setton, Aubrey Baring)
US title: *The Great Adventure*

In 1902, two Boers and a cashiered English officer set out to recover stolen diamonds.
Lethargic South African western in the wake of *Treasure of the Sierra Madre*; clumsy and unconvincing, with cardboard characters.
w Robert Westerby *d* David MacDonald *ph* Oswald Morris *m* Cedric Thorpe Davie

Dennis Price, Jack Hawkins, Siobhan McKenna, Peter Hammond, Bernard Lee, Grégoire Aslan

The Adventurers*
US 1970 170m Technicolor Panavision
Paramount / Avco Embassy / Adventurers Film (Lewis Gilbert)

A sensualist brought up amid Europe's luxuries returns to his Central American homeland to take vengeance on the brutal security chief who raped and murdered his mother.
Sprawling, sexy, bloodstained extravaganza from a Harold Robbins novel. Expensive to look at and riddled with sensation, but that's about all.
w Michael Hastings, Lewis Gilbert *d* Lewis Gilbert *ph* Claude Renoir *m* Antonio Carlos Jobim *pd* Tony Masters

Bekim Fehmiu, Alan Badel, Candice Bergen, Ernest Borgnine, Olivia de Havilland, Rossano Brazzi, Charles Aznavour, Sidney Tafler, Fernando Rey, Leigh Taylor-Young, Thommy Berggren, John Ireland
  'A three-hour slog through every imaginable cliché of writing and direction . . . in addition to an abundance of flaccid sex and violence, it offers drugs, sadism, orchids, fireworks, orgies, lesbianism, a miscarriage, a private torture chamber, and the hell of several fashion shows with loud pop music accompaniment. This might well be described as the film with everything; trouble is, it is difficult to imagine anybody wanting any of it.'—*MFB*
  'Lovers of rotten movies and close-up violence can revel in it.'—*Judith Crist*

The Adventures of Arsène Lupin*
France / Italy 1956 103m Eastmancolor
Chavane-SNE-Gaumont / Lambor-Costellazione (Robert Sussfeld)

In 1912, the famous jewel thief conducts several successful robberies and outwits the Kaiser.
The most stylish Lupin film, though not based on the original stories.
w Jacques Becker, Albert Simonin, based on the character created by Maurice Leblanc *d* Jacques Becker *ph* Edmond Séchan *ad* Rino Mondellini

Robert Lamoureux, Lisolotte Pulver, Otto Hasse, Henri Rolland

The Adventures of Barry Mackenzie*
Australia 1972 114m Eastmancolor
Columbia / Longford (Philip Adams)

A sex-hungry Australian gets into all kinds of trouble on a visit to the Old Country.
Occasionally funny, defiantly crude and tasteless, but poorly produced comedy-misadventure from the *Private Eye* comic strip. Australian slang combines with bad sound recording to make much of the film unintelligible.
w Barry Humphries, Bruce Beresford *d* Bruce Beresford *ph* Don McAlpine *m* Peter Best

Barry Crocker, Barry Humphries (as Dame Edna Everage), Peter Cook, Spike Milligan,

Dennis Price, Avice Landon, Dick Bentley, Joan Bakewell, William Rushton

'A wildly uneven concoction of antipodean bad taste, probably only fully appreciated by Earls Court exiles.'—*Sight and Sound*
† Sequel 1974: *Barry Mackenzie Holds His Own*.

The Adventures of Bullwhip Griffin**
US 1965   110m   Technicolor
Walt Disney (Bill Anderson)

In the 1849 California Gold Rush, two aristocrats and their butler head west.
Rather splendid spoof western with careful attention to detail and comedy pointing, well above the average Disney standard.

w *Lowell S. Hawley, novel* By the Great Horn Spoon by Sid Fleischman   *d* James Neilson   *ph* Edward Colman   *m* George Bruns   *titles Ward Kimball*

Roddy McDowall, Suzanne Pleshette, Bryan Russell, Karl Malden, Harry Guardino, Richard Haydn, Mike Mazurki, Hermione Baddeley, Cecil Kellaway

The Adventures of Captain Fabian
US 1951   100m   bw
Republic / Silver (William Marshall)

A sea captain returns to New Orleans to revenge himself on the family which had defrauded his father.
Stilted, old-fashioned *Monte Cristo*ish melodrama with some curiosity value but little verve in the playing or production. An awful warning to independent producers.

w Errol Flynn, *novel* Fabulous Ann Medlock by Robert Shannon   *d* William Marshall   *ph* Marcel Grignon   *m* René Cloerec

Errol Flynn, Micheline Presle, Agnes Moorehead, Vincent Price, Victor Francen, Jim Gerald
† Made in France.

Adventures of Casanova
US 1948   83m   bw

Casanova returns to Sicily and helps overthrow the tyrannical rule of the King of Naples. Robin Hood transplanted, with a few amorous asides; but this is a totally stilted production which fails to entertain. Arturo de Cordova, Lucille Bremer, Turhan Bey.
Written by Crane Wilbur, Walter Bullock and Ken de Wolf; directed by Roberto Gavaldon; for Eagle-Lion.

The Adventures of Don Juan**
US 1949   110m   Technicolor
Warner (Jerry Wald)
GB title: *The New Adventures of Don Juan*

A reformed 17th-century rake saves his queen from the machinations of her first minister.
Expensive, slightly uneasy, but generally very entertaining swashbuckler with elements of self-spoofery. Flynn's last big-budget extravaganza.

w George Oppenheimer, Harry Kurnitz   *d* Vincent Sherman   *ph* Elwood Bredell   *m* Max Steiner

Errol Flynn, Viveca Lindfors, Romney Brent, Robert Douglas, Alan Hale, Ann Rutherford, Robert Warwick, Jerry Austin, Douglas Kennedy, Una O'Connor, Aubrey Mather, Raymond Burr

The Adventures of Gerard**
GB 1970   91m   De Luxe   Panavision
UA / Sir Nigel Films (Peter Beale)

A hussar of Napoleon becomes involved in a double spy game but comes out trumps and wins a fair lady.
A lighthearted historical spoof of military pomp, with plenty of attractive elements which unfortunately fail to jell into a satisfying film.

w H. A. L. Craig and others, from stories by Arthur Conan Doyle   *d* Jerzy Skolimowski   *ph* Witold Sobocinski   *m* Riz Ortolani

Peter McEnery, Claudia Cardinale, Eli Wallach, Jack Hawkins, Mark Burns, Norman Rossington, John Neville

'Enormously graceful and witty . . . picks its way with amazing delicacy through the reefs of facetiousness.'—*Tom Milne*

The Adventures of Hajji Baba*
US 1954   93m   De Luxe   Cinemascope
Allied Artists / Walter Wanger

In ancient Arabia, a barber helps and falls in love with an escaping princess.
A reasonably dashing sword and sandal romp which no one takes very seriously.

w Richard Collins   *d* Don Weis   *ph* Harold Lipstein   *m* Dmitri Tiomkin   *pd* Gene Allen

John Derek, Elaine Stewart, Thomas Gomez, Amanda Blake, Paul Picerni, Rosemarie Bowe

The Adventures of Huckleberry Finn:
see Huckleberry Finn

The Adventures of Marco Polo*
US 1938   100m   bw
Samuel Goldwyn

The medieval Italian explorer discovers China, fireworks, and a beautiful maiden.
One gets the impression that this began as a standard adventure and that during production it switched to comedy; whatever the cause, lively and amusing scenes fail to add up to more than a thinly scripted pantomime.

w Robert E. Sherwood   *d* Archie Mayo   *ph* Rudolph Maté   *m* Hugo Friedhofer   *md* Alfred Newman   *ad* Richard Day

Gary Cooper, Sigrid Gurie, Basil Rathbone, Ernest Truex, Binnie Barnes, Alan Hale, George Barbier

'In spite of its elaborate settings and the presence of Gary Cooper, it never quite lives up to its promises.'—*New York Sun*

'Goldwyn's most ambitious endeavour . . . deserves and will get enthusiastic exhibitor plugging. Sherwood's more concerned with entertainment than with history.'—*Variety*
† Release prints were in sepiatone.

The Adventures of Mark Twain**
US 1944   130m   bw
Warner (Jesse L. Lasky)

The life of America's foremost humorous writer, from a Mississippi riverboat to his becoming an honorary fellow of Oxford University.
Conventional biopic, quite watchable and with unusual side turnings, but eventually lacking the zest of the subject.

w Harold M. Sherman, Alan le May, Harry Chandler   *d* Irving Rapper   *ph* Sol Polito   *m* Max Steiner

Fredric March, Alexis Smith, Donald Crisp, Alan Hale, C. Aubrey Smith, John Carradine, William Henry, Robert Barrat, Walter Hampden

'It's not that it's much worse than most cinematized biographies, because it does have its good moments. It's just that once more biographical inaccuracy is rampant, and once more the best dramatic possibilities have been overlooked, so it's hard to think of anything new, in the line of protest, to say.'—*David Lardner, New Yorker*

AAN: Max Steiner

The Adventures of Martin Eden
US 1942   87m   bw

A sailor exposes intolerable conditions on cargo ships. Low-budget hokum. Glenn Ford, Claire Trevor, Evelyn Keyes, Stuart Erwin, Dickie Moore. Written by W. L. River from the novel by Jack London; directed by Sidney Salkow; for B. P. Schulberg / Samuel Bronston / Columbia.

'Only the rainbow can duplicate its brilliance!'
The Adventures of Robin Hood****
US 1938   102m   Technicolor
Warner (Hal B. Wallis)

Rebel outlaw Robin Hood outwits Guy of Gisbourne and the Sheriff of Nottingham, and saves the throne for the absent King Richard.
A splendid adventure story, rousingly operatic in treatment, with dashing action highlights, fine comedy balance, and incisive acting all round. Historically notable for its use of early three-colour Technicolor; also for convincingly recreating Britain in California.

w *Seton I. Miller, Norman Reilly Raine   d William Keighley, Michael Curtiz   ph Tony Gaudio, Sol Polito, Howard Green   m Erich Wolfgang Korngold   ad Carl Jules Weyl*

Errol Flynn (Sir Robin of Locksley), *Basil Rathbone* (Sir Guy of Gisbourne), *Claude Rains* (Prince John), Olivia de Havilland (Maid Marian), *Alan Hale* (Little John), Patric Knowles (Will Scarlet), *Eugene Pallette* (Friar Tuck), *Ian Hunter* (King Richard), *Melville Cooper* (Sheriff of Nottingham), Una O'Connor (Bess), Herbert Mundin (Much the Miller's Son), Montagu Love (Bishop of Black Canons), Howard Hill (Captain of Archers)

PRINCE JOHN: 'Any objections to the new tax, from our Saxon friends?'

ROBIN to Gisbourne during duel: 'Did I upset your plans?'

THE ADVENTURES OF MARK TWAIN. Alan Hale in the jumping frog episode is watched critically by Frederic March in the first of many moustaches.

GISBOURNE: 'You've come to Nottingham once too often!'
ROBIN: 'When this is over, my friend, there'll be no need for me to come again!'
PRINCE JOHN: 'Ho, varlets, bring Sir Robin food! Such insolence must support a healthy appetite!'
ROBIN: 'It's injustice I hate, not the Normans!'
'Magnificent, unsurpassable . . . the film is lavish, brilliantly photographed, and has a great Korngold score.'—*NFT, 1974*
'Mostly the picture is full ot movement, some of it dashing in fine romantic costume style, some of it just sprightly. The excitement comes from fast action – galloping steeds, men swinging Tarzan-like from the trees, hurling tables and chairs, rapid running swordplay, the sudden whiz of Robin's arrows coming from nowhere to startle his enemies – more than from any fear that Robin might be worsted. Somehow the whole thing has the air of being a costume party, a jolly and rather athletic one, with a lot of well-bred Englishmen playing at being in the greenwood.'—*James Shelley Hamilton, National Board of Review*
† At the time of its release this was Warners' most expensive film, costing more than two million dollars. Chico, California, stood in for Sherwood Forest; the archery contest was shot at Busch Gardens, Pasadena. Curtiz took over direction when it was felt that the action lacked impact.
AA: Erich Wolfgang Korngold; Carl Jules Weyl
AAN: best picture
● *Video: Warner*

The Adventures of Robinson Crusoe***
Mexico 1953   89m   Pathecolor
Tepeyac (Oscar Dancigers, Henry F. Ehrlich)

A 17th-century mariner is shipwrecked on an uninhabited tropical island.
Fascinating version of a famous story, with only one character on screen until the belated arrival of Friday and the escape to civilization. Subtle and compelling, with only the colour unsatisfactory.

w Luis Bunuel, Phillip Roll, novel Daniel Defoe *d Luis Bunuel ph* Alex Phillips *m* Anthony Collins

Dan O'Herlihy, James Fernandez
'A film of which the purity, the tense poetic style, evokes a kind of wonder.'—*Gavin Lambert*
'Free of that deadly solicitude which usually kills off classics.'—*New Yorker, 1977*
AAN: Dan O'Herlihy

The Adventures of Sherlock Holmes***
US 1939   83m   bw
TCF (Gene Markey)
GB title: *Sherlock Holmes*

Moriarty sends Holmes on a false trail while he plots to steal the Crown jewels.
Highly engaging piece of Hollywood Victoriana, with all elements perfect except for an unconvincing plot.

w Edwin Blum, William Drake *d* Alfred Werker *ph Leon Shamroy m* Cyril Mockridge

Basil Rathbone (Holmes), *Nigel Bruce* (Dr Watson), *George Zucco* (Moriarty), Ida Lupino (Ann Brandon), Alan Marshal (Jerrold Hunter), Terry Kilburn (Billy), E. E. Clive (Inspector Bristol), Henry Stephenson (Sir Ronald Ramsgate), Mary Gordon (Mrs Hudson)
'The "elementary my dear Watson" type of dialogue is soft-pedalled for more modern phrases or understandable patter.'—*Variety*
'Told with more movie art per foot than seven reels of anything the intellectual men have been finding good this whole year or more.'—*Otis Ferguson*
† This was the second and last of Rathbone's costume outings as Holmes, and the one in which he sang a comic song in disguise.

The Adventures of Tartu*
GB 1943   103m   bw
MGM (Irving Asher)
US title: *Tartu*

During World War II, a British spy goes to Czechoslovakia to dismantle a poison gas factory.
Halting and artificial comedy-thriller, saved only by a graceful star performance.

w Howard Emmett Rogers, John Lee Mahin, Miles Malleson *d* Harold S. Bucquet *ph* John J. Cox *m* Hubert Bath *md* Louis Levy

Robert Donat, Valerie Hobson, Walter Rilla, Glynis Johns, Martin Miller
'You are seeing all it has, and bald spots as well, first time around, whereas with a good Hitchcock or even a good Carol Reed, the pleasures visible at a first seeing stand up, or intensify, at a third or a fifth.'—*James Agee*

Adventures of the Wilderness Family
US 1975   101m   colour

An urban family runs into trouble when it takes to the wilds. Naïve little four-wall family movie in which the pretty scenery (Utah and the Canadian Rockies) and the animals compensate for the dramatic inadequacies. Robert Logan, Susan Damante Shaw. Written and directed by Stewart Raffil; for Pacific International. (*Further Adventures of the Wilderness Family* appeared in 1977.)

The Adventures of Tom Sawyer***
US 1938   91m   Technicolor
David O. Selznick (William H. Wright)

Small-town Mississippi boy tracks down a murderer, Injun Joe.
Set-bound but excellent version of the children's classic by Mark Twain.
w John Weaver *d* Norman Taurog *ph* James Wong Howe, Wilfrid Cline *m* Max Steiner *ad* William Cameron Menzies

Tommy Kelly (Tom), *May Robson* (Aunt Polly), Walter Brennan (Muff Potter), Victor Jory (Injun Joe), Victor Kilian (Sheriff), Jackie Moran (Huckleberry Finn), Ann Gillis (Becky Thatcher), Donald Meek (Sunday School Superintendent), Margaret Hamilton (Mrs Sawyer), Marcia Mae Jones (Mary Sawyer)
'Another Selznick box office clean-up, an attraction destined for extended first runs, repeat bookings and heavy matinée take.'—*Variety*
'The familiar characters emerge in all their old amiability, the atmosphere is there and so is the excitement.'—*MFB*
'Should make Mark Twain circulate in his grave like a trout in a creel.'—*Otis Ferguson*
● *Video: Guild*

Advice to the Lovelorn
US 1933 62m bw

A reporter is demoted to the lonelyhearts column and becomes absorbed in it. Springy vehicle for Lee Tracy, with Sally Blaine, Sterling Holloway, Isabel Jewell; from Nathanael West's novel *Miss Lonelyhearts*; directed by Darryl Zanuck; for Fox. (Compare the Paul Muni vehicle *Hi Nellie*.)

'Are the men and women of Washington really like this?'
Advise and Consent**
US 1962 139m bw Panavision
Columbia / Alpha-Alpina / Otto Preminger

The President's choice of an unpopular secretary of state leads to divisions in the Senate and the blackmail and suicide of a senator.
Absorbing political melodrama from a novel which aimed to lift the lid on Washington. Many character actors make their mark, but the harsh-contrast photography seems misjudged.
w Wendell Mayes, *novel* Allen Drury *d* Otto Preminger *ph* Sam Leavitt *m* Jerry Fielding *titles* Saul Bass

Don Murray, *Charles Laughton,* Henry Fonda, Walter Pidgeon, Lew Ayres, Edward Andrews, Burgess Meredith, Gene Tierney, Franchot Tone, George Grizzard, Paul Ford, Peter Lawford, Inga Swenson, Will Geer
'The result is supremely ambivalent, a battle between fascinatingly real props and procedures and melodramatically unreal characters and situations.'—*Peter John Dyer*
'The parade of people helps to take one's mind off the overwrought melodrama.'—*New Yorker, 1980*

Aelita*
USSR 1924 70m approx bw silent
Mezhrabpom

Two Russian rocket pioneers land on Mars and start a revolution against the planet's queen.
Notable early space fiction, with footage of twenties Moscow as well as interesting set designs.
w Fedor Ozep, Alexei Faiko, *novel* Alexei Tolstoy *d* Yakov Protazanov *ph* Yuri Zhelabuzhsky *pd* Sergei Kozlovsky

Yulia Solntseva, Nikolai Batalov, Igor Ilinsky

Aerograd**
USSR 1935 81m bw
Mosfilm-Ukrainfilm
aka: *Frontier*

Guards keep Japanese spies out of Siberia, where an airport is being built.
An action film with style and pretensions.
wd Alexander Dovzhenko *ph* Edouard Tissé, Mikhail Gindin

Semyon Shagaida, Stepan Shkurat, Sergei Stolyarov

Affair in Trinidad*
US 1952 98m bw
Columbia / Beckworth (Vincent Sherman)

A nightclub singer whose husband is killed by gangsters works undercover for the police and routs the gang with the help of her husband's brother.
A tired tropical melodrama intended to follow up the success of *Gilda,* but without the verve. Some routine pleasures, though.
w Oscar Saul, James Gunn *d* Vincent Sherman *ph* Joseph Walker *m* Morris Stoloff, George Dunning

Rita Hayworth, Glenn Ford, Alexander Scourby, Torin Thatcher, Valerie Bettis, Steve Geray, Karel Stepanek, George Voskovec
'Improbable, foolish, but glossy.'—*Penelope Houston*

An Affair to Remember**
US 1957 114m Eastmancolor
Cinemascope
TCF (Leo McCarey)

An ex-nightclub singer falls in love with a wealthy bachelor on a transatlantic liner, but an accident prevents her from attending their subsequent rendezvous.
Remake of *Love Affair,* a surprisingly successful mixture of smart lines, sentiment and tears, all applied with style and assurance.
w Delmer Daves, Leo McCarey *d* Leo McCarey *ph* Milton Krasner *m* Hugo Friedhofer

Cary Grant, Deborah Kerr, Cathleen Nesbitt, Richard Denning, Neva Patterson
'A lush slice of Hollywood romanticism.'—*MFB*
'90 masterly minutes of entrancing light comedy and 25 beastly minutes of beastly, melodramatic, pseudo-tragic guff.'—*Paul Dehn*
AAN: Milton Krasner; Hugo Friedhofer; title song (*m* Harry Warren, *ly* Harold Adamson, Leo McCarey)

Affair with a Stranger*
US 1953 87m bw
RKO (Robert Sparks)

Five friends reminisce about a marriage which seems about to break up.
This would-be-smart comedy has a good idea unsatisfactorily worked out, and could have used a more sparkling cast.
w Richard Flournoy *d* Roy Rowland *ph* Harry J. Wild *m* Roy Webb

Jean Simmons, Victor Mature, Mary Jo Tarola, Monica Lewis, Jane Darwell, Nicholas Joy, Wally Vernon, Dabbs Greer

L'Affaire est dans le Sac*
France 1932 47m bw
Pathé / Nathan
aka: *It's in the Bag*

Two would-be kidnappers end up (a) married to and (b) employed by their intended victims.
Semi-professional nonsense comedy with political jokes.
w Jacques Prévert *d* Pierre Prévert *ph* A. Giboury, Eli Lotar *m* Maurice Jaubert

J.-P. Le Chanois, Jacques Brunius, Etienne Decroux, Lucien Raimbourg, Julien Carette, Lora Hays

Affairs of a Gentleman
US 1934 68m bw

A novelist who has used all his love affairs in his novels holds a reunion. Mild star vehicle which wastes an amusing idea. Paul Lukas, Leila Hyams, Onslow Stevens. Written by Cyril Hume, Peter Ruric and Milton Krims; directed by Edwin L. Marin; for Universal.

The Affairs of Anatol*
US 1921 95m approx (24 fps) bw
silent
Famous Players–Lasky / de Mille–Paramount

A socialite interrupts his honeymoon to go looking for romance.
Dated but historically very interesting sophisticated farce from a time when Hollywood was aping Viennese naughtiness.
w Jeanie MacPherson, Beulah Marie Dix, Lorna Moon, Elmer Harris, from Granville Barker's paraphrase of the play Anatol by Arthur Schnitzler *d* Cecil B. de Mille *ph* Alvin Wyckoff, Karl Struss *ed* Anne Bauchens

Wallace Reid, Gloria Swanson, Bebe Daniels, Elliott Dexter, Monte Blue, Wanda Hawley, Theodore Roberts
'Should be enormously popular, especially with those who think Schnitzler is a cheese.'—*Robert E. Sherwood*
'The man who doesn't sell out for every performance of a double run should turn his show shop into a Quaker meeting house.'—*Motion Picture Herald*

The Affairs of Annabel*
US 1938 69m bw
RKO (Lee Marcus, Lou Lusty)

A crackpot Hollywood press agent sends his star to jail as a publicity stunt.
An amusing frenetic comedy of its time, successful enough to warrant a sequel, *Annabel Takes a Tour*, in the same year.

w Bert Granet, Paul Yawitz d Lew Landers ph Russell Metty m Roy Webb

Lucille Ball, Jack Oakie, Ruth Donnelly, Bradley Page, Fritz Feld, Thurston Hall, Elizabeth Risdon, Granville Bates, James Burke

The Affairs of Cellini*
US 1934 90m bw
Twentieth Century (Darryl F. Zanuck)
The complex amours of a 16th-century Florentine rake.
Lively period bedroom farce somewhat hampered by censorship.

w Bess Meredyth, *play* The Firebrand by Edwin Justus Mayer d Gregory La Cava ph Charles Rosher m Alfred Newman

Fredric March, Constance Bennett, *Frank Morgan*, Fay Wray, Vince Barnett, Louis Calhern, Jessie Ralph
'Gay and entertaining though whipped up synthetically like circus ice cream.'—*Variety*
AAN: Charles Rosher; Frank Morgan

The Affairs of Dobie Gillis
US 1953 74m bw
MGM (Arthur M. Loew Jnr)
Adventures of an indolent and accident-prone university student.
Scatty comedy with good talent and musical numbers encased in a tatty production.

w Max Shulman d Don Weis ph William Mellor md Jeff Alexander

Bobby Van, Debbie Reynolds, Hans Conried, Barbara Ruick, Bob Fosse

The Affairs of Martha
US 1942 66m bw
A servant writes a scandalous book about her employers. Fairly amusing comedy with an ingratiating cast: Marsha Hunt, Richard Carlson, Spring Byington, Allyn Joslyn, Frances Drake, Margaret Hamilton, Melville Cooper, Virginia Weidler, Ernest Truex, Marjorie Main. Written by Isobel Lennart and Lee Gold; directed by Jules Dassin; for MGM. (GB title: *Once Upon a Thursday*.)

'She's so romantic she drives four men frantic!'
The Affairs of Susan**
US 1945 110m bw
Paramount (Hal B. Wallis)
Four men in Susan's life see her differently. Occasionally witty comedy designed as a champagne vehicle for its star. It seemed quite good at the time.

w Richard Flournoy, *original story* Laszlo Gorog, T. Monroe d William A. Seiter ph David Abel m Frederick Hollander

Joan Fontaine, George Brent, Walter Abel, Don Defore, Dennis O'Keefe

'The cast enters into the irresponsibilities with gusto.'—*MFB*
'A bright thing, a bit too long.'—*Richard Mallett, Punch*
AAN: Laszlo Gorog, T. Monroe

Affectionately Yours
US 1941 88m bw
Warner (Mark Hellinger)
A foreign correspondent hurries home when he hears that his wife plans to divorce him. Thin lightweight comedy, unsuitably cast.

w Edward Kaufman d Lloyd Bacon ph Tony Gaudio m Heinz Roemheld

Merle Oberon, Dennis Morgan, *Rita Hayworth*, George Tobias, Ralph Bellamy, James Gleason, Hattie McDaniel

Africa Screams
US 1949 79m bw
Two dumbbells go on safari with a treasure map. Lower-case Abbott and Costello comedy, with Hillary Brooke, Max Baer, Shemp Howard. Written by Earl Baldwin; directed by Charles Barton; for Edward Nassour / UA.
● *Video: European Video*

Africa Texas Style*
GB 1967 109m Eastmancolor
Paramount / Vantors (Andrew Marton)
A Kenyan settler hires two Texas cowboys to help in his scheme of wild game ranching. Excellent location sequences are dragged down by a very boring script, but it's a good family film nevertheless.

w Andy White d Andrew Marton ph Paul Beeson m Malcolm Arnold

John Mills, Hugh O'Brian, Nigel Green, Tom Nardini, Adrienne Corri, Ronald Howard
† Forerunner of TV series, *Cowboy in Africa*.
● *Video: Guild*

'They never dreamed of being in each other's arms, yet the mystic spell of the jungle swept them to primitive, hungry embrace! The greatest adventure a man ever had . . . with a woman!'
The African Queen***
GB 1951 103m Technicolor
IFD / Romulus–Horizon (Sam Spiegel)
In 1915, a gin-drinking river trader and a prim missionary make odd companions for a boat trip down a dangerous river, culminating in an attack on a German gunboat.
Despite some unfortunate studio sets mixed in with real African footage achieved through great hardship by all concerned, this is one of those surprising films that really work, a splendidly successful mixture of comedy, character and adventure.

w James Agee, *novel* C. S. Forester d John Huston ph Jack Cardiff m Allan Gray

Humphrey Bogart (Charlie Allnutt), *Katharine Hepburn* (Rose Sayer), Robert Morley (The Rev. Samuel Sayer), Peter Bull (Captain), Theodore Bikel (2nd Officer)

ROSE: 'I never dreamed that any experience could be so stimulating!'
'Entertaining but not entirely plausible or original.'—*Robert Hatch*
'The movie is not great art but it is great fun, essentially one long, exciting, old-fashioned movie chase.'—*Time*
'A Technicolor Cook's Tour of jungle wonders, enriched by performances unmatched by anything Hepburn or Bogart have yet contributed to the screen.'—*Cue*
† Peter Viertel's book, *White Hunter Black Heart*, is basically about Huston during the making of this film.
AA: Humphrey Bogart
AAN: James Agee; John Huston; Katharine Hepburn
● *Video: CBS / Fox*

After Office Hours
GB 1932 78m bw
A bird's-eye view of life in a City of London office. Popular film version of a popular play which would now seem almost Dickensian. Frank Lawton, Heather Angel, Viola Lyel, Garry Marsh, Eileen Peel, Frank Royde, Katie Johnson. Written by Thomas Bentley and Frank Launder, from the play *London Wall* by John Van Druten; directed by Thomas Bentley; for British International.

After Office Hours*
US 1935 75m bw
MGM (Bernard H. Hyman)
A newspaperman and his socialite reporter solve a murder mystery.
Crisply-written, fast-moving comedy melodrama; good stuff of its time and type.

w Herman J. Mankiewicz d Robert Z. Leonard ph Charles Rosher

Clark Gable, Constance Bennett, Stuart Erwin, Billie Burke, Harvey Stephens, Katherine Alexander, Henry Travers, Henry Armetta
'One of the best balanced pix of the season; it has practically everything.'—*Film Daily*
'Mildly satisfactory entertainment . . . story deficiencies are surprising . . . Gable and Bennett will have to carry this one.'—*Variety*

After the Ball*
GB 1957 89m Eastmancolor
IFD / Beaconsfield (Peter Rogers)
The life and loves of music-hall singer Vesta Tilley, who married into the nobility. Adequate if uninspired biopic with entertaining detail and songs.

w Hubert Gregg d Compton Bennett ph Jack Asher ad Norman Arnold md Muir Mathieson

Pat Kirkwood, Laurence Harvey, Clive Morton, Jerry Verno, June Clyde

After the Fox*
US / Italy 1966 103m Technicolor Panavision
UA / Nancy / CCM (John Bryan)
The Fox escapes from jail to execute a gold

bullion caper and save his young sister from the streets.

Unlikeable and unfunny farce which sets its star among excitable Italians and hopes for the best, adding a few wild stabs at satire on movie-making styles.

w Neil Simon, Cesare Zavattini d Vittorio de Sica ph Leonida Barboni m Burt Bacharach

Peter Sellers, Victor Mature (agreeably sending up his old image), Britt Ekland, Lilia Brazzi, Paola Stoppa, Akim Tamiroff, Martin Balsam

'Never even begins to get off the ground.'—MFB

After the Thin Man**
US 1936 113m bw
MGM (Hunt Stromberg)

Nick and Nora Charles, not forgetting Asta, solve another murder.

Overlong but well-carpentered sequel to The Thin Man, developing the thesis that a married couple, even if they are detectives and drink too much, can be interesting and lovable.

w Frances Goodrich, Albert Hackett d W. S. Van Dyke II ph Oliver T. Marsh m Herbert Stothart, Edward Ward

William Powell, Myrna Loy, James Stewart, Elissa Landi, Joseph Calleia, Jessie Ralph, Alan Marshal, Sam Levene

'It is evident that it was almost impossible to make a better mystery comedy than The Thin Man. Early speed would have helped, but . . . few films this season have contained more risibles.'—Variety

AAN: Frances Goodrich; Albert Hackett

After Tomorrow
US 1932 70m bw

Family troubles and small salaries prevent a young couple from getting married. Rather curious drama which was sold on the fact that it retained the sex discussion from its stage original. Charles Farrell, Marian Nixon, Minna Gombell, Josephine Hull, William Collier Snr, William Pawley. Written by Sonia Levien from the play by John Golden and Hugh Strange; directed by Frank Borzage; for Fox. 'In several sequences it pioneers for the picture business. That financial success is doubtful is rather unfortunate.'—Variety

After Tonight
US 1933 71m bw

During World War I a Russian lady spy falls for an Austrian officer. Tediously talky romantic vehicle which barely gets started before it bogs down. Constance Bennett, Gilbert Roland, Edward Ellis, Mischa Auer. Written by Jane Murfin; directed by George Archainbaud; for RKO. (GB title: Sealed Lips.)

Against All Flags*
US 1952 83m Technicolor
U-I (Howard Christie)

A daring British seaman routs Spanish ships at the request of the king.

Standard pirate yarn, almost Flynn's last swashbuckler; production below par.

w Aeneas Mackenzie, Joseph Hoffman d George Sherman ph Russell Metty m Hans Salter

Errol Flynn, Maureen O'Hara, Anthony Quinn, Mildred Natwick

† Remade as The King's Pirate (qv).

Against All Odds
US 1984 121m Metrocolor
Columbia / Delphi (Jerry Bick)

An unemployed football player is hired by a bookmaker to find his missing wife.

Complex and lugubrious remake of Out of the Past (qv), which long outstays its welcome.

w Eric Hughes d Taylor Hackford ph Donald Thorin, E. Pershing Flynn m Michel Colombier, Larry Carlton ad Richard James Lawrence

Jeff Bridges, Rachel Ward, James Woods, Richard Widmark, Jane Greer (from the original cast), Alex Karras, Dorian Harewood, Swoosie Kurtz

'It has so many convoluted double crosses that each time you are told what was really going on behind the scene you just witnessed, you care less.'—Time Out

'A tedious concatenation of narrative twists.'—MFB

Against the Wind**
GB 1947 96m bw
Ealing (Sidney Cole)

In London during World War II, men and women are trained as saboteurs, and one of them is a traitor.

Thoughtful, well-made spy thriller with good performances.

w T. E. B. Clarke, Michael Pertwee d Charles Crichton ph Lionel Banes m Leslie Bridgewater

Simone Signoret, Robert Beatty, Jack Warner, Gordon Jackson, Paul Dupuis, Gisele Preville, John Slater, Peter Illing, James Robertson Justice

Agatha*
GB 1978 105m Technicolor
Warner / First Artists / Sweetall / Casablanca (Jarvis Astaire, Gavrik Losey)

In 1926, Agatha Christie disappears after marital difficulties and tries to commit suicide in a Harrogate hotel under a pseudonym.

Lushly recreated but still imaginary and unconvincing solution to a real-life disappearance, complete with romantic encounter with an American newspaperman.

w Kathleen Tynan, Arthur Hopcraft d Michael Apted ph Vittorio Storaro m Johnny Mandel pd Shirley Russell

Vanessa Redgrave, Dustin Hoffman, Timothy Dalton, Helen Morse, Timothy West, Tony Britton, Alan Badel

'With its shadowy characters, paucity of plot, and an abundance of stylistic red herrings, one doubts whether Agatha would have met Mrs Christie's own requirements for a thriller, though she may well have enjoyed its sumptuous recreation of hotel interiors in the 1920s.'—Geoff Brown, MFB

'It has a general air of knowingness, but seems to be missing the scenes which would explain why it was made.'—New Yorker

L'Âge d'Or**
France 1930 63m bw
Vicomte de Noailles

A collection of strange events satirizing religion and the social order.

Deliberately shocking and possibly quite meaningless, this truly surrealist film is chiefly interesting now for its flashforwards to Bunuel's later work.

w Luis Bunuel, Salvador Dali d Luis Bunuel ph Albert Dubergen

Gaston Modot, Lya Lys, Max Ernst, Pierre Prévert, Jacques Brunius

'In some way the juxtaposition of images causes in almost every spectator a train of reactions of unprecedented violence.'—Basil Wright, 1972

'The story is also a sequence of moral and surrealist aesthetic. The sexual instinct and the sense of death form its substance.'—Luis Buñuel

'It retains its outrageous anarchic vitality, as though unwilling to admit its age.'—Observer 1980

The Age for Love
US 1931 81m bw
(UA) Howard Hughes

A wife does not want children; her husband leaves her and marries a woman who does. Shapeless and would-be shocking, this forgotten film was written off as soon as it was made.

w Robert E. Sherwood, Frank Lloyd, Ernest Pascal, from the latter's novel d Frank Lloyd

Billie Dove, Adrian Morris, Charles Starrett, Lois Wilson, Edward Everett Horton, Mary Duncan

'Everybody makes mistakes, and this is one by Howard Hughes.'—Variety

Age of Consent*
Australia 1969 103m Technicolor
Columbia / Nautilus (James Mason, Michael Powell)

An artist seduces the granddaughter of a drunken harridan with whom he shares a Barrier Reef island.

Mildly likeable but self-conscious and overlong South Pacific idyll.

w Peter Yeldham, novel Norman Lindsay d Michael Powell ph Hannes Staudinger m Stanley Myers

James Mason, Helen Mirren, Jack McGowran, Neva Carr-Glyn, Frank Thring

Age of Indiscretion
US 1935 80m bw

A high-minded publisher finds that his wife is unfaithful. Tolerable marital drama about child custody. Paul Lukas, Helen Vinson, May Robson, Madge Evans, Ralph Forbes. Written by Lenore Coffee; directed by Edward Ludwig; for MGM.

Age of Innocence
US 1934 71m bw

In the 1870s, a young attorney's career is threatened when he falls in love with a divorcee. Dated romantic drama, rather thinly performed and presented. Irene Dunne, John Boles, Lionel Atwill, Laura Hope Crews, Helen Westley, Julie Haydon. Written by Sarah Y. Mason, Victor Heerman, from the novel by Edith Wharton; directed by Philip Moeller; for RKO. 'It will take smart selling to protect it at the box office, especially away from the social registers of the land.'—Variety

Age of Innocence
Canada / GB 1977 101m Eastmancolor
Judson / Willoughby (Henning Jacobsen)

After World War I, an English teacher in Canada develops pacifist views which stir up local resentment and lead to violence. Rather uninteresting melodrama which never really comes to the boil despite care all round.

w Ratch Wallace d Alan Bridges ph Brian West m Lucio Agostini

David Warner, Honor Blackman, Trudy Young, Cec Linder, Tim Henry, Lois Maxwell, Robert Hawkins

The Agitator*
GB 1944 98m bw
British National (Louis H. Jackson)

An embittered mechanic becomes a loud-mouthed union spokesman, but fate eventually takes him into management. Fairly absorbing, modest narrative of the flaws of socialism.

w Edward Dryhurst, novel Peter Pettinger by William Riley d John Harlow ph James Wilson

William Hartnell (then being built into a star), Mary Morris, John Laurie, Moore Marriott, George Carney, Edward Rigby, Elliot Mason, Frederick Leister, Cathleen Nesbitt, Moira Lister

The Agony and the Ecstasy*
US 1965 140m De Luxe Todd-AO
TCF / International Classics Inc (Carol Reed)

Pope Julius II persuades Michelangelo to leave his sculptures and paint the ceiling of the Sistine Chapel. Dully reverent comic strip approach to art and history; generally heavy going, but good looking.

w Philip Dunne, novel Irving Stone d Carol Reed ph Leon Shamroy m Alex North pd John de Cuir

Charlton Heston, Rex Harrison, Diane Cilento, Harry Andrews, Alberto Lupo, Adolfo Celi

JULIUS: 'You dare to dicker with your pontiff?'

'The vulgarity of the whole concept has none of the joyfully enthusiastic philistinism of a de Mille; rather its tone is a dry, almost cynical, condescension.'—Brenda Davies

'All agony, no ecstasy.'—Judith Crist

'Not a strong and soaring drama but an illustrated lecture of a slow artist at work.'—Bosley Crowther

† Michelangelo was apparently both a dwarf and a homosexual. He is played by Charlton Heston.

AAN: Leon Shamroy; Alex North

● Video: CBS / Fox

Aguirre, Wrath of God**
West Germany 1972 95m colour
Werner Herzog / Hessicher Rundfunk

In 1560, one of Pizarro's lieutenants takes a party of forty down river by raft, and succumbs to megalomania. Absorbing conquistador melodrama, vividly assembled and impossible to forget.

wd Werner Herzog ph Thomas Mauch m Popol Vuh

Klaus Kinski, Ruy Guerra, Helena Rojo, Cecilia Rivera

'It ingeniously combines Herzog's gift for deep irony, his strong social awareness, and his worthy ambition to fashion a whole new visual perspective on the world around us via mystical, evocative, yet oddly direct imagery. It is a brilliant cinematic achievement.'—David Skerritt, Christian Science Monitor

● Video: Palace

'The play that startled the nation!'
Ah, Wilderness**
US 1935 101m bw
MGM (Hunt Stromberg)

Problems of a small-town family at the turn of the century. Well-acted, affectionately remembered version of a play later musicalized as Summer Holiday. The commercial success of this film led to the Hardy family series.

w Albert Hackett, Frances Goodrich, play Eugene O'Neill d Clarence Brown ph Clyde de Vinna m Herbert Stothart

Wallace Beery, Lionel Barrymore, Eric Linden, Spring Byington, Mickey Rooney, Aline MacMahon, Charley Grapewin, Cecilia Parker, Frank Albertson, Bonita Granville

'A job of picture making, in craftsmanship and feeling, that is wonderful to see.'—Otis Ferguson

'That it is a fine artistic effort will not be denied anywhere, but for the public at large it will need all the boosting it can get.'—Variety

Ai No Corrida*
France / Japan 1976 105m Eastmancolor
Argos / Oshima / Shibata (Anatole Dauman)
French title: L'Empire des Sens
aka: Empire of the Passions; Empire of the Senses

A sexually complicated servant girl has an intense affair with the master of the house, and finally murders and mutilates him. Strong but stylish stuff, a kind of Japanese Last Tango in Paris. Those who like this kind of thing will like it a lot.

wd Nagisa Oshima ph Hideo Ito m Minoru Miki

Tatsuya Fuji, Eiko Matsuda, Aoi Nakajima, Meika Seri

'By the final sequence, we are all implicated in the continuing social system which makes such love impossible. It is not Sade, but the censor in all of us who ultimately wields the knife.'—Jan Dawson, MFB

Aida
Italy 1953 95m Ferraniacolor
Oscar Film (Ferrucio de Martino, Federico Teti)

A young Egyptian army officer loves the captive princess of the Ethiopians. Stuffy, over-dressed, pantomimish version of the opera, with some pretension to cinematic vitality.

w various, from Verdi's opera d Clemente Fracassi ph Piero Portalupi ad Flavio Mogherini

Sophia Loren (sung by Renata Tebaldi), Lois Maxwell, Luciano della Marra

Ain't Misbehavin'*
US 1955 81m Technicolor
U-I (Samuel Marx)

A young millionaire marries a cabaret girl, who determines to improve her mind and manners. Lively American version of Pygmalion, with musical numbers and some bright lines.

w Edward Buzzell, Philip Rapp, Devery Freeman d Edward Buzzell ph Wilfrid Cline m Joseph Gershenson ch Kenny Williams, Lee Scott

Rory Calhoun, Piper Laurie, Reginald Gardiner, Jack Carson, Barbara Britton, Mamie Van Doren

'Are you going to let that boy go up alone?'
Air Cadet
US 1951 94m bw

Problems of an air force flight instructor. Routine flagwaver. Stephen McNally, Alex Nicol, Gail Russell, Richard Long, Charles Drake, Rock Hudson. Written by Robert L. Richards; directed by Joseph Pevney; for Universal-International. (GB title: Jet Men of the Air.)

Air Force*
US 1943 124m bw
Warner (Hal B. Wallis)

A Flying Fortress and its crew see action in Manila, Pearl Harbor and the Coral Sea. Propaganda piece concentrating on the characters of the crew members, with action set pieces largely provided by newsreel; but skilled direction still conveys plenty of punch.

w Dudley Nichols *d Howard Hawks*
ph James Wong Howe, Elmer Dyer, Charles
Marshall *m* Franz Waxman

John Garfield, Gig Young, Arthur Kennedy,
Charles Drake, John Ridgley, Harry Carey,
George Tobias, Stanley Ridges, Moroni
Olsen, Edward Brophy
'Maybe the story is high-flown, maybe it
overdraws a recorded fact a bit. We'd hate to
think it couldn't happen—or didn't—because
it leaves you feeling awfully good.'—*Bosley
Crowther*
'The film is one crisis after another, and the
director stages the air battles handsomely, but
for the rest it helps if you're interested in the
factors involved in getting a bomber
somewhere and back.'—*Pauline Kael, 70s*

AAN: Dudley Nichols; James Wong Howe,
Elmer Dyer, Charles Marshall

Air Hawks
US 1935 68m bw

Two aviation firms battle for airmail contracts.
Routine low-budget action drama inspired by
the stratosphere cross-continent flights of
Wiley Post (who appears as himself and was
killed later in the year along with Will
Rogers). Ralph Bellamy, Wiley Post, Tala
Birell, Douglass Dumbrille, Victor Kilian.
Written by Griffin Jay and Grace Neville;
directed by Albert Rogell; for Columbia.
'Word-of-mouth bally should help in face of
marquee weakness.'—*Variety*

Air Mail*
US 1932 84m bw

Brash young pilot effects a daring rescue and
gets the mail through. Moderate actioner of its
time. Pat O'Brien, Ralph Bellamy, Russell
Hopton, Gloria Stuart, Lillian Bond, Slim
Summerville. Written by Dale Van Every and
Frank Wead; directed by John Ford; for
Universal. 'Far short of a smash . . . it has no
sock name, it is weak on the romantic side and
the story material is directed at men.'—*Variety*

Air Raid Wardens*
US 1943 67m bw
MGM (B. F. Zeidman)

Rejected by the armed services, two
incompetent air raid wardens accidentally
round up Nazi spies.
Well below par star comedy: their
incomparable dignity has disappeared.

w Jack Jevne, Martin Rackin, Charles Rogers,
Harry Crane *d* Edward Sedgwick *ph* Walter
Lundin *m* Nathaniel Shilkret

Stan Laurel, Oliver Hardy, Edgar Kennedy,
Jacqueline White, Stephen McNally, Nella
Walker, Donald Meek

Airplane**
US 1980 88m Metrocolor
Paramount / Howard W. Koch (Jan
Davison)

A former pilot gets his nerve back when called
upon to land a passenger plane because the
crew all have food poisoning.
Arthur Hailey's play *Flight into Danger* and
the film *Zero Hour* which was made from it
get the zany parody treatment in this popular
movie which is often funny but sometimes
merely crude. It rang the box office bell more
loudly than most expensive epics of its year.

wd Jim Abrahams, David and Jerry Zucker
ph Joseph Biroc *m* Elmer Bernstein
pd Ward Preston

Robert Stack, Lloyd Bridges, Robert Hays,
Julie Hegerty, Peter Graves, Leslie Nielsen,
Lorna Paterson, Ethel Merman, Kareem
Abdul-Jabbar
'Parody may be the lowest form of humour,
but few comedies in ages have rocked the
laugh meter this hard.'—*Variety*
'It keeps going, like a dervish with skids
on.'—*Derek Malcolm, Guardian*
'Proof that the cinema is alive and well and
bursting with ingenuity.'—*David Hughes,
Sunday Times*
'It's compiled like a jokebook and has the
kind of pacing that goes with a laugh track.'—
Pauline Kael
'All pretty juvenile really, though the
relentless pace and sheer poor taste make up
for a lack of originality.'—*Time Out, 1984*
● *Video: CIC*

Airplane II: The Sequel
US 1982 85m Metrocolor
Paramount (Howard W. Koch)

A space shuttle gets into trouble but is rescued
in the nick of time.
Palsied sequel to a funny film, with some of
the same cast and some of the same jokes.

wd Ken Finkleman *ph* Joe Biroc *m* Elmer
Bernstein *pd* William Sandell *ed* Dennis
Virkler

Robert Hays, Julie Hagerty, Lloyd Bridges,
Peter Graves, William Shatner, Chad Everett,
Steven Stucker, Sonny Bono, Raymond Burr,
Chuck Connors, Rip Torn, John Dehner,
Kent McCord, John Vernon
'All the pleasure lies in the humour's
weakness.'—*Observer*
● *Video: CIC*

Airport***
US 1970 136m Technicolor Todd-AO
Universal / Ross Hunter (Jaque Mapes)

Events of one snowy night at a midwestern
international airport, culminating in airborne
melodrama when a mad bomber is killed and
the damaged plane has to be talked down.
Glossy, undeniably entertaining, all-star
version of a popular novel, with cardboard
characters skilfully deployed in Hollywood's
very best style.

w George Seaton, *novel* Arthur Hailey
d George Seaton *ph* Ernest Laszlo *m* Alfred
Newman

Burt Lancaster, Dean Martin, Jean Seberg,
Helen Hayes, Van Heflin, Jacqueline Bisset,

George Kennedy, Maureen Stapleton, Barry
Nelson, Dana Wynter, Lloyd Nolan, Barbara
Hale, Gary Collins, Jessie Royce Landis
'The best film of 1944.'—*Judith Crist*
'For sheer contentment there is nothing to
beat the sight of constant catastrophe
happening to others.'—*Alexander Walker*
'A *Grand Hotel* in the sky . . . every few
years or so some more show-biz types would
crowd onto a plane that would threaten to
crash, collide with another, meet with
terrorists, or otherwise be subjected to the
perils of Pauline.'—*Les Keyser, Hollywood in
the Seventies*

AA: Helen Hayes
AAN: best picture; George Seaton; Ernest
Laszlo; Alfred Newman; Maureen Stapleton

Airport 1975
US 1974 105m Technicolor
Panavision
Universal (Jennings Lang, William Frye)

A private aircraft collides with a jet plane and
kills or immobilizes its crew, so a stewardess
has to manoeuvre the jumbo to safety.
Inept airborne suspenser loaded with stars
who do nothing and marred by continuity
lapses and boring dialogue.

w Don Ingalls *d* Jack Smight *ph* Philip
Lathrop *m* John Cacavas

Charlton Heston, *Karen Black*, George
Kennedy, Helen Reddy, Efrem Zimbalist Jnr,
Susan Clark, Myrna Loy, Gloria Swanson,
Linda Blair, Dana Andrews, Roy Thinnes, Sid
Caesar, Ed Nelson, Nancy Olson, Martha
Scott
'Aimed squarely for the yahoo trade.'—
Variety
'Processed schlock. One can have a fairly
good time laughing at it, but it doesn't sit too
well as a joke, because the people on the
screen are being humiliated.'—*Pauline Kael,
New Yorker*

Airport '77
US 1977 114m Technicolor
Panavision
Universal (William Frye)

A private airliner loaded with guests and art
treasures hits an oil rig and settles underwater
on a sandbank.
Hysteria, rescue, and guest stars with nothing
to do; the mixture as before.

w Michael Scheff, David Spector *d* Jerry
Jameson *ph* Philip Lathrop *m* John Cacavas
pd George C. Webb

Jack Lemmon, James Stewart, Brenda
Vaccaro, Joseph Cotten, Olivia de Havilland,
Lee Grant, Darren McGavin, Christopher
Lee, Robert Foxworth, Robert Hooks, Monte
Markham, Kathleen Quinlan, James Booth
'Neither as riveting as it should be, nor as
much fun as its absurd plotline would
suggest.'—*Verina Glaessner, MFB*
† See also: *The Concorde—Airport '79.*

● *Video: CIC*

Akenfield
GB 1974   98m   Techniscope

Semi-dramatized film version of a book which documented a Suffolk village by interviewing its older inhabitants. An interesting venture ruined by imprecision, misty photography, lack of narrative drive or any compensating detail, and the appalling error of using a cheap wide screen process. Written by Ronald Blythe, from his book; directed by Peter Hall; for Angle Films and London Weekend Television.

Al Capone**
US 1959   105m   bw
Allied Artists (John H. Burrows, Leonard J. Ackerman)

An account of Chicago's most famous gangster, up to his arrest for income tax evasion.
Only slightly overplayed, semi-documentary retelling of a larger-than-life true story.

w Marvin Wald, Henry Greenberg   d Richard Wilson   ph Lucien Ballard   m David Raksin

Rod Steiger (a clever impersonation on the border of caricature), Fay Spain, Murvyn Vye, Nehemiah Persoff, Martin Balsam, James Gregory, Joe de Santis

'The most remarkable thing about it is its truth.'—*Daily Telegraph*

'This powerful production may turn out to be the definitive gangster film of all time.'—*Film Daily*

Al Jennings of Oklahoma
US 1950   78m   Technicolor

A lawyer becomes a western outlaw. Tolerable co-feature which strays from the truth. Dan Duryea, Gale Storm, Dick Foran, Gloria Henry, Guinn Williams. Written by George Bricker; directed by Ray Nazarro; for Columbia.

Alakazam the Great*
Japan 1960   88m   Eastmancolor
Toei (Hiroshi Okawa)
original title: *Saiyu-ki*

The arrogant monkey king of the animals is sent by his human master on a pilgrimage; he defeats evil King Gruesome and returns a hero.
Smartly animated, Disney-inspired cartoon based on the same legend as *Monkey*, translated by Arthur Waley.

w Osamu Tezuka, Keinosuke Uekusa   d Taiji Yabushita

The Alamo*
US 1960   193m   Technicolor   Todd-AO
UA / John Wayne

In 1836 a small southern fort becomes the centre of Texas' fight for independence, but it is suddenly annihilated by a Mexican raid, and all its defenders killed.
Sprawling historical epic with many irrelevant episodes and distracting changes of mood.

w James Edward Grant   d John Wayne
ph William H. Clothier   m Dmitri Tiomkin

John Wayne (as Crockett), Richard Widmark (Bowie), Laurence Harvey (Travis), Richard Boone (Houston), Frankie Avalon, Patrick Wayne, Linda Cristal, Chill Wills, Joseph Calleia

CROCKETT: 'Republic. I like the sound of the word. It means people can live free, talk free, go or come, buy or sell, be drunk or sober, however they choose. Some words give you a feeling. Republic is one of those words that makes you tight in the throat— the same tightness a man gets when his baby takes his first step or his first baby shaves and makes his first sound like a man. Some words can give you a feeling that makes your heart warm. Republic is one of those words.'

'Its sole redeeming feature lies in one of those crushing climaxes of total massacre which Hollywood can still pull off thunderingly well.'—*Peter John Dyer*

AAN: best picture; William H. Clothier; Dmitri Tiomkin; Chill Wills; song 'The Green Leaves of Summer' (m Dmitri Tiomkin, ly Paul Francis Webster)

● *Video: Warner*

Alaska Seas
US 1953   78m   bw
Paramount (Mel Epstein)

Alaska fishermen oppose the crooked owner of the local cannery.
Insipid remake of *Spawn of the North* (qv).

w Geoffrey Homes, Walter Doniger   d Jerry Hopper   ph William C. Mellor   md Irvin Talbot

Robert Ryan, Gene Barry, Jan Sterling, Brian Keith, Richard Shannon

Albert RN**
GB 1953   88m   bw
Dial (Daniel M. Angel)
US title: *Break to Freedom*

Prisoners of war construct a lifelike dummy to cover the absence of escaping prisoners. Competent, entertaining version of a successful play: an archetypal POW comedy drama.

w Guy Morgan, Vernon Harris, *play* Guy Morgan, Edward Sammis   d Lewis Gilbert ph Jack Asher   m Malcolm Arnold

Jack Warner, Anthony Steel, Robert Beatty, William Sylvester, Anton Diffring, Eddie Byrne, Guy Middleton, Paul Carpenter, Frederick Valk

Alcatraz Island
US 1937   64m   bw

The federal government decides to build a top-security prison on a rock in San Francisco Bay. Cheap routine treatment of what might have been an interesting subject. Ann Sheridan, Mary Maguire, Dick Purcell, Addison Richards, *George E. Stone*, Doris Lloyd, John Litel. Written by Crane Wilbur; directed by William McGann; for Warners / Cosmopolitan. 'Should about complete the Warner file on prisons.'—*Variety*

Alex and the Gypsy
US 1976   99m   De Luxe
TCF / Richard Shepherd

A cynical California bailbondsman involved in illicit activities chooses romantic freedom with a gypsy girl.
Incoherent hardbitten romance with an unconvincing set of characters.

w Lawrence B. Marcus, *novel* The Bailbondsman by Stanley Elkin   d John Korty ph Bill Butler   m Henry Mancini

Jack Lemmon, Genevieve Bujold, James Woods, Gino Ardito, Robert Emhardt

'Even if it were well done (which it is not) it would be banal, predictable and cloying.'—*Frank Rich*

'Off the beaten track, but that's just about the only thing you can give it points for.'—*Pauline Kael*

Alex in Wonderland
US 1970   109m   colour
MGM (Larry Tucker)

A Hollywood director finds life tedious. So did the small paying audiences who saw this pale imitation of Fellini. (Some wags called it *One and a Half*.)

w Paul Mazursky, Larry Tucker   d Paul Mazursky

Donald Sutherland, Jeanne Moreau, Ellen Burstyn, Federico Fellini

Alexander Hamilton*
US 1931   73m   bw
Warner

The life of America's 18th-century financier. Star biopic, highly satisfying in its day.

w Julian Josephson, Maude Howell, George Arliss   d John G. Adolfi   ph James Van Trees

George Arliss, Doris Kenyon, Montagu Love, Dudley Digges, Lionel Belmore, Ralf Harolde, Alan Mowbray

Alexander Nevsky****
USSR 1938   112m   bw
Mosfilm

In 1242, Prince Alexander Nevsky defeats the invading Teutonic Knights in a battle on the ice of Lake Peipus.
A splendid historical pageant which shows the director at his most inventively pictorial and climaxes in a superb battle sequence using music instead of natural sound.

w Pyotr Pavlenko, Sergei Eisenstein   d Sergei Eisenstein   ph Edouard Tissé   m Prokofiev ad I. Shpinel, N. Soloviov, K. Yeliseyev

Nikolai Cherkassov, Nikolai Okhlopkov, Andrei Abrikosov, Dmitri Orlov

'The picture will meet with good results wherever its political sentiments find established adherents. Otherwise it's almost nil for general appeal.'—*Variety*

'Superb sequences of cinematic opera that pass from pastoral to lamentation and end in a triumphal cantata.'—*Georges Sadoul*

'The colossus who conquered the world!
  The most colossal motion picture of all
  time!'

Alexander the Great°

US 1956 135m Technicolor
  Cinemascope
UA / Robert Rossen

The life and early death at thirty-three of the
Macedonian warrior who conquered the entire
known world.
Dour impassive epic which despite good
intelligent stretches makes one long for
Hollywood's usual more ruthless view of
history.

wd Robert Rossen *m* Mario Nascimbene
ph Robert Krasker *ad* Andrei Andreiev

Richard Burton, Fredric March, Danielle
Darrieux, Claire Bloom, Barry Jones, Harry
Andrews, Peter Cushing, Stanley Baker,
Michael Hordern, Niall MacGinnis

  'Not a scene is held for a second longer than
it is worth; greatness is pictured in constant
dissolve.'—*Alexander Walker*
  'Rossen has aimed for greatness and lost
honourably.'—*Andrew Sarris*

Alexander's Ragtime Band°°°

US 1938 106m bw
TCF (Darryl F. Zanuck, Harry Joe Brown)

Between 1911 and 1939, two songwriters vie
for the affections of a rising musical comedy
star.
Archetypal chronicle musical with 26 songs:
well-paced, smartly made, and bursting with
talent.

w Kathryn Scola, Lamar Trotti, Richard
Sherman *d* Henry King *ph* Peverell Marley
m / *ly* Irving Berlin *md* Alfred Newman

Tyrone Power, *Alice Faye*, Don Ameche,
Ethel Merman, Jack Haley, Jean Hersholt,
Helen Westley, John Carradine, Paul Hurst,
Wally Vernon, Ruth Terry, Eddie Collins,
Douglas Fowley, Chick Chandler

  'A grand filmusical which stirs and thrills,
finding response in the American heart to
memories of the exciting, sentimental and
patriotic moments of the past quarter of a
century.'—*Variety*

AA: Alfred Newman
AAN: best picture; Irving Berlin (for original
story); Irving Berlin (for song, 'Now It Can Be
Told')

Alf, Bill and Fred°

GB 1964 8m Eastmancolor

A man, a duck and a dog enjoy bouncing
together. Bittersweet cartoon fable which
pleases much more than its synopsis might
suggest. Written by Stan Hayward; produced,
directed and animated by *Bob Godfrey*; for
Biographic 4.

The Alf Garnett Saga

GB 1972 90m colour
Columbia / Associated London Films (Ned
  Sherrin, Terry Glinwood)

Bigoted Alf is exasperated by his council flat,
his son-in-law, and the possibility that his
daughter is pregnant by a black man.
Second inflation of the TV series, *Till Death
Us Do Part*, even cruder and less funny than
the first; listlessly written and developed.

w Johnny Speight *d* Bob Kellett *ph* Nic
Knowland *m* Georgie Fame

Warren Mitchell, Dandy Nichols, Adrienne
Posta, Mike Angelis, John Le Mesurier, Joan
Sims, John Bird, Roy Kinnear

  'One long, repetitive and unfunny
diatribe.'—*MFB*

Alfie°°

GB 1966 114m Techniscope
Paramount / Sheldrake (Lewis Gilbert)

A Cockney Lothario is proud of his amorous
conquests, but near-tragedy finally makes him
more mature.
Garish sex comedy, an immense box office
success because of its frankness and an
immaculate performance from its star.

w Bill Naughton, from his play *d* Lewis
Gilbert *ph* Otto Heller *m* Sonny Rollins

Michael Caine, Vivien Merchant, Shirley
Anne Field, Millicent Martin, Jane Asher,
Julia Foster, Shelley Winters, Eleanor Bron,
Denholm Elliott

  'Paramount thought it was a good bet
because it was going to be made for 500,000
dollars, normally the sort of money spent on
executives' cigar bills.'—*Lewis Gilbert*

AAN: best picture; Bill Naughton; Michael
Caine; Vivien Merchant; title song

Alfie Darling

GB 1975 102m Technicolor
EMI / Signal (Dugald Rankin)

Further repetitive amorous exploits of the
Cockney Lothario, now a continental truck
driver.
Soft porn adventures quite unworthy of the
writer–director, and tedious to sit through; the
touch of tragedy at the end only makes
matters worse.

wd Ken Hughes *ph* Ousama Rawi *m* Alan
Price

Alan Price, Jill Townsend, Paul Copley, Joan
Collins, Sheila White, Annie Ross, Hannah
Gordon, Rula Lenska

● *Video: Thorn EMI*

Alfred the Great°

GB 1969 122m Metrocolor Panavision
MGM / Bernard Smith

In AD 871 Alfred takes over kingship from his
weak elder brother.
A 'realistic' youth-oriented view of history:
blood and four-letter words alternate with
cliché to make a dispiriting, disunified whole,
though the background detail is interesting
and the battle scenes vivid.

w Ken Taylor, James R. Webb *d* Clive
Donner *ph* Alex Thomson *m* Ray Leppard
pd Michael Stringer

David Hemmings, Michael York, Prunella
Ransome, Colin Blakely, Julian Glover, Ian
McKellen, Alan Dobie

Alf's Button

GB 1930 96m bw

Not the first version (there was one in 1920
with Leslie Henson) but the first in sound of
W. A. Darlington's play about a soldier whose
button, when rubbed, summons an all-
powerful genie. It even had a colour sequence,
and featured Nervo and Knox (see below),
with Tubby Edlin, Alf Goddard, Nora
Swinburne and Polly Ward. Written by
L'Estrange Fawcett; directed by W. P.
Kellino; for Gaumont.

Alf's Button Afloat°

GB 1938 89m bw
Gainsborough (Edward Black)

Six itinerants encounter a genie, whose
granting of their wishes brings riches and
embarrassment.
Archetypal music hall farce descending at
moments into surrealism (the lovers are eaten
by a bear). All concerned are on top form.

w Marriott Edgar, Val Guest, Ralph Smart,
novel Alf's Button by W. A. Darlington
d Marcel Varnel *ph* Arthur Crabtree
md Louis Levy

Bud Flanagan, Chesney Allen, Jimmy Nervo,
Teddy Knox, Charles Naughton, Jimmy Gold
(the six original members of the Crazy Gang),
Alastair Sim, Wally Patch, Peter Gawthorne

Algiers°°

US 1938 95m bw
Walter Wanger

A romantic Casbah thief makes the mistake of
falling in love.
Seminal Hollywood romantic drama based
closely on a French original, *Pepe le Moko*;
laughed at for years because of the alleged line
'Come with me to the Casbah' (which is never
actually said), it holds up remarkably well in
its fashion.

w John Howard Lawson, James M. Cain
d John Cromwell *ph* James Wong Howe
m Vincent Scott, Mohammed Igorbouchen

*Charles Boyer, Hedy Lamarr, Sigrid Gurie,
Gene Lockhart, Joseph Calleia*, Alan Hale,
Johnny Downs

  'A quality of sustained suspense and
excitement . . . there is nothing makeshift
about the production.'—*Variety*
  'Few films this season, or any other, have
sustained their mood more brilliantly.'—*New
York Times*
  'The general tone is that of the decent
artistry we must demand and enjoy in pictures,
which should someday be as respectable as
books, only more near and vivid.'—*Otis
Ferguson*
  'This version is pure Hollywood, sacrificing
everything to glamour, and the heavy make-up
and studio lighting make it seem so artificial
one can get giggly.'—*New Yorker, 1977*
† Remake: *Casbah* (qv).

AAN: James Wong Howe; Charles Boyer;
Gene Lockhart

'Wild nights of sheer delights! Burning days of bold adventure! When beauty was the booty and the prize of all was love!'

Ali Baba and the Forty Thieves*
US 1944 87m Technicolor
U-I (Paul Malvern)

A deposed prince pretending to be a bandit regains his rightful throne.

Absurd but likeable wartime pantomime without much humour: a typical big-budget production of its studio and period.

w Edmund L. Hartmann d Arthur Lubin ph George Robinson m Edward Ward

Jon Hall, Maria Montez, Scotty Beckett, Turhan Bey, Frank Puglia, Andy Devine, Kurt Katch

† Remake: *Sword of Ali Baba*, which over twenty years later used much of the same footage.

Ali Baba and the Forty Thieves*
France 1954 90m Eastmancolor
Films du Cyclope

Ali Baba is sent to buy a new wife for his master, and accidentally finds a thieves' treasure cave . . .

Sporadically amusing but finally disappointing version of the Arabian Nights story; it looks hasty.

w Jacques Becker, Marc Maurette, Maurice Griffe d Jacques Becker ph Robert Le Fèbvre m Paul Misraki

Fernandel, Samia Gamal, Dieter Borsche, Henri Vilbert

Ali Baba Goes to Town*
US 1937 81m bw
TCF (Lawrence Schwab)

A hobo falls off a train into a film set and thinks he is back in the Arabian Nights. Rather flat star vehicle with a few compensations.

w Harry Tugend, Jack Yelten d David Butler ph Ernest Palmer m Louis Silvers songs Mack Gordon, Harry Revel

Eddie Cantor, Tony Martin, Roland Young, John Carradine, June Lang

'An elaborately produced filmusical which satirizes the New Deal policies, politicians and politics.'—*Variety*

Alias a Gentleman
US 1947 76m bw

An ex-convict tries to find his daughter and go straight. Sudsy star vehicle. Wallace Beery, Gladys George, Tom Drake, Leon Ames. Written by William Lipman; directed by Harry Beaumont; for MGM.

Alias French Gertie
US 1934 68m bw

A 'French maid' and her accomplice work a high society racket. Faded society comedy drama with Bebe Daniels and Ben Lyon in a rare teaming before their exile to England.

Written by Bayard Veiller; directed by George Archainbaud; for RKO. (GB title: *Love Finds a Way*.)

Alias Jesse James*
US 1958 92m De Luxe
Hope Enterprises (Jack Hope)

An incompetent insurance salesman sells a policy to Jesse James and has to protect his client until he can get it back.

Ho-hum star comedy saved by a climax in which Hope is protected by every cowboy star in Hollywood.

w William Bowers, D. D. Beauchamp d Norman Z. McLeod ph Lionel Lindon m Joseph J. Lilley

Bob Hope, Rhonda Fleming, Wendell Corey, Jim Davis, Will Wright

Alias Jimmy Valentine
US 1928 75m bw

Crook comedy drama previously made in 1920; this version is notable only as the first MGM sound film. William Haines, Karl Dane, Lionel Barrymore. Written by Sarah Y. Mason and A. P. Younger; directed by Jack Conway; for MGM.

Alias Mary Dow
US 1935 65m bw

A millionaire persuades a chorus girl to pose as his long-lost kidnapped daughter, to satisfy his wife. Obvious audience-pleaser of its time. Ray Milland, Sally Eilers, Henry O'Neill, Katherine Alexander. Written by Gladys Unger, Rose Franken and Arthur Caesar; directed by Kurt Neumann; for Universal.

'Not a bad picture . . . small towns should like it best.'—*Variety*

'No man ever held more terrible power over women than this tall dark handsome stranger from nowhere! The shock-filled story of a man whose love was more dangerous than a loaded gun!'

Alias Nick Beal***
US 1949 93m bw
Paramount (Endre Boehm)
GB title: *The Contact Man*

A politician is nearly corrupted by a mysterious stranger offering wealth and power.

Highly satisfactory modern version of *Faust*, done in gangster terms but not eschewing a supernatural explanation. Acting, photography and direction all in the right key.

w Jonathan Latimer, story Mindret Lord d John Farrow ph Lionel Lindon m Franz Waxman

Ray Milland, Thomas Mitchell, Audrey Totter, George Macready, Fred Clark

**9
Alias the Doctor**
US 1932 70m bw

A natural man of the soil tries to follow his mother's wish that he should become a doctor. Dated drama of family sentiment. Richard

Barthelmess, Laura la Plante, Marian Marsh, Norman Foster, Oscar Apfel. Written by Benjamin McGill, Houston Branch; directed by Michael Curtiz; for First National / Warners. 'It misses big league rating, but will satisfy on the average programme.'—*Variety*

Alibi*
US 1929 90m bw
Roland West

An ex-convict marries a policeman's daughter and uses her in his plan for the perfect murder.

Early talkie drama, mostly risible now but with interesting fragments of technique and imagination.

wd Roland West ph Ray June

Chester Morris, Eleanor Griffith, Regis Toomey, Mae Busch, Harry Stubbs

AAN: best picture; Chester Morris

Alibi
GB 1931 75m bw

Hercule Poirot proves that an apparent suicide was murder. Tame adaptation, without the narrative gimmick, of Agatha Christie's *The Murder of Roger Ackroyd*. Austin Trevor, Franklin Dyall, Elizabeth Allan, J. H. Roberts, Mary Jerrold. Written by H. Fowler Mear; directed by Leslie Hiscott; for Twickenham.

Alibi*
GB 1942 82m bw
Corona (Josef Somlo)

A nightclub mindreader forces the lady owner to give him a murder alibi.

Interesting but disappointing minor suspenser copied from a sharper French original.

w uncredited, novel Marcel Achard d Brian Desmond Hurst ph Otto Heller m Jack Beaver

Margaret Lockwood, Hugh Sinclair, James Mason, *Raymond Lovell*, Enid Stamp-Taylor, Hartley Power, Jane Carr, Rodney Ackland, Edana Romney, Elizabeth Welch, Olga Lindo, Muriel George

† The French film, *L'Alibi*, was made in 1939 by B-N Films. The girl was Jany Holt, with Erich Von Stroheim as the villain and Louis Jouvet as the inspector. Pierre Chenal directed.

Alibi Ike*
US 1935 73m bw
Warner

A baseball pitcher gets involved in all kinds of trouble.

Above average star comedy vehicle.

w William Wister Haines, story Ring Lardner d Ray Enright ph Arthur Todd md Leo F. Forbstein

Joe E. Brown, Olivia de Havilland, Ruth Donnelly, Roscoe Karns, William Frawley

Alice Adams***
US 1935 99m bw
RKO (Pandro S. Berman)

A social-climbing small-town girl falls in love. Dated but interesting star vehicle with good production values.

w Dorothy Yost, Mortimer Offner, *novel* Booth Tarkington *d* George Stevens *ph* Robert de Grasse *m* Max Steiner, Roy Webb

Katharine Hepburn, Fred MacMurray, Evelyn Venable, Frank Albertson, Fred Stone, Ann Shoemaker, Charles Grapewin, Grady Sutton, Hedda Hopper

'Sturdy cinematic substance, virtually audience proof.'—*Variety*

'A nice middle-class film, as trivial as a schoolgirl's diary, and just about as pathetically true.'—*C. A. Lejeune*

'What was in 1922 a biting and observant novel emerges in 1935 as a bitingly satiric portrait of an era.'—*Time*

AAN: best picture; Katharine Hepburn

Alice Doesn't Live Here Any More**
US 1974 112m Technicolor
Warner (David Susskind, Audrey Maas)

A widow sets off with her young son for Monterey and a singing career. Realistically squalid and foul-mouthed but endearing look at a slice of America today, with firm handling and excellent performances in a surprisingly old-fashioned theme.

w Robert Getchell d Martin Scorsese ph Kent L. Wakeford m various pd Toby Carr Rafelson

Ellen Burstyn, Alfred Lutter, Kris Kristofferson, Billy Green Bush, *Diane Ladd,* Lelia Goldoni, Jodie Foster

'What Scorsese has done is to rescue an American cliché from the bland, flat but much more portentous naturalism of such as *Harry and Tonto* and restore it to an emotional and intellectual complexity through his particular brand of baroque realism.'—*Richard Combs*

'Full of funny malice and breakneck vitality.'—*New Yorker*

'A tough weepie, redeemed by its picturesque locations and its eye for social detail.'—*Michael Billington, Illustrated London News*

AA: Ellen Burstyn
AAN: Robert Getchell; Diane Ladd
● *Video: Warner*

Alice in the Cities
West Germany 1974 110m bw

A German journalist in America reluctantly escorts a small girl back to Germany. Interesting but overlong collection of modern metaphors, occasionally reminiscent of *Paper Moon.* Rudiger Vogeler, Yella Röttlander. Written and directed by Wim Wenders; for Filmverlag der Autoren.
● *Video: Palace*

Alice in Wonderland**
US 1933 75m bw
Paramount (Louis D. Lighton)

ALICE IN WONDERLAND (1933). Charlotte Henry grows too big, too fast. The corridor decoration typifies the film's love of masks.

Intriguing but disappointing version of the nonsense classic, keeping to the Tenniel drawings by dressing an all-star cast in masks, thereby rendering them ineffective.

w Joseph L. Mankiewicz, William Cameron Menzies, *novel* Lewis Carroll *d* Norman Z. McLeod *ph* Henry Sharp, Bert Glennon *m* Dmitri Tiomkin

Charlotte Henry, W. C. Fields (Humpty Dumpty), Cary Grant (Mock Turtle), Gary Cooper (White Knight), Edward Everett Horton (Mad Hatter), Edna May Oliver (Red Queen), Jack Oakie (Tweedledum), Leon Errol (Uncle), Charles Ruggles (March Hare), May Robson (Queen of Hearts), Louise Fazenda (White Queen), Ned Sparks (Caterpillar), Alison Skipworth (Duchess)

'Nothing grows out of anything else in this phantasmagoria. It's like reading a whole volume of separate four-line gags.'—*Variety*

'Lavishly produced, with great care given to costumes and settings and make-up, but the spirit is missing.'—*New Yorker, 1977*

Alice in Wonderland*
US 1951 75m Technicolor
Walt Disney

Fully animated cartoon version which has good moments but modernizes and Americanizes the familiar characters.

w various d Clyde Geronomi, Hamilton Luske, Wilfred Jackson *supervisor* Ben Sharpsteen m Oliver Wallace

AAN: Oliver Wallace

Alice's Adventures in Wonderland*
GB 1972 101m Eastmancolor Todd-AO
TCF / Josef Shaftel (Derek Horne)

Live-action version which starts amiably enough but soon becomes flat and uninventive, with a star cast all at sea and tedium replacing the wit of the original.

wd William Sterling ph Geoffrey Unsworth m John Barry pd Michael Stringer

Fiona Fullerton, Michael Crawford (White Rabbit), Robert Helpmann (Mad Hatter), Dudley Moore (Dormouse), Spike Milligan (Gryphon), Peter Sellers (March Hare), Dennis Price (King of Hearts), Flora Robson (Queen of Hearts), Rodney Bewes (Knave of Hearts), Peter Bull (Duchess), Michael Hordern (Mock Turtle), Ralph Richardson (Caterpillar), etc

Alice's Restaurant*
US 1969 110m De Luxe
UA / Florin (Harold Levanthal)

Folk singer Arlo Guthrie. on the verge of being drafted, gets some varied experience of life among the drop-outs of Montana, Massachusetts and New York.
Typical of the freakish, anti-Vietnam, do-as-you-please movies which splurged from Hollywood in the wake of *Easy Rider*, this has the minor benefits of good production values and a few jokes.

w Venable Herndon, Arthur Penn *d* Arthur Penn *ph* Michael Nebbia *m* / songs Arlo Guthrie

Arlo Guthrie, Pat Quinn, James Broderick, Michael McClanathan, Geoff Outlaw

AAN: Arthur Penn
● *Video: MGM / UA*

'In space, no one can hear you scream!'
Alien*
GB 1979 117m Eastmancolor
  Panavision
TCF / Brandywine (Walter Hill, Gordon Carroll, David Giler)

Astronauts returning to earth visit an apparently dead planet and are infected by a violent being which has unexpected behaviour patterns and eliminates them one by one. Deliberately scarifying and highly commercial shocker with little but its art direction to commend it to connoisseurs.

w Dan O'Bannon *d* Ridley Scott *ph* Derek Vanlint, Denys Ayling *m* Jerry Goldsmith *chief designer* H. R. Giger

Tom Skerritt, Sigourney Weaver, John Hurt, Veronica Cartwright, Harry Dean Stanton, Ian Holm, Yaphet Kotto
'A sort of inverse relationship to *The Thing* invites unfavourable comparisons.'—*Sight and Sound*
'Empty bag of tricks whose production values and expensive trickery cannot disguise imaginative poverty.'—*Time Out*
'It was not, as its co-author admitted, a think piece. The message he intended was simple: Don't close your eyes or it will get ya.'—*Les Keyser, Hollywood in the Seventies*
● *Video: CBS / Fox*

Alive and Kicking*
GB 1958 94m bw
ABP (Victor Skuzetsky)

Three old ladies escape from a home to an Irish island.
Agreeable minor comedy, a showcase for its elderly but vigorous stars.

w Denis Cannan *d* Cyril Frankel *ph* Gilbert Taylor *m* Philip Green

Sybil Thorndike, Kathleen Harrison, Estelle Winwood, Stanley Holloway, Joyce Carey, Eric Pohlmann, Colin Gordon

'The most provocative picture of the year!'
All About Eve***
US 1950 138m bw
TCF (Darryl F. Zanuck)

An ageing Broadway star suffers from the hidden menace of a self-effacing but secretly ruthless and ambitious young actress.
A basically unconvincing story with thin characters is transformed by a screenplay scintillating with savage wit and a couple of waspish performances into a movie experience to treasure.

wd Joseph L. Mankiewicz *ph* Milton Krasner *m* Alfred Newman

Bette Davis (Margo Channing), *George Sanders* (Addison de Witt), Anne Baxter (Eve), Celeste Holm (Karen Richards), Thelma Ritter (Birdie), Gary Merrill (Bill Sampson), Hugh Marlowe (Lloyd Richards), Gregory Ratoff (Max Fabian), Marilyn Monroe (Miss Caswell), Barbara Bates (Girl at Mirror), Walter Hampden (Speaker at dinner)
  MARGO: 'Fasten your seat belts, it's going to be a bumpy night!'
  ADDISON: 'That I should want you at all suddenly strikes me as the height of improbability . . . you're an improbable person, Eve, but so am I. We have that in common. Also a contempt for humanity, an inability to love or be loved, insatiable ambition—and talent. We deserve each other.'
  BIRDIE: 'The bed looks like a dead animal act.'
  ADDISON: 'That's all television is, dear—just auditions.'
  BIRDIE: 'What a story! Everything but the bloodhounds snappin' at her rear end!'
  ADDISON: 'I have lived in the theatre as a Trappist monk lives in his faith. In it I toil not, neither do I spin. I am a critic and a commentator. I am essential to the theatre—as ants to a picnic, as the boll weevil to a cotton field.'
  'The wittiest, the most devastating, the most adult and literate motion picture ever made that had anything to do with the New York Stage.'—*Leo Mishkin*
  'The dialogue and atmosphere are so peculiarly remote from life that they have sometimes been mistaken for art.'—*Pauline Kael, 1968*
  'Plenty of surface cynicism, but no detachment, no edge and no satire. Boiled down it is a plush backstage drama.'—*Richard Winnington*
  'Long, but continuously, wonderfully entertaining in a way I had almost forgotten was possible for films.'—*Richard Mallett, Punch*
  'Someone remarked of this witty, exaggerated, cruel and yet wildly funny film that the secret of its success was the extreme bad taste shown throughout by all concerned (though I hope they didn't mean to include Milton Krasner's tactful camerawork in this).'—*Basil Wright, 1972*
  'The picture seemed long—though it was not by today's standards of length—and the crispness of the dialogue was not matched by equally crisp editing.'—*Hollis Alpert, 1962*
  † The idea for the film came from a short story, 'The Wisdom of Eve', by Mary Orr.

AA: best picture; Joseph L. Mankiewicz (as writer); Joseph L. Mankiewicz (as director); George Sanders

AAN: Milton Krasner; Alfred Newman; Bette Davis; Anne Baxter; Celeste Holm; Thelma Ritter
● *Video: CBS / Fox*

The All-American
US 1932 73m bw

A college football star finds his fame of little use to him in the outside world. Lively drama of its day, but with little permanent interest.
Richard Arlen, Andy Devine, Gloria Stuart, James Gleason, Preston Foster. Written by Frank Wead, Ferdinand Reyney, Richard Schayer, Dale Van Every; directed by Russell Mack; for Universal. 'A pleaser for all audiences, having more than the football stuff to recommend it.'—*Variety.* (GB title: *Sport of a Nation.*)

The All-American
US 1952 83m bw
U-I (Aaron Rosenberg)
GB title: *The Winning Way*

When his parents are killed on the way to a match, a college football hero rejects sport for the groves of *academe*.
Very modest formula drama.

w D. D. Beauchamp *d* Jesse Hibbs *ph* Maury Gertsman *m* Joseph Gershenson

Tony Curtis, Mamie Van Doren, Lori Nelson, Gregg Palmer, Richard Long, Paul Cavanagh

The All-American Boy
US 1973 118m colour

A young boxer has got to the top too fast, and is depressed by the future. Uninteresting character study. Jon Voight, Carol Androsky, Anne Archer. Written and directed by Charles Eastman; for Warner.

All Ashore
US 1952 80m Technicolor
Columbia (Jonie Taps)

Three sailors on shore leave work their passage to Catalina.
Very lightweight musical, no rival for *On the Town*.

w Blake Edwards, Richard Quine *d* Richard Quine *ph* Charles Lawton Jnr *m* Morris Stoloff, George Duning *ly* Robert Wells

Mickey Rooney, Dick Haymes, Ray McDonald, Peggy Ryan, Barbara Bates, Jody Lawrance

All Coppers Are . . .
GB 1972 87m colour

A crook and a cop both fancy the same girl. Pointlessly titled lowlife melodrama with no style whatever; any episode of *Z Cars* would be vastly preferable. Nicky Henson, Martin Potter, Julia Foster, Ian Hendry. Written by Allan Prior; directed by Sidney Hayers; for Peter Rogers / Rank.
● *Video: Rank*

All Creatures Great and Small*
GB1974 92m Eastmancolor
EMI / Venedon (David Susskind, Duane Bogie)

The pre-war Yorkshire life of a country vet. Simple-minded popular entertainment of a long-forgotten kind, oddly sponsored by American TV in the shape of Readers' Digest and the Hallmark Hall of Fame.

w Hugh Whitemore, *novel* James Herriot
d Claude Whatham ph Peter Suschitzky
m Wilfred Josephs

Anthony Hopkins, Simon Ward, Lisa Harrow, Freddie Jones, Brian Stirner, T. P. McKenna, Brenda Bruce, John Collin
† 1976 sequel: *It Shouldn't Happen to a Vet.*

All Fall Down*
US 1962 111m bw Panavision
MGM (John Houseman)

A young man reveres his ne'er-do-well elder brother but determines to shoot him when he causes a girl's death.
Another gallery of middle American failures, competently portrayed by a writer and actors very practised at this sort of thing.

w William Inge, *novel* James Leo Herlihy
d John Frankenheimer ph Lionel Lindon
m Alex North

Warren Beatty, Brandon de Wilde, Angela Lansbury, Karl Malden, Eva Marie Saint
 'That strange area of nostalgic Americana where the familiar is the Freudian grotesque.'—*New Yorker, 1982*

All for Mary*
GB 1955 82m Eastmancolor
Rank / Paul Soskin

Two rivals for the hand of the pretty daughter of a Swiss hotelier are struck down by chicken pox and cared for by the old nanny of one of them.
Simple-minded farce in which two grown men quail like children before a forceful old lady; on the strength of the latter characterization and a few funny lines the original play was a considerable West End success.

w Peter Blackmore, Paul Soskin, *play* Harold Brooke, Kay Bannerman d Wendy Toye
ph Reg Wyer m Robert Farnon

Kathleen Harrison, Nigel Patrick, David Tomlinson, Jill Day, David Hurst, Leo McKern

All Hands on Deck
US 1961 98m De Luxe Cinemascope
TCF (Oscar Brodney)

Romantic and farcical adventures of sailors on leave.
Tired musical comedy romp with a second team cast.

w Jay Sommars, *novel* Donald R. Morris
d Norman Taurog ph Leo Tover m Cyril Mockridge *songs* Jay Livingston, Ray Evans

Pat Boone, Buddy Hackett, Dennis O'Keefe, Barbara Eden, Warren Berlinger, Gale Gordon, Joe E. Ross

All I Desire
US 1953 79m bw
U-I (Ross Hunter)

A woman who had deserted her husband and family for a life on the stage returns for her daughter's graduation and is reconciled.
Resilient star melodrama with all stops out.

w James Gunn, Robert Blees d Douglas Sirk
ph Carl Guthrie m Joseph Gershenson

Barbara Stanwyck, Richard Carlson, Lyle Bettger, Maureen O'Sullivan, Richard Long, Lori Nelson

All in a Night's Work
US 1961 94m Technicolor
Paramount / Hal B. Wallis–Joseph Hazen

A publishing heir falls for a girl he suspects of having been his uncle's mistress.
Unpolished and not very amusing comedy which falters after an intriguing start.

w Edmund Beloin, Maurice Richlin, Sidney Sheldon d Joseph Anthony ph Joseph La Shelle m André Previn

Shirley Maclaine, Dean Martin, Charles Ruggles, Cliff Robertson, Norma Crane, Gale Gordon, Jerome Cowan, Jack Weston
 'Tame and aimless sex-and-big-business comedy.'—*MFB*

All Men Are Enemies
US 1934 78m bw

Sweethearts parted by the war are reunited at last, despite another woman. Tedious romantic drama which failed to make a Hollywood star of its British lead. Hugh Williams, Helen Twelvetrees, Mona Barrie, Herbert Mundin, Henry Stephenson, Walter Byron, Una O'Connor, Halliwell Hobbes. Written by Samuel Hoffenstein, Lenore Coffee from the novel by Richard Aldington; directed by George Fitzmaurice; for Rocket / Fox.

All Mine To Give*
US 1956 102m Technicolor RKOscope
RKO (Sam Wiesenthal)
GB title: *The Day They Gave Babies Away*

In 1856, a pioneer couple in Wisconsin train their children to carry on the family after their own deaths.
Weird sentimental sob story, even odder under its English title. Surprisingly, some of it works quite well.

w Dale and Katherine Eunson (apparently about their own ancestors) d Allen Reisner
ph William Skall m Max Steiner

Glynis Johns, Cameron Mitchell, Patty McCormack, Rex Thompson, Ernest Truex, Hope Emerson, Alan Hale
 'A strong mood of folksy western reminiscence.'—*MFB*

All My Sons*
US 1948 94m bw
U-I (Chester Erskine)

A young man establishes that his father sold defective airplanes during the war.
Heady family melodrama from a taut and topical stage play. The film is well-meaning but artificial and unconvincing.

w Chester Erskine, *play* Arthur Miller
d Irving Reis ph Russell Metty m Leith Stevens

Edward G. Robinson, Burt Lancaster, Mady Christians, Howard Duff

All Neat in Black Stockings
GB 1969 99m Eastmancolor
Anglo Amalgamated / Miton (Leon Clore)

Sex adventures of an amorous window cleaner.
Modish comedy drama with surface entertainment of a sort, but no depth.

w Jane Gaskell, Hugh Whitemore
d Christopher Morahan ph Larry Pizer
m Robert Cornford

Victor Henry, Susan George, Jack Shepherd, Anna Cropper, Clare Kelly, Terence de Marney

All Night Long*
GB 1961 95m bw
Rank / Bob Roberts (Michael Relph, Basil Dearden)

Because of rumour set about by a jealous rival, a jazz trumpeter at an all-night party tries to strangle his wife.
Cheeky updating of *Othello* with jazz accompaniment, played a shade too grimly by an excellent cast. An interesting misfire.

w Nel King, Peter Achilles d Basil Dearden
ph Ted Scaife m Philip Green

Patrick McGoohan, Richard Attenborough, Keith Michell, Betsy Blair, Marti Stevens, Paul Harris, Bernard Braden; and on the sound track Dave Brubeck, Tubby Hayes, Johnny Dankworth etc

All Night Long
US 1981 87m Technicolor
Universal (Leonard Goldberg, Jerry Weintraub)

The wife of the night manager of a supermarket has a hyperactive sex life.
Curiously misjudged and outdated farce which offers very few laughs.

w W. D. Richter d Jean-Claude Tramont
ph Philip Lathrop m Ira Newborn, Richard Hazard pd Peter Jamison

Barbra Streisand, Gene Hackman, Diane Ladd, Dennis Quaid, Kevin Dobson, William Daniels, Ann Doran
 'Neither screenplay nor direction seem very clear what they're trying to say, and large chunks of it make no sense at all.'—*Daily Mail*
● *Video: CIC*

'There are two kinds of women, but only one kind of love!'
All of Me
US 1934 70m bw
Paramount (Louis Lighton)

An engineering professor on his way to Boulder Dam finds his life affected by the problems of a criminal.

Confused and uninteresting romantic
melodrama with a good cast all at sea.

w Sidney Buchman, Thomas Mitchell, *play*
Chrysalis by Rose Porter *d* James Flood
ph Victor Milner *m / ly* Ralph Rainger, Leo
Robin

Fredric March, Miriam Hopkins, George Raft,
Helen Mack, Nella Walker, William Collier
Jnr, Gilbert Emery, Blanche Friderici, Edgar
Kennedy

'The most startling glorification of criminals
that even the movies have ever dared.'—*New
York Sun*

'The gags aren't thought out visually in
terms of the L.A. locations, and the film has
the bland ugliness of sitcoms.'—*Pauline Kael,
New Yorker*

All Over Town
US 1937 62m bw

A pair of vaudevillians with a trained seal save
a theatre on the skids. Routine knockabout
comedy. Ole Olsen, Chic Johnson, Mary
Howard, Harry Stockwell, James Finlayson,
Franklin Pangborn. Written by Jack Townley,
Jerome Chodorov; directed by James Horne;
for Republic.

All Over the Town*
GB 1949 88m bw
Rank / Wessex (Ian Dalrymple)

Two reporters revivify a West of England local
newspaper, and expose local corruption.
Fresh, agreeable romantic comedy on sub-
Ealing lines.

w Derek Twist and others *d* Derek Twist
ph C. Pennington-Richards *m* Temple Abady

Norman Wooland, Sarah Churchill, *Fabia
Drake* (as a local gorgon), Cyril Cusack,
James Hayter

All Quiet on the Western Front****
US 1930 130m approx. bw
Universal (Carl Laemmle Jnr)

In 1914, a group of German teenagers
volunteer for action on the Western Front, but
they become disillusioned, and none of them
survives.
A landmark of American cinema and
Universal's biggest and most serious
undertaking until the sixties, this highly
emotive war film with its occasional outbursts
of bravura direction fixed in millions of minds
the popular image of what it was like in the
trenches, even more so than *Journey's End*
which had shown the Allied viewpoint. Despite
dated moments, it retains its overall power
and remains a great pacifist work.

w Lewis Milestone, Maxwell Anderson, Del
Andrews, George Abbott, *novel* Erich Maria
Remarque *d* Lewis Milestone (in a manner
reminiscent of Eisenstein and Lang)
ph Arthur Edeson *m* David Broekman

Lew Ayres (Paul Baumer), Louis Wolheim
(Katczinsky), Slim Summerville (Tjaden), John
Wray (Himmelstoss), Raymond Griffith
(Gerard Duval), Russell Gleason (Muller),
Ben Alexander (Kemmerick), Beryl Mercer
(Mrs Baumer)

TJADEN: 'Me and the Kaiser, we are both
fighting. The only difference is, the Kaiser
isn't here.'

KATCZINSKY: 'At the next war let all the
Kaisers, Presidents and Generals and
diplomats go into a big field and fight it out
first among themselves. That will satisfy us
and keep us at home.'

PAUL: 'We live in the trenches out there. We
fight. We try not to be killed, but sometimes
we are. That's all.'

'A magnificent cinematic equivalent of the
book . . . to Mr Milestone goes the credit of
effecting the similitude in united and dynamic
picture terms. The sound and image mediums
blend as one, as a form of artistic expression
that only the motion screen can give.'—
National Board of Review

'Nothing passed up for the niceties; nothing
glossed over for the women. Here exhibited is
war as it is, butchery. The League of Nations
could make no better investment than to buy
up the master-print, reproduce it in every
language to be shown to every nation every
year until the word war is taken out of the
dictionaries.'—*Variety*

'A trenchant and imaginative audible
picture . . . most of the time the audience was
held to silence by its realistic scenes.'—*New
York Times*

AA: best picture; Lewis Milestone (as
director)
AAN: Lewis Milestone, Maxwell Anderson,
Del Andrews, George Abbott; Arthur Edeson
● *Video: CIC*

All That Heaven Allows
US 1955 89m Technicolor
U-I (Ross Hunter)

A sad widow falls in love with the gardener at
her winter home, and marries him despite
local prejudice.
Standard tearjerker in the tradition of
Magnificent Obsession, reuniting the same
stars, producer and director in the same rich
musical and photographic sauce.

w Peg Fenwick *d* Douglas Sirk *ph* Russell
Metty *m* Frank Skinner

Jane Wyman, Rock Hudson, Agnes
Moorehead, Conrad Nagel, Virginia Grey,
Charles Drake

'As laboriously predictable as it is fatuously
unreal.'—*MFB*

All That Jazz**
US 1979 123m Technicolor
TCF / Robert Alan Aurthur, Daniel Melnick

A stage musical director pushes himself too
hard, and dies of a surfeit of wine, women and
work.
Self-indulgent, semi-autobiographical tragi-
comic extravaganza complete with heart
operations and a recurring angel of death.
Flashes of brilliant talent make it a must for
Fosse fans.

w Robert Alan Aurthur, Bob Fosse *d* Bob
Fosse *ph* Giuseppe Rotunno *m* Ralph Burns
pd Philip Rosenberg, Tony Walton

Roy Scheider, Jessica Lange, Ann Rainking,
Leland Palmer, Ben Vereen, Cliff Gorman

'Egomaniacal, wonderfully choreographed,
often compelling . . . more an art item than a
broad commercial prospect.'—*Variety*

'An improbable mixture of crass gags, song
'n' dance routines and open heart surgery. Not
for the squeamish.'—*Time Out*

'By the end I felt I'd learned more about
Fosse than I actually cared to know.'—*Daily
Mail*

'High cholesterol hokum. Enjoyable, but
probably not good for you.'—*Pauline Kael,
New Yorker*

BFA: cinematography; editing (Alan Heim);
sound
● *Video: CBS / Fox*

All That Money Can Buy****
US 1941 106m bw
RKO / William Dieterle (Charles L. Glett)
aka: *The Devil and Daniel Webster; Daniel
and the Devil; Here Is a Man*

A hard-pressed farmer gives in to the Devil's
tempting, but is saved from the pit by a
famous lawyer's pleading at his 'trial'.
A brilliant Germanic *Faust* set in 19th-century
New Hampshire and using historical figures,
alienation effects, comedy asides and the
whole cinematic box of tricks which
Hollywood had just learned again through
Citizen Kane. A magic act in more ways than
one.

w Dan Totheroh, based on The Devil and
Daniel Webster by Stephen Vincent Benet
d William Dieterle *ph* Joseph August
m Bernard Herrmann *ad* Van Nest Polglase
sp Vernon L. Walker

Walter Huston ('Mr Scratch', a great
performance), James Craig, Anne Shirley,
Simone Simon, *Edward Arnold* (Daniel
Webster), Jane Darwell, Gene Lockhart, John
Qualen, H. B. Warner

MR SCRATCH: 'A soul. A soul is nothing. Can
you see it, smell it, touch it? No. Think of
it—this soul—your soul—a nothing, against
seven whole years of good luck! You will
have money and all that money can buy.'

'Some of those in the movie industry who
saw it restively called it a dog; but some of
them cried it was another catapult hurling the
cinema up to its glorious destiny.'—*Cecilia
Ager*

AA: Bernard Herrmann
AAN: Walter Huston

All the Brothers Were Valiant*
US 1953 94m Technicolor
MGM (Pandro S. Berman)

Rivalry between brothers on a whaling
schooner.
Remake of a silent melodrama with
predictable vengefulness and formula heroism,
capably but unmemorably portrayed.

w Harry Brown, *novel* Ben Ames Williams
d Richard Thorpe *ph* George Folsey
m Miklos Rozsa

Stewart Granger, Robert Taylor, Ann Blyth,
Betta St John, Keenan Wynn, James
Whitmore, Kurt Kasznar, Lewis Stone

AAN: George Folsey

All the Fine Young Cannibals
US 1960 122m Metrocolor
Cinemascope
MGM / Avon (Pandro S. Berman)

The son of a country clergyman loves the
daughter of another clergyman; they both find
the realities of life in New York a horrid
shock.
The glum joys of sex and dope in the big city
are revealed in this boring rather than daring
farrago which is not even unintentionally
funny.

w Robert Thom, *novel* The Bixby Girls by
Rosamond Marshall *d* Michael Anderson
ph William H. Daniels *m* Jeff Alexander

Robert Wagner, Natalie Wood, Pearl Bailey,
Susan Kohner, George Hamilton, Jack
Mullaney, Onslow Stevens, Anne Seymour

All the King's Horses
US 1935 87m bw

A Hollywood star revisiting his native
Langenstein turns out to be a double of the
king, and finds himself romancing the queen.
Operetta-style entertainment grafted onto the
plot of *The Prisoner of Zenda*; by no means
unacceptable even now. Carl Brisson, Mary
Ellis, Edward Everett Horton, Eugene
Pallette, Katherine de Mille. Written by Frank
Tuttle and Frederick Stephani, from a play by
Lawrence Clark and Max Giersberg; directed
by Frank Tuttle; for Paramount.

'He thought he had the world by the tail—
till it exploded in his face, with a bullet
attached!'
All the King's Men***
US 1949 109m bw
Columbia (Robert Rossen)

An honest man from a small town is elected
mayor and then governor, but power corrupts
him absolutely and he ruins his own life and
those of his friends before being assassinated.
Archetypal American political melodrama
based on the life of southern senator Huey
Long. The background is well sketched in and
there are excellent performances, but the
overall narrative is rather flabby.

w Robert Rossen, *novel* Robert Penn Warren
d Robert Rossen *ph* Burnett Guffey *m* Louis
Gruenberg *ad* Sturges Carne

*Broderick Crawford, John Ireland, Mercedes
McCambridge, Joanne Dru, John Derek,
Anne Seymour, Shepperd Strudwick*
'More conspicuous for scope and worthiness
of intention than for inspiration.'—*Gavin
Lambert*
'A superb pictorialism which perpetually
crackles and explodes.'—*Bosley Crowther*

'Realism comes from within as well as
without and the core of meaning that might
have made this film a step forward from
Boomerang does not exist amid all the
courageous camera-work.'—*Richard
Winnington*
'Broderick Crawford's Willie Stark might
just make you feel better about the President
you've got . . . By no means a great film, but
it moves along.'—*Pauline Kael, New Yorker*

AA: best picture; Broderick Crawford;
Mercedes McCambridge
AAN: Robert Rossen (as writer); Robert
Rossen (as director); John Ireland

All the Marbles . . .
US 1981 113m Metrocolor
MGM / Aldrich Company
GB title: *The California Dolls*

Problems of a women's wrestling team in the
midwest.
Tasteless and tedious exploitation comedy
with just a few flashes of the director's old
flair.

w Mel Frohman *d* Robert Aldrich *ph* Joseph
Biroc *m* Frank de Vol *pd* Carl Anderson
ed Irving C. Rosenblum, Richard Lane

Peter Falk, Vicki Frederick, Laurene Landon,
Burt Young, Tracy Reed

'The most devastating detective story of
the century!'
All the President's Men***
US 1976 138m Technicolor
Warner / Wildwood (Robert Redford,
Walter Coblenz)

A reconstruction of the discovery of the White
House link with the Watergate affair by two
young reporters from the *Washington Post*.
An absorbing drama from the headlines which
despite its many excellences would have been
better with a more audible dialogue track, less
murky photography and a clearer introduction
of the characters concerned. The acting
however is a treat.

w William Goldman, *book* Carl Bernstein,
Bob Woodward *d* Alan J. Pakula *ph* Gordon
Willis *m* David Shire *pd* George Jenkins

Robert Redford, Dustin Hoffman, Jason
Robards Jnr, Martin Balsam, Hal Holbrook,
Jack Warden, Jane Alexander, Meredith
Baxter
'It works as a detective thriller (even though
everyone knows the ending), as a credible (if
occasionally romanticized) primer on the
prosaic fundamentals of big league
investigative journalism, and best of all, as a
chilling tone poem that conveys the texture of
the terror in our nation's capital during that
long night when an aspiring fascist regime held
our democracy under siege.'—*Frank Rich,
New York Post*

AA: William Goldman; Jason Robards Jnr
AAN: best picture; Alan J. Pakula; Jane
Alexander
● *Video: Warner*

All the Right Noises*
GB 1969 91m Eastmancolor
(TCF) Trigon (Anthony Hope)

The electrician of a touring company has an
affair with a 15-year-old actress, but finally
returns to his wife.
Sharp, sensible treatment of a cliché situation,
as watchable as a superior television play.

wd Gerry O'Hara *ph* Gerry Fisher *m* John
Cameron

Tom Bell, Judy Carne, Olivia Hussey, John
Standing
'Built on a solid framework of disciplined
direction and animated performances.'—*MFB*

'Love is not a thing that grows only in the
dark!'
All the Way Home**
US 1963 107m bw
Paramount / Talent Associates (David
Susskind)

In 1916 Tennessee, the beloved father of a
family is killed in a car crash, and after the
trauma wears off, mother helps the children to
rebuild their lives.
Tactful, charming though finally depressing
slice of small town period Americana, with
generally eloquent performances.

w Philip Reisman Jnr, *play* Tad Mosel, *novel*
A Death in the Family by James Agee *d* Alex
Segal *ph* Boris Kaufman *m* Bernard Green

Robert Preston, Jean Simmons, Aline
MacMahon, Pat Hingle, Michael Kearney
'A heart-wrenching blend of nostalgia and
sorrow.'—*Judith Crist*
'Terribly earnest, pictorial, and well
intentioned. And a terrible mistake.'—*Pauline
Kael, New Yorker*

All the Way Up*
GB 1970 97m Technicolor
Granada / EMI (Philip Mackie)

Social-climbing Dad makes his way by
treachery and blackmail, but gets his come-
uppance when his son takes after him.
Crudely farcical adaptation of a thoughtful
comedy of its time; the treatment works in fits
and starts but leaves one in no mood for the
talkative finale.

w Philip Mackie, *play* Semi Detached by
David Turner *d* James MacTaggart *ph* Dick
Bush *m* Howard Blake

Warren Mitchell, Pat Heywood, Elaine
Taylor, Kenneth Cranham, Vanessa Howard,
Richard Briers, Adrienne Posta, Bill Fraser

All the Young Men
US 1960 87m bw
Columbia (Hall Bartlett / Jaguar)

A marine patrol in Korea is commanded by a
black man, and racial tensions take
precedence over fighting the enemy.
Simple-minded, parsimoniously-budgeted war
melodrama.

wd Hall Bartlett *ph* Daniel Fapp *m* George
Duning

Alan Ladd, Sidney Poitier, Ingemar Johansson, Glenn Corbett, James Darren, Mort Sahl

'Strenuously engaged in exploiting the entertainment values of nostalgia, fear, suspense, hatred and sex.'—*MFB*

All This and Heaven Too**
US 1940　143m　bw
Warner (Jack L. Warner, Hal B. Wallis)

A 19th-century French nobleman falls in love with his governess and murders his wife. Romantic, melodramatic soap opera from a mammoth best seller; well made for those who can stomach it, with excellent acting and production values.

w Casey Robinson, *novel* Rachel Field d Anatole Litvak *ph* Ernest Haller *m* Max Steiner

Charles Boyer, Bette Davis, Barbara O'Neil, Virginia Weidler, Jeffrey Lynn, Helen Westley, Henry Daniell, Harry Davenport, Walter Hampden, George Coulouris, Janet Beecher, Montagu Love

AAN: best picture; Ernest Haller; Barbara O'Neil

All This and World War Two*
US 1977　88m　De Luxe / bw

Wartime newsreels are interwoven with pop songs and clips from feature films. A messy mélange with obvious items of interest, but totally confusing and uninformative for the young historian. No writer credit; directed by Susan Winslow for Lou Reizner Productions / TCF. 'Desperately straining to make any kind of sense, it is reduced to making parallels that are either glib or facetious.'—*MFB*

'Killer Bogart takes the Gestapo for a ride!'
All Through the Night*
US 1942　107m　bw
Warner (Jerry Wald)

Gangsters help to track down fifth columnists in World War II New York.
Highly entertaining muddle of several styles which somehow works well and allows several favourites to do their thing.

w Leonard Spiegelgass, Edwin Gilbert d Vincent Sherman *ph* Sid Hickox *m* Adolph Deutsch

Humphrey Bogart, Conrad Veidt, Peter Lorre, Karen Verne, Judith Anderson, Jane Darwell, Frank McHugh, Jackie Gleason, William Demarest, Phil Silvers

'Exciting slaphappy stuff.'—*Kine Weekly*
'The thrills and the jokes have both been sharpened to a pin point.'—*New Statesman*

Allegheny Uprising
US 1939　98m　bw
RKO (P. J. Wolfson)
GB title: *The First Rebel*

A young frontiersman smashes liquor traffic with the Indians.
Modestly efficient western with an impressive cast.

w P. J. Wolfson, *story* Neil Swanson d William A. Seiter *ph* Nicholas Musuraca

John Wayne, Claire Trevor, Brian Donlevy, George Sanders, Wilfrid Lawson, Robert Barrat, Moroni Olsen, Eddie Quillan, Chill Wills

'Long on horsemanship and action, short on romance and suspense.'—*Variety*

● *Video: Kingston*

Allegro Ma Troppo*
France 1963　16m　Eastmancolor
Films Je Vois Tout

One night in Paris viewed through accelerated motion.
An amusing if not original conceit, smartly executed.

w, d, ph Paul de Roubaix *m* François de Roubaix *ed* Robert Enrico

Alligator*
US 1980　91m　De Luxe
Group 1 / Alligator Associates

A pet baby alligator is flushed down the toilet and later, grown to enormous size, goes on the rampage.
Jaws-type monster movie made tolerable by occasional flashes of humour but not otherwise remarkable.

w John Sayles d Lewis Teague *ph* Joseph Mangine *m* Craig Hundley *sp* Richard O. Helmer

Robert Forster, Robin Ryker, Michael Gazzo, Dean Jagger, Jack Carter, Henry Silva

'Hair raising, funny, shrewdly scripted and politically telling.'—*Margaret Hinxman, Daily Mail*

● *Video: Intervision*

An Alligator Named Daisy
GB 1955　88m　Technicolor　Vistavision
Rank (Raymond Stross)

A young songwriter finds himself saddled with a pet alligator.
The ultimate in silly animal comedies, this does score a few laughs.

w Jack Davies, *novel* Charles Terrot d J. Lee-Thompson *ph* Reg Wyer *m* Stanley Black

Donald Sinden, Diana Dors, Jean Carson, James Robertson Justice, Stanley Holloway, Roland Culver, Margaret Rutherford, Avice Landone, Richard Wattis, Frankie Howerd, Jimmy Edwards, Gilbert Harding

'Apart from a fairly Kafkaesque scene in which Daisy is discovered in an upright piano, the situation is treated with little wit or comic invention.'—*MFB*

The Alligator People
US 1959　73m　bw　Cinemascope

A doctor uses a revolutionary serum which unfortunately turns patients into the alligators from which it was derived. Moderately inventive 'B' chiller. George Macready, Frieda Inescort, Beverly Garland, Bruce Bennett, Lon Chaney Jnr. Written by Orville H. Hampton; directed by Roy del Ruth; for TCF.

Almonds and Raisins*
GB 1983　90m　bw

The story of the Yiddish cinema in thirties New York. Interesting documentary compilation majoring in the work of Edgar G. Ulmer. Written by Wolf Mankowitz; directed by Russ Karel; for Willowgold / Brook Productions and the National Center for Jewish Film.

Almost Married
US 1932　50m　bw

An insane Bolshevik breaks out of hospital when he hears of his wife's bigamous marriage. Oddly-titled melodrama with flashes of interest, previously filmed by MGM in 1919. Violet Heming, Ralph Bellamy, Alexander Kirkland, Alan Dinehart. Written by Wallace Smith from the novel Devil's Triangle by Andrew Soutar; directed by William Cameron Menzies; for TCF.

An Almost Perfect Affair*
US 1979　93m　De Luxe
Paramount / Terry Carr

A young film producer at the Cannes Festival falls for the wife of an Italian impresario. Lively detail lifts many scenes of this eccentric romance, but the routine plot is a downer.

w Walter Bernstein, Don Peterson d Michael Ritchie *ph* Henri Decae *m* Georges Delerue

Keith Carradine, Monica Vitti, Raf Vallone, Christian de Sica

Aloha Bobby and Rose
US 1975　89m　Metrocolor
(Warner) Cine Artists International

A Los Angeles motor mechanic becomes unwittingly involved in crime and finds himself fleeing for the Mexican border with a girl friend.
Warmed-over retread of *They Live By Night*, not badly done but of no abiding interest.

wd Floyd Mutrux *ph* William A. Fraker

Paul Le Mat, Dianne Hull, Tim McIntire, Leigh French, Noble Willingham, Robert Carradine

'As accurate a picture of Southern California as I've yet seen.'—*Guardian*

● *Video: VCL*

'Pagan love—in an exotic, exciting tropic paradise!'
Aloma of the South Seas
US 1941　77m　Technicolor
Paramount (Monte Bell)

A young Polynesian chieftain returns to quell trouble on his island after being educated in the US.
Hoary goings-on in gory colour, a remake of a silent epic devised to display the star's sarong and the backlot's expensive volcano.

w Frank Butler, Seena Owen, Lillie Hayward d Alfred Santell *ph* Karl Struss, Wilfrid M. Cline, William Snyder *m* Victor Young *sp* Gordon Jennings

Dorothy Lamour, Jon Hall, Lynne Overman, Philip Reed, Katherine de Mille, Fritz Leiber, Dona Drake, Esther Dale

'The mountain has the privilege of belching when it is dissatisfied, which is something no well-bred critic should do.'—*C. A. Lejeune*

† A silent version in 1926 had starred Gilda Gray. Directed by Maurice·Tourneur, it adhered more closely to the original play (by John B. Hymer and Leroy Clemens).

AAN: Karl Struss, Wilfrid M. Cline, William Snyder

Alone in the Dark
US 1982   93m   Cineffects

Maximum-security prisoners in a mental hospital are liberated by a power failure.
Pretentious but incompetent horror flick of the Halloween school, with a plot partly borrowed from *Spellbound*. Jack Palance, Donald Pleasence, Martin Landau, Dwight Schultz, Deborah Hedwall. Written and directed by Jack Shoder; for New Line / Masada.

Alone on the Pacific**
Japan 1963   104m   Eastmancolor
      Cinemascope
Ishihara-Nikkatsu (Akira Nakai)
original title: *Taiheiyo Hitoribochi*

A young man crosses from Osaka to San Francisco in a small yacht.
Fascinating Robinson-Crusoe-like exercise, with flashbacks to life on dry land.

w Natto Wada, based on the experiences of Kenichi Horie   *d* Kon Ichikawa   *ph* Yoshihiro Yamazaki   *m* Yasushi Akatagawa, Tohru Takemitsu

Yujiro Ishihara, Masayuki Mori, Kinuyo Tanaka, Ruriko Asaoko

'Wonderfully comic moments emerge, but they never overshadow the film's sheer pictorial value.'—*Brenda Davies, MFB*

Along Came Jones*
US 1945   90m   bw
(UA) Cinema Artists Corporation (Gary Cooper)

Two cowboys are mistaken for killers.
Very mild western comedy melodrama, with the star at his most self-effacing and production only mediocre.

w Nunnally Johnson, *novel* Alan le May   *d* Stuart Heisler   *ph* Milton Krasner   *m* Charles Maxwell, Arthur Lange, Hugo Friedhofer

Gary Cooper, Loretta Young, William Demarest, Dan Duryea, Russell Simpson

Along the Great Divide
US 1950   88m   bw
Warner (Anthony Veiller)

A marshal prevents an old man from being hanged for murder, and eventually discovers the real culprit.
Adequate, modest western with an unusual detective element.

w Walter Doniger, Lewis Meltzer   *d* Raoul Walsh   *ph* Sid Hickox   *m* David Buttolph

Kirk Douglas, Virginia Mayo, Walter Brennan, John Agar, Ray Teal

The Alphabet Murders
GB 1965   90m   bw
MGM (Ben Arbeid)

Hercule Poirot solves a series of murders by an apparent lunatic choosing his victims in alphabetical order.
Ruination of a classic whodunnit novel, misguided both in its attempt to mix slapstick with detection and in its terrible central performance.

w David Pursall, Jack Seddon, *novel* The ABC Murders by Agatha Christie   *d* Frank Tashlin   *ph* Desmond Dickinson   *m* Ron Goodwin

Tony Randall, Robert Morley, Anita Ekberg, Maurice Denham, Guy Rolfe, James Villiers, Clive Morton

Alphaville*
France / Italy 1965   98m   bw
Chaumiane / Filmstudio (André Michelin)

A special agent travels across space to find out what happened to his predecessor, and finds himself in a loveless society.
A rather chill futuristic fantasy on the lines of *1984* but with an outer space background and a hero borrowed from Peter Cheyney.
Interesting but not endearing.

wd Jean-Luc Godard   *ph* Raoul Coutard   *m* Paul Misraki

Eddie Constantine, Anna Karina, Akim Tamiroff, Howard Vernon, Laszlo Szabo

● *Video: Palace*

Altered States*
US 1980   102m   Technicolor
Warner / Howard Gottfried, Daniel Melnick

A psychophysiologist uses a sensory deprivation tank to hallucinate himself back into primitive states of human evolution, in which guise he emerges to kill. . . .
Amusing elaboration of Jekyll and Hyde, not to mention the Karloff mad doctor second features of the forties. All very po-faced now, and certainly impeccably done.

w Sidney Aaron, *novel* Paddy Chayevsky   *d* Ken Russell   *ph* Jordan Cronenweth   *m* John Corigliano   *pd* Richard McDonald

William Hurt, Blair Brown, Bob Balaban, Charles Haid

'Russell clomps from one scene to the next, the psychedelic visions come at you like choppy slide shows, and the picture has a dismal, tired, humanistic ending.'—*Pauline Kael, New Yorker*

● *Video: Warner*

'A herd of cattle against a herd of cannon!'
Alvarez Kelly
US 1966   116m   Technicolor
      Panavision
Columbia / Ray David (Sol C. Siegel)

The owner of a herd of 2500 cattle finds himself between two sides in the American Civil War.
Unusual if rather tepid western which balances historical interest against social conscience and throws in a variety of other elements.

w Franklin Coen   *d* Edward Dmytryk   *ph* Joseph MacDonald   *m* John Green

William Holden, Richard Widmark, Janice Rule, Patrick O'Neal, Victoria Shaw, Roger C. Carmel, Richard Rust

● *Video: RCA / Columbia*

Alvin Purple
Australia 1973   97m   colour

A young man who finds himself irresistible to women finally lands a job as gardener in a convent. Dismal sex farce which nevertheless helped to start the present world-wide popularity of Australian cinema. Graeme Blundell, Abigail, Lynette Curran, Christine Amor, Dina Mann. Written by Alan Hopgood; directed by Tim Burstall; for Hexagon.

Always Goodbye
US 1938   75m   bw
TCF (Raymond Griffith)

An unwed mother gives up her baby and later wants it back.
Tired sentimental warhorse, a remake of *Gallant Lady* (qv).

w Kathryn Scola, Edith Skouras   *d* Sidney Lanfield   *ph* Robert Planck   *md* Louis Silvers

Barbara Stanwyck, Herbert Marshall, Ian Hunter, Cesar Romero, Lynn Bari, Binnie Barnes

'A fair summer attraction . . . should do satisfactorily on the strength of its cast.'—*Variety*

Always in My Heart*
US 1942   92m   bw
Warner (Walter McEwen, William Jacobs)

A convict returns home to find his daughter a stranger and his wife about to marry again.
Well acted sentimental drama.

w Adele Commandini, *play* Fly Away Home by Dorothy Bennett, Irving White   *d* Joe Graham   *ph* Sid Hickox   *m* Heinz Roemheld

Walter Huston, Kay Francis, Gloria Warren, Frankie Thomas, Sidney Blackmer, Una O'Connor

AAN: title song (*m* Ernest Lucuona, *ly* Kim Gannon)

Always Leave Them Laughing*
US 1949   116m   bw
Warner (Jerry Wald)

A vaudeville comedian craves the spotlight at the expense of his private life.
Raucous backstage vehicle, crammed with sentimental and melodramatic cliché but affording tantalizing glimpses of the stage acts of its two stars.

w Jack Rose, Mel Shavelson   *d* Roy del Ruth   *ph* Ernest Haller   *ly* Sammy Cahn   *md* Ray Heindorf

Milton Berle, Bert Lahr, Virginia Mayo, Ruth Roman, Alan Hale, Jerome Cowan

Always Together*
US 1947 78m bw

Dying millionaire bequeaths his all to a working girl, then recovers and tries to retrieve it. Oddball comedy about a girl who has film fantasies, killed by dull title. Joyce Reynolds, Robert Hutton, Cecil Kellaway, Ernest Truex; guest appearances by Bogart and Flynn (among others). Written by Henry and Phoebe Ephron and I. A. L. Diamond; directed by Frederick de Cordova; for Warner.

Les Amants*
France 1958 88m bw Dyaliscope
Nouvelles Editions
aka: *The Lovers*

A rich provincial wife has a secret life in Paris, but finds real satisfaction in an affair with a young man.
A passionate romance which had some censorship difficulties at the time, this rather gloomy film never quite whirls one away as it should, and it doesn't have the eye for detail of *Brief Encounter*.

wd Louis Malle, *novel* Point de Lendemain by Dominique Vivant, Baron de Denon *ph* Henri Decaë *m* Brahms

Jeanne Moreau, Alain Cluny, Jean-Marc Bory, Judith Magre

Les Amants de Vérone*
France 1948 110m bw
CICC (Raymond Borderie)
aka: *The Lovers of Verona*

In modern Venice a film is being made of *Romeo and Juliet*, and the stand-ins for the stars feel they are re-enacting the old story. A superbly stylish if rather empty piece, the dazzling detail being much more interesting than the main story.

w André Cayatte, Jacques Prévert *d* André Cayatte *ph* Henri Alekan *m* Joseph Kosma *ad* Moulaert

Pierre Brasseur, Serge Reggiani, Anouk Aimée, Louis Salou, Marcel Dalio
'Visually exciting, immaculately made.'—*Penelope Houston*

Amarcord**
Italy / France 1973 123m Technicolor
FC Produzione / PECF (Franco Cristaldi)

Memories of a small Italian town during the fascist period.
A bizarre, intriguing mixture of fact, fantasy and obscurity, generally pleasing to watch though hardly satisfying. The title means I remember'.

w Federico Fellini, Tonino Guerra *d* Federico Fellini *ph* Giuseppe Rotunno *m* Nino Rota *ad* Danilo Donati

Puppela Maggio, Magali Noel, Armando Brancia, Ciccio Ingrassia
'A rich surface texture and a sense of exuberant melancholia.'—*Michael Billington, Illustrated London News*

'Peaks of invention separated by raucous valleys of low comedy.'—*Sight and Sound*
'Some idea of attitudes within the film business may be conveyed by the fact that this witty, tender, humane, marvellously photographed picture has been booked into a cinema with 132 seats.'—*Benny Green, Punch*
AA: best foreign film
AAN: script; direction

The Amateur
US 1982 111m Technicolor
TCF / Joel B. Michaels, Garth B. Drabinsky

A computer expert goes into action on his own account when his girl friend is killed in the Munich consulate and the CIA takes no reprisals.
Ho-hum espionage adventure which has its moments but barely got released.

w Robert Littell, Diana Maddox, *novel* Robert Littell *d* Charles Jarrott *ph* John Coquillon *m* Ken Wannberg

John Savage, Christopher Plummer, Marthe Keller, Arthur Hill, Ed Lauter
'Ill constructed and largely implausible, with occasional atmospheric touches.'—*Guardian*

Amateur Daddy
US 1932 71m bw

A promise to a dying friend leaves a construction engineer with four orphans to look after. Sentimental drama of the *Daddy Longlegs* school, with backwoods atmosphere which makes it seem even more dated than it is. Warner Baxter, Marian Nixon, Rita LaRoy, William Pawley, David Landau. Written by William Conselman, Doris Malloy and Frank Dolan, from the novel Scotch Valley by Mildred Cram; directed by John Blystone; for Fox. 'Strikes a strong human interest note . . . more than often very agreeable entertainment.'—*Variety*

The Amateur Gentleman*
GB 1936 102m bw
Criterion (Marcel Hellman, Douglas Fairbanks Jnr)

A Regency innkeeper's son poses as a travelling pugilist in order to clear his father's name of theft.
Dated but rather fascinating period adventure, quite a lively production of its time.

w Clemence Dane, Edward Knoblock, Sergei Nolbandov *d* Thornton Freeland *ph* Gunther Krampf

Douglas Fairbanks Jnr, Elissa Landi, Gordon Harker, Basil Sydney, Hugh Williams, Irene Browne, Margaret Lockwood, Coral Browne, Frank Pettingell, Athole Stewart, Esmé Percy

The Amazing Colossal Man*
US 1957 80m bw
AIP / Malibu (Bert I. Gordon)

A plutonium explosion causes an army colonel to grow at the rate of ten feet a day.
Modest, quite well written sci-fi let down by shaky trick work.

w Bert I. Gordon, Mark Hanna *d* Bert I. Gordon *ph* Joe Biroc *m* Albert Glasser

Glenn Langan, Cathy Downs, William Hudson, James Seay
† Sequel: *Revenge of the Colossal Man* (GB: *The Terror Strikes*).

The Amazing Dobermans
US 1976 99m colour

Most ambitious of three low-budget independent movies (others, *The Daring Dobermans* and *The Doberman Gang*) about a group of trained dogs; this one concerns an ex-con who hires them out for guard duty. A fair low-budget production for family audiences. Fred Astaire, James Franciscus, Parley Baer, Billy Barty. Written by Richard Chapman; directed by Byron Chudnow; for Doberman Associates.

The Amazing Dr Clitterhouse**
US 1938 87m bw
Warner (Robert Lord)

A criminologist researcher joins a gangster's mob and becomes addicted to crime.
Amusing, suspenseful, well acted comedy-melodrama.

w John Huston, John Wexley, *play* Barre Lyndon *d* Anatole Litvak *ph* Tony Gaudio *m* Max Steiner

Edward G. Robinson, Humphrey Bogart, Claire Trevor, Allen Jenkins, Gale Page, Donald Crisp, Maxie Rosebloom
'An unquestionable winner . . . the picture inculcates a bit of the sherlocking theme and modified romance.'—*Variety*
'The story is ingenious, but Anatole Litvak and his producing-acting crew have so thoroughly kept the larky mood of it while setting up the necessary mood of interest and suspense that it is hard to see where conception leaves off and the shaping of it into motion begins.'—*Otis Ferguson*

The Amazing Dr X
US 1948 78m bw
Eagle—Lion
GB title: *The Spiritualist*

A widow seeks comfort from a fraudulent medium.
'An interesting subject for a thriller is muffed by naïve handling.

w Muriel Roy Bolton, Ian McLellan Hunter, *story* Crane Wilbur *d* Bernard Vorhaus *ph* John Alton

Lynn Bari, Richard Carlson, Turhan Bey, Cathy O'Donnell

The Amazing Mr Blunden**
GB 1972 99m Eastmancolor
Hemdale / Hemisphere (Barry Levinson)

In 1918, a widow and her two children meet a kindly gentleman who offers them work in his old mansion. Here they meet two ghost children, discover that he is a ghost too, and travel a hundred years back in time to right a wicked wrong.
Involved ghost story for intellectual children, made generally palatable by oodles of period charm and good acting.

wd *Lionel Jeffries, story* The Ghosts by
Antonio Barker *ph* Gerry Fisher *m* Elmer
Bernstein *pd* Wilfrid Shingleton

Laurence Naismith, Diana Dors, James
Villiers, David Lodge, Lynne Frederick,
Dorothy Alison, Rosalyn Lander, Marc
Granger

'Easy period charm . . . fills every
crevice.'—*Clyde Jeavons*

● *Video: VCL*

The Amazing Mr Williams*
US 1939   86m   bw
Columbia (Everett Riskin)

About-to-be-marrieds investigate a murder.
Brisk comedy-thriller on *Thin Man* lines.

w Dwight Taylor, Sy Bartlett, Richard
Maibaum *d* Alexander Hall *ph* Arthur Todd
md Morris Stoloff

Melvyn Douglas, Joan Blondell, Ruth
Donnelly, Clarence Kolb, Ed Brophy, Donald
MacBride, Don Beddoe

The Amazing Mrs Holliday
US 1943   98m   bw
Universal (Bruce Manning, Frank Shaw)

Torpedoed in mid-Pacific, a missionary's
daughter arrives in San Francisco with eight
Chinese orphans.
Unusual sentimental vehicle for its star; of no
particular interest or merit in itself, but with
the usual interludes for song.

w Frank Ryan, John Jacoby *d* Bruce
Manning *ph* Elwood Bredell *m* Hans Salter,
Frank Skinner *md* Charles Previn

Deanna Durbin, Edmond O'Brien, Frieda
Inescort, Barry Fitzgerald

AAN: Hans Salter, Frank Skinner

The Amazing Quest of Ernest Bliss
GB 1936   80m   bw
Garrett–Klement (Robert Garrett, Otto
Klement)
US title: *Romance and Riches*

A millionaire accepts a wager that he can live
independently of his riches for one year.
Formulary comedy drama of its era on the
theme that money isn't everything. Very
dated.

w John L. Balderston *d* Alfred Zeisler
ph Otto Heller

Cary Grant (on home leave after his first
Hollywood success), Mary Brian, Henry
Kendall, Leon M. Lion, Garry Marsh, Moore
Marriott, Peter Gawthorne, Ralph Richardson

The Amazing Spiderman
The films released theatrically in the late
seventies were 'stretchouts' of television
episodes. See *Halliwell's Television
Companion*.

Ambassador Bill
US 1931   68m   bw

An Oklahoma cattle man is appointed US
ambassador to a foreign country ruled by a
regency. Poorly tailored star vehicle. Will

Rogers, Marguerite Churchill, Greta Nissen,
Gustav Von Seyffertitz, Ray Milland. Written
by Guy Bolton, from a story by Vincent
Sheean; directed by Sam Taylor; for Fox.
'Wilting yarn, illogical hoke.'—*Variety*

The Ambassador's Daughter*
US 1956   102m   Technicolor
    Cinemascope
UA / Norman Krasna

An American senator in Paris decides that the
presence of US forces in Paris constitutes a
moral danger. The ambassador's daughter
decides to investigate.
Thin comedy of the old-fashioned type: smart
lines and intimate playing not helped by the
vast screen.

wd Norman Krasna *ph* Michael Kelber
m Jacques Metehen

Olivia de Havilland, John Forsythe, Edward
Arnold, Adolphe Menjou, Myrna Loy,
Francis Lederer, Tommy Noonan, Minor
Watson

'An experienced cast approach the story's
frivolities with poise and style.'—*MFB*

Ambush*
US 1938   62m   bw

A girl proves her brother innocent and brings
gangsters to book. Brisk second feature with
an unexpected writing credit. Gladys
Swarthout, Lloyd Nolan, Ernest Truex.
Written by S. J. and Laura Perelman; directed
by Kurt Neumann; for Paramount. 'Hard
hitting, fast moving and at all times
plausible.'—*Variety*

Ambush*
US 1949   89m   bw
MGM (Armand Deutsch)

An army scout leads a posse to capture an
Indian chief who is holding a white woman
hostage.
Good, clean, robust western, well produced
and acted.

w Marguerite Roberts *d* Sam Wood *ph*
Harold Lipstein *m* Rudolph Kopp

Robert Taylor, John Hodiak, Arlene Dahl,
Don Taylor, Jean Hagen, Leon Ames

Ambush at Tomahawk Gap
US 1953   73m   Technicolor
Columbia (Wallace MacDonald)

Four ex-convicts seek hidden loot in a ghost
town.
Standard co-feature western with rather more
violence than usual for its date.

w David Lang *d* Fred F. Sears *ph* Henry
Freulich *m* Ross Di Maggio

John Hodiak, John Derek, David Brian,
Maria Elena Marques, Ray Teal, John Qualen

Ambush Bay
US 1966   109m   De Luxe
UA / Aubrey Schenck

In 1944, nine Marines try to escape from a
Japanese-held island.

Routine, lengthy, sub-standard heroics for
action addicts.

w Marve Feinberg, Ib Melchior *d* Ron
Winston *ph* Emanuel Rojas *m* Richard La
Salle

Hugh O'Brian, Mickey Rooney, James
Mitchum, Tisa Chang, Harry Lauter

The Ambushers
US 1967   102m   Technicolor
Columbia / Meadway / Claude (Irving Allen)

An experimental flying disc disappears on a
test run, and the trail leads Matt Helm to the
Mexican jungle.
The third Matt Helm adventure had such a
stupid script that all concerned decided to send
it up, unfortunately with too obvious a
tendency to smirk at their own bravado.

w Herbert Baker *d* Henry Levin *ph* Burnett
Guffey, Edward Colman *m* Hugo
Montenegro

Dean Martin, Senta Berger, Janice Rule, Kurt
Kasznar, James Gregory, Albert Salmi

'Plot, jokes and gadgets all well below
par.'—*MFB*

'Love of tender girlhood! Passionate deeds
    of heroes! A rushing, leaping drama of
    charm and excitement!'

America**
US 1924   122m (24 fps)   bw   silent
(UA)

Various characters experience the
Revolutionary War.
The Birth of a Nation, one war back. Much of
interest, but nothing new; Griffith was
basically repeating himself.

w John Pell *d* D. W. Griffith *ph* Billy Bitzer,
Hendrick Sartow, Marcel le Picard, Hal
Sintzenich

Neil Hamilton, Carol Dempster, Lionel
Barrymore, Erville Alderson

† As the English were the villains, the film was
banned in Britain, but later released under the
title *Love and Sacrifice*.

America, America*
US 1963   177m   bw
Warner (Elia Kazan)
GB title: *The Anatolian Smile*

In 1896 Turkey, a young Greek dreams of
emigrating to America, and finally does so.
A massive piece of self-indulgence by a one-
man band, fascinating for his family circle but
so poorly constructed as to be of very limited
interest elsewhere.

wd Elia Kazan *ph* Haskell Wexler *m* Manos
Hadjidakis

Stathis Giallelis, Frank Wolff, Harry Davis,
Elena Karam, Estelle Hemsley, Lou Antonio

'Kazan has failed to film the adventure
implicit in his material, and a potentially
exciting story has gone to waste.'—*MFB*

'If he sinks his teeth in a scene or a
sequence that he enjoys, the audience can just
sit around and be damned.'—*Stanley
Kauffmann*

'Every episode, almost every shot, has its own beginning, middle and end, and the numberless playlets are cemented together into a strip which after the first two hours threatens to stretch grimly into eternity.'—*Robert Hatch, The Nation*

AAN: best picture; Elia Kazan (as writer); Elia Kazan (as director)

An American Dream
US 1966   103m   Technicolor
Warner (William Conrad)
GB title: *See You in Hell, Darling*

A TV commentator is goaded into murdering his wife, becomes involved with gangsters and, tortured by guilt, allows them to kill him for shielding the girl friend of one of them. Ludicrously heavy-handed version of a semi-surrealist book which presumably had something to say about modern America, at least in its author's mind. Nothing comes through but relentless boredom at watching sordid and unlikely events, and sympathy for those involved.

w Mann Rubin, *novel* Norman Mailer *d* Robert Gist *ph* Sam Leavitt *m* Johnny Mandel

Stuart Whitman, Janet Leigh, Eleanor Parker (in a one-scene role of screaming bitchery that has to be seen to be believed), J. D. Cannon, Lloyd Nolan, Barry Sullivan, Murray Hamilton

AAN: song, 'A Time for Love' (*m* Johnny Mandel, *ly* Paul Francis Webster)

American Dreamer
US 1984   105m   Technicolor
Warner / CBS (Doug Chapin)

After a road accident, a dully married lady novelist begins to think she is the romantic creation of her favourite author.
Mildly amusing comedy of a curiously old-fashioned kind.

w Jim Kouf, David Greenwalt, Ann Biderman *d* Rick Rosenthal *ph* Giuseppe Rotunno *m* Lewis Furey *pd* Brian Eatwell

JoBeth Williams, Tom Conti, Coral Browne, Giancarlo Giannini, James Staley, Huckleberry Fox

American Empire
US 1942   82m   bw

Brothers fall out over management of their Texas ranch. Reasonable but forgettable semi-western. Richard Dix, Preston Foster, Frances Gifford, Leo Carrillo. Written by Ben Grauman Kohn, Gladys Atwater, Robert Bren; directed by William McGann; for Harry Sherman / UA. (GB title: *My Son Alone*.)

'He's the highest paid lover in Beverly Hills!'
American Gigolo
US 1980   117m   Metrocolor
Paramount / Pierre Associates (Freddie Fields)

A male prostitute finds that a client won't clear him when he is falsely charged with murder.

Thoroughly unattractive wallow on the seamy side of Los Angeles, with none of *Midnight Cowboy*'s compassion.

wd Paul Schraeder *ph* John Bailey *m* Giorgio Moroder

Richard Gere, Lauren Hutton, Hector Elizondo, Nina Van Pallandt
'A hot subject, cool style and overly contrived plotting don't all mesh.'—*Variety*
† Christopher Reeve allegedly refused one million dollars to play the lead.
● Video: CIC

'Where were you in '62?'
American Graffiti**
US 1973   110m   Techniscope
Universal / Lucasfilm / Coppola Company (Francis Ford Coppola, Gary Kurtz)

In 1962 California, four young men about to leave for college gather for a night's girl-chasing and police-baiting.
Nostalgic comedy recalling many sights and sounds of the previous generation and carefully crystallizing a particular time and place. Successful in itself, it led to many imitations.

wd George Lucas *ph* Ron Eveslage, Jan D'Alquen *m* popular songs

Richard Dreyfuss, Ronny Howard, Paul le Mat, Charlie Martin Smith, Cindy Williams, Candy Clark, Mackenzie Philips

AAN: best picture; George Lucas (as writer); George Lucas (as director); Candy Clark

An American Guerrilla in the Philippines*
US 1950   105m   Technicolor
TCF (Lamar Trotti)
GB title: *I Shall Return*

World War II, Pacific Zone: two American sailors try to make their way to Australia after MacArthur's surrender at Bataan.
Rather dull adventure story shot in the actual locations.

w Lamar Trotti, *novel* Ira Wolfert *d* Fritz Lang *ph* Harry Jackson *m* Cyril Mockridge

Tyrone Power, Micheline Presle, Tom Ewell, Bob Pattern, Tommy Cook, Robert Barrat (as MacArthur), Jack Elam
'Cannot be regarded as a serious war film.'—*Penelope Houston*

American Hot Wax
US 1978   91m   Metrocolor
Paramount (Art Limson)

The early days of rock and roll as seen by a prominent disc jockey of the time.
Mildly entertaining ragbag of semi-historical facts and authentic music, strictly for the youth market.

w John Kaye *d* Floyd Mutrux *ph* William A. Fraker *md* Kenny Vance

Tim McIntire (as Alan Freed), Fran Drescher, Jay Lena, Laraine Newman, Chuck Berry, Jerry Lee Lewis, Screamin' Jay Hawkins

An American in Paris****
US 1951   113m   Technicolor
MGM (*Arthur Freed*)

A carefree young artist scorns a rich woman's patronage and wins the love of a gamine. Altogether delightful musical holiday, one of the highspots of the Hollywood genre, with infectious enthusiasm and an unexpected sense of the Paris that was.

w Alan Jay Lerner d Vincente Minnelli ph Al Gilks, John Alton m George Gershwin ly Ira Gershwin ch Gene Kelly ad Cedric Gibbons, Preston Ames

Gene Kelly, Oscar Levant, Nina Foch, Leslie Caron, Georges Guetary

Songs include 'I Got Rhythm'; 'Embraceable You'; 'By Strauss'; 'Swonderful'; 'Tra La La'; 'Our Love Is Here to Stay'; 'Stairway to Paradise'; 'Concerto in F' (instrumental); 'An American in Paris' (ballet)
'Too fancy and overblown, but the principal performers are in fine form and the Gershwin music keeps everything good-spirited.'—*New Yorker, 1977*
† Chevalier was originally paged for the Georges Guetary role, but turned it down because he lost the girl. The production cost $2,723,903, of which $542,000 went on the final ballet.

AA: best picture; Alan Jay Lerner; Al Gilks, John Alton; musical arrangements (Saul Chaplin, Johnny Green)
AAN: Vincente Minnelli

American Madness**
US 1932   80m   bw
Columbia

When a bank failure threatens, hundreds of small savers increase their deposits to save the situation.
Vivid, overstressed topical melodrama with crowd scenes typical of its director's later output.

w Robert Riskin *d* Frank Capra *ph* Joseph Walker

Walter Huston, Pat O'Brien, Kay Johnson, Constance Cummings, Gavin Gordon, Berton Churchill
'It's a money picture. That goes both ways. It's about money and banks and spells dough for the box office. It's timely, topical, human, dramatic, punchy and good entertainment at one and the same time.'—*Variety*
'The sequence of the mounting panic and the storming of the bank are effectively staged, but the resolution is the usual Capra / Riskin populist hokum.'—*New Yorker, 1977*

An American Romance*
US 1944   151m   Technicolor
MGM (King Vidor)

The life of a European immigrant who becomes a master of industry.
Mind-boggling pageant of the American dream, coldly presented and totally humourless. Its saving grace is its smooth physical presentation.

AN AMERICAN IN PARIS. Georges Guetary danced up his famous stairway and was never seen again, not in an American film at least.

w Herbert Dalmas, William Ludwig *d* King Vidor *ph* Harold Rosson *m* Louis Gruenberg

Brian Donlevy, Ann Richards, John Qualen, Walter Abel, Stephen McNally

'A thousand chances to inform, excite or even interest have been flung away.'—*Richard Winnington*

'The whole aim of it is to boost The American Way.'—*Richard Mallett, Punch*

'Drama that happens around you every day—when the wild life of impetuous youth burns away age-old barriers!'

An American Tragedy**
US 1931 95m bw
Paramount

An ambitious young man murders his pregnant fiancée when he has a chance to marry a rich girl.
Dated but solidly satisfying adaptation of a weighty novel, more compelling than the 1951 remake *A Place in the Sun*.

wd Josef Von Sternberg, *novel* Theodore Dreiser *ph* Lee Garmes *ad* Hans Dreier

Phillips Holmes, *Sylvia Sidney*, Frances Dee, Irving Pichel, Frederick Burton, Claire McDowell

'It unreels as an ordinary programme effort with an unhappy ending . . . as Sternberg has seen fit to present it the celluloid structure is slow, heavy and not always interesting drama. Its box office success is very doubtful.'—*Variety*

'It is the first time, I believe, that the subjects of sex, birth control and murder have been put into a picture with sense, taste and reality.'—*Pare Lorentz*

'An aimless, lugubrious mess. The fireworks may dazzle to schoolboys of criticism, but they will add no permanent color to the motion picture.'—*Harry Alan Potamkin*

An American Werewolf in London*
GB 1981 97m Technicolor
Polygram / Lycanthrope (Peter Guber, Jon Peters)

Two American tourists are bitten by a werewolf.
Curious but oddly endearing mixture of horror film and spoof, of comedy and shock, with everything grist to its mill including tourist Britain and the wedding of Prince Charles. The special effects are notable, and signalled new developments in this field.

wd John Landis *ph* Robert Paynter *m* Elmer Bernstein *sp* Effects Associates, Rick Baker

David Naughton, Jenny Agutter, Griffin Dunne, John Woodvine

'The gear changes of tone and pace make for a very jerkily driven vehicle.'—*Sunday Times*

● *Video: Polygram*

The Americanization of Emily*
US 1964 115m bw
MGM / Filmways (John Calley)

World War II: just before the Normandy landings, a war widow driver falls for an American commander who is a self-confessed coward.
Bizarre comedy full of eccentric characters, an uneasy choice for its female star but otherwise successful in patches in its random distillation of black comedy, sex and the tumbling of old-fashioned virtues.

w Paddy Chayevsky, *novel* William Bradford Huie *d* Arthur Hiller *ph* Philip Lathrop, Chris Challis *m* Johnny Mandel

Julie Andrews, James Garner, *Melvyn Douglas*, James Coburn, Liz Fraser, Joyce Grenfell, Edward Binns, Keenan Wynn, William Windom

'Out of it all there comes the definite feeling that Hitler's war is incidental to Paddy Chayevsky's war of ideas . . . no plot synopsis could begin to suggest how much the characters talk.'—*MFB*

AAN: Philip Lathrop

The Americano
US 1916 60m approx (24 fps) bw silent
Triangle (D. W. Griffith)

A young American engineer becomes involved in a revolution in Patagonia.
Early star adventure vehicle, an immense popular success; the last film Fairbanks made for Griffith.

w Anita Loos, John Emerson, *novel* Blaze Derringer by Eugene P. Lyle Jnr *d* John Emerson *ph* Victor Fleming

Douglas Fairbanks, Alma Rubens, Spottiswoode Aitken, Lillian Langdon

The Americano
US 1955 85m Technicolor
(RKO) Robert Stillman

A westerner takes three prize bulls to Brazil, but finds the buyer has been murdered.
A western with a twist, but otherwise extremely dull, with poor pace, colour and use of settings.

w Guy Trosper *d* William Castle *ph* William Snyder *m* Roy Webb

Glenn Ford, Frank Lovejoy, Abbe Lane, Cesar Romero, Ursula Thiess

● *Video: BBC*

Un Ami Viendra ce Soir
France 1946 111m bw
CGC (R. Artus)

During World War II a French patriot uses a lunatic asylum as a resistance headquarters.
Rather glum wartime melodrama, lacking in tension.

w Jacques Companeez, Raymond Bernard *d* Raymond Bernard *ph* Robert Le Fèbvre *m* Arthur Honegger

Michel Simon, Louis Salou, Saturnin Fabre, Paul Bernard, Madeleine Sologne, Marcel André

Le Amiche*
Italy 1955   90m   bw
Trionfalcine
aka: *The Girl Friends*

The interaction of five girls living together in Turin.
Highbrow lending library stuff, quite watchable but equally forgettable.

w Suso Cecchi d'Amico, Alba de Cespedes, *story* Tra Donne Sole by Cesare Pavese *d* Michelangelo Antonioni *ph* Gianni di Venanzo *m* Giovanni Fusco

Eleanora Rossi Drago, Valentina Cortese, Yvonne Furneaux, Gabriele Ferzetti, Franco Fabrizi, Madeleine Fischer

The Amityville Horror
US 1979   118m   Movielab
AIP / Cinema 77 (Ronald Saland, Elliot Geisinger)

Newlyweds move into a house where a murder was committed, and experience strange manifestations which drive them away.
Sub-*Exorcist* goings on, a shameless exaggeration of some of the alleged facts retailed in the best-selling book. A shocker for the uncritical.

w Sandor Stern, *book* Jay Anson *d* Stuart Rosenberg *ph* Fred J. Koenekamp *m* Lalo Schifrin

James Brolin, Margot Kidder, Rod Steiger, Don Stroud, Murray Hamilton
● *Video:*·Guild

Amityville II: The Possession
US 1982   104m   De Luxe

The haunted house at Amityville gives the jitters to a second family. Everything but the kitchen sink is thrown into this ghoulish brew, and most of it is red; but the script is hopeless from the start. Burt Young, Rutanya Alda, James Olson, Jack Magner, Andrew Prine. Written by Tommy Lee Wallace; directed by Damiano Damiani; for Dino de Laurentiis / Orion. 'There probably isn't a more unsympathetic bunch on screen this year. They're sure to make audiences root for the house.'—*Variety*.
● *Video: Thorn EMI*

Amityville 3-D
US 1984   93m   colour   Arrivision

A sceptical journalist moves into the haunted house but is jolted out of his complacency. Ragbag of supernatural incident with neither cohesion nor plausibility, but good 3-D. Tony Roberts, Tess Harper, Robert Joy, Candy Clark, John Beal, Leora Dana. Written by William Wales; directed by Richard Fleischer; for Dino de Laurentiis / Orion. 'An assortment of unrelated happenings precedes the final appearance of a crude bug-eyed monster.'—*MFB*

Among the Living*
US 1941   68m   bw
Paramount (Sol C. Siegel)

In a small town live twin brothers, one of whom is a murderer.
Offbeat suspenser with effective performances.

w Lester Cole, Garrett Fort *d* Stuart Heisler *ph* Theodor Sparkuhl

Albert Dekker, Susan Hayward, Frances Farmer, Harry Carey, Gordon Jones
   'Head and shoulders above all the filler shows ground out by Hollywood to perpetuate the double feature system.'—*Howard Barnes, New York Herald Tribune*

L'Amore*
Italy 1948   79m   bw
Tevere Film (Roberto Rossellini)

Two short films. *The Human Voice*: a woman talks on the phone to the man who has forsaken her. *The Miracle*: a peasant woman is seduced and is convinced she will give birth to a new Messiah.
A *tour de force* by an actress to be reckoned with; but hardly compulsive as cinema.

play Jean Cocteau   *original script* Tullio Pinelli, Roberto Rossellini, Federico Fellini *d* Roberto Rossellini *ph* Robert Juillard, Aldo Tonti *m* Renzo Rossellini

Anna Magnani, Federico Fellini
† *The Miracle* was separately released in some countries.

'The rollicking story of a ribald century that should have been ashamed of itself!'
The Amorous Adventures of Moll Flanders
GB 1965   125m   Technicolor Panavision
Paramount / Winchester (Marcel Hellman)

An ambitious servant girl loses her virtue to a succession of rich gentlemen but finally settles for a highwayman.
The aim was to make a female *Tom Jones*, but this bawdy romp never achieves the freewheeling fluency of that surprise success, and a vacuous central performance makes the constant couplings more boring than exciting.

w Dennis Cannan, Roland Kibbee, *novel* Daniel Defoe *d* Terence Young *ph* Ted Moore *m* John Addison *pd* Syd Cain

Kim Novak, Richard Johnson, George Sanders, Lilli Palmer, Angela Lansbury, Leo McKern, Vittorio de Sica, Cecil Parker, Daniel Massey
   'Further from Defoe than *Tom Jones* was from Fielding, but with much the same combination of crude table manners and clean sets to stand in for period flavour.'—*MFB*

The Amorous Prawn*
GB 1962   89m   bw
BL / Covent Garden (Leslie Gilliat)
US title: *The Playgirl and the War Minister* (an attempt to cash in on the Profumo case)

A hard-up general's wife invites American paying guests to their official highland home.

This film version of a stage success seems very mild, but the cast is eager to please: the result is a frantic high class farce.

w Anthony Kimmins, Nicholas Phipps, *play* Anthony Kimmins *d* Anthony Kimmins *ph* Wilkie Cooper *m* John Barry

Joan Greenwood, Ian Carmichael, Cecil Parker, Dennis Price, Robert Beatty, Finlay Currie, Liz Fraser, Derek Nimmo

L'Amour à Mort*
France 1984   90m   colour
Dussart / Ariane / A2 (Philippe Dussart)

An archaeologist and his mistress come to the conclusion that their love will reach its fullest expression in death.
Chilly symbolic drama, a continuation of the same team's preoccupations with the meaning of life which were previously explored (via the same four actors) in *Mon Oncle d'Amérique* and *La Vie est un Roman*. Interesting but not especially rewarding.

w Jean Gruault *d* Alain Resnais *ph* Sacha Vierny *m* Hans Werner Henze

Sabine Azema, Fanny Ardant, Pierre Arditi, André Dussolier

Amsterdam Affair
GB 1968   91m   Eastmancolor
LIP / Trio / Group W (Gerry Willoughby)

Inspector Van der Valk investigates when a writer is accused of murdering his mistress.
Tolerable *roman policier*.

w Edmund Ward, *novel* Love in Amsterdam by Nicholas Freeling *d* Gerry O'Hara *ph* Gerry Fisher *m* Patrick John Scott

Wolfgang Kieling, William Marlowe, Caterina Von Schell

The Amsterdam Kill
Hong Kong 1977   93m   Technicolor Panavision
Golden Harvest / Fantastic Films / Raymond Chow

An American ex-Drug Enforcement Agency officer tries to protect an old friend caught in the Hong Kong drug wars.
Roughly made and uninventive thriller in which the Hong Kong film makers fail to consolidate the international ground they gained with kung fu films.

w Robert Clouse, Gregory Teifer *d* Robert Clouse *ph* Alan Hume *m* Hal Schaffer

Robert Mitchum, Bradford Dillman, Richard Egan, Leslie Nielsen, Keye Luke
● *Video: Rank*

Amy
US 1981   100m   Technicolor

A spinster is taught a little about life and love.
Unmemorable family comedy drama. Jenny Agutter, Barry Newman, Kathleen Nolan, Chris Robinson, Margaret O'Brien, Nanette Fabray. Written by Noreen Stone; directed by Vincent McEveety; for Walt Disney.

'The most amazing conspiracy the world has ever known, and love as it never happened to a man and woman before!'

Anastasia**
US 1956 105m Eastmancolor Cinemascope
TCF (Buddy Adler)

In 1928 Paris, a group of exiled White Russians claim to have found the living daughter of the Tsar, presumed executed in 1918; but the claimant is a fake schooled by a general, with whom she falls in love.
Slick, highly theatrical entertainment for the upper classes; it dazzles and satisfies without throwing any light on history.

w Arthur Laurents, *play* Marcelle Maurette, Guy Bolton *d* Anatole Litvak *ph* Jack Hildyard *m* Alfred Newman *ad* Andrei Andreiev, Bill Andrews

Ingrid Bergman (her Hollywood comeback after some years in Europe under a cloud for her 'immoral' behaviour), Yul Brynner, *Helen Hayes*, Martita Hunt, Akim Tamiroff, Felix Aylmer, Ivan Desny
'Little weight but considerable and urbane charm.'—*John Cutts*

AA: Ingrid Bergman
AAN: Alfred Newman

Anatahan
Japan 1953 92m bw
Daiwa (K. Takimura)
aka: *The Saga of Anatahan*

During World War II, Japanese seamen are shipwrecked on the same deserted island as a man and a woman; the latter causes jealousy and murder.
Downright peculiar studio-set melodrama, based on true events and directed by its creator through interpreters, with results far from happy.

wd, ph Josef Von Sternberg *m* A. Ifukube

Akemi Negishi, T. Sugunuma, K. Onoe, T. Bandoh
'The main impression is of tedium relieved by moments of far from intentional humour.'—*Penelope Houston*

'Last year's number one best seller. This year's (we hope) number one motion picture!'

Anatomy of a Murder**
US 1959 161m bw Cinemascope
Columbia / Carlyle / Otto Preminger

A small-town lawyer successfully defends an army officer accused of murdering a bartender who had assaulted his wife.
Overlong and over-faithful version of a highly detailed courtroom bestseller. The plot is necessarily equivocal, the characterizations overblown, but the trial commands some interest, and the use of 'daring' words in evidence caused controversy at the time.

w Wendell Mayes, *novel* Robert Traver *d* Otto Preminger *ph* Sam Leavitt *m* Duke Ellington *pd* Boris Leven

James Stewart, Ben Gazzara, Lee Remick, *Eve Arden*, Arthur O'Connell, *George C.*

Scott (his first notable role, as the prosecutor), Kathryn Grant, Orson Bean, Murray Hamilton
† The trial judge was played by Joseph N. Welch, a real-life judge who had gained fame in 1954 by representing the army against Senator McCarthy.

AAN: best picture; Wendell Mayes; Sam Leavitt; James Stewart; Arthur O'Connell; George C. Scott

Anchors Aweigh**
US 1945 139m Technicolor
MGM (Joe Pasternak)

Two sailors on leave in Los Angeles get involved with a small boy who wants to join the navy.
Rather droopy musical most notable as a forerunner of *On the Town*, though on much more conventional lines. Amiable performances, and a brilliant dance with a cartoon mouse, save the day.

w Isobel Lennart *d* George Sidney *ph* Robert Planck, Charles Boyle *principal songs* Jule Styne *ly* Sammy Cahn *m* George Stoll *pd* Cedric Gibbons

Frank Sinatra, Gene Kelly, Kathryn Grayson, Jose Iturbi, Sharon McManus, Carlos Ramirez, Dean Stockwell, Pamela Britton

Songs include 'We Hate to Leave'; 'What Makes the Sun Set?'; 'The Charm of You'; 'I Begged Her'; 'I Fall in Love Too Easily'; 'The Worry Song'

AA: George Stoll
AAN: best picture; Robert Planck; Gene Kelly; song 'I Fall in Love Too Easily' (*m* Jule Styne, *ly* Sammy Cahn)

● *Video: MGM / UA*

And Baby Makes Three
US 1950 83m bw
Columbia (Robert Lord)

A wife divorces her compromised husband before discovering that she is pregnant.
Thin marital comedy with minor compensations.

w Lou Breslow, Joseph Hoffman *d* Henry Levin *ph* Burnett Guffey *m* George Duning

Robert Young, Barbara Hale, Billie Burke, Robert Hutton, Janis Carter, Nicholas Joy, Lloyd Corrigan
'It has everything but a story that hangs together.'—*New York Herald Tribune*

And God Created Woman
France 1956 92m Eastmancolor Cinemascope
Iena / UCIL / Cocinor (Raoul Lévy)
original title: *Et Dieu Créa la Femme*; aka: *And Woman . . . Was Created*

An 18-year-old finds herself fatally attracted towards men.
Rather a feeble excuse for its star to strip on the St Tropez beach.

w Roger Vadim, Raoul Lévy *d* Roger Vadim *ph* Armand Thirard *m* Paul Misraki

Brigitte Bardot, Curt Jurgens, Jean-Louis Trintignant, Christian Marquand, Georges Poujouly, Jane Marken, Paul Faivre
'An open violation of conventional morality.'—*Catholic Legion of Decency*
'I'm prepared to bet an overcoat to a bikini that this film will make its star Miss Sex of the Universe.'—*Sketch*

And Hope To Die
US / Fr / Canada 1972 104m bw

A fugitive Frenchman in Canada runs foul of criminals and gypsies and causes several deaths. Muddled melodrama of the worst 'international' kind. Jean-Louis Trintignant, Robert Ryan, Aldo Ray, Tisa Farrow, Lea Massari. Written by Sebastien Japrisot; directed by René Clément; for Serge Silberman / TCF.

And Justice For All
US 1979 119m Metrocolor
Columbia / Walton (Joe Wizan)

An American lawyer gets into all kinds of trouble, including the defence of a judge on a rape charge.
Not so much a satire as a series of random pot-shots at the legal system, sometimes funny but cumulatively stultifying.

w Valerie Curtin, Barry Levinson *d* Norman Jewison *ph* Frank Holgate *m* Dave Grusin

Al Pacino, Jack Warden, John Forsythe, Lee Strasberg, Christine Lahti, Sam Levene, Jeffrey Taybor
'Most incriminating is its own hysterical imprecision and sentimental pleading.'—*Sight and Sound*

And Now For Something Completely Different*
GB 1971 88m colour
(Columbia) Kettledrum / Python (Victor Lownes / GSF) (Patricia Casey)

Useful round-up of the more famous sketches from BBC TV's zany comedy series *Monty Python*.
Side-splitting for those who want Groucho Marx updated; baffling for reactionaries; movie presentation perfunctory.

written by and starring *John Cleese, Graham Chapman, Terry Gilliam, Eric Idle, Michael Palin, Terry Jones* *d* Ian Macnaughton *ph* David Muir

And Now Miguel*
US 1965 95m Technicolor
Universal / Robert B. Radnitz

A 10-year-old Mexican boy proves himself worthy to work on the mountain with the sheep.
A children's film typical of its producer: good to look at, documentarily convincing, but too slight and too slow.

w Ted Sherdeman, Jane Clove, *novel* Joseph Krumgold *d* James B. Clark *ph* Clifford Stine *m* Phillip Lambro

Pat Cardi, Guy Stockwell, Clu Gulager,
Michael Ansara, Joe de Santis

And Now The Screaming Starts
GB 1973 91m colour
Amicus (Max J. Rosenberg, Milton
   Subotsky)

A new bride in a country house is haunted by
hallucinations of the past.
Grisly ghost story which overplays its hand
and outstays its welcome.

w Roger Marshall, *novel* Fengriffen by David
Case d Roy Ward Baker *ph* Denys Coop
m Douglas Gamley

Peter Cushing, Stephanie Beacham, Herbert
Lom, Patrick Magee, Ian Ogilvy, Geoffrey
Whitehead, Guy Rolfe, Rosalie Crutchley

● *Video: Guild*

'Who are you that a man can't make love to
   you?'
And Now Tomorrow*
US 1944 86m bw
Paramount (Fred Kohlmar)

A rich girl goes deaf, loses her fiancé, but wins
the poor doctor who cares for her.
Bestselling slush turned into a routine star
romance.

w Frank Partos, Raymond Chandler (!), *novel*
Rachel Field d Irving Pichel *ph* Daniel L.
Fapp *m* Victor Young

Loretta Young, Alan Ladd (his first film in
confirmed top-star status after a meteoric rise
interrupted by war service), Susan Hayward,
Beulah Bondi, Cecil Kellaway, Barry Sullivan.
   'A vernal sign of the boys getting back to
one of their favourite legends after the wintry
days of war.'—*Richard Winnington*

And So They Were Married
US 1935 74m bw
Columbia (B. P. Schulberg)

A widow and a widower try to get married
despite the ill-feeling of their children.
Predictable romantic farce.

w Doris Anderson, Joseph Anthony d Elliott
Nugent *ph* Henry Freulich *m* Howard
Jackson

Melvyn Douglas, Mary Astor, Edith Fellows,
Jackie Moran, Donald Meek, Dorothy
Stickney

And Soon the Darkness*
GB 1970 99m Technicolor
Associated British (Albert Fennell, Brian
   Clemens)

Of two young nurses on a cycling holiday in
France, one is murdered by a local sex maniac
and the other almost shares her fate.
Slow, overstretched, often risible suspenser on
vanishing lady lines; long on red herrings and
short on humour, but with some pretension to
style. The action all takes place along a mile or
two of sunlit country road.

w Brian Clemens, Terry Nation d Robert
Fuest *ph* Ian Wilson *m* Laurie Johnson

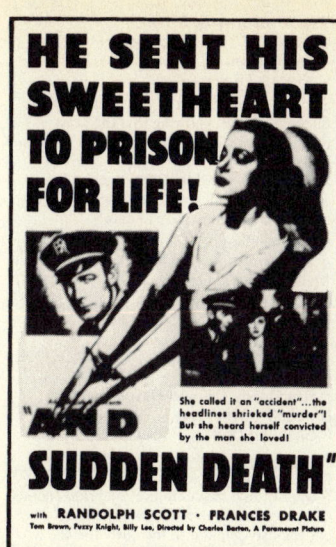

AND SUDDEN DEATH. A typical
Paramount 'crime support' of the thirties.
They often gave more satisfaction than the
main feature.

Pamela Franklin, Michele Dotrice, Sandor
Eles, John Nettleton
● *Video: Thorn EMI*

'There's nothing but trouble in Paradise
   when the bandleader tries to make love
   to a whole sister act—simultaneously!'
And the Angels Sing*
US 1943 95m bw
Paramount (E. D. Leshin)

Four singing sisters have hectic adventures
with a bandleader.
Mildly disarming romantic comedy with music,
more firmly set in a recognizable social milieu
than the usual fan product from this studio.

w Melvin Frank, Norman Panama, Claude
Binyon d George Marshall *ph* Karl Struss
m Victor Young *songs* Johnny Burke, Jimmy
Van Heusen

Dorothy Lamour, Diana Lynn, Betty Hutton,
Mimi Chandler, Fred MacMurray, Raymond
Walburn, Eddie Foy Jnr, Frank Albertson,
Mikhail Rasumny
   'Slapstick sophistication in a sub-Sturges
manner.'—*MFB*
   'Cruel, soggily professional, over-elaborate,
and inclined towards snobbish whimsy.'—
James Agee

And the Ship Sails On*
Italy / France 1983 132m Technicolor
RAI / Vides / Gaumont (Franco Cristaldi)
original title: *E la Nave Va*

From Naples in 1914 a luxurious liner sets
forth to scatter the ashes of an opera singer.
Less a Ship of Fools than a theatre of the
absurd, with familiar Fellini caricatures going
through their paces against studio sets.
Fascination alternates with boredom.

w Federico Fellini, Tonino Guerra d Federico
Fellini *ph* Giuseppe Rotunno *m* Gianfranco
Plenizio *ad* Dante Ferretti

Freddie Jones, Barbara Jefford, Victor Poletti,
Peter Cellier, Elisa Mainardi, Norma West

And Then There Were None****
US 1945 97m bw
Popular Pictures / Harry M. Popkin (René
   Clair)
GB title: *Ten Little Niggers*

Ten people are invited to a house party on a
lonely island, and murdered one by one.
A classic mystery novel is here adapted and
directed with the utmost care to provide
playful black comedy, stylish puzzlement, and
some splendid acting cameos.

w Dudley Nichols, *novel* Agatha Christie (aka
Ten Little Niggers) d René Clair *ph* Lucien
Andriot *m* Mario Castelnuovo-Tedesco

*Walter Huston, Barry Fitzgerald, Louis
Hayward, June Duprez, Roland Young,
Richard Haydn, C. Aubrey Smith, Judith
Anderson, Queenie Leonard, Mischa Auer*

MISS BRENT: 'Very stupid to kill the only
servant in the house. Now we don't even know
where to find the marmalade.'

   'Rich in the elements which have made
mystery melodramas popular, yet not in the
precise form of any previously made.'—
Hollywood Reporter
   'The efforts at sprightly, stylish comedy
don't gain much momentum.'—*Pauline Kael,
New Yorker, 70s*

And Then There Were None
GB 1974 98m Technicolor
EMI / Filibuster (Harry Alan Towers)

Ten people are lured to an isolated Persian
hotel and murdered one by one.
Listless remake, often so inept you could
scream.

w Peter Welbeck (Harry Alan Towers)
d Peter Collinson *ph* Fernando Arribas
m Bruno Nicolai

Oliver Reed, Richard Attenborough, Elke
Sommer, Herbert Lom, Gert Froebe,
Stéphane Audran, Charles Aznavour, Adolfo
Celi, Alberto de Mendoza, Maria Rohm
● *Video: Thorn EMI*

The Anderson Tapes*
US 1971 98m Technicolor Panavision
Columbia / Robert M. Weitman

An ex-con forms a gang to rob a building, not
knowing that police and others, for various
purposes, are making tape recordings of his
conversations.

Superficially slick and fashionable crime thriller, marred by unnecessarily flashy direction, a failure to explain enough about the tapes, and a climax which oddly mixes bloodshed and farce.

w Frank R. Pierson, *novel* Lawrence Sanders *d* Sidney Lumet *ph* Arthur J. Ornitz *m* Quincy Jones

Sean Connery, *Martin Balsam*, Dyan Cannon, Alan King, Ralph Meeker

● *Video: RCA / Columbia*

Andrei Rublev**
USSR 1966   181m   colour (part)
   Cinemascope
Mosfilm

Imaginary episodes from the life of a 15th-century icon painter.
A superb recreation of medieval life dramatizes the eternal problem of the artist, whether to take part in the life around him or merely comment on it.

w Andrei Mikhalkov-Konchalovsky, Andrei Tarkovsky *d* Andrei Tarkovsky *ph* Vadim Yusov *m* Vyacheslav Tcherniaiev
   'The one indisputable Russian masterpiece of the last decade.'—*Nigel Andrews, MFB, 1973*
   'With the exception of the great Eisenstein, I can't think of any film which has conveyed a feeling of the remote past with such utter conviction . . . a durable and unmistakable masterpiece.'—*Michael Billington, Illustrated London News*

Androcles and the Lion**
US 1952   96m   bw
RKO (Gabriel Pascal)

A slave takes a thorn from the paw of a lion which later, in the arena, refuses to eat him.
Shavian drollery, with interpolated discussions on faith, is scarcely ideal cinema material, but gusto in the performances keeps it going despite stolid direction.

w Chester Erskine, *play* Bernard Shaw *d* Chester Erskine *ph* Harry Stradling *m* Frederick Hollander *ad* Harry Horner

Alan Young, Jean Simmons, Robert Newton, Victor Mature, Maurice Evans (as Caesar), Reginald Gardiner, Elsa Lanchester, Alan Mowbray, Gene Lockhart
† Production had previously begun with Harpo Marx as Androcles and Rex Harrison as Caesar.

Android*
US 1982   80m   De Luxe
New World / Android (Mary Ann Fisher)

In 2036, a police transport vehicle is hijacked in space, and the scientists on board, some of them androids, react in unexpected ways.
Cheaply made, but a bobby dazzler for science fiction addicts.

w James Reigle, Don Opper   *d* Aaron Lipstadt *ph* Tim Suhrstedt *m* Don Preston

Klaus Kinski, Brie Howard, Norbert Weisser, Crofton Hardester, Kendra Kirchner, Don Opper
   'The best first feature since *Dark Star*.'—*Tom Milne, MFB*

The Andromeda Strain**
US 1970   131m   Technicolor
   Panavision
Universal / Robert Wise

Scientists work frantically to neutralize an infected village, knowing that the least infection will cause their laboratory to self-destruct.
Solemn and over-detailed but generally suspenseful thriller, with a sense of allegory about man's inhumanity to man.

w Nelson Gidding, *novel* Michael Crichton *d* Robert Wise *ph* Richard H. Kline *m* Gil Melle *ad* Boris Leven

Arthur Hill, David Wayne, James Olson, Kate Reid, Paula Kelly

● *Video: CIC*

Andy Hardy Comes Home*
US 1958   81m   bw
MGM (Red Doff)

Fortyish Andy returns to Carvel, his home town, to negotiate a land deal.
Rather dismal sequel to the celebrated series of Hardy family comedies which were enormously popular in the early forties: a thirteen-year gap is too long, and although most of the family is reunited the old Judge is sadly missed.

w Edward Everett Hutshing, Robert Morris Donley *d* Howard W. Koch *ph* William W. Spencer, Harold E. Wellman *m* Van Alexander

Mickey Rooney, Fay Holden, Cecilia Parker, Patricia Breslin, Sara Haden, Jerry Colonna
† See also under *Hardy Family*.

'I want love—and I'm going to get it!'
Angel*
US 1937   98m   bw
Paramount (Ernst Lubitsch)

The wife of an English diplomat finds herself neglected and almost has an affair with his old friend.
A curious romantic comedy in many ways typical of its time, yet with very few laughs, showing none of its director's usual cinematic sense, and compromised by the censor's refusal to let a spade be called a spade. Underplaying, and a sense that we watch a way of life about to be swept away, just about save it.

w Samson Raphaelson, *play* Melchior Lengyel *d* Ernst Lubitsch *ph* Charles Lang *m* Frederick Hollander

Marlene Dietrich, Herbert Marshall, Melvyn Douglas, Edward Everett Horton, Laura Hope Crews, Ernest Cossart
   MARIA: 'What's the matter, darling? Is it France?'
   SIR FREDERICK: 'No, no. Jugoslavia.'
   MARIA: 'Oh. I see.'
   'A rich Hollywood dish that copies foreign recipes. It's a good picture and in the keys, especially for the carriage trade, it can't miss.'—*Variety*

'Very sophisticated, very subtle, very chic, vastly polished and entertaining.'—*Literary Digest*
   'The production is performed with studied deliberation.'—*New York Times*
   'This movie isn't essentially different from the best of Lubitsch, but it's attenuated. It's the sort of cultivated triangular love affair in which each of the three has a turn at the piano.'—*Pauline Kael, 70s*

Angel*
Eire 1982   92m   Technicolor
Motion Picture Company of Ireland / Irish
   Film Board / Channel 4 (John Boorman)

Against a background of the Irish troubles, a saxophonist is drawn into a maze of violence when he attempts to avenge the murder of a mute girl.
Glumly Irish thriller with metaphysical overtones as well as references to the state of Ireland. Keen narrative style is dissipated by overkill.

wd Neil Jordan *ph* Chris Menges *m* Verdi

Stephen Rea, Veronica Quilligan, Alan Devlin, Peter Caffrey

'You're young, attractive and healthy—and swimming in a toilet bowl!'
Angel
US 1983   93m   CFI colour
New World / Adam's Apple / Angel (Sandy Howard)

A 15-year-old student doubles as a Hollywood hooker and takes on a psychopathic killer.
Yucky melodrama with no holds barred, not even moments of humour.

w Robert Vincent O'Neil, Joseph M. Cala *d* Robert Vincent O'Neil *ph* Andrew Davis *m* Craig Safan

Cliff Gorman, Donna Wilkes, Rory Calhoun, Susan Tyrrell, Dick Shawn, John Diehl, Elaine Giftos
   'A tasteless blend of realism and farce.'—*Sunday Times*

Angel and the Badman*
US 1947   100m   bw
Republic (John Wayne)

The love of a Quaker girl converts a wounded gunslinger to an honourable life.
Thoughtful western with good background detail and a fair measure of action.

wd James Edward Grant *ph* Archie Stout *m* Richard Hageman *pd* Ernest Fegte

John Wayne, Gail Russell, Harry Carey, Bruce Cabot, Irene Rich, Tom Powers
   'Unpretentious, sweet-tempered and quite likeable.'—*James Agee*

● *Video: World of Video 2000*

Angel Baby*
US 1960   97m   bw
Madera (Thomas F. Woods)

A mute girl is cured by an evangelist, and renounces her sins.
Strident, vigorous low-budget melodrama.

w Oris Borstem, Samuel Roeca, Paul Mason, *novel* Jenny Angel by Elsie Oaks Barbour *d* Paul Wendkos *ph* Haskell Wexler, Jack Marta *m* Wayne Shanklin

Salome Jens, George Hamilton, Joan Blondell, Mercedes McCambridge, Henry Jones, Burt Reynolds

Angel Face*
US 1952 91m bw
RKO (Otto Preminger)

A demented girl murders her father and stepmother, involving her chauffeur, whom she finally kills, and commits suicide.
Outrageous melodrama, so absurd as to be almost endearing.

w Frank Nugent, Oscar Millard *d* Otto Preminger *ph* Harry Stradling *m* Dmitri Tiomkin

Jean Simmons, Robert Mitchum, Herbert Marshall, Barbara O'Neil, Leon Ames, Mona Freeman, Kenneth Tobey, Raymond Greenleaf

'The one lyrical nightmare in the cinema.'—*Ian Cameron*

An Angel from Texas*
US 1940 69m bw
Warner

Misadventures of a country boy in New York.
Modest revamping of a much filmed farce, also made as *The Tenderfoot* (1928) and *Dance Charlie Dance* (1937).

w Fred Niblo Jnr, Bertram Millhauser, *play* The Butter and Egg Man by George F. Kaufman *d* Ray Enright *ph* Arthur L. Todd

Eddie Albert, Rosemary Lane, Wayne Morris, Ronald Reagan, Milburn Stone

Angel in Exile
US 1948 90m bw
Republic

An ex-con heads for an abandoned Arizona mine to recover stolen gold.
Modest, effective western about a baddie who reforms.

w Charles Larson *d* Allan Dwan, Philip Ford *ph* Reggie Lanning *m* Nathan Scott

John Carroll, Adele Mara, Thomas Gomez

Angel in My Pocket
US 1969 105m Technicolor
Universal (Ed Montagne)

A minister and his family arrive in a small town.
Simplistic comedy–drama with nothing to distinguish it from a dozen others in similar vein.

w Jim Fritzell, Everett Greenbaum *d* Alan Rafkin

Andy Griffith, Jerry Van Dyke, Kay Medford, Edgar Buchanan, Margaret Hamilton, Gary Collins, Lee Meriwether, Henry Jones

The Angel Levine*
US 1970 105m De Luxe
UA / Belafonte Enterprises (Chiz Schultz)

An elderly Jewish tailor complains to God of his bad luck; a black angel appears and seems to help him for a while.
Muddled and seemingly pointless parable with occasional felicities.

w Bill Gunn, Ronald Ribman, *story* Bernard Malamud *d* Jan Kadar *ph* Richard Kratina *pd* George Jenkins *m* Zdenck Linka

Zero Mostel, Harry Belafonte, Ida Kaminska, Milo O'Shea, Eli Wallach, Anne Jackson, Gloria Foster

'A prolonged variation on the theme that faith can produce miracles, but only if there is enough of it.'—*John Gillett*

Angel on My Shoulder**
US 1946 101m bw
UA / Charles R. Rogers

The devil promises leniency to a dead gangster if he will return to earth and take over the body of a judge who is stamping out evil.
Crude but lively fantasy on the tail-end of the *Here Comes Mr Jordan* cycle, and by the same author.

w Harry Segall, Roland Kibbee *d* Archie Mayo *ph* James Van Trees *m* Dmitri Tiomkin

Paul Muni, Claude Rains, Anne Baxter, Erskine Sanford, Hardie Albright

'The story is so imitative that it's hard to feel any more towards it than a mildly nostalgic regard.'—*Bosley Crowther*

Angel on the Amazon
US 1948 86m bw
Republic (John H. Auer)
GB title: *Drums Along the Amazon*

An elderly white lady resident of the Amazon jungle looks only 25 after being scared by a panther . . .
Ludicrous melodrama which the actors take seriously.

w Lawrence Kimble *d* John H. Auer *ph* Reggie Lanning *m* Nathan Scott

George Brent, Constance Bennett, Vera Hruba Ralston, Brian Aherne, Fortunio Bonanova, Alfonso Bedoya, Gus Schilling

The Angel Who Pawned Her Harp*
GB 1954 76m bw
Group Three (Sidney Cole)

A real angel arrives on a goodwill visit to scamy Islington, and manages to right a few wrongs.
Simple-minded whimsy, spottily effective, with good performances.

w Charles Terrot, Sidney Cole *d* Alan Bromly *ph* Arthur Grant *m* Antony Hopkins

Diane Cilento, Felix Aylmer, Robert Eddison, Jerry Desmonde, Sheila Sweet, Alfie Bass

The Angel with the Trumpet
GB 1949 98m bw
British Lion / London Films (Karl Hartl)

An Austrian lady has an affair with a crown prince but marries for security and dies in defiance of the Nazis.

Curious European cavalcade, dully directed to keep the budget down and accommodate long stretches of an Austrian original. An eccentricity.

w Karl Hartl, Franz Tassie, *novel* Ernst Lothar *d* Anthony Bushell *ph* Robert Krasker *m* Willy Schmidt-Gentner

Eileen Herlie, Basil Sydney, Norman Wooland, Anthony Bushell, Maria Schell, John Justin, Oskar Werner, Andrew Cruickshank

The Angel Wore Red
US 1960 105m bw
MGM / Titanus / Spectator (Gottfredo Lombardo)

The love story of a priest and a prostitute in the Spanish Civil War.
Turgid farrago, unsatisfactory both romantically and politically.

wd Nunnally Johnson *ph* Giuseppe Rotunno *m* Bronislau Kaper

Ava Gardner, Dirk Bogarde, Joseph Cotten, Vittorio de Sica, Aldo Fabrizi, Finlay Currie

'The stars show no apparent surprise that a film so empty of reward should take itself so seriously.'—*Peter John Dyer*

Angelina*
Italy 1947 98m bw
Lux

An impoverished housewife becomes the spokeswoman for her community on flooding, housing and other slum problems.
Reasonably rewarding star vehicle in the neo-realist tradition, this time angled for comedy.

w Suso Cecchi d'Amico, Piero Tellini, Luigi Zampa *d* Luigi Zampa *ph* Mario Craveri *m* Enzio Masetti

Anna Magnani, Nando Bruno, Gianni Glori, Franco Zeffirelli

Angélique
France / West Germany / Italy 1964
116m Eastmancolor Dyaliscope
Francos / CICC / Gloria /
Fona Roma (Francis Cosne)

Adventures of a nobleman's daughter at the court of Louis XIV.
Watchable swashbuckling nonsense, a kind of French *Forever Amber*. Several sequels were made.

w Claude Brûlé, Bernard Borderie, Francis Cosne, *novel* Serge and Anne Golon *d* Bernard Borderie *ph* Henri Pérsin *m* Michel Magne

Michèle Mercier, Robert Hossein, Giuliano Gemma, Jean Rochefort, François Maistre, Jacques Toja

Angelo My Love
US 1982 116m colour

Adventures of an eight-year-old gypsy boy in Manhattan. Angelo is a precocious little rogue, but two hours is a long haul for this kind of ethnic medley. Angelo Evans, Michael Evans, Ruthie Evans, Steve Tsigonoff. Written and directed by Robert Duvall; for

Lorton. 'Duvall has done wonders with his actors and then robbed them of their glory by mishandling the tempo of the piece.'—*Sunday Times*

Angel's Holiday
US 1937 74m bw

The niece of a newspaper editor rounds up a gang of racketeers. Smart comedy vehicle for Shirley Temple's only rival. Jane Withers, Robert Kent, Joan Davis, Sally Blane, Harold Huber, Frank Jenks, John Qualen, Lon Chaney Jnr. Written by Frank Fenton, Lynn Root; directed by James Tinling; for John Stone / TCF.

Angels in the Outfield
US 1952 99m bw
MGM (Clarence Brown)
GB title: *Angels and the Pirates*

The profane and bad-tempered manager of an unsuccessful baseball team gets help from an angel.
Unamusing, saccharine whimsy which does not deserve its excellent production values.

w Dorothy Kingsley, George Wells
d Clarence Brown ph Paul C. Vogel
m Daniele Amfitheatrof

Paul Douglas, Janet Leigh, Keenan Wynn, Lewis Stone, Donna Corcoran, Spring Byington, Bruce Bennett

Angels One Five*
GB 1952 98m bw
Associated British (Templar)

A slice of life in an RAF fighter station during the Battle of Britain.
Underplayed semi-documentary drama with stiff upper lips all round and the emphasis on characterization rather than action. A huge commercial success in Britain.

w Derek Twist d George More O'Ferrall
ph Christopher Challis m John Wooldridge

Jack Hawkins, John Gregson, Michael Denison, Andrew Osborn, Cyril Raymond, Humphrey Lestocq, Dulcie Gray, Veronica Hurst

Angels Over Broadway*
US 1940 80m bw
Columbia / Ben Hecht

During one rainy New York night, three of life's failures have one last stab at success.
Would-be poetic, moralizing melodrama very typical of its author; interesting but not a success.

w Ben Hecht d Ben Hecht, Lee Garmes
ph Lee Garmes m George Antheil

Douglas Fairbanks Jnr, Rita Hayworth, Thomas Mitchell, John Qualen, George Watts, Ralph Theodore
'There's a genial, original spirit to it.'—*New Yorker, 1978*
'It has excitement, fast talk, some knowable people, cynicism and sentiment.'—*Otis Ferguson*

† Sample dialogue: 'This town's a giant dice game . . . come on, seven!'
AAN: Ben Hecht (as writer)

Angels Wash Their Faces*
US 1939 86m bw
Warner (Max Siegel)

A bad boy joins the Dead End Kids, but they all reform in the end.
Routine programmer, hastily concocted after the success of *Angels with Dirty Faces*.

w Michael Fessier, Niven Busch, Robert Buckner d Ray Enright ph Arthur Todd
m Adolph Deutsch

Ann Sheridan, Ronald Reagan, the Dead End Kids, Bonita Granville, Frankie Thomas, Henry O'Neill, Berton Churchill, Eduardo Ciannelli
'Ray Enright's terrific meller pace makes it the sort of fare the average audience will eat up . . . he has an eye for the spectacular, including a thrilling fire sequence and a dramatic courtroom scene.'—*Variety*

† Original title: *The Battle of City Hall.*

Angels with Dirty Faces****
US 1938 97m bw
Warner (Sam Bischoff)

A Brooklyn gangster is admired by slum boys, but for their sake pretends to be a coward when he goes to the electric chair.
A shrewd, slick entertainment package and a seminal movie for all kinds of reasons. It combined gangster action with fashionable social conscience; it confirmed the Dead End Kids as stars; it provided archetypal roles for its three leading players and catapulted the female lead into stardom. It also showed the Warner style of film-making, all cheap sets and shadows, at its most effective.

w John Wexley, Warren Duff, *original story* Rowland Brown d Michael Curtiz
ph Sol Polito m Max Steiner

James Cagney (gangster with redeeming features), *Pat O'Brien* (priest), *Humphrey Bogart* (gangster with no redeeming features), *The Dead End Kids, Ann Sheridan,* George Bancroft, Edward Pawley
'Should do fair business, but the picture itself is no bonfire.'—*Variety*
'A rousing, bloody, brutal melodrama.'—*New York Mirror*

AAN: Rowland Brown; Michael Curtiz; James Cagney

Les Anges du Péché*
France 1943 73m bw
Synops / Robert Paul

A novice nun has trouble with the mother superior because of her obsessive interest in a rebellious delinquent girl, and dies before taking her vows.
Interesting study of an enclosed society, notable as its director's first film.

w R. P. Bruckberger, Jean Giraudoux, Robert Bresson d Robert Bresson ph Philippe Agostini m Jean-Jacques Grunenwald

Renée Faure, Jany Holt, Sylvie, Mila Parély, Marie-Hélène Dasté

Angora Love**
US 1929 20m bw silent

Laurel and Hardy keep a goat in their lodgings. Lively L & H comedy, even funnier when remade two years later as *Laughing Gravy*. With Edgar Kennedy, Charlie Hall. Written by Leo McCarey and H. M. Walker; directed by Lewis R. Foster; for Hal Roach.

The Angry Hills
GB 1959 105m bw
MGM / Raymond Stross

In 1940, an American war correspondent is helped by Greek freedom fighters.
Laboured war melodrama with pretentious dialogue but little characterization.

w A. I. Bezzerides, *novel* Leon Uris d Robert Aldrich ph Stephen Dade m Richard Rodney Bennett ad Ken Adam

Robert Mitchum, Gia Scala, Elisabeth Mueller, Stanley Baker, Donald Wolfit, Kieron Moore, Theodore Bikel, Sebastian Cabot, Peter Illing, Marius Goring, Leslie Phillips

The Angry Silence*
GB 1960 94m bw
British Lion / Beaver (Richard Attenborough, Bryan Forbes)

A worker who refuses to join an unofficial strike is 'sent to Coventry' by his mates; the matter hits national headlines, and the communists use it to their own advantage. Irresistibly reminding one of a po-faced *I'm All Right Jack*, this remains a fresh and urgent film which unfortunately lost excitement in its domestic scenes.

w Bryan Forbes, *story* Michael Craig, Richard Gregson d Guy Green ph Arthur Ibbetson
m Malcolm Arnold

Richard Attenborough, Michael Craig, Pier Angeli, Bernard Lee, Alfred Burke, Laurence Naismith, Geoffrey Keen
AAN: Bryan Forbes

Animal Crackers***
US 1930 98m bw
Paramount

Thieves covet a valuable oil painting unveiled at a swank party.
An excuse for the Marx Brothers, and a lively one in patches, though sedate and stage bound in treatment. The boys are all in top form, and many of the dialogue exchanges are classics.

w Morrie Ryskind, from musical play by himself and *George F. Kaufman* d Victor Heerman ph George Folsey m / ly Bert *Kalmar, Harry Ruby*

Groucho, Chico, Harpo, Zeppo, *Margaret Dumont,* Lillian Roth, Louis Sorin, Robert Greig, Hal Thompson

GROUCHO: 'You're the most beautiful woman I've ever seen, which doesn't say much for you.'

GROUCHO: 'One morning I shot an elephant in my pajamas. How he got into my pajamas I'll never know.'

GUESTS: 'Hooray for Captain Spaulding, the African explorer!'

GROUCHO: 'Did someone call me schnorrer?'

GUESTS: 'Hooray, hooray, hooray!'

ZEPPO: 'He went into the jungle, where all the monkeys *throw* nuts.'

GROUCHO: 'If I stay here, I'll *go* nuts.'

GUESTS: 'Hooray, hooray, hooray!
    He put all his reliance
    In courage and defiance
    And risked his life for science.'

GROUCHO: 'Hey, hey!'

MRS RITTENHOUSE: 'He is the only white man who covered every acre . . .'

GROUCHO: 'I think I'll try and make her . . .'

GUESTS: 'Hooray, hooray, hooray!'

'A hit on the screen before it opened, and in the money plenty.'—*Variety*

Animal Farm**
GB 1955   75m   Technicolor
Louis de Rochemont / Halas and Batchelor

Oppressed by the cruelty and inefficiency of their master, the animals take over a farm but find fresh tyrants among themselves.
George Orwell's political fable—'all animals are equal but some animals are more equal than others'—is faithfully followed in this ambitious but rather disappointingly flat cartoon version.

w, p, d John Halas and Joy Batchelor
voices Maurice Denham

● *Video: Rank*

The Animal Kingdom*
US 1932   95m   bw
RKO (David O. Selznick)
GB title: *The Woman in His House*

An intellectual publisher tries to justify keeping both a wife and a mistress.
Smart comedy-drama from a Broadway success, later bowdlerized as *One More Tomorrow* (qv).

w Horace Jackson, *play* Philip Barry
d Edward H. Griffith *ph* Lucien Andriot *m* Max Steiner

Leslie Howard, Ann Harding, Myrna Loy, Neil Hamilton, William Gargan, Henry Stephenson, Ilka Chase

'A wise and engaging picture addressed to the upper levels of fandom.'—*Variety*

'Two billion years in the making!'
The Animal World*
US 1956   80m   Technicolor
Warner / Windsor (Irwin Allen)

The evolution of animals from their primitive beginnings.
Ambitious documentary with a popular science approach; very variable, with poorish model work.

w, d Irwin Allen *ph* Harold Wellman *m* Paul Sawtell *sp* Willis O'Brien, Ray Harryhausen

The Animals Film*
GB / US 1981   136m   colour / bw

A hard-hitting documentary recording human ill-treatment of animals, with obvious hints that humans themselves will be next. Not for the squeamish. Narrated by Julie Christie; written and directed by Victor Schonfeld; for Slick Pix.

Animated Genesis*
GB 1952   22m   Technicolor (blown up from 16mm)

Greed and the machine enslave mankind.
Ambitious and decorative cartoon conceived and drawn by *Joan and Peter Foldes*, from whom little was subsequently heard. Music by Thomas Henderson; distributed by Korda / British Lion.

Ann Vickers*
US 1933   72m   bw
RKO (Pandro S. Berman)

A feminist social worker is taught a thing or two by life and settles down with a corrupt judge.
Reasonably effective version of a popular though heavy-going novel of the time.

w Jane Murfin, *novel* Sinclair Lewis *d* John Cromwell *ph* David Abel, Edward Cronjager *m* Max Steiner

Irene Dunne, Walter Huston, Conrad Nagel, Bruce Cabot, Edna May Oliver, Mitchell Lewis, Murray Kinnell

'Her sufferings are bearable and her ultimate happiness is assured, so this is vicarious enjoyment for any woman. Lovely romance, moderate penance, final respectability. All of which suggests that Ann Vickers should do moderately good biz.'—*Variety*

Anna
Italy 1952   100m   bw
Lux (Ponti / de Laurentiis)

A novice nun recalls her former life and almost gives up her vocation.
Soupy woman's picture of no particular merit.

w various *d* Alberto Lattuada *ph* Otello Martelli *m* Nino Rota

Silvana Mangano, Raf Vallone, Vittorio Gassman, Gaby Morlay, Jacques Dumesnil

Anna and the King of Siam**
US 1946   128m   bw
TCF (Louis D. Lighton)

In 1862 an English governess arrives in Bangkok to teach the 67 children of the king. Unusual and lavish drama, tastefully handled and generally absorbing despite miscasting and several slow passages.

w Talbot Jennings, Sally Benson, *book* Margaret Landon *d* John Cromwell *ph* Arthur Miller *m* Bernard Herrmann *ad* Lyle Wheeler, William Darling

Irene Dunne, Rex Harrison, Linda Darnell, Gale Sondergaard, Lee J. Cobb, Mikhail Rasumny

'A film that never touches the imagination, a film that leaves the mind uninformed and the memory unburdened.'—*Richard Winnington*

'It's pitifully unauthentic, and not a very good movie either, but the story itself holds considerable interest.'—*Pauline Kael, 70s*

AA: Arthur Miller
AAN: Talbot Jennings, Sally Benson; Bernard Herrmann; Gale Sondergaard

'Garbo talks!'
Anna Christie**
US 1930   86m   bw
MGM

A waterfront prostitute falls in love with a young seaman.
Primitive sound version of an earthy theatrical warhorse: it has a niche in history as the film in which Garbo first talked.

w Frances Marion, *play* Eugene O'Neill *d* Clarence Brown *ph* William Daniels

Greta Garbo, Charles Bickford, *Marie Dressler*, James T. Mack, Lee Phelps

'Great artistically and tremendous commercially . . . in all respects a wow picture.'—*Variety*

'A very talkie, uncinematic affair, more old-fashioned than the silent movies. If it were not so well acted it would be pretty tiresome.'—*National Board of Review*

AAN: Clarence Brown; William Daniels; Greta Garbo

Anna Karenina**
US 1935   95m   bw
MGM (David O. Selznick)

The wife of a Russian aristocrat falls for a dashing cavalry officer.
Well-staged but finally exasperating romantic tragedy, sparked by good performances and production.

w Clemence Dane, Salka Viertel, *novel* Leo Tolstoy *d* Clarence Brown *ph* William Daniels *m* Herbert Stothart

Greta Garbo (Anna), Fredric March (Vronsky), *Basil Rathbone* (Karenin), Freddie Bartholomew (Sergei), Maureen O'Sullivan (Kitty), May Robson (Countess), Reginald Owen (Silva), Reginald Denny (Yashvin)

'Cinch b.o. anywhere. In the foreign markets it should come close to establishing modern-day highs.'—*Variety*

'A dignified and effective drama which becomes significant because of that tragic, lonely and glamorous blend which is the Garbo personality.'—*André Sennwald*

'It reaches no great heights of tragedy or drama but rather moves forward relentlessly and a little coldly.'—*The Times*
† Previously filmed as a 1928 silent called *Love*, with Garbo and John Gilbert.

AAN: William Daniels

Anna Karenina*
GB 1947   139m   bw
London Films (Alexander Korda)

Tiresomely overlong but very handsomely staged remake marred by central miscasting.

w Jean Anouilh, Guy Morgan, Julien Duvivier d Julien Duvivier ph Henri Alekan m Constant Lambert

Vivien Leigh, Kieron Moore, *Ralph Richardson*, Marie Lohr, Sally Ann Howes, Niall MacGinnis, Michael Gough, Helen Haye, Mary Kerridge

'Vivien Leigh is lashed about by the tremendous role of Anna like a pussy cat with a tigress by the tail. She is not helped by a script which insists on sentimentally ennobling one of fiction's most vehemently average women.'—*James Agee*

● Video: Polygram

Anna Lucasta*
US 1949 86m bw
Columbia / Security (Philip Yordan)

The bad girl of a farming family comes home to marry, but her past catches up with her. Polish immigrant melodrama, a touring company staple, adequately transferred to the screen.

w Philip Yordan, Arthur Laurents, *play* Philip Yordan d Irving Rapper ph Sol Polito m David Diamond

Paulette Goddard, Oscar Homolka, Broderick Crawford, William Bishop, Gale Page, Mary Wickes

Anna Lucasta*
US 1958 97m bw
(UA) Longridge Enterprises (Sidney Harmon)

Black version of the long-running play; performances standard.

w Philip Yordan d Arnold Laven ph Lucien Ballard m Elmer Bernstein

Eartha Kitt, Frederick O'Neal, Sammy Davis Jnr, Henry Scott, Rex Ingram, James Edwards

Anna of Brooklyn
Italy / France / US 1958 106m
Technirama
Circeo Cinematografica / France Cinema / RKO (Milko Skofic)

An attractive widow returns from New York to her native Italian village in search of a husband.
Footling romantic drama which wastes its cast and budget.

w Ettore Margadonna, Dino Risi d Reginald Denham, Carlo Lasticati ph Giuseppe Rotunno m Alessandro Cicognini, Vittorio de Sica

Gina Lollobrigida, Dale Robertson, Vittorio de Sica, Amedeo Nazzari, Peppino de Felippo, Gabriella Palotta

Annabelle's Affairs
US 1931 74m bw

When her husband disappears, a young bride becomes head cook at his rival's home. Then the husband turns up. Standard farce which worked pretty well in its day. Jeanette MacDonald, Victor McLaglen, Roland Young, Sam Hardy, William Collier Snr. Written by anonymous hands from the play Good Gracious Annabelle by Clare Kummer; directed by Alfred Werker; for Fox.

Annabel Takes a Tour
US 1939 69m bw

A star on a publicity tour balks at the stunts she is expected to perform. Thinnish sequel to *The Affairs of Annabel*. Lucille Ball, Jack Oakie, Ruth Donnelly, Bradley Page, Ralph Forbes. Written by Bert Granet and Oliver Cooper; directed by Lew Landers; for RKO.

An Annapolis Story
US 1953 81m colour
Allied Artists / Walter Mirisch
GB title: *The Blue and the Gold*

Two cadets at the naval academy love the same girl.
Artless recruiting poster heroics.

w Dan Ullman d Don Siegel ph Sam Leavitt m Marlin Skiles

Diana Lynn, John Derek, Kevin McCarthy, Pat Dooley, L. Q. Jones

'Seldom have so many scrubbed, wholesome-looking young people thronged any picture.'—*New York Times*

Annapolis Farewell
US 1935 75m bw

A retired naval officer goes down with his ship in college manoeuvres. Fairly absurd stiff-upper-lip propaganda drama. *Sir Guy Standing*, Rosalind Keith, Tom Brown, Richard Cromwell, John Howard, Benny Baker, Louise Beavers, Minor Watson, Samuel S. Hinds. Written by Dale Van Every, Frank Craven, Grover Jones, William Slavens McNutt; directed by Alexander Hall; for Paramount.

Anne of Green Gables*
US 1934 79m bw
RKO (Kenneth MacGowan)

An orphan girl goes to the country to live with her aunt.
Standard version of the classic for young girls.

w Sam Mintz, *novel* L. M. Montgomery d George Nicholls Jnr ph Lucien Andriot m Max Steiner

Anne Shirley (who had been known as Dawn O'Day and legally adopted the name of her character in this, her first starring role), Tom Brown, O. P. Heggie, Helen Westley, Sara Haden, Charley Grapewin

'Made up and monotonous—tragedy having its breakfast in bed.'—*Otis Ferguson*
† *Anne of Windy Poplars*, with the same stars and production team, followed in 1940.

Anne of the Indies
US 1951 87m Technicolor
TCF (George Jessel)

Lady pirate Anne Bonney, the terror of the Caribbean, is at odds with her former master Blackbeard.

Routine swashbuckler, generally well handled.

w Philip Dunne, Arthur Caesar d Jacques Tourneur ph Harry Jackson m Franz Waxman

Jean Peters, Louis Jourdan, Debra Paget, Herbert Marshall, Thomas Gomez, James Robertson Justice, Sean McClory, Francis Pierlot

Anne of the Thousand Days*
GB 1969 146m Technicolor
Panavision
Universal / Hal B. Wallis

Henry VIII divorces his wife to marry Anne Boleyn, but soon finds evidence of adultery. A somewhat unlikely view of history, rather boringly presented on a woman's magazine level, but with occasional good moments from a cast of British notables.

w John Hale, Bridget Boland, *play* Maxwell Anderson d Charles Jarrott ph Arthur Ibbetson pd Maurice Carter m Georges Delerue

Richard Burton, Geneviève Bujold, John Colicos (as Cromwell), Irene Papas, Anthony Quayle, Michael Hordern, Katharine Blake, Peter Jeffrey, William Squire, Esmond Knight, Nora Swinburne

'The costumes, beautiful in themselves, have that unconvincing air of having come straight off the rack at Nathan's.'—*Brenda Davies*

'A decent dullness is, alas, the keynote.'—*Michael Billington, Illustrated London News*

'The quintessential work of art for people who haven't the foggiest notion of what art is.'—*John Simon*

'Intelligent from line to line, but the emotions supplied seem hypocritical, and the conception lacks authority . . . Burton's performance is colourless. It's as though he *remembered* how to act but couldn't work up much enthusiasm or involvement.'—*Pauline Kael*

AAN: best picture; John Hale, Bridget Boland; Arthur Ibbetson; Georges Delerue; Richard Burton; Geneviève Bujold; Anthony Quayle

Annie
US 1982 128m Metrocolor Panavision
Columbia / Ray Stark (Joe Layton)

In 1933 an orphan waif charms a munitions millionaire and is adopted by him. Misguided opening-out of a charming stage musical based on the comic strip which is basically a reversal of *Oliver Twist*. Some of the best numbers have been discarded, the dancing is ponderous, the acting distinctly uneasy, and the choice of director stupefying. None of it works at all.

w Carol Sobieski, from the stage play, *book* Thomas Meehan, *lyrics* Martin Charnin, *music* Charles Strouse; *comic strip* Harold Gray d John Huston ph Richard Moore pd Dale Hennesy m Ralph Burns

Albert Finney, Carol Burnett, Aileen Quinn, Ann Reinking, Bernadette Peters, Tim Curry, Geoffrey Holder, Edward Herrman (as Franklin D. Roosevelt)

'Whatever indefinable charm the stage show had is completely lost in this lumbering and largely uninteresting and uninvolving exercise, where the obvious waste reaches almost Pentagonian proportions.'—*Variety*

'The whole thing has the air of a vast, hollow Christmas tree bauble intended not so much for children as for the infantile-minded middle-aged.'—*Sunday Times*

'This is the film I want on my tombstone.'— *Ray Stark.*

'Funeral services may be held starting this week at a theatre near you.'—*Time*

† The cost of *Annie*, starting with $9,000,000 for the rights, rose to $35,000,000. It was not recovered.

AAN: art direction; original song score
● *Video: RCA / Columbia*

Annie Get Your Gun*
US 1950 107m Technicolor
MGM (Arthur Freed)

A young female hillbilly joins Frank Butler's sharpshooting act, and is sophisticated by her love for him.

Gaudy, stagey, generally uninspired screen version of the famous musical show based remotely on a historical character of post-wild-west days. There is a lack of dancing, the direction is stodgy, and in general flair the production falls disappointingly below MGM's usual standard.

w Sidney Sheldon, *musical play* Herbert and Dorothy Fields d George Sidney ph Charles Rosher m / ly Irving Berlin md Adolph Deutsch, Roger Edens ch Robert Alton ad Cedric Gibbons, Paul Grosse

Betty Hutton, *Howard Keel*, Edward Arnold, J. Carrol Naish, Louis Calhern

Songs include 'Colonel Buffalo Bill'; 'Doing What Comes Naturally'; 'The Girl That I Marry'; 'You Can't Get a Man with a Gun'; 'There's No Business Like Show Business'; 'My Defenses Are Down'; 'I'm an Indian Too'; 'I Got the Sun in the Morning'; 'Anything You Can Do'; 'They Say It's Wonderful'.

† The real Annie Oakley was born Phoebe Ann Oakley Mozic in 1860, and died in 1926. The role was to have been played by Judy Garland, who was fired after displays of temperament; also considered were Doris Day, Judy Canova and Betty Garrett.

†† Louis Calhern replaced Frank Morgan, who died during production

AA: music direction
AAN: Charles Rosher

Annie Hall***
US 1977 93m De Luxe
UA / Jack Rollins-Charles H. Joffe (Fred T. Gallo)
Sub-title: *A Nervous Romance*

Against the neuroses of New York and Los Angeles, a Jewish comedian has an affair with a midwestern girl.

Semi-serious collage of jokes and bits of technique, some of the former very funny and some of the latter very successful. For no very good reason it hit the box office spot and turned its creator, of whom it is very typical, from a minority performer to a superstar.

w Woody Allen, Marshall Brickman
d Woody Allen ph Gordon Willis m various

Woody Allen, Diane Keaton, Tony Roberts, Carol Kane, Paul Simon, Shelly Duvall

ALLEN: 'Hey, don't knock masturbation. It's sex with someone I love.'

'The film's priceless vignettes about the difficulties in chitchatting with strangers, the awkward moments in family visits, the frequent breakdowns in communication and failures in intimacy, its reminiscences about the palpable horrors of growing up in Brooklyn, and its comic encounters with lobsters in the kitchen or spiders in the bathroom, all seem like snapshots from Allen and Keaton's own romance.'—*Les Keyser, Hollywood in the Seventies*

† The narrative supposedly mirrors the real-life affair of the stars, who separated before the film came out. (Diane Keaton's family name is Hall.)

AA: best picture; script; direction; Diane Keaton
AAN: Woody Allen (as actor)
● *Video: Intervision*

Annie Oakley*
US 1935 90m bw
RKO (Cliff Reid)

The historical story, more or less, of the lady later immortalized in *Annie Get Your Gun*. Lively semi-western with good dialogue but gluey plot development.

w Joel Sayre, John Twist d George Stevens ph J. Roy Hunt m Alberto Columbo ad Van Nest Polglase

Barbara Stanwyck, Preston Foster, Melvyn Douglas, Moroni Olsen, Pert Kelton, Andy Clyde, Chief Thunderbird

'A swell idea that doesn't quite come through.'—*Variety*

Annie's Coming Out*
Australia 1984 93m Eastmancolor
Film Australia (Don Murray)

A physically handicapped child, wrongly characterized as mentally retarded also, is brought out by a devoted teacher. Fictionalized version of a true story: predictably well intentioned, shocking, and consistently watchable.

w John Patterson, Chris Borthwick, *book* Rosemary Crossley d Gil Brealey ph Mick Van Borneman m Simon Walker

Angela Punch McGregor, Drew Forsythe, Tina Arhondis, Liddy Clark, Monica Maughan

The Anniversary*
GB 1968 95m Technicolor
Hammer (Jimmy Sangster)

A malevolent one-eyed widow will stop at nothing to prevent her grown sons from leaving the family orbit, and they meet each year to mourn the death of the husband she really hated.

Agreeable but over-talkative black comedy with a splendid role for its star and some good scattered moments, marred by a general lack of style.

w Jimmy Sangster, *play* Bill MacIlwraith d Roy Ward Baker ph Harry Waxman m Philip Martell

Bette Davis, Jack Hedley, *James Cossins*, Sheila Hancock, Elaine Taylor, Christian Roberts, Timothy Bateson

'It all reminds one of a love scene in a funeral parlour.'—*Variety*

'Magisterially grotesque in elegantly tailored eye-patch and exotic gown, she snaps out her bitchy insults with all 57 varieties of relish.'— *MFB*

Another Country*
GB 1984 90m colour
TCF / Virgin / Goldcrest (Alan Marshall)

A homosexual defector to Russia reflects on the public school pressures which influenced him.

Upper-crust militarism, arrogance, sadism and homosexuality rolled up in a package which pleased the West End theatre crowds but seems faintly absurd on film. Not much of a recruiting poster for Eton.

w Julian Mitchell, from his play d Marek Kanievska ph Peter Biziou m Michael Storey pd Brian Morris

Rupert Everett, Colin Firth, Michael Jenn, Rupert Addie, Anna Massey, Rupert Wainwright, Betsy Brantley

'Inevitably it went down well at the Cannes Film Festival, where movies critical of their own country's shortcomings are always favoured.'—*Margaret Hinxman, Daily Mail*

Another Dawn
US 1937 73m bw
Warner (Harry Joe Brown)

In a British army post in Africa, a wife is torn between duty and romance.

Absurdly sudsy melodrama, a potboiler for stars between more important assignments.

w Laird Doyle d William Dieterle ph Tony Gaudio m Erich Wolfgang Korngold

Errol Flynn, Kay Francis, Ian Hunter, Frieda Inescort, Herbert Mundin

† In every Warner film where a cinema canopy was shown, the title advertised was *Another Dawn*, so its use here as an actual title is presumably a piece of cynicism.

Another Face
US 1935 72m bw

A gangster has his face lifted and becomes a film star. Rather heavy comedy with some good laughs. *Brian Donlevy, Wallace Ford, Phyllis Brooks, Erik Rhodes, Molly Lamont, Alan Hale.* Written by Garrett Graham, John Twist, Ray Mayer, Thomas Dugan; directed by Christy Cabanne; for RKO.

Another Fine Mess**
US 1930   30m   bw
On the run from a cop, Stan and Ollie masquerade as master and maid. Elaborate star comedy with spoken introduction instead of titles; very satisfying but not quite vintage.
Laurel and Hardy, James Finlayson, Thelma Todd, Charles Gerrard. Written by H. M. Walker, from a sketch by Stan Laurel's father; directed by James Parrott; for Hal Roach.

Another Language
US 1933   75m   bw
MGM (Walter Wanger)
A young wife does not fit in with her husband's snobby family and falls in love with his nephew.
Flat treatment of a dated play.
w Herman J. Mankiewicz, Gertrude Purcell, Donald Ogden Stewart, *play* Rose Franken d Edward H. Griffith *ph* Ray June
Helen Hayes, Robert Montgomery, John Beal, Louise Closser Hale, Henry Travers, Margaret Hamilton
'A very good picture that will get more than average box office attention . . . everything is handled with intellect and due restraint.'—*Variety*

Another Man, Another Chance
France / US 1977   132m   Eastmancolor
UA / Films 13 / Ariane (Alexandre Mnouchkine, George Dancigers)
French title: *Un Autre Homme, une Autre Chance*
aka: *Another Man, Another Woman*
A Yank vet and a French widow meet and fall in love in the old west.
Pretty, overlong, rather enervating romance with an unusual and not entirely convincing setting.
wd Claude Lelouch *ph* Jacques Lefrançois m Francis Lai
James Caan, Geneviève Bujold, Francis Huster, Susan Tyrrell

Another Man's Poison*
GB 1951   89m   bw
Douglas Fairbanks Jnr / Daniel M. Angel
A lady novelist poisons her husband and lover, then unwittingly takes a fatal dose herself.
Hysterical vehicle for a fading Hollywood star reduced to repeating her tantrums in an English studio on a low budget; she should have stayed home, as should her director.
w Val Guest, *play* Deadlock by Leslie Sands d Irving Rapper *ph* Robert Krasker *m* John Greenwood
Bette Davis, Anthony Steel, Gary Merrill, Emlyn Williams, Barbara Murray, Reginald Beckwith, Edna Morris

'Barnstormers as rich and improbable as this are rare . . . the general atmosphere takes one back to 1935.'—*Gavin Lambert*
'Like reading Ethel M. Dell by flashes of lightning.'—*Frank Hauser*

Another Part of the Forest*
US 1948   108m   bw
U-I (Jerry Bresler)
In the post-Civil War years, Marcus Hubbard leads his family to worldly success by cheating and the misuse of power; he lives to regret it, as the children learn their lessons all too well. This backwards sequel to *The Little Foxes*, showing how the characters of that play got to be their nasty selves, is quite absorbingly acted but stagily presented, with plenty of care but no style.
w Vladimir Pozner, *play* Lillian Hellman d Michael Gordon *ph* Hal Mohr *m* Daniele Amfitheatrof
Fredric March, Florence Eldridge, Ann Blyth, Dan Duryea, Edmond O'Brien, John Dall
'The Hubbards are the greatest collection of ghouls since *The Old Dark House*.'—*Pauline Kael, 70s*

Another Shore*
GB 1948   77m   bw
Ealing (Ivor Montagu)
A young Irishman dreams of life in the South Seas but gives up his fancies for love.
Curiously whimsical, artificial and unconvincing comedy drama from a famous studio, but not without its moments of interest.
w Walter Meade, *novel* Kenneth Reddin d Charles Crichton *ph* Douglas Slocombe m Georges Auric
Robert Beatty, Stanley Holloway, Moira Lister

'It's a blessed event!'
Another Thin Man
US 1939   102m   bw
MGM (Hunt Stromberg)
Nick Charles solves a murder on a Long Island weekend.
Overwritten and distinctly tedious star sequel to *The Thin Man* and *After the Thin Man*. The title refers (erroneously) to Nick and Nora's baby.
w Dashiell Hammett d W. S. Van Dyke II ph Oliver T. Marsh, William Daniels m Edward Ward
William Powell, Myrna Loy, Otto Kruger, C. Aubrey Smith, Virginia Grey, Nat Pendleton, Tom Neal, Ruth Hussey, Sheldon Leonard
'The screenplay tosses shootings and skulduggery and repartee at us before we're ready, and then Nick Charles takes an unconscionable amount of time sorting things out.'—*Pauline Kael, 70s*

Another Time, Another Place
GB 1958   98m   bw   Vistavision
Paramount / Kaydor (Lewis Allen, Smedley Aston)

During World War II an American newspaperwoman has an affair with a British war correspondent; when he is killed in action, she consoles his widow.
Drippy romance, unsympathetically played and artificially set in a Cornish village.
w Stanley Mann, *novel* Lenore Coffee d Lewis Allen *ph* Jack Hildyard *m* Douglas Gamley
Lana Turner, Barry Sullivan, Glynis Johns, Sean Connery, Sidney James

Anthony Adverse*
US 1936   141m   bw
Warner (Henry Blanke)
Adventures of an ambitious young man in early 19th-century America.
A rousing spectacle of its day, from a bestselling novel, this award-winning movie quickly dated and now seems very thin and shadowy despite the interesting talents involved.
w Sheridan Gibney, *novel* Hervey Allen d Mervyn Le Roy *ph* Tony Gaudio ad Anton Grot *m* Erich Wolfgang Korngold
Fredric March, Olivia de Havilland, Gale Sondergaard, Edmund Gwenn, Claude Rains, Anita Louise, Louis Hayward, Steffi Duna, Donald Woods, Akim Tamiroff, Ralph Morgan, Henry O'Neill
'A bulky, rambling and indecisive photoplay which has not merely taken liberties with the letter of the original but with its spirit.'—*Frank S. Nugent, New York Times*
'In the dramatizing there is shown no relish or conviction, only a retentive memory for all the old clothes of show business.'—*Otis Ferguson*
'A lavish gold-leaf from Hervey Allen's book, an earnest cinema endeavour, taxing alike its studio's purse and artistry.'—*Douglas Gilbert, New York World Telegram*
'The show is fairly glutted with plot and counter-plot and is apt to make one feel that one is witnessing a serial run off continuously at a single performance.'—*Howard Barnes, New York Herald Tribune*
'It goes on too long, otherwise it might have been the funniest film since *The Crusades*.'—*Graham Greene*
AA: Tony Gaudio; Erich Wolfgang Korngold; Gale Sondergaard
AAN: best picture; Anton Grot

Antoine et Antoinette*
France 1947   87m   bw
SNEG
A young married couple find they have won a lottery but lost the ticket.
A bubbly soufflé, most expertly served but leaving one still a little hungry; not quite in the Clair class.
w Françoise Giroud, M. Griffe, Jacques Becker d Jacques Becker *ph* Pierre Montazel *m* Jean-Jacques Grunenwald
Roger Pigaut, Claire Maffei

Antony and Cleopatra*
GB 1972   170m   Technicolor
   Todd-AO 35
Transac (Zurich) / Izaro (Madrid) / Folio
   Films (London)   (Peter Snell)

Well-meaning, well-mounted, but quite
uninspired rendering.

wd Charlton Heston, play William
Shakespeare ph Rafael Pacheco m John
Scott pd Maurice Pelling

Charlton Heston, Hildegarde Neil, Eric
Porter, John Castle (as Octavius), Fernando
Rey, Freddie Jones, Peter Arne, Roger
Delgado

† Olivier and Orson Welles were both sought
for the lead.

Any Number Can Play*
US 1949   103m   bw
MGM (Arthur Freed)

A gambling casino owner has health problems,
is reconciled with his son and retires from the
game.
Rather boring drama redeemed by slightly
offbeat dialogue and excellent star acting,
albeit in routine roles.

w Richard Brooks, novel E. H. Heth
d Mervyn Le Roy ph Harold Rosson
m Lennie Hayton

Clark Gable, Alexis Smith, Mary Astor,
Wendell Corey, Audrey Totter, Lewis Stone,
Frank Morgan, Marjorie Rambeau, Barry
Sullivan

Any Old Port*
US 1932   20m   bw

Stan and Ollie are sailors on leave, and Ollie
enters Stan for a boxing match. Minor star
comedy with good moments but a weak finish.
Laurel and Hardy, Walter Long. Written by
H. M. Walker; directed by James W. Horne;
for Hal Roach.

Any Wednesday*
US 1966   109m   Technicolor
Warner (Julius J. Epstein)
GB title: Bachelor Girl Apartment

A millionaire businessman spends every
Wednesday with his mistress, but
complications arise when his young associate is
accidentally sent to use the company flat.
Overlong screen version of a thinly scripted
Broadway success in which yawns gradually
overtake laughs.

w Julius J. Epstein, play Muriel Resnik
d Robert Ellis Miller ph Harold Lipstein
m George Duning

Jane Fonda, Dean Jones, Jason Robards Jnr,
Rosemary Murphy (a breath of air as the
deceived wife who doesn't mind), Ann
Prentiss, King Moody

Any Which Way You Can
US 1980   116m   De Luxe

The hero of Every Which Way But Loose
becomes involved in further brawls and car
crashes, with the help of his friendly orang-
utan. A sequel designed entirely for the box

office, its tone set by the scene in which the
villains on motorcycles are covered in tar.
Clint Eastwood, Ruth Gordon, Sondra Locke,
Geoffrey Lewis, William Smith, Harry
Guardino. Written by Stanford Sherman;
directed by Buddy Van Horn; for Malpaso /
Warner. 'This kind of thing is clearly beyond
or beneath criticism.'—Variety.
   'Where the previous comedy set up a zany
situation, this one ploughs it into the
ground.'—Daily Mail
● Video: Warner

Anybody's Woman
US 1930   80m   bw

A drunken lawyer marries a chorus girl and
regrets it, but she reforms him. Tedious
matrimonial drama. Ruth Chatterton, Clive
Brook, Paul Lukas, Huntley Gordon, Virginia
Hammond. Written by Zoe Akins, Doris
Anderson, Gouverneur Morris; directed by
Dorothy Arzner; for Paramount. 'It can't lose
through that title and the stars.'—Variety

Anything Can Happen*
US 1952   93m   bw
Paramount / William Perlberg, George
   Seaton

Adventures of a Russian immigrant family in
New York.
A standard Hollywood product based on a
sentimental best-seller.

w George Seaton, George Oppenheimer,
book George and Helen Papashvily d George
Seaton ph Daniel L. Fapp m Victor Young

Jose Ferrer, Kim Hunter, Kurt Kasznar, Alex
Danaroff, Oscar Beregi
   'Exploits to the hilt the somewhat limited
possibilities of quaintness and whimsicality
with a broken accent.'—Penelope Houston

Anything Goes**
US 1936   92m   bw
Paramount (Benjamin Glazer)
TV title: Tops is the Limit

Romantic adventures on board a transatlantic
liner.
Amiably batty musical comedy, zestfully
directed and blithely performed.

w Guy Bolton, P. G. Wodehouse, Howard
Lindsay, Russell Crouse, from their Broadway
show d Lewis Milestone ph Karl Struss
songs Cole Porter md Victor Young ad Hans
Dreier

Bing Crosby, Ethel Merman, Charles Ruggles,
Grace Bradley, Ida Lupino, Chill Wills, the
Avalon Boys, Arthur Treacher
† Only three of Cole Porter's songs were
retained from the Broadway show: 'Anything
Goes', 'You're the Top' and 'I Get a Kick out
of You'. Others by various hands include
'Moonburn', 'Sailor Beware', 'My Heart and
I', 'Am I Awake?', 'Hopelessly in Love'.

Anything Goes*
US 1956   106m   Technicolor
   Vistavision
Paramount (Robert Emmett Dolan)

The male stars of a musical comedy each sign
a girl to play the female lead; resulting
complications are ironed out during a
transatlantic voyage.
Below-par reworking of the 1936 film in which
technical gloss and dull sets virtually reduce
the characters to puppets. A few good
moments transcend the general lack of
imagination.

w Sidney Sheldon, from show as credited in
1936 version d Robert Lewis ph John F.
Warren songs Cole Porter md Joseph J.
Lilley ch Nick Castle, Roland Petit ad Hal
Pereira, Joseph M. Johnson

Bing Crosby, Donald O'Connor, Zizi
Jeanmaire, Mitzi Gaynor, Phil Harris, Kurt
Kasznar

Anzio
Italy 1968   117m   Technicolor
   Panavision
(Columbia) Dino de Laurentiis (Marcel
   Bebert)
GB title: The Battle for Anzio

A war correspondent joins American and
British troops preparing for the 1944 landing
in Italy.
Threadbare war film which wastes an all-star
American cast.

w H. A. L. Craig, book Anzio by Wynford
Vaughan Thomas d Edward Dmytryk
ph Giuseppe Rotunno m Riz Ortolani

Robert Mitchum, Peter Falk, Arthur
Kennedy, Robert Ryan, Earl Holliman, Mark
Damon, Reni Santoni, Anthony Steel, Patrick
Magee
   'It must be a long time since a script
managed to pack in so many crassly
portentous statements about why men fight
wars.'—MFB

Apache*
US 1954   91m   Technicolor
UA / Hecht–Lancaster (Harold Hecht)

After the surrender of Geronimo, one Apache
leader is unconquered; after creating much
havoc, he settles for domesticity, and the
white men let him go unharmed.
Sober western in the wake of Broken Arrow,
with a predictably sympathetic star
performance and a surprising happy ending.
More decency than excitement along the way.

w James R. Webb, novel Bronco Apache by
Paul I. Wellman d Robert Aldrich ph Ernest
Laszlo m David Raksin

Burt Lancaster, Jean Peters, John McIntire,
Charles Bronson, John Dehner, Paul
Guilfoyle, Walter Sande, Monte Blue

Apache Drums
US 1951   75m   Technicolor
U-I (Val Lewton)

A gambler helps a town under Indian attack.
Standard co-feature western, perfectly
adequate but showing no sign of its producer's
former tastes and skills.

w David Chandler d Hugo Fregonese
ph Charles Boyle m Hans Salter

Stephen McNally, Willard Parker, Coleen Gray, Arthur Shields, James Griffith

Apache Rifles
US 1964 92m De Luxe

In 1879 Arizona, an Indian-hating officer falls for a half-caste. Tolerable mid-budget western. Audie Murphy, Michael Dante, Linda Lawson, L. Q. Jones. Written by Charles B. Smith; directed by William H. Witney; for Admiral Pictures / TCF.

Apache Uprising
US 1965 90m Techniscope
Paramount / A. C. Lyles

Assorted passengers in a stagecoach survive an Indian attack at a way station.
It sounds like a remake, and almost is, but the handling is lively enough and the producer's usual cast of nostalgic stars is in evidence.

w Harry Sanford, Max Lamb d R. G. Springsteen ph W. Wallace Kelley m Jimmie Haskell

Rory Calhoun, Corinne Calvet, John Russell, Lon Chaney Jnr, Gene Evans, DeForest Kelley, Arthur Hunnicutt, Richard Arlen, Johnny Mack Brown, Jean Parker

Apache War Smoke
US 1952 67m bw

An Indian killer is among those sheltering in a desert outpost before an Apache raid.
Talkative but tense lower-berth western.
Gilbert Roland, Robert Horton, Glenda Farrell, Barbara Ruick, Henry Morgan. Written by Jerry Davis, from a story by Ernest Haycox; directed by Harold Kress; for MGM.

Aparajito***
India 1956 113m bw
Epic Films Private Ltd (Satyajit Ray)
aka: The Unvanquished

After his father's death, a poor country boy is helped by his mother to study for the university.
A detailed and moving study of two characters who are universally familiar despite an unusual background.

wd Satyajit Ray ph Subrata Mitra m Ravi Shankar

Pinaki Sen Gupta, Karuna Banerjee, Kanu Banerjee

'Movie-wise, there has never been anything like it—laugh-wise, love-wise, or otherwise-wise!'

The Apartment**
US 1960 125m bw Panavision
UA / Mirisch (Billy Wilder)

A lonely, ambitious clerk rents out his apartment to philandering executives and finds that one of them is after his own girl.
Overlong and patchy but agreeably mordant and cynical comedy with a sparkling view of city office life and some deftly handled individual sequences.

w Billy Wilder, I. A. L. Diamond d Billy Wilder ph Joseph La Shelle m Adolph Deutsch ad Alexander Trauner

Jack Lemmon (C. C. Baxter), Shirley Maclaine (Miss Kubelik), Fred MacMurray (Jeff D. Sheldrake), Ray Walston (Joe Dobisch), Jack Kruschen (Dr Dreyfuss), Joan Shawlee (Sylvia), Edie Adams (Miss Olsen), David Lewis (Al Kirkeby)

Baxter's opening narration: 'On November 1st, 1959, the population of New York City was 8,042,753. If you laid all these people end to end, figuring an average height of five feet six and a half inches, they would reach from Times Square to the outskirts of Karachi, Pakistan. I know facts like this because I work for an insurance company—Consolidated Life of New York. We are one of the top five companies in the country. Last year we wrote nine point three billion dollars worth of policies. Our home office has 31,259 employees, which is more than the entire population of Natchez, Mississippi, or Gallup, New Mexico. I work on the 19th floor—Ordinary Policy department—Premium Accounting division—Section W—desk number 861.'

BAXTER: 'Miss Kubelik, one doesn't get to be a second administrative assistant around here unless he's a pretty good judge of character, and as far as I'm concerned you're tops. I mean, decency-wise and otherwise-wise.'

BAXTER: 'You know, I used to live like Robinson Crusoe—shipwrecked among eight million people. Then one day I saw a footprint in the sand and there you were. It's a wonderful thing, dinner for two.'

MISS KUBELIK: 'Shut up and deal.' (Last line of film.')

'Without either style or taste, shifting gears between pathos and slapstick without any transition.'—Dwight MacDonald
'Billy Wilder directed this acrid story as if it were a comedy, which is a cheat, considering that it involves pimping and a suicide attempt and many shades of craven ethics.'—New Yorker, 1980

AA: best picture; Billy Wilder, I. A. L. Diamond (as writers); Billy Wilder (as director)

AAN: Joseph La Shelle; Jack Lemmon; Shirley Maclaine; Jack Kruschen

Apartment for Peggy*
US 1948 98m Technicolor
TCF (William Perlberg)

A retired professor finds a new lease of life through caring for the homeless family of an ex-GI.
Sentimental comedy with serious undertones (the professor twice attempts suicide). Signs of enterprise are smothered by regulation charm.

wd George Seaton, story Faith Baldwin ph Harry Jackson m David Raksin

Edmund Gwenn, Jeanne Crain, William Holden, Gene Lockhart, Henri Letondal, Charles Lane, Houseley Stevenson
'A first rate experience for observers with comprehending minds.'—Bosley Crowther, New York Times

The Ape
US 1940 61m bw
Monogram (Scott R. Dunlop)

Dr Adrian seeks to cure polio by means of a serum which can only be obtained from the spinal fluid of a human being. He kills an escaped ape and dresses in its skin to seek victims.
Silly and rather boring addition to the mad doctor cycle.

w Curt Siodmak, Richard Carroll, play Adam Shirk d William Nigh ph Harry Neumann m Edward Kay

Boris Karloff, Maris Wrixon, Gertrude Hoffman, Henry Hall

Ape and Super Ape
Netherlands / USA 1972 103m
Technicolor

An alleged documentary comparing human and animal behaviour seems regrettably to turn into a series of episodes depicting animal savagery in close-up. Written, directed, edited and produced by Bert Haanstra; photographed by Anton Van Munster; for Bert Haanstra Films / Unicorn. (Original title: Bij de Beesten Af.) 'It lacks even associational interest for the wild-life enthusiast, and is best written off as an inconclusive, unoriginal and often repellent exercise unworthy of its maker.'—John Baxter, MFB

The Ape Man
US 1943 64m bw
Monogram (Sam Katzman, Jack Dietz)
GB title: Lock Your Doors

A scientist injects himself with spinal fluid which turns him into an ape creature.
Cheap rubbish shot in a couple of corners and offering no thrill whatever.

w Barney A. Sarecky, story They Creep in the Dark by Karl Brown d William Beaudine ph Mack Stengler m Edward Kay

Bela Lugosi, Wallace Ford, Louise Currie, Minerva Urecal
† A supposed sequel the following year, Return of the Ape Man, had in fact no plot connection. In this Lugosi thawed out a neanderthal man, inserted John Carradine's brain, and the composite turned into George Zucco!

Apocalypse Now**
US 1979 153m Technicolor
Technovision
Omni Zoetrope (Francis Coppola)

A Vietnam captain is instructed to eliminate a colonel who has retired to the hills and is fighting his own war.
Pretentious war movie, made even more hollow-sounding by the incomprehensible performance of Brando as the mad martinet. Some vivid scenes along the way, and some interesting parallels with Conrad's Heart of Darkness, but these hardly atone for the director's delusion that prodigal expenditure of time and money will result in great art.

(The movie took so long to complete that it was dubbed *Apocalypse Later*.)

w John Milius, Francis Coppola *d* Francis Coppola *ph* Vittorio Storaro *m* Carmine Coppola, Francis Coppola *pd* Dean Tavoularis

Martin Sheen, Robert Duvall, Frederic Forrest, Marlon Brando, Sam Bottoms, Dennis Hopper

'The characters are living through Vietnam as pulp adventure fantasy, as movie, as stoned humour.'—*New Yorker*

† Coppola admitted the following at the Cannes Film Festival: 'It's more of an experience than a movie. At the beginning there's a story. Along the river the story becomes less important and the experience more important.'

● *Video: CIC*

The Appaloosa*
US 1966   99m   Techniscope
Universal (Alan Miller)
GB title: *Southwest to Sonora*

A cowboy's plan to start a stud farm with his magnificent horse is interrupted by badmen who think he has molested their girl. Mannered, slow western set on the Mexican border, with star and director apparently striving to upstage each other.

w James Bridges, Roland Kibbee, *novel* Robert MacLeod *d* Sidney J. Furie
ph Russell Metty *m* Frank Skinner

Marlon Brando, Anjanette Comer, John Saxon, Rafael Campos, Frank Silvera

'Seems intent less on telling a story than in carving out the incidental details.'—*MFB*

'The camerawork concentrates on beady eyes, sweaty foreheads, spurred boots and anonymous midriffs being studied through a variety of frames, ranging from tequila bottles to cook fires to grillwork to fingers to feet.'—*Judith Crist*

'A dog of a movie about a horse.'—*Pauline Kael*

'Is Kitty a mother?'
Applause***
US 1929   78m   bw
Paramount (Jesse L. Lasky, Walter Wanger)

A vaudeville star gradually loses the love of her daughter.
Absorbing treatment of a hasbeen tearjerking theme, full of cinematic touches and with unusual use of New York locations.

w Garrett Fort, *novel* Beth Brown *d* Rouben Mamoulian *ph* George Folsey

Helen Morgan, Joan Peers, Henry Wadsworth, Fuller Mellish Jnr

'An oasis of filmic sophistication in a desert of stage-bound early talkies.'—*William Everson, 1966*

'A cohesive, well integrated series of pictures. Its intensity, its sharp projection of tragedy, emerge from the eye of the camera; an omniscient, omnipresent eye that slides easily over the links of the story and emphasizes only the true and the relevant.'—*Thornton Delehanty, The Arts*

The Apple Dumpling Gang
US 1974   100m   Technicolor
Walt Disney (Bill Anderson)

Three orphan children strike gold in 1878 California.
Better-than-average Disney romp.

w Don Tait, *novel* Jack M. Bickham
d Norman Tokar *ph* Frank Phillips *m* Buddy Baker

Bill Bixby, Susan Clark, David Wayne, Don Knotts, Tim Conway, Slim Pickens, Harry Morgan, John McGiver, Marie Windsor, Iris Adrian

† *The Apple Dumpling Gang Rides Again*, a shoddy sequel under the direction of Vincent McEveety, appeared in 1979 with fragments of the old cast but no panache.

● *Video: Disney*

The Appointment*
US 1969   100m   colour
MGM (Martin Poll)

A businessman suspects his wife of spare time prostitution.
Unusual sophisticated fable, dressed to kill but rather stretched out for its substance. Shades of *El* and *The Chinese Room*.

w James Salter *d* Sidney Lumet *m* John Barry, Don Walker

Omar Sharif, Anouk Aimée, Lotte Lenya

Appointment for Love*
US 1941   89m   bw
Universal

A doctor and a playwright agree to marry 'without love'.
A familiar theme quite amusingly explored by a practised cast.

w Bruce Manning, Felix Jackson *d* William A. Seiter *ph* Joseph Valentine *m* Frank Skinner, Charles Previn

Charles Boyer, Margaret Sullavan, Eugene Pallette, Rita Johnson, Gus Schilling, Reginald Denny, Ruth Terry

Appointment in Berlin
US 1943   77m   bw
Columbia (Sam Bischoff)

An RAF wing commander expresses unpopular views and is recruited by the Nazis as a 'voice of truth' broadcaster.
World War II potboiler.

w Horace McCoy, Michael Hogan *d* Alfred E. Green *ph* Franz Planer *m* Werner Heymann

George Sanders, Marguerite Chapman, Gale Sondergaard, Onslow Stevens, Alan Napier, H. P. Sanders (the star's father)

Appointment in Honduras
US 1953   79m   Technicolor print
RKO / Benedict Bogeaus

Three assorted types and four criminals escape through the jungle from a revolution.
Predictable adventure drama sabotaged by poor colour.

w Karen deWolf *d* Jacques Tourneur
ph Joseph Biroc *m* Louis Forbes

Glenn Ford, Ann Sheridan, Zachary Scott, Rodolfo Acosta, Jack Elam

Appointment in London*
GB 1952   96m   bw
Mayflower (Aubrey Baring, Maxwell Setton)

The exploits of a squadron of Bomber Command during one month in 1943.
Dullish war film with standard credits.

w John Wooldridge, Robert Westerby
d Philip Leacock *ph* Stephen Dade *m* John Wooldridge

Dirk Bogarde, Ian Hunter, Dinah Sheridan, Bill Kerr, Bryan Forbes, William Sylvester, Charles Victor

Appointment with Crime
GB 1945   97m   bw

Ex-convict revenges himself on the former friends who shopped him. Stodgy melodrama which seemed about to make a big star of William Hartnell. Robert Beatty, Joyce Howard, Raymond Lovell, Herbert Lom. Written and directed by John Harlow; for British National.

Appointment with Danger*
US 1949   89m   bw
Paramount (Robert Fellows)

A nun becomes the government's chief witness in identifying the murderers of a US postal inspector.
Routine but entertaining star thick-ear.

w Richard Breen, Warren Duff *d* Lewis Allen *ph* John Seitz *m* Victor Young

Alan Ladd, Phyllis Calvert, Paul Stewart, Jan Sterling, Jack Webb, Henry Morgan

Appointment with a Shadow
US 1958   72m   bw   Cinemascope

An alcoholic reporter redeems himself by capturing a criminal single-handed. Maudlin melodrama which takes itself too seriously. George Nader, Joanna Moore, Brian Keith, Virginia Field. Written by Alec Coppel and Norman Jolley; directed by Richard Carlson; for Universal-International. (GB title: *The Big Story*.)

Appointment with Venus**
GB 1951   89m   bw
GFD / British Film Makers (Betty E. Box)
US title: *Island Rescue*

During World War II, a pedigree cow is rescued from the German-occupied Channel Islands.
Curious but generally agreeable mixture of comedy and war adventure, pleasantly shot on Sark.

w Nicholas Phipps, *novel* Jerrard Tickell
d Ralph Thomas *ph* Ernest Steward
m Benjamin Frankel

David Niven, Glynis Johns, George Coulouris, Barry Jones, Kenneth More, Noel Purcell, Bernard Lee, Jeremy Spenser

The Apprenticeship of Duddy Kravitz*
Canada 1974 121m Bellevue-Pathé
Panavision
Duddy Kravitz Syndicate (Gerald
Schneider)

An ambitious young Jew finds that it is best to
be liked.

Amusing adventures of an anti-hero; good
scenes but rather patchy technique.

w Mordecai Richler, from his novel d Ted
Kotcheff ph Miklos Lente m Stanley Myers

Richard Dreyfuss, Micheline Lanctot, Jack
Warden, Randy Quaid, Denholm Elliott,
Joseph Wiseman

AAN: Mordecai Richler

● Video: Guild

The April Fools*
US 1969 95m Technicolor Panavision
Cinema Center / Jalem (Gordon Carroll)

An unhappy New York husband elopes to
Paris with an unhappy wife.

Whimsical romantic comedy which rather
strains its resources without giving full value
for money in romance, humour or simple
charm. Good moments, though.

w Hal Dresner d Stuart Rosenberg
ph Michel Hugo m Marvin Hamlisch
pd Richard Sylbert

Jack Lemmon, Catherine Deneuve, Myrna
Loy, Charles Boyer, Peter Lawford, Jack
Weston, Harvey Korman, Sally Kellerman

'Painfully modish, from the opening party in
an apartment filled with fashionable objets
d'art to the final mad dash to the airport in an
expensive sports car.'—*MFB*

April in Paris*
US 1952 100m Technicolor
Warner (William Jacobs)

A chorus girl is mistakenly invited to a US
Arts Festival in Paris, and bewitches the
bureaucrat in charge.

Poorly produced star musical with a thin plot
and a few redeeming wisps of wit.

w Jack Rose, Melville Shavelson d David
Butler ph Wilfrid Cline md Ray Heindorf
ch Le Roy Prinz songs Sammy Cahn, Vernon
Duke, E. Y. Harburg

Doris Day, *Ray Bolger*, Claude Dauphin, Eve
Miller, George Givot

April Love
US 1957 99m Eastmancolor
Cinemascope
TCF (David Weisbart)

For stealing a car, a teenager is sent on
probation to his uncle's stud farm, where
circumstances seem once again to put him in
trouble with the law.

Easygoing star vehicle with little to
recommend it to adults.

w Winston Miller, novel George Agnew
Chamberlain d Henry Levin ph Wilfrid
Cline songs Sammy Fain, Paul Francis
Webster

Pat Boone, Shirley Jones, Dolores Michaels,
Arthur O'Connell, Jeanette Nolan

† A remake of *Home in Indiana*.

AAN: title song (m Sammy Fain, ly Paul
Francis Webster)

April Showers*
US 1948 94m bw
Warner (William Jacobs)

In a family vaudeville act, Dad takes to drink.

Hoary musical melodrama enlivened by
occasional acts.

w Peter Milne d James V. Kern ph Carl
Guthrie md Ray Heindorf m adaptation Max
Steiner songs various

Jack Carson, Robert Alda, Ann Sothern,
Robert Ellis, S. Z. Sakall

The Arab see The Barbarian

Arabella
US / Italy 1969 91m Technicolor

A female confidence trickster needs the money
to pay her grandmother's back taxes. Floppy,
tedious comedy adventure with an
international cast all at sea. Virna Lisi, James
Fox, Terry-Thomas, Margaret Rutherford.
Written by Adriano Barocco; directed by
Mauro Bolognini; for Cram Film / Universal.

Arabesque**
US 1966 118m Technicolor
Panavision
Universal (Stanley Donen)

An Oxford professor is asked by Middle
Eastern oil magnates to decipher a
hieroglyphic, and finds afterwards that he is
marked for assassination.

The ultimate in sixties spy kaleidoscopes, in
which the working out of the plot matters
much less than the stars, the jokes and the
lavish backgrounds. Fast moving, amusing and
utterly forgettable.

w Julian Mitchell, Stanley Price, Pierre
Marton, novel The Cipher by Gordon Votler
d Stanley Donen ph Christopher Challis
ad Reece Pemberton m Henry Mancini

Gregory Peck, Sophia Loren, *Alan Badel*,
Kieron Moore, Carl Duering

'Nothing could look more "with it", or
somehow matter less.'—*MFB*

'A strikingly visual chase and intrigue
yarn.'—*Robert Windeler*

'All rather too flashy for comfort.'—*Sight
and Sound*

† Pierre Marton was a pen name for Peter
Stone.

Arabian Adventure
GB 1979 98m colour
Badger Films / John Dark

The dictator of Jadur promises his daughter's
hand in marriage if a young prince will seek
and find a magic rose.

Artless juggling of elements from *The Thief of
Baghdad*, including magic carpets, monsters
and a bottle djinn.

w Brian Hayles d Kevin Connor ph Alan
Hume m Ken Thorne pd Elliot Scott

Christopher Lee, Oliver Tobias, Mickey
Rooney, Milo O'Shea, Elizabeth Welch, Peter
Cushing, Capucine

'Resolutely well mounted, but somehow
lacking that necessary fillip of Hollywood
vulgarity or exuberance.'—*John Pym, MFB*

● Video: Thorn EMI

Arabian Nights*
US 1942 86m Technicolor
Universal (Walter Wanger)

The Caliph of Baghdad is deposed by his
half-brother but wins back his throne with the
help of a dancer and an acrobat.

Well presented oriental adventure which has
nothing to do with its source material but
entertained multitudes in search of relief from
total war and was followed by several vaguely
similar slices of hokum with the same stars.

w Michael Hogan d John Rawlins ph Milton
Krasner, William V. Skall, W. Howard
Greene m Frank Skinner

Jon Hall, Maria Montez, Sabu, Leif Erickson,
Thomas Gomez, Turhan Bey, John Qualen,
Billy Gilbert, Shemp Howard

AAN: Milton Krasner, William V. Skall, W.
Howard Greene; Frank Skinner

'The story of an outcast and a killer!'
Arch of Triumph*
US 1948 120m bw
Enterprise (Lewis Milestone)

In postwar Paris, an embittered refugee seeks
his former Nazi tormentor and has a tragic
romance with a would-be suicide.

Doleful, set-bound melodrama knee-deep in
misery and artificial melodramatics. An
expensive, ambitious failure, both
commercially and artistically, but an
interesting one.

w Lewis Milestone, Harry Brown, novel Erich
Maria Remarque d Lewis Milestone
ph Russell Metty m Leonard Gruenberg
md Morris Stoloff

Ingrid Bergman, Charles Boyer, Charles
Laughton, Louis Calhern

† The story was remade for TV in 1984.

● Video: Intervision

Are Husbands Necessary?
US 1942 79m bw
Paramount

A bickering couple decide to adopt a baby.
Mild marital comedy in a familiar mould.

w Tess Slesinger, Frank Davis, novel Mr and
Mrs Cugat by Isabel Scott Rorick d Norman
Taurog ph Charles Lang m Robert Emmett
Dolan

Ray Milland, Betty Field, Patricia Morison,
Eugene Pallette, Charles Dingle, Cecil
Kellaway, Leif Erickson, Richard Haydn,
Elizabeth Risdon

'A chaos of farcical situations, conceived
without gusto and played without
conviction.'—*Richard Mallett, Punch*

Are These Our Children?
US 1931 75m bw

A teenager gets into bad company and ends up
facing the electric chair. Shapeless and

uncompelling moralistic farrago of no
entertainment value. Eric Linden, Rochelle
Hudson, Arline Judge, Ben Alexander,
Robert Quirk, Beryl Mercer. Written and
directed by Wesley Ruggles (screenplay by
Howard Estabrook); for RKO.

Are You a Mason?
GB 1934   70m   bw

A stockbroker has been pretending to be a
Masonic grand master so that he can get out
nights. Fairly simple-minded farce which could
have done with slicker production. Sonnie
Hale, Robertson Hare, Davy Burnaby,
Gwyneth Lloyd, Bertha Belmore. Written by
H. Fowler Mear from the farce by Leo
Dietrichstein and Emmanuel Lederer; directed
by Henry Edwards; for Twickenham.

Are You Being Served?
GB 1977   95m   Technicolor
EMI (Andrew Mitchell)

The staff of the clothing section of a
department store go on holiday to the Costa
Plonka.
Feeble enlargement of an old-fashioned but
very popular TV series relying heavily on
sexual badinage and ancient jokes.

w Jeremy Lloyd, David Croft d Bob Kellett
ph Jack Atcheler m various

John Inman, Frank Thornton, Mollie Sugden,
Trevor Bannister, Wendy Richard, Arthur
Brough, Nicholas Smith, Arthur English,
Harold Bennett, Glyn Houston
  'A withering selection of patent British
puns.'—John Pym, MFB
● Video: Thorn EMI

Are You Listening?
US 1932   73m   bw

A radio continuity announcer accidentally kills
his wife. Curious disjointed melodrama, the
sidelights on the new radio business being its
main interest. William Haines, Karen Morley,
Madge Evans, Anita Page, Neil Hamilton,
Wallace Ford, Jean Hersholt. Written by
Dwight Taylor from the Collier's serial by
J. P. McEvoy; directed by Harry Beaumont;
for MGM.

Are You With It?*
US 1948   90m   bw
Universal-International (Robert Arthur)

An insurance executive with doubts joins a fun
fair and has a whale of a time.
Pleasantly lively low-budget musical.

w Oscar Brodney, musical comedy Sam
Perrin, George Balzer d Jack Hively
ph Maury Gertsman md Walter Scharf
songs Sidney Miller, Inez James

Donald O'Connor, Olga San Juan, Martha
Stewart, Lew Parker

Arena
US 1953   83m   Anscocolor   3-D
MGM (Arthur M. Loew Jnr)

A rodeo rider regains his wife and his sense
when his best friend is killed.

Routine actioner, distinguished by 3-D
camerawork.

w Harold Jack Bloom d Richard Fleischer
ph Paul C. Vogel m Rudolph G. Kopp

Gig Young, Jean Hagen, Polly Bergen, Henry
Morgan, Barbara Lawrence, Robert Horton,
Lee Van Cleef

Aren't Men Beasts!*
GB 1937   66m   bw
BIP (Walter Mycroft)

A dentist poses as his aunt to stop a plot to
prevent his son's marriage.
Archetypal British star farce.

w Marjorie Deans, William Freshman, play
Vernon Sylvaine d Graham Cutts

Robertson Hare, Alfred Drayton, June Clyde,
Billy Milton, Judy Kelly

Aren't We All?
GB 1932   67m   bw

A society wife commits a momentary
indiscretion. A pale shadow of the theatrical
success of the twenties. Gertrude Lawrence,
Hugh Wakefield, Owen Nares, Harold Huth,
Marie Lohr, Renée Gadd, Aubrey Mather.
Written by Basil Mason from the play by
Frederick Lonsdale; directed by Harry
Lachman and Rudolf Maté; for Paramount
British.

L'Argent*
Switzerland / France 1983   84m   colour
EOS / Marion's Films / FR3 (Jean-Marc
Henchoz)

A tragic chain of events is started when a
forged note is passed in a photographer's
shop.
A bleak Bressonian study of conscience, fate
and atonement.

w,d Robert Bresson, story The False Note by
Leo Tolstoy ph Emmanuel Machuel,
Pasqualino de Santis m from Bach

Christian Patey, Sylvie Van Den Elsen, Michel
Briguet, Caroline Lang

Argentine Nights
US 1940   75m   bw

The Ritz Brothers and the Andrews Sisters
head for Argentina to avoid their creditors.
Fair low-budget musical. Written by Arthur
Horman, Ray Golden and Sid Kuller; directed
by Albert S. Rogell; for Universal.

Ariane
Germany 1931   78m   bw

An innocent young girl falls for a man of the
world and makes him think she is a cocotte.
Sophisticated comedy later remade as Love in
the Afternoon; this version is interesting chiefly
for its presentation of a new star. Elisabeth
Bergner, Rudolf Forster, Annemarie
Steinsieck, Hertha Guthmar. Written by Paul
Czinner and Carl Mayer from the novel by
Claude Anet; directed by Paul Czinner; for
Nerofilm.

'Here's the gay, glorious story of a war
  correspondent and a war ace . . . a
  romance that could happen only in
  1940!'

Arise My Love***
US 1940   113m   bw
Paramount (Arthur Hornblow Jnr)

American reporters in Europe and in love
survive the Spanish Civil War, a wrathful
editor in Paris and the sinking of the Athenia.
Unique sophisticated entertainment gleaned
from the century's grimmest headlines, ending
with a plea against American isolationism. A
significant and stylish comedy melodrama.

w Charles Brackett, Billy Wilder d Mitchell
Leisen ph Charles Lang m Victor Young

Claudette Colbert, Ray Milland, Walter Abel
(who as the harassed editor inaugurated his
celebrated line 'I'm not happy. I'm not happy
at all . . .'), Dennis O'Keefe, George Zucco,
Dick Purcell
† Joel McCrea was originally cast for the
Milland role.
AA: original story (Benjamin Glazer, John S.
Toldy)
AAN: Charles Lang; Victor Young

The Aristocats**
US 1970   78m   Technicolor
Walt Disney

Two cats are deliberately lost by a butler who
fears they will inherit his mistress's wealth; but
a variety of animal friends restore them to
their rightful place.
Cartoon feature, a moderate example of the
studio's work after Disney's death, with rather
too few felicitous moments.

d Wolfgang Reitherman

Arizona
US 1941   125m   bw
Columbia (Wesley Ruggles)

A Tucson wildcat meets her match in a
travelling Missourian who helps her outwit
villains who are sabotaging her wagon trains.
Loosely built, deliberately paced western
which for all its pretensions makes very little
impact.

w Claude Binyon d Wesley Ruggles
ph Joseph Walker, Harry Hollenberger, Fayte
Brown m Victor Young

Jean Arthur, William Holden, Warren
William, Porter Hall, Paul Harvey, George
Chandler, Byron Foulger, Regis Toomey,
Edgar Buchanan
  'Lacks the sweep and dramatic impulse that
would have made it a great picture.'—Variety
AAN: Victor Young

Arizona Bushwhackers
US 1968   86m   Techniscope
Paramount (A. C. Lyles)

A Confederate prisoner is given a chance as a
western sheriff.
Stolid western, notable only, as is usual with
this producer, for its gallery of ageing but still
reliable familiar faces.

ARISE MY LOVE. Ray Milland watches the only side of Claudette Colbert's face that he or the camera were ever allowed to see.

w Steve Fisher *d* Lesley Selander *ph* Lester Shorr *m* Jimmie Haskell

Howard Keel, Yvonne de Carlo, Brian Donlevy, John Ireland, Marilyn Maxwell, Scott Brady, Barton Maclane, James Craig

Arizona Raiders
US 1965 88m Techniscope

Two of Quantrell's Raiders are offered a pardon if they will round up renegades. Stereotyped western, poorly processed. Audie Murphy, Michael Dante, Ben Cooper, Buster Crabbe, Gloria Talbott. Written by Alex Gottlieb and Mary and Willard Willingham; directed by William Witney; for Admiral / Columbia.

The Arizonian
US 1935 72m bw

Lawless Silver City gets a reform marshal. Adequate first feature western, but not a spectacular. Richard Dix, Margot Grahame, Preston Foster, Louis Calhern. Written by Dudley Nichols; directed by Charles Vidor; for RKO. 'Through the names it can slip into the keys where westerns rarely treat, and where, therefore, horse operas are regarded as refreshing novelties.'—*Variety*

The Arkansas Traveller
US 1938 85m bw

A small-town widow is helped to keep her newspaper going by a stranger who happens to be passing through. Archetypal mid-American fantasy. Bob Burns, Fay Bainter, Jean Parker,

Irvin S. Cobb. Written by Viola Brothers Shore, George Sessions Perry, from a story by Jack Cunningham; directed by Alfred Santell; for Paramount.
    'It will get over nicely in the key spots, but its biggest b.o. will be in the nabes and smaller communities.'—*Variety*

Armored Car Robbery*
US 1950 67m bw
RKO (Herman Schlom)

A police lieutenant leads the recovery of half a million dollars stolen by gangsters.
Good competent second feature with Los Angeles locations and detailed observation of police methods.

w Earl Felton, Gerald Drayson Adams *d* Richard Fleischer *ph* Guy Roe *m* Constantin Bakaleinikoff

Charles McGraw, Adele Jergens, William Talman, Douglas Fowley, Steve Brodie

Armored Command
US 1961 105m bw
Allied Artists (Ron W. Alcorn)

During the Battle of the Bulge, a ravishing Nazi spy is infiltrated into an American army outpost.
Incredible Mata Hari melodrama posing as a war film, nicely shot in bleak snowscapes. Not exactly rewarding, but unusual.

w Ron W. Alcorn *d* Byron Haskin *ph* Ernest Haller *m* Bert Grund

Howard Keel, Tina Louise, Burt Reynolds, Earl Holliman, Warner Anderson, Carleton Young, Marty Ingels

Arms and the Man
GB 1932 85m bw

A soldier who finds discretion the better part of valour hides in a girl's bedroom. Faithful but uninspired version of Bernard Shaw's play. Barry Jones, Anne Grey, Angela Baddeley. Directed by Cecil Lewis; for BIP / Wardour.

Army Girl
US 1938 90m bw

Old loyalties flare at an army post when tanks replace cavalry troops. Modest flagwaver which got by at the time. Madge Evans, Preston Foster, James Gleason, H. B. Warner, Ruth Donnelly, Neil Hamilton, Billy Gilbert, Heather Angel, Ralph Morgan. Written by Barry Trivers and Sam Ornitz; directed by George Nicholls Jnr; for Republic. 'Thoroughly entertaining . . . suitable as single in smaller spots, or action half of double bill in keys.'—*Variety*. AAN: Ernest Miller, photography; Victor Young, music.

The Arnelo Affair
US 1946 86m bw

Lawyer's wife gets involved with nightclub owner. Yawnworthy murder melodrama. George Murphy, Frances Gifford, John Hodiak, Eve Arden. Written and directed by Arch Oboler; for MGM.

Arnold
US 1973 95m De Luxe
Avco / Fenady (Charles A. Pratt, Andrew Fenady)

Via cassette recordings, a dead man toys with his would-be heirs, and several are murdered. Unpleasant and very laboured black comedy on the lines of *And Then There Were None* and a hundred others, all better than this.

w Jameson Brewer, John Fenton Murray *d* Georg Fenady *ph* William Jurgenson *m* George Duning

Stella Stevens, Roddy McDowell, Elsa Lanchester, Shani Wallis, Farley Granger, Victor Buono, John McGiver, Bernard Fox, Patric Knowles
† Apparently made back to back with *Terror in the Wax Museum*, which has very similar credits.

Around the World
US 1943 81m bw
RKO (Allan Dwan)

Kay Kyser's band goes on a world tour to entertain troops overseas.
Typical wartime patriotic musical, now of sociological interest.

w Ralph Spence *d* Allan Dwan *ph* Russell Metty *md* Constantin Bakaleinikoff *m* George Duning *songs* Jimmy McHugh, Harold Adamson

Kay Kyser, Ish Kabibble, Ginny Simms, Joan Davis, Mischa Auer

'It's a wonderful world, if you'll only take the time to go around it!'

Around the World in Eighty Days***
US 1956 178m Technicolor Todd-AO
UA / Michael Todd

A Victorian gentleman and his valet win a bet that they can go round the world in eighty days.
Amiable large-scale pageant resolving itself into a number of sketches, which could have been much sharper, separated by wide screen spectacle. What was breathtaking at the time seems generally slow and blunted in retrospect, but the fascination of recognizing 44 cameo stars remains. The film is less an exercise in traditional skills than a tribute to its producer's energy.

w James Poe, John Farrow, S. J. Perelman, novel Jules Verne d Michael Anderson, Kevin McClory ph Lionel Lindon m Victor Young titles Saul Bass

David Niven, Cantinflas, Robert Newton, Shirley Maclaine, Charles Boyer, Joe E. Brown, Martine Carol, John Carradine, Charles Coburn, Ronald Colman, Melville Cooper, Noel Coward, Finlay Currie, Reginald Denny, Andy Devine, Marlene Dietrich, Luis Dominguin, Fernandel, John Gielgud, Hermione Gingold, Jose Greco, Cedric Hardwicke, Trevor Howard, Glynis Johns, Buster Keaton, Evelyn Keyes, Beatrice Lillie, Peter Lorre, Edmund Lowe, A. E. Matthews, Mike Mazurki, Tim McCoy, Victor McLaglen, John Mills, Alan Mowbray, Robert Morley, Jack Oakie, George Raft, Gilbert Roland, Cesar Romero, Frank Sinatra, Red Skelton, Ronald Squire, Basil Sidney, Harcourt Williams, Ed Murrow
'Michael Todd's "show", shorn of the ballyhoo and to critics not mollified by parties and sweetmeats, is a film like any other, only twice as long as most . . . the shots of trains and boats seem endless.'—David Robinson
AA: best picture; James Poe, John Farrow, S. J. Perelman; Lionel Lindon; Victor Young
AAN: Michael Anderson

Around the World in Eighty Minutes
US 1931 80m bw

An account of Douglas Fairbanks' travels, mainly in the Far East. Awfully padded travelogue which seems to have been a bore even at the time, despite a few magic-carpet tricks. Written by Robert E. Sherwood; directed by Douglas Fairbanks and Victor Fleming; for United Artists. 'Fairbanks enlivens much of the drab footage with his acrobatics.'—Variety

Around the World under the Sea
US 1966 110m Metrocolor Panavision
MGM / Ivan Tors (Andrew Marton)

An ultra-modern underwater craft travels around the seabed fixing sensors to give early warning of volcanoes.
Earnest, dullish, elementary sci-fi with cardboard characters providing routine five men-one woman skirmishes.

w Arthur Weiss, Art Arthur d Andrew Marton, Ricou Browning ph Clifford Poland, Lamar Boren m Harry Sukman
Lloyd Bridges, Shirley Eaton, Brian Kelly, David McCallum, Keenan Wynn, Marshall Thompson, Gary Merrill

The Arrangement**
US 1969 127m Technicolor Panavision
Warner / Athena (Elia Kazan)

A wealthy advertising man fails in a suicide attempt and spends his convalescence reflecting on his unsatisfactory emotional life. A lush, all-American melodrama, rich in technique but peopled by characters who have nothing to say; the film makes no discernible point except as a well-acted tirade against the compromises of modern urban living.

wd Elia Kazan, from his own novel ph Robert Surtees m David Amram pd Malcolm C. Bert
Kirk Douglas, Faye Dunaway, Deborah Kerr, Richard Boone, Hume Cronyn
'The sort of collage that won't fit together, no matter where you stand.'—PS
'As dead as a flower arrangement in an undertaker's parlour . . . all possible cinematic clevernesses—usually yesterday's—are dragged out in an endless parade, to illustrate a senseless and banal story that reels from platitude to platitude.'—John Simon

Arrest Bulldog Drummond: see Bulldog Drummond

Arrowhead
US 1953 105m Technicolor 3D
Paramount (Nat Holt)

Enmity between an army scout and an Indian chief is resolved by single combat.
Standard western, good-looking but rather lifeless.

w Charles Marquis Warren, novel W. R. Burnett d Charles Marquis Warren ph Ray Rennahan m Paul Sawtell
Charlton Heston, Jack Palance, Katy Jurado, Brian Keith, Milburn Stone

Arrowsmith*
US 1931 108m bw
Samuel Goldwyn

The self-sacrificing career of a doctor. Emotionally satisfactory, dramatically slow and unsurprising variation on a theme which has since been treated far too often.

w Sidney Howard, novel Sinclair Lewis
d John Ford ph Ray June m Alfred Newman
Ronald Colman, Helen Hayes, Richard Bennett, Myrna Loy, Charlotte Henry, Beulah Bondi, A. E. Anson
'Pictures would do better to stay clear of these elaborately biographical novels with their wealth of actionless detail. . . . That portion of the citizenry which read the Sinclair Lewis novel will probably be in sympathy with the film, those who didn't will not be prone to deem this macabre tale entertainment.'—Variety

† The negative was later cut to about 89m for reissue, and this version, virtually eliminating Myrna Loy, is the only one now available.
AAN: best picture; Sidney Howard; Ray June

Arsenal**
USSR 1929 99m (16 fps) bw silent
VUFKU

The 1914 war is made worse by strikes at home.
Patchy propagandist drama with brilliant sequences.

wd Alexander Dovzhenko ph Danylo Demutsky
S. Svashenko, A. Buchma, M. Nademsky
'A romantic and lyrical masterpiece.'—Georges Sadoul

The Arsenal Stadium Mystery
GB 1939 85m bw

A footballer is poisoned during a match. Brisk little mystery, with an amiable star performance. Leslie Banks, Greta Gynt, Esmond Knight, Brian Worth. Written by Thorold Dickinson and Donald Bull, from the novel by Leonard Gribble; directed by Thorold Dickinson; for G&S / GFD.
'This picture is as good to watch as either of the Thin Man films, and Dickinson gives us wit instead of facetiousness—wit of cutting and wit of angle.'—Graham Greene

Arsène Lupin**
US 1932 75m bw
MGM

The Parisian gentleman thief accomplishes some daring robberies and is almost caught stealing the Mona Lisa.
Amusing crook comedy with a few flat passages but much sparkle in between, and a lively finale.

w Carey Wilson, Lenore Coffee, Bayard Veiller d Jack Conway ph Oliver Marsh
John Barrymore, Lionel Barrymore, Karen Morley, Tully Marshall, John Miljan
'First screen appearance of John and Lionel together and their acting of this old standard detective story ensures its box office in spite of the absence of other qualities that make for notable screen successes. . . . At least it addresses itself to a higher class of fans than the lurid type of dime novel subject.'—Variety

Arsène Lupin Returns
US 1938 81m bw
MGM (John W. Considine Jnr)

The reformed jewel thief helps an American detective to track down a French criminal.
Smooth but disappointingly scripted sequel which never quite rises to a climax despite sympathetic casting.

w James Kevin McGuinness, Howard Emmett Rogers, George Harmon Coxe d George Fitzmaurice ph George Folsey m Franz Waxman
Melvyn Douglas, Warren William, Virginia Bruce, John Halliday, Nat Pendleton, Monty Woolley, George Zucco, E. E. Clive

'A first-class mystery jewel theft combo . . . for the top side of the marquee pairing, missing A classification quite a little, but still being okay.'—*Variety*

Arsenic and Old Lace***
US 1942 (released 1944) 118m bw
Warner (Frank Capra)

Two dear, well-meaning old ladies invite lonely old men to their Brooklyn home, poison them with elderberry wine, and have their mad brother, who believes the corpses are yellow fever victims, bury them in the cellar. A homicidal nephew then turns up with bodies of his own.
A model for stage play adaptations, this famous black farce provided a frenzy of hilarious activity, and its flippant attitude to death was better received in wartime than would have been the case earlier or later. The director coaxes some perfect if overstated performances from his star cast, and added his own flair for perpetuating a hubbub.
w Julius J. and Philip G. Epstein, from the play by Joseph Kesselring with help from Howard Lindsay and Russell Crouse *d* Frank Capra *ph* Sol Polito *m* Max Steiner

Cary Grant (Mortimer Brewster), *Josephine Hull* (Abby Brewster), *Jean Adair* (Martha Brewster), Priscilla Lane (Elaine Harper), Raymond Massey (Jonathan Brewster), *John Alexander* (Teddy Brewster), Peter Lorre (Dr Einstein), James Gleason (Lt Rooney), Jack Carson (Officer O'Hara), Edward Everett Horton (Mr Witherspoon), Grant Mitchell (Reverend Harper)

MORTIMER: 'Insanity runs in my family. It practically gallops.'

MARTHA: 'One of our gentlemen found time to say "How delicious!" before he died. . . .'

● *Video: Warner*

The Art of Love
US 1965 99m Technicolor
Universal / Cherokee / Ross Hunter

To stimulate interest in his work, a penniless artist fakes suicide, subsequently becoming so famous that he finds it difficult to reappear.
A pleasant black comedy idea is buried under lush production, dull direction and a host of unattractive Parisian sets.
w Carl Reiner *d* Norman Jewison *ph* Russell Metty *m* Cy Coleman

James Garner, Dick Van Dyke, Angie Dickinson, Elke Sommer, Ethel Merman, Pierre Olaf

The Arizona Kid
US 1930 84m bw

A wanted bandit finds a secret gold mine in Utah. Disappointing semi-sequel to *In Old Arizona*: same star, much less talent to back him up. Warner Baxter, Mona Maris, Carole Lombard, Mrs Jiminez, Theodore Von Eltz. Written by Ralph Block; directed by Alfred Santell; for Fox.

'I race cars, I play tennis, I fondle women, but I have weekends off and I am my own boss!'

Arthur*
US 1981 97m Technicolor
Warner / Orion (Robert Greenhut)

A rich New York layabout is forced to moderate his life style in order to qualify for his inheritance.
An unattractive excuse for the star to do his drunk act. In effect his thunder was stolen by Gielgud as the valet who is not above a few choice four-letter words; but over the whole enterprise hung a pall of desperation. It is a sign of its times that it made a lot of money.
wd Steve Gordon *ph* Fred Schuler *m* Burt Bacharach *pd* Stephen Hendrikson

Dudley Moore, *John Gielgud*, Liza Minnelli, Geraldine Fitzgerald, Jill Eikenberry, Stephen Elliott

'It comes as no surprise to find the funniest sequences packed into the first half-hour.'—*Martyn Auty, MFB*
'Gielgud may be the most poised and confident funnyman you'll ever see.'—*New Yorker*
'Arthur may be the surprise hit of 1981, but to me he's a pain in the neck.'—*Margaret Hinxman, Daily Mail*

AA: John Gielgud (supporting actor)
AAN: screenplay; Dudley Moore

● *Video: Warner*

Artistes at the Top of the Big Top: Disorientated**
West Germany 1968 103m bw / colour
Kairos Film

The daughter of a dead trapezist dreams of creating the ideal circus with a moral for mankind but step by step gives up her ambition.
A melancholy satire, told in fragmented fashion with some brilliant tricks and memorable sequences.
wd Alexander Kluge *ph* Gunther Hörmann, Thomas Mauch

Hannelore Hoger, Siegfried Graue, Alfred Edel, Bernd Höltz
'Those who interpret it simply as an allegory of German politics or of the present crisis in film-making narrow it unnecessarily.'—*Jan Dawson, MFB*

Artists and Models*
US 1937 97m bw
Paramount (Lewis E. Gensler)

An advertising man has to find the right girl as symbol for a silverware company.
Fairly stylish comedy musical with many elements typical of its studio.
w Walter de Leon, Francis Martin *d* Raoul Walsh *ph* Victor Milner *m* Victor Young *songs* various

Jack Benny, Ida Lupino, Richard Arlen, Gail Patrick, Ben Blue, Judy Canova, Martha Raye, Donald Meek, Hedda Hopper, André Kostelanetz and his Orchestra, Louis Armstrong and his Orchestra

'Should be a box-office bonanza for exhibitors. It holds enough variety, comedy, colour, spectacle, flash, dash and novelty for a couple of pictures.'—*Variety*

AAN: song 'Whispers in the Dark'
(*m* Frederick Hollander, *ly* Leo Robin)

Artists and Models*
US 1955 109m Technicolor
Vistavision
Paramount / Hal B. Wallis

A goonish young man receives telepathic top secret information in his nightmares, which are used by his artist friend in comic strips; foreign agents and the CIA get interested.
A good zany idea is worked into an overlong dyspeptic comedy which neither the stars nor frantic treatment can hope to save.
w Frank Tashlin, Don McGuire *d* Frank Tashlin *ph* Daniel Fapp *m* Walter Scharf

Dean Martin, Jerry Lewis, Shirley Maclaine, Dorothy Malone, Eddie Mayehoff, Eva Gabor, Anita Ekberg, George 'Foghorn' Winslow, Jack Elam

'It's an ooh-la-lalapalooza!'
Artists and Models Abroad*
US 1938 90m bw
Paramount (Arthur Hornblow Jnr)
GB title: *Stranded in Paris*

Stranded in Paris, a troupe of girls and their manager are helped by a Texas oil millionaire. Generally agreeable comedy musical with emphasis on fashion.
w Howard Lindsay, Russell Crouse, Ken Englund *d* Mitchell Leisen *ph* Ted Tetzlaff *md* Borris Morros *songs* various *ad* Hans Dreier, Ernest Fegte

Jack Benny, Joan Bennett, Mary Boland, Charley Grapewin, Joyce Compton, the Yacht Club Boys, Fritz Feld, G. P. Huntley, Monty Woolley
'Straight farce comedy. The models are in a fashion show and the artists are missing entirely.'—*Variety*

The Aryan*
US 1916 75m (16 fps) bw silent
Triangle (Thomas Ince)

A gold prospector is cheated by a woman and becomes an outlaw.
Striking early star western.
w C. Gardner Sullivan *d* William S. Hart, Clifford Smith *ph* Joseph August, Clyde de Vinna

William S. Hart, Bessie Love, Louise Glaum, Hershall Mayall

As Husbands Go
US 1934 65m bw

Lover and husband become friends, making infidelity impossible. Minor smart-set comedy from a then popular play. Warner Baxter, Helen Vinson, Warner Oland, G. P. Huntley Jnr, Catherine Doucet. Written by Sam Behrman and Sonia Levien from the play by

Rachel Crothers; directed by Hamilton
McFadden; for Jesse Lasky / Fox. 'Pleasant
entertainment all the way, but a lack of action
will bore children and annoy that not
inconsiderable body of Americans who
violently resent too much suavity of speech
and manner.'—*Variety*

As Long as They're Happy*
GB 1955   91m   Eastmancolor
Rank / Regroup (Raymond Stross)

The suburban home of a London stockbroker
is invaded by an American sob singer.
Frantic farce expanded from a stage satire of
the Johnnie Ray cult; a patchy but sometimes
funny star vehicle.

w Alan Melvile, *play* Vernon Sylvaine
d J. Lee-Thompson   *ph* Gilbert Taylor

Jack Buchanan, Brenda de Banzie, Diana
Dors, Jean Carson, Janette Scott, Susan
Stephen, Jerry Wayne, Hugh McDermott

As Long as You're Near Me
West Germany 1954   94m   colour

A film director almost ruins a small-part
actress's life by insisting on making her a star.
Reasonably absorbing drama (original title:
Solange Du da bist), chiefly remarkable for
being a great hit in the US when dubbed. O.
W. Fischer, Hardy Kruger, Maria Schell.
Written by Jochen Huth; directed by Harold
Braun; for Warner.

As the Earth Turns
US 1934   73m   bw

The problems of three farming families in
Maine. Reliable rustic soap opera, pretty well
presented. Jean Muir, Donald Woods, Emily
Lowry, William Janney, David Landau,
Dorothy Peterson. Written by Ernest Pascal
from the book by Gladys Hasty Carroll;
directed by Alfred E. Green; for Warners.
'What it may lack in box office, it makes up in
entertainment . . . the sort of story that
commands attention and favour.'—*Variety*

As You Desire Me*
US 1931   71m   bw
MGM (George Fitzmaurice)

The amnesiac mistress of a novelist rediscovers
her real husband and falls in love with him
again.
Interesting star vehicle with good cast and
production.

w Gene Markey, *play* Luigi Pirandello
d George Fitzmaurice   *ph* William Daniels

Greta Garbo, Melvyn Douglas, Erich Von
Stroheim, Owen Moore, Hedda Hopper,
Rafaela Ottiano

'Pretty subtle for the generality of fans. It
was more of a courageous gesture towards
production ideals than good business
judgement that dictated its choice for filming
in the first place.'—*Variety*

As You Like It*
GB 1936   96m   bw
TCF / Inter-Allied (Joseph M. Schenck, Paul
Czinner)

The fortunes of an exiled king take a turn in
the Forest of Arden.
Stylized, rather effete but often amusing
version of Shakespeare's pastoral comedy.

w J. M. Barrie, Robert Cullen, *play* William
Shakespeare   *d* Paul Czinner   *ph* Harold
Rosson   *m* William Walton

Elisabeth Bergner, Laurence Olivier, Sophie
Stewart, Leon Quartermaine, Henry Ainley,
Richard Ainley, Felix Aylmer, Mackenzie
Ward, Aubrey Mather, John Laurie, Peter
Bull

'Rather too respectably lighthearted, but by
no means a contemptible production.'—*New
Yorker, 1978*

'There are far too many dull middle-length
shots from a fixed camera, so that we might
just as well be seated in the circle above the
deep wide stage at Drury Lane.'—*Graham
Greene*

As Young as You Feel*
US 1951   77m   bw
TCF (Lamar Trotti)

An elderly employee, forced to retire,
impersonates the company president, saves the
firm from bankruptcy, and proves his
continued worth.
Good-natured comedy, ably presented.

w Lamar Trotti, *story* Paddy Chayevsky
d Harmon Jones   *ph* Joe MacDonald   *m* Cyril
Mockridge

Monty Woolley, Constance Bennett, Thelma
Ritter, David Wayne, Jean Peters, Marilyn
Monroe, Allyn Joslyn, Albert Dekker

Ascendancy*
GB 1982   85m   colour
British Film Institute Production Board
(Penny Clark, Ian Elsey)

In 1920 Belfast a shipyard owner's daughter,
shocked by the death of her brother in the
war, cannot come to terms with the sectarian
slaughter around her.
Unilluminatingly argumentative character
study which fails to make its purpose very
clear despite a stunning central performance.

w Edward Bennett, Nigel Gearing   *d* Edward
Bennett   *ph* Clive Tickner   *m* Ronnie Leahy

Julie Covington, Ian Charleson, John Phillips,
Susan Engel, Philip Locke

Ash Wednesday
US 1973   99m   Technicolor
Sagittarius (Dominick Dunne)

An ageing American beauty rejuvenates
herself via plastic surgery, leads a vivid sex
life, and leaves her stolid husband.
The bloodthirsty operation scenes are
revolting, yet this joyless saga seems meant as
a celebration of the wonders of cosmetic
surgery and Sex for the Aged. Hypnotic but
hardly rewarding.

w Jean Claude Tramont   *d* Larry Peerce
ph Ennio Guarnieri   *m* Maurice Jarre

Elizabeth Taylor, Henry Fonda, Helmut
Berger, Keith Baxter, Maurice Teynac

'Endless shots of Elizabeth Taylor
expensively attired against the plush
background of Cortina.'—*Michael Billington,
Illustrated London News*

'A long-drawn-out ghoulish commercial for
cosmetic surgery—made apparently for people
who can't think of anything to do with their
lives but go backwards.'—*Pauline Kael*

● *Video: Video Unlimited*

Ashanti
Switzerland 1979   117m   Panavision
Technicolor
Columbia / Beverly (Luciano Sacripanti)

In West Africa, the wife of a member of the
World Health Organization is seized by slave
traders.
Absurd and rather unattractively brutal
adventure story, decked out with appearances
by guest stars.

w Stephen Geller, *novel* Ebano by Alberto
Vasquez-Figueroa   *d* Richard Fleischer
ph Aldo Tonti   *m* Michael Melvoin

Michael Caine, Omar Sharif, Peter Ustinov,
Rex Harrison, Kabir Bedi, William Holden,
Zia Mohyeddin, Beverly Johnson

Ashes and Diamonds**
Poland 1958   104m   bw
Film Polski
original title: *Popiol y Diament*

A Polish partisan is confused by the apparent
need to continue killing after the war is over.
A chilling account of the intellectual
contradictions to which war leads, and a
moving and sensitive film in its own right.

wd Andrzej Wajda, *novel* Jerzy Andrzejewski
ph Jerzy Wojcik

Zbigniew Cybulski, Ewa Krzyzanowska,
Adam Pawlikowski

● *Video: Thorn EMI*

Ask a Policeman**
GB 1938   82m   bw
Gainsborough (Edward Black)

In a small coastal village, incompetent
policemen accidentally expose smugglers who
are scaring the locals with a headless horseman
legend.
One of the best comedies of an incomparable
team, with smart dialogue, good situations and
a measure of suspense.

w Marriott Edgar, Val Guest, J. O. C. Orton
d Marcel Varnel   *ph* Derek Williams

Will Hay, Moore Marriott, Graham Moffatt,
Glennis Lorimer, *Peter Gawthorne, Herbert
Lomas*, Charles Oliver

'A good laugh getter and safe second
feature on any programme.'—*Variety*

Ask Any Girl*
US 1959 98m Metrocolor
Cinemascope
MGM / Euterpe (Joe Pasternak)

A husband-hunting receptionist in New York catches the eye of a wealthy playboy but finally settles for his elder brother.
Predictable Cinderella story with a lively but forgettable script and actors going through familiar paces.

w George Wells, *novel* Winifred Wolfe
d Charles Walters *ph* Robert Bronner *m* Jeff Alexander

David Niven, Shirley Maclaine, Gig Young, Rod Taylor, Jim Backus, Claire Kelly

'Like a comic strip transposed to the glossy pages of *Vogue*.'—*MFB*

Asking for Trouble*
GB 1941 81m bw

A bookie poses as a big game hunter. The last opportunity to see a great music hall comic on film, his style admittedly bowdlerized. *Max Miller*, Carole Lynne, Wilfrid Hyde White, Mark Lester. Written by Oswald Mitchell and Con West; directed by Oswald Mitchell; for British National.

Aspern*
Portugal 1981 96m colour
VO / Oxala (Paulo Branco)

The French biographer of a deceased poet goes to Venice to get unpublished papers from his aged mistress.
This very well-known story (see also *The Lost Moment* and various theatrical versions) is styled with exceeding solemnity in this well-acted but boring version.

w Michael Graham, *story* Henry James
d Eduardo de Grigorio *ph* Acacio de Almeida *m* mainly from Mozart

Alida Valli, Jean Sorel, Bulle Ogier, Ana Marta

Asphalt*
Germany 1929 101m bw
UFA

A young policeman accidentally kills his rival for a worthless girl.
Heavily expressionist melodrama, overlong but good to watch.

w Rolf Vanloo, Fred Majo, Hans Szekely
d Joe May *ph* Günther Rittau

Gustav Fröhlich, Betty Amann, Else Heller, Louise Brooks

'So well produced that it is good entertainment in spite of itself.'—*Variety*

The Asphalt Jungle***
US 1950 112m bw
MGM (Arthur Hornblow Jnr)

An elderly crook comes out of prison and assembles a gang for one last robbery.
Probably the very first film to show a 'caper' from the criminals' viewpoint (a genre which has since been done to death several times over), this is a clever character study rather than a thriller, extremely well executed and indeed generally irreproachable yet somehow not a film likely to appear on many top ten lists; perhaps the writer-director stands too far back from everybody, or perhaps he just needed Humphrey Bogart.

w Ben Maddow, John Huston, *novel* W. R. Burnett *d* John Huston *ph* Harold Rosson *m* Miklos Rozsa

Sterling Hayden (Dix Handley), Louis Calhern (Alonzo D Emmerich), *Sam Jaffe* (Doc Erwin Riedenschneider), Jean Hagen (Doll Conovan), James Whitmore (Gus Minissi), John McIntire (Police Commissioner Hardy), Marc Lawrence (Cobby), Marilyn Monroe (Angela Phinlay), Barry Kelley (Lt Ditrich)

RIEDENSCHNEIDER: 'Crime is a left-handed form of human endeavour.'

'Where this film excels is in the fluency of its narration, the sharpness of its observation of character and the excitement of its human groupings.'—*Dilys Powell*

'That Asphalt Pavement thing is full of nasty, ugly people doing nasty things. I wouldn't walk across the room to see a thing like that.'—*Louis B. Mayer* (who was head of the studio which made it)

† Apart from imitations, the film has been directly remade as *The Badlanders*, *Cairo* and *A Cool Breeze*.

AAN: Ben Maddow, John Huston (writers); John Huston (as director); Harold Rosson; Sam Jaffe

The Asphyx
GB 1973 99m Eastmancolor
Todd AO 35
Glendale (John Brittany)

A Victorian aims to become immortal by separating the spirit of death from his body. Interminable hocus pocus with a plethora of talk, seldom exciting but watchable because of its remarkable cast and other credits.

w Brian Comport *d* Peter Newbrook
ph Freddie Young *m* Bill McGuffie *sp* Ted Samuels

Robert Stephens, Robert Powell, Jane Lapotaire

The Assassin**
Italy / France 1961 105m bw
Titanus-Vides-SGC (Franco Cristaldi)

A prosperous antique dealer is accused of murder and his unsavoury past is revealed; but when he is freed, he prides himself on his new personality.
A careful, detailed and wholly enjoyable character study, somewhere between comedy and drama.

w Elio Petri and others *d* Elio Petri *ph* Carlo di Palma *m* Piero Piccioni

Marcello Mastroianni, Salvo Randone, Micheline Presle, Andrea Checci

Assassin
GB 1973 83m Technicolor
Pemini (David M. Jackson)

MI5 arranges the liquidation of an Air Ministry spy.
Old hat espionage melodrama, topheavy with artiness which makes it look like an endless TV commercial.

w Michael Sloan *d* Peter Crane *ph* Brian Jonson *m* Zack Lawrence

Ian Hendry, Edward Judd, Frank Windsor, Ray Brooks, John Hart Dyke

Assassin for Hire*
GB 1951 67m bw

A professional killer is trapped into admitting a murder he didn't do. Taut little suspenser, quite watchable. Sydney Tafler, Ronald Howard, John Hewer, Martin Benson. Written by Rex Rienits; directed by *Michael McCarthy*; for Julian Wintle / Anglo Amalgamated.

The Assassination Bureau*
GB 1968 110m Technicolor
Paramount / Heathfield (Michael Relph)

In 1906 a lady journalist breaks up an international gang of professional killers by falling in love with their leader.
Black comedy period pastiche which resolves itself into a series of sketches leading up to a spectacular zeppelin climax. Plenty going on, but the level of wit is not high.

w Michael Relph, with Wolf Mankowitz
d Basil Dearden *ph* Geoffrey Unsworth
m Ron Grainer

Oliver Reed, Diana Rigg, Telly Savalas, Curt Jurgens, Philippe Noiret, Warren Mitchell, Clive Revill, Beryl Reid, Kenneth Griffith

The Assassination of the Duc de Guise*
France 1908 15m (16 fps) bw silent
Film d'Art

Henry III arranges the killing of the Duc de Guise when he comes to court.
Influential early story film.

w Henri Lavedan *d* Charles le Bargy
m Saint-Saëns

Charles le Bargy, Albert Lambert, Gabrielle Lavinne

'For one moment, they hold history in their hands. With one terrible blow, they make it'

The Assassination of Trotsky
Italy / GB / France 1972 103m
Technicolor
Dino de Laurentiis / Josef Shaftel / Cinetel (Norman Priggen, Joseph Losey)

In 1940, Trotsky is hiding out in Mexico; a Stalinist infiltrates his presence and kills him with an ice pick.
Glum historical reconstruction with much fictitious padding; basically undramatic.

w Nicholas Mosley, Masolino d'Amico
d Joseph Losey *ph* Pasquale de Santis
m Egisto Macchi

Richard Burton, Alain Delon, Romy Schneider, Valentina Cortese, Jean Desailly

'Not for anyone who knows, or cares, anything about Leon Trotsky.'—*New Yorker, 1977*

Les Assassins du Dimanche

France 1956 94m bw Cinepanoramic
EDIC
aka: *Every Second Counts*

Dozens of people help to track down a holiday car which has been driven away from a garage in a dangerous condition.
Watchable but artificial suspenser.

w Alex Joffe, Gabriel Arout d Alex Joffe ph Jean Bourgoin

Barbara Laage, Jean-Marc Thibault, Dominique Wilms, Paul Frankeur

Assault

GB 1970 91m Eastmancolor
Rank / Peter Rogers (George H. Brown)

An art mistress helps police to solve a case of multiple rape in an English village.
Old-fashioned police mystery with new-fangled shock treatment. Routine excitements.

w John Kruse, *novel* Kendal Young d Sidney Hayers ph Ken Hodges m Eric Rogers

Frank Finlay, Suzy Kendall, James Laurenson, Lesley-Anne Down, Freddie Jones, Tony Beckley, Anthony Ainley, Dilys Hamlett

'All right for that wet afternoon.'—*Michael Billington, Illustrated London News*

● Video: Rank

Assault on a Queen

US 1966 106m Technicolor
Panavision
Paramount / Seven Arts / Sinatra
Enterprises (William Goetz)

Crooks dredge up a submarine and use it to hi-jack the *Queen Mary*.
Strained caper film which remains uncertain whether to play for drama or thrills, and achieves neither. Special effects unconvincing.

w Rod Serling, *novel* Jack Finney d Jack Donohue ph William Daniels m Duke Ellington

Frank Sinatra, Virna Lisi, Tony Franciosa, Alf Kjellin, Errol John, Richard Conte, Murray Matheson, Reginald Denny

'Just about as enthralling as plastic boats in the bath.'—*MFB*

Assault on Precinct 13**

US 1976 91m Metrocolor Panavision
CKK (Joseph Kaufman)

Gang members on a vendetta attack a police station.
Violent but basically efficient and old-fashioned programmer which shows that not all the expertise of the forties in this then-familiar field has been lost.

wd / m John Carpenter ph Douglas Knapp

Austin Stoker, Darwin Joston, Laurie Zimmer, Martin West

'One of the most effective exploitation movies of the last ten years . . . Carpenter scrupulously avoids any overt socio-political pretensions, playing instead for laughs and suspense in perfectly balanced proportions.'—*Time Out*

● Video: Video Program Distributors

Assignment in Brittany

US 1943 96m bw
MGM (J. Walter Ruben)

A Free French soldier stays in occupied France to fight the Nazis.
Routine propagandist actioner, totally unbelievable.

w Anthony Veiller, William Wright, Howard Emmett Rogers, *novel* Helen MacInnes d Jack Conway ph Charles Rosher m Lennie Hayton

Jean Pierre Aumont, Signe Hasso, Susan Peters, Reginald Owen, Richard Whorf, Margaret Wycherly, John Emery, Miles Mander, George Coulouris

'Any moment the world might blow up in their double faces!'

Assignment K

GB 1968 97m Techniscope
Columbia / Mazurka (Ben Arbeid, Maurice Foster)

The European head of a toy firm is also head of a special spy unit.
Dreary espionage thriller, instantly forgettable, and only watchable at odd moments while it's on.

w Val Guest, Bill Strutton, Maurice Foster, *novel* Hartley Howard d Val Guest ph Ken Hodges m Basil Kirchen

Stephen Boyd, Michael Redgrave, Camilla Sparv, Leo McKern, Jeremy Kemp

Assignment Paris

US 1952 85m bw
Columbia (Sam Marx, Jerry Bresler)

A reporter on the Paris staff of the *New York Herald-Tribune* goes to Yugoslavia, is arrested as a spy, and has to be exchanged.
Dim cold war melodrama with occasional entertaining moments.

w William Bowers, *novel* Trial by Terror by Paul Gallico d Robert Parrish ph Burnett Guffey, Ray Cory m George Duning

George Sanders, Dana Andrews, Sandra Giglio, Marta Toren, Audrey Totter, Herbert Berghof

Assignment to Kill

US 1967 99m Technicolor Panavision
Warner Seven Arts (William Conrad)

A New York insurance company hires a private eye to investigate a dubious European financier.
Routine international intrigue with muddled plot and unusual cast. A nice production wasted.

wd Sheldon Reynolds ph Harold Lipstein m William Lava

Patrick O'Neal, John Gielgud, Peter Van Eyck, Joan Hackett, Herbert Lom, Eric Portman, Oscar Homolka, Leon Greene

The Astonished Heart*

GB 1949 89m bw
Gainsborough / Sydney Box (Antony Darnborough)

A psychiatrist is permitted by his wife to fall in love with another woman but finds the situation intolerable and kills himself.
The star, looking like a Chinese mandarin, reached his nadir in this unwise screen adaptation, inelegantly directed, of one of his slightest short plays about boring and effete people. It sank without trace.

w Noel Coward, from his play d Terence Fisher, Antony Darnborough ph Jack Asher m Noel Coward

Noel Coward, Margaret Leighton, Celia Johnson, Graham Payn, Joyce Carey, Ralph Michael, Michael Hordern

The Astounding She-Monster

US 1957 59m bw

In a remote spot, some crooks and a scientist combat a female space visitor with remarkable powers. An early sub-Corman pot-boiler with only its camp qualities to recommend it.
Robert Clarke, Kenne Duncan, Marilyn Harvey. Written by Frank Hall; directed and produced by Ronnie Ashcroft; for Hollywood International. (GB title: *Mysterious Invader*.)

'You have nothing to lose but your mind!'

Asylum*

GB 1972 88m Eastmancolor
Amicus (Max J. Rosenberg, Milton Subotsky)

A doctor applies for a job at an asylum, hears weird stories from four patients, and finds himself in the middle of a weirder one.
Lively horror compilation with echoes of *Caligari* and *Dead of Night*. Gruesomeness sometimes overdone.

w Robert Bloch d Roy Ward Baker ph Denys Coop m Douglas Gamley

Patrick Magee, Robert Powell, Geoffrey Bayldon, Barbara Parkins, Sylvia Syms, Richard Todd, Peter Cushing, Barry Morse, Britt Ekland, Charlotte Rampling, James Villiers, Megs Jenkins, Herbert Lom

● Video: Guild

At Gunpoint

US 1955 80m Technicolor
Cinemascope

A western storekeeper accidentally kills a bank robber, whose brothers seek revenge; will the townsfolk come to his aid? Fair western on the lines of *High Noon*. Fred MacMurray, Dorothy Malone, Walter Brennan, John Qualen, Skip Homeier. Written by Dan Ullman; directed by Alfred Werker; for Allied Artists. (GB title: *Gunpoint*.)

'A new kind of musical!'
At Long Last Love
US 1975 114m Technicolor
TCF / Copa de Oro (Peter Bogdanovich)

The 1935 romance of a New York millionaire and a musical star.
An attempt to recapture the simple pleasures of an Astaire–Rogers musical; unfortunately true professionalism is lacking and the wrong kind of talent is used. The result is awful to contemplate.

wd Peter Bogdanovich ph Laszlo Kovacs m Cole Porter pd Gene Allen

Burt Reynolds, Cybill Shepherd, Eileen Brennan, Madeleine Kahn, Duilio del Prete, John Hillerman, Mildred Natwick

'He works hard at reducing all his sets and costumes to variations of black against silver or white on white, and uncovers in his most oft-repeated visual motif—the elegant mirrors before which his cast seem at all times to be posed—the perfect metaphor for this endlessly narcissistic, thoroughly calcified enterprise.'—*Richard Combs*

'It just lies there, and it dies there.'—*Variety*
'Studios bury more films than the public or the critics. Fox gave up on *At Long Last Love* instantly. A six million dollar film was written off while it was doing well because their lawyers told them they could make more money that way.'—*Peter Bogdanovich*

'It is justly included on most lists of the ten worst films ever made.'—*Les Keyser, Hollywood in the Seventies*

'Stillborn . . . a relentlessly vapid pastiche.'—*Pauline Kael*

At Sword's Point
US 1951 81m Technicolor
RKO (Jerrold T. Brandt)
GB title: *Sons of the Musketeers*

The sons of the three musketeers rally round their ageing queen to prevent her daughter's marriage to a villain.
Adequate swashbuckler with plenty of pace and a sound cast.

w Walter Ferris, Joseph Hoffman d Lewis Allen ph Ray Rennahan m Roy Webb

Cornel Wilde, Maureen O'Hara, Gladys Cooper, Robert Douglas, Dan O'Herlihy, Alan Hale Jnr, Blanche Yurka, Nancy Gates

At the Circus**
US 1939 87m bw
MGM (Mervyn Le Roy)
aka: *The Marx Brothers at the Circus*

A shyster lawyer and two incompetents save a circus from bankruptcy.
This film began the decline of the Marx Brothers; in it nothing is ill done but nothing is very fresh either apart from the rousing finale which shows just what professionalism meant in the old Hollywood. Highlights include Groucho singing about Lydia the tattooed lady, his seduction of Mrs Dukesbury, and the big society party.

w Irving Brecher d Edward Buzzell
ph Leonard M. Smith m / ly Harold Arlen, E. Y. Harburg m Franz Waxman

Groucho, Chico, Harpo, Margaret Dumont, Florence Rice, Kenny Baker, Eve Arden, Nat Pendleton, Fritz Feld

Songs include 'Lydia', 'Two Blind Loves', 'Step up and Take a Bow'.

GROUCHO: 'I don't know what I'm doing here when I could be at home in bed with a hot toddy. That's a drink.'

'Rousing physical comedy and staccato gag dialogue . . . geared for fine b.o. and general audience appeal.'—*Variety*

'We must regretfully accept the fact that, thanks to the Metro millions, the Marx Brothers are finally imprisoned in the Hollywood world.'—*Graham Greene*

At the Earth's Core
GB 1976 90m Technicolor
Amicus (John Dark)

Scientists testing a geological excavator are carried by it to the centre of the earth, and find a prehistoric land inhabited by feuding tribes.
Mainly feeble science fiction for kids, with occasional amusing moments.

w Milton Subotsky, novel Edgar Rice Burroughs d Kevin Connor ph Alan Hume m Mike Vickers sp Ian Wingrove pd Maurice Carter

Doug McClure, Peter Cushing, Caroline Munro, Cy Grant, Godfrey James, Keith Barron

'Papier mâché people-eaters, idiotic situations, and a frequent sense of confusion as to what is going on.'—*David Stewart, Christian Science Monitor*

● *Video: Thorn EMI*

At the Stroke of Nine
GB 1957 72m bw

A mad concert pianist plots to murder a young girl reporter. Absurd and rather endearing melodrama of the very old school. Stephen Murray, Patricia Dainton, Patrick Barr, Dermot Walsh. Written by Tony O'Grady, Harry Booth, Jon Pennington and Michael Deeley; directed by Lance Comfort; for Tower / Grand National.

At the Villa Rose
This murder mystery by A. E. W. Mason has had three British filmings: in 1920 with Teddy Arundell as Inspector Hanaud; in 1930 with Austin Trevor; in 1939 with Keneth Kent. All were adequate to their time. The story concerns a medium framed for the murder of a rich widow.

At War with the Army
US 1951 93m bw
Paramount / Fred K. Finklehoffe

A couple of song and dance men have trouble as army recruits.
American service farce, based on a play and confined largely to one set; rather untypical of Martin and Lewis, yet oddly enough the film which sealed their success.

w Fred K. Finkelhoffe, play James Allardice d Hal Walker ph Stuart Thompson m Joseph Lilley

Dean Martin, Jerry Lewis, Mike Kellin, Polly Bergen, Jimmie Dundee

L'Atalante*
France 1934 89m bw
J. L. Nounez-Gaumont

A barge captain takes his new wife down river. One of those classics which no longer provides the authentic thrill; its lack of incident and plot leads quickly to boredom.

w Jean Guinée, Jean Vigo, Albert Riera d Jean Vigo ph Boris Kaufman, Louis Berger m Maurice Jaubert

Jean Dasté, Dita Parlo, *Michel Simon*, Giles Margarites

Athena
US 1954 96m Eastmancolor
MGM (Joe Pasternak)

A young lawyer falls in love with the eldest of seven sisters brought up to high standards of moral conduct and physical fitness.
Promising but unfulfilling light musical which smothers a good idea in routine treatment.

w William Ludwig, Leonard Spiegelgass d Richard Thorpe ph Robert Planck songs Hugh Martin, Ralph Blane

Edmund Purdom, Jane Powell, Debbie Reynolds, Louis Calhern, Evelyn Varden, Vic Damone, Linda Christian, Ray Collins

Atlantic
GB 1929 90m bw

A passenger liner sinks in mid-Atlantic. Veiled retelling of the *Titanic* story, here in a clumsy Anglo-German version with extremely primitive sound and a plethora of pregnant silences. Franklin Dyall, Madeleine Carroll, Monty Banks, John Stuart, John Longden, Ellaline Terriss. Written by Victor Kendall, from the play *The Berg* by Ernest Raymond; directed by E. A. Dupont; for BIP.

'If you want to be mentally shipwrecked or lost at sea, see Atlantic. . . . It's something unnecessary to see; something no one wants to see; something horrible to even think of.

'. . . It will draw to and drive away from the box office. Draw to because it holds horror, thrills and suspense; drive away through children not being permitted to see it and the suggested gruesomeness too strong for many, not only women.

'. . . A faint try at comedy with a valet was like a ghoul in a cemetery . . . but Franklin Dyall excelled as an aged invalid with John Longden as a ship's officer, making a splendid appearance.'—*Variety*

Atlantic Adventure*
US 1935 68m bw

A reporter captures a murderer on an ocean liner. Lively double-biller, better than average in all departments. Nancy Carroll, Lloyd Nolan, Harry Langdon, Arthur Hohl, Robert

Middlemass, John Wray, E. E. Clive. Written by John T. Neville and Nat Dorfman; directed by Albert Rogell; for Columbia. 'Only lack of cast names keeps this in dual pix classification.'—*Variety*

Atlantic City*
US 1944 87m bw
Republic (Albert J. Cohen)

Before World War I, a young showman aims to make Atlantic City the entertainment centre of the world.

Simple-minded romantic musical, quite pacy and effectively staged for a Republic product.

w Doris Gilbert, Frank Gill Jnr, George Carlton Brown *d* Ray McCarey *ph* John Alton *m / ly* various

Constance Moore, Brad Taylor, Jerry Colonna, Charley Grapewin

● *Video: Home Video*

Atlantic City USA*
Canada / France 1981 105m colour
Cine-Neighbour / Selta Films (Denis Heroux)

Small-time crooks congregate round Atlantic City's new casinos.

Elegiac character drama which often achieves the mood it seeks but on the whole remains too understated for its own good.

w John Guare *d* Louis Malle *ph* Richard Ciupka *m* Michel Legrand *pd* Anne Pritchard

Burt Lancaster, Susan Sarandon, Kate Reid, Michel Piccoli, Hollis McLaren

AAN: best picture; John Guare; Burt Lancaster; Susan Sarandon
BFA: best direction; Burt Lancaster; Louis Malle

Atlantic Ferry*
GB 1941 108m bw
Warner (Max Milder)
US title: *Sons of the Sea*

In 1837 Liverpool, two brothers build the first steamship to cross the Atlantic.

Ponderous historical romance with points of interest.

w Gordon Wellesley, Edward Dryhurst, Emeric Pressburger *d* Walter Forde *ph* Basil Emmott *m* Jack Beaver

Michael Redgrave, Valerie Hobson, Griffith Jones, Margaretta Scott, Hartley Power, Bessie Love, Milton Rosmer

'Probably the finest collection of model shots in captivity.'—*C. A. Lejeune*

L'Atlantide*
France 1921 125m approx (16 fps) bw
silent
Thalman

Two explorers find the lost continent of Atlantis and fall in love with its queen.

Highly commercial adventure fantasy of its day; it cost two million francs and ran in Paris for a year. Some scenes still sustain, and the desert scenes are impressive.

wd Jacques Feyder, *novel* Pierre Benoit *ph* Georges Specht, Victor Morin

Jean Angelo, Stacia Napierkowska, Georges Melchior

† Other versions include *Queen of Atlantis* (Germany 1932, *d* G. W. Pabst, with Brigitte Helm); *Siren of Atlantis* (US 1948, *d* Gregg Tallas, with Maria Montez); *L'Atlantide* (France / Italy 1961, *d* Edgar G. Ulmer).

Atlantis, the Lost Continent
US 1961 91m Metrocolor
MGM / Galaxy / George Pal

A Greek fisherman is imprisoned when he returns a maiden he has rescued to her island home of Atlantis, but escapes just before volcanic eruption overtakes the decadent nation.

Penny-pinching fantasy spectacle with very little entertainment value.

w Daniel Mainwaring, *play* Sir Gerald Hargreaves *d* George Pal *ph* Harold E. Wellman *m* Russell Garcia

Anthony Hall, Joyce Taylor, John Dall, Edward Platt, Frank de Kova, Jay Novello

The Atomic City*
US 1952 85m bw
Paramount (Joseph Sistrom)

The young son of a leading atomic scientist is kidnapped but his father and the FBI rescue him.

Routine but well-paced thriller with a documentary background of research at Los Alamos.

w Sidney Boehm *d* Jerry Hopper *ph* Charles B. Lang Jnr *m* Leith Stevens

Gene Barry, Lydia Clarke, Lee Aaker, Nancy Gates, Milburn Stone

AAN: Sidney Boehm

The Atomic Kid
US 1954 86m bw
Republic

After an atomic blast, a prospector accidentally left in the area proves immune to uranium, and after various adventures rounds up some communist spies.

Inane romp which raises a few laughs.

w Benedict Freeman, John Fenton Murray, *story* Blake Edwards *d* Leslie H. Martinson *ph* John L. Russell Jnr *m* Van Alexander

Mickey Rooney, Robert Strauss, Elaine Davis, Bill Goodwin, Whit Bissell

The Atonement of Gosta Berling**
Sweden 1924 200m approx (16 fps)
bw silent
Svensk Filmindustri
original title: *Gosta Berlings Saga*

A pastor is defrocked for drinking, becomes a tutor, and has various love affairs.

Lumpy but often engrossing picturization of a famous novel, veering mostly into melodrama but finding its way to a happy ending.

w Mauritz Stiller, Ragnar Hylten-Cavallius, *novel* Selma Lagerlof *d* Mauritz Stiller *ph* Julius Jaenzon

Lars Hanson, Gerda Lundeqvist, Ellen Cederstrom, Mona Martensson, Jenny Hasselqvist, Otto Elg-Lundberg, Greta Garbo.

'Stiller was a master at unifying visual beauty and emotional effect; the complicated narrative is blurry, but there are sequences as lovely and expressive as any on film.'—*New Yorker, 1980*

† It was her small role in this film which led directly to Greta Garbo's American stardom.

Attack**
US 1956 104m bw
UA / Associates and Aldrich

In 1944 Belgium, an American infantry command is led by a coward.

High-pitched, slick, violent and very effective war melodrama, even though by the end we seem to be in the company of raving lunatics rather than soldiers.

w James Poe, *play* Fragile Fox by Norman Brooks *d* Robert Aldrich *ph* Joseph Biroc *m* Frank de Vol

Jack Palance, Eddie Albert, Lee Marvin, Buddy Ebsen, Robert Strauss, Richard Jaeckel, William Smithers, Peter Van Eyck

'The film does not so much tackle a subject as hammer it down.'—*Penelope Houston*

Attack of the Crab Monsters
US 1957 65m bw

25-foot mutant crabs cause landslides on a Pacific island. Bottom-of-the-barrel monster mayhem from this tongue-in-cheek producer; now a cult. Richard Garland, Pamela Duncan, Russell Johnson. Written by Charles B. Griffith; produced and directed by Roger Corman; for Allied Artists.

The Attack of the Fifty Foot Woman
US 1958 72m bw

A neurotic woman is lured inside a space ship, becomes radio-active, and grows to alarming proportions. Hilarious tailpiece to the fifties monster cycle, a dismal movie worth remembering only for its title. Allison Hayes, William Hudson, Roy Gordon. Written by Mark Hanna; directed by Nathan Hertz; for Allied Artists.

Attack of the Puppet People
US 1957 79m bw

A doll-maker has also learned to shrink people. Inferior entry in the *Dr Cyclops* mould; mildly amusing moments are sandwiched between chunks of tedium. John Hoyt, John Agar, June Kenny. Written by George Worthing Yates; directed and produced by Bert I. Gordon; for Alta Vista. (GB title: *Six Inches Tall*.)

Attack on the Iron Coast
GB 1967 90m De Luxe
US / Mirisch (John Champion)

In World War II, a Canadian commando unit

destroys a German installation on the French coast.
Stagey low-budgeter with modest action sequences.

w Herman Hoffman d Paul Wendkos
ph Paul Beeson m Gerard Schurmann

Lloyd Bridges, Andrew Keir, Mark Eden, Sue Lloyd

Attila the Hun

Italy / France 1954 79m Technicolor
Lux Ponti de Laurentiis / LCCF
 (Georgio Andriani)
original title: *Attilo Flagello di Dio*

The barbarian chief attacks the forces of the Emperor Valentinian and marches on Rome. Predictably violent adventures after de Mille; a bit slow to start.

w Ennio de Concini, Primo Zeglio d Pietro Francisci ph Aldo Tonti m Enzo Masetti

Anthony Quinn, Sophia Loren, Henri Vidal, Irene Papas, Ettore Manni, Claude Laydu

● Video: Videomedia

Attorney for the Defense

US 1932 70m bw

A prosecutor's wiles result in an innocent man being executed, so he turns crusader and takes on defence cases. Punchy if unconvincing courtroom melodrama which would certainly satisfy at the time. Edmund Lowe, Evelyn Brent, Constance Cummings, Donald Dillaway, Dorothy Peterson, Dwight Frye, Nat Pendleton, Clarence Muse. Written by Jo Swerling and J. K. McGuinness; directed by Irving Cummings; for Columbia.

Au dela des Grilles

Italy / France 1949 90m bw
Italia Produzione / Francinex (Alfredo Guarini)
aka: *Beyond the Gates*; Italian title: *La mura de Malapaga*

A murderer on the run in Genoa falls in love with a waitress and loses his chance of escape. *Quai des Brumes* reworked against an Italian neo-realist setting; dramatic values less interesting now than historical ones.

w Jean Aurenche, Pierre Bost, Cesare Zavattini, Suso Cecchi d'Amico d René Clément ph Louis Page m Roman Vlad

Jean Gabin, *Isa Miranda*, Vera Talchi, Andrea Checci

Au Royaume des Cieux

France 1949 108m bw
Regina (Julien Duvivier)
aka: *Woman Hunt*

An 18-year-old girl suffers at a reform school. Shoddy melodrama, more sensational than Hollywood ever dared to be.

wd Julien Duvivier ph Victor Armenise

Suzanne Cloutier, Serge Reggiani, Monique Mélinand, Suzy Prim, Jean Davy, Juliette Greco

'A depressing exhibit from a director who once had a serious reputation.'—*Gavin Lambert*

Audrey Rose*

US 1977 113m De Luxe Panavision
United Artists / Robert Wise

A man believes that a 12-year-old girl is the reincarnation of his dead daughter.
Rather painful and not very persuasive spiritualist thriller in the wake of *The Exorcist*, only moments of dramaturgy survive.

w Frank de Felitta, from his novel d Robert Wise ph Victor J. Kemper m Michael Small pd Harry Horner

Anthony Hopkins, Marsha Mason, John Beck, Susan Swift, Norman Lloyd, John Hillerman, Robert Walden

Aunt Clara

GB 1954 84m bw
London Films (Colin Lesslie, Anthony Kimmins)

A pious old person inherits from a reprobate uncle five greyhounds, a pub and a brothel. Extremely mild star vehicle with a gallery of comedy character cameos.

w Kenneth Horne, *novel* Noel Streatfeild d Anthony Kimmins ph C. Pennington-Richards m Benjamin Frankel

Margaret Rutherford, Ronald Shiner, A. E. Matthews, Fay Compton, Nigel Stock, Jill Bennett, Reginald Beckwith, Raymond Huntley

Aunt Sally

GB 1933 84m bw
US title: *Along Came Sally*

A fake French star saves a nightclub owner from gangsters. Predictable star vehicle. Cicely Courtneidge, Sam Hardy, Billy Milton, Phyllis Clare, Hartley Power. Written by Austin Melford, Guy Bolton and A. R. Rawlinson; directed by Tim Whelan; for Gaumont.

Auntie Mame*

US 1958 144m Technirama
Warner (Morton da Costa)

An orphan boy is adopted by his volatile extravagant aunt, whose giddy escapades fill his memory of the twenties and thirties.
A rather unsatisfactory star revue from a book and play later turned into a musical, *Mame*. A few splendid moments, otherwise rather dull and irritating.

w Betty Comden, Adolph Green, *novel* Patrick Dennis, *play* Jerome Lawrence, Robert E. Lee d Morton da Costa ph Harry Stradling m Bronislau Kaper ad Malcolm Bert

Rosalind Russell, Forrest Tucker, *Coral Browne*, Fred Clark, Roger Smith, Patric Knowles, Peggy Cass, Lee Patrick, Joanna Barnes

AAN: best picture; Harry Stradling; Rosalind Russell; Peggy Cass

Une Aussi Longue Absence*

France / Italy 1961 96m bw
Procinex / Lyre / Galatea (Jacques Nahum)
aka: *The Long Absence*

A widow who owns a Paris café meets an amnesiac tramp who may be her long-lost husband.
Romantic character study which just about comes off thanks to good acting.

w Marguerite Duras, Gérald Jarlot d Henri Colpi ph Marcel Weiss m Georges Delerue

Alida Valli, Georges Wilson, Jacques Harden

Austerlitz

France / Italy / Liechtenstein / Yugoslavia
 1959 166m Eastmancolor
 Dyaliscope
CFPI / SCLF / Galatea / Michael Arthur / Dubrava (Alexander and Michael Salkind)
aka: *The Battle of Austerlitz*

Napoleon defeats the Austro-Russian army. Elaborate pageant with a hopelessly cluttered narrative line arranged to take in a roster of guest stars who merely distract from the central theme.

wd Abel Gance ph Henri Alekan, Robert Juillard m Jean Ledrut

Pierre Mondy, Jean Mercure, Jack Palance, Orson Welles, Michel Simon, Jean-Louis Trintignant, Martine Carol, Leslie Caron, Claudia Cardinale, Rossano Brazzi, Ettore Manni, Jean Marais, Vittorio de Sica

'Strictly for connoisseurs of Gance's brand of hyperbolic history.'—*Peter John Dyer, MFB*

Author, Author!*

US 1982 109m TVC
TCF (Irwin Winkler)

A Broadway playwright has worries about his wife's fidelity.
Like a sixties update of *All About Eve*, this thin but sometimes witty sex-behind-the-footlights comedy has nothing to offer the general audience of the eighties, and one can only speculate as to why it was made. The acting does help, but it's a long haul.

w Israel Horovitz d Arthur Hiller ph Victor J. Kemper m Dave Grusin pd Gene Rudolf ed William Reynolds

Al Pacino, Dyan Cannon, Tuesday Weld, Bob Dishy, Bob Elliott

'In trying to dig a little deeper than the average Neil Simon comedy, it only prepares its own grave.'—*Observer*

Automania 2000**

GB 1963 10m Eastmancolor

New cars have the ability to reproduce themselves: city dwellers of the future consequently live in stationary vehicles piled on top of each other. Amusing cartoon fantasy, neatly executed. Written by Joy Batchelor; directed by John Halas; for Halas and Batchelor.

Autumn Crocus
GB 1934   86m   bw

A British schoolmistress on holiday falls for
her Tyrolean innkeeper. Difficult now to
conceive the popularity in its day of this
novelettish romance, which seems frozen in
amber. Ivor Novello, Fay Compton, Jack
Hawkins, Diana Beaumont, Muriel Aked,
George Zucco. Written and directed by Basil
Dean, from the play by C. L. Anthony; for
ATP.

Autumn Leaves*
US 1956   108m   bw
Columbia / William Goetz

A middle-aged spinster marries a young man
who turns out to be a pathological liar and
tries to murder her.
Skilfully tailored star vehicle for female
audiences.
w Jack Jevne, Lewis Meltzer, Robert Blees
d Robert Aldrich ph Charles Lang m Hans
Salter
Joan Crawford, Cliff Robertson, Lorne
Greene, Vera Miles, Ruth Donnelly,
Shepperd Strudwick

Autumn Sonata*
Sweden / West Germany / GB 1978   97m
colour
Personafilm / ITC (Ingmar Bergman)

When her lover dies, a concert pianist visits
the daughter she has not seen for many years.
Typically Bergmanesque, understated
conversation piece with no obvious happy
ending for anybody.
wd Ingmar Bergman ph Sven Nykvist
Ingrid Bergman, Liv Ullmann, Halvar Bjork
'Professional gloom.'—*Time*
'It fills these middle-class rooms with the
deep music of conflict and reconciliation that
must strike home to any audiences in any
culture or society.'—*Jack Kroll, Newsweek*
AAN: script; Ingrid Bergman
● *Video: Precision Video*

Avalanche
US 1978   91m   Metrocolor
New World (Roger Corman)

Snow threatens holidaymakers at a ski lodge.
A disaster movie which, while quite competent
in most ways, is no better than TV movies of
this kind, especially as it resorts for its
climaxes to scratched old stock film.
w Claude Pola, Corey Allen d Corey Allen
ph Pierre-William Glenn m William Kraft
Rock Hudson, Mia Farrow, Robert Forster,
Jeanette Nolan, Rick Moses, Steve Franken,
Barry Primus

Avalanche Express
Eire 1979   88m   De Luxe   Panavision
TCF / Lorimar (Mark Robson)

Spies of all nations converge on a train from
Milan to Rotterdam.
Fitfully amusing hodgepodge which had to be
finished off in a hurry following the death of
its star and director in mid-production.

w Abraham Polonsky, *novel* Colin Forbes
d Mark Robson ph Jack Cardiff m Allyn
Ferguson
Robert Shaw, Lee Marvin, Linda Evans,
Maximilian Schell, Mike Connors, Joe
Namath, Horst Buchholz
'The most impressive work of montage to
emerge from a big-budget adventure movie.'—
Richard Combs, MFB
'Pell-mell direction and editing perform a
precarious, oddly suspenseful balancing act.'—
Sight and Sound
● *Video: CBS / Fox*

Avanti!**
US 1972   144m   De Luxe
UA / Mirisch / Phalanx / Jalem (Billy Wilder)

A young American goes to Ischia to collect the
body of his father who has died on holiday. He
finds that the fatal accident had also killed his
father's mistress, and amid overwhelming
bureaucratic problems proceeds to fall in love
with her daughter.
Absurdly overlong black comedy, with
compensations in the shape of a generally
witty script and some fine breakneck
sequences of culminating confusion.
w *Billy Wilder, I. A. L. Diamond, play*
Samuel Taylor d Billy Wilder ph Luigi
Kuveiller m Carlo Rustichelli
Jack Lemmon, Juliet Mills, Clive Revill,
Edward Andrews, Gianfranco Barra
● *Video: Warner*

The Avenging Conscience*
US 1914   58m (24 fps)   bw   silent

An elaboration of Poe's *The Tell Tale Heart* in
which Griffith first shows his ability to control
a feature-length movie, with many cinematic
devices. Henry B. Walthall, Blanche Sweet,
Spottiswoode Aiken, Mae Marsh. Written and
directed by D. W. Griffith; photographed by
Billy Bitzer; for Mutual.

The Aviator
US 1930   73m   bw

A timid clerk lends his name to a technical
book on aviation, and finds himself having to
back up the pretence by flying. Predictable
star comedy. Edward Everett Horton, Patsy
Ruth Miller, Johnny Arthur, Lee Moran.
From the play by James Montgomery; directed
by Roy del Ruth; for Warners. 'Peg this as a
good one.'—*Variety*

The Aviator's Wife*
France 1980   106m   Eastmancolor (blown
up from 16mm)
Les Films du Losange (Margaret Menegoz)
original title: *La Femme de L'Aviateur*

Anne and François are having an affair, but
each has other entanglements.
Meticulously arranged conversations in this
director's best style, but this time not seeming
to amount to very much.
wd Eric Rohmer ph Bernard Lutic m Jean-
Louis Valero

Philippe Marlaud, Marie Rivière, Anne-Laure
Maeury, Matthieu Carrière
'Does the aviator Christian's wife exist? It
really does not matter: she is a formal device
in a play of formalist devices.'—*Jill Forbes,
MFB*

L'Avventura**
Italy / France 1960   145m   bw
Cino del Duca / PCE / Lyre (Amato
Pennasilico)

Young people on a yachting holiday go ashore
on a volcanic island. One of them disappears;
this affects the life of the others, but she is
never found.
Aimless, overlong parable with lots of vague
significance; rather less entertaining than the
later *Picnic at Hanging Rock* (qv), it made its
director a hero of the highbrows.
w Michelangelo Antonioni, Elio Bartolini,
Tonino Guerra d *Michelangelo Antonioni*
ph Aldo Scavarda m Giovanni Fusco
Monica Vitti, Lea Massari, Gabriele Ferzetti,
Dominique Blanchar, James Addams, Lelio
Luttazi
'A film of complete maturity, sincerity and
creative intuition.'—*Peter John Dyer, MFB*

The Awakening
GB 1980   105m   Technicolor
EMI / Orion (Robert Solo)

An obsessed archaeologist believes that the
spirit of a long-dead Egyptian queen has
entered into the soul of his daughter.
Unpersuasive and humourless mumbo jumbo
from the same intractably complex novel
which provided the basis for *Blood from the
Mummy's Tomb*.
w Allan Scott, Chris Bryant, Clive Exton,
novel Jewel of the Seven Stars by Bram
Stoker d Mike Newell ph Jack Cardiff
m Claude Bolling pd Michael Stringer
Charlton Heston, Susannah York, Jill
Townsend, Stephanie Zimbalist, Patrick
Drury, Bruce Myers
'An almost total waste of the talents
involved.'—*Sunday Times*
'It is difficult to imagine a film more likely to
put you to sleep.'—*Guardian*
● *Video: Thorn EMI*

Away All Boats!
US 1956   114m   Technicolor
Vistavision
U-I (Howard Christie)

Adventures of a small transport boat during
the Pacific War.
Competent drum-beating war heroics with
expensive action sequences.
w Ted Sherdeman d Joseph Pevney
ph William Daniels, Clifford Stine m Frank
Skinner
Jeff Chandler, George Nader, Julie Adams,
Lex Barker, Keith Andes, Richard Boone,
Frank Faylen

The Awful Truth***
US 1937   90m   bw
Columbia (Leo McCarey)

A divorcing couple endure various adventures which lead to reconciliation.

Classic crazy comedy of the thirties, marked by a mixture of sophistication and farce and an irreverent approach to plot.

wd Leo McCarey, play Arthur Richman
ph Joseph Walker   *md* Morris Stoloff

Irene Dunne, Cary Grant, Ralph Bellamy, Alexander D'Arcy, Cecil Cunningham, Molly Lamont, Esther Dale, Joyce Compton

'Fast, smart comedy that will please everywhere and do strong general biz.'— *Variety*

'The funniest picture of the season.'—*Otis Ferguson*

'Among the ingredients the raising powder is the important thing and out of the oven comes a frothy bit of stuff that leaves no taste in the mouth and is easy on the stomach.'— *Marion Fraser, World Film News*

† Remade 1953 as *Let's Do It Again* (qv).

AA: Leo McCarey (as director)
AAN: best picture; script; Irene Dunne; Ralph Bellamy

B.F.'s Daughter*
US 1948 106m bw
MGM (Edwin A. Knopf)
GB title: *Polly Fulton*

The wife of a penniless lecturer secures her
husband's rise to fame without his knowing
that she is the daughter of a millionaire.
Solid upper class romantic drama with a touch
of Peg's Paper.

w Luther Davis, *novel* John P. Marquand
d Robert Z. Leonard *ph* Joseph Ruttenberg
m Bronislau Kaper

Barbara Stanwyck, Van Heflin, Charles
Coburn, Richard Hart, Keenan Wynn,
Margaret Lindsay, Spring Byington, Marshall
Thompson

B.S. I Love You
US 1970 98m De Luxe

A director of TV commercials is beset by
passionate women. Tiresomely trendy sex
comedy with a visual style that never lets up.
Peter Kastner, Joanna Cameron, Louise Sorel,
Gary Burghoff, Joanna Barnes, Richard B.
Shull. Written and directed by Steven Hillard
Stern; for Motion Pictures International /
TCF. (NB: The initials in the title are short for
bullshit.)

Babbitt*
US 1934 74m bw
Warner (Sam Bischoff)

Problems of a middle-aged man in a small
American town.
A minor attempt to film a major novel: quite
tolerable but lacking density.

w Mary McCall Jnr, *novel* Sinclair Lewis
d William Keighley *ph* Arthur Todd

Guy Kibbee, *Aline MacMahon*, Claire Dodd,
Maxine Doyle, Minor Watson, Minna
Gombell, Alan Hale, Berton Churchill,
Russell Hicks, Nan Grey
  'Smooth, pleasant but trite.'—*Variety*
† Previously filmed in 1924 with Willard Louis.

The Babe Ruth Story
US 1948 107m bw
Allied Artists

The biography of a baseball player who was
thought of as something of a saint.
Dim, sentimental and faintly mystical biopic,
throughout which the star presents his familiar
image.

w Bob Considine, George Callahan *d* Roy del
Ruth *ph* Philip Tunnura, James Van Trees
m Edward Ward

William Bendix, Claire Trevor, Charles
Bickford

Babes in Arms**
US 1939 96m bw
MGM (Arthur Freed)

The teenage sons and daughters of retired
vaudevillians put on a big show.
Simple-minded backstage musical which
marked the first enormously successful
teaming of its two young stars.

w Jack McGowan, Kay Van Riper, from the
Broadway show by Rodgers and Hart
d / *ch* Busby Berkeley *ph* Ray June
songs Rodgers and Hart and others *m* Roger
Edens, George Stoll

Judy Garland, Mickey Rooney, Charles
Winninger, Douglas Macphail, Leni Lynn,
June Preisser

Songs include 'Where or When'; 'The Lady Is
a Tramp'; 'Babes in Arms'; 'I Cried for You';
'God's Country'; 'Good Morning'; 'You Are
my Lucky Star'
  'A topflight filmusical entertainment. It will
click mightily in the key deluxers, and roll up
hefty profits for exhibs in the subsequent runs
and smaller situations.'—*Variety*

AAN: Roger Edens, George Stoll; Mickey
Rooney

Babes in Baghdad
US 1952 77m Exotic Color

Harem ladies go on strike. Embarrassing
attempt at satire by stars who are over the hill
and not helped by abysmal technique. Paulette
Goddard, Gypsy Rose Lee, Richard Ney,
John Boles, Sebastian Cabot. Written by Felix
E. Feist and Joe Anson; directed by Edgar G.
Ulmer; for the Danzigers.

Babes in Toyland**
US 1934 77m bw
Hal Roach
aka: *Wooden Soldiers; March of the
    Wooden Soldiers; Laurel and Hardy in
    Toyland*

Santa Claus's incompetent assistants
accidentally make some giant wooden soldiers,
which come in useful when a villain tries to
take over Toyland.

Comedy operetta in which the stars have
pleasant but not outstanding material; the
style and decor are however sufficient to
preserve the film as an eccentric minor classic.

w Nick Grinde, Frank Butler, *original book* /
ly Glen MacDonough *d* Gus Meins, Charles

Rogers *ph* Art Lloyd, Francis Corby
m Victor Herbert

Stan Laurel, Oliver Hardy, Charlotte Henry,
Henry Brandon, Felix Knight, Florence
Roberts, Johnny Downs, Marie Wilson
  'It is amusing enough to entertain older
persons who remember when they were
young.'—*Variety*

Babes in Toyland
US 1961 105m Technicolor
Walt Disney

A misfiring remake, all charm and no talent
apart from some excellent special effects at the
climax.

w Ward Kimball, Joe Rinaldi, Lowell S.
Hawley *d* Jack Donohue *ph* Edward
Colman *md* George Bruns *sp* Eustace
Lycett, Robert A. Mattey, Bill Justice, Xavier
Atencio, Yale Gracey

Ray Bolger (miscast as the villain), Annette
Funicello, Tommy Kirk, Gene Sheldon
(imitating Stan Laurel), Henry Calvin
(imitating Oliver Hardy), Ed Wynn, Kevin
Corcoran

AAN: George Bruns

Babes on Broadway**
US 1941 118m bw
MGM (Arthur Freed)

A sequel to *Babes in Arms*, in which the kids
get to Broadway and share some disillusion.
Inflated and less effective than the original,
but with good numbers.

w Fred Finkelhoffe, Elaine Ryan
d / *ch* Busby Berkeley *ph* Lester White
songs Burton Lane and Ralph Freed

Judy Garland, Mickey Rooney, Virginia
Weidler, Ray Macdonald, Richard Quine, Fay
Bainter
† The Virginia Weidler role was originally
intended for Shirley Temple, but TCF
wouldn't loan her.

AAN: song 'How About You' (*m* Burton
Lane, *ly* Ralph Freed)

Babette Goes to War

France 1959 103m Eastmancolor
Cinemascope
Iéna (Raoul Lévy)
original title: *Babette S'en Va-t-en Guerre*

In 1940 a French refugee girl is sent by British intelligence from London to Paris as bait in a plot to kidnap a German general and delay the Nazi invasion of England.
Witless war farce which goes on for ever.

w Raoul Lévy, Gérard Oury d Christian-Jaque ph Armand Thirard m Gilbert Bécaud

Brigitte Bardot, Jacques Charrier, Hannes Messemer, Yves Vincent, Ronald Howard, Francis Blanche

'A kind of *Private's Progress* without comedians.'—*MFB*

Baboona

US 1935 78m bw

Africa photographed from the air as well as the jungle; one of the better documentary features of the mid-thirties. Mr and Mrs Martin Johnson. Photographed and directed by Martin Johnson; for Fox.

The Baby and the Battleship

GB 1956 96m Eastmancolor
British Lion / Jay Lewis

Two sailors hide an Italian baby on their battleship.
Simple-minded lower decks farce, with lots of confusion and cooing over the baby, but not much to laugh at.

w Jay Lewis, Gilbert Hackforth-Jones, Bryan Forbes d Jay Lewis ph Harry Waxman

John Mills, Richard Attenborough, André Morell, Bryan Forbes, Michael Howard, Lisa Gastoni, Ernest Clark, Lionel Jeffries, Thorley Walters

Baby Blue Marine*

US 1976 90m Metrocolor
Columbia / Spelling—Goldberg (Robert LaVigne)

In 1943, a failed marine returns home and pretends to be a war hero.
Careful small-town drama with good period feel but not much dramatic punch: *Hail the Conquering Hero* did it better.

w Stanford Whitmore d John Hancock ph Laszlo Kovacs m Fred Karlin

Jan-Michael Vincent, Glynnis O'Connor, Katherine Helmond, Dana Elcar, Bert Remsen, Richard Gere

'A rickety structure of strange events.'— *New York Post*

'19 years old and married . . . but not really!'

Baby Doll**

US 1956 116m bw
Warner / Elia Kazan

In the deep South, the child wife of a broken-down cotton miller is seduced by her husband's revenge-seeking rival.
An incisive, cleverly-worked-out study of moral and physical decay; whether it was worth doing is another question, for it's a film difficult to remember with affection.

wd Elia Kazan, play Tennessee Williams ph Boris Kaufman m Kenyon Hopkins ad Richard Sylbert

Karl Malden, Eli Wallach, Carroll Baker, Mildred Dunnock, Lonny Chapman

'Just possibly the dirtiest American-made motion picture that has ever been legally exhibited, with Priapean detail that might well have embarrassed Boccaccio.'—*Time*

'He views southern pretensions with sardonic humor, and builds an essentially minor story into a magnificently humorous study of the grotesque and the decadent.'— *Hollis Alpert*

'A droll and engrossing carnal comedy.'— *Pauline Kael, 1968*

'A film in which everything works: narration, casting, tempo, rhythm, dramatic tension.'—*Basil Wright, 1972*

† Another publicity tag read: 'Condemned by Cardinal Spellman!'

AAN: script; Boris Kaufman; Carroll Baker; Mildred Dunnock

'She climbed the ladder of success—wrong by wrong!'

Baby Face**

US 1933 70m bw
Warner (Ray Griffith)

Amorous adventures of an ambitious working girl.
Sharp melodrama very typical of its time, with fast pace and good performances.

w Gene Markey, Kathryn Scola, Mark Canfield (Darryl F. Zanuck) d Alfred E. Green ph James Van Trees

Barbara Stanwyck, George Brent, Donald Cook, Margaret Lindsay, Arthur Hohl, John Wayne, Henry Kolker, Douglass Dumbrille

'Blue and nothing else. It possesses no merit for general or popular appeal, is liable to offend the family trade and can't count on any juve attendance.

'. . . This is reputed to be a remake on the first print, which was considered too hot. Anything hotter than this for public showing would call for an asbestos audience blanket.'— *Variety*

Baby Face Harrington

US 1935 63m bw

A timid man is mistakenly identified as a public enemy, and chased by both cops and rival gangsters. Thin but appealing comedy. Charles Butterworth, Una Merkel, Nat Pendleton, Eugene Pallette, Donald Meek. Written by Nunnally Johnson and Edwin Knopf; directed by Raoul Walsh; for MGM.

'Weak satire, grievously overacted.'— *Variety*

'Don't see it unless your nerves are bullet proof!'

Baby Face Nelson*

US 1957 85m bw
UA / Fryman—ZS (Al Zimbalist)
Fragmentary account of the life of a thirties public enemy, with the star over the top and the technicians doing what they can on an obviously low budget.

w Irving Shulman, Daniel Mainwaring d Don Siegel ph Hal Mohr m Van Alexander

Mickey Rooney, Cedric Hardwicke, Carolyn Jones, Chris Dark, Ted de Corsia, Leo Gordon, John Hoyt, Anthony Caruso, Jack Elam

Baby It's You*

US 1982 104m colour
Paramount / Double Play (Griffin Dunne, Andy Robinson)

In the sixties, a well-heeled high school girl is wooed and won by a greasy street sheik with ambitions.
Curious sweet-and-sour romance with a determination to be modern; agreeable in parts but basically empty, and rather undermined by a torrent of rock music on the sound track.

w,d John Sayles, from a story by Amy Robinson ph Michael Ballhaus md Joel Dorn pd Jeffrey Townsend

Rosanna Arquette, Vincent Spano, Joanna Merlin, Jack Davidson, Nick Ferrari, Leora Dana

Baby Love

GB 1968 93m Eastmancolor
(Avco) Avton / Michael Klinger (Guido Coen)

An orphaned nymphet causes trouble among the men in her foster home.
Ludicrous sexploiter which embarrasses a good cast and descends into bathos.

w Alastair Reid, Guido Coen, Michael Klinger, novel Tina Chad Christian d Alastair Reid ph Desmond Dickinson m Max Harris

Linda Hayden, Ann Lynn, Keith Barron, Derek Lamden, Diana Dors, Patience Collier, Dick Emery

● Video: Embassy

The Baby Maker

US 1970 109m Technicolor

A freewheeling girl agrees to have a baby for a childless couple. Stretched-out fable for our time which refrains from pointing a moral and is generally tastefully done but nevertheless outstays its welcome. Barbara Hershey, Collin Wilcox-Horne, Sam Groom, Scott Glenn, Jeannie Berlin. Written and directed by James Bridges; for National General.

Baby Take a Bow*

US 1934 76m bw

An ex-convict is accused of theft, but his small daughter unmasks the real culprit. *Shirley Temple*'s first star vehicle was a solid enough commercial property to take her right to the top. James Dunn, Claire Trevor, Alan Dinehart. Written by Philip Klein and E. E. Paramore Jnr; directed by Harry Lachman; for Fox. 'A pretty obvious and silly melodrama, but it has Shirley Temple, so it can go down in the books as a neat and sure b.o. hit.'— *Variety*

Baby, the Rain Must Fall
US 1964 100m bw
Columbia / Pakula–Mulligan (Alan Pakula)

A parolee rejoins his wife and daughter in a
Southern town, but his outbursts of violence
separate them again.
Hard work by all concerned scarcely produces
absorbing interest in this filmed play of the
Tennessee Williams school.

w Horton Foote, from his play The Travelling
Lady d Robert Mulligan ph Ernest Laszlo
m Elmer Bernstein

Steve McQueen, Lee Remick, Don Murray,
Paul Fix, Josephine Hutchinson, Ruth White,
Charles Watts

The Bachelor and the Bobbysoxer***
US 1947 95m bw
RKO (Dore Schary)
GB title: Bachelor Knight

A lady judge allows her impressionable young
sister to get over her crush on an errant
playboy by forcing them together.
Simple but unexpectedly delightful vehicle for
top comedy talents, entirely pleasant and with
several memorable moments.

w Sidney Sheldon d Irving Reis ph Robert
de Grasse, Nicholas Musuraca m Leigh
Harline

Cary Grant, Myrna Loy, Shirley Temple, Ray
Collins, Rudy Vallee, Harry Davenport,
Johnny Sands, Don Beddoe
'Sure-fire stuff guaranteed to do no
conceivable harm . . . the audience laughed so
loud I missed some of the lines.'—Shirley
O'Hara, New Republic
AA: Sidney Sheldon

Bachelor Apartment
US 1931 77m bw
RKO (William Le Baron)

A virtuous working girl in New York falls for a
rich woman-chasing bachelor.
Mildly agreeable early talking romantic
comedy.

w J. Walter Ruben, John Howard Lawson
d Lowell Sherman ph Leo Tover

Irene Dunne, Lowell Sherman, Mae Murray,
Norman Kerry, Claudia Dell, Ivan Lebedeff
'It oversteps the reasonable limits of
sophisticated art . . . thus the film is doubtful
for small towns.'—Variety

Bachelor Daddy*
US 1941 61m bw

Three bachelors find themselves in charge of a
baby. Best of the comedies starring Baby
Sandy. Edward Everett Horton, Franklin
Pangborn, Raymond Walburn, Donald
Woods, Evelyn Ankers. Written by Robert
Lees and Fred Rinaldo; directed by Harold
Young; for Universal.

Bachelor Father
US 1931 90m bw
MGM

A much-married elderly man visits his grown
children.
Unremarkable star comedy of its day.

w Laurence E. Johnson, play Edward Childs
Carpenter d Robert Z. Leonard ph Oliver T.
Marsh

Marion Davies, C. Aubrey Smith, Ray
Milland, Ralph Forbes, Halliwell Hobbes,
Guinn Williams, David Torrence
'Where they have used the old hoke they
have masked it with commendable skill.'—
Variety

Bachelor Flat
US 1961 91m De Luxe Cinemascope
TCF / Jack Cummings

An English professor at an American
university is unrelentingly pursued by girls.
Flat one-joke comedy which simply hasn't the
style to sustain itself.

w Frank Tashlin, Budd Grossman, from
Grossman's play d Frank Tashlin ph Daniel
L. Fapp m Johnny Williams

Terry-Thomas, Richard Beymer, Tuesday
Weld, Celeste Holm, Francesca Bellini,
Howard McNear

Bachelor in Paradise
US 1961 109m Metrocolor
       Cinemascope
MGM / Ted Richmond

A famous writer of advice to the lovelorn
settles incognito in a well-heeled Californian
community to observe its social habits.
Mildly amusing satire is too frequently
interrupted by unsuitable romantic interludes
in this rather ill-considered star comedy.

w Valentine Davies, Hal Kanter d Jack
Arnold ph Joseph Ruttenberg m Henry
Mancini

Bob Hope, Lana Turner, Janis Paige, Don
Porter, Paula Prentiss, Jim Hutton, Virginia
Grey, Reta Shaw, John McGiver, Agnes
Moorehead

AAN: title song (m Henry Mancini, ly Mack
David)

'Just ten tiny fingers and ten tiny toes . . .
    Trouble? Scandal? Gosh, nobody
    knows!'

Bachelor Mother***
US 1939 82m bw
RKO (B. G. De Sylva)

A shopgirl finds an abandoned baby and is
thought to be its mother; the department store
owner's son is then thought to be the father.
Blithely-scripted comedy which stands the test
of time and provided several excellent roles.

w Norman Krasna d Garson Kanin
ph Robert de Grasse m Roy Webb

Ginger Rogers, David Niven, Charles Coburn,
Frank Albertson, E. E. Clive, Ernest Truex
'Carries some rather spicy lines aimed at the
adult trade, but broad enough in implication
to catch the fancy of general audiences . . . a
surprise laugh hit that will do biz generally and
overcome hot weather box office lethargy.'—
Variety

'An excellent comedy, beautifully done.'—
Richard Mallett, Punch
'This is the way farce should be handled,
with just enough conviction to season its
extravagances.'—New York Times
† Remade as Bundle of Joy (qv).
AAN: Felix Jackson (for original story)

Bachelor of Hearts
GB 1958 94m Technicolor
Rank / Independent Artists (Vivian A. Cox)

Adventures of a German student at
Cambridge University.
Sometimes agreeable, sometimes annoying,
especially when romance gets in the way of the
possibilities for fun.

w Leslie Bricusse, Frederic Raphael d Wolf
Rilla ph Geoffrey Unsworth

Hardy Kruger, Sylvia Syms, Ronald Lewis,
Eric Barker, Newton Blick

The Bachelor Party***
US 1957 93m bw
UA / Norma (Harold Hecht)

New York book-keepers throw a wedding eve
party for one of their fellows, but drink only
brings to the fore their own private despairs.
Though the last half-hour lets it down, most of
this is a brilliantly observed social study of
New York life at its less attractive, and the
acting matches the incisiveness of the script.

w Paddy Chayevsky, from his TV play
d Delbert Mann ph Joseph La Shelle m Alex
North

Don Murray, E. G. Marshall, Jack Warden,
Philip Abbott, Larry Blyden, Patricia Smith,
Carolyn Jones

AAN: Carolyn Jones

Bachelor Party
US 1984 105m De Luxe

A bachelor party is beset by a series of
disasters. Crude, exploitative farce full of
physical mess and tending to get most of its
humour from the destruction of order and
some teetering on the brink of pornography.
Tom Hanks, Tawny Kitaen, Adrian Zmed,
George Grizzard, Barbara Stuart, Robert
Prescott. Written by Neal Israel, Pat Proft;
directed by Neal Israel; for Aspect Ratio /
Twin Continental / TCF.

Bachelor's Affairs
US 1931 64m bw

A middle-aged bachelor thinks he needs a
young wife, but can't keep up with the one he
gets. Strained star comedy of no surviving
interest. Adolphe Menjou, Minna Gombell,
Arthur Pierson, Joan Marsh, Alan Dinehart.
Written by Barry Conners and Philip Klein
from the play Precious by James Forbes;
directed by Alfred Werker; for Fox. 'Neither
farce nor a social problem development, it
misses throughout.'—Variety

The Bachelor's Daughters*
US 1946 90m bw
UA / Andrew Stone
GB title: Bachelor Girls

Four shopgirls and a floorwalker rent a Long

JUST TEN BABY FINGERS AND TEN BABY TOES— TROUBLES? SCANDAL?—GOSH—NOBODY KNOWS!

FUN and romance in the most DIFFERENT story to hit the screen in many a month! . . . Joyous Ginger as the glamorous shopgirl who found a baby on a doorstep and kept it for her own . . . David Niven, as the boss' son, who didn't believe her, but loved her anyhow . . . Charles Coburn, as the store owner who could forgive but not forget . . . Frank Albertson, as the jitterbug stock clerk . . . E. E. Clive, as the butler-turned-nursemaid! . . . ALL in the picture that will keep you on edge with deliciously tingling romantic suspense as you let yourself go in a heartfull of laughs!

GINGER ROGERS ★ DAVID NIVEN

in

"Bachelor Mother"

with

CHARLES COBURN
FRANK ALBERTSON
E. E. CLIVE

RKO RADIO Picture

"AND A LITTLE CHILD SHALL LEAD THEM"— into the most delightfully surprising complications you've seen on the screen!

Directed by GARSON KANIN. Produced by B. G. DeSYLVA. PANDRO S. BERMAN IN CHARGE OF PRODUCTION.
Screen Play by Norman Krasna. Story by Felix Jackson.

BACHELOR MOTHER.   A busy original advertisement for one of the brightest comedies of its year.

Island house and pass themselves off as a wealthy family in order to lure suitable husbands for the girls.
Mildly amusing comedy with good performances.

wd Andrew Stone *ph* Theodor Sparkuhl *m* Heinz Roemheld

Adolphe Menjou, Gail Russell, Claire Trevor, Billie Burke

Back Door to Heaven
US 1939 81m bw

A boy born on the wrong side of the tracks is prevented from going straight, and having escaped execution for murder, he is bumped off by gangsters. Heavy-going indictment of society; too glum to work, it seems to have finished off the career of its talented director. Wallace Ford, Aline MacMahon, Stuart Erwin, Jimmy Lydon, William Harrigan, Bert Frohman. Written by John Bright and Robert Tasker; produced, directed and original story by *William K. Howard* (who also appears as the prosecuting attorney); for Odessco / Paramount. 'Artistic drama, too heavy and slow-tempoed for general b.o.'—*Variety*

Back from Eternity
US 1956 97m bw
RKO (John Farrow)

An airliner is forced to crashland in headhunter country, and when repairs are made only five of the eight survivors can be carried.
Remake by the same producer-director of his own 1939 'B', *Five Came Back*, this time to considerably less effect despite superior production.

w Jonathan Latimer *d* John Farrow *ph* William Mellor *m* Franz Waxman

Robert Ryan, Anita Ekberg, Rod Steiger, Phyllis Kirk, Gene Barry, Keith Andes, Beulah Bondi, Fred Clark, Cameron Prud'homme, Jesse White
● *Video: Kingston*

Back from the Dead
US 1957 78m bw Regalscope
TCF / Regal (Robert Stabler)

A girl on honeymoon becomes possessed by the spirit of her husband's first wife.
Blithe Spirit played for real but getting just as many laughs, unintentional this time.

w Catherine Turney, from her novel The Other One *d* Charles Marquis Warren *ph* Ernest Haller *m* Raoul Kraushaar

Peggie Castle, Arthur Franz, Marsha Hunt, Don Haggerty

Back in Circulation
US 1937 80m bw

Girl news reporter wins her editor's attention by solving a murder. Sub-*Front Page* melodrama, of no intrinsic interest. Pat O'Brien, Joan Blondell, Margaret Lindsay. Written by Warren Duff; directed by Ray Enright; for Warner. 'The newspaper boys,

the goofy photographers and the hysterical city editor are on the murder trail, relentlessly pursuing the accused, telling coroners, district attorneys and defence counsel how to conduct their business.'—*Variety*

Back Roads
US 1981 95m De Luxe Panavision
CBS Theatrical / Meta Films (Ronald Shedlo)

A hooker and an ex-boxer hitch-hike to California.
Tiresomely with-it update of *It Happened One Night*, the humour and romance of the original are preferable to this dollop of bad language, boring people and bed-hopping.

w Gary Devore *d* Martin Ritt *ph* John A. Alonzo *m* Henry Mancini

Sally Field, Tommy Lee Jones, David Keith, Miriam Colon, Michael Gazzo
'Decidedly sticky, and instantly forgettable.'—*Guardian*

Back Room Boy*
GB 1942 82m bw
GFD / Gainsborough (Edward Black)

A timid meteorologist is sent to an Orkney lighthouse and unmasks a bunch of spies.
Fairly spirited star comedy of interest as a shameless rip-off of *The Ghost Train* and *Oh Mr Porter*, whose plotlines are milked but not improved: note also that Askey took over Will Hay's discarded stooges.

w Val Guest, Marriott Edgar *d* Herbert Mason

Arthur Askey, Moore Marriott, Graham Moffatt, Googie Withers, Vera Frances, John Salew

Back Street*
US 1932 93m bw
Universal (Carl Laemmle Jnr)

A married man has a sweet-tempered mistress who effaces herself for twenty years.
Popular version of a sudsy bestselling novel.

w Gladys Lehman, Lynn Starling, *novel* Fannie Hurst *d* John M. Stahl *ph* Karl Freund

Irene Dunne, John Boles, June Clyde, George Meeker, Zasu Pitts, Doris Lloyd
'Swell romance, a little tear-jerking, and a woman's picture—which means a money production.'—*Variety*

Back Street*
US 1941 89m bw
Universal (Bruce Manning)

Competent remake.

w Bruce Manning, Felix Jackson *d* Robert Stevenson *ph* William Daniels *m* Frank Skinner

Margaret Sullavan, Charles Boyer, Richard Carlson, Frank McHugh, Tim Holt, Frank Jenks, Esther Dale, Samuel S. Hinds

AAN: Frank Skinner

Back Street*
US 1961 107m Technicolor
U-I / Ross Hunter / Carrollton

Glossy remake typical of its producer: unfortunately it fails to work because the heroine suffers too luxuriously.

w Eleanore Griffin, William Ludwig *d* David Miller *ph* Stanley Cortez *m* Frank Skinner

Susan Hayward, John Gavin, Vera Miles, Virginia Grey, Charles Drake, Reginald Gardiner
'Though there is a lot to be said for this new version's thesis that one can be just as lonely in a series of apartments and lovers' nests apparently never less than a hundred yards wide, the illusion is quickly shattered the moment one gets the impression that the lovers prefer to keep much the same distance during their moments of passion.'—*Peter John Dyer*
'Ross Hunter has updated this old faithful and given it a contemporary lack of significance.'—*Hollis Alpert, Saturday Review*
'The bathrooms look like the lobby of the Beverly Hilton . . . the fallen woman falls, not into the pit of shame, but into the lap of luxury.'—*Time*

Back to Bataan
US 1945 97m bw
RKO (Robert Fellows)

When Bataan is cut off, a Marine colonel organizes guerrilla resistance.
Modestly made and rather dislikeable flagwaver.

w Ben Barzman, Richard Landau *d* Edward Dmytryk *ph* Nicholas Musuraca *m* Roy Webb

John Wayne, Anthony Quinn, Beulah Bondi, Fely Franquelli, Leonard Strong, Richard Loo, Philip Ahn, Lawrence Tierney, Paul Fix
● *Video: Kingston*

Back to God's Country
US 1953 78m Technicolor
U-I (Howard Christie)

A sea captain battles the Canadian winter and a villain who wants his wife and his cargo of furs.
Old-fashioned adventure story, moderately well presented.

w Tom Reed, *novel* James Oliver Curwood *d* Joseph Pevney *ph* Maury Gertsman *m* Frank Skinner

Rock Hudson, Steve Cochran, Marcia Henderson, Hugh O'Brian

Backfire
US 1949 90m bw
Warner (Anthony Veiller)

A war veteran solves the murder of which his best friend is accused.
Confusing murder mystery of a very familiar kind, adequately made but with no particular style. Flashbacks don't help.

w Larry Marcus, Ivan Goff, Ben Roberts *d* Vincent Sherman *ph* Carl Guthrie *ad* Anton Grot *m* Ray Heindorf

Gordon Macrae, Virginia Mayo, Edmond O'Brien, Dane Clark, Viveca Lindfors, Ed Begley

Background*
GB 1953 82m bw
Group Three (Herbert Mason)
US title: *Edge of Divorce*

Two people decide on divorce, but thoughts of their children bring them together again.
Low budget, stiff-upper-lip marriage guidance tract, well acted but more well-intentioned than memorable.

w Warren Chetham Strode, from his play, with Don Sharp d Daniel Birt ph Arthur Grant

Valerie Hobson, Philip Friend, Norman Wooland, Janette Scott, Mandy Miller, Jeremy Spenser, Richard Wattis

Background to Danger**
US 1943 80m bw
Warner (Jerry Wald)

An adventurer thwarts Nazi intrigue in Turkey.
Good routine war action yarn, well presented and performed.

w W. R. Burnett, *novel* Uncommon Danger by Eric Ambler d Raoul Walsh ph Tony Gaudio m Frederick Hollander

George Raft, Brenda Marshall, Sydney Greenstreet, Peter Lorre, Osa Massen, Turhan Bey, Kurt Katch
'You could use this film for one kind of measurement of the unconquerable difference between a good job by Hitchcock and a good job of the Hitchcock type.'—*James Agee*

Backlash*
US 1956 84m Technicolor
U-I (Aaron Rosenberg)

A gunman seeks the father he has never met, who turns out to be a villain who sold his partners for gold to attacking Indians.
Rather unusual suspense western, very watchable for its mystery elements.

w Borden Chase d John Sturges ph Irving Glassberg m Herman Stein

Richard Widmark, Donna Reed, John McIntire, William Campbell, Barton Maclane

The Bacon Grabbers*
US 1929 20m bw silent

Bailiffs fail to recover a radio on which the instalments are overdue. Modestly pleasing star comedy on the lines of *Big Business*.
Laurel and Hardy, Edgar Kennedy, Jean Harlow, Charlie Hall. Written by Leo McCarey and H. M. Walker; directed by Lewis R. Foster; for Hal Roach.

'The story of a blonde who wanted to go places, and a brute who got her there— the hard way!'
The Bad and the Beautiful**
US 1952 118m bw
MGM (John Houseman)

A director, a star, a screenwriter and an executive recall their experiences at the hands of a go-getting Hollywood producer.
Very much a Hollywood 'in' picture, this rather obvious flashback melodrama offers good acting chances and a couple of intriguing situations; never quite finding the style it seeks, it offers good bitchy entertainment along the way, and there are references back to it in *Two Weeks in Another Town*, made ten years later.

w Charles Schnee d Vincente Minnelli ph Robert Surtees m David Raksin ad Cedric Gibbons, Edward Carfagno

Kirk Douglas (Jonathan Shields), Lana Turner (Georgia Lorrison), Walter Pidgeon (Harry Pebbel), Dick Powell (James Lee Bartlow), Barry Sullivan (Fred Amiel), Gloria Grahame (Rosemary Bartlow), Gilbert Roland (Victor Ribera), Leo G. Carroll (Henry Whitfield), Vanessa Brown (Kay Amiel), Paul Stewart (Syd Murphy)
'For all the cleverness of the apparatus, it lacks a central point of focus.'—*Penelope Houston*
'Clever, sharply observed little scenes reflect the Hollywood surface: the egotistic babble at a party, the affectations of European directors, the sneak preview, the trying on of suits for catmen in a B picture.'—*MFB*
'It is a crowded and colourful picture, but it is choppy, episodic and vague. There does not emerge a clear picture of exactly how movies are made.'—*Bosley Crowther*

AA: Charles Schnee; Robert Surtees; art direction; Gloria Grahame
AAN: Kirk Douglas

Bad Bascomb*
US 1946 110m bw
MGM (Orville Dull)

A sentimental bank robber becomes the hero of a group of travelling Mormons.
Pleasing though overlong star western, with good production values.

w William Lipman, Grant Garrett d S. Sylvan Simon ph Charles Schoenbaum m David Snell

Wallace Beery, Margaret O'Brien, Marjorie Main, J. Carrol Naish, Russell Simpson, Sara Haden

Bad Boys
US 1983 123m Astro Color
EMI / Robert Solo

Delinquents get out of control in a Juvenile Correctional Facility.
Ugly but yawnworthy saga of up-to-date Dead End Kids.

w Richard di Lello d Rick Rosenthal ph Bruce Surtees, Don Thorin m Bill Conti

Sean Penn, Reni Santoni, Jim Moody, Eric Gurry, Esai Morales, Ally Sheedy

Bad Company**
US 1972 92m Technicolor
Paramount (Stanley R. Jaffe)

During the Civil War, two youths on the run team up and become outlaws.
A successful attempt to recreate the feeling of past time, by the writers of another criminal myth, *Bonnie and Clyde*.

w David Newman, Robert Benton d Robert Benton ph Gordon Willis m Harvey Schmidt

Jeff Bridges, Barry Brown, Jim Davis, David Huddleston, John Savage

Bad Day at Black Rock****
US 1954 81m Eastmancolor
       Cinemascope
MGM (Dore Schary)

A one-armed stranger gets off the train at a sleepy desert hamlet and is greeted with hostility by the townsfolk, who have something to hide.
Seminal suspense thriller—the guilty town motif became a cliché—with a terse script and professional presentation. The moments of violence, long awaited, are electrifying.

w Millard Kaufman, story Bad Time at Hondo by Howard Briskin d John Sturges ph William C. Mellor m André Previn

Spencer Tracy, Robert Ryan, Dean Jagger, Walter Brennan, Ernest Borgnine, Lee Marvin, Anne Francis, John Ericson, Russell Collins
'A very superior example of motion picture craftsmanship.'—*Pauline Kael*
'The movie takes place within twenty-four hours. It has a dramatic unity, an economy of word and action, that is admirable in an age of flabby Hollywood epics that maunder on forever.'—*William K. Zinsser, New York Herald Tribune*
'The skill of some sequences, the mood and symbiosis between man and nature makes this film sometimes superior to *High Noon*.'—*G. N. Fenin*

AAN: Millard Kaufman; John Sturges; Spencer Tracy

Bad for Each Other
US 1954 83m bw
Columbia (William Fadiman)

A doctor back from the army scorns his home town for high society, but a mine disaster reverses his decision.
Misleadingly titled cliché drama, patterned after *The Citadel*. Actors ill at ease, handling competent but routine.

w Irving Wallace, Horace McCoy, from the latter's novel d Irving Rapper ph Franz Planer md Mischa Bakaleinikoff

Charlton Heston, Lizabeth Scott, Dianne Foster, Mildred Dunnock, Arthur Franz, Ray Collins, Marjorie Rambeau

Bad Girl*
US 1931 90m bw
Fox

Two New York youngsters have to get married and find life bewildering.
Typical Borzage sentiment which was well received at the time.

w Edwin Burke, *novel* Vina Delmar *d Frank Borzage* ph Chester Lyons

Sally Eilers, James Dunn, Minna Gombell, William Pawley, Frank Darien

AAN: Frank Borzage; Edwin Burke; best picture

Bad Little Angel
US 1939 72m bw

A sad little girl flees an orphanage and brightens up several lives in a small town. Pollyanna-type period drama, definitely for small-town audiences but well enough done. Virginia Weidler, Gene Reynolds, Guy Kibbee, Ian Hunter, Elizabeth Patterson, Reginald Owen, Henry Hull, Lois Wilson. Written by Dorothy Yost from the novel Looking after Sandy by Margaret Turnbull; directed by William Thiele; for MGM. 'Homespunner for the nabes.'—*Variety*

The Bad Lord Byron*
GB 1948 85m bw
Rank / Sydney Box (Aubrey Baring)

Byron lies dying, and imagines his life and loves under review in a heavenly court. Thought risible at the time, this historical romance in flashback now seems no worse and even a little more stylish than most, though the script suffers from too many cooks.

w Terence Young, Anthony Thorne, Peter Quennell, Laurence Kitchin, Paul Holt *d* David MacDonald *ph* Stephen Dade *m* Cedric Thorpe Davie

Dennis Price, Mai Zetterling, Linden Travers, Joan Greenwood, Sonia Holm, Raymond Lovell, Leslie Dwyer

† The end of the British costume cycle which began with *The Man in Grey*.

The Bad Man
US 1940 70m sepia
MGM (J. Walter Ruben)
GB title: *Two Gun Cupid*

A Mexican outlaw helps a former friend and unites two lovers.
Forgettable western comedy drama with a sterling cast.

w Wells Root, *play* Porter Emerson Brown *d* Richard Thorpe *ph* Clyde de Vinna *m* Franz Waxman

Wallace Beery, Lionel Barrymore, Laraine Day, Ronald Reagan, Henry Travers

† Previously produced by First National in 1923, and in 1930 with Walter Huston and O. P. Heggie.

Bad Man of Brimstone
US 1937 89m bw

An old bandit discovers his long-lost son and sees the light. Hilariously predictable but enjoyable star vehicle, quite palatable when it isn't too lachrymose. Wallace Beery, Virginia Bruce, Noah Beery, Dennis O'Keefe, Lewis Stone, Guy Kibbee, Joseph Calleia. Written by Richard Maibaum and Cyril Hume; directed by J. Walter Ruben; for MGM.

Bad Man's River
Spain / Italy / France 1972 90m
   Eastmancolor Franscope
Zurbano / Apollo / Roitfeld (Bernard Gordon)

Four outlaws accept the job of blowing up a government arsenal in Mexico.
Lurid western with comedy leanings and a somewhat eccentric cast.

w Philip Yordan, Eugenio Martin *d* Eugenio Martin *ph* Alexander Ulloa *m* Waldo de Los Rios

Lee Van Cleef, James Mason, Gina Lollobrigida, Simon Andreu, Diana Lorys
   'When shooting a western in Spain one should not say to oneself, "Never mind, no one is going to see it," because that will be just the film which the Rank Organization will choose to release in England.'—*James Mason*

Bad Men of Missouri
US 1941 72m bw

The Younger brothers become outlaws when they fight the influence of carpetbaggers. Whitewashing of a family of western criminals; good double-bill entertainment. Dennis Morgan, Arthur Kennedy, Wayne Morris, Jane Wyman, Victor Jory, Walter Catlett. Written by Charles Grayson; directed by Ray Enright; for Warner.

Bad Men of Tombstone
US 1949 75m bw

Adventurers clash during gold rush days. Workaday western with some vigour. Broderick Crawford, Barry Sullivan, Marjorie Reynolds, Julie Gibson. Written by Philip Yordan and Arthur Strawn; directed by Kurt Neumann; for King Brothers / Allied Artists.

The Bad News Bears
US 1976 103m Movielab
Paramount (Stanley Jaffe)

An ex-baseball professional coaches a team of tough kids.
Rough-tongued, sentimental star comedy.

w Bill Lancaster *d* Michael Ritchie *ph* John A. Alonzo *m* Jerry Fielding (after Bizet)

Walter Matthau, Tatum O'Neal, Vic Morrow, Joyce Van Patten

The Bad News Bears in Breaking Training
US 1977 100m Movielab
Paramount / Leonard Goldberg (Fred T. Gallo)

The Bears are invited to play in the Houston Astrodome but have trouble finding a coach. Dimwitted and alarmingly sentimental sequel to a raucously vulgar oncer which should have been left alone.

w Paul Brickman *d* Michael Pressman *ph* Fred J. Koenekamp *m* Craig Safan from Tchaikovsky's 1812 Overture *ed* John W. Wheeler

William Devane, Clifton James, Jackie Earle Haley, Jimmy Baio, Chris Barnes

The Bad News Bears Go to Japan
US 1978 91m Movielab
Paramount

Yet another unnecessary sequel with a self-explanatory title.

w Bill Lancaster *d* John Berry *ph* Gene Polito *m* Paul Chihara

Tony Curtis, Jackie Earle Haley, Tomisaburo Wayakama, George Wyner

The Bad One
UA 70m bw

A prostitute falls for a client and saves him from prison. Artificial to the point of risibility, this incredible melodrama demeans all concerned with it. Dolores del Rio, Edmund Lowe, Don Alvarado, Blanche Friderici. Written by Carey Wilson, Howard E. Rogers and John Farrow; directed by George Fitzmaurice; for United Artists.

The Bad Seed*
US 1956 129m bw
Warner (Mervyn Le Roy)

A sweet-looking 8-year-old girl is a liar and a murderess; her mother finds out and attempts to kill her and commit suicide.
A real curiosity from an unexpected stage hit: absurd melodrama treated with astonishing high literary style and some censor-induced levity: at the end, after the little villainess has been struck by lightning, a curtain call shows her being soundly spanked.

w John Lee Mahin, *play* Maxwell Anderson, *novel* William March *d* Mervyn Le Roy *ph* Harold Rosson *m* Alex North

Nancy Kelly (rather uneasily recreating her stage role as the mother), *Patty McCormack,* Henry Jones, Eileen Heckart, Evelyn Varden, William Hopper, Paul Fix, Jesse White

AAN: Harold Rosson; Nancy Kelly; Patty McCormack; Eileen Heckart

Bad Sister
US 1931 71m bw
Universal (Carl Laemmle Jnr)

A small-town coquette falls for a city slicker, and her quiet sister gets her steady boy friend. A teenage potboiler of its day, remarkable only for its cast.

w Raymond L. Schrock, Tom Reed, *story* The Flirt by Booth Tarkington *d* Hobart Henley *ph* Karl Freund

Conrad Nagel, Sidney Fox, Bette Davis, Humphrey Bogart, Zasu Pitts, Slim Summerville, Emma Dunn, Bert Roach

Bad Timing
GB 1980 123m colour Technovision
Rank / Recorded Picture Company (Jeremy Thomas)

In Vienna, an American divorcee has a strange and unhappy affair with a psychoanalyst.
Weird and unsympathetic sex melodrama, presented with the disconnected style expected from this director as a series of flashbacks from the heroine's near-deathbed.

w Yale Udoff *d* Nicolas Roeg *ph* Anthony Richmond *m* Richard Hartley

Art Garfunkel, Theresa Russell, Harvey Keitel, Denholm Elliott, Daniel Massey

'An enervating experience. Technically flashy, and teeming with degenerate chic, the downbeat tale is unrelieved by its tacked-on thriller ending, and deals purely in despair.'—*Variety*

● Video: Rank

The Badge of Marshal Brennan
US 1957 75m bw

A man on the run takes on the identity of a dying marshal, and cleans up a corrupt town.
Satisfying lower-case western. Jim Davis, Arleen Whelan, Louis Jean Heydt, Lee Van Cleef. Written by Thomas G. Hubbard; directed by Albert C. Gannoway; for Allied Artists.

Badge 373
US 1973 116m Technicolor
Paramount (Howard W. Koch)

A police detective is enraged by the murder of his partner and his own suspension after the death of a suspect.
'Realistic' (i.e. violent and foul-mouthed) cop thriller in the wake of *The French Connection*, tolerable only for action highlights.

w Pete Hamill, from the exploits of Eddie Egan *d* Howard W. Koch *ph* Arthur J. Ornitz *m* J. J. Johnson

Robert Duvall, Verna Bloom, Henry Darrow, Eddie Egan, Felipe Luciano, Tina Christiana, Marina Durell

'A deeply divided and scarcely reassuring addition to the movies' composite portrait of the American police force.'—*John Gillett*

'Nasty, violent and humourless.'—*Sight and Sound*

'A movie well worth protesting about.'—*Michael Billington, Illustrated London News*

The Badlanders*
US 1958 83m Metrocolor
Cinemascope
MGM / Arcola (Aaron Rosenberg)

Crooked westerners plan to rob a goldmine.
Rather sloppy western remake of *The Asphalt Jungle*.

w Richard Collins *d* Delmer Daves *ph* John Seitz

Alan Ladd, Ernest Borgnine, Katy Jurado, Claire Kelly, Kent Smith, *Nehemiah Persoff*, Robert Emhardt

Badlands***
US 1973 94m Consolidated Color
(Columbia) Pressman / Williams /
Badlands (Terrence Malick)

A teenage girl and a young garbage collector wander across America leaving a trail of murder behind them.
A violent folk tale for moderns; very well put together if somewhat lacking in point, it quickly became a cult film.

wd Terrence Malick *ph* Brian Probyn, Tak Fujimoto, Stevan Larner *m* George Tipton

Martin Sheen, Sissy Spacek, Warren Oates, Ramon Bieri

'One of the finest literate examples of narrated cinema since the early days of Welles and Polonsky.'—*Jonathan Rosenbaum*

'So preconceived that there's nothing left to respond to.'—*New Yorker*

● Video: Warner

Badlands of Dakota
US 1941 75m bw

A young man steals his elder brother's girl and becomes sheriff of a corrupt western town.
Standard family fare. Robert Stack, Richard Dix, Broderick Crawford, Ann Rutherford, Frances Farmer, Hugh Herbert, Andy Devine, Lon Chaney Jnr. Written by Gerald Geraghty; directed by Alfred E. Green; for Universal.

Badman's Country
US 1958 72m bw

Pat Garrett, Wyatt Earp, Buffalo Bill Cody and Bat Masterson have a showdown with Butch Cassidy. Wildly unhistorical western.
George Montgomery, Buster Crabbe, Malcolm Attenbury, Gregory Walcott, Neville Brand. Written by Orville H. Hampton; directed by Fred F. Sears; for Warner.

Badman's Territory
US 1946 97m bw

The brutality of the Texas state police forces a sheriff to seek help from outlaws.
Unconvincing western with good moments.
Randolph Scott, Steve Brodie, Gabby Hayes, Ann Richards. Written by Jack Nettlefold and Luci Ward; directed by Tim Whelan; for RKO.

Bagdad
US 1949 81m Technicolor
U-I (Robert Arthur)

A chieftain's daughter seeks revenge for her father's death.
Thinly-conceived Arabian Nights modernization, unsure whether to take itself seriously.

w Robert Hardy Andrews *d* Charles Lamont *ph* Russel Metty *m* Frank Skinner, Jack Brooks

Maureen O'Hara, Vincent Price, Paul Christian, John Sutton, Jeff Corey, Frank Puglia

'The two most gorgeous humans you've ever beheld—caressed by soft tropic winds—tossed by the tides of love!'

Bahama Passage
US 1941 82m Technicolor
Paramount (Edward H. Griffith)

A sophisticated girl is determined to live on a salt-mining island in the West Indies.
Forgettable tropical romance in very pleasing early colour.

w Virginia Van Upp, *novel* Nelson Hayes *d* Edward H. Griffith *ph* Leo Tover

Madeleine Carroll, Sterling Hayden, Flora Robson, Leo G. Carroll, Cecil Kellaway, Dorothy Dandridge

La Baie des Anges**
France 1962 85m bw
Sud-Pacifique (Paul-Edmond Decharme)
GB title: *Bay of Angels*

A bank clerk who has had unexpected winnings at the Nice Casino falls in love with a compulsive gambler.
Good-looking romantic drama utilizing many of the cinema's most dazzling resources.

wd Jacques Demy *ph* Jean Rabier *m* Michel Legrand

Jeanne Moreau, Claude Mann, Paul Guers, Henri Nassiet

'Immense lightness, speed and gaiety . . . stunning visual texture.'—*Tom Milne, MFB*

'It's like a French attempt to purify, to get to the essence of, a Warners' movie of the 30s.'—*Pauline Kael*

Bail Out at 43,000
US 1957 82m bw

Airmen test ejection seats for jet bombers.
Humdrum flagwaver. John Payne, Paul Kelly, Karen Steele, Richard Eyer. Written by Paul Monash; directed by Francis D. Lyon; for Pine-Thomas-Shane / UA.

Bait
US 1954 79m bw
Columbia (Hugo Haas)

Gold prospectors fall out over a mine and a woman.
Antediluvian melodrama typical of this director, made more risible than usual by Cedric Hardwicke's introduction in the shape of Satan.

w Samuel W. Taylor *d* Hugo Haas *ph* Edward P. Fitzgerald *m* Vaclav Divina

Hugo Haas, Cleo Moore, John Agar, Emmett Lynn

Le Bal**
France / Italy / Algeria 1982 112m
Fujicolor
S.A. / A2 / Massfil / Oncic (Giorgio Silvagni)

Scenes from the history of a small Paris ballroom between 1936 and 1983.
Striking if overlong attempt at a totally speechless drama, with handling very nearly good enough to meet the challenge, though the result will not be to everyone's taste, and one's reaction in any case will depend very much on mood.

w Jean-Claude Penchenat, Ruggero Maccari, Furio Scarpelli, Ettore Scola, from an idea by the first-named and the stage production by the Théâtre du Campagnol *d* Ettore Scola *ph* Ricardo Aranovich *m* Vladimir Cosma

Jean-Claude Penchenat, Chantal Capron, Etienne Guichard and large company each playing several roles

Balalaika*
US 1939   102m   bw
MGM (Lawrence Weingarten)

Russian exiles gather in Paris.
Mildly pleasing star musical.

w Jacques Deval, Leon Gordon, *play* Eric
Maschwitz d Reinhold Schunzel ph Joseph
Ruttenberg, Karl Freund m Herbert Stothart

Nelson Eddy, Ilona Massey, Charles Ruggles,
Frank Morgan, C. Aubrey Smith, Lionel
Atwill, Walter Woolf King, Joyce Compton
Songs include 'At the Balalaika'; 'Tanya';
'Ride, Cossack, Ride'; 'Shadows on the Sand';
'Tale of the Tailors'; 'Beneath the Winter's
Snows'; 'In a Heart as Brave as Your Own';
'Soldiers of the Czar'; 'How Many Miles to
Go'; 'The Magic of Your Love'; 'My Heart Is
a Gypsy'
  'A sumptuously produced operetta in the
opulent MGM tradition.'—*Variety*

The Balcony*
US 1963   86m   bw
Walter Reade / Sterling / Allen Hodgdon /
  City Film (Joseph Strick, Ben Maddow)

In a war-torn world, a brothel continues to
attract customers of every variety.
Low-budget adaptation of a rather confused
allegorical play: vivid moments hardly atone
for reels of surrealist groping.

w Ben Maddow, *play* Jean Genet d Joseph
Strick ph George Folsey m Igor Stravinsky

Shelley Winters, Peter Falk, Lee Grant, Peter
Brocco, Kent Smith, Ruby Dee, Jeff Corey,
Leonard Nimoy
  'Relentlessly funny, shaggy, shocking.'—
Times
  'Unfit for exhibition to man, woman or
child.'—*The People*

AAN: George Folsey

Ball of Fire*
US 1942   111m   bw
Samuel Goldwyn
working title: *The Professor and the
  Burlesque Queen*

Seven professors compiling a dictionary give
shelter to a stripteaser on the run from
gangsters.
Rather overstretched but fitfully amusing
romp inspired by *Snow White and the Seven
Dwarfs*.

w Charles Brackett, Billy Wilder d Howard
Hawks ph Gregg Toland m Alfred Newman

Barbara Stanwyck, Gary Cooper, Oscar
Homolka, Henry Travers, S. Z. Sakall, Tully
Marshall, Leonid Kinskey, Richard Haydn,
Aubrey Mather, Allen Jenkins, Dana
Andrews, Dan Duryea
  'It's played as if it were terribly bright, but
it's rather shrill and tiresome.'—*New Yorker,
1982*

† Ginger Rogers was first choice for the
Stanwyck role.

AAN: original story (Theodore Monroe, Billy
Wilder); Alfred Newman; Barbara Stanwyck

Ballad in Blue
GB 1964   88m   bw
(Warner) Alexander and Miguel Salkind
  (Herman Blaser)
US title: *Blues for Lovers*

A famous pianist becomes friendly with a
blind boy and helps reconcile his parents.
Curious sentimental drama with the star
playing himself; competent but hardly rousing.

w Burton Wohl d Paul Henreid ph Ron
Taylor m Ray Charles, Stanley Black

Ray Charles, Mary Peach, Dawn Addams,
Tom Bell, Piers Bishop, Betty McDowell

Ballad of a Soldier**
USSR 1959   89m   bw
Mosfilm
original title: *Ballada o Soldate*

A soldier is granted four days' home leave
before returning to be killed at the front.
Lyrical tear-jerker most notable for its
impeccably photographed detail of Russian
domestic and everyday life.

w Valentin Yoshov, Grigori Chukrai
d Grigori Chukrai ph Vladimir Nikolayev,
Era Saveleva m Mikhail Ziv

Vladimir Ivashev, Sharma Prokhorenko,
Antonina Maximova
  'In an epoch when the entertainment in
most entertainment films is little more than
offensive, its persuasive charm is particularly
welcome.'—*MFB*

AAN: Valentin Yoshov, Grigori Chukrai

The Ballad of Cable Hogue*
US 1970   121m   Technicolor
Warner / Phil Feldman (Sam Peckinpah)

A gold prospector takes a lengthy and
ineffectual revenge on men who robbed him,
and dies trying to be a hero.
Curious peripatetic western with the director
in uncharacteristically experimental and
comparatively non-violent mood. All
concerned seem to be enjoying themselves,
but the fun is not always communicated.

w John Crawford, Edward Penney d Sam
Peckinpah ph Lucien Ballard m Jerry
Goldsmith

Jason Robards, David Warner, Strother
Martin, Slim Pickens, L. Q. Jones, Peter
Whitney, R. G. Armstrong, Gene Evans,
Stella Stevens

The Ballad of Joe Hill**
Sweden 1971   115m   Eastmancolor
Bo Widerberg Film (Waldemar Bergendahl)
aka: *Joe Hill*

In 1902, a Swedish immigrant in New York
becomes a revolutionary and is executed for
the murder of a grocer.
Romantic propaganda which incidentally gives
a delightfully detailed outsider's view of period
America.

w,d Bo Widerberg ph Peter Davidsson,
Jorgen Persson m Stefan Grossman ad Ulf
Axen

Thommy Berggren, Anja Schmidt, Evert
Anderson, Cathy Smith

● *Video: Thorn EMI*

The Ballad of Josie
US 1967   102m   Techniscope
Universal (Marty Melcher)

Cleared of the manslaughter of her husband, a
western widow renovates a derelict ranch and
sets up as a sheep´farmer.
Tediously whimsical, unsuitably cast women's
lib comedy with so few laughs that it may
require to be taken seriously.

w Harold Swanton d Andrew V. McLaglen
ph Milton Krasner m Frank de Vol

Doris Day, Peter Graves, George Kennedy,
William Talman, Andy Devine, Audrey
Christie

The Ballad of Narayama*
Japan 1983   130m   colour
Toei

In a remote village, local traditions include
burying alive for the theft of food, and this is
the fate of a pregnant woman and her family.
Primitivist ritual drama, totally distasteful to
those new to the myths. On its own terms,
some sort of classic.

w,d Shohei Imamura, from novels by Shichiro
Fukazawa ph Masao Tochizawa m Shinichiro
Ikebe

Ken Ogata, Sumiko Sakamoto, Tonpei Hidari
  'One of the most intense portraits of
personal fulfilment in all cinema.'—*Tony
Rayns, MFB*

Ballet Mécanique*
France 1924   10m   bw   silent

Famous experimental short in which everyday
images form abstract patterns. A key to all
subsequent surrealist experiments in the
cinema. Music by Georges Antheil; written,
directed and produced by *Fernand Léger* and
Dudley Murphy.

Balthazar*
France / Sweden 1966   95m   bw
Parc / Ardos / Athos / Svenska
  Filminstitutet (Mag Bodard)
original title: *Au Hasard, Balthazar*

The life of a talented donkey, born in the
Swiss alps and eventually killed during a
smuggling escapade.
Something between *Black Beauty* and a
Christian parable, this quiet, episodic film is
counted by some as its director's best work.

wd Robert Bresson ph Ghislain Cloquet
m Jean Wiener (and Schubert)

Anne Wiazemsky, François Lafarge, Walter
Green (amateur cast)

Baltic Deputy*
USSR 1937   100m   bw
Lenfilm

An old professor is finally reconciled to the
1917 revolution.
Propagandist biography (of scientist K. A.
Timiriazev) with interesting scenes and a
strong central performance.

w the directors and others d Alexander
Zharki, Josef Heifits ph M. Kaplan m M.
Timofeyev

Nikolai Cherkassov, M. Damasheva, A. Melnikov

The Baltimore Bullet
US 1980   103m   Eastmancolor
Avco Embassy / Filmfair (John F. Brescia)

Adventures of a pair of pool sharks. Flabby comedy attempting a lighthearted version of *The Hustler*. The rewards are meagre.

w John F. Brescia, Robert Vincent O'Neill *d* Robert Ellis Miller *ph* James A. Crabe *m* Johnny Mandel

James Coburn, Omar Sharif, Bruce Boxleitner, Ronee Blakely, Calvin Lockhart

'It manages to be stupidly macho and hopelessly incompetent at one and the same time.'—*Guardian*

● Video: Rank

Bambi**
US 1942   72m   Technicolor
Walt Disney

The story of a forest deer, from the book by Felix Salten.
Anthropomorphic cartoon feature, one of Disney's most memorable and brilliant achievements, with a great comic character in Thumper the rabbit and a climactic forest fire sequence which is genuinely thrilling. A triumph of the animator's art.

supervisor David Hand *m* Frank Churchill, Edward Plumb

AA: song 'Love Is a Song' (*m* Frank Churchill, *ly* Larry Morey)
AAN: Frank Churchill, Edward Plumb

The Bamboo Prison
US 1955   80m   bw

An American prisoner-of-war in Korea poses as a collaborator in order to get secret information. Forlorn war drama which makes little impact. Robert Francis, Brian Keith, E. G. Marshall, Dianne Foster, Jerome Courtland. Written by Edwin Blum and Jack de Witt; directed by Lewis Seiler; for Columbia.

Banana Ridge
GB 1941   87m   bw

A business man's old flame presents him with an alleged son. Stagey farce salvaged by star performances. Robertson Hare, Alfred Drayton, Isabel Jeans, Nova Pilbeam, Adele Dixon, Stewart Rome. From the play by Ben Travers; directed by Walter C. Mycroft; for ABPC.

Bananas*
US 1971   81m   De Luxe
UA / Rollins and Joffe (Jack Grossberg)

A meek and mild product tester for a New York corporation accidentally becomes a South American rebel hero.
Disjointed anarchic comedy with a few good jokes typical of their author.

w Woody Allen with Mickey Rose *d* Woody Allen *ph* Andrew M. Costikyan *m* Marvin Hamlisch

THE BAND WAGON.   Many famous trios have performed the 'Triplets' number. Here are Fred Astaire, Nanette Fabray and Jack Buchanan.

Woody Allen, Louise Lasser, Carlos Montalban, Jacobo Morales

'Full of hilarious comic ideas and lines, supplied by Allen and his collaborator; then Allen, the director and actor, murders them.'—*Stanley Kauffmann*

† Asked why his film was called *Bananas*, Allen replied: 'Because there are no bananas in it.'

● Video: Warner

'You're no blue blood any more, honey. The master bought you . . . and now he's waitin'!'

Band of Angels
US 1957   127m   Warnercolor
Warner (no producer credited)

In 1865, a Kentucky girl learns that her mother was black and is sold as a slave, but quickly becomes her owner's mistress.
Long-winded romantic adventure, rather lamely scripted and developed. The star's presence reinforces the impression of sitting through the ghost of *Gone with the Wind*.

w John Twist, Ivan Goff, Ben Roberts, *novel* Robert Penn Warren *d* Raoul Walsh *ph* Lucien Ballard *m* Max Steiner

Clark Gable, Yvonne de Carlo, Sidney Poitier, Efrem Zimbalist Jnr, Patric Knowles, Rex Reason, Torin Thatcher, Andrea King

'Too absurd to be dislikeable.'—*MFB*

The Band Plays On
US 1934   87m   bw

Four street kids are saved by football and eventually become national stars. Ho-hum sentimental melodrama with plot trouble. Robert Young, Stuart Erwin, Leo Carrillo, Betty Furness, Ted Healy, Preston Foster, Russell Hardie, William Tannen. Written by Bernard Schubert, Ralph Spence, Harvey Gates; directed by Russell Mack; for MGM.
'Slow, long, and weak on cast names.'—*Variety*

Band Waggon*
GB 1939   85m   bw
Gainsborough (Edward Black)

Comedians running a pirate TV station in a ghostly castle round up a gang of spies.
Film version of a long-running radio comedy series; quite a serviceable record of a phenomenon.

w Marriott Edgar, Val Guest *d* Marcel Varnel

Arthur Askey, Richard Murdoch, Jack Hylton and his band, Pat Kirkwood, Moore Marriott, Peter Gawthorne, Wally Patch, Donald Calthrop

The Band Wagon*
US 1953   112m   Technicolor
MGM (Arthur Freed)

A has-been Hollywood dancer joins forces

with a temperamental stage producer to put on a Broadway musical.
Simple but sophisticated musical with the bare minimum of plot, told mostly in jokes, and the maximum of music and song. Numbers include those listed below, as well as a spoof Mickey Spillane ballet finale. Level of technical accomplishment very high.

w *Adolph Green, Betty Comden* d *Vincente Minnelli* ph *Harry Jackson* songs *Howard Dietz, Arthur Schwarz* m *Adolph Deutsch* ad *Cedric Gibbons, Preston Ames*

Fred Astaire, Jack Buchanan, Oscar Levant, Cyd Charisse, Nanette Fabray

'The best musical of the month, the year, the decade, or for all I know of all time.'— *Archer Winsten*
† The Jack Buchanan character, Jeffrey Cordova, was first offered to Clifton Webb. It was loosely based on Jose Ferrer, who in the early fifties produced four Broadway shows all running at the same time, and acted in a fifth.
†† Songs include: 'A Shine on Your Shoes', 'By Myself', 'That's Entertainment', 'Dancing in the Dark', 'Triplets', 'New Sun in the Sky', 'I Guess I'll Have to Change My Plan', 'Louisiana Hayride', 'I Love Louisa', 'Girl Hunt' ballet.

AAN: Adolph Green, Betty Comden; Adolph Deutsch
● Video: MGM / UA

Bande à Part
France 1964 95m bw
Anouchka / Orsay (Philippe Dussart)
aka: *The Outsiders*
Aimless young people plan a robbery which ends in murder.
Despite the plot, the emphasis is on fragments of lyricism, and the film is not among its director's greatest successes.

wd *Jean-Luc Godard*, novel *Fool's Gold* by *Dolores and B. Hitchens* ph *Raoul Coutard* m *Michel Legrand*

Anna Karina, Claude Brasseur, Sami Frey, Louisa Colpeyn

'In a sense, the whole film is a metaphor illustrating this glancing collision, when fantasy and reality merge but one may still remain unsure which is which.'—*Tom Milne, MFB*

Bandido
US 1956 92m De Luxe Cinemascope
UA / Robert L. Jacks
Mexico 1916: an American adventurer helps a rebel leader to defeat a gun runner.
Standard action fare, rather slackly handled.

w *Earl Felton* d *Richard Fleischer* ph *Ernest Laszlo* m *Max Steiner*

Robert Mitchum, Gilbert Roland, Zachary Scott, Ursula Thiess

The Bandit*
Brazil 1953 119m bw
Companhia Cinematographica (Cid Leite da Silva)
original title: *O'Cangaceiro*

The leader of a gang of outlaws comes to grief after falling out with his second in command over a woman.
One of the few Brazilian films to achieve international popularity, mainly because of its memorable theme tune. The film itself looks attractive but becomes a bit of a bore.

wd *Lima Barreto* ph *Chick Fowle* m *Gabriel Migliori*

Alberto Ruschel, Milton Ribeiro, Marisa Prado

The Bandit of Sherwood Forest*
US 1946 87m Technicolor
Columbia (Leonard S. Picker, Clifford Sanforth)
Robin Hood frustrates the Regent who plans to usurp the throne from the boy king.
A lively romp through Sherwood Forest with a capable cast.

w *Wilfrid H. Pettit, Melvin Levy*, novel *Son of Robin Hood* by *Paul A. Castleton* d *George Sherman, Henry Levin* ph *Tony Gaudio, William Snyder, George Meehan* m *Hugo Friedhofer*

Cornel Wilde, Anita Louise, Edgar Buchanan, Jill Esmond, Henry Daniell, George Macready, Russell Hicks, John Abbott, Lloyd Corrigan

The Bandit of Zhobe
GB 1959 81m Technicolor
        Cinemascope
An Indian chieftain kidnaps a British major's daughter in retaliation for the death of his wife. Tinpot action melodrama in the wake of the rather better *Zarak*. Victor Mature, Anthony Newley, Anne Aubrey, Norman Wooland. Written and directed by John Gilling; for Warwick / Columbia.

The Bandit Queen
US 1950 69m bw
The daughter of murdered Spaniards in California takes revenge against violent settlers from the east. Predictable western adventure on a low budget. Barbara Britton, Willard Parker, Barton Maclane, Philip Reed, Victor Kilian, Thurston Hall. Written by Victor West and Budd Lesser; directed and produced by William Berke; for Lippert.

Bandits of Corsica: see The Corsican Brothers

Bandits of Orgosolo
Italy 1961 98m bw
Titanus
A Sardinian shepherd shelters some bandits and becomes one of them.
Rather slow character adventure which achieved some international reputation in its first release.

wd *Vittorio de Seta* m *Valentino Bucchi*

Michele Cossu, Peppeddu Cuccu, and amateur cast

Bandolero!*
US 1968 108m De Luxe Panavision
TCF (Robert L. Jacks)
In Texas, fugitive outlaw brothers run into trouble with their Mexican counterparts.
Dour and downbeat but well-staged western with emphasis on hanging and rape; an unusual mixture but smoothly assembled.

w *James Lee Barrett* d *Andrew V. McLaglen* ph *William H. Clothier* m *Jerry Goldsmith*

James Stewart, Dean Martin, Raquel Welch, George Kennedy, Will Geer, Andrew Prine

Bang the Drum Slowly
US 1973 96m Movielab
Paramount (Maurice and Lois Rosenfield)
A baseball star finds that he is dying of leukemia.
Cliché-ridden tearjerker in the modern style.

w *Mark Harris*, from his novel d *John Hancock* ph *Richard Shore* m *Stephen Lawrence*

Michael Moriarty, Robert de Niro, Vincent Gardenia, Phil Foster

AAN: Vincent Gardenia
● Video: Guild

Bang, You're Dead
GB 1954 88m bw
British Lion / Wellington (Lance Comfort)
A small boy accidentally shoots a local villain, and another man is arrested.
Singularly pointless and unattractive melodrama, a long way behind *The Window* and *The Yellow Balloon*.

w *Guy Elmes, Ernest Borneman* d *Lance Comfort* ph *Brendan J. Stafford* m *Eric Spear*

Jack Warner, Derek Farr, Veronica Hurst, Gordon Harker, Michael Medwin, Anthony Richmond, Philip Saville

Banjo on my Knee**
US 1936 95m bw
TCF (Nunnally Johnson)
In a Mississippi riverboat shanty town, a wedding night is interrupted when the groom is arrested during a brawl.
Unusual, easy-going comedy in which the stars sing and dance as well as fool around.

w *Nunnally Johnson*, novel *Harry Hamilton* d *John Cromwell* ph *Ernest Palmer* m *Arthur Lange* songs *Jimmy McHugh, Harold Adamson*

Barbara Stanwyck, Joel McCrea, Buddy Ebsen, Walter Brennan, Helen Westley, Walter Catlett, Tony Martin, Katherine de Mille

'Too complicated for any better than moderate reception.'—*Variety*

The Bank Dick**
US 1940 73m bw
Universal
GB title: *The Bank Detective*
In Lompoc, California, a ne'er-do-well accidentally stops a hold-up, is made a bank

detective, acquires deeds to a worthless mine and interferes in the production of a film. Imperfect, but probably the best Fields vehicle there is: the jokes sometimes end in mid-air, but there are delicious moments and very little padding. The character names are sometimes funnier than the script: they include Egbert Sousè (accent grave over the 'e'), J. Pinkerton Snoopington, Ogg Oggilbie and Filthy McNasty.

w Mahatma Kane Jeeves (W. C. Fields) d Eddie Cline ph Milton Krasner md Charles Previn

W. C. Fields, Franklin Pangborn, Shemp Howard, Jack Norton, Grady Sutton, Cora Witherspoon

'One of the great classics of American comedy.'—Robert Lewis Taylor

'When the man is funny he is terrific . . . but the story is makeshift, the other characters are stock types, the only pace discernible is the distance between drinks or the rhythm of the fleeting seconds it takes Fields to size up trouble coming and duck the hell out.'—Otis Ferguson

Bank Holiday*
GB 1938 86m bw
Gainsborough (Edward Black)
US title: Three on a Weekend

The lives of various people intertwine during a day out in Brighton.
Simple but effective slice-of-life comedy-drama, establishing several actors and a director. Still quite refreshing.

w Hans Wilhelm, Rodney Ackland, Roger Burford d Carol Reed ph Arthur Crabtree

Margaret Lockwood, Hugh Williams, Kathleen Harrison, Wally Patch, Rene Ray, Linden Travers, Garry Marsh, Wilfrid Lawson

The Bank Shot*
US 1974 83m De Luxe
UA / Hal Landers, Bobby Roberts

Using house-moving equipment, an escaped convict steals a whole bank.
Extended chase comedy with scenes of gleeful destruction. Acceptable for those in the mood, but a shade overdone.

w Wendell Mayes, novel Donald E. Westlake d Gower Champion ph Harry Stradling Jnr m John Morris

George C. Scott, Joanna Cassidy, Sorrell Brooke, G. Wood, Clifton James

Bannerline*
US 1951 87m bw
MGM (Henry Berman)

To comfort a dying old man, a young reporter prints a fake newspaper showing the indictment of the old man's gangster enemy. By an odd chain of events, the story becomes true.
Worthy but rather dull MGM 'B', typical of the regime of Dore Schary, boasting a pleasing small-town atmosphere and a remarkable cast of old actors.

w Charles Schnee, story Samson Raphaelson d Don Weis ph Harold Lipstein m Rudolph Kopp

Lionel Barrymore, Keefe Brasselle, Sally Forrest, Lewis Stone, Elizabeth Risdon, J. Carrol Naish, Spring Byington, Larry Keating

Banning*
US 1967 102m Techniscope
Universal (Dick Berg)

A golf pro has sporting and amorous adventures at a country club.
Tedious, complexly plotted melodrama of life among the idle rich; handling generally laboured. A showcase for the studio's young contract talent.

w James Lee d Ron Winston ph Loyal Griggs m Quincy Jones

Robert Wagner, Anjanette Comer, Jill St John, Guy Stockwell, James Farentino, Susan Clark, Howard St John, Mike Kellin, Sean Garrison, Gene Hackman

AAN: song 'The Eyes of Love' (m Quincy Jones, ly Bob Russell)

The Bar Sinister*
US 1955 87m Eastmancolor
Cinemascope
MGM (Henry Berman)
GB title: It's a Dog's Life

The rise in lifestyle of a Bowery bull terrier, as told by himself.
Tolerable whimsy, in MGM's best family manner; ten years earlier it might have been a hit.

w John Michael Hayes, story Richard Harding Davis d Herman Hoffman ph Paul Vogel m Elmer Bernstein

Edmund Gwenn, Jeff Richards, Jarma Lewis, Dean Jagger

Barabbas*
Italy / US 1962 144m Technirama
Columbia / Dino de Laurentiis

Pardoned instead of Christ, Barabbas is sentenced to the silver mines, turns Christian, and becomes a gladiator.
Overblown epic which starts with a genuine eclipse of the sun and has nowhere to go but down. The cast sparks a few moments, but it is generally a gaudy display of carnage.

w Christopher Fry, Nigel Balchin, Diego Fabbri, Ivo Perilli, novel Pär Lagerkvist d Richard Fleischer ph Aldo Tonti m Mario Nascimbene ad Mario Chiari

Anthony Quinn, Silvana Mangano, Vittorio Gassman, Ernest Borgnine, Jack Palance, Arthur Kennedy, Norman Wooland, Valentina Cortese, Harry Andrews, Katy Jurado, Michael Gwynn

'Unacceptable in its pain-preoccupation and its religiosity.'—Peter John Dyer

† The eclipse of the sun at the beginning is a real one, photographed at Nice.

● Video: RCA / Columbia

Barbarella*
France / Italy 1967 98m Technicolor
Panavision
Marianne / Dino de Laurentiis

A beautiful young 40th-century astronaut prevents the positronic ray from getting into the wrong hands.

Campy and slightly sick adventures with angels and other space people, from a highly censorable comic strip; some ingenious gadgetry and design, but not much of interest in the foreground.

w Terry Southern, book Jean-Claude Forest d Roger Vadim ph Claude Renoir pd Mario Garbuglia m Bob Crewe, Charles Fox

Jane Fonda, John Phillip Law, Anita Pallenberg, Milo O'Shea, David Hemmings, Marcel Marceau, Ugo Tognazzi, Claude Dauphin

'A leading science fiction authority has claimed that if Lewis Carroll were alive today he would inevitably have written not Alice's Adventures in Wonderland but Lolita. He might perhaps equally well have written Barbarella.'—Jack Ibberson

'A flaccid, jaded appeal to our baser appetites, always liberally doused with essence of cop-out, resulting in elucubrated, anaemic pornography.'—John Simon

● Video: CIC

The Barbarian*
US 1933 82m approx bw
MGM
GB title: A Night in Cairo

An American lady travelling in the Middle East falls for a local potentate.
Shades of The Sheik. Actually this version was first made in 1924 as The Arab, with the same leading man. Either version would seem fairly hysterical now.

w Anita Loos, Elmer Harris, play Edgar Selwyn d Sam Wood ph Harold Rosson

Ramon Novarro, Myrna Loy, Reginald Denny, C. Aubrey Smith, Louise Closser Hale, Edward Arnold

'An abrupt switch to melodrama at the halfway mark makes this a maudlin, doubtful desert melodrama.'—Variety

The Barbarian and the Geisha*
US 1958 105m Eastmancolor
Cinemascope
TCF (Eugene Frenke)

In 1856 the first US diplomat to visit Japan meets local opposition but is helped by a geisha.
Episodic semi-historical romance which scarcely suits the talents of those involved.

w Charles Grayson d John Huston ph Charles G. Clarke m Hugo Friedhofer

John Wayne, Eiko Ando, Sam Jaffe, So Yamamura

'It is saddening to think that the director of The Asphalt Jungle has gained professional freedom and international celebrity to become, at 51, yet another taskmaster who goes out in the midday sun.'—Arlene Croce

Barbarosa*
US 1981 90m Eastmancolor
ITC / Wittliff–Nelson–Busey (Paul N. Lazarus III)

An outlaw's legend grows along with his enemies.

Undercast but interestingly directed western, with more than enough elegiac qualities mixed with some nods to the old enjoyable style.

w William D. Wittliff *d* Fred Schepsi *ph* Ian Baker *m* Bruce Smeaton

Willie Nelson, Gary Busey, Isela Vega, Gilbert Roland, George Voskovec

'The most spirited and satisfying new western epic in several years.'—*New Yorker*

'More than its share of artistic merit.'—*Variety*

● *Video: Precision Video*

Barbary Coast••
US 1935 91m bw
Samuel Goldwyn

During San Francisco's gold rush days a ruthless club owner builds a lonely girl into a star attraction but cannot win her love.
Juicy melodrama tailored for its stars, but with excellent background detail, sets and lighting.

w Ben Hecht, Charles MacArthur *d* Howard Hawks *ph* Ray June *m* Alfred Newman

Edward G. Robinson, Miriam Hopkins, Joel McCrea, Walter Brennan, Frank Craven, Brian Donlevy, Donald Meek

'More than a year ago Sam Goldwyn picked Barbary Coast as a title and called in Hecht and MacArthur to write a story to fit. Result is a picture that has all it takes to get along in thoroughbred company.'—*Variety*

† David Niven made his first screen appearance as an extra.

AAN: Ray June

Barbary Coast Gent
US 1944 87m bw
MGM (Orville Dull)

A bandit from the Californian goldfields tries to go straight in San Francisco.
Star comedy drama, somewhat below par despite attractive settings and good production.

w William Lipman, Grant Garrett, Harry Ruskin *d* Roy del Ruth *ph* Charles Salerno Jnr *m* David Snell

Wallace Beery, Binnie Barnes, Frances Rafferty, Chill Wills, Ray Collins, John Carradine, Noah Beery, Morris Ankrum, Henry O'Neill, Donald Meek, Paul Hurst, Louise Beavers

Bardelys the Magnificent
US 1926 88m at 24 fps bw silent

A sixteenth-century French adventurer finally wins his fair lady. Laboured swashbuckler.
John Gilbert, Eleanor Boardman, George K. Arthur. Written by Dorothy Farnum, from the novel by Rafael Sabatini; directed by King Vidor; for MGM.

Barefaced Flatfoot•••
US 1952 7m Technicolor

Mr Magoo battles shortsightedly to save his nephew from the underworld. Archetypal Magoo cartoon. ('Didn't we meet in Heidelberg?' he murmurs to the dummy he is duelling with his umbrella.) The title is a spoof on a contemporary Columbia movie, *The Barefoot Mailman*. Designed by *John Hubley*; produced by *Stephen Bosustow*; for UPA.

Barefoot Battalion
Greece 1954 89m bw
Peter Boudoures

War orphans inhabit a derelict barge and band together to harass the Germans.
Unlikely true story, roughly dramatized and poorly produced.

w Nico Katsiotes *d* Gregg Tallas *ph* Mixalis Gaziadis *m* Mikis Theodorakis

Maria Costi, Nico Fermas, Stavros Krozos

'The world's most beautiful animal!'
The Barefoot Contessa•
US 1954 128m Technicolor
UA / Figaro (Forrest E. Johnston)

A glamorous barefoot dancer in a Spanish cabaret is turned into a Hollywood star, but her sexual frustrations lead to a tragic end.
A fascinating farrago of addled philosophy and lame wisecracks, very typical of a writer-director here not at his best, decorated by a splendid gallery of actors and some attractive settings.

wd Joseph L. Mankiewicz *ph* Jack Cardiff *m* Mario Nascimbene

Humphrey Bogart (Harry Dawes), Ava Gardner (Maria Vargas), Edmond O'Brien (Oscar Muldoon), Marius Goring (Alberto Bravano), Valentina Cortesa (Eleonora Torlato-Favrini), Rossano Brazzi (Vincenzo Torlato-Favrini), Elizabeth Sellars (Jerry), Warren Stevens (Kirk Edwards), Franco Interlenghi (Pedro), Mari Aldon (Myrna)

HARRY: 'Life, every now and then, behaves as though it had seen too many bad movies, when everything fits too well—the beginning, the middle, the end—from fade-in to fade-out.'

'This example of the Higher Lunacy must vie with *Johnny Guitar* for the silliest film of the year.'—*Gavin Lambert*

'A trash masterpiece: a Cinderella story in which the prince turns out to be impotent.'—*Pauline Kael, 1968*

AA: Edmond O'Brien
AAN: Joseph L. Mankiewicz (as writer)

The Barefoot Executive•
US 1970 96m Technicolor
Walt Disney (Bill Anderson)

A TV network discovers that its most infallible average viewer is a chimpanzee.
Quite a beguiling little farcical comedy with mild doses of satire.

w Joseph L. McEveety *d* Robert Butler *ph* Charles F. Wheeler *m* Robert F. Brunner

Kurt Russell, Harry Morgan, Joe Flynn, Wally Cox, Heather North, Alan Hewitt, Hayden Rorke

'Break the rules! Make love! Fall over laughing!'
Barefoot in the Park••
US 1967 109m Technicolor
Paramount / Hal B. Wallis

A pair of New York newlyweds rent a cold water flat at the top of a liftless building, and manage to marry the bride's mother to an eccentric neighbour.
Breezy but overlong adaptation of a stage play which succeeded through audience response to its one-liners, which on the screen sometimes fall flat. The people are nice, though.

w Neil Simon, from his play *d* Gene Saks *ph* Joseph La Shelle *m* Neal Hefti

Robert Redford (Paul Bratter), Jane Fonda (Corie Bratter), *Mildred Natwick* (Ethel Banks), *Charles Boyer* (Victor Velasco), Herb Edelman (Harry Pepper), Mabel Albertson (Aunt Harriet), Fritz Feld (restaurant owner)

ETHEL: 'Make him feel important. If you do that, you'll have a happy and wonderful marriage—like two out of every ten couples.'

ETHEL: 'I feel like we've died and gone to heaven—only we had to climb up.'

AAN: Mildred Natwick

● *Video: CIC*

The Barefoot Mailman
US 1951 82m Supercinecolor
Columbia (Robert Cohn)

In 19th-century Florida, the mailman is joined by a confidence trickster who later has a change of heart.
Inept comedy adventure which never really gets started.

w James Gunn, Francis Swann, *novel* Theodore Pratt *d* Earl McEvoy *ph* Ellis W. Carter *m* George Duning

Robert Cummings, Jerome Courtland, Terry Moore, John Russell, Will Geer, Arthur Shields, Trevor Bardette

† This is the title parodied by the Magoo cartoon *Barefaced Flatfoot*.

The Bargee•
GB 1964 106m Techniscope
AB / Galton–Simpson (W. A. Whitaker)

A canal barge Casanova is trapped into marriage.
The long-awaited comedy which was supposed to make a film star out of TV's Young Steptoe turned out to be rough and vulgar but not very funny.

w Ray Galton, Alan Simpson *d* Duncan Wood *ph* Harry Waxman *m* Frank Cordell

Harry H. Corbett, Ronnie Barker, Hugh Griffith, Eric Sykes, Julia Foster, Miriam Karlin, Eric Barker, Derek Nimmo, Norman Bird, Richard Briers

The Barkleys of Broadway•
US 1949 109m Technicolor
MGM (Arthur Freed)

A quarrelling couple of musical comedy stars split up, and she becomes a serious actress.

A rather flat and unattractive reunion for a famous pair, with a witless script, poorish numbers and very little style. The compensations are minor.

w Adolph Green, Betty Comden d Charles Walters ph Harry Stradling *songs* Harry Warren, Ira Gershwin

Fred Astaire, Ginger Rogers, Oscar Levant, Jacques François, Billie Burke

AAN: Harry Stradling

† Ginger Rogers was in fact second choice; Judy Garland was cast but withdrew through illness.

†† Songs include: 'They Can't Take That Away from Me', 'Shoes with Wings On', 'My One and Only Highland Fling', 'Swing Trot', 'Manhattan Downbeat', 'You'd be So Hard to Replace', 'A Weekend in the Country', 'Sabre Dance'.

● *Video: MGM / UA*

Barnacle Bill
US 1941 90m bw
MGM (Milton Bren)

A fishing boat skipper gets romantic in the hope of financing his enterprises.
Adequate waterfront comedy on *Min and Bill* lines, consolidating a popular star teaming.

w Jack Jevne, Hugo Butler d Richard Thorpe ph Clyde de Vinna m Bronislau Kaper

Wallace Beery, Marjorie Main, Leo Carrillo, Virginia Weidler, Donald Meek, Barton Maclaine, Connie Gilchrist, Sara Haden

Barnacle Bill*
GB 1957 87m bw
Ealing (Michael Balcon)
US title: *All at Sea*

The last of a long line of sailors suffers from seasickness, and takes command of a decaying Victorian pier at an English seaside resort.
Quite an amusing comedy which had the misfortune to come at the tag-end of the Ealing classics and so seemed too mild and predictable. Perhaps it was a little staid.

w T. E. B. Clarke d Charles Frend ph Douglas Slocombe m John Addison

Alec Guinness, Irene Browne, Percy Herbert, Harold Goodwin, Maurice Denham, George Rose, Lionel Jeffries, Victor Maddern

Le Baron Fantôme*
France 1943 100m bw
Consortium de Productions de Films (Robert Florat)
GB title: *The Phantom Baron*

In the early 19th-century, the disappearance of a nobleman causes problems for his heirs.
Macabre fairy tale with effective scenes which seem to relate to Cocteau's later fantasies; the film as a whole is less effective.

wd Serge de Poligny *dialogue* Jean Cocteau ph Roger Hubert m Louis Beydts

Jany Holt, Odette Joyeux, Alain Cuny, Gabrielle Dorziat

Baron Münchhausen*
Czechoslovakia 1962 81m Agfacolor
Ceskoslovensky Film
original title: *Baron Prasil*

An astronaut finds on the moon the famous liar Baron Münchhausen, who takes him back to earth and a variety of exaggerated adventures.
Amusing variation on the old stories, using live action against deliberately artificial backgrounds.

wd Karel Zeman, from the novel by Gottfried Burger and the illustrations by Gustave Doré ph Jiri Tarantik m Zdenek Liska

Milos Kopecky, Rudolf Jelinek, Jana Becjchova

The Baron of Arizona
US 1950 85m bw
Lippert (Carl Hittleman)

In the 19th century a clerk tries to claim the whole of Arizona by false land grants.
Initially appealing but basically rather feeble tall tale, ineffectively worked out and decidedly undernourished as a production.

wd Samuel Fuller ph James Wong Howe m Paul Dunlap

Vincent Price, Ellen Drew, Beulah Bondi, Vladimir Sokoloff, Reed Hadley, Robert Barrat

The Baroness and the Butler
US 1938 75m bw
TCF (Raymond Griffith)

The Hungarian prime minister's butler is loved by a princess.
Thin mittel-European romantic star whimsy.

w Sam Hellman, Lamar Trotti, Kathryn Scola, play The Lady Has a Heart by Ladislaus Bus-Fekete d Walter Lang ph Arthur Miller md Louis Silvers

William Powell, Annabella, Henry Stephenson, Nigel Bruce, Helen Westley, Joseph Schildkraut, J. Edward Bromberg, Lynn Bari

Barquero!
US 1970 114m De Luxe
Aubrey Schenck (Hal Klein)

A western ferryman is taken prisoner by bandits but turns the tables.
Long, violent, rather uninteresting western in the Spanish manner.

w George Schenck, William Marks d Gordon Douglas ph Jerry Finnermann m Dominic Frontiere

Lee Van Cleef, Forrest Tucker, Warren Oates, Kerwin Mathews, Mariette Hartley, Brad Weston, John Davis Chandler

'When poets love, heaven and earth fall back to watch!'

The Barretts of Wimpole Street**
US 1934 109m bw
MGM (Irving Thalberg)
TV title: *Forbidden Alliance*

Invalid Elizabeth Barrett plans to marry poet Robert Browning, against her tyrannical father's wishes.
Claustrophobic but well-acted adaptation of a stage play which has become more forceful than history. Stilted now, but still better than the remake.

w Ernst Vajda, Claudine West, Donald Ogden Stewart, *play* Rudolf Besier d Sidney Franklin ph William Daniels m Herbert Stothart

Norma Shearer (Elizabeth Barrett), Fredric March (Robert Browning), *Charles Laughton* (Edward Moulton-Barrett), Maureen O'Sullivan (Henrietta), Katherine Alexander (Arabel), Una O'Connor (Wilson), Ralph Forbes (Captain Surtees-Cook), Ian Wolfe (Harry Bevan)

'Box office for all its celluloid lethargy . . . truly an actor's picture, with long speeches and verbose philosophical observations.'—*Variety*

AAN: best picture; Norma Shearer

The Barretts of Wimpole Street
GB 1956 105m Metrocolor
Cinemascope
MGM (Sam Zimbalist)

Dreadful, miscast remake of the above, with emphasis on the Freudian father-daughter relationship. An unattractive and boring film.

w John Dighton d Sidney Franklin ph Frederick A. Young m Bronislau Kaper

Jennifer Jones, Bill Travers, John Gielgud, Virginia McKenna

Barricade
US 1939 71m bw
TCF (Edward Kaufman)

A newsman and a girl with a past fight Mongolian bandits in North China.
A bagful of clichés which does not quite add up to entertainment.

w Granville Walker d Gregory Ratoff ph Karl Freund m David Buttolph

Warner Baxter, Alice Faye, Charles Winninger, Arthur Treacher, Keye Luke, Willie Fung, Doris Lloyd

'Inadequate and confusing . . . it was launched as an A, but winds up as a B that will have to groove generally in the supporting spots.'—*Variety*

Barricade
US 1949 75m Technicolor
Warner (Saul Elkins)

A tough mine-owner who runs a camp miles from civilization meets his come-uppance when three strangers are forced to accept his hospitality.
Rough western only notable as an (almost) scene-for-scene steal from *The Sea Wolf*: a text-book adaptation.

w William Sackheim d Peter Godfrey ph Carl Guthrie m William Lava

Raymond Massey, Dane Clark, Ruth Roman, Robert Douglas, Morgan Farley

The Barrier

US 1926 79m at 24 fps bw silent

A brutal sea captain tries to prevent his
protégé's marriage. Brooding melodrama
climaxing in an Alaskan storm. Lionel
Barrymore (in his first film for the studio
where he spent the rest of his career), Henry
B. Walthall, Marceline Day, Norman Kerry.
Written by Rex Beach; directed by George
Hill; for MGM.

The Barrier

US 1937 90m bw

A gold rush prospector kidnaps a child and
brings her up in the belief that she is a
half-breed. Lyceum-like melodrama against
spectacular natural settings; somehow not of
interest. Leo Carrillo, Jean Parker, Robert
Barrat, James Ellison, Otto Kruger, Andy
Clyde, Addison Richards, Sara Haden.
Written by Bernard Schubert, Mordaunt
Shairp, Harrison Jacobs, from the novel by
Rex Beach; directed by Lesley Selander; for
Harry Sherman (Paramount).

Barry Lyndon**

GB 1975 187m Eastmancolor
Warner / Hawk / Peregrine (Stanley
    Kubrick)

Adventures of an 18th-century Irish gentleman
of fortune.
A curiously cold-hearted enterprise, like an art
gallery in which the backgrounds are sketched
in loving detail and the human figures totally
neglected; there is much to enjoy, but script
and acting are variable to say the least, and
the point of it all is obscure, as it certainly
does not tell a rattling good story.

wd *Stanley Kubrick,* novel W. M. Thackeray
ph John Alcott md Leonard Rosenman
pd Ken Adam

Ryan O'Neal, Marisa Berenson, Patrick
Magee, Hardy Kruger, Steven Berkoff, Gay
Hamilton, Marie Kean, Murray Melvin,
André Morell, Leonard Rossiter, Philip Stone
narrator Michael Hordern
'The motion picture equivalent of one of
these very large, very expensive, very elegant
and very dull books that exist solely to be seen
on coffee tables.'—*Charles Champlin*
'Watching the movie is like looking at
illustrations for a work that has not been
supplied.'—*John Simon*
'All art and no matter: a series of still
pictures which will please the retina while
denying our hunger for drama. And far from
re-creating another century, it more accurately
embalms it.'—*Michael Billington, Illustrated
London News*
AA: John Alcott; Leonard Rosenman
AAN: best picture; Stanley Kubrick (as
writer); Stanley Kubrick (as director)
● *Video: Warner*

Bartleby*

GB 1970 79m Eastmancolor
Pantheon (Rodney Carr-Smith)

A young clerk gradually refuses to take part in
life.

A non-action film from an independent
source, praiseworthy but overlong and fairly
lacking in any kind of appeal except to literary
connoisseurs.

w Anthony Friedmann, Rodney Carr-Smith,
story Herman Melville d Anthony
Friedmann ph Ian Wilson m Roger Webb
Paul Scofield, John McEnery, Thorley
Walters, Colin Jeavons

Les Bas-fonds*

France 1936 92m bw
Albatros (Alexander Kamenka)
aka: *The Lower Depths*

A clash of temperaments flares up between
derelicts in a dosshouse.
Uneven transposition of a famous work, with
patches of good acting.

w Jean Renoir, Charles Spaak and others,
play Maxim Gorky d *Jean Renoir* ph Jean
Bachelet m Jean Wiener
Jean Gabin, Louis Jouvet, Vladimir Sokoloff,
Robert Le Vigan, Suzy Prim

The Bat

US 1959 78m bw
AA / Liberty (C. J. Tevlin)

A lady mystery writer rents a spooky old
house and finds herself and her guests at the
mercy of a maniac in search of hidden loot.
Poor remake of a standard twenties stage
thriller; everyone chews the scenery.

wd *Crane Wilbur,* play Mary Roberts
Rinehart ph Joseph Biroc m Louis Forbes
Vincent Price, Agnes Moorehead, Gavin
Gordon, John Sutton, Lenita Lane, Darla
Hood
● *Video: Rank*

The Bat Whispers**

US 1930 82m bw
UA / Roland West

Classic early sound version of *The Bat* (qv) by
the director of the 1926 silent version.
Excellent use of camera, sets, and unusual
models.

wd *Roland West* ph Ray June, Robert Planck
Chester Morris, Una Merkel, Chancer Ward,
Grayce Hampton, Maude Eburne, Spencer
Charters, Gustav Von Seyffertitz
† Originally released in a 'wide screen'
process.
†† West had also made a silent version in
1926.

'The story America will never forget!'
Bataan*

US 1943 114m bw
MGM (Irving Starr)

Thirteen soldiers holding a bridge against the
Japanese die one by one.
Uncredited remake of *The Lost Patrol* (qv)
transposed to the Pacific war, with stereotyped
characters and much flagwaving. Very dated,
but a big box office film of its time, despite its
studio jungles.

w Robert D. Andrews d Tay Garnett
ph Sidney Wagner m Bronislau Kaper
Robert Taylor, George Murphy, Thomas
Mitchell, Lloyd Nolan, Lee Bowman, Robert
Walker, Desi Arnaz, Barry Nelson, Philip
Terry
'Naïve, coarse-grained, primitive, honest,
accomplished and true.'—*James Agee*

La Bataille du Rail**

France 1945 87m bw
CGCF

Reconstructions of heroic resistance work by
the French railwaymen during World War II.
Reasonably compulsive documentary fiction
which was plainly more inspiring at the time
than it seems now.

wd *René Clément* ph Henri Alekan m Yves
Baudrier
Salina, Daurand, Lozach, Tony Laurent

Bathing Beauty

US 1944 101m Technicolor
MGM (Jack Cummings)

A songwriter plans to retire and settle down,
but his publisher schemes to set his fiancée
against him.
Witless, artificial aqua-musical, with plenty of
unpersuasive high jinks but no real style
despite a capable cast.

w Dorothy Kingsley, Allen Boretz, Frank
Waldman d George Sidney ph Harry
Stradling m Johnny Green ch John Murray
Anderson
Esther Williams, Red Skelton, Basil
Rathbone, Keenan Wynn, Ethel Smith,
Xavier Cugat, Bill Goodwin
Songs include 'Faculty Row'; 'Tico Tico';
'Echo of a Serenade'; 'I Cried for You'; 'Bim
Bam Boom'; 'By the Waters of Minnetonka';
'Magic Is the Moonlight'; 'I've Got a
Problem'; 'I'll Take the High Note'
'I could not resist the wish that MGM had
topped its aquatic climax—a huge pool full of
girls, fountains and spouts of flame—by
suddenly draining the tank and ending the
show with the entire company writhing like
goldfish on a rug.'—*James Agee*

Batman*

US 1966 105m De Luxe
TCF / Greenlawn / National Periodical
    Publications (William Dozier)

The cloaked avenger saves an important
executive from the clutches of four of the
world's most notorious criminals.
Glossy feature version of the old and new
serials about the comic strip hero who scurries
around in his Batmobile making sure that
justice is done. The scriptwriter's invention
unfortunately flags halfway, so that despite a
fairly sharp production the result is more
childish than camp.

w Lorenzo Semple Jnr d Leslie Martinson
ph Howard Schwarz m Nelson Riddle
Adam West, Burt Ward, Cesar Romero,
Frank Gorshin, Burgess Meredith, Lee
Meriwether, Alan Napier, Neil Hamilton

The Battle*
France 1934 85m bw
Gaumont (Leon Garganoff)
English language version aka: *Thunder in the East, Hara Kiri*

A Japanese aristocrat urges his wife to befriend an English naval attaché and steal secrets from him; she does, and falls in love. Stagey but discreet melodrama of the old school, quite well made and acted.

w Nicolas Farkas, Bernard Zimmer, Robert Stevenson, *novel* Claude Farrère d Nicolas Farkas ph Roger Hubert

Charles Boyer, Merle Oberon, John Loder, Betty Stockfield, Miles Mander

The Battle at Apache Pass
US 1952 85m Technicolor

Cochise negotiates peace with the whites, but Geronimo won't agree. Standard cavalry-versus-Indians western, with Jeff Chandler repeating his famous Cochise impersonation. John Lund, Susan Cabot, Bruce Cowling, Richard Egan. Written by Gerald Drayson Adams; directed by George Sherman; for U-I.

The Battle at Bloody Beach
US 1961 80m bw Cinemascope
TCF / API (Richard Maibaum)
GB title: *Battle on the Beach*

Guerrillas fight Japs in the Philippines. Tedious war melodrama with interludes for an eternal triangle.

w Richard Maibaum, Willard Willingham d Herbert Coleman ph Kenneth Peach m Henry Vars

Audie Murphy, Gary Crosby, Dolores Michaels, Alejandro Rey

Battle beneath the Earth*
GB 1967 92m Technicolor
MGM / Reynolds / Vetter (Charles Reynolds)

Enemy agents burrow under the US by means of a giant laser.
Agreeable schoolboy science fiction with fair special effects.

w L. Z. Hargeaves d Montgomery Tully ph Kenneth Talbot m Ken Jones sp Tom Howard

Kerwin Mathews, Vivienne Ventura, Robert Ayres, Peter Arne, Martin Benson

Battle beyond the Stars*
US 1980 104m Metrocolor
New World / Roger Corman (Ed Carlin)

A small planet hires help to repel invaders. Impertinent and sometimes amusing space fiction rip-off of *Seven Samurai*, with plenty of in-jokes and quite pleasant special effects.

w John Sayles d Jimmy T. Murakami ph Daniel Lacambre m James Horner ad Jim Cameron, Charles Breen

Richard Thomas, Robert Vaughn, John Saxon, George Peppard, Sam Jaffe, Morgan Woodward, Darlanne Fluegel, Sybil Danning

● *Video: Warner*

Battle Circus
US 1952 90m bw
MGM (Pandro S. Berman)

A patriotic nurse and a disillusioned major fall in love at a mobile army hospital in Korea. A flat, studio-bound potboiler with miscast stars, bound to provoke hilarity now as a serious version of *M*A*S*H*.

wd Richard Brooks ph John Alton m Lennie Hayton

Humphrey Bogart, June Allyson, Keenan Wynn, Robert Keith, William Campbell

'It is disappointing that Brooks, whose early work . . . suggested considerable promise, should have descended to such a glib, uninteresting piece of film-making.'—*MFB*

Battle Cry
US 1954 148m Warnercolor
Cinemascope
Warner (producer not credited)

During World War II, marines endure tough training before combat in Saipan; their sex lives come a close second to the war. Interminable cheapie epic with both eyes on the box office: the cast salvages an odd moment or two, but violence of all kinds is the key to the entertainment.

w Leon Uris, from his novel d Raoul Walsh ph Sid Hickox m Max Steiner

Van Heflin, Aldo Ray, Mona Freeman, Dorothy Malone, Raymond Massey, Nancy Olson, James Whitmore, Tab Hunter, Anne Francis, William Campbell

AAN: Max Steiner

Battle for Music*
GB 1943 87m bw
Strand Films (Donald Taylor)

The story of the wartime ups and downs of the London Philharmonic Orchestra. Not many films feature a classical orchestra, and this simple tribute, a mediocre production at best, has considerable historical interest.

w St John L. Clowes d Donald Taylor

Hay Petrie, Joss Ambler, Charles Carson, Jack Hylton. J. B. Priestley, Eileen Joyce, Moiseiwitch, Sir Adrian Boult, Sir Malcolm Sargent

Battle for the Planet of the Apes
US 1973 86m De Luxe Panavision
TCF / APJAC (Frank Capra Jnr)

Following a nuclear war, apes are the only surviving leaders of society, but begin to fight among themselves.
Fifth and last in an increasingly confusing chronology, this is at least more thoughtful than violent.

w John William Corrington, Joyce Hooper Corrington d J. Lee Thompson ph Richard H. Kline m Leonard Rosenman make-up John Chambers

Roddy McDowall, Claude Akins, John Huston, Natalie Trundy, Severn Darden, Lew Ayres, Paul Williams

† See *Planet of the Apes*.

● *Video: CBS / Fox*

Battle Hymn
US 1957 108m Technicolor
Cinemascope
U-I (Ross Hunter)

An American preacher with a guilt complex volunteers to help the South Koreans and after many adventures founds an orphanage. Earnest, somnolent biopic of one Dean Hess; its mixture of drama, comedy, religion and war heroics is indigestible despite professional handling.

w Charles Grayson, Vincent B. Evans d Douglas Sirk ph Russell Metty m Frank Skinner

Rock Hudson, Anna Kashfi, Dan Duryea, Don Defore, Martha Hyer, Jock Mahoney, James Edwards, Carl Benton Reid

'The film seems to infer that heroic self-sacrifice, a little homely Eastern philosophy and a capacity for combining battle experience with an awareness of spiritual values are enough to overcome all emergencies.'—*John Gillett*

The Battle of Algiers*
Algeria / Italy 1965 135m bw
Casbah / Igor (Antonio Musi, Yacef Saadi)
original title: *La Battaglia di Algeri*

In 1954 Algiers, an ex-convict joins the terrorists in rebellion against the French government.
Politically oriented reconstruction of a bitter period of French colonial history, made better propaganda by its wealth of effective detail.

w Franco Solinas d Gillo Pontecorvo ph Marcello Gatti m Ennio Morricone, Gillo Pontecorvo

Brahim Haggiag, Jean Martin, Yacef Saadi, Tommaso Neri

AAN: best foreign film; Franco Solinas; Gillo Pontecorvo (as director)

● *Video: Capstan*

Battle of Britain*
GB 1969 131m Technicolor
Panavision
UA / Spitfire (Harry Saltzman, Ben Fisz)

Summer 1940: England defends itself against aerial onslaught.
Plodding attempt to cover an historic event from too many angles and with too many guest stars, all indistinguishable from each other when masked in the cockpit during the repetitive and interminable dogfight sequences. On the ground, things are even duller.

w James Kennaway, Wilfrid Greatorex d Guy Hamilton ph Frederick A. Young m William Walton, Ron Goodwin

Laurence Olivier (as Dowding), Robert Shaw, Michael Caine, Christopher Plummer, Kenneth More, Susannah York, Trevor Howard, Ralph Richardson, Patrick Wymark, Curt Jurgens, Michael Redgrave, Nigel Patrick, Robert Flemyng, Edward Fox

● *Video: Warner*

Battle of Broadway
US 1938 84m bw

Two American legionnaires at a New York convention try to break up the infatuation of their boss's son with a showgirl. Amiably rowdy Flagg-and-Quirt imitation. Victor McLaglen, Brian Donlevy, Gypsy Rose Lee, Raymond Walburn, Lynn Bari, Jane Darwell, Hattie McDaniel. Written by Lou Breslow and John Patrick; directed by George Marshall; for TCF. 'Flagg and Quirt shenanigans . . . rowdy, good-natured fun.'—*Variety*

The Battle of Neretva
Yugoslavia 1970 106m in dubbed version colour Cinemascope

In 1943, Yugoslav partisans resist German and Italian invaders. War spectacular with international cast; despite brilliant handling of the climaxes it didn't travel. Yul Brynner, Orson Welles, Hardy Kruger, Franco Nero. Written by Ugo Pirro and others; directed by Veljko Bulajic; for Jadran-Bosna.

The Battle of Paris
US 1929 71m bw
Paramount

A lady music seller teams up with a pickpocket and falls for an American artist.
Primitive sound musical notable chiefly for its cast.
w Gene Markey *d* Robert Florey *ph* Bill Steiner *songs* Cole Porter

Gertrude Lawrence, Charles Ruggles, Walter Petrie, Arthur Treacher, Gladys du Bois

The Battle of Rogue River
US 1954 71m Technicolor

A disciplinarian major at a western fort discovers that his friend is fanning hatred between Indians and whites, for personal reasons. Tatty western with little action, and that very lame. George Montgomery, Richard Denning, Martha Hyer, John Crawford. Written by Douglas Heyes; directed by William Castle; for Columbia.

Battle of the Bulge**
US 1965 167m Technicolor Ultra Panavision
Warner / United States Pictures (Sidney Harmon, Milton Sperling, Philip Yordan)

In December 1944, the Allies take longer than expected to win a land battle in the Ardennes because of a crack Nazi Panzer commander. Bloody and unbowed war spectacle, quite literate and handsome but deafeningly noisy and with emphasis on strategy rather than character.
w Philip Yordan, Milton Sperling, John Melson *d* Ken Annakin *ph* Jack Hildyard *m* Benjamin Frankel

Henry Fonda, Robert Shaw, Robert Ryan, Telly Savalas, Dana Andrews, George Montgomery, Ty Hardin, Pier Angeli, Barbara Werle, Charles Bronson, James MacArthur, Werner Peters
● *Video: Warner*

The Battle of the Century**
US 1927 20m bw silent

The manager of an unsuccessful boxer accidentally starts a marathon pie fight. The first reel is lost, but the pie sequence is what matters, being one of the most celebrated pieces of slapstick in cinema history. Laurel and Hardy, Eugene Pallette. Written by Hal Roach and H. M. Walker; directed by Clyde Bruckman; for Hal Roach.

Battle of the Coral Sea
US 1959 85m bw

During World War II a submarine commander, sent to photograph the Japanese fleet, is captured but escapes. Routine, unconvincing war heroics. Cliff Robertson, Gia Scala, Patricia Cutts. Written by Dan Ullman and Stephen Kandel; directed by Paul Wendkos; for Charles H. Schneer / Columbia.

The Battle of the River Plate*
GB 1956 119m Technicolor Vistavision
Rank / Powell and Pressburger
US title: *Pursuit of the Graf Spee*

Semi-documentary account of the 1939 trapping of the German pocket battleship *Graf Spee* in Montevideo Harbour, and of her subsequent scuttling.
A sympathetic view of a German hero, Commander Langsdorff (not unexpected from these producers) is the most notable feature of this disappointingly patchy and studio-bound war epic, with too many actors in ill-defined bit parts, too undisciplined a storyline, and too confusing scenes of battle.
wd Michael Powell, Emeric Pressburger *ph* Christopher Challis *m* Brian Easdale

John Gregson, Anthony Quayle, Peter Finch, Bernard Lee, Ian Hunter, Jack Gwillim, Lionel Murton, Anthony Bushell, Peter Illing
'It is difficult to understand how English film-makers can have done thus badly with material so apt to their gifts.'—*Stanley Kauffmann*
● Video: Rank

The Battle of the Sexes*
GB 1960 83m bw
Prometheus (Monja Danischewsky)

A lady efficiency expert upsets the even tenor of life at an Edinburgh tweed manufactory, and the chief accountant plans to eliminate her.
Sub-Ealing black comedy which tends to misfire despite effort all round.
w Monja Danischewsky, from James Thurber's story The Catbird Seat *d* Charles Crichton *ph* Freddie Francis *m* Stanley Black

Peter Sellers, Constance Cummings, Robert Morley, Jameson Clark, Moultrie Kelsall, Alex Mackenzie, Roddy McMillan, Donald Pleasance, Ernest Thesiger

The Battle of the V1
GB 1958 109m bw
Maynard–Sewell (George Maynard)
US titles: *Unseen Heroes; Missiles from Hell*

Polish patriots sabotage the German rocket installation at Peenemunde.
Effective though schoolboyish war adventure shot on a low budget: story development reasonably brisk though predictable.
w Jack Hanley, Eryk Wlodek, *book* Bernard Newman *d* Vernon Sewell *ph* Basil Emmott *m* Robert Sharples

Michael Rennie, Patricia Medina, Milly Vitale, David Knight, Esmond Knight, Christopher Lee

The Battle of the Villa Fiorita
GB 1964 111m Technicolor Panavision
Warner (Delmer Daves)
US title: *Affair at the Villa Fiorita*

Two children aim to break up their mother's romance with an Italian concert pianist. Quite lively, old-fashioned romantic comedy-drama largely set in a splendid Mediterranean villa; happy ending never in doubt.
wd Delmer Daves, *novel* Rumer Godden *ph* Oswald Morris *m* Mischa Spoliansky

Maureen O'Hara, Rossano Brazzi, Richard Todd, Phyllis Calvert, Olivia Hussey, Martin Stephens, Elizabeth Dear

Battle Stations
US 1956 81m bw

Life on an aircraft carrier as seen by the padre. Cliché-strewn, mini-budgeted war thriller. John Lund, William Bendix, Keefe Brasselle, Richard Boone. Written by Crane Wilbur; directed by Lewis Seiler; for Columbia.

Battle Taxi
US 1954 82m bw

A newcomer to the helicopter rescue service in Korea resents his non-combatant status, but becomes a hero. The story takes second place to one damned rescue after another in this lively but overlong second feature. Sterling Hayden, Arthur Franz, Marshall Thompson. Written by Malvin Wald; directed by Herbert L. Strock; for Ivan Tors / UA.

Battle Zone
US 1952 81m bw

Two official war photographers in Korea fall out over a girl. Very conventional war programmer. John Hodiak, Stephen McNally, Linda Christian, Martin Milner, Dave Willcock. Written by Steve Fisher; directed by Lesley Selander; for Walter Wanger / Allied Artists.

'The guts! The girls! The glory! of a lot of wonderful guys!'

Battleground*
US 1949 118m bw
MGM (Dore Schary)

How a group of American soldiers in 1944 endured the Battle of the Bulge.
Enormously successful at the box office, this studio-bound production now seems stilted and unpersuasive, despite some good writing and direction.

w Robert Pirosh *d* William Wellman *ph* Paul C. Vogel *m* Lennie Hayton

Van Johnson, John Hodiak, Ricardo Montalban, George Murphy, Marshall Thompson, Jerome Courtland, Don Taylor, Bruce Cowling, James Whitmore, Douglas Fowley, Leon Ames
  'Engrossingly well done.'—*Richard Mallett, Punch*

AA: Robert Pirosh; Paul C. Vogel
AAN: best picture; William Wellman; James Whitmore

Battles of Chief Pontiac
US 1953 75m bw
In the mid-18th century, peace talks with the Detroit Indians are sabotaged. Slightly unusual but undistinguished slice of western history. Lon Chaney Jnr, Lex Barker, Helen Westcott, Barry Kroeger, Roy Roberts. Written by Jack de Witt; directed by Felix E. Feist; for Jack Broder.

The Battleship Potemkin****
USSR 1925 75m approx (16 fps) silent; sound version 65m
Goskino
original title: *Bronenosets Potemkin*
A partly fictitious account of the mutiny at Odessa, an episode in the 1905 revolution. (The film was made as part of the 20th anniversary celebrations.)
A textbook cinema classic, and masterpiece of creative editing, especially in the famous Odessa Steps sequence in which innocent civilians are mown down in the bloodshed; the happenings of a minute are drawn into five by frenzied cross-cutting. The film contains 1,300 separate shots, and was judged the best film ever made in 1948 and 1958 by a panel of international judges.
wd Sergei Eisenstein *ph* Edouard Tissé, V. Popov
A. Antonov, Grigori Alexandrov, Vladimir Barsky, Levshin

Battling Butler*
US 1926 68m approx (24 fps) bw silent
MGM (Joseph M. Schenck)
A young millionaire pretends to be a boxer in order to win a sweetheart.
Middling star comedy.
w Al Boasberg, Charles Smith, Paul Gerard Smith, Lex Neal *d* Buster Keaton *ph* J. Devereux Jennings, Bert Haines
Buster Keaton, Sally O'Neil

The Bawdy Adventures of Tom Jones
GB 1976 94m Technicolor
Universal / Robert Sadoff
See *Tom Jones*, of which this is a musical version.
Not quite as bad as one would expect, but not up to the original.
w Jeremy Lloyd, *play* Don McPherson *songs* Paul Holden *d* Cliff Owen *ph* Douglas Slocombe *m* Ron Grainer

Nicky Henson, Trevor Howard, Terry-Thomas, Arthur Lowe, Georgia Brown, Joan Collins, William Mervyn, Murray Melvin, Geraldine McEwan, Michael Bates, James Hayter, Isabel Dean, Gladys Henson
  'A cheap, crude, sexed-up rehash with only three actual musical numbers . . . more boring than bawdy.'—*Kevin Thomas, Los Angeles Times*

Baxter*
GB 1972 100m Technicolor
(EMI) Performing Arts (Arthur Lewis)
An American son of divorced parents comes to London with his mother, meets tragedy in the shape of a friend's death, and responds to treatment for a speech defect.
Slight, appealing case history of a maladjusted 12-year-old; a rather unnecessarily uncommercial slice of life with no easy solution offered.
w Reginald Rose *d* Lionel Jeffries *ph* Geoffrey Unsworth *m* Michael J. Lewis
Patricia Neal (as the therapist), Scott Jacoby, Britt Ekland, Jean-Pierre Cassel, Lynn Carlin, Paul Eddington

The Bay of St Michel
GB 1963 73m bw
Commandos return to Normandy to seek hidden Nazi loot. Uninspired hokum programmer. Keenan Wynn, Mai Zetterling, Ronald Howard, Rona Anderson, Trader Faulkner, Edward Underdown. Written by Christopher David; produced and directed by John Ainsworth; for Trionyx / Rank.

Be Big*
US 1931 20m bw
Ollie feigns illness to avoid a trip with his wife, but Stan's help proves disastrous. Comedy warm-up for *Sons of the Desert*; Ollie spends most of the second reel trying to rid himself of a tight boot. Laurel and Hardy, Anita Garvin, Isabelle Keith. Written by H. M. Walker; directed by James Parrott; for Hal Roach.

Beach Party*
US 1963 104m Pathecolor Panavision
AIP / Alta Vista (James H. Nicholson)
An anthropologist sets up house on a California beach to study the mating habits of young people but becomes personally involved when one of them falls for him.
Vaguely satirical pop musical with relaxed performances; quite tolerable in itself, it started an excruciating trend.
w Lou Rusoff *d* William Asher *ph* Kay Norton *m* Les Baxter
Robert Cummings, Dorothy Malone, Annette Funicello, Frankie Avalon, Vincent Price, Harvey Lembeck, Morey Amsterdam, Jody McCrea

Beach Red*
US 1967 105m Technicolor
UA / Theodora (Cornel Wilde)
In 1943, American assault craft take a Jap-held Pacific island.

Brutal, pacifist war film, simply and clearly portrayed but not exactly entertaining.
w Clint Johnston, Donald A. Peters, Jefferson Pascal *d* Cornel Wilde *ph* Cecil R. Cooney *m* Antonio Buenaventura
Cornel Wilde, Rip Torn, Burr de Benning, Jean Wallace

The Beachcomber*
GB 1954 90m Technicolor
GFD / London Independent (William MacQuitty)
An alcoholic ne'er-do-well in the Dutch East Indies reforms after an unexpected adventure with a lady missionary.
Styleless remake of *Vessel of Wrath* (qv); the acting just about holds the interest, but all other contributions are flat.
w Sydney Box, from Somerset Maugham's story *d* Muriel Box *ph* Reg Wyer *m* Francis Chagrin
Robert Newton, Glynis Johns, Donald Sinden, Paul Rogers, Donald Pleasence, Walter Crisham, Michael Hordern, Ronald Lewis

Beachhead
US 1953 90m print by Technicolor
American marines land on a Pacific island to bring back a planter who has supplied information. World War II jungle thriller, not too badly done. Tony Curtis, Frank Lovejoy, Mary Murphy, Eduard Franz. Written by Richard Alan Simmons; directed by Stuart Heisler; for Aubrey Schenck / UA.

Be Mine Tonight
GB 1933 78m bw
A harassed opera star flees for quiet to a small town. Pleasing minor musical with first rate talent. Jan Kiepura, Sonnie Hale, Edmund Gwenn, Magda Schneider, Athene Seyler, Betty Chester, Aubrey Mather. Written by J. O. C. Orton; directed by Anatole Litvak; for Gaumont British. (Reproduced from a German film in which Kiepura and Schneider also appeared.)

Bear Country see The Living Desert

Bear Island
GB / Canada 1979 118m colour Panavision
Columbia / Bear Island / Selkirk (Peter Snell)
Meteorological experts on an Arctic island are menaced by neo-Nazis.
Highly implausible adventure yarn, indifferently presented.
w David Butler, Don Sharp, *novel* Alistair MacLean *d* Don Sharp *ph* Alan Hume *m* Robert Farnon
Vanessa Redgrave, Donald Sutherland, Richard Widmark, Christopher Lee, Barbara Parkins, Lloyd Bridges

● Video: RCA / Columbia

The Bears and I
US 1974 89m Technicolor
Walt Disney (Winston Hibler)

An army veteran goes to live near an Indian settlement and adopts three bear cubs, later becoming a Park Ranger.
Simple, pleasing outdoor family film.

w John Whedon, *novel* Robert Franklin Leslie d Bernard McEveety ph Ted D. Landon m Buddy Baker

Patrick Wayne, Chief Dan George, Andrew Duggan, Michael Ansara

The Beast from Twenty Thousand Fathoms
US 1953 80m bw
Warner (Hal Chester, Jack Dietz)

Heat generated by an atomic bomb test in the Arctic thaws out a prehistoric rhedosaurus which travels down the American coast to cause havoc in New York until cornered and destroyed on Coney Island.
Flat-footed addition to the monster cycle, with an interminable wait for the beast's appearance and inferior trick work when he goes on the rampage.

w Lou Morheim, Fred Freiburger d Eugène Lourié ph Jack Russell m David Buttolph sp Ray Harryhausen

Paul Christian, Paula Raymond, Cecil Kellaway (as a professor gobbled up in a bathysphere), Kenneth Tobey, Donald Woods, Lee Van Cleef

The Beast in the Cellar
GB 1970 87m Eastmancolor
Tigon-Leander (Tony Tenser, Graham Harris)

A rampaging killer in the Lancashire woods turns out to be the deranged ex-soldier brother of two elderly spinsters who have kept him locked up for thirty years.
Idiotically boring farrago, totally lacking in suspense and wasting good talent.

wd James Kelly ph Harry Waxman, Desmond Dickinson m Tony Macaulay

Flora Robson, Beryl Reid, Tessa Wyatt, John Hamill, T. P. McKenna

● *Video: Guild*

The Beast Must Die*
GB 1974 93m Technicolor
BL / Amicus (Milton Subotsky)

A millionaire big game hunter holds a weekend party to track down a werewolf, but his guest list rapidly gets smaller . . .
A savage variation on *Ten Little Niggers*, not badly done, with such gimmicks as a 'guess who' break near the end.

w Michael Winder, *story* James Blish d Paul Annett ph Jack Hildyard m Douglas Gamley

Calvin Lockhart, Peter Cushing, Charles Gray, Anton Diffring, Marlene Clark, Ciaran Madden, Michael Gambon

Beast of the City
US 1932 80m bw
MGM

A police captain is determined to get a

THE BEAST OF THE CITY.   A pre-Hays Office advertisement for a routine melodrama which promised more in the way of sin than it ever proposed to show.

ruthless racketeer by fair means or foul.
Curiously dour little crime melodrama with a high death rate; the cast does not quite save it.

w John Lee Mahin, *story* W. R. Burnett d Charles Brabin ph Barney McGill

Walter Huston, Jean Harlow, Wallace Ford, Jean Hersholt, Dorothy Petersen, Tully Marshall, John Miljan

'A gang story for rural and home circle consumption, preaching the gospel of civic righteousness and the glory of steadfast purpose. Aiming at domestic patronage, they even make Miss Harlow keep her skirts down.'—*Variety*

'Endowed with vitality and realism.'—*New York Times*

The Beast with a Million Eyes
US 1955 84m bw

A malicious space creature lands in the desert but is defeated by human love. Semi-professional would-be horror story, on a level with the Corman horrors of the period. Paul Birch, Lorna Thayer, Dick Sargent. Written by Tom Filer; directed by David Karminsky; for San Matteo / AIP.

The Beast with Five Fingers*
US 1946 88m bw
Warner (William Jacobs)

A famous pianist dies and his severed hand returns to commit murder.
Slow-moving, Italian-set horror thriller which wastes an excellent original; a superb central performance and clever trick effects can hardly

redeem the stodgy script or the ending which reveals the hauntings as an hallucination.

w Curt Siodmak, story W. F. Harvey
d Robert Florey ph Wesley Anderson
m Max Steiner

Peter Lorre, Andrea King, Robert Alda, J. Carrol Naish, Victor Francen, Charles Dingle

The Beastmaster
US 1982 118m colour

A royal child, stolen at birth by a witch, is rescued by a peasant who brings him up skilled in the martial arts. Comic strip sword and sorcery: fairly high budget but very low intelligence. Marc Singer, Tanya Roberts, Rip Torn, John Amos, Rod Loomis. Written by Don Coscarelli and Paul Pepperman; directed by Don Coscarelli; for Leisure Investments.

The Beat Generation
US 1959 95m bw Cinemascope
Albert Zugsmith
aka: This Rebel Age

A vicious rapist joins the beatniks. Bankrupt exploitation melodrama, not easy to sit through.

w Richard Matheson, Lewis Meltzer
d Charles Haas ph Walter H. Castle
m Albert Glasser

Ray Danton, Steve Cochran, Fay Spain, Mamie Van Doren, Jackie Coogan, Louis Armstrong, Maggie Hayes, Jim Mitchum, Irish McCalla, Maxie Rosenbloom
'An enervating mixture of slapstick, religiosity, psychological hokum and grubby sensationalism.'—MFB

Beat Girl
GB 1960 85m bw

An architect's teenage daughter goes to the dogs. Risible exposé-style melodrama. David Farrar, Noelle Adam, Christopher Lee, Gillian Hills, Adam Faith. Written by Dail Ambler; directed by Edmond T. Greville; for Renown.

Beat Street
US 1984 106m Movielab

An aspiring DJ from South Bronx has trouble getting into showbiz. For teenagers only; a rehash of Saturday Night Fever applied to the new fad of break-dancing. Rae Dawn Chong, Guy Davis, Jon Chardiet, Leon W. Grant, Saundra Santiago. Written by Andy Davis, David Gilbert, Paul Golding; directed by Stan Lathan; for Orion.

'Adventure at its boldest! Bogart at his best!'
Beat the Devil*
GB 1953 100m bw
Romulus / Santana (Jack Clayton)

In a small Mediterranean port, and subsequently on a boat bound for the African coast, oddly assorted travellers plan to acquire land known to contain uranium deposits. Unsatisfactory, over-talkative and inconsequential burlesque of the director's own The Maltese Falcon and Across the

Pacific. Good fun was obviously had by the cast, but audiences were mostly baffled by the in-jokes, the extra-strange characters, and the lack of attention to pace, suspense and plot development.

w Truman Capote, John Huston, novel James Helvick d John Huston ph Oswald Morris m Franco Mannino

Humphrey Bogart (Billy Dannreuther), Jennifer Jones (Gwendolen Chelm), Gina Lollobrigida (Maria Dannreuther), Edward Underdown (Harry Chelm), Peter Lorre (O'Hara), Robert Morley (Petersen), Ivor Barnard (Major Ross), Bernard Lee (Inspector), Marco Tulli (Ravello)

GWENDOLEN: 'Harry, we must beware of these men. They're desperate characters. Not one of them looked at my legs.'

DANNREUTHER: 'Trouble with England, it's all pomp and no circumstance. You're very wise to get out of it, escape while you can.'

O'HARA: 'Time! Time! What is time? The Swiss manufacture it. The French hoard it. Italians want it. Americans say it is money. Hindus say it does not exist. Do you know what I say? I say time is a crook.'

'A potential treat emerged as a wet firecracker . . . the incidents remain on a naggingly arch and lagging verbal keel.'—New York Times

'Each of its cinematic clichés appears to be placed in the very faintest of mocking quotation marks.'—Time

'Only the phonies liked it. It's a mess!'—Humphrey Bogart

'The formula of Beat the Devil is that everyone is slightly absurd.'—John Huston
† James Helvick was the pseudonym of Claud Cockburn.

● Video: CBS / Fox

Beau Brummell*
US 1924 104m approx at 24 fps bw silent

A Regency dandy becomes the right-hand man of the Prince of Wales, but falters through his own arrogance. Elegant period romance which marked the beginning of its star's great movie decade. John Barrymore, Mary Astor, Carmel Myers, Willard Louis. Written by Dorothy Farnum; directed by Harry Beaumont; for Warners.

Beau Brummell*
GB 1954 111m Eastmancolor
MGM (Sam Zimbalist)

A Regency dandy enjoys a close relationship with the Prince of Wales, and when this is eventually withdrawn he dies in penury. Stodgy historical romance with entertaining patches; the main story is too graceful and conventional to be believed.

w Karl Tunberg, play Clyde Fitch d Curtis Bernhardt ph Oswald Morris m Richard Addinsell ad Alfred Junge

Stewart Granger, Elizabeth Taylor, Peter Ustinov (as the Prince), Robert Morley (as George III), James Donald, James Hayter, Rosemary Harris, Paul Rogers, Noel Willman, Peter Bull, Peter Dyneley

Beau Geste**
US 1926 120m approx (24 fps) bw (colour sequences) silent
Paramount (Herbert Brenon)

Three English brothers join the Foreign Legion, suffer under a brutal sergeant, and die fighting the Arabs.
Although outmoded even when first filmed, this tale of derring-do and self sacrifice usually works, and in this case it gave its star a fresh image. One of the best remembered silents of the twenties.

w Paul Schofield, novel P. C. Wren d Herbert Brenon ph Roy Hunt ad Julian Boone Fleming

Ronald Colman, Neil Hamilton, Ralph Forbes, Alice Joyce, Mary Brian, Noah Beery, William Powell, Victor McLaglen
† Remade 1939 and 1966; sequel, Beau Ideal, 1931.

'Three against the world! Brothers and soldiers all!'
Beau Geste**
US 1939 120m bw
Paramount (William Wellman)

Spirited remake, with the famous flashback opening of the desert fort defended by corpses. Style and acting generally satisfactory.

w Robert Carson d William Wellman ph Theodor Sparkuhl, Archie Stout m Alfred Newman ad Hans Dreier, Robert Odell

Gary Cooper, Ray Milland, Robert Preston, Brian Donlevy, J. Carrol Naish, Susan Hayward, Heather Thatcher, James Stephenson, Donald O'Connor, G. P. Huntley Jnr, Albert Dekker, Broderick Crawford

FOREWORD: 'The love of a man for a woman waxes and wanes like the moon, but the love of brother for brother is steadfast as the stars and endures like the word of the prophet . . .' Arabian proverb

MARKOFF: 'Keep shooting, you scum! You'll get a chance yet to die with your boots on!'

'Its melodrama is sometimes grim but never harrowing, its pace is close to hectic and its suspense is constant.'—Herbert Cohn, Brooklyn Daily Eagle

'A morbid picture, but I doubt whether any morality council will take action, the whole story being so wrapped up in the school colours—in comradeship and loyalty and breeding, and the pure girl left behind; morbid because the brutality has no relation whatever to the real world; it is uncriticized day-dreaming.'—Graham Greene

'A handsome treatment of a well-loved adventure tale.'—New York Daily Mirror

'Will do nominal biz, but lacks punch for smash proportions.'—Variety
† Shot in Buttercup Valley, west of Yuma.
†† The nasty sergeant, originally Lejeune, became Markoff to avoid offending the French.

AAN: Brian Donlevy; Hans Dreier, Robert Odell

Beau Geste
US 1966 105m Techniscope
Universal (Walter Seltzer)

The central desert section of the story is here
augmented, with violence stressed, and Beau
allowed to survive at the end.
A cheap leery melodrama is what results from
the jettisoning of all the romantic portions of
the original.

wd Douglas Heyes ph Bud Thackery m Hans
Salter

Telly Savalas (rampant as the sadistic
sergeant), Guy Stockwell, Doug McClure,
Leslie Nielsen, Leon Gordon, Michael
Constantine

Beau Hunks**
US 1931 40m bw

A fool and his friend join the Foreign Legion
to forget. Patchy but amiable star comedy with
memorable high spots. In-joke: the woman the
whole legion wants to forget is Jean Harlow.
Laurel and Hardy, Charles Middleton.
Written by H. M. Walker; directed by James
W. Horne; for Hal Roach. (GB title: Beau
Chumps.)

Beau Ideal
US 1931 75m bw
RKO (William Le Baron)

John Geste and a new legionnaire friend
become involved in a religious war started by a
rascally emir.
Lame sequel to Beau Geste, fettered by
primitive dialogue.

w Paul Schofield, novel P. C. Wren d Herbert
Brenon ph J. Roy Hunt m Max Steiner

Lester Vail, Ralph Forbes, Don Alvarado,
Loretta Young, Irene Rich
'Ordinary programme picture with slight
romance. Doubtful draw for women.'—Variety

'He took New York for its wildest joy ride!'
Beau James*
US 1957 107m Technicolor
   Vistavision
Paramount / Hope Enterprises (Jack Rose)

The vaguely crooked career of Jimmy Walker,
mayor of New York in the twenties.
Romanticized biopic with few funny moments:
Hope cannot cope with the drama, and the
result is a creaking vehicle apart from a
well-recreated twenties atmosphere and
excellent production values.

w Jack Rose, Melville Shavelson, book Gene
Fowler d Melville Shavelson ph John F.
Warren m Joseph J. Lilley

Bob Hope, Paul Douglas, Vera Miles, Alexis
Smith, Darren McGavin, Joe Mantell, Walter
Catlett guest stars Jack Benny, George Jessel,
Jimmy Durante narrator Walter Winchell
(Alistair Cooke in GB)

Le Beau Mariage*
France 1981 97m colour
Les Films du Losange / Les Films du
   Carrosse (Margaret Menegoz)
GB title: A Good Marriage

An art student abandons her many affairs and
announces her intention of getting married,
but her intended proves reluctant . . .
Quietly amusing conversation piece in the
style expected of this director; an after-dinner
entertainment for the Sunday Times set.

wd Eric Rohmer ph Bernard Lutic m Ronan
Girre, Simon des Innocents

Beatrice Ronand, André Dussollier, Feodor
Atkine, Arielle Dombasle

Beau Sabreur
US 1928 85m (24 fps) bw silent

A French officer is sent to the Sahara to
negotiate a treaty with a powerful sheik.
Romantic adventure concocted to use up bits
and pieces left over from Beau Geste. Not a
hit. Gary Cooper, Evelyn Brent, Noah Beery,
William Powell, Roscoe Karns. Written by
Tom Geraghty; directed by John Waters; for
Paramount.

Le Beau Serge*
France 1958 97m bw
AYJM (Jean Cotet)

A student returns to his home town and tries
to redeem his old friend who has become a
drunkard.
Enjoyable character drama with well observed
village backgrounds. Credited with being the
spearhead of the 'new wave'.

wd Claude Chabrol ph Henri Decaë m Emile
Delpierre

Gérard Blain, Jean-Claude Brialy, Michèle
Meritz, Bernadette Lafont

La Beauté du Diable***
Italy / France 1949 96m bw
AYJM

The Faust story with the protagonists agreeing
to change places.
Dazzling plot twists and cinematic virtuosity
make this a richly enjoyable fantasy, though
perhaps not among Clair's greatest works.

w René Clair, Armand Salacrou d René
Clair ph Michel Kelber m Roman Vlad
ad Léon Barsacq

Michel Simon, Gérard Philipe, Raymond
Cordy, Nicole Besnard, Gaston Modot, Paolo
Stoppa

'She's got the biggest six-shooters in the
west!'
The Beautiful Blonde from Bashful
   Bend*
US 1949 77m Technicolor
TCF (Preston Sturges)

A temperamental saloon entertainer
accidentally shoots the sheriff and takes refuge
as a schoolmistress.
A dishevelled western farce unworthy of its
creator, but with the advantage of appearances
by many of his usual repertory of players.

wd Preston Sturges ph Harry Jackson
m Cyril Mockridge

Betty Grable, Cesar Romero, El Brendel,
Hugh Herbert, Rudy Vallee, Olga San Juan,
Sterling Holloway, Porter Hall, Esther
Howard, Margaret Hamilton

'It erects a fabric of roaring slapstick on a
conventional western foundation, and from
time to time it succeeds in being very
funny.'—Richard Mallett, Punch
'Somehow the ramshackle air of Bashful
Bend itself seems to have permeated the
whole film.'—MFB

Beautiful Stranger
GB 1954 89m bw
Maxwell Setton, John R. Sloan
US title: Twist of Fate

On the Riviera, an actress discovers that her
fiancé is a criminal.
Tawdry star melodrama of virtually no
interest.

w Robert Westerby, Carl Nystrom d David
Miller ph Robert Day, Ted Scaife
m Malcolm Arnold

Ginger Rogers, Jacques Bergerac, Herbert
Lom, Stanley Baker, Margaret Rawlings,
Eddie Byrne, Coral Browne

Beauty and the Boss
US 1932 75m bw

A girl down on her luck becomes secretary to
an amorous banker and eventually becomes
his wife. Artless Cinderella story in an uneasy
Viennese setting. Warren William, Marian
Marsh, Charles Butterworth, Frederick Kerr,
Lillian Bond. Written by Joseph Jackson from
the play The Church Mouse by Ladislas Fodor
and Paul Frank; directed by Roy del Ruth; for
Warners. 'Elementary stuff for the B houses,
titularly phrased for flap appeal.'—Variety

Beauty for Sale
US 1933 85m bw

An innocent girl snares a rich man while
working in a beauty parlour. Well-mounted
romantic comedy-drama with most of the
elements the 1933 public wanted. Madge
Evans, Alice Brady, Una Merkel, Otto
Kruger, May Robson, Phillips Holmes, Eddie
Nugent, Hedda Hopper. Written by Zelda
Sears and Eve Greene from the novel Beauty
by Faith Baldwin; directed by Richard
Boleslawski; for MGM. 'Pulp magazine fiction
made for subway-riding stenographers . . .
romantic hoke skilfully dressed up.'—Variety

Beauty for the Asking
US 1939 68m bw

Jealousies flourish among the women in a
cosmetics showroom. Average supporting
drama for female audiences. Lucille Ball,
Frieda Inescort, Patric Knowles, Donald
Woods, Inez Courtney. Written by Doris
Anderson and Paul Jarrico; directed by Glenn
Tryon; for RKO.

The Beauty Jungle*
GB 1964 114m Eastmancolor
   Cinemascope
Rank / Val Guest
US title: Contest Girl

A typist enters a beauty contest and step by
step becomes Miss Globe; but her descent is
equally rapid.
Wicked show biz and the road to ruin in one

glossy package, predictable, but not badly done; always something going on, and performed with gusto.

w Robert Muller, Val Guest *d* Val Guest *ph* Arthur Grant *m* Laurie Johnson

Janette Scott, Ian Hendry, Ronald Fraser, Edmund Purdom, Kay Walsh, Norman Bird, Janina Faye, Tommy Trinder, Francis Matthews

Because of Him*
US 1945 88m bw
U-I

A waitress pesters a Broadway author and actor for a leading role in their new show.
Moderately sprightly star vehicle with bonuses in the leading men; handling disappointingly routine.

w Edmund Beloin *d* Richard Wallace *ph* Hal Mohr *m* Miklos Rozsa

Deanna Durbin, Charles Laughton, Franchot Tone

'Even in the first wild joy of his arms, she realized that she would be . . . an unfit mother!'

Because of You
US 1952 95m bw
U-I (Albert J. Cohen)

A female ex-convict marries on parole but does not tell her husband of her past. Her old associates involve her innocently in another crime, and her husband divorces her; but years later she gets him and their child back.
Soap opera of the stickiest kind, made quite tolerable by good production.

w Ketti Frings *d* Joseph Pevney *ph* Russell Metty *m* Frank Skinner

Loretta Young, Jeff Chandler, Alex Nicol, Frances Dee, Lynne Roberts, Alexander Scourby, Mae Clarke

'Shows the most whole-hearted devotion to woman's magazine conventions.'— *MFB*

'Whoever you are, you're in this picture! Because this tells of youth's challenge to grown-ups who can't understand!'

Because They're Young
US 1960 98m bw
Columbia / Drexel (Jerry Bresler)

A high school teacher helps one of his tougher pupils not to slip into crime.
Routine sentimental melodrama, slightly redeemed by directorial expertise.

w James Gunn, *novel* Harrison High by John Farris *d* Paul Wendkos *ph* Wilfrid Cline *m* Johnny Williams

Dick Clark, Michael Callan, Tuesday Weld, Victoria Shaw, Warren Berlinger, Doug McClure

Because You're Mine
US 1952 103m Technicolor
MGM (Joe Pasternak)

An opera singer becomes a GI and wins the sergeant's sister.

Lumberingly inept star vehicle, giving the impression of nothing at all happening between the songs.

w Leonard Spiegelgass, Karl Tunberg *d* Alexander Hall *ph* Joseph Ruttenberg *md* Johnny Green

Mario Lanza, Doretta Morrow, James Whitmore, Dean Miller, Paula Corday, Jeff Donnell, Spring Byington

AAN: title song (*m* Nicholas Brodszky, *ly* Sammy Cahn)

'The screen explodes with rage and passion and greatness!'

Becket**
GB 1964 149m Technicolor Panavision
(Paramount) Hal B. Wallis

Henry II leans on his boisterous Saxon friend Thomas à Becket, but when the latter is made first chancellor and then archbishop a rift between them widens and ends in Becket's assassination by Henry's over-eager knights.
Jean Anouilh's bitter stage comedy is filmed literally and soberly as a rather anaemic epic, so that the point is lost and the edge blunted. The paucity of physical action causes good scenes to alternate with long stretches of tedium.

w Edward Anhalt *d* Peter Glenville *ph* Geoffrey Unsworth *m* Laurence Rosenthal

Richard Burton, Peter O'Toole, Donald Wolfit, *John Gielgud*, Martita Hunt, Pamela Brown, Sian Phillips, Paolo Stoppa

'Handsome, respectable and boring.'— *John Simon*

AA: Edward Anhalt
AAN: best picture; Peter Glenville; Geoffrey Unsworth; Laurence Rosenthal; Richard Burton; Peter O'Toole; John Gielgud

● *Video: Odyssey*

Becky Sharp**
US 1935 83m Technicolor
(RKO) Kenneth MacGowan

An ambitious girl makes her way into Regency society.
Chiefly notable as the first feature in three-colour Technicolor, this rather theatrical piece has its civilized enjoyments and the director made a few predictable cinematic experiments; the overall effect, however, is patchy.

w Francis Edward Faragoh, *play* Landon Mitchell, *novel* Vanity Fair by W. M. Thackeray *d* Rouben Mamoulian *ph* Ray Rennahan *m* Roy Webb *pd* Robert Edmond Jones

Miriam Hopkins, *Cedric Hardwicke*, Frances Dee, Billie Burke, Alison Skipworth, Nigel Bruce, Alan Mowbray, Colin Tapley, G. P. Huntley Jnr

'Beautiful cinematographically but weak on story. No cinch, and should be sold on colour angle.'— *Variety*

'As pleasing to the eye as a fresh fruit sundae, but not much more.'— *Otis Ferguson*

'If colour is to be of permanent importance a way must be found to use it realistically, not only as a beautiful decoration. It must be made to contribute to our sense of truth. The machine gun, the cheap striped tie, the battered Buick and the shabby bar will need a subtler colour sense than the Duchess of Richmond's ball, the girls of Miss Pinkerton's Academy, the Marquess of Steyne's dinner for two. Can Technicolor reproduce with the necessary accuracy the suit that has been worn too long, the oily hat?'— *Graham Greene*

AAN: Miriam Hopkins

'The girl who took a short cut down the primrose path!'

Bed of Roses
US 1933 67m bw

A reform-school graduate determines to be a scarlet woman but falls for an upright riverboat captain. Adequate vehicle for a fading star who had played too many such roles. Constance Bennett, Joel McCrea, Pert Kelton, Samuel S. Hinds, John Halliday. Written by Wanda Tuchok, Eugene Thackrey; directed by Gregory La Cava; for RKO.

The Bed Sitting Room*
GB 1969 .91m De Luxe
UA / Oscar Lewenstein (Richard Lester)

Surrealist romance; after a nuclear war, motley survivors in the waste lands turn into bed sitting rooms, cupboards and parakeets. Arrogantly obscure fantasy, a commercial flop which kept its director in the wilderness for four years. Fans of Monty Python may salvage a joke or two.

w John Antrobus, from the play by himself and Spike Milligan *d* Richard Lester *ph* David Watkin *m* Ken Thorne *pd* Assheton Gorton

Ralph Richardson, Rita Tushingham, Michael Hordern, Arthur Lowe, Mona Washbourne, Peter Cook, Dudley Moore, Spike Milligan, Harry Secombe, Marty Feldman, Jimmy Edwards

Bedazzled*
GB 1967 96m De Luxe Panavision
TCF / Stanley Donen

A short order cook is saved from suicide by Mr Spiggott, who offers him seven wishes in exchange for his soul.
A camped-up version of *Faust* which resolves itself into a series of threadbare sketches for the stars. All rather desperate apart from the leaping nuns.

w Peter Cook *d* Stanley Donen *ph* Austin Dempster *m* Dudley Moore

Peter Cook, Dudley Moore, Michael Bates, Raquel Welch, Eleanor Bron

● *Video: CBS / Fox*

Bedelia
GB 1946 90m bw
John Corfield (Isadore Goldsmith)

A psychotic woman is discovered to have poisoned three husbands.

Dreary upper-class British murder drama, totally devoid of style or suspense but a big star hit of the time.

w Vera Caspary, Moie Charles, Herbert Victor, Roy Ridley, Isadore Goldsmith, *novel* Vera Caspary d Lance Comfort ph F. A. Young

Margaret Lockwood, Ian Hunter, Barry K. Barnes, Anne Crawford, Jill Esmond, Ellen Pollock

Bedevilled
US 1955   86m   Eastmancolor
Cinemascope
MGM (Henry Berman)

In Paris, a novice priest befriends a girl on the run from gangsters. She turns out to be a murderess and is shot by her victim's brother. Absurd high-flown bosh, unsuitably cinemascoped in ugly colour, and surprisingly badly handled by old professionals.

w Jo Eisinger d Mitchell Leisen ph Frederick A. Young m William Alwyn

Anne Baxter, Steve Forrest, Simone Renant, Victor Francen, Maurice Teynac, Joseph Tomelty

'This mixture of melodrama and religion provides a most unedifying entertainment.'—*MFB*

The Bedford Incident*
GB 1965   102m   bw
Columbia / Bedford Productions (James B. Harris)

A ruthlessly efficient US destroyer captain in the Arctic chases a Russian submarine and accidentally fires an atomic weapon. Gripping mixture of themes from *Dr Strangelove* and *The Caine Mutiny*, very tense and forceful, with excellent acting.

w James Poe, *novel* Mark Rascovitch d James B. Harris ph Gilbert Taylor m Gerald Schurrmann

Richard Widmark, Sidney Poitier (his first role with no reference to his colour), James MacArthur, Eric Portman, Wally Cox, Martin Balsam, Phil Brown, Michael Kane, Garry Cockrell, Donald Sutherland

'Strong on virtues of a rather negative kind.'—*Penelope Houston*

Bedknobs and Broomsticks
US 1971   117m   Technicolor
Walt Disney (Bill Walsh)

In 1940 three evacuee children and a kindly witch ride on a magic bedstead and defeat the invasion of England. Extraordinarily dishevelled and incompetent Disney follow-up to *Mary Poppins*, a very muddled narrative with few high points and evidence of much cutting. Redeemed occasionally by camera trickery.

w Bill Walsh, Don DaGradi d Robert Stevenson ph Frank Phillips m / ly Richard M. Sherman, Robert B. Sherman sp Eustace Lycett, Alan Maley, Danny Lee

Angela Lansbury, David Tomlinson, Roy Smart, Cindy O'Callaghan, Sam Jaffe, Roddy McDowall, Bruce Forsyth, Tessie O'Shea, Reginald Owen

AAN: Richard M. Sherman, Robert B. Sherman; song 'The Age of Not Believing' by the Shermans

● *Video: Rank*

Bedlam*
US 1946   80m   bw
RKO (*Val Lewton*)

In 18th-century London, a sane girl is confined by the malevolent asylum master. Interesting but rather flatly handled addition to the Val Lewton gallery of horrors, perhaps too carefully and discreetly done for pace or suspense.

w Mark Robson, Carlos Keith d Mark Robson ph Nicholas Musuraca m Roy Webb

Boris Karloff, Anna Lee, Billy House, Richard Fraser, Glenn Vernon

† Carlos Keith was Val Lewton's pseudonym.
†† *Bedlam* was never granted a certificate in Britain.

Bedtime for Bonzo
US 1951   83m   bw
U-I (Michael Kraike)

To prove that environment determines character, a chimpanzee is brought up as a human baby. Very moderate fun and games which proved successful enough for a sequel, *Bonzo Goes to College*.

w Val Burton, Lou Breslow d Frederick de Cordova ph Carl Guthrie m Frank Skinner

Ronald Reagan, Diana Lynn, Walter Slezak, Lucille Berkely, Herbert Heyes

A Bedtime Story*
US 1933   89m   bw
Paramount (Emmanuel Cohen)

A breezy Frenchman has to interrupt his romances to look after an abandoned baby. Mild star vehicle in which the agreeable comedy is largely supplanted by sentimental cooing.

w Benjamin Glazer, *novel* Bellamy the Magnificent by Roy Horniman d Norman Taurog ph Charles Lang songs Ralph Rainger, Leo Robin

Maurice Chevalier, Helen Twelvetrees, Baby LeRoy, Edward Everett Horton, Adrienne Ames

Bedtime Story*
US 1941   85m   bw
Columbia (B. P. Schulberg)

A playwright's wife wants to retire instead of acting in his next play. Pleasantly sparkling comedy with good performances.

w Horace Jackson, Grant Garrett, Richard Flournoy d Alexander Hall ph Joseph Walker

Fredric March, Loretta Young, Robert Benchley, Allyn Joslyn, Eve Arden, Helen Westley, Joyce Compton, Tim Ryan

Bedtime Story*
US 1964   99m   Eastmancolor
U-I / Lankershim / Pennebaker (Stanley Shapiro)

Two Riviera confidence tricksters outwit each other. A fairly lively script is defeated by dull handling, but performances and backgrounds are attractive.

w Stanley Shapiro, Paul Henning d Ralph Levy ph Clifford Stine m Hans Salter

David Niven, Marlon Brando, Shirley Jones, Dody Goodman, Aram Stephan, Marie Windsor

'The most vulgar and embarrassing film of the year.'—*Daily Express*

Bees in Paradise
GB 1943   75m   bw

Four airmen find themselves on a South Sea island ruled by women who kill their spouses after the honeymoon. Saucy farce, too talkative to be very interesting even in the dark days of war. Arthur Askey, Peter Graves, Max Bacon, Anne Shelton, Jean Kent. Written by Val Guest and Marriott Edgar; directed by Val Guest; for Gainsborough.

Before Hindsight*
GB 1977   78m   Eastmancolor
Elizabeth Taylor-Mead

Interviews and clips show how inadequately cinema newsreels covered world events in the 1930s. Hard tack for entertainment seekers, but a clear exposition of a proven case of importance to film-makers and politicians.

w Elizabeth Taylor-Mead d Jonathan Lewis

'Certainly not the kind of picture people will pay money to see.'—*Variety*

Before I Hang*
US 1940   71m   bw
Columbia (Wallace MacDonald)

A research scientist experiments with a new serum which turns him into a murderer. Archetypal Karloff mad doctor flick, Jekyll and Hyde model: still quite tolerable.

w Robert D. Andrews d Nick Grinde ph Benjamin Kline md Morris Stoloff

Boris Karloff, Evelyn Keyes, Bruce Bennett, Pedro de Cordoba, Edward Van Sloan, Don Beddoe

Before the Nickelodeon*
US 1982   60m   bw / colour

The life, times and films of the pioneer Edwin S. Porter. Valuable documentary on a little-known figure, with films ranging from 1896 to 1907. Written by Warren D. Leight, Charles Musser; directed by Charles Musser; for Film for Thought.

Before Winter Comes*
GB 1968   107m   Technicolor
Columbia / Windward (Robert Emmett
  Ginna)

Austria 1945: a British major in charge of
displaced persons is helped and hindered by a
cheerful Yugoslav refugee who turns out to be
a Russian deserter.
Likeable, well-produced drama hampered by a
plot which becomes unnecessarily schematic,
coincidental and downbeat in its attempts to
tug at the heartstrings.
w Andrew Sinclair, *novel* The Interpreter by
Frederick L. Keefe   d J. Lee-Thompson
ph Gilbert Taylor   m Ron Grainer
David Niven, Topol, Ori Levi, Anna Karina,
John Hurt, Anthony Quayle
  'One of those films with a message on every
page of its script.'—*MFB*

Beg, Borrow or Steal
US 1937   70m   bw

An American expatriate lives by his wits in
Paris. Flabby comedy which misses on all
cylinders. Frank Morgan, Florence Rice, John
Beal, Janet Beecher, Herman Bing, Erik
Rhodes, E. E. Clive, Reginald Denny, George
Givot. Written by Leonard Lee, Harry
Ruskin, Marion Parsonnet; directed by
William Thiele; for MGM. 'Nothing quite so
incredible as this story has been tossed to the
double bills since the major studios started
competing among themselves to turn out low-
grade entertainment for the filler-in spots.'—
Variety

Beggars in Ermine
US 1934   70m   bw

A steelworker who loses his legs and his
livelihood organizes beggars into a wealthy
union. Curious semi-fantasy, probably worth a
mark for trying. Lionel Atwill, Henry B.
Walthall, Betty Furness, Jameson Thomas,
Astrid Allwyn. Written by Tristam Tupper
from the novel by Esther Lynd Daly; directed
by Phil Rosen; for Monogram.

The Beggar's Opera**
GB 1952   94m   Technicolor
British Lion / Imperadio (Herbert Wilcox,
  Laurence Olivier)

A highwayman in Newgate jail devises an
opera based on his own exploits.
Exuberant potted version of the 1728 low
opera, generally likeable but lacking a strong
coherent approach and marred by violent
colour and raggedly theatrical presentation. It
nearly but not quite comes off.
w Dennis Cannan, Christopher Fry, *opera*
John Gay   d Peter Brook   ph Guy Green
ad George Wakhevitch, William C. Andrews
musical arrangement and additions Arthur
Bliss
Laurence Olivier, Stanley Holloway, Dorothy
Tutin, Daphne Anderson, Mary Clare,
George Devine, Athene Seyler, Hugh Griffith,
Margot Grahame, Sandra Dorne, Laurence
Naismith

'The failure is equalled only by the
ambition.'—*Gavin Lambert*
● *Video: Thorn EMI*

The Beginning or the End
US 1947   112m   bw
MGM (Samuel Marx)

During World War II American scientists
continue to perfect the atom bomb despite
their own misgivings, and one dies in an
explosion.
Semi-documentary marred by sentimental
personal asides and of very little continuing
interest.
w Robert Considine   d Norman Taurog
ph Ray June   m Daniele Amfitheatrof
Brian Donlevy, Robert Walker, Tom Drake,
Beverly Tyler, Hume Cronyn, Audrey Totter,
Godfrey Tearle (as Roosevelt)

Begone Dull Care***
Canada 1953   9m   colour
National Film Board (Norman McLaren)

Abstract images drawn directly onto the film
are accompanied by three pieces of jazz
performed by the Oscar Peterson Trio.
The central movement is a little too slow, but
the first piece is witty and the climax is an
irresistible frenzy of sound and image.
Undeniably a classic short, and probably
McLaren's best.
conceived and made by Norman McLaren

The Beguiled*
US 1971   109m   Technicolor
Universal / Malpaso (Don Siegel)

A wounded Unionist soldier hides out in a
Confederate ladies' school; the teachers fend
for him until he causes trouble among the
sexually frustrated women, who eventually kill
him.
Eccentric melodrama which does not really
work despite its credentials and patient work
all round.
w John B. Sherry, Grimes Grice, *novel*
Thomas Cullinan   d Don Siegel   ph Bruce
Surtees   m Lalo Schifrin   pd Ted Haworth
Clint Eastwood, Geraldine Page, Elizabeth
Hartman, Jo Ann Harris, Darleen Carr, Mae
Mercer
  'A must for sadists and woman-haters.'—
Judith Crist

● *Video: CIC*

Behave Yourself*
US 1951   81m   bw
RKO (Jerry Wald, Norman Krasna)

A young married couple and their dog get
mixed up in a chain of murders.
Zany black comedy in the wake of *A Slight
Case of Murder* and *The Thin Man*. The
humour is spread too thin for success.
wd George Beck   ph James Wong Howe
m Leigh Harline
Farley Granger, Shelley Winters, William
Demarest, Francis L. Sullivan, Margalo
Gillmore, Lon Chaney, Hans Conried, Elisha
Cook Jnr
● *Video: VCL*

Behind the Eight Ball
US 1942   60m   bw

Actors are mistaken for spies. Very patchy but
commendably brief star comedy. The Ritz
Brothers, Carol Bruce, Dick Foran, William
Demarest. Written by Stanley Roberts and
Mel Ronson; directed by Edward F. Cline; for
Universal. (GB title: *Off the Beaten Track*.)

Behind the High Wall
US 1956   85m   bw
U-I (Stanley Rubin)

A prison warder, taken as hostage by escaping
convicts, steals some of the money they have
taken.
Glum melodrama, capably presented.
w Harold Jack Bloom   d Abner Biberman
ph Maury Gertsman   m Joseph Gershenson
Tom Tully, Sylvia Sidney, John Gavin, Betty
Lynn, John Larch, Barney Phillips, Don
Beddoe

Behind the Mask
US 1932   68m   bw

A crazy doctor operates fatally on those who
know too much. Semi-horror mystery using
two members of the Frankenstein cast. Jack
Holt, Constance Cummings, Edward Van
Sloan, Boris Karloff. Written by Jo Swerling;
directed by John Francis Dillon; for Columbia.

Behind the Mask*
GB 1958   99m   Eastmancolor
BL / GW Films (Sergei Nolbandov, Josef
  Somlo)

Political infighting causes tension on the board
of a local hospital.
Oddly titled social drama with interesting
detail but not much tension or conclusion.
w John Hunter, *novel* The Pack by John
Rowan Wilson   d Brian Desmond Hurst
ph Robert Krasker   m Geoffrey Wright
Michael Redgrave, Tony Britton, Carl
Mohner, Niall MacGinnis, Vanessa Redgrave,
Ian Bannen, Brenda Bruce, Lionel Jeffries,
Miles Malleson, John Welsh, Ann Firbank

Behind the Rising Sun*
US 1943   88m   bw
RKO

An American-educated Japanese goes home in
the thirties, comes under the influence of
war-mongers, and causes his father to commit
hara-kiri.
Outrageous wartime flagwaver designed to
vilify 'Uncle Tojo's dogs', from the writer and
director of the similar *Hitler's Children* (qv).
w Emmet Lavery, *novel* James R. Young
d Edward Dmytryk   ph Russell Metty   m Roy
Webb
J. Carrol Naish, Tom Neal, Margo, Robert
Ryan, Gloria Holden, Don Douglas, Adeline
de Walt Reynolds

Behold a Pale Horse*
US 1964   121m   bw
Columbia / Highland / Brentwood (Fred
  Zinnemann, Alexander Trauner)

A Spanish guerrilla goes into exile at the end of the Civil War. Twenty years later he is persuaded to return and kill a brutal police chief.

An action film which unfortunately insists on saying something significant about morality, destiny and death. Impeccably made, but somehow not very interesting apart from the action sequences.

w J. P. Miller, *novel* Killing a Mouse on Sunday by Emeric Pressburger *d* Fred Zinnemann *ph* Jean Badal *m* Maurice Jarre *ad* Alexander Trauner

Gregory Peck, Omar Sharif, Anthony Quinn, Raymond Pellegrin, Paolo Stoppa, Mildred Dunnock, Daniela Rocca, Christian Marquand
  'A fine example of a high class failure.'— *Judith Crist*

'Her savage heart pounded with revenge when her love went unwanted!'

Behold My Wife
US 1934 79m bw
Paramount (B. P. Schulberg)

A wealthy young man brings back and marries a New Mexico Indian girl to show up his snobbish family.
Dated melodrama, of interest solely for its racial theme.

w William R. Lippman, Oliver LaFarge, *novel* The Translation of a Savage by Sir Gilbert Parker *d* Mitchell Leisen *ph* Leon Shamroy

Sylvia Sidney, Gene Raymond, Juliette Compton, Laura Hope Crews, H. B. Warner, Monroe Owsley, Ann Sheridan
  'Frank melodrama of the hokiest sort.'— *Variety*

Being There**
US 1979 130m Metrocolor
Lorimar / North Star / CIP (Andrew Braunsberg)

An illiterate gardener is taken for a homespun philosopher and becomes a national celebrity. Overlong serio-comic parable hinging on a somewhat dubious star performance. Chance made it a popular urban success, but few who saw it were enthused.

w Jerzy Kosinski, from his novel *d* Hal Ashby *ph* Dianne Schroeder *m* John Mandel *pd* Michael Haller

Peter Sellers, Shirley Maclaine, *Melvyn Douglas*, Jack Warden, Richard Dysart, Richard Basehart
BFA: screenplay

● Video: MGM / UA

Bela Lugosi Meets a Brooklyn Gorilla
US 1952 74m bw

A tropical island scientist turns one half of a stranded comedy team into a gorilla. Stupid farce which never rises to the occasion. Bela Lugosi, Duke Mitchell, Sammy Petrillo, Ray 'Crash' Corrigan, Muriel Landers. Written by Tim Ryan; directed by William Beaudine; for Jack Broder. 'Neighbourhood and small-town audiences will get some laughs.'—*Box office*

Believe in Me
US 1971 90m colour
MGM (Irwin Winkler, Robert Chartoff)

Two young marrieds take to drugs.
Tedious and unenlightening modern drama which seems to think it's saying something new.

w Israel Horovitz *d* Stuart Hagmann *ph* Dick Kratina, Richard C. Brooks *m* Fred Karlin

Michael Sarrazin, Jacqueline Bisset, Jon Cypher, Allen Garfield

'A bewitching comedy about an enchanting subject!'

Bell, Book and Candle*
US 1958 103m Technicolor
Columbia / Phoenix (Julian Blaustein)

A publisher slowly becomes aware that his new girl friend is a witch.
A gossamer stage comedy has been fatally flattened in translation; most of the actors are miscast, and sentiment soaks the script. But it remains a civilized entertainment.

w Daniel Taradash, *play* John Van Druten *d* Richard Quine *ph* James Wong Howe *m* George Duning

James Stewart, Kim Novak, Jack Lemmon, Ernie Kovacs, *Hermione Gingold*, Elsa Lanchester, Janice Rule

Bell Bottom George
GB 1943 97m bw

A medically exempt waiter dons uniform and catches a ring of spies. Formula star comedy, too long and too familiar. George Formby, Anne Firth, Reginald Purdell, Peter Murray Hill. Written by Peter Fraser and Edward Dryhurst; directed by Marcel Varnel; for Columbia.

A Bell for Adano*
US 1945 104m bw
TCF (Louis D. Lighton, Lamar Trotti)

An American major takes over an Italian town and wins affection by replacing the local bell. Slight end-of-war mood piece, still quite pleasant but without the undercurrents of feeling it had at the time.

w Lamar Trotti, Norman Reilly Raine, *novel* John Hersey *d* Henry King *ph* Joseph La Shelle *m* Alfred Newman

John Hodiak, Gene Tierney, William Bendix, Glenn Langan, Richard Conte, Stanley Prager, Henry Morgan

The Bell Jar
US 1979 107m colour

A teenage girl becomes mentally ill when her father dies. Numbingly tedious case history without much apparent point. Marilyn Hassett, Julie Harris, Anne Jackson, Barbara Barrie. Written by Marjorie Kellog, from the novel by Sylvia Plath; directed by Larry Peerce; for Peerce-Goldston / Avco.

Belladonna
GB 1934 91m bw

A selfish woman tries to poison her husband for love of an Egyptian. Intriguingly-cast

version of the Robert Hichens novel dramatized by J. B. Fagan; later filmed in Hollywood as *Temptation* (qv). Mary Ellis, Conrad Veidt, Cedric Hardwicke, John Stuart, Michael Shepley. Written by H. Fowler Mear; directed by Robert Milton; for Twickenham.

Il Bell'Antonio*
Italy / France 1960 105m bw
Cina del Duca–Arco / Lyre Cinématographique (Alfredo Bini)
GB title: *Handsome Antonio*

A youngish man returns to his native town with the reputation of a lady-killer, but when married turns out to be impotent.
Amusing but finally exhausting Sicilian comedy with all the expected exaggeration of speech and gesture.

w Pier Paolo Pasolini, Gino Visentini, *novel* Vitaliano Brancati *d* Piero Piccioni

Marcello Mastroianni, Claudia Cardinale, Pierre Brasseur, Rina Morelli, Tomas Milian

The Bellboy*
US 1960 72m bw
Paramount / Jerry Lewis Productions (Jerry Lewis)

An incompetent bellboy causes havoc in a Miami hotel.
Plotless essence of a comedian who divides opinion and will never be better than variable. This ragbag of old gags at least prevents his usual sentimental excesses, and is mercifully short.

wd Jerry Lewis *ph* Haskell Boggs *m* Walter Scharf

Jerry Lewis, Alex Gerry, Bob Clayton, Herkie Styles, Milton Berle

La Belle Américaine*
France 1961 101m bw (colour finale)
CCFC / Film d'Art / Panorama / Corflor (Henri Diamant-Berger, Arthur Lesser)
GB / US titles: *What a Chassis; The American Beauty*

A Parisian factory worker gets into all kinds of trouble when he buys an American supercar for a ridiculously low price.
Some brilliant gags are separated by long dull spots of unnecessary storytelling.

w Robert Dhéry, Pierre Tchernia, Alfred Adam *d* Robert Dhéry *ph* Ghislain Cloquet *m* Gérard Calvi

Robert Dhéry, Louis de Funes, Colette Brosset, Alfred Adam, Bernard Lavalette, Annie Ducaux

Belle de Jour***
France / Italy 1967 100m Eastmancolor
Paris Film / Five Film (Robert and Raymond Hakim)

A surgeon's wife finds herself drawn to afternoon work in a brothel.
Fascinating Bunuel mixture of fact and fantasy, impeccably woven into a rich fabric.

w *Luis Bunuel, Jean-Claude Carrière* d *Luis Bunuel* ph *Sacha Vierny* m *none*

Catherine Deneuve, Jean Sorel, Michel Piccoli, Genevieve Page, Pierre Clémenti

La Belle Equipe°
France 1936 74m bw
Ciné Arts

Five unemployed Parisians win the lottery and open a restaurant, but things do not go smoothly.

Interesting but rather lumpy star drama which finally descends into melodrama; alternative tragic and happy endings were originally offered.

w *Charles Spaak, Julien Duvivier* d *Julien Duvivier* ph *Jules Kruger, Marc Fessard* m *Maurice Yvain*

Jean Gabin, Charles Vanel, Viviane Romance, Raymond Aimes, Robert Lynen, Raymond Cordy, Raphael Medina

La Belle et la Bête°°
France 1946 95m bw
André Paulvé

Beauty gives herself to the Beast who has kidnapped her father; through love the monster turns into a handsome prince.

Slightly heavy-handed though usually stunning-looking adaptation of the fairy tale.

wd *Jean Cocteau* ph *Henri Alekan* m *Georges Auric* ad *Christian Bérard*

Jean Marais, Josette Day, Mila Parély, Marcel André, Michel Auclair

'Perhaps the most sumptuously elegant of all filmed fairy tales.'—*New Yorker, 1980*

'Absolute magic: diamond cold and lunar bright.'—*CBS*

● *Video: Thorn EMI*

Belle le Grand
US 1951 89m bw
Republic

The proprietress of a Barbary Coast gambling house is plagued by an ex-husband on whose account she served a prison term.

Confused and incompetent period melodrama.

w *D. D. Beauchamp* d *Allan Dwan* ph *Reggie Lanning* m *Victor Young*

Vera Ralston, John Carroll, William Ching, Hope Emerson, Stephen Chase, Grant Withers, John Qualen

The Belle of New York°
US 1952 82m Technicolor
MGM (Arthur Freed)

A nineties playboy falls for a Salvation Army girl.

A rather dreary version of the old musical, with undistinguished additions.

w *Robert O'Brien, Irving Elinson* d *Charles Walters* ph *Robert Planck* m / *ly Johnny Mercer, Harry Warren* ad *Jack Martin Smith*

Fred Astaire, Vera-Ellen, Marjorie Main, Keenan Wynn, Alice Pearce, Clinton Sundberg, Gale Robbins

Songs include 'When I'm Out with the Belle of New York'; 'Oops'; 'Baby Doll'; 'Naughty but Nice'; 'Seeing's Believing'; 'Thank You Mr Currier, Thank You Mr Ives'; 'I Love to Beat a Big Bass Drum'; 'I Wanna Be a Dancing Man'; 'Let a Little Love Come In'

Belle of the Nineties°
US 1934 75m bw
Paramount (William Le Baron)

A saloon entertainer loves two men, one of whom is a crook.

Much-laundered star vehicle which despite superior production seems a pale shadow of the star's better pieces.

w *Mae West* d *Leo McCarey* ph *Karl Struss*

Mae West, Roger Pryor, John Miljan, John Mack Brown, Katherine de Mille, Duke Ellington and his Orchestra

'It's been sufficiently denatured from within, yet not completely emasculated.'—*Variety*

Belle of the Yukon°
US 1945 84m Technicolor
International

A troupe of saloon entertainers in the Yukon become involved with a bank robbery.

Threads of plot support comedy, dancing and songs in this thin but reasonably fresh musical imitation of *The Spoilers*.

w *James Edward Grant* d *William A. Seiter* ph *Ray Rennahan* md *Arthur Lange*

Gypsy Rose Lee, Randolph Scott, Dinah Shore, Charles Winninger, Bob Burns

AAN: Arthur Lange; song 'Sleigh Ride in July' (m *Jimmy Van Heusen*, ly *Johnny Burke*)

Belle Starr
US 1941 87m Technicolor
TCF (Kenneth MacGowan)

Absurdly laundered version of the life of the west's most notorious female outlaw, with the star laughably miscast.

w *Lamar Trotti* d *Irving Cummings* ph *Ernest Palmer, Ray Rennahan* m *Alfred Newman*

Gene Tierney, Randolph Scott, Dana Andrews, Shepperd Strudwick, Elizabeth Patterson, Chill Wills, Louise Beavers

Les Belles de Nuit°°
France / Italy 1952 89m bw
Franco London / Rizzoli

A discontented music teacher dreams of beautiful women through the ages.

Charming but very slight dream fantasy with many of the master's touches. (He claims to have intended a comic *Intolerance*.)

wd *René Clair* ph *Armand Thirard, Robert Juilliard, Louis Née* m *Georges Van Parys* ad *Léon Barsacq*

Gérard Philipe, Gina Lollobrigida, Martine Carol, Magali Vendeuil, Paolo Stoppa, Raymond Bussières, Raymond Cordy

The Belles of St Trinian's°
GB 1954 91m bw
BL / London Films / Launder and Gilliat

At an unruly and bankrupt school for girls, more time is spent backing horses than studying subjects, and the headmistress's bookmaker brother has a scheme or two of his own.

Fairly successful film version of Ronald Searle's awful schoolgirl cartoons, the emphasis shifted to a grotesque older generation with the star in drag. An enormous commercial success, but the three sequels *Blue Murder at St Trinian's, The Pure Hell of St Trinian's, The Great St Trinian's Train Robbery* went from bad to awful.

w *Frank Launder, Sidney Gilliat, Val Valentine* d *Frank Launder* ph *Stan Pavey* m *Malcolm Arnold*

Alastair Sim, George Cole, Joyce Grenfell, Hermione Baddeley, Betty Ann Davies, Renée Houston, Beryl Reid, Irene Handl, Mary Merrall

'Not so much a film as an entertainment on celluloid, a huge charade, a rich pile of idiot and splendidly senseless images.'—*David Robinson*

Belles on Their Toes
US 1952 89m Technicolor
TCF (Samuel G. Engel)

Further adventures in the growing up of the twelve Gilbreth children.

Flat sequel to *Cheaper by the Dozen* (qv) with sentimentality instead of Clifton Webb. Period atmosphere attractive.

w *Phoebe and Henry Ephron*, book *Frank B. Gilbreth Jnr and Ernestine Gilbreth Carey* d *Henry Levin* ph *Arthur E. Arling* m *Cyril Mockridge*

Myrna Loy, Jeanne Crain, Debra Paget, Jeffrey Hunter, Edward Arnold, Hoagy Carmichael, Barbara Bates, Robert Arthur

Bellissima°
Italy 1951 100m bw
Bellissima Films (Salvo d'Angelo)

A mother struggles to get a part in a film for her 7-year-old daughter.

Highly detailed, very noisy star vehicle with neo-realist working-class backgrounds. Exhausting.

w *Suso Cecchi d'Amico, Francesco Rosi, Luchino Visconti, Cesare Zavattini* d *Luchino Visconti* ph *Piero Portalupi* m *Franco Mannino*

Anna Magnani, Walter Chiari, Tina Apicella, Gastone Renzelli, Alessandro Blasetti

The Bells
GB 1931 75m bw

An Alsatian burgomaster is forced by conscience to confess to the killing of a Jew.

Only sound version of a famous melodrama played on stage by Henry Irving. Donald Calthrop, Jane Welsh, Edward Sinclair. (In a 1926 silent version Lionel Barrymore played the murderer and Boris Karloff the mesmerist.) Written by C. H. Dand, from the play by Erckmann and Chatrian; directed by Oscar M. Werndorff and Harcourt Templeman; in three language versions; for Isidore Schlesinger / BSFP.

Bells are Ringing*
US 1960   126m   Metrocolor
   Cinemascope
MGM (Arthur Freed)

A telephone answering service operator
becomes passionately involved in the lives of
her clients.
Dull, rather ugly and boring transcription of a
Broadway musical, with all talents below par,
not enough dancing and too much plot.

w / l Betty Comden, Adolph Green, from
their play d Vincente Minnelli ph Milton
Krasner m Jule Styne md André Previn
ad George W. Davis, Preston Ames
ch Charles O'Curran

Judy Holliday, Dean Martin, Fred Clark,
Eddie Foy Jnr, Jean Stapleton, Ruth Storey,
Frank Gorshin

AAN: André Previn

The Bells Go Down**
GB 1943   89m   bw
Ealing (S. C. Balcon)

The exploits of a London firefighting unit
during World War II.
Tragi-comedy with lively scenes, a good record
of the historical background of the blitz.

w Roger Macdougall, Stephen Black d Basil
Dearden ph Ernest Palmer m Roy Douglas

Tommy Trinder, James Mason, Mervyn
Johns, Philippa Hyatt, Finlay Currie, Philip
Friend, Meriel Forbes, Beatrice Varley, Billy
Hartnell

'Your heart will be wearing a smile!'
The Bells of St Mary's**
US 1945   126m   bw
RKO / Rainbow

At a big city Catholic school, Father O'Malley
and Sister Benedict indulge in friendly rivalry,
and succeed in extending the school through
the gift of a building.
Sentimental and very commercial sequel to
Going My Way, with the stars at their peak
and the handling as cosy and well-paced as
might be expected.

w Dudley Nichols d Leo McCarey
ph George Barnes m Robert Emmett Dolan

Bing Crosby, Ingrid Bergman, Henry Travers,
William Gargan, Ruth Donnelly, Rhys
Williams, Una O'Connor, Eva Novak
'The picture is full of shrewd and pleasant
flashes. It is also fascinating to watch as a
talented, desperate effort to repeat the
unrepeatable. But on the whole it is an
unhappy film.'—James Agee

AAN: best picture; Leo McCarey; Robert
Emmett Dolan; Bing Crosby; Ingrid Bergman;
song 'Aren't You Glad You're You' (m Jimmy
Van Heusen, ly Johnny Burke)

Beloved
US 1933   80m   bw

A composer ages from 10 to 90 while trying to
place his symphony; he dies happy. Curious
fictional biopic with plenty of incident but no
plot. John Boles, Gloria Stuart, Albert Conti,

Dorothy Peterson, Morgan Farley. Written by
Paul Gangelin and George O'Neil; directed by
Victor Schertzinger; for Bennie F. Zeidman /
Universal. 'Too hopelessly muddled in
conception to reach the important money
class.'—Variety

The Beloved Bachelor
US 1931   72m   bw

A man falls in love with his adopted daughter.
Innocuous tearjerker made with some style.
Paul Lukas, Dorothy Jordan, Betty Van
Allen, Charles Ruggles, Vivienne Osborne.
Written by Sidney Buchman, Raymond
Griffith and Agnes Brand Leahy, from the
play by Edward H. Peple; directed by Lloyd
Corrigan; for Paramount. 'A particularly
femme appealing yarn with apt dialogue and
natural continuity.'—Variety

Beloved Enemy*
US 1936   90m   bw
Samuel Goldwyn (George Haight)

During the 1921 Irish rebellion, the fiancée of
a British army officer falls in love with the
leading revolutionary.
Dreamy-eyed romance with little relevance to
the real situation; not badly done of its kind.

w John Balderston, Rose Franken, William
Brown Meloney, David Hart d H. C. Potter
ph Gregg Toland m Alfred Newman

Brian Aherne, Merle Oberon, David Niven,
Karen Morley, Jerome Cowan, Henry
Stephenson, Donald Crisp
'One of the most incredible screen yarns
which has been shown in many a day. . . . If
when the film is shown in Dublin a tidal wave
engulfs Hollywood, it will be caused by the
Emerald Isle turning somersaults.'—Variety

Beloved Infidel*
US 1959   123m   De Luxe   Cinemascope
TCF / Company of Artists (Jerry Wald)

Sheilah Graham, a British chorus girl turned
Hollywood columnist, lives with Scott
Fitzgerald but fails to cure him of alcoholism.
A bitter and even sordid true story becomes a
slice of Hollywood romance, with stars
unsuitably cast. On all levels it falls between
two stools, satisfying nobody.

w Sy Bartlett, book Sheilah Graham and
Gerald Frank d Henry King ph Leon
Shamroy m Franz Waxman

Gregory Peck, Deborah Kerr, Eddie Albert,
Philip Ober, Herbert Rudley, Karin Booth,
Ken Scott
'Catastrophically misguided.'—Penelope
Houston

The Beloved Rogue*
US 1927   99m at 24 fps   bw   silent

Fifteenth-century poet and thief François
Villon becomes a friend of the king, but is
banished when he falls for a lady of the court.
Stylish star vehicle remade as If I Were King
(qv). John Barrymore, Conrad Veidt,
Marceline Day, Mack Swain, Slim
Summerville. Written by Paul Bern; directed
by Alan Crosland; production design by
William Cameron Menzies; for UA.

The Beloved Vagabond*
GB 1936   78m   bw
Ludovico Toeplitz

At the turn of the century, a jilted French
artist becomes a vagabond and falls in love
with an orphan girl.
Mildly amusing bi-lingual production from a
bestselling picaresque novel; production quite
lively.

w Wells Root, Arthur Wimperis, Hugh Mills,
Walter Creighton, novel W. J. Locke d Curtis
Bernhardt ph Franz Planer

Maurice Chevalier, Margaret Lockwood,
Betty Stockfield, Desmond Tester, Austin
Trevor, Peter Haddon, Cathleen Nesbitt
'A weak sister, mostly for the duals.'—
Variety

Below Zero**
US 1930   20m   bw

Street musicians treat a policeman to lunch on
the contents of a found wallet which turns out
to be his. Slow-paced but likeable star comedy
from their best period. Laurel and Hardy,
Frank Holliday, Tiny Sandford. Written by H.
M. Walker; directed by James Parrott; for Hal
Roach.

The Belstone Fox*
GB 1973   103m   Eastmancolor   Todd-
   AO 35
Rank / Independent Artists (Sally Shuter)

A fox and a hound grow up together but the
fox leads to tragedy for its masters.
Good animal and countryside photography
barely compensate for a fragmentary story
with unpleasant moments or for a muddled
attitude towards humans and animals; one is
not clear what audience the result is supposed
to appeal to.

wd James Hill, novel David Rook ph John
Wilcox, James Allen m Laurie Johnson

Eric Porter, Rachel Roberts, Jeremy Kemp,
Bill Travers, Dennis Waterman
● Video: Rank

Ben
US 1972   92m   De Luxe
Cinerama / Bing Crosby (Mort Briskin)

A sickly boy inherits an army of trained rats.
Boring reprise of Willard in which the
audience knows only too well what to expect.
Production and development quite routine.

w Gilbert A. Ralston d Phil Karlson
ph Russell Metty m Walter Scharf

Lee Harcourt Montgomery, Arthur
O'Connell, Rosemary Murphy, Meredith
Baxter, Kaz Garas, Paul Carr, Kenneth Tobey

AAN: title song (m Walter Scharf, ly Don
Black)

'The great decade (1915–25) of the
   progress of motion picture art reaches its
   summit! A cast of 125,000!'
Ben Hur***
US 1926   170m approx (16 fps)   bw
   (colour sequence)   silent
MGM

In the time of Christ, a Jew suffers mightily under the Romans.

The American silent screen's biggest epic; the sea battle and the chariot race are its most famous sequences.

w Bess Meredyth, Carey Wilson, *novel* Lew Wallace *d* Fred Niblo *ph* Karl Struss, Clyde de Vinna, and others *ad* Horace Jackson, Ferdinand Pinney Earle

Ramon Novarro, Francis X. Bushman, Carmel Myers, May McAvoy, Betty Bronson

'Masterpiece of study and patience, a photodrama filled with artistry.'—*New York Times*

† Previously filmed in 1907.

Ben Hur**

US 1959 217m Technicolor Camera 65
MGM (Sam Zimbalist)

Solid, expensive, surprisingly unimaginative remake; generally less sprightly than the silent version.

w Karl Tunberg *d* William Wyler, *Andrew Marton ph* Robert L. Surtees *m* Miklos Rozsa *ad* William A. Horning, Edward Carfagno

Charlton Heston, Haya Harareet, Jack Hawkins, Stephen Boyd, Hugh Griffith, Martha Scott, Sam Jaffe, Cathy O'Donnell, Finlay Currie, Frank Thring, Terence Longdon, André Morell, George Relph

'Watching it is like waiting at a railroad crossing while an interminable freight train lumbers by, sometimes stopping altogether.'—*Dwight MacDonald*

'A Griffith can make a hundred into a crowd while a Wyler can reduce a thousand to a confused cocktail party.'—*Ibid.*

'The most tasteful and visually exciting film spectacle yet produced by an American company.'—*Albert Johnson, Film Quarterly*

'Spectacular without being a spectacle . . . not only is it not simple-minded, it is downright literate.'—*Saturday Review*

'A major motion picture phenomenon.'—*Films in Review*

† The production cost four million dollars, twice the maximum at the time. Rock Hudson, Marlon Brando and Burt Lancaster were all sought in vain for the lead before Heston was selected.

†† This version was subtitled 'A Tale of the Christ'.

AA: best picture; William Wyler; Robert L. Surtees; Miklos Rozsa; Charlton Heston; Hugh Griffith

AAN: Karl Tunberg

● *Video: MGM / UA*

Benchley

The one-reel shorts in which Robert Benchley, sitting behind a desk, delivered nonsensical lectures on aspects of modern life were very popular with better-class audiences, and launched Benchley onto his movie career as a light actor. Here is a list of them:

1928: THE TREASURER'S REPORT; THE SEX LIFE OF THE POLYP; THE SPELLBINDER.

1929: LESSON NUMBER ONE (2 reels); FURNACE TROUBLE (2 reels); STEWED, FRIED AND BOILED (2 reels).
1933: YOUR TECHNOCRACY AND MINE (2 reels).
1935: HOW TO BREAK 90 AT CROQUET; HOW TO SLEEP.
1936: HOW TO BEHAVE; HOW TO TRAIN A DOG; HOW TO VOTE; HOW TO BE A DETECTIVE.
1937: THE ROMANCE OF DIGESTION; HOW TO START THE DAY; A NIGHT AT THE MOVIES.
1938: HOW TO FIGURE INCOME TAX; MUSIC MADE SIMPLE; AN EVENING ALONE; HOW TO RAISE A BABY; THE COURTSHIP OF THE NEWT; HOW TO READ; HOW TO WATCH FOOTBALL; OPENING DAY; MENTAL POISE; HOW TO SUBLET.
1939: AN HOUR FOR LUNCH; DARK MAGIC; HOME EARLY; HOW TO EAT; THE DAY OF REST; SEE YOUR DOCTOR.
1940: THAT INFERIOR FEELING; HOME MOVIES; THE TROUBLE WITH HUSBANDS.
1941: WAITING FOR BABY; CRIME CONTROL; THE FORGOTTEN MAN; HOW TO TAKE A VACATION.
1942: NOTHING BUT NERVES; THE WITNESS; KEEPING IN SHAPE; THE MAN'S ANGLE.
1943: MY TOMATO; NO NEWS IS GOOD NEWS.
1944: IMPORTANT BUSINESS; WHY, DADDY?
1945: BOOGIE WOOGIE (2 reels); I'M A CIVILIAN HERE MYSELF.
In the late seventies a feature compilation was made under the title *Those Wonderful Benchley Shorts*.

Bend of the River**

US 1952 91m Technicolor
U-I (Aaron Rosenberg)
GB title: *Where the River Bends*

1880 wagon trains arrive in Oregon, and the pioneers have trouble with the local bad man. Good standard western with pace and period feeling.

w Borden Chase, *novel* Bend of the Snake by William Gulick *d* Anthony Mann *ph* Irving Glassberg *m* Hans Salter

James Stewart, Arthur Kennedy, Rock Hudson, Julia Adams, Lori Nelson, Jay C. Flippen, Henry Morgan, Royal Dano, Stepin Fetchit

Beneath the Planet of the Apes*

US 1969 94m De Luxe Panavision
TCF / APJAC (Mort Abrahams)

Astronauts on the ape planet discover that it is really Earth and that subterranean human mutants are nursing a live atom bomb. Violence replaces the thoughtfulness of the original, but this is not at all a bad sequel as sequels go.

w Paul Dehn, Mort Abrahams *d* Ted Post *ph* Milton Krasner *m* Leonard Rosenman

James Franciscus, Charlton Heston, Linda Harrison, Kim Hunter, Maurice Evans, Paul Richards, Victor Buono, Jeff Corey, James Gregory, Thomas Gomez

† See *Planet of the Apes*.

● *Video: CBS / Fox*

Beneath the Twelve Mile Reef

US 1953 102m Technicolor
Cinemascope
TCF (Robert Bassler)

Jealousy, tragedy and romance among the Florida sponge fishers.

Fox's early Cinemascope production involved much underwater shooting, a trick octopus, and predictable plot devices.

w A. I. Bezzerides *d* Robert D. Webb *ph* Edward Cronjager *m* Bernard Herrmann

Robert Wagner, Terry Moore, Gilbert Roland, Peter Graves, J. Carrol Naish, Richard Boone, Angela Clarke, Jay Novello

'The dead weight of a melodramatic script overtaxes the gallant attempts at conviction.'—*MFB*

AAN: Edward Cronjager

Bengal Brigade

US 1954 87m Technicolor
U-I (Ted Richmond)
GB title: *Bengal Rifles*

In 19th-century India, an officer is cashiered through false evidence, and becomes an undercover man with the wicked local rajah. Routine Hollywood heroics with a few unintended laughs.

w Richard Alan Simmons, *novel* Bengal Tiger by Hall Hunter *d* Laslo Benedek *ph* Maury Gertsman *m* Joseph Gershenson

Rock Hudson, Dan O'Herlihy, Ursula Thiess, Torin Thatcher, Michael Ansara, Arnold Moss

Bengazi

US 1955 79m bw Superscope
RKO / Panamint (Sam Wiesenthal, Eugene Tevlin)

Various unsavoury characters set out into the African desert to look for gold hidden by the Nazis.

Poor potboiler on predictable lines.

w Endre Boehm, Louis Vittes *d* John Brahm *ph* Joseph Biroc *m* Roy Webb

Richard Conte, Victor McLaglen, Richard Carlson, Mala Powers, Richard Erdman, Gonzales Gonzales, Hillary Brooke

Benjamin, or The Diary of an Innocent Young Man

France 1966 104m Eastmancolor
Paramount / Parc / Marianne (Mag Bodard)

In the 18th century, a 17-year-old orphan is taken in hand by his wealthy aunt and initiated into the mysteries of sex.

Imitation *Tom Jones*, quite good to look at but rather boring.

w Nina Companeez *d* Michel Déville *ph* Ghislain Cloquet

Pierre Clémenti, Michèle Morgan, Catherine Deneuve, Michel Piccoli, Francine Bergé, Anna Gaël, Odile Versois

'Heavy with Gallic naughtiness rather than airy charm . . . a plethora of colourful costumes, foliage and fireworks.'—*MFB*

'A marathon tease . . . an unending series of interrupted coitions . . . a gorgeously wrapped and beribboned Christmas package containing an empty box.'—*John Simon*

Benji*
US 1974   86m   CFI color
Mulberry Square (Joe Camp)

A stray mongrel dog saves two kidnapped children.
Family film par excellence which rang the box office bell in a big way in the US. Its modest merits are rather beside the point.

wd Joe Camp   *ph* Don Reddy   *m* Euel Box

Peter Breck, Edgar Buchanan, Terry Carter, Christopher Connelly

† A sequel, *For the Love of Benji*, followed in 1977.

AAN: song 'I Feel Love' (*m* Euel Box, *ly* Betty Box)

The Benny Goodman Story*
US 1955   117m   Technicolor
U-I (Aaron Rosenberg)

A clarinettist from the Jewish section of Chicago becomes internationally famous.
Sentimental biopic of a familiar figure which comes to life when the sound track is given its head (and the real Goodman's clarinet).

wd Valentine Davies   *ph* William Daniels
md Joseph Gershenson

Steve Allen, Donna Reed, *Berta Gersten*, Herbert Anderson, Robert F. Simon, Sammy Davis Snr, Harry James, Martha Tilton, Gene Krupa

'The customary fictional liberties appear to have been taken.'—*MFB*

Benvenuta*
Belgium / France / Italy 1982   106m
Eastmancolor
La Nouvelle Imagerie / UGC / FR3 / Opéra Film (Jean-Claude Batz)

A filmscript writer interviews a reclusive female novelist about a work which may be autobiographical.
Stylish but fairly incomprehensible romantic drama which makes the audience work rather harder than the material seems to warrant.

w,d André Delvaux, *novel* La Confession Anonyme by Suzanne Lilar   *ph* Charlie Van Damme   *m* Frédéric Devreese

Fanny Ardant, Vittorio Gassman, Françoise Fabian, Mathieu Carrière

Bequest to the Nation*
GB 1973   116m   Technicolor
Universal / Hal B. Wallis
US title: *The Nelson Affair*

The story of Nelson's long affair with the tempestuous Lady Hamilton.
Undistinguished historical drama from a thin

play which despite hard work all round makes very ordinary screen entertainment.

w Terence Rattigan, from his play   *d* James Cellan Jones   *ph* Gerry Fisher   *pd* Carmen Dillon   *m* Michel Legrand

Peter Finch, Glenda Jackson (way over the top), Michael Jayston, Anthony Quayle, Margaret Leighton, Dominic Guard, Nigel Stock, Roland Culver

'As empty as an out-of-town matinee.'—*MFB*

Berkeley Square**
US 1933   87m   bw
Fox (Jesse L. Lasky)

A London house reincarnates its owner as his 18th-century ancestor.
Romantic fantasy on a time lapse theme, the first of many and perhaps the most stylish and self-assured. Remade as *The House on the Square* (qv).

w Sonya Levien, John Balderston, from Balderston's play   *d* Frank Lloyd   *ph* Ernest Palmer   *m* Louis de Francesco   *ad* William Carling

Leslie Howard, Heather Angel, Valerie Taylor, Irene Browne, Beryl Mercer, Colin Keith-Johnson, Alan Mowbray

'Too far above the heads of ordinary theatregoers and too British in tempo and execution to break any box office records.'—*Variety*

AAN: Leslie Howard

Berlin Correspondent
US 1942   70m   bw
TCF (Bryan Foy)

In pre-war Germany an American reporter is kidnapped by the Nazis and replaced by a double . . .
Preposterous melodrama, so silly as to be often quite funny.

w Steve Fisher, Jack Andrews   *d* Eugene Forde   *ph* Virgil Miller   *m* Emil Newman

Dana Andrews, Virginia Gilmore, Mona Maris, Martin Kosleck, Sig Rumann, Kurt Katch, Torben Meyer

Berlin Express*
US 1948   87m   bw
RKO (Bert Granet)

Police of four nations guard a German VIP on a crack train to Berlin.
Rather muddled suspenser with attempts at political moralizing; the cast provides some good moments.

w Harold Medford   *d* Jacques Tourneur
ph Lucien Ballard   *m* Frederick Hollander

Merle Oberon, Robert Ryan, Charles Korvin, Paul Lukas, Robert Coote

● *Video: Kingston*

Berlin, Symphony of a Great City***
Germany 1927   78m   bw   silent
Fox-Europa
original title: *Berlin, die Symphonie einer Grosstadt*

An impression of the life of a city from dawn to midnight, expressed by cinematic montages, angles, sequences, etc, and set to music.
A leader in the field of 'impressionistic' documentaries which are now so familiar (*Rien que les Heures* did a similar job for Paris at around the same time), this still has moments of poetry which have seldom been equalled.

w Walter Ruttman, Karl Freund, Carl Mayer   *d* Walter Ruttman   *ph* Reimar Kuntze, Robert Baberske, Laszlo Schäffer   *m* Edmund Meisel   *ed* Walter Ruttman

Berliner Ballade*
Germany 1948   77m   bw
Comedia Film (Alf Teichs)
aka: *The Ballad of Berlin*

Otto Nobody, an unwilling soldier, returns home to find himself at the mercy of bureaucrats and black marketeers.
Melancholy satire presented as a series of sketches, almost a forerunner of *That Was the Week That Was*.

w Gunter Neumann   *d* Robert Stemmle
ph Georg Krause   *m / ly* Gunter Neumann, Werner Eisbrenner

Gert Fröbe, Anton Zeithammer, Tatjana Sais, O. E. Hasse

'Very much the film of a defeated people.'—*Penelope Houston*

Bermuda Affair
GB 1956   77m   bw

The pilot of a West Indian airline falls for his partner's wife but dies in an air accident.
Tedious and unconvincing marital drama with back-projected local colour. Kim Hunter, Gary Merrill, Ron Randell, Zena Walker. Written by Robert J. Shaw and Edward Sutherland; directed by Edward Sutherland; for Bermuda Studio Productions.

The Bermuda Mystery
US 1944   65m   bw

Friends who have invested in a joint insurance policy are murdered one by one. Competent lower-berth murder mystery. Preston Foster, Ann Rutherford, Charles Butterworth, Helene Reynolds, Richard Lane. Written by W. Scott Darling, from a story by John Larkin; directed by Ben Stoloff; for TCF.

Bernardine*
US 1957   95m   Eastmancolor
Cinemascope
TCF (Samuel G. Engel)

A college student forced to swot for exams asks a friend's elder brother to look after his girl.
Henry Aldrich-style high school comedy, showing the lighter side of *Rebel without a Cause*. Notable for the clean-living hero played by a clean-living singing star, and the reappearance of Janet Gaynor for the only time since 1939, in a routine mother role.

w Theodore Reeves, *play* Mary Chase
d Henry Levin *ph* Paul Vogel *m* Lionel
Newman

Pat Boone, Richard Sargent, Terry Moore,
Janet Gaynor, Walter Abel, Dean Jagger,
Natalie Schaefer, James Drury

Berserk!
GB 1967 96m Technicolor
Columbia (Herman Cohen)

A lady circus owner revels in the publicity
brought about by a series of murders.
Grisly and unattractive thriller with an ageing
star in a series of unsuitably abbreviated
costumes; the script is beyond redemption.

w Herman Cohen, Aben Kandel *d* Jim
O'Connolly *ph* Desmond Dickinson
m Patrick John Scott

Joan Crawford, Diana Dors, Ty Hardin, Judy
Geeson, Michael Gough, Robert Hardy,
Geoffrey Keen, Sidney Tafler, Philip Madoc

Berth Marks
US 1929 20m bw silent

Stan and Ollie, on a train, have to share an
upper berth. Overstretched single-situation
comedy, one of the team's poorest. Laurel and
Hardy. Written by Leo McCarey and H. M.
Walker; directed by Lewis R. Foster; for Hal
Roach.

The Bespoke Overcoat**
GB 1956 33m bw
Remus (Jack Clayton)

A clerk in a clothing warehouse is refused a
coat and asks a tailor friend to make him one.
But he dies of cold and his ghost persuades the
tailor to steal the coat he deserved.
The story seems stiff, but the production has a
rich Dickensian feel and may be the best short
drama filmed in Britain.

w Wolf Mankowitz, *story* Gogol *d* Jack
Clayton *ph* Wolfgang Suschitzky *m* Georges
Auric

Alfie Bass, David Kossoff

Best Boy*
US 1979 111m colour 16mm

A documentary, shot by his cousin, of the
problems of a mentally retarded 53-year-old
man whose elderly parents are ailing. A film
with very moving elements, though they would
have been even sharper at half the length.
Written, directed and produced by *Ira Wohl*.

Best Foot Forward
US 1943 94m Technicolor
MGM (Arthur Freed)

A glamorous publicity-seeking film star
accepts an invitation to a military college ball.
Old-fashioned formula musical based on a
lightweight Broadway success.

w Irving Brecher, Fred Finkelhoffe, *play* John
Cecil Holmes *d* Edward Buzzell *ph* Leonard
Smith *md* Lennie Hayton *songs* Hugh
Martin, Ralph Blane *ch* Charles Walters

Lucille Ball, William Gaxton, Virginia
Weidler, Harry James and his Orchestra, June
Allyson, Gloria de Haven

Best Friends*
US 1982 116m Technicolor
Warner / Joe Wizan / Norman Jewison

Two writers who have enjoyed a peaceful
professional relationship find problems when
they get married and visit their respective
families.
Rather a heavy comedy which seems to have
no real point, this gets by on enjoyable
sequences and star performances.

w Valerie Curtin, Barry Levinson *d* Norman
Jewison *ph* Jordan Cronenweth *m* Michel
Legrand *ad* Joe Russo *ed* Don Zimmerman

Burt Reynolds, Goldie Hawn, Jessica Tandy,
Barnard Hughes, Audra Lindley, Keenan
Wynn

'A print-out of a script conference at which
everyone collapsed at everyone else's
contributory sally.'—*Sunday Times*
AAN: song 'How Do You Keep the Music
Playing?' by John Williams, Alan and Marilyn
Bergman
● *Video: Warner*

The Best House in London*
GB 1968 96m Eastmancolor
MGM / Bridge / Carlo Ponti (Philip Breen,
Kurt Unger)

A Victorian publicity agent tries to organize a
government-sponsored brothel.
Cheerful slam-bang historical send-up with as
many dull thuds of banality as pleasant
witticisms.

w Denis Norden *d* Philip Savile *ph* Alex
Thompson *m* Mischa Spoliansky *pd* Wilfrid
Shingleton

David Hemmings, George Sanders, Joanna
Pettet, Warren Mitchell, Dany Robin, William
Rushton

The Best Little Whorehouse in Texas
US 1982 114m Technicolor
Panavision
Universal / RKO (Thomas L. Miller, Edward
K. Milkis, Robert L. Boyett)

A long-established Texas whorehouse
becomes the object of a clean-up campaign.
Flat and feeble screen version of a limp and
tuneless musical which astonishingly was a
Broadway hit, perhaps because people thought
it was naughty. Onscreen the acting is too
easy-going and the script too coy for anybody
to have a good time.

w Larry L. King, Peter Masterson from their
stage play *m* / *ly* Carol Hall *d* Colin Higgins
ph William A. Fraker *m* Patrick Williams
pd Robert F. Boyle

Burt Reynolds, Dolly Parton, Charles
Durning, Dom DeLuise, Jim Nabors, Robert
Mandan, Lois Nettleton, Noah Beery Jnr

'Rancid, self-deceiving, hypocritical stuff.'—
Observer
'A sanitized, coyly predictable piece of
brothel creeping, set to musak by a poorly
programmed computer.'—*Guardian*

'Almost everything about it is misjudged.'—
Daily Mail
'High on jollity, low on country and
western, and very uncertainly directed.'—*Sight
and Sound*
AAN: Charles Durning
● *Video: CIC*

The Best Man***
US 1964 104m bw
UA / Stuart Millar, Lawrence Turman

Two contenders for a presidential nomination
seek the support of the dying ex-president.
Brilliant political melodrama, ingeniously
adapted on a low budget from an incisive play,
with splendid dramatic scenes, memorable
performances and good convention detail.

w Gore Vidal from his play *d* Franklin
Schaffner *ph* Haskell Wexler *m* Mort
Lindsey

Henry Fonda, Cliff Robertson, *Lee Tracy*,
Margaret Leighton, Edie Adams, Kevin
McCarthy, *Shelley Berman*, Ann Sothern,
Gene Raymond, Mahalia Jackson

'A fine opportunity to watch pros at work in
a hard-hitting and cogent drama that seems to
become more topical and have more relevance
with each showing.'—*Judith Crist*
'Some of the wittiest lines since *Strangelove*
. . . the acting fairly crackled with
authenticity.'—*Isabel Quigly*
AAN: Lee Tracy

74
The Best Man Wins
US 1934 75m bw

A harbour cop finds himself tracking down the
friend who had saved his life. Predictable
tough-guy programmer. Edmund Lowe, Jack
Holt, Bela Lugosi, Florence Rice, Forrester
Harvey. Written by Ethel Hill and Bruce
Manning; directed by Erle C. Kenton; for
Columbia.

The Best of Enemies
US / Italy 1961 104m Technirama
Columbia / Dino de Laurentiis

During the Abyssinian campaign of 1941, an
Italian and a British officer learn mutual
respect.
Mild satirical comedy drama with a few points
to make about war; the elements blend rather
obviously and dispiritingly.

w Jack Pulman *d* Guy Hamilton *ph* Giuseppe
Rotunno *m* Nino Rota

David Niven, Alberto Sordi, Michael Wilding,
Amedeo Nazzari, Harry Andrews, David
Opatoshu, Kenneth Fortescue, Duncan
Macrae

The Best of Everything*
US 1959 121m De Luxe Cinemascope
TCF (Jerry Wald)

Personal problems of a New York publisher's
female staff.
Slick novelette on the lines of a naughty Peg's
Paper; pure Hollywood gossamer.

w Edith Sommer, Mann Rubin, *novel* Rona
Jaffe *d* Jean Negulesco *ph* William C.
Mellor *m* Alfred Newman

Hope Lange, Stephen Boyd, Joan Crawford,
Louis Jourdan, Suzy Parker, Martha Hyer,
Diane Baker, Brian Aherne, Robert Evans,
Brett Halsey, Donald Harron
  'A cautionary tale sensationally told.'—
Alexander Walker

AAN: title song (*m* Alfred Newman,
ly Sammy Cahn)

Best of the Badmen*
US 1951   84m   Technicolor
RKO (Herman Schlom)

At the end of the Civil War Jeff Clanton
organizes the break-up of Quantrell's Raiders,
but is himself arrested on a trumped-up charge
and needs the Raiders' help.
Standard western notable for a good cast and
for bringing in a remarkable number of
historical outlaws, doing rather unhistorical
things.

w Robert Hardy Andrews, John Twist
d William D. Russell *ph* Edward Cronjager
m Paul Sawtell

Robert Ryan, Claire Trevor, Jack Buetel,
Robert Preston, Walter Brennan, Bruce
Cabot, John Archer, Lawrence Tierney
● *Video: Kingston*

The Best Things in Life Are Free*
US 1956   103m   Eastmancolor
    Cinemascope
TCF (Henry Ephron)

From Broadway to Hollywood in the twenties,
the story of songwriting team De Sylva, Brown
and Henderson.
Gangsters, movie studios and the writing of
'Sonny Boy' for Al Jolson all figure in this
amiable musical which spends more time on
jokes than romance; the numbers are
disappointing despite good tunes.

w William Bowers, Phoebe Ephron *d* Michael
Curtiz *ph* Leon Shamroy *md* Lionel Newman

Ernest Borgnine, Gordon Macrae, Dan
Dailey, Sheree North, Jacques d'Amboise,
Norman Brooks, Murvyn Vye

AAN: Lionel Newman

'Three wonderful loves in the best picture
  of the year!'
The Best Years of Our Lives****
US 1946   182m   bw
Samuel Goldwyn

Three men come home from war to a small
middle-American community, and find it
variously difficult to pick up where they left
off.
The situations and even some of the characters
now seem a little obvious, but this was a
superb example of high-quality film-making in
the forties, with smiles and tears cunningly
spaced, and a film which said what was needed
on a vital subject.

w Robert Sherwood, novel *Glory for Me* by
Mackinlay Kantor *d* William Wyler *ph* Gregg
Toland *m* Hugo Friedhofer

Fredric March, Myrna Loy, Teresa Wright,
Dana Andrews, Virginia Mayo, Cathy
O'Donnell, *Hoagy Carmichael, Harold Russell*

THE BEST YEARS OF OUR LIVES.   Happy to be middle-aged, Myrna Loy and Fredric
March pick up right where they left off after five years of total war.

(a handless veteran whose only film this was),
Gladys George, Roman Bohnen, Ray Collins
  'One of the best pictures of our lives!'—
Variety
  'The result is a work of provocative and
moving insistence and beauty.'—*Howard
Barnes*
  'One recognizes everything and in the end
this recognition is all the excitement, for what
is on the screen becomes finally as accustomed
and undramatic as the shabby decor of the
theatre itself.'—*Robert Warshow, The
Immediate Experience*
  'One of the very few American studio-made
movies in years that seem to me profoundly
pleasing, moving and encouraging.'—*James
Agee*
† In 1977 came a TV remake *Returning Home*
but it did not lead to the expected series.

AA: best picture; Robert Sherwood; William
Wyler; Hugo Friedhofer; Fredric March;
Harold Russell

La Bête Humaine**
France 1938   99m   bw
Paris Films (Robert Hakim)
aka: *The Human Beast; Judas Was a
    Woman*

A psychopathic train driver falls for a married
woman, plans with her to kill her husband, but
finally strangles her instead.

Curious melodrama with strong visual
sequences, flawed by its ambivalent attitude to
its hero-villain.

wd Jean Renoir, novel Emile Zola *ph* Curt
Courant *m* Joseph Kosma

Jean Gabin, Simone Simon, Julien Carette,
Fernand Ledoux, Jean Renoir
  'French production at its best.'—*Variety*
  'Marvellous atmosphere and a fine cast, but
the material turns oppressive.'—*New Yorker,
1978*
  'What is most deft is the way Renoir works
the depot and the man's job into every scene—
conversations on platforms, in washrooms and
canteens, views from the station master's
window over the steaming metal waste: the
short sharp lust worked out in a wooden
platelayer's shed among shunted trucks under
the steaming rain.'—*Graham Greene*
† Remade in Hollywood as *Human Desire*.

Betrayal*
GB 1982   95m   colour
Horizon / Sam Spiegel (Eric Rattray)

The story of a publisher, his wife and her lover
is told in scenes that go backwards in time.
Sharply acted stuff very typical of its author,
for audiences with wideawake minds; but
more theatrical than cinematic.

w Harold Pinter from his play *d* David Jones
ph Mike Fash *m* Dominic Muldowney

Jeremy Irons, Ben Kingsley, Patricia Hodge,
Avril Elgar

AAN: Screenplay adaptation

● *Video: Virgin*

Betrayal from the East
US 1945 83m bw
RKO (Herman Schlom)

Japanese out to sabotage the Panama Canal
are thwarted by a carnival showman.
Extravagant but penny-pinching flagwaver.

w Kenneth Gamet, Aubrey Wisberg, *novel*
Alan Hynd *d* William Berke *ph* Russell
Metty *m* Roy Webb

Lee Tracy, Nancy Kelly, Richard Loo, Abner
Biberman, Regis Toomey, Philip Ahn,
Addison Richards, Sen Yung, Drew Pearson

Betrayed
US 1954 108m Eastmancolor
MGM (Gottfried Reinhardt)

In 1943 a Dutch intelligence officer works with
a resistance leader who turns out to be a
traitor.
Slow-moving, studio-set romantic melodrama
of the old school; not very lively.

w Ronald Millar, George Froeschel
d Gottfried Reinhardt *ph* Frederick A.
Young *m* Walter Goehr

Clark Gable, Victor Mature, Lana Turner,
Louis Calhern, O. E. Hasse, Wilfrid Hyde
White, Ian Carmichael, Niall MacGinnis,
Nora Swinburne

'The Harold Robbins people: what you
dream, they do!'
The Betsy
US 1977 125m Technicolor
Allied Artists / Harold Robbins International
  (Robert R. Weston)

Jockeying for power in the boardroom and the
family life of an aged car manufacturer.
Rather tame and obvious melodrama
enlivened by its star performance.

w William Bast, Walter Bernstein,
novel Harold Robbins *Daniel Petrie*
ph Mario Tosi *m* John Barry

Laurence Olivier, Robert Duvall, Tommy Lee
Jones, Katharine Ross, Jane Alexander,
Lesley-Anne Down, Joseph Wiseman, Edward
Herrmann
  'Almost compulsively dreadful.'—*Derek*
Malcolm, Guardian

The Better 'Ole
US 1926 97m (24 fps) bw silent

A British sergeant in Flanders proves that his
major is actually a German spy. Comedy–
drama based on the cartoons of Old Bill by
Bruce Bairnsfather. (The title comes from one
in which Old Bill, in the trenches, is saying to
a disgruntled soldier: 'If yer knows of a better
'ole, go to it.'). Criticism is irrelevant now, but
the piece has historical interest.

w Charles Reisner, Darryl F. Zanuck
d Charles Reisner *ph* Ed Du Par, Walter
Robinson

Syd Chaplin, Doris Hill, Harold Goodwin,
Edgar Kennedy

Between Heaven and Hell
US 1956 94m Eastmancolor
  Cinemascope
TCF (David Weisbart)

After Pearl Harbor a young southern
landowner is called up and finds himself on
active service with mixed racial types.
Vaguely anti-war, pro-understanding action
thriller which ends up going through
predictable heroics in a professional but not
too sympathetic manner.

w Harry Brown, *novel* The Day the Century
Ended by Francis Gwaltney *d* Richard
Fleischer *ph* Leo Tover *m* Hugo Friedhofer

Robert Wagner, Buddy Ebsen, Broderick
Crawford, Brad Dexter, Mark Damon, Robert
Keith, Ken Clark, Skip Homeier, Harvey
Lembeck

AAN: Hugo Friedhofer

Between Midnight and Dawn
US 1950 89m bw
Columbia (Hunt Stromberg)

Radio policemen track down a racketeer.
Competent, undistinguished programmer.

w Eugene Ling *d* Gordon Douglas
ph George E. Diskant *m* George Duning

Mark Stevens, Edmond O'Brien, Gale Storm,
Donald Buka, Gale Robbins, Roland Winters

Between Two Women
US 1937 88m bw

Romance between doctor and nurse is
interrupted by her alcoholic husband and his
infatuation with a patient. Incident-packed
men-in-white melodrama. Franchot Tone,
Maureen O'Sullivan, Virginia Bruce, Edward
Norris, Cliff Edwards, Janet Beecher. Written
by Carey Wilson, from a story by Erich Von
Stroheim; directed by George B. Seitz; for
MGM. (NB: Title later changed to
Surrounded by Women to avoid confusion with
a Dr Kildare episode.) 'Class B that almost
grew up. Eternal triangle in a hospital; okay
dualler for nabes.'—*Variety*

Between Two Worlds*
US 1944 112m bw
Warner (Mark Hellinger)

A number of air-raid victims, and two lovers
who have committed suicide, find themselves
on a luxury ship en route to the next world.
Nice-looking but slow and turgid remake of
Outward Bound (qv), largely sunk in its own
misery but redeemed by two performances.

w Daniel Fuchs, *play* Sutton Vane *d* Edward
A. Blatt *ph* Carl Guthrie *m* Erich Wolfgang
Korngold

John Garfield, *Edmund Gwenn*, Eleanor
Parker, Paul Henreid, *Sydney Greenstreet*,
Sara Allgood, George Tobias, Faye Emerson,
George Coulouris, Dennis King, Isobel Elsom

'For ferry service from a world so saturated
with death, the ship seems strangely empty—a
fact that was not obtrusive in a day when
death was not intrusive.'—*James Agee*

Between Us Girls
US 1942 89m bw
Universal

A mother and daughter are both involved in
romances which tend to cross.
Mild comedy, a disappointing bid for stardom
for a disappointing young star.

w Myles Connolly, True Boardman, *play* Le
Fruit Vert by Regis Gignoux, Jacques Thery
d Henry Koster *ph* Joseph Valentine
m Frank Skinner

Diana Barrymore, Kay Francis, Robert
Cummings, John Boles, Scotty Beckett, Ethel
Griffies

Beverly of Graustark
US 1926 85m approx at 24 fps bw
  silent

When a prince falls ill, his girl cousin
impersonates him at an important ceremony.
Cheerful Ruritanian comedy. Marion Davies,
Antonio Moreno, Roy D'Arcy, Creighton
Hale. Written by Agnes Christine Johnson;
directed by Sidney Franklin; for MGM.

Beverly Hills Cop*
US 1984 105m Technicolor
Paramount / Don Simpson / Jerry
  Bruckheimer

A cop tracks down the killers of his best
friend.
Ho-hum melodrama with farcical elements,
illuminated by the sudden star value of the
foul-mouthed Eddie Murphy and by a lively
music score.

w Daniel Petrie Jnr *d* Martin Brest *ph* Bruce
Surtees *m Harold Faltermeyer* *pd* Angelo
Graham

Eddie Murphy, Judge Reinhold, Lisa
Eilbacher, John Ashton, Ronny Cox, Steven
Berkoff, James Russo

Beware My Lovely
US 1952 77m bw
RKO / Filmmakers (Collier Young)

A handyman employed by a widow turns out
to be a mental defective who imprisons and
threatens to rape and murder her.
Dismal suspenser with a lot of screaming and
running around but very little flair.

w Mel Dinelli, from his play The Man
d Harry Horner *ph* George E. Diskant
m Leith Stevens

Ida Lupino, Robert Ryan, Taylor Holmes,
Barbara Whiting

'Inept characterization and ludicrously
repetitive situations will surely rank this
among the silliest films of the year.'—*MFB*

Beware of Pity*
GB 1946 106m bw
Two Cities (W. P. Lipscomb)

An officer courts a crippled girl out of pity.
She finds out and kills herself.

Ambitious but rather artificial and dreary drama, a shade too pleased with its own literariness; performances straitjacketed by production.

w W. P. Lipscomb, Elizabeth Baron, Margaret Steen, *novel* Stefan Zweig d Maurice Elvey *ph* Derick Williams

Lilli Palmer, Albert Lieven, Cedric Hardwicke, Gladys Cooper, Linden Travers, Ernest Thesiger, Emrys Jones

Beware Spooks!
US 1939 65m bw

A nervous policeman routs crooks operating from a fairground. Standard star comedy with some funny moments. Joe E. Brown, Mary Carlisle, Clarence Kolb, Marc Lawrence, Don Beddoe. Written by Richard Flournoy, Albert Duffy, Brian Marlow; directed by Edward Sedgwick; for Robert Sparks / Columbia.

Beware! The Blob
US 1971 88m De Luxe
Jack H. Harris
GB title: *Son of Blob*

A mysterious jelly from outer space consumes most of the population of a small town. Spoofy sequel to one of the original space monster movies of the fifties. It's all too laboured to raise a thrill or a smile.

w Jack Woods, Anthony Harris d Larry Hagman ph Al Hamm m Mort Garson sp Tim Baar

Robert Walker, Gwynne Gilford, Godfrey Cambridge, Richard Webb, Shelley Berman, Carol Lynley, Burgess Meredith, Gerrit Graham, Larry Hagman

Bewitched
US 1945 65m bw
MGM (Arch Oboler)

A girl with twin personalities has her murderous element exorcized by a spiritualist. Hilarious nonsense, ancestor of the Eve and Lizzie schizos of the fifties.

wd Arch Oboler, from his story Alter Ego ph Charles Salerno Jnr m Bronislau Kaper

Phyllis Thaxter, Edmund Gwenn, Addison Richards, Kathleen Lockhart

'Oboler manages the first persuasive imitations of stream of consciousness I know of in a movie. Much more often, he bores to desperation with the vulgarity and mere violence of his effects.'—*James Agee*

Beyond a Reasonable Doubt*
US 1956 80m bw
RKO (Bert Friedlob)

A novelist is persuaded by a crusading newspaper proprietor to fake circumstantial evidence incriminating himself in a murder, thus proving the uselessness of such evidence. He does it so well that he is convicted . . . but that doesn't matter as he was guilty all the time.

Ingenious but rather cheerless and mechanical thriller. The actors extract what they can from a script intent on sleight of hand, but the distinguished director is at his most flatulent.

w Douglas Morrow d Fritz Lang ph William Snyder m Herschel Burke Gilbert

Dana Andrews, Joan Fontaine, Sidney Blackmer, Philip Bourneuf, Shepperd Strudwick, Arthur Franz, Edward Binns

'An adventure which cowards quit early and weaklings never finish at all!'

Beyond Glory
US 1948 82m bw
Paramount (Robert Fellows)

The honour of a West Point cadet is vindicated.
Proficient but dramatically turgid vehicle for an absurdly over-age star.

w Jonathan Latimer, Charles Marquis Warren, William Wister Haines d John Farrow ph John F. Seitz m Victor Young

Alan Ladd, Donna Reed, George Coulouris, George Macready, Audie Murphy

Beyond Mombasa
GB1955 90m Technicolor
Columbia / Hemisphere (Adrian Worker)

In East Africa, an American avenges his brother's death at the hands of the Mau Mau (here called the Leopard Men and revealed to be run by a mad English missionary). Tasteless and rather humdrum jungle adventure using real-life problems purely as a backdrop.

w Richard English, Gene Levitt, *novel* Mark of the Leopard by James Eastwood d George Marshall ph Frederick A. Young m Humphrey Searle

Cornel Wilde, Donna Reed, Leo Genn, Ron Randell, Christopher Lee

Beyond Reasonable Doubt
New Zealand 1980 108m colour
Endeavour / New Zealand Film Commission (John Barnett)

A vengeful inspector convicts a farmer who may or may not be guilty of a triple murder. Sometimes striking but generally muddled crime story, which is based rather remotely on a real case but keeps shifting its angle.

w David Yallop, from his book d John Laing ph Alun Bollinger m Dave Fraser

David Hemmings, John Hargreaves, Tony Barry, Martyn Sanderson

'The queen of the tropics finds a new jungle man!'

Beyond the Blue Horizon*
US 1942 76m Technicolor
Paramount (Monta Bell)

An orphan white girl grows up on a tropical island with a chimpanzee and a swimming tiger; when rescued and her story doubted, she leads an expedition back to prove it.
The most tongue-in-cheek of the Lamour jungle extravaganzas, with plenty of simple fun.

w Frank Butler d Alfred Santell ph Charles Boyle m Victor Young

Dorothy Lamour, Richard Denning, Jack Haley, Patricia Morison, Walter Abel, Helen Gilbert, Elizabeth Patterson

Beyond the Curtain
GB 1960 88m bw
Rank / Welbeck (John Martin)

A flying officer rescues a stewardess whose plane has been forced down in East Germany. Inept, penny-pinching cold war melodrama in which very little happens.

w John Cresswell, Compton Bennett, *novel* Thunder Above by Charles F. Blair d Compton Bennett ph Eric Cross m Eric Pakeman

Richard Greene, Eva Bartok, Marius Goring, Lucie Mannheim, Andree Melly, George Mikell, John Welsh

'A twelve o'clock girl in a nine o'clock town!'

Beyond the Forest*
US 1949 96m bw
Warner (Henry Blanke)

The discontented wife of a small-town doctor has an affair with a wealthy Chicagoan, murders a witness, attempts suicide, and dies of fever.
The star caricatures herself in this overblown melodrama which marked the unhappy end of her association with the studio. The rest of the cast suffer more dumbly from the script's unintentional hilarities.

w Lenore Coffee, *novel* Stuart Engstrandt d King Vidor ph Robert Burks m Max Steiner

Bette Davis (Rosa Moline), Joseph Cotten (Dr Lewis Moline), David Brian (Neil Latimer); and Ruth Roman, Minor Watson, Dona Drake, Regis Toomey

ROSA: 'What a dump!'

ROSA: 'If I don't get out of here, I'll just die! Living here is like waiting for the funeral to begin.'

'Nobody's as good as Bette when she's bad!'—*publicity*

'This peerless piece of camp.'—*New Yorker, 1978*

'Miss Davis makes a regrettably melodramatic mess of what is undoubtedly one of the most unfortunate stories she has ever tackled.'—*Newsweek*

AAN: Max Steiner

Beyond the Poseidon Adventure
US 1979 114m Technicolor
Panavision
Warner / Irwin Allen

When rescuers reach the topsy-turvy passenger liner, one of them is intent on plunder.
Dreary alternative ending to *The Poseidon Adventure*, with cardboard character studies, cut-price action, and tenth-rate technicalities.

w Nelson Gidding d Irwin Allen ph Joseph Biroc m Jerry Fielding md Preston Ames

Michael Caine, Telly Savalas, Karl Malden, Sally Field, Peter Boyle, Jack Warden, Shirley Knight, Shirley Jones, Slim Pickens

● Video: Warner

Beyond the Time Barrier
US 1959 75m bw
AIP / Pacific International / Miller-Consolidated (Robert Clarke)

A test pilot crosses the fifth dimension and finds himself in 2024 when civilization has gone underground to avoid nuclear contamination.
Crude science fiction, roughly on the level of Flash Gordon but less entertaining.

w Arthur G. Pierce d Edgar G. Ulmer ph Meredith Nicholson m Darrell Calker

Robert Clarke, Darlene Tompkins, Adrienne Arden, Vladimir Sokoloff, Stephen Bekassy

Beyond the Valley of the Dolls
US 1970 109m De Luxe Panavision
TCF (Russ Meyer)

Three girls in Hollywood enjoy the wilder reaches of show biz high life.
The skinflick director's first film for a major studio, with positively no connection with *Valley of the Dolls*, is not explicitly pornographic but pussyfoots around with as many general excesses as can be crammed into two hours. If taken as high camp it provides a laugh or two, but is chiefly notable as marking a major studio's deepest dip into muddy waters.

w Roger Ebert d Russ Meyer ph Fred J. Koenekamp m Stu Phillips, William Loose

Dolly Read, Cynthia Myers, Marcia McBroom, John La Zar, Michael Blodgett, Edy Williams
　'If one can resist walking out, the last half hour is quite manic.'—*MFB*
　'A film whose total, idiotic, monstrous badness raises it to the pitch of near-irresistible entertainment.'—*Alexander Walker*
　'Awful, stupid and preposterous . . . also weirdly funny and a real curio, rather like a Grandma Moses illustration for a work by the Marquis de Sade.'—*John Simon*

● Video: CBS / Fox

Beyond This Place*
GB 1959 90m bw
Renown / Georgefield (Maxwell Setton, John R. Sloan)
US title: *Web of Evidence*

An American visiting London finds his supposedly dead father in prison serving a life sentence for murder; he delves into history and finds the real culprit.
Spiritless murder mystery with less serious intent than the original novel; tolerable entertainment.

w Kenneth Taylor, *novel* A. J. Cronin d Jack Cardiff ph Wilkie Cooper m Douglas Gamley ad Ken Adam

Van Johnson, Vera Miles, Bernard Lee, Emlyn Williams, Jean Kent, Moultrie Kelsall, Leo McKern, Ralph Truman

Beyond Tomorrow
US 1940 84m bw

Two elderly ghosts return at Christmas to help young lovers. An amiably modest example of the kind they don't do any more. Richard Carlson, Jean Parker, C. Aubrey Smith, Charles Winninger. Written by Adele Comandini from a story by Mildred Cram; directed by Edward Sutherland; for RKO.

Bezhin Meadow**
USSR 1937 31m bw
Mosfilm
original title: *Bezhin Lug*

Fragments from an incomplete Eisenstein film are held together by freeze frames.
Even this collection of bits and pieces shows the power of the master.

w Alexander Rozhdestvenski, *story* Ivan Turgenev d Sergei Eisenstein ph Edouard Tissé

Vitya Kartashov, Boris Zakhava, Igor Pavlenko
† The film was reconstructed in 1966.

Bhowani Junction*
GB 1956 110m Eastmancolor Cinemascope
MGM (Pandro S. Berman)

Adventures of an Anglo-Indian girl during the last years of British India.
Disappointingly anaemic semi-epic from a gutsy novel, variably handled by all concerned.

w Sonya Levien, Ivan Moffat, *novel* John Masters d George Cukor ph Frederick A. Young m Miklos Rozsa

Ava Gardner, Stewart Granger, *Francis Matthews*, Bill Travers, Abraham Sofaer, Marne Maitland, Peter Illing, Freda Jackson, Edward Chapman
　'An unwieldy, flatly-conceived charade.'—*MFB*
　'One may believe with Henry Ford that history is bunk; if so, be assured that the labour pains of India are not half as much bunk as the romance of Victoria Jones, daughter of a Hindu lady, and a Welsh engine driver.'—*Alexander Walker*

The Bible*
US / Italy 1966 174m De Luxe Dimension 150 (70mm)
TCF / Dino de Laurentiis (Luigi Luraschi)

Through the Old Testament from Adam to Isaac.
A portentous creation with whispered commentary gives way to a dull misty Eden with decorous nudes, a sprightly Noah's Ark, a spectacular Babel, a brooding Sodom and a turgid Abraham. The pace is killingly slow and the script has little religious sense, but the pictures are often pretty.

w Christopher Fry and others d John Huston ph Giuseppe Rotunno m Toshiro Mayuzumi ad Mario Chiari

Michael Parks (Adam), Ulla Bergryd (Eve), Richard Harris (Cain), *John Huston* (Noah), Stephen Boyd (Nimrod), George C. Scott (Abraham), Ava Gardner (Sarah), Peter O'Toole (the three angels)
　'An Old Testament spectacular like any other.'—*David Robinson*
　'At a time when religion needs all the help it can get, John Huston may have set its cause back a couple of thousand years.'—*Rex Reed*

AAN: Toshiro Mayuzumi

● Video: CBS / Fox

Les Biches**
France / Italy 1968 99m Eastmancolor
La Boétie / Alexandra (André Génovès)
aka: *The Does*

Two lesbians form an uneasy *ménage à trois* with a young architect, who loves both of them.
Fascinating and well-detailed character study with more depth than at first appears.

w Paul Gégauff, Claude Chabrol d Claude Chabrol ph Jean Rabier m Pierre Jansen

Stéphane Audran, Jacqueline Sassard, Jean-Louis Trintignant
　'You can almost see tubes attached to the heels of all the characters, through which the meaning has been sucked out of them and Chabrol pumped in.'—*John Simon*

Bicycle Thieves****
Italy 1948 90m bw
PDS-ENIC (Umberto Scarparelli)
original title: *Ladri di Biciclette*

An Italian workman, long unemployed, is robbed of the bicycle he needs for his new job, and he and his small son search Rome for it.
The epitome of Italian neo-realism, the slight human drama is developed so that it has all the force of *King Lear*, and both the acting and the backgrounds are vividly compelling.

w Cesare Zavattini d Vittorio de Sica ph Carlo Montuori m Alessandro Cicognini

Lamberto Maggiorani, Enzo Staiola
　'A film of rare humanity and sensibility.'—*Gavin Lambert*
　'A memorable work of art with the true flavour of reality. To see it is an experience worth having.'—*Richard Mallett, Punch*
　'My idea is to de-romanticize the cinema.'—*Vittorio de Sica*

AA: best foreign film; Cesare Zavattini

● Video: Longman

Les Bicyclettes de Belsize*
GB 1969 29m Eastmancolor
Delmore / Ullustria (Jacques de Lane Lea)

The way to true love for a Hampstead shop owner is found through his bicycle.
Mildly attractive whimsy, obviously patterned after *Les Parapluies de Cherbourg* but not quite hitting the spot.

w Michael Newling d Douglas Hickox ph Wolfgang Suschitzky m / ly Les Reed, Barry Mason

Anthony May, Judy Huxtable

Il Bidone••
Italy / France 1955   109m   bw
Titanus / SGC
aka: *The Swindlers*

A group of petty swindlers fails to move into
the higher criminal bracket.
Sharply observed but rather sentimental
melodrama with tragic pretensions.

w Federico Fellini, Ennio Flaiano, Tullio
Pinelli   *d* Federico Fellini   *ph* Otello Martelli
m Nino Rota

Broderick Crawford, Richard Basehart,
Franco Fabrizi, Giulietta Masina

Big Bad Mama
US 1974   85m   Metrocolor
Santa Cruz (Roger Corman)

In 1932 Texas, a desirable widow becomes a
bank robber. Fast moving, violent nonsense,
like a caricature of *Bonnie and Clyde*, which
was itself a caricature.

w William Norton, Frances Doel   *d* Steve
Carver   *ph* Bruce Logan   *m* David Grisman

Angie Dickinson, William Shatner, Tom
Skerritt, Susan Sennett, Robbie Lee.

The Big Blockade•
GB 1941   73m   bw
Ealing (Alberto Cavalcanti)

A semi-documentary showing the importance
of blockading Germany in winning the war.
A curious all-star propaganda revue with some
sketches more effective than others.

w Charles Frend, Angus Macphail   *d* Charles
Frend   *ph* Wilkie Cooper   *m* Richard
Addinsell

Leslie Banks, Michael Redgrave, John Mills,
Will Hay (his only serious role), Frank Cellier,
Robert Morley, Alfred Drayton, Michael
Rennie, Marius Goring, Bernard Miles

'Topical subject matter, graphic descriptive
work, pungent commentary, thrilling
spectacle, clever characterisation.'—*Kine
Weekly*

The Big Boodle
US 1957   83m   bw
UA / Monteflor (Lewis F. Blumberg)
GB Title: *Night in Havana*

A croupier in an Havana gambling casino is
suspected of knowing where counterfeited
plates are hidden . . .
An undistinguished chase film with the star
very tired and a long way from home.

w Jo Eisinger, *novel* Robert Sylvester
d Richard Wilson   *ph* Lee Garmes   *m* Raoul
Lavista

Errol Flynn, Pedro Armendariz, Gia Scala,
Rossana Rory

The Big Bounce
US 1969   102m   Technicolor
   Panavision
Warner / Greenway (Wiliam Dozier)

An ex-GI with a criminal record gets into
sexual and criminal trouble while working at a
Californian motel.

Unattractive melodrama with no discernible
point, certainly not to entertain.

w Robert Dozier, *novel* Elmore Leonard
d Alex March   *ph* Howard R. Schwartz
m Michael Curb

Ryan O'Neal, Leigh Taylor-Young, Van
Heflin, James Daly, Robert Webber, Lee
Grant

Big Boy
US 1930   68m approx   bw

A negro jockey wins a big race. Star musical
from a Broadway original; routine except that
Jolson plays in blackface, then comes on as
himself for the finale. Al Jolson. Lousie
Closser Hale, Noah Beery. Written by William
K. Wells and Perry Vekroff; directed by Alan
Crosland; for Warner. 'Comedy entertaining
in hoke way, but production inferior to
previous Jolson pictures.'—*Variety*

The Big Brawl
US 1980   95m   Technicolor   Panavision
Warner Brothers / Golden Harvest
   (Raymond Chow)

The son of a Chinese restaurateur in Chicago
outwits gangsters.
Silly but quite entertaining chopsocky
melodrama laced with comedy.

wd Robert Clouse   *ph* Robert Jessup   *m* Lalo
Schifrin

Jackie Chan, Jose Ferrer, Kristine de Bell,
Mako, David Sheiner

The Big Broadcast••
US 1932   78m   bw
Paramount

A failing radio station is saved by an all-star
show.
Revue-style show with a minimum of plot,
valuable as archive material covering many
stars of the time.

w George Marion Jnr, *novel* Wild Waves by
William Ford Manley   *d* Frank Tuttle
ph George Folsey

Bing Crosby, Kate Smith, George Burns,
Gracie Allen, Stuart Erwin, Leila Hyams, Cab
Calloway, the Mills Brothers, the Boswell
Sisters

Songs include 'Please'; 'Here Lies Love'; 'Hot
Toddy'; 'In the Blue of the Night'; 'Tiger
Rag'; 'Crazy People'; 'It Was So Beautiful';
'Kicking the Gong Around'
   'Flock of radio names ensures b.o. interest,
especially in hinterland.'—*Variety*

The Big Broadcast of 1936••
US 1935   97m   bw
Paramount (Ben Glazer)

The 'radio lover' of a small radio station is
kidnapped by a man-hungry countess.
Zany comedy with interpolated variety acts
and a totally Marxian climax.

w Walter de Leon, Francis Martin, Ralph
Spence   *d* Norman Taurog   *ph* Leo Tover
songs various   *ch* LeRoy Prinz

Jack Oakie, George Burns, Gracie Allen,
Henry Wadsworth, Wendy Barrie, Lyda
Roberti, C. Henry Gordon, Benny Baker,
Bing Crosby, Ethel Merman, Richard Tauber,
Amos 'n Andy, Mary Boland, Charles
Ruggles, Virginia Weidler, Guy Standing, Gail
Patrick, Bill Robinson, the Nicholas Brothers,
the Vienna Boys Choir, Akim Tamiroff

Songs include 'Miss Brown to You'; 'Through
the Doorway of Dreams'; 'Double Trouble';
'Why Dream?'; 'Amargura'; 'I Wished on the
Moon'; 'Crooner's Lullaby'; 'Why Stars Come
Out at Night'
   'Names are in and out as fast and as often as
a firefly's tail light.'—*Variety*

The Big Broadcast of 1937••
US 1936   100m   bw
Paramount (Lewis Gensler)

A radio station manager has trouble with his
sponsors.
More recorded acts separated by a measure of
plot.

w Edwin Gelsey, Arthur Kober, Barry
Travers, Walter de Leon, Francis Martin
d Mitchell Leisen   *ph* Theodor Sparkuhl
songs various

Jack Benny, George Burns, Gracie Allen, Bob
Burns, Martha Raye, Shirley Ross, Ray
Milland, Benny Fields, Benny Goodman and
his Orchestra, Leopold Stokowski and the
Philadelphia Orchestra, Eleanore Whitney,
Larry Adler, Louis da Pron

   'It isn't a comedy and it isn't a musical, but
it has a lot of laughs, the best in several types
of music, and I don't know where in the world
you will see anything like it.'—*Otis Ferguson*

The Big Broadcast of 1938••
US 1937   90m   bw
Paramount (Harlan Thompson)

A steamship owner engaged in a transatlantic
race is hampered by his practical joking twin
brother.
Glamorous, empty-headed all-star nonsense
with the expected bevy of interpolated acts.

w Walter de Leon, Francis Martin, Ken
Englund, Frederick Hazlitt Brennan
d Mitchell Leisen   *ph* Harry Fischbeck

W. C. Fields, Bob Hope (debut), Martha
Raye, Dorothy Lamour, Shirley Ross, Lynne
Overman, Ben Blue, Leif Erickson, Kirsten
Flagstad, Tito Guizar, Shep Fields and his
Rippling Rhythm Orchestra

Songs include 'Thanks for the Memory';
'Don't Tell a Secret to a Rose'; 'You Took the
Words Right Out of My Heart'; 'Mama That
Moon Is Here Again'; 'This Little Ripple Has
Rhythm'; 'The Waltz Lives On': 'Zuni Zuni';
'Sawing a Woman in Half'
   'Pictorially original and alluring, with the
rejuvenated W. C. Fields at his inimitable
best.'—*Variety*

AA: song 'Thanks for the Memory' (*m* Ralph
Rainger, *ly* Leo Robin)

Big Brown Eyes
US 1936   76m   bw
Paramount (Walter Wanger)

A private detective and his wisecracking girl
friend catch a jewel thief.

Minor league *Thin Man* stuff, quite acceptably done.

w Raoul Walsh, Bert Hanlon *d* Raoul Walsh
ph George Clemens *m* Gerald Carbonara
md Morris Stoloff

Cary Grant, Joan Bennett, Walter Pidgeon, Lloyd Nolan, Alan Baxter, Marjorie Gateson, Isabel Jewell, Douglas Fowley

The Big Bus

US 1976 88m Movielab Panavision
Paramount (Fred Freeman, Lawrence J. Cohen)

Misadventures of a giant atomic-powered bus on its first cross-country trip.
Rather feeble spoof on disaster pictures, with some good moments.

w Fred Freeman, Lawrence J. Cohen *d* James Frawley *ph* Harry Stradling Jnr *m* David Shire *pd* Joel Schiller

Joseph Bologna, Stockard Channing, John Beck, René Auberjonois, Ned Beatty, Bob Dishy, Jose Ferrer, Ruth Gordon, Harold Gould, Larry Hagman, Sally Kellerman, Richard Mulligan, Lynn Redgrave
'It's all fast, bright, surface stuff, almost obsessively intent on never letting a laugh get away, misfiring, backfiring, skidding and crashing gears gaily all the way, often quite as thrilling, if not always as ludicrous, as some of the films it mocks.'—*Alan Brien, Sunday Times*
'It has been produced with such consummate bad taste, schlock acting and feeble attempts at verbal and visual humour that whatever laughs are engendered are at it rather than with it.'—*Dave Pomeroy, Film Information*

Big Business****

US 1929 20m silent
Stan and Ollie fail to sell a Christmas tree to a belligerent householder. Classic silent comedy consisting largely of a brilliant tit-for-tat routine of reciprocal destruction, to which scripting, acting and editing equally combine. Laurel and Hardy, James Finlayson. Written by Leo McCarey and H. M. Walker; directed by James W. Horne; edited by Richard Currier; for Hal Roach.

The Big Cage

US 1933 71m bw
A lion tamer is worshipped by an orphan boy. Pretty awful programme filler capitalizing on the animal act from the Ringling Brothers circus. Clyde Beatty, Andy Devine, Mickey Rooney, Anita Page, Vince Barnett, Wallace Ford, Raymond Hatton. Written by Edward Anthony and Ferdinand Reyher; directed by Kurt Neumann; for Universal.

The Big Cat

US 1949 75m Technicolor
Feuding mountain families combine to track a marauding lion. Standard outdoor melodrama, almost a straight version of *Track of the Cat*.

Peggy Ann Garner, Lon McCallister, Preston Foster, Forrest Tucker, Skip Homeier, Sara Haden. Written by Morton Grant and Dorothy Yost; directed by Phil Karlson; for Eagle-Lion.

The Big Chill**

US 1983 105m Metrocolor
Columbia / Carson Productions (Michael Shamberg)

University contemporaries try to comfort each other after the death of a friend.
Wry satirical comedy which seems to be nostalgic for the sixties, but is funny anyway.

w Lawrence Kasdan, Barbara Benedek
d Lawrence Kasdan *ph* John Bailey
m various *pd* Ida Random *ed* Carol Littleton

Tom Berenger, Glenn Close, Jeff Goldblum, William Hurt, Kevin Kline, Mary Kay Place, Meg Tilly, JoBeth Williams, Don Galloway
'The final impression left is of a collage of small relishable moments.'—*Kim Newman, MFB*
'An entertainment in which humour and sentiment are finely balanced and profundities are artfully skirted.'—*Sight and Sound*
AAN: best picture; Glenn Close; screenplay

Big City Blues

US 1932 65m bw
A country boy gets into trouble on his first trip to New York. Predictable comedy drama which seems to have no point other than the obvious one. Joan Blondell, Eric Linden, Inez Courtney, Evalyn Knapp, Guy Kibbee, Walter Catlett, Humphrey Bogart, Ned Sparks. Written by Ward Morehouse and Lillie Hayward; directed by Mervyn Le Roy; for Warners.

The Big Circus*

US 1959 109m Technicolor
Cinemascope
AA (Irwin Allen)

A bankrupt circus owner tries to get his show back on the road despite the murderous schemes of his ex-partners.
Fast-paced melodrama which makes little sense but generally provides the expected thrills.

w Irwin Allen, Charles Bennett, Irving Wallace *d* Joseph Newman *ph* Winton C. Hoch *m* Paul Sawtell, Bert Shefter

Victor Mature, Red Buttons, Rhonda Fleming, Kathryn Grant, Vincent Price, Peter Lorre, *Gilbert Roland*, David Nelson, Adele Mara, Steve Allen

The Big City

US 1927 80m approx (24 fps) bw
silent
MGM

A cabaret owner has a jewel robbery gang as a sideline.
Minor star melodrama.

w Waldemar Young, Tod Browning *d* Tod Browning

Lon Chaney, Betty Compson, James Murray, Marceline Day

The Big City*

US 1937 80m bw
MGM (Norman Krasna)

An honest cab driver and his wife hold out against corruption.
Sentimental realism of the type expected of its director. Smooth and syrupy.

w Dore Schary, Hugo Butler *d* Frank Borzage *ph* Joseph Ruttenberg *m* William Axt

Spencer Tracy, Luise Rainer, Charley Grapewin, Janet Beecher, Irving Bacon, William Demarest, Eddie Quillan

Big City

US 1948 103m bw
MGM (Joe Pasternak)

In New York's East Side, a little girl is the adopted daughter of three bachelors, but trouble looms when they all get ideas of romance.
Later-day star vehicle for which the young star is really too old and all else is excessively sentimental and sprawling.

w Whitfield Cook, Ann Morrison *d* Norman Taurog *ph* Robert Surtees

Margaret O'Brien, Robert Preston, Danny Thomas, George Murphy, Karin Booth, Jackie Butch Jenkins, Betty Garrett

The Big City**

India 1963 131m bw
R. D. Bansal
original title: *Mahanagar*

A poverty-stricken Calcutta bank accountant sends his wife out to work; then the bank crashes, and she becomes the sole breadwinner.
Immensely detailed, overlong, but mainly fascinating account of modern urban India and its attitudes.

wd, m Satyajit Ray, *novel* Narendra Nath Mitra *ph* Subrata Mitra

Madhabi Mukherjee, Anil Chatterjee, Haren Chatterjee, Haradhan Banerjee

'The strangest and most savage manhunt in history!'

The Big Clock*

US 1947 95m bw
Paramount (John Farrow)

A publishing magnate murders his mistress and assigns one of his editors to solve the crime.
Slick but rather empty thriller with judicious use of adequate talent.

w Jonathan Latimer, *novel* Kenneth Fearing *d* John Farrow *ph* John Seitz *m* Victor Young

Charles Laughton, Ray Milland, Maureen O'Sullivan, Rita Johnson, Elsa Lanchester

The Big Combo*

US 1955 80m bw
Allied Artists / Security-Theodora (Sidney Harmon)

The police crush a crime syndicate.
An otherwise uninspired thriller memorable

for starting the new violence, with some ugly scenes of torture which suffered at the time from the censor.

w Philip Yordan *d* Joseph H. Lewis *ph* John Alton *m* David Raksin

Cornel Wilde, Richard Conte, Jean Wallace, Brian Donlevy, Robert Middleton, Lee Van Cleef, Ted de Corsia, Helen Walker, John Hoyt

● *Video: Video Unlimited*

The Big Country●●●
US 1958   165m   Technirama
UA / Anthony / Worldwide (William Wyler, Gregory Peck)

The Terills and the Hannesseys feud over water rights, and peace is brought about only with the deaths of the family heads.
Big-scale western with a few pretensions to say something about the Cold War. All very fluent, star-laden and easy to watch.

w James R. Webb, Sy Bartlett, Robert Wilder, *novel* Donald Hamilton *d* William Wyler *ph* Franz Planer *m* Jerome Moross

Gregory Peck, Jean Simmons, Charlton Heston, Carroll Baker, Burl Ives, Charles Bickford, Alfonso Bedoya, Chuck Connors

AA: Burl Ives
AAN: Jerome Moross

The Big Cube
US 1969   98m   Technicolor

Girl tries to murder her actress stepmother by feeding her overdoses of LSD. Stultifyingly boring melodrama. Lana Turner, George Chakiris, Dan O'Herlihy, Karin Mossberg, Richard Egan. Written by William Douglas Lansford; directed by Tito Davison; for Francisco Diez Barroso / Warner.

Big Executive
US 1933   70m   bw

A go-getting market operator finds himself competing with the grandfather of the girl he loves. Ho-hum melodrama with no compelling angles. Ricardo Cortez, Richard Bennett, Elizabeth Young, Sharon Lynn, Dorothy Peterson, Barton MacLane. Written by Laurence Stallings from a story by Alice Duer Miller; directed by Erle C. Kenton; for Paramount. 'It will be anything but big at the box office.'—*Variety*

Big Fella●
GB 1937   73m   bw
Fortune (J. Elder Wills)

In Marseilles, a black man returns a lost child to his English parents.
Pleasant light vehicle with the star in typical easy form.

w Fenn Sherie, Ingram d'Abbes, *novel* Banjo by Claude McKay *d* J. Elder Wills

Paul Robeson, Elizabeth Welch, Roy Emerton, Marcelle Rogez
'A very unpretentious vehicle.'—*Variety*

The Big Fisherman
US 1959   166m   Technicolor
    Panavision
Centurion (Rowland V. Lee)

An Arab princess meets disciple Simon Peter, who dissuades her from her plan to assassinate her stepfather Herod.
Well-meaning but leaden adaptation of a bestselling novel which followed on from *The Robe*. Too reverent by half, and in many respects surprisingly incompetent.

w Howard Estabrook, Rowland V. Lee, *novel* Lloyd C. Douglas *d* Frank Borzage *ph* Lee Garmes *m* Albert Hay Malotte *pd* John de Cuir

Howard Keel, Alexander Scourby, Susan Kohner, John Saxon, Martha Hyer, Herbert Lom, Ray Stricklyn, Beulah Bondi

'Its overall flatness of conception and execution is a stiff price to pay for the lack of spectacular sensationalism characterizing its fellow-epics.'—*MFB*

'The picture is three hours long, and, except for those who can be dazzled by big gatherings of props, horses and camels, it is hard to find three minutes of entertainment in it.'—*Hollywood Reporter*

AAN: Lee Garmes

The Big Fix
US 1978   108m   Technicolor
Universal (Carl Borack, Richard Dreyfuss)

An industrial investigator fancies himself as a private eye and gets involved in a political corruption case.
Hard to follow and harder still to care about, this rather sloppy, with-it movie is a little too pleased with itself from the word go.

w Roger L. Simon, from his novel *d* Jeremy Paul Kagan *ph* Frank Stanley *m* Bill Conti *pd* Robert F. Boyle

Richard Dreyfuss, Susan Anspach, Bonnie Bedelia, John Lithgow
'The strength of this film lies in the cool, meandering discretion with which its central theme is fleshed out: regret for lost illusions as the protest generation of the sixties finds its arteries hardening.'—*Tom Milne, MFB*

The Big Gamble●
US 1960   100m   De Luxe   Cinemascope
TCF / Darryl F. Zanuck

Three people drive an ailing truck to a remote African township where they hope to start a haulage business.
Curious comedy-drama-adventure which starts off with family matters in Dublin and gradually develops into a lighter-hearted *Wages of Fear*. It has its moments.

w Irwin Shaw *d* Richard Fleischer, Elmo Williams *ph* William Mellor, Henri Persin *m* Maurice Jarre

Stephen Boyd, Juliette Greco, David Wayne, *Gregory Ratoff*, Sybil Thorndike, Fernand Ledoux

The Big Gundown
Italy / Spain 1966   105m   Techniscope
PEA / PC (Alberto Grimaldi)
Italian title: *La Resa dei Conti*

A Texas lawman is hired to catch a Mexican outlaw, who repeatedly escapes and finally proves his innocence.
Violent but moderately enjoyable spaghetti western.

w Sergio Donati, Sergio Sollima *d* Sergio Sollima

Lee Van Cleef, Tomas Milian, Walter Barnes, Luisa Rivelli

The Big Guy
US 1939   78m   bw

A young convict becomes involved in a prison break which leads to murder. Suspenseful routine melodrama with adequate production values. Victor McLaglen, Jackie Cooper, Edward Brophy, Peggy Moran, Ona Munson, Russell Hicks, Jonathan Hale, Edward Pawley. Written by Lester Cole; directed by Arthur Lubin; for Universal.

'All the action you can take . . . all the adventure you can wish for!'

A Big Hand for the Little Lady●●
US 1966   96m   Technicolor
Warner / Eden (Fielder Cook)
GB title: *Big Deal at Dodge City* (though the action clearly takes place in Laredo)

Five rich poker players are outwitted by a family of confidence tricksters.
Diverting but thinly stretched acting-piece from a much shorter TV original; still, suspense builds nicely until the disappointingly handled revelation.

w Sidney Carroll, from his own TV play *d* Fielder Cook *ph* Lee Garmes *m* David Raksin

Henry Fonda, *Joanne Woodward*, Jason Robards, Paul Ford, Kevin McCarthy, *Charles Bickford*, Robert Middleton, *Burgess Meredith*, John Qualen

The Big Hangover
US 1950   82m   bw
MGM (Norman Krasna)

A lawyer struggling to mingle with the mighty finds he is allergic to strong drink.
Woefully unfunny comedy with virtually no plot.

wd Norman Krasna *ph* George Folsey *m* Adolph Deutsch

Van Johnson, Elizabeth Taylor, Percy Waram, Fay Holden, Leon Ames, Edgar Buchanan, Rosemary de Camp, Gene Lockhart, Selena Royle

Big Hearted Herbert
US 1934   60m   bw

A prosperous plumber becomes more concerned with money than with his family's happiness. Pleasing moral comedy, well cast. Guy Kibbee, Aline MacMahon, Patricia Ellis, Philip Reed, George Chandler. Written by Lillie Hayward and Ben Markson, from the play by Sophie Kerr and Anna Steese Richardson; directed by William Keighley; for Warners. (NB: 1940 brought a remake under the title *Father Is a Prince*, with Grant Mitchell.)

The Big Heat**
US 1953 90m bw
Columbia (Robert Arthur)

A police detective's wife is killed by a bomb meant for himself; he goes undercover to track down the gangsters responsible.

Considered at the time to reach a new low in violence (boiling coffee in the face), this dour little thriller also struck a new note of realism in crime films and produced one of Glenn Ford's most typical performances.

w Sydney Boehm, *novel* William P. McGivern d Fritz Lang ph Charles Lang m Arthur Morton md Mischa Bakaleinikoff

Glenn Ford, Gloria Grahame, Alexander Scourby, Jocelyn Brando, Lee Marvin, Jeanette Nolan, Peter Whitney

'The main impression is of violence employed arbitrarily, mechanically and in the long run pointlessly.'—*Penelope Houston*

'A hard cop and a soft dame!'—*publicity*

The Big House**
US 1930 88m bw
MGM

Tensions in prison lead to an attempted break-out and a massacre.

Archetypal prison melodrama and a significant advance in form for early talkies. Its sets were re-used by Laurel and Hardy in *Pardon Us*.

w *Frances Marion* d *George Hill* ph Harold Wenstrom

Chester Morris, Wallace Beery, Robert Montgomery, Lewis Stone, Leila Hyams, George F. Marion, J. C. Nugent, Karl Dane

'Not a two-dollar talker, but virile, realistic melodrama, a cinch for any week-stand and hold-overable generally.'—*Variety*

'We all gave our roles the best that was in us, and the virility and truthfulness of the picture were more satisfying than anything else I've done.'—*Chester Morris, 1953*

† The role played by Wallace Beery had been intended for Lon Chaney, who died during preparation

AA: Frances Marion
AAN: best picture; Wallace Beery

Big House USA
US 1954 82m bw
UA / Bel Air (Aubrey Schenck)

Convicts stage a break-out to get at hidden loot.

Though less explicit in its violence than many later films, this is a singularly unpleasant melodrama with not one attractive character.

w John C. Higgins d Howard W. Koch ph Gordon Avil m Paul Dunlap

Broderick Crawford, Ralph Meeker, Lon Chaney, Charles Bronson, William Talman, Reed Hadley

Big Jack
US 1949 85m bw
MGM (Gottfried Reinhardt)

Adventures of a couple of amiable scoundrels in 1890 Virginia.

The elements don't jell in this outdoor comedy-drama, which was its star's last film.

w Gene Fowler, Marvin Borowsky, Otto Van Eyss d Richard Thorpe ph Robert Surtees m Herbert Stothart

Wallace Beery, Marjorie Main, Richard Conte, Edward Arnold, Vanessa Brown, Clinton Sundberg, Charles Dingle, Clem Bevans

Big Jake*
US 1971 110m Technicolor
    Panavision
Batjac / Cinema Center (Michael A. Wayne)

An elderly Texas cattleman swings into action when his grandson is kidnapped.

Satisfactory example of the star's later vehicles, with efficient production and familiar cast and brawling.

w Harry Julian Fink, R. M. Fink d George Sherman ph William Clothier m Elmer Bernstein

John Wayne, Richard Boone, Maureen O'Hara, Patrick Wayne, Chris Mitchum, Bobby Vinton, Bruce Cabot, Glenn Corbett, Harry Carey Jnr, John Agar

'Another genial celebration of Big John's ability to carry a film practically single-handed.'—*MFB*

Big Jim McLain
US 1952 90m bw
Wayne / Fellows (Robert Fellows)

A special agent for the House of UnAmerican Activities Committee routs communists in Hawaii.

Curious and rather offensive star vehicle in which the right-wing political shading interferes seriously with the entertainment value.

w James Edward Grant d Edward Ludwig ph Archie Stout m Emil Newman

John Wayne, Nancy Olson, James Arness, Alan Napier, Veda Ann Borg, Hans Conried, Gayne Whitman

'Brings to the screen all the unattractively hysterical mentality of the witch hunt.'—*Penelope Houston*

The Big Knife*
US 1955 111m bw
UA / Aldrich and Associates

A depressed Hollywood star who wants better things for himself is blackmailed into signing a new contract.

Overheated argument between Art and Mammon, with rather disagreeable people shouting at each other, for too long a time. Limited interest is provided by the acting.

w James Poe, *play* Clifford Odets d Robert Aldrich ph Ernest Laszlo m Frank de Vol

Jack Palance, Ida Lupino, *Rod Steiger*, Everett Sloane, Jean Hagen, Shelley Winters, Wendell Corey, Ilka Chase, Wesley Addy

'Everything in it is garish and overdone: it's paced too fast and pitched too high, immorality is attacked with almost obscene relish, the knife turns into a buzz saw.'—*Pauline Kael, 1968*

The Big Land
US 1957 92m Warnercolor
(Warner) Jaguar
GB title: *Stampeded*

Cattlemen encourage the building of a rail link for Texas.

Undistinguished star western.

w David Dortort, Martin Rackin, *novel* Buffalo Grass by Frank Gruber d Gordon Douglas ph John F. Seitz m David Buttolph

Alan Ladd, Virginia Mayo, Edmond O'Brien, Anthony Caruso, Julie Bishop, John Qualen

'Hackneyed, humdrum western.'—*Howard Thompson*

● Video: Kingston

Big Leaguer
US 1953 73m bw
MGM (Matthew Rapf)

An ageing baseball player is given the job of running a youth training camp.

Even the synopsis is boring. A routine job from the doldrums of the star's career.

w Herbert Baker d Robert Aldrich ph William Mellor md Alberto Colombo

Edward G. Robinson, Vera-Ellen, Jeff Richards, William Campbell, Richard Jaeckel

'The film treats its subject with an almost hushed reverence and its appeal is restricted almost entirely to baseball enthusiasts.'—*MFB*

The Big Lift*
US 1950 119m bw
TCF (William Perlberg)

When the Russians blockade Berlin, British and American airmen get supplies there via a massive airlift; two men on one plane hold opposite views of the matter, and both have chastening experiences.

Rather heavy-going fiction based on fact, with earnest performances and good production.

wd George Seaton ph Charles G. Clarke m Alfred Newman

Montgomery Clift, Paul Douglas, Cornell Borchers, O. E. Hasse, Bruni Lobel

'There are some acute touches . . . just enough to make the slick evasions of the rest all the more regrettable.'—*Gavin Lambert*

The Big Money
GB 1956 86m Technicolor Vistavision
Rank

A family of petty crooks is ashamed of its eldest son, who is an incompetent thief.

A would-be high-spirited lark in which none of the jokes comes off, and a note of forced artificiality hangs over the whole production.

w John Baines d John Paddy Carstairs ph Jack Cox m Van Phillips

Ian Carmichael, Belinda Lee, Kathleen Harrison, Robert Helpmann, James Hayter, George Coulouris, Jill Ireland, Renée Houston, Leslie Phillips

The Big Mouth
US 1967 107m Pathecolor
Columbia (Jerry Lewis)

A meek bank auditor finds he is the double of

a dying gangster and is put on the trail of stolen diamonds.
The comedian at his worst, most repetitive and long drawn out.

w Jerry Lewis, Bill Richmond d Jerry Lewis
ph W. Wallace Kelley, Ernest Laszlo
m Harry Betts

Jerry Lewis, Harold J. Stone, Susan Day, Buddy Lester, Del Moore

The Big Night
US 1951 75m bw
(UA) Philip A. Waxman

A 17-year-old youth goes on the rampage in the underworld to avenge the beating up of his father by gangsters.
Hysterical melodrama presenting a rather false and dismal view of the world. Amazingly typical of its director's later output.

w Stanley Ellin, Joseph Losey, novel Dreadful Summit by Stanley Ellin d Joseph Losey
ph Hal Mohr m Lyn Murray

John Barrymore Jnr, Preston Foster, Howard St John, Philip Bourneuf, Howland Chamberlin, Emile Meyer, Dorothy Comingore, Joan Lorring
'We are in that familiar underworld of the American cinema: dark streets gleaming with rain, sleazy apartments, garish night clubs, with Negro singers, drunks who spout philosophy, discontented blondes and fierce pock-marked thugs.'—Gavin Lambert

The Big Noise
US 1944 74m bw
TCF (Sol M. Wurtzel)

Two incompetent detectives accidentally round up a spy gang.
Very thin star vehicle consisting largely of poorly staged and warmed up versions of a few old routines.

w Scott Darling d Mal St Clair ph Joe MacDonald m Cyril Mockridge

Stan Laurel, Oliver Hardy, Doris Merrick, Arthur Space, Jack Norton

The Big Operator
US 1959 91m bw Cinemascope
MGM / Albert Zugsmith-Fryman (Red Doff)

The racketeer head of a labour union goes berserk when the government has him investigated.
Unpleasant gangster exploitation melodrama from the bottom of the barrel.

w Robert Smith, Allen Rivkin d Charles Haas ph Walter H. Castle m Van Alexander

Mickey Rooney, Steve Cochran, Mamie Van Doren, Mel Tormé, Ray Danton, Jim Backus, Jackie Coogan, Ray Anthony, Charles Chaplin Jnr

'The epic of the American doughboy!'

The Big Parade***
US 1925 115m approx (24 fps) bw
   silent
MGM

A young American enlists in 1917, learns the realities of war, is wounded but survives.
Enormously successful commercially, this 'anti-war' film survives best as a thrilling spectacle and a well-considered piece of film-making.

w Lawrence Stallings, Harry Behn d King Vidor ph John Arnold m William Axt, David Mendoza

John Gilbert, Renee Adoree, Hobart Bosworth, Karl Dane, George K. Arthur
'The human comedy emerges from a terrifying tragedy.'—King Vidor
'A cinegraphically visualized result of a cinegraphically imagined thing . . . something conceived in terms of a medium and expressed by that medium as only that medium could properly express it.'—National Board of Review
'The extraordinary impression of the rush of lorries, the queer terror of the woods . . . it was amazing how much fear could be felt in the mere continuous pace of movement.'—Bryher, Close Up
† The biggest grossing silent film of all.

The Big Parade of Comedy**
US 1964 90m approx bw
MGM (Robert Youngson)
aka: MGM's Big Parade of Comedy

A compilation by Robert Youngson, including material as diverse as Ninotchka, Laurel and Hardy and the Marx Brothers.
One is grateful for the excerpts but the assembly of them is somewhat graceless.

The Big Pond*
US 1930 79m bw
Paramount (Monta Bell)

The son of an important French family acts as a tourist guide in Venice.
Reasonably lively, semi-satirical early musical with Americans the butt of the jokes.

w Robert Presnell, Garrett Fort, Preston Sturges, play George Middleton, A. E. Thomas d Hobart Henley ph George Folsey songs various

Maurice Chevalier, Claudette Colbert, George Barbier, Nat Pendleton, Marion Ballou
'An amiable and ingratiating comedy that will give the Chevalier momentum another good shove.'—Variety

AAN: Maurice Chevalier

The Big Punch
US 1948 80m bw

A boxer refuses to throw a fight and is framed for murder. Routine time-passer with a second team before and behind the camera. Gordon MacRae, Wayne Morris, Lois Maxwell, Mary Stewart. Written by Bernard Girard; directed by Sherry Shourds; for Warner.

Big Red
US 1962 89m Technicolor
Walt Disney (Winston Hibler)

An orphan boy protects a dog which later saves him from a mountain lion.

Simple boy-and-dog yarn with impressive Canadian settings.

w Louis Pelletier d Norman Tokar
ph Edward Colman m Oliver Wallace

Walter Pidgeon, Gilles Payant, Emile Genest

The Big Red One*
US 1980 111m colour
UA / Lorimar (Gene Corman)

Five foot-soldiers survive action in several theatres of war between 1940 and 1945
Symbolic action drama, very well made but finally lacking a cumulative impact.

wd Samuel Fuller ph Adam Greenberg m Dana Kaproff

Lee Marvin, Mark Hamill, Robert Carradine, Bobby DiCicco, Kelly Ward, Stéphane Audran, Serge Marquand
'A picture of palpable raw power which manages both intense intimacy and great scope at the same time.'—Variety
'Like all Fuller movies, about an inch from cliché all the way.'—Guardian

● Video: MGM / UA

The Big Shakedown
US 1934 64m bw
Warner (Sam Bischoff)

A racketeer finds a new gimmick: cut-price medicine.
Action programmer with emphasis on the young couple forced into helping the racket.

w Niven Busch, Rian James d John Francis Dillon ph Sid Hickox

Bette Davis, Ricardo Cortez, Charles Farrell, Glenda Farrell, Allen Jenkins, Henry O'Neill, Samuel S. Hinds
'A routine assortment of gang-film impedimenta.'—New York Times

The Big Shot*
US 1942 82m bw
Warner (Walter MacEwen)

An ill-fated criminal has trouble with women and his former companions.
Dullish star vehicle.

w Bertram Millhauser, Aben Finkel, Daniel Fuchs d Lewis Seiler ph Sid Hickox m Adolph Deutsch

Humphrey Bogart, Irene Manning, Richard Travis, Donald Crisp, Stanley Ridges, Henry Hull, Susan Peters, Howard da Silva

The Big Show
US 1961 113m De Luxe Cinemascope
TCF / API (Ted Sherdeman)

A circus proprietor dominates his sons; after his death they fight for supremacy.
Another remake of House of Strangers, which was also remodelled as Broken Lance. Not too bad as circus melodramas go.

w Ted Sherdeman d James B. Clark ph Otto Heller m Paul Sawtell, Bert Shefter

Esther Williams, Cliff Robertson, Nehemiah Persoff, Robert Vaughn, Carol Christensen, Margia Dean, David Nelson

The Big Sky*
US 1952 122m bw
RKO / Winchester (Howard Hawks)

In 1830 two Kentucky mountain men join an exploration up the Missouri and become preoccupied with Indian trouble.
A large-scale adventure, loaded with talent, which becomes oddly tedious.

w Dudley Nichols, *novel* A. B. Guthrie Jnr
d Howard Hawks *ph* Russell Harlan
m Dmitri Tiomkin

Kirk Douglas, Arthur Hunnicutt, Elizabeth Threatt, Dewey Martin, Buddy Baer, Steve Geray, Jim Davis

'It has the timeless, relentless quality of the long American historical novel.'—*Penelope Houston*

AAN: Russell Harlan; Arthur Hunnicutt

● *Video: Kingston*

The Big Sleep***
US 1946 114m bw
Warner (Howard Hawks)

Private eye Philip Marlowe is hired to protect General Sternwood's wild young daughter from her own indiscretions, and finds several murders later that he has fallen in love with her elder sister.
Inextricably complicated, moody thriller from a novel whose author claimed that even he did not know 'who done it'. The film is nevertheless vastly enjoyable along the way for its slangy script, star performances and outbursts of violence, suspense and sheer fun.

w *William Faulkner, Leigh Brackett, Jules Furthman, novel Raymond Chandler*
d *Howard Hawks ph* Sid Hickox *m Max Steiner*

Humphrey Bogart (Philip Marlowe), *Lauren Bacall* (Vivian Sherwood Rutledge), John Ridgely (Eddie Mars), Martha Vickers (Carmen Sternwood), Dorothy Malone (Proprietress), Regis Toomey (Bernie Ohls), Charles Waldron (General Sternwood), Charles D. Brown (Norris), Elisha Cook Jr (Harry Jones), Louis Jean Heydt (Joe Brody), Bob Steele (Canino), Peggy Knudsen (Mona Mars), Sonia Darrin (Agnes)

MARLOWE: 'My, my, my. Such a lot of guns around town and so few brains.'

GENERAL: 'You may smoke, too. I can still enjoy the smell of it. Nice thing when a man has to indulge his vices by proxy.'

VIVIAN: 'So you're a private detective. I didn't know they existed, except in books—or else they were greasy little men snooping around hotel corridors. My, you're a mess, aren't you?'

MARLOWE: 'I don't mind if you don't like my manners. I don't like 'em myself. They're pretty bad. I grieve over 'em on long winter evenings.'

GENERAL: 'If I seem a bit sinister as a parent, Mr Marlowe, it's because my hold on life is too slight to include any Victorian hypocrisy. I need hardly add that any man who has lived as I have and indulges for the first time in parenthood at the age of 55 deserves all he gets.'

THE BIG SLEEP.   Humphrey Bogart's toupé seems to be showing as he regards his recent real-life bride Lauren Bacall with considerable interest.

MARLOWE: 'Speaking of horses . . . you've got a touch of class, but I don't know how far you can go.'
VIVIAN: 'A lot depends on who's in the saddle. Go ahead, Marlowe. I like the way you work. In case you don't know it, you're doing all right.'

'A sullen atmosphere of sex saturates the film, which is so fast and complicated you can hardly catch it.'—*Richard Winnington*
'A violent, smoky cocktail shaken together from most of the printable misdemeanours and some that aren't.'—*James Agee*
'Harder, faster, tougher, funnier and more laconic than any thriller since.'—*NFT, 1974*
'Wit, excitement and glamour in generous doses.'—*Francis Wyndham*

● *Video: Warner*

The Big Sleep
GB 1977 39m De Luxe
ITC / Elliott Kastner, Michael Winner

Straight remake of the 1946 film, curiously and ineffectively set in London.

wd Michael Winner *ph* Robert Paynter
m Jerry Fielding

Robert Mitchum, Sarah Miles, Richard Boone, Candy Clark, Edward Fox, Joan Collins, John Mills, James Stewart, Oliver Reed, Harry Andrews, Richard Todd, James Donald, Colin Blakely

'The 1946 film takes on even more stature in light of this. For a Winner film, however, it's quite good.'—*Variety*

● *Video: Precision Video*

The Big Steal**
US 1949 72m bw
RKO (Jack J. Gross)

An army officer is framed for the theft of a payroll, and sets off across Mexico in hectic pursuit of the real culprit.
Unexpectedly enjoyable comedy melodrama with a plethora of twists and a pace that never lets up. Routine Hollywood at a level seldom achieved, and short enough to leave one asking for more.

w Gerald Drayson Adams, Geoffrey Homes, *story* The Road to Carmichael's by Richard Wormser *d* Don Siegel *ph* Harry J. Wild *m* Leigh Harline

Robert Mitchum, Jane Greer, William Bendix, Ramon Novarro, Patric Knowles, Don Alvarado, John Qualen

'Vigour and excellent craftsmanship.'—*Gavin Lambert*

● *Video: Kingston*

The Big Store*
US 1941 83m bw
MGM (Louis K. Sidney)

An eccentric private eye saves a department store from the hands of crooks.

Reckoned to be the Marx Brothers' weakest MGM vehicle, but it has its moments, especially the first reel and the bedding department scene, also Groucho's rendering of 'Sing While You Sell'.

w Sid Kuller, Hal Fimberg, Ray Golden d Charles Reisner ph Charles Lawton m George Stoll

Groucho, Chico, Harpo, Margaret Dumont, Douglass Dumbrille, Tony Martin, Virginia Grey, Virginia O'Brien, Henry Armetta

The Big Street*
US 1942   88m   bw
RKO (Damon Runyon)

A Broadway nightclub waiter falls in love with a crippled singer who selfishly accepts his help without loving him in return.
Unusual but mawkish material from an author who never really suited the screen; a mixture of laughs, tears and sentimentality, with a comic gangster background.

w Leonard Spiegelgass, *story* Little Pinks by Damon Runyon d Irving Reis ph Russell Metty m Roy Webb

Henry Fonda, Lucille Ball, Eugene Pallette, Virginia Weidler, Agnes Moorehead, Barton MacLane, Ozzie Nelson and his Orchestra, Sam Levene, Ray Collins, Marion Martin

Big Town Girl
US 1937   66m   bw

A night-club singer adopts a disguise to elude her escaped convict husband. Satisfactory supporting comedy-melodrama. Claire Trevor, Donald Woods, Alan Dinehart, Alan Baxter, Murray Alper, Spencer Charters. Written by Lou Breslow, John Patrick, Robert Ellis, Helen Logan; directed by Alfred Werker; for Milton H. Feld / TCF. 'First-class dualler which should please everywhere.'—*Variety*

The Big Trail*
US 1930   125m   bw
Fox

A wagon train struggles along the Oregon trail.
Simple-minded early talkie western spectacular with a new young star who took another nine years to make it big. Originally shown on a giant 70mm gauge and intended for big screens.

w Jack Peabody, Marie Boyle, Florence Postal d Raoul Walsh ph Lucien Andriot, Arthur Edeson

John Wayne, Marguerite Churchill, El Brendel, Tully Marshall, Tyrone Power Snr, David Rollins, Ward Bond, Helen Parrish

  'Failing to own a kick or a punch, other than scenically, and with no outstanding cast names, it remains only a western of the pioneering sort, so thoroughly made familiar by those pioneering epics preceding it.'—*Variety*

  'Printed upon the new wide film and projected upon the vastly large Grandeur screen, the landscapes, wagon trains, vistas and camp scenes achieve an incredibly greater

sweep [than *The Covered Wagon*]. *The Big Trail* is often stagey, melodramatic, ranty.'—*Theatre Magazine*

The Big Trees**
US 1952   89m   Technicolor
Warner (Louis F. Edelmann)

An unscrupulous lumberman tries to exploit California's giant redwood forests but is won over by the local Quakers who hold the trees in awe.
Pleasing, old-fashioned outdoor drama with a plot which allows the star much opportunity for derring-do.

w John Twist, James R. Webb d Felix Feist ph Bert Glennon m Heinz Roemheld

Kirk Douglas, Eve Miller, Patrice Wymore, Edgar Buchanan, John Archer, Alan Hale Jnr
† A remake of *Valley of the Giants* (qv)

Big Wednesday*
US 1978   119m   Metrocolor   Panavision
Warner / A-Team (Alex Rose, Tamara Asseyev)

Three California surfing friends of the early sixties get back together after the Vietnam war.
It isn't clear whether the intent is to extol or deride the mystical camaraderie of surfing, but for those who can stand rumbustious beach behaviour this curious movie may have at least as much to say as *The Deer Hunter*.

w John Milius, Dennis Aaberg d John Milius ph Bruce Surtees *surfing ph* Greg MacGillivray m Basil Poledouris

Jan-Michael Vincent, William Katt, Gary Busey, Darell Fetty

The Big Wheel
US 1949   92m   bw
(UA) Popkin / Stiefel / Dempsey (Samuel H. Stiefel)

The son of a racing driver is determined to follow in father's footsteps.
Grubby star actioner.

w Robert Smith d Edward Ludwig ph Ernest Laszlo m Nat W. Finston

Mickey Rooney, Spring Byington, Thomas Mitchell, Mary Hatcher, Allen Jenkins

'Wanted by two women!'
The Bigamist*
US 1953   80m   bw
Filmmakers (Collier Young)

A travelling salesman has two wives.
Minor melodrama which took its subject seriously but failed to make absorbing drama of it. Very much a family affair, starring the producer's present and past wives, the latter also directing.

w Collier Young d Ida Lupino ph George Diskant m Leith Stevens

Edmond O'Brien, Joan Fontaine, Ida Lupino, Edmund Gwenn, Jane Darwell

'The film seems to have summoned all its energy to shout defiantly that bigamous marriages exist and, finding no one to defy, retires deflated.'—*MFB*

The Bigamist*
Italy / France 1956   97m   bw
Royal / Filmel / Alba

An innocent young salesman is accused of bigamy and dragged into court.
Noisy comedy of mistaken identity; some laughs, but the talents are not at their best.

w Sergio Amidei, Age Scarpelli, Franco Rosi, Elio Talarico d Luciano Emmer ph Mario Montuori m Alessandro Cicognini

Marcello Mastroianni, Vittorio de Sica, Franca Valeri, Giovanna Ralli

Bigger than Life*
US 1956   95m   Eastmancolor   Cinemascope
TCF / James Mason

A small-town schoolteacher is prescribed cortisone for arthritis; it gradually turns him into a bullying megalomaniac full of grandiose schemes.
Exaggerated and sensationalized but still not very dramatic expansion of a genuine case history. A curious choice for all concerned.

w Cyril Hume, Richard Maibaum d Nicholas Ray ph Joe MacDonald m David Raksin

James Mason, Barbara Rush, Walter Matthau, Robert Simon, Roland Winters

'This is the world's sexiest robbery!'
The Biggest Bundle of Them All
US 1967   110m   Metrocolor   Panavision
MGM / Shaftel–Stewart

A retired gangster is kidnapped by other gangsters and shows them how to steal five million dollars worth of platinum.
Very moderately amusing international comedy caper.

w Josef Shaftel, Sy Salkowitz d Ken Annakin ph Piero Portalupi m Riz Ortolani

Raquel Welch, Robert Wagner, Vittorio de Sica, Edward G. Robinson, Godfrey Cambridge, Davy Kaye

  'It begins like one of these really bad movies that are unintentionally funny. Then it becomes clear that it intends to be funny, and it isn't.'—*Renata Adler*

Bikini Beach
US 1964   100m   Pathecolor

A California beach is disputed by surfers, motor bikers, and a businessman who wants to build a retirement community. Mindless youth nonsense with flashes of satire. Frankie Avalon, Annette Funicello, Martha Hyer, Don Rickles, Harvey Lembeck, Keenan Wynn, John Ashley, (guest appearance) Boris Karloff. Written by William Asher, Leo Townsend and Robert Diller; directed by William Asher; for American International.

Bill and Coo
US 1947   61m   colour

Trials and tribulations of the inhabitants of Chirpendale are enacted entirely by birds, mostly wearing hats and neckties. An eccentricity which won its creator, Ken

Murray, a special Academy Award. For Republic. 'By conservative estimate, the goddamnedest thing ever seen.'—*James Agee.*

A Bill of Divorcement**
US 1932 76m bw
RKO / David O. Selznick

A middle-aged man, released from a mental institution, comes home and meets his strong-willed daughter.
Pattern play which became a celebrated star vehicle; now very dated but the performances survive.

w Howard Estabrook, Harry Wagstaff Gribble, *play* Clemence Dane *d* George Cukor *ph* Sid Hickox *m* Max Steiner, W. Franke Harling

John Barrymore, Katharine Hepburn (her debut), Billie Burke, David Manners, Paul Cavanagh, Henry Stephenson, Elizabeth Patterson

'A money picture for all classes of houses . . . the most potent tear jerker in many a moon.'—*Variety*

● *Video: Guild*

A Bill of Divorcement*
US 1940 69m bw
RKO
GB title: *Never To Love*

Virtually a scene-for-scene remake of the above. Again the acting holds the material together.

w Dalton Trumbo *d* John Farrow *ph* Nicholas Musuraca *m* Roy Webb

Adolphe Menjou, Maureen O'Hara, Patric Knowles, Herbert Marshall, C. Aubrey Smith, Dame May Whitty

Billie
US 1965 87m Techniscope
UA / Peter Lawford (Don Weis)

A teenage tomboy runs into trouble because she is better at sport than her boy friends.
Routine American college / domestic comedy with a young star and good comedy support.

w Ronald Alexander, from his play *Time Out for Ginger d* Don Weis *ph* John Russell *m* Dominic Frontière

Patty Duke, Jim Backus, Jane Greer, Warren Berlinger, Billy de Wolfe, Charles Lane, Dick Sargent, Richard Deacon

Billion Dollar Brain
GB 1967 111m Technicolor
Panavision
UA / Lowndes (Harry Saltzman)

Ex-secret agent Harry Palmer agrees to take a mysterious canister to Finland and becomes involved in an American megalomaniac's bid to take over the world.
Incomprehensible spy story smothered in the kind of top dressing now expected from this director, but which almost killed his career at the time. Occasional pictorial pleasures, but the total kaleidoscopic effect is enough to drive most audiences to the exit.

w John McGrath, *novel* Len Deighton *d* Ken Russell *ph* Billy Williams *m* Richard Rodney Bennett *pd* Syd Cain

Michael Caine, *Oscar Homolka*, Françoise Dorléac, Karl Malden, Ed Begley

Billion Dollar Scandal
US 1932 81m bw

Ex-convicts are involved by a millionaire in a shady oil deal. Competent but complex and talky melodrama 'from the headlines'. Robert Armstrong, Constance Cummings, Frank Morgan, Olga Baclanova, James Gleason, Irving Pichel. From a story by Gene Towne and Graham Baker; directed by Harry Joe Brown; for Paramount.

Billy Budd*
GB 1962 125m bw Cinemascope
Anglo-Allied (A. Ronald Lubin, Peter Ustinov)

In 1797 the sadistic master at arms of a British warship terrorizes the crew and is killed by young Billy Budd, who must hang for his unpremeditated crime.
Handsomely photographed but obtusely scripted and variously acted attempt at the impossible, an allegory of good and evil more suited to opera or the printed page than film: in any case, a hopelessly and defiantly uncommercial enterprise. Some actors bore, others chew the scenery.

w Peter Ustinov, Robert Rossen, *novel* Herman Melville *d* Peter Ustinov *ph* Robert Krasker *m* Antony Hopkins

Peter Ustinov, Robert Ryan, Terence Stamp, Melvyn Douglas, Paul Rogers, John Neville, Ronald Lewis, David McCallum, Lee Montague, John Meillon, Thomas Heathcote, Niall MacGinnis, Cyril Luckham

AAN: Terence Stamp

Billy Jack*
US 1971 113m Technicolor
Warner / National Student Film Corporation (Mary Rose Solti)

A half-breed Vietnam veteran roams the Arizona desert protecting wild mustangs and a runaway teenager.
A trendy radical drama, virtually a one-man show which had an enormous success in the US and led to a sequel, *The Trial of Billy Jack.*

w Tom Laughlin, Delores Taylor *d* Tom Laughlin (T. C. Frank) *ph* Fred Koenekamp, John Stephens *m* Mundell Lowe

Tom Laughlin, Delores Taylor, Bert Freed, Clark Howat, Julie Webb, Ken Tobey, Victor Izay

'A plea for the alternative society with a format of the crudest melodrama.'—*MFB*

Billy Liar***
GB 1963 98m bw Cinemascope
Vic Films (Joe Janni)

In a drab North Country town, an undertaker's clerk lives in a world of fantasy.
Flawed only by its unsuitable Cinemascope

ratio, this is a brilliant urban comedy of its time, seminal in acting, theme, direction and permissiveness. From a novel and play no doubt inspired by Thurber's Walter Mitty, it was later turned into a TV series and a successful stage musical, making Billy a universal figure of the period.

w Keith Waterhouse, Willis Hall, from KW's novel and their play *d* John Schlesinger *ph* Denys Coop *m* Richard Rodney Bennett

Tom Courtenay, Julie Christie, Wilfred Pickles, Mona Washbourne, *Ethel Griffies*, Finlay Currie, Rodney Bewes, Leonard Rossiter

● *Video: Thorn EMI*

Billy the Kid*
US 1930 90m bw
MGM

A young western outlaw is relentlessly pursued by Sheriff Pat Garrett.
Mildly interesting early talkie western with the usual romanticized view of Billy. Originally made and shown in 70mm.

w Wanda Tuchock, Laurence Stallings, Charles MacArthur *d* King Vidor *ph* Gordon Avil

Johnny Mack Brown, Wallace Beery, Kay Johnson, Karl Dane, Roscoe Ates

'Should stand up for slightly better than average business where shown on Realife. Otherwise just an ordinary western.'—*Variety*

Billy the Kid*
US 1941 95m Technicolor
MGM (Irving Asher)

Remake of the above, equally false and rather less well acted, but a striking outdoor colour film of its period.

w Gene Fowler *d* David Miller *ph* Leonard Smith, William V. Skall *m* David Snell

Robert Taylor, Brian Donlevy, Ian Hunter, Mary Howard, Gene Lockhart, Henry O'Neill, Frank Puglia, Cy Kendall, Ethel Griffies

AAN: Leonard Smith, William V. Skall

Billy Two Hats
US 1973 99m Technicolor
UA / Algonquin (Norman Jewison, Patrick Palmer, Mitchell Lifton)
aka: *The Lady and the Outlaw*

The friendship of an old Scottish outlaw and a young half-breed is broken only by the old man's death.
Curiously miscast western shot in Israel; it makes no discernible point and is not very entertaining.

w Alan Sharp *d* Ted Kotcheff *ph* Brian West *m* John Scott

Gregory Peck, Desi Arnaz Jnr, Jack Warden, Sian Barbara Allen, David Huddleston

The Bingo Long Traveling All-Stars and Motor Kings
US 1976 111m Technicolor
Universal (Rob Cohen)

Adventures of a black baseball team in the 1940s.
High-spirited japes and exhibitions of athleticism which dramatically do not add up to very much.

w Hal Barwood, Matthew Robbins, *novel* William Brashler d John Badham ph Bill Butler m William Goldstein

Billy Dee Williams, James Earl Jones, Richard Pryor, Rico Dawson
'Modest pleasures and dull stretches co-exist in equal abundance.'—*Frank Rich, New York Times*

Biography (of a Bachelor Girl)*
US 1935   84m   bw
MGM

The biography of a sophisticated lady portrait painter reveals surprising details of her love life.
Leaden, bowdlerized screen version of a sparkling Broadway play, fragments of which do however survive.

w Anita Loos, *play* S. N. Behrman d Edward H. Griffith ph James Wong Howe

Ann Harding (miscast), Robert Montgomery, Edward Everett Horton, Edward Arnold, Una Merkel, Charles Richman, Donald Meek
'Smart entertainment for top houses.
Possibly too smart for the other end.'—*Variety*

Birch Interval
US 1976   105m   colour

A twelve-year-old girl goes to live with her Amish relations in the country. Simple-minded moral tale which needed some old-fashioned style to bring it off. Eddie Albert, Rip Torn, Susan McClung, Ann Wedgeworth, Bill Lucking. Written by Joanna Crawford, from her novel; directed by Delbert Mann; for Robert B. Radnitz / Gamma III.

Bird of Paradise
US 1932   80m   bw
RKO (David O. Selznick)

An adventurer on a South Sea island marries a native girl and causes trouble.
Never-never romance which remains stilted despite care obviously taken.

w Wells Root d King Vidor ph Clyde de Vinna m Max Steiner

Joel McCrea, John Halliday, *Dolores del Rio*, Skeets Gallagher
'The old tropical romance nicely done. OK for the main stem stands.'—*Variety*

Bird of Paradise
US 1951   100m   Technicolor
TCF (Harmon Jones)

Opulent remake of the above; the trappings make it even more absurd, and the ritual sacrifice of the heroine seems misplaced in what is otherwise a pantomime.

wd Delmer Daves ph Winton Hoch m Daniele Amfitheatrof

Louis Jourdan, Jeff Chandler, Debra Paget, Maurice Schwartz, Everett Sloane, Jack Elam

'The Kahuna is a naively grotesque figure, with a Central European accent and carrying what appears to be an outsize radish: he personifies the film's dubious approach to Polynesian myth and culture.'—*Gavin Lambert*

The Bird with the Crystal Plumage
Italy 1969   98m   colour

A supposed murderer is vindicated when his alleged next victim turns out to be a psychopath. Tolerable shocker which was popular in dubbed version. Suzy Kendall, Tony Musante. Written and directed by Dario Argento; for Salvatore Argento.

Birdy
US 1984   120m   Metrocolor
Tri-Star / Alan Marshall

A man tries to help his best friend, a war veteran who is shell-shocked and institutionalized.
Heavy-going, lugubrious and rather pointless canter over ground which has been well trodden before.

w Sandy Kroopf, Jack Behr, *novel* William Wharton d Alan Parker ph Michael Seresin m Peter Gabriel

Matthew Modine, Nicolas Cage, John Harkins, Sandy Baron, Karen Young

Birdman of Alcatraz*
US 1961   148m   bw
UA / Hecht–Lancaster (Stuart Millar, Guy Trosper)

An imprisoned murderer makes a name for himself as an ornithologist.
Overlong and rather weary biopic of Robert Stroud, who spent nearly sixty years in prison and became a *cause célèbre*. One cannot deny many effective moments, notably of direction, but it's a long haul.

w Guy Trosper, *book* Thomas E. Gaddis d John Frankenheimer ph Burnett Guffey m Elmer Bernstein

Burt Lancaster, Karl Malden, Thelma Ritter, Edmond O'Brien, Betty Field, Neville Brand, Hugh Marlowe, Telly Savalas, James Westerfield

AAN: Burnett Guffey; Burt Lancaster; Thelma Ritter; Telly Savalas

The Birds***
US 1963   119m   Technicolor
Universal / Alfred Hitchcock

In a Californian coastal area, flocks of birds unaccountably make deadly attacks on human beings.
A curiously absorbing work which begins as light comedy and ends as apocalyptic allegory, this piece of Hitchcockery has no visible point except to tease the audience and provide plenty of opportunity for shock, offbeat humour and special effects (which despite the drumbeating are not quite as good as might be expected). The actors are pawns in the master's hand.

w Evan Hunter, *story* Daphne du Maurier d Alfred Hitchcock ph Robert Burks sound consultant Bernard Herrmann sp Lawrence A. Hampton

Rod Taylor, Tippi Hedren, Jessica Tandy, Suzanne Pleshette, Ethel Griffies
'Enough to make you kick the next pigeon you come across.'—*Judith Crist*
'The dialogue is stupid, the characters insufficiently developed to rank as clichés, the story incohesive.'—*Stanley Kauffmann*
'We must sit through half an hour of pachydermous flirtation between Rod and Tippi before the seagull attacks, and another fifteen minutes of tedium . . . before the birds attack again. If one adds later interrelations between mother, girl friend and a particularly repulsive child actress, about two-thirds of the film is devoted to extraneous matters. Poe would have been appalled.'—*Dwight MacDonald*
● *Video: CIC*

The Birds and the Bees
US 1956   94m   Technicolor   Vistavision
Paramount (Paul Jones)

On a transatlantic voyage a wealthy simpleton is fleeced by a card sharp and his daughter; but the latter falls in love with her victim. Competent but uninspired reworking of *The Lady Eve* as a vehicle for a rather charmless comic. Lacking Preston Sturges at the helm, the mixture of slapstick and sentiment fails to jell.

w Sidney Sheldon after Preston Sturges d Norman Taurog ph Daniel Fapp m Walter Scharf

George Gobel, David Niven, Mitzi Gaynor, Fred Clark, Reginald Gardiner, Harry Bellaver, Hans Conried

Birds Come to Die in Peru
France 1968   98m   Technicolor   Franscope
Universal (Jacques Natteau)

On a Peruvian beach a tormented nymphomaniac makes love to several men and attempts suicide, but is rescued by her true love.
Elaborate high-flown bosh, quite fun to watch.

wd Romain Gary ph Christian Matras m Kenton Coe

Jean Seberg, Maurice Ronet, Danielle Darrieux, Pierre Brasseur

Birds Do It
US 1966   88m   colour
Columbia (Ivan Tors, Stanley Colbert)

A janitor at an atomic plant is accidentally ionized and finds he can fly, which enables him to catch a spy or two.
Childish stunt comedy.

w Arnie Kogen d Andrew Marton ph Howard Winner m Samuel Maltovsky

Soupy Sales, Tab Hunter, Arthur O'Connell, Edward Andrews, Doris Dowling, Beverly Adams, Louis Quinn

The Birds, the Bees and the Italians
Italy / France 1965   98m   colour
Dear Film / Films du Siècle (Robert
  Haggiag, Pietro Germi)
original title: *Signore e Signori*

Stories of adultery in an Italian provincial
town.
Mainly tedious sex comedy full of gesticulating
actors.

w Furio Scarpelli, Luciano Vincenzoni, Pietro
Germi *d* Pietro Germi *ph* Aiace Parolin
m Carlo Rustichelli

Gastone Moschin, Virna Lisi, Alberto
Lionello, Gigi Ballista, Beba Loncar, Franco
Fabrizi

Birth of a Legend*
US 1966   26m   bw

Sprightly compilation of clips from the films of
Mary Pickford and Douglas Fairbanks; the
treatment is cursory but sympathetic. Written
and directed by Matty Kemp; for the Mary
Pickford Corporation.

'The dawn of a new art!'
The Birth of a Nation****
US 1915   approx 185m (16 fps)   bw
    silent
Epoch (D. W. Griffith, Harry E. Aitken)

Northern and southern families are caught up
in the Civil War.
The cinema's first and still most famous epic,
many sequences of which retain their mastery
despite negro villains, Ku Klux Klan heroes,
and white actors in blackface. Originally
shown as *The Clansman*; a shorter version
with orchestral track was released in 1931.

w D. W. Griffith, Frank E. Woods, *novel* The
Klansman by Thomas Dixon Jnr *d* D. W.
Griffith ph G. W. Bitzer

Henry B. Walthall, Mae Marsh, Miriam
Cooper, Lillian Gish, Robert Harron, Wallace
Reid, Donald Crisp, Joseph Henaberry, Raoul
Walsh, Eugene Pallette, Walter Long

  'A film version of some of the melodramatic
and inflammatory material contained in *The
Clansman* . . . a great deal might be said
concerning the sorry service rendered by its
plucking at old wounds. But of the film as a
film, it may be reported simply that it is an
impressive new illustration of the scope of the
motion picture camera.'—*New York Times*
● *Video: Polygram*

The Birth of the Blues*
US 1941   85m   bw
Paramount (B. G. De Sylva, Monta Bell)

Trials and tribulations of a jazz band in New
Orleans.
Thin fiction on which is strung a multitude of
dark brown musical entertainment. Not bad,
even now.

w Harry Tugend, Walter de Leon *d* Victor
Schertzinger *ph* William C. Mellor
md Robert Emmett Dolan

Bing Crosby, Mary Martin, Brian Donlevy,
Jack Teagarden, Eddie Rochester Anderson,
Carolyn Lee

AAN: Robert Emmett Dolan

The Birthday Party*
GB 1968   126m   Technicolor
Palomar (Max Rosenberg, Milton
  Subotsky)

The down-at-heel lodger in a seaside boarding
house is menaced by two mysterious strangers,
who eventually take him away.
Overlong but otherwise satisfactory film
record of an entertaining if infuriating play,
first of the black absurdities which proliferated
in the sixties to general disadvantage,
presenting structure without plot and
intelligence without meaning.

w Harold Pinter, from his play *d* William
Friedkin *ph* Denys Coop *m* none
pd Edward Marshall

Sidney Tafler, Patrick Magee, Robert Shaw,
Dandy Nichols, Moultrie Kelsall
● *Video: Rank*

The Birthday Present*
GB 1957   100m   bw
BL / Jack Whittingham

A toy salesman's life is changed when he is
charged with smuggling a watch through the
customs.
Downcast, prolonged and rather uninteresting
domestic drama; attention is held by generally
good acting.

w Jack Whittingham *d* Pat Jackson *ph* Ted
Scaife *m* Clifton Parker
Tony Britton, Sylvia Syms, Jack Watling,
Walter Fitzgerald, Geoffrey Keen, Howard
Marion Crawford, John Welsh

The Biscuit Eater
Two versions exist of this story by James
Street about a white and a black boy who turn
a stray into a crack hunting dog. The first was
by Stuart Heisler for Paramount in 1940; it
starred Billy Lee and made quite a box-office
impact. The second was by Vincent McEveety
for Disney in 1972, with Johnny Whittaker;
despite the presence of Earl Holliman and
Lew Ayres it made no impact at all. (GB title,
1940 version: *God Gave Him a Dog*.)

The Bishop Misbehaves*
US 1935   87m   bw

A bishop gets on the wrong side of the law
when he helps a young girl to see justice done.
Amusing trifle with strong cast. Edmund
Gwenn, Maureen O'Sullivan, Lucile Watson,
Reginald Owen, Robert Greig, Reginald
Owen, Dudley Digges, Melville Cooper,
Lillian Bond. Written by Leon Gordon and
George Auerbach, from the play by Frederick
Jackson; directed by E. A. Dupont; for
MGM. (GB title: *The Bishop's
Misadventures*.) 'Reaches a grade above the
average programmer, but points mainly to
sophisticated patronage.'—*Variety*

The Bishop Murder Case
US 1930   91m   bw

Philo Vance unmasks a killer who sends
warning notes in rhyme. Mildly interesting
early talkie detection which moves at too

stately a pace. Basil Rathbone, Leila Hyams,
Alec B. Francis, Roland Young, George
Marion. Written by Lenore Coffee, from the
novel by S. S. Van Dine; directed by Nick
Grinde and David Burton; for MGM.

The Bishop's Wife**
US 1947   108m   bw
Samuel Goldwyn

An angel is sent down to mend the ways of a
bishop whose absorption with cathedral
buildings has put him out of touch with his
wife and parishioners.
Whimsical, stolid and protracted light comedy
saved by its actors and its old-fashioned
Hollywood style.

w Robert E. Sherwood, Leonardo Bercovici,
novel Robert Nathan *d* Henry Koster
ph Gregg Toland *m* Hugo Friedhofer

Cary Grant, Loretta Young, David Niven,
Monty Woolley, James Gleason, Gladys
Cooper, Elsa Lanchester, Sara Haden, Regis
Toomey

  'It is the Protestant comeback to the deadly
successful RC propaganda of *Going My Way*
and *The Bells of St Mary's*. It surpasses in
tastelessness, equals in whimsy and in
technique falls well below those crooning
parables. It is really quite a monstrous film.'—
Richard Winnington, News Chronicle
  'When a film undertakes to bring audiences
a spiritual message, we wonder whether the
director doesn't owe it to us to clothe such
messages in less muddled characterizations
and to dispense with caricature.'—*Scholastic
Magazine*
  'A sophisticated *Christmas Carol*.'—*Philip
Hartung*

AAN: best picture; Henry Koster; Hugo
Friedhofer

The Bitch
GB 1979   94m   colour

A woman of much influence in London's
underworld has a temporary liaison with a
young gangster wanted by the Mafia.
Intolerable sexed-up sequel to *The Stud*, hard
on both eyes and ears. Joan Collins, Kenneth
Haigh, Michael Coby, Ian Hendry, Carolyn
Seymour, Sue Lloyd, Mark Burns. Written
and directed by Gerry O'Hara; for Brent
Walker. 'Appropriately enough for a film
whose sole rationale seems to be its chic
consumerist decoration (and of course its disco
soundtrack), *The Bitch* ruthlessly pares away
any other elements of interest.'—*Richard
Combs, MFB.*

Bite the Bullet*
US 1975   131m   Metrocolor   Panavision
Columbia / Persky–Bright / Vista (Richard
  Brooks)

Several cowboys compete in a 700-mile
endurance horse race.
Episodic adventure story with too much
muddled chat and a very thin connecting story
line; good to look at, though.

wd Richard Brooks *ph* Harry Stradling
m Alex North

Gene Hackman, Candice Bergen, James Coburn, Ben Johnson, Ian Bannen, Jan-Michael Vincent, Paul Stewart

AAN: Alex North

'I want something good to happen to me before I die!'

Bitter Harvest
GB 1963　96m　Eastmancolor
Rank / Independent Artists (Albert Fennell)

An innocent Welsh girl comes to London, is deflowered, and sets off in search of wealth and luxury at any price.
Naive sixties version of the road to ruin, quite well done if you like that kind of thing.

w Ted Willis　d Peter Graham Scott
ph Ernest Steward　m Laurie Johnson

Janet Munro, John Stride, Anne Cunningham, Alan Badel, Thora Hird, Vanda Godsell, Terence Alexander

Bitter Rice*
Italy 1949　108m　bw
Lux Films
original title: Riso Amaro

In the rice fields of the Po valley, a thief on the run meets a girl who tries to steal his loot.
Well-made exploitation melodrama which made a star of the well-endowed Mangano but is not otherwise more memorable than its innumerable American counterparts.

w Carlo Lizzani, Carlo Musso, Gianni Puccini, Corrado Alvaro, Ivo Perillo, Giuseppe de Santis　d Giuseppe de Santis　ph Otello Martelli　m Goffredo Petrassi

Silvana Mangano, Raf Vallone, Doris Dowling, Vittorio Gassman

AAN: original story

Bitter Springs*
GB 1950　89m　bw
Ealing (Leslie Norman)

A pioneer family in Australia buys a patch of ground but has trouble with aborigines.
Thinnest of the Ealing attempts to make movies down under, suffering from a lack of pace and sharpness as well as obvious studio settings.

w Monja Danischewsky, W. P. Lipscomb
d Ralph Smart　ph George Heath　m Vaughan Williams

Chips Rafferty, Tommy Trinder, Gordon Jackson, Jean Blue, Charles Tingwell

Bitter Sweet
GB 1933　93m　bw
British and Dominion (Herbert Wilcox)

In 1875 Vienna, a violinist marries a girl dancer and is later killed by a gambler.
Rather feeble filming of Noel Coward's operetta: it pleased a lot of people at the time.

w Lydia Hayward, Herbert Wilcox, Monckton Hoffe　d Herbert Wilcox　ph F. A. Young

Anna Neagle, Fernand Gravet, Ivy St Helier, Miles Mander, Esmé Percy, Hugh Williams, Pat Peterson, Kay Hammond

Bitter Sweet
US 1940　94m　Technicolor
MGM (Victor Saville)

Remake of the above, retailored for unsuitable leads and with the story and music unattractively rearranged.

w Lesser Samuels, operetta Noel Coward
d W. S. Van Dyke II　ph Oliver T. Marsh, Allen Davey

Jeanette Macdonald, Nelson Eddy, George Sanders, Felix Bressart, Ian Hunter, Fay Holden, Sig Rumann, Herman Bing, Curt Bois

AAN: Oliver T. Marsh, Allen Davey

The Bitter Tea of General Yen**
US 1932　89m　bw
Columbia (Walter Wanger)

An American lady missionary in Shanghai is captured by a Chinese warlord and falls in love with him.
Arty miscegenation story which bids fair to become a cult film and certainly has a number of interesting sequences.

w Edward Paramore, story Grace Zaring Stone　d Frank Capra　ph Joseph Walker　m W. Frank Harling

Barbara Stanwyck, Nils Asther, Toshia Mori, Walter Connolly, Gavin Gordon, Lucien Littlefield

'It is doubtful whether this picture can make the grade without support . . . photographic advantages cannot overcome the queer story.'—Variety

† The film chosen to open Radio City Music Hall.

The Bitter Tears of Petra Von Kant
West Germany 1975　124m　colour

Lesbian jealousies in the fashion world.
Interesting but exhausting hothouse confection, no more likeable than the Hollywood kind for being more intelligent about its perversions. Margit Carstensen, Irm Hermann, Hanna Schygull. Written and directed by Rainer Werner Fassbinder for his own company. 'Dazzling in the brittle brilliance of its execution, the precision of its structure and movement, the total hermetic self-containment of the little world it creates.'—David Robinson, The Times.

● Video: Palace

Bitter Victory
US / France 1957　100m　bw
Cinemascope
Columbia / Transcontinental / Robert Laffont

Two officers sent on a document raid in Libya during World War II become poor soldiers because one suspects the other of an affair with his wife.
Glum desert melodrama, turgidly scripted and boringly made.

w René Hardy, Nicholas Ray, Gavin Lambert, novel Bitter Victory by René Hardy
d Nicholas Ray　ph Michel Kelber　m Maurice Le Roux

Richard Burton, Curt Jurgens, Ruth Roman, Raymond Pellegrin, Anthony Bushell, Andrew Crawford, Nigel Green, Christopher Lee

Bittersweet Love
US 1976　92m　colour

Newlyweds discover that they both had the same father. Old-fashioned family shocker which needed a lot more zip if it was going to shock anybody. Lana Turner, Robert Alda, Celeste Holm, Robert Lansing, Scott Hylands, Denise DeMirjian. Written by Adrian Morrall and D. A. Kellogg; directed by David Miller; for Zappala-Slott. 'Performances and settings are all very high class. I mean, when you have all that money and those great surroundings you can still suffer, but you do have multiple choices.'—Archer Winsten, New York Post.

Black and White in Colour*
France / Switzerland / Ivory Coast 1976　100m　Eastmancolor
Reggance / SFP / Artco / Société Ivorienne de Production (Arthur Cohn, Jacques Perrin, Giorgio Silvagni)
original title: La Victoire en Chantant

In French West Africa in 1915, easy-going colonials learn of the outbreak of war and prepare to attack a neighbouring German garrison.
Curious mixture of Ealing-style comedy and mordant satire; interesting without being wholly engaging.

w Georges Conchon, Jean-Jacques Annaud
d Jean-Jacques Annaud　ph Claude Agostini, Eduardo Serra, Nanamoudou Magassouda　m Pierre Bachelet, Mat Camison

Jean Carmet, Jacques Dufilho, Catherine Rouvel, Jacques Spiesser, Dora Doll

AA: best foreign film

Black Angel*
US 1946　80m　bw
U-I (Roy William Neill, Tom McKnight)

A drunk sets out to find the murderer of his wife, and finds it was himself.
Stylish but empty version of a tired theme, interesting for performances and atmosphere.

w Roy Chanslor, novel William Irish　d Roy William Neill　ph Paul Ivano　m Frank Skinner

Dan Duryea, Peter Lorre, Broderick Crawford, June Vincent, Wallace Ford, Hobart Cavanaugh, Constance Dowling

The Black Arrow
US 1948　76m　bw
Columbia
GB title: The Black Arrow Strikes

During the Wars of the Roses, an English knight seeks the murderer of his father.
Pennypinching swashbuckler which contrives to entertain despite total disregard of probability.

w Richard Schayer, David P. Sheppard, Thomas Seller, novel R. L. Stevenson
d Gordon Douglas　ph Charles Lawton Jnr

Louis Hayward, Janet Blair, George Macready, Edgar Buchanan, Paul Cavanaugh

Black Bart
US 1948   80m   Technicolor
U-I (Leonard Goldstein)
GB title: *Black Bart, Highwayman*

Lola Montez, on an American tour, falls for
an American bandit.
Acceptable western programmer with
historical trimmings and some evidence of
tongue-in-cheek attitudes.

w Luci Ward, Jack Natteford, William
Bowers d George Sherman ph Irving
Glassberg m Frank Skinner

Yvonne de Carlo, Dan Duryea, Jeffrey Lynn,
Percy Kilbride, Lloyd Gough, Frank Lovejoy,
John McIntire, Don Beddoe

Black Beauty
US 1946   74m   bw
(TCF) Edward L. Alperson

In Victorian England, a girl searches for her
lost colt.
Stilted children's film with little relation to the
book.

w Lillie Hayward, Agnes Christie Johnson,
novel Anna Sewell d Max Nosseck ph J. Roy
Hunt m Dmitri Tiomkin

Mona Freeman, Richard Denning, Evelyn
Ankers, J. M. Kerrigan, Terry Kilburn

Black Beauty*
GB 1971   106m   colour
Tigon / Chilton (Tony Tenser)

A luckless horse passes from hand to hand but
is finally restored to its original young master
and has a happy retirement.
Pleasant, episodic animal story which stays
pretty close to the book. A shade yawn-
inducing for adults, but fine for children.

w Wolf Mankowitz, *novel* Anna Sewell
d James Hill ph Chris Menges m Lionel
Bart, John Cameron

Mark Lester, Walter Slezak, Peter Lee
Lawrence, Patrick Mower, John Nettleton,
Maria Rohm

The Black Bird
US 1975   98m   colour
Columbia / Rastar (Michael Levee, Lou
Lombardo)

Sam Spade's son finds himself beset by crooks
still after the Maltese falcon.
Dismal, witless, boring parody of a classic
crime film, with none of the humour of the
original.

wd David Giler ph Philip Lathrop m Jerry
Fielding

George Segal, Stéphane Audran, *Lee Patrick*,
Elisha Cook Jnr, Lionel Stander, John
Abbott, Signe Hasso, Felix Silla

'A dumb comedy with an insecure tone and
some good ideas mixed up with some terrible
ones.'—*Variety*

'It doesn't work because it has nothing to
say.'—*Michael Billington, Illustrated London
News*

The Black Book*
US 1949   88m   bw
Eagle–Lion
GB title: *Reign of Terror*

A member of a secret organization which
plans to replace Robespierre with a moderate
goes undercover with the French
Revolutionaries.
Moderate period melodrama with an attractive
though artificial look.

w Philip Yordan, Aeneas Mackenzie
d Anthony Mann ph John Alton m Sol
Kaplan

Robert Cummings, Arlene Dahl, Richard
Basehart, Richard Hart, Arnold Moss

The Black Castle
US 1952   80m   bw
Universal-International (William Alland)

An 18th-century knight avenges the deaths of
two friends who have attended a hunting party
at the castle of a sadistic Viennese count.
A variation on *The Most Dangerous Game*,
and not a good one: the pace is far too
plodding and the atmosphere unpleasant.

w Jerry Sackheim d Nathan Juran ph Irving
Glassberg md Joseph Gershenson

Richard Greene, Stephen McNally, Boris
Karloff, Lon Chaney Jnr, Paula Corday, John
Hoyt, Michael Pate

'It's tremonstrous!'
The Black Cat*
US 1934   65m   bw
Universal (Carl Laemmle Jnr)
GB title: *House of Doom*

A revengeful doctor seeks out the Austrian
architect and devil-worshipper who betrayed
his country in World War I.
Absurd and dense farrago set in a modernistic
but crumbling castle which is eventually blown
to bits just as its owner is skinned alive.
Mostly rather dull despite the extraordinary
plot, but the thing has moments of style, a
delightful cod devil worship sequence
(especially for audiences with a rudimentary
knowledge of Latin) and nothing at all to do
with the title or Edgar Allan Poe.

w Peter Ruric d Edgar G. Ulmer ph John
Mescall m Heinz Roemheld ad Charles D.
Hall

Boris Karloff, *Bela Lugosi*, David Manners,
Jacqueline Wells, Egon Brecher

'On the counts of story, novelty, thrills and
distinction, the picture is sub-normal.'—
Variety

'A truly bizarre concoction of mayhem,
necrophilia, sadism and satanism.'—*Clive
Hirschhorn, 1980s*

The Black Cat*
US 1941   70m   bw
Universal

Murder follows the summoning of the family
to the spooky house of a cat-loving recluse.
Disappointing mystery which squanders a
splendid cast on a script full of non-sequiturs
and makes heavy weather of its light relief.

w Robert Lees, Fred Rinaldo, Eric Taylor,
Robert Neville d Albert S. Rogell ph Stanley
Cortez

Basil Rathbone, Gladys Cooper, Broderick
Crawford, Hugh Herbert, Gale Sondergaard,
Anne Gwynne, Alan Ladd, Cecilia Loftus,
Bela Lugosi

HUGH HERBERT (reading inscription): 'That
house is doubly blest, Which to our feline
friends gives rest.'
BRODERICK CRAWFORD (not impressed):
'Her hats are full of bats, For spending all her
dough on cats.'

'If this doesn't make your skin crawl . . . it's
on too tight!'
Black Christmas
Canada 1974   97m   Technicolor
aka: *Silent Night, Evil Night*

Girls in a college sorority house are attacked
by a lurking psychopath. Moderate suspense
chiller. Olivia Hussey, Keir Dullea, Margot
Kidder, Andre Martin, John Saxon, Marian
Waldman, Art Hindle. Written by Roy
Moore; directed by Robert Clark; for Film
Funding / Vision IV.

Black Eyes
GB 1939   72m   bw

A Moscow head waiter has raised his daughter
to believe he's a big wheel in the business
world. Well-made comedy drama from a
French original. Otto Kruger, Mary Maguire,
Walter Rilla, John Wood. Written by Dudley
Leslie (from the French original); directed by
Herbert Brenon; for Associated British.

Black Fox
US 1962   89m   bw

Slick documentary on the rise of Hitler, using
the expected newsreels reinforced not too
artfully by references to art and to the
medieval folk tale of Reynard the Fox.
Narrated by Marlene Dietrich. Written and
directed by Louis Clyde Stoumen; for Jack Le
Vien. (AA 1963; best documentary.)

Black Friday*
US 1940   70m   bw
Universal (Burt Kelly)

After an accident, a college professor is given
a gangster's brain, and the surgeon encourages
him to believe that he is the gangster so as to
find hidden loot.
Plot-packed melodrama which fails to provide
the chills suggested by the cast, but passes the
time agreeably enough.

w Curt Siodmak, Eric Taylor d Arthur Lubin
ph Woody Bredell m Hans Salter

Boris Karloff, Bela Lugosi, *Stanley Ridges*,
Anne Nagel, Anne Gwynne, Virginia Brissac,
Paul Fix

† Lugosi was originally cast as the professor,
but proved wrong for the part; Stanley Ridges
replaced him and walked off with the movie.

Black Fury*
US 1935   95m   bw
Warner (Robert Lord)

A coal miner comes up against union problems, unsafe conditions and corruption. Typical Warner social drama, good for its time but now very obvious.

w Abem Finkel, Carl Erickson, *play* Bohunk by Harry R. Irving d Michael Curtiz ph Byron Haskin md Leo Forbstein

Paul Muni, Karen Morley, William Gargan, Barton MacLane, John Qualen, J. Carrol Naish, Vince Barnett, Tully Marshall, Henry O'Neill
  'Basic box office, packed with promotional potentialities.'—*Variety*
  'The most powerful strike picture that has yet been made, and I am aware of the better-known Soviet jobs in the field.'—*Otis Ferguson*

Black Gold
US 1947 90m Cinecolor

An Indian couple on the reservation adopt a Chinese boy who becomes a famous jockey. Tears all round in this enterprising if rather muddled B picture with a social conscience. Anthony Quinn, Katherine de Mille, Elyse Knox, Kane Richmond, Ducky Louie, Raymond Hatton, Thurston Hall, Alan Bridge. Written by Agnes Christine Johnson from a story by Caryl Coleman; directed by Phil Karlson; for Allied Artists.

Black Gold
US 1963 98m bw

Novice wildcatter makes it rich in Oklahoma despite villains on every side. Absolutely predictable actioner which unspools like a remake even if it isn't. Philip Carey, Diane McBain, Claude Akins, Iron Eyes Cody, James Best. Written by Bob and Wanda Duncan; directed by Leslie H. Martinson; for Warner.

Black Hand*
US 1949 92m bw
MGM (William H. Wright)

In New York at the turn of the century, an Italian boy avenges his father's death at the hands of the Mafia.
Neatly produced, studio-set melodrama, unusual in subject but very stereotyped and artificial in treatment.

w Luther Davis d Richard Thorpe ph Paul C. Vogel m Alberto Colombo

Gene Kelly, J. Carrol Naish, Teresa Celli, Marc Lawrence, Frank Puglia, Barry Kelley

'A journey that begins where everything ends!'
The Black Hole*
US 1979 98m Technicolor
  Technovision
Walt Disney (Ron Miller)

A research team in space is welcomed aboard a mysterious survey ship poised on the edge of a black hole.
The special effects are superb, though achieved through a general gloom which is barely acceptable. But the story is an ill-worked-out remake of *Twenty Thousand*

Leagues Under the Sea, the characterization is ridiculously inept, and the final disclosure that black holes are doorways to hell sends one home rather bemused.

w Jeb Rosebrook, Gerry Day d Gary Nelson ph Frank Phillips pd Peter Ellenshaw m John Barry

Maximilian Schell, Robert Forster, Anthony Perkins, Joseph Bottoms, Yvette Mimieux, Ernest Borgnine
  'As pastiche, it sounds promising; as drama, encumbered with references to Cicero and Goethe, it is merely tedious.'—*John Halford, MFB*
  'Rated PG, but the only danger to children is that it may make them think that outer space is not much fun any more.'—*New Yorker*
● *Video: Disney*

Black Horse Canyon
US 1954 81m Technicolor

Two cowpunchers help a lady rancher to capture and train a wild black stallion. Slight but agreeable outdoor programmer. Joel McCrea, Mari Blanchard, Race Gentry, Murvyn Vye, Irving Bacon. Written by Geoffrey Homes; directed by Jesse Hibbs; for Universal-International.

Black Jack
GB 1979 110m colour

In 1750 Yorkshire, a rascally French sailor recovers from a hanging and has adventures on the road with a young apprentice. The purpose of this costume adventure, from these creators, is obscure, but the execution of it is muddled and amateurish. Jean Franval, Stephen Hirst, Louise Cooper. From the novel by Leon Garfield; directed by Kenneth Loach; for Tony Garnett / Kestrel. 'Ploddingly unpersuasive. Not only narrative clarity but simple credibility is lacking.'—*Tim Pulleine, MFB*

Black Joy*
GB 1977 109m Eastmancolor
Winkast / West One (Elliott Kastner, Martin Campbell)

A Guyanan immigrant in Brixton is tricked by a Jamaican good-for-nothing but later goes into partnership with him and learns to stand up for his rights.
Vivid but eventually wearying ethnic comedy-melodrama.

w Anthony Simmons, Jamal Ali, from the latter's play Dark Days and Light Nights d Anthony Simmons ph Philip Meheux md Lou Reizner from reggae songs

Norman Beaton, Trevor Thomas, Floella Benjamin, Dawn Hope
  'I wanted to show the reality of life in an immigrant area, angry and frustrated like so many parts of Britain—but full of hope and humour.'—*Anthony Simmons*

The Black Knight
GB 1954 85m Technicolor
Warwick (Irving Allen, Albert R. Broccoli)

A humble swordmaker reveals a traitor to King Arthur.
Hilarious travesty of English historical legend, meant seriously for Anglo-American consumption. Shades of *Zorro, Babes in the Wood* and *1066 and All That.*

w Alec Coppel d Tay Garnett ph John Wilcox m John Addison

Alan Ladd, Peter Cushing, Patricia Medina, Harry Andrews, André Morell, Anthony Bushell, Patrick Troughton, Laurence Naismith, John Laurie
  'Alan Ladd galahads with wild west *gentillesse* in this Technicolored rampage through British history.'—*MFB*

'Unmasking America's brotherhood of butchery!'
Black Legion**
US 1936 83m bw
Warner (Robert Lord)

A factory worker becomes involved with the Ku Klux Klan.
Social melodrama typical of its studio, and good of its kind.

w Robert Lord, Abem Finkel, William Wister Haines d Archie Mayo ph George Barnes

Humphrey Bogart, Erin O'Brien Moore, Dick Foran, Ann Sheridan, Robert Barrat, John Litel, Charles Halton
  'Powerful story of the horror spread by the hooded order; Surefire man's picture.'—*Variety*
  'An honest job of film work, and one of the most direct social pieces released from Hollywood.'—*Otis Ferguson*
AAN: Robert Lord (original story)

Black Limelight*
GB 1938 70m bw
ABPC (Walter C. Mycroft)

The wife of a man convicted of killing his mistress proves that a 'moon murderer' did it. Naive but effective little chiller.

w Dudley Leslie, Walter Summers, *play* Gordon Sherry d Paul Stein ph Claude Friese-Greene

Raymond Massey, Joan Marion, Walter Hudd, Henry Oscar, Coral Browne

'The biggest picture in ten years! The greatest cavalcade of intrigue, spectacle, adventure and excitement you'll ever see on the screen'

Black Magic*
US 1949 105m bw
Edward Small (Gregory Ratoff)

Cagliostro the magician becomes involved in a plot to supply a double for Marie Antoinette. Deliriously complicated historical romp which unfortunately suffers from a stolid script and production which kill all the flights of fancy.

w Charles Bennett d Gregory Ratoff ph Ubaldo Arata, Anchise Brizzi m Paul Sawtell

Orson Welles, Nancy Guild, Akim Tamiroff, Valentina Cortese, Margot Grahame, Charles Goldner, Frank Latimore, Stephen Bekassy

The Black Marble

US 1980 113m De Luxe
Avco / Frank Capra Jnr

A drunken cop redeems himself when teamed
with a policewoman who is less cynical about
the work.
Curious cop show with emphasis on child
murders and dog torturing. An unhappy film
with a garbled message.

w Joseph Wambaugh, from his novel
d Harold Becker ph Owen Roizman
m Maurice Jarre

Robert Foxworth, Paula Prentiss, Harry Dean
Stanton, Barbara Babcock, John Hancock

● Video: Embassy

Black Narcissus●●●

GB 1946 100m Technicolor
GFD / The Archers (Michael Powell, Emeric
Pressburger)

Anglo-Catholic nuns in the Himalayas have
trouble with climate, morale, and one of their
number who goes mad of sex frustration.
An unlikely theme produces one of the
cinema's most beautiful films, a visual and
emotional stunner despite some narrative
uncertainty.

wd Michael Powell, Emeric Pressburger, novel
Rumer Godden ph Jack Cardiff

Deborah Kerr, David Farrar, Sabu, Jean
Simmons, Kathleen Byron, Flora Robson,
Esmond Knight, Jenny Laird, May Hallatt,
Judith Furse

AA: Jack Cardiff

● Video: Rank

Black on White●

Finland 1967 95m Eastmancolor
Jorn Donner / FJ Film

A successful young executive falls in love with
a girl hitch-hiker, but when his wife leaves him
the girl is no longer interested.
Showy romantic melodrama which tries to
make rather too much of a slender theme.

wd Jorn Donner ph Esko Nevaleinen
m George Riedel

Jorn Donner, Kristina Halkola, Liisamaija
Laaksonen

The Black Orchid●

US 1958 95m bw Vistavision
Paramount (Carlo Ponti, Marcello Girosi)

A widower incurs hostility from his daughter
when he plans to marry a gangster's widow.
Rather solemn New York / Italian romantic
melodrama, with much gesticulation all round.

w Joseph Stefano d Martin Ritt ph Robert
Burks m Alessandro Cicognini

Sophia Loren, Anthony Quinn, Ina Balin,
Jimmy Baird, Mark Richman

Black Orpheus●

France / Italy / Brazil 1958 106m
Eastmancolor Cinemascope
Dispatfilm / Gemma / Tupan (Sacha
Gordine)
original title: Orfeu Negro

Against a background of the Rio carnival, a
black tram driver accidentally kills his girl
friend, and after seeking her in the nether
regions kills himself to be with her.
Rather irritating and noisy attempt to update a
legend, without showing very much reason for
doing so.

w Vinitius de Moraes d Marcel Camus
ph Jean Bourgoin m Luis Bonfa, Antonio
Carlos Jobim

Breno Mello, Marpessa Dawn, Ademar da
Silva, Lourdes de Oliviera

AA: best foreign film

The Black Panther

GB 1977 98m Technicolor

A small-time post office robber becomes a
kidnapper and murderer. Tasteless re-
enactment of a case which made headlines in
1975. Donald Sumpter, Debbie Farrington,
Marjorie Yates, David Swift. Written by
Michael Armstrong; directed and produced by
Ian Merrick; for Impics.

The Black Parachute

US 1944 65m bw

An American soldier parachutes into a
mythical European kingdom to free its king
from the Nazis. Thick-ear propaganda fare; it
has its moments. Larry Parks, John Carradine,
Osa Massen, Jeanne Bates, Jonathan Hale.
Written by Clarence Upson Young; directed
by Lew Landers; for Jack Fier / Columbia.

Black Patch

US 1957 84m bw

A marshal is wrongly suspected of murder.
Dour, dark western, occasionally worth
looking at. George Montgomery, Diane
Brewster, Tom Pittman, Leo Gordon. Written
and directed by Allen H. Miner; for
Montgomery / Warner.

The Black Pirate●●●

US 1926 76m approx (24 fps)
Technicolor silent
Douglas Fairbanks

A shipwrecked mariner swears revenge on the
pirates who blew up his father's ship.
Cheerful swashbuckler with the star in top
form.

w Douglas Fairbanks, Jack Cunningham
d Albert Parker ph Henry Sharp ad Oscar
Borg, Dwight Franklin

Douglas Fairbanks, Billie Dove, Donald
Crisp, Sam de Grasse

● Video: Polygram

The Black Room●

US 1935 70m bw
Columbia

A nobleman's power is claimed by his evil twin
brother.
Rather splendid old barnstormer with touches
of horror, a neatly produced star vehicle.

w Henry Myers, from the writings of Arthur
Strawn d Roy William Neill ph Al Siegler

Boris Karloff, Marian Marsh, Katherine de
Mille, Thurston Hall

'Eerie affair, dull and destined for negative
results. Its best qualities are scenic investiture
and photography, which do not excite dollars
to elope from people's pokes.'—Variety

'Mrs Radcliffe would not have been
ashamed of this wild and exciting film, of the
bones in the oubliette, the scene at the altar
when the dog leaps and the paralysed arm
comes to life in self-defence, of the Count's
wild drive back to the castle, of the rearing
horses, the rocketing coach, the strange valley
of rocks with its leaning cross and neglected
Christ, the graveyard with its owls and ivy.'—
Graham Greene

The Black Rose●

US 1950 120m Technicolor
TCF (Louis D. Lighton)

A 13th-century English scholar journeys to the
land of the Mongols, and after many
adventures returns to a knighthood for his
scientific discoveries.
Portentous and slow-moving adventure with
good things along the way.

w Talbot Jennings, novel Thomas B. Costain
d Henry Hathaway ph Jack Cardiff
m Richard Addinsell ad Paul Sheriff

Tyrone Power, Orson Welles, Cecile Aubry,
Jack Hawkins, Finlay Currie, Henry Oscar,
Michael Rennie

Black Sabbath

Italy 1963 99m Pathecolor

Three supernatural stories introduced by Boris
Karloff. Tolerable horror portmanteau. The
Drop of Water (Jacqueline Pierreux); The
Telephone (Michele Mercier); The Wurdelak
(Boris Karloff, Mark Damon). From stories by
Anton Chekhov, Howard Snyder, Leo
Tolstoy; directed by Mario Bava; for
American International.

'The management reserves the right to put
up the lights any time the audience
becomes too emotionally disturbed. We
urge you not to panic or bolt from your
seats.'

The Black Scorpion

US 1957 88m bw
Warner (Frank Melford, Jack Dietz)

Volcanic explosions uncover a nest of
prehistoric giant scorpions near a Mexican
village.
Apart from a genuinely terrifying sequence in
the scorpion's lair, this is a poor monster
movie in which excessively dark photography
seems intended to cover up very variable trick
work.

w David Duncan, Robert Bless d Edward
Ludwig ph Lionel Lindon m Paul Sawtell
sp Willis O'Brien

Richard Denning, Mara Corday, Carlos Rivas,
Mario Navarro

Black Sheep

US 1935 70m bw

A high-class gambler finds his forgotten son on a transatlantic liner. Mouldy compromise of sophistication and soul-searching. Edmund Lowe, Claire Trevor, Tom Brown, Eugene Pallette, Herbert Mundin, Adrienne Ames. Written and directed by Allan Dwan; for Fox. 'It doesn't rate as a solo performer.'—*Variety*

The Black Sheep of Whitehall*
GB 1941 80m bw
Ealing (S. C. Balcon)

An incompetent teacher is mistaken for an economics expert and saves the real expert from spies who run a nursing home.
Pretty good wartime star comedy, with a succession of briskly timed gags.

w Angus Macphail, John Dighton d Basil Dearden, Will Hay ph Gunther Krampf

Will Hay, John Mills, Basil Sydney, Frank Cellier, Felix Aylmer

The Black Shield of Falworth*
US 1954 99m Technicolor
   Cinemascope
U-I (Robert Arthur, Melville Tucker)

The film in which Tony Curtis says 'Yonda lies the castle of my fodda' (or something like it) is an amiable romp which alternates between comic strip dialogue and a surprisingly convincing sense of medieval custom. The training scenes are as sharp as the romantic asides are pallid.

w Oscar Brodney, *novel* Men of Iron by Howard Pyle d Rudolph Maté ph Irving Glassberg m Joseph Gershenson

Tony Curtis, Janet Leigh, David Farrar, Barbara Rush, Herbert Marshall, Rhys Williams, Dan O'Herlihy, Torin Thatcher

'A straightforward piece of hokum with no pretensions, and spoken in a variety of accents that only Hollywood could muster.'—*John Gillett*

The Black Sleep
US 1956 81m bw
UA / Bel Air (Howard W. Koch)

A Victorian brain surgeon experiments on human beings and produces freaks who eventually turn on him.
Gruesome and humourless horror film notable only for its gallery of wasted talent.

w John C. Higgins d Reginald Le Borg ph Gordon Avil m Les Baxter

Basil Rathbone, Bela Lugosi, Lon Chaney Jnr, John Carradine, Akim Tamiroff, Tor Johnson, Herbert Rudley, Patricia Blake

The Black Stallion*
US 1979 117m Technicolor
UA / Omni Zoetrope (Francis Coppola)

After a 1946 shipwreck, a boy and a stallion are cast up on the African shore; many years later, he rides the horse to victory at Santa Anita.
1980 seems a bit late for boy-and-horse pictures, but this one is so beautifully directed and photographed, if drastically overlong, that most adults thought their children should see it.

w Melissa Mathison, Jeanne Rosenberg, William D. Witliff, *novel* Walter Farley d Carroll Ballard ph Caleb Deschanel m Carmine Coppola

Kelly Reno, Mickey Rooney, Teri Garr, Clarence Muse, Hoyt Axton

'A perfect gem—the beautiful craftsmanship alone makes it a joy to behold.'—*Variety*

The Black Stallion Returns
US 1983 93m Technicolor

Rather desperate sequel in which a teenager loses his horse in Morocco and gets him back after various daredevil adventures. Tame, predictable and boring. Kelly Reno, Ferdy Mayne, Woody Strode, Vincent Spano, Allen Goorwitz. Written by Richard Kletter and Jerome Kass; directed by Robert Dalva; for Coppola / Zoetrope / MGM-UA. 'Well-intentioned, but overall it doesn't look like a winner.'—*Variety*

Black Sunday*
Italy 1960 83m bw

A beautiful witch is put to death in an iron maiden but rises from the dead to wreak vengeance. Stylish horror comic which started the Italian cult for such things. Barbara Steele, John Richardson, Ivo Garrani. From a story by Gogol; written and directed by Mario Bava; for Galatra / Jolly.

Black Sunday*
US 1977 143m Movielab Panavision
Paramount (Robert Evans)

The Black September movement threatens a football game to be held in Miami's Superbowl.
Spectacular, heavily detailed, but somehow unexciting disaster melodrama.

w Ernest Lehman, Kenneth Ross, Ivan Moffat, *novel* Thomas Harris d John Frankenheimer ph John A. Alonzo m John Williams

Robert Shaw, Marthe Keller, Bruce Dern, Fritz Weaver, Steven Keats, Bekim Fehmiu, Michael V. Gazzo, William Daniels, Walter Gotell

'There's only one real motivation for this movie, and that's the desire to make money. Why else would anyone make an ostensibly anti-terrorist film that in actuality could end up promoting terrorism?'—*Frank Rich, New York Post*

The Black Swan***
US 1942 85m Technicolor
TCF (Robert Bassler)

Morgan the pirate is made governor of Jamaica and enlists the help of his old friends to rid the Caribbean of buccaneers.
Rousing adventure story with comic asides: just what action hokum always aimed to be, with a spirited gallery of heroes and villains and an entertaining narrative taken at a spanking pace.

w Ben Hecht, Seton I. Miller, *novel* Rafael Sabatini d Henry King ph Leon Shamroy m Alfred Newman

Tyrone Power, Maureen O'Hara, *Laird Cregar, Thomas Mitchell, George Sanders*, Anthony Quinn, George Zucco, Edward Ashley

AA: Leon Shamroy
AAN: Alfred Newman

The Black Tent
GB 1956 93m Technicolor Vistavision
Rank / William MacQuitty

During a Libyan battle a wounded army captain is cared for by Arabs and marries the sheik's daughter. Ten years later, after his death, his son elects to live with the tribe.
Pleasantly shot but otherwise dull, formless and interminable romantic drama, all very stiff upper lip.

w Robin Maugham, Bryan Forbes d Brian Desmond Hurst ph Desmond Dickinson m William Alwyn

Anthony Steel, Donald Sinden, *André Morell*, Anna Maria Sandri, Ralph Truman, Donald Pleasence, Anthony Bushell, Michael Craig

The Black Torment*
GB 1964 85m Eastmancolor
Compton-Tekli (Robert Hartford-Davis)

The second wife of an 18th-century baronet investigates the hauntings which have followed the apparent suicide of his first.
Agreeably unpretentious period ghost story (with a rational explanation). Not exactly good, but better than one might expect.

w Donald and Derek Ford d Robert Hartford-Davis ph Peter Newbrook m Robert Richards

John Turner, Heather Sears, Ann Lynn, Joseph Tomelty, Peter Arne, Raymond Huntley

Black Tuesday*
US 1954 80m bw
UA / Leonard Goldstein (Robert Goldstein)

A killer escapes from Death Row and hides out with hostages in a disused warehouse.
Starkly melodramatic gangster vehicle with the star up to his oldest tricks. Good tension, but generally rather unpleasant.

w Sydney Boehm d Hugo Fregonese ph Stanley Cortez m Paul Dunlap

Edward G. Robinson, Jean Parker, Peter Graves, Milburn Stone, Warren Stevens, Jack Kelly, James Bell

The Black Widow
GB 1951 62m bw

A man succeeds in killing his would-be murderer; his wife schemes to bury the body as her real husband so that she can marry again. A whole lot less interesting than it sounds, acting and direction being alike laborious. Christine Norden, Robert Ayres, Anthony Forwood, John Longden. Written by Alan MacKinnon, from Lester Powell's BBC serial *Return from Darkness*; directed by Vernon Sewell; for Hammer / Exclusive.

THE JEALOUS ACTRESS

THE BROADWAY PRODUCER

THE PENTHOUSE WIFE

THE KEPT HUSBAND

GINGER **ROGERS**
VAN **HEFLIN**
GENE **TIERNEY**
GEORGE **RAFT**

One of them will kill her tonight!
and your guess is as good as ours!

20th Century-Fox presents

Black Widow
The First Crime-Of-Passion Story in
CinemaScope
Color by DeLuxe · In the wonder of High-Fidelity, Directional-STEREOPHONIC SOUND!

PLEASE! Don't reveal the ending!

with
PEGGY ANN GARNER · REGINALD GARDINER
OTTO KRUGER · VIRGINIA LEITH
CATHLEEN NESBITT · SKIP HOMEIER · HILDA SIMMS

Screen Play, Produced and Directed by
NUNNALLY JOHNSON

BLACK WIDOW. Cinemascope made this four-star mystery thriller a whole lot less interesting than it might have been in black and white on the old "square" screen.

'An electrifying drama about a predatory female! All the suspense your system can take!'

Black Widow*
US 1954 95m De Luxe Cinemascope
TCF (Nunnally Johnson)

A Broadway producer is suspected of the murder of an ambitious young girl.
Reasonably classy whodunnit with glamorous settings and an able cast, but a little lacking in wit and pace.

wd Nunnally Johnson, *novel* Fatal Woman by Patrick Quentin *ph* Charles G. Clarke *m* Leigh Harline

Ginger Rogers, Van Heflin, George Raft, Gene Tierney, Peggy Ann Garner, Reginald Gardiner, Virginia Leith, Otto Kruger, Hilda Simms, Cathleen Nesbitt

The Black Windmill*
GB 1974 106m Technicolor
Panavision
Universal / Zanuck–Brown (Don Siegel)

A secret service agent has to fight a lone battle when his young son is kidnapped by spies.
Unconvincing variant on *The Man Who Knew Too Much*, with an unwieldy and incoherent plot and more borrowings from Hitchcock than you can count. It ends up as fair predictable fun despite its jaded air.

w Leigh Vance, *novel* Seven Days to a Killing by Clive Egleton *d* Don Siegel *ph* Ousama Rawi *m* Roy Budd

Michael Caine, Janet Suzman, Joseph O'Conor, Donald Pleasence, Delphine Seyrig, John Vernon, Joss Ackland

'A flaccid spy thriller, vaguely reminiscent of Hitchcock and *Foreign Correspondent*, with direction as blank as the expression on Michael Caine's face throughout.'—*Sight and Sound*

Black Zoo
US 1962 88m Eastmancolor
Panavision
Allied Artists / Herman Cohen

The owner of a private Los Angeles zoo trains his animals to kill his enemies.
Stultifyingly inept and uninteresting horror film.

w Herman Cohen *d* Robert Gordon *ph* Floyd Crosby *m* Paul Dunlap

Michael Gough, Jeanne Cooper, Rod Lauren, Virginia Grey, Jerome Cowan, Elisha Cook Jnr, Marianna Hill

Blackbeard the Pirate*
US 1952 99m Technicolor
RKO (Edmund Grainger)

In the 17th century, reformed pirate Sir Henry Morgan is commissioned to rid the Caribbean of the rascally Blackbeard.
A farrago of action clichés with the star giving his eye-rolling all. The romantic element is dreary and the whole a shade bloodthirsty for family fare.

w Alan le May *d* Raoul Walsh *ph* William E. Snyder *m* Victor Young

Robert Newton, Linda Darnell, Keith Andes, William Bendix, Torin Thatcher, Irene Ryan, Alan Mowbray, Richard Egan

● *Video: Kingston*

Blackbeard's Ghost
US 1967 107m Technicolor
Walt Disney (Bill Walsh)

The famous pirate returns as a ghost to help the old ladies who own a hotel he loved.
Ponderous and lengthy comedy, partially salvaged by performances.

w Bill Walsh, Ben Da Gradi *d* Robert Stevenson *ph* Edward Colman *m* Robert F. Brunner

Peter Ustinov, Dean Jones, Suzanne Pleshette, Elsa Lanchester, Richard Deacon

● *Video: Rank*

The Blackbird
US 1925 70m at 24 fps bw silent

A Limehouse thief pretends to be a cripple, and after committing a murder finds that he is.
Standard star vehicle with recollections of several others. Lon Chaney, Renee Adoree, Owen Moore, Doris Lloyd. Written and directed by Tod Browning; for MGM.

'I'm a teacher. My pupils are the kind you don't turn your back on, even in class!'

The Blackboard Jungle*
US 1955 101m bw
MGM (Pandro S. Berman)

In a slum school, a teacher finally gains the respect of his class of young hooligans.

Seminal fifties melodrama more notable for its introduction of 'Rock Around the Clock' behind the credits than for any intrinsic interest.

wd Richard Brooks, *novel* Evan Hunter *ph* Russell Harlan *m* Bill Haley and the Comets

Glenn Ford, Anne Francis, Louis Calhern, Margaret Hayes, John Hoyt, Richard Kiley, Emile Meyer, Warner Anderson, Basil Ruysdael, *Sidney Poitier, Vic Morrow*, Rafael Campos

'It could just as well have been the first good film of this kind. Actually, it will be remembered chiefly for its timely production and release.'—*G. N. Fenin, Film Culture*

AAN: Richard Brooks (as writer); Russell Harlan

Blackjack Ketchum, Desperado
US 1956 76m bw

A former gunslinger turns sheriff and defeats the local badman. Standard lower-case western with predictable excitements. Howard Duff, Victor Jory, Maggie Mahoney, Angela Stevens. Written by Luci Ward and Jack Natteford, from a novel by Louis L'Amour; directed by Earl Bellamy; for Sam Katzman / Columbia.

Blackmail***
GB 1929 78m bw
BIP (John Maxwell)

A Scotland Yard inspector finds that his girl is involved in a murder; he conceals the fact and is blackmailed.
Hitchcock's first talkie is now a very hesitant entertainment but fully bears the director's stamp and will reward patient audiences in several excitingly staged sequences.

w Alfred Hitchcock, Benn W. Levy, Charles Bennett, *play* Charles Bennett *d* Alfred Hitchcock *ph* Jack Cox *m* Campbell and Connelly

Anny Ondra, Sara Allgood, John Longden, Charles Paton, Donald Calthrop, Cyril Ritchard

'Hitchcock's ending was to have been ironic, the detective seeing the cell door shut on the arrested girl, going home and then being asked if he was going out with his girl friend that evening. His answer: "Not tonight." This was unacceptable commercially and a happy ending was substituted.'—*George Perry*

● *Video: Thorn EMI*

Blackmail
US 1939 81m bw
MGM (John Considine Jnr)

A man is released from prison after serving a sentence for a crime he did not commit. Immediately a blackmailer pounces . . .
Co-feature drama for a star marking time; not bad in its way.

w David Hertz, William Ludwig
d H. C. Potter *ph* Clyde de Vinna

Edward G. Robinson, Ruth Hussey, Gene Lockhart, Guinn Williams, Esther Dale

'The family circuit will accept it as sufficient entertainment for a suspenseful evening.'—*Variety*

Blackmailed
GB 1950 85m bw
GFD / Harold Huth

Several victims of a blackmailer are involved in his murder.
Interestingly plotted and well cast melodrama which suffers from a flat script and production.

w Hugh Mills, Roger Vadim, *novel* Mrs Christopher by Elizabeth Myers *d* Marc Allégret *ph* George Stretton *m* John Wooldridge

Dirk Bogarde, Mai Zetterling, Fay Compton, Robert Flemyng, Michael Gough, James Robertson Justice, Joan Rice, Wilfrid Hyde White, Harold Huth

Blackout
GB 1950 73m bw

A man supposedly killed in an air crash turns out to be the head of a counterfeiting ring. Fairly entertaining British support of its time. Dane Clark, Belinda Lee, Betty Ann Davies, Andrew Osborn, Eleanor Summerfield. Written by John Gilling; directed and produced by Robert S. Baker and Monty Berman; for Tempean / Eros.

Blackwell's Island
US 1939 71m bw
Warner (Bryan Foy)

A reporter goes to jail to get the goods on a smart gangster.
Forgettable exposé of the lighter kind.

w Crane Wilbur *d* William McGann *ph* Sid Hickox

John Garfield, Rosemary Lane, Dick Purcell, Victor Jory, Stanley Fields

'An exploitation natural . . . a portrayal of incredible events taken from real life.'—*Variety*

Blacula
US 1972 93m Movielab
AIP (Joseph T. Naar)

In 1815 in Transylvania, an African prince falls victim to Dracula. A hundred and fifty years later, his body is shipped to Los Angeles and accidentally revivified.
Jaded semi-spoof notable chiefly as the first black horror film. The star's performance is as stately as could be wished in the circumstances.

w Joan Torres, Raymond Koenig *d* William Crain *ph* John Stevens *m* Gene Page

William Marshall, Vonetta McGee, Denise Nicholas, Gordon Pinsent, Charles Macaulay

Blade Runner*
US 1982 117m Technicolor
Panavision
Warner / Ladd / Blade Runner Partnership (Michael Deeley, Ridley Scott)

Los Angeles, AD 2019; a licensed-to-kill policeman tracks down and destroys a group

of intelligent robots who have hijacked a space shuttle and returned to earth.
Gloomy futuristic thriller, looking like a firework display seen through thick fog, and for all the tiring tricks and expense adding up to little more than an updated Philip Marlowe case.

w Hampton Fancher, David People, *novel* Do Androids Dream of Electric Sheep? by Philip K. Dick *d* Ridley Scott *ph* Jordan Cronenweth *ph* Lawrence G. Paull *m* Vangelis

Harrison Ford, Rutger Hauer, Sean Young, Edward James Olmos, M. Emmet Walsh, Daryl Hannah

'The sets are indeed impressive, but they are no compensation for a narrative so lame that it seems in need of a wheelchair.'—*Tom Milne, MFB*

'A richly detailed and visually overwhelming trip to 2019 which sticks with you like a recurrent nightmare.'—*Sunday Times*

'A massive assault on the senses which seems to have been launched from a madhouse equipped with all computerized mod cons.'—*Daily Mail*

'Glitteringly and atmospherically designed; but ultimately mechanics win out over philosophizing.'—*Sight and Sound*

AAN: art direction; visual effects (Douglas Trumbull, Richard Yuricich, David Dryer)

● *Video: Warner*

'She's the hottest thing on the beach. She's also his best friend's daughter!'
Blame It on Rio
US 1983 100m Metrocolor
Sherwood (Stanley Donen)

A businessman is enlisted by his best friend to find his daughter's seducer, who is in fact himself.
Totally joyless and witless comedy with a South American background which is supposedly presumed to take away the bad taste.

w Charlie Peters, Larry Gelbart, from Claude Berri's 1977 film Un Moment d'Egarement *d* Stanley Donen *ph* Reynaldo Villalobos *md* Ken Wannberg

Michael Caine, Joseph Bologna, Valerie Harper, Michelle Johnson

Blame It on the Night
US 1984 85m Technicolor

A rock star tries to make friends with the 13-year-old son he's only just met. Resolutely uninteresting pattern play which slouches its way to a predictable ending. Nick Mancuso, Byron Thames, Leslie Ackerman, Dick Bakalyan. Written by Len Jenkin; directed and produced by Gene Taft; for Tri-Star.

Blanche*
France 1971 92m Eastmancolor
Telepresse / Abel et Charton (Dominique Duvergé, Philippe d'Argila)

In 13th-century France, a baron's beautiful

young wife excites dark passions in her stepson and in the king.

An adult fairy tale full of symbols for those who seek them; but its main virtue is its highly decorative pictorialism.

wd Walerian Borowczyk, novel Mazepa by Juliusz Slowacki *ph* Guy Durban *m* 13th-century music

Ligia Branice, Michel Simon, Lawrence Trimble, Jacques Perrin

'Live-action *Jeux des Anges*, a brilliant, terrifying ballad of imprisonment.'—*Philip Strick, MFB*

Blanche Fury

GB 1948 95m Technicolor
GFD / Cineguild (Anthony Havelock-Allan)

A governess marries a wealthy heir, then with a steward connives at his murder.

Chilly Victorian melodrama without much interest outside the decor: the actors have unplayable roles and the handling is very flat.

w Audrey Erskine Lindop, Hugh Mills, Cecil McGivern, *novel* Joseph Shearing *d* Marc Allégret *ph* Guy Green, Geoffrey Unsworth *m* Clifton Parker

Valerie Hobson, Stewart Granger, Walter Fitzgerald, Michael Gough, Maurice Denham, Sybilla Binder

'She kept her love for one—by sharing it with all!'

Blaze of Noon

US 1947 91m bw
Paramount (John Farrow)

Three stunt flier brothers in the twenties leave their circus to start a commercial air-line.

Predictable romantic drama with little flying: tragic pretensions, routine performances.

w Frank Wead, Arthur Sheekman *d* John Farrow *ph* William C. Mellor *m* Adolph Deutsch

William Holden, Anne Baxter, Sonny Tufts, Sterling Hayden, William Bendix, Howard da Silva

'So long as it sticks to stunt flying and mild comedy it is pleasant enough, but the last half, during which the obsessed brothers come one by one to grief and the little woman waits it out, gets pretty monotonous.'—*James Agee*

The Blazing Forest

US 1952 90m Technicolor
Paramount / Pine–Thomas (William H. Pine, William C. Thomas)

A lady landowner has trouble with her rival timber bosses.

Fair period programmer.

w Lewis R. Foster, Winston Miller *d* Edward Ludwig *ph* Lionel Lindon *m* Lucien Caillet

John Payne, Agnes Moorehead, William Demarest, Richard Arlen, Susan Morrow, Roscoe Ates, Lynne Roberts

Blazing Magnum

Canada 1976 99m colour Panavision

A tough cop solves his sister's murder. Tired rehash of the *Dirty Harry* formula, with plenty of violent action. Stuart Whitman, John Saxon, Martin Landau, Tisa Farrow, Gayle Hunnicutt, Carole Laure. Written by Vincent Mann and Frank Clark; directed by Martin Herbert; for Security Investment Trust Inc.

Blazing Saddles*

US 1974 93m Technicolor Panavision
Warner / Crossbow (Michael Herzberg)

A black railroad worker and an alcoholic ex-gunfighter foil a crooked attorney and his henchmen.

Wild western parody in which the action eventually shifts to the Warner backlot, after which the actors repair to Grauman's Chinese Theatre to find out what happened at the end of the story. At least as many misses as hits, and all aimed squarely at film buffs.

w Norman Steinberg, Mel Brooks, Andrew Bergman, Richard Pryor, Alan Unger *d* Mel Brooks *ph* Joseph Biroc *m* John Morris

Cleavon Little, Gene Wilder, Slim Pickens, Harvey Korman, Madeline Kahn, Mel Brooks, Burton Gilliam, Alex Karras

'One suspects that the film's gradual disintegration derives not from the makers' inability to end it, so much as from their inability to stop laughing at their own jokes.'—*Jan Dawson*

'A surfeit of chaos and a scarcity of comedy.'—*Judith Crist*

' "I just about got everything out of me," said Brooks, "all my furor, my frenzy, my insanity, my love of life and hatred of death." Audiences flocked to this insane affirmation of dancing girls, Hollywood production numbers, stomach gas around the campfire, and gallows humor. Brooks had found the perfect vehicle for the age.'—*Les Keyser, Hollywood in the Seventies*

AAN: Madeline Kahn; title song (*m* John Morris, *ly* Mel Brooks)

● *Video: Warner*

Bleak Moments*

GB 1971 110m Eastmancolor
Autumn / Memorial / BFI (Leslie Blair)

Scenes from drab lives in a south London suburb.

Clearly not likely to appeal to the entertainment-seeking masses, and undeniably overlong, this small movie nevertheless has plenty of telling and even amusing detail about life as most of us recognize it.

wd Mike Leigh *ph* Bahram Manoochehri *songs* Mike Bradwell

Anne Raitt, Sarah Stephenson, Eric Allan, Mike Bradwell

'A prolonged poem to inhibitions, speechlessness, and social unease.'—*John Coleman, New Statesman*

Bless the Beasts and Children*

US 1973 110m colour
Columbia / Stanley Kramer

Six boys on an adventure holiday try to free a herd of buffalo earmarked for destruction.

Rather obviously pointed melodrama, well enough done but not very interesting.

w Mac Benoff, *novel* Glendon Swarthout *d* Stanley Kramer

Bill Mumy, Barry Robins, Miles Chapin, Jesse White, Ken Swofford

AAN: title song (*m* / *ly* Barry de Vorzon, Perry Botkin Jnr)

Bless This House

GB 1972 89m Eastmancolor

A suburbanite's multifarious frustrations culminate in preparations for his son's wedding. This tedious spin-off from a TV sitcom virtually abandons plot in favour of an endless series of slapstick gags which could have been better presented. Sid James, Diana Coupland, Terry Scott, June Whitfield, Peter Butterworth, Sally Geeson, Robin Askwith, Bill Maynard. Written by Dave Freeman; directed by Gerald Thomas; for Peter Rogers / Rank.

Blessed Event**

US 1932 84m bw
Warner (Ray Griffith)

A gossip columnist gets himself into hot water. Amusing vehicle for a fast-talking star, and quite an interesting historical document.

w Howard Green, *play* Manuel Seff, Forest Wilson *d* Roy del Ruth *ph* Sol Polito

Lee Tracy, Ned Sparks, Mary Brian, Dick Powell, Ruth Donnelly, Frank McHugh, Allen Jenkins

'A potential clean-up . . . a sustained hour and a half or so of smart entertainment.'—*Variety*

'Quick and pacy and very likeable.'—*Pauline Kael, 70s*

† A historically interesting note was small-part actress Emma Dunn's use of the expression 'Well I'll be damned', which was technically forbidden at the time.

Blighty*

GB 1926 93m (24 fps) bw silent
Gainsborough–Piccadilly (Michael Balcon, Carlyle Blackwell)

A chauffeur becomes an officer and after the war finds himself looking after the master's family.

Fairly unwatchable in a normal sense, but of historical interest as one of the key British films of the twenties to make a comment about the war.

w Eliot Stannard, Charles McEvoy, Ivor Montagu *d* Adrian Brunel

Jameson Thomas, Ellaline Terriss, Lilian Hall Davis, Godfrey Winn, Wally Patch, Seymour Hicks

Blind Adventure

US 1933 65m bw

An American in London gets mixed up with blackmailers and kidnappers. Light-hearted but ill-explained second feature. Robert Armstrong, Helen Mack, Roland Young, Ralph Bellamy, John Miljan, Laura Hope Crews, Henry Stephenson, Phyllis Barry. Written by Ruth Rose; directed by Ernest B. Schoedsack; music by Max Steiner; for RKO. 'Has some fine things but won't mean much more than a programmer in the split spots.'—*Variety*

†The film seems to have been undertaken as a diversion by the makers of *King Kong*.

Blind Alley**
US 1939   68m   bw
Columbia

An escaped killer takes refuge in the home of a psychiatrist, who explores his subconscious and tames him.
Unusual lowercase thriller with effective dream sequences; it was much imitated.

w Michael Blankfort, Albert Duffy, *play* James Warwick *d* Charles Vidor *ph* Lucien Ballard *m* Morris Stoloff

Chester Morris, Ralph Bellamy, Ann Dvorak, Melville Cooper, Rose Stradner, Marc Lawrence
'Psychoanalysis of a criminal provides a new twist to what would otherwise be another crime picture of general trend.'—*Variety*
'As un-Hollywood as anything that has come from France this year.'—*New York Daily News*
'Survive a sticky ten minutes and you have a thriller of quite unusual merit.'—*Graham Greene*
† Remake: *The Dark Past* (qv).

Blind Date
US 1934   71m   bw

A working girl jilts a man because he is not the marrying kind, then regrets it. Tedious homespun drama. Ann Sothern, Neil Hamilton, Paul Kelly, Mickey Rooney, Jane Darwell, Spencer Charters. Written by Ethel Hill; directed by Roy Willian Neill; for Columbia. 'Vida Hurst is credited with the basic story, but a lot of others used it before her. Used to be a favourite with Corinne Griffith.'—*Variety*

Blind Date*
GB 1959   95m   bw
Rank / Sydney Box / Independent Artists (David Deutsch)
US title: *Chance Meeting*

A young Dutch painter in London discovers his mistress's body and finds himself in a web of deceit.
Tolerable, comparatively sophisticated murder puzzle; rather glum looking, but the plot holds the interest.

w Ben Barzman, Millard Lampell, *novel* Leigh Howard *d* Joseph Losey *ph* Christopher Challis *m* Richard Rodney Bennett

Hardy Kruger, Stanley Baker, Micheline Presle, Robert Flemyng, Gordon Jackson, John Van Eyssen

The Blind Goddess
GB 1947   88m   bw
Gainsborough (Betty Box)

The private secretary to a public figure finds that his idol has feet of clay, and suffers in court for his discovery.
Courtroom drama from an old-fashioned stage play: surefire for addicts, but routine as a film.

w Muriel and Sydney Box, *play Patrick Hastings d* Harold French *ph* Ray Elton

Eric Portman, Anne Crawford, Hugh Williams, Michael Denison, Nora Swinburne, Claire Bloom, Raymond Lovell, Frank Cellier

Blind Husbands**
US 1919   90m approx (24 fps)   bw
          silent
Universal

An Austrian officer, on holiday in the Alps, seduces the wife of a rich American. Stroheim's first comedy of sexual manners, now of mainly archival interest.

w, d, ad Erich Von Stroheim *ph* Ben Reynolds

Erich Von Stroheim, Sam de Grasse, Gibson Gowland, Francella Billington

Blind Man's Buff
GB 1936   72m   bw

A doctor jealous of his wife does not reveal the fact that he has been cured of blindness. Yawnworthy melodrama. Basil Sydney, James Mason, Enid Stamp-Taylor, Barbara Greene, Iris Ashley. Written by Cecil Maiden, from the play *Smoked Glasses* by William Foster and B. Scott-Elder; directed by Albert Parker; for Present Day / Fox British.

Blind Terror
GB 1971   89m   colour
Columbia / Filmways / Genesis (Basil Appleby)
US title: *See No Evil*

A blind girl is the sole, hunted survivor of a maniac's rampage on a lonely estate.
Shocks, screams and starts fill a cliché-ridden but still effective script which is faithfully turned into a competent but routine heart-stopper.

w Brian Clemens *d* Richard Fleischer *ph* Gerry Fisher *m* Elmer Bernstein

Mia Farrow, Robin Bailey, Dorothy Alison, Diane Grayson, Norman Eshley, Brian Rawlinson
'For those who like to watch folks pull the wings off flies.'—*Judith Crist*

Blindfold**
US 1965   102m   Technicolor
          Panavision
Universal (Marvin Schwarz)

A society psychiatrist is enlisted by the CIA to make regular blindfold journeys to a secret destination where he treats a neurotic physicist. Discovering that his contacts are really enemy agents, he tracks down the destination by sound and guesswork, and routs the villains.

Lively spy spoof with rather too much knockabout between the Hitchcockian suspense sequences; it has indeed the air of a script which Hitchcock rejected, but provides reliable entertainment.

w Philip Dunne, W. H. Menger, *novel* Lucile Fletcher *d* Philip Dunne *ph* Joseph MacDonald *m* Lalo Schifrin

Rock Hudson, Claudia Cardinale, Jack Warden, Guy Stockwell, Brad Dexter

The Bliss of Mrs Blossom
GB 1968   93m   Technicolor
Paramount (Josef Shaftel)

The wife of a bra manufacturer keeps her lover in the attic.
Silly, wild-eyed sex comedy decorated with the flashy tinsel of swinging London's dying fall.

w Alec Coppel, Denis Norden *d* Joe McGrath *ph* Geoffrey Unsworth *m* Riz Ortolani *pd* Assheton Gorton

Richard Attenborough, Shirley Maclaine, James Booth, Freddie Jones, William Rushton, Bob Monkhouse, Patricia Routledge

Blithe Spirit***
GB 1945   96m   Technicolor
Two Cities / Cineguild (Anthony Havelock-Allan)

A cynical novelist's second marriage is disturbed when the playful ghost of his first wife materializes during a séance.
Direction and acting carefully preserve a comedy which on its first West End appearance in 1941 achieved instant classic status. The repartee scarcely dates, and altogether this is a most polished job of film-making.

w Noel Coward, from his play *scenario* David Lean, Anthony Havelock-Allan, Ronald Neame *d* David Lean *ph* Ronald Neame *m* Richard Addinsell

Rex Harrison, Kay Hammond, Constance Cummings, Margaret Rutherford, Hugh Wakefield, Joyce Carey, Jacqueline Clark
† After seeing this, Noël Coward reputedly told Rex Harrison: 'After me you're the best light comedian in the world.'

Blitz on Britain*
GB 1960   71m   bw

A very acceptable record of the Battle of Britain as it affected the home front, narrated by Alistair Cooke. Written by Patrick Brawn; directed and edited by Harry Booth; for Anglo-Continental / British Lion.

The Blob
US 1958   83m   De Luxe
Tonylyn / Jack H. Harris

A small town combats a slimy space invader. Padded hokum for drive-ins, with a few effective moments.

w Theodore Simonson, Kate Phillips *d* Irwin S. Yeaworth Jnr *ph* Thomas Spalding *m* Ralph Carmichael

Steve McQueen, Aneta Corseaut, Olin Howlin, Earl Rowe

† Sequel 1971: *Beware! The Blob* (GB: *Son of Blob*).

● *Video: Mountain*

Blockade*

US 1938 84m bw
Walter Wanger

During the Spanish Civil War, a peace-loving young farmer has to take up arms to defend his land.

Much touted as Hollywood's first serious contribution to international affairs, this dogged drama was in fact so bland that audiences had difficulty ascertaining which side it was on, especially as neither Franco nor the Fascists were mentioned. As a romantic action drama, however, it passed muster.

w John Howard Lawson *d* William Dieterle *m* Werner Janssen *ph* Rudolf Maté

Henry Fonda, Madeleine Carroll, Leo Carrillo, John Halliday, Vladimir Sokoloff, Robert Warwick, Reginald Denny

'It misses any claim to greatness because it pulls its punches . . . and it's going to be tough to sell.'—*Variety*

'The film has a curious unreality considering the grim reality behind it.'—*Frank S. Nugent*

'There is achieved a deadly numb level of shameless hokum out of which anything true or decent rises only for a second to confound itself.'—*Otis Ferguson*

† Original publicity carried this disclaimer: NOTE: Care has been taken to prevent any costume of the production from being accurately that of either side in the Spanish Civil War. The story does not attempt to favour any cause in the present conflict.

AAN: John Howard Lawson; Werner Janssen

Blockheads***

US 1938 60m bw
Hal Roach / Stan Laurel

Twenty years after World War I, Stan is still guarding a trench because nobody told him to stop. Olly takes him home to meet the wife, with disastrous consequences.

The last first-class Laurel and Hardy comedy is shapeless but hilarious, a fragmented reworking of earlier ideas, all of which work beautifully. Gags include encounters with a tip-up truck and an automatic garage, and a brilliantly worked out sequence up and down several flights of stairs.

w James Parrott, Harry Langdon, Felix Adler, Charles Rogers, Arnold Belgard *d* John G. Blystone *ph* Art Lloyd *m* Marvin Hatley

Stan Laurel, Oliver Hardy, Billy Gilbert, Patricia Ellis, Minna Gombell, James Finlayson

'Hodge-podge of old-fashioned slapstick and hoke.'—*Variety*

AAN: Marvin Hatley

Blonde Crazy*

US 1931 74m bw
Warner
GB title: *Larceny Lane*

A bellhop and a chambermaid set out to fleece all-comers.

Smart con man comedy with the star in excellent form.

w Kubec Glasmon, John Bright *d* Roy del Ruth *ph* Sid Hickox

James Cagney, Joan Blondell, Ray Milland, Louis Calhern, Guy Kibbee, Polly Walters, Charles Lane, Maude Eburne

'Naughty cracks galore, and one says "Nuts". But he doesn't push a grapefruit in the girl friend's face, though they expect it any time.'—*Variety*

'A chipper, hard-boiled, amusing essay in petty thieving.'—*Time*

The Blonde from Peking

US / France 1968 80m colour

The CIA thinks that a girl with amnesia may know Chinese nuclear secrets. Witless international spy stuff, neither funny nor thrilling. Mireille Darc, Claudio Brook, Edward G. Robinson, Pascale Roberts. Written by Nicolas Gessner and Marc Behm, from a story by James Hadley Chase; directed by Nicolas Gessner; for Paramount.

A Blonde in Love: see *Loves of a Blonde*

'What could she do but flee from love? She loved two men at once!'

Blonde Venus*

US 1932 97m bw
Paramount

A German café singer marries an English research chemist, but their marriage doesn't run smoothly.

Rather dreary, fragmented star vehicle with good moments, notably the star's opening appearance as a gorilla.

w Jules Furthman, S. K. Lauren *d* Josef Von Sternberg *ph* Bert Glennon *m* Oscar Poteker

Marlene Dietrich, Herbert Marshall, Cary Grant, Dickie Moore

'Weak story, inept direction and generally sluggish total count heavily against it . . . it'll require plenty of bally.'—*Variety*

'The story has all the dramatic integrity of a sashweight murderer's tabloid autobiography.'—*Pare Lorentz*

'There is more pleasure for the eye in *Blonde Venus* than in a hundred of its fellows. But what does beauty ornament? The story of a wife who becomes a kept woman for the sake of her husband, and a prostitute for the sake of her child.'—*Forsyth Hardy, Cinema Quarterly*

Blondes for Danger

GB 1938 68m bw

A cockney taxi driver takes an unwanted fare and becomes involved in a deep dark plot. Modest but effective vehicle for *Gordon Harker;* with Enid Stamp Taylor, Ivan Brandt. Written by Gerald Elliott, from the novel *Red for Danger* by Evadne Price; directed by Jack Raymond; for Herbert Wilcox.

Blondie*

US 1938 68m bw
Columbia

Misadventures of a harassed suburban family man.

Dagwood Bumstead and his wife Blondie were Mr and Mrs Small Town America throughout the thirties and forties, and received their perfect screen incarnations in this unambitious but quite watchable series, which provided familiar and often quite observant fun.

w Richard Flournoy, from the comic strip by *Chic Young d* Frank R. Strayer *ph* Henry Freulich

Arthur Lake, Penny Singleton, Larry Simms, Daisy the Dog, *Jonathan Hale* (as the boss, Mr Dithers), Gene Lockhart, Ann Doran, Irving Bacon (as the mailman)

'Light fare, but universal in appeal . . . could be clicko series.'—*Variety*

Other episodes were as follows:
1939: BLONDIE MEETS THE BOSS, BLONDIE TAKES A VACATION, BLONDIE BRINGS UP BABY
1940: BLONDIE ON A BUDGET, BLONDIE HAS SERVANT TROUBLE, BLONDIE PLAYS CUPID
1941: BLONDIE GOES LATIN, BLONDIE IN SOCIETY
1942: BLONDIE GOES TO COLLEGE, BLONDIE'S BLESSED EVENT, BLONDIE FOR VICTORY
1943: IT'S A GREAT LIFE, FOOTLIGHT GLAMOUR
1945: LEAVE IT TO BLONDIE
1946: BLONDIE KNOWS BEST, LIFE WITH BLONDIE, BLONDIE'S LUCKY DAY
1947: BLONDIE'S BIG MOMENT, BLONDIE'S HOLIDAY, BLONDIE IN THE DOUGH, BLONDIE'S ANNIVERSARY
1948: BLONDIE'S REWARD
1949: BLONDIE'S SECRET, BLONDIE'S BIG DEAL, BLONDIE HITS THE JACKPOT
1950: BLONDIE'S HERO, BEWARE OF BLONDIE
† TV series were started in the fifties and sixties, but both failed.

Blondie Johnson

US 1933 67m bw

The career of a female larcenist who eventually takes her medicine. Competent programmer very typical of its studio and year. Joan Blondell, Chester Morris, Allen Jenkins, Claire Dodd. Written by Earl Baldwin; directed by Ray Enright; for Warner. 'After she departs for the pen, she lets the public in on the fact that crime doesn't pay. Neither will the picture.'—*Variety*

Blondie of the Follies*

US 1932 97m bw
MGM (Marion Davies)

Two New York showgirls graduate from tenements to luxury.

Adequate comedy-melodrama with an interesting cast and good dialogue.

w Frances Marion, Anita Loos d Edmund
Goulding ph George Barnes m William Axt

Marion Davies, Jimmy Durante, Robert
Montgomery, Billie Dove, James Gleason,
Zasu Pitts, Sidney Toler, Douglass Dumbrille
  'Not bad, but not very good, with chances
that it will just get by. Length and slow pace
the drawbacks. . . . It isn't padded out, it's
just flatfooted.'—*Variety*
  'An unjustly forgotten film.'—*New Yorker,
1979*

Blood Alley
US 1955 115m Warnercolor
Cinemascope
Warner / Batjac (no producer credited)
An American sailor is helped by local people
to escape from a Chinese jail; he then escorts
them to Hong Kong.
Rudimentary anti-Red heroics with expensive
spectacle punctuating a tacky script.
w A. S. Fleischmann, from his novel
d William Wellman ph William H. Clothier
m Roy Webb pd Alfred Ybarra

John Wayne, Lauren Bacall, Paul Fix, Joy
Kim, Berry Kroger, Mike Mazurki, Anita
Ekberg

Blood and Black Lace
Italy 1964 90m Eastmancolor
Six women are nastily murdered in a fashion
house. Vaguely necrophiliac but trendy
suspense-horror flick in the wake of *Psycho*.
Cameron Mitchell, Thomas Reiner, Mary
Arden. Written by Marcel Fondato, Giuseppe
Barilla and Mario Bava; directed by Mario
Bava; for Emmepi. (Original title: *Sei Donne
per l'Assassino.*)

Blood and Roses
France / Italy 1960 87m Technirama
Eger / Documento (Raymond Eger)
original title: *Et Mourir de Plaisir*
Carmilla takes on the vampiric personality of
her ancestress Millarca, whom she closely
resembles.
A rather half-hearted attempt to make an
elegant horror story; boring rather than
charming or frightening.
w Claude Brûlé, Claude Martin, Roger
Vadim d Roger Vadim ph Claude Renoir
m Jean Prodromidès

Mel Ferrer, Elsa Martinelli, Annette Vadim,
Marc Allégret

Blood and Sand°
US 1922 80m (24 fps) bw silent
Paramount
A matador falls under the spell of an
aristocratic woman.
Elegant star vehicle which established his
image.
w June Mathis, *novel* Vicente Blasco Ibanez
d Fred Niblo

Rudolph Valentino, Nita Naldi, Lila Lee,
Walter Long

'Love flamed in the shadow of death!'
Blood and Sand°
US 1941 123m Technicolor
TCF (Darryl F. Zanuck, Robert T. Kane)
Rather boring remake, fine to look at but
dramatically deadly.
w Jo Swerling, *novel* Vicente Blasco Ibanez
d Rouben Mamoulian ph Ernest Palmer, Ray
Rennahan m Alfred Newman ad Richard
Day, Joseph C. Wright

Tyrone Power, Rita Hayworth, Linda Darnell,
Nazimova, Anthony Quinn, J. Carrol Naish,
John Carradine, Lynn Bari, Laird Cregar,
Monty Banks
AA: Ernest Palmer, Ray Rennahan
● *Video: CBS / Fox*

The Blood Beast Terror
GB 1967 88m Eastmancolor
Tigon (Arnold L. Miller, Tony Tenser)
A Victorian entomologist creates human
beings who can change themselves into
monster death's-head moths.
Unpersuasive and totally idiotic cheapjack
horror fare.
w Peter Bryan d Vernon Sewell ph Stanley
A. Long m Paul Ferris

Robert Flemyng, Peter Cushing, Wanda
Ventham, Vanessa Howard, David Griffin,
John Paul, Kevin Stoney, Roy Hudd

Blood from the Mummy's Tomb°
GB 1971 94m Technicolor
Hammer (Howard Brandy)
Twenty years after a female mummy is
brought back to England, members of the
expedition are killed one by one, and their
leader's daughter is possessed by the spirit of
the dead princess.
Interesting but over-complicated and hard-to-
enjoy attempt to maintain the mummy saga
without an actual marauding mummy.
Intelligently handled but sadly lacking in a
sense of humour.
w Christopher Wicking, *novel* Jewel of the
Seven Stars by Bram Stoker d Seth Holt
ph Arthur Grant m Tristam Cary

Andrew Keir, Valerie Leon, James Villiers,
Hugh Burden, George Coulouris, Mark
Edwards, Rosalie Crutchley, Aubrey Morris,
David Markham
  'Makes the genre seem like new.'—*Tony
Rayns*
† Seth Holt died when the shooting was still
incomplete, and Michael Carreras took over
for the last few days
● *Video: Thorn EMI*

Blood Money°
US 1933 66m bw
The decline of a bail-bond racketeer. Smartly
made melodrama with good work all round.
George Bancroft, Judith Anderson, Chick
Chandler, Frances Dee, Blossom Seeley.
Written and directed by Rowland Brown; for
Darryl F. Zanuck / Twentieth Century.

The Blood of a Poet°°
France 1930 58m bw
Vicomte de Noailles
original title: *Le Sang d'un Poète*
Aspects of a poet's vision, taking place while a
chimney is falling down.
An indescribable film full of striking imagery
which may, or may not, be meaningful. Its
author claims that it is not surrealist, but that
label for most people will do as well as any
other.
wd Jean Cocteau ph Georges Périnal
m Georges Auric ad Jean Gabriel d'Aubonne

Lee Miller, Pauline Carton, Odette Talazac
  'It must be placed among the classic
masterpieces of the seventh art.'—*Revue du
Cinéma*

Blood of the Vampire
GB 1958 85m Eastmancolor
An asylum keeper turns inmates into
vampires. Heavy-handed, crudely made horror
comic. Donald Wolfit, Barbara Shelley,
Vincent Ball, Victor Maddern, Andrew
Faulds. Written by Jimmy Sangster; directed
by Henry Cass; for Baker-Berman / Artistes
Alliance.

Blood on Satan's Claw
GB 1970 93m Eastmancolor
Tigon-Chilton (Tony Tenser, Malcolm B.
  Heyworth, Peter L. Andrews)
aka: *Satan's Skin*
A devil's claw wreaks havoc among children in
a 17th-century English village.
Moderately frightening, rather silly but at least
original period horror comic.
w Robert Wynne-Simmons d Piers Haggard
ph Dick Bush m Marc Wilkinson

Patrick Wymark, Linda Hayden, Barry
Andrews, Avice Landon, Simon Williams,
Tamara Ustinov, Anthony Ainley

Blood on the Arrow
US 1964 91m De Luxe
An outlaw is the only survivor of an Indian
raid, and later becomes a hero when the
Indians attack again. Unremarkable western,
with every turn of plot to order. Dale
Robertson, Martha Hyer, Wendell Corey,
Paul Mantee, Ted de Corsia. Written by
Robert E. Kent; directed by Sidney Salkow;
for Leon Fromkess / Allied Artists.

Blood on the Moon°
US 1948 88m bw
RKO
A homesteader finds that his best friend is the
villainous leader of a group of cattlemen.
Good-looking but rather pedestrian western,
generally well handled.
w Lillie Hayward d Robert Wise ph Nicholas
Musuraca m Roy Webb

Robert Mitchum, Barbara Bel Geddes,
Robert Preston, Walter Brennan

Blood on the Sun°
US 1945 94m bw
Cagney Productions (William Cagney)

In the twenties, the American editor of a Tokyo newspaper reveals a Japanese militarist plan for world conquest.
Satisfactory star actioner with good production and exciting highlights.

w Lester Cole d Frank Lloyd ph Theodor Sparkuhl m Miklos Rozsa

James Cagney, Sylvia Sidney, Wallace Ford, Rosemary de Camp, Robert Armstrong, John Emery, Leonard Strong, Frank Puglia
  'It ought to be fine for those who enjoy a good ninety-minute massacre.'—*New Yorker*
  'Tough, hard-hitting and explosive, with just enough rudimentary suspense.'—*Bosley Crowther*
  'Pure unadulterated melodrama has a safe niche in cinematic offerings, but this folderol is more pretentious than persuasive.'—*Howard Barnes*

Bloodbath at the House of Death
GB 1983 92m colour
EMI / Wildwood (Ray Cameron)

Scientists investigate a haunted house.
Spoof tailored to the requirements of a zany television comedian who never knows when enough is enough. Too much gore and far too much smut.

w Ray Cameron, Barry Cryer d Ray Cameron ph Brian West, Dusty Miller m Mike Moran, Mark London

Kenny Everett, Pamela Stephenson, Vincent Price, Gareth Hunt, Don Warrington, John Fortune, Sheila Steafel, Graham Stark
  'Presumably intended as high camp; looks like low-grade Carry On.'—*Martyn Auty, MFB*

Bloodbrothers
US 1978 116m Technicolor
Warner / Stephen Friedman / Kings Road

The disintegration through failure and inadequacy of a noisy Italian-American family. The kind of self-indulgence that has one seeking the exit before it's half over.

w Walter Newman, *novel* Richard Price d Robert Mulligan ph Robert Surtees m Elmer Bernstein pd Gene Callahan

Paul Sorvino, Tony Lo Bianco, Richard Gere, Lelia Goldoni
  'Why should filmgoers pay to see what they can already hear in the next apartment?'—
  'The director is trying for something crude, powerful, volatile . . . but it goes terribly wrong. People laugh with hysterical heartiness, or say things like: "Life can hurt. It's made me feel close to all those doing the hurting dance." '—*Pauline Kael, New Yorker*

Bloodhounds of Broadway*
US 1952 90m Technicolor
TCF (George Jessel)

With the help of a gangster, an orphan girl and her pet bloodhounds make a big hit in a cabaret.
Absurd but sporadically amusing gangster burlesque, typical of its author. Lively production values.

w Sy Gomberg, *story* Damon Runyon d Harmon Jones ph Edward Cronjager md Lionel Newman

Mitzi Gaynor, Scott Brady, Mitzi Green, Marguerite Chapman, Michael O'Shea, Wally Vernon, George E. Stone

Bloodline
US 1979 117m Movielab
Paramount / Geria (David V. Bicker, Sidney Beckerman)

A pharmaceutical tycoon is murdered and his daughter seems likely to be the next victim. Involved all-star suspense shocker which seems constantly about to be better than it ever is.

w Laird Koenig, *novel* Sidney Sheldon d Terence Young ph Freddie Young m Ennio Morricone pd Ted Haworth

Audrey Hepburn, Ben Gazzara, James Mason, Claudia Mori, Omar Sharif, Irene Papas, Maurice Ronet, Romy Schneider, Beatrice Straight, Gert Frobe, Micheline Phillips
  'Unutterably chic, inexpressibly absurd, and saved from being painfully tedious only by a personable cast doing their damnedest.'—*Tom Milne, MFB*

'The family that stays together slays together!'
Bloody Mama*
US 1969 90m Movielab
AIP (Roger Corman)

In the thirties, outlaw Kate Barker and her four sons conduct a reign of terror until what's left of the gang is riddled with machine gun bullets.
Violent gangster story with a star on the rampage; the attempt to philosophize is more than the facts will bear, but the production moves smartly enough.

w Robert Thom d Roger Corman ph John Alonzo m Don Randi

Shelley Winters, Pat Hingle, Don Stroud, Diane Varsi, Bruce Dern, Clint Kimbrough, Robert de Niro, Robert Walden, Alex Nicol

Bloomfield
GB 1969 95m Technicolor
World Film Services / Limbridge (John Heyman, Wolf Mankowitz)
US title: *The Hero*

A 10-year-old Israeli boy hitchhikes to Jaffa to see his football idol play his last game.
Sentimental whimsy, unattractively interpreted.

w Wolf Mankowitz d Richard Harris ph Otto Heller m Johnny Harris

Richard Harris, Romy Schneider, Kim Burfield, Maurice Kaufmann, Yossi Yadin

Blossom Time
GB 1934 90m bw

In old Vienna, a composer stands by while the girl he loves weds a dragoon. Stilted musical romance redeemed by its star's singing presence. Richard Tauber, Jane Baxter, Carl Esmond, Athene Seyler. Written by John Drinkwater, Walter Burford, Paul Perez and G. H. Clutsam; directed by Paul Stein; for BIP. (US title: *April Romance*.)

Blossoms in the Dust**
US 1941 99m Technicolor
MGM (Irving Asher)

A woman who loses her husband and child founds a state orphanage.
Archetypal tearjerker of the forties, a glossy 'woman's picture' which distorts the facts into a star vehicle. Excellent colour helped to make it an enormous success.

w Anita Loos, based on the life of Edna Gladney d Mervyn Le Roy ph Karl Freund, W. Howard Greene m Herbert Stothart

Greer Garson, Walter Pidgeon, Felix Bressart, Marsha Hunt, Fay Holden, Samuel S. Hinds

AAN: best picture; Karl Freund, W. Howard Greene; Greer Garson

'Heading for the laff round-up!'
Blossoms on Broadway
US 1937 88m bw

A girl who owns a Death Valley gold mine comes to New York and is hounded by confidence men. Tolerably fast-moving comedy. Edward Arnold, Shirley Ross, John Trent, Weber and Fields, Frank Craven, Rufe David, William Frawley. Written by Theodore Reeves; directed by Richard Wallace; for B. P. Schulberg / Paramount. 'Won't do much b.o. blossoming. Good songs, but story stumbles badly.'—*Variety*

Blotto*
US 1930 20m bw

Ollie helps Stan escape his wife for a night on the town, but the lady takes revenge. Palatable star comedy with a strained second half following a splendidly typical opening. Laurel and Hardy, Anita Garvin. Written by Leo McCarey and H. M. Walker; directed by James Parrott; for Hal Roach.

'Murder has a sound all of its own!'
Blow Out
US 1981 108m Technicolor Panavision
Filmways / Cinema 77 / Geria (George Litto)

A sound effects man accidentally captures on film what turns out to be a murder.
Showily unpleasant thriller concocted of equal parts of *The Conversation*, *Blow Up*, and *Kennedy at Chappaquiddick*; the work of a copycat talent operating below par.

wd Brian de Palma ph Vilmos Szigmond m Pino Donaggio pd Paul Sylbert

John Travolta, Nancy Allen, John Lithgow, Dennis Franz, John McMartin, John Aquino
  'The camera is better deployed than the script.'—*Guardian*
● Video: Rank

Blow Up**
GB 1966 110m Eastmancolor
MGM / Carlo Ponti

A London fashion photographer thinks he sees a murder, but the evidence disappears.
Not a mystery but a fashionable think-in on the difference (if any) between fantasy and reality. Agreeable to look at for those who can stifle their irritation at the non-plot and non-characters; a huge audience was lured by flashes of nudity and the trendy 'swinging London' setting.

wd Michelangelo Antonioni ph Carlo di Palma m Herbert Hancock ad Assheton Gorton

David Hemmings, Sarah Miles, Vanessa Redgrave

AAN: Michelangelo Antonioni (as writer and director)

● Video: MGM / UA

Blowing Wild•
US 1953 88m bw
(Warner) United States (Milton Sperling)

A Mexican oil driller becomes involved with the psychotic wife of an old friend; the triangle leads to murder and retribution.
Pot-boiling star vehicle with adequate melodramatic interest, full of reminiscences of other movies, with a wicked lady to end them all.

w Philip Yordan d Hugo Fregonese ph Sid Hickox m Dmitri Tiomkin

Gary Cooper, Barbara Stanwyck, Anthony Quinn, Ruth Roman, Ward Bond

Blue
US 1968 113m Technicolor Panavision
Paramount / Kettledrum (Judd Bernard, Irwin Winkler)

The white adopted son of a Mexican bandit prevents his cohorts from raping a white girl, and falls in love with her.
Pretentious, self-conscious, literary western without much zest.

w Meade Roberts, Ronald M. Cohen d Silvio Narizzano ph Stanley Cortez m Manos Hadjidakis

Terence Stamp, Joanna Pettet, Karl Malden, Ricardo Montalban
'I don't know which is worse—bad cowboy movies or bad arty cowboy movies. Blue is both.'—Rex Reed

The Blue Angel••••
Germany 1930 98m bw
UFA (Erich Pommer)

A fuddy-duddy professor is infatuated with a tawdry night-club singer. She marries him but is soon bored and contemptuous; humiliated, he leaves her and dies in his old classroom.
A masterwork of late twenties German grotesquerie, and after a slowish beginning an emotional powerhouse, set in a dark nightmare world which could be created only in the studio. Shot also in English, it was highly popular and influential in Britain and America.

w Robert Liebmann, Karl Zuckmayer, Karl Vollmoeller, novel Professor Unrath by Heinrich Mann d Josef Von Sternberg ph Günther Rittau, Hans Schneeberger m Frederick Hollander (inc 'Falling in Love Again', 'They Call Me Wicked Lola') ad Otto Hunte, Emil Hasler

Emil Jannings, Marlene Dietrich (who was instantly catapulted to international stardom), Kurt Gerron, Hans Albers
'It will undoubtedly do splendidly in the whole of Europe and should also appeal strongly in the States . . . only fault is a certain ponderousness of tempo which tends to tire.'—Variety

The Blue Angel
US 1959 107m De Luxe Cinemascope TCF (Jack Cummings)

Ill-advised attempt at a 'realistic', updated remake of the above; the result is a total travesty, with the actors aware that realistic melodrama is turning before their eyes into unintentional farce.

w Nigel Balchin d Edward Dmytryk ph Leon Shamroy m Hugo Friedhofer

Curt Jurgens, May Britt, Theodore Bikel, John Banner
'It totally lacks the stifling atmosphere of sordid and oppressive sexuality which is essential to give conviction to the German sadism of the story.'—Brenda Davies

The Blue Bird•••
US 1940 98m Technicolor (bw prologue)
TCF (Gene Markey)

In a Grimm's Fairy Tale setting, the two children of a poor woodcutter seek the bluebird of happiness in the past, the future and the Land of Luxury, but eventually discover it in their own back yard.
An imaginative and often chilling script clarifies Maurice Maeterlinck's fairy play, and the art direction is outstanding, but the children are necessarily unsympathetic and the expensive production paled beside the success of the more upbeat Wizard of Oz, which was released almost simultaneously. Slashed for re-release, the only existing prints now open with confusing abruptness and no scene-setting before the adventures begin.

w Ernest Pascal d Walter Lang ph Arthur Miller, Ray Rennahan m Alfred Newman

Shirley Temple, Johnny Russell, Gale Sondergaard (as the cat), Eddie Collins (as the dog), Nigel Bruce, Jessie Ralph, Spring Byington, Sybil Jason, Helen Ericson, Russell Hicks, Al Shean, Cecilia Loftus

AAN: Arthur Miller, Ray Rennahan

The Blue Bird
US / USSR 1976 99m Technicolor Panavision
TCF / Edward Lewis / Lenfilm

Abortive remake of the above, widely touted as the first Russian–American co-production, but sabotaged by a flabby script, unsuitable casting and unresolved production problems.

w Hugh Whitemore, Alfred Hayes d George Cukor ph Freddie Young, Ionas Gritzus m Irwin Kostal, Andrei Petrov

Elizabeth Taylor (as Mother, Maternal Love, Light and the Witch), Ava Gardner, Cicely Tyson, Jane Fonda, Harry Andrews, Will Geer, Mona Washbourne, George Cole
'It works so hard at making history that it forgets to make sense.'—David Sterritt, Christian Science Monitor
'If you have any naughty children you want to punish, take them to The Blue Bird and make them sit all the way through it.'—William Wolf, Cue
'It turns a work for adults that children can enjoy into a charade for children that must sicken adults.'—John Simon, New Yorker
'Senile and interminable.'—Stephen Farber, New West

Blue Blood
GB 1973 86m Technicolor
Mallard-Impact Quadrant

A German governess arrives at an English stately home and finds the malevolent butler plotting to show his supremacy over his effete master.
An extremely unattractive, would-be satirical melodrama which plays like a Grand Guignol version of The Servant.

wd Andrew Sinclair, novel The Carry-Cot by Alexander Thynne ph Harry Waxman m Brian Gascoigne

Oliver Reed, Derek Jacobi, Fiona Lewis, Anna Gael, Meg Wynn Owen

Blue Collar•
US 1978 114m Technicolor
Universal / TAT (Don Guest)

Three car factory workers try to improve their lot by unionization and robbery.
Salty, rough, downbeat but impressively realistic modern drama, a belated American equivalent of Saturday Night and Sunday Morning.

w Paul Schraeder, Leonard Schraeder d Paul Schraeder ph Bobby Byrne m Jack Nitzche

Richard Pryor, Harvey Keitel, Yaphet Kotto, Ed Begley Jnr, Harry Bellaver

● Video: CIC

'Tamed by a brunette—framed by a blonde—blamed by the cops!'

The Blue Dahlia••
US 1946 99m bw
Paramount (John Houseman)

A returning war veteran finds his faithless wife murdered and himself suspected.
Hailed on its first release as sharper than average, this mystery suspenser is now only moderately compelling despite the screenplay credit; direction and editing lack urgency and the acting lacks bounce.

w Raymond Chandler d George Marshall ph Lionel Lindon m Victor Young

Alan Ladd, Veronica Lake, William Bendix, Howard da Silva, Doris Dowling, Tom Powers, Hugh Beaumont, Howard Freeman, Will Wright

'It threatens to turn into something, but it never does.'—*New Yorker, 1978*

'The picture is as neatly stylized and synchronized, and as uninterested in moral excitement, as a good ballet; it knows its own weight and size perfectly and carries them gracefully and without self-importance; it is, barring occasional victories and noble accidents, about as good a movie as can be expected from the big factories.'—*James Agee*

AAN: Raymond Chandler

Blue Denim*

US 1959 89m bw Cinemascope
TCF (Charles Brackett)
GB title: *Blue Jeans*

Teenagers confronted with the prospect of illegitimate parenthood consult an abortionist, but all ends with wedding bells.

First of its rather dreary kind but better than most, this only slightly mawkish domestic drama has its heart in the right place and steers surprisingly towards a nick-of-time chase climax.

w Edith Sommer, Philip Dunne, *play* James Leo Herlihy, William Noble *d* Philip Dunne *ph* Leo Tover *m* Bernard Herrmann

Carol Lynley, Brandon de Wilde, Macdonald Carey, Marsha Hunt, Nina Shipman, Warren Berlinger

The Blue Gardenia

US 1953 90m bw
Warner / Gloria / Blue Gardenia (Alex Gottlieb)

A girl gets drunk and wakes up in a strange apartment with a dead man by her side. Totally undistinguished mystery which leaves egg on the actors' faces.

w Charles Hoffman *d* Fritz Lang *ph* Nicholas Musuraca *m* Raoul Krashaar

Anne Baxter, Richard Conte, Ann Sothern, Raymond Burr, Jeff Donnell, Richard Erdman, Nat King Cole

Blue Hawaii

US 1961 101m Technicolor
  Panavision
Hal B. Wallis

A GI comes home to Honolulu and becomes a beachcomber.

Lifeless star vehicle shot on glamorous locations.

w Hal Kanter *d* Norman Taurog *ph* Charles Lang Jnr *m* Joseph J. Lilley

Elvis Presley, Joan Blackman, Nancy Walters, Roland Winters, Angela Lansbury, John Archer, Howard McNear

● *Video: CBS / Fox*

The Blue Lagoon*

GB 1949 103m Technicolor
GFD / Individual (Frank Launder, Sidney Gilliat)

A shipwrecked boy and girl grow up on a desert island, ward off smugglers, have a baby, and eventually sail away in search of civilization.

THE BLUE LAGOON.   This is the more innocent British version of the forties. Donald Houston, Jean Simmons.

Rather lifeless, though pretty, treatment of a famous novel: the story never becomes vivid despite splendid Fijian locations.

w Frank Launder, John Baines, Michael Hogan, *novel* H. de Vere Stacpoole *d* Frank Launder *ph* Geoffrey Unsworth *m* Clifton Parker

Jean Simmons, Donald Houston, Noel Purcell, Cyril Cusack, James Hayter

The Blue Lagoon

US 1980 102m Colorfilm
Columbia / Randal Kleiser

Remake of the above with poor narrative balance and a great deal of nudity and adolescent frankness about sex. Adolescents are probably its only audience.

w Douglas Day Stewart *d* Randal Kleiser *ph* Nestor Almendros *m* Basil Poledouris

Brooke Shields, Christopher Atkins, Leo McKern, William Daniels

'At best a damp dream, a Sunday school fairy tale which makes the story of Adam and Eve seem like hard porn, as hygienically sanitized as a Hilton Hotel lavatory seat.'—*Sunday Times*

'A total fraud from beginning to end.'—*Guardian*

'The film has an inevitable, built-in prurience. All we have to look forward to is: when are these two going to discover fornication?'—*Pauline Kael, New Yorker*

AAN: Nestor Almendros

● *Video: RCA / Columbia*

The Blue Lamp***

GB 1949 84m bw
Ealing (Michael Relph)

A young man joins London's police force. The elderly copper who trains him is killed in a shootout, but the killer is apprehended. Seminal British police film which spawned not only a long line of semi-documentary imitations but also the twenty-year TV series *Dixon of Dock Green* for which the shot PC was happily revived. As an entertainment, pacy but dated; more important, it burnished the image of the British copper for a generation or more.

w T. E. B. Clarke *d* Basil Dearden *ph* Gordon Dines *md* Ernest Irving

Jack Warner, Jimmy Hanley, Dirk Bogarde, Meredith Edwards, Robert Flemyng, Bernard Lee, Patric Doonan, Peggy Evans, Gladys Henson, Dora Bryan

'The mixture of coyness, patronage and naive theatricality which has vitiated British films for the last ten years.'—*Gavin Lambert*

'A soundly made crime thriller which would not be creating much of a stir if it were American.'—*Richard Mallett, Punch*

The Blue Light*

Germany 1932 68m bw
H. R. Sokal / Leni Riefenstahl

In the early 19th century, a painter defies a local legend to climb a Dolomite mountain.

Romantic fairy tale with a story more suited to a ballet. It still takes the eye, and is recognizable as the work of its director.

wd Leni Riefenstahl *ph* Hans Schneeberger, Henry Jaworsky *m* Giuseppe Becce

Leni Riefenstahl, Matthias Wieman, Max Holsboer

† This version was put together in 1950 after the original negative had been lost; among other things, a flashback frame was removed.

The Blue Max*
US 1966   156m   De Luxe   Cinemascope
TCF (Christian Ferry)

In Germany after World War I an ambitious and skilful pilot causes the death of his comrades and steals the wife of his High Command superior, who eventually finds a means of revenge.
For once, an action spectacular not too badly let down by its connecting threads of plot, apart from some hilarious and unnecessary bedroom scenes in which the female star's bath towel seems to become conveniently adhesive.

w David Pursall, Jack Seddon, Gerald Hanley, *novel* Jack Hunter *d* John Guillermin *ph* Douglas Slocombe *m* Jerry Goldsmith

George Peppard, *James Mason*, Ursula Andress, Jeremy Kemp, Karl Michael Vogler, Anton Diffring, Derren Nesbitt
'Addicts of flying movies swear by this one, but for others, the monoplanes and biplanes can't smash or burn fast enough'—*Pauline Kael*

● Video: CBS / Fox

Blue Murder at St Trinians*
GB 1957   86m   bw
British Lion / John Marvel (Launder and Gilliat)

The awful schoolgirls win a UNESCO prize trip which takes them to Rome where they become involved with a jewel thief.
Possibly the best of this series, which isn't saying much. See *The Belles of St Trinians*.

w Frank Launder, Val Valentine, Sidney Gilliat *d* Frank Launder *ph* Gerald Gibbs *m* Malcolm Arnold

Terry-Thomas, George Cole, Joyce Grenfell, Alistair Sim, Judith Furse, Sabrina, Lionel Jeffries, Lloyd Lamble, Thorley Walters, Kenneth Griffith, Eric Barker, Richard Wattis

The Blue Peter
GB 1955   93m   Eastmancolor
British Lion / Beaconsfield (Herbert Mason)

A confused war hero becomes a trainer at an Outward Bound school for boys.
Pleasant but uninspired open air adventure for young people.

w Don Sharp, John Pudney *d* Wolf Rilla *ph* Arthur Grant *m* Antony Hopkins

Kieron Moore, Greta Gynt, Sarah Lawson, Mervyn Johns, Ram Gopal, Edwin Richfield, Harry Fowler, John Charlesworth

'It's the nearest thing to heaven!'
Blue Skies*
US 1946   104m   Technicolor
Paramount (Sol C. Siegel)

A dancing star and a nightclub owner fight for years over the same girl.
Thin musical with splendid Irving Berlin tunes and lively individual numbers.

w Arthur Sheekman *d* Stuart Heisler *ph* Charles Lang *md* Robert Emmett Dolan

Fred Astaire (dancing 'Putting On the Ritz'), Bing Crosby, Joan Caulfield, Billy de Wolfe, Olga San Juan, Robert Benchley, Frank Faylen, Victoria Horne, Jack Norton

AAN: Robert Emmett Dolan; song 'You Keep Coming Back Like a Song' (*m* / *ly* Irving Berlin)

Blue Thunder*
US 1983   110m   Technicolor
Panavision
Columbia / Rastar / Gordon Carroll

A policeman in Los Angeles' Astro Division is haunted by memories of Vietnam and goes berserk when using his new ultra-sophisticated helicopter to wage war against crime.
Slick but hollow thriller most remarkable for its helicopter stunting between city skyscrapers. Otherwise, it is too often fashionably inaudible and almost invisible.

w Dan O'Bannon, Don Jakoby *d* John Badham *ph* John A. Alonzo *m* Arthur B. Rubenstein *aerial ph* Frank Holgate

Roy Scheider, Warren Oates, Candy Clark, Daniel Stern, Malcolm McDowell
† A watered-down TV version was quickly assembled, but its comic-strip dialogue grounded it after 13 episodes.

AAN: editing (Frank Morriss, Edward Abroms)

The Blue Veil*
US 1951   114m   bw
(RKO) Wald–Krasna (Raymond Hakim)

The vocational career of a children's nurse who descends into poverty but is rescued by one of her own charges, now grown up.
Sober American remake of a French tearjerker (*Le Voile bleu*) with the star suffering nobly but being upstaged by the cameo players.

w Norman Corwin, from the original by François Campaux *d* Curtis Bernhardt *ph* Franz Planer *m* Franz Waxman

Jane Wyman, Charles Laughton, Richard Carlson, Joan Blondell, Agnes Moorehead, Don Taylor, Audrey Totter, Everett Sloane, Cyril Cusack, Natalie Wood, Warner Anderson

AAN: Jane Wyman; Joan Blondell

Blue Water, White Death*
US 1971   99m   Techniscope

A skilful and quite frightening documentary about the habits of the Great White Shark, with a lead-up showing events on the expedition which set out in search of it.

Written and directed by Peter Gimbel; photographed by James Lipscomb; for Blue Water Films / Cinema Center.

Bluebeard*
US 1944   73m   bw
PRC

A strangler of young girls is at large in Paris. Poverty Row chiller with effective moments; possibly the most interesting film ever to come from PRC (which isn't saying *very* much).

w Pierre Gendron *d* Edgar G. Ulmer *ph* Jockey Feindel

John Carradine, Jean Parker, Ludwig Stossel, Nils Asther, Iris Adrian

Bluebeard
France / Italy / Germany 1972   124m
Technicolor
Barnabé / Gloria / Geiselgasteig (Alexander Salkind)

The lady killer in this case is an Austrian aristocrat who has been driven to desperation and murder by a long line of mistresses whose bodies he keeps frozen in his cellar.
Would-be macabre comedy which becomes totally off-putting by its emphasis on close-up death agonies.

w Ennio di Concini, Edward Dmytryk, Maria Pia Fusco *d* Edward Dmytryk *ph* Gabor Pogany *m* Ennio Morricone

Richard Burton, Raquel Welch, Joey Heatherton, Virna Lisi, Nathalie Delon, Marilu Tolo
'Somewhere between (and a long way behind) *Kind Hearts and Coronets* and *The Abominable Dr Phibes*.'—*Clyde Jeavons, MFB*

● Video: Thorn EMI

Bluebeard's Eighth Wife*
US 1938   85m   bw
Paramount (Ernst Lubitsch)

The daughter of an impoverished French aristocrat marries for money a millionaire who has had seven previous wives, and determines to teach him a lesson.
Very thin sophisticated comedy with unsympathetic characters and little wit after the first scene; a disappointment from the talent involved.

w Charles Brackett, Billy Wilder, *play* Alfred Savoir *d* Ernst Lubitsch *ph* Leo Tover

Claudette Colbert, Gary Cooper, David Niven, Edward Everett Horton, Elizabeth Patterson, Herman Bing, Warren Hymer, Franklin Pangborn
'Light and sometimes bright, but it gets a bit tiresome.'—*Variety*
'In these days it is bad enough to have to admire millionaires in any circumstances; but a millionaire with a harem complex simply can't help starting the bristles on the back of a sensitive neck.'—*New York Times*
† A previous version, released by Paramount in 1923 and directed by Sam Wood, starred Gloria Swanson and Huntley Gordon.

Bluebeard's Ten Honeymoons
GB 1960 93m bw
Anglo-Allied (Roy Parkinson)

Another version of the story of Landru, alternating wildly between fantasy, farce and melodrama. Not a success in any of its moods.

w Myles Wilder *d* W. Lee Wilder
ph Stephen Dade *m* Albert Elms

George Sanders, Corinne Calvet, Patricia Roc, Ingrid Hafner, Jean Kent, Greta Gynt, Maxine Audley, Selma Vaz Diaz, George Coulouris

'The unedifying narrative is developed along the most obvious lines imaginable.'—*MFB*

The Bluebird see The Blue Bird

A Blueprint for Murder°
US 1953 77m bw
TCF (Michael Abel)

After the death of his brother and nephew, a man proves that his sister-in-law is a murderess.

Unpleasant but efficient murder story with enough twists to keep one watching.

wd Andrew Stone *ph* Leo Tover *m* Lionel Newman

Jean Peters, Joseph Cotten, Gary Merrill, Catherine McLeod, Jack Kruschen

Blueprint for Robbery°
US 1960 87m bw
Paramount (Bryan Foy)

Crooks plan and execute a robbery, agreeing not to touch the proceeds for two and a half years. But some get tired of waiting. . .

Minor but effective crime melodrama in semi-documentary vein.

w Irwin Winehouse, A. Sanford Wolf *d* Jerry Hopper *ph* Loyal Griggs *m* Van Cleave

J. Pat O'Malley, Robert Gist, Romo Vincent, Marion Ross, Tom Duggan

'A not uninteresting entry in the screen log-book on crime.'—*MFB*

The Blues Brothers
US 1980 133m Technicolor
Universal (Robert K. Weiss)

A massive car chase develops when two brothers collect money for their old orphanage without too much regard for law and order.

Fashionable chase comedy with so many stunts that its cost ran up to 33,000,000 dollars. The public stayed away.

w Dan Aykroyd, John Landis *d* John Landis *ph* Stephen M. Katz *md* Ira Newborn *pd* John Lloyd

John Belushi, Dan Aykroyd, Kathleen Freeman, James Brown, Henry Gibson, Cab Calloway, Carrie Fisher

'It meanders expensively like some pedigreed shaggy dog through 70s / 80s American cinema and 50s / 60s American rock, cocking its leg happily at every popular landmark on the way.'—*Paul Taylor, MFB*

'There's not a *soupçon* of wit or ingenuity in this brainless exercise in overspending.'—*Daily Mail*

● Video: CIC

Blues in the Night°
US 1941 88m bw
Warner (Henry Blanke)

Career and romantic problems for the members of a travelling jazz band.

Atmospheric little melodrama with good score and smart dialogue.

w Robert Rossen, *play* Hot Nocturne by Edwin Gilbert *d* Anatole Litvak *ph* Ernest Haller

Priscilla Lane, Richard Whorf, Lloyd Nolan, Betty Field, Jack Carson, Elia Kazan, Wallace Ford, Billy Halop, Peter Whitney

AAN: title song (*m* Harold Arlen, *ly* Johnny Mercer)

Blume in Love°
US 1973 116m Technicolor
Warner (Paul Mazursky)

A divorced American lawyer in Venice reminisces about his love life.

Shapeless but enjoyable 'serious comedy' with star and director in good form.

wd Paul Mazursky *ph* Bruce Surtees *m* various

George Segal, Susan Anspach, Kris Kristofferson, Marsha Mason, Shelley Winters

BMX Bandits
Australia 1983 90m colour Panavision

Bike enthusiasts become unpopular when they cause havoc in the streets, but become heroes when they capture bank robbers. Lively action piece with unacceptable behaviour followed by reformation and an old-fashioned moral for early teenagers. David Argue, John Ley, Nicole Brian Sloman, Peter Browne. Written by Patrick Edgeworth; directed by Brian Trenchard Smith; for BMX / Nilsen.

Boardwalk
US 1979 100m Eastmancolor
ITC / Stratford (Gerald T. Herrod)

An old couple in Coney Island are affected by escalating violence.

Well-meaning but somewhat absurd moral tale for our times, in which the harassed septuagenarian finally chokes the young punk leader to death.

w Stephen Verona, Leigh Chapman *d* Stephen Verona *ph* Billy Williams *m* various

Ruth Gordon, Lee Strasberg, Janet Leigh, Joe Silver, Eddie Barth

'One would probably have to reach as far back as *The Birth of a Nation* to find a more direct incitement to racial hatred.'—*Richard Combs, MFB*

The Boat°
West Germany 1981 149m Fujicolor
Columbia / Bavaria Atelier / Radiant Film (Gunter Röhrbach)
original and US title: *Das Boot*

Adventures of a German U-boat during World War II.

Well-crafted but totally unsurprising saga of heroism and self-sacrifice; a decent view of war from the German side, designed to impress world markets. It did so only moderately.

wd Wolfgang Petersen *ph* Jost Vacano *m* Klaus Doldinger *pd* Rolf Zehetbauer

Jürgen Prochnow, Herbert Grönemeyer, Klaus Wennemann, Hubertus Bengsch, Martin Semmelrogge

AAN: direction; screenplay (adaptation); cinematography; editing; sound; sound editing.

● Video: RCA / Columbia

The Boatniks°
US 1970 100m Technicolor
Walt Disney (Ron Miller)

An accident-prone coastguard officer creates havoc at a yachting marina but is acclaimed a hero after catching three jewel thieves. Simple fresh-air farce for the family, pleasantly set but flatly directed.

w Arthur Julian *d* Norman Tokar *ph* William Snyder *m* Robert F. Brunner

Phil Silvers, Robert Morse, Stefanie Powers, Norman Fell, Mickey Shaughnessey, Wally Cox, Don Ameche, Joey Forman

● Video: Disney

Bob and Carol and Ted and Alice°°
US 1969 105m Technicolor
Columbia / M. J. Frankovich (Larry Tucker)

Two California couples, influenced by a group therapy session advocating natural spontaneous behaviour, decide to admit their extra-marital affairs and narrowly avoid a wife-swapping party.

Fashionable comedy without the courage of its convictions: it starts and finishes very bashfully, but there are bright scenes in the middle. An attempt to extend it into a TV series was a failure.

w Paul Mazursky, Larry Tucker *d* Paul Mazursky *ph* Charles E. Lang *m* Quincy Jones

Natalie Wood, Robert Culp, Elliott Gould, Dyan Cannon, Horst Ebersberg

'An old-fashioned romantic comedy disguised as a blue picture.'—*Arthur Schlesinger Jnr*

AAN: Paul Mazursky, Larry Tucker; Charles E. Lang; Elliott Gould; Dyan Cannon

● Video: RCA / Columbia

The Bob Mathias Story
US 1954 80m bw

The biography of an American athlete who won the Decathlon in the 1952 Olympics. Predictable low-budgeter of no abiding interest. Bob Mathias, Ward Bond, Melba Mathias, Ann Doran, Howard Petrie. Written by Richard Collins; directed by Francis D. Lyon; for Allied Artists. (GB title: *The Flaming Torch*.)

Bobbikins
GB 1959 90m bw Cinemascope
TCF (Oscar Brodney, Bob McNaught)

A downtrodden variety artist finds that his baby can not only talk but also give him tips on the stock exchange.
Not at all a good idea, and feebly executed.

w Oscar Brodney d Robert Day ph Geoffrey Faithfull m Philip Green

Max Bygraves, Shirley Jones, Billie Whitelaw, Barbara Shelley, Colin Gordon, Charles Tingwell, Lionel Jeffries, Rupert Davies

Bobby Deerfield
US 1977 123m Metrocolor Panavision
Warner / First Artists (Sydney Pollack)

A depressive motor racing driver falls for a girl with an incurable illness.
A kind of understated *Love Story* for intellectuals; nicely made, but nothing that anybody will be wildly concerned about.

w Alvin Sargent, *novel* Heaven Has No Favourites by Erich Maria Remarque d Sydney Pollack ph Henri Decaë m Dave Grusin pd Stephen Grimes

Al Pacino, Marthe Keller, Anny Duperey, Walter McGinn, Romolo Valli, Jaime Sanchez

The Bobo
US 1967 105m Technicolor
Warner / Gina (Elliott Kastner, Jerry Gershwin) (David R. Schwarz)

An unsuccessful and timid bullfighter is offered a contract if within three days he can seduce the local belle.
Stylized, silly and boring comedy from an obviously dated play; Chaplinesque pathos was not this star's strong suit.

w David R. Schwarz, from his play and the novel *Olimpia* by Burt Cole d Robert Parrish ph Gerry Turpin m Francis Lai

Peter Sellers, Britt Ekland, Rossano Brazzi, Adolfo Celi, Hattie Jacques, Ferdy Mayne, Kenneth Griffith, John Wells

Boccaccio '70*
Italy / France 1962 210m Eastmancolor
TCF / CCC / Cineriz / Francinex / Gray Films (Antonio Cervi, Carlo Ponti)

Four modern stories which Boccaccio might have written (on an off day).
Overlong portmanteau with inevitable bright moments but many more longueurs.

'The Temptation of Dr Antonio': w Federico Fellini, Tullio Pinelli, Ennio Flaiano d Federico Fellini ph Otello Martelli; with Anita Ekberg
'The Job': w Suso Cecchi d'Amico, Luchino Visconti d Luchino Visconti ph Giuseppe Rotunno; with Romy Schneider, Tomas Milian
'The Raffle': w Cesare Zavattini d Vittorio de Sica ph Otello Martelli; with Sophia Loren
'Renzo and Luciana': d Mario Monichelli

Body and Soul
US 1931 82m bw

In the 1914–1918 war, a flier falls for the wife of his dead buddy. Tedious and often risible romantic melodrama. Charles Farrell, Elissa Landi, Humphrey Bogart, Myrna Loy, Donald Dillaway. From the play Squadrons by E. W.

Springs and A. E. Thomas; directed by Alfred Santell; for Fox. 'Kidding is almost bound to creep in.'—*Variety*

Body and Soul*
US 1947 104m bw
Enterprise (Bob Roberts)

A young boxer fights his way unscrupulously to the top.
Melodramatic but absorbing study of prizefighting's seamy side. (Is there any other?) Inventively studio-bound and almost impressionist in treatment.

w Abraham Polonsky d Robert Rossen ph James Wong Howe md Rudolph Polk m Hugo Friedhofer

John Garfield, Lilli Palmer, Hazel Brooks, Anne Revere, William Conrad, Joseph Pevney, Canada Lee

'Here are the gin and tinsel, squalor and sables of the depression era, less daring than when first revealed in *Dead End* or *Golden Boy* but more valid and mature because shown without sentiment or blur.'—*National Board of Review*

AAN: Abraham Polonsky; John Garfield
● *Video: Intervision*

Body and Soul
US 1981 122m colour
Cannon–Golan–Globus (Cliff Roquemore)

An amateur boxer turns professional to earn money for medical treatment for his kid sister.
Blood in the ring, sentimentality on the sidelines. Despite the credit, this repellent movie has virtually no connection with the previous 'version'.

w Leon Isaac Kennedy, from a *screenplay* by Abraham Polonsky d George Bowers ph James Forrest m Webster Lewis

Leon Isaac Kennedy, Jayne Kennedy, Muhammed Ali, Michael Gazzo, Perry Lang, Kim Hamilton, Peter Lawford

Body Double
US 1984 114m Metrocolor
Columbia / Delphia (Brian de Palma)

An out-of-work actor gets into deep trouble when he follows a lady who stripteases every night at her bedroom window.
Glum, slow suspenser with outbursts of violence; chiefly interesting for those who can spot its borrowings from other, better movies.

w Robert J. Avrech, Brian de Palma d Brian de Palma ph Stephen H. Burum m Pino Donaggio pd Ida Random

Craig Wasson, Gregg Henry, Melanie Griffith, Deborah Shelton, Guy Boyd

'A voyeur's delight and a feminist's nightmare.'—*Variety*

The Body Disappears
US 1941 72m bw
Warner (Ben Stoloff)

A professor invents an invisibility formula. Uninspired comedy switch on a familiar theme.

w Scott Darling, Erna Lazarus d D. Ross Lederman ph Allen G. Seigler

Edward Everett Horton, Jeffrey Dell, Jane Wyman, Herbert Anderson, Marguerite Chapman, Craig Stevens, David Bruce, Willie Best

'She taught him everything he knew— about passion and murder!'
Body Heat*
US 1981 113m Technicolor
Warner / Ladd (Fred T. Gallo)

A Florida lawyer becomes involved with a married woman and they plot to kill her businessman husband.
Oversexed and superfluous, not to mention uncredited, revamp of *Double Indemnity*. Some evidence of flair does not relieve that 'I have been here before' feeling.

wd Lawrence Kasdan ph Richard H. Kline m John Barry pd Bill Kenney ed Carol Littleton

William Hurt, *Kathleen Turner*, Richard Crenna, Ted Danson

'Film noir, if it is to be successfully reworked, needs to be approached with a sense of analysis, rather than simple excess.'—*Steve Jenkins, MFB*

● *Video: Warner*

The Body Snatcher***
US 1945 77m bw
RKO (Val Lewton)

In 19th-century Edinburgh a doctor obtains 'specimens' from grave-robbers, and murder results when supplies run short.
A familiar theme very imaginatively handled, and well acted, though the beginning is slow. The best of the Lewton thrillers.

w Philip MacDonald, Carlos Keith (Val Lewton), story R. L. Stevenson d Robert Wise ph Robert de Grasse m Roy Webb

Henry Daniell, Boris Karloff, Bela Lugosi, Edith Atwater, Russell Wade

'A humane sincerity and a devotion to good cinema . . . However, most of the picture is more literary than lively.'—*Time*

Boeing-Boeing
US 1965 102m Technicolor
(Paramount) Hal B. Wallis

By successfully juggling with plane schedules, a Paris journalist manages to live with three air hostesses at the same time.
Frenetic, paper-thin sex comedy from a one-joke play; film style generally undistinguished.

w Edward Anhalt, *play* Marc Camoletti d John Rich ph Lucien Ballard m Neal Hefti

Tony Curtis, Jerry Lewis (his only 'straight' part), Dany Saval, Christiane Schmidtner, Suzanna Leigh, *Thelma Ritter*

'A sort of jet-age French farce.'—*Judith Crist*
'The big comedy of nineteen sexty-sex!'—*publicity*

The Bofors Gun**
GB 1968 105m Technicolor
Rank / Everglades (Robert A. Goldson, Otto Plaschkes)

In 1954 Germany a British army unit runs into trouble when a violent and unstable Irish

THE BODY SNATCHER. A good poster, but the leading character is really Henry Daniell, whose name you have to search for and whose face isn't shown at all.

private picks on a weakly National Service
corporal.
Keen, fascinating, but often crude and
eventually rather silly expansion of a TV play
chiefly notable for the excellent acting
opportunities provided by its unattractive but
recognizable characters.

w John McGrath d Jack Gold ph Alan
Hume m Carl Davis

Nicol Williamson, John Thaw, *David Warner*,
Ian Holm

La Bohème
US 1926 75m approx at 24 fps bw
       silent

Mimi starves to death in a Paris garret.
Overacted straight version of the opera, with
two passionate star performances. Lillian
Gish, John Gilbert, Renee Adoree, Edward
Everett Horton. Written by Harry Behn and
Ray Doyle, after *Murger*; directed by King
Vidor; for MGM.

The Bohemian Girl*
US 1936 74m bw
Hal Roach

Gypsies kidnap a nobleman's daughter and
bring her up as their own.
One of several operettas reworked for Laurel
and Hardy, this is an inoffensive
entertainment which devotes too little care to
their need for slowly built-up gag structure;
their sequences tend to fizzle out and the
singing is a bore.

w Alfred Bunn, *operetta* William Balfe
d James Horne, Charles Rogers ph Art
Lloyd, Francis Corby

Stan Laurel, Oliver Hardy, Mae Busch,
Antonio Moreno, Jacqueline Wells, Darla
Hood, Zeffie Tilbury, James Finlayson,
Thelma Todd (for one song, apparently
dubbed: presumably before her sudden death
she had been cast as the heroine)
† There was in 1922 a British silent version
with a splendid cast including Ivor Novello,
Gladys Cooper, C. Aubrey Smith, Ellen Terry
and Constance Collier.

The Bold and the Brave
US 1956 87m bw Superscope
RKO / Hal E. Chester

An assortment of American types come
together in the Italian campaign of 1944.
Routine war heroics chiefly remembered (if at
all) for a crap game sequence.

w Robert Lewin d Lewis Foster ph Sam
Leavitt m Herschel Burke Gilbert

Wendell Corey, *Mickey Rooney*, Nicole
Maurey, Don Taylor

AAN: Robert Lewin; Mickey Rooney

'He rose to fame on a ladder of dancing
   ladies!'

Bolero*
US 1934 85m bw
Paramount

A New York dancer neglects his personal life

to become king of the European night club
circuit.
Lively romantic drama which performed
remarkably at the box office and led to a kind
of sequel, *Rumba*.

w Carey Wilson, Kubec Glasmon, Ruth
Ridenour, Horace Jackson d *Wesley Ruggles*
ph Leo Tover

George Raft, Carole Lombard, Sally Rand
(doing her fan dance), Frances Drake, William
Frawley, Ray Milland, Gertrude Michael
'A studio conference product: lots of
surefire elements. On screen it's a little
enervating . . . depends on Raft's popularity
with the women.'—*Variety*

Bolero
US 1984 104m colour
Cannon / City (Bo Derek)

In 1926, a wealthy romantic girl travels the
world in search of a man worthy of the
sacrifice of her virginity.
Ludicrous sexual charade with unpleasant
overtones resulting from the fact that the star's
husband wrote and photographed this
embarrassing piece of near-pornography.

w,ph,d John Derek m Peter Bernstein
pd Alan Roderick-Jones

Bo Derek, George Kennedy, Andrea
Occhipinti, Greg Bensen, Ana Obregon
'The only ecstatic moment a filmgoer might
derive will be at the discovery that it's over.'—
Philip Strick, MFB

Bomba the Jungle Boy
US 1949 71m bw or sepia
Monogram (Walter Mirisch)

Photographers in Africa meet a junior Tarzan
who rescues their girl friend.
Cut-rate hokum starring the lad who had
played Johnny Weissmuller's 'son' in earlier
Tarzan movies; it led to several tedious
sequels.

w Jack de Witt, from the comic strip by Roy
Rockwell d Ford Beebe ph William Sickner
m Edward Kay

Johnny Sheffield, Peggy Ann Garner, Onslow
Stevens, Charles Irwin
† Sequels were as follows:
1948: BOMBA ON PANTHER ISLAND
         (76m) with Allene Roberts
1949: BOMBA AND THE LOST
         VOLCANO (76m) with Donald Woods;
         BOMBA AND THE HIDDEN CITY
         (71m) with Paul Guilfoyle
1950: BOMBA AND THE ELEPHANT
         STAMPEDE (71m) with Myron Sealey
1951: BOMBA AND THE AFRICAN
         TREASURE (70m) with Lyle Talbot;
         BOMBA AND THE JUNGLE GIRL
         (70m) with Karen Sharpe; BOMBA
         AND THE LION HUNTERS (75m)
         with Morris Ankrum
1953: SAFARI DRUMS (71m) with Douglas
         Kennedy
1954: THE GOLDEN IDOL (71m) with Paul
         Guilfoyle; KILLER LEOPARD (70m)
         with Beverly Garland

1955: LORD OF THE JUNGLE (69m) with
         Wayne Morris

Bombardier
US 1943 99m bw
RKO (Robert Fellows)

Cadet bombardiers learn the realities of war
on raids over Japan.
Totally routine recruiting poster heroics.

w John Twist d Richard Wallace ph Nicholas
Musuraca m Roy Webb

Pat O'Brien, Randolph Scott, Anne Shirley,
Eddie Albert, Walter Reed, Robert Ryan,
Barton Maclane

Bombay Clipper
US 1941 54m bw

On a clipper bound for Bombay, a reporter
becomes involved in mystery and romance.
Capsule actioner with stock studio talent.
William Gargan, Irene Hervey, Maria
Montez, Charles Lang, Turhan Bey, Lloyd
Corrigan, Mary Gordon. Written by Roy
Chanslor and Stanley Rubin; directed by John
Rawlins; for Universal.

Bombay Mail
US 1933 66m bw

On a train between Calcutta and Bombay a
Scotland Yard detective solves the murder of
the Governor of Bengal. Very tolerable
mystery filler. Edmund Lowe, Shirley Grey,
Onslow Stevens, Ralph Forbes, Hedda
Hopper. Written by Tom Reed and L. G.
Blochman; directed by Edwin L. Marin; for
Universal. 'It mixes a colourful set of
characters and maintains a moderately
absorbing pace.'—*Variety*

Bombay Talkie*
India 1970 105m Eastmancolor
Merchant-Ivory (Ismail Merchant)

A sophisticated American woman comes to
Bombay and falls for two men involved in
film-making.
Interesting but unsatisfactory romantic drama,
rather pointlessly set against film studio
backgrounds.

w Ruth Prawer Jhabvala, James Ivory
d James Ivory ph Subrata Mitra m Shankar
Jaikishan

Jennifer Kendal, Shashi Kapoor, Zia
Mohyeddin

● *Video: Home Video*

Bombers B-52
US 1957 106m Warnercolor
       Cinemascope
Warner (Richard Whorf)
GB title: *No Sleep till Dawn*

A USAF sergeant considers applying for a
discharge so that he can earn more money in
civilian life.
Glossy domestic melodrama punctuated by
aircraft shots.

w Irving Wallace d Gordon Douglas
ph William Clothier m Leonard Rosenman

Karl Malden, Marsha Hunt, Natalie Wood, Efrem Zimbalist Jnr, Don Kelly

'No one questions the basic assumption—that the good life consists of servicing bigger and better bombers.'—*MFB*

Bomber's Moon
US 1943 70m bw

An American pilot crashlands into Germany and makes for the coast. Modestly budgeted war adventure with conventional thrills.

George Montgomery, Annabella, Kent Taylor, Walter Kingsford, Martin Kosleck. Written by Kenneth Gamet; directed by 'Charles Fuhr' (Edward Ludwig and Harold Schuster); for TCF.

Bombshell***
US 1933 91m bw
MGM (Hunt Stromberg)
GB and aka title: *Blonde Bombshell*

A glamorous film star yearns for a new image. Crackpot farce which even by today's standards moves at a fair clip and enabled the star to give her best comedy performance.

w Jules Furthman, John Lee Mahin, play Caroline Francke, Mack Crane d Victor Fleming ph Chester Lyons, Hal Rosson

Jean Harlow, Lee Tracy, Frank Morgan, Franchot Tone, Pat O'Brien, Ivan Lebedeff, Una Merkel, Ted Healy, Isabel Jewell, C. Aubrey Smith, Louise Beavers, Leonard Carey, Mary Forbes

'Bound to click and the best legitimate comedy in a long time.'—*Variety*

Bon Voyage*
US 1962 133m Technicolor
Walt Disney (Bill Walsh, Ron Miller)

An American family spends a holiday in Paris. Simple-minded, overlong comedy of mishaps, with daddy finally trapped in the sewer. Smoothly done of its kind.

w Bill Walsh, novel Marrijane and Joseph Hayes d James Neilson ph William Snyder m Paul Smith

Fred MacMurray, Jane Wyman, Michael Callan, Deborah Walley, Jessie Royce Landis, Tommy Kirk, Ivan Desny

Bond Street
GB 1948 107m bw
ABP / World Screenplays (Anatole de Grunwald)

Four stories, each concerning an item of an expensive wedding trousseau.
Mild and laboured short story compendium.

w Anatole de Grunwald d Gordon Parry ph Otto Heller m Benjamin Frankel

Roland Young, Jean Kent, Paula Valenska, Kathleen Harrison, Derek Farr, *Kenneth Griffith*, Hazel Court, Ronald Howard

'Even a glimpse of actual Bond Street makes little contact with reality.'—*MFB*

Le Bonheur*
France 1965 79m Eastmancolor
Parc / Mag Bodard

A young carpenter is happy with his wife and family, happier still when he finds a mistress, whom he marries when his wife is found drowned.
Slight, good looking, ambivalent little fable which finally expires in a surfeit of style.

wd Agnès Varda ph Jean Rabier, Claude Beausoleil m Mozart

Jean-Claude Drouot, Claire Drouot, Marie-France Boyer

Bonjour Tristesse*
GB 1957 93m Technicolor Cinemascope
(Columbia) Wheel Films (Otto Preminger)

A teenage girl becomes involved with her sophisticated father's amours and causes the death of his would-be mistress.
The novel's rather repellent characters are here played like royal personages against a background of Riviera opulence. The result is very odd but often entertaining, especially when it slips into self-parody.

w Arthur Laurents, novel Françoise Sagan d Otto Preminger ph Georges Périnal m Georges Auric pd Roger Furse

David Niven, Deborah Kerr, Jean Seberg, Mylene Demongeot, Geoffrey Horne, Juliette Greco, Martita Hunt, Walter Chiari, Jean Kent, Roland Culver

'An elegant, ice-cold charade of emotions.'—*Judith Crist*

'Sagan not so much translated as traduced—opened out, smartened up, the sickness overlaid with Riviera suntan.'—*Alexander Walker*

'Long, untidy, muddled and mushy.'—*Financial Times*
† Shot in monochrome for Paris, colour for the Riviera.

Bonne Chance
France 1935 75m bw

An artist who wins a lottery takes on holiday with him, on a purely platonic basis, the girl who gave him half her ticket. Modest star comedy which pleased at the time. Sacha Guitry, Jacqueline Delubac, Robert Darthez. Written and directed by Sacha Guitry for his own company.

La Bonne Soupe
France / Italy 1963 97m bw
Belstar / Du Siècle / Dear Film (André Hakim)

A high-class prostitute tells her life story. A saucy frolic complete with three-in-a-bed and rapidly closing doors; quite enjoyable of its kind.

wd Robert Thomas, play Félicien Marceau ph Roger Hubert m Raymond le Sénéchal

Annie Girardot, Marie Bell, Gérard Blain, Bernard Blier, Jean-Claude Brialy, Claude Dauphin, Sacha Distel, Daniel Gélin, Blanchette Brunoy, Jane Marken, Raymond Péllégrin, Franchot Tone

'They're young . . . they're in love . . . and they kill people!'

Bonnie and Clyde****
US 1967 111m Technicolor
Warner / Seven Arts / Tatira / Hiller (*Warren Beatty*)

In the early thirties, a car thief and the daughter of his intended victim team up to become America's most feared and ruthless bank robbers.
Technically brilliant evocation of sleepy mid-America at the time of the public enemies, using every kind of cinematic trick including fake snapshots, farcical interludes, dreamy soft-focus and a jazzy score. For all kinds of reasons a very influential film which even made extreme violence quite fashionable (and very bloody it is).

w David Newman, Robert Benton d Arthur Penn ph Burnett Guffey m Charles Strouse, using 'Foggy Mountain Breakdown' by Flatt and Scruggs

Warren Beatty, Faye Dunaway, Gene Hackman, Estelle Parsons, *Michael J. Pollard*, Dub Taylor, Denver Pyle, Gene Wilder

'It is a long time since we have seen an American film so perfectly judged.'—*MFB*

'. . . all to the rickety twang of a banjo and a saturation in time and place.'—*Judith Crist*

'The formula is hayseed comedy bursting sporadically into pyrotechnical bloodshed and laced with sentimental pop-Freudianism.'—*John Simon*

'A film from which we shall date reputations and innovations in the American cinema.'—*Alexander Walker*

AA: Burnett Guffey; Estelle Parsons
AAN: best picture; David Newman, Robert Benton; Arthur Penn; Warren Beatty; Faye Dunaway; Gene Hackman; Michael J. Pollard

The Bonnie Parker Story
US 1958 80m bw

A waitress joins up with a cheap crook in a series of bank raids. Tinpot 'B' gangster film chiefly notable for comparison with the later *Bonnie and Clyde*. All it really has is a certain exuberance in the action sequences. Dorothy Provine, Jack Hogan, Richard Bakalyan, Joseph Turkel. Written and produced by Stan Shpetner; directed by William Witney; for James H. Nicholson and Sam Arkoff.

Bonnie Prince Charlie
GB 1948 140m approx (later cut to 118m) Technicolor
British Lion / London Films (Edward Black)

The hope of the Stuarts returns from exile but is eventually forced to flee again.
Good highland photography combines with appalling studio sets, an initially confused narrative, a draggy script and uneasy performances to produce an ill-fated attempt at a British historical epic. Alexander Korda, who masterminded it, sulked in public at the critical roasting, but on this occasion the critics were right.

w Clemence Dane *d* Anthony Kimmins
ph Robert Krasker *m* Ian Whyte

David Niven, Margaret Leighton, Jack
Hawkins, Judy Campbell, Morland Graham,
Finlay Currie, John Laurie

'I have a sense of wonder about this film,
beside which *The Swordsman* seems like a
dazzling work of veracity and art. It is that
London Films, having surveyed the finished
thing, should not have quietly scrapped it.'—
Richard Winnington

'The picture is not lacking in moments of
unconscious levity, what with David Niven
rallying his hardy Highlanders to his standard
in a voice hardly large enough to summon a
waiter.'—*New Yorker*

'Time has made it the film industry's biggest
joke. But the joke turns a little sour when one
reflects how extravagance, recklessness and
sheer bungling administration during the fat
and prosperous years left the British film
industry so poor and vulnerable when the hard
times came along.'—*Gerald Garrett, 1975*

Bonnie Scotland**
US 1935 80m bw
MGM / Hal Roach

Two Americans journey to Scotland to collect
a non-existent inheritance, then follow their
friend in the army and wind up in India.
Generally disappointing star comedy which
still contains excellent sequences when it is not
vainly trying to preserve interest in a boring
plot. An obvious parody on *Lives of a Bengal
Lancer*, released earlier that year; Scotland
has almost nothing to do with it.

w Frank Butler, Jeff Moffitt *d* James Horne
ph Art Lloyd, Walter Lundin

Stan Laurel, Oliver Hardy, James Finlayson,
Daphne Pollard, William Janney, June Lang

The Boogie Man Will Get You
US 1944 66m bw
Columbia

Bodies accumulate when mad doctors get to
work creating supermen in a small village.
Desperately unfunny spoof notable only for
the fact that it was attempted with these
players and at that time.

w Edwin Blum *d* Lew Landers *ph* Colbert
Clark *md* Morris Stoloff

Boris Karloff, Peter Lorre, Maxie
Rosenbloom, Jeff Donnell, Larry Parks,
Maude Eburne, Don Beddoe

Boom!
GB 1968 113m Technicolor
Panavision
Universal / World Film Services / Moon
Lake Productions (John Heyman,
Norman Priggen)

On the volcanic Mediterranean island which
she owns, a dying millionairess plans to take as
her last lover a wandering poet who is the
angel of death.

Pretentious, boring nonsense, showing that
when talent goes awry it certainly goes boom.

w Tennessee Williams, from his play *The Milk
Train Doesn't Stop Here Any More d* Joseph
Losey *ph* Douglas Slocombe *m* John Barry

Elizabeth Taylor, Richard Burton, *Noel
Coward*, Michael Dunn, Joanna Shimkus

'It's a beautiful picture, the best ever made
of one of my plays.'—*Tennessee Williams*

'A pointless, pompous nightmare.'—*Paul
D. Zimmermann, Newsweek*

'An ordeal in tedium,'—*Hollywood
Reporter*

'Outright junk.'—*Saturday Review*

'The title could not be more apt: it is
precisely the sound of a bomb exploding.'—
Richard Schickel, Life

'*Boom!* isn't doing little business; it's doing
no business at all.'—*Universal executive*

Boom Town**
US 1940 120m bw
MGM (Sam Zimbalist)

Two friendly oil drillers strike it rich.
Enjoyable four-star, big-studio product of its
time: world-wide entertainment of assured
success, with a proven mix of romance, action,
drama and comedy.

w John Lee Mahin, *story* James Edward
Grant *d* Jack Conway *ph* Harold Rosson
m Franz Waxman *ad* Cedric Gibbons

Clark Gable, Spencer Tracy, Claudette
Colbert, *Hedy Lamarr, Frank Morgan,* Lionel
Atwill, Chill Wills

'Western high jinks, a wee child, and
courtroom speeches about individual
enterprise constitute the various come-ons in a
scrambled and inept picture.'—*New York
Herald Tribune*

'More colourful action in the oil fields and
less agitation indoors might have made it a
great picture.'—*Bosley Crowther*

AAN: Harold Rosson

Boomerang***
US 1947 88m bw
TCF (Louis de Rochemont)

In a New England town, a clergyman is shot
dead on the street. The DA prevents an
innocent man from being convicted, but
cannot track down the guilty party.
Incisive real life thriller: based on a true case,
it was shot in an innovative documentary style
which was much copied, and justice is not seen
to be done, though the murderer is known to
the audience. A milestone movie of its kind.

w Richard Murphy *d* Elia Kazan *ph* Norbert
Brodine *m* David Buttolph

Dana Andrews, Jane Wyatt, Lee J. Cobb,
Cara Williams, Arthur Kennedy, Sam Levene,
Taylor Holmes, Robert Keith, Ed Begley

'A study of integrity, beautifully developed
by Dana Andrews against a background of
political corruption and chicanery that is
doubly shocking because of its documentary
understatement.'—*Richard Winnington*

'For the first time in many a moon we are
treated to a picture that gives a good example
of a typical small American city—the people,
their way of living, their mode of government,
the petty politics practised, the power of the
press.'—*Frank Ward, National Board of
Review*

AAN: Richard Murphy

Boots Malone
US 1952 103m bw
Columbia (Milton Holmes)

A would-be jockey tags along with a down-at-
heel agent who gets him work and finally
persuades him not to throw a crooked race.
Dullish racetrack melodrama bogged down by
repetitive and unsympathetic plot twists.

w Milton Holmes *d* William Dieterle
ph Charles Lawton *m* Elmer Bernstein

William Holden, Johnny Stewart, Stanley
Clements, Basil Ruysdael, Carl Benton Reid,
Ed Begley, Henry Morgan

The Border
US 1981 108m Technicolor
Panavision
Universal / RKO (Neil Hartley)

A Los Angeles cop joins the border patrol in
El Paso and becomes involved in the squalor,
violence and double-dealing.
A rather solemn elaboration on a well-worn
theme, with nothing very memorable except
its excesses.

w Deric Washburn, Walon Green, David
Freeman *d* Tony Richardson *ph* Ric Waite
m Ry Cooder *pd* Toby Rafelson *ed* Robert
K. Lambert

Jack Nicholson, Harvey Keitel, Valerie
Perrine, Warren Oates, Elpidia Carrillo

● Video: CIC

Border Incident
US 1949 93m bw
MGM (Nicholas Nayfack)

Police stop the illegal immigration of labourers
from Mexico.
Routine semi-documentary cops and robbers,
well enough made.

w John C. Higgins *d* Anthony Mann *ph* John
Alton *m* André Previn

Ricardo Montalban, George Murphy, Howard
da Silva, James Mitchell, Alfonso Bedoya

Border River
US 1953 80m Technicolor

At the end of the Civil War, an ex-
Confederate officer gets involved with a gold
war in the Mexican free zone. Slightly unusual
western programmer. Joel McCrea, Yvonne
de Carlo, Pedro Armendariz, Ivan Triesault,
Alfonso Bedoya, Howard Petrie. Written by
William Sackheim and Louis Stevens; directed
by George Sherman; for Universal–
International.

Borderline
US 1980 97m colour
ITC (Martin Starger)

A Mexican border patrolman chases illegal
immigrants and the big time crooks making
money out of them.
Routine, quite effective action programmer.

w Steve Kline, Jerrold Freedman *d* Jerrold
Freedman *ph* Tak Fujimoto *m* Gil Melle

Charles Bronson, Bruno Kirby, Karmin
Murcelo, Michael Learner, Ed Harris

Bordertown*
US 1934 80m bw
Warner (Robert Lord)

In a North Mexican town, a shabby lawyer becomes infatuated with the neurotic wife of a businessman.
Satisfying melodrama whose plot climax was later borrowed for *They Drive by Night*.
w Laird Doyle, Wallace Smith, *novel* Carroll Graham *d* Archie Mayo *ph* Tony Gaudio *md* Leo Forbstein
Paul Muni, Bette Davis, Margaret Lindsay, Eugene Pallette, Robert Barrat, Henry O'Neill, Hobart Cavanaugh
'A strictly box office film, well written and paced.'—*Variety*
† *Blowing Wild* (qv) was also a partial uncredited remake.

Born Again
US 1978 110m Technicolor
Robert L. Munger / Frank Capra Jnr

Charles Colson, sent to prison after Watergate, becomes a devout Christian.
Part evangelism, part reconstruction through rose-tinted spectacles; not particularly entertaining or instructive as either.
w Walter Block *d* Irving Rapper *ph* Harry Stradling Jnr *m* Les Baxter
Dean Jones, Anne Francis, Jay Robinson, Dana Andrews, Raymond St Jacques, George Brent, Harry Spillman (as Nixon)

Born Free**
GB 1965 95m Technicolor Panavision
Columbia / Open Road (Carl Foreman) /
  High Road / Atlas (Sam Jaffe, Paul Radin)

A Kenyan game warden and his wife rear three lion cubs, one of which eventually presents them with a family.
Irresistible animal shots salvage this rather flabbily put together version of a bestselling book. An enormous commercial success, it was followed by the even thinner *Living Free*, by a TV series, and by several semi-professional documentaries.
w Gerald L. C. Copley, *book* Joy Adamson *d* James Hill *ph* Kenneth Talbot *m* John Barry
Virginia McKenna, Bill Travers, Geoffrey Keen
AA: John Barry; title song (*m* John Barry, *ly* Don Black)

Born Losers
US 1967 112m colour
AIP (Delores Taylor)

California teeny-boppers claim to have been gang-raped by wandering motorcyclists.
Teenage shocker, only notable for its credits, and for being the first Billy Jack film.
wd Tom Laughlin *ph* Gregory Sandor
Tom Laughlin, Jane Russell, Elizabeth James, Jeremy Slate, William Wellman Jnr
'It's so pokey and crudely obvious that it seems almost guileless—helplessly inept.'—*Pauline Kael*

Born Reckless
US 1930 73m bw

Doings of an Italian gangster bootlegger. A generally poorly regarded early work of its director. Edmund Lowe, Catherine Dale Owen, Lee Tracy, Marguerite Churchill, Warren Hymer, Frank Albertson. Written from the novel Louis Beretti by Donald Henderson Clarke; directed by John Ford; for Fox. 'A singularly full and sprawling scenario . . . Fox originally intended the yarn for Paul Muni. It's possible the script got kicked around the lot and came out as beef stew.'—*Variety*

Born Reckless
US 1937 60m bw

Big-town taxi drivers start a war among themselves. Second-feature actioner, well enough done. Brian Donlevy, Richelle Hudson, Barton MacLane, Robert Kent, Harry Carey, Pauline Moore, Chick Chandler. Written by John Patrick, Helen Logan, Robert Ellis; directed by Malcolm St Clair; for TCF. 'Houses in the knuckle districts will give it its best play.'—*Variety*

Born to be Bad
US 1934 61m bw
Twentieth Century (William Goetz, Raymond Griffith)

A girl schemes to seduce the man who has adopted her illegitimate son.
Batty mother-love melodrama.
w Ralph Graves *d* Lowell Sherman *ph* Barney McGill *m* Alfred Newman
Loretta Young, Cary Grant, Jackie Kelk, Henry Travers, Russell Hopton, Andrew Tombes, Harry Green

Born to be Bad
US 1950 70m bw
RKO (Robert Sparks)

An ambitious girl marries a millionaire but continues her affair with a novelist; finally both men discover her true character.
Tentative bad girl novelette, just about passable.
w Edith Sommer, *novel* All Kneeling by Anne Parrish *d* Nicholas Ray *ph* Nicholas Musuraca *m* Frederick Hollander
Joan Fontaine, Robert Ryan, Zachary Scott, Joan Leslie, Mel Ferrer
'Trash story too much for cast and director to live down.'—*Variety*

Born to Dance*
US 1936 108m bw
MGM (Jack Cummings)

A sailor meets a girl in New York.
Well remembered musical with good numbers but a rather lame look.
w Jack McGowan, Sid Silvers, B. G. De Sylva *d* Roy del Ruth *ph* Ray June *songs* Cole Porter
Eleanor Powell, James Stewart, Virginia Bruce, Una Merkel, Sid Silvers, Frances Langford, Raymond Walburn, *Reginald Gardiner*, Buddy Ebsen

Songs include 'I've Got You under My Skin'; 'Easy to Love'; 'I'm Nuts about You'; 'Rap Tap on Wood'; 'Swinging the Jinx Away'; 'Rolling Home'; 'Hey Babe Hey'; 'Love Me Love My Pekinese'
'Corking entertainment. . . . Cast is youthful, sight stuff is lavish, the specialties are meritorious, and as for songs, the picture is positively filthy with them.'—*Variety*
'The plot is a half-hearted reprise of *42nd Street* . . . this time Eleanor Powell is the understudy who replaces the star . . . and by the time she finishes the finale, you're overpowered and feel you should cheer.'—*Pauline Kael, 70s*
AAN: song 'I've Got You Under My Skin'

Born to Kill*
US 1947 92m bw
RKO
GB title: *Lady of Deceit*

A psychotic involves his new wife in his criminal pursuits.
Unusual, heavy-going, well acted melodrama.
w Eve Greene, Richard Macauley *d* Robert Wise *ph* Robert de Grasse *m* Paul Sawtell
Lawrence Tierney, Claire Trevor, Walter Slezak, Philip Terry, Elisha Cook Jnr

Born to Love
US 1931 84m bw
RKO

During World War I a nurse bears the child of an army pilot who is reported missing; but he turns up after she has married an English milord.
A useful compendium of thirties romantic clichés, quite attractively packaged.
w Ernest Pascal *d* Paul Stein *ph* John Mescall
Constance Bennett, Joel McCrea, Paul Cavanagh, Frederick Kerr, Anthony Bushell, Louise Closser Hale, Edmond Breon, Mary Forbes

Born to Sing
US 1941 82m bw

Kids put together a patriotic show. Curiously undernourished family musical in the wake of *Babes in Arms*: lots of talent but no star. Virginia Weidler, Douglas McPhail, Leo Gorcey, Ray McDonald, Rags Ragland, Sheldon Leonard, Margaret Dumont, Larry Nunn, Henry O'Neill. Written by Franz Spencer and Harry Clark; directed by Edward Ludwig; for Frederick Stephani / MGM.

Born to Win
US 1971 89m colour

A Times Square junkie with delusions of grandeur runs out of luck. Dim low-life drama unworthy of its talent. George Segal, Paula Prentiss, Karen Black, Hector Elizondo. Written by David Scott Milton; directed by Ivan Passer; for UA.

'A perfectly swell motion picture!'
Born Yesterday**
US 1950 103m bw
Columbia (S. Sylvan Simon)

The ignorant ex-chorus girl mistress of a scrap iron tycoon takes English lessons, falls for her tutor, and politically outmanoeuvres her bewildered lover.

Pleasant film version of a cast-iron box office play, subtle and intelligent in all departments yet with a regrettable tendency to wave the flag.

w Albert Mannheimer, *play Garson Kanin*
d George Cukor *ph* Joseph Walker
m Frederick Hollander

Judy Holliday, Broderick Crawford, William Holden, Howard St John
† The original choices for the Judy Holliday role were Rita Hayworth and Jean Parker (who had played it on tour).

AA: Judy Holliday
AAN: best picture; Albert Mannheimer; George Cukor

Borsalino*

France / Italy 1970   126m   Eastmancolor
Adel-Marianne-Mars (Alain Delon)

In the thirties two Marseilles gangsters become firm friends and join forces.

Semi-spoof, but with 'real' blood, and period atmosphere laid on thick. The stars just about keep it ticking over.

w Jean-Claude Carrière, Claude Sautet, Jacques Deray, Jean Cau *d* Jacques Deray
ph Jean-Jacques Tarbès *m* Claude Bolling

Jean-Paul Belmondo, Alain Delon, Michel Bouquet, Catherine Rouvel, Corinne Marchand
   'Rather like a Hollywood musical where someone has forgotten to insert the production numbers.'—*MFB*

The Boss*

US 1956   89m   bw
UA / Frank N. Seltzer

After World War I, a ne'er-do-well becomes a corrupt small town political boss.

Low budgeted, complexly plotted, occasionally quite powerful and efficient crime melodrama.

w Ben L. Parry *d* Byron Haskin *ph* Hal Mohr

John Payne, William Bishop, Gloria McGhee, Doe Avedon, Joe Flynn

Boston Blackie

An American second feature series made by Columbia between 1941 and 1949. There had been silent films about the character, a reformed crook and con man who has to solve crimes because he is suspected by the law. Cheap but sometimes vigorous productions, they had a loyal following, and starred Chester Morris with George E. Stone as his assistant the Runt.

The titles were:

1941: MEET BOSTON BLACKIE,
CONFESSIONS OF BOSTON BLACKIE
1942: ALIAS BOSTON BLACKIE,
BOSTON BLACKIE GOES TO
HOLLYWOOD

1943: AFTER MIDNIGHT WITH BOSTON
BLACKIE
1944: ONE MYSTERIOUS NIGHT
1945: BOSTON BLACKIE BOOKED ON
SUSPICION, BOSTON BLACKIE'S
RENDEZVOUS
1946: A CLOSE CALL FOR BOSTON
BLACKIE, THE PHANTOM THIEF
1947: BOSTON BLACKIE AND THE LAW
1948: TRAPPED BY BOSTON BLACKIE
1949: BOSTON BLACKIE'S CHINESE
VENTURE
† A television series starring Kent Taylor followed in 1951.

The Boston Strangler**

US 1968   118m   De Luxe   Panavision
TCF (Robert Fryer)

A semi-factual account of the sex maniac who terrified Boston in the mid-sixties.

Ambitious *policier* rendered less effective by pretentious writing and flashy treatment, including multi-image sequences; the investigation is more interesting than the psychoanalysis.

w Edward Anhalt, *book* Gerold Frank
d Richard Fleischer *ph* Richard Kline
m Lionel Newman

Henry Fonda, *Tony Curtis* (as the murderer), George Kennedy, Mike Kellin, Hurd Hatfield, Murray Hamilton, Sally Kellerman, Jeff Corey, George Voskovec
● *Video: CBS / Fox*

The Bostonians

GB 1984   122m   colour
Merchant Ivory / WGBH / Rediffusion / Almi (Ismail Merchant)

In 1876 Boston, the cause of female emancipation wrecks Verena Tarrant's relationship with the determined Basil Ransome.

Another sluggish literary adaptation from the heavily meaningful Merchant Ivory team: the material, one feels would have worked better as a TV bestseller.

w Ruth Prawer Jhabvala, *novel* Henry James
d James Ivory *ph* Walter Lassally *m* Richard Robbins *pd* Leo Austin

Christopher Reeve, Vanessa Redgrave, Madeleine Potter, Jessica Tandy, Nancy Marchand, Linda Hunt, Wesley Addy.
   'Although it's not so limp as some of their other collaborations, they don't dramatize the material, and Ivory doesn't shape the performances.'—*Pauline Kael, New Yorker*

Botany Bay

US 1952   94m   Technicolor
Paramount (Joseph Sistrom)

On a convict ship in 1787 an American student unjustly accused of robbery clashes with the brutal captain for the favours of the only woman aboard.

Cramped and brutal action melodrama, a let-down considering the talent involved.

w Jonathan Latimer, *novel* Charles Nordhof and James Hall *d* John Farrow *ph* John Seitz *m* Franz Waxman

James Mason, Alan Ladd, Patricia Medina, Cedric Hardwicke, Murray Matheson, Jonathan Harris

The Bottom of the Bottle

US 1956   86m   Eastmancolor
Cinemascope
TCF (Buddy Adler)
GB title: *Beyond the River*

A wealthy attorney is visited by his drunken brother, on the run from the police and needing help to escape into Mexico.

Dreary drama in muddy colour, a clearly misguided enterprise.

w Sydney Boehm, *novel* Georges Simenon
d Henry Hathaway *ph* Lee Garmes *m* Leigh Harline

Joseph Cotten, Van Johnson, Ruth Roman, Jack Carson

'For those who like to laugh and sing when
   tears get in their eyes!'
Bottoms Up

US 1934   85m   bw
Fox (B. G. De Sylva)

A slick promoter in Hollywood disguises his pals as British nobility and gets them lucrative jobs.

Mild musical with a rather interesting cast.

w B. G. De Sylva, David Butler, Sid Silvers
d David Butler *ph* Arthur Miller
md Constantin Bakaleinikoff

Spencer Tracy, Pat Patterson, John Boles, Harry Green, Herbert Mundin, Sid Silvers, Thelma Todd, Robert Emmett O'Connor
   'In the best 1934 filmusical manner and contributes handily toward the perpetuation of the cycle.'—*Variety*

Bottoms Up

GB 1960   89m   bw

A seedy schoolmaster passes off his bookie's son as an eastern prince. Rambling film version of a successful TV series, *Whacko!* Jimmy Edwards, Arthur Howard. Written by Frank Muir and Denis Norden; directed by Mario Zampi; for Transocean / Warner.

Le Boucher**

France / Italy 1969   94m   Eastmancolor
La Boétie / Euro International (André Génovès)
aka: *The Butcher*

Murders in a small French town are traced to the inoffensive-seeming young butcher who is courting the local schoolmistress.

Curious, mainly charming film which can't make up its mind whether to be an eccentric character study or a Hitchcock thriller, but has its moments as each.

wd Claude Chabrol *ph* Jean Rabier *m* Pierre Jansen

Stéphane Audran, Jean Yanne, Antonio Passalia, Mario Beccaria
   'A thriller, but a superlative example of the genre.'—*Times*
● *Video: VCL*

Boudu Sauvé des Eaux***
France 1932 87m bw
Michel Simon / Jean Gehret
aka: *Boudu Saved from Drowning*
A scruffy tramp is not grateful for being
rescued from suicide, and plagues the family
who invite him to stay.
A minor classic of black comedy, interesting
equally for its characterizations, its acting, and
its film technique.
wd Jean Renoir, *play* René Fauchois
ph Marcel Lucien *m* from Raphael and
Johann Strauss
Michel Simon, Charles Grandval, Marcelle
Hainia, Séverine Lerczinska, Jean Dasté,
Jacques Becker
  'A beautifully rhythmed film that makes one
nostalgic for the period when it was made.'—
New Yorker, 1977

Bought
US 1931 70m bw
Warner
An ambitious working girl rebels against her
slum existence and seeks a rich man.
Typical star vehicle of its time, with a
predictable and unlikely change of heart for a
finale.
w Charles Kenyon, Raymond Griffith, *novel*
Jackdaw's Strut by Harriet Henry *d* Archie
Mayo *ph* Ray June
Constance Bennett, Ben Lyon, Richard
Bennett, Dorothy Peterson, Ray Milland,
Doris Lloyd, Maude Eburne
  'It's an entertainment in itself to be seated
among women auditors during a Constance
Bennett picture. They love that girl and she
mustn't be worsted by men.'—*Variety*

Boulder Dam
US 1936 70m bw
A mechanic accidentally kills a man and seeks
anonymity among the crews building Boulder
Dam. Routine melo with an unusual setting.
Ross Alexander, Patricia Ellis, Lyle Talbot,
Eddie Acuff, Henry O'Neill. Written by Sy
Bartlett and Ralph Block; directed by Frank
McDonald; for Sam Bischoff / Warner.

Bound for Glory*
US 1976 148m De Luxe Panavision
UA / Robert F. Blumhofe, Harold Leventhal
In 1936 Woody Guthrie leaves the Texas dust
bowl for California, and after various
hardships his musical talent is recognized.
Care and occasional beauty in the
photography do not obscure memories of *The
Grapes of Wrath*, which told much the same
story more dramatically and succinctly, and
with less earnestness and self-pity.
w Robert Getchell, from Guthrie's
autobiography *d* Hal Ashby *ph* Haskell
Wexler *m* Leonard Rosenman *songs* Woody
Guthrie *pd* Michael Haller
David Carradine, Ronny Cox, Melinda Dillon,
Gail Strickland, John Lehne
  'The movie spends two-and-a-half hours and
seven million dollars gazing wistfully at a little
man and a big country, and it ends up prettily
embalming them both.'—*Janet Massin,
Newsweek*
AA: Haskell Wexler; Leonard Rosenman
AAN: best picture; Robert Getchell

The Bounty*
GB 1984 133m Technicolor
Dino de Laurentiis (Bernard Williams)
William Bligh is summoned before a court
martial to explain the events leading up to the
famous mutiny.
Rather independent version of the twice-told
movie tale, and the least compelling of all.
Despite the emphasis on character, only
occasionally interesting.
w Robert Bolt *d* Roger Donaldson
ph Arthur Ibbetson *m* Vangelis *pd* John
Graysmark
Anthony Hopkins (Bligh), Mel Gibson
(Fletcher Christian), Laurence Olivier
(Admiral Hood), Edward Fox (Captain
Greetham), Daniel Day-Lewis (John Fryer),
Bernard Hill (Cole)
  'A long voyage to nowhere.'—*Nick
Roddick, MFB*
  'This misshapen movie doesn't work as an
epic—it doesn't have the scope or the
emotional surge.'—*Pauline Kael, New Yorker*

The Bounty Hunter
US 1954 79m WarnerColor
Three respectable citizens are unmasked as
masterminds behind a series of train robberies.
Predictable but enjoyable star action fare.
Randolph Scott, Dolores Dorn, Marie
Windsor, Ernest Borgnine. Written by
Winston Miller; directed by André de Toth;
for Warners.

The Bowery***
US 1933 92m bw
Twentieth Century (Darryl F. Zanuck)
  (Raymond Griffith, William Goetz)
In nineties New York, two boisterous rivals
settle their differences after one has jumped
off the Brooklyn Bridge for a bet.
Roistering saga of cross and double cross on
the seamy side, splendidly vigorous in acting
and treatment.
w Howard Estabrook, James Gleason *d* Raoul
Walsh *ph* Barney McGill *m* Alfred Newman
ad Richard Day
Wallace Beery, George Raft, Pert Kelton,
Jackie Cooper, Fay Wray, Herman Bing
  'It delivers as entertainment. It should draw
by itself, while the cast will be a considerable
help.'—*Variety*
  'A model of skilful reconstruction and
ingenious research.'—*Times*
  'Fairly reeking with authentic, rowdy,
hurdy-gurdy atmosphere . . . a grand evening
of fun for everybody.'—*Photoplay*
† *The Bowery* was the first production of
Twentieth Century.
†† Gable was sought for the Raft role, but
proved unavailable.

Bowery at Midnight
US 1942 61m bw
A criminal by night doubles as a mission
proprietor by day. Star horror cheapie with
echoes of his previous *Dark Eyes of London*.
Bela Lugosi, John Archer, Wanda McKay,
Tom Neal, Dave O'Brien, Vince Barnett.
Written by Gerald Schnitzer; directed by
Wallace Fox; for Monogram.

The Bowery Boys
A cheap and cheerful series of American
second features, immensely popular between
1946 and 1958, these adventures of a group of
ageing Brooklyn layabouts had their origin in
the 1937 film *Dead End*, from which the Dead
End Kids graduated to other features at
Warner: *Crime School, They Made Me a
Criminal, Angels with Dirty Faces, Angels
Wash their Faces*, etc. A couple of the 'boys'
then defected to Universal and made *Little
Tough Guy* and a series of half a dozen
subsequent pictures; while in 1940 Monogram
took a couple more and built up another group
called the East Side Kids. In 1946 a formal
merger of talent at Monogram consolidated
the remaining members into the Bowery Boys.
The members were Leo Gorcey, Huntz Hall,
Bobby Jordan, Gabriel Dell (all from the
Dead End Kids), Bernard Gorcey, David
Gorcey, Billy Benedict, and Bennie Bartlett.
The films are:
1946: IN FAST COMPANY, BOWERY
BOMBSHELL, LIVE WIRES, SPOOK
BUSTERS, MR HEX
1947: BOWERY BUCKAROOS, HARD
BOILED MAHONEY, NEWS HOUNDS,
ANGELS' ALLEY
1948: JINX MONEY, SMUGGLER'S
COVE, TROUBLE MAKERS
1949: ANGELS IN DISGUISE, FIGHTING
FOOLS, HOLD THAT BABY, MASTER
MINDS
1950: BLONDE DYNAMITE, BLUES
BUSTERS, LUCKY LOSERS, TRIPLE
TROUBLE
1951: BOWERY BATALLION, CRAZY
OVER HORSES, GHOST CHASERS,
LET'S GO NAVY
1952: FEUDIN' FOOLS, HERE COME THE
MARINES, HOLD THAT LINE, NO
HOLDS BARRED
1953: CLIPPED WINGS, JALOPY, LOOSE
IN LONDON, PRIVATE EYES
1954: THE BOWERY BOYS MEET THE
MONSTERS, JUNGLE GENTS, PARIS
PLAYBOYS
1955: BOWERY TO BAGDAD, HIGH
SOCIETY, JAIL BUSTERS, SPY CHASERS
1956: DIG THAT URANIUM, CRASHING
LAS VEGAS, FIGHTING TROUBLE, HOT
SHOTS
1957: SPOOK CHASERS, HOLD THAT
HYPNOTIST, LOOKING FOR DANGER
1958: UP IN SMOKE, IN THE MONEY.

Bowery to Broadway
US 1944 94m bw
Universal (John Grant)

In the nineties, a Bowery songstress makes it to the big time.
Simple-minded musical in which the drama has no drive and the guest stars are given inferior material.

w Joseph Lytton, Arthur T. Horman d Charles Lamont ph Charles Van Enger md Edward Ward

Maria Montez, Turhan Bey, Susanna Foster, Jack Oakie, Donald Cook, Louise Allbritton, Andy Devine, Rosemary de Camp, Ann Blyth, Donald O'Connor, Peggy Ryan, Frank McHugh, Leo Carrillo, Evelyn Ankers, Mantan Moreland
Songs include 'The Love Waltz'; 'There'll Always Be a Moon'; 'My Song of Romance'; 'Montevideo'; 'Coney Island Waltz' (plus standards)

Boxcar Bertha*
US 1972 88m De Luxe
AIP (Roger Corman)

In early thirties Arkansas, an unhappy girl falls in with gangsters and train robbers.
Competent imitation of *Bonnie and Clyde*.

w Joyce H. and John W. Corrington d *Martin Scorsese* ph John Stephens m Gilb Guilbeau, Thad Maxwell

Barbara Hershey, David Carradine, Barry Primus, Bernie Casey, John Carradine

● *Video: Rank*

A Boy a Girl and a Bike
GB 1947 92m bw
Gainsborough (Ralph Keene)

Romantic jealousies arise between members of a Yorkshire cycling club.
Mild comedy drama with the advantage of fresh air locations.

w Ted Willis d Ralph Smart ph Ray Elton

John McCallum, Honor Blackman, Patrick Holt, Diana Dors, Leslie Dwyer, Thora Hird, Anthony Newley, Megs Jenkins, Maurice Denham

The Boy and the Bridge
GB 1959 91m bw
Xanadu (Kevin McClory)

A boy who believes he has committed a murder hides in the ramparts of Tower Bridge.
This tiny fable adds up to very weak entertainment, despite inventive photography, because it has virtually no plot development.

w Geoffrey Orme, Kevin McClory, Desmond O'Donovan d Kevin McClory ph Ted Scaife m Malcolm Arnold

Ian MacLaine, Liam Redmond, James Hayter, Norman Macowan, Geoffrey Keen, Jack MacGowran, Royal Dano, Rita Webb

The Boy and the Pirates
US 1960 84m Eastmancolor
Perceptovision

A small boy finds an old bottle on the seashore, wishes he could live in pirate days, and hey presto. Modest juvenile fantasy on the lines of *The Wizard of Oz* but without the

talent. Charles Herbert, Susan Gordon, Murvyn Vye, Paul Guilfoyle. Written by Lillie Hayward and Jerry Sackheim; directed and produced by Bert I. Gordon; for United Artists.

The Boy Cried Murder
GB / West Germany / Yugoslavia 1965 86m Eastmancolor

A small boy has such a vivid imagination that nobody except the criminal believes him when he says he has witnessed a murder. Flat and unnecessary remake of *The Window* (which was later done again as *Eye Witness*). Frazer MacIntosh, Veronica Hurst, Phil Brown, Tim Barrett. Written by Robin Estridge, from the story by Cornell Woolrich; directed by George Breakston; for CCC / Carlos / Avala.

'No more bubble bath, she screamed!'
Boy, Did I Get a Wrong Number
US 1966 99m De Luxe
UA / Edward Small (George Beck)

Trying to phone his wife, an estate agent gets involved with a runaway actress.
Lifeless and generally resistible star comedy, the first of several hard and unfunny vehicles for an ageing Bob Hope seeming to hark back to the least attractive aspects of burlesque rather than the sympathetic wisecracking which suits him best.

w Burt Styler, Albert E. Lewin, George Kennett d George Marshall ph Lionel Lindon m Richard Lasalle ly By Dunham

Bob Hope, Elke Sommer, Phyllis Diller, Marjorie Lord, Cesare Danova, Benny Baker

The Boy Friend*
GB 1971 125m Metrocolor Panavision
MGM / Russflix (Ken Russell)

On a wet Wednesday afternoon in Portsmouth in the late twenties, a tatty company with backstage problems puts on an empty-headed musical.
Russell the mastermind effectively destroys Sandy Wilson's charming period pastiche, sending up all the numbers (via badly staged dream sequences on the wrong shape screen) in a Busby Berkeley manner which had not yet been invented. Moments do work, but a non-star doesn't help, and the whole thing is an artistic disaster of some significance both to Russell's career and to the cinema of the early seventies.

w Ken Russell, from Sandy Wilson's musical play d Ken Russell ph David Watkin md Ian Whittaker, Peter Greenwell, Peter Maxwell Davies pd Tony Walton

Twiggy, Christopher Gable, *Max Adrian*, Tommy Tune, Barbara Windsor, Moyra Fraser, Bryan Pringle, Vladek Sheybal, *Antonia Ellis, Glenda Jackson*
'The glittering, joyless numbers keep coming at you: you never get any relief from Russell's supposed virtuosity.'—*New Yorker, 1977*

AAN: Ian Whittaker, Peter Greenwell, Peter Maxwell Davies

● *Video: MGM / UA*

The Boy from Oklahoma*
US 1953 88m Warnercolor
Warner (David Weisbart)

A genial plainsman studying law becomes sheriff of a small town and uncovers its mayor as a killer.
Modest, pleasing western with the star imitating his father.

w Frank David, Winston Miller d Michael Curtiz ph Robert Burks m Max Steiner

Will Rogers Jnr, Nancy Olson, Lon Chaney Jnr, Anthony Caruso, Wallace Ford, Clem Bevans, Merv Griffin

Boy Meets Girl**
US 1938 86m bw
Warner (George Abbott)

Two crazy Hollywood scenario writers make a star of an infant yet unborn.
Freewheeling film version of a hilarious play: fine crazy comedy and excellent Hollywood satire.

w Bella and Sam Spewack, from their play d Lloyd Bacon ph Sol Polito m Leo Forbstein

James Cagney, Pat O'Brien, Marie Wilson, Ralph Bellamy, Frank McHugh, Dick Foran, Bruce Lester, Ronald Reagan, James Stephenson
'Satisfactory, but not socko.'—*Variety*

Boy of the Streets
US 1937 75m bw

A city youngster falls in with racketeers.
Ho-hum Dead End melodrama. Jackie Cooper, Maureen O'Connor, Kathleen Byrke, Marjorie Main, Robert Emmett O'Connor. Written by Scott Darling and Wilson Brown; directed by William Nigh; for Monogram.
'Will do biz for independents . . . easily Monogram's most ambitious production effort to date.'—*Variety*

Boy on a Dolphin*
US 1957 111m Eastmancolor
Cinemascope
TCF (Samuel G. Engel)

A Greek girl diver discovers a sunken artifact of great value and the news spreads to an American archaeologist and an unscrupulous collector.
Likeable, sunswept Mediterranean adventure romance marred by the miscasting of the male lead.

w Ivan Moffatt, Dwight Taylor, novel David Divine d Jean Negulesco ph Milton Krasner m Hugo Friedhofer md Lionel Newman

Alan Ladd, Sophia Loren, *Clifton Webb*, Laurence Naismith, Alexis Minotis, Jorge Mistral

AAN: Hugo Friedhofer

Boy Slaves
US 1938 70m bw

A boy leaves home and ends up in a forced labour camp. Topical preachment drama which kicked up a bit of dust at the time.

Anne Shirley, Roger Daniel, James McCallion, Alan Baxter. Written by Albert Bein and Ben Orkow; directed by P. J. Wolfson; for RKO. 'Devoid of essential entertainment factors for general theatre showings.'—*Variety*

Boy Trouble
US 1939   75m   bw

A small-towner finds his life upset when his wife adopts two orphans. Sentimental comedy which caused a few tears to trickle. *Charles Ruggles*, Mary Boland, Donald O'Connor, Joyce Matthews, Billy Lee, Andrew Tombes. Written by Laura and S. J. Perelman from a story by Lloyd Corrigan and Monte Brice; directed by George Archainbaud; for Paramount. 'Good old hokum with an emotional wallop . . . Exhibitors can use more pictures of this type.'—*Variety*

'Those who don't believe—are dead!'
The Boy who Cried Werewolf
US 1973   93m   Technicolor

On a camping trip, a boy and his father are attacked by a werewolf, and later on dad starts acting mighty strange . . . Disappointingly straight rewrite of the old hokum. Kerwin Mathews, Elaine Devry, Scott Sealey. Written by Bob Homel; directed by Nathan Juran; for Universal.

The Boy Who Stole a Million
GB 1960   81m   bw

A young page in a Spanish bank 'borrows' some money to help his father but finds Dad, police and crooks all after him. Half-hearted attempt at a British *Bicycle Thieves*, oddly set in Spain and never quite managing to convince or interest us. Maurice Reyna, Virgilia Texera, Harold Kasket, George Coulouris, Edwin Richfield. Written by John Eldridge and Charles Crichton; directed by Charles Crichton; for Fanfare / George H. Brown / British Lion.

The Boy with Green Hair
US 1948   82m   Technicolor
RKO (Stephen Ames)

When he hears that his parents were killed in an air raid, a boy's hair turns green; other war orphans encourage him to parade himself publicly as an image of the horror and futility of war.
Muddled, pretentious and unpersuasive fantasy, typical of this producer's do-goodery. One of those oddities which make Hollywood endearing, but not very entertaining apart from Pat O'Brien's garrulous grandpa.
w Ben Barzman, Alfred Lewis Levitt, *story* Betsy Beaton *d* Joseph Losey *ph* George Barnes *m* Leigh Harline

Dean Stockwell, Pat O'Brien, Robert Ryan, Barbara Hale

The Boys
GB 1962   123m   Cinemascope
Gala / Columbia (Sidney J. Furie)

Four boys are on trial for killing a garage attendant.

Elaborate courtroom drama with flashbacks, stars for counsel, a tricksy director, and about forty minutes too much footage.
w Stuart Douglass *d* Sidney J. Furie *ph* Gerald Gibbs *m* The Shadows

Richard Todd, Robert Morley, Felix Aylmer, Dudley Sutton, Ronald Lacey, Tony Garnett, Jess Conrad, Wilfrid Brambell, Allan Cuthbertson, Colin Gordon

'94 men must die to keep alive a dream—or a nightmare!'
The Boys From Brazil**
US / GB 1978   124m   De Luxe
ITC / Producer Circle (Martin Richards, Stanley O'Toole)

A renegade Nazi in hiding has a sinister plot to reconquer the world.
Suspense fantasy firmly based on a gripping book; excellent performances, but a shade too long.
w Heywood Gould, *novel* Ira Levin *d* Franklin Schaffner *ph* Henri Decaë *m* Jerry Goldsmith *pd* Gil Parrando

Gregory Peck, Laurence Olivier, James Mason, Lilli Palmer, Uta Hagen, Steven Buttenberg, Denholm Elliott, Rosemary Harris, John Dehner, John Rubenstein, Anne Meara, David Hurst, Michael Gough

AAN: Jerry Goldsmith; Laurence Olivier
● *Video: Precision Video*

The Boys from Syracuse*
US 1940   74m   bw
Universal (Jules Levey)

The Comedy of Errors with modern wisecracks, and a few songs.
Predictable well-drilled confusion arises from master and slave having identical twins, but the general tone is a bit flat for an adaptation from a hilarious Broadway success. Still, the songs are lively and the chariot race finale shows spirit.
w Leonard Spiegelgass, Charles Grayson, Paul Gerard Smith, from the play by George Abbott and William Shakespeare *d* Edward A. Sutherland *ph* Joseph Valentine *m* Frank Skinner *md* Charles Previn *songs* Rodgers and Hart

Allan Jones, Joe Penner, Charles Butterworth, Rosemary Lane, Irene Hervey, Martha Raye, Alan Mowbray

Songs include 'Who Are You?'; 'This Can't be Falling in Love'; 'Falling in Love with Love'; 'The Greeks Have no Word for It'; 'Sing for Your Supper'; 'He and She'
† The writing credit on screen ends: 'After a play by William Shakespeare . . . long, long after!'

The Boys in Blue
GB 1983   91m   colour

Village policemen catch art thieves. Horribly incompetent remake of *Ask a Policeman*, with a totally untalented star team. Tommy Cannon, Bobby Ball, Suzanne Danielle, Roy Kinnear, Eric Sykes, Jack Douglas, Edward

Judd, Jon Pertwee, Arthur English. Written and directed by Val Guest; for Elstree / Rank. 'The perfect antidote to sweeping claims about the British renaissance.'—*Geoff Brown, MFB*

Boys in Brown
GB 1949   84m   bw
Gainsborough (Antony Darnborough)

Life in a Borstal institution.
The stars make elderly boys, but Jack Warner is a cuddly governor. Boring and unpersuasive non-documentary fiction in Britain's most tiresome style.
wd Montgomery Tully, *play* Reginald Beckwith *ph* Gordon Lang, Cyril Bristow *m* Doreen Carwithen

Jack Warner, Dirk Bogarde, Michael Medwin, Jimmy Hanley, Richard Attenborough, Alfie Bass, Barbara Murray, Thora Hird
† Made by the Independent Frame method, which blended real backgrounds with studio sets.

The Boys in Company C
Hong Kong 1977   125m   Technicolor Panavision
Golden Harvest (Andre Morgan)

Five marines find their lives changed by the Vietnam war.
Crude action melodrama.
w Rick Natkin, Sidney J. Furie *d* Sidney J. Furie *ph* Godfrey Godar *m* Jaime Mendoza-Nava

Stan Shaw, Andrew Stevens, James Canning, Michael Lembeck, Craig Wasson, James Whitmore Jnr
'Laden with barrack room dialogue and played at the enlisted man's level.'—*Variety*
'An exploitation war movie, like dirty TV.'—*New Yorker*

The Boys in the Band*
US 1970   120m   Technicolor
Cinema Center / Leo (Mart Crowley, Kenneth Utt)

Tempers fray and true selves are revealed when a heterosexual is accidentally invited to a homosexual party.
Careful but claustrophobic filming of a Broadway play, which at the screen's closer quarters becomes overpowering well before the end.
w Mart Crowley, from his play *d* William Friedkin *ph* Arthur J. Ornitz *m* none

Leonard Frey, Kenneth Nelson, Cliff Gorman, Frederick Combs, Reuben Greene, Robert La Tourneaux, Laurence Luckinbill, Keith Prentice, Peter White
'They crack jokes while their hearts are breaking.'—*New Yorker*
● *Video: Rank*

Boys' Night Out
US 1962   115m   Metrocolor Cinemascope
MGM / Filmways (Martin Ransohoff)

Three married men and their bachelor friend share a flat and a 'mistress'.

Would-be saucy comedy in which nothing sexy ever happens and the helpless players are as witless as the script.

w Ira Wallach *d* Michael Gordon *ph* Arthur E. Arling *m* Frank de Vol

James Garner, Kim Novak, Tony Randall, Howard Duff, Howard Morris, Oscar Homolka, Janet Blair, Patti Page, Jessie Royce Landis

Boys' Town**
US 1938 93m bw
MGM (John W. Considine Jnr)

The story of Father Flanagan and his school for juvenile delinquents.
Well-made, highly successful, but sentimental crowd pleaser.

w John Meehan, Dore Schary, *original story* Eleanor Griffin, Dore Schary *d* Norman Taurog *ph* Sidney Wagner *m* Edward Ward

Spencer Tracy, Mickey Rooney, Henry Hull, Gene Reynolds, Sidney Miller, Frankie Thomas, Bobs Watson, Tommy Noonan

'More laughs than Laurel and Hardy! More thrills than *Test Pilot*! More tears than *Captains Courageous*!'—*publicity*

'A production that should build goodwill for the whole industry.'—*Variety*

AA: Eleanor Griffin, Dore Schary; Spencer Tracy
AAN: best picture; John Meehan, Dore Schary; Norman Taurog

Boys Will Be Boys**
GB 1935 75m bw
Gaumont / Gainsborough (Michael Balcon)

An incompetent headmaster thwarts a jewel robber.
The first recognizable Will Hay vehicle, based in part on J. B. Morton's Narkover sketches.

w Will Hay, Robert Edmunds *d* William Beaudine *ph* Charles Van Enger *m* Louis Levy

Will Hay, Gordon Harker, Jimmy Hanley, Davy Burnaby, Norma Varden, Claude Dampier, Charles Farrell, Percy Walsh

'It is hard to see how his distinctive sketch writing could have found a satisfactory screen equivalent. Nevertheless, a good augury of the films to come.'—*Ray Seaton and Roy Martin, 1978*

The Brain
France / US 1969 115m colour
Paramount (Alain Poiré)

A British colonel leads an international crew in an attempt to rob NATO.
Exhausting and generally misfiring international crook comedy.

w Gérard Oury, Marcel Julian, Daniele Thompson *d* Gérard Oury *ph* Vladimir Ivanov, Armand Thirard *m* Georges Delerue

David Niven, Jean-Paul Belmondo, Bourvil, Eli Wallach, Silvia Monti

The Brain Machine*
GB 1954 83m bw

Through an electroencephalograph, a hospital psychiatrist recognizes a patient as a dangerous psychopath. Very tolerable crime thriller with a fresh angle. Elizabeth Allan, Patrick Barr, Maxwell Reed, Russell Napier, Vanda Gosell, Gibb McLaughlin. Written and directed by Ken Hughes; for Alec Snowden / Merton Park.

Brainstorm
US 1965 110m bw Panavision
Warner / Kodima (William Conrad)

A passer-by saves a married woman from suicide, has an affair with her, and conspires to murder her husband. This accomplished, she leaves him and he goes insane.
Overlong thriller which starts off agreeably in the *Double Indemnity* vein; but goes slow and solemn around the half way mark.

w Mann Rubin *d* William Conrad *ph* Sam Leavitt *m* George Duning

Jeffrey Hunter, Anne Francis, Dana Andrews, Viveca Lindfors, Stacy Harris

'A sub-B potboiler for those who find comic books too intellectual.'—*Judith Crist*

Brainstorm
US 1983 106m Metrocolor Super Panavision
MGM / UA / JF (Douglas Trumbull)

A technological device records emotions so faithfully as to make other people feel them through each of the five senses. The enemy is discovered to be using it for brainwashing purposes; but it has recorded the experience of death . . .
Scientific mumbo jumbo which went far too far as an attack on the audience's senses, and was jinxed by the death of its star during production.

w Robert Stitzel, Philip Frank Messina, Bruce Joel Rubin *d* Douglas Trumbull *ph* Richard Yuricich *m* James Horner *pd* John Vallone

Natalie Wood, Christopher Walken, Louise Fletcher, Cliff Roberston, Jordan Christopher, Alan Fudge

'A monstrous bore, with uninteresting characters buried beneath a mass of even less interesting technology.'—*Tom Milne, MFB*

The Bramble Bush
US 1960 105m Technicolor
Warner / United States (Milton Sperling)

A doctor returns to his home town and finds himself involved in old tragedies including the mercy killing of his friend.
Sordid small-town melodrama in the *Peyton Place* vein, with adequate production values but dispiriting treatment.

w Milton Sperling, Philip Yordan, *novel* Charles Mergendahl *d* Daniel Petrie *ph* Lucien Ballard *m* Leonard Rosenman

Richard Burton, Barbara Rush, Jack Carson, Angie Dickinson, James Dunn, Tom Drake, Henry Jones, Frank Conroy, Carl Benton Reid, William Hansen

Branded
US 1950 104m Technicolor
Paramount (Mel Epstein)

A gunman poses as a rancher's lost heir, but redeems himself by finding the real one.
Competent, brisk western.

w Sydney Boehm, Cyril Hume *d* Rudolph Maté *ph* Charles Lang Jnr *m* Roy Webb

Alan Ladd, Charles Bickford, Mona Freeman, Robert Keith, Joseph Calleia, Peter Hansen, Selena Royle, Tom Tully

Brandy for the Parson*
GB 1951 79m bw
Group Three (Alfred O'Shaughnessy)

A couple on a yachting holiday find themselves unwittingly smuggling brandy into Britain.
Pleasant little sub-Ealing comedy with agreeable locations but not much drive.

w John Dighton, Walter Meade, *story* Geoffrey Household *d* John Eldridge *ph* Martin Curtis *m* John Addison

James Donald, Kenneth More, Jean Lodge, Frederick Piper, Charles Hawtrey, Michael Trubshawe, Alfie Bass, Reginald Beckwith

'Detective-Lieutenant Brannigan is in London . . . God save the Queen!'
Brannigan*
GB 1975 111m De Luxe Panavision
UA / Wellborn (Jules Levy, Arthur Gardner)

A Chicago policeman is sent to London to pick up a gangster.
Cheerful crime pastiche and tour of London, quite an agreeable entertainment despite its obviously over-age star.

w Christopher Trumbo, Michael Butler, William P. McGivern, William Norton *d* Douglas Hickox *ph* Gerry Fisher *m* Dominic Frontière

John Wayne, Richard Attenborough, Judy Geeson, Mel Ferrer, John Vernon, Daniel Pilon, John Stride, James Booth, Barry Dennen

The Brasher Doubloon*
US 1946 72m bw
TCF
GB title: *The High Window*

Philip Marlowe investigates the theft of a rare coin and finds himself involved in a series of murders.
The poorest of the Chandler adaptations, previously filmed as *Time to Kill*, still contains good moments, though the star is lightweight and the production low-budget.

w Dorothy Bennett, *novel* The High Window by Raymond Chandler *d* John Brahm *ph* Lloyd Ahern *m* David Buttolph

George Montgomery, Nancy Guild, Florence Bates, Conrad Janis, Fritz Kortner

The Brass Bottle
US 1964 89m Eastmancolor
U-I / Scarus (Robert Arthur)

A young architect finds an old brass bottle which contains a troublesome genie.
Simple-minded farce with little invention and poor trickwork.

w Oscar Brodney, *novel* F. Anstey d Harry Keller ph Clifford Stine m Bernard Green sp Roswell Hoffman

Tony Randall, Burl Ives, Barbara Eden, Edward Andrews, Ann Doran

The Brass Legend
US 1956 79m bw

A sheriff finds himself in trouble when he tries to protect his fiancée's young brother. Stolid programmer of the *High Noon* school, but without the flair. Hugh O'Brian, Nancy Gates, Raymond Burr, Reba Tassell. Written by Don Martin; directed by Gerd Oswald; for Herman Cohen / Bob Goldstein / UA.

The Brass Monkey
GB 1948 84m bw

A radio singer thwarts the theft of a Buddhist idol. Flat thriller based round a radio 'discovery' programme. Carole Landis, Carroll Levis, Herbert Lom, Avril Angers, Ernest Thesiger. Written by Alec Coppel and Thornton Freeland; directed by Thornton Freeland; for Diadem / Alliance / UA. (Aka: *Lucky Mascot*.)

Brass Target
US 1978 111m Metrocolor
MGM (Berle Adams)

The alleged story behind the death of General Patton, who according to these sources was eliminated because he had discovered a bullion robbery attempt.
Good-looking but interminably complex and talkative, with nothing much for its star cast to do.

w Alvin Boretz, *novel* The Algonquin Project by Frederick Nolan d John Hough ph Tony Imi m Laurence Rosenthal

Sophia Loren, George Kennedy, Max Von Sydow, John Cassavetes, Patrick McGoohan, Robert Vaughn, Bruce Davison, Edward Herrmann, Ed Bishop

Brats*
US 1930 20m bw

Stan and Ollie have trouble baby-sitting their own mischievous kids. Fairly ambitious star comedy with trick sets and photography enabling Laurel and Hardy to play their own sons. About half the gags come off. Written by Leo McCarey, H. M. Walker and Hal Roach; directed by James Parrott; for Hal Roach.

The Bravados*
US 1958 98m Eastmancolor
Cinemascope
TCF (Herbert B. Swope)

A widower chases four killers who, he believes, raped and murdered his wife.
Dour western with a downbeat ending; production good, but entertainment uneasy.

w Philip Yordan, *novel* Frank O'Rourke d Henry King ph Leon Shamroy m Alfred Newman

Gregory Peck, Stephen Boyd, Joan Collins, Albert Salmi, Henry Silva, George Voskovec, Barry Coe, Lee Van Cleef

The Brave Bulls
US 1951 108m bw
Columbia (Robert Rossen)

A Mexican matador regains his courage but loses his girl in a car crash.
Muddled narrative with dollops of bull-fighting mystique; a rather miserable movie despite effort all round.

w John Bright, *novel* Tom Lea d Robert Rossen ph James Wong Howe, Floyd Crosby

Mel Ferrer, Miroslava, Anthony Quinn, Eugene Iglesias

The Brave Don't Cry*
GB 1952 90m bw
Group Three (John Baxter)

Over a hundred men are rescued in a Scottish mine disaster.
Semi-documentary based on a real incident; well done on a small budget, but hardly memorable.

w Montagu Slater d Philip Leacock ph Arthur Grant m none

John Gregson, Meg Buchanan, John Rae, Fulton Mackay, Andrew Keir, Russell Waters, Jameson Clark, Jean Anderson, Eric Woodburn

The Brave One*
US 1956 100m Technicolor
Cinemascope
King Brothers

A small boy saves the life of his pet bull when it is sent into the ring.
Mildly beguiling minor drama for those who adore small boys and bulls.

w Harry Franklin, Merrill G. White, *original story* Robert Rich d Irving Rapper ph Jack Cardiff m Victor Young

Michel Ray, Rodolfo Hoyos, Elsa Cardenas, Joi Lansing, Carlos Navarro

AA: Robert Rich. (There was much confusion when the mysterious Rich turned out to be Dalton Trumbo, who was blacklisted at the time.)

Brazil
US 1944 91m bw
Republic (Robert Worth)

A lady novelist goes to Brazil for material; a local composer poses as her guide in order to pay her back for her previous remarks about his country.
Acceptable lower case musical with pleasant tunes and humour.

w Frank Gill Jnr, Laura Kerr d Joseph Santley ph Jack Marta *songs* Bob Russell and others m Walter Scharf

Virginia Bruce, Tito Guizar, Edward Everett Horton, Roy Rogers

AAN: song 'Rio de Janeiro' (m Ary Barrosa, *ly* Ned Washington); Walter Scharf

Breach of Promise
GB 1941 79m bw

A girl chases the man she wants by filing a breach of promise suit against him. Dated but lively comedy with agreeable playing. Clive Brook, Judy Campbell, C. V. France, Margaret Allan, Percy Walsh. Written by Roland Pertwee; directed by Harold Huth and Roland Pertwee; for British Mercury / MGM.

Bread and Chocolate*
Italy 1973 112m Eastmancolor
Verona Cinematografica (Maurizio Lodo-Fe)

An Italian waiter in Switzerland is accused of murder and indecent exposure.
Amusing and often pathetic account of an inveterate loser, its flavour impossible to define.

w Franco Brusati, Iaia Fiastri, Nino Manfredi d Franco Brusati ph Luciano Tovoli md Daniele Patrucchi

Nino Manfredi, Anna Karina, Johnny Dorelli, Paolo Turco

Bread, Love and Dreams*
Italy 1953 90m bw
Titanus (Marcello Girosi)

The new sergeant of police in a small rural village comes looking for a wife.
Pleasant rather than exciting rural comedy which spun off a number of vaguely related sequels (*Bread, Love and Jealousy*, etc.).

w Luigi Comencini, *original story* Ettore Margadonna d Luigi Comencini ph Arturo Gallea m Alessandro Cicognini

Vittorio de Sica, Gina Lollobrigida, Marisa Merlini. Roberto Risso

AAN: Ettore Margadonna

Break of Hearts
US 1935 80m bw
RKO (Pandro S. Berman)

A girl composer falls in love with a distinguished conductor who becomes a dipsomaniac.
Well acted soap opera, not really worthy of its stars.

w Sarah Y. Mason, Victor Heerman, Anthony Veiller d Philip Moeller ph Robert de Grasse m Max Steiner

Katharine Hepburn, Charles Boyer, Jean Hersholt, John Beal, Sam Hardy

'A stale turnip story that relies entirely upon characterization to hide the basic dullness.'—*Variety*

'In spite of some capable acting, it lacks a certain compelling warmth. The audience's heart never breaks.'—*Eileen Creelman, New York Sun*

Break in the Circle
GB 1955 91m Eastmancolor

The owner of a cabin cruiser is hired to smuggle a scientist out of Germany. Routine action yarn of cross and double-cross, tolerably staged. Forrest Tucker, Eva Bartok, Marius Goring, Eric Pohlmann, Guy Middleton, Arnold Marle. Written and directed by Val Guest, from a novel by Philip Loraine; for Hammer / Exclusive.

Break the News*
GB 1938   78m   bw
GFD / Jack Buchanan

A dancer arranges his partner's 'death' for publicity reasons but is sent to jail when the partner disappears.
Thin but lively comedy with a remarkable couple of song and dance men. Negative apparently lost.

w Geoffrey Kerr, *novel* La Mort en Fuite by Loid de Gouriadec *d* René Clair *ph* Phil Tannura

Jack Buchanan, Maurice Chevalier, June Knight, Marta Labarr, Garry Marsh, Felix Aylmer, Robb Wilton
† Various remakes include *The Art of Love* (qv).

Breaker Morant*
Australia 1980   107m   Eastmancolor
   Panavision
South Australian Film Corporation
   (Matthew Carroll)

During the Boer War three Australian officers are courtmartialled for murdering prisoners. Careful, moving military drama which gives a more sympathetic view of the facts than history does.

w Jonathan Hardy, Bruce Beresford, David Stevens, *play* Kenneth Ross *d* Bruce Beresford *ph* Donald McAlpine *md* Phil Cuneen

Edward Woodward, Jack Thompson, John Waters, Charles Tingwell, Terence Donovan, Vincent Ball
   'It is impossible to suppress a feeling that the spirit of Stanley Kramer is abroad on the veldt.'—*Tim Pulleine, MFB*
AAN: screenplay
● *Video: Guild*

Breakfast at Tiffany's*
US 1961   115m   Technicolor
Paramount (Martin Jurow, Richard
   Shepherd)

A young New York writer has as neighbour the volatile Holly Golightly, a slightly crazy call girl with an exotic social and emotional life.
Impossibly cleaned up and asexual version of a light novel which tried to be the American *I Am a Camera*. Wild parties, amusing scenes and good cameos, but the pace is slow, the atmosphere is unconvincingly clean and luxurious, and the sentimentality kills it.

w George Axelrod, *novel* Truman Capote *d* Blake Edwards *ph* Franz Planer *m* Henry Mancini

Audrey Hepburn, George Peppard, Patricia Neal, Buddy Ebsen, Martin Balsam, *John McGiver* (as the Tiffany salesman), Mickey Rooney
AA: Henry Mancini; *song* 'Moon River' (*m* Henry Mancini, *ly* Johnny Mercer)
AAN: George Axelrod; Audrey Hepburn
● *Video: CIC*

Breakfast for Two*
US 1937   65m   bw
RKO (Edward Kaufman)

A Texas heiress turns a playboy into a businessman.
Star crazy comedy with some wildly funny scenes.

w Charles Kaufman, Paul Yawitz, Viola Brothers Shore *d* Alfred Santell *ph* J. Roy Hunt

Barbara Stanwyck, Herbert Marshall, Donald Meek, Glenda Farrell, Eric Blore, Etienne Girardot
   'Heaps of laughs in a breezily-paced farce.'—*Variety*

Breakheart Pass*
US 1975   94m   De Luxe
UA / Elliott Kastner (Jerry Gershwin)

Various mysterious passengers on an 1873 train across the frozen west to Fort Humboldt turn out to have smuggling and murder in mind.
Botched murder mystery on wheels: there are some exciting scenes, but the plot makes little sense and the 'action finale' is muddled.

w Alistair MacLean, from his book *d* Tom Gries *ph* Lucien Ballard *m* Jerry Goldsmith

Charles Bronson, Ben Johnson, Richard Crenna, Jill Ireland, Charles Durning, Archie Moore, Ed Lauter

Breakin'
US 1984   87m   Metrocolor

Youngsters promote a new form of dancing. Minor exploitation item, the form little improved on *Rock around the Clock* thirty years earlier. Lucinda Dickey, Adolfo Shabba-Doo Quinones, Michael Boogaloo-Shrimp Chambers, Ben Lokey, Phineas Newborn III. Written by Charles Parker, Allen DeBevoise, Gerald Scaife; directed by Joel Silberg; for Cannon. (GB title: *Breakdance*.)

Breaking Away*
US 1979   101m   De Luxe
TCF (Peter Yates)

An imaginative teenager has trouble adjusting to adult life after high school.
Andy Hardy would have felt at home in this fragmented comedy of the American hinterland; 1979 audiences found it a welcome relief from the stronger brews to which they had become accustomed.

w Steve Tesich *d* Peter Yates *ph* Matthew F. Leonetti *m* Lionel Newman

Dennis Christopher, Dennis Quaid, Daniel Stern, Jackie Earle Haley, Barbara Barrie, Paul Dooley

'Affection for the middle classes, the landscapes of Indiana, and bicycle racing.'— *New Yorker*
   'It is not devoid of pleasures . . . but it fatally lacks a clear purpose and identity.'— *Geoff Brown, MFB*
† An unsuccessful TV series followed in 1980.
● *Video: CBS / Fox*

'The experience is shattering!'
Breaking Glass
GB 1980   104m   Technicolor
   Panavision
GTO / Film and General (Dodi Fayed)

Vicissitudes of a pop band and of its singer who can't stand the pace.
Garish, freakish musical with unattractive characters strung along an oft-told tale. Some commendable vigour in the presentation, but it won't appeal to anybody over 21.

wd Brian Gibson *ph* Stephen Goldblatt *md* Tony Visconti

Hazel O'Connor, Phil Daniels, Jon Finch, Jonathan Pryce

● *Video: VCL*

'There's nothing more deadly than a gentle man pushed too far!'
The Breaking Point*
US 1950   97m   bw
Warner (Jerry Wald)

A charterboat owner becomes involved with crooks but turns them in when they have killed his friend.
Adequate if slightly humdrum attempt by Warners to atone for what they had done to a Hemingway novel, the infidelity of *To Have and Have Not* and the unauthorized variation of *Key Largo*. (See also: *The Gun Runners*.)

w Ranald MacDougall, *novel* To Have and Have Not by Ernest Hemingway *d* Michael Curtiz *ph* Ted McCord *m* (uncredited) William Lava, Max Steiner

John Garfield, Patricia Neal, Phyllis Thaxter, Juano Hernandez, Wallace Ford, Edmon Ryan, William Campbell

'Innocence and fury don't mix—they explode!'
Breaking Point
Canada 1976   92m   colour   Panavision
TCF / Astral Belle Vue (Harold Greenberg, Harold Pariser)

An innocent witness against the Mafia takes off against them vigilante style when his partner is murdered and his own life threatened.
Comic strip thuggery with performances to match; plenty of excitement for toughies.

w Roger E. Swaybill, Stanley Mann *d* Bob Clark *ph* Marc Champion *m* David McLey

Bo Svenson, Robert Culp, John Colicos, Belinda J. Montgomery, Stephen Young

Breaking the Ice
US 1938   80m   bw
(RKO) Sol Lesser

A Pennsylvania Dutch boy runs away to the

city so that his mother can afford her own farm.
Slim star musical which had its pleasing moments.

w Mary McCall Jnr, Manuel Seff, Bernard Schubert d Edward F. Cline ph Jack MacKenzie m Victor Young

Bobby Breen, Charles Ruggles, Dolores Costello, Robert Barrat, Dorothy Peterson, John King, Billy Gilbert, Margaret Hamilton
  'Moderately engrossing, combination folk drama and musical.'—*Variety*

AAN: Victor Young

Breakout

US 1975 96m colour Panavision
Columbia / Persky–Bright (Robert Chartoff, Irwin Winkler)

A professional rescuer gets an innocent man out of a Mexican jail.
Rough and ready adventure thriller which starts slowly and confusingly but later works up a fair head of steam.

w Howard B. Kreitsek, Frank Kowalski, from their novel Ten Second Jailbreak d Tom Gries ph Lucien Ballard m Jerry Goldsmith

Charles Bronson, Robert Duvall, John Huston, Jill Ireland, Randy Quaid, Sheree North

Breakthrough

US 1950 91m bw
Warner (Bryan Foy)

Adventures of a US army unit in Normandy after D-Day.
Routine low-budgeter which improves after a slow start.

w Bernard Girard, Ted Sherdeman, Joseph I. Breen Jnr d Lewis Seiler ph Edwin DuPar m William Lava

David Brian, John Agar, Frank Lovejoy, William Campbell, Paul Picerni, Greg McClure, Edward Norris, Matt Willis, Dick Wesson

A Breath of Scandal

US 1960 98m Technicolor
Paramount / Titanus / Ponti–Girosi (Carlo Ponti, Marcello Girosi)

A spirited Ruritanian princess falls for an American industrialist.
Exceedingly flat-footed and boring international co-production of an old Molnar play; if anyone concerned had bright ideas, they don't show.

w Sidney Howard (presumably in the thirties, for he died in 1939), play Olimpia by Ferenc Molnar d Michael Curtiz, Mario Russo ph Mario Montuori m Alessandro Cicognini

Sophia Loren, Maurice Chevalier, John Gavin, Isabel Jeans, Angela Lansbury, Roberto Risso, Frederick Ledebur, Tullio Carminati, Milly Vitale

Breathless

US 1983 101m De Luxe
Miko / Breathless Associates / Greenberg Brothers (Martin Erlichman)

A street-smart hustler steals a car in Las Vegas and heads for the coast.
Fashionable amalgam of sex and violence, borrowed from À Bout de Souffle but far too long after the event.

w L. M. Kit Carson, James McBride d James McBride ph Richard H. Kline m Jack Nitzsche pd Richard Sylbert

Richard Gere, Valerie Kaprinsky, William Tepper, John P. Ryan, Art Metrano
  'Not much more than an ego trip for a bankable star.'—*Daily Mail*

Breezy

US 1973 107m Technicolor
Universal / Malpaso (Robert Daley)

A divorced 50-year-old real estate agent is rejuvenated by an affair with a young girl hippy.
An abrasive veneer covers the most stereotyped of January/May love stories. Technically an attractive piece of work.

w Jo Heims d Clint Eastwood ph Frank Stanley m Michel Legrand

William Holden, Kay Lenz, Roger C. Carmel, Marj Dusay, Joan Hotchkis

Brewster McCloud

US 1970 105m Metrocolor Panavision
MGM / Adler–Phillips / Lion's Gate (Lou Adler)

A man hides out under the roof of the Houston Astrodrome, prepares to learn to fly with man-made wings, and refuses all offers of help; when he launches himself, he falls to his death.
Anarchic, allegorical fantasy, a delight no doubt for connoisseurs of way-out humour. Everyone else, forget it.

w Doran William Cannon d Robert Altman ph Lamar Boren, Jordan Cronenweth m Gene Page

Bud Cort, Sally Kellerman, Michael Murphy, William Windom, Shelley Duvall, René Auberjonois, Stacy Keach, John Shuck, Margaret Hamilton
  'Amorphous and rather silly . . . the idea seems to be left over from a Victorian fable, but the style is like a Road Runner cartoon.'—*New Yorker, 1974*

Brewster's Millions*

GB 1935 84m bw
British and Dominion (Herbert Wilcox)

If he can spend a million pounds within two months, a playboy will inherit many millions more.
Artless but lively version of a famous comedy which provided a good role for its star.

w Arthur Wimperis, Paul Gangelin, Douglas Furber, Clifford Grey, Donovan Pedelty, Wolfgang Wilhelm, play George Barr McCutcheon and Winchell Smith, original novel George Barr McCutcheon d Thornton Freeland ph Henry Harris, Barney McGill

Jack Buchanan, Lili Damita, Nancy O'Neil, Amy Veness, Sydney Fairbrother, Fred Emney, Sebastian Shaw
  'As near 100% film entertainment as can be expected.'—*Variety*

Brewster's Millions*

US 1945 79m bw
Edward Small

Competent American remake of the above.

w Sig Herzig, Charles Rogers d Allan Dwan ph Charles Lawton Jnr m Hugo Friedhofer

Dennis O'Keefe, Eddie 'Rochester' Anderson, Helen Walker
  † Remade as Three on a Spree (GB 1961).

AAN: Lou Forbes

The Bribe*

US 1949 98m bw
MGM (Robert Z. Leonard)

A US agent tracks down a group of criminals in Central America.
Steamy melodrama with pretensions but only moderate entertainment value despite high gloss. The rogues' gallery, however, is impressive.

w Marguerite Roberts d Robert Z. Leonard ph Joseph Ruttenberg m Miklos Rozsa

Robert Taylor, Ava Gardner, Charles Laughton, Vincent Price, John Hodiak

The Bridal Path*

GB 1959 95m Technicolor
British Lion / Sidney Gilliat, Frank Launder

A stalwart Hebridean islander journeys to the mainland in search of a wife.
Mild, episodic, very pleasant open-air comedy set amid splendid locations.

w Frank Launder, Geoffrey Willans, novel Nigel Tranter d Frank Launder ph Arthur Ibbetson m Cedric Thorpe Davie

Bill Travers, Fiona Clyne, George Cole, Duncan Macrae, Gordon Jackson, Dilys Laye, Bernadette O'Farrell

Bridal Suite

US 1939 70m bw

A playboy seldom turns up for his own weddings, but his new intended takes him and his mother in hand. Frothy comedy with dependable cast. Robert Young, Annabella, Walter Connolly, Billie Burke, Reginald Owen, Arthur Treacher. Written by Samuel Hoffenstein; directed by William Thiele; for MGM. 'Dull and uninteresting, with static direction, commonplace story and situations, and inability to catch audience attention except for brief moments.'—*Variety* (First known as Maiden Voyage.)

Bride by Mistake

US 1944 84m bw

An heiress tests her suitors by posing as her own secretary. Pleasant little comedy with hard-working cast. Laraine Day, Alan Marshall, Allyn Joslyn, Marsha Hunt. Written by Phoebe and Henry Ephron; directed by Richard Wallace; for RKO.

The Bride Came C.O.D.*

US 1941 92m bw
Warner (Hal B. Wallis)

A charter pilot agrees to kidnap a

temperamental heiress, but is stuck with her when they crashland in the desert.
Feeble comedy with a script totally unworthy of its stars. The mass of talent does however provide a smile or two towards the end.

w Julius J. and Philip G. Epstein *d* William Keighley *ph* Ernest Haller *m* Max Steiner

Bette Davis, James Cagney, Harry Davenport, Stuart Erwin, Eugene Pallette, Jack Carson, George Tobias, William Frawley, Edward Brophy, Chick Chandler

'Neither the funniest comedy ever made, nor the shortest distance between two points, but for the most part a serviceable romp.'—*Theodore Strauss*

'Both of them mug good-naturedly, and it's pleasantly fast.'—*New Yorker, 1977*

The Bride Comes Home*
US 1935   82m   bw
Paramount (Wesley Ruggles)

A penniless socialite helps a wealthy man and his roughneck bodyguard in a magazine venture.
Slight but freshly handled romantic comedy, still worth a look.

w Elizabeth Sanxay Holding, Claude Binyon *d* Wesley Ruggles *ph* Leo Tover

Claudette Colbert, Robert Young, Fred MacMurray, William Collier Snr, Donald Meek, Edgar Kennedy, Richard Carle, Jimmy Conlin

'Another galloping lithograph off the boy-and-girl-always-fighting woodblock.'—*Variety*

Bride for Sale
US 1949   87m   bw
RKO (Jack H. Skirball)

A practical-minded businesswoman has two admirers.
Skittish romantic comedy for ageing stars.

w Bruce Manning, Islin Auster *d* William D. Russell *ph* Joseph Valentine *m* Frederick Hollander

Claudette Colbert, George Brent, Robert Young, Max Baer, Gus Schilling, Charles Arnt, Thurston Hall

The Bride Goes Wild
US 1948   98m   bw
MGM (William H. Wright)

As his lady illustrator finds out, a writer of children's books is not quite the sober uncle she expected, especially when he has to pretend to adopt an unruly orphan.
Scatty comedy with farcical interludes, quite pleasantly played but lacking style.

w Albert Beich *d* Norman Taurog *ph* Ray June *m* Rudolf Kopp

June Allyson, Van Johnson, Jackie 'Butch' Jenkins, Hume Cronyn, Richard Derr

'The monster demands a mate!'
The Bride of Frankenstein****
US 1935   85–90m   bw
Universal (Carl Laemmle Jnr)

Baron Frankenstein is blackmailed by Dr

Praetorious into reviving his monster and building a mate for it.
Frankenstein was startlingly good in a primitive way; this sequel is the screen's sophisticated masterpiece of black comedy, with all the talents working deftly to one end. Every scene has its own delights, and they are woven together into a superb if wilful cinematic narrative which, of its gentle mocking kind, has never been surpassed.

w John L. Balderston, William Hurlbut *d* James Whale *ph* John Mescall *m* Franz Waxman

Boris Karloff, Colin Clive, *Ernest Thesiger*, Valerie Hobson, *E. E. Clive*, Dwight Frye, O. P. Heggie, Una O'Connor, *Elsa Lanchester* (as Mary Shelley and the monster's mate), Gavin Gordon (as Byron), Douglas Walton (as Shelley)

'It is perhaps because Whale was by now master of the horror film that this production is the best of them all.'—*John Baxter, 1968*

'An extraordinary film, with sharp humour, macabre extravagance, and a narrative that proceeds at a fast, efficient pace.'—*Gavin Lambert, 1948*

'A great deal of art has gone into it, but it is the kind of art that gives the healthy feeling of men with their sleeves rolled up and working, worrying only about how to put the thing over in the best manner of the medium—no time for nonsense and attitudes and long hair.'—*Otis Ferguson*

† The regular release version runs 75m, having dropped part of the Mary Shelley prologue and a sequence in which the monster becomes unsympathetic by murdering the burgomaster.
†† The title was originally to have been *The Return of Frankenstein*.

Bride of the Gorilla
US 1951   65m   bw

The manager of a rubber plantation is poisoned by a native woman and turns into a gorilla. Incredibly inane two-bit shocker, a strong contender for any list of the worst films of all time. Barbara Payton, Lon Chaney Jnr, Raymond Burr, Tom Conway, Paul Cavanagh (a rare cast of non-actors). Written and directed by Curt Siodmak; for Jack Broder Productions.

Bride of the Monster
US 1953   69m   bw

Dr Vornoff has an atomic machine which will convert people into beings of superhuman strength; it is turned on himself, but a giant octopus, also with superoctopus strength, gets him. A perfectly terrible movie, on a par with this director's other works. Written by Edward D. Wood Jnr and Alex Gordon; directed and produced by Edward D. Wood Jnr; for Rolling M.

Bride of the Regiment
US 1930   79m   Technicolor
First National

In northern Italy a band of aristocrats rises against the invading Austrians.
Early talkie operetta, well received at the time. No colour material survives.

w Ray Harris, *operetta* The Lady in Ermine by Rudolph Schanzer and Ernest Wellsch *d* John Francis Dillon *ph* Dev Jennings, Charles Schoenbaum *ch* Jack Haskell *songs* Al Bryan, Ed Ward

Vivienne Segal, Allan Prior, Walter Pidgeon, Louise Fazenda, Ford Sterling, Myrna Loy, Lupino Lane

'Entertaining all the way, deserves returns above the average.'—*Variety*

Bride of Vengeance*
US 1948   91m   bw
Paramount (Richard Maibaum)

The story of the Borgias (whitewashing Lucretia) and the Duke of Ferrara. Superb looking but appallingly acted and rather stodgily directed piece of historical melodrama. Totally studio-bound, but one of these days it could find a sympathetic audience.

w Cyril Hume, Michael Hogan *d* Mitchell Leisen *ph* Daniel L. Fapp *m* Hugo Friedhofer *ad* Hans Dreier, Roland Anderson, Albert Nozaki

Paulette Goddard, John Lund, Macdonald Carey, Albert Dekker, Raymond Burr

'A dud . . . it just couldn't be that bad by accident.'—*Los Angeles Times*

The Bride Walks Out
US 1936   81m   bw
RKO (Edward Small)

A successful mannequin tries to manage on her engineer husband's lowly salary.
Thin, pleasant marital comedy with no surprises.

w P. J. Wolfson, Philip G. Epstein *d* Leigh Jason *ph* J. Roy Hunt *m* Roy Webb

Barbara Stanwyck, Gene Raymond, Robert Young, Ned Sparks, Helen Broderick, Willie Best, Robert Warwick, Billy Gilbert, Hattie McDaniel, Irving Bacon

The Bride Wore Black*
France / Italy 1967   107m   Eastmancolor
Films du Carrosse / Artistes Associés / Dino de Laurentiis (Marcel Bébert)
original title: *La Mariée Était en Noir*

A melancholy lady traces and kills the five men responsible for her fiancé's death.
Uncertain and not very entertaining attempt to turn a Hitchcock situation into a character study.

w François Truffaut, Jean-Louis Richard, *novel* William Irish *d* François Truffaut *ph* Raoul Coutard *m* Bernard Herrmann

Jeanne Moreau, Jean-Claude Brialy, Michel Bouquet, Charles Denner, Claude Rich, Michel Lonsdale

'Truffaut has called the film a love story; others have taken it as a tribute to his master, a Hitchcockian thriller. In fact it is neither; it is a piece of junk.'—*John Simon*

The Bride Wore Boots
US 1946 86m bw
Paramount (Seton I. Miller)

A woman who loves horses is married to a man who does not.
Flimsy, silly, but mainly quite tolerable light comedy sustained by its stars.

w Dwight Mitchell Wiley d Irving Pichel ph Stuart Thompson m Frederick Hollander

Barbara Stanwyck, Robert Cummings, Diana Lynn, Patric Knowles, Peggy Wood, Robert Benchley, Willie Best, Natalie Wood

The Bride Wore Crutches
US 1941 55m bw

A young reporter witnesses a bank robbery and tracks down the criminals. Lightweight support. Ted North, Lynne Roberts, Edgar Kennedy, Lionel Stander, Richard Lane, Grant Mitchell, Horace MacMahon. Written by Ed Verdier; directed by Shepherd Traube; for TCF.

The Bride Wore Red*
US 1937 103m bw
MGM (Joseph L. Mankiewicz)

A whimsical count arranges for a chorus girl to spend two weeks at an aristocratic Tyrol resort, where she is pursued by two rich men. Cinderella retold in fancy dress; a typically unreal but quite entertaining star confection of its day.

w Tess Slesinger, Bradbury Foote, play The Girl from Trieste by Ferenc Molnar d Dorothy Arzner ph George Folsey m Franz Waxman

Joan Crawford, Robert Young, Franchot Tone, Billie Burke, Reginald Owen, George Zucco, Lynne Carver, Mary Phillips, Paul Porcasi

'Marquee values will have to bolster this one.'—Variety

'In the privacy of a girls' school he sought his prey—turning innocent beauty into a thing of unspeakable horror!'
Brides of Dracula**
GB 1960 Technicolor
U-I / Hammer / Hotspur (Anthony Hinds)

Baron Meinster, a disciple of Dracula, is locked up by his mother; but a servant lets him out and he goes on the rampage in a girls' school.
The best of the Hammer Draculas, with plenty of inventive action, some classy acting and a good sense of place and period.

w Jimmy Sangster, Peter Bryan, Edward Percy d Terence Fisher ph Jack Asher m Malcolm Williamson

David Peel (as Meinster), Peter Cushing, Freda Jackson, Martita Hunt, Yvonne Monlaur, Andrée Melly, Mona Washbourne, Henry Oscar, Miles Malleson

The Brides of Fu Manchu*
GB 1966 94m Eastmancolor

The yellow peril kidnaps twelve young women in order to blackmail their influential boy

friends. Very adequate sequel to The Face of Fu Manchu (qv for details of series), after which Fu Manchu went rapidly downhill. Christopher Lee, Douglas Wilmer, Howard Marion Crawford, Marie Versini, Tsai Chin, Rupert Davies. Written and produced by Harry Alan Towers (Peter Welbeck); directed by Don Sharp; for Anglo Amalgamated.

The Bridge*
West Germany 1959 106m bw
Fono / Jochen Severin (Hermann Schwerin)

In 1945, only a handful of 16-year-old schoolboys is left to defend the bridge of a small German town.
Painful but memorable war vignette, almost an updating of All Quiet on the Western Front.

w Michael Mansfield, Karl-Wilhelm Vivier, novel Manfred Gregor d Bernhard Wicki ph Gerd Von Bonen m Hans-Martin Majewski

Volker Bohnet, Fritz Wepper, Michael Hinz, Frank Glaubrecht, Karl Michael Balzer, Gunther Hoffman

The Bridge at Remagen*
US 1968 116m De Luxe Panavision
UA / Wolper (David L. Wolper)

February 1945: Germans and Americans fight over a Rhine bridge.
Disenchanted, violent war film in which incessant bang-bang, adroitly staged, is all that matters.

w Richard Yates, William Roberts d John Guillermin ph Stanley Cortez m Elmer Bernstein

George Segal, Robert Vaughn, Ben Gazzara, Bradford Dillman, E. G. Marshall, Peter Van Eyck

'Viable viewing if explosions and clichés are your shtick and exciting if you're not sure who won that war.'—Judith Crist

The Bridge of San Luis Rey*
US 1944 85m bw
(UA) Benedict Bogeaus

Five people die when a Peruvian rope bridge collapses; the film investigates why they were each on the bridge at the time.
An intriguing novel is turned into tedious film drama, with actors, director, scenarist and production designer all making heavy weather.

w Howard Estabrook, novel Thornton Wilder d Rowland V. Lee ph John Boyle m Dmitri Tiomkin

Lynn Bari, Francis Lederer, Nazimova, Louis Calhern, Akim Tamiroff, Blanche Yurka, Donald Woods

† A silent version, with a few minutes of hasty talk, was made in 1929 by Charles Brabin for MGM, from a script by Alice Duer Miller, Ruth Cummings and Marian Ainslee. The cast included Lili Damita, Ernest Torrence, Don Alvarado, Raquel Torres, and Henry B. Walthall.

AAN: Dmitri Tiomkin

The Bridge on the River Kwai***
GB 1957 161m Technicolor
  Cinemascope
Columbia / Sam Spiegel

British POWs in Burma are employed by the Japs to build a bridge; meanwhile British agents seek to destroy it.
Ironic adventure epic with many fine moments but too many centres of interest and an unforgivably confusing climax. It is distinguished by Guinness' portrait of the English CO who is heroic in his initial stand against the Japs but finally cannot bear to see his bridge blown up: and the physical detail of the production is beyond criticism.

w Carl Foreman, novel Pierre Boulle d David Lean ph Jack Hildyard m Malcolm Arnold

Alec Guinness (Colonel Nicholson), Shears (William Holden), Jack Hawkins (Major Warden), Sessue Hayakawa (Colonel Saito), James Donald (Major Clipton), Geoffrey Horne (Lieut. Joyce), Andre Morell (Col. Green), Percy Herbert (Grogan)

'It may rank as the most rousing adventure film inspired by the last World War.'—Alton Cook, New York World Telegram

† Cary Grant was originally sought for the William Holden role.

AA: best picture; Carl Foreman (credited as Michael Wilson); David Lean; Jack Hildyard; Malcolm Arnold; Alec Guinness
AAN: Sessue Hayakawa

Bridge to the Sun*
France / US 1961 112m bw
MGM / Cité Films (Jacques Bar)

Just before Pearl Harbor, an American girl marries a Japanese diplomat and goes to live in Tokyo.
Romantic drama which oddly sides with the Japanese and shows America in a poor light. Interesting if not very compelling, with some unfamiliar views of Japan.

w Charles Kaufman, autobiography Gwendolen Terasaki d Etienne Périer ph Marcel Weiss, Seiichi Kizuka, Bill Kelly m Georges Auric

Carroll Baker, James Shigeta, James Yagi, Tetsuro Tamba

'In yet another burst of national flagellation, Hollywood turns on itself and unthinking Americans for being so beastly about the wartime Japanese.'—MFB

A Bridge Too Far**
US / GB 1977 175m Technicolor
  Panavision
UA / Joseph E. Levine (John Palmer)

The story of the Allied defeat at Arnhem in 1944.
Like all large-scale military films, this one fails to make its tactics clear, and its sober intent conflicts with its roster of guest stars. For all that, there are impressive moments of acting and production.

w William Goldman, book Cornelius Ryan d Richard Attenborough (and Sidney Hayers) ph Geoffrey Unsworth, Harry Waxman, Robin Browne pd Terence Marsh

Dirk Bogarde, James Caan, Michael Caine,
Sean Connery, Edward Fox, Elliott Gould,
Gene Hackman, Anthony Hopkins, Hardy
Kruger, *Laurence Olivier*, Ryan O'Neal,
Robert Redford, Maximilian Schell, Liv
Ullmann, Arthur Hill, Wolfgang Preiss
  'A film too long.'—*Anon.*
  'So wearily, expensively predictable that by
the end the viewer will in all likelihood be too
enervated to notice Attenborough's prosaic
moral epilogue.'—*John Pym, MFB*

● *Video: Intervision*

The Bridges at Toko-Ri*
US 1954   104m   Technicolor
Paramount / Perlberg–Seaton

The comradeship and death of two jet pilots
during the Korean War.
Ambitiously staged action thriller with points
to make about war, death and politics: a
well-worn American formula pitched very
hard.

w Valentine Davies, *novel* James E.
Michener *d* Mark Robson *ph* Loyal Griggs
m Lyn Murray

William Holden, Mickey Rooney, Grace
Kelly, Fredric March, Robert Strauss, Charles
McGraw, Earl Holliman, Willis Bouchey
  'A taut, thrilling, top flight documentary
drama of men, war, ships and planes.'—*Cue*

● *Video: CIC*

Brief Encounter**
GB 1945   86m   bw
Cineguild (Anthony Havelock-Allan, Ronald
Neame)

A suburban housewife on her weekly shopping
visits develops a love affair with a local doctor;
but he gets a job abroad and they agree not to
see each other again.
An outstanding example of good middle-class
cinema turned by sheer professional craft into
a masterpiece; even those bored by the theme
must be riveted by the treatment, especially
the use of a dismal railway station and its
trains.

w Noel Coward, *from his one-act play* Still
Life *d* David Lean *ph* Robert Krasker
m Rachmaninov

Celia Johnson, Trevor Howard, Stanley
Holloway, Joyce Carey, Cyril Raymond
  'Both a pleasure to watch as a well-
controlled piece of work, and deeply
touching.'—*James Agee*
  'Polished as is this film, its strength does not
lie in movie technique, of which there is
plenty, so much as in the tight realism of its
detail.'—*Richard Winnington*
  'A celebrated, craftsmanlike tearjerker, and
incredibly neat. There's not a breath of air in
it.'—*Pauline Kael, 70s*
† A TV film version was made in 1975 by ITC,
starring Richard Burton and Sophia Loren and
directed by Alan Bridges. It was an
unqualified disaster.

AAN: script; David Lean; Celia Johnson

● *Video: Rank*

BRIEF ENCOUNTER.   A kindly gesture leads to unexpected complications. Celia Johnson,
Trevor Howard.

Brigadoon*
US 1954   108m   Anscocolor
  Cinemascope
MGM (Arthur Freed)

Two Americans in Scotland find a ghost village
which awakens only once every hundred years.
Likeable but disappointing adaptation of a
Lost Horizonish Broadway musical, marred by
artificial sets and jaded direction.

w Alan Jay Lerner, *from his play* *d* Vincente
Minnelli *ph* Joseph Ruttenberg *md* Johnny
Green *songs* Frederick Loewe, Alan Jay
Lerner

Gene Kelly, Cyd Charisse, Van Johnson,
Jimmy Thompson, Elaine Stewart, Barry
Jones, Eddie Quillan
  'The whimsical dream world it creates holds
no compelling attractions.'—*Penelope
Houston*

● *Video: MGM / UA*

The Brigand*
US 1952   93m   Technicolor
Columbia

A Moroccan adventurer looks like the king
and is reprieved from execution if he will
impersonate the latter and root out his
enemies.
Cheeky revamp of *The Prisoner of Zenda*,
quite acceptably done.

w Jesse Lasky Jnr *d* Phil Karlson *ph* W.
Howard Greene *m* Mario Castelnuovo-
Tedesco

Anthony Dexter, Jody Lawrance, Gale
Robbins, Anthony Quinn, Carl Benton Reid,
Ron Randell

The Brigand of Kandahar
GB 1965   81m   Technicolor   'Scope
EMI / Hammer (Anthony Nelson Keys)

A cashiered Bengal Lancer officer throws in
his lot with a troublesome bandit.
Feeble frontier adventure with nothing ringing
true.

wd John Gilling *ph* Reg Wyer *m* Don Banks
pd Bernard Robinson

Oliver Reed, Ronald Lewis, Duncan Lamont,
Yvonne Romain, Catherine Woodville, Glyn
Houston

Brigham Young**
US 1940   112m   bw
TCF (Kenneth MacGowan)

The story of the Mormon trek to Utah.
Ambitious but rather dull interpretation of
history, seen as a western with romantic
fictional trimmings.

w Lamar Trotti, *story* Louis Bromfield
d Henry Hathaway *ph* Arthur Miller
m Alfred Newman

Dean Jagger, Tyrone Power, Linda Darnell, Brian Donlevy, Jane Darwell, John Carradine, Mary Astor, Vincent Price, Moroni Olsen

Bright Eyes*
US 1934   84m   bw
TCF

An orphan finds herself torn between foster-parents.
The first of Shirley Temple's genuine star vehicles has a liveliness and cheerfulness hard to find today. As a production, however, it is decidedly economical.
w William Conselman   d David Butler   ph Arthur Miller   m Samuel Kaylin
Shirley Temple, James Dunn, Lois Wilson, *Jane Withers*, Judith Allen
'It seems a cinch to please generally, the family and sentimental strata particularly.'— *Variety*

Bright Leaf
US 1950   110m   bw
Warner (Henry Blanke)

A 19th-century tobacco farmer builds a cigarette empire.
Quite agreeable but disjointed fictional biopic, more about love than tobacco.
w Ranald MacDougall, *novel* Robert Wilder   d Michael Curtiz   ph Karl Freund   m Victor Young
Gary Cooper, Lauren Bacall, Patricia Neal, Jack Carson, Donald Crisp, Gladys George, Elizabeth Patterson, Jeff Corey, Taylor Holmes

Bright Lights*
US 1935   86m   bw

A vaudevillian lets success go to his head. The plot served for a score or more of thirties musicals, but this had Busby Berkeley routines and an unusual star role for Joe E. Brown; with Ann Dvorak, Patricia Ellis, William Gargan. Written by Bert Kalmar and Harry Ruby; directed by Busby Berkeley; for Warner. (GB title: *Funny Face*.) (The same title covered a 1925 MGM silent with Charles Ray as a country boy in love with a Broadway star.) 'Practically an 86-minute monologue, with the star doing everything but taking tickets.'—*Variety*

Bright Road*
US 1953   69m   bw
MGM (Sol Baer Fielding)

In an all-black school, a problem child finds himself when he helps to rid the school of a swarm of bees.
Slight but attractive second feature, unostentatiously set in a black community.
w Emmet Lavery   d Gerald Mayer   ph Alfred Gilks   m David Rose
Dorothy Dandridge, Harry Belafonte, Robert Horton, Philip Hepburn, Barbara Ann Sanders

Bright Victory*
US 1951   97m   bw
Universal (Robert Buckner)
GB title: *Lights Out*

A blinded soldier adjusts to civilian life.
Well-meaning if rather slow and sticky, this drama is more sentimental than realistic but has good performances.
w Robert Buckner, *novel* Bayard Kendrick   d Mark Robson   ph William Daniels   m Frank Skinner
Arthur Kennedy, Peggy Dow, Julia Adams, James Edwards, Will Geer, Minor Watson, Jim Backus
AAN: Arthur Kennedy

Brighton Rock***
GB 1947   92m   bw
Associated British / The Boultings
US title: *Young Scarface*

The teenage leader of a racetrack gang uses a waitress as alibi to cover a murder, and marries her. He later decides to be rid of her, but fate takes a hand in his murder plot.
A properly 'seedy' version of Graham Greene's 'entertainment', very flashily done for the most part but with a trick ending which allows the heroine to keep her illusions.
w Graham Greene, Terence Rattigan   d John Boulting   ph Harry Waxman   m Hans May
Richard Attenborough, Hermione Baddeley, *Harcourt Williams*, William Hartnell, Alan Wheatley, Carol Marsh
'The film is slower, much less compelling, and, if you get me, less cinematic than the book, as a child's guide to which I hereby offer it.'—*Richard Winnington*
'It proceeds with the efficiency, the precision and the anxiety to please of a circular saw.'—*Dilys Powell*
● Video: Thorn EMI

The Brighton Strangler
US 1945   67m   bw

An actor takes over in real life the part he is playing – of a murderer. This hoary plot had seen better days even in 1945, and was not helped by an establishing shot which put Parliament on the wrong side of the Thames. John Loder, June Duprez. Written by Arnold Philips and Max Nosseck; directed by Max Nosseck; for RKO.

Brimstone and Treacle*
GB 1982   87m   Technicolor
Namara / Alan E. Salke / Herbert Solow

A strange young man has a sinister effect on the family of a middle-aged writer of doggerel, whose crippled daughter he finally rapes.
Similar in mood to *Pennies from Heaven*, this is basically a television play very typical of its author. (Some years ago it was taped and then banned by the BBC.) In substance no more than a reversal of *The Passing of the Third Floor Back*, its points of interest are mainly technical.
w Dennis Potter, from his play   d Richard Loncraine   ph Peter Hannan   m Sting   pd Milly Burns

Sting, Denholm Elliott, Joan Plowright, Suzanna Hamilton, Benjamin Whitrow, Dudley Sutton
● Video: Brent Walker

Bring 'Em Back Alive
US 1932   65m   bw

A documentary showing how animal hunter Frank Buck scoured Malayan jungles for specimens to stock the world's zoos. Very dated now, but quite an attraction in its day. The title was used again in 1982 for a TV series in which Bruce Boxleitner played Buck; the emphasis now, however, was on serial-like intrigue. 'Will get money but needs alert exploitation.'—*Variety*

'It's got guts!'
Bring Me the Head of Alfredo Garcia
US 1974   112m   De Luxe
UA / Optimus / Churubusco (Martin Baum)

A wealthy Mexican offers a million dollars for the head of a man who seduced his daughter, and claimants find that grave robbing is involved.
Gruesome, sickly action melodrama with revolting detail; the nadir of a director obsessed by violence.
w Gordon Dawson, Sam Peckinpah   d Sam Peckinpah   ph Alex Phillips Jnr   m Jerry Fielding
Warren Oates, Gig Young, Isela Vega, Robert Webber, Helmut Dantine, Emilio Fernandez, Kris Kristofferson
'Few movies are as tedious. Bring me the head of the studio that released this one.'— *Gene Shalit*
'The only kind of analysis it really invites is psychoanalysis.'—*Wall Street Journal*
'Peckinpah clearly doesn't lack talent—what he lacks is brains.'—*John Simon*

Bring On the Girls
US 1945   92m   Technicolor
Paramount (Fred Kohlmar)

A millionaire joins the navy in the hope that a girl will love him for himself.
A good example of the gaily-coloured but witless drivel which occasionally came out of the big studios towards the end of the war.
w Karl Tunberg, Darrell Ware   d Sidney Lanfield   ph Karl Struss   md Robert Emmett Dolan
Veronica Lake, Eddie Bracken, Sonny Tufts, Marjorie Reynolds, Grant Mitchell, Alan Mowbray, Porter Hall

Bring Your Smile Along
US 1955   83m   Technicolor

A lady schoolteacher goes to New York to write songs. Amiable musical filler with rather flat jokes. Frankie Laine, Keefe Brasselle, Constance Towers, Lucy Marlow. Written and directed by Blake Edwards; for Columbia.

Bringing Up Baby***
US 1938   102m   bw
RKO (Howard Hawks)

A zany girl causes a zoology professor to lose a dinosaur bone and a pet leopard in the same evening.

Outstanding crazy comedy which barely pauses for romance and ends up with the whole splendid cast in jail.

w Dudley Nichols, Hagar Wilde d Howard Hawks ph Russell Metty m Roy Webb

Katharine Hepburn, Cary Grant, May Robson, Charles Ruggles, Walter Catlett, Fritz Feld, Jonathan Hale, Barry Fitzgerald

'Harum-scarum farce comedy . . . definite box-office.'—*Variety*

'I am happy to report that it is funny from the word go, that it has no other meaning to recommend it . . . and that I wouldn't swap it for practically any three things of the current season.'—*Otis Ferguson*

'It may be the American movies' closest equivalent to Restoration comedy.'—*Pauline Kael*

'Crazy comedies continue to become crazier, and there will soon be few actors and actresses left who have no straw in their hair.'—*Basil Wright*

† The dog George was played by Asta from *The Thin Man* movies.

● *Video: Thorn EMI*

Bringing Up Father
US 1928   approx 70m at 24 fps   bw silent

Mild domestic comedy about a henpecked husband, from the famous comic strip; it marked the successful comeback of Marie Dressler (as the maid). J. Farrell MacDonald, Polly Moran, Gertrude Olmsted, Grant Withers. Written by Frances Marion; directed by Jack Conway; for MGM. (Two or three second features about Jiggs and Maggie, featuring Renie Riano and Joe Yule, appeared in the late forties.)

The Brinks Job
US 1978   103m   Technicolor
Universal / Dino de Laurentiis (Ralph Serpe)

In 1944, amateur criminals bring off a raid on the vaults of a Boston security company. Farcical variation of a much-told true tale. Despite much mugging by the stars and a frantic narrative style, it does not come off.

w Walon Green d William Friedkin ph Norman Leigh m Richard Rodney Bennett pd Dean Tavoularis

Peter Falk, Warren Oates, Peter Boyle, Allen Goorwitz, Gena Rowlands, Paul Sorvino, Sheldon Leonard

Britannia Hospital
GB 1982   116m   colour
EMI / Film and General / NFFC (Davina Belling, Clive Parsons)

Problems besetting a British hospital celebrating its 500th anniversary include strikes, demonstrators, and a mad doctor who transplants heads.

Looking as crummy as a Carry On at the end of its tether, this intended lampoon of the state of the nation never warms up and can only fire off stale jokes in all directions while repelling the eye with its Frankenstein scenes.

w David Sherwin d Lindsay Anderson ph Mike Fash pd Norris Spencer m Alan Price

Malcolm McDowell, Leonard Rossiter, Graham Crowden, Fulton Mackay, Vivian Pickles, Joan Plowright, Peter Jeffrey, Robin Askwith, Dandy Nichols, Valentine Dyall, Roland Culver, Alan Bates, Arthur Lowe, Marsha Hunt

'It has all the intensity, along with the flailing incoherence, of a soapbox jeremiah.'—*Richard Combs, MFB*

'Having once created a general shambles, the film is at a loss to clean it up.'—*Margaret Hinxman, Daily Mail*

'Inexplicably muddled and inconclusive.'—*Guardian*

'It mentholates the tubes and oxygenates the brain.'—*Sunday Telegraph*

● *Video: Thorn EMI*

Britannia Mews
GB 1948   91m   bw
TCF (William Perlberg)
US title: *The Forbidden Street*

In Victorian times, the widow of a puppetmaster eventually marries his lookalike who rebuilds their puppet theatre.

Curious and uncertain comedy drama set among yesterday's high society, with poorly played leads but an interesting supporting cast and technical assurance.

w Ring Lardner Jnr, novel Margery Sharp d Jean Negulesco ph Georges Périnal ad Andrei Andreiev m Malcolm Arnold

Dana Andrews, Maureen O'Hara, Sybil Thorndike, Wilfrid Hyde White, Fay Compton, A. E. Matthews

British Agent*
US 1934   75m   bw
Warner (Henry Blanke)

In 1910 Russia, a Britisher falls in love with a lady spy.

Sluggish and dated romantic melodrama, notable only for Howard's performance and some directional felicities.

w Laird Doyle, novel H. Bruce Lockhart d Michael Curtiz ph Ernest Haller ad Anton Grot

Leslie Howard, Kay Francis, William Gargan, Irving Pichel, Philip Reed, Walter Byron, J. Carrol Naish, Halliwell Hobbes

'One of those rare cases of a film both artistically and cinematically good entertainment . . . an exciting story well told, excellent acting, draw names and production value.'—*Variety*

British Intelligence
US 1940   63m   bw
Warner
GB title: *Enemy Agent*

During World War I a German lady spy becomes a guest in the house of a British war official, the butler of which is the leader of a German spy ring.

Second feature remake of *Three Faces East* (qv); still quite an entertaining melodrama.

w Lee Katz, play Anthony Paul Kelly d Terry Morse ph Sid Hickox

Boris Karloff, Margaret Lindsay, Maris Wrixon, Bruce Lester, Leonard Mudie, Holmes Herbert

Broadminded*
US 1931   65m   bw

A bashful swain leaves town after a misunderstanding and becomes involved in an intercontinental chase. Modest star farce with some hilarious moments. Joe E. Brown, Ona Munson, William Collier Jnr, Marjorie White, Holmes Herbert, Bela Lugosi. Written by Bert Kalmar and Harry Ruby; directed by Mervyn Le Roy; for First National. 'Best he has ever done . . . any audience will enjoy it.'—*Variety*

Broadway
US 1942   90m   bw
Universal (Bruce Manning)

George Raft recalls his days as a hoofer in a New York speakeasy, and in particular a murder involving gangsters and chorus girls. Minor crime melodrama which after interminable scene-setting paints an effective picture of the twenties but has too slack a grip on narrative.

w Felix Jackson, John Bright, play Philip Dunning, George Abbott d William A. Seiter ph George Barnes md Charles Previn

George Raft, Pat O'Brien, S. Z. Sakall, Janet Blair, Broderick Crawford, Marjorie Rambeau

Broadway Bad
US 1933   59m   bw

A scheming chorus girl makes a rich marriage. Paper-thin melodrama, one of a hundred on similar lines. Joan Blondell, Ginger Rogers, Ricardo Cortez, Adrienne Ames, Spencer Charters, Donald Crisp. Written by Arthur Kober and Maude Fulton; directed by Sidney Lanfield; for Fox.

Broadway Bill**
US 1934   104m   bw
Columbia (Frank Capra)
GB title: *Strictly Confidential*

A cheerful horse trainer finds he has a winner. Easygoing romantic comedy with the energetic Capra style in fairly full bloom.

w Robert Riskin, story Mark Hellinger d Frank Capra ph Joseph Walker

Warner Baxter, Myrna Loy, Walter Connolly, Helen Vinson, Douglass Dumbrille, Raymond Walburn, Lynne Overman, Clarence Muse, Margaret Hamilton, Paul Harvey, Claude Gillingwater, Charles Lane, Ward Bond

'The effect of capable direction is discernible in every foot.'—*Variety*

'It will be a long day before we see so little made into so much: it is gay and charming and will make you happy, and I am sorry to say I do not know recommendations much higher.'—*Otis Ferguson*

† Remade as *Riding High* (qv).

Broadway Danny Rose*
US 1984 84m De Luxe
Orion (Robert Greenhut)

An artists' agent and former comic falls foul of the Mafia while promoting a client.
Generally appealing comedy-melodrama with rather less self-examination than has latterly been typical of its star.

w,d Woody Allen *ph* Gordon Willis *md* Nick Hyman *pd* Mel Bourne *ed* Susan E. Morse

Woody Allen, Mia Farrow, Nick Apollo Forte, Craig Vandenbergh, Herb Reynolds

Broadway Gondolier
US 1935 98m bw

A taxi driver wants to become a radio singer.
Rather tedious musical with second-rate elements. Dick Powell, Adolphe Menjou, Joan Blondell, Louise Fazenda, the Mills Brothers, Judy Canova, Ted Fiorito and his band. Written by Warren Duff and Sig Herzig; songs by Al Dubin and Harry Warren; directed by Lloyd Bacon; for Warner. 'Loose on story and even lethargic, it holds enough for gate values.'—*Variety*

Broadway Hostess
US 1935 69m bw

A small-town girl becomes a night-club singer.
Modest musical which failed to create a new star. Wini Shaw, Genevieve Tobin, Lyle Talbot, Allen Jenkins, Phil Regan, Marie Wilson, Spring Byington. Written by George Bricker; directed by Frank McDonald; for Warners. 'Adequate for family audience consumption.'—*Variety*

Broadway Limited*
US 1941 75m bw
Hal Roach
GB title: *The Baby Vanishes*

On an express train, a Hollywood publicity stunt backfires.
Wild farce which is not very funny as a whole but has entertaining comic performances.

w Rian James *d* Gordon Douglas *ph* Henry Sharp *m* Charles Previn

Victor McLaglen, Patsy Kelly, *Leonid Kinskey*, Marjorie Woodworth, Dennis O'Keefe, Zasu Pitts, George E. Stone

'The new wonder of the screen!'
Broadway Melody*
US 1929 110m bw (Technicolor scenes)
MGM (Lawrence Weingarten)

Chorus girls try to make it big on Broadway.
The screen's very first musical, exceedingly primitive by the standards of even a year later, but rather endearing and with a splendid score.

w James Gleason, Norman Houston, Edmund Goulding *d* Harry Beaumont *ph* John Arnold *songs* Nacio Herb Brown, Arthur Freed

Charles King, Anita Page, Bessie Love, Jed Prouty, Kenneth Thomson, Mary Doran, Eddie Kane

'A basic story with some sense to it, action, excellent direction, laughs, a tear, a couple of great performances and plenty of sex.'—*Variety*

AAN: best picture; Harry Beaumont; Bessie Love

'You have waited seven years for this!'
Broadway Melody of 1936**
US 1935 103m bw
MGM (John W. Considine Jnr)

A Broadway producer is at loggerheads with a columnist.
Fairly lively musical with lavish numbers.

w Jack McGowan, Sid Silvers, *original story* Moss Hart *d* Roy del Ruth *ph* Charles Rosher *songs* Nacio Herb Brown, Arthur Freed

Jack Benny, Robert Taylor, Una Merkel, *Eleanor Powell*, June Knight, Vilma and Buddy Ebsen, Nick Long Jnr
Songs include 'You Are My Lucky Star'; 'I've Gotta Feelin' You're Foolin''; 'Broadway Rhythm'; 'On a Sunday Afternoon'; 'Sing Before Breakfast'
'Smash musical with strong dancing and comedy framework.'—*Variety*

AAN: best picture; Moss Hart

Broadway Melody of 1938*
US 1937 110m bw
MGM (Jack Cummings)

Backstage problems threaten the opening of a musical show.
Lavish but fairly forgettable musical with top talent.

w Jack McGowan, Sid Silvers *d* Roy del Ruth *ph* William Daniels *songs* Nacio Herb Brown, Arthur Freed

Eleanor Powell, George Murphy, *Sophie Tucker*, Judy Garland, Robert Taylor, Buddy Ebsen, Sid Silvers, Billy Gilbert, Raymond Walburn

Songs include 'Your Broadway and My Broadway'; 'A Pair of New Shoes'; 'Yours and Mine'; 'Sun Showers'; 'I'm Feeling Like a Million'
'Explosion in the cash drawers . . . will do smash business everywhere.'—*Variety*

Broadway Melody of 1940*
US 1939 102m bw
MGM (Jack Cummings)

A dance team gets to the top.
Splendidly produced but thinly plotted extravaganza with good numbers.

w Leon Gordon, George Oppenheimer *d* Norman Taurog *ph* Oliver T. Marsh, Joseph Ruttenberg *songs* Cole Porter

Fred Astaire, Eleanor Powell, George Murphy, Douglas Macphail, Florence Rice, Frank Morgan, Ian Hunter

Broadway Musketeers
US 1938 62m bw

Three girls from the same orphanage meet again in New York. Uninspired remake of *Three on a Match*. Ann Sheridan, Marie Wilson, Margaret Lindsay, John Litel, Dick Purcell. Written by Don Ryan and Ken Gamet; directed by John Farrow; for Bryan Foy / Warner. 'A programmer of average distinction . . . ought to get by satisfactorily.'—*Variety*

Broadway Rhythm*
US 1943 113m Technicolor
MGM (Jack Cummings)

Originally intended as *Broadway Melody of 1944*, this putting-on-a-show extravaganza had only the numbers to commend it.

w Dorothy Kingsley, Harry Clark, from the Kern / Hammerstein operetta Very Warm for May *d* Roy del Ruth *ph* Leonard Smith *songs* various

George Murphy, Ginny Simms, Charles Winninger, Gloria de Haven, Lena Horne, Nancy Walker, Hazel Scott, Eddie Anderson, Ben Blue, Tommy Dorsey and his Orchestra
'It contains perhaps three minutes of good acrobatic dancing and lasts nearly two hours.'—*James Agee*

Broadway Serenade
US 1939 114m bw
MGM (Robert Z. Leonard)
GB title: *Serenade*

Career problems split the marriage of a songwriter and his singing wife.
Lavish but rather dull romantic drama with music.

w Charles Lederer, Lew Lipton, John T. Foote, Hans Kraly *d* Robert Z. Leonard *ph* Oliver T. Marsh *md* Herbert Stothart

Jeanette MacDonald, Lew Ayres, Frank Morgan, Ian Hunter, Rita Johnson, Virginia Grey, William Gargan, Katherine Alexander
Songs include 'No Time to Argue'; 'Time Changes Everything but Love'; 'For Every Lonely Heart'; 'Broadway Serenade'; 'High Flyin''; 'One Look at You'
'With all its lavishness, it impresses as only mild box office material.'—*Variety*

Broadway thru a Keyhole*
US 1933 90m bw
UA / William Goetz, Raymond Griffith

A tough New York gangster falls for a singer in his nightclub.
Reputed acid observation of the New York scene distinguishes this low-budget gangster drama.

w Gene Towne and Graham Baker *story* Walter Winchell *d* Lowell Sherman *ph* Barney McGill *songs* Mack Gordon, Harry Revel

Constance Cummings, Russ Columbo, Paul Kelly, *Blossom Seeley*, Gregory Ratoff, *Texas Guinan*, Hobart Cavanaugh, C. Henry Gordon
  'Not a big picture, but good entertainment.'—*Variety*

Broadway to Hollywood
US 1933 90m bw

A vaudeville family makes it in movies. Cliché-strewn rags-to-riches saga with songs; good moments. Frank Morgan, Alice Brady, Jackie Cooper, Madge Evans, Jimmy Durante, Nelson Eddy, May Robson, Una Merkel, Mickey Rooney. Written and directed by Willard Mack; for MGM. (GB title: *Ring Up the Curtain*.) 'A saga of the theatre that will please.'—*Variety*
† Some material was salvaged from an abandoned MGM musical of 1929, *The March of Time*.

Broken Arrow*
US 1950 92m Technicolor
TCF (Julian Blaustein)

A US army scout brings about peace between white man and Apache.
Solemn western which at the time was acclaimed for giving the Indian's point of view (something which had scarcely happened since silent days). As entertainment it was not exciting, but it set Jeff Chandler off on a career playing Cochise with variations, and a TV series of the same name surfaced in 1956.
w Michael Blankfort, *novel* Blood Brother by Elliott Arnold *d* Delmer Daves *ph* Ernest Palmer *m* Hugo Friedhofer *md* Alfred Newman

James Stewart, Jeff Chandler, Debra Paget, Basil Ruysdael, Will Geer, Arthur Hunnicutt, Jay Silverheels
  'It has probably done more to soften racial hostilities than most movies designed to instruct, indict and inspire.'—*Pauline Kael*
AAN: Michael Blankfort; Ernest Palmer; Jeff Chandler

Broken Blossoms**
US 1919 105m (16 fps) bw
UA / D. W. Griffith

In slummy Limehouse, a young Chinaman loves the daughter of a brute, who kills her; the Chinaman then kills him and commits suicide.
Victorian-style melodrama presented by Griffith with all the stops out; sometimes striking, but very dated even on its first appearance.
wd D. W. Griffith, *story* The Chink and the Child in Thomas Burke's Limehouse Nights *ph* G. W. Bitzer

Lillian Gish, Donald Crisp, Richard Barthelmess
  'This is a Limehouse which neither Mr Burke nor anybody else who knows his East End of London will be able to recognize . . . but *Broken Blossoms* is a genuine attempt to bring real tragedy onto the screen as opposed to machine-made drama, and for that Mr Griffith deserves the thanks of all who are

convinced of the potentialities of the film.'—*The Times*
  'I know of no other picture in which so much screen beauty is obtained . . . attributable to the Whistlerian fogs and shadows, with that dock in Limehouse recurring like some pedal point.'—*James Agate, 1928*
† Leslie Henson appeared in a parody, *Broken Bottles*, in 1920.

Broken Blossoms*
GB 1936 84m bw
Twickenham (Julius Hagen)

A remake originally intended to be directed by Griffith. Quite stylish, and in some ways more interesting than its predecessor.
w Emlyn Williams *d* John Brahm *ph* Curt Courant

Dolly Haas, Arthur Margetson, Emlyn Williams, Donald Calthrop, Ernest Sefton, Kathleen Harrison, Basil Radford
  'There isn't much reason for this one.'—*Variety*

Broken Journey
GB 1948 89m bw
Gainsborough (Sydney Box)

A plane crashes in the Alps, and the survivors take different attitudes to their situation.
Unpersuasive and stagey melodrama which wastes some good talent.
w Robert Westerby *d* Ken Annakin *ph* Jack Cox *m* John Greenwood

Phyllis Calvert, James Donald, Margot Grahame, Francis L. Sullivan, Raymond Huntley, Derek Bond, Guy Rolfe, David Tomlinson

Broken Lance*
US 1954 96m De Luxe Cinemascope
TCF (Sol C. Siegel)

An autocratic cattle baron causes dissension among his sons.
Western remake of *House of Strangers*, quite well done.
w Richard Murphy, *original story* Philip Yordan *d* Edward Dmytryk *ph* Joe MacDonald *m* Leigh Harline

Spencer Tracy, Richard Widmark, Robert Wagner, Jean Peters, Katy Jurado, Earl Holliman, Hugh O'Brian, Eduard Franz, E. G. Marshall

AA: Philip Yordan
AAN: Katy Jurado

Broken Lullaby*
US 1931 77m bw
Paramount
GB and original title: *The Man I Killed*

A young Frenchman goes to Germany to seek out the family of the man he killed in the war, and is accepted by them as a friend.
This most untypical Lubitsch film now seems very dated but was deeply felt at the time and has plenty of cinematic grip.
w Ernest Vajda, Samson Raphaelson, *play* L'Homme que J'ai Tué by Maurice Rostand *d* Ernst Lubitsch *ph* Victor Milner *ad* Hans Dreier

Lionel Barrymore, Phillips Holmes, Nancy Carroll, Tom Douglas, Zasu Pitts, Lucien Littlefield, Lois Carver, Emma Dunn
  'Well made, but heavy themes and actionless . . . hardly attuned to film patronage as a whole.'—*Variety*
  'The best talking picture that has yet been seen and heard.'—*Robert E. Sherwood*
  'I cannot remember a film so beautifully made, so completely fine in its execution.'—*John Grierson*
  'Lubitsch can't entirely escape his own talent, and the film is beautifully crafted, but he mistook drab, sentimental hokum for ironic, poetic tragedy.'—*Pauline Kael, 70s*

The Broken Wing
US 1932 71m bw
Paramount

A Mexican girl jilts a bandit for an American pilot.
Hokey romantic melodrama.
w Gordon Jones, William Slavens McNutt, *play* Paul Dickey, Charles Goddard *d* Lloyd Corrigan *ph* Henry Sharp

Lupe Velez, Leo Carrillo, Melvyn Douglas, George Barbier, Willard Robertson
  'Too much of a monologue to get far as a talker. Entire first half is just a stage-setter for what follows, and what follows isn't important.'—*Variety*

Bronco Billy*
US 1980 116m De Luxe Panavision
Warner / Second Street (Neal Dubrovsky, Dennis Hackin)

A New Jersey shoe salesman takes over a rundown wild west show.
Enjoyable, sentimental, satirical comedy which unaccountably let down its star's box office record.
w Dennis Hackin *d* Clint Eastwood *ph* David Worth *md* Snuff Garrett, Steve Dorff *ad* Eugene Lourie

Clint Eastwood, Sondra Locke, Geoffrey Lewis, Scatman Crothers, Bill McKinney, Sam Bottoms
  'Eastwood seems to have most enjoyed toying with some distinctly old-fashioned materials: a runaway heiress, a murder plot that isn't, some consequent punning on points of identity, and the most mischievously brittle set of greedy Eastern sophisticates since Frank Capra.'—*Richard Combs, MFB*
● Video: Warner

Bronco Buster
US 1952 80m Technicolor

A champion rodeo rider meets a challenge from a younger man. Totally routine programmer. John Lund, Scott Brady, Joyce Holden, Chill Wills, Don Haggerty. Written by Horace McCoy and Lillie Hayward; directed by Budd Boetticher; for Ted Richmond / Universal-International.

The Brood
Canada 1979 91m colour

The rage of a mentally disturbed woman produces homicidal 'babies'. Idiotic and repellent shocker. Oliver Reed, Samantha Eggar, Art Hindle, Cindy Hinds. Written and directed by David Cronenberg; for Mutual / Elgin.

Broth of a Boy
Eire 1958 77m bw
Emmet Dalton (Alec Snowden)

TV covers the village festivities celebrating an old poacher's 110th birthday.
Mildly amusing regional comedy.

w Patrick Kirwan, Blanaid Irvine, *play* The Big Birthday by Hugh Leonard d George Pollock ph Walter J. Harvey m Stanley Black

Barry Fitzgerald, June Thorburn, Tony Wright, Harry Brogan, Eddie Golden, Maire Kean, Godfrey Quigley, Dermot Kelly

Brother Can You Spare a Dime?
GB 1975 109m bw

A 'documentary' picture of America in the thirties, attempted by an apparently random collage of newsreel and feature film extracts, sometimes difficult to tell one from the other. Sometimes entertaining but mainly unpardonable. Written and directed by Philippe Mora; for VPS / Goodtimes.

The Brother from Another Planet
US 1984 108m Movielab

An alien lands in Harlem and is protected by locals from the horrors he finds there. Moderately amusing combination of science fiction, farce and satire, which outstays its welcome by at least half an hour. Joe Morton, Tom Wright, Caroline Aaron, Randy Sue Carter. Written and directed by John Sayles; for A-Train Films.

Brother John*
US 1970 94m Eastmancolor
Columbia / E and R (Joel Glickman)

A mysterious black man comes to town for a family funeral and is suspected by the townsfolk of various sinister motives, but when they imprison him he is freed by a sympathizer.
The humans are all mean-minded, the saintly visitor is either Christ or an emissary from another planet. Either way, we have been here before, but although this little fantasy has nothing clear to say on the surface, it is quite enjoyable on the surface.

w Ernest Kinoy d James Goldstone
ph Gerald Perry Finnerman m Quincy Jones

Sidney Poitier, Bradford Dillman, Will Geer, Beverly Todd, Ramon Pieri, Warren J. Kemmerling, Paul Winfield, Lincoln Kilpatrick

'It starts out as an engaging mystery with sociological overtones but ends up as a muddle-headed doomsday parable.'—*Judith Crist, 1977*

Brother Orchid*
US 1940 91m bw
Warner (Hal B. Wallis)

A gangster, 'taken for a ride' by his former friends, escapes and becomes a monk. Rather uneasy blend of comedy, drama and religion, with some good scenes.

w Earl Baldwin, *story* Richard Connell
d Lloyd Bacon ph Tony Gaudio m Heinz Roemheld

Edward G. Robinson, Humphrey Bogart, Donald Crisp, Ann Sothern, Ralph Bellamy, Allen Jenkins, Cecil Kellaway

Brother Rat*
US 1938 89m bw
Warner (Robert Lord)

Fun and games with the cadets at a military academy.
Brisk but dated farce from a highly successful Broadway original; remade as *About Face*.

w Richard Macaulay, Jerry Wald, *play* Fred Finklehoffe, John Monks d William Keighley ph Ernest Haller

Wayne Morris, Eddie Albert, Ronald Reagan, Priscilla Lane, Jane Bryan, Jane Wyman, Johnnie Davis, Henry O'Neill

'Exhibs who dig into exploitation fields will hit paydirt.'—*Variety*

Brother Rat and a Baby
US 1939 87m bw
Warner (Robert Lord)
GB title: *Baby Be Good*

Scatty follow-up to the above, with the cadets graduating.

w Jerry Wald, Richard Macauley d Ray Enright ph Charles Rosher

Wayne Morris, Eddie Albert, Ronald Reagan, Priscilla Lane, Jane Wyman, Jane Bryan, Arthur Treacher, Moroni Olsen

Brother Sun, Sister Moon
GB / Italy 1972 122m Technicolor Panavision
Paramount / Vic Films / Euro International (Luciano Perugia)

The life of Francis of Assisi.
Good-looking but relentlessly boring view of a medieval saint as a kind of early flower person.

w Suso Cecchi d'Amico, Kenneth Ross, Lina Wertmuller, Franco Zeffirelli d Franco Zeffirelli ph Ennio Guarnieri m Donovan

Graham Faulkner, Judi Bowker, Alec Guinness (as Pope Innocent III), Leigh Lawson, Kenneth Cranham, Lee Montague, Valentina Cortese

'If I were Pope, I would burn it.'—*Stanley Kauffmann*

The Brotherhood*
US 1968 96m Technicolor
Paramount / Brotherhood Company (Kirk Douglas)

A Mafia executive welcomes his younger brother into the syndicate, but is finally executed by him.

Dour melodrama with tragic pretensions: well made but rather tedious and violent.

w Lewis John Carlino d Martin Ritt ph Boris Kaufman m Lalo Schifrin

Kirk Douglas, Alex Cord, *Luther Adler*, Irene Papas, Susan Strasberg, Murray Hamilton, Eduardo Ciannelli

The Brotherhood of Satan*
US 1970 93m Techniscope
Columbia / LQJAF / Four Star Excelsior (L. Q. Jones, Alvy Moore)

A village is isolated by an outbreak of diabolism.
Fresh and intriguing minor horror film with imaginative touches.

w William Welch d Bernard McEveety
ph John Arthur Morril m Jaime Mendoza-Nava

Strother Martin, L. Q. Jones, Charles Bateman, Anna Capri, Charles Robinson, Alvy Moore, Geri Reischl

The Brothers**
GB 1947 98m bw
GFD / Sydney Box

An orphan girl comes to a Skye fishing family at the turn of the century, and causes superstition, sexual jealousy and tragedy. Wildly melodramatic but good-looking open-air melodrama, a surprising and striking British film of its time.

w Muriel and Sydney Box, *novel* L. A. G. Strong d David Macdonald ph Stephen Dade

Patricia Roc, Maxwell Reed, *Duncan Macrae* (a splendidly malevolent performance), Will Fyffe, Andrew Crawford, Finlay Currie

'Heavy breathing, heavier dialect, and any number of quaint folk customs . . . the island and its actual inhabitants are all right; the rest is Mary Webb with hair on her chest.'—*James Agee*

Brothers in Law*
GB 1957 97m bw
British Lion / the Boultings

A young barrister has comic misdemeanours in and out of court.
The lighter side of the law, from a bestseller by a judge; mechanically amusing and not in the same street as its predecessor *Private's Progress*, though it seemed hilarious at the time.

w Roy Boulting, Frank Harvey, Jeffrey Dell, *novel* Henry Cecil d John Boulting ph Max Greene m Benjamin Frankel

Ian Carmichael, Terry-Thomas, Richard Attenborough, *Miles Malleson, Eric Barker*, Irene Handl, John Le Mesurier, Olive Sloane, Kynaston Reeves

The Brothers Karamazov*
US 1958 146m Metrocolor
MGM / Avon (Pandro S. Berman)

In 19th-century Russia, the father of three sons is murdered and the wrong brother is found guilty.

Decent but decidedly unenthralling Hollywood compression of a classic, faithful to the letter but not the spirit of the book, and with few memorable moments or performances.

w Richard Brooks, novel Fedor Dostoievsky d Richard Brooks ph John Alton m Bronislau Kaper ad William A. Horning, Paul Groesse

Yul Brynner, Maria Schell, Richard Basehart, Claire Bloom, Lee J. Cobb, Albert Salmi, William Shatner, Judith Evelyn
† In 1968 came Ivan Pyryev's massive 220m Russian version, little seen in the west. See also The Murder of Dmitri Karamazov.
AAN: Lee J. Cobb

The Brothers Rico
US 1957   91m   bw
Columbia / William Goetz (Lewis J. Rachmil)

An accountant fails to retrieve his brothers from a life of crime.
Moderate gangster fare with good credentials but more talk than action.

w Lewis Meltzer, Ben Perry, novel Georges Simenon d Phil Karlson ph Burnett Guffey m George Duning

Richard Conte, James Darren, Dianne Foster, Kathryn Grant, Larry Gates, Lamont Johnson, Harry Bellaver

Brown of Harvard
US 1926   approx 70m at 24 fps   bw
silent

Two college students, one academic and one sporty, love the same girl. Best-known version of a 1909 play first filmed in 1917: archetypal campus drama. William Haines, Jack Pickford, Mary Brian. Written by Donald Ogden Stewart and A. P. Younger, from a play by Rida Johnson Young; directed by Jack Conway; for MGM.

Brown on Resolution*
GB 1935   80m   bw
Gaumont (Michael Balcon)
Later retitled: Forever England; US title: Born for Glory

In the 1914 war in the Mediterranean, a seaman holds a German warship at bay with a rifle.
Uneasy amalgam of adventure heroics and character study, interesting for its effort. Remade as Singlehanded (qv).

w Michael Hogan, Gerard Fairlie, J. O. C. Orton, novel C. S. Forester d Walter Forde ph Bernard Knowles

John Mills, Betty Balfour, Barry Mackay, Jimmy Hanley, Howard Marion Crawford, H. G. Stoker
'A milestone in British pictures . . . an attractive and interesting feature anywhere.'—Variety

The Browning Version*
GB 1951   90m   bw
GFD / Javelin (Teddy Baird)

Retiring through ill health, a classics master finds that he is hated by his unfaithful wife, his

headmaster and his pupils. An unexpected act of kindness gives him courage to face the future.
A rather thin extension of a one-act play, capped by a thank-you speech which is wildly out of character. Dialogue and settings are smooth, but the actors are not really happy with their roles.

w Terence Rattigan, from his play d Anthony Asquith ph Desmond Dickinson

Michael Redgrave, Jean Kent, Nigel Patrick, Wilfrid Hyde White, Bill Travers, Ronald Howard
'If the sustained anguish of the role does not allow Redgrave a great deal of room to move around in, it does give him a chance to show what he can do in tight quarters, and that, it turns out, is considerable.'—Pauline Kael, 70s

Brubaker*
US 1980   130m   De Luxe
TCF (Ron Silverman)

A new governor fails to make much headway with his reform plan at Wakefield Prison Farm.
Fairly brutal but unsurprising prison drama which takes itself somewhat too seriously.

w W. D. Richter d Stuart Rosenberg ph Bruno Nuytten m Lalo Schifrin

Robert Redford, Yaphet Kotto, Jane Alexander, Murray Hamilton, David Keith, Morgan Freeman
'It's hard to imagine a broad audience wanting to share the two hours of agony.'—Variety

AAN: screenplay

● Video: CBS / Fox

Brushfire!
US 1961   80m   bw

Planters in south-east Asia are attacked by rebel forces. Exploitation melodrama with a flat-footed script. John Ireland, Jo Morrow, Everett Sloane, Al Avalon, Carl Esmond. Written by Irwin R. Blacker; directed and produced by Jack Warner Jnr; for Obelisk / Paramount.

The Brute*
Mexico 1952   83m   bw
International Cinematografica
original title: El Bruto

Victimized slum tenants call for help to a slow-witted giant, who kills the landlord and falls in love with his daughter.
Eccentric melodrama which doesn't quite seem to make its point.

wd Luis Bunuel ph Augustin Jiminez m Rafael Larista

Pedro Armendariz, Katy Jurado, Rosita Arenas, Andres Soler

Brute Force**
US 1947   96m   bw
U-I (Mark Hellinger)

Six violent convicts revolt against a sadistic warden and try to escape.

Vivid and rather repellent prison melodrama leading up to an explosive climax; its savagery seemed at the time to break fresh ground.

w Richard Brooks d Jules Dassin ph William Daniels m Miklos Rozsa

Burt Lancaster, Charles Bickford, Hume Cronyn, Ella Raines, Yvonne de Carlo

The Brute Man
US 1946   60m   bw

A disfigured paranoic is helped by a blind pianist and kills again to help her. Schlock horror programmer. Rondo Hatton, Tom Neal, Jane Adams. Written by George Bricker and M. Coates Webster; directed by Jean Yarborough; for Universal (who were so ashamed of it that they farmed it out to PRC).

The Buccaneer*
US 1937   125m   bw
Paramount (Cecil B. de Mille)

During the 1812 war, pirate Jean Lafitte helps president Andrew Jackson to repel the British. Sprightly adventure romance with generally good production and acting.

w Jeanie Macpherson, Edwin Justus Mayer, Harold Lamb, C. Gardner Sullivan d Cecil B. de Mille ph Victor Milner md Boris Morros m Georges Antheil

Fredric March, Franciska Gaal, Akim Tamiroff, Margot Grahame, Walter Brennan, Ian Keith, Spring Byington, Douglass Dumbrille, Robert Barrat, Hugh Sothern, Beulah Bondi, Anthony Quinn, Montagu Love
'A cinch for big box-office returns around the world.'—Variety
'From de Mille's skilled craftsmanship have come other pictures quite as ambitious, none more adroitly fabricated, skilfully adjusted to the norm of appeal to the world audience that such imposing and costly productions must command.'—Terry Ramsaye
AAN: Victor Milner

The Buccaneer
US 1958   121m   Technicolor
Vistavision
Paramount / Cecil B. de Mille (Henry Wilcoxon)

Slow, slack and stolid remake of the 1938 film, with practically no excitement or interest and very obvious studio sets.

w Jesse L. Lasky Jnr, Berenice Mosk, from the earlier screenplay d Anthony Quinn ph Loyal Griggs m Elmer Bernstein

Yul Brynner, Claire Bloom, Charles Boyer, Inger Stevens, Henry Hull, Charlton Heston, E. G. Marshall, Douglass Dumbrille, Lorne Greene, Ted de Corsia, Robert F. Simon

Buccaneer's Girl
US 1949   77m   Technicolor

A New Orleans entertainer helps to free a pirate who was her friend. Cheerful action programmer. Yvonne de Carlo, Philip Friend, Robert Douglas, Elsa Lanchester. Written by Harold Shumate and Joseph Hoffman; directed by Frederick de Cordova; for Universal-International.

Buchanan Rides Alone
US 1958 78m colour

A wandering Texan helps a young Mexican accused of murder. Very moderate star western. Randolph Scott, Craig Stevens, Barry Kelley, Peter Whitney. Written by Charles Lang; directed by Budd Boetticher; for Columbia.

Buck and the Preacher
US 1971 103m colour
Columbia / E and R / Belafonte (Joel Glickman)

Nightriders chasing escaped slaves are outwitted by a wagon train guide and a con man.
Lively, easygoing western with a largely black cast, and a message of militancy sugar-coated by Hollywood hokum.

w Ernest Kinoy d Sidney Poitier ph Alex Phillips m Benny Carter

Sidney Poitier, Harry Belafonte, Ruby Dee, Cameron Mitchell, Denny Miller, Nita Talbot, John Kelly

Buck Privates*
US 1941 84m bw
Universal (Alex Gottlieb)
GB title: *Rookies*

Two incompetents in the army accidentally become heroes.
Abbott and Costello's first starring vehicle is a tired bundle of army jokes and old routines separated by plot and romance, but it sent the comedians right to the top, where they stayed for ten years.

w Arthur T. Horman d Arthur Lubin ph Milton Krasner md Charles Previn

Bud Abbott, Lou Costello, Lee Bowman, Alan Curtis, Jane Frazee, The Andrews Sisters, Nat Pendleton, Samuel S. Hinds, Shemp Howard

AAN: Charles Previn; song 'The Boogie Woogie Bugle Boy of Company B' (m Hugh Prince, ly Don Raye)

Buck Privates Come Home
US 1946 77m bw
U-I (Robert Arthur)
GB title: *Rookies Come Home*

Incompetent war veterans are demobilized and find civilian life tough.
Thin star comedy with a good final chase.

w John Grant, Frederic I. Rinaldo, Robert Lees d Charles T. Barton ph Charles Van Enger

Bud Abbott, Lou Costello, Beverly Simmons, Tom Brown, Nat Pendleton

A Bucket of Blood
US 1959 65m bw

A waiter becomes a renowned sculptor when he hits on the idea of moulding clay round corpses. Heavy-handed spoof with a few choice if bloody moments. Dick Miller, Barboura Morris, Anthony Carbone, Ed Nelson. Written by Charles B. Griffith; directed and produced by Roger Corman; for American International.

Buckskin
US 1968 97m Pathecolor
Paramount / A. C. Lyles

In the frontier town of Gloryhole a gambler is routed by the new marshal.
Routine old-fashioned western with this producer's predictable gallery of weatherbeaten familiar faces.

w Michael Fisher d Michael Moore ph W. Wallace Kelley m Jimmie Haskell

Barry Sullivan, Joan Caulfield, Lon Chaney Jnr, John Russell, Richard Arlen, Barbara Hale, Bill Williams, Barton Maclane

Buckskin Frontier
US 1943 75m bw

In the 1860s, cattle empires are born as the railroad stretches west. Ambitious mini-western; a bit stodgy. Richard Dix, Jane Wyatt, Lee J. Cobb, Albert Dekker, Victor Jory. Written by Norman Houston, from the novel *Buckskin Empire* by Harry Sinclair Drago; directed by Lesley Selander; for United Artists / George Sherman. (GB title: *The Iron Road.*)

Buddy Buddy
US 1981 96m Metrocolor Panavision
MGM (Jay Weston)

A hit man on a job is hampered by a woebegone fellow intent on committing suicide.
Painful remake of the French *L'Emmerdeur* (A Pain in the A . . .). Lugubriously funny at times, but generally much less attractive than the original.

w Billy Wilder, I. A. L. Diamond, play Francis Veber d Billy Wilder ph Harry Stradling Jnr m Lalo Schifrin pd Daniel A. Lomino

Walter Matthau, Jack Lemmon, Paula Prentiss, Klaus Kinski, Dana Elcar
'The saddest episode in Wilder's career.'— *Richard Combs, MFB*

The Buddy Holly Story
US 1978 113m colour
Columbia / Innavisions / ECA (Fred Bauer)

The life of a fifties rock-and-roller who died young in an accident.
Solidly carpentered showbiz biopic for the youth market.

w Robert Gitler d Steve Rash ph Stevan Larner md Joe Renzetti

Gary Busey, Dan Stroud, Charles Martin Smith, Bill Jordan, Maria Rochwine
'A B movie leavened by grade-A talent.'— *Les Keyser, Hollywood in the Seventies*

AA: Joe Renzetti
AAN: Gary Busey

Buffalo Bill*
US 1944 89m Technicolor
TCF (Harry Sherman)

A moderately fictitious account of the life of William Cody, from buffalo hunter to wild west showman.

Easygoing entertainment which turns from western excitements to domestic drama. Generally watchable.

w Aeneas Mackenzie, Clements Ripley, Cecile Kramer d William Wellman ph Leon Shamroy m David Buttolph

Joel McCrea, Maureen O'Hara, Linda Darnell, Thomas Mitchell, Edgar Buchanan, Anthony Quinn, Moroni Olsen

Buffalo Bill and the Indians, or Sitting Bull's History Lesson
US 1976 118m colour Panavision
UA / Robert Altman

During winter camp for his wild west show, Buffalo Bill Cody and his friends discuss life and his own myth.
Anti-action, alienation-effect talk piece which has some points of interest for sophisticates but is likely to set western addicts asking for their money back.

w Alan Rudolph, Robert Altman, play Indians by Arthur Kopit d Robert Altman ph Paul Lohmann m Richard Baskin

Paul Newman, Burt Lancaster, Joel Grey, Kevin McCarthy, Geraldine Chaplin, Harvey Keitel, John Considine, Denver Pyle
'The western is an enormously resilient form, but never has that resilience been tested quite so much as in this movie . . . it isn't really a movie, it's a happening.'—*Arthur Knight*
'Whereas Kopit's play offered a hallucinatory mosaic, Altman's script has the one-dimensional clarity of a cartoon.'— *Michael Billington, Illustrated London News*
'That American history is the creation of flamboyant lies and showmanship strikes us at first as an amusing trifle and then quickly becomes an epigram shaggy-dogging its way across two hours of eccentric Altmanship.'— *Will Aitken, Take One*

● *Video: Thorn EMI*

Buffet Froid
France 1979 93m Eastmancolor
Sara Films / Antenne 2 (Alain Sarde)
US title: *Cold Cuts*

A police inspector joins up with two new acquaintances: they discover that they all like killing people.
Satirical black comedy which goes on a little too long for its own good; invention gives way to glumness.

wd Bertrand Blier ph Jean Penzer m classical extracts

Gérard Depardieu, Bernard Blier, Jean Carmet, Geneviève Page

Bug
US 1975 101m Movielab
Paramount / William Castle

Large rocklike insects appear after an earthquake and set fire to themselves and their victims.
Absurd, overlong and rather nasty horror film with no visible redeeming features.

w William Castle, Thomas Page, *novel* The Hephaestus Plague by Thomas Page *d* Jeannot Szwarc *ph* Michel Hugo, Ken Middleham *m* Charles Fox

Bradford Dillman, Joanna Miles, Richard Gilliland, Jamie Smith Jackson, Alan Fudge, Patty McCormack

'The finer scientific points are to say the least elusive.'—*David Robinson*

● *Video: CIC*

The Bugle Sounds
US1941 101m bw
MGM (J. Walter Ruben)

An old cavalry sergeant, discharged for insubordination, rounds up fifth columnists and is reinstated.
Ho-hum star vehicle on familiar lines but at undue length.

w Cyril Hume *d* S. Sylvan Simon *ph* Clyde de Vinna *m* Lennie Hayton

Wallace Beery, Marjorie Main, Lewis Stone, George Bancroft, William Lundigan, Henry O'Neill, Donna Reed, Chill Wills, Roman Bohnen, Jerome Cowan, Tom Dugan, Guinn Williams, Jonathan Hale.

Bugles in the Afternoon
US 1952 85m Technicolor
William Cagney

In the US army at the time of Custer's last stand, a young officer is victimized by a jealous rival.
Modest, adequate western with nice scenery but no surprises.

w Geoffrey Homes, Harry Brown, *novel* Ernest Haycox *d* Roy Rowland *ph* Wilfrid Cline *m* Dmitri Tiomkin

Ray Milland, Hugh Marlowe, Helena Carter, Forrest Tucker, Barton Maclane, George Reeves, James Millican, Gertrude Michael

Bugsy Malone**
GB 1976 93m Eastmancolor •
Rank / Bugsy Malone Productions (David Puttnam, Allan Marshall)

New York 1929: gangster Fat Sam fights it out with Dandy Dan, and the best man wins the girl.
Extremely curious musical gangster spoof with all the parts played by children and the guns shooting ice cream. Very professionally done, but one wonders to whom it is supposed to appeal.

wd Alan Parker *ph* Michael Seresin, Peter Biziou *m / songs* Paul Williams *pd* Geoffrey Kirkland

Scott Baio, Jodie Foster, Florrie Digger, John Cassisi

'If for nothing else, you would have to admire it for the sheer doggedness of its eccentricity.'—*David Robinson, The Times*
'All the pizazz in the world couldn't lift it above the level of empty camp.'—*Frank Rich, New York Post*
'I only wish the British could make adult movies as intelligent as this one.'—*Michael Billington, Illustrated London News*

AAN: Paul Williams

● *Video: Rank*

Bulldog Drummond*
US 1929 90m bw
Samuel Goldwyn

After advertising for adventure, ex-war hero Drummond is approached by an American girl whose uncle is being held prisoner in a fake nursing home by villainous Carl Petersen.
This is the closest the screen ever came to the original Drummond character, debonair yet taking personal and unnecessary vengeance on the chief villain. A fairly primitive talkie with little movement, yet consistently interesting.

w Sidney Howard, *play* 'Sapper' (H. C. McNeile) *d* F. Richard Jones *ph* George Barnes, Gregg Toland *ad* William Cameron Menzies

Ronald Colman, Joan Bennett, *Claud Allister* (as Algy), Lilyan Tashman, Montagu Love, Lawrence Grant

AA: William Cameron Menzies
AAN: Ronald Colman

Bulldog Drummond Strikes Back*
US 1934 83m bw
UA / Twentieth Century (Darryl F. Zanuck)

Drummond gets married, but delays his honeymoon to investigate a mysterious London house with a disappearing body.
Slow-starting, then intriguing light mystery which becomes repetitive and silly.
Performances and production enjoyable.

w Nunnally Johnson *d* Roy del Ruth *ph* Peverell Marley *m* Alfred Newman

Ronald Colman, Loretta Young, C. Aubrey Smith, *Charles Butterworth* (Algy), Warner Oland, Mischa Auer, Una Merkel

'Zippy, snappy comedy melodrama with a swashbuckling flavour. Packed with what it takes.'—*Variety*

† The full complement of Drummond films is as follows:
BULLDOG DRUMMOND (GB 1922); silent with Carlyle Brackwell.
THE THIRD ROUND (GB 1925); silent with Jack Buchanan.
BULLDOG DRUMMOND (US 1929); see above.
TEMPLE TOWER (US 1930); lost Fox film with Kenneth MacKenna.
THE RETURN OF BULLDOG DRUMMOND (GB 1934); perhaps the most Fascist of the series, with Ralph Richardson.
BULLDOG JACK (GB 1934); amiable spoof with Jack Hulbert (and Richardson as the Moriarty-like villain). Finale in an Underground tunnel.
BULLDOG DRUMMOND STRIKES BACK (US 1934); see above.
BULLDOG DRUMMOND AT BAY (GB 1937); with John Lodge.
BULLDOG DRUMMOND ESCAPES (US 1937); start of minor series with Ray Milland, later replaced by John Howard (and Guy Standing as Colonel Neilson).
BULLDOG DRUMMOND COMES BACK (US 1937); John Howard takes over from Milland, John Barrymore from Standing.

BULLDOG DRUMMOND'S REVENGE (US 1938); Howard and Barrymore.
BULLDOG DRUMMOND'S PERIL (US 1938); ditto.
BULLDOG DRUMMOND IN AFRICA (US 1938); Howard and H. B. Warner.
ARREST BULLDOG DRUMMOND (US 1938); ditto.
BULLDOG DRUMMOND'S SECRET POLICE (US 1939); ditto.
BULLDOG DRUMMOND'S BRIDE (US 1939); ditto.
BULLDOG SEES IT THROUGH (GB 1939); imitation with Jack Buchanan.
BULLDOG DRUMMOND AT BAY (US 1947); second feature with Ron Randell.
BULLDOG DRUMMOND STRIKES BACK (US 1947); ditto.
THE CHALLENGE (US 1948); with Tom Conway.
THIRTEEN LEAD SOLDIERS (US 1948); ditto.
CALLING BULLDOG DRUMMOND (GB 1951); with Walter Pidgeon.
DEADLIER THAN THE MALE (GB 1967); Richard Johnson as a Bond-like Drummond.
SOME GIRLS DO (GB 1970); Johnson again in a feeble sequel.

Bullshot: See below.

Bulldog Jack*
GB 1934 72m bw
Gaumont (Michael Balcon)
US title: *Alias Bulldog Drummond*

A playboy poses as Bulldog Drummond when the real man is injured, and manages to foil the thieves and save the girl.
After a slowish start, this comedy thriller works up into a fine frenzy with exciting scenes on the London Underground and in the British Museum.

w H. C. McNeile, Gerard Fairlie, J. O. C. Orton, Sidney Gilliat *d* Walter Forde

Jack Hulbert, Ralph Richardson, Claude Hulbert, Fay Wray, Athole Fleming, Paul Graetz

'There is . . . a mad train ride towards the terminus and destruction, as good as anything in screen melodrama.'—*Peter John Dyer, 1965*
'A sense of showmanship that is rewarded in a full quota of thrills and laughs.'—*Kine Weekly*

Bullet for a Badman
US 1964 80m Technicolor

An ex-Texas Ranger escapes from prison to prove his innocence of murder. Lively western programmer. Audie Murphy, Darren McGavin, Ruta Lee, Skip Homeier, George Tobias. Written by Mary and Willard Winningham; directed by R. G. Springsteen; for Universal-International.

A Bullet for Joey
US 1955 85m bw
UA / Sam Bischoff, David Diamond

A Canadian policeman prevents the murder of an atomic scientist.
Listless low-budgeter with familiar stars below par.

w Geoffrey Homes, A. I. Bezzerides *d* Lewis Allen *ph* Harry Neumann *m* Harry Sukman

Edward G. Robinson, George Raft, Audrey
Totter, George Dolenz, Peter Hanson, Peter
Van Eyck

A Bullet is Waiting
US 1954 82m Technicolor
Columbia / Welsch (Howard Welsch)

A plane accident brings a policeman and his
prisoner to a lonely farm, where a girl and her
father bring a fresh twist to the situation.
Disappointing melodrama full of pretentious
moralizing and fey characterization.

w Thames Williamson, Casey Robinson
d John Farrow ph Franz Planer m Dmitri
Tiomkin

Jean Simmons, Rory Calhoun, Stephen
McNally, Brian Aherne

Bullet Scars
US 1942 59m bw

A doctor is kidnapped to patch up a bullet-
scarred gunman. Just another second feature.
Regis Toomey, Adele Longmire, Howard da
Silva, John Ridgley. Written by Robert E.
Kent; directed by D. Ross Lederman; for
Warner.

Bullets for O'Hara
US 1941 50m bw

A gangster's wife helps an FBI man to trap
her husband. Fast-moving filler with action
scenes lifted from its original, *Public Enemy's
Wife* (qv). Roger Pryor, Anthony Quinn, Joan
Perry, Maris Wrixon, Dick Purcell. Written by
Raymond L. Schrock; directed by William K.
Howard; for Warner.

'Every real citizen should see it!'
Bullets or Ballots°
US 1936 81m bw
Warner (Lou Edelman)

A city cop goes undercover to break the mob.
Vivid routine gangster thriller, not quite of the
top flight, but nearly.

w Seton I. Miller d William Keighley ph Hal
Mohr m Heinz Roemheld

Edward G. Robinson, Joan Blondell,
Humphrey Bogart, Barton Maclane, Frank
McHugh, Dick Purcell, George E. Stone
  'A good gangster film of the second class
. . . all the old chivalrous situations of *Chums*
and the *Boy's Own Paper* are agreeably
translated into sub-machine gun terms.'—
Graham Greene

The Bullfighter and the Lady
US 1950 87m bw
Republic / John Wayne (Budd Boetticher)

A young American in Mexico is fascinated by
bullfighting but during training accidentally
causes the death of a great matador.
Predictable, rather boring plot given routine
treatment: for aficionados only.

w James Edward Grant d Budd Boetticher
ph Jack Draper m Victor Young

Robert Stack, Gilbert Roland, Joy Page, Katy
Jurado, Virginia Grey, John Hubbard

AAN: original story (Budd Boetticher, Ray
Nazarro)

The Bullfighters°
US 1945 60m bw
TCF (William Girard)

Two detectives in Mexico find that one of
them resembles a famous matador.
Laurel and Hardy's last American feature is
poor enough as a whole, but at least has a few
sequences in their earlier style.

w Scott Darling d Mal St Clair ph Norbert
Brodine m David Buttolph

Stan Laurel, Oliver Hardy, Richard Lane,
Carol Woode

Bullitt°°
US 1968 113m Technicolor
Warner / Solar (Philip D'Antoni)

A San Francisco police detective conceals the
death of an underground witness in his charge,
and goes after the killers himself.
Routine cop thriller with undoubted charisma,
distinguished by a splendid car chase which
takes one's mind off the tedious plot.
Technical credits first class.

w Harry Kleiner, Alan R. Trustman, *novel*
Mute Witness by Robert L. Pike d Peter
Yates ph William A. Fraker m Lalo Schifrin

Steve McQueen, Jacqueline Bisset, Robert
Vaughn, Don Gordon, Robert Duvall, Simon
Oakland
  'It has energy, drive, impact, and above all,
style.'—*Hollis Alpert*
● *Video: Warner*

Bullshot
GB 1983 88m Technicolor
HandMade (Ian La Frenais)

In the twenties, Bullshot Crummond is pitted
against his arch enemy Count Otto von Bruno.
Very flat-footed spoof which belies the talents
involved.

w Ron House, Diz White, Alan Shearman
d Dick Clement ph Alex Thomson m John
Du Prez pd Norman Garwood

Alan Shearman, Diz White, Ron House,
Frances Tomelty, Michael Aldridge, Ron
Pember, Mel Smith, Billy Connelly, Geoffrey
Bayldon, Bryan Pringle
  'Unrelievedly ghastly . . . even canned
laughter would be hard pressed to raise a
titter.'—*Gilbert Adair, MFB*
  'Behind every mannered line you can hear
technicians laughing the fun to death on the
studio floor.'—*Sunday Times*

Bunco Squad
US 1950 67m bw

The police expose a fake medium. Slightly
unusual cop caper. Robert Sterling, Ricardo
Cortez, Joan Dixon. Written by George E.
Callahan; directed by Herbert Leeds; for
RKO.

Bundle of Joy
US 1956 98m Technicolor RKOscope
RKO / Edmund Grainger

A shopgirl finds an abandoned baby and
everyone thinks it is hers.
Tame musical remake of *Bachelor Mother*;
some laughs, but poor numbers.

w Norman Krasna, Arthur Sheekman, Robert
Carson d Norman Taurog ph William
Snyder m Josef Myrow

Debbie Reynolds, Eddie Fisher, Adolphe
Menjou, Melville Cooper, Tommy Noonan,
Nita Talbot, Una Merkel, Robert H. Harris
● *Video: Kingston*

Bunker Bean
US 1936 67m bw

A meek office clerk rises to power after a
personality course. Old-fashioned comedy
previously filmed in 1917 and 1924. Owen
Davis Jnr, Lucille Ball, Berton Churchill,
Louise Latimer, Jessie Ralph, Hedda Hopper.
Written by Edmund North, James Gow and
Dorothy Yost, from the novel by Harry Leon
Wilson; directed by William Hamilton and
Edward Killy; for RKO. (Also known as *His
Majesty Bunker Bean*.)

Bunny Lake is Missing°°
GB 1965 107m bw Panavision
Columbia / Wheel (Otto Preminger)

The 4-year-old illegitimate daughter of an
American girl in London disappears, and no
one can be found to admit that she ever
existed.
A nightmarish gimmick story, with more
gimmicks superimposed along the way to say
nothing of a *Psycho*ish ending; some of the
decoration works and makes even the
unconvincing story compelling, while the cast
is alone worth the price of admission.

w John and Penelope Mortimer, *novel* Evelyn
Piper d Otto Preminger ph Denys Coop
m Paul Glass pd Don Ashton titles Saul Bass

Laurence Olivier, Carol Lynley, Keir Dullea,
Noel Coward, Martita Hunt, Finlay Currie,
Clive Revill, Anna Massey, Lucie Mannheim
  'It has the enjoyable hallmarks of really high
calibre professionalism.'—*Penelope Houston*

Bunny O'Hare
US 1971 92m Movielab
AIP (Gerd Oswald, Norman T. Herman)

A middle-aged widow and an ex-con plumber
become bank robbers, dressed as hippies and
escaping on a motor cycle.
Unappealing, ill-thought-out comedy with
pretensions to satire, an unhappy venture for
both stars.

w Stanley Z. Cherry, Coslough Johnson
d Gerd Oswald ph Loyal Griggs, John
Stephens m Billy Strange

Bette Davis, Ernest Borgnine, Jack Cassidy,
Joan Delaney, Jay Robinson, John Astin

Buona Sera Mrs Campbell°
US 1968 113m Technicolor
UA / Connaught (Melvin Frank)

Wartime USAF comrades reassemble twenty
years later in an Italian village, and three find
that they have been paying paternity money to
the same local glamour girl.
Agreeably cast, pleasantly set and
photographed, quite funny in parts, this
comedy of middle age unfortunately outstays
its welcome and lets its invention peter out.

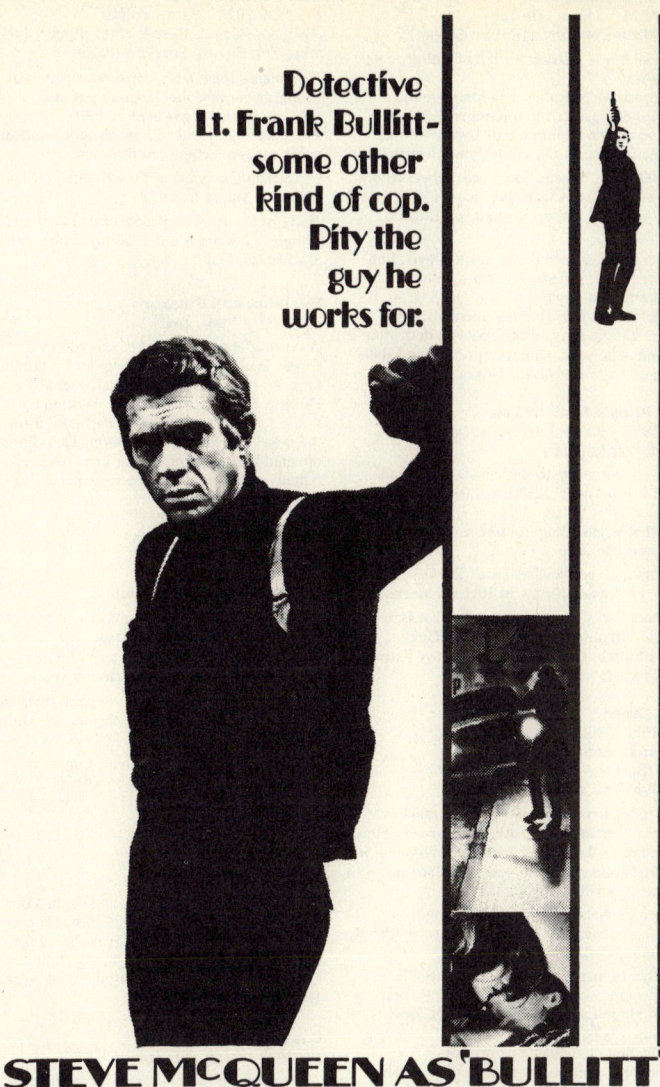

Detective
Lt. Frank Bullitt—
some other
kind of cop.
Pity the
guy he
works for:

STEVE McQUEEN AS 'BULLITT'
A SOLAR PRODUCTION   **ROBERT VAUGHN**

CO-STARRING
JACQUELINE BISSET · DON GORDON · ROBERT DUVALL · SIMON OAKLAND · NORMAN FELL   Screenplay by ALAN R.TRUSTMAN and HARRY KLEINER
Music by Lalo Schifrin · Based on the novel "Mute Witness" by Robert L. Pike · Executive Producer ROBERT E RELYEA · Produced by PHILIP D'ANTONI · Directed by PETER YATES **TECHNICOLOR® FROM WARNER BROS.-SEVEN ARTS**
                                                                  SUGGESTED FOR MATURE AUDIENCES

BULLITT. Just another cop story, the ad suggests. It was the car chase that made it a smash.

w Melvin Frank, Denis Norden, Sheldon Keller d Melvin Frank ph Gabor Pogany m Riz Ortolani

Gina Lollobrigida, Telly Savalas, Phil Silvers, Peter Lawford, Lee Grant, Marian Moses, Shelley Winters

Bureau of Missing Persons*
US 1933 73m bw
Police chief helps a girl find her husband, who turns out to have been murdered. Fast-moving potboiler typical of its studio. Pat O'Brien, Bette Davis, Lewis Stone, Glenda Farrell, Allen Jenkins, Hugh Herbert. Written by Robert Presnell; directed by Roy del Ruth; for Warner. 'Pretty fair entertainment. Nothing socko, but it will please.'—*Variety*

The Burglar*
US 1957 80m bw
Columbia (Louis W. Kellerman)
A burglar is shadowed by a policeman who is also after the loot.
Slightly pretentious but watchable low-budgeter.
w David Goodis from his novel d / ed Paul Wendkos ph Don Malkames m Sol Kaplan
Dan Duryea, Jayne Mansfield, Martha Vickers, Peter Capell

The Burglars
France / Italy 1971 120m Eastmancolor Panavision
Columbia / Vides (Henri Verneuil)
original title: *La Casse*
A determined policeman chases three burglars and their girl accomplice.
Expensive, camped-up version of *The Burglar*, with plenty going on, most of it borrowed from other films.
w Vahe Katcha, Henri Verneuil, *novel* The Burglar by David Goodis d Henri Verneuil ph Claude Renoir m Ennio Morricone
Omar Sharif, Jean-Paul Belmondo, Dyan Cannon, Robert Hossein, Nicole Calfan, Renato Salvatori
'Electronic equipment, wild action, exotic locales and bland villainy.'—*Tom Milne, MFB*

Burke and Hare
GB 1971 91m De Luxe
UA / Kenneth Shipman / Armitage (Guido Coen)
The story of anatomist Dr Knox and his body snatchers, retold with emphasis on the local brothel. Depressing in its childish attempts to be gruesome and perverted.
w Ernie Bradford d Vernon Sewell ph Desmond Dickinson m Roger Webb
Harry Andrews, Derren Nesbitt, Glynn Edwards, Yootha Joyce, Dee Sjendery, Alan Tucker

Burma Convoy
US 1941 72m bw
A trucking convoy on the Burma Road is terrorized by enemy smugglers. Adequately two-fisted second feature. Charles Bickford, Evelyn Ankers, Cecil Kellaway, Frank Albertson, Keye Luke, Turhan Bey, Willie

Fung. Written by Stanley Rubin and Roy Chanslor; directed by Noel M. Smith; for Universal.

The Burmese Harp***
Japan 1956   116m   bw
Nikkatsu (Masayuki Takagi)
original title: *Biruma no tategoto*

A shell-shocked Japanese soldier stays in the Burmese jungle to bury the unknown dead. Deeply impressive and horrifying war film with an epic, folk-tale quality, emphasized by superbly controlled direction.

w Natto Wada, *novel* Michio Takeyama
d Kon Ichikawa *ph* Minoru Yokoyama
m Akira Ifukube

Shoji Yasui, Rentaro Mikuni, Tatsuya Mihashi

Burn 'Em Up O'Connor
US 1938   70m   bw

The life and loves of a speedway ace. Modestly effective second from the time when the studios were trying to make a star of Dennis O'Keefe. Harry Carey, Cecilia Parker, Nat Pendleton, Charley Grapewin. Written by Milton Merlin and Byron Morgan, from Sir Malcolm Campbell's *Salute to the Gods*; directed by Edward Sedgwick; for MGM. 'Will fill better half of duals for good b.o.'—*Variety*

Burning an Illusion
GB 1981   111m   Eastmancolor
BFI (Vivien Pottersman)

A black secretary in London, reluctantly intrigued by the activities of her political boy friend, becomes a political militant. Most people would sigh at the thought of sitting through this decently made but rather earnest document which preaches only to the converted.

wd Menelik Shabazz *ph* Roy Cornwall
songs various

Cassie McFarlane, Victor Romero, Beverley Martin, Angela Wynter

The Burning Cross
US 1947   79m   bw

A frustrated war veteran succumbs temporarily to the wiles of the Ku Klux Klan. Cheap semi-documentary with a clear exploitation purpose. Hank Daniels, Virginia Patton, Raymond Bond. Written by Aubrey Wisberg; directed by Walter Colmes; for Screen Guild.

The Burning Hills
US 1956   92m   Warnercolor
Cinemascope

A young rancher gets even with a cattle baron who had his brother killed. Reasonable but unexciting star vehicle. Natalie Wood, Tab Hunter, Skip Homeier, Eduard Franz, Earl Holliman. Written by Irving Wallace, from a novel by Louis L'Amour; directed by Stuart Heisler; for Warner.

Burnt Offerings
US 1976   115m   De Luxe
UA / PEA–Dan Curtis (Robert Singer)

An evil house restores itself by feeding on its tenants.
An agreeably macabre idea for a five-page story is dragged out to interminable length, and seizes the attention only by a few shock moments. The title is mysteriously irrelevant.

w William F. Nolan, Dan Curtis, *novel* Robert Marasco *d* Dan Curtis *ph* Jacques Marquette *m* Robert Colbert *pd* Eugene Lourie

Oliver Reed, Karen Black, Bette Davis, Lee Montgomery, Burgess Meredith, Eileen Heckart, Dub Taylor
'Before the ludicrous dénouement, the movie merely piles on one special effect after another—none of them too special—and stalls for time.'—*Janet Maslin, Newsweek*

Bus Riley's Back in Town*
US 1965   93m   Eastmancolor
U-I (Elliott Kastner)

An ex-sailor wants to settle back into small-town life but finds that his girl friend has married.
Watchable, middling, routine small-town drama in the style of *Picnic*.

w Walter Gage (William Inge) *d* Harvey Hart *ph* Russell Metty *m* Richard Markowitz

Michael Parks, Ann-Margret, Jocelyn Brando, Janet Margolin, Kim Darby, Brad Dexter, Larry Storch, Crahan Denton, Mimsy Farmer, David Carradine

Bus Stop**
US 1956   96m   Eastmancolor
Cinemascope
TCF (Buddy Adler)
TV title: *The Wrong Kind of Girl*

In a rodeo town, a simple-thinking cowboy meets a café singer and asks her to marry him. Sex comedy-drama, a modest entertainment in familiar American vein, very well done but rather over-inflated by its star.

w George Axelrod, *play* William Inge
d Joshua Logan *ph* Milton Krasner *m* Alfred Newman, Cyril Mockridge

Marilyn Monroe, Don Murray, Betty Field, Arthur O'Connell, Eileen Heckart, Robert Bray, Hope Lange, Hans Conried, Casey Adams
'The film demands of its principal performers a purely physical display of their bodies viewed as sexual machinery.'—*David Robinson*

AAN: Don Murray
● *Video: CBS / Fox*

Bush Christmas
GB 1947   77m   bw

Australian children on holiday help catch horse thieves. Rather stolid family feature which got a reputation it hardly deserved. Chips Rafferty, John Fernside. Written and directed by Ralph Smart; for ABFD

The Bushido Blade
GB / US 1978   92m   colour
Trident / Rankin–Bass (Arthur Rankin Jnr)
aka: *The Bloody Bushido Blade*

Yokohama 1854; a US–Japanese treaty is in jeopardy because the Shogun's gift of a ceremonial sword has been stolen. Unappealing hybrid with much beheading and other random action, but little sense.

w William Overgard *d* Tom Katani *ph* Shaji Uedo *m* Maury Laws

Richard Boone, Frank Converse, Laura Gemser, Toshiro Mifune, Sonny Chibo, James Earl Jones, Mako

Business and Pleasure
US 1931   76m   bw

A down-to-earth husband is tempted by a *femme fatale*. Mild star comedy for his regular fans. Will Rogers, Jetta Goudal, Joel McCrea, Dorothy Peterson, Jed Prouty. Written by Gene Towne and William Conselman, from the novel The Plutocrat by Booth Tarkington; directed by David Butler; for Fox. 'West of Albany, perhaps, it will see some good business.'—*Variety*

Busman's Honeymoon*
GB 1940   99m   bw
MGM (Harold Huth)
US title: *Haunted Honeymoon*

Lord Peter Wimsey finds a murder to be solved in his honeymoon cottage.
Pleasant, slightly flat film version of a favourite old-fashioned detective novel.

w Monckton Hoffe, Angus Macphail, Harold Goldman, *novel* Dorothy L. Sayers *d* Arthur Woods *ph* F. A. Young

Robert Montgomery, Constance Cummings, Leslie Banks, *Seymour Hicks*, Robert Newton, Googie Withers, Frank Pettingell, Joan Kemp-Welch

Busses Roar
US 1942   61m   bw

A saboteur fixes a bomb to explode on a bus as it passes through an oilfield. Passable time-filler. Richard Travis, Eleanor Parker, Julie Bishop, Charles Drake. Written by Anthony Coldeway and George Bilson; directed by D. Ross Lederman; for Warner.

Buster and Billie
US 1973   99m   CFI colour

A sensitive high school senior elects to marry the school's derided 'easy lay', with tragic results. Unattractive reminiscences of rural Georgia with a rather desperate appeal to oversexed teenagers. Jan-Michael Vincent, Pamela Sue Martin, Joan Goodfellow, Clifton James. Written by Ron Turbeville; directed by Daniel Petrie; for Black Creek Billie / Columbia.

The Buster Keaton Story*
US 1957   91m   bw   Vistavision
Paramount (Sidney Sheldon, Robert Smith)

A biopic of the great silent comedian, with the emphasis on his years of downfall through drink.

An interesting recreation of Hollywood in the twenties and thirties is the main asset of this otherwise dismal tribute to a man whose greatness the star is unable to suggest apart from a few acrobatic moments.

w Robert Smith, Sidney Sheldon d Sidney Sheldon ph Loyal Griggs m Victor Young

Donald O'Connor, Rhonda Fleming, Ann Blyth, Peter Lorre, Larry Keating, Richard Anderson, Dave Willock

Busting
US 1973   92m   De Luxe
UA / Chartoff-Winkler (Henry Gellis)

Two Los Angeles vice squad officers fight corruption inside and outside the force.

Violent, exhausting, but totally routine police caper of the seventies.

wd Peter Hyams ph Earl Rath m Billy Goldenberg

Elliott Gould, Robert Blake, Allen Garfield, Antonio Fargas

'The farcical version of *Serpico*.'—*Michael Billington, Illustrated London News*

Bustin' Loose
US 1981   94m   Technicolor
Universal / Richard Pryor (William Greaves)

A thief on parole learns to look after a school for maladjusted children en route to a mountain retreat.

A fairly nauseous compendium of pratfalls and sentiment, not too bad while it keeps on the move.

w Roger L. Simon d Oz Scott ph Dennis Dalzell m Mark Davis, Roberta Flack

Richard Pryor, Cicely Tyson, Angel Ramirez, Jimmy Hughes

'The sort of forties-style warm experience I could well do without.'—*Derek Malcolm, Guardian*

Busy Bodies**
US 1933   20m   bw

Stan and Ollie are involved in various disasters in a sawmill. Though not among their most sympathetic comedies, this is a sustained and brilliantly contrived slapstick sequence. Laurel and Hardy, Tiny Sandford, Charlie Hall. Written by Anon (and Stan Laurel); directed by Lloyd French; for Hal Roach.

The Busy Body
US 1966   102m   Techniscope
Paramount / William Castle

A gangster is buried in a suit with a million dollar lining which various people are out to get.

Unfunny black comedy; laboured handling makes it a joke in poor taste.

w Ben Starr, *novel* Donald E. Westlake d William Castle ph Hal Stine m Vic Mizzy

Robert Ryan, Sid Caesar, Arlene Golonka, Anne Baxter, Kay Medford, Charles McGraw

But Not for Me
US 1959   105m   bw
Paramount (William Perlberg, George Seaton)

An ageing, washed-up Broadway producer is loved by his young drama student secretary. Rather heavy-going remake of *Accent on Youth*, efficiently performed but lacking the original gaiety.

w John Michael Hayes d Walter Lang ph Robert Burks m Leith Stevens

Clark Gable, Carroll Baker, Lilli Palmer, Lee J. Cobb, Barry Coe, Thomas Gomez

But The Flesh Is Weak
US 1932   82m   bw

A widower and his son both decide to marry wealthy widows. Amusing high society comedy from Ivor Novello's *The Truth Game*. Robert Montgomery, C. Aubrey Smith, Heather Thatcher, Edward Everett Horton, Nils Asther. Written by Ivor Novello; directed by Jack Conway; for MGM.

Butch and Sundance: The Early Days*
US 1979   112m   De Luxe
TCF (Gabriel Katzka, Stephen Bach)

Early episodes in the careers of the famous outlaws, culminating in a train robbery.

'Prequel' to a more celebrated but not a fresher or more lyrical western.

w Allan Burns d Richard Lester ph Laszlo Kovacs m Patrick Williams pd Brian Eatwell

Tom Berenger, William Katt, Jeff Corey, John Schuck, Michael C. Gwynne, Brian Dennehy, Peter Weller

● *Video: CBS / Fox*

'Not that it matters, but most of it is true!'
Butch Cassidy and the Sundance Kid***
US 1969   110m   De Luxe   Panavision
TCF / Campanile (John Foreman)

A hundred years ago, two western train robbers keep one step ahead of the law until finally tracked down to Bolivia.

Humorous, cheerful, poetic, cinematic account of two semi-legendary outlaws, winningly acted and directed. One of the decade's great commercial successes, not least because of the song 'Raindrops Keep Fallin' on My Head'.

w *William Goldman d George Roy Hill ph Conrad Hall m Burt Bacharach*

Paul Newman, Robert Redford, Katharine Ross, Strother Martin, Henry Jones, Jeff Corey, Cloris Leachman, Ted Cassidy, Kenneth Mars

'A mere exercise in smart-alecky device-mongering, chock-full of out of place and out of period one-upmanship, a battle of wits at a freshman smoker.'—*John Simon*

AA: William Goldman; Conrad Hall; Burt Bacharach; song 'Raindrops Keep Fallin' on My Head' (*m* Burt Bacharach, *ly* Hal David)
AAN: best picture; George Roy Hill

● *Video: CBS / Fox*

The Butler's Dilemma
GB 1943   83m   bw
British National / Shaftesbury

A jewel thief has to pose as his fiancée's butler.

Predictable comedy of pretence and mistaken identity; a tolerable co-feature of its day.

w Michael Barringer d Leslie Hiscott

Richard Hearne, Francis L. Sullivan, Judy Kelly, Hermione Gingold, Henry Kendall, Wally Patch

Butley*
US / GB 1973   130m   Eastmancolor
American Express / Ely Landau / Cinevision

Personal problems assail an English lecturer at a university college.

Adequate but not outstanding transcription (for the American Film Theatre) of a successful and percipient play.

w Simon Gray, from his play d Harold Pinter ph Gerry Fisher m none

Alan Bates, Jessica Tandy, Richard Callaghan, Susan Engel, Michael Byrne

The Butter and Egg Man
US

This pleasant George S. Kaufman comedy about a cowboy in New York was filmed as a silent in 1928, with Jack Mulhall; in 1932 as *The Tenderfoot* with Joe E. Brown; in 1937 as *Dance Charlie Dance* with Stuart Erwin; and in 1940 as *An Angel from Texas* with Eddie Albert; all for Warner in Hollywood.

The Buttercup Chain*
GB 1970   95m   Technicolor   Panavision
Columbia (Leslie Gilliat, John Whitney, Philip Waddilove)

A hothouse sex quartet changes partners with bewildering rapidity against a background of European splendour.

Chi-chi romance with a fashionably disillusioned and tragic ending. As watchable as the best TV commercials, but totally empty.

w Peter Draper, *novel* Janice Elliott d Robert Ellis Miller ph Douglas Slocombe m Richard Rodney Bennett

Hywel Bennett, Leigh Taylor-Young, Jane Asher, Sven-Bertil Taube, Clive Revill, Roy Dotrice

'British bathos about the unhappy overprivileged.'—*Variety*

'The most desirable woman in town, and the easiest to find!'
Butterfield Eight
US 1960   108m   Metrocolor
Cinemascope
MGM / Afton / Linebrook (Pandro S. Berman)

A society call girl has a complex love life.

This coy sex drama seemed mildly daring in 1960, but has since been well outclassed in that field and certainly has nothing else going for it except good production values.

w Charles Schnee, John Michael Hayes, *novel* John O'Hara d Daniel Mann ph Joseph Ruttenberg, Charles Harten m Bronislau Kaper

Elizabeth Taylor, Laurence Harvey, Eddie Fisher, Dina Merrill, Mildred Dunnock, Betty Field, Jeffrey Lynn, Kay Medford, Susan Oliver

'The mixture resolutely refuses to come to the boil.'—*John Gillett*

AA: Elizabeth Taylor

AAN: Joseph Ruttenberg, Charles Harten

Butterflies are Free
US 1972 109m Eastmancolor
Columbia / M. J. Frankovich

An aspiring actress falls for a blind neighbour but is handicapped by his possessive mother.
Three-character comedy-drama from a slight, sentimental but successful Broadway play.

w Leonard Gershe, from his play *d* Milton Katselas *ph* Charles B. Lang *m* Bob Alcivar

Goldie Hawn, Edward Albert, Eileen Heckart

AA: Eileen Heckart

AAN: Charles B. Lang

Butterfly
US 1981 108m Metrocolor
Par Par (Matt Cimber)

A 17-year-old sexpot reappears in her father's life, commits incest with him, and sets in train a grotesque series of plot developments.
Risible concatenation of murders, repentances, illegitimate sex and various kinds of lust, all revolving round butterfly marks and set in 1937 backwoods Arizona. *Tobacco Road* it ain't, though.

w John Goff, Matt Cimber, *novel* The Butterfly by James M. Cain *d* Matt Cimber *ph* Eddy Van Der Enden *m* Ennio Morricone

Stacy Keach, Pia Zadora, Orson Welles, Lois Nettleton, Edward Albert, Stuart Whitman, Ed MacMahon, June Lockhart, James Franciscus

● *video: Thorn EMI*

Buy Me That Town*
US 1941 70m bw
Paramount (Sol C. Siegel)

Gangsters take over a small town and pull the community out of bankruptcy.
Unusual comedy-drama, quite well done for a second feature.

w Gordon Kahn *d* Eugene Forde *ph* Theodor Sparkuhl

Lloyd Nolan, Albert Dekker, Constance Moore, Sheldon Leonard, Vera Vague, Edward Brophy, Horace MacMahon, Warren Hymer

Bwana Devil
US 1952 79m Anscocolor 3D
(UA) Arch Oboler

At the turn of the century, two man-eating lions threaten an African railroad.
Inept actioner notable only as the first film in 3-D ('Natural Vision'), advertised with the famous slogan 'A lion in your lap'.

wd Arch Oboler *ph* Joseph Biroc *m* Gordon Jenkins

Robert Stack, Barbara Britton, Nigel Bruce, Ramsay Hill

By Candlelight*
US 1933 70m bw
Universal (Carl Laemmle Jnr)

On a transcontinental train a woman meets a butler and takes him for a prince; he does not disillusion her.
Moderately pleasing romantic comedy of the old school.

w Hans Kraly, F. Hugh Herbert, Karen de Wolf, Ruth Cummings, *play* Siegfried Geyer *d* James Whale

Elissa Landi, *Paul Lukas,* Nils Asther

'A nice little class picture that should make money all round.'—*Variety*

'A dazzling display of romantic confidence trickery which takes on Lubitsch in his own territory.'—*Tom Milne, 1978*

By Love Possessed*
US 1961 116m De Luxe Panavision
UA / Miral (Walter Mirisch)

A Massachusetts lawyer reflects on the outlandish sexual mores of himself, his family and friends.
Peyton Place moved up in the social scale; a reasonably absorbing melodrama but hardly memorable.

w John Dennis, *novel* James Gould Cozzens *d* John Sturges *ph* Russell Metty *m* Elmer Bernstein

Lana Turner, Efrem Zimbalist Jnr, Jason Robards Jnr, Barbara Bel Geddes, George Hamilton, Susan Kohner, Thomas Mitchell, Yvonne Craig, Everett Sloane

'A talky succession of soap opera situations.'—*Robert Windeler*

By the Light of the Silvery Moon*
US 1953 101m Technicolor
Warner (William Jacobs)

In a small American town in 1918, the Winfield family has several problems arising from the return of daughter Marjorie's soldier boyfriend.
A sequel to *On Moonlight Bay* (qv), presenting further situations from the Penrod stories retailored for Doris Day. Inoffensive, well-made, old-fashioned entertainment with nostalgic songs and an archetypal family.

w Robert O'Brien, Irving Elinson, from stories by Booth Tarkington *d* David Butler *ph* Wilfrid M. Cline *m* Max Steiner

Doris Day, Gordon Macrae, *Leon Ames, Rosemary de Camp, Mary Wickes*

By Whose Hand?
US 1932 63m bw

Murder on a train between Los Angeles and San Francisco. Brisk little 'B' thriller. Ben Lyon, Barbara Weeks, Ethel Kenyon, Kenneth Thomson, Tom Dugan, Dwight Frye. Written by Isadore Bernstein, Stephen Roe, Harry Adler; directed by Ben Stoloff; for Columbia. 'The answer to a grind house exhib's prayer.'—*Variety*

By Your Leave
US 1934 81m bw

A restless husband tries to be a Don Juan. Very mild domestic comedy. Frank Morgan, Genevieve Tobin, Neil Hamilton, Marian Nixon, Glenn Anders, Gene Lockhart, Margaret Hamilton, Betty Grable, Charles Ray. Written by Allan Scott from the play by Gladys Hurlbut and Emma B. C. Wells; directed by Lloyd Corrigan; for RKO. 'Once the customers are in they'll get some laughs, but they're not going to be easy to entice.'—*Variety*

Bye Bye Birdie
US 1963 112m Eastmancolor
Panavision
Columbia / Fred Kohlmar / George Sidney

Havoc suffuses the last TV show of a pop star before he goes into the army.
Noisy, frenetic musical, hard to follow and even harder to like, with all the satire of the stage original subtracted. For young audiences who enjoy incoherence.

w Irving Brecher, from musical by Michael Stewart *d* George Sidney *ph* Joseph Biroc *md* Johnny Green *songs* Charles Strouse, Lee Adams

Janet Leigh, Dick Van Dyke, Maureen Stapleton, Ann-Margret, Bobby Rydell, Jesse Pearson, Ed Sullivan, Paul Lynde, Robert Paige

AAN: Johnny Green

Bye Bye Braverman*
US 1968 92m Technicolor
Warner / Sidney Lumet

New Yorkers get drunk and disillusioned on their way home from the funeral of a friend.
Witty, downbeat Jewish comedy which does not quite come off and would in any case be caviare to the general.

w Herbert Sargent, *novel* To an Early Grave by Wallace Markfield *d* Sidney Lumet *ph* Boris Kaufman *m* Peter Matz

George Segal, Jack Warden, Joseph Wiseman, Sorrell Booke, Jessica Walter, Phyllis Newman, Zohra Lampert, Alan King, Godfrey Cambridge

'You don't have to be Jewish to love it, but it helps a lot to be a New Yorker.'—*Robert Hatch, The Nation*

C Man
US 1949 75m bw

Customs agents track down a murderer. Lively little independent co-feature of its day. Dean Jagger, John Carradine, Lotte Elwen, Harry Landers. Written by Berne Giler; directed and produced by Irving Lerner; for Film Classics.

Cabaret*
US 1972 123m Technicolor
ABC Pictures / Allied Artists (Cy Feuer)

In the early thirties, Berlin is a hotbed of vice and anti-semitism. In the Kit Kat Klub, singer Sally Bowles shares her English lover with a homosexual German baron, and her Jewish friend Natasha has troubles of her own.
This version of Isherwood's Berlin stories regrettably follows the plot line of the play *I Am a Camera* rather than the Broadway musical on which it is allegedly based, and it lacks the incisive remarks of the MC, but the very smart direction creates a near-masterpiece of its own, and most of the songs are intact.

w Jay Presson Allen, from Goodbye to Berlin by Christopher Isherwood *d / ch* Bob Fosse *m* John Kander *ly* Fred Ebb *ph* Geoffrey Unsworth *md* Ralph Burns *pd* Rolf Zehetbauer

Liza Minnelli, Joel Grey, Michael York, Helmut Griem, Fritz Wepper, Marisa Berenson
'A stylish, sophisticated entertainment for grown-up people.'—*John Russell Taylor*
'Film journals will feast for years on shots from this picture; as it rolled along, I saw page after illustrated page from a not-too-distant book called *The Cinema of Bob Fosse*.'—*Stanley Kauffmann*

AA: Bob Fosse (as director); Geoffrey Unsworth; Ralph Burns; Liza Minnelli; Joel Grey
AAN: best picture; Jay Presson Allen
● Video: Rank

Cabin in the Cotton*
US 1932 79m bw
Warner (Hal B. Wallis)

A sharecropper is almost ruined by a southern belle.
Dated melodrama with interesting style and performances.

w Paul Green, *novel* Harry Harrison Knoll *d* Michael Curtiz *ph* Barney McGill

Richard Barthelmess, Dorothy Jordan, Bette Davis, David Landau, Tully Marshall, Henry B. Walthall, Hardie Albright
'Not well done . . . less than a moderate grosser all round.'—*Variety*
† The film in which Bette Davis drawled: 'Ah'd love to kiss yuh, but Ah just washed mah hair.'

Cabin in the Sky**
US 1943 99m bw
MGM (Arthur Freed)

An idle, gambling husband is reformed by a dream of his own death, with God and Satan battling for his soul.
Consistently interesting, often lively, but generally rather stilted all-black musical which must have seemed a whole lot fresher on the stage. Still, a good try.

w Joseph Schrank, *musical play* Lynn Root *d* Vincente Minnelli *ph* Sidney Wagner *md* George Stoll *new songs: m* Harold Arlen, *ly* E. Y. Harburg *show songs: m* Vernon Duke, *ly* John Latouche, Ted Fetter

Eddie 'Rochester' Anderson, Ethel Waters, Lena Horne, Cab Calloway, Louis Armstrong, John W. Bublett
'Broadway's big, fun-jammed music show is on the screen at last—crowded with stars and songs and spectacle in the famed MGM manner!'—*publicity*

AAN: song 'Happiness Is Just a Thing Called Joe' (*m* Harold Arlen, *ly* E. Y. Harburg)
Other songs: 'Li'l Black Sheep'; 'Ain't It De Truth'; 'Dat Ole Debbil Consequence'; 'Honey in the Honeycomb'; 'Taking a Chance on Love'; 'In My Old Virginia Home'; 'Going Up'; 'Things Ain't What They Used to be'; 'Shine'

The Cabinet of Caligari
US 1962 105m bw Cinemascope
TCF / Lippert (Roger Kay)

A young woman whose car breaks down near a country house is held prisoner by the sinister Caligari. Eventually it transpires that the mystery is all in her imagination: he is a psychiatrist and she an old lady whose sexual fantasies he has been curing.
Interminably talkative and frequently (unintentionally) funny trick film with the odd moment of effective suspense. The original ending, which cast some doubt on who was mad and who sane, is no longer available. The actors do not entirely escape absurdity.

w Robert Bloch *d* Roger Kay *ph* John Russell *m* Gerald Fried

Glynis Johns, Dan O'Herlihy, Constance Ford, Dick Davalos, Lawrence Dobkin
'It is impossible to be grateful for the film on any of its levels.'—*MFB*
'The most complete essay in the décor of delirium.'—*New Yorker, 1979*
† The fact that the story is told through the eyes of a mad person is the only link with the 1919 classic.

The Cabinet of Dr Caligari**
Germany 1919 90m approx (16 fps) bw silent
Decla-Bioscop (Erich Pommer)

A fairground showman uses a somnambulist for purposes of murder and is finally revealed to be the director of a lunatic asylum; but the whole story is only the dream of a madman.
Faded now, but a film of immense influence on the dramatic art of cinema, with its odd angles, stylized sets and hypnotic acting, not to mention the sting in the tail of its story (added by the producer).

w Carl Mayer, Hans Janowitz *d* Robert Wiene *ph* Willy Hameister *ad* Hermann Warm, Walter Röhrig, Walter Reiman

Werner Krauss, Conrad Veidt, Lil Dagover, Friedrich Feher, Hans von Twardowski
● Video: Thorn EMI

Cabiria**
Italy / France 1957 110m bw
Dino de Laurentiis / Les Films Marceau
original title: *Le Notti di Cabiria*; aka: *Nights of Cabiria*

A Roman prostitute has dreams of romance and respectability.
A bitter Cinderella story which was later turned into the Broadway musical *Sweet Charity*. Much of interest, but the leading lady is too Chaplinesque.

w Federico Fellini, Ennio Flaiano, Tullio Pinelli *d* Federico Fellini *ph* Aldo Tonti *m* Nino Rota

Giulietta Masina, François Périer, Amedeo Nazzari, Franca Marzi, Dorian Gray
'Any nobility in the original conception slowly suffocates in an atmosphere of subjective indulgence bordering dangerously on self-pity.'—*Peter John Dyer*

AA: best foreign film

Caboblanco

US 1981 87m colour Panavision
Avco / Martin V. Smith

A café proprietor in the Caribbean dodges
various groups of criminals.
Witless spoof of Casablanca which seems to
have been cobbled together from a half-
finished negative.

w Mort Fine, Milton Gelman *d* J. Lee
Thompson *ph* Alex Phillips Jnr *m* Jerry
Goldsmith

Charles Bronson, Jason Robards Jnr,
Dominique Sanda, Fernando Rey, Simon
MacCorkindale, Camilla Sparv, Denny Miller,
Gilbert Roland

Caccia Tragica°

Italy 1947 89m bw
Lux / ANPI
aka: *The Tragic Pursuit*

A bandit is hunted through the Po valley but
finally allowed to escape.
Minor peripatetic melodrama, well-handled
and exciting but uncertain in mood.

w Giuseppe de Santis, Michelangelo
Antonioni, Cesare Zavattini, Carlo Lizzani,
Unberto Barbaro *d Giuseppe de Santis*
ph Otello Martelli *m* Giuseppe Rosati

Massimo Girotti, Andrea Checci, Vivi Gioi

Cactus Flower°

US 1969 103m Technicolor
Columbia / M. J. Frankovich

To deceive his mistress, a dentist employs his
starchy secretary to pose as his wife, and falls
for her when she loosens up.
Amusing sophisticated comedy, generally well
handled.

w I. A. L. Diamond, *play* Abe Burrows,
French original by Pierre Barillet, Jean Pierre
Gredy *d* Gene Saks *ph* Charles E. Lang
m Quincy Jones *pd* Robert Clatworthy

Ingrid Bergman, Walter Matthau, Goldie
Hawn, Jack Weston, Rick Lenz, Vito Scotti,
Irene Hervey

AA: Goldie Hawn
● *Video: RCA / Columbia*

The Caddy

US 1953 95m bw
Paramount (Paul Jones)

A music hall comedy act recall how they got
together.
Less a feature than a series of short sketches,
this ragbag has its choice moments, but they
are few.

w Edmund Hartmann, Danny Arnold
d Norman Taurog *ph* Daniel L. Fapp
m Joseph L. Lilley

Dean Martin, Jerry Lewis, Donna Reed,
Barbara Bates, Joseph Calleia, Fred Clark,
Clinton Sundberg, Marshall Thompson

AAN: song 'That's Amore' (*m* Harry Warren,
ly Jack Brooks)

Caddyshack

US 1980 98m Technicolor

CAESAR AND CLEOPATRA. Apollodorus (Stewart Granger) makes a unique entrance.

Misadventures at a golf club. A relentlessly
crude and lumbering series of farcical incidents
which mainly fail to raise laughs. Chevy
Chase, Rodney Dangerfield, Ted Knight,
Michael O'Keefe. Written by Brian Doyle-
Murray, Harold Ramis and Douglas Kenney;
directed by Harold Ramis; for Jon Peters /
Orion. 'There are jests about vomiting and
nose-picking, while the most elaborate gag
sequence involves a chocolate bar falling into a
swimming pool and being mistaken for a turd
. . . a sustained exercise in tiresomeness.'—
Tim Pulleine, MFB

'Days of magnificent adventure . . . nights
of maddest revelry . . . a temptation in
Technicolor!'

Caesar and Cleopatra°°

GB 1945 135m Technicolor
Rank / Gabriel Pascal

An elaborate screen treatment of Bernard
Shaw's comedy about Caesar's years in
Alexandria.
Britain's most expensive film is an absurd
extravaganza for which the producer actually
took sand to Egypt to get the right colour. It
has compensations however in the sets, the
colour, the performances and the witty lines,
though all its virtues are theatrical rather than
cinematic and the play is certainly not a major
work.

w Bernard Shaw *d* Gabriel Pascal *ph* F. A.
Young, Robert Krasker, Jack Hildyard, Jack
Cardiff *m* Georges Auric *decor, costumes*
Oliver Messel *sets* John Bryan

*Claude Rains, Vivien Leigh, Cecil Parker,
Stewart Granger, Flora Robson, Francis L.
Sullivan, Raymond Lovell, Anthony Harvey,
Anthony Eustrel, Basil Sydney, Ernest*

Thesiger, Stanley Holloway, Leo Genn, Jean Simmons, Esmé Percy, Michael Rennie

'It cost over a million and a quarter pounds, took two and a half years to make, and well and truly bored one spectator for two and a quarter hours.'—*Richard Winnington*

'It is so wonderful as to make my other films look naive.'—*Bernard Shaw*

'When Rains played a small part he sometimes gave the impression that he was carrying the movie, but here his impish grin and his equanimity aren't enough.'—*Pauline Kael, 70s*

● *Video: Rank*

Café Colette
GB 1936   73m   bw
A diplomat in charge of a secret formula falls for a Russian princess. Old-hat spy melodrama, quite neatly staged. Paul Cavanagh, Greta Nissen, Sally Gray, Bruce Seton, Donald Calthrop, Dino Galvani. Written by Val Valentine and others; directed by Paul L. Stein; for Associated British.

Café Metropole
US 1937   83m   bw
TCF (Nunnally Johnson)
An heiress in Paris romances a Russian nobleman who is actually a penniless American.
Lighter-than-air romance which passed the time at the time.
w Jacques Duval *d* Edward H. Griffith *ph* Lucien Andriot *md* Louis Silvers
Loretta Young, Adolphe Menjou, Tyrone Power, Charles Winninger, Gregory Ratoff, Christian Rub, Helen Westley
'It's smart, sophisticated (not too much so), has the proper romantic ingredients, and will pull 'em in almost anywhere.'—*Variety*
'Here is a very amusing script, admirable acting . . . all thrown away by inferior direction. The camera is planked down four-square before the characters like a plain, honest, inexpressibly dull guest at a light and loony party.'—*Graham Greene*

Café Society
US 1939   84m   bw
Paramount
A publicity-seeking socialite impulsively marries a reporter who has annoyed her, but instead of making a fool of him she falls in love.
Faded light comedy which was never outstanding.
w Virginia Van Upp *d* Edward H. Griffith *ph* Ted Tetzlaff
Madeleine Carroll, Fred MacMurray, Shirley Ross, Claude Gillingwater
'Good cast will carry it nicely into okay if not wow business.'—*Variety*

La Cage aux Folles*
France / Italy 1978   91m   Eastmancolor
UA / PAA / Da Ma (Marcello Danon)
aka: *Birds of a Feather*

A homosexual nightclub owner is persuaded by his straight son to behave properly in front of his girl friend's parents, but chaos comes on the night of the party.
Internationally popular near-the-knuckle farce with excellent moments and some *longueurs*.
w Francis Veber, Edouard Molinaro, Marcello Danon, Jean Poiret, *play* Jean Poiret *d* Edouard Molinaro *ph* Armando Nannuzzi *m* Ennio Morricone
Ugo Tognazzi, Michel Serrault, Michel Galabru, Claire Maurier, Remi Laurent
AAN: Edouard Molinaro (as director)

● *Video: Warner*

La Cage aux Folles II
France / Italy 1980   99m   Technicolor
UA / PAA / DAMA (Marcello Danon)
An ageing homosexual tells his partner he is too old to be an effective female impersonator. Trying to prove the opposite, the partner becomes involved in a spy search for hidden microfilm.
Rather dimwitted sequel to a comedy which though deliberately 'naughty' showed some restraint; here, all is noise and excess.
w Jean Poiret, Francis Veber, Marcello Danon *d* Edouard Molinaro *ph* Armando Nannuzzi *m* Ennio Morricone
Ugo Tognazzi, Michel Serrault, Marcel Bozzuffi, Paola Borboni
'The juxtaposition of campy histrionics with the dreariest kind of espionage comedy offers quickly diminishing returns.'—*Gilbert Adair, MFB*

Cage of Gold*
GB 1950   83m   bw
Ealing (Michael Relph)
A girl's philandering ex-husband comes back into her life and is murdered.
Mild mystery melodrama in which the puzzle comes too late.
w Jack Whittingham *d* Basil Dearden *ph* Douglas Slocombe *m* Georges Auric
Jean Simmons, David Farrar, James Donald, Madeleine Lebeau, Maria Mauban, Herbert Lom, Bernard Lee, Gladys Henson, Harcourt Williams, Grégoire Aslan

'Will she come out woman or wildcat?'
Caged*
US 1950   96m   bw
Warner (Jerry Wald)
After being involved in a robbery a 19-year-old girl is sent to prison, and finds the staff more terrifying than the inmates.
Slick, superficial, hysterically harrowing women-in-prison melodrama; predictably overblown but also effective and powerful.
w Virginia Kellogg, Bernard Schoenfeld *d* John Cromwell *ph* Carl Guthrie *m* Max Steiner
Eleanor Parker, Agnes Moorehead, Ellen Corby, *Hope Emerson*, Betty Garde, Jan Sterling, Lee Patrick, Olive Deering, Jane Darwell, Gertrude Michael, Joan Miller

† Remade in 1962 as *House of Women*, directed by Walter Doniger, with Shirley Knight.
AAN: Virginia Kellogg, Bernard Schoenfeld; Eleanor Parker; Hope Emerson

'Break the law and he's the last man you'll want to see. And the last man you ever will!'
Cahill, US Marshal
US 1973   103m   Technicolor
Panavision
Warner / Batjac (Michael A. Wayne)
A stalwart western marshal finds that his own young sons are involved in a robbery he is investigating.
Satisfactory but sentimental John Wayne vehicle with the star too often yielding place to the rather boring young folk.
w Harry Julian Fink, Rita M. Fink *d* Andrew V. McLaglen *ph* Joseph Biroc *m* Elmer Bernstein
John Wayne, George Kennedy, Gary Grimes, Neville Brand, Clay O'Brien, Marie Windsor, Royal Dano, Denver Pyle, Jackie Coogan

● *Video: Warner*

'It's unlike any musical you've ever seen before—Timed to the Tantalizing Tempo of Today!'
Cain and Mabel*
US 1936   90m   bw
Warner (Sam Bischoff)
Tribulations of a prizefighter in love with a showgirl.
Generously produced but weakly written comedy drama with rather unexpected musical numbers; not a successful whole, but interesting.
w Laird Doyle, H. C. Witwer *d* Lloyd Bacon *ph* George Barnes
Clark Gable, Marion Davies, Allen Jenkins, Roscoe Karns, Walter Catlett, Hobart Cavanaugh, Pert Kelton, Ruth Donelly, E. E. Clive

'As big as the ocean!'
The Caine Mutiny**
US 1954   125m   Technicolor
Columbia / Stanley Kramer
Jealousies and frustrations among the officers of a peacetime destroyer come to a head when the neurotic captain panics during a typhoon and is relieved of his post. At the resulting trial the officers learn about themselves.
Decent if lamely paced version of a bestseller which also made a successful play; the film skates too lightly over the characterizations and even skimps the courtroom scene, but there are effective scenes and performances.
w Stanley Roberts, *novel* Herman Wouk *d* Edward Dmytryk *ph* Franz Planer *m* Max Steiner
Humphrey Bogart (Captain Queeg), Jose Ferrer (Lt Barney Greenwald), Van Johnson (Lt Steve Maryk), Fred MacMurray (Lt Tom

Keefer), Robert Francis (Ensign Willie Keith), May Wynn (May), Tom Tully (Captain DeVriess), E. G. Marshall (Lt Cdr Challee), Lee Marvin (Meatball), Claude Akins (Horrible)

QUEEG: 'There are four ways of doing things on board my ship. The right way, the wrong way, the navy way, and my way. If they do things my way, we'll get along.'

QUEEG: 'Ah, but the strawberries! That's where I had them. They laughed and made jokes, but I proved beyond the shadow of a doubt, and with geometric logic, that a duplicate key to the wardroom icebox did exist. And I'd have produced that key if they hadn't pulled the *Caine* out of action. I know now they were out to protect some fellow officer.'

KEEFER: 'There is no escape from the *Caine*, save death. We're all doing penance, sentenced to an outcast ship, manned by outcasts, and named after the greatest outcast of them all.'

AAN: best picture; Stanley Roberts; Max Steiner; Humphrey Bogart; Tom Tully

Cairo*
US 1941   100m   bw
MGM (Joseph L. Mankiewicz)

An American war reporter in Egypt meets a screen star and thinks she is a spy.
Mildly pleasing light comedy-drama with self-spoofing elements.

w John McClain d W. S. Van Dyke II ph Ray June md Herbert Stothart

Jeanette MacDonald, Robert Young, Ethel Waters, Reginald Owen, Lionel Atwill, Mona Barrie, Eduardo Ciannelli, Dennis Hoey, Dooley Wilson

Cairo
GB 1963   91m   bw
MGM (Ronald Kinnoch)

Crooks plan to steal Tutankhamun's jewels from the Cairo Museum.
Spiritless remake of *The Asphalt Jungle* (qv).

w Joanne Court d Wolf Rilla ph Desmond Dickinson m Kenneth V. Jones

George Sanders, Richard Johnson, Faten Hamama, John Meillon, Eric Pohlmann, Walter Rilla

Cairo Road
GB 1950   95m   bw
ABP (Aubrey Baring)

An Egyptian police chief lays traps for drug smugglers.
Oddly cast, reasonably lively but routine police adventure in an unfamiliar setting.

w Robert Westerby d David MacDonald ph Oswald Morris m Robert Gill

Eric Portman, Laurence Harvey, Maria Mauban, Karel Stepanek, Harold Lang, Camelia, Grégoire Aslan, Oscar Quitak

Cal*
GB 1984   102m   colour
Warner / Goldcrest / Enigma (Stuart Craig, David Puttnam)

A young Catholic in Ulster falls for the widow of the policeman in whose murder he has been an accomplice.
More clichés about the troubles: the film belies its publicity as 'a love story which happens to take place in Northern Ireland'. But it has style.

w Bernard MacLaverty, from his novel d Pat O'Connor ph Jerzy Zielinski m Mark Knopfler pd Stuart Craig

Helen Mirren, John Lynch, Donal McCann, John Kavanagh, Ray McAnally

Calabuch*
Spain / Italy 1956   93m   bw
Aguila / Constellaxione (Jose Luis Jerez)

An atomic scientist settles delightedly in a peaceful Spanish village, but sacrifices his own privacy when he invents a sky rocket.
Semi-satirical Ealing-type comedy which starts engagingly but runs out of steam.

w Leonardo Martin, Ennio Flaiano, Florentino Soria, Luis Berlanga d Luis Berlanga ph Francisco Sempere m Francesco Lavagnino

Edmund Gwenn, Valentina Cortese, Franco Fabrizi

Calamity Jane**
US 1953   101m   Technicolor
Warner (William Jacobs)

Calamity helps a saloon owner friend find a star attraction, and wins the heart of Wild Bill Hickok.
Agreeable, cleaned-up, studio-set western musical patterned after *Annie Get Your Gun*, but a much friendlier film, helped by an excellent score.

w James O'Hanlon d David Butler ph Wilfrid Cline songs Sammy Fain, Paul Francis Webster md Ray Heindorf ch Jack Donohue

Doris Day, Howard Keel, Allyn McLerie, Phil Carey, Dick Wesson, Paul Harvey

AA: song 'Secret Love' (m Sammy Fain, ly Paul Francis Webster)
AAN: Ray Heindorf

Calamity Jane and Sam Bass
US 1949   85m   Technicolor

Sam Bass murders the man who poisoned his horse, becomes an outlaw, and tangles with Jane Carraway. Routine western programmer from this stable. Yvonne de Carlo, Howard Duff, Dorothy Hart, Willard Parker, Houseley Stevenson, Ann Doran, Norman Lloyd. Written by Maurice Geraghty and Melvin Levy; directed by George Sherman; for Universal-International.

Calcutta
US 1946   83m   bw
Paramount (Seton I. Miller)

Two fliers seek the murderer of their friend in the hotels and bazaars of Calcutta.
Studio-bound action potboiler, simple-minded but quite good fun.

w Seton I. Miller d John Farrow ph John F. Seitz m Victor Young

Alan Ladd, Gail Russell, William Bendix, June Duprez, Lowell Gilmore

The Calendar
GB 1948   80m   bw

A girl trainer helps an owner to prove he didn't nobble his horse. Very average racecourse melodrama from a novel by Edgar Wallace, previously filmed in 1932 with Herbert Marshall and Edna Best. Here with Greta Gynt, John McCallum, Leslie Dwyer, Raymond Lovell, Charles Victor, Barry Jones. Written by Geoffrey Kerr; directed by Arthur Crabtree; for Gainsborough.

'No town would have her! No man could tame her!'

California
US 1946   97m   Technicolor
Paramount (Seton I. Miller)

An army deserter joins the 1848 California gold rush.
Standard glamorized star western; not bad if you accept the conventions.

w Frank Butler, Theodore Strauss d John Farrow ph Ray Rennahan m Victor Young

Ray Milland, Barbara Stanwyck, Barry Fitzgerald, Albert Dekker, George Coulouris, Anthony Quinn

'It quickly loses its stirrups and ends up caught by the chaps in a bed of cactus.'— *Newsweek*

California Conquest
US 1952   79m   Technicolor

Spanish Californians band together against Russian would-be invaders. Tedious and unsympathetic historical western on a 'B' budget. Cornel Wilde, Teresa Wright, Alfonso Bedoya, Lisa Ferraday, Ivan Lebedeff, John Dehner. Written by Robert E. Kent; directed by Lew Landers; for Sam Katzman / Columbia.

California Split*
US 1974   109m   Metrocolor   Panavision
Columbia / Persky–Bright / Reno (Robert Altman, Joseph Walsh)

Two cheerful gamblers get drunk, laid, cheated and happy.
Sporadically entertaining character comedy sunk in a sea of chatter.

w Joseph Walsh d Robert Altman ph Paul Lohman

Elliott Gould, George Segal, Gwen Welles, Ann Prentiss, Joseph Walsh

'The film seems to be being improvised . . . we catch at events and personalities by the ends of threads.'—*New Yorker*

† An end title reads: FOR BARBARA, 1933–1973. This was Barbara Ruick, who played the barmaid and died on location.

California Straight Ahead*
US 1937   57m   bw
Universal (Trem Carr)

A nationwide race is held between a special train and a convoy of high-powered trucks.
Unusual and quite lively second feature shot on location.

w Herman Boxer d Arthur Lubin ph Harry Neumann m Charles Previn

John Wayne, Louise Latimer, Robert McWade, Tully Marshall

'Everything happens as the audience expects and wishes, so in its field it will do okay.'—*Variety*

California Suite*
US 1978   103m   colour
Columbia / Ray Stark

Misadventures of four groups of guests at the Beverly Hills Hotel.
Two hits, two misses; closer intercutting might have helped. No doubt that Maggie Smith and Michael Caine come off best, with bitcheries about the Academy Awards; Walter Matthau and Elaine May also raise laughs in Jewish farce. But Alan Alda and Jane Fonda in stiff-upper-lip divorce drama are a bore; and the black farce with Richard Pryor and Bill Cosby is scuppered before it starts.

w Neil Simon, from his play d Herbert Ross ph David M. Walsh m Claude Bolling pd Albert Brenner

'By turns silly and thoughtful, tedious and charming, broad and delicate.'—*Frank Rich, Time*

AA: Maggie Smith

● *Video: RCA / Columbia*

'What would you have done if you had been given absolute power of life and death over everyone else in the whole wide world?'
Caligula
Italy / US 1979   150m   Eastmancolor
Penthouse Films (Bob Guccione)

The violent life and times of a decadent Roman emperor. What would have been a dull and worthless pseudo-epic has been perked up by violence and hardcore sex. The result is a vile curiosity of interest chiefly to sado-masochists.

w Bob Guccione, after a screenplay by Gore Vidal d Tinto Brass and others ph Silvano Ippoliti m Paul Clemente ph Danilo Donati

Malcolm McDowell, John Gielgud, Peter O'Toole, Helen Mirren, Teresa Ann Savoy, John Steiner

'An anthology of sexual aberrations in which incest is the only face-saving relationship . . . far more Gore than Vidal.'—*Variety*

'It just keeps rolling along at inordinate length, suggesting de Mille grinding slowly to a frequent stoppage for a display of bums, breasts and pubic hair.'—*Time Out*

Call a Messenger
US 1939   65m   bw

Working as telegraph messengers, the Little Tough Guys prevent a hold-up. Second-feature offshoot of the Dead End Kids, some of whom had now departed to become the East Side Kids (who later blossomed forth as the Bowery Boys). Billy Halop, Huntz Hall, Billy Benedict, David Gorcey, Robert Armstrong, Mary Carlisle, Anne Nagel, Victor Jory, El Brendel, Larry 'Buster' Crabbe. Written by Arthur T. Horman; directed by Arthur Lubin; for Universal.
'A rowdy, gripping production patterned as heavy bolstering in dual set-ups.'—*Variety*

Call Her Savage
US 1932   88m   bw
Paramount (Sam E. Rork)

Trials and tribulations of a half-breed Indian girl who marries a cad and later takes to the streets.
Rough and ready melodrama for female audiences; the penultimate appearance of a star who did not take to talkies.

w Edwin Burke, *novel* Tiffany Thayer d John Francis Dillon ph Lee Garmes

Clara Bow, Gilbert Roland, Monroe Owsley, Thelma Todd, Estelle Taylor

'The return of Clara Bow in a madcap role makes a natural . . . the result is bound to be money.'—*Variety*

Call It a Day*
US 1937   89m   bw
Warner (Henry Blanke)

An upper-class British family has problems during a single day.
Surprising, and not very effective, Hollywood treatment of a very British comedy.

w Casey Robinson, *play* Dodie Smith d Archie Mayo ph Ernest Haller

Olivia de Havilland, Ian Hunter, Anita Louise, Alice Brady, Roland Young, Frieda Inescort, Bonita Granville, Peggy Wood, Walter Woolf King, Una O'Connor, Beryl Mercer

'A fine cast rowing a very thin boat . . . charm, many a giggle but nary a sock laugh.'—*Variety*

Call Me Bwana*
GB 1962   93m   Eastmancolor
Rank / Eon (Harry Saltzman, Albert R. Broccoli)

A fake African explorer is sent to the jungle to recover a space capsule.
Moderate star farce with occasional bright moments.

w Nate Monaster, Johanna Harwood d Gordon Douglas ph Ted Moore m Monty Norman

Bob Hope, Anita Ekberg, Edie Adams, Lionel Jeffries, Percy Herbert, Paul Carpenter, Orlando Martins

Call Me Madam***
US 1953   114m   Technicolor
TCF (Sol C. Siegel)

A Washington hostess is appointed Ambassador to Lichtenberg and marries the foreign minister.
Studio-bound but thoroughly lively transcription of Irving Berlin's last big success, with most of the performers at their peak and some topical gags which may now be mystifying.

w Arthur Sheekman, *play* Howard Lindsay, Russel Crouse m / ly Irving Berlin md Alfred Newman ph Leon Shamroy d Walter Lang ch Robert Alton

Ethel Merman, Donald O'Connor, George Sanders, Vera-Ellen, Billy de Wolfe, Helmut Dantine, Walter Slezak, Steve Geray, Ludwig Stossel

AA: Alfred Newman

Call Me Mister
US 1951   95m   Technicolor
TCF (Fred Kohlmar)

A husband-and-wife dance team entertain the troops in Japan and after the war.
Passable musical of a very predictable kind.

w Albert E. Lewin, Burt Styler d Lloyd Bacon ph Arthur E. Arling m Leigh Harline ch Busby Berkeley songs various original show credits: m Harold Rome, book Arnold Auerbach, Arnold B. Horwitt

Betty Grable, Dan Dailey, Danny Thomas, Dale Robertson, Richard Boone

Call Northside 777**
US 1948   111m   bw
TCF (Otto Lang)

A Chicago reporter helps a washerwoman prove her son not guilty of murdering a policeman.
Overlong semi-documentary crime thriller based on a real case. Acting and detail excellent, but the sharp edge of *Boomerang* is missing.

w Jerome Cady, Jay Dratler d Henry Hathaway ph Joe MacDonald m Alfred Newman

James Stewart, Lee J. Cobb, Helen Walker, Kazia Orzazewski, Betty Garde, Richard Conte

'A most satisfying thriller, generously streaked with class.'—*Daily Mail*
'Absorbing, exciting, realistic.'—*Star*

Call of the Blood
GB 1947   88m   bw

A Sicilian fisherman takes revenge on his daughter's seducer. Antediluvian melodrama with stiff-upper-lip English looking on. John Clements, Kay Hammond, John Justin, Lea Padovani, Robert Rietti. Written by John Clements, Akos Tolnay and Basil Mason, from the novel by Robert Hichens; directed by John Clements and Ladislas Vajda; for Pendennis.

Call of the Flesh
US 1930   100m   bw (colour sequence)

A convent girl falls for a man of the world.
Would-be tempestuous melodrama which fails

through lack of pace. Ramon Novarro, Dorothy Jordan, Ernest Torrence, Nance O'Neil, Renee Adoree. Written by Dorothy Farnum and John Colton; directed by Charles Brabin; for MGM. 'Money picture, but can stand a lot of cutting.'—*Variety*

Call of the Wild*
US 1935 81m bw
Twentieth Century (Darryl F. Zanuck)
A young widow falls in love with a wild Yukon prospector.
Inaccurate but pleasing adaptation of an adventure novel with dog interest.

w Gene Fowler, Leonard Praskins, *novel* Jack London *d* William Wellman *ph* Charles Rosher *m* Alfred Newman

Clark Gable, Loretta Young, Jack Oakie, Reginald Owen, Frank Conroy

'The lion-hearted dog emerges as a stooge for a rather conventional pair of human love-birds . . . looks like box office.'—*Variety*

Call of the Wild
GB / Ger / Sp / It / Fr 1972   105m Eastmancolor
Massfilms / CCC / Izaro / Oceania / UPF (Harry Alan Towers)
During the Klondike gold rush, a stolen dog becomes a miner's best friend before joining the wolf-pack.
Closer to the book than the previous version, but curiously scrappy and unsatisfactory.

w Harry Alan Towers, Wyn Wells, Peter Yeldman *d* Ken Annakin *ph* John Vabrera, Dudley Lovell *m* Carlo Rustichelli

Charlton Heston, Michèle Mercier, Raimund Harmstorf, George Eastman

Call Out the Marines*
US 1942 67m bw
Two adventurers re-enlist in the Marines and foil a spy plot. The last of many action comedies featuring the original Flagg and Quirt from *What Price Glory?* Victor McLaglen, Edmund Lowe, Binnie Barnes, Paul Kelly, Franklin Pangborn. Written and directed by Frank Ryan and William Hamilton; for Universal.

Callan*
GB 1974 106m Eastmancolor
EMI / Magnum (Derek Horne)
A former secret agent is seconded to a government section devoted to the elimination of undesirables.
Expanded rewrite of the first episode of a long-running TV series, quite fresh and vivid in the circumstances, especially as it comes at the tail end of ten years of similar bouts of blood and thunder.

w James Mitchell, from A Magnum for Schneider *d* Don Sharp *ph* Ernest Steward *m* Wilfred Josephs

Edward Woodward, Eric Porter, Carl Mohner, Catherine Schell, Peter Egan, Russell Hunter, Kenneth Griffith

Callaway Went Thataway*
US 1951 81m bw
MGM (Melvin Frank, Norman Panama)
GB title: *The Star Said No*
The old movies of a Hollywood cowboy become popular on TV, but the star has become a hopeless drunk and an actor is hired to pose as him for public appearances.
Reasonably engaging comedy using charm rather than acid.

wd Melvin Frank, Norman Panama *ph* Ray June *m* Marlin Skiles

Dorothy McGuire, Fred MacMurray, Howard Keel, Jesse White, Natalie Schaefer

Calle Mayor*
Spain / France 1956 95m bw
Play Art Iberia / Cesareo Gonzales
aka: *Grande Rue*
In a small Spanish town, a young stud pretends for a bet to be in love with a plain spinster.
Interesting but rather unattractive and certainly unconvincing little comedy-drama, rather too obviously styled for its American star after her success in *Marty*.

wd Juan Antonio Bardem *ph* Michel Kelber *m* Joseph Kosma

Betsy Blair, Yves Massard, René Blancard, Lila Kedrova

Calling Bulldog Drummond
GB 1951 80m bw
MGM (Hayes Goetz)
Drummond goes undercover to catch a gang of thieves.
Minor-league quota quickie addition to the exploits of a long-running character (see *Bulldog Drummond*).

w Howard Emmett Rogers, Gerard Fairlie, Arthur Wimperis *d* Victor Saville *ph* F. A. Young *m* Rudolph Kopp

Walter Pidgeon, Margaret Leighton, Robert Beatty, David Tomlinson, Peggy Evans, Charles Victor, Bernard Lee, James Hayter

'Terror strikes as a madman rules!'
Calling Doctor Death
US 1943 63m bw
A doctor's wife is murdered; her lover is arrested; but did the doctor himself do it? Probably not, as the tendency of the tinpot *Inner Sanctum* series, of which this was the first, was to make its star look anguished for six reels and then show him to be as innocent as the film was (mercifully) short. Lon Chaney, Patricia Morison, Fay Helm, David Bruce, Ramsay Ames, J. Carrol Naish. Written by Edward Dein; directed by Reginald Le Borg; for Universal.

Calling Dr Gillespie*
US 1942 84m bw
A deranged ex-patient breaks into Blair Hospital for the purpose of killing Dr Gillespie, the man at which cranky old wheelchair-bound Dr Gillespie took over the Kildare series, its star (Lew Ayres) having

effectually abdicated from acting by declaring himself a conscientious objector. Production values up to par. Lionel Barrymore, Philip Dorn, Phil Brown, Donna Reed, Nat Pendleton, Mary Nash, Alma Kruger, Walter Kingsford. Written by Kubec Glasmon, Willis Goldbeck and Harry Ruskin; directed by Harold S. Bucquet; for MGM. (See *Dr Kildare* for titles in series.)

Calling Dr Kildare*
US 1939 86m bw
Kildare becomes innocently involved in murder and needs Dr Gillespie's help. The second in the Kildare series had the confidence that comes of box-office approval. Lew Ayres, Lionel Barrymore, Lana Turner, Nat Pendleton, Samuel S. Hinds, Laraine Day, Alma Kruger. Written by Harry Ruskin and Willis Goldbeck; directed by Harold S. Bucquet; for MGM.

Calling Philo Vance
US 1939 62m bw
A manufacturer is murdered and foreign agents are discovered among his servants. Essentially a remake of *The Kennel Murder Case*; inferior as a whole, but with an excellent new Vance in *James Stephenson*. Margot Stevenson, Henry O'Neill, Ed Brophy, Ralph Forbes, Martin Kosleck. Written by Tom Reed; directed by William Clemens; for Warner.

Calm Yourself
US 1935 70m bw
An advertising man helps solve a kidnapping. Spoofy comedy-drama which simply doesn't work. Robert Young, Madge Evans, Betty Furness, Nat Pendleton, Hardie Albright, Ralph Morgan. Written by Edward Hope, Arthur Kober; directed by George B. Seitz; for MGM. 'Strictly for the not too particular nabe clientele.'—*Variety*

Camelot**
US 1967 181m Technicolor Panavision 70
Warner (Jack L. Warner)
King Arthur marries Guinevere, loses her to Lancelot, and is forced into war.
A film version of a long-running Broadway show with many excellent moments. Unfortunately the director cannot make up his mind whether to go for style or realism, and has chosen actors who cannot sing. The result is cluttered and overlong, with no real sense of period or sustained imagination, but the photography and the music linger in the mind.

w Alan Jay Lerner *m* Frederick Loewe *d* Joshua Logan *ph* Richard H. Kline *pd / costumes* John Truscott *ad* Edward Carere *md* Ken Darby, Alfred Newman

Richard Harris, Vanessa Redgrave, David Hemmings, Lionel Jeffries, Laurence Naismith, Franco Nero
Songs include 'The Merry Month of May'; 'Camelot'; 'If Ever I Would Leave You'; 'Take Me to the Fair'; 'C'est Moi'

'One wonders whether the fashion for musicals in which only the chorus can actually sing may be reaching its final stage.'—*MFB*

'Three hours of unrelieved glossiness, meticulous inanity, desperate and charmless striving for charm.'—*John Simon*

'The sets and costumes and people seem to be sitting there on the screen, waiting for the unifying magic that never happens.'—*New Yorker, 1977*

AA: art direction; costumes; music direction
AAN: cinematography

● Video: Warner

The Camels are Coming
GB 1934   80m   bw

An officer in the camel corps catches Egyptian drug smugglers. Light, bouncy star vehicle. Jack Hulbert, Anna Lee, Hartley Power, Harold Huth, Allan Jeayes. Written by Jack Hulbert, Guy Bolton and W. P. Lipscomb; directed by Tim Whelan; for Gainsborough.

The Cameraman●●●
US 1928   78m approx (24 fps)   bw silent
MGM (Lawrence Weingarten)

In order to woo a film star, a street photographer becomes a newsreel cameraman. Highly regarded chapter of farcical errors, among the star's top features.

w Clyde Bruckman, Lex Lipton, Richard Schayer   *d* Edward Sedgwick   *ph* Elgin Lessley, Reggie Manning

Buster Keaton, Marceline Day, Harry Gribbon, Harold Goodwin
† The film was remade in 1948 for Red Skelton as *Watch the Birdie*, with Keaton sadly supervising the gags but getting no credit.

'You who are so young—where can you have learned all you know about women like me?'
Camille●●
US 1936   108m   bw
MGM (Irving Thalberg, Bernard Hyman)

A dying courtesan falls for an innocent young man who loves her, and dies in his arms. This old warhorse is an unsuitable vehicle for Garbo but magically she carries it off, and the production is elegant and pleasing.

w Frances Marion, James Hilton, Zoe Akins, *novel* Alexandre Dumas   *d George Cukor ph* William Daniels   *m* Herbert Stothart

Greta Garbo, Robert Taylor, Lionel Barrymore, *Henry Daniell*, Elizabeth Allan, Lenore Ulric, Laura Hope Crews, Rex O'Malley, Jessie Ralph, E. E. Clive

'Pretty close to the top mark in showmanship, direction, photography and box office names.'—*Variety*

'The slow, solemn production is luxuriant in its vulgarity: it achieves that glamor which MGM traditionally mistook for style.'—*Pauline Kael, 1968*

'The surprise is to find a story that should by rights be old hat coming to such insistent life on the screen.'—*Otis Ferguson*

'It steadily builds up an impression of being a spectacle of manners and fashions, a socially true background for its characters to move against.'—*National Board of Review*

'Their lips meet for the first time . . . a superb thrill seared in your memory forever!'—*publicity*

'This is not death as mortals know it. This is but the conclusion of a romantic ritual.'—*Bosley Crowther*

'Luxuriant in its vulgarity, it achieves that glamour which MGM traditionally mistook for style.'—*New Yorker 1982*

AAN: Greta Garbo

Il Cammino della Speranza●
Italy 1950   105m   bw
Lux (Luigi Rovere)
aka: *The Road to Hope*

Unemployed Sicilian miners travel to France in search of work.
Episodic location melodrama with a social conscience, a kind of Italian *Grapes of Wrath*. Very watchable, but not moving.

w Federico Fellini, Tullio Pinelli   *d* Pietro Germi   *ph* Leonido Barboni   *m* Carlo Rustichelli

Raf Vallone, Elena Varzi, Saro Urzi, Franco Navarra

The Camp on Blood Island
GB 1958   81m   bw   Megascope
Columbia / Hammer (Anthony Hinds)

The sadistic commandant of a Japanese POW camp swears to kill all the inmates. Japan surrenders, and a great effort is made to prevent the news from reaching him. Dubious melodrama parading sadism and brutality as entertainment.

w Jon Manchip White, Val Guest   *d* Val Guest   *ph* Jack Asher   *m* Gerard Schurmann

André Morell, Carl Mohner, Edward Underdown, Michael Goodliffe, Ronald Radd, Walter Fitzgerald, Phil Brown, Barbara Shelley, Michael Gwynn, Richard Wordsworth, Marne Maitland, Mary Merrall

Campbell's Kingdom●
GB 1957   102m   Eastmancolor
Rank (Betty E. Box)

A young man who thinks he is dying arrives in the Canadian Rockies to take over his father's oil valley, but a scheming contractor opposes him.
Competent and entertaining romantic thickear.

w Robin Estridge, *novel* Hammond Innes   *d* Ralph Thomas   *ph* Ernest Steward   *m* Clifton Parker

Dirk Bogarde, Michael Craig, Stanley Baker, Barbara Murray, Athene Seyler, Mary Merrall, James Robertson Justice

Can Can
US 1960   131m   De Luxe   Todd-AO
TCF / Suffolk-Cummings (Jack Cummings)

A Parisian nightclub dancer in the nineties is sued for performing the Can Can.
Flat film of a dull musical, with just a few

plums in the pudding.

w Dorothy Kingsley, Charles Lederer, *play* Abe Burrows   *songs* Cole Porter   *d* Walter Lang   *ph* William Daniels   *ch* Hermes Pan   *md* Nelson Riddle

Frank Sinatra, Shirley Maclaine, Maurice Chevalier, Louis Jourdan, Juliet Prowse, Marcel Dalio, Leon Belasco

AAN: Nelson Riddle

Can Heironymus Merkin Ever Forget Mercy Humppe and Find True Happiness?
GB 1969   117m   Technicolor
Universal / Taralex (Anthony Newley)

A performer on a beach assembles a huge pile of personal bric-à-brac and reminisces about his life in the style of a variety show. Obscure and pointless personal fantasy, financed at great expense by a major film company as a rather seedy monument to Anthony Newley's totally uninteresting sex life, and to the talent which he obviously thinks he possesses. The few mildly amusing moments are not provided by him.

w Herman Raucher, Anthony Newley   *d* Anthony Newley   *ph* Otto Heller   *m* Anthony Newley

Anthony Newley, Joan Collins, George Jessel, Milton Berle, Bruce Forsyth, Stubby Kaye, Patricia Hayes, Victor Spinetti

'If I'd been Anthony Newley I would have opened it in Siberia during Christmas week and called it a day.'—*Rex Reed*

'The kindest thing for all concerned would be that every available copy should be quietly and decently buried.'—*Michael Billington, Illustrated London News*

Can She Bake a Cherry Pie?
US 1983   90m   Du Art

An abandoned wife has an experimental affair with a hypochondriac divorcé. What the writer-director calls 'a bitter-sweet comedy about loneliness and love' has more to say to him than to an audience; but there are wryly amusing moments. Karen Black, Michael Emil Jaglom, Michael Margotta, Frances Fisher. Written and directed by Henry Jaglom; for Jagfilm / International Rainbow.

Can This Be Dixie?
US 1936   68m   bw

In the old south, a medicine showman and his daughter help a bankrupt Kentucky colonel. Agreeable supporting material, with elements of satire, spoof and musical comedy. Jane Withers, Slim Summerville, Claude Gillingwater, Helen Wood, Thomas Beck, Sara Haden, Donald Cook, Hattie McDaniel. Written by Lamar Trotti; directed by George Marshall; for Sol M. Wurtzel / TCF. 'Plenty of ingredients were thrown into the soup . . . it will hold its own in the duals.'—*Variety*

Canadian Pacific
US 1949   95m   Cinecolor

A surveyor discovers the vital pass through the Rockies, and chooses between a lady doctor and a wilful half-breed. Fairly unhistorical western; watchable, though. Randolph Scott, Jane Wyatt, Nancy Olson, J. Carrol Naish, Victor Jory, Robert Barrat. Written by Jack De Witt and Kenneth Gamet; directed by Edwin L. Marin; for Nat Holt (TCF).

The Canadians
GB / Canada 1961   85m   De Luxe
Cinemascope
TCF (Herman E. Webber)

After Custer's defeat at Little Big Horn, 6,000 Sioux flee north and are victimized by villainous Canadians; but the Mounties come to the rescue.
Dreary, stumbling semi-western which set back Canadian production by a year or two. The blame seems to be equally shared by all concerned.

wd Burt Kennedy *ph* Arthur Ibbetson
m none

Robert Ryan, John Dehner, Torin Thatcher, Burt Metcalfe, Teresa Stratas, Michael Pate, John Sutton

Canaries Sometimes Sing
GB 1930   90m   bw

Two unhappily married couples change partners. Mild sophisticated comedy, a shade daring for its time, but only in concept. Tom Walls, Yvonne Arnaud, Athole Stewart, Cathleen Nesbitt. From the play by Frederick Lonsdale; directed by Tom Walls; for British and Dominions.

Cancel My Reservation
US 1972   99m   Technicolor

A TV talk show host retreats to his ranch and finds himself mixed up with murder. Bob Hope's last film, though it reverted to farce and his bumbling coward persona, proved a sorry affair with egg on the face of everybody concerned. Bob Hope, Eva Marie Saint, Ralph Bellamy, Forrest Tucker, Anne Archer, Keenan Wynn, Doodles Weaver. Written by Arthur Marx and Robert Fisher, from the novel *The Broken Gun* by Louis L'Amour; directed by Paul Bogart; for Naho Enterprises.

The Candidate**
US 1972   110m   Technicolor
Warner / Redford–Ritchie (Walter Coblenz)

A young Californian lawyer is persuaded to run for senator; in succeeding, he alienates his wife and obscures his real opinions.
Put together in a slightly scrappy but finally persuasive style, this joins a select band of rousing, doubting American political films.

w Jeremy Larner *d* Michael Ritchie *ph* Victor J. Kemper *m* John Rubinstein

Robert Redford, Peter Boyle, *Don Porter*, Allen Garfield, Karen Carlson, Quinn Redeker, Morgan Upton, *Melvyn Douglas*
 'Decent entertainment . . . it is never boring, but it is never enlarging, informationally or emotionally or thematically.'—*Stanley Kauffmann*

AA: Jeremy Larner
● *Video: Warner*

Candide
France 1960   90m   bw
CLM / SN Pathé (Clément Duhour)

Ever optimistic, a 20th-century Candide tours Nazi prison camps, communist countries and various South American revolutions. Scrappily-made satire which soon overstays its welcome.

wd Norbert Carbonneaux, from Voltaire *ph* Robert Le Fèbvre *m* Hubert Rostaing

Jean-Pierre Cassel, Daliah Lavi, Pierre Brasseur, Nadia Gray, Michel Simon, Louis de Funès

Candlelight in Algeria
GB 1943   85m   bw

Spies seek whereabouts of Allied rendezvous. Elementary spy thriller using modest talents. Carla Lehmann, James Mason, Walter Rilla, Raymond Lovell, Enid Stamp Taylor. Written by Katherine Strueby and Brock Williams; directed by George King; for British Aviation.

Candles at Nine
GB 1944   86m   bw

A young heiress in her benefactor's old mansion is menaced by his housekeeper. Elementary *Cat and the Canary* reprise; cast understandably uneasy. Jessie Matthews, John Stuart, Beatrix Lehmann, Winifred Shotter, Reginald Purdell. Written by John Harlow and Basil Mason, from a novel by Anthony Gilbert; directed by John Harlow; for British National.

Candleshoe
GB 1977   101m   Technicolor
Walt Disney Productions (Hugh Attwooll)

An attempt to pass off a fake heiress to an English stately home is prevented by the resourceful butler.
Slackly handled comedy adventure full of easy targets and predictable incidents.

w David Swift, Rosemary Anne Sisson, *novel* Christmas at Candleshoe by Michael Innes *d* Norman Tokar *ph* Paul Beeson *m* Ron Goodwin

David Niven, Helen Hayes, Jodie Foster, Leo McKern, Veronica Quilligan, Ian Sharrock, Vivian Pickles
 'It might have been conceived by a computer called upon to produce the definitive pastiche of a Disney film of the 1970s.'—*Financial Times*

● *Video: Disney*

Candy
US 1968   124m   Technicolor
Selmur / Dear / Corona (Robert Haggiag)

An innocent girl defends herself from a fate worse than death in a variety of international situations.
Witless and charmless perversion of a sex satire in which the point (if any) was that the nymphet gladly surrendered herself to all the gentlemen for their own good. A star cast flounders helplessly in a morass of bad taste, bad film-making, and boredom.

w Buck Henry, *novel* Terry Southern *d* Christian Marquand *ph* Giuseppe Rotunno *m* Dave Grusin

Ewa Aulin, Richard Burton, Marlon Brando, James Coburn, Walter Matthau, Charles Aznavour, John Huston, Elsa Martinelli, Ringo Starr, John Astin
 'Hippy psychedelics are laid on with the self-destroying effect of an overdose of garlic.'—*MFB*
 'As an emetic, liquor is dandy, but *Candy* is quicker.'—*John Simon*

The Candy Man
US 1968   98m   Eastmancolor

A British drug pusher in Mexico City plots the kidnap of an American film star's child. Abysmal independent thriller with a star at the end of his tether. George Sanders, Leslie Parrish, Gina Roman, Manolo Fabregas. Written, produced and directed by Herbert J. Leder; for Sagittarius.

Cannery Row
US 1982   120m   Metrocolor
MGM / Michael Philips

Incidents in the life of a 1940s marine biologist who lives on the waterfront with bums and floozies.
Badly out of its time, this curious attempt at sentimental realism was long in the works but emerged as a bloodless, stultifying entertainment.

wd David S. Ward, *novel* John Steinbeck *ph* Sven Nykvist *m* Jack Nitzsche *ed* David Betherton *pd* Richard MacDonald

Nick Nolte, Debra Winger, Audra Lindley, Frank McRae, M. Emmet Walsh, John Huston (narrator)
 'Another MGM item in which the entertainment values are difficult to locate.'—*Variety*

† Raquel Welch, originally cast for the Winger role, was fired in mid-production.

Cannon for Cordoba
US 1970   104m   De Luxe   Panavision
UA / Mirisch (Stephen Kandel, Vincent Fenelly)

In 1912, the Mexican bandit Cordoba is outgunned and outwitted by a US army captain.
Fast-moving but rather uninteresting action adventure.

w Stephen Kandel *d* Paul Wendkos *ph* Antonio Macasoli *m* Elmer Bernstein

George Peppard, Raf Vallone, Giovanna Ralli, Pete Duel, Don Gordon, Nico Minardos, John Russell

Cannonball
US / Hong Kong 1976   93m   Metrocolor
Harbor / Shaw Brothers (Samuel W. Gelfman)
GB title: *Carquake*

Aggressive drivers compete in the Trans-American Grand Prix.
The plot is a thin excuse for multiple pile-ups and other road disasters. Moments amuse, but the violence quickly palls.

w Paul Bartel, Donald C. Simpson *d* Paul
Bartel *ph* Tak Fujimoto *m* David A.
Axelrod

David Carradine, Bill McKinney, Veronica
Hamel, Gerrit Graham, Judy Canova
  'A free-wheeling, stunt-studded, dented and
demented story of a road racer without
rules.'—*publicity*

The Cannonball Run
US 1980   95m   Technicolor
Golden Harvest (Albert S. Ruddy)

The adventures of ill-assorted contestants in
the illegal Cannonball coast-to-coast race.
Well-known stars are all at sea in this
comedy / disaster extravaganza, which seems
to have begun as a joke rather than a script.

w Brock Yates *d* Hal Needham *ph* Michael
Butler *md* Al Capps

Burt Reynolds, Roger Moore, Farrah Fawcett,
Dom DeLuise, Dean Martin, Sammy Davis
Jnr, Adrienne Barbeau, Jack Elam, Bert
Convy, Jamie Farr, Peter Fonda, Molly Picon,
Bianca Jagger
  'Lacking any recognizable plot or
characterization, or indeed incidental
invention, it merely offers a parade of inept
whimsy and lame intra-mural reference.'—*Tim
Pulleine, MFB*
  'Moviegoers who relish the screech of tyres
taking a fast turn on a narrow bend should
have a whale of a time.'—*Daily Mail*

Cannonball Run II
US 1983   108m   Technicolor

An Arab sheik puts up a million-dollar prize
for the Cannonball Run. Dispirited rehash of
number one, with poor technique and non-
performances by stars who should have known
better than to get involved. Burt Reynolds,
Dom DeLuise, Sammy Davis Jnr, Dean
Martin, Jamie Farr, Telly Savalas, Shirley
Maclaine, Frank Sinatra, Susan Anton,
Catherine Bach, Richard Kiel, Tim Conway,
Sid Caesar, Don Knotts, Ricardo Montalban,
Jim Nabors, Henry Silva. Written by Hal
Needham, Albert S. Ruddy, Harvey Miller;
directed by Hal Needham; for Golden
Harvest / Warners.

Canon City*
US 1948   82m   bw
Eagle Lion / Bryan Foy (Robert T. Kane)

Convicts break out of the Colorado State
Prison.
Minor semi-documentary melodrama, quite
effectively presented.

wd Crane Wilbur *ph* John Alton

Scott Brady, Jeff Corey, Whit Bissell, Stanley
Clements, De Forrest Kelley

Can't Help Singing*
US 1944   90m   Technicolor
Universal (Frank Ross)

A Washington heiress chases her army
lieutenant lover across the wild west to
California.
Lively star musical which could have used a
little more wit in its lighthearted script.

w Lewis Foster, Frank Ryan *d* Frank Ryan
ph Woody Bredell, W. Howard Greene
m Jerome Kern *ly* E. Y. Harburg
md Jerome Kern, Hans Salter

Deanna Durbin, David Bruce, Robert Paige,
Akim Tamiroff, Leonid Kinskey, Ray Collins,
Thomas Gomez
  'This could have been a beautiful and gay
picture, but it is made without much feeling
for beauty or gaiety.'—*James Agee*

AAN: Jerome Kern, Hans Salter; song 'More
and More' (*m* Jerome Kern, *ly* E. Y.
Harburg)
Other songs: 'Elbow Room'; 'Any Moment
Now'; 'Californ-i-ay'; 'Swing Your Sweetheart
round the Fire'; 'Finale Ultimo'

Can't Stop the Music
US 1980   124m   Metrocolor   Panavision
EMI / Allan Carr

A Greenwich Village pop group hits the
bigtime.
Curiously old-fashioned youth musical,
unwisely touted as something special, which it
isn't.

w Bronte Woodward, Allan Carr *d* Nancy
Walker
ph Bill Butler *m* Jacques Morali

The Village People, Valerie Perrine, Paul
Sand, Bruce Jenner, Tammy Grimes, June
Havoc, Barbara Rush, Jack Weston
  'The hype disaster of the 80s, a grisly rehash
of the let's-start-a-group-of-our-own plot,
peopled with butch gay stereotypes of both
sexes pretending to be straight. The pervasive
tackiness is unrelieved.'—*Time Out*
  'Desperately knowing about the eighties but
fixed remorselessly in a time warp of fifties
hokum.'—*Guardian*
  'All noise, lights, slogans, movement and
dazzle, like a 124m commercial devoted to
selling you a product you can't use.'—*Sunday
Times*
  'One doesn't watch it, one is attacked by
it.'—*New England Entertainment Digest*
  'Considering the low level of wit, perhaps
the Village People should consider renaming
themselves the Village Idiots.'—*Los Angeles
Magazine*
  'This shamefully tacky musical extravaganza
fails on every aesthetic level.'—*Los Angeles
Herald Examiner*
  'A forced marriage between the worst of
sitcom plotting and the highest of high camp
production numbers.'—*New West*
● *Video: Thorn EMI*

A Canterbury Tale*
GB 1944   124m   bw
Rank / Archers (Michael Powell, Emeric
  Pressburger)

A batty magistrate is unmasked by a land girl,
an army sergeant and a GI.
Curious would-be propaganda piece with Old
England bathed in a roseate wartime glow, but
the plot seems to have little to do with
Chaucer. Indeed, quite what Powell and
Pressburger thought they were up to is hard to
fathom, but the detail is interesting.

wd Michael Powell and Emeric Pressburger
ph Erwin Hillier

Eric Portman, Sheila Sim, John Sweet, Dennis
Price, Esmond Knight, Charles Hawtrey, Hay
Petrie, George Merritt, Edward Rigby
  'To most people the intentions of the film-
makers remained highly mysterious; nor did
this picture of the British administration of
justice commend itself to the authorities, who
showed some reluctance to encourage its
export to our allies.'—*Basil Wright, 1972*

The Canterbury Tales
Italy / France 1971   109m (English
  version)   Technicolor
UA / PEA / PAA (Alberto Grimaldi)

Medieval pilgrims amuse each other by telling
stories on the way to Canterbury.
A sweaty selection of the tales in their more
prurient aspects, with relentless emphasis on
excrement and sex perversions.

wd Pier Paolo Pasolini, after Chaucer
ph Tonino Delli Colli

Pier Paolo Pasolini (as Chaucer), Hugh
Griffith, Laura Betti, Tom Baker, Ninetto
Davoli, Franco Citti
  'Caricature Chaucer, with pilgrims losing
the way to Canterbury amid a forest of male
genitalia.'—*Sight and Sound*
  'The vivid depiction of taboo subjects
emerges less as an affirmation of the
Chaucerian belief that all human activity lies
within the artist's scope, than as a bludgeoning
over-emphasis on physical appetite as man's
primal motive for action.'—*Nigel Andrews,
MFB*

The Canterville Ghost*
US 1943   95m   bw
MGM (Arthur Field)

The young girl heiress of an English castle
introduces GIs to the resident ghost.
Leaden comedy a long way after Oscar Wilde,
sunk by slow script and direction, but partly
salvaged by the respective roguishness and
infant charm of its stars.

w Edwin Blum *d* Jules Dassin *ph* Robert
Planck *m* George Bassman

Charles Laughton, Margaret O'Brien, Robert
Young, William Gargan, Rags Ragland, Peter
Lawford, Una O'Connor, Mike Mazurki
† In the mid 1970s, a television version
starring David Niven was made by HTV.

Canyon Crossroads
US 1954   84m   bw

A uranium prospector is trailed by thieves.
Acceptable modern western. Richard
Basehart, Phyllis Kirk, Stephen Elliott,
Russell Collins, Charles Wagenheim. Written
by Emmett Murphy and Leonard Heideman;
directed by Alfred Werker; for MPT / UA.

Canyon Passage*
US 1946   99m   Technicolor
Universal (Walter Wanger)

In the 1850s along the pioneering tracks the
west's first towns were being built . . .

Simple, scrappy but generally pleasing film which gives a vivid picture of pioneering life while minimizing its hardships.

w Ernest Pascal, William Fosche d Jacques Tourneur ph Edward Cronjager m Frank Skinner

Dana Andrews, Patricia Roc, Hoagy Carmichael, Brian Donlevy, Susan Hayward, Ward Bond, Andy Devine, Lloyd Bridges
'Miles of beautiful scenery, lavishly punctuated with rough-and-tumble episodes, moments of tender romance and a smattering of folk customs.'—New York Times

AAN: song 'Ole Buttermilk Sky' (m Hoagy Carmichael, ly Jack Brooks)

Cape Fear
US 1962   106m   bw
U-I / Melville–Talbot (Sy Bartlett)

An ex-convict blames a lawyer for his sentence and threatens to rape the lawyer's wife. Unpleasant and drawn out suspenser with characters of cardboard and situations from stock.

w James R. Webb, novel The Executioners by John D. MacDonald d J. Lee-Thompson ph Sam Leavitt m Bernard Herrmann

Gregory Peck, Robert Mitchum, Polly Bergen, Martin Balsam, Lori Martin, Jack Kruschen, Telly Savalas

The Caper of the Golden Bulls
US 1966   104m   Pathecolor
Embassy (Clarence Greene)
GB title: Carnival of Thieves

Ex-air-aces rob banks in order to pay for the restoration of a French cathedral they had to bomb; to avoid incrimination they are blackmailed into doing one last job in Pamplona.
Ingeniously plotted, flatly executed suspenser set in Pamplona during the bull run.

w Ed Waters, William Moessinger, novel William P. McGivern d Russel Rouse ph Hal Stine m Vic Mizzy

Stephen Boyd, Giovanna Ralli, Yvette Mimieux, Walter Slezak, Vito Scotti

Capetown Affair
US / SA 1967   100m   De Luxe
TCF / Killarney (Robert D. Webb)

A pickpocket on a South African bus steals a purse containing secret microfilm.
Flatulent remake of Pickup on South Street with nothing but the unfamiliar locale to recommend it.

w Harold Medford, Samuel Fuller d Robert D. Webb ph David Millin m Bob Adams

James Brolin, Jacqueline Bisset, Claire Trevor, Bob Courtney, Jon Whiteley

'The man who made the twenties roar! Now, after 45 years, his true story can be told!'
Capone
US 1975   101m   De Luxe
TCF / Santa Fe (Roger Corman)

Exploitation version of the Capone story, with the emphasis on unpleasant violence.

w Howard Browne d Steve Carver ph Vilis Lapenieks m David Grisman

Ben Gazzara, Sylvester Stallone, Susan Blakely, Harry Guardino, John Cassavetes, John Davis Chandler, Peter Maloney, Royal Dano
† See also: Al Capone.

Caprice*
US 1967   98m   De Luxe   Cinemascope
TCF / Aaron Rosenberg, Marty Melcher

A career girl investigating the death of her boss discovers that a cosmetics empire is the front for international drug smuggling.
Incoherent kaleidoscope which switches from farce to suspense and Bond-style action, scattering in-jokes along the way. Bits of it however are funny, and it looks good.

w Jay Jayson, Frank Tashlin d Frank Tashlin ph Leon Shamroy (who also appears) m Frank de Vol

Doris Day, Richard Harris, Edward Mulhare, Ray Walston, Jack Kruschen, Lilia Skala, Irene Tsu, Michael Romanoff, Michael J. Pollard

Capricious Summer*
Czechoslovakia 1968   75m   Eastmancolor
Ceskoslovensky Film (Jan Libora)

The beautiful assistant of a wandering tightrope walker sets up sexual tensions when they stop at a sleepy riverside town.
Amusing little period comedy in a period setting.

wd Jiri Menzel ph Jaromir Sofr m Jiri Sust

Rudolf Hrusinsky, Vlastimil Brodsky, Frantisek Rehak, Jana Drchalova, Jiri Menzel

Capricorn One
US 1978   128m   CFI colour
Associated General / Lew Grade (Paul N. Lazarus III)

A reporter discovers that the first manned space flight to Mars was a hoax.
Smartly packaged topical adventure thriller rather marred by its all star cast.

wd Peter Hyams ph Bill Butler m Jerry Goldsmith pd Albert Brenner

Elliott Gould, James Brolin, Brenda Vaccaro, Sam Waterston, O. J. Simpson, Hal Holbrook, Telly Savalas, Karen Black, David Huddleston
'After weighing in with some Watergate / Bernstein pretensions, the makers then opt for boring, Bondish derring-do.'—Sight and Sound

● Video: Precision Video

Captain Apache
US / Spain 1971   94m   Technicolor
'Scope
Benmar (Milton Sperling, Philip Yordan, Irving Lerner)

An Indian serving with US army intelligence tracks down a gun runner.
An old formula tarted up with the new violence. Very ho-hum.

w Philip Yordan, Milton Sperling, novel S. E. Whitman d Alexander Singer ph John Cabrera m Dolores Claman

Lee Van Cleef, Carroll Baker, Stuart Whitman, Percy Herbert, Tony Vogel

Captain Applejack
US 1931   70m   bw

A timid man turns the tables on crooks who plan to find treasure beneath his ancestral home. Early talkie version of a well-worn play previously filmed in 1923. John Halliday, Kay Strozzi, Arthur Edmund Carewe, Mary Brian, Louise Closser Hale. Written by Maude Fulton, from Ambrose Applejohn's Adventure by Walter Hackett; directed by Hobart Henley; for Warner.

Captain Bill
GB 1935   81m   bw

A bargee saves a schoolmistress from trouble with crooks. By reputation the best of its star's modest comedies, which have not yet been rediscovered. Leslie Fuller, Georgie Harris, Judy Kelly, Hal Gordon, O. B. Clarence. Written by Val Valentine, Syd Courtenay and George Harris; directed by Ralph Ceder; for ABFD.

Captain Black Jack
US / France 1952   90m   bw

A Riviera socialite pretends to be an undercover agent but is really a smuggler; she is unmasked by a doctor who is really a detective. Trashy hodgepodge with a remarkable cast of ageing stars: George Sanders, Agnes Moorehead, Herbert Marshall, Patricia Roc, Marcel Dalio. Written by Julien Duvivier and Charles Spaak; directed by Julien Duvivier; for Walter Gould.

'A million dollars worth of adventure! To do justice in words to its fascination is impossible!'
'His sword carved his name across the continents—and his glory across the seas!'
Captain Blood**
US 1935   119m   bw
Warner (Harry Joe Brown)

A young British surgeon, wrongly condemned by Judge Jeffreys for helping rebels, escapes and becomes a Caribbean pirate.
Modestly produced but quite exhilarating pirate adventure notable for making a star of Errol Flynn. Direction makes the most of very limited production values.

w Casey Robinson, novel Rafael Sabatini d Michael Curtiz ph Hal Mohr m Erich Wolfgang Korngold ad Anton Grot

Errol Flynn, Olivia de Havilland, Basil Rathbone, Lionel Atwill, Guy Kibbee, Ross Alexander, Henry Stephenson, Forrester Harvey, Hobart Cavanaugh, Donald Meek
'A lavish, swashbuckling saga of the Spanish Main . . . it can't fail at the wickets.'—Variety

'Here is a fine spirited mix-up with clothes and wigs which sometimes hark back to the sixteenth century and sometimes forward to the period of Wolfe . . . one is quite prepared for the culminating moment when the Union Jack breaks proudly, anachronistically forth at Peter Blood's masthead.'—*Graham Greene*
'Magnificently photographed, lavishly produced, and directed with consummate skill.'—*Picturegoer*

AAN: best picture

Captain Boycott*
GB 1947 93m bw
GFD / Individual (Frank Launder, Sidney Gilliat)

In 1880, poor Irish farmers rebel against their tyrannical English landlords.
Modest historical drama in which a splendid cast is rather subdued.

w Wolfgang Wilhelm, Frank Launder, Paul Vincent Carroll, Patrick Campbell, *novel* Philip Rooney *d* Frank Launder *ph* Wilkie Cooper *m* William Alwyn

Stewart Granger, Kathleen Ryan, Alastair Sim, Robert Donat (a cameo as Parnell), Cecil Parker, Mervyn Johns, Noel Purcell, Niall MacGinnis

Captain Carey USA
US 1950 83m bw
Paramount (Richard Maibaum)
GB title: *After Midnight*

After the war, a military officer returns to an Italian village to expose the informer who betrayed his comrades.
Muddled and rather boring melodrama with a labyrinthine plot which seems to have stultified all concerned. It did produce a hit song, 'Mona Lisa'.

w Robert Thoeren, *novel* Dishonoured by Martha Albrand *d* Mitchell Leisen *ph* John F. Seitz *m* Hugo Friedhofer

Alan Ladd, Francis Lederer, Wanda Hendrix, Joseph Calleia, Celia Lovsky, Angela Clarke, Jane Nigh, Frank Puglia, Luis Alberni

AA: song 'Mona Lisa' (*m / ly* Ray Evans, Jay Livingston)

Captain Caution
US 1940 84m bw
Hal Roach

In 1812, a girl takes over her dead father's ship and fights the British.
Lively though unconvincing adventure with emphasis on comedy.

w Grover Jones, *novel* Kenneth Roberts *d* Richard Wallace *ph* Norbert Brodine *m* Phil Ohman

Victor Mature, Louise Platt, Bruce Cabot, Leo Carrillo, Robert Barrat, Vivienne Osborne, Alan Ladd

Captain China
US 1949 97m bw
Paramount / Pine-Thomas (William H. Pine, William C. Thomas)

A wandering seafarer seeks the mate who betrayed him.
Action melodrama with a second team look; all rather listless.

w Lewis R. Foster, Gwen Bagni *d* Lewis R. Foster *ph* John Alton *m* Lucien Caillet

John Payne, Gail Russell, Jeffrey Lynn, Lon Chaney Jnr, Michael O'Shea, Ellen Corby

Captain Clegg*
GB 1962 82m Technicolor
Universal / Hammer (John Temple-Smith)
US title: *Night Creatures*

The vicar of an 18th-century village in Romney Marsh is really a retired pirate, now doing a little smuggling on the side.
Mild remake of *Dr Syn* with a few moments of violence added; watchable for those who like totally predictable plot development.

w John Elder *d* Peter Graham Scott *ph* Arthur Grant *m* Don Banks

Peter Cushing, Patrick Allen, Michael Ripper, Oliver Reed, Derek Francis, Milton Reid, Martin Benson, David Lodge

Captain Eddie
US 1945 107m bw
TCF / Eureka

Eddie Rickenbacker, adrift on a life raft after a plane crash in the Pacific, thinks back on his adventurous life in aviation.
Flat and surprisingly poorly made biopic with little to hold the attention.

w John Tucker Battle *d* Lloyd Bacon *ph* Joe MacDonald *m* Cyril Mockridge

Fred MacMurray, Lynn Bari, Thomas Mitchell, Lloyd Nolan, Charles Bickford

Captain from Castile
US 1947 140m Technicolor
TCF (Lamar Trotti)

A young 15th-century Spaniard hopes for fame and fortune in the New World.
Rather empty and boring adventure epic from a bestseller; high production values produce moments of interest.

w Lamar Trotti, *novel* Samuel Shellabarger *d* Henry King *ph* Charles Clarke, Arthur E. Arling *m* Alfred Newman *ad* Richard Day, James Basevi

Tyrone Power, Jean Peters, Lee J. Cobb, Cesar Romero, John Sutton, Antonio Moreno, Thomas Gomez, Alan Mowbray, Barbara Lawrence, George Zucco, Roy Roberts, Marc Lawrence
'The first few reels have flow and a kind of boy's-book splendour; the rest is locomotor ataxia.'—*James Agee*

AAN: Alfred Newman

Captain Fury*
US 1939 91m bw
Hal Roach

In 19th-century Australia, an adventurer fights the evil head of a penal colony.
Shades of Zorro and Robin Hood in a brawling, comic actioner typical of this producer.

w Grover Jones, Jack Jevne, William de Mille *d* Hal Roach *ph* Norbert Brodine *m* Marvin Hatley

Brian Aherne, Victor McLaglen, Paul Lukas, June Lang, John Carradine
'Action, fast riding, gunplay, surprise attacks, some broad comedy and a few dashes of romance . . . will do pretty good biz in the keys, but will hit a more profitable stride in the subsequents.'—*Variety*

The Captain Hates the Sea*
US 1934 92m bw
Columbia

Crime and comedy on an ocean voyage.
Zany, rather endearing comedy which gave the star his last role.

w Wallace Smith *d* Lewis Milestone *ph* Joseph August

John Gilbert, Victor McLaglen, Walter Connolly, Alison Skipworth, Wynne Gibson, Helen Vinson, Leon Errol, Walter Catlett, Donald Meek, Arthur Treacher, Akim Tamiroff
'A fine cast, excellent comedy relief and expert direction.'—*Variety*
'The best neglected picture in two years.'—*Otis Ferguson, 1936*

Captain Horatio Hornblower RN
GB 1951 117m Technicolor
Warner (Raoul Walsh)

Events from the adventure novels about a 19th-century sailor who outwits the Spaniards and the French and marries his admiral's widow.
Sprawling, plotless sea saga with the cast ill at ease in highly unconvincing sets: no air seems to blow across the decks of the *Lydia*.

w Ivan Goff, Ben Roberts, Aeneas Mackenzie, *novels* C. S. Forester *d* Raoul Walsh *ph* Guy Green *m* Robert Farnon *ad* Tom Morahan

Gregory Peck, Virginia Mayo, Robert Beatty, James Robertson Justice, Terence Morgan, Moultrie Kelsall, Richard Hearne, Denis O'Dea
'No point makes a strong enough impression to suggest a main line of criticism.'—*Richard Mallett, Punch*

The Captain Is a Lady*
US 1940 63m bw

A sea captain is forced by ill-fortune to send his wife to an old ladies' home, but he dresses as a woman to be with her. Absurd-sounding comedy not without a certain lunatic charm. Charles Coburn, Billie Burke, Beulah Bondi, Dan Dailey, Virginia Grey, Helen Broderick, Helen Westley. Written by Harry Clark, from a play by Rachel Crothers; directed by Robert Sinclair; for MGM.

Captain January*
US 1936 74m bw
TCF (Darryl F. Zanuck)

A little girl is rescued from a shipwreck by a lighthouse keeper.

Standard Shirley Temple vehicle with pleasing dialogue and numbers.

w Sam Hellman, Gladys Lehman, Harry Tugend, *novel* Laura E. Richards *d* David Butler *ph* John F. Seitz *m* Louis Silvers *songs* Lew Pollack, Sidney Mitchell, Jack Yellen

Shirley Temple, Guy Kibbee, Buddy Ebsen, Slim Summerville, June Lang, Sara Haden, Jane Darwell

Captain Kidd
US 1945 90m bw
Benedict Bogeaus

A pirate tricks King William III into giving him royal orders, but enemies he believes dead return to see him hanged.
Rather poorly produced vehicle for a star who however rants and raves to some effect.

w Norman Reilly Raine *d* Rowland V. Lee *ph* Archie Stout *m* Werner Janssen

Charles Laughton, Randolph Scott, Barbara Britton, Reginald Owen, John Carradine, Gilbert Roland, Sheldon Leonard

AAN: Werner Janssen

Captain Kidd and the Slave Girl
US 1954 82m CFI Color

A scheming earl reprieves Captain Kidd so that he can steal his treasure. Cut-price swashbuckler with more vigour than some. Anthony Dexter, Eva Gabor, Alan Hale Jnr, James Seay. Written by Aubrey Wisberg and Jack Pollexfen; directed by Lew Landers; for Reliance / UA.

Captain Lightfoot
US 1955 92m Technicolor print Cinemascope
U-I (Ross Hunter)

Adventures of a 19th-century Irish rebel. Dullish adventure story with the star ill at ease.

w W. R. Burnett, Oscar Brodney *d* Douglas Sirk *ph* Irving Glassberg *m* Joseph Gershenson

Rock Hudson, Barbara Rush, Jeff Morrow, Kathleen Ryan, Finlay Currie, Denis O'Dea, Geoffrey Toone

Captain Nemo and the Underwater City
GB 1969 106m Metrocolor Panavision
MGM / Omnia (Steven Pallos, Bertram Ostrer)

Six survivors from an Atlantic shipwreck are picked up by a mysterious submarine and have adventures in a spectacular underwater city. Further adventures of Jules Verne's engaging Victorian character from *Twenty Thousand Leagues under the Sea*. Here however the general production values are stolid rather than solid, and the script makes heavy weather.

w Pip Baker, Jane Baker, R. Wright Campbell *d* James Hill *ph* Alan Hume, Egil Woxholt *m* Walter Stott *ad* Bill Andrews

Robert Ryan, Chuck Connors, Bill Fraser, Kenneth Connor, Nanette Newman, John Turner, Luciana Paluzzi, Allan Cuthbertson

Captain Newman MD*
US 1963 126m Eastmancolor
Universal–Brentwood–Reynard (Robert Arthur)

At an army air base during World War II, a psychiatrist has varied success with his patients.
A decidedly curious comedy drama on the fringe of bad taste; it should have turned out better than it does, but will entertain those who like hospital heroics drenched in bitter-sweet sentimentality.

w Richard L. Breen, Phoebe and Henry Ephron, *novel* Leo Rosten *d* David Miller *ph* Russell Metty *m* Joseph Gershenson

Gregory Peck, Tony Curtis, Angie Dickinson, Eddie Albert, Bobby Darin, James Gregory, Jane Withers, Bethel Leslie, Robert Duvall, Larry Storch, Robert F. Simon, Dick Sargent

AAN: script; Bobby Darin

Captain of the Guard
US 1930 83m bw

During the French Revolution, a guards captain changes sides. Unexciting historical melodrama which failed to make the intended impression. John Boles, Laura La Plante, Lionel Belmore, Sam de Grasse, James Marcus, Otis Harlan. Written by Arthur Ripley, from a story by Houston Branch; directed by Paul Fejos and John S. Robertson; music and songs by Charles Wakefield Cedman; for Carl Laemmle / Universal.
'Universal's most pretentious release of the season . . . liberal expenditure shows on the screen.'—*Variety*

Captain Pirate
US 1952 85m Technicolor
Columbia (Harry Joe Brown)
GB title: *Captain Blood, Fugitive*

A reformed pirate, accused of sacking Cartagena, returns to piracy to discover the perpetrators.
Lively buccaneering programmer with an adequate budget and plenty of high spirits.

w Robert Libbott, Frank Burt, John Meredyth Lucas, *novel* Captain Blood Returns by Rafael Sabatini *d* Ralph Murphy *ph* Charles Lawton Jnr *m* George Duning

Louis Hayward, Patricia Medina, John Sutton, George Givot, Rex Evans, Ted de Corsia, Charles Irwin

Captain Scarlett
US 1952 75m Technicolor
UA / Craftsman (Howard Dimsdale)

After the Napoleonic wars, southern France is in need of a protector against the villainous Duke of Corlaine. Captain Scarlett rides into action . . .
Robin Hood in all but name, an old tale retold without much flair.

w Howard Dimsdale *d* Thomas Carr *ph* Charles Carbajal *m* Elias Breeskin

Richard Greene, Leonora Amar, Nedrick Young, Eduardo Norriega

Captain Sinbad*
US / Germany 1963 88m
Eastmancolor Wonderscope
King Brothers

Sinbad returns to Baristan and by means of magic deposes a sultan.
Rather splendid adventure fantasy with a European flavour, good trick effects and full-blooded performances.

w Samuel B. West, Harry Relis *d* Byron Haskin *ph* Gunther Senftleben, Eugen Shuftan *m* Michel Michelet *sp* Tom Howard *ad* Werner and Isabell Schlicting

Guy Williams, Pedro Armendariz, Heidi Bruhl, Abraham Sofaer

Captain Tugboat Annie
US 1945 70m bw

Annie wants to adopt a small boy but by clerical error gets a young man instead. A silly story which prevented this reworking of the old Dressler–Beery vehicle from becoming a series. Jane Darwell, Edgar Kennedy, Charles Gordon. Written by C. Callahan; directed by Phil Rosen; for Republic.

Captains Courageous**
US 1937 116m bw
MGM (Louis D. Lighton)

A spoiled rich boy falls off a cruise liner and lives for a while among fisherfolk who teach him how to live.
Semi-classic Hollywood family film which is not all that enjoyable while it's on but is certainly a good example of the prestige picture of the thirties. (It also happened to be good box office.)

w John Lee Mahin, Marc Connelly, Dale Van Every, *novel* Rudyard Kipling *d* Victor Fleming *ph* Harold Rosson *m* Franz Waxman

Spencer Tracy, Lionel Barrymore, Freddie Bartholemew, Mickey Rooney, Melvyn Douglas, Charley Grapewin, Christian Rub, John Carradine, Walter Kingsford, Leo G. Carroll, Charles Trowbridge

'Will not have to go begging for patronage . . . one of the best pictures of the sea ever made.'—*Variety*

'Another of those grand jobs of movie-making we have come to expect from Hollywood's most profligate studio.'—*Frank S. Nugent, New York Times*

† 1977 brought a TV movie remake.

AA: Spencer Tracy
AAN: best picture; script

The Captain's Kid
US 1936 72m bw

In New England, a retired sea captain's blood-chilling tales thrill a little girl and involve him in a real-life court case. Slightly unusual tale which deserved better handling than this routine second feature allows. Guy Kibbee, May Robson, Sybil Jason, Jane Bryan, Dick Purcell. Written by Tom Reed; directed by Nick Grinde; for Warner.

Captains of the Clouds
US 1942 113m Technicolor
Warner (Hal. B. Wallis, William Cagney)

A flippant Canadian Air Force pilot proves his worth under fire.
Recruiting poster heroics, reasonably well done but lacking the vital spark.

w Arthur T. Horman, Richard Macauley, Norman Reilly Raine d Michael Curtiz
ph Sol Polito, Wilfrid M. Cline m Max Steiner

James Cagney, Dennis Morgan, Brenda Marshall, George Tobias, Alan Hale, Reginald Gardiner, Reginald Denny, Paul Cavanagh, Clem Bevans, J. M. Kerrigan
'Pure tribute to the unchanging forcefulness of James Cagney.'—*New York Post*

AAN: Sol Polito, Wilfrid M. Cline

The Captain's Paradise*
GB 1953 89m bw
BL / London (Anthony Kimmins)

The captain of a steamer plying between Gibraltar and Tangier has a wife in each port, one to suit each of his personalities.
Over-dry comedy in which the idea is much funnier than the script. One is left with the memory of a pleasant star performance.

w Alec Coppel, Nicholas Phipps d Anthony Kimmins ph Ted Scaife m Malcolm Arnold

Alec Guinness, Celia Johnson, Yvonne de Carlo, Charles Goldner, Miles Malleson, Bill Fraser, Nicholas Phipps, Ferdy Mayne, George Benson

AAN: original story (Alec Coppel)

The Captain's Table*
GB 1958 89m Eastmancolor
Rank (Joseph Janni)

A cargo skipper is given command of a luxury liner and has to watch his manners.
Lively adaptation of a frivolous book of obvious jokes, most of which come up quite funny amid the luxurious surroundings.

w John Whiting, Bryan Forbes, Nicholas Phipps, *novel* Richard Gordon d Jack Lee
ph Christopher Challis m Frank Cordell

John Gregson, Peggy Cummins, *Donald Sinden*, Reginald Beckwith, Nadia Gray, Richard Wattis, Maurice Denham, Nicholas Phipps, Joan Sims, Miles Malleson
● Video: Rank

The Captive City**
US 1951 91m bw
UA / Aspen (Theron Warth)

Small-town corruption imposed by the Mafia is revealed by a crusading editor who defies threats to his wife and family and tells all to the Kefauver Commission.
Excellent documentary melodrama made in a style then original, also notable for use of the Hoge deep focus lens.

w Karl Lamb, Alvin Josephy Jnr d Robert Wise ph Lee Garmes m Jerome Moross

John Forsythe, Joan Camden, Harold J. Kennedy, Marjorie Crossland, Victor Sutherland, Ray Teal, Martin Milner, Hal K. Dawson

The Captive Heart**
GB 1946 108m bw
Ealing (Michael Relph)

Stories of life among British officers in a German POW camp, especially of a Czech who has stolen the papers of a dead Britisher.
Archetypal POW drama lacing an almost poetic treatment with humour and melodrama.

w Angus Macphail, Guy Morgan d Basil Dearden ph Lionel Banes, Douglas Slocombe m Alan Rawsthorne

Michael Redgrave, *Jack Warner*, Basil Radford, Mervyn Johns, Jimmy Hanley, Gordon Jackson, Ralph Michael, Derek Bond, Karel Stepanek, Guy Middleton, Jack Lambert, Gladys Henson, Rachel Kempson, Meriel Forbes

Captive Wild Woman
US 1943 60m bw

A doctor finds a way of developing the glands of an ape and turning it into a beautiful girl.
Lamebrain horror item which amazingly spawned two sequels, *Jungle Woman* (1944) and *Jungle Captive* (1945). Evelyn Ankers, Aquanetta, John Carradine, Martha Vickers, Milburn Stone. Written by Griffin Jay and Henry Sucher; directed by Edward Dmytryk; for Universal.

Captured
US 1933 72m bw

A prisoner-of-war discovers that his best friend was his wife's lover. Turgid and heavy-going early variation on a theme which would become very familiar indeed; the stars couldn't save it. Leslie Howard, Paul Lukas, Douglas Fairbanks Jnr, Margaret Lindsay, J. Carrol Naish, Arthur Hohl. Written by Edward Chodorov, from a novel by Sir Philip Gibbs; directed by Roy Del Ruth; for Warner. 'Too many obviously adverse ingredients, chiefly story, to chalk this one up as a winner . . . at best its earnings shape up as spotty.'—*Variety*

'Is it a phantom, a demon, or the devil himself?'

The Car
US 1977 98m Technicolor Panavision
Universal (Peter Saphier)

A small southwestern town is terrorized by a driverless car which may be a creation of the devil.
Silly suspenser with a draggy midsection.

w Dennis Shyrack, Michael Butler, Lane Slate d Elliot Silverstein ph Gerald Hirschfeld m Leonard Rosenman

James Brolin, Kathleen Lloyd, John Marley, R. G. Armstrong, John Rubenstein

Car 99
US 1935 70m bw

A novice state trooper redeems early failure by capturing bank robbers. Competent routine programmer which helped to establish its star. Fred MacMurray, Ann Sheridan, Sir Guy Standing. Written by Karl Ditzer and C. Gardner Sullivan; directed by Charles Barton; for Paramount. 'Heaps of excitement and comedy make a swell hour of entertainment for the nabe element.'—*Variety*

Car of Dreams
GB 1935 72m bw

A rich man's son buys a car for one of his father's factory girls. Silly comedy with sillier music, remade from a German original. John Mills, Grete Mosheim, Mark Lester, Robertson Hare, Norah Howard. Written by Austin Melford; directed by Austin Melford and Graham Cutts; for Gaumont British.

Car Wash
US 1976 96m Technicolor

Various eccentrics congregate around the Dee Luxe Car Wash. Zany ethnic (black) comedy with little rhyme or reason in its development but a certain vigour in some of its sketches. A subsequent TV series didn't last. Franklyn Ajaye, Sully Boyar, Richard Pryor, Ivan Dixon, Antonio Fargas, Tracy Reed. Written by Joel Schumacher; directed by Michael Schultz; for Universal. 'Its specialty is yanking laughs by having blacks do dirtier versions of the standard pranks that naughty kids used to do in comedies.'—*Pauline Kael*

Caravan
US 1934 101m bw
Fox

A countess marries a gypsy.
Odd romantic drama with music: too whimsical to succeed.

w Samson Raphaelson d Erik Charell
ph Ernest Palmer, Theodor Sparkuhl
songs Werner B. Heymann, Gus Kahn

Loretta Young, Charles Boyer, Jean Parker, Phillips Holmes, Louise Fazenda, Eugene Pallette, C. Aubrey Smith, Charley Grapewin, Noah Beery, Dudley Digges
'Big, beautiful and boring . . . peasants come popping out of nowhere, in pairs, tens, hundreds, thousands, and burst into song.'—*Variety*

Caravan
GB 1946 122m bw
Gainsborough (Harold Huth)

A young man on a mission in Spain is left for dead by emissaries of his rival in love; he is nursed back to health by a gypsy girl who falls in love with him.
Artificial, romantic, high-flown period tosh without the courage of its lack of convictions. At the time, an exhibitor's dream.

w Roland Pertwee, *novel* Lady Eleanor Smith
d Arthur Crabtree ph Stephen Dade

Stewart Granger, Jean Kent, Anne Crawford, *Robert Helpmann*, Dennis Price, Gerard Heinz, Enid Stamp-Taylor, David Horne, John Salew

IS IT A PHANTOM, A DEMON,
OR THE DEVIL HIMSELF?

There's nowhere to turn, nowhere to hide, no way to stop...

THE CAR

UNIVERSAL PICTURES Presents
THE CAR
Starring JAMES BROLIN,
KATHLEEN LLOYD, JOHN MARLEY,
ELIZABETH THOMPSON and RONNY COX
Screenplay by DENNIS SHRYACK & MICHAEL BUTLER and LANE SLATE
Story by DENNIS SHRYACK & MICHAEL BUTLER   Music by LEONARD ROSENMAN   Directed by ELLIOT SILVERSTEIN
Produced by MARVIN BIRDT and ELLIOT SILVERSTEIN   A UNIVERSAL PICTURE · TECHNICOLOR ® PANAVISION ®
PG PARENTAL GUIDANCE SUGGESTED
SOME MATERIAL MAY NOT BE SUITABLE FOR PRE-TEENAGERS

THE CAR. One wonders what was original about the other demon car, *Christine*, which appeared several years later. Probably both movies borrowed the idea from a TV film called *Killdozer*, which at the time seemed very silly indeed.

Caravan to Vaccares
GB / France 1974 98m Eastmancolor
Panavision
Crowndale (Geoffrey Reeve)

An American drifter on the Riviera is
employed to escort a mysterious Hungarian to
New York.
Lumpy Alistair MacLean action thriller, all a
bit *déjà vu*.

w Paul Wheeler d Geoffrey Reeve
ph Frederic Tammes m Stanley Myers

David Birney, Charlotte Rampling, Michel
Lonsdale, Marcel Bozzuff, Michael Bryant
'An undernourished plot advanced only by a
series of venerable clichés.'—*MFB*
'The biggest load of schoolboy hokum since
Boy's Own Paper ceased circulation.'—
Michael Billington, Illustrated London News
● *Video: Rank*

Caravans
US / Iran 1978 123m Technicolor
Panavision
Ibex / FIDCI (Elmo Williams)

In the Middle East in 1948, a junior diplomat
is sent to bring back the daughter of a US
politician, who has married an arab, left him,
and joined a Bedouin caravan.
Curiously halting succession of pretty pictures
and not much plot; what there is tends to take
second place to philosophy and eastern
promise.

w Nancy Voyles Crawford, Thomas A.
MacMahon, Lorraine Williams, *novel* James
Michener d James Fargo ph Douglas
Slocombe m Mike Batt

Anthony Quinn, Michael Sarrazin, Jennifer
O'Neill, Christopher Lee, Joseph Cotten,
Barry Sullivan, Jeremy Kemp
'A tiresome exercise in anti-climax.'—*Tim
Pulleine, MFB*
● *Video: Guild*

Carbine Williams
US 1952 93m bw
MGM (Armand Deutsch)

An imprisoned bootlegger perfects a new gun
and is pardoned.
Flat fictionalization of a true story, with the
star miscast.

w Art Cohn d Richard Thorpe ph William
Mellor m Conrad Salinger

James Stewart, Jean Hagen, Wendell Corey,
Carl Benton Reid, Paul Stewart, Otto Hulett,
James Arness

Carbon Copy
US 1981 91m Metrocolor
Hemdale / RKO (Stanley Shapiro, Carter de
Haven)

An executive is shocked when his long-lost son
turns out to be black.
Stale comedy. The producers clearly think the
basic idea worth ramming home a score of
times; the characterization is thin and the
production undernourished.

w Stanley Shapiro d Michael Schultz ph Fred
J. Koenekamp m Bill Conti

George Segal, Susan Saint James, Jack
Warden, Dick Martin, Densel Washington,
Paul Winfield
'It makes *Guess Who's Coming to Dinner?*
look like a tract for the nineties.'—*Derek
Malcolm, Guardian*
● *Video: Guild*

The Card**
GB 1952 91m bw
Rank / British Film Makers (John Bryan)
US title: *The Promoter*

A bright young clerk from the potteries finds
many ingenious ways of improving his bank
account and his place in society.
Pleasing period comedy with the star in a
made-to-measure role and excellent
production values.

w Eric Ambler, *novel* Arnold Bennett
d Ronald Neame ph Oswald Morris ad T.
Hopwell Ash m William Alwyn

Alec Guinness, Glynis Johns, Petula Clark,
Valerie Hobson, Edward Chapman, Veronica
Turleigh, Gibb McLaughlin, Frank Pettingell
● *Video: Rank*

Card of Fate see Le Grand Jeu

Cardboard Cavalier*
GB 1949 96m bw
Rank / Two Cities (Walter Forde)

In Cromwellian England, royalists commission
a barrow boy to carry a secret letter. Helped
by Nell Gwynn, he succeeds after encounters
with a castle ghost and custard pies.
A pantomime crossed with an Aldwych farce
in a period setting. It failed at the time but
now seems a brave try, with nice judgment all
round.

w Noel Langley d Walter Forde ph Jack
Hildyard m Lambert Williamson

Sid Field, Margaret Lockwood, Mary Clare,
Jerry Desmonde, Claude Hulbert, Irene
Handl, Brian Worth, Edmund Willard (as
Cromwell)

The Cardinal*
US 1963 175m Technicolor
Panavision 70
Gamma / Otto Preminger

A 1917 ordinand becomes a Boston curate, a
fighter of the Ku Klux Klan, a Rome
diplomat, and finally gets a cardinal's hat.
Heavy-going documentary melodrama with
many interesting sequences marred by lack of
cohesion, too much grabbing at world
problems, and over-sensational personal
asides.

w Robert Dozier, *novel* Henry Morton
Robinson d Otto Preminger ph Leon
Shamroy m Jerome Moross pd Lyle
Wheeler titles Saul Bass

Tom Tryon, Carol Lynley, Dorothy Gish,
Maggie Macnamara, Cecil Kellaway, John
Saxon, John Huston, Robert Morse, Burgess
Meredith, Jill Haworth, Raf Vallone, Tullio
Carminati, Ossie Davis, Chill Wills, Arthur
Hunnicutt, Murray Hamilton, Patrick O'Neal,
Romy Schneider

'Very probably the last word in glossy
dishonesty posturing as serious art.'—*John
Simon*
'Mere and sheer wide screen Technicolor
movie.'—*Stanley Kauffmann*
AAN: Otto Preminger; Leon Shamroy; John
Huston

'To thwart a king's passion, he gambled
the fate of a nation!'
Cardinal Richelieu*
US 1935 83m bw
Twentieth Century (Darryl F. Zanuck)

Fictionalized biography of the unscrupulous
cardinal who was the grey eminence behind
Louis XIII.
One of George Arliss' better star vehicles,
with not much conviction but excellent
production values.

w Maude Howell, Cameron Rogers, W. P.
Lipscomb d Rowland V. Lee ph Peverell
Marley m Alfred Newman

George Arliss, Maureen O'Sullivan, Edward
Arnold, Cesar Romero
'In selecting the churchly cardinal of
Bulwer-Lytton rather than the cavalier-
cardinal beloved of Dumas, they have lost
romance and dash but gained compensating
dignity . . . a fine technical production.'—
Variety

Career
US 1939 80m bw
RKO (Robert Sisk)

A respected small-town storekeeper has old
scores to settle against the local banker.
Modest, pleasing, rather faded 'B' picture.

w Dalton Trumbo, Bert Granet, *novel* Phil
Stong d Leigh Jason ph Frank Redman

Edward Ellis, Samuel S. Hinds, Anne Shirley,
Janet Beecher, Leon Errol, Raymond Hatton,
Hobart Cavanaugh
'Small-town story will sell better outside
major playdates.'—*Variety*
† The film featured the winners of the
Gateway to Hollywood talent contest, John
Archer and Alice Eden.

Career*
US 1959 105m bw
Paramount / Hal B. Wallis (Paul Nathan)

An actor from the midwest finally gets his
chance in New York.
A location melodrama with the feel of a
documentary, well played but slow and rather
indeterminate.

w James Lee, from his play d Joseph
Anthony ph Joseph La Shelle m Franz
Waxman

Anthony Franciosa, Dean Martin, Shirley
Maclaine, Carolyn Jones, Joan Blackman,
Robert Middleton, Frank McHugh, Donna
Douglas

AAN: Joseph La Shelle

Career Woman
US 1936 75m bw

A shyster lawyer helps a girl student to win a murder case. Passable programme material which didn't bore. Michael Whalen, Claire Trevor, Isabel Jewell, Eric Linden, Virginia Field, Gene Lockhart, Ed Brophy, El Brendel. Written by Lamar Trotti from a story by Gene Fowler; directed by Lewis Seiler; for TCF. 'Teeters between farce and stark realism . . . not exactly for the family trade.'—*Variety*

Carefree*
US 1938 85m bw
RKO (Pandro S. Berman)

A humourless lawyer sends his undecided girl friend to an alienist, with whom she falls in love.
Slight, frothy comedy musical; quite palatable, but it signalled the end of the Astaire–Rogers series.

w Allan Scott, Ernest Pagano *d* Mark Sandrich *ph* Robert de Grasse *m / ly* Irving Berlin *ch* Hermes Pan *md* Victor Baravelle

Fred Astaire, Ginger Rogers, Ralph Bellamy, Luella Gear, Clarence Kolb, Jack Carson, Franklin Pangborne, Walter Kingsford, Hattie McDaniel
Songs: 'I Used to Be Colour Blind'; 'The Yam'; 'The Night Is Filled with Music'; 'Change Partners'
'Perhaps their poorest musical . . . a disappointing story and the stars alone may save it.'—*Variety*

AAN: Victor Baravelle; song 'Change Partners' (*m / ly* Irving Berlin)
● *Video: Kingston*

Careful, Soft Shoulder*
US 1942 69m bw
TCF (Walter Morosco)

A Washington socialite becomes a spy for both sides.
Modest, slightly unusual second feature which over the years has gathered for itself more reputation than it really deserves.

wd Oliver H. P. Garrett *ph* Charles Clarke *m* Leigh Harline

Virginia Bruce, James Ellison, Aubrey Mather, Sheila Ryan, Ralph Byrd

Careless Lady
US 1932 76m bw

A young girl from the country pretends to be a married society woman and finds herself with a husband she doesn't want. It was the scriptwriter who was careless: the story doesn't make much sense. Joan Bennett, John Boles, Minna Gombell, Weldon Heyburn, Raul Roulien, Fortunio Bonanova, Josephine Hull. Written by Guy Bolton from a story by Reita Lambert; directed by Kenneth MacKenna; for Fox. 'Reaching house averages will be beyond expectations regardless of campaign.'—*Variety*

The Caretaker*
GB 1964 105m bw
Caretaker Films (Michael Birkett)
US title: *The Guest*

Two brothers invite a revolting tramp to share their attic.
Rather doleful filming of the fashionable play with its non-plot, irregular conceits and interesting interplay of character. It remains a theatrical experience.

w Harold Pinter *d* Clive Donner *ph* Nicolas Roeg *m* Ron Grainer

Alan Bates, Robert Shaw, Donald Pleasence

The Caretakers*
US 1963 97m bw
UA / Hall Bartlett
GB title: *Borderlines*

The interrelationship of several cases in a state mental hospital.
Rather hysterical melodrama, lacking in the stature required for its subject, but sometimes perversely entertaining.

w Henry F. Greenberg, *novel* Daniel Telfer *d* Hall Bartlett *ph Lucien Ballard m* Elmer Bernstein

Polly Bergen, Robert Stack, Joan Crawford, Diane McBain, Janis Paige, Van Williams, Robert Vaughn, Herbert Marshall, Constance Ford

AAN: Lucien Ballard

The Carey Treatment*
US 1972 101m Metrocolor Panavision
MGM (William Belasco)

A Boston pathologist investigating the death of an abortion victim becomes the potential murder victim of a father turned killer.
Pretentious thriller with a tendency to make moral points among the bloodshed; vigorously but variably made.

w James P. Bonner, *novel* A Case of Need by Jeffrey Hudson *d* Blake Edwards *ph* Frank Stanley *m* Roy Budd

James Coburn, Jennifer O'Neill, Skye Aubrey, Pat Hingle, Dan O'Herlihy, Elizabeth Allen, Alex Dreier, Regis Toomey

Cargo to Capetown
US 1950 84m bw

A merchant ship captain Shanghais his friend on a long voyage. Routine, competently staged thick ear. Broderick Crawford, John Ireland, Ellen Drew, Edgar Buchanan, Ted de Corsia. Written by Lionel Houser; directed by Earl McEvoy; for Columbia.

Caribbean
US 1952 94m Technicolor
(Paramount) Pine–Thomas (William H. Pine, William C. Thomas)
GB title: *Caribbean Gold*

An 18th-century pirate captures the nephew of his old enemy.
Adequate but not very exciting swashbuckler with fair production values.

w Frank L. Moss, Edward Ludwig *d* Edward Ludwig *ph* Lionel Lindon *m* Lucien Cailliet

John Payne, Arlene Dahl, Cedric Hardwicke (incredibly cast as the pirate), Francis L. Sullivan, Dennis Hoey

The Caribbean Mystery
US 1945 65m bw

A Brooklyn detective arrives on a Caribbean island in search of a murderer. Good atmospheric second feature with local colour not getting in the way of the plot. James Dunn, Sheila Ryan, Edward Ryan, Roy Roberts. Written by Jack Andrews and Leonard Praskins; directed by Robert Webb; for TCF.

The Cariboo Trail
US 1949 80m Cinecolor

Prospectors get involved in a cattle war. Standard western full of predictable elements. Randolph Scott, Gabby Hayes, Bill Williams, Karin Booth, Victor Jory. Written by Frank Gruber; directed by Edwin L. Marin; for Nat Holt (TCF).

Carlton-Browne of the FO
GB 1958 88m bw
British Lion / Charter Films (John Boulting)
US title: *Man in a Cocked Hat*

When valuable mineral deposits are found in a small British colony, the diplomat sent to cement good relations does quite the reverse.
Hit-or-miss farcical comedy several rungs below the Ealing style, with all concerned in poor form.

wd Jeffrey Dell, Roy Boulting *ph* Max Greene *m* John Addison

Terry-Thomas, Peter Sellers, Ian Bannen, Thorley Walters, Raymond Huntley, John Le Mesurier, Luciana Paluzzi, Miles Malleson, Kynaston Reeves, Marie Lohr

Carmen**
Spain 1983 101m Eastmancolor

A rehearsal for the ballet *Carmen* finds dancers playing out in reality the parts of the drama. Enjoyable but exhausting melodrama with elements of *The Red Shoes*; meticulous choreography and direction are its chief assets. Antonio Gades, Laura del Sol, Paco de Lucia, Cristina Hoyos. Written by Carlos Saura, Antonio Gades; directed by *Carlos Saura*; for Emiliano Piedra Productions / Television Espanola. 'Extremely enjoyable, but lacks the edge that would make it in any way compelling.'—*Jill Forbes, MFB*

Carmen Jones*
US 1954 105m De Luxe Cinemascope
TCF (Otto Preminger)

A factory girl marries a pilot, and is strangled by him for infidelity.
Black American updating of Bizet's opera, not really satisfactory but given full marks for trying, though the main singing is dubbed and the effect remains doggedly theatrical.

w Harry Kleiner *d* Otto Preminger *ph* Sam Leavitt *ly* Oscar Hammerstein II *titles* Saul Bass *md* Herschel Burke Gilbert

Dorothy Dandridge, Harry Belafonte, Pearl Bailey, Olga James, Joe Adams, Roy Glenn, Nick Stewart, Diahann Carroll, Brock Peters

'All one regrets is that the director has been unable to impose a unifying style on this promising material.'—*Gavin Lambert*

AAN: Herschel Burke Gilbert; Dorothy Dandridge

Carnal Knowledge*
US 1971 97m Technicolor Panavision
Avco Embassy / Icarus (Mike Nichols)

A college student embarks on an enthusiastic and varied sex life but by middle age is bored and empty.

Hampered by an unsuitable wide screen, this pretentious but fragmented comedy drama is embarrassingly conscious of its own daring in subject and language, and good performances are weighed down by an unsubtle script and tricksy direction.

w Jules Feiffer *d* Mike Nichols *ph* Giuseppe Rotunno *m* various songs *pd* Richard Sylbert

Jack Nicholson, *Arthur Garfunkel*, Candice Bergen, *Ann-Margret*, Rita Moreno

AAN: Ann-Margret

● *Video: CBS / Fox*

Carnegie Hall
US 1947 134m bw
Federal Films (Boris Morros, William Le Baron)

The story of New York's music centre, based on a fiction about a cleaner who finally becomes a concert organizer when her son is a famous pianist.

Slim and risible excuse for a classical concert, featuring among others Bruno Walter, Leopold Stokowski, Artur Rubenstein, Jascha Heifitz, Lily Pons, Rise Stevens, Ezio Pinza, Jan Peerce, Harry James, Vaughn Monroe and the New York Philharmonic Symphony Orchestra.

w Karl Lamb *d* Edgar G. Ulmer *ph* William Miller

'The thickest and sourest mess of musical mulligatawny I have yet had to sit down to.'—*James Agee*

Un Carnet de Bal**
France 1937 135m bw
Lévy / Strauss / Sigma
aka: *Life Dances On*

A rich widow seeks her partners at a ball she remembers from her youth, finding that they are all failures and the ball a village hop.

Considering its fame, this is a lumpy porridge of a picture, good in parts but often slow, pretentious and banal. Its gallery of actors is, however, unique.

w Jean Sarment, Pierre Wolff, Bernard Zimmer, Henri Jeanson, Julien Duvivier *d* Julien Duvivier *ph* Michel Kelber, Philippe Agostini *m* Maurice Jaubert

Marie Bell, Françoise Rosay, *Louis Jouvet*, *Raimu*, Harry Baur, Fernandel, Pierre Blanchar

'Recent winner of the Mussolini Cup is loaded with top names, but it is not the film of the year . . . it tries to take in too much and takes too long to put across.'—*Variety*

† The film's international success took Duvivier to Hollywood, where he half-remade it as *Lydia* and went on to other multi-story films such as *Tales of Manhattan* and *Flesh and Fantasy.*

Carnival
US 1934 77m bw

A widowed puppeteer takes custody of his child, which is sought by the maternal grandfather, and seeks anonymity in a circus.

Curious sentimental melodrama with the stars shown in an unusual light. Lee Tracy, Jimmy Durante, Sally Eilers, Dickie Walters, Thomas Jackson, Florence Rice, Lucille Ball. Written by Robert Riskin; directed by Walter Lang; for Columbia. 'This should hold its own, though it probably will not climb to big grosses.'—*Variety*

Carnival
GB 1946 93m bw
Rank / Two Cities

In the nineties, a ballet dancer marries a dour Cornish farmer, who shoots her when her erstwhile lover comes after her.

Flimsy screen version of a solidly old-fashioned romantic drama.

w Eric Maschwitz, *novel* Compton Mackenzie *d* Stanley Haynes *ph* Guy Green

Sally Gray, Michael Wilding, Bernard Miles, Cathleen Nesbitt

† The story was previously filmed in 1931, as *Dance Pretty Lady*, with Ann Casson and Carl Harbord. The 1931 film *Carnival*, with Matheson Lang, is based on a story identical to *Men Are Not Gods* and *A Double Life:* an actor becomes obsessed with the part of Othello and strangles his wife.

Carnival in Costa Rica
US 1947 97m Technicolor
TCF (William A. Bacher)

A young Costa Rican, engaged to an American singer, returns home to find that his parents expect him to marry his childhood sweetheart.

Decidedly rundown musical in which incessant carnival largely supplants the wispy plot.

w John Larkin, Samuel Hoffenstein, Elizabeth Reinhardt *d* Gregory Ratoff *ph* Harry Jackson *ch* Leonide Massine *m / ly* Harry Ruby, Ernesto Lecuona

Dick Haymes, Vera-Ellen, Celeste Holm, J. Carrol Naish, Cesar Romero

Carnival Story
US / Germany 1954 95m Technicolor
The King Brothers

A starving girl becomes a trapezist at a German circus and stirs up jealousy among her partners.

Bleak reworking of *The Three Maxims* (qv), reworked again with more expertise in *Trapeze* (qv); this version is a cheap and unattractive co-production.

w Kurt Neumann, Hans Jacoby *d* Kurt Neumann *ph* Ernest Haller *m* Willi Schmidt-Genter

Anne Baxter, Steve Cochran, Lyle Bettger, George Nader, Jay C. Flippen

Carny
US 1980 105m Technicolor
Lorimar / Jonathan Taplin (Robbie Robertson)

Three wacky characters join a travelling carnival.

Sordid, sexy melodrama which seems to be doing a *Jules and Jim* with no holds barred. Not badly made, but full of people one would cross the road to avoid.

w Thomas Baum *d* Robert Kaylor *ph* Harry Stradling Jnr *m* Alex North

Gary Busey, Jodie Foster, Robbie Robertson, Kenneth McMillan, Meg Foster, Elisha Cook Jnr

'Too dark and turbulent a vision to be palatable to a large public.'—*Variety*

Carolina
US 1934 85m bw
Fox (Darryl F. Zanuck)
GB title: *House of Connelly*

A Yankee farmer's daughter falls in love with a Southern plantation owner.

Mildly pleasing period piece.

w Reginald Berkeley, *play* The House of Connelly by Paul Green *d* Henry King *ph* Hal Mohr

Janet Gaynor, Lionel Barrymore, Robert Young, Henrietta Crosman, Mona Barrie, Richard Cromwell, Steppin Fetchit

'An arresting saga of a proud old southern family that starts out threateningly strong but peters to the point where it misses being another *State Fair*.'—*Variety*

Carolina Blues
US 1944 81m bw

A bandleader needs a new singer. Wispy comedy musical towards the end of Kyser's unlikely popularity. Kay Kyser and his band, Ann Miller, Victor Moore. Written by M. M. Musselman, Kenneth Earl, Joseph Hoffman and Al Martin; directed by Leigh Jason; for Columbia.

Caroline Chérie
France 1951 115m approx bw
SNEG / Cinéphonie

Adventures of an attractive and willing young French girl in the days of the revolution.

A cheerful French imitation of *Forever Amber*; witless and not very entertaining despite good period sense and a certain amount of self-mockery.

w Jean Anouilh, *novel* Cécil Saint-Laurent *d* Richard Poitier *ph* Maurice Barry *m* Georges Auric

Martine Carol, Jacques Dacqmine, Marie Déa, Paul Bernard, Pierre Cressoy

† After several sequels, a colour remake appeared in 1967.

Carousel*
US 1956 128m Eastmancolor
  Cinemascope 55
TCF (Henry Ephron)

A ne'er-do-well dies while committing a hold-up. Fifteen years later he returns from heaven to set his family's affairs in order.
Based on a fantasy play with an honourable history, this super-wide-screen version of an effective stage musical is hollow and boring, a humourless whimsy in which even the songs seem an intrusion.

w Phoebe and Henry Ephron, from the musical based on Ferenc Molnar's play Liliom d Henry King ph Charles G. Clarke m / ly Rodgers and Hammerstein ch Rod Alexander, Agnes de Mille

Gordon Macrae, Shirley Jones, Cameron Mitchell, Gene Lockhart, Barbara Ruick, Robert Rounseville

'This is adult entertainment!'

The Carpetbaggers**
US 1964 150m Technicolor
  Panavision
Paramount / Embassy (Joseph E. Levine)

A young playboy inherits an aircraft business, becomes a megalomaniac tycoon, and moves to Hollywood in his search for power.
Enjoyable pulp fiction clearly suggested by the career of Howard Hughes. Lashings of old-fashioned melodrama, quite well pointed by all concerned.

w John Michael Hayes, novel Harold Robbins d Edward Dmytryk ph Joseph MacDonald m Elmer Bernstein ad Hal Pereira, Walter Tyler

George Peppard, Carroll Baker, Alan Ladd (his last film), Martin Balsam, Bob Cummings, Martha Hyer, Elizabeth Ashley, Lew Ayres, Ralph Taeger, Archie Moore, Leif Erickson, Audrey Totter

'One of those elaborate conjuring tricks in which yards and yards of coloured ribbon are spread all over the stage merely to prove that the conjuror has nothing up his sleeve.'—Tom Milne

Carrefour*
France 1938 75m bw

A French manufacturer, wounded during the war, finds himself the centre of blackmail plots. Intriguing melodrama which was later rather flatly remade in Hollywood as Crossroads. Charles Vanel, Jules Berry, Suzy Prim, Tania Fedor. Written by Hans Kofka; directed by Kurt Bernhardt; for BUP Tuscherer. 'One of the best French films of the late season, and worthy of American attention.'—Variety

Carrie**
US 1952 122m bw
Paramount (William Wyler)

In the early 1900s a country girl comes to Chicago, loses her innocence and goes on the stage, meanwhile reducing a wealthy restaurant manager to penury through love for her.

A famous satirical novel is softened into an unwieldy narrative with scarcely enough dramatic power to sustain interest despite splendid production values. Heavy pre-release cuts remain obvious, and the general effect is depressing; but it is very good to look at.

w Ruth and Augustus Goetz, novel Sister Carrie by Theodore Dreiser d William Wyler ph Victor Milner m David Raksin ad Hal Pereira, Roland Anderson

Laurence Olivier, Jennifer Jones, Miriam Hopkins, Eddie Albert, Basil Ruysdael, Ray Teal, Barry Kelley, Mary Murphy

'Olivier is so impassioned and so painfully touching that everything else in the movie, including the girl whose story it's meant to be, fades into insignificance.'—Variety

'They shot the later episodes for the strongest dramatic effect only, despite the fact that the story had stopped following a melodramatic line and become a sociological study . . . each additional episode exploits the audience's hope that things will be brought to a satisfactory conclusion, but they never are.'—Films in Review

Carrie*
US 1976 98m MGM-De Luxe
UA / Red Bank (Paul Monash)

A repressed teenager with remarkable mental powers takes a macabre revenge on classmates who taunt and persecute her.
Stylish but unattractive shocker which works its way up to a fine climax of gore and frenzy, and takes care to provide a final frisson just when the audience thinks it can safely go home.

w Laurence D. Cohen, novel Stephen King d Brian de Palma ph Mario Tosi m Pino Donaggio

Sissy Spacek, Piper Laurie, Amy Irving, William Katt, John Travolta

'Combining Gothic horror, offhand misogyny and an air of studied triviality, Carrie is de Palma's most enjoyable movie in a long while, and also his silliest.'—Janet Maslin, Newsweek

'The horror is effective only once, and the attempts at humour are never very successful and come almost when one is inclined to be moved by somebody's plight, so that the non-jokes yield authentic bad taste.'—John Simon, New York

AAN: Sissy Spacek; Piper Laurie

● Video: Intervision

Carrington VC*
GB 1954 106m bw
British Lion / Romulus (Teddy Baird)
US title: Court Martial

An army major is courtmartialled for embezzling mess funds.
Good courtroom drama with a few plot surprises, convincing characters, and very serviceable acting and direction.

w John Hunter, play Dorothy and Campbell Christie d Anthony Asquith ph Desmond Dickinson

David Niven, Margaret Leighton, Noelle Middleton, Laurence Naismith, Clive Morton, Mark Dignam, Allan Cuthbertson, Victor Maddern, John Glyn-Jones, Raymond Francis, Newton Blick, John Chandos

● Video: CBS / Fox

Carry on Sergeant
GB 1958 83m bw
Anglo Amalgamated / Insignia (Peter Rogers)

An army training sergeant accepts a bet that his last platoon of raw recruits will win the Star Squad award.
Shabby farce with humdrum script and slack direction, saved by energetic performances.

w Norman Hudis, play The Bull Boys by R. F. Delderfield d Gerald Thomas ph Peter Hennessy m Bruce Montgomery

Bob Monkhouse, William Hartnell, Kenneth Williams, Charles Hawtrey, Shirley Eaton, Eric Barker, Dora Bryan, Bill Owen, Kenneth Connor

† From this unlikely beginning sprang almost twenty years of Carry Ons, their jokes gradually disappearing under an accumulation of old jokes which grew steadily bluer. Colour did little to disguise their makeshift construction, and they never raised their sights as high as satire, but they became a British institution like fish and chips, and many of the regulars became stars. Apart from Williams, Hawtrey and Connor, those most regularly featured in the sequels were Sid James, Bernard Bresslaw, Jim Dale, Joan Sims, Hattie Jacques, Peter Butterworth, and Jack Douglas, with occasional guests such as Harry H. Corbett, Juliet Mills and even Phil Silvers. All were produced by Peter Rogers and directed by Gerald Thomas; most were written (or recollected) by Talbot Rothwell. Delivered at the rate of roughly two a year, the sequence of titles was CARRY ON NURSE (a surprising hit in the US), CARRY ON TEACHER, CARRY ON CONSTABLE, CARRY ON REGARDLESS, CARRY ON CRUISING, CARRY ON CABBY, CARRY ON JACK, CARRY ON SPYING, CARRY ON CLEO, CARRY ON COWBOY, CARRY ON SCREAMING, FOLLOW THAT CAMEL (Beau Geste), DON'T LOSE YOUR HEAD (the Scarlet Pimpernel), CARRY ON DOCTOR, CARRY ON UP THE KHYBER, CARRY ON CAMPING, CARRY ON AGAIN DOCTOR, CARRY ON LOVING, CARRY ON UP THE JUNGLE, CARRY ON HENRY (Henry VIII), CARRY ON AT YOUR CONVENIENCE, CARRY ON MATRON, CARRY ON ABROAD, CARRY ON GIRLS, CARRY ON DICK, CARRY ON BEHIND, CARRY ON ENGLAND, CARRY ON EMMANUELLE.
‡ CARRY ON ADMIRAL and WHAT A CARRY ON are not part of the series.

The Cars That Ate Paris*
Australia 1974 88m Eastmancolor
  Panavision
Saltpan / AFDC / Royce Smeal (Jim and Howard McElroy)

Car travellers become victims of a small town whose youthful inhabitants live on the pickings of engineered road accidents.
Another small town with a guilty secret, in this case more suitable to a half-hour than a feature, but with rewarding attention to detail.

wd Peter Weir *ph* John McLean *m* Bruce Smeaton

Terry Camillieri, John Meillon, Melissa Jaffa, Kevin Miles

Carson City*
US 1952   87m   Warnercolor
Warner (David Weisbart)

A stagecoach service suffers from bandit raids, so a local banker finances a railroad.
Agreeably conventional western with plenty of reliable plot and a satisfactory outcome for the goodies.

w Sloan Nibley, Winston Miller *d* André de Toth *ph* John Boyle *m* David Buttolph

Randolph Scott, Raymond Massey, Lucille Norman, Richard Webb, James Millican, Larry Keating, George Cleveland

Cartouche
Italy / US 1954   85m approx   bw
Venturini / RKO (John Nasht)

A French prince clears himself of a murder charge and brings the villain to book.
Flat costume drama.

w Louis Stevens, Tullio Pinelli *d* Steve Sekely, Gianni Vernuccio *ph* Massimo Dallamano *m* Bruce Montgomery

Richard Baseheart, Patricia Roc, Massimo Serato, Akim Tamiroff

Cartouche**
France / Italy 1961   114m
   Eastmancolor   Dyaliscope
Ariane / Filmsonor / Vides (Georges Danciger)
aka: *Swords of Blood*

An 18th-century cooper's son becomes a quick-witted and gallant thief.
Slightly bitter fairy tale based on a French legend, vigorously encompassing tragedy, farce, violence and high-flown adventure.

w Daniel Boulanger, Philippe de Broca *d* Philippe de Broca *ph* Christian Matras *m* Georges Delerue

Jean-Paul Belmondo, Claudia Cardinale, Odile Versois, Marcel Dalio, Philippe Lemaire, Jean Rochefort
   'A tour de force of virtuosity.'—*Peter John Dyer, MFB*

Carve Her Name with Pride*
GB 1958   119m   bw
Rank / Keyboard (Daniel M. Angel)

In 1940, the young British widow of a French officer is enlisted as a spy, and after various adventures dies before a German firing squad.
Slightly muddled if ultimately moving biopic in which initial light comedy gives way to romance, documentary, character study, blazing war action and finally tragedy.
Generally well made.

w Vernon Harris, Lewis Gilbert, *book* R. J. Minney *d* Lewis Gilbert *ph* John Wilcox *m* William Alwyn

Virginia McKenna (as Violette Szabo), *Paul Scofield*, Jack Warner, Sidney Tafler, Denise Grey, Alain Saury, Maurice Ronet, Nicole Stéphane, Noel Willman, Bill Owen, William Mervyn, Anne Leon
   'What is missing is the deeply charged passion which would have gone beyond the quietly decent statement intermittently achieved.'—*John Gillett*

'As big and timely a picture as ever you've seen! You can tell by the cast it's important! gripping! big!'

Casablanca****
US 1943   102m   bw
Warner *(Hal B. Wallis)*

Rick's Café in Casablanca is a centre for war refugees awaiting visas for America. Rick abandons his cynicism to help an old love escape the Nazis with her underground leader husband.
Cinema par excellence: a studio-bound Hollywood melodrama which after various chances just fell together impeccably into one of the outstanding entertainment experiences of cinema history, with romance, intrigue, excitement, suspense and humour cunningly deployed by master technicians and a perfect cast.

w Julius J. Epstein, Philip G. Epstein, Howard Koch, from an unproduced play, Everybody Comes to Rick's, by Murray Burnett and Joan Alison *d Michael Curtiz ph Arthur Edeson m Max Steiner*

Humphrey Bogart (Rick Blaine), *Ingrid Bergman* (Ilse Lund), Paul Henreid (Victor Laszlo), *Claude Rains* (Captain Louis Renault), Sydney Greenstreet (Ferrari), Peter Lorre (Ugarte), S. Z. Sakall (Carl), *Conrad Veidt* (Major Strasser), *Dooley Wilson* (Sam), *Marcel Dalio* (Croupier) and Madeleine LeBeau, Joy Page, John Qualen, Ludwig Stossel, Leonid Kinskey, Helmut Dantine, Ilka Gruning

Songs: 'As Time Goes By', 'Knock on Wood'

RICK: 'I stick out my neck for nobody. I'm the only cause I'm interested in.'

LOUIS: 'How extravagant you are, throwing away women like that. Someday they may be scarce.'

RICK: 'Ilse, I'm no good at being noble, but it doesn't take much to see that the problems of three little people don't amount to a hill of beans in this crazy world. Someday you'll understand that. Not now. Here's looking at you, kid.'

RICK: 'I came to Casablanca for the waters.'
LOUIS: 'What waters? We're in the desert.'
RICK: 'I was misinformed.'

RICK: 'Louis, I think this is the beginning of a beautiful friendship.'

'A picture which makes the spine tingle and the heart take a leap . . . they have so combined sentiment, humour and pathos with

taut melodrama and bristling intrigue that the result is a highly entertaining and even inspiring film.'—*New York Times*
   'Its humour is what really saves it, being a mixture of Central European irony of attack and racy Broadway–Hollywood Boulevard cynicism.'—*Herman G. Weinberg*
   'The happiest of happy accidents, and the most decisive exception to the *auteur* theory.'—*Andrew Sarris, 1968*
   'A film which seems to have been frozen in time . . . the sum of its many marvellous parts far exceeds the whole.'—*NFT, 1974*
   'It's far from a great film, but it has an appealingly schlocky romanticism, and you're never really pressed to take its melodramatic twists and turns seriously.'—*Pauline Kael, 70s*
   † Originally named for the leads were Ronald Reagan, Ann Sheridan and Dennis Morgan.

AA: best picture; Julius J. and Philip G. Epstein, Howard Koch; Michael Curtiz
AAN: Arthur Edeson; Max Steiner; Humphrey Bogart; Claude Rains

● *Video: Intervision*

Casanova
Italy 1976   163m (English version)
   Technicolor   Scope
TCF / PEA (Alberto Grimaldi)
aka: *Fellini's Casanova*

Episodes from the life of the eighteenth-century libertine, in the course of which he seduces, among others, a nun, a mechanical doll, and a hunchbacked nymphomaniac.
A curiously rarefied spectacle which seldom comes to anything like life and despite its vast expense seems more likely to provoke yawns than lust.

w Federico Fellini, Barnadino Zapponi *d* Federico Fellini *ph* Giuseppe Rotunno *m* Nino Rota *pd* Danilo Donati, Federico Fellini

Donald Sutherland, Tina Aumont, Cicely Browne, Carmen Scarpitta
   'It may well be the most ponderous specimen of imaginative vacuity ever devised.'—*John Simon, New York*

Casanova Brown
US 1944   99m   bw
International / Christie (Nunnally Johnson)

Just as his divorce comes through, a man discovers that his wife is pregnant.
Very mild star comedy which tiptoes round its subject.

w Nunnally Johnson, *play* Bachelor Father by Floyd Dell, Thomas Mitchell *d* Sam Wood *ph* John F. Seitz *m* Arthur Lange *ad* Perry Ferguson

Gary Cooper, Teresa Wright, Frank Morgan, Anita Louise, Patricia Collinge, Edmond Breon, Jill Esmond, Isobel Elsom, Mary Treen, Halliwell Hobbes
   'There is so much clowning with so little subject that one is exposed to the impression that anything went for a laugh.'—*Bosley Crowther, New York Times*

AAN: Arthur Lange; Perry Ferguson

Casanova in Burlesque
US 1944 74m bw

A professor has a secret summer life as a
burlesque performer. Unusual, amiable
comedy. Joe E. Brown, June Havoc. Written
by Frank Gill; directed by Leslie Goodwins;
for Republic.

Casanova's Big Night
US 1954 86m Technicolor
Paramount (Paul Jones)

In old Italy, the great lover is fleeing from his
creditors and changes places with a tailor's
apprentice.
The last of Bob Hope's big-budget, big-studio
burlesques is a lumbering vehicle which wastes
its star cast and mistimes its laughs.
w Hal Kanter, Edmund Hartmann d Norman
Z. McLeod ph Lionel Lindon

Bob Hope, Joan Fontaine (an unhappy
comedy foil), Basil Rathbone, Vincent Price,
Audrey Dalton, Hugh Marlowe, John
Carradine, Primo Carnera, Arnold Moss, Lon
Chaney Jnr

Casbah
US 1948 94m bw
Universal (Erik Charell)

Remake of *Algiers* (qv) with songs added.
Not too bad in the circumstances, but a wholly
artificial exercise, and another version was
really not needed. The sets seem overlit and
claustrophobic.
w (not credited) d John Berry ph Irving
Glassberg m Harold Arlen

Tony Martin, Yvonne de Carlo, Marta Toren,
Peter Lorre, Hugo Haas

AAN: song 'For Every Man There's a
Woman' (*m* Harold Arlen, *ly* Leo Robin)

The Case against Brooklyn
US 1958 81m bw

An undercover cop smashes a gambling
syndicate. Competent second feature
treatment of a story we have heard somewhere
before. Darren McGavin, Marrie Hayes,
Warren Stevens, Emile Meyer, Nestor Paiva.
Written by Raymond T. Marcus; directed by
Paul Wendkos; for Charles H. Schneer /

'Is she an unfit mother?'
The Case against Mrs Ames
US 1936 85m bw
Paramount (Walter Wanger)

The prosecutor in a murder case is convinced
of the defendant's innocence.
Tired rehash of a familiar theme.
w Gene Towne, Graham Baker d William A.
Seiter ph Lucien Andriot

Madeleine Carroll, George Brent, Arthur
Treacher, Alan Baxter, Beulah Bondi, Alan
Mowbray, Esther Dale, Ed Brophy

The Case of Charles Peace
GB 1949 88m bw

The story of a burglar and murderer of the
1870s whose career caught the public fancy.

Antediluvian and largely fictitious treatment of
a Victorian *cause célèbre*. Michael Martin
Harvey, Chili Bouchier, Valentine Dyall,
Bruce Belfrage, Ronald Adam. Written by
Doris Davison and Norman Lee; directed by
Norman Lee; for John Argyle.

The Case of Sergeant Grischa
US 1930 82m bw

A Russian no-good escapes from a German
prison camp and after many adventures is shot
as a spy. Oddball entertainment to come from
Hollywood at any time, this seems to have no
intent to please. Chester Morris, Betty
Compson, Alec B. Francis, Gustav Von
Seyffertitz, Jean Hersholt, Leyland Hodgson.
From the story by Arnold Zweig; directed by
Herbert Brenon; for RKO. 'No sympathy, no
fan appeal and no entertainment. Can only be
exploited as "a fine production" or "a new era
in pictures".'—*Variety*

The Case of the Black Cat
US 1936 66m bw

An old man is murdered after changing his
will: Perry Mason investigates. One of the
better tales of the lawyer sleuth, here
impersonated by Ricardo Cortez; with Harry
Davenport, June Travis, Jane Bryan. Written
by F. Hugh Herbert; directed by William
McGann; for Warner.

The Case of the Black Parrot
US 1941 60m bw

Was it the butler who murdered to steal a case
of diamonds? This sounds like a Perry Mason
but is not; William Lundigan stars as a
reporter who solves the puzzle; with Maris
Wrixon, Eddie Foy Jnr, Paul Cavanagh.
Written by Robert E. Kent, from a play by
Burton Stevenson; directed by Noel Smith; for
Warner.

The Case of the Curious Bride
US 1935 80m bw

Perry Mason helps a woman who is being
blackmailed by her 'dead' husband. Smoothish
mystery, with Warren William, Margaret
Lindsay, Donald Woods, Claire Dodd, Allen
Jenkins and—briefly—Errol Flynn. Written by
Tom Reed, from an Erle Stanley Gardner
original; directed by Michael Curtiz; for
Warner.

The Case of the Frightened Lady
GB 1940 81m bw

A dowager knows that her son is mad and tries
to prevent him from strangling his cousin.
Quite a lively suspenser of its time. Marius
Goring, Penelope Dudley Ward, Helen Haye,
Patrick Barr, Felix Aylmer. Written by
Edward Dryhurst, from the novel by Edgar
Wallace; directed by George King; for
Pennant. A previous version was released in
1932 as *The Frightened Lady* (qv).

The Case of the Howling Dog
US 1934 75m bw

Two men claim the same woman as their wife.
Adequate Perry Mason mystery. Warren
William, Mary Astor, Allen Jenkins, Grant
Mitchell, Helen Trenholme. Written by Ben
Markson, from an Erle Stanley Gardner
original; directed by Alan Crosland; for
Warner.

The Case of the Lucky Legs
US 1935 77m bw

Perry Mason chases a beauty contest promoter
who skips town with the winnings. Fair light-
hearted mystery, with Warren William as a
somewhat dissipated sleuth; also Genevieve
Tobin, Allen Jenkins, Patricia Ellis, Lyle
Talbot, Barton Maclane. Written by Ben
Markson and Brown Holmes, from an Erle
Stanley Gardner original; directed by Archie
Mayo; for Warner.

The Case of the Stuttering Bishop
US 1937 70m bw

Perry Mason investigates an heiress who may
be an impostor. Thin mystery with another
different star in the lead: Donald Woods. Also
Ann Dvorak, Anne Nagel, Linda Perry.
Written by Don Ryan and Kenneth Gamet,
from an Erle Stanley Gardner original;
directed by William Clemens; for Warner.

The Case of the Velvet Claws
US 1936 63m bw

Perry Mason's honeymoon is postponed when
he finds himself on a murder charge. Moderate
light-hearted mystery, but they should have
awarded prizes to anyone who could explain
the title. Warren William, Claire Dodd, Wini
Shaw, Gordon Elliott, Addison Richards.
Written by Tom Reed, from an Erle Stanley
Gardner original; directed by William
Clemens; for Warner.

Casey's Shadow
US 1978 116m Metrocolor Panavision
Columbia / Ray Stark (Michael Levee)

A Cajun family in New Mexico breeds a
champion horse which wins the annual race.
Shades of *Maryland*: an old-fashioned movie
of the kind which absolutely nobody should
want to revive, at least not so ineptly or at
such length.

w Carol Sobieski, *story* Ruidoso by John
McPhee d Martin Ritt ph John A. Alonzo
m Patrick Williams

Walter Matthau, Alexis Smith, Robert
Webber, Murray Hamilton, Andrew A.
Rubin, Stephan Burns, Michael Hershewe

Cash McCall
US 1960 102m Technicolor
Warner (Henry Blanke)

A Napoleon of the stock market gets into
trouble for the first time when love interferes
with business.
Slightly unusual comedy drama, quite sharply
made and played, but not adding up to much.
w Lenore Coffee, Marion Hargrove, *novel*
Cameron Hawley d Joseph Pevney
ph George Folsey m Max Steiner

James Garner, Natalie Wood, Nina Foch, Dean Jagger, E. G. Marshall, Henry Jones, Otto Kruger, Roland Winters

Cash on Demand*
GB 1963   86m   bw
Columbia / Woodpecker / Hammer (Michael Carreras)

A fussy bank manager outwits a classy robber. Quietly effective suspenser with an admirable middle-aged cast and no love interest.

w Lewis Greifer, David T. Chantler, from Jacques Gillies' TV play d Quentin Lawrence ph Arthur Grant m Wilfred Josephs

Peter Cushing, André Morell, Richard Vernon, Norman Bird, Edith Sharpe

The Casino Murder Case
US 1935   85m   bw

Philo Vance solves a murder in a family of neurotics. Rather heavy-going detection. Paul Lukas, Rosalind Russell, Eric Blore, Donald Cook, Louise Fazenda, Ted Healy, Isabel Jewell, Leo G. Carroll. Written by Florence Ryerson and Edgar Allen Woolf, from an S. S. Van Dine original; directed by Edwin Marin; for MGM.

Casino Royale
GB 1967   130m   Technicolor Panavision
Columbia / Famous Artists (Charles K. Feldman, Jerry Bresler)

The heads of the allied spy forces call Sir James Bond out of retirement to fight the power of *SMERSH*.
Woeful all-star kaleidoscope, a way-out spoof which generates far fewer laughs than the original. One of the most shameless wastes of time and talent in screen history.

w Wolf Mankowitz, John Law, Michael Sayers, novel Ian Fleming d John Huston, Ken Hughes, Val Guest, Robert Parrish, Joe McGrath, Richard Talmadge ph Jack Hildyard m Burt Bacharach pd Michael Stringer

David Niven, Deborah Kerr, Orson Welles, Peter Sellers, Ursula Andress, Woody Allen, William Holden, Charles Boyer, John Huston, Joanna Pettet, Daliah Lavi, Kurt Kasznar, Jacqueline Bisset, Derek Nimmo, George Raft, Ronnie Corbett, Peter O'Toole, Jean-Paul Belmondo, Geoffrey Bayldon, Duncan Macrae

'One of those wild wacky extravaganzas in which the audience is expected to have a great time because everybody making the film did. It seldom works out that way, and certainly doesn't here.'—*John Russell Taylor*
'The dialogue is witless and unhampered by taste, and the interminable finale is a collection of clichés in a brawl involving the cavalry, parachuted Indians, split-second appearances by George Raft and Jean-Paul Belmondo, every variety of mayhem, and Woody Allen burping radiation as a walking atom bomb.'—*Judith Crist*
'The worst film I ever enjoyed.'—*Donald Zec*

AAN: song 'The Look of Love' (m Burt Bacharach, ly Hal David)

Casque d'Or***
France 1952   96m   bw
Speva / Paris
aka: *Golden Marie*

1898. In the Paris slums, an Apache finds passionate love but is executed for murder. A tragic romance which on its first release seemed bathed in a golden glow and is certainly an impeccable piece of film-making.

w Jacques Becker, Jacques Companeez d Jacques Becker ph Robert Le Fèbvre m Georges Van Parys

Simone Signoret, Serge Reggiani, Claude Dauphin, Raymond Bussières, Gaston Modot
'Takes its place alongside *Le Jour Se Lève* among the masterpieces of the French cinema.'—*Karel Reisz*
'A screen alive with sensuousness and luminous figures.'—*Dilys Powell*

Cass Timberlane*
US 1947   119m   bw
MGM (Arthur Hornblow Jnr)

A judge marries a working class girl, who is unsettled at first but finally comes to realize her good fortune.
Solid drama with an understanding star performance and good production values.

w Donald Ogden Stewart, novel Sinclair Lewis d George Sidney ph Robert Planck m Roy Webb

Spencer Tracy, Lana Turner, Zachary Scott, Tom Drake, Mary Astor, Albert Dekker, Selena Royle, Josephine Hutchinson, Margaret Lindsay

The Cassandra Crossing
GB / Italy / West Germany 1976   129m Technicolor Panavision
AGF / CCC / International Cine (Lew Grade, Carlo Ponti)

A terrorist carrying a deadly plague virus boards a transcontinental train.
Disaster spectacular with a number of fashionable interests but no observable film-making technique.

w Tom Mankiewicz, Robert Katz, George Pan Cosmatos d George Pan Cosmatos ph Ennio Guarnieri m Jerry Goldsmith pd Aurelio Crugnola

Sophia Loren, Richard Harris, Ava Gardner, Burt Lancaster, Martin Sheen, Ingrid Thulin, Lee Strasberg, John Phillip Law, Lionel Stander, Ann Turkel, O. J. Simpson, Alida Valli

● Video: Precision Video

Cast a Dark Shadow*
GB 1955   82m   bw
Frobisher / Daniel M. Angel (Herbert Mason)

A wife-murderer marries an ex-barmaid and tries again.
Unambitious but enjoyable melodrama, well acted though with directorial opportunities missed.

w John Cresswell, play Murder Mistaken by Janet Green d Lewis Gilbert ph Jack Asher m Antony Hopkins

Dirk Bogarde, Margaret Lockwood, Kay Walsh, Kathleen Harrison, Robert Flemyng, Mona Washbourne, Walter Hudd

'Outnumbered—unarmed—unprepared— they hurled back their answer in flesh and flame!'

Cast a Giant Shadow*
US 1966   141m   De Luxe   Panavision
UA / Mirisch / Llenroc / Batjac (Melville Shavelson)

An American military lawyer and ex-colonel goes to Israel in 1947 to help in the fight against the Arabs.
Spectacular war biopic with all concerned in good form but lacking the clarity and narrative control of a real smash.

w Melville Shavelson, from Ted Berkman's biography of Col. David Marcus d Melville Shavelson ph Aldo Tonti m Elmer Bernstein pd Michael Stringer

Kirk Douglas, Angie Dickinson, Senta Berger, Luther Adler, Stathis Giallelis, Chaim Topol, John Wayne, Frank Sinatra, Yul Brynner, James Donald, Gordon Jackson, Michael Hordern, Gary Merrill, Allan Cuthbertson, Jeremy Kemp

Cast a Long Shadow
US 1959   82m   colour

A hard-drinking drifter thinks he may be the illegitimate son of a dead cattle baron. Would-be psychological western with not enough going for it. Audie Murphy, John Dehner, Terry Moore, James Best, Denver Pyle. Written by Martin H. Goldsmith and John McGreevey, from the novel by Wayne D. Overholser; directed by Thomas Carr; for Mirisch / UA.

The Castaway Cowboy*
US 1974   91m   Technicolor
Walt Disney (Ron Miller, Winston Hibler)

In 1850, a Shanghaied sailor on Hawaii helps a lady potato farmer to turn her land into a cattle ranch.
Unexciting and unexceptional family fare.

w Don Tait d Vincent McEveety ph Andrew Jackson m Robert F. Brunner

James Garner, Vera Miles, Robert Culp, Eric Shea, Elizabeth Smith

Castle in the Desert*
US 1942   62m   bw

Murders take place at the remote castle of an eccentric millionaire. One of the sharpest Charlie Chan mysteries, with a lively plot and some good lines. Sidney Toler, Arleen Whelan, Richard Derr, Douglass Dumbrille, Henry Daniell, Steve Geray, Sen Yung, Ethel Griffies, Milton Parsons. Written by John Larkin; directed by Harry Lachman; for TCF.

'A one-eyed major and his oddball heroes
fight a twentieth-century war in a tenth-
century castle!'

Castle Keep°

US 1969 107m Technicolor
Panavision
Columbia / Filmways (Martin Ransohoff,
John Calley)

During World War II seven battle-weary
American soldiers occupy a 10th-century castle
filled with art treasures, then die defending it.
Or are they dead all the time? The film version
of this fantastic novel never seems quite sure,
and the uncertainty finally deadens it despite
careful work all round.

w Daniel Taradash, David Rayfiel, *novel*
William Eastlake *d* Sydney Pollack *ph* Henri
Decaë *m* Michel Legrand

Burt Lancaster, Peter Falk, Jean Pierre
Aumont, Patrick O'Neal, Al Freeman Jnr,
Scott Wilson, Tony Bill, Bruce Dern, Astrid
Heeren

Castle of Evil

US 1966 81m Eastmancolor

A disfigured industrialist summons six people
to a remote Caribbean island for the reading
of his will. Tedious variation on *Ten Little
Niggers* and *The Cat and the Canary*, with
horror asides and the lowest of budgets.
Virginia Mayo, Scott Brady, David Brian, Lisa
Gaye, Hugh Marlowe. Written by Charles A.
Wallace; directed by Francis D. Lyon; for
NTA.

CAST A GIANT SHADOW. John Wayne was one of several guest stars in this biopic based on the career of Mickey Marcus (Kirk Douglas).

Castle of Fu Manchu

West Germany / Spain / Italy / GB 1968
92m Eastmancolor

The yellow peril wrecks an ocean-going liner
by turning water into ice, and keeps the
inventor a prisoner. Extraordinarily tatty entry
in a series which started off well. (See *Fu
Manchu* for list.) Christopher Lee, Richard
Greene, Howard Marion Crawford, Gunther
Stoll, Maria Perschy. Written by Harry Alan
Towers (Peter Welbeck); directed by Jesus
Franco; for Terra Finkunst / Balcazar / Italian
International / Towers of London.

Castle on the Hudson°

US 1940 77m bw
Warner (Sam Bischoff)
GB title: *Years without Days*

A hardened criminal is not helped by his years
in prison.
Adequate, gloomy remake of *Twenty
Thousand Years in Sing Sing*.

w Seton I. Miller, Brown Holmes, Courtney
Terrett *d* Anatole Litvak *ph* Arthur Edeson
m Adolph Deutsch

John Garfield, Pat O'Brien, Ann Sheridan,
Burgess Meredith, Jerome Cowan, Henry
O'Neill, Guinn Williams, John Litel

The Cat°

France 1973 88m colour

After twenty-five years of marriage an
embittered trapeze star and her husband

simply don't talk to each other. Absorbing
drama for two characters, brilliantly acted by
Jean Gabin and Simone Signoret, but with a
somewhat unsatisfactory conclusion. Written
by Pascal Jardin; directed by Pierre Granier-
Deferre; for Raymond Danon.

Cat and Mouse°

GB 1958 79m bw
(Eros) Anvil (Paul Rotha)

The daughter of a man executed for murder is
threatened by criminals seeking hidden loot.
Interesting rather than exciting second feature
thriller directed by a documentary maker.

wd Paul Rotha, *novel* Michael Halliday
ph Wolfgang Suschitsky

Lee Patterson, Ann Sears, Hilton Edwards,
Victor Maddern, George Rose, Roddy
McMillan

The Cat and the Canary°°°

US 1927 84m (24 fps) bw silent
Universal

Greedy relatives assemble in an old house to
hear an eccentric's will, and a young girl's
sanity is threatened.
Archetypal spooky house comedy horror, here
given an immensely stylish production which
influenced Hollywood through the thirties and
was spoofed in *The Old Dark House*.

w Alfred Cohn, Robert F. Hill, *play* John
Willard *d* Paul Leni *ph* Gilbert Warrenton
ad Charles D. Hall

Creighton Hale, Laura La Plante, Forrest
Stanley, Tully Marshall, Flora Finch, Gertrude
Astor, Arthur Carewe
† Remade for sound by Rupert Julian in 1930
as *The Cat Creeps*, with Raymond Hackett,
Helen Twelvetrees and Jean Hersholt. This
title was also used for a grade Z 1946 second
feature with a different plot.

The Cat and the Canary°°°

US 1939 72m bw
Paramount (Arthur Hornblow Jnr)

A superbly staged remake, briskly paced,
perfectly cast and lusciously photographed.
The comedy-thriller par excellence, with Bob
Hope fresh and sympathetic in his first big star
part.

w Walter de Leon, Lynn Starling *d* Elliott
Nugent *ph* Charles Lang *m* Dr Ernst Toch
ad Hans Dreier, Robert Usher

Bob Hope (Wally Campbell), *Paulette
Goddard* (Joyce Norman), *Gale Sondergaard*
(Miss Lu), *Douglass Montgomery* (Charlie
Wilder), *John Beal* (Fred Blythe), *George
Zucco* (Lawyer Crosby), *Nydia Westman*
(Cicily), *Elizabeth Patterson* (Aunt Susan),
John Wray (Hendricks)

CICILY: 'Do you believe people come back from the dead?'
WALLY: 'You mean like republicans?'
CICILY: 'Don't these big empty houses scare you?'
WALLY: 'Not me, I was in vaudeville.'
WALLY: 'I get goose pimples. Even my goose pimples have goose pimples'.

'The objective is carried out briskly and to our complete satisfaction.'—*New York Times*
'A top programmer for upper-bracket bookings in the keys, and will hit a consistent stride down the line in the subsequents.'—*Variety*
'Beautifully shot, intelligently constructed.'—*Peter John Dyer, 1966*

The Cat and the Canary
GB 1979 98m Technicolor
Gala / Grenadier (Richard Gordon)
An overpoweringly cast but half-heartedly scripted remake of the above, which after a spirited beginning bores more than it thrills.
wd Radley Metzger *ph* Alex Thomson *m* Steven Cagan
Honor Blackman, Michael Callan, Edward Fox, Wendy Hiller, Beatrix Lehmann, Olivia Hussey, Daniel Massey, Carol Lynley, Peter McEnery, Wilfrid Hyde-White
'So mechanically are characters shunted through the indistinguishable rooms and corridors that one is surprised not to see the parquet marked off in neat little squares, as on a Cluedo board.'—*Gilbert Adair, MFB*

The Cat and the Fiddle
US 1933 90m bw (colour sequence)
In a taxi in Brussels, a leading lady of Broadway musicals meets a European composer. Very lightweight musical comedy.
Jeanette MacDonald, Ramon Novarro, Charles Butterworth, Frank Morgan, Jean Hersholt, Vivienne Segal, Henry Armetta. Written by Sam and Bella Spewack, from the show by Jerome Kern and Otto Harbach; directed by William K. Howard; for MGM.
'The only thing remaining of merit is the music.'—*Variety*

Cat Ballou••
US 1965 96m Technicolor
Columbia (Harold Hecht)
Young Catherine Ballou hires a drunken gunfighter to protect her father from a vicious gunman, but despite her efforts he is shot, so she turns outlaw.
Sometimes lively, sometimes somnolent western spoof which considering the talent involved should have been funnier than it is. The linking ballad helps.
w Walter Newman, Frank R. Pierson, *novel* Roy Chanslor *d* Eliot Silverstein *ph* Jack Marta *m* Frank de Vol
Jane Fonda, *Lee Marvin*, Michael Callan, Dwayne Hickman, Nat King Cole, Stubby Kaye, Tom Nardini, John Marley, Reginald Denny
'Uneven, lumpy, coy and obvious.'—*Pauline Kael*

AA: Lee Marvin
AAN: Walter Newman, Frank R. Pierson; Frank de Vol; song 'The Ballad of Cat Ballou' (*m* Jerry Livingston, *ly* Mack David)

The Cat Creeps see The Cat and the Canary (1927)

The Cat Creeps
US 1930 71m bw
A sound remake of *The Cat and the Canary*; not in any way memorable. Helen Twelvetrees, Raymond Hackett, Neil Hamilton, Lilyan Tashman, Jean Hersholt, Montagu Love, Lawrence Grant, Theodore Von Eltz, Blanche Friderici, Elizabeth Petterson (playing Aunt Susan as she did in the later version). Written by Gladys Lehman and William Hurlbut; directed by Rupert Julian; for Universal. 'In the translation from silent to sound it has been badly slowed up.'—*Variety*

The Cat from Outer Space
US 1978 103m Technicolor
Walt Disney Productions (Ron Miller)
A superintelligent extraterrestrial cat is forced to land on earth for running repairs. Fairly modest studio offering which pleased its intended market but could have been sharper.
w Ted Key *d* Norman Tokar *ph* Charles F. Wheeler *m* Lalo Schifrin *sp* Eustace Lycett, Art Cruickshank, Danny Dee
Ken Berry, Roddy McDowall, Sandy Duncan, Harry Morgan, McLean Stevenson, Jesse White, Alan Young, Hans Conried
● *Video: Rank*

Cat o'Nine Tails
Italy / France / Germany 1971 112m Techniscope
A blind reporter overhears an industrial espionage plot that turns into murder. Smart surface mechanics camouflage poor storytelling. Karl Malden, James Franciscus, Catherine Spaak. Written and directed by Dario Argento; for Spettacoli / Mondial / Terra / Labrador.

Cat on a Hot Tin Roof••
US 1958 108m Metrocolor
MGM / Avon (Lawrence Weingarten)
A rich plantation owner, dying of cancer, finds his two sons unsatisfactory: one is a conniver, the other a neurotic who refuses to sleep with his wife.
Slightly bowdlerized version of Tennessee Williams' most straightforward melodrama, watchable for the acting but still basically a theatrical experience.
w Richard Brooks, James Poe *d* Richard Brooks *ph* William Daniels *m* uncredited
Paul Newman, Burl Ives, Elizabeth Taylor, Jack Carson, Judith Anderson, Madeleine Sherwood, Larry Gates
BIG DADDY: 'Truth is pain and sweat and paying bills and making love to a woman that you don't love any more. Truth is dreams that don't come true and nobody prints your name in the paper until you die.'

MAGGIE: 'Win what? What is the victory of a cat on a hot tin roof?'
BRICK: 'Just staying on it, I guess.'
AAN: best picture; Richard Brooks, James Poe; Richard Brooks (as director); William Daniels; Paul Newman; Elizabeth Taylor
● *Video: MGM / UA*

Cat People••
US 1942 73m bw
RKO (*Val Lewton*)
A beautiful Yugoslavian girl believes she can turn into a panther; before she is found mysteriously dead, several of her acquaintances are attacked by such a beast. The first of Lewton's famous horror series for RKO is a slow starter but has some notable suspense sequences. It was also the first monster film to refrain from showing its monster.
w De Witt Bodeen *d Jacques Tourneur* *ph* Nicholas Musuraca *m* Roy Webb
Simone Simon, Kent Smith, Tom Conway, Jane Randolph, Jack Holt
'(Lewton) revolutionized scare movies with suggestion, imaginative sound effects and camera angles, leaving everything to the fear-filled imagination.'—*Pauline Kael, 1968*
† *Curse of the Cat People* (qv) was a very unrelated sequel.

Cat People
US 1982 118m Technicolor
Universal (Charles Fries)
A kinky version of the 1942 horrorpic. The feline lady now has an incestuous relationship with her brother, only changes after sex, and then must kill to become human again. (It is therefore safe to mate only with relatives.) One presumes that among the eroticism and bloodlust a statement is being made, but it is never evident.
w Alan Ormsby *d* Paul Schraeder *ph* John Bailey *m* Giorgio Moroder *ed* Jacqueline Cambas *sp* Tom Burman, Albert Whitlock *visual consultant* Ferdinando Scarfiotti
Nastassja Kinski, Malcolm McDowell, John Heard, Annette O'Toole, Ruby Dee, Ed Begley Jnr
'The final impression is of a phantasmagoric indulgence in sound and vision by a film-maker who fears sex and is excited by violence.'—*Sunday Times*
'The hobgoblins of an actual horror movie aren't easily translatable into the demons that haunt a Schrader hero on his way to a religious transcendence that is also a renunciation.'—*Richard Combs, MFB*

The Cat That Hated People••
US 1948 7m Technicolor
A weary Manhattan cat rockets to the moon but finds it even noisier and is glad to come home. Violent but dazzlingly inventive cartoon from this madcap director; a little classic of its kind. Written by Heck Allen; directed by *Tex Avery*; for MGM.

Cat Women of the Moon
US 1953 63m bw 3D

Five American astronauts find the moon inhabited solely by ravenous cat women. One of the top claimants to film history's booby prize, along with such other space fiction entrants as *Fire Maidens from Outer Space*, *Planet Seven from Outer Space* and *Santa Claus Conquers the Martians*. It has more than a chance. Sonny Tufts, Victor Jory, Marie Windsor, William Phipps, Douglas Fowley. Written by Roy Hamilton; directed by Arthur Hilton; for Three Dimensional Pictures. (Aka: *Rocket to the Moon*.)

Catacombs
GB 1964 90m bw

A rich woman is murdered by her husband and her male secretary. Involved melodrama with rather too many twists. Gary Merrill, Neil McCallum, Georgina Cookson, Jane Merrow, Rachel Thomas, Jack Train. Written by Dan Mainwaring; directed by Gordon Hessler; for Parroch / McCallum.

Catch As Catch Can
GB 1937 71m bw

Crooks after a valuable diamond converge on a transatlantic liner. Modest comedy-thriller. James Mason, Viki Dobson, Eddie Pola, Finlay Currie. Written by Richard Llewellyn; directed by Roy Kellino; for Fox British. (Aka: *Atlantic Episode*.)

Catch Me a Spy
GB 1971 94m Technicolor
Rank / Ludgate / Capitol / Films de la Pleiade (Steven Pallos)

A British agent smuggling Russian manuscripts into England falls for the wife of a Russian spy and finally gets his money as well. Complex, patchy comedy thriller with dispirited action scenes in Bucharest and Scotland. Technical credits rather dim.

w Dick Clement, Ian La Frenais, *novel* George Marton, Tibor Meray *d* Dick Clement *ph* Christopher Challis *m* Claude Bolling

Kirk Douglas, Trevor Howard, Tom Courtenay, Marlene Jobert, Patrick Mower, Bernadette Lafont, Bernard Blier

Catch 22*
US 1970 122m Technicolor Panavision
Paramount / Filmways (John Calley, Martin Ransohoff)

At a US Air Force base in the Mediterranean during World War II, one by one the officers are distressingly killed; a survivor paddles towards neutral Sweden.
Intensely black comedy, more so than *M*A*S*H* and less funny, effectively mordant in places but too grisly and missing several tricks.

w Buck Henry, *novel* Joseph Heller *d* Mike Nichols *ph* David Watkin *m* none *pd* Richard Sylbert

Alan Arkin, Martin Balsam, Richard Benjamin, Art Garfunkel, Jack Gilford, Buck Henry, Bob Newhart, Anthony Perkins, Paula Prentiss, Jon Voight, Martin Sheen, Orson Welles

'There are startling effects and good revue touches here and there, but the picture keeps going on and on, as if it were determined to impress us.'—*New Yorker, 1977*

'As hot and heavy as the original was cool and light.'—*Richard Schickel*

'It goes on so long that it cancels itself out, even out of people's memories; it was long awaited and then forgotten almost instantly.'—*Pauline Kael*

● *Video: CIC*

Catch Us If You Can
GB 1965 91m bw
Anglo Amalgamated / Bruton (David Deutsch)
US title: *Having a Wild Weekend*

Freelance stuntmen have various adventures in the west of England.
The first film of a pretentious director is a bright but wearisomely high-spirited imitation of *A Hard Day's Night*.

w Peter Nichols *d* John Boorman *ph* Manny Wynn *m* Dave Clark

The Dave Clark Five, Barbara Ferris, David Lodge, Robin Bailey, Yootha Joyce

The Catered Affair*
US 1956 93m bw
MGM (Sam Zimbalist)
GB title: *Wedding Breakfast*

When the daughter of a New York taxi driver gets married, her mother insists on a bigger function than they can afford.
Rather heavy-going comedy with amusing dialogue, from the period when Hollywood was seizing on TV plays like *Marty* and *Twelve Angry Men*.

w Gore Vidal, TV play Paddy Chayevsky *d* Richard Brooks *ph* John Alton *m* André Previn

Bette Davis, Ernest Borgnine, Debbie Reynolds, Barry Fitzgerald, Rod Taylor, Robert Simon, Madge Kennedy, Dorothy Stickney

Catherine the Great*
GB 1934 93m bw
Alexander Korda

How Catherine married the mad prince and slowly conquered the Russian court.
Dated but well acted and written account, sober by comparison with *The Scarlet Empress* which came out at the same time.

w Lajos Biro, Arthur Wimperis, Marjorie Deans, *play* The Czarina by Melchior Lengyel, Lajos Biro *d* Paul Czinner *ph* Georges Périnal *md* Muir Matheson

Elisabeth Bergner, Douglas Fairbanks Jnr, Flora Robson, Gerald du Maurier, Irene Vanbrugh, Griffith Jones, Joan Gardner, Diana Napier

'It rates no raves but is a good piece of merchandise.'—*Variety*

† The style is typified by a speech given to Grand Duke Peter: 'If she wasn't on the throne she'd be on the street.'

Catlow*
GB 1971 101m Metrocolor
MGM / Euan Lloyd

A likeable outlaw tries to avoid problems while recovering his hidden gold.
Light-hearted, cheerfully cast, fast-moving, Spanish-located western.

w Scot Finch, J. J. Griffith, *novel* Louis L'Amour *d* Sam Wanamaker *ph* Ted Scaife *m* Roy Budd

Yul Brynner, Leonard Nimoy, Richard Crenna, Daliah Lavi, Jo Ann Pflug, Jeff Corey, Bessie Love, David Ladd

The Cat's Paw*
US 1936 101m bw
Harold Lloyd

The son of a Chinese missionary returns home and finds himself in the middle of a Tong war. Very moderate star comedy from the time when he was considering himself a character comedian rather than a slapstick ace.

w Harold Lloyd, Sam Taylor, *story* Clarence Budington Kelland *d* Sam Taylor

Harold Lloyd, George Barbier, Una Merkel, Nat Pendleton, Grant Mitchell, Vince Barnett

'The picture gets its laughs all right, but it approaches them at a crawl.'—*Variety*

Cattle Annie and Little Britches
US 1980 98m CFI colour
Hemdale / UATC (David Korda)

In 1893, two girls head west in search of adventure.
Rather winsome family western, with too little real action and too much romping about.

w Robert Ward, from his novel *d* Lamont Johnson *ph* Larry Pizer *m* Sanh Berti, Tom Slocum

Burt Lancaster, John Savage, Rod Steiger, Diane Lane, Amanda Plummer, Scott Glenn, Steven Ford

Cattle Drive
US 1951 78m Technicolor

The spoiled teenage son of a magnate finds humanity and friendship with a cowhand during a cattle drive. *Captains Courageous* out west, not badly done. Joel McCrea, Dean Stockwell, Chill Wills, Leon Ames, Bob Steele. Written by Jack Natteford and Lillie Hayward; directed by Kurt Neumann; for Aaron Rosenberg / Universal-International.

Cattle Empire
US 1958 82m De Luxe Cinemascope

A trail boss out of prison gets a new assignment and signs up helpers who had previously made life difficult for him. Fair general western, entirely dependent on its star. Joel McCrea, Gloria Talbott, Don Haggerty, Phyllis Coates, Paul Brinegar.

Written by Endre Boehm and Eric Norden;
directed by Charles Marquis Warren; for TCF.

Cattle King
US 1963   90m   Metrocolor
MGM / Missouri (Nat Holt)
GB title: *Guns of Wyoming*

A big rancher opposes a cattle trail and starts
a range war.
Moderately expert but very familiar star
western.

w Thomas Thompson *d* Tay Garnett
ph William E. Snyder *m* Paul Sawtell

Robert Taylor, Joan Caulfield, Robert
Middleton, Robert Loggia, Larry Gates,
Malcolm Atterbury

Cattle Queen of Montana
US 1954   88m   Technicolor

A tough woman inherits her father's rangeland
and resists cattle rustlers. A western which
runs in predictable grooves, and could have
done with more vigour. Barbara Stanwyck,
Ronald Reagan, Gene Evans, Lance Fuller,
Anthony Caruso, Jack Elam. Written by
Robert Blees and Howard Estabrook; directed
by Allan Dwan; for RKO / Benedict Bogeaus.

Cattle Town
US 1952   71m   bw

After the Civil War, returning ranch owners
find their land appropriated by squatters.
Reach-me-down western programmer. Dennis
Morgan, Amanda Blake, Rita Moreno, Ray
Teal, Philip Carey. Written by Tom
Blackburn; directed by Noel Smith; for
Warner.

Caught!
US 1931   71m   bw

A US cavalry officer discovers that Calamity
Jane is his mother. Curious mother-love
western. Richard Arlen, Louise Dresser,
Frances Dee. Written by Agnes Brand Leahy,
Keane Thompson, Sam and Bella Spewack;
directed by Edward Sloman; for Paramount.

Caught*
US 1948   88m   bw
Enterprise (Wolfgang Reinhardt)

The ill-treated wife of a vicious millionaire
leaves him for a doctor, but finds she is to
have the millionaire's baby.
Pretentious *film noir*, rather typical of its time,
with much talent squandered on a very boring
plot.

w Arthur Laurents, *novel* Wild Calendar by
Libbie Block *d* Max Ophuls *ph* Lee Garmes
m Frederick Hollander

James Mason (the doctor), Robert Ryan (the
millionaire), Barbara Bel Geddes, Natalie
Schaefer, Curt Bois

'Ophuls had suffered at Hughes' hands . . .
had wasted time on worthless projects . . . and
had been referred to as "the oaf". Laurents
built the script on stories which Ophuls told
him about Hughes, and on the accounts given
by one of Hughes' girls.'—*Pauline Kael*

● *Video: Intervision*

Caught in the Draft**
US 1941   82m   bw
Paramount (B. G. De Sylva)

A nervous film star cannot avoid being drafted
into the army.
Sprightly comedy from the star's best period,
with gags and supporting cast well up to form.

w Harry Tugend *d* David Butler *ph* Karl
Struss *m* Victor Young

Bob Hope, Lynne Overman, Dorothy
Lamour, Clarence Kolb, Eddie Bracken, Paul
Hurst, Irving Bacon

Caught Short
US 1930   approx 75m   bw

Feuding boarding house landladies play the
stock market—and win. Lumbering comedy
which marked the first big success for the
team of Marie Dressler and Polly Moran;
featuring Charles Morton, Anita Page.
Written by Willard Mack and Robert
Hopkins; directed by Charles Reisner; for
Cosmopolitan / MGM. 'A gold mine . . . the
apex of the career of this pair of sublimated
film-makers . . . a box office smash for all
classes everywhere.'—*Variety*
† A credit reads: Story suggested by Eddie
Cantor's gag book.

Cause for Alarm*
US 1951   74m   bw
MGM (Tom Lewis)

A housewife tries frantically to retrieve a
posted letter containing manufactured
evidence which may put her on a murder
charge.
Minor-league suspenser, watchable but
disappointingly handled.

w Mel Dinelli, Tom Lewis *d* Tay Garnett
ph Joe Ruttenberg *m* André Previn

Loretta Young, Barry Sullivan, Bruce
Cowling, Margalo Gillmore, Irving Bacon

Caught Plastered
US 1931   68m   bw

In helping an old lady save her drug store, two
hams get mixed up with bootleggers. Tedious
star farce. Bert Wheeler, Robert Woolsey,
Dorothy Lee, Lucy Beaumont, Jason
Robards. Written by Ralph Spence, Douglas
MacLean; directed by William Seiter; for
RKO. 'Best for combo and three-dayers.'—
Variety.

'A love that suffered and rose triumphant
above the crushing events of this
modern age! The march of time
measured by a mother's heart!'

Cavalcade**
US 1932   109m   bw
Fox (Winfield Sheehan)

The story of an upper-class English family
between the Boer War and World War I.
Rather static version of the famous stage
spectacular, very similar in setting and style to
TV's later *Upstairs Downstairs*. Good
performances, flat handling.

w Reginald Berkeley, *play* Noel Coward
d Frank Lloyd *ph* Ernest Palmer *war scenes*
William Cameron Menzies *ad* William
Darling *m* Louis de Francesco

Clive Brook, Diana Wynyard, Ursula Jeans,
Herbert Mundin, Una O'Connor, Irene
Browne, Merle Tottenham, Beryl Mercer,
Frank Lawton, Billy Bevan

'Dignified and beautiful spectacle that will
demand respect.'—*Variety*
'If there is anything that moves the ordinary
American to uncontrollable tears, it is the
plight—the constant plight—of dear old
England . . . a superlative newsreel, forcibly
strengthened by factual scenes, good music,
and wonderful photography.'—*Pare Lorentz*
'Greater even than *Birth of a Nation*!'—
Louella Parsons
'An orgy of British self-congratulation.'—
Pauline Kael, 70s

AA: best picture; Frank Lloyd; William
Darling
AAN: Diana Wynyard

The Cave Man
US 1926   approx 78m at 24 fps   bw
silent

A bored socialite cuts a high denomination
note in half, throws one half away, and offers
riches to the first man to find it. Typical
twenties comedy which seemed very modern
at the time. Marie Prevost, Matt Moore,
Phyllis Haver, Myrna Loy. Written by Darryl
F. Zanuck; directed by Lewis Milestone; for
Warner.

Cave of Outlaws
US 1951   76m   Technicolor

After surviving a long prison term, a bandit
returns to the caves where his partners hid
their booty. Modest western with scenes shot
in the Carlsbad Caverns. Macdonald Carey,
Alexis Smith, Edgar Buchanan, Victor Jory,
Hugh O'Brian, Houseley Stevenson. Written
by Elizabeth Wilson; directed by William
Castle; for Universal-International.

Caveman
US 1981   91m   Technicolor

Adventures of a prehistoric man. Witless
farrago of puns and farts on a lower level than
Mel Brooks, if such a thing were possible.
Ringo Starr, Dennis Quaid, Jack Gilford,
Barbara Bach, Avery Schreiber. Written by
Rudy de Luca and Carl Gottlieb; directed by
Carl Gottlieb; for Laurence Turman, David
Foster / UA. 'Too gross and leery for children
and not nearly sprightly or sly enough for
adults.'—*Daily Mail*. 'Worth about half an
hour of anybody's time. Unfortunately it runs
97 minutes.'—*Guardian*

The Cavern
US / Italy 1966   96m   bw

In the last days of World War II, six soldiers
and a girl are trapped by aerial bombardment
in a cave in the Italian mountains. Enervating

psychological drama, glum to look at and listen to. John Saxon, Rosanna Schiaffino, Larry Hagman, Brian Aherne, Nino Castelnuovo. Written by Michael Pertwee and Jack Davis; directed and produced by Edgar G. Ulmer; for Ulmer / TCF.

Ceiling Zero°
US 1935 95m bw
Warner / Cosmopolitan (Harry Joe Brown)

Amorous and airborne adventures of an irresponsible but brilliant civil airlines pilot.
Splendid star vehicle which turns maudlin in the last reel but until then provides crackling entertainment.

w Frank 'Spig' Wead, from his play
d Howard Hawks ph Arthur Edeson

James Cagney, Pat O'Brien, June Travis, Stuart Erwin, Henry Wadsworth, Isabel Jewell, Barton Maclane
  'An entertainment wallop of extraordinary power.'—Variety
  'The best of all airplane pictures.'—Otis Ferguson, 1939
  'Directed at a breakneck pace which emphasizes its lean fibre and its concentration on the essentials of its theme.'—Andrew Sarris, 1963
† Remade in 1939 as International Squadron.

Cela s'appelle l'Aurore°
France / Italy 1955 108m bw
Marceau / Laetitia

A Corsican company doctor falls for a young widow while his wife is on holiday, and events lead to tragedy.
Efficient melodrama, given an extra dimension by its auteur.

w Luis Bunuel, Jean Ferry, novel Emmanuel Robles d Luis Bunuel ph Robert Le Fèbvre m Joseph Kosma

Georges Marchal, Lucia Bose, Gianni Esposito, Julien Bertheau, Henri Nassiet

Céleste°
West Germany 1981 106m
  Eastmancolor
Pelemele / Bayerische Rundfunk (Eleonore Adlon)

During his last years, Marcel Proust is looked after by his voluntary housekeeper.
Subdued and only partially effective memoir from Céleste's biography; not for action seekers, but with a fascination of its own if one can give in to its pace.

wd Percy Adlon, book Monsieur Proust by Céleste Albaret, ph Jurgen Martin, Horst Becker, Helmo Sahliger, Hermann Ramelow, m César Franck

Eva Mattes, Jürgen Arndt

Celine and Julie Go Boating°
France 1974 192m Eastmancolor
Les Films du Losange (Barbet Schroeder)

Two girls change the outcome of a drama played daily in a haunted house.
Odd, dreamlike, absurdly long and semi-improvisational mood piece, with

reverberations from Alice in Wonderland and Orphée. Not an unpleasant experience, but sometimes a tiresome one.

w Eduardo de Gregorio, Juliet Berto, Dominique Labourier, Bulle Ogier, Marie-France Pisier, Jacques Rivette, partly suggested by two stories by Henry James ph Jacques Renard m Jean-Marie Senia

Juliet Berto, Dominique Labourier, Bulle Ogier, Marie-France Pisier, Barbet Schroeder
  'Rivette uncannily combines slapstick, suspense and tears in his most watchable assault on the narrative form.'—Jan Dawson
† Shot in 16mm.

Cell 2455 Death Row
US 1955 77m bw
Columbia (Wallace MacDonald)

A convicted murderer staves off execution with appeal after appeal.
Cheap run-off of the case of Caryl Chessman, who was executed ten years after his trial for rape and murder. Retold in a 1977 TV movie, Kill Me If You Can.

w Jack de Witt, book Caryl Chessman d Fred F. Sears ph Fred Jackman Jnr md Mischa Bakaleinikoff

William Campbell, Kathryn Grant, Harvey Stephens, Marian Carr, Vince Edwards

Centennial Summer°°
US 1946 102m Technicolor
TCF (Otto Preminger)

A Philadelphia family responds to the Great Exposition of 1876.
Pleasing family comedy with music, the kind of harmless competence Hollywood used to throw off with ease but can no longer manage.

w Michael Kanin, novel Albert E. Idell d Otto Preminger ph Ernest Palmer m Alfred Newman songs Jerome Kern, Oscar Hammerstein II, E. Y. Harburg, Leo Robin

Jeanne Crain, Cornel Wilde, Linda Darnell, William Eythe, Walter Brennan, Constance Bennett, Dorothy Gish

AAN: Alfred Newman; song 'All Through the Day' (m Jerome Kern, ly Oscar Hammerstein II)

Central Airport
US 1933 75m bw

After the war the only job an ace pilot can get is as 'chauffeur' to a lady parachutist. Rather stiff romantic drama with aeronautics thrown in. Richard Barthelmess, Sally Eilers, Tom Brown, Glenda Farrell, Harold Huber. Written by Rian James and James Seymour; directed by William A. Wellman; for Warner.
'The aerial excitement should bring sufficient response to bring it over to the right side of the box office.'—Variety

The Ceremony
US / Spain 1963 107m bw
UA / Magla (Laurence Harvey)

In a Tangier jail, a bank robber awaits the firing squad, but he and his brother have an escape plan.

Murky and pretentious melodrama with aspirations to high style and symbolism. A bore.

w Ben Barzman, novel Frederic Grendel d Laurence Harvey ph Oswald Morris m Gerard Schurmann

Laurence Harvey, Sarah Miles, Robert Walker, John Ireland, Ross Martin, Lee Patterson, Jack McGowran, Murray Melvin, Fernando Rey

A Certain Smile°
US 1958 105m Eastmancolor
  Cinemascope
TCF (Henry Ephron)

A girl student falls in love with her philandering uncle.
Another sordid novella by Françoise Sagan (see Bonjour Tristesse), transformed by Hollywood into a glowing romantic saga of life among the Riviera rich. On this level, very competent.

w Frances Goodrich, Albert Hackett d Jean Negulesco ph Milton Krasner m Alfred Newman

Christine Carere, Rossano Brazzi, Joan Fontaine, Bradford Dillman, Eduard Franz, Kathryn Givney, Steve Geray

AAN: title song (m Sammy Fain, ly Paul Francis Webster)

Cervantes
Spain / Italy / France 1968 119m
  Eastmancolor Supertotalvision
Prisma / Protor / Procinex (Alexander Salkind)

Cervantes, an assistant papal envoy, helps persuade Philip of Spain to join the Holy League, then turns soldier and has various adventures.
Rather boring spectacular with conventional set pieces.

w Enrique Llovet, Enrico Bomba, novel Bruno Frank d Vincent Sherman ph Edmond Richard m Jean Ledrut

Horst Buchholz, Gina Lollobrigida, Louis Jourdan, Jose Ferrer, Fernando Rey, Francisco Rabal

César see Marius

César and Rosalie°
France / Italy / West Germany 1972
  105m Eastmancolor
Fildebroc / UPS / Mega Paramount / Orion (Michèle de Broca)

A divorcee living with a rich merchant becomes attracted to a young artist. Unexpectedly, the two men become friends . . .
Wryly amusing comedy for adults.

w Jean-Loup Dabadie, Claude Sautet d Claude Sautet ph Jean Boffety m Philippe Sarde

Yves Montand, Romy Schneider, Sami Frey, Umberto Orsini

Chad Hanna*
US 1940 86m Technicolor
TCF (Darryl F. Zanuck, Nunnally Johnson)

Life in a New York state circus in the 1840s.
Mild romantic drama from a bestseller; local
colour excellent, dramatic interest thin.

w Nunnally Johnson, *novel* Red Wheels
Rolling by Walter D. Edmonds *d* Henry
King *ph* Ernest Palmer *m* David Buttolph

Henry Fonda, Dorothy Lamour, Linda
Darnell, Guy Kibbee, Jane Darwell, John
Carradine, Ted North, Roscoe Ates

Chain Lightning
US 1950 94m bw
Warner (Anthony Veiller)

After World War II a bomber pilot learns how
to control the new jets.
Absolutely routine romance and heroics.

w Liam O'Brien, Vincent Evans *d* Stuart
Heisler *ph* Ernest Haller *m* David Buttolph

Humphrey Bogart, Eleanor Parker, Raymond
Massey, Richard Whorf, James Brown, Roy
Roberts, Morris Ankrum

Chained*
US 1934 77m bw
MGM (Hunt Stromberg)

A devoted wife has a shipboard romance with
another man.
Moderate star romantic drama.

w John Lee Mahin *d* Clarence Brown
ph George Folsey *m* Herbert Stothart

Joan Crawford, Clark Gable, Otto Kruger,
Stuart Erwin, Una O'Connor. Akim Tamiroff
  'Simple in story and unoriginal in idea, its
weight is in words rather than action and
dramatic potency.'—*Variety*

A Chairy Tale**
Canada 1957 10m bw

A young man finds that a kitchen chair is
unwilling for him to sit on it, but they arrive at
a compromise. The simplest and most effective
of fantasies is told at somewhat excessive
length but remains among its director's more
memorable creations. Written and directed by
Norman McLaren (with Claude Jutra, who
plays the young man); for the National Film
Board of Canada.

The Chalk Garden*
GB 1964 106m Technicolor
U-I / Quota Rentals (Ross Hunter)

The governess in a melancholy household has
an effect on the lives of her aged employer and
the young granddaughter.
Sub-Chekhovian drama in a house by the sea,
flattened by routine handling into something
much less interesting than it was on the stage.

w John Michael Hayes, *novel* Enid Bagnold
d Ronald Neame *ph* Arthur Ibbetson
m Malcolm Arnold

Edith Evans, Deborah Kerr, Hayley Mills,
John Mills, Felix Aylmer, Elizabeth Sellars,
Lally Bowers, Toke Townley

  'Crashing symbolism, cracker-motto
sententiousness.'—*MFB*
AAN: Edith Evans

The Challenge
GB 1938 75m bw

On the Matterhorn in 1865, a guide proves
that an English climber did not sacrifice his
friends. Fictionalized mountain climbing
history, a little dull. Luis Trenker, Robert
Douglas, Joan Gardner, Mary Clare, Ralph
Truman. Written by Emeric Pressburger,
Milton Rosmer and Patrick Kirwan; directed
by Milton Rosmer and Luis Trenker; for
Alexander Korda. 'A rather simple story, yet
seldom dull.'—*Variety*

The Challenge
US 1948 69m bw

Bulldog Drummond solves the mystery of a
yacht which is stolen after its owner is
murdered. Modest addition to a long-running
series. Tom Conway, June Vincent, Richard
Stapley. Written by Frank Gruber and Irving
Elman; directed by Jean Yarbrough; for
Reliance (TCF).

The Challenge
GB 1960 89m bw

In search of buried loot, a lady gangster
kidnaps a convict's son. Murky and
unsympathetic melodrama. Jayne Mansfield,
Anthony Quayle, Carl Mohner, Barbara
Mullen, Peter Reynolds, Dermot Walsh.
Written and directed by John Gilling; for John
Temple-Smith / Alexandra.

The Challenge
US 1982 112m Eastmancolor
CBS Theatrical Film Group (Lyle Poncher,
  Robert L. Rosen, Ron Beckman)

An American boxer in Japan becomes
involved in a feud between two brothers.
Belated martial arts saga with a good deal of
head-lopping and plenty of pretensions but no
apparent message to spike its dismal
entertainment values.

w Richard Maxwell, John Sayles *d* John
Frankenheimer *ph* Kozo Okazaki *m* Jerry
Goldsmith *pd* Yoshiyuki Ishida *ed* Jack
Wheeler

Scott Glenn, Toshiro Mifune, Donna Kei
Benz, Atsuo Nakamura, Calvin Young, Clyde
Kusatsu
  'Ridiculous, demeaning stuff.'—*Guardian*

A Challenge for Robin Hood*
GB 1967 96m Technicolor
Hammer (Clifford Parkes)

A retelling of the original Robin Hood legend.
Unassuming, lively, predictable adventure
hokum.

w Peter Bryan *d* C. Pennington-Richards
ph Arthur Grant *m* Gary Hughes

Barrie Ingham, James Hayter, Leon Greene,
John Arnatt

  'The unspeakable vengeance of the crazed
  Baltimore strangler!'
Chamber of Horrors
US 1966 99m Warnercolor
Warner (Hy Averback)

A maniacal murderer is finally trapped by two
amateur criminologists who run a wax museum
in Baltimore.
Zany horror thriller originally meant for TV; it
turned out a shade too harrowing. Advertised
as 'the picture with the Fear Flasher and the
Horror Horn', shock gimmicks which proved
much more startling than the crude events
they heralded.

w Stephen Kandel *d* Hy Averback
ph Richard Kline *m* William Lava

Patrick O'Neal, Cesare Danova, Wilfrid Hyde
White, Laura Devon, Patrice Wymore, Suzy
Parker, Jeanette Nolan, Tony Curtis (guest)

  'Don't fail to get a ringside seat!'
The Champ*
US 1931 87m bw
MGM (Harry Rapf)

A young boy has faith in a washed-up
prizefighter.
Maudlin drama, highly commercial in its day
and a box office tonic for its two stars.
Remade as *The Clown* (qv).

w Leonard Praskins, Frances Marion *d* King
Vidor *ph* Gordon Avil

Wallace Beery, Jackie Cooper, Irene Rich,
Roscoe Ates, Edward Brophy
  'The knockout picture of the year!'—
publicity
  'This picture will hit 'em all, large or small,
and that means lots of money.'—*Variety*

AA: original story (Frances Marion); Wallace
Beery
AAN: best picture; King Vidor

The Champ*
US 1979 122m Metrocolor
MGM (Dyson Lovell)

A remake of the above, with Florida racetrack
asides.
A lush version, so little updated in mood that
its tearfulness seems to have strayed from
another age.

w Walter Newman *d* Franco Zeffirelli
ph Fred J. Koenekamp *m* Dave Grusin
pd Herman A. Blumenthal

Jon Voight, Faye Dunaway, *Ricky Schroeder*,
Jack Warden, Arthur Hill, Strother Martin,
Joan Blondell, Elisha Cook
● Video: MGM / UA

Champagne
GB 1928 90m (24 fps) bw silent

A millionaire pretends to be bankrupt so that
his daughter won't marry. Tedious comedy
drama with very few of the master's touches.
Betty Balfour, Jean Bradin, Gordon Harker,
Theodore Von Alten. Written by Eliot
Stannard, Walter C. Mycroft and Alfred
Hitchcock; directed by Alfred Hitchcock; for
BIP. 'Dreadful.'—*Alfred Hitchcock*

Champagne Charlie*
GB 1944 107m bw
Ealing (John Croydon)

The life of Victorian music hall singer George Leybourne and his rivalry with the Great Vance.
Careful period reconstruction and good songs and acting are somehow nullified by unsympathetic handling and photography.

w Austin Melford, Angus Macphail, John Dighton d Alberto Cavalcanti ph Wilkie Cooper md Ernest Irving

Tommy Trinder, Stanley Holloway, Betty Warren, Austin Trevor, Jean Kent, Guy Middleton, Frederick Piper, Harry Fowler
'Cavalcanti's taste for the bizarre and the vigour of the performances make it something more than a museum piece.'—*Time Out, 1984*

Champagne for Caesar*
US 1950 99m bw
Cardinal (George Moskov)

A self-confessed genius with a grudge against a soap company determines to win astronomical sums on its weekly radio quiz.
Agreeable, mildly satirical star comedy which tends to peter out halfway.

w Hans Jacoby, Fred Brady d Richard Whorf ph Paul Ivano m Dmitri Tiomkin

Ronald Colman, Vincent Price, Celeste Holm, Barbara Britton, Art Linkletter

The Champagne Murders
France 1967 107m Techniscope
Universal (France) (Jacques Natteau)
original title: *Le Scandale*

A disturbed champagne millionaire thinks he may be a murderer.
Complex but uninvolving mystery story in which the director's eye seems to be more on satire than on narrative.

w Claude Brûlé, Derek Prouse, Paul Gégauff d Claude Chabrol ph Jean Rabier m Pierre Jansen

Anthony Perkins, Maurice Ronet, Stéphane Audran, Yvonne Furneaux, Suzanne Lloyd

'As gay and sparkling as a champagne cocktail!'

Champagne Waltz
US 1937 90m bw

A press agent takes a swing band to Vienna. Rather tedious romantic comedy with music. Fred MacMurray, Gladys Swarthout, Jack Oakie. Written by Don Hartman, Frank Butler from a story by Billy Wilder, H. S. Kraft and Vienna Hall; directed by Edward Sutherland; for Paramount. 'On the slow side, but should do fairly.'—*Variety*

'This is the only sport in the world where two guys get paid for doing something they'd be arrested for if they got drunk and did it for nothing.'

Champion**
US 1949 99m bw
Stanley Kramer

An ambitious prizefighter alienates his friends and family, and dies of injuries received in the ring.

Interesting exposé of the fight racket, presented in good cinematic style and acted with great bravura.

w Carl Foreman, story Ring Lardner d Mark Robson ph Franz Planer m Dmitri Tiomkin

Kirk Douglas, Arthur Kennedy, Marilyn Maxwell, Paul Stewart, Ruth Roman, Lola Albright, Luis Van Rooten

AAN: Carl Foreman; Franz Planer; Dmitri Tiomkin; Kirk Douglas; Arthur Kennedy

Champions*
GB 1983 115m colour
Embassy / Archerwest / Ladbroke / United British Artists (Peter Shaw, Eva Monley)

A leading jockey develops cancer and his horse receives a leg injury, but both survive to win the Grand National.
Gruelling factual story which could have done with a little more drama, not to mention a more sympathetic hero.

w Evan Jones, book Bob Champion and Jonathan Powell d John Irvin ph Ronnie Taylor m Carl Davis

John Hurt, Edward Woodward, Ben Johnson, Jan Francis, Peter Barkworth, Ann Bell, Judy Parfitt
'It ignores any inner aspect, the better to concentrate on tearjerking externals.'—*Tom Milne, MFB*
'Told as an indecent tearjerker, directed with the discretion of a rampaging steamroller.'—*Sight and Sound*

Chance of a Lifetime*
GB 1950 93m bw
Pilgrim Pictures (Bernard Miles)

The owner of a small engineering works, impatient with the unionism of his men, gives them a chance to run the factory themselves. Quiet comedy-drama on sub-Ealing lines; always interesting, it never quite catches fire despite a reliable cast.

w Walter Greenwood, Bernard Miles d Bernard Miles ph Eric Cross

Bernard Miles, Basil Radford, Niall MacGinnis, Geoffrey Keen, Julien Mitchell, Josephine Wilson, Kenneth More, Hattie Jacques

Chances*
US 1931 72m bw

In wartime London, two soldiers on leave fall for the same girl. Unexpectedly sensitive and pleasing romance, generally well handled. Douglas Fairbanks Jnr, Anthony Bushell, Rose Hobart. Written by Waldemar Young, from a novel by Hamilton Gibbs; directed by Allan Dwan; for Warner. 'Enough contributing sidelights to keep the emphasis away from the combat . . . should be pleasant b.o.'—*Variety*

Chandler
US 1971 88m Metrocolor Panavision

An ex-private eye becomes a security guard and an alcoholic but even worse befalls when he agrees to keep an eye on a government witness. Downbeat, generally unamusing and

little seen piece of thick ear which harks back unsuccessfully to the forties. Warren Oates, Leslie Caron, Alex Dreier, Mitchell Ryan, Gordon Pinsent, Charles McGraw, Richard Loo, Walter Burke, Gloria Grahame, Royal Dano, Scatman Crothers. Written by John Sacret Young; directed by Paul Magwood; for MGM.

Chandu the Magician*
US 1932 74m bw
Fox

A spiritualist battles against a madman with a death ray which could destroy the world. Rather dim serial-like thriller, with interesting talent not at its best.

w Philip Klein, Barry Conners d Marcel Varnel, William Cameron Menzies ph James Wong Howe

Edmund Lowe, Bela Lugosi, Irene Ware, Herbert Mundin, Henry B. Walthall
† Sequels (whittled down from serials) include *The Return of Chandu* and *Chandu and the Magic Isle*.

Chanel Solitaire
France / GB 1981 124m colour
Gardenia / Todrest (Larry G. Spangler)

Fashion designer Coco Chanel thinks back on her long career.
Moderately elegant but frigid autobiopic with very little entertainment value.

w Julian More, *novel* Claude Dulay d George Kaczender ph Ricardo Aronovich m Jean Musy

Marie-France Pisier, Timothy Dalton, Rutger Hauer, Karen Black, Brigitte Fossey
'The producer says the film is devoted to providing what every woman wants—men, money, jewellery, castles, caviare, champagne and love, love, love. I never realized they could be so boring.'—*Sunday Times*

Chang**
US 1927 71m (24 fps) bw silent
Paramount

The life of a rice-grower in Thailand. Influential but now rather boring documentary with animal interest.

wd, ph, ed Merian C. Cooper, Ernest B. Schoedsack

Change of Habit
US 1969 97m colour

A young doctor working in a ghetto has his opinions changed by three nuns. A notably unsuccessful attempt by a star to change his image. Elvis Presley, Mary Tyler Moore, Barbara McNair, Ed Asner, Leora Dana, Jane Elliot, Robert Emhardt. Written by James Lee, S. S. Schweltzer and Eric Bercovici; directed by William Graham; for Universal.

Change of Heart
US 1934 74m bw
Fox

Four young California students make good in New York.

Minor fairy tale which marked the last of twelve teamings for Gaynor and Farrell.

w Sonya Levien, James Gleason, Samuel Hoffenstein, *novel* Kathleen Norris *d* John G. Blystone *ph* Hal Mohr

Janet Gaynor, Charles Farrell, Ginger Rogers, James Dunn, Beryl Mercer, Gustav Von Seyffertitz, Shirley Temple
'They are on the back of a nag that never quite gets started . . . most of the time it causes that tired feeling.'—*Variety*

Change of Heart
US 1937 65m bw

A bored man and wife go their separate ways but are eventually reconciled. Bright little comedy on a tired old theme. Michael Whalen, Gloria Stuart, Lyle Talbot, Jane Darwell. Written by Frances Hyland, Albert Ray; directed by James Tinling; for Sol M. Wurtzel / TCF. 'More originality, freshness of treatment and solid entertainment than in half the more expensive efforts from the Hollywood studios.'—*Variety*

Change of Heart
US 1943 87m bw

A country girl writes songs and a publisher steals them. Slim basis for a so-so musical. Susan Hayward, John Carroll, Eve Arden, Gail Patrick, Walter Catlett, Melville Cooper, Count Basie and his Orchestra. Written by Frank Gill Jnr; directed by Albert S. Rogell; for Republic. (Original title: *Hit Parade of 1943*.)

Change of Mind
US 1969 98m Eastmancolor
Sagittarius (Seeleg Lester, Richard Wesson)

The life of a liberal white DA can only be 'saved' by transplanting his brain into the body of a dead black man.
Fantasy melodrama with a social conscience, about a half-and-half which is acceptable to neither whites nor blacks. Very obvious and rather boring.

w Seeleg Lester, Richard Wesson *d* Robert Stevens *ph* Arthur J. Ornitz *m* Duke Ellington

Raymond St Jacques, Susan Oliver, Janet McLachlan, Leslie Nielsen.

A Change of Seasons
US 1980 102m De Luxe
TCF / Martin Ransohoff / Film Finance Group Ltd

A college professor takes a mistress and his wife retaliates.
Zestless and unhumorous rehash of *Who's Afraid of Virginia Woolf?* and *Bob and Carol and Ted and Alice*. Not a new thought anywhere.

w Erich Segal, Ronni Kern, Fred Segal *d* Richard Lang *ph* Philip Lathrop *m* Henry Mancini *pd* Bill Kenney

Shirley Maclaine, Anthony Hopkins, Bo Derek, Michael Brandon, Mary Beth Hurt, Ed Winter

'A tired rehash of themes that might have been provocative a decade ago . . . it would take a Lubitsch to do justice to the incredibly tangled relationships.'—*Variety*
'The situation soon melts into a gooey mess, like a Mars bar left too long in a trouser pocket.'—*Sunday Times*

The Changeling
Canada 1979 107m colour Panavision
Chessman Palk Productions

A widowed academic takes on an old house haunted by the spirit of a murdered child. Tedious and not very brief, this uninspired ghost story comes very late in the horror stakes and contains very little to make one care about its outcome.

w William Gray, Diana Maddox *d* Peter Medak *ph* John Coquillon *m* Rick Wilkins

George C. Scott, Melvyn Douglas, Trish Van Devere, John Colicos, Jean Marsh, Barry Morse
'None of its most eerily untoward occurrences proceed from any spectral intervention, but from the worst abuses of Peter Medak's infuriatingly fidgety camera.'—*Gilbert Adair, MFB*

Channel Crossing°
GB 1933 70m bw

Various characters converge on a ferry boat to France. Somewhat stilted potboiler with interesting cast: Matheson Lang, Max Miller, Constance Cummings, Edmund Gwenn, Anthony Bushell, Dorothy Dickson, Nigel Bruce. Written by W. P. Lipscomb and Cyril Campion; directed by Milton Rosmer; for Gaumont.

The Chant of Jimmie Blacksmith
Australia 1978 122m Eastmancolor Panavision

In 1900, a half-caste mingles with high class whites, goes berserk, and slaughters several of them with an axe. Hard-to-take moral tale for philosophers with strong stomachs. Tommy Lewis, Ray Barrett, Jack Thompson, Freddy Reynolds. Written and directed by Fred Schepsi, from the novel by Thomas Keneally; for Film House.

Chapayev°
USSR 1934 94m bw
Lenfilm

Exploits of a Red Army commander during the 1919 battles.
Moderately striking propaganda piece.

wd Sergei and Georgy Vasiliev *ph* Alexander Sigayev *m* Gavril Popov

Boris Babochkin, B. Blinov, Leonid Kmit
'Easily the best film turned out in Russia since sound.'—*Variety*

The Chapman Report
US 1962 125m Technicolor
(Warner) Darryl F. Zanuck (Richard D. Zanuck)

Dr Chapman conducts a study of female sex behaviour in an American suburb.

Influenced by the Kinsey report, this melodramatic compendium takes itself far too seriously, and the director's smooth style is barely in evidence.

w Wyatt Cooper, Don M. Mankiewicz, *novel* Irving Wallace *d* George Cukor *ph* Harold Lipstein *m* Leonard Rosenman

Shelley Winters, Claire Bloom, *Glynis Johns*, Efrem Zimbalist Jnr, Jane Fonda, Ray Danton, Ty Hardin, Andrew Duggan, John Dehner, Henry Daniell, Corey Allen, Harold J. Stone
'We had a preview which went very well, and then it was sent over to Mr Zanuck, who did what I thought was a most horrendous job of cutting it up.'—*George Cukor*

Chapter Two°
US 1979 127m Metrocolor
Columbia / Rastar (Margaret Booth)

A widowed novelist reluctantly embarks on an affair with a divorcee.
Simon in sad mood means that the wisecracks are still there but the pauses between them are longer. The thin but heavy-going plot finally militates against enthusiasm.

w Neil Simon *d* Robert Moore *ph* David M. Walsh, Richard Kratina *m* Marvin Hamlisch *pd* Gene Callahan

James Caan, Marsha Mason, Joseph Bologna, Valerie Harper, Alan Fudge
'The regular Neil Simon Broadway takeaway for people who watch movies with their ears. Over two hours of theatrical smart talk and unfailing wit-under-pressure as Simon-surrogate Caan and the real Mrs Simon swap marital repartee in front of a reverent camera.'—*Time Out*
'All the couple have to do is swap wisecracks and nurse their rather pretty emotional bruises.'—*Observer*

Charade°°
US 1964 113m Technicolor
Universal / Stanley Donen

A Parisienne finds her husband murdered. Four strange men are after her, and she is helped by a handsome stranger . . . but is he hero, spy or murderer?
Smoothly satisfying sub-Hitchcock nonsense, effective both as black romantic comedy and macabre farce.

w Peter Stone *d* Stanley Donen *ph* Charles Lang Jnr *m* Henry Mancini

Cary Grant (sixty but concealing the fact by taking a shower fully clothed), *Audrey Hepburn, Walter Matthau*, James Coburn, George Kennedy, Ned Glass, Jacques Marin
'One hesitates to be uncharitable to a film like *Charade*, which seeks only to provide a little innocent merriment and make a pot of money. . . . Of itself, it is a stylish and amusing melodrama, but in the context of the bloodlust that seems unloosed in our land it is as sinister as the villains who stalk Miss Hepburn through the cobbled streets of Paris.'—*Arthur Knight*

AAN: song 'Charade' (*m* Henry Mancini, *ly* Johnny Mercer)

The Charge at Feather River*
US 1953 96m Warnercolor
Warner (David Weisbart)

An army platoon composed of men from the
guardhouse tries to rescue two women
kidnapped by Indians.
Formula western distinguished by 3-D
photography, probably the best to be achieved
in the brief life of the medium. Warnerphonic
sound was less successfully added; the sum
total would be trying for nervous people.

w James R. Webb d Gordon Douglas
ph Peverell Marley m Max Steiner

Guy Madison, Frank Lovejoy, Vera Miles,
Helen Westcott, Dick Wesson, Onslow
Stevens, Steve Brodie
  'From the start we are involved in a whirl of
frenzied activity: a cavalry charge, knife
throwing, sabre practice, flaming arrows—not
a trick missed.'—MFB

Charge of the Lancers
US 1953 74m Technicolor

During the Crimean War, the Russians
capture an English major who knows the
details of a new cannon. Action cheapie which
seems to be largely shot in the producer's back
garden but provides a laugh or two. Paulette
Goddard, Jean-Pierre Aumont, Richard
Stapley, Karin Booth, Lester Matthews.
Written by Robert E. Kent; directed by
William Castle; for Sam Katzman / Columbia.

'The reckless lancers sweep on and on—so
  that a woman's heart might not be
  broken! You're not fighting a single
  legion—you're fighting the entire British
  army, Surat Khan!'
The Charge of the Light Brigade*
US 1936 115m bw
Warner (Hal B. Wallis, Sam Bischoff)

An army officer deliberately starts the
Balaclava charge to even an old score with
Surat Khan, who's on the other side.
Though allegedly 'based on the poem by
Alfred Lord Tennyson', this is no more than a
travesty of history, most of it taking place in
India. As pure entertainment however it is a
most superior slice of Hollywood hokum and
the film which set the seal on Errol Flynn's
superstardom.

w Michael Jacoby, Rowland Leigh d Michael
Curtiz ph Sol Polito, Fred Jackman m Max
Steiner

Errol Flynn, Olivia de Havilland, Patric
Knowles, Donald Crisp, C. Aubrey Smith,
David Niven, Henry Stephenson, Nigel Bruce,
C. Henry Gordon, Spring Byington, E. E.
Clive, Lumsden Hare, Robert Barrat, J.
Carrol Naish
AAN: Max Steiner

The Charge of the Light Brigade
GB 1968 141m De Luxe Panavision
UA / Woodfall (Neil Hartley)

An historical fantasia with comic, sociological
and cartoon embellishments.
This version for the swinging sixties has a few

splendid moments but apes Tom Jones all too
obviously and leaves audiences with an even
dimmer view of history than they started with.

w Charles Wood d Tony Richardson
ph David Watkin, Peter Suschitsky m John
Addison animation Richard Williams
ad Edward Marshall

Trevor Howard, John Gielgud, David
Hemmings, Vanessa Redgrave, Jill Bennett,
Harry Andrews, Peter Bowles, Mark Burns
  'Considering the lucid book on which it is
largely based, it is almost as inexcusably
muddled as the British commanders at
Balaclava.'—John Simon
  'The point of the film is to recreate mid-
Victorian England in spirit and detail.'—
Stanley Kauffmann
  'Notions for at least three interesting films
are on view . . . what seems signally lacking is
a guiding hand, an overriding purpose.'—John
Coleman
  'This epic has so little feeling for the
courage that went with the idiocies of the past
that it diminishes itself along with its
targets.'—Pauline Kael

Charing Cross Road
GB 1935 72m bw

Struggling boy and girl singers try to move into
high society. Dated and artificial filler. John
Mills, June Clyde, Derek Oldham, Jean Colin,
Judy Kelly. Written by Con West and Clifford
Grey; directed by Albert de Courville; for
British Lion.

'Two men chasing dreams of glory!'
Chariots of Fire*
GB 1981 121m colour
TCF / Allied Stars / Enigma (David Puttnam)

In the 1924 Paris Olympics, a Jew and a
Scotsman run for Britain.
A film of subtle qualities, rather like those of a
BBC classic serial. Probably not quite worth
the adulation it received, but full of pleasant
romantic touches and sharp glimpses of the
wider issues involved.

w Colin Welland d Hugh Hudson ph David
Watkin m Vangelis

Ben Cross, Ian Charleson, Nigel Havers,
Nicholas Farrell, Daniel Gerroll, Cheryl
Campbell, Alice Krige, John Gielgud, Lindsay
Anderson, Nigel Davenport, Ian Holm,
Patrick Magee
  'The whole contradictory bundle is
unexpectedly watchable.'—Jo Imeson, MFB
  'A piece of technological lyricism held
together by the glue of simple-minded heroic
sentiment.'—Pauline Kael

AA: best picture; Colin Welland; Vangelis;
costume design (Milera Canonero)
AAN: Hugh Hudson; editing (Terry
Rawlings); Ian Holm (supporting actor)
BFA: best picture; costume design; Ian Holm

● Video: CBS / Fox

Charley and the Angel*
US 1974 93m Technicolor
Walt Disney (Bill Anderson)

A small-town sporting goods storekeeper in
the thirties escapes death three times and finds
an impatient angel waiting for him.
Mild sentimental whimsy on the lines of On
Borrowed Time, but with a happy ending and
attractive period trappings.

w Roswell Rogers, novel The Golden
Evenings of Summer by Will Stanton
d Vincent McEveety ph Charles F. Wheeler
m Buddy Baker

Fred MacMurray, Cloris Leachman, Harry
Morgan, Kurt Russell, Kathleen Cody,
Edward Andrews, Barbara Nichols

Charley Moon*
GB 1956 92m Eastmancolor
Colin Lesslie, Aubrey Baring

A music hall comic becomes swollen-headed
but returns to his home village and marries his
childhood sweetheart.
Faltering musical lacking the gusto of its
background, but providing a generally
believable impression of life on the halls.

w / songs Leslie Bricusse, novel Reginald
Arkell d Guy Hamilton ph Jack Hildyard

Max Bygraves, Dennis Price, Michael
Medwin, Florence Desmond, Shirley Eaton,
Patricia Driscoll, Reginald Beckwith

'When he runs out of dumb luck he always
  has genius to fall back on!'
Charley Varrick**
US 1973 111m Technicolor
Universal (Don Siegel)

A bank robber discovers he has stolen Mafia
money, and devises a clever scheme to get
himself off the hook.
Sharp, smart, well-observed but implausible
thriller, astringently handled and agreeably set
in Californian backlands. Accomplished,
forgettable entertainment.

w Howard Rodman, Dean Reisner, novel The
Looters by John Reese d Don Siegel
ph Michael Butler m Lalo Schifrin

Walter Matthau, Joe Don Baker, Felicia Farr,
Andy Robinson, John Vernon, Sheree North,
Norman Fell
  'It proves there is nothing wrong with an
auteur director that a good script can't cure.'—
Stanley Kauffmann
  'The narrative line is clean and direct, the
characterizations economical and functional,
and the triumph of intelligence gloriously
satisfying.'—Andrew Sarris

Charley's Aunt**
US 1941 81m bw
TCF (William Perlberg)
GB title: Charley's American Aunt

For complicated reasons, an Oxford
undergraduate has to impersonate his own rich
aunt from Brazil (where the nuts come from).
Very adequate version of the Victorian farce,
with all concerned in excellent form.

w George Seaton, play Brandon Thomas
d Archie Mayo ph Peverell Marley m Alfred
Newman ad Richard Day, Nathan Juran

Jack Benny, Kay Francis, James Ellison, Anne Baxter, *Laird Cregar*, Edmund Gwenn, Reginald Owen, Richard Haydn, Arleen Whelan, Ernest Cossart
† See also: *Where's Charley?*

Charley's Big-Hearted Aunt
GB 1940 76m bw
Gainsborough (Edward Black)

Rather disappointing British version of the famous farce, dully assembled and rather unsuitably cast.

w Marriott Edgar, Val Guest d Walter Forde
ph Jack Cox

Arthur Askey, Phyllis Calvert, Moore Marriott, Graham Moffatt, Richard Murdoch, Jeanne de Casalis, J. H. Roberts, Felix Aylmer, Wally Patch

Charlie Bubbles***
GB 1968 91m Technicolor
Universal / Memorial (Michael Medwin, George Pitcher)

A successful novelist loathes the pointlessness of the good life and tries unsuccessfully to return to his northern working class background.
A little arid and slow in its early stages, and with a rather lame end (our hero escapes by air balloon), this is nevertheless a fascinating, fragmentary character study with a host of wry comedy touches and nimbly sketched characters; in its unassuming way it indicts many of the symbols people lived by in the sixties.

w Shelagh Delaney d Albert Finney ph Peter Suschitsky m Mischa Donat

Albert Finney, Billie Whitelaw, Liza Minnelli, Colin Blakely, Timothy Garland, Diana Coupland, Alan Lake, Yootha Joyce, Joe Gladwin

'A modest thing, but like all good work in minor keys it has a way of haunting the memory.'—*Richard Schickel*
'The supreme deadweight is Liza Minnelli, whose screen debut proves easily the most inauspicious since Turhan Bey's.'—*John Simon*

Charlie Chan
The Oriental detective created by Earl Derr Biggers began his film career as a minor character (played by George Kuwa) in a 1926 serial called HOUSE WITHOUT A KEY. In 1928 Kamiyama Sojin had a bigger role in THE CHINESE PARROT, but in 1929 E. L. Park did almost nothing in BEHIND THAT CURTAIN. In 1931 however began the fully-fledged Chan movies, which entertained a generation. Chan, based on a real-life Chinese detective named Chang Apana, became a citizen of Honolulu and was developed as a polite family man, aided by his impulsive number one or number two son (out of a family of fourteen), in solving murder puzzles. He had a treasury of aphorisms (a whole book of which has been published), and his technique was to gather all the suspects into one room before unmasking one as the

murderer. The films built to a peak around 1936–9, but tailed off disastrously in the mid-forties. They were never noted for production values, but many retain interest for their scripts, their puzzles, and their casts of budding stars, as well as the central character. This is a complete list:
For Fox (later Twentieth Century Fox), with *Warner Oland* as Chan:
1931: CHARLIE CHAN CARRIES ON*, THE BLACK CAMEL
1932: CHARLIE CHAN'S CHANCE
1933: CHARLIE CHAN'S GREATEST CASE
1934: CHARLIE CHAN'S COURAGE, CHARLIE CHAN IN LONDON
1935: CHARLIE CHAN IN PARIS*, CHARLIE CHAN IN EGYPT, CHARLIE CHAN IN SHANGHAI
1936: CHARLIE CHAN'S SECRET*, CHARLIE CHAN AT THE CIRCUS*, CHARLIE CHAN AT THE RACE TRACK, CHARLIE CHAN AT THE OPERA**
1937: CHARLIE CHAN AT THE OLYMPICS, CHARLIE CHAN ON BROADWAY*, CHARLIE CHAN AT MONTE CARLO
For Twentieth Century Fox, with *Sidney Toler*:
1938: CHARLIE CHAN IN HONOLULU
1939: CHARLIE CHAN IN RENO, CHARLIE CHAN ON TREASURE ISLAND**, CITY OF DARKNESS
1940: CHARLIE CHAN IN PANAMA, CHARLIE CHAN'S MURDER CRUISE, CHARLIE CHAN AT THE WAX MUSEUM*, MURDER OVER NEW YORK
1941: DEAD MEN TELL, CHARLIE CHAN IN RIO, CASTLE IN THE DESERT*
For Monogram, with Sidney Toler:
1944: CHARLIE CHAN IN THE SECRET SERVICE, THE CHINESE CAT, BLACK MAGIC
1945: THE SCARLET CLUE, THE JADE MASK, SHANGHAI COBRA, RED DRAGON
1946: SHADOWS OVER CHINATOWN, DANGEROUS MONEY
1947: THE TRAP
For Monogram, with Roland Winters:
1947: THE CHINESE RING
1948: DOCKS OF NEW ORLEANS, SHANGHAI CHEST, THE GOLDEN EYE, THE FEATHERED SERPENT
1949: SKY DRAGON

In the late fifties J. Carrol Naish appeared in a half-hour TV series as Chan, but the episodes were dull. In 1971 Universal tried to revive the character in a 96-minute pilot film *Happiness is a Warm Clue*, but Ross Martin was woefully miscast. See also below.

Charlie Chan and the Curse of the Dragon Queen
US 1980 95m CFI Color
UA / American Cinema / Jerry Sherlock

The villainous Dragon Queen puts a curse on Chan and his descendants, and works it out some years later in San Francisco.

The targets in this spoof are somewhat elementary (the sinister housekeeper is Mrs Danvers, the wheelchair-bound butler Gillespie) and almost all the jokes fall flat on their faces.

w Stan Burns, David Axelrod d Clive Donner ph Paul Lohmann m Patrick Williams

Peter Ustinov, Angie Dickinson, Richard Hatch, Brian Keith, Roddy McDowall, Rachel Roberts, Johnny Sekka

Charlie McCarthy, Detective
US 1939 65m bw

Ventriloquist Edgar Bergen helps to solve a murder. Slightly tiresome mystery comedy with no real place for the wisecracking dummy. Edgar Bergen, Robert Cummings, Constance Moore, John Sutton, Louis Calhern, Edgar Kennedy, Samuel S. Hinds, Warren Hymer, Harold Huber. Written by Edward Eliscu; directed and produced by Frank Tuttle; for Universal. 'Looks like a corner-cutter . . . will have to struggle as top half of the duallers.'—*Variety*

Charlotte's Web
US 1972 96m Technicolor
Hanna-Barbera for Sagittarius

Farmyard animals who sense their fate are stimulated and encouraged by a resourceful spider.
Interesting but overlong and rather plodding version of a stylish book for children; the animation has no style at all.

w Earl Hanmer Jnr, *novel* E. B. White
d Charles A. Nichols, Iwao Takamoto
m / ly Richard and Robert Sherman

Charming Sinners
US 1929 66m bw

A society wife schemes to regain the attention of her wayward husband. Early talkie version of Somerset Maugham's *The Constant Wife*; of historical interest only. Ruth Chatterton, Clive Brook, William Powell, Mary Nolan, Florence Eldridge. Written by Doris Anderson; directed by Robert Milton; for Paramount.

Charly*
US 1968 106m Techniscope
Selmur / Robertson Associates (Ralph Nelson)

New methods of surgery cure a mentally retarded young man, who becomes a genius, but the effects wear off.
Smooth, unconvincing, rather pointless fantasy which ultimately leaves a bad taste in the mouth.

w Sterling Silliphant, *novel* Flowers for Algernon by Daniel Keyes d Ralph Nelson
ph Arthur J. Ornitz m Ravi Shankar

Cliff Robertson, Claire Bloom, Leon Janney, Lilia Skala

'The most distressing thing about *Charly* is not its ticklish subject, nor yet its clumsily modish surface, but its insistent, persistent sentimentality.'—*Tom Milne*

AA: Cliff Robertson

Charro

US 1969 98m Technicolor Panavision
National General (Charles Marquis Warren)

A reformed outlaw is framed for the theft of a cannon.

Dismal western with a singing star playing straight. A bad experience.

wd Charles Marquis Warren ph Ellsworth Fredericks m Hugo Montenegro

Elvis Presley, Ina Balin, Barbara Werle, Lynn Kellogg, Victor French, Solomon Sturges

Chartroose Caboose

US 1960 76m Eastmancolor·
Panavision

A runaway couple take refuge with a retired train conductor in his converted rolling stock home. Old-fashioned to the point of seeming half-witted, this comedy has little to offer but geniality. Molly Bee, Ben Cooper, Edgar Buchanan, O. Z. Whitehead, Slim Pickens. Written by Rod Peterson; directed by William Reynolds; for Red-Bill / U-I.

The Chase°

US 1947 84m bw
Nero Pictures (Seymour Nebenzal)

A shell-shocked ex-serviceman foils a criminal and falls for his wife.

Weird Cuban-set film noir with a strange cast and stranger atmosphere. A genuine bomb, but worth a look for its pretensions, its cast, and its trick ending.

w Philip Yordan, novel The Black Path of Fear by Cornell Woolrich d Arthur Ripley ph Franz Planer m Michel Michelet

Robert Cummings, Michèle Morgan, Peter Lorre, Steve Cochran, Lloyd Corrigan, Jack Holt

The Chase°

US 1966 135m Technicolor
Panavision
Columbia / Sam Spiegel

When a convict escapes and heads for his small Texas home town, almost all the inhabitants are affected in one way or another. Expensive but shoddy essay in sex and violence, with Brando as a masochistic sheriff lording it over Peyton-Place-in-all-but-name. Literate moments do not atone for the general pretentiousness, and we have all been here once too often.

w Lillian Hellman, novel Horton Foote d Arthur Penn ph Joseph La Shelle pd Richard Day m John Barry

Marlon Brando, Jane Fonda, Robert Redford, Angie Dickinson, Janice Rule, James Fox, Robert Duvall, E. G. Marshall, Miriam Hopkins, Henry Hull

'The worst thing that has happened to movies since Lassie played a war veteran with amnesia.'—Rex Reed

'Considering all the talent connected with it, it is hard to imagine how The Chase went so haywire.'—Philip T. Hartung

Chase a Crooked Shadow**

GB 1957 87m bw
ABP / Associated Dragon Films (Douglas Fairbanks Jnr)

An heiress finds her home invaded by a stranger posing as her dead brother.
Tricksy, lightly controlled suspense melodrama with a perfectly fair surprise ending. Handling equivocal but competent.

w David D. Osborn, Charles Sinclair d Michael Anderson ph Erwin Hillier m Matyas Seiber

Richard Todd, Anne Baxter, Faith Brook, Herbert Lom, Alexander Knox, Alan Tilvern

† The plot was borrowed from an episode in The Whistler TV series, and later reversed for a 1975 TV film, One of my Wives is Missing.

Chasing Rainbows

US 1929 100m bw (colour sequence)

True love finds a way while a big musical is rehearsing. Naïve attempt to repeat the success of Broadway Melody. Bessie Love, Charles King, Marie Dressler, Polly Moran, Jack Benny. Written by Bess Meredyth; directed by Charles Riesner; for MGM.

Songs include 'Happy Days Are Here Again'; 'Everybody Tap'; 'Lucky Me, Loveable You'; 'Poor but Honest'; 'Dynamic Personality'; 'Love Ain't Nothing but the Blues'; 'Gotta Feeling for You'

'Numerous exploitable names and a snappy set of tunes.'—Variety

Chasing Yesterday

US 1935 78m bw

An elderly archaeologist seeks to renew his lost youth through the daughter of the woman he once loved but lost. Slow and old-fashioned melodrama. O. P. Heggie, Anne Shirley, Elizabeth Patterson, Helen Westley, John Qualen, Etienne Girardot. Written by Francis E. Faragoh from The Crime of Sylvestre Bonnard by Anatole France; directed by George Nicholls Jnr; for RKO. 'Prospects not bright.'—Variety

The Chastity Belt

Italy 1967 110m Eastmancolor
Warner / Julia (Francesco Mazzei)
aka: On My Way to the Crusades I Met a Girl Who . . .

A 12th-century knight is called to the Crusades just as he is consummating his marriage, and when he locks his wife in a chastity belt she follows him.
Abysmal international romp which looks nice but is killed stone dead by writing, dubbing and direction.

w Luigi Magni, Larry Gelbart d Pasquale Festa Campanile ph Carlo di Palma m Riz Ortolani

Tony Curtis, Virna Lisi, Hugh Griffith, John Richardson, Nino Castelnuovo

Chato's Land

GB 1971 100m Technicolor
UA / Scimitar (Michael Winner)

An Apache half-breed kills a man in self-defence, subsequently eluding and destroying the sheriff's posse.
Exhaustingly violent western in which the audience is spared no gory detail; efficiently put together for those who like this kind of fracas.

w Gerald Wilson d Michael Winner ph Robert Paynter m Jerry Fielding

Charles Bronson, Jack Palance, Richard Basehart, James Whitmore, Simon Oakland, Richard Jordan, Ralph Waite, Victor French, Lee Patterson

Chatterbox

US 1935 68m bw

A country maiden aspires to the stage. Mildly likeable comedy for family audiences. Anne Shirley, Phillips Holmes, Edward Ellis, Erik Rhodes, Margaret Hamilton, Granville Bates. Written by Sam Mintz from a play by David Carb; directed by George Nicholls Jnr; for RKO. 'Discounting the nice job all around, the picture isn't there.'—Variety

Chatterbox

US 1943 77m bw
Republic (Albert J. Cohen)

A radio cowboy gets a film contract but can't stand horses.
Flat star comedy which borrows some well-worn situations but handles them badly.

w George Carleton Brown, Frank Gill Jnr d Joseph Santley ph Ernest Miller md Walter Scharf

Joe E. Brown, Judy Canova, Rosemary Lane, John Hubbard, Chester Clute

'With a dream of justice, he created a nightmare of violence!'

Che!

US 1969 94m De Luxe Panavision
TCF (Sy Bartlett)

Fidel Castro is helped in his subversion of Batista's Cuban regime by an Argentinian doctor named Che Guevara.
Fictionalized biography, and a dull one, of a man who became a myth.

w Michael Wilson, Sy Bartlett d Richard Fleischer ph Charles Wheeler m Lalo Schifrin

Omar Sharif, Jack Palance (as Castro), Cesare Danova, Robert Loggia, Woody Strode, Barbara Luna

'It goes at the pace of a drugged ox, and hasn't an ounce of political or historical sense in its nut.'—New Yorker

The Cheap Detective

US 1978 92m Metrocolor Panavision
Columbia / Ray Stark

Forties private eye Lou Peckinpaugh is involved in a complex case with echoes of Casablanca, The Big Sleep, The Maltese Falcon and Farewell My Lovely.
Lame spoof which might have seemed funnier on a small screen in black and white; as it is, the strain is evident and desperate.

w Neil Simon d Robert Moore ph John A. Alonzo m Patrick Williams

Peter Falk (Bogart), John Houseman (Greenstreet), Nicol Williamson (Veidt), *Louise Fletcher* (Bergman), Fernando Lamas (Henreid), Madeleine Kahn (Astor), Dom de Luise (Lorre), Paul Williams (Cook), Marsha Mason (Gladys George), Ann-Margret (Claire Trevor), Eileen Brennan (Bacall), Stockard Channing (Lee Patrick), Sid Caesar (Miles Mander), Scatman Crothers (Dooley Wilson); and James Coco, Phil Silvers, Abe Vigoda, Vic Tayback

'Frankly they did this sort of thing just as well, and a lot more quickly, on *The Carol Burnett Show*.'—*Richard Shickel, Time*

'There is about enough talent around for a twenty-minute sketch at the Edinburgh fringe.'—*Derek Malcolm, Guardian*

† The film was a follow-up to the not much more effective but at least more controlled *Murder by Death*.

Cheaper by the Dozen••
US 1950 86m Technicolor
TCF (Lamar Trotti)

Efficiency expert Frank Gilbreth and his wife Lillian have twelve children, a fact which requires mathematical conduct of all their lives.

Amusing family comedy set in the twenties, unconvincing in detail though based on a book by two of the children. A great commercial success and a Hollywood myth-maker. Sequel: *Belles on their Toes* (qv).

w Lamar Trotti, *book* Frank B. Gilbreth Jnr, Ernestine Gilbreth Carey d *Walter Lang* ph Leon Shamroy m Cyril Mockridge md Lionel Newman ad Lyle Wheeler, Leland Fuller

Clifton Webb, Myrna Loy, Jeanne Crain, Edgar Buchanan, Barbara Bates, Betty Lynn, Mildred Natwick, Sara Allgood

The Cheat•
US 1915 95m (16 fps) bw silent
Famous Players Lasky / Paramount

A society lady borrows from a rich Japanese, and he brands her when she refuses to become his mistress.

Hoary melodrama which caused a sensation in its day.

w Hector Turnbull d Cecil B. de Mille ph Alvin Wyckoff

Fanny Ward, Jack Dean, Sessue Hayakawa, James Neill

† Remade in 1923 by George Fitzmaurice, in 1931 by George Abbott, and in 1937 (in France, as *Forfaiture*) by Marcel L'Herbier.

The Cheaters•
US 1945 86m bw
Republic

A selfish and ostentatious family is reformed by the ministrations of a down-and-out actor. Fairly engaging variation on *The Passing of the Third Floor Back*, with sweetness and light brought into people's lives by a fireside recital of *A Christmas Carol*.

w Francis Hyland d Joseph Kane ph Reggie Lanning m Walter Scharf

Joseph Schildkraut, Billie Burke, Eugene Pallette, Ona Munson, Raymond Walburn

Cheating Cheaters
US 1934 67m bw

Two groups of jewel thieves clash when posing as society swells. Tolerable programmer from an old stage hit. Fay Wray, Cesar Romero, Minna Gombell, Hugh O'Connell, Henry Armetta, Francis L. Sullivan, Ann Shoemaker. Written by Gladys Unger and Allen Rivkin, from the play by Max Marcin; directed by Richard Thorpe; for Universal. 'Rather creaky entertainment, but it will about get by.'—*Variety*

Check and Double Check
US 1930 71m bw
RKO

Comic adventures of a couple of black handymen.

Feeble comedy notable only for the film appearance of radio's immensely popular Amos 'n Andy, played by white actors in blackface.

w Bert Kalmar, Harry Ruby, J. Walter Ruben d Melville Brown ph William Marshall m Max Steiner

Freeman F. Gosden, Charles V. Correll, Sue Carol, Charles Morton, Irene Rich, Ralf Harolde, Duke Ellington and his Orchestra

'The best picture for children ever put on the screen . . . as a freak talking picture it's in the money immediately.'—*Variety*

Checkers
US 1937 79m bw

The niece of a ne'er-do-well horse owner brings him success. One of the most successful vehicles of Shirley Temple's arch rival. Jane Withers, Stuart Erwin, Una Merkel, Marvin Stephens, Andrew Tombes, Minor Watson. Written by Lynn Root, Frank Fenton and Karen de Wolf, from the play by Rida Johnson Young; directed by H. Bruce Humberstone; for TCF. 'Will delight the moppet's following . . . due for heavy dual booking.'—*Variety*

Checkpoint•
GB 1956 84m Eastmancolor
Rank (Betty Box)

A tycoon sends an industrial spy to Italy in search of new motor racing car designs. Acceptable hokum, cleanly assembled, with motor race highlights.

w Robin Estridge d Ralph Thomas ph Ernest Steward m Bruce Montgomery

Anthony Steel, Stanley Baker, James Robertson Justice, Odile Versois, Maurice Denham, Michael Medwin, Lee Patterson

Cheech and Chong's Next Movie
US 1980 95m Technicolor

Two dopers have various rude adventures. Totally repulsive comedy which gives a bad name to self-indulgence. Richard Marin, Thomas Chong, Evelyn Guerrero, Betty Kennedy, Sy Kramer. Written by Cheech and Chong; directed by Chong; for Howard Brown / Universal. (GB title: *High Encounters of the Ultimate Kind*.)

Cheer Boys Cheer
GB 1939 84m bw

Brewery owners hate each other but their children fall in love. A highly predictable plot provides some incidental pleasures in this modest precursor of the Ealing comedies. Nova Pilbeam, Edmund Gwenn, Jimmy O'Dea, Moore Marriott, Graham Moffatt, C. V. France, Alexander Knox. Written by Roger MacDougall and Allan MacKinnon; directed by Walter Forde; for ATP.

Cheers for Miss Bishop•
US 1941 94m bw
Paramount (Richard A. Rowland)

The life of a schoolmistress in a small midwestern town.

Acceptable sentimental hokum, quite pleasantly done.

w Adelaide Heinbron, *novel* Bess Streeter Aldrich d Tay Garnett ph Hal Mohr m Edward Ward

Martha Scott, William Gargan, Edmund Gwenn, Sterling Holloway, Sidney Blackmer, Mary Anderson, Dorothy Petersen

AAN: Edward Ward

'America's favourite two-gun star battles for love and glory!'
Cherokee Strip
US 1940 86m bw

A marshal brings law and order to a frontier town. Competent western programmer. Richard Dix, Florence Rice, William Henry, Victor Jory, Andy Clyde. Written by Herman Houston and Bernard McConville; directed by Lesley Selander; for Harry Sherman / Paramount.

Chess Fever•
USSR 1925 20m (24 fps) bw silent

A chess fanatic is so absorbed that he misses his wedding. Spirited visual comedy which still raises the intended laughs. Vladimir Fogel, Anna Zemtsova. Written and co-directed by Nikolai Shpikovsky; co-directed by Vsevolod Pudovkin; for Mezhrabpom-Russ.

The Chess Players•
India 1977 129m Eastmancolor

In 1856 Lucknow, two noblemen are more interested in playing chess than in their state's imminent annexation by the British. Patchy but frequently charming historical piece with more specifically Indian elements than are usual from its director. Sanjeev Kumar, Saeed Jaffrey, Richard Attenborough, Amjad Khan. Written and directed by Satyajit Ray; for Devki Chitra.

Cheyenne

US 1947   100m   bw

A gambler turns lawman, catches a robber and marries his wife. Rather sluggish western which later inspired a long-running TV series.
Dennis Morgan, Bruce Bennett, Jane Wyman, Arthur Kennedy, Janis Paige, Alan Hale. Written by Alan Le May and Thames Williamson; directed by Raoul Walsh; for Warner. (Later retitled: *The Wyoming Kid.*)

Cheyenne Autumn*

US 1964   170m   Technicolor
Panavision 70
Warner / Ford-Smith (Bernard Smith)

In the 1860s, Cheyenne Indians are moved to a new reservation 1500 miles away; wanting aid, they begin a trek back home, and various battles follow.
Dispirited, shapeless John Ford western with little of the master's touch; good to look at, however, with effective cameos, notably an irrelevant and out-of-key comic one featuring James Stewart as Wyatt Earp.

w James R. Webb, *novel* Mari Sandoz   *d* John Ford   *ph* William H. Clothier   *m* Alex North

Richard Widmark, Carroll Baker, Karl Malden, *Dolores del Rio*, Sal Mineo, Edward G. Robinson, *James Stewart*, Ricardo Montalban, Gilbert Roland, Arthur Kennedy, Patrick Wayne, Elizabeth Allen, Victor Jory, John Carradine, Mike Mazurki, John Qualen, George O'Brien

  'Although one would like to praise the film for its high-minded aims, it is hard to forget how ponderous and disjointed it is.'—*Moira Walsh*
  'The acting is bad, the dialogue trite and predictable, the pace funereal, the structure fragmented and the climaxes puny.'—*Stanley Kauffmann*

AAN: William H. Clothier

The Cheyenne Social Club*

US 1970   102m   Technicolor
Panavision
National General (James Lee Barrett, Gene Kelly)

Two itinerant cowboys inherit a high-class brothel.
Disappointing star comedy western with pleasing moments and a lively climactic shoot-out. Perhaps the girls are just a shade too winsome.

w James Lee Barrett   *d* Gene Kelly
ph William H. Clothier   *m* Walter Scharf

James Stewart, Henry Fonda, Shirley Jones, Sue Anne Langdon, Robert Middleton, Arch Johnson
  'Co-starring Shirley Jones and Rigor Mortis, who enters early and stays through the very last scene.'—*Rex Reed*

Chicago Calling*

US 1951   75m   bw
UA / Arrowhead / Joseph Justman (Peter Berneis)

A drunk cannot pay his phone bill and is waiting for a vital call about his daughter's involvement in a car crash.

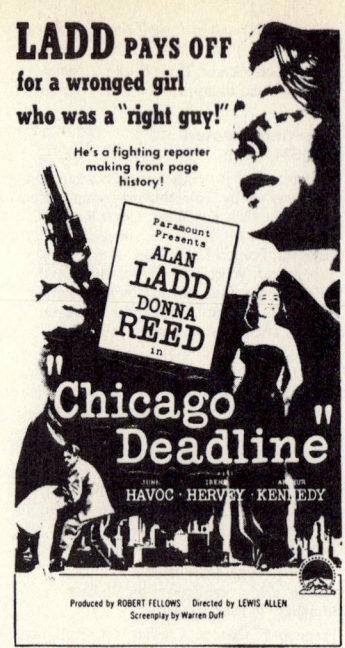

LADD PAYS OFF
for a wronged girl
who was a "right guy!"

He's a fighting reporter
making front page
history!

Paramount
Presents
ALAN
LADD
DONNA
REED
in

Chicago
Deadline

JUNE   IRENE   ARTHUR
HAVOC · HERVEY · KENNEDY

Produced by ROBERT FELLOWS   Directed by LEWIS ALLEN
Screenplay by Warren Duff

CHICAGO DEADLINE.   Hollywood never wastes a good story. When MCA bought up the Paramount library, they remade this one as the TV pilot of *The Name of the Game.*

Moderate, location-shot minor melodrama with a few good ideas.

w John Reinhardt, Peter Berneis   *d* John Reinhardt   *ph* Robert de Grasse

Dan Duryea, Mary Anderson, Gordon Gebert, Ross Elliot

Chicago Confidential

US 1957   74m   bw

A gambling syndicate takes over a labour union and frames its incorruptible president for murder. Very routine gangster potboiler.
Brian Keith, Beverly Garland, Dick Foran, Elisha Cook Jnr. Written by Raymond T. Marcus; directed by Sidney Salkow; for Peerless / UA.

Chicago Deadline

US 1949   87m   bw
Paramount (Robert Fellows)

A reporter researches the life of a lonely girl who died of tuberculosis.
Flat star vehicle consisting mainly of overplayed cameos.

w Warren Duff, Tiffany Thayer   *d* Lewis Allen   *ph* John F. Seitz   *m* Victor Young

Alan Ladd, Donna Reed, *June Havoc*, Berry Kroeger, Arthur Kennedy, Gavin Muir, Shepperd Strudwick
† Remade as the TV pilot of *The Name of the Game.*

Chicago Syndicate

US 1955   86m   bw

A young accountant breaks up an outwardly respectable crime syndicate. Formula racket-busting melodrama. Dennis O'Keefe, Abbe Lane, Paul Stewart, Xavier Cugat, Alison Hayes. Written by Joseph Hoffman; directed by Fred F. Sears; for Clover / Columbia.

The Chicken Chronicles

US 1977   94m   CFI Color

Problems of a teenager in an American small town. Extremely boring comedy drama, obsessed with sex and lacking background detail. Phil Silvers, Ed Lauter, Steven Guttenberg, Meridith Baer, Lisa Reeves. Written by Paul Diamond; directed by Francis Simon; for Chicken Enterprises / Avco Embassy.

Chicken Every Sunday*

US 1949   94m   bw
TCF

The Hefferans have run a boarding house for twenty years, but dad's wild schemes run away with any possible profit.
Archetypal, folksy, American small-town chronicle, reasonably well made, for an audience that now watches *The Waltons.*

w George Seaton, Valentine Davies   *d* George Seaton   *ph* Harry Jackson   *m* Alfred Newman

Dan Dailey, Celeste Holm, Colleen Townsend, Alan Young, Natalie Wood

The Chicken Wagon Family

US 1939   81m   bw

Louisiana backwooders make a trip to New York. Feeble country cousin comedy. Jane Withers, Leo Carrillo, Marjorie Weaver, Spring Byington, Kane Richmond, Hobart Cavanaugh. Written by Viola Brothers Shore; directed by Herbert I. Leeds; for TCF. 'Nabes and second runs will write best ledger marks.'—*Variety*

Chickens Come Home*

US 1931   30m   bw

Stan helps his boss Ollie to evade the attentions of an old flame. Rather heavy and untypical, but mainly very enjoyable star comedy, a remake of *Love 'Em and Weep* in which all three leading players had appeared four years earlier in different roles. Laurel and Hardy, James Finlayson, Mae Busch, Thelma Todd. Written by H. M. Walker, from a story by Hal Roach; directed by James W. Horne; for Hal Roach.

The Chief

US 1933   80m   bw

A fireman's son becomes a Bowery candidate for alderman. Feeble comedy with the star ill at ease. Ed Wynn, Dorothy Mackaill, Charles 'Chic' Sale, William Boyd, George Givot, C. Henry Gordon. Written by Arthur Caesar and R. E. Hopkins; directed by Charles F. Reisner; for MGM. (GB title: *My Old Man's a Fireman*.) 'With the radio draw angle discarded it is weak entertainment.'—*Variety*

Chief Crazy Horse
US 1954 86m Technicolor
Cinemascope
U-I (William Alland)
GB title: *Valley of Fury*

The tribal problems of the Indian chief who defeated Custer at Little Big Horn. Competent pro-Indian western.

w Franklin Coen, Gerald Drayson Adams *d* George Sherman *ph* Harold Lipstein *m* Frank Skinner

Victor Mature, Suzan Ball, John Lund, Ray Danton, Keith Larsen, Paul Guilfoyle, David Janssen

Un Chien Andalou*
France 1928 17m bw silent
Luis Bunuel

Famous surrealist short which includes dead donkeys on pianos and starts with a woman's eyeball being cut by a razor blade.
It had meaning for its makers, but very few other people saw anything in it but sensationalism.

w Luis Bunuel, Salvador Dali *d, ed* Luis Bunuel *ph* Albert Dubergen

Simone Mareuil, Pierre Batcheff, Jaime Miravilles, Salvador Dali, Luis Bunuel

La Chienne*
France 1931 85m bw
Braunberger-Richebé

A bank clerk falls for a prostitute and later kills her; her pimp is executed for the crime and the bank clerk becomes a tramp.
Heavy-going, old-fashioned melodrama with some interesting detail.

wd Jean Renoir, *novel* Georges de la Fouchardière *ph* Theodor Sparkuhl, Roger Hubert

Michel Simon, Janie Marèze, Georges Flament, Jean Gehret
'If the English translation of the title is unfit to print, the film's dialogue cannot be translated into English. Okay for sophisticated audiences that look for a taste of spice in a ritzy spot.'—*Variety*
† Remade as *Scarlet Street* (qv).

Child in the House
GB 1956 88m bw
Eros / Golden Era (Ben Fisz)

When her mother is ill and her father in hiding from the police, a 12-year-old girl goes to stay with her fussy uncle and aunt.
Modest family drama of the novelette type in which adult problems are put right by the wisdom of a child.

wd C. Raker Endfield, *novel* Janet McNeill *ph* Otto Heller *m* Mario Nascimbene *ad* Ken Adam

Eric Portman, Phyllis Calvert, Stanley Baker, Mandy Miller, Dora Bryan, Joan Hickson, Victor Maddern, Percy Herbert

A Child is Born
US 1939 79m bw
Warner (Sam Bischoff)

A slice of life in the maternity ward. Adequately dramatic sequence of cameos, with mothers-to-be including a gangster's moll: a remake of *Life Begins*.

w Robert Rossen, *play* Mary M. Axelson *d* Lloyd Bacon *ph* Charles Rosher

Geraldine Fitzgerald, Jeffrey Lynn, Gladys George, Gale Page, Spring Byington, Henry O'Neill, John Litel, Gloria Holden, Eve Arden, Nanette Fabares, Hobart Cavanaugh, Johnny Downs, Johnnie Davis

A Child is Waiting**
US 1963 104m bw
UA / Stanley Kramer

A mixed-up spinster joins the staff of a school for mentally handicapped children.
Worthy semi-documentary marred by having a normal boy play the central character (albeit very well). A little over-dramatized but cogent and unsentimental.

w Abby Mann *d* John Cassavetes *ph* Joseph La Shelle *m* Ernest Gold

Burt Lancaster, *Judy Garland, Bruce Ritchey*, Steven Hill, Gena Rowlands, *Paul Stewart*, Lawrence Tierney

Child of Manhattan
US 1933 70m bw

A night-club hostess has an affair with a millionaire, but her baby dies. Hokey melodrama on familiar lines (at the time).
John Boles, Nancy Carroll, Warburton Gamble, Clara Blandick, Jane Darwell, Betty Grable. Written by Gertrude Purcell from a play by Preston Sturges; directed by Edward Buzzell; for Columbia. 'Programme fodder, with more simplicity than purity.'—*Variety*

The Childhood of Maxim Gorky***
USSR 1938–40 bw
Soyuzdetfilm

Orphan Gorky is raised by his grandparents, and becomes a ship's cook and a painter before going on to university.
This simple and direct story is told in three beautifully detailed if rather overlong films:
'The Childhood of Maxim Gorky': 101m
'Out in the World': 98m
'My Universities': 104m

w Mark Donskoi, I. Grudzev *d* Mark Donskoi *ph* Pyotr Yermolov *m* Lev Schwartz *ad* I. Stepanov

Alexei Lyarsky, Y. Valbert, M. Troyanovski, Valeria Massalitinova

Children of Hiroshima**
Japan 1952 97m bw
Kendai Eiga Lyokai / Gekidan Mingei

A young teacher returns to Hiroshima seven years after the bomb.
Restrained yet harrowing social documentary

in fiction form, with the most effective use of flashbacks to show the horror of the bomb and its aftermath.

wd Kaneto Shindo, *novel* Arata Osada *ph* Takeo Itoh *m* Akira Ifukube

Nobuko Otowa, Chikako Hoshawa, Niwa Saito

The Children of Sanchez
US / Mexico 1978 126m colour
Hall Bartlett

A macho Mexican and one of his daughters have ideas above the semi-slum in which they live.
The star is still looking for another *Zorba the Greek*, but this isn't it. Glum, glum, glum.

w Cesare Zavattini, Hall Bartlett, *novel* Oscar Lewis *d* Hall Bartlett *ph* Gabriel Figueroa *m* Chuck Mangione

Anthony Quinn, Dolores del Rio, Lupita Ferrer, Katy Jurado, Stathis Giallelis

Children of the Corn
US 1984 92m CFI colour
New World / Angeles / Cinema Group (Donald P. Borchers, Terence Kirby)

A doctor and his girl friend run down a child, discover that his throat has been cut, and find themselves in a community of murderous adolescents.
Nightmarish modern fantasy with style but very little to like.

w George Goldsmith, *story* Stephen King *d* Fritz Kiersch *ph* Raoul Lomas *m* Jonathan Elias

Peter Horton, Linda Hamilton, R. G. Armstrong, John Franklin
'The aim seems to be to reassure rather than to disturb.'—*Robert Murphy, MFB*

'So young, so innocent, so deadly—they came to conquer the world!'
Children of the Damned*
GB 1964 90m bw
MGM (Ben Arbeid)

Six super-intelligent children of various nations are brought to London by UNESCO, and turn out to be invaders from another planet.
Moderate sequel to *Village of the Damned*, well made but with no new twists.

w John Briley *d* Anton M. Leader *ph* David Boulton *m* Ron Goodwin

Ian Hendry, Alan Badel, Barbara Ferris, Alfred Burke, Sheila Allen, Ralph Michael, Martin Miller, Harold Goldblatt

The Children's Hour*
US 1961 108m bw
UA / Mirisch (William Wyler)
GB title: *The Loudest Whisper*

A spoilt schoolgirl spreads a rumour that her schoolmistresses are lesbians.
Frank sixties version of a play originally filmed in a much bowdlerized version as *These Three*. Unfortunately frankness in this case leads to dullness, as nothing is done with the theme once it is stated, and the treatment is heavy-handed.

w Lillian Hellman, from her play d William Wyler ph Franz Planer m Alex North

Audrey Hepburn, Shirley Maclaine, James Garner, Miriam Hopkins, Fay Bainter, Karen Balkin

'All very exquisite, and dead as mutton.'—Tom Milne

AAN: Franz Planer; Fay Bainter

Child's Play*
US 1972 100m Movielab
Paramount (David Merrick)

In a Catholic boarding school for boys, an unpopular master is hounded and discredited by another whose motives may be diabolic. Enjoyable overblown melodrama with hints of many nasty goings on, rather spoiled by too much talk and too little local colour.

w Leon Prochnik, play Robert Marasco d Sidney Lumet ph Gerald Hirschfeld m Michael Small

James Mason, *Robert Preston*, Beau Bridges, Ronald Weyand

The Chiltern Hundreds*
GB 1949 84m bw
Rank / Two Cities (George H. Brown)
US title: The Amazing Mr Beecham

An aged earl is bewildered when his son fails to be elected to parliament as a socialist but his butler gets in as a tory.
Satisfactory filming of an amusing stage comedy, with the aged A. E. Matthews repeating his delightful if irrelevant act as the dotty earl.

w William Douglas Home, Patrick Kirwan, play William Douglas Home d John Paddy Carstairs ph Jack Hildyard m Benjamin Frankel

A. E. Matthews, Cecil Parker, David Tomlinson, Marjorie Fielding, Joyce Carey

Chimes at Midnight*
Spain / Switz 1966 119m bw
Internacional Films Espanola / Alpine (Alessandro Tasca)
aka: Falstaff

Prince Hal becomes King Henry V and rejects his old friend Falstaff.
Clumsy adaptation of Shakespeare with brilliant flashes and the usual Welles vices of hasty production, poor synchronization and recording, etc. One wonders why, if he wanted to make a telescoped version of the plays, he did not spare the time and patience to make it better.

w Orson Welles d Orson Welles ph Edmond Richard m Angelo Francesco Lavagnino

Orson Welles, Keith Baxter, John Gielgud (Henry IV), Margaret Rutherford (Mistress Quickly), Jeanne Moreau (Doll Tearsheet), Norman Rodway, Alan Webb, Marina Vlady, Tony Beckley, Fernando Rey

The Chimp*
US 1932 30m bw

Stan and Ollie try to get lodgings without revealing that their friend is a chimp, their share of a bankrupt circus. The circus scenes are better than the rather tired farce which follows, especially as it is so similar to *Laughing Gravy*. Laurel and Hardy, James Finlayson, Billy Gilbert, Tiny Sandford. Written by H. M. Walker; directed by James Parrott; for Hal Roach.

'Alan Ladd and twenty girls—trapped by the rapacious Japs!'

China
US 1943 79m bw
Paramount (Richard Blumenthal)

An oil salesman joins a Chinese guerrilla force and sacrifices himself.
Solemnly nilarious propaganda piece tailored to its star, showing the immense superiority of one lone American to the entire Japanese army.

w Frank Butler, novel The Fourth Brother by Reginald Forbes d John Farrow ph Leo Tover m Victor Young

Alan Ladd, Loretta Young, William Bendix, Philip Ahn, Iris Wong, Sen Yung, Richard Loo, Tala Birell

China Clipper*
US 1936 89m bw
Warner (Sam Bischoff)

An aviator neglects his wife while building up a trans-Pacific civil aviation link.
Solid entertainment feature of its day, with adequate production and performance.

w Frank 'Spig' Wead d Ray Enright ph Arthur Edeson m Bernhard Kaun, W. Franke Harling

Pat O'Brien, Beverly Roberts, Ross Alexander, Humphrey Bogart, Marie Wilson, Henry B. Walthall, Joseph Crehan, Addison Richards

China Doll
US 1958 99m bw
Romina / Batjac (Frank Borzage)

In 1943 an American air force officer accidentally buys the services of a young Chinese housekeeper. He marries her but they are both killed in action; years later their daughter is welcomed to America by members of his old air crew.
Incurably sentimental and icky romantic drama in the style of the director's silent films; something of a curiosity for historians.

w Kitty Buhler d Frank Borzage ph William H. Clothier m Henry Vars

Victor Mature, Li Li Hua, Bob Mathias, Ward Bond, Stuart Whitman

'An American dynamiter love-locked in war-locked China!'

China Gate
US 1957 90m bw Cinemascope
TCF (Samuel Fuller)

A Eurasian girl guides her American husband to a communist arms dump.
Anti-Red thick ear, slick but undistinguished.

wd Samuel Fuller ph Joseph Biroc m Victor Young, Max Steiner

Gene Barry, Angie Dickinson, Nat King Cole, Paul Dubov, Lee Van Cleef, George Givot

China Girl
US 1943 95m bw
TCF (Ben Hecht)

A newsreel cameraman in China falls in love with a Eurasian schoolteacher.
Routine adventure romance with splodges of love and self-sacrifice.

w Ben Hecht d Henry Hathaway ph Lee Garmes m Hugo Friedhofer

Gene Tierney, George Montgomery, *Lynn Bari*, Victor McLaglen, Alan Baxter, Sig Rumann, Myron McCormick, Philip Ahn

China Seas**
US 1935 89m bw
MGM (Albert Lewin)

Luxury cruise passengers find themselves involved with piracy.
Omnibus shipboard melodrama, tersely scripted and featuring a splendid cast all somewhere near their best; slightly dated but very entertaining.

w Jules Furthman, James Kevin McGuinness, novel Crosbie Garstin d Tay Garnett ph Ray June m Herbert Stothart

Clark Gable, Jean Harlow, Wallace Beery, Rosalind Russell, Lewis Stone, C. Aubrey Smith, Dudley Digges, Robert Benchley

'It will do double-barrelled duty, drawing business and providing ace entertainment.'—Variety

'The hell with art this time. I'm going to produce a picture that will make money.'—Irving Thalberg

China Sky
US 1945 78m bw
RKO (Maurice Geraghty)

Two American doctors live with Chinese guerrillas; the jealousy of the wife of one of them causes problems.
Routine adventure romance with generally unconvincing production and performance.

w Brenda Weisberg, Joseph Hoffman, novel Pearl Buck d Ray Enright ph Nicholas Musuraca m Roy Webb

Randolph Scott, Ellen Drew, Ruth Warrick, Anthony Quinn, Carol Thurston, Richard Loo, Philip Ahn

The China Syndrome**
US 1979 122m Metrocolor
Columbia / IPC (Bruce Gilbert)

The controller of a nuclear power plant discovers an operational flaw which could lead to disaster, but the unscrupulous authorities want to cover it up.
Topical thriller-with-a-moral, absorbingly done in the old style but perhaps in the end a shade too hysterical and self-congratulatory.

w Mike Gray, T. S. Cook, James Bridges d James Bridges ph James Crabe m various pd George Jenkins

Jane Fonda, *Jack Lemmon*, Michael Douglas, Scott Brady, Peter Donat, James Hampton

'The performances are so good, and the screen so bombarded with both action and informative images . . . that it's only with considerable hindsight that one recovers sufficient breath to reproach the script with the occasional glib symmetry.'—*Jan Dawson, MFB*

China Venture
US 1953   83m   bw

In 1945, American marines are sent into the Chinese jungle to recover a Japanese admiral held captive there. Topical thick-ear, played and presented without conviction. Edmond O'Brien, Barry Sullivan, Jocelyn Brando, Richard Loo. Written by George Worthing Yates and Richard Collins; directed by Don Siegel; for Anson Bond / Columbia.

Chinatown•••
US 1974   131m   Technicolor
    Panavision
Paramount / Long Road (Robert Evans)

In 1937, a Los Angeles private eye takes on a simple case and burrows into it until it leads to murder and a public scandal.
Pretentious melodrama which is basically no more serious than the Raymond Chandler mysteries from which it derives; the tragic ending is merely an irritation, and the title only allusive. Superficially, however, it is eminently watchable, with effective individual scenes and performances and photography which is lovingly composed though tending to suggest period by use of an orange filter.

w Robert Towne d Roman Polanski ph John A. Alonso m Jerry Goldsmith pd Richard Sylbert

Jack Nicholson, Faye Dunaway, John Huston, Perry Lopez, John Hillerman, Roman Polanski, Darrell Zwerling, Diane Ladd

AA: Robert Towne
AAN: best picture; Roman Polanski; John A. Alonso; Jerry Goldsmith; Jack Nicholson; Faye Dunaway

The Chinese Bungalow
GB 1939   72m   bw
George King
US title: *Chinese Den*

A Chinese merchant plots to kill the lover of his English wife.
Stolid version of an old melodrama which can hardly fail; previously filmed in 1926 with Matheson Lang and Genevieve Townsend (directed by Sinclair Hill) and in 1930 with Matheson Lang and Anna Neagle (directed by J. B. Williams).

w A. R. Rawlinson, George Wellesley, play Matheson Lang, Marian Osmond *d George King ph* Hone Glendinning

Paul Lukas, Jane Baxter, Robert Douglas, Kay Walsh, Jerry Verno

Chinese Roulette•
West Germany / France 1976   86m
    Eastmancolor
Albatros / Losange (Rainer Werner Fassbinder)

Various related people, mainly adulterous, meet in a country château and play a truth game which ends in violence.
Interestingly enigmatic character melodrama reminiscent of Bergman at his prime, but concerning people who barely seem to matter.

wd Rainer Werner Fassbinder ph Michael Ballhaus *m* Peer Raben

Margit Carstensen, Andrea Schober, Ulli Lommel, Anna Karina, Macha Meril

'Locked into their private hell . . . this vicious octet form their own coherent and compelling universe.'—*Jan Dawson, MFB*

Chino
US / Italy 1973   98m   colour

A runaway boy helps a half-breed run a ranch in New Mexico. Undistinguished western. Charles Bronson, Jill Ireland, Vincent Van Petten. Written by Clair Huffaker, from a novel by Lee Hoffman; directed by John Sturges; for Dino de Laurentiis.

Chisum•
US 1970   110m   Technicolor
    Panavision
Warner / Batjac (Michael Wayne, Andrew J. Fenady)

A corrupt businessman plots against the head of a vast cattle empire, who is saved by the intervention of numerous friends including Pat Garrett and Billy the Kid.
Desultory, overlong, friendly western in the Ford manner. Easy to watch and easier to forget.

w Andrew J. Fenady d Andrew V. McLaglen ph William H. Clothier m Dominic Frontière

John Wayne, Forrest Tucker, Christopher George, Ben Johnson, Glenn Corbett, Bruce Cabot, Andrew Prine, Patric Knowles, Richard Jaeckel, Linda Day George, John Agar, Ray Teal, Glenn Langan, Alan Baxter, Abraham Sofaer, Pete Duel

'A curious mixture of styles and myths.'— *John Gillett*

● *Video: Warner*

Chitty Chitty Bang Bang
GB 1968   145m   Technicolor   Super
    Panavision 70
UA / Warfield / DFI (Albert R. Broccoli)

An unsuccessful inventor rescues a derelict car and gives it magical properties, then helps the children who own it to overthrow the government of a country which hates children.
A bumpy ride. Sentiment, slapstick, whimsy and mild scares do not combine but are given equal shares of the limelight, while poor trickwork prevents the audience from being transported.

w Roald Dahl, Ken Hughes d Ken Hughes ph Christopher Challis m Irwin Kostal songs the Sherman Brothers *ad* Ken Adam *decor* Rowland Emmett

Dick Van Dyke, Sally Ann Howes (as Truly Scrumptious), Lionel Jeffries, Robert Helpmann, Gert Frobe, Benny Hill, James Robertson Justice

AAN: title song
● *Video: Intervision*

The Chocolate Soldier•
US 1941   102m   bw
MGM (Victor Saville)

Married opera singers fall out backstage. Talky musical remake of *The Guardsman*: nearly comes off but not quite.

w Keith Winter, Leonard Lee d Roy del Ruth ph Karl Freund songs Oscar Straus *m* Herbert Stothart, Bronislau Kaper

Nelson Eddy, Rise Stevens, Nigel Bruce, Florence Bates, Nydia Westman

AAN: Karl Freund; Herbert Stothart, Bronislau Kaper

The Choirboys
US 1978   119m   Technicolor
Lorimar / Airone (Lee Rich, Merv Adelson)

Members of a police department are if anything more delinquent, vicious and mentally retarded than their quarries.
A vulgar and repellent anti-establishment display, apparently intended as black comedy. Just the thing to put an end to the art of the movie once and for all.

w Christopher Knopf, novel Joseph Wambaugh *d Robert Aldrich ph* Joseph Biroc *m* Frank de Vol

Charles Durning, Lou Gossett Jnr, Perry King, Stephen Macht, Tim McIntyre, Clyde Kusatu, Randy Quaid, Don Stroud, Robert Webber, Blair Brown

The Chosen
US 1981   108m   Movielab
The Chosen Film Company (Edie and Ely Landau)

In New York in the early forties, a family feud between Zionist and Hassidic Jews interferes with a friendship between two boys.
A sentimental minority piece which does what it has to do quite effectively.

w Edwin Gordon, novel Chaim Potok *d Jeremy Paul Kagan ph* Arthur Ornitz *m* Elmer Bernstein *pd* Stuart Wurtzel

Maximilian Schell, Rod Steiger, Robby Benson, Barry Miller, Hildy Brooks, Kaethe Fine

● *Video: Embassy*

Chosen Survivors
US 1974   98m   colour
Alpine / Metromedia (Charles Fries)

Ten people with special skills are chosen to test human reaction to thermo-nuclear war, but find themselves at the mercy of vampire bats.
Another misfit group united by disaster; more shocks than suspense, and not much characterization, but for adventure / horror addicts it will pass the time.

·w H. B. Cross, Joe Red Moffly d Sutton Roley ph Gabriel Torres m Fred Karlin

Jackie Cooper, Alex Cord, Richard Jaeckel, Diana Muldaur, Lincoln Kilpatrick, Bradford Dillman, Pedro Armendariz Jnr, Gwen Mitchell, Barbara Babcock, Christina Moreno

Les Choses de la Vie*
France / Italy 1969　89m　Eastmancolor
Lira / Fida (Raymond Danon)
aka: *These Things Happen; The Things of
Life*

An architect has his wife and mistress neatly
balanced when an accident upsets his scheme
of things.
Nicely observed tragi-comedy in the best
French manner; since it starts with the car
crash, a mini-*Bridge of San Luis Rey*.

w Paul Guimard, Claude Sautet, Jean-Loup
Dabadie, *novel* Paul Guimard *d* Claude
Sautet *ph* Jean Boffety *m* Philippe Sarde

Michel Piccoli, Romy Schneider, Lea Massari,
Gérard Lartigau, Jean Bouise

Christ Stopped at Eboli*
Italy / France 1979　155m　Technospes
colour
Vides Cinematografica / RAI / Action Film /
Gaumont (Franco Cristaldi, Nicola
Carraro)

In 1935 an Italian doctor is exiled because of
his political views to a remote southern part of
the country.
An attractively faithful account of a book
which was part personal statement, part
symbolism, part political opinion and part
local colour. Non-Italians will be unable to
extract the full flavour.

w Francesco Rosi, Tonino Guerra, Raffaele
La Capria, *book* Carlo Levi *d* Francesco
Rosi *ph* Pasqualino de Santis *m* Piero
Piccioni

Gian Maria Volonte, Alain Cuny, Paolo
Bonacelli, Lea Massari, Irene Papas, François
Simon

BFA: best foreign film

Christiane F*
West Germany 1981　131m　colour

A teenage girl becomes a drug addict. Slick
melodrama hoked up from 'true' confessions
with excellent background detail. Natja
Brunckhorst, Thomas Haustein, Jens Kuphal.
Written by Herman Weigel; directed by Ulrich
Edel; for Maran Film / Popular Film / Hans
H. Kaden / TCF.

Christine
US 1983　110m　Technicolor
Panavision
Columbia / Delphi (Richard Kobritz)

A diabolical car maims and kills its owner's
girl friends.
Thin and gruesomely extended horror flick
which never begins to be convincing. For
teenagers only.

w Bill Phillips, *novel* Stephen King *d* John
Carpenter *ph* Donald M. Morgan *m* John
Carpenter *pd* Daniel Lomino

Keith Gordon, John Stockwell, Alexandra
Paul, Robert Prosky, Harry Dean Stanton,
Christine Belford

A Christmas Carol*
US 1938　69m　bw
MGM (Joseph L. Mankiewicz)

Scrooge the miser is reformed when four
ghosts visit him on Christmas Eve.
Standard Dickensian frolic, quite well
mounted.

w Hugo Butler *d* Edwin L. Marin *ph* Sidney
Wagner *m* Franz Waxman

Reginald Owen, Gene Lockhart, Kathleen
Lockhart, Terry Kilburn, Leo G. Carroll,
Lynne Carver
　'Top production, inspired direction, superb
acting.'—*Variety*
† See also *Scrooge*.

Christmas Eve*
US 1947　92m　bw
Benedict Bogeaus
aka: *Sinners' Holiday*

An old lady needs the help of her three
adopted sons to prevent herself from being
swindled.
Basically three short stories sealed by a
Christmas Eve reunion, this is old-fashioned
sentimental stuff, but it works on its level and
the cast is interesting.

w Lawrence Stallings *d* Edwin L. Marin
ph Gordon Avil *m* Heinz Roemheld

Ann Harding, George Raft, Randolph Scott,
George Brent, Joan Blondell, Virginia Field,
Reginald Denny

Christmas Holiday
US 1944　93m　bw
Universal (Felix Jackson)

A young girl marries a murderer, and later, as
a shady songstress in a nightclub, is forced to
help him escape.
A weird change of pace for Deanna Durbin,
whose forte had been sweetness and light, this
relentlessly grim and boring melodrama was
also a travesty of the novel on which it was
based.

w Herman J. Mankiewicz, *novel* Somerset
Maugham *d* Robert Siodmak *ph* Elwood
Bredell *m* Hans Salter

Deanna Durbin, Gene Kelly, Dean Harens,
Gladys George, Richard Whorf, Gale
Sondergaard

AAN: Hans Salter

Christmas in Connecticut*
US 1945　101m　bw
Warner (William Jacobs)
GB title: *Indiscretion*

The spinster writer of a successful column
about love and marriage has to conjure up a
family for herself in the cause of publicity.
Predictable but fairly brisk comedy with
excellent talent well deployed.

w Lionel Houser, Adele Commandini *d* Peter
Godfrey *ph* Carl Guthrie *m* Frederick
Hollander

Barbara Stanwyck, Dennis Morgan, Sydney
Greenstreet, Reginald Gardiner, S. Z. Sakall,
Robert Shayne, Una O'Connor, Frank Jenks

'If you can't sleep at night, it isn't the
　coffee—it's the bunk!'
Christmas in July**
US 1940　67m　bw
Paramount

A young clerk and his girl win first prize in a
big competition.
Slightly unsatisfactory as a whole, this Preston
Sturges comedy has echoes of Clair and a dully
predictable plot line, but is kept alive by
inventive touches and a gallery of splendid
character comedians.

wd Preston Sturges *ph* Victor Milner
m Sigmund Krumgold

Dick Powell, Ellen Drew, Ernest Truex, Al
Bridge, Raymond Walburn, William Demarest
　'The perfect restorative for battered humors
and jangled nerves.'—*Bosley Crowther*
　'Agreeable enough, but it lacks the full-
fledged Sturges lunacy.'—*New Yorker, 1977*

A Christmas Story*
US 1983　93m　colour
MGM / UA (René Dupont, Bob Clark)

In an Indiana suburb during the 1940s, a
schoolboy hopes to get a rifle for Christmas.
Curious, almost plotless family comedy of the
old school, with the difference that some
grotesquerie and tastelessness is added. On
the whole, however, an amusing
entertainment for adults who don't mind their
mood of sentimental nostalgia being tilted at
by the director of *Porky's*.

w Jean Shepherd, Leigh Brown, Bob Clark
d Bob Clark

Peter Billingsley, Melinda Dillon, Darren
McGavin, Ian Petrella

The Christmas Tree
France / Italy 1969　110m　Eastmancolor
Corona / Jupiter (Robert Dorfmann)

The small son of a millionaire widower is
fatally infected by radioactivity.
Painfully sentimental and overdrawn weepie,
the most lachrymose film of the sixties.

wd Terence Young, *novel* Michel Bataille
ph Henri Alekan *m* Georges Auric

William Holden, Virna Lisi, Brook Fuller,
Bourvil
　'Depending on your taste threshold, there
may not be a dry eye—nor a full stomach—in
the house.'—*Judith Crist*

Christopher Bean*
US 1933　80m　bw
aka: *Her Sweetheart*

A dying artist appoints his housekeeper as his
executor. Solid family entertainment very
typical of its studio. *Marie Dressler* (her last
film), Lionel Barrymore, Beulah Bondi, Helen
Mack, George Coulouris, H. B. Warner, Jean
Hersholt. Written by Laurence Johnson and
Sylvia Thalberg, from Sidney Howard's play
The Late Christopher Bean; directed by Sam
Wood; for MGM.

Christopher Columbus
US 1949   104m   Technicolor
Rank / Gainsborough / Sydney Box (Betty
E. Box)

Columbus seeks and receives the patronage of
the Spanish court for his voyage to the west.
An extraordinarily tediously paced historical
account of basically undramatic events;
interesting without being stimulating.

w Muriel and Sydney Box, Cyril Roberts
d David MacDonald ph Stephen Dade
m Arthur Bliss

Fredric March, Florence Eldridge, Francis L.
Sullivan, Linden Travers
   'Even ten-year-olds will find it about as
thrilling as an afternoon spent looking at
Christmas cards.'—*Time*

'She gave herself to the great God speed,
   and tried to run away from the fires
   within her!'
'The personal story of a million daughters!'
Christopher Strong*
US 1933   72m   bw
RKO (Pandro S. Berman)

A daring lady aviator has an affair with a
married businessman and commits suicide
when she finds herself pregnant.
A curious and unsatisfactory yarn for
Hepburn's second film; well enough made, it
died at the box office.

w Zoe Akins, *novel* Gilbert Frankau
d Dorothy Arzner ph Bert Glennon m Max
Steiner

Katharine Hepburn, Colin Clive, Billie Burke,
Helen Chandler, Ralph Forbes, Irene Browne,
Jack La Rue
   'Draggy society play with circusy aeroplane
stunt incidentals . . . interest in the star will
outweigh other elements.'—*Variety*

Chronique d'un Eté*
France 1961   90m   bw
Argos

Parisians talk about their lives.
Curious but rather stimulating acted
documentary, with two interviewers
pontificating; saved by shrewd editing to keep
interest at its maximum.

wd Jean Rouch, Edgar Morin ph various

Chu Chin Chow*
GB 1934   102m   bw
Gaumont British / Gainsborough (Michael
Balcon)

In old Arabia, a slave girl foils a robber posing
as a dead mandarin.
Second screen version (the first was silent) of
the old Arabian Nights stage musical. A
curiosity.

w Edward Knoblock, L. DuGarde Peach,
Sidney Gilliat, *play* Oscar Asche and
Frederick Norton d Walter Forde
songs Frederick Norton md Louis Levy
ph Max Greene ch Anton Dolin

George Robey, Fritz Kortner, Anna May
Wong, John Garrick, Pearl Argyle, Malcolm
MacEachern, Dennis Hoey, Francis L.
Sullivan, Sydney Fairbrother
   'A colourful, extravagant costume film that
makes its bid for attention purely on an

extravaganza platform, and makes the
grade.'—*Variety*
   'Gaumont British have broken away for the
first time from their careful refinement, and
produced something that has guts as well as
grace.'—*C. A. Lejeune*

Chubasco
US 1967   100m   Technicolor
   Panavision
Warner Seven Arts (William Conrad)

A wild beach boy takes a job on a tuna fishing
boat.
Old-fashioned boy-makes-good melodrama à
la Captains Courageous. Excellent action
sequences at sea.

wd Allen H. Miner ph Louis Jennings, Paul
Ivano m William Lava

Chris Jones, Richard Egan, Susan Strasberg,
Ann Sothern, Simon Oakland, Preston Foster,
Audrey Totter, Peter Whitney

Chuka
US 1967   105m   Technicolor
Paramount / Rod Taylor

A wandering gunfighter defends the
inhabitants of a fort against Indian attack.
Ill-assorted characters under stress is the
theme of this rather pedestrian and slightly
pretentious western.

w Richard Jessup d Gordon Douglas
ph Harold Stine m Leith Stevens

Rod Taylor, Ernest Borgnine, John Mills,
Luciana Paluzzi, James Whitmore, Louis
Hayward, Angela Dorian

A Chump at Oxford**
US 1939   63m   bw
Hal Roach

Two street cleaners foil a bank hold-up and
are presented with an Oxford education.
Patchy but endearing Laurel and Hardy romp,
starting with an irrelevant two reels about
their playing butler and maid, but later
including Stan's burlesque impersonation of
Lord Paddington.

w Charles Rogers, Harry Langdon, Felix
Adler d Alfred Goulding ph Art Lloyd
Stan Laurel, Oliver Hardy, James Finlayson,
Forrester Harvey, Wilfrid Lucas, Peter
Cushing
   'Ranks with their best pictures—which, to
one heretic, are more agreeable than
Chaplin's. Their clowning is purer; they aren't
out to better an unbetterable world; they've
never wanted to play Hamlet.'—*Graham
Greene*

'Earth-shaking in its grandeur! A titanic
   canvas sprung to life!'
Cimarron*
US 1930   130m   bw
RKO (Louis Sarecky)

The life of an Oklahoma homesteader from
1890 to 1915.
Sprawling western family saga; a big early
talkie, it dates badly.

w Howard Estabrook, *novel* Edna Ferber
d Wesley Ruggles ph Edward Cronjager
m Max Steiner

Richard Dix, Irene Dunne, Estelle Taylor,
Nance O'Neill, William Collier Jnr, Roscoe
Ates, George E. Stone, Stanley Fields, Edna
May Oliver
   'An elegant example of super film-making
. . . big money feature for all classes.'—
Variety

AA: best picture; Howard Estabrook
AAN: Wesley Ruggles; Edward Cronjager;
Richard Dix; Irene Dunne

Cimarron*
US 1961   147m   Metrocolor
   Cinemascope
MGM (Edmund Grainger)

Flabby, relentlessly boring remake of the
above.

w Arnold Schulman d Anthony Mann
ph Robert L. Surtees m Franz Waxman

Glenn Ford, Maria Schell, Anne Baxter, Lili
Darvas, Russ Tamblyn, Henry Morgan, David
Opatoshu, Charles McGraw, Aline
MacMahon, Edgar Buchanan, Arthur
O'Connell, Mercedes McCambridge, Vic
Morrow, Robert Keith, Mary Wickes, Royal
Dano, Vladimir Sokoloff

The Cincinnati Kid**
US 1965   113m   Metrocolor
MGM / Filmways (Martin Ransohoff, John
Calley)

In New Orleans in the late thirties, stud poker
experts compete for supremacy.
This is to poker what *The Hustler* was to pool,
a fascinating suspense study of experts at
work; as before, the romantic asides let down
the effectiveness of the others.

w Ring Lardner Jnr, Terry Southern, *novel*
Richard Jessup d Norman Jewison ph Philip
Lathrop m Lalo Schifrin

Steve McQueen, *Edward G. Robinson*, Karl
Malden, Ann-Margret, Tuesday Weld, Joan
Blondell, Rip Torn, Jack Weston, Cab
Calloway, Jeff Corey
● Video: MGM / UA

Cinderella**
US 1950   75m   Technicolor
Walt Disney

The Perrault fairy tale embroidered with
animal characters.
A feature cartoon rather short on inspiration,
though with all Disney's solid virtues. The
mice are lively and the villainous cat the best
character.

supervisor Ben Sharpsteen d Wilfred Jackson,
Hamilton Luske, Clyde Geronomi m Oliver
Wallace, Paul J. Smith

AAN: Oliver Wallace, Paul J. Smith; song
'Bibbidy Bobbidy Boo' (m / ly Mack David,
Al Hoffman, Jerry Livingston)

Cinderella Jones
US 1946   89m   bw
Warner (Alex Gottlieb)

To collect an inheritance, a girl must marry a
brainy man.
Witless comedy for the easily pleased.

w Charles Hoffman, *story* Philip Wylie
d Busby Berkeley ph Sol Polito m Frederick
Hollander

Joan Leslie, Robert Alda, S. Z. Sakall, Edward Everett Horton, Julie Bishop, William Prince, Charles Dingle, Ruth Donnelly, Elisha Cook Jnr, Hobart Cavanaugh, Chester Clute

'A movie for every woman who thinks she can never fall in love again!'

Cinderella Liberty
US 1974 117m De Luxe Panavision
TCF / Sanford (Mark Rydell)

A sailor on shore leave picks up a prostitute and falls in love with her.
Assertively 'modern' yet glutinously sentimental love story in squalid settings. It presumably has an audience.

w Darryl Ponicsan, from his novel d Mark Rydell ph Vilmos Zsigmond m John Williams

James Caan, Marsha Mason, Eli Wallach, Kirk Calloway, Allyn Ann McLerie
'A sordid, messy affair which wants to jerk tears but just doesn't have the knack.'—*New Yorker*

AA: song 'Nice To Be Around' (m John Williams, ly Paul Williams)
AAN: John Williams; Marsha Mason

Cinderfella
US 1960 91m Technicolor
Paramount / Jerry Lewis

Luxury pantomime featuring a male Cinderella.
Annoyingly lavish and empty star vehicle with precious little to laugh at: Lewis' own jokes are strung out to snapping point and no one else gets a look in.

wd Frank Tashlin ph Haskell Boggs m Walter Scharf

Jerry Lewis, Ed Wynn, Judith Anderson, Anna Maria Alberghetti, Henry Silva, Robert Hutton, Count Basie
'A drought of comic inspiration, followed by a flood of mawkish whimsy, gradually increases one's early misgivings to a degree which finally verges on revulsion.'—*Peter John Dyer*

The Circle

Somerset Maugham's brittle play contrasting noble breeding with vulgar riches was filmed by Frank Borzage as a Hollywood silent, in 1925 for MGM, with Elinor Boardman, Creighton Hale and Alec B. Francis. In 1930 the same studio made it as a talkie under the title *Strictly Unconventional,* with Catherine Dale Owen, Tyrrell Davis and Lewis Stone; directed by David Burton. Neither version really worked.

Circle of Danger*
GB 1951 89m bw
Coronado / David Rose (Joan Harrison)

An American in England investigates the strange death some years earlier of his brother during a commando raid.
Individual scenes are well milked for suspense and dramatic emphasis, but the plot line has virtually no mystery and absolutely no danger. It all seems mildly reminiscent of several Hitchcock films.

w Philip MacDonald d Jacques Tourneur ph Oswald Morris m Robert Farnon

Ray Milland, Patricia Roc, Marius Goring, Hugh Sinclair, Naunton Wayne, Marjorie Fielding, Edward Rigby, Colin Gordon, Dora Bryan

Circle of Deceit*
West Germany / France 1981 109m Eastmancolor
Bioskop / Artemis / Hessicher Rundfunk / Argos (Eberhard Junkersdorf)
original title: *Die Fälschung*

A German journalist has a crisis of conscience while covering the war in Beirut.
Fashionable self-scrutiny based on a published 'faction'. As a film, quite engrossing and occasionally hair-raising.

w Volker Schlöndorff and others, book Nicolas Born d Volker Schlöndorff ph Igor Luther m Maurice Jarre

Bruno Ganz, Hanna Schygulla, Jerzy Skolimowski, Gila von Weitershausen
'Rarely can a fiction film about war have had such a vividly authentic background, with real corpses and real destruction lending a bleak chill never captured by staged reconstructions.'—*Tom Milne, MFB*

Circle of Deception
GB 1960 100m bw Cinemascope
TCF (T. H. Morahan)

An officer is parachuted into Germany with the intention that he should crack under interrogation and reveal false information.
Depressing World War II tall tale, with suspense sacrificed by flashback structure.

w Nigel Balchin, Robert Musel, novel Alec Waugh d Jack Lee ph Gordon Dines m Clifton Parker

Bradford Dillman, Harry Andrews, Suzy Parker, Robert Stephens, John Welsh, Paul Rogers, Duncan Lamont, Michael Ripper

Circle of Two
Canada 1980 105m colour
Film Consortium of Canada (Henk Van der Kolk)

A 60-year-old artist falls for a teenage student. Dreary and uninteresting star drama which never really gets going.

w Thomas Hedley, from A Lesson in Love by Marie Terese Baird d Jules Dassin ph Lazlo George m Paul Hoffert

Richard Burton, Tatum O'Neal, Nuala Fitzgerald, Kate Reid, Robin Gammell, Patricia Collins

Circonstances Atténuantes*
France 1939 85m bw

A retired magistrate becomes innocently involved with a gang of crooks. Nimble farce, most skilfully acted. Michel Simon, Arletty, Suzanne Dantes, Arnoux, Mila Parely. Written by Jean-Pierre Feydeau from a novel by Marcel Arnac; directed by Jean Boyer; for CCFC.

The Circus*
US 1928 72m (24 fps) bw silent (UA) Charles Chaplin

A tramp on the run from the police takes refuge in a circus and falls for an equestrienne. Pathos often descends to bathos in this self-constructed star vehicle which has far too few laughs.

wd Charles Chaplin ph Rollie Totheroh, Jack Wilson, Mark Marlott

Charles Chaplin, Merna Kennedy, Allan Garcia, Harry Crocker

AAN: Charles Chaplin (as actor and director)
● Video: Polygram

Circus of Horrors
GB 1960 91m Eastmancolor
Anglo Amalgamated / Lynx / Independent Artists (Norman Priggen)

A plastic surgeon staffs a semi-derelict circus with criminals whose faces he has altered, and murders any who try to flee.
Stark horror comic; quite professionally made, but content-wise a crude concoction of sex and sadism.

w George Baxt d Sidney Hayers ph Douglas Slocombe m Franz Reizenstein, Muir Mathieson

Anton Diffring, Erika Remberg, Yvonne Monlaur, Donald Pleasance, Jane Hylton, Kenneth Griffith, Conrad Phillips, Jack Gwyllim

Circus World
US 1964 138m Super Technirama
Bronston / Midway (Samuel Bronston)
GB title: *The Magnificent Showman*

An American circus owner tours Europe in search of his alcoholic ex-wife who left him when her lover fell to death from the trapeze. Lethargic big-screen epic which exhausts its spectacle in the first hour and then settles down to a dreary will-daughter-guess-who-the-strange-lady-is plot, without even the plus of an exciting finale.

w Ben Hecht, Julian Halevy, James Edward Grant d Henry Hathaway ph Jack Hildyard pd John de Cuir m Dmitri Tiomkin

John Wayne, *Rita Hayworth*, Claudia Cardinale, John Smith, Lloyd Nolan, Richard Conte, Wanda Rotha, Kay Walsh
'To sit through this film is something like holding an elephant on your lap for two hours and fifteen minutes.'—*Time*
● Video: Intervision

The Cisco Kid

The Cisco Kid, a ruthless Mexican bandit originally created by O. Henry in a short story, was turned by Hollywood into a dashing wild western Robin Hood in twenty-three sound features (following a few silent ones) and a long-running TV series. In most of them he was accompanied by his fat side-kick Pancho.

For Fox:
1929: IN OLD ARIZONA (Warner Baxter)
1931: THE CISCO KID (Baxter)

For Twentieth Century Fox:
1939: THE RETURN OF THE CISCO KID (Baxter), THE CISCO KID AND THE LADY (Cesar Romero: who played the role in all the remaining TCF movies).
1940: VIVA CISCO KID, LUCKY CISCO KID, THE GAY CABALLERO
1941: ROMANCE OF THE RIO GRANDE, RIDE ON, VAQUERO

For Monogram:
1945: THE CISCO KID RETURNS (Duncan Renaldo), THE CISCO KID IN OLD NEW MEXICO (Renaldo), SOUTH OF THE RIO GRANDE (Renaldo)
1946: THE GAY CAVALIER (Gilbert Roland), SOUTH OF MONTEREY (Roland), BEAUTY AND THE BANDIT (Roland)
1947: RIDING THE CALIFORNIA TRAIL (Roland), ROBIN HOOD OF MONTEREY (Roland), KING OF THE BANDITS (Roland)

For United Artists (all with Renaldo):
1949: THE VALIANT HOMBRE, THE GAY AMIGO, THE DARING CABALLERO, SATAN'S CRADLE
1950: THE GIRL FROM SAN LORENZO
† The fifties TV series starred Renaldo with Leo Carrillo.

Cisco Pike
US 1971 94m Eastmancolor
Columbia / Acrobat (Gerald Ayres)

A former pop group leader and drug pusher is blackmailed by a cop into selling heroin.
Low-key, would-be realistic study of a section of life in seventies LA. Flashy, boring and almost plotless.

wd Bill L. Norton *ph* Vilis Lapenieks
m various

Kris Kristofferson, Gene Hackman, Karen Black, Harry Dean Stanton
'A moody, melancholy little film whose strength lies in its evocation of the rootless, aimless, irresponsible life-style of the pop / drug culture.'—*Brenda Davies*

'Secrets of a doctor as told by a doctor!'
The Citadel••
GB 1938 113m bw
MGM (Victor Saville)

A young doctor has a hard time in the mining villages but is later swayed by the easy rewards of a Mayfair practice.
Solidly produced adaptation of a bestseller; the more recent deluge of doctors on television make it appear rather elementary, but many scenes work in a classical way. One of the first fruits of MGM's British studios which were closed by World War II.

w Elizabeth Hill, Ian Dalrymple, Emlyn Williams, Frank Wead, *novel* A. J. Cronin *d* King Vidor *ph* Harry Stradling *m* Louis Levy

Robert Donat, Rosalind Russell, Ralph Richardson, Emlyn Williams, Penelope Dudley Ward, Francis L. Sullivan
'General audience limited . . . strong for the Anglo market.'—*Variety*

'I think any doctor will agree that here is a medical picture with no *Men in White* hokum, no hysterical, incredible melodrama, but with an honest story, honestly told. And that's a rare picture.'—*Pare Lorentz*
'We are grateful that a worthy idea has been handled with intelligence and imagination, that Vidor has shown respect both for his talent and for the sensibilities of the audience.'—*Robert Stebbins*
† The parts played by Russell and Richardson were originally intended for Elizabeth Allan and Spencer Tracy

AAN: best picture; script; King Vidor; Robert Donat

Citizen Kane••••
US 1941 119m bw
RKO (Orson Welles)

A newspaper tycoon dies, and a magazine reporter interviews his friends in an effort to discover the meaning of his last words.
A brilliant piece of Hollywood cinema using all the resources of the studio; despite lapses of characterization and gaps in the narrative, almost every shot and every line is utterly absorbing both as entertainment and as craft. See *The Citizen Kane Book* by Pauline Kael, and innumerable other writings.

w Herman J. Mankiewicz, Orson Welles *d* Orson Welles *ph* Gregg Toland *m* Bernard Herrmann *ad* Van Nest Polglase *sp* Vernon L. Walker

Orson Welles (Kane), *Joseph Cotten* (Jedediah Leland), *Dorothy Comingore* (Susan Alexander), *Everett Sloane* (Bernstein), *Ray Collins* (Boss Jim Geddes), *Paul Stewart* (Raymond), *Ruth Warrick* (Emily Norton), *Erskine Sanford* (Herbert Carter), *Agnes Moorehead* (Kane's mother), *Harry Shannon* (Kane's father), *George Coulouris* (Walter Parks Thatcher), *William Alland* (Thompson), *Fortunio Bonanova* (music teacher)
'What is his name? It's Charlie Kane!
'I'll bet you five you're not alive if you don't know his name!'
NEWSREEL: 'Then, last week, as it must to all men, death came to Charles Foster Kane.'
BERNSTEIN: 'Old age . . . it's the only disease you don't look forward to being cured of.'
THOMPSON: 'Mr Kane was a man who got everything he wanted, and then lost it. Maybe Rosebud was something he couldn't get, or something he lost. Anyway, I don't think it would have explained everything. I don't think any word can explain a man's life. No, I guess Rosebud is just a piece in a jigsaw puzzle . . . a missing piece.'
SUSAN: 'Forty-nine acres of nothing but scenery and statues. I'm lonesome.'
KANE: 'You're right, Mr Thatcher. I did lose a million dollars last year. I expect to lose a million dollars this year. I expect to lose a million dollars next year. You know, Mr Thatcher, at the rate of a million dollars a year, I'll have to close this place—in sixty years.'
KANE: 'I run a couple of newspapers. What do you do?'

BERNSTEIN: 'One day back in 1896 I was crossing over to Jersey on the ferry, and as we pulled out, there was another ferry pulling in, and on it there was a girl waiting to get off. A white dress she had on. She was carrying a white parasol. I only saw her for one second. She didn't see me at all, but I'll bet a month hasn't gone by since then that I haven't thought of that girl.'
'On seeing it for the first time, one got a conviction that if the cinema could do that, it could do anything.'—*Penelope Houston*
'What may distinguish *Citizen Kane* most of all is its extracting the mythic from under the humdrum surface of the American experience.'—*John Simon, 1968*
'Probably the most exciting film that has come out of Hollywood for twenty-five years. I am not sure it isn't the most exciting film that has ever come out of anywhere.'—*C. A. Lejeune*
'At any rate Orson Welles has landed in the movies, with a splash and a loud yell.'—*James Shelley Hamilton*
'More fun than any great movie I can think of.'—*Pauline Kael, 1968*
'It is a fascinating picture, but because of its congestion of technical stunts, it fails to move us.'—*Egon Larsen*
'A quite good film which tries to run the psychological essay in harness with the detective thriller, and doesn't quite succeed.'—*James Agate*

AA: Herman J. Mankiewicz, Orson Welles (script)
AAN: best picture; Orson Welles (as director); Gregg Toland; Bernard Herrmann; Orson Welles (as actor)
● Video: Thorn EMI

La Città Si Difende
Italy 1951 90m bw
Cines (Carlo Civallero)

A gang is recruited to rob a football stadium.
Moderate forerunner of *The Good Die Young*, *The Killing*, and a hundred other caper films.

w Federico Fellini, Tullio Pinelli, Luigi Comencini *d* Pietro Germi *ph* Carlo Montuori *m* Carlo Rustichelli

Fausto Tozzi, Gina Lollobrigida, Patrizia Manca, Enzo Maggio
'As anonymous as the average B picture.'—*Gavin Lambert*

The City•
US 1939 32m bw

A historical, social and psychoanalytical study of urban living. Slightly guarded but convention-breaking documentary which though of its time still fascinates mildly by its style. Written by Henwar Rodakiewicz, from the book *The Culture of Cities* by Lewis Mumford; photographed and directed by Ralph Steiner and Willard Van Dyke; for the American Institute of Planners.

City across the River
US 1949 91m bw
U-I (Howard Christie)

Brooklyn delinquents get involved in murder. Semi-documentary throwback to the Dead End Kids, with location shooting influenced by *The Naked City*. Dull.

w Maxwell Shane, Dennis Cooper, *novel* The Amboy Dukes by Irving Shulman d Maxwell Shane *ph* Maury Gertsman *m* Walter Scharf

Stephen McNally, Barbara Whiting, Peter Fernandez, Al Ramsen, Joshua Shelley, Anthony Curtis (Tony Curtis in his first film role)

City beneath the Sea
US 1953 87m Technicolor
U-I (Albert J. Cohen)

Deep sea divers fall out over a sunken treasure.
Adequate double-biller with little to stir the interest.

w Jack Harvey, Ramon Romero d Budd Boetticher *ph* Charles P. Boyle

Robert Ryan, Anthony Quinn, Mala Powers, Suzan Ball, George Mathews, Karel Stepanek, Lalo Rios

City beneath the Sea
US 1970 98m De Luxe TVM
Warner / Kent / Motion Pictures International (Irwin Allen)
GB theatrical release title: *One Hour to Doomsday*

An undersea city is threatened by an errant planetoid.
Futuristic adventure from a familiar stable; it will satisfy followers of *Voyage to the Bottom of the Sea*.

w John Meredyth Lucas d Irwin Allen *ph* Kenneth Peach *m* Richard La Salle *ad* Roger E. Maus, Stan Jolley

Stuart Whitman, Robert Wagner, Rosemary Forsyth, Robert Colbert, Burr de Benning, Richard Basehart, Joseph Cotten, James Darren, Sugar Ray Robinson, Paul Stewart

City for Conquest**
US 1940 106m bw
Warner (Anatole Litvak)

An East Side truck driver becomes a boxer but is blinded in a fight; meanwhile his composer brother gives up pop music for symphonies.
Phony but oddly persuasive melodrama set in a studio in New York and heavily influenced by the pretensions of the Group theatre.

w John Wexley, but *novel* Aben Kandel d Anatole Litvak *ph* Sol Polito, James Wong Howe *m* Max Steiner

James Cagney, Ann Sheridan, Frank Craven, Donald Crisp, *Arthur Kennedy*, Frank McHugh, George Tobias, Anthony Quinn, Jerome Cowan, Lee Patrick, Blanche Yurka, Thurston Hall

'Sometimes we wonder whether it wasn't really the Warner brothers who got New York from the Indians, so diligent and devoted have they been in feeling the great city's pulse, picturing its myriad facets and recording with deep compassion the passing life of its seething population.'—*Bosley Crowther*

City Girl°
US 1930 77m bw
Fox

A city girl finds rural life has its own drama.
Rural drama distinguished by directorial touches.

w Berthold Viertel, Marion Orth, *play* The Mud Turtle by Elliot Lester d F. W. Murnau *ph* Ernest Palmer *m* Arthur Kay

Charles Farrell, Mary Duncan, David Torrence, Edith Yorke, Dawn O'Day

City Girl
US 1937 60m bw

A slightly dumb waitress becomes a gangster's moll. Fast-moving B picture which undoubtedly gave satisfaction. Phyllis Brooks, Ricardo Cortez, Robert Wilcox, Douglas Fowley, Chick Chandler, Esther Muir. Written by Frances Hyland, Robin Harris, Lester Ziffren; directed by Alfred Werker; for TCF.

City Heat
US 1984 97m Technicolor
Warner / Malpaso / Deliverance (Fritz Manes)

A cop tracks the killer of his partner, with the help of another old colleague who has turned private eye.
Lightweight star turn which doesn't quite deliver, though it manages to be more entertaining than either of the participants' previous half-dozen films.

w Sam O. Brown (Blake Edwards), Joseph C. Stinson d Richard Benjamin *ph* Nick McLean *m* Lennie Niehaus *pd* Edward Carfagno

Clint Eastwood, Burt Reynolds, Jane Alexander, Madeline Kahn, Rip Torn, Irene Cara, Richard Roundtree, Tony Lo Bianco

City Lights***
US 1931 87m bw silent (with music and effects)
(UA) Charles Chaplin

A tramp befriends a millionaire and falls in love with a blind girl.
Sentimental comedy with several delightful sequences in Chaplin's best manner.

wd, m Charles Chaplin *ph* Rollie Totheroh, Mark Marlott, Gordon Pollock

Charles Chaplin, Virginia Cherrill, Harry Myers

'Chaplin has another good picture, but it gives indications of being short-winded, and may tire fast after a bombastic initial seven days . . . he has sacrificed speed to pathos, and plenty of it.'—*Variety*
'Even while laughing, one is aware of a faint and uneasy feeling that Chaplin has been pondering with more than a bit of solemnity on conventional story values, and it has led him further than ever into the realms of what is often called pathetic.'—*National Board of Review*

● *Video: Polygram*

City of Bad Men°
US 1953 82m Technicolor
TCF (Leonard Goldstein)

In Carson City during the Corbett/ Fitzsimmons boxing match, outlaws plan to rob the arena of its receipts.
Slightly unusual western suspenser with generally accomplished handling.

w George W. George, George Slavin d Harmon Jones *ph* Charles G. Clarke *md* Lionel Newman

Dale Robertson, Jeanne Crain, Richard Boone, Lloyd Bridges, Carl Betz, Carole Mathews, Whitfield Connor

The City of Beautiful Nonsense
GB 1935 88m bw

A poor composer wins the girl he loves from a rich man. Thin and dated version of a fashionable novel by E. Temple Thurston. Emlyn Williams, Sophie Stewart, Eve Lister, George Carney. Written by Donovan Pedelty; directed by Adrian Brunel; for Butcher's.

City of Fear°
US 1958 81m bw
Columbia / Orbit (Leon Chooluck)

A convict escapes with a canister of radioactive cobalt, which he believes to be heroin. After terrifying the city, he finally dies of exposure to it.
Rough-edged but occasionally gripping minor thriller from an independent company.

w Steven Ritch, Robert Dillon d Irving Lerner *ph* Lucien Ballard *m* Jerry Goldsmith

Vince Edwards, John Archer, Patricia Blair, Steven Ritch, Lyle Talbot

City of Gold**
Canada 1957 23m bw

The story of Dawson City, capital of the Klondike in 1897–8, is told by an accumulation of details from still photographs. A film with much to answer for, being the first documentary exclusively using the rostrum camera, a technique later adopted extensively by television. The subject matter is fascinating. Written and narrated by Pierre Berton; photographed and directed by Colin Low and Wolf Koenig; for National Film Board of Canada.

City of the Dead°
GB 1960 78m bw
Vulcan (Donald Taylor)
US title: *Horror Hotel*

In Massachusetts, a woman burned as a witch 250 years ago is still 'alive', running a local hotel and luring unwary strangers into becoming sacrificial victims.
A deadly first half gives way to splendid cinematic terror when the scene shifts to the village by night, all dry ice and limpid fog, and the heroine becomes a human sacrifice. A superior horror comic.

w George Baxt d John Moxey *ph* Desmond Dickinson *m* Douglas Gamley, Ken Jones

CITY OF BAD MEN. Not a bad little melodrama, but the advertising makes it look like an epic.

Patricia Jessel, Betta St John, Christopher
Lee, Dennis Lotis, Valentine Dyall, Venetia
Stevenson, Norman Macowan, Fred Johnson
● Video: Intervision

City of Women*
Italy-France 1980 140m Eastmancolor
Opera Film-Gaumont (Renzo Rossellini)
Original title: La Città delle Donne

A businessman finds himself trapped and
threatened by women en masse.
Often leaden but sometimes spectacular
fantasy in which the director spews out his
views of the war between men and women.
Fascinating in patches, but generally
indigestible.

w Federico Fellini, Bernardino Zapponi
d Federico Fellini ph Giuseppe Rotunno
m Luis Bacalov

Marcello Mastroianni, Anna Prucnal, Bernice
Stegers, Ettore Manni, Donatella Damiani
  'Another visual tour de force in an elaborate
dream framework; narrative thin, overlong,
and finally overweight.'—Variety

City on Fire
Canada / US 1979 106m colour
A slum fire threatens an entire city. Shoddy

disaster movie which does its cast no favour.
Barry Newman, Susan Clark, Shelley Winters,
Henry Fonda, Leslie Nielsen, James
Franciscus, Ava Gardner. Written by Jack
Hill, David P. Lewis and Celine La Freniere;
directed by Alvin Rakoff; for Astral-Bellevue-
Pathe / Sandy Howard.

'Love and courage pitted against a ruthless
    hate!'
City Streets**
US 1931 86m bw
Paramount (Rouben Mamoulian)

A gangster's daughter is sent to jail for a
murder she did not commit, and on release
narrowly escapes being 'taken for a ride'.
Tense, dated gangland melodrama of primary
interest because of its director's very cinematic
treatment.

w Max Marcin, Oliver H. P. Garrett, Dashiell
Hammett, *story* Ladies of the Mob by Ernest
Booth d Rouben Mamoulian ph Lee Garmes

Sylvia Sidney, Gary Cooper, Paul Lukas, Guy
Kibbee, William (Stage) Boyd, Stanley Fields,
Wynne Gibson

  'Too much attempt to artify hurts though
the sophisticated treatment and elegant
settings will help.'—*Variety*
  'A love story in a gangster setting which got
carried away into so much fancy expressionism
and symbolism that it seems stylized out of all
relationship to the actual world.'—*Pauline
Kael, 70s*

City That Never Sleeps
US 1953 90m bw
Republic (John H. Auer)

The work of the Chicago police force during
one night.
Adequate minor semi-documentary police
yarn.

w Steve Fisher d John H. Auer ph John I.
Russell m R. Dale Butts

Gig Young, Mala Powers, William Talman,
Edward Arnold, Chill Wills, Paula Raymond,
Marie Windsor

'They dared the most romantic journey that
    has ever challenged the imagination!'
City under the Sea
GB 1965 84m Eastmancolor
    Colorscope
Bruton / AIP (Daniel Haller)
US title: *War Gods of the Deep*

An American heiress in Cornwall meets
Victorian smugglers who have lived a hundred
years under the sea in Lyonesse.
Childlike, unpersuasive nonsense which wastes
some good talent.

w Charles Bennett, Louis M. Heyward
d Jacques Tourneur ph Stephen Dade
m Stanley Black

Vincent Price, David Tomlinson, Susan Hart,
Tab Hunter, Henry Oscar, John Le Mesurier

City Without Men
US 1943 75m bw

A boarding house near a prison is filled with
women awaiting the parole of their menfolk.

Stereotyped programmer. Linda Darnell,
Michael Duane, Sara Allgood, Edgar
Buchanan, Glenda Farrell, Leslie Brooks,
Margaret Hamilton, Sheldon Leonard.
Written by W. L. River, George Skier and
Donald Davis; directed by Sidney Salkow; for
Columbia.

Civilization***
US 1916 68m (1931 'sound' version)
    bw silent
Triangle

A mythical country starts war, but one of the
principals has a vision of Christ on the
battlefields and the king is persuaded to sign a
peace treaty.
Surprisingly impressive parable showing this
early director at his best; intended as a pacifist
tract in the middle of World War I.

w C. Gardner Sullivan d Thomas Ince
ph Irwin Willat

Enid Markey, Howard Hickman, J. Barney
Sherry

The Clairvoyant*
GB 1934 80m bw
Gainsborough (Michael Balcon)

A fraudulent mindreader predicts a disaster
which comes true.
Effective minor suspenser on predictable but
enjoyable lines.

w Charles Bennett, Bryan Edgar Wallace,
Robert Edmunds d Maurice Elvey ph Glen
MacWilliams

Claude Rains, Fay Wray, Jane Baxter, Mary
Clare, Athole Stewart, Ben Field, Felix
Aylmer, Donald Calthrop

● *Video: Rank*

Clambake
US 1967 98m Techniscope
UA / Rhodes (Laven–Gardner–Levy)

The son of an oil millionaire sets out to see
life.
Painless, forgettable star vehicle.

w Arthur Browne Jnr d Arthur H. Nadel
ph William Margulies m Jeff Alexander

Elvis Presley, Shelley Fabares, Bill Bixby,
James Gregory, Will Hutchins, Gary Merrill

Clarence the Cross-Eyed Lion
US 1965 98m Metrocolor
MGM (Leonard Kaufman)

Adventures of animal farmers in Africa.
Amiable theatrical 'pilot' for the *Daktari* TV
series.

w Alan Caillou, Marshall Thompson, Art
Arthur d Andrew Marton ph Lamar Boren

Marshall Thompson, Betsy Drake, Richard
Haydn, Cheryl Miller

'Livin' in my house! Lovin' another man! Is
    that what you call honest? That's just
    givin' it a nice name!'
Clash by Night*
US 1952 105m bw
RKO (Harriet Parsons) (A Wald–Krasna
    Production)

In a northern fishing village, jealousy and
near-tragedy are occasioned by the return
home of a hardened girl from the big city.
Absurdly overblown melodrama of the *Anna
Christie* school, burdened with significance and
doggedly acted by a remarkable cast.

w Alfred Hayes, *play* Clifford Odets d Fritz
Lang ph Nicholas Musuraca m Roy Webb

Barbara Stanwyck, Paul Douglas, Robert
Ryan, Marilyn Monroe, J. Carrol Naish, Keith
Andes

  'When Stanwyck snarls into a pub and belts
down a straight shot, we think we're watching
a remake of *Anna Christie*; when she is shyly
and ineptly courted by Douglas we think it's a
remake of *Min and Bill*; a sub-plot involving
Monroe and Andes plays like *Gidget Faces an
Identity Crisis*.'—*Kit Parker catalogue*

● *Video: VCL*

Clash of the Titans
GB 1981 118m Metrocolor Dynarama
MGM / Charles H. Schneer, Ray
    Harryhausen

Perseus sets out to win Andromeda despite the
impossible obstacles set for him by Thetis,
which include a number of mythical monsters.
Star-packed but feebly imagined mythological
spectacular, further hampered by gloomy
photography which is presumably required to
offset the jerkiness of the monsters. A very
few moments provide the right kind of elation.

w Beverley Cross d Desmond Davis ph Ted
Moore m Laurence Rosenthal sp Ray
Harryhausen pd Frank White

Laurence Olivier, Claire Bloom, Maggie
Smith, Ursula Andress, Jack Gwyllim, Harry
Hamlin, Judy Bowker, Burgess Meredith, Siân
Phillips, Flora Robson, Freda Jackson,
Donald Houston

  'There's a real possibility some audiences
will be turned to stone before Medusa even
appears.'—*Geoff Brown, MFB*
  'Unspeakable dialogue, muddy photography
and a motley, lacklustre cast.'—*Sight and
Sound*

● *Video: MGM / UA*

Class
US 1983 98m Astro Color
Orion / Martin Ransohoff

A shy student has an affair with an older
woman who turns out to be his best friend's
mother.
Ghastly travesty of *The Graduate* which
aspires to every kind of sophistication it can
think of but ends nowhere.

w Jim Kouf, David Greenwalt d Lewis John
Carlino ph Ric Waite m Elmer Bernstein
ad Jack Poplin

Jacqueline Bisset, Cliff Robertson, Rob Lowe,
Andrew McCarthy, Stuart Margolin, John
Cusack.

  'It is not often that one comes across a film
of such muddled aspirations and widely
divergent achievements.'—*Nick Roddick,
MFB*

Class of '44
US 1973 95m Technicolor Panavision
Warner (Paul Bogart)

Sex problems of college students during World
War II.

Thin sequel to *Summer of '42*, nostalgic to
Americans over forty but not much of a trip
for anyone else.

w Herman Raucher d Paul Bogart
ph Andrew Laszlo m David Shire

Gary Grimes, Jerry Houser, Oliver Conant,
William Atherton, Sam Bottoms, Deborah
Winters

Class of 84
Canada 1981 98m colour

A new teacher finds his students involved in
drug and vice rackets. *The Blackboard Jungle*
goes several steps further, to general
indifference. Perry King, Merrie Lynn Ross,
Timothy Van Patten, Roddy McDowall.
Written by Mark Lester, John Saxton, Tom
Holland; directed by Mark Lester; for
Guerrilla High.

● *Video: Thorn EMI*

The Class of Miss McMichael
GB 1978 90m colour
Brut / Kettledrum (Judd Bernard)

A dedicated schoolmistress has no chance
against her slum surroundings.
The Blackboard Jungle lives on, very boringly.

w Judd Bernard, *novel* Sandy Hutson
d Silvio Narizzano ph Alex Thomson
m Stanley Myers

Glenda Jackson, Oliver Reed, John Standing,
Michael Murphy, Rosalind Cash

'Poorly mannered, simple minded, badly
disciplined . . . gives social science a bad
name.'—*Variety*

Claudelle Inglish
US 1961 99m bw
Warner (Leonard Freeman)
GB title: *Young and Eager*

A poor farmer's daughter scorns a wealthy
man for a succession of young studs.
Would-be sensational novelette from the
author of *Tobacco Road*; it does not begin to
be interesting.

w Leonard Freeman, *novel* Erskine Caldwell
d Gordon Douglas ph Ralph Woolsey
m Howard Jackson

Diane McBain, Arthur Kennedy, Constance
Ford, Chad Everett, Claude Akins, Will
Hutchins, Robert Colbert, Ford Rainey,
James Bell

Claudia**
US 1943 92m bw
TCF (William Perlberg)

A middle-class husband helps his child-wife to
mature.
Typical of the best of Hollywood's 'woman's
pictures' of the period, this is a pleasant
domestic comedy-drama featuring
recognizably human characters in an agreeable
setting.

w Morrie Ryskind, *novel and play* Rose
Franken d Edmund Goulding ph Leon
Shamroy m Alfred Newman

Dorothy McGuire (her film debut), *Robert
Young, Ina Claire*, Reginald Gardiner, Olga
Baclanova, Jean Howard, Elsa Janssen

† Cary Grant was sought for the Robert
Young part.

Claudia and David*
US 1946 78m bw
TCF (William Perlberg)

Claudia and her husband survive assorted
crises including their son's illness and David's
involvement in a car crash.
Patchwork sequel to *Claudia*, quite pleasant
but obviously contrived quickly from scraps.

w Rose Franken, William Brown Meloney
d Walter Lang ph Joseph La Shelle m Cyril
Mockridge

Dorothy McGuire, Robert Young, Mary
Astor, John Sutton, Gail Patrick, Florence
Bates

The Clay Pigeon**
US 1949 63m bw
RKO (Herman Schlom)

An amnesiac sailor finds himself
courtmartialled for treason, but discovers the
real culprit.
Tidily efficient second feature thriller; good
enjoyable stuff of its kind.

w Carl Foreman d Richard Fleischer
ph Robert de Grasse m Paul Sawtell

Bill Williams, Barbara Hale, Richard Quine,
Richard Loo, Frank Fenton

Cleo from Five to Seven*
France / Italy 1961 90m part colour
Rome / Paris (Bruno Drigo)

A girl waiting for the result of a medical
examination wanders around Paris thinking
she has cancer.
Impressively handled character sketch with
gratifying attention to detail.

wd Agnès Varda ph Jean Rabier m Michel
Legrand

Corinne Marchand, Antoine Bourseiller,
Dorothée Blanck, Michel Legrand

'The love affair that shook the world!'
Cleopatra**
US 1934 101m bw
Paramount / Cecil B. de Mille

After Julius Caesar's death, Cleopatra turns
her attention to Mark Antony.
More of the vices than the virtues of its
producer are notable in this fustian epic, which
is almost but not quite unwatchable because of
its stolid pace and miscasting. Some of the
action montages and the barge scene,
however, are superb cinema.

w Waldemar Young, Vincent Lawrence
d Cecil B. de Mille ph Victor Milner
m Rudolph Kopp

Claudette Colbert, Henry Wilcoxon (Antony),
Warren William (Caesar), Gertrude Michael,
Joseph Schildkraut, Ian Keith, C. Aubrey
Smith, Leonard Mudie, Irving Pichel, Arthur
Hohl

'He has certainly made the most sumptuous
of Roman circuses out of Roman history . . . a
constant succession of banquets, dancers,
triumphs, and a fleet set on fire.'—*The Times*

'Gorgeous optically but mentally weak . . . .
a handpicked audience was polite but not
over-enthusiastic.'—*Variety*

'A great cinematic achievement, a spectacle
of breathtaking brilliance.'—*Daily Express*

'It is remarkable how Cecil B. de Mille can
photograph so much on such a vast scale and
still say nothing . . . it reeks of so much
pseudo-artistry, vulgarity, philistinism, sadism,
that it can only be compared with the lowest
form of contemporary culture: Hitlerism. This
is the type of "culture" that will be fed to the
audience of Fascist America.'—*Irving Lerner,
1968*

AA: Victor Milner
AAN: best picture

'The motion picture the world has been
waiting for!'
Cleopatra
US 1963 243m De Luxe Todd-AO
TCF (Walter Wanger)

The unsurprising story is told at inordinate
length and dullness in this ill-starred epic, one
of the most heralded, and mismanaged, in film
history. (Its story is best told in the producer's
My Life with Cleopatra.) The most expensive
film ever made, for various reasons which do
not appear on the screen.

w Joseph L. Mankiewicz, Ranald
MacDougall, Sidney Buchman, and others
d Joseph L. Mankiewicz (and others)
ph Leon Shamroy m Alex North ad John de
Cuir, Jack Martin Smith, and others

Elizabeth Taylor, Richard Burton, Rex
Harrison, Pamela Brown, George Cole, Hume
Cronyn, Cesare Danova, Kenneth Haigh,
Andrew Keir, Martin Landau, Roddy
McDowall, Robert Stephens, Francesca
Annis, Martin Benson, Herbert Berghof,
Grégoire Aslan, Richard O'Sullivan

'Whatever was interesting about it clearly
ended up somewhere else: on the cutting room
floor, in various hotel rooms, in the newspaper
columns . . . it lacks not only the intelligent
spectacle of *Lawrence of Arabia* but the
spectacular unintelligence of a Cecil B. de
Mille product . . .'—*John Simon*

'The small screen does more than justice to
this monumental mouse.'—*Judith Crist*

'I only came to see the asp.'—*Charles
Addams*

'Surely the most bizarre piece of
entertainment ever to be perpetrated.'—
Elizabeth Taylor

AA: Leon Shamroy
AAN: best picture; Alex North; Rex Harrison

Cleopatra Jones
US 1973 89m Technicolor Panavision

A black female CIA agent eliminates a ring of dope peddlers. Grotesque comic strip fantasy with a high mortality rate. Tamara Dobson, Shelley Winters, Bernie Casey, Brenda Sykes. Written by Max Julien and Sheldon Keller; directed by Jack Starrett; for Warner. 'It hampers the cause of racial entente more effectively than any work since *Uncle Tom's Cabin*.'—*John Baxter, MFB.*

The Climax*
US 1944 86m Technicolor
Universal (George Waggner)

A young opera singer is hypnotized by a mad doctor, who has kept his murdered mistress embalmed for ten years.
Gothic romantic melodrama invented to capitalize on the success—and the sets—of *Phantom of the Opera*. Curiously endearing, with a good eye-rolling part for Karloff.

w Curt Siodmak, Lynn Starling, *play* Edward Cochran d George Waggner ph Hal Mohr, W. Howard Greene m Edward Ward

Boris Karloff, Susanna Foster, Gale Sondergaard, Turhan Bey, Thomas Gomez, Scotty Beckett
    'All quite unalarming, which is a bit of a handicap.'—*New Yorker, 1978*

Climbing High*
GB 1938 78m bw
Gaumont

A rich man pretends to be a male model in order to win a girl.
Light-hearted romantic musical with interesting credits.

w Stephen Clarkson, *story* Lesser Samuels, Marian Dix d Carol Reed

Jessie Matthews, Michael Redgrave, Noel Madison, Alistair Sim, Margaret Vyner, Mary Clare, Francis L. Sullivan

The Clinging Vine*
US 1926 71m (24 fps) bw silent
Cecil B. de Mille

The president's secretary is the real driving force of a paint company, but finds that love is more important than business.
Interesting silent predecessor of many career girl comedies of the thirties and forties.

w Jeannie McPherson d Paul Sloane

Leatrice Joy, Tom Moore, Toby Claude, Robert Edeson

'People are going to **** whether you like it or not—and this place is here to see that they enjoy it!'
The Clinic*
Australia 1982 92m colour

One day in the life of a clinic for venereal diseases. Slightly dishevelled comedy-drama which will be generally remembered as a very naughty carry-on. Chris Haywood, Simon Burke, Gerda Nicolson, Rona McLeod, Suzanne Roylance. Written by Greg Millin; directed by David Stevens; for Film House / Generation Films.

'Six words from a woman changed the map of Asia!'
Clive of India*
US 1934 90m bw
Twentieth Century (Darryl F. Zanuck, William Goetz, Raymond Griffith)

The life of the 18th-century empire builder, with special emphasis on his marriage.
A very tame and now faded epic, with more romance than adventure. The production relies more on stars than technique, but it works.

w W. P. Lipscomb, R. J. Minney, from their play d Richard Boleslawski ph Peverell Marley m Alfred Newman

Ronald Colman, Loretta Young, Colin Clive, Francis Lister, Montagu Love, Robert Greig, Leo G. Carroll, C. Aubrey Smith, Mischa Auer
    'It may be spoken of as another of the best British pictures made in Hollywood. . . . Should be strong b.o.'—*Variety*
    'Patriotic pageantry, undistorted by facts.'—*J. R. Parish*

Cloak and Dagger*
US 1946 106m bw
United States Pictures (Milton Sperling)

A physics professor joins the secret service and is parachuted into Germany to interview a kidnapped scientist.
Supposedly authoritative espionage adventure which turned out dull and humourless; plot routine, direction absent-minded.

w Albert Maltz, Ring Lardner Jnr d Fritz Lang ph Sol Polito m Max Steiner

Gary Cooper, Lilli Palmer, Robert Alda, Vladimir Sokoloff, J. Edward Bromberg, Ludwig Stossel, Helene Thimig, Marc Lawrence
    'Just a B plot dressed up in A trimmings.'—*Newsweek*
    'The moment he fell in love was his moment of greatest danger!'—*ad line*

Clochemerle
France 1948 93m bw
Cinéma Productions (Ralph Baum)

The progressive mayor of a French village erects a gentlemen's convenience in the main street and shocks the local reactionaries.
Most of the book's political satire was ironed out in this cheap and opportunist production which got a few easy laughs but failed to sustain itself.

w Gabriel Chevalier, from his novel d Pierre Chénal ph Robert Le Fèbvre m Henri Sauguet

Brochard, Maximilienne, Simone Michels, Jane Marken, Paul Demange, Felix Oudart, Saturnin Fabre

The Clock**
US 1945 90m bw
MGM (Arthur Freed)
GB title: *Under the Clock*

A girl meets a soldier at New York's Grand Central Station and marries him during his 24-hour leave.

Everyone now seems far too nice in this winsome romance full of comedy cameos and real New York locations, but if you can relive the wartime mood it still works as a corrective to the Betty Grable glamour pieces.

w Robert Nathan, Joseph Schrank, *story* Paul and Pauline Gallico d Vincente Minnelli ph George Folsey m George Bassman

Judy Garland, Robert Walker, James Gleason, Lucile Gleason, Keenan Wynn, Marshall Thompson, Chester Clute
    'Sweetly charming, if maybe too irresistible . . . fortunately the director fills the edges with comic characters.'—*New Yorker, 1978*
    'The emotion may have been honest, but the method was too rich for my eyes, and the writing as used on the screen too weak for my mind.'—*Stephen Longstreet*
    'Strictly a romance . . . safely told, disappointing and angering in the thought of the great film it might have been.'—*James Agee*
    'Amazingly, it was all shot in the studio, using street sets and back projection; even the old Penn Station, where so much of the action takes place, is a set.'—*Pauline Kael, 70s*

'The adventures of a young man whose interests are rape, ultra-violence, and Beethoven!'
A Clockwork Orange*
GB 1971 136m colour
Warner / Polaris (Bernard Williams)

In a future Britain of desolation and violence, a young gangster guilty of rape and murder obtains a release from prison after being experimentally brainwashed: he finds society more violent than it was in his time.
A repulsive film in which intellectuals have found acres of social and political meaning; the average judgement is likely to remain that it is pretentious and nasty rubbish for sick minds who do not mind jazzed-up images and incoherent sound.

wd Stanley Kubrick, *novel* Anthony Burgess ph John Alcott m Walter Carlos pd John Barry

Malcolm McDowell, Michael Bates, Adrienne Corri, Patrick Magee, Warren Clarke
    'Very early there are hints of triteness and insecurity, and before half an hour is over it begins to slip into tedium . . . Inexplicably the script leaves out Burgess' reference to the title.'—*Stanley Kauffmann*
    'It might be the work of a strict and exacting German professor who set out to make a porno violent sci-fi comedy.'—*New Yorker, 1980*

AAN: best picture; Stanley Kubrick (as writer and director)

'We are not alone . . .
Close Encounters of the Third Kind*
US 1977 135m Metrocolor Panavision
Columbia / EMI (Julia and Michael Phillips)

A series of UFOs takes Indiana by surprise, and a workman is led by intuition and

detection to the landing site which has been
concealed from the public.
There's a lot of padding in this slender fantasy,
which has less plot and much less suspense
than *It Came from Outer Space* which was
made on a tiny budget in 1955; but the
technical effects are masterly though their
exposure is over-prolonged, and the
benevolent mysticism filled a current
requirement of popular taste, accounting for
the enormous box-office success of a basically
flawed film. Much of the dialogue is inaudible.

wd Steven Spielberg *ph* Vilmos Zsigmond
m John Williams *sp* Douglas Trumbull
pd Joe Alves

Richard Dreyfuss, Françoise Truffaut, Teri
Garr, Melinda Dillon, Cary Guffey

'It somehow combines Disney and 1950s SF
and junk food into the most persuasive (if
arrested) version of the American dream
yet.'—*Time Out*

† The cost of this film was estimated at
20,000,000 dollars.

†† In 1980 a 'special edition' was released with
some success: this pared down the idiotic
middle section and extended the final scenes of
the space ship, including some new interiors.

††† This film used the largest set in film
history: the inside of an old dirigible hangar.

Of the special edition, Derek Malcolm in the
Guardian wrote: 'One is inclined to feel that
with all the money at his disposal, Spielberg
might have got it right the first time.'

AA: Vilmos Zsigmond
AAN: direction; John Williams; Melinda
Dillon

Close to My Heart
US 1951   90m   bw
Warner (William Jacobs)

An adopted baby is discovered to have a
murderer for a father; but environment is
proved to be more important than heredity.
Routine sentimental drama.

wd William Keighley, *story* A Baby for Midge
by James R. Webb *ph* Robert Burks *m* Max
Steiner

Ray Milland, Gene Tierney, Fay Bainter,
Howard St John, Mary Beth Hughes

Closely Observed Trains**
Czechoslovakia 1966   92m   bw
Ceskoslovensky Film (Zdenek Oves)

During World War II, an apprentice railway
guard at a country station falls in love and
becomes a saboteur.
Warm, amusingly detailed comedy with a
disconcerting downbeat ending.

wd Jiri Menzel, *novel* Bohumil Hrabal
ph Jaromir Sofr *m* Jiri Pavlik

Vaclav Neckar, Jitka Bendova, Vladimir
Valenta, Josef Somr

'Like Forman, Menzel seems incapable of
being unkind to anybody.'—*Tom Milne*

AA: best foreign film

Cloud Dancer
US 1977   108m   colour

Episodes in the life of a stunt flyer.
Technically proficient, loosely assembled
amble through the problems of a man with an
obsession for danger; not a great crowd-puller.
David Carradine, Jennifer O'Neill, Joseph
Bottoms, Albert Salmi, Salome Jens, Colleen
Camp. Written by William Goodhart; directed
by Barry Brown; for Melvin Simon.

Cloudburst
GB 1951   92m   bw

A vengeful code expert goes after the
criminals who ran down his wife in making a
getaway. Watchable potboiler. Robert
Preston, Elizabeth Sellars, Colin Tapley,
Sheila Burrell, Harold Lang. Written by Leo
Marks; directed by Francis Searle; for
Hammer.

The Clouded Yellow*
GB 1950   96m   bw
Sydney Box (Betty Box)

A sacked secret service agent gets work
tending a butterfly collection and finds that
this involves him in a murder plot.
Implausible but quite engaging thriller in the
Hitchcock style, involving a chase across the
Lake District.

w Janet Green, Eric Ambler *d* Ralph
Thomas *ph* Geoffrey Unsworth

Trevor Howard, Jean Simmons, Barry Jones,
Sonia Dresdel, Maxwell Reed, Kenneth More,
André Morell

The Clown
US 1952   91m   bw
MGM (William H. Wright)

A drunken clown, once a great star, is idolized
by his son who believes in a comeback.
Maudlin reworking of *The Champ* (qv), with
not a surprise in the plot and a star way over
the top.

w Martin Rackin *d* Robert Z. Leonard
ph Paul C. Vogel *m* David Rose

Red Skelton, Jane Greer, Tim Considine,
Loring Smith, Philip Ober

Club Havana
US 1946   62m   bw

Several stories come to a head in a night club.
Slight musical multi-drama with moments of
interest. Tom Neal, Margaret Lindsay, Don
Douglas, Isabelita, Ernest Truex, Renee
Riano, Paul Cavanagh, Marc Lawrence.
Written by Raymond L. Schrock and Fred
Jackson; directed by Edgar G. Ulmer; for
PRC.

Cluny Brown**
US 1946   100m   bw
TCF (Ernst Lubitsch)

A plumber's niece goes into service and falls
for a Czech refugee guest.
Romantic comedy in a never-never pre-war
England; it does no more than poke casual fun
at upper-class conventions, but the smooth
direction and some excellent character comedy
keep it well afloat.

w Samuel Hoffenstein, Elizabeth Reinhardt,
novel Margery Sharp *d* Ernst Lubitsch
ph Joseph La Shelle *m* Cyril Mockridge, Emil
Newman

Jennifer Jones, Charles Boyer, *Richard
Haydn, Una O'Connor*, Peter Lawford, Helen
Walker, Reginald Gardiner, Reginald Owen,
C. Aubrey Smith, Sara Allgood, Ernest
Cossart, Florence Bates, Billy Bevan

'A lovely, easygoing comedy, full of small
surprising touches.'—*Pauline Kael, 70s*

Coal Miner's Daughter*
US 1980   124m   Technicolor
Universal (Bob Larson)

The wife of a Kentucky hillbilly becomes a
pop star.
'With-it' version of the old show business
story: gradual success, stardom, nervous
breakdown, reconciliation. Based on the life
of Loretta Lynn, but mainly notable for its
depiction of backwoods Kentucky.

w Tom Rickman *d* Michael Apted *ph* Ralf D.
Bode *md* Owen Bradley *pd* John W. Corso

Sissy Spacek, Tommy Lee Jones, Levon Helm,
Jennifer Beasley, Phyllis Boyens

AA: Sissy Spacek
AAN: best film; Tom Rickman; Ralf D. Bode;
editing (Arthur Schmidt); art direction (John
W. Corso, John M. Dwyer)

Coast to Coast
US 1980   94m   Movielab
Paramount (Terry Carr)

A Los Angeles wife flees her husband and
hitches a lift from a truck driver with
problems.
Comedy for easy watching: pleasant characters
are given very little of interest to do.

w Stanley Weiser *d* Joseph Sargent *ph* Joel
King *m* Charles Bernstein

Dyan Cannon, Robert Blake, Quinn Redeker,
Michael Lerner, Bill Lucking, Maxine Stuart

Cobra Woman
US 1944   71m   Technicolor
U-I (George Waggner)

A South Seas girl is abducted by snake
worshippers ruled by her evil twin.
A monument of undiluted hokum with some
amusing sets and performances but not enough
self-mockery in the script.

w Richard Brooks, Gene Lewis *d* Robert
Siodmak *ph* George Robinson, W. Howard
Greene *m* Edward Ward

Maria Montez, Jon Hall, Sabu, Lon Chaney
Jnr, Mary Nash, Edgar Barrier, Lois Collier,
Samuel S. Hinds, Moroni Olsen

'Among the exotic treats: a rumbling
volcano, a pet chim, ominous gong sounds,
forest glade love scenes, human sacrifices,
handmaidens in high-heeled pumps, Tollea's
imperious writhing during a demonic dance,
and the good Nadja's plea for the symbol of
the power that is rightly hers: "Gif me the
cobra jool." '—*Pauline Kael, 70s*

The Cobweb
US 1955 124m Eastmancolor
Cinemascope
MGM (John Houseman)

Tensions among the staff of a private mental clinic reach a new high over the purchase of curtains.
The patients seem saner than the doctors in this strained and verbose character drama which despite its cast and big studio look never begins to engage the interest.

w John Paxton, novel William Gibson
d Vincente Minnelli ph George Folsey
m Leonard Rosenman

Richard Widmark, Lauren Bacall, Charles Boyer, Lillian Gish, Gloria Grahame, John Kerr, Susan Strasberg, Oscar Levant, Tommy Rettig, Paul Stewart, Adèle Jergens
'An overwrought and elaborately artificial exercise, made scarcely more plausible by reliance on the basic jargon of psychiatry.'—Penelope Houston
'By the mid-50s, nobody was surprised that the new variant on Grand Hotel was an expensive, exclusive loony bin.'—Pauline Kael, 70s

Cockeyed Cavaliers
US 1934 72m bw

Two idiots have various adventures in medieval England. Fairly tolerable slapstick from a team which never seemed quite at its best. Bert Wheeler, Robert Woolsey, Thelma Todd, Noah Beery, Dorothy Lee, Franklyn Pangborn, Robert Greig. Written by Edward Kaufman, Ben Holmes; directed by Mark Sandrich; for RKO. 'With a fair quota of laughs, it eclipses their previous releases.'—Variety

The Cockeyed Cowboys of Calico County
US 1969 99m Technicolor

A western blacksmith stops working when his mail order bride doesn't arrive. Styleless American rehash of La Femme du Boulanger, with all concerned trying too hard. Dan Blocker, Nanette Fabray, Mickey Rooney. Written by Ranald MacDougall; directed by Tony Leader; for Universal.

The Cockeyed Miracle
US 1946 92m bw

Family ghosts return to sort out domestic chaos. Moderate 'Topper'-style comedy with amiable cast: Frank Morgan, Cecil Kellaway, Gladys Cooper, Audrey Totter, Marshall Thompson, Leon Ames. Written by Karen de Wolf, from a play by George Seaton; directed by S. Sylvan Simon; for MGM. (GB title: Mr Griggs Returns.)

The Cockeyed World*
US 1929 115m bw
Fox

Further adventures of Sergeants Flagg and Quirt, the boisterous heroes of What Price Glory.

Lively early talkie; the adventure comedy remains interesting, though the technique is badly faded.

w William K. Wells, Laurence Stallings, Michael Anderson, Wilson Mizner, Tom Barry d Raoul Walsh ph Arthur Edeson

Victor McLaglen, Edmund Lowe, Lili Damita, Lelia Karnelly, El Brendel, Bobby Burns, Stuart Erwin

Cockfighter
US 1974 83m Metrocolor
Rio Pinto / New World / Artists
Entertainment Complex (Roger Corman)
aka: Born to Kill

A professional cockfighter ends a run of bad luck but loses his girl.
Not badly made but rather seedy film about appalling people.

w Charles Willeford, from his novel d Monte Hellman ph Nestor Almendros m Michael Franks

Warren Oates, Richard B. Shull, Harry Dean Stanton, Ed Begley Jnr, Laurie Bird, Troy Donahue

Cockleshell Heroes
GB 1955 97m Technicolor
Cinemascope
Columbia / Warwick (Phil C. Samuel)

During World War II, ten marines are trained to travel by canoe into Bordeaux harbour and attach limpet mines to German ships.
Absolutely predictable semi-documentary war heroics, with barrack-room humour turning eventually into tragedy. The familiar elements, including a display of stiff upper lips, ensured box office success.

w Bryan Forbes, Richard Maibaum d Jose Ferrer ph John Wilcox, Ted Moore m John Addison

Jose Ferrer, Trevor Howard, Dora Bryan, Victor Maddern, Anthony Newley, Peter Arne, David Lodge, Walter Fitzgerald, Beatrice Campbell

Cocoanut Grove
US 1938 85m bw
Paramount (George Arthur)

A band is fired from an excursion boat but makes it big in a Los Angeles night club.
Vacuous comedy musical with a watchable number or two.

w Sy Bartlett, Olive Cooper d Alfred Santell ph Leo Tover songs various

Fred MacMurray, Harriet Hilliard, The Yacht Club Boys, Ben Blue, Eve Arden, Billy Lee, Rufe Davis
'No mind-wearier as to plot, it shapes up as nice summer film fare.'—Variety

The Cocoanuts**
US 1929 96m bw
Paramount (Walter Wanger, James R. Cown)

A chiselling hotel manager tries to get in on the Florida land boom.
Considering its age and the dismal prints which remain, this is a remarkably lively if

primitive first film by the Marxes, with some good routines among the excess footage.

w George S. Kaufman, Morrie Ryskind d Robert Florey, Joseph Santley ph George Folsey m / ly Irving Berlin

The Four Marx Brothers, Margaret Dumont, Oscar Shaw, Mary Eaton, Kay Francis, Basil Ruysdael
'The camerawork showed all the mobility of a concrete fire hydrant caught in a winter freeze.'—Paul D. Zimmermann

Code of the Secret Service
US 1939 58m bw

Agents track a gang who stole treasury banknote plates. Serial-like adventures, one of several from the same stable, all featuring the future president of the US. Ronald Reagan, Eddie Foy Jnr, Rosella Towne, Moroni Olsen, Edgar Edwards. Written by Lee Katz, Dean Franklin; directed by Noel Smith; for Warners. 'Filler fodder; a wild actioner for lower dual bookings.'—Variety

The Cohens and the Kellys

Seven comedies were made, all for Universal, about the friendly rivalry of Jewish and Irish neighbours. They were:
1927: THE COHENS AND KELLYS IN NEW YORK
1928: THE COHENS AND KELLYS IN PARIS
1929: THE COHENS AND KELLYS IN ATLANTIC CITY
1930: THE COHENS AND KELLYS IN SCOTLAND, THE COHENS AND KELLYS IN AFRICA, THE COHENS AND KELLYS IN HOLLYWOOD
1933: THE COHENS AND KELLYS IN TROUBLE
In all cases the leading roles were played by Charles Murray and George Sidney

Coiffeur pour Dames
France 1952 87m approx bw
Hoche (Jean Boyer)
GB title: An Artist with Ladies

A Provençal sheep shearer becomes a fashionable ladies' hairdresser with a Champs-Élysées salon, and finds that his clients are all susceptible to his charms.
Obvious star comedy with a fair measure of laughs; more in fact than the much later Shampoo.

w Serge Véber, Jean Boyer, play P. Armont, M. Gerbidon d Jean Boyer ph Charles Suin m Paul Misraki

Fernandel, Blanchette Crunoy, Renée Devillers, Arlette Poirier

Cold Turkey*
US 1970 102m De Luxe
UA / Tandem / DFI (Bud Yorkin, Norman Lear)

A tobacco company offers 25 million dollars to any town which can give up smoking for thirty days.

THE COCOANUTS.   Probably the earliest all-talking film which can still be revived without too much audience discomfort.

Rather wild and strained but sporadically amusing satirical comedy, aggressively littered with unpleasant detail.

w Norman Lear, *novel* I'm Giving Them Up for Good by Margaret and Neil Rau
d Norman Lear *ph* Charles F. Wheeler
m Randy Newman

Dick Van Dyke, Pippa Scott, Tom Poston, Edward Everett Horton, Bob Newhart, Vincent Gardenia, Jean Stapleton
  'An eager desire to debunk and shock at the same time.'—*David McGillivray*

A Cold Wind in August*
US 1960 77m bw
UA / Troy Films (Robert L. Ross, Philip Hazleton)

An ageing stripper seduces a 17-year-old janitor but the affair ends when he sees her do her act.
Roughly-made, well-acted sex drama which at the time seemed mildly shocking but can only survive for its central acting performance.

w Burton Wohl, from his novel *d* Alexander Singer *ph* Floyd Crosby *m* Gerald Fried
Lola Albright, Scott Marlowe, Joe de Santis, Herschel Bernardi

The Colditz Story**
GB 1954 97m bw
British Lion / Ivan Foxwell

Adventures of British POWs in the German maximum security prison in Saxony's Colditz Castle during World War II.
Probably the most convincing of the British accounts of POW life, with a careful balance of tragedy and comedy against a background of humdrum, boring daily existence. A TV series followed in 1972.

w Guy Hamilton, Ivan Foxwell, *book* P. R. Reid *d* Guy Hamilton *ph* Gordon Dines *m* Francis Chagrin

John Mills, Eric Portman, Christopher Rhodes, Lionel Jeffries, Bryan Forbes, Ian Carmichael, Richard Wattis, Frederick Valk, Anton Diffring, Eugene Deckers, Theodore Bikel

'It has all the realism, dignity and courage of the men it commemorates.'—*News of the World*
● *Video: Thorn EMI*

'You won't dare open your mouth, but you'll be screaming for her to escape!'
The Collector*
US 1965 119m Technicolor
Columbia (Jud Kinberg, John Kohn)

An inhibited young butterfly specialist kidnaps a girl to add to his collection.
Talkative and unrewarding suspenser with pretensions, sluggishly handled and not very interestingly acted.

w Stanley Mann, John Kohn, *novel* John Fowles *d* William Wyler *ph* Robert L. Surtees, Robert Krasker *m* Maurice Jarre

Terence Stamp, Samantha Eggar, Mona Washbourne

AAN: Stanley Mann, John Kohn; William Wyler; Samantha Eggar

Colleen*
US 1936 89m bw
Warner (Robert Lord)

Boy meets Irish girl in New York.
Typical light musical of the period with standard studio talent.

w Peter Milne, F. Hugh Herbert, Sig Herzig
d Alfred E. Green ph Byron Haskin, Sol Polito m / ly Harry Warren, Al Dubin
ch Bobby Connolly gowns Orry-Kelly

Dick Powell, Ruby Keeler, Jack Oakie, Joan Blondell, Hugh Herbert, Louise Fazenda, Paul Draper, Marie Wilson, Luis Alberni, Hobart Cavanaugh, Berton Churchill

College*
US 1927 65m (24 fps) bw silent
Buster Keaton Productions (Joseph M. Schenck)

A brainy high school student becomes a college football star.
Disappointing comedy from this great stone-faced clown: the plums are there, but few and far between.

w Carl Harbaugh, Bryan Foy d James W. Horne ph J. Devereux Jennings, Bert Haines

Buster Keaton, Ann Cornwall, Harold Goodwin, Snitz Edwards, Florence Turner

● Video: Polygram

College Coach
US 1933 75m bw

A tough football coach finds that his best star is a timid chemistry student. Unremarkable studio programmer despite a strong cast. Dick Powell, Pat O'Brien, Ann Dvorak, Arthur Byron, Lyle Talbot, Hugh Herbert, Guinn Williams, Donald Meek. Written by Niven Busch, Manuel Seff; directed by William A. Wellman; for Warners. 'Hasn't enough punch for real sock grosses.'—Variety

College Holiday
US 1936 87m bw
Paramount (Harlan Thompson)

Bright young specimens are invited to spend a summer with a lady hotelier interested in eugenics.
Boisterous fun and games which may have seemed funny at the time.

w J. P. McEvoy, Harlan Ware, Jay Gorney, Henry Myers d Frank Tuttle ph Theodor Sparkuhl songs various

Jack Benny, George Burns, Gracie Allen, Mary Boland, Martha Raye, Etienne Girardot, Marsha Hunt, Leif Erickson, Eleanore Whitney, Johnny Downs, Olympe Bradna, Ben Blue, Jed Prouty
'For a picture that permits the cast to run around practically on the loose, it gets along remarkably well.'—Variety

College Humor
US 1933 84m bw
Paramount

A freshman discovers that football and necking are at least as important as studies.
Easy-going comedy-musical which helped to establish its star.

w Claude Binyon, Frank Butler, story Dean Fales d Wesley Ruggles ph Leo Tover

Bing Crosby, Jack Oakie, George Burns, Gracie Allen, Richard Arlen, Mary Carlisle
'A light frothy musical that doesn't give the customers much of a mental workout.'—Variety

College Rhythm
US 1934 75m bw

A college football team fights to help an old-fashioned department store to modernize itself. Of its time, a pleasant 'youth' movie, but with nothing for posterity. Jack Oakie, Joe Penner, Mary Brian, Lanny Ross, Helen Mack, Lyda Roberti, George Barbier, Franklin Pangborn, Dean Jagger. Written by Walter De Leon, John McDermott, Francis Martin, George Marion Jnr; directed by Norman Taurog; for Paramount. 'Entertaining semi-musical with bright box-office possibilities.'—Variety
† Songs, composed by Mack Gordon and Harry Revel, include: 'Stay as Sweet as you Are'; 'Goo Goo'; 'Let's Give Three Cheers for Love'; 'Take a Number from One to Ten'.

College Scandal
US 1935 75m bw

A killer attacks three male students. After College Humor and College Rhythm, this amounts to College Murder. With stars, it could have been memorable. Arline Judge, Kent Taylor, Wendy Barrie, Mary Nash, William Stack, William Frawley, Benny Baker, Johnny Downs. Written by Frank Partos, Charles Brackett, Marguerite Roberts; directed by Elliott Nugent; for Paramount. 'Worthwhile summer fare for high-grade dual houses.'—Variety

College Swing
US 1938 86m bw
Paramount (Lewis Gensler)
GB title: Swing, Teacher, Swing

A dumb girl must graduate if a college is to inherit a fortune.
Mild comedy more notable for its cast than its script.

w Walter de Leon, Francis Martin d Raoul Walsh ph Victor Milner songs various

George Burns, Gracie Allen, Martha Raye, Bob Hope, Edward Everett Horton, Florence George, Ben Blue, Betty Grable, Jackie Coogan, John Payne, Cecil Cunningham, Robert Cummings
'A medley of vaude specialties, bits and numbers strung together in not too happy a manner.'—Variety

Collegiate
US 1935 80m bw

A girls' college is kept going by the whim of an amnesiac. Mild comedy in the vein of College

Rhythm. Jack Oakie, Joe Penner, Frances Langford, Ned Sparks, Betty Grable, Lynne Overman, Mack Gordon, Harry Revel, Julius Tannen. Written by Walter de Leon, Francis Martin, from the play The Charm School by Alice Duer Miller; directed by Ralph Murphy; for Paramount. 'Light, diverting, no sock, but no bore.'—Variety

Colonel Effingham's Raid
US 1946 70m bw
TCF (Lamar Trotti)
GB title: Man of the Hour

A retired southern colonel tries to straighten out a corrupt Georgia town.
Competent, unsurprising programmer.

w Kathryn Scola, novel Berry Fleming
d Irving Pichel ph Edward Cronjager
m Cyril Mockridge

Charles Coburn, Joan Bennett, William Eythe, Allyn Joslyn, Elizabeth Patterson, Donald Meek, Frank Craven, Thurston Hall, Cora Witherspoon, Emory Parnell, Henry Armetta, Roy Roberts, Charles Trowbridge

Colorado Territory*
US 1949 93m bw
Warner (Anthony Veiller)

An outlaw escapes from prison planning one last robbery but is shot in the attempt.
Moderate western remake of High Sierra.

w John Twist, Edmund H. North d Raoul Walsh ph Sid Hickox m David Buttolph

Joel McCrea, Virginia Mayo, Dorothy Malone, Henry Hull, John Archer, James Mitchell, Morris Ankrum, Basil Ruysdael, Frank Puglia

The Colossus of New York
US 1958 70m bw

An international scientist is killed in an accident; his father puts his brain into a robot, which goes on the rampage. Absurd horror comic for kids, with hilariously unexplained detail and poor technical effects. Otto Kruger, Ross Martin, Robert Hutton, John Baragrey, Mala Powers. Written by Thelma Schnee; directed by Eugene Lourie; for William Alland / Paramount.

The Colossus of Rhodes
Italy 1960 129m Technicolor
SuperTotalScope

In 300 BC, a huge statue doubles as a fortress to prevent the Phoenicians from invading. Good-looking spectacle with the usual muddled script. Rory Calhoun, Lea Massari, Georges Marchal. Written by Sergio Leone and seven others; directed by Sergio Leone; for Michele Scaglione / MGM.

Colt 45
US 1950 74m Technicolor

A new kind of gun, intended to bring law and order to the west, gets into the wrong hands. Routine, watchable western which achieved a surprising popularity. Randolph Scott, Zachary Scott, Ruth Roman, Lloyd Bridges.

Written by Thomas Blackburn; directed by Edwin L. Marin; for Warner. (American TV title: *Thundercloud*.)

Coma*
US 1978 113m Metrocolor
MGM (Martin Erlichman)

A lady doctor suspects that patients are being put deliberately into coma so that their organs can be sold, and finds herself in deadly peril. Hitchcockian suspense thriller with nobody but the audience believing the heroine; the fact that there are more dead than living characters makes it slightly too ghoulish at times.

wd Michael Crichton, *novel* Robin Cook *ph* Victor J. Kemper, Gerald Hirschfeld *m* Jerry Goldsmith *pd* Albert Brenner

Geneviève Bujold, Michael Douglas, Richard Widmark, Elizabeth Ashley, Rip Torn, Lois Chiles, Harry Rhodes

● *Video: MGM / UA*

Comanche
US 1955 87m De Luxe Cinemascope

In 1875 New Mexico, a renegade Indian prevents peace between white and red man. Cheerful action western, satisfying to the easily pleased. Dana Adrews, Kent Smith, Nestor Paiva, Henry Brandon, John Litel, Lowell Gilmore, Mike Mazurki. Written by Carl Krueger; directed by George Sherman; for Carl Krueger / UA.

Comanche Station
US 1960 74m Technicolor
Cinemascope

A man seeks his wife, taken prisoner by Indians. Below par star western, indifferently plotted. Randolph Scott, Nancy Gates, Claude Akins, Skip Homeier. Written by Burt Kennedy; directed by Budd Boetticher; for Harry Joe Brown / Columbia.

Comanche Territory
US 1950 76m Technicolor

Jim Bowie assists the Comanches against treacherous whites. Double bill western, adequate for its purpose. Maureen O'Hara, Macdonald Carey, Will Geer, Charles Drake. Written by Oscar Brodney and Louis Meltzer; directed by George Sherman; for Universal-International.

The Comancheros**
US 1961 107m De Luxe Cinemascope
TCF (George Sherman)

A Texas Ranger and his gambler prisoner join forces to clean up renegade gunmen operating from a remote armed compound.
Easy-going, cheerfully violent western with lively roughhouse sequences.

w James Edward Grant, Clair Huffaker *d* Michael Curtiz *ph* William H. Clothier *m* Elmer Bernstein

John Wayne, Stuart Whitman, Nehemiah Persoff, Lee Marvin, Ina Balin, Bruce Cabot

Come and Get It*
US 1936 99m bw
Samuel Goldwyn (Merritt Hulburd)

The life and loves of a lumber tycoon in 19th-century Wisconsin.

Disappointingly conventional, mainly studio-bound action drama using top talent of the period.

w Jules Furthman, Jane Murfin, *novel* Edna Ferber *d* Howard Hawks, William Wyler *ph* Gregg Toland, Rudolph Maté *m* Alfred Newman

Edward Arnold, Joel McCrea, Frances Farmer, Walter Brennan, Andrea Leeds

AA: Walter Brennan

Come Back Charleston Blue*
US 1972 101m Technicolor
Warner / Formosa (Samuel Goldwyn Jnr)

Harlem detectives Coffin Ed Johnson and Gravedigger Jones investigate the case of a long-dead gangster who seems to be still taking vengeance.
Occasionally funny but disturbingly violent crime kaleidoscope with a black ambience, more sophisticated and therefore more generally acceptable than its predecessor *Cotton Comes to Harlem* (qv).

w Bontche Schweig, Peggy Elliott, *novel* The Heat's On by Chester Himes *d* Mark Warren *ph* Dick Kratina *m* Donny Hathaway

Godfrey Cambridge, Raymond St Jacques, Peter de Anda, Jonelle Allen, Percy Rodrigues, Minny Gentry

'That girl in their house spelled trouble!'
Come Back Little Sheba*
US 1952 99m bw
Paramount (Hal B. Wallis)

An ex-alcoholic is let down not only by his slovenly wife but by the young girl he idolizes. Stagey but theatrically effective transcription of a popular domestic drama, with one outstanding performance.

w Ketti Frings, *play William Inge d* Daniel Mann *ph* James Wong Howe *m* Franz Waxman

Shirley Booth, Burt Lancaster, Terry Moore, Richard Jaeckel

AA: Shirley Booth
AAN: Terry Moore

Come Back to the Five and Dime, Jimmy Dean, Jimmy Dean
US 1983 110m Du Art Color
Sandcastle 5 / Mark Goodman / Viacom

Misfits meet to celebrate the twentieth anniversary of the death of James Dean. Filmed play which descends from cynicism through gloom to hysteria and is never very revealing.

w Ed Graczyk, from his play *d* Robert Altman *ph* Pierre Mignot *m* various

Sandy Dennis, Karen Black, Cher, Sudie Bond, Kathy Bates

'It may seem perverse to describe as Altman's masterpiece so self-contained and "alien" a work, with an existence pre-dating his own involvement and a thrusting (if perverse) biological life that owes nothing to the audience's willingness to participate. But the irony depends solely on which side of Altman's own two-way world one stands.'— *Richard Combs, MFB*

Come Blow Your Horn*
US 1962 112m Technicolor
Panavision
Paramount / Lear and Yorkin

A country boy in New York is envious of his older brother's sophisticated life.
Amusing characters and funny lines permeate this stolid transcription of an early Neil Simon success; the big screen is not the place for them.

w Norman Lear, *play Neil Simon d* Bud Yorkin *ph* William Daniels *m* Nelson Riddle

Frank Sinatra, Tony Bill, Lee J. Cobb, Molly Picon, Jill St John, Barbara Rush, Dan Blocker

Come Clean**
US 1931 20m bw

Two much-married men go out for ice-cream and bring back a woman of the streets they have saved from suicide. Splendid star comedy with the famous characterizations fully rounded. Laurel and Hardy, Mae Busch, Charlie Hall, Gertrude Astor, Linda Loredo. Written by H. M. Walker; directed by James W. Horne; for Hal Roach. (NB: Remade in 1942 as *Brooklyn Orchid*, with William Bendix and Joe Sawyer.)

Come Fill the Cup*
US 1951 113m bw
Warner (Henry Blanke)

An alcoholic newspaperman cures himself, then his boss's alcoholic son who is involved with gangsters.
Unlikely but solidly entertaining melodrama, powerfully cast.

w Ivan Goff, Ben Roberts, *novel* Harlan Ware *d* Gordon Douglas *ph Robert Burks m* Ray Heindorf

James Cagney, Gig Young, Raymond Massey, Phyllis Thaxter, James Gleason, Selena Royle, Larry Keating

AAN: Gig Young

Come Fly with Me
US 1962 109m Metrocolor Panavision
MGM / Anatole de Grunwald

The romantic adventures of three air hostesses.
Good-looking girls and airplanes but little else make thin entertainment.

w William Roberts *d* Henry Levin *ph* Oswald Morris *m* Lyn Murray

Hugh O'Brian, Dolores Hart, Karl Malden, Pamela Tiffin, Lois Nettleton, Karl Boehm

Come Live with Me*
US 1941 86m bw
MGM (Clarence Brown)

In order to stay in America, a girl refugee from Vienna arranges a strictly platonic marriage with a struggling author.
Hypnotically predictable comedy, quite well presented and performed.

w Patterson McNutt, Virginia Van Upp *d* Clarence Brown *ph* George Folsey *m* Herbert Stothart

James Stewart, Hedy Lamarr, Ian Hunter, Verree Teasdale, Donald Meek, Barton MacLane, *Adeline de Walt Reynolds*

Come Next Spring*

US 1955 92m Trucolor
Republic

A drunkard returns to his Arkansas farm family and wins the respect of them and the community.

D. W. Griffith-type pastoral melodrama which surprisingly works pretty well and leaves one with the intended warm glow.

w Montgomery Pittman d R. G. Springsteen
ph Jack Marta m Max Steiner

Ann Sheridan, Steve Cochran, Walter Brennan, Sherry Jackson, Richard Eyer, Edgar Buchanan, Sonny Tufts, Mae Clarke
   'An unpretentious film with a good deal of charm.'—*MFB*

The Come On

US 1956 83m bw Superscope
AA (Lindley Parsons)

Husband and wife confidence tricksters get homicidal when she falls in love.

In trade parlance, strictly a lower berth item; but with points of mild interest.

w Warren Douglas, *novel* Whitman Chambers d Russell Birdwell ph Ernest Haller m Paul Dunlap

Anne Baxter, Sterling Hayden, John Hoyt, Jesse White, Paul Picerni

Come on George*

GB 1939 88m bw
ATP / Ealing (Jack Kitchin)

A stableboy calms a nervous racehorse and rides him to victory.

Standard comedy vehicle, well mounted, with the star at his box office peak.

w Anthony Kimmins, Leslie Arliss, Val Valentine d Anthony Kimmins ph Ronald Neame, Gordon Dines m Ernest Irving

George Formby, Pat Kirkwood, Joss Ambler, Meriel Forbes, Cyril Raymond, George Carney, Ronald Shiner

Come Out of the Pantry

GB 1935 73m bw

An English milord is forced by circumstance to take a job as his boss's footman. Pleasing if obvious comedy, later remodelled as *Spring in Park Lane*. Jack Buchanan, Fay Wray, James Carew, Ronald Squire, Olive Blakeney, Fred Emney. Written by Austin Parker from a story by Alice Duer Miller; directed by Jack Raymond; for British and Dominions.

Come September

US 1961 112m Technicolor
CinemaScope
Universal / 7 Pictures Corporation / Raoul Walsh Enterprises (Robert Arthur)

A wealthy American discovers that his Italian villa is being used as a hotel by his once-a-year mistress, who is about to marry.

Clumsy sex farce with lush trimmings and generation gap asides; effort more noticeable than achievement.

w Stanley Shapiro, Maurice Richlin d Robert Mulligan ph William Daniels m Hans J. Salter

Rock Hudson, Gina Lollobrigida, Sandra Dee, Bobby Darin, Walter Slezak, Brenda de Banzie, Joel Grey, Rosanna Rory, Ronald Howard

Come to the Stable*

US 1949 94m bw
TCF (Samuel G. Engel)

Two French nuns arrive in New England to build a local hospital, and melt the hearts of the local grumps.

This old-time charmer simply brims with sweetness and light and is produced with high-class studio efficiency.

w Oscar Millard, Sally Benson, *story* Clare Boothe Luce d Henry Koster ph Joseph La Shelle md Lionel Newman m Cyril Mockridge

Loretta Young, Celeste Holm, Hugh Marlowe, Elsa Lanchester, Thomas Gomez, Dorothy Patrick, Basil Ruysdael, Dooley Wilson, Regis Toomey, Henri Letondal

AAN: Clare Boothe Luce; Joseph La Shelle; Loretta Young; Celeste Holm; Elsa Lanchester; song 'Through a Long and Sleepless Night' (m Alfred Newman, ly Mack Gordon)

The Comedians*

US / Bermuda / France 1967 160m
   Metrocolor Panavision
MGM / Maximilian / Trianon (Peter
   Glenville)

A variety of English-speaking eccentrics are caught up in the violent events of Haiti under Papa Doc Duvalier.

Clumsy and heavy-going compression of a too-topical novel, with most of the plot left in at the expense of character. Neither entertaining nor instructive, but bits of acting please.

w Graham Greene, from his novel d Peter Glenville ph Henri Decaë m Laurence Rosenthal

Richard Burton, Elizabeth Taylor, *Alec Guinness*, Peter Ustinov, Lillian Gish, Paul Ford, Roscoe Lee Browne, James Earl Jones, Raymond St Jacques, Cicely Tyson
   'So thick and fast do the clichés come that one feels the script can only have been salvaged from some *New Statesman* competition.'—*Tom Milne*
   'It's pleasant to spend two hours again in Greenland, still well-stocked with bilious minor crucifixions, furtive fornication, cynical politics, and reluctant hope.'—*Stanley Kauffmann*

The Comedy Man*

GB 1964 92m bw
British Lion–Gray–Consort (Jon
   Pennington)

A middle-aged actor on the skids desperately rounds up his contacts and becomes the star of a TV commercial.

Determinedly depressing satirical melodrama with engaging moments; comedy emphasis would have better suited the talents.

w Peter Yeldham, *novel* Douglas Hayes
d Alvin Rakoff ph Ken Hodges m Bill McGuffie

Kenneth More, Cecil Parker, Dennis Price, Billie Whitelaw, Norman Rossington, Angela Douglas, Edmund Purdom, Frank Finlay, Alan Dobie

The Comedy of Terrors*

US 1963 88m Pathecolor Panavision
Alta Vista / AIP (Anthony Carras, Richard
   Matheson)

Two impecunious funeral directors decide to speed up the demise of their prospective clients.

Disappointingly slackly-handled and rather tiresome macabre frolic, notable for a few splendid moments and an imperishable cast.

w Richard Matheson d Jacques Tourneur
ph Floyd Crosby m Les Baxter

Vincent Price, Peter Lorre, Boris Karloff, Basil Rathbone, Joe E. Brown, Joyce Jameson

Comes a Horseman

US 1978 118m Technicolor
Panavision
UA / Chartoff-Winkler (Robert Caan)

In the forties, Montana ranchers have a hard time holding onto their land against the pressures of progress and a villainous cattle baron.

Portentous and wholly unexciting modern western, not helped by a loftily unexplained title and show-off photography.

w Dennis Lynton Clark d Alan J. Pakula
ph Gordon Willis m Michael Small
pd George Jenkins

Jane Fonda, Jason Robards Jnr, James Caan, George Grizzard, Richard Farnsworth, Jim Davis
   'It's a film of few words (and about a quarter of them mangled by the sound recording). The melodrama is smothered under sullen, overcast skies. How can you get involved in the conflict between the good guys and the bad guys if you can't even see them?'—*Pauline Kael*
● Video: Warner

Comet over Broadway

US 1938 65m bw

An actress, having been involved in a murder, is torn between burning ambition and mother love. Arrant melodrama which overtaxes its star. Kay Francis, Ian Hunter, John Litel, Donald Crisp, Minna Gombell, Sybil Jason, Melville Cooper. Written by Mark Hellinger and Robert Buckner, from a story by Faith Baldwin; directed by Busby Berkeley; for Warners. 'A backstage yarn that goes overboard on assorted heartbreaks.'—*Variety*

Comfort and Joy*

GB 1984 106m colour
Lake / EMI / STV (Davina Belling, Clive
   Parsons)

A Scottish radio disc jockey becomes involved in a war between two ice-cream firms.

Heavy comedy, short of laughs and sympathy; a distinct descent from *Local Hero*, which was a comedown after *Gregory's Girl*.

w,d Bill Forsyth *ph* Chris Menges *m* Mark Knopfler

Bill Paterson, Eleanor David, C. P. Grogan, Alex Norton

The Comic**
US 1969 95m Technicolor
Columbia (Carl Reiner)

The success, downfall and old age of a silent film comedian in Hollywood.
Remarkably bright and cinematic tragi-comedy obviously based on Buster Keaton, with a *Citizen Kane*-type framework. Not a commercial success, but a must for professionals.

w Carl Reiner, Aaron Rubin *d* Carl Reiner *ph* W. Wallace Kelley *m* Jack Elliott

Dick Van Dyke, Mickey Rooney (more or less playing Ben Turpin), Cornel Wilde, Carl Reiner, Michele Lee, Pert Kelton
  'Offers a variety of delights.'—*Judith Crist*

Comin' at Ya!
US 1981 101m Technicolor 3D

An ex-outlaw goes in search of three outlaws who kidnapped his wife-to-be. Determined three-dimensional attack on the sensibilities, with nothing to interest in story or acting.
Tony Anthony, Gene Quintano, Victoria Abril. Written by Wolf Lowenthal, Lloyd Battista and Gene Quintano; directed by Ferdinando Baldi; for CAU.

'A man who believed in war! A man who believed in nothing! And a woman who believed in both of them!'
Coming Home*
US 1978 128m De Luxe
UA / Jerome Hellman

An embittered Vietnam veteran falls for the wife of a serving soldier.
Self-pitying romantic wallow which must mean more to American audiences than to others. Goodish acting.

w Waldo Salt, Robert C. Jones, *story* Nancy Dowd *d* Hal Ashby *ph* Haskell Wexler *pd* Mike Haller *m* various

Jane Fonda, Jon Voight, Bruce Dern, Robert Carradine, Penelope Milford
 AA: Jon Voight; Jane Fonda
 ● Video: Intervision

Comin' Thro' the Rye
GB 1923 approx 85m (24 fps) bw
    silent
Hepworth Picture Plays

In Victorian England, lovers meet periodically in a rye field, but events move against them. Statuesque romantic drama whose reputation may be largely due to its accidental survival. (There was a previous version from the same producer in 1916, with the same leading actress.)

w Blanche McIntosh, *novel* Helen Mathers *d* Cecil M. Hepworth *ph* Geoffrey Faithfull

Alma Taylor, Shayle Garner, Eileen Dennes, Ralph Forbes, Francis Lister
  'My best and most important film.'—*Cecil M. Hepworth*
  'Hepworth's directorial style matches his material in simplicity.'—*Geoff Brown, MFB, 1976*

The Command
US 1954 94m Warnercolor
    Cinemascope
Warner (David Weisbart)

A cavalry troop escorts a wagon train through Indian country.
Competent but unsurprising 'second team' western.

w Russell Hughes, *novel* James Warner Bellah *d* David Butler *ph* Wilfrid M. Cline *m* Dmitri Tiomkin

Guy Madison, Joan Weldon, James Whitmore, Carl Benton Reid, Harvey Lembeck, Ray Teal, Bob Nichols

'Heroes, cowards, fighters, braggarts, liars . . . and what goes on in their hearts!'
Command Decision*
US 1949 111m bw
MGM (Sidney Franklin)

War among the back-room boys; a general, his staff and his peers debate the aerial bombardment of Germany.
Plainly reproduced version of a determinedly serious play, with a remarkable cast partly at sea.

w William R. Laidlaw, George Froeschel, *play* William Wister Haines *d* Sam Wood *ph* Harold Rosson *m* Miklos Rozsa

Clark Gable, Walter Pidgeon, Van Johnson, Brian Donlevy, John Hodiak, Charles Bickford, Edward Arnold, Marshall Thompson, Richard Quine, Cameron Mitchell, Clinton Sundberg, Ray Collins, Warner Anderson, John McIntire, Moroni Olsen

The Commandos Strike at Dawn*
US 1942 98m bw
Columbia (Lester Cowan)

Norwegian commandos outwit the Nazis with the help of the British navy.
Standard war adventure shot on Vancouver Island.

w Irwin Shaw, *story* C. S. Forester *d* John Farrow *ph* William C. Mellor *m* Louis Gruenberg

Paul Muni, Anna Lee, Lillian Gish, Cedric Hardwicke, Robert Coote, Ray Collins, Rosemary de Camp, Richard Derr, Alexander Knox, Rod Cameron
 AAN: Louis Gruenberg

Common Clay
US 1930 68m bw
Fox

A speakeasy hostess becomes maid in a wealthy household and falls in love with her betters.

Archetypal soap opera which caused a mild sensation and sent its star into half a dozen imitations.

w Jules Furthman, *novel* Cleves Kincaid *d* Victor Fleming *ph* Glen MacWilliams

Constance Bennett, Lew Ayres, Tully Marshall, Matty Kemp, Purnell Pratt, Beryl Mercer
  'Emotional play of 1916 bearing the marks of that artificial school . . . heavy for fan diet.'—*Variety*

The Common Touch*
GB 1941 104m bw
British National (John Baxter)

A rich young man poses as a tramp to save a dosshouse from destruction.
Naive drama with a social conscience, remade from the 1932 talkie *Dosshouse*. A brave try.

w Barbara K. Emery, Geoffrey Orme, *novel* Herbert Ayres *d* John Baxter

Geoffrey Hibbert, Greta Gynt, Joyce Howard, Harry Welchman, Edward Rigby, George Carney, Bransby Williams, Wally Patch, Eliot Makeham, Bernard Miles, Bill Fraser, John Longden; *guests* Sandy Macpherson, Scott Sanders, Mark Hambourg, Carrol Gibbons

Company Limited*
India 1971 112m bw
Bharat Shumshere Rana
original title: *Seemabadha*

The young export sales manager of a firm of Delhi electrical appliance manufacturers is saved from boredom by his wife's younger sister.
Quietly pleasing but overlong comedy-drama of modern urban India, very typical of its director.

wd Satyajit Ray, *novel* Shankar *ph* Soumendu Roy *m* Satyajit Ray

Barun Chanda, Sharmilla Tagore, Parumita Chowdhary
  'Subtle, witty, intelligent, and beautifully acted.'—*Michael Billington, Illustrated London News*

The Company of Wolves**
GB 1984 95m colour
ITC / Palace (Chris Brown, Stephen Woolley)

A young girl dreams of wolves and werewolves.
Fragmentary adult fantasy which had an unexpected box office success, chiefly because of its sexual allusiveness, its clever make-up and its pictorial qualities.

w Angela Carter, Neil Jordan, from stories by Angela Carter *d* Neil Jordan *ph* Bryan Loftus *m* George Fenton *special make-up effects* Christopher Tucker *pd* Anton Furst

Angela Lansbury, David Warner, Graham Crowden, Brian Glover, Sarah Patterson, Micha Bergese, Stephen Rea

The Company She Keeps
US 1950 83m bw
RKO (John Houseman)

A self-sacrificing parole officer allows a parolee to steal her fiancé.
Considering the credits, a dismally novelettish drama of almost no interest.

w Ketti Frings d John Cromwell ph Nicholas Musuraca m Leigh Harline

Lizabeth Scott, *Jane Greer*, Dennis O'Keefe, Fay Baker, John Hoyt, James Bell, Don Beddoe, Bert Freed

The Competition*
US 1980 129m Metrocolor
Columbia / Rastar / William Sackheim

An ageing piano prodigy has one last shot at fame in a San Francisco piano competition.
Slightly curious, old-fashioned but heavy-handed romance which aims to do for the piano what *The Turning Point* did for ballet. It doesn't sustain its length but at least the milieu is interesting.

wd Joel Oliansky ph Richard H. Kline
m,md Lalo Schifrin pd Dale Hennesy

Richard Dreyfuss, Lee Remick, Amy Irving, Sam Wanamaker, Joseph Cali

AAN: editing (David Blewitt); best song ('People Alone')

Compulsion**
US 1959 103m bw Cinemascope
TCF / Darryl F. Zanuck Productions (Richard F. Zanuck)

In the twenties, two Chicago students kidnap and murder a young boy for kicks.
Rather dogged but earnest fictionalization of the Leopold-Loeb case with solid performances and production.

w Richard Murphy, *play* Meyer Levin
d Richard Fleischer ph William C. Mellor
m Lionel Newman

Dean Stockwell, Bradford Dillman, Orson Welles (in a cameo court appearance as Clarence Darrow), Diane Varsi, E. G. Marshall, Martin Milner, Richard Anderson, Robert Simon

The Computer Wore Tennis Shoes
US 1970 90m Technicolor

While mending a computer a college student gets an electric shock and becomes omniscient.
Ho-hum Disney comedy, eager to please but instantly forgotten. Kurt Russell, Cesar Romero, Joe Flynn, William Schallert, Alan Hewitt. Written by Joseph L. McEveety; directed by Robert Butler; for Disney.

Comrade X*
US 1940 89m bw
MGM (Gottfried Reinhardt)

An American correspondent in Russia is blackmailed into smuggling a girl out of the country.
Lame satirical comedy in the wake of *Ninotchka*; a few good moments, but generally heavy-handed.

w Ben Hecht, Charles Lederer, *original story* Walter Reisch d King Vidor ph Joseph L. Ruttenberg m Bronislau Kaper

Clark Gable, Hedy Lamarr, Felix Bressart, Oscar Homolka, Eve Arden, Sig Rumann

AAN: Walter Reisch

Comradeship*
GB 1919 67m (24 fps) bw silent

Two friends endure varying fortunes during World War I. An early British 'A' feature which was highly popular in its day. Lily Elsie, Gerald Ames, Guy Newall, Peggy Carlisle. Written by Jeffrey Bernerd; directed by Maurice Elvey; for Stoll.

Conan the Barbarian
US 1981 129m Technicolor Todd AO
Dino de Laurentiis / Edward R. Pressman (Buzz Feitshans, Raffaella de Laurentiis)

In the Dark Ages, a young stalwart seeks out the barbarian tribe which murdered his parents.
Intolerably doomladen, slow-moving and mainly unintelligible rubbish which failed to put a lift into the long-announced sword-and-sorcery cycle.

w John Milius, Oliver Stone, from a character created by Robert E. Howard d John Milius ph Duke Callaghan m Basil Poedouris pd Ron Cobb ed C. Timothy O'Meara

Arnold Schwarzenegger, James Earl Jones, Max Von Sydow, Sandahl Bergman, Ben Davidson, Mako, Gerry Lopez

'A ragbag of half-witted kitsch, where even locations resemble a set, actors look like extras, violence like a stunt and life a bad dream.'—*Sunday Times*
'An indigestible blend of anti-liberal braggadocio, post-60s mysticism and echt-60s blockbusting.'—*Sight and Sound*

● Video: Thorn EMI

Conan the Destroyer
US 1984 101m Technicolor Scope

An evil queen offers to bring Conan's last love back to life, if he will undertake a magical quest for her. More heavy-handed and unpleasant nonsense, with a slightly better pace than before. Arnold Schwarzenegger, Grace Jones, Wilt Chamberlain, Mako, Tracey Walter, Sarah Douglas. Written by Stanley Mann; directed by Richard Fleischer; photographed by Jack Cardiff; for Dino de Laurentiis.

The Concorde: Airport '79
US 1979 113m Technicolor
Universal (Jennings Lang)
GB title: *Airport '80: The Concorde*

Various disasters befall the Concorde on its way from Washington to Paris.
Stultified final (one presumes) effort in the *Airport* series; it could hardly be funnier if it were intended as a comedy, but somehow it entertains.

w Eric Roth d David Lowell Rich ph Philip Lathrop m Lalo Schifrin

Alain Delon, Susan Blakely, Robert Wagner, Sylvia Kristel, George Kennedy, Eddie Albert, Bibi Andersson, John Davidson,

Martha Raye, Cicely Tyson, Mercedes McCambridge

'Larger-than-life characters are thrown together on a storyboard and must fend for themselves against attacks, chases and assorted escapades . . . this would be soporific even as a transatlantic inflight movie.'—*Martyn Auty, MFB*

● Video: CIC

'A kiss that cannot be forgotten!'
Condemned*
US 1930 86m bw
Samuel Goldwyn
aka: *Condemned to Devil's Island*

A bank robber is sent to Devil's Island and falls in love with the wife of the brutal warden.
Slow-moving but pictorially attractive melodrama with old-style performances.

w Sidney Howard, *novel* Condemned to Devil's Island by Blair Niles d Wesley Ruggles ph George Barnes, Gregg Toland sets William Cameron Menzies

Ronald Colman, Ann Harding, Louis Wolheim, Dudley Digges, William Elmer

'A piece of nonsense from which it would appear that French convicts on Devil's Island live a life consisting entirely of hot-towel shaves and flirtations with the governor's wife.'—*James Agate*

AAN: Ronald Colman

The Condemned of Altona*
Italy / France 1962 113m bw
(TCF) Titanus / SGC (Carlo Ponti)

The head of a German shipping empire discovers he has only a few months to live and tries to bring his family to order.
Strident intellectual melodrama whose credits tell all. Watchable for the acting, but very glum.

w Abby Mann, Cesare Zavattini, *play* Jean-Paul Sartre d Vittorio de Sica ph Roberto Gerardi m Dmitri Shostakovich

Fredric March, Sophia Loren, Robert Wagner, Maximilian Schell, Françoise Prévost, Alfredo Franchi

'This film is such a hopeless mess that it is difficult to know where to begin criticizing it.'—*Tom Milne*

Condemned to Death*
GB 1932 75m bw
Twickenham (Julius Hagen)

A condemned killer hypnotizes a judge into murdering those who turned him in.
Irresistible nonsense of the old school, with spirited direction and a good cast.

w Bernard Merivale, Harry Fowler Mear, Brock Williams, *play* Jack O'Lantern by George Goodchild and James Dawson d Walter Forde ph Sidney Blythe, William Luff

Arthur Wontner, Gillian Lind, Edmund Gwenn, Gordon Harker, Jane Welsh, Cyril Raymond

'A weak daily changer with double-headed programming its merited rating.'—*Variety*
'It would be difficult to find a dull moment.'—*The Bioscope*

Condemned Women
US 1938 77m bw

Murder in a prison for women. Rough-and-tumble melodrama with predictable elements.
Sally Eilers, Anne Shirley, Louis Hayward, Esther Dale, Lee Patrick. Written by Lionel Houser; directed by Lew Landers; for RKO.
'Indelicate stuff and doubtful b.o.'—*Variety*

Condorman
US 1981 90m Technicolor Panavision
Walt Disney (Jan Williams)

The author of a 'superman' comic tries to act like his hero in real life.
Very mildly amusing spy spoof with inadequate special effects.
w Marc Sturdivant, Glen Caron, Mickey Rose, *novel* The Game of X by Robert Sheckley d Charles Jarrott ph Charles F. Wheeler m Henry Mancini ph Albert Witherick sp Art Cruickshank
Michael Crawford, Oliver Reed, Barbara Carrera, James Hampton, Jean-Pierre Kalfon
● *Video: Rank*

Conduct Unbecoming*
GB 1975 107m Technicolor
British Lion / Crown (Michael Deeley, Barry Spikings)

In an officers' mess in India in the nineties, a cadet is accused of assault on a lady but the real culprit is a paranoic who has taken to pigsticking in quite the wrong way.
Disappointingly flatly-handled and quite unatmospheric picturization of an absorbing West End melodrama. The cast is largely wasted, but stretches of dialogue maintain their interest.
w Robert Enders, *play* Barry England d Michael Anderson ph Bob Huke m Stanley Myers
Michael York, Stacy Keach, Trevor Howard, Christopher Plummer, Richard Attenborough, Susannah York, James Faulkner, James Donald
● *Video: Thorn EMI*

The Conductor*
Poland 1979 102m Orwocolor
PRF / X Films of Poland
original title: *Dyrygent*

A Polish girl violinist finds her life affected when an elderly international conductor returns to her town.
Initially interesting but finally tedious and muddled allegory, further handicapped by stilted post-synching of the English version.
w Andrzej Kijowski d Andrzej Wajda ph Slawomir Idziak m from Beethoven
John Gielgud, Krystyna Janda, Andrzej Seweryn

Cone of Silence*
GB 1960 92m bw
British Lion / Bryanston (Aubrey Baring)
US title: *Trouble in the Sky*

A seasoned pilot is condemned for an error which caused a crash and later dies in similar circumstances. A flying examiner discovers scientific reasons for exonerating him.
Tolerable suspense drama let down by thin dialogue and confused characterization.
w Robert Westerby, *novel* David Beaty d Charles Frend ph Arthur Grant m Gerhard Schurmann
Michael Craig, Bernard Lee, Peter Cushing, George Sanders, Elizabeth Seal, André Morell, Gordon Jackson, Delphi Lawrence, Noel Willman, Charles Tingwell

Coney Island**
US 1943 96m Technicolor
TCF (William Perlberg)

Two fairground showmen vie for the affections of a songstress.
Brassy, simple-minded, entertaining musical. Very typical of its time; later remade as *Wabash Avenue* (qv).
w George Seaton d Walter Lang ph Ernest Palmer songs Leo Robin, Ralph Rainger m Alfred Newman ch Hermes Pan ad Richard Day, Joseph C. Wright
Betty Grable, George Montgomery, Cesar Romero, Charles Winninger, Phil Silvers, Matt Briggs, Paul Hurst, Frank Orth, Andrew Tombes, Alec Craig, Hal K. Dawson
AAN: Alfred Newman

Confession
US 1937 90m bw
Warner (Henry Blanke)

An errant mother shoots her former lover to protect her daughter.
Stilted romantic melodrama copied scene for scene from a 1936 German film *Mazurka*.
w Julius J. Epstein, Margaret Le Vino, *original screenplay* Hans Rameau d Joe May ph Sid Hickox m Peter Kreuder md Leo F. Forbstein ad Anton Grot
Kay Francis, Ian Hunter, Basil Rathbone, Jane Bryan, Donald Crisp, Dorothy Peterson, Laura Hope Crews, Robert Barrat
'Distinctly in the upper bracket and made to order for important first runs.'—*Variety*

Confession
GB 1955 90m bw

A murderer stalks the priest who knows his guilt through the confessional but may not reveal it. So-so reworking of the theme that daunted Hitchcock in *I Confess*; some pleasant touches are nullified by slow pacing. Sydney Chaplin, Audrey Dalton, John Welsh, John Bentley, Peter Hammond. Written and directed by Ken Hughes; for Anglo Amalgamated.

The Confession*
France / Italy 1970 160m Eastmancolor
Films Corona / Films Pomereu / Selena Cinematografica (Robert Dorfmann)
original title: *L'Aveu*

In Prague in 1951, a minister is secretly imprisoned and interrogated, and finally confesses under duress to anti-communist activities.

Brutally long but frequently impressive anti-Soviet tract, extremely well acted but less exciting than *Z*. Based on a true account.
w Jorge Semprun, *book* Lise and Artur London d Costa-Gavras ph Raoul Coutard m not credited
Yves Montand, Simone Signoret, Gabriele Ferzetti, Michel Vitold

Confessions of a Nazi Spy***
US 1939 110m bw
Warner (Robert Lord)

How G-men ferreted out Nazis in the United States.
Topical exposé with all concerned in top form; a semi-documentary very typical of Warner product throughout the thirties and forties, from *G-Men* to *Mission to Moscow* and *I Was a Communist for the FBI*: well made, punchy, and smartly edited, with a loud moral at the end.
w Milton Krims, John Wexley, from materials gathered by former FBI agent Leon G. Turrou d Anatole Litvak ph Sol Polito m Max Steiner
Edward G. Robinson, Paul Lukas, George Sanders, Francis Lederer, Henry O'Neill, Lya Lys, James Stephenson, Sig Rumann, Dorothy Tree, Joe Sawyer
'Its social implications are far more important than the immediate question of how much money the release makes for Warner Brothers.'—*Variety*
'The Warner brothers have declared war on Germany with this one . . . with this precedent there is no way any producer could argue against dramatizing any social or political theme on the grounds that he's afraid of domestic or foreign censorship. Everybody duck.'—*Pare Lorentz*
'Has a remarkable resemblance to a full-length *Crime Does Not Pay*.'—*David Wolff*
'One of the most sensational movie jobs on record, workmanlike in every respect and spang across the headlines.'—*Otis Ferguson*

Confessions of an Opium Eater
US 1962 85m bw
Albert Zugsmith
GB title: *Evils of Chinatown*

In San Francisco in the nineties, a seaman falls into the clutches of a tong.
The hero is called De Quincey, but that is the only association with the famous book of the same title. This absurd melodrama is just about bad enough to be funny, but not very.
w Robert Hill d Albert Zugsmith ph Joseph Biroc m Albert Glasser ad Eugene Lourié
Vincent Price, Linda Ho, Richard Loo, Philip Ahn, June Kim
'Has to be seen to be believed . . . starved girls captive in cages, secret panels, sliding doors, sewer escape routes, opium dens and nightmares . . .'—*MFB*

Confidential Agent**
US 1945 122m bw
Warner (Robert Buckner)

An emissary of Franco's Spain comes to England in the late thirties to make a munitions deal, and falls in love with the tycoon's daughter.
Heavy-going simplification of Graham Greene's lowering novel, with cast and (especially) set designers all at sea but nevertheless providing striking moments.

w Robert Buckner d Herman Shumlin ph James Wong Howe m Franz Waxman

Charles Boyer, Lauren Bacall, Katina Paxinou, Peter Lorre, Victor Francen, George Coulouris, Wanda Hendrix, George Zucco, Miles Mander
　'In some ways an exciting and good picture, the best attempt yet, though still inadequate, to make the best of a Greene novel.'—James Agee

Confidential Report*

Spain 1955 99m bw
Sevilla Studios (Louis Dolivet, Orson Welles)
aka: Mr Arkadin

A wealthy and powerful financier employs a young American to seek out figures from his own past, who are soon found dead . . .
Silly melodrama which might have been suspenseful if done by Hitchcock, or even by Welles at his peak; as it is, weak writing and sloppy production remove most of the interest and reveal it as a very obvious bag of tricks.

wd Orson Welles ph Jean Bourgoin m Paul Misraki

Orson Welles, Michael Redgrave, Katina Paxinou, Akim Tamiroff, Mischa Auer, Patricia Medina, Jack Watling, Peter Van Eyck, Paola Mori, Robert Arden, Grégoire Aslan, Suzanne Flon
　'Tilted camera angles, heavy atmospheric shots, overlapping dialogue—all the trademarks are here, sometimes over-used to an almost hysterical degree, but they have little significance . . . (the film) springs not from life but from the earlier cinematic world of Welles himself and from the kind of thriller written about thirty years ago by E. Philips Oppenheim.'—Gavin Lambert
　'The quality of the soundtrack is quite disastrous, but there is a certain grandeur about the carelessness of the film's construction which makes one forget everything except the immediacy of the moment.'—Basil Wright, 1972

Confirm or Deny*

US 1941 78m bw
TCF (Len Hammond)

An American reporter falls for a wireless operator in wartime London.
Artificial but watchable minor romantic melodrama.

w Jo Swerling, Henry Wales, Samuel Fuller d Archie Mayo ph Leon Shamroy

Don Ameche, Joan Bennett, Roddy McDowall, Arthur Shields, Raymond Walburn, John Loder
† Fritz Lang directed some scenes.

Conflict*

US 1945 86m bw
Warner (William Jacobs)

A man murders his wife and is apparently haunted by her; but the odd happenings have been arranged by a suspicious psychiatrist.
Leaden and artificial melodrama with both stars miscast; a few effective moments.

w Arthur T. Horman, Dwight Taylor d Curtis Bernhardt ph Merritt Gerstad m Frederick Hollander

Humphrey Bogart, Sydney Greenstreet, Alexis Smith, Rose Hobart, Charles Drake, Grant Mitchell
† The film was completed in August 1943.

Conflict of Wings*

GB 1953 84m Eastmancolor
Group Three (Herbert Mason)
US title: Fuss over Feathers

East Anglian villagers fight to save a bird sanctuary from being taken over by the RAF as a rocket range.
Sub-Ealing comedy-drama with a highly predictable outcome; generally pleasant but without much bite.

w Don Sharp, John Pudney d John Eldridge ph Arthur Grant m Philip Green

John Gregson, Muriel Pavlow, Kieron Moore, Niall MacGinnis, Sheila Sweet, Harry Fowler, Barbara Hicks, Charles Lloyd Pack

The Conformist**

Italy / France / West Germany 1969
108m Technicolor
Mars / Marianne / Maran (Giovanni Bertolucci)
original title: Il Conformista

In 1938 an inhibited young man tries to conform to the prevailing mood of Fascism, but gets out of his depth when he turns informer.
Psychologically confusing but brilliantly realized recreation of an age.

wd Bernardo Bertolucci, novel Alberto Moravia ph Vittorio Storaro m Georges Delerue

Jean-Louis Trintignant, Stefania Sandrelli, Gastone Moschin, Enzo Taroscio, Dominique Sanda, Pierre Clementi

Congo Crossing

US 1956 85m Technicolor
U-I (Howard Christie)

Assorted fugitives from justice gather at Congotanga, which has no extradition laws.
The poor man's Casablanca, quite good looking but dully written and presented.

w Richard Alan Simmons d Joseph Pevney ph Russell Metty m Joseph Gershenson

George Nader, Virginia Mayo, Peter Lorre, Michael Pate, Rex Ingram

Congorilla*

US 1932 74m bw

A record of two years spent in the Belgian Congo by Mr and Mrs Martin Johnson.

Excellent exploration documentary of its time. Written and directed by the Johnsons; for Fox.
'Replete with thrills, adventure and laughs, making withal for an excellent entertainment.'—Variety

Congress Dances*

Germany 1931 92m bw
UFA (Erich Pommer)
original title: Der Kongress Tanzt

At the Congress of Vienna, Metternich attempts to decoy the Tsar with a countess; but the Tsar has a double.
Lubitsch-like treatment of sexual dalliance in high places; no doubt a stunner in its time, but rather faded now.

w Norbert Falk, Robert Liebmann d Erik Charrell ph Carl Hoffmann m Werner Heymann

Conrad Veidt, Henri Garat / Willy Fritsch, Lilian Harvey
　'A revue more than a story . . . grace, taste and a light hand.'—Variety

A Connecticut Yankee*

US 1931 96m bw
Fox

A man dreams himself back to the court of King Arthur, and teaches the Middle Ages a thing or two about modern living.
First sound version of Mark Twain's classic fantasy, also filmed in 1921 and 1949. Creaky now, but amiable.

w William Conselman d David Butler ph Ernest Palmer

Will Rogers, Maureen O'Sullivan, Myrna Loy, Frank Albertson, William Farnum
　'Good deluxe comedy . . . should draw substantial grosses.'—Variety

'Its laughter will ring through the centuries!'

A Connecticut Yankee in King Arthur's Court*

US 1948 106m Technicolor
Paramount (Robert Fellows)
GB title: A Yankee in King Arthur's Court

Gossamer musical version of the above with the emphasis on song and knockabout.
Palatable, with the 'Busy Doin' Nothin' ' sequence the most memorable.

w Edmund Beloin d Tay Garnett ph Ray Rennahan md Victor Young
songs Johnny Burke, Jimmy Van Heusen

Bing Crosby, Rhonda Fleming, William Bendix, Cedric Hardwicke, Murvyn Vye
　'The tacky pageantry is more suited to the opening of a West Coast supermarket than to an English court in the 6th century.'—Pauline Kael, 70s

Connecting Rooms

GB 1969 103m Technicolor
Telstar / Franklin Gollings (Harry Field)

In a seedy Bayswater boarding house, a dismissed schoolmaster befriends a failed cellist whose protégé is a sponging songwriter.

Aggressively dismal melodrama which would be hilarious if it were not so sadly slow and naive.

wd Franklin Gollings, *play* The Cellist by Marion Hart *ph* John Wilcox *m* Joan Shakespeare

Bette Davis, Michael Redgrave, Alexis Kanner, Kay Walsh, Gabrielle Drake, Leo Genn, Olga Georges-Picot, Richard Wyler, Brian Wilde

● Video: VCL

The Connection
US 1961   110m   bw
Shirley Clarke / Lewis Allen

Junkies hang around waiting for a fix and are filmed by a documentary unit.
Unattractive low-budgeter with occasional impressive moments.

w Jack Gelber *d* Shirley Clarke *ph* Arthur J. Ornitz *m* Freddie Redd *ad* Richard Sylbert

Warren Finnerty, Jerome Raphael, Jim Anderson, Carl Lee, Roscoe Browne

The Conquering Horde
US 1931   73m   bw

In Texas after the Civil War, resistance to railroads hampers the movement of cattle.
Strongish western of its period, but of no continuing interest. Richard Arlen, Fay Wray, Claude Gillingwater, Ian MacLaren. Written by Grover Jones, William Slavens McNutt; directed by Edward Sloman; for Paramount.
'Good story, plenty of love interest, action and comedy . . . will do above average.'—*Variety*

'Spectacular as its barbaric passions and savage conquests!'
The Conqueror
US 1955   112m   Technicolor
   Cinemascope
Howard Hughes (Dick Powell)

A romance of the early life of Genghis Khan, who captures and is enamoured by the daughter of an enemy.
Solemn pantomime with a measure of bloodthirsty action and dancing girls, but featuring too many dull spots between, especially as the star is the most unlikely of eastern warriors and the production values careful but not too steady.

w Oscar Millard *d* Dick Powell *ph* Joseph La Shelle, Leo Tover, Harry J. Wild *m* Victor Young

John Wayne, Susan Hayward, Pedro Armendariz, Agnes Moorehead, Thomas Gomez, John Hoyt, William Conrad, Ted de Corsia, Lee Van Cleef

GENGHIS KHAN: 'This tartar woman is for me, and my blood says, take her!'

'Simply an oriental western.'—*New York Times*

'History has not been well served and nor has the popcorn public.'—*Richard Hatch, Nation*

'It's all that its makers wanted it to be.'—*Manchester Guardian*

'John Wayne as Genghis Khan—history's most improbable piece of casting unless Mickey Rooney were to play Jesus in *King of Kings*.'—*Jack Smith, L.A. Times*

† The location was Utah's Escalante Desert, and three local mountains were renamed Mount Wayne, Mount Hughes and Mount Powell. The desert had been used for atom bomb tests, and twenty-five years after the production, questions were asked when several members of the cast died of cancer.
†† Wayne asked for his role. 'The way the screenplay reads, this is a cowboy picture, and that's how I am going to play Genghis Khan. I see him as a gunfighter.'

The Conquerors
US 1932   88m   bw
RKO (David O. Selznick)
TV title: *Pioneer Builders*

Nebraska settlers in the 1870s set the seeds of a banking empire.
Routine family epic with the star playing himself and his own grandson.

w Robert Lord, *story* Howard Estabrook *d* William Wellman *ph* Edward Cronjager *m* Max Steiner

Richard Dix, Ann Harding, Edna May Oliver, Guy Kibbee, Donald Cook, Julie Haydon, Jed Prouty

'As good as a depression story can be, which isn't much box office.'—*Variety*

Conquest**
US 1937   115m   bw
MGM (Bernard Hyman)
GB title: *Marie Walewska*

The life of Napoleon's most enduring mistress. Measured, dignified, and often rather dull historical fiction, lightened by excellent performances and production.

w Samuel Hoffenstein, Salka Viertel, S. N. Behrman, from a Polish play dramatized by Helen Jerome *d* Clarence Brown *ph* Karl Freund *m* Herbert Stothart

Greta Garbo, *Charles Boyer*, Reginald Owen, Alan Marshal, Henry Stephenson, Dame May Whitty, Leif Erickson

'For special first-run openings—and then the clean up.'—*Variety*

'Ornate, unexpectedly tasteful, carefully detailed—and lifeless.'—*Pauline Kael, 70s*

AAN: Charles Boyer

Conquest of Cochise
US 1953   78m   Technicolor

An army major is sent to make peace with Cochise, the Apache. Feeble western cheapie. Robert Stack, John Hodiak, Joy Page. Written by Arthur Lewis and De Vallon Scott; directed by William Castle; for Sam Katzman / Columbia.

Conquest of Space
US 1955   80m   Technicolor
Paramount (George Pal)

In 1980, the Americans have built a space station in the atmosphere, and plan a voyage

to the moon but are sent to Mars instead.
So history catches up with science fiction. This sober prophecy looks good but very little happens and the result is as dull as it is bright and shiny.

w James O'Hanlon *d* Byron Haskin *ph* Lionel Lindon *m* Van Cleave *ad* Hal Pereira, James McMillan Johnson *sp* John P. Fulton, Irmin Roberts, Paul Lerpae, Ivyl Burks, Jan Domella

Eric Fleming, Walter Brooke, Mickey Shaughnessy, William Hopper, Ross Martin

Conquest of the Air
GB 1936   71m   bw

A history of man's discovery of the power of flight. Curious schoolbook documentary, of historical interest. Laurence Olivier (as Lunardi), Franklin Dyall, Henry Victor, Hay Petrie, John Turnbull. Written by Hugh Gray and Peter Bezencenet; directed by Zoltan Korda and others; for Alexander Korda.

Conrack*
US 1974   106m   De Luxe   Panavision
TCF (Martin Ritt, Irving Ravetch)

A young white teacher is assigned to an all-black school in South Carolina, and after some difficulty makes friends with children and parents.
Nostalgically mellow happy-film, lit by bright smiles all round.

w Irving Ravetch, Harriet Frank Jnr, *novel* The Water Is Wide by Pat Conroy *d* Martin Ritt *ph* John Alonzo *m* John Williams

Jon Voight, Paul Winfield, Hume Cronyn, Madge Sinclair, Tina Andrews

'For all its craftsman-like virtues, it seems a conscious turning aside from the complexities of modern cinema to the simpler alternatives of yesteryear. Indeed, with underprivileged white children instead of black and Greer Garson substituting for Jon Voight, the film might have been made all of thirty years ago.'—*John Raisbeck*

Consider Your Verdict
GB 1938   40m   bw

A juror proves an accused man not guilty by falsely confessing to the crime himself. Fairly smart little entry into the feature film scene for the Boulting Brothers, from a popular radio play of the time. Marius Goring, Manning Whiley, Olive Sloane, Hay Petrie, George Carney. Written by Francis Miller, from the play by Laurence Housman; directed by Roy Boulting; for Charter.

Consolation Marriage
US 1931   62m   bw

A wife keeps a stiff upper lip when her husband strays. Ho-hum domestic drama with attempts at comedy relief. Irene Dunne, Pat O'Brien, John Halliday, Matt Moore, Myrna Loy. Written by Humphrey Pearson; directed by Paul Sloane; for RKO. 'Fair entertainment; will satisfy with good stage support.'—*Variety*

'What conflict in the heart of a nun would make her break her vows?'

Conspiracy of Hearts*
GB 1960 113m bw
Rank (Betty E. Box)

During World War II, Italian nuns smuggle Jewish children across the border from a nearby prison camp.

Highly commercial combination of exploitable sentimental elements: Germans, Jews, nuns, children, war, suspense. Remarkably, it gets by without causing nausea.

w Robert Presnell Jnr d Ralph Thomas
ph Ernest Steward m Angelo Lavagnino

Lilli Palmer, Sylvia Syms, Yvonne Mitchell, Albert Lieven, Ronald Lewis, Peter Arne, Nora Swinburne, Michael Goodliffe, Megs Jenkins, David Kossoff, Jenny Laird, George Coulouris, Phyllis Neilson-Terry

Conspirator
GB 1949 87m bw
MGM (Arthur Hornblow Jnr)

A guards officer, unknown to his young wife, is a communist spy.

Singularly awful romantic melodrama which never convinces or entertains for a moment.

w Sally Benson, Gerard Fairlie, novel Humphrey Slater d Victor Saville ph F. A. Young m John Wooldridge

Robert Taylor, Elizabeth Taylor, Harold Warrender, Robert Flemyng, Marie Ney

The Conspirators*
US 1944 101m bw
Warner (Jack Chertok)

A Dutch underground leader escapes to Lisbon and clears up international intrigue.

Interestingly cast but often listless wartime melodrama, a doomed attempt to reprise Casablanca without Humphrey Bogart.

w Vladimir Pozner, Leo Rosten, novel City of Shadows by Frederick Prokosch d Jean Negulesco ph Arthur Edeson m Max Steiner

Hedy Lamarr, Paul Henreid, Sydney Greenstreet, Peter Lorre, Victor Francen, Carol Thurston, Vladimir Sokoloff, Joseph Calleia, Edward Ciannelli, Steve Geray, Kurt Katch, George Macready

SYDNEY GREENSTREET (as Quintanilla): 'This may seem to you melodramatic, but indulge me, please, I like melodrama.'

'As exciting as baseball and almost as gentlemanly as cricket.'—New Statesman
'I enjoyed it as much as any Warner melodrama since Casablanca.'—Observer

The Constant Husband*
GB 1954 88m Technicolor print
British Lion / London Films (Frank Launder, Sidney Gilliat)

An amnesiac discovers that he is a multiple bigamist, still wanted by each of his five wives.

Flimsy comedy which never really gets going despite an attractive cast.

w Sidney Gilliat, Val Valentine d Sidney Gilliat ph Ted Scaife m Malcolm Arnold

Rex Harrison, Kay Kendall, Margaret Leighton, Cecil Parker, Nicole Maurey, George Cole, Raymond Huntley, Michael Hordern, Eric Pohlmann, Robert Coote

The Constant Nymph*
GB 1933 98m bw
Gaumont (Michael Balcon)

In the Tyrol, a composer leaves his rich wife for a schoolgirl suffering from a heart condition.

Archetypal romantic drama from Margaret Kennedy's book, first filmed in 1928 by the same producer (directed by Adrian Brunel, with Ivor Novello and Mabel Poulton). A standard production of its time, which seems to have vanished with the literary copyright.

w Margaret Kennedy, Basil Dean, from their play based on her novel d Basil Dean ph Max Greene

Brian Aherne, Victoria Hopper, Leonora Corbett, Lyn Harding, Mary Clare, Jane Baxter

'Beautifully done artistic success from England, of doubtful box office for America.'—Variety
'One can say that it has a beginning, a middle and an end, but it lacks something vital.'—E. V. Lucas, Punch

The Constant Nymph*
US 1943 112m bw
Warner (Henry Blanke)

Artificially well-produced, overlong Hollywood version of the above.

w Kathryn Scola d Edmund Goulding ph Tony Gaudio m Erich Wolfgang Korngold

Charles Boyer, Joan Fontaine, Alexis Smith, Brenda Marshall, Charles Coburn, Dame May Whitty, Peter Lorre, Joyce Reynolds, Jean Muir, Edward Ciannelli, Montagu Love, André Charlot

AAN: Joan Fontaine

Continental Divide
US 1981 103m Technicolor
Universal / Amblin (Bob Larson)

A national columnist finds himself banished to the wilds with a lady ornithologist studying the bald eagle.

Old-fashioned comedy, a cross between Bringing Up Baby and Woman of the Year. Not actually bad, but somewhat lacking in personality.

w Lawrence Kasdan d Michael Apted ph John Bailey m Michael Small

John Belushi, Blair Brown, Allen Goorwitz, Carlin Glynn

Contraband**
GB 1940 92m bw
British National (John Corfield)
US title: Blackout

A Danish merchant captain and a girl in wartime London expose a gang of spies using a cinema as headquarters.

Enjoyable lightweight comedy melodrama on Hitchcock lines, reuniting the unlikely star team from The Spy in Black.

w Emeric Pressburger, Michael Powell, Brock Williams d Michael Powell ph F. A. Young

Conrad Veidt, Valerie Hobson, Esmond Knight, Hay Petrie, Raymond Lovell, Harold Warrender, Charles Victor, Manning Whiley

Contraband Spain
GB 1955 82m Eastmancolor

An American agent in Barcelona investigates the death there of a compatriot involved in drug smuggling. Pretty awful formula thick-ear with bland stars and a boring look. Richard Greene, Anouk Aimée, Michael Denison, John Warwick. Written and directed by Laurence Huntingdon; for Diadem / ABP.

Convention City*
US 1933 78m bw
Warner (Henry Blanke)

Extra-marital fun and games at a Chicago convention.

Amusing and rather risqué comedy which helped to bring down on Hollywood the wrath of the Legion of Decency.

w Robert Lord d Archie Mayo ph William Rees

Joan Blondell, Guy Kibbee, Adolphe Menjou, Dick Powell, Mary Astor, Frank McHugh, Ruth Donnelly, Hugh Herbert, Hobart Cavanaugh

'Not a dull foot . . . probably the fastest complex comedy of the year and a certain money picture.'—Variety

The Conversation**
US 1974 113m Technicolor
Paramount / Francis Ford Coppola

A bugging device expert lives only for his work, but finally develops a conscience. Absorbing but extremely difficult to follow in detail, this personal, timely (in view of Watergate) Kafkaesque suspense story centres almost entirely on director and leading actor, who have a field day.

wd Francis Ford Coppola ph Bill Butler m David Shire

Gene Hackman, John Cazale, Allen Garfield, Frederick Forrest

'A private, hallucinatory study in technical expertise and lonely guilt.'—Sight and Sound
'A terrifying depiction of a ransacked spirit.'—New Yorker, 1977
'Alert, truthful, unarty and absolutely essential viewing.'—Michael Billington, Illustrated London News

AAN: best picture; Francis Ford Coppola (as writer)

Conversation Piece
Italy / France 1974 121m Technicolor
Todd AO 35
Rusconi / Gaumont (Giovanni Bertolucci)
original title: Gruppo di Famiglia in un Interno

When a reclusive professor is persuaded to let his top floor to a young couple he is brought face to face with his latent homosexuality and his approaching death.

Death in Venice revisited, but with much less style and even more obscurity.

w Luchino Visconti, Suso Cecchi d'Amico, Enrico Medioli d Luchino Visconti ph Pasqualino de Santis m Franco Mannino

Burt Lancaster, Helmut Berger, Claudia Marsani, Silvana Mangano

Convict 99**
GB 1938 91m bw
Gainsborough (Edward Black)

A seedy schoolmaster accidentally becomes a prison governor and lets the convicts run the place.
Patchily funny if overlong and in some ways rather serious Will Hay comedy, not quite typical of him.

w Marriott Edgar, Val Guest, Ralph Smart, Jack Davies d Marcel Varnel ph Arthur Crabtree md Louis Levy

Will Hay, Graham Moffatt, Moore Marriott, Googie Withers, Garry Marsh, Peter Gawthorne, Basil Radford, Kathleen Harrison

Convicted*
US 1950 91m bw
Columbia (Jerry Bresler)

When a prison informer is killed, one convict knows who did it.
Routine, over-plotted, strongly cast prison melodrama.

w William Bowers, Fred Niblo Jnr, Seton I. Miller, *play* Martin Flavin d Henry Levin ph Burnett Guffey m George Duning

Glenn Ford, Broderick Crawford, Millard Mitchell, Dorothy Malone, Frank Faylen, Carl Benton Reid, Will Geer

Convicts Four*
US 1962 106m bw
Allied Artists–Lubin–Kaufman (A. Ronald Lubin)
original and GB title: *Reprieve*

A convict reprieved from the electric chair spends eighteen years in prison, becomes a painter, and is rehabilitated.
Odd and unsatisfactory mixture of documentary, melodrama, sentimentality and character study, with stars unexpectedly popping in for cameo appearances. Something worthier was obviously intended.

wd Millard Kaufman, from the autobiography of John Resko ph Joseph Biroc m Leonard Rosenman

Ben Gazzara, Vincent Price, Rod Steiger, Broderick Crawford, Stuart Whitman, Ray Walston, Jack Kruschen, Sammy Davis Jnr

Convoy*
GB 1940 90m bw
Ealing (Sergei Nolbandov)

A German pocket battleship menaces a British convoy, and a merchant ship sacrifices itself to prevent disaster.
Fluent British war film of the early days, the only substantial work of a much vaunted director who was subsequently killed.

w Pen Tennyson, Patrick Kirwan d Pen Tennyson ph Gunther Krampf, Roy Kellino m Ernest Irving

Clive Brook, John Clements, Edward Chapman, Judy Campbell, Penelope Dudley Ward, Edward Rigby, Allan Jeayes, Albert Lieven

Convoy
US 1978 110m De Luxe Panavision
UA / EMI (Robert M. Sherman)

A folk hero truck driver survives several crashes and his policeman nemesis.
A virtually plotless anthology of wanton destruction. Too noisy to sleep through.

w B. W. L. Norton, based on the song by C. W. McCall d Sam Peckinpah ph Harry Stradling Jnr

Kris Kristofferson, Ali MacGraw, Ernest Borgnine, Burt Young, Madge Sinclair

'There's a whole lot of nothing going on here . . . strictly a summer popcorn picture for the nondiscriminating.'—*Variety*

'Roughly as much fun as a ride on the New Jersey turnpike with the window open. It not only numbs the brain but pollutes the senses.'—*Richard Schickel, Time*

● Video: Thorn EMI

Coogan's Bluff**
US 1968 94m Technicolor
Universal (Don Siegel)

An Arizona sheriff takes an escaped killer back to New York, and when the man escapes uses western methods to recapture him.
Violent, well-done police story which inspired the TV series *McCloud*.

w Herman Miller, Dean Riesner, Howard Rodman d Don Siegel ph Bud Thackery m Lalo Schifrin

Clint Eastwood, Lee J. Cobb, Susan Clark, Don Stroud, Tisha Sterling, Betty Field, Tom Tully

Cool Breeze
US 1972 102m Metrocolor
MGM / Penelope (Gene Corman)

A miscellaneous gang of crooks is rounded up to commit a robbery, which ultimately fails.
Third, all-black remake of *The Asphalt Jungle* (the others being *The Badlanders* and *Cairo*). Fashionable violence against a Los Angeles backdrop, but not at all memorable.

wd Barry Pollack ph Andy Davis m Solomon Burke

Thalmus Rasulala, Judy Pace, Jim Watkins, Raymond St Jacques, Lincoln Kilpatrick

'What we've got here is a failure to communicate.'

Cool Hand Luke**
US 1967 126m Technicolor
Panavision
Warner / Jalem (Gordon Carroll)

Sentenced to two years' hard labour with the chain gang, a convict becomes a legend of invulnerability but is eventually shot during an escape.

Allegedly a Christ-allegory, this well-made and good-looking film is only partially successful as an entertainment; slow stretches of soul-searching alternate with brutality, and not much acting is possible.

w Donn Pearce, Frank R. Pierson, *novel* Donn Pearce d Stuart Rosenberg ph Conrad Hall m Lalo Schifrin

Paul Newman, George Kennedy, Jo Van Fleet, J. D. Cannon, Lou Antonio, Robert Drivas, Strother Martin, Clifton James

AA: George Kennedy
AAN: Donn Pearce, Frank R. Pierson; Lalo Schifrin; Paul Newman
● Video: Warner

The Cool Ones
US 1967 96m Technicolor Panavision
Warner (William Conrad)

Former pop singer makes a comeback.
Zazzy showbiz saga with ear-splitting track, quite professionally assembled.

w Joyce Geller d Gene Nelson ph Floyd Crosby m Ernie Freeman

Roddy McDowall, Debbie Watson, Robert Coote, Phil Harris, Nita Talbot

The Co-Optimists*
GB 1929 83m bw
New Era (Gordon Craig)

A revue by a popular pierrot troupe of the time.
Famous as Britain's first musical, this is a dated but valuable record of a stage performance of the kind long vanished.

d Edwin Greenwood, Laddie Cliff ph Basil Emmott

Davy Burnaby, Stanley Holloway, Laddie Cliff, Phyllis Monkman, Melville Gideon, Gilbert Childs, Betty Chester, Elsa MacFarlane, Peggy Petronella, Harry S. Pepper

Copacabana
US 1947 91m bw
(UA) Sam Coslow

A quick-thinking agent forms two acts out of one client, which makes things awkward when both are needed at once.
Thinly produced comedy with both stars doing what is expected of them in surroundings less glamorous than those to which they were previously accustomed.

w Laslo Vadnay, Allen Boretz, Howard Harris d Alfred E. Green ph Bert Glennon m Edward Ward

Groucho Marx, Carmen Miranda, Steve Cochran, Gloria Jean, Andy Russell

Copper Canyon
US 1949 84m Technicolor

After the Civil War, southern veterans trying to rebuild their homes are helped by a gunslinger. Shiny unpersuasive western with stars ill at ease. Ray Milland, Hedy Lamarr, Macdonald Carey, Mona Freeman, Harry Carey Jnr. Written by Jonathan Latimer; directed by John Farrow; for Paramount.

Cops•••
US 1922 20m (24 fps) bw silent
First National / Comique Film (Joseph M.
  Schenck)

An innocent disrupts a parade and is pursued
by a horde of policemen.
The perfect Keaton short, a careful assembly
of perfectly timed gags.

wd Buster Keaton *ph* Elgin Lessley

Buster Keaton, Virginia Fox

Cops and Robbers•
US 1973 89m De Luxe
UA / EK Corp (Elliott Kastner)

Two New York cops turn crook and pull off a
job for the Mafia.
Trendily anti-establishment comedy, quite
snappy and smart when you can follow it.

w Donald E. Westlake *d* Aram Avakian
ph David L. Quaid *m* Michel Legrand

Cliff Gorman, Joe Bologna, Dick Ward,
Shepperd Strudwick, Ellen Holly, John P.
Ryan

Le Corbeau••
France 1943 92m bw
L'Atelier Français
US title: *The Raven*

Poison pen letters disturb a small provincial
town.
Impressively characterized whodunnit with the
usual French qualities of detail and discretion.
Remade in Hollywood to less effect as *The
Thirteenth Letter* (qv).

w Louis Chavance *d* Henri-Georges Clouzot
ph Nicholas Hayer *m* Tony Aubain

Pierre Fresnay, Pierre Larquey, Ginette
Leclerc, Hélène Manson
  'By no means as malign or as brilliant as it's
cracked up to be, but a sour, clever, amusing
job.'—*James Agee*

Corky
US 1971 88m colour

An arrogant auto mechanic becomes a stock
car racer. Noisy and unattractive movie about
an anti-hero. Robert Blake, Patrick O'Neal,
Charlotte Rampling, Christopher Connolly,
Laurence Luckinbill, Ben Johnson. Written by
Eugene Price; directed by Leonard Horn; for
Bruce Geller / MGM.

The Corn is Green•
US 1945 118m bw
Warner (Jack Chertok)

In 1895 Miss Moffat starts a village school for
Welsh miners, and after some tribulations sees
one of them off to Oxford.
A very theatrical production with
unconvincing sets and mannered acting, but
the original play has its felicities.

w Casey Robinson, Frank Cavett, *play Emlyn
Williams d* Irving Rapper *ph* Sol Polito
m Max Steiner *ad* Carl Jules Weyl

Bette Davis, John Dall, Nigel Bruce, Joan
Lorring, Rhys Williams, Rosalind Ivan,
Mildred Dunnock, Arthur Shields

THE CORN IS GREEN.   Bette Davis inspires John Dall in an idealized Welsh cottage.

  'It's very apparent that Hollywood isn't
Wales . . . but the film lingers in the memory
anyway.'—*New Yorker, 1978*
† Remade as a TV movie in 1978, with
Katharine Hepburn.
AAN: John Dall; Joan Lorring

Cornered•
US 1945 102m bw
RKO

After demobilization, a French-Canadian pilot
tracks down the collaborationist responsible
for the death of his wife. Well-made but
humourless revenge thriller.

w John Paxton, *story* John Wexley *d* Edward
Dmytryk *ph* Harry J. Wild *m* Roy Webb

Dick Powell, Micheline Cheirel, Walter
Slezak, Morris Carnovsky

● *Video: Kingston*

Coronado
US 1935 77m bw

Marital misunderstandings abound at a swanky
beach hotel. Thinly plotted but star-spotted
comedy musical, notable now for the talent.
Jack Haley, Leon Errol, Eddy Duchin and his
Orchestra, Johnny Downs, Betty Burgess,
Andy Devine, Alice White, Jameson Thomas.
Written by Don Hartman, Frank Butler;
directed by Norman McLeod; for Paramount.

Corps Profond•
France 1963 21m Technicolor

A tour inside the human body by courtesy of
micro-photography. Spellbinding and
educative documentary of a new kind, and just
the right length; the later British imitation,
The Body, outstayed its welcome. Written and
directed by Igor Barrière and Etienne Lalou;
for Delpire.

The Corpse Came COD
US 1947 87m bw
Columbia (Sam Bischoff)

Rival reporters try to solve the mystery of a
wandering body.
Routine crime comedy with too few smart
lines.

w George Bricker, Dwight Babcock,
novel Jimmy Starr *d* Henry Levin *ph* Lucien
Andriot *m* George Duning

George Brent, Joan Blondell, Adele Jergens,
Jim Bannon, Leslie Brooks, Grant Mitchell,
Una O'Connor

Corridor of Mirrors
GB 1948 105m bw
Cartier–Romney–Apollo (Rudolph Cartier)

An eccentric art collector believes that he and
his mistress are reincarnations of 400-year-old
lovers in a painting; but they are separated by
murder.

Pretentious melodrama of no urgent narrative interest, with all concerned sadly at sea.

w Rudolph Cartier, Edana Romney
d Terence Young ph André Thomas
m Georges Auric

Eric Portman, Edana Romney, Barbara Mullen, Hugh Sinclair
'It has aimed at Art. It is, in fact, Effect. Some members of the cast wander in and out of the scenes as if they are not quite sure what has happened to them. Their confusion is not beyond comprehension.'—MFB

Corridors of Blood*
GB 1958   86m   bw
Producers' Associates (John Croydon)
original title: Doctor from Seven Dials

Seeking to discover anaesthetics, a Victorian doctor falls a prey to resurrection men.
Unpleasant but well-mounted semi-horror backed by strong cast and art direction.

w Jean Scott Rogers   d Robert Day
ph Geoffrey Faithfull   m Buxton Orr
ad Anthony Masters

Boris Karloff, Christopher Lee, Finlay Currie, Frank Pettingell, Betta St John, Francis Matthews, Adrienne Corri, Marian Spencer
† Not released until 1964.

Corruption
GB 1967   91m   Technicolor
Columbia / Titan (Peter Newbrook)

A surgeon kills for pituitary gland fluid to restore his fiancée's beauty.
Highly derivative shocker with no inspiration of its own except an accumulation of gory detail.

w Donald and Derek Ford   d Robert Hartford Davis   ph Peter Newbrook   m Bill McGuffie

Peter Cushing, Sue Lloyd, Noel Trevarthen, Kate O'Mara, David Lodge

Corsair*
US 1931   75m   bw

A college football hero turns hi-jacker.
Modest gangster saga with signs of style smothered by the script. Chester Morris, Alison Loyd, William Austin, Frank McHugh, Ned Sparks. Written by Josephine Lovett from the novel by Walon Green; directed by Roland West; for his own company. NB: Alison Loyd was a name momentarily adopted by Thelma Todd. 'A bit out-dated . . . will take a lot of nursing to reach average grosses.'—Variety

The Corsican Brothers*
US 1942   111m   bw
Edward Small

Siamese twins are separated but remain spiritually tied through various adventures.
Adequately exciting picturization of the Dumas swashbuckler.

w George Bruce, Howard Estabrook
d Gregory Ratoff   ph Harry Stradling
m Dmitri Tiomkin

Douglas Fairbanks Jnr, Akim Tamiroff, Ruth Warrick, J. Carrol Naish, H. B. Warner, Henry Wilcoxon

† In 1953 came an undistinguished sequel, Bandits of Corsica (GB: The Return of the Corsican Brothers), with Richard Greene, Paul Raymond, Raymond Burr and Dona Drake. Written by Richard Schayer; directed by Ray Nazarro; for Global / UA.

AAN: Dmitri Tiomkin

Corvette K 225*
US 1943   97m   bw
Universal (Howard Hawks)
GB title: The Nelson Touch

A Canadian corvette commander encounters submarines and bombers in mid-Atlantic.
Good war film of its period, marred by romantic interest.

w Lt John Sturdy   d Richard Rosson   ph Tony Gaudio   m David Buttolph

Randolph Scott, James Brown, Ella Raines, Barry Fitzgerald, Andy Devine, Richard Lane

AAN: Tony Gaudio

Corvette Summer
US 1979   104m   Metrocolor
MGM / Plotto (Hal Barwood)
GB title: The Hot One

A Los Angeles student spends the summer looking for his stolen customized car, and has various adventures around Las Vegas.
There are a few choice moments in this disconnected comedy drama, but the appeal is almost entirely to moonstruck teenagers.

w Hal Barwood, Matthew Robbins
d Matthew Robbins   ph Frank Stanley
m Craig Safan

Mark Hamill, Annie Potts, Eugene Roche, Kim Milford, Richard McKenzie

Cottage on Dartmoor
GB 1929   75m   bw
BIP (Bruce Woolfe)

A farmer's wife shelters her ex-lover when he breaks jail.
Crude early talkie notable only as an immature work of its director.

wd Anthony Asquith   ph Stanley Rodwell

Norah Baring, Uno Hemming, Hans Schlettow, Judd Green

Cottage to Let*
GB 1941   90m   bw
Gainsborough (Edward Black)
US title: Bombsight Stolen

Evacuated to Scotland, a Cockney helps prevent spies from kidnapping his inventor foster-father.
Stagey but often amusing comedy-thriller which after a shaky start becomes agreeably Hitchcockian.

w Anatole de Grunwald, J. O. C. Orton, play Geoffrey Kerr   d Anthony Asquith   ph Jack Cox   md Louis Levy

Leslie Banks, Alastair Sim, John Mills, Jeanne de Casalis, George Cole, Carla Lehmann, Michael Wilding, Frank Cellier, Wally Patch, Muriel Aked, Muriel George, Catherine Lacey, Hay Petrie

The Cotton Club*
US 1984   127m   Technicolor
Orion / Zoetrope (Robert Evans)

A fanciful melodrama of girls and gangsters at the famous Harlem musical club.
Whole books have been written on the traumas behind this shamefully wasteful production, and if the result is not entirely the disaster that might have been feared, nor is it any sort of masterpiece. The Roaring Twenties in 1939 was ten times more entertaining.

w William Kennedy, Francis Coppola
d Francis Coppola   ph Stephen Goldblatt
m John Barry   pd Richard Sylbert   ed Barry Malkin, Robert Lovett

Richard Gere, Gregory Hines, Diane Lane, Lonette McKee, Bob Hoskins, James Remar, Nicolas Cage, Allen Garfield, Fred Gwynne, Gwen Verdon
† The reputed production cost was 47,000,000 dollars.

Cotton Comes to Harlem
US 1970   97m   De Luxe

Two black detectives try to beat the police to a bale of cotton containing a fortune in stolen dollars. Rickety vehicle for two amiable black characters presented rather more surely in Come Back Charleston Blue (qv). Godfrey Cambridge, Raymond St Jacques, Calvin Lockhart, Judy Pace, Redd Foxx. Written by Arnold Perl and Ossie Davis, from the novel by Chester Himes; directed by Ossie Davis; for Formosa / UA.

The Couch
US 1962   100m   bw

A psychiatrist's patient goes on the rampage with an ice pick. Overstretched suspenser which never really holds the interest. Grant Williams, Shirley Knight, Onslow Stevens. Written by Robert Bloch; directed and produced by Owen Crump; for Warner.

Council of the Gods*
Germany 1950   106m   bw
DEFA (Adolf Fischer)

A research chemist working for a big chemical company denounces them after the war when he finds they have been producing poison gas for the concentration camps.
Self-flagellatory expiation of war crimes encased in an absorbing drama.

w Friedrich Wolff, Philipp Gebb   d Kurt Maetzig   ph Friedl Behn-Grund   m Hanns Eisler, Erwin Lehn

Paul Bildt, Agnes Windeck, Yvonne Merin, Fritz Tillman

Counsel for Crime
US 1937   61m   bw

A crooked lawyer fixes alibis for his clients before they commit a crime, until he finds his own son on the other side of one of his cases. Adequate programmer. Otto Kruger, Douglass Montgomery, Jacqueline Wells, Thurston Hall, Nana Bryant. Written by Fred Niblo Jnr, Grace Neville, Lee Loeb, Harold

Buchman; directed by John Brahm; for Columbia. 'Won't disappoint those who get caught with it on a dual.'—*Variety*

Counsellor at Law*
US 1933 78m bw
Universal (Henry Henigson)

Life in the New York office of a successful Jewish lawyer.
Practised film-making from a Broadway hit.

w Elmer Rice, from his play *d* William Wyler *ph* Norbert Brodine

John Barrymore, Bebe Daniels, Melvyn Douglas, Doris Kenyon, Onslow Stevens, Isabel Jewell, Thelma Todd, Mayo Methot

'Good drama, well produced and with strong b.o. potentialities.'—*Variety*
† Paul Muni was the first choice for the lead, but refused to play a Jewish role.

Counsel's Opinion
GB 1933 76m bw

A widow wins a barrister by pretending to be a flighty socialite. Semi-sophisticated comedy; this rather thin quickie version was done over four years later and became *The Divorce of Lady X* (qv). Henry Kendall, Binnie Barnes, Cyril Maude, Laurence Grossmith. Written by Dorothy Greenhill and Arthur Wimperis, from a play by Gilbert Wakefield; directed by Allan Dwan; for Alexander Korda.

Count Five and Die*
GB 1957 92m bw Cinemascope
TCF / Zonic (Ernest Gartside)

British intelligence seeks to give the Nazis false information about the 1944 invasion, but conviction grows that a double agent is among them.
Terse, downbeat war suspenser, gripping in parts but quite forgettable.

w Jack Seddon, David Pursall *d* Victor Vicas *ph* Arthur Grant *m* John Wooldridge

Nigel Patrick, Jeffrey Hunter, Anne-Marie Duringer, David Kossoff

The Count of Monte Cristo***
US 1934 114m bw
Edward Small / Reliance

After spending years in prison, Edmond Dantes escapes and avenges himself on those who framed him.
Classic swashbuckler, extremely well done with due attention to dialogue as well as action; a model of its kind and period.

w Philip Dunne, Dan Totheroh, Rowland V. Lee, *novel* Alexandre Dumas *d* Rowland V. Lee *ph* Peverell Marley *m* Alfred Newman

Robert Donat, Elissa Landi, Louis Calhern, Sidney Blackmer, Raymond Walburn, O. P. Heggie, William Farnum

'A near-perfect blend of thrilling action and grand dialogue.'—*Variety*

Count the Hours
US 1952 74m bw

A man's wife and lawyer fight to save him from the gallows. Stiff and unconvincing suspenser. Teresa Wright, Macdonald Carey,

Dolores Moran, Adele Mara, Edgar Barrier, John Craven, Jack Elam. Written by Doane R. Hoag and Karen DeWolf; directed by Don Siegel; for Benedict Bogeaus / RKO. (GB title: *Every Minute Counts*.)

Count Three and Pray
US 1955 92m Technicolor
        Cinemascope
Columbia / Copa (Ted Richmond)

After the Civil War a roistering Southerner comes home to rebuild his town and become its parson.
Moderate semi-western, fresh and pleasing but not memorable.

w Herb Meadow *d* George Sherman *ph* Burnett Guffey *m* George Duning

Van Heflin, Joanne Woodward (debut), Phil Carey, Raymond Burr, Allison Hayes, Myron Healey, Nancy Kulp, James Griffiths

'Don't dare come alone!'
Count Yorga Vampire
US 1970 90m Movielab
Erica / AIP (Michael Macready)

Inquisitive Los Angeles teenagers are vampirized by a suave foreign visitor.
A semi-professional film that looks it but amid the longueurs provides one or two nasty frissons.

wd Bob Kelljan *ph* Arch Archambault *m* William Marx

Robert Quarry, Roger Perry, Michael Murphy, Michael Macready, Donna Anders, Judith Lang
† *The Return of Count Yorga* followed a year later.

Count Your Blessings
US 1959 102m Metrocolor
        Cinemascope
MGM (Karl Tunberg)

An English girl marries an aristocratic Frenchman, but the war and other considerations make them virtual strangers until their son is nine years old, when it becomes clear that daddy is a philanderer.
Slight upper-crust comedy, basically rather tedious but kept buoyant by Chevalier as commentator.

w Karl Tunberg, *novel* The Blessing by Nancy Mitford *d* Jean Negulesco *ph* Milton Krasner, George Folsey *m* Franz Waxman

Deborah Kerr, *Maurice Chevalier*, Rossano Brazzi, Martin Stephens, Tom Helmore, Ronald Squire, Patricia Medina, Mona Washbourne

'Negulesco's aspirations to elegance are now familiar . . . this is far too absurd an example of Hollywood's infatuation with Old Europe to arouse much interest.'—*MFB*
● *Video: Warner*

Countdown*
US 1967 101m Technicolor
        Panavision
Warner (William Conrad)

Russian and American spaceships race for the moon.

Earnest, simply-plotted science-fiction in which technology is the centre of interest.

w Loring Mandel *d* Robert Altman *ph* William W. Spencer *m* Leonard Rosenman *ad* Jack Poplin

James Caan, Robert Duvall, Barbara Baxley, Joanna Moore, Charles Aidman, Steve Ihnat
● *Video: Warner*

Counterattack
US 1945 89m bw
Columbia
GB title: *One against Seven*

Resistance fighters go behind enemy lines for purposes of sabotage.
Standard World War II actioner, the star appearing above his surroundings.

w John Howard Lawson, *play* Janet and Philip Stevenson *d* Zoltan Korda *ph* James Wong Howe *m* Louis Gruenberg

Paul Muni, Marguerite Chapman, Larry Parks, George Macready, Roman Bohnen

Counterblast
GB 1948 99m bw

An escaped Nazi poses as a British scientist in a research laboratory. Overlong espionage thick ear with some compensations. Robert Beatty, Mervyn Johns, Nova Pilbeam, Margaretta Scott, Marie Lohr, Karel Stepanek, Alan Wheatley. Written by Jack Whittingham, from a story by Guy Morgan; directed by Paul Stein; for British National.

The Counterfeit Traitor*
US 1962 140m Technicolor
Paramount / Perlberg–Seaton

An oil importer, a naturalized Swede born in America, is blackmailed by the Allies into becoming a spy.
Heavy-going espionage drama which divides its time between action and moralizing. Excellent production does not quite make it exciting.

wd George Seaton, *book* Alexander Klein *ph* Jean Bourgoin *m* Alfred Newman

William Holden, Lilli Palmer, Hugh Griffith, Werner Peters, Eva Dahlbeck

'The picture is too long, it is also incessantly exciting, occasionally witty . . . and in its expression of organized sadism comparatively subtle.'—*Time*

Counterpoint*
US 1967 107m Techniscope
Universal (Dick Berg)

In 1944, an American symphony orchestra is captured by the Germans and threatened with execution.
Bizarre war suspenser, quite unconvincing but with effectively suspenseful moments and an old-fashioned portrayal of the Nazis as sadistic music-loving Huns.

w James Lee, Joel Oliansky, *novel* The General by Alan Sillitoe *d* Ralph Nelson *ph* Russell Metty *m* Bronislau Kaper

Charlton Heston, Maximilian Schell, Anton Diffring, Kathryn Hays, Leslie Nielsen

Countess Dracula

GB 1970　93m　Eastmancolor
Rank / Hammer (Alexander Paal)

A Hungarian noblewoman restores her youth by bathing in the blood of young virgins.
Risibly sub-Freudian addition to a grotesque Hammer gallery of monsters, indistinguishable from the others once it gets going.

w Jeremy Paul, Alexander Paal, Peter Sasdy, Gabriel Ronay　d Peter Sasdy　ph Ken Talbot　m Harry Robinson

Ingrid Pitt, Nigel Green, Sandor Eles, Maurice Denham, Patience Collier, Peter Jeffrey, Lesley-Anne Down

'At its best the film employs the kind of romantic imagery one associates with Keats; and if it doesn't quite live up to that comparison, it is at least a worthy companion to Corman's Bloody Mama.'—David Pirie, MFB

● Video: Rank

A Countess from Hong Kong

GB 1967　120m　Technicolor
Universal (Jerome Epstein)

An American millionaire diplomat is followed from Hong Kong by his Russian émigrée girl friend, and complications mount when his wife boards the ship at Hawaii.
Flatulent comedy with neither the sparkle of champagne nor even the fizz of lemonade: Chaplin's writing, direction and music are alike soporific, and commiserations are due to the cast.

wd / m Charles Chaplin　ph Arthur Ibbetson　pd Don Ashton

Marlon Brando, Sophia Loren, Patrick Cargill, Margaret Rutherford, Charles Chaplin, Sydney Chaplin, Oliver Johnston, John Paul

'An unfunny, mindless mess.'—Robert Windeler

'So old-fashioned and dull that one can hardly believe it was made now.'—Philip T. Hartung

The Countess of Monte Cristo

US 1933　74m　bw

A bit player in a musical convinces her friends she is a countess. Mild comedy remade in 1948 as an even dimmer vehicle for Sonja Henie. Fay Wray, Paul Lukas, Patsy Kelly, Reginald Owen. Written by Karen de Wolf and Gene Lewis; directed by Karl Freund; for Universal.

Country Dance

GB 1969　112m　Metrocolor
MGM / Keep—Windward (Robert Emmett Ginna)
aka: Brotherly Love

An eccentric baronet's incestuous love for his sister finally breaks up her marriage.
Rambling melodrama with O'Toole going mad in squire's tweeds; tediously fashionable but too pallid for general success, it was barely released.

w James Kennaway, from his novel Household Ghosts　d J. Lee-Thompson　ph Ted Moore　m John Addison

Peter O'Toole, Susannah York, Michael Craig, Harry Andrews, Cyril Cusack, Judy Cornwell, Brian Blessed

The Country Doctor*

US 1936　94m　bw
TCF (Darryl F. Zanuck)

A rural physician becomes famous when quintuplets are born to one of his patients. Fictionalization of the birth of the Dionne Quintuplets; pleasantly nostalgic even forty years after its raison d'être.

w Sonya Levien　d Henry King　ph John F. Seitz, Daniel B. Clark

Jean Hersholt, the Dionne Quins, Dorothy Petersen, June Lang, Slim Summerville, Michael Whalen, Robert Barrat
† Sequels: Reunion (1936), Five of a Kind (1938).

Country Gentlemen

US 1936　66m　bw

A couple of con men help a widow who runs a small-town hotel. Strained comedy in which the gag men misguidedly try to play straight. Ole Olsen, Chic Johnson, Joyce Compton, Lila Lee, Pierre Watkin. Written by Milton Ralson, Jack Harvey, Jo Graham; directed by Ralph Staub; for Republic. 'Missing is the rapidfire buffoonery with which they have been identified in vaudeville.'—Variety

'How far should a woman go to redeem the man she loves?'

The Country Girl*

US 1954　104m　bw
Paramount (William Perlberg)

The wife of an alcoholic singer blossoms when he is stimulated into a comeback.
Theatrically effective but highly unconvincing, this rather glum stage success made a cold film, miscast with an eye on the box office.

w George Seaton, play Clifford Odets　d George Seaton　ph John F. Warren　m Victor Young　songs Ira Gershwin, Harold Arlen

Bing Crosby, Grace Kelly, William Holden, Anthony Ross, Gene Reynolds
'The dramatic development is not really interesting enough to sustain a film of the intensity for which it strives.'—Karel Reisz
'Rather inexplicably, this sado-masochist morass was one of the biggest box office hits of its year.'—Pauline Kael, 70s

AA: George Seaton (as writer); Grace Kelly
AAN: best picture; John F. Warren; Bing Crosby

The County Chairman

US 1934　85m　bw

A small-town attorney competes with his prospective son-in-law for the post of public prosecutor. Small-town period comedy drama, not among its star's best. Will Rogers, Evelyn Venable, Kent Taylor, Louise Dresser, Mickey Rooney, Stepin Fetchit, Berton Churchill. Written by Sam Hellman, Gladys Lehman, from the novel by George Ade; directed by John Blystone; for Fox.

County Hospital**

US 1932　20m　bw

Ollie is in hospital; Stan brings him some hardboiled eggs and some nuts, and nearly wrecks the place. Archetypal star comedy with brilliant character and slapstick sequences, let down by a badly processed car ride home. Laurel and Hardy, Billy Gilbert. Written by H. M. Walker; directed by James Parrott; for Hal Roach.

Coup de Torchon

France 1981　128m　colour
Les Films de la Tour / Les Films A2 / Little Bear (Adolphe Viezzi)
GB title: Clean Slate

In French West Africa in 1938, an apparently easy-going police officer is inspired to commit a series of murders.
Well-made, heavy-going study of mania.

w Jean Aurenche, Bertrand Tavernier, novel POP. 1280 by Jim Thompson　d Bertrand Tavernier　ph Pierre William Glenn　m Philippe Sarde

Philippe Noiret, Isabelle Huppert, Jean-Pierre Marielle, Stéphane Audran, Eddy Mitchell

Courage

US 1930　65m　bw

A widow has a large family of which the one sweet-natured son is left a fortune by the old lady next door. Glutinous mother-love saga from a popular play. Belle Bennett, Marian Nixon, Rex Bell, Leon Janney, Blanche Friderici. Written by Walter Anthony; directed by Archie Mayo; for Warners.
'Should be certain in neighbourhood houses. For abroad, a perfect picture for a glimpse of a real American boy of breeding and the sort of mother who lives in every nation.'—Variety

Courage Fuyons*

France 1979　98m　Eastmancolor
Gaumont / Gueville (Yves Robert)

A middle-aged man embarks on a series of surprising romantic adventures.
A mainly enjoyable exercise in wish-fulfilment, sharply written and acted.

w Jean-Loup Dabadie, Yves Robert　d Yves Robert　ph Yves Lafaye　m Vladimir Cosma

Jean Rochefort, Catherine Deneuve, Robert Webber, Philippe Leroy-Beaulieu

The Court Jester***

US 1955　101m　Technicolor
Vistavision
Paramount / Dena (Melvin Frank, Norman Panama)

Opposition to a tyrannical king is provided by the Fox, but it is one of the rebel's meekest men who, posing as a jester, defeats the usurper.
One of the star's most delightful vehicles, this medieval romp has good tunes and lively action, not to mention an exceptional cast and the memorable 'chalice from the palace' routine.

THE COURT JESTER. Danny Kaye tells Cecil Parker what the duke did to the doge with his dirk.

wd Norman Panama, Melvin Frank *ph* Ray June *songs* Sylvia Fine, Sammy Cahn *ad* Hal Pereira, Roland Anderson

Danny Kaye, Glynis Johns, *Basil Rathbone*, Cecil Parker, *Mildred Natwick*, Angela Lansbury, Edward Ashley, Robert Middleton, Michael Pate, Alan Napier

The Court Martial of Billy Mitchell*

US 1955 100m Warnercolor
Cinemascope
United States Pictures (Milton Sperling)
GB title: *One Man Mutiny*

In the early twenties, an American general of the Army Air Service is court-martialled for accusing the war department of criminal negligence.

Adequate recreation of a historical incident, with a cast of excellent actors converging for a courtroom scene of some effectiveness.

w Milton Sperling, Emmet Lavery *d* Otto Preminger *ph* Sam Leavitt *m* Dmitri Tiomkin

Gary Cooper, *Rod Steiger*, Ralph Bellamy, Charles Bickford, Elizabeth Montgomery, Fred Clark, Darren McGavin, James Daly

AAN: Milton Sperling, Emmet Lavery

The Courtneys of Curzon Street*

GB 1947 120m bw
British Lion / Herbert Wilcox
US title: *The Courtney Affair*

In Victorian times, a baronet's son marries a lady's maid . . . and many years later, their grandson marries a factory worker.

Unbelievable upstairs-downstairs romantic drama spanning three generations; all to be taken with a gigantic pinch of salt, but a huge success when released.

w Nicholas Phipps, *novel* Florence Tranter *d* Herbert Wilcox *ph* Max Greene

Anna Neagle, Michael Wilding, Gladys Young, Coral Browne, Michael Medwin, Daphne Slater, Jack Watling, Helen Cherry, Bernard Lee

'The dignity of Curzon Street is Hollywoodized, and it is rare in 1945 that people in their sixties look as though they have one foot in the grave.'—*MFB*

'If my livelihood depended on booking the right film into the average cinema, this is one I would not dare to miss.'—*Observer*

The Courtship of Eddie's Father*

US 1962 117m Metrocolor Panavision
MGM / Joe Pasternak

The small son of a widower tries to interest Dad in another woman.

Fairly icky American-style sentimental comedy with most of the stops pulled out; way over-length and too self-indulgently solemn in the last part, but with professional touches.

w John Gay, *novel* Muriel Toby *d* Vincente Minnelli *ph* Milton Krasner *m* George Stoll

Glenn Ford, Ronnie Howard, Shirley Jones, Stella Stevens, Dina Merrill
† A TV series starring Bill Bixby followed in 1971.

Cousin, Cousine**

France 1975 95m Eastmancolor
Pomereu / Gaumont (Bertrand Javal)

Various furtive love affairs centre on a family wedding.

Sprightly satirical comedy full of pleasing touches, mostly jibes at French bourgeois standards.

wd Jean-Charles Tacchella *ph* Georges Lendi *m* Gerard Anfosso

Marie-France Pisier, Marie-Christine Barrault, Victor Lanoux, Guy Marchand, Ginette Garcin

'One of those rare delights you want to see again and again just to share the sheer joy of living, zest for love, genuine affection, all-too-human absurdity, and pure happiness of all those delicious people on screen.'—*Judith Crist, Saturday Review*

Les Cousins*

France 1958 110m bw
AJYM (Claude Chabrol)

A law student stays with his sophisticated cousin in Paris, and his life is altered.

The country cousin fable filled with undramatic detail and given a rather perverse ending without any apparent point.

wd Claude Chabrol *ph* Henri Decaë *m* Paul Misraki

Jean-Claude Brialy, Gérard Blain, Juliette Mayniel, Claude Cerval

A Covenant with Death

US 1966 97m Technicolor
Warner (William Conrad)

A half-Mexican judge in a border town convicts a man who accidentally kills the hangman just as the real murderer confesses.

Dreary moral melodrama with accents, nicely photographed but cold, remote and drawn out.

w Larry Marcus, Saul Levitt, *novel* Stephen Becker *d* Lamont Johnson *ph* Robert Burks *m* Leonard Rosenman

George Maharis, Katy Jurado, Earl Holliman, Sidney Blackmer, Laura Devon, Gene Hackman

'Too thrilling for words, so they set it to music!'

Cover Girl**

US 1944 107m Technicolor
Columbia (Arthur Schwartz)

The road to success for magazine cover models.

Wartime glamour musical with a stronger reputation than it really deserves apart from Kelly's solos; it does however manage a certain *joie de vivre* which should not be despised.

w Virginia Van Upp *d* Charles Vidor *ph* Rudolph Maté *md* Morris Stoloff, Carmen Dragon *songs* Jerome Kern, Ira Gershwin

Rita Hayworth, Gene Kelly, Phil Silvers, Lee Bowman, Jinx Falkenberg, Otto Kruger, Eve Arden, Ed Brophy

'Kelly and Silvers are better than Kelly and Hayworth, though she does look sumptuous, and her big smile could be the emblem of the period.'—*New Yorker, 1977*

'Much of it is not as fresh as it may seem; but its second-handedness and its occasional failures cannot obliterate the pleasure of seeing the work of a production company which obviously knows, cares about and enjoys what it is doing.'—*James Agee*

AA: Morris Stoloff, Carmen Dragon
AAN: Rudolph Maté; song 'Long Ago and Far Away'

Cover Girl Killer
GB 1959   61m   bw

A trap is set for the mad murderer of cover models. Good unpretentious second feature with plenty of suspense. Harry H. Corbett, Felicity Young, Spencer Teakle, Victor Brooks. Written and directed by Terry Bishop; for Parroch / Eros.

Cover Up
US 1948   82m   bw

An insurance investigator finds senior officials conspiring to obscure the facts of a small-town murder. Modest mystery, initially intriguing but finally unsatisfying. Dennis O'Keefe, William Bendix, Barbara Britton, Art Smith. Written by Jerome Odlum and Jonathan Ritz; directed by Alfred E. Green; for Strand / UA.

The Covered Wagon*
US 1923   103m (24 fps)   bw   silent
Paramount / Famous Players-Lasky

Pioneer settlers travel west by wagon train. A classic western which now seems painfully undernourished in terms of plot and character but still retains moments of epic sweep.

w Jack Cunningham, *novel* Emerson Hough *d* James Cruze *ph* Karl Brown

Ernest Torrence, Tully Marshall, J. Warren Kerrigan, Lois Wilson, Alan Hale

'There wasn't a false whisker in the film.'—*James Cruze*

'Forthright, impressive and vigorous, it brought a breath of fresh air into the jazz-ridden film world.'—*Lewis Jacobs*

The Cow and I
France 1959   119m   bw
Cyclope / Omnia (Walter Rupp)
original title: *La Vache et le Prisonnier*

A French soldier escapes from a prison camp and takes a farm cow as cover.
Curiously overlong war adventure which hovers uncertainly between comedy and suspense.

w Henri Verneuil, Henri Jeanson, Jean Manse *d* Henri Verneuil *ph* Roger Hubert *m* Paul Durand

Fernandel, René Havard, Albert Remy, Bernard Musson

Cowboy*
US 1957   92m   Technicolor
Columbia / Phoenix (Julian Blaustein)

Frank Harris becomes a cattle herder for love of a lady but is quickly disillusioned with the outdoor life.
Fashioned from a lively autobiography, this has interesting moments but is never as fascinating as one would expect.

w Edmund H. North, *book* On the Trail by Frank Harris *d* Delmer Daves *ph* Charles Lawton Jnr *m* George Duning

Jack Lemmon, Glenn Ford, Brian Donlevy, Anna Kashfi, Dick York, Richard Jaeckel, King Donovan

The Cowboy and the Lady
US 1938   91m   bw
Samuel Goldwyn

The daughter of a presidential candidate becomes infatuated with a rodeo cowboy. Insubstantial and witless romantic comedy which suffered many sea changes from script to screen.

w Leo McCarey, S. N. Behrman, Sonya Levien *d* H. C. Potter *ph* Gregg Toland *m* Alfred Newman

Gary Cooper, Merle Oberon, Patsy Kelly, Walter Brennan, Fuzzy Knight, Henry Kolker, Harry Davenport

'By and large only mildly diverting . . . the interest and promise of the early reels is not sustained in the latter half.'—*Variety*

'Just a lot of chestnuts pulled out of other people's dead fires.'—*Otis Ferguson*

AAN: Alfred Newman; title song (*m* Alfred Newman, *ly* Arthur Quenzer)

Cowboy from Brooklyn
US 1938   80m   bw

A supposed cowboy crooner is taken out west and proves to be terrified of animals. Genial but witless spoof of a trend of the times. Pat O'Brien, Dick Powell, Priscilla Lane, Dick Foran, Ann Sheridan, Ronald Reagan, Johnnie Davis, James Stephenson. Written by Earl Baldwin from the play Howdy Stranger by Robert Sloane and Louis Pelletier Jnr; directed by Lloyd Bacon; for Warners.

The Cowboys*
US 1972   128m   Technicolor
Panavision 70
Sanford / Warner (Mark Rydell)

Deserted by his ranch hands, a cattle drover on a long trail enlists the help of eleven schoolboys, who later avenge his death. Ambling, climactically violent, extremely unlikely western with good scenes along the way.

w Irving Ravetch, Harriet Frank Jnr, *novel* William Dale Jennings *d* Mark Rydell *ph* Robert Surtees *m* John Williams

John Wayne, Roscoe Lee Browne, Bruce Dern, Colleen Dewhurst, Slim Pickens, Sarah Cunningham

† A TV series followed in 1974 but was shortlived.

Crack in the Mirror
US 1960   97m   bw   Cinemascope
TCF / Darryl F. Zanuck

A young lawyer and his ageing mentor are at opposite sides of a murder case.
Pointless Paris-set melodrama in which for no obvious reason each of the three stars plays two roles. Relentlessly boring.

w Mark Canfield (Darryl F. Zanuck) *d* Richard Fleischer *ph* William C. Mellor *m* Maurice Jarre

Orson Welles, Bradford Dillman, Juliette Greco, William Lucas, Alexander Knox, Catherine Lacey

'Thank God it's only a motion picture!'
Crack in the World
US 1965   96m   Technicolor
Paramount / Security (Philip Yordan, Bernard Glasser, Lester A. Sansom)

A dying scientist fires a missile into the earth's centre, and nearly blows the planet apart. Jaded science-fiction melodrama, overburdened with initial chat but waking up when the special effects take over.

w Jon Manchip White, Julian Halevy *d* Andrew Marton *ph* Manuel Berenguer *m* John Douglas *ad* Eugene Lourié *sp* John Douglas

Dana Andrews, Janette Scott, Kieron Moore, Alexander Knox, Peter Damon, Gary Lasdun

Crack Up
US 1936   65m   bw

Espionage agents try to corrupt a test pilot. Modestly efficient thriller. Peter Lorre, Brian Donlevy, Helen Wood, Ralph Morgan, Thomas Beck. Written by Charles Kenyon and Sam Mintz; directed by Mal St Clair; for TCF.

Crack Up*
US 1946   93m   bw
RKO

A museum curator with an eye for forgery is discredited by crooks who make him appear drunk or half-crazed when he recounts a set of strange events which have happened to him . . .
The intriguing mystery of the opening reels, when solved, is replaced by rather dull detection, but this remains a thriller with a difference, generally well presented.

w John Paxton *d* Irving Reis *ph* Robert de Grasse *m* Leigh Harline

Pat O'Brien, Claire Trevor, Herbert Marshall, Ray Collins

Cracked Nuts
US 1931   65m   bw

Two Americans get mixed up in a revolution in a mythical country. Padded farce vehicle for a comedy team. Bert Wheeler, Robert Woolsey, Ben Turpin, Edna May Oliver, Dorothy Lee. Written by Al Boasberg, Ralph Spence; directed by Edward Cline; for RKO.
'As a two-reeler it would be fair entertainment.'—*Variety*

Crackerjack*
GB 1938 79m bw
US title: The Man with a Hundred Faces

A gentleman thief poses as butler at a stately home. Fairly smart sardonic star vehicle. Tom Walls, Lilli Palmer, Noel Madison, Leon M. Lion, Edmund Breon, Charles Heslop. Written by A. R. Rawlinson, Michael Pertwee and Basil Mason; directed by Albert de Courville; for Gainsborough. 'Carelessly made but fairly engrossing.'—Variety

Crackers
US 1984 92m Technicolor
Universal / Edward Lewis

Incompetent crooks run a pawnshop. Insufficiently rethought, San Francisco set, updating of Monicelli's 1956 comedy Big Deal on Madonna Street (I Soliti Ignoti). No longer at all funny.

w Jeffrey Fiskin d Louis Malle ph Laszlo Kovacs m Paul Chihara pd John L. Lloyd

Donald Sutherland, Jack Warden, Sean Penn, Wallace Shawn, Larry Riley, Trinidad Silva, Charlaine Woodard, Irwin Corey
'One can sense that it would all sound much funnier in Italian.'—Variety

The Cracksman
GB 1963 112m Technicolor
Cinemascope

A master locksmith becomes the unwitting dupe of a gang of safecrackers. The most elaborate vehicle devised for this diminutive star; despite bright moments, conventional mounting and over-generous length finally defeat it. Charlie Drake, George Sanders, Dennis Price, Nyree Dawn Porter, Eddie Byrne, Finlay Currie, Percy Herbert. Written by Lew Schwartz and Charlie Drake; directed by Peter Graham Scott; for ABPC.

Cradle Song*
US 1933 78m bw
Paramount (E. Lloyd Sheldon)

A nun adopts a foundling.
Stately transcription of a once-fashionable play, too concerned with its own artistic background and handicapped by a star who didn't travel well, except to those partial to Jewish nuns.

w Marc Connelly, play G. M. Martinez Sierra d Mitchell Leisen ph Charles Lang m W. Franke Harling

Dorothea Wieck, Evelyn Venable, Sir Guy Standing, Louise Dresser, Kent Taylor, Gertrude Michael, Nydia Westman, Eleanor Wesselhoeff
'It moves slowly, laboriously . . . as a commercial entry decidedly dubious.'—Variety

Craig's Wife*
US 1936 77m bw
Columbia

A middle-class wife lets her house take precedence over her husband.
Capable picturization of a Broadway success, later remade as Harriet Craig (qv).

w Mary McCally Jnr, George Kelly, play George Kelly d Dorothy Arzner ph Lucien Ballard md Morris Stoloff

Rosalind Russell, John Boles, Billie Burke, Jane Darwell, Dorothy Wilson, Alma Kruger, Thomas Mitchell, Elizabeth Risdon, Raymond Walburn

Crainquebille*
France 1922 70m approx (16 fps) bw
silent
Trarieux Films

A street trader is unjustly accused and imprisoned, afterwards finding happiness as a tramp.
Somewhere between Chaplin and Kafka, this fable was long admired for its style.

wd Jacques Feyder, story Anatole France ph Léonce Burel

Maurice de Féraudy, Françoise Rosay, Felix Oudart
† Remade 1933 by Jacques de Baroncelli with Maurice Tramel; 1954 by Ralph Habib with Yves Deniaud.

The Cranes Are Flying**
USSR 1957 94m bw
Mosfilm
original title: Letyat Zhuravli

When her lover goes to war, a girl refuses to believe later reports of his death even though she has suffered much, including marriage to a bully, in the interim.
Sleek, moving love story with most of the Hollywood production virtues plus an attention to detail and a realism which are wholly Russian.

w Victor Rosov d Mikhail Kalatozov ph Sergei Urusevski

Tatiana Samoilova, Alexei Batalov, Vasili Merkuriev

The Crash
US 1932 59m bw

An unfaithful wife finds her life changed by the stock market crash. Dim high-society goings-on make a poor star vehicle. Ruth Chatterton, George Brent, Paul Cavanagh, Henry Kolker, Barbara Leonard. Written by Earl Baldwin from the novel Children of Pleasure by Larry Barratto; directed by William Dieterle; for Warners. 'A weak sister . . . nothing happens to pique interest or capture sympathy or even provoke hostility.'—Variety

Crash Dive*
US 1943 105m Technicolor
TCF (Milton Sperling)

A submarine lieutenant and his commander love the same girl.
Well-staged war thrills in the final reels are prefaced by a long romantic comedy build-up, which probably seemed good propaganda at the time.

w Jo Swerling, story W. R. Burnett d Archie Mayo ph Leon Shamroy m David Buttolph md Emil Newman sp Fred Sersen

Tyrone Power, Anne Baxter, Dana Andrews, James Gleason, Dame May Whitty, Henry Morgan, Frank Conroy, Minor Watson
'One of those films which have no more sense of reality about this war than a popular song.'—Bosley Crowther

Crashing Hollywood*
US 1937 60m bw

A studio screenwriter selects a criminal as collaborator, and gets into all kinds of trouble. Lively melodramatic star vehicle with a reasonably vivid background. Lee Tracy, Joan Woodbury, Paul Guilfoyle, Lee Patrick, Richard Lane, Jack Carson, Tom Kennedy. Written by Paul Yawitz and Gladys Atwater, from a play by Paul Dickey and Mann Page; directed by Lew Landers; for RKO. 'Completely satisfactory programme picture.'—Variety

Crashout
US 1955 83m bw

Six convicts escape from prison, but most of them die en route. Watchable melodrama, fairly savage for its day. William Bendix, Arthur Kennedy, Luther Adler, William Talman, Gene Evans, Marshall Thompson, Beverly Michaels. Written by Hal E. Chester and Lewis R. Foster; directed by Lewis R. Foster; for Hal E. Chester / Standard.

Craze
GB 1973 95m Technicolor
(EMI) Harbour (Herman Cohen)

An African idol accidentally causes a death which brings money to its owner, who kills again and again in the hope of more loot. Crude shocker from the bottom of even this producer's barrel, notable for the star cast which was surprisingly roped in.

w Aben Kandel, Herman Cohen, novel Infernal Idol by Henry Seymour d Freddie Francis ph John Wilcox m John Scott

Jack Palance, Diana Dors, Julle Ege, Edith Evans, Hugh Griffith, Trevor Howard, Michael Jayston, Suzy Kendall, Martin Potter, Percy Herbert, Kathleen Byron

Crazy House
US 1943 80m bw
Universal (Erle C. Kenton)

Olsen and Johnson go to Hollywood to make a film.
Lame sequel to Hellzapoppin; after an explosively well edited first reel of panic in the studio, it degenerates into a slew of below-par variety turns.

w Robert Lees, Frederic I. Rinaldo d Edward Cline ph Charles Van Enger md George Hale, Milt Rosen

Ole Olsen, Chic Johnson, Martha O'Driscoll, Patric Knowles, Percy Kilbride, Cass Daley, Thomas Gomez, Edgar Kennedy
† Sherlock Holmes fans may or may not wish to record a two-line comic bit by Basil Rathbone and Nigel Bruce in character.

Crazy Joe
US / Italy 1973   99m   Technicolor

The rise and fall of a Mafia hood in New York.
Noisy, violent, reasonably proficient gangster
movie which seems to have some pretensions
to play against stereotype. Peter Boyle, Paula
Prentiss, Fred Williamson, Charles Cioffi, Rip
Torn, Luther Adler, Eli Wallach, Henry
Winkler. Written by Lewis John Carlino;
directed by Carlo Lizzani; for Bright-Persky /
De Laurentiis.

Crazy Mama
US 1975   80m   colour
New World (Julie Corman)

In 1958 Arkansas, mother and daughter set off
on a series of robberies and kidnaps which end
in violence.
Exploitation crime movie with no apparent
basis in fact; as such, occasionally exciting for
those who can tolerate this kind of thing.
w Robert Thom d Jonathon Demme ph Tak
Fujimoto m Snotty Scotty and the Hankies
Cloris Leachman, Ann Sothern, Stuart
Whitman, Jim Backus, Linda Purl, Brian
Englund

The Crazy World of Laurel and Hardy°°
US 1964   83m   bw
Hal Roach / Jay Ward

A compilation of Laurel and Hardy extracts
from their classic period.
Although the material is in itself excellent and
some of the build-up sequences well done, the
clips are all too short to achieve maximum
impact, and virtually none is identified.
w Bill Scott m Jerry Fielding narrator Garry
Moore

The Creature from the Black Lagoon
US 1954   79m   bw   3-D
U-I (William Alland)

Up the Amazon, scientists encounter a fearful
fanged creature who is half man, half fish.
Unpersuasive and unsuspenseful horror
hokum from the bottom drawer of
imagination: it did, however, coin enough
pennies to generate two even worse sequels,
Revenge of the Creature (1955) and *The
Creature Walks Among Us* (1956). And the
underwater photography is super.
w Harry Essex, Arthur Ross d Jack Arnold
ph William E. Snyder md Joseph Gershenson
Richard Carlson, Julie Adams, Richard
Denning, Antonio Moreno, Nestor Paiva,
Ricou Browning (in the rubber suit)

Creatures the World Forgot
GB 1970   95m   Technicolor
Columbia / Hammer (Michael Carreras)

Quarrels break out between rival tribes of
Stone Age men.
Feeble follow-up to *One Million Years BC* and
When Dinosaurs Ruled the Earth: someone
forgot to order any monsters.
w Michael Carreras d Don Chaffey
ph Vincent Cox m Mario Nascimbene
Julie Ege, Brian O'Shaughnessy, Robert John,
Marcia Fox, Rosalie Crutchley

The Creeper
US 1948   63m   bw

Scientists disagree over a serum which changes
humans into cats. Nonsense horror item with
stalwart cast. Ralph Morgan, Eduardo
Ciannelli, Onslow Stevens, June Vincent,
Richard Lane. Written by Maurice
Tombragel; directed by Jean Yarbrough; for
TCF.

The Creeping Flesh°
GB 1972   91m   Eastmancolor
Tigon / World Film Services (Michael
   Redbourn)

A Victorian scientist discovers that water
causes the recomposing of tissue on the
skeleton of a Neanderthal man.
Absurd but persuasive horror film, quite well
done in all departments.
w Peter Spenceley, Jonathan Rumbold
d Freddie Francis ph Norman Warwick
m Paul Ferris
Peter Cushing, Christopher Lee, Lorna
Heilbron, George Benson, Kenneth J.
Warren, Duncan Lamont, Michael Ripper

Creepshow
US 1982   120m   colour
United Film Distribution / Laurel Show
   (Richard P. Rubenstein)

A boy reads five gruesome stories from a
horror comic.
Supposedly funny but mainly rather nasty
recreation of a famous 'comic' style; far too
extended for its own good.
w Stephen King d George A. Romero
ph Michael Gornick m John Marrison
pd Tom Savini
Carrie Nye, Viveca Lindfors, Stephen King,
Leslie Nielsen, Hal Holbrook, Adrienne
Barbeau, E. G. Marshall
'Robert Bloch and Freddie Francis did it all
so much better in *Torture Garden*.'—Tom
Milne, MFB
● Video: Intervision

Crescendo°
GB 1969   95m   Technicolor
Warner / Hammer (Michael Carreras)

A girl researcher goes to stay with the widow
of a famous composer, and finds herself in
mortal danger . . .
Lunatic Hammer horror with the courage of
its shameless borrowings from *Taste of Fear,
Fanatic, Nightmare, Maniac* and all the films
about mad twin brothers, to which this chaotic
brew adds dollops of sex and heroin addiction.
w Jimmy Sangster, Alfred Shaughnessy
d Alan Gibson ph Paul Beeson m Malcolm
Williamson
Stefanie Powers, James Olson, Margaretta
Scott, Jane Lapotaire, Joss Ackland

Cries and Whispers°°°
Sweden 1972   91m   Eastmancolor
Cinematograph (Ingmar Bergman)
original title: *Viskingar och Rop*

A young woman dying of cancer in her family
home is tended by her two sisters.
Quiet, chilling, classical chapter of doom
which variously reminds one of Chekhov,
Tolstoy and Dostoievsky but is also essential
Bergman. Tough but important viewing, it
lingers afterwards in the mind like a picture
vividly painted in shades of red.
wd Ingmar Bergman ph Sven Nykvist
m Chopin and Bach
Harriet Andersson, Kari Sylwan, Ingrid
Thulin, Liv Ullmann
'Harrowing, spare and perceptive, but
lacking the humour that helps to put life and
death into perspective.'—*Michael Billington,
Illustrated London News*
AA: Sven Nykvist
AAN: best picture; Ingmar Bergman (as
writer); Ingmar Bergman (as director)
● Video: Longman

Crime and Punishment°
US 1935   88m   bw
Columbia

A student kills a pawnbroker and is tortured
by remorse.
Heavy-going rendering of Dostoievsky with
some pictorial interest.
w S. K. Lauren, Joseph Anthony d Josef Von
Sternberg ph Lucien Ballard m Arthur
Honegger md Louis Silvers
Peter Lorre, Edward Arnold, Tala Birell,
Marian Marsh, Elizabeth Risdon, Mrs Patrick
Campbell
'Will have to be sold, but should average
fair takings.'—*Variety*

Crime and Punishment°
France 1935   110m   bw

Incisive, well-acted French version.
w Marcel Aymé d Pierre Chenal m Artur
Honegger
Pierre Blanchar, Harry Baur, Marcelle Geniat,
Madeleine Ozeray
'There's a real picture in this Dostoievsky
book, and the French have proved it.'—
Variety

Crime and Punishment USA
US 1958   96m   bw
Allied Artists / Sanders Associates (Terry
   Sanders)

A student murders an old pawnbroker and is
driven mad by guilt.
Pointless updating of Dostoievsky by two
young film-makers who seemed for years to be
on the brink of a masterpiece but never
actually produced it. Some points of interest,
but the low budget is cramping.
w Walter Newman d Denis Sanders ph Floyd
Crosby m Herschel Burke Gilbert
George Hamilton, Frank Silvera, Mary
Murphy, John Harding, Marian Seldes
'There is about it a strange quality of
aimlessness which nullifies much of its
effect.'—*MFB*

Crime by Night*
US 1944 72m bw
Warner (William Jacobs)

A private detective reluctantly solves a small-town murder, and finds a spy.
Second feature which was thought at the time to have established a new pair of married detectives in the tradition of *The Thin Man*. However, one poor sequel, *Find the Blackmailer*, put paid to the idea.

w Richard Weil, Joel Malone, *novel* Forty Whacks by Geoffrey Homes d William Clemens ph Henry Sharpe

Jerome Cowan, Jane Wyman, Faye Emerson, Charles Lang, Eleanor Parker, Cy Kendall, Creighton Hale

Crime Doctor
US 1934 75m bw

A criminologist uses his special knowledge to wreak vengeance on his wife's lover. Smart co-feature which doubtless pleased a good many audiences. Otto Kruger, Karen Morley, Nils Asther, Judith Wood, William Frawley, Donald Crisp. Written by Jane Murfin from a story by Israel Zangwill; directed by John Robertson; for RKO. 'Good in every department, with mounting suspense.'—*Variety*

Crime Doctor*
US 1943 66m bw
Columbia

An amnesiac becomes a successful psychiatrist, then discovers that he was once a wanted gangster.
Time-passing second feature from a popular radio series. Ten *Crime Doctor* films were made between 1943 and 1949, all starring Warner Baxter, all except the first being locked room mysteries which seldom played fair with the audience.

w Graham Baker, Louise Lantz d Michael Gordon m Louis Silvers

Warner Baxter, Margaret Lindsay, John Litel, Ray Collins, Harold Huber, Leon Ames, Don Costello

The sequels:
1943: CRIME DOCTOR'S STRANGEST CASE
1944: SHADOWS IN THE NIGHT, CRIME DOCTOR'S COURAGE
1945: CRIME DOCTOR'S WARNING
1946: CRIME DOCTOR'S MANHUNT, JUST BEFORE DAWN
1947: THE MILLERSON CASE
1948: CRIME DOCTOR'S GAMBLE
1949: CRIME DOCTOR'S DIARY

Crime Does Not Pay**
A celebrated series of two-reel shorts made by MGM between 1935 and 1947. In a hard-driving, tensely commentated manner more reminiscent of Warner filmmaking, they gave ample scope to trainee actors and directors in allegedly truthful re-enactments of contemporary crimes, often introduced by the state governor or police commissioner.

The titles were as follows:
BURIED LOOT (1935); d George B. Seitz; with Robert Taylor, Robert Livingston.
ALIBI RACKET (1935); d George B. Seitz.
DESERT DEATH (1935); d George B. Seitz; with Raymond Hatton, Harvey Stephens.
A THRILL FOR THELMA (1935); d Edward Cahn; with Irene Hervey, Robert Warwick.
HIT AND RUN DRIVER (1935); d Edward Cahn; with Morgan Wallace, Jonathan Hale.
PERFECT SET-UP (1936); d Edward Cahn.
FOOLPROOF (1936); d Edward Cahn; with Niles Welch, Alonzo Price.
THE PUBLIC PAYS (1936); d Errol Taggart; with Paul Stanton, Cy Kendall.
TORTURE MONEY (1936); d Harold S. Bucquet; AA.
IT MAY HAPPEN TO YOU (1937); d Harold S. Bucquet.
SOAK THE POOR (1937); d Harold S. Bucquet.
GIVE TILL IT HURTS (1937); d Felix Feist; with Janet Beecher, Howard Hickman.
BEHIND THE CRIMINAL (1937); d Harold S. Bucquet; with Edward Emerson, Walter Kingsford.
WHAT PRICE SAFETY (1938); d Harold S. Bucquet; with John Wray, George Huston.
MIRACLE MONEY (1938); d Leslie Fenton; with John Miljan, Claire DuBrey.
COME ACROSS (1938); d Harold S. Bucquet; with Bernard Nedell, Donald Douglas.
A CRIMINAL IS BORN (1938); d Leslie Fenton; with George Breakston, David Durand.
THEY'RE ALWAYS CAUGHT (1938); d Harold S. Bucquet; with Stanley Ridges, John Eldredge.
THINK IT OVER (1938); d Jacques Tourneur; with Lester Matthews, Dwight Frye.
THE WRONG WAY OUT (1938); d Gustav Machaty; with Linda Terry, Kenneth Howell.
MONEY TO LOAN (1939); d Joe Newman; with Alan Dinehart, Paul Guilfoyle.
WHILE AMERICA SLEEPS (1939); d Fred Zinnemann; with Dick Purcell, Roland Varno.
HELP WANTED (1939); d Fred Zinnemann; with Tom Neal, Jo Ann Sayers.
THINK FIRST (1939); d Roy Rowland; with Laraine Day, Marc Lawrence, Sara Haden.
DRUNK DRIVING (1939); d David Miller; with Dick Purcell, Jo Ann Sayers.
POUND FOOLISH (1940); d Felix Feist; with Neil Hamilton, Lynne Carver.
KNOW YOUR MONEY (1940); d Joe Newman; with Dennis Moore, Noel Madison.
JACKPOT (1940); d Roy Rowland; with Tom Neal, Ann Morriss.
WOMEN IN HIDING (1940); d Joe Newman; with Marsha Hunt, C. Henry Gordon.
BUYER BEWARE (1940); d Joe Newman; with Charles Arnt.
SOAK THE OLD (1940); d Sammy Lee; with Ralph Morgan, Kenneth Christy.
YOU THE PEOPLE (1940); d Roy Rowland; with C. Henry Gordon, Paul Everton.
RESPECT THE LAW (1941); d Joe Newman.

FORBIDDEN PASSAGE (1941); d Fred Zinnemann; with Harry Woods; AAN.
COFFINS ON WHEELS (1941); d Joe Newman; with Cy Kendall, Darryl Hickman.
SUCKER LIST (1941); d Roy Rowland; with Lynne Carver, John Archer.
FOR THE COMMON DEFENSE (1942); d Allen Kenward; with Van Johnson, Douglas Fowley.
KEEP 'EM SAILING (1942); d Basil Wrangell; with Jim David, Lou Smith.
PLAN FOR DESTRUCTION (1943); d Edward Cahn; with Lewis Stone.
PATROLLING THE ETHER (1944); d Paul Burnford.
EASY LIFE (1944); d Walter Hart; with Bernard Thomas, Steve Geray.
DARK SHADOWS (1944); d Paul Burnford; with Arthur Space, Henry O'Neill.
FALL GUY (1945); d Paul Burnford; with Leon Ames.
THE LAST INSTALLMENT (1945); d Walter Hart; with Cameron Mitchell, Walter Sande.
PHANTOMS INC. (1945); d Harold Young; with Frank Reicher, Ann Shoemaker.
A GUN IN HIS HAND (1945); d Joseph Losey; with Anthony Caruso, Richard Gaines.
PURITY SQUAD (1945); d Harold Kress; with Byron Foulger, Dick Elliott.
LUCKIEST GUY IN THE WORLD (1947); d Joe Newman; with Barry Nelson, Eloise Hardt; AAN.

Crime in the Streets*
US 1956 91m bw
Allied Artists (Vincent M. Fenelly)

Rival knife gangs bring havoc to tenement dwellers.
Lively semi-documentary low-life melodrama; routine subject, excellent credits.

w Reginald Rose, from his TV play d Don Siegel ph Sam Leavitt m Franz Waxman

John Cassavetes, James Whitmore, Sal Mineo, Mark Rydell

The Crime of Dr Crespi
US 1935 64m bw

A surgeon induces suspended animation in a hated rival, and has him buried. Crude and tasteless variation on Poe's 'The Premature Burial'. Erich Von Stroheim, Dwight Frye, Paul Guilfoyle, Harriet Russell. Written by Lewis Graham, Edward Olmstead; directed by John H. Auer; for Republic. 'As a baby scarer it's a weak entry.'—*Variety*

The Crime of Dr Forbes
US 1936 75m bw

A gravely injured scientist asks to be put out of his misery, and a colleague is accused of murder. Competently handled minor item, more a mystery story than a consideration of euthanasia. Robert Kent, J. Edward Bromberg, Gloria Stuart, Henry Armetta, Sara Haden, Alan Dinehart. Written by Frances Hyland and Saul Elkins; directed by George Marshall; for TCF.

The Crime of Dr Hallet
US 1938 68m bw

A doctor working on jungle fever finds it
convenient to disappear and take over a dead
colleague's identity. Implausible time-passer.
Ralph Bellamy, Josephine Hutchinson,
William Gargan, Barbara Read. Written by
Lester Cole and Brown Holmes; directed by S.
Sylvan Simon; for Universal. (Remade in 1946
as *Strange Conquest*, with Lowell Gilmore and
Jane Wyatt.)

The Crime of Monsieur Lange**
France 1935 85m bw
Obéron (André Halley des Fontaines)

When the hated boss of a publishing house is
believed killed, the workers turn it into a
successful co-operative. When he reappears,
they kill him.
The political elements of this fable now seem
unimportant, but it still shows its original
charm and cinematic skill.

w *Jacques Prévert* d *Jean Renoir* ph Jean
Bachelet m Jean Wiener

René Lefèbvre, Jules Berry, Florelle, Sylvie
Bataille, Henri Guisol

Crime of Passion
US 1956 86m bw
UA / Bob Goldstein (Herman Cohen)

An executive's wife sleeps his way to the top,
but when the boss does not come through with
promotion she shoots him.
Old-fashioned star melodrama on a low
budget.

w Jo Eisinger d Gerd Oswald ph Joseph La
Shelle m Paul Dunlap

Barbara Stanwyck, Sterling Hayden, Raymond
Burr, Fay Wray, Royal Dano, Virginia Grey

Crime of the Century
US 1933 74m bw

A doctor commits a robbery by hypnotism,
but is himself assaulted and the money
disappears. Smart exploitation mystery with an
intermission for the audience to check the
clues, and a revelation that the police
investigator is the guilty man. Jean Hersholt,
Robert Elliott, Wynne Gibson, Stuart Erwin,
Frances Dee, David Landau. Written by
Florence Ryerson and Brian Marlow from the
play The Grootman Case by Walter Maria
Espe; directed by William Beaudine; for B. P.
Schulberg / Paramount. 'Can be built up into a
better than average below the de luxe
theatres.'—*Variety*

Crime School*
US 1938 86m bw
Warner (Bryan Foy)

Problems of the warden of a reform school.
Predictable vehicle for the Dead End Kids;
watchable at the time.

w Crane Wilbur, Vincent Sherman d Lewis
Seiler ph Arthur Todd m Max Steiner

Humphrey Bogart, Gale Page, Billy Halop,
Huntz Hall, Leo Gorcey, Bobby Jordan,
Gabriel Dell, Bernard Punsley, Paul Porcasi,
Al Bridge

'A rough entertainment, sometimes brutal
. . . should do well where audiences like 'em
tough.'—*Variety*

Crime Wave
US 1954 74m bw

An ex-con is prevented from going straight.
Basically humdrum programmer with lively
detail. Sterling Hayden, Gene Nelson, Phyllis
Kirk, Ted De Corsia, Charles Bronson.
Written by Crane Wilbur; directed by André
de Toth; for Warner. (GB title: *The City Is
Dark*.)

'He had tired of her—and for that he was
     sorry! He was tied to her—and for that
     he hated her!'

Crime without Passion**
US 1934 82m bw
Paramount (Ben Hecht, Charles MacArthur)

A lawyer is driven to commit murder.
Effective melodrama notable for then-new
techniques which were blended into the
mainstream of movie-making, and for the first
appearance in Hollywood of a smart new
writer-producer-director team.

wd *Ben Hecht, Charles MacArthur*, from their
story Caballero of the Law ph Lee Garmes
sp Slavko Vorkapitch

Claude Rains, Margo, Whitney Bourne,
Stanley Ridges

'It turns a lot of established motion picture
conventions topsy-turvy . . . shouldn't have
much trouble at the box office, and inside the
theatre it is safe.'—*Variety*
'The whole venture seems to take a long
stride forward for the movies.'—*Otis Ferguson*
'A flamboyant, undisciplined, but
compulsively fascinating film classic.'—*Peter
John Dyer, 1966*

Crimes at the Dark House
GB 1939 69m bw
Pennant (George King)

A Victorian landowner kills his wife and
conceals the fact by using a lunatic as her
double.
Cheeky adaptation of a classic to make one of
the star's most lip-smacking barnstormers.

w Edward Dryhurst, Frederick Hayward, H.
F. Maltby from The Woman in White by
Wilkie Collins d George King

Tod Slaughter, Hilary Eaves, Sylvia Marriott,
Hay Petrie, David Horne

Crimes of Passion
US 1984 101m colour
New World (Barry Sandler, Donald P.
  Borchers)

A sportswear designer is a hooker by night.
Risible sex melodrama with adolescent smut.

w Barry Sandler d Ken Russell ph Dick
Bush m Rick Wakeman pd Richard
MacDonald

Kathleen Turner, Anthony Perkins, John
Laughlin, Annie Potts

'One keeps waiting for Cheech and Chong
to enter this clumsily contrived boudoir.'—
Variety

The Crimes of Stephen Hawke
GB 1936 69m bw

A nineteenth-century moneylender is exposed
as the mysterious murderer who had terrorized
London. Amusing barnstormer, a vehicle for
Tod Slaughter; with Eric Portman, Marjorie
Taylor, Gerald Barry. Written by H. F.
Maltby; directed by George King; for George
King / MGM.

The Criminal*
GB 1960 97m bw
Merton Park (Jack Greenwood)
US title: *The Concrete Jungle*

Sent to jail for a racecourse snatch, a gangster
comes out fifteen years later to regain the loot
and is followed by other criminals who kill
him.
Relentlessly grim saga of prison life, with a
few sensational trimmings.

w Alun Owen, Jimmy Sangster d Joseph
Losey ph Robert Krasker m Johnny
Dankworth

Stanley Baker, Sam Wanamaker, Margit Saad,
Patrick Magee, Noel Willman, Grégoire
Aslan, Jill Bennett, Kenneth J. Warren, Nigel
Green, Patrick Wymark, Murray Melvin

'A savage, almost expressionistic picture of
English underworld life.'—*NFT, 1973*

The Criminal Code*
US 1930 97m bw
Columbia (Harry Cohn)

A young man kills in self-defence, is
railroaded into jail and becomes involved in
another murder.
Impressive melodrama with good
performances and sharp handling.

w Seton I. Miller, Fred Niblo Jnr, *play* Martin
Flavin d Howard Hawks ph James Wong
Howe, William O'Connell

Walter Huston, Phillips Holmes, Constance
Cummings, Mary Doran, De Witt Jennings,
John Sheehan, Boris Karloff

'It can play to any type of audience: they'll
understand it and talk about it. A corking
picture.'—*Variety*
† Remade as *Penitentiary* (1938) with Walter
Connolly and *Convicted* (1950) with Broderick
Crawford.

AAN: Seton I. Miller, Fred Niblo Jnr

Criminal Court
US 1946 63m bw

A lawyer is blackmailed by a crooked club
owner. Stock crime and lawcourt yarn, rather
stodgily put together but with interesting
moments. Tom Conway, Martha O'Driscoll,
Robert Armstrong, Addison Richards.
Written by Lawrence Kimble; directed by
Robert Wise; for RKO.

Criminal Lawyer
US 1936 72m bw

A smart lawyer who has devoted his career to
getting criminals off the hook has a change of
heart when appointed district attorney.
Standard programmer with a first-rate star

performance. *Lee Tracy*, Margot Grahame, Eduardo Ciannelli, Erik Rhodes. Written by G. V. Atwater, Thomas Lennon, from a story by Louis Stevenson; directed by Christy Cabanne; for RKO. 'Strong fronter for a dual, but can go solo where Tracy's name will draw.'—*Variety*

The Criminal Life of Archibaldo de la Cruz*
Mexico 1955 91m bw
Alianza Cinematografica (Roberto Figueroa)
original title: *Ensayo de un Crimen*

A fantasist determines to kill all women who cross his path, but fate intervenes.
Cheaply made macabre joke, one of its director's throwaway oddities: not too smooth, but often amusing.

w Luis Bunuel, E. Ugarte *d Luis Bunuel ph* Augusto Jimenez *md* Jorge Perez

Ernesto Alonso, Ariadna Welter, Miroslava Stern, Rita Macedo

The Crimson Circle
GB 1936 76m bw

Scotland Yard rounds up a blackmail gang.
Lively Edgar Wallace adaptation. Hugh Wakefield, Alfred Drayton, Noah Beery, June Duprez, Niall MacGinnis. Written by Howard Irving Young; directed by Reginald Denham; for Wainwright. 'Considerably superior to pictures of its kind coming out of the tight little isle.'—*Variety*

The Crimson Curtain*
France 1952 43m bw
Argos
original title: *Le Rideau Cramoisi*

An officer billeted with a bourgeois family is visited at night by the beautiful daughter, who finally dies in his arms.
A curious polished fragment with narration replacing spoken dialogue. For those in the mood, it works.

wd Alexandre Astruc, from a story by Barbey d'Aurevilly *ph* Eugene Schufftan *m* Jean-Jacques Grunenwald

Jean-Claude Pascal, Anouk Aimée, Madeleine Garcia, Jim Gerald
'In its limited time, with the greatest economy of means, it evokes an authentic sense of the past, as well as telling a story movingly and dramatically.'—*Richard Roud*

The Crimson Kimono
US 1959 82m bw
Columbia / Globe (Samuel Fuller)

Detectives seeking the murderer of a stripper in Los Angeles' Little Tokyo both fall in love with a witness.
Self-conscious local colour, though quite freshly observed and well photographed, finally overwhelms an ordinary little murder mystery.

wd Samuel Fuller *ph* Sam Leavitt *m* Harry Sukman

Glenn Corbett, James Shigeta, Victoria Shaw, Anna Lee, Paul Dubov

'Ask me no questions: believe only what you see!'
The Crimson Pirate*
GB 1952 104m Technicolor
Warner / Harold Hecht

An 18th-century pirate and an eccentric inventor lead an island's people in rebellion against a tyrant.
One suspects that this started off as a straight adventure and was turned halfway through production into a spoof; at any rate, the effect is patchy but with spirited highlights, and the star's acrobatic training is put to good use.

w Roland Kibbee *d* Robert Siodmak *ph* Otto Heller *m* William Alwyn

Burt Lancaster, Nick Cravat, Eva Bartok, Torin Thatcher, James Hayter, Margot Grahame, Noel Purcell, Frank Pettingell

Crimson Romance
US 1934 70m bw

Two Americans join the German Air Force and one is killed fighting Americans. Very curious action drama which does not make its actual sympathies very clear. Ben Lyon, James Bush, Erich Von Stroheim, Sari Maritza, Bodil Rosing, Herman Bing. Written by Al Martin, Sherman Lowe; directed by David Howard; for Mascot. 'By indie standards a pretentious production . . . but not very promising for localities where resentment is rife.'—*Variety*

Crin Blanc**
France 1953 47m bw
Albert Lamorisse
aka: *Wild Stallion*

A small boy befriends and rides a wild horse in the Camargue.
A favourite short film of great beauty, but a shade overlong for its content.

wd Albert Lamorisse *ph* Edmond Séchan *m* Maurice Le Roux

Alain Emery, Pascal Lamorisse

Crisis*
US 1950 96m bw
MGM (Arthur Freed)

A brain surgeon is forced to operate secretly on a South American dictator, and his wife is kidnapped by revolutionaries.
Dour intellectual suspense piece, in key with the genteel enlightenment of the Dore Schary regime at MGM. Well made but cold.

wd Richard Brooks, *story* George Tabori *ph* Ray June *m* Miklos Rozsa

Cary Grant, Jose Ferrer, Signe Hasso, Paula Raymond, Ramon Navarro, Antonio Moreno, Leon Ames, Gilbert Roland
'Original, arresting and considered . . . so far the most striking example of Dore Schary's policy of encouraging the development of new talents.'—*Gavin Lambert*
'A bold piece of movie adventuring.'—*L.A. Mirror*

Criss Cross*
US 1948 87m bw
U-I (Michael Draike)

An armoured car guard and his double-crossing ex-wife get mixed up with vicious gangsters.
Sordid *film noir* with a poor plot but suspenseful sequences.

w Daniel Fuchs, *novel* Don Tracy *d* Robert Siodmak *ph* Franz Planer *m* Miklos Rozsa

Burt Lancaster, Yvonne de Carlo, Dan Duryea, Stephen McNally, Richard Long, Tom Pedi, Alan Napier
'Siodmak's talent for brooding violence and the sombre urban setting gives the film a relentlessly mounting tension.'—*Peter John Dyer*

Critic's Choice
US 1963 100m Technicolor Panavision
Warner / Frank P. Rosenberg

A ruthless Broadway critic is forced by his scruples to write a bad review of his wife's play.
Unsuitable vehicle for stars who have shorn a good comedy of wit and strive vainly for sentiment, wisecracks and pratfalls.

w Jack Sher, *play* Ira Levin *d* Don Weis *ph* Charles Lang *m* George Duning

Bob Hope, Lucille Ball, Marilyn Maxwell, Rip Torn, Jessie Royce Landis, John Dehner, Jim Backus, Marie Windsor
'For instant stultification.'—*Judith Crist*

Cromwell*
GB 1970 141m Technicolor Panavision
Columbia / Irving Allen (Andrew Donally)

An account of the rise of Cromwell to power, the execution of Charles I, and the Civil War.
Disappointingly dull schoolbook history, with good production values but glum handling.

wd Ken Hughes *ph* Geoffrey Unsworth *m* Frank Cordell *pd* John Stoll

Richard Harris, Alec Guinness, Robert Morley, Dorothy Tutin, Frank Finlay, Timothy Dalton, Patrick Wymark, Patrick Magee, Nigel Stock, Charles Gray, Michael Jayston, Anna Cropper, Michael Goodliffe
'It tries to combine serious intentions with the widest kind of popular appeal and falls unhappily between the two. It will offend the purists and bore the kiddies.'—*Brenda Davies*
'Shakespeare spoiled us for this sort of thing. We wait for great speeches and witty remarks, for rage and poetry, and we get dedicated stodginess.'—*Pauline Kael*

AAN: Frank Cordell

The Crooked Billet
GB 1929 82m bw

Spies and detectives converge on an old inn where documents are hidden. Fairly unwatchable now, this once-entertaining melodrama was shot as a silent and had sound clumsily added. Its cast remains notable: Carlyle Blackwell, Madeleine Carroll, Miles Mander, Gordon Harker. Written by Angus Macphail, from the play by Dion Titherage; directed by Adrian Brunel; for Michael Balcon / Gainsborough.

HURTLING OUT OF A VAST ARENA OF BREATHLESS ADVENTURE!

WARNER BROS. PRESENT

BURT LANCASTER AS **The Crimson Pirate**

An astounding exhibition of daredevil deeds never before seen on the screen——and all FILMED IN THE MEDITERRANEAN

"RAM THE TYRANTS OUT OF THE SEA! Follow me mates--we'll eat the smoke of their broadsides to steal the woman from the king!"

Death-defying Balloon Attack --one of its 1000 surprises!

COLOR BY TECHNICOLOR

NICK CRAVAT · ROLAND KIBBEE · HAROLD HECHT · ROBERT SIODMAK · A NORMA PRODUCTION · DISTRIBUTED BY WARNER BROS.

THE CRIMSON PIRATE. The star had himself a splendid time in this all-action spoof of every Hollywood swashbuckler the writer could think of.

The Crooked Road
GB / Yugoslavia 1964   92m   bw

An American journalist plans to expose as a crook the dictator of a small Balkan state, but finds himself framed for murder. Lugubrious and too-talkative melodrama of political intrigue. Robert Ryan, Stewart Granger, Marius Goring, Nadia Gray, Catherine Woodville, George Coulouris. Written by J. Garrison and Don Chaffey, from the novel *The Big Story* by Morris West; directed by Don Chaffey; for Argo / Triglav.

The Crooked Way
US 1949   87m   bw

An amnesiac ex-veteran finds that he was once a minor gangster. Predictable thick ear with film noir aspirations. John Payne, Sonny Tufts, Ellen Drew, Rhys Williams. Written by Richard Landau, from a radio play *No Blade Too Sharp* by Robert Monroe; directed by Robert Florey; photographed by John Alton; for Benedict Bogeaus.

The Crooked Web
US 1955   77m   bw

A restaurant owner is lured into a scheme to recover buried Nazi gold from Germany, but finds it is a means of arresting him on an old murder charge. Ingenious but somehow uninteresting puzzle melodrama. Frank Lovejoy, Richard Denning, Mari Blanchard. Written by Lou Breslow; directed by Nathan Juran; for Sam Katzman / Columbia.

Crooks and Coronets
GB 1969   106m   Technicolor
Warner Seven Arts / Herman Cohen
US title: *Sophie's Place*

American gangsters plan to rob a stately home but are taken over by the dowager in charge. Overlong and mainly flatulent comedy, with a good climax involving a vintage plane.

wd Jim O'Connelly *ph* Desmond Dickinson *m* Patrick John Scott

Telly Savalas, Edith Evans, Warren Oates, Nicky Henson, Cesar Romero, Harry H. Corbett

Crooks Anonymous*
GB 1962   87m   bw
Anglo Amalgamated (Nat Cohen)

A petty thief joins an organization for reforming criminals, but is tempted again . . . and so are they. Amusingly devised and plotted minor comedy with an exceptional cast.

w Jack Davies, Henry Blyth *d* Ken Annakin *ph* Ernest Steward *m* Muir Mathieson, Henry Martin

Leslie Phillips, Stanley Baxter, Wilfrid Hyde White, Julie Christie, James Robertson Justice, Robertson Hare, Charles Lloyd Pack

Crooks in Cloisters
GB 1963   97m   Technicolor   Scope

Forgers pose as monks but are reformed by the country life. Busy comedy full of familiar faces; perhaps a small cut above the *Carry Ons*. Ronald Fraser, Barbara Windsor, Grégoire Aslan, Bernard Cribbins, Davy

Kaye, Wilfred Brambell. Written by Mike Watts; directed by Jeremy Summers; for ABPC.

Crooks' Tour*
GB 1940 84m bw
British National (John Corfield)

English tourists are mistaken for spies by Nazis in Baghdad.
Amusing vehicle for two comic actors who excelled at portraying the English abroad.

w John Watt, Max Kester, from the radio serial by Sidney Gilliat and Frank Launder d John Baxter ph James Wilson m Kennedy Russell

Basil Radford, *Naunton Wayne*, Greta Gynt, Abraham Sofaer, Gordon McLeod

Crooner
US 1932 64m bw

A radio singer who is more than something of a prig gets his come-uppance. Would-be satire with more bore than bite. David Manners, Ann Dvorak, Ken Murray, William Janney, Eddie Nugent, J. Carrol Naish. Written by Charles Kenyon from a story by Rian James; directed by Lloyd Bacon; for Warners. 'A general slap at that ether pest who for a time held popular sway . . . but there is no sympathy for anybody in the cast.'—*Variety*

Cross Country
Canada 1983 104m colour

The boy friend of a murdered girl finds himself being driven west at gunpoint by a mad nymphomaniac and her protector. No-holds-barred 'adult' thriller whose excesses become risible. Richard Beymer, Nina Axelrod, Michael Ironside, Brent Carver. Written by Logan N. Danforth (John Hunter); directed by Paul Lynch; for Filmline / Yellowbill.

Cross Creek*
US 1983 122m Technicolor
EMI / Radnitz / Ritt (Robert B. Radnitz)

In 1928 Marjorie Kinnan Rawlings leaves her journalist husband and goes to live in the Florida backwoods, where she hopes to write a Gothic romance.
Elongated study of writer's block (though the subject did eventually write *The Yearling*). Altogether too typical of its producer and director—and too slow—to hold much surprise or interest.

w Dalene Young *memoir* Marjorie Kinnan Rawlings d Martin Ritt ph John A. Alonzo m Leonard Rosenman pd Walter Scott Herndon

Mary Steenburgen, Rip Torn, Peter Coyote, Dana Hill, Ike Eisenmann, Alfre Woodard
'The landscapes are attractive, but much too lushly filmed with lyrical inserts in which the wonders of the bayou are contemplated. Good performances fail to mask the fact that the characters are stereotypes from start to finish.'—*Tom Milne, MFB*
'Everything is lighted to look holy, and when the score isn't shimmering and burnishing, nature is twittering.'—*New Yorker*
AAN: Rip Torn, Alfre Woodard

Cross My Heart*
US 1945 83m bw
Paramount (Harry Tugend)

A romantic girl confesses to murder, is acquitted, and finds the real murderer.
Modest remake of *True Confession* (qv), with frenetic pace but not much style.

w Claude Binyon, Harry Tugend, Charles Schnee d John Berry ph Charles Lang Jnr m Robert Emmett Dolan

Betty Hutton, Sonny Tufts, Michael Chekhov, Rhys Williams, Ruth Donnelly, Al Bridge, Howard Freeman, Iris Adrian

Cross of Iron*
GB / West Germany 1976 133m Technicolor
EMI–Rapid Film / Terra Filmkunst (Wolf C. Hartwig)

Militarily and emotionally at the end of its tether, a German battalion is decimated while fighting the Russians in 1943.
Painful to follow, occasionally beautiful to watch, this quite horrid film offers too much opportunity for its director to wallow in unpleasant physical details, and its main plot of bitter rivalry offers no relief.

w Julius J. Epstein, Herbert Asmodi d Sam Peckinpah ph John Coquillon m Ernest Gold

James Coburn, James Mason, Maximilian Schell, David Warner, Klaus Löwitch, Senta Berger
'Morally dubious but technically brilliant.'—*Michael Billington, Illustrated London News*
● *Video: Thorn EMI*

The Cross of Lorraine*
US 1944 91m bw
MGM (Edwin Knopf)

In a German camp for French prisoners, an escape leads to a rising by local villagers.
Standard war propaganda piece, made with enthusiasm on unconvincing sets.

w Michael Kanin, Ring Lardner Jnr, Alexander Esway, Robert Andrews d Tay Garnett ph Sidney Wagner m Bronislau Kaper

Gene Kelly, Jean-Pierre Aumont, Cedric Hardwicke, Peter Lorre, Joseph Calleia, Richard Whorf, Hume Cronyn
'Half a football team worked on the story, yet except for a foolish coda it is one of the most edged, well-characterized, and naturally cinematic scripts of the year.'—*James Agee*

Crossed Swords
Italy / USA 1954 83m Pathecolor
Viva Films (J. Barrett Mahon, Vittorio Vassarotti)
original title: *Il Maestro di Don Giovanni*

The son of an Italian duke prevents an uprising.
A thin swashbuckler showing the perils of early co-production.

wd Milton Krims ph Jack Cardiff

Errol Flynn, Gina Lollobrigida, Cesare Danova, Nadia Gray, Paola Mori

'Sensational? No, it's dynamite!'
Crossfire**
US 1947 86m bw
RKO (Adrian Scott)

A Jew is murdered in a New York hotel, and three soldiers are suspected.
Tense, talky thriller shot entirely at night with pretty full expressionist use of camera technique; notable for style, acting, experimentation, and for being the first Hollywood film to hit out at racial bigotry.

w John Paxton, *novel* The Brick Foxhole by Richard Brooks ph J. Roy Hunt d Edward Dmytryk m Roy Webb

Robert Young, Robert Mitchum, *Robert Ryan*, Gloria Grahame, *Paul Kelly*, Sam Levene, Jacqueline White, Steve Brodie

AAN: best picture; John Paxton; Edward Dmytryk; Robert Ryan; Gloria Grahame
● *Video: Thorn EMI*

The Crossing of the Rhine*
France / Italy / West Germany 1960 125m bw
Franco-London-Gibe-Jonia-UFA (Ralph Baum)
original title: *Le Passage du Rhin*

Two French soldiers escape from the Germans in 1940 and after various adventures meet up again in Paris in 1945.
Two crowded plots and not a great deal of point emerge from this watchable war film full of conventional set pieces.

w André Cayatte, Armand Jammot d André Cayatte ph Roger Fellous m Louiguy

Charles Aznavour, Nicole Courcel, Georges Rivière, Cordula Trantow

Crossplot
GB 1969 97m Eastmancolor
UA / Tribune (Robert S. Baker)

An advertising executive gets involved in a spy ring.
Old-fashioned, London-set amalgam of secret codes, disappearing bodies, helicopter attacks, and a finale frustrating the assassination of a statesman in Hyde Park.

w Leigh Vance d Alvin Rakoff ph Brendan J. Stafford m Stanley Black

Roger Moore, Martha Hyer, Alexis Kanner, Francis Matthews, Bernard Lee

Crossroads**
Japan 1928 80m approx bw silent
Shochiku
original title: *Jujiro*

A woman kills her seducer. Her brother thinks he has killed a man and takes refuge with her, only to die of shock when he sees the man alive.
The only widely distributed Japanese silent film, this curious piece is fragmentarily told and will remind many of *Rashomon* with its mixture of flashbacks and dreams.

wd Teinosuke Kinugasa *ph* Kohei Sugiyama
J. Bandoha, A. Tschihaya, Yujiko Ogawa, I.
Sohma

Crossroads°
US 1942 84m bw
MGM (Edwin Knopf)

A French diplomat who once lost his memory
is blackmailed by crooks who claim he was
once a criminal.
Smooth mystery melodrama adapted from the
French film *Carrefour*.

w Howard Emmett Rogers, John Kafka
d Jack Conway *ph* Joseph Ruttenberg
m Bronislau Kaper

William Powell, Hedy Lamarr, Basil
Rathbone, Claire Trevor, Margaret Wycherly,
Felix Bressart, Sig Rumann

Crosswinds
US 1951 93m Technicolor

Treasure-hunting boatmen fall out in New
Guinea. Adequate outdoor thick-ear; good
value for money as the lower half of a double
bill. John Payne, Rhonda Fleming, Forrest
Tucker, Robert Lowery, Alan Mowbray, John
Abbott. Written and directed by Lewis R.
Foster; for Pine / Thomas (Paramount).

The Crowd°°°
US 1928 98m bw silent
MGM (King Vidor)

Episodes in the life of a city clerk.
A deliberately humdrum story, chosen to show
that drama can exist in the lowliest
surroundings, retains much of its original
power, though some of the director's
innovations have become clichés.

w King Vidor, John V. A. Weaver, Harry
Behn *d* King Vidor *ph* Henry Sharp
ad Cedric Gibbons, Arnold Gillespie
ed Hugh Wynn

James Murray, Eleanor Boardman, Bert
Roach, Estelle Clark
  'No picture is perfect, but this comes as near
to reproducing reality as anything you have
ever witnessed.'—*Photoplay*

AAN: King Vidor

The Crowd Roars°
US 1932 85m bw
Warner

A star motor-racing driver tries to prevent his
young brother from following in his footsteps.
Typical early Cagney vehicle, still
spectacularly pacy but dated in its dialogue
scenes.

w Kubec Glasmon, John Bright, Niven Busch
d Howard Hawks *ph* Sid Hickox, John
Stumar *md* Leo Forbstein

James Cagney, Joan Blondell, Ann Dvorak,
Eric Linden, Guy Kibbee, Frank McHugh,
Regis Toomey
  'A thin and uneventful story, but a majority
of the footage is devoted to three stirring
contests.'—*Variety*
  'As so often Hawks seems bitter at the
world men have created but respects those
who have to attempt to live it to the full.'—
NFT, 1963

'The story is not precisely exciting . . . the
closing episode is the best, for it reveals a
certain originality in having the injured
automobile racers eager to continue the race
in ambulances on the way to hospital.'—
Mordaunt Hall, New York Times
† Remade in 1939 as *Indianapolis Speedway*.

The Crowd Roars°
US 1938 90m bw
MGM (Sam Zimbalist)

A young boxer becomes involved with the
underworld.
Standard star vehicle with efficient trimmings.

w Thomas Lennon, George Bruce, George
Oppenheimer *d* Richard Thorpe *ph* John
Seitz *m* Edward Ward

Robert Taylor, Frank Morgan, Edward
Arnold, Maureen O'Sullivan, William Gargan,
Frank Craven, Jane Wyman, Lionel Stander,
Nat Pendleton
  'Exciting melodrama with plenty of ring
action, some plausible romance and several
corking good characterizations.'—*Variety*
† Remade as *Killer McCoy*.

The Crowded Day
GB 1954 82m bw

Problems of five assistants in a department
store during the Christmas rush. Naïve little
portmanteau which suited its purpose. Joan
Rice, John Gregson, Freda Jackson, Patricia
Marmont, Josephine Griffin, Sonia Holm,
Rachel Roberts, Thora Hird, Dora Bryan,
Edward Chapman, Sid James, Richard Wattis.
Written by Talbot Rothwell; directed by John
Guillermin; for Adelphi.

The Crowded Sky
US 1960 104m Technicolor
Warner (Michael Garrison)

As two planes fly unwittingly towards each
other, the passengers muse on their personal
problems. An emergency landing averts total
disaster.
The format goes back as far as *Friday the
Thirteenth*, and forward to *Airport 75*, but this
was in fact a cut-rate rehash of *The High and
the Mighty*, with dull characters and
insufficiently tense handling, not to mention a
second tense cast.

w Charles Schnee *d* Joseph Pevney *ph* Harry
Stradling *m* Leonard Rosenman

Dana Andrews, Rhonda Fleming, Efrem
Zimbalist Jnr, John Kerr, Anne Francis,
Keenan Wynn, Troy Donahue, Joe Mantell,
Patsy Kelly

The Cruel Sea°°
GB 1953 126m bw
Ealing (Leslie Norman)

Life and death on an Atlantic corvette during
World War II.
Competent transcription of a bestselling book,
cleanly produced and acted; a huge box office
success.

w Eric Ambler, *novel* Nicholas Monsarrat
d Charles Frend *ph* Gordon Dines, Jo Jago,
Paul Beeson *m* Alan Rawsthorne

Jack Hawkins, Donald Sinden, Stanley Baker,
John Stratton, Denholm Elliott, John Warner,
Bruce Seton, Virginia McKenna, Moira Lister,
June Thorburn
  'This is a story of the battle of the Atlantic,
a story of an ocean, two ships and a handful of
men. The men are the heroes.. The heroines
are the ships. The only villain is the sea—the
cruel sea—that man has made even more
cruel.'—*opening narration*
  'One is grateful nowadays for a film which
does not depict war as anything but a tragic
and bloody experience, and it is this quality
which gives the production its final power to
move.'—*John Gillett*
  'Sensitivity, faithfulness, and almost
inevitable tedium.'—*Time Out, 1984*

AAN: Eric Ambler
● *Video: Thorn EMI*

Cruising
US 1980 106m Technicolor
Lorimar (Jerry Weintraub)

A New York cop becomes degraded in his
search among homosexuals for a sadistic killer.
Alleged thriller with phoney pretensions and
repellent detail.

wd William Friedkin *ph* James Contner
m Jack Nitzsche

Al Pacino, Paul Sorvino, Karen Allen,
Richard Cox, Don Scardino, Joe Spinell
  'Like any approach to the bizarre, it's
fascinating for about fifteen minutes. After
that, it suffers from the same boring repetition
that makes porno so uninteresting
generally.'—*Variety*

● *Video: MGM / UA*

'Wonders to dazzle the human
imagination—in a flaming love story set
in titanic world conflict!'

The Crusades°°
US 1935 127m bw
Paramount / Cecil B. de Mille

Spurred by his wife Berengaria, Richard the
Lionheart sets off on his holy wars.
Heavily tapestried medieval epic, spectacular
sequences being punctuated by wodges of
uninspired dialogue. A true de Mille pageant.

w Harold Lamb, Waldemar Young, Dudley
Nichols *d* Cecil B. de Mille *ph* Victor Milner
sp Gordon Jennings *m* Rudolph Kopp

Henry Wilcoxon, Loretta Young, C. Aubrey
Smith, Ian Keith, Katherine de Mille, Joseph
Schildkraut, Alan Hale, C. Henry Gordon,
George Barbier, Montagu Love, Lumsden
Hare, William Farnum, Hobart Bosworth,
Pedro de Cordoba, Mischa Auer
  'Mr de Mille's evangelical films are the
nearest equivalent today to the glossy German
colour prints which decorated mid-Victorian
bibles. There is the same lack of a period
sense, the same stuffy horsehair atmosphere of
beards and whiskers, and, their best quality, a
childlike eye for detail.'—*Otis Ferguson*
  'Cinema addicts by now have some idea
what to expect in a de Mille version of the
Holy Wars. *The Crusades* should fulfil all

WONDERS TO DAZZLE THE HUMAN IMAGINATION...IN A FLAMING LOVE STORY SET IN TITANIC WORLD CONFLICT!

You need ten eyes to see...
ten ears to hear...ten hearts
to feel...the tumultuous
surge and glory of this mighty
spectacle, this shining
romance... as impassioned
now as when it first awed
the world with its perfection!

Adolph Zukor presents
CECIL B. DeMILLE'S
The CRUSADES
with
LORETTA YOUNG
HENRY WILCOXON
Ian Keith · Katherine DeMille · C. Aubrey Smith
Joseph Schildkraut · Cast of 10,000 · A Paramount Picture

THE CRUSADES. With de Mille, the human drama was usually dwarfed by the extras, and never so obviously as in this case.

expectations. As a picture it is historically worthless, didactically treacherous, artistically absurd. None of these defects impairs its entertainment value. It is a hundred-million-dollar sideshow which has at least three features to distinguish it from the long line of previous de Mille extravaganzas. It is the noisiest; it is the biggest; it contains no baths.'—*Time*

'Probably only de Mille could make a picture like this and get away with it. It's long, and slow, and the story is not up to some of his previous films, but the production has sweep and spectacle.'—*Variety*

AAN: Victor Milner

Cry Danger*
US 1951 79m bw
RKO / Olympic (Sam Wiesenthal,
W. R. Frank)

After serving five years for robbery, a man gets out on parole and clears his name.
Slick little slice of thick ear, very lively all round.

w William Bowers, *story* Jerome Cady
d Robert Parrish *ph* Joseph F. Biroc *m* Emil Newman, Paul Dunlap *ad* Richard Day

Dick Powell, Rhonda Fleming, Richard Erdman, William Conrad, Regis Toomey, Jay Adler

Cry for Happy
US 1961 110m Eastmancolor
Cinemascope
Columbia (William Goetz)

Four navy cameramen in Japan help geishas to found an orphanage.
As bad as it sounds, a repellent mixture of sentiment and knockabout.

w Irving Brecher *d* George Marshall
ph Burnett Guffey *m* George Duning

Glenn Ford, Donald O'Connor, Miiko Taka, James Shigeta, Mikoshi Umeki, Joe Flynn, Howard St John

'Any film which expends most of its energies on a protracted joke about how far you can go with a geisha could hardly fail to be as charmless and witless as this.'—*MFB*

A Cry from the Streets
GB 1958 100m bw
Film Traders (Ian Dalrymple)

Episodes from the work of child welfare officers.
Mildly pleasing but unconvincing semi-documentary, with children competing with the star at scene-stealing.

w Vernon Harris, *novel* The Friend in Need by Elizabeth Coxhead *d* Lewis Gilbert
ph Harry Gillan *m* Larry Adler

Max Bygraves, Barbara Murray, Colin Petersen, Dana Wilson, Elizabeth Harrison, Eleanor Summerfield, Mona Washbourne

Cry Havoc
US 1943 97m bw
MGM (Edwin Knopf)

War nurses are caught up in the Bataan retreat.
An all-woman cast adequately handles a stagey melodrama about a tragic situation.

w Paul Osborn, *play* Proof thro' the Night by Allen R. Kenward *d* Richard Thorpe
ph Karl Freund *m* Daniele Amfitheatrof

Margaret Sullavan, Joan Blondell, Ann Sothern, Fay Bainter, Marsha Hunt, Ella Raines, Frances Gifford, Diana Lewis, Heather Angel, Connie Gilchrist

'A sincere fourth-rate film made from a sincere fifth-rate play.'—*James Agee*

'Its popularity will stem less from its probably factual record of nurses starving, sweating and dying in the beleaguered Philippine jungle than from the impressive all-woman cast which MGM has rounded up for the occasion.'—*Newsweek*

A Cry in the Night
US 1956 75m bw
Warner / Jaguar (George C. Bertholon)

A peeping Tom, caught by a teenage couple, abducts the girl and threatens rape.
Odd little domestic thriller, with parents and police working together. Watchable, but a bit over the top.

w David Dortort d Frank Tuttle ph John Seitz m David Buttolph

Edmond O'Brien, Brian Donlevy, Natalie Wood, Raymond Burr, Richard Anderson, Irene Hervey, Anthony Caruso

Cry of the Banshee
GB 1970 87m Movielab
AIP (Gordon Hessler)

A 16th-century magistrate is cursed by a witch, who sends a devil in the form of a young man to destroy him.
Modest horror film which fails to do justice to its interesting plot.

w Tim Kelly, Christopher Wicking d Gordon Hessler ph John Coquillon m Les Baxter

Vincent Price, Elisabeth Bergner, Patrick Mower, Essy Persson, Hugh Griffith, Hilary Dwyer, Sally Geeson

Cry of the City**
US 1948 96m bw
TCF

A ruthless gangster on the run is pursued by a policeman who was once his boyhood friend.
Very well produced but relentlessly miserable New York thriller on the lines of *Manhattan Melodrama* and *Angels with Dirty Faces*.

w Richard Murphy, *novel* The Chair for Martin Rome by Henry Helseth d Robert Siodmak ph Lloyd Aherne m Alfred Newman

Victor Mature, Richard Conte, Mimi Agulia, Shelley Winters, Tommy Cook, Fred Clark, Debra Paget

'When the city cries in a movie, it's with the desolate wail of police sirens and with rain-streaked sidewalks; but most of all with poetic justification.'—*Paul Taylor, Time Out, 1980*

Cry Terror**
US 1958 96m bw
MGM / Andrew Stone

As security against ransom money being delivered, an airline bomber kidnaps a family.
Unabashed suspenser which screws panic situations as far as they will go and farther.

wd Andrew Stone ph Walter Strenge m Howard Jackson

James Mason, Rod Steiger, Inger Stevens, Neville Brand, Angie Dickinson, Kenneth Tobey, Jack Klugman, Jack Kruschen

Cry the Beloved Country*
GB 1951 96m bw
London Films (Alan Paton)
US title: *African Fury*

In South Africa, a white farmer and a black preacher find friendship through linked family tragedies.
Well-intentioned, earnest, rather high-flown racial drama.

w Alan Paton, from his novel d Zoltan Korda ph Robert Krasker m Raymond Gallois-Montbrun

Canada Lee, Sidney Poitier, Charles Carson, Charles McRae, Joyce Carey, Geoffrey Keen, Michael Goodliffe, Edric Connor

Cry Vengeance
US 1954 81m bw
Allied Artists (Lindsley Parsons)

An innocent man is released from jail and seeks vengeance against the man who framed him and killed his wife and child.
Adequate toughie with no particular flair.

w Warren Douglas, George Brinker d Mark Stevens ph William Sickner m Paul Dunlap

Mark Stevens, Martha Hyer, Skip Homeier, Joan Vohs, Douglas Kennedy

Cry Wolf
US 1947 83m bw
Warner (Henry Blanke)

A widow claims her husband's estate and finds his mysterious uncle very difficult to deal with . . .
Rather obvious old dark house mystery with a not very interesting solution, all relying too heavily on star performances.

w Catherine Turney, *novel* Marjorie Carleton d Peter Godfrey ph Carl Guthrie m Franz Waxman

Barbara Stanwyck, Errol Flynn (as the apparent heavy), Geraldine Brooks, Richard Basehart, Helene Thimig

Cry Wolf
GB 1980 31m bw

A scientist accidentally imbibes a canine serum and turns into a werewolf. Flattish comedy which is mainly indistinguishable from the low-budget British shockers it satirizes, but manages a few good moments. Paul Maxwell, Rosalind Ayres, Stephen Greif. Written by Stan Hey; directed by Leszek Burzynski; photographed by Robert Krasker; for Picture Partnership / Paramount.

The Crystal Ball*
US 1943 82m bw
(Richard Blumenthal)

A failed beauty contestant becomes a fortune teller and is involved in a land swindle.
Pleasant comedy with fanciful moments, ending with a pie-throwing contest.

w Virginia Van Upp d Elliott Nugent ph Leo Tover m Victor Young

Paulette Goddard, Ray Milland, Gladys George, Virginia Field, Cecil Kellaway, William Bendix, Ernest Truex

Cuba
US 1979 122m Technicolor
UA / Alex Winitsky, Arlene Sellers

Upper-crust characters are caught in Havana when the Castro revolution starts.
Aimless romantic melodrama which gets absolutely nowhere and might have been better played in the *Casablanca* vein.

w Charles Wood d Richard Lester ph David Watkin m Patrick Williams pd Gil Parrando

Sean Connery, Brooke Adams, Jack Weston, Hector Elizondo, Denholm Elliott, Martin Balsam, Chris Sarandon

Cuba Si!*
France 1961 58m bw
Films de la Pléïade

A documentary on the Cuban revolution and Castro's rise to power.
Remarkable and influential at the time for its use of techniques which are now the commonplaces of television, this documentary still has its flashes of interest.

wd, ph Chris Marker m E. G. Mantici, J. Calzada ed Eva Zora

'An eloquent, personal record of history in the making.'—*Georges Sadoul*

Cuban Love Song
US 1931 86m bw
MGM (Albert Lewin)

A marine on leave in Cuba falls in love; years later he returns to retrieve his illegitimate child, whose mother has died.
Pathetic musical melodrama which did not advance its singing star's film career.

w John Lynch d W. S. Van Dyke ph Harold Rosson songs various

Lawrence Tibbett, Lupe Velez, Jimmy Durante, Ernest Torrence, Karen Morley, Louise Fazenda

'Tibbett may be a sensation on the concert stage, but it's not the same in pictures.'—*Variety*

A Cuckoo in the Nest*
GB 1933 85m bw
Gaumont (Ian Dalrymple, Angus MacPhail)

A newlywed husband is forced to spend a night at an inn with an old flame pretending to be his wife.
Classic Aldwych farce with the stage company in excellent form; directorial style on the stagey side.

w Ben Travers, A. R. Rawlinson, *play Ben Travers* d Tom Walls

Ralph Lynn, Tom Walls, Yvonne Arnaud, Mary Brough, Veronica Rose, Gordon James, Cecil Parker, Roger Livesey

† Remade 1955 as *Fast and Loose*.

The Cuckoos
US 1930 90m bw (Technicolor sequences)

Two tramps become fortune tellers. The most ambitiously staged, and probably the most popular of this team's gag marathons. Bert Wheeler, Robert Woolsey, Jobyna Howland, June Clyde, Hugh Trevor, Dorothy Lee. Written by Cy Woods from the musical comedy The Ramblers by Philip H. Goodman; directed by Paul Sloane; for RKO. 'It holds little between the laughs and doesn't need anything else.'—*Variety*

Cujo
US 1983 91m CFI colour

A St Bernard dog is bitten by a rabies-infected bat, and becomes a vicious killer. Not much of a basis for a horror film, and this is not much of a horror film. Dee Wallace, Daniel-Hugh Kelly, Danny Pintauro, Ed Lauter, Christopher Stone. Written by Don Carlos Dunaway, Lauren Currier, from the novel by Stephen King; directed by Lewis Teague; for Sunn Classic / Taft.

Cul de Sac
GB 1966   111m   bw
Compton—Tekli (Gene Gutowski)

Two gangsters on the run take refuge in an old castle on a desolate Northumbrian island, but find their nemesis in the effeminate owner and his voluptuous wife.
Overlong, eccentric black comedy, more perplexing than entertaining.

w Roman Polanski, Gerard Brach d Roman Polanski ph Gilbert Taylor m Komeda

Lionel Stander, Donald Pleasence, Jack MacGowran, Françoise Dorléac, William Franklyn, Robert Dorning, Renée Houston

● Video: Video Media

The Culpeper Cattle Company*
US 1972   92m   De Luxe
TCF (Paul A. Helmick)

A 16-year-old would-be cowboy joins a cattle trail but is shocked at the harsh realities of western life.
Excellent moody photography helps to convince us that the old west was really like this, but the story is more brutal than interesting.

w Eric Bercovici, Gregory Prentiss d Dick Richards ph Lawrence Edward Williams, Ralph Woolsey m Tom Scott, Jerry Goldsmith

Gary Grimes, Billy 'Green' Bush, Luke Askew, Bo Hopkins, Geoffrey Lewis, Wayne Sutherlin

● Video: CBS / Fox

Cult of the Cobra
US 1955   79m   bw

Six GIs are cursed by the high priest of an Indian cobra cult. Back in New York, a mysterious woman brings about their deaths, and when the survivor kills a cobra, it turns into her. Glossy but wholly unconvincing and unexciting non-horror potboiler. Faith Domergue, Richard Long, Marshall Thompson, Kathleen Hughes, Jack Kelly. Written by Jerry Davis, Cecil Maiden and Richard Collins; directed by Francis D. Lyon; for Universal–International.

A Cup of Kindness
GB 1934   81m   bw

Young lovers marry despite parental disapproval on both sides. Farcical updating of *Romeo and Juliet*; it hasn't worn too well, but the stars are at their peak. Tom Walls, Ralph Lynn, Robertson Hare, Claude Hulbert, Dorothy Hyson, Eva Moore. Written by Ben Travers, from his play; directed by Tom Walls; for Michael Balcon / Gaumont.

The Cure***
US 1917   20m approx   bw   silent
Mutual / Charles Chaplin

A dipsomaniac sent to a spa gets his booze mixed up with the spa water.
One of the funniest of the Chaplin shorts, with no pathos intervening (nor come to that much plot); it is simply a succession of balletic slapstick scenes of the highest order.

wd Charles Chaplin ph William C. Foster, Rollie Totheroh

Charles Chaplin, Edna Purviance, Eric Campbell, Henry Bergman

The Cure*
GB 1950   18m   bw

A health nut tries every possible remedy for lumbago. Richard Massingham huffs and puffs in his endearing way through a short which is too long by far to be effective in his particular vein; but it does identify his particular persona. Written, directed and produced by Richard and Betty Massingham (with Michael Law).

The Cure for Love
GB 1949   98m   bw
London Films (Robert Donat)

An ex-soldier goes home and tries to get married.
Thin Lancashire comedy which seemed an astonishing choice for Robert Donat, whose acting and direction are equally ill at ease.

w Robert Donat, Alexander Shaw, Albert Fennell, play Walter Greenwood d Robert Donat ph Jack Cox m William Alwyn

Robert Donat, Renée Asherson, Dora Bryan, Marjorie Rhodes, Charles Victor, Thora Hird, Gladys Henson
  'Antediluvian regional farce.'—*MFB*

Curly Top*
US 1935   78m   bw
TCF (Darryl F. Zanuck, Winfield Sheehan)

An orphan waif is adopted by a playboy, and not only sets his business right but fixes his romantic interest in her sister.
Archetypal Temple vehicle, a loose remake of *Daddy Longlegs*.

w Patterson McNutt, Arthur Beckhard d Irving Cummings ph John Seitz songs Ray Henderson, Ted Koehler, Edward Heyman, Irving Caesar

Shirley Temple, John Boles, Rochelle Hudson, Jane Darwell, Rafaela Ottiano, Esther Dale, Arthur Treacher, Etienne Girardot
  'Cinch b.o. for almost any house.'—*Variety*

'The creature created by man is forgotten by nature!'

The Curse of Frankenstein**
GB 1957   83m   Eastmancolor
Warner / Hammer (Anthony Hinds)

A lurid revamping of the 1931 *Frankenstein*, this time with severed eyeballs and a peculiarly unpleasant and uncharacterized creature, all in gory colour. It set the trend in nasty horrors

from which we have all suffered since, and launched Hammer Studios on a long and profitable career of charnelry. But it did have a gruesome sense of style.

w Jimmy Sangster d Terence Fisher ph Jack Asher m James Bernard ad Ted Marshall

Peter Cushing, Christopher Lee, Hazel Court, Robert Urquhart, Valerie Gaunt, Noel Hood

The Curse of the Cat People*
US 1944   70m   bw
RKO (Val Lewton)

A child is haunted by the spirit of the cat people.
A gentle film ordered by the studio as a sequel to *Cat People* but turned by Lewton into a fantasy of childhood. Slow to start but finally compelling, it's a pleasing and unusual film in a minor key.

w De Witt Bodeen d Robert Wise, Gunther Fritsch ph Nicholas Musuraca m Roy Webb

Kent Smith, Simone Simon, Jane Randolph, Julia Dean, Ann Carter, Elizabeth Russell
  'Full of the poetry and danger of childhood.'—*James Agee*
  'A clumsy coming together of unrealized ideas, gothic effects, and stiff, dull acting.'—*New Yorker, 1979*

Curse of the Crimson Altar
GB 1968   89m   Eastmancolor
Tigon / AIP (Tony Tenser)
aka: *The Crimson Cult*

Witchcraft, diabolism and mystery in an English country house.
A derivative, muddled scribble of a horror film, making no sense and wasting much talent.

w Mervyn Haisman, Henry Lincoln d Vernon Sewell ph John Coquillon m Peter Knight

Boris Karloff, Christopher Lee, Rupert Davies, Mark Eden, Barbara Steele, Michael Gough

Curse of the Pink Panther
GB 1983   110m   Technicolor
Panavision
MGM-UA / Titan / Jewel (Blake Edwards, Gerald T. Nutting)

Inspector Clouseau has disappeared, and Dreyfus selects the world's worst detective to replace him.
Unspeakably awful attempt at prolonging a series whose star died two episodes ago. Crude, tasteless and unfunny throughout.

w Blake Edwards, Geoffrey Edwards d Blake Edwards ph Dick Bush pd Peter Mullins m Henry Mancini

Ted Wass, Joanna Lumley, Herbert Lom, David Niven, Robert Wagner, Capucine, Harvey Korman, Burt Kwouk
  'Another bout of film-making as grave robbing.'—*Sight and Sound*
  'The ultimate version of deadpan humour . . . the most tedious of the whole series.'—*Richard Combs, MFB*

Curse of the Undead
US 1959 79m bw

A black-clad stranger in a western town turns
out to be a vampire of Spanish origin.
Abysmal attempt to substitute Wyoming for
Transylvania; more skill and sensitivity were
required. Michael Pate, Eric Fleming,
Kathleen Crowley, John Hoyt. Written and
directed by Edward Dein; for Universal-
International.

Curse of the Werewolf
GB 1961 92m Technicolor
U-I / Hammer (Anthony Hinds)

A beggar rapes a servant girl and their
offspring grows up to be a werewolf.
Doleful Hammer horror in a Spanish setting,
with an absurd but predictable plot and a lack
of sympathy for its fancy, hairy hero.

w John Elder (Anthony Hinds) *d* Terence
Fisher *ph* Arthur Grant *m* Benjamin Frankel

Oliver Reed, Clifford Evans, Catherine Feller,
Yvonne Romain, Anthony Dawson, Richard
Wordsworth, Warren Mitchell

The Curse of the Wraydons
GB 1946 94m bw

The Victorian story of Spring-heeled Jack,
here depicted as a mad inventor out for
revenge. Too long and stagey to be one of its
star's better barnstormers, especially as by this
time his girth made the notion of his springing
about somewhat hilarious. Tod Slaughter,
Bruce Seton, Gabriel Toyne. Written by
Michael Barringer; directed by Victor M.
Gover; for Bushey.

THE CURSE OF THE MUMMY'S TOMB. Ronald Howard (left) and John Paul (right)
survey the results of a long night's work.

Curtain Call°
US 1940 63m bw
RKO

Two Broadway producers buy an awful play in
order to get even with a temperamental star,
but she likes it.
Amusing second feature, a kind of
flashforward to *The Producers*. A reprise the
following year, *Footlight Fever*, did not work.

w Dalton Trumbo *d* Frank Woodruff
ph Russell Metty *m* Roy Webb

Alan Mowbray, Donald MacBride, Helen
Vinson, Barbara Read, John Archer

Curtain Call at Cactus Creek°
US 1949 83m Technicolor
U-I (Robert Arthur)
GB title: *Take the Stage*

A travelling repertory company in the old west
exposes a gang of bank robbers.
Cheerful minor comedy with good pace and
amusing burlesques of old melodramas.

w Oscar Brodney *d* Charles Lamont
ph Russell Metty *m* Walter Scharf

Donald O'Connor, Gale Storm, Eve Arden,
Vincent Price, Walter Brennan, Chick
Chandler

Curtain Up°
GB 1952 85m bw
Rank / Constellation (Robert Garrett)

A seaside repertory company runs into trouble
when the producer is at loggerheads with the
author of next week's play.
Fairly amusing farce which has now acquired
historical value for the light it throws on the
old weekly reps.

w Michael Pertwee, Jack Davies, *play* On
Monday Next by Philip King *d* Ralph Smart
ph Stanley Pavey *m* Malcolm Arnold

Margaret Rutherford, Robert Morley, Olive
Sloane, Joan Rice, Charlotte Mitchell, Kay
Kendall, Liam Gaffney, Michael Medwin

Custer of the West
US 1967 146m Super Technirama 70
Cinerama / Security (Louis Dolivet, Philip
Yordan, Irving Lerner)

After the Civil War, Custer is offered a
cavalry command, becomes disillusioned, and
is massacred with his troops at Little Big
Horn.
Gloomily inaccurate spectacular with pauses
for Cinerama carnival thrills and dour bits of
melodrama.

w Bernard Gordon, Julian Halevy *d* Robert
Siodmak *ph* Cecilio Paniagua *m* Bernardo
Segall

Robert Shaw, Mary Ure, Robert Ryan,
Jeffrey Hunter, Ty Hardin, Lawrence Tierney,
Kieron Moore

Cutter and Bone
US 1981 109m Technicolor
United Artists / Gurian
GB title: *Cutter's Way*

A California failure witnesses the aftermath of
murder, and with a crippled ex-Vietnam
veteran turns detective.
Heavy-going melodrama which tries very hard
to be something more than a thriller, and
manages only to imply that the world stinks;
so it might as well have stuck to Philip
Marlowe.

w Jeffrey Alan Fiskin, *novel* Newton
Thornburg *d* Ivan Passer *ph* Jordan
Cronenweth *m* Jack Nitzsche *ed* Caroline
Ferriol

Jeff Bridges, John Heard, Lisa Eichhorn, Ann
Dusenberry, Stephen Elliott, Nina Van
Pallandt

The Cyclops
US 1956 65m bw
B and H (Bert I. Gordon)

Explorers in Mexico find animals turned by
radiation into monsters, plus a one-eyed 25-
foot-tall human.
Modest monster movie, quite palatable of its
kind.

wd Bert I. Gordon *ph* Ira Morgan *m* Albert
Glasser

James Craig, Lon Chaney Jnr, Gloria Talbot,
Tom Drake

Cynara**

US 1933   78m   bw

Samuel Goldwyn

A London barrister has an affair with a young girl who commits suicide when he goes back to his wife.

Solidly carpentered, effective star vehicle of the old school, now dated but preserving its dignity.

w Frances Marion, Lynn Starling, *novel* An Imperfect Lover by Robert Gore Brown *d* King Vidor *ph* Ray June *m* Alfred Newman

Ronald Colman, Kay Francis, Phyllis Barry, *Henry Stephenson*, Paul Porcasi

'The values it involves are wholly unlike those which US audiences are usually called upon to comprehend.'—*Time*

Cynthia

US 1947   98m   bw

MGM (Edwin H. Knopf)

GB title: *The Rich Full Life*

An over-protected girl finds an outlet in music and her parents finally allow her to lead her own life.

An overlong domestic drama in which thin writing and acting are backed by unsound psychology.

w Harold Buchman, Charles Kaufman, *play* Vina Delmar *d* Robert Z. Leonard *ph* Charles Schoenbaum *m* Bronislau Kaper

Elizabeth Taylor, George Murphy, Mary Astor, S. Z. Sakall, James Lydon, Gene Lockhart, Spring Byington

Cyrano de Bergerac*

US 1950   112m   bw

Stanley Kramer

In the 17th century a long-nosed poet, philosopher and buffoon writes letters enabling a friend to win the lady he loves himself.

The classic romantic verse play does not take kindly to a hole-in-corner black-and-white production, but at the time it was lapped up as a daring cultural breakthrough.

w Brian Hooker, *play* Edmond Rostand *d* Michael Gordon *ph* Franz Planer *m* Dmitri Tiomkin

Jose Ferrer, Mala Powers, William Prince, Morris Carnovsky, Ralph Clanton, Virginia Farmer, Edgar Barrier, Elena Verdugo

AA: Jose Ferrer

D. C. Cab
US 1983 99m Technicolor

Cab drivers for a run-down Washington company capture kidnappers. Brainless extravaganza with aspirations somewhere between *Taxi* and *Carry On*. Mr T, Max Gail, Adam Baldwin, Charlie Barnett, Gary Busey, Gloria Gifford. Written and directed by Joel Schumacher; for Guber-Peters / RKO-Universal. (GB title: *Street Fleet*.) 'Artificial energy used to bolster wretched material.'—*Steve Jenkins, MFB*

Daddy Longlegs*
US 1931 80m bw
Fox

An orphan girl grows up to fall in love with her mysterious benefactor.
Cinderella-like romance, adequately adapted from a novel which became the classic American version of the January–May romance.

w Sonya Levien, *novel* Jean Webster *d* Alfred Santell *ph* Lucien Andriot

Janet Gaynor, Warner Baxter, Una Merkel, John Arledge, Claude Gillingwater, Louise Closser Hale
'A smash . . . one of those rare talkers with universal appeal.'—*Variety*
† Other versions were made in 1919 with Mary Pickford and Mahlon Hamilton, directed by Marshal Neilan; in 1935 disguised as *Curly Top* (qv) and in 1955 (see below).

Daddy Longlegs*
US 1955 126m Technicolor
Cinemascope
TCF (Samuel G. Engel)

Overlong and unsuitably wide-screened musical version of a popular story (see above). Generally clumsy and dispirited, but Astaire is always worth watching and a couple of the dances are well staged.

w Phoebe and Henry Ephron *d* Jean Negulesco *ph* Leon Shamroy *m* Alfred Newman *songs* Johnny Mercer

Fred Astaire, Leslie Caron, *Fred Clark*, Thelma Ritter, Terry Moore, Charlotte Austin, Larry Keating

AAN: Alfred Newman; song 'Something's Gotta Give' (m / ly Johnny Mercer)

Daddy's Gone A-Hunting
US 1969 108m Technicolor
Warner / Red Lion (Mark Robson)

A child and its mother are threatened by her deranged ex-husband.
Unpleasant and protracted suspenser with the emphasis on sex rather than thrills.

w Larry Cohen, Lorenzo Semple Jnr *d* Mark Robson *ph* Ernest Laszlo *m* John Williams

Carol White, Paul Burke, Scott Hylands, Mala Powers, Andrea King

Dad's Army**
GB 1971 95m Technicolor
Columbia / Norcon (John R. Sloan)

Misadventures of a number of elderly gents in Britain's wartime Home Guard.
Expanded big-screen version of the long-running TV series, a pleasant souvenir but rather less effective than was expected because everything is shown—the town, the Nazis, the wives—and thus the air of gentle fantasy disappears, especially in the face of much coarsened humour.

w Jimmy Perry, David Croft *d* Norman Cohen *ph* Terry Maher *m* Wilfred Burns

Arthur Lowe, John Le Mesurier, John Laurie, *James Beck*, Ian Lavender, *Arnold Ridley*, Liz Fraser, *Clive Dunn*, Bill Pertwee, Frank Williams, Edward Sinclair

Daisy Kenyon*
US 1947 99m bw
TCF (Otto Preminger)

A fashion designer has two men in her life.
Adequate woman's picture which hardly justifies its cast.

w David Hertz, *novel* Elizabeth Janeway *d* Otto Preminger *ph* Leon Shamroy *m* David Raksin

Joan Crawford, Henry Fonda, Dana Andrews, Ruth Warrick, Martha Stewart, Peggy Ann Garner

Daisy Miller*
US 1974 92m Technicolor
Paramount / Copa de Oro (Peter Bogdanovich)

In the 19th century, an American girl tourist in Europe falls in love but dies of the Roman fever.
Curious attempt to film a very mild and uneventful Henry James story, with careful production but inadequate leads. The first sign that Bogdanovich was getting too big for his boots.

w Frederic Raphael *d* Peter Bogdanovich *ph* Alberto Spagnoli *m* classical themes *ad* Ferdinando Scarfiotti

Cybill Shepherd, Barry Brown, Cloris Leachman, Mildred Natwick, Eileen Brennan, James MacMurtry
'A historical film bereft of any feeling for history, and a literary adaptation which reveals a fine contempt for literary subtlety.'—*Jan Dawson*
'Appallingly crass . . . directed with all the subtlety of a sledgehammer.'—*Michael Billington, Illustrated London News*
'Trying to make that little thing he's with into Daisy Miller was hilarious. God almighty couldn't do that. She's so coy.'—*Henry Hathaway*

Dakota
US 1945 82m bw
Republic (Joseph Kane)

The daughter of a railroad tycoon elopes with a cowboy and becomes involved in a land war. Adequate star western.

w Lawrence Hazard, *story* Carl Foreman *d* Joseph Kane *ph* Jack Marta *m* Walter Scharf

John Wayne, Vera Hruba Ralston, Walter Brennan, Ward Bond, Ona Munson, Hugo Haas, Mike Mazurki, Paul Fix, Grant Withers, Jack La Rue

Daleks: Invasion Earth 2150 AD see Dr Who and the Daleks

Dallas*
US 1950 94m Technicolor
Warner (Anthony Veiller)

A renegade ex-Confederate colonel is pardoned for bringing law and order to Dallas. Routinely competent top-of-the-bill western.

w John Twist *d* Stuart Heisler *ph* Ernest Haller *m* Max Steiner

Gary Cooper, Ruth Roman, Raymond Massey, Steve Cochran, Barbara Payton, Leif Erickson, Antonio Moreno, Jerome Cowan

The Dam Busters**
GB 1954 125m bw
ABPC (Robert Clark)

In 1943 the Ruhr dams are destroyed by Dr Barnes Wallis' bouncing bombs.
Understated British war epic with additional scientific interest and good acting and model work, not to mention a welcome lack of love interest.

w R. C. Sheriff, books by Guy Gibson and
Paul Brickhill *d* Michael Anderson *ph* Eric
Hillier *m* Leighton Lucas, *Eric Coates*
sp George Blackwell

Michael Redgrave, books Richard Todd, Basil
Sydney, Derek Farr, Patrick Barr, Ernest
Clark, Raymond Huntley, Ursula Jeans

● Video: *Thorn EMI*

Damaged Goods
US 1937   56m   bw

A young man infects his wife and child with
syphilis. An 'awful warning' which seemed
naive even at the time; there had been a silent
version in 1914. Pedro de Cordoba, Douglas
Walton, Arletta Duncan, Esther Dale, Phyllis
Barry. Written by Upton Sinclair from the
play by Eugene Brieux; directed by Phil
Stone; for Grand National.

Damaged Lives
US 1937   61m (plus a 29m lecture)   bw

A young man infects his wife with syphilis.
One of a rival pair of moral tales (see above);
both had trouble with the censors on subject
matter alone. Not otherwise notable. Diane
Sinclair, Lyman Williams, Cecilia Parker,
George Irving, Jason Robards. Written by
Donald Davis and Edgar C. Ulmer; directed
by Edgar G. Ulmer; for Weldon.

Dames**
US 1934   90m   bw
Warner (Robert Lord)

A millionaire purity fanatic tries to stop the
opening of a Broadway show.
Typical Warner musical of the period: its real
raison d'être is to be found in the splendidly
imaginative numbers at the finale, but it also
gives very full rein to the roster of comic
actors under contract at the time.

w Delmer Daves *d* Ray Enright *ch* Busby
Berkeley *ph* Sid Hickox, George Barnes
m various

*Joan Blondell, Hugh Herbert, Guy Kibbee,
Zasu Pitts,* Dick Powell, Ruby Keeler
   'That Warners was able to fashion so zestful
an entertainment under post-Haysian
restrictions is a credit to the collective
ingenuities of the studio artificers. . . . Swell
entertainment, no matter how you slice it.'—
Variety
† Originally intended as *Gold Diggers of 1934.*

Les Dames du Bois de Boulogne*
France 1946   90m   bw
Films Raoul Ploquin

Hélène revenges herself on her bored lover by
arranging for him to marry a prostitute.
Spare, symbolic melodrama which has
occasioned as much irritation as applause.

w Robert Bresson, Jean Cocteau, from
Diderot's *Jacques Le Fataliste* *d Robert
Bresson* *ph* Philippe Agostini *m* Jean-
Jacques Grunenwald

Maria Casarès, Elina Labourdette, Lucienne
Bogaert, Paul Bernard

'Through abstraction, Bresson has been able
to make a film in which the tragedy is implicit
not only in the plot but also in the form.'—
Richard Roud, MFB, 1966

Damien: Omen Two
US 1978   109m   De Luxe   Panavision
TCF (Harvey Bernhard)

The antichrist who got rid of the entire cast of
The Omen now, as a teenager, starts in on his
foster parents.
Once was enough.

w Stanley Mann, Michael Hodges *d* Don
Taylor *ph* Bill Butler *m* Jerry Goldsmith
William Holden, Lee Grant, Jonathan Scott-
Taylor, Robert Foxworth, Lucas Donat, Lew
Ayres, Sylvia Sidney, Elizabeth Shepherd

● Video: *CBS Fox*

Damn Yankees**
US 1958   110m   Technicolor
Warner (George Abbott, Stanley Donen)
GB title: *What Lola Wants*

The devil interferes in the fortunes of a failing
baseball team.
Smartly-styled but very American musical
based on *Faust;* brilliant moments but some
tedium.

w George Abbott, *novel* Douglas Wallop
d George Abbott, Stanley Donen *ph* Harold
Lipstein *m / ly* Richard Adler, Jerry Ross
md Ray Heindorf

Gwen Verdon, Tab Hunter, Ray Walston,
Russ Brown, Shannon Bolin

AAN: Ray Heindorf

Damnation Alley
US 1977   95m   De Luxe
TCF / Hal Landers, Bobby Roberts, Jerome
   M. Zeitman

Four survivors from World War Three try to
reach a colony of fellow-survivors in New
York.
Feeble attempt at a low-budget blockbuster.

w Alan Sharp, Lukas Heller, *novel* Roger
Zelazny *d* Jack Smight *ph* Harry Stradling
Jnr *m* Jerry Goldsmith *pd* Preston Ames

Jan-Michael Vincent, George Peppard,
Dominique Sanda, Paul Winfield

The Damned*
France 1947   105m   bw
Speva Film
original title: *Les Maudits*

In 1945 fanatical Nazis escape in a submarine
but make the mistake of stopping to sink a
freighter.
Unusual melodrama with a brilliant sense of
claustrophobia, good characterization and
much suspense.

w Jacques Remy, René Clément, Henri
Jeanson *d René Clément* *ph* Henri Alekan
m Yves Baudrier

Paul Bernard, Henri Vidal, Marcel Dalio,
Michel Auclair, Florence Marly

The Damned*
GB 1961   87m   bw   Hammerscope
Columbia / Hammer–Swallow (Anthony
   Hinds)
US title: *These Are the Damned*

A scientist keeps radioactive children in a cliff
cave, sealed off from the world's corruption.
Absurdly pompous, downcast and confused
sci-fi melodrama set in Weymouth, with a
secondary plot about motor-cycling thugs.

w Evan Jones, *novel* The Children of Light by
H. L. Lawrence *d* Joseph Losey *ph* Arthur
Grant *m* James Bernard

Macdonald Carey, Shirley Ann Field,
Alexander Knox, Viveca Lindfors, Oliver
Reed, Walter Gotell, James Villiers
   '*A folie de grandeur.*'—*Tom Milne*
   'Out of this wild mishmash some really
magnificent images loom.'—*John Coleman*

The Damned**
West Germany / Italy 1969   164m
   Eastmancolor
Praesidens / Pegaso
original title: *Götterdämmerung*

A family of German industrialists divides and
destroys itself under Nazi influence.
A film which has been called baroque,
Wagnerian, and just plain unpleasant; it is also
rather a strain to watch, with exaggerated
colour and make-up to match the rotting
theme.

w Nicola Badalucco, Enrico Medioli, Luchino
Visconti *d Luchino Visconti* *ph* Armando
Nannuzzi, Pasquale de Santis *m* Maurice
Jarre *ad* Enzo del Prato, Pasquale Romano

Dirk Bogarde, Ingrid Thulin, Helmut Berger,
Renaud Verley, Helmut Griem, René
Kolldehof, Albrecht Schönhals, Umberto
Orsini

   'One is left lamenting that such a quondam
master of realism as Visconti is making his
films look like operas from which the score has
been inexplicably removed.'—*MFB*
   'The ludicrous flailings of puny puppets in
inscrutable wooden frenzies.'—*John Simon*

AAN: script

● Video: *Warner*

The Damned Don't Cry
US 1950   103m   bw
Warner (Jerry Wald)

A middle-class housewife leaves her husband
for a gambler, and becomes involved with
gangsters, but eventually reforms.
Rather dreary stimulation for female
audiences who like safe dreams of danger.

w Harold Medford, Jerome Weidman, *novel*
Case History by Gertrude Walker *d* Vincent
Sherman *ph* Ted McCord *m* Daniele
Amfitheatrof

Joan Crawford, Kent Smith, David Brian,
Steve Cochran, Hugh Sanders, Selena Royle,
Morris Ankrum, Richard Egan
   'The private lady of a public enemy!'—
publicity

'Mad adventure! Daring deeds! White hot love with music!'
A Damsel in Distress*
US 1937   101m   bw
RKO (Pandro S. Berman)

An American dancing star falls for an aristocratic young Englishwoman.
Astaire without Rogers, but the style is the same and there are some very good numbers.

w P. G. Wodehouse, S. K. Lauren, Ernest Pagano d George Stevens ph Joseph H. August m / ly George and Ira Gershwin ch Hermes Pan

Fred Astaire, George Burns, Gracie Allen, Joan Fontaine, Reginald Gardiner, Constance Collier, Ray Noble, Montagu Love
  'Plenty for the b.o.—dancing, comedy, marquee values, the usual sumptuous investiture accorded by Pandro Berman, and those Gershwin songs.'—*Variety*
† Rogers had demanded a break from musicals, so she was replaced by the demure Miss Fontaine, who was generally thought disappointing.

● *Video: Kingston*

Dance Band
GB 1935   75m   bw

A band leader who croons falls for the boss of an all-ladies orchestra. Fairly slick light musical fare of its period. Buddy Rogers, June Clyde, Fred Duprez, Richard Hearne, Steve Geray, Magda Kun. Written by Roger Burford; directed by Marcel Varnel; for BIP. 'Popular entertainment from start to finish, cut to a point where there is hardly a draggy moment.'—*Variety*

Dance Fools Dance
US 1931   82m   bw
MGM

A lady reporter in Chicago proves her worth. Bizarrely-titled gangster thriller based on the Jake Lingle killing. Very moderate of its kind.

w Richard Schayer, Aurania Rouverol d Harry Beaumont ph Charles Rosher

Joan Crawford, Lester Vail, Cliff Edwards, William Bakewell, William Holden (the other one), Clark Gable, Earle Foxe, Joan Marsh
  'It will rock the b.o. . . . sex, romance, punch, suspense, and everything a deluxer can sell.'—*Variety*

Dance Girl Dance*
US 1940   88m   bw
RKO (Erich Pommer)

Private problems of the members of a nightclub dance troupe.
Competent and sometimes interesting formula drama with a harder edge than usual.

w Tess Slesinger, Frank Davis, *story* Vicki Baum d Dorothy Arzner ph Russell Metty m Edward Ward

Maureen O'Hara, Louis Hayward, Lucille Ball, Maria Ouspenskaya, Ralph Bellamy, Virginia Field, Mary Carlisle, Walter Abel, Edward Brophy, Harold Huber

Dance Hall*
GB 1950   80m   bw
Ealing (E. V. H. Emmett)

Four factory girls seek relaxation and various kinds of romance at the local palais.
Untypically flat Ealing slice of life, now watchable only with a smile as musical nostalgia.

w E. V. H. Emmett, Diana Morgan, Alexander Mackendrick d Charles Crichton ph Douglas Slocombe md Ernest Irving

Natasha Parry, Donald Houston, Diana Dors, Bonar Colleano, Jane Hylton, Petula Clark, Gladys Henson, Sydney Tafler; the bands of Geraldo and Ted Heath

Dance Little Lady
GB 1954   87m   Eastmancolor

An ambitious man tries to turn his balletomane daughter into a film star. Artless melodrama in poor colour. Terence Morgan, Mai Zetterling, Mandy Miller, Guy Rolfe, Eunice Gayson. Written by Val Guest and Doreen Montgomery; directed by Val Guest; for George Minter / Renown.

Dance Pretty Lady
GB 1932   64m   bw

Ballerina loves artist but settles unwisely for respectability. Stilted early talkie from Compton Mackenzie's *Carnival*, qv under its own title. Ann Casson, Carl Harbord, Michael Hogan. Written and directed by Anthony Asquith; for H. Bruce Woolfe / British Instructional.

The Dance of Death*
GB 1968   149m   Technicolor
BHE / National Theatre (John Brabourne)

Edgar and Alice live alone on an island, their marriage having become a constant war.
Too-literal film transcription of an applauded theatrical production, with the camera anchored firmly in the middle of the stalls.

w August Strindberg (*translation* by C. D. Locock) d David Giles ph Geoffrey Unsworth

Laurence Olivier, Geraldine McEwan, Robert Lang, Carolyn Jones

Dance Team
US 1931   80m   bw

Struggles of a couple to become top ballroom dancers. Easy-going star fare which needed tightening. James Dunn, Sally Eilers, Minna Gombell, Ralph Morgan. Written by Edwin Burke from the novel by Sarah Addington; directed by Sidney Lanfield; for Fox. 'Its comedy overcomes drawn-out sequences laden with sentimentality.'—*Variety*

Dancers in the Dark
US 1932   76m   bw

A taxi dancer with a shady past tries to prove that she's really in love. Banal show business melodrama with authentic-seeming nightclub background. Miriam Hopkins, Jack Oakie, George Raft, William Collier Jnr, Lyda

Roberti, Eugene Pallette. Written by Herman J. Mankiewicz; directed by David Burton; for Paramount. 'Only fair for Times Square, looks surefire in the hinterland.'—*Variety*

Dancing Co-ed
US 1939   90m   bw
MGM (Edgar Selwyn)
GB title: *Every Other Inch a Lady*

A college girl makes it in show business as well as the groves of academe.
Mindless vehicle for a 19-year-old star.

w Albert Mannheimer, *story* Albert Treynor d S. Sylvan Simon ph Alfred Gilks

Lana Turner, Richard Carlson, Artie Shaw, *Leon Errol*, Ann Rutherford, Lee Bowman, Monty Woolley, Roscoe Karns, June Preisser, Walter Kingsford
  'Better than average programme entertainment.'—*Variety*

Dancing in the Dark*
US 1949   92m   Technicolor
TCF (George Jessel)

A silent movie idol makes a comeback as a talent scout, and spots his own daughter.
Thin but unusual Hollywood drama with music; in the long run too sentimental.

w Mary C. McCall Jnr, *play* The Band Wagon by George F. Kaufman, Howard Dietz, Arthur Schwarz d Irving Reis ph Harry Jackson m Alfred Newman

William Powell, Adolphe Menjou, Mark Stevens, Betsy Drake, Hope Emerson, Lloyd Corrigan, Walter Catlett, Jean Hersholt

Dancing Lady*
US 1933   94m   bw
MGM (David O. Selznick)

A successful dancer chooses between a playboy and her stage manager.
Routine backstage semi-musical with interesting talent applied rather haphazardly.

w Allen Rivkin, P. J. Wolfson, *novel* James Warner Bellah d Robert Z. Leonard ph Oliver T. Marsh m various

Joan Crawford, Clark Gable, *Fred Astaire*, Franchot Tone, May Robson, Ted Healy and his Stooges (the Three Stooges), Winnie Lightner, Robert Benchley, Nelson Eddy
  'Very potent b.o. in the screen musical cycle.'—*Variety*

The Dancing Masters
US 1943   63m   bw
TCF (Lee Marcus)

Laurel and Hardy run a ballet school, and get involved with gangsters and inventors.
Insubstantial star comedy featuring reworkings of old routines, and a back-projected runaway bus climax.

w Scott Darling, George Bricker d Mal St Clair ph Norbert Brodine m Arthur Lange

Stan Laurel, Oliver Hardy, Trudy Marshall, Bob Bailey, Margaret Dumont, Matt Briggs, Robert Mitchum

With Sword in Hand He Goes to the Head of the Clash!

Mad adventure . . . daring deeds . . . white hot love with music! Your toes will tingle as you laugh through your cheers!

FRED ASTAIRE
GEORGE BURNS ★ GRACIE ALLEN

By George, they're Gracier than ever . . . in this tune filled, girl thrilled, rousing show!

"A Damsel in Distress"

WITH JOAN FONTAINE REGINALD GARDINER RAY NOBLE

CONSTANCE COLLIER · MONTAGU LOVE · HARRY WATSON

P. G. WODEHOUSE *did the dizzy drama* GEORGE *and* IRA GERSHWIN *wrote the bluezy tunes and rippling songs:* "Foggy Day," "Nice Work If You Can Get It," "Things Are Looking Up," "I Can't Be Bothered Now"

PANDRO S. BERMAN PRODUCTION · *Directed by* GEORGE STEVENS Screen play by P. G. Wodehouse, Ernest Pagano, S. K. Lauren R K O · R A D I O PICTURE

A DAMSEL IN DISTRESS. One of the dancing star's lesser-known but most delightful musicals, made at a time when he was trying to show that he could if necessary get along without Ginger Rogers.

Dancing with Crime
GB 1947 83m bw

A dance hall is the front for black marketeers, who are exposed by a resourceful taxi driver. Tolerable post-war melodrama aping Hollywood. Richard Attenborough, Barry K. Barnes, Sheila Sim, Garry Marsh, John Warwick, Barry Jones. Written by Brock Williams; directed by John Paddy Carstairs; for Coronet-Alliance.

The Dancing Years
GB 1949 97m Technicolor
ABPC (Warwick Ward)

A composer loves a singer who leaves him after a misunderstanding but later bears his son . . . all in the Alps pre-1914. Lamentable transcription of an operetta; precisely the ingredients which worked so well on stage seem embarrassing on film, and the performances and direction do not help.

w Warwick Ward, Jack Whittingham, from Ivor Novello's operetta *d* Harold French *ph* Stephen Dade *m* Ivor Novello

Dennis Price, Gisèle Préville, Patricia Dainton, Anthony Nicholls, Grey Blake, Muriel George, Olive Gilbert

Dandy Dick
GB 1935 72m bw

A country vicar becomes innocently involved with racehorse doping. Flatly-handled farce which helped to introduce Will Hay to the screen, though not in his accustomed role; with Nancy Burne, Esmond Knight, Davy Burnaby. Written by William Beaudine, Frank Miller, Clifford Grey and Will Hay, from the play by Sir Arthur Wing Pinero; directed by William Beaudine; for Twickenham.

'His mission is murder! His victim— himself!'
A Dandy in Aspic
GB 1968 107m Technicolor Panavision
Columbia (Anthony Mann)

A double agent in Berlin is given orders to kill himself.
Muddled, pretentious spy thriller; flat, nebulous and boring.

w Derek Marlowe, from his novel *d* Anthony Mann *ph* Christopher Challis *m* Quincy Jones

Laurence Harvey, Tom Courtenay, Lionel Stander, Mia Farrow, Harry Andrews, Peter Cook, Per Oscarsson
† Anthony Mann died during shooting, and Laurence Harvey completed the direction.

Dandy the All-American Girl
US 1976 90m Metrocolor Panavision

A much convicted woman car thief determines to become the legitimate owner of a Dino Ferrari. The American dream gone sour again, this time offering in its wake a curious stream of moral values. Stockard Channing, Sam Waterston, Richard Doughty, Franklin Ajaye. Written by B. J. Perla and Marilyn Goldin; directed by Jerry Schatzberg; for MGM. (GB title: *Sweet Revenge*.)

Danger: Diabolik
Italy / France 1967 105m Technicolor
Dino de Laurentiis / Marianne (Bruno Todini)

International police bait a golden trap for a master criminal.
Superior Batman-type adventures with a comic strip hero-villain.

w Dino Maiuri, Adriano Baracco, Mario Bava *d* Mario Bava *ph* Antonio Rinaldi *m* Ennio Morricone

John Phillip Law, Marisa Mell, Michel Piccoli, Adolfo Celi, Terry-Thomas

Danger, Love at Work°
US 1937 84m bw
TCF (Harold Wilson)

A young lawyer needs the signature of a rich crazy family to conclude a land sale.

The title doesn't suggest it, but this is a not inconsiderable comedy in the tradition of *My Man Godfrey* and *You Can't Take It With You*. A highly competent cast does its best.

w James Edward Grant, Ben Markson *d* Otto Preminger *ph* Virgil Miller *md* David Buttolph

Ann Sothern, Jack Haley, Edward Everett Horton, Mary Boland, Walter Catlett, John Carradine, Maurice Cass, Alan Dinehart, E. E. Clive

'Not important enough to be a main feature but a very good dualler.'—*Variety*

Danger Route

GB 1967   92m   De Luxe
UA / Amicus (Max J. Rosenberg, Milton Subotsky)

An 'eliminator' for the British secret service finds after a series of adventures that he must dispose of his own girl friend.
Dour sub-Bondian thriller with little to commend it.

w Meade Roberts, *novel* The Eliminator by Andrew York *d* Seth Holt *ph* Harry Waxman *m* John Mayer

Richard Johnson, Diana Dors, Sylvia Syms, Carol Lynley, Barbara Bouchet, Gordon Jackson, Sam Wanamaker, Maurice Denham, Harry Andrews

Danger Within**

GB 1958   101m   bw
British Lion / Colin Lesslie
US title: *Breakout*

Escape plans of officers in a prisoner-of-war camp are threatened by an informer.
Familiar comedy and melodrama with an added whodunnit element, smartly handled and very entertaining.

w Bryan Forbes, Frank Harvey, *novel* Michael Gilbert *d* Don Chaffey *ph* Arthur Grant *m* Francis Chagrin

Richard Todd, Bernard Lee, Michael Wilding, Richard Attenborough, Dennis Price, Donald Houston, William Franklyn, Vincent Ball, Peter Arne

Dangerous*

US 1935   78m   bw
Warner (Harry Joe Brown)

An alcoholic actress is rehabilitated.
Unconvincing and only adequately handled melodrama which won the star her first Oscar, presumably from sympathy at her losing it the previous year for *Of Human Bondage*.

w Laird Doyle *d* Alfred E. Green *ph* Ernest Haller

Bette Davis, Franchot Tone, Margaret Lindsay, Alison Skipworth, John Eldridge, Dick Foran

'Well-acted and directed drama with *femme* appeal.'—*Variety*

† Remade 1941 as *Singapore Woman*.

AA: Bette Davis

Dangerous Corner*

US 1934   67m   bw
RKO

After dinner conversation reveals what might have been if friends had spoken the truth about a long-ago suicide.
A fascinating trick play makes interesting but scarcely sparkling cinema.

w Anne Morrison Chapin, Madeleine Ruthven, *play* J. B. Priestley *d* Phil Rosen *ph* J. Roy Hunt *m* Max Steiner

Melvyn Douglas, Conrad Nagel, Virginia Bruce, Erin O'Brien Moore, Ian Keith, Betty Furness, Henry Wadsworth

'Confusing mixture of a mystery and problem play . . . doubtful as to general fan appeal.'—*Variety*

Dangerous Crossing*

US 1953   75m   bw
TCF (Robert Bassler)

At the start of an Atlantic sea voyage a woman's husband disappears, and she is assured that he never existed. He does, and is trying to murder her.
Adequately handled twist on the vanishing lady story: grade A production covers lapses of grade B imagination.

w Leo Townsend, *story* John Dickson Carr *d* Joseph M. Newman *ph* Joseph La Shelle *md* Lionel Newman

Jeanne Crain, Michael Rennie, Carl Betz, Casey Adams, Mary Anderson, Willis Bouchey

Dangerous Curves

US 1929   75m   bw
Paramount

A bareback rider loves a high wire artist.
Obvious circus melodrama, a modest star vehicle.

w Donald David, Florence Ryerson *d* Lothar Mendes *ph* Harry Fischbeck.

Clara Bow, Richard Arlen, Kay Francis, David Newell, Anders Randolf

Dangerous Exile

GB 1957   90m   Eastmancolor
Vistavision
Rank (George H. Brown)

After the French Revolution, the young would-be Louis XVII is brought across the Channel and hidden in Pembrokeshire, where enemies attack him.
Historical romance, ineptly plotted but quite well produced.

w Robin Estridge, *novel* Vaughan Wilkins *d* Brian Desmond Hurst *ph* Geoffrey Unsworth *m* Georges Auric

Louis Jourdan, Belinda Lee, Keith Michell, Richard O'Sullivan, Martita Hunt, Finlay Currie, Anne Heywood, Jacques Brunius

Dangerous Millions

US 1946   69m   bw

Eight would-be inheritors of a millionaire's estate find themselves at the mercy of a warlord in the Chinese mountains. Odd little

second feature confusion of *The Cat and the Canary* and *Shanghai Express*; quite watchable. Kent Taylor, Dona Drake, Tala Birell, Leonard Strong, Konstantin Shayne. Written by Irving Cummings Jnr and Robert G. North; directed by James Tinling; for TCF. (GB title: *The House of Tao Ling*.)

Dangerous Mission

US 1954   75m   Technicolor   3-D
RKO (Irwin Allen)

In Montana's Glacier National Park, a policeman tries to protect an innocent girl witness from big city gangsters.
Tolerable routine double-bill thriller with a predictable cable car climax.

w Horace McCoy, W. R. Burnett, Charles Bennett, James Edmiston *d* Louis King *ph* William Snyder *m* Roy Webb

Victor Mature, Piper Laurie, Vincent Price, William Bendix, Betta St John, Dennis Weaver

'The scenery received the best notices.'—*James Robert Parish 1976*

● *Video: Kingston*

'This is your melody—you gave it to me. I'll never play it again without thinking of you!'

Dangerous Moonlight*

GB 1941   98m   bw
RKO (William Sistrom)
US title: *Suicide Squadron*

A Polish pianist escapes from the Nazis and loses his memory after flying in the Battle of Britain.
Immensely popular wartime romance which introduced Richard Addinsell's Warsaw Concerto. Production values and script somewhat below par.

w Shaun Terence Young, Brian Desmond Hurst, Rodney Ackland *d* Brian Desmond Hurst *ph* Georges Périnal, Ronald Neame

Anton Walbrook, Sally Gray, Derrick de Marney, Cecil Parker, Percy Parsons, Kenneth Kent, Guy Middleton, John Laurie, Frederick Valk

Dangerous Number

US 1937   71m   bw

A showgirl is confused by her husband's rich relations. Rather tedious comedy drama which never really gets anywhere. Robert Young, Ann Sothern, Reginald Owen, Cora Witherspoon, Dean Jagger, Barnett Parker. Written by Carey Wilson from a story by Leora Dalrymple; directed by Richard Thorpe; for MGM. 'A compact piece of entertainment, though pretty shallow on the drama end.'—*Variety*

A Dangerous Profession

US 1949   79m   bw

An ex-detective tries to help a beautiful woman and becomes involved in murder and the bail bond racket. Undistinguished crime melodrama providing a satisfactory vehicle for its stars: Pat O'Brien, George Raft, Ella

Raines, Jim Backus, Bill Williams. Written by Martin Rackin and Warren Duff; directed by Ted Tetzlaff; for RKO.

Dangerous to Know°
US 1938 70m bw
Paramount

A ruthless Chicago gangster comes a cropper when his Chinese mistress discovers he has fallen for a socialite.
Flatly handled but mildly interesting adaptation of a highly successful play, the potential of which seems to have been thrown away.
w William R. Lippmann, Horace McCoy, *play* On the Spot by Edgar Wallace d Robert Florey ph Theodor Sparkuhl

Akim Tamiroff, Anna May Wong, Gail Patrick, Lloyd Nolan, Harvey Stephens, Anthony Quinn, Porter Hall

Dangerous When Wet°°
US 1953 95m Technicolor
MGM (George Wells)

An entire Arkansas family is sponsored to swim the English Channel.
A bright and lively vehicle for an aquatic star, who in one sequence swims with Tom and Jerry. Amusing sequences give opportunities to a strong cast.
w Dorothy Kingsley d Charles Walters ph Harold Rosson songs Johnny Mercer, Arthur Schwarz
Esther Williams, Charlotte Greenwood, William Demarest, Fernando Lamas, Jack Carson, Denise Darcel, Barbara Whiting

Dangerously They Live
US 1941 77m bw
Warner (Ben Stoloff)

American Nazi agents try to get a secret memorized by a British girl agent injured in a car crash.
Watchable, routine spy propaganda fare.
w Marion Parsonnet d Robert Florey ph William O'Connell

John Garfield, Raymond Massey, Nancy Coleman, Moroni Olsen, Lee Patrick, Christian Rub, Frank Reicher

Dangerously Yours
US 1933 74m bw

A gentleman crook falls for a lady detective.
Ho-hum society crook drama. Warner Baxter, Miriam Jordan, Herbert Mundin, Florence Eldredge, Florence Roberts, Mischa Auer. Written by Horace Jackson from a story by Paul Hervey Fox; directed by Frank Tuttle; for Fox. 'None too potent.'—*Variety*

Dangerously Yours
US 1937 60m bw

On board ship a detective captures a lady jewel thief but reforms her. Very tolerable programme filler with watchable performances. Cesar Romero, Phyllis Brooks, Jane Darwell, Alan Dinehart, Douglas Wood,

Leon Ames. Written by Lou Breslow, John Patrick; directed by Mal St Clair; for TCF. 'Fox is turning out a pretty good quality of B product.'—*Variety*

Daniel
US 1983 129m Technicolor
World Film Services (John Van Eyssen)

The children of executed spies are traumatized by the past.
Patchwork vision of thirties America, with Jewishness thrown in for added weight. Not easy to watch.
w E. L. Doctorow from his novel The Book of Daniel d Sidney Lumet ph Andrzej Bartkowiak m Bob James pd Philip Rosenberg

Timothy Hutton, Mandy Patinkin, Lindsay Crouse, Ed Asner, Ellen Barkin, Tovah Feldshuh
'Only with the last scene does one realize that it has collapsed into an empty liberal squeak.'—*Tom Milne, MFB*

Danny Boy
GB 1941 80m bw

A singer searches for her estranged husband and small son who have become street entertainers. Sentimental drama with music; not for the critical. Ann Todd, Wilfrid Lawson, Grant Tyler, John Warwick, David Farrar. Written by Oswald Mitchell and A. Barr-Carson; directed by Oswald Mitchell; for Butcher's.

Dante's Inferno°°
US 1935 89m bw
TCF (Sol M. Wurtzel)

A ruthless carnival owner gets too big for his boots, and has a vision of hell induced by one of his own attractions.
Curiously unpersuasive melodrama with a moral, but the inferno sequence is one of the most unexpected, imaginative and striking pieces of cinema in Hollywood's history.
w Philip Klein, Robert Yost d Harry Lachman ph Rudolph Maté
Spencer Tracy, Claire Trevor, Henry B. Walthall, Alan Dinehart, Scotty Beckett, Rita Hayworth (her first appearance, as a dancer)
'A pushover for vigorous exploitation . . . accentuate the inferno sequence and forget the rest, including the story.'—*Variety*
'We depart gratefully, having seen papier mache photographed in more ways than we had thought possible.'—*Robert Herring*
'One of the most unusual and effectively presented films of the thirties.'—*John Baxter, 1968*

Danton°
France / Poland 1982 136m colour
Losange / Group X (for Gaumont / TFI)

Robespierre quarrels with his colleague Danton, who hopes for a new spirit of tolerance.

Vivid historical re-creation which finally exhausts the spectator and is a little too concerned to make political points.
w Jean-Claude Carrière from the play The Danton Affair by Stanislawa Przybyszewska d Andrzej Wajda ph Igor Luther m Jean Prodromides

Gérard Depardieu, Wojciech Pszoniak, Anne Alvaro, Roland Blanche
'The temptation to see it in terms of Solidarity is unavoidable.'—*Philip Strick, MFB*
'By any reasonable standard, terrible.'— *New Yorker*
BFA: best foreign-language film

Darby O'Gill and the Little People°
US 1959 90m Technicolor
Walt Disney

An Irish caretaker falls down a well and is captured by leprechauns, who allow him three wishes to rearrange his life.
Pleasantly barmy Irish fantasy with brilliant trick work but some tedium in between.
w Lawrence Edward Watkin, *stories* H. T. Kavanagh d Robert Stevenson ph Winton C. Hoch m Oliver Wallace sp Peter Ellenshaw, Eustace Lycett, Joshua Meador

Albert Sharpe, Jimmy O'Dea, Sean Connery, Janet Munro, Kieron Moore, Estelle Winwood, Walter Fitzgerald, Denis O'Dea, J. G. Devlin, Jack MacGowran
'One of the best fantasies ever put on film.'—*Leonard Maltin*

Darby's Rangers
US 1957 121m bw
Warner (Martin Rackin)
GB title: *The Young Invaders*

A tough American commando unit is trained in Britain before seeing action in Africa and Sicily.
Standard World War II actioner, adequately executed.
w Guy Trosper, *book* Major James Altieri d William Wellman ph William H. Clothier m Max Steiner

James Garner, Etchika Choureau, Jack Warden, Edward Byrnes, Venetia Stevenson, Torin Thatcher, Stuart Whitman, Andrea King, Frieda Inescort, Reginald Owen, Adam Williams

The Daring Game
US 1967 101m Eastmancolor
Paramount / Tors (Gene Levitt)

A commercial group experiments with airborne and underwater inventions, and rescues a scientist from a police state.
Well photographed but haphazardly assembled adventures, aimed at TV.
w Andy White d Laslo Benedek ph Edmund Gibson m George Bruns

Lloyd Bridges, Nico Minardos, Joan Blackman, Michael Ansara

The Dark Angel°
US 1925 83m (24 fps) bw silent
First National (Samuel Goldwyn)

During World War I, a blinded officer tries to persuade his fiancée to marry another man, without her knowing of his own infirmity. Vilma Banky's first American film, her first teaming with Colman and a mid-twenties hit of colossal proportions.

w Frances Marion, *play* Guy Bolton
d George Fitzmaurice *ph* George Barnes

Ronald Colman, Vilma Banky, Wyndham Standing, Frank Elliott, Charles Lane, Florence Turner, Helen Jerome Eddy

The Dark Angel°
US 1935   105m   bw
Samuel Goldwyn

Tearstained melodrama from another age (see above), neatly packaged for the romantic 1935 public.

w Lillian Hellman, Mordaunt Shairp *d* Sidney Franklin *ph* Gregg Toland *m* Alfred Newman *ad* Richard Day

Merle Oberon, Fredric March, Herbert Marshall, Janet Beecher, John Halliday, Henrietta Crosman, Frieda Inescort, George Breakston, Claud Allister

'A sockaroo woman's picture.'—*Variety*
'A highly literate screen adaptation, telling the story with feeling and good taste.'—*New York Times*
'It makes a systematic and skilful appeal to those untrustworthy emotions which may suddenly cause the most hardened intellects to dissolve before the most obvious sentimentality.'—*The Times*

AAN: Merle Oberon
AA: Richard Day

The Dark at the Top of the Stairs°°
US 1960   124m   Technicolor
Warner (Michael Garrison)

Twenties small town drama about a young boy's awakening to the sexual tensions around him.
Archetypal family drama set in that highly familiar American street. The perfect essence of this playwright's work, with high and low spots, several irrelevancies, but a real feeling for the people and the place.

w Harriet Frank Jnr, Irving Ravetch, *play* William Inge *d* Delbert Mann *ph* Harry Stradling *m* Max Steiner

Robert Preston, Dorothy McGuire, Angela Lansbury, Eve Arden, Shirley Knight, Frank Overton, Lee Kinsolving, Robert Eyer

'Every time a woman turns her face away because she's tired or unwilling, there's someone waiting like me . . .'—*publicity*
† The curious title turns out to be a synonym for life, which one should never be afraid of.

AAN: Shirley Knight

The Dark Avenger°
GB 1955   85m   Eastmancolor
            Cinemascope
Allied Artists
US title: *The Warriors*

The Black Prince quells some French rebels. Good-humoured historical romp with the

ageing star in his last swashbuckling role, helped by a good cast and brisk pace.

w Daniel B. Ullman *d* Henry Levin *ph* Guy Green *m* Cedric Thorpe Davie

Errol Flynn, Peter Finch, Joanne Dru, Yvonne Furneaux, Patrick Holt, Michael Hordern, Moultrie Kelsall, Robert Urquhart, Noel Willman

Dark City
US 1950   97m   bw
Paramount / Hal B. Wallis

A bookmaker finds himself on the run from a revenge-seeking psychopath.
Unattractive and heavily-handled underworld melodrama, a disappointment from the talents involved.

w John Meredyth Lucas, Larry Marcus *d* William Dieterle *ph* Victor Milner *m* Franz Waxman

Charlton Heston (his first Hollywood appearance), Lizabeth Scott, Viveca Lindfors, Dean Jagger, Don DeFore, Jack Webb, Ed Begley, Henry Morgan, Mike Mazurki

'A jaded addition to a type of thriller which has become increasingly tedious and unreal.'—*MFB*

Dark Command°
US 1940   92m   bw
Republic (Sol C. Siegel)

In pre-Civil War Kansas, an ambitious ex-schoolteacher named Cantrill organizes guerrilla bands to pillage the countryside. Semi-historical hokum, quite well done with a good cast.

w Grover Jones, Lionel Houser, F. Hugh Herbert, *novel* W. R. Burnett *d* Raoul Walsh *ph* Jack Marta *m* Victor Young

John Wayne, Claire Trevor, Walter Pidgeon, Roy Rogers, George 'Gabby' Hayes, Porter Hall, Marjorie Main

AAN: Victor Young

● *Video: World of Video 2000*

The Dark Corner°
US 1946   98m   bw
TCF (Fred Kohlmar)

A private eye with a criminal record thinks he is being menaced by an old adversary, but the latter is found murdered.
Moody, brutish, well-made thriller with a plot put together from bits and pieces of older, better movies, notably Clifton Webb's reprise of his *Laura* performance and William Bendix ditto *The Glass Key*.

w Jay Dratler, Bernard Schoenfeld, *story* Leo Rosten *d* Henry Hathaway *ph* Joe MacDonald *m* Cyril Mockridge

Mark Stevens, Clifton Webb, Lucille Ball, William Bendix, Kurt Kreuger, Cathy Downs, Reed Hadley, Constance Collier

JARINE (Clifton Webb): 'I hate the dawn. The grass always looks as though it's been left out all night.'

BRAD (Mark Stevens): 'There goes my last lead. I feel all dead inside. I'm backed up in a dark corner, and I don't know who's hitting me.'

'Not so much a whodunnit as a whodunnwhat . . . all seem bent on "getting" each other and their internecine plottings add up to an alpha thriller.'—*Daily Mail*

The Dark Crystal°°
GB 1982   94m   Technicolor Panavision
Universal / AFD / ITC (David Lazer)

Two young people defeat the evil creatures who have taken over the world by replacing a shard which has been taken from the Dark Crystal.
Surprisingly effective piece of mysticism performed entirely by hand puppets from the Muppet stable.

w David Odell *d* Jim Henson, Frank Oz *conceptual designer* Brian Froud *ph* Oswald Morris *pd* Harry Lange *ed* Ralph Kemplen

'A dazzling technological and artistic achievement . . . could teach a lesson in morality to youngsters at the same time as it is entertaining their parents.'—*Variety*

Dark Delusion
US 1947   90m   bw

A neurotic girl may have to be committed to an asylum. Last episode of the Dr Gillespie series; not a sensation on its own account. Lionel Barrymore, James Craig, Lucille Bremer, Edward Arnold, Keye Luke. Written by Jack Andrews and Harry Ruskin; directed by Willis Goldbeck; for MGM. (GB title: *Cynthia's Secret*.)

Dark Eyes of London°
GB 1939   75m   bw
Pathe / Argyle (John Argyle)
US title: *The Human Monster*

The proprietor of a home for the blind uses a mute giant to drown insured victims. Reasonably effective British horror, a rarity at the time.

w John Argyle, Walter Summers, Patrick Kirwan, *novel* Edgar Wallace *d* Walter Summers *ph* Bryan Langley

Bela Lugosi, Hugh Williams, Greta Gynt, Wilfrid Walter, Edmon Ryan

Dark Hazard
US 1934   72m   bw

A compulsive gambler loses his wife as well as his money. Modest star drama, remade in 1937 as *Wine, Women and Horses*. Edward G. Robinson, Glenda Farrell, Robert Barrat, Hobart Cavanagh. Written by Ralph Block and Brown Holmes; directed by Alfred E. Green; for Warner.

The Dark Horse
US 1932   75m   bw

A nitwit runs for governor and nearly makes it. Mild political satire; closer to farce, really. Guy Kibbee, Bette Davis, Warren William, Frank McHugh. Written by Joseph Jackson and Wilson Mizner; directed by Alfred E. Green; for Warner.

DARK HAZARD. New Yorkers Glenda Farrell and Edward G. Robinson seem happy together under their Warner contracts; one wonders why they didn't play together more often.

Dark Journey*
GB 1937 82m bw
London Films / Victor Saville

In 1915 Stockholm, a French woman spy masquerading as a traitor falls in love with her German spy contact.
Unconvincing but entertaining romantic adventure with good star performances.

w Lajos Biro, Arthur Wimperis, *play* Lajos Biro *d* Victor Saville *ph* Georges Périnal, Harry Stradling *m* Richard Addinsell

Conrad Veidt, Vivien Leigh, Joan Gardner, Anthony Bushell, Ursula Jeans, Eliot Makeham, Austin Trevor, Edmund Willard
  'An exceptional quantity of carefully thought out direction . . . the financial success will depend on whether the general public will understand and keep pace with the plot.'—
Variety

The Dark Man
GB 1950 91m bw
Rank / Independent Artists (Julian Wintle)

A mysterious murderer haunts a seaside resort.
Limp, disappointing location police thriller, with too much chat and generally mishandled moments of suspense

wd Jeffrey Dell *ph* Eric Cross *m* Hubert Clifford

Maxwell Reed, Edward Underdown, Natasha Parry, Barbara Murray, William Hartnell, Cyril Smith, Geoffrey Sumner
  'The contrivances of the script are not helped by stilted dialogue.'—*MFB*

'One twin loves—and one twin loves to kill!'
The Dark Mirror**
US 1946 85m bw
International

A police detective works out which of identical twin girls is a murderer.
Unconvincing but highly absorbing thriller with all credits plus; the best brand of Hollywood moonshine.

w Nunnally Johnson, *original story* Vladimir Posner *d* Robert Siodmak *ph* Milton Krasner

Olivia de Havilland, Lew Ayres, Thomas Mitchell, Garry Owen
  'Smooth and agreeable melodrama . . . the detective work involves inkblot and word association tests and an amusingly sinister tandem of oscillating pens which register concealed emotions as one of the sisters talks.'—*James Agee*

AAN: Vladimir Posner

● *Video: Intervision*

Dark Passage**
US 1947 106m bw
Warner (Jerry Wald)

A convicted murderer escapes from jail and proves his innocence.
Loosely assembled, totally unconvincing star thriller which succeeds because of its professionalism, some good cameos, and a number of narrative tricks including subjective camera for the first half hour.

w Delmer Daves, *novel* David Goodis *d* Delmer Daves *ph* Sid Hickox *m* Franz Waxman

Humphrey Bogart, Lauren Bacall, Agnes Moorehead, Bruce Bennett, *Tom D'Andrea, Houseley Stevenson*
  'An almost total drag.'—*New Yorker, 1977*

The Dark Past**
US 1948 75m bw
Columbia (Buddy Adler)

A psychiatrist turns the tables on convicts who break into his home.
Tense, economical remake of *Blind Alley* (qv); a fresh look at a familiar situation (*The Small Voice, The Desperate Hours*, etc) helped by excellent performances.

w Philip Macdonald, Malvin Wald, Oscar Saul *d* Rudolph Maté *ph* Joseph Walker *m* George Duning

William Holden, Lee J. Cobb, Nina Foch, Adele Jergens, Stephen Dunne
  'A picture so packed with skill and imagination that every minute is absorbing.'—*Richard Mallett, Punch*

'The mission of the Strangelove generation!'
Dark Star*
US 1974 83m Metrocolor
Jack H. Harris (John Carpenter)

In the 22nd century, the bored crew of a starship on an intergalactic mission become prey to their own phobias and to the alien mascot they are taking back to earth.
A semi-professional film which turned out to be one of the screen's neatest low-budget entries in the pulp science fiction genre. That doesn't make it wholly entertaining, but its credentials are impeccable.

w John Carpenter, Dan O'Bannon *d* John Carpenter *pd, ed* Dan O'Bannon *ph* Douglas Knapp *m* John Carpenter

Brian Narelle, Dre Pahich, Cal Kuniholm, Dan O'Bannon

● *Video: Iver Film*

The Dark Tower
GB 1943 93m bw
Warner

A circus hypnotist possessively controls a girl trapezist.
Heavy-handed but quite effective melodrama.

w Brock Williams, Reginald Purdell, *play* Alexander Woolcott, George S. Kaufman *d* John Harlow *ph* Otto Heller

Ben Lyon, Anne Crawford, David Farrar, Herbert Lom, William Hartnell, Frederick Burtwell, Josephine Wilson

'Never a love so exquisite! She smiled at the cost, and bravely paid the reckoning when her heart's happy dancing was ended!'

Dark Victory**
US 1939 106m bw
Warner (David Lewis)

A good-time society girl discovers she is dying of a brain tumour.

A highly commercial tearjerker of its day, this glutinous star vehicle now works only fitfully.

w Casey Robinson, *play* George Brewer Jnr, Bertram Bloch d Edmund Goulding *ph* Ernest Haller *m* Max Steiner

Bette Davis, George Brent, Humphrey Bogart, Ronald Reagan, Geraldine Fitzgerald, Henry Travers, Cora Witherspoon, Dorothy Peterson

JUDITH (Bette Davis): 'Nothing can hurt us now. What we have can't be destroyed. That's our victory—our victory over the dark. It is a victory because we're not afraid.'

'If it were an automobile, it would be a Rolls-Royce with the very best trimmings.'— *Time*

'Will turn in a good account of itself at the box office, though not rating socko proportions.'—*Variety*

'A completely cynical appraisal would dismiss it all as emotional flim-flam . . . but it is impossible to be that cynical about it.'— *Frank S. Nugent*

'A gooey collection of clichés, but Davis slams through them in her nerviest style.'— *New Yorker, 1976*

† Remade 1963 as *Stolen Hours*, with Susan Hayward; 1975 as *Dark Victory* (TV movie) with Elizabeth Montgomery.

AAN: best picture; Bette Davis; Max Steiner
● *Video:* Warner

Dark Water*
GB 1980 28m colour

A girl locked in a swimming pool is terrorized by a mad killer. Agreeably watchable thriller full of shadows and shocks. Phil Davis, Gwyneth Strong, David Beames. Written by Andrew Bogle and Tony Grisoni; directed by Andrew Bogle; for Dragonfly / ITC.

Dark Waters**
US 1944 90m bw
Benedict Bogeaus

Recovering from being torpedoed, an orphan girl visits her aunt and uncle in Louisiana and has some terrifying experiences.

Competent frightened-lady melodrama helped by its bayou surroundings. Possibly discarded by Hitchcock, but with sequences well in his manner.

w Joan Harrison, Marian Cockrell d André de Toth ph John Mescall m Miklos Rozsa

Merle Oberon, Franchot Tone, *Thomas Mitchell, Fay Bainter, John Qualen,* Elisha Cook Jnr, Rex Ingram

Darker than Amber
US 1970 96m Technicolor
Cinema Center / Major Films (Walter Seltzer)

A Florida private eye rescues a girl who is subsequently murdered and turns out to be part of a confidence racket.

Routine suspenser from the Travis McGee books; not very stimulating.

w Ed Waters, *novel* John D. MacDonald d Robert Clouse *ph* Frank Phillips *m* John Parker

Rod Taylor, Suzy Kendall, Theodore Bikel, James Booth, Jane Russell, Janet McLachlan, William Smith

'When she was good she was very very good. When she was bad, she was . . .'

Darling**
GB 1965 127m bw
Anglo-Amalgamated / Vic / Appia (Joseph Janni, Victor Lyndon)

An ambitious young woman deserts her journalist mentor for a company director, an effeminate photographer and an Italian prince. Fashionable mid-sixties concoction of smart swinging people and their amoral doings. Influential, put over with high style, and totally tiresome in retrospect.

w Frederic Raphael d John Schlesinger ph Ken Higgins m John Dankworth

Julie Christie, Dirk Bogarde, Laurence Harvey, Roland Curram, Alex Scott, Basil Henson, Pauline Yates

BOGARDE to Christie: 'Your idea of being fulfilled is having more than one man in bed at the same time.'

'As empty of meaning and mind as the empty life it's exposing.'—*Pauline Kael*

AA: Frederic Raphael; Julie Christie
AAN: best picture; John Schlesinger

Darling How Could You
US 1951 96m bw
Paramount (Harry Tugend)
GB title: *Rendezvous*

Children long separated from their parents have fantasies about them.

Faded-looking Edwardian comedy which does not quite have the style or the cast for success. (Or the title, come to that.)

w Dodie Smith, Lesser Samuels, *play* Alice Sit by the Fire by J. M. Barrie d Mitchell Leisen ph Daniel L. Fapp m Frederick Hollander

Joan Fontaine, John Lund, Mona Freeman, Peter Hanson, David Stollery, Lowell Gilmore, Robert Barrat, Gertrude Michael

Darling Lili*
US 1970 136m Technicolor
Panavision
Paramount / Geoffrey (Owen Crump)

During World War I, an American air ace falls for a German lady spy, and waits till the war is over to marry her.

Farce and romance mix oddly with aerial acrobatics in this expensive and dull extravaganza which bore the sub-title *Where*

Were You the Night I Shot Down Baron Von Richthofen? (which probably sums up its aims and its failure). A coffee table film, good to look at and with occasional striking moments.

wd Blake Edwards ph Russell Harlan, Harold E. Wellman m Henry Mancini pd Fernando Carrere

Julie Andrews, Rock Hudson, Jeremy Kemp, Lance Percival, Michael Witney, Jacques Marin, André Maranne

AAN: Henry Mancini; song 'Whistling Away the Dark' (m Henry Mancini, ly Johnny Mercer)

The Darwin Adventure*
GB 1971 91m Eastmancolor
(TCF) Palomar (Joseph Strick, Irving Lerner)

In 1831, Charles Darwin becomes ship's naturalist on the *Beagle* and studies wild life in South America.

Rather naive biopic of Darwin which tries to cover too much with too slender resources but makes a pleasant introduction to the subject.

w William Fairchild d Jack Couffer ph Denys Coop, Jack Couffer m Marc Wilkinson

Nicholas Clay, Susan Macready, Ian Richardson, Christopher Martin, Robert Flemyng, Aubrey Woods, Hugh Morton

'The biopic plague, which has ravaged the screen lives of Pasteur, Juarez, Cole Porter and countless others, has now struck down the memory of famed naturalist Charles Darwin. The filmgoing public's own version of Darwin's natural selection theory will immediately weed out this inferior species.'— *Variety*

A Date with Judy
US 1948 113m Technicolor
MGM (Joe Pasternak)

A teenager wrongly suspects her friend of an illicit affair.

Ambitious but flat comedy musical which neatly wraps up all kinds of forties people and institutions: teenagers, small towns, families, Carmen Miranda and Miss Taylor, not to mention the producer.

w Dorothy Cooper, Dorothy Kingsley d Richard Thorpe ph Robert Surtees m / ly various md George Stoll

Wallace Beery, Elizabeth Taylor, Jane Powell, Carmen Miranda, Xavier Cugat, Robert Stack, Selena Royle, Scotty Beckett, Leon Ames

Daughter of Darkness
GB 1947 91m bw
Kenilworth–Alliance (Victor Hanbury)

A murderous Irish servant girl has a fatal flair for men.

Absurd melodrama, almost Grand Guignol, louringly set on the Yorkshire moors but lethargically handled all round.

w Max Catto, from his play They Walk Alone d Lance Comfort ph Stanley Pavey

Siobhan McKenna, Anne Crawford, Maxwell Reed, George Thorpe, Barry Morse, Honor Blackman, Liam Redmond, David Greene

Daughter of Dr Jekyll
US 1957 74m bw

An evil doctor tells his ward that she is the daughter of the unfortunate Dr Jekyll and therefore responsible for a series of werewolf killings. Bathetic cheapie with risible views of England and a tendency to mix up several myths in one package. Arthur Shields, John Agar, Gloria Talbott, John Dierkes. Written by Jack Pollexfen; directed by Edgar C. Ulmer; for Allied Artists.

The Daughter of Rosie O'Grady*
US 1950 104m Technicolor
Warner (William Jacobs)

A girl determines to follow in her dead mother's musical comedy footsteps against the wishes of her still-grieving father.
Absolutely standard period musical, quite pleasantly handled but with below-par musical numbers.

w Jack Rose, Mel Shavelson, Peter Milne d David Butler ph Wilfred M. Cline md David Buttolph

June Haver, Gordon Macrae, James Barton, S. Z. Sakall, Gene Nelson, Debbie Reynolds, Sean McClory, Jane Darwell

Daughter of Shanghai*
1937 63m bw

The daughter of a wealthy merchant revenges herself on smugglers who kill him. Pacy lower-berth melodrama packed with good talent. Anna May Wong, Charles Bickford, Philip Ahn, Larry Crabbe, Cecil Cunningham, Anthony Quinn, J. Carrol Naish, Evelyn Brent. Written by Gladys Unger and Garnett Weston; directed by Robert Florey; for Paramount. 'Meaningless title to a routine crime meller . . . downstairs dualler, but not half bad.'—Variety

Daughter of the Dragon
US 1931 70m bw

Fu Manchu continues to seek revenge on Dr Petrie for the loss of his wife in the Boxer rebellion. Muddled thriller with too much plot and too little action. Warner Oland, Anna May Wong, Sessue Hayakawa, Bramwell Fletcher, Holmes Herbert. Written by Lloyd Corrigan and Monte Katterjohn; directed by Lloyd Corrigan; for Paramount. 'Chinese blunderings, murders, and silly acting. Best for the combos where the kids may get a kick out of it.'—Variety

Daughters Courageous*
US 1939 107m bw
Warner (Hal B. Wallis)

A prodigal father returns to his family and sorts out their problems.
Following the success of Four Daughters (qv) the cast was reassembled to make this amiable rehash about a different family.

w Julius and Philip Epstein, play Fly Away Home by Dorothy Bennett, Irving White d Michael Curtiz ph James Wong Howe Claude Rains, John Garfield, Jeffrey Lynn, Fay Bainter, Priscilla Lane, Rosemary Lane, Lola Lane, Gale Page, Donald Crisp, May Robson, Frank McHugh, Dick Foran, Berton Churchill

'Suited to the family trade anywhere . . . but there's something to be said against a running time of an hour and 47 minutes.'—Variety
'For its intelligent use of small town locations, its skilled acting, fine camerawork and evenly paced, sympathetic direction, it surpasses everything of its type.'—John Baxter, 1968
'Attractive people, good dialogue and camerawork, and skilful direction can work wonders.'—Richard Mallett, Punch

'For this woman—he broke God's own commandments! The fire and tempest of their love still flames across 3000 years!'

David and Bathsheba*
US 1951 116m Technicolor
TCF (Darryl F. Zanuck)

King David loves the wife of one of his captains, and ensures that the latter is killed in battle.
Deliberately sober bible-in-pictures, probably intended as a riposte to Cecil B. de Mille. Somewhat lacking in excitement, but you can't call it gaudy.

w Philip Dunne d Henry King ph Leon Shamroy m Alfred Newman

Gregory Peck, Susan Hayward, James Robertson Justice, Raymond Massey, Kieron Moore, Jayne Meadows, John Sutton, Dennis Hoey, Francis X. Bushman, George Zucco

'Hardly a single unintentional laugh.'—Richard Mallett, Punch

AAN: Phillip Dunne; Leon Shamroy; Alfred Newman

David and Lisa*
US 1963 94m bw
Continental (Paul M. Heller)

Two disturbed adolescents at a special school fall in love.
Case history drama, earnest and well meaning rather than exciting.

w Eleanor Perry, book Theodore Isaac Rubin d Frank Perry ph Leonard Hirschfield m Mark Lawrence

Keir Dullea, Janet Margolin, Howard da Silva, Neva Patterson, Clifton James, Richard McMurray

AAN: Eleanor Perry; Frank Perry

'One of the greatest stories of love and adventure ever told is brought to the screen as Dickens himself would wish it!'

David Copperfield****
US 1934 132m bw
MGM (David O. Selznick)

Disliked by his cruel stepfather and helped by his eccentric aunt, orphan David grows up to

become an author and eventually to marry his childhood sweetheart.
Only slightly faded after forty-five years, this small miracle of compression not only conveys the spirit of Dickens better than the screen has normally managed but is a particularly pleasing example of Hollywood's handling of literature and of the deployment of a great studio's resources. It also overflows with memorable character cameos, and it was a box office giant.

w Hugh Walpole, Howard Estabrook, novel Charles Dickens d George Cukor ph Oliver T. Marsh m Herbert Stothart montages Slavko Vorkapitch ad Cedric Gibbons

Freddie Bartholomew (young David), Frank Lawton (David as a man), W. C. Fields (Micawber), Roland Young (Uriah Heep), Edna May Oliver (Aunt Betsy), Lennox Pawle (Mr Dick), Basil Rathbone (Mr Murdstone), Violet Kemble Cooper (Miss Murdstone), Maureen O'Sullivan (Dora), Madge Evans (Agnes), Elizabeth Allan (Mrs Copperfield), Jessie Ralph (Peggotty), Lionel Barrymore (Dan Peggotty), Hugh Williams (Steerforth), Lewis Stone (Mr Wickfield), Herbert Mundin (Barkis), Elsa Lanchester (Clickett), Jean Cadell (Mrs Micawber), Una O'Connor (Mrs Gummidge), John Buckler (Ham), Hugh Walpole (the Vicar), Arthur Treacher (donkey man)

'One of the best ensembles ever . . . unusually good production which will win general approval.'—Variety
'Though half the characters are absent, the whole spectacle of the book, Micawber always excepted, is conveyed.'—James Agee
'The most profoundly satisfying screen manipulation of a great novel that the camera has ever given us.'—André Sennwald
'Perhaps the finest casting of all time.'—Basil Wright, 1972

AAN: best picture

David Harum*
US 1934 83m bw
Fox

A wily old rancher plays matchmaker.
Simple, pleasing small-town comedy-drama, ably fashioned for its star.

w Walter Woods, play Edward Westcott d James Cruze ph Hal Mohr m Louis de Francesco

Will Rogers, Evelyn Venable, Kent Taylor, Louise Dresser, Stepin Fetchit, Charles Middleton, Noah Beery

'Looks like a sugar picture.'—Variety

Davy*
GB 1957 84m Technirama
Ealing (Basil Dearden)

A member of a family music hall act auditions at Covent Garden.
Curiously unsuccessful vehicle for a popular singing comic; the script and continuity are simply poor, and swamped by the wide screen.

w William Rose d Michael Relph ph Douglas Slocombe m various classics

Harry Secombe, Ron Randell, George Relph, Alexander Knox, Susan Shaw, Bill Owen

Davy Crockett°
US 1955   93m   Technicolor
Walt Disney

Episodes in the career of the famous Tennessee hunter and Indian scout who died at the Alamo.
Disjointed and naive but somehow very fresh and appealing adventures; made for American television (as 3 × 50m episodes) but elsewhere an enormous hit in cinemas.

w Tom Blackburn d Norman Foster
ph Charles Boyle m George Bruns

Fess Parker, Buddy Ebsen, Basil Ruysdael, William Bakewell, Hans Conried, Kenneth Tobey, Nick Cravat
† 1956 sequel on similar lines: *Davy Crockett and the River Pirates*.

● Video: Disney

Dawn at Socorro
US 1954   80m   Technicolor

A gunfighter is trapped into one last duel. Moderate western programmer. Rory Calhoun, David Brian, Alex Nicol, Piper Laurie, Edgar Buchanan. Written by George Zuckerman; directed by George Sherman; for Universal-International.

'When there's no more room in Hell, the dead will walk the earth . . .'

Dawn of the Dead
US 1979   127m   Technicolor

America is filled by legions of carnivorous zombies. Seemingly endless horror comic with absurd pretensions to be an allegory of something or other; occasionally laughable, otherwise sickening or boring. David Emge, Ken Foree, Scott H. Reininger, Gaylen Ross. Written and directed by George A. Romero; for Laurel Group. (GB title: *Zombies*.)

'Forty youngsters sporting with fate!'

The Dawn Patrol°°
US 1930   90m   bw
Warner

In France during World War I, flying officers wait their turn to leave on missions which may mean death.
The second version (see below) is more watchable today, but this early talkie was highly effective in its time, and much of its aerial footage was re-used.

w John Monk Saunders d Howard Hawks
ph Ernest Haller

Richard Barthelmess, Douglas Fairbanks Jnr, Neil Hamilton, William Hanney, *James Finlayson*, Clyde Cook, Edmund Breon, Frank McHugh
  'No women and few laughs, so needs good surrounding comedy shorts.'—*Variety*
  'Bare, cleancut, uncluttered technique, a stark story line, terse dialogue . . . and a pervasive atmosphere of hopelessness captured with economy and incisiveness.'—*Andrew Sarris, 1963*

† TV title is *Flight Commander*, which was the title of Saunders' original story.
AAN: John Monk Saunders

'There's no chance for a flight to get through, but one man—flying low, hedgehopping—might make it!'

The Dawn Patrol°°
US 1938   103m   bw
Warner (Hal B. Wallis)

A remarkably early but trim and competent remake of the above, using much of the same aerial footage.

w Seton I. Miller, Dan Totheroh d Edmund Goulding ph Tony Gaudio m Max Steiner

Errol Flynn, Basil Rathbone, David Niven, Melville Cooper, Donald Crisp, Barry Fitzgerald, Carl Esmond
  'A powerful, red-corpuscled drama . . . geared for top grosses.'—*Variety*
  'A great deal of self-pity and romanticism have gone into the making of this excellent ham sandwich.'—*Graham Greene*

The Day
GB 1960   26m   bw

A young Ibizan travels a long way to collect his relatives for the celebration of the birth of a baby. Vivid and yet rather boring short which could have done with a twist in the tail. Written, directed and produced by Peter Finch.

A Day at the Races°°°°
US 1937   109m   bw (blue-tinted ballet sequence)
MGM (Lawrence Weingarten)

The Marxes help a girl who owns a sanatorium and a racehorse.
Fashions in Marxism change, but this top quality production, though lacking their zaniest inspirations, does contain several of their funniest routines and a spectacularly well integrated racecourse climax. The musical and romantic asides are a matter of taste but delightfully typical of their time.

w Robert Pirosh, George Seaton, George Oppenheimer d Sam Wood ph Joseph Ruttenberg m Franz Waxman

Groucho, Chico, Harpo, Margaret Dumont, Maureen O'Sullivan, Allan Jones, *Douglass Dumbrille, Esther Muir, Sig Rumann*
  'The money is fairly splashed about; the capitalists have recognized the Marx Brothers; ballet sequences, sentimental songs, amber fountains, young lovers. Easily the best film to be seen in London, but all the same I feel a nostalgia for the old cheap rickety sets.'—*Graham Greene*

Day for Night°°°
France / Italy 1973   116m   Eastmancolor
Films du Carrosse / PECF / PIC (Marcel Bébert)
original title: *La Nuit Américaine*

Frictions and personality clashes beset the making of a romantic film in Nice. Immensely enjoyable, richly detailed,

insider's-eye-view of the goings-on in a film studio. A fun film with melodramatic asides.

w François Truffaut, Jean-Louis Richard, Suzanne Schiffman d François Truffaut
ph Pierre-William Glenn m Georges Delerue

Jacqueline Bisset, Valentina Cortese, Jean-Pierre Aumont, Jean-Pierre Léaud, Dani, Alexandra Stewart, Jean Champion, François Truffaut, David Markham
  'I thought I'd had my last dram of enjoyment out of the Pagliacci theme and studio magic, and Truffaut shows there's life in the old whirl yet.'—*Stanley Kauffmann*
  'Made with such dazzling craftsmanship and confidence that you can never quite believe Truffaut's point that directing a movie is a danger-fraught experience.'—*Michael Billington, Illustrated London News*
† Graham Greene, as Henry Graham, played an insurance representative.

AA: best foreign film
AAN: script; François Truffaut (as director); Valentina Cortese

● Video: Warner

A Day in the Death of Joe Egg°°
GB 1971   106m   Eastmancolor
Columbia / Domino (David Deutsch)

A teacher and his wife are frustrated by their own inability to cope with the problem of their spastic daughter.
A well-filmed version of a sincerely human play, with humour and fantasy sequences leavening the gloom.

w Peter Nichols, from his play d Peter Medak
ph Ken Hodges m Elgar

Alan Bates, Janet Suzman, Peter Bowles, Sheila Gish, *Joan Hickson*
  'It's unsatisfying, and it's not to be missed.'—*Stanley Kauffmann*

The Day of the Animals
US 1976   98m   De Luxe   Todd AO 35
Film Ventures International (Edward L. Montero)

In the Californian High Sierras, animals of all kinds suddenly turn on human beings, but a day later are all found dead.
Irritatingly pointless horror fable borrowing heavily from *The Birds*; basically an exploitation shocker, most efficient when most unpleasant.

w William and Eleanor Norton d William Girdler ph Tom McHugh m Lalo Schifrin

Christopher George, Lynda Day George, Leslie Nielsen, Robert Sorrentino, Richard Jaeckel, Michael Ansara, Ruth Roman, Paul Mantee, Gil Lamb

Day of the Badman
US 1957   82m   Eastmancolor
Cinemascope

A circuit judge stands up against threatening outlaws. Uninvolving western which can't fill the wide screen. Fred MacMurray, Joan Weldon, John Ericson, Robert Middleton, Edgar Buchanan. Written by Irving Glassberg;

directed by Harry Keller; for Universal-International.

The Day of the Dolphin*
US 1973 104m Technicolor
Panavision
Avco–Embassy / Icarus (Robert E. Relyea)

A marine biologist researching dolphins off the Florida coast discovers they are being used in a plot to blow up the President's yacht.
A strangely unexpected and unsuccessful offering from the talent involved: thin and repetitive as scientific instruction (the dolphins' language in any case topples it into fantasy), and oddly childlike as spy adventure.

w Buck Henry, *novel* Robert Merle *d* Mike Nichols *ph* William A. Fraker *m* Georges Delerue *pd* Richard Sylbert

George C. Scott, Trish Van Devere, Paul Sorvino, Fritz Weaver

'The whole thing seems to have been shoved through the cameras as glibly as possible, so that everyone concerned could grab the money and run.'—*Stanley Kauffmann*

'An eight and a half million dollar Saturday afternoon special for sheltered nine-year-olds.'—*Judith Crist*

'Dolphins may live in a state of ecstasy, but the cast of this film seems lost in a state of confusion, wondering whether they are in an enlightened documentary, juvenile fantasy, or lurid soap opera.'—*Les Keyser, Hollywood in the Seventies*

'The most expensive Rin Tin Tin movie ever made.'—*Judith Crist*

AAN: Georges Delerue

● Video: CBS / Fox

The Day of the Evil Gun*
US 1968 93m Metrocolor Panavision
MGM (Jerry Thorpe)

Returning home after three years, a rancher finds that his wife and child have been carried off by Indians.
Competent standard western which resolves itself into a duel of wits between the hero and his rival.

w Charles Marquis Warren, Eric Bercovici *d* Jerry Thorpe *ph* W. Wallace Kelley *m* Jeff Alexander

Glenn Ford, Arthur Kennedy, Dean Jagger, Paul Fix, John Anderson, Nico Minardos

The Day of the Jackal**
GB / France 1973 142m Technicolor
Universal / Warwick / Universal France
(John Woolf, David Deutsch)

British and French police combine to prevent an OAS assassination attempt on de Gaulle by use of a professional killer.
An incisive, observant and professional piece of work based on a rather clinical bestseller.
Lack of a channel for sympathy, plus language confusions, are its main drawbacks.

w Kenneth Ross, *novel* Frederick Forsyth *d* Fred Zinnemann *ph* Jean Tournier *m* Georges Delerue

Edward Fox, Michel Lonsdale, Alan Badel, Eric Porter, Cyril Cusack, Delphine Seyrig, Donald Sinden, Tony Britton, Timothy West, Olga Georges-Picot, Barrie Ingham, Maurice Denham, Anton Rodgers

'Before *Jackal* is five minutes old, you know it's just going to be told professionally, with no flavour and no zest.'—*Stanley Kauffmann*

'All plot, with scarcely a character in sight.'—*Michael Billington, Illustrated London News*

'A better than average thriller for those who haven't read the book.'—*Judith Crist*

'A rare lesson in film-making in the good old grand manner.'—*Basil Wright, 1972*

● Video: CIC

'It happened in Hollywood—but it could have happened in Hell!'

The Day of the Locust**
US 1975 143m Technicolor
Paramount / Long Road (Jerome Hellman, Sheldon Shrager)

In Hollywood in the 1930s, a novice art director is bewildered by the eccentricities of life and an innocent man is martyred by the crowd.
A curious and interesting work from a savagely satirical novel; full of stimulating scenes and characters, it barely succeeds as a whole and was a disaster at the box office.

w Waldo Salt, *novel* Nathanael West *d* John Schlesinger *ph* Conrad Hall *m* John Barry *pd* Richard MacDonald

Donald Sutherland, William Atherton, Karen Black, Burgess Meredith, Geraldine Page, Richard A. Dysart, Bo Hopkins, Lelia Goldoni

AAN: Conrad Hall; Burgess Meredith

The Day of the Outlaw**
US 1958 96m bw
UA / Security Pictures (Sidney Harmon)

Two rival cattlemen forget their differences to fight six outlaws who ride into town.
Bleak and wintry western, well done and sufficiently unusual to stick in the mind.

w Philip Yordan, *novel* Lee Wells *d* André de Toth *ph* Russell Harlan *m* Alexander Courage

Robert Ryan, Burl Ives, Tina Louise, Nehemiah Persoff, David Nelson, Venetia Stevenson, Jack Lambert, Lance Fuller

'In the best William S. Hart tradition.'—*MFB*

The Day of the Triffids*
GB 1962 95m Eastmancolor
Cinemascope
Philip Yordan (George Pitcher)

Almost everyone in the world is blinded by meteorites prior to being taken over by intelligent plants.
Rough and ready adaptation of a famous sci-fi novel, sometimes blunderingly effective and with moments of good trick work.

w Philip Yordan, *novel* John Wyndham *d* Steve Sekely *ph* Ted Moore *m* Ron Goodwin

Howard Keel, Nicole Maurey, Kieron Moore, Janette Scott, Alexander Knox

● Video: IPC

Day of Wrath***
Denmark 1943 105m bw
Palladium
original title: *Vredens Dag*

In a 17th-century village an old woman is burned as a witch and curses the pastor who judged her. He dies and his mother accuses her daughter-in-law, in love with another man, of using witchcraft to kill him.
Harrowing, spellbinding melodrama with a message, moving in a series of Rembrandtesque compositions from one horrifying sequence to another. Depressing, but marvellous.

w Carl Dreyer, Poul Knudsen, Mogens Skot-Hansen, *play* Anne Pedersdotter by Hans Wiers Jenssen *d* Carl Dreyer *ph* Carl Andersson *m* Poul Schierbeck *ad* Erik Ases, Lis Fribert

Thorkild Roose, Lisbeth Movin, Sigrid Neiiendam, Preben Lerdoff Rye, Anna Svierkier

The Day the Earth Caught Fire**
GB 1961 99m bw with filters
Dyaliscope
British Lion / Pax (Val Guest)

Nuclear tests knock the world off its axis and send it careering towards the sun.
A smart piece of science fiction told through the eyes of Fleet Street journalists and showing a sharp eye for the London scene. Rather exhaustingly talkative, but genuinely frightening at the time.

w Wolf Mankowitz, Val Guest *d* Val Guest *ph* Harry Waxman *m* Monty Norman

Edward Judd, Janet Munro, Leo McKern, *Arthur Christiansen* (ex-editor of the Daily Express), Michael Goodliffe, Bernard Braden, Reginald Beckwith, Austin Trevor, Renée Asherson, Edward Underdown

● Video: Intervision

'From out of space—a warning and an ultimatum!'

The Day the Earth Stood Still**
US 1951 92m bw
TCF (Julian Blaustein)

A flying saucer arrives in Washington and its alien occupant, aided by a robot, demonstrates his intellectual and physical power, warns the world what will happen if wars continue, and departs.
Cold-war wish-fulfilment fantasy, impressive rather than exciting but very capably put over with the minimum of trick work and the maximum of sober conviction.

w Edmund H. North *d* Robert Wise *ph* Leo Tover *m* Bernard Herrmann

Michael Rennie, Patricia Neal, Hugh Marlowe, Sam Jaffe, Billy Gray

'Quite wry and alarmingly smooth.'—*New Yorker, 1977*

● Video: CBS / Fox

The Day the Fish Came Out

GB / Greece 1967 109m De Luxe
TCF / Michael Cacoyannis

Atomic material contaminates a
Mediterranean island.
Addle-pated, would-be satirical mod fantasy
with establishment figures cast as world
villains.

wd Michael Cacoyannis *ph* Walter Lassally
m Mikis Theodorakis

Tom Courtenay, Colin Blakely, Sam
Wanamaker, Candice Bergen, Ian Ogilvy,
Patricia Burke

The Day the Hot Line Got Hot

US 1968 92m Eastmancolor

Russian and American agents are outwitted by
their go-between. Feeble espionage comedy
teaming two big stars at the end of their
careers. Charles Boyer, Robert Taylor,
George Chakiris, Marie Dubois. Written by
Paul Jarrico, Dominique Fabre and M.
Trueblood; directed by Etienne Périer; for
Commonwealth United.

The Day They Robbed the Bank of England°

GB 1960 85m bw
MGM / Summit (Jules Buck)

In 1901 Irish patriots plan a coup against the
British government . . .
Small-scale, well-detailed period caper story,
marred by a slow-starting script and
unsympathetic acting.

w Howard Clewes, Richard Maibaum, *novel*
John Brophy *d* John Guillermin *ph* Georges
Périnal *m* Edwin Astley

Peter O'Toole, Aldo Ray, Elizabeth Sellars,
Kieron Moore, Albert Sharpe, Hugh Griffith,
John Le Mesurier, Joseph Tomelty, Miles
Malleson, Colin Gordon

The Day Will Dawn°

GB 1942 98m bw
Paul Soskin
US title: *The Avengers*

Norwegian freedom fighters destroy a U-boat
base and are saved by commandos.
Dated propaganda piece with an interesting
cast.

w Terence Rattigan, Anatole de Grunwald,
Patrick Kirwan *d* Harold French *ph* Bernard
Knowles *m* Richard Addinsell

Ralph Richardson, Deborah Kerr, Hugh
Williams, Griffith Jones, Francis L. Sullivan,
Roland Culver, Niall MacGinnis, Finlay
Currie, Bernard Miles, Patricia Medina

Daybreak°

US 1931 85m approx bw
MGM

An Austrian guardsman falls in love out of his
class.
Elegant romantic fable comparable with *Letter
From an Unknown Woman*; equally unpopular
and quite forgotten.

w Ruth Cummings, Zelda Sears, Cyril Hume,
play Arthur Schnitzler *d Jacques Feyder*
ph J. Merrit Gerstad

Ramon Novarro, Helen Chandler, C. Aubrey
Smith, Karen Morley, Kent Douglass, Jean
Hersholt, Glenn Tryon

'One of those pictures that won't draw after
opening . . . pretty flat all the way . . . good
only insofar as Novarro will draw
anywhere.'—*Variety*

Daybreak

GB 1946 81m bw
GFD / Triton (Sydney Box)

A barber and part-time hangman marries a
destitute girl, loses her to a Swedish seaman,
and kills himself in such a way as to implicate
the other man.
Dockside melodrama of extraordinary
pretentious gloominess; laughable in most
respects. A curious follow-up from the *Seventh
Veil* team.

w Muriel and Sydney Box, *play* Monckton
Hoffe *d* Compton Bennett *ph* Reg Wyer

Ann Todd, Eric Portman, Maxwell Reed,
Edward Rigby, Bill Owen, Jean Hylton,
Maurice Denham

Days of Glory

US 1944 86m bw
RKO (Casey Robinson)

Russian peasants fight the invading Nazis.
Lower-berth wartime propaganda piece chiefly
notable for introducing Gregory Peck to the
screen.

w Casey Robinson, *story* Melchior Lengyel
d Jacques Tourneur *ph* Tony Gaudio
m Daniele Amfitheatrof

Tamara Toumanova, Gregory Peck, Alan
Reed, Maria Palmer, Lowell Gilmore, Hugo
Haas

Days of Heaven°°

US 1978 95m Metrocolor
Paramount / OP (Bert and Harold
  Schneider)

In the early 20th century, three young
immigrants leave Chicago for the wheatfields.
Visually a superb slice of period life, let down
by obsessively self-important and symbolic
drama; also by imperfect sound recording.

wd Terrence Malick *ph* Nestor Almendros
m Ennio Morricone

Richard Gere, Brooke Adams, Sam Shepard,
Linda Manz

AAN: Ennio Morricone

● *Video: CIC*

Days of Thrills and Laughter°°°

US 1961 93m bw
(TCF) *Robert Youngson*

Appealing if rather miscellaneous silent film
compilation with the accent on action and
thrills as well as comedy. Like the other
Youngson histories, a boon to film archivists
despite a facetious commentary.

m Jack Shaindlin *narrator* Jay Jackson

Stan Laurel, Oliver Hardy, Snub Pollard,
Douglas Fairbanks, Charles Chaplin, Pearl
White, Houdini, Harry Langdon, Ben Turpin,
Charlie Chase, Boris Karloff, Warner Oland,
Fatty Arbuckle, Keystone Kops

Days of Wine and Roses°°

US 1962 117m bw
Warner (Martin Manulis)

A PR man becomes an alcoholic; his wife
gradually reaches the same state, but he
recovers and she does not.
Smart satirical comedy confusingly gives way
to melodrama, then sentimentality; quality is
evident throughout, but all concerned are
happiest with the first hour.

w J. P. Miller *d* Blake Edwards *ph* Philip
Lathrop *m* Henry Mancini

*Jack Lemmon, Lee Remick, Charles Bickford,
Jack Klugman*, Alan Hewitt, Debbie
Megowan, Jack Albertson

AA: title song (*m* Henry Mancini, *ly* Johnny
Mercer)
AAN: Jack Lemmon; Lee Remick

A Day's Pleasure°

US 1919 20m bw silent
First National / Charles Chaplin

Mishaps of a family picnic.
Very mild Chaplin, reaching for but not
achieving a kind of lyric quality. Amusing bits
rather than scenes.

wd Charles Chaplin *ph* Rollie Totheroh

Charles Chaplin, Edna Purviance, Henry
Bergman, Babe Lincoln

Daytime Wife

US 1939 71m bw

A young wife finds that her husband is still
dating his secretary, and retaliates by dating
his colleague. Hollywood version of a French
farce; not terrific, but watchable. Tyrone
Power, Linda Darnell, Warren William,
Binnie Barnes, Wendy Barrie, Joan Davis,
Leonid Kinskey. Written by Art Arthur,
Robert Harari; directed by Gregory Ratoff;
for TCF. 'Will give a good account of itself in
the key runs.'—*Variety*

Dayton's Devils

US 1968 103m Eastmancolor
Madison / Harold Goldman (Robert W.
  Stabler)

A former USAF colonel assembles a group of
misfits and adventurers to steal an army
payroll.
Overlong, routine caper film with a
surprisingly crisp climax (when it comes).

w Fred de Gorter *d* Jack Shea *ph* Brick
Marquard *m* Marlin Skiles

Leslie Nielsen, Rory Calhoun, Lainie Kazan,
Hans Gudegast

D-Day the Sixth of June

US 1956 106m Eastmancolor
  Cinemascope
TCF (Charles Brackett)

On the way to invade France in 1944, a British
colonel and an American captain reminisce
about their love for the same woman.
Turgid war romance with some good action
scenes and the usual hilarious Hollywood view
of London. General effect very wooden.

w Ivan Moffat, Harry Brown, *novel* Lionel Shapiro *d* Henry Koster *ph* Lee Garmes *m* Lyn Murray

Robert Taylor, Richard Todd, Dana Wynter, Edmond O'Brien, John Williams, Jerry Paris, Richard Stapley

'Reminiscent of *Mrs Miniver* in style and feeling.'—*MFB*

'He made evil an art, vice a virtue and pain a pleasure!'

De Sade*
US / Germany 1969 113m Movielab
AIP / CCC / Transcontinental (Louis M. Heyward, Artur Brauner)

The unbalanced Marquis de Sade is tormented by his wicked uncle with thoughts of his past. Mildly interesting attempt by AIP at European debauchery, with a good theatrical framework for the fantasies but too much flailing about by all concerned, especially in the slow motion orgy sequences, which are relentlessly boring, as is the film.

w Richard Matheson *d* Cy Endfield *ph* Heinz Pehlke *ad* Jurgen Kiebach *m* Billy Strange

Keir Dullea, *John Huston*, Lilli Palmer, Senta Berger, Anna Massey, Uta Levka

Dead End***
US 1937 92m bw
Samuel Goldwyn

A slice of life in New York's east side, where slum kids and gangsters live in a river street next to a luxury apartment block.
Highly theatrical film of a highly theatrical play, more or less preserving the single set and overcoming the limitations of the script and setting by sheer cinematic expertise. It is chiefly remembered, however, for introducing the Dead End Kids to a delighted world.

w Lillian Hellman, *play Sidney Kingsley*
d William Wyler *ph* Gregg Toland
ad Richard Day *m* Alfred Newman

Joel McCrea, Sylvia Sidney, *Humphrey Bogart*, Wendy Barrie, Claire Trevor, Allen Jenkins, *Marjorie Main*, James Burke, Ward Bond, *The Dead End Kids* (Billy Halop, Leo Gorcey, Bernard Punsley, Huntz Hall, Bobby Jordan, Gabriel Dell)

'Tense and accurate transcription, but sordid and depressing . . . in for a disappointing career.'—*Variety*

AAN: best picture; Gregg Toland; Claire Trevor

The Dead End Kids
The films in which the original gang of young 'hooligans' (see above) appeared were as follows:
1937: DEAD END
1938: CRIME SCHOOL, ANGELS WITH DIRTY FACES
1939: THEY MADE ME A CRIMINAL, HELL'S KITCHEN, ANGELS WASH THEIR FACES
1940: THE DEAD END KIDS ON DRESS PARADE

Subsequently they broke up into the LITTLE TOUGH GUYS, the EAST SIDE KIDS, and the BOWERY BOYS (all qv)

Dead Heat on a Merry Go Round
US 1967 108m Technicolor
Columbia (Carter de Haven)

An ex-con breaks parole and plans to rob Los Angeles Airport.
Boringly arty caper comedy-melodrama, concentrating less on the robbery than on its hero's sexual prowess. All very superficially flashy, and what the title means is anybody's guess.

wd Bernard Girard *ph* Lionel Lindon *m* Stu Phillips

James Coburn, Camilla Sparv, Aldo Ray, Nina Wayne, Robert Webber, Rose Marie, Todd Armstrong, Marian Moses, Severn Darden

'Just fills the space between a frisky title and a tricky TV-comedy ending, but doesn't fill it with any revels that require a viewer's complete attention.'—*Time*

Dead Man's Eyes
US 1944 64m bw

In order to trap a murderer, a blind artist pretends to have recovered his sight. Cheerless lower-case thriller from the disappointing *Inner Sanctum* series. Lon Chaney Jnr, Jean Parker, Paul Kelly. Written by Dwight V. Babcock; directed by Reginald LeBorg; for Universal.

Dead Man's Shoes
GB 1939 67m bw

A wealthy Paris manufacturer is accused of being a criminal who once disappeared. Sufficiently absorbing courtroom / amnesia melodrama, with British actors in a French setting. Leslie Banks, Joan Marion, Geoffrey Atkins, Wilfred Lawson, Judy Kelly, Nancy Price, Peter Bull, Walter Hudd, Ludwig Stossel. Written by Hans Kafka, Nina Jarvis; directed by Thomas Bentley; for Associated British. 'Goes straight into tense situations, and there are unexpected twists . . . should do well.'—*Variety*

Dead Men Are Dangerous
GB 1938 69m bw

A down-and-out changes clothes with a corpse and is accused of murder. Lethargic thriller, unconvincing in detail. Robert Newton, Betty Lynne, John Warwick, Peter Gawthorne. Written by Victor Kendall, Peter Hughes and Vernon Clancy; directed by Harold French; for Pathé.

Dead Men Don't Wear Plaid*
US 1982 88m bw
Universal / Aspen Film Society (David V. Picker, William E. McEuen)

A private eye is hired by a beautiful girl to find her father's murderer.
Ingenious but overstretched prank in which the hero apparently (by intercutting) gets

involved with famous crime stars of the forties: Bogart, Ladd, Bacall, Stanwyck, etc. The basic script is simply not funny enough to support the superstructure, though the selection of lines from the oldies is often ingenious.

w Carl Reiner, George Gipe, Steve Martin *d* Carl Reiner *ph* Michael Chapman *m* Miklos Rozsa *ed* Bud Molin *pd* John DeCuir

Steve Martin, Rachel Ward, Carl Reiner, Reni Santoni

'The content is undergraduate facetiousness at its worst, but at least the excerpts themselves provide a pleasant *noir* anthology.'—*Sight and Sound*

● *Video: Rank*

Dead Men Tell No Tales
GB 1938 80m bw

The matron of a school for boys is murdered after winning a lottery. Reasonably intriguing mystery. Emlyn Williams, Hugh Williams, Marius Goring, Lesley Brook, Sara Seegar. Written by Walter Summers and others, from the novel *The Norwich Victims* by Francis Beeding; directed by David MacDonald; for British National.

Dead Men Walk
US 1943 64m bw

A vampire returns from death to destroy his twin brother. Incompetent chiller partly sustained by its star performance. George Zucco, Mary Carlisle. Written by Fred Myton; directed by Sam Newfeld; for PRC.

Dead of Night****
GB 1945 104m bw
Ealing (Sidney Cole, John Croydon)

An architect is caught up in an endless series of recurring dreams, during which he is told other people's supernatural experiences and finally murders the psychiatrist who is trying to help him.
Chillingly successful and influential compendium of the macabre, especially effective in its low-key handling of the linking sequence with its circular ending.

w John Baines, Angus Macphail, based on stories by themselves, H. G. Wells, E. F. Benson *d* Cavalcanti, Charles Crichton, Robert Hamer, Basil Dearden *ph* Douglas Slocombe, Stan Pavey *m* Georges Auric *ad* Michael Relph

Mervyn Johns, Roland Culver, Mary Merrall, Judy Kelly, Anthony Baird, *Sally Ann Howes, Frederick Valk, Googie Withers*, Ralph Michael, Esmé Percy, Basil Radford, Naunton Wayne, Miles Malleson, *Michael Redgrave*, Hartley Power, Elizabeth Welch

'In a nightmare within a nightmare are contained five separate ghost stories . . . they have atmosphere and polish, they are eerie, they are well acted.'—*Richard Winnington*

'One of the most successful blends of laughter, terror and outrage that I can remember.'—*James Agee*

'The five ghost stories accumulate in intensity until the trap closes in the surrealist climax.'—*Pauline Kael, 1968*

Dead or Alive
Italy / US 1967   89m   Eastmancolor
Documento / Selmur (Albert Band)
US title: *A Minute to Pray, a Second to Die*

A gunman with a paralysed right arm helps a state governor rid a town of bandits.
Semi-spaghetti western with a strong cast and violent action scenes.

w Ugo Liberatore, Louis Garfinkle d Franco Giraldi ph Aiace Parolin m Carlo Rustichelli

Robert Ryan, Arthur Kennedy, Alex Cord, Nicoletta Machiavelli

Dead Pigeon on Beethoven Street
West Germany 1972   103m   De Luxe

An American private eye is shot dead in Germany by an international extortion gang, and his partner arrives to seek revenge.
Cheapskate thriller of interest only to addicts of the director. Glenn Corbett, Christa Lang, Anton Diffring. Written and directed by Samuel Fuller; for Bavaria Atelier. (NB: Filmed in English.)
● Video: Thorn EMI

Dead Reckoning*
US 1947   100m   bw
Columbia (Sidney Biddell)

Two war veterans are on their way to be decorated in Washington when one disappears.
Dour, complexly plotted thriller, a typical Hollywood *film noir* of the post-war years but a long way behind *Gilda* in likeability. The hero confesses the plot to a priest, and all the way it is more glum than fun.

w Oliver H. P. Garrett, Steve Fisher d John Cromwell ph Leo Tover m Marlin Skiles md Morris Stoloff

Humphrey Bogart, Lizabeth Scott, *Morris Carnovsky*, Charles Cane, William Prince, Marvin Miller, Wallace Ford, James Bell

Dead Ringer*
US 1964   116m   bw
Warner (William H. Wright)
GB title: *Dead Image*

A woman shoots her rich twin sister and assumes her identity.
High camp star vehicle, full of memories of long ago but rather drearily assembled and far too long, though Miss Davis as ever is in fighting form.

w Albert Beich, Oscar Millard d Paul Henreid ph Ernest Haller m André Previn

Bette Davis, Karl Malden, Peter Lawford, Philip Carey, Jean Hagen, Estelle Winwood, George Chandler, Cyril Delevanti

The Dead Zone*
US 1983   103m   Technicolor
Lorimar / Dino de Laurentiis (Cebra Hill)

The survivor of a road accident discovers that he has psychic powers.

Glum thriller with a fairly predictable outcome but some well-staged episodes

w Jeffrey Boan, *novel* Stephen King d David Cronenberg ph Mark Irwin m Michael Kamen pd Carol Spier

Christopher Walken, Brooke Adams, Tom Skerritt, Herbert Lom, Anthony Zerbe, Colleen Dewhurst

Deadfall
GB 1968   120m   De Luxe
TCF / Salamanda (Paul Monash, Jack Rix)

Robbery turns sour when a cat burglar falls in love with the wife of his homosexual partner.
Drearily fashionable romantic melodrama with far too few high spots and generally dull performances.

w Bryan Forbes, *novel* Desmond Cory d Bryan Forbes ph Gerry Turpin m John Barry

Michael Caine, Eric Portman, Giovanna Ralli, Nanette Newman, David Buck
'Exhausted no doubt by their past passions and childhood traumas, the principal protagonists move like so many somnambulists through the turgid labyrinth . . . whatever the intention, *Deadfall* merely falls flat on its somewhat ludicrous face.'—*MFB*

Deadlier Than the Male
GB 1967   101m   Techniscope
Rank / Sydney Box (Betty E. Box)

Bulldog Drummond traces the death of oil company executives to a master criminal using glamorous female assassins.
Just about tolerable recreation of Drummond in the modern world, with too little style, too much violence and sex, and an almost total lack of self-mockery. A sequel *Some Girls Do* (qv), was an unmitigated disaster.

w Jimmy Sangster, David Osborn, Liz Charles-Williams d Ralph Thomas ph Ernest Steward m Malcolm Lockyer ad Alex Vetchinsky

Richard Johnson, Nigel Green, Elke Sommer, Sylva Koscina, Suzanna Leigh, Zia Mohyeddin, Steve Carlson
'The original Drummond would have found the whole thing rather distasteful.'—*MFB*

Deadline at Dawn
US 1946   82m   bw
RKO

A sailor on leave passes out, finds the girl he was with has been murdered, and is helped by a philosophical taxi driver and a girl.
This could have been another *Crossfire*, but is smothered by pretentious writing and uncertain direction. The credits are interesting, though.

w Clifford Odets d Harold Clurman ph Nicholas Musuraca

Paul Lukas, Bill Williams, Susan Hayward, Osa Massen, Lola Lane
● Video: Kingston

Deadline USA*
US 1952   87m   bw
TCF (Sol C. Siegel)
GB title: *Deadline*

Despite threats and the killing of a witness, a crusading newspaper editor goes ahead with a story about the crimes of a powerful gangster.
Watchable newspaper melodrama with nothing much to say except that America must wake up to the enemy within. Smooth production, but too much semi-pretentious talk.

wd Richard Brooks ph Milton Krasner m Cyril Mockridge

Humphrey Bogart, Kim Hunter, Ethel Barrymore, Ed Begley, Paul Stewart, Warren Stevens, Martin Gabel, Joe de Santis, Audrey Christie, Jim Backus

The Deadly Affair**
GB 1966   106m   Technicolor
Columbia / Sidney Lumet

A Foreign Office man apparently commits suicide; his colleague is unconvinced and finally uncovers a spy ring.
Compulsive if heavy-going thriller from the sour-about-spies era, deliberately glum, photographed against the shabbiest possible London backgrounds in muddy colour. Solidly entertaining for sophisticated grown-ups.

w Paul Dehn, *novel* Call for the Dead by John Le Carré d Sidney Lumet ph Frederick A. Young m Quincy Jones

James Mason, Simone Signoret, Harry Andrews, Maximilian Schell, Harriet Andersson, Kenneth Haigh, *Max Adrian*, Robert Flemyng, Roy Kinnear, Lynn Redgrave

The Deadly Bees
GB 1966   83m   Technicolor

A pop singer goes on holiday to a remote farm and finds herself menaced by killer bees. Flat little thriller with one very obvious twist and no monster: just those bees. Frank Finlay, Guy Doleman, Suzanna Leigh, Catherine Finn. Written by Robert Bloch and Anthony Marriott; directed by Freddie Francis; for Amicus.

'To the valley of mystery came the shadow of death!'
Deadly Blessing
US 1981   102m   Metrocolor
Polygram / Interplanetary (William Gilmore)

A strict Hittite sect in Pennsylvania is disrupted by the murderous activities of an incubus.
Further developments from the school of *Alien, Omen* and *The Exorcist*; basically a succession of well-engineered shocks punctuated by long periods of boredom.

w Glenn M. Benest, Matthew Barr, Wes Craven d Wes Craven ph Robert Jessup m James Horner sp Jack Bennett

Maren Jensen, Susan Buckner, Jeff East, Ernest Borgnine, Lisa Hartman, Lois Nettleton

● Video: Polygram

The Deadly Companions*

US 1961 90m Pathecolor Panavision
Warner / Pathe America (Charles B.
  Fitzsimmons)

An army sergeant, a deserter, a trigger-happy
gunman and a saloon hostess join forces to rob
a bank.
Disjointed but rather attractive little western
let down by corny moments in the script.

w A. S. Fleishman d Sam Peckinpah
ph William H. Clothier m Martin Skiles,
Raoul Kraushaar

Brian Keith, Maureen O'Hara, Chill Wills,
Steve Cochran

The Deadly Mantis

US 1957 78m bw

A 'prehistoric' mantis escapes from Arctic ice
and travels rapidly towards New York. Absurd
and poorly crafted monster movie. Craig
Stevens, Alix Talton, William Hopper.
Written by Martin Berkeley; directed by
Nathan Juran; for Universal-International.

Deadly Strangers

GB 1974 93m Eastmancolor
Rank / Silhouette (Peter Miller)

A girl accepts a lift from a motorist at a time
when a mad strangler is on the loose.
Sub-Hitchcock melo-thriller with enough red
herrings to sink a ship. Smartly enough done,
but the grisliness needed balancing by
humour.

w Philip Levene d Sidney Hayers
ph Graham Edgar m Ron Goodwin

Hayley Mills, Simon Ward, Sterling Hayden,
Ken Hutchison, Peter Jeffrey

The Deadly Trackers

US 1973 104m Technicolor
Warner / Cine Film (Ed Rosen, Fouad Said)

A sheriff stalks the bandits who killed his wife
and son.
Lurid and ludicrous western started, and
abandoned, by Samuel Fuller; the challenge
need not have been taken up.

w Lukas Heller d Barry Shear ph Gabriel
Torres m various

Rod Taylor, Richard Harris, Al Lettieri,
Neville Brand, William Smith

  'It is no more than the outline of a
shadow.'—Tony Rayns

  'An incoherent, blood-soaked chase
story.'—New Yorker, 1977

The Deadly Trap

France / Italy 1971 100m Eastmancolor

The children of an American couple in Paris
are kidnapped. Smoothly made thriller which
spends rather too much time being chic. Faye
Dunaway, Frank Langella, Barbara Parkins.
Written by Sidney Buchman and Eleanor
Perry, from the novel The Children are Gone
by Arthur Cavanaugh; directed by René
Clément; for Corona / Pomereu / Oceania.

Dear Brigitte

US 1965 100m De Luxe Cinemascope
TCF (Henry Koster)

The small son of an American professor writes
a love letter to Brigitte Bardot, and when they
finally go to Paris she is charming to them.
Mild family comedy quaintly set around a
decaying Mississippi riverboat home; despite
assured performances, it all gets a bit icky at
times.

w Hal Kanter, novel Erasmus with Freckles by
John Haase d Henry Koster ph Lucien
Ballard m George Duning

James Stewart, Glynis Johns, Fabian, Cindy
Carol, Billy Mumy, John Williams, Jack
Kruschen, Brigitte Bardot, Ed Wynn, Alice
Pearce

Dear Heart*

US 1964 114m bw
Warner (Martin Manulis)

At a postmasters' convention in New York,
two middle-aged delegates fall in love.
Charming, understated, overlong romantic
drama in the Marty tradition; all quite
professional and satisfying.

w Tad Mosel d Delbert Mann ph Russell
Harlan m Henry Mancini

Glenn Ford, Geraldine Page, Angela
Lansbury, Michael Anderson Jnr, Barbara
Nichols, Patricia Barry, Charles Drake, Ruth
McDevitt, Neva Patterson, Alice Pearce,
Richard Deacon

AAN: title song (m Henry Mancini, ly Jay
Livingston, Ray Evans)

Dear Inspector*

France 1977 105m Eastmancolor
Ariane / Mondex (Alexander Mnouchkine)
Original title: Tendre Poulet

A female detective chases a murderer, helped
by her professor boyfriend.
Very likeable comedy-thriller with neat
performances. Popular in America, it was
translated into a series for television, but
didn't run.

w Michel Audiard, Philippe de Broca,
novel Jean-Paul Rouland and Claude Olivier
d Philippe de Broca ph Jean-Paul Schwartz
m Georges Delerue

Annie Girardot, Philippe Noiret, Catherine
Alric, Hubert Deschamps

Dear John*

Sweden 1964 111m bw
Sandrew (Bo Jonsson)
original title: Kare John

An unmarried mother in a seaside village falls
for a seaman.
A slight story effectively tricked out with all
manner of cinematic devices including a
multitude of flashbacks. Very watchable if a
little self-conscious.

wd Lars Magnus Lindgren, novel Olle
Lansburg ph Rune Ericson m Bengt-Arne
Wallin

Jarl Kulle, Christina Schollin, Helena Nilsson,
Morgan Anderson

  'It shines with the cool clear light of the
Swedish summer, and despite its glossy surface
manages also to convey strong sensual
pleasure.'—Brenda Davies

Dear Mr Prohack

GB 1949 91m bw
GFD / Wessex (Ian Dalrymple, Dennis Van
  Thal)

A treasury official copes admirably with public
money but is helpless when he comes into a
private fortune.
Flat little comedy in which the minor
amusements are incidental to the story.

w Ian Dalrymple, Donald Bull, novel Arnold
Bennett d Thornton Freeland ph H. E.
Fowle m Temple Abady

Cecil Parker, Hermione Baddeley, Dirk
Bogarde, Sheila Sim, Glynis Johns, Heather
Thatcher, Henry Edwards, Judith Furse

Dear Murderer

GB 1947 94m bw
GFD / Gainsborough (Betty E. Box)

Plot and counterplot among an adulterous
triangle.
Thoroughly artificial pattern play set among
the unreal rich, from one of those
unaccountable West End successes, here
boringly filmed.

w Muriel and Sydney Box, Peter Rogers, play
St John L. Clowes d Arthur Crabtree
ph Stephen Dade

Eric Portman, Greta Gynt, Dennis Price,
Maxwell Reed, Jack Warner, Hazel Court,
Andrew Crawford, Jane Hylton

Dear Octopus**

GB 1943 86m bw
GFD / Gainsborough (Edward Black)
US title: The Randolph Family

Members of a well-to-do British family reunite
for Golden Wedding celebrations.
Traditional upper-class British comedy drama,
and very well done too, with opportunities for
excellent character acting.

w R. J. Minney, Patrick Kirwan, play Dodie
Smith d Harold French ph Arthur Crabtree

Margaret Lockwood, Michael Wilding, Helen
Haye, Frederick Leister, Celia Johnson,
Roland Culver, Athene Seyler, Basil Radford,
Nora Swinburne, Jean Cadell, Kathleen
Harrison, Ann Stephens, Muriel George,
Antoinette Cellier, Graham Moffatt

'The screen's gayest love story!'

Dear Ruth*

US 1947 95m bw
Paramount (Paul Jones)

A schoolgirl causes confusion when she writes
love letters to a soldier using her elder sister's
photograph.
Smoothly amusing family comedy from a
Broadway success.

w Arthur Sheekman, play Norman Krasna
d William D. Russell ph Ernest Laszlo
m Robert Emmett Dolan

Joan Caulfield, William Holden, Mona
Freeman, Billy de Wolfe, Edward Arnold,
Mary Philips, Virginia Welles

'It is unlikely that 1947 will bring a more satisfying comedy . . . so many surprising and funny twists.'—*John Thompson, New York Mirror*

† Two less amusing sequels were made using virtually the same cast: *Dear Wife* (1949, 88m, d Richard Haydn); *Dear Brat* (1951, 82m, d William A. Seiter).

Death at Broadcasting House*
GB 1934   71m   bw
ABFD / Phoenix (Hugh Perceval)

A radio actor is murdered during a broadcast. Intriguing little murder mystery with an unusual background.

w Basil Mason, *novel* Val Gielgud   d Reginald Denham

Ian Hunter, Austin Trevor, Mary Newland, Henry Kendall, Val Gielgud, Peter Haddon, Betty Ann Davies, Jack Hawkins, Donald Wolfit

Death Hunt
US 1981   97m   Technicolor
Golden Harvest (Murray Shostak)

In 1931 Yukon, a reclusive trapper turns to violence when goaded by other wanderers and drunken mounties.
An arctic cross between *Straw Dogs* and *Death Wish*, and not even so good as either.

w Michael Grais, Mark Victor   d Peter Hunt   ph James Devis   m Jerrold Immel

Charles Bronson, Lee Marvin, Angie Dickinson, Andrew Stevens, Ed Lauter, Carl Weathers, Henry Beckman

● Video: CBS / Fox

Death in Venice**
Italy 1971   128m   Technicolor
Panavision
Warner / Alfa (Mario Gallo)
original title: *Morte a Venezia*

In a lush Venetian hotel one summer in the early years of the century, a middle-aged German composer on holiday falls for the charms of a silent young boy, and stays in the city too long to escape the approaching plague.
Incredibly extended and rather pointless fable enriched by moments of great beauty and directorial style; these do not quite atone for the slow pace or the muddled storyline.

w Luchino Visconti, Nicola Bandalucco, *novel* Thomas Mann   d Luchino Visconti   ph Pasquale de Santis   m Gustav Mahler   md Franco Mannino   ad Ferdinando Scarfiotti

Dirk Bogarde, Bjorn Andresen, Silvana Mangano, Marisa Berenson, Mark Burns
'Maybe a story as elusive as *Death in Venice* simply can't be filmed. Visconti has made a brave attempt, always sensitive to the original; but it's finally not quite the same thing.'— *David Wilson, MFB*

● Video: Warner

The Death Kiss
US 1932   74m   bw

During the making of a film an actor is

murdered. Promising murder mystery which becomes more and more muddled as it progresses; it wasn't helped by advertising suggesting that Lugosi was again playing a vampire instead of a red herring. David Manners, Adrienne Ames, Bela Lugosi, John Wray, Vince Barnett, Edward Van Sloan. Written by Barry Barringer and Gordon Kahn from the novel by Madelon St Dennis; directed by Edwin L. Marin; for KBS / World Wide.

Death of a Champion
US 1939   67m   bw

A champion show dog is murdered, and a memory expert and a small boy solve the mystery. Medium support with few opportunities for its star. Lynne Overman, Donald O'Connor, Virginia Dale, Joseph Allen Jnr, Harry Davenport, Robert Paige. Written by Stuart Palmer and Cortland Fitzsimmons, from a story by Frank Gruber; directed by Robert Florey; for Paramount.
'Skimpy on plot; fair dualler.'—*Variety*

Death of a Cyclist*
Spain / Italy 1955   85m   bw
Guion-Suevia / Trionfalcine
original title: *Muerte de un Ciclista*

An accident – a cyclist is knocked down and killed by an adulterous couple – tragically affects the lives of many people.
Rather like a politically conscious version of *An Inspector Calls*, this mannered and unemotional film was most interesting because of its almost Hollywoodian self-assurance.

wd Juan Antonio Bardem   *story* Luis de Igoa   ph Alfredo Fraile   m Isrido Maiztegui

Lucia Bose, Alberto Closas, Otello Toso, Carlos Casaravilla

Death of a Gunfighter*
US 1969   100m   Technicolor
Universal (Richard E. Lyons)

An unpopular marshal refuses to resign, and the situation leads to gunplay.
Downcast character western set in the early years of the century.

w Joseph Calvelli   d Robert Totten, Don Siegel   ph Andrew Jackson   m Oliver Nelson

Richard Widmark, Lena Horne, John Saxon, Carroll O'Connor, Larry Gates, Kent Smith

'A salesman's got to dream—it comes with the territory!'
'One mistake—seen by his son—unleashes with overwhelming power the great drama of our day!'

Death of a Salesman***
US 1951   112m   bw
Columbia (Stanley Kramer)

An ageing travelling salesman recognizes the emptiness of his life and commits suicide.
A very acceptable screen version of a milestone play which has become an American classic; stage conventions and tricks are cleverly adapted to cinematic use, especially

when the hero walks from the present into the past and back again.

w Stanley Roberts, *play* Arthur Miller   d Laslo Benedek   ph Franz Planer   m Alex North   md Morris Stoloff

Fredric March, Kevin McCarthy, Cameron Mitchell, Mildred Dunnock, Howard Smith, Royal Beal, Jesse White

MRS LOMAN: 'Attention must finally be paid to such a man. He's not to be allowed to fall into his grave like an old dog.'

WILLY LOMAN: 'A salesman is somebody way up there in the blue, riding on a smile and a shoeshine . . .'

'Its time shifts with light, which were poetic in the theatre, seemed shabby in a medium that can dissolve time and space so easily.'— *Stanley Kauffmann*

AAN: Franz Planer; Alex North; Fredric March; Kevin McCarthy; Mildred Dunnock

Death of a Scoundrel*
US 1956   119m   bw
RKO / Charles Martin

A Czech in New York becomes rich by fraud. Unconvincing but intermittently entertaining melodrama, a vehicle for a male Bette Davis.

wd Charles Martin   ph James Wong Howe   m Max Steiner

George Sanders, Yvonne de Carlo, Coleen Gray, Victor Jory, Zsa Zsa Gabor, Nancy Gates, John Hoyt, Tom Conway
'Vague moralizing and some attempts at social comment scarcely enliven this protracted study in megalomania.'—*MFB*

The Death of Mario Ricci*
Switzerland / France / West Germany
1983   101m   Eastmancolor
Pegase / TSR / Swanie / FR3 / Tele München

A Swiss TV journalist arrives in a remote village to record an interview with a malnutrition expert, and finds himself in the middle of a mystery about the death of an Italian immigrant worker.
A rather uncontrolled drama which begins by suggesting *Bad Day at Black Rock* but becomes less interesting as it proceeds.

w Claude Goretta, Georges Haldas   d Claude Goretta   ph Hans Liechti   m Arie Dzierlatka

Gian-Maria Volonte, Magali Noel, Mimsy Farmer, Heinz Bennent, Jean-Michael Dupuis

Death on the Diamond
US 1934   69m   bw

Murder during a baseball game. The story isn't much, so the picture's appeal depends on one's addiction to baseball. Robert Young, Madge Evans, Nat Pendleton, Ted Healy, C. Henry Gordon, Paul Kelly, Edward Brophy, Mickey Rooney, David Landau. Written by Harvey Thew, Joseph Sherman and Ralph Spence from the novel by Courtland Fitzsimmons; directed by Edward Sedgwick; for MGM. 'Due to plot, miscasting and some minor league technical preparation, it was two strikes to the bad before the cameras started to grind.'—*Variety*

Death on the Nile°
GB 1978 140m Technicolor
EMI (John Brabourne, Richard Goodwin)

Hercule Poirot solves the mystery of who killed the spoilt heiress on a steamer cruising down the Nile.
A pleasant thirties atmosphere and the travel poster backgrounds are the chief assets of this rather hesitant whodunnit which plays fair enough with the audience but gives its popular cast too little to do, while its constant repetitions of the crime become rather ghoulish. On the whole, though, a very passable representation of an old-fashioned genre, and a few points up on *Murder on the Orient Express.*

w Anthony Shaffer, *novel* Agatha Christie d John Guillermin ph Jack Cardiff pd Peter Murton m Nino Rota

Peter Ustinov, Bette Davis, Mia Farrow, Angela Lansbury, Jane Birkin, David Niven, George Kennedy, Jack Warden, Simon MacCorkindale, Lois Chiles, Jon Finch, Maggie Smith, Olivia Hussey, Harry Andrews, I. S. Johar
● *Video: Thorn EMI*

Death Race 2000°
US 1975 79m colour
New World (Roger Corman)

In the year 2000, the world's most popular sport involves motor racers who compete for the highest total of human casualties.
Cheaply made macabre satire, quite well enough made to please addicts of the blackest of black comedy.

w Robert Thom, Charles Griffith, Ib Melchior d Paul Bartel ph Tak Fujimoto m Paul Chihara

David Carradine, Simone Griffeth, Sylvester Stallone, Mary Woronov
  'The script is hardly Swiftian and therefore treads a thin delicate line between mockery and exploitation.'—*Michael Billington, Illustrated London News*

Death Ship
Canada 1980 91m CFI color

Survivors of a shipwreck take refuge on a mysterious empty ship which sets about killing them one by one. Yes, that's the synopsis, in the wake of *Killdozer* and *The Car*, and this film is stupider than either. George Kennedy, Richard Crenna, Nick Mancuso, Sally Ann Howes, Kate Reid. Written by John Robins; directed by Alvin Rakoff; for Astral Bellevue Pathé / Bloodstar.

'No woman ever loved such a man! The whole world waited while he made love!'
Death Takes a Holiday°
US 1934 78m bw
Paramount (E. Lloyd Sheldon)

In the form of a mysterious prince, Death visits an Italian noble family to see why men fear him so.

A somewhat pretentious classic from a popular play of the twenties; interesting handling and performances, but a slow pace by modern standards.

w Maxwell Anderson, Gladys Lehman, Walter Ferris based on plays by Maxwell Anderson and Alberto Casella d Mitchell Leisen ph Charles Lang ad Ernst Fegte

Fredric March, Evelyn Venable, Sir Guy Standing, Katherine Alexander, Gail Patrick, Helen Westley, Kathleen Howard, Henry Travers, Kent Taylor
  'Highly fantastic, but well done . . . likely to have greater appeal among the intelligentsia.'—*Variety*

Death Trap
US 1976 89m colour
Mars (Mohammed Rustam)

The proprietor of a motel on the edge of a swamp is a maniac who murders his guests and feeds them to his pet crocodile.
Pretty sick rip-off of *Psycho*, with no holds barred; a typical and regrettable example of the so-called Gothic horrors of the independent American cinema in the late seventies.

w Alvin L. Fast, Mardi Rustam d Tobe Hooper ph Jack Beckett m Tobe Hooper, Wayne Bell

Neville Brand, Mel Ferrer, Carolyn Jones, Marilyn Burns, William Finley, Stuart Whitman

Death Trap (1982): see Deathtrap

Death Valley
US 1981 88m Technicolor
Universal (Elliott Kastner)

A boy on vacation in Arizona finds himself being chased by a murderer.
Tedious shocker with little in the way of scenic background to relieve the unpleasant monotony.

w Richard Rothstein d Dick Richards ph Stephen H. Burum m Dana Kaproff ed Joel Cox

Paul Le Mat, Catherine Hicks, Stephen McHattie, A. Wilford Brimley, Edward Herrman
● *Video: CIC*

Death Weekend
Canada 1976 94m Eastmancolor

Four louts take revenge on a lady driver by following her to a secluded country house. Hoary shocker chiefly concerned with rape, the threat of rape, and various unpleasant methods of murder. Brenda Vaccaro, Don Stroud, Chuck Shamata. Written and directed by William Fruet; for Quadrant.
  'Exploitation of the emptiest and most blatant kind.'—*MFB.*

'Vigilante, city style . . . judge, jury and executioner!'
Death Wish°
US 1974 94m Technicolor
Paramount / Dino de Laurentiis (Hal Landers, Bobby Roberts, Michael Winner)

When his wife dies and his daughter becomes a vegetable after an assault by muggers, a New York businessman takes the law into his own hands.
After a highly unpleasant and sensational opening, this curious and controversial film settles down into what amounts to black comedy, with the audience well on the vigilante's side. It's not very good, but it keeps one watching.

w Wendell Mayes, *novel* Brian Garfield d Michael Winner ph Arthur J. Ornitz m Herbie Hancock

Charles Bronson, Hope Lange, Vincent Gardenia, Stuart Margolin, Stephen Keats, William Redfield
  'This urban version of *Walking Tall* transcends its violence to satisfy every base instinct that "we liberals" are heir to.'—*Judith Crist*
● *Video: CIC*

Death Wish II
US 1981 95m colour
Golan–Globus / Landers–Roberts

His maid gang-raped and killed, his handicapped daughter driven to her death, Paul Kersey resumes his stalking of urban thugs.
A badly made exercise in the exploitation of the most repellent aspects of violence, without the first film's saving grace of slickness and humour.

w David Engelbach d Michael Winner ph Richard L. Kline, Tom Del Ruth m Jimmy Page

Charles Bronson, Jill Ireland, Vincent Gardenia, J. D. Cannon, Anthony Franciosa
  'Bad art is one thing, but *Death Wish II* is ludicrous.'—*Variety*
  'The sort of sequel which makes you realize that the original wasn't half so bad as you thought.'—*Margaret Hinxman, Daily Mail*

The Deathmaster
US 1973 88m De Luxe

California surfers cheerfully adopt a local mystic, not knowing that he is a vampire. Modestly budgeted teenage screamer, competently made but of interest only to avid bibliographers of Count Dracula. Robert Quarry, Brenda Dickson, Bill Ewing, John Fiedler. Written by R. L. Grove; directed by Ray Danton; for RF World Entertainment / AIP.

Deathsport
US 1978 83m Metrocolor
New World (Roger Corman)

A popular game of the future involves

DEATH WISH.   Charles Bronson dares the cops to prove anything against him in this notorious vigilante movie.

gladiators willing to lose their lives against lethal motorcyclists.
Low-budget shocker for teenagers, by *Rollerball* out of *Death Race*. Of no possible interest except as exploitation.

w Henry Suso, Donald Stewart *d* Henry Suso, Allan Arkush *ph* Gary Graver *m* Andrew Stein

David Carradine, Claudia Jennings, Richard Lynch, William Smithers

Deathtrap*

US 1982   116m   Technicolor
Warner / LAH (Burtt Harris)

A playwright past his best conceives a plan to murder an upcoming rival and steal his script. This thriller on the lines of *Sleuth* was enjoyable enough on stage, but on the screen, despite pretensions to style, it takes far too long to unravel its very few twists, the last of which is badly fumbled.

w Jay Presson Allen, *play* Ira Levin *d* Sidney Lumet *ph* Andrzej Bartkowiak *m* Johnny Mandel *pd* Tony Walton

Michael Caine, Christopher Reeve, Dyan Cannon, Irene Worth, Henry Jones
● Video: Warner

Decameron Nights

GB 1952   94m   Technicolor
Film Locations (M. J. Frankovich)

Young Boccaccio entertains a glamorous widow and her three guests with stories.

Feeble costume charade with all the cuckolding off-screen: insipid and artificial.

w George Oppenheimer *d* Hugo Fregonese *ph* Guy Green *m* Antony Hopkins

Louis Jourdan, Joan Fontaine, Binnie Barnes, Joan Collins, Godfrey Tearle, Eliot Makeham, Noel Purcell
    'The sort of hybrid international production of which experience has made one mistrustful.'—*Gavin Lambert*

Deception**

US 1946   112m   bw
Warner (Henry Blanke)

A European cellist returning to America after the war finds that his former girl friend has a rich and jealous lover.
Downcast melodrama made when its star was beginning to slide; today it seems irresistible bosh with a background of classical music, done with intermittent style especially by Claude Rains as the egomaniac lover.

w John Collier, *play* Monsieur Lamberthier by Louis Verneuil *d* Irving Rapper *ph* Ernest Haller *m* Erich Wolfgang Korngold

Bette Davis, *Claude Rains*, Paul Henreid, John Abbott, Benson Fong
    'It's like grand opera, only the people are thinner . . . I wouldn't have missed it for the world.'—*Cecelia Ager*
    'Exquisitely foolish: a camp classic.'—*New Yorker, 1977*
† Previously filmed in 1929 as *Jealousy*, with Fredric March and Jeanne Eagels.

Decision at Sundown

US 1957   77m   Technicolor

A cowboy tracks down the badman who has seduced his wife. Routine small-town western, efficiently done. Randolph Scott, John Carroll, Karen Steele, Valerie French, Noah Beery Jnr, Andrew Duggan. Written by Charles Lang Jnr; directed by Budd Boetticher; for Harry Joe Brown / Columbia.

Decision before Dawn*

US 1951   119m   bw
TCF (Anatole Litvak, Frank McCarthy)

In 1944, anti-Nazi German POWs are parachuted into Germany to obtain information.
Meticulous, well made but unexciting spy story which seldom comes vividly to life.

w Peter Viertel, *novel* Call It Treason by George Howe *d* Anatole Litvak *ph* Franz Planer *m* Franz Waxman

Oskar Werner, Richard Basehart, Gary Merrill, Hildegarde Neff, Dominique Blanchar, Helene Thimig, O. E. Hasse, Hans Christian Blech

AAN: best picture

The Decision of Christopher Blake

US 1948   75m   bw
Warner (Ranald MacDougall)

A 12-year-old boy reunites his divorcing parents.
Sentimental slop, surprisingly ill done, but with a few good lines.

w Ranald MacDougall, *play* Moss Hart *d* Peter Godfrey *ph* Karl Freund *m* Max Steiner

Alexis Smith, Robert Douglas, *Cecil Kellaway*, Ted Donaldson, *Harry Davenport*, John Hoyt, Mary Wickes, Art Baker, Lois Maxwell

The Decks Ran Red

US 1958   84m   bw
MGM / Andrew and Virginia Stone

Unscrupulous sailors plan to murder the entire crew of a freighter and claim the salvage money.
Solidly crafted but basically uninteresting melodrama.

w Andrew and Virginia Stone *d* Andrew Stone *ph* Meredith M. Nicholson

James Mason, Broderick Crawford, Dorothy Dandridge, Stuart Whitman

Decline and Fall

GB 1968   113m   De Luxe
TCF / Ivan Foxwell
aka: *Decline and Fall of a Birdwatcher*

An innocent, accident-prone Oxford undergraduate is expelled and after various adventures in high and low society is convicted as a white slaver.
Flabby, doomed attempt to film a satirical classic which lives only on the printed page. Odd moments amuse.

w Ivan Foxwell, *novel* Evelyn Waugh *d* John Krish *ph* Desmond Dickinson *m* Ron Goodwin

Robin Phillips, Donald Wolfit, Genevieve Page, Robert Harris, Leo McKern, Colin Blakely, Felix Aylmer, Donald Sinden, Griffith Jones

'The British *Graduate*.'—*New Yorker*

'Literate, lavishly furnished, tastefully faithful.'—*Observer*

Decoy
US 1947 76m bw

The girl friend of an executed gangster tries to get her hands on his buried loot. Surprisingly tough little co-feature of its day; even more surprisingly, the leading lady is British. Jean Gillie, Edward Norris, Herbert Rudley, Robert Armstrong. Written by Nedrick Young; directed by Jack Bernhard; for Monogram.

Dédée d'Anvers*
France 1948 95m bw
Sacha Gordine (André Paulvé)
aka: *Woman of Antwerp; Dédée*

A dockside prostitute falls for a sailor and arouses the jealousy of her protector. Seamy low life melodrama, presented *con brio*, but rather like a tenth copy of *Quai des Brumes*.

w Yves Allégret, Jacques Sigurd *d* Yves Allégret *ph* Jean Bourgoin *m* Jacques Besse

Simone Signoret, Marcel Pagliero, Bernard Blier, Marcel Dalio, Jane Marken

The Deep
US 1977 124m Metrocolor Panavision
Columbia / EMI / Casablanca (Peter Guber)

Underwater treasure seekers off Bermuda clash with black villains seeking a lost consignment of morphine.

An expensive action picture which is singularly lacking in action and even in plot, but oozes with brutality and overdoes the splendours of submarine life, forty per cent of it taking place under water.

w Peter Benchley, Tracy Keenan Wynn, *novel* Peter Benchley *d* Peter Yates *ph* Christopher Challis, Al Giddings, Stan Waterman *m* John Barry *pd* Tony Masters

Jacqueline Bisset, Robert Shaw, Nick Nolte, Lou Gossett, Eli Wallach

'The ultimate disco experience . . . it dances on the spot for two hours, taking voodoo, buried treasure, morphine, violence and sea monsters in its stride.'—*Time Out*

'Peter Yates has knocked himself out doing masterly underwater action sequences in the service of a woefully crummy book.'—*Russell Davies, Observer*

● *Video: RCA / Columbia*

The Deep Blue Sea*
GB 1955 99m Eastmancolor
Cinemascope
TCF / London Films (Anatole Litvak)

A judge's wife attempts suicide when jilted by her ex-RAF lover.

Undistinguished adaptation of a very good play, hampered by wide screen and muddy colour, helped by thoughtful performances.

w Terence Rattigan, from his play *d* Anatole Litvak *ph* Jack Hildyard *m* Malcolm Arnold

Vivien Leigh, Kenneth More, Eric Portman, *Emlyn Williams*, Moira Lister, Arthur Hill, Dandy Nichols, Jimmy Hanley, Miriam Karlin

Deep End*
West Germany / USA 1970 88m
Eastmancolor
Maran / Kettledrum / Bavaria Atelier (Judd Bernard)

Sexual problems of two young people on the staff of a London municipal bathhouse. Interestingly made but rather dreary and vaguely symbolic modern fable.

w Jerzy Skolimowski, Jerzy Gruza, Boleslaw Sulik *d* Jerzy Skolimowski *ph* Charly Steinberger *m* Cat Stevens

Jane Asher, John Moulder-Brown, Diana Dors, Karl Michael Vogler, Christopher Sandford

'A study in the growth of obsession that is both funny and frighteningly exact.'—*Nigel Andrews, MFB*

Deep in My Heart*
US 1954 132m Eastmancolor
MGM (Roger Edens)

Sigmund Romberg, a composer-waiter in New York, is helped by writer Dorothy Donnelly and showman Florenz Ziegfeld to become a famous writer of musicals.

Standard fictionalized biopic with plenty of good turns and a sharper script than usual.

w Leonard Spiegelgass *d* Stanley Donen *ph* George Folsey *m* Sigmund Romberg *ad* Cedric Gibbons, Edward Carfagno *ch* Eugene Loring

Jose Ferrer, Merle Oberon, Paul Henreid (as Ziegfeld), Walter Pidgeon, Helen Traubel, Doe Avedon, Tamara Toumanova, Paul Stewart, Isobel Elsom, David Burns, Jim Backus . . . and Gene Kelly, Fred Kelly, Rosemary Clooney, Jane Powell, Ann Miller, Cyd Charisse, James Mitchell, Howard Keel, Tony Martin, Joan Weldon

The Deep Six
US 1958 110m Warnercolor
Jaguar (Martin Rackin)

A Quaker is unhappy at being drafted into the submarine service, but after initial unpopularity becomes a hero.

An ageing star contends with many hazards: slipshod production, poor colour, a dull script, and an unplayable part.

w John Twist, Martin Rackin, Harry Brown *d* Rudolph Maté *ph* John Seitz *m* David Buttolph

Alan Ladd, William Bendix, Efrem Zimbalist Jnr, Dianne Foster, Keenan Wynn, James Whitmore, Joey Bishop, Jeanette Nolan

Deep Valley
US 1947 104m bw
Warner (Henry Blanke)

The daughter of a poor California farmer falls for a convict on a work gang.

Downright peculiar melodrama, a cross between *Tobacco Road* and *Cold Comfort Farm*, with touches of *High Sierra*. For collectors.

w Salka Viertel, Stephen Morehouse Avery, *novel* Dan Totheroh *d* Jean Negulesco *ph* Ted McCord *m* Max Steiner

Ida Lupino, Dane Clark, Wayne Morris, Henry Hull, Fay Bainter, Willard Robertson

Deep Waters
US 1948 85m bw
TCF

A problem orphan boy is content when adopted by a lobster fisherman.

Forgettable family film, smoothly directed and photographed.

w Richard Murphy *d* Henry King *ph* Joseph La Shelle *m* Cyril Mockridge

Jean Peters, Dana Andrews, Dean Stockwell, Cesar Romero, Anne Revere

The Deer Hunter*
US 1978 182m Technicolor
Panavision
Universal / EMI (Barry Spikings, Michael Deeley, Michael Cimino, John Peverall)

Three friends from a small Pennsylvania town go to fight in Vietnam.

The three-hour running time is taken up with crosscutting of a wedding, a deer hunt and a game of Russian roulette. Presumably the audience has to guess the point, if any; meanwhile it may be repelled by this long and savage if frequently engrossing film.

w Deric Washburn, *story* Michael Cimino, Louis Garfinkle, Quinn K. Redeker and Washburn *d* Michael Cimino *ph* Vilmos Zsigmond *m* Stanley Myers

Robert De Niro, John Cazale, John Savage, Christopher Walken, Meryl Streep

'A hollow spectacle, less about war than its effect on a community, full of specious analogies, incoherent sentimentality and belief in its own self-importance.'—*Time Out*

AA: best picture; direction; Christopher Walken

AAN: Deric Washburn; Vilmos Zsigmond; Robert de Niro; Meryl Streep

● *Video: Thorn EMI*

The Defector
France / West Germany 1966 101m
Eastmancolor
PECF / Rhein Main (Raoul Lévy)
original title: *L'Espion*

An American physicist in East Germany gets involved in the spy game.

Disenchanted espionage 'realism', not very well styled and hampered by a star at the end of his tether.

w Robert Guenette, Raoul Lévy, *novel* The Spy by Paul Thomas *d* Raoul Lévy *ph* Raoul Coutard *m* Serge Gainsbourg

Montgomery Clift, Hardy Kruger, Macha Meril, Roddy McDowall, David Opatoshu, Christine Delaroche, Jean-Luc Godard

Defiance

US 1980 102m Movielab

A young seaman staying in New York fights back against the power of an urban gang. Belated and unnecessary addition to the gang cycle; violent nonsense. Jan Michael Vincent, Theresa Saldana, Danny Lopez. Written by Thomas Michael Donnelly; directed by John Flynn; for AIP.

The Defiant Ones**

US 1958 96m bw

UA / Stanley Kramer

A black and a white convict escape from a chain gang, still linked together but hating each other.
Schematic melodrama with a moral, impeccably done and with good performances.

w Nathan E. Douglas, Harold Jacob Smith *d* Stanley Kramer *ph* Sam Leavitt *m* Ernest Gold

Tony Curtis, Sidney Poitier, Theodore Bikel, Charles McGraw, Lon Chaney Jnr, King Donovan, Claude Akins, Lawrence Dobkin, Whit Bissell, Carl 'Alfalfa' Switzer, Cara Williams
'Probably Kramer's best picture. The subject matter is relatively simple, though "powerful"; the action is exciting; the acting is good. But the singleness of purpose behind it all is a little offensive.'—*Pauline Kael*

AA: Nathan E. Douglas, Harold Jacob Smith; Sam Leavitt
AAN: best picture; Stanley Kramer; Tony Curtis; Sidney Poitier; Theodore Bikel; Cara Williams

Le Défroqué*

France 1953 111m bw

SFC / SNEG

A defrocked priest performs a gallant action which persuades an acquaintance to become a priest himself and try to draw his friend back into the fold.
Curious but holding moral melodrama embellished by good acting.

w Leo Joannon, Denys de la Patellière *d* Leo Joannon *ph* Nicolas Torporkoff *m* Jean-Jacques Grunenwald

Pierre Fresnay, Pierre Trabaud, Nicole Stéphane, Marcelle Geniat, Guy Decomble, Leo Joannon, René Blancard

The Delavine Affair

GB 1954 64m bw

A reporter is framed for killing an informer. Routine British second feature. Honor Blackman, Peter Reynolds, Gordon Jackson, Michael Balfour. Written by George Fisher, from the story 'Winter Wears a Shroud' by Robert Chapman; directed by Douglas Pierce; for John Croydon / Monarch. (US title: *Murder Is News*.)

A Delicate Balance*

US 1975 134m colour

American Express / Ely Landau / Cinevision

A quarrelsome Connecticut family is dominated by an ageing matriarch, and tensions mount to a climax of fear and threats. Honourable but slightly boring film version of an essentially theatrical play: the acting is the thing.

w Edward Albee, from his play *d* Tony Richardson *ph* David Watkin *m* none

Katharine Hepburn, Paul Scofield, Joseph Cotten, Lee Remick, Kate Reid, Betsy Blair

The Delicate Delinquent

US 1956 101m bw Vistavision

Paramount / Jerry Lewis

A New York policeman tries to make friends with an eccentric youth who mixes with thugs; the boy decides to train as a policeman.
Jerry Lewis' first film without Dean Martin: a sobering experience combining zany comedy, sentiment, pathos and social comment. The mixture fails to rise.

wd Don McGuire *ph* Haskell Boggs *m* Buddy Bregman

Jerry Lewis, Darren McGavin, Martha Hyer, Robert Ivers, Horace McMahon

Delicious

US 1931 106m bw

Fox

An Irish girl in New York falls for a rich man. Early musical, very thin, but an agreeable museum piece for collectors.

w Guy Bolton, Sonya Levien *d* David Butler *ph* Ernest Palmer *songs* George and Ira Gershwin

Janet Gaynor, Charles Farrell, El Brendel, Lawrence O'Sullivan, Virginia Cherrill, Mischa Auer
'Cream puffs, applesauce, and plenty of nuts . . . should do the team's business on its name strength.'—*Variety*

Delightfully Dangerous

US 1945 93m bw

A straitlaced girl discovers that her eldest sister is a burlesque dancer. Mild family comedy with music. Jane Powell, Constance Moore, Ralph Bellamy, Arthur Treacher. Written by Walter De Leon and Arthur Phillips; directed by Arthur Lubin; for Buddy Rogers / UA.

Deliverance**

US 1972 109m Technicolor Panavision

Warner / Elmer Enterprises (John Boorman)

Four men spend a holiday weekend canoeing down a dangerous river, but find that the real danger to their lives comes from themselves and other humans.
Vigorous, meaningful, almost apocalyptic vision of man's inhumanity, disguised as a thrilling adult adventure.

w James Dickey, from his novel *d* John Boorman *ph* Vilmos Zsigmond *m* Eric Weissberg

Burt Reynolds, Jon Voight, Ned Beatty, Ronny Cox, James Dickey

'There is fundamentally no view of the material, just a lot of painful grasping and groping.'—*Stanley Kauffmann*
AAN: best picture; John Boorman
● *Video: Warner*

Dementia 13*

US / Eire 1963 81m bw

Filmgroup / AIP (Roger Corman)

GB title: *The Haunted and the Hunted*

An axe murderer attacks members of a noble Irish family at their lonely castle.
Nastily effective macabre piece with interesting credits.

wd Francis Ford Coppola *ph* Charles Hannawalt *m* Ronald Stein

Luana Anders, William Campbell, Bart Patton, Mary Mitchell, Patrick Magee, Eithne Dunn

Demetrius and the Gladiators**

US 1954 101m Technicolor Cinemascope

TCF (Frank Ross)

A Greek slave who keeps Christ's robe after the crucifixion is sentenced to be one of Caligula's gladiators and becomes involved in Messalina's wiles.
Lively, efficient sequel to *The Robe*, with emphasis less on religiosity than on the brutality of the arena and our hero's sexual temptations and near-escapes. Good Hollywood hokum.

w Philip Dunne *d* Delmer Daves *ph* Milton Krasner *m* Franz Waxman

Victor Mature, Susan Hayward, Michael Rennie (as Peter), Debra Paget, Anne Bancroft, Jay Robinson, Barry Jones, William Marshall, Richard Egan, Ernest Borgnine
'An energetic attempt to fling the mantle of sanctity over several more millions of the entertainment dollar.'—*The Times*

The Demi-Paradise*

GB 1943 114m bw

Two Cities (Anatole de Grunwald)

US title: *Adventure for Two*

In 1939, a Russian inventor is sent to observe the British way of life.
Pleasant, aimless little satirical comedy in which this blessed plot seems to be peopled entirely by eccentrics.

w Anatole de Grunwald *d* Anthony Asquith *ph* Bernard Knowles *m* Nicholas Brodszky

Laurence Olivier, Penelope Dudley Ward, *Margaret Rutherford*, Leslie Henson, Marjorie Fielding, Felix Aylmer, Guy Middleton, Michael Shepley, George Thorpe, Edie Martin, Muriel Aked, Joyce Grenfell
'A backhanded way of showing us poor juvenile-minded cinemagoers that the England of Mr Punch and Mrs Malaprop lives forever.'—*Richard Winnington*

Demon Seed

US 1977 95m Metrocolor Panavision

MGM (Herb Jaffe)

A scientist invents too perfect a computer: it locks up his wife, rapes her, and incubates a child . . .

Science fiction at the end of its tether, all very smart and self-conscious, but at this length very tasteless. Hitchcock would have got it into a television half-hour.

w Robert Jaffe, Roger O. Hirson, *novel* Dean R. Koontz d Donald Cammell *ph* Bill Butler *m* Jerry Fielding *pd* Edward Carfagno

Julie Christie, Fritz Weaver, Gerrit Graham, Berry Kroeger, Lisa Lu

● Video: MGM / UA

The Dentist••
US 1932 19m bw

Classic star short with W. C. Fields working up briskly to a dentist sketch in which he deals summarily with a variety of patients. Directed by Leslie Pearce; for Paramount / Sennett.

Denver and Rio Grande
US 1952 89m Technicolor

Railroad companies compete to lay track through a narrow gorge. Adequate western thick-ear. Edmond O'Brien, Sterling Hayden, Dean Jagger, Laura Elliot, Zasu Pitts, Lyle Bettger, J. Carrol Naish. Written by Frank Gruber; directed by Byron Haskin; for Nat Holt / Paramount.

Deported
US 1950 88m bw

A gangster is sent back to his native Italy and tries to smuggle in his stolen money, but is finally redeemed. Slightly unusual from this studio at this time, but not very interesting. Jeff Chandler, Marta Toren, Claude Dauphin, Marina Berti, Richard Rober. Written by Robert Buckner; directed by Robert Siodmak; for Universal-International.

The Depraved
GB 1957 63m bw

An American officer helps his beloved kill her unattractive husband. Shades of *Double Indemnity*, but only shades. Anne Heywood, Robert Arden, Carroll Levis, Basil Dignam. Written by Brian Clemens; directed by Paul Dickson; for the Danzigers.

Derby Day
GB 1952 84m bw
British Lion / Wilcox-Neagle (Maurice Cowan)
US title: *Four Against Fate*

Intercut comic and melodramatic stories of four people who go to the Derby. Quietly efficient, class-conscious entertainment on the lines of *Friday the 13th* and *The Bridge of San Luis Rey*. No surprises, but plenty of familiar faces.

w John Baines, Monckton Hoffe, Alan Melville d Herbert Wilcox *ph* Max Greene *m* Anthony Collins

Anna Neagle, Michael Wilding, Googie Withers, Gordon Harker, John McCallum, Peter Graves, Suzanne Cloutier, Gladys Henson, Ralph Reader, Alfie Bass, Edwin Styles, Nigel Stock

'Excessive loyalty to a formula has produced far from happy results.'—*Penelope Houston, MFB*

Derelict
US 1930 73m bw

Two sea dogs battle over a ship and a girl. Well-filmed melodrama, with plenty of location work. George Bancroft, William Boyd, Jessie Royce Landis, Donald Stuart. Written by Max Marcin, William Slavens McNutt, Grover Jones; directed by Rowland V. Lee; for Paramount. 'One of the best sea pictures filmed . . . a cinch for the deluxers.'—*Variety*

Le Dernier Milliardaire•
France 1934 100m bw
Pathé-Natan

The queen of a small principality invites a financial wizard to pay court to her daughter. The girl elopes with a bandleader, the financier is engaged to the queen, and is then revealed as a sham.
Rather too determined to be satirical, this comedy sadly lacks the pace and flair of the director's best work but there are several sequences of interest.

wd René Clair *ph* Rudolph Maté, Louis Née *m* Maurice Jaubert

Max Dearly, Renée Saint-Cyr, Marthe Mellot, Raymond Cordy

'This film is so unpopular here that the crowd is rioting against it nightly—partly because they think it's rotten and partly because they don't like the way it kids the State . . . despite flop here, American specialized houses should do well with it.'—*Variety, Paris*

● Video: Thorn EMI

Le Dernier Tournant•
France 1939 90m bw

A French version of *The Postman Always Rings Twice, qv* for plot. Interesting but not remarkable. Fernand Gravet, Corinne Luchaire, Michel Simon, Marcel Vallée, Florence Marly. Written by Charles Spaak and Henry Torres from the novel by James M. Cain; directed by Pierre Chenal; for Lux. 'Class B at best.'—*Variety*

Les Dernières Vacances•
France 1947 95m bw
Pathé

During a country house holiday in the twenties, the last before the house is sold, old friends conduct amorous intrigues and so do their teenage progeny.
A moderately charming little fable making a rather obscure social point.

w R. Breuil, Roger Leenhardt d Roger Leenhardt *ph* Philippe Agostini

Berthe Bovy, Renée Devillers, Pierre Dux, Jean d'Yd, Odile Versois, Michel François

Derrière la Façade•
France 1939 90m bw

A judge, his son, a soldier and a prostitute are

involved in a night of attempted and actual murders. Complex puzzle drama which made its mark. Lucien Baroux, Jacques Baumer, Jules Berry, Gaby Morlay, Michel Simon, Betty Stockfield, Erich Von Stroheim, Carette, André Lafaur. Directed by Yves Mirade and Georges Lacombe; for Filmsonor.

Dersu Uzala•
USSR / Japan 1975 140m colour

A Russian surveyor mapping Siberian wastes becomes friendly with a wily Mongolian hunter.
Magnificent vistas punctuate an essentially plodding propaganda piece which does not rank with its director's best work. Maxim Munzuk, Juri Solomine. Written by Yuri Nagibin and Akira Kurosawa; directed by Akira Kurosawa; for Mosfilm / Toho.
AA: best foreign film.

The Desert Fox••
US 1951 88m bw
TCF (Nunnally Johnson)
GB title: *Rommel, Desert Fox*

Rommel returns, disillusioned, to Hitler's Germany after his North African defeat, and is involved in the July plot.
Vivid but scrappy account of the last years of a contemporary hero. At the time it seemed to show a new immediacy in film-making, and was probably the first film to use an action sequence to arrest attention before the credit titles.

w Nunnally Johnson, *book* Rommel by Desmond Young d Henry Hathaway *ph* Norbert Brodine *m* Daniele Amfitheatrof

James Mason, Jessica Tandy, Cedric Hardwicke, Luther Adler (as Hitler), Everett Sloane, Leo G. Carroll, George Macready, Richard Boone, Eduard Franz, Desmond Young

● Video: CBS / Fox

'Two men wanted her love—the third wanted her life!'
Desert Fury
US 1947 96m Technicolor
Paramount (Hal B. Wallis)

Against advice, a girl is attracted to a neurotic gambler who may have murdered his first wife. Muddled melodrama slightly helped by Arizona colour settings; unconvincing characters mouth unspeakable lines in an airless tedium.

w Robert Rossen, *novel* Desert Town by Ramona Stewart d Lewis Allen *ph* Charles Lang, Edward Cronjager *m* Miklos Rozsa

Lizabeth Scott, Wendell Corey, Burt Lancaster, John Hodiak, Mary Astor, Kristine Miller

'The only fury I could sense was in my corner of the balcony.'—*C. A. Lejeune*

The Desert Hawk
US 1950 77m Technicolor

Against an Arabian Nights background, a cheerful outlaw abducts a princess. Tolerable cloak-and-sandal action comedy. Richard

Greene, Yvonne de Carlo, Jackie Gleason, George Macready, Rock Hudson, Carl Esmond. Written by Aubrey Wisberg, Jack Pollexfen and Gerald Drayson Adams; directed by Frederick de Cordova; for Universal-International.

'The Legion's my life. A girl doesn't fit into it. Especially a girl like you!'

Desert Legion
US 1953   86m   Technicolor
Universal (Ted Richmond)

A Foreign Legion captain rids a lost city of menacing bandits.
Schoolboy stuff, impudent in its silly story and its unconvincing Shangri-La, but quite entertaining for those prepared to let their hair down.

w Irving Wallace, Lewis Meltzer d Joseph Pevney ph John Seitz m Frank Skinner

Alan Ladd, Richard Conte, Arlene Dahl, Akim Tamiroff, Leon Askin

Desert Mice
GB 1959   83m   bw
Artna / Welbeck / Sydney Box (Michael Relph, Basil Dearden)

Adventures of a concert party sent to entertain the troops in North Africa during World War II.
A most promising idea is wasted on a singularly unfunny script which leaves its actors all at sea.

w David Climie d Michael Relph ph Ken Hodges m Philip Green

Alfred Marks, Sid James, Patricia Bredin, Dick Bentley, Dora Bryan, Irene Handl, Kenneth Fortescue, Reginald Beckwith, Joan Benham, Marius Goring

The Desert Rats*
US 1953   88m   bw
TCF (Robert L. Jacks)

An English captain commands an Australian detachment in the siege of Tobruk, and survives an encounter with Rommel.
Actioner made to cash in on the success of *The Desert Fox* (qv). Stars and battle scenes survive a studio look.

w Richard Murphy d Robert Wise ph Lucien Ballard m Leigh Harline md Nathaniel Finston

James Mason (as Rommel), Richard Burton, Robert Newton, Robert Douglas, Torin Thatcher, Chips Rafferty

AAN: Richard Murphy

The Desert Song
US 1929   106m   bw (Technicolor sequences)

A romantic and mysterious figure leads North African natives against evil Arabs.
Primitive sound version of the highly successful 1926 operetta.

w Harvey Gates, *play* Otto Harbach, Lawrence Schwab, Frank Mandel d Roy del Ruth ph Barney McGill m Sigmund Romberg ly Oscar Hammerstein II

John Boles, Carlotta King, Louise Fazenda, Johnny Arthur, Edward Martindel, Jack Pratt

The Desert Song
US 1943   96m   Technicolor
Warner (Robert Florey)

Updated version with Nazis as the real villains.
adaptation Robert Buckner d Robert Florey ph Bert Glennon m Heinz Roemheld

Dennis Morgan, Irene Manning, Bruce Cabot, Lynne Overman, Gene Lockhart, Victor Francen, Faye Emerson, Curt Bois, Jack La Rue, Marcel Dalio, Nestor Paiva, Gerald Mohr

The Desert Song
US 1953   110m   Technicolor
Warner (Rudi Fehr)

Well staged straight version of the musical, with full score.
adaptation Roland Kibbee d Bruce Humberstone ph Robert Burks *m adaptation* Max Steiner

Gordon Macrae, Kathryn Grayson, Steve Cochran, Raymond Massey, Dick Wesson, Allyn McLerie, Ray Collins, Paul Picerni, William Conrad

The Deserter
Italy / Yugoslavia / USA 1970   99m   Technicolor   Panavision
Dino de Laurentiis / Jadran / Heritage (Norman Baer, Ralph Serpe)
original title: *La Spina Dorsale del Diavolo*

In the southwest in 1886, a cavalry captain tracks down the Apaches who tortured his wife to death.
Brutal revenge western, as muddled as its international credits would suggest.

w Clair Huffaker d Burt Kennedy ph Aldo Tonti m Piero Piccione pd Mario Chiari

Bekim Fehmiu, John Huston, Richard Crenna, Chuck Connors, Ricardo Montalban, Ian Bannen, Brandon de Wilde, Slim Pickens, Albert Salmi, Woody Strode, Patrick Wayne, Fausto Tozzi

'Three people who loved each other very much!'

Design for Living**
US 1933   88m   bw
Paramount (Ernst Lubitsch)

Two friends love and are loved by the same worldly woman, and they set up house together.
Elegant but miscast version of a scintillating play, with all the sex and the sting removed (at the insistence of the Legion of Decency, then coming into power). Ben Hecht claimed to have removed all but one line of Coward's dialogue: 'For the good of our immortal souls!'

w Ben Hecht, *play* Noel Coward d Ernst Lubitsch ph Victor Milner m Nathaniel Finston ad Hans Dreier

Gary Cooper, Fredric March, Miriam Hopkins, Edward Everett Horton, Franklin Pangborn, Isabel Jewell

'Can't miss because it holds plenty . . . an improvement on the original.'—*Variety*
'A delightfully smart, crisp piece of entertainment, cleverly conceived and delightfully executed.'—*New York American*
'A partial cleansing for the screen of a stage story notorious for its wealth and variety of moral code infractions.'—*Martin Quigley*

Design for Scandal
US 1941   85m   bw

A reporter is assigned by his boss to get a lady judge disbarred. Mechanical star comedy
Rosalind Russell, Walter Pidgeon, Edward Arnold, Guy Kibbee, Lee Bowman. Written by Lionel Houser; directed by Norman Taurog; for MGM.

Designing Woman*
US 1957   118m   Metrocolor Cinemascope
MGM (Dore Schary)

A sports reporter marries a dress designer and finds that their common interests are few.
Lumbering comedy which aims for sophistication but settles for farce: tolerable for star watchers who have dined well.

w George Wells d Vincente Minnelli ph John Alton m André Previn

Gregory Peck, Lauren Bacall, Dolores Gray, Sam Levene, Tom Helmore, Mickey Shaughnessey, Jesse White, Chuck Connors, Jack Cole

AAN: George Wells

Desirable
US 1934   68m   bw

An actress keeps her daughter at school rather than admit she is 19. Mildly amusing comedy-drama of its day. Verree Teasdale, Jean Muir, George Brent, John Halliday. Written by Mary McCall Jnr; directed by Archie Mayo; for Edward Chodorov / Warner. 'The purity seal is remembered throughout.'—*Variety*

Desire**
US 1936   89m   bw
Paramount (Ernst Lubitsch)

In Spain, an American car designer falls for a glamorous jewel thief.
Romantic comedy which the producer should have worked on longer: it begins brilliantly and keeps its style, but the pace and wit ebb away.

w Edwin Justus Mayer, Waldemar Young, Samuel Hoffenstein, from a German film *Die schönen Tage von Aranjuez* and a play by Hans Szekely and R. A. Stemmle d Frank Borzage ph Charles Lang, Victor Milner m Frederick Hollander ad Hans Dreier, Robert Usher

Marlene Dietrich, Gary Cooper, *John Halliday*, William Frawley, Ernest Cossart, Akim Tamiroff, Alan Mowbray, Zeffie Tilbury

'It sparkles and twinkles . . . one of the most engaging pictures of the season.'—*Frank S. Nugent, New York Times*

'A sure, beautifully written piece about the usual Lubitsch trifles, about crooks and fake countesses breathless before the dawn of romance.'—*Alistair Cooke*

Desire in the Dust

US 1960 102m bw Cinemascope
TCF / Associated Producers (William F. Claxton)

A wealthy southern aristocrat is involved in a fatal car crash and persuades a young farmhand to take the blame.
Derivative hothouse drama, a little better than its title, with a cast breathing heavily in imitation of refugees from Tennessee Williams or William Faulkner.

w Charles Lang, *novel* Harry Whittington
d William F. Claxton ph Lucien Ballard
m Paul Dunlap

Raymond Burr, Martha Hyer, Joan Bennett, Ken Scott, Brett Halsey, Anne Helm, Jack Ging, Edward Binns

Desire Me

US 1947 91m bw
MGM (Arthur Hornblow Jnr)

The wife of a Normandy villager hears that he has died in a concentration camp. She marries the bearer of the news, who turns out to be a psychotic who has left her husband for dead . . . but he is not.
Dreary drama, troubled during production and offering little for the actors to chew on.

w Marguerite Roberts, Zoe Akins, Casey Robinson, *novel* Leonhard Frank d not credited, but mostly by George Cukor, Melvyn Le Roy, Jack Conway ph Joseph Ruttenberg m Herbert Stothart

Greer Garson, Robert Mitchum, Richard Hart, George Zucco, Morris Ankrum
'The supporting cast includes a number of characters who give the appearance of having come out of a dusty cupboard marked "French Types—Assorted".'—*MFB*
† Robert Montgomery shot a few scenes before bowing out to be replaced by Richard Hart.

Desire under the Elms

US 1958 111m bw Vistavision
Paramount (Don Hartman)

A New England farmer brings home a young bride and causes friction with his son.
This bid for culture turns out like a hoary and very slow melodrama, not exactly risible but annoying because it teeters between several styles.

w Irwin Shaw, *play* Eugene O'Neill d Delbert Mann ph Daniel L. Fapp m Elmer Bernstein

Sophia Loren, Burl Ives, Anthony Perkins, Frank Overton, Pernell Roberts, Anne Seymour
'The film is consistently and unhappily out of its depth.'—*Penelope Houston*
AAN: Daniel L. Fapp

Desirée

US 1954 110m De Luxe Cinemascope
TCF (Julian Blaustein)

Fictionalized biopic of one of Napoleon's mistresses.
Heavy-going costume piece, with all contributors distinctly uncomfortable.

w Daniel Taradash, *novel* Annemarie Selinko
d Henry Koster ph Milton Krasner m Alex North

Jean Simmons, Marlon Brando, Merle Oberon, Michael Rennie, Cameron Mitchell, Elizabeth Sellars, Cathleen Nesbitt, Isobel Elsom
'Their story is not in the history books. It has never been seen on the screen—until now!'—*publicity*

The Desk Set**

US 1957 103m Eastmancolor Cinemascope
TCF (Henry Ephron)
GB title: *His Other Woman*

Ladies in a broadcasting company's reference section are appalled when an electronics expert is sent to improve their performance.
Thin comedy, altered from a Broadway success; patchy as a whole, but with several splendid dialogue scenes for the principals.

w Phoebe and Henry Ephron, *play* William Marchant d Walter Lang ph Leon Shamroy m Cyril Mockridge

Spencer Tracy, Katharine Hepburn, Joan Blondell, Gig Young, Dina Merrill, Neva Patterson
'They lope through this trifling charade like a couple of oldtimers who enjoy reminiscing with simple routines.'—*Bosley Crowther, New York Times*

Despair*

West Germany / France 1978 119m Eastmancolor
NF Geria / Bavaria / SFP (Peter Märthesheimer)
West German title: *Eine Reise ins Licht*

In 1930 Berlin, a Russian immigrant businessman leads a fantasy life which drives him to murder and insanity.
Filmed in English, this curious cross between *Lolita* and *Repulsion* found surprisingly little critical favour, considering its participants.

w Tom Stoppard, *novel* Vladimir Nabokov
d Rainer Werner Fassbinder ph Michael Ballhaus m Peer Raben pd Rolf Zehetbauer

Dirk Bogarde, Andrea Ferreol, Volker Spengler, Klaus Löwitsch, Berhard Wicki
'It begins magnificently, remains sporadically brilliant throughout, but grows heavier and heavier until it finally sinks into inertia.'—*Tom Milne, MFB*
● Video: Thorn EMI

Desperadoes

US 1943 85m Technicolor

A gunman rides into town to cause trouble, but finds romance and renews an old friendship. Lively star western of its day.
Randolph Scott, Glenn Ford, Evelyn Keyes, Edgar Buchanan, Claire Trevor, Guinn Williams. Written by Max Brand, Robert Carson; directed by Charles Vidor; for Harry Joe Brown / Columbia

The Desperados

US 1968 90m Technicolor
Columbia / Meadway (Irving Allen)

After the Civil War, a fanatic 'parson' leads a tribe of violent outlaws including his three sons.
Rough-and-tumble western in the modern savage manner; made in Spain.

w Walter Brough d Henry Levin ph Sam Leavitt m David Whitaker

Vince Edwards, Jack Palance, George Maharis, Neville Brand, Sylvia Syms, Christian Roberts, Kate O'Mara, Kenneth Cope, John Paul

Desperate*

US 1947 73m bw
RKO (Michel Kraike)

A trucker becomes innocently involved in a robbery and goes on the run.
Lively second feature from the studio's best period, with plenty of burgeoning talent.

w Harry Essex d Anthony Mann ph George E. Diskant m Paul Sawtell

Steve Brodie, Audrey Long, Raymond Burr, Jason Robards Snr, Douglas Fowley, William Challee, Ilka Gruning
'Amazingly watchable within its formulary limits.'—*Tom Milne, MFB, 1982*

Desperate Characters*

US 1971 106m colour
ITC / TDJ (Frank D. Gilroy)

Residents of New York's east side find the rigours of life hard to take.
Curious but interesting suburban drama, a kind of deglamorized and updated *City for Conquest.*

wd Frank D. Gilroy, *novel* Paula Fox ph Urs Furrer m Lee Konitz, Ron Carter, Jim Hall

Shirley Maclaine, Gerald S. O'Loughlin, Kenneth Mars, Sada Thompson, Jack Somack
'The most blistering indictment of New York City since *Midnight Cowboy*.'—*Rex Reed*
'A film of authenticity, of delicately realized intangibles.'—*Stanley Kauffmann*

The Desperate Hours*

US 1955 112m bw Vistavision
Paramount (William Wyler)

Three escaped convicts take over a suburban house but are finally outwitted by the family.
Ponderous treatment of an over-familiar situation with only the acting and an 'A' picture look to save it.

w Joseph Hayes, from his novel and play
d William Wyler ph Lee Garmes m Gail Kubik

Fredric March, Humphrey Bogart, Martha Scott, Arthur Kennedy, Gig Young, Dewey Martin, Mary Murphy, Robert Middleton, Richard Eyer
'A solid, deliberate and long-drawn-out exercise in the mechanics of suspense.'—*Penelope Houston*

Desperate Journey**
US 1942 109m bw
Warner (Hal B. Wallis)

Three POWs in Nazi Germany fight their way
back to freedom.
When you pit Errol Flynn against the Nazis,
there's no doubt who wins; and the last line is
'Now for Australia and a crack at those Japs!'
Exhilarating adventure for the totally
uncritical; professional standards high.

w Arthur Horman d Raoul Walsh ph Bert
Glennon m Max Steiner

Errol Flynn, Alan Hale, Ronald Reagan,
Nancy Coleman, Raymond Massey, Arthur
Kennedy, Ronald Sinclair, Albert Basserman,
Sig Rumann, Ilka Gruning, Pat O'Moore

Desperate Moment
GB 1953 88m bw
Rank / George H. Brown

In Poland, a man imprisoned for murder finds
he didn't do it, escapes, and tracks down the
real criminal, his best friend.
Cliché-ridden melodrama climaxing in a car
chase; poor in all departments.

w Patrick Kirwan, George H. Brown,
novel Martha Albrand d Compton Bennett
ph C. Pennington-Richards m Ronald Binge

Dirk Bogarde, Mai Zetterling, Philip Friend,
Albert Lieven, Carl Jaffe, Gerald Heinz

Destination Gobi*
US 1953 90m Technicolor
TCF (Stanley Rubin)

American soldiers get Mongol help against the
Japanese in the Gobi desert.
A curious war adventure, a kind of camel
opera, apparently based on fact; mildly
enjoyable, though the outlandish is gradually
replaced by the predictable.

w Everett Freeman d Robert Wise
ph Charles G. Clarke m Sol Kaplan

Richard Widmark, Don Taylor, Casey Adams,
Murvyn Vye, Darryl Hickman, Martin Milner,
Ross Badgasarian, Rodolfo Acosta

Destination Moon*
US 1950 91m Technicolor
Universal / George Pal

An American inventor gets private backing to
build a rocket so that the US can reach the
moon before the Russians.
Semi-documentary prophecy with impressive
gadgetry encased in a tedious and totally
unsurprising script.

w Rip Van Ronkel, Robert Heinlein, James
O'Hanlon d Irving Pichel ph Lionel Lindon
m Leith Stevens

Warner Anderson, John Archer, Tom Powers,
Dick Wesson
'Heavy-handed, unimaginative and very
badly acted.'—MFB

Destination Tokyo*
US 1943 135m bw
Warner (Jerry Wald)

A US submarine is sent into Tokyo harbour.
Solid, well acted war suspenser, but overlong.

w Delmer Daves, Albert Maltz, original
story Steve Fisher d Delmer Daves ph Bert
Glennon m Franz Waxman

Cary Grant, John Garfield, Alan Hale, John
Ridgely, Dane Clark, Warner Anderson,
William Prince, Robert Hutton, Tom Tully,
Peter Whitney, Faye Emerson, John Forsythe

'We don't say it is credible; we don't even
suggest that it makes sense. But it does make a
pippin of a picture from a purely melodramatic
point of view.'—Bosley Crowther
'Even moviegoers who have developed a
serious allergy for service pictures should find
it high among the superior films of the war.'—
Newsweek

AAN: Steve Fisher

Destination Unknown
US 1933 69m bw

Bootleggers, in a crippled ship with a
mutinous crew, are saved by a mysterious
stranger. Curious melodrama which turns
halfway through into The Passing of the Third
Floor Back. Pat O'Brien, Ralph Bellamy,
Alan Hale, Russell Hopton, Tom Brown,
Betty Compson, Noel Madison. Written by
Tom Buckingham; directed by Tay Garnett;
for Universal. 'Good sea melodrama ruined by
change of intent.'—Variety

Destiny*
Germany 1921 100m approx bw silent
Decla-Bioscop
original title: Der Müde Tod

In the 19th-century a young woman tries to
save her lover from the presence of Death,
who shows her that whatever she does it is
inevitable.
A solemn fantasy on the lines of Appointment
in Samarra, the framing story being more
effective than the 'illustrations'.

w Thea Von Harbou, Fritz Lang d Fritz
Lang ph Fritz Arno Wagner, Erich
Nitschmann, Hermann Saalfrank

Lil Dagover, Rudolph Klein-Rogge, Bernhard
Götzke, Walter Janssen

Destiny*
US 1944 65m bw
Universal (Roy William Neill)

An escaped convict on the run finds refuge
with a blind girl on a lonely farm.
Curious second feature, interesting because it
began as a story eliminated from Flesh and
Fantasy (qv); extra footage was added to bring
it up to the required length. The original
footage is mainly the nightmare suffered by
the girl.

w Roy Chanslor (F and F Ernest Pascal)
d Reginald Le Borg (F and F Julien Duvivier)
ph George Robinson (F and F Paul Ivano)
m Frank Skinner

Gloria Jean, Alan Curtis (who died in the
original but here survives), Frank Craven,
Grace McDonald

Destiny of a Man**
USSR 1959 98m bw
Sovexportfilm / Mosfilm (G. Kuznetsov)
original title: Sudba Cheloveka

During World War II a Russian is captured by
Nazis but escapes and returns home only to
find his family dead.
Strikingly styled sob story whose very
glumness prevented it from being hailed as a
masterpiece; in technique however it is in the
best Russian tradition.

w Y. Lukin, F. Shakhmagonov, story Mikhail
Sholokhov d Sergei Bondarchuk ph Vladimir
Monakhov m V. Basnov

Sergei Bondarchuk, Zinaida Kirienko, Pavlik
Boriskin
'Of all Soviet post-war films, this will be
looked on as the greatest and most original
work of the period.'—MFB

'Her only rival is his ship!'
Destroyer
US 1943 99m bw
Columbia (Louis F. Edelmann)

An old sea dog talks himself into a job on a
World War II destroyer but works his men too
hard.
Flat propaganda piece, not too well made.

w Frank Wead, Lewis Meltzer, Borden Chase
d William A. Seiter ph Franz Planer
m Anthony Collins

Edward G. Robinson, Glenn Ford,
Marguerite Chapman, Edgar Buchanan, Leo
Gorcey, Regis Toomey, Ed Brophy

Destry*
US 1954 95m Technicolor
U-I (Stanley Rubin)

Almost scene-for-scene remake of Destry
Rides Again (qv). Well enough made and
tolerably acted, but it doesn't have the
sparkle, despite employing the same director.

w Edmund H. North, D. D. Beauchamp
d George Marshall ph George Robinson
m Joseph Gershenson

Audie Murphy, Mari Blanchard, Lyle Bettger,
Thomas Mitchell, Edgar Buchanan, Wallace
Ford, Lori Nelson, Alan Hale Jnr, Mary
Wickes
'The impression is of a school revival of the
original production.'—MFB

'They make the fighting sinful west blaze
into action before your eyes!'
Destry Rides Again****
US 1939 94m bw
Universal (Joe Pasternak)

A mild-mannered sheriff finally gets mad at
local corruption and straps on his guns.
Classic western which manages to encompass
suspense, comedy, romance, tenderness, vivid
characterization, horseplay, songs and
standard western excitements, without moving
for more than a moment from a studio main
street set. It starts with a sign reading
'Welcome to Bottleneck' and an outburst of
gunfire; it ends with tragedy followed by a
running joke. Hollywood expertise at its very
best.

DESTRY RIDES AGAIN.   Marlene Dietrich leads the saloon singalong in the perfect western entertainment.

w Felix Jackson, Gertrude Purcell, Henry Myers, novel Max Brand d George Marshall ph Hal Mohr songs Frederick Hollander, Frank Loesser m Frank Skinner

James Stewart, Marlene Dietrich, Brian Donlevy, Charles Winninger, Samuel S. Hinds, Mischa Auer, Irene Hervey, Jack Carson, Una Merkel, Allen Jenkins, Warren Hymer, Billy Gilbert

'Makes the b.o. grade in a big way . . . just plain, good entertainment.'—Variety

'I think it was Lord Beaverbrook who said that Marlene Dietrich standing on a bar in black net stockings, belting out See What the Boys in the Back Room Will Have, was a greater work of art than the Venus de Milo.'—Richard Roud

† An early sound version in 1932 starred Tom Mix; Frenchie (1950) was a slight variation. See also Destry.

The Detective**
US 1968 114m De Luxe Panavision
TCF / Arcola / Millfield (Aaron Rosenberg)

A New York police detective fights crime and corruption.
Determinedly sleazy and 'frank' cop stuff, quite arrestingly narrated and with something to say about police methods. Good violent entertainment, with just a shade too many homosexuals and nymphomaniacs for balance.

w Abby Mann, novel Roderick Thorp
d Gordon Douglas ph Joseph Biroc m Jerry Goldsmith

Frank Sinatra, Lee Remick, Jacqueline Bisset, Ralph Meeker, Jack Klugman, Horace MacMahon, Lloyd Bochner, William Windom, Tony Musante, Al Freeman Jnr, Robert Duvall

'It vacillates uncertainly between murder mystery, political allegory, and a psychological study of the hero.'—Jan Dawson

● Video: CBS / Fox

'A man whose wife was more woman than angel!'

Detective Story***
US 1951 103m bw
Paramount (William Wyler)

A day in a New York precinct police station, during which a detective of almost pathological righteousness discovers a stain on his family and himself becomes a victim of violence.
Clever, fluent transcription of a Broadway play with some of the pretensions of Greek tragedy; it could have been the negation of cinema, but professional handling makes it the essence of it.

w Philip Yordan, Robert Wyler, play Sidney Kingsley d William Wyler ph Lee Garmes

Kirk Douglas, Eleanor Parker, William Bendix, Cathy O'Donnell, George Macready,

Horace MacMahon, Gladys George, Joseph Wiseman, Lee Grant, Gerald Mohr, Frank Faylen, Luis Van Rooten

'The admirably directed interaction of movement and talk all over the big room is what gives the thing its satisfying texture.'—Richard Mallett, Punch

AAN: Philip Yordan, Robert Wyler; William Wyler; Eleanor Parker; Lee Grant

Detour*
US 1945 68m bw
PRC (Leon Fromkess)

On his way to Hollywood to meet a girl friend, a night club pianist assumes the identity of a dead man.
A minor cult movie with as much doomladen dialogue and film noir angles as could be shovelled into a Poverty Row 'B' at the time. On the whole, less than meets the eye.

w Martin Goldsmith d Edgar G. Ulmer
ph Benjamin H. Kline m Leo Erdody

Tom Neal, Ann Savage, Claudia Drake, Edmund MacDonald, Tim Ryan

Devi*
India 1960 93m bw
Satyajit Ray Productions
aka: The Goddess

While his son is away at university, a farmer persuades his daughter-in-law that she is a goddess, and the events which follow, including the death of her son, are too much for her reason.
A curious, 'foreign' story which does not have the usual Ray tempo or feeling for character, but wins one's attention by its very strangeness.

wd Satyajit Ray, story Prabhat Kumar Mukherjee ph Subrata Mitra m Ali Akbar Khan

Chhabi Biswas, Sharmila Tagore, Soumitra Chatterjee, Karuna Bannerjee

The Devil and Max Devlin
US 1981 95m Technicolor
Walt Disney (Jerome Courtland)

An unscrupulous apartment manager is knocked down by a bus. Finding himself in hell, he is offered freedom if he can buy three young souls within two months.
Frowsty Freudian comedy, a very unhappy indication of the depths to which Disney productions have sunk since Walt's death. To carry this kind of thing off requires a hundred times more style than is evidenced here.

w Mary Rodgers d Steven Hilliard Stern
ph Howard Schwartz m Buddy Baker

Elliott Gould, Bill Cosby, Susan Anspach, Adam Rich, Charles Shamata, Ronnie Schell

● Video: Disney

The Devil and Miss Jones**
US 1941 97m bw
RKO / Frank Ross, Norman Krasna

A millionaire masquerades as a clerk in his

own department store to investigate worker complaints.
Attractive comedy with elements of the crazy thirties and the more socially conscious forties.

w Norman Krasna d Sam Wood ph Harry Stradling

Jean Arthur, *Charles Coburn*, Robert Cummings, Spring Byington, S. Z. Sakall, William Demarest

AAN: Norman Krasna; Charles Coburn

'Her sin—their death?'
Devil and the Deep*
US 1932 73m bw
Paramount (Emmanuel Cohen)

A submarine commander goes mad with jealousy of his faithless wife.
A turgid melodrama notable for its stars.

w Benn Levy d Marion Gering ph Charles Lang

Tallulah Bankhead, Charles Laughton, Gary Cooper, Cary Grant, Paul Porcasi

'Of femme interest despite lukewarm performance of Tallulah Bankhead . . . a fair commercial release.'—*Variety*

The Devil and the Nun*
Poland 1960 108m bw
Kadr
original title: *Matka Joanna od Aniolow;*
aka: *Mother Joan of the Angels*

In a 17th-century convent nuns are possessed by devils. A priest who tries to help is burned at the stake; another becomes possessed himself.
Reasonably dispassionate and fairly stylized version of the same facts that were treated so hysterically by Ken Russell in *The Devils*.

w Tadeusz Konwicki, Jerzy Kawalerowicz, novel Jaroslav Iwaszkiewicz d Jerzy Kawalerowicz ph Jerzy Wojcik m Adam Walacinski

Lucyna Winnicka, Mieczyslaw Voit, Anna Ciepielewska

The Devil at Four o'Clock*
US 1961 126m Eastmancolor
Columbia / Leroy / Kohlmar (Fred Kohlmar)

A drunken missionary and three convicts save a colony of leper children from a South Seas volcano.
Muddled adventure melodrama with a downbeat ending long delayed.

w Liam O'Brien, novel Max Catto d Mervyn Le Roy ph Joseph Biroc m George Duning

Spencer Tracy, Frank Sinatra, Kerwin Mathews, Jean-Pierre Aumont, Grégoire Aslan, Alexander Scourby, Barbara Luna

The Devil Bat*
US 1942 70m bw

A crazed scientist trains bats to kill at the scent of a certain perfume. Horror comic hokum from the bottom of the barrel. Bela Lugosi, Suzanne Kaaren, Dave O'Brien. Written by John Neville; directed by Jean

Yarbrough; for PRC. *Devil Bat's Daughter* (1946), with Rosemary La Planche, was an even tamer sequel.

The Devil Commands*
US 1941 65m bw
Columbia (Wallace MacDonald)

An electrical scientist tries to communicate with his dead wife through a medium.
Modestly effective horror thriller, though rather too deliberately paced.

w Robert D. Andrews, Milton Gunzberg, story The Edge of Running Water by William Sloane d Edward Dmytryk ph Allan G. Siegler md Morris Stoloff

Boris Karloff, Richard Fiske, Amanda Duff, Anne Revere, Ralph Penney

Devil Dogs of the Air*
US 1935 86m bw
Warner (Lou Edelman)

Rivalry and romance in the Marine Flying Corps.
Standard, lively vehicle for Cagney and O'Brien, with excellent stunt flying sequences.

w Malcolm Stuart Boylan, Earl Baldwin, novel John Monk Saunders d Lloyd Bacon ph Arthur Edeson md Leo F. Forbstein

James Cagney, Pat O'Brien, Margaret Lindsay, Frank McHugh, Helen Lowell, John Arledge, Robert Barrat, Russell Hicks, Ward Bond

'Exhibs should have no squawks and may even cheer if they put a little steam behind their selling.'—*Variety*

'A loud and roughneck screen comedy, both amusing and exciting.'—*André Sennwald*

The Devil Doll**
US 1936 79m bw
MGM (E.J.Mannix)

A refugee from Devil's Island disguises himself as an old lady who sells human dolls which murder those responsible for his imprisonment.
Interesting rather than exciting tall tale with a Paris backdrop; despite impressive moments it does not quite have the right *frisson*.

w Tod Browning, Garrett Fort, Erich Von Stroheim, Guy Endore, novel Burn Witch Burn by A. A. Merritt d Tod Browning ph Leonard Smith m Franz Waxman ad Cedric Gibbons

Lionel Barrymore, Maureen O'Sullivan, Frank Lawton, Henry B. Walthall, Rafaela Ottiano, Grace Ford, Arthur Hohl

'Grotesque, slightly horrible and consistently interesting.'—*Frank Nugent, New York Times*

The Devil Is a Sissy*
US 1936 92m bw
MGM (Frank Davis)
aka: *The Devil Takes the Count*

The young son of divorcing parents gets into bad company.
Adequate juvenile melodrama

w John Lee Mahin, Richard Schayer, Roland Brown d W. S. Van Dyke ph Harold Rosson, George Schneidermann m Herbert Stothart

Freddie Bartholomew, Jackie Cooper, Mickey Rooney, Ian Hunter, Peggy Conklin, Katherine Alexander, Gene Lockhart, Dorothy Peterson

'Men are my slaves—and glad to be!'
The Devil Is a Woman*
US 1935 82m bw
Paramount

In Seville in the 1890s a *femme fatale* has several admirers.
The last Dietrich vehicle to be directed by Von Sternberg, and rather splendid in its highly decorative and uncommercial way; a treat for addicts.

w John Dos Passos, S. K. Winston, novel La Femme et le Pantin by Pierre Louÿs d Josef Von Sternberg ph Josef Von Sternberg, Lucien Ballard ad Hans Dreier m from Rimsky-Korsakov

Marlene Dietrich, Lionel Atwill, Cesar Romero, Edward Everett Horton, Alison Skipworth, Don Alvarado, Morgan Wallace, Tempe Pigott

'A somewhat monotonous picture . . . sophisticated audiences are its best bet.'—*Variety*

'One of the most sophisticated films ever produced in America.'—*André Sennwald, New York Times*

'Light and shadow are splashed liberally around over the white-painted sets; cafés, tobacco factories, stairs and balconies are decorated with every conceivable device and camera-level.'—*Peter John Dyer, 1964*

'A clever, perversely dehumanized picture said to be one of Von Sternberg's favourites.'—*New Yorker, 1977*

The Devil is Driving*
US 1937 69m bw

An attorney protects a friend's son from a drunk driving charge, but finally indicts himself for perjury. Standard moral melodrama with the star in good form.
Richard Dix, Joan Perry, Nana Bryant, Frank C. Wilson, Ian Wolfe, Elisha Cook Jnr, Henry Kolker, Ann Rutherford, Walter Kingsford. Written by Jo Milward, Richard Blake; directed by Harry Lachman; for Columbia.
'Carries a good deal of punch, but not enough to lug it above the moderate biz bracket.'—*Variety*

The Devil Makes Three*
US 1952 90m bw
MGM (Richard Goldstone)

An American intelligence officer in post-war Germany becomes involved with neo-Nazis.
A curious break from dancing for Gene Kelly, this obscurely titled thriller has little to commend it but authentic locations.

w Jerry Davis, story Lawrence Bachmann d Andrew Marton ph Vaclav Vich m Rudolph G. Kopp

Gene Kelly, Pier Angeli, Richard Rober, Richard Egan, Claus Clausen

Devil on Horseback

GB 1954   89m   bw
Group 3 (John Grierson, Isobel Pargiter)

A teenage jockey gets to the top the hard way.
Highly resistible compendium of racetrack clichés and sentiment, not at all what one expected from Group 3.

w Neil Paterson, Montagu Slater   d Cyril Frankel   ph Denny Densham   m Malcolm Arnold

Googie Withers, John McCallum, Jeremy Spenser, Meredith Edwards, Liam Redmond, Sam Kydd

The Devil, Probably*

France 1977   95m   Eastmancolor
Sunchold / GMF (Stéphane Tchalgadchieff)
original title: Le Diable, Probablement

A young Parisian goes to the devil and arranges to have himself shot.
A despairing vision of an arid world, seen through unpleasant details of city life. A fascinating but enervated film very typical of its director.

wd Robert Bresson   ph Pasqualino de Santis   m Philippe Sarde   pd Eric Simon

Antoine Monnier, Tina Irissari, Henri de Maublanc

The Devil Rides Out*

GB 1967   95m   Technicolor
Hammer (Anthony Nelson Keys)
US title: The Devil's Bride

The Duc de Richleau rescues a friend from a group of Satanists.
Rather stodgy adaptation of a frightening novel; moments of suspense.

w Richard Matheson, novel Dennis Wheatley   d Terence Fisher   ph Arthur Grant   m James Bernard

Christopher Lee, Charles Gray, Leon Greene, Patrick Mower, Gwen Ffrangcon Davies

Devil Ship Pirates

GB 1963   96m   Technicolor
   Hammerscope
ABP / Hammer (Anthony Nelson Keyes)

At the time of the Armada, Spanish privateers terrorize a Cornish seaside village.
Lacklustre pirate yarn with not much action and some elements of Hammer horror.

w Jimmy Sangster   d Don Sharp   ph Michael Reed   m Gary Hughes

Christopher Lee, John Cairney, Barry Warren, Ernest Clark, Andrew Keir, Duncan Lamont

The Devil Thumbs a Ride

US 1947   63m   bw

A commercial traveller gives a lift to a man who turns out to be wanted for murder.
Predictable suspenser without much entertainment value. Ted North, Lawrence Tierney, Nan Leslie. Written and directed by Felix Feist; for RKO.

The Devil to Pay*

US 1930   72m   bw
Samuel Goldwyn

The prodigal son of a snooty English family returns to cheer them all up.
Agreeably lighthearted star comedy in the drawing-room tradition.

w Frederick Lonsdale   d George Fitzmaurice   ph Gregg Toland, George Barnes   m Alfred Newman

Ronald Colman, Loretta Young, Myrna Loy, Frederick Kerr

'Snappy British comedy that should please everywhere . . . a set-up for femmes.'—Variety

'Six reels of Mr Colman being charming . . . a polished, tasteful and entirely likeable screen comedy.'—New York Herald Tribune

A Devil with Women

US 1930   76m   bw
Fox (George Middleton)

Soldiers of fortune in a banana republic end the regime of a notorious bandit and compete for a fair señorita.
Primitive Flagg-and-Quirt style knockabout.

w Dudley Nichols, Henry M. Johnson, novel Dust and Sun by Clements Ripley   d Irving Cummings   ph Arthur Todd   m Peter Brunelli

Victor McLaglen, Humphrey Bogart, Mona Maris, Michael Vavitch

'No real plot or continuity, but has some laughs. Best for neighbourhood grinds.'—Variety

'Hell holds no surprises . . . for them!'

The Devils*

GB 1970   111m   Technicolor
   Panavision
Warner / Russo (Robert H. Solo, Ken Russell)

An account of the apparent demoniacal possession of the 17th-century nuns of Loudun, climaxing in the burning of their priest as a sorcerer.
Despite undeniable technical proficiency this is its writer-director's most outrageously sick film to date, campy, idiosyncratic and in howling bad taste from beginning to end, full of worm-eaten skulls, masturbating nuns, gibbering courtiers, plague sores, rats and a burning to death before our very eyes . . . plus a sacrilegious dream of Jesus. A pointless pantomime for misogynists.

wd Ken Russell, play John Whiting, book The Devils of Loudun by Aldous Huxley   ph David Watkin   m Peter Maxwell Davies   ad Robert Cartwright

Vanessa Redgrave, Oliver Reed, Dudley Sutton, Max Adrian, Gemma Jones, Murray Melvin, Michael Gothard, Graham Armitage

'Ken Russell doesn't report hysteria, he markets it.'—New Yorker, 1976

'Russell's swirling multi-colored puddle . . . made me glad that both Huxley and Whiting are dead, so that they are spared this farrago of witless exhibitionism.'—Stanley Kauffmann

'A garish glossary of sado-masochism . . . a taste for visual sensation that makes scene after scene look like the masturbatory fantasies of a Roman Catholic boyhood.'—Alexander Walker

● Video: Warner

The Devil's Advocate

West Germany 1977   109m   colour
Geria (Lutz Hengst)

A dying priest is summoned to Rome to investigate the cult of a dead partisan nominated for sainthood.
Well-meaning but rather tepid and inconclusive adaptation of a bestseller which presumably made its points more firmly.

w Morris West, from his novel   d Guy Green   ph Billy Williams   m Bert Grund

John Mills, Stéphane Audran, Jason Miller, Timothy West, Patrick Mower, Paola Pitagora, Daniel Massey, Leigh Lawson, Raf Vallone, Jack Hedley

The Devil's Agent

GB 1962   77m   bw
British Lion / Emmet Dalton

A wine salesman in Germany is duped by Soviet agents.
Scrappy cold war adventures which look as though they were originally intended as episodes in a TV series.

w Robert Westerby   d John Paddy Carstairs   ph Gerald Gibbs   m Philip Green

Peter Van Eyck, Marianne Koch, Macdonald Carey, Christopher Lee, Billie Whitelaw, David Knight, Marius Goring, Helen Cherry, Colin Gordon, Niall MacGinnis, Eric Pohlmann, Peter Vaughan

The Devil's Brigade

US 1968   132m   De Luxe   Panavision
UA / David L. Wolper

For combat in Norway and Italy during World War II a US officer assembles a platoon of thugs and misfits to work with crack Canadian commandos.
Flagrant but routine imitation of The Dirty Dozen, quite undistinguished.

w William Roberts   d Andrew V. McLaglen   ph William Clothier   m Alex North

William Holden, Cliff Robertson, Vince Edwards, Andrew Prine, Claude Akins, Carroll O'Connor, Richard Jaeckel

'After nearly three decades of World War II films, it is hardly surprising that Hollywood is beginning to suffer from combat fatigue.'—Time

Devil's Canyon

US 1953   92m   Technicolor   3-D
RKO / Edmund Grainger

Life in a notorious Arizona prison in the 1880s; a marshal is unjustly convicted but wins his pardon.
Fairly brutal western, quite unmemorable.

w Frederick Hazlitt Brennan   d Alfred Werker   ph Nicholas Musuraca   m Daniele Amfitheatrof

Dale Robertson, Virginia Mayo, Stephen McNally, Arthur Hunnicutt, Robert Keith, Jay C. Flippen, Whit Bissell

● Video: Kingston

The Devil's Disciple*
GB 1959   82m   bw
UA / Hecht–Hill–Lancaster / Brynaprod (Harold Hecht)

In 1777 an American ne'er-do-well almost allows himself to be hanged by the British in mistake for a rebel pastor.
Star-studded but indifferently staged adaptation of a minor Shavian frolic. Patchy, with good moments.

w John Dighton, Roland Kibbee, play Bernard Shaw d Guy Hamilton ph Jack Hildyard m Richard Rodney Bennett ad Terence Verity, Edward Carere

Burt Lancaster, Kirk Douglas, Laurence Olivier (as General Burgoyne), Eva Le Gallienne, Janette Scott, Harry Andrews, Basil Sidney, George Rose, Neil McCallum, David Horne, Mervyn Johns

Devil's Doorway
US 1950   84m   bw
MGM (Nicholas Nayfack)

A Shoshone Indian fights valiantly in the Civil War but on his return to Wyoming finds himself hated and threatened by his former colleagues.
Dull pro-Indian western with a most unsuitable star.

w Guy Trosper d Anthony Mann ph John Alton m Daniele Amfitheatrof

Robert Taylor, Louis Calhern, Paula Raymond, Marshall Thompson, James Mitchell, Edgar Buchanan, Rhys Williams, Spring Byington

The Devil's Eight
US 1968   98m   Pathecolor
AIP / Burt Topper

A federal agent on the trail of a moonshine gang recruits a gang of hardened convicts and arranges for them to escape.
The Dirty Dozen all over again, and not good.

w James Gordon White, Willard Huyck, John Milius d Burt Topper ph Richard C. Glouner m Mike Curb

Christopher George, Ralph Meeker, Fabian, Tom Nardini, Leslie Parrish, Ross Hagen

The Devil's Eye*
Sweden 1960   90m   bw
Svensk Filmindustri

An old proverb says that a woman's chastity is a stye in the devil's eye. So when Satan has a sore eye he comes down to earth to put things right.
Surprisingly shoddily-made comedy with just a few of the sharpnesses of technique and mystifications of plot which one had come to expect from this maestro.

wd Ingmar Bergman ph Gunnar Fischer m Domenico Scarlatti

Jarl Kulle, Bibi Andersson, Nils Poppe, Stig Järrel, Gunnar Björnstrand

The Devil's General
West Germany 1955   121m   bw
Ryal (Gyula Trebitsch)

In 1941 a German air ace becomes estranged from the high command and is tortured by the Gestapo. On release he helps a Jewish couple . . .
Heavy-going melodrama which nevertheless paints a convincing picture of Berlin during the war.

w George Hurdalek, Helmut Kautner, play Carl Zuckmayer d Helmut Kautner ph Albert Benitz

Curt Jurgens, Victor de Kowa, Karl John, Eva-Ingeborg Scholz

The Devil's Hairpin
US 1957   83m   Technicolor   Vistavision
Paramount / Cornel Wilde

A former motor racing champion makes a comeback, and redeems his past boorish behaviour.
Efficient routine melodramatics with good action sequences.

w James Edmiston, Cornel Wilde d Cornel Wilde ph Daniel Fapp m Van Cleave

Cornel Wilde, Jean Wallace, Arthur Franz, Mary Astor, Paul Fix

Devil's Holiday*
US 1930   80m   bw

A mercenary lady repents her life on the make. Very dated moral story which at the time was showered with praise. Nancy Carroll, Phillips Holmes, James Kirkwood, Hobart Bosworth, Ned Sparks, Jed Prouty, Paul Lukas, Zasu Pitts. Written and directed by Edmund Goulding; for Paramount. 'It is pictures such as this which revive the drooping confidence in the screen as a mirror of things as they really are.'—Variety

AAN: Nancy Carroll.

The Devil's in Love
US 1933   70m   bw

At a French Foreign Legion post, an outcast doctor falls in love with the niece of a mission father. Old-fashioned and predictable romantic drama. Victor Jory, Loretta Young, Vivienne Osborne, David Manners, C. Henry Gordon, Herbert Mundin, J. Carrol Naish. Written by Howard Estabrook from a story by Harry Hervey; directed by William Dieterle; for Fox. 'Given any kind of a break returns should be fair.'—Variety

Devil's Island*
US 1939   63m   bw
Warner (Bryan Foy)

A surgeon is sent to Devil's Island for aiding an escaped convict.
Sharply-made exposé of the notorious French penal colony; commendable pace and vigour all round.

w Kenneth Gamet, Don Ryan d William Clemens

Boris Karloff, James Stephenson, Nedda Harrigan, Adia Kuznetzoff, Robert Warwick, Pedro de Cordoba

The Devil's Mask
US 1946   66m   bw

An unclaimed parcel containing a shrunken head is found after a plane crash; murder follows. Involved but amusing entry in the I Love a Mystery series. Jim Bannon, Anita Louise, Michael Duane, Mona Barrie, Byron Foulger. Written by Charles O'Neal; directed by Henry Levin; for Columbia.

The Devil's Playground*
Australia 1976   107m   Eastmancolor
The Feature Film House (Fred Schepsi)

Tensions between masters and boys in a Catholic seminary in the fifties.
Well made but rather dislikeable intrusion into Mr Perrin and Mr Traill country with the addition of modern frankness.

wd Fred Schepsi ph Ian Baker m Bruce Smeaton

Arthur Dignam, Nick Tate, Simon Burke, Charles McCallum, John Frawley

The Devil's Rain
US 1975   86m   colour   Todd-AO 35
Sandy Howard

Witchcraft in the modern west causes victims to melt; the son of one of them takes arms against the leading Satanist.
Interestingly cast example of the low-budget seventies exploitation picture, with more nastiness than logic.

w Gabe Essoe, James Ashton, Gerald Hopman d Robert Fuest ph Alex Phillips Jnr m Al de Lory

Ernest Borgnine, Ida Lupino, Eddie Albert, William Shatner, Keenan Wynn, Tom Skerritt

Devils of Darkness
GB 1964   90m   Eastmancolor

A vampire disguises himself as a French count and preys on young girls. Mainly tatty shocker with a few lively scenes. William Sylvester, Hubert Noel, Tracy Reed, Diana Decker, Rona Anderson. Written by Lyn Fairhurst; directed by Lance Comfort; for Tom Blakeley / Planet.

The Devil's Wanton*
Sweden 1949   80m   bw
Terrafilm
original title: Fängelse
aka: Prison

Film-makers discuss some rather unpleasant projects but put them aside as unsatisfactory.
A bit of a Scandinavian wallow, with heavy expressionism and low-life themes.

wd Ingmar Bergman ph Göran Strindberg m Erland von Koch

Doris Svedlund, Birger Malmsten, Eva Henning, Hasse Ekman
'It employs all the paraphernalia associated with Scandinavian angst.'—John Gillett, MFB

Devotion

US 1931   84m   bw

A woman falls in love with a barrister and
takes a job as governess to his son. Rather
winsome tear-jerker entirely dependent on its
stars. Ann Harding, Leslie Howard, Robert
Williams, O. P. Heggie, Louise Closser Hale,
Dudley Digges. Written by Graham John and
Horace Jackson, from the novel *A Little Flat
in the Temple* by Pamela Wynne; directed by
Robert Milton; for RKO-Pathé. 'Much talk
and little action. Star's name its best chance of
rating more than mild financially.'—*Variety*

'It tells ALL about those Brontë sisters! . . .
    They didn't dare call it love—they tried to
    call it devotion!'

Devotion**

US 1943 (released 1946)   107m   bw
Warner (Robert Buckner)

A highly romanticized account of the lives of
the Brontë sisters and their brother Branwell.
An enjoyably bad example of a big-budget
Hollywood production which tampers with
things it cannot understand, in this case life in
a Yorkshire parsonage in Victorian times. An
excuse is found to give the curate an Austrian
accent to fit the available actor, but this and
other *faux pas* are atoned for by the vividness
of Emily's recurrent dream of death as a
silhouetted man on horseback. In general, an
interesting period piece in more senses than
one.

w Keith Winter *d* Curtis Bernhardt *ph* Ernest
Haller *m* Erich Wolfgang Korngold

Ida Lupino (Emily), Olivia de Havilland
(Charlotte), Nancy Coleman (Anne), Arthur
Kennedy (Branwell), Montagu Love (Revd
Brontë), Paul Henreid (Revd Nicholls), Ethel
Griffies (Aunt Branwell), Sidney Greenstreet
(Thackeray), Eily Malyon, Forrester Harvey,
Victor Francen

'I found it painless. It never got nearer to
the subject than names and consequently
didn't hurt. But I would like to know who was
devoted to whom and why.'—*Richard
Winnington*

† More items from the extraordinary publicity
campaign devised by Warners for this placid
Victorian romance:

Emily: she ruled in that strange quiet house!
None could resist the force of her will!

The man in black (i.e. the Revd Nicholls):
he fled from her demands into her sister's
arms!

Charlotte: the sweetness of love and the
meaning of torment—she learned them both
together!

The 'friend'—the furious fat man (i.e.
William Makepeace Thackeray): they couldn't
fool him—they couldn't trust him!

†† Dialogue includes the celebrated exchange
between two celebrated London literary
figures:

THACKERAY: 'Morning, Dickens.'
DICKENS: 'Morning, Thackeray.'

The DI

US 1957   106m   bw
Warner / Mark VII (Jack Webb)

A tough marine drill instructor takes a special
interest in a backward member of his platoon.
Noisy recruiting poster heroics in which the
producer gives himself a loud but boring part.
The drill sequences are well done, but the film
is overlong and repetitive.

w James Lee Barrett *d* Jack Webb
ph Edward Colman *m* David Buttolph

Jack Webb, Don Dubbins, Jackie Loughery,
Lin McCarthy, Monica Lewis

Le Diable au Corps*

France 1947   110m   bw
Transcontinental
US title: *Devil in the Flesh*

When her husband is away at war, a young
married woman falls for a college student and
dies bearing his child.
A love story of World War I; a great
commercial success, but tending to be slow
and dreary.

w Jean Aurenche, Pierre Bost,
novel Raymond Radiguet *d* Claude Autant-
Lara *ph* Michel Kelber *m* René Cloërc

Micheline Presle, Gérard Philipe, Jean
Debucourt, Denise Grey, Jacques Tati

Les Diaboliques***

France 1954   114m   bw
Filmsonor (Henri-Georges Clouzot)
aka: *Diabolique; The Fiends*

A sadistic headmaster's wife and mistress
conspire to murder him; but his body
disappears and evidence of his presence haunts
them.

Highly influential, suspenseful and scary
thriller with a much-copied twist typical of its
authors. Slow to start and shabby-looking as
befits its grubby school setting, it gathers
momentum with the murder and turns the
screw with fine professionalism.

w Henri-Georges Clouzot, G. Geronimi,
novel The Woman Who Was by Pierre
Boileau and Thomas Narcejac *d* Henri-
Georges Clouzot *ph* Armand Thirard
m Georges Van Parys

Simone Signoret, Vera Clouzot, Charles
Vanel, Paul Meurisse

'Scary, but so calculatedly sensational that
it's rather revolting.'—*New Yorker, 1978*

'It depends very much on the intimate
details of the seedy fourth-rate school, with its
inadequate education and uneatable food, its
general smell of unwashed children, hatred
and petty perversions.'—*Basil Wright, 1972*

† Remade in 1976 as a TV movie, *Reflections
of Murder*.

Diagnosis: Murder

GB 1974   90m   Eastmancolor
Silhouette (Patrick Dromgoole, Peter Miller)

A psychiatrist's wife disappears, and the police
suspect her husband.
Well-upholstered but sadly old-fashioned
domestic crime thriller; one is vaguely
surprised to see it in colour, having seen it so
often in black-and-white.

w Philip Levene *d* Sidney Hayers *ph* Bob
Edwards *m* Laurie Johnson

LES DIABOLIQUES.   Vera Clouzot gets her come-uppance in the startling climax.

Jon Finch, Judy Geeson, Christopher Lee, Tony Beckley, Dilys Hamlett, Jane Merrow, Colin Jeavons

'If a woman answers—hang on for dear life!'

Dial M For Murder**
US 1954   105m   Warnercolor   3-D
Warner (Alfred Hitchcock)

An ageing tennis champion tries to arrange the death of his wife so that he will inherit, but his complex plan goes wrong.
Hitchcock did not try very hard to adapt this highly commercial play for the cinema, nor did he exploit the possibilities of 3-D. But for a one-room film with a not very exciting cast the film holds its grip pretty well.

w *Frederick Knott*, from his play d *Alfred Hitchcock* ph Robert Burks m Dmitri Tiomkin

Ray Milland, John Williams, Grace Kelly, Robert Cummings, Anthony Dawson
  'All this is related with Hitchcock's ghoulish chic but everyone in it seems to be walking around with tired blood.'—*Pauline Kael, 1968*

● *Video: VTC*

Dial 1119*
US 1950   75m   bw
MGM (Richard Goldstone)
GB title: *The Violent Hour*

An assortment of people are held up in a bar by a maniac.
Suspenseful thriller when it sticks to its central theme; dullish when it tries characterization. A good second feature.

w John Monks Jnr d Gerald Mayer ph Paul Vogel m André Previn

Marshall Thompson, Virginia Field, Andrea King, Leon Ames, Keefe Brasselle, Richard Rober, James Bell, William Conrad

Diamond City
GB 1949   90m   bw
GFD / Gainsborough (A. Frank Bundy)

Law and order is maintained during the working of a South African diamond field. British imitation of a Wyatt Earp western; very milk-and-water.

w Roger Bray, Roland Pertwee d David MacDonald ph Reginald Wyer m Clifton Parker

David Farrar, Honor Blackman, Diana Dors, Niall MacGinnis, Andrew Crawford, Mervyn Johns, Bill Owen, Phyllis Monkman

Diamond Frontier
US 1940   72m   bw

An honest diamond dealer is framed and sent to prison. Co-feature action stuff, with South Africa standing in for the west. Victor McLaglen, Anne Nagel, John Loder, Philip Dorn, Cecil Kellaway. Written by Edmund L. Hartmann and Stanley Rubin; directed by Harold Schuster; for Universal.

Diamond Head
US 1962   107m   Eastmancolor
   Panavision
Columbia (Jerry Bresler)

A domineering Hawaiian landowner almost ruins the lives of his family.
Predictable, heavy-going transcription of a bestseller.

w Marguerite Roberts, *novel* Peter Gilman d Guy Green ph Sam Leavitt m Johnny Williams

Charlton Heston, Yvette Mimieux, George Chakiris, France Nuyen, James Darren, Aline MacMahon, Elizabeth Allen, Richard Loo

Diamond Horseshoe
US 1945   104m   Technicolor
TCF (William Perlberg)
aka: *Billy Rose's Diamond Horseshoe*

A nightclub singer gives up her career for a medical student.
Lavish but humourless star vehicle with standard numbers.

wd George Seaton, *play* The Barker by Kenyon Nicholson ph Ernest Palmer songs Mack Gordon, Harry Warren

Betty Grable, Dick Haymes, *William Gaxton*, Phil Silvers, Beatrice Kay, Carmen Cavallero, Margaret Dumont

Diamond Jim*
US 1935   93m   bw
Universal (Edmund Grainger)

A fantasia on the life of the nineties millionaire who sailed pretty close to the wind in business, adored Lillian Russell, and developed a gargantuan appetite.
Cheerful period comedy drama with plenty of gusto.

w Preston Sturges d A. Edward Sutherland ph George Robinson m Ferde Grofe, Franz Waxman

Edward Arnold, Jean Arthur, Binnie Barnes, Cesar Romero, Eric Blore
  'Good picture and title. Lacks real pull names.'—*Variety*

The Diamond Queen
US 1953   80m   Supercinecolor
Warner / Melson (Frank Melford, Edward L. Alperson Jnr)

Frenchmen journey to India to bring back a diamond for the crown of Louis XIV.
The adventures are basically lively enough to warrant a better production.

w Otto Englander d John Brahm ph Stanley Cortez m Paul Sawtell

Fernando Lamas, Arlene Dahl, Gilbert Roland, Sheldon Leonard, Michael Ansara

The Diamond
GB 1954   83m   bw   3D
Gibraltar Films (Stephen Pallos)
US title: *The Diamond Wizard*

An American agent in London investigates a million-dollar treasury robbery involving a process for making synthetic diamonds.

Leaden cops-and-robbers which went out on the bottom of a bill instead of being shown in three dimensions.

w John C. Higgins, *story* The Bowstring Murders by Maurice Procter m Montgomery Tully m Matyas Seiber

Dennis O'Keefe, Margaret Sheridan, Philip Friend, Alan Wheatley, Francis de Wolff

Diamonds
US 1975   108m   Eastmancolor
Avco Embassy / AmeriEuro (Menahem Golan)

A London diamond merchant sets himself up to be robbed so that he can blackmail the culprits into a raid on the Tel Aviv diamond repository.
Cheerful but unremarkable caper movie with an upbeat ending.

w David Paulsen, Menahem Golan d Menahem Golan ph Adam Greenberg m Roy Budd

Robert Shaw, Richard Roundtree, Barbara Seagull, Shelley Winters

● *Video: Embassy*

Diamonds Are Forever*
GB 1971   120m   Technicolor
   Panavision
UA / Eon / Danjaq (Harry Saltzman, Albert R. Broccoli)

Seeking a diamond smuggler, James Bond has adventures in Amsterdam, a Los Angeles crematorium, various Las Vegas gambling parlours, and a secret installation in the desert.
Campy, rather vicious addition to a well-worn cycle, with an element of nastiness which big-budget stunts cannot conceal. Panavision does not help, and Connery's return to the role for a final throw is disappointing.

w Richard Maibaum, Tom Mankiewicz, *novel* Ian Fleming d Guy Hamilton ph Ted Moore m John Barry pd Ken Adam

Sean Connery, Jill St John, Charles Gray, Lana Wood, Jimmy Dean, Bruce Cabot, Bernard Lee, Lois Maxwell

● *Video: Warner*

Diamonds for Breakfast
GB 1968   102m   Eastmancolor
Paramount / Bridge Films (Carlo Ponti, Pierre Rouve)

An impoverished Russian aristocrat decides to retrieve from a museum the crown jewels of his ancestors, and seduces seven female accomplices.
Yawning caper yarn embellished with sex and slapstick.

w N. F. Simpson, Pierre Rouve, Ronald Harwood d Christopher Morahan ph Gerry Turpin m Norman Kay

Marcello Mastroianni, Rita Tushingham, Elaine Taylor, Warren Mitchell, Nora Nicholson, Bill Fraser, Leonard Rossiter

Diane

US 1956 110m Eastmancolor
Cinemascope
MGM (Edwin H. Knopf)

Diane de Poitier becomes a consultant to the
king and falls in love with his son.
Solidly boring slice of Hollywood history, with
all concerned out of their depth.

w Christopher Isherwood d David Miller
ph Robert Planck m Miklos Rozsa

Lana Turner, Roger Moore, Cedric
Hardwicke, Pedro Armendariz, Marisa Pavan

The Diary of a Chambermaid*

US 1946 86m bw
Benedict Bogeaus (Burgess Meredith,
Paulette Goddard)

A 19th-century serving girl causes sexual
frustration and other troubles in two
households.
Hollywood notables were all at sea in this
wholly artificial and unpersuasive adaptation
of a minor classic.

w Burgess Meredith, novel Octave Mirbeau
d Jean Renoir ph Lucien Andriot pd Eugene
Lourié

Paulette Goddard, Burgess Meredith, Hurd
Hatfield, Francis Lederer, Judith Anderson,
Florence Bates, Irene Ryan, Reginald Owen,
Almira Sessions

The Diary of a Chambermaid*

France / Italy 1964 98m bw Franscope
Speva / Ciné Alliance / Filmsonor / Dear
(Serge Silberman, Michel Sabra)
original title: Le Journal d'une Femme de
Chambre

Interesting but not especially successful
Bunuel version: the subject is certainly up his
street, but the novel seems to restrict him and
the visual quality is unattractive.

w Luis Bunuel, Jean-Claude Carrière d Luis
Bunuel ph Roger Fellous m none

Jeanne Moreau, Georges Géret, Michel
Piccoli, Françoise Lugagne

The Diary of a Country Priest***

France 1950 120m bw
Union Générale Cinématographique (Léon
Carré)
original title: Journal d'un Curé de
Campagne

A lonely young priest fails to make much
impression in his first parish; and, falling ill, he
dies alone.
Striking, depressing, slow and austere, with
little dialogue but considerable visual beauty;
a very typical work of its director.

wd Robert Bresson, novel Georges Bernanos
ph L. Burel m Jean-Jacques Grunenwald

Claude Laydu, Jean Riveyre, Armand
Guibert, Nicole Ladmiral

Diary of a Lost Girl**

Germany 1929 110m approx bw silent
G. W. Pabst Film
original title: Tagebuch einer Verlorenen

A rich man's daughter is seduced, has an
illegitimate child, is placed in a house of
correction and finds herself later in a brothel.
Heavily Germanic Road to Ruin, superbly
mounted in best cinematic style, with several
memorable sequences. Heavily mutilated by
censors; according to the screenwriter the film
ends just after the middle of his script.

w Rudolf Leonhardt, novel Margaret Böhme
d G. W. Pabst ph Sepp Allgeier

Louise Brooks, Fritz Rasp, Josef Ravensky
† A previous version had been made in 1918,
written and directed by Richard Oswald.

Diary of a Mad Housewife**

US 1970 95m Technicolor
Universal / Frank Perry

The bored and repressed wife of a lawyer tries
an affair, walks out on her husband, and opts
for group therapy.
An agreeably mordant view of the
contemporary American scene, with good
dialogue and performances, but the little bits
of satire do not really add up to a satisfactory
film.

w Eleanor Perry, novel Sue Kaufman d Frank
Perry ph Gerald Hirschfeld

Carrie Snodgress, Richard Benjamin, Frank
Langella, Lorraine Cullen, Frannie Michel
  'A prototypical contemporary American
artifact . . . all its assorted talents and
technological smartness are turned to the
varnishing of mediocrity.'—Stanley Kauffmann

AAN: Carrie Snodgress

The Diary of a Madman

US 1962 96m Technicolor
UA / Admiral (Robert E. Kent)

A murderer explains to a magistrate that he
was possessed by an evil spirit.
Ponderous transcription of a Maupassant story
with a few moments of horror.

w Robert E. Kent d Reginald Le Borg
ph Ellis W. Carter m Richard La Salle

Vincent Price, Nancy Kovack, Chris Warfield,
Stephen Roberts

The Diary of a Married Woman

Germany 1953 83m bw
Magna
original title: Tagebuch einer Verliebten

A wife divorces her adulterous husband, but
their small son brings them together again.
One long Hollywood cliché, assembled with
some spirit; notable only as one of the rare
post-war German films to get distribution in
English-speaking countries.

w Emil Burri, Johann Mario Simmel d Josef
Von Baky ph Oskar Snirch m Alois Melichar

Maria Schell, O. W. Fischer, Franco Andrei

Diary of a Shinjuku Thief*

Japan 1969 94m bw / Eastmancolor
Sozosha (Masayuki Nakajima)
original title: Shinjuku Dorobo Nikki

A minor theft in a bookstore brings a young
man in contact with a mysterious girl who
leads him into various sexual experiments.

Inexplicable but quite fascinating piece of
oriental mystification in which sex equates to
some extent with revolution.

w Tsutomu Tamura and others d Nagisa
Oshima ph Yasuhiro Yamaguchi m none

Tadanori Yokoo, Rie Yokoyama, Moichi
Tanabe

The Diary of Anne Frank**

US 1959 170m bw Cinemascope
TCF / George Stevens

In 1942, a family of Dutch Jews hides in an
attic from the Nazis; just before the war ends
they are found and sent to concentration
camps.
Based on the famous diaries of a girl who died
at Auschwitz, this solemn adaptation is
elephantine in its length, its ponderousness
and its use of Cinemascope when the
atmosphere is supposed to be claustrophobic.

w Frances Goodrich, Albert Hackett, from
their play based on Anne Frank's diaries
d George Stevens ph William C. Mellor
m Alfred Newman

Millie Perkins, Joseph Schildkraut, Shelley
Winters, Ed Wynn, Richard Beymer, Gusti
Huber, Lou Jacobi, Diane Baker

AA: William C. Mellor; Shelley Winters
AAN: best picture; George Stevens; Alfred
Newman; Ed Wynn

● Video: CBS / Fox

The Diary of Major Thompson

France 1955 83m bw
SNE Gaumont / Paul Wagner
original title: Les Carnets de Major
Thompson; US title: The French They
Are a Funny Race

An Englishman married to a Frenchwoman
keeps notes on the French way of life.
Tatty filming of a mildly amusing book; it falls
away into a number of badly-timed and
presented gags, and one can't believe that its
creator was once the top comedy genius of
Hollywood.

wd Preston Sturges ph Maurice Barry,
Christian Matras m Georges Van Parys

Jack Buchanan, Martine Carol, Noel-Noel,
Genevieve Brunet
  'Even allowing for the appalling editing and
the frequently incomprehensible dubbed
soundtrack, there is little evidence to suggest
that this film could ever have been anything
but a shambles.'—Peter John Dyer, MFB

Dick Barton

The radio detective was created by Edward J.
Mason in the mid-forties, and three rough-
and-ready film versions were subsequently
made by Hammer / Exclusive. They were
Dick Barton Special Agent (1948); Dick
Barton Strikes Back (1949); and Dick Barton
at Bay (1950); all with Don Stannard. Critical
comment would be irrelevant.

Dick Deadeye, or Duty Done

GB 1975 81m Technicolor
Bill Melendez Productions (Leo Rost)

A naval officer is commissioned by Queen Victoria to retrieve the Ultimate Secret from the Wicked Sorcerer.
Fairly joyless animated amalgam of several Gilbert and Sullivan operas, fussily designed by Ronald Searle and with modernized lyrics. Sure to infuriate G and S devotees and to bewilder everyone else.

w Robin Miller, Leo Rost d Bill Melendez animation d Dick Horn

Dick Tracy

US 1945 61m bw
RKO (Herman Schlom)
GB title: *Splitface*

The jut-jawed detective routs a disfigured criminal named Splitface.
Vigorous second feature from the comic strip.

w Eric Taylor, *strip* Chester Gould d William Berke ph Frank Redman m Roy Webb

Morgan Conway, Jane Greer, Mike Mazurki, Anne Jeffreys, Lyle Latell, Joseph Crehan, Trevor Bardette

† Sequels: *Dick Tracy vs Cueball* (1946) with Morgan Conway, *d* John Rawlins; *Dick Tracy Meets Gruesome* (1947) with Ralph Byrd, Boris Karloff, *d* John Rawlins; *Dick Tracy's Dilemma* (1947), with Ralph Byrd, *d* John Rawlins. There had been several Republic serials featuring Tracy, and in the fifties a cartoon series appeared.

Dick Turpin

GB 1933 79m bw
Stoll-Stafford (Clyde Cook)

In this version the highwayman's ride to York is to prevent an enforced marriage.
Mild British costume piece which sent its star to Hollywood.

w Victor Kendall, *novel* Rookwood by Harrison Ainsworth d Victor Hanbury, John Stafford ph Desmond Dickinson

Victor McLaglen, Jane Carr, Frank Vosper, James Finlayson, Gillian Lind

The Dictator*

GB 1935 86m bw
Toeplitz
aka: *For Love of a Queen; The Loves of a Dictator*

In 18th-century Denmark, a country doctor falls in love with his queen and overthrows the mad king.
Stiff-backed middle-class romance, an interesting example of English-German co-production at the time.

w Benn Levy, Hans Wilhelm, H. G. Lustig, Michael Hogan d Victor Saville, Alfred Santell ph Franz Planer

Clive Brook, Madeleine Carroll, Helen Haye, Emlyn Williams, Isabel Jeans, Alfred Drayton, Frank Cellier

'One of the most lavish costume pictures that has yet come out of England: supposed to have cost 500,000 dollars. It's great pictorially, but not moving enough.'—*Variety*

Did You Hear the One about the Travelling Saleslady?

US 1967 96m Techniscope
Universal (Si Rose)

In a Kansas town in 1910 an eccentric saleslady offers pianolas which tend to go berserk.
Cornbelt comedy vehicle for an unappealing star.

w John Fenton Murray d Don Weis ph Bud Thackery m Vic Mizzy

Phyllis Diller, Bob Denver, Joe Flynn, Jeanette Nolan

Die Laughing

US 1980 108m Technicolor

After the murder of a nuclear scientist, a young musician who knows too much is chased by the murderers and the FBI. Witless black comedy rehash of *The 39 Steps*. Robby Benson, Linda Grovenor, Charles Durning, Elsa Lanchester, Bud Cort. Written by Jerry Segal, Robby Benson and Scott Parker; directed by Jeff Werner; for Jon Peters / Orion / Warner.

Dieu A Besoin des Hommes*

France 1950 100m bw
Transcontinental (Paul Graetz)
aka: *Isle of Sinners; God Needs Men*

The priest of a Breton island leaves in horror at the sinfulness of his flock, and the fisherfolk appoint one of their number as priest.
Cold, gloomy, rather pointless fable, often a pleasure to look at.

w Jean Aurenche, Pierre Bost, *novel* Un Recteur de l'Ile de Sein by H. Queffléc d Jean Delannoy ph Robert Le Fèbvre m René Cloërc

Pierre Fresnay, Madeleine Robinson, Daniel Gélin, Andrée Clément, Sylvie, Jean Brochard

A Different Story

US 1978 106m CFI color
Avco / Alan Belkin

A homosexual falls in love with a lesbian. One supposes it had to come, but one doesn't really have to watch it.

w Henry Olek d Paul Aaron ph Philip Lathrop m David Frank

Perry King, Meg Foster, Valerie Curtin, Peter Donat

'There's something in *A Different Story* to turn off audiences of every sexual persuasion—and movie lovers most of all.'—*Richard Schickel, Time*

Digby: the Biggest Dog in the World

GB 1973 88m Technicolor
TCF / Walter Shenson

An old English sheepdog accidentally eats a chemical intended to increase the size of vegetables . . .
Nice to see this kind of gimmick used for comedy instead of horror, but the result is rather tame and old-fashioned, though for several years it made a pleasant television offering for Christmas.

w Michael Pertwee d Joseph McGrath ph Harry Waxman sp Tom Howard m Edwin T. Astley

Jim Dale, Spike Milligan, Angela Douglas, Milo O'Shea, Dinsdale Landen, Garfield Morgan, Victor Spinetti, Bob Todd

Dillinger*

US 1945 70m bw
Monogram (Frank and Maurice King)

The life of American public enemy number one who was shot by the police in 1934.
Slick, speedy gangster thriller, possibly the most tolerable movie to come from this low-budget studio.

w Philip Yordan d Max Nosseck ph Jackson Rose m Dmitri Tiomkin

Lawrence Tierney, Edmund Lowe, Anne Jeffreys

AAN: Philip Yordan

Dillinger*

US 1973 107m Movielab
AIP (Buzz Feitshans)

Violence-soaked version, with black comedy touches, of the last year of Dillinger's life. Not badly done, with a style reminiscent of *Bonnie and Clyde*.

wd John Milius ph Jules Brenner m Barry Devorzon

Warren Oates, Ben Johnson (as Melvin Purvis), Michelle Philips, Cloris Leachman, Harry Dean Stanton, Richard Dreyfuss

Dimension 5

US 1966 88m colour

CIA agents use a time converter to jump ahead three weeks and prevent the Chinese from bombing Los Angeles. Silly spy fantasy with inadequate effects. Jeffrey Hunter, France Nuyen, Harold Sakata, Donald Woods. Written by Arthur C. Pierce; directed by Franklin Adreon; for United Pictures Corporation.

Dimples**

US 1936 82m bw
TCF (Darryl F. Zanuck, Nunnally Johnson)

In the New York Bowery in pre-Civil War days, a child and her reprobate grandfather win the hearts of high society.
Excellent Temple vehicle with good period flavour.

w Arthur Sheekman, Nat Perrin d William A. Seiter ph Bert Glennon m Louis Silvers songs Jimmy McHugh, Ted Koehler

Shirley Temple, Frank Morgan, Helen Westley, Berton Churchill, Robert Kent, Delma Byron, Astrid Allwyn

Diner**

US 1982 110m Technicolor
MGM / SLM (Jerry Weintraub)

In 1959 Baltimore, college students congregate at their old meeting place and find themselves more occupied by adult problems than of yore.
Generally amusing group character study, an awkward attempt to divine the meaning of life

through the accumulation of detail. A little masterpiece of observation, for those with ears to hear; but not necessarily a great film.

wd Barry Levinson *ph* Peter Sova *m* Bruce Brody, Ivan Kral *pd* Leon Harris *ed* Stu Linder

Steve Guttenberg, Daniel Stern, Mickey Rourke, Kevin Bacon, Timothy Daly, Ellen Barkin, Paul Reiser, Kathryn Dowling, Michael Tucker, Jessica James

AAN: original screenplay

● Video: *MGM / UA*

Dingaka
South Africa 1965   97m   Technicolor Cinemascope
Embassy (Jamie Uys)

Tribal antagonisms cause a simple native to seek revenge in the city.
Unconvincing and now very dated melodrama with rather too much local colour.

wd Jamie Uys *ph* Manie Botha *m* Bertha Egnos, Eddie Domingo, Basil Gray

Ken Gampu, Stanley Baker, Juliet Prowse, Siegfried Mynhardt, Paul Makgoba

Dinky
US 1935   65m   bw

The mother of a military school cadet is framed into a prison term. Sentimental drama of little interest. Jackie Cooper, Mary Astor, Roger Pryor, Henry Armetta, Henry O'Neill, Edith Fellowes. Written by Harry Sauber; directed by D. Ross Lederman and Howard Bretherton; for Warners. 'A rapidly maturing Jackie Cooper is revealed here as lacking the strength to stand alone.'—*Variety*

Dinner at Eight***
US 1933   113m   bw
MGM (David O. Selznick)

Guests at a society dinner party all find themselves in dramatic circumstances.
Artificial but compelling pattern play from a Broadway success.

-*w* Frances Marion, Herman J. Mankiewicz, *play* George S. Kaufman, Edna Ferber *d* George Cukor *ph* William Daniels *m* William Axt

Marie Dressler, John Barrymore, Lionel Barrymore, Billie Burke, Wallace Beery, *Jean Harlow*, Lee Tracy, Edmund Lowe, Madge Evans, Jean Hersholt, Karen Morley, Louise Closser Hale, Phillips Holmes, May Robson, Grant Mitchell, Elizabeth Patterson

KITTY (Jean Harlow): 'You know, I read a book the other day. It's all about civilization or something—a nutty kind of a book. Do you know that the guy said machinery is going to take the place of every profession?'
CARLOTTA (Marie Dressler): 'Oh, my dear. That's something *you* need *never* worry about!'

'Marquee speaks for itself. It spells money, and couldn't very well be otherwise.'—*Variety*

Dinner at the Ritz
GB 1937   77m   bw
New World (Robert T. Kane)

A French girl exposes swindlers who faked her father's suicide.
Once-diverting comedy melodrama with an international cast.

w Roland Pertwee, Romney Brent *d* Harold Schuster *ph* Philip Tannura

Annabella, Paul Lukas, David Niven, Romney Brent, Stewart Rome, Francis L. Sullivan, Nora Swinburne, Frederick Leister
'Slow and shoddily made British product.'—*Variety*
'It moves with old world decorum and occasional touches of gout.'—*New York Times*

Diplomaniacs
US 1933   59m   bw

Two halfwits are offered a fortune to go to Geneva and make the peace delegates stop fighting. Fatuous comedy which never gets going. Bert Wheeler, Robert Woolsey, Hugh Herbert, Marjorie White, Phyllis Barry, Louis Calhern. Written by Joseph Mankiewicz and Henry Meyers; directed by William Seiter; for RKO. 'A baddie; rhymed dialogue no help for inane plot.'—*Variety*

Diplomatic Courier*
US 1952   98m   bw
TCF (Casey Robinson)

American and Russian agents clash on a train between Salzburg and Trieste; an unexpected master spy is revealed after several chases.
Lively cold war intrigue, well produced and played with relish.

w Casey Robinson, Liam O'Brien, *novel* Sinister Errand by Peter Cheyney *d* Henry Hathaway *ph* Lucien Ballard *md* Lionel Newman *m* Sol Kaplan

Tyrone Power, Patricia Neal, Stephen McNally, Hildegarde Neff, Karl Malden, James Millican, Herbert Berghof
'A reversion to the oldest tradition of spy fiction.'—*Penelope Houston*

Dirigible*
US 1931   102m   bw
Columbia

The story of an airship disaster.
Economical epic with a few Capra touches.

w Jo Swerling, Dorothy Howell, *story* 'Spig' Wead *d* Frank Capra *ph* Joe Wilbur, Elmer Dyer, Joseph Walker

Jack Holt, Fay Wray, Ralph Graves, Hobart Bosworth, Roscoe Karns
'Plenty of everything expected in a flying film spectacle.'—*Variety*

Dirty Dingus Magee
US 1970   91m   Metrocolor   Panavision
MGM (Burt Kennedy)

A likeable western outlaw crosses swords with an old enemy.
Fair burlesque western often stooping to vulgarity.

w Tom Waldman, Frank Waldman, Joseph Heller, *novel* David Markson *d* Burt Kennedy *ph* Harry Stradling *m* Jeff Alexander

Frank Sinatra, George Kennedy, Anne Jackson, Lois Nettleton, Jack Elam, John Dehner, Henry Jones, Harry Carey Jnr, Paul Fix
'Skittish burlesque, scripted in the brash and undisciplined style of a TV show . . . heavily reliant on the *Carry On* brand of humour.'—*David McGillivray*

'Damn them or praise them—you'll never forget them!'

The Dirty Dozen**
US / Spain 1967   150m   Metrocolor 70mm
MGM / Kenneth Hyman (Raymond Anzarut)

In 1944, twelve convicts serving life sentences are recruited for a commando suicide mission.
Professional, commercial but unlikeable slice of wartime thick ear; pretensions about capital punishment are jettisoned early on in favour of frequent and violent bloodshed. Much imitated, e.g. by *The Devil's Brigade, A Reason to Live, a Reason to Die*, etc.

w Nunnally Johnson, Lukas Heller *d* Robert Aldrich *ph* Edward Scaife *m* Frank de Vol

Lee Marvin, Ernest Borgnine, Robert Ryan, Charles Bronson, Jim Brown, John Cassavetes, George Kennedy, Richard Jaeckel, Trini Lopez, Telly Savalas, Ralph Meeker, Clint Walker, Robert Webber, Donald Sutherland

AAN: John Cassavetes

● Video: *MGM / UA*

'You don't assign him to murder cases— you just turn him loose!'

Dirty Harry**
US 1971   103m   Technicolor Panavision
Warner / Malpaso (Don Siegel)

A violently inclined San Francisco police inspector is the only cop who can bring to book a mad sniper. When the man is released through lack of evidence, he takes private revenge.
A savage cop show which became a cult and led to a spate of dirty cop movies, including two sequels, *Magnum Force* (qv) and *The Enforcer*. Well done for those who can take it.

w Harry Julian Fink, Rita M. Fink, Dean Riesner *d* Don Siegel *ph* Bruce Surtees *m* Lalo Schifrin

Clint Eastwood, Harry Guardino, Reni Santoni, John Vernon, Andy Robinson, John Larch, John Mitchum

● Video: *Warner*

Dirty Little Billy
US 1972   92m   Eastmancolor
Columbia / WRG / Dragoti (Jack L. Warner)

The violent young life of Billy the Kid.
Squalid little western with few attractive aspects except that it presents its hero as the mentally retarded delinquent which history says he was.

w Charles Moss, Stan Dragoti d Stan
Dragoti ph Ralph Woolsey m Sascha
Burland

Michael J. Pollard, Lee Purcell, Richard
Evans, Charles Aidman

'The gap between its ostensible aims and its
manner of realizing them continually leaves
the film bogged down in its own scrupulously
realistic mud.'—Tony Rayns

Dirty Mary, Crazy Larry
US 1974 92m De Luxe
Academy Pictures Corporation (Norman T.
Herman)

Two racing drivers and a kooky groupie rob a
supermarket and almost elude their police
pursuers.
Elaborately stunted chase film, agreeable
enough to watch if the characters were not so
disagreeable.

w Leigh Chapman, Antonio Santean, novel
The Chase by Richard Unekis d John Hough
ph Mike Margulies m Jimmie Haskell

Peter Fonda, Susan George, Adam Roarke,
Vic Morrow, Kenneth Tobey, Roddy
McDowall, Eugene Daniels

'The film's general delight in destruction and
despoliation makes one wonder if it is the
cinema that reflects the ugliness of modern
society or the ugliness of modern society that
reflects trends in the cinema.'—Michael
Billington, Illustrated London News

● Video: CBS / Fox

Dirty Work•••
US 1933 20m bw
Chimney sweeps cause havoc in the house of
an eccentric scientist. Hilarious star comedy
with splendid timing and comedy touches.
Laurel and Hardy, Lucien Littlefield, Sam
Adams. Written by H. M. Walker; directed by
Lloyd French; for Hal Roach.

Dirty Work
GB 1934 78m bw
Gaumont (Michael Balcon)

Shop assistants pose as crooks in order to
catch thieves.
Rather thin Ben Travers farce with some
authentic moments.

w Ben Travers, from his play d Tom Walls

Ralph Lynn, Gordon Harker, Robertson
Hare, Lillian Bond, Basil Sydney, Cecil
Parker, Margaretta Scott, Gordon James,
Peter Gawthorne

The Disappearance
GB / Canada 1977 102m Eastmancolor
Trofar / Tiberius (David Hemmings)

An international hit man finds that his wife has
disappeared.
Confusing and pretentious thriller which
spends more time on introspection than action
and ends up not satisfying anybody.

w Paul Mayersberg, novel Echoes of
Celandine by Derek Marlowe d Stuart
Cooper ph John Alcott m Robert Farnon

Donald Sutherland, Francine Racette, David
Hemmings, John Hurt, David Warner, Peter
Bowles, Virginia McKenna, Christopher
Plummer

Disbarred
US 1938 58m bw
A lady lawyer is paid by a crime czar to defend
a gangster. Slick mini-melo of the kind at
which this studio excelled at the time. Otto
Kruger, Gail Patrick, Robert Preston, Sidney
Toler, Charles D. Brown. Written by Lillie
Hayward and Robert Presnell; directed by
Robert Florey; for Paramount. 'Moderately
entertaining drama; nicely fills the lower
brackets.'—Variety

The Discreet Charm of the
Bourgeoisie•••
France / Spain / Italy 1972 105m
Eastmancolor
Greenwich (Serge Silberman)
original title: Le Charme Discret de la
Bourgeoisie

The efforts of a group of friends to dine
together are continually frustrated.
A frequently hilarious, sometimes savage
surrealist fable which makes all its points
beautifully and then goes on twenty minutes
too long. The performances are a joy.

w Luis Bunuel, Jean-Claude Carrière d Luis
Bunuel ph Edmond Richard

Fernando Rey, Delphine Seyrig, Stéphane
Audran, Bulle Ogier, Jean-Pierre Cassel, Paul
Frankeur, Julien Bertheau

'A perfect synthesis of surreal wit and
blistering social assault.'—Jan Dawson, MFB

AA: best foreign film
AAN: Luis Bunuel, Jean-Claude Carrière
(script)

The Disembodied
US 1957 73m bw
In the tropics, a doctor's wife is really a
voodoo queen who is trying to kill him by
supernatural means. Verbose rubbish with
more yawns than thrills. Allison Hayes, Paul
Burke, John Wengraf. Written by Jack
Townley; directed by Walter Grauman; for
Allied Artists.

Dishonored••
US 1931 91m bw
Paramount

An officer's widow turned streetwalker is hired
by the German government as a spy.
Rather gloomy melodrama which helped to
establish its star as a top American attraction;
but the heavy hand of her Svengali, Von
Sternberg, was already evident.

w Daniel H. Rubin d Josef Von Sternberg
ph Lee Garmes m Karl Hajos

Marlene Dietrich, Victor McLaglen, Lew
Cody, Gustav Von Seyffertitz, Warner Oland,
Barry Norton, Wilfred Lucas

'Miss Dietrich rises above her director . . .
should make the money grade of an A1 draw
talker.'—Variety

'The most exciting movie I have seen in
several months . . . yet I hope I may die young
if I ever again have to listen to a manuscript so
full of recusant, stilted, outmoded theatrical
mouthings.'—Pare Lorentz

'The whole film has a kind of magnificent
grandeur embellished, of course, by its shining
central performance.'—John Gillett, 1964

'She insulted her soul!'
Dishonored Lady
US 1947 85m bw
Mars Film (Hedy Lamarr)

A girl with a past is cleared of a murder charge
by her psychiatrist.
Melodramatic showpiece designed for herself
by a glamorous star; OK for the silly season.

w Edmund H. North, play Edward Sheldon,
Margaret Ayer Barnes d Robert Stevenson
ph Lucien Andriot m Carmen Dragon

Hedy Lamarr, John Loder, Dennis O'Keefe,
Paul Cavanagh, William Lundigan, Natalie
Schaefer, Morris Carnovsky

Dishonour Bright•
GB 1936 82m bw
GFD / Cecil (Herman Fellner, Max Schach)

An ageing playboy is blackmailed about a past
affair.
Interesting semi-smart comedy of the period,
tailored for its star.

w Ben Travers d Tom Walls

Tom Walls, Eugene Pallette, Betty Stockfeld,
Diana Churchill, Arthur Wontner, Cecil
Parker, George Sanders, Henry Oscar, Basil
Radford

The Disorderly Orderly
US 1964 89m Technicolor
Paramount / York (Paul Jones)

A hospital orderly creates havoc by his
inefficiency and his sympathy for other
people's predicaments.
Spasmodic farce with far too much pathos
between its highlights.

wd Frank Tashlin ph W. Wallace Kelley
m Joseph Lilley

Jerry Lewis, Glenda Farrell, Everett Sloane,
Kathleen Freeman, Karen Sharpe, Susan
Oliver, Alice Pearce

Disorderly Conduct
US 1932 82m bw
A cop turns crook after being demoted.
Heavy-going melodrama apparently intended
as a tribute to the New York police. Spencer
Tracy, Sally Eilers, El Brendel, Dickie Moore,
Ralph Bellamy, Ralph Morgan, Alan
Dinehart. Written by William Anthony
McGuire; directed by John W. Considine Jnr;
for Fox. 'Good entertainment . . . mother-
love sentiment with some kid atmosphere.'—
Variety

Les Disparus de St Agil•
France 1938 95m bw
Students disappear in a school whose
headmaster is a forger and murderer. Curious

black comedy: a half-success. Michel Simon,
Erich Von Stroheim, Aimé Clariond, Armand
Bernard. Written by J. H. Blanchon, from a
novel by Pierre Véry; directed by Christian-
Jaque; for Vog Films.

A Dispatch from Reuters**
US 1940   90m   bw
Warner (Henry Blanke)
GB title: *This Man Reuter*

The story of the man who provided Europe's
first news service.
Acceptable if slightly dull addition to Warner's
prestige biopics; well made and acted.

w Milton Krims *d* William Dieterle *ph* James
Wong Howe *m* Max Steiner

Edward G. Robinson, Edna Best, Eddie
Albert, Albert Basserman, Gene Lockhart,
Otto Kruger, Montagu Love, Nigel Bruce,
James Stephenson

Disputed Passage*
US 1939   90m   bw
Paramount (Harlan Thompson)

A young scientist who wants to marry meets
resistance from his mentor.
Adequate screen version of a bestseller.

w Anthony Veiller, Sheridan Gibney, *novel*
Lloyd C. Douglas *d* Frank Borzage
ph William C. Mellor *m* Frederick Hollander,
James Leopold

Dorothy Lamour, John Howard, Akim
Tamiroff, Judith Barrett, William Collier Snr,
Victor Varconi, Keye Luke, Elizabeth Risdon
  'Fine drama of medical science: a top-of-
the-bill attraction.'—*Variety*
  'I should describe the flavour as a rather
nauseating blend of iodine and glucose.'—
Graham Greene

'It dwarfs the stage!'
Disraeli*
US 1929   89m   bw
Warner

Fictionalized episodes in the life of the
Victorian statesman, including his activities as
a matchmaker.
Very early star talkie, of primarily archival
interest; Arliss had appeared in a silent
version in 1921.

w Julian Josephson, *play* Louis N. Parker
d Alfred E. Green *ph* Lee Garmes *md* Louis
Silvers

George Arliss, Joan Bennett, Florence Arliss,
Anthony Bushell, David Torrence, Ivan
Simpson, Doris Lloyd
  'Those seeking a fuller assessment of the
man and his work would have been better off
in a library.'—*Clive Hirschhorn, 1982*

AA: George Arliss
AAN: best picture; Julian Josephson

'The rescue . . . the throbbing jungle drums
  . . . the man-devouring marsh wilderness
  aflame with unseen menace!'
Distant Drums
US 1951   101m   Technicolor
United States Pictures (Milton Sperling)

A DISPATCH FROM REUTER'S.   Eddie Albert learns the theory of the pigeon post from
Edward G. Robinson.

In 1840 Florida, an army officer rescues
prisoners from an Indian fort and decimates
the Seminoles who threaten their return
journey.
Overlong action saga, with dull stretches
compensated by a dominating star and some
lively incident.

w Niven Busch, Martin Rackin *d* Raoul
Walsh *ph* Sid Hickox *m* Max Steiner

Gary Cooper, Mari Aldon, Richard Webb,
Ray Teal, Arthur Hunnicutt, Robert Barrat
  'Don't look for surprises. Mr Cooper is kept
steady and laconic throughout, the action is
serio-comic, and the pace is conventionally
maintained.'—*Bosley Crowther, New York
Times*

A Distant Trumpet
US 1964   116m   Technicolor
  Panavision
Warner (William H. Wright)

The new commander of a cavalry outpost
tightens up discipline, which serves him well
when Indian trouble erupts.
Moderate western, quite well staged but with a
second team cast.

w John Twist, *novel* Paul Horgan *d* Raoul
Walsh *ph* William Clothier *m* Max Steiner

Troy Donahue, Suzanne Pleshette, James
Gregory, Diane McBain, William Reynolds,
Claude Akins, Kent Smith, Judson Pratt

Ditte, Child of Man*
Denmark 1946   106m   bw
Nordisk
original title: *Ditte Menneskebarn*

An unmarried mother abandons her daughter,
who grows up to be a servant and to be
seduced in her turn.
Impressive, doom-laden Scandinavian saga,
highly thought of on its release.

wd Astrid and Bjarne Henning-Jensen,
novel Martin Andersen *ph* Werner Jenssen
m Herman Koppel

Tove Maes, Rasmus Ottesen, Karen Poulsen

Diva*
France 1981   117m   Eastmancolor
Galaxie / Greenwich / Antenne 2 (Irene
  Silberman)

A black prima donna in Paris becomes
accidentally involved in drug smuggling and
murder.
A curious hybrid of violence and surrealism
which doesn't seem to know what effect it's
aiming at, or at least doesn't let the viewer in
on the secret, being content to entertain in a
flashy and sometimes shocking way.

w Jean-Jacques Beineix, Jean Van Hamme,
novel Delacorta *d* Jean-Jacques Beineix
ph Philippe Rousselot *m* Vladimir Cosma
pd Hilton McConnico

Frederic Andrei, Roland Bertin, Richard Bohringer, Wilhelmenia Wiggins Fernandez, Jean-Jacques Moreau, Chantal Deruaz

● *Video: Palace*

Dive Bomber*
US 1941 133m Technicolor
Warner (Hal B. Wallis)

Aviation scientists work to eliminate pilot blackout.
Somewhat rarefied propaganda piece with too many reels of romantic banter but tense climactic scenes and good star performances.

w Frank 'Spig' Wead, Robert Buckner d Michael Curtiz ph Bert Glennon, Winton C. Hoch m Max Steiner md Leo F. Forbstein

Errol Flynn, Fred MacMurray, Ralph Bellamy, Alexis Smith, Regis Toomey, Robert Armstrong, Allen Jenkins, Craig Stevens, Moroni Olsen, Gig Young, William Hopper, Charles Drake, Russell Hicks, Addison Richards, Ann Doran, Herbert Anderson

AAN: Bert Glennon, Winton C. Hoch

The Divided Heart**
GB 1954 89m bw
Ealing (Michael Truman)

A boy believed to be a war orphan is lovingly brought up by foster parents; then his real mother turns up and wants him back.
Effective 'woman's picture' set in Europe and giving a genuine sense of post-war feelings and problems.

w Jack Whittingham d Charles Crichton ph Otto Heller m Georges Auric

Cornell Borchers, Yvonne Mitchell, Armin Dahlen, Alexander Knox, Geoffrey Keen, Michel Ray, Liam Redmond, Eddie Byrne

The Divine Lady*
US 1929 100m bw
Warner

The adventures of Emma, Lady Hamilton.
Historical charade which titillated at the time.

w Agnes Christine Johnson, Forrest Halsey d Frank Lloyd ph John Seitz

Corinne Griffith, Victor Varconi, H. B. Warner, Montagu Love, Marie Dressler

AA: Frank Lloyd
AAN: John Seitz

Divine Madness
US 1980 93m Technicolor Panavision

A record of a Bette Midler concert performance. 'Since this is the time capsule version of my show, I may as well do everything I know.' It certainly isn't a movie. Directed by Michael Ritchie; photographed by William A. Fraker; for Ladd Company / Warner.

● *Video: Warner*

The Divine Woman*
US 1927 95m approx (24 fps) bw silent
MGM

The loves of Sarah Bernhardt.

Garbo's first star role; a typical Hollywood melodramatization of facts.

w Dorothy Farnum, play Starlight by Gladys Unger d Victor Sjostrom

Greta Garbo, Lars Hanson, Lowell Sherman, John Mack Brown, Polly Moran

Divorce American Style**
US 1967 109m Technicolor
Columbia / Tandem (Norman Lear)

Well-heeled Los Angeles suburbanites toy with divorce but eventually resume their domestic bickering.
Rather arid and patchy but often sharply sardonic comedy about a society in which people can't afford to divorce.

w Norman Lear d Bud Yorkin ph Conrad Hall m David Grusin pd Edward Stephenson

Dick Van Dyke, Debbie Reynolds, Jean Simmons, Jason Robards Jnr, Van Johnson, Joe Flynn, Shelley Berman, Martin Gabel, Lee Grant, Tom Bosley, Dick Gautier

AAN: Norman Lear

A Divorce in the Family
US 1932 78m bw

A boy is affected by his parents' divorce.
Dated drama, an odd choice of vehicle for a boy star fresh from The Champ. Jackie Cooper, Conrad Nagel, Lois Wilson, Lewis Stone, Jean Parker, Lawrence Grant. Written by Delmer Daves, Maurice Rapf; directed by Charles Reisner; for MGM. 'Not more than medium box office; Cooper fans will not be attracted by the title.'—Variety

'A delightfully daring plan to give marriage a surprise ending!'
Divorce Italian Style**
Italy 1961 108m bw
Lux / Vides / Galatea (Franco Cristaldi)
original title: Divorzio all'Italiana

A Sicilian nobleman explains how, wishing to be rid of his wife, he arranged for her to be seduced and later shot by a jealous lover.
Sardonic, stylized comedy which, rather in the manner of Kind Hearts and Coronets, manages while retailing a black comedy plot to satirize Italian manners and institutions.

w Ennio de Concini, Pietro Germi, Alfredo Gianetti d Pietro Germi ph Leonida Barboni m Carlo Rustichelli

Marcello Mastroianni, Daniela Rocca, Stefania Sandrelli, Leopoldo Trieste

AA: script
AAN: Pietro Germi; Marcello Mastroianni

The Divorce of Lady X**
GB 1938 92m Technicolor
London Films (Alexander Korda)

A nobleman's daughter wins a barrister by posing as a divorce client.
Pleasing comedy with high production standards of its time, deftly performed by a distinguished cast.

w Lajos Biro, Arthur Wimperis, Ian Dalrymple, play Counsel's Opinion by Gilbert Wakefield d Tim Whelan ph Harry Stradling m Miklos Rozsa

Laurence Olivier, Merle Oberon, Binnie Barnes, Ralph Richardson, Morton Selten, J. H. Roberts

'Her sin was no greater than his, but she was a woman! If the world permits the husband to philander—why not the wife?'
The Divorcee*
US 1930 83m bw
MGM

Would-be liberal young marrieds divorce when she puts up with his affairs but he can't tolerate hers. She falls in love with another married man but sends him back to his wife.
Rather wan illustration of the double standard which was being much discussed in society at the time.

w John Meehan, Nick Grinde, Zelda Sears, novel Ex-Wife by Ursula Parrott d Robert Z. Leonard ph Norbert Brodine ad Cedric Gibbons

Norma Shearer, Chester Morris, Conrad Nagel, Robert Montgomery, Florence Eldridge

'Shearer's specialty was sexy suffering in satin gowns by Adrian; here, she almost seems to want to abandon herself to naughtiness, but one line after another stops her.'—Pauline Kael, 70s

AA: Norma Shearer
AAN: best picture; Robert Z. Leonard; John Meehan, Nick Grinde, Zelda Sears

Dixiana
US 1930 100m bw (Technicolor sequences)

A Dutchman from Pennsylvania tries to run a plantation in Louisiana. Lavish but utterly witless musical comedy which just lies there and dies there. Bebe Daniels, Bert Wheeler, Robert Woolsey, Everett Marshall, Joseph Cawthorn, Jobyna Howland, Dorothy Lee, Bill Robinson. Written and directed by Luther Reed from a play by Ann Caldwell; for RKO. 'Not much but bigness for exploiting.'—Variety

Dixie*
US 1943 90m Technicolor
Paramount (Paul Jones)

The life of old-time minstrel man Dan Emmett.
Lighter-than-air fictionalized biography with pleasing mid-19th-century settings.

w Karl Tunberg, Darrell Ware d A. Edward Sutherland ph William C. Mellor m Robert Emmet Delan songs Johnny Burke, Jimmy Van Heusen

Bing Crosby, Dorothy Lamour, Marjorie Reynolds, Lynne Overman, Eddie Foy Jnr, Billy de Wolfe, Raymond Walburn, Grant Mitchell

DOA**
US 1949 81m bw
Cardinal Pictures (Leo C. Popkin)

A businessman discovers that he has

effectively been murdered by a slow-acting poison. In the few hours left to him he tracks down and kills his murderer, and confesses to the police.

Unusual and effective thriller, well photographed on location in San Francisco and Los Angeles.

w *Russell Rouse, Clarence Greene* d *Rudolph Maté* ph *Ernest Laszlo* m *Dmitri Tiomkin*

Edmond O'Brien, Luther Adler, Pamela Britton, William Ching

† Remade 1970 as *Colour Me Dead*, with Tom Tryon.

The Do It Yourself Cartoon Kit**
GB 1961 6m Eastmancolor

A commercial for the kit in question, poking fun at all comers in a Monty Pythonish way. Great stuff for those who like zany humour well controlled. Written by *Colin Pearson*; directed by *Bob Godfrey*; for Biographic.

Do Not Disturb
US 1965 102m De Luxe Cinemascope
TCF / Melcher / Arcola (Aaron Rosenberg, Martin Melcher)

An American wool executive is posted to London; his dizzy wife makes him jealous by flirting with a French antique dealer.

Silly farce which paints a lunatic picture of English and French life but occasionally raises a wild laugh or two. Thin script and production.

w *Milt Rosen, Richard Breen, play* William Fairchild d *Ralph Levy* ph *Leon Shamroy* m *Lionel Newman*

Doris Day, Rod Taylor, *Sergio Fantoni*, Reginald Gardiner, Hermione Baddeley, Leon Askin

Do You Like Women?
France / Italy 1964 100m bw
Francoriz / Number One / Federiz (Pierre Kalfon)
original title: *Aimez-Vous Les Femmes?*

Secret rival sects of woman-eaters cause an outbreak of murders in Paris.

Bizarre black comedy that doesn't quite work but provides ghoulish fun along the way.

w *Roman Polanski, Gérard Brach, novel* Georges Bardawil d *Jean Léon* ph *Sacha Vierny* m *Ward Swingle*

Sophie Daumier, Guy Bédos, Edwige Feuillère, Grégoire Aslan, Roger Blin

'It has the provoking quality of a carefully-prepared firework display which, due to faulty timing or bad connections, is never actually ignited.'—*MFB*

Do You Love Me?
US 1946 91m Technicolor
TCF (George Jessel)

The lady dean of a music school gets herself glamorized.

Thin, mildly agreeable but forgettable musical.

w *Robert Ellis, Helen Logan* d *Gregory Ratoff* ph *Edward Cronjager* songs various

Maureen O'Hara, Dick Haymes, Harry James and his Orchestra, Reginald Gardiner, Richard Gaines, Stanley Prager

Doc*
US 1971 96m De Luxe
UA / Frank Perry

Doc Holliday goes to Tombstone to die of TB, but is drawn into the feud between the Clantons and his friend Wyatt Earp, whose motives are not of the highest.

A somewhat glum debunking of the west's most heroic myth, backing dour character study with grubby pictures. The result lacks excitement but maintains interest.

w *Pete Hamill* d *Frank Perry* ph *Gerald Hirschfeld* m *Jimmy Webb*

Stacy Keach (Doc), Harris Yulin (Earp), Faye Dunaway (Kate Elder), Mike Witney, Denver John Collins, Dan Greenberg

'The physical realism that *Doc* is at pains to establish becomes simply a convention of its own.'—*Richard Combs*

Doc Savage, Man of Bronze
US 1975 100m Technicolor
Warner (George Pal)

A thirties superman and his assistants the Amazing Five fly to South America to avenge the death of Doc's father.

Stolid, humourless adaptation from a comic strip, totally lacking in the necessary panache.

w *George Pal, Joe Morhaim, stories* Kenneth Robeson d *Michael Anderson* ph *Fred Koenekamp* m *John Philip Sousa*

Ron Ely, Paul Gleason, Bill Lucking, Michael Miller, Eldon Quick

'A slick, ultra-self-conscious camp that denies the material its self-respect.'—*Colin Pahlow*

'Nothing in this unfortunate enterprise is likely to please anyone: former Savage fans will be enraged, newcomers bored, and children will probably feel superior to the whole mess . . .'—*New Yorker*

The Dock Brief
GB 1962 88m bw
(MGM) Dimitri de Grunwald
US title: *Trial and Error*

An incompetent barrister defends his client on a murder charge. The client is found guilty but the sentence is quashed on the grounds of inadequate defence.

Flat filming of a TV play which was a minor milestone; the film is twice the length and half as funny, and both stars quickly become tiresome.

w *John Mortimer, Pierre Rouve, play* John Mortimer d *James Hill* ph *Ted Scaife* m *Ron Grainer*

Peter Sellers, Richard Attenborough

Docks of New York**
US 1928 80m (24 fps) bw silent
Paramount

A stoker marries a girl he has saved from suicide. Further unfortunate incidents result in his going to prison, but she waits for him.

Glum melodrama chiefly remarkable for its

sets and lighting, reminiscent of the later *Quai des Brumes*.

w *Jules Furthman, story* The Dock Walloper by John Monk Saunders d *Josef Von Sternberg* ph *Harold Rosson* ad Hans Dreier

George Bancroft, Betty Compson, Olga Baclanova, Clyde Cooke, Gustav Von Seyffertitz

'One comes away with the memory of a film impregnated with a life whose essential is in its energy and force.'—*Louis Chavance*

The Doctor and the Girl
US 1949 98m bw
MGM (Pandro S. Berman)

A young doctor renounces specialization to help the poor.

Antediluvian medical romance full of the nicest people. Technically very competent.

w *Theodore Reeves, from 'a literary work' by* Maxene Van Der Meersch d *Curtis Bernhardt* ph *Robert Planck* m R. G. Kopp

Glenn Ford, Charles Coburn, Gloria de Haven, Janet Leigh, Bruce Bennett, Warner Anderson

Doctor at Large
GB 1957 104m Eastmancolor
Rank (Betty E. Box)

Simon Sparrow tries two country practices, but returns at last to St Swithin's.

Hit-or-miss medical comedy with honours about even.

w *Nicholas Phipps, novel* Richard Gordon d *Ralph Thomas* ph *Ernest Steward* m *Bruce Montgomery*

Dirk Bogarde, Muriel Pavlow, James Robertson Justice, Donald Sinden, Shirley Eaton, Derek Farr, Michael Medwin, Edward Chapman, Barbara Murray, Gladys Henson, Lionel Jeffries, A. E. Matthews, Athene Seyler, George Coulouris

Doctor at Sea*
GB 1955 93m Technicolor VistaVision
Rank / Group Films (Betty E. Box)

Simon Sparrow becomes medical officer on a cargo steamer.

Reasonably lively comedy of errors with nice seascapes and predictable jokes.

w *Nicholas Phipps, Jack Davies, d* Ralph Thomas *ph* Ernest Steward *m* Bruce Montgomery

Dirk Bogarde, Brigitte Bardot, Brenda de Banzie, James Robertson Justice, Maurice Denham, Michael Medwin, Hubert Gregg, Raymond Huntley, Geoffrey Keen, George Coulouris, Jill Adams, James Kenney

'Brisk professional humour has given way to the more elementary business of traditional British farce.'—*Penelope Houston, MFB*

● *Video: Rank*

Doctor Blood's Coffin
GB 1960 92m Eastmancolor
UA / Caralan (George Fowler)

A disbarred doctor sets up in a Cornish tin mine and begins to emulate Dr Frankenstein.

Lurid horror piece which makes no sort of sense.

w Jerry Juran d Sidney J. Furie ph Stephen Dade m Buxton Orr

Kieron Moore, Hazel Court, Ian Hunter, Gerald C. Lawson, Kenneth J. Warren, Fred Johnson
'It lacks style, suspense and imagination and will scarcely satisfy even the most naive necrophiliac.'—MFB

'He's the main stem's specialist in heart trouble—and lead poisoning!'
Dr Broadway
US 1942 75m bw
A young medico gets involved with guns, girls and gangsters. Adequate filler which failed to spawn the intended series. Macdonald Carey, Jean Phillips, J. Carrol Naish, Richard Lane, Eduardo Ciannelli. Written by Art Arthur, from a story by Borden Chase; directed by Anthony Mann; for Paramount.

Dr Bull
US 1933 75m bw
A genial country doctor triumphs over his own lack of medical knowledge. Rather lumpy star vehicle which paid its way. Will Rogers, Vera Allen, Marian Nixon, Berton Churchill, Louise Dresser, Andy Devine, Ralph Morgan. Written by Paul Green from The Last Adam by James Gould Cozzens; directed by John Ford; for Fox. 'Drips with human interest and can scarcely miss.'—Variety

Dr Christian
Following the success of THE COUNTRY DOCTOR (qv), a rival studio (RKO) made a series of second features about a fictional country doctor, the rights to Dr Dafoe's life story being unavailable. Jean Hersholt again played the leading role and the films were immensely popular in small towns. A TV series followed in the fifties, starring Macdonald Carey.

1939: MEET DR CHRISTIAN
1940: THE COURAGEOUS DR CHRISTIAN, DR CHRISTIAN MEETS THE WOMEN, REMEDY FOR RICHES
1941: MELODY FOR THREE, THEY MEET AGAIN

Dr Crippen*
GB 1962 98m bw
ABP / John Clein
A quiet doctor murders his wife and elopes with a typist.
Straightforward account of a famous and rather unsurprising Edwardian murder case; well enough made but with no special raison d'être.

w Leigh Vance d Robert Lynn ph Nicolas Roeg

Donald Pleasence, Coral Browne, Samantha Eggar, Donald Wolfit

'Diabolical dictator . . . devastating discoverer of the most frightening invention in the history of civilized man!'
Dr Cyclops*
US 1940 76m Technicolor
Paramount (Merian C. Cooper)
Jungle travellers are captured and miniaturized by a mad scientist.
Splendid special effects and an appropriately sombre atmosphere are hampered by a slow-paced narrative in this minor horror classic.

w Tom Kilpatrick d Ernest Schoedsack
ph Henry Sharp, Winton Hoch m Ernst Toch, Gerard Carbonera, Albert Hay Malotte

Albert Dekker, Janice Logan, Victor Kilian, Thomas Coley, Charles Halton
'The picture made behind locked doors!'—publicity

Dr Dolittle
US 1967 152m De Luxe Todd-AO
TCF / APJAC (Arthur P. Jacobs)
In a Victorian English village, Dr Dolittle is a veterinary surgeon who talks to his patients; escaping from a lunatic asylum, he travels with friends to the South Seas in search of the Great Pink Sea Snail.
Lumpish family spectacular with no imagination whatever, further handicapped by charmless performances and unsingable songs.

w / songs Leslie Bricusse, novels Hugh Lofting d Richard Fleischer ph Robert Surtees pd Mario Chiari md Lionel Newman, Alex Courage

Rex Harrison, Anthony Newley, Samantha Eggar, Richard Attenborough, William Dix, Peter Bull

AA: song 'Talk to the Animals'
AAN: best picture; Robert Surtees; Lionel Newman, Alex Courage; Leslie Bricusse (m)

● Video: CBS / Fox

Dr Ehrlich's Magic Bullet***
US 1940 103m bw
Warner (Wolfgang Reinhardt)
aka: The Story of Dr Ehrlich's Magic Bullet
A German scientist develops a cure for venereal disease.
Excellent period biopic: absorbing, convincing and extremely well put together.

w John Huston, Heinz Herald, Norman Burnside d William Dieterle ph James Wong Howe m Max Steiner

Edward G. Robinson, Ruth Gordon, Otto Kruger, Donald Crisp, Maria Ouspenskaya, Montagu Love, Sig Rumann, Donald Meek, Henry O'Neill, Albert Basserman, Edward Norris, Harry Davenport, Louis Calhern, Louis Jean Heydt
'A superb motion picture.'—Pare Lorentz

AAN: John Huston, Heinz Herald, Norman Burnside

Dr Faustus
GB 1967 93m Technicolor
Columbia / Oxford University Screen Productions / Nassau Films / Venfilms (Richard Burton, Richard McWhorter)
A medieval scholar conjures up

Mephistopheles and offers his soul in exchange for a life of voluptuousness.
Marlowe's play has been adapted and 'improved', and there is some good handling of the poetry, but the production is flat, dingy and uninspired, as well as ludicrous when Miss Taylor makes her silent appearances.

w Nevill Coghill, play Christopher Marlowe d Richard Burton, Nevill Coghill ph Gabor Pogany m Mario Nascimbene pd John de Cuir

Richard Burton, Andreas Teuber, Ian Marter, Elizabeth Donovan, Elizabeth Taylor (as Helen of Troy)
'It is of an awfulness that bends the mind. The whole enterprise has the immense vulgarity of a collaboration in which academe would sell its soul for a taste of the glamour of Hollywood, and the stars are only too happy to appear a while in academe.'—John Simon
'It turns out to be the story of a man who sold his soul for Elizabeth Taylor.'—Judith Crist

● Video: Rank

Dr Gillespie's Criminal Case
US 1943 89m bw
The elderly doctor solves a murder for which an innocent man is in prison. Skilled programme filler with beloved characters. Lionel Barrymore, Margaret O'Brien, Donna Reed, Van Johnson, Keye Luke, Marilyn Maxwell. Written by Martin Berkeley, Harry Ruskin and Lawrence Bachmann; directed by Willis Goldbeck; for MGM. (GB title: Crazy to Kill.) See also Dr Kildare.

Dr Gillespie's New Assistant
US 1942 88m bw
Shorn of young Dr Kildare, Gillespie chooses a new support from three interns, and meanwhile concentrates on an amnesia case. Slick series entry which played widely as top of the bill. Lionel Barrymore, Van Johnson, Keye Luke, Richard Quine, Susan Peters. Written by Willis Goldbeck, Harry Ruskin and Lawrence Bachmann; directed by Willis Goldbeck; for MGM. See also Dr Kildare.

Dr Goldfoot and the Bikini Machine
US 1965 90m Pathecolor Panavision
AIP (Anthony Carras)
Dr G. makes girl robots programmed to lure wealthy men into their clutches.
Way-out farce for the jaded end of the teenage market; a few lively touches and a climactic chase partly atone for the general tastelessness.

w Elwood Ullman, Robert Kaufman d Norman Taurog ph Sam Leavitt m Les Baxter ad Daniel Haller

Vincent Price, Fred Clark, Frankie Avalon, Dwayne Hickman, Susan Hart, Jack Mullaney

'Meet the girls with the thermo-nuclear navels! The most titillating time bombs you've ever been tempted to trigger!'
Dr Goldfoot and the Girl Bombs
US / Italy 1966 86m colour

The evil mastermind teams up with Red China to cause trouble between Russia and the USA. Inane teenage nonsense, almost enough to make one swear off movies. Vincent Price, Fabian Forte, Franco Franchi, Laura Antonelli. Written by Louis M. Heyward and Robert Kaufmann; directed by Mario Bava; for AIP.

Dr Heckyl and Mr Hype
US 1980 99m Metrocolor

An ugly scientist is transformed into a handsome young sadist. Would-be comic variation on a well-worn theme; the level of comedy is indicated by the title. Oliver Reed, Sunny Johnson, Mel Wells, Maia Danziger. Written and directed by Charles B. Griffith; for Golan-Globus.

Doctor in Clover
GB 1966 101m Eastmancolor
Rank / Betty E. Box–Ralph Thomas

Grimsdyke goes back to his old hospital for a refresher course and finds a rejuvenating drug useful in his philandering.
Depressing mixture of smut and slapstick.

w Jack Davies, *novel* Richard Gordon
d Ralph Thomas ph Ernest Steward m John Scott

Leslie Phillips, James Robertson Justice, Shirley Anne Field, Joan Sims, John Fraser, Arthur Haynes, Fenella Fielding, Noel Purcell, Jeremy Lloyd, Eric Barker, Terry Scott, Alfie Bass

Doctor in Distress
GB 1963 102m Eastmancolor
Rank / Betty E. Box–Ralph Thomas

Simon Sparrow goes back to work for Sir Lancelot Spratt and finds his old mentor in love.
Tedious flummery whose characters fail to perform with the old pizazz.

w Nicholas Phipps, Ronald Scott Thorn
d Ralph Thomas ph Ernest Steward
m Norrie Paramour

Dirk Bogarde, James Robertson Justice, Mylene Demongeot, Samantha Eggar, Barbara Murray, Donald Houston, Jessie Evans, Ann Lynn, Leo McKern, Dennis Price

● *Video: Rank*

Doctor in Love
GB 1960 97m Eastmancolor
Rank / Betty E. Box–Ralph Thomas

Dr Burke and Dr Hare have various adventures, mostly amorous, in city and country practices.
Virtually plotless collection of weak sketches based on schoolboy smut.

w Nicholas Phipps, *novel* Richard Gordon
d Ralph Thomas ph Ernest Steward m Bruce Montgomery

Michael Craig, Leslie Phillips, James Robertson Justice, Virginia Maskell, Nicholas Phipps, Reginald Beckwith, Joan Sims, Liz Fraser, Ambrosine Philpotts, Irene Handl

DR JEKYLL AND MR HYDE. There seems to have been plenty of time for joking on the set of the 1931 film. Here Fredric March takes tea, Hyde fashion, with Miriam Hopkins and director Rouben Mamoulian.

Doctor in the House**
GB 1954 91m Eastmancolor
Rank (Betty Box)

Amorous and other misadventures of medical students at St Swithin's Hospital.
A comedy with much to answer for: several sequels and an apparently endless TV series. The original is not bad, as the students, though plainly over age, constitute a formidable mass of British talent at its peak.

w Nicholas Phipps, *book* Richard Gordon
d Ralph Thomas ph Ernest Steward m Bruce Montgomery

Dirk Bogarde, Kenneth More, Donald Sinden, Donald Houston, Kay Kendall, Muriel Pavlow, *James Robertson Justice*, Geoffrey Keen

'Works its way with determined high spirits through the repertoire of medical student jokes.'—*MFB*
† Sequels, of increasing inanity and decreasing connection with the original characters, were: *Doctor at Sea, Doctor at Large, Doctor in Love, Doctor in Distress, Doctor in Clover* and *Doctor in Trouble. Carry on Doctor* and *Carry on Again Doctor* were horses of a different colour.

● *Video: Rank*

Doctor in the Village*
Holland 1958 92m bw
Nationale Filmproductie Maatschappij (Bobby Roosenboom)
original title: Dorp aan de Rivier

Stories are recalled of an eccentric but respected country doctor at the turn of the century.
Tragi-comic incidents in the vein of Pagnol, a little too rich in farce and melodrama to be convincingly human.

w Hugo Claus, *novel* Antoon Coolen d Fons Rademakers ph Eduard J. R. van der Enden m Jurriaan Andriessen

Max Croiset, Mary Dresselhuys, Bernhard Droog, Jan Teulings

'Scenes which should have had disturbing power crowd one upon another with an almost repellent relish which falls over into parody.'—*Peter John Dyer, MFB*

Doctor in Trouble
GB 1970 90m Technicolor
Rank / Betty Box

Dr Burke inadvertently becomes a stowaway on an Atlantic cruise.
Witless tailpiece to the Doctor saga, like a half-hearted wrapping-up of discarded jokes from the other episodes.

w Jack Davies, *novel* Doctor on Toast by
Richard Gordon *d* Ralph Thomas *ph* Ernest
Steward *m* Eric Rogers

Leslie Phillips, Harry Secombe, Angela
Scoular, Irene Handl, Robert Morley, Simon
Dee, Freddie Jones, James Robertson Justice,
Joan Sims, John Le Mesurier, Fred Emney

Doctor Jack*
US 1922   72m approx (24 fps)   bw
silent
Pathé / Rolin

A quack country doctor does more good than
the licensed medicos.
Pleasing but not hilariously funny star vehicle.

w Sam Taylor, Jean Havez *d* Fred Newmeyer

Harold Lloyd, Mildred Davis, John Prince,
Eric Mayne

Dr Jekyll and Mr Hyde**
US 1921   63m (24 fps)   bw   silent
Paramount Artcraft

A respected London physician experiments
with a drug which separates out the evil part of
his soul.
A lively star vehicle which renewed John
Barrymore's popularity with film audiences.
Some scenes still grip, and Barrymore
accomplished some transformations in full
view of the camera, by facial contortions.

w Clara S. Beranger, *novel* Robert Louis
Stevenson *d* John S. Robertson

John Barrymore, Nita Naldi, Martha
Mansfield, Louis Wolheim

● *Video: Polygram*

'Strange desires! Loves and hates and
    secret yearnings . . . hidden in the
    shadows of a man's mind!'
Doctor Jekyll and Mr Hyde****
US 1931   98m   bw
Paramount (Rouben Mamoulian)

A Victorian research chemist finds a formula
which separates the good and evil in his soul;
when the latter predominates, he becomes a
rampaging monster.
The most exciting and cinematic version by far
of the famous horror story; the make-up is
slightly over the top, but the gas-lit London
settings, the pace, the performances and clever
camera and sound tricks make it a film to
enjoy over and over again. Subjective camera
is used at the beginning, and for the first
transformation the actor wore various layers of
make up which were sensitive to different
colour filters and thus produced instant
change.

w Samuel Hoffenstein, Percy Heath, *novel*
Robert Louis Stevenson *d* Rouben
Mamoulian *ph* Karl Struss *ad* Hans Dreier

Fredric March, Miriam Hopkins, Rose
Hobart, Holmes Herbert, Halliwell Hobbes,
Edgar Norton

'Promises abundant shocks and returns now
that the fan public is horror conscious.
Probably loses something on popular appeal
by highbrow treatment.'—*Variety*

'As a work of cinematic imagination this
film is difficult to fault.'—*John Baxter, 1968*
† The screenplay with 1,400 frame blow-ups
was published in 1976 in the Film Classics
Library (editor Richard J. Anobile).
†† The film was subsequently edited down to
80m, and this is the only version remaining.
AA: Fredric March
AAN: Samuel Hoffenstein, Percy Heath; Karl
Struss

● *Video: Polygram*

Dr Jekyll and Mr Hyde**
US 1941   122m   bw
MGM (Victor Saville, Victor Fleming)

Curiously misconceived, stately, badly cast
version with elaborate production including
Freudian dream sequences. Always worth
watching, but not a success.

w John Lee Mahin *d* Victor Fleming
ph Joseph Ruttenberg *m* Franz Waxman

Spencer Tracy, Ingrid Bergman, Lana Turner,
Ian Hunter, C. Aubrey Smith, Donald Crisp,
Sara Allgood

'Not so much evil incarnate as ham rampant
. . . more ludicrous than dreadful.'—*New
York Times*
'A romantic gentleman by day—a love-mad
beast at night!'—*publicity*
† Other versions: *The Two Faces of Dr Jekyll*
(1960), *I Monster* (1970). Variations: *Daughter
of Dr Jekyll* (1957), *Abbott and Costello Meet
Dr Jekyll and Mr Hyde* (1954), *Son of Dr
Jekyll* (1951), *The Ugly Duckling* (1960),
House of Dracula (1945), *The Nutty Professor*
(1963), *Dr Jekyll and Sister Hyde* (1971).

AAN: Joseph Ruttenberg; Franz Waxman

Dr Jekyll and Sister Hyde*
GB 1971   97m   Technicolor
Hammer (Albert Fennell, Brian Clemens)

A twist: Jekyll now turns into a young and
beautiful woman, and kills prostitutes so that
he can continue his research.
Half-successful attempt to link the legend with
Jack the Ripper, killed by gore and
overlength.

w Brian Clemens *d* Roy Ward Baker
ph Norman Warwick *m* David Whitaker

Ralph Bates, Martine Beswick, Gerald Sim,
Lewis Fiander, Dorothy Alison

● *Video: Thorn EMI*

Dr Kildare
This long-running screen hero was a young
intern at Blair Hospital, under the cranky
tutelage of old Dr Gillespie. Created by Max
Brand in a series of novels, he first appeared
on the screen in a 1937 Paramount double-
biller called INTERNS CAN'T TAKE
MONEY, played by Joel McCrea with
Barbara Stanwyck, no less, providing the love
interest. Kildare came up against gangsters;
Gillespie did not appear. MGM then took
over the property and went to town with it,
making fifteen films in ten years. They were as
follows:

1938: YOUNG DR KILDARE
1939: CALLING DR KILDARE, THE
SECRET OF DR KILDARE
1940: DR KILDARE'S STRANGE CASE
(qv), DR KILDARE GOES HOME (qv), DR
KILDARE'S CRISIS (qv)
1941: THE PEOPLE vs DR KILDARE
1942: DR KILDARE'S WEDDING DAY
(qv)
1942: DR KILDARE'S VICTORY (qv),
CALLING DR GILLESPIE, DR
GILLESPIE'S NEW ASSISTANT (qv)
1943: DR GILLESPIE'S CRIMINAL CASE
(qv)
1944: THREE MEN IN WHITE, BETWEEN
TWO WOMEN
1947: DARK DELUSION

Lew Ayres played Kildare, but in 1942
declared himself a conscientious objector and
was dropped. The emphasis shifted to
Gillespie, played by Lionel Barrymore from a
wheelchair, and he proceeded to deal with a
whole series of interns. The films were well
enough made on medium budgets; nine were
directed by Harold S. Bucquet and the last five
by Willis Goldbeck, one by W. S. Van Dyke.
In 1961 a TV series began with Richard
Chamberlain and Raymond Massey, and ran
for seven years.

Dr Kildare Goes Home
US 1940   79m   bw

Young Dr Kildare temporarily deserts Blair
Hospital to help his father establish a small-
town clinic. Rather below par episode with
obvious outcome. Lew Ayres, Lionel
Barrymore, Laraine Day, Samuel S. Hinds,
Gene Lockhart. Written by Willis Goldbeck
and Harry Ruskin; directed by Harold S.
Bucquet; for MGM.

Dr Kildare's Strange Case
US 1940   77m   bw

The young doctor cures a mental patient by
the newest methods. Crisp series episode. Lew
Ayres, Lionel Barrymore, Laraine Day,
Shepperd Strudwick, Samuel S. Hinds.
Written by Willis Goldbeck and Harry Ruskin;
directed by Harold S. Bucquet; for MGM.

Dr Kildare's Crisis
US 1940   75m   bw

Dr Kildare's fiancée may have epilepsy in the
family. The series at its peak. Lew Ayres,
Lionel Barrymore, Robert Young, Laraine
Day, Nat Pendleton, Marie Blake. Written by
Willis Goldbeck and Harry Ruskin; directed
by Harold S. Bucquet; for MGM.

Dr Kildare's Victory
US 1942   92m   bw
GB title: *The Doctor and the Débutante*

Back at Blair, Dr Kildare fights ambulance
zoning regulations. Rather heavy-going
episode, its star's last before becoming a
conscientious objector and leaving Hollywood
for the duration. Lew Ayres, Lionel
Barrymore, Ann Ayars, Robert Sterling.
Written by Harry Ruskin and Willis Goldbeck;
directed by W. S. Van Dyke; for MGM.

Dr Kildare's Wedding Day
US 1941 83m bw

Dr Kildare's fiancée is killed in a road accident. Rather deliberately downbeat episode, well enough assembled. Lew Ayres, Lionel Barrymore, Laraine Day, Red Skelton, Nils Asther. Written by Lawrence Bachmann and Ormond Ruthven; directed by Harold S. Bucquet; for MGM. (GB title: *Mary Names the Day*.)

Dr Knock*
France 1936 74m bw

A sly young doctor takes over a country practice and turns the townsfolk into hypochondriacs. Amusing version of a modern French comedy classic. *Louis Jouvet*, Palau, Le Vigan, Moor, Alexandre Rignault. Written by *Jules Romains* from his play; directed by Louis Jouvet and Roger Goupillières; for Pathé-Natan. 'Once under way it scoots along like a Bermuda sloop, and holds right till the surprise fadeout.'—*Variety*

Doctor Mabuse the Gambler***
Germany 1922 101m (24 fps) bw silent
UFA
original title: *Doktor Mabuse, der Spieler*

A criminal mastermind uses hypnotism and blackmail in his efforts to obtain world domination, but when finally cornered is discovered to be a raving maniac.
A real wallow in German post-war depression and melodrama, in the form of a Fu Manchu / Moriarty type thriller. Fascinating scene by scene, but by now a slightly tiresome whole.
w Thea Von Harbou, Fritz Lang, *novel* Norbert Jacques *d Fritz Lang ph* Carl Hoffman *ad* Otto Hunte, Stahl-Urach, Erich Kettelhut, Karl Vollbrecht
Rudolph Klein-Rogge, Alfred Abel, Gertrude Welcker, Lil Dagover, Paul Richter
† Originally issued in Germany in two parts, *Der Grosse Spieler* and *Inferno*, adding up to a much longer running time.
†† See sequels, *The Testament of Dr Mabuse* and *The Thousand Eyes of Dr Mabuse*.

● Video: Thorn EMI

Dr Monica
US 1934 80m bw
Warner (Henry Blanke)

A lady doctor allows her husband to fall for another woman.
Heavy-handed 'woman's picture' which did well at the time.
w Charles Kenyon, *play* Marja Morozowicz
d William Keighley
Kay Francis, Warren William, Jean Muir, Verree Teasdale, Philip Reed, Emma Dunn

Doctor No***
GB 1962 111m Technicolor
UA / Eon (Harry Saltzman, Albert R. Broccoli)

A British secret service agent foils a master criminal operating in the West Indies.

First of the phenomenally successful James Bond movies, mixing sex, violence and campy humour against expensive sets and exotic locales. Toned down from the original novels, they expressed a number of sixties attitudes, and proved unstoppable box office attractions for nearly fifteen years. The first was, if not quite the best, reasonably representative of the series.
w Richard Maibaum, Johanna Harwood, Berkely Mather, *novel* Ian Fleming *d* Terence Young *ph* Ted Moore *m* Monty Norman
Sean Connery, Ursula Andress, Jack Lord, Joseph Wiseman, John Kitzmiller, Bernard Lee, Lois Maxwell, Zena Marshall, Eunice Gayson, Anthony Dawson
† The subsequent titles, all qv, were *From Russia with Love* (1963), *Goldfinger* (1964), *Thunderball* (1965), *You Only Live Twice* (1967), *On Her Majesty's Secret Service* (1969), *Diamonds Are Forever* (1971), *Live and Let Die* (1973), *The Man with the Golden Gun* (1974), *The Spy Who Loved Me* (1977), *Moonraker* (1979), *For Your Eyes Only* (1981), *Octopussy* (1983), *Never Say Never Again* (1984).
Casino Royale (1967) was a Bond spoof made by other hands.
● Video: Warner

Dr Phibes Rises Again*
GB 1972 89m De Luxe
AIP (Richard Dalton)

The immortal Phibes and his wife rise from the dead to seek an Egyptian elixir of life, and cross swords with a satanic Egyptologist. Uncertainly paced but generally zippy comic strip for adults, with all concerned entering gleefully into the evil spirit of the thing. See prequel, *The Abominable Dr Phibes*.
w Robert Fuest, Robert Blees *d* Robert Fuest *ph* Alex Thomson *m* John Gale *ad* Brian Eatwell
Vincent Price, Robert Quarry, Valli Kemp, Fiona Lewis, Peter Cushing, Beryl Reid, Terry-Thomas, Hugh Griffith, *Peter Jeffrey*, Gerald Sim, John Thaw, John Cater, Lewis Fiander
'It's refreshing to find a sequel which is better than its prototype.'—*Philip Strick, MFB*

Dr Renault's Secret
US 1942 58m bw

A scientist turns an ape into a semi-human, which runs amok. Fairly well done horror support. George Zucco, J. Carrol Naish, John Shepperd, Lynne Roberts. Written by William Bruckner and Robert F. Metzler; directed by Harry Lachman; for TCF.

Dr Rhythm*
US 1938 80m bw

A veterinary surgeon goes into show business. Easy-going star musical with pleasant songs. Bing Crosby, Beatrice Lillie, Mary Carlisle, Andy Devine, Laura Hope Crews, Rufe Davis. Written by Jo Swerling, Richard Connell, from a story by O. Henry; directed by Frank Tuttle; for Paramount.

Dr Socrates*
US 1935 70m bw
Warner (Robert Lord)

A small-town doctor is forced to help wounded gangsters, and becomes involved. Good star melodrama.
w Robert Lord, *novel* W. R. Burnett
d William Dieterle *ph* Tony Gaudio *md* Leo F. Forbstein
Paul Muni, Ann Dvorak, Barton Maclane, Robert Barrat, John Eldridge, Hobart Cavanaugh, Mayo Methot, Samuel S. Hinds, Henry O'Neill
'Arriving at the tail end of the G-man and gangster cycle, Dr Socrates is a graceful valedictory.'—*Variety*
'Rapid, strong and exciting.'—*Sunday Times*
† Remade as *King of the Underworld* and *Bullet Scars*.

'The hot line suspense comedy!'
Dr Strangelove; or, How I Learned to Stop Worrying and Love the Bomb***
GB 1963 93m bw
Columbia / Stanley Kubrick (Victor Lyndon)

A mad USAF general launches a nuclear attack on Russia, and when recall attempts fail, and retaliation is inevitable, all concerned sit back to await the destruction of the world. Black comedy resolving itself into a series of sketches, with the star playing three parts (for no good reason): the US president, an RAF captain, and a mad German-American scientist. Historically an important film in its timing, its nightmares being those of the early sixties, artistically it clogs its imperishable moments by untidy narrative and unattractively contrasty photography.
w Stanley Kubrick, Terry Southern, Peter George, *novel* Red Alert by Peter George *d* Stanley Kubrick *ph* Gilbert Taylor *m* Laurie Johnson *ad* Ken Adam
Peter Sellers, George C. Scott, Peter Bull, Sterling Hayden, Keenan Wynn, Slim Pickens, James Earl Jones, Tracy Reed
GENERAL (George C. Scott): 'I don't say we wouldn't get our hair mussed, but I do say no more than ten to twenty million people killed.'
'Scarcely a picture of relentless originality; seldom have we seen so much made over so little.'—*Joan Didion*
† *Fail Safe* (qv), which took the same theme more seriously, was released almost simultaneously.
AAN: best picture; script; Stanley Kubrick (as director); Peter Sellers

Dr Syn*
GB 1937 80m bw
Gaumont

The vicar of Dymchurch in 1780 is really a pirate believed dead.
This now obscure, lively pirate yarn was its star's last film.
w Michael Hogan, Roger Burford, *novel* Russell Thorndike *d* Roy William Neill *ph* Jack Cox *md* Louis Levy

George Arliss, Margaret Lockwood, John Loder, Roy Emerton, Graham Moffatt, Frederick Burtwell, Meinhart Maur, George Merritt

'With Arliss in the name part it doesn't ring true.'—*Variety*

Dr Syn Alias the Scarecrow
GB 1962 98m Technicolor
Walt Disney (Bill Anderson)

The vicar of Dymchurch is really a smuggler who manages to outwit a rascally general and save a prisoner from Dover Castle.
Oddly released the same year as another version of the story, *Captain Clegg*, this rather set-bound adventure yarn turns its hero into a Robin Hood figure. It was originally made to be shown in three parts on American TV.

w Robert Westerby, *novel* Christopher Syn by Russell Thorndike, William Buchanan d James Neilson ph Paul Beeson m Gerard Schurmann

Patrick McGoohan, George Cole, Tony Britton, Geoffrey Keen, Kay Walsh, Patrick Wymark, Alan Dobie, Eric Pohlmann

The Doctor Takes a Wife*
US 1940 89m bw
Columbia (William Perlberg)

A young doctor has to pretend to be the husband of a socialite.
Typical high life comedy of its period, quite brisk and diverting.

w George Seaton, Ken Englund d Alexander Hall ph Sid Hickox m Frederick Hollander md Morris Stoloff

Loretta Young, Ray Milland, Edmund Gwenn, Reginald Gardiner, Gail Patrick, Frank Sully, George Metaxa, Charles Halton, Chester Clute

Dr Terror's House of Horrors
GB 1965 98m Techniscope
Amicus (Milton Subotsky)

An eccentric, who turns out to be Death himself, tells the fortunes of five men in a railway carriage.
One of the first Amicus horror compendiums and a weak one, not helped by wide screen, a couple of naïve scripts and ho-hum acting. The book-ends are quite pleasant, though.

w Milton Subotsky d Freddie Francis ph Alan Hume m Elisabeth Lutyens
Peter Cushing, Ursula Howells, Max Adrian, Roy Castle, Alan Freeman, Bernard Lee, Jeremy Kemp, Kenny Lynch, Christopher Lee, Michael Gough, Donald Sutherland
† Later collections from the same stable include *Torture Garden, Tales from the Crypt, Vault of Horror* and *Asylum*.

Dr Who and the Daleks
GB 1965 83m Techniscope
British Lion / Regal / Aaru (Milton Subotsky, Max J. Rosenberg)

Three children and their grandfather accidentally start his time machine and are whisked away to a planet where villainous robots rule.

Junior science fiction from the BBC series. Limply put together, and only for indulgent children.

w Milton Subotsky d Gordon Flemyng ph John Wilcox m Malcolm Lockyer

Peter Cushing, Roy Castle, Jennie Linden, Roberta Tovey, Barrie Ingham
† A sequel, no better, emerged in 1966: *Daleks: Invasion Earth 2150 AD*, with similar credits except that Bernard Cribbins instead of Roy Castle provided comic relief.

Dr X**
US 1932 82m Technicolor
Warner (Hal Wallis)

A reporter investigates a series of moon murders and narrows his search to one of several doctors at a medical college.
Fascinating, German-inspired, overblown and generally enjoyable horror mystery whose armless villain commits murders by growing limbs from 'synthetic flesh'.

w Earl Baldwin, Robert Tasker, *play* Howard W. Comstock, Allen C. Miller d Michael Curtiz ph Richard Tower, Ray Rennahan md Leo Forbstein

Lee Tracy, Lionel Atwill, Preston Foster, Fay Wray, George Rosener, Mae Busch, Arthur Edmund Carewe, John Wray

'The settings, lighting and final battle with the man-monster are quite stunning.'—*NFT, 1974*
'It almost makes Frankenstein seem tame and friendly.'—*New York Times*

Doctor You've Got to be Kidding
US 1967 93m Metrocolor Panavision
MGM / Trident (Douglas Laurence)

A girl arrives at a maternity hospital chased by three prospective husbands.
Wild and wacky farce which leaves little impression.

w Phillip Shuken, *novel* Patte Wheat Mahan d Peter Tewkesbury ph Fred Koenekamp m Kenyon Hopkins

Sandra Dee, George Hamilton, Celeste Holm, Bill Bixby, *Dwayne Hickman*, Dick Kallman, Mort Sahl, Allen Jenkins

'A love caught in the fire of revolution!'
Doctor Zhivago***
US 1965 192m Metrocolor
Panavision 70
MGM / Carlo Ponti

A Moscow doctor is caught up in World War I, exiled for writing poetry, forced into partisan service and separated from his only love.
Beautifully photographed and meticulously directed, this complex epic has been so reduced from the original novel that many parts of the script simply do not make any kind of sense. What remains is a collection of expensive set pieces, great for looking if not listening.

w Robert Bolt, *novel* Boris Pasternak d David Lean ph Frederick A. Young m Maurice Jarre

Omar Sharif, Julie Christie, Rod Steiger, Alec Guinness, Rita Tushingham, Ralph Richardson, Tom Courtenay, Geraldine Chaplin, Siobhan McKenna, Noel Willman, Geoffrey Keen, Adrienne Corri

'A long haul along the road of synthetic lyricism.'—*MFB*
'David Lean's *Doctor Zhivago* does for snow what his *Lawrence of Arabia* did for sand.'—*John Simon*
'It isn't shoddy (except for the music); it isn't soap opera; it's stately, respectable, and dead. Neither the contemplative Zhivago nor the flow of events is intelligible, and what is worse, they seem unrelated to each other.'—*Pauline Kael*

AA: Robert Bolt; Frederick A. Young; Maurice Jarre
AAN: best picture; David Lean; Tom Courtenay

● *Video: MGM / UA*

A Doctor's Diary
US 1937 77m bw

The resident physician of a privately-endowed hospital is impatient with the niceties of procedure. Unsurprising medical drama which adequately filled half a bill. George Bancroft, John Trent, Helen Burgess, Ruth Coleman, Charles Waldron, Ra Hould, Sidney Blackmer. Written by Sam Ornitz, Joseph Anthony; directed by Charles Vidor; for Paramount. 'Packs enough drama to hold attention.'—*Variety*

The Doctor's Dilemma*
GB 1958 99m Metrocolor
MGM / Anatole de Grunwald

Eminent Harley Street surgeons debate the case of a devoted wife and her tubercular artist husband.
Well acted but curiously muffled filming of Shaw's Edwardian play about ethics and human values.

w Anatole de Grunwald, *play* Bernard Shaw d Anthony Asquith ph Robert Krasker m Joseph Kosma ad Paul Sheriff

Leslie Caron, Dirk Bogarde, *John Robinson*, Alastair Sim, Felix Aylmer, Robert Morley, Michael Gwynn, Maureen Delany, Alec McCowen

Doctors' Wives
US 1970 102m Eastmancolor
Columbia / M. J. Frankovich

When Dr Dellman shoots his unfaithful wife, his colleagues reconsider their sex lives.
Adult soap opera from talents who at other times have found better things to do. In the sensational circumstances, two sanguinary operation sequences are tastelessly irrelevant.

w Daniel Taradash, *novel* Frank G. Slaughter d George Schaefer ph Charles B. Lang m Elmer Bernstein

Richard Crenna, Janice Rule, Gene Hackman, John Colicos, Dyan Cannon, Diana Sands, Rachel Roberts, Carroll O'Connor, Cara Williams, Ralph Bellamy, Richard Anderson

'Crisis follows hard on crisis to breathlessly ludicrous effect.'—*Tom Milne*

'West of Chicago there was no law! West
of Dodge City there was no God!'

Dodge City***
US 1939   104m   Technicolor
Warner (Robert Lord)

An ex-soldier and trail boss helps clean up the
west's great railroad terminus.
Standard, satisfying big-scale western with all
clichés intact and very enjoyable, as is the soft,
rich early colour. The story is plainly inspired
by the exploits of Wyatt Earp.

w Robert Buckner d Michael Curtiz ph Sol
Polito, Ray Rennahan m Max Steiner

Errol Flynn, Olivia de Havilland, Ann
Sheridan, Bruce Cabot, Alan Hale, Frank
McHugh, John Litel, Victor Jory, William
Lundigan, Henry Travers, Henry O'Neill,
Guinn Williams, Gloria Holden
  'A lusty western, packed with action,
including some of the dandiest mêlée stuff
screened.'—Variety
  'It looks programmed and underpopulated,
though in an elegantly stylized way.'—New
Yorker, 1980

Dodsworth***
US 1936   101m   bw
Samuel Goldwyn

An American businessman takes his wife on a
tour of Europe, and their lives are changed.
Satisfying, well-acted drama from a bestselling
novel; production values high.

w Sidney Howard, novel Sinclair Lewis
d William Wyler ph Rudolph Maté m Alfred
Newman

Walter Huston, Mary Astor, Ruth Chatterton,
David Niven, Paul Lukas, Gregory Gaye,
Maria Ouspenskaya, Odette Myrtil, Spring
Byington, John Payne
  'No one, I think, will fail to enjoy it, in spite
of its too limited and personal plot, the sense
it leaves behind of a very expensive, very
contemporary, Bond Street vacuum flask.'—
Graham Greene
  'William Wyler has had the skill to execute
it in cinematic terms, and a gifted cast has
been able to bring the whole alive to our
complete satisfaction.'—New York Times
  'A smoothly flowing narrative of substantial
interest, well-defined performances and good
talk.'—New York Times
AAN: best picture; Sidney Howard; William
Wyler; Walter Huston; Maria Ouspenskaya

Dog Day Afternoon**
US 1975   130m   Technicolor
Warner / AEC (Martin Bregman, Martin
Elfland)

Two incompetent robbers are cornered in a
Brooklyn bank.
Recreation of a tragi-comic episode from the
newspaper headlines; for half its length a
fascinating and acutely observed film which
then bogs itself down in a surplus of talk and
excessive sentiment about homosexuality.

w Frank Pierson, book Patrick Mann
d Sidney Lumet ph Victor J. Kemper m none
Al Pacino, John Cazale, Charles Durning,
Sully Boyar, James Broderick, Chris Sarandon

DODGE CITY. The railroad, cause of many a fracas . . .

  'There is plenty of Lumet's vital best here in
a film that at least glancingly captures the
increasingly garish pathology of our urban
life.'—Jack Kroll
  'Scattered moments of wry humour, sudden
pathos and correct observation.'—John Simon
  'The mask of frenetic cliché doesn't spoil
moments of pure reporting on people in
extremity.'—New Yorker
  'A long and wearying case history of the
beaten, sobbing, despairing and ultimately
powerless anti-hero.'—Karyn Kay, Jump Cut
  'Full of galvanic mirth rooted in human
desperation.'—Michael Billington, Illustrated
London News
  'Brisk, humorous and alive with urban
energies and angers fretting through the 92
degree heat.'—Sight and Sound

AA: Frank Pierson
AAN: best picture; Sidney Lumet; Al Pacino;
Chris Sarandon

● Video: Warner

A Dog of Flanders
US 1959   97m   De Luxe   Cinemascope
TCF / Associated Producers (Robert B.
Radnitz)

A small boy wants to be an artist; when he
runs away in frustration, his shaggy dog,
formerly a stray, leads his family to him.

Old-fashioned tear-jerker for well-brought-up
children, previously filmed as a silent; quite
accomplished in presentation.

w Ted Sherdeman, novel Ouida d James B.
Clark ph Otto Heller m Paul Sawtell, Bert
Shefter

David Ladd, Donald Crisp, Theodore Bikel,
Max Croiset, Monique Ahrens

A Dog's Life*
US 1918   30m approx   bw   silent
First National / Charles Chaplin

A tramp and a stray mongrel help each other
towards a happy ending.
Threatening sentiment is kept at bay by
amusing sight gags in this pleasing star
featurette.

wd Charles Chaplin ph Rollie Totheroh
Charles Chaplin, Edna Purviance, Chuck
Riesner, Henry Bergman, Albert Austin,
Scraps

Dogpound Shuffle
Canada 1974   97m   Eastmancolor

An old Irish hobo lives on the earnings of his
dancing dog. Dog-eared 'family film' which
didn't seem to entertain many families. Ron
Moody, David Soul, Ray Stricklyn. Written
and directed by Jeffrey Bloom; for Elliott
Kastner / Bulldog. (Aka: Spot.)

... is regarded thoughtfully by Alan Hale and Errol Flynn.

The Dogs of War
GB 1980   118m   Technicolor
UA / Silverwold (Norman Jewison, Patrick Palmer)

A disenchanted mercenary becomes involved in a plot to take over an impoverished West African state.
Tough but seemingly dated modern irony, somewhat lacking in action and surprise.

w Gary DeVore, George Malko novel Frederick Forsyth d John Irvin ph Jack Cardiff m Geoffrey Burgon

Christopher Walken, Tom Berenger, Colin Blakely, Hugh Millais, Paul Freeman, Robert Urquhart

● Video: Warner

La Dolce Vita**
Italy / France 1960   173m   bw   Totalscope
Riama / Pathé Consortium (Giuseppe Amato)
aka: The Sweet Life

A journalist mixes in modern Roman high society and is alternately bewitched and sickened by what he sees.
Episodic satirical melodrama, a marathon self-indulgent wallow with a wagging finger never far away. Not a successful whole, but full of choice moments such as a statue of Christ being flown by helicopter over the city.

w Federico Fellini, Tullio Pinelli, Ennio Flaiano, Brunello Rondi d Federico Fellini ph Otello Martelli m Nino Rota ad Piero Gherardi

Marcello Mastroianni, Anita Ekberg, Anouk Aimée, Alain Cuny, Yvonne Furneaux, Magali Noel, Nadia Gray, Lex Barker
'Its personification of various familiar symbols—love, death, purity, sin, reason and so on—never succeeds in reflecting human values or creating intellectual excitement . . . Its actual significance rests in the way its (albeit specious) social attack has stirred the imagination of other Italian film-makers, as well as public interest in their work.'—Robert Vas, MFB

AAN: script; Federico Fellini

Doll Face
US 1945   80m   bw
TCF (Bryan Foy)
GB title: Come Back to Me

A burlesque queen goes to Broadway. Lower case musical of minimal interest.

w Leonard Praskins d Lewis Seiler ph Joseph La Shelle songs Harold Adamson, Jimmy McHugh

Vivian Blaine, Dennis O'Keefe, Carmen Miranda, Perry Como, Martha Stewart, Michael Dunne, Reed Hadley, George E. Stone, Donald McBride, Edgar Norton

The Dollar Bottom
GB 1981   33m   Eastmancolor

A sharp-witted public schoolboy sells his friends insurance against being beaten. Ingenious but thinly acted short, with the added hazard of impenetrable accents. Rikki Fulton, Robert Urquhart, Jonathan McNeil. Written by Shane Connaughton, from the story by James Kennaway; directed by Roger Christian; for Rocking Horse Films / Paramount.

Dollars*
US 1971   120m   Technicolor
Columbia / M. J. Frankovich
GB title: The Heist

An American security expert installs an electronic system in a Hamburg bank which he plans to rob himself.
Overlong caper comedy-drama which is quite good to watch when it starts moving, though the quick cutting, short takes and deliberately obscure narrative leave one breathless.

wd Richard Brooks ph Petrus Schloemp m Quincy Jones

Warren Beatty, Goldie Hawn, Gert Frobe, Robert Webber, Scott Brady, Arthur Brauss
'An essay in virtuoso film construction . . . rather as if one were watching a perfect machine in full throttle but with nowhere to go.'—John Gillet

A Doll's House*
GB 1973   95m   Eastmancolor
Elkins / Freeward (Hillard Elkins)

A wife begins to resist her husband's will. Ibsen's feminist play was always good value; set in Norway in the nineties, it was taken up eighty years later as a precursor of women's lib, which accounts for two film versions in one year. This one is simply staged and well performed, but suffers from a bad translation.

w Christopher Hampton, play Henrik Ibsen d Patrick Garland ph Arthur Ibbetson m John Barry

Claire Bloom, Anthony Hopkins, Ralph Richardson, Denholm Elliott, Anna Massey, Edith Evans

A Doll's House
GB / France 1973   106m   Eastmancolor
World Film Services / Les Films de la Boétie (Joseph Losey)

Opened out but less effective version of the above, with too much solemnity and the central part miscast.

w David Mercer, play Henrik Ibsen d Joseph Losey ph Gerry Fisher m Michel Legrand

Jane Fonda, David Warner, Trevor Howard, Edward Fox, Delphine Seyrig, Anna Wing

The Dolly Sisters**
US 1945 114m Technicolor
TCF (George Jessel)

The lives of a Hungarian sister act in American vaudeville.
Fictionalized biographical musical, only fair in the script department but glittering to look at in superb colour, and enriched by splendid production values. Undoubtedly among the best of its kind.

w John Larkin, Marian Spitzer d Irving Cummings ph Ernest Palmer md Alfred Newman, Charles Henderson songs various ch Seymour Felix ad Lyle Wheeler, Leland Fuller

Betty Grable, June Haver, John Payne, S. Z. Sakall, Reginald Gardiner, Frank Latimore, Gene Sheldon, Sig Rumann, Trudy Marshall

AAN: song 'I Can't Begin to Tell You' (m Johnny Monaco, ly Mack Gordon)

w Alfred Machard, Leonide Moguy d Leonide Moguy ph Mario Craveri, Renato del Frate m Alessandro Cicognini

Vittorio de Sica, Lois Maxwell, Gabrielle Dorziat, Anna Maria Pierangeli, Gino Leurini

Domani è Troppo Tardi
Italy 1950 101m bw
Rizzoli (Giuseppe Amato)
GB title: Tomorrow Is Too Late

Inquisitive pupils and repressive teachers at a co-educational school almost cause a tragedy.
Possibly well intentioned, but in effect an old-fashioned melodrama which works well enough on its level.

w Alfred Machard, Leonide Moguy d Leonide Moguy ph Mario Craveri, Renato del Frate m Alessandro Cicognini

Vittorio de Sica, Lois Maxwell, Gabrielle Dorziat, Anna Maria Pierangeli, Gino Leurini

Domenica d'Agosto**
Italy 1950 75m bw
Colonna (Sergio Amidei)
GB title: Sunday in August

Various Romans enjoy Sunday by the sea at Ostia.
Fragmented comedy-drama which succeeds in being charming throughout, every detail being freshly observed through an inquisitive eye.

w Franco Brusati, Luciano Emmer, Giulio Macchi, Cesare Zavattini d Luciano Emmer ph Domenico Scala, Leonida Barboni, Ubaldo Marelli m Roman Vlad ed Jolanda Benvenuti

Anna Baldini, Franco Interlenghi, Elvy Lissiak, Massimo Serato, Marcello Mastroianni, Corrado Verga

The Dominant Sex
GB 1937 71m bw

A woman demands the right to her own individuality after marriage. Tepid comedy drama from a popular stage play. Phillips Holmes, Diana Churchill, Carol Goodner, Romney Brent, Hugh Miller, Billy Milton. Written by Vino de Vesci, John Fernald, from the play by Michael Kean: directed by Herbert Brenon; for Associated British.

Dominique
GB 1978 100m colour
Grand Prize / Melvin Simon (Milton Subotsky, Andrew Donally)

A woman who was convinced that her husband was deliberately driving her mad is found dead, and buried, but seemingly returns . . .
The old Diabolique syndrome revamped in a very parsimonious production with little to hold the interest.

w Edward and Valerie Abraham, novel What Beckoning Ghost by Harold Lawlor d Michael Anderson ph Ted Moore m David Whitaker

Cliff Robertson, Jean Simmons, Jenny Agutter, Simon Ward, Ron Moody, Judy Geeson, Michael Jayston, Flora Robson, David Tomlinson, Jack Warner.

● Video: Guild

The Domino Principle
US 1977 100m CFI color
Associated General Films (Lew Grade, Martin Starger) / Stanley Kramer
GB title: The Domino Killings

A murderer is offered his freedom if he will assassinate a national figure.
Fashionable, complex and rather boring political thriller.

w Adam Kennedy, from his novel d Stanley Kramer ph Fred Koenekamp, Ernest Laszlo m Billy Goldenberg

Gene Hackman, Richard Widmark, Candice Bergen, Mickey Rooney, Edward Albert, Eli Wallach, Ken Swofford, Neva Patterson

'Terrible movies tend to start with a preposterous premise and then laboriously work their way to an impossible conclusion. This one however starts with an arrant impossibility and works its way to whatever lies beyond and below that.'—John Simon

● Video: Precision

Don Camillo's Last Round*
Italy 1955 98m bw
Rizzoli
original title: Don Camillo e l'Onorevole Peppone

The village Catholic priest tries to stop the re-election of the communist mayor.
Pleasant third collection of encounters with familiar characters.

w Giovanni Guareschi and others, from his books d Carmine Gallone ph Anchise Brizzi m Alessandro Cicognini

Fernandel, Gino Cervi, Claude Silvain, Leda Gloria

'The episodic narrative is full of mildly amusing incident.'—MFB

Don Giovanni
France-Italy-Germany 1979 184m colour
Gaumont-Opera-Camera One (Michel Seydoux)

Grandiose but artistically somewhat hesitant version of Mozart's opera; little here for film buffs.

cinematic conception Rolf Lieberman d Joseph Losey ph Gerry Fisher ad Alexander Trauner

Ruggero Raimondi, John Macurdy, Edda Moser, Kiri Te Kanawa

The Don is Dead
US 1973 117m Technicolor
Universal / Hal B. Wallis (Paul Nathan)

Cross and double cross among Mafia families. A failed attempt to cash in on The Godfather, this endless melodrama is boringly violent and totally predictable.

w Marvin H. Albert, from his novel d Richard Fleischer ph Richard H. Kline m Jerry Goldsmith

Anthony Quinn, Frederic Forrest, Robert Forster, Al Lettieri, Angel Tompkins, Charles Cioffi

Don Juan**
US 1926 126m (synchronized) bw
Warner

Exploits of the famous lover and adventurer at Lucretia Borgia's court.
Lithe swashbuckler in the best silent tradition, but with a synchronized score (by William Axt) which made it a sensation and led directly to the talkie revolution.

w Bess Meredyth d Alan Crosland ph Byron Haskin

John Barrymore, Mary Astor, Warner Oland, Estelle Taylor, Myrna Loy, Phyllis Haver, Willard Louis, Montagu Love

Don Juan Quilligan
US 1945 76m bw

A would-be romantic bargee becomes engaged to two girls simultaneously, one on each side of the Hudson. Thin comedy of bigamy, similar to The Captain's Paradise, which came later. William Bendix, Phil Silvers, Joan Blondell, Mary Treen, Anne Revere, George Macready. Written by Arthur Kober and Frank Gabrielson; directed by Frank Tuttle; for TCF.

Don Q Son of Zorro*
US 1925 170m (16 fps) bw silent
United Artists

Further adventures in the manner of the star's 1920 hit (see The Mark of Zorro).

w K. and H. Pritchard d Donald Crisp w Jack Cunningham, novel K. and H. Pritchard ph Henry Sharp

Douglas Fairbanks, Mary Astor, Donald Crisp, Jack McDonald, Jean Hersholt

Don Quixote*
France 1933 82m bw
Vandor / Nelson / Wester

An adequate potted version starring Fedor Chaliapin and in the English version George Robey (French version: Dorville).

w Paul Morand, Alexandre Arnoux, from Cervantes d G. W. Pabst ph Nikolas Farkas, Paul Portier ad André Andreiev m Jacques Ibert

'Strictly for the arty clientele . . . for general consumption tedious and dull. Americans in general may feel that the story scarcely rates retelling.'—*Variety*

Don Quixote**
USSR 1957   105m   Agfacolor   Sovscope
Lenfilm

An extremely handsome version with a commanding star performance.

w E. Schwarz   *d* Grigori Kozintsev   *ph* Andrei Moskvin, Apollinari Dudko   *ad* Yevgeny Yenei   *m* Kara-Karayev

Nikolai Cherkassov, Yuri Tolubeyev
† Other versions came from France in 1902 and 1908, Italy in 1910, France in 1911, USA in 1915, Britain in 1923, Denmark in 1926, Spain in 1927, Britain in 1972, and Britain (ballet version with Nureyev) in 1975.

Dona Flor and Her Two Husbands
Brazil 1976   110m   Eastmancolor
Carnaval (Luis Carlos Barreto)

A young widow remarries, and has to share her bed with her late husband's ghost.
Semi-pornographic comedy which achieved some fashionable success.

wd Bruno Barreto, *novel* Jorge Amado *ph* Maurito Salles   *m* Chico Buarque de Holanda

Sonia Braga, Jose Wilker, Mauro Mendonca

Dondi
US 1960   80m   bw

GIs in Italy adopt an orphan boy, who stows away to be with them in America. Glutinous, sentimental comedy-drama. David Janssen, Patti Page, Walter Winchell, Mickey Shaughnessy, Robert Strauss, Arnold Stang, Gale Gordon. Written by Albert Zugsmith and Gus Edson, from a comic strip; directed by Albert Zugsmith; for Allied Artists.

Donovan's Brain*
US 1953   81m   bw
UA / Dowling (Tom Gries)

An unscrupulous tycoon is fatally injured, but his brain is kept alive by a surgeon who finds himself dominated by it.
Modest competence marks this version of a much filmed novel, with quiet suspense and a firm central performance.

w Felix Feist, *novel* Curt Siodmak   *d* Felix Feist   *ph* Joseph Biroc   *m* Eddie Dunstedter

Lew Ayres, Gene Evans, Nancy Davis, Steve Brodie, Lisa K. Howard

Donovan's Reef
US 1963   108m   Technicolor
Paramount (John Ford)

War veterans settle down on a South Sea island; when the daughter of one of them comes to visit, his reputation must be protected.
Good-humoured but finally enervating mixture of rough-house and slapstick, with the appearance of an old friends' benefit and the director in familiar sub-standard form.

w Frank Nugent, James Edward Grant *d* John Ford   *ph* William H. Clothier   *m* Cyril Mockridge

John Wayne, Lee Marvin, Jack Warden, Elizabeth Allen, Dorothy Lamour, Cesar Romero, Mike Mazurki

Don's Party*
Australia 1976   90m   Eastmancolor

In suburban Sydney, a political celebration party turns into a pretence of wife-swapping. Fairly acute observation of middle-class antipodean mores, interrupted with predictable bouts of antipodean crudeness. Ray Barrett, Clare Binney, Pat Bishop, Graeme Blundell, John Hargreaves. Written by David Williamson, from his own play; directed by Bruce Beresford; for Double Head / AFC.

Don't Bother to Knock*
US 1952   76m   bw
TCF (Julian Blaustein)

A deranged girl gets a baby-sitting job in a hotel and terrifies all concerned by threatening to kill her charge.
Curious vehicle for the emergent Monroe, who is not up to it, as who would be? Technical credits par, but entertainment value small.

w Daniel Taradash, *novel* Charlotte Armstrong   *d* Roy Baker   *ph* Lucien Ballard *m* Lionel Newman

Marilyn Monroe, Richard Widmark, Anne Bancroft, Donna Corcoran, Jeanne Cagney, Lurene Tuttle, Jim Backus, Elisha Cook Jnr

Don't Bother to Knock
GB 1961   89m   Technicolor
Cinemascope
ABP / Haileywood (Frank Godwin)
US title: *Why Bother to Knock*

A Casanova travel agent gives each of his girl friends a key to his Edinburgh flat.
Poorly developed and self-conscious sex farce.

w Dennis Cannan, Frederick Gotfurt, Frederic Raphael, *novel* Clifford Hanley   *d* Cyril Frankel   *ph* Geoffrey Unsworth   *m* Elisabeth Lutyens

Richard Todd, *Judith Anderson*, Elke Sommer, June Thorburn, Nicole Maurey, Rik Battaglia, Eleanor Summerfield, John Le Mesurier

Don't Ever Leave Me
GB 1949   85m   bw

A kidnapped teenager falls for her abductor. *No Orchids for Miss Blandish* played as a family comedy; quite unmemorable. Jimmy Hanley, Petula Clark, Edward Rigby, Hugh Sinclair, Linden Travers, Anthony Newley. Written by Robert Westerby, from Anthony Armstrong's novel *The Wide Guy*; directed by Arthur Crabtree; for Triton / Rank.

Don't Give Up the Ship
US 1959   89m   bw

A dim-witted naval lieutenant is accused of stealing a destroyer. Feeble American service

farce. Jerry Lewis, Dina Merrill, Diana Spencer, Mickey Shaughnessey, Robert Middleton, Gale Gordon. Written by Herbert Baker, Edmund Beloin and Henry Garson; directed by Norman Taurog; for Hal Wallis (Paramount).

Don't Go Near the Water*
US 1957   107m   Metrocolor
Cinemascope
MGM / Avon (Lawrence Weingarten)

The US Navy sets up a public relations unit on a South Pacific island.
Loosely cemented service farce full of fumbling lieutenants and bumbling commanders, a more light-hearted *M*A*S*H*. Boring romantic interludes separate some very funny farcical sequences.

w Dorothy Kingsley, George Wells, *novel* William Brinkley   *d* Charles Walters *ph* Robert Bronner   *m* Bronislau Kaper

Glenn Ford, Fred Clark, Gia Scala, Romney Brent, Mickey Shaughnessey, Earl Holliman, Anne Francis, Keenan Wynn, Eva Gabor, Russ Tamblyn, Jeff Richards, Mary Wickes

'Drop everything! And see the cheekiest comedy of the year!'
Don't Just Lie There, Say Something!
GB 1973   91m   Eastmancolor

By a strange chapter of accidents, a politician finds himself in bed with his under-secretary and a lady not his wife. Stupefying from-the-stalls rendering of a successful stage farce; in this form it simply doesn't work. Brian Rix, Leslie Phillips, Joan Sims, Joanna Lumley, Derek Royle, Peter Bland. Written by Michael Pertwee, from his play; directed by Bob Kellett; for Comocroft / Rank.

Don't Just Stand There
US 1967   99m   Techniscope
Universal (Stan Margulies)

A mild-mannered watch smuggler gets himself involved with kidnapping, murder, and finishing a sex novel.
Frantic but ineffective farce which keeps on the move but does not arrive anywhere.

w Charles Williams, from his novel The Wrong Venus   *d* Ron Winston   *ph* Milton Krasner   *m* Nick Perito

Mary Tyler Moore, Robert Wagner, *Barbara Rhoades*, Glynis Johns, Harvey Korman
'Paris locations might have helped, but we're stuck with the San Fernando Valley.'—*Robert Windeler*

Don't Look Now***
GB 1973   110m   Technicolor
BL / Casey / Eldorado (Peter Katz)

After the death of their small daughter, the Baxters meet in Venice two old sisters who claim mediumistic connection with the dead girl. The husband scorns the idea, but repeatedly sees a little red-coated figure in shadowy passages by the canals. When he confronts it, it proves to be a maniac dwarf who stabs him to death.
A macabre short story has become a

pretentious and puzzling piece of high cinema art full of vague suggestions and unexplored avenues. Whatever its overall deficiencies, it is too brilliant in surface detail to be dismissed. Depressingly but fascinatingly set in wintry Venice, it has to be seen to be appreciated.

w Allan Scott, Chris Bryant, *story* Daphne du Maurier *d* Nicolas Roeg *ph* Anthony Richmond *m* Pino D'Onnagio *ad* Giovanni Soccol

Donald Sutherland, Julie Christie, Hilary Mason, Clelia Matania, Massimo Serrato
'The fanciest, most carefully assembled enigma yet seen on the screen.'—*New Yorker*
'A powerful and dazzling visual texture.'—*Penelope Houston*

● *Video:* Thorn EMI

Don't Look Now . . . We're Being Shot At!*
France 1966 130m Eastmancolor Panavision
Les Films Corona (Robert Dorfmann)
original title: *La Grande Vadrouille*
During World War II three members of a British bomber crew bale out over Paris and make a frantic escape to the free zone by means of various wild disguises.
Freewheeling star farce, a shade lacking in control, but with some funny sequences.

wd Gérard Oury *ph* Claude Renoir *m* Georges Auric

Terry-Thomas, Bourvil, Louis de Funès, Claudio Brook, Mike Marshall
'Both the sight gags and the characters evoke pale echoes of Laurel and Hardy, but it is not familiarity that breeds contempt here so much as the debasement of the familiar.'—*MFB*

Don't Make Waves
US 1967 97m Metrocolor Panavision
MGM / Filmways (Julian Bercovici)
A swimming-pool salesman attempts to get his own back on an impulsive young woman who has wrecked his car.
Malibu beach farce for immature adults, made by professionals helpless in the face of a weak script, but boasting a funny climax with a house teetering on the edge of a cliff.

w Ira Wallach, George Kirgo, *novel* Muscle Beach by Ira Wallach *d* Alexander Mackendrick *ph* Philip Lathrop *m* Vic Mizzy

Tony Curtis, Claudia Cardinale, Robert Webber, Joanna Barnes, Sharon Tate, Jim Backus, Mort Sahl

Don't Open till Christmas
GB 1983 86m colour
A maniac goes about killing Father Christmases. Tawdry horror film of marginal interest because of subject and cast. Edmund Purdom, Alan Lake, Gerry Sundquist, Belinda Mayne, Mark Jones. Written by Derek Ford and Al McGoohan; directed by Edmund Purdom; for 21st Century.

Don't Panic, Chaps!
GB 1959 85m bw
British and German units are sent to set up observation posts on the same Adriatic island, and agree to sit out the war in comfort. An ingenious idea is ill-served by a poorly written script and a rather bored cast. Dennis Price, George Cole, Thorley Walters, Harry Fowler, Nicholas Phipps, Percy Herbert, Nadja Regin. Written by Jack Davies; directed by George Pollock; for Hammer / ACT.

'The fun never sets on the British Empire!'
Don't Raise the Bridge, Lower the River
GB 1967 100m Technicolor
Columbia / Walter Shenson
An American turns his English wife's home into a discotheque.
Dreary comedy apparently intent on proving that its star can be just as unfunny abroad as at home.

w Max Wilk *d* Jerry Paris *ph* Otto Heller *m* David Whitaker

Jerry Lewis, Terry-Thomas, Jacqueline Pearce, Bernard Cribbins, Patricia Routledge, Nicholas Parsons, Michael Bates

Don't Take it to Heart*
GB 1944 90m bw
GFD / Two Cities (Sydney Box)
A genial castle ghost is unleashed by a bomb and affects the love affair of a researcher with the daughter of the house.
Amiably lunatic British-upper-class extravaganza with eccentric characters and some felicitous moments.

wd Jeffrey Dell *ph* Eric Cross

Richard Greene, *Edward Rigby*, Patricia Medina, Alfred Drayton, Richard Bird, Wylie Watson, Moore Marriott, Brefni O'Rourke, Amy Veness, Claude Dampier, Joan Hickson, Joyce Barbour, Ronald Squire, Ernest Thesiger
'A cheerful and rewarding entertainment.'—*Richard Mallett, Punch*

Don't Trust Your Husband
US 1948 90m bw
An executive conceals from his wife the sex of the client with whom he has to spend a lot of time. Ho-hum comedy with a laborious plotline and a flagging cast. Fred MacMurray, Madeleine Carroll, Charles Rogers. Written by Lou Breslow and Joseph Hoffman; directed by Lloyd Bacon; for James Nasser / United Artists.

The Doolins of Oklahoma
US 1949 90m bw
When his old gang claims his return to lawlessness, Bill Doolin walks into the sheriff's guns rather than cause his wife unhappiness. Moderate western with an unusually less-than-sympathetic role for its star. Randolph Scott, George Macready, Louise Allbritton, John Ireland, Noah Beery Jnr, Dona Drake. Written by Kenneth Gamet; directed by Gordon Douglas; for Harry Joe Brown / Columbia. (GB title: *The Great Manhunt*.)

The Doomed Battalion*
US / Germany 1932 74m bw
Austrians fight Italians high in the Alps. Interesting but not very effective attempt to internationalize a German 'bergfilm'. Luis Trenker, Tala Birell, Victor Varconi, Albert Conti, C. Henry Gordon, Gibson Gowland, Henry Armetta, Gustav Von Seyffertitz. Written by Luis Trenker and Carl Hartl; directed by Cyril Gardner; for Universal. 'Beaucoup snow and ice stuff for hot weather appeal . . . capable of sustaining bally.'—*Variety*

Doomed to Die: see Mr Wong

Doomwatch
GB 1972 92m colour
Tigon (Tony Tenser)
An investigator of coastal pollution discovers a village in which dumped chemicals have given all the inhabitants a distorting disease called acromegaly.
An unsatisfactory horror film is drawn from a moderately serious TV series about ecology.

w Clive Exton *d* Peter Sasdy *ph* Kenneth Talbot *m* John Scott

Ian Bannen, Judy Geeson, John Paul, Simon Oates, George Sanders, Percy Herbert, Geoffrey Keen, Joseph O'Conor

The Door in the Wall*
GB 1956 29m Technicolor Vistavision
AB Pathé / BFI / Lawrie (Howard Thomas)
A man is obsessed by a childhood dream of a green door which leads into a beautiful garden.
The story is chosen to experiment with Dynamic Frame, a system in which the picture changes shape and size according to the subject matter. In this case the results are entertaining enough.

wd Glenn H. Alvey Jnr *ph* Jo Jago *m* James Bernard

Stephen Murray, Ian Hunter

The Door with Seven Locks
GB 1940 89m bw
Rialto (John Argyle)
US title: *Chamber of Horrors*
A mad doctor abducts an heiress in the hope of gaining her wealth.
Old-fashioned barnstormer, ineptly made.

w Norman Lee, John Argyle, Gilbert Gunn, *novel* Edgar Wallace *d* Norman Lee

Leslie Banks, Lilli Palmer, Romilly Lunge, Gina Malo, Richard Bird, David Horne, Cathleen Nesbitt

Doorway to Hell
US 1930 79m (approx) bw
Warner
GB title: *A Handful of Clouds*
A young gangster tries to go straight but is driven back into crime.
Vividly written but dramatically evasive crime-does-not-pay story, trying to eat its cake and have it.

w George Rosener, *story* A Handful of Clouds by Rowland Brown *d* Archie Mayo *ph* Barney McGill *md* Leo Forbstein

Lew Ayres, Charles Judels, James Cagney, Dorothy Matthews, Leon Janney, Robert Elliott
'Swell gang picture, handled so as to just slip by the censors.'—*Variety*

AAN: original story

Dosshouse*
GB 1933 53m bw
Sound City (John Baxter)
An escaped convict is captured by a reporter and detective posing as tramps.
Low-budget featurette which deserves a footnote in film history for its social consciousness, rare at the time, especially in the dosshouse scenes.
w Herbert Ayres *d* John Baxter
Frank Cellier, Arnold Bell, Herbert Franklyn, J. Hubert Leslie

Double Confession
GB 1950 85m bw
ABP / Harry Reynolds
At a seaside resort, a man finds his wife dead and tries to frame her lover, but becomes confused with two real murderers with a different purpose.
Confused and unlikely melodrama which signally lacks the ancient mariner's eye.
w William Templeton, *novel* All on a Summer's Day by John Garden *d* Ken Annakin *ph* Geoffrey Unsworth *m* Benjamin Franklin
Derek Farr, Peter Lorre, William Hartnell, Joan Hopkins, Naunton Wayne, Ronald Howard, Kathleen Harrison, Leslie Dwyer, Edward Rigby

Double Crime in the Maginot Line
France 1939 83m bw
A spy is discovered in the French system of international fortifications. A topical melodrama which quickly became very dated indeed. Victor Francen, Jacques Baumer, Vera Korene, Fernand Fabre. Written by Felix Gandera and Robert Bibal from a novel by Pierre Nord; directed by Felix Gandera for his own company.

Double Crossbones
US 1950 75m Technicolor
Circumstances force our hero to assume the identity of a pirate, in which disguise he rescues a fair lady. Lamebrained burlesque unworthy of its star. Donald O'Connor, Helena Carter, Will Geer, John Emery, Hope Emerson, Charles McGraw, Alan Napier. Written by Oscar Brodney; directed by Charles R. Barton; for Universal-International.

'Frankenstein, Dracula and other screen monsters pale by comparison with this fiendish, decadent woman!'

Double Door
US 1934 75m bw
A selfish, wealthy Fifth Avenue spinster takes a dislike to her brother's girlfriend and locks her up in a vault. Silly, rather boring melodrama which may have worked on the stage but did not take to the screen. Mary Morris (the American one), Evelyn Venable, Kent Taylor, Sir Guy Standing, Anne Revere, Colin Tapley, Halliwell Hobbes. Written by Gladys Lehman, Jack Cunningham from the play by Elizabeth McFadden; directed by Charles Vidor; for Paramount. 'Not likely to get anywhere at the b.o. . . . dull, drab and incredible.'—*Variety*

Double Dynamite
US 1951 (produced 1948) 80m bw
RKO (Irving Cummings)
aka: *It's Only Money*
A bank teller wins a fortune at the race track but is afraid his winnings will be thought the proceeds of a bank robbery.
Insultingly mild comedy, nearly saved by a few quips from Groucho.
w Melville Shavelson, Harry Crane, Leo Rosten *d* Irving Cummings *ph* Robert de Grasse *m* Leigh Harline
Frank Sinatra, Jane Russell, Groucho Marx, Don McGuire, Howard Freeman

Double Harness
US 1933 70m bw
A girl sets out to trick a rich man into marriage. Mildly amusing comedy which in its time was considered risqué. Ann Harding, William Powell, Henry Stephenson, Lillian Bond, Reginald Owen, George Meeker, Kay Hammond. Written by Jane Murfin from the play by Edward Montgomery; directed by John Cromwell; for RKO. 'Managed with such reticence that at no time is there a note of offence . . . this class actress again triumphs over her surroundings, and the picture will please her large following.'—*Variety*

Double Indemnity: see River's End

'You can't kiss away a murder!'

Double Indemnity****
US 1944 107m bw
Paramount (Joseph Sistrom)
An insurance agent connives with the glamorous wife of a client to kill her husband and collect.
Archetypal *film noir* of the forties, brilliantly filmed and incisively written, perfectly capturing the decayed Los Angeles atmosphere of a Chandler novel but using a simpler story and more substantial characters. The hero / villain was almost a new concept.
w Billy Wilder, Raymond Chandler, *novel* James M. Cain *d* Billy Wilder *ph* John Seitz *m* Miklos Rozsa
Fred MacMurray, Barbara Stanwyck, Edward G. Robinson, Tom Powers, Porter Hall, Jean Heather, Byron Barr, Richard Gaines

Opening narration: Office memorandum. Walter Neff to Barton T. Keyes, Claims Manager, Los Angeles, July 16, 1938. Dear Keyes: I suppose you'll call this a confession when you hear it. Well, I don't like the word confession. I just want to set you right about something you couldn't see because it was smack up against your nose . . . I killed Dietrichson. Me, Walter Neff, insurance salesman, 35 years old, unmarried, no visible scars. Until a while ago, that is . . .
'The sort of film which revives a critic from the depressive effects of bright epics about the big soul of America or the suffering soul of Europe and gives him a new lease of faith.'— *Richard Winnington*
'Masturbation fantasy triple distilled.'— *James Agee*
'The most pared-down and purposeful film ever made by Billy Wilder.'—*John Coleman, 1966*
'Profoundly, intensely entertaining,'— *Richard Mallett, Punch*
'One of the highest summits of *film noir* . . . without a single trace of pity or love.'— *Charles Higham, 1971*
AAN: best picture; script; direction; John Seitz; Miklos Rozsa; Barbara Stanwyck

'This woman inspired him—this woman feared him!'
A Double Life**
US 1947 103m bw
(Universal) Kanin Productions (Michael Kanin)
An actor playing Othello is obsessed by the role and murders a woman he imagines to be Desdemona.
An old theatrical chestnut (cf *Men Are Not Gods*) is decked out with smartish backstage dialogue but despite a pleasant star performance remains unrewarding if taxing, and the entertainment value of the piece is on the thin side considering the mighty talents involved.
w Ruth Gordon, Garson Kanin *d* George Cukor *ph* Milton Krasner *m* Miklos Rozsa
Ronald Colman, Shelley Winters, Signe Hasso, Edmond O'Brien, Millard Mitchell
AA: Miklos Rozsa; Ronald Colman
AAN: Ruth Gordon, Garson Kanin; George Cukor
● *Video: Intervision*

The Double McGuffin
US 1979 100m colour
Kids turn into amateur detectives when they find that a visiting foreign leader is to be assassinated. Barely tolerable lightweight mystery for an audience which probably doesn't exist. Ernest Borgnine, George Kennedy, Elke Sommer, Rod Browning. Written, directed and produced by Joe Camp for Mulberry Square.

The Double Man*
GB 1967 105m Technicolor
Warner / Hal E. Chester
A CIA agent investigates the death of his son

on a Swiss skiing holiday and finds the murder was a lure to get him there so that an enemy lookalike can substitute for him.
Rather ruthless but good-looking and generally watchable spy melodrama.

w Frank Tarloff, Alfred Hayes, *novel* Henry S. Maxfield *d* Franklin Schaffner *ph* Denys Coop *m* Ernie Freeman

Yul Brynner, Clive Revill, Anton Diffring, Britt Ekland, Moira Lister

Double Negative
Canada 1980 96m colour

A photo journalist tries to find the murderer of his wife, and discovers he's an amnesiac and did it himself. Ho-hum mystery thriller centring on an ancient wheeze; treatment resolutely plodding. Michael Sarrazin, Susan Clark, Anthony Perkins, Howard Duff, Kate Reid. Written by Thomas Hedley Jnr, Janis Allen and Charles Dennis, from *The Three Roads* by Ross Macdonald; directed by George Bloomfield; for Quadrant.

Double or Nothing
US 1937 90m bw

Inheritors under a trick will must double their bequests or lose them. Flat comedy with music; none of the elements are really up to scratch. Bing Crosby, Martha Raye, Andy Devine, William Frawley, Mary Carlisle, Benny Baker. Written by Charles Lederer and others; directed by Theodore Reed; for Paramount. 'Due for big openings and tapering-off business. Will squeeze through.'—*Variety*

Double Wedding
US 1937 87m bw
MGM (Joseph L. Mankiewicz)

A bohemian artist makes a play for the lady of his choice by romancing her sister.
Zany star comedy which doesn't quite come off.

w Jo Swerling, *play* Great Love by Ferenc Molnar *d* Richard Thorpe *ph* William Daniels *m* Edward Ward

William Powell, Myrna Loy, John Beal, Florence Rice, Jessie Ralph, Edgar Kennedy, Sidney Toler, Barnett Parker, Katherine Alexander, Donald Meek
'OK for topflight business . . . would be funnier if it were shorter.'—*Variety*

Double Whoopee**
US 1928 20m bw silent

Incompetent doormen at a swank hotel cause havoc. Simple-minded but pleasing star farce. Laurel and Hardy, Jean Harlow, Charlie Hall. Written by Leo McCarey and H. M. Walker; directed by Lewis R. Foster; for Hal Roach.

Doubting Thomas
US 1935 78m bw

Small-town 'society' puts on an amateur show. Slight but attractive star vehicle. Will Rogers, Billie Burke, Alison Skipworth, Sterling

Holloway, Andrew Tombes, Gail Patrick. Written by William Conselman and Bartlett Cormack from the play The Torch Bearers by George Kelly; directed by David Butler; for Fox. 'There is one thing that Rogers knows, and that is how to get laughs with any sort of a situation, and he didn't learn that just from reading the papers.'—*Variety*

Douce*
France 1943 106m bw
Société Parisienne de l'Industrie Cinématographique

In 1887 Paris a sheltered young rich girl falls for a steward and encounters family opposition.
A charming old-fashioned story which provides a well-taken opportunity for a portrait of the old bourgeoisie.

w Jean Aurenche, Pierre Bost *d* Claude Autant-Lara *ph* Gaston Thonnart *m* René Cloërc

Odette Joyeux, Jean Debucourt, Marguerite Moreno, Roger Pigaut, Madeleine Robinson
'Direction and camerawork constantly reveal touches of felicity.'—*MFB*

Doughboys*
US 1930 80m approx bw
MGM / Buster Keaton (Lawrence Weingarten)
GB title: *Forward March*

A young eccentric joins the army.
Simple-minded farce with a few good routines for the star.

w Richard Schayer *d* Edward Sedgwick *ph* Leonard Smith

Buster Keaton, Sally Eilers, Cliff Edwards, Edward Brophy
'Keaton's first talker is comedy with a kick.'—*Variety*

The Doughgirls*
US 1944 102m bw
Warner (Mark Hellinger)

In a crowded wartime Washington hotel, a honeymoon is frustrated by constant interruption, not to mention the discovery that the wedding was not legal.
Frantic farce, generally well adapted, and certainly played with gusto.

w James V. Kern, Sam Hellman, *play* Joseph Fields *d* James V. Kern *ph* Ernest Haller *m* Adolph Deutsch

Alexis Smith, Jane Wyman, Jack Carson, Ann Sheridan, Irene Manning, *Eve Arden*, Charlie Ruggles, John Alexander, John Ridgely, Craig Stevens, Alan Mowbray, Donald MacBride
'There's nothing so good in it that you must attend, just as there is nothing bad enough to keep you away.'—*Archer Winsten*

The Dove*
US 1968 15m bw

Back in the countryside of his childhood, a Nobel prize winner recalls the events of a summer . . . Elaborate Ingmar Bergman spoof

complete with sub-titles and pidgin Swedish. Hilarious at the time for those who had just seen *Wild Strawberries*. David Zirlin, George Coe, Pamela Burrell. Written by Sidney Davis; directed by George Coe and Anthony Lover; for Coe / Davis Ltd.
● Video: Thorn EMI

The Dove*
US 1974 104m Technicolor Panavision
St George Productions (Gregory Peck)

Yachtsman Robin Lee Graham makes a five-year voyage around the world.
Bland, rather stolid adventure story for boatniks, based on real incidents; good to look at.

w Peter Beagle, Adam Kennedy *d* Charles Jarrott *ph* Sven Nykvist *m* John Barry

Joseph Bottoms, Deborah Raffin, John McLiam, Dabney Coleman
'Postcard views flick by to the strains of a saccharine score.'—*David McGillivray*

Down Among the Sheltering Palms
US 1952 86m Technicolor
TCF (Fred Kohlmar)

An American army unit takes over a south sea island, but fraternization is forbidden.
Tolerable comedy-musical with familiar jokes and situations.

w Claude Binyon, Albert Lewin, Burt Styler *d* Edmund Goulding *ph* Leon Shamroy *m* Leigh Harline *songs* Harold Arlen, Ralph Blane

William Lundigan, Jane Greer, Mitzi Gaynor, David Wayne, Gloria de Haven, Gene Lockhart, Jack Paar, Billy Gilbert

Down Argentine Way*
US 1940 94m Technicolor
TCF (Harry Joe Brown)

A wealthy American girl falls in love with an Argentinian horse-breeder.
A very moderate musical which happened to bring both Grable and Miranda to star stature and set Fox off on their successful run of forties extravaganzas, reasonably pleasant to look at but empty-headed.

w Karl Tunberg, Darrell Ware *d* Irving Cummings *ph* Ray Rennahan, Leon Shamroy *songs* Harry Warren, Mack Gordon

Betty Grable, Carmen Miranda, Don Ameche, Charlotte Greenwood, J. Carrol Naish, Henry Stephenson, Leonid Kinskey, The Nicholas Brothers
'I dislike Technicolor in which all pinks resemble raspberry sauce, reds turn to sealing wax, blues shriek of the washtub, and yellows become suet pudding.'—*James Agate*
'So outrageous—that it's hard to believe it isn't at least partly intentional—but why would anybody make this picture on purpose.'—*New Yorker, 1976*

AAN: Ray Rennahan, Leon Shamroy; title song (*m* Harry Warren, *ly* Mack Gordon)

Down Three Dark Streets°
US 1954 85m bw
UA / Edward Small (Arthur Gardner, Jules V. Levy)

An FBI agent is shot on duty, and his friend avenges him in the course of clearing up three cases in which he was involved.
Competent, enjoyable police film with three cases for the price of one.

w The Gordons, Bernard C. Schoenfeld, book Case File FBI by the Gordons d Arnold Laven ph Joseph Biroc m Paul Sawtell

Broderick Crawford, Ruth Roman, Martha Hyer, Marisa Pavan, Casey Adams, Kenneth Tobey
† One of the first collaborations of the prolific production company Laven-Gardner-Levy.

Down to Earth
US 1932 79m bw

Nouveau riche Americans return from Europe and find themselves misfits at home. Thin sequel to They Had to See Paris. Will Rogers, Dorothy Jordan, Irene Rich, Matty Kemp, Mary Carlisle. Written by Edwin Burke, from a story by Homer Croy. 'Will need support . . . the least powerful in draw of all Rogers' pictures.'—Variety

Down to Earth°
US 1947 101m Technicolor
Columbia (Don Hartman)

The muse Terpsichore comes down to help a Broadway producer fix a new show in which she is featured.
Pleasant but undistinguished musical fantasy, a sequel to Here Comes Mr Jordan. The heavenly sequences promise more amusement than they produce.

w Edwin Blum, Don Hartman d Alexander Hall ph Rudolph Maté m Heinz Roemheld
Rita Hayworth, Larry Parks, Roland Culver (as Mr Jordan), Edward Everett Horton (repeating as Messenger 7013), Marc Platt, James Gleason
'Just the film to make the spectator forget the troubles of life.'—MFB
'Celestial whimsy musical, with arch acting and a dull score.'—New Yorker, 1977

Down to the Sea in Ships°
US 1948 120m bw
TCF

An old whaling skipper wants his grandson to follow in his footsteps.
Seagoing spectacle with strong characters; all concerned show Hollywood in its most professional form, but the film somehow fails to catch the imagination or live in the memory.

w John Lee Mahin, Sy Bartlett d Henry Hathaway ph Joe MacDonald m Alfred Newman
Lionel Barrymore, Dean Stockwell, Richard Widmark, Cecil Kellaway, Gene Lockhart

Downhill
GB 1927 80m approx (24 fps) bw silent
Gainsborough (Michael Balcon)
US title: When Boys Leave Home

A sixth-form schoolboy, accused of theft, is expelled and goes to the bad in Marseilles before being found innocent.
Absurd novelette with only marginal glimpses of the director's emerging talent.

w Eliot Stannard, play Ivor Novello and Constance Collier d Alfred Hitchcock ph Claude McDonnell ed Ivor Montagu
Ivor Novello, Ben Webster, Robin Irvine, Sybil Rhoda, Lillian Braithwaite, Isabel Jeans, Ian Hunter
   Famous line: 'Does this mean, sir, that I shall not be able to play for the Old Boys?'

Downhill Racer°
US 1969 101m Technicolor
Paramount / Wildwood (Richard Gregson)

An ambitious American skier gains a place on the team competing in Europe.
Virtually plotless, casually assembled study of a man and a sport, good to look at, often exciting, but just as frequently irritating in its throwaway style.

w James Salter, novel Oakley Hall d Michael Ritchie ph Brian Probyn m Kenyon Hopkins
Robert Redford, Gene Hackman, Camilla Sparv, Joe Jay Jalbert, Timothy Kirk, Dabney Coleman

Downstairs°
US 1932 84m bw

Life below stairs: a butler clashes with a chauffeur over the love of a maid. Surprisingly sharp little drama from a story by the star.
John Gilbert, Paul Lukas, Virginia Bruce, Hedda Hopper, Reginald Owen. Written by Lenore Coffee and Melville Baker; directed by Monta Bell; for MGM.
'Gilbert too unsympathetically cast in a role of his own writing.'—Variety

'The strangest love a woman has ever known . . . a livid face bent over her in the ghostly mist!'

Dracula°°°
US 1931 84m bw
Universal (Carl Laemmle Jnr)

A Transylvanian vampire count gets his come-uppance in Yorkshire.
A film which has much to answer for. It started its star and its studio off on horror careers, and it launched innumerable sequels (see below). In itself, after two eerie reels, it becomes a pedantic and slow transcription of a stage adaptation, and its climax takes place offscreen; but for all kinds of reasons it remains full of interest.

w Garrett Fort, play Hamilton Deane, John Balderston, novel Bram Stoker d Tod Browning ph Karl Freund m Tchaikovsky
Bela Lugosi, Helen Chandler, David Manners, Dwight Frye, Edward Van Sloan

'Must have caused much uncertainty as to the femme fan reaction . . . as it turns out the signs are that the woman's angle is all right and that sets the picture for better than average money . . . it comes out as a sublimated ghost story related with all surface seriousness and above all with a remarkably effective background of creepy atmosphere.'—Variety

'A too literal adaptation of the play (not the book) results in a plodding, talkative development, with much of the vital action taking place off-screen.'—William K. Everson
'The mistiest parts are the best; when the lights go up the interest goes down.'—Ivan Butler
† Sequels include Dracula's Daughter (qv), Son of Dracula (qv); the later Hammer sequence consists of Dracula (see below), Brides of Dracula (qv), Dracula Prince of Darkness (qv), Dracula Has Risen From the Grave (qv), Taste the Blood of Dracula (qv), Scars of Dracula (qv), Dracula AD 1972 (qv), The Satanic Rites of Dracula (qv). Other associated films in which the Count or a disciple appears include (all qv) Return of the Vampire (1944), House of Frankenstein (1945), House of Dracula (1945), Abbott and Costello Meet Frankenstein (1948), The Return of Dracula (1958), Kiss of the Vampire (1963), The Fearless Vampire Killers (1967), Count Yorga Vampire (1969), Countess Dracula (1970), Vampire Circus (1970), The House of Dark Shadows (1970), Vampire Lovers (1971), Blacula (1972). Minor potboilers are legion.
● Video: CIC

Dracula°°°
GB 1958 82m Technicolor
Hammer (Anthony Hinds)
US title: Horror of Dracula

A remake of the 1930 film.
Commendably brief in comparison with the later Hammer films, this was perhaps the best horror piece they turned out as well as the most faithful to its original. Decor and colour were well used, and the leading performances are striking.

w Jimmy Sangster d Terence Fisher ph Jack Asher m James Bernard ad Bernard Robinson
Peter Cushing (as Van Helsing), Christopher Lee (as Dracula), Melissa Stribling, Carol Marsh, Michael Gough, John Van Eyssen, Valerie Gaunt, Miles Malleson

Dracula°
GB 1979 112m Technicolor Panavision
Universal / Mirisch (Marvin Mirisch / Tom Pevsner)

A lush, expensive and romantic version which presents the count as a matinée idol and spends too much time on the romantic scenes to distract attention from an old old story.

w W. D. Richter d John Badham ph Gilbert Taylor pd Peter Murton m John Williams

Frank Langella, Laurence Olivier, Donald Pleasence, Kate Nelligan, Trevor Eve

'A triumphantly lurid creation that seems bound to be either under-valued for its circus effects or over-valued for the stylishness with which it steers between the reefs of camp and theatrical indulgence.'—*Richard Combs, MFB*
● *Video: CIC*

'The Count is back, with an eye for London's hot pants, and a taste for everything!'
Dracula AD 1972
GB 1972 95m Eastmancolor
Warner / Hammer (Josephine Douglas)

Dracula reappears among Chelsea teenagers practising black magic.
Depressed attempt to update a myth; the link with modern sin makes it seem not only tarnished but tasteless, and the film itself is lamentably short on excitement.

w Don Houghton *d* Alan Gibson *ph* Richard Bush *m* Michael Vickers

Peter Cushing, Christopher Lee, Stephanie Beacham, Michael Coles, Christopher Neame, William Ellis

'You just can't keep a good man down!'
Dracula Has Risen from the Grave
GB 1968 92m Technicolor
Hammer (Aida Young)

Dracula again terrorizes the village in the shadow of his castle, and is routed by a bishop.
Tedious, confined and repetitive shocker with little conventional action and an unusual emphasis on sex.

w John Elder (Anthony Hinds) *d* Freddie Francis *ph* Arthur Grant *m* James Bernard
Christopher Lee, Rupert Davies, Veronica Carlson, Barbara Ewing, Barry Andrews, Ewan Hooper
'A bloody bore.'—*Judith Crist*

Dracula Prince of Darkness
GB 1965 90m Techniscope
Warner / Hammer (Anthony Nelson Keys)

Stranded travellers are made welcome at the late count's castle by his sinister butler, who proceeds to use the blood of one of them to revivify his master.
Ingenious rehash of incidents from the original story, largely dissipated by poor colour and unsuitable wide screen.

w John Sansom *d* Terence Fisher *ph* Michael Reed *m* James Bernard
Christopher Lee, *Philip Latham*, Barbara Shelley, Thorley Walters, Andrew Keir, Francis Matthews, Suzan Farmer, Charles Tingwell
'Run-of-the-coffin stuff . . . only for ardent fang-and-cross fans.'—*Judith Crist*

'More sensational than her unforgettable father!'
Dracula's Daughter**
US 1936 70m bw
Universal (E. M. Asher)

The daughter of the old count follows his remains to London.

DRACULA'S DAUGHTER. Gloria Holden presides over papa's cremation. Actually, we thought he withered away like all staked vampires, at the end of the first episode.

Lively sequel which develops in the manner of a Sherlock Holmes story.

w Garrett Fort *d* Lambert Hillyer *ph* George Robinson *m* Heinz Roemheld

Otto Kruger, Marguerite Churchill, Edward Van Sloan, Gloria Holden, Irving Pichel, Nan Grey, Hedda Hopper, Gilbert Emery, Claud Allister, E. E. Clive, Halliwell Hobbes, Billy Bevan

Dracula's Dog
US 1977 88m De Luxe
Vic (Albert Band, Frank Ray Perelli)
GB title: *Zoltan, Hound of Dracula*

The resurrected servant of Dracula tries to use his vampire dog to create a new master.
Ingenious but unattractive addition to the saga, with dogs as chief villains; the style varies between spoof and rather nasty horror.

w Frank Ray Perelli *d* Albert Band *ph* Bruce Logan *m* Andrew Belling

Jose Ferrer, Reggie Nalder, Michael Pataki, Jan Shutan

Draegerman Courage
US 1937 59m bw

Problems of a Nova Scotian gold mine cave-in.
Adequate action fare inspired by a real event. (Draegermen are burrowers.) Jean Muir, Barton MacLane, Henry O'Neill, Robert Barrat, Addison Richards, Gordon Oliver.

Written by Anthony Coldeway; directed by Louis King; for Warners. 'Vivid and often thrilling.'—*Variety*

The Dragnet*
US 1928 77m approx (24 fps) bw
silent
Paramount

When his buddy is killed, a detective resigns from the force and takes to the bottle.
Obviously interesting sequel to *Underworld*. It can't be evaluated because no print is known to exist.

w Jules and Charles Furthman, *story* Night Stick by Oliver H. P. Garrett *d* Josef von Sternberg *ph* Harold Rosson *ad* Hans Dreier

George Bancroft, Evelyn Brent, William Powell, Fred Kohler, Francis MacDonald, Leslie Fenton

Dragnet*
US 1954 93m Warnercolor
Mark VII (Jack Webb)

Sgt Joe Friday solves the murder of an ex-convict.
Moderately interesting but overlong attempt to transfer television techniques to the big screen; laconic dialogue, question and answer, cheap sets, close-ups and convenient Los Angeles locations.

w Richard Breen *d Jack Webb* *ph* Edward Colman

Jack Webb, Ben Alexander, Richard Boone, Stacy Harris, Ann Robinson, Virginia Gregg

Dragon Seed°
US 1944 144m bw
MGM (Pandro S. Berman)

Chinese peasants fight the Japs.
Ill-advised attempt to follow the success of *The Good Earth*; badly cast actors mouth propaganda lines in a mechanical script which provokes more boredom and unintentional laughter than sympathy.

w Marguerite Roberts, Jane Murfin, *novel* Pearl S. Buck *d* Jack Conway, Harold S. Bucquet *ph* Sidney Wagner *m* Herbert Stothart

Katharine Hepburn, Walter Huston, Turhan Bey, Aline MacMahon, Akim Tamiroff, Hurd Hatfield, Frances Rafferty, Agnes Moorehead, Henry Travers, J. Carrol Naish

'A kind of slant-eyed *North Star*. Often awkward and pretentious, it nevertheless has moments of moral and dramatic grandeur.'—*Time*

AAN: Sidney Wagner; Aline MacMahon

'Only sorcery can destroy it!'
Dragonslayer
US 1981 110m Metrocolor Panavision
Walt Disney / Paramount (Howard W. Koch, Hal Barwood)

A sorcerer's apprentice uses his master's magic amulet to ward off various dangers.
Heavy-going sword-and-sorcery fable, not helped at all by slow plotting and dark photography. The dragons however are genuinely fierce.

w Hal Barwood, Matthew Robbins *d* Matthew Robbins *ph* Derek Vanlint *m* Alex North *pd* Elliot Scott *sp* Thomas Smith

Peter MacNichol, Caitlin Clarke, Ralph Richardson, John Hallam, Peter Eyre, Albert Salmi

'Verges on the nasty for the nippers; sails too close to *déjà vu* for fantasy fans.'—*Time Out*

AAN: Alex North; make-up

● *Video:* Disney

Dragonwyck°
US 1946 103m bw
TCF (Darryl F. Zanuck)

In the 1840s a farmer's daughter marries her rich cousin, not knowing that he has poisoned his first wife.
Good-looking but rather tedious romance of the Jane Eyre / Rebecca school: tyrannical recluse, mystery upstairs, spooky house, etc. Heavy going.

w Joseph L. Mankiewicz, *novel* Anya Seton *d* Joseph L. Mankiewicz *ph* Arthur Miller *m* Alfred Newman

Gene Tierney, Vincent Price, Glenn Langan, Walter Huston, Anne Revere, Spring Byington, Henry Morgan, Jessica Tandy

Drake of England
GB 1935 104m bw
Wardour (Walter C. Mycroft)
US titles: *Drake the Pirate; Elizabeth of England*

Sir Francis Drake is knighted by Queen Elizabeth for his seafaring exploits, and defeats the Spanish Armada.
Stiffly moving historical pageant; you can smell the mothballs.

w Clifford Grey, Akos Tolney, Marjorie Deans, Norman Watson *d* Arthur Woods *ph* Claude Friese-Greene

Matheson Lang, Athene Seyler, Jane Baxter, Donald Wolfit, Henry Mollison, George Merritt, Amy Veness, Sam Livesey, Ben Webster

Dramatic School°
US 1938 80m bw
MGM (Mervyn Le Roy)

Young actresses compete for success.
Another, less lively, *Stage Door*; tolerable but not exciting.

w Ernst Vajda, Mary McCall Jnr, *play* School of Drama by Hans Szekely, Zoltan Egyed *d* Robert B. Sinclair Jnr *ph* William Daniels *m* Franz Waxman

Luise Rainer, Paulette Goddard, Alan Marshal, Lana Turner, Anthony Allan (later John Hubbard), Henry Stephenson, Genevieve Tobin, Gale Sondergaard, Melville Cooper, Erik Rhodes, Ann Rutherford, Margaret Dumont, Virginia Grey, Hans Conried

'A disappointing effort which arouses little interest in its unfolding.'—*Variety*

Drango
US 1957 92m bw
UA / Hall Bartlett

After the Civil War, a Union Army officer is assigned to bring law and order to a Georgia community.
Eccentric, downbeat semi-western with aspirations to be some kind of *film noir*; does not come off.

wd Hall Bartlett *ph* James Wong Howe *m* Elmer Bernstein

Jeff Chandler, Ronald Howard, Joanne Dru, Julie London, Donald Crisp, John Lupton, Morris Ankrum

The Draughtsman's Contract°°
GB 1982 108m colour
BFI / Channel Four (David Payne)

In 1694 a young draughtsman receives a curious commission from a country gentlewoman, his rewards to include bed and bawd.
Pleasantly unusual, stylized puzzle film which involves both sex and murder while maintaining a detached attitude to both. The period costumes help to give it an air of fantasy which was presumably intended.

wd Peter Greenaway *ph* Curtis Clark *m* Michael Nyman *ed* John Wilson

Anthony Higgins, Janet Suzman, Anne Louise Lambert, Neil Cunningham, Hugh Fraser, Dave Hill

'Mannered and idiosyncratic, the speeches are so arch and twitty that they seem to be pitched higher than a dog whistle.'—*Pauline Kael, New Yorker*
'Perhaps the four-hour version which may one day become available is clearer if not more concise.'—*Guardian*
'Best enjoyed as a sly piece of double bluff, a puzzle without a solution, an *avant garde* hoax in the spirit of Dada and the surrealists.'—*Observer*

Dream Girl
US 1947 86m bw
Paramount (P. J. Wolfson)

A girl revels in her own romantic dreams, one of which nearly comes true.
Potentially pleasant comedy about a female Walter Mitty does not work because the director has run out of ideas, the star is miscast and Hollywood has insisted on making the girl rich to begin with, which robs the dreams of any point.

w Arthur Sheekman, *play* Elmer Rice *d* Mitchell Leisen *ph* Daniel L. Fapp *m* Victor Young

Betty Hutton, Macdonald Carey, Walter Abel, Patric Knowles, Virginia Field, Peggy Wood, Lowell Gilmore

The Dream of a Rarebit Fiend°
US 1906 4m (24 fps) bw silent

Early trick film depicting a nightmare resulting from overeating. Written by Winsor McKay; directed and produced by Edwin S. Porter.

A Dream of Kings
US 1969 110m Technicolor
National General (Jules Schermer)

Episodes in the life of an improvident, lusty, poetical Chicago Greek with a dying son.
The part screamed for Anthony Quinn and got him, with the result that it has all been seen before, too frequently. Well made, with strong appeal to Chicago Greeks.

w Harry Mark Patrakis, Ian Hunter, *novel* Harry Mark Patrakis *ph* Richard H. Kline *m* Alex North

Anthony Quinn, Irene Papas, Inger Stevens, Sam Levene, Val Avery, Tamara Daykarhanova

A Dream of Passion
Greece 1978 110m Eastmancolor
Branfilm / Melinafilm (Jules Dassin)

A woman who, Medea-like, has killed her children is drawn into an eccentric relationship with an actress playing Medea on the stage.
Weird and ineffective character drama which badly needs discipline.

wd Jules Dassin *ph* George Arvanitis *m* Ionnis Markopoulos

Melina Mercouri, Ellen Burstyn, Andreas Voutsinas, Despo Diamantidou

Dream Street°
US 1921 89m (at 24 fps) bw silent
D. W. Griffith Inc

Three Limehouse folk, torn between good and evil, act out their dreams.
Trilogy of moral tales, fancifully and often charmingly assembled by the master director who often reminds one of a Victorian lace maker.

wd D. W. Griffith, from stories by Thomas Burke *ph Henrik Sartov*

Carol Dempster, Ralph Graves, Charles Emmett Mack, Edwart Peil, Tyrone Power Snr, W. J. Ferguson

Dream Wife
US 1953 99m bw
MGM (Dore Schary)

An executive leaves his ambitious wife for a sheik's daughter schooled in the art of pleasing men, but naturally finds drawbacks.
Very moderate comedy with strained situations and few laughs. The stars work hard.

w Sidney Sheldon, Herbert Baker, Alfred L. Levitt *d* Sidney Sheldon *ph* Milton Krasner *m* Conrad Salinger

Cary Grant, Deborah Kerr, Walter Pidgeon, Betta St John, Eduard Franz, Buddy Baer, Les Temayne

Dreamboat*
US 1952 83m bw
TCF (Sol C. Siegel)

A romantic star of the silent film era is embarrassed when his old movies turn up on television.
Hollywood rather blunderingly makes fun of its arch enemy in this sometimes sprightly but often disappointing comedy which should have been a bulls-eye.

wd Claude Binyon *ph* Milton Krasner *m* Cyril Mockridge

Clifton Webb, Ginger Rogers, Anne Francis, Jeffrey Hunter, Elsa Lanchester, Fred Clark, Ray Collins, Paul Harvey
'A merry comedy filled with uproarious laughter from beginning to end.'—*Hollywood Reporter*

Dreaming
GB 1944 78m bw

A soldier on leave gets a bump on the head, and dreams . . . Rather elementary series of sketches with a few good laughs and interesting guest appearances. Flanagan and Allen, Hazel Court, Dick Francis, Philip Wade, Teddy Brown, Reginald Foort, Gordon Richards, Alfredo Campoli. Written by Bud Flanagan and Reginald Purdell; directed by John Baxter; for Ealing.

Dreaming Lips*
GB 1936 94m bw
Trafalgar (Paul Czinner)

The wife of an invalid musician has an affair with another man and commits suicide.
Standard star fare, possibly Miss Bergner's most notable film, also available in a German version.

w Margaret Kennedy, Lady Cynthia Asquith, Carl Mayer, *play* Henry Bernstein *d* Paul Czinner, Lee Garmes *ph* Lee Garmes *m* William Walton

Elisabeth Bergner, Romney Brent, Raymond Massey, Joyce Bland, Sydney Fairbrother, Felix Aylmer, Donald Calthrop
'In many respects one of the finest productions ever made in England . . . made in Hollywood, the story would be whitewashed and much of its strength weakened.'—*Variety*

Dreams That Money Can Buy*
US 1946 81m Technicolor
Art of the Century (Hans Richter, Peggy Guggenheim, Kenneth MacPherson)

A young itinerant sells dreams to people who need them.
Semi-underground surrealist film, momentarily of interest, but disjointed and with no real apparent purpose.

wd Hans Richter *ph* Arnold Eagle *md* Louis Applebaum

'Arch, snobbish and sycophantic, about as genuinely experimental as a Chemcraft set.'—*James Agee*
† The individual dreams are directed by Max Ernst, Man Ray, Fernand Leger, Marcel Duchamp and Alexander Calder as well as Richter.

Dreamscape
US 1984 99m CFI color

Experiments prove that it is possible for a dreamer to enter the dreams of others, and a subject finds himself being used for a plot against the president of the US. Complex fantasy melodrama with a cold war basis; neither exciting nor praiseworthy. Dennis Quaid, Max Von Sydow, Christopher Plummer, Eddie Albert. Kate Capshaw. Written by David Loughery, Joseph Ruben, Chuck Russell; directed by Joseph Ruben; for Zupnik-Curtis / Bella.

Drei von der Tankstelle*
Germany 1930 80m bw
UFA

Three penniless young men find happiness as petrol station attendants.
Light-hearted operetta of the Depression era, well received at the time.

w Franz Schultz, Paul Frank *d* William Thiele *ph* Franz Planer *m* Werner Heymann

Willy Fritsch, Lilian Harvey, Oskar Karlweis, Heinz Ruhmann, Olga Tchekhova
'When leaving this charming talker operetta, one feels in good humour, humming the catchy hits of its talented composer . . . constant laughter and enthusiasm.'—*Variety*
† Remade 1955 by Hans Wolff, with a cast still led by Willy Fritsch.

Die Dreigroschenoper**
Germany 1931 114m bw
Warner / Tobis / Nero
US title: *The Threepenny Opera*

In turn-of-the-century London, Mack the Knife marries the daughter of the beggar king and runs into trouble.
Heavy-footed but interesting updating of *The Beggar's Opera*, with splendid sets.

w Bela Balazs, Leo Lania, Ladislas Vajda, from Bertolt Brecht's version *d* G. W. Pabst *ph* Fritz Arno Wagner *m* Kurt Weill *ad* Andrei Andreiev

Lotte Lenya, Rudolf Forster, Fritz Rasp, Caroline Neher, Reinhold Schunzel, Valeska Gert, Vladimir Sokoloff
† Brecht disliked the film and sued the makers, but lost.
†† A French version was also released under the title *L'Opéra de Quat'sous*, with Albert Préjean.

Dressed to Kill (1946): see Sherlock Holmes

'Every nightmare has a beginning. This one never ends!'
Dressed to Kill**
US 1980 105m Technicolor
Filmways / Samuel Z. Arkoff / Cinema 77 (George Litto)

A sexually disturbed matron under analysis is murdered by a transvestite slasher, who then goes after a witness.
Occasionally brilliant, generally nasty suspenser clearly derived from many viewings of *Psycho*. Certainly not for the squeamish.

wd Brian de Palma *ph* Ralf Bode *m* Pino Donaggio *pd* Gary Weist

Michael Caine, Angie Dickinson, Nancy Allen, Keith Gordon, Dennis Franz
'De Palma goes right for the audience jugular . . . it fully milks the boundaries of its "R" rating.'—*Variety*
'By casting a halo of excitement around killing, a glow of degradation around living, and linking the two in a queasy, guilty partnership, de Palma is asking us to celebrate the joys of barbarism in a world already drunk on rape, torture, murder and war.'—*Sunday Times*

● *Video: Guild*

The Dresser*
GB 1983 118m colour
Columbia / Goldcrest / World Film Services (Peter Yates)

An exhausted Shakespearean actor-manager has a wild last day on tour, comforted and restrained by his homosexual dresser.
A strained film, but a valuable record of a play based on the touring career of Donald Wolfit, whose dresser the author was. The leading performances are too strident for the close-ups.

w Ronald Harwood from his own play *d* Peter Yates *ph* Kelvin Pike *pd* Stephen Grimes *m* James Horner

Albert Finney, Tom Courtenay, Edward Fox, Zena Walker, Eileen Atkins, Michael Gough, Betty Marsden, Lockwood West

AAN: best picture; Tom Courtenay; Albert Finney; Peter Yates as director; Ronald Harwood (adaptation)

Dreyfus°
GB 1931 80m bw
Wardour (F. W. Kraemer)
In 1894 France, a Jewish officer is accused of spying.
Primitive version of a much-filmed story (cf *The Life of Emile Zola, I Accuse*).
w Rehfisch Herzog, Reginald Berkeley, Walter C. Mycroft *d* F. W. Kraemer, Milton Rosmer *ph* Willy Minterstein
Cedric Hardwicke, George Merritt (as Zola), Charles Carson, Sam Livesey, Garry Marsh (as Esterhazy), Randle Ayrton, George Zucco
  'A picture of the documentary class, well out of the ordinary.'—*Variety*

Drifters°
GB 1929 40m approx bw
Empire Marketing Board (John Grierson)
A documentary of the North Sea fishing fleet. A highly influential documentary, made at a time when British films were totally unrealistic and studio-bound. Unfortunately it now seems extremely dull.
wd, ed John Grierson *ph* Basil Emmott

Driftwood
US 1947 90m bw
An orphan is adopted by a kindly doctor.
Lavender-scented family yarn with pleasant backgrounds and expert performances. Natalie Wood, Ruth Warrick, Walter Brennan, Dean Jagger, Charlotte Greenwood. Written by Mary Loos and Richard Sale; directed by Allan Dwan; for Republic.

Drive a Crooked Road
US 1954 82m bw
Columbia (Jonie Taps)
A garage mechanic falls in with bank robbers. Terse crime melodrama, quite watchable.
w Blake Edwards *d* Richard Quine *ph* Charles Lawton Jnr *md* Ross di Maggio
Mickey Rooney, Kevin McCarthy, Dianne Foster

Drive He Said
US 1970 90m colour
Columbia / Drive Productions / BBS (Steve Blauner)
An easygoing college basketball star is helped by an eccentric rebel to ensure his own unfitness for military service. Both run into trouble.
Flabby celebration of against-the-government attitudes, expressed partly through sex and bad language. Defiantly hard to like.
w Jeremy Larner, Jack Nicholson *d* Jack Nicholson *ph* Bill Butler *m* David Shire
Michael Margotta, William Tepper, Bruce Dern, Karen Black, Robert Towne, Henry Jaglom

Drive-in
US 1976 96m Technicolor
Columbia (George Litto)
In Texas, various illicit activities find their climax at a drive-in movie.

Mild sex-and-destruction comedy which raises few laughs and makes little sense.
w Bob Peete *d* Rod Amateau *ph* Robert Jessup *m* various
Lisa Lemole, Glen Morshower, Gary Cavagnaro, Billy Milliken, Lee Newsome, Regan Kee

The Driver°
US 1978 91m De Luxe
TCF / EMI / Lawrence Gordon
A detective determines to catch an old enemy, a getaway driver.
Noisy melodrama, very proficient in the screeching tyre department but extremely empty as a character.
wd Walter Hill *ph* Philip Lathrop *m* Michael Small
Ryan O'Neal, Bruce Dern, Isabelle Adjani, Ronee Blakeley
● *Video: Thorn EMI*

Drôle de Drame°
France 1936 100m approx bw
aka: *Bizarre, Bizarre* (84m American version)
A complicated chain of bizarre events is set in motion when a botanist pretends not to be a detective story writer, a bishop tries to be a detective, and a murderer seeks revenge for libel.
A curious satirical comedy which is never quite as funny as it seems about to be, but should be seen for its downright peculiar London sets and its array of actors in top form.
w Jacques Prévert, *novel* The Lunatic at Large by J. Storer Clouston *d* Marcel Carné
Françoise Rosay, Michel Simon, Louis Jouvet, Jean-Louis Barrault, Jean-Pierre Aumont
  'Art theatres and foreign-language houses will do fair business.'—*Variety*
  'No one with any taste for nonsense should miss it.'—*Richard Mallett, Punch*

Drop Dead Darling
GB 1966 100m Technicolor
Panavision
Seven Arts (Ken Hughes)
US title: *Arrivederci Baby*
A con man who marries and murders rich women meets a con lady with similar intentions.
Loud, restless black comedy which squanders its moments of genuine inventiveness among scenes of shouting, confusion and action for action's sake.
wd Ken Hughes, *story* The Careful Man by Richard Deeming *ph* Denys Coop *m* Dennis Farnon
Tony Curtis, Rosanna Schiaffino, Lionel Jeffries, Zsa Zsa Gabor, Nancy Kwan, Fenella Fielding, Anna Quayle, Warren Mitchell, Mischa Auer

The Drowning Pool
US 1975 108m Technicolor
Panavision
Warner / Coleytown (Lawrence Turman, David Foster)
Private eye Lew Harper goes to New Orleans to investigate an anonymous letter which ends in murder.
Dreary sequel to *Harper* (qv), full of boring characters uninventively deployed.
w Tracy Keenan Wynn, Lorenzo Semple Jnr, Walter Hill, *novel* John Ross MacDonald *d* Stuart Rosenberg *ph* Gordon Willis *m* Michael Small
Paul Newman, Joanne Woodward, Coral Browne, Tony Franciosa, Murray Hamilton, Gail Strickland, Linda Hayes, Richard Jaeckel
  'The impenetrable mystery is not particularly gripping; and the general air of pointlessness is only intensified by the sudden rush of clarifications at the end.'—*Tom Milne*
  'It recycles every private eye cliché known to civilized man as it crawls through Louisiana talking all the way.'—*Paul D. Zimmermann*
  'All the clichés of cheapjack TV private eye capers have been added to MacDonald's book; whatever separates him from the paperback hacks has been deleted.'—*Judith Crist*

The Drum°
GB 1938 96m Technicolor
London Films (Alexander Korda)
US title: *Drums*
The British army helps an Indian prince to resist his usurping uncle.
Reasonably entertaining story of the Raj, with adequate excitement after a meandering start.
w Lajos Biro, Arthur Wimperis, Patrick Kirwan, Hugh Gray, *novel* A. E. W. Mason *d* Zoltan Korda *ph* Georges Périnal *m* John Greenwood, Miklos Rozsa
Sabu, Roger Livesey, Raymond Massey, Valerie Hobson, Desmond Tester, David Tree, Francis L. Sullivan, Roy Emerton, Edward Lexy
  'Looks like a 100% commercial bet.'—*Variety*
● *Video: Polygram*

Drum
US 1976 100m Metrocolor Panavision
Dino de Laurentiis (Ralph Serpe)
In 1860 New Orleans, a bordello house slave faces all manner of sexual predators.
Tediously single-minded sequel to the appalling *Mandingo*.
w Norman Wexler, *novel* Kyle Onstott *d* Steve Carver *ph* Lucien Ballard *m* Charles Smalls
Warren Oates, Ken Norton, Isela Vega, Yaphet Kotto, John Colicos
  'Shamelessly it exploits the factors which explain the success of the prototype: a feeble pretence at outraged historical exposé of the abuses of the slave trade provides the excuse for an orgy of wish dreams, of sadism, flagellation, domination, sexuality of all tastes, popular fantasies of negro potency.'—*David Robinson, The Times*
● *Video: Guild*

Drumbeat

US 1954   111m   Warnercolor
Jaguar (no producer credited)

An Indian fighter sets out to make peace with a renegade.
Long, dull western, stolid all round.

wd Delmer Daves *ph* J. Peverell Marley
m Victor Young

Alan Ladd, Audrey Dalton, Marisa Pavan, Robert Keith, Rodolpho Acosta, Charles Bronson, Warner Anderson, Elisha Cook Jnr, Anthony Caruso

● *Video: Kingston*

Drums Across the River

US 1954   78m   Technicolor
Universal-International (Melville Tucker)

A young westerner who hates Indians finally helps them to overthrow a white crook.
Slick little western with almost every familiar ingredient.

w John K. Butler, Lawrence Roman
d Nathan Juran *ph* Harold Lipstein
m Joseph Gershenson

Audie Murphy, Walter Brennan, Lyle Bettger, Lisa Gaye, Hugh O'Brian, Jay Silverheels, Emile Meyer

Drums along the Mohawk**

US 1939   103m   Technicolor
TCF (Raymond Griffith)

Colonists survive Indian attacks in upstate New York during the Revolutionary War.
Patchy, likeable period adventure story with domestic and farming interludes; in its way a key film in the director's canon.

w Lamar Trotti, Sonya Levien, *novel* Walter Edmonds *d* John Ford *ph* Bert Glennon, Ray Rennahan *m* Alfred Newman

Claudette Colbert, Henry Fonda, *Edna May Oliver*, Eddie Collins, John Carradine, Dorris Bowdon, Jessie Ralph, Arthur Shields, Robert Lowery, Roger Imhof, Ward Bond

'Outdoor spec, a top-bracketer, though not in the smash division.'—*Variety*

'No one appears to know why the picture is being made, or what its point is, exactly.'—
Pauline Kael, 70s

AAN: Edna May Oliver

Drums in the Deep South

GB 1951   87m   Supercinecolor

A Confederate officer finds himself fighting a lonely battle with his best friend from West Point. Barely stimulating semi-western in appalling colour. James Craig, Barbara Payton, Guy Madison, Barton Maclane, Craig Stevens, Tom Fadden, Taylor Holmes. Written by Philip Yordan and Sidney Harmon; directed by William Cameron Menzies (also production designer); for King Brothers / RKO.

'A volcano erupts! A hurricane strikes! A man . . . a woman . . . discover passion in each other's arms!'

Drums of Tahiti

US 1953   73m   Technicolor   3D

In 1877 an American helps the queen of Tahiti, who doesn't want to become a French possession. Cheapskate potboiler with an extended volcanic climax (courtesy of older, better movies). Dennis O'Keefe, Patricia Medina, Francis L. Sullivan, Sylvia Lewis. Written by Douglas Heyes and Robert E. Kent; directed by William Castle; for Sam Katzman / Columbia.

Dry Rot

GB 1956   87m   bw
Romulus (Jack Clayton)

Three bookmakers plot to make a fortune by substituting a doped horse for the favourite.
Flat filming of a long-running theatrical farce.

w John Chapman, from his play *d* Maurice Elvey *ph* Arthur Grant *m* Peter Akister

Ronald Shiner, Brian Rix, Sid James, Michael Shepley, Joan Haythorne, Joan Sims, Heather Sears, Lee Patterson, Peggy Mount.

Dual Alibi

GB 1947   81m   bw
British National (Louis H. Jackson)

Twin trapezists fall out over a lottery ticket and a worthless woman, but later extract a unique revenge.
Sprightly circus melodrama, shot on a shoestring.

w Alfred Travers, Stephen Clarkson *d* Alfred Travers *ph* James Wilson

Herbert Lom, Phyllis Dixey, Ronald Frankau, Terence de Marney, Abraham Sofaer, Eugene Deckers

Du Barry, Woman of Passion

US 1930   88m   bw

Incidents in the life of the mistress of Louis XV. Tedious early talkie which marked the virtual end of its star's career. Norma Talmadge, William Farnum, Hobart Bosworth, Conrad Nagel, Alison Skipworth. From the play by David Belasco; directed by Sam Taylor; for Talmadge / United Artists.

'Wholly unimpressive . . . nix for kids and the sticks.'—*Variety*

Dubarry Was a Lady

US 1943   101m   Technicolor
MGM (Arthur Freed)

A New Yorker imagines himself back at the court of Louis XIV.
Dull, stiff adaptation of a Broadway musical comedy, with changed songs.

w Irving Brecher, *book* B. G. De Sylva, Herbert Fields *d* Roy del Ruth *ph* Karl Freund *md* George Stoll *songs* Cole Porter

Gene Kelly, Lucille Ball, Red Skelton, Virginia O'Brien, Zero Mostel, Rags Ragland, Tommy Dorsey and his Orchestra

'If the rustlers didn't get you . . . the hustlers did!'

The Duchess and the Dirtwater Fox

US 1976   104m   De Luxe   Panavision
TCF (Melvin Frank)

A Barbary Coast con man and a saloon singer have various hectic adventures.

Wild and woolly spoof western which fires off aimlessly in a variety of styles and becomes merely tiresome despite good scenes.

w Melvin Frank, Barry Sandler *d* Melvin Frank *ph* Joseph Biroc *m* Charles Fox

George Segal, Goldie Hawn, Conrad Janis, Thayer David, Roy Jenson, Bob Hoy, Bennie Dobbins

'The classic western has now been shot to death by Sam Peckinpah, laughed to death by Mel Brooks and pondered to death by Arthur Penn, and Frank is like a scavenger picking up stray relics from its body.'—*Newsweek*

'The relentless vulgarity of the enterprise suggests that Mr Frank, having been so long constrained by the Hollywood Production Code when churning out vehicles for Bob Hope and Danny Kaye, is still making up for lost time.'—*Philip French, The Times*

● *Video: CBS / Fox*

The Duchess of Idaho

US 1950   98m   Technicolor
MGM (Joe Pasternak)

Romantic misunderstandings among candidates for Miss Idaho Potato.
Lightweight musical, quite pleasant if routine, with guest spots.

w Dorothy Cooper, Jerry Davis *d* Robert Z. Leonard *ph* Charles Schoenbaum
md Georgie Stoll

Esther Williams, Van Johnson, John Lund, Paula Raymond, Clinton Sundberg; guests Red Skelton, Eleanor Powell, Lena Horne

Duck Soup****

US 1933   68m   bw
Paramount

An incompetent becomes President of Fredonia and wages war on its scheming neighbour.
The satirical aspects of this film are fascinating but appear to have been unintentional. Never mind, it's also the most satisfying and undiluted Marx Brothers romp, albeit the one without instrumental interludes. It does include the lemonade stall, the mirror sequence, and an endless array of one-liners and comedy choruses.

w Bert Kalmar, Harry Ruby, Arthur Sheekman, Nat Perrin *d* Leo McCarey *ph* Henry Sharp *m / ly* Bert Kalmar, Harry Ruby *ad* Hans Dreier, Wiard Ihnen

The Four Marx Brothers, Margaret Dumont, Louis Calhern, Edgar Kennedy, Raquel Torres

'It should make practically everybody laugh.'—*Variety*

'So much preliminary dialogue is necessary that it seems years before Groucho comes on at all; and waiting for Groucho is agony.'
—*E. V. Lucas, Punch*

'The most perfect of all Marxist masterpieces.'—*Time Out, 1984*

● *Video: CIC*

Due Soldi di Speranza*

Italy 1952   98m   bw
Universalcine (Sandro Ghenzi)
GB title: *Two Pennyworth of Hope*

Demobilized after World War II, Antonio finds life in his native village hard to take. Neo-realist comedy-melodrama full of gesticulating rustics; good for those who like this sort of thing.

w Renato Castellani, Titina de Filippo *d* Renato Castellani *ph* Arturo Gallea *m* Alessandro Cicognini

Vincenzo Musolino, Maria Fiore, Filumena Russo, Luigi Astarita

Duel: see *Television Companion*

Duel at Diablo*
US 1966 103m De Luxe
UA / Nelson / Engel / Cherokee / Rainbow / Brien

White and black man fight together as Apaches attack.
Well-paced, old-fashioned, shoot-em-up star western.

w Marvin H. Albert, Michel M. Grilikhes *d* Ralph Nelson *ph* Charles F. Wheeler *m* Neal Hefti

Sidney Poitier, James Garner, Bibi Andersson, Bill Travers, William Redfield, John Hoyt, John Hubbard

Duel at Silver Creek
US 1952 77m Technicolor
U-I (Leonard Goldstein)

An honest man is murdered by claim jumpers, and the Silver Kid is suspected.
Modest, efficient western.

w Gerald Drayson Adams, Joseph Hoffman *d* Don Siegel *ph* Irving Glassberg *m* Hans Salter

Audie Murphy, Stephen McNally, Faith Domergue, Susan Cabot, Gerald Mohr, Eugene Iglesias, Lee Marvin, Walter Sande

Duel in the Jungle
GB 1954 101m Technicolor
ABP / Marcel Hellman

An African explorer intends to defraud an insurance company and sets traps for the investigator who pursues him.
Lackadaisical romp in the studio jungle, none of it with much style or film sense.

w Sam Marx, T. J. Morrison *d* George Marshall *ph* Erwin Hillier *m* Mischa Spoliansky

Dana Andrews, Jeanne Crain, David Farrar, Patrick Barr

Duel in the Sun***
US 1946 135 or 138m Technicolor
David O. Selznick

A half-breed girl causes trouble between two brothers.
Massive western, dominated and fragmented by its producer, who bought the best talent and proceeded to interfere with it, so that while individual scenes are marvellous, the narrative has little flow. The final gory shoot-up between two lovers was much discussed at the time.

w David O. Selznick, Oliver H. P. Garrett, *novel* Niven Busch *d* King Vidor (and others) *second unit* B. Reeves Eason, Otto Brower *ph* Lee Garmes, Harold Rosson, Ray Rennahan *m* Dmitri Tiomkin *ad* James Basevi *pd* J. McMillan Johnson

Jennifer Jones, Joseph Cotten, Gregory Peck, Lionel Barrymore, Lillian Gish, Walter Huston, Herbert Marshall, Charles Bickford, Tilly Losch, Joan Tetzel, Harry Carey, Otto Kruger, Sidney Blackmer
  'A razzmatazz of thunderous naïvety simmering into a kind of majestic dottiness.'—*Basil Wright, 1972*
  'A lavish, sensual spectacle, so heightened it becomes a cartoon of passion.'—*Pauline Kael, 70s*

† The uncredited directors included Joseph Von Sternberg, William Dieterle, B. Reeves Eason, and Selznick himself.

AAN: Jennifer Jones; Lillian Gish

● *Video: Guild*

Duel on the Mississippi
US 1955 72m Technicolor

A river planter owes money to pirates.
Standard second feature excitements with romantic interludes. Patricia Medina, Lex Barker, Craig Stevens, Warren Stevens. Written by Gerald Drayson Adams; directed by William Castle; for Sam Katzman / Columbia.

The Duellists*
GB 1977 101m colour
Scott Free / NFFC / David Puttnam

In the early 1800s, two Hussar Officers challenge each other to a series of duels; after sixteen years an ironic truce is called. A singularly pointless anecdote; its main virtue is that it is coldly attractive to look at.

w Gerald Vaughan-Hughes, *story* The Point of Honour by Joseph Conrad *d* Ridley Scott *ph* Frank Tidy *m* Howard Blake *pd* Peter J. Hampton

Keith Carradine, Harvey Keitel, Albert Finney, Edward Fox, Cristina Raines, Tom Conti, Robert Stephens, John McEnery

● *Video: CIC*

'Some helpful hints for those who are very rich, very beautiful, very hip, elaborately oversexed, tuned in, turned on and bored to death!'

Duffy
GB 1968 101m Technicolor
Columbia / Martin Manulis

Two half-brothers plan to rob their millionaire father.
Would-be with-it caper film, all flashy fragments and pop art, like sitting through a feature-length commercial. Exasperating.

w Donald Cammell, Harry Joe Brown Jnr *d* Robert Parrish *ph* Otto Heller *m* Ernie Freeman

James Coburn, James Mason, James Fox, Susannah York, John Alderton, Guy Deghy,

Tutte Lemkow, Carl Duering, Marne Maitland

Duffy of San Quentin
US 1953 78m bw
Allied Artists (Berman Swarttz, Walter Doniger)
GB title: *Men Behind Bars*

An elderly warden institutes prison reforms which cause him problems.
Semi-true melodrama with standard excitements and too much talk.

wd Walter Doniger *ph* John Alton *m* Paul Dunlap

Paul Kelly, Louis Hayward, Maureen O'Sullivan, Joanne Dru, George Macready, Horace MacMahon

Duffy's Tavern
US 1945 97m bw
Paramount (Danny Dare)

The owner of a bar is helped by Hollywood stars.
Flat comedy based on a radio show and not helped by dismal guest star appearances.

w Melvin Frank, Norman Panama *d* Hal Walker *ph* Lionel Lindon *m* Robert Emmet Dolan

Ed Gardner, Victor Moore, Marjorie Reynolds, Barry Sullivan and guests including Bing Crosby, Bob Hope, Betty Hutton, Alan Ladd, Dorothy Lamour, Veronica Lake, William Bendix, Joan Caulfield

The Duke of West Point*
US 1938 112m bw
Edward Small

An extrovert army cadet finds the going tough. Dated romantic flagwaver which pleased at the time.

w George Bruce *d* Alfred E. Green *ph* Robert Planck

Louis Hayward, Joan Fontaine, Tom Brown, Richard Carlson, Alan Curtis, Donald Barry, Gaylord Pendleton, Jed Prouty, Marjorie Gateson
  'Fairly good entertainment. Much human interest, but the comedy relief is rather light.'—*Variety*

The Duke Wore Jeans
GB 1958 89m bw

An aristocrat persuades his cockney double to woo a princess on his behalf. Moderately lively comedy with songs, tailored for Britain's new musical star. Tommy Steele, June Laverick, Michael Medwin, Alan Wheatley, Eric Pohlmann. Written by Norman Hudis; directed by Gerald Thomas; for Peter Rogers / Insignia.

Dulcima
GB 1971 98m Technicolor
EMI (Basil Rayburn)

A farmer's daughter reluctantly moves in with a persistent, lecherous old miser.

Weird sex melodrama from *Cold Comfort Farm* country, more risible than interesting.

wd Frank Nesbitt, *story* H. E. Bates *ph* Tony Imi *m* Johnny Douglas

John Mills, Carol White, Stuart Wilson, Bernard Lee, Dudley Foster

Dumbo***
US 1941 64m Technicolor
Walt Disney

A baby circus elephant finds that his big ears have a use after all.
Delightful cartoon feature notable for set pieces such as the drunken nightmare and the crows' song.

w various *d* Ben Sharpsteen *m* Frank Churchill, Oliver Wallace

AA: music
AAN: song, 'Baby Mine' (*m* Frank Churchill, *ly* Ned Washington)

The Dummy Talks
GB 1943 85m bw

A ventriloquist turns to blackmail and is murdered backstage. Curious, oddly cast murder mystery, not unentertaining at the time. Jack Warner, Claude Hulbert, Beryl Orde, G. H. Mulcaster, Ivy Benson, Manning Whiley. Written by Michael Barringer; directed by Oswald Mitchell; for British National.

Dune
US 1984 140m Technicolor Todd-AO
Dino de Laurentiis (Raffaella de Laurentiis)

Armies from several planets descend on another which has valuable spice guarded by monster worms.
A basically simple space fiction plot is immensely complicated by a welter of characters who are not properly introduced and who indeed are mostly irrelevant. The result, which cost nearly 50 million dollars, is inaudible, invisible (because of dim lighting) and unentertaining: a disaster of the very first order.

w,d David Lynch, *novel* Frank Herbert *ph* Freddie Francis *m* Toto *pd* Anthony Masters *ed* Antony Gibbs

Francesca Annis, Jose Ferrer, Sian Phillips, Brad Dourif, Dean Stockwell, Freddie Jones, Linda Hunt, Kenneth McMillan, Richard Jordan, Kyle MacLachlan, Silvana Mangano, Jurgen Prochnow, Max Von Sydow, Sting

Dunkirk**
GB 1958 135m bw
MGM / Ealing (Michael Balcon)

In 1940 on the Normandy beaches, a small group gets detached from the main force. Sober, small-scale approach to an epic subject; interesting but not inspiring, with performances to match.

w W. P. Lipscomb, David Divine *d* Leslie Norman *ph* Paul Beeson *m* Malcolm Arnold

John Mills, Richard Attenborough, Bernard Lee, Robert Urquhart, Ray Jackson

'Men invoke its horror! Women invite its shame!'
The Dunwich Horror*
US 1970 90m Movielab
AIP (Roger Corman, Jack Bohrer)

A young warlock plans to use his girl friend in a fertility rite.
Bookish horror story, quite well done against a village background.

w Curtis Lee Hanson, Henry Rosenbaum, Ronald Silkosky, *story* H. P. Lovecraft *d* Daniel Haller *ph* Richard C. Glouner *m* Les Baxter

Dean Stockwell, Sandra Dee, Ed Begley, Sam Jaffe, Lloyd Bochner

● Video: Guild

Duped Till Doomsday*
East Germany 1957 97m bw
DEFA (Adolf Fischer)
original title: *Betrogen bis zum Jüngsten Tag*

Three Nazi NCOs go to the bad.
Propagandist anti-Nazi war melodrama, very well made in parts.

w Kurt Bortfeldt, *novel* Kameraden by Franz Fuhmann *d* Kurt Jung-Alsen *ph* Walter Fehdmer

Wolfgang Kieling, Rudolph Ulrich, Hans-Joachim Martens

During One Night
GB 1961 80m bw

During World War II, a country girl helps a USAAF deserter dispel his fear of impotence. Glum sex drama, a curious and unsuccessful attempt. Don Borisenko, Susan Hampshire, Sean Sullivan, Joy Webster. Written and directed by Sidney J. Furie; for Galaworldfilm.

Dust Be My Destiny*
US 1939 88m bw
Warner (Lou Edelman)

A young misfit tries to find himself in the country.
Dated but well made social melodrama.

w Robert Rossen, *story* Jerome Odlum *d* Lewis Seiler *ph* James Wong Howe *m* Max Steiner

John Garfield, Priscilla Lane, Alan Hale, Frank McHugh, John Litel, Charles Grapewin, Billy Halop, Bobby Jordan, Stanley Ridges

'Strong programmer, though overlong and episodic.'—*Variety*

'You can tell from the title that John Garfield has his usual part—the angry, bitter, tough, poor young man with slight persecution mania.'—*Richard Mallett, Punch*

† Remade 1942 as *I Was Framed*, with Michael Ames.

Dusty Ermine
GB 1938 74m bw

Scotland Yard chases counterfeiters to Switzerland, and the hunt ends in a ski chase. Modestly effective melodrama with dated romantic leads. Jane Baxter, Anthony Bushell, Ronald Squire, Margaret Rutherford, Athole Stewart, Katie Johnson, Austin Trevor, Felix Aylmer. Written by Paul Hervey Fox from a play by Neil Grant; directed by Bernard Vorhaus; for Julius Hagen. 'The humour is of the British kind – not too hilarious but still tickling.'—*Variety* (US title: *Hideout in the Alps.*)

Dutchman*
GB 1966 56m bw
Gene Persson

On a New York subway train a woman humiliates a black man and finally knifes him. An allegory for addicts who can ferret out the meaning; on the surface, vaguely Pinterish and mainly boring.

w LeRoi Jones, from his play *d* Anthony Harvey *ph* Gerry Turpin *m* John Barry

Shirley Knight, Al Freeman Jnr

Dynamite**
US 1929 129m bw
MGM (Cecil B. de Mille)

In order to gain an inheritance, a socialite marries a man about to be executed . . . but he is reprieved.
Dated but still dynamic social melodrama of the early talkie period.

w Jeanie Macpherson *d* Cecil B. de Mille *ph* Peverell Marley *m* Herbert Stothart

Kay Johnson, Charles Bickford, Conrad Nagel, Julia Faye, Joel McCrea

'A pot-pourri of all previous de Mille efforts crammed into one picture.'—*Variety*

'Exuberant, wonderfully vigorous, the film skilfully evokes the look and character of the Jazz Age.'—*Charles Higham*

'An astonishing mixture, with artificiality vying with realism and comedy hanging on the heels of grim melodrama.'—*Mordaunt Hall, New York Times*

E.T.*
US 1982 115m De Luxe
Universal (Steven Spielberg, Kathleen
  Kennedy)

When an alien spacecraft is disturbed in a Los
Angeles suburb, one of its crew members is
left behind and befriended by a small boy.
Stupefyingly successful box office fairy tale by
the current wonder kid Spielberg, taken to the
world's heart because he dares to make films
without sex, violence or bad language. This
one could hardly be simpler, but it works; and
the ailing cinema would love to know how to
repeat the trick several times a year.

*w Melissa Mathison d Steven Spielberg
ph Allen Daviau m John Williams pd James
D. Bissell creator of E.T. Carlo Rimbaldi*

Dee Wallace, Henry Thomas, Peter Coyote,
Robert MacNaughton, Maxie Rosenbloom, Drew Barrymore,
K. C. Martel
† E.T. = extra-terrestrial.

AA: visual effects; music; sound
AAN: best picture; direction; original
screenplay; cinematography; editing
BFA: best score

Each Dawn I Die*
US 1939 84m bw
Warner (David Lewis)

A crusading reporter is framed for
manslaughter and becomes a hardened
prisoner.
Efficient, vigorous yet slightly disappointing
star vehicle; the talents are in the right
background, but the script is wobbly.

*w Norman Reilly Raine, Warren Duff,
Charles Perry, novel Jerome Odlum
d William Keighley ph Arthur Edeson
m Max Steiner*

James Cagney, George Raft, Jane Bryan,
George Bancroft, Maxie Rosenbloom, Stanley
Ridges, Alan Baxter, Victor Jory
  'Rich in horror and brutality.'—*New York
Sunday Mirror*
  'In addition to its crackling screenplay, it is
made memorable by the easy mastery of its
two principals.'—*Time*
  'Towards the end of the thirties Warners
underworld pictures began to get hazy and
high-minded, and in this one the pre-Second
World War spiritual irradiation blurs the
conventions of the prison genre.'—*Pauline
Kael, 70s*
† Original title: *Killer Meets Killer.*

The Eagle**
US 1925 80m approx (24 fps) bw
  silent
United Artists

A Cossack lieutenant turns masked outlaw
when his father's lands are annexed.
Enjoyable romp in the wake of Robin Hood,
the Scarlet Pimpernel and Zorro; the eye-
flashing star is somewhere near his best.

*w Hans Kraly, story Dubrowsky by Alexander
Pushkin d Clarence Brown ph George Barnes*

Rudolph Valentino, Vilma Banky, Louise
Dresser

The Eagle and the Hawk**
US 1933 72m bw
Paramount

In 1918 France, two American army fliers
dislike each other but come together before
the death of one of them.
Dawn Patrol melodrama, well done with
unusually vivid dialogue and acting.

*w Bogart Rogers, Seton I. Miller, story John
Monk Saunders d Stuart Walker ph Harry
Fischbeck*

Fredric March, Cary Grant, Carole Lombard,
Sir Guy Standing, Jack Oakie, Forrester
Harvey
  'Will make good with those it attracts, but is
handicapped by the mass of earlier flight
pictures.'—*Variety*

The Eagle and the Hawk
US 1949 86m bw
(Paramount) Pine-Thomas

During the Mexican wars, a US government
agent tracks down a traitor who is supplying
arms to the rebel Juarez.
Stolid adventure yarn, energetically played.

*w Geoffrey Homes, Lewis R. Foster d Lewis
R. Foster ph James Wong Howe m David
Chudnow*

John Payne, Dennis O'Keefe, Rhonda
Fleming, Thomas Gomez, Fred Clark, Frank
Faylen, Eduardo Noriega

The Eagle Has Landed*
GB 1976 135m Eastmancolor
  Panavision
ITC / Associated General (Jack Wiener,
  David Niven Jnr)

During World War II, enemy aliens infiltrate
an English village in the hope of killing
Churchill.

Elaborately plotted but uninvolving spy
melodrama, lethargically directed, muddily
coloured and too concerned to create some
good Germans.

*w Tom Mankiewicz, novel Jack Higgins
d John Sturges ph Anthony Richmond
m Lalo Schifrin*

Michael Caine, Donald Sutherland, Robert
Duvall, Jenny Agutter, Donald Pleasence,
Anthony Quayle, Jean Marsh, Sven-Bertil
Taube, John Standing, Judy Geeson, Larry
Hagman, Maurice Roeves

● *Video: Precision*

Eagle in a Cage*
GB 1970 103m Eastmancolor
Group W / Ramona (Millard Lampell, Albert
  Schwarz)

In 1815, a professional soldier becomes
governor of St Helena and jailer to Napoleon.
Talkative, anecdotal, heavily serious historical
reconstruction with good acting but little
control.

*w Millard Lampell d Fielder Cook ph Frano
Vodopivec m Marc Wilkinson*

John Gielgud, Ralph Richardson, Kenneth
Haigh, Billie Whitelaw, Moses Gunn, Ferdy
Mayne, Lee Montague

Eagle Squadron
US 1942 102m bw
Universal (Walter Wanger)

During World War II, American fliers join the
RAF.
Studio-bound air epic, leavened with
conventional romance but little humour or
sympathy.

*w Norman Reilly Raine, story C. S. Forester
d Arthur Lubin ph Stanley Cortez m Frank
Skinner*

Robert Stack, Diana Barrymore, John Loder,
Eddie Albert, Nigel Bruce, Leif Erickson,
Edgar Barrier, Jon Hall, Evelyn Ankers,
Isobel Elsom, Alan Hale Jnr, Don Porter,
Frederick Worlock, Gladys Cooper

Eagle's Wing
GB 1979 111m Eastmancolor
  Panavision
Rank / Peter Shaw (Ben Arbeid)

A Comanche chief pursues a white man who
has stolen a prize Indian horse.
Would-be poetic western which emerges as

THE EAGLE HAS LANDED. Nazi infiltration of an English village in wartime was a film subject as long ago as 1942 in *Went the Day Well?*, but Michael Caine, Donald Sutherland and Jean Marsh were among the actors who gave it freshness.

very pretty but stultifyingly dull; an odd thing indeed to come from a moribund British studio.

w John Briley *d* Anthony Harvey *ph* Billy Williams *m* Marc Wilkinson *pd* Herbert Westbrook

Martin Sheen, Sam Waterston, Harvey Keitel, Stephane Audran, John Castle

Earl Carroll Vanities
US 1945 91m bw
Republic (Albert J. Cohen)

A Ruritanian princess in need of a loan becomes the singing star of a New York night club.
Nit-witted musical with no style but an engaging cast.

w Frank Gill Jnr *d* Joseph Santley *ph* Jack Marta *md* Walter Scharf *songs* Walter Kent, Kim Gannon

Constance Moore, Dennis O'Keefe, Alan Mowbray, Eve Arden, Otto Kruger (as Earl Carroll), Pinky Lee, Mary Forbes, Stephanie Bachelor, Parkyakarkus, Leon Belasco, Robert Greig

AAN: song 'Endlessly' (*ly* Kim Gannon, *m* Walter Kent)

The Earl of Chicago*
US 1940 87m bw
MGM (Victor Saville)

An American gangster accedes to an English earldom but is tried for murder.
Unusual but unsatisfactory comedy-drama which rambles to a dismal conclusion but has entertaining passages.

w Lesser Samuels, *novel* Brock Williams *d* Richard Thorpe *ph* Ray June *m* Werner Heymann

Robert Montgomery, Edward Arnold, Reginald Owen, Edmund Gwenn

The Early Bird
GB 1965 98m Eastmancolor
Rank / Hugh Stewart

A milkman gets involved in an inter-company war.
Star farcical comedy; not the worst of Wisdom, but overlong and mainly uninventive.

w Jack Davies, Norman Wisdom, Eddie Leslie, Henry Blyth *d* Robert Asher *ph* Jack Asher *m* Ron Goodwin

Norman Wisdom, Edward Chapman, Jerry Desmonde, Paddie O'Neil, Bryan Pringle, Richard Vernon, John Le Mesurier, Peter Jeffrey

● *Video: Rank*

Early to Bed
US 1928 20m bw silent

Stan becomes Ollie's butler but rebels when his friend's fortune goes to his head. One of the most untypical and seldom seen Laurel and Hardy comedies, with both stars prankishly out of characters. On its own account however it is mainly very funny.
Written by H. M. Walker; directed by Emmett Flynn; for Hal Roach.

Earth•••
USSR 1930 63m approx (24 fps) bw
silent
VUFKU
original title: *Zemlya*

Trouble results in a Ukrainian village when a landowner refuses to hand over his land for a collective farm.
The melodramatic little plot takes second place to lyrical sequences of rustic beauty, illustrating life, love and death in the countryside.

wd, ed Alexander Dovzhenko *ph* Danylo Demutsky

Semyon Svashenko, Stephan Shkurat, Mikola Nademsky, Yelena Maximova

'Stories in themselves do not interest me. I choose them in order to get the greatest expression of essential social forms.'— *Dovzhenko*
'A picture for filmgoers who are prepared to take their cinema as seriously as Tolstoy took the novel.'—*James Agate*

Earth Versus the Flying Saucers
US 1956 83m bw

Saucermen from another planet try to disintegrate the earth. Elementary science fiction with special effects in a similar if enthusiastic vein. Hugh Marlowe, Joan Taylor, Donald Curtis, Morris Ankrum. Written by George Worthing Yates and Raymond T. Marcus, from a story by Curt Siodmak; directed by Fred F. Sears; special effects by Ray Harryhausen; for Charles H. Schneer / Columbia.

Earthbound*
US 1940 67m bw

The ghost of a murdered man helps his widow to bring the murderer to justice. Curious attempt at *Topper* without laughs, nicely done once you get used to the idea. Warner Baxter, Lynn Bari, Andrea Leeds, Charles Grapewin, Henry Wilcoxon, Elizabeth Patterson. Written by John Howard Lawson and Samuel Engel, from a story by Basil King; directed by Irving Pichel; for Sol M. Wurtzel / TCF.

Earthquake*
US 1974 123m Technicolor
Panavision
Universal / Jennings Lang / Mark Robson

Various personal stories intertwine in a Los Angeles earthquake.
Dreary drama with very variable special effects, gimmicked up by Sensurround. A box office bonanza.

w George Fox, Mario Puzo *d* Mark Robson
ph Philip Lathrop *m* John Williams
pd Alexander Golitzen *sp* Albert Whitlock

Charlton Heston, Ava Gardner, Lorne
Greene, Marjoe Gortner, Barry Sullivan,
George Kennedy, Richard Roundtree,
Geneviève Bujold, Walter Matthau (under the
alias of his real name)
'The picture is swell, but it isn't a cheat. It's
an entertaining marathon of Grade A
destruction effects, with B-picture stock
characters spinning through it.'—*Pauline Kael*

AAN: Philip Lathrop

● Video: CIC

Earthworm Tractors
US 1936   69m   bw

A salesman whose fiancée wants him to think
big turns to tractors. One of the star's livelier
comedies. *Joe E. Brown,* June Travis, Guy
Kibbee, Dick Foran. Written by Richard
Macauley, Joe Traub and Hugh Cummings;
directed by Ray Enright; for Warner.(GB
title: *A Natural Born Salesman*.)

'The frank fearless drama of a woman who
sinned!'
The Easiest Way
US 1931   86m   bw
MGM

A hard-working slum girl falls into the lap of
luxury but her easy virtue finally causes her to
be rejected.
Familiar moral melodrama which got past the
Hays Office only after some heavy deletions.

w Edith Ellis, *play* Eugene Walter *d* Jack
Conway *ph* John Mescall

Constance Bennett, Robert Montgomery,
Adolphe Menjou, Anita Page, Marjorie
Rambeau, J. Farrell MacDonald, Clark
Gable, Clara Blandick
'Gilded wickedness played by flawless cast:
will entice.'—*Variety*

East Is West
US 1930   72m   bw

Half-caste Big Time Charlie Young lords it
over San Francisco's Chinatown. Muddled
melodrama reminiscent of many silent films.
Edward G. Robinson, Lupe Velez, Lew
Ayres, Henry Kolker, Mary Forbes, Edgar
Norton. Written by Tom Reed from the play
by Sam Shipman and John Hymer; directed by
Monta Bell; for Universal. 'Good daily change
grind meller.'—*Variety*

East Lynne
US 1931   102m   bw
Fox

A Victorian lady is unjustly divorced by her
husband, and later loses both her lover and
her sight.
Much caricatured melodrama, here presented
in stolidly acceptable form.

w Bradley King, Tom Barry, *novel* Mrs Henry
Wood *d* Frank Lloyd *ph* John Seitz
m Richard Fall

Ann Harding, Clive Brook, O. P. Heggie,
Conrad Nagel, Cecilia Loftus, Beryl Mercer,
Flora Sheffield
'A lavish production, some corking
direction, and the elemental appeal of all
dramatic hokum.'—*Variety*

† Previous versions had been made by Fox, in
1916 with Theda Bara and in 1925 with Alma
Rubens.

AAN: best picture

East Lynne on the Western Front
GB 1931   85m   bw

War rookies produce *East Lynne* to relieve
boredom. Slapstick army farce which tickled a
few fancies at the time.
Herbert Mundin, Wilfred Lawson, Mark Daly,
Harold French. Written by George Pearson
and T. A. Welsh; directed by George Pearson;
for Gaumont-Welsh-Pearson. 'Recording is
not good and the production shoddy, but it's
crammed with hoke and will do good business
for juvenile matinées and in the
neighbourhoods.'—*Variety*

East Meets West
GB 1936   74m   bw

A proud sultan learns that his son is having an
affair with the wife of a crook. Derivative star
vehicle, very stagey even then. George Arliss,
Godfrey Tearle, Lucie Mannheim, Romney
Brent, Ballard Berkeley, John Laurie. Written
by Maude Howell, from Edwin Greenwood's
play *The Lake of Life*; directed by Herbert
Mason; for Gaumont.

'Of what a boy did . . . what a girl did . . . of
ecstasy and revenge!'
'The most shocking revenge a girl ever let
one brother take on another!'
East of Eden*'
US 1955   115m   Warnercolor
Cinemascope
Warner (Elia Kazan)

In a California farming valley in 1917 a wild
adolescent rebels against his stern father and
discovers that his mother, believed dead, runs
a nearby brothel.
Turgid elaboration of Genesis with strong
character but nowhere to go. Heavily overdirected and rousingly acted.

w Paul Osborn, *novel* John Steinbeck *d* Elia
Kazan *ph* Ted McCord *m* Leonard
Rosenman *ad* James Basevi, Malcolm Bert

Raymond Massey, James Dean (his first star
role), Julie Harris, Dick Davalos, *Jo Van
Fleet,* Burl Ives, Albert Dekker
'The first distinguished production in
Cinemascope.'—*Eugene Archer*

AA: Jo Van Fleet
AAN: Paul Osborn; Elia Kazan; James Dean

East of Elephant Rock
GB 1976   92m   colour
Boyd's Company / Kendon (Don Boyd)

In 1948 Malaya a womanizing civil servant is
shot by his jealous mistress.

Style-less and quite uncredited re-hash of *The
Letter*, striving vainly to recreate the spirit of
Somerset Maugham.

wd Don Boyd *ph* Keith Goddard *m* Peter
Skellern

Judi Bowker, Jeremy Kemp, John Hurt,
Christopher Cazenove, Anton Rodgers,
Vajira, Tariq Yunus
'Punishingly inept in every department.'—
David Badder, MFB

East of Java
US 1935   72m   bw

After a shipwreck, menagerie animals take
refuge along with the passengers on a tropic
island. The synopsis says it all; the production
is sub-standard. Charles Bickford, Elizabeth
Young, Frank Albertson, Sig Rumann.
Written by James Ashmore, Sam Creelman
and Paul Perez, from the story 'Tiger Island'
by Goeverneur Morris; directed by George
Melford; for Universal. 'Highly thrilling, weak
on names.'—*Variety*

East of Piccadilly
GB 1940   79m   bw
ABPC (Walter C. Mycroft)
US title: *The Strangler*

A novelist and a girl reporter catch a silk
stocking murderer.
Adequate lower case mystery with good
atmosphere.

w Lesley Storm, J. Lee-Thomson,
novel Gordon Beckles *d* Harold Huth

Sebastian Shaw, Judy Campbell, Henry
Edwards, Niall MacGinnis, George Pughe,
Martita Hunt, George Hayes, Cameron Hall,
Edana Romney

East of Sudan
GB 1964   94m   Techniscope
Columbia / Ameran (Charles H. Schneer)

A trooper, a governess and others escape
downriver from one of General Gordon's
outposts.
Shameless borrowing of plot from *The African
Queen* and footage from *The Four Feathers*.
The purest hokum.

w Jud Kinberg *d* Nathan Juran *ph* Wilkie
Cooper *m* Laurie Johnson

Anthony Quayle, Sylvia Syms, Jenny Agutter.
'Nathan Juran could direct this kind of thing
blindfold, and for once would appear to have
done so.'—*MFB*

East of Sumatra*
US 1953   82m   Technicolor
U-I (Albert J. Cohen)

A mining engineer has trouble with the
ruthless chief of a Pacific island.
A good example of routine Hollywood
hokum, efficiently staged and acted.

w Frank Gill Jnr *d* Budd Boetticher
ph Clifford Stine

Jeff Chandler, Anthony Quinn, Marilyn
Maxwell, John Sutton

East of the River
US 1940 73m bw

A young gangster and his respectable brother both love the same girl. Tedious formula melodrama in a studio New York. John Garfield, William Lundigan, Brenda Marshall, Marjorie Rambeau, George Tobias. Written by Fred Niblo Jnr; directed by Alfred E. Green; for Warner.

East Side of Heaven
US 1939 85m bw

A singing taxi driver looks after an abandoned baby. Modestly pleasing comedy with music and sentiment; Baby Sandy subsequently starred in her own series. Bing Crosby, Joan Blondell, Mischa Auer, C. Aubrey Smith, Irene Hervey. Written by William Consetman; directed by David Butler; for Universal. 'A grand package of entertainment that will play a merry tune at the b.o.'—*Variety*

East Side West Side*
US 1949 108m bw
MGM (Voldemar Veltuguin)

A New York businessman is torn between his wife and another woman.
High class soap opera with all the production stops pulled out; generally well acted and reasonably entertaining.
w Isobel Lennart, *novel* Marcia Davenport d Mervyn Le Roy ph Charles Rosher m Miklos Rozsa

James Mason, Barbara Stanwyck, Van Heflin, Ava Gardner, *Gale Sondergaard*, Cyd Charisse, Nancy Davis, William Conrad
'No company is quite so adept as MGM at presenting basically uninteresting material with such style, and such a strong cast, that it cannot fail to entertain.'—*Penelope Houston*

Easter Parade**
US 1948 109m Technicolor
MGM (Arthur Freed)

A song and dance man quarrels with one partner but finds another.
A musical which exists only in its numbers, which are many but variable. All in all, an agreeable lightweight entertainment without the style to put it in the top class.
w Sidney Sheldon, Frances Goodrich, Albert Hackett d Charles Walters ph Harry Stradling m / ly Irving Berlin md Roger Edens, Johnny Green

Fred Astaire, Judy Garland, Ann Miller, Peter Lawford, Clinton Sundberg, Jules Munshin
'The important thing is that Fred Astaire is back, with Irving Berlin calling the tunes.'—*Newsweek*
† Fred Astaire was actually second choice, replacing Gene Kelly who damaged an ankle.
AA: Roger Edens, Johnny Green

● *Video: MGM / UA*

Easy Come, Easy Go
US 1947 78m bw
Paramount

An old Irishman gambles away the money his daughter earns.

Whimsical sentimental comedy with an unattractive central character.
w Francis Edward Faragoh, John McNulty, Anne Froelich d John Farrow ph Daniel L. Fapp m Roy Webb

Barry Fitzgerald, Diana Lynn, Sonny Tufts, Dick Foran, Frank McHugh, Allen Jenkins, John Litel, Arthur Shields

Easy Come, Easy Go
US 1966 97m Technicolor
(Paramount) Wallis–Hazen

A frogman tries to salvage a treasure from a wreck off the Californian coast.
Empty-headed star vehicle, almost indistinguishable from many of the others.
w Allan Weiss, Anthony Lawrence d John Rich ph William Margulies m Joseph J. Lilley

Elvis Presley, Dodie Marshall, Pat Priest, Pat Harrington, Skip Ward, Frank McHugh, Elsa Lanchester

Easy Living***
US 1937 91m bw
Paramount (Arthur Hornblow Jnr)

A fur coat is thrown out of a window and lands on a typist . . .
Amusing romantic comedy with farcical trimmings; it now stands among the classic crazy comedies of the thirties.
w Preston Sturges d Mitchell Leisen ph Ted Tetzlaff md Boris Morros

Jean Arthur, Ray Milland, *Edward Arnold*, Luis Alberni, Mary Nash, Franklin Pangborn, William Demarest, Andrew Tombes
'Slapstick farce which does not fulfil the box office possibilities of its stars.'—*Variety*
'Secretaries, millionaires, jokes, sight gags, furies, attacks of cool sense—there are always three things going on at once.'—*New Yorker, 1977*

Easy Living
US 1949 77m bw
RKO (Robert Sparks)

An ageing football star wants to retire but has to satisfy the living standards of his ambitious wife.
Dim drama.
w Charles Schnee, *story* Irwin Shaw d Jacques Tourneur ph Harry J. Wild m Roy Webb

Victor Mature, Lucille Ball, Lizabeth Scott, Sonny Tufts, Lloyd Nolan, Paul Stewart, Jack Paar, Jeff Donnell

Easy Money
GB 1948 93m bw
GFD / Gainsborough (A. Frank Bundy)

Four people win big prizes on the football pools.
Short story compendium; very average.
w Muriel and Sydney Box, *play* Arnold Ridley d Bernard Knowles m Temple Abady

Edward Rigby, Greta Gynt, Dennis Price, Jack Warner, Mervyn Johns, Petula Clark, Marjorie Fielding, Bill Owen, Raymond Lovell

'A man went looking for America and couldn't find it anywhere!'

Easy Rider***
US 1969 94m Technicolor
Columbia / Pando / Raybert (Peter Fonda)

Two drop-outs ride across America on motorcycles.
Happening to please hippies and motor-cycle enthusiasts as well as amateur politicians, this oddball melodrama drew freakishly large audiences throughout the world and was much imitated though never equalled in its casual effectiveness, nor did promising careers ensue for the actors mainly concerned.
w Peter Fonda, Dennis Hopper, Terry Southern d Dennis Hopper ph Laszlo Kovacs m various recordings

Peter Fonda, Dennis Hopper, *Jack Nicholson*
'Cinéma-vérité in allegory terms.'—*Peter Fonda*
'Ninety-four minutes of what it is like to swing, to watch, to be fond, to hold opinions and to get killed in America at this moment.'—*Penelope Gilliatt*
AAN: script; Jack Nicholson

● *Video: RCA / Columbia*

Easy Street****
US 1917 22m approx bw silent
Mutual / Charles Chaplin

In a slum street, a tramp is reformed by a dewy-eyed missionary, becomes a policeman, and tames the local bully.
Quintessential Chaplin, combining sentimentality and social comment with hilarious slapstick.
wd Charles Chaplin ph William C. Foster, Rollie Totheroh

Charles Chaplin, Edna Purviance, Albert Austin, Eric Campbell

Easy to Love*
US 1933 62m bw

A pair of couples get into a romantic mix-up.
Innocent predecessor of *Bob and Carol and Ted and Alice*; come to think of it, quite sophisticated for its year. Adolphe Menjou, Genevieve Tobin, Mary Astor, Edward Everett Horton, Guy Kibbee, Patricia Ellis, Hugh Herbert. Written by Carl Erickson and Manuel Seff from a play by Thompson Buchanan; directed by William Keighley; for Warners. 'Adaptation, direction and able performances make an old story amusing entertainment.'—*Variety*

Easy to Love
US 1953 96m Technicolor
MGM (Joe Pasternak)

The romances of an aqua-queen in Florida's Cypress Gardens.
Thin, humourless and forgettable musical vehicle sustained by spectacular water ballets.
w Laslo Vadnay, William Roberts d Charles

Walters *ph* Ray June *md* Lennie Hayton,
George Stoll; numbers staged by *Busby
Berkeley*

Esther Williams, Tony Martin, Van Johnson

Easy to Wed*
US 1946   110m   Technicolor
MGM (Jack Cummings)

A socialite threatens a newspaper editor with
libel; he postpones his own wedding and sets a
friend to compromise her.
Bright but tasteless remake of *Libelled Lady*,
with a second team cast trying hard.

w Dorothy Kingsley, Maurine Watkins,
Howard Emmett Rogers, George
Oppenheimer *d* Edward Buzzell *ph* Harry
Stradling *m* Johnny Green

Van Johnson, Esther Williams, *Lucille Ball*,
Keenan Wynn, Cecil Kellaway, Carlos
Ramirez, Ben Blue, Ethel Smith

Easy Virtue
GB 1927   73m (24 fps)   bw   silent
Gainsborough (Michael Balcon)

A drunkard's wife falls for a young man who
kills himself. Her past then prevents her
attempts to lead a respectable life.
Vapid social melodrama with minimal points
of interest despite its credits.

w Eliot Stannard, *play* Noël Coward *d* Alfred
Hitchcock *ph* Claude McDonnell *ed* Ivor
Montagu

Isabel Jeans, Franklyn Dyall, Eric Bransby
Williams, Ian Hunter, Violet Farebrother,
Robin Irvine

Eating Raoul*
US 1982   83m   Pacific Color
Bartel Film (Anne Kimmel)

A restaurateur kills a drunken swinger, and
finds that he has a profitable sideline on his
hands . . .
Black comedy with insufficient humour to
offset tastelessness.

w Richard Blackburn, Paul Bartel *d* Paul
Bartel *ph* Gary Thieltges *m* Arlon Ober

Paul Bartel, Mary Woronov, Robert Beltran,
Susan Saiger, Richard Blackburn.

'I wanted to make a film about two greedy,
uptight people who are at the same time not so
unlike you and me and Nancy and Ronnie, to
keep it funny and yet communicate something
about the psychology and perversity of those
values . . . My movie touches on many things:
the perversion of middle class values, the
resurgence of Nixonism, machismo versus
WASP fastidiousness, *film noir* . . .'—*Paul
Bartel*

● Video: *Palace*

Ebb Tide**
US 1937   92m   Technicolor
Paramount (Lucien Hubbard)

Sailors are stranded with a dangerous fanatic
on a South Sea island.
Interesting adaptation of Stevenson, notable
both for its early colour and its genuinely sour,
anti-romantic mood, almost unique for
Hollywood in this period.

w Bertram Millhauser, *novel* R. L. Stevenson
and Lloyd Osbourne *d* James Hogan *ph* Leo
Tover *m* Victor Young

Ray Milland, Frances Farmer, Oscar
Homolka, Barry Fitzgerald, Lloyd Nolan

'More pretentious as to production than
dramatically. Does not suggest big b.o.'—
Variety

† Remade 1946 as *Adventure Island*.

Echo of Barbara
GB 1958   58m   bw

A stripper poses as the daughter of an ex-con
in a plot to retrieve hidden loot. Taut little
crime support, not bad at all. Mervyn Johns,
Maureen Connel, Paul Stassino, Ronald
Hines, Tom Bell. Written by John Kruse,
from a novel by Jonathan Burke; directed by
Sidney Hayers; for Independent Artists.

Echoes of a Summer
US / Canada 1975   98m   Eastmancolor
Beata / Castle / Astral / Bryanston (Robert L.
Joseph)

An 11-year-old girl dying of heart disease
spends her last summer with her parents on
holiday in a Nova Scotian village.
Excruciating.

w Robert L. Joseph *d* Don Taylor *ph* John
Coquillon *m* Terry James

Jodie Foster, Richard Harris, Lois Nettleton,
Geraldine Fitzgerald, William Windom, Brad
Savage

'The only honest thing about this movie is
its desire to make a buck.'—*Frank Rich, New
York Post*

The Eclipse*
Italy / France 1962   125m   bw
Interopa-Cineriz / Paris Film (Robert and
Raymond Hakim)
original title: *L'Eclisse*

A young Roman woman breaks off one affair
and begins another.
A portrait in depth, rather tiresomely long and
with at least one totally irrelevant stock-
market sequence; but superbly done for
connoisseurs.

wd Michelangelo Antonioni, Tonino Guerra,
Elio Bartolini, Ottiero Ottieri *ph* Gianni di
Venanzo *m* Giovanni Fusco

Monica Vitti, Alain Delon, Francisco Rabal

L'Ecole Buissonière*
France 1948   89m   bw
UGC / CGCF
US title: *I Have a New Master*

At a provincial village school, a new teacher
introduces new methods and takes a while to
win over the locals.
Rustic comedy-drama of a kind the French do
well.

w Jean-Paul Le Chanois, Elise Freinet
d Jean-Paul Le Chanois *ph* Marc Fossard,
Maurice Pecqueux, André Dumaître
m Joseph Kosma

Bernard Blier, Juliette Fabre, Edouard
Delmont

'It's big and bright as those banjo eyes!'
The Eddie Cantor Story
US 1953   116m   Technicolor
Cinemascope
Warner (Sidney Skolsky)

After a tough childhood on New York's east
side, Israel Iskowitz becomes a famous
entertainer.
Deliberately patterned after the success of *The
Jolson Story*, this is an unhappy example of
how close are success and failure; the elements
are the same, but this film suffers from unsure
timing, lack of humour, rather apologetic
numbers, a really dismal script and a
caricature performance in the lead.

w Jerome Weidman, Ted Sherdeman, Sidney
Skolsky *d* Alfred E. Green *ph* Edwin DuPar
md Ray Heindorf *songs* various *ch* Le Roy
Prinz

Keefe Brasselle, Marilyn Erskine, Aline
MacMahon, Arthur Franz, Alex Gerry,
Gerald Mohr, William Forrest (as Ziegfeld),
Will Rogers Jnr (as Will Rogers), and Eddie
Cantor (who also sings the songs off screen)

Eddie Macon's Run
US 1983   95m   Technicolor
Universal / Martin Bregman (Louis A.
Stroller)

A man innocently convicted escapes and
hotfoots it back home. Old-style chase film
marred by passages of sex and crude
backwoods violence.

w,d,ed Jeff Kanew, *novel* James McLendon
ph James A. Contner *m* Norton Buffalo

John Schneider, Kirk Douglas, Lee Purcell,
Leah Ayres

The Eddy Duchin Story
US 1956   123m   Technicolor
Cinemascope
Columbia (Jonie Taps, Jerry Wald)

The success story of a pianist who died of
leukemia.
Predictable, glossy, sentimental musical
biopic.

w Samuel Taylor, *original story* Leo Katcher
d George Sidney *ph* Harry Stradling
md George Duning *piano* Carmen Cavallero

Tyrone Power, Kim Novak, *Victoria Shaw*,
James Whitmore, Shepperd Strudwick, Frieda
Inescort, Gloria Holden, Larry Keating

AAN: Leo Katcher; Harry Stradling; George
Duning

Edgar Wallace

Between 1960 and 1963 no fewer than 47
second features emerged from Jack
Greenwood's production unit at the London
suburban studios of Merton Park, under the
Edgar Wallace banner and prefaced by a
sinister revolving bust of the author (though
few had very much to do with his original
stories). All maintained a better standard than
any other crime second features of the period,
and a few were seized on with delight by the
critics. They were subsequently popular on
television, though the Independent

EDGE OF DARKNESS. World War II films about the Norwegian resistance were usually disappointing, and despite its all-star cast this was no exception. Ann Sheridan and Errol Flynn lead the rebels.

Broadcasting Authority banned repeats on the grounds that they were without merit. In this complete list, details are given for the more interesting items:

THE CLUE OF THE TWISTED CANDLE
A MARRIAGE OF CONVENIENCE
THE MALPAS MYSTERY
THE MAN WHO WAS NOBODY
THE CLUE OF THE NEW PIN*
(w Philip Mackie, d Allan Davis, with Paul Daneman, Bernard Archard)
PARTNERS IN CRIME
THE FOURTH SQUARE
THE MAN AT THE CARLTON TOWER
THE CLUE OF THE SILVER KEY
ATTEMPT TO KILL
THE SINISTER MAN*
(w Philip Mackie, d Clive Donner, with Patrick Allen, John Bentley)
NEVER BACK LOSERS
MAN DETAINED
RICOCHET
THE DOUBLE
THE RIVALS
TO HAVE AND TO HOLD
THE PARTNER
FIVE TO ONE
ACCIDENTAL DEATH
WE SHALL SEE
DOWNFALL
THE VERDICT
WHO WAS MADDOX?*

(w Roger Marshall, d Geoffrey Nethercott, with Bernard Lee, Finlay Currie)
ACT OF MURDER*
(w Lewis Davidson, d Alan Bridges, with John Carson, Anthony Bate)
FACE OF A STRANGER
NEVER MENTION MURDER*
(w Robert Banks Stewart, d John Nelson Burton, with Maxine Audley, Dudley Foster)
THE MAIN CHANCE
GAME FOR THREE LOSERS
DEAD MAN'S CHEST
CHANGE PARTNERS
STRANGLER'S WEB*
(w George Baxt, d John Moxey, with Griffith Jones, Gerald Harper)
BACKFIRE
CANDIDATE FOR MURDER*
(w Lukas Heller, d David Villers, with Michael Gough, John Justin)
FLAT TWO
THE SHARE-OUT
NUMBER SIX
TIME TO REMEMBER
PLAYBACK*
(w Robert Banks Stewart, d John Nelson Burton, with Maxine Audley, Dudley Foster)
SOLO FOR SPARROW
LOCKER 69
DEATH TRAP
THE SET-UP

ON THE RUN
THE £20,000 KISS
INCIDENT AT MIDNIGHT
RETURN TO SENDER

Edge of Darkness*
US 1943 124m bw
Warner (Henry Blanke)

Norwegian village patriots resist the Nazis. High-intentioned, ambitiously cast but ultimately bathetic resistance melodrama, high principled down to its tragic finale but compromised by backlot shooting and the presence of Errol Flynn.

w Robert Rossen d Lewis Milestone ph Sid Hickox m Franz Waxman

Errol Flynn, Ann Sheridan, Walker Huston, Judith Anderson, Ruth Gordon, Nancy Coleman, Helmut Dantine, Morris Carnovsky, Charles Dingle, John Beal, Richard Fraser, Helene Thimig

Edge of Doom
US 1950 97m bw
Samuel Goldwyn
GB title: *Stronger than Fear*

A desperate youth kills a priest and struggles with his conscience.
A sanctimonious weirdie, extremely odd coming from this producer, and unhappily re-edited before release. Someone was interested enough to want to make it, but it seems to have been killed by the cast and the front office.

w Philip Yordan, novel Leo Brady d Mark Robson ph Harry Stradling m Hugo Friedhofer

Dana Andrews, Farley Granger, Joan Evans, Robert Keith, Paul Stewart, Mala Powers, Adele Jergens, Harold Vermilyea, Mabel Paige

Edge of Eternity*
US 1959 80m Technicolor
Cinemascope
Columbia / Thunderbird (Kendrick Sweet)

A Grand Canyon sheriff traces three murders to an ownership struggle over a disused mine. Routine but suspenseful thriller with splendid locations.

w Knut Swenson, Richard Collins d Don Siegel ph Burnett Guffey m Daniele Amfitheatrof

Cornel Wilde, Victoria Shaw, Edgar Buchanan, Mickey Shaughnessy, Jack Elam

Edge of Hell
US 1956 76m bw

In a slummy rooming house, a beggar who lives by his dog's talents falls for the new lodger. Self-parodying sub-Jannings melodrama with an unlikely star. Hugo Haas, Francesca de Scaffa, Ken Carlton, June Hammerstein. Written, directed and produced by Hugo Haas; for Universal-International.

Edge of the City**
US 1957 85m bw
MGM / Jonathan (David Susskind, Jim di
Ganci)
GB title: *A Man is Ten Feet Tall*
Racial tensions lead to tragedy in the railroad
yards of New York's waterfront.
Tense, brutal melodrama, which has historical
interest as an effective opening-up in cinematic
terms of a TV play, in its imitation of *On the
Waterfront*, and in its rebel hero and relaxed
black friend.
w Robert Alan Arthur, from his play *d Martin
Ritt ph* Joseph Brun *m* Leonard Rosenman
Sidney Poitier, John Cassavetes, Jack Warden,
Kathleen Maguire, Ruby Dee, Robert Simon,
Ruth White

Edge of the World**
GB 1937 80m bw
GFD / Rock (Joe Rock)
Life, love and death on Foula, a remote
Shetland island.
Rare for its time, a vigorous location drama in
the Flaherty tradition; sometimes naïve,
usually exhilarating.
wd Michael Powell ph Ernest Palmer and
others
Niall MacGinnis, Belle Chrystal, John Laurie,
Finlay Currie, Eric Berry
  'Scant of plot and unlikely to be hailed by
the public at large.'—*Variety*

'The love of a woman . . . the courage of a
    fighting America . . . lifted him from
    obscurity to thrilling fame!'
Edison the Man**
US 1940 107m bw
MGM (John W. Considine Jnr)
Edison struggles for years in poverty before
becoming famous as the inventor of the
electric light bulb.
Standard, well-made biopic following on from
Young Tom Edison; reasonably absorbing, but
slightly suspect in its facts.
w Dore Schary, Talbot Jennings, Bradbury
Foote, Hugo Butler *d Clarence Brown
ph* Harold Rosson *m* Herbert Stothart
Spencer Tracy, Rita Johnson, Lynne
Overman, Charles Coburn, Gene Lockhart,
Henry Travers. Felix Bressart
AAN: Dore Schary, Hugo Butler (original
story)

Edouard et Caroline**
France 1951 99m bw
UGC / CICC
A young pianist and his wife quarrel while
preparing for an important recital.
Gay, slight, charming comedy, a two-hander
taking place within the course of a few hours.
*w Annette Wademant, Jacques Becker
d Jacques Becker ph* Robert Le Fèbvre
m Jean-Jacques Grunenwald

Daniel Gélin, Anne Vernon, Jacques François,
William Tubbs, Jean Galland, Elina
Labourdette, Betty Stockfield
  'It lifts its weighty trivialities into a world of
enchantment.'—*Sunday Times*

Educated Evans
GB 1936 86m bw
A racetrack bookie becomes a trainer. Rather
unyielding vehicle for a fast-talking star. Max
Miller, Nancy O'Neil, Clarice Mayne, Albert
Whelan, Hal Walters. Written by Frank
Launder and Robert Edmunds, from an Edgar
Wallace character; directed by William
Beaudine; for Warner.

Educating Rita*
GB 1983 110m Technicolor
Rank / Acorn (Lewis Gilbert)
A cheerful young hairdresser improves her
knowledge of English Literature by enrolling
on an Open University course.
Rather dismal, thinly characterized and ill-lit
variation on *Pygmalion*, with endless talk
leading nowhere (it was originally a two-
character play). Due to its Liverpudlian
modishness it achieved surprising box office
success.
w Willy Russell from his play *d* Lewis
Gilbert *ph* Frank Watts *m* David Hentschel
Michael Caine, Julie Walters, Michael
Williams, Maureen Lipman

Edward My Son
GB 1949 112m bw
MGM (Edwin H. Knopf)
A rich, unscrupulous man remembers the
people he has made unhappy, and the son to
whom he never behaved as a father should.
Unsatisfactory, rather ugly-looking adaptation
of a gripping piece of theatre, with casting and
direction remarkably uncertain from such
professionals.
w Donald Ogden Stewart, *play* Robert
Morley *d* George Cukor *ph* F. A. Young
m John Woolbridge, Malcolm Sargent
Spencer Tracy, Deborah Kerr, Ian Hunter,
James Donald, Leueen McGrath, Mervyn
Johns
AAN: Deborah Kerr

The Effect of Gamma Rays on
Man-in-the-Moon Marigolds
US 1972 101m De Luxe
Newman–Foreman
A slatternly middle-aged woman dreams of
better times for herself and her children.
Well-written but essentially banal and
pretentious domestic drama, the kind of film
that only gets made when powerful stars see in
it a juicy role.
w Alvin Sargent, *play* Paul Zendel *d* Paul
Newman *ph* Adam Holender *m* Maurice
Jarre
Joanne Woodward, Nell Potts, Roberta
Wallach, Judith Lowry

Effi Briest*
West Germany 1974 140m bw
Tango Film (Rainer Werner Fassbinder)
original title: *Fontane Effi Briest*
A teenage girl is married to a rich baron, but
fails to understand what is expected of her.
Overlong but often fascinating picture of a
vanished society in which not the slightest
weakening of structure is permitted.
wd Rainer Werner Fassbinder, *novel* Theodor
Fontane *ph* Jürgen Jürges, Dietrich
Lohmann *m* from Saint-Saens
Hanna Schygulla, Wolfgang Schenck, Ulli
Lommel, Karl-Heinz Böhm, Ursula Strätz

The Egg and I*
US 1947 104m bw
U-I (Chester Erskine)
A city couple try to become gentleman
farmers.
Mild, pleasant comedy notable chiefly for
introducing a hillbilly couple, Ma and Pa
Kettle, who went on, in the personae of Main
and Kilbride, to make several later features.
(See under *Kettles*.)
w Chester Erskine, Fred Finkelhoffe,
novel Betty Macdonald *d* Chester Erskine
ph Milton Krasner *m* Frank Skinner
Claudette Colbert, Fred MacMurray, *Marjorie
Main, Percy Kilbride,* Louise Allbritton,
Richard Long, Billy House, Ida Moore,
Donald MacBride
  'Marjorie Main, in an occasional fit of fine,
wild comedy, picks the show up and
brandishes it as if she were wringing its neck. I
wish to God she had.'—*James Agee*
AAN: Marjorie Main

'10,965 pyramids! 5,337 dancing girls! One
million swaying bulrushes! 802 sacred
bulls!'
The Egyptian*
US 1954 140m De Luxe Cinemascope
TCF (Darryl F. Zanuck)
In ancient Egypt an abandoned baby grows up
to be physician to the pharaoh.
More risible than reasonable, sounding more
like a parody than the real thing, this
pretentious epic from a bestseller flounders
helplessly between its highlights but has
moments of good humour and makes an
excellent example of the pictures they don't
make 'em like any more.
w Philip Dunne, Casey Robinson, *novel* Mika
Waltari *d* Michael Curtiz *ph* Leon Shamroy
m Bernard Herrmann, Alfred Newman
ad Lyle Wheeler, George W. Davis
Edmund Purdom, Victor Mature, *Peter
Ustinov,* Bella Darvi, Gene Tierney, Michael
Wilding, Jean Simmons, Judith Evelyn, Henry
Daniell, John Carradine, Carl Benton Reid
  'The novel . . . supplied the reader with
enough occurrences and customs of
Akhnaton's time . . . to hide some of the more
obvious contrivances of the story. The film
does not do this.'—*Carolyn Harrow, Films in
Review*
AAN: Leon Shamroy

The Eiger Sanction*
US 1975   125m   Technicolor
Panavision
Universal / Malpaso (Jennings Lang)

An art teacher returns to the CIA as an
exterminator, and finds himself in a party
climbing the Eiger.
Silly spy melodrama with some breathtaking
mountain sequences.

w Warren B. Murphy, Hal Dresner, Rod
Whitaker, *novel* Trevanian   d Clint Eastwood
ph Frank Stanley, John Cleare, Jeff
Schoolfield, Peter Pilafian, Pete White
m John Williams

Clint Eastwood, George Kennedy, Vonetta
McGee, Jack Cassidy, Heidi Bruhl, Thayer
David
    'All the villains have been constructed from
prefabricated Bond models.'—*Richard Combs*

Eight and a Half**
Italy 1963   138m   bw
Cineriz (Angelo Rizzoli)
original title: *Otto e Mezzo*

A successful film director on the verge of a
nervous breakdown has conflicting fantasies
about his life.
A Fellini self-portrait in which anything goes.
Some of it is fascinating, some not worth the
trouble of sorting out.

w Federico Fellini, Ennio Flaiano, Tullio
Pinelli, Brunello Rondi   d Federico Fellini
ph Gianni di Venanzo   m Nino Rota   ad Piero
Gherardi

Marcello Mastroianni, Claudia Cardinale,
Anouk Aimée, Sandra Milo, Rossella Falk,
Barbara Steele, Madeleine Lebeau
    'The whole may add up to a magnificent
folly, but it is too singular, too candid, too
vividly and insistently alive to be judged as
being in any way diminishing.'—*Peter John
Dyer, MFB*
    'Fellini's intellectualizing is not even like
dogs dancing; it is not done well, nor does it
surprise us that it is done at all. It merely palls
on us, and finally appals us.'—*John Simon*
    'A de luxe glorification of creative crisis,
visually arresting but in some essential way
conventional-minded.'—*Pauline Kael, 70s*

AAN: best foreign film; script; direction

Eight Iron Men
US 1952   80m   bw
Columbia / Stanley Kramer

In the ruins of an Italian village, eight
American infantrymen wait for relief.
Quickie war film in which everyone talks a lot
and they all survive; from the time when
Kramer was discovering how fast he could turn
'em out.

w Harry Brown, from his play A Sound of
Hunting   d Edward Dmytryk   ph Roy Hunt
m Leith Stevens   pd Rudolph Sternad

Bonar Colleano, Lee Marvin, Arthur Franz,
Richard Kiley, Nick Dennis, James Griffith,
Dick Moore, George Cooper

Eight O'Clock Walk
GB 1953   87m   bw
British Lion / George King

A young barrister proves a taxi driver innocent
of murder.
Minor-league courtroom stuff, an adequate
time-passer.

w Katherine Strueby, Guy Morgan, *story* Jack
Roffey, Gordon Harbord   d Lance Comfort
ph Brendan Stafford   m George Melachrino

Richard Attenborough, Derek Farr, Cathy
O'Donnell, Ian Hunter, Maurice Denham,
Bruce Seton, Harry Welchman

Eight on the Lam
US 1966   107m   De Luxe
United Artists / Hope Enterprises (Bill
    Lawrence)
GB title: *Eight on the Run*

A bank teller is suspected of embezzlement
and goes on the run with his seven children.
Feeble comedy punctuated by even feebler
chases; the star had lost his comic character.

w Albert E. Lewin, Burt Styler, Bob Fisher,
Arthur Marx   d George Marshall   ph Alan
Stensvold   m George Romanis

Bob Hope, Phyllis Diller, Jonathan Winters,
Shirley Eaton, Jill St John

Eighty Thousand Suspects*
GB 1963   113m   bw   Cinemascope
Rank / Val Guest

A smallpox epidemic terrorizes the city of
Bath.
Predictable melodrama which adequately
passes the time.

w Val Guest, *novel* Pillars of Midnight by
Elleston Trevor   d Val Guest   ph Arthur
Grant   m Stanley Black

Claire Bloom, Richard Johnson, Yolande
Donlan, Cyril Cusack, Michael Goodliffe,
Mervyn Johns, Kay Walsh, Basil Dignam, Ray
Barrett

El**
Mexico 1952   91m   bw
Nacional Film (Oscar Dancigers)
aka: *This Strange Passion; Torments*

A middle-aged aristocrat marries a beautiful
young girl and falls victim to insane jealousy.
A tragi-comic case history with chilling and
memorable details; not one of its director's
great works, but an engaging minor one.

w Luis Bunuel, Luis Alcoriza,
novel Pensamientos by Mercedes Pinto   d Luis
Bunuel   ph Gabriel Figueroa   m Luis
Hernandez Breton

Arturo de Cordova, Delia Garces, Luis
Beristain, Aurora Walker

El Cid*
US / Spain 1961   184m   Super
    Technirama
Samuel Bronston

A legendary 11th-century hero drives the
Moors from Spain.
Endless glum epic with splendid action
sequences as befits the high budget.

w Frederic M. Frank, Philip Yordan
d Anthony Mann   ph Robert Krasker
m Miklos Rozsa

Charlton Heston, Sophia Loren, Raf Vallone,
Geraldine Page, John Fraser, Gary Raymond,
Herbert Lom, Hurd Hatfield, Massimo Serato,
Andrew Cruickshank, Michael Hordern,
Douglas Wilmer, Frank Thring

AAN: Miklos Rozsa; song 'The Falcon and
the Dove' (m Miklos Rozsa, ly Paul Francis
Webster)

● Video: Intervision

El Condor
US 1970   102m   Technicolor
National General / Carthay Continental
    (André de Toth)

An escaped convict and a con man seek a
fortune in gold believed to be hidden in a
fortress in the Mexican desert.
Blood and guts western with few moments of
interest.

w Larry Cohen, Steven Carabatsos   d John
Guillermin   ph Henri Persin   m Maurice Jarre

Jim Brown, Lee Van Cleef, Patrick O'Neal,
Marianna Hill, Iron Eyes Cody, Elisha Cook
Jnr
    'The kind of fun you can find at your
friendly neighbourhood abattoir.'—*Judith
Crist, 1977*

'The big one with the big two!'

El Dorado*
US 1966   126m   Technicolor
Paramount / Laurel (Howard Hawks)

A gunfighter and a drunken sheriff tackle a
villainous cattle baron.
Easy-going, semi-somnolent, generally
likeable but disappointing western . . . an old
man's movie all round.

w Leigh Brackett, *novel* The Stars in their
Courses by Harry Joe Brown   d Howard
Hawks   ph Harold Rosson   m Nelson Riddle

John Wayne, Robert Mitchum, James Caan,
Charlene Holt, Michele Carey, Ed Asner,
Arthur Hunnicutt, R. G. Armstrong, Paul
Fix, Christopher George
    'A rumbustious lament for the good days of
the bad old west.'—*Tom Milne*
    'A claustrophobic, careless and cliché-
ridden thing, wavering constantly between
campy self-deprecation and pretentious
pomposity.'—*Richard Schickel*
    'Wayne and Mitchum, parodying themselves
while looking exhausted.'—*Pauline Kael, 70s*

El Greco
Italy / France 1964   94m   Eastmancolor
    Cinemascope
(TCF) Artistiche Internazionale / Arco-Films
    du Siècle (Alfredo Bini, Mel Ferrer)

In the 16th century, a Greek-Italian painter
finds favour in Spain and falls in love with an
aristocratic girl.
Heavily embellished history with a few good
scenes.

w Guy Elmes, Massimo Franciosa, Luigi
Magni, Luciano Salce   d Luciano Salce
ph Leonida Barboni   m Ennio Morricone

Mel Ferrer, Rosanna Schiaffino, Adolfo Celi, Angel Aranda

El Paso
US 1949 92m Cinecolor
Paramount / Pine–Thomas

After the civil war, a young lawyer brings a corrupt township to its senses by learning to outshoot the badmen.
Lively, fairly tough western with all the familiar ingredients.

wd Lewis R. Foster *ph* Ellis Carter *m* Darrell Calker

John Payne, Gail Russell, Dick Foran, Sterling Hayden, George 'Gabby' Hayes

El Topo*
Mexico 1971 124m Eastmancolor
Producciones Panic

An evil gunfighter rides through the old west and has various encounters, after which he sets himself on fire.
Curious, perverse, powerful surrealist allegory which takes in the life of Christ and the fate of man among some exceedingly unpleasant violence. A treat for connoisseurs of the unpleasantly absurd.

w, d, m, ad Alexandro Jodorowsky *ph* Raphael Corkidi

Alexandro Jodorowsky, Brontis Jodorowsky, Mara Lorenzio, David Silva

'He's a good cop on a big bike on a bad road!'
Electra Glide in Blue*
US 1973 113m De Luxe Panavision
UA / James William Guercio / Rupert Hitzig

A small-town motor-cycle cop becomes disillusioned.
Agreeable desert melodrama in the wake of *Easy Rider*, freshly observed with mordant humour, marred by a fashionable downbeat ending.

w Robert Boris *d / m* James William Guercio *ph* Conrad Hall

Robert Blake, Billy Green Bush, Mitch Ryan, Jeannine Riley, Elisha Cook Jnr, Royal Dana

Electric Dreams
GB 1984 112m Metrocolor
Virgin / MGM-UA (Rusty Lemorande, Larry de Waay)

A computer becomes jealous of its owner's love affair.
Gruesomely extended revue sketch which totally fails to develop its characters and offers instead a very sparing amount of cleverness.

w Rusty Lemorande *d* Steve Barron *ph* Alex Thomson *m* Giorgio Moroder *pd* Richard MacDonald

Lenny Von Dohlen, Virginia Madsen, Maxwell Caulfield, Bud Cort, Don Fellows

The Electric Horseman*
US 1979 120m Technicolor
Panavision
Columbia / Universal (Ray Stark / Wildwood)

A horseman advertising breakfast cereal in Las Vegas suddenly tires of it all and heads for the wilderness.
Pretty but slightly sheepish moral saga with too much technique for its own good.

w Robert Garland *d* Sydney Pollack *ph* Owen Roizman *m* Dave Grusin *pd* Stephen Grimes

Robert Redford, Jane Fonda, Valerie Perrine, Willie Nelson, John Saxon, Nicholas Coster
'Overlong, talky and diffused.'—*Variety*

● Video: CIC

Elephant Boy**
GB 1937 91m bw
Alexander Korda

In India, a boy elephant keeper helps government conservationists.
Documentary drama which seemed fresh and extraordinary at the time, has dated badly since, but did make an international star of Sabu.

w John Collier, Akos Tolnay, Marcia de Sylva, *novel* Toomai of the Elephants by Rudyard Kipling *d* Robert Flaherty, Zoltan Korda *ph* Osmond Borradaile *m* John Greenwood

Sabu, Walter Hudd, Allan Jeayes, W. E. Holloway, Wilfrid Hyde White
'Should draw anywhere in the world.'—*Variety*
'This is a fractured film, its skeleton is awry, its bones stick out through the skin.'—*Richard Griffith, 1941*
'It has gone the way of *Man of Aran*: enormous advance publicity, director out of touch with the press for months, rumours of great epics sealed in tins, and then the disappointing diminutive achievement.'—*Graham Greene*

● Video: Palace

The Elephant Man**
US 1980 124m bw Panavision
EMI / Brooksfilms (Stuart Cornfield)

In 1884 London, a penniless man deformed by a rare illness is rescued by a doctor from a fairground freak show, and becomes a member of fashionable society.
A curious story which happens to be true; the film sets its scene superbly, has splendid performances and a fascinating make-up. Yet it fails to move quite as it should, perhaps because the central figure is treated as a horrific come-on, like the hunchback of Notre Dame.

w Christopher de Core, Eric Bergren, David Lynch, from various memoirs *d* David Lynch *ph* Freddie Francis *m* John Morris *pd* Stuart Craig

Anthony Hopkins, *John Hurt*, John Gielgud, Anne Bancroft, Freddie Jones, Wendy Hiller, Michael Elphick, Hannah Gordon
'If there's a wrong note in this unique movie—in performance, production design, cinematography or anywhere else—I must have missed it.'—*Paul Taylor, Time Out*

'In an age of horror movies this is a film which takes the material of horror and translates it into loving kindness.'—*Dilys Powell, Punch*
AAN: best film; screenplay; David Lynch; editing (Anne V. Coates); art direction (Stuart Craig, Bob Cartwright, Hugh Scaife); John Morris; costume design (Patricia Norris); John Hurt
BFA: best film; production design; John Hurt

● Video: Thorn EMI

Elephant Walk*
US 1954 103m Technicolor
Paramount (Irving Asher)

The owner of a Ceylon tea plantation takes back an English wife who finds the atmosphere strange and turns to a friendly overseer for comfort.
Echoes of *Jane Eyre* and *Rebecca*, with stampeding elephants instead of a mad or dead wife. Grade A fiction for ladies.

w John Lee Mahin, *novel* Robert Standish *d* William Dieterle *ph* Loyal Griggs *m* Franz Waxman

Elizabeth Taylor, Peter Finch, Dana Andrews, Abraham Sofaer
'The climactic elephant stampede's a rouser—if you're still awake.'—*Judith Crist*

Eleven Harrowhouse*
GB 1974 108m De Luxe Panavision
TCF / Harrowhouse (Elliott Kastner)

An American diamond merchant is robbed of a valuable jewel, and finds himself in the middle of an ingenious plot.
Amusing caper story marred by sudden changes of mood.

w Jeffrey Bloom, *novel* Gerald A. Browne *d* Aram Avakian *ph* Arthur Ibbetson *m* Michael J. Lewis

Charles Grodin, *James Mason*, Trevor Howard, John Gielgud, Candice Bergen, Peter Vaughan, Helen Cherry, Jack Watson, Jack Watling
'This lackadaisical caper comedy is inoffensive, but the comic ideas don't build or erupt, and since the director fails to get any suspense going, it becomes a bumbling and stupid romp.'—*Pauline Kael*

Elinor Norton
US 1935 71m bw

A wife has a jealous husband and a South American lover. Underwritten triangle drama which never comes to boiling point. Claire Trevor, Gilbert Roland, Hugh Williams, Henrietta Crossman, Norman Foster. Written by Rose Franken and Philip Klein from the novel The State versus Elinor Norton by Mary Roberts Rinehart; directed by Hamilton McFadden; for Fox. 'No cast for b.o. and results look mild.'—*Variety*

Elizabeth and Essex: see The Private Lives of Elizabeth and Essex

Elizabeth of Ladymead
GB 1948   97m   Technicolor
BL / Imperadio (Herbert Wilcox)

Four husbands of different generations come
home from war (1854, 1903, 1919, 1946) to
find their wives altered.
Thin star vehicle turns into an amateur-night
compendium with a few funny moments.

w Frank Harvey, from his play d Herbert
Wilcox ph Max Greene

Anna Neagle, Hugh Williams, Bernard Lee,
Michael Laurence, Nicholas Phipps, Isobel
Jeans, Michael Shepley, Jack Allen

Ellery Queen
The debonair detective created by Manfred B.
Lee and Frederic Dannay was seen in several
unremarkable second features, usually with his
secretary Nikki and his police inspector father.
The first two were made for Republic, the rest
for Columbia.
1935: THE SPANISH CAPE MYSTERY with
Donald Cook
1936: THE MANDARIN MYSTERY (Eddie
Quillan)
1940: ELLERY QUEEN MASTER
DETECTIVE (Ralph Bellamy)
1941: ELLERY QUEEN'S PENTHOUSE
MYSTERY, ELLERY QUEEN AND THE
PERFECT CRIME, ELLERY QUEEN AND
THE MURDER RING (all Bellamy)
1942: A CLOSE CALL FOR ELLERY
QUEEN, A DESPERATE CHANCE FOR
ELLERY QUEEN, ENEMY AGENTS
MEET ELLERY QUEEN (all William
Gargan)
In 1971 Peter Lawford starred in a TV pilot,
Don't Look behind You, and in 1975 a one-
season series starred Jim Hutton. The books,
pseudonymously authored by Ellery Queen,
were far more popular than any of the movies.

Elmer and Elsie
US 1934   65m   bw

A wife harbours big ideas for her meek-and-
mild husband. Unsuccessful attempt to find a
change of pace for a fading star. George
Bancroft, Frances Fuller, Roscoe Karns,
George Barbier, Nella Walker. Written by
Humphrey Pearson from the play To the
Ladies by George S. Kaufman and Marc
Connelly; directed by Gilbert Pratt; for
Paramount. 'Screen version has not only
removed most of the verve, pace and bite but
has loaded itself down with a couple of
maladroit cases of miscasting.'—Variety

Elmer Gantry**
US 1960   146m   Eastmancolor
UA / Bernard Smith

The exploits of an American evangelist in the
twenties.
Mainly gripping but overlong exposé of
commercialized small-town religion

wd Richard Brooks, novel Sinclair Lewis
ph John Alton m André Previn ad Edward
Carrere

Burt Lancaster, Jean Simmons, Arthur
Kennedy, Shirley Jones, Dean Jagger, Edward
Andrews, Patti Page, John McIntire
AA: Richard Brooks (as writer); Burt
Lancaster; Shirley Jones
AAN: best picture; André Previn

● Video: Warner

Elmer the Great
US 1933   74m   bw
Warner (Ray Griffith)

A country hick turns out to be a great baseball
hitter.
Best and most farcical version of a play also
filmed in 1929 as Fast Company and in 1939 as
The Cowboy Quarterback.

w Tom Geraghty, play Ring Lardner, George
M. Cohan d Mervyn Le Roy

Joe E. Brown, Patricia Ellis, Frank McHugh,
Claire Dodd, Sterling Holloway, Emma Dunn,
Douglass Dumbrille, Jessie Ralph, J. Carrol
Naish

Elopement
US 1951   82m   bw
TCF (Fred Kohlmar)

A girl student eloping with her professor is
chased by her father.
Unconvincing domestic comedy with some
lively chase sequences.

w Bess Taffell d Henry Koster ph Joseph La
Shelle m Cyril Mockridge

Clifton Webb, Charles Bickford, Anne
Francis, William Lundigan, Margalo Gillmore,
Evelyn Varden, Reginald Gardiner
'A picture that goes beyond what men think
about . . . because no man ever thought about
it in quite this way!'—publicity

Elstree Calling**
GB 1930   95m   bw and colour
Wardour / BIP (John Maxwell)

A film studio mounts a television show.
Slender excuse for an all-star revue which
luckily preserves much light entertainment
talent of the time.

w Adrian Brunel, Walter C. Mycroft, Val
Valentine d Adrian Brunel, Alfred
Hitchcock, Jack Hulbert, André Charlot, Paul
Murray ph Claude Friese-Greene

Tommy Handley, Jack Hulbert, Cicely
Courtneidge, Will Fyffe, Lily Morris, Teddy
Brown, Anna May Wong, Gordon Harker,
Donald Calthrop, John Longden, Jameson
Thomas, Bobbie Comber

The Elstree Story*
GB 1952   61m   bw
ABPC (Gilbert Gunn)

A compilation drawn from 25 years of film-
making at Elstree Studios. Highlights include
Hitchcock's Number Seventeen; The White
Sheik; Piccadilly; Bulldog Drummond; Arms
and the Man; The Informer; Blossom Time;
and Poison Pen. Commentary and
presentation are adequate.

d Gilbert Gunn m Philip Green

The Elusive Pimpernel*
GB 1950   109m   Technicolor
BL / London Films (Michael Powell, Emeric
Pressburger)

A foppish 18th-century London dandy is
actually the hero who rescues French
aristocrats from the guillotine.
Expensive remake of The Scarlet Pimpernel
which fails to please, apparently because the
talents were not congenial to the subject.
Interesting detail, though.

wd Michael Powell, Emeric Pressburger,
novel Baroness Orczy ph Christopher Challis
m Brian Easdale ph Hein Heckroth

David Niven, Margaret Leighton, Cyril
Cusack, Jack Hawkins, David Hutcheson,
Robert Coote
'The quality of excitement which should
carry the film is quite lost. The Elusive
Pimpernel is highly—often too highly—
coloured, and has an artificiality quite
different in character from that of the
original.'—Penelope Houston
'I never thought I should feel inclined to
leave a Powell and Pressburger film before the
end; but I did here.'—Richard Mallett, Punch
'Niven plays the Scarlet Pimpernel with the
sheepish lack of enthusiasm of a tone deaf
man called upon to sing solo in church. His
companions lumber through their parts like
schoolboys about to go down with mumps.'—
Daily Express

Elvira Madigan*
Sweden 1967   95m   Eastmancolor
Europa Film (Waldemar Bergendahl)

A married army officer runs off with a
tightrope dancer; when they run out of money
they live in the woods and finally commit
suicide rather than part.
A simple Victorian romantic idyll, based on a
true incident; a director's and photographer's
piece which entrances the eyes and ears while
starving the mind.

wd Bo Widerberg ph Jorgen Persson
m Mozart

Thommy Berggren, Pia Degermark

Embassy*
US 1972   90m   colour
Hemdale / Triad / Weaver (Mel Ferrer)

At the US Embassy in Beirut, a Soviet official
seeking asylum is in danger from a KGB
killer.
Goodish suspenser with reasonably literate
dialogue and several Hitchcockian sequences.

w William Fairchild d Gordon Hessler
ph Raoul Coutard m Jonathan Hodge

Richard Roundtree, Chuck Connors, Max
Von Sydow, Broderick Crawford, Ray Milland

Embraceable You
US 1948   80m   bw

A gangster on the run fatally injures a young
girl, and stays to nurse her during her last
weeks. Incredible heavy-handed romantic
melodrama. Dane Clark, Geraldine Brooks,
Wallace Ford, S. Z. Sakall, Richard Rober.
Written by Edna Anhalt; directed by Felix
Jacoves; for Warner.

Embryo
US 1976   104m   colour
Cine Artists

A researcher experiments on foetuses with
growth hormones, and lives to regret it.
Rather unpleasant mixture of science fiction
and old-fashioned horror; slickness can't
conceal a total lack of taste.

w Anita Doohan, Jack W. Thomas d Ralph
Nelson ph Fred Koenekamp m Gil Melle

Rock Hudson, Diane Ladd, Barbara Carrera,
Roddy McDowall

Emergency Call*
GB 1952   90m   bw
Butcher's / Nettlefold (Ernest G. Roy)
US title: Emergency!

Inspector Lane tracks down several people
who share a rare blood group needed to save a
life.
Now a boringly predictable collection of mild
anecdotes, but then a rather smart idea, much
better executed than one would normally
expect of Britain's Poverty Row.

w Vernon Harris, Lewis Gilbert d Lewis
Gilbert ph Wilkie Cooper m Wilfred Burns

Jack Warner, Joy Shelton, Anthony Steel,
Sidney James, Freddie Mills, Earl Cameron,
John Robinson, Thora Hird

The Emigrants*
Sweden 1970   191m   Technicolor
Svensk Filmindustri (Bengt Forslund)
original title: Utvandrarna

A family of farmers leaves famine-stricken
19th-century Sweden for America, and builds
a homestead in Minnesota.
Solemn, forceful, overlong epic which while
full of trial and tribulation is sufficiently well
made to cast a hypnotic spell and was a major
hit among Swedish-Americans.

w Jan Troell, Bengt Forslund, from four
novels by Vilhelm Moberg d, ph, ed Jan
Troell m Erik Nordgren

Max Von Sydow, Liv Ullmann, Eddie Axberg,
Svenolof Bern
  'A Fordian canvas without the Fordian
warmth.'—Sight and Sound
† A sequel, The New Land, shortly appeared,
and this was also the title of a short-lived TV
series on the subject.

AAN: best picture; Jan Troell (direction and
script); Liv Ullmann

Emil and the Detectives*
Germany 1931   80m   bw
UFA

City children discover and chase a crook, who
is finally arrested.
A pleasing fable for children which has
survived several subsequent versions; the
original is probably the best.

w Billy Wilder, novel Erich Kästner
d Gerhard Lamprecht ph Werner Brandes
m Allan Grey

Fritz Rasp, Kathe Haack

† Other versions: Britain 1934, directed by
Milton Rosmer, with George Hayes; West
Germany 1954, directed by R. A. Stemmle,
with Kurt Meisel; US 1964 (Walt Disney),
directed by Peter Tewkesbury, with Walter
Slezak.

Emma*
US 1932   73m   bw
MGM

A servant marries into the family.
Predictably cosy family drama tailored for its
star.

w Frances Marion, Leonard Praskins, Zelda
Sears d Clarence Brown ph Oliver T. Marsh

Marie Dressler, Richard Cromwell, Jean
Hersholt, Myrna Loy, John Miljan, Purnell E.
Pratt
  'A hoke story saved by the star.'—Variety

AAN: Marie Dressler

Emmanuelle*
France 1974   94m   Eastmancolor
Trinacra / Orphée (Yves Rousset-Rouard)

The bored bride of a French Embassy official
in Siam is initiated by well-meaning friends
into various forms of sexual activity.
Not much sexier than a Sunday colour
supplement, this fashionable piece of sub-
eroticism took off like a bomb and spawned
half-a-dozen so-called sequels. Future students
may well wonder why.

w Jean-Louis Richard, novel Emmanuelle
Arsan d Just Jaeckin ph Richard Suzuki,
Marie Saunier m Pierre Bachelet

Sylvia Kristel, Marika Green, Daniel Sarky,
Alain Cuny
  'Much hazy, soft-focus coupling in
downtown Bangkok.'—Michael Billington,
Illustrated London News

The Emperor Jones*
US 1933   72m   bw

A train porter becomes king of the Haitian
jungle. Stagey transcript of a stagey play, with
acting of some interest at the time. Paul
Robeson, Dudley Digges, Frank Wilson. From
the play by Eugene O'Neill; directed by
Dudley Murphy; for UA. 'For the classes
rather than the masses, and questionable
commercially.'—Variety

Emperor of the North Pole*
US 1973   119m   De Luxe
TCF / Inter Hemisphere (Robert Aldrich)
GB title: Emperor of the North

In 1933 Oregon, freeloading hobos are
brutally attacked by a sadistic train guard.
Unlikely melodrama with vicious but
exhilarating high spots separating acres of
verbiage.

w Christopher Knopf d Robert Aldrich
ph Joseph Biroc m Frank de Vol

Lee Marvin, Ernest Borgnine, Keith
Carradine, Charles Tyner, Malcolm
Atterbury, Elisha Cook Jnr
  'It's hard, contrived, pointless in its thesis,
repulsive in its people, and it's singularly

joyless and contemptible in its glorification of
the bum and freeloader.'—Judith Crist

● Video: CBS / Fox

'The biggest thing that ever happened to
Bing—or to you!'
The Emperor Waltz
US 1948   106m   Technicolor
Paramount (Charles Brackett)

In 1901 Austria, a countess falls for an
American phonograph salesman.
Thin to the point of emaciation, this witless
comedy with music, dully set-bound, proved
its director's strangest and most unsatisfactory
choice.

w Charles Brackett, Billy Wilder d Billy
Wilder ph George Barnes m Victor Young
songs Johnny Burke, Jimmy Van Heusen
ad Hans Dreier, Franz Bachelin

Bing Crosby, Joan Fontaine, Roland Culver,
Lucile Watson, Richard Haydn, Harold
Vermilyea, Sig Rumann, Julie Dean

AAN: Victor Young

The Emperor's Candlesticks*
US 1937   89m   bw
MGM (John Considine Jnr)

In old Russia, spies on opposite sides fall in
love.
Lavish romantic comedy drama, generally well
handled; superior Hollywood moonshine.

w Monckton Hoffe, Herman J. Mankiewicz,
Harold Goldman, novel Baroness Orczy
d George Fitzmaurice ph Harold Rosson
m Franz Waxman

William Powell, Luise Rainer, Maureen
O'Sullivan, Robert Young, Frank Morgan,
Douglass Dumbrille
  'It's about international spies in evening
dress during that long ago period when Russia
had a Czar, Vienna was the scene of brilliant
valasques, and the favour of royalty was
something to get excited over . . . it's acted
with unusual seriousness midst settings of
unusual extravagance.'—Variety

Empire of the Ants
US 1977   89m   Movielab
AIP / Cinema 77 (Bert I. Gordon)

Giant ants menace a stretch of the Florida
coast.
A long way behind Them, but as exploitation
it could be worse.

w Jack Turley, story H. G. Wells d Bert I.
Gordon ph Reginald Morris m Dana Kaproff

Joan Collins, Robert Lansing, John David
Carson, Albert Salmi, Jaqueline Scott

The Empire Strikes Back**
US 1980   124m   Eastmancolor
Panavision
TCF / Lucasfilm (Gary Kurtz)

The Rebel Alliance takes refuge from Darth
Vader on a frozen planet.
More exhilarating interplanetary adventures,
as mindless as Star Wars but just as enjoyable
for aficionados.

w Leigh Brackett, Lawrence Kasdan, *story*
George Lucas *d* Irvin Kershner *ph* Peter
Suschitzky *m* John Williams *pd Norman
Reynolds*

Mark Hamill, Harrison Ford, Carrie Fisher,
Billy Dee Williams

'Slightly encumbered by some mythic and
neo-Sophoclean overtones, but its
inventiveness, humour and special effects are
scarcely less inspired than those of its
phenomenally successful predecessor.'—*New
Yorker*

AAN: art direction
BFA: music

Employees' Entrance*
US 1933 75m bw

A ruthless department store manager gets his
comeuppance. Smart comedy-melodrama with
solidly familiar cast. *Warren William*, Loretta
Young, Alice White, Wallace Ford, Allen
Jenkins, Marjorie Gateson. Written by Robert
Presnell, from a play by David Boehm;
directed by Roy del Ruth; for Warner.

'Here's one that calls for preferred dating
. . . plenty to sell for the mobs.'—*Variety*

The Empty Canvas
Italy / France 1964 118m bw
CC Champion / Concordia (Joseph E.
   Levine, Carlo Ponti)
original title: *La Noia*

A young painter, obsessed by his own spiritual
emptiness, becomes paranoically jealous of his
promiscuous young mistress.
An extraordinarily boring film version of a
novel which needed Bunuel, if anybody, to
handle it.

w Tonino Guerra, Ugo Liberatore, Damiano
Damiani, *novel* Alberto Moravia *d* Damiano
Damiani *ph* Roberto Gerardi *m* Luis
Enriquez Bacalov

Horst Buchholz, Catherine Spaak, Bette
Davis, Isa Miranda, Lea Padovani

En Cas de Malheur*
France / Italy 1958 120m bw
Iena / UCIL / Incom
aka: *Love Is My Profession*

A wealthy, middle-aged lawyer leaves his wife
for a worthless young wanton whom he is
defending on a robbery charge.
Good solid melodrama with excellent credits:
it caught all concerned on top form and had
international success, but the theme is not in
itself very interesting.

w Jean Aurenche, Pierre Bost, *novel* Georges
Simenon *d Claude Autant-Lara ph* Jacques
Natteau *m* René Cloërc

Jean Gabin, Edwige Feuillère, Brigitte Bardot,
Franco Interlenghi

En Rade*
France 1927 60m approx bw silent
Neofilm

A Marseilles docker dreams of escaping his
pent-in existence and fleeing with his mistress
to the South Seas.

More realistic than Pagnol's *Marius* trilogy,
which used the same setting, this remains an
interesting slice of romantic realism, with good
attention to detail.

w Alberto Cavalcanti, Claude Heymann
d Alberto Cavalcanti *ph* Jimmy Rogers, A.
Fairli, P. Enberg

Catherine Hessling, Philippe Heriat, Georges
Charlia

Enchanted April
US 1935 66m bw

A woman becomes lonely when her husband
turns into a successful novelist. Thin marital
comedy-drama for fans of the star. Ann
Harding, Frank Morgan, Katharine
Alexander, Reginald Owen, Jane Baxter,
Jessie Ralph. Written by Samuel Hoffenstein
and Ray Harris, from the novel by 'Elizabeth';
directed by Harry Beaumont; for RKO. 'Very
British in background and proceeding at all
times with a lifted eyebrow.'—*Variety*

The Enchanted Cottage*
US 1945 92m bw
RKO

A plain girl and a disfigured man are beautiful
to each other.
Wartime updating of a sentimental old play;
insufficiently well considered to be more than
tolerable.

w De Witt Bodeen, Herman J. Mankiewicz,
play Sir Arthur Wing Pinero *d* John
Cromwell *ph* Ted Tetzlaff *m* Roy Webb

Dorothy McGuire, Robert Young, Herbert
Marshall, Mildred Natwick

AAN: Roy Webb

The Enchanted Forest*
US 1945 77m Cinecolor
PRC

Old John the Hermit talks to trees and
animals, and rescues a lost child.
Surprising piece of Victorian whimsy,
remarkably effective in its unambitious way,
especially as a product of this studio. The best
known example of Cinecolor.

w Robert Lee Johnson, John Le Bar, Lou
Brock *d* Lew Landers *ph* Marcel Le Picard
m Alfred Hay Malotte

Harry Davenport, Edmund Lowe, Brenda
Joyce, Billy Severn

Enchanted Island
US 1958 94m Technicolor
Waverly (Benedict Bogeaus)

In the 1840s two sailors jump ship and settle
on what they later discover to be a cannibal
island.
Tame adaptation of a minor classic, with the
actors all at sea.

w James Leicester, Harold Jacob Smith, *novel*
Typee by Herman Melville *d* Allan Dwan
ph George Stahl *m* Raul Lavista

Jane Powell (an unconvincing Polynesian),
Dana Andrews, Don Dubbins, Arthur Shields,
Ted de Corsia, Friedrich Ledebur

Enchantment*
US 1948 101m bw
Samuel Goldwyn

A London house tells the story of three
generations.
Yes, a house tells the story, and the leading
characters are called Rollo and Lark, but this
is a very appealing piece of period romantic
nonsense, with the highest possible gloss upon
it.

w *John Patrick, novel* A Fugue in Time by
Rumer Godden *d Irving Reis ph* Gregg
Toland *m* Hugo Friedhofer

David Niven, Teresa Wright, Evelyn Keyes,
Farley Granger, Jayne Meadows, Leo G.
Carroll

'Deliberate in pace, and artfully contrived as
an emotional holiday, yet genuinely moving on
its own terms.'—*Newsweek*

Encore*
GB 1951 88m bw
GFD / Two Cities (Antony Darnborough)

Three more Somerset Maugham short stories
introduced by the author.
The final follow-up to the success of *Quartet*
and *Trio*; television playlets quickly made this
kind of short story seem old-fashioned, but the
standard here was high.

w T. E. B. Clarke, Arthur Macrae, Eric
Ambler, *stories* The Ant and the Grasshopper,
Winter Cruise, Gigolo and Gigolette *d* Pat
Jackson, Anthony Pelissier, Harold French
ph Desmond Dickinson *m* Richard Addinsell

Nigel Patrick, Ronald Culver, *Kay Walsh*,
Noel Purcell, Ronald Squire, John Laurie,
Glynis Johns, Terence Morgan, David
Hutcheson

'A comedy for you and your next of kin!'
The End
US 1978 100m De Luxe
UA / Lawrence Gordon (Hank Moonjean)

A selfish man finds he is dying and
unsuccessfully tries to change what remains of
his life.
Presumably intended as an ironic black
comedy, this comes over as tasteless ham;
nobody involved, least of all the director-star,
has any idea how to handle it.

w Jerry Belson *d* Burt Reynolds *ph* Bobby
Byrne *m* Paul Williams *pd* Jan Scott

Burt Reynolds, Dom de Luise, Sally Field,
Strother Martin, David Steinberg, Joanne
Woodward, Norman Fell, Myrna Loy, Pat
O'Brien, Robby Benson, Carl Reiner

The End of August*
US 1981 107m Metrocolor
Sewanee (Martin Jurow)

In 1900, a bored young wife takes a lover
beneath her station.
Unexpectedly nostalgic wallow in days gone
by, the background seeming more
important than the personal story, and
certainly very good to look at.

w Eula Seaton, Leon Heller, *novel* The Awakening by Kate Chopin *d* Bob Graham *ph* Robert Elswit *m* Shirley Walker *pd* Warren Jacobson, Erin Jo Jurow

Sally Sharp, Lilia Skala, David Marshall Grant, Kathleen Widdoes, Paul Roebling, Paul Shenar

'Reminiscent of nothing so much as the turning of pages in a family album.'—*Jo Imeson, MFB*

The End of St Petersburg**

USSR 1927   110m approx   bw   silent
Mezhrabpom-Russ
original title: *Konyets Sankt-Peterburga*

A peasant comes to live in St Petersburg in 1914, understands the workers' problems, and joins in the revolution.

Exhilarating propaganda, reprehensible but superbly conceived, with an especially rousing climax.

w Nathan Zarkhi   *d V. I. Pudovkin*
ph Anatoli Golovnya, K. Vents
ad S. Kozlovsky

Ivan Chuvelov, Vera Baranovskaya, A. P. Christiakov

† The film was officially commissioned as part of the 10th anniversary celebrations.

The End of the Affair

GB 1954   106m   bw
Columbia / Coronado (David Lewis)

In wartime London, a repressed wife has an affair with a writer but develops religious guilt which leads indirectly to her death.

Glum sinning in Greeneland; over-ambitious, miscast, and poor-looking.

w Lenore Coffee, *novel* Graham Greene *d* Edward Dmytryk *ph* Wilkie Cooper *m* Benjamin Frankel

Deborah Kerr, Van Johnson, Peter Cushing, John Mills, Stephen Murray, Nora Swinburne, Charles Goldner

End of the Game*

US / West Germany 1976   104m   colour
TCF / Maximilian Schell

A retiring police inspector intensifies his vendetta against the crooked industrialist who thirty years earlier killed the woman they both loved.

Chess-like revenge melodrama very typical of its author, with no light relief and a few existentialist touches added for general confusion. Well made and sometimes fascinating, but finally annoying.

w Maximilian Schell and Friedrich Durrenmatt, from Durrenmatt's novel *The Judge and his Hangman* *d* Maximilian Schell *ph* Ennio Guarnieri, Klaus Koenig, Roberto Gerardi

Jon Voight, Robert Shaw, Martin Ritt, Jacqueline Bisset

'A more addled, overreaching, misjudged, ill-made, wasteful, posturizing, uninteresting and tedious little epic has not toddled into town in years.'—*Charles Champlin, Los Angeles Times*

The End of the River*

GB 1947   83m   bw
GFD / The Archers (Michael Powell, Emeric Pressburger)

A South American Indian boy flees to the outside world and finds life in the city as dangerous as in the jungle.

Strange but oddly impressive departure for British film-makers at this time. A commercial and critical disaster.

w Wolfgang Wilhelm   *d* Derek Twist
ph Christopher Challis   *m* Lambert Williamson

Sabu, Esmond Knight, Bibi Ferreira, Robert Douglas, Antoinette Cellier, Raymond Lovell, Torin Thatcher

The End of the Road

GB 1936   71m   bw

A travelling singer loses heart when he hears of the death of his daughter. Stilted star vehicle of archival interest. *Harry Lauder,* Ruth Haven, Ethel Glendinning, Bruce Seton. Written by Edward Dryhurst; directed by Alan Bryce; for Fox British.

The End of the Road*

GB 1954   77m   bw
Group Three (Alfred Shaughnessy)

A retired engineer becomes frustrated by idleness, and his family contemplate sending him to an old people's home.

Reasonably absorbing study of old age, suffering from a contrived end.

w James Forsyth, Geoffrey Orme   *d* Wolf Rilla   *ph* Arthur Grant   *m* John Addison

Finlay Currie, Duncan Lamont, Naomi Chance, David Hannaford

End of the World*

France 1930   105m   bw
Ecran d'Art (Abel Gance)
Original title: *La Fin du Monde*

Social and economic panic is caused when a comet is about to hit the earth.

Massive attempt by Gance to rival his Napoleon in scope. Made in German, French and English, it cost a phenomenal sum which it never regained; Gance found work hard to get in future, especially since he set himself up as a prophet.

w,d Abel Gance

Abel Gance, Colette Darfeuil, Sylvia Grenade, Victor Francen

'A megalomaniac's effort turned out without consideration for financial results, and containing a strange mixture of crazy stuff, with successfully directed spectacular sequences.'—*Variety*

† The full title is *The End of the World as Seen, Heard and Rendered by Abel Gance*

Endangered Species

US 1982   97m   Metrocolor
MGM / Alive Enterprises (Carolyn Pfeiffer)

Citizens of a small Wyoming town discover that their cattle are being systematically murdered.

Curious melodrama which never really explains itself but seems to be carrying a message about chemical warfare. With a proper ending it could have been a good suspenser.

w Alan Rudolph, John Binder, *story* Judson Kinger, Richard Woods   *d* Alan Rudolph *ph* Paul Lohmann   *m* Gary Wright   *pd* Trevor Williams

Robert Urich, Jobeth Williams, Paul Dooley, Hoyt Axton, Peter Coyote

Endless Love

'It's not over . . . it's not over!'

US 1981   110m   Technicolor
Polygram (Keith Barish)

A high school student's love for a 15-year-old girl is thwarted by circumstance and accident.

Overheated melodrama with unbelievable and unlikeable characters. Why this director should choose to make it is mysterious.

w Judith Rascoe, *novel* Scott Spencer *d* Franco Zeffirelli   *ph* David Watkin *m* Jonathan Tunick   *pd* Ed Wittstein

Brooke Shields, Martin Hewitt, Shirley Knight, Don Murray, Richard Kiley, Beatrice Straight

● *Video: Spectrum*

Endless Night*

GB 1971   99m   Eastmancolor
BL / EMI (Leslie Gilliat)

An American girl buys an English stately home and marries a chauffeur, but is later frightened to death.

Bumpy British thriller, structurally weak and peopled by the dullest conceivable characters, but with watchably scary sequences.

wd Sidney Gilliat, *novel* Agatha Christie *ph* Harry Waxman   *m* Bernard Herrmann

Hayley Mills, Hywel Bennett, George Sanders, Britt Ekland, Per Oscarsson, Lois Maxwell

The Endless Summer

US 1966   95m   Technicolor

A study of surfing round the world. A documentary which became a cult for those influenced by this Californian obsession; smashing photography hardly atones for an approach so naïve as to become fatuous. Written, directed, photographed and edited by *Bruce Brown,* for Bruce Brown Films / Columbia.

Enemy Agent

US 1940   64m   bw

An aircraft worker is framed as a spy. Nifty little topical support with not much sense but plenty of zest. Richard Cromwell, Philip Dorn, Helen Vinson, Marjorie Reynolds, Robert Armstrong, Vinton Haworth, Abner Biberman, Jack Carson, Jack La Rue. Written by Sam Robbins and Edmund L. Hartmann; directed by Lew Landers; for Universal.

The Enemy Below°
US 1957 98m Technicolor
Cinemascope
TCF (Dick Powell)

During World War II an American destroyer in the South Atlantic is involved in a cat-and-mouse operation with a U-boat.
Well-staged, unsurprising naval thriller with good pace and a pat let's-not-be-nasty-to-each-other ending.

w Wendell Mayes, *novel* Commander D. A. Rayner d Dick Powell ph Harold Rosson m Leigh Harline

Robert Mitchum, Curt Jurgens, Theodore Bikel, David Hedison

● Video: CBS / Fox

The Enemy General
US 1960 74m bw
Columbia (Sam Katzman)

An American officer takes revenge on the German general who executed his fiancée.
Routine World War II heroics with a plot deserving a rather better production.

w Dan Pepper, Burt Picard d George Sherman ph Basil Emmott md Mischa Bakaleinikoff

Van Johnson, Jean-Pierre Aumont, John Van Dreelen, Dany Carrel, Françoise Prévost

An Enemy of the People°
US 1977 103m Metrocolor
First Artists (George Schaefer)

A small-town doctor discovers that for commercial reasons his colleagues propose to conceal the fact that the local spa is contaminated by tannery waste.
Ibsen's plot is well intentioned but well worn – it more or less served as the starting point for *Jaws* – so in any modern version the acting is all. Here it isn't enough, though the star so badly wanted to do it that arguments and sulks kept him off the screen for three years.

w Alexander Jacobs, from Arthur Miller's version of the play by Henrik Ibsen d George Schaefer ph Paul Lohmann m Leonard Rosenman

Steve McQueen, Charles Durning, Bibi Andersson, Eric Christmas, Richard Bradford, Richard A. Dysart

L'Enfant Sauvage°
France 1969 84m bw
UA / Films du Carrosse (Marcel Berbert)
US title: *The Wild Child*

In 1797, a scientist tames and studies a young boy who has mysteriously been living wild in the forest.
Slightly flat but generally interesting reconstruction of a true event, the same one which subsequently inspired TV projects such as *Stalk the Wild Child* and *Lucan*.

w François Truffaut, Jean Gruault d François Truffaut ph Nestor Almendros m Vivaldi

Jean-Pierre Cargol, François Truffaut, Jean Dasté, Françoise Seigner

Les Enfants du Paradis°°°°
France 1945 195m bw
Pathé (Fred Orain, Raymond Borderic)
US title: *Children of Paradise*

In the 'theatre street' of Paris in the 1840s, a mime falls in love with the elusive Garance, but her problems with other men keep them apart.
A magnificent evocation of a place and a period, this thoroughly enjoyable epic melodrama is flawed only by its lack of human warmth and of a real theme. It remains nevertheless one of the cinema's most memorable films.

w Jacques Prévert d Marcel Carné ph Roger Hubert m Maurice Thiriet, Joseph Kosma, G. Mouque ad Alexandre Trauner, Léon Barsacq, Raymond Gabutti

Arletty, Jean-Louis Barrault, Pierre Brasseur, Marcel Herrand, Maria Casarès, Louis Salou, Pierre Renoir, Gaston Modot, Jane Marken
'A magnificent scenario . . . Prévert is as adept with wit as with poignancy . . . I don't believe a finer group of actors was ever assembled on film'—*John Simon*

AAN: Jacques Prévert

● Video: Thorn EMI

Les Enfants Terribles°
France 1950 100m bw
Jean-Pierre Melville
aka: *The Strange Ones*

The hothouse relationship of an adolescent brother and sister leads to tragedy.
Rough-edged, stage-bound but occasionally quite powerful exploration into familiar Cocteau territory.

wd Jean-Pierre Melville, *novel* Jean Cocteau ph Henri Decaë m Bach, Vivaldi

Nicole Stéphane, Edouard Dermithe, Renée Cosima, Jacques Bernard

'The first story of the double-fisted DA who tore apart the evil dynasty that peddled murder for a price!'

The Enforcer°°°
US 1950 87m bw
United States Pictures (Milton Sperling)
GB title: *Murder, Inc*

A crusading District Attorney tracks down the leader of a gang which murders for profit.
Extremely suspenseful and well-characterized police yarn based on fact. One of the very best of its kind.

w Martin Rackin d Bretaigne Windust ph Robert Burks m David Buttolph

Humphrey Bogart, Everett Sloane, Zero Mostel, Ted de Corsia, Roy Roberts, King Donovan
'A tough, very slickly-made thriller with a host of fine character parts.'—*NFT, 1969*
'Absorbing and exciting, with little of the violence that so often disfigures films of this kind.'—*Richard Mallett, Punch*

The Enforcer
US 1976 96m De Luxe Panavision
Warner / Malpaso (Robert Daley)

Brutal Inspector Callahan of the San Francisco police redeems himself by rounding up a group of psychopathic hoodlums.
Dirty Harry, phase three: for hardened veterans only.

w Stirling Silliphant, Dean Riesner d James Fargo ph Richard Glouner m Jerry Fielding

Clint Eastwood, Tyne Daly, Harry Guardino, Bradford Dillman, John Mitchum, DeVeren Brookwalter, John Crawford
'A new low in mindless violence is reached in this film, which is so bad it would be funny if it were not for the gut-thumping killings from beginning to end.'—*William F. Fore, Film Information*

The Engagement°
GB 1970 44m Technicolor
Memorial (David Barber)

A young executive spends a devastating afternoon trying to borrow money to pay for an engagement ring which cost more than he expected.
Brisk little comedy which doesn't wear out its welcome.

w Tom Stoppard d Paul Joyce ph Tony Spratling m John Dankworth

David Warner, Michael Bates, George Innes, Juliet Harmer, Paul Curran, Barbara Couper, Peter Copley

England Made Me°°
GB 1972 100m Eastmancolor
Hemdale / Atlantic (Jack Levin)

In 1935 a sponging Englishman becomes involved through his sister with a German financier.
Somewhat altered from the novel, this unusual film remains a lively, intelligent character melodrama.

w Desmond Cory, Peter Duffell, *novel* Graham Greene d Peter Duffell ph Ray Parslow m John Scott

Peter Finch, Michael York, Hildegarde Neil, Michael Hordern, Joss Ackland

English without Tears°
GB 1944 89m bw
GFD / Two Cities (Anatole de Grunwald, Sydney Box)
US title: *Her Man Gilbey*

World War II a rich ATS girl falls for her butler who has become a lieutenant.
Wispy satirical comedy with amusing moments, chiefly interesting for the pre-war League of Nations sequences.

w Terence Rattigan, Anatole de Grunwald d Harold French

Lilli Palmer, Michael Wilding, Margaret Rutherford, Penelope Dudley Ward, Albert Lieven, Roland Culver, Peggy Cummins

An Englishman's Home
GB 1939 79m bw

An English family plays unwitting host to a foreign spy. Hilarious clinker, far too unintentionally funny to make the effective propaganda intended. Edmund Gwenn, Mary

Maguire, Paul Von Hernreid, Geoffrey Toone, Richard Ainley, Desmond Tester. Written by (catch them all) Dennis Wheatley, Edward Knoblock, Ian Hay, Robert Edmunds, Dora Nirva, Clifford Grey, Richard Llewellyn and Rodney Ackland; directed by Albert de Courville; for Aldwych. 'There is nothing to be said for this film—though it might prove useful propaganda in enemy countries, purporting to illustrate the decadence of English architecture and taste.'—*Graham Greene.*

Enigma

GB / France 1982   101m   colour
Embassy / Filmcrest / Peter Shaw

An East German refugee is recruited by the CIA to return to East Berlin.
Threadbare spy stuff with an indecipherable plot.

w John Briley, *novel* Michael Barak d Jeannot Szwarc ph Jean-Louis Picavet m Marc Wilkinson

Martin Sheen, Brigitte Fossey, Sam Neill, Derek Jacobi, Michel Lonsdale, Frank Finlay, Michael Williams, Warren Clarke
    'Well made but insufficiently exciting.'—*Variety*
    'The mystery is why they bothered.'—*Guardian*
● *Video: Guild*

Ensign Pulver

US 1964   104m   Technicolor
Panavision
Warner (Joshua Logan)

Further naval misadventures of the character from *Mr Roberts.*
Threadbare naval comedy with every expected cliché.

w Joshua Logan, Peter S. Feibleman, *play* Joshua Logan, Thomas Heggen d Joshua Logan ph Charles Lawton m George Duning

Robert Walker, Burl Ives, Walter Matthau, Tommy Sands, Millie Perkins, Kay Medford, Larry Hagman, James Farentino, James Coco, Al Freeman Jnr

Entente Cordiale*

France 1939   95m   bw
Max Glass

A history of relations between England and France from Victorian times to the present day.
Ambitious pageant from the French point of view.

w Steve Passeur, Max Glass, *book* Edward VII and His Times by André Maurois d Marcel l'Herbier ph Ted Pahle, Marc Fossard m Darius Milhaud

Victor Francen (Edward VII), Gaby Morlay (Queen Victoria), André Lefaur, Jean Perier, Jean d'Yd, Jean Worms
    'One of the most outstanding productions of its type ever made in France.'—*Variety*

Enter Arsène Lupin

US 1944   72m   bw

A master thief protects a beautiful girl's

emerald. Stiff little second which failed to bring forth a series. Charles Korvin, Ella Raines, J. Carrol Naish, George Dolenz, Gale Sondergaard, Miles Mander. Written by Bertram Millhauser; directed by Ford Beebe; for Universal.

Enter Laughing*

US 1967   111m   Technicolor
Columbia / Acre / Sajo (Carl Reiner, Joseph Stein)

In New York in the thirties, a young man about to train as a pharmacist decides to become an actor instead.
Strident Jewish comedy based on the writer-director's own youthful experiences, which might have been more effectively strained by another hand. The talent is there, though.

w Joseph Stein, Carl Reiner, *play* Carl Reiner d Carl Reiner ph Joseph Biroc m Quincy Jones

Reni Santoni, Jose Ferrer, Shelley Winters, Elaine May, Jack Gilford, Janet Margolin, David Opatoshu, Michael J. Pollard

Enter Madame

US 1934   83m   bw

A millionaire is humbled when he marries a glamorous opera singer. Modest comedy operetta, with the star's voice dubbed by Nina Koshetz. Elissa Landi, Cary Grant, Lynne Overman, Sharon Lynne, Paul Porcasi. Written by Charles Brackett and Gladys Lehmann, from the play by Gilda Varesi Archibald and Dorothea Donn-Byrne; directed by Elliott Nugent; for Paramount.

Enter the Dragon*

US / Hong Kong 1973   99m
Technicolor   Panavision
Warner / Concord (Fred Weintraub, Paul Heller)

A master of martial arts is enlisted by British intelligence to stop opium smuggling.
The first Hollywood-based Kung Fu actioner; not bad, on the lines of a more violent James Bond.

w Michael Allin d Robert Clouse ph Gilbert Hubbs m Lalo Schifrin

Bruce Lee, John Saxon, Shih Kien, Jim Kelly, Bob Wall
    'A good-natured example of the pleasures of schlock art.'—*Pauline Kael*
● *Video: Warner*

The Entertainer*

GB 1960   96m   bw
BL / Bryanston / Woodfall / Holly (John Croydon)

A faded seaside comedian reflects on his failure as an entertainer and as a man.
Even with Olivier repeating his stage triumph, or perhaps because of it, this tragi-comedy remains defiantly theatrical and does not take wing on film.

w John Osborne, Nigel Kneale, *play* John Osborne d Tony Richardson ph Oswald Morris m John Addison

Laurence Olivier, Joan Plowright, Brenda de Banzie, *Roger Livesey*, Alan Bates, Shirley Anne Field, Albert Finney, Thora Hird, Daniel Massey
    'No amount of deafening sound effects and speciously busy cutting can remove one's feeling that behind this distracting façade of heightened realism lurks a basic lack of confidence.'—*Peter John Dyer*
† For the television version starring Jack Lemmon and Ray Bolger, see *Television Companion.*

AAN: Laurence Olivier

Entertaining Mr Sloane*

GB 1969   94m   Technicolor
Pathe / Canterbury (Douglas Kentish)

A lodger attracts the amorous attention of both the middle-aged daughter and older son of the house.
A Gothic *tour de force* of bad taste which worked better on the stage but has its moments.

w Clive Exton, *play* Joe Orton d Douglas Hickox ph Wolfgang Suschitzky m Georgie Fame

Beryl Reid, Harry Andrews, Peter McEnery, Alan Webb
● *Video: Thorn EMI*

The Entity

US 1981   125m   Technicolor
Panavision
(TCF) Pelleport Investors / American Cinema (Harold Schneider)

A young mother is attacked and raped by an invisible entity which may come from her own id.
Unpleasant nonsense, way overlong but with the occasional well-staged scene for those who can stay the course.

w Frank DeFelitta, from his novel d Sidney J. Furie ph Stephen H. Burum m Charles Bernstein pd Charles Rosen ed Frank J. Urioste

Barbara Hershey, Ron Silver, David Labiosa, George Coe, Jacqueline Brookes
● *Video: CBS / Fox*

Entr'acte**

France 1924   20m approx   bw   silent
Ballets Suédois

Various eccentric characters become involved in a crazy chase.
Hilarious nonsense short, devised originally to be shown between the acts of a Dadaist ballet. Very clearly the start of a famous directorial career.

w Francis Picabia d, ed René Clair ph J. Berliet

Jean Borlin, Inge Fries, Francis Picabia, Man Ray, Georges Auric, Marcel Achard, Marcel Duchamps

Entre Onze Heures et Minuit*

France 1948   103m   bw
Francinex (Jacques Roitfeld)

A police detective solves his case by impersonating one of the victims.

Twisty, elaborate murder mystery, very competently performed but a little overlong.

w Henri Decoin, Marcel Rivet, *novel* Le Sosie de la Morgue by Claude Luxel *d* Henri Decoin *ph* Nicolas Hayer *m* Henri Saguet

Louis Jouvet, Madeleine Robinson, Robert Arnoux, Gisèle Casadeus

Entrée des Artistes*
France 1938 100m bw

Jealousies among the students at the Paris Conservatory lead to murder. Predictable but well-made audience pleaser. Louis Jouvet, Odette Joyeux, Claude Dauphin, Janine Darcey, Carette, Dalio, Sylvie. Written by Henri Jeanson, André Cayatte; directed by Marc Allegret; for Regina.

L'Equipage*
France 1935 107m bw

A World War I flier finds that the love of his wife is the wife of his colleague. Tense romantic drama with aerial sequences, subsequently remade in Hollywood as *The Woman Between. Charles Vanel, Jean-Pierre Aumont,* Annabella. From a story by Joseph Kessel; directed by *Anatole Litvak;* for Pathé-Natan. 'A gripping human story, beautifully told.'—*Variety*

Equus*
GB 1977 137m colour
UA / Winkast (Denis Holt)

A middle-aged psychiatrist tries to find out why a 17-year-old boy blinded six horses. Overlong film version of a play which was a *succès d'estime;* it makes the fatal mistake of showing the tragic events realistically instead of stylistically as was done on the stage, and as a study in abnormal psychology it is scarcely gripping or revealing.

w Peter Shaffer, from his play *d* Sidney Lumet *ph* Oswald Morris *m* Richard Rodney Bennett *pd* Tony Walton

Richard Burton, Peter Firth, Colin Blakely, Joan Plowright, Harry Andrews, Eileen Atkins, Jenny Agutter, Kate Reid

'It sets Peter Shaffer's worst ideas on a pedestal.'—*Pauline Kael*

AAN: Peter Shaffer; Richard Burton; Peter Firth

● *Video: Warner*

Eraserhead
US 1976 89m bw

A nondescript man has a number of increasingly nightmarish experiences including becoming pregnant and being consumed by a planet. Tediously elongated piece of schlock surrealism. At least Bunuel and Dali didn't take so long about their nonsense. John Nance, Charlotte Stewart, Allen Joseph. Written, produced and directed by David Lynch; photographed by David Elmes and Herbert Cardwell; for David Lynch.

● *Video: Palace*

Eroica*
Poland 1957 83m bw
Kadr
aka: *Heroism*

Two ironic episodes of war; in the 1944 Warsaw uprising and in a POW camp. Nicely-judged little stories with a sting.

w Jerzy Stefan Stawinski, from his novels *d* Andrzej Munk *ph* Jerzy Wojcik *m* Jan Krenz

Barbara Polomska, L. Niemszyk, Edward Dziewonski, K. Rudzki, Roman Klosowski, Josef Nowak

Erotikon*
Sweden 1920 85m approx bw silent
Svensk Filmindustri

When a professor discovers that his wife is unfaithful, he consoles himself with his young niece.

Sophisticated comedy drama filled with material which might later have appealed to Lubitsch; a little faded now, but it still has charm.

w Gustav Molander, Mauritz Stiller, *play* Franz Herzog *d* Mauritz Stiller *ph* Henrik Jaenzon

Lars Hanson, Karin Molander, Tora Teje, Anders de Wahl

Erotikon*
Czechoslovakia 1929 85m approx bw silent
Gem Film

A stationmaster's daughter takes a rich lover. Atmospheric little sex drama which sufficiently justified its title to be a big international success.

wd Gustav Machaty *ph* Vaclav Vich

Ita Rina, Karel Schleichert, Olaf Fjord, Theo Pistek

The Errand Boy
US 1961 92m bw
Paramount / Jerry Lewis (Ernest D. Glucksman)

A dimwit paperhanger causes havoc in a Hollywood studio but is eventually signed up as a comic to rival Jerry Lewis.

Feeble comedy with the star at his self-satisfied worst.

wd Jerry Lewis *ph* W. Wallace Kelley *m* Walter Scharf

Jerry Lewis, Brian Donlevy, Sig Rumann, Fritz Feld, Isobel Elsom, Iris Adrian

Escapade
US 1935 87m bw
MGM (Bernard Hyman)

Affairs of a Viennese artist.
Turgid romantic drama copied from the more successful German film *Maskerade.*

w Herman J. Mankiewicz, *original* Walter Reisch *d* Robert Z. Leonard *ph* Ernest Haller *m* Bronislau Kaper, Walter Jurmann

William Powell, Luise Rainer, Virginia Bruce, Mady Christians, Reginald Owen, Frank Morgan, Laura Hope Crews, Henry Travers

'A triumph of studio slickness.'—*Variety*

Escapade*
GB 1955 87m bw
Pinnacle (Daniel Angel)

Parents row with a headmaster when their three sons steal an aeroplane, but all is well when it turns out that they are on a peace mission.

Whimsical comedy-drama with a rather foolish point; the cast however can hardly fail to provide entertaining moments.

w Gilbert Holland (Donald Ogden Stewart), *play* Roger MacDougall *d* Philip Leacock *ph* Eric Cross *m* Bruce Montgomery

John Mills, Alastair Sim, Yvonne Mitchell, Colin Gordon, Marie Lohr

Escapade in Florence
US 1962 80m Technicolor
Walt Disney (Bill Anderson)

Two American students in Florence uncover art thefts.

Cheerful adventure for children, well enough produced on location, but quite unmemorable.

w Maurice Tombragel *d* Steve Previn *ph* Kurt Grigoleit *m* Buddy Baker

Ivan Desny, Tommy Kirk, Annette Alliotto, Nino Castelnuovo

Escapade in Japan
US 1957 93m Technirama
RKO (Arthur Lubin)

An American boy survives a plane crash in Tokyo and the crisis reunites his parents. Nicely photographed travelogue with a thread of plot; pleasant but hardly sustaining.

w Winston Miller *d* Arthur Lubin *ph* William Snyder *m* Max Steiner

Cameron Mitchell, Teresa Wright, Jon Prevost, Philip Ober

Escape
GB 1930 69m bw
ATP (Basil Dean)

An escaped convict on Dartmoor is helped and hindered by various chance encounters. Episodic, unsatisfactory drama from a stilted play.

wd Basil Dean, *play* John Galsworthy *ph* Jack Mackenzie

Gerald du Maurier, Edna Best, Madeleine Carroll, Gordon Harker, Horace Hodges, Mabel Poulton, Lewis Casson, Ian Hunter, Felix Aylmer

'A more careful work than most of the British talker product, but as an entertainment proposition it doesn't mean much.'—*Variety*

Escape**
US 1940 104m bw
MGM (Lawrence Weingarten)
reissue title: *When the Door Opened*

An American gets his mother out of a Nazi concentration camp before World War II. Ingenious but somewhat slow-moving melodrama with an exciting climax and good production values.

w Arch Oboler, Marguerite Roberts, *novel* Ethel Vance *d* Mervyn Le Roy *ph* Robert Planck *m* Franz Waxman

Norma Shearer, Robert Taylor, *Conrad Veidt*, *Nazimova*, Felix Bressart, Albert Basserman, Philip Dorn, Bonita Granville

'It takes an hour to get started and makes just another feeble fable from headlines.'— *Otis Ferguson*

'Far and away the most dramatic and hair-raising picture yet made on the sinister subject of persecution in a totalitarian land.'—*Bosley Crowther, New York Times*

'One of the most poignant dramatic films of the year.'—*Modern Screen*

'The director takes forever to set up the manoeuvres, and the villain is so much more attractive than the hero that the whole thing turns into a feeble, overproduced joke.'— *Pauline Kael, 70s*

'Some men are born to imperilled adventure! Some women are drawn to the most dangerous of loves!'

Escape
GB 1948   79m   bw
TCF (William Perlberg)

Wholly artificial, predictable and uninteresting remake of the 1930 film.

w Philip Dunne *d* Joseph L. Mankiewicz *ph* Frederick A. Young *m* William Alwyn

Rex Harrison, Peggy Cummins, William Hartnell, Norman Wooland, Jill Esmond

The Escape Artist*
US 1982   93m   Technicolor
Zoetrope Studios (Doug Claybourne, Buck Houghton)

A young boy justifies his descent from 'the world's greatest escape artist'.
Curiously unfulfilled fable, too vague to satisfy the family audience it seems to aim at, but with pleasant moments.

w Melissa Mathison, Stephen Zito, *novel* David Wagoner *d* Caleb Deschanel *ph* Stephen H. Burum *m* Georges Delerue *pd* Dean Tavoularis

Griffin O'Neal, Raul Julia, Teri Garr, Joan Hackett, Gabriel Dell, Desi Arnaz

Escape by Night
GB 1953   79m   bw
Tempean (Robert S. Baker, Monty Berman)

A tough reporter tries to get the inside story on a vice ring.
Formula thick ear with what now seems the world's most unlikely villain—Sid James.

wd John Gilling *ph* Monty Berman *m* Stanley Black

Bonar Colleano, Andrew Ray, Sidney James, Ted Ray, Simone Silva, Avice Landone, Patrick Barr

Escape from Alcatraz*
US 1979   112m   De Luxe
Paramount / Malpaso (Don Siegel)

The allegedly true story of a 1960 escape from the prison on a rock in San Francisco Bay.
A dour, terse, depressing prison movie which

makes an uncomfortable star vehicle and not very much of an entertainment, but does preserve a certain integrity right to its ambiguous ending.

w Richard Tuggle, *book* J. Campbell Bruce *d* Don Siegel *ph* Bruce Surtees *m* Jerry Fielding *pd* Allen Smith

Clint Eastwood, Patrick McGoohan, Roberts Blossom, Jack Thibeau, Larry Hankin

'An almost entirely interior film masquerading as an exterior one.'—*Tom Milne, MFB*

● Video: CIC

Escape from Dartmoor*
GB 1930   77m   bw

A barber murders his wife's lover. Stilted melodrama, of interest only as an early British part-talkie. (The only words heard are from a film in a cinema which the characters visit.)
Nora Baring, Uno Henning, Hans Schlettow. Written by Herbert Price; directed by *Anthony Asquith*; for Pro Patria. 'Morbid material, interesting only because of clever direction.'— *Variety*

Escape from East Berlin
Germany / US 1962   94m   bw
MGM / Walter Wood / Hans Albin
aka: *Tunnel 28*

An East German chauffeur is persuaded to help an escape attempt by digging and tunnelling under the Berlin Wall.
Cheerless escape melodrama, thinly based on fact but without much suspense.

w Gabrielle Upton, Peter Berneis, Millard Lampell *d* Robert Siodmak *ph* Georg Krause *m* Hans-Martin Majewski

Don Murray, Christine Kaufmann, Werner Klemperer, Ingrid van Bergen

Escape from Fort Bravo*
US 1953   98m   Anscocolor
MGM (Nicholas Nayfack)

A girl helps her Confederate lover to escape from a Yankee fort in Arizona; the commander then tries to save them from Indians.
Grade A western, effectively shot in Death Valley.

w Frank Fenton *d* John Sturges *ph* Robert Surtees *m* Jeff Alexander

William Holden, Eleanor Parker, John Forsythe, William Demarest

Escape from New York*
US 1981   99m
      Metrocolor Panavision
Avco Embassy / International Film Investors / Goldcrest (Larry Franco, Debra Hill)

In 1997 the whole of Manhattan Island has become a vast security prison; a president has to bale out over it and is taken hostage.
Inventive but too complex melodrama with unattractive detail; its director's biggest production but not his most rewarding.

w John Carpenter, Nick Castle *d* John Carpenter *ph* Jim Lucas *m* John Carpenter *pd* Joe Alves

Kurt Russell, Lee Van Cleef, Ernest Borgnine, Donald Pleasence, Isaac Hayes, Season Hubley, Adrienne Barbeau, Harry Dean Stanton

● Video: Embassy

Escape from the Dark
GB 1976   104m   Technicolor
Walt Disney (Ron Miller)

In 1909 Yorkshire, two boys save pit ponies from the slaughterhouse.
Efficient family fare with plenty of suspense and good character cameos.

w Rosemary Anne Sisson *d* Charles Jarrott *ph* Paul Beeson *m* Ron Goodwin

Alastair Sim, Peter Barkworth, Maurice Colbourne, Susan Tebbs, Geraldine McEwan, Prunella Scales, Leslie Sands, Joe Gladwin

Escape from the Planet of the Apes
US 1971   97m   De Luxe   Panavision
TCF / APJAC (Arthur P. Jacobs, Frank Capra Jnr)

Three educated apes travel back from the disaster-strewn future to warn mankind of what lies ahead. Mankind naturally misunderstands. Predictable third in the series, with infantile humour alternating with a downbeat trend.

w Paul Dehn *d* Don Taylor *ph* Joseph Biroc *m* Jerry Goldsmith

Roddy McDowall, Kim Hunter, Bradford Dillman, Ricardo Montalban, Natalie Trundy, Eric Braeden, William Windom, Sal Mineo
† See also *Planet of the Apes*.

Escape from Zahrain
US 1961   93m   Technicolor   Panavision
Paramount (Ronald Neame)

Prisoners escape across the desert from an oil sheikdom.
Slow, boring adventure film; good to look at, with James Mason unbilled in a tiny part.

w Robin Estridge *d* Ronald Neame *ph* Ellsworth Fredericks *m* Lyn Murray

Yul Brynner, Sal Mineo, Madlyn Rhue, Jack Warden, Jay Novello

Escape in the Desert
US 1945   81m   bw
Warner (Alex Gottlieb)

An American flier outwits renegade Nazis.
Oddball remake of *The Petrified Forest*, with Nazis sitting in for gangsters. Of no interest in itself.

w Thomas Job, *play* Robert E. Sherwood *d* Edward A. Blatt *ph* Robert Burks *m* Adolph Deutsch

Philip Dorn, Helmut Dantine, Alan Hale, Jean Sullivan, Irene Manning, Samuel S. Hinds

Escape in the Fog
US 1945   65m   bw

A nurse sees a man attacked in a dream, and helps to save him when the events recur in real life. Muddy little spy story with premonition used as a book-end. Nina Foch, Otto Kruger, William Wright. Written by Aubrey Wisberg; directed by Budd Boetticher; for Columbia.

Escape Me Never*
GB 1935   95m   bw
B and D (Herbert Wilcox)

The mother of an illegitimate baby marries a composer who loves someone else.
Archetypal romantic weepie which has probably the star's most memorable and likeable performance.

w Carl Zuckerman, Robert Cullen, *play* Margaret Kennedy *d* Paul Czinner
ph Georges Périnal

Elisabeth Bergner, Hugh Sinclair, Griffith Jones, Penelope Dudley Ward, Irene Vanbrugh, Leon Quartermaine, Lyn Harding
  'Story stirs audience resentment, yet its able presentation commands attention.'—*Variety*
  'That it is a thoroughly British film is proved by the fact that among the staff one can see names like Andrejiev, Allgeier and Strassner, that the principal actress is German, and the producer is German too.'—*James Agate*
AAN: Elisabeth Bergner

Escape Me Never
US 1947   104m   bw
Warner (Henry Blanke)

Muddled remake of the above with shifted emphasis. So ill-conceived it's like watching through frosted glass.

w Thomas Williamson *d* Peter Godfrey
ph Sol Polito *m* Erich Wolfgang Korngold

Errol Flynn, Ida Lupino, Eleanor Parker, Gig Young, Reginald Denny, Isobel Elsom, Albert Basserman, Ludwig Stossel, Helene Thimig

Escape Route
GB 1952   79m   bw

Man on the run turns out to be FBI agent on the spy trail. A moderate co-feature, as unremarkable as its plot. George Raft, Sally Gray, Clifford Evans, Reginald Tate. Written by John Baines and Nicholas Phipps; directed by Seymour Friedman and Peter Graham Scott; for Banner / Eros.

Escape to Athena
GB 1979   117m   Eastmancolor Panavision
ITC / Pimlico (David Niven Jnr, Jack Wiener)

Prisoners-of-war on a Greek island during World War II recruit the aid of their sympathetic camp commandant in harassing the SS.
Expensive but not very involving thick-ear, hampered by tediously typecast actors and an uninventive script.

w Edward Anhalt, Richard S. Lochte
d George Pan Cosmatos *ph* Gil Taylor
m Lalo Schifrin

Roger Moore, David Niven, Elliott Gould, Sonny Bono, Telly Savalas, Claudia Cardinale, Stefanie Powers, Richard Roundtree, Anthony Valentine

'Performing as though they had met up by chance on holiday . . . the clutch of box office stars do what they can in a situation where they are the stand-ins and the stuntmen (especially the motorcyclists) dominate the screen.'—*Martyn Auty, MFB*

Escape to Burma
US 1955   88m   Technicolor Superscope
Benedict Bogeaus

An adventurer suspected of murder hides out on the tea plantation of an indomitable American woman.
Far Eastern hokum in which the heroine has a way with elephants.

w Talbot Jennings, Herbert Donovan *d* Allan Dwan *ph* John Alton *m* Louis Forbes

Barbara Stanwyck, Robert Ryan, David Farrar, Murvyn Vye, Reginald Denny

Escape to Danger
GB 1943   92m   bw
RKO (William Sistrom)

A British schoolmistress becomes a spy.
Adequate propaganda hokum.

w Wolfgang Wilhelm, Jack Whittingham
d Lance Comfort *ph* Max Greene *m* William Alwyn

Eric Portman, Ann Dvorak, Karel Stepanek, Ronald Ward, Ronald Adam, Lily Kann, David Peel, Felix Aylmer, A. E. Matthews

Escape to Glory
US 1940   74m   bw
Columbia (Sam Bischoff)
aka: *Submarine Zone*

A merchant ship with a variety of passengers is stalked by a Nazi submarine.
Minor *Grand Hotel* afloat: quite brisk and watchable.

w P. J. Wolfson *d* John Brahm *ph* Franz Planer

Pat O'Brien, Constance Bennett, John Halliday, Alan Baxter, Melville Cooper, Edgar Buchanan, Marjorie Gateson

Escape to Witch Mountain*
US 1974   97m   Technicolor
Walt Disney (Jerome Courtland)

Two mysterious orphan children have extraordinary powers, are chased by a scheming millionaire, and prove to come from another planet.
Mildly ingenious story frittered away by poor scripting and special effects. A stimulating change in children's films, however.

w Robert Malcolm Young, *novel* Alexander Key *d* John Hough *ph* Frank Phillips
m Johnny Mandel *sp* Art Cruickshank, Danny Lee

Ray Milland, Donald Pleasence, Eddie Albert, Kim Richards, Ike Eisenmann, Walter Barnes, Reta Shaw, Denver Pyle

● *Video: Disney*

Escort West
US 1958   75m   bw   Cinemascope
An ex-Confederate soldier helps the survivors

of a Union wagon train attack. Watchable lower-berth western. Victor Mature, Elaine Stewart, Faith Domergue, Noah Beery Jnr, Rex Ingram, John Hubbard. Written by Leo Gordon and Fred Hartsook; directed by Francis D. Lyon; for Batjac / Romina / UA.

Eskimo*
US 1933   120m   bw

The life of an Eskimo hunter and his family.
Curious fated attempt by a major studio to do a northern version of the successful *White Shadows in the South Seas*. Despite a melodramatic plot and gripping documentary sequences, the locale chilled audiences to the marrow. Mala, Peter Freuchen. Written by John Lee Mahin from books by Peter Freuchen; directed by W. S. Van Dyke; for MGM. 'Igloo whoopee variations not sufficiently hotcha to spell b.o.'—*Variety*

Espionage*
US 1937   67m   bw
MGM (Harry Rapf)

Spies and counter spies mingle on the Orient Express.
Lively second feature on familiar lines.

w Manuel Seff, Leonard Lee, Ainsworth Morgan, *play* Walter Hackett *d* Kurt Neumann *ph* Ray June

Edmund Lowe, Madge Evans, Paul Lukas, Ketti Gallian, Skeets Gallagher, Leonid Kinskey, Barnett Parker, Frank Reicher
  'Quite some laughs but chiefly for the duals.'—*Variety*

Espionage Agent
US 1939   83m   bw
Warner (Louis F. Edelmann)

An American diplomat falls in love with a spy. Anti-isolationist, semi-documentary exposé, a rather sketchy cross between *Foreign Correspondent* and *Confessions of a Nazi Spy*.

w Warren Duff, Michael Fessier, Frank Donaghue, Robert Buckner *d* Lloyd Bacon *ph* Charles Rosher

Joel McCrea, Brenda Marshall, Jeffrey Lynn, George Bancroft, Stanley Ridges, James Stephenson, Nana Bryant
  'War headlines dramatized. Lots of openings for exploitation.'—*Variety*

Les Espions
France 1957   136m   bw
Cinedis (L. de Mazure)
aka: *The Spies*

Spies from all sides converge on a psychiatric clinic where an atomic scientist is being hidden.
Unsatisfactory thriller with some aims to be both a whimsy and a parable. Not one of its director's successes.

w Henri-Georges Clouzot, Gerome Geronomi *d* Henri-Georges Clouzot
ph Christian Matras *m* Georges Auric

Martita Hunt, Peter Ustinov, Sam Jaffe, Vera Clouzot, Gabrielle Dorziat, Curt Jurgens, Gerard Sety, O. E. Hasse

Espoir*
France / Spain 1938–45   73m   bw
Cornignion / Moligniec
aka: *Days of Hope; Man's Hope*

Events of the Spanish Civil War, recreated by surviving combatants.

Anti-fascist propaganda which seems a good deal less inspiring than on its first release, but has some vivid cinematic ideas.

wd André Malraux ph Louis Page   *m* Darius Milhaud

Mejuto, Nicolas Rodriguez, Jose Lado

'And it was written—gather together all the fair young virgins unto the palace—and let the maiden which pleaseth the king be queen.'

Esther and the King
US 1960   109m   Technicolor
   Cinemascope
TCF / Galatea (Raoul Walsh)

A Persian king selects a new bride who helps defend him from his enemies.

Tedious biblical hokum with a muddled script and the usual co-production deficiencies.

w Raoul Walsh, Michael Elkins   *d* Raoul Walsh   *ph* Mario Bava   *m* Francesco Lavagnino, Roberto Nicolosi

Richard Egan, Joan Collins, Dennis O'Dea, Sergei Fantoni, Rik Battaglia

Esther Waters
GB 1947   108m   bw
GFD / Wessex (Ian Dalrymple)

In the 1870s, a maid is seduced by a squire but insists on bringing up her child without help. Faded costumer with tentative performances and little else to recommend it.

w Michael Gordon, William Rose, Gerard Tyrrell, *novel* George Moore   *d* Ian Dalrymple, Peter Proud
ph C. Pennington-Richards, H. E. Fowle   *m* Gordon Jacob

Kathleen Ryan, Dirk Bogarde, Cyril Cusack, Ivor Barnard, Fay Compton, Mary Clare, Morland Graham

The Eternal Sea
US 1955   96m   bw
Republic (John H. Auer)

The career of an aircraft carrier captain in World War II and Korea.

Solemn biopic of John Hoskins: competent but quite uninspired.

w Allen Rivkin   *d* John H. Auer   *ph* John L. Russell Jnr   *m* Elmer Bernstein

Sterling Hayden, Alexis Smith, Dean Jagger, Virginia Grey

Eternally Yours*
US 1939   95m   bw
Walter Wanger

A magician's wife thinks he is too interested in his tricks.

Slightly scatty romantic comedy, amiable if not quite good enough to stand the test of time, but with a great cast.

w Gene Towne, Graham Baker   *d* Tay Garnett   *ph* Merritt Gerstad   *m* Werner Janssen

Loretta Young, David Niven, Broderick Crawford, Hugh Herbert, Billie Burke, C. Aubrey Smith, Raymond Walburn, Zasu Pitts, Virginia Field, Eve Arden, Herman the Rabbit

'Will have to depend on the name power to get it by.'—*Variety*

'An amusing and irresponsible picture, though on the whole more irresponsible than amusing.'—*New York Times*

AAN: Werner Janssen

L'Etoile du Nord*
France 1982   124m   Fujicolor
Sara Films / Antenne 2 (Alain Sarde)

On a transcontinental train, a petty con man finds a new lover but is involved in an argument which leads to murder.

Curious semi-thriller with good credentials, compromised by the fact that having changed most of the original novel it tries to make new statements of its own.

w Jean Aurenche, Michel Grisolia, Pierre Granier-Deferre   *novel* Le Locataire by Georges Simenon   *d* Pierre Granier-Deferre   *ph* Pierre-William Glenn   *m* Philippe Sarde

Philippe Noiret, Simone Signoret, Fanny Cottençon, Julie Jezequel

Eureka
GB / USA 1982   129m   Technicolor
MGM / UA / RPC / JF (Jeremy Thomas)

An immensely rich gold striker becomes a recluse and is murdered by Mafia hoods.

Unpleasant in detail and obscure in meaning, this is the sort of film of which the fact that it was financed at all is the most interesting thing about it.

w Paul Mayersberg, *book* Who Killed Sir Harry Oakes? by Marshall Houts   *d* Nicolas Roeg   *ph* Alex Thomson   *m* Stanley Myers   *pd* Michael Seymour

Gene Hackman, Theresa Russell, Rutger Hauer, Jane Lapotaire, Mickey Rourke, Ed Lauter

'A Roeg elephant film.'—*Variety*

'Between them Roeg and Mayersberg have worked an astonishing alchemy through which an abstraction of the basic patterns of human intercourse is rendered wholly concrete. Embodying Vico's cyclical theory of history, it expounds the despair of humanity's vicious circle from ecstasy to agony, as the impulse to love and possession leads inevitably to loss and destruction.'—*Tom Milne, Monthly Film Bulletin*

'I've a feeling it will become a cult movie, but no one will convince me that it isn't just the poshest kind of tosh.'—*Margaret Hinxman, Daily Mail*

Eureka Stockade
GB 1948   103m   bw
Ealing (Leslie Norman)
US title: *Massacre Hill*

In 1854, Australian gold miners revolt against a harsh governor.

Unconvincingly made historical actioner from Ealing's antipodean period.

w Harry Watt, Walter Greenwood, Ralph Smart   *d* Harry Watt   *ph* Gerald Heath   *m* John Greenwood

Chips Rafferty, Jane Barrett, Gordon Jackson, Jack Lambert, Peter Illing, Ralph Truman, Peter Finch

Europa 51*
Italy 1952   110m   bw
Ponti / de Laurentiis

An American society woman living in Rome seeks vainly for truth in the chaotic post-war world and is committed to an asylum by her husband.

A despairing, ironic comment on a period which unfortunately does not convince on the personal level.

w Roberto Rossellini and others   *d* Roberto Rossellini   *ph* Aldo Tonti   *m* Renzo Rossellini

Ingrid Bergman, Alexander Knox, Ettore Giannini, Giulietta Masina

The Europeans*
GB 1979   83m   colour
Merchant Ivory (Ismail Merchant)

In 1850, a European baroness arrives in Boston in search of a husband.

Charming if rather tentative period mood piece, probably the most professional and judicious of all the overpraised Merchant Ivory offerings.

w Ruth Prawer Jhabvala, *novel* Henry James   *d* James Ivory   *ph* Larry Pizer   *m* Richard Robbins   *ad* Jeremiah Rusconi

Lee Remick, Robin Ellis, Tim Woodward, Wesley Addy, Lisa Eichhorn

'A film of astonishing delicacy and richness in which the tiniest gesture or intonation reverberates with a world of meanings.'—*Tom Milne, MFB*

● Video: Virgin

Eva
France / Italy 1962   135m   bw
Paris / Interopa (Robert and Raymond Hakim)

A raw Welsh novelist in Venice is humiliated by a money-loving Frenchwoman who erotically ensnares him.

Foolish story of a *femme fatale*; elegantly Freudian at moments, it long outstays its welcome.

w Hugo Butler, Evan Jones, *novel* James Hadley Chase   *d* Joseph Losey   *ph* Gianni di Venanzo   *m* Michel Legrand

Stanley Baker, Jeanne Moreau, Virna Lisi, James Villiers

The Eve of St Mark
US 1944   95m   bw
TCF (William Perlberg)

A small-town boy goes to war and his sweetheart waits for him.

Poetic propaganda based on a sticky play which however had a tragic ending which the film eschews. Smartly made is all one can say.

w George Seaton, *play* Maxwell Anderson *d* John M. Stahl *ph* Joseph La Shelle *m* Cyril Mockridge

William Eythe, Anne Baxter, Michael O'Shea, Vincent Price, Ruth Nelson, Ray Collins, Stanley Prager, Henry Morgan

Eve Wants to Sleep*
Poland 1957 98m bw
Film Polski (Wislaw Mincer)

An innocent country girl arrives in a city overrun by subversives.
Curious yet sympathetic black farce, like a cross between *Hellzapoppin* and *M.* One on its own.

wd Tadeusz Chmielewski *ph* Stefan Matyjaskiewicz *m* Henryk Czyz

Barbara Kwiatkowska, Stanislaw Mikulski, Ludwik Benoit

Evel Knievel
US 1971 90m Metrocolor
(MGM) Fanfare (George Hamilton)

Episodes from the life of a motor-cycle stuntman.
Mildly entertaining ragbag of action sequences and fragments of philosophy which might have been more tolerable had EK played himself.

w Alan Caillou, John Milius *d* Marvin Chomsky *ph* David Walsh *m* Pat Williams

George Hamilton, Sue Lyon, Bert Freed, Rod Cameron

Evelyn Prentice
US 1934 80m bw
MGM (John W. Considine Jnr)

The wife of a criminal lawyer has an affair with a man who blackmails her.
Moderate domestic-cum-courtroom melodrama, heavily reliant on its popular stars.

w Lenore Coffee, *novel* W. E. Woodward *d* William K. Howard *ph* Charles G. Clarke *md* Oscar Radin

Myrna Loy, William Powell, Una Merkel, Harvey Stephens, Isabel Jewell, Rosalind Russell, Henry Wadsworth, Edward Brophy
  'Uneven film but extra heavy cast and strong femme sob yarn will put it in the money class.'—*Variety*

Evenings for Sale
US 1932 68m bw

An impoverished count becomes a dancing master. Scented Viennese romance intended to extend the star's success in *Trouble in Paradise*. Herbert Marshall, Sari Maritza, Mary Boland, Charles Ruggles. Written by S. K. Lauren, Agnes Brand Leahy from a novel by I. A. R Wylie; directed by Stuart Walker; for Paramount. 'Fair entertainment but extremely doubtful on the draw.'—*Variety*

Evensong*
GB 1934 84m bw
Gaumont (Michael Balcon)

At the turn of the century, an Austrian prima donna gives up her career for love.
Well-made romantic drama of its type, notable as the best of its star's few films.

w Edward Knoblock, Dorothy Farnum, *play* Beverly Nichols *d* Victor Saville *ph* Max Greene

Evelyn Laye, Fritz Kortner, Carl Esmond, Alice Delysia, Emlyn Williams, Muriel Aked
  'A highly absorbing and intelligently produced musical . . . looks like money.'—*Variety*

Ever in My Heart
US 1933 70m bw

A Daughter of the American Revolution finds that her husband is a German spy. Heavy romantic drama with a tragic finish. One for the ladies. Barbara Stanwyck, Otto Kruger, Ralph Bellamy, Ruth Donnelly, Frank Albertson. Written by Bertram Millhauser from a story by Beulah Marie Dix; directed by Archie Mayo; for Warners. 'A clean picture, more for the nabes than the first runs.'—*Variety*

'She'd say yes, but she no's him too well!'
Ever Since Eve
US 1937 80m bw
Warner (Earl Baldwin)

A publisher falls for a pretty girl, not realizing that she is his own plain secretary in disguise.
Silly romantic comedy which sadly lacks wit, style and believability.

w Lawrence Riley, Earl Baldwin, Lillie Hayward *d* Lloyd Bacon *ph* George Barnes *m* Heinz Roemheld

Marion Davies (her last film), Robert Montgomery, Frank McHugh, Patsy Kelly, Louise Fazenda, Barton MacLane, Mary Treen
  'A highly incredible script, and badly handled . . . it just doesn't jell.'—*Variety*

Evergreen**
GB 1934 90m bw
Gaumont (Michael Balcon)

A star's daughter takes her mother's place, with romantic complications.
Pleasant musical with more wit and style than might be expected.

w Emlyn Williams, Marjorie Gaffney, *play* Benn W. Levy *d* Victor Saville *ph* Glen MacWilliams *songs* Rodgers and Hart: 'Dancing on the Ceiling'; 'Harry Woods'

Jessie Matthews, Sonnie Hale, Betty Balfour, Barry Mackay, Ivor McLaren, Hartley Power

Every Day's a Holiday*
US 1937 79m bw
Paramount (Emmanuel Cohen)

A confidence girl in the old Bowery sells Brooklyn Bridge to suckers.
The most satisfactory example of post-Legion of Decency Mae West, the smut being replaced by a lively cast of comedians.

w Mae West *d* A. Edward Sutherland *ph* Karl Struss *songs* various

Mae West, Edmund Lowe, Charles Butterworth, Charles Winninger, Walter Catlett, Lloyd Nolan, Herman Bing, Roger Imhof, Chester Conklin
  'A lively, innocuously bawdy, and rowdy entertainment.'—*Variety*

Every Girl Should be Married
US 1948 84m bw
RKO (Don Hartman, Dore Schary)

A determined girl sets her cap at a bachelor pediatrician.
Woefully thin star comedy with few laughs.

w Stephen Morehouse Avery, Don Hartman *d* Don Hartman *ph* George E. Diskant *m* Leigh Harline

Cary Grant, Betsy Drake, Franchot Tone, Diana Lynn, Alan Mowbray, Elizabeth Risdon, Richard Gaines
  'In the past, Cary Grant has shown a talent for quietly underplaying comedy. In this picture, he has trouble finding comedy to play.'—*Time*

Every Home Should Have One
GB 1970 94m Eastmancolor
British Lion / Example (Ned Sherrin)

An advertising man goes berserk when he tries to think up an erotic way of selling porridge.
Tiresomely frenetic star comedy with the emphasis on smut.

w Marty Feldman, Barry Took, Denis Norden *d* James Clark *ph* Ken Hodges *m* John Cameron

Marty Feldman, Shelley Berman, Judy Cornwell, Julie Ege, Patrick Cargill, Jack Watson, Patience Collier, Penelope Keith, Dinsdale Landen

Every Little Crook and Nanny
US 1972 92m Metrocolor
MGM (Leonard J. Ackerman)

A Mafia chief finds his child's new nanny has a grudge against him.
Sporadically amusing farce.

w Cy Howard, Jonathan Axelrod, Robert Klane *d* Cy Howard *ph* Philip Lathrop *m* Fred Karlin

Victor Mature, Lynn Redgrave, Paul Sand, Maggie Blye, Austin Pendleton, John Astin, Dom De Luise

Every Night at Eight
US 1935 80m bw
Paramount (Walter Wanger)

Three sisters become a successful radio singing team.
Forgettable comedy musical with a mildly interesting cast.

w Gene Towne, Graham Baker *d* Raoul Walsh *ph* James Van Trees *songs* Dorothy Fields, Jimmy McHugh

George Raft, Alice Faye, Frances Langford, Patsy Kelly, The Radio Rogues, Walter Catlett, Herman Bing

'Looks like another case of missed opportunity . . . a routine show world romance.'—*Variety*

Every Saturday Night: see The Jones Family

Every Which Way But Loose
US 1978   114m   De Luxe
Warner / Malpaso

A Los Angeles trucker wins an orang-utan in a prize fight and becomes involved in sundry brawls and chases.
Easy-going, shambling star vehicle which was liked by nobody but the public.

w Jeremy Joe Kronsberg *d* James Fargo *ph* Rexford Metz *md* Steve Dorff

Clint Eastwood, Sondra Locke, Ruth Gordon, Geoffrey Lewis, Walter Barnes
† The 1980 sequel, almost indistinguishable, was *Any Which Way You Can.*

Everybody Dance
GB 1936   74m   bw

A nightclub singer is forced to pose as a rural do-gooder. Thin comedy vehicle. Cicely Courtneidge, Ernest Truex, Charles Riesner Jnr, Billie de la Volta, Percy Parsons. Written by Stafford Dickens, Ralph Spence and Leslie Arliss; directed by Charles Riesner; for Gaumont.

Everybody Does It
US 1949   98m   bw
TCF (Nunnally Johnson)

A stage-struck wife is chagrined to see her dull husband accidentally become an opera singer.
Very mild remake of *Wife, Husband and Friend*; everyone tries to be zany, but the result is often just silly.

w Nunnally Johnson *d* Edmund Goulding *ph* Joseph La Shelle *m* Alfred Newman

Paul Douglas, Celeste Holm, Linda Darnell, Charles Coburn, Millard Mitchell, Lucile Watson, John Hoyt, George Tobias, Leon Belasco
'For sheer momentary enjoyment it would be hard to beat.'—*Richard Mallett, Punch*

Everybody Sing°
US 1937   80m   bw
MGM (Harry Rapf)

An eccentric theatrical family is upstaged by its servants, who put on a Broadway show.
Agreeably zany comedy with music.

w Florence Ryerson, Edgar Allan Woolf *d* Edwin L. Marin *ph* Joseph L. Ruttenberg *m* William Axt

Allan Jones, *Fanny Brice, Judy Garland*, Reginald Owen, Billie Burke, Lynne Carver, Monty Woolley, Reginald Gardiner, Henry Armetta
'Excellent film musical with fresh ideas and a corking cast . . . for the top spots.'—*Variety*

Everything But the Truth
US 1956   83m   Technicolor
U-I (Howard Christie)

A small boy embarrasses his family by telling the truth at all times.
Dum-dum formula comedy made with jaded professionalism.

w Herb Meadow *d* Jerry Hopper *ph* Maury Gertsman *m* Milton Rosen

Maureen O'Hara, John Forsythe, Tim Hovey, Frank Faylen, Barry Atwater

Everything Happens at Night
US 1939   77m   bw
TCF (Harry Joe Brown)

Two reporters fall for the daughter of a Nobel Peace Prize winner on the run from the Gestapo.
The star's sixth American film plays down the music and skating in favour of rather jaded spy comedy. Modest entertainment.

w Art Arthur, Robert Harari *d* Irving Cummings *ph* Edward Cronjager *m* various

Sonja Henie, Ray Milland, Robert Cummings, Maurice Moscovitch, Leonid Kinskey, Alan Dinehart, Fritz Feld, Victor Varconi
'At no time does very much happen that is of interest.'—*Variety*

Everything I Have Is Yours
US 1952   92m   Technicolor
MGM (George Wells)

A song and dance team is disrupted when the wife decides to become a mother.
Uninventive but lively musical vehicle for the Champions.

w George Wells *d* Robert Z. Leonard *ph* William V. Skall *md* David Rose *ch* Nick Castle, Gower Champion

Marge and Gower Champion, Dennis O'Keefe, Eduard Franz

Everything Is Rhythm
GB 1936   73m   bw

A dance band leader wins a European princess. Modest programme filler remarkable only for its record of a top band of its time. Harry Roy and his Band, Princess Pearl, Ivor Moreton, Dave Kaye. Written by Syd Courtenay, Jack Byrd and Stanley Haynes; directed by Alfred Goulding; for Joe Rock.

Everything Is Thunder°
GB 1936   76m   bw
Gaumont-British

A German girl helps a British prisoner of war to escape.
Tolerable let's-not-be-beastly melodrama, quite unusual in its time.

w Marion Dix, John Orton, *novel* J. B. Hardy *d* Milton Rosmer *ph* Gunther Krampf

Constance Bennett, Douglass Montgomery, Oscar Homolka, Roy Emerton, Frederick Lloyd, George Merritt

Everything You Always Wanted to Know About Sex°
US 1972   87m   De Luxe
UA (Charles H. Joffe)

Seven sketches on sexual themes.
Dishevelled revue with a reasonable number of laughs for broadminded audiences.

wd Woody Allen, *book* Dr David Reuben *ph* David M. Walsh *m* Mundell Lowe *pd* Dale Hennesy

Woody Allen, Lynn Redgrave, Anthony Quayle, John Carradine, Lou Jacobi, Louise Lasser, Tony Randall, Burt Reynolds, Gene Wilder

● *Video: Warner*

Everything's Ducky
US 1961   81m   bw

Two naval ratings adopt a talking duck.
Anything-goes service farce, with material below the standard of the talent available.
Mickey Rooney, Buddy Hackett, Jackie Cooper, Joanie Summers, Roland Winters. Written by John Fenton Murray and Benedict Freedman; directed by Don Taylor; for Barboo / Columbia.

The Evictors
US 1979   92m   Movielab

Axe murders abound when a young couple move into an old house with a history. Old-hat horror, out of *Psycho* and *The Amityville Horror*: strictly for drive-ins. Michael Parks, Jessica Harper, Vic Morrow, Sue Ane Langdon. Written by Charles B. Pierce; directed by Charles B. Pierce; for AIP.

The Evil
US 1978   89m   Movielab
New World / Rangoon (Ed Carlin)

A psychologist takes a team to investigate a haunted house, and is soon sorry he meddled.
Another variation on the theme of *The Haunting* and *The Legend of Hell House*; more this time on the horror comic level, but reasonably effective.

w Donald G. Thompson *d* Gus Trikonis *ph* Mario Di Leo *m* Johnny Harris

Richard Crenna, Joanna Pettet, Andrew Prine, Cassie Yates, Victor Buono, Lynne Moody

The Evil Dead
US 1980 (released 1983)   85m   Du Art

Five youngsters in a remote cabin find an old book which helps them summon up dormant demons from a nearby forest. Semi-professional horror rubbish, blown up from 16mm and looking it. When released in England, it was prosecuted as unsuitable for public showing. Bruce Campbell, Ellen Sandweiss, Betsy Baker. Written and directed by Sam M. Raimi; for Renaissance. 'The *ne plus ultra* of low-budget gore and shock effects.'—*Variety*

The Evil of Frankenstein
GB 1964   94m   Technicolor
U-I / Hammer (Anthony Hinds)

Frankenstein returns to his derelict castle and finds the Monster preserved in a glacier.
For their third Frankenstein film Hammer made a distribution deal with Universal and

EVERY DAY'S A HOLIDAY.   Mae West was forced by the Hays Office to clean up her act, but instead of innuendo she hired some fine supporting comedians for this one.

thus for the first time were able to use fragments of the old plots as well as something approximating to the Karloff make-up. Production and writing, however, are sadly dispirited except when relying on sadism.

w John Elder (Anthony Hinds) d Freddie Francis ph John Wilcox m Don Banks

Peter Cushing, Peter Woodthorpe, Sandor Eles, Kiwi Kingston (as the monster), Duncan Lamont, Katy Wild, David Hutcheson

The Evil that Men Do
US 1984   90m   CFI color
ITC / Capricorn / Zuleika Farms (Pancho Kohner)

A professional killer is asked to eliminate a sadistic political torturer in Guatemala. More than usually turgid and unpleasant vehicle for a star who is now too old for this kind of thing.

w David Lee Henry, John Crowther, *novel* R. Lance Hill　*d* J. Lee Thompson　*ph* Javier Ruvalcaba Cruz　*m* Ken Thorne

Charles Bronson, Theresa Saldana, Joseph Maher, Jose Ferrer, René Enriquez, John Glover, Raymond St Jacques

Evil Under the Sun
GB 1982　117m　Technicolor
Panavision
EMI / Mersham / Titan (John Brabourne, Richard Goodwin)

Hercule Poirot solves the murder of a film star on an Adriatic holiday island.
Very competent but somehow too bland package in the Agatha Christie series, not quite so lively as *Death on the Nile*.
w Anthony Shaffer, *novel* Agatha Christie　*d* Guy Hamilton　*ph* Christopher Challis　*m* Cole Porter　*pd* Elliot Scott

Peter Ustinov, James Mason, Diana Rigg, Maggie Smith, Colin Blakely, Jane Birkin, Nicholas Clay, Roddy McDowall, Sylvia Miles, Dennis Quilley
'They have swapped elegant English menace for a splurge of theatrical camp.'—*Time Out*
'Temperance beverage Noël Coward.'—*Sunday Times*
● *Video: Thorn EMI*

Ex-Champ
US 1939　72m　bw

A retired boxer works as a doorman and has trouble with his ungrateful and semi-criminal son. Father-love weepie, rather hard to take.
Victor McLaglen, Tom Brown, Nan Grey, William Frawley, Constance Moore. Written by Alex Gottleib, Edmund L. Hartmann, Gordon Kahn; directed by Phil Rosen; for Universal. 'Pathos and sentiment expertly mixed for satisfactory dualler.'—*Variety*

Ex-Flame
US 1930　68m　bw

A modernized version of *East Lynne*. With so many American accents attached to the British peerage, this is mainly for laughs – unintentional ones. Neil Hamilton, Marian Nixon, Norman Kerry, Roland Drew, Snub Pollard. Written and directed by Victor Halperin; for Liberty. 'Old-fashioned mush stuff for the woman.'—*Variety*

'We don't dare tell you how daring it is!'
Ex-Lady°
US 1933　70m　bw

A lady artist has ultra-modern views on sex and marriage, but turns conventional when she falls in love. Mildly shocking in its day, this romantic drama was one of the contributing factors to the onslaught of the Legion of Decency which transformed Hollywood output in the following year. Bette Davis (her first starring role), Gene Raymond, Frank McHugh, Monroe Owsley, Clare Dodd. Written by David Boehm from a story by Edith Fitzgerald and Robin Riskin (previously filmed in 1931 as *Illicit*); directed by Robert Florey; for Warner.

The Ex-Mrs Bradford°
US 1936　87m　bw
MGM (Edward Kaufman)

A doctor's scatty ex-wife involves him in solving a murder plot.
Amusing crime comedy, just a little way behind *The Thin Man*.
w Anthony Veiller, James Edward Grant　*d* Stephen Roberts　*ph* J. Roy Hunt　*m* Roy Webb

William Powell, Jean Arthur, James Gleason, Eric Blore, Robert Armstrong, Lila Lee, Grant Mitchell, Ralph Morgan

'Forged by a god! Foretold by a wizard! Found by a king!'
'No mortal could possess it! No kingdom could command it!'
Excalibur
US 1981　140m　Technicolor
Warner / Orion (John Boorman)

The story of King Arthur, Merlin, Uther Pendragon, the Holy Grail and the Lady of the Lake.
Curiously pointless retelling of a legend with unexplained flashes of realism and bouts of gore alternating with romance and modern wisecracks. Of mainly visual interest.
w Rospo Pallenberg, John Boorman　*d* John Boorman　*ph* Alex Thomson　*m* Trevor Jones　*pd* Anthony Pratt

Nigel Terry, Helen Mirren, Nicol Williamson, Nicholas Clay, Cherie Lunghi, Paul Geoffrey
'Left entirely to his own devices, Boorman seems to run in self-defeating circles.'—*Richard Combs, MFB.*
'It tries overhard to be simultaneously critical and credulous, magical and earthy, inspiring and entertaining.'—*Sunday Times*
AAN: Alex Thomson

● *Video: Warner*

'Racket rule sweeps midwest city!'
Exclusive
US 1937　76m　bw

Journalist sacrifices himself for daughter whose views he despises. Solid newspaper drama jinxed by the excellent tragic performance of a star too long regarded as a comedian. *Charles Ruggles*, Fred MacMurray, Frances Farmer, Lloyd Nolan. Written by John C. Moffitt, Sidney Salkow, Rian James; directed by Alexander Hall; for Paramount. 'Hokey newspaper-gangster yarn of old-fashioned meller calibre.'—*Variety*. 'In the tough kid it falls behind—it can't make the 1937 speed in murder, and the result, like lavender, is not unagreeable.'—*Graham Greene*.

Exclusive Story
US 1934　75m　bw

A newspaperman has a go at the numbers racket. Tolerable anti-gangster crusade.
Franchot Tone, Madge Evans, *Joseph Calleia*, Stuart Erwin, J. Carrol Naish. Written by Michael Fessier and Martin Mooney; directed by George B. Seitz; for MGM. 'Publicity possibilities should put this one over, but it also has plenty of excitement to sell.'—*Variety*

Excuse My Dust°
US 1951　82m　Technicolor
MGM (Jack Cummings)

The inventor of a horseless carriage loves the daughter of a livery stable owner.
Innocuous small-town nineties comedy with a race climax. Quite pleasant.
w George Wells　*d* Roy Rowland　*ph* Alfred Gilks　*m* Arthur Schwarz

Red Skelton, Sally Forrest, Macdonald Carey, William Demarest

'Every day he loves, somebody else dies!'
The Executioner°
GB 1970　107m　Technicolor
Panavision
Columbia / Ameran (Charles H. Schneer)

A British spy suspects a colleague of being a double agent.
Dour espionage thriller with a reasonably holding narrative and predictable performances.
w Jack Pulman　*d* Sam Wanamaker　*ph* Denys Coop　*m* Ron Goodwin

George Peppard, Nigel Patrick, Joan Collins, Judy Geeson, Oscar Homolka, Charles Gray, Keith Michell, George Baker, Alexander Scourby, Peter Bull, Ernest Clark, Peter Dyneley
'Does not escape from the well-worn shallow groove in which the contemporary spy film is in danger of becoming stuck.'—*Russell Campbell*

Executive Action°
US 1973　91m　colour
EA Enterprises / Wakefield Orloff (Edward Lewis)

An imaginative version of the facts behind the 1963 assassination of President Kennedy. Interesting but rather messy mixture of fact and fiction; makes one sit up while it's unreeling.
w Dalton Trumbo, *story* Mark Lane, Donald Freed　*d* David Miller　*ph* Robert Steadman　*m* Randy Edelman

Burt Lancaster, Robert Ryan, Will Geer, Gilbert Green, John Anderson
'A dodo bird of a movie, the winner of the *Tora Tora Tora* prize.'—*Variety*
● *Video: Warner*

'High up in the skyscraper beauty and power clash in conflict!'
Executive Suite°°°
US 1954　104m　bw
MGM (John Houseman)

When the president of a big company dies, the boardroom sees a battle for control.
First of the boardroom films of the fifties, a calculatedly commercial mixture of business ethics and domestic asides, with an all-star cast working up effective tensions.
w *Ernest Lehman, novel* Cameron Hawley　*d* Robert Wise　*ph* George Folsey

Fredric March, William Holden, June Allyson, *Barbara Stanwyck*, Walter Pidgeon, Shelley Winters, Paul Douglas, *Louis Calhern*, Dean Jagger, *Nina Foch*, Tim Considine

'Not a classic, not a milestone in movie making, but it does suggest a standard of product that could bring back to the box office those vast audiences long alienated by trivia.'—*Arthur Knight*

'The only trouble with all these people is that they are strictly two-dimensional. They give no substantial illusion of significance, emotion or warmth.'—*Bosley Crowther, New York Times*

† A TV series followed in 1976.

AAN: George Folsey; Nina Foch

The Exile°
US 1948 90m bw
U-I (Douglas Fairbanks Jnr)

The man who is to return to the English throne as Charles II hides in Holland, receives his friends and despatches his enemies.
Curious, talkative swashbuckler with only a few moments of action; the available talents are simply not used, though the director imposes a nice pictorial style.

w Douglas Fairbanks Jnr, *novel* His Majesty the King by Cosmo Hamilton *d* Max Ophuls *ph* Franz Planer *m* Frank Skinner

Douglas Fairbanks Jnr, Maria Montez, Paula Corday, Henry Daniell, Nigel Bruce, Robert Coote

† Originally released in sepia.

Exile Express
US 1939 70m bw

A lab assistant is innocently involved in the murder of her boss by a spy gang. Lumpy comedy thriller taking place mainly on a train; very forgettable. Anna Sten, Alan Marshal, Jerome Cowan, Jed Prouty, Stanley Fields, Walter Catlett, Leonid Kinskey, Harry Davenport, Irving Pichel. Written by Edwin Justus Mayer, Ethel La Blanche; directed by Otis Garrett; for Grand National. 'Both story and direction take it up all sorts of dull and impossible alleys.'—*Variety*

Exit Smiling°°
US 1926 71m (24 fps) bw silent
MGM (Sam Taylor)

The worst actress in a stock company saves the show.
Amusing comedy for a star who never quite made it in films: this is the best of her vehicles.

w Sam Taylor, Tim Whelan, *play* Marc Connelly *d* Sam Taylor *ph* Andre Barlatier

Beatrice Lillie, Jack Pickford, Harry Myers, Doris Lloyd, DeWitt Jennings, Louise Lorraine, Franklin Pangborn

Exodus°
US 1960 220m Technicolor Super Panavision 70
UA / Carlyle / Alpha (Otto Preminger)

The early years of the state of Israel, seen through various eyes.
Heavy-going modern epic, toned down from a passionate novel.

w Dalton Trumbo, *novel* Leon Uris *d* Otto Preminger *ph* Sam Leavitt *m* Ernest Gold

Paul Newman, Eva Marie Saint, Ralph Richardson, Peter Lawford, Lee J. Cobb, Sal Mineo, John Derek, Hugh Griffith, Gregory Ratoff, Felix Aylmer, David Opatoshu, Jill Haworth, Alexandra Stewart, Martin Benson, Martin Miller

'Professionalism is not enough—after three and a half hours the approach seems more exhausting than exhaustive.'—*Penelope Houston*

† Jewish comedian Mort Sahl, invited by the director to a preview, is said to have stood up after three hours and said: 'Otto—let my people go!'

AA: Ernest Gold
AAN: Sam Leavitt; Sal Mineo

The Exorcist°
US 1973 122m Metrocolor
Warner / Hoya (William Peter Blatty)

A small girl is unaccountably possessed by the devil and turned into a repellent monster who causes several violent deaths before she is cured.
Spectacularly ludicrous mishmash with uncomfortable attention to physical detail and no talent for narrative or verisimilitude. Its sensational aspects, together with a sudden worldwide need for the supernatural, assured its enormous commercial success.

w William Peter Blatty, from his novel *d* William Friedkin *ph* Owen Roizman *m* George Crumb and others *pd* Bill Malloy

Ellen Burstyn, Max Von Sydow, Jason Miller, Linda Blair, Lee J. Cobb, Kitty Winn, Jack McGowran

'No more nor less than a blood and thunder horror movie, foundering heavily on the rocks of pretension.'—*Tom Milne*

'*The Exorcist* makes no sense, [but] if you want to be shaken, it will scare the hell out of you.'—*Stanley Kauffmann*

'It exploits the subject of diabolic possession without telling you anything about it . . . just a stylistic exercise.'—*Michael Billington, Illustrated London News*

'There is a little exposition, some philosophy and theology, a quiet interlude, and then pandemonium reigns: rooms shake, heads turn full circle on bodies, wounds fester, vomit spews forth in bilious clouds besmirching a saintly priest, a possessed adolescent girl masturbates bloodily on a crucifix as she barks blasphemies and obscenities, and hoary demons freeze the soul.'—*Les Keyser, Hollywood in the Seventies*

'I know how to do it. I just throw everything at the audience and give them a real thrill. That's what they want. They don't want to go into a theater and treat it like a book. They don't even read books!'—*William Peter Blatty*

† Published 1974: *The Story Behind the Exorcist* by Peter Travers and Stephanie Reiff.

AA: William Peter Blatty
AAN: best picture; William Friedkin; Owen Roizman; Ellen Burstyn; Jason Miller; Linda Blair

Exorcist II: The Heretic
US 1977 117m Technicolor
Warner (Richard Lederer, John Boorman)

Father Lamont, investigating the case related in *The Exorcist*, finds that the evil in Regan, apparently exorcized, is only dormant.
Highly unsatisfactory psychic melodrama which, far from the commercial route of the shocker followed by its predecessor, falls flat on its face along some wayward path of metaphysical and religious fancy. A commercial disaster, it was released in two versions and is unintelligible in either.

w William Goodhart *d* John Boorman *ph* William A. Fraker *m* Ennio Morricone *pd* Richard MacDonald

Richard Burton, Linda Blair, Louise Fletcher, Kitty Winn, Max Von Sydow, Paul Henreid, James Earl Jones, Ned Beatty

Experiment in Terror°°
US 1962 123m bw
Columbia / Geoffrey-Kate Productions (Blake Edwards)
GB title: *The Grip of Fear*

An asthmatic stranger threatens the life of a bank teller and her sister if she does not help him commit a robbery.
Detailed, meticulous police thriller with San Francisco locations. Good stuff, a bit long.

w The Gordons, from their novel Operation Terror *d* Blake Edwards *ph* Philip Lathrop *m* Henry Mancini

Glenn Ford, Lee Remick, Ross Martin

Experiment Perilous°
US 1944 91m bw
RKO (Warren Duff)

A woman's wealthy husband is killed in mysterious circumstances, and she is suspected.
Enjoyable mystery melodrama which takes itself with a pinch of salt.

w Warren Duff, *novel* Margaret Carpenter *d* Jacques Tourneur *ph* Tony Gaudio *m* Roy Webb

Hedy Lamarr, Paul Lukas, George Brent, Albert Dekker, Margaret Wycherly

The Exploits of Elaine°
US 1914 14 episodes, each 20m approx bw silent
Pathé / Wharton

Detective Craig Kennedy helps his girl friend avenge her father's murder.
Archetypal cliffhanger serial following on the success of *The Perils of Pauline*. It was itself followed within a year by *The New Exploits of Elaine* and *The Romance of Elaine*. Chapter headings included such now familiar clichés as 'The Clutching Hand', 'The Vanishing Jewels', 'The Poisoned Room', 'The Death Ray' and 'The Devil Worshippers'. The films were much praised by critics for their pace and inventiveness.

w Charles W. Goddard, George B. Seitz, from stories by Arthur B. Reeve *d* Louis Gasnier, George B. Seitz

Pearl White, Creighton Hale, Sheldon Lewis, Arnold Daly

Exposed
US 1983 99m Metrocolor

A fashion model falls for a concert violinist who turns out to be a notorious terrorist. A glossy absurdity confected from reading too many indigestible headlines, Nastassja Kinski, Rudolf Nureyev, Harvey Keitel, Ian McShane, Bibi Andersson, Ron Randell, Pierre Clementi. Written and directed by James Toback; for MGM-UA. 'It often seems to be working out of a tension between sophisticated ambition and the capabilities of a tyro director, a kind of neo-primitivism (with a hint, perhaps, of Fuller, especially in its cultural name-dropping – Bach, Bosch, Dostoievsky, Heifetz, Perlman, Stern, to name a few).'—*Richard Combs, MFB*

Expresso Bongo*
GB 1959 111m bw Dyaliscope
BL / Britannia / Conquest (Val Guest)

A Soho agent turns a nondescript teenage singer into an international star.
Heavily vulgarized version of a stage skit on the Tommy Steele rock phenomenon, divested of most of its satirical barbs and only intermittently amusing.

w Wolf Mankowitz, from his play d Val Guest ph John Wilcox songs David Heneker, Monty Norman

Laurence Harvey, Sylvia Syms, Yolande Donlan, Cliff Richard, *Meier Tzelniker*, Gilbert Harding, Ambrosine Philpotts, Eric Pohlmann, Wilfrid Lawson, Hermione Baddeley, Reginald Beckwith, Martin Miller

● *Video: Video Media*

The Exquisite Sinner
US 1926 80m approx at 24 fps bw
  silent

A young French industrialist becomes bored with his society and takes off with a band of gypsies. Curious and unsatisfactory farrago originally directed by Josef von Sternberg, but with extensive retakes by Phil Rosen (who also took credit the following year for an almost exactly similar film with a different title, *Heaven on Earth*, but featuring the same stars: Conrad Nagel and Renee Adoree). Written by Josef von Sternberg and Alice Duer Miller; for MGM.

Extase*
Czechoslovakia 1932 90m bw
Universal Elektra Film
aka: *Ecstasy*

A country girl takes a lover.
Simple love story with Freudian sequences, quite successfully and cinematically done. It caused a sensation at the time and was issued in various censored versions; the star's husband later tried to destroy all the copies.

w Gustav Machaty, story Viteslav Nezval d Gustav Machaty ph Jan Stallich m Giuseppe Becce

Hedy Kiesler (later Hedy Lamarr), Aribert Mog
'The first important film to come out of Czechoslovakia since *Erotikon*, and what a

hornet's nest it has stirred up! Critics and public are divided into two camps. Some proclaim it the world's worst, others rank it among the best productions of the year. It would never get by the censor in America.'—*Variety*

The Exterminating Angel***
Mexico 1962 95m bw
Uninci-Films 59
original title: *El Angel Exterminador*

High society dinner guests find themselves unable to leave the room, stay there for days, and go totally to the bad before the strange spell is broken; when they go to church to give thanks, they find themselves unable to leave. Fascinating surrealist fantasia on themes elaborated with even more panache in *The Discreet Charm of the Bourgeoisie*. Nevertheless, one of its director's key films.

wd Luis Bunuel (story assistance from Luis Alcoriza) ph Gabriel Figueroa ad Jesus Bracho

Silvia Pinal, Enrique Rambal, Jacqueline Andere, Jose Baviera
'An unsound and unsightly mixture of spurious allegory and genuine craziness.'—*John Simon*

The Exterminator
US 1980 102m Movielab
Interstar Corporation

An ex-Vietnam vet goes berserk when his friend is killed by a street gang, and vows revenge.
Vigilante movie with aspects of the modern horror-comic tradition; not much doubt that its real purpose is exploitation. It aroused some anger in America when a murder seemed to be based on its methods, but it was quickly succeeded by even more violent films.

wd James Glickenhaus ph Robert M. Baldwin m Joe Renzetti

Robert Ginty, Christopher George, Samantha Eggar, Steve James
'Glickenhaus has plundered the iconographic treasury of recent American cinema, wrenching the images of war, sexuality and street crime out of their contexts and deploying them portentously so as to lend spurious significance to his film.'—*Martyn Auty, MFB*

Exterminator 2
US 1984 90m TVC colour

An unemployed Vietnam veteran in New York eliminates punks with a flame thrower. Violence fantasy, an extreme form of *Death Wish*; quite reprehensible, and not for the squeamish. Robert Ginty, Deborah Geffner, Mario Van Peebles, Frankie Faison. Written by Mark Buntzman, William Sachs; directed by Mark Buntzman; for Cannon.

The Extra Day
GB 1956 83m Eastmancolor
British Lion / William Fairchild (E. M. Smedley Aston)

The personal problems of five film extras who are recalled when a scene has to be reshot. Thin excuse for portmanteau drama, only amusing in its depiction of a British movie being made with mostly foreign talent.

wd William Fairchild ph Arthur Grant m Philip Green

Richard Basehart, Simone Simon, Sid James, Josephine Griffin, George Baker, Colin Gordon, Laurence Naismith, Charles Victor, Olga Lindo, Beryl Reid, Dennis Lotis

The Extra Girl*
US 1923 69m bw silent
Mack Sennett

A small town girl wins a beauty contest and goes to Hollywood.
A comparatively restrained comedy with slapstick interludes, this charming film shows its star at her best and admirably illustrates Hollywood in the early twenties.

d Mack Sennett m Jack Ward

Mabel Normand, Max Davidson, Ralph Graves, George Nicholls

The Extraordinary Seaman
US 1968 80m Metrocolor Panavision
MGM / John Frankenheimer / Edward Lewis (John H. Cushingham, Hal Dresner)

Four stranded sailors come upon the ghostly Royal Navy captain of a ghostly World War II ship.
Curious sixties attempt at forties fantasy; obviously, from its short running time and fragmented style, something went sadly adrift during its making, and the wide screen does not help, but there are scattered funny moments.

w Philip Rock, Hal Dresner d John Frankenheimer ph Lionel Lindon m Maurice Jarre

David Niven, Faye Dunaway, Alan Alda, Mickey Rooney, Jack Carter, Juano Hernandez, Barry Kelley
'A cleverly made curiosity, not so much produced as manufactured.'—*Marjorie Bilbow*

An Eye for an Eye
France / Italy 1956 93m Technicolor VistaVision
UGC / Jolly (André Cayatte)

A doctor finds himself trekking across the desert with a demented man whose wife has died in his care.
Initially striking melodrama which becomes increasingly unconvincing and has a tendency to harp on unpleasant detail.

wd André Cayatte, novel Vahe Katcha ph Christian Matras m Louiguy

Curt Jurgens, Folco Lulli, Lea Padovani

An Eye for an Eye
US 1981 104m CFI Color

An undercover cop resigns from the force but uncovers a drug ring. Tedious and violent actioner with a martial arts champion for hero. Chuck Norris, Christopher Lee, Richard

Roundtree, Matt Clark, Mako. Written by William Gray and James Bruner; directed by Steve Carver; for Wescom.

Eye of the Cat*
US 1969 102m Technicolor
Universal / Joseph M. Schenck (Bernard Schwarz, Philip Hazelton)

A young man who hates cats goes to stay with his crippled aunt who keeps a house full of them.

Odd, *Psycho*-like thriller (from the same screen writer) with plenty of scary sequences but an inadequate resolution.

w Joseph Stefano d David Lowell Rich
ph Russell Metty, Ellsworth Fredericks m Lalo Schifrin cat trainer Ray Berwick

Eleanor Parker, Michael Sarrazin, Gayle Hunnicutt, Tim Henry, Laurence Naismith
  'Not so much a good film as an extravagantly enjoyable one.'—*MFB*

Eye of the Devil*
GB 1967 92m bw
MGM / Filmways (John Calley, Ben Kadish)

A French nobleman is obsessed by a family tradition of pagan self-sacrifice.

Diabolical goings-on in a spooky castle, not really helped by a glittering supporting cast any more than by miscast stars, sluggish direction or a general atmosphere of gloom rather than suspense.

w Robin Estridge, Dennis Murphy, *novel* Day of the Arrow by Philip Loraine d J. Lee-Thompson ph Erwin Hillier m Gary McFarland

David Niven, Deborah Kerr, Emlyn Williams, Flora Robson, Donald Pleasence, Edward Mulhare, David Hemmings, Sharon Tate, John Le Mesurier, Donald Bisset
  'It is hard to say why the total effect is so constantly hilarious.'—*MFB*
† The film had a chequered career. The first attempt to make it was abandoned because of Kim Novak's inadequacy; it then went through three titles and a lot of trouble with the censor.

'To love a stranger is easy . . . to kill a lover is not!'

Eye of the Needle
GB 1981 113m Technicolor
UA / Kings Road (Stephen Friedman)

In London in 1940 a German agent murders his landlady but is eventually cornered by a girl on a Scottish island.

Listless espionage narrative with very little drive or interest: the shape of the story defies suspense.

w Stanley Mann, *novel* Ken Follett d Richard Marquand ph Alan Hume m Miklos Rozsa

Donald Sutherland, Kate Nelligan, Christopher Cazenove, Ian Bannen, Alex McCrindle

Eye Witness
GB 1956 82m bw
Rank / Sydney Box

A maniacal burglar pursues a witness of his crime into the emergency ward of a local hospital.

Naïve but adequate suspenser with too many character cameos getting in the way of the plot.

w Janet Green d Muriel Box ph Reg Wyer m Bruce Montgomery

Donald Sinden, Muriel Pavlow, Belinda Lee, Michael Craig, Nigel Stock, Susan Beaumont, David Knight, Ada Reeve

Eye Witness
US 1981 108m Technicolor
TCF (Peter Yates)
GB title: The Janitor

A bashful janitor with a crush on a TV star finds himself hunted down by a murderer afraid of identification.

Odd little character thriller which despite pleasant touches never really seems to have its mind on its plot.

w Steve Tesich d Peter Yates ph Matthew F. Leonetti m Stanley Silverman pd Philip Roseberg

William Hurt, Christopher Plummer, Sigourney Weaver, Irene Worth, James Woods, Kenneth McMillan, Steven Hill

● Video: CBS / Fox

Eyes in the Night*
US 1942 80m bw
MGM (Jack Chertok)

A blind detective sets out to discover whether a mysterious man engaged to an heiress is really a Nazi spy.

Tolerable wartime puzzler.

w Guy Trosper, Howard Emmett Rogers, *novel* Odor of Violets by Bayard Kendrick d Fred Zinnemann ph Robert Planck, Charles Lawton m Lennie Hayton

Edward Arnold, Ann Harding, Donna Reed, Allen Jenkins, John Emery, Stephen McNally, Reginald Denny, Rosemary de Camp, Stanley Ridges
† Edward Arnold appeared once more as Duncan Maclain, in *The Hidden Eye* (1944).

Eyes of Laura Mars
US 1978 104m Metrocolor
Columbia / Jon Peters (Jack H. Harris)

A fashion photographer has violent premonitions about a series of murders.

Silly and often unpleasant suspenser which despite its chic appearance never bothers to explain itself.

w John Carpenter, David Zelag Goodman d Irvin Kershner ph Victor J. Kemper m Artie Kane

Faye Dunaway, Tommy Lee Jones, Brad Dourif, René Auberjonois, Raul Julia, Frank Adonis
  'Long on trendy settings, high-priced actors and vicious murders, but devoid of narrative thrills.'—*Richard Schickel, Time*
  'Perhaps the most austerely elegant horror film ever made.'—*New Yorker*

● Video: RCA / Columbia

Eyes of the Underworld
US 1941 61m bw

A crusading lawyer exposes an auto theft ring. Efficient little support which smart enough to play top on its original release. Richard Dix, Lon Chaney Jnr, Wendy Barrie, Don Porter, Bill Lee, Lloyd Corrigan. Written by Michael L. Simmons and Arthur Strawn; directed by Roy William Neill; for Universal.

Eyes without a Face*
France / Italy 1959 90m bw
Champs Elysées / Lux (Jules Borkon)
original title: Les Yeux sans Visage

When his daughter is mutilated in a car accident, a mad professor murders young girls in the process of grafting their faces onto hers.

Unpleasant horror film which its director seems to have made as a joke; the years have made it a cult.

w Jean Redon, from his novel d Georges Franju ph Eugen Schufftan m Maurice Jarre

Pierre Brasseur, Alida Valli, Edith Scob, François Guérin

● Video: Thorn EMI

Eyewitness*
GB 1970 91m Technicolor
ITC / ABP (Paul Maslansky)

A boy is the sole witness to an assassination, but no one believes him except the assassins. *The Window* all over again, the standard clichés being tricked out with fancy photography, sub-Hitchcock set-ups and Mediterranean locations, which make it all very tolerable.

w Ronald Harwood, *novel* Mark Hebden d John Hough ph David Holmes m Fairfield Parlour, David Whitaker

Mark Lester, Lionel Jeffries, Susan George, Tony Bonner, Jeremy Kemp, Peter Vaughan, Peter Bowles, Betty Marsden

F for Fake*
France / Iran / West Germany 1973   85m
colour
Astrophore / Saco / Janus (Dominique
Antoine, François Reichenbach)
French title: *Vérités et Mensonges*

Orson Welles, at a railway station, lectures the
audience in truth and falsehood, in art, in films
and in life.
A ragbag of an entertainment, cannibalizing as
it does more than one unsold documentary,
shredded at the editing table to match the
narrator's illusionist style. Despite the raptures
of some critics, this is an irritating effusion,
and Welles now looks more like a clever
charlatan than a master film-maker.

w Orson Welles, Oja Palinkas   *d* Orson
Welles   *ph* Gary Graver, Christian Odasso
m Michel Legrand
   'Welles stretches his material and his legend
just about as thin as possible in this tedious
treatise on truth and illusion.'—*Kevin
Thomas, Los Angeles Times*

F.P.1*
GB / Germany 1933   93m   bw
Gaumont / UFA (Erich Pommer)

Financiers try to destroy the first floating
aerodrome.
'Futuristic' melodrama about an aircraft
carrier. Very well done, and shot in two
languages, but now dated in most respects.

w Curt Siodmak, Walter Reisch, Robert
Stevenson, Peter Macfarlane   *d* Karl Hartl
ph Gunther Rittau, Konstantin Tochet

Conrad Veidt, Leslie Fenton, Jill Esmond,
George Merritt, Donald Calthrop, Nicholas
Hannen, Francis L. Sullivan

The Fabulous Adventures of Marco Polo
France / Italy / Yugoslavia / Egypt /
Afghanistan 1964   115m
Eastmancolor   Franscope
Ittac / Prodi / Avala / Mounir Rafla / Italaf
Kaboul (Raoul Lévy)
aka: *Marco the Magnificent*

In 1271 Marco Polo carries a message of peace
to Kubla Khan.
Curious mixture of melodrama and
pantomime, with a star cast half playing for
laughs.

w Raoul Lévy, Denys de la Patellière
d Denys de la Patellière, Noel Howard
ph Armand Thirard   *m* George Garvarentz

Horst Buchholz, Anthony Quinn, Orson
Welles, Akim Tamiroff, Robert Hossein,
Omar Sharif, Elsa Martinelli, Grégoire Aslan,
Massimo Girotti, Folco Lulli

The Fabulous Dorseys
US 1947   91m   bw
UA (Charles R. Rogers)

Two quarrelling bandleader brothers are
reunited on the death of their father.
Slight, comedic biopic with the Dorseys
playing well and trying hard.

w Richard English, Art Arthur, Curtis
Kenyon   *d* Alfred E. Green   *ph* James Van
Trees   *m* Leo Shuken

Tommy Dorsey, Jimmy Dorsey (and their
bands), Janet Blair, Paul Whiteman, William
Lundigan

The Face***
Sweden 1958   103m   bw
Svensk Filmindustri
original title: *Ansiktet;* US title: *The
Magician*

In 19th-century Sweden, a mesmerist and his
troupe are halted at a country post to be
examined by three officials. Partly exposed as
a fraud, he takes a frightening revenge.
A virtually indecipherable parable which may
be about the survival of Christianity (and may
not), this wholly personal Bergman fancy has
to be enjoyed chiefly for its surface frissons,
for its acting and its look, which are almost
sufficient compensation.

wd Ingmar Bergman   *ph* Gunnar Fischer
m Erik Nordgren

Max Von Sydow, Ingrid Thulin, *Gunnar
Bjornstrand*, Naima Wifstrand, Ake Fridell,
Lars Ekborg, Bengt Ekerot

The Face at the Window*
GB 1939   65m   bw
Pennant / Ambassador (George King)

In 1880 Paris, a murderer uses his moronic
half-brother to distract his victims but is foiled
when a dead man apparently incriminates him.
Roistering melodrama which provided Tod
Slaughter with one of his juiciest roles and is
here effectively presented, which is more than
can be said for the screen treatments of most
of his other vehicles.

w A. R. Rawlinson, Randall Faye, *play* F.
Brooke Warren   *d* George King

Tod Slaughter, Marjorie Taylor, John
Warwick, Leonard Henry, Aubrey Mallalieu

'One of the best English pictures I have seen
. . . leaves the American horror films far
behind.'—*Graham Greene*

The Face behind the Mask*
US 1941   69m   bw
Columbia (Wallace MacDonald)

When his face is disfigured in a fire, an
immigrant turns to a life of crime.
Effective second feature melodrama with a
good star performance.

w Allen Vincent, Paul Jarrico, *play* Thomas
O'Connell   *d* Robert Florey   *ph* Franz Planer
md Sidney Cutner

Peter Lorre, Evelyn Keyes, *Don Beddoe*,
George E. Stone

A Face in the Crowd***
US 1957   126m   bw
(Warner) Newton (Elia Kazan)

A small-town hick becomes a megalomaniac
when television turns him into a cracker-barrel
philosopher.
Brilliantly cinematic melodrama of its time
which only flags in the last lap and paints a
luridly entertaining picture of modern show
business.

w Budd Schulberg, from his story Your
Arkansas Traveller   *d* Elia Kazan   *ph* Harry
Stradling, Gayne Rescher   *m* Tom Glazer
*Andy Griffith, Lee Remick, Walter Matthau,
Patricia Neal*, Anthony Franciosa, Percy
Waram, Marshall Neilan
   'Savagery, bitterness, cutting humour.'—
Penelope Houston
   'If Kazan and Schulberg had been content to
make their case by implication, it might have
been a completely sophisticated piece of
movie-making. Instead, everything is
elaborately spelled out, and the film
degenerates into preposterous liberal
propaganda.'—*Andrew Sarris*
   'Some exciting scenes in the first half, but
the later developments are frenetic, and by the
end the film is a loud and discordant mess.'—
Pauline Kael, 70s

A Face in the Rain*
US 1963   80m   bw
Filmways / Calvic (John Calley)

During World War II an American spy in Italy
bungles his mission, and hides in the
apartment of a professor's wife.
Offbeat, talkative melodrama with a few neat
touches.

w Hugo Butler, Jean Rouverol d *Irvin Kershner* ph *Haskell Wexler* m Richard Markowitz

Rory Calhoun, Marina Berti, Niall MacGinnis

Face in the Sky
US 1932 68m bw

A sign painter falls for a farmer's daughter.
Curious, whimsical comedy romance which didn't work at any level. Spencer Tracy, Marian Nixon, Stuart Erwin, Sam Hardy, Lila Lee. Written by Humphrey Pearson from a story by Myles Connolly; directed by Harry Lachman; for Fox. 'Why it was considered feature-length picture material is hard to understand.'—*Variety*

Face of a Fugitive*
US 1959 81m Eastmancolor
Columbia / Morningside

A man falsely accused of murder makes a new life in a frontier town.
Lively western melodrama with good atmosphere.

w David T. Chantler d *Paul Wendkos* ph Wilfrid M. Cline m Jerry Goldsmith

Fred MacMurray, Lin McCarthy, Alan Baxter, James Coburn

The Face of Fu Manchu**
GB 1965 96m Techniscope
Anglo–EMI / Hallam (Harry Alan Towers)

In the twenties, Nayland Smith of Scotland Yard links an oriental crime wave with evil mastermind Fu Manchu.
A splendidly light touch and attention to detail make this entertaining spoof like a tuppenny blood come to life.

w Peter Welbeck (Harry Alan Towers) d *Don Sharp* ph Ernest Steward m Chris Whelan ad *Frank White*

Nigel Green, Christopher Lee, Tsai Chin, Howard Marion Crawford

● *Video: Thorn EMI*

Faces*
US 1968 130m bw
Maurice McEndree

A discontented Los Angeles executive tries but fails to go through with a divorce.
A personal, probing study of middle-aged loneliness, made with the director's usual long-winded relentlessness but quite frequently compelling.

wd John Cassavetes ph Al Ruban m Jack Ackerman

John Marley, Gena Rowlands, Lynn Carlin, Fred Draper, Seymour Cassell
  'The cast are all painfully and overpoweringly real.'—*Jan Dawson*

AAN: John Cassavetes (as writer); Lynn Carlin; Seymour Cassell

Faces in the Dark*
GB 1960 85m bw
Rank / Welbeck / Penington Eady (Jon Penington)

A blind man survives a plot against his life.

Unlikely but watchable puzzler, betrayed by lifeless handling. Hitchcock could have worked wonders with such a plot.

w Ephraim Kogan, John Tulley, *novel* Pierre Boileau, Thomas Narcejac d David Eady ph Ken Hodges m Edwin Astley

John Gregson, Mai Zetterling, Michael Denison, John Ireland, Tony Wright, Nanette Newman

The Facts of Life*
US 1960 103m bw
(UA) HLP (Norman Panama)

Two middle-aged married suburbanites have an abortive affair.
Star comedy with muted slapstick and earnest acting, a good try, but less effective than their normal pratfalls.

w Norman Panama, Melvin Frank d *Melvin Frank* ph Charles Lang Jnr m Leigh Harline

Bob Hope, Lucille Ball, Ruth Hussey, Don Defore, Louis Nye, Philip Ober
  'Random shots of mockery aimed effectively at the American middle-class way of life.'—*Peter John Dyer*

AAN: Norman Panama, Melvin Frank (script); Charles Lang Jnr; title song (*m / ly* Johnny Mercer)

Fahrenheit 451*
GB 1966 112m Technicolor
Rank / Anglo Enterprise / Vineyard (Lewis M. Allen)

In a fascist future state, a fireman's job is to burn books.
1984 stuff, a little lacking in plot and rather tentatively directed, but with charming moments.

w François Truffaut, Jean-Louis Richard, *novel* Ray Bradbury d *François Truffaut* ph Nicolas Roeg m Bernard Herrmann *design consultant* Tony Walton

Oskar Werner, Julie Christie, Cyril Cusack, Anton Diffring, Jeremy Spenser
  'He barely dramatizes the material at all, and though there are charming, childlike moments, the performers seem listless, and the whole enterprise is a little drab.'—*Pauline Kael*

† All the credits in this film are spoken.

Fail Safe***
US 1964 111m bw
Columbia / Max E. Youngstein / Sidney Lumet

An American atomic bomber is accidentally set to destroy Moscow, and the president has to destroy New York in retaliation.
Despite a confusing opening, this deadly earnest melodrama gets across the horror of its situation better than the contemporaneous *Dr Strangelove* which treated the same plot as black comedy. Here the details are both terrifying and convincing.

w Walter Bernstein, *novel* Eugene Burdick, Harvey Wheeler d *Sidney Lumet* ph Gerald Hirschfeld m none

Henry Fonda, Walter Matthau, Dan O'Herlihy, Walter Overton, Fritz Weaver, Edward Binns, Larry Hagman, Russell Collins
  'It will have you sitting on the brink of eternity.'—*publicity*

Fair Warning
US 1937 70m bw

A sheriff solves the murder of a Death Valley miner. Very watchable little second feature.
J. Edward Bromberg, Betty Furness, John Howard Payne, Victor Kilian, Gavin Muir, Andrew Tombes. Written and directed by Norman Foster, from a story by Philip Wylie; for TCF. 'Stereotype whodunit comedy.'—*Variety*

Fair Wind to Java
US 1952 92m Trucolor
Republic (Joseph Kane)

A sailor with a mutinous crew seeks a South Sea treasure.
Routine adventure culminating in a volcanic explosion.

w Richard Tregaskis, *novel* Garland Roark d *Joseph Kane* ph Jack Marta m Victor Young

Fred MacMurray, Vera Hruba Ralston, Robert Douglas, Victor McLaglen

Faithful in My Fashion
US 1946 81m bw

A soldier on leave causes havoc in a department store where his girl friend is manager. Sentimental comedy, forgettable for itself but containing endearing performances by a number of favourite character actors.
Tom Drake, Donna Reed, Edward Everett Horton, Spring Byington, Harry Davenport, Sig Rumann, Margaret Hamilton, Hobart Cavanaugh. Written by Lionel Houser; directed by Sidney Salkow; for MGM.

Faithless
US 1932 76m bw
MGM

A spoiled rich girl and her beau both descend to working-class level and almost further.
Would-be sensational drama ruined by censorship and miscasting.

w Carey Wilson, *novel* Tinfoil by Mildred Cram d *Harry Beaumont* ph Oliver T. Marsh

Tallulah Bankhead, Robert Montgomery, Hugh Herbert, Maurice Murphy, Louise Closser Hale, Lawrence Grant, Henry Kolker
  'They pile the suffering on so thick that any but the most naive theatregoers are going to revolt and scoff.'—*Variety*

The Fake
GB 1953 81m bw

The Tate Gallery hires an American investigator who discovers that one of their da Vincis is a substitute. Very standard co-feature mystery with pleasant touches. Dennis O'Keefe, Coleen Gray, Hugh Williams, John Laurie, Guy Middleton. Written by Patrick Kirwan; directed by Godfrey Grayson; for Steven Pallos / Pax.

The Falcon
A debonair solver of crime puzzles allegedly created by Michael Arlen but owing much to The Saint and resulting from a need by RKO for more of the same. Helped by a tough / comic manservant, he flourished during the forties in sixteen second features (the last three for Film Classics). After three episodes George Sanders tired of the role and was written out by being 'shot' and having his real-life brother Tom Conway take over as his fictional one. The performances of these two actors are pleasant, though the films are now fairly unwatchable, but John Calvert who took over for the last three was not a success.

1941: THE GAY FALCON, A DATE WITH THE FALCON
1942: THE FALCON TAKES OVER (the plot was borrowed from Raymond Chandler's FAREWELL MY LOVELY), THE FALCON'S BROTHER
1943: THE FALCON STRIKES BACK, THE FALCON AND THE CO-EDS, THE FALCON IN DANGER
1944: THE FALCON IN HOLLYWOOD, THE FALCON IN MEXICO, THE FALCON OUT WEST
1945: THE FALCON IN SAN FRANCISCO
1946: THE FALCON'S ALIBI, THE FALCON'S ADVENTURE
1948: THE DEVIL'S CARGO, APPOINTMENT WITH MURDER, SEARCH FOR DANGER

The Fall°
Argentina 1958   86m   bw
Argentine Sono (Leopoldo Torre Nilsson)
original title: *La Caída*

A strictly brought-up college girl lodges with an eccentric family whose strange world comes to mean more to her than the love of a young lawyer.
Odd, claustrophobic melodrama from a very personal film-maker.

w Beatriz Guido, Leopoldo Torre Nilsson, *novel* Beatriz Guido *d* Leopoldo Torre Nilsson *ph* Alberto Etchebehere *m* Juan Carlos Paz

Elsa Daniel, Duilio Marzia, Lydia Lamaison, Carlos Lopez Monet

The Fall of Berlin°
USSR 1949   160m   Agfacolor
Mosfilm

A steel worker turns soldier, sees all the major Russian battles of World War II, and has his hand shaken by Stalin.
Out-and-out propaganda, with caricatures of famous people and magnificently staged battles.

w M. Chiaureli, P. A. Pavlenko
d M. Chiaureli *ph* L. V. Kosmatov *m* Dmitri Shostakovich

B. Andreyev, M. Gelovani (as Stalin), V. Stanitsine (as Churchill), M. Kovaleva

The Fall of the House of Usher
France 1928   48m (24 fps)   bw   silent
Roderick Usher's sister, prone to catalepsy, is

buried alive; her unexpected return to life is instrumental in setting the house ablaze. The original story is not so much stated as inferred in this very impressionistic version, of limited interest only to art movie buffs. Marguerite Gance, Jean Debucourt, Charles Lamy. Written and directed by Jean Epstein and Luis Bunuel; art direction by Pierre Kefer.

The Fall of the House of Usher
GB 1949   70m   bw
Dismally inept low-budgeter, a pain to sit through. Gwen Watford, Kay Tendeter, Irving Steen. Directed by Ivan Barnett; for Valiant.

The Fall of the House of Usher: for the Vincent Price version, see House of Usher

The Fall of the Roman Empire°°
US / Spain 1964   187m   Technicolor
   Ultra Panavision 70
Samuel Bronston

After poisoning the Emperor Marcus Aurelius his mad son Commodus succumbs to dissipation and allows Rome to be ravaged by pestilence and the Barbarians.
Would-be distinguished epic with an intellectual first hour; unfortunately the hero is a priggish bore, the villain a crashing bore, the heroine a saintly bore, and the only interesting character is killed off early. A chariot race, a javelin duel, some military clashes and a mass burning at the stake keep one watching, and the production values are high indeed.

w Ben Barzman, Philip Yordan *d* Anthony Mann *ph* Robert Krasker, John Moore *m* Dmitri Tiomkin *pd* Venerio Colasanti

Alec Guinness, Christopher Plummer, Stephen Boyd, James Mason, Sophia Loren, John Ireland, Eric Porter, Anthony Quayle, Mel Ferrer, Omar Sharif
  'The film works from a restricted palette, and the result is weirdly restraining and severe, a dignified curb on absurdities.'—*John Coleman*

† The forum set in this film is said to be the largest ever built.

AAN: Dmitri Tiomkin

● *Video: Intervision*

'Even now she stood between us—the taunt of her smile like a black curse on our love!'

Fallen Angel°
US 1945   97m   bw
TCF (Otto Preminger)

A man plans to get rid of his wife and marry another woman, but it is the latter who is murdered.
Oddly sleazy melodrama, not more successful then because it was unexpected than now because it is miscast. Some good sequences, though.

w Harry Kleiner, *novel* Marty Holland *d* Otto Preminger *ph* Joseph La Shelle *m* David Raksin

Dana Andrews, Alice Faye, Linda Darnell, Charles Bickford, Anne Revere, Bruce Cabot, John Carradine, Percy Kilbride

'It holds you by its undertones of small-town life and frustration.'—*Richard Winnington*

'It isn't in the class of *Laura*, but it's tolerable, in a tawdry sort of way.'—*Pauline Kael, 70s*

The Fallen Idol°°°
GB 1948   94m   bw
British Lion / London Films (Carol Reed)
US title: *The Lost Illusion*

An ambassador's small son nearly incriminates his friend the butler in the accidental death of his shrewish wife.
A near-perfect piece of small-scale cinema, built up from clever nuances of acting and cinematic technique.

w Graham Greene, from his story The Basement Room *d* Carol Reed *ph* Georges Périnal *m* William Alwyn

Ralph Richardson, Michèle Morgan, *Bobby Henrey*, Sonia Dresdel, Jack Hawkins
  'A short story has become a film which is compact without loss of variety in pace and shape.'—*Dilys Powell*
  'It's too deliberate and hushed to be much fun . . . you wait an extra beat between the low-key lines of dialogue.'—*Pauline Kael, 70s*

AAN: Graham Greene; Carol Reed

● *Video: Thorn EMI*

The Fallen Sparrow°
US 1943   93m   bw
RKO (Robert Fellows)

An American veteran of the Spanish Civil War finds himself hounded in New York by Nazis seeking the Spanish flag of freedom.
Obscure melodrama, very good to look at but hardly worth unravelling; a precursor of Hollywood's post-war *films noirs*.

w Warren Duff, *novel* Dorothy B. Hughes *d* Richard Wallace *ph* Nicholas Musuraca *md* Roy Webb, Constantin Bakaleinikoff

John Garfield, Maureen O'Hara, Walter Slezak, Martha O'Driscoll, Patricia Morison, Bruce Edwards, John Banner, John Miljan

AAN: Roy Webb, Constantin Bakaleinikoff

Falling in Love°
US 1984   107m   Technicolor
Paramount / Marvin Worth

Two people, each married to someone else, have a furtive love affair.
By present-day standards this is a rather tame rip-off of *Brief Encounter*, and even includes the trains. However, very little happens and we are left with nothing but star personalities in a vacuum.

w Michael Cristofer *d* Ulu Grosbard *ph* Peter Suschitzky *m* Dave Grusin *pd* Santo Loquasto *ed* Michael Kahn

Robert de Niro, Meryl Streep, Harvey Keitel, Jane Kaczmarek, George Martin

Falling in Love Again°
US 1980   103m   colour
International Picture Show of Atlanta
   (Steven Paul)

A middle-aged New Yorker remembers his
young romances and his dreams of success.
Warm little independent production harking
back to the days of *H. M. Pulham Esquire* and
none the worse for that.

w Steven Paul, Ted Allan, Susannah York
d Steven Paul ph Michael Mileham, Dick
Bush, Wolfgang Suschitzky m Michel
Legrand

Elliott Gould, Susannah York, Stuart Paul,
Kaye Ballard

Falling for You*
GB 1933 88m bw
Gainsborough (Michael Balcon)

Fleet Street journalists in Switzerland try to
outsmart each other.
Dated comedy very typical of the stars'
extremely casual style, with immaculate set
pieces.

w Jack Hulbert, Douglas Furber, Robert
Stevenson, *story* Sidney Gilliat d Jack
Hulbert, Robert Stevenson ph Bernard
Knowles *songs* Vivian Ellis, Douglas Furber

Jack Hulbert, Cicely Courtneidge, Tamara
Desni, Garry Marsh, Alfred Drayton, O. B.
Clarence, Morton Selten

Fame*
US 1980 133m Metrocolor
MGM (David de Silva, Alan Marshall)

Assorted teenagers attend Manhattan's High
School for the Performing Arts.
Cleverly shot and edited slice of life which
unfortunately features people whose language
and personalities are fairly repellent. The
result is like *A Chorus Line* without the music.

w Christopher Gore d Alan Parker
ph Michael Seresin m Michael Gore and
others pd Geoffrey Kirkland

Irene Cara, Lee Curreri, Laura Dean, Paul
McCrane, Barry Miller, Gene Anthony Ray

'Our film, I hope, will be a microcosm of
New York . . . a dozen races pitching in and
having their own crack at the American
dream.'—*Alan Parker*

'Its soft-centred view of human relationships
is periodically undercut by what can only be
described as the grotesque.'—*John Pym*

AA: screenplay; best original song (Michael
Gore, Dean Pitchford); editing (Gerry
Hambling)

● *Video: MGM / UA*

Fame Is the Spur*
GB 1947 116m bw
GFD / Two Cities / Charter Films (John
Boulting)

The rise to political eminence of a working-
class socialist.
Disappointingly flat historical drama from a
novel allegedly based on the career of Ramsay
MacDonald. Interesting moments.

w Nigel Balchin, *novel* Howard Spring d Roy
Boulting ph Gunther Krampf, Harry
Waxman

Michael Redgrave, Rosamund John, Bernard
Miles, Carla Lehmann, Hugh Burden,
Marjorie Fielding, Seymour Hicks

A Family Affair*
US 1937 69m bw
MGM (Lucien Hubbard)

A small-town judge faces a few family
problems.
The second feature that started the highly
successful Hardy family series (qv under
Hardy). In this case the judge and his wife
were played by actors who did not persevere
into the series, but the stage was otherwise set
for a long run, and the town of Carvel came to
mean home to many Americans abroad.

w Kay Van Riper, *play* Skidding by Aurania
Rouverol d George B. Seitz ph Lester White

Lionel Barrymore, Spring Byington, *Mickey
Rooney*, Eric Linden, Cecilia Parker, Sara
Haden, Charles Grapewin, Julie Haydon

'Family trade and tops in dual locations.'—
Variety

Family Honeymoon*
US 1948 90m bw
U-I (John Beck, Z. Wayne Griffin)

A college professor marries a widow whose
three children join them on their Grand
Canyon honeymoon.
Very ordinary and predictable star comedy.

w Dane Lussier, Homer Croy d Claude
Binyon ph William Daniels m Frank Skinner

Claudette Colbert, Fred MacMurray, Rita
Johnson, Gigi Perreau, Peter Miles, Jimmy
Hunt, Hattie McDaniel, Chill Wills

The Family Jewels*
US 1965 100m Technicolor
Paramount / York / Jerry Lewis

A child heiress chooses a new father from
among her five uncles.
Unfunny star farce with multiple
impersonations.

w Jerry Lewis, Bill Richmond d Jerry Lewis
ph W. Wallace Kelley m Pete King

Jerry Lewis, Donna Butterworth, Sebastian
Cabot, Robert Strauss

Family Life*
GB 1971 108m Technicolor
EMI / Kestrel (Tony Garnett)

A 19-year-old girl is driven into a mental
collapse by emotional and family problems.
A slice of suburban life and an indictment of
it, put together with unknown actors and
probing TV techniques. Somewhat too
harrowing for fiction, but extraordinarily vivid.

w David Mercer, from his play In Two Minds
d Ken Loach ph Charles Stewart m Marc
Wilkinson

Sandy Ratcliff, Bill Dean, Grace Cave

● *Video: Thorn EMI*

'There's no body in the family plot!'
Family Plot*
US 1976 126m Technicolor
Universal (Alfred Hitchcock)

A fake medium tries for easy money by
producing a lost heir.
Talkative, complex, patchy, low-key but
always interesting Hitchcock suspenser in an
unusually friendly vein.

w Ernest Lehman, *novel* The Rainbird Pattern
by Victor Canning d Alfred Hitchcock
ph Leonard J. South m John Williams
pd Henry Bumstead

Karen Black, Bruce Dern, Barbara Harris,
William Devane, Ed Lauter, Cathleen Nesbitt

'Full of benign mischief, beautiful
craftsmanship and that elusive sense of
cinematic rhythm that has always been
Hitchcock's trump card.'—*Michael Billington,
Illustrated London News*

'The picture bogs down in one talky,
undramatic sequence after another, and the
plot, with all its exposition and loose ends, is
involved beyond belief.'—*De Witt Bodeen,
Films in Review*

● *Video: CIC*

Family Portrait*
GB 1950 24m bw
Festival of Britain / Wessex (Ian Dalrymple)

A study of the English tradition and spirit
through history.
The last work of a director–poet; not his most
vivid movie, yet an accurate distillation of the
themes which concerned him and of a dreamlike patriotism which now seems lost.

wd Humphrey Jennings ph Martin Curtis
ed Stewart MacAllister comm Michael
Goodliffe

'Perhaps the most polished in style of all
Jennings' films . . . continuously fascinating,
sharp and evocative.'—*MFB*

The Family Secret*
US 1951 85m bw
Columbia / Santana (Robert Lord, Henry S.
Kesler)

The son of a suburban family kills his best
friend in a brawl, and his mother insists he
conceal the truth even when another man is
charged.
Television-style pattern play, not even very
interesting at the time.

w Francis Cockrell, Andrew Solt d Henry
Levin ph Burnett Guffey m George Duning

John Derek, Lee J. Cobb, Erin O'Brien
Moore, Jody Lawrance, Henry O'Neill, Carl
Benton Reid

'The general atmosphere is one of outward
torment unbacked by inner emotion.'—*MFB*

The Family Way*
GB 1966 115m Eastmancolor
BL / Jambox (John Boulting)

There is consternation in a Lancashire family
when the son cannot consummate his
marriage.
Overstretched domestic farce-drama. Good
scenes and performances, but it was all much
sharper as a one-hour TV play.

w Bill Naughton, from his play Honeymoon
Deferred d Roy Boulting ph Harry Waxman
m Paul McCartney

John Mills, *Marjorie Rhodes*, Hywel Bennett,
Hayley Mills, *Avril Angers*, Murray Head,
Wilfred Pickles, Barry Foster, Liz Fraser

The Famous Ferguson Case
US 1932   80m   bw

Reporters on a small town paper expose their own hang-ups as they argue over the outcome of a current murder trial. Generally unsuccessful attempt to do something mildly different. Joan Blondell, Tom Brown, Adrienne Dore, Walter Miller, Leslie Fenton, J. Carrol Naish, Grant Mitchell. Written by Harvey Thew from a story by Courtenay Terrett and Granville Moore; directed by Lloyd Bacon; for Warners. 'Dull, trite, talky exposé of yellow journalism.'—*Variety*

The Fan*
US 1949   79m   bw
TCF (Otto Preminger)
GB title: *Lady Windermere's Fan*

Scandal almost results when Lady Windermere loses her fan.
Reasonably polished, rather dull version of an old play, not really helped by modern bookends.
w Walter Reisch, Dorothy Parker, Ross Evans, *play* Lady Windermere's Fan by Oscar Wilde d Otto Preminger ph Joseph La Shelle m Daniele Amfitheatrof
George Sanders, Madeleine Carroll, Jeanne Crain, Richard Greene, Martita Hunt, John Sutton, Hugh Dempster, Richard Ney

The Fan
US 1981   95m   Technicolor
Paramount / Robert Stigwood / Filmways

A Broadway actress is threatened by a disturbed admirer.
Ruthless, witless thriller with no suspense cliché unturned.
w Priscilla Chapman, John Hartwell d Edward Bianchi ph Dick Bush m Pino Donaggio pd Santo Loquasto
Lauren Bacall, James Garner, Maureen Stapleton, Hector Elizondo, Michael Biehn, Anna Maria Horsford
'Horror comic mechanics . . . the theatrical milieu fails to register, either individually or collectively.'—*Gilbert Adair, MFB*
● *Video: CIC*

Fanatic*
GB 1965   96m   Technicolor
Hammer / Seven Arts (Anthony Hinds)
US title: *Die! Die! My Darling*

An American girl in England visits the mother of her dead fiancé and finds herself the prisoner of a religious maniac.
Boringly overlong Grand Guignol which even defeats its gallantly unmade-up and deathly-looking star; mildly notable however as a record of one of her last performances.
w Richard Matheson, *novel* Nightmare by Anne Blaisdell d Silvio Narizzano ph Arthur Ibbetson m Wilfrid Josephs pd Peter Proud
Tallulah Bankhead, Stefanie Powers, Peter Vaughan, Yootha Joyce, Donald Sutherland

The Fanatics*
France 1957   92m   bw
Cinégraphe-Regent (Pierre Lévy)

Patriots quarrel over the assassination by bomb of a South American dictator when he travels by public plane.
Suspense melodrama with many artificial twists, but slick and well acted.
w Alex Joffé, Jean Levitte d Alex Joffé ph L. H. Burel m Paul Misraki
Pierre Fresnay, Michel Auclair, Grégoire Aslan, Betty Schneider

Fancy Pants**
US 1950   92m   Technicolor
Paramount (Robert Welch)

A British actor stranded in the far west poses as a butler.
Lively western comedy remake of *Ruggles of Red Gap* (qv), one of the star's better vehicles.
w Edmund Hartman, Robert O'Brien d George Marshall ph Charles Lang Jnr m Van Cleave
Bob Hope, Lucille Ball, Bruce Cabot, Jack Kirkwood, Lea Penman, Eric Blore, John Alexander, Norma Varden

Fanfan la Tulipe*
France 1951   98m   bw
Filmsonor-Ariane-Amato

Recruited into the army of Louis XV by a prophecy that he will marry the king's daughter, a young braggart does everything he can to live up to it.
Rather like a spoof Errol Flynn effort, this likeable swashbuckler can't quite summon up enough buckle or swash to be the minor classic it clearly intends.
w René Wheeler, Jean Fallet d Christian-Jaque ph Christian Matras m Georges Van Parys, Maurice Thiriet
Gérard Philipe, Gina Lollobrigida, Noel Roquevert, Marcel Herrand
'A daring and delightful piece of work.'—*Times*

Fanny (Pagnol) see Marius

Fanny*
'There are three men in her life. The one she married . . . the young adventurer . . . and the baby they all shared!'

US 1960   133m   Technicolor
Warner / Mansfield (Joshua Logan)

Life on the Marseilles waterfront, and in particular the story of two old men and two lovers.
Lumbering adaptation of three Pagnol films of the thirties (*Marius, Fanny, César*—see *Marius*) previously seen as a 1938 Hollywood film (*Port of Seven Seas*) and later as a Broadway musical. This is the dullest version despite fine photography and a couple of good performances.
w Julius J. Epstein, *play* S. N. Behrman, Joshua Logan, *films* Marcel Pagnol d Joshua Logan ph Jack Cardiff m Harold Rome md Morris Stoloff, Harry Sukman
Charles Boyer, Maurice Chevalier, Leslie Caron, Horst Buchholz, Georgette Anys, Salvatore Baccaloni, Lionel Jeffries, Raymond Bussières, Victor Francen

† The film was proudly advertised as 'Joshua Logan's *Fanny*' until the press pointed out the double meaning.
AAN: best picture; Jack Cardiff; Morris Stoloff, Harry Sukman; Charles Boyer

Fanny and Alexander**
Sweden / France / West Germany 1982
188m   Eastmancolor
AB Cinematograph / Swedish Film Institute / Swedish TV One / Gaumont / Persona Film / Tobis (Jorn Donner)

A well-to-do Uppsala family comes together to celebrate Christmas 1907.
An interesting mixture of *Dear Octopus* and *Wild Strawberries* turns into something more akin to *The Face* or *The Night Comers*. A kind of Bergman compendium, and impossible to describe exactly for those who have not seen it.
wd Ingmar Bergman ph Sven Nykvist m Daniel Bell pd Anna Asp
Gunn Walgren, Ewa Froeling, Jarl Kulle, Erland Josephson, Allan Edwall, Boerje Ahlstedt, Mona Malm, Gunnar Bjornstrand, Jan Malmsjoe
'It's as if Bergman's neuroses had been tormenting him for so long that he cut them off and went sprinting back to Victorian health and domesticity.'—*New Yorker*
AA: cinematography; best foreign-language film; screenplay; art direction; costume
AAN: direction

Fanny by Gaslight**
GB 1944   108m   bw
GFD / Gainsborough (Edward Black)
US title: *Man of Evil*

The illegitimate daughter of a cabinet minister is saved from a lustful Lord.
Highly-coloured Victorian romantic melodrama, enjoyably put over with no holds barred and a pretty high budget for the time.
w Doreen Montgomery, Aimée Stuart, *novel* Michael Sadleir d Anthony Asquith ph Arthur Crabtree m Cedric Mallabey
James Mason, Phyllis Calvert, Stewart Granger, Wilfrid Lawson, John Laurie, Margaretta Scott, Stuart Lindsell, Jean Kent
'Seldom have I seen a film more agreeable to watch, from start to finish.'—*William Whitebait*
'Mr Asquith does not seem to have made much effort to freshen it by interesting treatment, so that the rare unusual device seems quite out of key among so much that is simple, obvious, hackneyed.'—*Richard Mallett, Punch*
† One of several costume melodramas patterned after the success of *The Man in Grey* (qv).

Fanny Foley Herself
US 1931   73m   Technicolor

A female vaudeville entertainer chooses between her profession and looking after her two daughters. Rather disappointing comedy drama. Edna May Oliver, Hobart Bosworth, Helen Chandler, Rochelle Hudson, John Darrow. Written by Carey Wilson from a story by Juliet Wilbur Tompkins; directed by Melville Brown; for RKO.

Fanny Hill
West Germany 1965   104m   bw
Adventures of an 18th-century woman of pleasure. Tacky exploitation piece half-spoofing a suddenly fashionable piece of pornography. Miriam Hopkins, Laetitia Roman, Walter Giller, Alex D'Arcy, Helmut Weiss. Written by Robert Heel; directed by Russ Meyer; for Albert Zugsmith / Pan World.

Fantasia**
US 1940   135m   Technicolor
Walt Disney
A concert of classical music is given cartoon interpretations. The pieces are:
   Bach: Toccata and Fugue in D Minor
   Tchaikovsky: The Nutcracker Suite
   Dukas: The Sorcerer's Apprentice
   Stravinsky: The Rite of Spring
   Beethoven: The Pastoral Symphony
   Ponchielli: Dance of the Hours
   Moussorgsky: Night on a Bare Mountain
   Schubert: Ave Maria
Brilliantly inventive for the most part, the cartoons having become classics in themselves. The least part (the Pastoral Symphony) can be forgiven.
supervisor Ben Sharpsteen *md* Edward H. Plumb
Leopold Stokowski, the Philadelphia Orchestra, Deems Taylor
   'Dull as it is towards the end, ridiculous as it is in the bend of the knee before Art, it is one of the strange and beautiful things that have happened in the world.'—*Otis Ferguson*
   'It is ambitious, and finely so, and one feels that its vulgarities are at least unintentional.'—*James Agate*
† Multiplane cameras, showing degrees of depth in animation, were used for the first time.

Fantastic Voyage*
US 1966   100m   De Luxe   Cinemascope
TCF (Saul David)
When a top scientist is shot and suffers brain damage, a team of doctors and a boat are miniaturized and injected into his blood stream . . . but one is a traitor.
Engagingly absurd science fiction which keeps its momentum but is somewhat let down by its decor.
w Harry Kleiner *d* Richard Fleischer *ph* Ernest Laszlo *m* Leonard Rosenman *ad* Dale Hennesy, Jack Martin Smith *sp* L. B. Abbott, Art Cruickshank, Emil Kosa Jnr
Stephen Boyd, Raquel Welch, Edmond O'Brien, Donald Pleasence, Arthur Kennedy, Arthur O'Connell, William Redfield
   'The process shots are so clumsily matted . . . that the actors look as if a child has cut

them out with blunt scissors.'—*Pauline Kael*
AA: art direction
AAN: Ernest Laszlo
● *Video: CBS / Fox*

The Far Country*
US 1954   97m   Technicolor
U-I (Aaron Rosenberg)
Two cowboys on their way to the Alaska goldfields are beset by swindlers.
Sturdy star western with good production values.
w Borden Chase *d* Anthony Mann
ph William Daniels *m* Joseph Gershenson
James Stewart, Walter Brennan, Ruth Roman, Corinne Calvet, John McIntire

Far from the Madding Crowd*
GB 1967   175m   Technicolor
   Panavision 70
EMI / Vic / Appia (Joseph Janni)
In Victorian Wessex a headstrong girl causes unhappiness and tragedy.
Good-looking but slackly handled version of a melodramatic and depressing novel.
w Frederic Raphael, *novel* Thomas Hardy *d* John Schlesinger *ph* Nicolas Roeg *m* Richard Rodney Bennett *pd* Richard Macdonald
Julie Christie, Peter Finch, Alan Bates, Terence Stamp, Prunella Ransome
   'In this rather plodding film the insufficiency of the foreground is partly offset by the winsomeness of the backgrounds. The very sheep are so engaging as to entice our gaze into some extremely amiable woolgathering.'—*John Simon*
AAN: Richard Rodney Bennett
● *Video: Thorn EMI*

The Far Horizons
US 1955   108m   Technicolor
   Vistavision
(Paramount) Pine–Thomas
The story of Lewis and Clark's 1803 expedition west through the Louisiana Purchase territory.
Flabbily-handled historical hokum; potential interest quickly dissipated.
w Winston Miller, Edmund H. North *d* Rudolph Maté *ph* Daniel L. Fapp *m* Hans Salter
Fred MacMurray, Charlton Heston, Donna Reed, Barbara Hale, William Demarest

Farewell Again**
GB 1937   85m   bw
Pendennis / London Films (Erich Pommer)
US title: *Troopship*
Soldiers returning from India have six hours' shore leave to sort out their problems.
Dated but sharply made compendium drama, a solid success of its time.
w Clemence Dane, Patrick Kirwan *d* Tim Whelan *ph* James Wong Howe, Hans Schneeberger *m* Richard Addinsell

Flora Robson, Leslie Banks, Robert Newton, René Ray, Patricia Hilliard, Sebastian Shaw, Leonora Corbett, Anthony Bushell, Edward Lexy, Wally Patch, Edmund Willard, Martita Hunt, John Laurie

Farewell My Lovely***
US 1944   95m   bw
RKO (Adrian Scott)
aka: *Murder My Sweet*
A private eye searches for an ex-convict's missing girl friend.
A revolutionary crime film in that it was the first to depict the genuinely seedy milieu suggested by its author. One of the first *films noirs* of the mid-forties, a minor masterpiece of expressionist film making, and a total change of direction for a crooner who suddenly became a tough guy.
w John Paxton, *novel* Raymond Chandler *d* Edward Dmytryk *ph* Harry J. Wild *m* Roy Webb
Dick Powell, Claire Trevor, Anne Shirley, *Mike Mazurki, Otto Kruger*, Miles Mander, Douglas Walton, Ralf Harolde, Don Douglas, Esther Howard
   MARLOWE (Dick Powell): ' "Okay Marlowe," I said to myself. "You're a tough guy. You've been sapped twice, choked, beaten silly with a gun, shot in the arm until you're crazy as a couple of waltzing mice. Now let's see you do something really tough—like putting your pants on." '
   MARLOWE: 'I caught the blackjack right behind my ear. A black pool opened up at my feet. I dived in. It had no bottom.'
   MARLOWE: 'My fingers looked like a bunch of bananas.'
   'A nasty, draggled bit of dirty work, accurately observed.'—*C. A. Lejeune*

Farewell My Lovely**
US 1975   95m   Technicolor
Avco Embassy / Elliott Kastner / ITC
   (George Pappas, Jerry Bruckheimer)
A pretty sharp remake of the above, with the plot slightly rewritten but tightened, and an excellent performance from a rather over-age star.
w David Zelag Goodman *d* Dick Richards *ph* John A. Alonzo *m* David Shire *pd* Dean Tavouraris
Robert Mitchum, Charlotte Rampling, John Ireland, Sylvia Miles, Anthony Zerbe, Jack O'Halloran, Kate Murtagh
   'A moody, bluesy, boozy recreation of Marlowe's tacky, neon-flashed Los Angeles of the early forties.'—*Judith Crist*
   'A delicious remake with a nice, smoky 1940s atmosphere.'—*Michael Billington, Illustrated London News*
AAN: Sylvia Miles
● *Video: Precision*

A Farewell to Arms**
US 1932   78m   bw
(Paramount) Frank Borzage
In World War I, a wounded American

FAREWELL MY LOVELY (1975). Robert Mitchum was really too old to play Marlowe, but he gave the best acting performance. John Ireland looks on.

ambulance driver falls in love with his nurse. Now very dated but important in its time, this romantic drama was one of the more successful Hemingway adaptations to be filmed.

w Benjamin Glazer, Oliver H. P. Garrett, *novel* Ernest Hemingway *d* Frank Borzage *ph* Charles Lang *m* W. Franke Harling

Gary Cooper, *Helen Hayes*, Adolphe Menjou, Mary Philips, Jack La Rue, Blanche Frederici, Henry Armetta

'Too much sentiment and not enough strength.'—*Mordaunt Hall, New York Times*

'Borzage has invested the war scenes with a strange, brooding expressionist quality . . . indeed, the overall visual style is most impressive.'—*NFT, 1974*

'Corking femme film fare at any angle or price.'—*Variety*

† Remade as *Force of Arms* (qv) and see below.

AA: Charles Lang
AAN: best picture

● *Video: VCL*

A Farewell to Arms
US 1957 150m De Luxe Cinemascope
TCF / David O. Selznick

Elaborate ill-fated remake which tried to make an adventure epic out of a low-key war drama. Its failure caused David O. Selznick to produce no more films.

w Ben Hecht *d* Charles Vidor *pd* Alfred Junge *ph* Piero Portalupi, Oswald Morris *m* Mario Nascimbene

Rock Hudson, Jennifer Jones, Vittorio de Sica, Alberto Sordi, Kurt Kasznar, Mercedes McCambridge, Oscar Homolka, Elaine Stritch, Victor Francen

AAN: Vittorio de Sica

● *Video: CBS / Fox*

Fargo
US 1964 99m Technicolor
Universal / Pennebaker (Al Ruddy)
aka: *Wild Seed*

A teenage girl hitch-hikes from New York to Los Angeles and is befriended by a young tramp.
Peripatetic romance in the modern manner, with no conclusions drawn and not much entertainment value beyond the scenery.

w Les Pine *d* Brian G. Hutton *ph* Conrad Hall *m* Richard Markowitz

Michael Parks, Celia Kaye, Ross Elliott, Woodrow Chambliss, Eva Novak

The Farmer Takes a Wife*
US 1935 91m bw
TCF (Winfield Sheehan)

By the Erie Canal in the 1820s, a wandering girl finds security with a farmer.

Pleasantly 'different' romantic drama, quite ably executed and introducing Henry Fonda to the screen.

w Edwin Burke, *play* Frank B. Elser and Marc Connelly, *novel* Rome Haul by Walter D. Edmonds *d* Victor Fleming *ph* John Seitz *m* Arthur Lange

Janet Gaynor, Henry Fonda, Charles Bickford, Slim Summerville, Andy Devine, Roger Imhof, Jane Withers, Margaret Hamilton, Sig Rumann, John Qualen

'It will pull in the Gaynor fans, and do much to return her to favour.'—*Variety*

The Farmer Takes a Wife*
US 1953 81m Technicolor
TCF (Frank P. Rosenberg)

Musical remake with an agreeably stylized look, hampered by a slowish script and dull cast.

w Walter Bulloch, Sally Benson, Joseph Fields *d* Henry Levin *ph* Arthur E. Arling *m* Cyril Mockridge *ad* Lyle Wheeler, Addison Hehr *songs* Harold Arlen, Dorothy Fields

Betty Grable, Dale Robertson, Thelma Ritter, Eddie Foy Jnr, John Carroll

The Farmer's Daughter
US 1940 60m bw
Paramount (William C. Thomas)

A stage struck country girl tries to horn in on a Broadway musical rehearsing nearby.
Feeble comedy for the sticks.

w Lewis R. Foster, Delmer Daves *d* James Hogan *ph* Leo Tover

Martha Raye, Charles Ruggles, Richard Denning, Gertrude Michael, William Frawley, William Demarest, Jack Norton

'Now she's raising eyebrows instead of corn!'

The Farmer's Daughter**
US 1947 97m bw
David O. Selznick (Dore Schary)

The Swedish maid of a congressman becomes a political force.
Well-made Cinderella story with a touch of asperity and top notch production values and cast.

w Allen Rivkin, Laura Kerr *d* H. C. Potter *ph* Milton Krasner *m* Leigh Harline

Loretta Young, Joseph Cotten, Ethel Barrymore, Charles Bickford, Rose Hobart, Rhys Williams, Harry Davenport, Tom Powers

'Patricians, politicians, even peasants are portrayed with unusual perception and wit.'—*James Agee*

AA: Loretta Young
AAN: Charles Bickford

● *Video: Guild*

The Farmer's Wife
GB 1928 67m approx bw silent
BIP (John Maxwell)

A farmer seeks a wife and after three disappointments settles for his housekeeper.

A simple and not very interesting silent screen version of a stage success which depended largely on dialogue.

wd Alfred Hitchcock, play Eden Phillpotts ph Jack Cox

James Thomas, Gordon Harker, Lillian Hall-Davis

'Some pleasant photography and a subtle impression of rural life rescued the picture from complete failure.'—George Perry, 1966

The Farmer's Wife

GB 1940 82m bw

Talkie remake of the above, a perfectly adequate photographed play. Basil Sydney, Wilfrid Lawson, Nora Swinburne, Patricia Roc, Michael Wilding. Written by Norman Lee, Leslie Arliss and J. E. Hunter; directed by Norman Lee and Leslie Arliss; for Pathé.

Farrebique**

France 1947 85m bw

L'Ecran Français / Les Films Etienne Lallier

Problems of a peasant family in central France.

Superbly-filmed semi-documentary, acted by a real family.

wd Georges Rouquier ph André Dantan m Henri Sauguet

'Definitely a film for posterity.'—MFB

Fashions of 1934*

US 1934 78m bw

Warner (Henry Blanke)

A confidence trickster conquers the French fashion world.

Slight musical comedy with a couple of splendid Berkeley numbers.

w F. Hugh Herbert, Carl Brickson d William Dieterle ch Busby Berkeley ph William Rees m / ly Sammy Fain, Irving Kahal ad Jack Okey

William Powell, Bette Davis, Verree Teasdale, Frank McHugh, Reginald Owen, Hugh Herbert, Henry O'Neill

Fast and Furious: see Fast Company (1938)

Fast and Loose

US 1930 70m bw

Paramount

A spoiled rich girl falls in love with a car mechanic.

Tiresome melodrama, dully scripted.

w Doris Anderson, Jack Kirkland, Preston Sturges, play The Best People by Avery Hopwood, David Gray d Fred Newmeyer ph William Steiner

Miriam Hopkins, Carole Lombard, Frank Morgan, Charles Starrett, Henry Wadsworth, David Hutcheson, Ilka Chase

Fast and Loose*

US 1939 80m bw

MGM (Frederick Stephani)

Married detectives and rare book experts solve the mystery of a missing Shakespeare manuscript.

Pleasing comedy mystery in the wake of The Thin Man.

w Harry Kurnitz d Edwin L. Marin ph George Folsey

Robert Montgomery, Rosalind Russell, Ralph Morgan, Reginald Owen, Etienne Girardot, Alan Dinehart, Joan Marsh, Sidney Blackmer

Fast and Loose

GB 1954 75m bw

By a series of accidents, a married man has to spend a night at an inn with an old flame.

Spiritless and miscast remake of A Cuckoo in the Nest; all talents below form. Brian Reece, Stanley Holloway, Kay Kendall, Reginald Beckwith, Charles Victor, June Thorburn. Written by A. R. Rawlinson and Ben Travers, from the latter's play; directed by Gordon Parry; for Group Films / Rank.

Fast Company*

US 1938 75m bw

A couple in the rare book business are implicated in the murder of a rival. First of three whodunnits featuring Joel and Garda Page, whose style was not at all dissimilar from that of Nick and Nora Charles in the Thin Man series. A polished time-passer. Melvyn Douglas, Florence Rice, Clare Dodd, Louis Calhern, George Zucco. Written by Marco Page (Harry Kurnitz); directed by Edward Buzzell; for MGM. (NB: The follow-ups had different stars as the pair of sleuths. Fast and Loose (qv) featured Robert Montgomery and Rosalind Russell; Sidney Blackmer, Ralph Morgan and Reginald Owen supported. Fast and Furious, also released in 1939, starred Franchot Tone and Ann Sothern, with Ruth Hussey, Lee Bowman and Allyn Joslyn.)

Fast Company

US 1953 67m bw

A girl inherits a racing stable and discovers a little chicanery. Ho-hum support wasting a good cast. Howard Keel, Nina Foch, Polly Bergen, Marjorie Main. Written by William Roberts; directed by John Sturges; for MGM.

The Fast Lady**

GB 1962 95m Eastmancolor

Rank / Group Films (Teddy Baird)

A bashful suitor buys an old Bentley, becomes a roadhog, passes his test, captures some crooks and gets the girl.

Spirited if aimless farcical comedy which crams in all the jokes about cars anyone can think of.

w Jack Davies, Henry Blyth d Ken Annakin ph Reg Wyer m Norrie Paramor

Stanley Baxter, James Robertson Justice, Leslie Phillips, Julie Christie, Dick Emery

● Video: Rank

Fast Times at Ridgemont High

US 1982 92m Technicolor

Universal / Refugee (C. O. Erickson)

Students at a California high school aim to lose their virginity.

The tiresome content of this teen comedy is slightly offset by bright handling. But only slightly.

w Cameron Crowe, from his book d Amy Heckerling ph Matthew F. Leonetti m / songs Rob Fahey

Sean Penn, Jennifer Jason Leigh, Judge Reinhold, Phoebe Cates, Brian Backus, Robert Romanus, Ray Walston

Fast-Walking

US 1981 116m Metrocolor

Racial disharmony and violence prevail at a midwest state prison. Curious black comedy dealing entirely with unpleasant types. James Woods, Tim McIntire, Kay Lenz, Robert Hooks, M. Emmet Walsh. Written and directed by James B. Harris from the novel The Rap by Ernest Brawley; for Lorimar. 'What do people think of when they write a script these days? Don't they have any sense of human values or human decency?'—Arthur Knight

Fast Workers

US 1933 68m bw

Rivalries erupt among skyscraper workers.

Standard action programmer with which MGM terminated John Gilbert's contract after an illustrious rise and dramatic fall. Also cast: Mae Clarke, Willard Mack, Robert Armstrong. Written by Laurence Stallings; directed by Tod Browning; for MGM.

The Fastest Guitar Alive

US 1966 87m Metrocolor

Inept confederate soldiers are sent on a spy mission. Ham-handed farce with music, unappealing on either count. Roy Orbison, Sammy Jackson, Maggie Pierce, Joan Freeman, Lyle Bettger. Written by Robert E. Kent; directed by Michael Moore; for Sam Katzman / MGM.

The Fastest Gun Alive*

US 1956 89m bw

MGM (Clarence Greene)

A mild-mannered western storekeeper proves to be the son of a famous gunfighter, and is put to the test.

Flimsily contrived mini-western helped by good performances.

w Frank D. Gilroy, Russel Rouse d Russel Rouse ph George Folsey m André Previn

Glenn Ford, Broderick Crawford, Jeanne Crain, Russ Tamblyn, Allyn Joslyn, Leif Erickson, John Dehner

Fat City*

US 1972 96m Eastmancolor

Columbia / Rastar (Ray Stark)

In a small Californian town, a has-been boxer tries to get back to the top, but loses his self respect and becomes a hobo.

Vivid but over-casual exploration of failure, with more interest in the characters than the sport.

w Leonard Gardner, from his novel d John
Huston ph Conrad Hall md Marvin
Hamlisch pd Richard Sylbert

Stacy Keach, Jeff Bridges, Susan Tyrell

AAN: Susan Tyrell

The Fat Man
US 1950 77m bw
U-I (Aubrey Schenck)

The murder of a dentist leads to the circus.
Dense murder mystery featuring a gourmet
17-stone detective; understandably, no series
resulted.

w Harry Essex, Leonard Lee d William
Castle ph Irving Glassberg m Bernard Green

J. Scott Smart, Rock Hudson, Julie London,
Clinton Sundberg, Jerome Cowan, Jayne
Meadows

The Fatal Glass of Beer°
US 1933 18m bw

The prodigal son returns to a snowbound
cabin in the Yukon. Absurd star comedy with
appeal to addicts only: most of the humour
consists of repeats of one line, ' 'Taint a fit
night out for man nor beast.' W. C. Fields,
Rosemary Theby, Rychard Cramer, George
Chandler. Written by Fields; directed by
Clyde Bruckman; for Paramount / Sennett.

Fatal Lady
US 1936 77m bw

An opera singer has trouble with men and
becomes involved with murder. Lively
melodrama with songs, very much of its
period. Mary Ellis, Walter Pidgeon, John
Halliday, Ruth Donnelly, Alan Mowbray,
Edgar Kennedy. Written by Jules Furthman;
directed by Edward Ludwig; for Walter
Wanger / Paramount.

The Fatal Night°
GB 1948 49m bw
(Columbia) Mario Zampi

A joke haunting has unfortunate
consequences.
A small, cheaply-made film which really
thrilled.

w Gerald Butler, story The Gentleman from
America by Michael Arlen d Mario Zampi
ph Cedric Williams m Stanley Black

Lester Ferguson, Jean Short, Leslie
Armstrong, Brenda Hogan, Patrick MacNee

Fate Is the Hunter
US 1964 106m bw Cinemascope
TCF / Arcola (Aaron Rosenberg)

An airline executive investigates the cause of a
fatal crash in which his friend the pilot was a
victim.
Watchable how-did-it happen melodrama
marred by pretentious dialogue.

w Harold Medford, novel Ernest K. Gann
d Ralph Nelson ph Milton Krasner m Jerry
Goldsmith

Glenn Ford, Rod Taylor, Nehemiah Persoff,
Nancy Kwan, Suzanne Pleshette, Jane Russell

AAN: Milton Krasner

FATHER BROWN. Alec Guinness proves to Bernard Lee that clerical detectives are not
immune from seasickness.

Father Brown°°°
GB 1954 91m bw
(Columbia) Facet (Vivian A. Cox)
US title: The Detective

A Catholic clergyman retrieves a priceless
church cross from master thief Flambeau.
Delightfully eccentric comedy based closely on
the famous character, with a sympathetic if
rather wandering script, pointed direction and
some delicious characterizations. A thoroughly
civilized entertainment.

w Thelma Schnee, story The Blue Cross by
G. K. Chesterton d Robert Hamer ph Harry
Waxman m Georges Auric

Alec Guinness, Joan Greenwood, Peter Finch,
Sidney James, Cecil Parker, Bernard Lee,
Ernest Thesiger, Marne Maitland

Father Brown Detective°
US 1934 67m bw

Flambeau, the thief, decides to steal Father
Brown's blue cross. Early attempt at the same
story used in the 1954 Father Brown with Alec
Guinness; quite pleasantly interesting. Walter
Connolly, Paul Lukas, Gertrude Michael,
Robert Loraine, Halliwell Hobbes, Una
O'Connor, E. E. Clive. 'Clean, but not strong
enough to stand solo.'—Variety

Father Came Too°
GB 1963 93m Eastmancolor
Rank / Independent Artists

Honeymooners agree to live with her
overbearing actor manager father.
Less funny sequel to The Fast Lady, with
comic household disasters striking every
couple of minutes. Easy-going, and
predictably amusing in spots.

w Jack Davies, Henry Blyth d Peter Graham
Scott ph Reg Wyer m Norrie Paramor

Stanley Baxter, James Robertson Justice, Sally
Smith, Ronnie Barker, Timothy Bateson,
Philip Locke

Father Goose°
US 1964 116m Technicolor
U-I / Granox (Robert Arthur)

During World War II a South Seas wanderer is
compelled by the Australian navy to act as sky
observer on a small island, where he finds
himself in charge of six refugee schoolchildren
and their schoolmistress.
Eager-to-please but unsatisfactory film which
wanders between farce, adventure and sex
comedy, taking too long about all of them.

w Peter Stone, Frank Tarloff d Ralph Nelson
ph Charles Lang Jnr m Cy Coleman

Cary Grant, Leslie Caron, Trevor Howard

(Cary Grant): 'Let me tell you I am not a
father figure. I am not a brother figure or an
uncle figure or a cousin figure. In fact, the only
figure I intend being is a total stranger figure.'

'Reasoning would indicate a made-to-order Christmas package for the family trade. However, the more sophisticated may be bored and exasperated after some of the initial brightness wears off.'—*Cue*

'Cary Grant wrings what there is to be wrung from the role, but never quite enough to conceal the fact that *Father Goose* is a waste of his talent and the audience's time.'—*Arthur Knight*

AA: Peter Stone, Frank Tarloff

Father Is a Bachelor
US 1950 85m bw
Columbia (S. Sylvan Simon)

A young tramp cares for a family of orphaned children.
Boringly sentimental semi-western.

w Aleen Leslie, James Edward Grant
d Norman Foster, Abby Berlin ph Burnett Guffey m Arthur Morton

William Holden, Coleen Gray, Charles Winninger, Stuart Erwin, Sig Rumann

'Saccharine, paper thin. At least one spectator at the Palace yesterday couldn't take it—a tot of about four, wearing a cowboy suit, who aimed a toy pistol at the screen and popped off the cast one by one.'—*New York Times*

Father Is a Prince: see Big Hearted Herbert

'The bride gets the thrills! Father gets the bills!'
Father of the Bride**
US 1950 93m bw
MGM (Pandro S. Berman)

A dismayed but happy father surveys the cost and chaos of his daughter's marriage.
Fragmentary but mainly delightful suburban comedy which finds Hollywood in its best light vein and benefits from a strong central performance.

w Frances Goodrich, Albert Hackett, novel Edward Streeter d Vincente Minnelli ph John Alton m Adolph Deutsch

Spencer Tracy, Joan Bennett, Elizabeth Taylor, Don Taylor, Billie Burke, Moroni Olsen, Leo G. Carroll, Taylor Holmes, Melville Cooper

'The idealization of a safe sheltered existence, the good life according to MGM: 24 carat complacency.'—*New Yorker, 1980*

† Jack Benny badly wanted the role but was thought unsuitable.

AAN: best picture; Frances Goodrich, Albert Hackett; Spencer Tracy

Father Takes a Wife*
US 1941 80m bw
RKO (Lee S. Marcus)

A famous actress marries a shipping magnate and runs into resentment from her children.
Disappointing comedy with a script too flat for the stars to make interesting.

w Dorothy and Herbert Fields d Jack Hively ph Robert de Grasse m Roy Webb

Gloria Swanson, Adolphe Menjou, Desi Arnaz, John Howard, Helen Broderick, Florence Rice, Neil Hamilton

Father Was a Fullback
US 1949 84m bw
TCF (Fred Kohlmar)

The coach of a college football team has domestic problems.
Thin star comedy, strictly double bill.

w Aleen Leslie, Casey Robinson, Richard Sale, Mary Loos, play Clifford Goldsmith d John M. Stahl ph Lloyd Ahern m Cyril Mockridge

Fred MacMurray, Maureen O'Hara, Betty Lynn, Natalie Wood, Rudy Vallee, Jim Backus

Father's Doing Fine
GB 1952 83m Technicolor

An impoverished lady has trouble with her daughters, one of whom is pregnant.
Agreeable madcap farce from a long-running stage success (so why did they change the title?). Heather Thatcher, Richard Attenborough, Susan Stephen, Noel Purcell, George Thorpe. Written by Anne Burnaby, from the play *Little Lambs Eat Ivy* by Noel Langley; directed by Henry Cass; for Marble Arch / ABP.

Father's Little Dividend
US 1951 81m bw
MGM (Pandro S. Berman)

Sequel to *Father of the Bride*, in which the newlyweds have a baby.
A very flat follow-up, palatable enough at the time but quite unmemorable.

w Frances Goodrich, Albert Hackett d Vincente Minnelli ph John Alton m Albert Sandrey

Spencer Tracy, Joan Bennett, Elizabeth Taylor, Don Taylor, Billie Burke, Moroni Olsen, Frank Faylen, Marietta Canty, Russ Tamblyn

'The world's most uncovered undercover agent!'
Fathom
GB 1967 99m De Luxe Franscope
TCF (John Kohn)

Adventures of a glamorous sky-diving spy.
Watchable romp with nothing memorable about it.

w Lorenzo Semple Jnr, novel Larry Forrester d Leslie Martinson ph Douglas Slocombe, Ken Vos m Johnny Dankworth

Raquel Welch, Tony Franciosa, Clive Revill, Ronald Fraser, Greta Chi, Richard Briers, Tom Adams

'Belongs not in the category of High Camp but in that of Good Wholesome Fun.'—*MFB*

Fatso
US 1980 93m De Luxe

A fat man fails to make much headway at slimming, and gives up. Unappealing mixture

of sentiment, satire, shouting and crude humour. Dom DeLuise, Anne Bancroft, Ron Carey, Candice Azzara. Written and directed by Anne Bancroft; for Brooksfilms / TCF. 'As bumbling and sluggish as its title might suggest, a lamentable affair which ricochets uncontrollably between attempts at hilarity and pathos.'—*Variety*.

Faust**
Germany 1926 100m approx bw silent
UFA

A superbly stylish version of the legend about a man who sells his soul to the devil. The best of many silent versions; see also *All That Money Can Buy*.

w Hans Kyser d F. W. Murnau ph Carl Hoffman

Emil Jannings, Gosta Ekman, Camilla Horn, Yvette Guilbert, William Dieterle

The FBI Story*
US 1959 149m Technicolor
Warner (Mervyn Le Roy)

An FBI agent thinks back on his career with the bureau.
Predictable mix of domestic sentimentality (very trying) and competent crime capsules: mad bomber, Ku Klux Klan, thirties hoodlums, Nazi spy rings and the cold war.

w Richard L. Breen, John Twist d Mervyn Le Roy ph Joseph Biroc m Max Steiner ad John Beckman

James Stewart, Vera Miles, Larry Pennell, Nick Adams, Murray Hamilton

'Insufferably cosy.'—*MFB*

● *Video: Warner*

Fear
US 1946 68m bw
Monogram

A student kills his professor, and a detective taunts him to the point of confession.
Cheeky second feature version of *Crime and Punishment*, with a twist ending. Not too bad in its way.

w Alfred Zeisler, Dennis Cooper d Alfred Zeisler ph Jackson Rose

Warren William, Peter Cookson, Anne Gwynne, Nestor Paiva

Fear Eats the Soul*
West Germany 1973 92m colour
Tango Film (Christian Hohoff)

A Moroccan immigrant in Munich comes up against social and racial prejudice when he marries a sixty-year-old charwoman.
Unexceptional moral tale which can hardly have been necessary in view of the infrequency of such cases.

wd Rainer Werner Fassbinder ph Jürgen Jürges

Brigitti Mira, El Hedi Ben Salem, Barbara Valentin, Irm Hermann, Rainer Werner Fassbinder

● *Video: Palace*

Fear in the Night**
US 1947 72m bw
Maxwell Shane

A man suffering from a strange nightmare discovers he has been hypnotized into committing a murder.

Intriguing small-scale puzzler later remade to less effect as *Nightmare* (qv). Adequate performances and handling, but the plot's the thing.

wd Maxwell Shane *ph* Jack Grennhalgh *m* Rudy Schraeger

Paul Kelly, De Forrest Kelley, Ann Doran, Kay Scott

Fear in the Night*
GB 1972 85m Technicolor
Hammer (Jimmy Sangster)

A girl recovering from a nervous breakdown is deluded into committing a murder.

Yet another variant on *Les Diaboliques*, ingeniously worked out with good touches of detail to produce an air of general competence.

w Jimmy Sangster, Michael Syson *d* Jimmy Sangster *ph* Arthur Grant *m* John McCabe

Peter Cushing, Judy Geeson, Joan Collins, Ralph Bates

● *Video: Thorn EMI*

Fear Is the Key*
GB 1972 108m Technicolor
  Panavision
EMI / KLK (Alan Ladd Jnr, Elliott Kastner)

A man conceives an elaborate plot to track down those responsible for killing his wife and family in a plane crash.

Reasonably absorbing, surprise-plotted thriller.

w Robert Carrington, *novel* Alistair MacLean *d* Michael Tuchner *ph* Alex Thomson *m* Roy Budd

Suzy Kendall, Barry Newman, John Vernon, Dolph Sweet, Ben Kingsley, Ray McAnally

● *Video: Thorn EMI*

Fear Strikes Out
US 1957 100m bw Vistavision
Paramount / Alan Pakula

A father wants his son to become a professional baseball player, and the son in consequence suffers a nervous breakdown. Rather flat biopic of Jim Piersall; well-intentioned and careful in its psychological insights, but too often just plain dull.

w Ted Berkman, Raphael Blau *d* Robert Mulligan *ph* Haskell Boggs *m* Elmer Bernstein

Anthony Perkins, Karl Malden, Norma Moore, Perry Wilson

Fearless Fagan
US 1952 78m bw

A circus clown is enlisted and takes his pet lion along. Rather silly comedy padded out with sentimentality. Carleton Carpenter, Janet

Leigh, Keenan Wynn, Richard Anderson, Ellen Corby. Written by Charles Lederer; directed by Stanley Donen; for MGM.

The Fearless Vampire Killers, or Pardon Me, Your Teeth Are in My Neck*
US 1967 124m Metrocolor Panavision
MGM / Cadre Films / Filmways (Gene
  Gutowski)
aka: *Dance of the Vampires*

A professor and his assistant stake a Transylvanian vampire.

Heavy, slow spoof of *Dracula*, most of which shows that sense of humour is very personal; a few effective moments hardly compensate for the prevailing stodge.

w Gerard Brach, Roman Polanski *d* Roman Polanski *ph* Douglas Slocombe *m* Krzystof Komeda *pd* Wilfrid Shingleton

Jack McGowran, Roman Polanski, Alfie Bass, Sharon Tate, *Ferdy Mayne*, Iain Quarrier, Terry Downes

'An engaging oddity . . . long stretches might have been lifted intact from any Hammer horror.'—*Tom Milne*
† A credit ran: Fangs by Dr Ludwig von Krankheit.

The Fearmakers
US 1958 85m bw
Pacemaker (Martin H. Lancer)

A brainwashed Korean War veteran returns to Washington and finds that his PR firm has been taken over by communist racketeers. Unusual but cheaply made anti-Red propaganda, too talkative to be very entertaining.

w Elliot West, Chris Appley, *novel* Darwin Teilhet *d* Jacques Tourneur *ph* Sam Leavitt *m* Irving Gertz

Dana Andrews, Dick Foran, Mel Tormé

A Feather in Her Hat
US 1935 72m bw
Columbia

A London widow with delusions of grandeur tells her son that his real mother was a famous actress.

Outmoded mother-love drama, interestingly cast.

w Lawrence Hazard, *story* I. A. R. Wylie *d* Alfred Santell *ph* Joseph Walker

Pauline Lord, Basil Rathbone, Louis Hayward, Billie Burke, Wendy Barrie, J. M. Kerrigan, Victor Varconi, Nydia Westman, Thurston Hall

'Too British for general appeal, though well acted.'—*Variety*

Feather Your Nest*
GB 1937 86m bw
ATP (Basil Dean)

A gramophone record technician substitutes his own voice for a star and becomes world famous.

The star in less farcical vein than usual; this is the one in which he sings 'Leaning on a Lamp-post'.

w Austin Melford, Robert Edmunds, Anthony Kimmins *d* William Beaudine

George Formby, Polly Ward, Enid Stamp Taylor, Val Rosing, Davy Burnaby

Fedora*
West Germany / France 1978 110m
  Eastmancolor
Geria / SFP (Billy Wilder)

An ageing star who seems miraculously to have kept her beauty comes out of retirement. *Sunset Boulevard* revisited, with a less bitter approach and less effectiveness; but any civilized film is welcome in the late seventies.

w I. A. L. Diamond, Billy Wilder, from a story in Crowned Heads by Tom Tryon *d* Billy Wilder *ph* Gerry Fisher *m* Miklos Rozsa

William Holden, Marthe Keller, Hildgarde Knef, Jose Ferrer, Mario Adorf, Henry Fonda, Michael York

'Rife with Wilderean gallows humour and a sumptuous sense of decay in never-never land.'—*Sight and Sound*

● *Video: Thorn EMI*

'A thrill a minute! A laugh a second! A comedy cyclone!'

Feet First**
US 1930 88m bw
Harold Lloyd

A shoe salesman gets entangled with crooks and has a narrow escape when hanging from the side of a building.

Very funny early talkie comedy, probably the comedian's last wholly satisfactory film.

w Lex Neal, Felix Adler, Paul Gerard Smith *d* Clyde Bruckman *ph* Walter Ludin, Henry Kohler

Harold Lloyd, Robert McWade, Barbara Kent

'That Lloyd was a bit pressed for laughs may be guessed from the fact that he is again dangling from the front of a skyscraper.'—*Variety*

Female*
US 1933 60m bw

A high-powered lady president of a motor car company has a secret night life. Slick star vehicle reminiscent of *Peg's Paper* but absorbing while on screen. *Ruth Chatterton*, George Brent, Johnny Mack Brown, Ruth Donnelly, Douglass Dumbrille, Lois Wilson. Written by Gene Markey and Kathryn Scola, from a story by Donald Henderson Clarke; directed by Michael Curtiz and William Dieterle; for Warner. 'The story is worthy neither of this actress nor of the high-grade production.'—*Variety*

The Female Animal
US 1957 82m bw Cinemascope
U-I (Albert Zugsmith)

A beach bum becomes the lover of a film star, then falls in love with her daughter.

Dreary and humourless melodrama notable only for the comeback appearance of one of the screen's legendary glamour queens.

w Robert Hill d Harry Keller ph Russell Metty m Hans Salter

Hedy Lamarr, Jan Sterling, Jane Powell, George Nader, James Gleason

'Once she was too hungry for love to be afraid—but now—it was too late!'
The Female on the Beach
US 1955 97m bw
U-I (Albert Zugsmith)

A wealthy widow visits her late husband's beach house and falls for the gigolo next door, who later seems intent on murdering her.
Absurd and jaded melodrama, a rehash of *Love from a Stranger*, enlivened by some hilarious love-hate dialogue.

w Robert Hill, Richard Alan Simmons d Joseph Pevney ph Charles Lang m Joseph Gershenson

Joan Crawford, Jeff Chandler, Jan Sterling, Cecil Kellaway, Natalie Schaefer
(Joan Crawford) to Jeff Chandler: 'I would have you if you were hung with diamonds, upside down!'

The Feminine Touch
US 1941 97m bw
MGM (Joseph L. Mankiewicz)

A professor gets into woman trouble when he writes a book about jealousy.
Matrimonial comedy rather less interesting than its credits suggest.

w George Oppenheimer, Edmund L. Hartmann, Ogden Nash d W. S. Van Dyke m Franz Waxman

Rosalind Russell, Don Ameche, Kay Francis, Van Heflin, Donald Meek, Henry Daniell, Sidney Blackmer

The Feminine Touch
GB 1956 91m Technicolor
Ealing (Jack Rix)

Five young student nurses arrive at St Augustine's Hospital.
Portmanteau soap opera of no absorbing interest.

w (anon.) from the novel A Lamp is Heavy by Sheila Mackay Russell d Pat Jackson ph Paul Beeson m Clifton Parker

George Baker, Belinda Lee, Delphi Lawrence, Adrienne Corri, Henryetta Edwards, Barbara Archer, Diana Wynyard, Mandy Miller

La Femme de Nulle Part*
France 1922 70m approx bw silent
aka: *The Woman from Nowhere*

A woman who feels that her life has been ruined through love returns home and persuades a young girl not to do the same.
A minor atmospheric piece of some power, comparable with *Partie de Campagne* and cinematically very interesting.

wd *Louis Delluc* ph Lucas Gibory ad F. Jourdain

Eve Francis, Roger Karl, Gine Avril

La Femme du Boulanger**
France 1938 110m bw
Marcel Pagnol
aka: *The Baker's Wife*

Villagers put a stop to the infidelity of the baker's wife because her husband no longer has the heart to make good bread.
Best-known of Pagnol's rustic fables, this rather obvious and long-drawn-out joke is important because international critics hailed it as a work of art (which it isn't) and because it fixed an image of the naughty bucolic French.

wd *Marcel Pagnol, novel* Jean Le Bleu by Jean Giono ph G. Benoit, R. Lendruz, N. Daries m Vincent Scotto

Raimu, Ginette Leclerc, Charles Moulin, Charpin, Maximilienne
'It is a long film with a small subject, but the treatment is so authentic that it seems over far too soon, and the acting is superb.'—*Graham Greene*

La Femme Infidèle**
France / Italy 1968 98m Eastmancolor
La Boétie / Cinégai (André Génovès)
aka: *The Unfaithful Wife*

A middle-aged insurance broker, set in his ways, murders his wife's lover; when she suspects the truth, they are drawn closer together.
Almost a Bunuel-like black comedy, spare and quiet, with immaculate performances.

wd *Claude Chabrol* ph Jean Rabier m Pierre Jansen

Stéphane Audran, Michel Bouquet, Maurice Ronet
'On any level, this bizarre murder framed by whiskies emerges as Chabrol's most flawless work to date.'—*Jan Dawson, MFB*

Femmes de Paris*
France 1954 85m approx Agfacolor
Optimax-Lux (Edgar Bacquet)
aka: *Ah! Les Belles Bacchantes*

A touring revue is almost run out of town for indecency.
A rather crude but quite valuable record of Dhéry's stage revue, which convulsed London in the fifties.

w Robert Dhéry d Jean Loubignac ph René Colas m Gérard Calvi

Robert Dhéry, Colette Brosset, Louis de Funès, Raymond Bussières, the Bluebell Girls

La Ferme du Pendu*
France 1946 90m bw
Corona
aka: *Hanged Man's Farm*

The lecherous son of a farming family brings tragedy to the lives of himself and his brothers and sister.
Cold Comfort Farm with a vengeance, appropriately played: arrant melodrama, but watchable.

w André-Paul Antoine d Jean Dréville ph André Thomas

Alfred Adam, Charles Vanel, Arlette Merry

Ferry to Hong Kong
GB 1958 113m Eastmancolor
Cinemascope
Rank (George Maynard)

An Austrian layabout can land at neither of the Hong Kong ferry's ports of call, but shows his true worth when a typhoon strikes.
Silly storyline and rampant bad acting ruin the Rank Organization's first attempt at an international epic.

w Vernon Harris, Lewis Gilbert d Lewis Gilbert ph Otto Heller m Kenneth V. Jones

Curt Jurgens, Sylvia Syms, Orson Welles, Jeremy Spenser, Noel Purcell

La Fête à Henriette*
France 1952 113m bw
Regina-Filmsonor
aka: *Holiday for Henrietta*

Two screenwriters disagree whether or not to give their hero and heroine a happy ending.
A rather heavy-handed romantic joke which does have its moments and was later—fatally—Americanized as *Paris When It Sizzles*.

w Julien Duvivier, Henri Jeanson d Julien Duvivier ph Roger Hubert m Georges Auric

Dany Robin, Michel Auclair, Hildegarde Neff, Michel Roux, Saturnin Fabre, Julien Carette

Feudin', Fussin' and A-fightin'
US 1948 78m bw

A fast-running travelling salesman is kidnapped by a hillbilly town which needs him in its annual sports. Unpretentious lower-berth comedy for middle America. Donald O'Connor, Marjorie Main, Percy Kilbride, Penny Edwards, Joe Besser. Written by D. D. Beauchamp; directed by George Sherman; for Universal-International.

Le Feu Follet*
France / Italy 1963 110m bw
Nouvelles Editions / Arco
aka: *Will o' the Wisp; A Time to Live and a Time to Die*

The last 24 hours, before his suicide, in the life of an ex-alcoholic playboy.
Not quite as weary as it sounds, and full of admirable touches, this is nevertheless a fairly downbeat film and a pointless one.

wd *Louis Malle, ph* Ghislain Cloquet m Erik Satie

Maurice Ronet, Léna Skerla, Yvonne Clech, Hubert Deschamps, Jeanne Moreau

A Fever in the Blood
US 1960 117m bw
Warner (Roy Huggins)

Candidates for governor sharpen their campaigns on a murder trial.
Interestingly-cast, flabbily-written melodrama.

w Roy Huggins, Harry Kleiner, *novel* William Pearson d Vincent Sherman ph J. Peverell Marley m Ernest Gold

Efrem Zimbalist Jnr, Angie Dickinson, Don
Ameche, Herbert Marshall, Jack Kelly, Ray
Danton, Jesse White, Rhodes Reason, Robert
Colbert

Fiddler on the Roof**
US 1971   180m   Technicolor
Panavision 70
UA / Mirisch (Norman Jewison)

In a pre-revolutionary Russian village, Tevye
the Jewish milkman survives family and
political problems and when the pogroms
begin cheerfully emigrates to America.
Self-conscious, grittily realistic adaptation of
the stage musical, with slow and heavy patches
in its grossly overlong celebration of a
vanished way of life. The big moments still
come off well though the songs tend to be
thrown away and the photography is
unnecessarily murky.

w Joseph Stein, from his play and Sholom
Aleichem's story Tevye and his Daughters
d Norman Jewison ph Oswald Morris
m Jerry Bock md John Williams pd Robert
Boyle ly Sheldon Harnick

Topol, Norma Crane, Leonard Frey, Molly
Picon
  'Jewison hasn't so much directed a film as
prepared a product for world consumption.'—
Stanley Kauffmann

AA: Oswald Morris; John Williams
AAN: best picture; Norman Jewison (as
director); Topol; Leonard Frey

● Video: Intervision

Fiddlers Three*
GB 1944   87m   bw
Ealing (Robert Hamer)

Sailors struck by lightning on Salisbury Plain
are transported back to ancient Rome.
Sequel to Sailors Three; despite a harsh and
unattractive look, every conceivable joke
about old Romans is deftly mined and the
good humour flows free.

w Diana Morgan, Angus Macphail d Harry
Watt ph Wilkie Cooper m Spike Hughes

Tommy Trinder, Sonnie Hale, Frances Day,
Francis L. Sullivan, Ernest Milton, Diana
Decker, Elizabeth Welch, Mary Clare

'Don't be ashamed to scream! Everyone in
   the theatre will be screaming with you!'
The Fiend Who Walked the West
US 1958   101m   bw   Cinemascope
TCF (Herbert B. Swope Jnr)

A sadistic killer released from prison tracks
down the associates of a cellmate and
terrorizes the district.
Western remake of Kiss of Death, with
babyface Robert Evans in the Widmark role.
Violent and dull.

w Harry Brown, Philip Yordan d Gordon
Douglas ph Joe MacDonald m Leon
Klatzkin

Hugh O'Brian, Dolores Michaels, Robert
Evans, Linda Cristal, Stephen McNally,
Edward Andrews

The Fiend without a Face
GB 1957   75m   bw
Producers' Associates (John Croydon)

A scientist working on materialized thought
produces monsters from his own id.
Tepid shocker with well-organized mobile
brains.

w H. J. Leder d Arthur Crabtree ph Lionel
Banes m Buxton Orr sp Ruppel and
Nordhoff

Kynaston Reeves, Terry Kilburn, Marshall
Thompson

The Fiendish Plot of Dr Fu Manchu
US 1980   108m   Technicolor
Warner / Orion / Playboy (Hugh Hefner)

The 'yellow peril' returns to the western world
to mastermind diamond thefts.
Feeble spoof with a history of production
troubles; clearly the only thing in anybody's
mind was to get it over with.

w Jim Moloney, Rudy Dochtermann d Piers
Haggard ph Jean Tournier m Marc
Wilkinson pd Alexander Trauner

Peter Sellers, Helen Mirren, David
Tomlinson, Sid Caesar, Simon Williams, Steve
Franken, Stratford Johns, John Le Mesurier,
Clive Dunn

● Video: Warner

The Fiercest Heart
US 1961   90m   De Luxe   Cinemascope
TCF (George Sherman)

A British army deserter joins a Boer trek into
South Africa.
Pioneer 'western', poorly done but with
novelty value.

w Edmund H. North, novel Stuart Cloete
d George Sherman ph Ellis Carter m Irving
Gertz

Stuart Whitman, Juliet Prowse, Raymond
Massey, Ken Scott, Geraldine Fitzgerald,
Rafer Johnson

Fiesta
US 1947   102m   Technicolor
MGM (Jack Cummings)

A young Mexican wants to be a musician
though his father insists he should be a
bullfighter.
An extremely boring idea for a musical which
at best is a tedious time-passer.

w George Bruce, Lester Cole d Richard
Thorpe ph Sidney Wagner, Charles Rosner,
William Cline m Aaron Copland

Esther Williams, Ricardo Montalban, Cyd
Charisse, Mary Astor, John Carroll, Akim
Tamiroff, Hugo Haas

Fièvre*
France 1921   50m approx   bw   silent
Alhambra

A brawl in a Marseilles bar ends in murder.
A dramatic sketch, filmed with remarkable
detail and artistry.

wd Louis Delluc ph A. Gibory ad Bécan

Eve Francis, Edmond Van Daele, Gaston
Modot

Fifi la Plume
France 1964   80m   bw
Les Films Montsouris (Albert Lamorisse)

A burglar becomes a circus bird-man, learns to
fly, and is everywhere mistaken for an angel.
A likeable fantasy idea which doesn't quite
come off, alternating uneasily between
slapstick and sentiment.

wd Albert Lamorisse ph Pierre Petit m Jean-
Michel Defaye

Philippe Avron, Mireille Nègre, Henri
Lambert, Raoul Delfosse

Fifth Avenue Girl*
US 1939   83m   bw
RKO (Gregory La Cava)

An unemployed girl is persuaded by a
millionaire to pose as a gold digger and annoy
his avaricious family.
Brightish comedy of the Cinderella kind.

w Allan Scott d Gregory La Cava ph Robert
de Grasse

Ginger Rogers, Walter Connolly, Verree
Teasdale, Tim Holt, James Ellison, Franklin
Pangborn, Kathryn Adams, Louis Calhern
  'Substantial comedy drama for top
grosses.'—Variety

The Fifth Musketeer
Austria 1978   106m   Eastmancolor
Sascha-Wien Film / Ted Richmond

Louis XIII and his twin brother Philippe vie
for the crown of France.
Virtually a remake of The Man in the Iron
Mask, with patchy style and a few excisable
sex scenes added. The 1939 version was better.

w David Ambrose d Ken Annakin ph Jack
Cardiff m Riz Ortolani

Beau Bridges, Sylvia Kristel, Ursula Andress,
Cornel Wilde (as D'Artagnan), Lloyd Bridges,
Alan Hale Jnr, Jose Ferrer (the ageing
musketeers), Rex Harrison (Colbert), Olivia
de Havilland (Queen Anne), Ian McShane,
Helmut Dantine

55 Days at Peking*
US / Spain 1962   154m   Super
Technirama 70
Samuel Bronston

In 1900 Peking, Boxer fanatics are encouraged
by the Empress to take over the city and
besiege the international diplomatic quarter;
an American major leads the defence.
Spasmodically lively action spectacular
weighed down by romantic stretches.

w Philip Yordan, Bernard Gordon d Nicholas
Ray, Andrew Marton ph Jack Hildyard,
Manuel Berenguer m Dmitri Tiomkin
ad Venerio Colasanti, John Moore

Charlton Heston, David Niven, Ava Gardner,
Flora Robson, Robert Helpmann, Leo Genn,
Paul Lukas, John Ireland, Harry Andrews,
Elizabeth Sellars, Massimo Serrato, Jacques
Sernas, Geoffrey Bayldon
  'An open-air western in Chinese.'—David
Niven

'Pictorially this is a beautiful film, but the characters are conventional siege figures.'—*Sunday Times*

AAN: Dmitri Tiomkin; song 'So Little Time' (*m* Dmitri Tiomkin, *ly* Paul Francis Webster)

Fifty Million Frenchmen
US 1931 68m Technicolor

A rich American in Paris tries to prove that he was able to win a blonde without the aid of his bankroll. Much changed and enfeebled version of a Broadway musical, with the Broadway talent transplanted. Olsen and Johnson, William Gaxton, John Halliday, Helen Broderick, Claudia Dell, Lester Crawford. Written by Al Boasberg, Eddie Welch, Joseph Jackson; directed by Lloyd Bacon; for Warners. 'Will have to depend mostly on its title for b.o. attraction.'—*Variety*

Fifty Roads to Town*
US 1937 80m bw

Mistaken identities abound in a snowbound cabin. Fairly funny minor comedy. Don Ameche, Ann Sothern, Slim Summerville, Jane Darwell, John Qualen, Douglas Fowley, Stepin Fetchit. Written by George Marion Jnr and William Conselman; directed by Norman Taurog; for TCF. 'Just about right for summer audiences . . . pleasant light romantic comedy demanding a minimum of concentration.'—*Variety*

52nd Street
US 1937 83m bw

A strictly-brought-up young woman shocks her family by falling for a singer. Tame romantic comedy with musical items. Kenny Baker, Ella Logan, Ian Hunter, Zasu Pitts, Leo Carrillo. Written by Grover Jones; directed by Harold Young; for Walter Wanger. 'It may have been a good idea to make a film about the metamorphosing of 52nd Street into a lane of niteries, but the conception doesn't come through . . . filmgoers are likely to wonder what it's all about, and why.'—*Variety*

Fight for Your Lady*
US 1937 67m bw

A jilted tenor is helped by a wrestling trainer. Odd little comedy which contrives to amuse. John Boles, Jack Oakie, Ida Lupino, Margot Grahame, Erik Rhodes, Billy Gilbert. Written by Ernest Pagano, Harry Segall, Harold Kusell; directed by Ben Stoloff; for RKO. 'This picture is going to entertain whether it sells or not.'—*Variety*

The Fighter
US 1952 78m bw
GH (Alex Gottlieb)

A Mexican fisherman whose family is murdered by government troops becomes a prizefighter to earn money for the rebels. A rather glum attempt to turn a few ringside clichés.

w Aben Kandel, Herbert Kline, *story* The Mexican by Jack London *d* Herbert Kline *ph* James Wong Howe *m* Vincente Gomez

Richard Conte, Vanessa Brown, Lee J. Cobb, Frank Silvera

Fighter Squadron
US 1948 96m Technicolor
Warner (Seton I. Miller)

In World War II, a dedicated flier risks his friends' lives.
Routine aerial actioner.

w Seton I. Miller *d* Raoul Walsh *ph* Sid Hickox, Wilfrid M. Cline *m* Max Steiner

Edmond O'Brien, Robert Stack, John Rodney, Tom D'Andrea, Henry Hull, Walter Reed, Shepperd Strudwick, Rock Hudson

Fighting Back
US 1982 98m Technicolor
Dino de Laurentiis (D. Constantine Conte)
GB title: *Death Vengeance*

After his wife and mother are both injured in crimes of violence, a delicatessen owner forms a vigilante group and is backed to some extent by police and businessmen.
Smartly made but ethically muddled urban shocker.

w Tom Hedley, David Zelag Goodman *d* Lewis Teague *ph* Franco DiGiacomo *m* Piero Piccioni

Tom Skerritt, Michael Sarrazin, Patti LuPone, Yaphet Kotto, David Rasche

Fighting Back
Australia 1982 100m Eastmancolor

A teenager runs riot at home and at school. Tolerable problem picture with no surprises. Lewis FitzGerald, Kris McQuade, Caroline Gillmer, Paul Smith. Written by Tom Jeffrey, Michael Cove, from the book Tom by John Embling; directed by Michael Caulfield; for Samson.

● *Video: Iver*

Fighting Caravans
US 1931 91m bw

A covered wagon party faces various dangers. Slow-moving western. Gary Cooper, Lily Damita, Ernest Torrence, Fred Kohler, Tully Marshall, Eugene Pallette. Written by E. E. Paramore Jnr, Keene Thompson, Agnes Leahy, from the novel by Zane Grey; directed by Otto Brower and David Burton; for Paramount. 'Very mild western, rating de luxe house attention on the cast names . . . lacks a punch.'—*Variety*

Fighting Father Dunne
US 1948 93m bw
RKO (Phil L. Ryan)

A clergyman looks after unfortunate boys. A slum melodrama which all concerned could have made with their eyes closed, and probably did.

w Martin Rackin, Frank Davis *d* Ted Tetzlaff *ph* George E. Diskant *m* Roy Webb

Pat O'Brien, Darryl Hickman, Charles Kemper, Una O'Connor

Fighting Man of the Plains
US 1949 94m Cinecolor

A reformed outlaw becomes marshal but is exposed. Tolerable western with familiar elements. Randolph Scott, Bill Williams, Victor Jory, Jane Nigh, Douglas Kennedy. Written by Frank Gruber; directed by Edwin L. Marin; for Nat Holt / (TCF).

The Fighting Guardsman
US 1945 84m bw

Under the tyrannical reign of Louis XVI a young nobleman leads a peasants' revolt. Stiff swashbuckler in which the actors appear to have been only recently introduced to their clothes. Willard Parker, Anita Louise, George Macready, John Loder. Written by Franz Spencer and Edward Dein; directed by Henry Levin; for Columbia.

The Fighting Kentuckian
US 1949 100m bw
Republic (John Wayne)

In 1810 a farmer combats land-grabbing criminals.
Standard star western for the family.

wd George Waggner *ph* Lee Garmes *m* George Antheil

John Wayne, Vera Ralston, Oliver Hardy, Philip Dorn, Marie Windsor, Mae Marsh

Fighting Mad
US 1976 90m De Luxe
TCF / Santa Fe (Roger Corman)

A rancher and his son are murdered by a local industrialist who wants their land, and the rancher's city-bred son takes revenge.
Another vigilante western in modern dress, very laborious and violent without being very exciting.

wd Jonathan Demme *ph* Bill Birch *m* Bruce Langhorne

Peter Fonda, Lynn Lowry, John Doucette, Philip Carey, Scott Glen

'Demme has allowed violence to outweigh ideas to such a degree that the picture becomes a turnoff, little more than a blatantly obvious play to the yahoo mentality.'—*Kevin Thomas, Los Angeles Times*

The Fighting O'Flynn
US 1949 94m bw
U-I (Douglas Fairbanks Jnr)

In 18th-century Ireland, a penniless young adventurer aborts Napoleon's plan for invasion.
Lively minor-league adventure.

w Douglas Fairbanks Jnr, Robert Thoeren, *novel* Justin Huntly McCarthy *d* Arthur Pierson *ph* Arthur Edeson *m* Frank Skinner

Douglas Fairbanks Jnr, Helena Carter, Richard Greene, Patricia Medina, Arthur Shields, J. M. Kerrigan

'Fairbanks plays the irrepressible O'Flynn with unflagging energy and tongue in cheek good humour; the rest of the cast stolidly refuses to see the joke.'—*MFB*

The Fighting Prince of Donegal
GB 1966   104m   Technicolor
Walt Disney (Bill Anderson)

Adventures of an Irish rebel in the reign of Elizabeth I.
Adequate Boys' Own Paper romp.

w Robert Westerby, *novel* Red Hugh, Prince of Donegal by Robert T. Reilly d Michael O'Herlihy ph Arthur Ibbetson m George Bruns

Peter McEnery, Susan Hampshire, Tom Adams, Gordon Jackson, Andrew Keir, Norman Woolland, Richard Leech

The Fighting Seabees
US 1944   100m   bw
Republic (Albert J. Cohen)

During World War II in the Pacific, construction workers attack the Japanese.
Routine, studio-staged war melodrama, heavily fleshed out with love interest.

w Borden Chase, Aeneas Mackenzie d Edward Ludwig ph William Bradford m Walter Scharf, Roy Webb

John Wayne, Susan Hayward, Dennis O'Keefe, William Frawley, Duncan Renaldo, Addison Richards, Leonid Kinskey, Paul Fix

AAN: Walter Scharf, Roy Webb

The Fighting 69th*
US 1940   89m   bw
Warner (Hal B. Wallis)

During World War I in the trenches, a cocky recruit becomes a hero and loses his life in the process.
Recruiting poster stuff, all well enough done but bewildering in its changes of mood.

w Norman Reilly Raine, Fred Niblo Jnr, Dean Franklin d William Keighley ph Tony Gaudio m Adolph Deutsch

James Cagney, Pat O'Brien, George Brent, Jeffrey Lynn, Alan Hale, Frank McHugh, Dennis Morgan, Dick Foran, William Lundigan, Guinn Williams, John Litel, Henry O'Neill

  'The picture is better if you can manage to forget the plot and think of it instead as the human, amusing and frequently gripping record of a regiment marching off to war.'— *Frank Nugent, New York Times*

Fighting Stock
GB 1935   68m   bw

The family gets together to save a girl from a blackmailer. Fair example of the Aldwych farces, with the trio in good form. Tom Walls, Ralph Lynn, Robertson Hare, Marie Lohr, Lesley Waring. Written by Ben Travers; directed by Tom Walls; for Gaumont.

The Figurehead*
GB 1952   8m   Technicolor

A carved saint is turned into a figurehead and can't respond when a mermaid falls in love with him. Pleasant whimsy, one of the better jobs from this team of animators. Narrated by Robert Beatty; animation and production by John Halas and Joy Batchelor; from a poem by Crosbie Garstin.

Figures in a Landscape
GB 1970   110m   Technicolor
  Panavision
Cinecrest (John Kohn)

Two men on the run are pursued by soldiers and helicopters; only one crosses the frontier.
Portentous Pinterish parable, very long-winded and relentlessly boring though good to look at. Everything is symbolic, nothing is specific, not even the country.

w Robert Shaw, *novel* Barry England d Joseph Losey ph Henri Alekan m Richard Rodney Bennett

Robert Shaw, Malcolm McDowell

The File of the Golden Goose
GB 1969   109m   De Luxe
UA / Theme / Caralan / Dador (David E. Rose)

An American agent works with Scotland Yard to track down counterfeiters.
Incredibly predictable spy thriller which almost makes an eccentricity out of collecting so many clichés and so many tourist views of London. Like ten TV episodes cut together.

w John C. Higgins, James B. Gordon d Sam Wanamaker ph Ken Hodges m Harry Robinson

Yul Brynner, Edward Woodward, Charles Gray, John Barrie, Bernard Archard, Ivor Dean, Adrienne Corri, Graham Crowden, Karel Stepanek

  'The film plods wearily homewards through an exceptionally uninteresting batch of fights, intrigues and sinister encounters.'—*MFB*

The File on Thelma Jordon*
US 1949   100m   bw
Paramount (Hal B. Wallis)
aka: *Thelma Jordon*

A district attorney falls for a murder suspect and has her acquitted by losing the case.
Stylishly made, murkily plotted melodrama and a superior star vehicle of its time.

w Ketti Frings d Robert Siodmak ph George Barnes m Victor Young

Barbara Stanwyck, Wendell Corey, Paul Kelly, Joan Tetzel, Stanley Ridges, Richard Rober, Minor Watson, Barry Kelley

La Fille du Puisatier*
France 1946   131m   bw
Marcel Pagnol
aka: *The Well-Digger's Daughter*

A stern old well-digger feels bound to send his daughter away when she becomes pregnant.
More country matters from Pagnol, this time with an East Lynne type plot getting in the way of some fine acting. Not much comedy.

wd Marcel Pagnol

Raimu, Fernandel, Charpin, Josette Day
  'There is a feeling in France that such films are made for the foreigner and exploit the eccentricities of French rural life rather than the realities.'—*MFB*

Film
GB 1979   26m   Eastmancolor
No synopsis is possible for this speechless

parable about a poor old man fighting (presumably) against personal obscurity, but its credits make it interesting; it was originally written for Buster Keaton. Max Wall, Patricia Hayes. Written by Samuel Beckett; directed by David Rayner Clark; photographed by Mike Tomlinson; designed by Ariane Gastambide; for BFI.

Film ohne Titel*
West Germany 1947   100m   bw
Camera Film (Erwin Gitt)
aka: *Film without Title*

Scriptwriters discuss how it is possible to make a comedy film in post-war Germany, and evolve a story with alternative endings.
Elegantly conceived but rather humourlessly executed, this interesting film was one of the first post-war German exports, but failed to start a trend. It has similarities to *La Fête à Henriette* and *Rashomon*.

w Helmut Kautner, Ellen Fechner, Rudolf Jugert d Rudolf Jugert ph Igor Oberberg m Bernard Eichhorn

Hans Söhnker, Hildegarde Knef, *Irene Von Meyendorff*, Willy Fritsch

La Fin du Jour**
France 1939   106m   bw
Filmsonor / Regina

Tensions mount in a home for retired actors.
Fascinating opportunity for three fine actors to play off each other.

w Charles Spaak, Julien Duvivier d Julien Duvivier ph Christian Matras m Maurice Jaubert

Michel Simon, Louis Jouvet, Victor Francen, Gabrielle Dorziat, Madeleine Ozeray, Sylvie

  'The power of evil is no longer in the hands of a child!'

The Final Conflict
US 1981   108m   De Luxe   Panavision
TCF / Mace Neufeld (Harvey Bernhard)

The Antichrist, now head of Thorn Industries, arranges to become US Ambassador in London.
The devil as an adult proves somehow less chilling than the devil as a child, and all the elaborate mayhem seems decidedly old hat in this sequel to *The Omen* and *Damien: Omen II*.

w Andrew Birkin d Graham Baker ph Robert Paynter, Phil Meheux m Jerry Goldsmith pd Herbert Westbrook

Sam Neill, Rossano Brazzi, Don Gordon, Lisa Harrow, Mason Adams, Robert Arden

The Final Countdown*
US 1980   105m   TVC colour   Panavision
UA / Bryna (Peter Vincent Douglas)

An aircraft carrier on manoeuvres near Hawaii passes through a strange storm and finds itself back at Pearl Harbor.
Quite an enjoyable bit of schoolboy science fiction, but containing no more body than an episode of *Twilight Zone*. The ending, as so often, is impenetrable.

w David Ambrose, Gerry Davis, Thomas
Hunter, Peter Powell d Don Taylor
ph Victor J. Kemper m John Scott
pd Fernando Carrere

Kirk Douglas, Martin Sheen, Katherine Ross,
James Farentino, Ron O'Neal, Charles
Durning

The Final Programme
GB 1973 89m Technicolor
Goodtimes / Gladiole (John Goldstone,
Sanford Lieberson)
US title: *The Last Days of Man on Earth*

In the future, when the world is torn by
famine and war, a scientist awaits a new
messiah.
Intellectualized sci-fi, hard to take as
entertainment but very glossy.

wd Robert Fuest, *novel* Michael Moorcock
ph Norman Warwick m Paul Beaver, Bernard
Krause

Jon Finch, Jenny Runacre, Sterling Hayden,
Hugh Griffith
'Clumsy and almost incomprehensible.'—
Sight and Sound

The Final Test
GB 1953 90m bw
Rank / ACT (R. J. Minney)

A cricketer looks forward to his last game but
is out for a duck; he is however cheered by the
crowd and comforted by his son.
Flat character study some way below the
author's best style, cluttered up with real
cricketers and stymied by lack of action.

w Terence Rattigan d Anthony Asquith
ph Bill McLeod m Benjamin Franklin

Jack Warner, Robert Morley, George Relph

Finally, Sunday*
France 1983 111m bw
Films du Carrosse / Films A2 / Soprofilms
(Armand Barbault)
French title: *Vivement Dimanche*

When his friend is murdered, a small-town
estate agent becomes a prime suspect.
Agreeable Hitchcock parody which goes on
too long and runs out of steam.

w François Truffaut, Suzanne Schiffman, Jean
Aurel, *novel* The Long Saturday Night by
Charles Williams d François Truffaut
ph Nestor Almendros m Georges Delerue
pd Hilton McConnico

Fanny Ardant, Jean-Louis Trintignant,
Philippe Laudenbach, Caroline Sihol
'Devoid of interest or distinction, a comedy-
thriller that is not funny and most emphatically
not thrilling. Ardant and Trintignant fancy
themselves as Carole Lombard and Fredric
March, an illusion not likely to be shared by
anyone else . . .'—*Gilbert Adair, MFB*
● *Video: Thorn EMI*

Finders Keepers
GB 1966 94m Eastmancolor
UA / Interstate (George H. Brown)

The Americans lose an atomic bomb off the
Spanish coast, and it's found by a pop group.

Harmless youth musical without much style.
Tunes poor, comedy rather too easy-going.

w Michael Pertwee d Sidney Hayers ph Alan
Hume m The Shadows, Norrie Paramor

Cliff Richard, The Shadows, Robert Morley,
Peggy Mount, Viviane Ventura, Graham
Stark, John Le Mesurier, Robert Hutton

Finders Keepers
US 1984 96m Technicolor
CBS (Sandra Marsh, Terence Marsh)

On a train from California to New York,
various factions try to grab stolen money
hidden in a coffin.
Yawnworthy comedy-thriller with a zany
streak; all the elements have been better done
in other movies.

w Ronny Graham, Charles Dennis, Terence
Marsh from Dennis' novel The Next to Last
Train Ride d Richard Lester ph Brian West
m Ken Thorne pd Terence Marsh

Michael O'Keefe, Beverly D'Angelo, Lou
Gossett Jnr, Pamela Stephenson, Ed Lauter,
David Wayne, Brian Dennehy, John Schuck

A Fine Madness*
US 1966 104m Technicolor
Warner Seven Arts (Jerome Hellman)

A frustrated New York poet has outbursts of
violence.
Patchy, interesting, with-it comedy which
suffers from too many changes of mood.

w Elliot Baker, from his novel d Irvin
Kershner ph Ted McCord m John Addison

Sean Connery, Jean Seberg, Joanne
Woodward, Patrick O'Neal, Colleen
Dewhurst, Clive Revill
'Straddling a no man's land somewhere
between the *nouvelle vague* and the crazy
comedies of Old Hollywood.'—*Tom Milne*

A Fine Pair
Italy 1968 115m Technicolor
Panavision
Vides (Franco Cristaldi)
original title: *Ruba al Prossimo Tua*

A New York detective falls for an Italian girl
jewel thief.
Tedious, meandering comedy-thriller with
nothing to offer apart from a good robbery
sequence.

w Francesco Maselli, Luisa Montagnana,
Larry Gelbart, Virgil C. Leone d Francesco
Maselli ph Alfio Contino m Ennio
Morricone

Rock Hudson, Claudia Cardinale, Tomas
Milian, Leon Askin, Ellen Corby

The Finest Hours*
GB 1964 116m Technicolor

The life of Winston Churchill is built up from
newsreels plus a few feature film clips and
some original location shooting. Generally
excellent documentary, a handy introduction
to Churchill's own writing and rather more
entertaining than the later *Young Winston*.
Written by Victor Wolfson; directed by Peter
Baylis; for *Jack Le Vien*.
● *Video: Thorn EMI*

The Finger Points
US 1931 88m bw

A crime reporter succumbs to pressures from
the underworld. Humourless and low-geared
exposé-style melodrama. Richard
Barthelmess, Clark Gable, Fay Wray, Regis
Toomey. Written by John Monk Saunders, W.
R. Burnett and Robert Lord; directed by John
Francis Dillon; for Warner.

Fingers*
US 1977 90m Technicolor

A would-be concert pianist gets involved with
his father's gangster friends, and violence
results. Lively and interesting skirmish with an
overworked and essentially downbeat subject.
Harvey Keitel, Tisa Farrow, Jim Brown,
Marion Seldes. Written and directed by *James
Toback*; for Brut.

Fingers at the Window
US 1942 90m bw
MGM (Irving Starr)

A stage magician hypnotizes lunatics into
murdering all those who stand between him
and an inheritance.
Slow-starting thriller which never achieves top
gear.

w Rose Caylor, Lawrence P. Bachmann
d Charles Lederer ph Harry Stradling,
Charles Lawton m Bronislau Kaper

Basil Rathbone, Lew Ayres, Laraine Day,
Walter Kingsford, Miles Mander, Russell
Gleason
'The kind of picture actors do when they
need work.'—*Lew Ayres*

Finian's Rainbow*
US 1968 140m Technicolor
Panavision 70
Warner Seven Arts (Joseph Landon)

A leprechaun tries to retrieve a crock of gold
from an old wanderer who has taken it to
America.
Musical whimsy-whamsy, a long way after a
1947 Broadway success; in this overlong and
overblown screen version the elements and the
style do not jell and there is too much
sentimental chat, but moments of magic shine
through.

w E. Y. Harburg, Fred Saidy, from their play
d Francis Ford Coppola ph Philip Lathrop
m Burton Lane ly E. Y. Harburg pd Hilyard
M. Brown md Ray Heindorf

Fred Astaire, Petula Clark, Tommy Steele,
Don Francks, Keenan Wynn, Barbara
Hancock, Al Freeman Jnr

AAN: Ray Heindorf

Finis Terrae*
France 1929 90m approx bw silent
Société Générale des Films

A re-enacted account of the lives of fishermen
on remote Brittany islands.
A feature documentary which was impressive
at the time; very similar to Flaherty's *Man of
Aran*.

wd Jean Epstein ph Joseph Barth, Joseph
Kottula

Finishing School
US 1934 73m bw
RKO (Kenneth MacGowan)

A girl at an exclusive school falls for an intern.
Modest pap for the teenage audience.

w Wanda Tuchock, Laird Doyle d George
Nicholls Jnr ph J. Roy Hunt m Max Steiner

Frances Dee, Ginger Rogers, Billie Burke,
Bruce Cabot, John Halliday, Beulah Bondi,
Sara Haden

The Finishing Touch*
US 1928 20m bw; silent

Stan and Ollie accidentally destroy the house
they are building. Excellent early star slapstick
with predictable but enjoyable gags. Laurel
and Hardy, Edgar Kennedy, Dorothy Coburn.
Written by H. M Walker; directed by Clyde
Bruckman; for Hal Roach.

Finn and Hattie
US 1930 77m bw

A newly rich American takes his family to
Paris. Dodsworth-like comedy, fairly well
regarded in its time but now looking very thin.
Leon Errol, Zasu Pitts, Mitzi Green, Jackie
Searl, Regis Toomey, Lilyan Tashman.
Written by Sam Mintz, Joseph L. Mankiewicz,
from the story by Donald Ogden Stewart;
directed by Norman Taurog, Norman
McLeod; for Paramount.

Fire and Ice
US 1982 82m colour

Evil Lord Nekron uses black magic to subdue
the good King Jarol. Fair cartoon feature in
the mould of *Conan the Barbarian*. Written by
Roy Thomas, Jerry Conway; directed by
Ralph Bakshi; for Polyc International.

'Three of the biggest in one of the best!'
Fire Down Below
GB 1957 116m Technicolor
    Cinemascope
Columbia / Warwick (Irving Allen, Albert
    Broccoli)

Partners in a Caribbean fishing and smuggling
business fall out over a woman.
Overheated melodrama with thin characters,
predictable incident and ill-advised casting.

w Irwin Shaw, novel Max Catto d Robert
Parrish ph Desmond Dickinson m Arthur
Benjamin

Rita Hayworth, Robert Mitchum, Jack
Lemmon, Herbert Lom, Bonar Colleano,
Bernard Lee, Edric Connor, Peter Illing

A Fire Has Been Arranged
GB 1935 70m bw
Twickenham (Julius Hagen)

Ex-convicts find a building in the field where
they buried the loot.
Modest star comedy. Was this the first use of
this well-worn plot?

w H. Fowler Mear, Michael Barringer
d Leslie Hiscott

Bud Flanagan, Chesney Allen, Alastair Sim,
Robb Wilton, Mary Lawson, Harold French,
C. Denier Warren

THE FINISHING TOUCH. This Laurel and Hardy silent saw the boys at their best, and
nobody could wish for better support than Edgar Kennedy's.

'A world of women seeking male partners
  to carry on their race!'
Fire Maidens from Outer Space
GB 1956 80m bw

Space explorers find that the thirteenth moon
of Jupiter is inhabited solely by sixteen
beautiful girls and an aged patriarch. A strong
contender for the title of worst movie ever
made, with diaphanously clad English gals
striking embarrassed poses against cardboard
sets. Must be seen to be believed. Susan Shaw,
Anthony Dexter, Harry Fowler, Sidney Tafler,
Owen Berry, Paul Carpenter. Written and
directed by Cy Roth; for Criterion Films /
Eros. 'Even the most dedicated connoisseurs
of the artless are likely to find this something
of a strain on their patience.'—*MFB*.

Fire Over England**
GB 1937 92m bw
London Films / Pendennis

Elizabeth I and her navy overcome the
Spanish Armada.
Though the film has a faded air and the action
climax was always a bath-tub affair, the
splendid cast keeps this pageant afloat and
interesting.

w Clemence Dane, Sergei Nolbandov, novel
A. E. W. Mason d William K. Howard
ph James Wong Howe m Richard Addinsell

Flora Robson, Laurence Olivier, Leslie
Banks, Vivien Leigh, Raymond Massey,
Tamara Desni, Morton Selten, Lyn Harding,
James Mason

'Should bring much artistic acclaim but,
outside of the urban class spots, business will
be stubborn . . . if it had marquee strength it
would stand an excellent chance.'—*Variety*

'Pommer and Howard have done one
remarkable thing: they have caught the very
spirit of an English public schoolmistress's
vision of history.'—*Graham Greene*

'Swashbuckling nonsense, but with a fine
spirit.'—*Pauline Kael, 70s*

● *Video: Video Media*

Fire Sale*
US 1977 88m De Luxe
TCF (Marvin Worth)

Misadventures of a frantic, eccentric New
York-Jewish family who own a department
store.
Frenzied black farce for ethnic audiences.

w Robert Klane, from his novel d Alan
Arkin ph Ralph Woolsey m Dave Grusin

Alan Arkin, Rob Reiner, Vincent Gardenia,
Anjanette Comer, Kay Medford, Sid Caesar,
Alex Rocco

'It moves fast enough to carry the occasional
lapses from its own high standards of
tastelessness.'—*Jan Dawson, MFB*

The Fireball
US 1950 84m bw

A juvenile delinquent becomes a ruthless roller-skating champion. Predictable and unattractive star character drama with sporting asides. Mickey Rooney, Pat O'Brien, Beverly Tyler, Glenn Corbett. Written by Tay Garnett and Horace McCoy; directed by Tay Garnett; for Thor / TCF.

Firecreek
US 1968 104m Technicolor
  Panavision
Warner Seven Arts (Philip Leacock)

The people of Firecreek protect themselves from wandering gunmen.
Dour, predictable little western which does not show its stars at their best.

w Calvin Clements d Vincent McEveety
ph William Clothier m Alfred Newman

James Stewart, Henry Fonda, Inger Stevens, Gary Lockwood, Dean Jagger, Ed Begley, Jay C. Flippen, Jack Elam, James Best, Barbara Luna

'This cramped and clumsy western grinds to a standstill in its attempts to give Firecreek symbolic status . . . while the gunmen roister like mad and the townsfolk rhubarb glumly in the background.'—MFB

Fired Wife
US 1943 75m bw

A radio actress has to keep her marriage a secret in order to preserve her job. Decidedly humdrum comedy. Louise Allbritton, Diana Barrymore, Robert Paige, Walter Abel, George Dolenz, Walter Catlett, Ernest Truex, Rex Ingram, Richard Lane. Written by Michael Fessier and Ernest Pagano; directed by Charles Lamont; for Universal.

The Firebird
US 1934 75m bw

An actor with the reputation of a Lothario is murdered. Well cast but rather disappointing murder mystery. Verree Teasdale, Ricardo Cortez, Lionel Atwill, C. Aubrey Smith, Anita Louise, Dorothy Tree, Hobart Cavanaugh. Written by Charles Kenyon from the play by Lajos Zilahy; directed by William Dieterle; for Warners. 'Padding in late reels keeps it from ace rating.'—Variety

The Firefly*
US 1937 131m bw
MGM (Hunt Stromberg)

Adventures of a Spanish lady spy during the Napoleonic war.
Solid production of a romantic operetta; splendid stuff for connoisseurs.

w Frances Goodrich, Albert Hackett, Ogden Nash d Robert Z. Leonard ph Oliver Marsh
original book / ly Otto Harbach m Rudolf Friml md Herbert Stothart

Jeanette MacDonald, Allan Jones (who sings the Donkey Serenade), Warren William, Billy Gilbert, Henry Daniell, George Zucco, Douglass Dumbrille

'The sepia tint is monotonous . . . the length will seriously militate against popularity.'—Variety
'A lavish musical monstrosity.'—New Yorker, 1978
'It will make 1937 remembered always as the year of the first romantic dramatic musical film!'—publicity

Firefox
US 1982 136m De Luxe Panavision
Warner (Clint Eastwood)

An American pilot is disguised as a businessman and sent to Moscow to steal a new supersonic Soviet fighter.
Dreary melodrama with doleful acting and very little action or suspense.

w Alex Lasker, Wendell Willman, novel Craig Thomas d Clint Eastwood ph Bruce Surtees
m Maurice Jarre sp John Dykstra

Clint Eastwood, Freddie Jones, David Huffman, Warren Clarke, Ronald Lacey, Kenneth Colley, Nigel Hawthorne

'What is most curious about this farrago is that Eastwood, the actor and the director, should have walked through it all with scarcely a thought for each other.'—Richard Combs, MFB
'Despite the tense mission being depicted, there's no suspense, excitement or thrills to be had, and lackadaisical pacing gives the viewer plenty of time to ponder the gaping implausibilities that skilful execution could have rendered irrelevant.'—Variety
'Immensely long, unfailingly dull, and not even silly enough to be funny.'—Sunday Times

Fireman Save My Child
US 1932 67m bw

A fireman is more interested in baseball but becomes a hero all the same. Thin star comedy. Joe E. Brown, Evalyn Knapp, Lillian Bond, Guy Kibbee. Written by Ray Enright, Robert Lord and Arthur Caesar; directed by Lloyd Bacon; for Warner / First National.

Fireman Save My Child
US 1954 80m bw
U-I (Howard Christie)

In 1910 San Francisco, incompetent firemen accidentally catch a gang of crooks.
Slapstick farce intended for Abbott and Costello, taken over by a new team which did not catch on, played like the Keystone Kops. Mildly funny during the chases.

w Lee Loeb, John Grant d Leslie Goodwins
ph Clifford Stine m Joseph Gershenson

Buddy Hackett, Spike Jones and the City Slickers, Hugh O'Brian, Adèle Jergens

The Firemen's Ball*
Czechoslovakia / Italy 1967 73m
  Eastmancolor
Barrandov / Carlo Ponti
original title: Hori, Ma Panenko

In a small provincial town, arrangements for the firemen's annual ball go wrong at every turn.

Vaguely amusing Tati-esque comedy with not quite enough funny moments and a prevailing atmosphere of pessimism.

w Milos Forman, Ivan Passer, Jaroslav Papousek d Milos Forman ph Miroslav Ondricek m Karel Mares

Jan Vostrcil, Josef Kolb, Josef Svet, Frantisek Debelka

'A compendium of superb items.'—Philip Strick

AAN: best foreign film

Firepower
GB 1979 104m Technicolor
ITC / Michael Winner

A chemist about to expose contaminated drugs is murdered; his widow persuades the US Justice Department to hire her ex-lover, a gangster, to track down his killers.
Globe-trotting kaleidoscope of the familiar patterns of violence; tolerable for those who haven't been here a hundred times before.

w Gerald Wilson d Michael Winner
ph Robert Paynter, Dick Kratina md Jay Cattaway

Sophia Loren, James Coburn, Anthony Franciosa, O. J. Simpson, Eli Wallach, George Grizzard, Vincent Gardenia, Victor Mature

'The nearest thing yet to film-making by numbers, with identikit characters jet-setting across a travel brochure landscape to an orchestration of gunfire, car smashes and colourful explosions.'—Clyde Jeavons, MFB

● Video: Precision

Fires on the Plain**
Japan 1959 108m bw
Daiei (Masaichi Nagata)
original title: Nobi

In the Philippines during World War II, a half-demented Japanese private takes to the hills, becomes a cannibal, and is shot by the Americans when he tries to surrender.
Stomach-turning anti-war epic with fine scenes and performances but dubious intent.

w Natto Wada, novel Shohei O-oka d Kon Ichikawa ph Setsuo Kobayashi m Yasushi Akatagawa

Eiji Funakoshi, Osamu Takizawa, Micky Curtis

Fires Were Started**
GB 1942 63m bw
Crown Film Unit (Ian Dalrymple)
aka: I Was a Fireman

One day and night in the life of a National Fire Service unit during the London blitz.
Thoughtful, slow-moving, poetic documentary originally intended as a training film but generally released to boost morale. Not its director's finest work, but perhaps his most ambitious.

wd Humphrey Jennings ph C. Pennington-Richards m William Alwyn

'An astonishingly intimate portrait of an isolated and besieged Britain . . . an unforgettable piece of human observation, affectionate, touching, and yet ironic.'—*Georges Sadoul*

'It transforms its observation into a personal, epic celebration of the courage and dignity of ordinary people in times of stress.'—*Time Out, 1984*

† The firemen were real firemen, but the scenes were re-enacted.

Firestarter
US 1984 114m Technicolor
Universal (Frank Capra Jnr)

A young girl is capable of starting fires by pyrokinesis, and the government wants to use her as a weapon.
Complicated and dislikeable piece of political science fiction.

w Stanley Mann, from the novel by Stephen King d Mark L. Lester ph Giuseppe Ruzzolini m Tangerine Dream

Drew Barrymore, George C. Scott, David Keith, Martin Sheen, Freddie Jones, Heather Locklear, Art Carney, Louise Fletcher, Moses Gunn

First a Girl
GB 1935 94m bw

A messenger girl attracts attention by posing as a boy, and becomes a star. Moderate light star vehicle. Jessie Matthews, Sonnie Hale, Griffith Jones, Anna Lee, Alfred Drayton, Martita Hunt, Eddie Gray. Written by Marjorie Gaffney, from the play *Viktor und Viktoria* by Reinhold Schunzel; directed by Victor Saville; for Gaumont.

First Blood
US 1982 94m Technicolor Panavision
Carolco (Buzz Feitshans)

A former Green Beret gets into trouble in a small Californian community and sets himself against the forces of law.
Pure blood and thunder with some decent action sequences.

w Michael Kazall, William Sackheim, Sylvester Stallone, *novel* David Marell d Ted Kotcheff ph Andrew Laszlo m Jerry Goldsmith

Sylvester Stallone, Richard Crenna, Brian Dennehy, David Caruso, Jack Starrett

'Socially irresponsible . . . there are enough nuts out there without giving them a hero to cheer for.'—*Variety*

● Video: Thorn EMI

Firstborn
US 1984 100m Technicolor
Paramount / Paul Junger Witt, Tony Thomas

A divorced woman thinking of remarriage has trouble with her resentful teenage sons, and her intended proves to be a psychotic.
Part drama, part suspenser, all adding up to very little.

w Ron Koslow d Michael Apted ph Ralf D. Bode m Michael Small pd Paul Sylbert

ed Arthur Schmidt

Teri Garr, Peter Weller, Christopher Collet, Corey Haim, Sara Jessica Parker

First Comes Courage
US 1943 88m bw
Columbia (Harry Joe Brown)

During World War II, a Norwegian girl appears to be a Quisling but is really a spy getting information from the Nazis by fraternizing with them.
Doleful war drama with little to commend it except propaganda.

w Lewis Meltzer, Melvin Levy, *novel* The Commandos by Elliott Arnold d Dorothy Arzner ph Joseph Walker m Ernst Toch

Merle Oberon, Brian Aherne, Carl Esmond, Fritz Leiber, Erik Rolf, Reinhold Schunzel, Isobel Elsom

The First Deadly Sin
US 1980 112m TVC color
Filmways / Artanis / Cinema Seven (Elliott Kastner)

A police lieutenant tracks down a homicidal lunatic but is unable to save his own wife who is dying in hospital from an obscure ailment. The two halves of this depressing cop show don't seem to relate, and it offers little in the way of entertainment value beyond the traditional tracking down of the murderer.

w Mann Rubin, *novel* Lawrence Sanders d Brian G. Hutton ph Jack Priestley m Gordon Jenkins

Frank Sinatra, Faye Dunaway, David Dukes, George Coe, Brenda Vaccaro, Martin Gabel, Anthony Zerbe, James Whitmore

'An odd collection of pretensions seem to be rattling round in an overlength TV film.'—*Mark Lefanu, MFB*

'Mystery without meaning, despite a froth of intercutting and religious iconography.'—*Sight and Sound*

The First Gentleman*
GB 1948 111m bw
Columbia (Joseph Friedman)
US title: *Affairs of a Rogue*

The affairs and foibles of the Prince Regent. Dullish adaptation of a successful West End play about 18th-century court life; script and performances still entertain.

w Nicholas Phipps, Reginald Long, *play* Norman Ginsbury d Cavalcanti ph Jack Hildyard

Cecil Parker, Jean-Pierre Aumont, Joan Hopkins, Margaretta Scott, Jack Livesey, Ronald Squire, Athene Seyler, Hugh Griffith

The First Great Train Robbery*
GB 1978 108m Technicolor
UA / Starling (John Foreman)

In 1855, an elegant but ruthless crook picks out a gang to help him rob the Folkestone express of gold bullion.
Patchy but generally very likeable period crime story, with just a few lapses of pace and taste.

wd Michael Crichton, from his novel *ph* Geoffrey Unsworth *m* Jerry Goldsmith *ph* Maurice Carter

Sean Connery, Donald Sutherland, Lesley-Anne Down, Alan Webb, Robert Lang, Malcolm Terris

'My dream was that the historical world was going to be lovingly recreated, and then I was going to shoot *The French Connection* inside it.'—*Michael Crichton*

● Video: Warner

The First Hundred Years
US 1938 75m bw

A self-supporting wife is reluctant to give up her career. Tolerable matrimonial comedy resolved by pregnancy. Robert Montgomery, Virginia Bruce, Warren William, Binnie Barnes, Alan Dinehart, Harry Davenport, Nydia Westman. Written by Melville Baker from a story by Norman Krasna; directed by Richard Thorpe; for MGM.

First Lady*
US 1937 82m bw
Warner (Hal B. Wallis)

The President's wife is a power behind the scenes.
Solidly entertaining Washington comedy.

w Rowland Leigh, *play* George S. Kaufman, Katherine Dayton d Stanley Logan ph Sid Hickox

Kay Francis, Preston Foster, Anita Louise, Walter Connolly, Verree Teasdale, Victor Jory, Marjorie Rambeau, Louise Fazenda

'Smart stuff but generally palatable.'—*Variety*

The First Legion*
US 1951 86m bw
Sedif (Douglas Sirk)

Priests are bewildered when one of their number is the centre of an apparent miracle. Talkative religious drama of a peculiarly American kind which likes to have its cake and eat it; watchable for the performances.

w Emmet Lavery, from his play d Douglas Sirk ph Robert de Grasse m Hans Sommer

Charles Boyer, William Demarest, Lyle Bettger, Barbara Rush, Leo G. Carroll, Walter Hampden, George Zucco, Taylor Holmes

First Love*
US 1939 84m bw
Universal (Joe Pasternak)

An orphaned teenager goes to live with her uncle and his snobbish family, and falls for a local bigwig's son.
A vehicle carefully conceived to introduce its star to grown-up romance. The compromises show, but it's palatable enough.

w Bruce Manning, Lionel Houser d Henry Koster ph Joseph Valentine m Frank Skinner md Charles Previn

Deanna Durbin, Robert Stack, Eugene Pallette, Helen Parrish, Lewis Howard, Leatrice Joy

'A top-bracketer for general audiences in keys and subsequents.'—*Variety*

'The most obvious Cinderella story I ever met with, apart from *Cinderella*.'—*Richard Mallett, Punch*

'There is nothing at all to resent in the picture: it is admirably directed, amusingly written, and acted with immense virtuosity by a fine cast.'—*Graham Greene*

AAN: Charles Previn

First Man into Space
GB 1958 78m bw
Producers' Associates (John Croydon)

An astronaut runs into a cloud of meteor dust and returns to earth a vampirish killer.
Quatermass-like shocker with modest budget but firm control.

w John C. Cooper, Lance Z. Hargreaves d Robert Day ph Geoffrey Faithfull m Buxton Orr

Marshall Thompson, Marla Landi, Bill Edwards

First Men in the Moon*
GB 1964 103m Technicolor Panavision
Columbia / Ameran (Charles H. Schneer)

A Victorian eccentric makes a voyage to the moon and is forced to stay there.
Rather slack in plot development, but an enjoyable schoolboy romp with a good eye for detail and tongue firmly in cheek.

w Nigel Kneale, Jan Read, *novel* H. G. Wells d Nathan Juran ph Wilkie Cooper m Laurie Johnson sp Ray Harryhausen

Lionel Jeffries, Edward Judd, Martha Hyer
† Uncredited, Peter Finch played the bit part of a process server.

'In the Supreme Court, there are only eight of them against all of her!'

First Monday in October
US 1981 99m Metrocolor Panavision
Paramount (Paul Heller, Martha Scott)

Ruth Loomis becomes the first woman to be appointed to the US Supreme Court, and wins over her severest critic.
Fairly yawnworthy comedy which has nowhere to go from its initial situation, and has detail too complex for any but politically minded Americans.

w Jerome Lawrence, Robert E. Lee, from their play d Ronald Neame ph Fred J. Koenekamp m Sousa, Handel, arr. Ian Fraser pd Philip M. Jefferies

Jill Clayburgh, Walter Matthau, Barnard Hughes, Jan Sterling, James Stephens, Joshua Bryant

'Any attempts to inject a little healthy subversion or a few dangerous thoughts are soon smothered by the plot demands of middle-aged romantic whimsy.'—*Sunday Times*

● *Video: CIC*

The First of the Few**
GB 1942 117m bw
Melbourne / British Aviation (Leslie Howard, George King, Adrian Brunel, John Stafford)
US title: *Spitfire*

The story of R. J. Mitchell who saw World War II coming and devised the Spitfire.
Low-key but impressive biopic with firm acting and good dialogue scenes. Production values slightly shaky.

w Anatole de Grunwald, Miles Malleson, Henry C. James, Katherine Strueby d Leslie Howard ph Georges Perinal m William Walton

Leslie Howard, David Niven, Rosamund John, Roland Culver, David Horne
'Full of action, Schneider Trophy races, test flying and flashes from the Battle of Britain.'—*Sunday Times*

● *Video: Precision*

The First Texan
US 1956 82m Technicolor Cinemascope
Allied Artists (Walter Mirisch)

The Governor of Tennessee helps Texas win its independence.
Generally well done biopic of Sam Houston, with the usual western excitements.

w Daniel B. Ullman d Byron Haskin ph Wilfrid Cline m Roy Webb

Joel McCrea, Felicia Farr, Jeff Morrow, Wallace Ford, Abraham Sofaer

The First Time
US 1968 90m De Luxe
UA / Mirisch / Rogallan (Roger Smith, Allan Carr)
GB title: *You Don't Need Pajamas at Rosie's*

Three teenage boys who fantasize about sex help a stranded girl under the impression that she is a prostitute.
Embarrassingly sentimental teenage sex comedy, all the more irritating by its restraint. Not a patch on *Summer of '42*.

w Jo Heims, Roger Smith d James Nielson ph Ernest Laszlo m Kenyon Hopkins

Jacqueline Bisset, Wes Stern, Rick Kelman, Wink Roberts, Sharon Acker

First to Fight
US 1967 97m Technicolor Panavision
Warner (William Conrad)

A World War II hero is taken home and fêted, but on returning to the front he loses his nerve.
War film in the guise of a psychological study; competently done but very American in its sentiments and a bit shaky on period detail.

w Gene L. Coon d Christian Nyby ph Harold Wellman m Fred Steiner

Chad Everett, Gene Hackman, Dean Jagger, Marilyn Devon, Claude Akins

The First Travelling Saleslady
US 1956 92m Technicolor
RKO (Arthur Lubin)

Two women set out to sell barbed wire in the old west.
Strained comedy with very few effective moments.

w Devery Freeman, Stephen Longstreet d Arthur Lubin ph William Snyder m Irving Gertz

Ginger Rogers, Carol Channing, Barry Nelson, James Arness, David Brian, Clint Eastwood

First Yank into Tokyo
US 1945 82m bw

An army pilot undergoes plastic surgery so that he can infiltrate the Japanese lines. Highly unconvincing spy fiction ripped off from the headlines as the war ended. Tom Neal, Richard Loo, Marc Cramer, Barbara Hale, Keye Luke. Written and produced by J. Robert Bren; directed by Gordon Douglas; for RKO.

The First Year*
US 1932 80m bw

Problems of a couple in their first year of married life. Pleasant star vehicle. Janet Gaynor, Charles Farrell, Minna Gombell, Dudley Digges, Leila Bennett. Written by Lynn Starling from the play by Frank Craven; directed by William K. Howard; for Fox.
'Gaynor and Farrell in a story that's as close to perfection for them as any piece of screenwriting could be.'—*Variety*

Fisherman's Wharf
US 1939 72m bw

The relationship of a boy and his foster father is upset by the arrival of relations on their fishing boat. Family fare for addicts of the singing boy star. Bobby Breen, Leo Carrillo, Lee Patrick, Henry Armetta, Tommy Bupp. Written by Bernard Schubert, Ian Hunter, Herbert Clyde Lewis; directed by Bernard Vorhaus; for Sol Lesser / RKO. 'Lightweight entertainment which will find its level in the duals.'—*Variety*

F.I.S.T.*
US 1978 145m Technicolor
UA / Norman Jewison (Gene Corman)

The rise and fall of a union boss.
Reminiscent of *All the King's Men* and *On the Waterfront*, this much overlong melodrama has compelling passages, but the star is not quite equal to it and parts are both repetitive and obscure.

w Joe Eszterhas, Sylvester Stallone d Norman Jewison ph Laszlo Kovacs m Bill Conti pd Richard MacDonald

Sylvester Stallone, Rod Steiger, Peter Boyle, Melinda Dillon, David Huffman, Tony L. Bianco, Cassie Yates, Peter Donat, Henry Wilcoxon

● *Video: Warner*

A Fistful of Dollars*
Italy / Germany / Spain 1964   100m
Techniscope
UA / Jolly / Constantin / Ocean (Arrigo
Colombo, Georgio Papi)

An avenging stranger, violent and mysterious,
cleans up a Mexican border town.
A film with much to answer for: it began the
craze for 'spaghetti westerns', took its director
to Hollywood, and made a TV cowboy into a
world star. In itself it is simple, noisy, brutish
and actionful.

w Sergio Leone, Duccio Tessari d Sergio
Leone ph Massimo Dallamano m Ennio
Morricone

Clint Eastwood, Gian Maria Volonte,
Marianne Koch
† Direct sequels by Leone, apart from
numerous imitations, are For a Few Dollars
More and The Good, the Bad and the Ugly.

● Video: Warner

A Fistful of Dynamite
Italy 1971   150m   Techniscope
UA / Rafran / San Marco / Miura (Fulvio
Morsella)
aka: Duck, You Sucker

In 1913 a Mexican bandit and an ex-IRA
explosives expert join forces to rob a bank.
Overblown action spectacular, far too long to
be sustained by its flashes of humour and
excitement. A good instance of what happens
to a small talent when success goes to its head.

wd Sergio Leone ph Giuseppe Ruzzolini
m Ennio Morricone

Rod Steiger, James Coburn

Fists in the Pocket*
Italy 1965   113m   bw
Doria (Ezio Passadore)
original title: I Pugni in Tasca

One of a family of epileptics murders most of
the others in order to help his normal eldest
brother.
Complex black melodrama which makes its
points, if it has any, with great style.

wd Marco Bellocchio ph Alberto Marrama
m Ennio Morricone

Lou Castel, Paola Pitagora, Liliona Gerace
'There have been few debuts as exciting as
this in recent years.'—Tom Milne, MFB

Fitzcarraldo***
West Germany 1982   158m   colour
Werner Herzog / Project Filmproduktion /
Zweite Deutsches Fernsehen / Wildlife
Films, Peru (Werner Herzog, Lucki
Stipetic)

In Peru at the turn of the century, an eccentric
Irishman succeeds against all odds in
establishing an opera house in the jungle.
A strange and brilliant film centring on the
hero's successful attempt to drag his massive
boat from one river to another.

wd Werner Herzog ph Thomas Mauch
m Popol Vuh

Klaus Kinski, Claudia Cardinale, Jose
Lewgoy, Paul Hittscher

† 'Fitzcarraldo' is the nearest the natives can
get to 'Fitzgerald'.
● Video: Palace

Fitzwilly*
US 1967   102m   De Luxe   Panavision
UA / Dramatic Features Inc / Walter Mirisch
GB title: Fitzwilly Strikes Back

A New York butler, in order to keep his lady
in style, has to organize the staff into a crime
syndicate.
Moderately inventive, good-looking comedy
with rather too much plot and not enough
funny lines.

w Isobel Lennart, novel A Garden of
Cucumbers by Poyntz Tyler d Delbert Mann
ph Joseph Biroc m Johnny Williams

Dick Van Dyke, Edith Evans, Barbara Feldon,
John McGiver, Harry Townes, John Fiedler,
Norman Fell, Cecil Kellaway, Anne Seymour,
Sam Waterston, Billy Halop

Five
US 1951   89m   bw
Columbia (Arch Oboler)

There are only five survivors of an atomic
holocaust, and their political and racial
tensions soon reduce the number to two.
Gutless talkfest which becomes interesting
only when the camera moves out of doors;
otherwise, too pretentious and dull by half.

wd Arch Oboler ph Lou Stoumen, Ed
Spiegel, Sid Lubow m Henry Russell

William Phipps, Susan Douglas, James
Anderson, Charles Lampkin, Earl Lee
'The talk leaves one with a strong
impression that in this case the fittest did not
survive.'—Penelope Houston

Five Against the House
US 1955   84m   bw
Columbia (Sterling Silliphant, John
Barnwell)

College students try to rob a casino.
Meandering caper melodrama with too much
flabby dialogue.

w Sterling Silliphant, John Barnwell, novel
Jack Finney d Phil Karlson ph Leslie White
m George Duning

Guy Madison, Kim Novak, Brian Keith,
Kerwin Mathews, William Conrad

Five and Ten
US 1931   88m   bw

A chain store heiress elopes with a married
man, but is tamed by family misfortune. Solid
star drama which maintains points of interest.
Marion Davies, Leslie Howard, Richard
Bennett, Irene Rich, Kent Douglass, Halliwell
Hobbes. Written by A. P. Younger and Edith
Fitzgerald, from the novel by Fannie Hurst;
directed by Robert Z. Leonard; for MGM.
(GB title: Daughter of Luxury.)

Five Boys from Barska Street*
Poland 1953   115m   Agfacolor
Film Polski
original title: Piatka z Ulicy Barskiej

Five city boys are placed on probation and

gradually change their attitudes towards life
and society.
Rather dated propaganda piece with a plot
which surprisingly follows western models.

wd Aleksander Ford, novel Kazimierz
Kozniewski ph Jaroslav Tuzar m Kazimierz
Serocki

Tadeusz Janczar, Aleksandra Slaska, Andrzej
Kozak

Five Branded Women
Italy / US 1960   100m   bw
Paramount / Dino de Laurentiis

Five Yugoslav girls have their heads shaved
for associating with German soldiers, and after
various adventures join the partisans.
Rough, tough war adventure which makes a
few boring points about love and war.

w Ivo Perelli, novel Ugo Pirro d Martin Ritt
ph Giuseppe Rotunno m Francesco
Lavagnino

Silvana Mangano, Van Heflin, Vera Miles,
Barbara Bel Geddes, Jeanne Moreau, Richard
Basehart, Harry Guardino, Steve Forrest,
Alex Nicol
'For the most part the film is devoted to
unexciting guerrilla action and uninviting
partisan life . . . obstinately unreal despite
lashings of blood, mutilation, childbirth and
death.'—MFB

Five Came Back**
US 1939   75m   bw
RKO (Robert Sisk)

A passenger plane crashlands in the jungle. It
can carry back only five survivors, and
headhunters are coming closer . . .
A minor film which gradually achieved cult
status and was remade as Back to Eternity as
well as being the starting point for many
variations. Still gripping in its dated way.

w Jerry Cady, Dalton Trumbo, Nathanael
West d John Farrow ph Nicholas Musuraca
m Roy Webb

Chester Morris, Lucille Ball, C. Aubrey
Smith, Elizabeth Risdon, Wendy Barrie, John
Carradine, Joseph Calleia, Allen Jenkins,
Kent Taylor, Patric Knowles
'Exceptionally well-made adventure yarn,
out of the B category and almost rates A . . .
looks like a solid click.'—Variety

Five Card Stud
US 1968   103m   Technicolor
Paramount / Hal. B. Wallis

Members of a lynching party are murdered
one by one.
Would-be nonchalant murder mystery
western: the stars just about hold it together,
but it's an uphill fight.   ·

w Marguerite Roberts, novel Ray Gaulden
d Henry Hathaway ph Daniel L. Fapp
m Maurice Jarre

Dean Martin, Robert Mitchum, Inger Stevens,
Roddy McDowall, Katherine Justice, John
Anderson, Yaphet Kotto
'Marginally watchable . . . but destined to
sink without trace minutes after one leaves the
cinema.'—Gavin Millar
'So mediocre you can't get mad at it.'—
Judith Crist

Five Days One Summer*
US 1982 108m Technicolor
Warner / Ladd (Fred Zinnemann)

In 1932 a middle-aged Scots doctor takes his young mistress on an Alpine climbing holiday, and she falls for the guide.
Superbly photographed and crafted mountain movie, akin to the German epics of the early thirties. Alas, the content is very thin.

w Michael Austin, *story* Maiden Maiden by Kay Boyle d Fred Zinnemann ph Giuseppe Rotunno m Elmer Bernstein pd Willy Holt ed Stuart Baird

Sean Connery, Betsy Brantley, Lambert Wilson, Jennifer Hilary, Isabel Dean, Anna Massey
'Dawdling and eventually silly, though the veteran director's tenacity and craftsmanship provide muted applause.'—*Variety*
● Video: Warner

Five Easy Pieces**
US 1970 98m Technicolor
Columbia / Bert Schneider (Bob Rafelson, Richard Wechsler)

A middle-class drifter jilts his pregnant mistress for his brother's fiancée, but finally leaves both and hitches a ride to nowhere in particular.
Echoes of *Easy Rider*, *The Graduate* and *Charlie Bubbles* abound in this generally likeable but insubstantial modern anti-drama which at least takes place in pleasant surroundings and is firmly directed.

w Adrien Joyce d Bob Rafelson ph Laszlo Kovacs m various

Jack Nicholson, Karen Black, Susan Anspach, Lois Smith, Billy 'Green' Bush, Fannie Flagg
AAN: best picture; Adrien Joyce; Jack Nicholson; Karen Black

Five Finger Exercise
US 1962 109m bw
Columbia / Sonnis (Frederick Brisson)

A snobbish wife falls in love with a young house guest, with dire effect on her husband and son.
This West End study of a neurotic family is probably not good film material, certainly not adaptable to California, and above all not suitable to this star's whizzbang dramatics. Numbing hysteria arrives early and stays till the end.

w Frances Goodrich, Albert Hackett, *play* Peter Shaffer d Daniel Mann ph Harry Stradling m Jerome Moross

Rosalind Russell, Jack Hawkins, Maximilian Schell, Richard Beymer
'There are many kinds of love, but are there any without guilt?'—*publicity*

Five Fingers***
US 1952 108m bw
TCF (Otto Lang)

The valet of the British ambassador in Ankara sells military secrets to the Germans, who pay him but never use the information.

Absorbing, lightweight film adaptation of a true story of World War II; civilized suspense entertainment with all talents contributing nicely.

w Michael Wilson, *book* Operation Cicero by L. C. Moyzich d Joseph L. Mankiewicz ph Norbert Brodine m Bernard Herrmann ad Lyle Wheeler, George W. Davis

James Mason, Danielle Darrieux, Michael Rennie, Walter Hampden, Oscar Karlweis, Herbert Berghof, John Wengraf, Michael Pate
'One of the highest, fastest and most absorbing spy melodramas since Hitchcock crossed the Atlantic.'—*Arthur Knight*
AAN: Michael Wilson; Joseph L. Mankiewicz

Five Gates to Hell
US 1959 98m bw Cinemascope

A Vietcong warlord carries off a nun and seven nurses; the latter escape by brutal means. Unpleasant shocker showing no signs of talent in any department. Dolores Michaels, Patricia Owens, Neville Brand, Kevin Scott, Nobu McCarthy, Nancy Kulp, Shirley Knight, Irish McCalla. Written, directed and produced by James Clavell; for TCF. 'This grimly amateurish war film exploits sex and violence with an emotional arrest bordering on paranoia.'—*MFB*.

Five Golden Dragons
GB 1965 92m Techniscope

An American playboy in Hong Kong becomes involved in the affairs of five master criminals preparing to sell out to the Mafia. Anything-goes comedy-thriller, patchy at best, unintelligible at worst, and filled with ageing stars. Robert Cummings, Rupert Davies, Margaret Lee, Maria Perschy, Klaus Kinski, Dan Duryea, Brian Donlevy, Christopher Lee, George Raft. Written by Harry Alan Towers; directed by Jeremy Summers; for Harry Alan Towers.

Five Golden Hours
GB / Italy 1960 90m bw
(Columbia) Anglofilm / Fabio Jegher (Mario Zampi)

A con man tries to murder three widows who have invested money in one of his schemes. Ill-judged black comedy, sadly lacking style.

w Hans Wilhelm d Mario Zampi ph Christopher Challis m Stanley Black

Ernie Kovacs, Cyd Charisse, Kay Hammond, George Sanders, Dennis Price, Reginald Beckwith, Martin Benson, Ron Moody, Finlay Currie, Avis Landone, Sidney Tafler, John Le Mesurier, Clelia Matania

Five Graves to Cairo***
US 1943 96m bw
Paramount (Charles Brackett)

During the North Africa campaign, British spies try to destroy Rommel's secret supply dumps.
Intriguing spy melodrama set in a desert hotel, a notable example of Hollywood's ability to snatch polished drama from the headlines.

w Charles Brackett, Billy Wilder, *play* Lajos Biro d Billy Wilder m Miklos Rozsa ph John Seitz

Franchot Tone, Anne Baxter, *Erich Von Stroheim* (as Rommel), Akim Tamiroff, Peter Van Eyck, Miles Mander
'Von Stroheim has all the other movie Huns backed completely off the screen.'—*Variety*
'Billy Wilder must have had something a little grander in mind: the cleverness lacks lustre.'—*New Yorker, 1978*
'A fabulous film fable, but it has been executed with enough finesse to make it a rather exciting pipe dream.'—*Howard Barnes, New York Herald Tribune*
† Locations representing the African desert include California's Salton Sea and Yuma, Arizona.
AAN: John Seitz

Five Guns West
US 1955 78m Pathecolor

Five criminals are recruited into the southern army to catch a traitor and some Union gold.
Western trial run for *The Dirty Dozen*; cheapjack actioner, quite tolerable of its kind. John Lund, Dorothy Malone, Chuck Connors, Paul Birch. Written by R. Wright Campbell; directed and produced by Roger Corman; for Palo Alto.

Five Miles to Midnight*
France / Italy 1962 110m bw
UA / Filmsonor / Dear Film (Anatole Litvak)

A neurotic believed dead forces his terrified wife to collect his life insurance.
Hysterical melodrama, smoothly made with all the familiar expressionist devices, but far too long for its content.

w Peter Viertel, Hugh Wheeler d Anatole Litvak ph Henri Alekan m Mikis Theodorakis

Sophia Loren, Anthony Perkins, Gig Young, Jean-Pierre Aumont, Yolande Turner, Tommy Norden
'From the polished immediacy of the cars, streets, shop windows and café tables to the off-focus vertigo shots of panic, from the overhead view of neighbours on stairs . . . to the close-ups of hands in filing trays touching off the details of fear and guilt, there is a thread of colour to keep you watching.'—*MFB*
'One of those movies without a country that are becoming as fixed a part of the international scene as the Duke and Duchess of Windsor.'—*Arthur Schlesinger Jnr, Show*

Five of a Kind
US 1938 83m bw

Two reporters compete for the best stories about the Dionne Quintuplets. Third effort to exploit the famous quins, then four years old. Not otherwise remarkable. Jean Hersholt, Claire Trevor, Cesar Romero, Slim Summerville, Henry Wilcoxon, John Qualen, Jane Darwell. Written by Lou Breslow, John Patrick; directed by Herbert I. Leeds; for TCF. 'Will find difficulty in generating much audience enthusiasm except in spots where women patronage predominates.'—*Variety*

The Five Pennies*
US 1959 117m Technicolor
  Vistavision
Paramount / Dena (Jack Rose)

The rags-to-riches success story of cornet
player Red Nichols.
The only touch of originality in this biopic is
that the subject is given touches of irascibility.
Production values reach a good standard.

w Jack Rose, Melville Shavelson d Melville
Shavelson ph Daniel L. Fapp md Leith
Stevens ad Hal Pereira, Tambi Larsen
songs Sylvia Fine trumpet solos Red Nichols

Danny Kaye, Barbara Bel Geddes, *Louis
Armstrong*, Bob Crosby, Harry Guardino,
Tuesday Weld, Ray Anthony

AAN: Daniel L. Fapp; Leith Stevens; title
song (m / ly Sylvia Fine)

Five Star Final**
US 1931 89m bw
Warner

A sensation-seeking newspaper editor causes
tragedy.
Dated but still powerful melodrama which set
the pattern for all the newspaper films of the
thirties.

w *Robert Lord, Byron Morgan, play* Louis
Weitzenkorn d *Mervyn Le Roy* ph Sol
Polito md Leo F. Forbstein

Edward G. Robinson, H. B. Warner, Marian
Marsh, Anthony Bushell, George E. Stone,
Ona Munson, Aline MacMahon, Boris Karloff
  'All the elements to make a hit
attraction.'—*Variety*
† Remade in 1936 with Humphrey Bogart, as
Two Against the World.

AAN: best picture

Five Steps to Danger
US 1956 80m bw
UA / HSK

A girl possessing secret information from her
dead scientist brother has a mental
breakdown, and is pursued by spies.
Lively if cliché-ridden espionage melodrama,
like an old-time serial.

wd Henry S. Kesler, *novel* Donald Hamilton
ph Kenneth Peach m Paul Sawtell, Bert
Shefter

Sterling Hayden, Ruth Roman, Werner
Klemperer, Richard Gaines

**The Five Thousand Fingers of
Doctor T****
US 1953 88m Technicolor
Columbia / *Stanley Kramer*

A boy who hates piano lessons dreams of his
teacher as an evil genius who keeps five
hundred boys imprisoned in a castle of musical
instruments.
Badly scripted fantasy with gleaming
sophisticated dream sequences which deserve
a better frame. A real oddity to come from
Hollywood at this time, even though Dr Seuss'
books were and are bestsellers.

w Dr Seuss (Theodore Geisel), Alan Scott
d Roy Rowland ph Franz Planer
m Frederick Hollander ly Dr Seuss
pd Rudolph Sternad ch Eugene Loring

Hans Conried, Tommy Rettig, Peter Lind
Hayes, Mary Healy

AAN: Frederick Hollander

Five Weeks in a Balloon
US 1962 101m De Luxe Cinemascope
TCF (Irwin Allen)

In 1862 a professor is financed on a balloon
trip into central Africa.
Would-be humorous semi-fantasy which
strives to equal *Journey to the Center of the
Earth* but unfortunately falls flat on its face
despite the interesting talent available. Limp
comedy situations, poor production values.

w Charles Bennett, Irwin Allen, Albert Gail,
novel Jules Verne d Irwin Allen ph Winton
Hoch m Paul Sawtell ad Jack Martin Smith,
Alfred Ybarra

Cedric Hardwicke, Peter Lorre, Red Buttons,
Fabian, Richard Haydn, Billy Gilbert, Herbert
Marshall, Reginald Owen, Henry Daniell

Fixed Bayonets
US 1951 93m bw
TCF (Jules Buck)

An American division in Korea fights a
rearguard action.
Downbeat war melodrama of a familiar kind,
with more characterization than action.

wd Samuel Fuller ph Lucien Ballard m Roy
Webb

Richard Basehart, Gene Evans, Michael
O'Shea, Richard Hylton, Craig Hill

The Fixer
US 1968 130m Metrocolor
MGM / Edward Lewis, John Frankenheimer

A Jew in Tsarist Russia denies his race but
becomes a scapegoat for various crimes and is
imprisoned without trial until he becomes a
cause célèbre.
Worthy but extremely dreary realist
melodrama.

w Dalton Trumbo, *novel* Bernard Malamud
d John Frankenheimer ph Marcel Grignon
m Maurice Jarre

Alan Bates, Dirk Bogarde, Georgia Brown,
Jack Gilford, Hugh Griffith, Elizabeth
Hartman, Ian Holm, David Warner, Carol
White, Murray Melvin, Peter Jeffrey, Michael
Goodliffe
  'The kind of film in which one has to admire
much of the acting simply because it is all
there is to admire.'—*David Pirie*
  'A totally false film, devoid of a breath of
human life or truth.'—*Arthur Schlesinger Jnr*
  'Alan Bates's bare posterior, known to us
from *Georgy Girl* and *King of Hearts*, makes
another timely appearance here, thus
becoming one of the most exposed arses in
cinematic annals.'—*John Simon*

AAN: Alan Bates

The Fixer Uppers
US 1935 20m bw

Christmas card salesmen try to help a bored

wife, but her jealous husband challenges Ollie
to a duel. Rather flat comedy marking a
tailing-off from the stars' best period. Laurel
and Hardy, Mae Busch, Charles Middleton,
Arthur Housman. Writer uncredited; directed
by Charles Rogers; for Hal Roach. (NB: A
remake of an early silent, *Slipping Wives*.)

The Flag Lieutenant
GB 1933 85m bw
British and Dominions (Herbert Wilcox)

A naval lieutenant, thought to be a coward,
shows his true courage when a fort is
beleaguered.
Boy's Own Paper stuff from a popular play
previously filmed in 1919 (with George Wynn)
and 1926 (with Henry Edwards).

w W. P. Drury, Leo Tover, from their play
d Henry Edwards

Henry Edwards, Anna Neagle, Joyce Bland,
Peter Gawthorne, Sam Livesey, O. B.
Clarence, Abraham Sofaer

The Flame
US 1947 97m bw
Republic (John H. Auer)

A nurse marries for money, but her ailing
spouse recovers and she falls in love with him.
Turgid melodrama, ineptly presented.

w Lawrence Kimble d John H. Auer
ph Reggie Lanning m Heinz Roemheld

Vera Hruba Ralston, John Carroll, Robert
Paige, Broderick Crawford, Henry Travers,
Blanche Yurka, Constance Dowling, Hattie
McDaniel, Sen Yung
  'A good picture to stay away from, with or
without a good book.'—*Cue*

The Flame and the Arrow*
US 1950 88m Technicolor
(Warner) Harold Hecht, Frank Ross

In medieval Italy, a rebel leader seeks victory
over a tyrant.
Good-humoured Robin Hood stuff with the
star at his most acrobatic.

w Waldo Salt d Jacques Tourneur ph Ernest
Haller ad Edward Carrere

Burt Lancaster, Virginia Mayo, Robert
Douglas, Aline MacMahon, Frank Allenby,
Nick Cravat
  'I never found a Technicolor costume
picture so entertaining.'—*Richard Mallett,
Punch*

AAN: Ernest Haller; Max Steiner

The Flame and the Flesh
US 1954 104m Technicolor
MGM (Joe Pasternak)

An unscrupulous American woman in Naples
has a fatal fascination for the local menfolk.
Dreary remake of *Naples au Baiser du Feu*
(France 1937), with the dullest possible
handling all round.

w Helen Deutsch, *novel* Auguste Bailly
d Richard Brooks ph Christopher Challis
m Nicholas Brodszky

Lana Turner, Carlos Thompson, Bonar Colleano, Pier Angeli, Charles Goldner, Peter Illing

Flame in the Streets
GB 1961 93m colour Cinemascope
Rank / Somerset (Roy Baker)

A liberal-minded union man erupts when his daughter proposes to marry a black man.
Predictable East End problem picture, unconvincingly set and acted and boring into the bargain.

w Ted Willis, from his TV play Hot Summer Night d Roy Baker ph Christopher Challis m Phil Green

John Mills, Brenda de Banzie, Sylvia Syms, Earl Cameron, Johnny Sekka, Ann Lynn, Wilfred Brambell
  'Its methods belong more to the writer's study than to life.'—John Gillett

Flame of Calcutta
US 1953 70m Technicolor

In 18th-century India a mysterious girl leads attacks against a usurper. Saturday matinee historical romp without much flair. Denise Darcel, Patric Knowles, Paul Cavanagh, George Keymas. Written by Robert E. Kent; directed by Seymour Friedman; for Sam Katzman / Columbia.

The Flame of New Orleans*
US 1941 79m bw
Universal (Joe Pasternak)

A European adventuress settles in America. Fluffy comedy romance with the exiled director scarcely in top form.

w Norman Krasna d René Clair ph Rudolph Maté m Frank Skinner

Marlene Dietrich, Roland Young, Bruce Cabot, Mischa Auer, Andy Devine, Frank Jenks, Eddie Quillan, Laura Hope Crews, Franklin Pangborn
† Remade as Scarlet Angel.

Flame of the Barbary Coast
US 1945 97m bw
Republic (Joseph Kane)

In old San Francisco, a cowboy becomes involved with a night club queen, and their fortunes are resolved by the earthquake. Tolerable period melodrama, and the one in which Wayne played a character named Duke: the nickname stuck.

w Borden Chase d Joseph Kane ph Robert de Grasse m Dale Butts sp Howard and Theodore Lydecker

John Wayne, Ann Dvorak, Joseph Schildkraut, William Frawley, Virginia Grey, Russell Hicks, Jack Norton, Paul Fix, Marc Lawrence

AAN: Dale Butts

Flame of the Islands
US 1955 90m Trucolor
Republic (Edward Ludwig)

A girl invests a bequest in a Bahamas night club, and there becomes involved with four men.
Barely competent time-filler.

w Bruce Manning d Edward Ludwig ph Bud Thackery m Nelson Riddle

Yvonne de Carlo, Howard Duff, Zachary Scott, Kurt Kasznar, Barbara O'Neil, James Arness, Frieda Inescort

The Flame Within
US 1935 73m bw

A lady psychiatrist falls for the husband of one of her patients. Decent star melodrama. Ann Harding, Maureen O'Sullivan, Louis Hayward, Henry Stephenson, Herbert Marshall. Written, directed (and produced) by Edmund Goulding; for MGM.

Flaming Feather
US 1951 78m Technicolor

Arizona is harassed by an outlaw called The Sidewinder who leads a troupe of pillaging Indians. Spot-the-villain western; not much to detain one. Sterling Hayden, Forrest Tucker, Barbara Rush, Richard Arlen, Victor Jory, Edgar Buchanan. Written by Gerald Drayson Adams; directed by Ray Enright; for Nat Holt / Paramount.

Flaming Star*
US 1960 92m De Luxe Cinemascope
TCF (David Weisbart)

A half-breed family is torn between two loyalties.
Solemn, unusual Civil War western with a downbeat ending.

w Clair Huffaker, Nunnally Johnson d Don Siegel ph Charles G. Clarke m Cyril Mockridge

Elvis Presley, Dolores del Rio, Steve Forrest, Barbara Eden, John McIntire, Rodolpho Acosta
  'Despite familiar absurdities, it has more than its share of good moments.'—MFB

The Flamingo Kid
US 1984 100m De Luxe
TCF / ABC (Michael Phillips)

An 18-year-old becomes a man rather quickly when he works the summer at a beach club. Reliable but not very interesting sketch of teenage uncertainty, certainly no better than a TV movie.

w Neal Marshall, Garry Marshall d Garry Marshall ph James A. Contner m various pd Lawrence Miller ed Priscilla Nedd

Matt Dillon, Richard Crenna, Hector Elizondo, Jessica Walter

'A wrong girl from the right side of the tracks!'
Flamingo Road*
US 1949 94m bw
Warner (Jerry Wald)

A tough carnival dancer is stranded in a small town and soon affects the lives of the local politicians.
Standard melodrama from a bestseller, absurd but well performed.

w Robert Wilder, from his novel d Michael Curtiz ph Ted McCord m Max Steiner

Joan Crawford, David Brian, Sidney Greenstreet, Zachary Scott, Gladys George, Virginia Huston, Fred Clark

The Flanagan Boy
GB 1953 81m bw

A young merchant seaman becomes a boxer and is corrupted by a hard-boiled blonde. Competent British imitation of an American B movie. Tony Wright, Barbara Payton, Sidney James, John Slater, Frederick Valk, Marie Burke. Written by Guy Elmes; directed by Reginald LeBorg; for Exclusive.

Flap
US 1970 106m Technicolor
  Panavision
Warner (Jerry Adler)
GB title: The Last Warrior

A drunken Indian on a dilapidated modern reservation starts a public relations war and leads a march on the city.
Unendearing comedy with a tragic end tacked on, not very entertaining as whimsy, farce or social conscience.

w Clair Huffaker, from his novel Nobody Loves a Drunken Indian d Carol Reed ph Fred Koenekamp m Marvin Hamlisch

Anthony Quinn, Claude Atkins, Tony Bill, Victor Jory, Shelley Winters

Flare Up
US 1969 98m Metrocolor
MGM / GMF (Leon Fromkes)

A man kills his wife and threatens her friends who he feels are responsible for the break-up of his marriage.
Sensationally violent melodrama with a plot that goes back to Sudden Fear and further. Adequately made.

w Mark Rodgers d James Neilson ph Andrew J. McIntyre m Les Baxter

Raquel Welch, James Stacy, Luke Askew, Don Chastain, Ron Rifkin

'Don't you understand? When you give up the dream, you die!'
Flashdance*
US 1983 98m Movielab
Paramount / Polygram (Don Simpson, Jerry Bruckheimer)

A female welder in a Pittsburgh factory has ambitions to be a ballet dancer.
Slickly-made, disco-style but dramatically empty entertainment.

w Tom Hedley, Joe Eszterhas d Adrian Lyne ph Don Peterman m Giorgio Moroder ed Bud Smith, Walt Mulconery

Jennifer Beals, Michael Nouri, Lilia Skala, Sunny Johnson, Kyle T. Heffner, Belinda Bauer
  'It resembles an extended video for a record album.'—Observer
  'A preposterous success.'—Guardian
  'Basically, a series of rock videos.'—New Yorker
AA: song, 'What a feeling!'
AAN: cinematography; editing; song, 'Maniac'
● Video: CIC

Flash Gordon

The hero of the 25th century was created in comic strip form by Alex Raymond and his chief claims to film fame are three wild and woolly serials made by Universal: *Flash Gordon* (1936), *Flash Gordon's Trip to Mars* (1938), and *Flash Gordon Conquers the Universe* (1940), all starring Buster Crabbe with Charles Middleton as the wily Emperor Ming. Their cheap and cheerful futuristic sets and their non-stop action have kept them popular with film buffs through the years. In 1974 a semi-porno spoof, *Flesh Gordon*, appeared.

Flash Gordon*

GB 1980   115m   Technicolor   Todd-AO
EMI / Famous / Starling (Dino de Laurentiis)

A football hero, his girl friend, and Dr Zarkov have adventures on the planet Mongo.
Lively comic strip addition to the increasing numbers of such things being restaged at enormous expense fifty years after their prime.

w Lorenzo Semple Jnr, from characters created by Alex Raymond *d* Michael Hodges *ph* Gil Taylor *m* Queen *pd* Danilo Donati

Sam J. Jones, Melody Anderson, Topol, Max Von Sydow, Timothy Dalton, Brian Blessed, Peter Wyngarde

'An expensively irrelevant gloss on its sources.'—*Richard Combs, MFB*

● *Video: Thorn EMI*

Flaxy Martin

US 1948   86m   bw
Warner

A lawyer falls for a racketeer's girl friend and finds himself framed for murder.
Flatly-handled melodrama with unsympathetic characters.

w David Lang *d* Richard Bare *ph* Carl Guthrie

Zachary Scott, Virginia Mayo, Dorothy Malone, Tom d'Andrea, Elisha Cook Jnr

A Flea in Her Ear*

US / France 1968   94m   De Luxe   Panavision
TCF (Fred Kohlmar)

Various suspicious wives and husbands converge on the notorious Hotel Coq d'Or.
Disappointing filming of a Feydeau farce, which needs to be much more cleverly handled to come over with its full theatrical force.

w John Mortimer, *play* La Puce à l'Oreille by Georges Feydeau *d* Jacques Charon *ph* Charles Lang *m* Bronislau Kaper *pd* Alexander Trauner

Rex Harrison, Rachel Roberts, Rosemary Harris, Louis Jourdan, John Williams, Grégoire Aslan, Edward Hardwicke, Frank Thornton, Victor Sen Yung

'The plunge into madness never comes, and one is left with the sight of a group of talented players struggling with alien material.'—*Michael Billington, Illustrated London News*

'Gobs of glee! A boatload of beauties! A shipful of songs!'

The Fleet's In*

US 1942   93m   bw
Paramount (Paul Jones)

A sailor on leave in San Francisco takes a bet that he can kiss the glamorous singer at a swank nightclub.
Mindless wartime musical which happened to set the seal of success on a number of young talents. Previously a Clara Bow vehicle.

w Walter de Leon, Sid Silvers *d* Victor Schertzinger *ph* William Mellor *m / ly* Victor Schertzinger, Johnny Mercer

Dorothy Lamour, William Holden, *Eddie Bracken, Betty Hutton*, Cass Daley, Gil Lamb, Leif Erickson, Betty Jane Rhodes

Songs: 'I Remember You'; 'When You Hear the Time Signal'; 'The Fleet's In'; 'Tomorrow You Belong to Uncle Sam'; 'Arthur Murray Taught Me Dancing in a Hurry'; 'If Somebody Builds a Better Mousetrap'; 'Somebody Else's Moon'; 'Tangerine'; 'Conga from Honga'

'A slim and obvious comedy with some good tunes. Much of the film is a roughhouse; several reels towards the end are turned over to straight vaudeville.'—*Eileen Creelman, New York Sun*

The Flemish Farm

GB 1943   82m   bw
Two Cities (Sydney Box)

An attempt is made to retrieve a buried flag from occupied Belgium.
Tolerable wartime flagwaver.

w Jeffrey Dell, Jill Craigie *d* Jeffrey Dell

Clive Brook, Clifford Evans, Jane Baxter, Philip Friend, Brefni O'Rourke

Flesh*

US 1932   95m   bw
MGM

A German wrestler in the US falls for a street waif.
Unusual, rather unattractive, but vivid melodrama.

w Leonard Praskins, Edgar Allen Woolf, Moss Hart, *story* Edmund Goulding *d* John Ford *ph* Arthur Edeson

Wallace Beery, Ricardo Cortez, Karen Morley, John Miljan, Jean Hersholt, Herman Bing, Edward Brophy

'Not bad, could have been better . . . that it takes 95 minutes to get home is the big fault.'—*Variety*

Flesh and Blood

GB 1951   102m   bw
BL / Harefield (Anatole de Grunwald)

Three generations of a family suffer from the effects of heredity.
Fragmented Scottish period piece which never settles down long enough to make an impact with any group of characters.

w Anatole de Grunwald, *play* A Sleeping Clergyman by James Bridie *d* Anthony Kimmins *ph* Otto Heller *m* Charles Williams

Richard Todd, Glynis Johns, Joan Greenwood, André Morell, Ursula Howells,

Freda Jackson, George Cole, James Hayter, Ronald Howard, Muriel Aked

Flesh and Fantasy*

US 1943   94m   bw
Universal (Charles Boyer, Julien Duvivier)

A club bore tells three strange stories.
A portmanteau with ingredients of varying interest, attempting to emulate the success of *Tales of Manhattan*. The fourth episode planned was deleted and turned up as *Destiny* (qv). All quite stylish, the best section being *Lord Arthur Savile's Crime*.

w Ernest Pascal, Samuel Hoffenstein, Ellis St Joseph, *stories* Ellis St Joseph, Oscar Wilde, Laslo Vadnay *d* Julien Duvivier *ph* Paul Ivano, Stanley Cortez *m* Alexandre Tansman

Robert Benchley, *Edward G. Robinson*, Barbara Stanwyck, Charles Boyer, Betty Field, Robert Cummings, *Thomas Mitchell*, C. Aubrey Smith, Dame May Whitty, Edgar Barrier, David Hoffman

Flesh and Fury

US 1952   82m   bw

A young deaf mute becomes a successful prizefighter. Totally unremarkable programmer with a happy ending. Tony Curtis, Jan Sterling, Mona Freeman, Wallace Ford, Connie Gilchrist. Written by Bernard Gordon; directed by Joseph Pevney; for Leonard Goldstein / Universal-International.

Flesh and the Devil*

US 1926   109m   bw   silent
MGM

A temptress toys with three men.
Hokey but good-looking star melodrama, climaxing with death on an ice floe. A huge commercial success because of the off-screen Garbo-Gilbert romance.

w Benjamin Glazer, *novel* The Undying Past by Hermann Sudermann *d* Clarence Brown

Greta Garbo, John Gilbert, Lars Hanson, Marc McDermott, Barbara Kent

'A film of more than passing cleverness . . . the theme is sheer undiluted sex, and Brown uses a series of close-ups to get this across with considerable effect.'—*Paul Rotha, The Film Till Now*

The Flesh and the Fiends

GB 1959   97m   bw   Dyaliscope
Regal / Triad (Robert Baker, Monty Berman)

In 1820 Edinburgh, 'resurrection men' commit murders to keep anatomists supplied.
Dr Robert Knox rides again, in a version more bloody but less entertaining than *The Body Snatcher*.

w John Gilling, Leon Griffiths *d* John Gilling *ph* Monty Berman *m* Stanley Black

Peter Cushing, June Laverick, George Rose, Donald Pleasence, Renée Houston, Billie Whitelaw, Dermot Walsh

The Flesh Is Weak

GB 1957   88m   bw

A girl goes from bad to worse when she finds

that her boy friend is head of a vice ring. Road to Ruin, fifties style; competently made, but neither shocking nor entertaining, just an exploitation piece. John Derek, Milly Vitale, William Franklyn, Martin Benson, Freda Jackson, Norman Wooland, Harold Lang, Patricia Jessel, John Paul. Written by Leigh Vance; directed by Don Chaffey; for Raymond Stross / Eros.

'What would you do if the man you loved wanted you to love his pal?'

Flight
US 1929 110m bw
Columbia (Harry Cohn)

Two rival flyers join a mission to rescue US Marines ambushed in Nicaragua.
Pale stuff now, but in its time an ambitious action movie showing a new suppleness in its young director.

w Frank Capra, Ralph Graves d Frank Capra ph Joseph Walker ad Harrison Wiley

Jack Holt, Lila Lee, Ralph Graves, Alan Roscoe, Harold Goodwin, Jimmy de la Cruze
'The first all-talking drama of the air!'— publicity

Flight Command
US 1940 116m bw
MGM (J. Walter Ruben)

A cocky recruit makes good in the naval air arm.
Routine flagwaver.

w Wells Root, Cmdr Harvey Haislip d Frank Borzage ph Harold Rosson m Franz Waxman

Robert Taylor, Ruth Hussey, Walter Pidgeon, Paul Kelly, Nat Pendleton, Red Skelton, Shepperd Strudwick, Dick Purcell

Flight Commander see The Dawn Patrol, for which this is the TV title (1930 version).

Flight for Freedom
US 1943 101m bw
RKO (David Hempstead)

Biography of an intrepid aviatrix and her husband.
Patchy job based on the life of Amelia Earhart, suggesting that her final disappearance was on a government mission. Dull production.

w Oliver H. P. Garrett, S. K. Lauren d Lothar Mendes ph Lee Garmes m Roy Webb

Rosalind Russell, Fred MacMurray, Herbert Marshall, Eduardo Ciannelli, Walter Kingsford

Flight from Ashiya*
US / Japan 1963 102m Eastmancolor Panavision
UA / Harold Hecht / Daiei

When a cargo vessel sinks off the coast of Japan during a typhoon, the helicopter rescue service springs into action.
Conventional Grade A action thriller with flashbacks to earlier disasters in the lives of its heroes.

w Elliot Arnold, Waldo Salt d Michael Anderson ph Joe MacDonald, Burnett Guffey m Frank Cordell pd Eugène Lourié

Yul Brynner, Richard Widmark, George Chakiris, Shirley Knight, Daniele Gaubert, Suzy Parker

Flight from Destiny
US 1941 74m bw

An elderly professor with six months to live determines on one good deed . . . which includes murder. Likeable minor melodrama, well put together. Thomas Mitchell, Geraldine Fitzgerald, Jeffrey Lynn, Mona Maris. Written by Barry Trivers, from a play by Anthony Berkeley; directed by Vincent Sherman; for Warner.

Flight from Folly
GB 1944 93m bw

A chorus girl cures a playwright's amnesia. Leadenly-titled and played variation on Random Harvest, with dreary musical numbers. Pat Kirkwood, Hugh Sinclair, Sydney Howard, Marian Spencer, Tamara Desni, Jean Gillie, A. E. Matthews. Written by Basil Woon, Lesley Storm and Katherine Strueby; directed by Herbert Mason; for Warner.

Flight from Glory*
US 1937 66m bw

Tensions mount among fliers who cross the Andes daily between secluded mines and their supply base. Tense 'B' picture which looks like a trial run for Only Angels Have Wings. Chester Morris, Whitney Bourne, Onslow Stevens, Van Heflin, Richard Lane, Paul Guilfoyle. Written by David Silverstein, John Twist; directed by Lew Landers; for Robert Sisk / RKO. 'Better than the average programmer and worth strong exhibitor plugging. In tone the picture may be fairly described as semi-sophisticated, which for rank and file purposes is probably just the right amount of sophistication.'—Variety

Flight of the Doves*
US 1971 101m colour
Columbia / Rainbow (Ralph Nelson)

Two children run away from their bullying stepfather to join their Irish grandmother, but are chased by a wicked uncle who knows they are heirs to a fortune.
Pantomimish whimsy which works in fits and starts, but has little real humour or charm.

wd Ralph Nelson, novel Walter Macken ph Harry Waxman m Roy Budd

Ron Moody, Dorothy McGuire, Helen Raye, Dana, Jack Wild, Stanley Holloway, William Rushton

The Flight of the Phoenix*
US 1965 149m De Luxe
TCF / Associates and Aldrich

A cargo passenger plane crashes in the desert, and the survivors try to avert disaster.
Achingly slow character adventure; an all-star cast works desperately hard but the final flight of the rebuilt plane seems almost an anti-climax after the surfeit of personal melodramatics.

w Lukas Heller, novel Elleston Trevor d Robert Aldrich ph Joseph Biroc m Frank de Vol

James Stewart, Richard Attenborough, Hardy Kruger, Peter Finch, Dan Duryea, Ernest Borgnine, Ian Bannen, Ronald Fraser, Christian Marquand, George Kennedy

AAN: Ian Bannen

The Flight that Disappeared
US 1961 73m bw
UA / Harvard (Robert E. Kent)

Atomic scientists on an airliner find themselves in 'heaven' being tried by people of the future.
Eccentric anti-bomb curiosity, a second feature Outward Bound.

w Ralph Hart, Judith Hart, Owen Harris d Reginald Le Borg ph Gilbert Warrenton m Richard La Salle

Gregory Morton, Addison Richards, Craig Hill, Paula Raymond, Dayton Lummis

Flight to Mars
US 1951 75m Cinecolor

After a rocket flight, four scientists discover that the inhabitants of Mars speak perfect American, learned by radio. Pioneering science-fiction entry with nothing going for it but being first: writing, production and acting are alike abysmal. Cameron Mitchell, Marguerite Chapman, Arthur Franz, Virginia Huston, John Litel. Written by Arthur Strawn; directed by Lesley Selander; for Monogram.

Flight to Tangier
US 1953 90m Technicolor 3-D
Paramount (Nat Holt)

A female FBI agent chases a three million dollar letter of credit.
Forced and boring action romance without much of either element.

wd Charles Marquis Warren ph Ray Rennahan m Paul Sawtell

Joan Fontaine, Jack Palance, Corinne Calvet, Robert Douglas, Marcel Dalio, Jeff Morrow, Murray Matheson, John Doucette

The Flim Flam Man*
US 1967 104m De Luxe Panavision
TCF / Lawrence Turman
GB title: One Born Every Minute

An army deserter joins forces with an elderly con man.
Folksy comedy in a small-town setting; none of it really comes to the boil after a couple of early chase sequences.

w William Rose, novel Guy Owen d Irvin Kershner, Yakima Canutt ph Charles Lang m Jerry Goldsmith

George C. Scott, Michael Sarrazin, Sue Lyon, Harry Morgan, Jack Albertson, Alice Ghostley, Albert Salmi

Flipper
US 1963 87m Metrocolor
(MGM) Ivan Tors

A fisherman's son on the Florida Keys
befriends a dolphin.
Harmless boy-and-animal adventure which
spawned two sequels and a TV series.

w Arthur Weiss d James B. Clark ph Lamar
Boren, Joseph Brun m Henry Vars

Chuck Connors, Luke Halpin, Kathleen
Maguire, Connie Scott

Flirtation Walk°
US 1934 97m bw
Warner (Frank Borzage)

Love affairs of West Point cadets.
Light musical very typical of its period, with a
few agreeable numbers.

w Delmer Daves d Frank Borzage ch Bobby
Connelly ph Sol Polito, George Barnes
m / ly Allie Wrubel, Mort Dixon

Dick Powell, Ruby Keeler, Pat O'Brien, Ross
Alexander, John Arledge, Henry O'Neill,
Guinn Williams

'A rousing recruiting poster . . . and a
splendid laboratory specimen of the adolescent
cinema.'—André Sennwald, New York Times

AAN: best picture

The Flirting Widow
US 1930 70m bw

A girl invents a lover, then kills him off . . .
but his friend shows up. Whimsical comedy
which outstays its welcome. Dorothy Mackaill,
Basil Rathbone, Leila Hyams, Claude
Gillingwater, William Austin. Written by John
F. Goodrich from the story Green Stockings
by A. E. W. Mason; directed by William A.
Seiter; for First National. 'Slim for the key
houses and really built for neighbourhoods.'—
Variety

Flirting with Fate
US 1938 70m bw

A trailerized vaudeville troupe tours South
America. The setting is the only surprising
thing about this rather dim comedy. Joe E.
Brown, Leo Carrillo, Beverly Roberts, Wynne
Gibson, Steffi Duna, Stanley Fields, Leonid
Kinskey, Charles Judels. Written by Joseph
Moncure March, Ethel La Blanche, Charlie
Melson, Harry Clork; directed by Frank
McDonald; for David L. Loew.

Floods of Fear°
GB 1958 84m bw
Rank / Sydney Box

Two escaped convicts, a warder, and a pretty
girl are trapped by floods in a lonely house.
Adequate melodrama with impressively
gloomy production and performances but not
many surprises.

wd Charles Crichton, novel Joan and Ward
Hawkins ph Christopher Challis m Alan
Rawsthorne

Howard Keel, Anne Heywood, Harry H.
Corbett, Cyril Cusack

Floodtide
GB 1949 90m bw

A Clydebank apprentice becomes a ship
designer. Boring inspirational drama hindered
by the Independent Frame method. Gordon
Jackson, Rona Anderson, John Laurie, Jack
Lambert, Elizabeth Sellars. Written by
Donald B. Wilson and George Blake; directed
by Frederick Wilson; for Aquila / Rank.

The Floradora Girl
US 1930 75m bw (Technicolor
    sequence)

The romance of the last remaining Floradora
girl. Not a musical but a period farce which
laughs at rather than with the fashions of 1900.
It doubtless succeeded with the audiences of
its time. Marion Davies, Lawrence Gray,
Walter Catlett, Ilka Chase, Vivian Oakland,
Jed Prouty. Written by Gene Markey, Ralph
Spence, Al Boasberg, Robert Hopkins;
directed by Harry Beaumont; for MGM.
'Good hoke entertainment . . . an all-type
audience picture with no limitations.'—Variety
(GB title: The Gay Nineties.)

The Florentine Dagger
US 1935 69m bw

A mysterious Borgia influence is brought to
bear on the murder of an art dealer. Vaguely
unsatisfactory whodunnit with some intriguing
and some pretentious elements. Margaret
Lindsay, Donald Woods, C. Aubrey Smith,
Robert Barrat, Henry O'Neill. Written by
Brown Holmes and Tom Reed, from the novel
by Ben Hecht; directed by Robert Florey; for
Warner.

Florian
US 1940 91m bw
MGM (Winfield Sheehan)

In 1910 Austria, a poor boy and a rich girl are
united by their love of a Lippizaner stallion.
Not kinky, but strangely dull.

w Noel Langley, Geza Herczeg, James K.
McGuinness d Edwin L. Marin ph Karl
Freund, Richard Rosson m Franz Waxman

Robert Young, Helen Gilbert, Charles
Coburn, Lee Bowman, Reginald Owen, S. Z.
Sakall, Lucile Watson, Irina Baronova

Flower Drum Song°
US 1961 133m Technicolor
    Panavision
U-I / Rodgers and Hammerstein / Joseph
Fields (Ross Hunter)

Romantic problems among the immigrants in
San Francisco's Chinatown.
A Broadway musical which on the screen
seems old-fashioned, remorselessly cute, and
even insulting to the Chinese characters.
Within its limits, however, it is well enough
staged and performed.

w Joseph Fields d Henry Koster m / ly
Richard Rodgers, Oscar Hammerstein II
md Alfred Newman, Ken Darby ph Russell
Metty ad Alexander Golitzen, Joseph Weight
costumes Irene Sharaff ch Hermes Pan

Nancy Kwan, James Shigeta, Juanita Hall,
Myoshi Umeki, James Soo, Sen Yung

AAN: Alfred Newman, Ken Darby; Russell
Metty

Flowing Gold
US 1940 82m bw

A fugitive from justice finds himself in a
western oilfield. Routine melodrama with
climactic heroics and nothing to remember
next day. John Garfield, Pat O'Brien, Frances
Farmer, Raymond Walburn, Cliff Edwards.
Written by Kenneth Gamet; directed by
Alfred E. Green; for Warner.

Fluffy
US 1964 92m Eastmancolor
U-I / Scarus (Gordon Kay)

A biologist manages to tame a lion.
Mindless, cheerful animal comedy.

w Samuel Rocca d Earl Bellamy ph Clifford
Stine m Irving Gertz

Tony Randall, Shirley Jones, Edward
Andrews, Ernest Truex, Howard Morris, Jim
Backus, Frank Faylen

The Flute and the Arrow°
Sweden 1957 75m Technicolor
    Agascope
Sandrews (Arne Sucksdorff)
original title: En Djungelsaga

The story of a remote Indian tribe and a
prowling leopard thought to be possessed by a
demon.
Superbly photographed but rather dull:
Sucksdorff failed to provide enough story for a
feature.

wd, ph Arne Sucksdorff m Ravi Shankar

'Once it was human . . . even as you and I
    . . . this monster created by atoms gone
    wild!'
The Fly
US 1958 94m Eastmancolor
    Cinemascope
TCF (Kurt Neumann)

A scientist invents a method of transmitting
and reassembling atoms. He transmits himself
and does not notice a fly in the
compartment . . .
Unpleasant horror film which becomes
ludicrous but not funny.

w James Clavell d Kurt Neumann ph Karl
Struss m Paul Sawtell

David Hedison, Patricia Owens, Herbert
Marshall, Vincent Price

† Sequels were Return of the Fly (1959) and
Curse of the Fly (1965), neither worth noting
in detail.

'Action that makes every pulse beat sound
    like thunder!'
Fly By Night°
US 1942 74m bw

A doctor, accused of murdering a scientist,
goes on the run and uncovers a Nazi spy ring.
Hoary 39 Steps imitation, commendably done
on a low budget to furnish wartime
propaganda. Richard Carlson, Nancy Kelly,

Albert Basserman, Walter Kingsford, Martin Kosleek, Miles Mander. Written by Jay Dratler and F. Hugh Herbert; directed by Robert Siodmak; for Paramount. (GB title: *Secrets of G32.*)

The Flying Deuces*
US 1939 67m bw
Boris Morros

Laurel and Hardy join the Foreign Legion.
Patchy comedy from the end of the comedians' period of glory, and showing signs of decline.

w Ralph Spence, Harry Langdon, Charles Rogers, Alfred Schiller d Edward Sutherland ph Art Lloyd, Elmer Dyer

Stan Laurel, Oliver Hardy, Jean Parker, James Finlayson, Reginald Gardiner, Charles Middleton

'Mechanical stuff . . . seemed like *Beau Hunks* and *Bonnie Scotland* all over again.'— *William K. Everson*

● Video: Mountain

Flying Devils
US 1933 62m bw

Three war veteran pilots join a flying circus.
Smart little programmer which certainly provided money's worth and has no axe to grind. Arline Judge, Bruce Cabot, Ralph Bellamy, Eric Linden, Cliff Edwards. Written by Byron Morgan, Louis Stevens; directed by Russell Birdwell; photographed by Nicholas Musuraca; music by Max Steiner; for RKO. (GB title: *The Flying Circus.*)

Flying Down to Rio**
US 1933 89m bw
RKO (Merian C. Cooper, Lou Brock)

A dance band is a big success in Rio de Janeiro.
A thin musical electrified by the finale in which girls dance on the wings of moving airplanes, and by the teaming of Astaire and Rogers for the first time. Now an irresistible period piece.

w Cyril Hume, H. W. Hannemann, Erwin Gelsey, *play* Anne Caldwell d Thornton Freeland ph J. Roy Hunt m Vincent Youmans ly Edward Eliscu, Gus Kahn ch Dave Gould

Dolores del Rio, Gene Raymond, Raul Roulien, *Ginger Rogers, Fred Astaire*, Blanche Frederici, Walter Walker, Franklin Pangborn, Eric Blore

'Its main point is the screen promise of Fred Astaire . . . the others are all hoofers after him.'—*Variety*
Other songs: 'Music Makes Me'; 'Orchids in the Moonlight'; 'Flying Down to Rio'

AAN: song 'The Carioca'

Flying Elephants
US 1927 20m bw silent

A caveman has the toothache. Fragmentary and generally unsatisfactory comedy starring Laurel and Hardy before they properly teamed, but released after their joint success. Written by Hal Roach and H. M. Walker; directed by Fred Butler and Hal Roach; for Hal Roach.

Flying Fortress
GB 1942 104m bw
Warner

A Canadian becomes a hero of bombing missions over Berlin.
Cardboard propaganda with silly love interest and a hilarious climax in which the hero does his stuff on the wing of a flying plane.

w Brock Williams, Gordon Wellesley, Edward Dryhurst d Walter Forde ph Gus Drisse, Basil Emmott

Richard Greene, Carla Lehmann, Betty Stockfield, Donald Stewart, Charles Heslop, Sidney King, Basil Radford, John Stuart

Flying High
US 1931 80m bw

A zany inventor breaks a long-distance flight record because he doesn't know how to land.
Primitive comedy musical with inept dialogue and a static camera, partially salvaged by two early Busby Berkeley routines. Bert Lahr, Charlotte Greenwood, Pat O'Brien, Charles Winninger, Guy Kibbee, Hedda Hopper. Written by Robert Hopkins, A. P. Younger and Charles Riesner; directed by Charles Riesner; for MGM. (GB title: *Happy Landing.*)

Flying Leathernecks
US 1951 102m Technicolor
RKO (Edmund Grainger)

Two marine officers fight the Japs and each other on Guadalcanal.
Empty, violent war actioner full of phoney heroics.

w James Edward Grant d Nicholas Ray ph William E. Snyder m Roy Webb

John Wayne, Robert Ryan, Janis Carter, Don Taylor, Jay C. Flippen, William Harrigan, James Bell

'Ray's treatment is depressingly second rate and does nothing to alleviate the unpleasant impression of this disturbingly violent production.'—*Penelope Houston*

● Video: Kingston

The Flying Missile
US 1950 92m bw
Columbia (Jerry Bresler)

A submarine commander defies authority to prove that rockets can be launched from the deck of a submarine.
Dated semi-documentary melodrama which was pretty flat on first viewing.

w Richard English, James Gunn d Henry Levin ph William Snyder m George Duning

Glenn Ford, Viveca Lindfors, Henry O'Neill, Carl Benton Reid, Joe Sawyer, John Qualen

The Flying Scotsman
GB 1929 63m bw

An ex-employee tries to wreck a crack train.
Fairly presentable example of an early talkie film originally shot silent; one or two climactic thrills. Moore Marriott, Pauline Jameson, Ray Milland, Dino Galvani. Written by Victor Kendal and Garnett Weston; directed by Castleton Knight; for BIP.

'A bomber squadron wouldn't get through . . . but one ship might make it!'

Flying Tigers
US 1942 100m bw
Republic (Edmund Grainger)

American airmen fight the Japs over World War II China.
More mock heroics with noisy but unconvincing action sequences.

w Kenneth Gamet, Barry Trivers d David Miller ph Jack Marta m Victor Young

John Wayne, John Carroll, Anna Lee, Paul Kelly, Mae Clarke

AAN: Victor Young

FM (aka *Citizens' Band*)
US 1978 104m Technicolor

Problems of a commercial radio station whose disc jockeys seek integrity above commerce.
Footling cause-pleading is all this 'with-it' movie has to offfer apart from its picture of commercial radio in the late seventies, which should be of interest to social historians.
Michael Brandon, Eileen Brennan, Alex Karras, Cleavon Little, Martin Mull. Written by Ezra Sacks; directed by John A. Alonzo; for Universal.

Fog
US 1933 70m bw

Three murders occur on an ocean liner enveloped in fog. Promising but increasingly inept mystery with an unconvincing solution.
Donald Cook, Mary Brian, Reginald Denny, Robert McQuade, Maude Eburne. Written by Ethel Hill and Dore Schary from a magazine story by Valentine Williams and Dorothy Rice Sims; directed by Albert Rogell; for Columbia. 'Ably directed but deficient on casting and story.'—*Variety*

The Fog*
US 1979 91m Metrocolor Panavision
Avco / Debra Hill

A small Californian town is invaded by the leprous ghosts of mariners wrecked on the coast a hundred years before.
Silly but beguiling horror film with shock effects typical of its director.

w John Carpenter, Debra Hill d John Carpenter ph Dean Cundey m John Carpenter pd Tommy Lee Wallace

Adrienne Barbeau, Hal Holbrook, John Houseman, Janet Leigh, Jamie Lee Curtis, Tom Atkins

'An uneasy venture down a blind alley.'— *Tom Milne, MFB*

● Video: Embassy

Fog over Frisco***
US 1934 68m bw
Warner (Henry Blanke)

A San Francisco heiress gets herself murdered.
Silly whodunnit highly notable for its cinematic style, all dissolves, wipes and quick takes. Probably the fastest moving film ever made, and very entertaining despite its plot inadequacy.

w Robert N. Lee, *novel* George Dyer
d William Dieterle *ph* Tony Gaudio *md* Leo
F. Forbstein *ed* Harold McLernon

Bette Davis, Donald Woods, Margaret
Lindsay, Lyle Talbot, Hugh Herbert, Arthur
Byron, Robert Barrat, Douglass Dumbrille,
Henry O'Neill, Irving Pichel, Alan Hale

'Another racketeering story, mild in
entertainment. No marked names of
strength.'—*Variety*

'It reveals those qualities of pace and
velocity and sharpness which make the
Hollywood product acceptable even when the
shallow content of ideas makes you want to
scream.'—*Robert Forsythe*

'Its speed is artificially created by pacing,
wipes, opticals, overlapping sound, camera
movement and placing of characters, and by
its habit of never having time really to begin or
end scenes.'—*William K. Everson*

† Remade 1942 as *Spy Ship*, a second feature.

Folies Bergère***
US 1935 84m bw
Twentieth Century (William Goetz,
  Raymond Griffith)
GB title: *The Man from the Folies Bergère*

A Parisian banker persuades a music hall artist
to impersonate him, but the wife and girl
friend become involved in the confusion.
Amusing star vehicle with inventive
Berkeleyish numbers and some remarkably
sexy dialogue.

w Bess Meredyth, Hal Long, *play* The Red
Cat by Rudolph Lothar, Hans Adler *d* Roy
del Ruth *ph* Barney McGill, Peverell Marley
md Alfred Newman *ch* Dave Gould

Maurice Chevalier, Merle Oberon, Ann
Sothern, Eric Blore

† Remade as *That Night in Rio*, with Don
Ameche, and *On the Riviera*, with Danny
Kaye (both qv).

Follow a Star
GB 1959 104m bw
Rank (Hugh Stewart)

A shy amateur singer allows a fading star to
mime to his voice.
Star comedy with an antique plot and a
superfluity of pathos.

w Jack Davies, Henry Blyth, Norman
Wisdom *d* Robert Asher *ph* Jack Asher
m Philip Green

Norman Wisdom, Jerry Desmonde, June
Laverick, Hattie Jacques, Richard Wattis,
John Le Mesurier, Fenella Fielding, Ron
Moody

'Such comedy as there is is mostly muffed by
the lack of any sense of comic timing.'—*MFB*

Follow Me
GB 1971 93m Technicolor Panavision
Universal / Hal B. Wallis (Paul Nathan)
US title: *The Public Eye*

An eccentric private eye is hired to follow an
accountant's wife, and she finds him
fascinating.
Dullish, whimsical rendering of a dullish,
whimsical one-act play; it never springs to life
or interest.

FOG OVER FRISCO.   Arthur Byron finds two headstrong girls (Margaret Lindsay and Bette
Davis) too much for one head of family to cope with.

w Peter Shaffer, from his play *d* Carol Reed
ph Christopher Challis *m* John Barry

Topol, Michael Jayston, Mia Farrow

'An uneasy mixture of broad comedy and
high romance.'—*Sight and Sound*

Follow Me Boys
US 1966 132m Technicolor
Walt Disney (Winston Hibler)

The domestic trials and tribulations of a small-
town schoolmaster.
Sentimental family saga full of patriotic
fervour.

w Louis Pelletier, *novel* God and My Country
by Mackinlay Kantor *d* Norman Tokar
ph Clifford Stine *m* George Bruns

Fred MacMurray, Vera Miles, Lillian Gish,
Charlie Ruggles, Elliott Reid, Kurt Russell,
Luana Patten, Ken Murray

'Demands an extremely strong stomach.'—
MFB

Follow That Camel
GB 1967 95m Eastmancolor

An English gentleman is accused of fraud and
joins the Foreign Legion. A Carry On in all
but name, and not the best of them despite an
American co-star and better-than-average
production values. Phil Silvers, Jim Dale,
Charles Hawtrey, Kenneth Williams, Anita
Harris, Joan Sims, Bernard Bresslaw. Written
by Talbot Rothwell; directed by Gerald
Thomas; for Peter Rogers / Rank. (Reissue
title: *Carry On, Follow That Camel*.)

Follow That Dream
US 1962 110m De Luxe Panavision
UA / Mirisch (David Weisbart)

A wandering family sets up house on a Florida
beach.
Tiresomely cute comedy vehicle for a resistible
star.

w Charles Lederer, *novel* Pioneer Go Home
by Richard Powell *d* Gordon Douglas
ph Leo Tover *m* Hans Salter

Elvis Presley, Arthur O'Connell, Joanna
Moore, Anne Helm, Jack Kruschen

Follow the Boys*
US 1944 109m bw
Universal (Charles K. Feldman)

A song and dance man organizes
entertainment for the US troops during World
War II.
Scrappy, unattractive propaganda tribute by
the stars to the stars, enlivened only by a few
guest spots.

w Lou Breslow, Gertrude Purcell
d A. Edward Sutherland *ph* David Abel
m Leigh Harline and others

George Raft, Vera Zorina, Charley Grapewin,
Grace MacDonald, Charles Butterworth,
George Macready, Elizabeth Patterson; and
Orson Welles, Marlene Dietrich, Jeanette
MacDonald, Dinah Shore, Donald O'Connor,
Peggy Ryan, W. C. Fields, the Andrews
Sisters, Artur Rubenstein, Sophie Tucker, Ted
Lewis and his band, etc

AAN: song 'I'll Walk Alone' (*m* Jule Styne, *ly* Sammy Cahn)

Follow the Boys

US 1963 95m Metrocolor Panavision
MGM / Franmet (Laurence P. Bachmann)

An American warship is diverted from Cannes to Santa Margarita, and the waiting wives have to follow by road.
Harmless star comedy musical.

w David T. Chantler, David Osborn
d Richard Thorpe *ph* Ted Scaife

Connie Francis, Paula Prentiss, Dany Robin, Russ Tamblyn, Richard Long

Follow the Fleet**

US 1936 110m bw
RKO (Pandro S. Berman)

Sailors on shore leave romance a couple of girl singers.
Amiable star musical which makes heavy weather of a listless and overlong script, but has good numbers for those who can wait.

w Dwight Taylor, *play* Shore Leave by Hubert Osborne, Allan Scott *d* Mark Sandrich
ph David Abel *m* / *ly* Irving Berlin

Fred Astaire, Ginger Rogers, Randolph Scott, Harriet Hilliard, Astrid Allwyn, Harry Beresford, Lucille Ball, Betty Grable, Tony Martin

Songs: 'I'm Putting All My Eggs in One Basket'; 'We Saw the Sea'; 'Let's Face the Music and Dance'; 'Let Yourself Go'; 'But Where Are You?'; 'I'd Rather Lead a Band'; 'Get Thee Behind Me Satan'

'The running time is way overboard . . . dialogue is good and can be depended on for laughs, with the Astaire-Rogers dancing sure to do the rest. But cutting it would have helped a lot more.'—*Variety*

Follow the Leader

US 1930 76m bw

A saucy understudy replaces a kidnapped leading lady. Broadway spoof rather tediously designed as a vehicle for the star's face-pulling. Ed Wynn, Ginger Rogers, Ethel Merman, Lou Holtz, Stanley Smith. Written by Sid Silvers and Gertrude Purcell from the Broadway musical Manhattan Mary; directed by Norman Taurog; for Paramount. 'First-run material and above average.'—*Variety*

Follow the Sun

US 1951 93m bw
TCF (Samuel G. Engel)

Ben Hogan, a professional golfer, recovers slowly and painfully from a car crash and for the first time gains the affection of the crowd.
Modest sporting biopic, generally watchable but rising to no great heights.

w Frederick Hazlitt Brennan *d* Sidney Lanfield *ph* Leo Tover *m* Cyril Mockridge

Glenn Ford, Anne Baxter, Dennis O'Keefe, June Havoc, Larry Keating, Nana Bryant, Roland Winters

Follow Thru

US 1930 93m Technicolor

Two women are after the same pro golfer. Flat film version of a Broadway show. Charles Rogers, Nancy Carroll, Zelma O'Neal, Jack Haley, Eugene Pallette, Thelma Todd. Written from their show by De Sylva, Brown and Henderson; directed by Laurence Schwab and Lloyd Corrigan; for Paramount. 'Paramount has tossed away a heavy money picture.'—*Variety*

Songs: 'Button Up Your Overcoat'; 'You Wouldn't Fool Me Would You'; 'I'm Hard to Please'; 'A Peach of a Pair'; 'It Must be You'.

Folly to be Wise*

GB 1952 91m bw
London Films / Launder and Gilliat

A brains trust at an army unit starts off a battle of the sexes.
Typical James Bridie comedy which starts brightly and whimsically, then peters out and is saved by the acting.

w Frank Launder, John Dighton, *play* It Depends What You Mean by James Bridie
d Frank Launder *ph* Jack Hildyard
m Temple Abady

Alastair Sim, Roland Culver, Elizabeth Allan, Martita Hunt, Colin Gordon

'It seems to get funnier the longer it's spun out.'—*Pauline Kael, 70s*

The Food of the Gods

US 1976 88m Movielab
AIP (Bert I. Gordon)

A curious substance which oozes out of the ground turns common beasts into monsters. Rather crude horror movie which has little affinity with its literary original.

wd Bert I. Gordon, *story* H. G. Wells
ph Reginald Morris *m* Elliot Kaplan

Marjoe Gortner, Pamela Franklin, Ida Lupino, Ralph Meeker, John McLiam

'Not only sick, but sickening.'—*Arthur Knight*

'I wish I hadn't seen the movie, so I could avoid it like the plague.'—*John Simon*

'More plot holes than any movie in recent memory, and enough dopey lines to make a Saturday night audience howl in all the wrong places.'—*David Sterritt, Christian Science Monitor*

A Fool There Was*

US 1914 67m (24 fps) bw silent
William Fox

A financier in Europe forsakes all for a *femme fatale*, and dies in her arms.
Antediluvian moral melodrama which made a star of Bara and added the word 'vamp' to the language.

wd Frank Powell, play Porter Emerson Browne suggested by Rudyard Kipling's poem The Vampire

Theda Bara, Edward Jose, Mabel Frenyer, May Allison

Foolin' Around

US 1979 101m De Luxe
Columbia / Arnold Kopelson

A country bumpkin wins a runaway heiress. Uneasy harkback to the innocence of It Happened One Night, with willing performers in search of a script and setting.

w Mike Kane, David Swift *d* Richard T. Heffron *ph* Philip Lathrop *m* Charles Bernstein

Gary Busey, Annette O'Toole, John Calvin, Eddie Albert, Cloris Leachman, Tony Randall

Foolish Wives**

US 1921 85m approx (24 fps); originally much longer bw silent
Universal

In Monte Carlo, a fake count seduces and blackmails rich women.
Weird melodrama with memorable moments and a vast set; Stroheim's most vivid star performance and one of his most lavish productions.

wd Erich Von Stroheim *ph* Ben Reynolds, William Daniels *ad* Erich Von Stroheim, *Richard Day*

Erich Von Stroheim, Mae Busch, Maud George, Cesare Gravina

'A very superior piece of photoplay craftsmanship, original in ideas and treatment and deserving of higher rating than *Orphans of the Storm, Loves of Pharaoh, The Storm* and other second-class material which however brought forth applause and bravos from screen public and scribes.'—*Tamar Lane, What's Wrong with the Movies*

† The film was released in Latin America at a length of 6hrs 48m.

Fools

US 1970 93m Eastmancolor

An unsuccessful actor has an idyllic love affair with a girl he meets in a park; but her jealous millionaire husband shoots her dead. Foolish is the word for those who concocted this tedious parable about the innocence of love and the sickness of society. Jason Robards Jnr, Katharine Ross, Scott Hylands. Written by Robert Rudelson; directed by Tom Gries; for Translor.

Fools for Scandal*

US 1938 81m bw
Warner (Mervyn Le Roy)

A Hollywood movie star falls in love with a French nobleman.
Disappointingly leaden romantic comedy.

w Herbert and Joseph Fields, *play* Return Engagement by Nancy Hamilton, Rosemary Casey, James Shute *d* Mervyn Le Roy
ph Ted Tetzlaff *m* Richard Rodgers, Lorenz Hart

Carole Lombard, Fernand Gravet, Ralph Bellamy, Allen Jenkins, Isabel Jeans, Marie Wilson, Ottola Nesmith

'Many diverting moments . . . will do average business.'—*Variety*

Fools Parade**

US 1971 98m Eastmancolor
Columbia / Stanmore / Penbar (Andrew V. McLaglen)
GB title: *Dynamite Man from Glory Jail*

An ex-con has trouble cashing a cheque for his prison savings, especially as outlaws are after it.

Curious admixture of comedy, adventure and violence with a thirties setting, from the author of *Night of the Hunter*; generally gripping entertainment.

w James Lee Barrett, novel Davis Grubb d Andrew V. McLaglen ph Harry Stradling Jnr m Henry Vars

James Stewart, George Kennedy, Strother Martin, Anne Baxter, Kurt Russell, William Windom, Mike Kellin

'A quintessentially American tribute to the quiet heroism of the self-made man.'—*Nigel Andrews*

Fools Rush In
GB 1949   82m   bw

A girl changes her mind on her wedding day, and causes repercussions through the family.
Thin, flat film version of a successful play.
Sally Ann Howes, Guy Rolfe, Nora Swinburne, Nigel Buchanan, Raymond Lovell, Thora Hird. Written by Geoffrey Kerr, from the play by Kenneth Horne; directed by John Paddy Carstairs; for Rank.

'Can you even think of missing it?'

Footlight Parade***
US 1933   104m   bw
Warner (Robert Lord)

A determined producer of cine-variety numbers gets the show going despite great difficulty.
Classic putting-on-a-show musical distinguished by rapid-fire dialogue, New York setting, star performances and some of the best Busby Berkeley numbers.

w Manuel Seff, James Seymour d Lloyd Bacon ch Busby Berkeley ph George Barnes ad Anton Grot, Jack Okey m / ly Harry Warren, Al Dubin, Sammy Fain, Irving Fahal

James Cagney, Joan Blondell, Ruby Keeler, Dick Powell, Frank McHugh, Guy Kibbee, Ruth Donnelly, Hugh Herbert, Claire Dodd, Herman Bing
Songs: 'By a Waterfall'; 'Ah, the Moon Is Here'; 'Sitting on a Backyard Fence'; 'Shanghai Lil'; 'Honeymoon Hotel'

'1,000 surprises! 300 beauties! 20 big stars!'—*publicity*

'Bevies of beauty and mere males disport themselves in a Honeymoon Hotel, by (and in) a Waterfall, and over several acres of Shanghai.'—*C. A. Lejeune*

† The Chester Kent studio was a take-off of Fanchon and Marco, who had just such a studio on Sunset Boulevard.

Footlight Serenade
US 1942   80m   bw
TCF (William LeBaron)

A boxer romances a showgirl.
Indifferent star musical.

w Robert Ellis, Helen Logan, Lynn Starling d Gregory Ratoff ph Lee Garmes md Charles Henderson songs Ralph Rainger, Leo Robin

Betty Grable, John Payne, Victor Mature, James Gleason, Phil Silvers, Jane Wyman, Cobina Wright Jnr, June Lang, Mantan Moreland

Footloose
US 1984   107m   Movielab
Paramount / Indieprod (Lewis J. Rachmil, Craig Sedan)

The domination of an old-fashioned local preacher is slackened by a young newcomer who insists on arranging a dance.
Odd fable which seeks to combine *Flashdance* with *Rebel without a Cause*, and misses out on both.

w Dean Pitchford d Herbert Ross ph Ric Waite pd Ron Hobbs m various

Kevin Bacon, Lori Singer, John Lithgow, Dianne Wiest, Christopher Penn

'The celebration of teenage frustration as dance reduces the issues to the level of platitude.'—*Donald Greig, MFB*

Footsteps in the Dark
US 1941   96m   bw
Warner (Robert Ford)

A would-be detective novelist on the lookout for story material finds himself solving a murder.
Lethargic modern vehicle for Flynn between his swashbucklers, a poor imitation of the *Thin Man* style.

w Lester Cole, John Wexley, play Blondie White by Ladislas Fodor d Lloyd Bacon ph Ernest Haller m Frederick Hollander

Errol Flynn, Brenda Marshall, Ralph Bellamy, Alan Hale, Lucile Watson, Allen Jenkins, Lee Patrick, William Frawley, Roscoe Karns, Grant Mitchell

'The footsteps were those of restless patrons on their way out to buy popcorn.'—*Clive Hirschhorn*

'When he comes to her room at midnight, is it to kiss or kill?'

Footsteps in the Fog*
GB 1955   90m   Technicolor
Columbia / Mike Frankovich (Maxwell Setton)

A Victorian murderer plans to eliminate a blackmailing maid.
This variation on *Gaslight* turns into a black comedy without laughs, but it has effective moments and is efficiently if charmlessly made.

w Dorothy Reid, Lenore Coffee, story The Interruption by W. W. Jacobs d Arthur Lubin ph Christopher Challis m Benjamin Frankel ad Wilfrid Shingleton

Stewart Granger, Jean Simmons, Bill Travers, Ronald Squire, Finlay Currie, Peter Bull

For a Few Dollars More
Italy / Spain / West Germany 1965   130m
Techniscope
PEA / Gonzales / Constantin (Alberto Grimaldi)

Bounty hunters in El Paso agree to work together.
Vague, inflated, sometimes good-looking sequel to *A Fistful of Dollars*, with customary violence and predictably mean performances.

w/d Sergio Leone ph Massimo Dallamano m Ennio Morricone

Clint Eastwood, Lee Van Cleef, Gian Maria Volonte, Klaus Kinski
● *Video: Warner*

For Better For Worse
GB 1954   84m   Eastmancolor

Tribulations of a young married couple.
Undernourished comedy with an agreeable cast but no surprises. Dirk Bogarde, Susan Stephen, Cecil Parker, Dennis Price, Athene Seyler, Eileen Herlie, Thora Hird, James Hayter, Pia Terri, Sid James, Charles Victor. Written and directed by J. Lee-Thompson, from the play by Arthur Watkyn; for Kenneth Harper/ABP.

For Freedom
GB 1940   88m   bw
GFD / Gainsborough (Edward Black, Castleton Knight)

Events surrounding the Battle of the River Plate and the sinking of the Graf Spee.
Economical wartime potboiler with much use of newsreel.

w Miles Malleson, Leslie Arliss d Maurice Elvey

Will Fyffe, Anthony Hulme, E. V. H. Emmett, Guy Middleton, Albert Lieven

For Heaven's Sake
US 1950   92m   bw
TCF (William Perlberg)

Two angels are sent to earth to mend a Broadway producer's marriage.
Silly, flat whimsy of the *Here Comes Mr Jordan* school, and originating from the same author. Stale beer, but historically interesting.

w George Seaton, play Harry Segall d George Seaton ph Lloyd Ahern m Alfred Newman

Clifton Webb, Edmund Gwenn, Robert Cummings, Joan Bennett, Joan Blondell, Gigi Perreau, Jack La Rue

For Love of Ivy
US 1968   100m   Perfectcolor
Cinerama / Palomar (Edgar J. Scherick, Jay Weston)

An invaluable coloured maid gives notice, and the family blackmails a likeable black ne'er-do-well to make love to her so that she will stay.
Unhappy whimsy with an extremely laboured script and no jokes, notable only as Hollywood's first bow towards a black love affair.

w Robert Alan Aurthur, story Sidney Poitier d Daniel Mann ph Joseph Coffey m Quincy Jones

Sidney Poitier, Abby Lincoln, Beau Bridges, Carroll O'Connor, Nan Martin, Lauri Peters

AAN: title song (m Quincy Jones, ly Bob Russell)

● *Video: Guild*

For Love or Money
US 1963   108m   Technicolor
U-I (Robert Arthur)

A rich widow hires a lawyer to look after the affairs of her three wayward daughters; he picks the eldest for himself.

Slow, thin, overlong comedy with a surfeit of witless chat.

w Larry Marks, Michael Morris d Michael Gordon ph Clifford Stine m Frank de Vol

Kirk Douglas, Mitzi Gaynor, Thelma Ritter, William Bendix, Gig Young

For Me and My Gal***
US 1942 104m bw
MGM (Arthur Freed)

Just before World War I, a girl vaudevillian chooses between two partners.

A routine musical romance at the time of its production, this film now stands out because of its professional execution, its star value, and the fact that they don't make 'em like that any more.

w Richard Sherman, Sid Silvers, Fred Finkelhoffe d Busby Berkeley ph William Daniels md Georgie Stoll, Roger Edens

Judy Garland, Gene Kelly, George Murphy, Marta Eggerth, Ben Blue, Richard Quine, Stephen McNally

'A touch of imagination and a deal more than a touch of energy.'—The Times

AAN: Georgie Stoll, Roger Edens

For Men Only
US 1952 95m bw

A college professor is shocked when a death ensues from a freshman 'hazing' ceremony. Weird exploitation study of supposed college rites. Paul Henreid, Robert Sherman, Russell Johnson, Margaret Field, Vera Miles. Written by Lou Morheim and Herbert Margolies; directed and produced by Paul Henreid; for Lippert. 'Henreid allots himself an over-generous proportion of screen time—walking in and out of doors, smiling at the camera, being charming.'—MFB

For Pete's Sake*
US 1974 90m Eastmancolor
Columbia / Rastar / Persky–Bright–Barclay (Martin Erlichmann, Stanley Shapiro)

A New York taxi driver's wife borrows money and finds herself heavily committed to work off the debt.

Involved farcical comedy with amusing passages.

w Stanley Shapiro, Martin Richlin d Peter Yates ph Laszlo Kovacs m Artie Butler

Barbra Streisand, Michael Sarrazin, Estelle Parsons, William Redfield, Molly Picon

'Revives memories of how much more inventively they used to do it thirty years ago.'—Sight and Sound

For the Defense*
US 1930 62m bw

Exploits of a New York criminal lawyer. Slick programme picture of its day; it gave a lift to its star's career. William Powell, Kay Francis, Scott Kolk, Thomas E. Jackson, William H. Davidson. Written by Oliver H. P. Garrett

(based on the career of William J. Fallon); directed by John Cromwell; for Paramount. 'Certain to hold its head up on grosses.'— Variety

For the First Time
US 1959 97m Technirama
MGM / Corona / Orion (Alexander Gruter)

A famous tenor slips off incognito to Capri and falls in love with a deaf girl.

Slipshod co-production (with West Germany) with a hoary sentimental plot, a fat star, and some agreeable picture postcard views.

w Andrew Solt d Rudolph Maté ph Aldo Tonti md Georgie Stoll

Mario Lanza, Johanna von Koczian, Kurt Kasznar, Zsa Zsa Gabor, Hans Sohnker

For the Love of Benji
US 1977 84m colour

A small dog gets lost in the Greek islands. Adequate follow-up to Benji; what more can one say? Patsy Garrett, Cynthia Smith, Peter Bowles, Ed Nelson. Written by Ben Vaughn and Joe Camp; directed by Joe Camp; for Mulberry Square.

For the Love of Mary
US 1948 90m bw
Universal (Robert Arthur)

A White House switchboard operator gets tangled up in politics when the president helps cure her hiccups.

Tedious comedy with music, a hasty vehicle for a star past her peak.

w Oscar Brodney d Frederick de Cordova ph William Daniels m Frank Skinner

Deanna Durbin, Edmond O'Brien, Harry Davenport, Don Taylor, Jeffrey Lynn, Ray Collins, Hugo Haas

'A warning to all interfering presidents.'— MFB

For the Love of Mike
US 1927 74m (24 fps) bw silent

Three bachelors adopt an abandoned baby boy, who nearly (but not quite) lets them down when he grows up. Sentimental comedy most notable now as the leading lady's first movie. Claudette Colbert, Ben Lyon, George Sidney, Ford Sterling, Hugh Cameron, Skeets Gallagher. Written by Leland Hayward and J. Clarkson Miller, from the story 'Hell's Kitchen' by John Moroso; directed by Frank Capra; photographed by Ernest Haller; for First National.

For the Love of Mike*
US 1960 84m De Luxe Cinemascope
TCF / Shergari (George Sherman)
GB title: None But the Brave

An Indian boy in New Mexico is helped by a priest to care for sick animals.

Sentimental outdoor film for young people with a pleasantly light touch.

w D. D. Beauchamp d George Sherman ph Alex Phillips m Raul La Vista

Richard Basehart, Stuart Erwin, Arthur Shields, Armando Silvestre

For Them That Trespass
GB 1948 93m bw
ABP (Victor Skutezky)

A man proves himself innocent of the crime for which he has served fifteen years in prison. Tedious melodrama which served to introduce Richard Todd to the screen.

w J. Lee-Thompson d Alberto Cavalcanti ph Derick Williams m Philip Green

Richard Todd, Stephen Murray, Joan Dowling, Patricia Plunkett, Michael Laurence, Rosalyn Boulter

For Those in Peril
GB 1943 67m bw

Exploits of the air / sea rescue service. Standard semi-documentary morale-raiser. David Farrar, Ralph Michael, Robert Wyndham, John Slater. Written by Harry Watt, J. O. C. Orton and T. E. B. Clarke; directed by Charles Crichton; for Ealing.

For Those Who Think Young
US 1964 96m Techniscope
UA / Aubrey Schenck-Howard W. Koch (Hugh Benson)

College students save their favourite club from closure.

Tedious beach party frolic, very typical of its day, with some odd cameo appearances.

w James and George O'Hanlon, Dan Beaumont d Leslie H. Martinson ph Harold E. Stine m Jerry Fielding

James Darren, Pamela Tiffin, Woody Woodbury, Nancy Sinatra, Tina Louise, Paul Lynde, Bob Denver, Jack La Rue, George Raft, Allen Jenkins, Robert Armstrong, Roger Smith

For Valour*
GB 1937 95m bw
GFD / Capitol (Max Schach)

Adventures in two wars of a major, his shady friend, and their sons.

Agreeable adult farce with the stars each playing father and son.

w Ben Travers d Tom Walls

Tom Walls, Ralph Lynn, Veronica Rose, Joan Marion, Hubert Harben

'A very pleasant antidote to the Coronation, though a little marred by its inability to remain wholly flippant.'—Graham Greene

'168 minutes of breathless thrills and romance!'

For Whom the Bell Tolls**
US 1943 168m Technicolor
Paramount (Sam Wood)

An American joins partisan fighters in the Spanish Civil War and falls in love with a refugee girl before going on a suicide mission. Portentous, solemn adventure story based on a modern classic but without much cinematic impetus despite careful handling and useful performances. It looks expensive, though.

w Dudley Nichols, novel Ernest Hemingway d Sam Wood ph Ray Rennahan m Victor Young pd William Cameron Menzies

Gary Cooper, Ingrid Bergman, Akim Tamiroff, Arturo de Cordova, *Katina Paxinou*, Vladimir Sokoloff, Mikhail Rasumny, Victor Varconi, Joseph Calleia, Alexander Granach

MARIA (Ingrid Bergman): 'I do not know how to kiss, or I would kiss you. Where do the noses go?'

'Everybody must have thought they were making a classic . . . but what with the typical Hollywood compromises, plus the political pressures from Spain and from Catholics—or the fears of such pressures—the whole thing became amorphous and confused.'—*Pauline Kael, 70s*

'The rhythm of this film is the most defective I have ever seen in a super-production . . . colour is very nice for costume pieces and musical comedies, and has a great aesthetic future in films, but it still gets fatally in the way of any serious imitation of reality.'—*James Agee*

AA: Katina Paxinou
AAN: best picture; Ray Rennahan; Victor Young; Gary Cooper; Ingrid Bergman; Akim Tamiroff

For You Alone
GB 1944 98m bw

Romance of a naval officer and a vicar's daughter. Sentimental drama with music; you can smell the lavender a mile off, but it was probably the most ambitious production of this indefatigable Poverty Row production company. Lesley Brook, Jimmy Hanley, Dinah Sheridan, G. H. Mulcaster, Manning Whiley. Written by Montgomery Tully; directed by Geoffrey Faithfull; for Butcher's.

For Your Eyes Only*
GB 1981 127m Technicolor
Panavision
UA / Eon (Albert R. Broccoli)

James Bond traces a top secret device sunk in a surveillance vehicle off the Greek coast. Lively set pieces can't quite redeem this wholly uninventive addition to the Bond canon. Fun while it's on, but next morning there's nothing left to remember.

w Richard Maibaum, Michael G. Wilson d John Glen ph Alan Hume m Bill Conti pd Peter Lamont

Roger Moore, Carole Bouquet, Topol, Lynn-Holly Johnson, Julian Glover, Jill Bennett, Jack Hedley, Lois Maxwell, Desmond Llewellyn, Geoffrey Keen
'Roger Moore fronts for a succession of stunt men with all the relaxed, lifelike charm of a foyer poster of himself.'—*Sunday Times*
'Pretty boring between the stunts, as if the director isn't interested in actors, and Broccoli forgot to commission a screenplay.'—*Guardian*
† The first Bond in which original author Ian Fleming doesn't even rate a credit.

● *Video: Warner*

Forbidden
US 1931 83m bw

Our heroine loves the DA, but to save his marriage she marries someone else. Turgid renunciation drama with some interest added by stars and director. Barbara Stanwyck, Adolphe Menjou, Ralph Bellamy. Written by Frank Capra and Jo Swerling; directed by Frank Capra; for Columbia. 'A cry picture for the girls, and on that presumption stands a good chance of going out and getting itself and the theatre some coin.'—*Variety*

Forbidden
GB 1949 87m bw

A man in love with another woman tries to poison his extravagant wife. Turgid melodrama with funfair background. Douglass Montgomery, Hazel Court, Patricia Burke, Garry Marsh, Ronald Shiner, Kenneth Griffith. Written by Katherine Strueby; directed by George King; for Pennant / British Lion.

Forbidden
US 1953 85m bw

A detective falls in love with the woman a mobster has hired him to find. Would-be intense *film noir*; talent does not enable it to register. Tony Curtis, Joanne Dru, Lyle Bettger, Marvin Miller, Sen Yung. Written by William Sackheim and Gil Doud; directed by Rudolph Maté; for Universal-International.

Forbidden Cargo
GB 1954 85m bw
Rank / London Independent Productions (Sydney Box)

A customs investigator prevents a large consignment of drugs from reaching its English outlets.
Routine British thick ear.

w Sydney Box d Harold French ph C. Pennington-Richards m Lambert Williamson

Nigel Patrick, Elizabeth Sellars, Terence Morgan, Jack Warner

Forbidden Fruit*
France 1952 103m bw
Gray Film
original title: *Le Fruit Défendu*

A widowered doctor marries again, then falls for a prostitute.
One of the rather solemn romantic melodramas in which the star insisted from time to time in becoming involved.

w Jacques Companeez, Henri Verneuil, Jean Manse, *novel* Lettre à Mon Juge by Georges Simenon d Henri Verneuil ph Henri Alekan m Paul Durand

Fernandel, Claude Nollier, Françoise Arnoul, Sylvie

Forbidden Paradise
US 1924 60m (24 fps) bw silent
Paramount

The amorous intrigues of Catherine the Great of Russia.

Seldom seen these days, this was judged at the time a scintillating satire, with its sly innuendo and modern references such as motor cars and bobbed hair. Remade, more or less, as *Czarina*.

w Hans Kraly, Agnes Christine Johnson, *play* The Czarina by Melchior Lengyel, Lajos Biro d Ernst Lubitsch ph Charles Van Enger ad Hans Dreier

Pola Negri, Adolphe Menjou, Rod La Rocque, Pauline Starke, Fred Malatesta
'Lubitsch's most brilliant film'—*Paul Rotha, 1949*

'More than a year in production!'
Forbidden Planet**
US 1956 98m Eastmancolor
Cinemascope
MGM (Nicholas Nayfack)

In AD 2200 a space cruiser visits the planet Altair Four to discover the fate of a previous mission.
Intriguing sci-fi with a plot derived from *The Tempest* and a Prospero who unwittingly creates monsters from his own id. High spirits and suspense sequences partially cancelled out by wooden playing from the younger actors and some leaden dialogue.

w Cyril Hume d Fred M. Wilcox ph George Folsey m Louis and Bebe Barron ad Cedric Gibbons, Arthur Lonergan

Walter Pidgeon, Anne Francis, Leslie Nielsen, Warren Stevens, Jack Kelly, Richard Anderson, Earl Holliman
'It's a pity they didn't lift some of Shakespeare's language.'—*New Yorker, 1977*

● *Video: MGM / UA*

The Forbin Project**
US 1969 100m Technicolor
Panavision
Universal (Stanley Chase)
GB title: *Colossus, The Forbin Project*

An enormous computer takes over the defence of the western world; but it goes into collaboration with the Russian one.
Good-looking sci-fi for intellectual addicts.

w James Bridges, *novel* Colossus by D. F. Jones d Joseph Sargent ph Gene Polito m Michel Columbier

Eric Braeden, Gordon Pinsent, Susan Clark, William Schallert

Force of Arms*
US 1951 100m bw
Warner (Anthony Veiller)

A soldier in the Italian campaign falls in love with his nurse.
Routine variation on *A Farewell to Arms*, adequately but unexcitingly mounted.

w Orin Jannings, *story* Richard Tregaskis d Michael Curtiz ph Ted McCord m Max Steiner

William Holden, Nancy Olson, Frank Lovejoy, Gene Evans, Dick Wesson, Paul Picerni
'The romance rings true and the battle scenes are dangerously alive.'—*Variety*

Force of Evil***
US 1948 78m bw
MGM / Enterprise (Bob Roberts)

A racketeer's lawyer finds that his boss has killed the lawyer's brother.
Involved, atmospheric melodrama about the numbers racket, moodily and brilliantly photographed in New York streets, gloweringly well acted and generally almost as hypnotic as *Citizen Kane*.

w Abraham Polonsky, Ira Wolfert, *novel* Tucker's People by Ira Wolfert *d* Abraham Polonsky *ph* George Barnes *m* David Raksin

John Garfield, *Thomas Gomez*, Beatrice Pearson, Marie Windsor
'It credits an audience with intelligence in its ears as well as its eyes.'—*Dilys Powell*

Force Ten from Navarone
GB 1978 118m Technicolor
Panavision
Columbia / AIP / Guy Hamilton (Oliver A. Unger)

During World War II, commandos are detailed to blow up a vital bridge separating the Germans and partisans in Yugoslavia.
Routine war hokum with plenty of explosions and sudden death, but not much sense. Nothing, really, to do with *The Guns of Navarone*.

w Robin Chapman, *novel* Alistair MacLean *d* Guy Hamilton *ph* Chris Challis *m* Ron Goodwin *pd* Geoffrey Drake

Robert Shaw, Edward Fox, Franco Nero, Harrison Ford, Barbara Bach, Richard Kiel

A Foreign Affair**
US 1948 116m bw
Paramount (Charles Brackett)

A deputation of American politicians goes to visit post-war Berlin and a congresswoman finds herself in an emotional triangle with a captain and his German mistress.
Bleakly sophisticated comedy from this team's headline-grabbing period; full of interest and amusement, it never quite sparkles enough to remove the doubtful taste.

w Charles Brackett, Billy Wilder, Richard Breen *d* Billy Wilder *ph* Charles Lang Jnr *m* Frederick Hollander

Jean Arthur, Marlene Dietrich, John Lund, Millard Mitchell, Peter Von Zerneck, Stanley Prager
'This deliberately cynical political farce . . . often seems on the verge of being funny, but the humour is too clumsily forced.'—*New Yorker, 1980*

AAN: script; Charles Lang Jnr

Foreign Affaires
GB 1935 71m bw
Gainsborough (Michael Balcon)

A gambler and a car salesman get mixed up with a phoney casino.
Mild star farce.

w Ben Travers *d* Tom Walls

Tom Walls, Ralph Lynn, Robertson Hare, Norma Varden, Marie Lohr, Diana Churchill, Cecil Parker

Foreign Correspondent****
US 1940 120m bw
Walter Wanger

An American journalist is sent to Europe in 1938 and becomes involved with spies.
Thoroughly typical and enjoyable Hitchcock adventure with a rambling script which builds up into brilliantly managed suspense sequences: an assassination, a windmill, an attempted murder in Westminster Cathedral, a plane crash at sea. The final speech was an attempt to encourage America into the war.

w Charles Bennett, Joan Harrison, James Hilton, Robert Benchley, from Personal History by Vincent Sheean *d* Alfred Hitchcock *ph* Rudolph Maté *m* Alfred Newman *sp* Lee Zavitz *ad* Alexander Golitzen *pd* William Cameron Menzies

Joel McCrea, Laraine Day, Herbert Marshall, Albert Basserman, Edmund Gwenn, George Sanders, Eduardo Ciannelli, Robert Benchley, Harry Davenport, Martin Kosleck

HAVERSTOCK (Joel McCrea): 'I've been watching a part of the world blown to pieces! I can't read the rest of the speech I had because the lights have gone out. It is as if the lights were out everywhere, except in America. Keep those lights burning there! Cover them with steel! Ring them with guns! Build a canopy of battleships and bombing planes around them! Hello, America! Hang on to your lights, they're the only lights left in the world!'

'If you have any interest in the true motion and sweep of pictures, watching that man work is like listening to music . . . If you would like a seminar in how to make a movie travel the lightest and fastest way, in a kind of beauty that is peculiar to movies alone, you can see this once, and then again to see what you missed, and then study it twice.'—*Otis Ferguson*

'The most excitingly shot and edited picture of the year.'—*Basil Wright*

'A masterpiece of propaganda, a first class production which no doubt will make a certain impression upon the broad masses of the people in enemy countries.'—*Joseph Goebbels*

'This juxtaposition of outright melodramatics with deadly serious propaganda is eminently satisfactory . . . Hitchcock uses camera tricks, cinematic rhythm and crescendo to make his points.'—*Howard Barnes, New York Herald Tribune*

'Easily one of the year's finest pictures.'—*Time*

AAN: best picture; script; Rudolph Maté; Albert Basserman

Foreign Intrigue*
US 1956 100m Eastmancolor
UA / Sheldon Reynolds

A press agent investigates the death of a man who had been blackmailing potential traitors.
Location espionage melodrama of the cold war fifties, quite well done in a rather dismal vein, but a long way from *Foreign Correspondent*.

wd Sheldon Reynolds *ph* Bertil Palmgrem *m* Paul Durand

Robert Mitchum, Genevieve Page, Ingrid Thulin, Eugene Deckers

The Foreman Went to France**
GB 1941 87m bw
Ealing (Alberto Cavalcanti)
US title: *Somewhere in France*

Before Dunkirk, a Welsh foreman is sent on a mission to salvage secret French machinery.
Fresh, appealing comedy drama based on a true incident of World War II.

w John Dighton, Angus Macphail, Leslie Arliss, Roger Macdougall, Diana Morgan, *story* J. B. Priestley *d* Charles Frend *ph* Wilkie Cooper *m* William Walton

Tommy Trinder, Constance Cummings, Clifford Evans, Robert Morley, Gordon Jackson, Ernest Milton

'The thrilling story of women who play with fire, and men who fight it!'
The Forest Rangers*
US 1942 85m Technicolor
Paramount (Robert Sisk)

A socialite marries a district ranger and rescues her disgruntled rival during a forest blaze.
Routine, competent, box office actioner of its time, with popular stars, adequate plot, but precious little inventiveness.

w Harold Shumate *d* George Marshall *ph* Charles Lang *m* Victor Young

Fred MacMurray, Paulette Goddard, Susan Hayward, Lynne Overman, Albert Dekker, Eugene Pallette, Regis Toomey, Rod Cameron
'Another tale of the tall timbers, complete with conflagrations, he-men, and women like cats.'—*New York Times*

Forever Amber*
US 1947 137m Technicolor
TCF (William Perlberg)

Adventures of a desirable young lady during the reign of Charles II.
Much-bowdlerized version of a sensational novel of the forties; pretty but rather thin, with a colourless cast, saved by lively action sequences.

w Philip Dunne, Ring Lardner Jnr, *novel* Kathleen Winsor *d* Otto Preminger *ph* Leon Shamroy *m* David Raksin *ad* Lyle Wheeler

Linda Darnell, Cornel Wilde, *George Sanders* (as Charles II), Richard Greene, Glenn Langan, Richard Haydn, Jessica Tandy, Anne Revere, Robert Coote, John Russell, Leo G. Carroll

AAN: David Raksin

Forever and a Day**
US 1943 104m bw
RKO (Herbert Wilcox, Victor Saville)
The history of a London house from 1804 to the blitz of World War II.
Made for war charities by a combination of the European talents in Hollywood, this series of sketches was unavoidably patchy but gave

good opportunities to several familiar performers and stands as a likeable quick reference to their work at this period.

w Charles Bennett, C. S. Forester, Lawrence Hazard, Michael Hogan, W. P. Lipscomb, Alice Duer Miller, John Van Druten, Alan Campbell, Peter Godfrey, S. M. Herzig, Christopher Isherwood, Gene Lockhart, R. C. Sherriff, Claudine West, Norman Corwin, Jack Hartfield, James Hilton, Emmet Lavery, Frederick Lonsdale, Donald Ogden Stewart, Keith Winter *ph* Robert de Grasse, Lee Garmes, Russell Metty, Nicholas Musuraca *m* Anthony Collins *d* René Clair, Edmund Goulding, Cedric Hardwicke, Frank Lloyd, Victor Saville, Robert Stevenson, Herbert Wilcox *ad* Albert D'Agostino, Lawrence Williams, Al Herman

Anna Neagle, Ray Milland, *Claude Rains*, *C. Aubrey Smith*, Dame May Whitty, Gene Lockhart, Ray Bolger, Edmund Gwenn, Charles Coburn, Ian Hunter, *Jessie Matthews*, *Charles Laughton*, Montagu Love, *Cedric Hardwicke*, Reginald Owen, *Buster Keaton*, Wendy Barrie, Ida Lupino, *Brian Aherne*, Edward Everett Horton, June Duprez, Eric Blore, Merle Oberon, Una O'Connor, Nigel Bruce, *Roland Young*, *Gladys Cooper*, Robert Cummings, Richard Haydn, Elsa Lanchester, Sara Allgood, Robert Coote, Donald Crisp, Ruth Warrick, Kent Smith, Herbert Marshall, Victor McLaglen, many others in bit parts

'One of the most brilliant casts of modern times has been assembled to bolster up one of the poorest pictures.'—*James Agate*
† The film is notable for having the longest-ever list of credited co-writers.

Forever Darling
US 1956 91m Eastmancolor
MGM / Zanra (Desi Arnaz)

A couple's matrimonial difficulties are solved by her guardian angel.
Cutesy-pie comedy with all concerned embarrassed by their material.

w Helen Deutsch *d* Alexander Hall *ph* Harold Lipstein *m* Bronislau Kaper

Lucille Ball, Desi Arnaz, James Mason (as the angel), John Emery, Louis Calhern, John Hoyt, Natalie Schaefer

Forever England see Brown on Resolution

Forever Female
US 1953 93m bw
Paramount (Pat Duggan)

A young writer sells his play to a Broadway producer who wants to transform it into a vehicle for his ex-wife; she falls for the writer but eventually discourages him.
Talky romantic comedy without much style or sense of Broadway; a long way from *All About Eve*.

w Julius J. Epstein, Philip G. Epstein, *play* Rosalind by J. M. Barrie *d* Irving Rapper *ph* Harry Stradling *m* Victor Young

Ginger Rogers, William Holden, Paul Douglas, James Gleason, Pat Crowley

Forever Young
GB 1984 84m colour
Goldcrest (Chris Griffin)

Father Michael finds himself influenced by sexual tensions among his flock.
Rather slight drama chiefly concerning a twelve-year-old boy who idolizes his fallible priest.

w Ray Connolly *d* David Drury *ph* Norman Langley *md* Anthony King

James Aubrey, Nicholas Gecks, Alec McCowen, Karen Archer

Forfaiture see The Cheat

Forget Me Not
GB 1936 72m bw
London Films (Alexander Korda)
US title: *Forever Yours*

On board ship, a young girl falls for a widowed tenor.
Bland romance, notable only for the star's singing.

w Hugh Gray, Arthur Wimperis *d* Zoltan Korda, Stanley Irving *ph* Hans Schneeberger *m* Mischa Spoliansky

Beniamino Gigli, Joan Gardner, Ivan Brandt, Hugh Wakefield

'As a larynx exercise it possesses an appeal for those audiences which go for singing.'—*Variety*

Forgotten Commandments*
US 1932 75m bw

In a Russia which has renounced Christianity, a scientist who considers himself above emotion is led by jealousy into the murder of his mistress. Vague, feeble and absurd modern parable which takes in its stride a 20-minute excerpt from de Mille's 1923 *The Ten Commandments*. Gene Raymond, Sari Maritza, Irving Pichel, Marguerite Churchill, Edward Van Sloan, Harry Beresford. Written by J. B. Fagan, Agnes Brand Leahy; directed by Louis Gasnier and William Schoor; for Paramount. 'Hardly a single dramatic sequence and not over three laughs at the New York opening – and one of them at, not with, the picture.'—*Variety*

Forgotten Woman
US 1939 68m bw

A woman wrongfully imprisoned has a baby in prison and emerges embittered. Heavygoing tearjerker. Sigrid Gurie, Eve Arden, Donald Briggs, William Lundigan, Elizabeth Risdon. Written by Lionel Houser, Harold Buchman, John Kobler; directed by Harold Young; for Edmund Grainger / Universal.

The Formula
US 1980 117m Metrocolor
MGM / CIP (Steve Shagan)

A cop follows a murder trail to West Germany and finds that it all hinges on a secret formula for turning coal into petrol.
Convoluted thriller which is all McGuffin and no interest.

w Steven Shagan, from his novel *d* John G. Avildsen *ph* James Crabe *m* Bill Conti

George C. Scott, Marlon Brando, Marthe Keller, John Gielgud, Beatrice Straight, Richard Lynch

AAN: James Crabe
● *Video: MGM / UA*

Forsaking All Others*
US 1934 84m bw
MGM (Bernard H. Hyman)

A wife nearly breaks up her rather dull marriage, but thinks better of it.
Star power carries this thin comedy drama.

w Joseph L. Mankiewicz, *play* Edward Barry Roberts, Frank Morgan Cavett *d* W. S. Van Dyke *ph* Gregg Toland, George Folsey *m* William Axt

Clark Gable, Joan Crawford, Robert Montgomery, *Charles Butterworth*, Billie Burke, Frances Drake, Rosalind Russell, Arthur Treacher

'Sock romantic comedy despite some messy hokum.'—*Variety*

'Where a woman meant more to a man than anywhere else in the world!'
Fort Algiers
US 1952 85m bw

A female French agent loves a fellow spy who turns up as a Foreign Legionnaire, working against an evil Emir. Quite lively old-fashioned hokum, satisfactory on its level. Yvonne de Carlo, Carlos Thompson, Raymond Burr, Leif Erickson, Anthony Caruso. Written by Theodore St John; directed by Lesley Selander; for Erco / UA.

Fort Apache**
US 1948 127m bw
RKO (John Ford, Merian C. Cooper)

In the old west, a military martinet has trouble with his family as well as the Indians.
Rather stiff and unsatisfactory epic western which yet contains sequences in its director's best manner.

w Frank S. Nugent, *story* Massacre by James Warner Bellah *d John Ford ph* Archie Stout *m* Richard Hageman

Henry Fonda, John Wayne, Shirley Temple, Pedro Armendariz, Ward Bond, Irene Rich, George O'Brien, John Agar, Victor McLaglen, Anna Lee, Dick Foran, Guy Kibbee

'A visually absorbing celebration of violent deeds.'—*Howard Barnes*

'The whole picture is bathed in a special form of patriotic sentimentality: scenes are held so that we cannot fail to appreciate the beauty of the American past.'—*New Yorker, 1976*

'Shirley Temple and her husband handle the love interest as though they were sharing a soda fountain special, and there is enough Irish comedy to make me wish Cromwell had done a more thorough job.'—*James Agee*

● *Video: Thorn EMI*

Fort Apache, the Bronx
US 1980 123m De Luxe
Time Life / Producer Circle (David
Susskind)

A veteran policeman deals with various violent
crimes in New York.
This instantly forgettable movie unspools like
an ultra-violent *Dixon of Dock Green*, but
Newman is no Jack Warner.

w Heywood Gould d Daniel Petrie ph John
Alcott m Jonathan Tunick pd Ben Edwards

Paul Newman, Ed Asner, Ken Wahl, Danny
Aiello, Rachel Ticotin, Pam Grier, Kathleen
Beller

● *Video: VTC*

Fort Defiance
US 1981 81m Cinecolor

Ben Shelby comes back from the Civil War to
avenge his brother's death. Complicated
lower-berth western, crudely executed. Dane
Clark, Ben Johnson, Peter Graves, Tracey
Roberts, George Cleveland. Written by Louis
Lantz; directed by John Rawlins; for Ventura /
UA.

Fort Dobbs
US 1957 90m bw

Man on the run rescues widow from
Comanches and clears his name. Very routine
medium-scale western showcasing a TV star.
Clint Walker, Virginia Mayo, Brian Keith,
Richard Eyer. Written by George W. George
and Burt Kennedy; directed by Gordon
Douglas; for Warner.

Fort Massacre
US 1958 80m De Luxe Cinemascope

A cavalry sergeant becomes reckless when he
has to lead to safety the survivors of an Indian
attack. Psychological western without the skill
necessary to realize its pretensions. Joel
McCrea, Forrest Tucker, Susan Cabot, John
Russell. Written by Martin N. Goldsmith;
directed by Joseph Newman; for Mirisch /
UA.

Fort Ti
US 1953 73m Technicolor 3-D
Columbia (Sam Katzman)

In 1759 a platoon of Rogers' Rangers marches
north to defend their territory against Indians.
Cheap and feeble western memorable only for
the amount of miscellaneous objects thrown at
the audience via 3-D photography.

w Robert E. Kent d William Castle
ph Lester E. White, Lathrop B. Worth
md Ross di Maggio

George Montgomery, Joan Vohs, Irving
Bacon, James Seay
'The lack of restraint is remarkable. To the
injury of tomahawks, rifle shots, cannon balls,
flaming arrows, broken bottles and blazing
torches is added the insult of grubby redskins
hurled judo style into one's lap.'—*David
Robinson*

Fort Vengeance
US 1953 75m Cinecolor

A new Mountie recruit is an Indian killer.
Uninteresting western with stock cast and
situations. James Craig, Rita Moreno, Keith
Larsen, Reginald Denny, Morris Ankrum.
Written by Dan Ullman; directed by Lesley
Selander; for Walter Wanger / Allied Artists.

Fort Worth
US 1951 80m Technicolor

A newspaper editor combats a would-be
dictator. Satisfying star western. Randolph
Scott, Phyllis Thaxter, David Brian, Dick
Jones, Paul Picerni. Written by John Twist;
directed by Edwin L. Marin; for Warner.

The Fortune
US 1975 88m Technicolor Panavision
Columbia (Hank Moonjean)

A twenties heiress elopes with her lover and
his dim-witted friend but discovers that they
mean to murder her for her money.
Bungled black comedy with top talent over-
confident of carrying it.

w Adrien Joyce (Carol Eastman) d Mike
Nichols ph John A. Alonzo m various songs
pd Richard Sylbert

Jack Nicholson, Warren Beatty, Stockard
Channing, Florence Stanley, Richard B. Shull,
John Fiedler
'Like the ill-assorted styles of the film
generally, the stars themselves frequently
seem to belong in different movies.'—*Richard
Combs*
'A silly, shallow, occasionally enjoyable
comedy trifle . . . classy 20's production values
often merit more attention than the plot.'—
Variety

Fortune and Men's Eyes
Canada / US 1971 102m Metrocolor
MGM / Cinemex / CFD (Lester Persky,
Lewis M. Allen)

Life among homosexuals in a Canadian jail.
A welter of sensational incident outweighs any
point the author may have had; this prison
seems to be beyond reform.

w John Herbert, from his play d Harvey
Hart ph Georges Dufaux m Galt McDermot

Wendell Burton, Michael Greer

The Fortune Cookie*
US 1966 125m bw Panavision
UA / Mirisch / Phalanx / Jalem (Billy Wilder)
GB title: *Meet Whiplash Willie*

A crooked lawyer forces his slightly injured
client to sue for a million dollars.
Flat, stretched-out, only occasionally effective
comedy which relies too much on mordant
attitudes and a single star performance.

w Billy Wilder, I. A. L. Diamond d Billy
Wilder ph Joseph La Shelle m André Previn

Walter Matthau, Jack Lemmon, Ron Rich,
Cliff Osmond, Lurene Tuttle
'A jackhammer of a film savagely applied to
those concrete areas of human spirit where
cupidity and stupidity have been so long
entrenched.'—*Richard Schickel*

AA: Walter Matthau
AAN: Billy Wilder, I. A. L. Diamond (script);
Joseph La Shelle

Fortune Is a Woman*
GB 1956 95m bw
Columbia / Frank Launder, Sidney Gilliat
US title: *She Played with Fire*

An insurance assessor investigates a fire, finds
a murder, marries the victim's widow, and is
blackmailed . . .
Slackly-handled mystery thriller, a
disappointment from the talents involved.

w Frank Launder, Sidney Gilliat, novel
Winston Graham d Sidney Gilliat ph Gerald
Gibbs m William Alwyn

Jack Hawkins, Arlene Dahl, Dennis Price,
Geoffrey Keen, Violet Farebrother, John
Robinson, Bernard Miles, Greta Gynt

Fortunes of Captain Blood
US 1950 91m bw

The famous Caribbean pirate eludes his
pursuers by taking over their own ship.
Lethargic adventures on a low budget; the cast
was there for something better. Louis
Hayward, Patricia Medina, George Macready,
Dona Drake, Alfonso Bedoya. Written by
Michael Hogan, Robert Libbott and Frank
Burt; directed by Gordon Douglas; for Harry
Joe Brown / Columbia.

Forty Carats*
US 1973 109m Metrocolor
Columbia / M. J. Frankovich

A 40-year-old divorcee on holiday in Greece
has a brief affair with a 22-year-old man.
Curiously miscast and mishandled comedy for
the smart set; scores a laugh or two but never
really takes off.

w Leonard Gershe, play Pierre Barillet, Jean-
Pierre Gredy d Milton Katselas ph Charles
Lang Jnr m Michel Legrand

Liv Ullmann, Edward Albert, Gene Kelly,
Billy 'Green' Bush, Binnie Barnes, Nancy
Walker, Deborah Raffin, Don Porter, Natalie
Schaefer, Rosemary Murphy

Forty Eight Hours
US 1982 96m Movielab
Paramount / Lawrence Gordon

A cop and a criminal on parole combine to
track down the latter's former associates.
Reasonable action melodrama with comedy
asides and San Francisco locations; but too
violent for its own good.

w Roger Spottiswoode, Walter Hill, Larry
Gross d Walter Hill ph Ric Waite m James
Horner pd John Vallone

Nick Nolte, Eddie Murphy, Annette O'Toole,
Frank McRae
'It's like *The French Connection*, *Dirty
Harry* and *Butch Cassidy* all put in a
compactor and pressed into cartoon form.'—
New Yorker

● *Video: CIC*

The Forty First*
USSR 1927 80m approx bw silent
Mezhrabpom
original title: *Sorok Pervyi*

During the Civil War in Turkestan, a girl

sniper for the Reds becomes the companion in adventure of a White lieutenant. But in the end he becomes her 41st victim.

Strong action melodrama which found an international audience.

w Boris Lavryenov, from his novel d Yakov Protazanov ph Pyotr Yermolov

Ada Voitsik, Ivan Kovan-Samborsky
† Remade in 1956 by Grigori Chukrai, in colour.

Forty-Five Fathers
US 1937 71m bw

A show business orphan becomes the personal ward of the Gun and Spear Club. Palatable vehicle for a growing child star. Jane Withers, Paul and Grace Hartman, Thomas Beck, Louise Henry, Richard Carle, Nella Walker, Andrew Tombes. Written by Frances Hyland, Albert Ray, Mary Bickel; directed by James Tinling; for John Stone / TCF.

Forty Guns
US 1957 80m bw Cinemascope
TCF / Globe (Samuel Fuller)

A powerful ranchwoman protects her hoodlum brother.

Heavily melodramatic and slow-moving western with a few effective moments.

wd Samuel Fuller ph Joseph Biroc m Harry Sukman

Barbara Stanwyck, Barry Sullivan, Dean Jagger, Gene Barry, John Ericson

Forty Guns to Apache Pass
US 1967 95m Technicolor

A cavalry captain protects homesteaders when Cochise attacks. Flat and overlong star western compounded of excessively familiar elements. Audie Murphy, Michael Burns, Kenneth Tobey, Laraine Stephens. Written by Willard and Mary Willingham; directed by William Witney; for Admiral / Columbia.

Forty Little Mothers
US 1940 90m bw
MGM (Harry Rapf)

A teacher in a girls' school finds himself in charge of a baby.

Ill-advised star vehicle composed largely of whimsy . . . and no musical numbers.

w Dorothy Yost, Ernest Pagano d Busby Berkeley ph Charles A. Lawton Jnr

Eddie Cantor, Judith Anderson, Bonita Granville, Rita Johnson, Diana Lewis, Nydia Westman, Martha O'Driscoll

Forty Naughty Girls
US 1937 68m bw

Hildegarde Withers solves a murder backstage. Weak addition to a faltering series. Zasu Pitts, James Gleason, Marjorie Lord, George Shelley, Joan Woodbury. Written by John Grey, Stuart Palmer; directed by Edward Cline; for William Sistrom / RKO. 'Decidedly tame, and won't cause much ripple on nether side of duals, where it'll undoubtedly land.'—Variety

The Forty Niners
US 1954 70m bw

A marshal tracks down three men who were accomplices to a murder. Very tolerable minor western. Wild Bill Elliott, Virginia Grey, Henry Morgan, John Doucette, Lane Bradford. Written by Dan Ullman; directed by Thomas Carr; for Allied Artists.

Forty Ninth Parallel•••
GB 1941 123m bw
GFD / Ortus (John Sutro, Michael Powell)
US title: The Invaders

In Canada, five stranded U-boat men try to escape into the US.

Episodic, effective propaganda piece which develops some nice Hitchcockian touches and allows a range of star actors to make impact.

w Emeric Pressburger, Rodney Ackland d Michael Powell ph F. A. Young m Ralph Vaughan Williams

Eric Portman, Laurence Olivier, Anton Walbrook, Leslie Howard, Raymond Massey, Glynis Johns, Niall MacGinnis, Finlay Currie, Raymond Lovell, John Chandos

'Some of the plotting and characterization look rather rusty at this remove, but the sense of landscape and figures passing through it remains authoritatively dynamic.'—Tony Rayns, Time Out, 1979

'An admirable piece of work from every point of view.'—MFB

AA: original story (Emeric Pressburger)
AAN: best picture; script

Forty Pounds of Trouble•
US 1963 105m Eastmancolor
Panavision
U-I / Curtis Enterprises (Stan Margulies)

A casino manager is chased by his ex-wife's detective for alimony payments, and also has to look after an abandoned six-year-old girl. Standard sentimental comedy with some verve and a lively climactic chase through Disneyland.

w Marion Hargrove d Norman Jewison ph Joe MacDonald m Mort Lindsey

Tony Curtis, Phil Silvers, Suzanne Pleshette, Edward Andrews

'Mightier than Broadway ever beheld!'
Forty-Second Street••••
US 1933 89m bw
Warner (Hal B. Wallis)

A Broadway musical producer has troubles during rehearsal but reaches a successful opening night.

Archetypal Hollywood putting-on-a-show musical in which the leading lady is indisposed and a chorus girl is told to go out there and come back a star. The clichés are written and performed with great zest, the atmosphere is convincing, and the numbers when they come are dazzlers.

w James Seymour, Rian James, novel Bradford Ropes d Lloyd Bacon ch Busby Berkeley ph Sol Polito m / ly Al Dubin, Harry Warren

Warner Baxter, Ruby Keeler, Bebe Daniels, George Brent, Una Merkel, Guy Kibbee, Dick Powell, Ginger Rogers (as Anytime Annie), Ned Sparks, George E. Stone, Allen Jenkins

Songs: 'Forty-Second Street'; 'Shuffle Off to Buffalo'; 'Young and Healthy'; 'You're Getting to Be a Habit with Me'

(Warner Baxter): 'Sawyer, you listen to me, and you listen hard. Two hundred people, two hundred jobs, two hundred thousand dollars, five weeks of grind and blood and sweat depend upon you. It's the lives of all these people who've worked with you. You've got to go on, and you've got to give and give and give. They've got to like you. Got to. Do you understand? You can't fall down. You can't because your future's in it, my future and everything all of us have is staked on you. All right, now I'm through, but you keep your feet on the ground and your head on those shoulders of yours and go out, and Sawyer, you're going out a youngster but you've got to come back a star!'

'The story has been copied a hundred times since, but never has the backstage atmosphere been so honestly and felicitously caught.'—John Huntley, 1966

'It gave new life to the clichés that have kept parodists happy.'—New Yorker, 1977

AAN: best picture

● Video: Warner

Foul Play•
US 1978 116m Movielab
Paramount / Thomas L. Miller, Edward K. Milkis

Two innocents in San Francisco get involved in a plot to assassinate the visiting pope. Sometimes sprightly, sometimes tired rehash of Hitchcock elements, rather on the level of the similar Silver Streak.

wd Colin Higgins ph David M. Walsh m Charles Fox

Goldie Hawn, Chevy Chase, Burges Meredith, Rachel Roberts, Eugene Roche, Dudley Moore, Billy Barty

AAN: song, 'Ready to Take a Chance Again'

The Fountain
US 1934 84m bw
RKO (Pandro S. Berman)

During World War I a British woman is tempted to forsake her mangled German air ace husband for her childhood sweetheart. A slice of impenetrable gloom from an intractable novel.

w Jane Murfin, Samuel Hoffenstein, novel Charles Morgan d John Cromwell ph Henry W. Gerrard m Max Steiner

Ann Harding, Brian Aherne, Paul Lukas, Jean Hersholt, Ralph Forbes, Violet Kemble-Cooper, Sara Haden

'One of the talkiest talkies yet.'—Variety
'Long and solemn and wonderfully empty.'—Otis Ferguson

The Fountainhead**
US 1949 114m bw
Warner (Henry Blanke)

An idealistic architect clashes with big business.
Overripe adaptation of a rather silly novel, full of Freudian symbols and expressionist techniques with which the star really can't cope; but an enjoyable field day for the director and the rest of the cast.

w Ayn Rand, from her novel d King Vidor
ph Robert Burks m Max Steiner

Gary Cooper, *Patricia Neal, Raymond Massey*, Kent Smith, Robert Douglas, Henry Hull, Ray Collins, Moroni Olson, Jerome Cowan

'If you like deep thinking, hidden meanings, plus pure modern architecture, then this is something for which you have been waiting a long time.'—*Screenland*

'The most bizarre movie in both Vidor's and Cooper's filmographies, this adaptation mutes Ms Rand's neo-Nietzschian philosophy of "objectivism" but lays on the expressionist symbolism with a "free enterprise" trowel.'—*Time Out, 1980*

Four Clowns**
US 1970 96m bw
Robert Youngson Productions (Herb Gelbspan)

Studies of four silent comedians. Laurel and Hardy in excerpts from *Putting Pants on Philip*, *The Second Hundred Years*, *Their Purple Moment*, *Big Business*, *Two Tars* and *Double Whoopee*; Charley Chase in *Us*, *What Price Goofy*, *Fluttering Hearts*, *The Family Group* and *Limousine Love*; Buster Keaton in *Seven Chances*.
An essential compendium, especially for the Charley Chase revaluation which was long overdue.

w Robert Youngson m Manny Alban
narr Jay Jackson

Four Daughters***
US 1938 90m bw
Warner (Henry Blanke)

Domestic and romantic adventures of a small-town family.
Standard small-town hearth-fire hokum, impeccably done and really quite irresistible.

w Julius Epstein, Lenore Coffee, *novel* Sister Act by Fannie Hurst d Michael Curtiz
ph Ernest Haller m Max Steiner

Claude Rains, John Garfield (a sensation in his first role), Priscilla Lane, Rosemary Lane, Lola Lane, Gale Page, Jeffrey Lynn, Frank McHugh, *May Robson*, Dick Foran

'It may be sentimental, but it's grand cinema.'—*New York Times*

† An immediate sequel was required, but the Garfield character had been killed off, so to accommodate him a variation was written under the title *Daughters Courageous*; then came two proper sequels without him, *Four Wives* and *Four Mothers*. In 1955 the original was remade as *Young at Heart* (qv).

AAN: best picture; script; Michael Curtiz; John Garfield

THE FOUR FEATHERS (1939). A frame of the location photography, shot on the Nile, which later turned up as stock footage in so many inferior adventure films.

The Four Days of Naples*
Italy 1962 119m bw
Titanus-Metro (Goffredo Lombardo)

A reconstruction of the 1943 city battle in which the Nazis were driven out by civilian fury.
A kind of update of *Open City*: much admired, but a little ill-timed.

w Nanni Loy and others d Nanni Loy
ph Marcello Gatti m Carlo Rustichelli

Lea Massari, Frank Wolff, Domenico Formato, Raffaele Barbato

AAN: script

The Four Feathers**
US 1929 83m bw
Paramount (David O. Selznick)

During the Sudan campaign of the nineties, a stay-at-home receives four white feathers as a symbol of cowardice; but he goes undercover, becomes a hero, and rescues his best friend.
Ambitious early talkie based on a famous adventure novel, partly filmed in Africa; interesting but now very stilted.

w Howard Estabrook, *novel* A. E. W. Mason
d Lothar Mendes, Merian C. Cooper, Ernest Schoedsack ph Robert Kurlle, Merian C. Cooper, Ernest Schoedsack m William F. Peters

Richard Arlen, Fay Wray, Clive Brook, William Powell, George Fawcett, Theodore Von Eltz, Noah Beery

The Four Feathers****
GB 1939 130m Technicolor
London (Alexander Korda, Irving Asher)

The standard version of the above, perfectly cast and presented, with battle scenes which have since turned up in a score of other films from *Zarak* to *Master of the World*; also a triumph of early colour.

w R. C. Sheriff, Lajos Biro, Arthur Wimperis
d Zoltan Korda ph Georges Périnal, Osmond Borradaile, Jack Cardiff m Miklos Rozsa

John Clements, Ralph Richardson, C. Aubrey Smith, June Duprez, Allan Jeayes, Jack Allen, Donald Gray, Henry Oscar, John Laurie

'It cannot fail to be one of the best films of the year . . . even the richest of the ham goes smoothly down, savoured with humour and satire.'—*Graham Greene*

† Remade 1956 as *Storm over the Nile* (qv).

● Video: Polygram

The Four Feathers: see *Television Companion* for the TV movie

Four for Texas
US 1963 124m Technicolor
Warner / Sam Company (Robert Aldrich)

Two survivors of a stagecoach raid doublecross each other for the loot and become rival saloon owners.
Flabby western comedy, tediously directed and casually performed.

w Teddi Sherman, Robert Aldrich *d* Robert Aldrich *ph* Ernest Laszlo *m* Nelson Riddle

Dean Martin, Frank Sinatra, Anita Ekberg, Ursula Andress, Charles Bronson, Victor Buono, the Three Stooges

'The major laughs come from the Three Stooges doing an ancient routine and an old lady falling out of her wheelchair. Zowie.'—*Judith Crist*

'One suspects that the most amusing antics were those that went on off-screen.'—*Films and Filming*

Four Friends
US 1981 115m Technicolor
Filmways / Cinema 77 / Geria (Arthur Penn, Gene Lasko)
GB title: *Georgia's Friends*

A Yugoslavian boy grows up in Indiana and is influenced by the adult behaviour of his three friends.
Mildly interesting semi-autobiographical nostalgia movie, a vein which has been mined twice too often.

w Steve Tesich *d* Arthur Penn *ph* Ghislain Cloquet *m* Elizabeth Swados *pd* David Chapman

Craig Wasson, Jodi Thelen, Michael Huddleston, Jim Metzler

● *Video: Rank*

'They threw away conventions with their tattered clothes!'
Four Frightened People*
US 1934 78m bw
Paramount / Cecil B. de Mille

A bubonic plague outbreak on board ship causes four survivors to escape via a lifeboat and trek through dangerous jungle.
Studio-bound but interesting action melodrama, of a type unusual from this director.

w Bartlett Cormack, Lenore Coffee, *novel* E. Arnot Robertson *d* Cecil B. de Mille *ph* Karl Struss *m* Karl Hajos and others

Claudette Colbert, Herbert Marshall, William Gargan, Mary Boland, Leo Carrillo, Nella Walker, Tetsu Komai, Ethel Griffies

'The adventures are episodic and disjointed, running the gamut from stark tragedy to unbelievable farce.'—*Variety*

'A cumbersome sort of melodrama . . . despite some mildly entertaining jungle scenes.'—*Literary Digest*

Four Girls in Town
US 1956 85m Technicolor
Cinemascope
U-I (Aaron Rosenberg)

Girls from various countries are chosen for Hollywood screen tests.
Formula romantic comedy adequately exposing young talent.

wd Jack Sher *ph* Irving Glassberg *m* Alex North

George Nader, Julie Adams, Marianne Cook, Elsa Martinelli, Gia Scala, Sidney Chaplin, Grant Williams, John Gavin

Four Girls in White
US 1938 88m bw
MGM (Nat Levine)

Drama among the student nurses.
Standard hospital fare designed as a try-out for budding talent.
w Nathalie Bucknall, Endre Boehm *d* S. Sylvan Simon

Florence Rice, Alan Marshal, Ann Rutherford, Una Merkel, Buddy Ebsen, Mary Howard, Kent Taylor, Jessie Ralph, Sara Haden, Philip Terry, Tom Neal

Four Guns to the Border
US 1954 83m Technicolor

Things go wrong for four bank robbers after a raid. Rather downbeat western with insufficient excitement. Rory Calhoun, Walter Brennan, Coleen Miller, George Nader, Nina Foch, John McIntire, Charles Drake. Written by George Van Marter and Franklin Coen; directed by Richard Carlson; for Universal-International.

The Four Horsemen of the Apocalypse**
US 1921 150m approx bw silent
Metro

A young Argentinian fights for his father's country, France, in World War I.
Highly derivative dramatic spectacle, almost a pageant, from a fairly unreadable novel. Despite its variable if exotic style, it made a star of Rudolph Valentino.

w June Mathis, *novel* Vicente Blasco-Ibanez *d* Rex Ingram *ph* John F. Seitz

Rudolph Valentino, Alice Terry, Nigel de Brulier, Alan Hale, Jean Hersholt, Wallace Beery

'A blend of exotic settings, striking composition, dramatic lighting, and colourful if sordid atmosphere.'—*Lewis Jacobs*

'Not only was it marvellously effective in its appeal to the eye, but the logical and dramatic unfolding of the basic story was a striking revelation of the valuable service that an expert scenario-writer may render to the professional writer of novels.'—*Edward S. Van Zile, That Marvel the Movie*

The Four Horsemen of the Apocalypse*
US 1961 153m Metrocolor
Cinemascope
MGM (Julian Blaustein)

In this ill-fated modernization, the idle grandson of an Argentinian beef tycoon finds his manhood at last as a member of the French resistance during World War II. The visionary skyriding figures of death and pestilence simply do not fit in with bombs and concentration camps. Glum acting by a too elderly company, ugly colour and the usual hindrances of Cinemascope.

w Robert Ardrey, John Gay *d* Vincente Minnelli *ph* Milton Krasner *m* André Previn

Glenn Ford, Ingrid Thulin, Charles Boyer, Paul Henreid, Lee J. Cobb, Paul Lukas, Karl Boehm, Yvette Mimieux

'An elephantine helping of hysteria and hokum.'—*Judith Crist, 1973*

Four Hours to Kill**
US 1935 74m bw
Paramount (Arthur Hornblow Jnr)

A psychopathic gangster gets loose during an evening at the theatre.
Tense, well-handled melodrama making full use of its setting.

w Norman Krasna, from his play Small Miracle *d* Mitchell Leisen *ph* Theodor Sparkuhl

Richard Barthelmess, Ray Milland, Gertrude Michael, Joe Morrison, Helen Mack, Dorothy Tree, Roscoe Karns, Henry Travers

'It fails to grip and isn't long on laughs.'—*Variety*

The Four Hundred Blows**
France 1958 94m bw Dyaliscope
Films du Carrosse / SEDIF
original title: *Les Quatre Cents Coups*

A 12-year-old boy, unhappy at home, finds himself in a detention centre but finally escapes and keeps running.
Little more in plot terms than a piece of character observation, this engaging film is so controlled and lyrical as to be totally refreshing, and it gives a very vivid picture of the Paris streets.

wd François Truffaut *ph* Henri Decaë *m* Jean Constantin

Jean-Pierre Léaud, Claire Maurier, Albert Rémy

† The film is said to be based on Truffaut's own childhood.

AAN: script

Four in a Jeep*
Switzerland 1951 96m bw
Praesensfilm (Lazar Wechsler)

In the post-war international zone of Vienna, the four nationals of a police patrol come to blows over the cases they encounter.
Historically interesting but rather bland illustration of an untenable and even tragic political situation which was treated more melodramatically in *The Third Man*.

w Richard Schweizer *d* Leopold Lindtberg *ph* Emil Barna *m* Robert Blum

Viveca Lindfors, Ralph Meeker, Yoseph Yadin, Michael Medwin

Four in the Morning*
GB 1965 94m bw

Four personal stories are intercut during one London night. Attractive minor effort which takes the eye without engaging the mind. Ann Lynn, Judi Dench, Norman Rodway, Brian Phelan, Joe Melia. Written and directed by *Anthony Simmons*; for John Morris / West One.

Four Jacks and a Jill
US 1941 68m bw
RKO (John Twist)

Four struggling musicians adopt a down-and-out girl.

Flimsy remake of *That Girl from Paris*; the talent is given little opportunity to rise.

w John Twist d Jack Hively ph Russell Metty songs Mort Greene, Harry Revel

Anne Shirley, Ray Bolger, Desi Arnaz, Jack Durant, June Havoc, Eddie Foy Jnr, Fritz Feld

Four Jills in a Jeep
US 1944 89m bw
TCF (Irving Starr)

Four Hollywood glamour girls entertain the troops.
Condescending, dispirited 'semi-documentary' war musical.

w Robert Ellis, Helen Logan, Snag Werris d William A. Seiter ph Peverell Marley md Emil Newman

Kay Francis, Martha Raye, Carole Landis, Mitzi Mayfair, Jimmy Dorsey and his band, John Harvey, Phil Silvers, Dick Haymes; guest stars Alice Faye, Betty Grable, Carmen Miranda, George Jessel
'It gives the painful impression of having been tossed together in a couple of hours.'—*Bosley Crowther*

The Four Just Men*
GB 1939 85m bw
Ealing–Capad (S. C. Balcon)
US title: *The Secret Four*

To save the Empire, four stalwart Britishers agree to murder a villainous MP.
Bright, unusual but dated thriller from a popular novel.

w Roland Pertwee, Angus Macphail, Sergei Nolbandov, *novel* Edgar Wallace d Walter Forde ph Ronald Neame m Ernest Irving

Hugh Sinclair, Francis L. Sullivan, Frank Lawton, Griffith Jones, Anna Lee, Basil Sidney, Alan Napier, Athole Stewart, Edward Chapman, Garry Marsh, Ellaline Terriss, Lydia Sherwood, George Merritt
† The TV series of the late fifties restrained its heroes from criminal acts; the men were Jack Hawkins, Richard Conte, Dan Dailey, Vittorio de Sica.

Four Men and a Prayer*
US 1938 85m bw
TCF (Kenneth MacGowan)

Four young Englishmen set out to clear the name of their dishonoured father.
Pleasantly performed mystery which improves after a slowish start.

w Richard Sherman, Sonya Levien, Walter Ferris, *novel* David Garth d John Ford ph Ernest Palmer md Louis Silvers

Loretta Young, Richard Greene, George Sanders, David Niven, William Henry, C. Aubrey Smith, J. Edward Bromberg, John Carradine, Alan Hale, Reginald Denny, Barry Fitzgerald, Berton Churchill, John Sutton
'Better cast than story . . . the pace is so uneven that the general effect at times is bewildering.'—*Variety*
'Energetically told, compactly presented.'—*New York Times*

Four Mothers
US 1940 86m bw
Warner (Henry Blanke)

The four Lemp sisters, all happily married, have financial problems.
Third and last in the *Four Daughters* trilogy; quite attractively made but very routine.

w Stephen Morehouse Avery d William Keighley

Priscilla Lane, Rosemary Lane, Lola Lane, Gale Page, Claude Rains, Dick Foran, Frank McHugh, Jeffrey Lynn, Eddie Albert, Vera Lewis

'What has eight legs, feathers, and is usually seen coming to the rescue?'

The Four Musketeers (The Revenge of Milady)*
Panama 1974 103m Technicolor
TCF / Film Trust / Este (Alexander Salkind, Michael Salkind)

Athos, Porthos, Aramis and D'Artagnan have a final battle with Rochefort.
Perfunctory sequel to the same team's *The Three Musketeers*; allegedly the two films were intended as one, but if so the first ten reels were by far the best, though this section has its regulation quota of high spirits and lusty action.

w George MacDonald Fraser d Richard Lester ph David Watkin m Lalo Schifrin pd Brian Eatwell

Michael York, Oliver Reed, Frank Finlay, Richard Chamberlain, Raquel Welch, Faye Dunaway, Charlton Heston, Christopher Lee, Simon Ward, Geraldine Chaplin, Jean-Pierre Cassel, Roy Kinnear
'The whole sleek formula has rolled over to reveal a very soft, very flabby underside.'—*Tony Rayns*
● Video: Thorn EMI

The Four-Poster
US 1952 103m bw
Columbia / Stanley Kramer

The history of a marriage told in a series of bedroom scenes.
Hastily shot and rather tatty looking version of a stage play; unfortunately film can't contrast the comedy of the opening and the tragedy of the close within one small set, and the UPA cartoon bridges, though smart in themselves, are merely an irritation.

w Allan Scott, *play* Jan de Hartog d Irving Reis ph Hal Mohr m Dmitri Tiomkin

Rex Harrison, Lilli Palmer

AAN: Hal Mohr

'Here's to our friends—and the strength to put up with them!'

The Four Seasons**
US 1981 108m Technicolor
Universal (Martin Bregman)

Three married couples take seasonal holidays together, and remain united despite various tensions.
Rueful sexual comedy which maintains considerable momentum and actually makes us laugh at its sympathetic characters.

wd Alan Alda ph Victor J. Kemper m Antonio Vivaldi

Alan Alda, Carol Burnett, Len Cariou, Sandy Dennis, Rita Moreno, Jack Weston, Bess Armstrong
'An odd mingling of perspicuity and histrionics . . . a real middle-of-the-road film.'—*Geoff Brown, MFB*
'Unfailingly amusing, touchingly honest, and in the end refreshingly decent.'—*Margaret Hinxman, Daily Mail*

'See! a strange and beautiful woman created before your eyes!'

Four Sided Triangle
GB 1952 81m bw
Hammer (Michael Carreras, Alexander Paal)

When a scientist's girl friend marries another, he creates a clone but finds that it has the same preferences.
A very early entry in this field; not too well done, but faithful to its silly theme.

w Paul Tabori, Terence Fisher, *novel* William F. Temple d Terence Fisher ph Reg Wyer m Malcolm Arnold

Stephen Murray, Barbara Payton, James Hayter, John Van Eyssen, Percy Marmont, Kynaston Reeves

The Four Skulls of Jonathan Drake
US 1959 70m bw
UA / Vogue (Robert E. Kent)

A family is cursed by a head-hunting Equadorian medicine man.
Cheaply made but full-blooded occult horror, rather effectively done by a cast that knows how.

w Orville H. Hampton d Edward L. Cahn ph Maury Gertsman m Paul Dunlap

Henry Daniell, Eduard Franz, Valerie French, Grant Richards, Paul Cavanagh
'Amazonian Indians may find the plot a shade far-fetched.'—*MFB*

Four Sons*
US 1940 89m bw
TCF

A Czech family is divided when the Nazis take over.
Predictable po-faced anti-Hitler melodrama released to an indifferent public well before America entered the war. A remake of a silent film set during World War I.

w John Howard Lawson d Archie Mayo ph Leon Shamroy m David Buttolph

Don Ameche, Eugenie Leontovich, Mary Beth Hughes, Alan Curtis, George Ernest, Robert Lowery, Sig Rumann, Lionel Royce, Ludwig Stossel
'It partakes more of sentimental melodrama than of tragedy. . . . Neither in its performance nor its writing does the film ever rise to any passion.'—*New York Times*

Four Steps in the Clouds*
Italy 1942 90m bw
Cines Amato
original title: *Quattro Passi fra le Nuvole*

A travelling salesman on a bus gets involved with the problems of a pregnant girl, but misunderstandings are finally cleared up to general satisfaction.

A comedy on the American model which was a great success in wartorn Italy. Not particularly remarkable in itself, it was remade in 1957, as *The Virtuous Bigamist*, with Fernandel. It does show the lighter side of Italian neo-realism.

w Cesare Zavattini, Giuseppe Amato, Piero Tellini, Aldo de Benedetti *d* Alessandro Blasetti *ph* Vaclav Vich *m* Alessandro Cicognini

Gino Cervi, Adriana Benetti, Giuditta Rissone

Four Wives*
US 1939   110m   bw
Warner (Henry Blanke)

Three of the Lemp girls find a new husband for their widowed sister.

Lively and thickly textured sequel to *Four Daughters*; predecessor of the less interesting *Four Mothers*.

w Julius J. and Philip G. Epstein, Maurice Hanline, *novel* Sister Act by Fannie Hurst *d* Michael Curtiz

Claude Rains, Priscilla Lane, Rosemary Lane, Lola Lane, Gale Page, Jeffrey Lynn, Eddie Albert, May Robson, Frank McHugh, Dick Foran, John Garfield (briefly)

'Will ride along on momentum to excellent box office.'—*Variety*

Four's a Crowd
US 1938   91m   bw
Warner (Hal B. Wallis / David Lewis)

A public relations man has the job of promoting a mean-spirited millionaire, and falls in love with his daughter.

Floppy comedy, neither very witty nor as crazy as might have been expected. However, it ambles along quite engagingly.

w Casey Robinson, Sig Herzig *d* Michael Curtiz *ph* Ernest Haller *m* Heinz Roemheld, Ray Heindorf

Errol Flynn, Rosalind Russell, Olivia de Havilland, Patric Knowles, Walter Connolly, Hugh Herbert, Melville Cooper, Franklin Pangborn, Herman Bing, Margaret Hamilton

'Goofy click comedy that moves along to a whirlwind laugh finish.'—*Variety*

Fourteen Hours***
US 1951   92m   bw
TCF (Sol C. Siegel)

A man stands on the ledge of a tall building and threatens to jump.

Well-made documentary drama based on a true occurrence but given a happy ending. First class detail gives an impression of realism.

w John Paxton, article Joel Sayre *d* Henry Hathaway *ph* Joe MacDonald *m* Alfred Newman

Richard Basehart, Paul Douglas, Barbara Bel Geddes, Grace Kelly, Debra Paget, Agnes Moorehead, Robert Keith, Howard da Silva, Jeffrey Hunter, Martin Gabel, Jeff Corey

'A model of craftsmanship in all departments.'—*Penelope Houston*

'A highly enjoyable small scale picture, with a strength immensely greater than its size would suggest.'—*Richard Mallett, Punch*

'Between Ellen and Jill came Paul . . .'
The Fox*
US / Canada 1967   110m   De Luxe
Warner / Raymond Stross / Motion Pictures International (Howard Koch)

On an isolated farm, two lesbians are disturbed by the arrival of a wandering seaman.

Rather obvious sexual high jinks full of symbolism and heavy breathing.

w Lewis John Carlino, Howard Koch, *novel* D. H. Lawrence *d* Mark Rydell *ph* Bill Fraker *m* Lalo Schifrin

Anne Heywood, Sandy Dennis, Keir Dullea

AAN: Lalo Schifrin

Fox*
West Germany 1975   123m
Eastmancolor
Tango Film (Rainer Werner Fassbinder)
aka: *Fox and His Friends*
original title: *Faustrecht der Freiheit*

The decline of a homosexual sideshow performer.

Ironic, semi-autobiographical melodrama in the *Blue Angel* tradition, with sidelong glances at Hollywood glamour. In its way very memorable, but overlong.

w Rainer Werner Fassbinder, Christian Hohoff *d* Rainer Werner Fassbinder *ph* Michael Ballhaus *m* Peer Raben

Rainer Werner Fassbinder, Karl-Heinz Boehm, Peter Chatel, Harry Bär, Adrian Hoven, Ulla Jacobsen

● *Video: Palace*

The Fox and the Hound*
US 1981   83m   Technicolor
Walt Disney (Wolfgang Reitherman, Art Stevens)

A fox cub makes friends with a hound puppy, but their friendship is tested when they grow up.

Not unpleasant but somewhat heavy-going for a feature cartoon, made with some of the old Disney style but none of the old inventiveness.

w various, *novel* Daniel P. Mannix *d* Art Stevens, Ted Berman, Richard Rich

voices: Mickey Rooney, Kurt Russell, Pearl Bailey, Jack Albertson, Sandy Duncan, Jeanette Nolan

'Laughs are few and far between . . . the whole enterprise lacks vitality.'—*Brenda Davies, MFB*

Fox Follies of 1929
US 1929   82m   bw (sequence in colour)
Fox
GB title: *Movietone Follies of 1929*

An all-star review.

Every studio had its early talkie musical using up its contract stars; this was perhaps the least interesting.

wd David Butler, William K. Wells
ph Charles Van Enger

Sue Carol, Lola Lane, Dixie Lee, Sharon Lynn, Stepin Fetchit

Foxes
US 1980   106m   Technicolor

Four teenage girls battle with sex, drugs and life in general. Well-meaning but entirely resistible melodrama from behind the headlines. Jodie Foster, Scott Baio, Sally Kellerman, Randy Quaid, Adam Faith. Written by Gerald Ayres; directed by Adrian Lyne; for Casablanca / UA. 'Almost nil adult appeal.'—*Variety*

The Foxes of Harrow
US 1947   117m   bw
TCF (William A. Bacher)

In 1820 New Orleans, a philanderer seeks advancement by breaking up his marriage. Tolerable but rather flat adaptation of a bestseller, stultified by central miscasting.

w Wanda Tuchock, *novel* Frank Yerby *d* John M. Stahl *ph* Joseph La Shelle *m* Alfred Newman

Rex Harrison, Maureen O'Hara, Richard Haydn, Victor McLaglen, Vanessa Brown, Patricia Medina, Gene Lockhart, Hugo Haas
† Rex Harrison's role had been turned down by Tyrone Power.

'I don't care what they call you! I only care that you are all man—and all mine!'
Foxfire
US 1955   92m   Technicolor
U-I (Aaron Rosenberg)

A rich New York girl on holiday in Arizona is attracted to a half-Apache miner.
Romantic melodrama with action asides; watchable for women who like that sort of thing.

w Ketti Frings, *novel* Anya Seton *d* Joseph Pevney *ph* William Daniels *m* Frank Skinner

Jane Russell, Jeff Chandler, Frieda Inescort, Dan Duryea

Foxhole in Cairo
GB 1960   80m   bw
Omnia (Steven Pallos, Donald Taylor)

A German agent in Libya is allowed to get back to Rommel with false information. Interesting true spy story deflated by muddled handling.

w Leonard Mosley, from his book The Cat and the Mice *d* John Moxey *ph* Desmond Dickinson *m* Wolfram Rohrig, Douglas Gamley, Ken Jones

James Robertson Justice, Adrian Hoven, Albert Lieven (as Rommel), Niall MacGinnis, Peter Van Eyck, Robert Urquhart, Fenella Fielding

Fra Diavolo**
US 1933 90m bw
MGM / Hal Roach
aka: *The Devil's Brother*

Two incompetent bandits are hired as
manservants by a real bandit.
Auber's 1830 operetta becomes a vehicle for
Laurel and Hardy, setting a pattern they
followed with *Babes in Toyland* and *The
Bohemian Girl*. They have excellent
sequences, but overall the film lacks pace.

w Jeanie McPherson d Hal Roach, Charles
Rogers ph Art Lloyd, Hap Depew md Le
Roy Shield

Stan Laurel, Oliver Hardy, Dennis King,
James Finlayson, Thelma Todd
'An early 19th-century comic opera doesn't
make for particularly good film fare despite its
hoking.'—*Variety*

Fragment of an Empire*
USSR 1929 100m approx bw silent
Sovkino

A young man who lost his memory in World
War I regains it in 1928 and surveys the
changed social order.
Mildly satirical propaganda piece with a vivid
impression of Leningrad at the time.

w Friedrich Ermier, Katerina Vinogradskaya
d Friedrich Ermler ph Yevgeni Schneider

Fyoder Nikitin, Yakov Gudkin, Ludmila
Semyonova

Fragment of Fear*
GB 1970 95m Technicolor
Columbia (John R. Sloan)

A young writer investigates the murder of his
aunt, but finds that he may himself be mad.
What appears to be a whodunnit turns into a
flashy, fashionable, sub-Antonioni puzzle with
no ending, but despite the considerable
irritation this causes, the details and character
cameos are excellent.

w Paul Dehn, *novel* John Bingham d Richard
C. Sarafian ph Oswald Morris m Johnny
Harris

David Hemmings, Gayle Hunnicutt, Roland
Culver, Daniel Massey, Flora Robson, Wilfrid
Hyde White, Adolfo Celi, Mona Washbourne

Framed
US 1947 82m bw

A drunken out-of-work engineer is used as fall
guy by two thieves planning an elaborate
coup. Lugubrious mixture of puzzle, character
drama and gloomy philosophizing, complete
with femme fatale who is handed over to the
cops at the end. Glenn Ford, Janis Carter,
Barry Sullivan. Written by Ben Maddow;
directed by Richard Wallace; for Columbia.
(GB title: *Paula*.)

Framed
US 1974 106m Metrocolor

A Tennessee gambler inadvertently kills a
sheriff, is sent to prison, gets out on parole
and wreaks revenge on those who framed him.
Violent thick-ear update of *The Count of
Monte Cristo*, of interest only to connoisseurs

of gratuitous nastiness. Joe Don Baker, Conny
Van Dyke, Gabriel Dell, Brock Peters, John
Marley, John Larch. Written by Mort Briskin;
directed by Phil Karlson; for Paramount.

Frances
US 1982 140m Technicolor
EMI / Brooksfilm (Jonathan Sanger)

The downhill career of 30s actress Frances
Farmer.
Long, glum, and not particularly convincing in
its inferences, this exhaustive study of a person
who didn't deserve all this fuss is illuminated
only by a strong star performance.

w Eric Bergren, Christopher Devore, Nicholas
Kazan d Graeme Clifford ph Laszlo Kovacs
m John Barry pd Richard Sylbert

Jessica Lange, Kim Stanley, Sam Shepard,
Bart Burns, Jeffrey de Munn

AAN: Jessica Lange; Kim Stanley
● *Video: Thorn EMI*

The Franchise Affair*
GB 1950 88m bw
ABP (Robert Hall)

A young girl accuses two gentlewomen of
kidnapping and ill-treating her.
Unusual and absorbing mystery based on a
true 18th-century case; the treatment however
is rather too mild.

w Robert Hall, Lawrence Huntington. *novel*
Josephine Tey d Lawrence Huntington
ph Gunther Krampf m Philip Green

Michael Denison, Dulcie Gray, Anthony
Nicholls, Marjorie Fielding, Athene Seyler,
Ann Stephens, Hy Hazell, John Bailey,
Kenneth More

Francis*
US 1950 90m bw
U-I (Robert Arthur)

An army private makes friends with a talking
mule who causes him some embarrassment.
Simple-minded, quite agreeable if rather slow-
moving fantasy farce which was popular
enough to spawn several sequels and later a
TV series called *Mister Ed*.

w David Stern, from his novel d Arthur
Lubin ph Irving Glassberg m Frank Skinner

Donald O'Connor, Patricia Medina, Zasu
Pitts, Ray Collins, John McIntyre, Eduard
Franz, Robert Warwick, and Chill Wills as
Francis' voice.

Sequels (the first six with Donald O'Connor):
1951: FRANCIS GOES TO THE RACES
1952: FRANCIS GOES TO WEST POINT
1953: FRANCIS COVERS BIG TOWN
1954: FRANCIS JOINS THE WACS
1955: FRANCIS IN THE NAVY
1956: FRANCIS IN THE HAUNTED
HOUSE (with Mickey Rooney)

Francis of Assisi
US 1961 107m De Luxe Cinemascope
TCF / Perseus (Plato A. Skouras)

The son of a medieval cloth merchant takes a
vow of poverty, cares for animals and dies a
hermit.
Tedious biopic.

w Eugene Vale, Jack Thomas, James Forsyth
d Michael Curtiz ph Piero Portalupi m Mario
Nascimbene

Bradford Dillman, Dolores Hart, Stuart
Whitman, Eduard Franz, Pedro Armendariz,
Cecil Kellaway, Finlay Currie, Mervyn Johns,
Athene Seyler

'To have seen it is to wear a badge of
courage!'
'A monster science created but could not
destroy!'

Frankenstein****
US 1931 71m bw
Universal (Carl Laemmle Jnr)

A research scientist creates a living monster
from corpses, but it runs amok.
Whole books have been written about this film
and its sequels. Apart from being a fascinating
if primitive cinematic work in its own right, it
set its director and star on interesting paths
and established a Hollywood attitude towards
horror (mostly borrowed from German silents
such as *The Golem*). A seminal film indeed,
which at each repeated viewing belies its age.

w Garrett Fort, Francis Edward Faragoh, John
L. Balderston, from the play by Peggy
Webling and the novel by Mary Wollstonecraft
Shelley d James Whale, ph Arthur Edeson
m David Broekman ad Charles D. Hall

Boris Karloff, Colin Clive, Mae Clarke, John
Boles, Edward Van Sloan, Frederick Kerr,
Dwight Frye
'Still the most famous of all horror films,
and deservedly so.'—*John Baxter, 1968*
'The horror is cold, chilling the marrow but
never arousing malaise.'—*Carlos Clarens*
† Direct sequels by the same studio (all qv)
include *The Bride of Frankenstein, Son of
Frankenstein, Ghost of Frankenstein,
Frankenstein Meets the Wolf Man, House of
Frankenstein, House of Dracula, Abbott and
Costello Meet Frankenstein*. The later Hammer
series, which told the story all over again in
gorier vein, includes (all qv) *The Curse of
Frankenstein, The Revenge of Frankenstein,
The Evil of Frankenstein, Frankenstein Created
Woman, Frankenstein Must be Destroyed,
Horror of Frankenstein, Frankenstein and the
Monster from Hell*. Other Frankenstein films
date from as early as 1908, and scores have
been made in various languages. *Young
Frankenstein* (qv) is a partly effective spoof on
the Hollywood series; *The Munsters* was a
sixties comedy series for TV which used the
monster as its leading character in a domestic
setting.
†† Robert Florey is said to have contributed to
the script, having been the first choice for
director.
● *Video: CIC*

Frankenstein and the Monster from
Hell
GB 1973 99m Technicolor

The Baron turns an injured lunatic into a hairy
ape man. Cheaply made and very ghoulish
horror comic in the unattractive setting of an
asylum; very little entertainment is provided.
Peter Cushing, Shane Briant, Madeleine

Smith, John Stratton, Bernard Lee, Dave
Prowse. Written by John Elder (Anthony
Hinds); directed by Terence Fisher; for
Hammer / Avco.

'A beautiful woman with the soul of a
    devil!'
Frankenstein Created Woman
GB 1966   86m   Technicolor

The Baron invests the body of a dead girl with
the soul of her dead lover, and a murder spree
results. Crude and gory farrago, with the
central laboratory sequence apparently excised
at the last moment. Peter Cushing, Thorley
Walters, Susan Denberg, Robert Morris,
Duncan Lamont. Written by John Elder
(Anthony Hinds); directed by Terence Fisher;
for Hammer / Warner.

'Titans of terror, clashing in mortal
    combat!'
Frankenstein Meets the Wolf Man**
US 1943   73m   bw
Universal (George Waggner)

Lawrence Talbot, the wolf man, travels to
Vasaria in the hope of a cure, and finds the
Frankenstein monster being reactivated.
Once one recovered from the bargain
basement combination of two monsters in one
picture, this was a horror comic with stylish
sequences, weakened by cuts in the script and
a miscast Bela Lugosi.

w Curt Siodmak d Roy William Neill
ph George Robinson m Hans Salter

Lon Chaney Jnr, Ilona Massey, Bela Lugosi
(as the monster), Patric Knowles, Maria
Ouspenskaya

FRANKENSTEIN.   Mae Clarke meets the original Boris Karloff monster, way back in 1931.

Frankenstein Must Be Destroyed
GB 1969   96m   Technicolor

The Baron transplants the brain of one
colleague into the body of another. Spirited
but decidedly unpleasant addition to the cycle,
made more so by a genuine note of pathos.
Peter Cushing, Freddie Jones, Veronica
Carlson, Simon Ward, Thorley Walters,
Maxine Audley. Written by Bert Batt;
directed by Terence Fisher; for Hammer /
Warner-Pathé.

Frankenstein '70
US 1958   83m   bw   Cinemascope
Allied Artists (Aubrey Schenck)

Television film-makers descend on Castle
Frankenstein; the current Count needs the
money to finance some monster making of his
own.
Boringly talkative and very silly 'futuristic'
blot on an honourable name, apart from a
rather frightening pre-credits sequence.

w Richard Landau, G. Worthing Yates
d Howard W. Koch ph Carl Guthrie m Paul
Dunlap

Boris Karloff, Tom Duggan, Jana Lund

Frankie and Johnny*
US 1966   87m   Technicolor
UA / F and J (Edward Small)

On a Mississippi riverboat, a gambling singer

is the despair of his lady partner.
Mildly amusing pastiche both of the old song
and of the various riverboat dramas.

w Alex Gottlieb d Frederick de Cordova
ph John Marquette m Fred Karger

Elvis Presley, Donna Douglas, Sue Ane
Langdon, Harry Morgan, Nancy Kovack,
Audrey Christie, Jerome Cowan

Fräulein
US 1958   100m   Eastmancolor
    Cinemascope
TCF (Walter Reisch)

During World War II an American prisoner of
war escapes and is helped by the daughter of a
German professor.
Studio-bound war heroics with little conviction
achieved or aimed at.

w Lee Townsend, novel James McGowan
d Henry Koster ph Leo Tover m Daniele
Amfitheatrof

Dana Wynter, Mel Ferrer, Margaret Hayes,
Dolores Michaels, Theodore Bikel, Helmut
Dantine

Fräulein Doktor
Italy / Yugoslavia 1968   104m
    Technicolor
(Paramount) Dino de Laurentiis / Avala

In World War I, a German lady spy outwits
British intelligence.

Rather glum international action melodrama.

w Diulio Coletti, H. A. L. Craig, Stanley
Mann, Vittoriano Petrilli, Alberto Lattuada
d Alberto Lattuada ph Luigi Kuveiller
m Ennio Morricone

Suzy Kendall, Kenneth More, James Booth,
Capucine, Alexander Knox, Nigel Green,
Roberto Bisacco
† A similar story was filmed in 1936 as
Mademoiselle Docteur.

Freaks**
US 1932   64m   bw
MGM (Tod Browning)

A lady trapeze artist marries a midget, then
poisons him for his money; his abnormal
friends take revenge by turning her into a
freak.
Made but disowned by MGM after accusations
of tastelessness, this strident and silly
melodrama has dated badly but has sequences
of great power, especially the final massing of
the freaks, slithering to their revenge in a
rainstorm. It would have been better as a
silent; the dialogue kills it.

w Willis Goldbeck, Leon Gordon, novel Spurs
by Tod Robbins d Tod Browning ph Merrit
B. Gerstad

Wallace Ford, Olga Baclanova, Leila Hyams,
Roscoe Ates

'Either too horrible or not sufficiently so.'—
Variety

'It is a skilfully presented production but of
a character which in consideration of the
susceptibilities of mass audiences should be
avoided.'—*Martin Quigley*

'For pure sensationalism it tops any picture
yet produced.'—*Louella Parsons*

'I want something that out-horrors
Frankenstein.'—*Irving Thalberg*

'Touching and funny and made with a
miraculous delicacy.'—*Evening Standard, 1964*

Freaky Friday
US 1976 100m Technicolor
Walt Disney (Ron Miller)

A 13-year-old and her mother, each
discontented with their lot, express a wish to
change places—and do.
A trendy update of *Vice Versa*, padded out
with Disney irrelevancies and long outstaying
its welcome.

w Mary Rodgers, from her novel d Gary
Nelson ph Charles F. Wheeler m Johnny
Mandel

Jodie Foster, Barbara Harris, John Astin,
Patsy Kelly, Dick Van Patten, Sorrell Booke,
Marie Windsor

● *Video: Rank*

Freckles
US 1935 69m bw

A mild teenager gets a job as a timber guard.
Unsensational version of a rustic classic.
Written by Dorothy Yost from the novel by
Gene Stratton-Porter; directed by Edward
Killy and William Hamilton; for Pandro S.
Berman / RKO. 'The novel, published in
1875, is shown to have sold 2,000,000 copies.
It will have a tough time making the same
grade as a picture . . . its appeal is of a past
generation.'—*Variety*

Free and Easy
US 1930 75m bw
MGM

A beauty contest winner is taken to
Hollywood by her accident-prone manager.
Primitive talkie showing a great silent
comedian all at sea with the new techniques,
and the MGM studio offering entertainment
on the level of a very bad school concert.

w Al Boasberg, Richard Schayer d Edward
Sedgwick ph Leonard Smith

Buster Keaton, Anita Page, Robert
Montgomery, Trixie Freganza

Free for All
US 1949 83m bw
U-I (Robert Buckner)

A young inventor finds a way of turning water
into petrol.
Scatty comedy with mildly amusing moments.

w Robert Buckner d Charles T. Barton
ph George Robinson m Frank Skinner

Robert Cummings, Ann Blyth, Percy Kilbride,
Ray Collins, Donald Woods, Mikhail
Rasumny

A Free Soul*
US 1931 91m bw
MGM

An unconventional lawyer regrets allowing his
daughter to consort with a gangster.
Heavy melodrama with outdated attitudes, but
an impressive example of the studio's style in
the early thirties.

w John Meehan, *novel* Adela Rogers St John
d Clarence Brown ph William Daniels
m William Axt

Lionel Barrymore, Norma Shearer, Leslie
Howard, Clark Gable, Lucy Beaumont, James
Gleason

'An ungainly, rambling and preposterous
theme, awkwardly brought to the screen.'—
Variety
† Remade 1953 as *The Girl Who Had
Everything*.
AA: Lionel Barrymore (who had a 14-minute
speech)
AAN: Clarence Brown; Norma Shearer

'Today they demolished 23 cars, four
 motor cycles and one apartment
 building. But don't call the cops. They
 are the cops!'
Freebie and the Bean*
US 1974 113m Technicolor
 Panavision
Warner (Richard Rush)

Two vaguely incompetent cops try to link a
mobster with the numbers racket.
Violent comedy melodrama with a high
mortality rate, amoral outlook, and the usual
seventies reliance on incoherent plot, bumbled
dialogue and excessive background noise.
Occasionally funny all the same.

w Richard Kaufman d Richard Rush
ph Laszlo Kovacs m Dominic Frontière

Alan Arkin, James Caan, Loretta Swit, Jack
Kruschen, Mike Kellin

'It summarizes Hollywood's favourite
thematic elements of the early seventies:
platonic male love affair, police corruption,
comic violence, cynicism in high places, San
Francisco, gay villains, the car chase. A return
to the Keystone Kops, with character
trimmings and lashings of sado-masochistic
mayhem.'—*Clyde Jeavons*

'A tasteless film from a spitball script.'—
Variety

'There is a beating or a killing, or at least a
yelling scene, every couple of minutes.'—*New
Yorker, 1980*
● *Video: Warner*

Freedom Radio
GB 1941 95m bw
Columbia / Two Cities (Mario Zampi)
US title: *A Voice in the Night*

In Vienna during World War II, the husband
of a Nazi actress runs a secret radio
transmitter for Allied propaganda.
Moderate wartime flagwaver.

w Basil Wood, Gordon Wellesley, Louis
Golding, Anatole de Grunwald, Jeffrey Dell,
Bridget Boland, Roland Pertwee d Anthony
Asquith ph Bernard Knowles

Diana Wynyard, Clive Brook, Raymond
Huntley, Joyce Howard, Derek Farr, Howard
Marion Crawford, Morland Graham

French Can-Can**
France / Italy 1955 105m Technicolor
Franco-London / Jolly (Louis Wipf)

How the can-can was launched in Paris night
clubs.
A dramatically thin vehicle splendidly evoking
a vision of vanished Paris: a feast for the eyes.

w André-Paul Antoine d Jean Renoir
ph Michel Kelber m Georges Van Parys

Jean Gabin, Françoise Arnoul, Maria Félix,
Jean-Roger Caussimon, Edith Piaf, Patachou

'Doyle is bad news . . . but a good cop!'
The French Connection***
US 1971 104m De Luxe
TCF / Philip D'Antoni

New York police track down a consignment of
drugs entering the country in a car.
Lively semi-documentary based on the true
exploits of a tough cop named Eddie Egan
who liked to break a few rules. Most
memorable for a car chase scene involving an
elevated railway, for showing the seamy side
of New York more or less as it is, and for the
most mumbled dialogue and the poorest sound
track in years.

w Ernest Tidyman, *book* Robin Moore
d William Friedkin ph Owen Roizman
m Don Ellis

Gene Hackman, Roy Scheider, *Fernando Rey*,
Tony Lo Bianco

AA: best picture; Ernest Tidyman; William
Friedkin; Gene Hackman
AAN: Owen Roizman; Roy Scheider
● *Video: CBS / Fox*

French Connection II
US 1975 119m De Luxe
TCF (Robert L. Rosen)

The New York cop who in *The French
Connection* smashed most of a drug ring
arrives in Marseilles to track down its elusive
leader.
Sleazy, virtually plotless and unattractive
sequel which rises to a few good action
moments but is bogged down by bad language,
unconvincing characterization and an
interminable and irrelevant 'cold turkey'
sequence.

w Robert Dillon, Laurie Dillon, Alexander
Jacobs d John Frankenheimer ph Claude
Renoir m Don Ellis

Gene Hackman, Fernando Rey, Bernard
Fresson, Jean-Pierre Castaldi

'Visually as well as morally the film makes
you uncertain where its feet are.'—*New
Yorker*

● *Video: CBS / Fox*

French Dressing
GB 1963 86m bw
ABP / Kenwood (Kenneth Harper)

A deckchair attendant and a local reporter
believe that what Bardot can do for St Tropez

they can do for Gormleigh-on-Sea.
Cinema's *enfant terrible* directs this his first
theatrical film at breakneck speed with echoes
of Tati, Keaton and the Keystone Kops. Alas,
lack of star comedians and firm control make
its exuberance merely irritating.

w Peter Myers, Ronald Cass, Peter Britt
d Ken Russell *ph* Ken Higgins *m* Georges
Delerue

James Booth, Roy Kinnear, Marisa Mell,
Bryan Pringle

'She was lost from the moment she saw
him . . . '

The French Lieutenant's Woman°
GB 1981 123m Technicolor
UA / Juniper (Leon Clore)

In 1867 Lyme Regis, a gentleman forsakes his
fiancée for the abandoned mistress of a French
seaman.
Vaguely unsatisfactory and muddily coloured
adaptation of a novel which set its thin story
against the entire social background of the
Victorian age as related to our own. The
attempt to replace this by an equally thin
modern story about actors playing the
Victorian roles fails rather dismally; but the
enterprise supplies points of interest along the
way.

w Harold Pinter, *novel* John Fowles *d* Karel
Reisz *ph* Freddie Francis *m* Carl Davis
pd Assheton Gorton

Jeremy Irons, Meryl Streep, Leo McKern,
Patience Collier, Peter Vaughan, Hilton
McRae
    'Pinter's reduction not only shears away the
sliding historical perspective, but robs the
narrative of its Victorian charisma.'—*Tom
Milne, MFB*
    'There are some lovely moments, and a few
have magical undertones, but most of the
picture might be taking place in a glass
case.'—*Pauline Kael*
AAN: Harold Pinter; editing (John Bloom);
Meryl Streep
BFA: best sound; Carl Davis; Meryl Streep
● *Video: Warner*

The French Line
US 1953 102m Technicolor 3-D
RKO (Edmund Grainger)

A cheery Texas oil heiress finds a husband
while travelling to France.
Very thinly plotted but quite attractive light
musical with a good-humoured star wearing
costumes once thought censorable.

w Mary Loos, Richard Sale *d* Lloyd Bacon
ph Harry J. Wild *m* Walter Scharf *md* Lionel
Newman *ch* Jack Cole

Jane Russell, Gilbert Roland, Arthur
Hunnicutt, Mary McCarty
    'A slouching Amazon, her clothes appear to
stay put just as long as she agrees not to burst
out of them; essentially a good sort, she has an
ever-annihilating sneer for the false, the
pretentious and the fresh.'—*MFB*

● *Video: Kingston*

HOW TO WIN A MAN...
IN **4** EASY LESSONS!

LESSON No. 1
IS ME ROMANTIC? Then get him out under the moon...and he's yours!

LESSON No. 2
IS HE JEALOUS? Tell him he's the only one in the world...and you're irresistible!

LESSON No. 3
IS ME WORLDLY? Just let him talk about himself...and wait for the proposal!

LESSON No. 4
IS ME JOLLY? Listen to his stories, even if it kills you. He's yours for life!

Yessir, Ellen sure knows how to land her
man...and she gets more of them than the
Canadian Mounted Police. Learn all about
love from a gal who takes this Leap Year
business seriously. It's the fastest, funniest
screen romance ever!

"**FRENCH** *WITHOUT* **TEARS**"

...*but with laughs...and laughs...and laughs!*

Starring
**RAY MILLAND
ELLEN DREW**

From the Stage Play by Terence Rattigan · Directed by
ANTHONY ASQUITH · Produced by MARIO ZAMPI
A Paramount Picture

FRENCH WITHOUT TEARS.   Ellen Drew was not enough of a comedienne to bring a
central spark to this version, the only one we have, of Rattigan's long-running stage
comedy.

A French Mistress
GB 1960 98m bw
British Lion / Charter (John Boulting)

An attractive new mistress causes havoc at a
boys' school.
Sloppy, predictable comedy with practised
performers getting a few easy laughs. The
producers tried to excuse its imperfections by
promoting it as 'a romp'.

w Roy Boulting, Jeffrey Dell, *play* Robert
Monro (Sonnie Hale) *d* Roy Boulting
ph Max Greene *m* John Addison

James Robertson Justice, Cecil Parker,
Raymond Huntley, Ian Bannen, Agnes
Laurent, Thorley Walters, Edith Sharpe,
Athene Seyler, Kenneth Griffith

French without Tears°
GB 1939 85m bw
Paramount / Two Cities (David E. Rose)

Young Britons at a French crammers fall for
the young sister of one of their number.
Pleasant light comedy from a successful West
End play.

w Terence Rattigan, Anatole de Grunwald,
Ian Dalrymple, *play Terence Rattigan*
d Anthony Asquith *ph* Bernard Knowles

Ray Milland, Ellen Drew, *Guy Middleton,
Ronald Culver*, David Tree, Jim Gerald,
Janine Darcy, Kenneth Morgan
    'There is always something a little shocking
about English levity. The greedy exhilaration
of these blithe young men when they learn

that another fellow's girl is to join them at the establishment where they are learning French, the scramble over her luggage, the light-hearted badinage, the watery and libidinous eye—that national mixture of prudery and excitement—would be unbearable if it were not for Mr Asquith's civilized direction.'—*Graham Greene*

† Incredibly, Paramount had purchased the property as a vehicle for Marlene Dietrich.

Frenchie
US 1950   80m   Technicolor
U-I (Michael Kraike)

A saloon queen sets up shop in Bottleneck, her real aim being to track down her father's murderers.
Modest western of the *Destry Rides Again* school.

w Oscar Brodney d Louis King ph Maury Gertsman m Hans Salter

Shelley Winters, Joel McCrea, Paul Kelly, Elsa Lanchester, Marie Windsor, John Emery, George Cleveland, John Russell

'For 24 reckless hours the arms of adventure embraced her—and she knew the thrill of true love!'

Frenchman's Creek*
US 1944   112m   Technicolor
Paramount (B. G. De Sylva)

In Restoration England, a lady flees from a lascivious nobleman to her family home in Cornwall, where she falls in love with a French pirate.
Enjoyable Girls' Own Paper romance, dressed to kill and entertaining despite its many palpable absurdities.

w Talbot Jennings, *novel* Daphne du Maurier d Mitchell Leisen ph George Barnes m Victor Young ad Hans Dreier, Ernest Fegte

Joan Fontaine, Arturo de Cordova, Basil Rathbone, Nigel Bruce, *Cecil Kellaway*, Ralph Forbes, Moyna McGill

'As infallible as any real-life dream.'—*James Agee*

Frenzy*
Sweden 1944   101m   bw
Svensk Filmindustri
original title: *Hets*; aka: *Torment*

A sadistic Latin teacher and his sensitive pupil find themselves competing for the same girl.
Hothouse melodrama of the *Blue Angel* school: it seemed pretty powerful at the time.

w Ingmar Bergman d Alf Sjöberg ph Martin Bodin m Hilding Rosenberg

Stig Jarrel, Alf Kjellin, Mai Zetterling

'From the master of shock, a shocking masterpiece!'

Frenzy*
GB 1972   116m   Technicolor
Universal / Alfred Hitchcock

A disillusioned and aggressive ex-RAF officer is suspected through circumstantial evidence of being London's 'necktie murderer'.
Has-been, unconvincing, cliché-ridden thriller,

an old man's sex suspenser, which would have been derided if anyone but Hitchcock had made it. As it is, a few comic and suspenseful touches partly atone for the implausibilities and lapses of taste.

w Anthony Shaffer, *novel* Goodbye Piccadilly, Farewell Leicester Square by Arthur La Bern d Alfred Hitchcock ph Gilbert Taylor m Ron Goodwin

Jon Finch, *Alec McCowen, Barry Foster*, Vivien Merchant, Anna Massey

'Hitchcock's most stodgy piece since *Dial M for Murder* and possibly his least interesting film from any period.'—*William S. Pechter*

● *Video: CIC*

The Freshman**
US 1925   75m (24 fps)   bw   silent
Harold Lloyd

An awkward college student accidentally becomes a star football player.
A rather slow but striking star vehicle with assured set-pieces. The football game climax was later used as the first reel of *Mad Wednesday*.

w Sam Taylor, Ted Wilde, Time Whelan, John Grey d Fred Newmeyer, Sam Taylor ph Walter Lundin, Henry Kohler

Harold Lloyd, Jobyna Ralston, Brooks Benedict

Freud**
GB 1962   140m   bw
U-I (Wolfgang Reinhardt)

Vienna 1885; Dr Sigmund Freud, a neurologist, uses hypnotism to treat hysteria, and finds new interest in the case of a boy whose hatred of his father springs from incestuous love of his mother, a failing which Freud finds in himself.
Earnest and competent biopic harking back to Warners' similar films of the thirties, with the addition of franker language. Generally absorbing, but undeniably hard tack.

w Charles Kaufman, Wolfgang Reinhardt d John Huston ph Douglas Slocombe m Jerry Goldsmith

Montgomery Clift, Larry Parks, Susannah York, Eileen Herlie, Susan Kohner, David McCallum

'The dream sequences, photographed mostly in negative or overexposure, belong not on the couch of Dr Freud but in the Cabinet of Dr Caligari.'—*John Simon*

'It is impossible, I would think, for any educated person to sit through *Freud* without bursting into laughter at least once.'—*Ernest Callenbach, Film Quarterly*

AAN: script; Jerry Goldsmith

Fric Frac*
France 1939   95m   bw

A provincial jeweller's assistant falls in with underworld characters. Well-prized French comedy with dialogue entirely in thieves' slang. Michel Simon, Fernandel, Arletty, Helene Robert. Written by Michel Duran from the play by Edouard Bourdet; directed by Maurice Lehmann; for his own company.

Friday the Thirteenth***
GB 1933   84m   bw
Gainsborough (Michael Balcon)

Several people are involved in a bus crash, and we turn back the clock to see how they came to be there.
Highly competent compendium of comedies and dramas looking back to *The Bridge of San Luis Rey* and forward to the innumerable all-star films of the forties.

w G. H. Moresby-White, Sidney Gilliat, Emlyn Williams d Victor Saville ph Charles Van Enger

Sonnie Hale, Cyril Smith, *Eliot Makeham*, Ursula Jeans, *Emlyn Williams*, Frank Lawton, Belle Chrystal, *Max Miller*, Alfred Drayton, Edmund Gwenn, Mary Jerrold, Gordon Harker, *Robertson Hare*, Martita Hunt, Leonora Corbett, Jessie Matthews, Ralph Richardson

Friday the Thirteenth
US 1980   95m   colour
Georgetown (Sean S. Cunningham)

When a summer camp is reopened after many years, the grisly murders which closed it down begin again.
Horror suspense story with no *raison d'être* but a series of inventively gory shock moments, which were enough however for it to ring the box office bell.

w Victor Miller d Sean S. Cunningham ph Barry Abrams

Betsy Palmer, Adrienne King, Jeannine Taylor, Robbi Morgan

'An oversexed couple makes love in the bottom bunk, there's a dead body in the top bunk and the rest of the bunk is in the television commercials.'—*Variety*

Friday the Thirteenth Part Two
US 1981   87m   De Luxe

The sole survivor of the massacre at Camp Crystal Lake is murdered, and five years later the mayhem begins again, the villain being the son of the woman who committed the former killings. Virtually a remake of the first film, starting with a long flashback to it; short sharp shocks punctuate slabs of tedium. Amy Steel, John Furey, Adrienne King, Kirsten Baker. Written by Ron Kurz; directed by Steve Miner; for Georgetown Productions.

Friday the Thirteenth Part Three
US 1982   95m   Movielab   3D

Crazy Jason is still murdering kids up at Crystal Lake. No better than its predecessors for being in three dimensions; in fact, half as bad again. Dana Kimmell, Richard Brooker, Catherine Parks, Paul Kratka. Written by Martin Kitrosser and Carol Watson; directed by Steve Miner; for Georgetown productions.
'The first was dreadful and took seventeen million. The second was just as bad and took more than ten million. No doubt the distributor will be happy to learn that the third is terrible too.'—*Variety*

Friday the Thirteenth: Final Chapter
US 1984   91m   Movielab

Supposedly dead Jason escapes from cold storage at the morgue and goes on another rampage. The awful mixture as before: would the title meant what it says. E. Erich Anderson, Judie Aronson, Peter Barton, Kimberly Beck. Written by Barney Cohen; directed by Joseph Zito; for Paramount. 'Yet another catalogue of mindless slaughter which doesn't even offer the courtesy of a story.'— *Daily Mail.* 'The censor says you have to be 18 to see it. I would suggest you merely have to be daft.'—*Sunday Times*

Frieda*
GB 1947   97m   bw
Ealing (Michael Relph)

An RAF officer marries and takes home a girl who helped him escape from a POW camp. Stuffy and dated drama about how one English family learned to love one particular German. Timely when it appeared, however, and well made within its conventions.

w Angus Macphail, Ronald Millar, *play* Ronald Millar *d* Basil Dearden *ph* Gordon Dines *m* John Greenwood

Mai Zetterling, David Farrar, Glynis Johns, Flora Robson, Albert Lieven

Friendly Enemies
US 1925   70m (24 fps)   bw   silent

Two German immigrants are divided when the United States enters the war. Curious comedy-drama for two vaudevillians, based on a topical play of the time. Joe Weber, Lew Fields, Virginia Brown Faire, Jack Mulhall. Written by Alfred A. Cohn, from the play by Samuel Shipman and Aaron Hoffman; directed by George Melford; for PDC. (Remade in 1942 with Charles Winninger.)

Friendly Persuasion**
US 1956   139m   De Luxe
AA (William Wyler)

At the outbreak of the Civil War, a family of Quakers has to consider its position. Sentimental, homespun western fare, well done without being especially engrossing.

w Michael Wilson, *novel* Jessamyn West *d William Wyler ph* Ellsworth Fredericks *m* Dmitri Tiomkin

Gary Cooper, Dorothy McGuire, Anthony Perkins, Marjorie Main, Richard Eyer, Robert Middleton, Walter Catlett

'The material is a little tenuous . . . but Wyler's sure-handed direction constantly illuminates it with a humour, a gentle charm and a feeling for fundamental values that are rare indeed.'—*Moira Walsh, America*
† For TV movie remake, see *Television Companion.*

AAN: best picture; Michael Wilson; William Wyler; Anthony Perkins; song 'Thee I Love' (*m* Dmitri Tiomkin, *ly* Paul Francis Webster)

'Who needs the world when you own the moon and stars?'

Friends
GB 1971   102m   Technicolor
Paramount (Lewis Gilbert)

Teenage lovers run away to a country cottage and have a child.
Peculiar idyll given corny 'poetic' treatment: a real non-starter.

w Jack Russell, Vernon Harris *d* Lewis Gilbert *ph* Andrew Winding *m* Elton John

Sean Bury, Anicee Alvina, Toby Robbins, Ronald Lewis

Friends and Lovers
US 1931   67m   bw
RKO (William Le Baron)

A society wife causes several hearts to flutter illicitly. Unsatisfactory comedy-drama which lurches along from one mood to another and may have been intended as satire.

w Wallace Smith, *novel* The Sphinx Has Spoken by Maurice Dekobra *d* Victor Schertzinger *ph* J. Roy Hunt *m* Victor Schertzinger, Max Steiner

Adolphe Menjou, Laurence Olivier, Lily Damita, Erich Von Stroheim, Hugh Herbert, Frederick Kerr, Blanche Friderici
'Dumb sentimental romance . . . the people never once display motives that are understandable or reasonable.'—*Variety*

The Friends of Eddie Coyle*
US 1973   102m   Technicolor
Paramount (Paul Monash)

An ageing hoodlum agrees to become a police informer and is hunted down by his former associates.
Dour gangster melodrama held together by its central performance.

w Paul Monash, *novel* George V. Higgins *d* Peter Yates *ph* Vernon J. Kemper *m* Dave Grusin

Robert Mitchum, Peter Boyle, Richard Jordan, Steven Keats, Mitch Ryan, Alex Rocco

Friends of Mr Sweeney*
US 1934   68m   bw

A brow-beaten reporter gets drunk, faces life, and changes his personality. Amusing minor comedy of a kind no longer made. *Charles Ruggles,* Eugene Pallette, Berton Churchill, Robert Barrat, Ann Dvorak. Written by Warren Duff and Sidney Sutherland, from the novel by Elmer Davis; directed by Edward Ludwig; for Warner. 'Old situations given a new comedy coating . . . positive all-round fun for every family.'—*Variety*

Fright
GB 1971   87m   Eastmancolor

A babysitter is menaced by a psychotic. Unattractive screamer which starts on a hysterical note and never lets up. Susan George, Ian Bannen, Dennis Waterman, Honor Blackman, John Gregson, Maurice Kaufman. Written by Tudor Gates; directed by Peter Collinson; for Fantale / British Lion.

● *Video: Thorn EMI*

Frightened City
GB 1961   98m   bw
Anglo Amalgamated / Zodiac (John Lemont)

Gangsters fall out over a protection racket. Reasonably terse racketeer melodrama rather surprisingly set in London.

w Leigh Vance *d* John Lemont *ph* Desmond Dickinson *m* Norrie Paramour

Herbert Lom, Sean Connery, John Gregson, Alfred Marks, Yvonne Romain, Kenneth Griffith

The Frightened Lady
GB 1932   87m   bw

A mad young lord is protected by his mother. Modest chiller remade later as *The Case of the Frightened Lady* (qv). Norman McKinnel, Cathleen Nesbitt, Emlyn Williams, Gordon Harker, Belle Chrystall, Finlay Currie. Written by Angus McPhail and Bryan Edgar Wallace, from the play by Edgar Wallace; directed by T. Hayes Hunter; for Gainsborough.

Frisco Jenny
US 1933   73m   bw

A Barbary Coast lady is prosecuted for murder by her own son. Antediluvian melodramatic plot, borrowed from *Madame X*, provides an adequate star vehicle. Ruth Chatterton, Donald Cook, Louis Calhern, J. Carrol Naish, James Murray. Written by Wilson Mizner and Robert Lord; directed by William A. Wellman; for Warner.

The Frisco Kid*
US 1935   77m   bw
Warner (Samuel Bischoff)

A Shanghaied sailor rises to power among the riff raff of the Barbary Coast in the 1860s. Fair melodrama with the star in action and (less interestingly) in love.

w Warren Duff, Seton I. Miller *d* Lloyd Bacon *ph* Sol Polito *md* Leo F. Forbstein

James Cagney, Margaret Lindsay, Ricardo Cortez, Lili Damita, Donald Woods, Barton MacLane, George E. Stone, Addison Richards
'So similar to *Barbary Coast* as almost to be its twin . . . nevertheless, good entertainment.'—*Variety*

● *Video: Warner*

The Frisco Kid
US 1979   108m   Technicolor
Warner (Howard W. Koch Jnr)

In the old west, a rabbi heading for San Francisco makes friends with an outlaw. Unsuccessful episodic comedy, unreasonably alternating farce with sentimentality.

w Michael Elias, Frank Shaw *d* Robert Aldrich *ph* Robert B. Hauser *m* Frank De Vol

Gene Wilder, Harrison Ford, Ramon Bieri, Leo Fuchs, Penny Peyser
'A very forced comedy, made all the worse by the fact that Aldrich seems to time and edit

comedy as though it were a melodrama only played a little slower.'—*Richard Combs, MFB*

Frisco Lil
US 1942 62m bw

A girl law student traps a killer and clears her dad. Formula second feature, quite adequate in its way. Irene Hervey, Kent Taylor, Minor Watson, Jerome Cowan. Written by George Bricker and Michael Jacoby; directed by Erle C. Kenton; for Universal.

Frisco Sal
US 1945 63m bw

A New England girl goes to California to avenge her brother's murder. Minor musical vehicle for a star being groomed as a rival to Deanna Durbin. Susanna Foster, Turhan Bey, Alan Curtis, Andy Devine, Thomas Gomez, Samuel S. Hinds. Written by Curt Siodmak and Gerald Geraghty; directed by George Waggner; for Universal.

Fritz the Cat••
US 1971 78m De Luxe
Fritz Productions / Aurica (Steve Krantz)

An alleycat student in New York seeks new and varied experience.
Cartoon feature which applies the old anthropomorphism to the contemporary scene, and whips up more obscenity and violence than Disney ever dreamed of. A fast-moving orgy of outrage which could never have got by in live form.

wd / animator Ralph Bakshi, *comic strip* R. H. Crumb
'A bitter and snarling satire that refuses to curl up in anyone's lap.'—*Bruce Williamson*

The Frog•
GB 1937 75m bw
Herbert Wilcox

The mysterious leader of a criminal organization is unmasked.
Lively old-fashioned mystery melodrama.

w Ian Hay, Gerald Elliott, *novel* The Fellowship of the Frog by Edgar Wallace *d* Jack Raymond

Gordon Harker, Carol Goodner, Noah Beery, Jack Hawkins, Richard Ainley, Esmé Percy, Felix Aylmer
'Badly directed, badly acted, it is like one of those plays produced in country towns by stranded actors. It has an old-world charm: Scotland Yard is laid up in lavender.'—*Graham Greene*
† Sequel 1938: *The Return of the Frog.*

The Frogmen
US 1951 96m bw
TCF (Samuel G. Engel)

Underwater demolition experts pave the way for the invasion of a Japanese-held island. Standard, efficient war fare.

w John Tucker Battle *d* Lloyd Bacon *ph* Norbert Brodine *m* Cyril Mockridge

Richard Widmark, Dana Andrews, Gary Merrill, Jeffrey Hunter, Warren Stevens, Robert Wagner, Harvey Lembeck

'Competent, unpretentious and free from jingoism.'—*MFB*
AAN: original story (Oscar Millard); Norbert Brodine

'Frogs lay millions and millions of eggs each year! What if they all hatched? Today the pond—tomorrow the world!'

Frogs•
US 1972 91m Movielab
AIP (George Edwards, Peter Thomas)

A remote, inhabited island in the southern States is overtaken by reptiles.
As Hitchcock might have said, the frogs is coming; instead of monsters, ordinary creepy-crawlies in their thousands devour most of the cast. Well enough done for those with strong stomachs.

w Robert Hutchison, Robert Blees *d* George McCowan *ph* Mario Tosi *m* Les Baxter

Ray Milland, Joan Van Ark, Sam Elliott, Adam Roarke, Judy Pace
'One of the most remarkable and impressive onslaughts since *King Kong*.'—*David Pirie*

● Video: Guild

From Beyond the Grave•
GB 1973 98m Technicolor
Warner / Amicus (Milton Subotsky)

The proprietor of an East End antique shop involves his customers in horrific situations. Reasonably lively portmanteau of tall tales from a familiar stable.

w Robin Clarke, Raymond Christodoulou *d* Kevin Connor *ph* Alan Hume *m* David Gamley *pd* Maurice Carter

David Warner, Donald Pleasence, Ian Bannen, Diana Dors, Margaret Leighton, Ian Carmichael, Nyree Dawn Porter, Ian Ogilvy

From Headquarters
US 1933 63m bw
Warner

The police solve a murder by scientific methods.
Efficient, rather boring programmer.

w Robert N. Lee, Peter Milne *d* William Dieterle *ph* William Reese

George Brent, Margaret Lindsay, Eugene Pallette, Hugh Herbert, Hobart Cavanaugh, Robert Barrat, Henry O'Neill, Edward Ellis

From Hell It Came
US 1957 71m bw

An executed native of Kalai returns to life in the form of a vengeful tree stump. Absolute rubbish, just about worth sitting through for the unintentional laughs. Tod Andrews, Tina Carver, Linda Watkins. Written by Richard Bernstein; directed by Dan Milner; for Milner Brothers / Allied Artists.

From Hell to Texas
US 1958 100m Eastmancolor Cinemascope
TCF (Robert Buckner)
GB title: *Manhunt*

After accidentally killing a man, a cowboy is

vengefully pursued by the victim's father. Competent chase western with a stand against violence.

w Robert Buckner, Wendell Mayes *d* Henry Hathaway *ph* Wilfrid Cline *m* Daniele Amfitheatrof

Don Murray, Diane Varsi, Chill Wills, Dennis Hopper, R. G. Armstrong, Margo, Jay C. Flippen

From Here to Eternity•••
US 1953 118m bw
Columbia (Buddy Adler)

Life in a Honolulu barracks at the time of Pearl Harbor.
Cleaned up and streamlined version of a bestseller in which the mainly sexual frustrations of a number of unattractive characters are laid bare. As a production, it is Hollywood in good form, and certainly took the public fancy as well as establishing Sinatra as an acting force.

w Daniel Taradash, *novel* James Jones *d* Fred Zinnemann *ph* Burnett Guffey *m* George Duning

Burt Lancaster, Deborah Kerr, *Frank Sinatra*, Donna Reed, Ernest Borgnine, Montgomery Clift, Philip Ober, Mickey Shaughnessy
'This is not a theme which one would expect Zinnemann to approach in the hopeful, sympathetic mood of his earlier films; but neither could one expect the negative shrug of indifference with which he seems to have surrendered to its hysteria.'—*Karel Reisz, Sight and Sound*
† The story was remade for TV in 1979 as a six-hour mini-series.
†† Frank Sinatra got his key role after Eli Wallach dropped out.

AA: best picture; Daniel Taradash; Fred Zinnemann; Burnett Guffey; Frank Sinatra; Donna Reed
AAN: George Duning; Burt Lancaster; Deborah Kerr; Montgomery Clift

From Noon Till Three
US 1976 99m De Luxe
UA / Frankovich-Self

A bank robber becomes a local legend when he interrupts a raid to dally with an attractive widow. Later, when someone else is shot in mistake for him, he is reduced to penury, unable to prove his identity or live up to his own legend.
Curious, shapeless, lumpy western satire, difficult to synopsize or analyse. Despite effort all round, it's just plain unsatisfactory.

wd Frank D. Gilroy, from his novel *ph* Lucien Ballard *m* Elmer Bernstein

Charles Bronson, Jill Ireland, Douglas Fowley, Stan Haze, Damon Douglas
'It squanders its early sparkle for a pot of message.'—*Michael Billington, Illustrated London News*
'The main thing—hell, the only thing—worth noting about *From Noon Till Three* is that it is profoundly weird, which is not quite the same thing as being good.'—*Frank Rich, New York Post*

From Russia with Love***
GB 1963   118m   Technicolor
UA / Eon (Harry Saltzman, Albert Broccoli)

A Russian spy joins an international crime organization and develops a plan to kill James Bond and steal a coding machine.
The second Bond adventure and possibly the best, with Istanbul and Venice for backdrops and climaxes involving a speeding train and a helicopter. Arrant nonsense with tongue in cheek, on a big budget.

w Richard Maibaum, Johanna Harwood, novel Ian Fleming d Terence Young ph Ted Moore m John Barry titles Robert Brownjohn

Sean Connery, Robert Shaw, Pedro Armendariz, Daniela Bianchi, Lotte Lenya, Bernard Lee, Eunice Gayson, Lois Maxwell

● Video: Warner

From Soup to Nuts*
US 1928   20m   bw   silent

Two temporary waiters wreck a dinner party.
Very funny slapstick which the stars subsequently reworked into A Chump at Oxford. Laurel and Hardy, Anita Garvin, Tiny Sandford. Written by H. M. Walker; directed by Edgar Kennedy; for Hal Roach.

From the Earth to the Moon
US 1958   100m   Technicolor
Waverley (Benedict Bogeaus)

In the 1880s an armaments millionaire finances a trip to the moon in a projectile fired by his own invention.
Cardboard science fiction, with an imposing cast at sea in an unspeakable script and an unseaworthy production.

w Robert Blees, James Leicester, novel Jules Verne d Byron Haskin ph Edwin DuPar m Louis Forbes ad Hal Wilson Cox

Joseph Cotten, George Sanders, Henry Daniell, Carl Esmond, Melville Cooper, Don Dubbins, Debra Paget, Patric Knowles

● Video: Kingston

From the Life of the Marionettes*
West Germany 1980   104m   colour / bw
ITC / Martin Starger

An inquiry into the killing of a prostitute by a rich businessman.
A film somehow very typical of its director, but far from his most interesting work.

wd Ingmar Bergman ph Sven Nykvist m Rols Wilhelm pd Rolf Zechetbauer

Robert Atzorn, Christine Buchegger, Martin Benrath

● Video: Precision

From the Terrace
US 1960   144m   De Luxe   Cinemascope
TCF / Linebrook (Mark Robson)

Life among Pennsylvania's idle rich.
Heavy-going family melodrama from a bestseller peopled with boorish characters.

w Ernest Lehman, novel John O'Hara d Mark Robson ph Leo Tover m Elmer Bernstein

Paul Newman, Joanne Woodward, Myrna Loy, Ina Balin, Leon Ames, Felix Aylmer, George Grizzard, Patrick O'Neal, Elizabeth Allen

From This Day Forward***
US 1946   95m   bw
RKO (William L. Pereira)

After World War II, a New York couple think back to their early years in the poverty-stricken thirties.
Effective sentimental realism coupled with Hollywood professionalism made this film more memorable than it may sound.

w Hugo Butler, Garson Kanin, novel All Brides Are Beautiful by Thomas Bell d John Berry ph George Barnes m Leigh Harline

Joan Fontaine, Mark Stevens, Rosemary de Camp, Henry Morgan, Wally Brown, Arline Judge, Bobby Driscoll, Mary Treen

'Distinguished from the usual film about Young Love and Young Marriage by irony, poetry and realism.'—Richard Winnington

The Front*
US 1976   95m   Metrocolor
Columbia / Persky-Bright, Devon (Martin Ritt, Charles H. Joffe)

For a small commission, a bookmaker puts his name to scripts by blacklisted writers.
Rather bland satire on the communist witch hunts of the fifties; interesting, but neither funny nor incisive enough.

w Walter Bernstein d Martin Ritt ph Michael Chapman m Dave Grusin

Woody Allen, Zero Mostel, Herschel Bernardi, Michael Murphy, Andrea Marcovicci, Lloyd Gough

'The pacing is off, the sequences don't flow, and the film seems sterile, unpopulated and flat.'—New Yorker

'A light comedy forged out of dark and authentic pain.'—Frank Rich, New York Post

'It catches the anguish of America's creative community with wit and feeling.'—Sunday Express

AAN: Walter Bernstein

The Front Page***
US 1931   101m   bw
Howard Hughes

A Chicago reporter wants to retire and marry, but is tricked by his scheming editor into covering one last case.
Brilliant early talkie perfectly transferring into screen terms a stage classic of the twenties.
Superficially a shade primitive now, its essential power remains.

w Bartlett Cormack, Charles Lederer, play Charles MacArthur, Ben Hecht d Lewis Milestone ph Glen MacWilliams

Adolphe Menjou (Walter Burns), Pat O'Brien (Hildy Johnson), Mary Brian (Peggy), Edward Everett Horton (Bensinger), Walter Catlett (Murphy), George E. Stone (Earl Williams), Mae Clarke (Molly), Slim Summerville (Pincus), Matt Moore (Kruger), Frank McHugh (McCue)

'Sure money-getter . . . it will universally entertain and please.'—Variety

'The most riproaring movie that ever came out of Hollywood.'—Pare Lorentz

'It excelled most of the films of its day by sheer treatment. The speedy delivery of lines and business and the re-emphasis upon cutting as a prime structural element made the film a model of mobility for confused directors who did not know yet how to handle sound.'—Lewis Jacobs, The Rise of the American Film
† Remade 1940 as His Girl Friday (qv).

AAN: best picture; Lewis Milestone; Adolphe Menjou

The Front Page**
US 1974   105m   Technicolor
    Panavision
U-I (Paul Monash)

Disappointing Billy Wilder remake, relying overmuch on bad language and farcical intrusions, while tending to jettison the plot in the latter half. Some laughs nevertheless.

w Billy Wilder, I. A. L. Diamond d Billy Wilder ph Jordan S. Cronenweth m Billy May

Walter Matthau, Jack Lemmon, Susan Sarandon, David Wayne, Carol Burnett, Vincent Gardenia, Allen Garfield, Herb Edelmann, Charles Durning, Austin Pendleton

'The signs of coarsening in Wilder's comedy technique are unmistakable.'—MFB

'I can't think of a better tonic for the winter glooms.'—Michael Billington, Illustrated London News

Front Page Story*
GB 1953   99m   bw
British Lion / Jay Lewis

A day in the life of a Fleet Street newspaper, when the editor is torn between several big stories and nearly loses his wife.
Dogged 'slice of life' drama with few excitements but some incidental entertainment and a production of routine competence.

w Jay Lewis, Jack Howells d Gordon Parry ph Gilbert Taylor m Jackie Brown

Jack Hawkins, Elizabeth Allan, Derek Farr, Michael Goodliffe, Martin Miller

Front Page Woman**
US 1935   82m   bw
Warner (Samuel Bischoff)

Rival reporters try to outshine each other.
Lively comedy-melodrama very typical of its style and time.

w Laird Doyle, Lillie Hayward, Roy Chanslor d Michael Curtiz ph Tony Gaudio m Heinz Roemheld md Leo Forbstein

Bette Davis, George Brent, Roscoe Karns, Wini Shaw, J. Carroll Naish, Walter Walker

'Completely screwy but will get fair b.o.'—Variety

Frontier Gal
US 1945   84m   Technicolor
Universal (Michael Fessier, Ernest Pagano)
GB title: The Bride Wasn't Willing

An outlaw weds a saloon girl at pistol point; emerging five years later from prison, he finds he has a daughter.

Rambling western with some pretensions to humour and sentiment; not a success, but it established de Carlo as a star.

w Michael Fessier, Ernest Pagano d Charles Lamont ph George Robinson, Charles Boyle m Frank Skinner

Yvonne de Carlo, Rod Cameron, Sheldon Leonard, Andy Devine, Fuzzy Knight, Andrew Tombes, Clara Blandick

Frontier Marshal°
US 1933 66m bw

A marshal cleans up Tombstone. Interesting trial run for the 1939 film, which was subsequently done over as *My Darling Clementine*. George O'Brien, Irene Bentley, George E. Stone, Ruth Gillette. Written by William Conselman and Stuart Anthony, from the book by Stuart N. Lake; directed by Lew Seiler; for Fox. (NB: For legal reasons in this version the marshal is called Michael Wyatt instead of Wyatt Earp.)

Frontier Marshal°
US 1939 70m bw
TCF (Sol M. Wurtzel)

Wyatt Earp cleans up Tombstone. Simple-minded, pleasing western, later worked over by Ford as *My Darling Clementine*.

w Sam Hellman book Stuart N. Lake d Allan Dwan ph Charles Clarke m Samuel Kaylin

Randolph Scott, Nancy Kelly, Cesar Romero (as Doc Holliday), Binnie Barnes, John Carradine, Joe Sawyer, Lon Chaney Jnr, Ward Bond, Edward Norris, Eddie Foy Jnr

'Strong programme western, in-betweener for key duals, but a top biller in subsequents.'—*Variety*

† Eddie Foy Jnr appeared as his father, who historically did perform in Tombstone at the time. The equivalent in *My Darling Clementine* was the Shakespearean actor played by Alan Mowbray.

The Frozen Dead
GB 1966 95m Eastmancolor

In an English laboratory, a scientist is trying to revive the frozen corpses of Nazi leaders. Flatfooted horror piece providing very little of interest to pass the time. Dana Andrews, Anna Palk, Philip Gilbert, Karel Stepanek, Kathleen Breck. Written, directed and produced by Herbert J. Leder; for Goldstar / Seven Arts.

The Frozen Ghost
US 1945 61m bw

When a drunk dies while under his influence, a hypnotist fears he has the will and power to kill. Absurdly titled and insufficiently vigorous entry in the *Inner Sanctum* series. Lon Chaney Jnr, Evelyn Ankers, Martin Kosleck, Milburn Stone, Tala Birell, Douglass Dumbrille. Written by Bernard Schubert and Luci Ward; directed by Harold Young; for Universal.

HYPNOTIC EYES...CRAWLING WITH MADNESS!

Nameless Terror!...creeping from the walls of a Museum for Murder!

Screen's NEWEST INNER SANCTUM MYSTERY!

LON CHANEY

THE FROZEN GHOST

with
EVELYN ANKERS
ELENA VERDUGO
TALA BIRELL
MARTIN KOSLECK
DOUGLASS DUMBRILLE
MILBURN STONE

Screen Play by Bernard Schubert and Luci Ward   Original Story by Harrison Carter and Henry Sucher   Adaptation by Henry Sucher
Directed by HAROLD YOUNG   A UNIVERSAL PICTURE   Associate Producer WILL COWAN

THE FROZEN GHOST.   One of the Inner Sanctum mysteries which filled half a bill in the forties and usually disappointed.

The Frozen Limits°
GB 1939 84m bw
Gainsborough (Edward Black)

Six impecunious comedians hear of the Yukon gold rush, and join it . . . forty years too late. The Crazy Gang not quite at its best, but working hard, with a few hilarious moments and a special assist from Moore Marriott.

w Marriott Edgar, Val Guest, J. O. C. Orton d Marcel Varnel ph Arthur Crabtree

Flanagan and Allen, Nervo and Knox, Naughton and Gold, *Moore Marriott*, Eileen Bell, Anthony Hulme, Bernard Lee, Eric Clavering

'The funniest English picture yet produced . . . it can bear comparison with *Safety Last* and *The General*.'—*Graham Greene*

Fu Manchu

The Yellow Peril, or evil Oriental master criminal, was created by Sax Rohmer in a 1911 novel, which led to 13 more plus some short stories. A long series of British two-reelers was made in the twenties, and talking films are as follows:

1929: THE MYSTERIOUS DR FU MANCHU, with Warner Oland (Paramount)
1930: THE RETURN OF DR FU MANCHU (ditto)
1931: DAUGHTER OF THE DRAGON (ditto)
1932: THE MASK OF FU MANCHU (qv) with Boris Karloff (MGM)
1939: DRUMS OF FU MANCHU, with Henry Brandon (Republic serial).

The remainder are British productions by Harry Alan Towers, with Christopher Lee:
1965: THE FACE OF FU MANCHU (qv)
1966: BRIDES OF FU MANCHU
1968: THE VENGEANCE OF FU MANCHU
1969: THE BLOOD OF FU MANCHU
1970: THE CASTLE OF FU MANCHU

Fuddy Duddy Buddy**
US 1952   7m   Technicolor

Mr Magoo mistakes a walrus for his friend the colonel. Top drawer Magoo adventure climaxing with the celebrated line: 'I don't care if he *is* a walrus. I like him. I like him!' Written and directed by *John Hubley*; music by *William Lava*; for UPA.

The Fugitive*
US 1947   104m   bw
Argosy (Merian C. Cooper, John Ford)

In an anti-clerical country, a priest is on the run.
Ford's attempt to do a Mexican *Informer* is slow and rather boring, but the pictures are nice to look at even though the original novel has been totally emasculated.

w Dudley Nichols, *novel* The Power and the Glory by Graham Greene *d* John Ford *ph* Gabriel Figueroa *m* Richard Hageman

Henry Fonda, Dolores del Rio, Pedro Armendariz, J. Carrol Naish, Leo Carrillo, Ward Bond, Robert Armstrong, John Qualen
'A symphony of light and shade, of deafening din and silence, of sweeping movement and repose.'—*Bosley Crowther*
'The most pretentious travesty of a literary work since *For Whom the Bell Tolls*.'—*Richard Winnington*

● *Video: Kingston*

The Fugitive Kind
US 1960   121m   bw
UA / Martin Jurow / Richard A. Shepherd / Pennebaker

A Mississippi drifter in a small strange town runs into trouble with women.
Doom-laden melodrama, almost a parody of the author's works, full of cancer patients, nympho-dipsos, and cemetery seductions; we are however spared the final castration.

w Tennessee Williams, Meade Roberts, *play* Orpheus Descending by Tennessee Williams *d* Sidney Lumet *ph* Boris Kaufman *m* Kenyon Hopkins *pd* Richard Sylbert

Marlon Brando, Anna Magnani, Joanne Woodward, Victor Jory, Maureen Stapleton, R. G. Armstrong
'A series of mythological engravings, determined by a literary text and a lurid concept of hell on earth.'—*Peter John Dyer*
'Sidney Lumet is usually clever at least part of the time—an acquisitive magpie who has picked up, along with the selly trash, a few small gems. This time he brings us nothing but bits of coloured glass.'—*Stanley Kauffmann*

Fugitive Lovers
US 1933   74m   bw

A convict escapes on a transcontinental bus.
Unsatisfactory comedy drama with a miscast star; chiefly interesting for showing the form of travel, but *It Happened One Night* did it better in the following year. Robert Montgomery, Madge Evans, Ted Healy and the 3 Stooges, Nat Pendleton, C. Henry Gordon. Written by Ferdinand Reyher, Frank Wead; directed by Richard Boleslawski; for MGM. 'Acceptable for lesser houses but not de luxe quality.'—*Variety*

Fugitive Road
US 1934   69m   bw

A would-be immigrant into Austria has trouble with the patrol captain of a border garrison. Curious, aimless, cheaply made drama which doesn't even provide a coherent role for its fallen star. Erich Von Stroheim, Vera Evgeles, Leslie Fenton, George Humbert. Written by Charles S. Belden, Robert Ellis; directed by Frank Strayer; for Chesterfield. 'Picture won't rate solo in many places.'—*Variety*

Full Circle
GB / Canada 1976   97m   Eastmancolor
Paramount / Fetter-Classic (Peter Fetterman, Alfred Parisier)

After the death of her small daughter, a woman leaves home to live in an old house which is haunted by the malevolent spirit of another dead child.
Unpleasant and incompetent supernatural nonsense, seeking a niche somewhere between *Don't Look Now* and *The Exorcist*.

w Dave Humphries, *novel* Julia by Peter Straub *d* Richard Loncraine *ph* Peter Hannan *m* Colin Towns

Mia Farrow, Keir Dullea, Tom Conti, Jill Bennett, Robin Gammell, Cathleen Nesbitt, Mary Morris, Edward Hardwicke

Full Confession
US 1939   73m   bw

A priest bound by the sanctity of confession urges a murderer to give himself up. Neat little melodrama with a plot much copied subsequently. Victor McLaglen, Barry Fitzgerald, Sally Eilers. Written and directed by John Farrow; for RKO. 'Rather interesting, but not strong enough for the upper bracket.'—*Variety*

Full of Life*
US 1956   91m   bw
Columbia (Fred Kohlmar)

A poor New York / Italian couple expect a baby.
Domestic comedy drama with good scenes but fatally uncertain mood.

w John Fante, from his novel *d* Richard Quine *ph* Charles Lawton Jnr *m* George Duning

Judy Holliday, Richard Conte, Esther Minciotti, Salvatore Baccaloni

The Full Treatment
GB 1960   109m   bw   Megascope
Columbia / Hilary / Falcon (Val Guest)
US title: *Stop Me Before I Kill*

A racing driver crashes and subsequently tries to murder his wife; psychiatric help leads to further gruesome goings-on.
Variation on *Les Diaboliques*, with very little mystery and too much talk from boring characters.

w Val Guest, Ronald Scott Thorn, *novel* Ronald Scott Thorn *d* Val Guest *ph* Gilbert Taylor *m* Stanley Black

Ronald Lewis, Diane Cilento, Claude Dauphin, Françoise Rosay, Bernard Braden

The Fuller Brush Girl*
US 1950   85m   bw
Columbia (S. Sylvan Simon)
GB title: *Affairs of Sally*

A cosmetics saleslady gets involved in murder. Fairly amusing slapstick mystery with the star in good form.

w Frank Tashlin *d* Lloyd Bacon *ph* Charles Lawton *m* Heinz Roemheld

Lucille Ball, Eddie Albert, Carl Benton Reid, Gale Robbins, Jeff Connell, John Litel, Jerome Cowan, Lee Patrick

The Fuller Brush Man*
US 1948   93m   bw
Columbia (S. Sylvan Simon)
GB title: *That Mad Mr Jones*

A door-to-door salesman gets involved in homicide.
Bright star comedy with slow patches.

w Frank Tashlin, Devery Freeman *d* S. Sylvan Simon *ph* Leslie White *m* Heinz Roemheld

Red Skelton, Janet Blair, Don McGuire, Adele Jergens

Fun and Fancy Free*
US 1947   73m   Technicolor
Walt Disney (Ben Sharpsteen)

Cartoon stories told by and to Jiminy Cricket and Edgar Bergen.
Variable Disney ragbag including *Bongo* the Bear, and a lengthy version of *Jack and the Beanstalk*.

w various *d* various
● *Video: Rank*

Fun in Acapulco
US 1963   97m   Technicolor
Paramount / Hal B. Wallis

A trapeze artist becomes a lifeguard and is pursued by a lady bullfighter.
Dim comedy musical.

w Allan Weiss *d* Richard Thorpe *ph* Daniel Fapp *m* Joseph J. Lilley

Elvis Presley, Ursula Andress, Paul Lukas

Fun with Dick and Jane
US 1976   100m   Metrocolor
Columbia / Peter Bart, Max Pelevsky

When an aerospace executive is fired, in order to keep up with the Joneses he and his wife embark on a life of crime.

This being a 1970s satire, they actually get away with it, providing some, but not enough, fun on the way.

w David Giler, Jerry Belson, Mordecai Richler, *story* Gerald Gaiser d Ted Kotcheff ph Fred J. Koenekamp m Ernest Gold

George Segal, Jane Fonda, Ed McMahon, Dick Gautier, Alan Miller

'A nitwit mixture of counterculture politics, madcap comedy and toilet humour.'—*New Yorker*

† The sequence in which the heroine discusses the family predicament while sitting on a toilet was later deleted, reducing the running time by two minutes.

Funeral in Berlin*
GB 1967 102m Technicolor
Paramount / Harry Saltzman (Charles Kasher)

Harry Palmer is sent to Berlin to check a story that a Russian colonel wants to defect.
Initially intriguing, finally confusing, always depressing spy yarn in the sixties manner, i.e. with every character devious and no one a hero. Good production.

w Evan Jones, *novel* The Berlin Memorandum by Len Deighton d Guy Hamilton ph Otto Heller m Konrad Elfers pd Ken Adam

Michael Caine, *Oscar Homolka*, Eva Renzi, Paul Hubschmid, *Hugh Burden*, Guy Doleman, Rachel Gurney

'So many twists that even Sherlock Holmes might have been baffled . . . before long it becomes difficult to remember who is watching whom and why, or indeed whether anybody *was* watching anybody at any given moment.'—*Tom Milne*

† Second in the Harry Palmer series, of which the first was *The Ipcress File* and the third *Billion Dollar Brain* (both qv).

The Funniest Man in the World*
US 1967 102m bw

Moderately intelligent compilation of sequences from the films of Charlie Chaplin, including *Making a Living*, *Kid Auto Races at Venice*, *Tillie's Punctured Romance*, *The Tramp*, *A Night Out*, *The Rink*, *The Immigrant* and *Easy Street*. The later shorts and features, on which Chaplin himself claimed full copyright, are not included.
Written and directed by Vernon P. Becker; for Funnyman Inc.

Funny Face**
US 1956 103m Technicolor
Vistavision
Paramount (Roger Edens)

A fashion editor and photographer choose a shy bookstore attendant as their 'quality woman'.
Stylish, wistful musical with good numbers but drawn-out dialogue; finally a shade too sophisticated and a whole lot too fey.

w Leonard Gershe d Stanley Donen ph Ray June m / ly George and Ira Gershwin

Fred Astaire, Audrey Hepburn, Kay Thompson, Michel Auclair, Robert Flemyng

AAN: Leonard Gershe; Ray June

Funny Girl**
US 1968 169m Technicolor
Panavision 70
Columbia / Rastar (Ray Stark)

Fanny Brice, an ugly Jewish girl from New York's east side, becomes a big Broadway star but loses her husband in the process.
Interminable cliché-ridden musical drama relieved by a few good numbers, high production gloss and the unveiling of a new powerhouse star.

w Isobel Lennart, from her play d William Wyler ph Harry Stradling md Walter Scharf m Jule Styne ly Bob Merrill pd Gene Callahan

Barbra Streisand, Omar Sharif, Walter Pidgeon, Kay Medford, Anne Francis, Lee Allen, Gerald Mohr, Frank Faylen

AA: Barbra Streisand
AAN: best picture; Harry Stradling; Walter Scharf; Kay Medford; title song

Funny Lady*
US 1975 138m Eastmancolor
Columbia / Rastar / Persky–Bright / Vista (Ray Stark)

Fanny Brice marries Billy Rose.
Unnecessary sequel to the above, entirely predictable and far from the truth, but with the occasional pleasures that a high budget brings.

w Jay Presson Allen, Arnold Schulman d Herbert Ross ph James Wong Howe m / ly various md Peter Matz pd George Jenkins

Barbra Streisand, James Caan, *Ben Vereen*, Omar Sharif, Roddy McDowall, Larry Gates

'The plot line is as slackly handled as the milieu.'—*Geoff Brown*

'As Fanny Brice, Streisand is no longer human; she's like a bitchy female impersonator imitating Barbra Streisand.'—*New Yorker*

AAN: James Wong Howe; Peter Matz; song 'How Lucky Can You Get' (m / ly Fred Ebb, John Kander)

A Funny Thing Happened on the Way to the Forum**
GB 1966 99m De Luxe
UA / Quadrangle (Melvin Frank)

In ancient Rome, a conniving slave schemes to win his freedom.
Bawdy farce from a Broadway musical inspired by Plautus but with a New York Jewish atmosphere. The film pays scant attention to the comic numbers that made the show a hit, but adds some style of its own, including a free-for-all slapstick climax.

w Melvin Frank, Michael Pertwee, *musical comedy* Burt Shevelove, Larry Gelbart m / ly Stephen Sondheim md Ken Thorne d Richard Lester ph Nicolas Roeg pd Tony Walton titles Richard Williams

Zero Mostel, Phil Silvers, Michael Crawford, Jack Gilford, *Michael Hordern*, Buster Keaton, Patricia Jessel, Leon Greene, Beatrix Lehmann

'Actors have to be very fast and very sly to make themselves felt amid the flash and glitter of a characteristic piece of Lester film-mosaic.'—*John Russell Taylor*

'He proceeds by fits and starts and leaves jokes suspended in mid-air . . . like coitus interruptus going on forever.'—*Pauline Kael*

AA: Ken Thorne

Funnyman
US 1967 100m bw and colour
Korty Films (Hugh McGraw, Stephen Schmidt)

A satirical comedian seeks some better occupation in life, but finally agrees he's best as a comic.
One suspects Korty has seen *Sullivan's Travels* several times; but even though his film tries hard, it finally provides more yawns than appreciative chuckles.

w John Korty, Peter Bonerz d John Korty ph John Korty m Peter Schickele

Peter Bonerz, Sandra Archer, Carol Androsky, Gerald Hiken

'It has its dull patches, but it made me laugh louder and more often than any other film this year.'—*Michael Billington, Illustrated London News*

The Furies*
US 1950 109m bw
Paramount / Hal B. Wallis

A cattle baron feuds with his tempestuous daughter.
Interesting but heavy-going western, more solemn than stimulating despite its Freudian excesses.

w Charles Schnee, *novel* Niven Busch d Anthony Mann ph Victor Milner m Franz Waxman

Barbara Stanwyck, *Walter Huston*, Wendell Corey, Judith Anderson, Gilbert Roland, Thomas Gomez, Beulah Bondi, Wallace Ford, Albert Dekker, Blanche Yurka

'An immoral saga, capably mounted, with some pretentious psychological trimmings.'—*MFB*

AAN: Victor Milner

The Further Perils of Laurel and Hardy***
US 1967 99m bw
TCF / Robert Youngson

A compilation of longish extracts from the stars' silent comedies, including *Early to Bed*, *The Second Hundred Years*, *Should Married Men Go Home*, *You're Darn Tootin'*, *Habeas Corpus*, *That's My Wife*, and *Leave 'Em Laughing*. The producer is to be congratulated on refurbishing so many deteriorating negatives, though the commentary leaves much to be desired.

w, ed Robert Youngson m John Parker

Fury•••
US 1936   94m   bw
MGM (Joseph L. Mankiewicz)

A traveller in a small town is mistaken for a murderer and apparently lynched; he escapes in a fire but determines to have his persecutors hanged for his murder.

Powerful drama which becomes artificial in its latter stages but remains its director's best American film.

w Bartlett Cormack, Fritz Lang, *story* Norman Krasna *d* Fritz Lang *ph* Joseph Ruttenberg *m* Franz Waxman

Spencer Tracy, Sylvia Sidney, Bruce Cabot, Walter Abel, Edward Ellis, Walter Brennan, Frank Albertson

'The surface of American life has been rubbed away: *Fury* gets down to the bones of the thing and shows them for what they are.'—*C. A. Lejeune*

'Since the screen began to talk, no other serious film except *The Front Page* has so clearly shown that here is a new art and what this new art can do.'—*John Marks*

'Everyday events and people suddenly took on tremendous and horrifying proportion; even the most insignificant details had a pointed meaning.'—*Lewis Jacobs*

'For half its length a powerful and documented piece of fiction about a lynching, and for the remaining half a desperate attempt to make love, lynching and the Hays Office come out even.'—*Otis Ferguson*

'Astonishing, the only film I know to which I have wanted to attach the epithet of *great*.'—*Graham Greene*

AAN: Norman Krasna

The Fury•
US 1978   117m   De Luxe
TCF / Frank Yablans (Ron Preissman)

The head of a government institute for psychic research finds that his own son is wanted by terrorists who wish to use his lethal psychic powers.

Flashy, kaleidoscopic nonsense which never even begins to make sense but is used as the basis for the director's showing-off, which is occasionally worth a glance for those with hardened stomachs.

w John Farris, from his novel *d* Brian de Palma *ph* Richard H. Kline *m* John Williams

Kirk Douglas, John Cassavetes, Carrie Snodgress, Charles Durning, Andrew Stevens, Amy Irving, Fiona Lewis

'A conception of cinema that is closer to Ken Russell than Alfred Hitchcock.'—*Richard Combs, MFB*

● *Video: CBS / Fox*

Fury at Furnace Creek•
US 1948   88m   bw
TCF

A westerner clears the name of his father, a general accused of diverting a wagon train into hostile Indian territory.

Adequate old-fashioned western with a good story line and standard excitements.

w Charles G. Booth *d* H. Bruce Humberstone *ph* Harry Jackson *m* David Raksin *md* Alfred Newman

Victor Mature, Coleen Gray, Glenn Langan, Reginald Gardiner

Fury at Smugglers' Bay
GB 1960   96m   Eastmancolor
Panascope
(Regal) Mijo (Michael Green, Joe Vegoda)

The squire of a Cornish village is being blackmailed by the vicious leader of a gang of wreckers.

Watchable, then forgettable variation on *Jamaica Inn*.

wd John Gilling *ph* Harry Waxman *m* Harold Geller

Peter Cushing, John Fraser, Bernard Lee, William Franklyn, June Thorburn, Miles Malleson, Michele Mercier, George Coulouris

Futtock's End•
GB 1969   49m   Eastmancolor

Adventures of a weekend in an English country mansion. A collection of visual gags, rather thinly spread, with dialogue replaced by squeaks and mumblings. Like all Barker's

subsequent comedies on similar lines (*The Picnic, By the Sea*, etc) one chuckles in constant anticipation of guffaws which never come. Ronnie Barker, Michael Hordern, Roger Livesey, Julian Orchard, Kika Markham, Mary Merrall, Richard O'Sullivan. Written by Ronnie Barker; directed by Bob Kellett; for Paradine / Gannet / British Lion.

Futureworld•
US 1976   107m   Metrocolor
AIP (James T. Aubrey Jnr, Paul Lazarus III)

The robot factory seen in *Westworld* (qv) now aims at world domination by duplicating influential figures.

Amusing and fairly suspenseful fantasy with a bigger budget than its predecessor.

w Mayo Simon, George Schenck *d* Richard T. Heffron *ph* Howard Schwarz, Gene Polito *m* Fred Karlin

Peter Fonda, Blythe Danner, Arthur Hill, Yul Brynner, John Ryan, Stuart Margolin, Jim Antonio

Fuzz•.
US 1972   93m   De Luxe
UA / Filmways / Javelin (Jack Farren)

Detectives of Boston's 87th precinct try to catch a rapist.

A black farce devoted to police incompetence, though taken from a straight 'Ed McBain' story. Brisk and sometimes funny.

w Evan Hunter ('Ed McBain') *d* Richard A. Colla *ph* Jacques Marquette *m* Dave Grusin

Burt Reynolds, Raquel Welch, Jack Weston, Yul Brynner, Tom Skerritt, James McEachin

The Fuzzy Pink Nightgown
US 1957   88m   bw
UA / Russ–Field (Robert Waterfield)

A glamorous film star falls in love with her kidnapper.

Unendurable cheap romantic farce.

w Richard Alan Simmons, *novel* Sylvia Tate *d* Norman Taurog *ph* Joseph La Shelle *m* Billy May

Jane Russell, Ralph Meeker, Keenan Wynn, Fred Clark

GI Blues
US 1960 104m Technicolor
Paramount / Hal B. Wallis (Paul Nathan)

A guitar-playing gunner with the American army in West Germany falls for a cabaret dancer.

Routine star vehicle marking Presley's return from military service.

w Edmund Beloin, Henry Garson d Norman Taurog ph Loyal Griggs m Joseph J. Lilley

Elvis Presley, Juliet Prowse, Robert Ivers, Leticia Roman, Arch Johnson

G Men***
US 1935 85m bw
Warner (Lou Edelman)

A young lawyer becomes a G-man to avenge the murder of his best friend, and finds himself tracking down another old friend who is a gangster.

In the face of mounting criticism of their melodramas making heroes of gangsters, Warners pulled a clever switch by showing the same crimes from a different angle, that of the law enforcer. As an action show it became pretty good after a slow start.

w Seton I. Miller d William Keighley ph Sol Polito md Leo F. Forbstein

James Cagney, Ann Dvorak, Margaret Lindsay, Robert Armstrong, Barton MacLane, Lloyd Nolan, William Harrigan

'Cagney joins the government and cleans up the gangsters. Just loads of action, knocked off in bing-bang manner. Strong b.o.'—Variety

'The gangster is back, racing madly through one of the fastest melodramas ever made.'—New York Sun

'The headiest dose of gunplay that Hollywood has unleashed in recent months.'—André Sennwald, New York Times

'It is not violence alone which is in the air; there is also a skilfully contrived and well-maintained suspense, and throughout a feeling of respect for the men who are paid to die in the execution of necessary work.'—The Times

'A swell show: the construction is swift and staccato.'—New York World Telegraph

'They had more than love . . . they had fame!'
Gable and Lombard
US 1976 131m Technicolor
Universal (Harry Korshak)

After Carole Lombard's death in a 1942 air crash, Clark Gable recalls their years together. Vulgar and inaccurate representation of two Hollywood stars of the thirties; it fails even as titillation.

w Barry Sandler d Sidney J. Furie ph Jordan S. Cronenweth m Michel Legrand pd Edward Carfagno

James Brolin, Jill Clayburgh, Allen Garfield (as Louis B. Mayer), Red Buttons, Joanne Linville

'A limply raunchy, meaningless movie with nothing to say about the movies, about love, or about stardom.'—New Yorker

'An uneven combination of smut and sentimentality.'—Les Keyser, Hollywood in the Seventies

'The picture that will make 1933 famous!'
Gabriel over the White House*
US 1933 87m bw
MGM / Walter Wanger

A crook becomes president and mysteriously reforms.

Pleasing, dated New Deal fantasy.

w Carey Wilson, Bertram Bloch, novel Rinehard by T. F. Tweed d Gregory La Cava ph Bert Glennon m William Axt

Walter Huston, Karen Morley, Franchot Tone, C. Henry Gordon, Samuel S. Hinds, Jean Parker, Dickie Moore

'Flag-waving flapdoodle, shrewdly dished up for the man in the street and his best girl. Beautifully produced, cannily hoked, and looks like money all round.'—Variety

Gabriela
Brazil 1983 99m colour

In a coastal town in 1925, the sensual Gabriela marries a bar owner but becomes involved again with her old gangster cronies. Ethnic melodrama of familiar type, a spin-off from an immensely popular Brazilian TV series. Sonia Braga, Marcello Mastroianni, Antonio Cantafora. Written by Leopoldo Sarran, Bruno Barreto, from the novel by Jorge Amada; directed by Bruno Barreto; for Sultana.

Gaby
US 1956 97m Eastmancolor
Cinemascope
MGM (Edwin H. Knopf)

Flabby remake of Waterloo Bridge (qv); saccharine, fussy and outmoded, despite updated settings and a happy ending.

w Albert Hackett, Frances Goodrich, Charles Lederer d Curtis Bernhardt ph Robert Planck m Conrad Salinger

Leslie Caron, John Kerr, Cedric Hardwicke, Taina Elg, Margalo Gillmore

Gaiety George
GB 1946 98m bw
Embassy (George King)
US title: Showtime

The career in the London theatre of Irish impresario George Howard in the early part of the century.

Tepid musical biopic.

w Katherine Strueby d George King ph Otto Heller

Richard Greene, Ann Todd, Peter Graves, Hazel Court, Leni Lynn, Ursula Jeans, Morland Graham, Frank Pettingell

Gaily, Gaily**
US 1969 117m De Luxe
UA / Mirisch / Cartier
GB title: Chicago, Chicago

The early life on a Chicago newspaper of Ben Hecht.

Busy, farcical, melodramatic, always interesting biopic of the formative years of a celebrated literary figure.

w Abram S. Ginnes, book Ben Hecht d Norman Jewison ph Richard Kline m Henry Mancini pd Robert Boyle

Beau Bridges, Melina Mercouri, Brian Keith, George Kennedy, Hume Cronyn, Margot Kidder, Wilfrid Hyde White, Melodie Johnson, John Randolph

The Gal Who Took the West `
US 1949 84m Technicolor

In 1890, an opera singer travels west and is the object of romantic rivalry. Lame attempt to equal the splendid idiocy of Salome Where She Danced. Yvonne de Carlo, Charles Coburn, Scott Brady, John Russell, James Millican. Written by William Bowers and Oscar Brodney; directed by Frederick de Cordova; for Universal-International.

Galileo*
GB 1975 145m Eastmancolor
Ely Landau / Cinevision

In the 17th century, a poor Italian mathematics teacher has trouble establishing his 'heretical' astronomical theories.

Overlong play-on-celluloid for the American Film Theatre: very decently made and acted, it lacks inspiration.

w Barbara Bray, Joseph Losey, *play* Bertolt Brecht d Joseph Losey ph Michael Reed m Hanns Eisler

Topol, Edward Fox, Michel Lonsdale, Richard O'Callaghan, Tom Conti, Judy Parfitt, Patrick Magee, Michael Gough, John Gielgud, Colin Blakely, Margaret Leighton, Clive Revill

Gallant Bess

US 1946 99m Cinecolor

A soldier's horse saves his life and becomes his peacetime friend. Boy-and-horse story with a wartime setting; good for small towns.
Marshall Thompson, George Tobias, Clem Bevans, Donald Curtis. Written by Jeanne Bartlett; directed by Andrew Marton; for MGM.

The Gallant Blade

US 1948 81m Cinecolor

In France in 1648, a dashing young lieutenant rescues his general from the plot of a would-be revolutionary. Pinchpenny swashbuckler which maintains a commendable verve. Larry Parks, Marguerite Chapman, Victor Jory, George Macready. Written by Walter Ferris and Morton Grant; directed by Henry Levin; for Columbia.

The Gallant Hours*

US 1959 115m bw
UA / James Cagney / Robert Montgomery

Episodes in the career of Admiral William F. Halsey.
Adulatory but physically restrained biopic which covers World War II with barely a scene outside control room sets: interesting but finally too talky.

w Beirne Lay Jnr, Frank D. Gilroy d Robert Montgomery ph Joe MacDonald m Roger Wagner

James Cagney, Dennis Weaver, Richard Jaeckel, Ward Costello, Carl Benton Reid
'Imaginatively conceived but erroneously realized.'—*Robert Vas*

Gallant Journey

US 1946 86m bw
Columbia

The life of an early American aviation pioneer.
Curious biopic, very tentatively done, about an inventor so obscure as to be virtually fictitious. Sentimental, artificial, but harmless.

w Byron Morgan, William A. Wellman d William A. Wellman ph Burnett Guffey m Marlin Skiles

Glenn Ford, Janet Blair, Charles Ruggles, Henry Travers, Arthur Shields

Gallant Lady

US 1933 84m bw
(UA) Twentieth Century (Darryl F. Zanuck)

A woman allows her illegitimate son to be adopted, but years later marries his stepfather.

A tearjerker very typical of its time, moderately well assembled; later remade as *Always Goodbye* (qv).

w Sam Mintz, *story* Gilbert Emery, Doug Doty d Gregory La Cava ph Peverell Marley m Alfred Newman

Ann Harding, Clive Brook, Otto Kruger, Tullio Carminati, Dickie Moore, Janet Beecher

Gallipoli*

Australia 1981 111m Eastmancolor Panavision
Associated R and R (Martin Cooper, Ben Gannon)

In 1915, two friends trek from Perth across the desert to join up, and one dies in the Dardanelles.
Consistently interesting aspects of the 1914–18 war, but rather broken-backed as a story.

w David Williamson d Peter Weir ph Russell Boyd md Brian May

Mark Lee, Mel Gibson, Bill Hunter, Robert Grubb, Tim McKenzie, Bill Kerr
'Like so many of Weir's films it promises more than it delivers.'—*Time Out, 1984*

The Galloping Major*

GB 1951 82m bw
British Lion / Romulus (Monja Danischewsky)

A group of suburbanites form a syndicate to buy a racehorse.
Rather contrived and imitative sub-Ealing comedy which fails to generate much steam.

w Monja Danischewsky, Henry Cornelius d Henry Cornelius ph Stan Pavey m Georges Auric

Basil Radford, Janette Scott, Hugh Griffith, Jimmy Hanley, René Ray, Joyce Grenfell, Sidney Tafler, Charles Victor, A. E. Matthews

Gambit**

US 1966 109m Techniscope
Universal (Leo L. Fuchs)

A cockney thief conspires with a Eurasian girl to rob a multi-millionaire of a prize statue.
An enjoyably light pattern of cross and double cross is well sustained to the end.

w Jack Davies, Alvin Sargent d Ronald Neame ph Clifford Stine m Maurice Jarre

Michael Caine, Shirley Maclaine, Herbert Lom, John Abbott, Roger C. Carmel, Arnold Moss

'He's been bruised, blackmailed, sliced and slammed. But nothing can stop him from going after the big money!'

The Gambler*

US 1975 111m Eastmancolor
Paramount (Irwin Winkler, Robert Chartoff)

A compulsive gambler has a will to lose.
Flashily made but basically uninteresting sub-Freudian study, vaguely based on Dostoievsky.

w James Tomack d Karel Reisz ph Victor J. Kemper m Mahler md Jerry Fielding

James Caan, Paul Sorvino, Lauren Hutton, Morris Carnovsky, Jacqueline Brookes, Burt Young

● Video: CIC

Gambler from Natchez

US 1954 88m Technicolor
TCF / Panoramic

A professional gambler returns to New Orleans to avenge his father's murder, and disposes of his enemies one by one.
Mildly watchable semi-western with a plot borrowed from *The Count of Monte Cristo*.

w Gerald Drayson Adams, Irving Wallace d Henry Levin ph Lloyd Ahern md Lionel Newman

Dale Robertson, Debra Paget, Thomas Gomez, Kevin McCarthy

Gambling*

US 1934 82m bw

A professional gambler ferrets out the killer of his ward. Transcript of a George M. Cohan play, with the star in good form; but the presentation is uncinematic and tedious.
George M. Cohan, Wynne Gibson, Dorothy Burgess, Theodore Newton. Written by Garrett Graham, from Cohan's play; directed by Rowland V. Lee; for Harold B. Franklin.
'It moves too slowly towards an intelligent but almost wholly mental climax.'—*Variety*

Gambling House

US 1950 80m bw

An immigrant gambler is threatened with deportation when involved in a murder. Heavy melodrama with assumed social conscience.
Victor Mature, Terry Moore, William Bendix, Basil Ruysdael. Written by Marvin Borowsky and Allen Rivkin; directed by Ted Tetzlaff; for RKO.

Gambling Lady*

US 1934 66m bw
Warner

The daughter of a gambling suicide follows in father's footsteps and becomes involved in murder.
Fast-paced melodrama with a happy ending: smart entertainment of its time.

w Ralph Block, Doris Malloy d Archie Mayo ph George Barnes

Barbara Stanwyck, Joel McCrea, Pat O'Brien, Claire Dodd, C. Aubrey Smith, Robert Barrat, Philip Reed

Gambling on the High Seas

US 1940 56m bw

A reporter proves that a gambling ship owner is a murderer. Unsurprising filler. Wayne Morris, Jane Wyman, Gilbert Roland, William Pawley, John Litel. Written by Robert E. Kent; directed by George Amy; for Warner.

Gambling Ship
US 1933 70m bw

A big shot gambler annoys rivals by opening a gambling ship off Long Beach. Any freshness this once had wore off long ago. Cary Grant, Benita Hume, Roscoe Karns, Glenda Farrell, Jack La Rue. Written by Marcia and Seton I. Miller; directed by Max Marcin; for Paramount. 'A fair flicker . . . but in toto it's a familiar formula of mob vs mob.'—*Variety*

A Game for Vultures
GB 1979 106m colour

In Rhodesia, a sanctions-buster comes to understand a black freedom fighter. After a lot of violence and attitudinizing, that is, in this unattractively pretentious piece of bloodthirsty hokum. Richard Harris, Richard Roundtree, Ray Milland, Joan Collins, Sven Bertil Taube, Denholm Elliott. Written by Phillip Baird, from a novel by Michael Hartmann; directed by James Fargo; for Columbia.

A Game of Death
US 1945 72m bw
RKO

Cheap remake of *The Most Dangerous Game* (qv); excitement dissipated by poor handling.
w Norman Houston *d* Robert Wise
ph J. Roy Hunt *m* Paul Sawtell

John Loder, Audrey Long, Edgar Barrier, Russell Wade, Russell Hicks

Games*
US 1967 100m Techniscope
Universal (George Edwards)

A sophisticated New York couple play complex games, one of which turns out to have a deadly edge.
Tedious variation on *Les Diaboliques*, with interesting moments.
w Gene Kearney *d* Curtis Harrington
ph William A. Fraker *m* Samuel Matlovsky

Simone Signoret, James Caan, Katharine Ross, Don Stroud, Kent Smith, Estelle Winwood, Marjorie Bennett

The Games*
GB 1970 97m De Luxe Panavision
TCF (Lester Linsk)

Four men in various parts of the world prepare to take part in the marathon at the Rome Olympics.
Tepid multi-drama with good locations and a well-shot and exciting climactic race.
w Erich Segal, *novel* Hugh Atkinson
d Michael Winner *ph* Robert Paynter
m Francis Lai

Stanley Baker, Michael Crawford, Ryan O'Neal, Charles Aznavour, Jeremy Kemp, Elaine Taylor, Kent Smith, Mona Washbourne

● *Video: CBS / Fox*

The Gamma People
GB 1955 79m bw

Journalists in a Balkan state uncover a plot by a mad scientist to control the minds of children by gamma rays. Artless serial-like thriller with little suspense. Paul Douglas, Leslie Phillips, Eva Bartok, Walter Rilla, Philip Leaver. Written by John Gilling and John Gossage; directed by John Gilling; for Warwick / Columbia.

'His goal was freedom . . . his strategy was peace . . . his weapon was his humanity!'

Gandhi***
GB 1982 188m Technicolor
Panavision
Columbia / Goldcrest / Indo-British / International Film Investors / National Film Development Corporation of India (*Richard Attenborough*)

The life of the young Indian advocate who became a revolutionary, a saint and a martyr.
A straightforward treatment with the odd twists and turns expected of this director; but the remarkable things about the film are first, that it was made at all in an age which regards inspirational epics as very old hat; and secondly, that it has brought into life so splendid a leading performance. Beside these factors the sluggish pace and the air of schoolbook history seem comparatively unimportant.
w John Briley *d* Richard Attenborough
ph Billy Williams, Ronnie Taylor *m* George Fenton *pd* Stuart Craig *ed* John Bloom

Ben Kingsley, Candice Bergen, Edward Fox, John Mills, John Gielgud, Trevor Howard, Martin Sheen, Ian Charleson, Athol Fugard, Saeed Jaffrey
† Opening dedication: 'No man's life can be encompassed in one telling . . . what can be done is to be faithful in spirit to the record and try to find one's way to the heart of the man.'
AA: best picture; Ben Kingsley; Richard Attenborough as director; John Briley; cinematography; costume design (John Mollo, Bhanu Athalya); art direction (Stuart Craig, Bob Laing); editing (John Bloom)
AAN: music
BFA: best film; best direction; best actor; best supporting actress (Rohini Hattangady); outstanding newcomer (Ben Kingsley)

Gang Buster*
US 1931 65m bw

A small-town sap defeats gangsters by accident. Lively comedy which scored in the middle of the first gangster cycle. Jack Oakie, Jean Arthur, William Boyd, Wynne Gibson, Tom Kennedy. Written by Joseph L. Mankiewicz from a story by Percy Heath; directed by A. Edward Sutherland; for Paramount. 'First-rate week-stander . . . inlaid with surefire comic devices.'—*Variety*

The Gang That Couldn't Shoot Straight
US 1971 96m Metrocolor
MGM (Robert Chartoff, Irwin Winkler)

Members of the New York Mafia organize a cycle race and start antagonisms that end in mass murder.
Unfunny black comedy with all concerned gesticulating wildly.
w Waldo Salt, *novel* Jimmy Breslin *d* James Goldstone *ph* Owen Roizman *m* Dave Grusin

Jerry Orbach, Leigh Taylor-Young, Jo Van Fleet, Lionel Stander, Robert de Niro, Herve Villechaize, Joe Santos

● *Video: MGM / UA*

The Gang's All Here*
GB 1939 77m bw
ABP (Walter C. Mycroft, Jack Buchanan)
US title: *The Amazing Mr Forrest*

An insurance investigator goes undercover among gangsters.
Lively comedy-melodrama.
w Ralph Spence *d* Thornton Freeland

Jack Buchanan, Googie Withers, Edward Everett Horton, Syd Walker, Otto Kruger, Jack La Rue. Walter Rilla

The Gang's All Here**
US 1943 103m Technicolor
TCF (William Le Baron)
GB title: *The Girls He Left Behind*

A serviceman is caught between a fiery entertainer and a Park Avenue socialite.
Frenetic wartime musical with some of Busby Berkeley's most outré choreography (e.g. The Lady in the Tutti Frutti Hat) and gleamingly effective Technicolor.
w Walter Bullock *d / ch* Busby Berkeley
ph Edward Cronjager *md* Alfred Newman
songs Leo Robin, Harry Warren

Alice Faye, Carmen Miranda, James Ellison, Phil Baker, Benny Goodman, Charlotte Greenwood, Eugene Pallette, Edward Everett Horton

'Those who consider Berkeley a master consider this film his masterpiece.'—*New Yorker, 1976*
'Mainly made up of Busby Berkeley's paroxysmic production numbers, which amuse me a good deal.'—*James Agee*

Gangs of New York*
US 1938 67m bw

A cop infiltrates the mob and impersonates a tough gangster. Highly unlikely but entertaining programmer, a good shot for a B studio. Charles Bickford, Ann Dvorak, Alan Baxter, Wynne Gibson, Harold Huber, Willard Robertson, Maxie Rosenbloom, John Wray. Written by Wellyn Totman, Sam Fuller, Charles Francis Royal; directed by James Cruze; for Republic. 'Rapid-fire gangster meller . . . sure to be a strong entry.'—*Variety*

The Gangster
US 1947 84m bw

Rival gangs rub each other out. Shoddy-looking Poverty Row melodrama with little rhyme, reason or interest. Barry Sullivan, Akim Tamiroff, Belita, John Ireland. Written by Daniel Fuchs; directed by Gordon Wiles; for Monogram / King Bros.

Gangway*

GB 1937 89m bw

GFD / Gaumont

A girl reporter poses as a star's maid and is accused of theft.

Mildly pleasing star vehicle.

w Lesser Samuels, Sonnie Hale d Sonnie Hale ph Glen MacWilliams

Jessie Matthews, Barry Mackay, Pat Pendleton, Noel Madison, Alastair Sim

Gangway for Tomorrow

US 1943 69m bw

Five defence workers with problematical pasts unite in the cause of war. Naïve but oddly stirring little propaganda piece. Robert Ryan, Margo, John Carradine. Written by Arch Oboler: directed by John H. Auer; for RKO.

Garbo Talks*

US 1984 103m Technicolor

MGM-UA / Elliott Kastner

An eccentric woman spends her life worshipping Greta Garbo, and when she finds herself mortally ill expresses a last wish to meet her idol.

Curious low-key comedy, very New Yorkish and rather easily pleased with its own wit; but certainly a banquet for certain tastes.

w Larry Grusin d Sidney Lumet ph Andrzej Bartkowiak m Cy Coleman pd Philip Rosenberg ed Andrew Mondshein

Anne Bancroft, Ron Silver, Carrie Fisher, Catherine Hicks, Steven Hill, Howard Da Silva, Harvey Fierstein, Dorothy Loudon, Hermione Gingold

Garde a Vue*

France 1981 88m Eastmancolor

Ariane / TF1 (Georges Dancigers, Alexandre Mnouchkine)

GB title: *The Inquisitor*

In a French provincial town a wealthy lawyer is interrogated by police, who think he may be implicated in a rape case.

Basically a talk-piece, though with a twist ending, this is a smart little film which would undoubtedly have its best effect when not understood through sub-titles.

w Claude Miller, Jean Herman, novel Brainwash by John Wainwright d Claude Miller ph Bruno Nuytten m Georges Delerue

Lino Ventura, Michel Serrault, Guy Marchand, Romy Schneider

'Not unlike a *Twelve Angry Men* from which all comfortable certainties have been withdrawn.'—*Tom Milne, MFB*

'Dangerous love in a desert paradise!'

The Garden of Allah*

US 1936 80m Technicolor

David O. Selznick

A disenchanted socialite falls in love with a renegade monk in the Algerian desert.

Arty old-fashioned romantic star vehicle; great to look at, and marking a genuine advance in colour photography, but dramatically a bit of a drag.

w W. P. Lipscomb, Lynn Riggs, novel Robert Hichens d Richard Boleslawski ph W. Howard Greene, Harold Rosson m Max Steiner ad Sturges Carne, Lyle Wheeler, Edward Boyle

Marlene Dietrich, Charles Boyer, Basil Rathbone, Tilly Losch

'The last word in colour production, but a pretty dull affair.'—*Variety*

'Hopelessly dated folderol.'—*J. R. Parish*

'The juiciest tale of woe ever, produced in poshly lurid colour, with a Max Steiner score poured on top.'—*Judith Crist*

'Alas! my poor church, so picturesque, so noble, so superhumanly pious, so intensely dramatic. I really prefer the *New Statesman* view, shabby priests counting pesetas on their dingy fingers before blessing tanks.'—*Graham Greene*

† Previous, silent, versions had been made in 1917, with Tom Santochi and Helen Ware, and in 1927 with Ivan Petrovich and Alice Terry.

AA: photography

AAN: Max Steiner

● *Video: Guild*

Garden of Evil*

US 1954 100m Technicolor Cinemascope

TCF (Charles Brackett)

En route to the Californian goldfields an ex-sheriff and a gambler help a woman to rescue her husband from a mine, but are trapped by Indians.

High-flying western melodrama with the principals glowering at each other. Stock situations quite skilfully compiled.

w Frank Fenton d Henry Hathaway ph Milton Krasner m Bernard Herrmann

Susan Hayward, Gary Cooper, Richard Widmark, Hugh Marlowe, Cameron Mitchell

The Garden of the Finzi-Continis**

Italy / West Germany 1970 95m Eastmancolor

Documento Film / CCC Filmkunst (Gianni Hecht Lucari, Arthur Cohn)

In 1938, a family of wealthy Italian Jews sees its world collapse, with a concentration camp as the next destination.

A dreamlike, poignant, and very beautiful film.

w Tullio Pinelli, Valerio Zurlini, Franco Brusati, Ugo Pirro, Vittorio Bonicelli, Alain Katz, novel Giorgio Bassani d Vittorio de Sica ph Ennio Guarnieri m Manuel de Sica

Dominique Sanda, Lino Capolicchio, Helmut Berger, Romolo Valli, Fabio Testi

AAN: script

Garden of the Moon

US 1938 94m bw

Warner (Lou Edelman)

A night club owner vies with his bandleader for the affections of his leading singer.

Pleasant talent can't turn this script into

anything but a tedious small-scale musical, especially since both director and songwriters are operating below par.

w Jerry Wald, Richard Macauley d Busby Berkeley songs Al Dubin, Harry Warren

Pat O'Brien, Margaret Lindsay, John Payne, Melville Cooper, Isabel Jeans

The Garment Jungle*

US 1957 88m bw

Columbia (Harry Kleiner)

Union and gangster problems abound for a family in the New York clothing business. Reasonably powerful melodrama fashioned from familiar material in the wake of *On the Waterfront*.

w Harry Kleiner d Robert Aldrich, Vincent Sherman ph Joseph Biroc m Leith Stevens

Lee J. Cobb, Kerwin Mathews, Gia Scala, Richard Boone, Valerie French, Robert Loggia, Joseph Wiseman

Gas! or It Became Necessary to Destroy the World in Order to Save It

US 1970 79m Movielab

AIP / San Jacinto (Roger Corman)

A gas which speeds up the ageing process is accidentally released and kills everyone over twenty-five.

Psychedelic sci-fi for the Easy Rider set. Very mildly diverting.

w Graham Armitage d Roger Corman ph Ron Dexter m Country Joe and the Fish

Robert Corff, Elaine Giftos, Pat Patterson, Graham Armitage, Alex Wilson, Ben Vereen, Bud Cort

Gasbags*

GB 1940 77m bw

Gainsborough (Edward Black)

Airmen stranded in Germany by a barrage balloon return in a captured secret weapon. Fast-moving knockabout from the Crazy Gang; often inventive despite reach-me-down script and production.

w Val Guest, Marriott Edgar d Marcel Varnel

Flanagan and Allen, Nervo and Knox, Naughton and Gold, Moore Marriott, Wally Patch, Peter Gawthorne, Frederick Valf

Gaslight***

GB 1939 88m bw

British National (John Corfield)

US title: *Angel Street*

A Victorian schizophrenic drives his wife insane when she seems likely to stumble on his guilty secret of an old murder and hidden rubies.

Modest but absolutely effective film version of a superb piece of suspense theatre.

w A. R. Rawlinson, Bridget Boland, play Patrick Hamilton d Thorold Dickinson ph Bernard Knowles m Richard Addinsell

Anton Walbrook, Diana Wynyard, Frank Pettingell, Cathleen Cordell, Robert Newton, Jimmy Hanley

'The electric sense of tension and mid-Victorian atmosphere are entirely cinematic.'—*Sequence, 1950*

'A melodrama of a strange love!'

Gaslight**
US 1944 114m bw
MGM (Arthur Hornblow Jnr)
GB title: *The Murder in Thornton Square*

Grossly overblown and less effective version of the above, but with moments of power, effective performances and superior production.

w John Van Druten, Walter Reisch, John L. Balderston d George Cukor ph Joseph Ruttenberg m Bronislau Kaper ad Cedric Gibbons

Charles Boyer, Ingrid Bergman, Joseph Cotten, Dame May Whitty, Barbara Everest, *Angela Lansbury*, Edmund Breon, Halliwell Hobbes

'This is love . . . clouded by evil . . . darkened by a secret no one dared to guess! The strange drama of a captive sweetheart!'—*publicity*

† Irene Dunne and Hedy Lamarr were previously offered the Ingrid Bergman part, and turned it down.

AA: Ingrid Bergman

AAN: best picture; script; Joseph Ruttenberg; Charles Boyer; Angela Lansbury

Gate of Hell*
Japan 1953 90m Eastmancolor
original title: *Jigokumon*

After a 12th-century war, a soldier demands as his prize a woman who has helped him; but she is married.

Curious traditional Japanese saga, its emphases strange to western eyes and ears. Its colour, however, is devastatingly beautiful.

wd Teinosuke Kinugasa, *novel* Kan Kikuchi ph Kohei Sugiyama m Yasushi Akutagawa

Machiko Kyo, Kazuo Hasegawa, Isao Yamagata

AA: best foreign film

Gateway*
US 1938 75m bw
TCF (Darryl F. Zanuck)

An Irish girl emigrating to the US is helped on board ship by a war correspondent.

Brisk romantic drama which provides an interesting recreation of the Ellis Island procedures still effective in the thirties.

w Lamar Trotti d Alfred Werker ph Edward Cronjager

Don Ameche, Arleen Whelan, Gregory Ratoff, Raymond Walburn, Binnie Barnes, Gilbert Roland, John Carradine, Harry Carey

'*Grand Hotel* treatment applied to Ellis Island . . . should look to fair b.o.'—*Variety*

A Gathering of Eagles
US 1962 115m Eastmancolor
U-I (Sy Bartlett)

A colonel becomes unpopular when he strives to improve the efficiency of a Strategic Air Command base.

Tame revamp of *Twelve O'clock High* without the justification of war; all strictly routine and perfectly dull.

w Robert Pirosh d Delbert Mann ph Russell Harlan m Jerry Goldsmith

Rock Hudson, Mary Peach, Rod Taylor, Barry Sullivan, Kevin McCarthy

Gator
US 1976 116m De Luxe Todd AO 35
UA / Levy-Gardner-Laven

A convicted moonshiner is blackmailed into becoming a government undercover man in the organization of a hoodlum.

Shambling mixture of action, violence, and raw humour.

w William Norton d Burt Reynolds ph William A. Fraker m Charles Bernstein

Burt Reynolds, Jack Weston, Lauren Hutton, Jerry Reed, Alice Ghostley, Dub Taylor, Mike Douglas

'The relentless violence, the sentimentality, the raucous stag party humour, the inability to cut off a scene once it has made its point, attest to the influence of Robert Aldrich.'—*Philip French, The Times*

The Gaunt Stranger*
GB 1938 73m bw
Northwood / Capad (Ealing) (S. C. Balcon)
US title: *The Phantom Strikes*

A criminal master of disguise threatens to kill a much more despicable criminal at an appointed hour . . . and does so despite police protection.

A highly reliable suspenser of which this is perhaps the best film version.

w Sidney Gilliat, *novel and play* The Ringer by Edgar Wallace d Walter Forde ph Ronald Neame

Sonnie Hale, Wilfrid Lawson, Alexander Knox, Louise Henry, Patricia Roc, Patrick Barr, John Longden, George Merritt

† Other versions, as *The Ringer*, appeared in 1931 and 1953.

The Gauntlet*
US 1977 109m De Luxe Panavision
Warner / Malpaso (Robert Daly)

A disreputable cop is assigned to escort a foul-mouthed prostitute to a courtroom across country, through the gauntlet of baddies who want them both dead.

The epitome of seventies violence, with no excuse except to stage one detailed shoot-up or explosion after another. Well done for those who like this sort of thing.

w Michael Butler, Dennis Shryack d Clint Eastwood ph Rexford Metz m Jerry Fielding

Clint Eastwood, Sondra Locke, Pat Hingle, William Prince

'At times the whole world seems to be firing at them. Buildings and cars are turned to lace. You look at the screen even though there's nothing to occupy your mind . . .'—*Pauline Kael*

† This was the first film to give a credit for first aid.

● *Video: Warner*

Gawain and the Green Knight*
GB 1973 93m Technicolor Panavision
UA / Sancrest (Philip Breen)

The medieval legend of a supernatural knight who challenges the king's men to kill him. Enterprising if unsuccessful low-budget attempt to create a medieval world; too long by half.

w Philip Green, Stephen Weeks d Stephen Weeks ph Ian Wilson m Ron Goodwin ad Anthony Woollard

Murray Head, Ciaran Madden, Nigel Green, Anthony Sharp, Robert Hardy, Murray Melvin

The Gay Bride
US 1934 80m bw
MGM (John Considine Jnr)

A gold-digging chorus girl marries a racketeer but soon becomes a widow.

Misfiring satirical melodrama which quickly becomes tedious.

w Bella and Samuel Spewack, *story* Repeal by Charles Francis Coe d Jack Conway ph Ray June

Carole Lombard, Chester Morris, Zasu Pitts, Nat Pendleton, Leo Carrillo

'Gangster pictures are gone, and this won't do anything to bring them back.'—*Variety*

The Gay Deception*
US 1935 79m bw
TCF (Jesse L. Lasky)

A Ruritanian prince becomes a doorman at a swank New York hotel, and marries a secretary.

Lightly-handled Cinderella story showing most of its director's accomplishment.

w Stephen Morehouse Avery, Don Hartman d William Wyler ph Joseph Valentine m Louis de Francesco

Francis Lederer, Frances Dee, Benita Hume, Alan Mowbray, Akim Tamiroff, Lennox Pawle, Richard Carle, Lionel Stander

'Doesn't lean too much to sophistication to miss appreciation in the hamlet houses.'—*Variety*

AAN: script

The Gay Desperado**
US 1936 85m bw
Mary Pickford

An heiress is held for ransom by a romantic bandit.

Very light, quite amusing, sometimes irritatingly skittish musical spoof sparked by the director's ideas.

w Wallace Smith, *story* Leo Birinski d Rouben Mamoulian m Alfred Newman ph Lucien Andriot

Ida Lupino, Nino Martini, Leo Carrillo, Harold Huber, Mischa Auer

'Fairly diverting Mexican western . . . it'll do spotty trade, depending on locale.'—*Variety*

'One of the best light comedies of the year . . . Mr Mamoulian's camera is very persuasive.'—*Graham Greene*

Introducing "THE GAY FALCON"

The bold adventurer who's as smooth with the ladies as he's clever with crime! . . . Fiction's slickest super sleuth, created by Michael Arlen and portrayed by the star who thrilled you as "The Saint".

THE GAY FALCON

with
GEORGE
SANDERS
WENDY
BARRIE

ALLEN JENKINS • ANNE HUNTER
GLADYS COOPER • EDWARD BROPHY

See "The Falcon" solve the double murder and diamond robbery that turned society upside down. Try and outguess the man who seems to know all the answers even before the questions are asked. Don't miss
THE FIRST OF A GREAT NEW SERIES!

R K O RADIO PICTURES

Produced by HOWARD BENEDICT • Directed by IRVING REIS.
Screen Play by Lynn Root and Frank Fenton.

THE GAY FALCON.   They'd have to retitle that these days, unless they wanted a very different kind of film. George Sanders soon got bored with the role and handed it over to his real brother Tom Conway.

'While some of the show is fetching, the ideas mostly misfire and the spell is fitful and unsure.'—*Otis Ferguson*

'It has the lightness of touch which goes into the making of the perfect meringue.'—*Basil Wright*

'The gayest of mad musicals!'
'The dance-mad musical triumph of two continents!'
The Gay Divorcee****
US 1934 107m bw
RKO (Pandro S. Berman)
GB title: *The Gay Divorce*

A would-be divorcee in a Brighton hotel mistakes an author who loves her for a professional co-respondent.
Wildly and hilariously dated comedy musical with splendidly archaic comedy routines supporting Hollywood's great new dance team in their first big success. Not much dancing, but 'The Continental' is a show-stopper.

w George Marion Jnr, Dorothy Yost, Edward Kaufman, *musical comedy* Dwight Taylor d Mark Sandrich ph David Abel md Max Steiner *songs* various sp Vernon Walker ad Van Nest Polglase, Carroll Clark

Fred Astaire, Ginger Rogers, Edward Everett Horton, Alice Brady, Erik Rhodes, Eric Blore, Lillian Miles, Betty Grable
'Cinch box office anywhere and certain of big foreign grosses.'—*Variety*
'The plot is trivial French farce, but the dances are among the wittiest and most lyrical expressions of American romanticism on the screen.'—*New Yorker, 1977*

AA: song 'The Continental' (*m* Con Conrad, *ly* Herb Magidson)
AAN: best picture; musical adaptation (Ken Webb, Samuel Hoffenstein)

The Gay Diplomat
US 1931 66m bw

A Russian officer is sent to Bucharest to combat a woman superspy. Thoroughly confused and inane mixture of romance, presumed sophistication and dark doings. Ivan Lebedeff, Genevieve Tobin, Ilka Chase, Betty Compson. Written by Doris Anderson from a story by Benn W. Levy; directed by Richard Boleslawski; for RKO. 'A picture almost without a merit.'—*Variety*

The Gay Dog
GB 1954 87m bw

A miner trains a pet greyhound to win races. Modest, set-bound regional comedy. Wilfred Pickles, Petula Clark, Megs Jenkins, John Blythe. Written by Peter Rogers, from the play by Joseph Colton; directed by Maurice Elvey; for Coronet / Eros.

The Gay Intruders
US 1948 68m bw

Quarrelling stage marrieds consult psychiatrists, who end up more confused than the patients. Unusual second feature comedy

with a few good laughs; allegedly based on Tallulah Bankhead. Tamara Geva, John Emery, Leif Erickson, Virginia Gregg. Written by Francis Swann; directed by Ray McCarey; for TCF.

Gay Purree*
US 1962 85m Technicolor
UPA

A country cat goes to Paris and is Shanghaied. Feature cartoon similar to Disney's later *The Aristocats* and about as good, i.e. not quite up to the best standards.

w Dorothy and Chuck Jones d Abe Levitow md Mort Lindsey

voices Judy Garland, Robert Goulet, Hermione Gingold

The Gay Sisters*
US 1942 110m bw
Warner (Henry Blanke)

Three sisters refuse to sell their aristocratic New York mansion to make way for development.
Slowish but quite interesting family drama with Chekhovian touches.

w Lenore Coffee, *novel* Stephen Longstreet d Irving Rapper ph Sol Polito m Max Steiner

Barbara Stanwyck, George Brent, Geraldine Fitzgerald, Donald Crisp, *Gig Young* (so named after his part in this film; formerly Byron Barr), Nancy Coleman, Gene Lockhart, Larry Simms, Donald Woods, Grant Mitchell

The Gazebo*
US 1959 102m bw
MGM / Avon (Lawrence Weingarten)

A TV writer kills a blackmailer (he thinks) and hides his body in the garden.
Frenetic black comedy which must have worked better on the stage but produces a few laughs.

w George Wells, *play* Alec Coppel d George Marshall ph Paul C. Vogel m Jeff Alexander

Glenn Ford, Debbie Reynolds, Carl Reiner, John McGiver, Mabel Albertson, Doro Merande, Zasu Pitts, Martin Landau

The Geisha Boy
US 1958 98m Technicolor Vistavision
Paramount (Jerry Lewis)

A third-rate magician joins a USO entertainment tour in Japan.
Disconnected farce which amuses only fitfully, and actively displeases when it becomes sentimental with the star drooling over a baby.

wd Frank Tashlin ph Haskell Boggs m Walter Scharf

Jerry Lewis, Marie MacDonald, Barton MacLane, Sessue Hayakawa, Suzanne Pleshette

The Gene Krupa Story
US 1959 101m bw
Columbia (Philip A. Waxman)
GB title: *Drum Crazy*

A successful jazz drummer is convicted on a drugs charge and falls from grace.

Dreary biopic with the expected music track.

w Orin Jannings d Don Weis ph Charles Lawton Jnr m Leith Stevens

Sal Mineo, Susan Kohner, James Darren, Susan Oliver, Yvonne Craig, Lawrence Dobkin, Celia Lovsky; and Red Nichols, Shelly Manne, Buddy Lester

The General****
US 1926 80m approx (24 fps) bw silent
UA / Buster Keaton (Joseph M. Schenck)

A confederate train driver gets his train and his girl back when they are stolen by Union soldiers.
Slow-starting, then hilarious action comedy, often voted one of the best ever made. Its sequence of sight gags, each topping the one before, is an incredible joy to behold.

w Al Boasberg, Charles Smith d Buster Keaton, Clyde Bruckman ph J. Devereux Jennings, Bert Haines

Buster Keaton, Marian Mack, Glen Cavander
'It has all the sweet earnestness in the world. It is about trains, frontier America, flower-faced girls.'—*New Yorker, 1977*
'The production itself is singularly well mounted, but the fun is not exactly plentiful . . . here he is more the acrobat than the clown, and his vehicle might be described as a mixture of cast iron and jelly.'—*Mordaunt Hall, New York Times*
† The story is based on an actual incident of the Civil War, treated more seriously in *The Great Locomotive Chase.*
†† The screenplay with 1,400 freeze frames was issued in 1976 in the Film Classics Library (editor, Richard Anobile).
● Video: Polygram

'He strides recklessly into the vortex of cyclonic romantic adventure, sweeping monarchs from their thrones to suit a gypsy's whim!'
General Crack
US 1930 100m approx bw (colour sequences)

Exploits of an eighteenth-century brigand prince. Elaborate swashbuckler which provided the star with his first talkie but boringly demonstrates the technical problems of films of this period, however highly budgeted. John Barrymore, Marian Nixon, Hobart Bosworth, Armida, Lowell Sherman. Written by J. Grubb Alexander and others; directed by Alan Crosland; for Warner.

'Gary goes to town for the best-looking gal in China!'
The General Died at Dawn**
US 1936 93m bw
Paramount (William le Baron)

A mercenary in China overcomes an evil warlord and falls in love with a spy.
Heavy-going but very decorative studio-bound intrigue which seems to take place on the old *Shanghai Express* sets with an extra infusion of dry ice. An intellectual's picture of its day.

w Clifford Odets, *novel* Charles Booth
d Lewis Milestone *ph* Victor Milner
m Werner Janssen, Gerard Carbonara

Gary Cooper, Madeleine Carroll, *Akim Tamiroff*, *Dudley Digges*, Porter Hall, *William Frawley*

'If it were not for a rather ludicrous ending, this would be one of the best thrillers for some years.'—*Graham Greene*
'In terms of cinematic invention, a fascinating technical exercise.'—*John Baxter, 1968*
'A curious study in exoticism.'—*NFT, 1974*
'In direction and photography it has undeniable class . . . but like most movies, it is empty of any ideas or characters that stay with you longer than it takes to reach the nearest subway entrance.'—*Brooklyn Daily Eagle*

AAN: Victor Milner; Werner Janssen; Akim Tamiroff

The General Line**
USSR 1929   90m (24 fps)   bw   silent
Sovkino
original title: *Staroye i Novoye;* aka: *Old and New*

A country woman helps to start a village co-operative.
A slight piece of propaganda, put together with all of Eisenstein's magnificent cinematic resources: the cream separator demonstration is one of the most famous montage sequences in cinema history.

wd Sergei Eisenstein   *co-d* Grigori Alexandrov   *ph* Edouard Tissé.

Marta Lapkina and a cast of non-professionals

General Spanky
US 1936   73m approx   bw

A small boy is instrumental in a famous Civil War victory. Uneasy sentimental melodrama vehicle for one of the moppet stars of 'Our Gang'. Spanky McFarland, Phillips Holmes, Hobart Bosworth, Ralph Morgan, Irving Pichel. Written by Richard Flournoy, Hal Yates and John Guedal; directed by Gordon Douglas and Fred Newmeyer; for Hal Roach / MGM. 'Desultory, overlong . . . built for the lesser family trade.'—*Variety*

Il Generale della Rovere
Italy / France 1959   137m   bw
Zebra / Gaumont (Morris Ergas)

During World War II, a con man is persuaded to impersonate a dead general, and becomes so imbued with the latter's code of honour that he goes before a firing squad rather than expose a partisan.
An unlikely piece of tragic whimsy with some good acting, but imperfectly assembled and at too great length.

w Sergio Amidei, Diego Fabbri, Indro Montanelli, Roberto Rossellini *d* Roberto Rossellini *ph* Carlo Carlini *m* Renzo Rossellini

Vittorio de Sica, Hannes Messemer, Sandra Milo, Giovanna Ralli, Anne Vernon

AAN: script

Generation*
Poland 1954   90m   bw
Film Polski
original title: *Pokolenie*

In occupied Warsaw in 1942 a teenager becomes hardened by life and joins the resistance.
Heavy-going but quite striking propaganda piece, amply demonstrating its director's talents.

w Bohdan Czeszko, from his novel   *d* Andrzej Wajda   *ph* Jerzy Lipman   *m* Andrzej Markowski

Tadeusz Lomnicki, Urszula Modrzynska, Roman Polanski, Zbigniew Cybulski

Generation
US 1969   104m   Technicolor
Avco Embassy / Frederick Brisson
GB title: *A Time for Giving*

A Denver advertising executive is horrified by his daughter's ideas of modern marriage. Lame generation-gap comedy centring on a couple who intend to deliver their own baby.

w William Goodheart, from his play
d George Schaefer *ph* Lionel Lindon
m Dave Grusin

David Janssen, Kim Darby, Carl Reiner, Pete Duel, Andrew Prine, James Coco, Sam Waterston, Don Beddoe
'Slightly too sticky for comfort.'—*MFB*
● Video: Thorn EMI

Genevieve****
GB 1953   86m   Technicolor
GFD / Sirius (Henry Cornelius)

Two friendly rivals engage in a race on the way back from the Brighton veteran car rally. One of those happy films in which for no very good or expected reason a number of modest elements merge smoothly to create an aura of high style and memorable moments. A charmingly witty script, carefully pointed direction, attractive actors and locations, an atmosphere of light-hearted British sex and a lively harmonica theme turned it, after a slowish start, into one of Britain's biggest commercial hits and most fondly remembered comedies.

w William Rose   *d* Henry Cornelius
ph Christopher Challis   *m* Larry Adler (who also played it) *md* Muir Mathieson
ad Michael Stringer

Dinah Sheridan, John Gregson, Kay Kendall, Kenneth More, Geoffrey Keen, Joyce Grenfell, Reginald Beckwith, Arthur Wontner
'One of the best things to have happened to British films over the last five years.'—*Gavin Lambert*

AAN: William Rose; Muir Mathieson
● Video: Rank

'In the eight centuries since he ruled the world, no man has matched the magnificence of his adventure!'
Genghis Khan*
US 1964   126m   Technicolor
Panavision
Columbia / Irving Allen / CCC / Avala

Temujin raises a Mongol army and revenges himself on his old enemy Jamuga.

Meandering epic in which brutality alternates with pantomimish comedy and bouts of sex. Necessarily patchy but reasonably watchable.

w Clarke Reynolds, Beverly Cross   *d* Henry Levin *ph* Geoffrey Unsworth *m* Ducan Radic

Omar Sharif, Stephen Boyd, Françoise Dorléac, *James Mason*, Robert Morley, Telly Savalas, Woody Strode, Eli Wallach, Yvonne Mitchell

Les Gens du Voyage*
France 1938   123m   bw

Trials and tribulations of circus people on the road. Interesting but overlong multi-drama. Françoise Rosay, André Brule, Fabien Loris, Marie Glory, Sylvia Bataille. Written by Jacques Feyder and Jacques Viol; directed by Jacques Feyder; for Tobis. 'Boredom is unavoidably the impression.'—*Variety*

Gentle Annie
US 1944   80m   bw

A marshal deals with a lady rancher who sees no harm in an occasional bank robbery to augment her income. Tidy MGM second-string western, originally intended for Robert Taylor. James Craig, Marjorie Main, Donna Reed, Henry Morgan, Paul Langton, Barton MacLane. Written by Lawrence Hazard, from the novel by Mackinlay Kantor; directed by Andrew Marton; for MGM.

The Gentle Giant
US 1967   93m   Eastmancolor

A small boy in Florida befriends a bear, which later saves his disapproving father's life. Lumbering family movie which provided the impetus for a TV series. Dennis Weaver, Clint Howard, Vera Miles, Ralph Meeker, Huntz Hall. Written by Edward J. Lakso and Andy White, from the novel *Gentle Ben* by Walt Morey; directed by James Neilson; for Ivan Tors / Paramount.

The Gentle Gunman
GB 1952   88m   bw
GFD / Ealing (Michael Relph)

Tensions mount in an IRA family where one brother believes in peace.
Stilted and unconvincing pattern play which wouldn't have done at all once the Troubles restarted.

w Roger MacDougall, from his play   *d* Basil Dearden *ph* Gordon Dines *m* John Greenwood *ed* Peter Tanner

John Mills, Dirk Bogarde, Elizabeth Sellars, Barbara Mullen, Robert Beatty, Eddie Byrne, Joseph Tomelty, Gilbert Harding, Liam Redmond, Jack MacGowran

The Gentle Sex**
GB 1943   93m   bw
Rank / Two Cities / Concanen (Leslie Howard, Derrick de Marney)

Seven girls from different backgrounds are conscripted into the ATS.

Unassuming war propaganda, quite pleasantly done and historically very interesting.

w Moie Charles, Aimée Stuart, Phyllis Rose, Roland Pertwee d Leslie Howard, Maurice Elvey

Rosamund John, Joan Greenwood, Joan Gates, Jean Gillie, Lilli Palmer, Joyce Howard, Barbara Waring, John Justin, Frederick Leister, Mary Jerrold, Everley Gregg

A Gentleman after Dark
US 1942 74m bw
Edward Small

A jewel thief comes out of prison to pay back his vindictive wife for shopping him.
Efficient melodrama of a dated kind.

w Patterson McNutt, George Bruce, *story* A Whiff of Heliotrope by Richard Washburn Child d Edwin L. Marin ph Milton Krasner m Dmitri Tiomkin

Brian Donlevy, Miriam Hopkins, Preston Foster, Harold Huber, Philip Reed, Gloria Holden, Douglass Dumbrille, Ralph Morgan
† Previously filmed in 1920 as *Heliotrope* with Fred Burton; in 1928 as *Forgotten Faces* with Clive Brook; and in 1936 as *Forgotten Faces* with Herbert Marshall.

A Gentleman at Heart
US 1942 66m bw

A racetrack bookie has aspirations to the art business but finds there are crooks there too.
Fairly lively second feature. Cesar Romero, Carole Landis, Milton Berle, J. Carrol Naish, Rose Hobart, Jerome Cowan, Elisha Cook Jnr, Steve Geray. Written by Lee Loeb and Harold Buchman, from a story by Paul Hervey Fox; directed by Ray Macarey; for Walter Morosco / TCF.

The Gentleman in Room Six*
US 1951 11m bw

In a seedy room in South America, a man we can't see gives orders to old associates. As he finally goes to shave, we see in the mirror that he is—Adolf Hitler! A fairly sensational novelty at the time, and historically interesting thirty years later. Written by Sidney Carroll; directed by Alexander Hammid; produced by George Brest for Meteor Films.

Gentleman Jim**
US 1942 104m bw
Warner (Robert Buckner)

The rise to fame of boxer Jim Corbett.
Cheerful biopic of a nineties show-off, mostly played for comedy.

w Vincent Lawrence, Horace McCoy, *book* The Roar of the Crowd by James J. Corbett d Raoul Walsh ph Sid Hickox m Heinz Roemheld

Errol Flynn, *Alan Hale*, Alexis Smith, John Loder, Jack Carson, *Ward Bond*, William Frawley, Rhys Williams, Arthur Shields
  'Good-natured enough, but it lacks flavour.'—*New Yorker, 1976*

● *Video: Warner*

A Gentleman of Paris
GB 1931 76m bw

A philandering French judge knows that the girl before him is innocent of murder, but dare not say so. Tolerable melodrama of its time.
Arthur Wontner, Hugh Williams, Vanda Greville, Phyllis Konstam, Sybil Thorndike. Written by Sydney Gilliat, Sewell Collins, from the novel *His Honour the Judge* by Niranjan Pal; directed by Sinclair Hill; for Stoll / Gaumont.

'Now! It comes to the screen with nothing left unsaid and no emotion unstressed!'
Gentleman's Agreement**
US 1947 118m bw
TCF (Darryl F. Zanuck)

A journalist poses as a Jew in order to write about anti-semitism.
Worthy melodrama which caused a sensation at the time but as a film is alas rather dull and self-satisfied.

w Moss Hart, *novel* Laura Z. Hobson d Elia Kazan ph Arthur Miller m Alfred Newman

Gregory Peck, Dorothy McGuire, *John Garfield*, Celeste Holm, *Anne Revere*, June Havoc, Albert Dekker, Jane Wyatt, Dean Stockwell

AA: best picture; Elia Kazan; Celeste Holm
AAN: Moss Hart; Gregory Peck; Dorothy McGuire; Anne Revere

Gentleman's Fate
US 1930 90m bw

A man goes to the bad after his wife walks out on him. Dismal early talkie, one of several which killed off its star's career. John Gilbert, Louis Wolheim, Leila Hyams, Anita Page, John Miljan, Marie Prevost. Written from a story by Ursula Parrott; directed by Mervyn Le Roy; for MGM. 'It got a laugh at the Strand Saturday afternoon, where all of the audience probably thought the same thing, that Gilbert died too late as the picture had been dying since its start.'—*Variety*

A Gentleman's Gentleman
GB 1939 70m bw

A valet thinks his master is a murderer, and tries a little blackmail. Uneasy serio-comic vehicle for a London stage character who had made his name in Hollywood. Eric Blore, Peter Coke, Marie Lohr, David Hutcheson. Written by Austin Melford and Elizabeth Meehan, from the play by Philip MacDonald; directed by Roy William Neill; for Warner.

Gentlemen Are Born
US 1934 74m bw

College graduates find it hard to get jobs. Tedious and uninventive quartet of linked stories. Franchot Tone, Ross Alexander, Dick Foran, Robert Light, Jean Muir, Margaret Lindsay, Ann Dvorak, Charles Starrett. Written by Eugene Solow and Robert Lee Johnson; directed by Alfred E. Green; for Warner.

Gentlemen Marry Brunettes
US 1955 95m Technicolor Cinemascope
UA / Russ–Field (Richard Sale, Robert Waterfield)

Two American shopgirls seek rich husbands in Paris, and find that their aunts were notorious there.
Jaded sequel to *Gentlemen Prefer Blondes*; it barely raises a smile and the numbers are dismal.

w Mary Loos, Richard Sale d Richard Sale ph Desmond Dickinson m Robert Farnon ad Paul Sheriff ch Jack Cole

Jane Russell, Jeanne Crain, Alan Young, Scott Brady, Rudy Vallee

Gentlemen Prefer Blondes*
US 1953 91m Technicolor
TCF (Sol. C. Siegel)

A dumb blonde and a showgirl go to Paris in search of rich husbands.
Musicalized and updated version of the twenties satire; no real vigour, but not too bad.

w Charles Lederer, *novel* Anita Loos d Howard Hawks ph Harry J. Wild md Lionel Newman songs Jule Styne, Leo Robin ch Jack Cole

Jane Russell, Marilyn Monroe, Charles Coburn, Tommy Noonan, Norma Varden, Elliott Reid, George Winslow

● *Video: CBS / Fox*

Geordie*
GB 1955 99m Technicolor
British Lion / Argonaut (Sidney Gilliat, Frank Launder)
US title: *Wee Geordie*

A weakly Scottish boy takes a physical culture course and becomes an Olympic hammer-thrower.
Slight comic fable, good to look at but without the necessary style to follow it through.

w Sidney Gilliat, Frank Launder, *novel* David Walker d Frank Launder ph Wilkie Cooper m William Alwyn

Bill Travers, Alastair Sim

George and Margaret
GB 1940 77m bw

The frictions of a suburban family come to boiling point. Fairly spruce film version of a stage comedy in which the title pair were much talked of but never seen. Judy Kelly, Marie Lohr, Oliver Wakefield, Noel Howlett, Ann Casson, Arthur Macrae. Written by Brock Williams and Rodney Ackland, from the play by Gerald Savory; directed by George King; for Warner.

George and Mildred
GB 1980 93m colour

A suburban husband on a weekend package holiday is mistaken for a hired killer. Abysmal TV spinoff, seeming even more lugubrious since it was released after the death of the female star. Yootha Joyce, Brian Murphy, Stratford Johns, Norman Eshley, Sheila Fearn, Kenneth Cope. Written by Dick Sharples; directed by Peter Frazer Jones; for Chips / ITC. 'Flaccid entertainment even by routine sit-com standards.'—*Martyn Auty, MFB*.

George in Civvy Street
GB 1946 79m bw
Columbia (Marcel Varnel, Ben Henry)

A soldier returns to his country pub and finds himself in the middle of a beer war.
The star's last film was oddly lacklustre and compared very badly with his earlier successes.

w Peter Fraser, Ted Kavanaugh, Max Kester, Gale Pedrick *d* Marcel Varnel *ph* Phil Grindrod

George Formby, Rosalyn Boulter, Ronald Shiner, Ian Fleming, Wally Patch

The George Raft Story
US 1961 105m bw
Allied Artists (Ben Schwab)
GB title: *Spin of a Coin*

In twenties New York, a dancer falls in with gangsters, but eludes them when he goes to Hollywood, where his acting career is harmed by temperament.
Tepid, unconvincing biopic, rather shoddily made but with flashes of interest.

w Crane Wilbur *d* Joseph M. Newman *ph* Carl Guthrie *m* Jeff Alexander

Ray Danton, Julie London, Jayne Mansfield, Frank Gorshin, Neville Brand (as Al Capone)

George Washington Slept Here
US 1942 93m bw
Warner (Jerry Wald)

A New York couple move to a dilapidated country house.
Disappointingly stiff and ill-timed version of a play that should have been a natural.

w Everett Freeman, *play* George Kaufman, Moss Hart *d* William Keighley *ph* Ernest Haller *m* Adolph Deutsch

Jack Benny, Ann Sheridan, Percy Kilbride, Charles Coburn, Hattie McDaniel, William Tracy, Lee Patrick, John Emery, Charles Dingle

George White's Scandals*
US 1934 79m bw
Fox (Winfield Sheehan)

Romance blossoms backstage during the production of a big musical.
Revue with minimum plot and some impressive numbers.

w Jack Yellen, from the Broadway show directed by George White *d* Thornton Freeland, Harry Lachman, George White *ph* Lee Garmes, George Schneiderman *songs* various

George White, Rudy Vallee, Alice Faye, Jimmy Durante, Dixie Dunbar, Adrienne Ames, Cliff Edwards, Gertrude Michael, Gregory Ratoff

George White's 1935 Scandals*
US 1935 83m bw
Fox (Winfield Sheehan)

A small-town star is discovered by a Broadway producer.
Again, basic plot serves to introduce some pretty good acts.

w Jack Yellen, Patterson McNutt *d* George White *ph* George Schneiderman
songs various

George White, Alice Faye, James Dunn, Eleanor Powell, Ned Sparks, Lyda Roberti, Cliff Edwards, Arline Judge

George White's Scandals*
US 1945 95m bw
RKO (Jack J. Gross, Nat Holt, George White)

Ex-Scandals girls get together, and one disappears.
Lively comedy-musical with vaudeville orientations.

w Hugh Wedlock, Parker Levy, Howard Green *d* Felix E. Feist *m* Leigh Harline *ph* Robert de Grasse *songs* various

Joan Davis, Jack Haley, Philip Terry, Martha Holliday, Ethel Smith, Margaret Hamilton, Glenn Tryon, Jane Greer, Fritz Feld, Rufe Davis

Georgy Girl*
GB 1966 100m bw
Columbia / Everglades (Otto Plaschkes, Robert A. Goldston)

An unattractive girl is fancied by her middle-aged employer but escapes to look after the illegitimate baby of her ungrateful friend.
Frantic black farce which seems determined to shock, but has a few good scenes once you get attuned to the mood. A censorship milestone.

w Margaret Forster, Peter Nichols, *novel* Margaret Forster *d* Silvio Narizzano *ph* Ken Higgins *m* Alexander Faris

James Mason, Lynn Redgrave, Charlotte Rampling, Alan Bates, Bill Owen, Clare Kelly, Rachel Kempson
'Another swinging London story filled with people running through London late at night, dancing madly in the rain, and visiting deserted children's playgrounds to ride on the roundabouts.'—*MFB*
'So glib, so clever, so determinedly kinky that everything seems to be devalued.'—*Pauline Kael*
'Its barrage of fashionable tricks proves exhausting.'—*Sight and Sound*
AAN: Ken Higgins; James Mason; Lynn Redgrave; title song (*m* Tom Springfield, *ly* Jim Dale)

Gerald McBoing Boing***
US 1951 7m Technicolor

A small boy becomes famous because he can't speak words: 'he goes boing-boing instead'.
Highly influential cartoon in what was then a new style; told with a light touch which is still extremely funny. Followed less successfully by *Gerald McBoing Boing's Symphony* and

Gerald McBoing Boing On Planet Moo. Written by *Dr Seuss* (Theodore Geisel); directed by *Robert Cannon*; designed by *John Hubley*; music by *Gail Kubik*; for UPA.

The German Sisters*
West Germany 1981 107m Fujicolor
Bioskop Film / (Eberhard Junkersdorf)
original title: *Die Bleierne Zeit*

Based on a real-life case, this is a suppositional account of how two well-brought-up girls can develop so differently.

wd Margarethe von Trotta *ph* Franz Rath *m* Nicolas Economou *ed* Dagmar Hirtz

Jutte Lampe, Barbara Sukowa, Rudiger Vogler, Doris Schade, Verenice Rudolph
'Beautifully acted and strikingly shot, it all has a calculated, crowd-pleasing fervour.'—*Tom Milne, MFB*

Germany Year Zero*
France / Italy 1947 78m bw
Union Générale Cinématographique / DEFA

Life in post-war Germany is so appalling that a boy kills his father and then himself.
Both realistic and pessimistic, this depressing film has a savage power of its own but totally fails to be constructive.

wd Roberto Rossellini *ph* Robert Juillard *m* Renzo Rossellini

Franz Gruger and a cast of non-professionals

'Ten thousand red raiders roar into battle!'
Geronimo!
US 1939 89m bw
Paramount

The seventh cavalry gives the Indians a run for their money.
Muddled western of no discernible merit.

wd Paul H. Sloane *ph* Henry Sharp *m* Gerald Carbonara

Ellen Drew, Preston Foster, Andy Devine, Gene Lockhart, Ralph Morgan, William Henry
'Lusty and actionful melodrama geared to hit popular appeal.'—*Variety*

Geronimo
US 1962 101m Technicolor
Panavision
UA / Laven–Gardner–Levy

In 1883 Geronimo and his remaining Apaches seek peace but are betrayed.
Moderate western held back by script and performances.

w Pat Fielder *d* Arnold Laven *ph* Alex Phillips *m* Hugo Friedhofer

Chuck Connors, Ross Martin, Kamala Devi

Gervaise*
France 1956 116m bw
Agnès Delahaye–Silver Films–CLCC

In 19th-century Paris, a laundrymaid is deserted by her lover, settles with another man and is able to open her own laundry, but they both take to drink.
The French equivalent of David Lean's Dickens films, superbly detailed and

GEORGE WASHINGTON SLEPT HERE. Percy Kilbride tells the tale to Jack Benny and Ann Sheridan.

wonderful to look at, but with a plot which finally seems worthless and depressing.

w Jean Aurenche, Pierre Bost, *novel* L'Assommoir by Emile Zola *d* René Clément *ph* René Juillard *m* Georges Auric *decor* Paul Bertrand

Maria Schell, François Périer, Suzy Delair, Mathilde Casadeus

'A tremendous *tour de force* of literal realism . . . a piece for the admiration of technicians, or for those whose consciences are purged and hands kept clean by the vicarious contemplation of how the other half lived— once upon a time.'—*David Robinson, MFB*
† Other French versions were made in 1902, 1909, 1911 and 1933.

Get Carter*
GB 1971 112m Metrocolor
MGM / Mike Klinger

A racketeer goes to Newcastle to avenge his brother's death at the hands of gangsters. He kills those responsible but is himself shot by a sniper.
Brutal British crime melodrama with faint echoes of Raymond Chandler. Sex and thuggery unlimited, narrative disjointed, rewards few.

wd Mike Hodges, *novel* Jack's Return Home by Ted Lewis *ph* Wolfgang Suschitzky *m* Roy Budd

Michael Caine, John Osborne, Ian Hendry, Britt Ekland

'TV on the big screen—more sex, more violence, but no more attention to motivation or plot logic.'—*Arthur Knight*
'So calculatedly cool and soulless and nastily erotic that it seems to belong to a new era of virtuoso viciousness.'—*Pauline Kael*

Get Cracking*
GB 1942 96m bw
Columbia (Ben Henry)

George joins the home guard.
Adequate star comedy.

w L. DuGarde Peach *d* Marcel Varnel

George Formby, Edward Rigby, Frank Pettingell, Dinah Sheridan, Ronald Shiner, Wally Patch, Irene Handl

Get Off My Foot
GB 1935 83m bw
Warner (Irving Asher)

A Smithfield porter becomes a butler, and later finds himself heir to a fortune.
The nearest Max Miller came to being a genuine film star was in this first of eight Warner comedies, but the screen simply couldn't contain him.

w Frank Launder, Robert Edmunds, *play* Money By Wire by Edward Paulton *d* William Beaudine *ph* Basil Emmott

Max Miller, Chili Bouchier, Morland Graham, Jane Carr, Norma Varden, Reginald Purdell, Wally Patch

The Getaway
US 1941 89m bw

A lawman goes to jail, gets to know an imprisoned mob leader, and breaks out with him. Routine rehash of 1935's *Public Hero Number One*. Robert Sterling, Dan Dailey, Donna Reed, Charles Winninger, Henry O'Neill. Written by Wells Root and W. R. Burnett; directed by Edward Buzzell; for MGM.

The Getaway**
US 1972 122m Technicolor Todd-AO 35
Solar / First Artists (David Foster, Mitchell Brower)

A convict leaves jail and promptly joins his wife in a bank robbery.
Violent, amoral, terse and fast-moving action melodrama which generally holds the interest despite its excesses.

w Walter Hill, *novel* Jim Thompson *d* Sam Peckinpah *ph* Lucien Ballard *m* Quincy Jones

Steve McQueen, Ali MacGraw, Ben Johnson, Sally Struthers, Al Lettieri, Slim Pickens

'This pair have no mission or "meaning". As in all romances, *The Getaway* simply extracts one element of reality and dwells on it. Nor is the violence "American". Pictures like this don't fail overseas.'—*Stanley Kauffmann*
● Video: Warner

Getting Gertie's Garter
US 1945 73m bw

A businessman tries all manner of wiles to retrieve an incriminating garter. Silly variation on *Up in Mabel's Room*, with similar team and cast. A few laughs are inevitable. Dennis O'Keefe, Marie McDonald, Mischa Auer. Written by Allan Dwan and Karen de Wilf, from the play by Wilson Collinson and Avery Hopwood; directed by Allan Dwan; for Edward Small / UA.

The Getting of Wisdom**
Australia 1977 101m Eastmancolor
Southern Cross / AFC / Victorian Film Corporation / 9 Television Network (Phillip Adams)

In 1897 a backwoods girl is sent to an exclusive Melbourne ladies' college and eventually wins a music scholarship.
Praiseworthy period piece which thankfully seems to have no axe to grind and is all the better for it.

w Eleanor Witcombe, *novel* Henry Handel Richardson (Ethel Richardson) *d* Bruce Beresford *ph* Donald McAlpine *m* various *pd* John Stoddart

Susannah Fowle, Sheila Helpman, Patricia Kennedy, John Waters, Barry Humphries, Kerry Armstrong
● Video: Guild

Getting Straight*
US 1970 125m Eastmancolor
Columbia / The Organization (Richard
Rush)

A political activist returns to college in order
to teach and discovers the foolishness of most
contemporary attitudes.
Modish comedy, too long, far too pleased with
itself, and now irrevocably dated.

w Robert Kaufman novel Ken Kolb
d Richard Rush ph Laszlo Kovacs m Ronald
Stein

Elliott Gould, Candice Bergen, Robert F.
Lyons, Jeff Corey, Max Julien, Cecil Kellaway

The Ghost and Mr Chicken
US 1965 90m Techniscope
Universal (Edward J. Montagne)

An incompetent small-town reporter finds
ghosts in a local murder mansion.
Old-fashioned scare comedy starring a highly
resistible comic. A big hit in American small
towns.

w James Fritzell, Everett Greenbaum d Alan
Rafkin ph William Margulies m Vic Mizzy

Don Knotts, Skip Homeier, Joan Staley, Liam
Redmond, Dick Sargent, Reta Shaw

'Doin' what comes supernaturally . . . it's
the man-woman affair that's like nothing
on earth!'

The Ghost and Mrs Muir*
US 1947 104m bw
TCF (Fred Kohlmar)

A widow refuses to be frightened away from
her seaside home by the ghost of a sea captain,
with whom she falls in love.
Charming sentimental fable in Hollywood's
best style.

w Philip Dunne, novel R. A. Dick d Joseph
L. Mankiewicz ph Charles Lang m Bernard
Herrmann ad Richard Day and George Davis
Gene Tierney, Rex Harrison, George Sanders,
Edna Best, Vanessa Brown, Anna Lee,
Robert Coote, Natalie Wood, Isobel Elsom
'A not at all disagreeable piece of
whimsy.'—News Chronicle
'A jolly caper, gently humorous and often
sparkling.'—New York Times
† A half-hour TV series followed in 1968.

AAN: Charles Lang

The Ghost Breakers*
US 1940 85m bw
Paramount (Arthur Hornblow Jnr)

A girl inherits a West Indian castle and finds
herself up to her neck in ghosts, zombies and
buried treasure.
Archetypal comedy horror, very well done; a
follow-up to the success of The Cat and the
Canary, and just about as entertaining.

w Paul Dickey, Walter de Leon, play Paul
Dickey, Charles W. Goddard d George
Marshall ph Charles Lang m Ernst Toch
ad Hans Dreier

Bob Hope, Paulette Goddard, Paul Lukas,
Willie Best, Richard Carlson, Lloyd Corrigan,
Anthony Quinn, Noble Johnson, Pedro de
Cordova

† Previously filmed in 1914 with H. B.
Warner; in 1922 with Wallace Reid; and
remade in 1953 as Scared Stiff.

Ghost Catchers
US 1944 68m bw

A southern colonel and his beautiful daughters
have spooks in their mansion—or bats in the
belfry. Lower-case farce made when the stars'
contract was being allowed to run out. Ole
Olsen, Chic Johnson, Gloria Jean, Leo
Carrillo, Martha O'Driscoll, Andy Devine,
Lon Chaney Jnr, Walter Catlett, Henry
Armetta. Written by Edmund L. Hartmann,
from a story by Milt Gross and Edward Cline;
directed by Edward Cline; for Universal.

The Ghost Comes Home
US 1940 79m bw

The return of a long-lost father causes
embarrassment to his family. Hoary hide-in-
the-closet farce with all concerned straining at
the leash. Frank Morgan, Billie Burke, Ann
Rutherford, John Shelton, Reginald Owen,
Donald Meek, Nat Pendleton. Written by
Richard Maibaum and Harry Ruskin; directed
by William Thiele; for MGM.

The Ghost Goes West*
GB 1935 85m bw
London Films (Alexander Korda)

When a millionaire buys a Scottish castle and
transports it stone by stone to America, the
castle ghost goes too.
Amusing whimsy which is always pleasant but
never quite realizes its full potential; fondly
remembered for its star performance.

w Robert E. Sherwood, Geoffrey Kerr, story
Eric Keown d René Clair ph Harold Rosson
m Mischa Spoliansky

Robert Donat, Jean Parker, Eugene Pallette,
Elsa Lanchester, Ralph Bunker, Patricia
Hilliard, Morton Selten
'Fine business likely in the keys, but not for
the tanks.'—Variety
'Although the film is not cast in the fluid,
rapidly paced style of Clair's typical work, it
has a sly wit and an adroitness of manner that
make it delightful.'—André Sennwald, New
York Times
'It is typical of the British film industry that
M. René Clair should be brought to this
country to direct a Scottish film full of what
must to him be rather incomprehensible jokes
about whisky and bagpipes, humorous fantasy
without any social significance, realistic
observation, or genuine satire.'—Graham
Greene

The Ghost in the Invisible Bikini
US 1966 82m Pathecolor

A motor cycle gang gets mixed up with a
rejuvenated corpse in a haunted mansion.
Mindless beach party stuff suffering under one
of Hollywood's most inane titles. Boris
Karloff, Basil Rathbone, Patsy Kelly, Tommy
Kirk, Deborah Walley, Aron Kincaid, Quinn
O'Hara, Jesse White. Written by Louis M.
Heyward and Elwood Ullman; directed by
Don Weis; for American International.

The Ghost of Frankenstein
US 1942 67m bw
Universal (George Waggner)

Frankenstein's second son implants evil
shepherd Igor's brain into the monster.
The rot set in with this flatly-handled
potboiler, which had none of the literary mood
or cinematic interest of Bride or Son which
preceded it, and suffered from a particularly
idiotic script.

w W. Scott Darling, story Eric Taylor d Erle
C. Kenton ph Milton Krasner, Woody
Bredell m Charles Previn md Hans J. Salter

Cedric Hardwicke, Lon Chaney Jnr (as the
monster), Bela Lugosi, Lionel Atwill, Evelyn
Ankers, Ralph Bellamy
'You can't keep a good monster down!'—
publicity
† See Frankenstein for other episodes in series

The Ghost of St Michael's**
GB 1941 82m bw
Ealing (Basil Dearden)

A school is evacuated to the Isle of Skye, and
the local ghost turns out to be an enemy agent.
The star's schoolmaster character is here at its
seedy best, and he is well supported in a
comedy-thriller plot.

w Angus Macphail, John Dighton d Marcel
Varnel ph Derek Williams

Will Hay, Claude Hulbert, Felix Aylmer,
Raymond Huntley, Elliot Mason, Charles
Hawtrey, John Laurie, Hay Petrie, Roddy
Hughes, Manning Whiley

The Ghost Ship
US 1943 69m bw
RKO (Val Lewton)

The captain of a merchant ship is driven mad
by isolation.
Long unavailable because of legal problems,
this very minor Val Lewton thriller inevitably
disappoints because it has no supernatural
elements and must compare unfavourably with
both The Caine Mutiny and The Sea Wolf,
which plotwise it closely resembles.

w Donald Henderson Clarke d Mark Robson
ph Nicholas Musuraca m Roy Webb

Richard Dix, Russell Wade, Edith Barrett,
Ben Bard, Edmund Glover, Skelton Knaggs

The Ghost Ship
GB 1952 74m bw

A motor yacht proves to be haunted by the
previous owner's murdered wife. Mildly
unusual second feature. Dermot Walsh, Hazel
Court, Hugh Burden, John Robinson. Written
and directed by Vernon Sewell; for Anglo
Amalgamated.

'She'll never rest till her tale is told!'
Ghost Story*
GB 1974 89m Fujicolor
Stephen Weeks

Former college acquaintances spend a
weekend at a country house, and one of them
is drawn into tragic events of forty years
before.
Overlong chiller, ingeniously shot in India but

very variably acted; aims for the M. R. James style and sometimes achieves it, but badly needs cutting.

w Rosemary Sutcliff, Stephen Weeks d Stephen Weeks ph Peter Hurst m Ron Geesin

Murray Melvin, Larry Dann, Vivian Mackerall, Marianne Faithfull, Anthony Bate, Leigh Lawson, Barbara Shelley

Ghost Story
US 1981 110m Technicolor
Universal (Ronald G. Smith)

Four old men tell each other ghost stories, but are haunted by a guilty secret of their own. Bizarre vehicle for four welcome old actors, ruined by the director's insistence on frequent shock cuts to the rotting spectre. A subtler treatment akin to that of *The Uninvited* might have produced a little masterpiece.

w Lawrence D. Cohen, *novel* Peter Straub d John Irvin ph Jack Cardiff m Philippe Sarde

Fred Astaire, Melvyn Douglas, John Houseman, Douglas Fairbanks Jnr, Craig Wasson, Patricia Neal, Alice Krige, Jacqueline Brookes
● Video: CIC

The Ghost That Never Returns*
USSR 1929 80m approx (24 fps) bw
silent
Sovkino
original title: *Prividenie, Kotoroe ne Vozvrashchaetsya*

After ten years' imprisonment for leading a strike, a South American worker is given a day's leave which may result in his death. Unsatisfactory communist propaganda of its time, probably rescued from obscurity by its title. A few strikingly visual moments stand out, but the narrative is needlessly obscure.

w Valentin Turkin, *story* Henri Barbusse d Abram Room ph Dmitri Feldman

B. Ferdinandov, Olga Zhizneva, Maxime Straukh

The Ghost That Walks Alone
US 1943 63m bw

Honeymooners find a dead radio producer in their suite. Ho-hum second feature mystery. Arthur Lake, Janis Carter, Frank Sully, Lynne Roberts. Written by Doris Shattuck and Clarence Upson Young; directed by Lew Landers; for Columbia.

Ghost Town
US 1956 72m bw

Stagecoach passengers are forced to spend the night in a ghost town beset by Indians. Thin western second with a few effectively restrained moments. Kent Taylor, John Smith, Marian Carr, John Doucette. Written by Jameson Brewer; directed by Allen Miner; for Bel Air / UA.

The Ghost Train***
GB 1931 72m bw
Gainsborough (Michael Balcon)

Passengers stranded at a haunted station in Cornwall include a detective posing as a silly ass in order to trap smugglers.
Excellent early sound version of a comedy-thriller play which has not only been among the most commercially successful ever written but also provided the basic plot for many another comedy: *Oh Mr Porter, The Ghost of St Michael's, Back Room Boy, Hold That Ghost*, etc. Previously filmed as a silent in 1927, with Guy Newall.

w Angus Macphail, Lajos Biro, play Arnold Ridley d Walter Forde

Jack Hulbert, Cicely Courtneidge, Donald Calthrop, Ann Todd, Cyril Raymond, Angela Baddeley, Allan Jeayes

The Ghost Train**
GB 1941 85m bw
Gainsborough (Edward Black)

Adequate remake with the lead split into two characters, which doesn't work quite so well.

w Marriott Edgar, Val Guest, J. O. C. Orton d Walter Forde ph Jack Cox

Arthur Askey, Richard Murdoch, Kathleen Harrison, Morland Graham, Linden Travers, Peter Murray Hill, *Herbert Lomas*
● Video: Rank

The Ghost Walks
US 1934 70m bw

A hired 'ghost' engaged for a party is scared off by a real one. Cheeseparing spooky house comedy-thriller. John Miljan, June Collyer, Richard Carle. Written by Edward T. Lowe; directed by Frank Strayer; for Chesterfield.
'Above the indie norm all round.'—*Variety*

Ghostbusters*
US 1984 105m Metrocolor Panavision
Columbia / Delphi (Ivan Reitman)

Unemployed academic parapsychologists set themselves up as ghostbusters and destroy several monstrous apparitions on the streets of New York.
Crude farce with expensive special effects. It took more money—millions more—than *Indiana Jones and the Temple of Doom*, which must say something about the age we live in.

w Dan Aykroyd, Harold Ramis d Ivan Reitman ph Laszlo Kovacs, Herb Wagreitch m Elmer Bernstein pd John De Cuir ed Sheldon Kahn, David Blewitt

Bill Murray, Dan Aykroyd, Harold Ramis, Sigourney Weaver, Rick Moranis, Annie Potts, William Atherton

The Ghosts of Berkeley Square*
GB 1947 89m bw
British National (Louis H. Jackson)

Two 18th-century ghosts are doomed to haunt a London house until royalty visits.
Thin, skittish whimsy with pleasant moments.

w James Seymour, *novel* No Nightingales by S. J. Simon, Caryl Brahms d Vernon Sewell

Robert Morley, Claude Hulbert, Felix Aylmer, Yvonne Arnaud, Abraham Sofaer, Ernest Thesiger, Marie Lohr, Martita Hunt, A. E. Matthews, John Longden, Ronald Frankau, Wilfrid Hyde White, Esmé Percy, Mary Jerrold, Wally Patch. Martin Miller

The Ghoul**
GB 1933 79m bw
Gaumont (Michael Balcon)

An Egyptologist returns from the tomb to uncover stolen jewels and a murderer. Fascinating minor horror piece reminiscent of *The Old Dark House*, with many effective moments and a ripe cast.

w Frank King, Leonard Hines, L. DuGarde Peach, Roland Pertwee, John Hastings Turner, Rupert Downing, *novel* Frank King d T. Hayes Hunter ph Gunther Krampf make-up Heinrich Heitfeld

Boris Karloff, Cedric Hardwicke, Ralph Richardson, Kathleen Harrison, Ernest Thesiger, Dorothy Hyson, Anthony Bushell, D. A. Clarke-Smith
'Lacks general US appeal because of bad plot mechanics, mostly bad acting, and colourless camerawork.'—*Variety*
† Remade after a fashion as *What A Carve Up* (1962).

The Ghoul
GB 1975 87m Eastmancolor
Tyburn (Kevin Francis)

In the twenties, a group of stranded travellers is reduced in number when they take shelter in the house of a former clergyman.
The build-up is too slow, the revelation too nasty, and the whole thing is a shameless rip-off of the structure of *Psycho*.

w John Elder d Freddie Francis ph John Wilcox m Harry Robinson

Peter Cushing, Alexandra Bastedo, John Hurt, Gwen Watford, Veronica Carlson, Don Henderson
'Peter Cushing brings out his violin for a soothing spot of the classics, the local copper mutters veiled warnings before trundling off on his bike, and thick fog swirls round the exterior sets at the drop of a canister.'—*Geoff Brown*

Giant**
US 1956 197m Warnercolor
Warner (George Stevens, Henry Ginsburg)

The life of a Texas cattle rancher through two generations.
Sprawling, overlong family saga with unconvincing acting but good visual style.

w Fred Guiol, Ivan Moffat, *novel* Edna Ferber d George Stevens ph William C. Mellor, Edwin DuPar m Dmitri Tiomkin

Rock Hudson, Elizabeth Taylor, James Dean, Mercedes McCambridge, Carroll Baker, Chill Wills, Jane Withers, Dennis Hooper, Sal Mineo, Rod Taylor, Judith Evelyn, Earl Holliman, Alexander Scourby, Paul Fix

AA: George Stevens
AAN: best picture; script; Dmitri Tiomkin;
Rock Hudson; James Dean; Mercedes
McCambridge

The Giant Behemoth
GB 1959   70m   bw

A radioactive palaeosaurus menaces London.
Underfed monster, undercast melodramatics.
Gene Evans, André Morell, Leigh Madison,
John Turner, Jack MacGowran. Written by
Eugene Lourie; directed by Eugene Lourie
and Douglas Hickox; for Artistes Alliance /
Stratford. (Aka: *Behemoth the Sea Monster*.)

The Giant Claw
US 1957   71m   bw

A monstrous bird threatens New York.
Incompetent horror item: the bird is mostly
talons and sound track. Jeff Morrow, Mara
Corday, Morris Ankrum. Written by Samuel
Newman and Paul Gargelin; directed by Fred
F. Sears; for Sam Katzman / Clover.

The Giant Spider Invasion
US 1975   76m   Eastmancolor

Nuclear fall-out causes giant spiders to breed
and go on the rampage. Thinly scripted reprise
of one of those small-town horror thrillers of
the fifties. Barbara Hale, Steve Brodie, Leslie
Parrish, Alan Hale. Written by Richard L.
Huff and Robert Easton; directed by Bill
Rebane; for Transcentury Pictures.

Gideon's Day*
GB 1958   91m   Technicolor
Columbia / John Ford (Michael Killanin)
US title: *Gideon of Scotland Yard*

A Scotland Yard Inspector has an eventful but
frustrating day.
Pleasant, ordinary little TV style police yarn
showing no evidence of its director's particular
talents.
w T. E. B. Clarke, *novel* John Creasey
d John Ford *ph* Frederick A. Young
m Douglas Gamley *ad* Ken Adam
Jack Hawkins, Dianne Foster, Anna Lee,
Andrew Ray, Anna Massey, Frank Lawton,
John Loder, Cyril Cusack

Gidget
US 1959   95m   Eastmancolor
Cinemascope
Columbia (Lewis J. Rachmil)

A 16-year-old girl falls for a surfer; her parents
disapprove until he turns out to be the son of
their best friend.
Commercial mixture of domestic comedy and
beach athletics, for nice teenagers and their
moms and pops.
w Gabrielle Upton, *novel* Frederick Kohner
d Paul Wendkos *ph* Burnett Guffey
m George Duning *md* Morris Stoloff
Sandra Dee, Cliff Robertson, James Darren,
Arthur O'Connell
† Sequels include *Gidget Goes Hawaiian*
(1961) with Deborah Walley; *Gidget Goes to
Rome* (1962) with Cindy Carol; and two TV
movies.

The Gift Horse*
GB 1952   100m   bw
British Lion / Molton (George Pitcher)
US title: *Glory at Sea*

In 1940 an old US destroyer is given to
Britain, and an officer reluctantly takes charge
of it.
Conventional, popular seafaring war
adventure.
w William Fairchild, Hugh Hastings, William
Rose *d* Compton Bennett *ph* Harry
Waxman *m* Clifton Parker
Trevor Howard, Richard Attenborough,
Sonny Tufts, James Donald, Joan Rice,
Bernard Lee, Dora Bryan, Hugh Williams,
Robin Bailey

The Gift of Gab
US 1934   71m   bw
Universal

A conceited radio announcer gets his
comeuppance.
Odd little comedy drama notable only for its
long list of stars making cameo appearances.
w Rian James, Lou Breslow *d* Karl Freund
m Albert Von Tilzer, Con Conrad, Charles
Tobias
Edmund Lowe, Gloria Stuart, Ruth Etting,
Phil Baker, Alexander Woollcott, Ethel
Waters, Victor Moore, Boris Karloff, Bela
Lugosi, Paul Lukas, Chester Morris, Binnie
Barnes, Douglass Montgomery, Wini Shaw
'A hodge-podge, an elongated short.'—
Variety

The Gift of Love
US 1958   105m   Eastmancolor
Cinemascope
TCF (Charles Brackett)

A dying wife adopts an orphan girl so that her
husband will not be lonely.
Incredibly cloying and miscast remake of
Sentimental Journey (qv).
w Luther Davis *d* Jean Negulesco *ph* Milton
Krasner *m* Cyril Mockridge
Lauren Bacall, Robert Stack, Evelyn Rudie,
Lorne Greene

Gigi*
France 1948   109m   bw
Codo Cinema (Claude Dolbert)

In Paris in the nineties, a young girl is trained
by her aunt to be a cocotte, but when married
off to a rake she reforms him.
Charming, overlong, non-musical version of a
famous story, chiefly memorable for its local
colour.
w Pierre Laroche, *novel* Colette *d* Jacqueline
Audry *ph* Gérard Perrin *m* Marcel
Landowski
Daniele Delorme, *Gaby Morlay, Yvonne de
Bray*, Frank Villard, Jean Tissier, Madeleine
Rousset

Gigi***
US 1958   119m   Metrocolor
Cinemascope
MGM (Arthur Freed)

Laundered and musicalized version;
delightfully set, costumed and performed, but
oddly lacking dance numbers.
w / ly Alan Jay Lerner *m* Frederick Loewe
d Vincente Minnelli *ph* Joseph Ruttenberg
md André Previn *pd* / cost Cecil Beaton
Leslie Caron, Louis Jourdan, Maurice
Chevalier, Hermione Gingold, Isabel Jeans,
Jacques Bergerac, Eva Gabor, John Abbott
'It has the sureness expected when a group
of the most sophisticated talents are able to
work together on material entirely suited to
them.'—*Penelope Houston*
AA: best picture; Alan Jay Lerner; Vincente
Minnelli; Joseph Ruttenberg; André Previn;
Cecil Beaton; Adrienne Fazan (editing);
Preston Ames and Keogh Gleason (art
directors); title song (*m* Frederick Loewe,
ly Alan Jay Lerner); Maurice Chevalier
(special award)
● Video: MGM / UA

Gigot
US 1962   104m   De Luxe
TCF / Seven Arts (Kenneth Hyman)

The mute caretaker of a Montmartre boarding
house looks after an ailing prostitute and her
child.
From Paris, Hollywood, comes a grotesque
piece of self-indulgence, the arch example of
the clown who wanted to play Hamlet.
Plotless, mawkish and wholly unfunny.
w John Patrick, Jackie Gleason *d* Gene
Kelly *ph* Jean Bourgoin *m* Jackie Gleason
md Michael Magne *ad* Auguste Capelier
Jackie Gleason, Katherine Kath, Gabrielle
Dorziat, Jean Lefebvre, Jacques Marin
'Chaplinesque pretensions have proved fatal
before to artists who will not accept their own
limitations.'—*Gavin Lambert*
AAN: Michael Magne

Gilda****
US 1946   110m   bw
Columbia (Virginia Van Upp)

A gambler in a South American city resumes a
love-hate relationship with an old flame . . .
but she is now married to his dangerous new
boss.
Archetypal Hollywood *film noir*, wholly
studio-bound and the better for it, with
dialogue that would seem risible if it did not
happen to be dealt with in this style and with
these actors, who keep the mood balanced
between suspense and absurdity.
w Marion Parsonnet, *story* E. A. Ellington
d Charles Vidor *ph* Rudolph Maté *m* Hugo
Friedhofer *md* Morris Stoloff, Marlin Skiles
Rita Hayworth, Glenn Ford, George
Macready, Steve Geray, Joseph Calleia, Joe
Sawyer, Gerald Mohr, Ludwig Donath
'There never was a woman like Gilda!'—
publicity
'From a quietly promising opening the film
settles into an intractable obscurity of
narrative through which as in a fog three
characters bite off at each other words of
hate.'—*Richard Winnington*

'He fed her popcorn and kisses on a park bench!'

The Gilded Lily*
US 1935 85m bw
Paramount (Albert Lewis)

A poor stenographer who meets her reporter boy friend on a park bench is wooed by a British peer.
Good depression era romantic comedy with the heroine inevitably choosing poverty.

w Claude Binyon d Wesley Ruggles
ph Victor Milner

Claudette Colbert, Fred MacMurray, Ray Milland, C. Aubrey Smith, Luis Alberni, Donald Meek

'Breezy romance . . . should carry box-office draught.'—*Variety*

A Girl, a Guy and a Gob
US 1941 91m bw
Harold Lloyd
GB title: *The Navy Steps Out*

A secretary and her sailor boy friend teach her stuffy boss how to enjoy life.
Did producer Lloyd intend himself for the role played by O'Brien? If so, he would have needed a stronger script to prevent this Capraesque comedy from falling flat.

w Frank Ryan, Bert Granet d Richard Wallace ph Russell Metty m Roy Webb

Lucille Ball, Edmond O'Brien, George Murphy, George Cleveland, Henry Travers, Franklin Pangborn, Marguerite Churchill, Lloyd Corrigan

The Girl and the General
Italy / France 1967 113m Technicolor
MGM / Champion / Corcordia (Carlo Ponti)

During World War I, a captured Austrian general escapes with a girl partisan.
Turgid war epic veering from melodrama to comedy.

w Luigi Malerba, Pasquale Festa Campanile d Pasquale Festa Campanile ph Ennio Guarnieri m Ennio Morricone

Rod Steiger, Virna Lisi, Umberto Orsini

The Girl Can't Help It*
US 1956 97m Eastmancolor
  Cinemascope
TCF (Frank Tashlin)

A theatrical agent grooms a gangster's dumb girl friend for stardom.
Scatty, garish pop scene spoof with a plot borrowed from *Born Yesterday* and a lot of jokes about its new star's superstructure. Some scenes are funny, and it puts the first rock and roll stars in pickle for all time.

w Frank Tashlin, Herbert Baker, story Do Re Mi by Garson Kanin d Frank Tashlin ph Leon Shamroy md Lionel Newman

Jayne Mansfield, Tom Ewell, Edmond O'Brien, Henry Jones, John Emery; and Julie London, Ray Anthony, Fats Domino, Little Richard, the Platters

Girl Crazy
US 1932 75m bw

Romance at a desert college. Early talkie version of the musical comedy (see below), here redesigned as a weak vehicle for two comedy stars. Bert Wheeler, Robert Woolsey, Eddie Quillan, Dorothy Lee, Mitzi Green, Arline Judge. Written by Tim Whelan, Herman J. Mankiewicz; directed by William A. Seiter; for RKO. 'A weak sister . . . after a while it all becomes too silly.'—*Variety*

Girl Crazy*
US 1943 99m bw
MGM (Arthur Freed)
aka: *When the Girls Meet the Boys*

Romance at a desert college.
Predictable star musical with good tunes.

w Fred F. Finkelhoffe, play Guy Bolton, Jack McGowan d Norman Taurog ph William Daniels, Robert Planck md Georgie Stoll songs George and Ira Gershwin

Judy Garland, Mickey Rooney, Guy Kibbee, Gil Stratton, Robert E. Strickland, Rags Ragland, June Allyson, Nancy Walker, Tommy Dorsey and his band
† Remade 1965 as *When the Boys Meet the Girls*.

The Girl Downstairs
US 1938 77m bw

A rich bachelor in Europe chooses the maid instead of the mistress. Feeble rewrite of *Cinderella*. Franchot Tone, Franciska Gaal, Walter Connolly, Rita Johnson, Reginald Owen, Reginald Gardiner, Franklin Pangborn, Robert Coote. Written by Harold Goldman, Felix Jackson and Karl Noti; directed by Norman Taurog; for MGM.
'Keen direction and fine performances highlight moderate programmer.'—*Variety*

The Girl Friend
US 1935 67m bw

An actor and two songwriters become rural con men. Thin comedy with music. Ann Sothern, Jack Haley, Roger Pryor, Thurston Hall, Victor Kilian. Written by Gertrude Purcell, Benny Rubin; directed by Eddie Buzzell; for Columbia. 'Enough hoke to make it a welcome laugh picture for lesser towns.'—*Variety*

The Girl from Jones Beach
US 1949 78m bw

A commercial artist meets a schoolteacher who is the real-life counterpart of his 'perfect girl'. Predictable comedy with only the dimmest professional sparkle. Ronald Reagan, Virginia Mayo, Eddie Bracken, Dona Drake, Henry Travers, Florence Bates. Written by I. A. L. Diamond; directed by Peter Godfrey; for Warner.

The Girl from Manhattan
US 1948 81m bw
UA / Benedict Bogeaus

A model returns home to help her uncle with his mortgaged boarding house.

Mouldy comedy-drama full of kind thoughts, charming failures and worldly priests. Interesting for cast.

w Howard Estabrook d Alfred E. Green ph Ernest Laszlo md David Chudnow m Heinz Roemheld

Dorothy Lamour, Charles Laughton, George Montgomery, Ernest Truex, Hugh Herbert, Constance Collier, Sara Allgood, Frank Orth, Howard Freeman, Adeline de Walt Reynolds, George Chandler, Maurice Cass

The Girl from Maxim's
GB 1933 79m bw

Circumstances force a doctor to pass off a singer as his wife. Tolerable period farce from a Feydeau original. Leslie Henson, Francis Day, George Grossmith, Lady Tree, Stanley Holloway. Written by Arthur Wimperis and Harry Graham; directed by Alexander Korda; for London Films.

The Girl from Mexico see Mexican Spitfire

The Girl from Missouri*
US 1934 75m bw
MGM (Bernard H. Hyman)
aka: *100% Pure*
original titles: *Born to be Kissed, Eadie was a Lady*

A chorus girl determines to remain virtuous until the right millionaire comes along.
Smart, amusing comedy very typical of its period.

w Anita Loos, John Emerson d Jack Conway ph Ray June m William Axt

Jean Harlow, Franchot Tone, Lionel Barrymore, Lewis Stone, Patsy Kelly, Alan Mowbray, Clara Blandick, Henry Kolker

'It's going to be in the money . . . one that plenty of purity crusaders will see and like.'—*Variety*

'Noisily defiant, rip-roaring and raucous in spots . . . fast and furious adult fare.'—*Photoplay*

The Girl from Petrovka
US 1974 103m Technicolor
Universal / Richard Zanuck, David Brown

An American correspondent in Moscow falls for a Russian girl.
Lugubrious and lethargic romantic comedy-drama.

w Allan Scott, Chris Bryant d Robert Ellis Miller m Henry Mancini

Goldie Hawn, Hal Holbrook. Anthony Hopkins, Grégoire Aslan, Anton Dolin

The Girl from Scotland Yard
US 1937 61m bw

A female agent tracks down the cause of mysterious explosions. Lacklustre second feature. Karen Morley, Robert Baldwin, Katherine Alexander, Eduardo Ciannelli. Written by Doris Anderson, Dore Schary; directed by Robert Vignola; for Paramount. 'Weak thriller . . . only for the back seat in duals.'—*Variety*

The Girl from Tenth Avenue
US 1935   69m   bw
Warner (Robert Lord)
GB title: *Men on Her Mind*

A jilted attorney drowns his sorrows and marries on the rebound.
Watchable 'woman's picture'.

w Charles Kenyon, *play* Hubert Henry Davies *d* Alfred E. Green *ph* James Van Trees

Bette Davis, Ian Hunter, Colin Clive, Alison Skipworth, Katherine Alexander, John Eldredge, Philip Reed

'Bette Davis' first starring venture . . . she should pull the picture through to good returns.'—*Variety*

The Girl Habit
US 1931   77m   bw

A mild Lothario tries to get arrested as protection from the gangster husband who has threatened him. Easy-going farce which established Ruggles in Hollywood. Charles Ruggles, Tamara Geva, Margaret Dumont, Allen Jenkins, Donald Meek, Sue Conroy. Written by Owen Davis and Gertrude Purcell from a play by A. E. Thomas and Clayton Hamilton; directed by Eddie Cline; for Paramount. 'Hardly a dynamic b.o. prospect, but nice entertainment.'—*Variety*

Girl Happy
US 1965   96m   Metrocolor   Panavision
MGM / Euterpe (Joe Pasternak)

A pop singer in Florida is forced to chaperone a group of college girls including a gangster's daughter.
Standard star vehicle, quite professionally made and totally forgettable.

w Harvey Bullock, R. S. Allen *d* Boris Sagal *ph* Philip Lathrop *m* George Stoll

Elvis Presley, Harold J. Stone, Shelley Fabares, Gary Crosby, Nita Talbot

The Girl He Left Behind
US 1956   103m   bw
Warner (Frank P. Rosenberg)

The army makes a man of a spoiled youth. Platitudinous recruiting comedy for dim American teenagers.

w Guy Trosper, *book* Marion Hargrove *d* David Butler *ph* Ted McCord *m* Ray Heindorf

Tab Hunter, Natalie Wood, Jessie Royce Landis, Jim Backus, Henry Jones, Murray Hamilton, Alan King, James Garner, David Janssen

The Girl Hunters
GB 1963   100m   bw   Panavision
Present Day (Robert Fellows)

Private eye Mike Hammer solves a few murders plus the disappearance of his own ex-secretary.
Comic strip thuggery with the author playing his own slouchy hero; the general incompetence gives this cheap production an air of Kafkaesque menace.

w Mickey Spillane, Roy Rowland, Robert Fellows *d* Roy Rowland *ph* Ken Talbot *m* Phil Green

Mickey Spillane, Shirley Eaton, Lloyd Nolan

A Girl in a Million
GB 1946   90m   bw

Having divorced a nagging wife, a chemist marries a dumb girl, but when he cures her . . . Thin comedy which must have seemed funnier on the page than it does on the screen. Joan Greenwood, Hugh Williams, Basil Radford, Naunton Wayne, Wylie Watson, Yvonne Owen. Written by Muriel and Sydney Box; directed by Francis Searle; for Boca / British Lion.

The Girl in Black
Greece 1955   93m   bw
Hermes
original title: *To Koritsi me ta Mavra*

A writer holidaying on a remote fishing island causes tension and tragedy when he falls for a local maiden.
Watchable mood piece benefiting from its star female performance.

wd Michael Cacoyannis *ph* Walter Lassally *m* Argyris Kounadis, Manos Hadjidkis

Elle Lambetti, George Foundas, Dimitri Horna

The Girl in Black Stockings
US 1957   71m   bw

Suspects abound when a young woman is killed in a Utah hotel. Tolerable murder mystery. Anne Bancroft, Lex Barker, Mamie Van Doren, John Dehner, Ron Randell, Marie Windsor. Written by Richard Landau, from the story 'Wanton Murder' by Peter Godfrey; directed by Howard W. Koch; for Bel Air / UA.

A Girl in Every Port*
US 1928   62m (24 fps)   bw   silent
Fox

Two sailors brawl over women.
Adventure comedy with themes typical of its director.

w Seton Miller, James K. McGuinness *d* Howard Hawks *ph* R. J. Bergquist, L. W. O'Connel *m* William Perry

Victor McLaglen, Natalie Joyce, Dorothy Matthews, Maria Casajuana, Louise Brooks, Francis McDonald

'Brief and essentially anecdotal, it now looks more than anything else like a preliminary sketch for concerns which Hawks would later elaborate.'—*Tim Pulleine, MFB*

A Girl in Every Port
US 1951   87m   bw
RKO (Irwin Allen, Irving Cummings Jnr)

Two accident-prone sailors have trouble with a racehorse.
Dismally mechanical farce.

wd Chester Erskine *ph* Nicholas Musuraca *m* Roy Webb

Groucho Marx, William Bendix, Marie Wilson, Don Defore, Gene Lockhart
● *Video: Kingston*

The Girl in the Headlines*
GB 1963   93m   bw
Bryanston / Viewfinder (John Davis)
US title: *The Model Murder Case*

Scotland Yard investigates the murder of a model.
Standard police mystery, well enough done.

w Vivienne Knight, Patrick Campbell, *novel* The Nose on My Face by Laurence Payne *d* Michael Truman *ph* Stan Pavey *m* John Addison

Ian Hendry, Ronald Fraser, Margaret Johnston, Natasha Parry

The Girl in the Kremlin
US 1957   81m   bw

An OSS agent infiltrates the Iron Curtain to assist a plot to overthrow Stalin. Boring cold war nonsense with the leading lady for some reason playing three parts. Lex Barker, Zsa Zsa Gabor, Jeffrey Stone, Maurice Manson, William Schallert. Written by Gene L. Coon and Robert Hill; directed by Russell Birdwell; for Universal.

The Girl in the News*
GB 1940   78m   bw
TCF (Edward Black)

A nurse is framed for the death of her employer.
Easy-going British mystery of the Agatha Christie school.

w Sidney Gilliat, *novel* Roy Vickers *d* Carol Reed *ph* Otto Kanturek *md* Louis Levy

Margaret Lockwood, Barry K. Barnes, Emlyn Williams, Margaretta Scott, Roger Livesey, Basil Radford, Wyndham Goldie, Irene Handl, Mervyn Johns, Kathleen Harrison, Richard Bird, Michael Hordern, Roland Culver, Edward Rigby

The Girl in the Red Velvet Swing*
US 1955   109m   De Luxe   Cinemascope
TCF (Charles Brackett)

In New York at the turn of the century, a rich unstable man shoots his mistress's former lover.
Plushy but not very interesting recounting of a celebrated murder case in which the victim was a famous architect, Stanford White.

w Walter Reisch, Charles Brackett *d* Richard Fleischer *ph* Milton Krasner *m* Leigh Harline *ad* Lyle R. Wheeler, Maurice Ransford

Ray Milland, Farley Granger, Joan Collins, Glenda Farrell, Luther Adler, Cornelia Otis Skinner, Philip Reed, John Hoyt

'A needlessly long-winded piece of lush sensationalism.'—*Penelope Houston*

The Girl in the Taxi
GB 1937   72m   bw

The head of the purity league is drawn into an adulterous flirtation. Moderately piquant comedy shot in English and French versions. Frances Day, Henri Garat, Lawrence Grossmith, Jean Gillie, Mackenzie Ward, Helen Haye, Albert Whelan. Written by Austin Melford, Val Valentine and Fritz

Gottfurcht, from the play by George Okonowski; directed by André Berthomieu; for British Unity.

The Girl in White*
US 1952 93m bw
MGM (Armand Deutsch)
GB title: So Bright the Flame

The story of Dr Emily Dunning, the first woman to become an intern in one of New York's hospitals.
Bland biopic, modestly produced, with predictable plot crises.

w Irmgard Von Cube, Allen Vincent, book Bowery to Bellevue by Emily Dunning Barringer d John Sturges ph Paul C. Vogel m David Raksin

June Allyson, Arthur Kennedy, Gary Merrill, Mildred Dunnock, Jesse White, Marilyn Erskine

The Girl Most Likely
US 1956 98m Technicolor RKOscope
RKO (Stanley Rubin)

A girl finds herself engaged to three men at the same time, and envisions marriage with each.
Dully cast, quite brightly handled remake of Tom, Dick and Harry, with modest songs and dances.

w Devery Freeman d Mitchell Leisen ph Robert Planck m Nelson Riddle songs Ralph Blane, Hugh Martin

Jane Powell, Cliff Robertson, Keith Andes, Tommy Noonan, Kaye Ballard, Una Merkel
† For Mitchell Leisen and RKO studios, their last film.

A Girl Must Live**
GB 1939 92m bw
Gainsborough (Edward Black)

A runaway schoolgirl falls among chorus girls planning to marry into the nobility.
Light, peppery comedy with a strong cast.

w Frank Launder, Michael Pertwee, novel Emery Bonnet d Carol Reed ph Jack Cox md Louis Levy

Margaret Lockwood, Renée Houston, Lilli Palmer, George Robey, Hugh Sinclair, Naunton Wayne, Moore Marriott, Mary Clare, David Burns, Kathleen Harrison, Martita Hunt, Helen Haye
'An unabashed display of undressed femininity, double-meaning dialogue alternating between piquancy and vulgarity, and hearty knockabout involving scantily attired young viragos who fight furiously in a whirligig of legs and lingerie.'—Kine Weekly

'He was half-oriental . . . but he used the women of two continents without shame or guilt!'

A Girl Named Tamiko
US 1962 119m Technicolor Panavision
Paramount / Hal B. Wallis (Paul Nathan)

A Eurasian photographer uses his women in an attempt to get American nationality.
Humdrum romantic melodrama with dim performances.

w Edward Anhalt, novel Ronald Kirkbride d John Sturges ph Charles Lang Jnr m Elmer Bernstein

Laurence Harvey, France Nuyen, Martha Hyer, Michael Wilding, Miyoshi Umeki

The Girl Next Door
US 1953 92m Technicolor
TCF (Robert Bassler)

A Broadway musical star falls for her suburban neighbour.
Mild musical linked by UPA cartoon sequences.

w Isobel Lennart d Richard Sale ph Leon Shamroy md Lionel Newman songs Josef Myrow, Mack Gordon ch Richard Barstow

Dan Dailey, June Haver, Natalie Schaefer, Dennis Day, Cara Williams

The Girl of the Golden West
US 1930 81m bw
Warner (Robert North)

A gun-toting, saloon-owning girl marries an outlaw and saves him from the sheriff.
Straight version of a dusty old Broadway success, later musicalized under the same title (see below).

w Waldemar Young, play David Belasco d John Francis Dillon ph Sol Polito

Ann Harding, James Rennie, Harry Bannister, Ben Hendricks Jnr, J. Farrell MacDonald
† A silent version was made in 1923 by First National, with Sylvia Breamer and J. Warren Kerrigan, directed by Edwin Carewe.

The Girl of the Golden West
US 1938 121m bw (sepia release)
MGM (William Anthony McGuire)

In backwoods Canada, a girl loves a bandit who is being chased by the Mounties.
Solemn musical melodrama in which the stars seem miscast and a bit of pep is badly needed.
Taken from a hoary David Belasco spectacular, and looks it.

w Isobel Dawn, Boyce DeGaw d Robert Z. Leonard ph Oliver Marsh songs Sigmund Romberg, Gus Kahn

Jeanette MacDonald, Nelson Eddy, Walter Pidgeon, Leo Carrillo, Buddy Ebsen, Olin Howland
'This musical mustanger finds the stars not only out of their element, but hemmed in by a two-hour mélange of the great outdoors, Mexican bandits, early Spanish-Californian atmosphere and musical boredom . . . a spotty entry.'—Variety

Girl of the Limberlost
US 1934 86m bw

A girl of the swamps becomes a high school graduate. Tearful rehash of an old sentimental warhorse. Louise Dresser, Ralph Morgan, Marian Marsh, Henry B. Walthall, Helen Jerome Eddy, Betty Blythe. Written by Adele Comandini from the novel by Gene Stratton Porter; directed by Christy Cabanne; for

Monogram. 'Wholesome to a fault. A family film good enough for anybody to see, but the fault lies in that not everybody will want to see it.'—Variety

Girl on a Motorcycle
GB / France 1968 91m Technicolor
Mid Atlantic / Ares (William Sassoon)
US title: Naked under Leather; French title: La Motocyclette

A married woman leaves her husband, zooms off on her motorcycle to see her lover, and crashes to her death while indulging in sexual reverie.
An incredibly plotless and ill-conceived piece of sub-porn claptrap, existing only as a long series of colour supplement photographs.

w Ronald Duncan, novel La Motocyclette by André Pieyre de Mandiargues d Jack Cardiff ph Jack Cardiff, René Guissart m Les Reed

Marianne Faithfull, Alain Delon, Roger Mutton

The Girl on the Boat
GB 1962 91m bw
UA / Knightsbridge (John Bryan)

On a transatlantic liner in the twenties, two Englishmen fall in love.
Curious attempt to do something different with a star comic, who is clearly outclassed by the lighter talents at hand.

w Reuben Ship, story P. G. Wodehouse d Henry Kaplan ph Denys Coop m Kenneth V. Jones

Norman Wisdom, Richard Briers, Millicent Martin, Athene Seyler, Sheila Hancock, Philip Locke

The Girl on the Front Page
US 1936 74m bw

The lady owner of a newspaper gets a job on it under an assumed name, and helps the editor solve a mystery. Fairly pleasing programmer. Edmund Lowe, Gloria Stuart, Spring Byington, Reginald Owen. Written by Austin Parker, Albert R. Perkins and Alice Duer Miller; directed by Harry Beaumont; for Universal.

The Girl Rosemarie
West Germany 1958 100m bw
Roxy
original title: Das Mädchen Rosemarie

Corrupt industrialists and investigators alike are relieved when a girl who had been the mistress of all of them is murdered .
Slick melodrama based on an actual case; almost a documentary exposé.

w Erich Kuby, Rolf Thiele, Joe Herbst, Rolf Urich d Rolf Thiele ph Klaus von Rautenfeld m Norbert Schultze

Nadja Tiller, Peter Van Eyck, Carl Raddatz, Gert Frobe, Mario Adorf, Horst Frank

The Girl Rush
US 1955 85m Technicolor Vistavision
Paramount (Frederick Brisson, Robert Alton)

A gambler's daughter inherits a half share in a Las Vegas hotel.

Dull charmless semi-musical vehicle for a star who can't quite carry it.

w Phoebe and Henry Ephron d Robert Pirosh ph William Daniels m Herbert Spencer, Earle Hagen ch Robert Alton

Rosalind Russell, Eddie Albert, Fernando Lamas, James Gleason, Gloria de Haven, Marion Lorne

Girl Stroke Boy
GB 1971   88m   Eastmancolor
Hemdale / Virgin (Ned Sherrin, Terry Glinwood)

A well-to-do couple try to find out whether their son's house guest is male or female. Initially funny but appallingly extended one-joke comedy which many will find merely embarrassing.

w Caryl Brahms, Ned Sherrin, play Girlfriend by David Percival d Bob Kellett ph Ian Wilson m John Scott

Joan Greenwood, Michael Hordern, Clive Francis, Patricia Routledge, Peter Bull, Rudolph Walker, Elizabeth Welch

Girl Trouble
US 1942   82m   bw

A South American in New York rents the apartment of a socialite who pretends to be his maid. Thin romantic comedy with half-hearted screwball touches. Don Ameche, Joan Bennett, Billie Burke, Frank Craven, Alan Dinehart. Written by Ladislas Fodor and Robert Riley Crutcher; directed by Harold Schuster; for Robert Bassler / TCF.

The Girl Who Couldn't Quite
GB 1950   85m   bw

Talk, that is. A tramp cures a teenager's amnesia and she fails to recognize him afterwards. Sentimental bosh from a mildly popular play of its time. Bill Owen, Iris Hoey, Elizabeth Henson, Betty Stockfield. Written by Norman Lee and Marjorie Deans, from the play by Leo Marks; directed by Norman Lee; for Argyle.

The Girl Who Couldn't Say No
Italy 1968   104m   Techniscope

A medical assistant has an on-off relationship with an eccentric girl. Downright peculiar romantic comedy with an American star all at sea in the Mediterranean. George Segal, Virna Lisi, Lila Kedrova. Written by Franco Brusati and Ennio de Concini; directed by Franco Brusati; for INC / PC / Fulcro. (Original title: Il Suo Modo di Fari.)

The Girl Who Had Everything
US 1953   69m   bw
MGM (Armand Deutsch)

The daughter of a wealthy criminal lawyer falls in love with one of her father's crooked clients.
Glossy melodrama of purely superficial interest.

w Art Cohn, novel Adela Rogers St John d Richard Thorpe ph Paul Vogel m André Previn

Elizabeth Taylor, William Powell, Fernando Lamas, Gig Young
† Remake of A Free Soul.

Girl with Green Eyes**
GB 1963   91m   bw
UA / Woodfall (Oscar Lewenstein)

An artless young Dublin girl falls for a middle-aged writer.
Lyrical romance which just about preserves its charm by good location sense.

w Edna O'Brien, from her novel The Lonely Girl d Desmond Davis ph Manny Wynn m John Addison

Peter Finch, Rita Tushingham, Lynn Redgrave
● Video: Thorn EMI

A Girl with Ideas
US 1937   70m   bw

A rich girl takes control of a daily paper which libelled her. Lively comedy on familiar lines. Wendy Barrie, Walter Pidgeon, Kent Taylor, George Barbier, Dorothea Kent, Samuel S. Hinds. Written by Bruce Manning, Robert T. Shannon; directed by S. Sylvan Simon; for Universal. 'Bright and original comedy, suitable for the more important first runs.'— Variety

Girlfriends*
US 1978   86m   Du Art
Cyclops (Claudia Weill, Jan Saunders)

A Jewish girl photographer in New York is ditched by her girl friend and considers men. Mild, amusing, well-observed little comedy-drama which goes nowhere in particular and slightly outstays its welcome.

w Vicki Polon d Claudia Weill ph Fred Murphy m Michael Small

Melanie Mayron, Eli Wallach, Anita Skinner, Bob Balaban

Les Girls*
US 1957   114m   Metrocolor
             Cinemascope
MGM (Sol. C. Siegel)

Two members of a girl dancing troupe sue over a memoir written by the third. Disappointing, talent-laden comedy-musical with a Rashomon-like flashback plot and a curious absence of the expected wit and style.

w John Patrick, novel Vera Caspary d George Cukor ph Robert Surtees m / ly Cole Porter ch Jack Cole

Gene Kelly, Kay Kendall, Mitzi Gaynor, Taina Elg, Jacques Bergerac, Leslie Phillips, Henry Daniell, Patrick MacNee
● Video: MGM / UA

Girls about Town
US 1931   80m   bw

Gold diggers find true love. A laugh, a tear

and a wisecrack in the big city: very dated, but may have seemed fresh at the time. Kay Francis, Joel McCrea, Lilyan Tashman, Eugene Pallette, Alan Dinehart, George Barbier. Written by Raymond Griffith, Brian Marlow from a story by Zoe Akins; directed by George Cukor; for Paramount. 'Generally only fair b.o. as ultra sophistication may be small-town setback.'—Variety

Girls' Dormitory*
US 1936   66m   bw
TCF

A college girl falls for her headmaster. Old-fashioned romance for nice young people, smoothly produced in the Fox mid-thirties manner.

w Gene Markey, story Ladislaus Fodor d Irving Cummings m Arthur Lange ph J. Merrit Gerstad

Herbert Marshall, Simone Simon, Ruth Chatterton, Constance Collier, J. Edward Bromberg, Dixie Dunbar, Tyrone Power

Girls, Girls, Girls
US 1962   106m   Technicolor
Wallis–Hazen (Hal B. Wallis)

A nightclub singer runs a fishing boat as a hobby.
Empty-headed, lighter than air vehicle for star fans.

w Edward Anhalt, Allan Weiss d Norman Taurog ph Loyal Griggs m Joseph J. Lilley

Elvis Presley, Stella Stevens, Laurel Goodwin, Jeremy Slate

Girls in the Night
US 1953   82m   bw

The son of a New York tenement family falls under suspicion of murder. Very mildly sensational low-life melodrama, like a citified Tobacco Road. Glenda Farrell, Harvey Lembeck, Joyce Holden, Glen Roberts, Don Gordon. Written by Ray Buffum; directed by Jack Arnold; for Universal. (GB title: Life After Dark.)

The Girls of Pleasure Island
US 1953   96m   Technicolor
Paramount (Paul Jones)

In 1945 the Marines land on a tiny Pacific island, disturbing the life of an English gentleman and his three inexperienced but beautiful daughters.
Tedious and wholly artificial comedy with a leaden touch, devised as a try-out for young talent.

w F. Hugh Herbert d F. Hugh Herbert, Alvin Ganzer ph Daniel Fapp m Lyn Murray

Leo Genn, Gene Barry, Don Taylor, Elsa Lanchester, Dorothy Bromiley, Audrey Dalton, Joan Elan

Girls on Probation
US 1937 62m bw

The child of wealthy parents is neglected. Formula social conscience piece, a programme filler. Dolores Costello, Bonita Granville, Natalie Moorehead, Donald Crisp, Emmett Vogan. Written by Lawrence Kimble from a story by Jean Negulesco; directed by Arthur Lubin; for Warners. 'A creditable job.'—*Variety*

Giro City°
GB 1982 102m colour
Silvarealm / Rediffusion / Channel 4
(Sophie Balhetchet, David Payne)

A television documentary team tries to present honest programmes about Ireland and about local government corruption.
Smartly made if somewhat predictably and stridently left-wing slice of so-called realism.

wd Karl Francis *ph* Curtis Clark *m* Alun Francis *ed* Kent Pan

Glenda Jackson, Jon Finch, Kenneth Colley, James Donnelly, Emrys James, Simon Jones

Giuseppina°
GB 1960 32m Technicolor

The daughter of an Italian petrol station proprietor has an amusing afternoon watching customers. Pleasing little Tatiesque sponsored comedy. Written, directed and produced by James Hill; for British Petroleum.

Give a Girl a Break°
US 1953 84m Technicolor
MGM (Jack Cummings)

A Broadway star walks out on a show and three girls audition as replacements.
Minor musical vehicle for the Champions; an agreeable time-passer.

w Frances Goodrich, Albert Hackett *d* Stanley Donen *ph* William Mellor *md* André Previn *songs* Ira Gershwin, Burton Lane *ch* Stanley Donen, Gower Champion

Marge and Gower Champion, Debbie Reynolds, Bob Fosse, Kurt Kasznar

Give Her a Ring
GB 1934 79m bw

A telephonist falls for her employer. Curious romantic comedy attempting to woo continental audiences. Clifford Mollison, Wendy Barrie, Zelma O'Neal, Erik Rhodes, Bertha Belmore, Stewart Granger (in a bit). Written by Clifford Grey, Ernst Wolff, Marjorie Deans and Wolfgang Wilhelm, from a play by H. Rosenfeld; directed by Arthur Woods; for BIP. 'Delightful and unassuming'—*National Film Theatre, 1970.*

Give Me a Sailor
US 1938 80m bw
Paramount (Jeff Lazarus)

An ugly girl envies her sister her beaux, but ends up winning a competition for beautiful legs.
One of the double bill comedies which got Bob Hope's career off to a shaky start.

w Doris Anderson, Frank Butler, *play* Anne Nichols *d* Elliott Nugent *ph* Victor Milner *md* Boris Morros *songs* Leo Robin, Ralph Rainger

Martha Raye, Bob Hope, Betty Grable, Jack Whiting, Clarence Kolb
'Not so funny farce.'—*Variety*

Give Me the Stars
GB 1944 90m bw

An American girl takes charge of her Scottish grandfather. Half-hearted comedy of the music halls. Will Fyffe, Leni Lynn, Jackie Hunter, Olga Lindo, Stanelli, Ronald Chesney. Written by Maclean Rogers and Austin Melford; directed by Maclean Rogers; for British National.

'Daringly intimate—it's strictly adult entertainment! The picture every woman will want some man to see!'

Give Me Your Heart
US 1936 88m bw

A socialite has a child by a married man. Dated tearjerker. Kay Francis, George Brent, Patric Knowles, Roland Young, Henry Stephenson, Frieda Inescort. Written by Casey Robinson, from the play *Sweet Aloes* by Joyce Carey; for Warner. (GB title: *Sweet Aloes*.)

Give My Regards to Broad Street°
GB 1984 108m colour
TCF / MPL (Andros Epimanondas)

An international rock star fears that the priceless tapes of his new album have been stolen, and searches London for them.
An absurdly thin premise even for a musical which is essentially an ego trip for Paul McCartney, who at least squandered his own money on it and not the bank's. Some of the numbers have merit but the mood never connects.

w Paul McCartney *d* Peter Webb *ph* Ian McMillan *m* Paul McCartney *pd* Anthony Pratt

Paul McCartney, Bryan Brown, Ringo Starr, Barbara Bach, Tracey Ullman, Ralph Richardson, George Martin, John Bennett

Give My Regards to Broadway°
US 1948 89m Technicolor
TCF (Walter Morosco)

An old-time vaudevillian yearns to get back into show business.
Pleasantly performed, sentimental family musical with familiar tunes.

w Samuel Hoffenstein, Elizabeth Reinhardt *d* Lloyd Bacon *ph* Harry Jackson

Dan Dailey, *Charles Winninger*, Fay Bainter, Charles Ruggles, Nancy Guild
'Vaudeville is dead. I wish to God someone would bury it.'—*James Agee*

Give Out, Sisters
US 1942 65m bw

For reasons of pure plot, the Andrews Sisters pose as wealthy old maids. One of scores of musical seconds produced by Universal at this time; this one has an unusually strong cast. The Andrews Sisters, Grace McDonald, Dan Dailey, Charles Butterworth, Walter Catlett, William Frawley, Donald O'Connor, Peggy Ryan. Written by Paul Gerard Smith and Warren Wilson; directed by Edward F. Cline; for Universal.

Give Us the Moon
GB 1944 95m bw
GFD / Gainsborough (Edward Black)

In post-war London a club is opened for idle members only.
Whimsical comedy which fell with a dull thud.

wd Val Guest, *novel* The Elephant is White by Caryl Brahms, S. J. Simon

Margaret Lockwood, Vic Oliver, Peter Graves, Max Bacon, Roland Culver, Frank Cellier, Jean Simmons

Give Us This Day
GB 1949 120m bw
Plantagenet (Rod E. Geiger, N. A. Bronsten)
US title: *Salt to the Devil*

Depression struggles of an Italian immigrant family in New York.
An unconvincing, self-pitying wallow, a very curious enterprise for a British studio.

w Ben Barzman, *story* Christ in Concrete by Pietro di Donato *d* Edward Dmytryk *ph* C. Pennington Richards *m* Benjamin Frankel

Sam Wanamaker, Lea Padovani, Kathleen Ryan, Charles Goldner, Bonar Colleano, William Sylvester, Karel Stepanek, Sidney James
'Dmytryk insisted on cutting the film himself and he has left in at least three spare reels.'—*Richard Winnington*
'Worth making and worth seeing, but cramped by its symbolism and its language.'—*Richard Mallett, Punch*

The Gladiator
US 1938 70m bw

A poor boy wins a prize and becomes a college football hero. Elementary star farce. Joe E. Brown, Man Mountain Dean, June Travis, Dickie Moore, Lucien Littlefield. Written by Charles Melson, Arthur Sheekman, from the novel by Philip Wylie; directed by Edward Sedgwick; for Columbia. 'Goofy but a lot of fun.'—*Variety*

Glamorous Night
GB 1937 81m bw
ABP (Walter C. Mycroft)

An opera singer and her gypsy friends save a Ruritanian king from his scheming prime minister.
Modest transcription of a popular stage musical.

w Dudley Leslie, Hugh Brooke, William Freshman, *play* Ivor Novello *d* Brian Desmond Hurst *m* Ivor Novello

Mary Ellis, Otto Kruger, Victor Jory, Barry Mackay, Trefor Jones

GIVE ME A SAILOR. Hope and Grable were on their way to stardom, but the rest didn't amount to very much, though Martha Raye had a long career on the second level.

Glamour

US 1934 74m bw
Universal

A day in the life of a Broadway star.
Competent minor entertainment.

w Doris Anderson, *story* Edna Ferber
d William Wyler *ph* George Robinson

Constance Cummings, Paul Lukas, Philip
Reed, Joseph Cawthorne, Doris Lloyd, Olaf
Hytten

'A good b.o. number with special pull for
the femmes.'—*Variety*

'Underwater . . . undercover . . . under any
  circumstances . . . you must see the
  wildest, funniest new comedy!'

The Glass Bottom Boat

US 1966 110m Metrocolor Panavision
MGM / Arwin–Reame (Martin Melcher)

A young widow gets involved with spies.
Frantic spy spoof, pleasantly set on the
Californian coast, but overflowing with
pratfalls, messy slapstick and pointless guest
appearances.

w Everett Freeman *d* Frank Tashlin *ph* Leon
Shamroy *m* Frank de Vol

Doris Day, Rod Taylor, Arthur Godfrey, Paul
Lynde, John McGiver, Edward Andrews, Eric
Fleming, Dom De Luise

'He carries his love in his iron fists!'

The Glass Key**

US 1935 87m bw
Paramount (E. Lloyd Sheldon)

A slightly corrupt but good-natured politician
is saved by his henchman from being
implicated in a murder.
Lively transcription of a zesty crime novel.

w Kathryn Scola, Kubec Glasmon, Harry
Ruskin, *novel* Dashiell Hammett *d* Frank
Tuttle *ph* Henry Sharp

Edward Arnold, George Raft, Claire Dodd,
Rosalind Keith, Guinn Williams, Ray Milland
'Will have to struggle to strike above-
average grosses.'—*Variety*

The Glass Key**

US 1942 85m bw
Paramount (Fred Kohlmar)

Nifty remake of the above which finds some
limited talents in their best form, helped by a
plot which keeps one watching.

w Jonathan Latimer *d* Stuart Heisler
ph Theodor Sparkuhl *m* Victor Young

Brian Donlevy, Alan Ladd, *Veronica Lake*,
Bonita Granville, *William Bendix*, Richard
Denning, Joseph Calleia, Moroni Olsen

  MADVIG (Brian Donlevy): 'I'm going to
  society. He's practically given me the key to
  his house.'
  BEAUMONT (Alan Ladd): 'Yeah, a glass
  key. Be sure it doesn't break up in your hand.'

The Glass Menagerie**

US 1950 107m bw
Warner (Jerry Wald, Charles K. Feldman)

A shy crippled girl seeks escape from the
shabby reality of life in St Louis and from her
mother's fantasies.
Pleasantly moody version of one of its author's
lighter and more optimistic plays; fluent and
good-looking production, memorable
performances.

w Tennessee Williams (with Peter Berneis)
from his play *d* Irving Rapper *ph* Robert
Burks *m* Max Steiner

Gertrude Lawrence, Jane Wyman, Kirk
Douglas, Arthur Kennedy
† For the TV movie starring Katharine
Hepburn, see *Television Companion*.

The Glass Mountain

GB 1949 98m bw
Victoria (John Sutro, Joseph Janni, Fred
Zelnik)

In the Dolomites, a married composer loves
an Italian girl who saved his life during the
war.
Tedious sudser, ineptly produced; an
enormous British box office success because of
its theme music.

w Joseph Janni, John Hunter, Emery Bonnet,
Henry Cass, John Cousins *d* Henry Cass
ph Otello Martelli, William McLeod *m* Nino
Rota

Michael Denison, Dulcie Gray, Valentina
Cortese, Tito Gobbi, Sebastian Shaw

The Glass Slipper

US 1954 94m Eastmancolor
MGM (Edwin H. Knopf)

The story of Cinderella.
To those used to the pantomime version this is
dull, dreary, high-flown stuff: limbo sets,
ballets, psychological rationalization and
virtually no comedy.

w / ly Helen Deutsch *d* Charles Walters
ph Arthur E. Arling *m* Bronislau Kaper
ch Roland Petit

Leslie Caron, Michael Wilding, Elsa
Lanchester, Barry Jones, *Estelle Winwood* (as
Fairy Godmother)

The Glass Sphinx

Spain / Italy 1968 98m colour

An archaeologist is in danger because of his
discoveries. Multi-national mish-mash only
notable as one of the last films of its star.
Robert Taylor, Anita Ekberg, Gianna Sera,
Jack Stuart. Written by Adriano Bolzoni and
Louis M. Heyward; directed by Fulvio
Lucisano; for AIP.

The Glass Web

US 1953 81m bw 3-D
U-I (A. J. Cohen)

A TV executive kills a blackmailing actress
and allows a young scriptwriter to be accused.
Boring thriller set in a TV studio.

w Robert Blees, Leonard Lee *d* Jack Arnold
ph Maury Gertsman *m* Joseph Gershenson

Edward G. Robinson, John Forsythe, Marcia
Henderson, Richard Denning

The Glenn Miller Story**

US 1954 116m Technicolor
U-I (Aaron Rosenberg)

The life of the unassuming trombonist and
bandleader whose plane disappeared during
World War II.
Competent musical heartwarmer with a well-
cast star and successful reproduction of the
Miller sound. A big box office hit.

w Valentine Davies, Oscar Brodney
d Anthony Mann *ph* William Daniels
md Henry Mancini, Joseph Gershenson

James Stewart, June Allyson, Harry Morgan,
Charles Drake, Frances Langford, Louis
Armstrong, Gene Krupa

AAN: script; music direction

A Global Affair

US 1963 84m bw
Seven Arts / Hall Bartlett

A United Nations official has to look after an
abandoned baby.
Flat sentimental farce which embarrassingly
tries to say something about the UN.

w Arthur Marx, Bob Fisher, Charles Lederer
d Jack Arnold *ph* Joseph Ruttenberg
m Dominic Frontière

Bob Hope, Lilo Pulver, Michèle Mercier,
Yvonne de Carlo
'Squaresville incarnate, with a side trip into
Leersville.'—*Judith Crist, 1973*

Gloria*

US 1980 121m Technicolor
Columbia (Sam Shaw)

In the Bronx, an innocent woman finds she has
to meet violence with violence in order to
protect a small boy from the mob.
Overlong but lively and oddly entertaining;
however, one is never quite sure what if
anything it is getting at.

wd John Cassavetes *ph* Fred Schuler *m* Bill
Conti

Gena Rowlands, John Adames, Bucky Henry

AAN: Gena Rowlands

Glorifying the American Girl*

US 1929 87m bw, colour sequence
Paramount (Florenz Ziegfeld)

A chorus girl rejects her boy friend for the
sake of stardom.
Archetypal show-must-go-on musical.

w J. P. McEvoy, Millard Webb *d* Millard
Webb, John Harkrider *ph* George Folsey
md Frank Tours

Mary Eaton, Edward Crandall; and as guests
Eddie Cantor, Helen Morgan, Rudy Vallee,
Florenz Ziegfeld, Adolph Zukor, Otto Kahn,
Texas Guinan, Mayor Jimmy Walker, Ring
Lardner, Noah Beery, Johnny Weissmuller

The Glorious Adventure*

GB 1921 100m (approx) Prizmacolor
  silent
Stoll / J. Stuart Blackton

Various lives are affected by the Great Fire of
London in 1666.

Stagey costume drama, notable only as the
first British film in colour.

w Felix Orman d J. Stuart Blackton
ph William T. Crespinal

Lady Diana Manners, Victor McLaglen,
Gerald Lawrence, Cecil Humphreys, Alex
Crawford, Lennox Pawle (as Pepys)

Glorious Betsy

US 1928 90m approx bw silent

Napoleon's younger brother loves an
American girl. Popular period romance of its
day. Conrad Nagel, Dolores Costello, John
Miljan, Betty Blythe. Written by Anthony
Coldeway, from the play by Rida Johnson
Young; directed by Alan Crosland; for
Warner. (NB: Remade as *Hearts Divided*.)

† The happy ending is not historical.

AAN: Anthony Coldeway

Glory

US 1955 100m Technicolor
  Superscope
RKO (David Butler)

Girl loves horse more than boy.
Conventional young love / Kentucky Derby
marshmallow.

w Peter Milne d David Butler ph Wilfrid
Cline m Frank Perkins

Margaret O'Brien, Walter Brennan, Charlotte
Greenwood, John Lupton

Glory Alley

US 1952 79m bw
MGM (Nicholas Nayfack)

A sullen young boxer has trouble with his girl,
her father and the demon rum.
Flat, boring second feature with musical
interludes.

w Art Cohn d Raoul Walsh ph William
Daniels md Georgie Stoll

Leslie Caron, Ralph Meeker, Kurt Kasznar,
Gilbert Roland, John McIntire, Louis
Armstrong, Jack Teagarden

'This is the kind of film that contains bits of
everything. New Orleans night life and an
episode of the Korean war; an arty French
ballet sequence and jazz from Louis
Armstrong; a boxer who acquired a neurosis
in childhood when his father hit him over the
head and a blind old father with a French
accent, who knows all about everything.'—
MFB

The Glory Brigade

US 1953 82m bw
TCF (William Bloom)

Greek soldiers fight in Korea alongside the
Americans.
Modest war adventure with predictable racial
tensions.

w Franklin Coen d Robert D. Webb
ph Lucien Andriot md Lionel Newman

Victor Mature, Alexander Scourby, Lee
Marvin, Richard Egan

The Glory Guys*

US 1965 112m De Luxe Panavision
UA / Levy–Gardner–Laven

Officers of the US cavalry disagree about
dealing with the Indians.
Standard big-budget western.

w Sam Peckinpah, *novel* The Dice of God by
Hoffman Birney d Arnold Laven ph James
Wong Howe m Riz Ortolani

Tom Tryon, Harve Presnell, Senta Berger,
Andrew Duggan, James Caan, Slim Pickens,
Michael Anderson Jnr

The Gnome-Mobile*

US 1967 90m Technicolor
Walt Disney (James Algar)

A millionaire and his family go for a forest
picnic and help a colony of gnomes.
Cheerful adventures for small children, with
good trick work.

w Ellis Kadison, *novel* Upton Sinclair
d Robert Stevenson ph Edward Colman
m Buddy Baker

Walter Brennan, Matthew Garber, Karen
Dotrice, Richard Deacon, Sean McClory, Ed
Wynn, Jerome Cowan, Charles Lane

The Go-Between**

GB 1970 116m Technicolor
EMI / World Film Services (John Heyman,
  Norman Priggen)

Staying at a stately home around the turn of
the century, 12-year-old Leo carries love
letters from a farmer to his friend's sister.
A rather tiresome plot sustains a rich picture
of the Edwardian gentry, a milieu with which
however the director is not at home and treats
far too slowly and tricksily.

w Harold Pinter, *novel* L. P. Hartley
d Joseph Losey ph *Geoffrey Fisher* m Michel
Legrand ad Carmen Dillon

Alan Bates, Julie Christie, Michael Redgrave,
Dominic Guard, Michael Gough, Margaret
Leighton, Edward Fox

'It's an almost palpable recreation of a past
environment, and that environment is the
film's real achievement, not the drama enacted
within it.'—*Stanley Kauffmann*

AAN: Margaret Leighton

● *Video: Thorn EMI*

Go Chase Yourself

US 1938 70m bw

A bank teller unwittingly aids robbers but
turns up trumps. Flat, limited comedy with a
star who didn't take. Joe Penner, Lucille Ball,
June Travis, Richard Lane, Fritz Feld, Tom
Kennedy. Written by Paul Yawitz, Bert
Granet; directed by Eddie Cline; for RKO.
'Aimed at the duals, where it will do a
modicum of biz.'—*Variety*

The Go-Getter

US 1937 90m bw
Warner (Sam Bischoff)

A one-legged navy veteran is determined that
his injury will not prevent him from becoming
a success.
Moderate comedy-drama, agreeably played.

w Delmer Daves, Peter B. Kyne d Busby
Berkeley ph Arthur Edeson md Leo F.
Forbstein

George Brent, Charles Winninger, Anita
Louise, John Eldredge, Henry O'Neill,
Willard Robertson, Eddie Acuff

'A fair amount of comedy within a story
bordering on the ridiculous.'—*Variety*

Go for a Take

GB 1972 90m colour
Rank / Century Films (Roy Simpson)

Two waiters in debt to a gangster take refuge
in a film studio.
Painful British farce.

w Alan Hackney d Harry Booth ph Mark
McDonald m Glen Mason

Reg Varney, Norman Rossington, Sue Lloyd,
Dennis Price, Julie Ege, Patrick Newell,
David Lodge

Go for Broke

US 1951 93m bw
MGM (Dore Schary)

World War II exploits of Japanese-American
soldiers.
Absolutely unsurprising war film with all the
anti-Japs converted by the end. Production
quite good.

wd Robert Pirosh ph Paul C. Vogel
m Alberto Columbo

Van Johnson, Lane Nakano, George Miki,
Akira Fukunaga, Warner Anderson, Don
Haggerty

AAN: Robert Pirosh (as writer)

Go into Your Dance**

US 1935 89m bw
Warner (Sam Bischoff)
GB title: *Casino de Paree*

A big-headed star gets his come-uppance and
finds happiness.
Moderate backstage musical notable for the
only teaming of Jolson and Keeler, who were
then married.

w Earl Baldwin d Archie Mayo ph Tony
Gaudio, Sol Polito songs Harry Warren, Al
Dubin

Al Jolson, Ruby Keeler, Glenda Farrell,
Benny Rubin, Phil Regan, Barton MacLane,
Sharon Lynne, Akim Tamiroff, Helen
Morgan, Patsy Kelly

'It has everything for the box office.'—
Variety

Go Man Go

US 1954 82m bw
Alfred Palca (Anton M. Leader)

How Abe Saperstein moulded and trained the
Harlem Globetrotters basketball team.
Not so much a film as an athletic
demonstration with some actors round the
edges.

w Arnold Becker d *James Wong Howe*
ph Bill Steiner m Alex North

Dane Clark, Sidney Poitier, Pat Breslin,
Edmond Ryan

Go Naked in the World
US 1960 103m Metrocolor
  Cinemascope
MGM / Arcola (Aaron Rosenberg)

A prostitute causes a rift between son and
millionaire father.
Antediluvian melodrama with overblown
performances.

wd Ranald MacDougall, *novel* Tom Chanales
ph Milton Krasner *m* Adolph Deutsch

Gina Lollobrigida, Tony Franciosa, Ernest
Borgnine, Luana Patten, Will Kuluva, Philip
Ober
  'A good example of how the increased
liberation of Hollywood can be misused.'—
MFB

Go Tell the Spartans
US 1978 114m CFI color
Spartan Company (Allan F. Badah, Mitchell
  Cannold)

In Vietnam, a seasoned commander tries to
get a platoon of raw soldiers out of a Vietcong
ambush.
We have been here before, in other wars, and
since there is little heroism to be had from
Vietnam it is difficult to see why we are invited
again.

w Wendell Mayes, *story* Daniel Ford *d* Ted
Post *ph* Harry Stradling Jnr *m* Dick Halligan

Burt Lancaster, Craig Wasson, Jonathan
Goldsmith, Marc Singer

Go to Blazes
GB 1961 84m Technicolor
  Cinemascope
ABP (Kenneth Harper)

Ex-convicts become firemen, intending to use
the engine for smash and grab raids.
Mild comedy ruined by wide screen.

w Patrick Campbell, Vivienne Knight
d Michael Truman *ph* Erwin Hillier *m* John
Addison

Dave King, Daniel Massey, Norman
Rossington, Wilfrid Lawson, Maggie Smith,
Robert Morley, Coral Browne

Go West°
US 1925 70m (24 fps) bw silent
Metro-Goldwyn / Buster Keaton (Joseph M.
  Schenck)

A tenderfoot makes friends with a cow and
takes it everywhere.
Disappointingly slow star comedy with
splendid moments.

w Raymond Cannon *d* Buster Keaton
ph Bert Haines, E. Lessley

Buster Keaton, Howard Truesdall, Kathleen
Myers

Go West°°
US 1940 82m bw
MGM (Jack Cummings)

Three zanies tackle a western villain.
Minor Marx comedy with a good start (the
ticket office sketch) and a rousing finale as
they take a moving train to bits, but some
pretty soggy stuff in between.

w Irving Brecher *d* Edward Buzzell
ph Leonard Smith *m* Bronislau Kaper
md Georgie Stoll

Groucho, Harpo, Chico, John Carroll, Diana
Lewis, Robert Barrat

Go West Young Lady
US 1940 70m bw

A lawless western town expects a sheriff who
turns out to be a girl. Mildly pleasing variation
on *Destry Rides Again*. Glenn Ford, Penny
Singleton, Charles Ruggles. Written by Karen
de Wolf and Richard Flournoy; directed by
Frank Strayer; for Columbia.

'How you gonna keep 'em down on the
  farm, after they've seen Mae West?'

Go West Young Man
US 1936 80m bw
Paramount (Emanuel R. Cohen)

A movie star has a car breakdown in
Pennsylvania and falls for a local lad.
Cleaned-up Mae West vehicle, all rather
boring.

w Mae West, *play* Personal Appearance by
Lawrence Riley *d* Henry Hathaway *ph* Karl
Struss *m* George Stoll

Mae West, Randolph Scott, Warren William,
Lyle Talbot, Alice Brady, Isabel Jewell,
Elizabeth Patterson
  'On the way to snug profits.'—*Variety*
  'Quite incredibly tedious, as slow and
wobbling in its pace as Miss West's famous
walk. The wisecracks lack the old impudence,
and seldom have so many feet of film been
expended on a mere dirty look.'—*Graham
Greene*

God Is My Co-Pilot
US 1945 89m bw
Warner (Robert Buckner)

Pacific air adventures during World War II.
Adequate flagwaver.

w Peter Milne, Abem Finkel, *book* Col.
Robert Lee Scott Jnr *d* Robert Florey *ph* Sid
Hickox *m* Franz Waxman

Dennis Morgan, Dane Clark, Raymond
Massey, Alan Hale, Andrea King, John
Ridgely, Stanley Ridges, Craig Stevens
  'A slapped-together attraction . . . all the
flashbacks, supposedly emotional scenes, and
fragments of philosophy which punctuate the
aerial action vitiate a tale which might have
been a notable addition to the screen's
extensive considerations of the far-flung
theatres of the war.'—*Howard Barnes, New
York Herald Tribune*

God Is My Partner
US 1957 82m bw Regalscope

A surgeon retires and begins to give his money
away to religious causes; members of his
family file suit against him. Rather obvious
fable in the *Mr Deeds* tradition. Walter
Brennan, John Hoyt, Marion Ross, Jesse
White. Written by Charles Francis Royal;
directed by William F. Claxton; for Sam
Hersh / TCF.

God Told Me To
US 1976 89m colour

A detective investigates the death of a mad
sniper and finds it to be a case of demonic
possession. Unsavoury mix of several genres,
insufficiently well written to compel. Tony Lo
Bianco, Deborah Raffin, Sandy Dennis, Sylvia
Sidney, Sam Levene, Robert Drivas, Richard
Lynch, Harry Bellaver. Written, directed and
produced by Larry Cohen; for Larco. (GB
title: *Demon*.)

The Goddess°
US 1958 105m bw
Columbia (Milton Perlman)

A small-town girl becomes a Hollywood sex
symbol and lives to regret it.
Savage attack on the Marilyn Monroe cult, a
bit lachrymose and compromised by
miscasting, but with interesting detail.

w Paddy Chayevsky *d* John Cromwell
ph Arthur J. Ornitz *m* Virgil Thompson

Kim Stanley, Lloyd Bridges, Steven Hill,
Betty Lou Holland

AAN: Paddy Chayevsky

The Godfather°°°
US 1972 175m Technicolor
Paramount / Alfran (Albert S. Ruddy)

When, after ruling for two generations, the
Mafia's New York head dies of old age, his
son takes over reluctantly but later learns how
to kill.
A brilliantly-made film with all the fascination
of a snake pit: a warm-hearted family saga
except that the members are thieves and
murderers. Cutting would help, but the duller
conversational sections do heighten the
cunningly judged moments of suspense and
violence.

w Francis Ford Coppola, Mario Puzo, *novel*
Mario Puzo *d* Francis Ford Coppola
ph Gordon Willis *m* Nino Rota *pd* Dean
Tavoularis

Marlon Brando (unintentionally comic in an
absurd make-up), Al Pacino, Robert Duvall,
James Caan, Richard Castellano, Diane
Keaton, Talia Shire, Richard Conte, John
Marley
  'The immorality lies in his presentation of
murderers as delightful family men—the
criminal is the salt of the earth—and to our
shame we rub it into the wounds of our
Watergate-world morality and even ask for
more.'—*Judith Crist, 1974*
  'They have put pudding in Brando's cheeks
and dirtied his teeth, he speaks hoarsely and
moves stiffly, and these combined mechanics
are hailed as great acting . . . Like star, like
film, the keynote is inflation. *The Godfather*
was made from a big bestseller, a lot of money
was spent on it, and it runs over three hours.
Therefore it's important.'—*Stanley Kauffmann*

AA: best picture; script; Marlon Brando
AAN: Francis Ford Coppola (as director); Al
Pacino; Robert Duvall; James Caan

● *Video: CIC*

GO WEST YOUNG MAN. Mae West tried the rustic life, but it really didn't suit her.

The Godfather, Part Two***
US 1974   200m   Technicolor
Paramount / the Coppola Company
  (Francis Ford Coppola)

In 1958, Michael Corleone reflects on the
problems of himself and his father before him.
Curious rehash of part of the original with new
scenes, a shade difficult to follow but full of
good scenes and performances.

w Francis Ford Coppola, Mario Puzo
d Francis Ford Coppola ph Gordon Willis
m Nino Rota pd Dean Tavoularis

Al Pacino, Robert de Niro, Diane Keaton,
Robert Duvall, John Cazale, Lee Strasberg,
Michael V. Gazzo, Talia Shire, Troy Donahue
  'The complete work is an epic vision of the
corruption of America.'—New Yorker
† The two films were eventually combined and
extended for television into a ten-hour serial,
The Godfather Saga.

AA: best picture; script; Francis Ford
Coppola (as director); Nino Rota; Robert de
Niro
AAN: Al Pacino; Lee Strasberg; Michael V.
Gazzo; Talia Shire

God's Country and the Woman
US 1936   80m   Technicolor
Warner (Lou Edelman)

The junior partner of a lumber company goes
to work undercover in an opponent's camp,
causes trouble, and falls in love.
Adequate outdoor melodrama in early colour.

w Norman Reilly Raine, novel James Oliver
Curwood d William Keighley ph Tony
Gaudio m Max Steiner

George Brent, Beverly Roberts, Barton
MacLane, Robert Barrat, Alan Hale, Addison
Richards, El Brendel, Roscoe Ates, Billy
Bevan
  'Great outdoors in Technicolor, but not
likely for much b.o.'—Variety

God's Gift to Women
US 1931   72m   bw

In Paris, a descendant of Don Juan is pursued
by numerous women but falls for an American
girl. Tedious comedy with a star out of his
element. Frank Fay, Joan Blondell, Laura la
Plante, Charles Winninger, Louise Brooks.
Written by Joseph Jackson and Raymond
Griffith from the play The Devil Was Sick by
Jane Hinton; directed by Michael Curtiz; for
Warners. 'No gift to audiences.'—Variety

'The story that no one dared film till now
  becomes the most adult motion picture
  ever made!'
God's Little Acre*
US 1958   110m   bw
Security (Sidney Harmon)

A poor white farmer in Georgia neglects his
land in a fruitless search for gold.
Tobacco Road under another name, and not
so lively: bowdlerized and eventually tedious
despite a welter of sensational incident and
depraved characters.

w Philip Yordan, novel Erskine Caldwell
d Anthony Mann ph Ernest Haller m Elmer
Bernstein

Robert Ryan, Aldo Ray, Tina Louise, Buddy
Hackett, Jack Lord, Vic Morrow, Rex Ingram
● Video: Video Unlimited

The Gods Must Be Crazy
South Africa 1980   109m   colour
Panavision

A Coca Cola bottle falls from a plane and
becomes a religious object to Kalahari
bushmen. Unexpected throwback farce with
the blacks behaving almost as stupidly as
Mantan Moreland in an old Charlie Chan
movie. One for the Race Relations Board.
N'Xau, Marius Weyers, Sandra Prinsloo.
Written, directed and produced by Jamie Uys;
for Mimosa / CAT.

'The gospel according to today!'
Godspell*
US 1973   102m   TVC color
Columbia / Lansbury / Duncan / Beruh
  (Edgar Lansbury)

The Gospel according to St Matthew played
out musically by hippies in the streets of New
York.
Wild and woolly film version of the successful
theatrical fantasy, surviving chiefly by virtue of
its gleaming photography.

w David Greene, John Michael Tebelak,
play John Michael Tebelak d David Greene
ph Richard G. Heimann m / ly Stephen
Schwarz

Victor Garber, David Haskell, Jerry Sroka,
Lynne Thigpen, Robin Lamont
  'A patch of terra incognita somewhere
between Sesame Street and the gospel
according to Laugh-In.'—Bruce Williamson

Godzilla
Japan 1955   80m (dubbed version)   bw
Toho (Tomoyuki Tanaka)
original title: Gojira

A prehistoric monster is awakened by H-bomb
tests and menaces Tokyo.
Tepid forerunner of scores of Japanese
monster movies peopled by men in rubber
suits.

w Takeo Murato, Inoshiro Honda d Inoshiro
Honda

Raymond Burr, Takashi Shimura, Momoko
Kochi
† Sequels included Godzilla vs the Thing, King
Kong vs Godzilla, Godzilla vs the Sea
Monster, Godzilla vs the Smog Monster,
Destroy All Monsters. Other monstrous
creations included Rodan, Manda and Mothra.

Gog*
US 1954   85m   Color Corporation   3D
Ivan Tors

In an underground laboratory in New Mexico,
a giant computer controls two robots, and a
spy programmes it to kill.
Brisk, imaginative low-budget sci-fi in
gleaming colour, well staged and developed.

w Tom Taggart d Herbert B. Strock
ph Lothrop B. Worth m Harry Sukman

Richard Egan, Constance Dowling, Herbert
Marshall

Goha
France / Tunisia 1957   90m   Agfacolor
Films Franco-Africains

A young Arab helps a blind musician and falls
in love with a wise man's young bride.
Curiously winning, good-looking little
romance which, apart from an unexpected sad
ending, plays like an update of the Arabian
Nights.

w Georges Schéhadé, novel Le Livre de Goha
le Simple by A. Ades, A. Jospiovici
d Jacques Baratier ph Jean Bourgoin
m Maurice Ohana

Omar Chérif (later Sharif), Zina Bouzaiane,
Lauro Gazzolo

Going Bye Bye**
US 1934   20m   bw

A violent convict escapes to take vengeance
on the two innocents whose evidence sent him
up. Splendid star comedy displaying most of
the team's most endearing aspects. Laurel and
Hardy, Walter Long, Mae Busch. Written by
Anon; directed by Charles Rogers; for Hal
Roach.

Going Highbrow
US 1935   68m   bw

Two nouveaux riches people try to trick their
way into society. Agreeably cast farce that
outstays its welcome. Edward Everett Horton,
Guy Kibbee, Zasu Pitts, Ross Alexander,
Judy Canova. Written by Edward Kaufmann,
Sy Bartlett, Ralph Spence; directed by Robert
Florey; for Warners. 'So-so flicker for the
lesser spots.'—Variety

Going Hollywood*
US 1933   80m   bw

A crooner is pursued by a girl who poses as a
French maid. Lively comedy with a studio
setting; anything goes. Bing Crosby, Marion
Davies, Patsy Kelly, Stuart Erwin. Written by
Donald Ogden Stewart; directed by Raoul
Walsh; for MGM. 'Lavishly produced musical
with everything but a story.'—Variety

Going Home
US 1971   98m   colour

An ex-convict who killed his wife while drunk
assumes an ambivalent relationship with his
son. Thoroughly uninteresting melodrama
which was barely released. Robert Mitchum,
Jan-Michael Vincent, Brenda Vaccaro.
Written by Lawrence Marcus; directed by
Herbert B. Leonard; for MGM.

Going in Style
US 1979   97m   Technicolor
Warner / Tony Bill

Three bored elderly men decide to plan a bank
robbery.

Curiously aimless sentimental comedy-drama which is simply neither funny enough, thrilling enough or moving enough to hold the interest.

wd Martin Brest *ph* Billy Williams *m* Michael Small

George Burns, Art Carney, Lee Strasberg

Going My Way**
US 1944 126m bw
Paramount (Leo McCarey)

A young priest comes to a New York slum parish and after initial friction charms the old pastor he is to succeed.

Sentimental comedy which got away with it wonderfully at the time, largely through careful casting, though it seems thin and obvious now.

w Frank Butler, Frank Cavett, Leo McCarey *d* Leo McCarey *ph* Lionel Lindon *m* Robert Emmett Dolan *songs* Johnny Burke, James Van Heusen, J. R. Shannon

Bing Crosby, Barry Fitzgerald, Rise Stevens, Frank McHugh, James Brown, Gene Lockhart, Jean Heather, Porter Hall

'I should not feel safe in recommending it to anyone but a simple-hearted sentimentalist with a taste for light music.'—*Richard Mallett, Punch*

'The lessons, if I read them right, are that leisureliness can be excellent, that if you take a genuine delight in character the universe is opened to you, and perhaps above all that a movie, like any other genuine work of art, must be made for love. But I am willing to bet that the chief discernible result of *Going My Way* will be an anxiety-ridden set of vaudeville sketches about Pat and Mike in cassocks.'—*James Agee*

† Father O'Malley reappeared in *The Bells of St Mary's* and *Say One for Me* (both qv).

AA: best picture; script; original story (Leo McCarey); Leo McCarey (direction); Bing Crosby; Barry Fitzgerald; song, 'Swinging on a Star' (*m* James Van Heusen, *ly* Johnny Burke)
AAN: Lionel Lindon

Going Places
US 1939 84m bw

A sporting goods salesman poses as a jockey and has to ride a horse to victory. Thin musical spurred by the hit song 'Jeepers Creepers'. Dick Powell, Anita Louise, Ronald Reagan, Louis Armstrong, Allen Jenkins, Walter Catlett. Written by Jerry Wald, Sig Herzig and Maurice Leo, from the play *The Hottentot* (filmed thrice previously) by Victor Mapes and William Collier; directed by Ray Enright; for Warner. 'Satisfactory but not smash.'—*Variety*.

AAN: song 'Jeepers Creepers', by Al Dubin and Harry Warren.

Goin' South
US 1978 101m Metrocolor
Paramount (Henry Gittes, Harold Schneider)

An unwashed outlaw is saved from the rope when a young girl promises to marry and reform him . . .

. . . for no very good reason. Curious semi-comic western which might have made a good two-reeler.

w John Herman Shaner, Al Ramrus, Charles Shyer, Alan Mandel *d* Jack Nicholson *ph* Nestor Almendros *m* Van Dyke Parks, Perry Botkin Jnr

Jack Nicholson, Mary Steenburgen, Christopher Lloyd, John Belushi, Veronica Cartwright, Richard Bradford

● *Video: CIC*

'Mae's a lady now and she'll lick anyone in the house who says she ain't!'
Goin' to Town*
US 1935 74m bw
Paramount (William Le Baron)

A western oil heiress moves into society. Reasonably satisfactory Mae West vehicle, but not in the old bawdy style.

w Mae West *d* Alexander Hall *ph* Karl Struss *songs* Sammy Fain, Irving Kahal

Mae West, Paul Cavanagh, Ivan Lebedeff, Tito Coral, Marjorie Gateson, Fred Kohler Snr, Monroe Owsley

'No amount of epigrammatic hypoing can offset the silly story.'—*Variety*

Gold*
Germany 1934 105m bw

Scientists invent a machine that will make synthetic gold. Overlong melodrama made in German and French, boring when the equipment is off the screen. Hans Albers, Brigg Helm, Lien Deyers, Michael Bohnen. Written by Rolf E. Vanloo; directed by Karl Hartl; for UFA.

NB: the central sequences were reused years later for the climax of *The Magnetic Monster* (qv).

Gold**
GB 1974 124m Technicolor
      Panavision
Hemdale / Avton (Michael Klinger)

A South African mining engineer falls for the boss's granddaughter and exposes a conspiracy.

Old-fashioned thick ear with spectacular underground sequences and a rousing finale.

w Wilbur Smith, Stanley Price, *novel* Goldmine by Wilbur Smith *d* Peter Hunt *ph* Ousama Rawi *m* Elmer Bernstein

Roger Moore, Susannah York, Ray Milland, Bradford Dillman, John Gielgud, Tony Beckley

AAN: song 'Wherever Love Takes Me' (*m* Elmer Bernstein, *ly* Don Black)

● *Video: VCL*

Gold Diggers of Broadway*
US 1929 98m Technicolor
Warner

Three Broadway chorus girls seek rich husbands.

Fascinating primitive musical.

w Robert Lord, *play* The Gold Diggers by Avery Hopwood *d* Roy del Ruth *ph* Barney McGill, Ray Rennahan *songs* Al Dubin, Joe Burke

Nancy Welford, Conway Tearle, Winnie Lightner, Ann Pennington, Lilyan Tashman, William Bakewell, Nick Lucas

'Exceeds in pretentiousness and beauty anything which has yet appeared on the screen!'—*publicity*
† Other versions of the play include *The Gold Diggers* (1923), *Gold Diggers of 1933* (qv), *Painting the Clouds with Sunshine* (qv).

Gold Diggers of 1933***
US 1933 96m bw
Warner (Robert Lord)

Cheerful, competent, well-cast remake of the above; numbers include 'My Forgotten Man', 'We're in the Money' and 'Pettin' in the Park'.

w Erwin Gelsey, James Seymour, David Boehm, Ben Markson *d* Mervyn Le Roy *ch* Busby Berkeley *songs* Harry Warren, Al Dubin *ph* Sol Polito

Warren William, Joan Blondell, Aline MacMahon, Ruby Keeler, Dick Powell, Guy Kibbee, Ned Sparks, Ginger Rogers, Clarence Nordstrom

'It sums up what is meant by the phrase "pure thirties": electrically wired chorus girls singing "In the Shadows Let Me Come and Sing to You" merge to form a big illuminated violin.'—*New Yorker, 1979*

'It is memorable chiefly because Busby Berkeley created a mad geometry of patterned chorines. . . . The innocent vulgarity of the big numbers is charming and uproarious, and aesthetically preferable to the pretentious ballet finales of fifties musicals like *An American in Paris*. Even those of us who were children at the time did not mistake *Gold Diggers* for art—and certainly no one took it for life.'—*Pauline Kael, 1968*

'Your dream of perfect beauty come true!'—*publicity*

Gold Diggers of 1935**
US 1935 95m bw
Warner (Robert Lord)

A socialite puts on a Broadway show at her country home, and is taken in by a swindler. Heavy-handed but laugh-provoking comedy with familiar faces of the day, climaxed by big numbers including 'Lullaby of Broadway'.

w Manuel Seff, Peter Milne, Robert Lord *d* / *ch* Busby Berkeley *ph* George Barnes *songs* Al Dubin, Harry Warren

Dick Powell, Adolphe Menjou, Gloria Stuart, Alice Brady, Hugh Herbert, Glenda Farrell, Frank McHugh, Grant Mitchell, Wini Shaw

'Busby Berkeley, the master of scenic prestidigitation, continues to dazzle the eye and stun the imagination.'—*André Sennwald, New York Times*

'A decidedly heady mixture.'—*Pare Lorentz*

AA: song 'Lullaby of Broadway'

Gold Diggers of 1937*
US 1936 100m bw
Warner (Hal B. Wallis)

A group of insurance salesmen back a show.
Mild tailing-off of the Gold Diggers series,
though with the accustomed production
polish.

w Warren Duff, *play* Richard Maibaum,
Michael Wallach, George Haight *d* Lloyd
Bacon *ch Busby* Berkeley *ph* Arthur Edeson
songs Harry Warren, Al Dubin, E. Y. Harburg,
Harold Arlen

Dick Powell, Joan Blondell, Glenda Farrell,
Victor Moore, Lee Dixon, Osgood Perkins,
Charles D. Brown

Gold Diggers in Paris*
US 1938 95m bw
Warner (Sam Bischoff)
GB title: *The Gay Imposters*

Three girls chase rich husbands abroad.
A thin end to the series, saved by an agreeable
cast.

w Earl Baldwin, Warren Duff *d* Ray Enright
ph Sol Polito, George Barnes *ch Busby
Berkeley songs* Harry Warren, Al Dubin,
Johnny Mercer

Rudy Vallee, Rosemary Lane, Hugh Herbert,
Allen Jenkins, Gloria Dickson, Melville
Cooper, Fritz Feld, Ed Brophy, Curt Bois

Gold Dust Gertie
US 1931 66m bw

A tough divorcee tries to sponge on her
former spouses. Silly and unattractive comedy.
Winnie Lightner, Chic Johnson, Ole Olsen,
Dorothy Carlisle, Claude Gillingwater.
Written by W. K. Wells and Ray Enright;
from the play The Life of the Party by Len D.
Hollister; directed by Lloyd Bacon; for
Warners. 'Roughest kind of comedy dialogue;
in need of careful surgery.'—*Variety*

Gold Is Where You Find It*
US 1938 90m Technicolor
Warner (Sam Bischoff)

Gold rush miners settle as California farmers.
Agreeable western in excellent early colour.

w Warren Duff, Clements Ripley, Robert
Buckner *d* Michael Curtiz *ph* Sol Polito
m Max Steiner

George Brent, Olivia de Havilland, Claude
Rains, Margaret Lindsay, John Litel, Marcia
Ralston, Barton MacLane, Tim Holt, Sidney
Toler

Gold of Naples
Italy 1955 135m bw
Ponti-de Laurentiis
original title: *L'Oro di Napoli*

Six sketches, comic and tragic, give an
impression of Naples today.
A variable collection, mainly shown around
the world in abridged versions.

w Cesare Zavattini, Vittorio de Sica,
Giuseppe Marotta *d* Vittorio de Sica
ph Otello Martelli *m* Alessandro Cicognini

Vittorio de Sica, Eduardo de Filippo, Toto,
Sophia Loren, Paolo Stoppa, Silvana Mangano

Gold of the Seven Saints
US 1961 89m bw Warnerscope
Warner (Leonard Freeman)

Cowboys compete in a search for lost gold.
Adequate minor western using TV stars.

w Leigh Brackett, Leonard Freeman
d Gordon Douglas *ph* Joseph Biroc
m Howard Jackson

Clint Walker, Roger Moore, Leticia Roman,
Robert Middleton, Chill Wills, Gene Evans

The Gold Rush***
US 1925 72m (sound version 1942) bw
Charles Chaplin

A lone prospector in the Yukon becomes rich
after various adventures.
Essentially a succession of slowly but carefully
built visual gags, this is Chaplin's finest
example of comedy drawn from utter
privation; as such it appealed vastly to the
poor of the world. As a clown, Chaplin
himself is near his best, though as usual there
is rather too much straining for pathos.

w, d, p, m *Charles Chaplin ph* Rollie
Totheroh, Jack Wilson

Charles Chaplin, Georgia Hale, Mack Swain,
Tom Murray

● Video: *Spectrum*

The Golden Age of Buster Keaton**
US 1975 97m bw
Jay Ward (Raymond Rohauer)

A useful introductory package to the shorts
and features of Buster Keaton, with most of
the great silent scenes present.

commentary Bill Scott

The Golden Age of Comedy****
US 1957 78m bw
Robert Youngson Productions

First of the scholarly compilations of silent
comedy which saved many negatives from
destruction, this is a fast-paced general survey
which despite a facetious sound track does
provide a laugh a minute. It particularly
brought Laurel and Hardy back into public
notice, and includes sections from *Two Tars*
and *The Battle of the Century*.

wd Robert Youngson *narrators* Dwight
Weist, Ward Wilson *m* George Steiner

Stan Laurel, Oliver Hardy, Harry Langdon,
Ben Turpin, Will Rogers, Billy Bevan, Charlie
Chase, Andy Clyde

Golden Arrow
US 1936 68m bw

An heiress tricks a newspaper reporter into a
marriage of convenience. Dull, schematic
romantic comedy. Bette Davis, George Brent,
Eugene Pallette, Dick Foran. Written by
Charles Kenyon, from the play by Michael
Arlen; directed by Alfred E. Green; for
Warner.

Golden Arrow
GB 1949 82m bw

On a transcontinental train, three men have
different daydreams about the same girl.

Transparent portmanteau comedy which didn't
click. Jean Pierre Aumont, Paula Valenska,
Richard Murdoch, Kathleen Harrison, Karel
Stepanek, Edward Lexy. Written by Paul
Darcy and Sid Colin; directed by Gordon
Parry; for Anatole de Grunwald. (Alternative
title: *Three Men and a Girl*.)

The Golden Blade
US 1953 80m Technicolor
U-I (Richard Wilson)

With the help of a magic sword, Harun saves a
princess and captures a rebel.
Standard cut-rate Arabian Nights adventure,
very typical of its studio during the fifties.

w John Rich *d* Nathan Juran *ph* Maury
Gertsman *m* Joseph Gershenson

Rock Hudson, Piper Laurie, George
Macready, Gene Evans, Kathleen Hughes

Golden Boy*
US 1939 101m bw
Columbia (William Perlberg)

A poor boy is torn between two absorbing
interests: prizefighting and the violin.
Personalized version of a socially conscious
play; moderately effective with smooth
production and good cast.

w Lewis Meltzer, Daniel Taradash, Sarah Y.
Mason, Victor Heerman, *play* Clifford Odets
d Rouben Mamoulian *ph* Nicholas Musuraca,
Karl Freund *m* Victor Young *md* Morris
Stoloff

Barbara Stanwyck, *William Holden*, Adolphe
Menjou, Joseph Calleia, *Lee J. Cobb*, Sam
Levene, Edward Brophy, Don Beddoe

'Strong entertainment with general audience
appeal.'—*Variety*
  'A slick, swift, exciting but insensitive
movie.'—*Gordon Sager*
  'Interesting, entertaining, dramatic, but
scarcely first-rate.'—*Frank Nugent, New York
Times*

AAN: Victor Young

The Golden Coach
Italy / France 1953 100m Technicolor
Hoche / Panaria (Valentine Brosio,
   Giuseppe Bordognoi)
original title: *Le Carrosse d'Or*

In Spanish South America in the 18th century,
the leading lady of a band of strolling players
turns all heads including that of the viceroy,
who scandalizes all by making her a present of
his official golden coach.
The director seems to have been chiefly
interested in the colour and the backgrounds:
the story is a bore and the leading lady
ill-chosen.

w Jean Renoir, Jack Kirkland, Renzo Avanzo,
Giulio Macchi, *play* Prosper Merimée *d* Jean
Renoir *ph* Claude Renoir *m* Vivaldi

Anna Magnani, Duncan Lamont, Paul
Campbell, Ricardo Rioli, William Tubbs

Golden Dawn
US 1930 81m Technicolor

An English regiment holds the blacks at bay.
An operetta outmoded even in 1930, stagily
brought to the screen. Walter Woolf, Vivienne
Segal, Noah Beery, Alice Gentle, Lupino

Lane. Adapted by Walter Anthony; songs by Emmerich Kalman and Herbert Stothart; directed by Ray Enright; for Warners.

'Everybody seems to sing, even Noah Beery in blackface.'—*Variety*

'Now you know the way a gypsy loves!'
Golden Earrings*
US 1947   95m   bw
Paramount (Harry Tugend)

A British Intelligence officer is helped by a gypsy to sneak a poison gas formula out of Nazi Germany.

One of the silliest stories of all time, despite the presence of Quentin Reynolds asserting that he believed it; also lacking in the humour which might have saved it, but produced with polish and interesting for the two stars at this stage in their careers.

w Abraham Polonsky, Frank Butler, Helen Deutsch, *novel* Yolanda Foldes d *Mitchell Leisen* ph Daniel L. Fapp m Victor Young

Ray Milland, Marlene Dietrich, Murvyn Vye, Bruce Lester, Dennis Hoey, Reinhold Schuntzel, Ivan Triesault

'A good deal of torso work goes on which I can't help feeling they're a bit old for.'—*Richard Winnington*

The Golden Fleecing
US 1940   84m approx   bw

A timid insurance salesman becomes embroiled with gangsters. Modestly effective double-bill comedy. Lew Ayres, Lloyd Nolan, Virginia Grey, Leon Errol, Rita Johnson, Nat Pendleton, William Demarest, Marc Lawrence. Written by S. J. and Laura Perelman; directed by Edgar Selwyn; for MGM.

Golden Girl*
US 1951   108m   Technicolor
TCF (George Jessel)

The story of Lotta Crabtree, who after the Civil War determined to become a great musical star.

Harmless semi-western biopic with good tunes.

w Walter Bullock, Charles O'Neal, Gladys Lehman d Lloyd Bacon ph Charles G. Clarke md Lionel Newman ch Seymour Felix

Mitzi Gaynor, Dale Robertson, Dennis Day, James Barton, Una Merkel, Raymond Walburn, Gene Sheldon

AAN: song 'Never' (m Lionel Newman, ly Eliot Daniel)

Golden Gloves
US 1939   69m   bw

A sports reporter cleans up a boxing racket. Competent second feature. Richard Denning, Jeanne Cagney, William Frawley, Robert Ryan. Written by Maxwell Shane and Lewis R. Foster; directed by Edward Dmytryk; for Paramount.

The Golden Hawk
US 1952   83m   Technicolor

A pirate determines to avenge his mother's death at the hands of the governor of

Cartagena. Clean-cut period romp for boys who don't demand realism. Sterling Hayden, Rhonda Fleming, John Sutton, Helena Carter, Paul Cavanagh. Written by Robert E. Kent, from the novel by Frank Yerby; directed by Sidney Salkow; for Columbia.

The Golden Head
US / Hungary 1964   115m
     Technirama 70
Cinerama / Hungarofilm (Alexander Paal)

Passengers on a Danube pleasure boat become involved in the theft of the golden head of St Laszlo.

Travelogue with a thin plot, somewhat slow moving but suitable for children.

w Stanley Boulder, Ivan Boldizsar d Richard Thorpe ph Istvan Hildebrand m Peter Fenyes

George Sanders, Buddy Hackett, Douglas Wilmer, Jess Conrad, Robert Coote

The Golden Horde
US 1951   76m   Technicolor
U-I (Howard Christie)
aka: *The Golden Horde of Genghis Khan*

Crusaders meet Mongols in Samarkand, and Sir Guy wins a princess.

Rather priceless idiocies are perpetrated in this variation on the studio's favourite Arabian Nights theme, but somehow they fail to make one laugh, which should be the only possible response to such a farrago.

w Gerald Drayson Adams d George Sherman ph Russell Metty m Hans Salter

David Farrar, Ann Blyth, George Macready, Henry Brandon, Richard Egan, Marvin Miller

The Golden Madonna
GB 1949   88m   bw
IFP / Pendennis (John Stafford)

Two young people search Italy for a religious painting stolen by thieves.

Stilted but eager to please, this romantic comedy-drama seemed a bit lacking in drive.

w Akos Tolnay d Ladislas Vajda ph Anchise Brizzi

Phyllis Calvert, Michael Rennie, Tullio Carminati, David Greene, Aldo Silvani

The Golden Mistress*
US 1954   80m   Technicolor
UA / RK (Richard Kay, Harry Rybnick)

An American and his girl friend search the sea bed for the forbidden treasure of a Haitian tribe.

Curious independent production, an adventure in the style of silent serials; amateur in many ways, yet with a freshness of photography and location plus some powerful voodoo scenes.

wd Fred Judge ph William C. Thompson m Raoul Kraushaar

John Agar, Rosemarie Bowe, Abner Biberman

'Whoever owns them can rule the world!'
Golden Needles
US 1974   92m   Movielab   Panavision
AIP / Sequoia (Fred Weintraub, Paul Heller)

Various factions seek a Hong Kong statue

showing seven miraculous acupuncture points. Youth / sex / Kung Fu / James Bond action amalgam.

w S. Lee Pogostin, Sylvia Schneble d Robert Clouse ph Gilbert Hubbs m Lalo Schifrin

Joe Don Baker, Elizabeth Ashley, Jim Kelly, Burgess Meredith, Ann Sothern

Golden Rendezvous
US 1977   109m   colour
Film Trust / Milton Okun (Andre Pieterse)

Murderous mercenaries take over a freighter, but reckon without the courageous first officer. Blood-and-thunder hokum with many casualties but not much sense.

w Stanley Price, *novel* Alistair MacLean d Ashley Lazarus ph Ken Higgins m Jeff Wayne

Richard Harris, Ann Turkel, David Janssen, Burgess Meredith, John Vernon, Gordon Jackson, Keith Baxter, Dorothy Malone, John Carradine, Robert Flemyng, Leigh Lawson, Robert Beatty

● *Video: Rank*

The Golden Salamander
GB 1949   87m   bw
GFD / Pinewood (Ronald Neame, Alexander Galperson)

An Englishman in Tunis defeats gun runners. Boring and unconvincing action hokum.

w Lesley Storm, Victor Canning, Ronald Neame, *novel* Victor Canning d Ronald Neame ph Oswald Morris m William Alwyn

Trevor Howard, Anouk Aimée, Herbert Lom, Miles Malleson, Walter Rilla, Jacques Sernas, Wilfrid Hyde White, Peter Copley

The Golden Seal*
US 1983   94m   Metrocolor
Samuel Goldwyn Jnr (Russell Thatcher)

On a bleak Aleutian island a boy stops hunters from killing a seal once thought mythical. Rather chilling and thinly plotted moral fable for children, who may, however, be bored. The seals, the scenery and the music just about save it.

w John Groves, *novel* A River Ran Out of Eden by James Vance Marshall d Frank Zuniga ph Eric Saarinen m Dana Kaproff, John Barry

Steve Railsback, Michael Beck, Penelope Milford, Torquil Campbell

The Golden Voyage of Sinbad*
GB 1973   105m   Eastmancolor
Columbia / Morningside (Charles H. Schneer)

Sinbad finds a strange map and crosses swords with a great magician.

Routine, rather uninspired fantasy enlivened by grotesque trick effects.

w Brian Clemens, Ray Harryhausen d Gordon Hessler ph Ted Moore m Miklos Rozsa sp Ray Harryhausen pd John Stoll

John Philip Law, Caroline Munro, Tom Baker, Douglas Wilmer, Grégoire Aslan

Goldfinger***
GB 1964 112m Technicolor
UA / Eon (Harry Saltzman, Albert R.
  Broccoli)

James Bond prevents an international gold
smuggler from robbing Fort Knox.
Probably the liveliest and most amusing of the
Bond spy spoofs, with a fairly taut plot
between the numerous highlights. The big
budget is well used.

w Richard Maibaum, Paul Dehn, novel Ian
Fleming d Guy Hamilton ph Ted Moore
m John Barry pd Ken Adam titles Robert
Brownjohn

Sean Connery, Honor Blackman, Gert Frobe,
Harold Sakata, Shirley Eaton, Bernard Lee,
Lois Maxwell, Desmond Llewellyn

 'A dazzling object lesson in the principle
that nothing succeeds like excess.'—Penelope
Gilliatt
 'A diverting comic strip for grown-ups.'—
Judith Crist

● Video: Warner

The Goldwyn Follies**
US 1938 115m Technicolor
Samuel Goldwyn

A Hollywood producer seeks the average girl
to test his scripts.
Goldwyn's failure to become Ziegfeld, chiefly
due to a lack of humour in the script, still has
a soupçon of effective Hollywood satire and
some excellent numbers.

w Ben Hecht d George Marshall ph Gregg
Toland m Alfred Newman ch George
Balanchine ad Richard Day

Kenny Baker, Vera Zorina, the Ritz Brothers,
Adolphe Menjou, Edgar Bergen and Charlie
McCarthy, Helen Jepson, Phil Baker, Ella
Logan, Bobby Clark, Jerome Cowan, Nydia
Westman, Andrea Leeds

 'An advance glimpse at next Sunday's
amusement section from any metropolitan
newspaper.'—Variety
 'The bizarre in musical pretentiousness.'—
Commonweal
 'Many features to suit all tastes and not
enough of them to suit anybody's.'—Time

AAN: Alfred Newman

The Golem***
Germany 1920 75m approx bw silent
UFA

In 16th-century Prague a Jewish Rabbi
constructs a man of clay to defend his people
against a pogrom.
There were several versions of this story
(Germany 1913, sequel 1917; Czechoslovakia
1935 and 1951), but this is almost certainly the
best, its splendid sets, performances and
certain scenes all being clearly influential on
later Hollywood films, especially Frankenstein.

w Paul Wegener, Henrik Galeen d Paul
Wegener, Carl Boese ph Karl Freund, Guido
Seeber ad Hans Poelzig

Paul Wegener, Albert Steinruck, Ernst
Deutsch

The Golem*
Czechoslovakia 1936 95m bw

Rather disappointing remake with entirely
French crew. Harry Baur, Roger Karl,
Ferdinand Hart, Charles Dorat. Written by
André Paul Antoine and Julien Duvivier;
directed by Julien Duvivier; for AB.
'Sequences are scattered; there's no build-up,
and no human interest is created.'—Variety

The Golf Specialist**
US 1930 18m bw

A film version of W. C. Fields in his classic
vaudeville golfing sketch (also reprised in
You're Telling Me). Directed by Monte Brice;
for RKO.

Golgotha*
France 1935 100m bw

The trial and passion of Jesus Christ.
Impressive version made at a time when the
portrayal of Christ was still virtually taboo.
Harry Baur (Herod), Jean Gabin (Pilate),
Robert le Vigan (Jesus), Charles Granval
(Caiaphas), Edwige Feuillère (Claudia).
Written and directed by Julien Duvivier; music
by Jacques Ibert; for D'Agular. 'An
accomplishment that should bring world-wide
prestige to the French film industry.'—Variety

Gone to Earth
GB 1948 110m Technicolor
London Films / David O. Selznick
US title: The Wild Heart

In the 1890s, a wild Shropshire girl is desired
by the local squire.
Unintentionally funny film version of an
intractable novel.

w / p / d Michael Powell and Emeric
Pressburger, novel Mary Webb
ph Christopher Challis m Brian Easdale
pd Hein Heckroth

Jennifer Jones, David Farrar, Cyril Cusack,
Esmond Knight, Sybil Thorndike, Edward
Chapman, George Cole, Hugh Griffith,
Beatrice Varley

 'It tries hard to be a powerful work of art,
but it is intrinsically artificial and
pretentious.'—Richard Mallett, Punch

Gone with the Wind****
US 1939 220m Technicolor
MGM / David O. Selznick

An egotistic Southern girl survives the Civil
War but finally loses the only man she cares
for.
The only film in history which could be
profitably revived for forty years: 'still pure
gold', said the Daily Mirror in 1975. Whole
books have been written about it; its essential
appeal is that of a romantic story with strong
characters and an impeccable production. The
widescreen version produced in the late sixties
ruined its composition and colour, but it is to
be hoped that the original negative still
survives.

w Sidney Howard (and others), novel
Margaret Mitchell d Victor Fleming (and
George Cukor, Sam Wood) ph Ernest Haller,

Ray Rennahan m Max Steiner pd William
Cameron Menzies ad Lyle Wheeler

Clark Gable, Vivien Leigh, Olivia de
Havilland, Leslie Howard, Thomas Mitchell,
Barbara O'Neil, Hattie McDaniel, Butterfly
McQueen, Victor Jory, Evelyn Keyes, Ann
Rutherford, Laura Hope Crews, Harry
Davenport, Jane Darwell, Ona Munson, Ward
Bond

 'A major event in the history of the industry
but only a minor event in motion picture art.
There are moments when the two categories
meet on good terms, but the long stretches
between are filled with mere spectacular
efficiency.'—Franz Hoellering, The Nation
 'Shakespeare's The Taming of the Shrew
seems to have got mixed up with one of the
novels of Ethel M. Dell.'—James Agate
 'Perhaps the key plantation movie.'—Time
Out, 1980
 'Forget it, Louis, no Civil War picture ever
made a nickel.'—Irving Thalberg to Louis B.
Mayer, 1936
† The best account of the film's making is in
Gavin Lambert's 1975 book, GWTW.
†† In the early seventies a stage musical
version toured the world; music by Harold
Rome.

AA: best picture; Sidney Howard; Victor
Fleming; Ernest Haller, Ray Rennahan; Lyle
Wheeler; Vivien Leigh; Hattie McDaniel; Hal
C. Kern and James E. Newcom (editors)
AAN: Max Steiner; Clark Gable; Olivia de
Havilland

● Video: MGM / UA

The Good Companions***
GB 1932 113m bw
Gaumont / Welsh–Pearson (T. A. Welsh,
  George Pearson)

Three ill-assorted people take to the road and
in various capacities join the Dinky Doos
pierrot troupe.
Gallant, mini-budgeted version of Priestley's
popular picaresque novel. A little faded now,
it retains some of its vigour, and the
performances please.

w W. P. Lipscomb, Angus Macphail, Ian
Dalrymple novel J. B. Priestley d Victor
Saville ph Bernard Knowles

Edmund Gwenn, Mary Glynne, John Gielgud,
Jessie Matthews, Percy Parsons, A. W.
Baskomb, Dennis Hoey, Richard Dolman,
Frank Pettingell, Finlay Currie, Max Miller,
Jack Hawkins, George Zucco

The Good Companions*
GB 1956 104m Technicolor
  Cinemascope
ABP (Hamilton Inglis, J. Lee-Thompson)

Faint-hearted remake of the above, unwisely
Cinemascoped and leaving no impression.

w T. J. Morrison d J. Lee-Thompson
ph Gilbert Taylor m Laurie Johnson

Eric Portman, Celia Johnson, John Fraser,
Janette Scott, Hugh Griffith, Bobby Howes,
Rachel Roberts, John Salew, Thora Hird
† A stage musical version (music by André
Previn) had moderate success in London in
1974.

Good Dame
US 1934   77m   bw

A penniless chorus girl falls for a cardsharp.
Unsurprising pattern play for two miscast
stars. Sylvia Sidney, Fredric March, Jack La
Rue, Noel Francis, Russell Hopton. Written
by William K. Lipman, Vincent Lawrence,
Frank Partos and Sam Hellman; directed by
Marion Gering; for Paramount. (GB title:
Good Girl.)

Good Day for a Hanging
US 1959   85m   Columbia Color

A young outlaw is arrested and seems destined
to be lynched; the marshal tries to see fair
play. Moody western in which the protected
hero turns out to be very guilty after all. Fred
MacMurray, Robert Vaughn, Maggie Hayes,
Joan Blackman, James Drury. Written by
Daniel B. Ullman and Maurice Zimm;
directed by Nathan Juran; for Columbia.

The Good Die Young*
GB 1954   98m   bw
Remus (Jack Clayton)

Four crooks, all with private problems, set out
to rob a mail van.
Glum all-star melodrama which set a pattern
for such things; worth waiting for is the
climactic chase through underground stations.

w Vernon Harris, Lewis Gilbert *d* Lewis
Gilbert *ph* Jack Asher *m* Georges Auric

Laurence Harvey, Margaret Leighton, Gloria
Grahame, Richard Basehart, Joan Collins,
John Ireland, René Ray, Stanley Baker,
Robert Morley

● *Video: CBS / Fox*

'To the memory of Irving Grant Thalberg
   we dedicate this picture—his last great
   achievement!'

The Good Earth***
US 1937   138m   bw
MGM (*Irving Thalberg*)

A Chinese peasant grows rich but loses his
beloved wife.
A massive, well-meaning and fondly
remembered production which is nevertheless
artificial, unconvincing and pretty undramatic
in the second half. The star performances
impress to begin with, then wear thin, but the
final locust attack is as well done as it
originally seemed. Historically valuable as a
Hollywood prestige production of the thirties.

w Talbot Jennings, Tess Schlesinger, Claudine
West, *play* Owen and Donald Davis, *novel*
Pearl S. Buck *d* Sidney Franklin *ph* Karl
Freund *m* Herbert Stothart *montage* Slavko
Vorkapitch *ad* Cedric Gibbons

Paul Muni, *Luise Rainer*, Walter Connolly,
Tilly Losch, Jessie Ralph, Charley Grapewin,
Keye Luke, Harold Huber

'A true technical achievement with names
enough to send it across. But it's not going to
be easy to get the three-million-dollar
investment back. And if it does come back it's
going to take a long time.'—*Variety*

'One of the superb visual adventures of the
period.'—*John Baxter, 1968*
'Prestigious boredom, and it goes on for a
very long time.'—*New Yorker, 1977*
AA: Karl Freund; Luise Rainer
AAN: best picture; Sidney Franklin

The Good Fairy*
US 1935   90m   bw
Universal (Henry Henigson)

A beautiful but naïve cinema usherette
ensnares three rich men.
Unusual, rather lumpy romantic comedy using
top talent.

w Preston Sturges, *play* Ferenc Molnar
d William Wyler *ph* Norbert Brodine

Margaret Sullavan, Herbert Marshall, Frank
Morgan, Reginald Owen, Alan Hale, Beulah
Bondi, Cesar Romero, Eric Blore, Al Bridge

'It's rather slapsticking a master but it's for
the box office. Will not please those who
cherish memories of the play but it will please
a more important audience.'—*Variety*
† Remade as *Because of Him* (qv).

The Good Fellows
US 1943   70m   bw

A family man spends too much time with his
fraternal order. Mild, pleasant family comedy.
Cecil Kellaway, Helen Walker, James Brown,
Mabel Paige. Written by Hugh Wedlock Jnr
and Howard Snyder, from a play by George S.
Kaufman and Herman Mankiewicz; directed
by Jo Graham; for Paramount.

Good Girls Go To Paris*
US 1939   75m   bw
Columbia (William Perlberg)

After several zany adventures, a Greek
professor marries a gold digger.
Amusingly crazy comedy, one of the last of its
type.

w Gladys Lehman, Ken Englund *d* Alexander
Hall *ph* Henry Freulich *md* Morris Stoloff

Melvyn Douglas, Joan Blondell, Walter
Connolly, Alan Curtis, Joan Perry, Isabel
Jeans, Alexander D'Arcy, Clarence Kolb

'It can't stand analysis much, but it pleases
while you're there.'—*Variety*

The Good Guys and the Bad Guys*
US 1969   90m   Technicolor   Panavision
Warner (Robert M. Goldstein)

An ageing sheriff and a train robber have one
last showdown.
Good-humoured, black-flavoured western set
in the early days of automobiles.

w Ronald M. Cohen, Dennis Shyrack *d* Burt
Kennedy *ph* Harry Stradling Jnr *m* William
Lava

Robert Mitchum, George Kennedy, David
Carradine, Tina Louise, Douglas Fowley,
Martin Balsam, Lois Nettleton, John Davis
Chandler, John Carradine, Marie Windsor

Good Morning Boys**
GB 1937   79m   bw
GFD / Gainsborough (Edward Black)

A schoolmaster takes his troublesome pupils

to Paris and becomes involved with an art
theft.
Sprightly vehicle for the star's seedy
schoolmaster persona: it established him as a
major draw in British films.

w Marriott Edgar, Val Guest, Anthony
Kimmins *d* Marcel Varnel

Will Hay, Graham Moffatt, Lilli Palmer, Mark
Daly, Peter Gawthorne, Martita Hunt,
Charles Hawtrey, Will Hay Jnr
† Remade with Ronald Shiner as *Top of the
Form.*

Good Morning Miss Dove
US 1955   107m   Eastmancolor
   Cinemascope
TCF (Samuel G. Engel)

While recovering from an operation, a small-
town schoolmistress looks back on her career.
A fairly spirited weepie with a happy ending
and a strong sense of cynicism behind the
scenes.

w Eleanore Griffin, *novel* Frances Gray
Patton *d* Henry Koster *ph* Leon Shamroy
m Leigh Harline

Jennifer Jones, Robert Stack, Robert
Douglas, Kipp Hamilton, Peggy Knudsen,
Marshall Thompson, Chuck Connors, Mary
Wickes

'Mr Chips has changed sex and habitat while
preserving intact his ability to provoke
epidemics of sentimentality.'—*MFB*

Good Neighbour Sam
US 1964   130m   Eastmancolor
Columbia / David Swift

A prissy suburban advertising man becomes
innocently involved in a pretence to be the
husband of the divorcee next door.
A promising comic idea is here ruined by
lengthiness, lack of funny lines, and no
apparent idea of how to film a farce. The
actors are driven to repeating every trick a
dozen times.

w James Fritzell, Everett Greenbaum, David
Swift, *novel* Jack Finney *d* David Swift
ph Burnett Guffey *m* Frank de Vol

Jack Lemmon, Romy Schneider, Dorothy
Provine, Senta Berger, Edward G. Robinson,
Mike Connors, Edward Andrews, Louis Nye

Good News
US 1930   85m approx   bw
MGM

Fraternity tensions are sorted out in time for
the big football game.
Spirited early talkie musical.

w Frances Marion, Joe Farnham *d* Nick
Grinde, Edgar McGregor *ph* Percy Hilburn
songs De Sylva, Brown and Henderson

Bessie Love, Stanley Smith, Gus Shy, Mary
Lawlor, Lola Lane, Dorothy McNulty, Cliff
Edwards

Songs: 'He's a Ladies' Man'; 'The Best Things
in Life Are Free'; 'Varsity Drag'; 'Good
News'; 'Tait Song'; 'Students Are We'; 'If
You're Not Kissing Me'; 'Football'; 'I Feel
Pessimistic'; 'I'd Like to Make You Happy'

'Not the smash hit the show was. Too fast, too peppy, too entertaining to flop, though.'—
Variety

Good News*
US 1947 83m Technicolor
MGM (Arthur Freed)

Bright, good-humoured remake of the above.

w Betty Comden, Adolph Green *d* Charles Walters *ph* Charles Schoenbaum *md* Lennie Hayton

June Allyson, Peter Lawford, Patricia Marshall, *Joan McCracken*, Mel Tormé

AAN: song 'Pass that Peace Pipe' (*m / ly* Ralph Blane, Hugh Martin, Roger Edens)

The Good Old Days
GB 1939 79m bw
Warner

A noble child is kidnapped by a chimney sweep and saved by strolling players.
Curious Victorian vehicle for a snappy 20th-century star.

w Austin Melford, John Dighton *d* Roy William Neill

Max Miller, Hal Walters, Kathleen Gibson, H. F. Maltby, Martita Hunt, Allan Jeayes, Roy Emerton

Good Old Soak
MGM 1937 67m bw

A small-town drunk beats a teetotal banker guilty of a shady transaction. Amiable star comedy. *Wallace Beery*, Una Merkel, Eric Linden, Judith Barrett, Betty Furness, Janet Beecher, Robert McWade, Margaret Hamilton. Written by A. E. Thomas from the play The Old Soak by Don Marquis; directed by J. Walter Ruben; for MGM. 'A melodramatic sentimentality that will probably do okay.'—*Variety*

Good Sam
US 1948 114m bw
Rainbow (Leo McCarey)

A small-town business man is so charitable that he finds himself bankrupt.
Poor, disjointed, overlong and obvious comedy in the Capra style.

w Ken Englund *d* Leo McCarey *ph* George Barnes *m* Robert Emmett Dolan

Gary Cooper, Ann Sheridan, Ray Collins, Edmund Lowe, Joan Lorring, Ruth Roman, Clinton Sundberg
'A bit too long, but in its incidentals often very enjoyable.'—*Richard Mallett, Punch*

Good Time Girl
GB 1948 93m bw

A girl escapes from a remand home and starts on the road to ruin.
Risible vehicle for a rising star; at the time it set the box offices clicking. Jean Kent, Dennis Price, Flora Robson, Griffith Jones, Herbert Lom, Bonar Colleano. Written by Muriel and Sidney Box and Ted Willis, from the novel *Night Darkens the Street* by Arthur La Bern; directed by David MacDonald; for Triton / Rank.

The Good, the Bad and the Ugly
Italy 1966 180m Techniscope
PEA (Alberto Grimaldi)
original title: *Il Buono, il Bruto, il Cattivo*

During the American Civil War, three men seek hidden loot.
Intermittently lively, very violent, and interminably drawn out western with a number of rather hilarious stylistic touches.

w Age Scarpelli, Luciano Vincenzoni, Sergio Leone *d* Sergio Leone *ph* Tonino delli Colli *m* Ennio Morricone

Clint Eastwood, Eli Wallach, Lee Van Cleef

● Video: Intervision

Goodbye Again
US 1933 66m bw

An author's secretary is jealous of his rekindled interest in an old flame. Unassuming star comedy which entertained at the time. Warren William, Joan Blondell, Genevieve Tobin, Hugh Herbert, Helen Chandler, Ruth Donnelly. Written by Ben Markson, from the play by George Haight and Allan Scott; directed by Michael Curtiz; for Warner. (NB: *Honeymoon for Three* in 1941 [qv] was a leaden remake.)

Goodbye Again*
US 1961 120m bw
UA / Mercury / Argus / Anatole Litvak

A woman of forty swaps her rich lover for a young law student.
Melancholy romantic drama, well produced and staged on Paris locations.

w Samuel Taylor, *novel* Aimez-vous Brahms by Françoise Sagan *d* Anatole Litvak *ph Armand Thirard m* Georges Auric

Ingrid Bergman, Anthony Perkins, Yves Montand, Jessie Royce Landis, Jackie Lane
'A grey-toned Sagan novella, spread wide and lush over two hours of screen time.'—*MFB*
'The kind of "woman's picture" that gives women a bad name.'—*Judith Crist, 1973*

Goodbye Charlie*
US 1964 116m De Luxe Cinemascope
TCF / Venice (David Weisbart)

A philandering gangster, shot dead by an irate husband, is reincarnated in his friend's house as a dishy blonde.
Overlong but amusing Broadway comedy for wisecrackers, uninventively adapted.

w Harry Kurnitz, *play* George Axelrod *d* Vincente Minnelli *ph* Milton Krasner *m* André Previn

Debbie Reynolds, Pat Boone, Walter Matthau, Tony Curtis

'Every father's daughter is a virgin!'

Goodbye Columbus**
US 1969 105m Technicolor
Paramount / Willow Tree (Stanley Jaffe)

A young Jewish librarian has an affair with the wilful daughter of a *nouveau riche* family.
An amusing and well-observed delineation of two kinds of Jewish life in New York; the

story, despite its frank talk of penises and diaphragms, leaves much to be desired, and the style is post-*Graduate*.

w Arnold Schulman, *novel* Philip Roth *d* Larry Peerce *ph* Gerald Hirschfeld *m* Charles Fox

Richard Benjamin, Ali MacGraw, Jack Klugman, Nan Martin, Michael Meyers, Lori Shelle

AAN: Arnold Schulman

Goodbye Gemini
GB 1970 89m colour
Cinerama / Josef Shaftel (Peter Snell)

A 20-year-old brother and sister share a world of petulant fantasy which leads to murder. Abysmally over-the-top melodrama with a swinging London backdrop. Its immaculate appearance only makes matters worse.

w Edmund Ward, *novel* Ask Agamemnon by Jenni Hall *d* Alan Gibson *ph* Geoffrey Unsworth *m* Christopher Gunning *pd* Wilfrid Shingleton

Judy Geeson, Martin Potter, Michael Redgrave, Alexis Kanner, Mike Pratt, Freddie Jones, Peter Jeffrey

'Every man she ever loved thought a permanent relationship was a three-day weekend!'
The Goodbye Girl*
US 1977 110m Metrocolor
Warner / Rastar (Ray Stark)

A misunderstanding about the lease of an apartment results in a girl dancer agreeing to share it with a would-be actor.
A very moderate script assisted by excellent acting and the usual array of Neil Simon one-liners. Nothing at all new, but enjoyable.

w Neil Simon *d* Herbert Ross *ph* David M. Walsh *m* Dave Grusin

Richard Dreyfuss, Marsha Mason, Quinn Cummings, Paul Benedict, Barbara Rhoades

AA: Richard Dreyfuss
AAN: best picture; Neil Simon; Marsha Mason; Quinn Cummings

● Video: Warner

Goodbye Mr Chips***
GB 1939 114m bw
MGM (Victor Saville)

The life of a shy schoolmaster from his first job to his death.
Sentimental romance in MGM's best style, a long-standing favourite for its performances and humour; but the production seems slightly unsatisfactory these days.

w R. C. Sherriff, Claudine West, Eric Maschwitz, *novel* James Hilton *d* Sam Wood *ph* Frederick A. Young *m* Richard Addinsell

Robert Donat, Greer Garson, Paul Henreid, Lyn Harding, Austin Trevor, Terry Kilburn, John Mills, Milton Rosmer, Judith Furse

'Charming, quaintly sophisticated . . . more for the big situations than the smaller towns.'—*Variety*

'The whole picture has an assurance, bears a glow of popularity like the face of a successful candidate on election day. And it is wrong to despise popularity in the cinema.'—*Graham Greene*

'The picture has no difficulty in using two hours to retell a story that was scarcely above short story length. *Mr Chips* is worth its time.'—*New York Times*

'The novel became an American best seller when that old sentimentalist Alexander Woollcott touted it on the radio . . . the movie clogs the nose more than necessary.'—*Pauline Kael, 70s*

AA: Robert Donat

AAN: best picture; script; Sam Wood; Greer Garson

'He is a shy schoolmaster. She is a music hall star. They marry and immediately have 283 children—all boys!'

Goodbye Mr Chips*
GB 1969   147m   Metrocolor
Panavision 70
MGM / APJAC (Arthur P. Jacobs)

Elaborate musical remake of the above. Slow and slushy, with no improvement visible whatever; but a few of the trimmings please.

w Terence Rattigan *d* Herbert Ross
ph Oswald Morris *m* Leslie Bricusse *pd* Ken Adam *ad* John Williams

Peter O'Toole, Petula Clark, Michael Bryant, Michael Redgrave, George Baker, Jack Hedley, Sian Phillips, Alison Leggatt

'The sum total is considerably less than the parts.'—*Variety*

'An overblown version with songs where they are not needed (and Leslie Bricusse's songs are never needed).'—*Pauline Kael, New Yorker*

† Originally sought for the title role, in order of preference, were Richard Burton and Rex Harrison; for the female lead, Samantha Eggar and Lee Remick.

AAN: Leslie Bricusse; John Williams; Peter O'Toole

Goodbye My Fancy
US 1951   107m   bw
Warner (Henry Blanke)

A congresswoman returns to her old college for an honorary degree, and falls in love. Tolerable romantic flim-flam.

w Ivan Goff, Ben Roberts, *play* Fay Kanin
d Vincent Sherman *ph* Ted McCord
m Daniele Amfitheatrof

Joan Crawford, Robert Young, Frank Lovejoy, Eve Arden, Janice Rule

Goodbye My Lady*
US 1956   95m   bw
Batjac

A Mississippi swamp boy finds a valuable dog but eventually returns it to its owner. Reliable, slightly unusual family film.

w Sid Fleischman, *novel* James Street
d William Wellman *ph* William H. Clothier, Archie Stout *m* Laurindo Almeida, George Field

ENTER THE WEIRD, TERRIFYING WORLD OF THE GEMINI TWINS!

CINERAMA RELEASING presents   A JOSEF SHAFTEL PRODUCTION
JUDY GEESON · MARTIN POTTER · ALEXIS KANNER
MICHAEL REDGRAVE
"GOODBYE GEMINI"
MIKE PRATT · FREDDIE JONES · EDMUND WARD   screenplay by Ask Agamemnon   from the novel by JENNI HALL   executive producer JOSEF SHAFTEL
produced by PETER SNELL · ALAN GIBSON   directed by   FROM CINERAMA RELEASING   COLOR   [R]
Original Soundtrack Available on DJM Records.

GOODBYE GEMINI.   An eccentric relic of swinging London, this psychopathic nonsense was a strange waste of Michael Redgrave.

Brandon de Wilde, Walter Brennan, Phil Harris, Sidney Poitier, William Hopper, Louise Beavers

The Goodbye People

US 1984 104m De Luxe

Middle-aged eccentrics meet on a beach. Saroyanesque talk piece which never quite comes off, and will probably be seen only at festivals. Martin Balsam, Judd Hirsch, Pamela Reed, Ron Silver, Michael Tucker, Gene Saks. Written and directed by Herb Gardner, from his stage play; for Coney Island Productions.

Goodbye Pork Pie*

New Zealand 1980 105m Eastmancolor
NZ Film Commission / NZ United
  Corporation / Nigel Hutchinson, Geoff
  Murphy

Three young people go on an illegal road spree and are arrested one by one.
Familiar high jinks with a moral conclusion. Fun up to a point, and good to look at.

w Geoff Murphy, Ian Mune d Geoff Murphy ph Alun Bollinger m John Charles

Tony Barry, Kelly Johnson, Claire Oberman
  'Displays encouraging physical flair in its cross-country sweep of action.'—*Tim Pulleine, MFB*

● *Video: Brent Walker*

Goodnight Vienna

GB 1933 76m bw
British and Dominions (Herbert Wilcox)
US title: *Magic Night*

In 1913 Vienna, a general's son falls for a shopgirl.
Already dated when it was made, this thin musical romance nevertheless made a star of Anna Neagle and re-established Jack Buchanan on the screen.

w Holt Marvel, George Posford, from their radio play d Herbert Wilcox ph F. A. Young

Jack Buchanan, Anna Neagle, Gina Malo, Clive Currie, William Kendall

The Goose and the Gander

US 1935 65m bw

A divorcee can't leave her ex-husband's life alone. Tolerable farcical goings-on which just fail to come to the boil. Kay Francis, George Brent, Genevieve Tobin, John Eldredge, Claire Dodd. Written by George Kenyon; directed by Alfred E. Green; for Warners. 'Well-played little farce with too much story for its own good.'—*Variety*

The Goose Steps Out*

GB 1942 79m bw
Ealing (S. C. Balcon)

To steal a secret weapon, an incompetent teacher is sent into Germany in place of his Nazi double.
Quite amusing star vehicle, not up to his best standards.

w Angus Macphail, John Dighton d Will Hay, Basil Dearden ph Ernest Palmer m Bretton Byrd

Will Hay, Charles Hawtrey, Frank Pettingell, Julien Mitchell, Peter Croft, Jeremy Hawk, Peter Ustinov, Raymond Lovell, Barry Morse

The Goose Woman

US 1925 90m approx bw silent
Universal

A young actress falls for the son of an embittered old one.
Interesting character melodrama of which prints have survived.

w Melville Brown, *story* Rex Beach d Clarence Brown ph Milton Moore

Louise Dresser, Jack Pickford, Constance Bennett, James Barrows

Gordon's War

US 1973 90m TVC color
TCF / Palomar (Robert L. Schaffel)

A black Vietnam veteran returns to Harlem and avenges the death of his wife.
Violent vigilante melodrama with vivid locations.

w Howard Friedlander, Ed Spielman d Ossie Davis ph Victor J. Kemper m Andy Bodale, Al Ellis

Paul Winfield, Carl Lee, David Downing

'An unbeatable cast in an unequalled drama! Metro's successor to The Great Ziegfeld!'

The Gorgeous Hussy*

US 1936 105m bw
MGM (Joseph L. Mankiewicz)

The love life of Peggy O'Neal, protégée of President Andrew Jackson.
Bowdlerized all-star historical drama; the production values are better than the script.

w Ainsworth Morgan, Stephen Morehouse Avery, *novel* Samuel Hopkins Adams d Clarence Brown ph George Folsey m Herbert Stothart

Joan Crawford, Lionel Barrymore, Franchot Tone, Melvyn Douglas, Robert Taylor, James Stewart, Alison Skipworth, Louis Calhern, Beulah Bondi, Melville Cooper, Sidney Toler, Gene Lockhart

† A Foreword read: 'This story of Peggy Eaton and her times is not presented as a precise account of either, rather as fiction founded upon historical fact.'

AAN: George Folsey; Beulah Bondi

'This is the big one! Two years in the making!'

Gorgo

GB 1960 78m Technicolor
King Brothers (Wilfrid Eades)

A prehistoric monster is caught in Irish waters and brought to London, but rescued by its mother.
Amiable monster hokum with a happy ending but not much technical resource.

w John Loring, Daniel Hyatt d Eugene Lourié ph Frederick A. Young m Angelo Lavagnino sp Tom Howard

Bill Travers, William Sylvester, Vincent Winter, Christopher Rhodes, Joseph O'Conor, Bruce Seton, Martin Benson

The Gorgon*

GB 1964 83m Technicolor
Hammer (Anthony Nelson Keys)

A castle ruin near a German village is infested by Megaera, the gorgon of ancient myth, whose gaze turns people to stone and who can take over the form of an unknowing villager.
Writhing snakes in the hair-do being too great a challenge to the make-up man, the monster is barely glimpsed and the film becomes a who-is-it, all quite suspenseful despite the central idea being too silly for words.

w John Gilling d Terence Fisher ph Michael Reed m James Bernard

Peter Cushing, Christopher Lee, Barbara Shelley, Richard Pasco, Patrick Troughton

The Gorilla*

US 1939 66m bw
TCF

A murderer blames an escaped gorilla for his crimes.
Spooky house mystery comedy revamped as a Ritz Brothers vehicle; not much suspense, but it all looks good and the cast is highly satisfactory.

w Rian James, Sid Silvers, *play* Ralph Spence d Allan Dwan ph Edward Cronjager m David Buttolph

The Ritz Brothers, Bela Lugosi, Lionel Atwill, Patsy Kelly, Joseph Calleia, Anita Louise, Edward Norris, Wally Vernon

  'A good programmer that will get by for normal biz where the Ritzes can attract.'—*Variety*

† There were two previous versions, in 1927 with Charlie Murray and 1931 with Joe Frisco.

Gorilla at Large

US 1954 93m Technicolor 3-D
TCF / Panoramic (Robert L. Jacks)

A circus gorilla is used as a cover for murder.
Silly thriller with the gorilla as unconvincing as the story.

w Leonard Praskins, Barney Slater d Harmon Jones ph Lloyd Aherne m Lionel Newman

Anne Bancroft, Lee J. Cobb, Cameron Mitchell, Lee Marvin, Raymond Burr, Charlotte Austin, Peter Whitney, Warren Stevens

The Gorilla Man

US 1942 63m bw

A wounded commando discovers that his hospital is run by Nazis, who then try to prove him insane so that he won't be believed. There must have been less laborious ways, one assumes, but at least this farrago is good for a few unintentional laughs. John Loder, Ruth Ford, Richard Fraser, Paul Cavanagh, John Abbott. Written by Anthony Coldeway; directed by D. Ross Lederman; for Warner.

THE GORGON.   Richard Pasco makes the mistake of looking at the malignant lady, a fatal thing to do even through a mirror. Sadly the snakes in her hair were poor actors.

Gorky Park
US 1983   128m   Technicolor
Orion / Eagle (Gene Kirkwood, Howard W. Koch Jnr)

The Moscow police link murders with a sable-smuggling operation.
Bleak thriller which doggedly makes its way through a conventional plot but fails to convey the book's detail of life in Moscow today. (The film was shot in Helsinki.)

w Dennis Potter, *novel* Martin Cruz Smith
d Michael Apted *ph* Ralf D. Bode *m* James Horner *pd* Paul Sylbert

Lee Marvin, William Hurt, Brian Dennehy, Ian Bannen, Joanna Pacula, Michael Elphick, Richard Griffiths, Alexander Knox

The Gospel According to St Matthew*
Italy / France 1964   142m   bw
Arco / Lux (Alfredo Bini)
original title: *Il Vangelo Secondo Matteo*

The life of Christ seen almost as a ciné-vérité documentary: the tone is realist but not notably iconoclastic.

wd Pier Paolo Pasolini *ph* Tonino delli Colli *m* Bach, Mozart, Prokofiev *md* Luis Enrique Bacalov

Enrique Irazoqui, Susanna Pasolini, Mario Socrate

AAN: Luis Enrique Bacalov

Goupi Mains Rouges*
France 1943   95m   bw
Minerva
US title: `It Happened at the Inn`

A French village is largely populated by members of the same family, and one of them murders another.
An odd little black comedy which strengthened its director's reputation.

w Pierre Véry, Jacques Becker, *novel* Pierre Véry *d* Jacques Becker *ph* Pierre Montazel, Jean Bourgoin *m* Jean Alfaro

Fernand Ledoux, Georges Rollin, Blanchette Brunoy, Robert Le Vigan

Government Girl
US 1943 94m bw

War Department secretaries find their love lives confused in wartime Washington, where rooms have to be shared. Thin variation on a theme curiously dear to Hollywood at the time. Olivia de Havilland, Sonny Tufts, Anne Shirley, James Dunn, Paul Stewart, Agnes Moorehead, Harry Davenport, Una O'Connor, Sig Rumann, Jane Darwell. Written and directed by Dudley Nichols; from an adaptation by Budd Schulberg of a story by Adela Rogers St John; for RKO.

The Gracie Allen Murder Case*
US 1939 74m bw

Gracie Allen helps Philo Vance solve the murder of an escaping convict. At the time of Gracie Allen's radio eminence, this was a cute comedy idea. Gracie Allen, Warren William, Ellen Drew, Kent Taylor, Jed Prouty, Jerome Cowan, Donald McBride, H. B. Warner, William Demarest. Written by Nat Perrin from a novel by S. S. Van Dine; directed by Alfred E. Green; for George K. Arthur / Paramount. 'Smacko for general audiences . . . one of the top comedies of the season.'—*Variety*

'This is Benjamin . . . he's a little worried about his future!'
The Graduate***
US 1967 105m Technicolor Panavision
UA / Embassy (Lawrence Turman)

A rich Californian ex-student is led into an affair with the wife of his father's friend, then falls in love with her daughter.
Richly reflecting the anything-goes mood of the late sixties, this lushly-filmed sex comedy opened a few new doors, looked ravishing, was well acted and had a popular music score, so that few people noticed that only the first half was any good.

w Calder Willingham, Buck Henry, *novel Charles Webb* d Mike Nichols *ph Robert Surtees songs Paul Simon singers Simon and Garfunkel* m Dave Grusin *pd Richard Sylbert*

Dustin Hoffman, Anne Bancroft, Katharine Ross, Murray Hamilton, William Daniels, Elizabeth Wilson

BENJAMIN: 'Mrs Robinson, if you don't mind my saying so, this conversation is getting a little strange.'

'Seeing *The Graduate* is a bit like having one's most brilliant friend to dinner, watching him become more witty and animated with every moment, and then becoming aware that what one may really be witnessing is the onset of a nervous breakdown.'—*Renata Adler*

'Yes, there are weaknesses . . . But in cinematic skill, in intent, in sheer connection with us, *The Graduate* is a milestone in American film history.'—*Stanley Kauffmann*

AA: Mike Nichols
AAN: best picture; script; Robert Surtees; Dustin Hoffman; Anne Bancroft; Katharine Ross
● *Video: Warner*

Grand Canary
US 1934 76m bw

In the Canary Islands, a missionary girl tries to reform a derelict doctor, who finds true love elsewhere. Curiously slack adaptation; one feels that something grandly philosophical was attempted and failed. Warner Baxter, H. B. Warner, Madge Evans, Marjorie Rambeau, Juliette Compton, Zita Johann. Written by Ernest Pascal from the novel by A. J. Cronin; directed by Irving Cummings; for Jesse Lasky / Fox. 'Essentially dull and slow . . . nothing very much happens.'—*Variety*

Grand Central Murder
US 1942 72m bw
MGM (B. F. Zeidman)

A murder is solved in New York's giant railway station.
Very moderate time-filler with a rather lethargic script.

w Peter Ruric, *novel* Sue McVeigh d S. Sylvan Simon *ph* George F. Folsey m David Snell

Van Heflin, Cecilia Parker, Sam Levene, Connie Gilchrist, Millard Mitchell, Tom Conway, Virginia Grey, Samuel S. Hinds

Grand Exit
US 1935 68m bw

An insurance company sleuth traps an arson fiend. Lively co-feature mystery. Edmund Lowe, Ann Sothern, Onslow Stevens, Robert Middlemass, Selmer Jackson, Edward Van Sloan. Written by Gene Towne, Graham Baker, Bruce Manning, Lionel Houser; directed by Erle C. Kenton; for Columbia. 'Novel story, crisp dialogue, distinguished direction.'—*Variety*

'The greatest cast in stage or screen history!'
Grand Hotel**
US 1932 115m bw
MGM (Irving Thalberg)

The lives of various hotel guests become intertwined and reach their climaxes.
It's a little faded now, but much of the magic still works in this first of the portmanteau movies; the production is opulent yet somehow stiff, and the performances have survived with varying success.

w William A. Drake, *novel* Vicki Baum d Edmund Goulding *ph* William Daniels *ad* Cedric Gibbons

Greta Garbo, *John Barrymore,* Lionel Barrymore, Joan Crawford, Wallace Beery, Jean Hersholt, Lewis Stone

DOCTOR (Lewis Stone): 'Grand Hotel. Always the same. People come, people go. Nothing ever happens.'

GRUSINSKAYA (Greta Garbo): 'I want to be alone . . . I think I have never been so tired in my life.'

† Remade as *Weekend at the Waldorf* (qv).

AA: best picture

Le Grand Jeu*
France 1934 115m bw

A young man joins the Foreign Legion to forget a woman, meets another who reminds him of her, and is condemned to death for murdering the second woman's lover.
Hokey melodrama whose great interest lay in its picture of life in the Legion.

w Charles Spaak, Jacques Feyder d Jacques Feyder *ph* Harry Stradling, Maurice Forster m Hanns Eisler

Pierre-Richard Wilm, Marie Bell (in a dual role), Françoise Rosay, Charles Vanel

'At last a good French film.'—*Variety*
† A remake appeared in 1953, directed by Robert Siodmak and starring Jean-Claude Pascal, Gina Lollobrigida and Arletty. Sometimes known as *Card of Fate*, it is of little interest.

Le Grand Méliès*
France 1952 30m bw

Georges Méliès, conjuror and pioneer film maker, is played by his own son André in a series of vignettes separated by clips from the films. An interesting documentary reconstruction. Written and directed by Georges Franju; for Fred Orain / Armor Films.

Grand National Night
GB 1953 80m bw
Talisman (George Minter)
US title: *The Wicked Wife*

A stable owner accidentally kills his drunken wife, but fate and a complex series of events clear him.
Slightly dubious morally, but otherwise an adequate detective story with the outcome hinging on train timetables and the like.

w Dorothy and Campbell Christie, from their play d Bob McNaught *ph* Jack Asher m John Greenwood

Nigel Patrick, Moira Lister, Beatrice Campbell, Betty Ann Davies, Michael Hordern, Noel Purcell, Leslie Mitchell, Barry Mackay, Colin Gordon

Grand Prix*
US 1966 179m Metrocolor Super Panavision
MGM / Douglas and Lewis (Edward Lewis)

Motor racers converge on Monte Carlo and other European centres.
Seemingly endless montage, mostly in multi-split screens, of motor races, with some very jaded personal footage between. It looks a dream but quickly becomes a bore.

w Robert Alan Arthur d John Frankenheimer *ph* Lionel Lindon m Maurice Jarre *pd* Richard Sylbert

James Garner, Eva Marie Saint, Brian Bedford, Yves Montand, Toshiro Mifune, Jessica Walter, Françoise Hardy, Adolfo Celi, Claude Dauphin, Genevieve Page

'The same old story with the same types we've seen flying planes and riding horses in dozens of fast, cheap, hour-and-a-quarter movies.'—*Pauline Kael*

'Nothing more nor less than a paean to the racing car . . . off the track, though, the film is firmly stuck in bottom gear.'—*MFB*

Grand Slam
US 1933   65m   bw

A Russian waiter is called in to make a fourth at bridge and proves to be an expert. Able spoof of the bridge craze then sweeping America; precise knowledge unnecessary. Paul Lukas, Loretta Young, Frank McHugh, Glenda Farrell, Helen Vinson, Walter Byron, Ferdinand Gottschalk. Written by David Boehm and Ernest Gelsey from the novel by B. Russell Herts; directed by William Dieterle; for Warners. 'It just about makes three spades doubled, which isn't bad when you're vulnerable, and that should be enough to show a profit.'—*Variety*

Grand Slam
Italy / Spain / West Germany 1967   120m   Techniscope
(Paramount) Jolly-Coral-Constantin (Harry Columbo, George Papi)
original title: *Ad Ogni Costo*

A retired professor has a plan for a diamond robbery, but recruits his aides unwisely. Long-drawn-out caper melodrama with good sequences but nothing at all new; a very poor man's *Rififi*.

w Mino Roli, Caminito, Marcello Fondato, Antonio de la Loma d Giuliano Montaldo ph Antonio Macasoli m Ennio Morricone

Janet Leigh, Edward G. Robinson, Klaus Kinski, Robert Hoffman, Georges Rigaud, Adolfo Celi

La Grande Illusion***
France 1937   117m   bw
RAC

During World War I, three captured French pilots have an uneasy relationship with their German commandant.
Celebrated mood piece with much to say about war and mankind; more precisely, it is impeccably acted and directed and has real tragic force.

w Jean Renoir, Charles Spaak d Jean Renoir ph Christian Matras, Claude Renoir, Bourgoin, Bourreaud m Joseph Kosma

Pierre Fresnay, Erich Von Stroheim, Jean Gabin, Julien Carette, Marcel Dalio, Gaston Modot, Jean Dasté, Dita Parlo

'Artistically masterful.'—*Variety*
'The story is true. It was told to me by my friends in the war . . . notably by Pinsard who flew fighter planes. I was in the reconnaissance squadron. He saved my life many times when the German fighters became too persistent. He himself was shot down seven times. His escapes are the basis for the story.'—*Jean Renoir*
'One of the true masterpieces of the screen.'—*Pauline Kael, 70s*
AAN: best picture

Les Grandes Manoeuvres*
France / Italy 1955   106m   Eastmancolor
Filmsonor / Rizzoli
aka: *Summer Manoeuvres*

In 1913, an army lieutenant takes a bet that he can win any woman in the town in which his regiment is quartered during manoeuvres.
An elegant, but surprisingly unwitty film from this director, saddled with a well-worn and very predictable plot.

wd René Clair ph Robert Le Fèbvre, Robert Juillard m Georges Van Parys

Gérard Philipe, Michèle Morgan, Brigitte Bardot, Yves Robert, Jean Desailly, Pierre Dux

Grandma's Boy*
US 1922   50m approx (24 fps)   bw   silent

Inspired by the heroism of his own grandpa, a meek and mild young fellow subdues a terrifying tramp. Modest second-feature-length comedy of a burgeoning star, no great shakes by his later standards. Harold Lloyd, Dick Sutherland, Anna Townsend. Directed by Fred Newmeyer; for Associated Exhibitors.

Granny Get Your Gun
US 1939   56m   bw

An indomitable old lady turns sheriff to get her granddaughter off the hook for murder. Energetic second feature comedy mystery from a Perry Mason story; pleasant performances. May Robson, Harry Davenport, Margot Stevenson, Hardie Albright. Written by Kenneth Gamet; directed by George Amy; for Warner.

'The thousands who have read the book will know why WE WILL NOT SELL ANY CHILDREN TICKETS to see this picture!'

The Grapes of Wrath****
US 1940   128m   bw
TCF (Nunnally Johnson)

After the dust-bowl disaster of the thirties, Oklahoma farmers trek to California in the hope of a better life.
A superb film which could scarcely be improved upon. Though the ending is softened from the book, there was too much here for filmgoers to chew on. Acting, photography, direction combine to make this an unforgettable experience, a poem of a film.

w Nunnally Johnson, *novel* John Steinbeck d John Ford ph Gregg Toland m Alfred Newman

Henry Fonda, Jane Darwell, John Carradine, Charley Grapewin, Dorris Bowdon, Russell Simpson, Zeffie Tilbury, O. Z. Whitehead, John Qualen, Eddie Quillan, Grant Mitchell

TOM (Henry Fonda) reading grave marker: 'This here's William James Joad, died of a stroke, old, old man. His fokes bured him because they got no money to pay for funerls. Nobody kilt him. Just a stroke and he died.'

MA (Jane Darwell): 'Rich fellas come up, an' they die, an' their kids ain't no good, an' they die out. But we keep a-comin'. We're the people that live. Can't lick us. We'll go on forever, Pa, because we're the people.'

MA: 'Well, Pa, woman can change bettern a man. Man lives—well, in jerks. Baby born or somebody dies, that's a jerk. Gets a farm or loses one, an' that's a jerk. With a woman, it's all one flow, like a stream—little eddies, little waterfalls—but the river, it goes right on. Woman looks at it that way.'

'A genuinely great motion picture which makes one proud to have even a small share in the affairs of the cinema.'—*Howard Barnes*
'The most mature motion picture that has ever been made, in feeling, in purpose, and in the use of the medium.'—*Otis Ferguson*
'A sincere and searing indictment of man's cruel indifference to his fellows.'—*Basil Wright*
AA: John Ford; Jane Darwell
AAN: best picture; Nunnally Johnson; Henry Fonda

Grass*
US 1925   50m approx   bw   silent
Famous Players-Lasky

Nomadic Iranian tribes make an annual migration in search of fresh pasture.
Striking early documentary marred by facetious sub-titles.

w, d, ph Merian C. Cooper, Ernest Schoedsack titles Terry Ramsaye

The Grass Is Greener*
GB 1960   104m   Technirama
Grandon (Stanley Donen)

The wife of an English earl falls for an American millionaire tourist.
Heavy-going and unsuitably widescreened version of an agreeable piece of West End fluff. Performances just about save it.

w Hugh and Margaret Williams, from their play d Stanley Donen ph Christopher Challis m / ly Noel Coward md Muir Mathieson

Cary Grant, Deborah Kerr, Robert Mitchum, *Jean Simmons, Moray Watson*

'It's too bad Coward couldn't have written the wisecracks too.'—*Philip T. Hartung*
'The stars do not glitter or even glow. Instead of being liberated and propelled by the screenplay, they are chained and sunk. It is one of the year's most disappointing films.'—*James Powers, Hollywood Reporter*
● Video: BBC

The Grasshopper
US 1969   98m   Technicolor
NGP (Jerry Belson, Barry Marshall)

A small-town girl goes from man to man in Los Angeles and Las Vegas, finally becoming a call girl.
The road to ruin in modern dress; nicely made and quite entertaining in its gaudy way.

w Jerry Belson, *novel* The Passing of Evil by Mark MacShane d Jerry Paris ph Sam Leavitt m Billy Goldenberg

Jacqueline Bisset, Jim Brown, Joseph Cotten, Corbett Monica

Gray Lady Down

US 1978   111m   Technicolor
Panavision
Universal / Mirisch (Walter Mirisch)

After a collision, an American submarine
lodges in the neck of an underwater canyon.
A rather boring update of *Morning Departure*
with added technology.

w James Whittaker, Howard Sackler, *novel*
Event 1000 by David Levallee *d* David
Greene *ph* Stevan Larner *m* Jerry Fielding

Charlton Heston, David Carradine, Stacy
Keach, Ned Beatty, Stephen McHattie, Ronny
Cox, Dorian Harewood, Rosemary Forsyth
  'The crew eventually reach the surface, but
the film deserves to sink without trace.'—
Nicholas Wapshott, The Times
● *Video: CIC*

Grease**

US 1978   110m   Metrocolor   Panavision
Paramount / Robert Stigwood, Allan Carr

The path of true love in a fifties high school
does not run smoothly.
Amiable 'period' musical for teenagers: a
highly fashionable exploitation of the new star
John Travolta, its commercialism was
undeniable, and it carefully built in appeal to
older age groups.

w Bronte Woodard, *stage musical play* Jim
Jacobs, Warren Casey *d* Randal Kleiser
ph Bill Butler *pd* Phil Jefries *titles* John
Wilson

John Travolta, Olivia Newton-John, Stockard
Channing, Eve Arden, Frankie Avalon, Joan
Blondell, Edd Byrnes, Sid Caesar, Alice
Ghostley, Sha Na Na, Jeff Conaway, Barry
Pearl, Michael Tucci
  'A bogus, clumsily jointed pastiche of late
fifties high school musicals, studded with
leftovers from *West Side Story* and *Rebel
Without A Cause.*'—*New Yorker*
AAN: song, 'Hopelessly Devoted to You'
● *Video: CIC*

Grease 2

US 1982   114m   Metrocolor   Panavision
Paramount (Robert Stigwood, Allan Carr)

In 1961 an English boy causes emotional
problems when he joins the senior class of
Rydell High School.
Despite the mixture as before, this sequel was
a resounding flop in all departments, perhaps
proving that the success of the original was
only a fluke of timing.

w Ken Finkleman *d* Patricia Birch *ph* Frank
Stanley *m* Louis St Louis *songs* various

Maxwell Caulfield, Michele Pfeiffer, Adrian
Zmed, Lorna Luft, Eve Arden, Sid Caesar,
Tab Hunter, Connie Stevens
  'It's like being cooped up for two hours
inside a combination of juke box and pinball
machine, with you as the ball.'—*Daily Mail*
● *Video: CIC*

Greased Lightning

US 1977   96m   Movielab
Third World (Hannah Weinstein)

A black Virginian moonshiner becomes a
famous stock car racer.

Fashionable action hokum based on a real
character.

w Kenneth Vose, Lawrence DuKore, Melvin
Van Peebles, Leon Capetanos *d* Michel
Schultz *ph* George Bouillet *m* Fred Karlin

Richard Pryor, Beau Bridges, Pam Grier,
Cleavon Little, Vincent Gardenia

The Great Adventure**

Sweden 1953   73m   bw
Arne Sucksdorff

Two boys on a farm rescue an otter and keep
it as a pet.
Superbly photographed wild life film featuring
a variety of small animals.

w, d, ph, ed Arne Sucksdorff

Anders Norberg, Kjell Sucksdorff, Arne
Sucksdorff

The Great American Broadcast*

US 1941   90m   bw
TCF (Kenneth MacGowan)

A romantic triangle set against the burgeoning
years of the radio industry.
Pleasant musical, amusing if historically
inaccurate.

w Don Ettlinger, Edwin Blum, Robert Ellis,
Helen Logan *d* Archie Mayo *ph* Leon
Shamroy, Peverell Marley *songs* Mack
Gordon, Harry Warren

Alice Faye, John Payne, Jack Oakie, Cesar
Romero, The Ink Spots, The Nicholas
Brothers, The Wiere Brothers

The Great American Pastime

US 1956   89m   bw
MGM (Henry Berman)

A mild lawyer takes over a junior baseball
team but incurs parental jealousy.
Thin lower-bracket comedy.

w Nathaniel Benchley *d* Herman Hoffman
ph Arthur E. Arling *m* Jeff Alexander

Tom Ewell, Anne Francis, Ann Miller, Dean
Jones, Raymond Bailey

The Great Bank Robbery*

US 1969   98m   colour   Panavision
Warner (Malcolm Stuart)

Would-be bank robbers turn up in a western
town disguised as priests.
Western spoof without the courage of its
convictions, but easy enough to watch.

w William Peter Blatty, *novel* Frank
O'Rourke *d* Hy Averback *ph* Fred J.
Koenekamp *m* Nelson Riddle

Kim Novak, Zero Mostel, Clint Walker,
Claude Akins, Akim Tamiroff, Larry Storch,
John Anderson, Sam Jaffe, Ruth Warrick,
Elisha Cook Jnr

The Great Barrier

GB 1937   85m   bw

A professional cardplayer gets involved in the
building of the Canadian Pacific Railway.
Forgotten epic which has scenes of some
grandeur. Richard Arlen, Antoinette Cellier,
Lilli Palmer, Barry Mackay, Roy Emerton.

Written by Michael Barringer, Milton
Rosmer, from the novel The Great Divide by
Alan Sullivan; directed by Milton Rosmer; for
Gaumont British. 'Authentic history done
sensitively . . . ranks with the best made
anywhere . . . will certainly achieve
commercial and artistic success throughout the
world.'—*Variety*

The Great Caruso**

US 1950   109m   Technicolor
MGM (Joe Pasternak)

Semi-fictional biography of the Italian tenor.
Dramatically flat but opulently staged biopic,
turned into a star vehicle and a huge
commercial success.

w Sonya Levien, William Ludwig *d* Richard
Thorpe *ph* Joseph Ruttenberg *md* Johnny
Green, Peter Herman Adler

Mario Lanza, Ann Blyth, Dorothy Kirsten,
Jarmila Novotna, Carl Benton Reid, Eduard
Franz, Richard Hageman, Ludwig Donath,
Alan Napier

AAN: Johnny Green, Peter Herman Adler
● *Video: MGM / UA*

Great Catherine

GB 1968   98m   Technicolor
Warner / Keep Films (Jules Buck)

An English captain visits the court of
Catherine the Great.
Chaos results from the attempt to inflate an
ill-considered Shavian whimsy into a feature
film: the material is simply insufficient and the
performances flounder in irrelevant production
values.

w Hugh Leonard, *play* Bernard Shaw
d Gordon Flemyng *ph* Oswald Morris
m Dmitri Tiomkin *pd* John Bryan

Jeanne Moreau, Peter O'Toole, Zero Mostel,
Jack Hawkins, Marie Lohr, Akim Tamiroff,
Marie Kean, Kenneth Griffith
  'All Shaw's jokes work very well, but the
film has been padded out with Cossack dances,
frantic chases, and unfunny slapstick.'—
Michael Billington, Illustrated London News

The Great Chase

US 1963   82m   bw

A compendium of chase sequences from silent
films, including William S. Hart, Douglas
Fairbanks Snr, and Buster Keaton (in *The
General*). Written by Harvey Kort, Paul
Killiam and Saul Turrell; for Continental.

Great Day

GB 1945   79m   bw
RKO British (Victor Hanbury)

A village Women's Institute prepares for a
visit by Mrs Roosevelt.
Modestly pleasing little drama from a
successful play.

w Wolfgang Wilhelm, John Davenport,
play Lesley Storm *d* Lance Comfort
ph Erwin Hillier

Eric Portman, Flora Robson, Sheila Sim,
Isabel Jeans, Walter Fitzgerald, Philip Friend,
Marjorie Rhodes, Maire O'Neill, Beatrice
Varley

Great Day in the Morning
US 1955 92m Technicolor Superscope
RKO (Edmund Grainger)

At the outbreak of the Civil War, Denver has divided loyalties.
Solemn semi-western without much excitement.

w Lesser Samuels, *novel* Robert Hardy Andrews *d* Jacques Tourneur *ph* William Snyder *m* Leith Stevens

Robert Stack, Virginia Mayo, Ruth Roman, Alex Nicol, Raymond Burr, Regis Toomey

The Great Diamond Robbery
US 1954 69m bw

Crooks convince a dumb jewellery apprentice to help them. Tedious second feature comedy, the star's last for the studio. Red Skelton, Cara Williams, James Whitmore, Kurt Kasznar, Reginald Owen. Written by Laslo Vadnay; directed by Robert Z. Leonard; for MGM.

The Great Dictator**
US 1940 129m bw
Charles Chaplin

A Jewish barber is mistaken for dictator Adenoid Hynkel.
Chaplin's satire on Hitler has a few funny moments, but the rest is heavy going, the production is cheeseparing, and the final speech to the world is a grave mistake.

wd Charles Chaplin *ph* Karl Struss, Rollie Totheroh *md* Meredith Willson *ad* J. Russell Spencer

Charles Chaplin, Paulette Goddard, *Jack Oakie* (as Napaloni), Reginald Gardiner, Henry Daniell, Billy Gilbert, Maurice Moscovitch

'For this film he takes on more than a mimed representation of common humanity; he states, and accepts, the responsibility of being one of humanity's best and most widely-known representatives.'—*Basil Wright*
'The last impassioned speech about peace and serenity still wrecks everything that has gone before: Chaplin mawkish can always overrule Chaplin the innocent mime.'—*New Yorker, 1978*
'You must go back to *Intolerance* for another motion picture that is so completely one man's personal expression of his attitude on something about which he feels deeply and passionately.'—*James Shelley Hamilton, National Board of Review*
'No time for comedy? Yes, I say, time for comedy. Time for Chaplin comedy. No time ever for Chaplin to preach as he does in those last six minutes, no matter how deeply he may feel what he wrote and says. He is not a good preacher. Indeed, he is frighteningly bad.'—*John O'Hara*
'Some moments actually work, but they are very few and far between.'—*Time Out, 1984*

AAN: best picture; Charles Chaplin (as writer and actor); Meredith Willson; Jack Oakie

● *Video: Polygram*

The Great Escape**
US 1963 173m De Luxe Panavision
UA / Mirisch / Alpha (John Sturges)

Allied prisoners plan to escape from a German prison camp.
Pretty good but overlong POW adventure with a tragic ending.

w James Clavell, W. R. Burnett, *book* Paul Brickhill *d* John Sturges *ph* Daniel Fapp *m* Elmer Bernstein

James Garner, *Steve McQueen*, Richard Attenborough, James Donald, Charles Bronson, Donald Pleasence, James Coburn, David McCallum, Gordon Jackson, John Leyton, Nigel Stock

● *Video: Warner*

Great Expectations
US 1934 100m bw
Universal

A poor boy becomes unexpectedly rich and mistakes the source of his good fortune. Solidly carpentered but never inspired version of a sprawling novel later tackled with much more style by David Lean. See below.

w Gladys Unger *novel* Charles Dickens *d* Stuart Walker

Phillips Holmes (Pip), Jane Wyatt (Estella), Henry Hull (Magwitch), Florence Reed (Miss Havisham), Alan Hale (Joe Gargery), Rafaela Ottiano (Mrs Joe), Francis L. Sullivan (Jaggers)

'First half represents a fine achievement . . . and then it all falls apart.'—*Variety*

Great Expectations****
GB 1946 118m bw
Rank / Cineguild (Anthony Havelock-Allan)

A boy meets an escaped convict on the Romney Marshes, with strange consequences for both of them.
Despite the inevitable simplifications, this is a superbly pictorial rendering of a much-loved novel, with all the famous characters in safe hands and masterly judgement in every department.

w Ronald Neame, David Lean, Kay Walsh, Cecil McGivern, Anthony Havelock-Allan *d* David Lean *ph* Guy Green *ad* John Bryan

John Mills, Bernard Miles, *Finlay Currie, Martita Hunt*, Valerie Hobson, *Jean Simmons*. Alec Guinness, Francis L. Sullivan, Anthony Wager, Ivor Barnard, Freda Jackson, Hay Petrie, O. B. Clarence, George Hayes, Torin Thatcher, Eileen Erskine

'The first big British film to have been made, a film that sweeps our cloistered virtues out into the open.'—*Richard Winnington*
'The best Dickens adaptation, and arguably David Lean's finest film.'—*NFT, 1969*
'It does for Dickens what *Henry V* did for Shakespeare. That is, it indicates a sound method for translating him from print to film . . . almost never less than graceful, tasteful and intelligent, and some of it better than that.'—*James Agee*

† See *Television Companion* for the later TV version with Michael York.

AA: Guy Green; John Bryan
AAN: best picture; script; David Lean (as director)

● *Video: Rank*

The Great Flamarion
US 1945 78m bw

A jealous vaudeville sharpshooter hunts down and kills the woman he loves because she prefers another. Heavy-handed melodrama reminiscent of German silents but without their flair. Erich Von Stroheim, Dan Duryea, Mary Beth Hughes. Written by Heinz Harald, Ann Widton and Richard Weil; directed by Anthony Mann; for Republic.

The Great Flirtation
US 1934 71m bw

An actor is jealous of his wife's stardom. Would-be sophisticated comedy with far too many loose ends. Adolphe Menjou, Elissa Landi, David Manners, Lynne Overman, Raymond Walburn, Paul Porcasi, Akim Tamiroff. Written by Humphrey Pearson from a story by Gregory Ratoff; directed by Ralph Murphy; for Paramount. 'Hardly a picture of strong audience appeal.'—*Variety*

The Great Gabbo
US 1929 88m bw

A ventriloquist's personality is taken over by that of his dummy. Yes, that old chestnut, here in tedious and primitive early talkie form. Erich Von Stroheim, Betty Compson, Margie Kane. Written by F. Hugh Herbert from a story by Ben Hecht; directed by James Cruze; for Sono Art.

The Great Gambini
US 1937 70m bw

A mindreader's efforts to solve a murder only point to his own guilt. Talkative twister which doesn't quite work. Akim Tamiroff, John Trent, Marian Marsh, Genevieve Tobin, Reginald Denny, William Demarest, Edward Brophy. Written by Frederick Jackson, Frank Partos, Howard Irving Young; directed by Charles Vidor; for Paramount. 'Not enough punch to produce better than ordinary entertainment.'—*Variety*

The Great Game
GB 1952 80m bw

A football club chairman gets involved in crooked deals. Dismal comedy drama which gives few opportunities to anybody. James Hayter, Diana Dors, Thora Hird, Sheila Shand Gibbs, John Laurie, Glyn Houston. Written by Wolfgang Wilhelm, from the play *Shooting Star* by Basil Thomas; directed by Maurice Elvey; for Adelphi.

The Great Garrick**
US 1937 91m bw
Warner (Mervyn Le Roy)

When Garrick goes to act in Paris, members of the Comédie Française take over a wayside inn and try to teach him a lesson, but the plan goes awry.

GREAT EXPECTATIONS. A formidable trio: Alec Guinness as Herbert Pocket, Finlay Currie as Magwitch, John Mills as Pip.

A pleasant unhistorical conceit makes a rather literary film to have come from Hollywood, but it is all very winning and cast and director keep the fun simmering happily.

w *Ernest Vajda* d *James Whale* ph Ernest Haller m Adolph Deutsch

Brian Aherne, Edward Everett Horton, Olivia de Havilland, Lionel Atwill, *Melville Cooper*, *Luis Alberni*, *Étienne Girardot*, Marie Wilson, Lana Turner, Albert Dekker, Fritz Leiber, Dorothy Tree, Chester Clute

'Finely made period romantic comedy, but its reception at the paygate is extremely problematical.'—*Variety*

'As elegantly witty as anything Whale ever did.'—*Tom Milne*

'A jestful and romantic piece.'—*Frank S. Nugent, New York Times*

The Great Gatsby*

US 1949 90m bw
Paramount (Richard Maibaum)

Events leading to the death of a retired gangster and mysterious Long Island plutocrat.
Rather bland and uninteresting attempt to accommodate a unique author to a formula star.

w Richard Maibaum, *novel* F. Scott Fitzgerald d Elliott Nugent ph John Seitz m Robert Emmett Dolan

Alan Ladd, Macdonald Carey, Betty Field, Barry Sullivan, Howard da Silva

The Great Gatsby**

US 1974 146m Eastmancolor
Paramount / Newdon (David Merrick)

Plush version with lavish production values and pleasing period sense but not much grip on the story or characters. Overlong footage is not made to seem shorter by snail's pace and dull performances.

w Francis Ford Coppola d Jack Clayton ph Douglas Slocombe m Nelson Riddle pd John Box

Robert Redford, Mia Farrow, Karen Black, Scott Wilson, *Sam Waterston*, Lois Chiles

'Pays its creator the regrettable tribute of erecting a mausoleum over his work.'—*Richard Combs*

'Leaves us more involved with six-and-a-half-million dollars' worth of trappings than with human tragedy.'—*Judith Crist*

'A total failure of every requisite sensibility.'—*Stanley Kauffmann*

'Profoundly unfilmable: a poetic and ultimately pessimistic comment on the American dream is transformed by cinematic realism into pure prose.'—*Michael Billington, Illustrated London News*

AA: Nelson Riddle

Great Guns*

US 1941 74m bw
TCF (Sol M. Wurtzel)

A young millionaire's retainers join the army with him.
Disappointing Laurel and Hardy comedy, their first for Fox and the beginning of their decline. A few good jokes, but no overall control or inventiveness.

w Lou Breslow d Monty Banks ph Glen MacWilliams m Emil Newman

Stan Laurel, Oliver Hardy, Sheila Ryan, Dick Nelson, Edmund Macdonald, Charles Trowbridge, Ludwig Stossel, Mae Marsh

Great Guy*

US 1936 73m bw
Grand National (Douglas Maclean)
GB title: *Pluck of the Irish*

An ex-prizefighter joins the bureau of weights and measures and fights corruption.
Rather tame racket film, Cagney's first independent venture away from Warners. He atones for rather thin production values.

w Henry McCarthy, Henry Johnson, James Edward Grant, Harry Ruskin d John G. Blystone ph Jack McKenzie m Marlin Skiles

James Cagney, Mae Clarke, James Burke, Edward Brophy, Henry Kolker

'It's all typical Cagney stuff, and that's the trouble with it. Cagney apparently is doing the things he likes best, but they're repetitious and apt to disappoint a public anticipating something finer from this star after his quite lengthy absence.'—*Variety*

● *Video: European*

The Great Hospital Mystery

US 1937 59m bw

The lady superintendent of a hospital has a busy night including impersonation and murder. Confused but watchable second feature. Jane Darwell, Joan Davis, Sig Rumann, Sally Blane, Thomas Beck, William Demarest. Written by Bess Meredyth, William Conselman and Jerry Cady, from a novel by Mignon G. Eberhardt; directed by James Tinling; for TCF.

The Great Hotel Murder

US 1934 70m bw

Rival sleuths find the truth about a murder less important than being first to find it out. Lively programme filler of its day, with the stars still doing their Flagg and Quirt act. Edmund Lowe, Victor McLaglen, Rosemary Ames, Mary Carlisle. Written by Arthur Kober from a story by Vincent Starrett; directed by Eugene Forde; for TCF.

The Great Impersonation*

US 1935 81m bw
Universal (Edmund Grainger)

During World War I, a German murders an English nobleman and, being his double, takes over.
Reliable espionage melodrama with atmospheric country house asides, from a

sturdily compelling novel, previously filmed in 1921 with James Kirkwood.

w Frank Wead, Eve Greene, *novel* E. Phillips Oppenheim *d* Alan Crosland *ph* Milton Krasner *m* Franz Waxman

Edmund Lowe, Valerie Hobson, Vera Engels, Henry Mollison, Lumsden Hare, Spring Byington, Charles Waldron, Dwight Frye

'They giggled a bit when Lowe went to bed with candles, and an hour later a sliding panel attempt on his life has him pushing an electric light switch . . . probably doesn't matter that the 1914 characters are dressed throughout in 1935 modishness and drive around in streamlined automobiles.'—*Variety*

The Great Impersonation*
US 1942 71m bw
Universal (Paul Malvern)

Okay quickie updating of the above, serviceable rather than inventive.

w W. Scott Darling *d* John Rawlins *ph* George Robinson *m* Hans Salter

Ralph Bellamy, Evelyn Ankers, Aubrey Mather, Edward Norris, Karen Verne, Henry Daniell, Ludwig Stossel

The Great Imposter*
US 1961 112m bw
U-I (Robert Arthur)

The career of Ferdinand Waldo Demara, a marine and Trappist monk who also impersonated a Harvard research fellow, a prison warden, a naval doctor and a schoolteacher.
Uncertain mood hampers this biopic of a likeable fantasist.

w Liam O'Brien, *book* Robert Crichton *d* Robert Mulligan *ph* Robert Burks *m* Henry Mancini

Tony Curtis, Raymond Massey, Karl Malden, Edmond O'Brien, Arthur O'Connell, Gary Merrill, Frank Gorshin, Joan Blackman, Robert Middleton

Great—Isambard Kingdom Brunel*
GB 1975 28m Eastmancolor

A musical biography of the great Victorian engineer. Quite unexpected, and therefore the more delightful. Conceived and directed by *Bob Godfrey*; for British Lion.

The Great Jasper
US 1933 83m bw

An Irish motorman becomes a fortune teller, and has his way with lots of women. Curious comedy-melodrama which never quite hits the right style. Richard Dix, Wera Engels, Edna May Oliver, Florence Eldredge, Bruce Cabot. Written by Sam Ornitz and H. W. Hanemann, from the novel by Fulton Oursler; directed by J. Walter Ruben; for RKO. 'Okay as a critics' film but looks like an in-and-outer.'—*Variety*

The Great Jesse James Raid
US 1953 70m Ansco Color

Jesse James comes out of retirement for one last haul. Boring two-bit western, all

preparation and no action. Willard Parker, Barbara Payton, Tom Neal, Wallace Ford, Jim Bannon. Written by Richard Landau; directed by Reginald Le Borg; for Lippert.

The Great Jewel Robber
US 1950 91m bw

The exploits of real-life society thief Gerald Graham Dennis. Surprisingly acceptable and entertaining reconstruction. David Brian, Marjorie Reynolds, John Archer, Jacqueline de Wit. Written by Borden Chase; directed by Peter Godfrey; for Warner.

The Great John L.
US 1945 96m bw
UA (Frank Mastroly, James Edward Grant)
GB title: *A Man Called Sullivan*

Women in the life of prizefighter John L. Sullivan.
Very mild period biopic without the zest of *Gentleman Jim*.

w James Edward Grant *d* Frank Tuttle *ph* James Van Trees *m* Victor Young

Greg McClure, Linda Darnell, Barbara Britton, Lee Sullivan, Otto Kruger, Wallace Ford, Robert Barrat

'Sometimes there's a terrible penalty for telling the truth . . .'

The Great Lie***
US 1941 107m bw
Warner (Hal B. Wallis, Henry Blanke)

A determined girl loses the man she loves, believes him dead in a plane crash, and takes over the baby which his selfish wife does not want.
Absurd melodrama becomes top-flight entertainment with all concerned in cracking form and special attention on the two bitchy female leads, splendidly played. Classical music trimmings, too.

w Leonore Coffee, *novel* January Heights by Polan Banks *d* Edmund Goulding *ph* Tony Gaudio *m* Max Steiner

Bette Davis, Mary Astor, George Brent, Lucile Watson, Hattie McDaniel, Grant Mitchell, Jerome Cowan

AA: Mary Astor

The Great Locomotive Chase*
US 1956 76m Technicolor
Cinemascope
Walt Disney (Lawrence Edward Watkin)

During the Civil War, Union spies steal a train and destroy track and bridges behind them.
A serious version of Buster Keaton's *The General*, based on a true incident; good sequences but no overall pace.

w Lawrence Edward Watkin *d* Francis D. Lyon *ph* Charles Boyle *m* Paul Smith

Fess Parker, Jeffrey Hunter, Jeff York, John Lupton, Kenneth Tobey

The Great Lover
US 1931 77m bw

Capers of a philandering opera star.
Satisfactory drama-comedy vehicle for a

durable star. Adolphe Menjou, Irene Dunne, Neil Hamilton, Olga Baclanova. Written by Gene Markey; directed by Harry Beaumont; for MGM. 'Appeal limited to the mature fan.'—*Variety*

The Great Lover*
US 1949 80m bw
(Paramount) Hope Enterprises (Edmund Beloin)

On a transatlantic liner, a timid scoutmaster catches a strangler.
Amusing suspense comedy, a good star vehicle.

w Edmund Beloin, Melville Shavelson, Jack Rose *d* Alexander Hall *ph* Charles Lang *m* Joseph J. Lilley

Bob Hope, Rhonda Fleming, *Roland Young*, Jim Backus, Roland Culver, George Reeves

'He'll give you the biggest heart sock, laugh shock you ever thrilled to!'

The Great McGinty**
US 1940 83m bw
Paramount
GB title: *Down Went McGinty*

A hobo and a crook have a hectic political career.
Lively comedy-drama which signalled the arrival as director of a new and stimulating Hollywood talent.

wd Preston Sturges *ph* William C. Mellor *m* Frederick Hollander

Brian Donlevy, Akim Tamiroff, Muriel Angelus, Louis Jean Heydt, Arthur Hoyt

PROLOGUE: 'This is the story of two men who met in a banana republic. One of them never did anything dishonest in his life except for one crazy minute. The other never did anything honest in his life except for one crazy minute. They both had to leave the country.'

'This is his first directing job and where has he been all our lives? He has that sense of the incongruous which makes some of the best gaiety.'—*Otis Ferguson*

'The tough dialogue is matched by short, snappy scenes; the picture seems to have wasted no time, no money.'—*Gilbert Seldes*

'A director as adroit and inventive as any in the business . . . it starts like a five-alarm fire and never slackens pace for one moment until its unexpected conclusion.'—*Pare Lorentz*

'Sturges takes the success ethic and throws it in the face of the audience.'—*James Orsini*

'Capra with the gloves off.'—*Raymond Durgnat*

AA: script

The Great Man**
US 1956 92m bw
U-I (Aaron Rosenberg)

A memorial programme to a much-loved TV personality turns into an exposé.
Patchy melodrama with a *Citizen Kane* framework; the best bits are very effective.

w *Jose Ferrer, Al Morgan, novel* Al Morgan *d* Jose Ferrer *ph* Harold Lipstein *m* Herman Stein

Jose Ferrer, Dean Jagger, Keenan Wynn, *Julie London*, Joanne Gilbert, *Ed Wynn*, Jim Backus

'Its distinction is in its unwavering tone— one of blunt and frequently savage irony and cynicism.'—*MFB*

'The movie is almost over before one realizes what a slick, fast sell it is (resembling nothing so much as what it is attacking).'— *Pauline Kael, 1968*

The Great Man Votes*
US 1938 72m bw
RKO

A drunken professor turns out to have the casting vote in a local election.
Slow-starting but progressively funny political comedy with some favourite talents in good form.

w John Twist, *story* Gordon Malherbe Hillman *d Garson Kanin ph* Russell Metty *m* Roy Webb

John Barrymore, Virginia Weidler, Peter Holden, *William Demarest, Donald MacBride*
'It will be hailed by class audiences as a fine example of the film art, yet carrying sock appeal for mass patronage.'—*Variety*

The Great Man's Lady*
US 1941 90m bw
Paramount (William A. Wellman)

A western pioneer is inspired and encouraged by his wife.
Adequate but unsurprising flashback family drama starting with its star as a lady of 109.

w W. L. Rivers, *story* Vina Delmar *d* William L. Wellman *ph* William C. Mellor *m* Victor Young

Barbara Stanwyck, Joel McCrea, Brian Donlevy, Katharine Stevens, Thurston Hall, Lloyd Corrigan

The Great Meadow
US 1931 80m bw

Early settlers from Virginia walk to Kentucky. Dim pioneering fable, without even a covered wagon. John Mack Brown, Eleanor Boardman, Lucille La Verne, Anita Louise, Gavin Gordon, Guinn Williams. Written by Edith Ellis, Charles Brabin, from the novel by Elizabeth Madox Roberts; directed by Charles Brabin; for MGM. 'Rather a sorry mess . . . cannot be depended on for an average gross.'—*Variety*

The Great Missouri Raid
US 1950 81m Technicolor

Jesse and Frank James are seen as Civil War guerrillas, subsequently forced into crime by a vengeful officer. Unsuccessful whitewash job, tediously told. Macdonald Carey, Wendell Corey, Ward Bond, Ellen Drew, Bruce Bennett, Bill Williams, Anne Revere, Edgar Buchanan. Written by Frank Gruber; directed by Gordon Douglas; for Nat Holt / Paramount.

The Great Mr Handel*
GB 1942 103m Technicolor
Rank / GHW (James B. Sloan)

How the 18th-century composer came to write the Messiah.
Earnest, unlikely biopic, naïve but rather commendable.

w Gerald Elliott, Victor MacClure, *play* L. DuGarde Peach *d* Norman Walker *ph* Claude Friese-Greene

Wilfrid Lawson, Elizabeth Allan, Malcolm Keen, Michael Shepley, Hay Petrie, A. E. Matthews

'They booed him to greatness!'
The Great Moment**
US 1944 83m bw
Paramount

How anaesthetics may have been invented.
Curious biopic of Dr W. T. G. Morgan, poised somewhere between utter seriousness and pratfall farce. The beginning of its director's decline, but always interesting in itself.

wd Preston Sturges, *book* Triumph over Pain by René Fulop-Miller *ph* Victor Milner *m* Victor Young

Joel McCrea, Betty Field, William Demarest, Harry Carey, Franklin Pangborn, Porter Hall, Grady Sutton

The Great Muppet Caper**
GB 1981 97m Technicolor
ITC (David Lazer, Frank Oz)

Kermit and Fozzie are reporters sent to solve a jewel robbery.
Considerably livelier than *The Muppet Movie* but a badly timed flop at the box office, this genial caper has a pleasant collection of guest stars as well as showing the familiar puppets at their most typical.

w Tom Patchett, Jay Tarses, Jerry Juhl, Jack Rose *d* Jim Henson *ph* Oswald Morris *m* Joe Raposo *pd* Harry Lange

Diana Rigg, Charles Grodin, John Cleese, Robert Morley, Trevor Howard, Peter Ustinov, Jack Warden
'Large chunks are pleasingly daft.'—*Sight and Sound*

● Video: Precision

The Great Northfield Minnesota Raid*
US 1971 91m Technicolor
Universal / Robertson and Associates / Jennings Lang

In 1876 a gang of bandits, technically pardoned, plan a bank robbery.
'Realistic' western in which the settings and photography have an impressively rough look but the script leaves much to be desired.

wd Philip Kaufman *ph* Bruce Surtees *m* Dave Grusin

Cliff Robertson, Robert Duvall, Luke Askew, Elisha Cook Jnr

The Great O'Malley
US 1937 77m bw
Warner (Harry Joe Brown)

An overzealous cop cares for the wife and

child of a petty criminal whom he has sent to prison.
Considering the talent involved, an astonishingly routine programmer.

w Milton Krims, Tom Reed, *story* The Making of O'Malley by Gerald Beaumont *d* William Dieterle *ph* Ernest Haller *m* Heinz Roemheld

Pat O'Brien, Humphrey Bogart, Ann Sheridan, Sybil Jason, Frieda Inescort, Donald Crisp, Henry O'Neill, Hobart Cavanagh, Mary Gordon
'Familiar sentimental police theme: little action or appeal.'—*Variety*
† Previously filmed in 1923 with Milton Sills, as *The Making of O'Malley*.

The Great Profile*
US 1940 82m bw
TCF (Raymond Griffith)

A dissipated actor disgraces his family and becomes an acrobat.
Shapeless farce in which a great talent on his last legs parodies himself.

w Milton Sperling, Hilary Lynn *d* Walter Lang *ph* Ernest Palmer *m* Cyril Mockridge

John Barrymore, Mary Beth Hughes, Gregory Ratoff, Anne Baxter, John Payne, Lionel Atwill, Edward Brophy, Willie Fung

'The greatest comedy ever made!'
The Great Race***
US 1965 163m Technicolor
Super Panavision
Warner / Patricia / Jalem / Reynard (Martin Jurow)

In 1908, the Great Leslie and Professor Fate are leading contenders in the first New York to Paris car race.
Elaborate comedy spectacular with many good moments, notably the early disasters, a western saloon brawl, and a custard pie fight. Elsewhere, there is more evidence of an oversize budget than of wit or finesse, and the entire Prisoner of Zenda spoof could have been omitted. Excellent production detail and general good humour.

w Arthur Ross *d* Blake Edwards *ph* Russell Harlan *m* Henry Mancini *pd* Fernando Carrere

Jack Lemmon, Tony Curtis, Peter Falk, Natalie Wood, George Macready, Ross Martin, Vivian Vance, Dorothy Provine
AAN: Russell Harlan; song 'The Sweetheart Tree' (*m* Henry Mancini, *ly* Johnny Mercer)
● Video: Warner

The Great Rupert
US 1950 87m bw

A family of impoverished acrobats are assisted by a pet squirrel which proves lucky in more ways than one. Modest whimsical comedy which outstays its welcome. Jimmy Durante, Terry Moore, Tom Drake, Sara Haden, Frank Orth. Written by Laslo Vadnay; directed by Irving Pichel; for George Pal / Eagle Lion. (NB: The squirrel was part puppet.)

The Great St Trinian's Train Robbery
GB 1966   94m   Eastmancolor
British Lion / Braywild (Leslie Gilliat)

The staff of St Trinian's is infiltrated by
would-be train robbers.
Flat-footed farce with a sense of strain evident
from first to last shot.

w Frank Launder, Ivor Herbert d Frank
Launder, Sidney Gilliat ph Ken Hodges
m Malcolm Arnold

Frankie Howerd, Dora Bryan, Reg Varney,
Desmond Walter-Ellis, Raymond Huntley,
Richard Wattis, George Benson, Eric Barker,
Godfrey Winn, George Cole, Colin Gordon,
Barbara Couper, Elspeth Duxbury

The Great Santini*
US 1979   115m   Technicolor
Warner / Orion / Bing Crosby Productions

A crack fighter pilot has difficulty adjusting to
peacetime domestic life.
Overlong but generally absorbing star
character drama.

wd Lewis John Carlino, novel Pat Conway
ph Ralph Woolsey m Elmer Bernstein
pd Jack Poplin

Robert Duvall, Blythe Danner, Michael
O'Keefe, Lisa Jane Perskey, Julie Anne
Haddock

AAN: Robert Duvall; Michael O'Keefe
(supporting actor)

'They were not forgotten by history—they
were left out on purpose!'
**The Great Scout and Cathouse
Thursday**
US 1976   102m   Technicolor
AIP (Jules Buck and David Korda)
reissue title: Wildcat

While trying to revenge himself on an
absconding partner, an old cowboy falls for a
young prostitute.
Downright peculiar comedy western which
never seems to make up its mind what it's
trying to be, and too often is merely
embarrassing.

w Richard Shapiro d Don Taylor ph Alex
Phillips Jnr m John Cameron pd Jack Martin
Smith

Lee Marvin, Oliver Reed, Kay Lenz, Robert
Culp, Elizabeth Ashley, Strother Martin,
Sylvia Miles
'It takes more than a dollop or two of
sentiment and acres of dirty talk to make a
movie.'—Michael Billington, Illustrated
London News
'It sounds like the latest in the cute twosome
series launched by Butch Cassidy and the
Sundance Kid. In fact it features not two but
seven wacky westerners who all seem addicted
to stealing, hee-hawing, falling into puddles
and punching each other in the privates.'—
Janet Maslin, Newsweek

The Great Sinner*
US 1949   110m   bw
MGM (Gottfried Reinhardt)

A serious young writer becomes a compulsive
gambler.
Rather pointless and heavy-handed but

extremely good-looking and splendidly cast
period drama vaguely based on Dostoievsky.

w Ladislas Fodor, Christopher Isherwood
d Robert Siodmak ph George Folsey
m Bronislau Kaper ad Cedric Gibbons, Hans
Peck

Gregory Peck, Walter Huston, Ava Gardner,
Agnes Moorehead, Ethel Barrymore, Melvyn
Douglas, Frank Morgan

The Great Sioux Massacre
US 1965   93m   Eastmancolor
      Cinemascope
Columbia / FF (Leon Fromkess)

Two officers are court-martialled after Custer's
last stand.
Fragmentary flashback western let down by
production and performances.

w Fred C. Dobbs d Sidney Salkow ph Irving
Lippman m Emil Newman, Edward B.
Powell

Joseph Cotten, Darren McGavin, Phil Carey,
Nancy Kovack, Julie Sommars, Michael Pate

The Great Sioux Uprising
US 1953   80m   Technicolor
U-I (Albert J. Cohen)

Indians rebel when their horses are stolen for
sale to the commander of Fort Laramie.
Moderate western programmer.

w Richard Breen, Gladys Atwater d Lloyd
Bacon ph Maury Gertsman m Joseph
Gershenson

Jeff Chandler, Faith Domergue, Lyle Bettger

The Great Smokey Roadblock
US 1976   106m   colour
Marvista (Allan F. Bodon)

A truckdriver avoiding the finance company
picks up an assortment of eccentrics and starts
on a wild chase.
What possessed Henry Fonda to appear in this
hick action melodrama will be forever unclear.

w,d John Leone ph Ed Brown Snr m Craig
Safan

Henry Fonda, Eileen Brennan, John Byner,
Dub Taylor, Susan Sarandon, Dana House,
Robert Englund, Melanie Mayron, Valerie
Curtin

The Great Stone Face*
US 1968   93m   bw

A very acceptable biography of Buster
Keaton, with unusual emphasis on the very
early films. Written and directed by Vernon P.
Becker; for Funnyman Productions.

The Great Train Robbery***
US 1903   10m approx   bw   silent
Edison

Bandits tie up a telegraph operator and rob a
train, but are arrested.
In its day this was a real pioneer. It was among
the longest films then made, it had the most
complicated story line, it was the first western
and it used new technical tricks such as the
pan and the close-up. Needless to say, it must
now be viewed with sympathy.

wd Edwin S. Porter

Marie Murray, Broncho Billy Anderson,
George Barnes

The Great Train Robbery (1978, Sean
Connery): see The First Great Train
Robbery

The Great Victor Herbert*
US 1939   91m   bw
Paramount (Andrew L. Stone)

At the turn of the century a famous composer
plays cupid to two young singers.
Pleasant minor musical with excellent songs
and an infectious cheerfulness.

w Russel Crouse, Robert Lively d Andrew L.
Stone ph Victor Milner md Phil Boutelje,
Arthur Lange

Walter Connolly, Allan Jones, Mary Martin,
Susanna Foster, Lee Bowman
'Elaborately produced, visually effective
. . . but audiences will learn from it very little
about Victor Herbert.'—Variety

AAN: Phil Boutelje, Arthur Lange

The Great Waldo Pepper**
US 1975   108m   Technicolor   Todd-
      AO 35
Universal (George Roy Hill)

In the twenties, a World War I flier becomes
an aerial stuntman.
Whimsical spectacular which concentrates less
on the mystique of flying than on a series of
splendid stunts.

w William Goldman d George Roy Hill
ph Robert Surtees m Henry Mancini

Robert Redford, Bo Svenson, Bo Brundin,
Susan Sarandon, Geoffrey Lewis
'Charged with enthralling balletic
precision.'—Tom Milne
'One hundred per cent pure plastic
adolescent male fantasy.'—New Yorker

'Miliza Korjus—rhymes with gorgeous!'
The Great Waltz**
US 1938   103m   bw
MGM (Bernard Hyman)

Young Johann Strauss becomes Vienna's waltz
king.
Exhilarating old-fashioned studio-set musical
located in Hollywood's endearing vision of
Old Vienna, assisted by streamlined
production and excellent cast. Musical
schmaltz.

w Walter Reisch, Samuel Hoffenstein, story
Gottfried Reinhardt d Julien Duvivier
ph Joseph Ruttenberg m Dmitri Tiomkin

Fernand Gravet, Luise Rainer, Miliza Korjus,
Lionel Atwill, Hugh Herbert, Herman Bing,
Curt Bois
'Should click nicely, but in these swingaroo
days the waltz part may slow down anticipated
b.o. enthusiasm.'—Variety

AA: Joseph Ruttenberg
AAN: Miliza Korjus

The Great Waltz*

US 1972 . 134m Metrocolor
Panavision 70
MGM (Andrew L. Stone)

Heavy-going remake set on real locations and hampered by them, styled in the manner of the same director's *Song of Norway*, i.e. with no real style at all. The music survives.

wd Andrew L. Stone ph David Boulton
ad William Albert Havenmeyer ch Onna White

Horst Buchholz, Nigel Patrick, Mary Costa, Rossano Brazzi, Yvonne Mitchell

'Take a box of chocolates—soft-centred, of course.'—*Michael Billington, Illustrated London News*

The Great White Hope**

US 1970 103m De Luxe Panavision
TCF (Lawrence Turman)

In 1910, a black boxer becomes world heavyweight champ but has trouble through his affair with a white girl.
Vivid, slightly whitewashed biopic of Jack Johnson (called Jefferson). Dramatic deficiencies outweighed by excellent period detail and a spellbinding central performance.

w Howard Sackler, from his play d Martin Ritt ph Burnett Guffey m negro traditionals
pd John de Cuir

James Earl Jones, Jane Alexander, Lou Gilbert, Joel Fluellen, Chester Morris, Robert Webber, Hal Holbrook

AAN: James Earl Jones; Jane Alexander

The Great Ziegfeld**

US 1936 179m bw
MGM (Hunt Stromberg)

The growth and Broadway fame of impresario Florenz Ziegfeld.
Mammoth biopic which despite a few show-stopping numbers never takes off dramatically and becomes something of an endurance test; interesting, however, as a spectacular of its time.

w William Anthony McGuire d Robert Z. Leonard ph Oliver T. Marsh, Ray June, George Folsey md Arthur Lange ad Cedric Gibbons

William Powell, Luise Rainer (as Anna Held), Myrna Loy (as Billie Burke), Frank Morgan, Reginald Owen, Nat Pendleton, Virginia Bruce, *Ray Bolger*, Harriett Hoctor, Ernest Cossart, *Fanny Brice*, Robert Greig, Gilda Gray, Leon Errol, Stanley Morner (Dennis Morgan)

'This huge inflated gas-blown object bobs into the critical view as irrelevantly as an airship advertising somebody's toothpaste at a south coast resort. It lasts three hours. That is its only claim to special attention.'—*Graham Greene*

'Everything should have been tightened— not in the team job of cutting those miles of negative, but in boiling down the script, saving a line here, combining two scenes into one.'—*Otis Ferguson*

AA: best picture; Luise Rainer
AAN: William Anthony McGuire; Robert Z. Leonard

The Greatest

US / GB 1977 101m Metrocolor
Columbia / EMI (John Marshall)

The life and times of Muhammed Ali.
Bland confection of rags to riches in the boxing ring, its only plus being that Ali plays himself and offers a predictable array of enjoyable one-liners.

w Ring Lardner Jnr, from Ali's autobiography *The Greatest* d Tom Gries ph Harry Stradling m Michael Masser

Muhammed Ali, Ernest Borgnine, Roger E. Mosley, Lloyd Haynes, Malachi Throne, John Marley, Robert Duvall, David Huddleston, Ben Johnson, James Earl Jones, Dina Merrill, Paul Winfield

The Greatest Show on Earth*

US 1952 153m Technicolor
Paramount / Cecil B. de Mille (Henry Wilcoxon)

Various dramas come to a head under the big top.
Moribund circus drama with bad acting, stilted production, an irrelevant train crash climax and a few genuinely spectacular and enjoyable moments.

w Fredric M. Frank, Theodore St John, Frank Cavett, Barre Lyndon d Cecil B. de Mille ph George Barnes, Peverell Marley, Wallace Kelley m Victor Young ad Hal Pereira, Walter Tyler

Betty Hutton, Cornel Wilde, James Stewart, Charlton Heston, Dorothy Lamour, Gloria Grahame, Lyle Bettger, Henry Wilcoxon, Emmett Kelly, Lawrence Tierney, John Kellogg, John Ringling North

AA: best picture
AAN: original story (Fredric M. Frank, Theodore St John, Frank Cavett); Cecil B. de Mille (as director)

The Greatest Story Ever Told**

US 1965 225m Technicolor Ultra Panavision 70
UA / George Stevens

Solemn spectacular with an elephantine pace, shot in Utah because allegedly it looked more like Palestine than Palestine did. All frightfully elegant and reverent, but totally unmoving, partly because of the fatal casting of stars in bit parts. (John Wayne looks in merely to say 'Truly this man was the son of God.')

w James Lee Barrett, George Stevens, from various sources d George Stevens ph William C. Mellor, Loyal Griggs m Alfred Newman ad Richard Day, William Creber

Max Von Sydow, Dorothy McGuire, Claude Rains, Jose Ferrer, David McCallum, Charlton Heston, Sidney Poitier, Donald Pleasence, Roddy McDowall, Gary Raymond, Carroll Baker, Pat Boone, Van Heflin, Sal Mineo, Shelley Winters, Ed Wynn, John Wayne, Telly Savalas, Angela Lansbury, Joseph Schildkraut, Victor Buono, Nehemiah Persoff

'George Stevens was once described as a water buffalo of film art. What this film more precisely suggests is a dinosaur.'—*MFB*

'God is unlucky in *The Greatest Story Ever Told*. His only begotten son turns out to be a bore . . . the photography is inspired mainly by Hallmark Cards . . . as the Hallelujah Chorus explodes around us stereophonically and stereotypically it becomes clear that Lazarus was not so much raised from the tomb as blasted out of it. As for pacing, the picture does not let you forget a single second of its four hours.'—*John Simon*

'No more than three minutes have elapsed before we suspect that Stevens' name and fame have been purchased by the Hallmark Greeting Card Company, and that what we are looking at is really a lengthy catalogue of greeting cards for 1965—for Those Who Care Enough to Send the Very Best.'—*Stanley Kauffmann*

'Who but an audience of diplomats could sit through this thing? As the picture ponderously unrolled, it was mainly irritation that kept me awake.'—*Shana Alexander, Life*

'If the subject-matter weren't sacred, we would be responding to the picture in the most charitable way by laughing at it from start to finish.'—*Brendan Gill, New Yorker*

'A big windy bore.'—*Bruce Williamson, Playboy*

† The film was originally released at 4 hours 20 minutes. Subsequent versions were at 3 hours 58 minutes, 3 hours 17 minutes, 2 hours 27 minutes and 2 hours 7 minutes.

AAN: William C. Mellor, Loyal Griggs; Alfred Newman

Greed***

US 1923 110m (24 fps) bw silent
Metro-Goldwyn (Erich Von Stroheim, Irving Thalberg)

An ex-miner dentist kills his avaricious wife. Later in Death Valley he also kills her lover, but is bound to him by handcuffs.
This much-discussed film is often cited as its director's greatest folly: the original version ran eight hours. Re-edited by June Mathis, it retains considerable power sequence by sequence, but is necessarily disjointed in development. However, it must be seen to be appreciated.

wd Erich Von Stroheim, novel McTeague by Frank Norris ph Ben Reynolds, William Daniels, Ernest B. Schoedsack ad Richard Day, Cedric Gibbons, Erich Von Stroheim

Gibson Gowland, Zasu Pitts, *Jean Hersholt*, Chester Conklin, Dale Fuller

'The end leaves one with an appalling sense of human waste, of futility, of the drabness and cruelty of lives stifled by genteel poverty. Every character in the film is overwhelmed by it.'—*Gavin Lambert*

'Von Stroheim is a genius—*Greed* established that beyond all doubt—but he is badly in need of a stopwatch.'—*Robert E. Sherwood*

† In 1972 Herman G. Weinberg published a complete screenplay with 400 stills.

†† The original length at the première is said to have been 420m.

The Greed of William Hart
GB 1948 78m bw
Bushey (Gilbert Church)

In old Edinburgh, grave robbers procure
corpses for an anatomist.
Cheapie version of a much filmed subject. This
scenario was refurbished eleven years later by
the same writer as *The Flesh and the Fiends*;
see also *The Body Snatcher, Burke and Hare.*

w John Gilling d Oswald Mitchell ph S. D.
Onions

Tod Slaughter, Henry Oscar, Aubrey Woods,
Arnold Bell

The Greek Tycoon
US 1978 106m Technicolor
  Panavision
Universal / ABKCO (Allan Klein, Ely
  Landau)

A billionaire shipping tycoon marries the
widow of an American president.
Rather messy 'faction' based on Onassis and
Jacqueline Kennedy; entirely uninteresting
save for glossy backgrounds and the
relentlessness with which the characters swear
at each other.

w Mort Fine d J. Lee Thompson ph Tony
Richmond m Stanley Myers pd Michael
Stringer

Anthony Quinn, Jacqueline Bisset, Raf
Vallone, Edward Albert, James Franciscus,
Camilla Sparv
† Among its other idiocies, this is the first film
to credit 'Assistant to the assistant to the Unit
Publicist'.

The Greeks Had a Word for Them*
US 1932 77m bw
UA (Samuel Goldwyn)

Adventures of three New York gold diggers.
Smart early talkie which helped launch the
Gold Diggers series and TCF's parallel *Three
Little Mice / Moon over Miami / How to
Marry a Millionaire* series.

w Sidney Howard, *play* Zoe Akins d Lowell
Sherman ph George Barnes m Alfred
Newman

Joan Blondell, Madge Evans, Ina Claire,
David Manners, Lowell Sherman, Phillips
Smalley, Betty Grable
  'Grand rowdy comedy . . . a revel in femme
clothes and a picture calculated to fascinate
women. Backwater clienteles questionable.'—
Variety

'Their badge of honour was a green beret,
and it said they had lived it all . . . the
night jumps, the ambushes, the hand-to-
hand combat, and the long nights of
terror they filled with courage!'
The Green Berets
US 1968 141m Technicolor
  Panavision
Warner / Batjac (Michael Wayne)

After extensive training, two tough army
detachments see service in Vietnam.
Overlong actioner criticized for
unquestioningly accepting the Vietnam cause;
in itself, violent, exhausting and dull.

w James Lee Barrett, *novel* Robin Moore
d John Wayne, Ray Kellogg ph Winton C.
Hoch m Miklos Rozsa

John Wayne, David Janssen, Jim Hutton,
Aldo Ray, Raymond St Jacques, Jack Soo,
Bruce Cabot, Patrick Wayne, Irene Tsu, Jason
Evers, Luke Askew
  'Propaganda as crude as this can only do
damage to its cause.'—*David Wilson*
  'A film best handled from a distance and
with a pair of tongs.'—*Penelope Gilliatt*

The Green Buddha
GB 1954 62m bw

A charter pilot finds his clients are thieves and
rounds them up. Fair second feature thick-ear.
Wayne Morris, Mary Germaine, Walter Rilla,
Arnold Marle. Written by Paul Erickson;
directed by John Lemont; for Republic.

The Green Cockatoo
GB 1937 65m bw
TCF / New World (Robert T. Kane)
aka: *Four Dark Hours; Race Gang*

A man seeks revenge on the gangsters who
killed his brother.
Sleazy little Soho-set thriller, mainly
remarkable for cast and credits.

w Edward O. Berkman, Arthur Wimperis,
story Graham Greene d William Cameron
Menzies

John Mills, Robert Newton, Rene Ray, Bruce
Seton, Charles Oliver

'A fiery girl dares the dangers of the sea
and a strange land—fighting for the love
of a bold adventurer!'
Green Dolphin Street
US 1947 141m bw
MGM (Carey Wilson)

A Channel Islander emigrates to New Zealand
and sends home for the wrong bride.
Silly 19th-century romance climaxed by rather
a good earthquake. Expensively but falsely
produced.

w Samson Raphaelson, *novel* Elizabeth
Goudge d Victor Saville ph George Folsey
m Bronislau Kaper

Lana Turner, Richard Hart, Edmund Gwenn,
Van Heflin, Donna Reed
  'The actors in this stupefyingly flimsy epic
seem to be in competition for booby prizes.'—
Pauline Kael, 70s

AAN: George Folsey

Green Fingers
GB 1946 83m bw

An unqualified osteopath tries to achieve
respectability. Unsurprising and flatly made
drama of eventual success against all odds.
Robert Beatty, Carol Raye, Nova Pilbeam,
Felix Aylmer, Moore Marriott, Edward
Rigby. Written by Jack Whittingham, from
the novel *Persistent Warrior* by Edith
Arundel; directed by John Harlow; for
British National.

Green Fire
US 1954 100m Eastmancolor
  Cinemascope
MGM (Armand Deutsch)

Two engineers disagree over their mining of
Colombia emeralds.
Routine adventure story with good action
highlights including landslide, flood and storm,
all deadened by dull dialogue and romantic
complications.

w Ivan Goff, Ben Roberts d Andrew Marton
ph Paul Vogel m Miklos Rozsa

Stewart Granger, Paul Douglas, Grace Kelly

Green for Danger***
GB 1946 93m bw
Rank / Individual (Frank Launder, Sidney
  Gilliat)

A mysterious murderer strikes on the
operating table at a wartime emergency
hospital.
Classic comedy-thriller, with serious detection
balanced by excellent jokes and performances,
also by moments of fright.

w Sidney Gilliat, Claud Gurney, *novel*
Christianna Brand d Sidney Gilliat ph Wilkie
Cooper m William Alwyn

Alastair Sim, Sally Gray, Rosamund John,
Trevor Howard, Leo Genn, Megs Jenkins,
Judy Campbell, Ronald Ward, Moore
Marriott
  'Slick, witty and consistently
entertaining.'—*Daily Telegraph*
  'Launder and Gilliat have told an exciting
story excitingly.'—*Times*

The Green Glove
US / France 1952 89m bw
UA / Benagoss (George Maurer)

A paratrooper against all odds returns a
jewelled relic to its proper place in a French
church.
An unsatisfactory concoction by people who
have clearly seen *The Maltese Falcon* as well as
lots of Hitchcock films, this interestingly cast
and credited independent production never
really takes off.

w Charles Bennett d Rudolph Maté
ph Claude Renoir m Joseph Kosma

Glenn Ford, Cedric Hardwicke, Geraldine
Brooks, George Macready, Gaby André,
Roger Treville

The Green Goddess*
US 1930 80m bw
Warner

An Indian potentate holds Britishers prisoner.
Early talkie star vehicle which was also
successful on the stage and as a silent but has
little appeal now.

w Julian Josephson, *play* William Archer
d Alfred E. Green ph James Van Trees

George Arliss, Alice Joyce, H. B. Warner,
Ralph Forbes, David Tearle
  'Nice programme fare, but it suggests too
many synthetic thrillers that have gone
before.'—*Variety*
† Remade 1942 as *Adventure in Iraq.*
AAN: George Arliss

She was the most famous woman in the world.
He was a peasant, a pirate, a shark.
What he couldn't buy with money he stole with charm.

ALLEN KLEIN Presents

ANTHONY JACQUELINE QUINN BISSET

THE GREEK TYCOON

also starring RAF VALLONE · EDWARD ALBERT · CHARLES DURNING
LUCIANA PALUZZI · CAMILLA SPARV · MARILU TOLO
and JAMES FRANCISCUS as President James Cassidy

Screenplay by MORT FINE · Story by NICO MASTORAKIS & WIN WELLS and MORT FINE · Co-Producers
NICO MASTORAKIS and LAURENCE MYERS · Directed by J. Lee THOMPSON · Produced by ALLEN KLEIN
and ELY LANDAU · An abkco Films Production · A Universal Release · Technicolor®

Now a WARNER Book

©1978 UNIVERSAL CITY STUDIOS INC
ALL RIGHTS RESERVED

R RESTRICTED
UNDER 17 REQUIRES ACCOMPANYING
PARENT OR ADULT GUARDIAN

THE GREEK TYCOON. A piece of total fiction based rather obviously on a real-life romance.

Green Grass of Wyoming

US 1948 88m Technicolor
TCF

A rancher captures his runaway white stallion
and wins the local trotting races.
Predictable, good-looking family film shot on
location; a second sequel to *My Friend Flicka*.

w Martin Berkeley, *novel* Mary O'Hara
d Louis King ph Charles G. Clarke m Cyril
Mockridge

Peggy Cummins, Charles Coburn, Robert
Arthur, Lloyd Nolan

AAN: Charles G. Clarke

Green Grow the Rushes

GB 1951 77m bw
ACT Films

Civil servants discover that a Kentish village is
devoted to smuggling.
Amiable but disappointingly feeble imitation
of Ealing comedy by a company formed from
the technicians' union; it simply hasn't got the
right snap in any department.

w Derek Twist, Howard Clewes,
novel Howard Clewes d Derek Twist
ph Harry Waxman m Lambert Williamson

Roger Livesey, Richard Burton, Honor
Blackman, Frederick Leister, John Salew,
Colin Gordon, Geoffrey Keen, Harcourt
Williams, Vida Hope

● *Video: Video Unlimited*

Green Hell*

US 1940 87m bw
Universal (Harry Edgington)

Explorers seek Inca treasure in the South
American Jungle.
Studio-bound potboiler unworthy of its
director but mainly enjoyable as a romp.

w Frances Marion d James Whale ph Karl
Freund

Douglas Fairbanks Jnr, Joan Bennett, George
Sanders, Vincent Price, Alan Hale, Gene
Garrick, George Bancroft, John Howard
† The temple set was re-used the same year in
The Mummy's Hand.

The Green Helmet

GB 1961 88m bw
MGM (Charles Francis Vetter)

A race driver with shattered nerves makes his
last job the introduction of an American car of
new design.
Totally conventional motor racing thriller.
Most of the work could just as effectively have
been phoned in.

w Jon Cleary, from his novel d Michael
Forlong ph Geoffrey Faithfull m Ken Jones

Bill Travers, Ed Begley, Sidney James, Nancy
Walters, Ursula Jeans, Megs Jenkins

Green Ice

GB 1981 116m colour
ITC / Lew Grade (Jack Wiener)

An aimless American in Mexico becomes
involved with emerald thieves.
Dismally routine punch-ups and car chases are
enlivened by a mildly original theft by balloon,
but the overall effect is soporific.

w Edward Anhalt, Ray Hassett, Anthony
Simmons, Robert de Laurentis, *novel* Gerald
Browne d Ernest Day ph Gilbert Taylor
m Bill Wyman

Ryan O'Neal, Anne Archer, Omar Sharif,
Philip Stone

'It should not tempt anyone away from
doubtlessly superior versions of the same
material on television.'—*Geoff Brown, MFB*

● *Video: Precision*

The Green Light*

US 1937 85m bw
Warner (Henry Blanke)

A dedicated doctor gives up his practice when
a patient dies.
Adequate star melodrama.

w Milton Krims, *novel* Lloyd C. Douglas
d Frank Borzage ph Byron Haskin m Max
Steiner

Errol Flynn, Anita Louise, Margaret Lindsay,
Cedric Hardwicke, Henry O'Neill, Spring
Byington

'Customer lure in the title and the player
names . . . it will carry a weak sister nicely.'—
Variety

The Green Man*

GB 1956 80m bw
BL / Grenadier (Frank Launder, Sidney
Gilliat)

A professional assassin stalks a pompous
politician.
Cheerful but not very subtle black comedy,
suffering from the attempt to make a star part
out of a very minor character.

w Sidney Gilliat, Frank Launder, from their
play Meet a Body d Robert Day ph Gerald
Gibbs m Cedric Thorpe Davie

Alastair Sim, George Cole, Jill Adams, Terry-
Thomas, Avril Angers, John Chandos, Dora
Bryan, Colin Gordon, Raymond Huntley

Green Mansions

US 1959 104m Metrocolor
Cinemascope
MGM / Avon (Edmund Grainger)

In a remote Amazon forest an adventurer
encounters Rima, a child of nature who takes
him on a quest for truth.
Absurd studio-bound Shangri-La story based
on an Edwardian fantasy that may well have
suited the printed page, but not the wide
screen. Dismally photographed in shades of
green, with all concerned looking acutely
uncomfortable.

w Dorothy Kingsley, *novel* W. H. Hudson
d Mel Ferrer ph Joseph Ruttenberg
m Bronislau Kaper, Hector Villa-Lobos

Anthony Perkins, Audrey Hepburn, Lee J.
Cobb, Henry Silva

The Green Pastures****

US 1936 93m bw
Warner (Henry Blanke)

Old Testament stories as seen through simple-
minded negro eyes.
Though recently attacked as setting back the
cause of black emancipation, this is a
brilliantly sympathetic and humorous film,
very cunningly adapted for the screen in a
series of dramatic scenes which make the
material work even better than it did on the
stage.

w Marc Connelly, from his play and stories by
Roark Bradford d William Keighley, Marc
Connelly ph Hal Mohr m Erich Wolfgang
Korngold

Rex Ingram, Oscar Polk, Eddie Anderson,
Frank Wilson, George Reed

'I imagine God has a sense of humour, and I
imagine that He is delighted with *The Green
Pastures*.'—*Don Herold*

'That disturbance around the Music Hall
yesterday was the noise of shuffling queues in
Sixth Avenue and the sound of motion picture
critics dancing in the street.'—*Bosley
Crowther, New York Times*

'This is as good a religious play as one is
likely to get in this age from a practised New
York writer.'—*Graham Greene*

Green Promise

US 1949 88m bw
RKO / Glenn McCarthy (Robert Paige,
Monty F. Collins)
GB title: *Raging Waters*

A farmer refuses to move from the dust bowl
area, and a landslide causes a flood.
Curiously stilted independent production
which doesn't really bear comparison with *The
Grapes of Wrath*.

w Monty F. Collins d William D. Russell
ph John Russell m David Chudnow

Marguerite Chapman, Walter Brennan,
Robert Paige, Natalie Wood, Ted Donaldson,
Connie Marshall

The Green Scarf

GB 1954 96m bw
B and A (Bertram Ostrer, Albert Fennell)

An elderly French lawyer takes on the defence
of a blind, deaf and dumb murder suspect.
Plodding courtroom drama with familiar faces
in unconvincing French guise.

w Gordon Wellesley, *novel* The Brute by Guy
des Cars d George More O'Ferrall ph Jack
Hildyard m Brian Easdale

Michael Redgrave, Ann Todd, Leo Genn,
Kieron Moore

The Green Years*

US 1946 127m bw
MGM (Leon Gordon)

A young boy brought up strictly in Ireland
makes friends with his mischievous
grandfather.
Period family film in familiar style, sparked
only by its scene-stealing star performance.

w Robert Ardrey, Sonya Levien, *novel* A. J.
Cronin d Victor Saville ph George Folsey
m Herbert Stothart ad Cedric Gibbons, Hans
Peters

Charles Coburn, Dean Stockwell, Tom Drake,
Beverly Tyler, Hume Cronyn, Gladys Cooper,
Selena Royle, Jessica Tandy, Richard Haydn,
Andy Clyde

GREEN FOR DANGER. Saved in the nick of time, Sally Gray looks for comfort to Trevor Howard and Alastair Sim.

'It has been described in the ads as "wonderful" by everyone within Louis B. Mayer's purchasing power except his horses, so I hesitate to ask you to take my word for it: the picture is awful.'—*James Agee*
AAN: George Folsey; Charles Coburn

The Greengage Summer*
GB 1961 99m Technicolor
Columbia / PKL (Victor Saville, Edward Small)
US title: *Loss of Innocence*

A young girl staying at a hotel falls in love with a jewel thief but is accidentally responsible for his capture.
Old-fashioned and not very interesting story with an appeal, one supposes, to well-brought-up young women. Decently made.

w Howard Koch, *novel* Rumer Godden
d Lewis Gilbert *ph* Frederick A. Young
m Richard Addinsell

Kenneth More, Danielle Darrieux, Susannah York, Claude Nollier, Jane Asher, Elizabeth Dear, Maurice Denham

Greenwich Village*
US 1944 82m Technicolor
TCF (William Le Baron)

In the twenties, a hick composer in New York allows his concerto to be used in a jazz musical.
Lightweight musical romp.

w Michael Fessier, Ernest Pagano *d* Walter Lang *ph* Leon Shamroy, Harry Jackson
songs Leo Robin, Nacio Herb Brown

Carmen Miranda, Don Ameche, William Bendix, Vivian Blaine, Felix Bressart, Tony and Sally De Marco, Adolph Green, Betty Comden, Alvin Hammer, Judy Holliday

Greetings*
US 1968 88m Eastmancolor

A draftee tries every which way to be exempted, then subjects himself to a whirl of physical experience. Kaleidoscopic stringing together of fleeting satirical bits; talent undeniable but equally uncontrolled. Jonathan Warden, Robert de Niro, Gerrit Graham, Megan McCormick. Written by Charles Hirsch and Brian de Palma; directed and edited by Brian de Palma; for West End Films.

Gregory's Girl**
GB 1980 91m colour
Lake / NFFC / STV (Davina Belling, Clive Parsons)

In a Scottish new town, a school footballer becomes aware of sex.
Curiously diverting comedy peopled by dreamers but handicapped by impenetrable accents. An unexpected world-wide success.

wd Bill Forsyth *ph* Michael Coulter *m* Colin Tully

Gordon John Sinclair, Dee Hepburn, Jake D'Arcy, Claire Grogan
BFA: best script
● *Video: Hokushin*

Gremlins*
US 1984 106m Technicolor
Warner / Amblin (Michael Finnell)

Small furry creatures called mogwais prove to be immensely prolific and dangerous when wet.
Juvenile horror comic, a kind of deliberate inversion of *E.T.* Slow to start, and a little too knowingly nasty, with variable special effects; but a pretty hot commercial success.

w Chris Columbus *d* Joe Dante (with Steven Spielberg as a presumably involved producer) *ph* John Hora *m* Jerry Goldsmith *gremlin designer* Chris Walas *ed* Tina Hirsch

Zach Galligan, Phoebe Cates, Hoyt Axton, Polly Holliday, Keye Luke, Scott Brady, Edward Andrews

Greyfriars Bobby*
GB 1960 91m Technicolor
Walt Disney (Hugh Attwooll)

A Skye terrier keeps persistent vigil over his master's grave and is made a freeman of the city of Edinburgh.
Adequately produced film of a charming old Victorian story.

w Robert Westerby *d* Don Chaffey *ph* Paul Beeson *m* Francis Chagrin

Donald Crisp, Laurence Naismith, Alexander Mackenzie, Kay Walsh, Andrew Cruickshank, Vincent Winter, Moultrie Kelsall, Duncan Macrae
'The better Disney qualities of exact period detail and childlike directness are apparent.'—*MFB*
† The story was previously filmed as *Challenge to Lassie*.

Greystoke: The Legend of Tarzan, Lord of the Apes
GB 1984 130m Eastmancolor
Panavision

In the 1880s, an English lord and lady are killed in Africa, and their son is brought up by apes.
An absurd attempt to treat the story seriously after 70 years of hokum, this meandering chronicle, cut down from something much longer and even less endurable, has men in ape suits, an eye for unpleasant detail, and Ralph Richardson sliding down the stairs on a tray. The attempt to moralize at the end is emetic.

w P. H. Vazak (Robert Towne), Michael Austin, *novel* Tarzan of the Apes by Edgar Rice Burroughs *d* Hugh Hudson *ph* John Alcott *m* John Scott *pd* Stuart Craig

Ralph Richardson, Ian Holm, James Fox, Christopher Lambert, Andie MacDowell, Cheryl Campbell, Paul Geoffrey, John Wells, Nigel Davenport, Ian Charleson, Richard Griffiths

'A unique mixture of pomposity and ineptitude . . . in the second half the movie simply loses its mind, and dribbles to a pathetically indecisive conclusion.'—*Pauline Kael, New Yorker*

Il Grido*

Italy 1957   102m   bw
SPA Cinematografica / Robert Alexander
aka: *The Cry*

A man whose wife has left him travels across the Po Valley with his daughter in search of new happiness, but fails to find it and commits suicide.
Watchable but rather aimlessly depressing character drama.

w Michelangelo Antonioni, Elio Bartolini, Ennio de Concini d Michelangelo Antonioni ph Gianni di Venanzo m Giovanni Fusco

Steve Cochran, Alida Valli, Dorian Gray, Betsy Blair, Lynn Shaw

Grip of the Strangler*

GB 1958   78m   bw
Producers' Associates (John Croydon)
US title: *The Haunted Strangler*

A novelist investigating an old murder case finds that he was himself the murderer.
Moderate thriller with a predictable but efficient plot.

w Jan Read d Robert Day ph Lionel Banes m Buxton Orr

Boris Karloff, Elizabeth Allan, Jean Kent, Vera Day, Anthony Dawson
● *Video: Kingston*

The Grissom Gang

US 1971   128m   Metrocolor
Associates and Aldrich / ABC

In 1931, a New York heiress is kidnapped by gangsters and comes to like it.
Unpleasant remake of *No Orchids for Miss Blandish* (previously filmed under that title, incredibly badly, in GB in 1948), with too much footage of lush blonde being slobbered over by psychotic thug, and an inevitable emphasis on violence.

w Leon Griffiths, *novel* James Hadley Chase d Robert Aldrich ph Joseph Biroc m Gerald Fried ad James Dowell Vance

Scott Wilson, Kim Darby, Tony Musante, Robert Lansing, Irene Dailey, Connie Stevens, Wesley Addy
'Offensive, immoral and perhaps even lascivious.'—*Vincent Canby*
● *Video: Guild*

Grizzly

US 1976   91m   Movielab   Todd AO 35
Film Ventures International (David Sheldon, Harvey Flaxman)
aka: *Killer Grizzly*

A mammoth bear preys upon campers in a national park.
Inept and boring shocker in the wake of *Jaws*.

w Harvey Flaxman, David Sheldon d William Girdler ph William Asman m Robert O. Ragland

Christopher George, Andrew Prine, Richard Jaeckel, Joan McCall

Grounds for Marriage

US 1950   90m   bw

A divorced couple meet again and find they have strange effects on each other. Stolid romantic comedy with second team talent.
Van Johnson, Kathryn Grayson, Paula Raymond, Lewis Stone, Reginald Owen, Barry Sullivan. Written by Allen Rivkin and Laura Kerr; directed by Robert Z. Leonard; for MGM.

'We challenge you to guess the ending!'
The Groundstar Conspiracy*

US 1972   96m   Technicolor   Panavision
Universal / Hal Roach International (Trevor Wallace)

An explosion rips apart a top secret space project, and the surviving scientist loses his memory.
Gimmicky but generally compulsive sci-fi mystery yarn, with an effective though predictable climax.

w Matthew Howard, *novel* The Alien by L. P. Davies d Lamont Johnson ph Michael Reed m Paul Hoffert

George Peppard, Michael Sarrazin, James Olson, Christine Belford, Tim O'Connor, James McEachin

The Group***

US 1966   152m   De Luxe
UA / Famous Artists (Sidney Buchman)

The subsequent love lives of a group of girls who graduate from Vassar in 1933.
Patchy but generally fascinating series of interwoven sketches and character studies, with mainly tragic overtones; good attention to period detail, and dazzling array of new talent.

w Sidney Buchman, *novel* Mary McCarthy d Sidney Lumet ph Boris Kaufman m Charles Gross pd Gene Callahan

Joanna Pettet, Candice Bergen, *Jessica Walter, Joan Hackett*, Elizabeth Hartman, Mary Robin-Redd, *Kathleen Widdoes*, Shirley Knight, Larry Hagman, *Hal Holbrook, Robert Emhardt*, Robert Mulligan, James Congdon, James Broderick

'Although it is a strange, inclusive, no-holds-barred movie that runs the gamut from scenes that are almost soap-operaish, to amusing scenes that are almost satire, to outrageously frank scenes that are almost voyeuristic, it is still greatly exhilarating while it provokes thought and pushes the viewer into examining his own conscience.'—*Philip T. Hartung, Commonweal*

Grumpy

US 1930   74m   bw

A very elderly gentleman is still in control of his family. Interesting but not exciting transcript of a production which was having

surprising success on Broadway with English players, though a very musty vehicle even then. Cyril Maude, Phillips Holmes, Paul Cavanagh, Frances Dade, Halliwell Hobbes, Paul Lukas. Written by Doris Anderson from a play by Horace Hodges and Thomas Wigney Percyval; directed by George Cukor and Cyril Gardner; for Paramount. 'Its box office fate is in the balance.'—*Variety*

Guadalcanal Diary*

US 1943   93m   bw
TCF (Bryan Foy)

Marines fight for a vital Pacific base.
Standard war propaganda, with good action scenes.

w Lamar Trotti, *book* Richard Tregaskis d Lewis Seiler ph Charles G. Clarke m David Buttolph

Preston Foster, Lloyd Nolan, William Bendix, Richard Conte, Anthony Quinn, Richard Jaeckel, Roy Roberts, Minor Watson, Ralph Byrd, Lionel Stander, Miles Mander, Reed Hadley

The Guardsman*

US 1931   83m   bw
MGM (Albert Lewin)

A jealous actor tests his wife's fidelity.
Theatrically effective comedy filmed for the sake of its stars; later remade as a musical, *The Chocolate Soldier* (qv).

w Ernest Vajda, Claudine West, *play* Ferenc Molnar d Sidney Franklin ph Norbert Brodine

Alfred Lunt, Lynn Fontanne, Roland Young, Zasu Pitts, Maude Eburne, Herman Bing, Ann Dvorak

'Looks like a smash engagement on Broadway and less than moderate returns on general release.'—*Variety*

AAN: Alfred Lunt; Lynn Fontanne

La Guerre Est Finie

France / Sweden 1966   122m   bw
Sofracima / Europa Film
aka: *The War Is Over*

A Spanish revolutionary maintains his ideals even though he is warned that he will be sold out.
Dreary drama with romantic interludes and a fussy technique involving what appears to be the first use of flashforwards.

w Jorge Semprun d Alain Resnais ph Sacha Vierny m Giovanni Fusco

Yves Montand, Ingrid Thulin, Geneviève Bujold, Michel Piccoli

AAN: Jorge Semprun

Guess Who's Coming to Dinner**

US 1967   112m   Technicolor
Columbia / Stanley Kramer

A well-to-do San Francisco girl announces that she is going to marry a black man, and her parents find they are less broad-minded than they thought.

The problem picture that isn't really, since everyone is so nice and the prospective bridegroom is so eligible. It looks like a photographed play, but isn't based on one; the set is unconvincing; but the acting is a dream.

w William Rose d Stanley Kramer ph Sam Leavitt md Frank de Vol pd Robert Clatworthy

Spencer Tracy, Katharine Hepburn, Katharine Houghton (Hepburn's niece), *Sidney Poitier*, Cecil Kellaway, Roy E. Glenn Snr, Beah Richards, Isabell Sanford, Virginia Christine

'Suddenly everybody's caught up in a kind of integrated drawing-room comedy, and unable to decide whether there's anything funny in it or not.'—*Ann Birstein, Vogue*

'A load of embarrassing rubbish. In the circumstances there is little that director Stanley Kramer can do but see that his camera plod from room to room and make the most of people sitting down and getting up again.'—*Penelope Mortimer*

'What Rose and Kramer have done is to create a number of elaborate Aunt Sallies, arrange them in attractive patterns, and dispose of them with the flick of a feather.'—*Basil Wright, 1972*

'Mendacious and sanctimonious drivel.'—*John Simon*

AA: William Rose; Katharine Hepburn
AAN: best picture; Stanley Kramer; Frank de Vol; Spencer Tracy; Cecil Kellaway; Beah Richards

Guest in the House*
US 1944 121m bw
Hunt Stromberg

A seemingly pleasant young woman is invited to stay with a family and brings tragedy and hatred to them.
Theatrical and rather unconvincing melodrama.

w Ketti Frings, *play* Dear Evelyn by Dale Eunson, Hagar Wilde d John Brahm ph Lee Garmes m Werner Janssen pd Nicolai Remisoff

Anne Baxter, Ralph Bellamy, Aline MacMahon, Ruth Warrick, Scott McKay, Jerome Cowan, Marie McDonald, Percy Kilbride, Margaret Hamilton

AAN: Werner Janssen

Guest Wife
US 1945 90m bw
(UA) Jack H. Skirball

For business purposes a man allows his wife to pretend to be the wife of another.
Stereotyped star farce which seemed tolerable at the time.

w Bruce Manning, John Klorer d Sam Wood ph Joseph Valentine md Daniele Amfitheatrof

Claudette Colbert, Don Ameche, Dick Foran, Charles Dingle, Grant Mitchell

'Mr Wood is a big gun to be trained on so trivial a target, but the result justifies the choice.'—*Richard Mallett, Punch*

AAN: Daniele Amfitheatrof

A Guide for the Married Man**
US 1967 91m De Luxe Panavision
TCF (Frank McCarthy)

A practised wolf explains to a perfect husband how to be unfaithful.
Generally funny revue with as many hilarious moments as flat spots.

w Frank Tarloff d Gene Kelly ph Joe Macdonald m Johnny Williams

Walter Matthau, Inger Stevens, *Robert Morse*, Sue Anne Langdon, Lucille Ball, Art Carney, Jack Benny, Polly Bergen, Joey Bishop, Sid Caesar, Wally Cox, Jayne Mansfield, Carl Reiner, Phil Silvers, Jeffrey Hunter, Terry-Thomas, Ben Blue

'One of the funniest films of the last several seasons . . . it has sense enough to sit down when it's through.'—*Robert Windeler*

Guilt Is My Shadow
GB 1950 86m bw

A girl kills her villainous husband and is helped by a farmer. Tedious melodrama, stiffly told and not helped by rural surroundings. Patrick Holt, Elizabeth Sellars, Peter Reynolds, Lana Morris, Avice Landone. Written by Ivan Foxwell, Roy Kellino and John Gilling, from the novel *You're Best Alone* by Peter Curtis; directed by Roy Kellino; for Ivan Foxwell.

The Guilt of Janet Ames
US 1947 83m bw
Columbia

A paralysed war widow seeks to discover whether her husband's sacrifice was worthwhile.
Embarrassing attempt by a comedienne to play Hamlet.

w Louella Macfarlane, Allen Rivkin, Devery Freeman, *story* Lenore Coffee d Henry Levin ph Joseph Walker m Morris Stoloff

Rosalind Russell, Melvyn Douglas, Sid Caesar, Betsy Blair, Nina Foch, Harry Von Zell, Arthur Space

Guilty?
GB 1956 93m bw
Grand National / Gibraltar (Charles A. Leeds)

An ex-resistance heroine is on trial for murder at the Old Bailey; her young solicitor goes to Avignon to prove her innocence.
Solidly cast old-fashioned mystery with a courtroom climax.

w Maurice J. Wilson, *novel* Death Has Deep Roots by Michael Gilbert d Edmond Greville ph Stan Pavey m Bruce Montgomery

John Justin, Barbara Laage, Donald Wolfit, Stephen Murray, Norman Wooland, Frank Villard, Sydney Tafler, Betty Stockfield

Guilty as Hell*
US 1932 82m bw

A doctor commits what he hopes is the perfect murder. Smart murder story with two points of interest: the audience knows who done it from

the start, and the detective and reporter roles are worked over to fit the actors who played Flagg and Quirt. It certainly pleased at the time, and was remade in 1937 as *Night Club Scandal*, with John Barrymore in the lead as the doctor. Edmund Lowe, Victor McLaglen, Richard Arlen, Ralph Ince, Adrienne Ames, Henry Stephenson, Elizabeth Patterson. Written by Arthur Kober and Frank Partos, from the play Riddle Me This by Daniel Rubin; directed by Erle C. Kenton; for Paramount. 'Excellent entertainment and should do a good business where the title does not hurt.'—*Variety*

The Guilty Generation
US 1931 82m bw

A gangster has social ambitions for his daughter's sake. Rather heavy melodrama which didn't catch on. Leo Carrillo, Constance Cummings, Robert Young, Boris Karloff, Emma Dunn. From the play by Jo Milward and J. Kerby Hawkes; directed by Rowland V. Lee; for Columbia. 'Merits a fair showing . . . will do average or better.'—*Variety*

Guilty Hands
US 1931 60m bw

A district attorney commits murder and tries to frame a girl, but is killed when rigor mortis makes the gun go off in his victim's hand. Risible melodrama which might with better writing have been effective. Lionel Barrymore, Kay Francis, Madge Evans, William Bakewell, C. Aubrey Smith, Polly Moran, Alan Mowbray. Written by Bayard Veiller; directed by W. S. Van Dyke; for MGM. 'Someone missed here, and plenty.'—*Variety*

Guilty of Treason
US 1950 86m bw

An account of the trial by the Russians of the Hungarian primate Cardinal Mindzenty. Gutter press version of real events, with cheap production and fictional frills. Charles Bickford, Paul Kelly, Bonita Granville, Richard Derr, Barry Kroeger, Elisabeth Risdon. Written by Emmet Lavery; directed by Felix Feist; for Eagle Lion. (GB title: *Treason*.)

The Guinea Pig**
GB 1948 97m bw
Pilgrim (The Boultings)
US title: *The Outsider*

The first poor boy to win a scholarship to a famous public school has a hard time. Enjoyable though unrealistic school drama with chief interest centring on the staff. A rude word ('kick up the arse') ensured its popularity.

w Bernard Miles, Warren Chetham Strode, from the latter's play d Roy Boulting ph Gilbert Taylor m John Wooldridge

Richard Attenborough, *Robert Flemyng, Cecil Trouncer*, Sheila Sim, Bernard Miles, Joan Hickson

Gulliver's Travels**
US 1939 74m Technicolor
(Paramount) Max Fleischer

Animated cartoon version which invents a
Romeo-Juliet romance between Lilliput and
Blefuscu and has the usual trouble with
romantic humans. At the time it represented a
genuine challenge to Disney, but has not worn
well in terms of pace or inventiveness.
Fleischer made one more feature cartoon, Mr
Bug Goes to Town.

d Dave Fleischer m Victor Young
songs Ralph Rainger, Leo Robin
   'Effective entertainment, but may not reach
the grosses of Snow White.'—Variety

AAN: song 'Faithful Forever'; Victor Young
● Video: BBC

Gulliver's Travels
GB 1976 81m Eastmancolor
EMI / Valeness-Belvision (Josef Shaftel)

An ineffective treatment, again aimed at
children, in which Gulliver is the only human
element and all the Lilliputians are cartooned.

w Don Black d Peter Hunt ph Alan Hume
pd Michael Stringer m Michel Legrand

Richard Harris, Catherine Schell, Norman
Shelley
   'Bonelessly inoffensive.'—Sight and Sound

The Gumball Rally
US 1976 107m Technicolor
Warner / First Artists (Chuck Bail)

A variety of vehicles take part in a crazy race
from New York to Long Beach.
The stuntmen are the real stars of this good-
looking but dramatically deficient chase and
destruction extravaganza.

w Leon Capetanos d Chuck Bail ph Richard
Glouner m Dominic Frontière stunt co-
ordinator Eddie Donno

Michael Sarrazin, Normann Burton, Gary
Busey, John Durren, Susan Flannery

Gumshoe**
GB 1971 85m Eastmancolor
Columbia / Memorial (David Barber)

A Liverpool bingo caller dreams of becoming
a Bogart-like private eye and finds himself in
the middle of a murder case.
A likeable spoof which is never quite as funny
as it means to be. Billy Liar did it better, but
there's plenty of amusing detail.

w Neville Smith d Stephen Frears ph Chris
Menges m Andrew Lloyd Webber

Albert Finney, Billie Whitelaw, Fulton
Mackay, Frank Finlay, Janice Rule

Gun Crazy*
US 1950 87m bw
King Brothers
reissue title: Deadly is the Female

A boy and girl set off on a trail of armed
robbery and murder.
Modernized Bonnie and Clyde story which has
become a minor cult film.

w Dalton Trumbo, story Mackinlay Kantor
d Joseph H. Lewis ph Russell Harlan
m Victor Young

John Dall, Peggy Cummins, Morris
Carnovsky, Barry Kroger, Annabel Shaw,
Harry Lewis

Gun for a Coward
US 1956 88m Technicolor
   Cinemascope

Three brothers join forces on a cattle drive,
but one is killed. Slightly pretentious western
co-feature. Fred MacMurray, Jeffrey Hunter,
Dean Stockwell, Chill Wills, Janice Rule.
Written by R. Wright Campbell; directed by
Abner Biberman; for Universal-International.

Gun Fury
US 1953 80m Technicolor 3-D
Columbia (Lewis J. Rachmil)

Outlaws rob a stagecoach and abduct a girl;
her fiancé follows and takes revenge.
Adequate western programmer.

w Irving Wallace, Roy Huggins d Raoul
Walsh ph Lester H. White md Mischa
Bakaleinikoff

Rock Hudson, Donna Reed, Phil Carey, Lee
Marvin, Neville Brand

Gun Glory
US 1957 89m Metrocolor
   Cinemascope
MGM (Nicholas Nayfack)

A gunfighter returns home to settle down, but
finds his wife dead and his son resentful.
Dull, unexciting star western.

w William Ludwig, novel Man of the West by
Philip Yordan d Roy Rowland ph Harold J.
Marzorati m Jeff Alexander

Stewart Granger, Rhonda Fleming, Chill
Wills, Steve Rowland, James Gregory

The Gun Runners*
US 1958 82m bw
UA / Seven Arts (Clarence Greene)

The owner of a Florida motor cruiser
innocently rents it to a gun merchant.
Modestly effective action melodrama, the
third version of To Have and Have Not (qv).

w Daniel Mainwaring, d Don
Siegel ph Hal Mohr m Leith Stevens

Audie Murphy, Eddie Albert, Patricia Owens,
Everett Sloane

A Gunfight*
US 1970 94m Technicolor
Harvest / Thoroughbred / Bryna (Ronnie
Lubin, Harold Jack Bloom)

Two famous gunfighters on their uppers stage
a duel for money.
Austere and anti-climactic western supposedly
against popular blood lust.

w Harold Jack Bloom d Lamont Johnson
ph David M. Walsh m Laurence Rosenthal

Kirk Douglas, Johnny Cash, Karen Black, Raf
Vallone, Jane Alexander
● Video: Rank

Gunfight at Comanche Creek
US 1963 90m De Luxe Panavision

In 1875 a detective goes undercover to unmask
the brains behind a robber gang with complex
methods. Ingenious but over-emphatic western
programmer. Audie Murphy, Ben Cooper,
Coleen Miller, John Hubbard, DeForrest
Kelley. Written by Edward Bernds; directed
by Frank McDonald; for Allied Artists.

Gunfight at Dodge City
US 1958 81m De Luxe Cinemascope
UA / Mirisch

After various problems, Bat Masterson is
elected sheriff of Dodge City.
Fair standard western with emphasis on plot
and character.

w Daniel B. Ullman, Martin M. Goldsmith
d Joseph M. Newman ph Carl Guthrie
m Hans Salter

Joel McCrea, Julie Adams, John McIntire,
Richard Anderson, Nancy Gates

Gunfight at the OK Corral**
US 1957 122m Technicolor
   Vistavision
Paramount / Hal Wallis

Wyatt Earp and Doc Holliday defeat the
Clanton Gang.
Watchable, ambitious, but vaguely
disappointing super-western.

w Leon Uris d John Sturges ph Charles B.
Lang m Dmitri Tiomkin

Burt Lancaster, Kirk Douglas, Jo Van Fleet,
Rhonda Fleming, John Ireland, Frank Faylen,
Kenneth Tobey, Earl Holliman
   'Carefully and lavishly mounted, but
overlong and overwrought.'—John Cutts

Gunfight in Abilene
US 1967 86m Technicolor

After the Civil War, an officer goes home to
find strife between farmers and cattlemen.
Fairly sensible and pleasing lower-berth
western. Bobby Darin, Emily Banks, Leslie
Nielsen, Donnelly Rhodes, Don Galloway,
Michael Sarrazin. Written by Berne Giler and
John D. F. Black; directed by Joseph Kenny;
for Universal.

'His only friend was his gun—his only
   refuge, a woman's heart!'
The Gunfighter**
US 1950 84m bw
TCF (Nunnally Johnson)

A gunfighter fails to shake off his past.
Downbeat, small-scale but very careful adult
western set in a believable community.

w William Bowers, William Sellers d Henry
King ph Arthur Miller m Alfred Newman

Gregory Peck, Helen Westcott, Millard
Mitchell, Jean Parker, Karl Malden, Skip
Homeier, Mae Marsh
   'Preserves throughout a respectable level of
intelligence and invention.'—Lindsay
Anderson
   'Not merely a good western, a good film.'—
Richard Mallett, Punch

'The movie is done in cold, quiet tones of gray, and every object in it—faces, clothing, a table, the hero's heavy moustache—is given an air of uncompromising authenticity, suggesting those dim photographs of the nineteenth-century west. . .'—*Robert Warshow, The Immediate Experience*

AAN: original story (William Bowers)

Gunfighters
US 1947 87m Cinecolor

A retired gunfighter is suspected of the murder of his best friend. Presentable star western.
Randolph Scott, Barbara Britton, Dorothy Hart, Bruce Cabot, Forrest Tucker. Written by Alan Le May, from the novel *Twin Sombreros* by Zane Grey; directed by George Waggner; for Columbia. (GB title: *The Assassin.*)

Gung Ho!
US 1943 88m bw
Universal / Walter Wanger

Adventures of the Marines in the Pacific War.
Trite flagwaver, popular at the time.

w Lucien Hubbard, based on the experiences of Captain W. S. LeFrancois USMC *d* Ray Enright *ph* Milton H. Krasner *m* Frank Skinner, Hans Salter

Randolph Scott, Grace MacDonald, Alan Curtis, Noah Beery Jnr, J. Carrol Naish, David Bruce, Peter Coe, Robert Mitchum

'Thrills for a thousand movies plundered for one mighty show!'
'Romance aflame through dangerous days and nights of terror! In a land where anything can happen—most of all to a beautiful girl alone!'

Gunga Din***
US 1939 117m bw
RKO (George Stevens)

Three cheerful army veterans meet adventure on the North-West Frontier.
Rousing period actioner with comedy asides, one of the most entertaining of its kind ever made.

w Joel Sayre, Fred Guiol, Ben Hecht, Charles MacArthur, *poem* Rudyard Kipling *d* George Stevens *ph* Joseph H. August *m* Alfred Newman *ad* Van Nest Polglase

Cary Grant, Victor McLaglen, Douglas Fairbanks Jnr, Sam Jaffe, Eduardo Ciannelli, Joan Fontaine, Montagu Love, Robert Coote, Cecil Kellaway, Abner Biberman, Lumsden Hare

'One of the big money pictures this year . . . will recoup plenty at the box office window.'—*Variety*
'One of the most enjoyable nonsense-adventure movies of all time.'—*Pauline Kael, 1968*
'Bravura is the exact word for the performances, and Stevens' composition and cutting of the fight sequences is particularly stunning.'—*NFT, 1973*

Gunman's Walk*
US 1958 97m Technicolor
Cinemascope
Columbia (Fred Kohlmar)

A tough westerner has two sons, one of whom follows too literally in his footsteps.
Competent action melodrama with good characterization.

w Frank Nugent *d* Phil Karlson *ph* Charles Lawton *m* George Duning

Van Heflin, Tab Hunter, James Darren, Kathryn Grant

Gunn*
US 1967 95m Technicolor
Paramount / Geoffrey (Owen Crump)

A private eye is hired to find a gangster's killer.
Tongue-in-cheek violence from the television series, with Craig Stevens doing a Cary Grant imitation.

w Blake Edwards, William Peter Blatty *d* Blake Edwards *ph* Philip Lathrop *m* Henry Mancini

Craig Stevens, Laura Devon, Ed Asner, Sherry Jackson, Helen Traubel, J. Pat O'Malley, Regis Toomey
'Falters between parody and straight action.'—*MFB*

Gunpoint
US 1966 86m Technicolor

A Colorado sheriff goes after train robbers.
Simple-minded but quite professional and good-looking western programmer. Audie Murphy, Joan Staley, Warren Stevens, Edgar Buchanan, Denver Pyle. Written by Mary and Willard Willingham; directed by Earl Bellamy; for Universal.

Guns at Batasi*
GB 1964 103m bw Cinemascope
TCF / George H. Brown

The headquarters of an Anglo-African regiment is threatened by rebels.
Basically the old chestnut about a group of disparate types trapped in a dangerous situation, this is given shape and stature by the star's lively performance as the martinet of an RSM.

w Robert Hollis, from his novel The Siege of Battersea *d* John Guillermin *ph* Douglas Slocombe *m* John Addison

Richard Attenborough, Flora Robson, Mia Farrow, Jack Hawkins, Cecil Parker, Percy Herbert, Errol John, John Leyton, Earl Cameron

Guns for San Sebastian
France / Mexico / Italy 1967 111m
Eastmancolor Franscope
MGM / Cipra / Filmes / Ernesto Enriques (Jacques Bar)

In Mexico in 1746, a rebel on the run stays to defend a besieged village.
Multi-national actioner, violent but quite undistinguished.

w Serge Ganz, Miguel Morayta, Ennio de Concini *d* Henri Verneuil *ph* Armand Thirard *m* Ennio Morricone

Anthony Quinn, Charles Bronson, Sam Jaffe, Anjanette Comer, Silvia Pinal

Guns in the Heather
US 1968 90m Technicolor

An American schoolboy in Ireland finds that his elder brother is a CIA agent. Tolerable kiddie-fodder from the Disney treadmill; later desiccated for TV. Glenn Corbett, Alfred Burke, Kurt Russell, Patrick Barr. Written by Herman Groves; directed by Robert Butler; for Walt Disney.

Guns of Darkness
GB 1962 102m bw
ABP / Cavalcade (Thomas Clyde)

A British plantation boss in Latin America escapes with his wife when rebels strike.
Chase / escape film with a few tiny comments about violence.

w John Mortimer, *novel* Act of Mercy by Francis Clifford *d* Anthony Asquith *ph* Robert Krasker *m* Benjamin Frankel

David Niven, Leslie Caron, James Robertson Justice, David Opatoshu

The Guns of Fort Petticoat
US 1957 79m Technicolor
Columbia / Brown-Murphy (Harry Joe Brown)

During the Civil War, a wandering Texan trains townswomen into a fighting force.
Unlikely western which passes the time.

w Walter Doniger *d* George Marshall *ph* Ray Rennahan *m* Mischa Bakaleinikoff

Audie Murphy, Kathryn Grant, Hope Emerson, Jeff Donnell, Isobel Elsom

The Guns of Loos*
GB 1927 89m (24 fps) bw silent
Stoll / New Era

A blinded hero of the war returns home to run an industrial empire and is confronted by a strike.
One of the better British silents, with a strong plot and an interesting cast.

w L. H. Gordon, Reginald Fogwell, Sinclair Hill *d* Sinclair Hill *ph* Desmond Dickinson

Henry Victor, Madeleine Carroll, Bobby Howes, Hermione Baddeley

The Guns of Navarone**
GB 1961 157m Technicolor
Cinemascope
Columbia / Carl Foreman (Cecil F. Ford)

In 1943 a sabotage team is sent to destroy two giant guns on a Turkish Island.
Ambitiously produced Boy's Own Paper heroics, with lots of noise and self-sacrifice; intermittently exciting but bogged down by philosophical chat.

w Carl Foreman, *novel* Alistair Maclean *d* J. Lee-Thomson *ph* Oswald Morris *m* Dmitri Tiomkin *ad* Geoffrey Drake

OUT of the stirring glory of Kipling's seething world of battle they roar —red-blood and gunpowder heroes all! ..The stalwart, lusty, swaggering Sergeants Three . . . Rash and reckless battalioneers, who'd rather fight than and the lips they're always seeking!...Like towering giants astride the bristling hills that hide the bandit hordes of India . . . Headlong through the terrors of the Temples of Tantrapur ...Onward pushing the thin red line of Empire through a land the white man rules, but never conquers! . . . It's big! ...It's grand!...It's glorious!...No wonder it was more than a year in the making! . . . No wonder it taxed all Hollywood's resources to give the screen a sweep and a scope and an emotional blaze that it never had before! ...DON'T LET ANYTHING KEEP YOU FROM SEEING IT!

"GUNGA DIN"

CARY GRANT · VICTOR McLAGLEN

DOUGLAS FAIRBANKS, Jr.

RKO RADIO'S GIANT SHOW OF SHOWS!

Sam Jaffe · Eduardo Ciannelli · Joan Fontaine

Armies and elephants...Love and Laughter...Breathless adventure tuned to the rolling thunder of red drumfire in a land where men fight to live, and women love and weep!

PANDRO S. BERMAN in charge of production. Produced and directed by GEORGE STEVENS. From a story by Ben Hecht and Charles MacArthur. Screen Play by Joel Sayre and Fred Guiol.

GUNGA DIN.   Original advertising for a 1939 epic . . . . very wordy, but that was the way the customers liked it.

Gregory Peck, David Niven, Stanley Baker, Anthony Quinn, Anthony Quayle, James Darren, Gia Scala, James Robertson Justice, Richard Harris, Irene Papas, Bryan Forbes

'A desperate imbalance: the moral arguments cut into the action without extending it.'—*Penelope Houston*

AAN: best picture; Carl Foreman; J. Lee-Thompson; Dmitri Tiomkin

● *Video: RCA / Columbia*

Guns of the Magnificent Seven
US 1969 106m De Luxe Panavision
UA / Mirisch (Vincent M. Fennelly)

Seven mercenaries rescue a Mexican Robin Hood.
Stale, flat and unprofitable third serving of this particular hash.

w Herman Hoffman *d* Paul Wendkos
ph Antonio Macasoli *m* Elmer Bernstein

George Kennedy, Monte Markham, Joe Don Baker, James Whitmore, Bernie Casey, Scott Thomas, Reni Santoni, Michael Ansara, Wende Wagner, Fernando Rey, Frank Silvera

Guns of the Timberland
US 1960 91m Technicolor
Jaguar (Aaron Spelling)

Loggers are opposed by cattle interests.
Routine star western with tolerable production values.

w Joseph Petracca, Aaron Spelling *d* Robert D. Webb *ph* John Seitz *m* David Buttolph

Alan Ladd, Jeanne Crain, Gilbert Roland, Frankie Avalon, Lyle Bettger, Noah Beery Jnr

Gunsmoke
US 1953 79m Technicolor

A cowboy befriends the rancher he has been hired to kill. Moderate western with too many pauses for sentiment. Audie Murphy, Paul Kelly, Susan Cabot, Mary Castle, Charles Drake. Written by D. D. Beauchamp; directed by Nathan Juran; for Universal.

The Guru
US / India 1969 112m De Luxe
TCF / Arcadia (Ismail Merchant)

In India, an English pop singer succumbs to the local atmosphere.
Pleasant, affectionate but forgettable anecdote of modern India.

w Ruth Prawer Jhabvala, James Ivory
d James Ivory *ph* Subrata Mitra *m* Ustad Vilayat Khan

Michael York, Rita Tushingham, Utpal Dutt, Aparna Sen, Barry Foster

Gus
US 1976 96m Technicolor
Walt Disney (Ron Miller)

A football team co-opts a mule which can kick a hundred yard ball.
Predictable Disney fantasy comedy with a direct line back to *The Absent Minded Professor*.

w Arthur Alsberg, Don Nelson *d* Vincent McEveety *ph* Frank Phillips *m* Robert F. Brunner

Ed Asner, Don Knotts, Gary Grimes, Tim Conway, Liberty Williams, Bob Crane, Harold Gould, Tom Bosley, Dick Van Patten

'In the current comedy climate, when humour so often hinges on a four-letter word or its lengthier variant, a light-hearted football game spoof is a breath of fresh air.'—*Tatiana Balkoff Lipscomb, Films in Review*

The Guvnor
GB 1935 88m bw
Gaumont (Michael Balcon)
US title: *Mr Hobo*

By chance a tramp becomes a bank director.
Predictable star vehicle with Arliss a most unlikely tramp.

w Maude Howell, Guy Bolton *d* Milton Rosmer *ph* Max Greene

George Arliss, Gene Gerrard, Viola Keats, Patric Knowles, Frank Cellier, Mary Clare, George Hayes

'His admirers need not fear that he has lost any of his usual refinement or sentiment, his cultured English accent, his Universal certificate.'—*Graham Greene*

A Guy Named Joe
US 1944 120m bw
MGM (Everett Riskin)

A flier is killed but comes back as a ghost to supervise his ex-girl's new romance.
Icky romantic comedy-drama with strong propaganda intent; the stars make it tolerable.

w Dalton Trumbo *d* Victor Fleming
ph George Folsey, Karl Freund *m* Herbert Stothart

Spencer Tracy, Irene Dunne, Ward Bond, Van Johnson, James Gleason, Lionel Barrymore, Barry Nelson, Don Defore, Henry O'Neill

'As far as I could judge, the audience loved it: melodrama, farce, fake philosophy, swimming eyes and all.'—*Richard Mallett, Punch*

'It neatly obtunds death's sting as ordinary people suffer it by not only assuming but photographing a good, busy, hearty hereafter.'—*James Agee*
† The title was explained by one of the characters who observed that 'in the Army Air Corps, any fellow who is a right fellow is called Joe'.

AAN: original story (David Buchan, Chandler Sprague)

The Guy Who Came Back
US 1951 92m bw

A pro football player hates the thought of retiring. Sentimental sporting drama without much life in it. Paul Douglas, Joan Bennett, Linda Darnell, Don Defore, Zero Mostel. Written by Allan Scott; directed by Joseph Newman; for TCF.

Guys and Dolls[*]
US 1955 149m Eastmancolor
Cinemascope
Samuel Goldwyn

A New York gangster takes a bet that he can romance a Salvation Army lady.
The artifices of Runyonland are made more so by a defiantly studio-bound production and thoroughly flat handling; but the songs and sometimes the performances survive.

wd Joseph L. Mankiewicz, *musical* Jo Swerling and Abe Burrows *ph* Harry Stradling, *songs* Frank Loesser *md* Cyril Mockridge, Jay Blackton *ch* Michael Kidd *ad* Joseph Wright *pd* Oliver Smith

Frank Sinatra, Marlon Brando, Jean Simmons, *Vivian Blaine, Stubby Kaye*, B. S. Pully, Robert Keith, Sheldon Leonard, George E. Stone

'Quantity has been achieved only at the cost of quality.'—*Penelope Houston*

AAN: Harry Stradling; Cyril Mockridge, Jay Blackton

● *Video: CBS / Fox*

Gypsy
GB 1936 78m bw

An ageing playboy marries a gypsy but gives her back to her true love. Hard-to-swallow drama with insufficient comedy relief for its star. Roland Young, Chili Bouchier, Hugh Williams, Frederick Burtwell. Written by Brock Williams and Terence Rattigan, from the novel *Tsigane* by Lady Eleanor Smith; directed by Roy William Neill; for Warner.

'The girl who became the greatest show in show business!'
Gypsy[*]
US 1962 149m Technirama
Warner (Mervyn Le Roy)

The early days of stripteaser Gypsy Rose Lee, and the exploits of her ambitious mother.
A vaudeville musical that is nowhere near raucous enough, or brisk enough, for its subject, and is miscast into the bargain. The songs are great, but not here: Miss Russell is as boring as an electric drill in a role that should have been reserved for Ethel Merman.

w Leonard Spiegelgass, *book* Arthur Laurents *d* Mervyn Le Roy *m* Jule Styne *ly* Stephen Sondheim *ph* Harry Stradling *md* Frank Perkins *ad* John Beckman

Rosalind Russell, Natalie Wood, *Karl Malden*, James Milhollin

AAN: Harry Stradling; Frank Perkins

The Gypsy and the Gentleman
GB 1957 107m Eastmancolor
Rank (Maurice Cowan)

A penniless Regency rake marries a tempestuous gypsy, with melodramatic and tragic results.
Expensive and typically mistimed Rank attempt to re-do *The Man in Grey*; a barnstormer notable only for waste of talent.

w Janet Greene, *novel* Darkness I Leave You
by Nina Warner Hooke *d* Joseph Losey
ph Jack Hildyard *m* Hans May *ad* Ralph
Brinton

Melina Mercouri, Keith Michell, Patrick
McGoohan, June Laverick, Flora Robson,
Helen Haye

Gypsy Colt
US 1954   72m   Ansco Color

A cherished colt has to be sold, but makes its
way back home. Disguised second feature
remake of *Lassie Come Home*; good for
children. Donna Corcoran, Ward Bond,
Frances Dee, Larry Keating, Lee Van Cleef.
Written by Martin Berkeley; directed by
Andrew Marton; for MGM.

The Gypsy Moths*
US 1969   110m   Metrocolor
MGM / Frankenheimer-Lewis (Hal Landers,
  Bobby Roberts)

Sky-diving stuntmen find love and death on a
small-town tour.
Brilliantly breathtaking actioner which too
frequently gets grounded, and does not find a
reason for being so glum.

w William Hanley, *novel* James Drought
d John Frankenheimer *ph* Philip Lathrop
aerial ph Carl Boenisch *m* Elmer Bernstein

Burt Lancaster, Deborah Kerr, Gene
Hackman, Scott Wilson, William Windom,
Bonnie Bedelia, Sheree North
  'A Bergmanesque world of inner emotions
and ambiguous means. . . . As in many of
Frankenheimer's films it rains, and the wind in
the trees in the park and the sound of traffic
all contribute to the realism that makes his
work so satisfying.'—*Gerald Pratley*

Gypsy Wildcat
US 1944   77m   Technicolor
Universal (George Waggner)

A Transylvanian gypsy girl is really a long lost
countess.
Universal's Frankenstein sets are put to lighter
use in a quite incredible piece of downright
hokum.

w James Hogan, Gene Lewis, James M. Cain
d Roy William Neill *ph* George Robinson,
W. Howard Greene *m* Edward Ward

Maria Montez, Jon Hall, Leo Carrillo, Gale
Sondergaard, Douglass Dumbrille, Nigel
Bruce, Peter Coe, Curt Bois
  'The picture's so bad, it's bound to make
money.'—*Cue*
  'Never rises to the wild camp of *Cobra
Woman*; it's just *opéra bouffe* without
music.'—*Pauline Kael, 70s*

H. M. Pulham Esquire**
US 1940 120m bw
MGM (King Vidor)
A moderately successful Bostonian
businessman looks back over his rather stuffy
life and has a fling.
Solidly upholstered drama which does not
quite do justice to the book on which it is
based.
w King Vidor, Elizabeth Hill, *novel* John P.
Marquand *d* King Vidor *ph* Ray June
Robert Young, Ruth Hussey, Hedy Lamarr,
Charles Coburn, Van Heflin, Fay Holden,
Bonita Granville

Habeas Corpus*
US 1928 20m bw silent
A mad professor sends two vagabonds out to
look for a body. Unusual star comedy, more
grotesque and pantomimish than any of the
others. Laurel and Hardy, Richard Carle.
Written by H. M. Walker; directed by James
Parrott; for Hal Roach.

Hail the Conquering Hero***
US 1944 101m bw
Paramount (Preston Sturges)
An army reject is accidentally thought a hero
when he returns to his small-town home.
Skilfully orchestrated Preston Sturges romp,
slightly marred by an overdose of sentiment
but featuring his repertory of comic actors at
full pitch.
wd Preston Sturges *ph* John Seitz *m* Werner
Heymann
Eddie Bracken, William Demarest, Ella
Raines, *Franklin Pangborn,* Elizabeth
Patterson, *Raymond Walburn, Alan Bridge,*
Georgia Caine, Freddie Steele, Jimmy Conlin,
Torben Meyer
'Mob scenes, rough-houses and sharply
serious passages are played for all the
pantomime they are worth . . . one of the
happiest, heartiest comedies in a
twelvemonth.'—*Otis L. Guernsey Jnr*
'First rate entertainment, a pattern of film
making, not to be missed.'—*Richard Mallett,
Punch*
'The energy, the verbal density, the rush of
Americana and the congestion seen
periodically in *The Miracle of Morgan's Creek*
stagger the senses in this newest film.'—*James
Ursini*

'He uses verbal as well as visual slapstick,
and his comic timing is so quirkily effective
that the dialogue keeps popping off like a
string of firecrackers.'—*New Yorker, 1977*
AAN: Preston Sturges (as writer)

Hair*
US 1979 121m Technicolor
UA / CIP (Lester Persky, Michael Butler)
An Oklahoman on his way to enlist for
Vietnam service stops off in New York and
becomes embroiled with the flower people.
Slick, vigorous but eventually unsatisfying
version of a quickly dated musical frolic with
some obvious points to make.
w Michael Weller, *musical play* Galt
MacDermot (music) and Gerome Ragni /
James Rado (book) *d* Milos Forman
ph Miroslav Ondricek, Richard Kratina, Jean
Talvin
John Savage, Treat Williams, Beverly
D'Angelo, Annie Golden, Dorsey Wright
● Video: Intervision

The Hairy Ape
US 1944 91m bw
Jules Levy
A ship's stoker aims to kill a socialite who has
insulted him.
Patchy treatment of an intractable and dated
play.
w Jules Levy, *play* Eugene O'Neill *d* Alfred
Santell *ph* Lucien Andriot *m* Michel
Michelet, Edward Paul
William Bendix, Susan Hayward, John Loder,
Dorothy Comingore, Roman Bohnen, Alan
Napier
AAN: Michel Michelet, Edward Paul

Half a Hero
US 1953 71m bw
A timid journalist has problems with wife,
baby, boss and new house. Aimless comedy
quite unsuited to its star. Red Skelton, Jean
Hagen, Charles Dingle, Mary Wickes, Polly
Bergen. Written by Max Shulman; directed by
Don Weis; for MGM.

Half a Sinner
US 1934 70m bw
A cheerful elderly cardsharp masquerades as a
deacon. Midwestern pleaser not too well made
here, but later remade under its original title

as a Bob Burns vehicle. Berton Churchill, Joel
McCrea, Sally Blane, Mickey Rooney,
Spencer Charters. Written by Earle Snell,
Clarence Marks, from the play Alias the
Deacon by John B. Hymer and LeRoy
Clemens; directed by Kurt Neumann; for
Universal. 'Little marquee strength, but
sufficient punch to please 'em once they're
in.'—*Variety*

Half a Sixpence*
GB 1967 148m Technicolor
 Panavision
Paramount / Ameran (Charles H. Schneer,
 George Sidney)
A draper's assistant inherits a fortune and
moves into society.
Mildly likeable but limp and overlong musical
which would have benefited from more
intimate, sharper treatment than the wide
screen can give. The period decor and lively
numbers seem insufficient compensation for
the longueurs.
w Beverly Cross, from his play based on Kipps
by H. G. Wells *d* George Sidney
ph Geoffrey Unsworth *m* / *ly* David
Heneker *pd* Ted Haworth *ch* Gillian Lynne
Tommy Steele, Julia Foster, Cyril Ritchard,
Penelope Horner, Elaine Taylor, Hilton
Edwards, Pamela Brown, James Villiers

Half Angel
US 1951 80m Technicolor
A prim and proper nurse has a more forthright
personality when she sleepwalks. Silly
romantic comedy with amusing moments.
Loretta Young, Joseph Cotten, Cecil
Kellaway, Basil Ruysdael, Jim Backus, Irene
Ryan. Written by Robert Riskin; directed by
Richard Sale; for TCF.

The Half-Breed
US 1952 81m Technicolor
A gambler helps a half-breed and wins the
respect of the Apaches. Half-hearted western
which could never be more than the bottom
half of a double bill. Robert Young, Jack
Buetel, Janis Carter, Barton MacLane, Reed
Hadley, Porter Hall, Connie Gilchrist.
Written by Harold Shumate and Richard
Wormser; directed by Stuart Gilmore; for
RKO.

The Half Naked Truth*
US 1932 67m bw
RKO (David O. Selznick)

A publicity agent has trouble with a temperamental actress whose schemes are always over the top.
Amusing wisecracking comedy.

w Bartlett Cormack, Corey Ford d Gregory La Cava ph Bert Glennon m Max Steiner

Lee Tracy, Lupe Velez, Eugene Pallette, Frank Morgan, Bob McKenzie

Half Shot at Sunrise*
US 1930 78m bw

Allegedly one of the best representations of a star comedy duo who went into a decline after 1932. Bert Wheeler, Robert Woolsey, Edna May Oliver, Dorothy Lee, John Rutherford. Written by James Ashmore Creelman; directed by Paul Sloane; for RKO. 'Laugh programmer beyond ordinary . . . it will do business, including de luxers.'—*Variety*

The Halfway House*
GB 1944 99m bw
Ealing (Cavalcanti)

Overnight guests at an inn find it was bombed a year before and they have all been given a supernatural chance to reconsider their lives. Interesting pattern play which would have benefited from lighter handling.

w Angus Macphail, Diana Morgan, *play* Denis Ogden d Basil Dearden ph Wilkie Cooper m Lord Berners

Françoise Rosay, Tom Walls, Alfred Drayton, Sally Ann Howes, Mervyn Johns, Glynis Johns, Esmond Knight, Richard Bird, Guy Middleton

Hallelujah!**
US 1929 106m bw
MGM (King Vidor)

A black cotton worker accidentally kills a man and decides to become a preacher.
Hollywood's unique black melodrama now seems stilted because of its early talkie technique, but at the time its picture of negro life had a freshness and truth which was not reached again for thirty years.

w Wanda Tuchock, King Vidor d King Vidor ph Gordon Avil md Eva Jessye

Daniel Haynes, Nina Mae McKinney, William Fountaine, Fannie Belle De Knight, Harry Gray
'The central theme became swamped by the forty or so singing sequences of folk songs, spirituals, baptism wails, love songs and blues.'—*Peter Noble, The Negro in Films*

AAN: King Vidor

Hallelujah, I'm a Bum**
US 1933 80m bw
Lewis Milestone
GB titles: *Hallelujah I'm a Tramp; Lazy Bones*

The leader of a group of Central Park tramps smartens himself up for love of a lady who lost her memory. When she recovers it, he becomes a tramp again.

Curious whimsy expressed mainly in recitative, with embarrassing stretches relieved by moments of visual and verbal inspiration. Very typical of the Depression, with the tramps knowing best how life should be lived.

w S. N. Behrman, Ben Hecht d Lewis Milestone ph Lucien Andriot ad Richard Day rhymes / m / ly Richard Rodgers, Lorenz Hart

Al Jolson, Harry Langdon, Madge Evans, Frank Morgan, Chester Conklin

Songs: 'Hallelujah I'm a Bum'; 'You Are Too Beautiful'; 'I'll Do It Again'; 'What Do You Want with Money?'; 'I've Got to Get Back to New York'
'It must rise or fall by Al Jolson's rep . . . it won't bore, once in, but it's not a mass play picture.'—*Variety*
● Video: Intervision

The Hallelujah Trail
US 1965 167m Technicolor
Ultra Panavision 70
UA / Mirisch / Kappa (John Sturges)

In 1867 a wagonload of whisky bound for Denver is waylaid by Indians, temperance crusaders and the civilian militia.
Absurdly inflated, prolonged, uninventive comedy western with poor narrative grip; all dressed up and nowhere to go.

w John Gay, *novel* Bill Gulick d John Sturges ph Robert Surtees m Elmer Bernstein

Burt Lancaster, Lee Remick, Brian Keith, Jim Hutton, Donald Pleasence, Martin Landau

The Halliday Brand*
US 1956 78m bw
UA / Collier Young

A tough farmer / sheriff conflicts with his son over his attitude to Indians.
Dour, reliable western melodrama with a good cast.

w George W. George, George S. Slavin d Joseph H. Lewis ph Ray Rennahan m Stanley Wilson

Joseph Cotten, Viveca Lindfors, Ward Bond, Betsy Blair, Bill Williams, Jay C. Flippen

Halloween*
US 1978 91m Metrocolor Panavision
Falcon International (Irwin Yablans)

In a small Illinois town, a mad killer escapes from the asylum.
Single-minded shocker with virtually no plot, just a succession of bloody attacks in semi-darkness. Very well done if you like that kind of thing, though the final suggestion of the supernatural is rather baffling.

w John Carpenter, Debra Hill d John Carpenter ph Dean Cundy m John Carpenter pd Tommy Wallace

Donald Pleasence, Jamie Lee Curtis, Nancy Loomis, P. J. Soles
'One of the cinema's most perfectly engineered devices for saying Boo!'—*Richard Combs, MFB*

● Video: VPD

Halloween Two
US 1981 92m Metrocolor Panavision
Dino de Laurentiis (Debra Hill, John Carpenter)

The motiveless murderer from *Halloween* escapes from the asylum fifteen years later. A totally unnecessary sequel which seems merely an excuse for assorted mayhem at close quarters.

w John Carpenter, Debra Hill d Rick Rosenthal ph Dean Cundey m John Carpenter, Alan Howarth

Donald Pleasence, Jamie Lee Curtis, Charles Cyphers, Jeffrey Kramer
● Video: Thorn EMI

Halloween Three: Season of the Witch
US 1983 98m Technicolor Panavision
Dino de Laurentiis (Debra Hill, John Carpenter)

A malicious toy maker intends to restore Halloween to its witch cult origins through magic masks made at his Santa Mira factory. The Halloween zombie-killer makes no appearance: this is a fresh story inspired by *Invasion of the Body Snatchers*. Alas, its good intentions flounder in a bath of gore.

w,d Tommy Lee Wallace ph Dean Cundey m John Carpenter, Alan Howarth pd Peter Jamison

Tom Atkins, Stacey Nelkin, Dan O'Herlihy, Ralph Strait, Michael Currie
†Nigel Kneale wrote the original script but asked to have his name removed from the credits.

Halls of Anger
US 1969 99m De Luxe
UA / Mirisch (Herbert Hirschman)

A black basketball star goes to teach in his home town and faces segregation problems. Schematic melodrama, as well meaning as it is boring.

w John Shaner, Al Ramrus d Paul Bogart ph Burnett Guffey m Dave Grusin

Calvin Lockhart, Janet McLachlan, Jeff Bridges

Halls of Montezuma*
US 1950 113m Technicolor
TCF (Robert Bassler)

Marines fight World War II in the Pacific. Well-mounted, simple-minded actioner.

w Michael Blankfort d Lewis Milestone ph Winton C. Hoch, Harry Jackson m Sol Kaplan md Lionel Newman

Richard Widmark, Jack Palance, Reginald Gardiner, Robert Wagner, Karl Malden, Richard Hylton, Richard Boone, Skip Homeier, Jack Webb, Bert Freed, Neville Brand, Don Hicks, Martin Milner
'By far the noisiest war film I ever encountered.'—*Richard Mallett, Punch*

Ham and Eggs at the Front
US 1927 70m approx at 24 fps bw silent

Two black soldiers have adventures in the trenches. Irresistibly-titled war farce with our

heroes played by whites in blackface. Tom
Wilson, Charlie Conklin, Myrna Loy. Written
by Darryl F. Zanuck; directed by Roy Del
Ruth; for Warner.

Hambone and Hillie

US 1983 90m colour Panavision
Sandy Howard / Adams Apple (Gary
   Gillingham)

A small dog is lost at New York airport and
tracks his aged mistress on foot to California.
Basically a revamp of *Lassie Come Home*,
with a cute dog and some attractive exteriors,
but made unsuitable for its presumably
intended family audience by the death of a
second dog and a horrific pitchfork sequence
in which a heavily pregnant woman is attacked
by marauders.

w Sandra K. Bailey, Michael Murphey, Joel
Soisson d Roy Watts *ph* Jon Kranhouse
m George Garvarentz

Lillian Gish, Timothy Bottoms, Candy Clark,
Robert Walker, O. J. Simpson, Jack Carter,
Alan Hale

Hamlet**

GB 1948 142m bw
Rank / Two Cities (Laurence Olivier)

Prince Hamlet takes too long making up his
mind to revenge his father's death.
The play is sharply cut, then time is wasted
having the camera prowl pointlessly along
gloomy corridors . . . but much of the acting is
fine, some scenes compel, and the production
has a splendid brooding power.

w William Shakespeare d Laurence Olivier
ph Desmond Dickinson *pd* Roger Furse
m William Walton *ad* Carmen Dillon

*Laurence Olivier, Eileen Herlie, Basil Sydney,
Jean Simmons, Felix Aylmer,* Norman
Wooland, Terence Morgan, *Stanley Holloway*,
Peter Cushing, Esmond Knight, Anthony
Quayle, Harcourt Williams, John Laurie, Niall
MacGinnis, Patrick Troughton

AA: best picture; Laurence Olivier (as actor)
AAN: Laurence Olivier (as director); William
Walton; Jean Simmons
● *Video: Rank*

Hamlet*

USSR 1964 150m bw Sovscope
Lenfilm

A Russian version of the play, with lowering
sets, brooding photography and strong acting.

translation Boris Pasternak d Grigori
Kozintsev *ph* I. Gritzys *m* Dmitri
Shostakovich

Innokenti Smoktunovsky, Mikhail Nazvanov,
Elsa Radzin, Anastasia Vertinskaya
   'An opportunity almost deliberately
missed.'—*Basil Wright, 1972*

Hammerhead

GB 1968 99m Technicolor
Columbia / Irving Allen

An American secret agent captures a master
criminal.

Jaded James Bond imitation, full of would-be
fashionable detail.

w William Bast, Herbert Baker, *novel* James
Mayo d David Miller *ph* Kenneth Talbot,
Wilkie Cooper *m* David Whitaker

Vince Edwards, Peter Vaughan, Judy Geeson,
Diana Dors, Michael Bates, Beverly Adams,
Patrick Cargill, Patrick Holt

Hammersmith Is Out*

US 1972 114m Du Art Color
Cinerama / J. Cornelius Cream (Alex Lucas)

With the help of a male nurse, a homicidal
mental inmate escapes and becomes the most
influential man in the country.
Pretentious updating of Faust into a kind of
black farce that seldom amuses but is
interesting in fits and starts.

w Stanford Whitmore d Peter Ustinov
ph Richard Kline *m* Dominic Frontière

Richard Burton, Elizabeth Taylor, Peter
Ustinov, Beau Bridges, Leon Ames, John
Schuck, George Raft

Hammett*

US 1982 97m Technicolor
Orion / Zoetrope (Francis Coppola)

San Francisco 1928: Dashiell Hammett is
asked to locate a missing Chinese girl and gets
involved in sinister goings-on which provide
the basis for another mystery book.
Careful and interesting crime thriller in which,
however, the rather pretentious framework is
largely irrelevant, leaving a detective story
slightly off-beat in treatment but otherwise
indistinguishable from many others.

w Ross Thomas, Dennis O'Flaherty, *novel* Joe
Gores d Wim Wenders *ph* Philip Lathrop,
Joseph Biroc *m* John Barry *pd* Dean
Tavoularis, Eugene Lee *ed* Barry Malkin,
Marc Laub, Robert Q. Lovett, Randy Roberts

Frederic Forrest, Peter Boyle, Marilu Henner,
Roy Kinnear, Elisha Cook Jnr, R. G.
Armstrong, Richard Bradford, Sylvia Sidney,
Royal Dano, Samuel Fuller
   'A symbolic liquidation by Wenders of the
massive, but ambivalent patrimony of the
American cinematic and cultural tradition that
has increasingly dominated his work.'—*Sheila
Johnston, MFB*
† The film was actually in pre-production from
1975, though shooting did not begin until
1980. This version was abandoned in rough cut
and two-thirds of it was shot again in 1981 with
a different crew. Sylvia Miles and Brian Keith
were in the first version and not the second.
● *Video: 3M*

The Hand

GB 1960 60m bw

When an old man has his hand severed and is
subsequently murdered, the trail leads to a
doctor who subsequently commits suicide.
Confused second feature which seems to have
been badly edited but might otherwise have
been quite entertaining. Derek Bond, Ronald
Leigh-Hunt, Reed de Rouen, Ray Cooney,
Harold Scott. Written by Ray Cooney and
Tony Hilton; directed by Henry Cass; for Bill
and Michael Luckwell / Butcher's.

The Hand

US 1981 104m Technicolor
Warner / Orion (Edward R. Pressman)

A cartoonist loses his hand, which takes on a
life of its own to wreak vengeance on his
enemies.
Pale imitation of *The Beast with Five Fingers*,
which wasn't all that good to begin with.

wd Oliver Stone, from his novel The Lizard's
Tail *ph* King Baggot *m* James Horner
pd John Michael Riva *sp* Carlo Rambaldi
ed Richard Marks

Michael Caine, Andrea Marcovicci, Viveca
Lindfors, Rosemary Murphy, Bruce McGill

Hand in Hand*

GB 1960 80m bw
ABP / Helen Winston

The friendship of two 7-year-olds is affected
by racial prejudice because one is Catholic and
the other Jewish; but after misunderstandings
their friendship is confirmed by priest and
rabbi.
Pleasant, well-meaning drama apparently
intended for older children.

w Diana Morgan d Philip Leacock
ph Frederick A. Young *m* Stanley Black

Lorette Parry, Phillip Needs, Sybil Thorndike,
John Gregson, Finlay Currie

Handgun

US 1982 101m Du Art
EMI / Kestrel (Tony Garnett)

A schoolmistress, raped at gunpoint, takes her
revenge.
Overlong, unpleasant, uninteresting
exploitation melodrama.

w,d Tony Garnett *ph* Charles Stewart
m Mike Post *pd* Lilly Kilvert

Karen Young, Clayton Day, Suzie
Humphreys, Helena Humann
● *Video: Thorn EMI*

Handle with Care*

US 1958 82m bw
MGM (Morton Fine)

Small-town college students stage a mock trial
and come up with some embarrassing answers.
Interesting melodrama with a disappointing
ending; a well done second feature.

w Morton Fine, David Friedkin d David
Friedkin *ph* Harold J. Marzorati
m Alexander Courage

Dean Jones, Joan O'Brien, Thomas Mitchell,
Walter Abel, John Smith

Hands across the Table**

US 1935 81m bw
Paramount (E. Lloyd Sheldon)

A manicurist determines to marry a rich man.
Lively romantic comedy, smoothly made and
typical of its time.

w Norman Krasna, Vincent Lawrence,
Herbert Fields d Mitchell Leisen *ph* Ted
Tetzlaff *m* Sam Coslow, Frederick Hollander

Carole Lombard, Fred MacMurray, Ralph
Bellamy, Astrid Allwyn, Ruth Donnelly,
Marie Prévost, William Demarest, Ed Gargan

'Snappy comedy that should satisfy all over.'—*Variety*

'A happy mixture of brainwork and horseplay and a reminder that when intelligence goes for a walk among even the oldest props, the props may come to life.'—*Otis Ferguson*

† Ray Milland was originally cast, but bowed out saying that he couldn't play comedy.

The Hands of Orlac
GB / France 1960   105m   bw
Riviera / Pendennis (Steven Pallos, Don Taylor)

A concert pianist's hands are crushed in an accident, and a mad surgeon grafts on those of an executed murderer.

Flatulent remake of the 1926 German silent and the 1935 American *Mad Love*. Stilted, hammy, threadbare and overlong.

w John Baines, Edmond T. Gréville, *novel* Maurice Renard *d* Edmond T. Gréville *ph* Desmond Dickinson *m* Claude Bolling

Mel Ferrer, Donald Wolfit, Christopher Lee

Hands of the Ripper
GB 1971   85m   Technicolor
Hammer (Aida Young)

Jack the Ripper stabs his wife to death in view of his small daughter, who grows up a sexually repressed murderess.

Gory Hammer horror with well done scenes.

w L. W. Davidson *d* Peter Sasdy *ph* Kenneth Talbot *m* Christopher Gunning *ad* Roy Stannard

Angharad Rees, Eric Porter, Dora Bryan, Jane Merrow, Derek Godfrey

● *Video: Rank*

Hands over the City
Italy 1963   105m   bw
Galatea
original title: *Le Mani sulla Città*

A property tycoon wangles local politicians so that he gets development on the property he controls.

An angry political film which is too strident to have much entertainment value.

w Enzo Provencale, Enzo Forcella, Raffaele La Capria, Francesco Rosi *d* Francesco Rosi *m* Piero Piccioni *ph* Gianni di Venanzo

Rod Steiger, Salvo Randone, and non-professionals

Hands Up°
US 1926   65m (24 fps)   bw   silent

General Lee assigns a spy to prevent a Union man from getting his hands on a gold cache. Pleasant Civil War comedy with a curious Mormon happy ending. *Raymond Griffith*, Marion Nixon, Virginia Lee Corbin, Mack Swain, Montagu Love. Written by Monty Brice, Lloyd Corrigan; directed by Clarence Badger; for Paramount.

Handy Andy
US 1934   82m   bw
Fox

A midwestern druggist is married to a snob. Competent star vehicle overflowing with crackerbarrel philosophy.

w William Counselman, Henry Johnson, *play* Merry Andrew by Lewis Beach *d* David Butler *ph* Arthur Miller

Will Rogers, Peggy Wood, Conchita Montenegro, Mary Carlisle, Roger Imhof, Robert Taylor (his first film), Paul Harvey

'They made two mistakes—they hanged the wrong man, and they didn't finish the job!'

Hang 'em High
US 1967   114m   De Luxe
UA / Malpaso / Leonard Freeman

A cowboy is rescued from lynching and takes revenge on his persecutors.

Hollywood's first attempt to imitate the gore and brutality of spaghetti westerns and to take back its own errant star. Emetic and interminable.

w Leonard Freeman, Mel Goldberg *d* Ted Post *ph* Leonard South, Richard Kline *m* Dominic Frontière

Clint Eastwood, Inger Stevens, Ed Begley, Pat Hingle, James MacArthur, Arlene Golonka, Charles McGraw, Ben Johnson, L. Q. Jones

Hangar 18
US 1980   97m   Technicolor

A UFO crashlands and is cared for in secret by the American government. A cinematic equivalent to the yellow press, supposing villainous behaviour by all concerned but eager only to provide low grade thriller entertainment. Darren McGavin, Robert Vaughn, Gary Collins, Philip Abbott. Written by Steven Thornley; directed by James L. Conway; for Sunn Classic.

The Hanging Tree°
US 1958   106m   Technicolor
Warner / Baroda (Martin Jurow, Richard Shepherd)

Life is tough in a Montana gold-mining camp, especially for a doctor who has killed his unfaithful wife.

Lowering western with a feeling for place and period, plus a welter of melodramatic incident.

w Wendell Mayes, Halstead Welles, *novel* Dorothy M. Johnson *d* Delmer Daves *ph* Ted McCord *m* Max Steiner

Gary Cooper, Maria Schell, Karl Malden, Ben Piazza, George C. Scott

AAN: title song (*m* Jay Livingston, *ly* Ray Evans)

The Hangman
US 1959   86m   bw
Paramount (Frank Freeman Jnr)

A marshal with a reputation for getting his man deliberately allows one to escape.

Dour, low-key western, competent but rather flat and uninteresting.

w Dudley Nichols *d* Michael Curtiz *ph* Loyal Griggs *m* Harry Sukman

Robert Taylor, Jack Lord, Fess Parker, Tina Louise, Mickey Shaughnessy

Hangman's House
US 1928   72m (24 fps)   bw   silent
Fox

To please her dying father, an Irish girl marries a wastrel instead of the man she loves, but her husband is killed in a duel.

Blarney-filled melodrama, like a sober *Quiet Man*. John Wayne can be glimpsed as an extra.

w Marion Orth, *story* Don Byrne *d* John Ford *ph* George Schneiderman

June Collyer, Larry Kent, Earle Foxe, Victor McLaglen, Hobart Bosworth

Hangman's Knot
US 1952   81m   Technicolor

Confederate soldiers returning home with Union booty are waylaid at a way station by renegades. Adequate suspense western. Randolph Scott, Donna Reed, Claude Jarman Jnr, Frank Faylen, Glenn Langan, Richard Denning, Lee Marvin, Jeanette Nolan. Written and directed by Roy Huggins; for Harry Joe Brown / Columbia.

Hangmen Also Die°
US 1943   131m   bw
Arnold Pressburger / Fritz Lang (T. W. Baumfield)
Reissue title: *Lest We Forget*

The Nazis take revenge for the killing of Heydrich.

Disappointingly heavy-handed, though deeply felt war propaganda in Hollywood's idea of Czechoslovakia. Only moments of interest remain.

w John Wexley, *story* Fritz Lang, Bertolt Brecht *d Fritz Lang ph James Wong Howe m* Hanns Eisler

Brian Donlevy, Anna Lee, Walter Brennan, Gene Lockhart, Dennis O'Keefe, Alexander Granach, Margaret Wycherly, Nana Bryant, Hans von Twardowski (as Heydrich), Jonathan Hale, Lionel Stander

'Lang, working with American actors on an American theme, has produced *Fury*. Lang trying to recreate his own Central Europe on a Hollywood set is completely at sea.'—*Paul Rotha, 1949*

'Directed with a skill which excites and delights . . . brilliant use of the tiny, shocking detail.'—*Dilys Powell*

'They have chosen to use brutality, American gangster idiom, and middle high German cinematic style to get it across, and it is rich with clever melodrama, over-*maestoso* directional touches, and the sort of Querschnitt sophistication for detail which Lang always has.'—*James Agee*

† Working titles included *The Silent City* and *Never Surrender*.

AAN: Hanns Eisler

Hangover Square*
US 1944 77m bw
TCF (Robert Bassler)

In 1903 London, a psychopathic composer murders pretty women.
This rather empty melodrama has almost nothing to do with the book from which it is allegedly taken, but the Hollywoodian evocation of gaslit London is richly entertaining and good to look at.

w Barre Lyndon, *novel* Patrick Hamilton
d John Brahm *ph* Joseph La Shelle
m Bernard Herrmann *ad* Lyle Wheeler,
Maurice Ransford

Laird Cregar, Linda Darnell, George Sanders, Glenn Langan, Faye Marlowe, Alan Napier, Frederick Worlock

'Cregar lumbers around with a Karloffian glare in the spacious mists which happily blur the architectural decor.'—*Richard Winnington*
'Distinguished photography gets the last glint of fancy fright out of the pomps and vanities of the turn of the century.'—*Time*
'A half-chewed collection of reminiscences of *Dr Jekyll and Mr Hyde* and *The Lodger.*'—*Richard Mallett, Punch*
'The worst betrayal of a first class novel that I can remember.'—*James Agate*
'A better than average horror picture up to, but not including, its wildly overloaded climax.'—*James Agee*
† Tragically, Laird Cregar died after slimming for this role, to which he was in any case unsuited.

Hanky Panky
US 1982 107m Metrocolor
Columbia (Martin Ransohoff)

A girl on a spy mission is pursued by assassins and enlists the reluctant aid of an architect she meets in a taxi.
Frantic spoof of *North by Northwest*, which was itself as spoofy as all get out. This strained effort lacks wit, substituting shouting, violence and an exasperating hero.

w Henry Rosenbaum, David Taylor *d* Sidney Poitier *ph* Arthur Ornitz *m* Tom Scott *pd* Ben Edwards *ed* Harry Keller
Gene Wilder, Gilda Radner, Kathleen Quinlan, Richard Widmark

'The plot, rather like Mr Wilder, rushes hither and yon at the slightest excuse without ever adding up to very much. Even McGuffins are supposed to make more sense than this'.—*Richard Combs, MFB*
'A comedy thriller designed solely as a vehicle for Wilder's uninhibited hysteria is bad enough; one that so thoroughly submerges everyone else is so much worse.'—*Sight and Sound*

Hannibal
Italy 1959 103m Technicolor
Superscinescope
Liber Film (Ottavio Poggi)

Hannibal crosses the Alps and falls for the daughter of a Roman senator.
Unhistorical farrago which totally fails to entertain on any level.

w Mortimer Braus *d* Carlo Ludovico Bragaglia, Edgar G. Ulmer *ph* Raffaele Masciocchi *m* Carlo Rustichelli
Victor Mature, Rita Gam, Gabriele Ferzetti, Milly Vitale, Rik Battaglia

'Not even the elephants emerge with dignity.'—*MFB*

Hannibal Brooks
GB 1968 102m De Luxe
UA / Scimitar (Michael Winner)

A British POW in Germany escapes over the Alps with an elephant.
Curious action adventure which seems undecided whether to take itself seriously. Some passable sequences.

w Dick Clement, Ian La Frenais *d* Michael Winner *ph* Robert Paynter *m* Francis Lai
Oliver Reed, Michael J. Pollard, Wolfgang Preiss, Karen Baal

Hannie Caulder
GB 1971 85m colour Panavision
Tigon / Curtwel (Tony Tenser)

Raped by three outlaws who murdered her husband, a western woman takes revenge.
Unintentionally comical action melodrama with the star defeating all comers.

w Z. X. Jones (Burt Kennedy, David Haft) *d* Burt Kennedy *ph* Ted Scaife *m* Ken Thorne
Raquel Welch, Robert Culp, Ernest Borgnine, Strother Martin, Jack Elam, Christopher Lee, Diana Dors

Hanover Street
GB 1979 108m Technicolor
Columbia (Paul N. Lazarus III)

In 1943, an American bomber pilot meets a Red Cross nurse in a bus queue.
Wartime romance of a rather sticky sort, which turns with little warning into escape adventure, with our hero rescuing his loved one's husband from certain death.

wd Peter Hyams *ph* David Watkin *m* John Barry *pd* Philip Harrison
Harrison Ford, Lesley-Anne Down, Christopher Plummer, Alec McCowen, Richard Masure, Michael Sacks, Max Wall

Hans Christian Andersen*
US 1952 112m Technicolor
Samuel Goldwyn

A storytelling cobbler leaves his village to make shoes for the prima ballerina in Copenhagen.
Artificial, sugary confection with little humour and far too little magic of any kind; the star carries it nicely, but he is on his own apart from the songs.

w Moss Hart *d* Charles Vidor *ph* Harry Stradling *md* Walter Scharf *songs* Frank Loesser *ad* Richard Day *ch* Roland Petit
Danny Kaye, Zizi Jeanmaire, Farley Granger, John Qualen, Joey Walsh

AAN: Harry Stradling; Walter Scharf; song 'Thumbelina' (*m / ly* Frank Loesser)

The Happening
US 1967 101m Technicolor
Columbia / Horizon / Dover (Jud Kinberg)

Four young hippies kidnap a wealthy businessman and don't know what to do with him; he turns the tables.
Freewheeling irresponsible comedy which even at the time of swinging cities seemed very irritating.

w Frank R. Pierson, James D. Buchanan, Ronald Austin *d* Eliot Silverstein *ph* Philip Lathrop *m* Frank de Vol *pd* Richard Day
Anthony Quinn, George Maharis, Michael Parks, Faye Dunaway, Robert Walker, Oscar Homolka, Martha Hyer, Milton Berle, Jack Kruschen

'A wacky comedy à la mode, oddly mixed and only spasmodically effective.'—*Variety*

The Happiest Days of Your Life***
GB 1950 81m bw
British Lion / Individual (Frank Launder)

A ministry mistake billets a girls' school on a boys' school.
Briskly handled version of a semi-classic post-war farce, with many familiar talents in excellent form.

w Frank Launder, John Dighton, *play* John Dighton *d* Frank Launder *ph* Stan Pavey *m* Mischa Spoliansky
Alastair Sim, Margaret Rutherford, Joyce Grenfell, Richard Wattis, Edward Rigby, Guy Middleton, Muriel Aked, John Bentley, Bernadette O'Farrell

'Absolutely first rate fun.'—*Richard Mallett, Punch*

The Happiest Millionaire
US 1967 159m Technicolor
Walt Disney (Bill Anderson)

In 1916, a sporting millionaire has several surprising interests but finds time to sort out family problems.
Drearily inept family entertainment with a couple of good songs and an amusing alligator sequence but acres of yawning boredom in between.

w A. J. Carothers, *play* Kyle Crichton, *book* My Philadelphia Father by Cornelia Drexel Biddle *d* Norman Tokar *ph* Edward Colman *m / ly* Richard M. and Robert B. Sherman
Fred MacMurray, *Tommy Steele*, Greer Garson, John Davidson, Gladys Cooper, Lesley Anne Warren, Geraldine Page, Hermione Baddeley

Happiness Ahead
US 1934 80m bw

A rich girl finds her true love in a singing window cleaner. Not anybody's idea of a big attraction, but it passed the time for small towns. Dick Powell, Josephine Hutchinson, John Halliday, Dorothy Dare, Frank McHugh, Allen Jenkins, Ruth Donnelly. Written by Ralph Spence, Philip Dunne; directed by Charles F. Reisner; for First National. 'Pleasant comedy, bound to amuse.'—*Variety*

The Happiness of Three Women
GB 1954   78m   bw

A village postman and busybody adopts
various subterfuges to improve the future
happiness of his clients. Minor Welsh waffle
which pleased naïve audiences at the time.
Brenda de Banzie, Eynon Evans, Petula
Clark, Donald Houston, Patricia Burke,
Patricia Cutts. Written by Eynon Evans, from
his play *Wishing Well*; directed by Maurice
Elvey; for Adelphi.

Happy Anniversary
US 1959   83m   bw
UA / Ralph Fields

A television set causes family trouble.
Marital farce designed to take a few sideswipes
at TV.

w Joseph Fields, Jerome Chodorov, from their
play Anniversary Waltz *d* David Miller
ph Lee Garmes *m* Sol Kaplan, Robert Allan

David Niven, Mitzi Gaynor, Carl Reiner,
Loring Smith, Patty Duke, Phyllis Povah

Happy Anniversary*
France 1961   13m   bw

A husband is late for his anniversary dinner
because of a traffic jam. Amusing gag comedy,
virtually silent and all the better for it. *Pierre
Etaix*, Loriot, Nono Zammit. Written and
directed by *Pierre Etaix*; for Capac.

Happy Birthday to Me
Canada 1980   111m   Metrocolor
Birthday / CFDC / Famous Players (John
Dunning, Andre Link)

Members of the senior class at Crawford
Academy are killed off one at a time by one of
their number.
Abysmal teenage shocker which grinds on
relentlessly for nearly two hours.

w Timothy Bond, Peter Jobin, John Saxton
d J. Lee Thompson *ph* Miklos Lente *m* Bo
Harwood, Lance Rubin

Melissa Sue Anderson, Glenn Ford, Laurence
Dane, Sharon Acker, Frances Hyland

Happy Birthday Wanda June*
US 1971   105m   Technicolor
Columbia (Lester Goldsmith)

An adventurer believed dead returns just as
his wife is about to choose one of two suitors.
A farcical situation becomes in this writer's
hands an investigation of the hero cult, with
many zany jokes, episodes in heaven, and bad
language. Interesting in spots, but it would
have worked better with a more fluent
cinematic technique.

w Kurt Vonnegut Jnr, from his play *d* Mark
Robson *ph* Fred J. Koenekamp

Rod Steiger, Susannah York, George
Grizzard, Don Murray
 'We can only assume that Mr Robson
deserted the filmic instincts that brought him
commercial success because here he was,
finally, in the presence of Art.'—*Hollis Alpert*
 'Nothing more than a miscast film record of
the dialogue and plot outline of the stage
work.'—*Judith Crist*

Happy Days
US 1930   86m   bw   Grandeur
Fox

A showboat singer is a hit in New York and
helps her old friends.
Virtually a revue, with spectacular effects on
the giant screen.

w Sidney Lanfield, Edwin Burke *d* Benjamin
Stoloff *ph* Lucien Andriot and others *music*
various

Marjorie White; and Janet Gaynor, Charles
Farrell, Victor McLaglen, Edmund Lowe, El
Brendel, Walter Catlett, James J. Corbett,
Tom Patricola, Dixie Lee, Sharon Lynn,
Whispering Jack Smith

'We don't love. We just make love. And
damn little of that!'

The Happy Ending*
US 1969   112m   Technicolor
Panavision
UA / Pax Films (Richard Brooks)

A middle-aged woman reflects over sixteen
years of unhappy marriage.
Sometimes glib, sometimes trenchant
sophisticated drama with enough interesting
scenes to make it more than merely a
'woman's picture'.

wd Richard Brooks *ph* Conrad Hall
m Michel Legrand

Jean Simmons, John Forsythe, Shirley Jones,
Lloyd Bridges, Teresa Wright, Dick Shawn,
Nanette Fabray, Bobby Darin, Tina Louise
 'Packed with punchy little epigrams floating
in a vacuum of glossy superficiality.'—*David
Wilson*
 'The truth about the process of ageing is
what binds this film together like cement.'—
Alexander Walker

AAN: Jean Simmons; song 'What Are You
Doing the Rest of Your Life' (*m* Michel
Legrand, *ly* Alan and Marilyn Bergman)

Happy Ever After
GB / Germany 1932   86m   bw
UFA (Erich Pommer)

Window-cleaners put a young actress on the
way to stardom.
Cheerful comedy, set and made in Germany
by mainly British talent.

w Jack Hulbert, Douglas Furber, from a story
by Walter Reisch and Billy Wilder *d* Paul
Martin, Robert Stevenson

Lilian Harvey, Jack Hulbert, Cicely
Courtneidge, Sonnie Hale, Edward Chapman

Happy Ever After*
GB 1954   87m   Technicolor
ABP / Mario Zampi
US title: *Tonight's the Night*

Irish villagers draw lots for the privilege of
murdering their rascally squire.
Fairly hilarious black comedy with a good cast
entering into the spirit of the thing.

w Jack Davies, Michael Pertwee, L. A. G.
Strong *d* Mario Zampi *ph* Stan Pavey
m Stanley Black

David Niven, Yvonne de Carlo, A. E.
Matthews, Michael Shepley, George Cole,
Barry Fitzgerald

The Happy Family
GB 1952   86m   bw

A shopkeeper refuses to move and provide a
site for the Festival of Britain. Pale Ealing
imitation with amiable cast. Stanley Holloway,
Kathleen Harrison, Naunton Wayne, George
Cole, Dandy Nichols, Miles Malleson. Written
by Muriel and Sydney Box, from a play by
Michael Clayton Hutton; directed by Muriel
Box; for London Independent. (US title: *Mr
Lord Says No*.)

Happy Go Lovely
GB 1950   97m   Technicolor
ABP (Marcel Hellman)

A chorus girl meets a millionaire during the
Edinburgh Festival.
For a semi-official contribution to the Festival
of Britain this is a lamentably unspontaneous
musical with no use of cinema techniques or
natural locales. Even allowing for the flat
handling, it is tedious.

w Val Guest *d* Bruce Humberstone
ph Erwin Hillier *m* Mischa Spoliansky

David Niven, Vera-Ellen, Cesar Romero,
Bobby Howes, Diane Hart, Gordon Jackson,
Barbara Couper, Gladys Henson, Joyce Carey

Happy Go Lucky
US 1943   81m   Technicolor
Paramount (Harold Wilson)

A cigarette girl chases a millionaire to a
Caribbean island.
Flimsy musical for those who like the stars.

w Walter de Leon, Melvin Frank, Norman
Panama *d* Curtis Bernhardt *ph* Karl Struss,
Wilfrid Cline *songs* Frank Loesser, Jimmy
McHugh

Mary Martin, Dick Powell, Betty Hutton
(singing 'Murder He Says'), Rudy Vallee,
Eddie Bracken, Mabel Paige, Eric Blore,
Clem Bevans

Happy Gypsies*
Yugoslavia 1967   90m   Eastmancolor
Avala
aka: *I Even Knew Happy Gypsies*

A handsome, cruel-natured gypsy and his wife
have violent adventures and find themselves
on the run from the police.
The first film in the gypsy language does not
make one too sympathetic to their cause, but
some scenes are well managed and the colour
is fine.

wd Alexander Petrovic *ph* Tomislav Pinter
m gypsy melodies

Bekim Fehmiu, Olivera Vuco, Bata
Zivojinovic

The Happy Hooker
US 1975   98m   Movielab
Double H / Cannon-Happy (Fred Caruso)

A Dutch girl in New York starts a career as a
prostitute and finds she enjoys it.

Glum sex comedy based on the supposed exploits of a real madam; crude and not very funny. If this is emancipation, Shirley Temple seems more attractive by the minute.

w William Richert, *book* Xaviera Hollander d Nicholas Sgarro *ph* Dick Kratina *m* Don Elliott

Lynn Redgrave (hilariously miscast), Jean-Pierre Aumont, Lovelady Powell, Nicholas Pryor, Elizabeth Wilson, Tom Poston, Conrad Janis, Richard Lynch

Happy Is the Bride*
GB 1957 84m bw
British Lion / Paul Soskin

A couple planning a quiet summer wedding reckon without the intervention of her parents.
Tame remake of *Quiet Wedding*; the right spirit but not much sparkle.

w Jeffrey Dell, Roy Boulting, *play* Esther McCracken d Roy Boulting *ph* Ted Scaife *m* Benjamin Frankel

Ian Carmichael, Janette Scott, Cecil Parker, Joyce Grenfell, Terry-Thomas, John Le Mesurier, Eric Barker, Edith Sharpe, Athene Seyler

Happy Land*
US 1943 75m bw
TCF (Kenneth MacGowan)

Grandfather's ghost comes back to comfort a family which has lost its son at war.
Sentimental flagwaver very typical of its time; well made, it ensured not a dry eye in the house.

w Kathryn Scola, Julien Josephson, *novel* Mackinlay Kantor d Irving Pichel *ph* Joseph La Shelle *m* Cyril Mockridge

Don Ameche, Frances Dee, Harry Carey, Ann Rutherford, Cara Williams, Henry Morgan, Richard Crane, Dickie Moore

Happy Landing*
US 1938 102m bw
TCF (David Hempstead)

A Norwegian girl falls for an American flier who crashes near her home.
Lightweight skating musical, well put together.

w Milton Sperling, Boris Ingster d Roy del Ruth *ph* John Mescall *md* Louis Silvers

Sonja Henie, Don Ameche, Cesar Romero, Ethel Merman, Jean Hersholt, Billy Gilbert, Wally Vernon, El Brendel
'Just about everything to ensure entertainment value, shrewdly blended.'— *Variety*

Happy New Year*
France / Italy 1973 115m Eastmancolor
Films 13 / Rizzoli (Claude Lelouch)
original title: *La Bonne Année*

A thief is paroled on New Year's Eve in the hope that he will lead police to his confederates. In fact he learns a lot about the world and himself.
Bitter comedy apparently intended to distance the director from the romantic fervour of *A*

Man and a Woman, a clip from which is screened for the convicts at the beginning.

w, d, *ph* Claude Lelouch *m* Francis Lai

Lino Ventura, Françoise Fabian, Charles Gérard, André Falcon

The Happy Road*
US / France 1956 100m bw
MGM / Thor (Gene Kelly)

Two children run away from a Swiss school and are pursued by the American father of one of them.
Whimsical peripatetic comedy which fails to come off despite charming passages.

w Arthur Julian, Joseph Morhain, Harry Kurnitz d Gene Kelly *ph* Robert Juillard *m* Georges Van Parys

Gene Kelly, Barbara Laage, Michael Redgrave, Bobby Clark, Brigitte Fossey

The Happy Thieves
US 1962 88m bw
UA / Hillworth (James Hill, Rita Hayworth)

A gentleman thief and his accomplice become unwittingly involved in murder.
Dreary comedy which turns into equally dreary drama and makes its European backgrounds look ugly.

w John Gay, *novel* The Oldest Confession by Richard Condon d George Marshall *ph* Paul Beeson *m* Mario Nascimbene

Rex Harrison, Rita Hayworth, Grégoire Aslan, Joseph Wiseman, Alida Valli

The Happy Time***
US 1952 94m bw
Columbia / Stanley Kramer (Earl Felton)

Domestic misadventures of a family of French Canadians during the twenties.
Basically concerned with adolescent sexual stirrings, this very agreeable film has a light touch and is most deftly directed and acted.

w Earl Felton, *play* Samuel A. Taylor d Richard Fleischer *ph* Charles Lawton Jnr *m* Dmitri Tiomkin *pd* Rudolph Sternad

Charles Boyer, Louis Jourdan, Bobby Driscoll, Marsha Hunt, Marcel Dalio, Kurt Kasznar, Linda Christian, Jeanette Nolan, Jack Raine, Richard Erdman

The Happy Years
US 1950 86m bw
MGM (Carey Wilson)

The taming of an unruly pupil at a turn-of-the-century American school.
A curiously unrealized piece of Americana, with only moments to suggest what was being aimed at.

w Harry Ruskin, from 'The Lawrenceville School Stories' by Owen Johnson d William Wellman *ph* Paul C. Vogel *m* Leigh Harline

Dean Stockwell, Leo G. Carroll, Darryl Hickman, Scotty Beckett, Leon Ames, Margalo Gillmore

Hara Kiri*
Japan 1962 135m bw Grandscope
Shochiku
original title: *Seppuku*

17th-century samurai often pretend to commit hara kiri so that a grand lord will have sympathy and take them on. One of them is forced to go through with it.
Strange, traditional, slow and explicitly brutal costume piece, for specialized western eyes only.

w Shinodu Hashimoto d Masaki Kobayashi *ph* Yoshio Miyajima *m* Toru Takemitsu *ad* Junichi Ozumi

Tatsuya Nakadai, Shimai Iwashita, Akira Isahama

Hard Contract
US 1969 106m De Luxe Panavision
TCF (Marvin Schwarz)

A professional killer has sexual hang-ups.
Heavy-going modern thriller with lively scenes separated by too much self-analytical chat, not to mention a tour of Europe.

wd S. Lee Pogostin *ph* Jack Hildyard *m* Alex North

James Coburn, Lilli Palmer, Lee Remick, Burgess Meredith, Patrick Magee, Sterling Hayden, Helen Cherry, Karen Black, Claude Dauphin
'Behind it one glimpses a much better film than its surface suggests.'—*MFB*
'Like a flat-footed James Bond story that soaked its feet in a hot bath of existentialism.'—*John Simon*

Hard Country
US 1981 104m CFI Color
AFD (David Greene, Mack Bing)

An urban cowboy has no ambitions until he falls in love.
Simple modern western with music, not at all bad but with a scant potential audience.

w Michael Kane d David Greene *ph* Dennis Dalzell *m* Michael Martin Murphey, Jimmie Haskell *ed* John A. Martinelli *pd* Edward Richardson

Jan-Michael Vincent, Kim Basinger, Michael Parks, Tanya Tucker, Gailard Sartain
● *Video: Precision*

A Hard Day's Night****
GB 1964 85m bw
(UA) Proscenium (Walter Shenson)

Harassed by their manager and Paul's grandpa, the Beatles embark from Liverpool by train for a London TV show.
Comic fantasia with music; an enormous commercial success with the director trying every cinematic gag in the book, it led directly to all the kaleidoscopic swinging London spy thrillers and comedies of the later sixties, and so has a lot to answer for; but at the time it was a sweet breath of fresh air, and the Beatles even seemed willing and likeable.

w Alun Owen d Richard Lester *ph* Gilbert Taylor *songs* The Beatles *md* George Martin

The Beatles, Wilfrid Brambell, Norman Rossington, *Victor Spinetti*

'A fine conglomeration of madcap clowning . . . with such a dazzling use of camera that it tickles the intellect and electrifies the nerves.'—*Bosley Crowther*

'All technology was enlisted in the service of the gag, and a kind of nuclear gagmanship exploded.'—*John Simon*

AAN: Alun Owen; George Martin

Hard, Fast and Beautiful

US 1951　76m　bw
RKO / The Filmmakers (Collier Young)

A girl tennis player is influenced by her ambitious mother.
Unusual but not very effective melodrama.

w Martha Wilkerson, *novel* John R. Tunis d Ida Lupino ph Archie Stout m Roy Webb

Claire Trevor, Sally Forrest, Carleton Young, Robert Clarke, Kenneth Patterson, Joseph Kearns

Hard Steel

GB 1942　86m　bw
GFD / GHW (James B. Sloan)
reissue title: *What Shall It Profit*

A steel worker is promoted and loses his humanity, but comes to his senses when his wife leaves him.
Modest moral drama from the uplift side of the Rank empire.

w Lydia Hayward, *novel* Steel Saraband by Roger Dataller d Norman Walker

Wilfrid Lawson, Betty Stockfield, John Stuart, George Carney, Joan Kemp-Welch, Hay Petrie

Hard Times*

US 1975　93m　Metrocolor　Panavision
Columbia (Lawrence Gordon)
GB title: *The Streetfighter*

In New Orleans in the Depression-hit thirties, a prizefighter and a promoter help each other. Interesting, atmospheric melodrama on the lone stranger theme.

w Walter Hill, Bryan Gindorff, Bruce Henstell d Walter Hill ph Philip Lathrop m Barry DeVorzon

Charles Bronson, James Coburn, Jill Ireland, Strother Martin, Maggie Blye

Hard to Get

US 1938　80m　bw

An architect is reduced to working at a gas station; here he meets and falls in love with a millionairess. Arch romantic comedy which failed to enhance its stars. Dick Powell, Olivia de Havilland, Charles Winninger, Thurston Hall, Isabel Jeans, Penny Singleton, Allen Jenkins. Written by Jerry Wald, Maurice Leo and Richard Macauley; directed by Ray Enright; for Warner. 'Will carry in top brackets mainly due to selling names.'—*Variety*

Hard to Handle**

US 1933　75m　bw
Warner (Robert Lord)

The success story of a cheerful public relations man.
Punchy star comedy with interesting sidelights on the social fads of the early thirties including marathon dancing, get-rich-quick schemes and grapefruit diets.

w Wilson Mizner, Robert Lord d Mervyn Le Roy ph Barney McGill

James Cagney, Ruth Donnelly, Mary Brian, Allen Jenkins, Claire Dodd
'Hokum this time instead of the realism that boosted him to stardom.'—*Variety*
'A violent, slangy, down-to-the-pavement affair which has many a mirthful moment.'—*Mordaunt Hall*

'There are two sides to every story—and every woman!'

The Hard Way*

US 1942　109m　bw
Warner (Jerry Wald)

A strong-willed girl pushes her reluctant sister to the heights of show business.
Unconvincing but well-mounted drama.

w Daniel Fuchs, Peter Viertel d Vincent Sherman ph James Wong Howe m Heinz Roemheld md Leo F. Forbstein

Ida Lupino, Joan Leslie, Dennis Morgan, Jack Carson, Gladys George, Faye Emerson, Paul Cavanagh, Roman Bohnen

Hardcore*

US 1978　108m　Metrocolor
Columbia / A-Team (John Milius)
GB title: *The Hardcore Life*

A religious man from Michigan journeys to Los Angeles in search of his daughter, who has taken to acting in porno films.
Intense and solemn treatment of a situation that could have gone over the top, and very nearly does; the acting saves it.

wd Paul Schraeder ph Michael Chapman m Jack Nitzsche

George C. Scott, Peter Boyle, Season Hubley, Dick Sargent, Leonard Gaines
● Video: RCA / Columbia

The Harder They Fall*

US 1956　109m　bw
Columbia (Philip Yordan)

A press agent exposes the crooked fight game. Wearily efficient sporting melodrama.

w Philip Yordan, *novel* Budd Schulberg d Mark Robson ph Burnett Guffey m Hugo Friedhofer

Humphrey Bogart (his last performance), Rod Steiger, Jan Sterling, Mike Lane, Max Baer, Edward Andrews, Harold J. Stone

AAN: Burnett Guffey

The Hardy Family

America's favourite fictional characters just before and during World War II were the family of a small-town judge, who seemed to personify all that everyone was fighting for, especially as the young son was always getting into amusing scrapes. Designed by a delighted MGM as low-budgeters, they paid for many an expensive failure, and introduced, as young Andy's girl friends, a series of starlets who went on to much bigger things. The basic family was Lewis Stone, Fay Holden, Mickey Rooney, Cecilia Parker and Sara Haden (as the spinster aunt); but in the very first episode Lionel Barrymore and Spring Byington played the judge and his wife.

A FAMILY AFFAIR (1936); 69m; d George B. Seitz; w Kay Van Riper, *play* Aurania Rouverol

YOU'RE ONLY YOUNG ONCE (1938); 78m; d George B. Seitz; w Kay Van Riper; introducing Ann Rutherford (who became a regular)

JUDGE HARDY'S CHILDREN (1938); 78m; d George B. Seitz; w Kay Van Riper; *with* Ruth Hussey

LOVE FINDS ANDY HARDY (1938); 90m; d George B. Seitz; w William Ludwig; *with* Judy Garland, Lana Turner

OUT WEST WITH THE HARDYS (1938); 90m; d George B. Seitz; w Kay Van Riper, Agnes Christine Johnson, William Ludwig

THE HARDYS RIDE HIGH (1939); 81m; d George B. Seitz; w as above

ANDY HARDY GETS SPRING FEVER (1939); 85m; d W. S. Van Dyke II; w Kay Van Riper

JUDGE HARDY AND SON (1939); 90m; d George B. Seitz; w Carey Wilson; *with* June Preisser, Maria Ouspenskaya

ANDY HARDY MEETS A DEBUTANTE (1940); 89m; d George B. Seitz; w Annalee Whitmore, Thomas Seller; *with* Judy Garland

ANDY HARDY'S PRIVATE SECRETARY (1941); 101m; d George B. Seitz; w Jane Murfin, Harry Ruskin; *with* Kathryn Grayson, Ian Hunter

LIFE BEGINS FOR ANDY HARDY (1941); 100m; d George B. Seitz; w Agnes Christine Johnson; *with* Judy Garland

THE COURTSHIP OF ANDY HARDY (1942); 93m; d George B. Seitz; w Agnes Christine Johnson; *with* Donna Reed

ANDY HARDY'S DOUBLE LIFE (1942); 92m; d George B. Seitz; w Agnes Christine Johnson; *with* Esther Williams, Susan Peters

ANDY HARDY'S BLONDE TROUBLE (1944); 107m; d George B. Seitz; w Harry Ruskin, William Ludwig, Agnes Christine Johnson; *with* Bonita Granville, Jean Porter, Herbert Marshall, the Wilde twins

LOVE LAUGHS AT ANDY HARDY (1946); 94m; d Willis Goldbeck; w Harry Ruskin, William Ludwig; *with* Bonita Granville

ANDY HARDY COMES HOME (1958); 80m; d Howard Koch; w Edward Everett Hutshing, Robert Morris Donley; *without* Lewis Stone

Harem Girl

US 1952　70m　bw

The secretary to a princess vanquishes her employer's Arab ill-wishers. Dispirited pratfall farce, its star's last movie. Joan Davis, Peggie Castle, Arthur Blake, Paul Marion. Written by Edward Bernds and Ellwood Ullman; directed by Edward Bernds; for Columbia.

Harlequin
Australia 1980 93m Eastmancolor
Panavision

A faith healer cures a politician's son, seduces his wife, and proves to be of supernatural origin. Muddled and unsatisfactory fantasy in the manner of *The Passing of the Third Floor Back*; in this case far too much is left unexplained, and the film is scarcely entertaining despite effort all round. Robert Powell, David Hemmings, Carmen Duncan, Broderick Crawford. Written by Everett de Roche; directed by Simon Wincer; for FG Films.

● *Video: VCL*

'She was famous for light dresses, loose living, and trips to the bottom between pictures!'

Harlow
US 1965 125m Technicolor
Panavision
Paramount / Embassy / Prometheus
(Joseph E. Levine)

In 1929, starlet Jean Harlow is shot to fame by her agent Arthur Landau.
Absurdly whitewashed and excruciatingly boring rags-to-riches yarn with most of the characters fictitious and little to do with the real Jean Harlow. Only the studio scenes are mildly interesting.
w John Michael Hayes *d* Gordon Douglas *ph* Joseph Ruttenberg *m* Neal Hefti *ad* Hal Pereira, Roland Anderson *costumes* Edith Head

Carroll Baker, Peter Lawford, Mike Connors, Red Buttons, Raf Vallone, Angela Lansbury, *Martin Balsam*
'Hollywood once again succeeds in reducing one of its few fascinating realities to the sleazy turgid level of its more sordid fictions.'—*Judith Crist*
† A rather better television tape drama of the same title, starring Carol Lynley and Ginger Rogers, was made almost simultaneously. It was converted to film ('Electronovision') but had few bookings.

Harmony Heaven*
GB 1930 61m colour
BIP

A composer becomes famous with the help of his girl friend.
Unbelievably naïve musical, notable only as British and in colour. Not tolerable today as entertainment.
w Arthur Wimperis, Randall Faye *d* Thomas Bentley *ph* Theodor Sparkuhl *songs* Edward Brandt, Eddie Pola

Polly Ward, Stuart Hall, Trilby Clark, Jack Raine

Harmony Lane
US 1935 85m bw

The life of Stephen Foster. Heavygoing biopic from an independent studio; for rural audiences only. Douglass Montgomery, Evelyn Venable, Adrienne Ames, Joseph Cawthorn, William Frawley, Clarence Muse. No writing credit; directed by Joseph Santley; for Colbert Clark / Mascot.

Harold and Maude*
US 1971 92m Technicolor
Paramount / Mildred Lewis / Colin Higgins

A repressed young man, fixated on death and funerals, has an affair with an 80-year-old woman.
Often hilarious black comedy for those who can stand it; the epitome of bad taste, splashed around with wit and vigour, it became a minor cult.
w Colin Higgins *d* Hal Ashby *ph* John A. Alonzo *m* Cat Stevens

Bud Cort, Ruth Gordon, Vickie Pickles, Cyril Cusack

● *Video: CIC*

Harold Lloyd's Funny Side of Life***
US 1963 99m bw
Harold Lloyd (Duncan Mansfield)

Excerpts from twenties comedies plus a shortened version of *The Freshman* (1925). Excellent compilation, though the mini-feature makes it a little unbalanced.
w Arthur Ross *m* Walter Scharf
Harold Lloyd

Harold Lloyd's World of Comedy****
US 1962 97m bw
Harold Lloyd

Generous clips from the comic climaxes of Lloyd's best silent and sound comedies including *Safety Last, The Freshman, Hot Water, Why Worry, Girl Shy, Professor Beware, Movie Crazy* and *Feet First*.
As Lloyd's work lends itself well to extract, this can hardly fail to be a superb anthology capsuling the appeal of one of America's greatest silent comedians. The timing is just perfect.
m Walter Scharf *commentary* Art Ross

Harold Teen
US 1934 66m bw

A young reporter saves a small-town bank from collapse. Teenage romantic comedy previously filmed in 1928 (with Arthur Lake and Mary Brian, directed by Mervyn Le Roy) and here reduced to second feature status. Hal Le Roy, Rochelle Hudson, Patricia Ellis, Guy Kibbee, Hobart Cavanagh. Written by Paul Gerard Smith and Al Cohn, from the comic strip by Carl Ed; directed by Murray Roth; for Warner. (GB title: *Dancing Fool*.)

Harper*
US 1966 121m Technicolor
Panavision
Warner / Gershwin–Kastner
GB title: *The Moving Target*

A Los Angeles private eye is hired by a rich woman to find her missing husband.

Formula Californian detection distinguished by its cast rather than by any special talent in the writing or presentation. It seemed likely to produce a new Chandleresque school, but imitations proved very sporadic; the star repeated the role less successfully in *The Drowning Pool* (qv).

w William Goldman, *novel* The Moving Target by John Ross Macdonald *d* Jack Smight *ph* Conrad Hall *m* Johnny Mandel

Paul Newman, Lauren Bacall, Shelley Winters, Arthur Hill, Julie Harris, Janet Leigh, Pamela Tiffin, Robert Wagner, Robert Webber, Strother Martin

'It isn't a bad try, but it never really slips into overdrive.'—*Penelope Houston*
'Nothing needs justification less than entertainment; but when something planned only to entertain fails, it has no justification. A private-eye movie without sophistication and style is ignominious.'—*Pauline Kael, 1968*

The Harrad Experiment
US 1973 97m Eastmancolor
Cinerama / Cinema Arts (Dennis F. Stevens)

A college professor conducts a series of tests on sexual relationships.
Low-keyed Kinsey Report for the seventies, pleasantly made but not very stimulating.
w Michael Werner, Ted Cassidy, *novel* Robert H. Rimmer *d* Ted Post *ph* Richard Kline *m* Artie Butler

James Whitmore, Tippi Hedren, Don Johnson, Laurie Walters, Robert Middleton
'Ludicrously sober-sided amalgam of nude yoga and extra-curricular groping, which should set sex educational theory back ten years.'—*Sight and Sound*

Harriet Craig
US 1950 94m bw
Columbia (William Dozier)

A wife's only real love is her meticulously kept and richly appointed house.
Ho-hum remake of a sturdy thirties film *Craig's Wife* (qv).
w Anne Froelick, James Gunn, *play* Craig's Wife by George Kelly *d* Vincent Sherman *ph* Joseph Walker *m* George Duning *md* Morris Stoloff

Joan Crawford, Wendell Corey, Allyn Joslyn, Lucile Watson, William Bishop, K. T. Stevens, Raymond Greenleaf

Harry and Son
US 1984 117m Technicolor
Orion / Paul Newman

An ageing construction worker is at odds with his twenty-one-year-old son, who lives with him.
One can't imagine why Paul Newman wanted to make this boring shouting match between people no one can care for.
w Ronald L. Buck, Paul Newman, suggested by the novel A Lost King by Raymond DeCapite *d* Paul Newman *ph* Donald McAlpine *m* Henry Mancini

Paul Newman, Robby Benson, Ellen Barkin, Wilford Brimley
● *Video: Rank*

Harry and Tonto°
US 1974   115m   De Luxe
TCF (Paul Mazursky)

An elderly New York widower and his cat are evicted and trek to Chicago.
Amiable character study, very watchable but rather pointless.

w Paul Mazursky, Josh Greenfield   *d* Paul Mazursky   *ph* Michael Butler   *m* Bill Conti

Art Carney, Ellen Burstyn, Chief Dan George, Geraldine Fitzgerald, Larry Hagman, Arthur Hunnicutt, Herbert Berghof
  'A vivacious and affectionate folk tale.'—*New Yorker*
  'It has a life-affirming quality as welcome contrast to the destructive delirium of most modern movies.'—*Michael Billington, Illustrated London News*
AA: Art Carney
AAN: Paul Mazursky (as writer)

Harry and Walter go to New York
US 1976   120m   Metrocolor   Panavision
Columbia (Don Devlin, Harry Gittes)

In oldtime New York, two carnival entertainers get involved with suffragettes and a safecracker.
Extended period romp in which the high humour soon palls and a general lack of talent makes itself felt.

w John Byrum, Robert Kaufman   *d* Mark Rydell   *ph* Laszlo Kovacs   *m* David Shire   *pd* Harry Horner

James Caan, Elliott Gould, Michael Caine, Diane Keaton, Charles Durning, Lesley Ann Warren, Jack Gilford
  'A charmless mishmash.'—*Sight and Sound*
  'This film fails to work as a light comedy, as a period piece, as a jigsaw puzzle . . . mainly, it just sits there and dies.'—*Frank Rich, New York Post*
  'Strictly for those who'll laugh at anything.'—*Kevin Thomas, Los Angeles Times*
● *Video: RCA / Columbia*

'The woman or the tiger? He can't have them both!'
Harry Black and the Tiger
GB 1958   117m   Technicolor
Cinemascope
TCF (John Brabourne)
US title: *Harry Black*

A famous tiger hunter allows his best friend to prove himself a hero, and falls in love with the friend's wife.
Lethargic melodrama with good Indian backgrounds.

w Sydney Boehm, *novel* David Walker   *d* Hugo Fregonese   *ph* John Wilcox   *m* Clifton Parker

Stewart Granger, Anthony Steel, Barbara Rush, I. S. Johar

Harry in Your Pocket
US 1973   103m   De Luxe   Panavision
UA / Cinema Video (Bruce Geller)

Adventures of a young, a middle-aged and an old pickpocket.
Partly pleasant but rather aimless comedy drama, agreeably set in Seattle and Salt Lake City.

w Ron Austin, James Buchanan   *d* Bruce Geller   *ph* Fred Koenekamp   *m* Lalo Schifrin

James Coburn, *Walter Pidgeon*, Michael Sarrazin, Trish Van Devere

Harum Scarum
US 1965   95m   Metrocolor

An American star on the way to the middle eastern première of his latest film is kidnapped by assassins. Flavourless comedy with music; before dull backgrounds the star performs adequately. Elvis Presley, Mary Ann Mobley, Fran Jeffries, Michael Ansara, Theo Marcuse, Jay Novello, Billy Barty. Written by Gerald Drayson Adams; directed by Gene Nelson; for Sam Katzman / MGM. (GB title: *Harem Holiday*.)

Harvest
France 1937   122m   bw   Marcel Pagnol
original title: *Regain*

A poacher and an itinerant girl set up house in a deserted village and bring it back to life.
Somewhat charming but interminably slow rustic parable.

wd Marcel Pagnol, *novel* Jean Giono   *ph* Willy   *m* Arthur Honegger

Gabriel Gabrio, Fernandel, Orane Demazis, E. Delmont

Harvey°°°
US 1950   104m   bw
U-I (John Beck)

A middle-aged drunk has an imaginary white rabbit as his friend, and his sister tries to have him certified.
An amiably batty play with splendid lines is here transferred virtually intact to the screen and survives superbly thanks to understanding by all concerned, though the star is as yet too young for a role which he later made his own.

w Mary Chase (with Oscar Brodney) from her play   *d* Henry Koster   *ph* William Daniels   *m* Frank Skinner

James Stewart, Josephine Hull, Victoria Horne, Peggy Dow, *Cecil Kellaway*, Charles Drake, *Jesse White*, Nana Bryant, Wallace Ford

VETA LOUISE (Josephine Hull): 'Myrtle Mae, you have a lot to learn, and I hope you never learn it.'

ELWOOD (James Stewart): 'I've wrestled with reality for 35 years, and I'm happy, doctor. I finally won out over it.'

ELWOOD: 'Harvey and I have things to do . . . we sit in the bars . . . have a drink or two . . . and play the juke box. Very soon the faces of the other people turn towards me and they smile. They say: "We don't know your name, mister, but you're all right, all right."

Harvey and I warm ourselves in these golden moments. We came as strangers—soon we have friends. They come over. They sit with us. They drink with us. They talk to us. They tell us about the great big terrible things they've done and the great big wonderful things they're going to do. Their hopes, their regrets. Their loves, their hates. All very large, because nobody ever brings anything small into a bar. Then I introduce them to Harvey, and he's bigger and grander than anything they can offer me. When they leave, they leave impressed. The same people seldom come back.'

ELWOOD (describing his first meeting with Harvey): 'I'd just helped Ed Hickey into a taxi. Ed had been mixing his drinks, and I felt he needed conveying. I started to walk down the street when I heard a voice saying: "Good evening, Mr Dowd". I turned, and there was this big white rabbit leaning against a lamp-post. Well, I thought nothing of that! Because when you've lived in a town as long as I've lived in this one, you get used to the fact that everybody knows your name . . .'

AA: Josephine Hull
AAN: James Stewart

The Harvey Girls°°
US 1946   101m   Technicolor
MGM (Arthur Freed)

A chain of 19th-century restaurants hires young ladies to go out west as waitresses.
Sprightly if overlong musical based on fact; a good example of an MGM middle-budget extravaganza.

w Edmund Beloin, Nathaniel Curtis   *d* George Sidney   *ph* George Folsey   *md* Lennie Hayton   *songs* Johnny Mercer, Harry Warren

Judy Garland, Ray Bolger, John Hodiak, Preston Foster, Virginia O'Brien, Angela Lansbury, Marjorie Main, Chill Wills, Kenny Baker, Selena Royle
  'Anybody who did anything at all in America up to 1900 is liable to be made into a film by MGM.'—*Richard Winnington*
  'An abundance of chromatic spectacle and an uncommonly good score.'—*New York Times*
  'A perfect example of what Hollywood can do with its vast resources when it wants to be really showy.'—*New York Herald Tribune*
AA: song 'On the Atcheson, Topeka and the Santa Fe'
AAN: Lennie Hayton

Harvey Middleman Fireman°
US 1965   76m   Eastmancolor
Columbia (Robert L. Lawrence)

A frustrated middle-aged fireman begins an affair; the resulting guilt complex drives him to a psychiatrist.
Grotesque satirical comedy from one of the sixties' most fashionable cartoonists. Mild, quite pleasing, occasionally crude.

wd / m Ernest Pintoff   *ph* Karl Malkames

Gene Troobnick, Hermione Gingold, Pat Harty

Has Anybody Seen My Gal?**
US 1952 89m Technicolor
U-I (Ted Richmond)

A multi-millionaire pretends to be poor and
moves in with distant relatives to test their
worthiness.
Very agreeable comedy set in the twenties and
centring on a satisfying star performance.

w Joseph Hoffman d Douglas Sirk
ph Clifford Stine m Joseph Gershenson
ad Bernard Herzbrun, Hilyard Brown

Charles Coburn, Piper Laurie, Rock Hudson,
Gigi Perreau, Lynn Bari, Larry Gates,
William Reynolds, Skip Homeier, James Dean

The Hasty Heart*
GB 1949 104m bw
ABP (Vincent Sherman)

At an army hospital in Burma, attitudes to an
arrogant young Scot change when it is learned
that he has only a few weeks to live.
Flat, adequate filming of a successful
sentimental stage play.

w Ranald MacDougall, play John Patrick
d Vincent Sherman ph Wilkie Cooper
m Jack Beaver

Richard Todd, Patricia Neal, Ronald Reagan,
Orlando Martins, Howard Marion-Crawford

AAN: Richard Todd

Hat, Coat and Glove
US 1934 64m bw

A New York lawyer accidentally kills an old
flame. Tiresome courtroom melodrama, told
in a rather stilted manner. Ricardo Cortez,
Barbara Robbins, John Beal, Margaret
Hamilton, Sara Haden, Samuel S. Hinds.
Written by Francis Faragoh, from a play by
Wilhelm Speyer; directed by Worthington
Miner; for RKO.

Hatari!*
US 1962 158m Technicolor
Paramount / Malabar (Howard Hawks)

International hunters in Tanganyika catch
game to send to zoos.
Plotless adventure film with good animal
sequences but no shape or suspense; a typical
folly of its director, whose chief interest is
seeing smart men and women in tough action.
The elephants steal this overlong show.

w Leigh Brackett d Howard Hawks
ph Russell Harlan m Henry Mancini

John Wayne, Elsa Martinelli, Red Buttons,
Hardy Kruger

'Hawks was taking his friends and cast and
crew on a trip he wanted to make personally,
and the film is both the incidental excuse for
and the record of that experience.'—Joseph
Gelmis, 1970

AAN: Russell Harlan

The Hatchet Man
US 1932 74m bw
Warner
GB title: The Honourable Mr Wong

The executioner of a San Francisco tong
dutifully kills his best friend but promises to
care for his daughter.

Unconvincing Chinese-American melodrama.

w J. Grubb Alexander, play Achmed
Abdullah, David Belasco d William A.
Wellman ph Sid Hickox

Edward G. Robinson, Loretta Young, Dudley
Digges, Leslie Fenton, Edmund Breese, Tully
Marshall, J. Carrol Naish, Noel Madison,
Blanche Frederici

'Mild gang stuff in oriental trappings . . .
dynamic action or high voltage drama is
missing.'—Variety

A Hatful of Rain*
US 1957 108m bw Cinemascope
TCF / (Buddy Adler)

A war veteran becomes a drug addict and
upsets his wife and family.
One of the first drug dramas: straightforward,
well acted, and quite powerful.

w Michael V. Gazzo (with Alfred Hayes),
from his play d Fred Zinnemann ph Joe
Macdonald m Bernard Herrmann

Eva Marie Saint, Don Murray, Anthony
Franciosa, Lloyd Nolan, Henry Silva

AAN: Anthony Franciosa

'Are you shockproof? Then you will dare to
   see this famous drama of violence—of
   hate—of men who teach women the
   terror of cruelty and mad obsession!'

Hatter's Castle**
GB 1941 102m bw
Paramount British (Isadore Goldsmith)

In the nineties, a megalomaniac Scottish hatter
ruins the lives of his wife and daughter.
Enjoyable period melodrama with a rampant
star performance and pretty good detail.

w Rodney Ackland, novel A. J. Cronin
d Lance Comfort ph Max Greene m Horace
Shepherd

Robert Newton, Deborah Kerr, James Mason,
Beatrice Varley, Emlyn Williams, Henry
Oscar, Enid Stamp-Taylor, Brefni O'Rourke

The Haunted Palace
US 1963 85m Pathecolor Panavision
AIP / Alta Vista (Roger Corman)

In 1875 a New Englander claims an old
mansion as his inheritance and is haunted by
his vicious ancestor.
Plodding horror comic, too slow to give
opportunities to its stalwart cast.

w Charles Beaumont, from material by H. P.
Lovecraft and Edgar Allan Poe d Roger
Corman ph Floyd Crosby m Ronald Stein

Vincent Price, Lon Chaney Jnr, Debra Paget,
Frank Maxwell, Leo Gordon, Elisha Cook
Jnr, John Dierkes

'For those of ghoulish bent, or lovers of the
perfectly awful.'—Judith Crist
● Video: Rank

The Haunting*
GB 1963 112m bw Panavision
MGM / Argyle (Robert Wise)

An anthropologist, a sceptic and two mediums
spend the weekend in a haunted Boston
mansion.

Quite frightening but exhausting and
humourless melodrama with a lot of suspense,
no visible spooks, and not enough plot for its
length. The wide screen is a disadvantage.

w Nelson Gidding, novel The Haunting of Hill
House by Shirley Jackson d Robert Wise
ph David Boulton m Humphrey Searle
pd Elliot Scott

Richard Johnson, Claire Bloom, Russ
Tamblyn, Julie Harris, Lois Maxwell,
Valentine Dyall

'You may not believe in ghosts, but you
cannot deny terror!'—publicity

Havana Widows*
US 1933 63m bw

Gold diggers seek millionaires in Havana.
Lively second feature with the Warner
repertory company. Joan Blondell, Glenda
Farrell, Guy Kibbee, Lyle Talbot, Allen
Jenkins, Frank McHugh, Ruth Donnelly,
Hobart Cavanagh. Written by Stanley Logan,
Earl Badwin; directed by Ray Enright; for
First National. 'Hasn't been a picture in weeks
with the same content of rapid-fire laughs, all
legitimately gained and inescapable.'—Variety

Have a Heart
US 1934 75m bw

A dancing instructress becomes a cripple and
is deserted by her boy friend. Family drama
with comedy asides, plus a dog and a mystery
element. Jean Parker, James Dunn, Una
Merkel, Stuart Erwin, Willard Robertson.
Written by Florence Ryerson and Edgar Allen
Woolf; directed by David Butler; for MGM.
'Such a barrage of sobbing hokum is a novelty
in itself in this supposedly sophisticated
age.'—Variety

Having a Wonderful Crime
US 1945 70m bw

Three amateur detectives solve the mystery of
a disappearing magician. Easy-going comedy
thriller. Pat O'Brien, Carole Landis, George
Murphy. Written by Howard J. Green,
Stewart Sterling and Parke Levy; directed by
Eddie Sutherland; for RKO.

Having Wonderful Time
US 1938 70m bw
RKO (Pandro S. Berman)

A New York girl falls in love at a summer
camp.
Mild comedy which, robbed of its original
Jewish milieu, falls resoundingly flat.

w Arthur Kober, from his play d Alfred
Santell ph Robert de Grasse m Roy Webb

Ginger Rogers, Douglas Fairbanks Jnr, Peggy
Conklin, Lucille Ball, Lee Bowman, Eve
Arden, Red Skelton, Donald Meek, Jack
Carson

Hawaii*
US 1966 186m De Luxe Panavision
UA / Mirisch (Lewis J. Rachmil)

In 1820 a pious Yale divinity student becomes
a missionary to the Hawaiian islands.

Ambitious attempt to contrast naïve dogma with native innocence, ruined by badly handled sub-plots, storms, a childbirth sequence and other distractions, all fragments of an immense novel. Heavy going.

w Daniel Taradash, Dalton Trumbo, *novel* James A. Michener d George Roy Hill ph Russell Harlan m Elmer Bernstein *2nd unit* Richard Talmadge pd Cary Odell

Max Von Sydow, Julie Andrews, Richard Harris, *Jocelyn la Garde*, Carroll O'Connor, Torin Thatcher, Gene Hackman

'Consistently intelligent humanism gives it a certain stature among the wide screen spectacles.'—*Brenda Davies*

AAN: cinematography; Jocelyn La Garde

Hawaii Calls
US 1938 73m bw

Boy stowaways catch a steamer from San Francisco to Hawaii. Slight vehicle for a singing star. Bobby Breen, Ned Sparks, Irvin S. Cobb, Warren Hull, Gloria Holden, Pua Lani. Written by Wanda Tuchock, from the novel Stowaways in Paradise by Don Blanding; directed by Edward F. Cline; for Sol Lesser / RKO. 'Okay musically but light on romance.'—*Variety*

The Hawaiians
US 1970 132m De Luxe Panavision
UA / Mirisch (Walter Mirisch)
GB title: *Master of the Islands*

A young scion of a shipping business leaves after an argument and strikes oil in terrain supposedly barren.
More fragments from Michener, covering 1870 to 1900 and comprising an absolutely uninteresting family chronicle with moments of spectacle.

w James R. Webb d Tom Gries ph Philip Lathrop m Henry Mancini pd Cary Odell

Charlton Heston, Tina Chen, Geraldine Chaplin, John Philip Law, Alec McCowen, Mako, Ann Knight, Lyle Bettger, Keye Luke

'A quickfire succession of corruption, revolution, plague, fire and questions of moral responsibility.'—*MFB*

'Total relaxation—preferably of the brain—is recommended.'—*Judith Crist*

Hawk the Slayer
GB 1980 93m colour
ITC / Chips (Harry Robertson)

Good and evil brothers compete for possession of a magical flying sword.
Curiously unexciting and rather gloomy sword-and-sorcery epic.

w Terry Marcel, Harry Robertson d Terry Marcel ph Paul Beeson m Harry Robertson

Jack Palance, John Terry, Bernard Bresslaw, Ray Charleson, Annette Crosbie, Cheryl Campbell, Peter O'Farrell

● *Video: Precision*

Hawmps
US 1976 127m colour

The Texas cavalry experiments with the use of camels in the southwestern desert. Incredibly

overstretched and tedious period comedy with some bright patches. James Hampton, Christopher Connelly, Slim Pickens, Denver Pyle, Jennifer Hawkins, Jack Elam. Written by William Bickley and Michael Warren; directed by Joe Camp; for Mulberry Square.

Hazard
US 1948 95m bw
Paramount (Mel Epstein)

A compulsive lady gambler agrees to marry the winner of a dice game, but runs away and is chased by a private detective.
Silly, unamusing romantic comedy-drama.

w Arthur Sheekman, Roy Chanslor d George Marshall ph Daniel L. Fapp m Frank Skinner

Paulette Goddard, Macdonald Carey, Fred Clark, Stanley Clemens, Maxie Rosenbloom, Charles McGraw

'A good bit this side of inspired.'—*New York Times*

He Found a Star
GB 1941 88m bw

A theatrical agent loses his star singer and thinks again about his secretary. A strong contender for the Golden Turkey Award (British Division); the ineptitude has to be sampled to be believed. Vic Oliver, Sarah Churchill, Joan Greenwood, Evelyn Dall, Robert Atkins. Written by Austin Melford and Bridget Boland; directed by John Paddy Carstairs; for John Corfield.

He Knows You're Alone
US 1980 92m Metrocolor

A sex-starved maniac attacks teenage girls. Cheapjack horror comic full of fashionable slashing and screaming; of no cinematic interest whatever. Don Scardino, Elizabeth Kemp. Written by Scott Parker; directed by Armand Mastroianni; for Lansbury-Beruh / MGM. 'At this point in the killer-with-a-knife sweepstakes, every company in Hollywood is getting into the act . . . more ingenuity is going into the titles and campaigns than into the films.'—*Variety*

He Laughed Last*
US 1956 77m Technicolor
Columbia (Jonie Taps)

In the twenties, New York gangsters battle for control of a night club.
Small-scale gangster burlesque which comes off rather better than its credits suggest.

wd Blake Edwards ph Henry Freulich m Arthur Morton

Frankie Laine, Lucy Marlow, Anthony Dexter, *Jesse White*

He Ran All the Way*
US 1951 78m bw
UA / Bob Roberts

A hoodlum on the run from the police virtually picks up a girl and hides in her family's apartment.
Uninteresting situation melodrama helped by intelligent acting and handling.

w Guy Endore, Hugo Butler, *novel* Sam Ross d John Berry ph James Wong Howe m Franz Waxman

John Garfield, Shelley Winters, Wallace Ford, Selena Royle, Gladys George, Norman Lloyd, Bobby Hyatt

He Rides Tall
US 1964 84m bw

A marshal postpones his marriage after being forced to kill his stepbrother. Semi-adult western, of no particular consequence. Tony Young, Dan Duryea, Madlyn Rhue, Jo Morrow, R. G. Armstrong. Written by Charles W. Irwin and Robert Creighton; directed by R. G. Springsteen; for Universal.

He Snoops to Conquer
GB 1944 103m bw
Columbia (Ben Henry, Marcel Varnel)

A local handyman exposes a corrupt council. Spotty star comedy with insufficient zest for its great length.

w Stephen Black, Howard Irving Young, Norman Lee, Michael Vaughan, Langford Reed d Marcel Varnel ph Roy Fogwell

George Formby, Robertson Hare, Elizabeth Allen, Aubrey Mallalieu

He Stayed for Breakfast
US 1940 89m bw
Columbia (B. P. Schulberg)

A Parisian communist waiter hides out in the apartment of American capitalists, and learns from them.
Post-*Ninotchka* comedy, not bad but somehow rather uninteresting and mechanical.

w P. J. Wolfson, Michael Fessier, Ernest Vajda, *play* Liberté Provisoire by Michel Duran d Alexander Hall ph Joseph Walker m Werner Heymann

Melvyn Douglas, Loretta Young, Alan Marshal, Eugene Pallette, Una O'Connor, Curt Bois, Leonid Kinskey

He Walked by Night*
US 1948 80m bw
Eagle–Lion / Bryan Foy

A burglar becomes a cop-killer and is hunted down by the police.
Interesting if rather flatly handled documentary melodrama in clear imitation of *Naked City*.

w John C. Higgins, Crane Wilbur d Alfred Werker ph John Alton m Leonid Raab

Richard Basehart, Scott Brady, Roy Roberts, Whit Bissell

He Was Her Man
US 1934 70m bw

A safecracker goes straight in order to get even with old rivals. Sassy comedy-drama, not quite smart enough to match its star. James Cagney, Joan Blondell, Victor Jory, Frank Craven, Harold Huber. Written by Niven Busch and Tom Buckingham; directed by Lloyd Bacon; for Warner. 'No help will be President Roosevelt's pronunciamento of last

Saturday (May 19) in which he decried the public penchant for romanticizing crime.'—*Variety*

He Who Gets Slapped*
US 1924   80m approx (24 fps)   bw
  silent
MGM

A scientist starts a new life as a circus clown.
Odd poetic tragedy, Metro-Goldwyn-Mayer's very first production; the public took to it surprisingly well.

w Victor Sjostrom, Carey Wilson, *play* Leonid Andreyev *d* Victor Sjostrom

Lon Chaney, Norma Shearer, John Gilbert, Tully Marshall, Ford Sterling
'For dramatic value and a faultless adaptation of a play, this is the finest production we have yet seen.'—*New York Times*

He Who Must Die*
France / Italy 1957   126m   bw
  Cinemascope
original title: *Celui Qui Doit Mourir*

In a Greek village in 1921, preparations for a passion play are interrupted by the arrival of refugees from the mountains.
Occasionally striking, but mainly arty and pretentious parable; however well meant, a bore to watch.

w Ben Barzman, Jules Dassin, *novel* Nikos Kazantzakis *d* Jules Dassin *ph* Jacques Natteau *m* Georges Auric

Jean Servais, Carl Mohner, Pierre Vaneck, Melina Mercouri, Fernand Ledoux

He Who Rides a Tiger
GB 1965   103m   bw
British Lion / David Newman

A feckless burglar comes out of prison and returns to the old life.
Cliché crime yarn which tries rather desperately after fresh detail but bogs down in romantic asides.

w Trevor Peacock *d* Charles Crichton *ph* John Von Kotze *m* Alexander Faris

Tom Bell, Judi Dench, Paul Rogers, Kay Walsh, Ray McAnally, Jeremy Spenser

Head*
US 1968   85m   Technicolor
Columbia (Bert Schneider)

Fantasia on the life of a sixties pop group.
A psychedelic trip of a movie which does for the Monkees what *A Hard Day's Night* and *Yellow Submarine* did for the Beatles, and what *Monty Python* did for us all. Sometimes funny, slick and clever; often just plain silly.

w Jack Nicholson, Bob Rafaelson *d* Bob Rafaelson *ph* Michael Hugo *m* Ken Thorne *sp* Chuck Gaspar

The Monkees, Victor Mature, Annette Funicello, Timothy Carey
'Random particles tossed around in some demented jester's wind machine.'—*Richard Combs, MFB, 1978*

Head Over Heels*
GB 1937   81m   bw
Gaumont (S. C. Balcon)
US title: *Head Over Heels in Love*

A singing star can't make up her mind between two men.
Interestingly dated light star vehicle.

w Dwight Taylor, Fred Thompson, Marjorie Gaffney, *play* Francois de Croisset *d* Sonnie Hale *ph* Glen McWilliams

Jessie Matthews, Robert Flemyng, Louis Borell, Romney Brent, Helen Whitney Bourne, Eliot Makeham

Head Over Heels
US 1980   97m   Technicolor
aka: *Chilly Scenes of Winter*

A government office worker thinks back on his on-again off-again relationship with the woman he loves. Quirky comedy drama without the zest of *Annie Hall*, which it much resembles; too much like a television play for box office success. John Heard, Mary Beth Hurt, Peter Riegert, Kenneth McMillan, Gloria Grahame. Written and directed by Joan Macklin Silver, from the novel *Chilly Scenes of Winter* by Ann Beattie; for Triple Play / UA.

Heads Up
US 1930   76m   bw

A coastguard ensign is assigned to a private yacht under suspicion of rum-running.
Tedious, flat musical, only interesting for starring the 'boop boop a doop girl', who soon outstays her welcome. Charles Rogers, Helen Kane, Victor Moore, Margaret Breen. Written from the musical play by Jack McGowan and Jack Kirkland; directed by Victor Schertzinger; for Paramount. 'Holds nothing to pull above average grosses and will slide many a house below that mark.'—*Variety*

Health*
US 1979   102m   De Luxe
TCF / Robert Altman

Complications result when a health foods convention is staged in a Florida hotel.
Zany satirical all-star romp on the lines of *A Wedding* but by no means as likeable or laughable, considering its cast, as it should be.

w Robert Altman, Paul Dooley, Frank Barhydt *d* Robert Altman *ph* Edmond L. Koons *m* Joseph Byrd

Lauren Bacall, Glenda Jackson, James Garner, Dick Cavett, Carol Burnett, Paul Dooley, Henry Gibson, Donald Moffat

Hear Me Good
US 1957   82m   bw   VistaVision

Adventures of a confidence trickster in the beauty contest racket. Sub-Damon Runyon goings on, featuring a brash new comedian who was subsequently little heard from. Hal March, Jean Willes, Joe E. Ross, Merry Anders, Milton Frome. Written and directed by Don McGuire; for Paramount.

Heart Beat
US 1979   109m   Technicolor

The literary career of Jack Kerouac is paralleled with his curious sex life. Hesitant and generally unsatisfactory analysis of the so-called beat generation. John Heard, Nick Nolte, Sissy Spacek, Ray Sharkey, Tony Bill. Written and directed by John Byrun; for Orion / Warner.

The Heart is a Lonely Hunter*
US 1968   123m   Technicolor
Warner Seven Arts (Joel Freeman)

Incidents in the life of a gentle deaf mute in a small southern town.
Wispy film of a wistful novel; quite well done but overlong and hard to cheer at.

w Thomas C. Ryan, *novel* Carson McCullers *d* Robert Ellis Miller *ph* James Wong Howe *m* Dave Grusin

Alan Arkin, Sondra Locke, Stacy Keach, Laurinda Barrett, Chuck McCann, Biff McGuire, Percy Rodriguez, Cicely Tyson

AAN: Alan Arkin; Sondra Locke

Heart like a Wheel*
US 1983   113m   CFI colour
Aurora (Charles Rovin)

The wife of a service station owner stops at nothing to become a racing driver.
Well-made study of an obsession, with the usual racing thrills.

w Ken Friedman *d* Jonathan Kaplan *ph* Tak Fujimoto *m* Laurence Rosenthal *pd* James William Newport

Bonnie Bedelia, Beau Bridges, Leo Rossi, Hoyt Axton, Bill McKinney
'An Americanized *Chariots of Fire* for the drive-in market.'—*Observer*

Heart of Glass*
West Germany 1976   94m   Eastmancolor
Werner Herzog

A wandering herdsman with special powers supplies a factory owner with the secret of making a very precious glass.
Apocalyptic visionary parable which may mean everything, or nothing, but amuses fitfully while it's on the screen.

wd Werner Herzog, *text* Herbert Achternbusch *ph* Jorg Schmidt-Reitwin *m* Popol Vuh

Josef Bierbichler, Stefan Guttler, Clemens Scheitz, Sepp Müller

Heart of New York*
US 1932   74m   bw

A plumber invents a washing machine and becomes a millionaire. Ethnic farce set in New York's Jewish quarter; of considerable curiosity value. Smith and Dale, George Sidney, Anna Apfel, Aline MacMahon, Donald Cook. Written by Arthur Caesar and Houston Branch from the play *Mendel Inc* by David Freedman; directed by Mervyn Le Roy; for Warners. 'Gabby to an extreme . . . too much dialect and too little animation.'—*Variety*

The Heart of the Matter*
GB 1953 105m bw
British Lion / London Films (Ian Dalrymple)

In 1942 in an African colony a police officer
has an affair while his wife is away, is
blackmailed, and plans suicide despite his
staunch Catholic belief.
Rather stodgy attempt to film Graham
Greene; perhaps everyone tries a little too
hard, and in any case the ending is
compromised.

w Ian Dalrymple, Lesley Storm, *novel*
Graham Greene d George More O'Ferrall
ph Jack Hildyard m Brian Easdale

Trevor Howard, Maria Schell, Elizabeth
Allan, Denholm Elliott, Peter Finch, Gérard
Oury, George Coulouris, Earl Cameron,
Michael Hordern, Colin Gordon, Cyril
Raymond, Orlando Martins
  'A curious choice for commercial filming.'—
Lindsay Anderson

Heartbeat*
US 1946 102m bw
RKO / Robert and Raymond Hakim

A French gamin released from reform school
becomes a professional pickpocket.
Unamusing remake of *Battement de Coeur*,
with script and most performances very
strained.

w Hans Wilhelm, Max Kolpe, Michel Druan,
Morrie Ryskind d Sam Wood ph Joe
Valentine m Paul Misraki

Ginger Rogers, Jean-Pierre Aumont, Adolphe
Menjou, Basil Rathbone, Mikhail Rasumny,
Melville Cooper, Mona Maris, Henry
Stephenson
  'The heartbeat is irregular and sadly
ailing.'—*Photoplay*

The Heartbreak Kid*
US 1972 106m De Luxe
(TCF) Palomar (Edgar J. Scherick)

Disappointed with his honeymoon, a sporting
goods salesman promptly sets his cap at a
richer, prettier prospective spouse.
Heartless modern comedy reminiscent of *The
Graduate*; quite well done but unsympathetic
and somehow too American to export
satisfactorily.

w Neil Simon, *story* A Change of Plan by
Bruce Jay Friedman d Elaine May ph Owen
Roizman m Garry Sherman

Charles Grodin, Cybill Shepherd, Jeannie
Berlin, Eddie Albert, Audra Lindley, William
Prince, Art Metrano
  'The latest in a relatively new kind of
American film—glittery trash.'—*Stanley
Kauffmann*

AAN: Jeannie Berlin; Eddie Albert
● *Video: CBS / Fox*

Heartland*
US 1979 96m Du Art
Wilderness Women Productions / Filmhaus
  (Annick Smith)

In 1910 Wyoming, a woman with a small
daughter takes up her arduous duties as
housekeeper to a dour rancher.

Impressive if not very likeable semi-
documentary which certainly rubs one's nose
in the unfairness of life.

w Beth Ferris, from the papers of Elmore
Randall Stewart d Richard Pearce ph Fred
Murphy m Charles Gross

Conchata Ferrell, Rip Torn, Barry Primus,
Lila Skala
● *Video: Thorn EMI*

Heart's Desire
GB 1935 82m bw

In old Vienna, a tenor finds that a glamorous
socialite wants him for his voice rather than
himself. Dated operetta, but the star still
reigns supreme. *Richard Tauber*, Leonora
Corbett, Diana Napier, Frank Vosper.
Written by Clifford Grey, L. DuGarde Peach,
Jack Davies, Roger Burford and Bruno Frank;
directed by Paul Stein; for BIP.

Hearts Divided
US 1936 76m bw

Napoleon's brother weds a Baltimore beauty.
Uneasy remake of *Glorious Betsy* (qv) with a
couple of musical numbers added; a splendid
cast retires defeated. Marion Davies, Dick
Powell, Edward Everett Horton, Claude
Rains, Charles Ruggles, Arthur Treacher,
Henry Stephenson. Written by Laird Doyle
and Casey Robinson; directed by Frank
Borzage; for Warner.

Hearts of the West*
US 1975 103m Metrocolor
MGM / Bill–Zieff (Tony Bill)
GB title: *Hollywood Cowboy*

In the early thirties a naïve mid-westerner
almost accidentally becomes a Hollywood star.
Overstretched comedy poking gentle fun at
old Hollywood: likeable but finally
disappointing, as it obviously needed a Buster
Keaton.

w Rob Thompson d Howard Zieff ph Mario
Tosi m Ken Lauber

Jeff Bridges, Alan Arkin, Andy Griffith,
Blythe Danner, Donald Pleasence, Richard B.
Shull, Herb Edelman

Hearts of the World*
US 1918 80m (24 fps) bw silent
Artcraft (David Wark Griffith)

Of various people involved in World War I,
the patriotic and dutiful ones come out best.
Rather dim patriotic propaganda made by
Griffith at the request of the British
government and using a good deal of newsreel
as well as reconstruction. The personal stories
are on the predictable side.

wd David Wark Griffith ph Billy Bitzer
ed James Smith

Lillian Gish, Dorothy Gish, Robert Harron,
Josephine Crowell, Erich Von Stroheim, Noel
Coward
  'Here we have an art of pure emotion which
can go beneath thought, beneath belief,
beneath ideals, down to the brute fact of
emotional psychology, and make a man or a
woman who has hated war, all war, even this

war, feel the surge of group emotion, group
loyalty and group hate.'—*Kenneth
MacGowan, The New Republic (1918)*
† For the screenplay credit Griffith used the
pseudonym of Gaston de Tolignac.

Heat and Dust**
GB 1982 130m colour
Merchant Ivory Productions (Ismail
  Merchant)

A woman discovers India's past through her
great-aunt's letters.
Much praised by those who admire the work
of this team, but found (as usual) mildly
bewildering by others, this has at least a large
enough budget to produce interest in its
historically re-created backgrounds if not its
complex plot structure.

w Ruth Prawer Jhabvala from her novel
d James Ivory ph Walter Lassally m Richard
Robbins

Julie Christie, Christopher Cazenove, Shashi
Kapoor, Greta Scacchi, Nickolas Grace,
Jennifer Kendal, Julian Glover, Susan
Fleetwood
  'A likeable patchwork of concepts and
cameos.'—*Philip Strick, MFB*

BFA: screenplay
● *Video: 3M*

Heat Lightning
US 1934 63m bw

A lady gas station attendant in the hot
southwest becomes involved with two
murderers on the run. Cautionary tale which
does not quite jell despite effort all round.
Aline MacMahon, Ann Dvorak, Preston
Foster, Lyle Talbot, Glenda Farrell, Frank
McHugh, Ruth Donnelly. Written by Brown
Holmes and Warren Duff, from the play by
George Abbott and Leon Abrams; directed by
Mervyn Le Roy; for Warner. (NB: remade in
1941 as *Highway West*.) 'Drab background,
little sex appeal and not enough tension. It's a
sluffo for deluxers, but can get by
elsewhere.'—*Variety*

The Heat's On
US 1943 79m bw
Columbia (Milton Carter)
GB title: *Tropicana*

A star seeks financial backing from an elderly
angel whose sister runs the Legion of Purity.
Dim musical vehicle for a fading star; her last
film for twenty-seven years.

w Fitzroy Davis, George S. George, Fred
Schiller d Gregory Ratoff ph Franz Planer
md Yasha Bunchuk

Mae West, Victor Moore, William Gaxton,
Almira Sessions, Lester Allan, Mary Roche,
Hazel Scott, Alan Dinehart, Lloyd Bridges,
Xavier Cugat and his Orchestra
  'A stale-ale musical in which a lot of good
people apathetically support the almost
equally apathetic Mae West.'—*James Agee*

Heatwave*

Australia 1982   95m   Eastmancolor
M and L Enterprises / Preston Crothers
(Hilary Linstead)

Community activists move to prevent the schemes of a Sydney developer.
Rather like an Ealing drama descending into melodrama; a polished piece of committed film journalism masquerading as fiction.

w Marc Rosenberg, Phillip Noyce *d* Phillip Noyce *ph* Vincent Monton *m* Cameron Allan *pd* Ross Major

Judy Davis, Richard Moir, Chris Haywood, Bill Hunter, John Meillon, John Gregg
† A similarly themed Australian film, *The Killing of Angel Street*, came out almost simultaneously.

Heaven Can Wait***

US 1943   112m   Technicolor
TCF (Ernst Lubitsch)

On arrival in Hades, an elderly playboy reports his peccadilloes to Satan, who sends him Upstairs.
Charming period piece with fantasy bookends; the essence of the piece is its evocation of American society in the nineties, and in its director's waspish way with a funny scene.

w Samson Raphaelson, play Birthday by Lazlo Bus-Fekete *d* Ernst Lubitsch *ph* Edward Cronjager *m* Alfred Newman *ad* James Basevi, Leland Fuller

Don Ameche, Gene Tierney, *Laird Cregar*, Charles Coburn, Marjorie Main, Eugene Pallette, *Allyn Joslyn*, Spring Byington, Signe Hasso, Louis Calhern
'It was so good I half believed Lubitsch could still do as well as he ever did, given half a chance.'—*James Agee*

AAN: best picture; Ernst Lubitsch; Edward Cronjager

Heaven Can Wait*

US 1978   100m   Movielab
Paramount / Warren Beatty (Howard W. Koch Jnr, Charles H. McGuire)

A football star finds himself accidentally in heaven after a car accident; when he is allowed to return, his body has been cremated, so he has to find another.
Unexpectedly commercially successful (the late seventies clearly needed religion) remake of 1941's *Here Comes Mr Jordan*. It lacks the sharpness and style of its predecessor, and despite amusing moments is often merely tacky.

w Warren Beatty, Elaine May, *play* Harry Segall *d* Warren Beatty, Buck Henry *ph* William A. Fraker *m* Dave Grusin *pd* Paul Sylbert

Warren Beatty, Julie Christie, James Mason (as Mr Jordan), Jack Warden, Charles Grodin, *Dyan Cannon*, Buck Henry, Vincent Gardenia, Joseph Maher

AAN: best picture; script; direction; photography; music; Warren Beatty (as actor); Jack Warden; Dyan Cannon
● *Video: CIC*

Heaven Fell That Night

France / Italy 1958   90m   Eastmancolor
Cinemascope
IENA / CEIAP (Raoul Levy)
original title: *Les Bijoutiers du Clair de Lune*

A young girl becomes involved in a revenge plot and finds herself on the run with a killer.
Heavy going sex-and-violence hokum.

w Roger Vadim, Peter Viertel, *novel* Albert Vidalie *d* Roger Vadim *ph* Armand Thirard *m* Georges Auric

Brigitte Bardot, Alida Valli, Stephen Boyd, Pepe Nieto

Heaven Is Round the Corner

GB 1943   94m   bw

A war veteran is helped to find his long-lost love. Sentimental tosh with music, a second team effort which went down well enough in wartime. Will Fyffe, Leni Lynn, Austin Trevor, Magda Kun, Peter Glenville. Written by Austin Melford; directed by Fred Zelnick; for British National.

Heaven Knows Mr Allison*

US 1957   105m   Technicolor
Cinemascope
TCF (Buddy Adler, Eugene Franks)

Marooned on a small Pacific island during World War II, a marine and a nun, antagonistic to each other, combine to outwit the Japs.
Silly adventure story with predictably well-handled action sequences separated by even more predictable dialogue, lots of it.

w John Lee Mahin, John Huston, *novel* Charles Shaw *d* John Huston *ph* Oswald Morris *m* Georges Auric

Robert Mitchum, Deborah Kerr

AAN: script; Deborah Kerr

Heaven on Earth

US 1931   78m   bw

Mississippi steamship owners feud with the shanty houseboaters who line the riverbank. Oddly titled melodrama with a conscience; it doesn't really work. Lew Ayres, Anita Louise, Harry Beresford, Elizabeth Patterson, Slim Summerville. Written by Ray Doyle from the novel Mississippi by Ben Lucian Burman; directed by Russel Mack; for Universal. 'Needs strong stage support wherever chanced.'—*Variety*

Heaven on Earth: see The Exquisite Sinner

Heaven Only Knows

US 1947   98m   bw
(UA) Seymour Nebenzal

An angel is sent to the old west to reform a bad man.
Whimsical comedy-drama which doesn't work at all, even as a distant cousin of *Here Comes Mr Jordan*.

w Art Arthur, Rowland Leigh *d* Albert S. Rogell *ph* Karl Struss *m* Heinz Roemheld

Robert Cummings, Brian Donlevy, Marjorie Reynolds, Bill Goodwin, John Litel, Stuart Erwin

Heaven with a Barbed Wire Fence

US 1939   61m   bw

A New York clerk hitch-hikes his way to Arizona, where he has bought a piece of land. Subdued flagwaver with everybody behaving just swell in God's own country. Glenn Ford (his first film), Jean Rogers, Richard Conte, Marjorie Rambeau, Raymond Walburn, Eddie Collins, Ward Bond. Written by Dalton Trumbo, Leonard Hoffman and Ben Grauman Kohn; directed by Ricardo Cortez; for TCF. 'A slightly clouded title, with little possibility of propelling many customers through the front door.'—*Variety*

Heaven with a Gun

US 1969   101m   Metrocolor   Panavision

The determined new preacher of a small western town is an ex-gunfighter. Solidly carpentered half-a-bill western. Glenn Ford, Carolyn Jones, David Carradine, J. D. Cannon, Barbara Hershey, Noah Beery Jnr. Written by Richard Carr; directed by Lee Katzin; for King Brothers / MGM.

The Heavenly Body

US 1943   93m   bw
MGM (Arthur Hornblow Jnr)

An astronomer is too busy to notice his wife, so she takes up astrology and meets a dark handsome stranger as predicted.
Thin romantic comedy which despite crazy touches never actually makes one laugh.

w Michael Arlen, Walter Reisch *d* Alexander Hall *ph* Robert Planck *m* Bronislau Kaper

William Powell, Hedy Lamarr, James Craig, Fay Bainter, Henry O'Neill, Spring Byington, Morris Ankrum, Connie Gilchrist

Heavens Above*

GB 1963   118m   bw
British Lion / Charter (Roy Boulting)

A northern parson with proletarian sympathies is accidentally appointed to a snobby village where he converts the dowager aristocrat to works of absurd charity. Eventually he has the whole country in an uproar and takes the place of an astronaut.
Patchy satirical comedy which takes unsteady aim at too many targets but scores some predictable laughs.

w Frank Harvey, John Boulting *d* John Boulting *ph* Max Greene *m* Richard Rodney Bennett

Peter Sellers, Isabel Jeans, Cecil Parker, Brock Peters, Ian Carmichael, Irene Handl, Eric Sykes, Bernard Miles
● *Video: Thorn EMI*

'What one loves about life are the things
that fade . . .'
'The most talked-about film of the decade!'
'The only thing greater than their passion
for America . . . was their passion for
each other!'

Heaven's Gate

US 1980 219m Technicolor
UA / Michael Cimino

1890 Wyoming: established cattlemen fight
immigrants.
Totally incoherent, showy western which was
lambasted by the critics and quickly
withdrawn. A vital turning point in Hollywood
policy, hopefully marking the last time a whiz
kid with one success behind him is given a
blank cheque to indulge in self-abuse.

wd Michael Cimino *ph* Vilmos Zsigmond
m David Mansfield

Kris Kristofferson, Christopher Walken, John
Hurt, Sam Waterston, Brad Dourif, Isabelle
Huppert, Joseph Cotten, Jeff Bridges
  'The trade must marvel that directors now
have such power that no one, in the endless
months since work on the picture began, was
able to impose some structure and sense.'—
Variety
  'All too much and not enough.'—*Sunday
Times*
  'A film which John Ford would have
brought in on time and on budget with quite as
much social, critical and political comment—
and much more entertainment value.'—
Margaret Hinxman, Daily Mail
  'It fails so completely that you might suspect
Mr Cimino sold his soul to the devil to obtain
the success of *The Deer Hunter*, and the devil
has just come around to collect.'—*Vincent
Canby, New York Times*

'A step beyond science fiction!'

Heavy Metal°

US 1981 90m Metrocolor
Columbia / Ivan Reitman, Leonard Vogel

A complicated comic strip / science fiction
story, with soft core jokes in the modern
manner, is told by international teams of
animators each working on an episode.
The experiment is interesting rather than
successful.

w Dan Goldberg, Len Blum *d* Gerald
Potterton
  'Something of a hodge-podge . . . the script
is a skeletal, whimsically mystical affair . . .'—
John Pym, MFB

Hedda°

GB 1975 102m Technicolor
Brut (Robert Enders)

A selfish pregnant woman is bored by her
husband and revolted at the idea of carrying
his child. She takes an opportunity to revenge
herself on an old lover, but the scheme
rebounds on herself.
Rather flat rendering of a play which has
received more than its due share of attention.

wd Trevor Nunn, *play* Henrik Ibsen
ph Douglas Slocombe *m* Laurie Johnson

Glenda Jackson, Peter Eyre, Timothy West,
Jennie Linden, Patrick Stewart
AAN: Glenda Jackson

Heidi°

US 1937 88m bw
TCF (Raymond Griffith)

An orphan is sent to stay with her crusty
grandfather in a mountain village.
Star-tailored version of a favourite children's
story; just what the box office ordered at the
time.

w Walter Ferris, Julian Josephson, *novel*
Johanna Spyri *d* Allan Dwan *ph* Arthur
Miller *md* Louis Silvers

Shirley Temple, Jean Hersholt, Arthur
Treacher, Helen Westley, Pauline Moore,
Mary Nash, Thomas Beck, Sidney Blackmer,
Mady Christians, Sig Rumann, Marcia Mae
Jones, Christian Rub
  'Good for the average Temple draw or
better.'—*Variety*
  ● *Video: CBS / Fox*

'She was taught to love and hate—by
masters!'

The Heiress°°

US 1949 115m bw
Paramount (William Wyler)

A plain but rich young woman takes revenge
on her fortune-seeking lover.
Richly-decorated and generally pleasing
version of a stage success based on a Henry
James story set in the nineties.

w Ruth and Augustus Goetz, from their play
and Henry James's Washington Square
d William Wyler *ph* Leo Tover *m* Aaron
Copland *ad* John Meehan

Olivia de Havilland, Ralph Richardson,
Montgomery Clift, Miriam Hopkins, Vanessa
Brown, Mona Freeman, Ray Collins
  'Wyler is that rarest of craftsmen who can
take such a drama, already completely fulfilled
in theatre terms, and convert it to film without
ever permitting the play-form to dominate the
screen.'—*Hermione Isaacs, Films in Review*
AA: Aaron Copland; Olivia de Havilland
AAN: best picture; William Wyler; Leo
Tover; Ralph Richardson

'No star ever climbed higher—no woman
ever fell lower!'

The Helen Morgan Story

US 1957 118m bw Cinemascope
Warner (Martin Rackin)
GB title: *Both Ends of the Candle*

A young singer rises from vaudeville to
Broadway but becomes an alcoholic.
Moderately truthful biopic with effective
twenties trimmings.

w Oscar Saul, Dean Riesner, Stephen
Longstreet, Nelson Gidding *d* Michael Curtiz
ph Ted McCord *m* various *ad* John Beckman

Ann Blyth, Paul Newman, Richard Carlson,
Gene Evans, Alan King, Cara Williams,
Walter Woolf King (as Ziegfeld)

'All the tumultuous wonder and
tremendous drama in the story of
history's most famous runaway lovers!
Soon the whole world will know of its
greatness!'

Helen of Troy

US / Italy 1955 118m Warnercolor
Cinemascope
Warner (Robert Wise)

Helen is kidnapped by Paris and regained by
use of the Trojan Horse.
Dingy historical spectacular, stultifyingly
boring until the final spectacle, with the actors
obviously wishing themselves doing anything
but mouthing the doggerel dialogue.

w John Twist, Hugh Gray *d* Robert Wise
ph Harry Stradling *m* Max Steiner

Rosanna Podesta, Jacques Sernas, Cedric
Hardwicke, Niall MacGinnis, Stanley Baker,
Nora Swinburne, Robert Douglas, Torin
Thatcher, Harry Andrews, Janette Scott,
Ronald Lewis, Brigitte Bardot

Hell and High Water

US 1954 103m Technicolor
Cinemascope
TCF (Raymond A. Klune)

A privately-financed anti-Red scientific
expedition sets off for Alaska to prevent a
Chinese anti-American plot.
Early scoper which mixes deviously plotted
schoolboy fiction with submarine spectacle and
cold war heroics.

wd Samuel Fuller *ph* Joe MacDonald
m Alfred Newman

Richard Widmark, Bella Darvi, Victor
Francen, David Wayne, Cameron Mitchell,
Gene Evans

Hell Below

US 1933 105m bw
MGM

Tensions mount at a Mediterranean submarine
base during World War I.
Adequate war actioner with appropriate
trimmings of heroism, tragedy, comedy and
romance.

w John Lee Mahin, John Meehan, Laird
Doyle, Raymond Schrock, *novel* Pigboats by
Commander Edward Ellsberg *d* Jack
Conway *ph* Harold Rosson

Robert Montgomery, Walter Huston, Madge
Evans, Jimmy Durante, Eugene Pallette,
Robert Young, Edwin Styles, John Lee
Mahin, Sterling Holloway
  'Not a two dollar picture, but will be more
than oke in the grinds.'—*Variety*

Hell Below Zero

GB 1954 91m Technicolor
Columbia / Warwick (Irving Allen, Albert
Broccoli)

An American adventurer accompanies the
daughter of a whaling captain to the Antarctic
to discover who killed her father.
Adequate outdoor thick ear with an unusual
setting and lively cast.

w Alec Coppel, Max Trell, *novel* The White South by Hammond Innes *d* Mark Robson *ph* John Wilcox *m* Clifton Parker

Alan Ladd, Joan Tetzel, Basil Sydney, Stanley Baker, Jill Bennett, Niall MacGinnis

Hell Divers*

US 1931 113m bw

MGM

Friendly rivalry exists between two officers in the Naval Air Force.
Routine romantic melodrama with action highlights; a crowdpuller of its day.

w Harvey Gates, Malcolm Stuart Boylan, *story* Spig Wead *d* George Hill *ph* Harold Wenstrom

Wallace Beery, Clark Gable, Conrad Nagel, Dorothy Jordan, Marjorie Rambeau, Marie Prévost, Cliff Edwards
'Fine technical naval aviation display, and no story . . . unusually long on footage and short on entertainment.'—*Variety*
'It's a matter of squadron after squadron of planes, the mechanics attached thereto, the cutting in and around newsreel material, which Metro does so well, and Beery's excellent personal performance.'—*Hollywood Reporter*

Hell Drivers*

GB 1957 108m bw Vistavision

Rank / Aqua (Ben Fisz)

Fast driving on death-trap roads is required of rival lorry drivers for a cheapjack haulage firm.
Absurd, violent, hilarious and constantly surprising melodrama with the silliest of premises backed by a good cast and well handled thrill sequences.

w John Kruse, C. Raker Endfield *d* C. Raker Endfield *ph* Geoffrey Unsworth *m* Hubert Clifford

Stanley Baker, Patrick McGoohan, Herbert Lom, Peggy Cummins, William Hartnell, Wilfrid Lawson, Sidney James, Jill Ireland, Alfie Bass, Gordon Jackson
'This extraordinary film may interest future historians for its description of road haulage and masculine social behaviour in the mid-20th century . . . though produced with efficiency and assurance it is disagreeable and occasionally vicious.'—*MFB*

● Video: Rank

Hell Harbour

US 1930 90m bw

Derelicts congregate in a Caribbean harbour. Low-life dramatics and scenery, but not much story interest. Lupe Velez, Jean Hersholt, Gibson Gowland, John Holland, Al St John. Written by Clarke Silvernall from a story by Rida Johnson Young; directed by Henry King; for United Artists. 'Production of great beauty retarded by a story which fails to retain interest.'—*Variety*

Hell in the Heavens

US 1934 79m bw

In the 1918 air war, an American helps a French unit to get an ace German flier.

Routine *Dawn Patrol* stuff which somehow fails to make an impact. Warner Baxter, Conchita Montenegro, Herbert Mundin, Russell Hardie, Andy Devine, Ralph Morgan. Written by Byron Morgan and Ted Parsons, from the play The Ace by Herman Rossmann; directed by John G. Blystone; for Fox. 'Interesting but probably too familiar at this date.'—*Variety*

Hell in the Pacific*

US 1969 104m Technicolor

Panavision

Cinerama / Selmur (Reuben Bercovitch)

During World War II, an American pilot and a Japanese naval officer who are stranded on the same tiny Pacific island almost become friends.
Highly artificial and pretentious allegorical two-parter which is occasionally well acted and good to look at.

w Alexander Jacobs, Eric Bercovici *d* John Boorman *ph* Conrad Hall *m* Lalo Schifrin

Lee Marvin, Toshiro Mifune
'No real reverberation and no real excitement, intellectual or physical.'—*Tom Milne*

● Video: Guild

Hell Is a City*

GB 1959 93m bw Hammerscope

ABP / Hammer (Michael Carreras)

A jewel thief breaks jail and is hunted by the Manchester police.
Lively semi-documentary, cameo-filled cop thriller filmed on location.

wd Val Guest, *novel* Maurice Proctor *ph* Arthur Grant *m* Stanley Black

Stanley Baker, John Crawford, Donald Pleasence, Maxine Audley, Billie Whitelaw, Joseph Tomelty, George A. Cooper, Vanda Godsell
'A hectic pace, with frequent scene changes, mobility of camera and performers, and much rapid, loud, intense dialogue.'—*MFB*

Hell Is for Heroes*

US 1962 90m bw

Paramount (Henry Blanke)

In 1944, embittered GIs fight and die while taking a German pillbox near the Siegfried line.
Fairly routine anti-war film with a strong cast and effectively-directed moments battling a generally artificial look.

w Robert Pirosh, Richard Carr *d* Don Siegel *ph* Harold Lipstein *m* Leonard Rosenman

Steve McQueen, Bobby Darin, Fess Parker, James Coburn, Bob Newhart, Harry Guardino

Hell Is Sold Out

GB 1951 84m bw

A novelist returns from the supposed dead to find that a glamorous woman is posing as his widow and issuing best-sellers under his name. Downright peculiar comedy-drama which never jells for long enough to be enjoyable. ('Hell Is Sold Out' is the title of a book in the

story.) Herbert Lom, Mai Zetterling, Richard Attenborough. Written by Guy Morgan and Moie Charles; directed by Michael Anderson; for Raymond Stross / Eros.

Hell on Frisco Bay

US 1955 98m Warnercolor

Cinemascope

Jaguar (George Berthelon)

An ex-cop sets out to find the man who framed him for manslaughter.
Tedious actioner enlivened by the character parts and a violent climax.

w Sidney Boehm, Martin Rackin, *novel* William P. McGivern *d* Frank Tuttle *ph* John Seitz *m* Max Steiner

Alan Ladd, Edward G. Robinson, Joanne Dru, *Paul Stewart*, William Demarest, Fay Wray

● Video: Kingston

Hell to Eternity

US 1960 132m bw

Allied Artists / Atlantic (Irving H. Levin)

Marine Guy Gabaldon, brought up by Japanese foster parents, has divided loyalties after Pearl Harbor.
Battle-strewn biopic which after two hours seems to lose its point, if it ever had one, but is efficiently made.

w Ted Sherdeman, Walter Roeber Schmidt *d* Phil Karlson *ph* Burnett Guffey *m* Leith Stevens

Jeffrey Hunter, David Janssen, Vic Damone, Patricia Owens, Richard Eyer, Sessue Hayakawa

'They all had something to sell—courage— sex—corruption!'

The Hell with Heroes

US 1968 102m Techniscope

Universal (Stanley Chase)

Air cargo experts find themselves unwittingly smuggling cigarettes into France, and American counter-intelligence steps in. Unremarkable, totally predictable action melodrama.

w Halsted Welles, Harold Livingston *d* Joseph Sargent *ph* Bud Thackery *m* Quincy Jones

Rod Taylor, Claudia Cardinale, Harry Guardino, Kevin McCarthy, Pete Deuel, William Marshall

Hellcats of the Navy

US 1957 82m bw

Exploits of a daring submarine commander in the war against Japan. Flimsy jingoistic potboiler. Ronald Reagan, Nancy Davis, Arthur Franz, Robert Arthur. Written by David Lang; directed by Nathan Juran; for Charles H. Schneer / Columbia.

Helldorado

US 1934 75m bw

A penniless hitchhiker finds a ghost town with a gold mine. Feeble fable unpersuasively presented. Richard Arlen, Madge Evans, Henry B. Walthall, Ralph Bellamy, James Gleason, Helen Jerome Eddy. Written by Frances Hyland, Rex Taylor, from a story by Frank M. Dazey; directed by James Cruze; for Jesse L. Lasky / Fox. 'Incredible story poorly cast and not at all likely at the b.o.'—*Variety*

Heller in Pink Tights*
US 1960   100m   Technicolor
    Vistavision
Paramount / Ponti–Girosi

Adventures of a dramatic company touring the west in the 1880s.
Genteel spoof western which does not quite come off.

w Dudley Nichols, Walter Bernstein, *novel* Louis L'Amour d George Cukor ph Harold Lipstein m Daniele Amfitheatrof ad Hal Pereira, Eugene Allen

Sophia Loren, Anthony Quinn, Steve Forrest, Eileen Heckart, Edmund Lowe, Margaret O'Brien, Ramon Novarro

'It has a welcome individuality which is never quite smothered by its lapses into convention.'—*Penelope Houston*

Hellfighters
US 1969   120m   Technicolor
    Panavision
Universal (Robert Arthur)

Oil well fire-fighting specialists have problems among themselves and with their womenfolk.
Ham-fisted story line and performances are slightly, but only slightly, compensated by excellent special effects.

w Clair Huffaker d Andrew V. McLaglen ph William H. Clothier m Leonard Rosenman

John Wayne, Jim Hutton, Katharine Ross, Vera Miles, Jay C. Flippen, Bruce Cabot, Barbara Stuart
'The overall effect is unpardonably tedious.'—*MFB*

The Hellfire Club*
GB 1960   93m   Eastmancolor
    Dyaliscope
Regal / New World (Robert S. Baker, Monty Berman)

In the 18th century, a nobleman's child escapes from his degenerate father, joins a travelling circus, and later returns to claim his inheritance.
Sprightly historical romantic melodrama lightly based on the nefarious activities of the real Hellfire Club; energetic and entertaining if slightly too jokey.

w Leon Griffiths, Jimmy Sangster d / ph Robert S. Baker, Monty Berman m Clifton Parker

Keith Michell, Peter Arne, Adrienne Corri, Kai Fischer, Bill Owen, Peter Cushing, David Lodge, Francis Matthews

Hellgate
US 1952   87m   bw

In the 1860s a veterinary surgeon is wrongly convicted and sent to a savage prison.

Competent exploitation melodrama, not apparently based on truth. Sterling Hayden, Ward Bond, Joan Leslie, Jim Arness, Peter Coe. Written and directed by Charles Marquis Warren; for Commander Films / Lippert.

The Hellions
GB 1961   80m   Technirama
Columbia / Irving Allen, Jamie Uys (Harold Huth)

In the 1860s, a family of South African outlaws starts a reign of terror in a small village.
A British attempt to restage the OK Corral; it goes sadly awry.

w Harold Swanton, Patrick Kirwan, Harold Huth d Ken Annakin ph Ted Moore m Larry Adler

Richard Todd, Lionel Jeffries, James Booth, Jamie Uys, Ronald Fraser, Anne Aubrey, Zena Walker, Marty Wilde, Colin Blakely
'Unconvincingly staged and plotted, tediously violent, uncertainly directed and very badly acted.'—*MFB*

Hello Dolly**
US 1969   129m   De Luxe   Todd-AO
TCF / Chenault (Ernest Lehman)

In 1890 New York, a widowed matchmaker has designs on a wealthy grain merchant.
Generally agreeable but overblown musical based on a slight but much worked-over farce, fatally compromised by the miscasting of a too-young star. Some exhilarating moments.

w Ernest Lehman, *musical Jerry Herman* (m / ly) and Michael Stewart (*book*), from *Thornton Wilder's* play The Matchmaker d Gene Kelly ph Harry Stradling md Lennie Hayton, Lionel Newman pd John de Cuir ch Michael Kidd

Barbra Streisand, Walter Matthau, *Michael Crawford, Marianne McAndrew*, E. J. Peaker, Tommy Tune, David Hurst
'The film leaves an oddly negative impression; a good deal of synthetic effervescence . . . but very little real vitality.'—*David Wilson*

AA: music direction; art direction; set decoration
AAN: best picture; photography
● Video: CBS / Fox

Hello Down There
US 1969   98m   Eastmancolor

The designer of an underwater house volunteers to live in it for a month. Curious comedy with predictable obstacles to the happy ending. Tony Randall, Janet Leigh, Jim Backus, Roddy McDowall, Merv Griffin, Ken Berry, Richard Dreyfuss. Written by Frank Telford and John McGreevey; directed by Jack Arnold; for Ivan Tors / MGM.

'A lady bountiful with a ready song on her
    lips to hide the ache of emptiness in her
    own heart!'

Hello Everybody
US 1932   69m   bw

An overweight girl becomes a national radio celebrity. Slim vehicle in which its star sings

nine times. *Kate Smith*, Randolph Scott, Sally Blane, Jerry Tucker, George Barbier. Written by Dorothy Yost, Lawrence Hazard, from a story by Fannie Hurst; directed by William Seiter; for Paramount. 'Should do okay outside big cities.'—*Variety*

Hello Frisco Hello*
US 1943   98m   Technicolor
TCF (Milton Sperling)

On the Barbary Coast, a girl singer becomes a star.
Moderately pleasing period musical with plenty going on but nothing very striking.

w Robert Ellis, Helen Logan, Richard Macauley d Bruce Humberstone ph Charles Clarke, Allen Davey *songs* various ad James Basevi, Boris Leven

Alice Faye, John Payne, Jack Oakie, Lynn Bari, Laird Cregar, June Havoc, Ward Bond, Aubrey Mather, George Barbier, Frank Orth

AA: song 'You'll Never Know' (m Harry Warren, *ly* Mack Gordon)
AAN: Charles Clarke, Allen Davey

Hello Goodbye
US 1970   101m   De Luxe
TCF (André Hakim)

A cheerful young Englishman falls for a mysterious Frenchwoman who turns out to be the wife of a Baron.
Modest, aimless, forgettable romantic comedy, full of old-fashioned clichés imperfectly remembered.

w Roger Marshall d Jean Negulesco ph Henri Decaë m Francis Lai pd John Howell ad Auguste Capelier

Michael Crawford, Geneviève Gilles, Curt Jurgens, Ira Furstenberg

Hello Sister*
US 1933   62m   bw
Fox (Winfield Sheehan)
aka: *Walking down Broadway*

Boy meets girl in New York.
A mild little romance, only notable because it was edited down from an original by Erich Von Stroheim, and touches of his work remain.

w Erich Von Stroheim, Leonard Spiegelass, *novel* Dawn Powell d Erich Von Stroheim, Alfred Werker ph James Wong Howe

James Dunn, Boots Mallory, Zasu Pitts, Minna Gombell

Hell's Angels****
US 1930   135m   bw (some scenes in
    colour)
Howard Hughes

Two Americans become fliers in World War I.
Celebrated early talkie spectacular, with zeppelin and flying sequences that still thrill. The dialogue is another matter, but all told this expensive production, first planned as a silent, is a milestone of cinema history.

w Howard Estabrook, Harry Behn d Howard Hughes ph Tony Gaudio, Harry Perry, E. Burton Steene m Hugo Reisenfeld

Ben Lyon, James Hall, Jean Harlow, John Darrow, Lucien Prival

'That it will ever pay off for its producer is doubtful . . . he's in so deep it can't really matter to him now. Minus blue nose interference, it can't miss, but it's up to the brim with sex.'—*Variety*

'It is not great, but it is as lavish as an eight-ring circus, and when you leave the theatre you will know you have seen a movie and not a tinny reproduction of a stage show.'—*Pare Lorentz*

AAN: Tony Gaudio, Harry Perry, E. Burton Steene

Hell's Five Hours
US 1958 75m bw

A psychopath takes hostages and threatens to blow up a rocket fuel plant. Standard suspense programmer, tolerable but entirely forgettable. Stephen McNally, Vic Morrow, Coleen Gray. Written and directed by Jack L. Copeland; for Allied Artists.

Hell's Half Acre
US 1953 91m bw

A soldier missing after Pearl Harbor turns up years later in Hawaii under a different identity. Complex melodrama ending in self-sacrifice; amusing bits don't hang together. Wendell Corey, Evelyn Keyes, Elsa Lanchester, Nancy Gates, Philip Ahn, Keye Luke. Written by Steve Fisher; directed by John H. Auer; for Republic.

Hell's Heroes
US 1930 65m bw
Universal

Three cowboys find an abandoned baby. Yet another version of *Three Godfathers*; maybe not the best but the shortest.

w Tom Reed, *novel* Peter Kyne d William Wyler ph George Robinson

Charles Bickford, Raymond Hatton, Fred Kohler, Fritzi Ridgeway
† Photographed in the Mojave and Panamint Deserts.

Hell's Highway*
US 1932 62m bw

A convict plans escape from a forced labour gang, under the threat of the lash and the sweatbox. Well-made but heavy-going melodrama without light relief. Richard Dix, Rochelle Hudson, Tom Brown, C. Henry Gordon, Louise Carter. Written by Samuel Ornitz, Robert Tasker, Rowland Brown; directed by Rowland Brown; for RKO. 'The story is too sodden to carry a general appeal.'—*Variety*

Hell's House
US 1932 72m bw

A boy is wrongly sentenced to a corrupt reform school. Primitive cheapie notable only for the early appearance of Bette Davis; with Pat O'Brien, Junior Durkin, Junior Coghlan, Emma Dunn, Charley Grapewin. Written by Paul Gangelin and B. Harrison Orkow; directed by Howard Higgins; for Capital Films.

Hell's Island*
US 1955 84m Technicolor Vistavision
Paramount / Pine–Thomas

Crooks congregate on a Caribbean island in search of a famous ruby.
Cheeky rehash of *The Maltese Falcon*, not bad in its own routine way.

w Maxwell Shane d Phil Karlson ph Lionel Lindon md Irvin Talbot

John Payne, Mary Murphy, *Francis L. Sullivan*, Arnold Moss

Hell's Kitchen
US 1939 82m bw

Boys revolt under the cruel headmaster of a reformatory. Dreary vehicle for the Dead End Kids. Billy Halop, Leo Gorcey, Bobby Jordan, Huntz Hall, Gabriel Dell, Bernard Punsley, Ronald Reagan, Margaret Lindsay, Stanley Fields, Grant Mitchell. Written by Crane Wilbur, Fred Niblo Jnr; directed by Lewis Seiler and E. A. Dupont; for Warners. 'A quagmire of misplaced sentimentality, hokum and general incredulousness.'—*Variety*

The Hellstrom Chronicle
US 1971 90m CFI colour

A scientist explains the range and variety of insect life. Odd documentary in fictional bookends; smart and quite sensational for those with strong stomachs. Laurence Pressman as Nils Hellstrom. Written by David Seltzer; directed by Walon Green; for David Wolper.

Hellzapoppin***
US 1942 84m bw
Universal / Mayfair (Glenn Tryon, Alex Gottlieb)

Two incompetent comics make a picture. Zany modification of a smash burlesque revue; the crazy jokes are toned down and a romantic interest is added (and tentatively sent up). The result is patchy but often hilarious, and the whole is a handy consensus of forties humour and pop music.

w Nat Perrin, Warren Wilson d H. C. Potter ph Woody Bredell md Charles Previn

Ole Olsen, Chic Johnson, Hugh Herbert, Martha Raye, Mischa Auer, Robert Paige, Jane Frazee, Shemp Howard, Elisha Cook Jnr, Richard Lane

Help!*
GB 1965 92m Eastmancolor
(UA) Walter Shenson / Suba Films

An oriental high priest chases the Beatles around the world because one of them has a sacred ring.
Exhausting attempt to outdo *A Hard Day's Night* in lunatic frenzy, which goes to prove that some talents work better on low budgets. The humour is a frantic cross between *Hellzapoppin*, the Goons, Bugs Bunny and the shade of Monty Python to come. It looks good but becomes too tiresome to entertain.

w Charles Wood, Marc Behm d Dick Lester ph David Watkin m The Beatles ad Ray Simm

The Beatles, Leo McKern, Eleanor Bron, Victor Spinetti

Helpmates***
US 1932 20m bw

Stan helps Ollie clean up after a wild party while the wife was away. A brilliant succession of catastrophe gags in the stars' best tradition. Laurel and Hardy. Written by H. M. Walker; directed by James Parrott; for Hal Roach.

Helter Skelter
GB 1949 75m bw
GFD / Gainsborough

An heiress with hiccups is helped by the staff of the BBC.
Scatty comedy which tries everything, from custard pies and guest stars to a clip from a silent Walter Forde comedy. It isn't the British *Hellzapoppin* it sets out to be, but hardened buffs will find it worth a look.

w Patrick Campbell d Ralph Thomas ph Jack Asher m Francis Chagrin

Carol Marsh, David Tomlinson, Mervyn Johns, Peter Hammond, Jimmy Edwards, Richard Hearne, Jon Pertwee, Terry-Thomas

Hemingway's Adventures of a Young Man*
US 1962 145m De Luxe Cinemascope
TCF (Jerry Wald)
aka: *Adventures of a Young Man*

The son of a weak doctor and a religious mother breaks away from his family circle on a voyage of discovery.
Curious mélange of ill-assimilated Hemingway stories based on his Nick Adams character. The film has good intentions but no shape or style, and the guest stars don't help.

w A. E. Hotchner, *stories* Ernest Hemingway d Martin Ritt ph Lee Garmes m Franz Waxman

Richard Beymer, Diane Baker, Corinne Calvet, Fred Clark, Dan Dailey, James Dunn, Juano Hernandez, Arthur Kennedy, Ricardo Montalban, Susan Strasberg, Paul Newman, Jessica Tandy, Eli Wallach

'They had killed a woman and destroyed his life. Now he will kill a woman and destroy their nation!'

Hennessy
GB 1975 104m colour
AIP / Marseilles (Peter Snell)

Angered at the death of his family in the Belfast troubles, an Irish revolutionary hurries to London to blow up the Houses of Parliament.
Unattractive, uninventive thriller with a silly script and not an ounce of real suspense.

w John Gay, *story* Richard Johnson *d* Don Sharp *ph* Ernest Steward *m* John Scott *pd* Ray Simm

Rod Steiger, Richard Johnson, Lee Remick, Trevor Howard, Eric Porter, Peter Egan, David Collings

Henry Aldrich

Henry was originally a radio character created by Ezra Stone, an awkward small-town youth who like Andy Hardy was always getting into scrapes. Clifford Goldsmith wrote the original play which hit Broadway as well as the radio waves before starting a Hollywood series of amiable Paramount second features, most of them starring Jimmy Lydon with Charles Smith as his friend Dizzy.

1939: WHAT A LIFE (with Jackie Cooper)
1941: LIFE WITH HENRY (with Jackie Cooper), HENRY ALDRICH FOR PRESIDENT
1942: HENRY AND DIZZY, HENRY ALDRICH EDITOR
1943: HENRY ALDRICH GETS GLAMOUR, HENRY ALDRICH SWINGS IT, HENRY ALDRICH HAUNTS A HOUSE
1944: HENRY ALDRICH BOY SCOUT, HENRY ALDRICH PLAYS CUPID, HENRY ALDRICH'S LITTLE SECRET

Henry Nine Till Five*
GB 1970   6m   colour

A commuter spends his working days fantasizing about sex. Typical and very lively cartoon by *Bob Godfrey*; written by Stan Heyward; for British Lion.

Henry V••••
GB 1944   137m   Technicolor
Rank / Two Cities (Laurence Olivier)

Shakespeare's historical play is seen in performance at the Globe Theatre in 1603; as it develops, the scenery becomes more realistic.
Immensely stirring, experimental and almost wholly successful production of Shakespeare on film, sturdy both in its stylization and its command of more conventional cinematic resources for the battle.

w Laurence Olivier, Alan Dent, *play* William Shakespeare *d* Laurence Olivier *ph* Robert Krasker *m* William Walton *ad* Paul Sheriff

Laurence Olivier, *Robert Newton, Leslie Banks, Esmond Knight,* Renée Asherson, George Robey, *Leo Genn,* Ernest Thesiger, Ivy St Helier, Ralph Truman, Harcourt Williams, Max Adrian, Valentine Dyall, Felix Aylmer, John Laurie, Roy Emerton

'His production—it was his first time out as a director—is a triumph of colour, music, spectacle, and soaring heroic poetry, and, as actor, he brings lungs, exultation, and a bashful wit to the role.'—*Pauline Kael, 70s*

AAN: best picture; William Walton; Laurence Olivier (as actor)
● *Video: Rank*

Henry VIII and His Six Wives*
GB 1972   125m   Technicolor
EMI (Roy Baird)

Dullish historical account of the king's reign, staged as recollections from his deathbed but lacking any of the sparkle of *The Private Life of Henry VIII* made forty years previously. Accurate sets and costumes fail to compensate for lack of film flair.

w Ian Thorne *d* Waris Hussein *ph* Peter Suschitsky *m* David Munro
Keith Michell, Frances Cuka (Aragon), Charlotte Rampling (Boleyn), Jane Asher (Seymour), Jenny Bos (Cleves), Lynne Frederick (Howard), Barbara Leigh-Hunt (Parr), Donald Pleasence (Thomas Cromwell)
† The production was stimulated by a highly successful BBC TV series, *The Six Wives of Henry VIII*
● *Video: Thorn EMI*

Her Cardboard Lover*
US 1942   93m   bw
MGM (J. Walter Ruben)

A flirtatious lady hires a lover to make her fiancé jealous.
Paper-thin comedy previously filmed in silent days as *The Passionate Plumber* (with Buster Keaton). It did nobody any good, but preserves some style despite a witless script.

w Jacques Deval, John Collier, Anthony Veiller, William H. Wright, *play* Jacques Deval *d* George Cukor *ph* Harry Stradling, Robert Planck *m* Franz Waxman

Norma Shearer, Robert Taylor, George Sanders, Frank McHugh, Elizabeth Patterson, Chill Wills

Her Favourite Husband
GB 1950   79m   bw

A wife finds that her husband has been replaced by a gangster who aims to rob a bank. Rather tiresome Italian-set comedy with funny moments. Jean Kent, Robert Beatty, Gordon Harker, Margaret Rutherford, Rona Anderson, Max Adrian. Written by Noel Langley and W. F. Templeton, from a play by Pepine de Felipe; directed by Mario Soldati; for Orlux / Renown.

Her Highness and the Bellboy
US 1945   112m   bw
MGM (Joe Pasternak)

A hotel bellboy forsakes his crippled sweetheart to woo a visiting princess. Glutinous sentimental mishmash; one waits for musical numbers which never happen.

w Richard Connell, Gladys Lehmann *d* Richard Thorpe *ph* Harry Stradling *m* Georgie Stoll

Hedy Lamarr, Robert Walker, June Allyson, Rags Ragland, Agnes Moorehead, Carl Esmond, Warner Anderson, Ludwig Stossel

Her Husband Lies
US 1937   74m   bw

A New York gambler tries to ensure that his kid brother is not contaminated. Adequate

remake of *Street of Chance*. Ricardo Cortez, Gail Patrick, Akim Tamiroff, Tom Brown, Louis Calhern. Written by Wallace Smith, Eve Brown, from a story by O. H. P. Garrett; directed by Edward Ludwig; for Paramount. 'Superb direction and expert acting.'—*Variety*

Her Husband's Affairs*
US 1947   83m   bw
Columbia (Raphael Hakim)

A husband and wife team of advertising agents promote a depilatory which turns out to grow hair instead.
Mildly amiable crazy comedy.

w Ben Hecht *d* S. Sylvan Simon *ph* Charles Lawton Jnr *m* George Duning

Lucille Ball, Franchot Tone, Edward Everett Horton, Mikhail Rasumny, Gene Lockhart, Nana Bryant, Jonathan Hale, Mabel Paige

'See the mystical hypnotic rites of the white goddess of the jungle! See the plane crash in the tragic typhoon! See the ravening charge of the hundred sacred crocodiles!'

Her Jungle Love*
US 1938   81m   Technicolor
Paramount (George M. Arthur)

An aviator crashlands in the jungle, where he is comforted by a lovely lady, a chimp and a lion but distressed by an earthquake, a volcano and assorted villains.
Second of Dorothy Lamour's jungle hokum shows, and the first in colour; despite its fair technical proficiency, the fact that it once packed 'em in is tribute to the changing tastes of mankind.

w Joseph M. March, Lillie Hayward, Eddie Welch *d* George Archainbaud *ph* Ray Rennahan *m* Gregory Stone

Dorothy Lamour, Ray Milland, Lynne Overman, J. Carrol Naish, Dorothy Howe
'Splendid colour job, but there's little more . . . only slightly varied from the type of a bygone era.'—*Variety*
† The Lynne Overman character wisecracks: 'Those *Esquire* cartoons must be right: there's always just one girl on a desert island.'
†† The lion cub in this case is called Meewa, the chimp Gaga.

Her Kind of Man
US 1946   78m   bw

A singer finds a gangster irresistible but eventually settles for a newspaper columnist. Shiny, nondescript forties copy of a thirties style; more yawns than thrills. Dane Clark, Zachary Scott, Janis Paige, Faye Emerson, George Tobias, Sheldon Leonard. Written by Gordon Kahn and Leopold Atlas; directed by Frederick de Córdova; for Warner.

Her Man*
US 1930   85m   bw

The story of Frankie and Johnnie is transposed to a French apache setting. Comedy melodrama which has its adherents. Helen

HENRY ALDRICH SWINGS IT. One of a second-feature series which never seemed to wear out its welcome.

Twelvetrees, Ricardo Cortez, Marjorie Rambeau, James Gleason, Franklin Pangborn, Phillips Holmes, Thelma Todd. Written by Howard Higgins and Tay Garnett; directed by Tay Garnett; for Pathé. 'Looks like box office ... full of action.'—*Variety*

Her Majesty Love
US 1931 76m bw
A well-born Berliner finds it easier to court the barmaid he loves after she has married a baron. Heavy-handed musical comedy worth excavating for the odd talents involved.

Marilyn Miller, Ben Lyon, W. C. Fields, Leon Errol, Chester Conklin, Ford Sterling. Written by Robert Lord and Arthur Caesar; directed by William Dieterle; for Warner. 'An exceptionally dismal musical.'—*Clive Hirschhorn 1983*

Her Master's Voice
US 1936   75m   bw

Henpecked by his wife and her mother, a man makes a name for himself as a radio troubadour. Mild comedy from a stage success. Edward Everett Horton, Peggy Conklin, Laura Hope Crews, Elizabeth Patterson, Grant Mitchell. Written by Dore Schary, Harry Sauber from the play by Clare Kummer; directed by Joseph Santley; for Walter Wanger / Paramount. 'Suitable because of frothy humour for family and nabe audiences solo.'—*Variety*

Her Primitive Man
US 1944   87m   bw

An author disguises himself as a savage in order to denounce a woman trying to prove his theories a fraud. Very silly comedy partly salvaged by a few good lines. Robert Paige, Louise Allbritton, Robert Benchley, Edward Everett Horton, Helen Broderick, Ernest Truex, Walter Catlett, Nydia Westman. Written by Michael Fessier and Ernest Pagano; directed by Charles Lamont; for Universal.

Her Twelve Men
US 1954   91m   Anscocolor
MGM (John Houseman)

A woman teacher in a boys' school reforms a difficult class.
Predictable, sugary and artificial school story with the star exuding sweetness and light.

w William Roberts, Laura Z. Hobson d Robert Z. Leonard ph Joseph Ruttenberg m Bronislau Kaper

Greer Garson, Robert Ryan, Richard Haydn, Barry Sullivan

Her Wedding Night
US 1930   78m   bw

On the Italian riviera a man marries his friend's wife under the impression that they are only booking rooms for the night. Spicy bedroom farce which crested the wave of its star's notoriety. Clara Bow, *Charles Ruggles*, Ralph Forbes, Skeets Gallagher. Written by Henry Myers from the play by Avery Hopwood; directed by Frank Tuttle; for Paramount. 'Deftly handled for smartness and taste . . . ought to make women talk.'—*Variety*

Herbie Goes Bananas
US 1980   100m   Technicolor

Two Americans take their magical Volkswagen on a South American holiday. Listless addition to a series which has already gone on too long. Charles Martin Smith, Stephan W. Burns, Cloris Leachman, John Vernon. Written by Don Tait; directed by Vincent McEveety; for Walt Disney.
● Video: Rank

Herbie Goes to Monte Carlo
US 1977   105m   Technicolor
Walt Disney (Ron Miller)

The Volkswagen with a mind of its own enters the Monte Carlo rally and routs a gang of thieves.
Utterly predictable, patchily made family comedy.

w Arthur Alsberg, Don Nelson d Vincent McEveety ph Leonard J. South m Frank de Vol

Dean Jones, Don Knotts, Julie Sommars, Jacques Marin, Roy Kinnear, Bernard Fox
† Second sequel to *The Love Bug*.

Hercules
Italy 1957   105m   Eastmancolor
  Dyaliscope
Oscar / Galatea
original title: *Le Fatiche di Ercole*

Hercules helps Jason find the golden fleece. The strong man epic which started a genre; of little interest in itself.

w Pietro Francisci, Ennio de Concini, Gaio Frattini d Pietro Francisci ph Mario Bava m Enzo Masetti

Steve Reeves, Sylva Koscina, Gianna Maria Canale, Fabrizio Mione

Hercules Unchained
Italy / France 1959   105m
  Eastmancolor   Dyaliscope
Lux / Galatea
original title: *Ercole e la Regina di Lidia*

Hercules has problems with the king of Thebes and the queen of Lidia.
More comic-strip versions of old legends. This item had more spent on it in publicity than in production cost, and consequently was seen by vast audiences around the world. It isn't very good.

w Pietro Francisci, Ennio di Concini d Pietro Francisci ph Mario Bava m Enzo Masetti

Steve Reeves, Sylva Koscina, Sylvia Lopez, Primo Carnera
† Many sequels followed, the hero sometimes being known as Ursus or Goliath.

Here Come the Coeds
US 1945   88m   bw
Universal (John Grant)

Janitors help to forestall a mortgage foreclosure on a college for women.
Routine star vehicle with few highlights.

w Arthur T. Horman, John Grant d Jean Yarbrough ph George Robinson songs Jack Brooks, Edgar Fairchild

Bud Abbott, Lou Costello, Lon Chaney Jnr, Peggy Ryan, Martha O'Driscoll, Donald Cook, June Vincent, Charles Dingle

Here Come the Girls*
US 1953   78m   Technicolor
Paramount (Paul Jones)
original title: *Champagne for Everybody*

In the nineties an ageing chorus boy traps a mysterious murderer.
Spotty, ineptly titled star comedy with music; in fact among the last of his passable vehicles, with excellent production backing.

w Edmund Hartmann, Hal Kanter d Claude Binyon ph Lionel Lindon md Lyn Murray ad Hal Pereira, Roland Anderson

Bob Hope, Rosemary Clooney, Tony Martin, Arlene Dahl, Millard Mitchell, Fred Clark, William Demarest, Robert Strauss

Here Come the Huggetts*
GB 1948   93m   bw
Rank / Gainsborough (Betty Box)

A suburban family has its ups and downs. Cosy domestic comedy drama, a presage of TV soap operas to come, or Britain's answer to the Hardys, depending how you look at it. Tolerable at the time.

w Mabel and Denis Constanduros, Muriel and Sydney Box, Peter Rogers d Ken Annakin ph Reg Wyer

Jack Warner, Kathleen Harrison, Jane Hylton, Susan Shaw, Petula Clark, Jimmy Hanley, David Tomlinson, Diana Dors, Peter Hammond, John Blythe
† The Huggetts had actually originated in *Holiday Camp* the previous year, and appeared again in *Vote for Huggett* and *The Huggetts Abroad*; Warner and Harrison became an inseparable duo for many years.

Here Come the Nelsons
US 1951   76m   bw

The sons of an advertising agent get involved with gangsters. Empty-headed family comedy based on the long-running TV show *The Adventures of Ozzie and Harriet*. Ozzie Nelson, Harriet Hilliard, David and Ricky Nelson, Rock Hudson, Barbara Lawrence, Ann Doran, Jim Backus. Written by Ozzie Nelson, Donald Nelson and William Davenport; directed by Frederick de Cordova; for Universal.

Here Come the Waves
US 1944   98m   bw
Paramount (Mark Sandrich)

A sailor falls in love with identical twin Waves.
Empty-headed, professionally executed musical recruiting poster.

w Allen Scott, Ken Englund, Zion Myers d Mark Sandrich ph Charles Lang md Robert Emmett Dolan songs Harold Arlen, Johnny Mercer

Bing Crosby, Betty Hutton, Sonny Tufts, Ann Doran, Gwen Crawford
  'An almost totally negligible musical.'—*James Agee*

AAN: song 'Accentuate the Positive' (m Harold Arlen, ly Johnny Mercer)

Here Comes Cookie
US 1935   65m   bw

Gracie comes into money and opens a theatre-cum-hotel for vaudevillians. Slight star comedy with its share of laughs. George Burns, Gracie Allen, George Barbier, Betty Furness, Andrew Tombes. Written by Sam Mintz and Don Hartman; directed by Norman Z. McLeod; for William le Baron / Paramount. 'Situation and gag pounding without an ounce of seriousness or sense.'—*Variety*

HERE COMES MR JORDAN.   Edward Everett Horton seemed somewhat miscast as a heavenly messenger, but he seems to be convincing Robert Montgomery. Claude Rains's role consisted chiefly of quizzical smiles.

Here Comes Mr Jordan***
US 1941 93m bw
Columbia (Everett Riskin)

A prizefighter who is also an amateur saxophonist crashes in his private plane and goes to heaven by mistake: he was supposed to survive and live another forty years. Unfortunately when he goes back for his body it has been cremated, so he has to find another one, recently deceased . . .

Weird heavenly fantasy which succeeded because of its novelty and because heaven in wartime was a comforting vision. As a movie taken on its own merits, it suffers from illogicalities, a miscast star and a wandering plot, but scene for scene there is enough firmness and control to make it memorable. It certainly had many imitations, including *Angel on My Shoulder, Down to Earth, A Guy Named Joe, Heaven Only Knows, The Horn Blows at Midnight* and *That's the Spirit.*

w *Seton I. Miller, Sidney Buchman, play Halfway to Heaven by Harry Segall*
d *Alexander Hall* ph Joseph Walker
m *Frederick Hollander* md Morris Stoloff

Robert Montgomery, Evelyn Keyes, Rita Johnson, *Claude Rains, James Gleason, Edward Everett Horton*, John Emery, *Donald MacBride*, Halliwell Hobbes, Don Costello

'There is something about this original so sweet-spirited and earnest that it transcends its plot devices and shines through its comedic asides to become a true morality play without once becoming either preachy or mawkish.'—*Kit Parker catalogue, 1980*

'Audiences loved this chunk of whimsy . . . the slickly hammy Rains gives Mr Jordan a sinister gloss, as if he were involved in some heavenly racket, like smuggling Chinese.'—*Pauline Kael, 70s*

† Remade 1978 as *Heaven Can Wait.*

AA: original story (Harry Segall); script
AAN: best picture; Seton I. Miller, Sidney Buchman; Alexander Hall; Joseph Walker; Robert Montgomery; James Gleason

Here Comes the Band
US 1935 82m bw

Buddies from an army band are stuck in the taxi business. Shapeless comedy with interesting numbers. But not very. *Ted Lewis* and his Band, Ted Healy, Nat Pendleton, Virginia Bruce, Harry Stockwell, Donald Cook, Spanky McFarland. Written by Paul Sloane, Ralph Spence, Victor Mansfield; directed by Paul Sloane; for MGM. 'Not punchy enough for the de luxe trade . . . best as second stringer.'—*Variety*

Here Comes the Groom*
US 1951 114m bw
Paramount (Frank Capra)

A journalist adopts war orphans and reforms his selfish fiancée.
Tired attempt by Capra to recapture his pre-war mood; despite intermittent pleasures it has neither the right style nor the topical substance.

w Virginia Van Upp, Myles Connelly, Liam O'Brien, *story* Robert Riskin *d Frank Capra ph* George Barnes *md* Joseph Lilley *songs* Jay Livingston, Ray Evans

Bing Crosby, Jane Wyman, Franchot Tone, Alexis Smith, James Barton, Connie Gilchrist, Robert Keith, Anna Maria Alberghetti
   'The general impression is of a loud, strident, rather vulgar comedy in which technique is used to disappointingly mechanical ends, and which a few bright lines of dialogue cannot rescue from tedium.'— *Penelope Houston*
AA: song 'In the Cool Cool Cool of the Evening' (*m* Hoagy Carmichael, *ly* Johnny Mercer)
AAN: Robert Riskin

Here Comes the Navy*
US 1934 86m bw
Warner

An aggressive young naval rating fights with his former friend, now Petty Officer.
Breezy comedy melodrama teaming Cagney and O'Brien for the first time and offering star heroics as a sop to the Legion of Decency.

w Ben Markson, Earl Baldwin *d* Lloyd Bacon *ph* Arthur Edeson *m* Leo F. Forbstein

James Cagney, Pat O'Brien, Dorothy Tree, Gloria Stuart, Frank McHugh, Robert Barrat
   'It's a bit too masculine for matinée appeal and it'll have to be a case of the kids and men dragging the womenfolk along.'— *Variety*
   'Rapid and reasonably authentic, a satisfactory addition to a series of cinema cartoons which, because their colour and mood are indigenous and timely, may be more interesting twenty years from now.'— *Time*
AAN: best picture

Here Comes the Sun
GB 1945 91m bw

Racetrack touts help to breathe fresh life into a provincial newspaper. Amiable comedy with a touch of do-goodery, very typical of this producer. Bud Flanagan, Chesney Allen, Joss Ambler, Dick Francis. Written by Geoffrey Orme; directed and produced by John Baxter.

Here I Am a Stranger
US 1939 81m bw

A rich woman tries to prevent her son being influenced by her once-drunken ex-husband. Predictable family drama which was catnip to 1939 audiences. Gladys George, Richard Dix,

Richard Greene, Brenda Joyce, Roland Young, Russell Gleason, George Zucco. Written by Sam Hellman and Milton Sperling from a story by Gordon Malherbe Hillman; directed by Roy del Ruth; for Harry Joe Brown / TCF. 'Strong programme drama will catch many top key spots.'— *Variety*

Here Is My Heart
US 1934 73m bw

An American radio crooner on the riviera pretends to be a waiter in order to court a princess. Musical remake of *The Grand Duchess and the Waiter*; not bad of its type. Bing Crosby, Kitty Carlisle, Roland Young, Alison Skipworth, Reginald Owen, Akim Tamiroff. Written by Edwin Justus Mayer and Harlan Thompson; directed by Frank Tuttle; for Paramount. 'First-class entertainment . . . though it seems they adapted it by running it through the electric fan.'— *Variety*. Songs by Leo Robin and Ralph Rainger: 'Love Is Just Around the Corner'; 'With Every Breath I Take'; 'June in January'; 'Here Is my Heart'; 'You Can't Make a Monkey of the Moon'.

Here We Go round the Mulberry Bush*
GB 1967 96m Technicolor
UA / Giant (Larry Kramer, Clive Donner)

A school-leaver is obsessed by sex and determines to lose his virginity.
Repetitive comedy which certainly opened new avenues in British humour and seemed pretty permissive at the time (pre-*Graduate*). In itself, however, more modish than sympathetic.

w Hunter Davies (with Larry Kramer), from his novel *d Clive Donner ph* Alex Thomson *m* various groups

Barry Evans, Judy Geeson, Angela Scoular, Adrienne Posta, Sheila White, Vanessa Howard, Denholm Elliott, Maxine Audley, Moyra Fraser, Michael Bates
   'The only incongruity is that it should have been made by adults, so completely does it enter into the teenager's view of himself.'— *MFB*

Here's to Romance
US 1935 82m bw

A young tenor who finds a patron in Paris is pursued by the wealthy wife. Amiable piece of musical froth which somehow failed to make a big singing star of Martini. Nino Martini, Genevieve Tobin, Reginald Denny, Anita Louise, Mme Schumann-Heink, Maria Gambarelli. Written by Ernest Pascal and Arthur Richman; directed by Alfred E. Green; for Jesse L. Lasky / TCF. 'Given a sturdier story he might have emerged as a Grace Moore for talkers.'— *Variety*

A Hero Ain't Nothing but a Sandwich
US 1977 107m CFI color
New World / Radnitz-Mattel (Robert B. Radnitz)

Problems for an urban family in the black ghetto.

Well-intentioned but ultimately wearisome and cliché-strewn melodrama.

w Alice Childress, from her novel *d* Ralph Nelson *ph* Frank Stanley *m* Tom McIntosh

Cicely Tyson, Paul Winfield, Larry B. Scott, Helen Martin, Glynn Turman
   'The sort of dreaded wholesome film that cultural and societal groups heavily endorse but nobody pays money to go see.'— *Variety*

Hero at Large
US 1980 98m Metrocolor

An actor playing Captain Avenger accidentally becomes a real-life hero, but his fans turn against him when they find he's just an ordinary guy. Muddled satirical comedy-melodrama with too many pauses for love interest. John Ritter, Anne Archer, Bert Convy, Kevin McCarthy, Harry Bellaver. Written by A. J. Carothers; directed by Martin Davidson; for Stephen Freedman / MGM.

Heroes
US 1977 113m Technicolor
Universal (David Foster, Lawrence Turman)

A Vietnam veteran, made slightly kooky by his experiences, settles down after several adventures when he falls in love.
Just plain awful: a would-be star vehicle that doesn't work.

w James Carabatsos (and, uncredited, David Freeman) *d Jeremy Paul Kagan ph* Frank Stanley *m* Jack Nitzche, Richard Hazard

Henry Winkler, Sally Field, Harrison Ford, Val Avery

The Heroes Are Tired
France 1955 101m bw
Cila-Terra
original title: *Les Héros Sont Fatigués*

Two ex-wartime pilots, one Free French and the other German, set up an air charter service in Liberia but come to grief over stolen diamonds.
Gloomy post-war *film noir* set in a peculiarly depressing atmosphere, and not really sharp enough to overcome its squalid plot.

w Yves Ciampi, Jacques-Laurent Bost, *novel* Christine Garnier *d* Yves Ciampi *ph* Henri Alekan *m* Louiguy

Yves Montand, Maria Félix, Jean Servais, Curt Jurgens, Gérard Oury

Heroes for Sale
US 1933 73m bw

A war veteran becomes in turn a drug addict, a millionaire and the central figure in a labour dispute. Minor social-conscience melodrama with watchable elements. Richard Barthelmess, Aline MacMahon, Loretta Young, Berton Churchill, Robert Barrat. Written by Robert Lord and Wilson Mizner; directed by William A. Wellman; for Warner. 'This attempted satire on unemployment conditions just prior to the Roosevelt election is not well told . . . b.o. doubtful.'— *Variety*

The Heroes of Telemark*
GB 1965   131m   Technicolor
Panavision
Rank / Benton (Ben Fisz)

Norwegian resistance workers in World War II
help the Allies to smash a heavy water plant.
Ambling narrative with big action sequences
which often seem irrelevant, so that the story
as a whole fails to excite.

w Ivan Moffat, Ben Barzman d Anthony
Mann ph Robert Krasker m Malcolm Arnold

Kirk Douglas, Richard Harris, Ulla Jacobsson,
Roy Dotrice, Anton Diffring, Michael
Redgrave

● Video: Rank

Hero's Island*
US 1962   94m   Technicolor   Panavision
UA / Daystar / Portland (James Mason,
Leslie Stevens)

In 1718 bondslaves settle on a Carolina island,
are attacked by fishermen and protected by
Blackbeard the Pirate.
An oddly personal, patchy, rather mysterious
film with a rhetorical script and rather good
action sequences.

wd Leslie Stevens ph Ted McCord
m Dominic Frontière

James Mason, Kate Manx, Neville Brand, Rip
Torn

Herr Puntila and his Servant Matti*
Austria 1955   95m   Agfacolor
Bauerfilm

A rich landowner, usually drunk, is rescued
from scrapes by his patient valet.
A cogent comedy which its author is said to
have approved in this version.

w Alberto Cavalcanti, Vladimir Pozner, Ruth
Wieden, play Bertolt Brecht d Alberto
Cavalcanti ph André Bac, Arthur Hämmerer
m Hanns Eisler

Curt Bois, Hans Engelmann, Maria Emo,
Edith Prager

Hers to Hold
US 1943   94m   bw
Universal (Felix Jackson)

A girl decides whether or not to marry a
serviceman.
Limp star vehicle, a sequel to Three Smart
Girls (qv).

w Lewis R. Foster d Frank Ryan ph Elwood
Bredell md Charles Previn m Frank Skinner

Deanna Durbin, Joseph Cotten, Charles
Winninger, Nella Walker, Gus Schilling,
Ludwig Stossel

AAN: song 'Say a Prayer for the Boys Over
There' (m Jimmy McHugh, ly Herb
Magidson)

He's a Cockeyed Wonder
US 1950   77m   bw

An orange sorter goes into the magic business.
Energetic low-budget comedy vehicle for

unsophisticated audiences. Mickey Rooney,
Terry Moore, William Demarest, Charles
Arnt, Mike Mazurki. Written by Jack Henley;
directed by Peter Godfrey; for Columbia.

Hester Street*
US 1974   89m   bw
Midwest Films (Raphael D. Silver)

How Jewish immigrants settled in East Side
New York in the nineties.
Modest, humorous, but not always smooth or
dramatically emphatic chronicle of a familiar
background; the detail however is excellent.

wd Joan Macklin Silver, story Yeki by
Abraham Cahan ph Kenneth Van Sickle
m William Bolcom

Steven Keats, Carol Kane, Mel Howard,
Dorrie Kavanaugh, Doris Roberts

'A small, beautifully detailed, slightly
shaggy independent film of charm and
substance.'—Judith Crist

'For old diehards who still go to the cinema
seeking humanity, tenderness and insight.'—
Michael Billington, Illustrated London News

AAN: Joan Macklin Silver (as writer); Carol
Kane

Hey, Good-Lookin'
US 1982   76m   Technicolor

Life in 1953 Brooklyn centres round two
young womanizers. Enterprising attempt to
use animation to tell a youth melodrama;
interesting but not successful. Written,
directed and produced by Ralph Bakshi; for
Warners.

Hey! Hey! USA
GB 1938   92m   bw

An education expert sails to America, falls in
with gangsters, and saves a boy from being
kidnapped by them. Misconceived star vehicle
which provides some laughs, but not of the
expected kind. Will Hay, Edgar Kennedy,
David Burns, Fred Duprez. Written by J. O.
C. Orton; directed by Marcel Varnel; for
Gainsborough.

Hi Diddle Diddle*
US 1943   72m   bw
UA / Andrew Stone
aka: Try and Find It

Young lovers are hampered by con artist
parents.
Scatty comedy with amusing patches and some
zest in the telling.

w Edmund L. Hartmann d Andrew L. Stone
ph Charles Van Enger m Phil Boutelje

Adolphe Menjou, Pola Negri, Dennis
O'Keefe, Billie Burke, Martha Scott, June
Havoc

AAN: Phil Boutelje

Hi Gang
GB 1941   100m   bw
Rank / Gainsborough (Edward Black)

American expatriates in London get involved
in a case of mistaken identity.

Icky farce based faintly on a wartime radio
variety series, notable only for preserving the
three stars involved.

w Val Guest, Marriott Edgar, J. O. C. Orton,
Howard Irving Young d Marcel Varnel
ph Jack Cox

Bebe Daniels, Ben Lyon, Vic Oliver, Graham
Moffatt, Moore Marriott, Felix Aylmer, Sam
Browne

Hi, Mom!*
US 1969   86m   Movielab

Adventures of a young porno film maker and
of the eccentrics who live in the same building.
Busy comedy of the drop-out life, full of
random satirical jabs and hommages to other
film makers. Robert de Niro, Allen Garfield,
Gerrit Graham, Jennifer Salt. Written and
directed by Brian de Palma; for West End
films.

Hi Nellie*
US 1934   79m   bw
Warner (Robert Presnell)

An ex-editor is demoted to advice to the
lovelorn and gets involved in city rackets.
Minor, effective star comedy-melodrama.

w Abem Finkel, Sidney Sutherland d Mervyn
Le Roy ph Sol Polito

Paul Muni, Glenda Farrell, Ned Sparks,
Robert Barrat, Hobart Cavanaugh, Berton
Churchill, Donald Meek, Douglass Dumbrille,
Edward Ellis

'Barely gets by as fair entertainment . . . it's
a better Muni performance than a picture.'—
Variety

† Remade in 1935 as Front Page Woman; 1937
as Love Is on the Air; 1942 as You Can't
Escape Forever; 1949 as The House across the
Street.

Hi Ya Chum
US 1943   61m   bw

On their way to Hollywood, variety
performers are stranded in a small town. Thin
star comedy support. The Ritz Brothers, Jane
Frazee, Robert Paige, June Clyde. Written by
Edmund L. Hartmann; directed by Harold
Young; for Universal. (GB title: Everything
Happens to Us.)

Hiawatha
US 1952   80m   Cinecolor

A young brave prevents war between three
Indian tribes. Muddled actioner which has
little to do with Longfellow's poem. Vincent
Edwards, Yvette Dugay, Keith Larsen, Morris
Ankrum, Ian MacDonald. Written by Arthur
Strawn and Dan Ullman; directed by Kurt
Neumann; for Allied Artists.

Hickey and Boggs
US 1972   111m   De Luxe
UA / Film Guarantors Ltd (Fouad Said)

Two down and out private eyes, hired to find a
girl, keep falling over dead bodies.
Extraordinarily confused thriller with
moments of humour and well staged action
sequences.

w Walter Hill *d* Robert Culp *ph* Wilmer Butler *m* Ted Ashford

Robert Culp, Bill Cosby, Rosalind Cash

The Hidden Eye
US 1945 69m bw

A blind detective gets on the trail of a murderer who deliberately leaves confusing clues. Thin successor to *Eyes in the Night*: no style at all. Edward Arnold, Frances Rafferty, William Phillips, Ray Collins, Thomas Jackson. Written by George Harmon Coxe and Harry Ruskin; directed by Richard Whorf; for MGM.

Hidden Fear
US 1957 83m bw

An American cop in Copenhagen clears his sister of a murder charge. Patchy, tough thriller with some pretensions to style sabotaged by a muddled script. John Payne, Anne Neyland, Alexander Knox, Conrad Nagel, Elsy Albiin. Written by André de Toth and John Ward Hawkins; directed by André de Toth; for St Aubrey-Kohn / UA.

The Hidden Fortress*
Japan 1958 123m bw Tohoscope
Toho (Masumi Fujimoto)
original title: *Kakushi Toride No San-Akunin*

In medieval Japan, the heiress of a feudal lord is saved from a bandit by a samurai. Roistering eastern western.

w Ryuzo Kikushima, Hideo Oguni, Shinobu Hashimoto, Akira Kurosawa *d* Akira Kurosawa *ph* Ichio Yamazaki *m* Masaru Sato

Toshiro Mifune, Misa Uehara, Minoru Chiaki

The Hidden Hand
US 1942 67m bw

Murders proliferate in the house of a wealthy old spinster. Heavy-going spoof of the thunderstorm mystery; sometimes amusing for connoisseurs of the genre. Craig Stevens, Elizabeth Fraser, Julie Bishop, Willie Best, Milton Parsons. Written by Anthony Coldeway; directed by Ben Stoloff; for Warner.

Hide and Seek
GB 1963 90m bw
British Lion / Albion / Spectrum (Hal E. Chester)

A research scientist is the centre of a kidnap plan designed to make it appear that he has defected.

Too many mysterious happenings with too little explanation sink this comedy-thriller from the start.

w David Stone *d* Cy Endfield *ph* Gilbert Taylor *m* Muir Mathieson, Gary Campbell

Ian Carmichael, Janet Munro, Curt Jurgens, Hugh Griffith, George Pravda, Kieron Moore, Edward Chapman

Hide in Plain Sight
US 1980 92m Metrocolor
MGM (Robert Christiansen, Rick Rosenberg)

A factory worker searches for his children when his former wife is hidden by the government to protect her husband, an informer.

Unpersuasive melodrama with little more than its unusual plot to commend it.

w Spencer Eastman *book* Leslie Waller *d* James Caan *ph* Paul Lohmann *m* Leonard Rosenman

James Caan, Jill Eikenberry, Robert Viharo

Hideaway Girl
US 1936 71m bw

A girl suspected of stealing a necklace goes on the run. Humdrum comedy melodrama with songs: a hotchpotch. Martha Raye, Shirley Ross, Robert Cummings, Monroe Owsley. Written by Joseph Moncure March; directed by George Archainbaud; for A. M. Botsford / Paramount. 'Rowdy, nonsensical lightweight, geared for doubles.'—*Variety*

Hideout
US 1934 83m bw

An injured racketeer takes refuge with a farm family and is reformed by the simple life and true love. Schematic eat-your-cake-and-have-it melodrama which pleased audiences at the time. Robert Montgomery, Maureen O'Sullivan, Mickey Rooney, Edward Arnold, C. Henry Gordon, Elizabeth Patterson, Edward Brophy, Herman Bing. Written by Frances Goodrich and Albert Hackett; directed by W. S. Van Dyke; for MGM.

The Higgins Family
US 1938 65m bw

An advertising man is driven almost to divorce when his wife becomes a radio personality. Modest family comedy which ran to a short series. James Gleason, Lucile Gleason, Russell Gleason, Lynne Roberts, Harry Davenport. Written by Paul Gerard Smith, Jack Townley, Richard English; directed by Gus Meins; for Republic. 'Shows fine promise.'—*Variety*

High and Low*
Japan 1963 142m bw Tohoscope
Toho (Tomoyuki Tanaka)

A wealthy shoe manufacturer's chauffeur's son is kidnapped in mistake for his own, and he faces a moral dilemma.

Interesting, rather gloomy Japanese version of a light American thriller with all the style expected of the director.

w Hideo Oguni, Ryuzo Kikushima, Eijiro Hisaito, Akira Kurosawa, *novel* The King's Ransom by Ed McBain *d* Akira Kurosawa *ph* Asakazu Makai, Takao Saito *m* Masaru Sato

Toshiro Mifune, Kyoko Kagawa, Tatsuya Nakadai

The High and the Mighty*
US 1954 147m Warnercolor
Cinemascope
Wayne–Fellows

A big passenger plane is in trouble over the Pacific, and its occupants react in various ways to the prospect of a crash landing. Compendium fiction with even the pilot having a personal problem which could cloud his judgment. Tolerable, well made hokum.

w Ernest K. Gann, from his novel *d* William Wellman *ph* William Clothier *m* Dmitri Tiomkin

John Wayne, Robert Newton, Robert Stack, Doe Avedon, Claire Trevor, Laraine Day, Jan Sterling, Phil Harris, Sidney Blackmer, John Howard

AA: Dmitri Tiomkin
AAN: William Wellman; Claire Trevor; Jan Sterling; title song (*m* Dmitri Tiomkin, *ly* Ned Washington)

High Anxiety*
US 1977 94m De Luxe
TCF / Crossbow (Mel Brooks)

A psychologist taking up a new appointment suspects that his predecessor may have been murdered.

Elementary but somewhat entertaining spoof of various Hitchcock movies (*Spellbound, North by Northwest, The Birds*), with the level of humour as unsubtle and lavatorial as one has come to expect.

w Mel Brooks, Ron Clark, Rudy DeLuca, Barry Levinson *d* Mel Brooks *ph* Paul Lohmann *m* John Morris

Mel Brooks, Madeline Kahn, Cloris Leachman, Harvey Korman, Ron Carey, Howard Morris, Dick Van Patten

'It basically just shambles along, in search of the next big set-piece to send up.'—*Richard Combs, MFB*

'Brooks has no idea of how to build a sequence, how to tell a story, when to leave well enough (or ill enough) alone.'—*Philip French, Observer*

'A child's idea of satire—imitations, with a comic hat and a leer.'—*New Yorker*

● *Video: CBS / Fox*

High-Ballin'
US 1978 100m Movielab
AIP / Stanley Chase / Pando (Jan Slan)

An independent trucker battles hijackers as well as pressures from a giant trucking firm. Routine action hokum, a long way behind 1948's *Thieves' Highway* and even less entertaining than TV's *Movin' On*.

w Paul Edwards *d* Peter Carter *ph* René Verzier *m* Paul Hoffert

Peter Fonda, Jerry Reed, Helen Shaver, Chris Wiggins

High Barbaree
US 1947 91m bw
MGM (Everett Riskin)

A pilot crashlands in the Pacific and finds himself drifting towards a Utopian island fancifully described by his favourite uncle. Thin Hollywood mysticism on Shangri-La lines but without the solid virtues of plot, dialogue and imagination.

w Anne Morrison Chapin, Whitfield Cook, Cyril Hume d Jack Conway ph Sidney Wagner m Herbert Stothart

Van Johnson, June Allyson, Thomas Mitchell, Marilyn Maxwell

The High Bright Sun
GB 1965   114m   Technicolor
Rank (Betty Box)
US title: *McGuire Go Home*

In 1957 Cyprus the British army is beleaguered by partisans, and an officer tries to contact a leading rebel.
Confused and boring attempt to make romantic drama out of an intractably sad situation.

w Ian Stuart Black, from his novel d Ralph Thomas ph Ernest Steward m Angelo Lavagnino

Dirk Bogarde, Susan Strasberg, George Chakiris, Denholm Elliott

The High Command*
GB 1936   88m   bw
ABFD / Fanfare / Wellesley (Gordon Wellesley)

The general of a West African garrison has a guilty secret known to his young medical officer.
Dated melodrama, rather interestingly performed and directed.

w Katherine Strueby, *novel* The General Goes Too Far by Lewis Robinson d Thorold Dickinson ph Otto Heller m Ernest Irving

James Mason, Lionel Atwill, Lucie Mannheim, Steve Geray, Leslie Perrins

The High Cost of Loving*
US 1958   87m   bw   Cinemascope
MGM (Milo O. Frank Jnr)

A happily married middle class couple have doubts about their future.
Pleasant, mildly satirical romantic comedy which doesn't really get anywhere.

w Rip Van Ronkel d Jose Ferrer ph George J. Folsey m Jeff Alexander

Jose Ferrer, Gena Rowlands, Joanne Gilbert, Jim Backus, Bobby Troup, Philip Ober, Edward Platt, Werner Klemperer

High Flight
GB 1957   102m   Technicolor
    Cinemascope
Columbia / Warwick (Phil C. Samuel)

Cadets train at the Royal Air Force College.
Simple-minded peacetime flagwaver.

w Joseph Landon, Ken Hughes d John Gilling ph Ted Moore md Muir Mathieson m Kenneth V. Jones, Douglas Gamley title march Eric Coates

Ray Milland, Bernard Lee, Kenneth Haigh, Anthony Newley, Kenneth Fortescue, Sean Kelly, Helen Cherry

High Flyers
US 1937   70m   bw
RKO (Lee Marcus)

Two incompetents are duped into smuggling contraband gems.
Feeble finale to the career of two comedians.

w Benny Rubin, Bert Granet, *play* Victor Mapes d Edward Cline ph Jack Mackenzie *songs* Herman Ruby, Dave Dreyer

Bert Wheeler, Robert Woolsey, Lupe Velez, Marjorie Lord, Margaret Dumont, Jack Carson, Paul Harvey

High Lonesome
US 1950   80m   Technicolor

A young man believed to be crazed and homicidal flees into the desert and returns to establish his innocence. Thinly-stretched western not helped by an exhibitionist star performance. John Barrymore Jnr, Chill Wills, Kristine Miller, Lois Butler. Written and directed by Alan Le May; for Eagle Lion.

'When the hands point up . . . the
    excitement starts!'
High Noon****
US 1952   85m   bw
Stanley Kramer

A marshal gets no help when he determines to defend his town against revengeful badmen.
A minor western with a soft-pedalled message for the world, this turned out to be a classic simply because it was well done, with every scene and performance clearly worked out. Cinematically it was pared to the bone, and the theme tune helped.

w Carl Foreman, *story* The Tin Star by John W. Cunningham d Fred Zinnemann ph Floyd Crosby m Dimitri Tiomkin *singer* Tex Ritter

Gary Cooper, Grace Kelly, Thomas Mitchell, Lloyd Bridges, Katy Jurado, Otto Kruger, Lon Chaney, Henry Morgan

'The western form is used for a sneak civics lesson.'—*Pauline Kael, 70s*

'Like nearly all the Kramer productions, this is a neat, well-finished and literate piece of work, though its limitations are more conventional than most.'—*Gavin Lambert*

'A western to challenge *Stagecoach* for the all-time championship.'—*Bosley Crowther*

'A series of crisp and purposeful scenes that interpret each other like the pins on a strategist's war map.'—*Robert L. Hatch*

'It is astonishing how much of the simple western story is told visually by rapid cross-cutting.'—*Films in Review*

'Few recent westerns have gotten so much tension and excitement into the classic struggle between good and evil.'—*Life*

AA: Dimitri Tiomkin; Gary Cooper; title song (m Dimitri Tiomkin, ly Ned Washington)
AAN: best picture; Carl Foreman; Fred Zinnemann

● Video: BBC

'They'll never forget the day he drifted into
    town!'
High Plains Drifter*
US 1972   105m   Technicolor
    Panavision
Universal / Malpaso (Robert Daley)

A mysterious stranger rides into town and terrifies the inhabitants.
Semi-supernatural, mystical revenge western with an overplus of violence. Very watchable, but irritating.

w Ernest Tidyman d Clint Eastwood ph Bruce Surtees m Dee Barton ad Henry Bumstead

Clint Eastwood, Verna Bloom, Marianna Hill, Mitch Ryan, Jack Ging

'Ritualized violence and plodding symbolism make for heavy going.'—*Sight and Sound*

'A nervously humorous, self-conscious near-satire on the prototype Eastwood formula.'—*Variety*

● Video: CIC

High Pressure*
US 1932   74m   bw

A would-be tycoon believes there's a fortune to be made in artificial rubber. Amusing con man comedy with good work all round. *William Powell*, Evelyn Brent, George Sidney, Guy Kibbee, Frank McHugh. Written by Joseph Jackson, from Abem Kandel's play *Hot Money*; directed by Mervyn Le Roy; for Warner. 'Well acted, but lacks strength to attract much business.'—*Variety*

High Risk
US 1981   94m   colour
American Cinema (Joe Raffill, Gerard Green)

A documentary film-maker enlists three buddies to steal a million dollars from a South American drugs dealer.
Moderately entertaining caper movie which stops too often for action and occasionally for comedy.

wd Stewart Raffill ph Alex Phillips Jnr m not credited ed Tom Walls Jnr

James Brolin, Cleavon Little, Lindsay Wagner, Ernest Borgnine, Bruce Davison, Chick Vennera, Anthony Quinn, James Coburn

High Road to China
US 1983   105m   Technicolor
Golden Harvest / Pan Pacific (Fred Weintraub)

In the twenties, an American heiress in Afghanistan has adventures with a drunken flier.
Abysmal attempt to mate James Bond with a cut-price *Raiders of the Lost Ark*. It comes up with nothing at all, and is on the lowest level for continuity, dialogue and direction.

w Sandra Weintraub Roland, S. Lee Pogostin, *novel* Jon Cleary d Brian G. Hutton ph Ronnie Taylor m John Barry pd Robert Laing

Tom Selleck, Bess Armstrong, Jack Weston, Robert Morley, Wilford Brimley, Brian Blessed

'An attempt to revive the sort of comedy-adventure romance in which Clark Gable and Jean Harlow would squabble furiously but you knew they were really in love. But as scripted and abominably directed, the thing is as flat as a pancake.'—*Guardian*

'The blazing mountain manhunt for Killer Mad-Dog Earle!'

High Sierra*

US 1941 96m bw
Warner (Hal. B. Wallis, Mark Hellinger)

An ex-con gangster plans one last heist in the Californian mountains, but is mortally wounded through his involvement with two women.
Rather dreary action melodrama which gave Bogart his first real star part (after George Raft turned it down). Remade 1955 as *I Died a Thousand Times* (qv); also in 1949 as a western, *Colorado Territory*.

w John Huston, W. R. Burnett, *novel* W. R. Burnett *d* Raoul Walsh *ph* Tony Gaudio *m* Adolph Deutsch

Humphrey Bogart, Ida Lupino, Joan Leslie, Alan Curtis, Arthur Kennedy, Henry Hull, Henry Travers, Jerome Cowan

'The last swallow, perhaps, of the gangsters' summer.'—*William Whitebait*
'Like it or not, I'll be damned if you leave before the end, or go to sleep.'—*Otis Ferguson*
'As gangster pictures go, this one has everything—speed, excitement, suspense, and that ennobling suggestion of futility which makes for irony and poetry.'—*New York Times*

High Society

US 1956 107m Technicolor
Vistavision
MGM (Sol C. Siegel)

A haughty rich girl chooses between several suitors.
Cold, flat, dull musical reworking of *The Philadelphia Story* (qv), with ill-cast performers and just a few bright moments.

w John Patrick *d* Charles Walters *ph* Paul C. Vogel *m / ly* Cole Porter *md* Johnny Green, Saul Chaplin *ad* Cedric Gibbons, Hans Peters

Bing Crosby, Grace Kelly, Frank Sinatra, Celeste Holm, Louis Armstrong, Sidney Blackmer, Margalo Gillmore, Louis Calhern, Lydia Reed, John Lund

Songs include 'Swell Party'; 'High Society'; 'Who Wants to be a Millionaire?'
AAN: Johnny Green, Saul Chaplin; song 'True Love'

● *Video: MGM / UA*

High Society Blues

US 1930 102m bw
Fox

A girl ditches a French count in favour of an all-American hero.

Frothy musical romance which did nothing for its stars and is now unwatchable.

w Howard J. Green *d* David Butler *ph* Charles Van Enger *songs* Joe McCarthy, James Hanley

Janet Gaynor, Charles Farrell, William Collier Snr, Hedda Hopper, Louise Fazenda, Lucien Littlefield, Joyce Compton

'Certain to please the average fan . . . commercial product of the first programme grade.'—*Variety*

High Tension

US 1936 63m bw

Exploits of a cable layer in Hawaii. Routine brawling comedy. Brian Donlevy, Norman Foster, Glenda Farrell, Helen Wood, Robert McWade. Written by Lou Breslow, Edward Eliscu and John Patrick; directed by Allan Dwan; for TCF.

The High Terrace

GB 1956 82m bw

A theatrical producer is murdered, and members of the cast protect their leading lady; but she is guilty. Rather solemn, enclosed little mystery which evokes no compulsion to go on watching. Lois Maxwell, Dale Robertson, Derek Bond, Eric Pohlmann, Mary Laura Wood, Lionel Jeffries. Written by Alfred Shaughnessy and Norman Hudis; directed by Henry Cass; for CIPA / Robert S. Baker.

High Tide at Noon

GB 1957 111m bw
Rank (Julian Wintle)

Passions run high among lobster fishermen in Nova Scotia.
Neat, clean romantic melodrama in agreeable surroundings.

w Neil Paterson *d* Philip Leacock *ph* Eric Cross *m* John Veale

Betta St John, Michael Craig, Patrick McGoohan, William Sylvester, Flora Robson, Alexander Knox, Peter Arne, Patrick Allen, Susan Beaumont

High Time

US 1960 103m De Luxe Cinemascope
TCF / Bing Crosby (Charles Brackett)

A middle-aged widower goes back to college.
Flaccid comedy-musical with some undergraduatish jokes.

w Tom and Frank Waldman *d* Blake Edwards *ph* Ellsworth Fredericks *m* Henry Mancini *songs* Sammy Cahn, Jimmy Van Heusen

Bing Crosby, Tuesday Weld, Fabian, Richard Beymer, Nicole Maurey

AAN: song 'The Second Time Around' (*m* Jimmy Van Heusen, *ly* Sammy Cahn)

High Treason

GB 1929 90m bw

In 1940, women unite to prevent a second world war. Tired little prophetic fable with primitive techniques. Jameson Thomas, Benita Hume, Basil Gill, Humberston Wright.

Written by L'Estrange Fawcett, from the play by Noel Pemberton-Billing; directed by Maurice Elvey; for Gaumont.

High Treason*

GB 1951 93m bw
GFD / Conqueror (Paul Soskin)

Saboteurs are routed by the London police.
Unconvincing documentary melodrama which moves fast enough to be entertaining.

w Frank Harvey, Roy Boulting *d* Roy Boulting *ph* Gilbert Taylor *m* John Addison

Liam Redmond, André Morell, Anthony Bushell, Kenneth Griffith, Patric Doonan, Joan Hickson, Anthony Nicholls, Mary Morris, Geoffrey Keen, Dora Bryan

High Wall

US 1947 99m bw
MGM (Robert Lord)

A war veteran is put in an asylum after confessing to killing his wife, but later events prove that he was drugged into saying so.
Adequately entertaining, supremely unconvincing mystery melodrama.

w Sydney Boehm *d* Curtis Bernhardt *ph* Paul C. Vogel *m* Bronislau Kaper

Robert Taylor, Herbert Marshall, Audrey Totter, Dorothy Patrick, H. B. Warner, Warner Anderson

High, Wide and Handsome*

US 1937 110m bw
Paramount (Arthur Hornblow Jnr)

Pennsylvania 1859: a travelling showgirl falls in love with a farmer.
Disappointingly stilted period musical with most of the talent ill at ease until the final reel.

w Oscar Hammerstein II *d* Rouben Mamoulian *ph* Victor Milner, Theodore Sparkuhl *ch* LeRoy Prinz *songs* Jerome Kern, Oscar Hammerstein II *md* Boris Morros *ad* Hans Dreier, John Goodman

Irene Dunne, Randolph Scott, Dorothy Lamour, Raymond Walburn, Alan Hale, Elizabeth Patterson, Charles Bickford, William Frawley, Akim Tamiroff, Ben Blue, Irving Pichel, Lucien Littlefield

'Not a road show, but a big picture, and should get nice returns.'—*Variety*
'There are two hours of this long, dumb and dreary picture . . . one is left with a few dim distressing memories.'—*Graham Greene*
'Irene Dunne at her cornball primmest, singing alongside a farmhorse when Randolph Scott isn't around.'—*Pauline Kael, 70s*

A High Wind in Jamaica*

GB 1965 104m De Luxe Cinemascope
TCF (John Croydon)

In Victorian days, English children en route home from Jamaica are captured by pirates and influence their lives.
Semi-serious adventure story with a highly unlikely ending in which the chief pirate allows himself to be executed for a murder committed by a child. There are however pleasures along the way.

w Stanley Mann, Ronald Harwood, Denis
Cannan, *novel* Richard Hughes *d* Alexander
Mackendrick *ph* Douglas Slocombe *m* Larry
Adler

Deborah Baxter, Anthony Quinn, James
Coburn, Isabel Dean, Nigel Davenport, Gert
Frobe, Lila Kedrova

Higher and Higher*
US 1943   90m   bw
RKO (Tim Whelan)

Servants have an elaborate plan to restore the
family fortune.
Unamusing musical which undernourishes
several talents.

w Jay Dratler, Ralph Spence, *play* Gladys
Hurlbut, Joshua Logan *d* Tim Whelan
ph Robert de Grasse *md* Constantin
Bakaleinikoff *songs* Jimmy McHugh, Harold
Adamson

Michele Morgan, Jack Haley, *Frank Sinatra*,
Leon Errol, Marcy McGuire, *Victor Borge*,
Mary Wickes, Barbara Hale, Elizabeth Risdon

AAN: Constantin Bakaleinikoff; song 'I
Couldn't Sleep a Wink Last Night (*m* Jimmy
McHugh, *ly* Harold Adamson)
● *Video: Kingston*

The Highest Honour
Australia 1982   143m   colour
aka: *Southern Cross*

In 1942, an Australian spy befriends his captor
and finally executioner. Sombre true story, far
too long in the telling. John Howard, Atsuo
Nakamura, Stuart Wilson, Steve Bisley.
Written by Lee Robinson; directed by Peter
Maxwell; for Southern International Films.
'Largely fails to ignite.'—*Julian Petley, MFB*

Highly Dangerous
GB 1950   88m   bw
Rank / Two Cities (Anthony Darnborough)

A lady entomologist in a Balkan country is
suspected of spying but manages to outwit her
enemies.
Odd blend of straight adventure and spoof; it
doesn't quite come off.

w Eric Ambler *d* Roy Baker *ph* Reg Wyer
m Richard Addinsell

Margaret Lockwood, Dane Clark, Marius
Goring, Naunton Wayne, Eugene Deckers,
Wilfrid Hyde White, Michael Hordern, Gladys
Henson

Highpoint
Canada 1984 (filmed 1979)   88m
   Eastmancolor

An industrialist is on the run from both the
Mafia and the CIA. Routine thriller with a
finale atop Toronto's CN Tower. Richard
Harris, Christopher Plummer, Beverly
D'Angelo, Kate Reid, Peter Donat. Written
by Richard Guttman, Ian Sutherland; directed
by Peter Carter; for Highpoint / New World.

Highway Dragnet
US 1954   71m   bw

A lady photographer gives a lift to an ex-
marine who may or may not be a murderer.
Twisty lower-berth thriller in which all is not
as it seems. Joan Bennett, Richard Conte,
Wanda Hendrix, Reed Hadley, Mary Beth
Hughes, Iris Adrian. Written by Herb
Meadow and Jerome Odlum; directed by
Nathan Juran; for William F. Broidy / Allied
Artists.

Highway 301*
US 1950   83m   bw
Warner (Bryan Foy)

The Tri-State Gang is apprehended by police.
Actionful gangster melodrama of the *Bonnie
and Clyde* type, with plenty of suspenseful
situations and slick camerawork.

wd Andrew Stone *ph* Carl Guthrie
m William Lava

Steve Cochran, Virginia Grey, Gaby Andre,
Edmon Ryan, Richard Egan, Robert Webber
  'Several good suspense sequences, some
good comic observation, and many pleasing
visual moments of the wet-streets-at-night
category.'—*Richard Mallett, Punch*

The Highwayman
US 1951   82m   Cinecolor
Allied Artists / Jack Dietz (Hal. E. Chester)

A 17th-century nobleman disguises himself as
a Quaker and becomes a highwayman to right
wrongs.
Curious Poverty Row period actioner with
ideas generally above its station, not to
mention an unexpected tragic ending.

w Jan Jeffries, *poem* Alfred Noyes *d* Lesley
Selander *ph* Harry Neumann *m* Herschel
Burke Gilbert

Philip Friend, Charles Coburn, Victor Jory,
Wanda Hendrix, Cecil Kellaway, Scott
Forbes, Virginia Huston, Dan O'Herlihy

'I want to live like a man—and still be a
   woman!'
Hilda Crane
US 1956   87m   Technicolor
   Cinemascope
TCF (Herbert B. Swope Jnr)

An unhappy woman marries for the third time
and convinces herself it won't work.
Emotional melodrama of the old school: very
moderate in all departments.

wd Philip Dunne, *play* Samson Raphaelson
ph Joe MacDonald *m* David Raksin

Jean Simmons, Guy Madison, Jean-Pierre
Aumont, *Evelyn Varden*, Judith Evelyn,
Peggy Knudsen

'They went up like men! They came down
   like animals!'
The Hill**
GB 1965   122m   bw
MGM / Seven Arts (Kenneth Hyman)

Prisoners rebel against the harsh discipline of a
British military detention centre in North
Africa during World War II.
Lurid melodrama which descends fairly
quickly into black farce with a number of
sweaty actors outshouting each other.
Enjoyable on this level when you can hear the
dialogue through the poor sound recording.

w Ray Rigby, from his TV play *d* Sidney
Lumet *ph* Oswald Morris *m* none
Sean Connery, Harry Andrews, Michael
Redgrave, Ian Bannen, Alfred Lynch, *Ossie
Davis*, Roy Kinnear, Jack Watson, Ian
Hendry

A Hill in Korea
GB 1956   81m   bw
British Lion / Wessex (Anthony Squire)
US title: *Hell in Korea*

During the Korean war, a small patrol guards
a hill.
Minor war talk-piece, shot in Surrey and
looking it.

w Ian Dalrymple, Anthony Squire, Ronald
Spencer, *novel* Max Catto *d* Julian Amyes
ph Freddie Francis *m* Malcolm Arnold

George Baker, Harry Andrews, Stanley
Baker, Michael Medwin, Ronald Lewis,
Stephen Boyd, Victor Maddern, Harry Landis
  'Character is adequately sketched into a
suitably laconic script.'—*MFB*

Hill 24 Doesn't Answer
Israel 1954   101m   bw
Sikor (Thorold Dickinson, Peter Frye)

Four friends defend Hill 24 against the Arabs
on the eve of the cease-fire, and are all killed.
Israel's first feature film, a curious amalgam of
the slick and the amateur, with long flashbacks
which make it resemble *The Bridge of San
Luis Rey*.

w Zvi Kolitz, Peter Frye, Joanna and Thorold
Dickinson *d* Thorold Dickinson *ph* Gerald
Gibbs *m* Paul Ben-Haim

Michael Wager, Edward Mulhare, Haya
Hararit, Arie Lavi, Michael Shilo

The Hills Have Eyes
US 1977   90m   Movielab

Holidaymakers are waylaid and killed by a
family of desert cannibals. Low-grade shocker
which mysteriously achieved some cult status.
John Steadman, Janus Blythe, Arthur King,
Russ Grieve. Written and directed by Wes
Craven; for Blood Relations. 'Simultaneously
risible and nauseating.'—*Tim Pulleine, MFB.*

The Hills of Home
US 1948   95m   Technicolor

A doctor returns to his Scottish village to
practise medicine, and brings his faithful
collie. Adequate addition to the Lassie saga,
with competent work all round. Edmund
Gwenn, Tom Drake, Donald Crisp, Rhys
Williams, Reginald Owen. Written by William
Ludwig; directed by Fred Wilcox; for MGM.
(GB title: *Master of Lassie*.)

The Hindenburg*
US 1975   125m   Technicolor
   Panavision
Universal / Filmakers (Robert Wise)

In 1937, sabotage causes the airship
Hindenburg to crash on arrival at New York.
An extremely uninteresting guess at the cause
of this famous disaster. The plot and dialogue
are leaden, and such actors as have more than
a couple of lines look extremely glum. The

KING of the OUTLAWS!

ROBIN HOOD! JESSE JAMES! DON JUAN!... No rogue, robber or ravager ever equalled history's boldest firebrand!

The Highwayman

SEE The capture of a beauty whose love rocks a kingdom!

SEE Torture dungeons where secrets are torn from captives!

SEE The ambush of The Highwayman by 100 armed guardsmen!

SEE History made at night by a Prince of Lovers!

starring

CHARLES **COBURN** PHILIP **FRIEND**

WANDA **HENDRIX**

co-starring

CECIL **KELLAWAY** VICTOR **JORY**

Running Time: 82 Minutes

with Scott Forbes · Virginia Huston · Dan O'Herlihy · Henry Morgan · Albert Sharpe · Alan Napier

A JACK DIETZ Production   Produced by HAL E. CHESTER   Directed by LESLEY SELANDER   Screenplay by JAN JEFFRIES

THE HIGHWAYMAN.   A forgotten film now, but one which didn't do badly by its material.

special effects, however, are fine despite curious blue-rinse photographic processing.

w Nelson Gidding, *novel* Michael M. Mooney *d* Robert Wise *ph* Robert Surtees *pd* Edward Carfagno *sp* Albert Whitlock *m* David Shire

George C. Scott, Anne Bancroft, Burgess Meredith, William Atherton, Roy Thinnes, Gig Young, Charles Durning, Robert Clary, René Auberjonois

'The tackiest disaster movie yet—a cheap and chaotic collage of painted drops, wooden actors and not-so-special effects that manages to make one of this century's most sensational real-life catastrophes seem roughly as terrifying as a badly stubbed toe.'—*Frank Rich*

AAN: Robert Surtees

Hindle Wakes
GB 1952 82m bw

A Lancashire millgirl spends a week at Blackpool with the master's son but causes a scandal when she refuses to marry him. Modestly competent version of a semi-classic play about class distinctions. Lisa Daniely, Leslie Dwyer, Brian Worth, Sandra Dorne, Ronald Adam. Written by John Baines, from the play by Stanley Houghton; directed by Arthur Crabtree; for Monarch. (NB: A probably better, but unavailable version was made in 1931 by Victor Saville for Gaumont, with Belle Chrystall, Edmund Gwenn, John Stuart, Ruth Peterson, Norman McKinnel and Sybil Thorndike.)

Hips Hips Hooray
US 1934 68m bw

Two salesmen pitch flavoured lipstick to a beauty parlour chain. Tired star comedy. Bert Wheeler, Robert Woolsey, Ruth Etting, Thelma Todd, Dorothy Lee, George Meeker. Written by Harry Ruby and Bert Kalmar; directed by Mark Sandrich; for RKO. 'Femme display chief asset.'—*Variety*

The Hired Hand
US 1971 93m Technicolor
Universal / Pando (William Hayward)

Two western drifters avenge the killing of their friend and settle down to work on a farm; but violence follows them.
A potentially enjoyable small-scale western is spoiled by pretentious direction and effects which bore the spectator to death.

w Alan Sharp *d* Peter Fonda *ph* Vilmos Zsigmond *m* Bruce Langhorne

Peter Fonda, Warren Oates, Verna Bloom, Severn Darden

'The first slow-motion western, with endless artsy photography not quite succeeding in obscuring the rambling plot.'—*Judith Crist, 1973*

'When a film begins with a "lyrical" shot, your heart has a right to sink.'—*Stanley Kauffmann*

Hired Wife
US 1940 96m bw

A secretary who loves her boss saves his company by marrying him so that it can be transferred to her name. After which the plot has absolutely nowhere to go. Rosalind Russell, Brian Aherne, Virgina Bruce, Robert Benchley, John Carroll, Hobart Cavanagh. Written by Richard Connell and Gladys Lehman; directed by William A. Seiter; for Universal.

The Hireling*
GB 1973 108m colour
Columbia / World Film Services (Ben Arbeid)

In the twenties, a lady's chauffeur falls in love with her.
Talkative drama, elegant but not much fun.

w Wolf Mankowitz, *novel* L. P. Hartley *d* Alan Bridges *ph* Michael Reed *m* Marc Wilkinson *pd* Natasha Kroll

Sarah Miles, Robert Shaw, Peter Egan, Elizabeth Sellars, Caroline Mortimer

Hiroshima Mon Amour*
France / Japan 1959 91m bw
Argos / Comei / Pathé / Daiei

A French actress working in Hiroshima falls for a Japanese architect and remembers her tragic love for a German soldier during the occupation.
Jumbled mixture of flashbacks and flashforwards which can now be recognized as typical of this director and on its first appearance was hailed as a work of art in an innovative new style.

w Marguerite Duras *d* Alain Resnais *ph* Sacha Vierny, Takahashi Michio *m* Giovanni Fusco, Georges Delerue

Emmanuele Riva, Eiji Okada

AAN: Marguerite Duras

His and Hers
GB 1960 90m bw

An author gets lost with the Bedouin while on a research trip, and by the time he gets home his personality is transformed. The thinnest of comedy ideas becomes a film of almost no substance at all. Terry-Thomas, Janette Scott, Wilfrid Hyde White, Nicole Maurey, Joan Sims, Kenneth Connor, Kenneth Williams, Meier Tzelniker, Joan Hickson, Colin Gordon, Oliver Reed, Francesca Annis. Written by Stanley Mann and Jan and Mark Lowell; directed by Brian Desmond Hurst; for Hal E. Chester / Eros.

His Brother's Wife
US 1936 91m bw
MGM (Lawrence Weingarten)

A young scientist is helped out of trouble by his brother, on condition he disappears; the brother then weds the scientist's girl friend. Heavy romantic melodrama containing everything including jungle fever, flung together to take advantage of the stars' real-life romance.

w Leon Gordon, John Meehan, *story* George Auerbach *d* W. S. Van Dyke II *ph* Oliver T. Marsh *m* Franz Waxman

Robert Taylor, Barbara Stanwyck, Joseph Calleia, John Eldredge, Jean Hersholt, Samuel S. Hinds, Leonard Mudie, Jed Prouty

His Butler's Sister*
US 1943 94m bw
Universal (Felix Jackson)

A temporary maid falls for her sophisticated boss.
Pleasant comedy musical: no great shakes, but the principals give the air of enjoying themselves.

w Samuel Hoffenstein, Betty Reinhardt *d* Frank Borzage *ph* Elwood Bredell *m* Hans Salter

Deanna Durbin, Franchot Tone, Pat O'Brien, Evelyn Ankers, Walter Catlett, Alan Mowbray, Akim Tamiroff, Else Janssen, Iris Adrian

His Double Life*
US 1933 63m bw

A famous painter, when his valet dies, takes his identity. Adequate transcription of an Arnold Bennett novel later redone as *Holy Matrimony*. Roland Young, Lillian Gish, Lumsden Hare, Lucy Beaumont. Written by Arthur Ellis; directed by Arthur Hopkins; for Eddie Dowling / Paramount. 'Pleasant little film; big grosses unlikely.'—*Variety*

His Excellency
GB 1951 84m bw
Ealing (Michael Truman)

The Labour government sends a trade union official to govern a Mediterranean colony. Disappointingly tacky-looking and stagebound version of an unpersuasive West End comedy.

w Robert Hamer, W. P. Lipscomb, *play* Dorothy and Campbell Christie *d* Robert Hamer *ph* Douglas Slocombe *m* selections from Handel

Eric Portman, Cecil Parker, Helen Cherry, Susan Stephen, Edward Chapman, Clive Morton, Robin Bailey, Geoffrey Keen

His Family Tree
US 1935 59m bw

An Irishman migrates to America and gets involved in politics. Lively second feature for the Irish halls. James Barton, Margaret Callahan, Maureen Delany, Addison Randall, William Harrigan. Written by Joel Sayre and John Twist from the play Old Man Murphy by Patrick Kearney and Henry Wagstaff Gribble; directed by Charles Vidor; for RKO. 'With more care, this might have been much better.'—*Variety*

His Girl Friday**
US 1940 92m bw
Columbia (Howard Hawks)

A remake of *The Front Page* (qv), with Hildy Johnson turned into a woman.
Frantic, hilarious black farce with all participants at their best; possibly the fastest comedy ever filmed, and one of the funniest.

HIS GIRL FRIDAY. Typical expressions are exchanged by stars who at the time could do no wrong: Cary Grant and Rosalind Russell.

w Charles Lederer, *play* The Front Page by Charles MacArthur, Ben Hecht *d* Howard Hawks *ph* Joseph Walker *m* Sydney Cutner *md* Morris Stoloff

Rosalind Russell, Cary Grant, Ralph Bellamy, Gene Lockhart, Porter Hall, Ernest Truex, Cliff Edwards, Clarence Kolb, Roscoe Karns, Frank Jenks, Abner Biberman, Frank Orth, John Qualen, Helen Mack, Billy Gilbert, Alma Kruger

'The kind of terrific verbal slam-bang that has vanished from current film-making.'—*New Yorker, 1975*

'One of the fastest of all movies, from line to line and from gag to gag.'—*Manny Farber, 1971*

'Overlapping dialogue carries the movie along at breakneck speed; word gags take the place of the sight gags of silent comedy, as this vanished race of brittle, cynical, childish people rush around on corrupt errands.'—*Pauline Kael, 1968*

'The main trouble is that when they made *The Front Page* the first time, it stayed made.'—*Otis Ferguson*

His Glorious Night

US 1929 85m bw
MGM
GB title: *Breath of Scandal*

A princess falls in love with a commoner. Soporific early talkie, remade in 1960 as *A Breath of Scandal*. The movie which first

exposed its star's high-pitched voice, it is credited with killing his career.

w Willard Mack, *play* Olimpia by Ferenc Molnar *d* Lionel Barrymore *ph* Percy Hilburn

John Gilbert, Catherine Dale Owen, Hedda Hopper, Gustav von Seyffertitz, Nance O'Neil

His Kind of Woman*

US 1951 120m bw
RKO (Howard Hughes, Robert Sparks)

At a remote Mexican ranch resort, a gangster on the run holds up residents including a fortune-hunting girl and a fading matinee idol. Agreeable tongue-in-cheek melodrama which slightly outstays its welcome but is generally good fun.

w Frank Fenton, *d* John Farrow *ph* Harry J. Wild *m* Leigh Harline *md* Constantin Bakaleinikoff

Robert Mitchum, Jane Russell, *Vincent Price*, Raymond Burr, Tim Holt, Charles McGraw, Marjorie Reynolds, Jim Backus

His Lordship*

GB 1936 71m bw
Gaumont (S. C. Balcon)
US title: *Man of Affairs*

A politician's twin takes his place to expose an old murder.
Comfortable star comedy-drama.

w Maude Howell, Edwin Greenwood, L. DuGarde Peach, *play* The Nelson Touch by Neil Grant *d* Herbert Mason

George Arliss, Rene Ray, Romilly Lunge, Jessie Winter, Allan Jeayes

His Majesty O'Keefe

GB 1954 90m Technicolor
Warner / Norma (Harold Hecht)

Native islanders are taught by an easygoing mariner how to exploit their natural resources and defend themselves against pirates. Thin adventure romance with too little for its star to do.

w Borden Chase, James Hill, *novel* Lawrence Kingman and Gerald Green *d* Byron Haskin *ph* Otto Heller *m* Robert Farnon

Burt Lancaster, Joan Rice, André Morell, Abraham Sofaer, Benson Fong, Archie Savage

His Night Out

US 1935 74m bw

A henpecked office help saves the bonds from gangsters. Typical star farce, a remake of *The Mollycoddle*. Edward Everett Horton, Irene Hervey, Robert McWade, Jack La Rue, Willard Robertson. Written by Doris Malloy, Harry Cock; directed by William Nigh; for Universal.

'From the ends of the earth . . . a darling baby brings them together!'

His Woman

US 1931 80m bw
Paramount

The captain of a tramp freighter finds himself in charge of an abandoned baby and a runaway girl.
Slow, indifferent comedy drama, previously filmed in 1929 as *Sal of Singapore*.

w Adelaide Heilbron, Melville Baker, *novel* The Sentimentalist by Dale Collins *d* Edward Sloman *ph* William Steiner, Arthur Ellis

Gary Cooper, Claudette Colbert, Averill Harris, Richard Spiro, Douglass Dumbrille, Joseph Calleia, Harry Davenport

'Actionless picture . . . too many barnacles cling to the script.'—*Variety*

Une Histoire D'Amour*

France 1951 95m bw
Jacques Roitfeld / Cité Films
GB title: *Love Story*

A police inspector discovers that a young couple killed themselves because of parental opposition.
A rather soggy little drama made watchable by its careful detail and immaculate leading performance.

w Michel Audiard *d* Robert Clavel *ph* Louis Page *m* Paul Misraki

Louis Jouvet, Daniel Gélin, Dany Robin

History Is Made at Night*
US 1937 97m bw
Walter Wanger

A divorcee and her new love have trouble from her ex-husband.
Atmospheric, artificial, generally entertaining romantic comedy-drama of a kind which went out of fashion long ago.

w Gene Towne, Graham Baker d Frank Borzage ph Gregg Toland m Alfred Newman

Charles Boyer, Jean Arthur, *Leo Carrillo*, Colin Clive

'A weird and unbelievable melodrama . . . mildly entertaining with good scenes.'—*Variety*

'So souped up with demonic passions and tender glances and elegant photography that it's rather fun.'—*New Yorker, 1978*

'Frank Borzage, who could turn *Frankenstein Meets the Wolf Man* into a romantic reverie, is quite undeterred by the venality rampant in the script and interjects his vision of what Andrew Sarris called love over probability. Oh, there's an iceberg disaster too.'—*Kit Parker catalogue*

The History of Mr Polly*
GB 1949 94m bw
GFD / Two Cities (John Mills)

A draper's assistant buys a small shop but tires of his nagging wife and decides the time has come for a change.
Patchy but generally amusing version of a popular comic novel, very English and rather appealingly done.

w Anthony Pelissier, *novel* H. G. Wells
d Anthony Pelissier ph Desmond Dickinson m William Alwyn

John Mills, Sally Ann Howes, Megs Jenkins, Finlay Currie, Betty Ann Davies, Edward Chapman

History of the World Part One
US 1981 92m De Luxe Panavision
Brooksfilms (Mel Brooks)

Episodes from world history are presented with the author's usual lack of taste or wit: a woeful collection of schoolboy scatology.

wd Mel Brooks ph Woody Omens, Paul Wilson m John Morris

Mel Brooks, Dom De Luise, Madeleine Kahn, Cloris Leachman, Harvey Korman, Ron Carey, Sid Caesar, Pamela Stephenson, Henny Youngman

● *Video: CBS / Fox*

Hit!
US 1973 134m Technicolor Panavision
Paramount (Harry Korshak)

A federal agent takes personal action against a drug ring which caused his daughter's death.
Black vigilante melodrama, very violent and interminably padded out with irrelevancies.

w Alan Trustman, David M. Wolf d Sidney J. Furie ph John A. Alonzo m Lalo Schifrin

Billy Dee Williams, Richard Pryor, Paul Hampton, Gwen Welles

'No more under-the-armpit shots, but obscurity is still the keynote of this Sidney Furie effort in the urban vigilante genre.'—*Sight and Sound*

The Hit
GB 1984 98m Technicolor
Zenith / Central / The Recorded Picture Company (Jeremy Thomas)

A supergrass hiding in Spain is sought by two gang executioners.
Old hat thuggery shown in new-style detail. Violently suspenseful but not otherwise interesting.

w Peter Prince d Stephen Frears ph Mike Molloy m Paco de Lucia pd Andrew Sanders

John Hurt, Terence Stamp, Tim Roth, Laura del Sol, Fernando Rey, Bill Hunter

'Sensitive editing and seductive camerawork can't disguise that the exercise is heading nowhere, a road movie without fuel.'—*Philip Strick, MFB*

● *Video: Palace*

The Hit Parade
US 1937 77m bw

An agent tries to get a new star into radio. An excuse for a line-up of acts, some quite tolerable. Frances Langford, Phil Regan, Louise Henry, Pert Kelton, Al Pearce, Ed Brophy, William Demarest, Duke Ellington and his Band, Eddy Duchin and his Band, Max Terhune, Monroe Owsley, Inez Courtney, the Tic Toc Girls. Written by Bradford Ropes and Sam Ornitz; directed by Gus Meins; for Nat Levin / Republic. 'Should gather plenty of de luxe dates . . . the tempo guarantees that the average fan will find it diverting.'—*Variety*

Hit the Deck
US 1930 93m bw (colour sequences)

Navy recruits have girl trouble. Lumpy production of a stage musical already well worn. Jack Oakie, Polly Walker, Roger Gray, Harry Sweet. No writer credit; directed by Luther Reed; for RKO. 'No reason why this one should run into trouble on week stands or less.'—*Variety*

Hit the Deck
US 1954 112m Eastmancolor Cinemascope
MGM (Joe Pasternak)

Romantic adventures of three sailors on shore leave in San Francisco.
Boring situations and performances reduce the temperature of this youth musical which is not another *On the Town*.

w Sonya Levien, William Ludwig, *musical play* Herbert Fields, *novel* Shore Leave by Hubert Osborn ph George Folsey m Vincent Youmans ly Leo Robin ch Hermes Pan

Tony Martin, Jane Powell, Ann Miller, Debbie Reynolds, Walter Pidgeon, Vic Damone, Gene Raymond

Hitch-hike Lady
US 1935 77m bw

An English housekeeper saves enough money to visit her son in the US, not aware that he is in San Quentin. Easy-going sentimental comedy, shot on the road. Alison Skipworth, Arthur Treacher, Mae Clarke, James Ellison, Warren Hymer, Beryl Mercer. Written by Gordon Rigby and Lester Cole from a story by Wallace MacDonald; directed by Aubrey Scotto; for Republic. 'Happy intermingling of humour and heart tugs.'—*Variety*

Hitler
US 1961 107m bw
Three Crown / E. Charles Straus

A sex-oriented, semi-fictional biopic of the German dictator, from the murder of his niece to his final madness and suicide.
Enterprising sensationalism which deserves a nod for sheer audacity.

w Sam Neuman d Stuart Heisler ph Joseph Biroc m Hans Salter

Richard Basehart, Maria Emo, Martin Kosleck, John Banner

Hitler—Beast of Berlin
US 1939 87m bw

A spy among Hitler's storm troopers escapes to Switzerland. Feeble exploitation item which succeeded only as propaganda. Hitler is not seen. Roland Drew, Steffi Duna, Alan Ladd, Greta Granstedt, Lucien Prival. Written by Shepard Traube from his story Goose Step; directed by Sherman Scott; for PRC. 'There are doubtless powerful pictures to be made on the anti-Nazi theme, but this isn't one.'—*Variety* (aka: *Beasts of Berlin*.)

'More morphine for Herr Goering! The greatest gangster picture of all!'
'Did Hitler kill the one woman he loved? What was Hess to Hitler?'

The Hitler Gang**
US 1944 101m bw
Paramount (B. G. De Sylva)

The rise to power of Hitler and his henchmen.
Though at the time it seemed rather like a serious cabaret turn, this fictionalization of historical fact has some good impersonations and dramatically effective scenes.

w Frances Goodrich, Albert Hackett d John Farrow ph Ernest Laszlo m David Buttolph

Robert Watson, Martin Kosleck (Goebbels), Victor Varconi (Hess), Luis Van Rooten (Himmler), Alexander Pope (Goering), Roman Bohnen, Ivan Triesault, Helene Thimig, Reinhold Schunzel, Sig Rumann, Alexander Granach

Hitler—The Last Ten Days
GB / Italy 1973 104m Technicolor
MGM / Wolfgang Reinhardt / Westfilm

With Adolf and Eva in the bunker.
Claustrophobic historical reconstruction with an uncomfortable star.

w Ennio de Concini, Maria Pia Fusco,
Wolfgang Reinhardt, Ivan Moffat *d* Ennio de
Concini *ph* Ennio Guarnieri *m* Mischa
Spoliansky

Alec Guinness, Simon Ward, Doris
Kunstmann, Adolfo Celi, Diane Cilento, Eric
Porter, Joss Ackland

Hitler's Children*
US 1943 83m bw
RKO (Edward A. Golden)

A family reacts to Hitler and the Hitler Youth.
Artificial melodrama set in an unlikely
Germany but successful at the time because of
its topicality and its refusal to play the Nazis as
idiots, which was the usual Hollywood line.

w Emmet Lavery, *book* Education for Death
by Gregor Ziemer *d* Edward Dmytryk
ph Russell Metty *m* Roy Webb

Tim Holt, Bonita Granville, Otto Kruger,
Kent Smith, H. B. Warner, Lloyd Corrigan,
Erford Gage, Gavin Muir, Hans Conried

'A curiously compromised production . . .
strong anti-Nazi propaganda, it has not been
woven into a defined and moving show.'—
Howard Barnes, New York Herald Tribune
'The truth about the Nazis from the cradle
to the battlefront!'—*publicity*

Hitler's Madman*
US 1943 84m bw
(MGM) PRC / Seymour Nebenzal
aka: *Hitler's Hangman*

Heydrich is assassinated in Czechoslovakia
and the Nazis take revenge on the village of
Lidice.
Cheapjack sensationalism based on a
horrifying incident of World War II; despite its
imperfections it generates a certain raw power.

w Peretz Hirshbein, Melvin Levy, Doris
Malloy *d* Douglas Sirk *m* Karl Hajos

Patricia Morison, *John Carradine*, Alan
Curtis, Ralph Morgan, Ludwig Stossel, Edgar
Kennedy, Al Shean, Jimmy Conlin, Blanche
Yurka, Victor Kilian

'Newspaper accounts of the bombing of
German cities will be pleasant antidotes for
the unhappy feeling brought on by the final
grim scenes of *Hitler's Madman*.'—*New York
Herald Tribune*
'Even in its poorly depicted scenes of
brutality, it inflames a common anger.'—
Theodore Strauss, New York Times

HMS Defiant*
GB 1962 101m Technicolor
        Cinemascope
Columbia / GW (John Brabourne)
US title: *Damn the Defiant*

Mutiny erupts on an 18th-century British
sailing ship.
Rather unpleasant and unenterprising sea fare
reminiscent of the goings-on aboard the
Bounty. Well enough staged and acted but not
very remarkable or memorable.

w Nigel Kneale, Edmund H. North, *novel*
Mutiny by Frank Tilsley *d* Lewis Gilbert
ph Christopher Challis *m* Clifton Parker

Alec Guinness, Dirk Bogarde, Anthony
Quayle, Tom Bell, Nigel Stock, Murray
Melvin, Victor Maddern, Maurice Denham,
Walter Fitzgerald

'It authentically if superficially recreates the
days of press gangs, maggots and the cat.'—
Peter John Dyer

Hobson's Choice***
GB 1953 107m bw
British Lion / London (Norman Spencer)

In the 1890s a tyrannical Lancashire
bootmaker is brought to heel by his plain-
speaking daughter and her simple-minded
husband.
Brilliantly played version of a famous working-
class comedy, memorably set and
photographed; one regrets only the slight
decline of the predictable third act.

w Norman Spencer, Wynard Browne, *play*
Harold Brighouse *d* David Lean *ph* Jack
Hildyard *m* Malcolm Arnold *ad* Wilfrid
Shingleton

*Charles Laughton, Brenda de Banzie, John
Mills*, Richard Wattis, Helen Haye, Daphne
Anderson, Prunella Scales
† Previously filmed in 1931 by Thomas
Bentley for BIP from a screenplay by Frank
Launder, with James Harcourt, Viola Lyel and
Frank Pettingell.

● Video: Thorn EMI

Hoffman
GB 1970 113m Technicolor
ABP / Longstone (Ben Arbeid)

A middle-aged misfit blackmails a typist into
spending a week with him.
Interminable sex comedy padded out from a
short TV play; it quickly becomes
claustrophobic, tasteless, and boring.

w Ernest Gebler, from his novel and play
d Alvin Rakoff *ph* Gerry Turpin *m* Ron
Grainer

Peter Sellers, Sinead Cusack, Jeremy Bulloch,
Ruth Dunning

'Hope never dies for a man with a good
dirty mind.'—*publicity*

Hog Wild***
US 1930 20m bw

Stan helps Ollie to put a radio aerial on the
roof of his house. Brilliantly sustained
slapstick makes this one of the best star
comedies of Laurel and Hardy. Written by H.
M. Walker and Leo McCarey; directed by
James Parrott; for Hal Roach.

● Video: Thorn EMI

'Master of love! He is to all women what
each desires him to be!'

Hold Back the Dawn*
US 1941 115m bw
Paramount (Arthur Hornblow Jnr)

A would-be immigrant into the US via Mexico
marries a schoolteacher he does not love.
Surprisingly effective romantic melodrama
with a nice style and some mordant lines in the
script.

w *Charles Brackett, Billy Wilder d* Mitchell
Leisen *ph* Leo Tover *m* Victor Young

Charles Boyer, Olivia de Havilland, Paulette
Goddard, Victor Francen, Walter Abel, Curt
Bois, Rosemary de Camp, Nestor Paiva,
Mitchell Leisen

'All those years with all the others I closed
my eyes and thought of you.'—*sample
dialogue spoken by Paulette Goddard*
AAN: best picture; Charles Brackett, Billy
Wilder; Leo Tover; Victor Young; Olivia de
Havilland

Hold Back the Night
US 1956 80m bw

From World War II to Korea, a marine
commander carries with him a lucky whisky
bottle. Pointlessly titled war heroics,
competently mounted. John Payne, Mona
Freeman, Peter Graves, Chuck Connors,
Audrey Dalton. Written by John C. Higgins
and Walter Doniger, from the novel by Pat
Frank; directed by Allan Dwan; for Allied
Artists.

Hold Back Tomorrow
US 1956 75m bw

A convicted killer's last request is for a woman
to spend his last night with him. They fall in
love before he is executed. A ripe example of
the higher tosh, indifferently made and acted.
Cleo Moore, John Agar, Frank de Kova,
Dallas Boyd. Written, directed and produced
by Hugo Haas; for Universal-International.

Hold 'em Yale
US 1935 61m bw

Four con men find themselves looking after a
disinherited heiress. Thin filming of a Damon
Runyon story; strictly supporting material.
Patricia Ellis, Cesar Romero, Larry Crabbe,
William Frawley, Andy Devine, George E.
Stone, Warren Hymer. Written by Paul
Gerard Smith, Eddie Welch; directed by
Sidney Lanfield; for Paramount.

Hold Everything
US 1930 78m Technicolor

A comedian becomes a prizefighter. Pleasant
comedy musical which established Joe E.
Brown in Hollywood, as it had established
Bert Lahr on stage. Joe E. Brown, Winnie
Lightner, Georges Carpentier, Sally O'Neill,
Bert Roach. From the play by B. G. De Sylva
and John McGowan; directed by Roy del
Ruth; for Warners. 'Pip laugh picture, the best
comedy Warners has turned out since talkers
came in.'—*Variety*

Hold That Blonde
US 1945 75m bw
Paramount (Paul Jones)

A psychiatrist suggests that romance may cure
a kleptomaniac, but the patient unfortunately
chooses a jewel thief.
Thin comedy which erupts into frantic farce,
with some energetic slapstick and a Harold
Lloyd style finale.

w Walter de Leon, Earl Baldwin, E. Edwin
Moran d George Marshall ph Daniel L.
Fapp m Werner Heymann

Eddie Bracken, Veronica Lake, Albert
Dekker, Frank Fenton, George Zucco,
Donald MacBride, Norma Varden, Willie Best

Hold That Co-Ed*
US 1938 80m bw
TCF (David Hempstead)
GB title: *Hold That Girl*

A girl dressed as a boy wins a university
football match and thereby helps a governor
get re-elected.
Intriguingly-cast crazy comedy which works up
into a fine frenzy.

w Karl Tunberg, Don Ettinger, Jack Yellen
d George Marshall ph Robert Planck
md Arthur Lange

John Barrymore, Joan Davis, George Murphy,
Marjorie Weaver, Jack Haley, George
Barbier, Donald Meek, Johnny Downs, Guinn
Williams
 'On the wacky side and fairly amusing, but
not quite making the big league.'—*Variety*

Hold That Ghost*
US 1941 86m bw
Universal (Burt Kelly, Glenn Tryon)

A group of strangers are stranded in an
apparently haunted house.
Long thought of as Abbott and Costello's best
comedy, this now seems pretty strained and
slow to start, but it has its classic moments.

w Robert Lees, Fred Rinaldo, John Grant
d Arthur Lubin ph Elwood Bredell, Joe
Valentine m Hans Salter

Bud Abbott, Lou Costello, Joan Davis, the
Andrews Sisters, Richard Carlson, *Ted Lewis*
and his band, Evelyn Ankers, Marc Lawrence,
Mischa Auer

Hold That Kiss
US 1938 75m bw

A man and woman each believe the other to
be wealthy. Elementary comedy of
misunderstandings, of no abiding interest.
Maureen O'Sullivan, Dennis O'Keefe, Mickey
Rooney, George Barbier, Jessie Ralph, Ed
Brophy. Written by Stanley Rauh; directed by
Edwin S. Marin; for MGM. 'Pleasant but
undistinguished.'—*Variety*

Hold Your Man*
US 1933 89m bw
MGM (Sam Wood)

A hard-boiled young woman falls for a
confidence man, has his baby, and waits for
him to emerge from prison.
Briskly-fashioned star comedy-drama with
entertaining moments.

w Anita Loos, Howard Emmett Rogers
d Sam Wood ph Harold Rosson

Jean Harlow, Clark Gable, Stuart Erwin,
Dorothy Burgess, Muriel Kirkland, Paul Hurst
 'A real money picture . . . most promising
box office prospect in months.'—*Variety*

'The sudden transition from wise-cracking
romance to sentimental penitence provides a
jolt.'—*Frank S. Nugent*

The Hole*
France / Italy 1959 123m bw
Play-Art / Filmsonor / Titanus (Serge
 Silberman)
original title: *Le Trou*

Four convicts in a Paris prison dig a tunnel to
freedom and almost make it.
Meticulous escape drama nicely shot in very
limited sets: hypnotic for those with the
patience to adjust to its pace.

w Jacques Becker, José Giovanni, Jean Aurel,
novel José Giovanni d Jacques Becker
ph Ghislain Cloquet

Philippe Leroy, Mark Michel, Jean Kéraudy,
Michel Constantine

A Hole in the Head*
US 1959 120m De Luxe Cinemascope
UA / Sincap (Frank Sinatra)

A Miami hotelier is threatened with
foreclosure and tries to raise the money from
his provident elder brother.
Easy-going comedy without much point, but
various amusing facets artfully deployed.

w Arnold Shulman, from his TV and stage
play d Frank Capra ph William H. Daniels
m Nelson Riddle

Frank Sinatra, Edward G. Robinson, Eleanor
Parker, Eddie Hodges, Carolyn Jones, Thelma
Ritter, Keenan Wynn, Joi Lansing

AA: song 'High Hopes' (m Jimmy Van
Heusen, ly Sammy Cahn)

The Hole in the Wall
US 1929 73m bw
Paramount

A gangster falls for a phony fortune teller on a
revenge scheme.
Involved melodrama, a primitive talkie
notable chiefly for its stars.

w Pierre Collings, *play* Fred Jackson
d Robert Florey ph George Folsey

Edward G. Robinson, Claudette Colbert,
David Newell, Nelly Savage, Donald Meek,
Louise Closser Hale

Holiday*
US 1930 99m bw
Pathe (E. B. Derr)

A bright-minded rich girl steals her sister's
fiancé, a struggling young lawyer.
Competent early talkie version of a hit play.

w Horace Jackson, *play* Philip Barry
d Edward H. Griffith ph Norbert Brodine
m Josiah Zuro

Ann Harding, Robert Ames, Mary Astor,
Edward Everett Horton, Hedda Hopper,
Monroe Owsley, William Holden
 'A comedy of wide appeal in a finished
style.'—*Variety*

AAN: Horace Jackson; Ann Harding

'So daring—so tender—so human—so
 true—that everyone in love will want to
 see it!'
Holiday***
US 1938 93m bw
Columbia (Everett Riskin)
GB titles: *Free to Live; Unconventional
Linda*

Elegant, highly successful remake of the
above; still a stage play on film, but subtly
devised to make the very most of the lines and
performances.

w Donald Ogden Stewart d George Cukor
ph Franz Planer m Sidney Cutner

*Katharine Hepburn, Cary Grant, Doris Nolan,
Edward Everett Horton* (same role), *Ruth
Donnelly, Lew Ayres*, Henry Kolker, Binnie
Barnes
 'Corking comedy . . . exhibitors will pencil
in some extra days.'—*Variety*
 'The comedy is full of the best of humour,
edged with pathos never allowed to drop into
sentimentality. It is played with the greatest
cheerfulness and a winning skill.'—*Arthur
Pollock, Brooklyn Daily Eagle*
 'I suppose actually it is a neat and
sometimes elegant job, but under its surface of
too much brightness and too many words it
seems so deadly bored and weary. Hell, save
your money and yawn at home.'—*Otis
Ferguson*

Holiday Affair
US 1949 87m bw
RKO (Don Hartman)

A young widow falls for an easy-going boat
builder.
Flimsy star-shaped romantic comedy with nice
touches.

w Isobel Lennart d Don Hartman ph Milton
Krasner m Roy Webb

Robert Mitchum, Janet Leigh, Wendell
Corey, Griff Barnett, Esther Dale, Gordon
Gebert, Henry O'Neill, Harry Morgan

Holiday Camp*
GB 1947 97m bw
GFD / Gainsborough (Sydney Box)

At a summer holiday camp, a murderer on the
prowl affects people's enjoyment in various
ways.
Seminal compendium comedy drama, a bore
in itself but establishing several post-war
norms of the British cinema, including the
Huggetts.

w Muriel and Sidney Box, Ted Willis, Peter
Rogers, Mabel and Denis Constanduros
d Ken Annakin

Jack Warner, Kathleen Harrison, Flora
Robson, Dennis Price, Hazel Court, Emrys
Jones, Yvonne Owen, Esmond Knight, Jimmy
Hanley, Peter Hammond, Esma Cannon, John
Blythe, Susan Shaw

Holiday for Lovers
US 1959 103m De Luxe Cinemascope
TCF (David Weisbart)

To distract his teenage daughter from boys, a

Boston psychiatrist organizes a family holiday in South America.
Frail old-fashioned family comedy with entirely predictable situations culminating in a drunk scene for stuffy father.

w Luther Davis d Henry Levin ph Charles G. Clarke m Leigh Harline

Clifton Webb, Jane Wyman, Paul Henreid, Carol Lynley, Jill St John, Gary Crosby, José Greco

Holiday for Sinners

US 1952 72m bw
MGM (John Houseman)

In New Orleans during the Mardi Gras three old friends meet crises in their lives.
Slightly curious but not very interesting portmanteau drama.

w A. I. Bezzerides, *novel* Hamilton Basso d Gerald Mayer ph Paul Vogel md Alberto Columbo

Gig Young, Keenan Wynn, Janice Rule, Richard Anderson, William Campbell, Michael Chekhov, Sandro Giglio, Edith Barrett, Porter Hall
'It gives an impression of blurred, rather heavy-going sincerity.'—*MFB*

Holiday in Mexico

US 1946 127m Technicolor
MGM (Joe Pasternak)

The daughter of the American Ambassador to Mexico falls for Jose Iturbi.
Travel brochure musical in which the occasional plums do not redeem the sogginess of the pudding.

w Isobel Lennart d George Sidney ph Harry Stradling

Walter Pidgeon, Ilona Massey, Jane Powell, Jose Iturbi, Roddy McDowall

Holiday Inn**

US 1942 101m bw
Paramount (Mark Sandrich)

The joint proprietors of a roadhouse hotel love the same girl.
Plain, simple-minded musical which provided a peg for pleasant performances and good numbers. It hit the box office spot, especially as it introduced 'White Christmas'.

w Claude Binyon, Elmer Rice d Mark Sandrich ph David Abel m / ly Irving Berlin md Robert Emmett Dolan

Bing Crosby, Fred Astaire, Walter Abel, Marjorie Reynolds, Virginia Dale, Louise Beavers, Irving Bacon, James Bell
'The best musical drama of the year.'—*New York Post*
† Marjorie Reynolds was dubbed by Martha Mears.
AA: song 'White Christmas'
AAN: original story (Irving Berlin); Robert Emmett Dolan

The Holly and the Ivy*

GB 1952 83m bw
British Lion / London (Anatole de Grunwald)

Christmas brings family revelations in a remote Norfolk rectory.
A badly-filmed stage success which succeeds because of its performances.

w Anatole de Grunwald, *play* Wynard Browne d George More O'Ferrall ph Ted Scaife m Malcolm Arnold

Ralph Richardson, Celia Johnson, Margaret Leighton, Denholm Elliott, John Gregson, Hugh Williams, Margaret Halstan, Maureen Delany, William Hartnell, Robert Flemyng, Roland Culver
'This type of direct translation to the screen, using none of the cinema's resources, can only do harm to the play itself.'—*Penelope Houston*

Hollywood Boulevard*

US 1936 75m bw
Paramount (A. M. Botsford)

A washed-up Hollywood actor writes a sensational memoir for publication, but lives to regret it.
Entertaining melodrama with famous names in bit parts.

w Marguerite Roberts d Robert Florey ph Karl Struss m Gregory Stone

John Halliday, Marsha Hunt, Robert Cummings, C. Henry Gordon, Frieda Inescort, Esther Dale; and Gary Cooper, Francis X. Bushman, Maurice Costello, Mae Marsh, Charles Ray, Jane Novak, Bryant Washburn, Jack Mulhall, Creighton Hale, Bert Roach
'A pretty hoary melodrama and a slight enough excuse for a whole series of homilies upon the uncertainty of fame and fortune in the glamour city.'—*New York Times*

Hollywood Canteen*

US 1944 123m bw
Warner (Alex Gottlieb)

The stars give their evenings to entertaining soldiers.
Shoddily made but sociologically fascinating record of Hollywood doing its bit in World War II.

wd Delmer Daves ph Bert Glennon m Ray Heindorf md Leo F. Forbstein

Joan Leslie, Robert Hutton, Dane Clark, Janis Paige; and The Andrews Sisters, Jack Benny, Joe E. Brown, Eddie Cantor, Joan Crawford, Bette Davis, John Garfield, Sidney Greenstreet, Paul Henreid, Peter Lorre, Ida Lupino, Dennis Morgan, Roy Rogers, S. Z. Sakall, Alexis Smith, Barbara Stanwyck, Jane Wyman, etc etc
'The corporal steps slowly backwards, in his eyes that look of glazed ecstasy which Jennifer Jones wore all through *The Song of Bernadette*. He has just been kissed by Joan Leslie.'—*Richard Winnington*

AAN: Ray Heindorf; song 'Sweet Dreams, Sweetheart' (m M. K. Jerome, ly Ted Koehler)

'It does for the motion picture what Alexander's Ragtime Band did for popular music!'

Hollywood Cavalcade*

US 1939 96m Technicolor
TCF (Harry Joe Brown)

The career of an old-time Hollywood producer.
A lively first half with amusing re-staging of early slapstick comedies gives way depressingly to personal melodrama, but there is enough historical interest to preserve the balance.

w Ernest Pascal d Irving Cummings ph Allen M. Davey, Ernest Palmer ad Richard Day, Wiard B. Ihnen md Louis Silvers

Don Ameche, Alice Faye, *J. Edward Bromberg*, Alan Curtis, Stuart Erwin, Jed Prouty, Buster Keaton, Donald Meek, and the original Keystone Kops
'Surefire . . . should score heavily in theatres of every type.'—*Variety*
† Alice Faye did not sing. The Keystone Kops sequence was directed by Mal St Clair. The Ameche / Faye characters were supposedly based on Mack Sennett and Mabel Normand; Mack Sennett's appearance under his own name seemed to be an effort to throw people off the scent.

Hollywood Hotel

US 1937 109m bw
Warner (Sam Bischoff)

A Hollywood radio show has its problems.
Half-hearted, overlong Warner musical with little of the expected zip.

w Jerry Wald, Maurice Leo, Richard Macauley d Busby Berkeley ph Charles Rosher, George Barnes m / ly Johnny Mercer, Richard Whiting

Dick Powell, Rosemary Lane, Lola Lane, Hugh Herbert, Ted Healy, Glenda Farrell, Louella Parsons, Alan Mowbray, Frances Langford, Allyn Joslyn, Benny Goodman, Edgar Kennedy

Hollywood or Bust

US 1956 95m Technicolor Vistavision
(Paramount) Hal Wallis

Two halfwits win a car and drive across country to Hollywood.
Dopey comedy with more misses than hits; the last film of Martin and Lewis as a team.

w Erna Lazarus d Frank Tashlin ph Daniel Fapp m Walter Scharf

Dean Martin, Jerry Lewis, Pat Crowley, Maxie Rosenbloom, Anita Ekberg

Hollywood Party

US 1934 68m bw (Technicolor sequence)
MGM (Harry Rapf)

A mad Russian throws a party which ends in disaster.
Dismal 'all-star' comedy relieved by guest appearances.

w Howard Dietz, Arthur Kober
d (uncredited) Richard Boleslawski, Allan
Dwan, Roy Rowland *ph* James Wong Howe

Laurel and Hardy, Jimmy Durante, Lupe
Velez, Charles Butterworth, Eddie Quillan,
Ted Healy and the Stooges, Polly Moran

'A big short . . . averagely passable screen
divertissement.'—*Variety*

The Hollywood Revue of 1929**
US 1929 116m part-Technicolor
MGM (Harry Rapf)

A variety show featuring most of MGM's
talent in slightly surprising acts, this is
something of a bore to sit through but an
archival must; and just occasionally it boasts
surprising vitality.

w Al Boasberg, Robert E. Hopkins *d* Charles
F. Reisner *ph* John Arnold, Irving Ries,
Maximillian Fabian *ch* Sammy Lee
m / ly various

Jack Benny, Buster Keaton, Joan Crawford,
John Gilbert, Norma Shearer, Laurel and
Hardy, Marion Davies, Marie Dressler,
William Haines, Lionel Barrymore, Conrad
Nagel, Bessie Love, Cliff Edwards, Nils
Asther

AAN: best picture

Hollywood Speaks
US 1932 71m bw

A Los Angeles columnist exposes Hollywood
corruption. Superficial exploitation piece of no
interest apart from glimpses of studios. Pat
O'Brien, Genevieve Tobin, Lucien Prival,
Rita Leroy. Written by Norman Krasna with
Jo Swerling; directed by Eddie Buzzell; for
Columbia. 'Its field is really the split weeks
. . . good bet for the less educated
clientele.'—*Variety*

Hollywood Story*
US 1951 76m bw
U-I (Leonard Goldstein)

A young producer solves a 20-year-old studio
murder mystery.
Adequate potboiler with a reasonably
absorbing plot and glimpses of silent stars.

w Frederick Kohner, Fred Brady *d* William
Castle *ph* Carl Guthrie *m* Joseph
Gershenson

Richard Conte, Julia Adams, Richard Egan,
Henry Hull, Fred Clark, Jim Backus, Paul
Cavanagh; and Francis X. Bushman, William
Farnum, Betty Blythe, Helen Gibson, Joel
McCrea

Holocaust 2000
GB / Italy 1977 102m Technicolor
Technovision
(Rank) Aston / Embassy (Edmondo Amati)
aka: *The Chosen*

The executive in charge of a thermonuclear
plant in the Middle East is drawn into a legend
about the rebirth of the anti-Christ, and
discovers that the evil one is his own son.
Extraordinary mishmash of horror, religiosity
and social conscience which scarcely works on
any level.

w Sergio Donati, Alberto de Martino, Michael
Robson *d* Alberto de Martino *ph* Erico
Menczer *m* Ennio Morricone

Kirk Douglas, Simon Ward, Agostina Belli,
Anthony Quayle, Virginia McKenna, Spiros
Focas, Alexander Knox, Adolfo Celi

'The wildest farrago yet to have come out of
the demonology genre.'—*Richard Combs,
MFB*

Holy Matrimony*
US 1943 87m bw
TCF (Nunnally Johnson)

A famous painter comes back from exile for a
knighthood; but when his valet dies of
pneumonia, has him buried as himself in
Westminster Abbey.
Slightly stilted but generally warmly amusing
version of a favourite novel, with excellent star
performances.

w Nunnally Johnson, *novel* Buried Alive by
Arnold Bennett *d* John Stahl *ph* Lucien
Ballard *m* Cyril Mockridge

Monty Woolley, Gracie Fields, Laird Cregar,
Eric Blore, Una O'Connor

'A pleasant hour and a half, very well
produced and acted.'—*James Agate*

AAN: Nunnally Johnson

The Holy Terror
US 1936 66m bw

A child is a mischief-maker at a naval air
station. Lightweight star vehicle for Shirley
Temple's only competitor. Jane Withers, Tony
Martin, Leah Ray, Joan David, El Brendel,
John Eldredge. Written by Lou Breslow and
John Patrick; directed by James Tinling; for
TCF. 'Nicely paced for laughs . . . strong dual
bill attraction.'—*Variety*

Hombre**
US 1967 111m De Luxe Panavision
TCF / Hombre Productions (Martin Ritt,
Irving Ravetch)

Stagecoach passengers at the mercy of a
robber are helped by a despised half-caste.
Slow but suspenseful western melodrama
which works up to a couple of good climaxes
but falls away in an unnecessary tragic ending.

w Irving Ravetch, Harriet Frank, *novel*
Elmore Leonard *d* Martin Ritt *ph* James
Wong Howe *m* David Rose

Paul Newman, *Diane Cilento, Fredric March*,
Richard Boone, Martin Balsam, Barbara
Rush, Cameron Mitchell

'A fine array of quirkish characters . . . and
some unusually literate dialogue.'—*Tom Milne*

● Video: CBS / Fox

Home at Seven
GB 1952 85m bw
British Lion / London (Maurice Cowan)
US title: *Murder on Monday*

A clerk suffers a 24-hour loss of memory and
may have been involved in a murder.
Intriguing suburban mystery, well acted but all
too flatly transferred from the stage, and with
a weak solution.

w Anatole de Grunwald, *play* R. C. Sherriff
d Ralph Richardson *ph* Jack Hildyard,
Edward Scaife *m* Malcolm Arnold

Ralph Richardson, Margaret Leighton, Jack
Hawkins, Campbell Singer, Michael Shepley,
Margaret Withers, Meriel Forbes, Frederick
Piper

'A film with a notable absence of
imagination in conception, direction and
acting is not vindicated because it was made
very cheaply in fifteen days . . . it seems
ominous that the technique closely resembles
that of television.'—*MFB*

Home before Dark
US 1958 137m bw
Warner (Mervyn Le Roy)

A college professor brings his wife home after
a year in a mental hospital, but trouble starts
again as the circumstances are unchanged.
Overlong, heavygoing, well-made soap opera,
quite unconvincing despite firm performances
and a suitably gloomy *mise-en-scène*.

w Eileen and Robert Bassing *d* Mervyn Le
Roy *ph* Joseph Biroc *m* Franz Waxman
md Ray Heindorf

Jean Simmons, Efrem Zimbalist Jnr, Dan
O'Herlihy, Rhonda Fleming, Mabel Albertson

Home from the Hill
US 1959 150m Metrocolor
Cinemascope
MGM / Sol C. Siegel (Edmund Grainger)

A southern landowner with a voracious sexual
appetite has trouble with his two sons,
legitimate and illegitimate.
Shades of *Cold Comfort Farm* and *Tobacco
Road* . . . and this solemn family saga does go
on a bit.

w Irving Ravetch, Harriet Frank, *novel*
William Humphrey *d* Vincente Minnelli
ph Milton Krasner *m* Bronislau Kaper

Robert Mitchum, George Hamilton, George
Peppard, Eleanor Parker, Luana Patten,
Everett Sloane, Constance Ford, Ray Teal

Home in Indiana
US 1944 103m Technicolor
TCF (André Daven)

Farmers compete in trotting races and their
progeny fall in love.
Archetypal homespun Americana, well
enough made according to its lights, but now
like something from another world . . . an
innocent one.

w Winston Miller, *novel* The Phantom Filly by
George Agnew Chamberlain *d* Henry
Hathaway *ph* Edward Cronjager *m* Hugo
Friedhofer *md* Emil Newman

Jeanne Crain, June Haver, Lon McCallister,
Walter Brennan, Charlotte Greenwood, Ward
Bond, Charles Dingle, Willie Best
† Remade as *April Love*.

AAN: Edward Cronjager

Home of the Brave*
US 1949 86m bw
Stanley Kramer

During World War II, a black man finds

himself the butt of racist behaviour from the rest of his platoon.

One of the first films to touch the subject of anti-black bias, this now seems pretty tame and dated, and in fact never was much more than a filmed play (in which the butt was originally a Jew).

w Carl Foreman, *play* Arthur Laurents d Mark Robson *ph* Robert de Grasse m Dmitri Tiomkin

Frank Lovejoy, Lloyd Bridges, Douglas Dick, James Edwards, Steve Brodie, Jeff Corey, Cliff Clark

A Home of Your Own*
GB 1965   44m   bw

Calamities pile up on a building site. Genuinely funny silent comedy, with bits from a variety of familiar faces. Ronnie Barker, George Benson, Richard Briers, Janet Brown, Peter Butterworth, Bernard Cribbins, Fred Emney, Bill Fraser, Ronnie Stevens. Written by Jay Lewis and John Whyte; directed by Bob Kellett; for Dormar / British Lion.

Home Sweet Homicide
US 1946   90m   bw
TCF

Children solve a murder mystery with the help of their mother, a detective novelist. Mild family fare.

w F. Hugh Herbert, *novel* Craig Rice d Lloyd Bacon *ph* John Seitz m David Buttolph

Lynn Bari, Randolph Scott, Peggy Ann Garner, Connie Marshall, Dean Stockwell, Barbara Whiting

Home to Danger
GB 1951   66m   bw

An heiress returns after her father's death and finds herself pursued by a murderer. Tuppenny shocker, quite amusing in its way. Rona Anderson, Guy Rolfe, Stanley Baker, Francis Lister, Alan Wheatley. Written by Francis Edge and Guy Temple-Smith; directed by Terence Fisher; for Lance Comfort / Eros.

The Home Towners
US 1928   84m   bw

A wealthy man falls for a girl half his age and is warned by a hometown friend that she may be a gold digger. Fairly fluent early talkie which pleased at the time. Richard Bennett, Robert McWade, Doris Kenyon, Stanley Taylor. Written by Addison Burkhart, from the play by George M. Cohan; directed by Bryan Foy; for Warner. (Remakes include *Times Square Playboy* [1936] with Warren William, Gene Lockhart and June Travis, directed by William McGann; and *Ladies Must Live* [1940] with Wayne Morris, Priscilla Lane and Roscoe Karns; both for Warner.)

Homecoming
US 1948   113m   bw
MGM (Sidney Franklin)

A ruthless society doctor is called up in World War II and has his life changed by a brief affair with a nurse who is killed in action.

Ho-hum romantic melodrama which stumbles most badly when it aims to be serious.

w Paul Osborn d Mervyn Le Roy ph Harold Rosson md Charles Previn m Bronislau Kaper

Clark Gable, Lana Turner, Anne Baxter, John Hodiak, Ray Collins, Gladys Cooper, Cameron Mitchell, Marshall Thompson

'Its basic substance, like the base of a perfume, has a terrible smell; but to many moviegoers the end-product will seem quite pleasant.'—*Time*

The Homecoming*
GB 1973   114m   colour
American Express / Ely Landau

Tensions mount and sexual revelations abound in the house of a retired London butcher. Plain treatment of an anything-but-plain Pinter play. The result is a record of a performance rather than a film.

w Harold Pinter, from his play d Peter Hall ph David Watkin m Thelonious Monk pd John Bury

Paul Rogers, Cyril Cusack, Michael Jayston, Ian Holm, Vivien Merchant, Terence Rigby

'Shocking in its own lucidity, and fascinating as an arrangement of mutually reflecting prisms . . . the remarkable control of Pinter's language guarantees that the dramatic situations are revealed to be even *more* abstract and diagrammatic as they steadily accumulate psychological density.'—*Jonathan Rosenbaum*

The Homestretch
US 1947   97m   Technicolor

A racing enthusiast neglects his wife. Thin romantic drama, handsomely photographed on various racecourses. Cornel Wilde, Maureen O'Hara, Glenn Langan, Helen Walker, James Gleason, Henry Stephenson. Written by Wanda Tuchock; directed by H. Bruce Humberstone; for TCF.

'Can your heart stand the challenge when the clock starts the countdown?'
Homicidal
US 1961   87m   bw
Columbia / William Castle

A murderous blonde and a very strange young man both live in the house of a paralysed old lady.

Transvestite horror comic allegedly based on a true case; made on a low budget and played for cheap shocks.

w Robb White d William Castle ph Burnett Guffey m Hugo Friedhofer

Jean Arless, Glenn Corbett, Patricia Breslin, Eugenie Leontovich, Alan Bunce, Richard Rust

† The film was played with a 'fright break' during which faint-hearted members of the audience might leave before the final onslaught.

Homicide
US 1949   76m   bw

A murder witness is intimidated by the killers.

Stiff little crime yarn which slowly recovers after a dull beginning. Robert Douglas, Robert Alda, Helen Westcott. Written by William Sackheim; directed by Felix Jacoves; for Warner.

Homicide Bureau
US 1938   56m   bw

A tough small-town cop deals with racketeers. Routine programme filler. Bruce Cabot, Rita Hayworth, Marc Lawrence, Moroni Olsen. Written by Earle Snell; directed by C. C. Coleman Jnr; for Columbia. 'Hits new low . . . every department of production way below par.'—*Variety*

L'Homme au Chapeau Rond*
France 1946   91m   bw
Alcina

When his wife dies, a man becomes obsessed with causing the downfall of her two lovers. Heavy-going melodrama without much in the way of light relief; chiefly memorable for its central performance.

w Charles Spaak, Jean Loubignic, *novel* The Eternal Husband by Dostoevsky d Pierre Billon ph Nicolas Torporkoff m Maurice Thiriet

Raimu, Aimé Clariond, Lucy Valnor

Hondo*
US 1954   93m   Warnercolor   3-D
Wayne–Fellows

In 1874 New Mexico a cavalry despatch rider stops to defend a lonely widow and her son against Indians.

Overwritten but pleasant-looking western, clearly patterned after *Shane*.

w James Edward Grant d John Farrow ph Robert Burks, Archie Stout m Emil Newman, Hugo Friedhofer

John Wayne, Geraldine Page, Ward Bond, Michael Pate

AAN: Geraldine Page

Honey
US 1930   75m   bw

A brother and sister rent out their southern mansion and decide to become the butler and cook. Comedy with music, a little heavier than it should have been. Nancy Carroll, Skeets Gallagher, Stanley Smith, Lillian Roth, Harry Green, Mitzi Green, Zasu Pitts. Written by Herman J. Mankiewicz from the play Come Out of the Kitchen by Alice Duer Miller and A. E. Thomas; directed by Wesley Ruggles; for Paramount. 'Not worthy of a big rave but should satisfy the mob.'—*Variety*

'You are cordially invited to a perfectly elegant case of murder!'
The Honey Pot*
US 1966   150m   Technicolor
UA / Famous Artists (Charles K. Feldman) (Joseph L. Mankiewicz)

A millionaire pretends to be dying in order to trick three former mistresses; but one of them is murdered.

Uneasy variation, via two other variations, on Ben Jonson's *Volpone*; despite bright moments, the mood is fatally inconsistent, and a cloud of pseudo-sophisticated dialogue hangs over the whole thing like a pall.

wd Joseph L. Mankiewicz, *play* Mr Fox of Venice by Frederick Knott, *novel* The Evil of the Day by Thomas Sterling *ph* Gianni di Venanzo *m* John Addison *pd* John De Cuir

Rex Harrison, Susan Hayward, *Maggie Smith*, Cliff Robertson, Capucine, Edie Adams, Adolfo Celi, Herschel Bernardi

'One of the talkiest pictures ever made.'— *Stephen Farber*

Honeychile
US 1951 89m Trucolor

A music publisher tries to cheat a country composer. Hayseed shenanigans for small-town consumption. Judy Canova, Eddie Foy Jnr, Alan Hale Jnr, Walter Catlett, Claire Carleton, Leonid Kinskey. Written by R. G. Springsteen; for Republic.

Honeymoon
US 1947 74m bw
RKO (Warren Duff)
GB title: *Two Men and a Girl*

An 18-year-old elopes to Mexico City with an army corporal but meets a sophisticated older man.
Emaciated comedy, one of the reasons for Shirley Temple's early retirement.

w Michael Kanin, *story* Vicki Baum *d* William Keighley *ph* Edward Cronjager *m* Leigh Harline

Shirley Temple, Franchot Tone, Guy Madison, Lina Romay, Gene Lockhart, Grant Mitchell

Honeymoon
Spain / GB 1959 109m Technicolor
Technirama / Dimension 180
Suevia / Everdene (Cesario Gonzalez, Michael Powell)
Spanish title: *Luna de Miel*

An ex-ballerina in Spain with her new husband is tempted to return to the boards.
Incredibly shapeless travel poster with some dancing and two interpolated ballets to provide moments of musical interest. An unbelievable disaster from the co-creator of *The Red Shoes*.

w Michael Powell, Luis Escobar *d* Michael Powell *ph* Georges Périnal, Gerry Turpin *m* Mikis Theodorakis

Anthony Steel, Ludmilla Tcherina, Antonio, Leonide Massine

Honeymoon Deferred
US 1940 84m bw

An insurance investigator is called away from honeymoon when his boss is murdered.
Unremarkable star programmer. Edmund Lowe, Margaret Lindsay, Elizabeth Risdon, Joyce Compton, Chick Chandler. Written by Roy Chanslor and Eliot Gibbons; directed by Lew Landers; for Universal.

Honeymoon Deferred
GB 1951 79m bw

A war veteran returns for his honeymoon to the Italian village he helped to liberate, but finds himself accused of ruining the crops. Curious hybrid comedy which fails to jell on all levels. Griffith Jones, Sally Ann Howes, Kieron Moore, Lea Padovani. Written by Suso d'Amico and A. Pietrangeli; directed by Mario Camerini; for Vic Films.

Honeymoon for Three
US 1941 77m bw

An author is protected from adoring females by his secretary. Fairly flaccid romantic comedy, a remake of *Goodbye Again* (1933). George Brent, Ann Sheridan, Osa Massen, Charles Ruggles, Jane Wyman, Lee Patrick. Written by Julius J. Epstein, Philip G. Epstein and Earl Baldwin; directed by Lloyd Bacon; for Warner.

Honeymoon Hotel
US 1964 98m Metrocolor
    Cinemascope
MGM / Avon (Lawrence Weingarten)

A jilted swain goes off with a philandering friend on what was to have been his honeymoon trip . . . only to be followed by his repentant fiancée.
Rather unattractive farce with insufficient funny moments.

w R. S. Allen, Harvey Bulloch *d* Henry Levin *ph* Harold Lipstein *m* Walter Scharf

Nancy Kwan, Robert Goulet, Robert Morse, Jill St John, Elsa Lanchester, Keenan Wynn

Honeymoon in Bali
US 1939 95m bw

A department store head intends to pursue her career without marriage, but two swains try to prove her wrong. Thin romantic comedy which got by on its stars. Madeleine Carroll, Fred MacMurray, Allan Jones, Akim Tamiroff, Helen Broderick, Osa Massen. Written by Virginia Van Upp; directed by Edward H. Griffith; for Jeff Lazarus / Paramount.
'Infectiously sparkling . . . will click substantially in the regular runs.'—*Variety*
NB. The original title, *Are Husbands Necessary?*, was discarded when Miss Carroll became involved in a divorce suit.

The Honeymoon Machine
US 1961 91m Metrocolor
    Cinemascope
MGM / Avon (Lawrence Weingarten)

A naval lieutenant uses the ship's computer to break the bank at the Venice casino.
Stolid, expensive-looking comedy which barely raises a laugh.

w George Wells, *play* The Golden Fleecing by Lorenzo Semple Jnr *d* Richard Thorpe *ph* Joseph La Shelle *m* Leigh Harline

Steve McQueen, Brigid Bazlen, Jim Hutton, Paula Prentiss, Dean Jagger, Jack Weston, Jack Mullaney

Honeysuckle Rose
US 1980 119m Technicolor

A happily married country and western star takes to the bottle whenever he goes on the road. Glum modern drama with music, a semi-autobiographical star vehicle; for fans only. Willie Nelson, Dyan Cannon, Amy Irving, Slim Pickens. Written by Carol Sobieski, William D. Wittliff and John Binder; directed by Jerry Schatzberg; for Sydney Pollack / Warner.

Hong Kong
US 1951 91m Technicolor
Paramount / Pine–Thomas

An ex-GI has various adventures with a Chinese orphan and a golden idol.
And a plot that seems to make itself up as they go along. Corn-fed hokum.

w Winston Miller *d* Lewis R. Foster *ph* Lionel Lindon *m* Lucien Cailliet

Ronald Reagan, Rhonda Fleming, Nigel Bruce, Marvin Miller, Lowell Gilmore

The Honkers*
US 1971 102m De Luxe
UA / Levy–Gardner–Laven

An ageing rodeo rider has trouble with his wife.
Quiet, carefully accomplished study of a man and his milieu.

w Steve Ihnat, Stephen Lodge *d* Steve Ihnat *ph* John Crabe *m* Jimmie Haskell

James Coburn, Lois Nettleton, Slim Pickens, Richard Anderson

Honky Tonk
US 1929 80m bw

A nightclub entertainer sacrifices everything for her daughter's education. Primitive cross between *Applause* and *Imitation of Life*, with spirited moments from Sophie Tucker the only plus; also Lila Lee, Audrey Ferris, George Duryea, Mahlon Hamilton. Written by C. Graham Baker and Jack Yellen; directed by Lloyd Bacon; for Warner.

'Every kiss a thrill!'
Honky Tonk*
US 1941 104m bw
MGM (Pandro S. Berman)

A western con man meets his match in the daughter of a fake judge.
Generally amusing comedy melodrama that ambles along between two styles but leaves a pleasant after-effect.

w Marguerite Roberts, John Sandford *d* Jack Conway *ph* Harold Rosson *m* Franz Waxman

Clark Gable, Lana Turner, Frank Morgan, Claire Trevor, Marjorie Main, Albert Dekker, Henry O'Neill, Chill Wills, Betty Blythe
'A lively, lusty western that makes you wish you had been there.'—*Variety*

HONKY TONK.   Lana Turner and Clark Gable were two more stars at the sound of whose names a queue would form.

Honky Tonk Freeway

US 1981   107m   Technicolor
EMI / Kendon / HTF Company (Don Boyd, Howard W. Koch Jnr)

The mayor of a small Florida resort town has it painted pink to attract tourists . . . but too many of the wrong kind come in.
Zany farce, rather like *It's a Mad Mad Mad Mad World* without a proper hook to the story. Not an audience-pleaser, and very expensive.

w Edward Clinton d John Schlesinger
ph John Bailey m George Martin, Elmer Bernstein

William Devane, Beau Bridges, Teri Garr, Beverly D'Angelo, Hume Cronyn, Jessica Tandy, Howard Hesseman, Geraldine Page, George Dzundza

'A shambles, and a more convincing one than the half-hearted affair which brings it to a close.'—*Richard Combs, MFB*

'A film for "now" which seems almost endearingly bereft of any real ideas about the messed-up contemporary world it inhabits.'—*Guardian*

● *Video: Thorn EMI*

Honkytonk Man

US 1982   122m   Technicolor
Warner / Malpaso (Clint Eastwood)

In the thirties, an ageing and alcoholic country singer turns to his rural family for help.
Yet another occasion when the star should have asked for help instead of doing all the chores himself. Not much real entertainment here, just a very few moments that amuse.

w Clancy Carlile, from his novel d Clint Eastwood ph Bruce Surtees m Steve Dorff pd Edward Carfagno

Clint Eastwood, Kyle Eastwood, John McIntire, Verna Bloom, Alexa Kenin, Matt Clark

Honolulu

US 1938   83m   bw
MGM (Jack Cummings)

A movie star is mistaken for his double.
Sloppy comedy with a few musical numbers.

w Herbert Fields, Frank Partos d Edward Buzzell ph Ray June m Franz Waxman

Robert Young, Eleanor Powell, George Burns, Gracie Allen, Rita Johnson, Ruth Hussey, Clarence Kolb, Sig Rumann, Eddie Anderson

'Fairly amusing comedy for top brackets in duals.'—*Variety*

'The whole thing seems to have been thrown together so that Eleanor Powell can do a frenetic hula.'—*New Yorker, 1977*

Honor Among Lovers

US 1931   76m   bw

A young businessman complicates his life when he decides to marry his secretary. Smart comedy unfolding a complex plot, but slow by modern standards. Claudette Colbert, Fredric March, Monroe Owsley, Charlie Ruggles, Ginger Rogers. Written by Austin Parker and Gertrude Purcell; directed by Dorothy Arzner; for Paramount. 'A sweet piece of work hiding behind a faulty title.'—*Variety*

Honor of the Family

US 1931   66m   bw

The young mistress of an aged Budapest resident is after his money. Tiresome comedy drama. Bebe Daniels, Warren William, Frederick Kerr, Alan Mowbray, Blanche Friderici. Written from a play by Emil Fabre and a story by Balzac; directed by Lloyd Bacon; for First National.

The Honorary Consul

GB 1983   104m   Movielab
World Film Services (Norma Heyman)
US title: *Beyond the Limit*

In northern Argentina, a doctor is drawn into the kidnapping by activists of a drunken British consul.
Self-parodic visit to Greeneland, with everybody drunk or depressed. Bouts of explicit sex don't help much, if at all.

w Christopher Hampton, *novel* Graham Greene d John MacKenzie ph Phil Meheux m Stanley Myers pd Allan Cameron

Michael Caine, Richard Gere, Bob Hoskins, Elpidia Carrillo, Joaquim de Almeida

'Some very old friends: exhausted passion, moral betrayal and relics of religious faith.'—*Sight and Sound*

'All it takes is the character to decide he is a burnt-out case, sleeping with all women but capable of loving none, for all the familiar icons to be ranged in battle array.'—*Tom Milne, MFB*

An Honourable Murder*

GB 1959   70m   bw
Danziger

Boardroom executives scheme to be rid of their chairman.
Oddball, interesting attempt to play *Julius Caesar* in modern dress. Not entirely successful, but full marks for trying.

w Brian Clemens, Eldon Howard d Godfrey Grayson

Norman Wooland, Margaretta Scott, Lisa Daniely, Douglas Wilmer, Philip Saville, John Longden

The Hoodlum

US 1951 63m bw

A convict is paroled but continues his criminal career. Toughish crime support with interesting moments. Lawrence Tierney, Liza Golm, Edward Tierney, Allene Roberts. Written by Sam Neumann and Nat Tanchuck; directed by Max Nosseck; for Jack Schwarz Productions.

Hoodlum Empire

US 1952 98m bw
Republic (Joseph Kane)

A Congressional committee investigates a racketeer.
Moderate semi-documentary potboiler inspired by the Kefauver investigations.
w Bruce Manning, Bob Considine d Joseph Kane ph Reggie Lanning m Nathan Scott

Brian Donlevy, Forrest Tucker, Claire Trevor, Vera Ralston, Luther Adler, John Russell, Gene Lockhart, Grant Withers, Taylor Holmes

'Familiar gangster melodramatics and repentances, played out in a rigmarole of flashbacks.'—MFB

The Hoodlum Priest*

US 1961 100m bw
UA / Don Murray–Walter Wood

A Jesuit teacher tries to help young criminals, especially a condemned murderer.
Moderately well done, very depressing and downbeat chunk of social conscience based on the life of Charles Dismas Clark.
w Don Mankiewicz, Joseph Landon d Irvin Kershner ph Haskell Wexler m Richard Markowitz

Don Murray, Keir Dullea, Larry Gates, Cindi Wood, Logan Ramsey

The Hoodlum Saint

US 1946 93m bw
MGM (Cliff Reid)

A cynical newspaperman turns to religion and succours thieves.
Hard-boiled sentimentality, a downright peculiar and doleful comedy drama in deflated post-war mood.
w Frank Wead, James Hill d Norman Taurog ph Ray June m Nathaniel Shilkret

William Powell, Esther Williams, Angela Lansbury, James Gleason, Lewis Stone, Rags Ragland, Frank McHugh, Slim Summerville, Roman Bohnen, Louis Jean Heydt, Charles Arnt, Charles Trowbridge, Henry O'Neill

The Hook

US 1962 98m bw Panavision
MGM / Perlberg–Seaton

Three GIs escaping from Korea are ordered to execute a prisoner but cannot bring themselves to do it.
Predictable, claustrophobic drama which becomes a slick exercise in morality.
w Henry Denker, novel The Hameçon by Vahe Katcha d George Seaton ph Joe Ruttenberg

Kirk Douglas, Robert Walker, Nick Adams, Nehemiah Persoff

Hook Line and Sinker

US 1930 72m bw

Two insurance agents run a derelict hotel.
Feeble comedy vehicle. Bert Wheeler, Robert Woolsey, Hugh Herbert, Dorothy Lee, Jobyna Howland, Ralf Harolde. Written by Tim Whelan, Ralph Spence; directed by Eddie Cline; for RKO. 'Will tickle most in those spots where the price is least.'—Variety

Hook, Line and Sinker

US 1968 92m Technicolor
Columbia / Jerry Lewis

A salesman who thinks he is dying goes on a spending spree; when he learns the truth, he has to disappear because of his huge debts.
Miserable comedy with frantic slapstick interludes. The plot might have served Preston Sturges.
w Rod Amateau d George Marshall ph W. Wallace Kelley m Dick Stabile

Jerry Lewis, Peter Lawford, Anne Francis, Pedro Gonzales Gonzales

Hooper*

US 1978 99m Metrocolor
Warner / Burt Reynolds, Lawrence Gordon (Hank Moonjean)

An ageing stunt man decides on one last sensational stunt before retiring.
There are some agreeably striking moments, but you can't make a movie out of stunts and loud camaraderie. This one palls half way through.
w Thomas Rickman, Bill Kerby d Hal Needham ph Bobby Byrne m Bill Justis

Burt Reynolds, Sally Field, Brian Keith, Jan-Michael Vincent, John Marley, Robert Klein, James Best, Adam West

'Burt Reynolds's annual Kleenex of a movie: something to use and throw away without any thought beyond a certain gratitude for the convenience of the thing.'—Richard Schickel, Time

● Video: Warner

'Clara Bow . . . red-headed warm-blooded dynamite . . . again releases the torrent of her genius in the most colorful performance of her life.'

Hoopla

US 1933 85m bw

A hardboiled carnival dancer agrees to seduce the son of the show's manager, but ends by marrying him. Strained melodrama with the star, in her last film, at the end of her tether. Clara Bow, Richard Cromwell, Preston Foster, Herbert Mundin, James Gleason, Minna Gombell, Roger Imhof. Written by Bradley King and J. M. March, from the play The Barker by Kenyon Nicholson; directed by Frank Lloyd; for Fox. 'Miss Bow seems ripe to come back strongly.'—Variety

Hooray for Love

US 1935 75m bw

A rich college boy plays angel to a musical comedy. Thin pot-pourri of familiar elements. Ann Sothern, Gene Raymond, Bill Robinson, Thurston Hall, Pert Kelton, Lionel Stander, Fats Waller. Written by Lawrence Hazard, Ray Harris; directed by Walter Lang; for RKO. 'Trouble is entirely traceable to its terribly lethargic tempo and lack of any real production numbers.'—Variety

The Hoosegow**

US 1929 20m bw

Stan and Ollie, in prison, contrive to fell a tree on the cook's tent and to smother the governor in boiled rice. Splendid slapstick leading up to one of their best tit-for-tat routines. Laurel and Hardy, James Finlayson, Tiny Sandford. Written by Leo McCarey and H. M. Walker; directed by James Parrott; for Hal Roach.

Hoosier Schoolboy

US 1937 62m bw

A rural boy defends his drunken father, shell-shocked in the war. Simple tale for rural audiences. Mickey Rooney, Anne Nagel, Frank Shields, Edward Pawley. Written by Robert Lee Johnson from the novel by Edward Eggleston; directed by William Nigh; for Ken Goldsmith / Monogram. 'A compelling film which word of mouth might turn into a sleeper.'—Variety

Hoots Mon*

GB 1939 77m bw

A cockney comedian starts a popularity contest with a female impressionist. Tolerable comedy whose value is that it preserves, albeit in cleaned-up form, portions of Max Miller's variety act. Florence Desmond isn't bad either. With Hal Walters, Davina Craig, Garry Marsh. Written by Roy William Neill, Jack Henley and John Dighton; directed by Roy William Neill; for Warner.

Hopalong Cassidy

Cassidy, a creation of Clarence E. Mulford, was a fictitious gentleman cowboy who oddly enough wore black; 26 books about him were published between 1912 and 1956 when Mulford died. 66 films were made starring William Boyd as Hoppy, with either George Gabby Hayes or Andy Clyde as comic sidekick: Harry Sherman produced them, first for Paramount and then for UA, and they were later edited down for TV, in which medium Boyd became a folk hero and eventually made a further series. The films were easy-going, slow-moving second features which always pointed an admirable moral for children; their main directors were Howard Bretherton, Nate Watt, Lesley Selander and George Archainbaud.

1935: HOPALONG CASSIDY, THE EAGLE'S BROOD, BAR 20 RIDES AGAIN

1936: CALL OF THE PRAIRIE, THREE
ON THE TRAIL, HEART OF THE WEST,
HOPALONG CASSIDY RETURNS, TRAIL
DUST
1937: BORDERLAND, HILLS OF OLD
WYOMING, NORTH OF THE RIO
GRANDE, RUSTLERS' VALLEY,
HOPALONG RIDES AGAIN, TEXAS
TRAIL
1938: HEART OF ARIZONA, BAR 20
JUSTICE, PRIDE OF THE WEST, IN OLD
MEXICO, SUNSET TRAIL, THE
FRONTIERSMAN, PARTNERS OF THE
PLAINS, CASSIDY OF BAR 20
1939: RANGE WAR, LAW OF THE
PAMPAS, SILVER ON THE SAGE,
RENEGADE TRAIL
1940: SANTA FE MARSHAL, THE
SHOWDOWN, HIDDEN GOLD,
STAGECOACH WAR, THREE MEN
FROM TEXAS
1941: DOOMED CARAVAN, IN OLD
COLORADO, BORDER VIGILANTES,
PIRATES ON HORSEBACK, WIDE OPEN
TOWN, OUTLAWS OF THE DESERT,
RIDERS OF THE TIMBERLINE,
SECRETS OF THE WASTELAND, STICK
TO YOUR GUNS, TWILIGHT ON THE
TRAIL
1942: UNDERCOVER MAN
1943: COLT COMRADES, BAR 20, LOST
CANYON, HOPPY SERVES A WRIT,
BORDER PATROL, THE LEATHER
BURNERS, FALSE COLOURS, RIDERS
OF THE DEADLINE
1944: MYSTERY MAN, FORTY THIEVES,
TEXAS MASQUERADE, LUMBERJACK
1946: THE DEVIL'S PLAYGROUND
1947: FOOL'S GOLD, HOPPY'S
HOLIDAY, MARAUDERS,
UNEXPECTED GUEST, DANGEROUS
VENTURE
1948: SINISTER JOURNEY, SILENT
CONFLICT, STRANGE GAMBLE,
BORROWED TROUBLE, THE DEAD
DON'T DREAM, FALSE PARADISE

Hopscotch°
US 1980 104m Movielab
Avco / Edie and Ely Landau (Otto
    Plaschkes)

An ex-CIA man writes a revealing book and
foils the consequent attempts on his life.
Genial but patchy spy comedy caper; a filler
for all concerned.

w Brian Garfield, Bryan Forbes, from
Garfield's novel d Ronald Neame ph Arthur
Ibbetson m Ian Fraser

Walter Matthau, Glenda Jackson, Ned Beatty,
Sam Waterston, Herbert Lom, George Baker

● Video: Thorn EMI

Horizons West
US 1952 81m Technicolor
U-I (Albert J. Cohen)

After the Civil War, a rancher builds an
empire on greed and ruthlessness, and his
brother has to bring him to trial.
Rather lugubrious western with the usual
quota of effective action scenes.

w Louis Stevens d Budd Boetticher
ph Charles P. Boyle md Joseph Gershenson
Rock Hudson, Robert Ryan, Julia Adams,
John McIntire, Raymond Burr, Dennis
Weaver, Judith Braun

The Horizontal Lieutenant
US 1962 90m Metrocolor
    Cinemascope
MGM / Euterpe (Joe Pasternak)

World War II Hawaii; an amorous intelligence
officer accidentally captures a Japanese
guerrilla.
Very moderate army farce of no great skill or
memorability.

w George Wells d Richard Thorpe
ph Robert Bronner m George Stoll
Jim Hutton, Paula Prentiss, Jim Backus,
Miyoshi Umeki, Jack Carter

The Horn Blows at Midnight°
US 1945 80m bw
Warner (Mark Hellinger)

An angel is sent to earth to destroy the planet
with Gabriel's horn.
Wacky comedy inspired by Here Comes Mr
Jordan, but on a broader slapstick level; much
better than its star always pretended.

w Sam Hellman, James V. Kern d Raoul
Walsh ph Sid Hickox m Franz Waxman

Jack Benny, Alexis Smith, Dolores Moran,
Allyn Joslyn, Guy Kibbee, Reginald Gardiner,
Franklin Pangborn, John Alexander, Margaret
Dumont

Hornet's Nest
US 1969 109m De Luxe
UA / Triangle (Stanley S. Kanter)

In World War II Italy, a wounded US army
demolitions expert is nursed back to health by
child partisans, who help him destroy a
German-held dam.
Overlong war exploits with the children used
as a tiresome gimmick.

w S. S. Schweitzer d Phil Karlson ph Gabor
Pogani m Ennio Morricone
Rock Hudson, Sergio Fantoni, Sylva Koscina,
Jacques Sernas

Horror Express
Spain / GB 1972 90m Technicolor

In 1906 China a fossilized missing link comes
to violent life on a train. Rather nasty horror
film which manages to keep one watching
despite some obvious fakery. Peter Cushing,
Christopher Lee, Telly Savalas, Jorge Rigaud.
Written by Arnaud D'Usseau and Julian
Halevy; directed by Eugenio Martin; for
Granada Madrid / Benmar. (Spanish title:
Pánico en el Transiberiano.)

Horror Island
US 1941 60m bw

Various people travel to an island where
buried treasure might be hidden. Feeble little
mystery with very little interest in who done
what to whom. Dick Foran, Leo Carrillo,

Peggy Moran, Fuzzy Knight, John Eldredge,
Walter Catlett, Hobart Cavanaugh. Written by
Maurice Tombragel and Victor McLeod;
directed by George Waggner; for Universal.

The Horror of Frankenstein
GB 1970 95m Technicolor

Victor Frankenstein is not above murdering
his acquaintances for the sake of his
experiments in bringing the dead back to life.
Ill-advised attempt to remake the original
story as a black comedy, with Frankenstein
frankly villainous from the start. The last in
the Hammer series. Ralph Bates, Kate
O'Mara, Graham James, Veronica Carlson,
Bernard Archard, Dennis Price, Joan Rice,
Dave Prowse. Written and directed by Jimmy
Sangster; for Hammer / EMI.

● Video: Thorn EMI

Horrors of the Black Museum
GB 1959 81m Eastmancolor
    Cinemascope

A crime writer is fascinated by murder, and
works out his own plots by practice
beforehand. Crude shocker. Michael Gough,
Graham Curnow, Shirley Ann Field, Geoffrey
Keen. Written by Aben Kandel and Herman
Cohen; directed by Arthur Crabtree; for
Herman Cohen.

'A scandalous record of low Marx at
    college—or life among the thirsty co-
    eds!'

Horse Feathers****
US 1932 69m bw
Paramount (Herman J. Mankiewicz)

A college needs to win at football, and its
corrupt new president knows just how to do it.
Possibly the Marxes' wildest yet most
streamlined kaleidoscope of high jinks and
irreverence, with at least one bright gag or line
to the minute and lively musical interludes to
boot. A classic of zany comedy.

w Bert Kalmar, Harry Ruby, S. J. Perelman,
Will B. Johnstone d Norman Z. McLeod
ph Ray June m / ly Bert Kalmar, Harry Ruby
Groucho, Chico, Harpo, Zeppo, Thelma
Todd, Robert Greig

GROUCHO: 'You have the brain of a four-
year-old child, and I'll bet he was glad to get
rid of it.'
CHICO: 'There's a man outside with a big
black moustache.'
GROUCHO: 'Tell him I've got one.'
GROUCHO (to Zeppo): 'You're a disgrace to
our family name of Wagstaff, if such a thing is
possible.'
GROUCHO: 'For years before my son was
            born
    I used to yell from night till
            morn
    Whatever it is—I'm against it!
    And I've been yelling since I first
            commenced it—I'm against it!'

'The current Marx comedy is the funniest talkie since the last Marx comedy, and the record it establishes is not likely to be disturbed until the next Marx comedy comes along. As for comparisons, I was too busy having a good time to make any.'—*Philip K. Scheuer*

The Horse in the Grey Flannel Suit
US 1969   112m   Technicolor

A teenager's horse beomes the central figure in an advertising campaign for a stomach pill. Interminable kiddie movie which in its virtual absence of plot or excitement is likely to bore kiddies to death. Dean Jones, Fred Clark, Diane Baker, Lloyd Bochner, Morey Amsterdam. Written by Louis Pelletier, from the novel *The Year of the Horse* by Eric Hatch; directed by Norman Tokar; for Walt Disney.

The Horse Soldiers*
US 1959   119m   De Luxe
UA / Mirisch (John Lee Mahin, Martin Rackin)

In 1863 a Union cavalry officer is sent three hundred miles into Confederate territory to demolish a railroad junction.
Typically sprawling John Ford cavalry western with not too many high spots and more sombre ingredients than usual.
w John Lee Mahin, Martin Rackin *d* John Ford *ph* William Clothier *m* David Buttolph

John Wayne, William Holden, Constance Towers, Hoot Gibson

The Horse without a Head**
GB 1963   89m   Technicolor
Walt Disney (Hugh Attwooll)

Stolen money is hidden in an old toy horse, and crooks trying to get it back clash with police and children.
Excellent children's adventure with scenes on trains and in a toy factory.
w T. E. B. Clarke *d* Don Chaffey *ph* Paul Beeson *m* Eric Rogers

Leo McKern, Jean-Pierre Aumont, Herbert Lom, Pamela Franklin, Vincent Winter

The Horsemen
US 1970   109m   colour
Super Panavision
Columbia / John Frankenheimer–Edward Lewis

An Afghan tribesman is determined to rival his father at horsemanship.
Rather tedious variant on *Taras Bulba*; plenty of action but not much characterization, or taste, or interest.
w Dalton Trumbo, *novel* Joseph Kessel *d* John Frankenheimer *ph* Claude Renoir *m* Georges Delerue

Omar Sharif, Jack Palance, Leigh Taylor-Young, Peter Jeffrey, Eric Pohlmann, Despo, David De Keyser

The Horse's Mouth*
GB 1958   93m   Technicolor
UA / Knightsbridge (John Bryan)

An obsessive painter is a liability to his friends.
Thin but fitfully amusing light study of a social outcast, with a background of London river and streets. Too slight for real success.
w Alec Guinness, *novel* Joyce Cary *d* Ronald Neame *ph* Arthur Ibbetson *m* K. V. Jones from Prokofiev *paintings* John Bratby

Alec Guinness, Kay Walsh, Renée Houston, Robert Coote, Arthur Macrae, Michael Gough, Ernest Thesiger

AAN: Alec Guinness (as writer)

The Hospital**
US 1971   101m   De Luxe   Panavision
UA / Simcha (Howard Gottfried)

A city hospital is beset by weird mishaps, and it transpires that a killer is on the loose.
Black comedy with the emphasis on sex and medical ethics; in the same genre as *M*A*S*H*, and very funny if you can take it.
w Paddy Chayevsky *d* Arthur Hiller *ph* Victor Kemper *m* Morris Surdin

George C. Scott, Diana Rigg, Barnard Hughes, Nancy Marchand, Richard Dysart

AA: Paddy Chayevsky
AAN: George C. Scott

The Hostage
GB 1956   86m   bw

A South American president condemns a revolutionary to death; in London, sympathizers kidnap the president's daughter. Tolerable support. Ron Randell, Mary Parker, Carl Jaffe, Margaret Diamond, Cyril Luckham. Written by Alfred Shaughnessy; directed by Harold Huth; for Westridge / Eros.

'They're blasting the Nazis—from inside!'
Hostages
US 1943   88m   bw
Paramount (Sol C. Siegel)

In occupied Prague, the Nazis seize a variety of hostages and threaten them with death as a reprisal for underground activities.
Modest morale-builder, unfortunately padded out with melodramatics and overacting.
w Lester Cole, Frank Butler, *novel* Stefan Heym *d* Frank Tuttle *ph* Victor Milner *m* Victor Young

Luise Rainer, Paul Lukas, William Bendix, Oscar Homolka, Arturo de Cordova, Katina Paxinou, Roland Varno

Hostile Guns
US 1967   91m   Techniscope

A marshal has to deliver four dangerous convicts to the penitentiary. Rather crude addition to the A. C. Lyles series distinguished only by nostalgic casting. George Montgomery, Tab Hunter, Yvonne de Carlo, Brian Donlevy, Fuzzy Knight, John Russell, Leo Gordon, Robert Emhardt, Richard Arlen. Written by Steve Fisher and Sloan Nibley; directed by R. G. Springsteen; for A. C. Lyles / Paramount.

Hostile Witness
GB 1968   101m   De Luxe
UA / Caralan / Dador (David E. Rose)

A barrister suffers a nervous breakdown after the death of his daughter and finds himself accused of murder.
Complex courtroom thriller, filmed in a flatly boring way with stagey sets and performances. The plot is the only interest.
w Jack Roffey, from his play *d* Ray Milland *ph* Gerry Gibbs

Ray Milland, Sylvia Sims, Felix Aylmer, Raymond Huntley, Geoffrey Lumsden, Norman Barrs, Percy Marmont, Ewan Roberts

'If you'd hit me and given me orders on our wedding night, I would have kissed your hand!'
Hot Blood
US 1955   85m   Technicolor Cinemascope
Columbia (Howard Welsch)

A dying gypsy king wants his young brother to get married and succeed him.
What promises to be a boring musical proves to be a boring melodrama. Artificial Romany hokum.
w Jesse Lasky Jnr *d* Nicholas Ray *ph* Ray June *m* Les Baxter

Cornel Wilde, Jane Russell, Joseph Calleia, Helen Westcott, Mikhail Rasumny
'Be there when Jane Russell shakes her tambourines!'—*publicity*

Hot Enough for June
GB 1963   98m   Eastmancolor
Rank (Betty E. Box)
US title: *Agent 8¾*

A penniless writer is sent to Czechoslovakia on a goodwill mission and finds himself being used as a spy.
Very moderate spoof, neither very funny nor very thrilling.
w Lukas Heller, *novel* The Night before Wenceslas by Lionel Davidson *d* Ralph Thomas *ph* Ernest Steward *m* Angelo Lavagnino

Dirk Bogarde, Sylva Koscina, Robert Morley, Leo McKern, John Le Mesurier

Hot Millions*
US 1968   106m   colour
MGM / Mildred Freed Alberg

A confidence trickster makes a fortune out of fictitious companies.
Elaborate, talky, overlong comedy with irresistible star performances.
w Ira Wallach, Peter Ustinov *d* Eric Till

Peter Ustinov, Maggie Smith, Bob Newhart, Karl Malden, Robert Morley, Cesar Romero

AAN: Ira Wallach, Peter Ustinov (script)

Hot Pepper
US 1933   76m   bw
Fox

Ex-Marines Flagg and Quirt become
bootleggers and quarrel over a fiery South
American entertainer.
Fourth and last in the comedy-melodrama
series stemming from *What Price Glory?* Mild,
stereotyped entertainment.
w Barry Connors, Philip Klein, Dudley
Nichols d John G. Blystone ph Charles G.
Clarke

Edmund Lowe, Victor McLaglen, Lupe Velez,
El Brendel, Lillian Bond

The Hot Rock*
US 1972   105m   De Luxe   Panavision
TCF (Hal Landers, Bobby Roberts)
GB title: *How to Steal a Diamond in Four
Uneasy Lessons*

Four crooks plan to rob the Brooklyn Museum
of a priceless diamond.
Enjoyable variation on the caper theme, with
relaxed comic performances and highly skilled
technical back-up. It's refreshing to come
across a film which hits its targets so precisely.
w *William Goldman, novel* Donald E.
Westlake d *Peter Yates* ph Ed Brown
m Quincy Jones

Robert Redford, George Segal, Zero Mostel,
Paul Sand, Ron Leibman, Moses Gunn,
William Redfield
'A funny, fast-paced, inventive and infinitely
clever crime comedy, almost as if *The French
Connection* had been remade as a piece of
urban humour.'—*Michael Korda*
● *Video: CBS / Fox*

'Her lips offered what her heart denied!'
Hot Saturday
US 1932   73m   bw

Malicious gossip in a small town causes a girl
to lose her job. Small town, small potatoes:
interesting chiefly for its two budding male
stars. Nancy Carroll, Cary Grant, Randolph
Scott, Edward Woods, Lillian Bond, Jane
Darwell, William Collier Snr. Written by
Seton I. Miller from the novel by Harvey
Ferguson; directed by William A. Seiter; for
Paramount. 'Fairly agreeable as
entertainment, but will not get preferred
playing time.'—*Variety*

Hot Spell*
US 1958   86m   bw   Vistavision
Paramount / Hal Wallis

In a small southern town, a husband seeks to
leave his wife and family for a 20-year-old girl.
Overwrought domestic drama slipping
perilously close to farce at times, but a good
theatrical vehicle for its stars.
w James Poe, *play* Next of Kin by Lonnie
Coleman d Daniel Mann ph Loyal Griggs
m Alex North

Anthony Quinn, Shirley Booth, Shirley
Maclaine, Earl Holliman, Eileen Heckart

Hot Stuff
US 1979   91m   Metrocolor
Columbia / Rastar / Mort Engleberg

Members of a Burglary Task Force need
convictions, so they set up fences in order to
lure criminals, and are embarrassed by the
results.
Slightly unusual but rather frantically
assembled comedy which wears out its
welcome long before the end.
w Michael Kane, Donald E. Westlake d Dom
DeLuise ph James Pergola m Patrick
Williams

Dom DeLuise, Suzanne Pleshette, Ossie
Davis, Jerry Reed, Luis Avalos, Marc
Lawrence
'Heavy farce in which a bright comedy is
struggling to escape.'—*Tom Milne, MFB*

Hot Summer Night*
US 1957   85m   bw
MGM (Morton S. Fine)

A foolhardy reporter determines on an
interview with a notorious outlaw, and has to
be rescued.
Interesting but disappointing low-budget
experiment.
w Morton S. Fine, David Friedkin d David
Friedkin ph Harold S. Marcorati m André
Previn

Leslie Nielsen, Colleen Miller, Edward
Andrews, Jay C. Flippen, James Best, Paul
Richards, Robert Wilke, Claude Akins

Hot Water*
US 1924   50m approx (24 fps)   bw
silent

A young husband has trouble with a turkey, a
new car and his in-laws. Casually structured
star comedy with brilliant sequences. *Harold
Lloyd*, Jobyna Ralston, Josephine Crowell.
Written by Harold Lloyd and Sam Taylor;
directed by Fred Newmeyer and Sam Taylor;
for Harold Lloyd.

Hotel*
US 1967   124m   Technicolor
Warner (Wendell Mayes)

Guests at a luxurious New Orleans hotel have
various problems.
Old-fashioned omnibus drama from a
bestseller, quite brightly done.
w Wendell Mayes, *novel* Arthur Hailey
d Richard Quine ph Charles Lang m Johnny
Keating

Rod Taylor, Catherine Spaak, Karl Malden,
Melvyn Douglas, Merle Oberon, Richard
Conte, Michael Rennie, Kevin McCarthy,
Alfred Ryder

Hotel Berlin*
US 1945   98m   bw
Warner (Louis F. Edelman)

Various lives intertwine in a Berlin hotel
towards the end of the war.
After five years of total war this view of life on
the other side can hardly fail to be

unconvincing, but the actors gleefully seize on
moments of melodrama.
w Thomas Job, *novel* Vicki Baum d Peter
Godfrey ph Carl Guthrie m Franz Waxman

Raymond Massey, Peter Lorre, Faye
Emerson, Helmut Dantine, Andrea King,
Alan Hale, George Coulouris, Henry Daniell,
Helene Thimig, Kurt Kreuger, Steve Geray,
Frank Reicher
'The most heavily routine of Warners'
political melodramas, stuffed with sympathetic
veterans.'—*James Agee*

Hotel du Nord**
France 1938   110m   bw
Sedif / Imperial

People with problems congregate at a small
hotel.
Melancholy, studio-confined character drama
which has its adherents but technically seemed
a throwback to earlier standards. The acting
rescues it.

Annabella, *Louis Jouvet*, Jean-Pierre
Aumont, *Arletty*, Jeanne Marken, Bernard
Blier
w Henri Jeanson, Eugene Dabit d Marcel
Carné ph Armand Thirard m Maurice
Jaubert
'An outstander in this country and possesses
good chance abroad.'—*Variety (Paris)*

Hotel for Women
US 1939   83m   bw
TCF (Raymond Griffith)

Young city gold diggers are encouraged by a
matron.
Slight comedy drama notable for the acting
debut of hostess Elsa Maxwell.
w Katherine Scola, Darrell Ware d Gregory
Ratoff ph Peverell Marley m David Buttolph

Elsa Maxwell, Linda Darnell, Ann Sothern,
James Ellison, John Halliday, Lynn Bari, Alan
Dinehart
'Synthetic Cinderella story . . . fluffed up
with a generous display of latest fashions.'—
Variety

Hotel Haywire
US 1937   66m   bw
Paramount (Harold Hurley)

An astrologer makes eyes at a dentist's wife,
and causes much confusion in a hotel.
Frantic farce which might have been funnier if
it had stuck to the original script and cast (it
was intended for Burns and Allen).
w Preston Sturges (before studio revision)
d George Archainbaud ph Henry Sharp

Leo Carrillo, Lynne Overman, Mary Carlisle,
Benny Baker, Spring Byington, George
Barbier, Porter Hall, Lucien Littlefield, John
Patterson
'Broad comedy applied with sufficient skill
and effect to make the journey on the dual
route fairly safe.'—*Variety*

891-50

HOTEL. Vaguely derived from *Grand Hotel*, this was also the precursor of a TV series of the eighties. Those trapped in the lift include Michael Rennie and Karl Malden.

'Flaming love drama of the war-torn Balkans!'

'Her beauty sent men marching to their death with a smile!'

Hotel Imperial

US 1939 78m bw
Paramount

Balkans, 1916: a Polish dancer suspects a Hungarian officer of being responsible for her sister's death.

Dim romantic melodrama with espionage trimmings.

w Gilbert Gabriel, Robert Thoeren, *play* Lajos Biro *d* Robert Florey *ph* William Mellor *md* Boris Morros

Ray Milland, Isa Miranda, Reginald Owen, Gene Lockhart, J. Carrol Naish, Curt Bois, Henry Victor, Albert Dekker

'Nothing much to be done about this one . . . a weak sister, dated and inconclusive . . . never seems to generate any interest.'— *Variety*

'A very competent rehash . . . for the unexacting the picture has its moments.'— *Graham Greene*

† Previously made in 1926 by Erich Pommer, with Pola Negri. This version was originally announced in 1936 as *I Loved a Soldier*, to star Marlene Dietrich (or Margaret Sullavan) and Charles Boyer.

The Hotel New Hampshire

US 1984 108m Technicolor
Orion / Woodfall (Neil Hartley, Pieter Kroonenburg, David Patterson)

A schoolmaster and his family are obsessed by the fantasy of living in a hotel, and this fantasy is performed with variations.

A parable of life in the manner of Thornton Wilder's *The Skin of Our Teeth*, and sometimes even more obscure, but generally quite entertaining along the way.

w,d Tony Richardson, *novel* John Irving *ph* David Watkin *m* Jacques Offenbach *pd* Jocelyn Herbert *ed* Robert K. Lambert

Rob Lowe, Jodie Foster, Paul McCrane, Beau Bridges, Nastassja Kinski, Wallace Shawn, Wilford Brimley

Hotel Paradiso*

US 1966 99m Metrocolor Panavision
MGM (Peter Glenville)

Various romantic affairs come to a head one evening at a seedy hotel.

A famous boulevard farce seems jellied in aspic in this good-looking but very flatly handled film version, in which famous artists are left to caper about on an unsuitable wide screen with no help from the director.

w Peter Glenville, Jean-Claude Carrière, *play* Georges Feydeau *d* Peter Glenville *ph* Henri Decaë *m* Laurence Rosenthal *pd* François de Lamothe

Alec Guinness, Gina Lollobrigida, Robert Morley, Peggy Mount, Douglas Byng, Akim Tamiroff, Robertson Hare

Hotel Reserve
GB 1944 89m bw
RKO (Victor Hanbury)

An Austrian refugee in the south of France is asked by the police to track down a spy among his fellow hotel guests.
Slow, obvious and poorly made suspenser from a good novel.

w John Davenport, novel Epitaph for a Spy by Eric Ambler d Victor Hanbury, Lance Comfort, Max Greene ph Max Greene

James Mason, Lucie Mannheim, Raymond Lovell, Julien Mitchell, Martin Miller, Herbert Lom, Frederick Valk, Valentine Dyall

Hotel Sahara*
GB 1951 96m bw
GFD / Tower (George H. Brown)

In North Africa during World War II, a small hotel changes its loyalties to suit its occupiers.
Overstretched, studio-bound, fitfully amusing comedy.

w George H. Brown, Patrick Kirwan d Ken Annakin ph David Harcourt m Benjamin Franklin

Peter Ustinov, Yvonne de Carlo, David Tomlinson, Roland Culver, Albert Lieven, Bill Owen, Sidney Tafler, Ferdy Mayne

'Cheerful, uncomplicated empty stuff . . . no more subtle than a music hall sketch.'— Richard Mallett, Punch

The Hottentot
US 1929 77m bw

A horse lover is forced to masquerade as a champion jockey. Early talkie version of a well-worn theme which had previously appeared as a silent in 1923 with Douglas MacLean; it later turned up as a Joe E. Brown vehicle and in 1938 became Going Places, a Dick Powell musical. The 1929 version also starred Patsy Ruth Miller and Douglas Gerrard; written by Harvey Thew, from the play by Victor Mapes and Willie Collier; directed by Roy del Ruth; for Warner.

Houdini*
US 1953 106m Technicolor
Paramount (George Pal)

In the 1890s a fairground magician shows a passionate talent for escapology and finally kills himself by undertaking increasingly impossible tricks.
Superficial biopic with more attention to romance than to interesting detail. Some zest in the playing is killed by claustrophobic studio sets.

w Philip Yordan d George Marshall ph Ernest Laszlo m Roy Webb

Tony Curtis, Janet Leigh, Torin Thatcher, Sig Rumann, Angela Clarke

The Hound Dog Man
US 1959 87m colour Cinemascope
TCF / Company of Artists (Jerry Wald)

An irresponsible country boy gets his come-uppance.

Mild, competent backwoods comedy drama introducing a teenage rave.

w Fred Gipson, Winston Miller d Don Siegel ph Charles G. Clarke m Cyril Mockridge

Fabian, Stuart Whitman, Carol Lynley, Arthur O'Connell, Betty Field, Royal Dano, Jane Darwell, Edgar Buchanan, Claude Akins

The Hound of the Baskervilles**
US 1939 80m bw
(TCF) Gene Markey

Sherlock Holmes solves the mystery of a supernatural hound threatening the life of a Dartmoor baronet.
Basil Rathbone's first appearance as Sherlock Holmes is in a painstaking studio production which achieves good atmosphere and preserves the flavour if not the letter of the book but is let down by a curious lack of pace.

w Ernest Pascal, novel Arthur Conan Doyle d Sidney Lanfield ph Peverell Marley m Cyril Mockridge ad Thomas Little

Basil Rathbone, Nigel Bruce, Richard Greene, Wendy Barrie, Lionel Atwill, Morton Lowry, John Carradine, Barlowe Borland, Beryl Mercer, Ralph Forbes, E. E. Clive, Eily Malyon, Mary Gordon

'A startling mystery-chiller . . . will find many bookings on top spots of key duallers.'— Variety

'Lush dialogue, stagey sets and vintage supporting cast make it a delectable Hollywood period piece.'—Judith Crist, 1980
† For Rathbone's other appearances as Holmes see under Sherlock Holmes.

The Hound of the Baskervilles*
GB 1959 86m Technicolor
UA / Hammer (Anthony Hinds)

Spirited remake let down by dogged Hammer insistence on promises of horror and sex; good atmosphere also let down by poor colour.

w Peter Bryan d Terence Fisher ph Jack Asher m James Bernard

Peter Cushing, André Morell, Christopher Lee, Marla Landi, Ewen Solon, Francis de Wolff

The Hound of the Baskervilles
GB 1977 85m Technicolor
Hemdale / Michael White Ltd (John Goldstone)

A pointless, pitiful and vulgar spoof of an enjoyable original.

w Dudley Moore, Peter Cook, Paul Morrissey d Paul Morrissey ph Dick Bush, John Wilcox m Dudley Moore

Peter Cook (Sherlock Holmes), Dudley Moore (Watson), Denholm Elliot (Stapleton), Terry-Thomas (Mortimer), Joan Greenwood, Max Wall, Irene Handl, Kenneth Williams, Hugh Griffith, Roy Kinnear, Penelope Keith, Dana Gillespie, Prunella Scales, Jessie Matthews, Spike Milligan

'As I held her in my arms, how could I know that she was as vicious as she was beautiful?'

The Hour before the Dawn
US 1944 75m bw
Paramount (William Dozier)

When a pacifist English nobleman discovers during World War II that he has married a Nazi spy, he strangles her and joins the forces.
Stultifyingly absurd, badly made and acted melodrama which its author clearly wished he had never written, as it was later withdrawn from his canon.

w Michael Hogan, Lester Samuels, novel W. Somerset Maugham d Frank Tuttle ph John F. Seitz m Miklos Rozsa

Franchot Tone, Veronica Lake, John Sutton, Binnie Barnes, Henry Stephenson, Philip Merivale, Nils Asther, Edmund Breon

The Hour of Decision
GB 1957 81m bw

A reporter is assigned to investigate the death of a columnist. A familiar type of second feature whodunit, with little about it to spark enthusiasm. Jeff Morrow, Hazel Court, Lionel Jeffries, Anthony Dawson, Mary Laura Wood. Written by Norman Hudis; directed by C. Pennington-Richards; for Tempean / Eros.

'Wyatt Earp—hero with a badge, or cold-blooded killer?'

Hour of the Gun**
US 1967 101m De Luxe Panavision
UA / Mirisch / Kappa (John Sturges)

After the gunfight at the OK corral, Wyatt Earp tracks down the rest of the Clanton gang. Vividly set, slowly developed western which makes an ambiguous but forceful figure of Earp. Generally confident and interesting.

w Edward Anhalt d John Sturges ph Lucien Ballard m Jerry Goldsmith

James Garner, Jason Robards Jnr, Robert Ryan, Steve Ihnat, Michael Tolan, Frank Converse, Sam Melville, Monte Markham, Albert Salmi, Jon Voight, William Windom, Charles Aidman

The Hour of the Wolf*
Sweden 1967 89m bw
Svensk Filmindustri (Lars-Owe Carlberg)
original title: Vargtimmen

A painter, at his summer island home with his wife, is terrorized by monstrous nightmares and by memories of his own adulterous past. Rather like the gloomy side of Smiles of a Summer Night, this very typical Bergman melodrama doesn't quite flow as intended, and whatever its meaning may be, its surface is less entertaining than usual.

wd Ingmar Bergman ph Sven Nykvist m Mars Johan Werle

Max Von Sydow, Liv Ullmann, Ingrid Thulin, Erland Josephson

The Hour of Thirteen
GB 1952 78m bw
MGM (Hayes Goetz)

Edwardian London is shocked when
policemen are stabbed one by one.
Jaded Hollywood-English thriller, a remake of
The Mystery of Mr X (qv).

w Leon Gordon, Howard Emmett Rogers,
novel X vs Rex by Philip MacDonald
d Harold French ph Guy Green m John
Addison

Peter Lawford, Dawn Addams, Roland
Culver, Derek Bond, Leslie Dwyer, Michael
Hordern, Colin Gordon, Heather Thatcher
† Originally to be called *T for Terror*.

The House across the Bay
US 1940 88m bw
(UA) Walter Wanger

To protect her racketeer husband from his
enemies, his wife has him convicted of income
tax evasion.
Unpersuasive melodrama, a star potboiler.

w Kathryn Scola d Archie Mayo ph Merritt
Gerstad m Werner Janssen

Joan Bennett, George Raft, Lloyd Nolan,
Walter Pidgeon, Gladys George, June Knight

House Calls*
US 1978 98m Technicolor
Universal / Jennings Lang (Alex Winitsky,
Arlene Sellers)

A middle-aged doctor finds himself widowed
and seeks a new mate.
Spotty comedy which tries to combine
conventional romantic spats with medical
satire, and comes off only in fits and starts.

w Max Shulman, Julius J. Epstein, Alan
Mandel, Charles Shyer d Howard Zieff
ph David M. Walsh m Henry Mancini

Walter Matthau, Glenda Jackson, Art Carney,
Richard Benjamin, Candice Azzara, Thayer
David, Dick O'Neill

A House Divided*
US 1931 70m bw
Universal (Paul Kohner)

A tough widowed fisherman seeks a new wife,
but she falls in love with his son.
Glum variation on *Desire under the Elms*,
interesting for early Wyler touches.

w John P. Clymer, Dale Van Every, John
Huston, *story* Heart and Hand by Olive
Edens d William Wyler ph Charles Stumar

Walter Huston, Kent Douglass, Helen
Chandler, Vivian Oakland, Frank Hagney,
Mary Foy

The House in Nightmare Park*
GB 1973 95m Technicolor
EMI / Associated London / Extonation
(Clive Exton, Terry Nation)

In 1907, a ham actor is asked to perform at an
old dark house in the country where an axe
murderer prowls during the night.
Standard creepy house comedy thriller, well

enough done though it would have been better
with Bob Hope.

w Clive Exton, Terry Nation d Peter Sykes
ph Ian Wilson m Harry Robinson

Frankie Howerd, Ray Milland, Hugh Burden,
Kenneth Griffith, John Bennett, Rosalie
Crutchley, Ruth Dunning

The House in the Square*
GB 1951 91m Technicolor
   (b / w endpieces)
TCF (Sol C. Siegel)
US title: *I'll Never Forget You*

An American atomic chemist living in London
becomes his own ancestor of two hundred
years ago, and falls in love.
Slow-starting but thereafter quite acceptable
remake of *Berkeley Square* (qv), with some
interesting dialogue and a genuinely affecting
fade-out.

w Ranald MacDougall, *play* John L.
Balderston d Roy Baker ph Georges Périnal
m William Alwyn ad C. P. Norman

Tyrone Power, Ann Blyth, Michael Rennie,
Beatrice Campbell, Dennis Price, Raymond
Huntley, Irene Browne, Robert Atkins (as Dr
Johnson)

A House Is Not a Home
US 1964 98m bw
(Paramount) Embassy (Clarence Greene)

The life story of New York's most famous
madam, Polly Adler.
Dismal, unappealing, laundered biopic,
cheaply made in an unconvincing period
setting.

w Russel Rouse, Clarence Greene d Russel
Rouse ph Harold Stine m Joseph Weiss

Shelley Winters, Robert Taylor, Cesar
Romero, Ralph Taeger, Broderick Crawford

The House of a Thousand Candles
US 1936 54m bw

A young man must live in an unfinished
mansion to inherit under the terms of his
grandfather's will. Odd but basically
unremarkable little mystery; the title is more
interesting than the movie. Phillips Holmes,
Mae Clarke, Irving Pichel, Rosita Moreno.
Written by H. W. Hanemann and Endre
Boehm from the novel by Meredith Nicholson;
directed by Arthur Lubin; for Republic.

'The story Tokyo couldn't hide, and
   Washington couldn't hold back!'
House of Bamboo
US 1955 102m De Luxe Cinemascope
TCF (Buddy Adler)

Japanese and American authorities move into
undercover action against Tokyo gangsters.
Routine big-budget crime drama with only the
location in its favour; a time passer, vaguely
adapted from *The Street with No Name* (qv).

w Harry Kleiner d Samuel Fuller ph Joe
MacDonald m Leigh Harline

Robert Stack, Robert Ryan, Shirley
Yagamuchi, Cameron Mitchell, Sessue
Hayakawa

House of Cards
US 1968 100m Techniscope
Universal / Westward (Dick Berg)

An American becomes tutor in the Paris
household of a French general's widow, and
finds himself a pawn in a high-powered game
of international intrigue.
Good-looking location thriller which after an
intricate opening settles into a *39 Steps*-style
chase, but makes little of it.

w James P. Bonner, *novel* Stanley Ellin
d John Guillermin ph Piero Portalupi
m Francis Lai

George Peppard, Inger Stevens, Orson
Welles, Keith Michell, William Job, Maxine
Audley, Peter Bayliss

House of Dracula*
US 1945 67m bw
U–I (Paul Malvern)

As a result of being visited in one evening by
Count Dracula, the Wolf Man and the
Frankenstein monster, a sympathetic doctor
goes on the rampage.
Mind-boggling finale to the first Universal
monster cycle, with a happy ending for the
Wolf Man. Cheaply made and not really
inventive, but has to be seen to be believed.

w Edward T. Lowe d Erle C. Kenton
ph George Robinson m Edgar Fairchild

Onslow Stevens, John Carradine, Lon Chaney
Jnr, Glenn Strange, Lionel Atwill, Martha
O'Driscoll, Jane Adams

The House of Fear see The Last Warning (1929)

The House of Fear
US 1939 65m bw

Murder in a haunted theatre: an actor dies and
the corpse disappears. Lively Crime Club
whodunit, a remake of *The Last Warning*
(1929). William Gargan, Irene Hervey,
Dorothy Arnold, Alan Dinehart, Harvey
Stephens, Walter Woolf King, Robert Coote,
El Brendel, Tom Dugan. 'Sufficient edge-of-
seat suspense to catch lower-bracket bookings
in the nabe duallers.'—*Variety*

The House of Fear*
US 1945 68m bw

Members of a club are murdered one by one.
A knotty problem for Sherlock Holmes, but
rather tediously unravelled. Despite the
orange pips it owes virtually nothing to Conan
Doyle. Basil Rathbone, Nigel Bruce, Dennis
Hoey, Aubrey Mather, Paul Cavanagh,
Holmes Herbert, Gavin Muir. Written by Roy
Chanslor; directed by Roy William Neill; for
Universal.

House of Frankenstein*
US 1944 71m bw
U–I (Paul Malvern)

A mad doctor thaws out the monster and the
Wolf Man (frozen at the end of *Frankenstein
Meets the Wolf Man*) but comes to a sticky
end.

463

When in Southern California visit Universal Studios

who holds the deadly key to the

HOUSE OF CARDS

The Blood-Hot Diary of the People who Fight the War of Intrigue Across the Face of the Globe!

GEORGE PEPPARD · INGER STEVENS · ORSON WELLES in

"HOUSE OF CARDS"

G Suggested for GENERAL audiences.

CO STARRING KEITH MICHELL · Screenplay by JAMES P. BONNER · Directed by JOHN GUILLERMIN · Produced by DICK BERG · A UNIVERSAL RELEASE in TECHNICOLOR*

HOUSE OF CARDS. Not too many people could follow the plot of this movie, but the cast gave good value.

Originally called *Chamber of Horrors*, this was the studio's first attempt to package its monsters (the first two reels are about Dracula). It could have been pacier in view of the possibilities, but it has its interest.

w Edward T. Lowe, Curt Siodmak *d* Erle C. Kenton *ph* George Robinson *m* Hans Salter

Boris Karloff, John Carradine, Lon Chaney Jnr, George Zucco, J. Carrol Naish, Anne Gwynne, Elena Verdugo, Lionel Atwill, Sig Rumann, Glenn Strange

House of Horrors
US 1946 65m bw

An incompetent sculptor tricks a psychopathic killer into murdering his critics. Grade Z thriller with a monster element; crude beyond belief. Martin Kosleck, Rondo Hatton, Robert Lowery, Virginia Grey, Bill Goodwin. Written by George Bricker; directed by Jean Yarbrough; for Universal. (GB title: *Joan Medford Is Missing*.)

House of Numbers
US 1957 92m bw Cinemascope
MGM (Charles Schnee)

A man helps his thuggish twin brother escape from prison.
An original melodramatic idea is frittered away through slow pacing.

w Russel Rouse, Don M. Mankiewicz, *novel* Jack Finney *d* Russel Rouse *ph* George J. Folsey *m* André Previn

Jack Palance, Barbara Lang, Harold J. Stone, Edward Platt

The House of Rothschild••
US 1934 87m bw (Technicolor sequence)
Twentieth Century (William Goetz, Raymond Griffith)

The chronicles of the famous banking family at the time of the Napoleonic Wars.
Lavish historical pageant with interesting scenes and performances.

w Nunnally Johnson, *play* George Hembert Westley *d* Alfred Werker *ph* Peverell Marley *m* Alfred Newman

George Arliss, Loretta Young, Boris Karloff, Robert Young, C. Aubrey Smith, Arthur Byron, Helen Westley, Reginald Owen, Florence Arliss, Alan Mowbray, Holmes Herbert

'A fine picture on all counts . . . one of those occasional 100% smashes which Hollywood achieves.'—*Variety*
'A good dramatic photoplay, finely presented, packed with ripe incident and quite beautiful photography.'—*C. A. Lejeune*

AAN: best picture

House of Secrets
GB 1956 97m Technicolor Vistavision
Rank / Julian Wintle (Vivian A. Cox)

A naval officer is asked to impersonate a lookalike counterfeiter and work undercover to expose the gang.
Old-hat Boys' Own Paper adventure story, mindlessly watchable.

w Robert Buckner, Bryan Forbes *d* Guy Green *ph* Harry Waxman *m* Hubert Clifford

Michael Craig, Julia Arnall, Brenda de Banzie, David Kossoff, Barbara Bates, Gerard Oury, Geoffrey Keen, Anton Diffring

The House of Seven Gables
US 1940 89m bw
Universal

In 17th-century New England, a jealous brother sends his sister's fiancé to prison.
Flat adaptation of a grim, brooding novel; it never grips.

w Lester Cole, *novel* Nathaniel Hawthorne *d* Joe May *ph* Milton Krasner *m* Frank Skinner

George Sanders, Margaret Lindsay, Vincent Price, Alan Napier, Nan Grey, Cecil Kellaway, Dick Foran, Miles Mander

AAN: Frank Skinner

House of Strangers••
US 1949 101m bw
TCF (Sol C. Siegel)

An Italian-American banker who rigidly controls his three sons is arrested for illegal practices, and the family ties slacken.
Interesting ethnic melodrama with good script and performances; much remade, e.g. as *Broken Lance*.

w Philip Yordan, *novel* Jerome Weidman *d* Joseph L. Mankiewicz *ph* Milton Krasner *m* Daniele Amfitheatrof

Edward G. Robinson, Richard Conte, Susan Hayward, *Luther Adler*, Paul Valentine, Efrem Zimbalist Jnr, Debra Paget, Hope Emerson, Esther Minciotti, Diana Douglas

The House of the Angel••
Argentina 1957 73m bw
Argentina Sono Film (Leopoldo Torre Nilsson)
original title: *La Casa del Angel*

A repressed girl is obsessed for life by the shame of her first love affair.
Fascinating minor classic in a heavily Wellesian style.

w Beatriz Guido, Leopoldo Torre Nilsson, Martin Rodriguez Mentasti, *novel* Beatriz Guido *d* Leopoldo Torre Nilsson *ph* Anibal Gonzalez Paz *m* Juan Carlos Paz

Elsa Daniel, Lautaro Murua, Guillermo Battaglia

'The first major work of a director of individual vision and strongly national style.'—*Robert Vas, MFB*

The House of the Arrow
GB 1940 66m bw

A wealthy Frenchwoman is murdered and her English companion is under suspicion. A case for Inspector Hanaud; very tolerable whodunnit. Keneth Kent, Diana Churchill, Belle Chrystall, Peter Murray Hill, Clifford Evans, Catherine Lacey. Written by Doreen Montgomery, from the novel by A. E. W. Mason; directed by Harold French; for ABPC. (A previous version in 1930 starred Dennis Neilson Terry and was directed by Leslie Hiscott.)

House of the Damned•
US 1963 63m bw
TCF / Associated Producers (Maury Dexter)

An architect is asked to make a survey of an old empty castle, but he and his wife find that someone or something is in hiding there.
Corny but mildly effective second feature with a few neat touches.

w Harry Spalding *d Maury Dexter* *ph* John Nickolaus Jnr *m* Henry Vars

Ronald Foster, Merry Anders

House of the Long Shadows
GB 1983 101m colour
Cannon (Jenny Craven)

An author takes a bet to isolate himself in a dilapidated house and write a Gothic novel within 24 hours . . .
Semi-spoof variation on an old chestnut, with aged horror practitioners interrupting the silence. Too restricted in script and production to be really effective.

w Michael Armstrong, *play* Seven Keys to Baldpate by George M. Cohan and *novel* by Earl Derr Biggers *d* Pete Walker *ph* Norman Langley *m* Richard Harvey

Christopher Lee, Peter Cushing, Vincent Price, Desi Arnaz Jnr, John Carradine, Sheila Keith, Julie Peasgood, Richard Todd

'Golan and Globus seem to have inherited Lord Grade's habit of assembling advertising packages with movies appended as an afterthought.'—*Kim Newman, MFB*
'A horror flick which basks in the Hammer tradition without in any way understanding it.'—*Guardian*

● *Video: Guild*

House of the Seven Hawks
GB 1959 92m bw
MGM / David E. Rose

An American adventurer becomes involved in a search by criminals for buried Nazi loot.
Cliché-ridden thick ear, adequately produced but of no interest.

w Jo Eisinger, *novel* The House of Seven Flies by Victor Canning *d* Richard Thorpe *ph* Ted Scaife *m* Clifton Parker

Robert Taylor, Nicole Maurey, Linda Christian, Donald Wolfit, David Kossoff, Eric Pohlmann, Gerard Heinz

House of Usher•
US 1960 85m Eastmancolor Cinemascope
AIP / Alta Vista (Roger Corman)
GB title: *The Fall of the House of Usher*

The last of the Usher line, prone to catalepsy, is buried alive by her brother and returns to wreak vengeance.
Stylish but grottily-coloured low-budget horror which started the Poe cycle of the sixties. A bit slow, it would have worked better in the standard screen ratio, but there is a tense and spectacular finale.

w Richard Matheson, *story* Edgar Allan Poe *d* Roger Corman *ph* Floyd Crosby *m* Les Baxter *ad* Daniel Haller

Vincent Price, Myrna Fahey, Mark Damon, Harry Ellerbe

'The most astounding motion picture since motion pictures began! Man turned monster stalking show-world beauties! The ultimate dimension in terror!'

House of Wax**
US 1953 88m Warnercolor 3-D
Warner (Bryan Foy)

Mutilated in a fire at his wax museum, a demented sculptor arranges a supply of dead bodies to be covered in wax for exhibition at his new showplace.
Spirited remake of *The Mystery of the Wax Museum* (qv); as a piece of screen narrative it leaves much to be desired, but the sudden shocks are well managed, perhaps because this is the first Grade-A 3-D film, packed with gimmicks irrelevant to the story and originally shown with stereophonic sound.

w Crane Wilbur d André de Toth ph Bert Glennon m David Buttolph

Vincent Price (whose horror career began here), Carolyn Jones, Paul Picerni, Phyllis Kirk, Frank Lovejoy
† The director could not see the 3-D effect, being blind in one eye.
● *Video: Warner*

House of Women
US 1962 85m bw

A pregnant woman is sent to prison for a robbery she didn't commit. Loose remake of *Caged*, with very little sense or vigour. Shirley Knight, Andrew Duggan, Constance Ford, Barbara Nichols, Margaret Hayes. Written by Crane Wilbur; directed by Walter Doniger; for Warner.

House on Haunted Hill
US 1958 75m bw
Allied Artists / William Castle

An old house which has seen several murders is the setting for a millionaire's party. Gimmick ghost story with some (unexplained) gruesome moments; the most outlandish of its producer's cheapjack trick films (*Thirteen Ghosts, The Tingler, Macabre*, etc), it was originally billed as being in Emergo, which meant that at an appropriately horrific moment an illuminated skeleton on wires was suddenly trundled over the heads of the audience.

w Robb White d William Castle ph Carl Guthrie m Von Dexter

Vincent Price, Richard Long, Carol Ohmart, Alan Marshal, Elisha Cook Jnr

The House on 92nd Street****
US 1945 88m bw
TCF (*Louis de Rochemont*)

During World War II in New York, the FBI routs Nazi spies after the atomic bomb formula.
Highly influential documentary-style 'now it can be told' spy drama, which borrowed the feel of its producer's *March of Time* series and applied them to a fairly true story set on genuine locations though with a modicum of fictional mystery and suspense.

Highly effective in its own right, it looked forward to *The Naked City* three years later; the later film unaccountably got most of the credit for taking Hollywood out into the open air.

w Barre Lyndon, Charles G. Booth, John Monks Jnr d Henry Hathaway ph Norbert Brodine m David Buttolph

William Eythe, Lloyd Nolan, Signe Hasso, *Leo G. Carroll*, Gene Lockhart, Lydia St Clair, Harry Bellaver
'Recommended entertainment for those who believe that naïve Americans are no match for wily Europeans in the spy trade, and for those who just like their movies to move.'—*Time*
'Imagine an issue of *The March of Time*. The hard agglomeration of fact; the road drill style; the voice. Prolong it to four times its usual length, throw in a fictional climax, and there you have *The House on 92nd Street*.'—*William Whitebait, New Statesman*
AA: original story (Charles G. Booth)

The House on Telegraph Hill
US 1951 93m bw
TCF (Robert Bassler)

A woman in a concentration camp assumes her dead friend's identity so that on release she can be sent to America; but murder threatens there.
Modernized amalgam of *Gaslight* and *Suspicion*, not as good as either, but the complexities of the story hold adequate interest.

w Elick Moll, Frank Partos, *novel* Dana Lyon d Robert Wise ph Lucien Ballard m Sol Kaplan

Richard Basehart, Valentina Cortesa, William Lundigan, Fay Baker, Gordon Gebert, Steve Geray

The House that Dripped Blood*
GB 1970 102m Eastmancolor
Amicus (Milton Subotsky)

A Scotland Yard man investigating a disappearance is led to a house with a murderous history.
Quartet of stories in *Dead of Night* style, neatly made and generally pleasing despite a low level of originality in the writing.

w Robert Bloch d Peter John Duffell ph Robert Parslow m Michael Dress

John Bennett, Christopher Lee, Peter Cushing, Denholm Elliott, Joanna Dunham, Nyree Dawn Porter, Jon Pertwee, Ingrid Pitt

Houseboat
US 1958 110m Technicolor
Vistavision
Paramount / Scribe (Jack Rose)

A widower with three children engages a maid who is really a socialite, and they all set up house on a boat.
Artificial sentimental comedy with A-1 credits but little style or bite.

w Melville Shavelson, Jack Rose d Melville Shavelson ph Ray June m George Duning

Cary Grant, Sophia Loren, Martha Hyer, Eduardo Ciannelli, Harry Guardino
'The kind of picture to which you can take your stuffy maiden aunt, your wicked sophisticated uncle and your ten-year-old child, and they will all have a wonderful time.'—*Ruth Waterbury, Los Angeles Examiner*
AAN: script; song 'Almost In Your Arms' (*m / ly* Jay Livingston, Ray Evans)

The Housekeeper's Daughter*
US 1939 71m bw
Hal Roach

A gangster's moll returns to mama for a visit and falls in love with the stuffy son of the household.
Zany crime farce which too often lets its zip fade, but atones in a crazy firework finale.

w Rian James, Gordon Douglas, *novel* Donald Henderson Clarke d Hal Roach ph Norbert Brodine m Amedeo de Filippi

Joan Bennett, John Hubbard, Adolphe Menjou, William Gargan, George E. Stone, Peggy Wood, Donald Meek, Marc Lawrence, Lilian Bond, Victor Mature, Luis Alberni
'A smacko laugh generator due for profitable biz up and down the line.'—*Variety*

Housemaster*
GB 1938 95m bw
ABPC (Walter C. Mycroft)

A schoolmaster sides with his boys against the new headmaster's dictatorial methods.
Pleasing photographed play with all concerned in good form.

w Dudley Leslie, Elizabeth Meehan, *play* Bachelor Born by Ian Hay d Herbert Brenon

Otto Kruger, Diana Churchill, Phillips Holmes, Joyce Barbour, Kynaston Reeves, Rene Ray, Walter Hudd, John Wood, Cecil Parker, Michael Shepley, Jimmy Hanley

Housewife
US 1934 69m bw
Warner (Robert Lord)

For an advertising copywriter, success almost brings divorce.
Modestly efficient romantic programmer of its day.

w Manuel Seff, Lillie Hayward d Alfred E. Green ph William Rees m Leo F. Forbstein

Bette Davis, George Brent, Ann Dvorak, John Halliday, Ruth Donnelly, Hobart Cavanaugh, Robert Barrat, Phil Regan
'The dramatic punches are not merely telegraphed, but radioed.'—*Frank S. Nugent*

The Houston Story
US 1956 80m bw

An oil worker has a plan for stealing oil, and is employed by the syndicate. Racketeering melodrama of the least interesting kind. Gene Barry, Barbara Hale, Edward Arnold, Paul Richards, Frank Jenks. Written by James B. Gordon; directed by William Castle; for Sam Katzman / Columbia.

How Do I Love Thee
US 1970 109m Metrocolor
ABC (Robert Enders, Everett Freeman)

A philosophy professor recalls the odd career of his atheist father.
Curious comedy about an eccentric and his family relationships, a kind of *Cheaper by the Dozen* with religion added. Not on in 1970.

w Everett Freeman, *novel* Let Me Count the Ways by Peter De Vries d Michael Gordon ph Russell Metty m Randy Sparks

Jackie Gleason, Maureen O'Hara, Shelley Winters, Rick Lenz, Rosemary Forsyth
'Nauseated embarrassment for participants and onlookers alike.'—*Judith Crist*

' "What are you? A man or a saint? I don't want him, I want you!" Her desire scorched both their lives with the vicious breath of scandal!'

How Green Was My Valley***
US 1941 118m bw
TCF (Darryl F. Zanuck)

Memories of childhood in a Welsh mining village.
Prettified and unconvincing but dramatically very effective tearjerker in the style which lasted from Cukor's *David Copperfield* to *The Green Years*. High production values here add a touch of extra class, turning the result into a Hollywood milestone despite its intrinsic inadequacies.

w Philip Dunne, *novel* Richard Llewellyn d John Ford ph Arthur Miller m Alfred Newman

Walter Pidgeon, Maureen O'Hara, Roddy McDowall, Donald Crisp, Sara Allgood, Anna Lee, John Loder, Barry Fitzgerald, Patric Knowles, Morton Lowry, Arthur Shields, Frederic Worlock
'Perfection of cinematic narrative . . . pure visual action, pictures powerfully composed, dramatically photographed, smoothly and eloquently put together.'—*James Shelley Hamilton*
† The unseen narrator was Irving Pichel.

AA: best picture; John Ford; Arthur Miller; Donald Crisp
AAN: Philip Dunne; Alfred Newman; Sara Allgood

How He Lied to Her Husband
GB 1930 33m bw

An early film version of Bernard Shaw's playlet about a minor flirtation. Of historical interest only. Edmund Gwenn, Robert Harris, Vera Lennox. Written by Frank Launder; directed by Cecil Lewis; for BIP.

How I Won the War
GB 1967 110m Eastmancolor
UA / Petersham (Richard Lester)

During World War II an earnest young man becomes an officer and survives many tribulations including the death of his comrades.
Appalling kaleidoscope of black comedy and the director's own brand of uncontrolled cinematic zaniness, with echoes of *Candide* and *Oh What a Lovely War!* Just the way to alienate a paying audience.

w Charles Wood, *novel* Patrick Ryan d Richard Lester ph David Watkin m Ken Thorne

Michael Crawford, John Lennon, Roy Kinnear, Lee Montague, Jack McGowran, Michael Hordern, Jack Hedley, Karl Michael Vogler, Ronald Lacey, James Cossins, Alexander Knox
'Pretentious tomfoolery.'—*John Simon*
'One feels that Lester has bitten off more than he can chew . . . the ideas misfire, lost somewhere between the paper on which they were conceived and the celluloid on which they finally appear.'—*MFB*

How Sweet It Is*
US 1968 98m Technicolor Panavision
Warner / Cherokee / National General
(Garry Marshall, Jerry Belson)

Suspicious of their son's intentions towards his girl friend on a European holiday, a middle-aged American couple decide to follow.
Good-looking, rather silly comedy, plain spoken in the modern manner but without much entertainment value except when farce gets the upper hand.

w Garry Marshall, Jerry Belson, *novel* The Girl in the Turquoise Bikini by Muriel Resnik d Jerry Paris ph Lucien Ballard m Pat Williams

James Garner, Debbie Reynolds, Maurice Ronet, Paul Lynde, Marcel Dalio, Terry-Thomas, Donald Losby, Hilarie Thompson
'One of those slender marital farces in which the behaviour of the adults is consistently more juvenile than that of the teenagers.'—*MFB*

How the West Was Won*
US 1962 162m Technicolor Cinerama
MGM / Cinerama (Bernard Smith)

Panoramic western following the daughter of a pioneering family from youth (1830) to old age, with several half-relevant stories along the way.
Muddled spectacular with splendid set-pieces but abysmal dullness in between, especially if not seen in three-strip Cinerama (the Cinemascope prints are muddy and still show the dividing lines). An all-star fairground show of its time.

w James R. Webb d Henry Hathaway (first half), John Ford (Civil War), George Marshall (train) ph William Daniels, Milton Krasner, Charles Lang Jnr, Joseph La Shelle m Alfred Newman and George W. Davis, William Ferrari, Addison Hehr

Debbie Reynolds, Carroll Baker, Lee J. Cobb, Henry Fonda, Carolyn Jones, Karl Malden, Gregory Peck, George Peppard, Robert Preston, James Stewart, Eli Wallach, John Wayne, Richard Widmark, Brigid Bazlen, Walter Brennan, David Brian, Andy Devine, Raymond Massey, Agnes Moorehead, Henry Morgan, Thelma Ritter, Russ Tamblyn, Spencer Tracy (narrator)

'That goddamned Cinerama . . . do you know a waist shot is as close as you could get with that thing?'—*Henry Hathaway*

AA: James R. Webb
AAN: best picture; photography; music

How to Be Very Very Popular
US 1955 89m De Luxe Cinemascope
TCF (Nunnally Johnson)

Two belly dancers on the run from gangsters hide out in a co-ed college.
Wacky remake of *She Loves Me Not* (qv); tries hard for a vein of freewheeling lunacy but only occasionally achieves it. A few numbers might have helped.

wd Nunnally Johnson ph Milton Krasner m Cyril Mockridge

Betty Grable, Sheree North, *Charles Coburn*, Robert Cummings, Orson Bean, Fred Clark, Tommy Noonan

How to Beat the High Cost of Living
US 1980 110m Movielab

Three middle-class women take to robbery when they can't make the housekeeping balance. Undercast, reprehensible and almost totally unfunny alleged comedy. Susan Saint James, Jane Curtin, Jessica Lange, Richard Benjamin, Fred Willard, Eddie Albert. Written by Robert Kaufman; directed by Robert Scheerer; for Filmways.

How to Commit Marriage
US 1969 98m Technicolor
Cinerama / Naho (Bill Larence)

A couple decide to divorce, with repercussions on their family and in-laws.
Tiresome generation-gap comedy.

w Ben Starr, Michael Kanin d Norman Panama ph Charles Lang m Joseph J. Lilley

Bob Hope, Jackie Gleason, Jane Wyman, Leslie Nielsen, Maureen Arthur, Paul Stewart, Tina Louise

How to Marry a Millionaire**
US 1953 96m Technicolor
Cinemascope
TCF (Nunnally Johnson)

Three girls rent an expensive New York apartment and set out to trap millionaires.
Cinemascope's first attempt at modern comedy was not quite as disastrous as might have been expected, largely because of the expensiveness of everything and the several stars still brightly twinkling, but the handling of this variation on the old *Golddiggers* theme, while entirely amiable, is dramatically very slack.

w Nunnally Johnson d Jean Negulesco ph Joe MacDonald md Alfred Newman m Cyril Mockridge

Lauren Bacall, *Marilyn Monroe*, Betty Grable, *William Powell*, Cameron Mitchell, David Wayne, Rory Calhoun, Alex D'Arcy, Fred Clark
● Video: CBS / Fox

'The last word in do-it-yourself!'
How to Murder a Rich Uncle
GB 1957   80m   bw   Cinemascope
Columbia / Warwick (Ronald Kinnoch)

An impoverished nobleman decides to murder
his rich old uncle.
Feebly-handled black comedy which does not
come off at all despite a highly talented cast.

w John Paxton, *play* Il faut tuer Julie by Dider
Daix   d Nigel Patrick   ph Ted Moore

Nigel Patrick, Charles Coburn, *Katie Johnson*,
Wendy Hiller, Anthony Newley, Athene
Seyler, Michael Caine, Noel Hood, Kenneth
Fortescue

How to Murder Your Wife*
US 1964   118m   Technicolor
UA / Murder Inc (George Axelrod)

A strip cartoonist tests out his violent scenes in
real life; when his wife disappears he finds
himself accused of murder.
Amusing preliminaries give way to dreary plot
complications and an overlong courtroom
scene. Leave after the first hour.

w George Axelrod   d Richard Quine
ph Harry Stradling   m Neal Hefti   pd Richard
Sylbert

Jack Lemmon, Virna Lisi, *Terry-Thomas*,
Eddie Mayehoff, Sidney Blackmer, Claire
Trevor

How to Save a Marriage and Ruin Your
Life
US 1968   102m   Technicolor
  Panavision
Columbia / Nob Hill (Stanley Shapiro)

An attorney takes it upon himself to convince
his friend of the infidelity of the friend's
mistress . . .
Tedious sex antics without any sex; a few
smiles are not enough to endear it.

w Stanley Shapiro, Nate Monaster   d Fielder
Cook   ph Lee Garmes   m Michel Legrand

Dean Martin, Eli Wallach, Stella Stevens,
Anne Jackson, Betty Field, Jack Albertson,
Katharine Bard
   'Another variation on Hollywood's patent
version of the Restoration comedy, which as
usual abandons the lustiness of its 17th-century
prototype in favour of guilt-ridden lechery and
a fundamental respect for the married state.'—
MFB

How to Steal a Million*
US 1966   127m   De Luxe   Panavision
TCF / World Wide (Fred Kohlmar)

The daughter of an art forger mistakenly
involves a private detective in a robbery.
High-class but rather boring romantic comedy;
the credits promise much but interest wanes
quickly owing to uncertain handling.

w Harry Kurnitz   d William Wyler   ph Charles
Lang   m Johnny Williams

Audrey Hepburn, Peter O'Toole, Charles
Boyer, Hugh Griffith, Eli Wallach, Fernand
Gravet, Marcel Dalio
   'Terribly wordy and slow . . . Wyler hasn't
got the touch nowadays.'—*Sight and Sound*

'The picture isn't offensive, and it's
handsome enough, but it's just blah.'—*Pauline
Kael, New Yorker*

How to Succeed in Business without
Really Trying**
US 1967   121m   De Luxe   Panavision
UA / Mirisch (David Swift)

A window cleaner cajoles his way to the top of
a New York company.
Cinematically uninventive but otherwise brisk
and glowing adaptation of a sharp, slick
Broadway musical.

w David Swift, *musical book* Abe Burrows,
Jack Weinstock, Willie Gilbert, *book*
Shepherd Mead   d David Swift   ph Burnett
Guffey   m / ly Frank Loesser   ch Dale Moreda
after Bob Fosse

Robert Morse, Rudy Vallee, Michele Lee,
Anthony Teague, Maureen Arthur, Murray
Matheson
   'Shows how taste and talent can succeed in
bringing a stage musical to the screen with its
virtues intact.'—*John Cutts*

The Howards of Virginia
US 1940   117m   bw
Columbia (Frank Lloyd)
GB title: *The Tree of Liberty*

A Virginian surveyor finds himself involved in
the Revolutionary War.
Historical cavalcade in which central
miscasting seems to cast a shadow of artifice
over the whole. Interesting but seldom
stimulating.

w Sidney Buchman, *novel* The Tree of Liberty
by Elizabeth Page   d Frank Lloyd   ph Bert
Glennon   m Richard Hageman

Cary Grant, Martha Scott, Cedric Hardwicke,
Alan Marshal, Richard Carlson, Paul Kelly,
Irving Bacon, Elizabeth Risdon

AAN: Richard Hageman

'Imagine your worst fear a reality!'
The Howling*
US 1980   90m   CFI Color
Avco Embassy / International Film
  Investors / Wescom (Ron Bottin)

A lady newscaster discovers that the medical
retreat at which she stays to recover from a
nervous breakdown is likely to give her
another.
A plethora of werewolves and a glut of in-
jokes pale beside a gallery of convincing and
horrifying special effects.

w John Sayles, Terence H. Winkless,
novel Gary Brander   d Joe Dante   ph John
Hora   m Pino Donaggio   make-up Rick Baker

Dee Wallace, Patrick MacNee, Dennis Dugan,
Christopher Stone, Kevin McCarthy, John
Carradine, Slim Pickens
† Some of the character names: George
Waggner, R. William Neill, Sam Newfield,
Fred Francis, Terry Fisher, Erle Kenton,
Charlie Barton, Lew Landers . . .

● *Video: Embassy*

Huckleberry Finn
US 1931   71m   bw
Paramount

The river adventures of Mark Twain's
scapegrace hero.
Adequate early talkie family film.

w Grover Jones, William Slavens McNutt
d Norman Taurog   ph David Abel

Jackie Coogan, Junior Durkin, Mitzi Green,
Jackie Searl, Eugene Pallette

Huckleberry Finn**
US 1939   90m   bw
MGM (Joseph L. Mankiewicz)

Solidly competent remake with excellent
production values and several entertaining
sequences.

w Hugo Butler   d Richard Thorpe   ph John
Seitz   m Franz Waxman

Mickey Rooney, Walter Connolly, William
Frawley, Rex Ingram

Huckleberry Finn*
US 1960   107m   Metrocolor
MGM (Samuel Goldwyn Jnr)
aka: *The Adventures of Huckleberry Finn*

Another patchy remake.

w James Lee   d Michael Curtiz   ph Ted
McCord   m Jerome Moross

Eddie Hodges, Tony Randall, Archie Moore,
Neville Brand, Judy Canova, Buster Keaton,
Andy Devine

Huckleberry Finn
US 1974   118m   De Luxe   Panavision
UA / Apjac / Readers Digest (Robert
  Greenhut)

Ambitious but lustreless version of the famous
story, with songs.

w / ly / m Richard M. Sherman, Robert B.
Sherman   d J. Lee-Thompson   ph Laszlo
Kovacs   pd Philip Jeffries

Jeff East, Paul Winfield, David Wayne,
Harvey Korman, Arthur O'Connell, Gary
Merrill, Natalie Trundy
   'It expires in a morass of treacle.'—*Tom
Milne*
   'It transforms a great work of fiction into
something bland, boring and tasteless.'—
Michael Billington, Illustrated London News

The Hucksters**
US 1947   115m   bw
MGM (Arthur Hornblow Jnr)

Back from the war, an advertising executive
finds it difficult to put up with his clients'
tantrums.
Good topical entertainment which still
entertains and gives a good impression of its
period.

w Luther Davis, *novel* Frederic Wakeman
d Jack Conway   ph Harold Rosson   m Lennie
Hayton

Clark Gable, Deborah Kerr, Ava Gardner,
Sidney Greenstreet, Adolphe Menjou, Keenan
Wynn, Edward Arnold, Aubrey Mather
   'A good picture, quick and to the point.'—
Photoplay

Hud•••

US 1963 112m bw Panavision
Paramount / Salem / Dover (Martin Ritt,
Irving Ravetch)

Life is hard on a Texas ranch, and the veteran
owner is not helped by his sexually arrogant
ne'er-do-well son, who is a bad influence on
the household.
Superbly set in an arid landscape, this incisive
character drama is extremely well directed and
acted but somehow lacks the touch of
greatness.

w Irving Ravetch, Harriet Frank, novel
Horseman Pass By by Larry McMurty
d Martin Ritt ph James Wong Howe m Elmer
Bernstein

Paul Newman, Patricia Neal, Melvyn Douglas,
Brandon de Wilde

AA: James Wong Howe; Patricia Neal;
Melvyn Douglas
AAN: script; Martin Ritt; Paul Newman

Huddle

US 1932 104m bw
GB title: The Impossible Lover.

A steel worker's son makes good at Harvard,
and wants to marry out of his class. Would-be
serious class drama which fell over its own
feet. Ramon Novarro, Madge Evans, Una
Merkel, Conrad Nagel, Arthur Byron, Cliff
Edwards. Written by Robert Johnson, C.
Gardner Sullivan, Arthur Hyman and Walton
Smith; directed by Sam Wood; for MGM.

'Football film doing much to defeat its own
purpose by extreme length . . . the Metro
foreign production end is substituting soccer
for the football portions for European
screenings.'—Variety

Hudson's Bay••

US 1940 95m bw
TCF (Kenneth MacGowan)

Pierre Radisson, a French Canadian trapper,
opens up millions of acres of northern
wilderness for England.
Well-made historical saga with good
production and performances.

w Lamar Trotti d Irving Pichel ph Peverell
Marley, George Barnes m Alfred Newman
ad Richard Day, Wiard B. Ihnen

Paul Muni, Laird Cregar, Gene Tierney, John
Sutton, Virginia Field, Vincent Price (as King
Charles II), Nigel Bruce, Morton Lowry,
Robert Greig, Frederic Worlock, Montagu
Love

Hue and Cry•••

GB 1946 82m bw
Ealing (Henry Cornelius)

East End boys discover that their favourite
boys' paper is being used by crooks to pass
information.
The first 'Ealing comedy' uses vivid London
locations as background for a sturdy comic
plot with a climax in which the criminals are
rounded up by thousands of boys swarming
over dockland.

w T. E. B. Clarke d Charles Crichton
ph Douglas Slocombe, John Seaholme
m Georges Auric

Alastair Sim, Jack Warner, Harry Fowler,
Valerie White, Frederick Piper

'Refreshing, bloodtingling and disarming.'—
Richard Winnington

● Video: Thorn EMI

Hugo the Hippo

US 1975 78m colour
Brut (Robert Halmi)

An independently-minded hippo combats a
Zanzibar magician.
Uninventive cartoon feature, endearing
neither in characterization nor in
draughtsmanship.

w Thomas Baum d William Feigenbaum
md Bert Keyes

Hugs and Kisses•

Sweden 1966 96m bw
Sandrews (Göran Lindgren)
original title: Puss och Kram

A destitute bohemian takes over the house
and the wife of the old executive friend who
shelters him out of pity.
Rather like a comedy version of the Dirk
Stroeve section of The Moon and Sixpence,
this sophisticated film came under censorship
fire for depicting the first full frontal female.

wd Jonas Cornell ph Lars Swanberg m Bengt
Ernryd

Sven-Bertil Taube, Agneta Ekmanner, Hakan
Serner

'The brilliance of the film lies in the way
humour and sadness are kept in perfect
equilibrium.'—MFB

Huis Clos•

France 1954 99m bw
Films Marceau

Two women and a man die, go to hell, and are
locked up for ever in an elegant room.
Rather flat intellectual fantasy from a play
which made great waves when first performed.

w Pierre Laroche, play Jean-Paul Sartre
d Jacqueline Audry ph Robert Juillard
m Joseph Kosma

Arletty, Frank Villard, Gaby Sylvia
'Without the ecstasy, terror and poetic
imagination of a Cocteau, the subject becomes
a fatally stationary one.'—Peter John Dyer,
MFB

Huk!

US 1956 83m Eastmancolor

In 1951, an American fights Philippine
guerrillas who murdered his father. Crude
action melodrama which served a purpose.
George Montgomery, Mona Freeman, John
Baer, James Bell. Written by Stirling
Silliphant, from his novel; directed by John
Barnwell; for Collier Young / UA.

The Human Comedy•

US 1943 117m bw
MGM (Clarence Brown)

In a small town during the war, a telegram boy

brings tragedy to others and is touched by it
himself.
Gooey, sentimental morale booster in the best
MGM tradition, a variant on the Hardy family
series but with all the pretensions of its author.

w Howard Estabrook, novel William Saroyan
d Clarence Brown ph Harry Stradling
m Herbert Stothart

Mickey Rooney, Frank Morgan, James Craig,
Marsha Hunt, Jackie Jenkins, Fay Bainter,
Ray Collins, Van Johnson, Donna Reed

Opening narration by Ray Collins: 'I am
Matthew Macauley. I have been dead for two
years. So much of me is still living that I know
now the end is only the beginning. As I look
down on my homeland of Ithaca, California,
with its cactus, vineyards and orchards, I see
that so much of me is still living there—in the
places I've been, in the fields and streets and
church and most of all in my home, where my
hopes, my dreams, my ambitions still live in
the daily life of my loved ones.'

'The dignity and simplicity of the ideas
shade off into cheap pretentiousness.'—Bosley
Crowther

'The best one can say of it . . . is that it tries
on the whole to be "faithful" to Saroyan; not
invariably a good idea.'—James Agee

'The Saroyan touch leaves nothing ordinary:
the film is electric with the joy of life.'—Time

AA: original story
AAN: best picture; Clarence Brown; Harry
Stradling; Mickey Rooney

Human Desire

US 1954 90m bw
Columbia (Lewis J. Rachmil)

A jealous railway official forces his wife to
help him murder her suspected lover.
Drab and unattractive remake of La Bête
Humaine.

w Alfred Hayes d Fritz Lang ph Burnett
Guffey m Daniele Amfitheatrof

Gloria Grahame, Glenn Ford, Broderick
Crawford, Edgar Buchanan

The Human Factor

GB 1979 114m Technicolor
Panavision
(Rank) Wheel / Sigma / Otto Preminger

An innocent man is suspected of being the
'mole' in the Foreign Office.
Quietly sardonic scenes of diplomatic chess are
played far too broadly and literally in this
ill-advised and poorly executed foray into the
serious spy scene, which despite its stars
becomes merely risible before the end.

w Tom Stoppard, novel Graham Greene
d Otto Preminger ph Mike Malloy
m Richard and Gary Logan

Nicol Williamson, Richard Attenborough,
Derek Jacobi, Robert Morley, John Gielgud,
Ann Todd, Richard Vernon, Joop Doderer,
Iman

'Unfortunately, Preminger stages it all as if
he was just trying to get all the actors through
their line readings in under two hours,
allowing no breathing room or time for
character nuance in a tale which resolutely
calls for quiet moments.'—Variety

● Video: Rank

The Human Jungle
US 1954   82m   bw

A new police captain cleans up a gangster-ridden slum district. Adequate low-life actioner of the kind later taken over by TV.
Gary Merrill, Jan Sterling, Paula Raymond, Emile Meyer, Regis Toomey, Lamont Johnson, Chuck Connors. Written by William Sackheim and Daniel Fuchs; directed by Joseph M. Newman; for Allied Artists.

The Human Side
US 1934   60m   bw

A philandering theatrical producer returns to his family. Pleasant light comedy, instantly forgettable. Adolphe Menjou, Doris Kenyon, Charlotte Kenyon, Dickie Moore, Reginald Owen, Joseph Cawthorn. Written by Frank Craven and Ernest Pascal, from the play by Christine Ames; directed by Eddie Buzzell; for Universal. 'Homely, wholesome domestic comedy that should find beaucoup favour with the family trade.'—*Variety*

Humanoids of the Deep
US 1980   81m   Metrocolor
New World (Martin B. Cohen)
GB title: *Monster*

Gruesome amphibious creatures rise from the ocean to stalk and destroy the most nubile women in sight.
Lurid, nonsensical but very violent horror flick, with much rape and nudity; like a Corman quickie of the fifties but with added gore.
w Frederick James *d* Barbara Peeters (*sic*)
ph Daniele Lacambre *m* James Horner
costumes Rob Bottin

Vic Morrow, Doug McClure, Ann Turkel

Humoresque**
US 1947   125m   bw
Warner (Jerry Wald)

An ambitious violinist gets emotionally involved with his wealthy patroness.
Lush soaper about suffering in high society, complete with tragic end and lashings of classical music (Isaac Stern on the sound track).
w Clifford Odets, Zachary Gold, *novel* Fannie Hurst *d* Jean Negulesco *ph* Ernest Haller
md Franz Waxman

Joan Crawford, John Garfield, Oscar Levant, J. Carrol Naish, Joan Chandler, Tom D'Andrea, Craig Stevens, Ruth Nelson

AAN: Franz Waxman

The Hunchback of Notre Dame**
US 1923   120m approx (24 fps)   bw
silent
Universal

The deformed Notre Dame bellringer rescues a gypsy girl from the evil intentions of her guardian.
Victorian gothic version with a riveting star performance.

HUMORESQUE.   Isaac Stern, off-screen, played for John Garfield; Oscar Levant played for himself.

w Percy Poore Sheehan, Edward T. Lowe Jnr, *novel* Notre Dame de Paris by Victor Hugo *d* Wallace Worsley *ph* Robert S. Newhard, Tony Kornman

Lon Chaney, Patsy Ruth Miller, Norman Kerry, Ernest Torrence, Gladys Brockwell, Kate Lester, Brandon Hurst, Tully Marshall
● *Video: Polygram*

The Hunchback of Notre Dame****
US 1939   117m   bw
RKO (Pandro S. Berman)

This superb remake is one of the best examples of Hollywood expertise at work: art direction, set construction, costumes, camera, lighting and above all direction brilliantly support an irresistible story and bravura acting.
w Sonya Levien, Bruno Frank *d* William Dieterle *ph* Joseph H. August *m* Alfred Newman *ad* Van Nest Polglase

Charles Laughton, Cedric Hardwicke, Maureen O'Hara, Edmond O'Brien, Thomas Mitchell, Harry Davenport, Walter Hampden, Alan Marshal, George Zucco, Katherine Alexander, Fritz Leiber, Rod la Rocque
'A super thriller-chiller. Will roll up healthy grosses at the ticket windows.'—*Variety*
'Has seldom been bettered as an evocation of medieval life.'—*John Baxter, 1968*

'It exceeds in sheer magnificence any similar film in history. Sets are vast and rich in detail, crowds are immense, and camera uses of both are versatile, varied and veracious.'—*Motion Picture Herald*
† Other versions: *Esmeralda* (1906, French); *Notre Dame de Paris* (1911, French); *The Darling of Paris* (1917, US, with Theda Bara); and see above and below.

AAN: Alfred Newman
● *Video: Thorn EMI*

The Hunchback of Notre Dame
France / Italy 1956   107m
Eastmancolor   Cinemascope
Paris Films / Panitalia (Robert and Raymond Hakim)

Crude international rehash with nothing to commend it, though the script before dubbing may have been interesting.
w Jacques Prévert, Jean Aurenche *d* Jean Delannoy *ph* Michel Kelber *m* Georges Auric

Anthony Quinn, Gina Lollobrigida, Jean Danet, Alain Cuny, Robert Hirsch

The Hundred Pound Window
GB 1943 84m bw
Warner

A racecourse clerk becomes involved with gamblers who bribe him to rig the totalizator, but he finally exposes them.
Routine programmer notable only for giving a leading role to an old character actor.

w Abem Finkel, Brock Williams, Rodney Ackland d Brian Desmond Hurst ph Otto Heller

Frederick Leister, Mary Clare, Anne Crawford, Richard Attenborough, David Farrar, Niall MacGinnis, David Hutcheson

'The Hunger is a mood, a look, an ambience created by Tony Scott. It is the lighting of Stephen Goldblatt, it is the production design of Brian Morris, it is the clothes created by Milena Canonero.'

The Hunger
US 1983 99m Metrocolor Panavision
MGM-UA / Richard Shepherd

A couple of ageless vampires are desperate for blood.
Absurd attempt to update Dracula with lashings of sex, rock music and flashy photography. An ordeal.

w Ivan Davis, Michael Thomas, novel Whitley Strieber d Tony Scott ph Stephen Goldblatt, Tom Mangravite m Michael Rubini, Denny Jaeger pd Brian Morris

Catherine Deneuve, Susan Sarandon, David Bowie, Cliff de Young
'One of the most incoherent and foolish pictures of recent months.'—Observer
● Video: MGM / UA

Hungry Hill
GB 1946 92m bw
GFD / Two Cities (William Sistrom)

An Irish family feud spans three generations. Rather uninteresting costume melodrama.

w Daphne du Maurier, Terence Young, Francis Crowdy d Brian Desmond Hurst ph Desmond Dickinson

Margaret Lockwood, Dennis Price, Cecil Parker, Michael Denison, F. J. McCormick, Dermot Walsh, Jean Simmons, Eileen Herlie, Siobhan McKenna, Eileen Crowe, Dan O'Herlihy

Hunted*
GB 1952 84m bw
GFD / Independent Artists (Julian Wintle)
US title: The Stranger in Between

A runaway boy joins forces with a runaway murderer, and the latter sacrifices himself for the boy's safety.
Predictable pattern melodrama, nicely made and acted.

w Jack Whittingham d Charles Crichton ph Eric Cross m Hubert Clifford

Dirk Bogarde, Jon Whiteley, Kay Walsh, Elizabeth Sellars, Frederick Piper, Geoffrey Keen, Julian Somers

Hunted Men*
US 1938 67m bw
Paramount

A killer on the run moves into a private home and is outwitted by the head of the house. Competent second feature which sticks in the memory.

w Horace McCoy, William R. Lipman d Louis King ph Victor Milner

Lloyd Nolan, Lynne Overman, Mary Carlisle, J. Carrol Naish, Anthony Quinn, Dorothy Peterson

The Hunter
US 1980 117m Metrocolor
Paramount / Rastar / Mort Engelberg

Episodes in the violent career of an urban bounty hunter.
The action scenes salvage a mysteriously banal screenplay full of continuity lapses and unexplained characters.

w Ted Leighton, Peter Hyams book Christopher Keane, and the life of Ralph Thorson d Buzz Kulik ph Fred J. Koenekamp m Michel Legrand

Steve McQueen (his last film), Eli Wallach, Kathryn Harrold, LeVar Burton, Ben Johnson
'The final impression is of an extended TV pilot for yet another police-boosting serial with more action than sense.'—Sunday Times
● Video: CIC

The Hunters
US 1958 108m De Luxe Cinemascope
TCF (Dick Powell)

A fearless American pilot is sent to Korea on a special mission.
Standard war thriller, good to look at when airborne but pretty boring on the ground; propaganda element very strong.

w Wendell Mayes d Dick Powell ph Charles G. Clarke m Paul Sawtell

Robert Mitchum, Robert Wagner, Richard Egan, Mai Britt

The Hunting Party
US 1971 108m De Luxe
UA / Brighton / Levy–Gardner–Levy

A sadistic Texas baron sets out to shoot one by one the outlaws who have kidnapped his wife.
Crude, brutish and repellent melodrama: the epitome of permissiveness, replete with gore, rape and sadism.

w William Norton, Gilbert Alexander, Lou Morheim d Don Medford ph Cecilio Paniagua m Riz Ortolani

Gene Hackman, Candice Bergen, Oliver Reed

'Through miles of raging ocean he defied man's law!'

The Hurricane**
US 1937 110m bw
Samuel Goldwyn (Merritt Hulburd)

The simple life on a South Pacific island is disrupted, not only by a vindictive governor but by a typhoon.

Tolerable island melodrama with a spectacular climax and a generally good cast.

w Dudley Nichols, Oliver H. P. Garrett, novel Charles Nordhof, James Norman Hall d John Ford, Stuart Heisler ph Bert Glennon m Alfred Newman

Dorothy Lamour, Jon Hall, C. Aubrey Smith, Mary Astor, Raymond Massey, Thomas Mitchell, John Carradine, Jerome Cowan
'A big money picture . . . a production masterpiece.'—Variety
† Remade in 1979.
AAN: Alfred Newman; Thomas Mitchell

Hurricane
US 1979 120m Technicolor Todd AO 70
Dino de Laurentiis / Famous Films (Lorenzo Semple Jnr)

A remake of the 1937 film, lacking the style, the innocence, and even the technical splendour.

w Lorenzo Semple Jnr d Jan Troell ph Sven Nykvist m Nino Rota pd Danilo Donati

Jason Robards, Mia Farrow, Trevor Howard, Max Von Sydow, Dayton Ka'ne, Timothy Bottoms, James Keach

Hurricane Island
US 1951 71m Supercinecolor

Spaniards colonizing Florida are beset by evil spirits. Saturday matinee hokum in poor colour. Jon Hall, Edgar Barrier, Marie Windsor, Marc Lawrence. Written by David Matthews; directed by Lew Landers; for Sam Katzman / Columbia.

Hurricane Smith
US 1952 90m Technicolor
Paramount / Nat Holt

An adventurer charters a boat to find a South Sea treasure but the boat owner turns the tables on him.
Standard thick ear with plenty of action.

w Frank Gruber d Jerry Hopper ph Ray Rennahan m Paul Sawtell

John Ireland, Yvonne de Carlo, James Craig, Forrest Tucker

'Will the south overcome the bigotry of the hate-laden white aristocrats?'

Hurry Sundown
US 1967 146m Technicolor Panavision
Paramount / Sigma (Otto Preminger)

Post-war racial problems in Georgia farmland, with degenerate whites and noble blacks.
Incredibly cliché-ridden epic melodrama with action and sex asides, from a rock bottom bestseller. It long outstays its welcome even for unintentional hilarity.

w Thomas C. Ryan, Horton Foote, novel K. B. Gilden d Otto Preminger ph Loyal Griggs, Milton Krasner m Hugo Montenegro

THE HURRICANE.   Dorothy Lamour and Jon Hall withstand all the punishment the studio wind machines can give.

Jane Fonda, Michael Caine, Rex Ingram, Diahann Carroll, Burgess Meredith, John Philip Law, Robert Hooks, Faye Dunaway, Beah Richards, George Kennedy, Madeleine Sherwood

'Critic Wilfrid Sheed wrote recently that no film is ever so bad that you can't find some virtue in it. He must not have seen *Hurry Sundown*.'—*Rex Reed*

'To criticize it would be like tripping a dwarf.'—*Wilfrid Sheed*

'A pantomime version of Greek tragedy.'—*MFB*

'Preminger's taste is atrocious. His idea of erotic symbolism is Jane Fonda caressing Michael Caine's saxophone.'—*Cue*

'A comedy about love, death, and freedom!'
Husbands*
US 1970 154m De Luxe
Columbia / Faces Music Inc (Al Ruban)

Three married men, shocked by the death of their friend, impulsively get drunk, fly to London and set out on a weekend of dissipation.
Irritatingly rough hewn and insanely overlong, this half-improvised tragi-comedy forces three good actors to overplay embarrassingly; but its best moments are memorable.

wd John Cassavetes *ph* Victor Kemper
m none

Peter Falk, John Cassavetes, Ben Gazzara

Husband's Holiday
US 1931 70m bw

A wife takes a passive attitude to her husband's affair. Tepid sophisticated comedy which doesn't register. Clive Brook, Vivienne Osborne, Charles Ruggles, Juliette Compton, Charles Winninger, Elizabeth Patterson. Written by Ernest Pascal from his play The Marriage Bed; directed by Robert Milton; for Paramount. 'Mild drawing-room problem play made even milder by repressed acting.'—*Variety*

Hush Hush Sweet Charlotte*
US 1964 133m bw
TCF / Associates and Aldrich

A southern belle lives thirty-seven years in a lonely mansion tormented by nightmarish memories of her fiancé's murder. Suddenly, after a series of apparent hauntings and other strange events, she finds she didn't do it. Padded but generally enjoyable replay of elements from *Whatever Happened to Baby Jane*, with a large helping of *Les Diaboliques*. The stars help more than the director.

w Henry Farrell, Lukas Heller *d* Robert Aldrich *ph* Joseph Biroc *m* Frank de Vol *ad* William Glasgow

Bette Davis, Olivia de Havilland, Joseph Cotten, Cecil Kellaway, Victor Buono, William Marshall, Mary Astor, Agnes Moorehead

'The blood is on the cleaver, the madwoman is on the loose, the headless corpse is on the prowl and the Guignol is about as grand as it can get.'—*Judith Crist*
AAN: Joseph Biroc; Frank de Vol; Agnes Moorehead; title song (*m* Frank de Vol, *ly* Mack David)

Hush Money
US 1931 68m bw

A girl serves a jail term, but afterwards gets involved with a racketeer. Underworld comedy-drama which paid its way. Joan Bennett, Owen Moore, Hardie Albright, Myrna Loy, C. Henry Gordon, George Raft. Written by Dudley Nichols and Courtney Terret; directed by Sidney Lanfield; for Fox. 'A light programmer for fair grosses.'—*Variety*

Hussy
GB 1979 94m Eastmancolor

A high-class prostitute becomes involved with gangsters but eventually finds a new life for herself and her offspring. Tedious exploitation melodrama, shot like a ninety-minute commercial. Helen Mirren, John Shea, Daniel Chasin, Jenny Runacre. Written and directed by Matthew Chapman; for Boyd's Company.

Hustle
US 1975 118m Eastmancolor
Paramount / RoBurt (Robert Aldrich)

A police lieutenant lives with a call girl and is drawn into her corrupt life.
Doleful crime melodrama with both eyes in the gutter.

w Steve Shagan *d* Robert Aldrich *ph* Joseph Biroc *m* Frank de Vol

Burt Reynolds, Catherine Deneuve, Ben Johnson, Paul Winfield, Eddie Albert, Ernest Borgnine, Catherine Bach, Jack Carter

'A fine companion piece to *Kiss Me Deadly* in its vision of a journey to the end of the night in quest of a myth.'—*Tim Milne*

'Even with such a meandering script as this, one expects more than the paltry fare Aldrich offers.'—*Paul Coleman*

The Hustler**
US 1961 135m bw Cinemascope
TCF / Robert Rossen

A pool room con man comes to grief when he falls in love.
Downbeat melodrama with brilliantly handled and atmospheric pool table scenes; the love interest is redundant.

w Robert Rossen, Sidney Carroll, *novel*
Walter Tevis *d* Robert Rossen *ph* Eugen
Schufftan *m* Kenyon Hopkins

*Paul Newman, Jackie Gleason, George C.
Scott, Piper Laurie, Myron McCormick,
Murray Hamilton, Michael Constantine*
  'There is an overall impression of intense
violence, and the air of spiritual decadence has
rarely been conveyed so vividly.'—*David
Robinson*

AA: Eugen Schufftan
AAN: best picture; script; Robert Rossen (as
director); Paul Newman; Jackie Gleason;
George C. Scott; Piper Laurie

● *Video: CBS / Fox*

Hyde Park Corner
GB 1935 84m bw

Events of 1780 at Hyde Park Corner seem to
happen again in modern times. Half-hearted
reincarnation romance with good moments.
Gordon Harker, Binnie Hale, Gibb
McLaughlin, Harry Tate, Eric Portman,
Donald Wolfit. Written by D. B. Wyndham-
Lewis, from the play by Walter Hackett;
directed by Sinclair Hill; for Grosvenor.

The Hypnotic Eye
US 1960 79m bw

A mad killer hypnotizes pretty girls into
defacing themselves. Unattractive thriller
including much mumbo-jumbo about
hypnotism. Jacques Bergerac, Allison Hayes,
Merry Anders, Marcia Henderson. Written by
Gitta and William Read Woodfield; directed
by George Blair; for Allied Artists.

Hysteria
GB 1964 85m bw
MGM / Hammer (Jimmy Sangster)

An American suffering from amnesia is
discharged from a London clinic and walks
into a murder plot.
Complicated and rather unsympathetic
Hammer twister.

w Jimmy Sangster *d* Freddie Francis *ph* John
Wilcox *m* Don Banks

Robert Webber, Lelia Goldoni, Anthony
Newlands, Jennifer Jayne, *Maurice Denham*,
Peter Woodthorpe

● *Video: MGM / UA*

I Accuse*
GB 1958 99m bw Cinemascope
MGM (Sam Zimbalist)

In 1894 Paris, Alfred Dreyfus is tried for
treason and later defended by Emile Zola.
A well tried historical incident is stolidly retold
and unsuitably wide-screened; the star cast
tends to flounder for lack of assistance.

w Gore Vidal d Jose Ferrer ph Frederick A.
Young m William Alwyn

Jose Ferrer (Dreyfus), *Anton Walbrook*
(Esterhazy), Emlyn Williams (Zola), Viveca
Lindfors, David Farrar, Leo Genn, Herbert
Lom, Harry Andrews, Felix Aylmer, George
Coulouris, Donald Wolfit

I Aim at the Stars
US 1960 107m bw
Columbia / Morningside / Fama (Charles H.
Schneer)

The story of German rocket expert Wernher
Von Braun and his later work on American
space vehicles.
Shaky biopic of a controversial scientist who
changed sides.

w Jay Dratler d J. Lee-Thompson ph Wilkie
Cooper m Laurie Johnson

Curt Jurgens, Herbert Lom, James Daly, Gia
Scala, Victoria Shaw, Adriah Hoven, Karel
Stepanek
  'Mannered panning shots and crafty cutting
abound, leading to a stylistic St Vitus'
Dance.'—*John Gillett*

'The biggest double exposure since Adam
and Eve!'

I Am a Camera
GB 1955 99m bw
Romulus (Jack Clayton)

A young English writer observes life in Berlin
in the early thirties, and has a platonic
relationship with an amoral and reckless young
English girl.
A rather flat and flabby treatment of the
stories by Christopher Isherwood and the play
by John Van Druten, all better known these
days in the form of *Cabaret*. Disappointingly
unstylish.

w John Collier d Henry Cornelius ph Guy
Green m Malcolm Arnold

Julie Harris, Laurence Harvey, Shelley
Winters, Ron Randell, Anton Diffring
● *Video: CBS / Fox*

'Six sticks of dynamite that blasted his way
to freedom . . . and awoke America's
conscience!'

I Am a Fugitive from a Chain Gang**
US 1932 90m bw
Warner (Hal B. Wallis)

An innocent man is convicted and after brutal
treatment with the chain gang becomes a
vicious criminal on the run.
Horrifying story in the semi-documentary
manner; a milestone in Hollywood history and
still a fairly compelling piece of shock
entertainment.

w *Sheridan Gibney, Brown Holmes, Robert E.
Barns* d *Mervyn Le Roy* ph *Sol Polito*

Paul Muni, Glenda Farrell, Helen Vinson,
Preston Foster, Allen Jenkins, Edward J.
Macnamara, Berton Churchill, Edward Ellis
  'A picture with guts . . . everything about it
is technically 100% . . . shy on romantic
angles, but should get nice money all over.'—
Variety
  'To be enthusiastically commended for its
courage, artistic sincerity, dramatic vigour,
high entertainment concept and social
message.'—*Wilton A. Barrett*
  'I quarrel with the production not because it
is savage and horrible, but because each step
in an inevitable tragedy is taken clumsily, and
because each character responsible for the
hero's doom is shown more as a caricature
than as a person.'—*Pare Lorentz*

AAN: best picture; Paul Muni

I Am a Thief
US 1934 64m bw

Robbery and murder on the Orient Express.
Involved programmer which becomes as
tiresome as its library footage. Mary Astor,
Ricardo Cortez, Dudley Digges, Robert
Barrat, Irving Pichel. Written by Ralph Block
and Doris Malloy; directed by Robert Florey;
for Warners. 'Should be able to top on a
double bill but will have a tough time
singling.'—*Variety*

I Am Not Afraid
US 1939 59m bw

An old man testifies against political terrorists.
Tepid remake of *Star Witness*. Charley
Grapewin, Jane Bryan, Henry O'Neill,
Elizabeth Risdon. Written by Lee Katz;
directed by Crane Wilbur; for Warners. 'Filler
for the duals.'—*Variety*

I Am Suzanne*
US 1933 99m bw

A dancer in love with a puppeteer comes
under the influence of gangsters. Curious but
vaguely endearing mixture of music and
mayhem, with the puppets used as symbolic
furtherers of the plot. Lilian Harvey, Gene
Raymond, Leslie Banks, Georgia Caine,
Halliwell Hobbes. Written by Edwin Justus
Mayer and Rowland V. Lee; directed by
Rowland V. Lee; for Jesse L. Lasky / Fox.
'Not a wow, but rates fairly well.'—*Variety*

I Am the Law*
US 1938 83m bw
Columbia (Everett Riskin)

A law professor is asked by a civic leader to
become a special prosecutor cleaning up
rackets.
Adequate star potboiler, quite enjoyable.

w Jo Swerling d Alexander Hall ph Henry
Freulich md Morris Stoloff

Edward G. Robinson, Otto Kruger, John
Beal, Barbara O'Neil, Wendy Barrie, Arthur
Loft, Marc Lawrence
  'A slam-bang, rip-roaring meller that has all
the elements of previous films inspired by
District Attorney Thomas E. Dewey's
career.'—*Variety*

I Believed in You
US 1934 69m bw

A wife is driven to leave her radical agitator
husband. Initially interesting but
unsatisfactory romantic melodrama. Rosemary
Ames, Victor Jory, John Boles, Gertrude
Michael, George Meeker. Written by William
Conselman; directed by Irving Cummings;
for Fox. 'Some idea, but lacking punch in plot
and direction.'—*Variety*

I Believe in You*
GB 1952 95m bw
Ealing (Michael Relph)

Interwoven stories of probation officers;
watchable and reasonable but not very
compelling.

w Michael Relph, Basil Dearden, Jack
Whittingham, Nicholas Phipps d Basil
Dearden ph Gordon Dines m Ernest Irving

Celia Johnson, Cecil Parker, Godfrey Tearle,
Harry Fowler, George Relph, Joan Collins,
Laurence Harvey, Ernest Jay, Ursula Howells,
Sidney James, Katie Johnson, Ada Reeve,
Brenda de Banzie

I Bury the Living
US 1957 77m bw

The honorary chairman of a cemetery seems to have the power to mark people for death.
Unusual enough to be encouraging, sloppy enough to disappoint even mystery lovers.
Richard Boone, Theodore Bikel, Herbert Anderson, Peggy Maurer. Written by Louis Garfinkle; directed by Albert Band; for Maxim / UA.

I Can Get It for You Wholesale*
US 1951 89m bw
TCF (Sol C. Siegel)
GB title: *This Is My Affair*
American TV title: Only the Best

An ambitious young mannequin starts her own dressmaking firm and sets her sights high.
Watchable comedy-drama which quickly sheds the edge of satire which might have made it the dressmaker's *All About Eve*.

w Abraham Polonsky, *novel* Jerome Weidman d Michael Gordon ph Milton Krasner m Sol Kaplan md Lionel Newman

Susan Hayward, Dan Dailey, George Sanders, Sam Jaffe, Randy Stuart, Marvin Kaplan, Harry Von Zell

'Crushed lips don't talk!'
I Confess**
US 1953 94m bw
Warner / Alfred Hitchcock

A priest hears the confession of a murderer and cannot divulge it to the police even though he is himself suspected.
Hitchcock is always worth watching, and although this old chestnut gives him very restricted scope he imbues the story with a strong feeling for its setting (Quebec) and an overpowering sense of doom.

w George Tabori, William Archibald, *play* Paul Anthelme d *Alfred Hitchcock* ph Robert Burks m Dmitri Tiomkin

Montgomery Clift, Anne Baxter, Brian Aherne, Karl Malden, Dolly Haas, O. E. Hasse
    'Whatever its shortcomings, it has the professional concentration of effect, the narrative control, of a story teller who can still make most of his rivals look like amateurs.'— *MFB*
● *Video: Warner*

I Could Go on Singing*
GB 1963 99m Eastmancolor
    Panavision
UA / Barbican (Lawrence Turman)

An American singing star in Britain looks up an old lover and tries to take over their illegitimate son, but the call of the footlights proves stronger.
The star enjoys her last specially-tailored role; a banal, old-fashioned agreeable one-woman show.

w Mayo Simon d Ronald Neame ph Arthur Ibbetson m Mort Lindsey

Judy Garland, Dirk Bogarde, Aline MacMahon, Jack Klugman
    'Merely standard fare in an age without standards.'—*John Simon*

I Cover the Waterfront*
US 1933 75m bw
(UA) Twentieth Century (Edward Small)

A reporter uses a girl's friendship to expose her father's smuggling activities.
In its time a tough, even daring melodrama, this plot has now become the stuff of every other TV series episode.

w Wells Root, Jack Jevne, Max Miller d James Cruze ph Ray June m Alfred Newman

Claudette Colbert, Ben Lyon, Ernest Torrence, Hobart Cavanaugh
    'Combination of title, picturesque background and three good performances should offset inferior story for favourable business.'—*Variety*
    'A bit raw and a bit sentimental and a bit routine, the film does let life in through the cracks.'—*Graham Greene*
† Credited with being the origin of the phrase, 'Not tonight, Josephine!'

I Didn't Do It
GB 1945 97m bw
Columbia (Ben Henry, Marcel Varnel)

Murder in a theatrical boarding house, with suspicion pointing at Our George.
One of the star's last vehicles: not too bad at all, but without the sweet smell of success.

w Howard Irving Young, Stephen Black, Norman Lee, Peter Fraser, Michael Vaughan d Marcel Varnel ph Roy Fogwell

George Formby, Billy Caryll, Hilda Mundy, Gaston Palmer, Jack Daly, Carl Jaffe, Marjorie Browne, Wally Patch

I Died a Thousand Times
US 1955 109m Warnercolor
    Cinemascope
Warner (Willis Goldbeck)

An ex-convict plans a big hotel robbery, but things go wrong within his gang.
Overlong, heavygoing, tedious gangster melodrama with too much talk.

w W. R. Burnett d Stuart Heisler ph Ted McCord m David Buttolph

Jack Palance, Shelley Winters, Lori Nelson, Lon Chaney Jnr, Lee Marvin, Gonzales Gonzales, Earl Holliman, Perry Lopez
    'This remake of *High Sierra* is scarcely more inspired than its title.'—*MFB*
    'It is an insult to the intelligence to pull this old mythological hero out of the archives and set him on a mountaintop again.'—*New York Times*

The I Don't Care Girl*
US 1953 78m Technicolor
TCF (George Jessel)

The life of musical entertainer Eva Tanguay, at her height during World War I, as told by three men in her life.
Breezy, conventional backstage musical biopic.

w Walter Bullock d Lloyd Bacon ph Arthur Arling md Lionel Newman ch Jack Cole, Seymour Felix

Mitzi Gaynor, David Wayne, Oscar Levant, *George Jessel*, Warren Stevens

I Don't Want to be Born
GB 1975 94m Eastmancolor
(Rank) Unicapital (Norma Corney)
US title: *The Devil within Her*

An ex-stripper gives birth to a monstrous baby which goes on a murderous rampage.
Sick horror stuff with a high death rate and no notable credits.

w Stanley Price d Peter Sasdy ph Ken Talbot m Ron Grainer

Joan Collins, Ralph Bates, Donald Pleasence, Eileen Atkins, George Claydon

I Dood It!
US 1943 102m bw
MGM (Jack Cummings)
GB title: *By Hook or by Crook*

A tailor falls for a Hollywood star.
Boring star comedy with interpolated musical numbers.

w Sig Herzig, Fred Saidy d Vincente Minnelli ph Ray June md Georgie Stoll

Red Skelton, Eleanor Powell, John Hodiak, Lena Horne, Jimmy Dorsey and his Orchestra, Hazel Scott, Richard Ainley

I Dream of Jeannie
US 1952 90m Trucolor

The loves and financial problems of songwriter Stephen Foster. Low-key musical biopic covering exactly the same ground as *Swanee River*. Ray Middleton (as E. P. Christy), Bill Shirley, Muriel Lawrence, Rex Allen. Written by Alan Le May; directed by Allan Dwan; for Republic.

I Dream Too Much
US 1935 95m bw
RKO (Pandro S. Berman)

A French girl singer marries an American composer.
Forgettable vehicle for an operatic star.

w Edmund North, James Gow d John Cromwell ph David Abel songs Jerome Kern, Dorothy Fields

Lily Pons, Henry Fonda, Eric Blore, Osgood Perkins, Lucien Littlefield, Lucille Ball, Esther Dale, Mischa Auer, Paul Porcasi
    'It will be a winner at the box office without breaking any records.'—*Variety*

I Escaped from Devil's Island
US 1973 81m De Luxe
UA Roger Corman, Gene Corman

In 1918, a black convict makes his plans for escape.
Rough, brutish melodrama which plainly aimed to beat *Papillon* to the box office.

w Richard L. Adams d William Witney ph Rosalio Solano m Les Baxter

Jim Brown, Christopher George, Rick Ely, James Luisi, Richard Rust
    'Exploitation's own *Papillon*, mercifully free from big brother's pretentiousness.'—*Sight and Sound*

I Found Stella Parish
US 1935 85m bw

An actress tries to keep her naughty past from her child, but a blackmailer strikes. One for the ladies, who flocked to it in its day. Kay Francis, Paul Lukas, Ian Hunter, Sybil Jason, Jessie Ralph, Barton MacLane. Written by Casey Robinson; directed by Mervyn Le Roy; for Warners. 'Will receive widespread support at the box office all the way from the best runs down to the subsequents, in the big keys and in the smallest towns.'—*Variety*

I Give My Love
US 1934 68m bw

A mother goes to prison for killing her no-good husband. Tedious mother-love story with a happy ending. Paul Lukas, Wynne Gibson, Eric Linden, Anita Louise. Written by Doris Anderson from a novel by Vicki Baum; directed by Karl Freund; for Universal. 'Good, clean, wholesome, although wholly unoriginal entertainment.'—*Variety*

I, Jane Doe
US 1948 85m bw

A French girl comes to America in search of the flyer she married during the war. When she finds he was already married, she shoots him. Melodrama for women, culminating in an unconvincing trial scene. Ruth Hussey, John Carroll, Vera Ralston, Gene Lockhart, John Howard. Written by Lawrence Kimble; directed by John H. Auer; for Republic. (GB title: *Diary of a Bride*).

I Killed Rasputin
France / Italy 1967 100m
Eastmancolor Franscope
Copernic / CGC (Raymond Danon)

The evil monk of the Russian court is killed by Prince Yusopov.
Dull version of a much told story. One of the big international films that never seems to get shown anywhere.

w Alain Decaux, Claude Desailly, Robert Hossein d Robert Hossein ph Henri Persin m André Hossein

Gert Frobe, Peter McEnery, Robert Hossein, Geraldine Chaplin, Ira Furstenberg, Patrick Balkany
'A tedious illustrated history lesson which actually manages to obscure the motivation behind the murder.'—*MFB*
† The script was authorized by Prince Yusopov

I Killed the Count
GB 1939 89m bw
Grafton (Isadore Goldschmidt)

Four people confess to the murder of a philanderer.
Inept version of a West End success.

w Alec Coppel, Lawrence Huntington, play Alec Coppel d Fred Zelnik

Syd Walker, Ben Lyon, Terence de Marney, Barbara Blair, Antoinette Cellier, Kathleen Harrison, Athole Stewart, Leslie Perrins, Ronald Shiner

I Know Where I'm Going**
GB 1945 91m bw
GFD / The Archers (Michael Powell, Emeric Pressburger)

A determined girl travels to the Hebrides to marry a wealthy old man, but is stranded on Mull and marries a young naval officer instead.
A strange assembling of attractive but disparate elements: romance, comedy, bleak scenery, a trained hawk and a dangerous whirlpool. At the time it seemed to represent the Elizabethan age of the British cinema, and remains entertaining for its parts though a bit of a puzzle as a whole.

wd Michael Powell, Emeric Pressburger ph Erwin Hillier

Wendy Hiller, Roger Livesey, Pamela Brown, Nancy Price, Finlay Currie, John Laurie, George Carney, Walter Hudd
'Continuously fresh and interesting, intelligently written and played, and full of beautiful photography.'—*Richard Mallett, Punch*
'The sensitive photography and the intelligent if not very imaginative use of sound do more than enough to make eloquent the influence of place on people; and the whole thing is undertaken with taste and modesty.'—*James Agee*

I Like Your Nerve
US 1931 70m bw

A bookworm goes to Central America and becomes a romantic adventurer. Junior aspiring to Senior's seven league boots; he doesn't quite make it, and that's the script's fault. Douglas Fairbanks Jnr, Loretta Young, Claude Allister, Henry Kolker, Edmund Breon, Boris Karloff. Written by Houston Branch from a story by Roland Pertwee; directed by William McGann; for First National. 'Mediocre, unimpressive and implausible story . . . strictly an off-day booking.'—*Variety*

I Live for Love
US 1935 83m bw
Warner (Bryan Foy)
GB title: *I Live For You*

A socialite has show business leanings.
Minor musical.

w Jerry Wald, Julius Epstein, Robert Andrews d / ch Busby Berkeley ph George Barnes md Leo F. Forbstein

Dolores del Rio, Everett Marshall, Allen Jenkins, Eddie Conrad, Guy Kibbee, Berton Churchill

I Live in Grosvenor Square
GB 1945 113m bw
ABP (Herbert Wilcox)
US title: *A Yank in London*

A duke's daughter falls in love with an American air force sergeant.
Sloppily-made topical romance which was hot box office at the time and started the producer's 'London' romances: *Piccadilly Incident, Spring in Park Lane, Maytime in Mayfair,* etc.

w Nicholas Phipps, William D. Bayles, Maurice Cowan d Herbert Wilcox ph Max Greene

Anna Neagle, *Dean Jagger*, Rex Harrison, Robert Morley, Jane Darwell, Nancy Price, Irene Vanbrugh, Edward Rigby, Walter Hudd

I Live My Life
US 1935 85m bw
MGM (Bernard H. Hyman)

A bored society girl falls for a working class archaeologist.
Standard star romance.

w Joseph L. Mankiewicz, story Claustrophobia by A. Carter Goodloe d W. S. Van Dyke II ph George Folsey m Dmitri Tiomkin

Joan Crawford, Brian Aherne, Frank Morgan, Aline MacMahon, Eric Blore, Jessie Ralph, Arthur Treacher, Hedda Hopper, Etienne Girardot, Ed Brophy
'An amusing romance is backgrounded by clothes, cocktails and butlers.'—*Variety*

I Lived with You
GB 1933 100m bw

A cockney family find that their lodger is an exiled Russian prince. Overlong whimsy from a successful West End play. Ivor Novello, Ursula Jeans, Ida Lupino, Minnie Rayner, Eliot Makeham, Jack Hawkins. Written by H. Fowler Mear, from the play by Ivor Novello; directed by Maurice Elvey; for Twickenham.

I Love a Mystery*
US 1945 68m bw
Columbia

An eastern secret society offers a businessman a large sum for his head when he dies, as he resembles their founder whose embalmed head is deteriorating.
Start of a short series of mysteries from a radio series; the production was never up to the ingenious plots.

w Charles O'Neal d Henry Levin ph Burnett Guffey

George Macready, Jim Bannon, Nina Foch

'She kissed the boys goodbye—until Sonny said hello!'

I Love a Soldier
US 1944 106m bw
Paramount (Mark Sandrich)

A San Francisco girl thinks hard before embarking on a wartime marriage.
Glossy, insubstantial sudser chiefly memorable for casting its leading lady as a welder.

w Allan Scott d Mark Sandrich ph Charles Lang m Robert Emmett Dolan

Paulette Goddard, Sonny Tufts, Beulah Bondi, Walter Sande, Mary Treen, Ann Doran, Barry Fitzgerald

I Love Melvin*
US 1953 77m Technicolor
MGM (George Wells)

A photographer's assistant falls for a high-born chorus girl.
Zippy little musical with all concerned working hard with thin material.

w George Wells d Don Weis ph Harold Rosson m / ly Josef Myrow, Mack Gordon md George Stoll ch Robert Alton

Donald O'Connor, Debbie Reynolds, Una Merkel, Allyn Joslyn

I Love My Wife
US 1970 95m Technicolor
Universal (Robert Kaufman)

The affairs of a successful doctor with a guilt complex about sex.
Frantic, fashionable comedy drama with wildly erratic treatment and performances.

w Robert Kaufman d Mel Stuart ph Vilis Lapenieks m Lalo Schifrin

Elliott Gould, Brenda Vaccaro, Angel Tompkins
  'A leer-laden, anti-feminist tract disguised as a comedy.'—Judith Crist

I Love You Again*
US 1940 99m bw
MGM (Lawrence Weingarten)

A much married man gets amnesia and turns into a gay Lothario.
Sprightly romantic comedy with all concerned letting rip until the pace slows.

w Charles Lederer, George Oppenheimer, Harry Kurnitz d W. S. Van Dyke II ph Oliver T. Marsh m Franz Waxman

William Powell, Myrna Loy, Frank McHugh, Edmund Lowe, Donald Douglas, Nella Walker, Pierre Watkin

I Love You, Alice B. Toklas*
US 1968 93m Technicolor
Warner Seven Arts / Paul Mazursky, Larry Tucker

An asthmatic Los Angeles lawyer escapes his bullying fiancée by joining the flower people.
Quite amusing satirical farce about the dangers of marijuana. Gertrude Stein and Jewish mothers, thrown together with no great sense of style but achieving hilarious moments among the longueurs.

w Paul Mazursky, Larry Tucker d Hy Averback ph Philip Lathrop m Elmer Bernstein pd Pato Guzman

Peter Sellers, Jo Van Fleet, Joyce Van Patten, Leigh Taylor-Young, David Arkin, Herb Edelman

'Lips of thunder on lips of fire!'
I Loved a Woman*
US 1933 90m bw
Warner (Henry Blanke)

The career of a Chicago meat packer is hampered by his social-climbing wife.
Potboiling star melodrama which still holds some interest.

w Charles Kenyon, Sidney Sutherland d Alfred E. Green ph James Van Trees

Edward G. Robinson, Kay Francis, Genevieve Tobin, J. Farrell MacDonald, Henry Kolker, Robert Barrat
  'E.G.R. out of his class; may cut biz.'— Variety

I Loved You Wednesday
US 1933 77m bw

A man vies with a married friend for a lady's favour. Mildly amusing comedy of the second rank. Warner Baxter, Elissa Landi, Victor Jory, Miriam Jordan, Laura Hope Crews. Written by Philip Klein and Horace Jackson from the play by Molly Ricardei and William Dubois; directed by Henry King and William Cameron Menzies; for Fox. 'A romantic comedy-drama of first-rate possibilities, beautifully made and abundantly provided with class.'—Variety

I Married a Doctor
US 1936 87m bw

An idealistic city girl marries a small-town doctor. Solidly carpentered version of Sinclair Lewis's Main Street (filmed under its own title in 1923, with Florence Vidor, directed by Harry Beaumont). Josephine Hutchinson, Pat O'Brien, Ross Alexander, Guy Kibbee, Louise Fazenda. Written by Casey Robinson, Harriet Ford and Harvey O'Higgin; directed by Archie Mayo; for Warner.

I Married a Monster from Outer Space*
US 1958 78m bw
Paramount / Gene Fowler Jnr

A young man is taken over by alien invaders but his wife helps to destroy them and bring him back to normal.
Decent, plodding, reasonably effective low-budget science fiction on a well-trampled theme; its minor virtues have been effaced by its silly title.

w Louis Vittes d Gene Fowler Jnr ph Haskell Boggs sp John P. Fulton

Tom Tryon, Gloria Talbott, Robert Ivers

'She knows all about love potions . . . and lovely motions!'
I Married a Witch***
US 1942 82m bw
(UA) Cinema Guild / René Clair

A Salem witch and her sorcerer father come back to haunt the descendant of the Puritan who had them burned.
Delightful romantic comedy fantasy which shows all concerned at the top of their form. Hollywood moonshine, impeccably distilled.

w Robert Pirosh, Marc Connelly, novel The Passionate Witch by Thorne Smith d René Clair ph Ted Tetzlaff m Roy Webb

Fredric March, Veronica Lake, Cecil Kellaway, Robert Benchley, Susan Hayward, Elizabeth Patterson, Robert Warwick
  'A delightful sense of oddity and enchantment.'—New York World Telegram
AAN: Roy Webb

I Married a Woman
US 1956 85m bw (colour sequence)
RKOscope
RKO

A nervous young advertising executive neglects his wife, who determines to make him jealous.
Simple-minded comedy tailored to unsympathetic stars.

w Goodman Ace d Hal Kanter ph Lucien Ballard m Cyril Mockridge

George Gobel, Diana Dors, Adolphe Menjou, Jessie Royce Landis, Nita Talbot

'It brings laughter and song to the screen as this pair from paradise is joyously reunited!'
I Married an Angel
US 1942 84m bw
MGM (Hunt Stromberg)

An attractive angel lures a playboy from his earthly girl friends.
Silly musical fantasy which spelled the end of a great musical star partnership.

w Anita Loos, play Vilismary Janos d W. S. Van Dyke ph Ray June m / ly Richard Rodgers, Lorenz Hart

Jeanette MacDonald, Nelson Eddy, Edward Everett Horton, Binnie Barnes, Reginald Owen, Douglass Dumbrille
  'As bland as operetta but without its energy.'—New Yorker, 1978

I Met a Murderer*
GB 1939 78m bw
Grand National / Gamma (Roy Kellino, Pamela Kellino, James Mason)

A murderer on the run meets a girl novelist who is touring in her motor caravan.
Semi-professional location melodrama which won commendation at the time but now seems very faded.

w Pamela Kellino, James Mason d Roy Kellino ph Roy Kellino m Eric Ansell

James Mason, Pamela Kellino, Sylvia Coleridge, William Devlin, Peter Coke
  'Graceful, gallant, resourceful . . . better and more enjoyable than most studio pictures.'—James Agee
  'That it has a number of defects does not mean that it is not worthy of serious consideration.'—Basil Wright

I Met Him in Paris*
US 1937 86m bw
Paramount (Wesley Ruggles)

A fashion designer spends five years' savings on a fling in Paris and finds herself pursued to Switzerland by two philanderers.
Not very witty but likeable romantic comedy with polished performers near their best.

w Claude Binyon d Wesley Ruggles ph Leo Tover m John Leopold md Boris Morros

Claudette Colbert, Melvyn Douglas, Robert Young, Lee Bowman, Mona Barrie
  'A moncy picture . . . laughs are piled on laughs.'—Variety
  'At least half the footage is a perfect scream, and if you miss it you are an old sobersides, and who cares.'—Otis Ferguson

I Met My Love Again
US 1937 77m bw
Walter Wanger

A small-town girl marries a drunken writer, but on his death returns to her first love, a biology professor.

Mildly pleasing, rather dated romantic drama with good local colour.

w David Hertz, *novel* Summer Lightning by Aileen Corliss *d* Joshua Logan, Arthur Ripley *ph* Hal Mohr

Henry Fonda, Joan Bennett, Alan Marshal, Dorothy Stickney, Dame May Whitty, Alan Baxter, Louise Platt, Tim Holt, Florence Lake
'Sentimentally as sticky as a gum drop, this sugar-coated romance will have to find its favour with the femmes.'—*Variety*

I, Mobster
US 1958 80m bw Cinemascope
Edward L. Alperson

A slum teenager becomes a top gangster.
Routine gangland thriller.

w Steve Fisher, *novel* Joseph Hilton Smith *d* Roger Corman *ph* Floyd Crosby *m* Gerald Fried

Steve Cochran, Lita Milan, Robert Strauss, Celia Lovsky, Grant Withers

I, Monster*
GB 1970 75m Eastmancolor
Amicus (Milton Subotsky)

A straight remake of *Dr Jekyll and Mr Hyde*, holding closely to the original novel but mysteriously using different names. Interesting minor work.

w Milton Subotsky *d* Stephen Weeks *ph* Moray Grant *m* Carl Davis *ad* Tony Curtis

Christopher Lee, Peter Cushing, Richard Hurndall, George Merritt

● *Video: Thorn EMI*

I Never Promised You a Rose Garden
US 1977 96m colour
New World / Imorh / Fadsin (Roger Corman)

A suicidal teenage girl is treated in a psychiatric hospital.
Careful, thoughtful case history which can't help, after so many TV movies of the kind, seeming rather too simple for a theatrical feature, as well as too heavy-going despite the upbeat ending.

w Gavin Lambert, Lewis John Carlino, *novel* Hannah Green *d* Anthony Page *ph* Bruce Logan *m* Paul Chihara *pd* Toby Rafelson

Kathleen Quinlan, Bibi Andersson, Sylvia Sidney, Ben Piazza, Lorraine Gary, Reni Santoni, Signe Hasso

I Never Sang for My Father*
US 1969 92m Technicolor
Columbia / Jamel (Gilbert Cates)

When his mother dies, a middle-aged widower is saddled with his cantankerous father, who tries to prevent him from remarrying.
Literal transcription of a Eugene O'Neillish play, a fascinating if depressing character study.

w Robert Anderson, from his play *d* Gilbert Cates *ph* Morris Hartzband, George Stoetzel *m* Al Gorgoni, Barry Mann

I MARRIED A WITCH. Fredric March watches with awe as Veronica Lake stoppers up her father.

Melvyn Douglas, Gene Hackman, Dorothy Stickney, Estelle Parsons

AAN: Robert Anderson; Melvyn Douglas; Gene Hackman

I Ought to Be in Pictures*
US 1982 107m De Luxe
TCF (Herbert Ross, Neil Simon)

A young actress hitch-hikes to Hollywood to break into pictures and also to see her estranged scriptwriter father.
Fairly agreeable comedy-drama in the Neil Simon manner, with the studio background an extra plus.

w Neil Simon, from his play *d* Herbert Ross *ph* David M. Walsh *m* Marvin Hamlisch *pd* Albert Brenner

Walter Matthau, Ann-Margret, Dinah Manoff, Lance Guest, Lewis Smith

I Passed for White
US 1960 92m bw
Allied Artists (Fred M. Wilcox)

A light-skinned Negress comes to New York but fails to achieve happiness by pretending to be white.
Earnest, rather dreary social drama which doesn't get anywhere.

d Fred M. Wilcox *ph* George J. Folsey *m* Johnny Williams

Sonya Wilde, James Franciscus, Pat Michon, Elizabeth Council

I Promise to Pay
US 1937 68m bw

An office worker finds himself at the wrong end of the loan shark racket. Competent programmer from the headlines. Chester Morris, Leo Carrillo, Helen Mack, Thomas Mitchell, Thurston Hall. Written by Mary McCall Jnr and Lionel Houser; directed by D. Ross Lederman; for Columbia. 'Just average . . . if placed on a dual bill, it'll be found more than enough to float its end.'—*Variety*

'The sweetest movie anyone would ever wish to see!'
I Remember Mama**
US 1948 134m bw
RKO (Harriet Parsons)

A novelist remembers some of the adventures of growing up with her Norwegian–American family.
Overlong, but well-upholstered nostalgia: warm-hearted, sentimental, nicely detailed, richly acted but just a little boring in spots.

w De Witt Bodeen, *play* John Van Druten, *book* Mama's Bank Account by Kathryn Forbes *d* George Stevens *ph* Nicholas Musuraca *m* Roy Webb

Irene Dunne, Barbara Bel Geddes, Oscar Homolka, Edgar Bergen, Philip Dorn, Ellen Corby, Florence Bates, Cedric Hardwicke, Barbara O'Neil, Rudy Vallee

AAN: Nicholas Musuraca; Irene Dunne; Barbara Bel Geddes; Oscar Homolka; Ellen Corby

I Saw What You Did
US 1965 82m bw
Universal / William Castle

A murderer thinks that two playful teenagers have witnessed his deed, and sets out to kill them too.
Predictable and long-winded suspenser, very short of inventive detail.
w William McGivern, *novel* Ursula Curtiss d William Castle ph Joseph Biroc m Van Alexander

John Ireland, Joan Crawford, Leif Erickson

I See a Dark Stranger**
GB 1945 112m bw
GFD / Individual
US title: *The Adventuress*

An Irish colleen who hates the English comes to England to spy for the Germans but falls in love with a young English officer.
Slipshod plotting does not quite destroy the jolly atmosphere of this comedy-thriller which has the cheek to take an IRA member as its heroine. Good fun, very well staged.
w *Frank Launder, Sidney Gilliat, Wolfgang Wilhelm & Frank Launder* ph Wilkie Cooper m William Alwyn

Deborah Kerr, Trevor Howard, Raymond Huntley, Norman Shelley, Michael Howard, Brenda Bruce, Liam Redmond, Brefni O'Rourke
'It is the cinematic equivalent of Irish blarney which inspires most of this picture.'—*MFB*
'There is some intelligence, grace and fun here, but essentially this seems to me a supercilious drama, as if it had been made by bright young men who had decided to package and toss a bone to the groundlings.'—*James Agee*

I See Ice
GB 1938 81m bw

The property man in an ice ballet company is a keen amateur photographer who accidentally snaps crooks at work. Fair star comedy with good production. George Formby, Kay Walsh, Betty Stockfeld, Cyril Ritchard, Garry Marsh. Written by Anthony Kimmins and Austin Melford; directed by Anthony Kimmins; for ATP.

I Sell Anything
US 1935 70m bw

An auctioneer rises in the business. Mildly interesting comedy-drama with character progress but not much plot. Pat O'Brien, Ann Dvorak, Claire Dodd, Roscoe Karns, Hobart Cavanaugh. Written by Brown Holmes, Sidney Sutherland; directed by Robert Florey; for First National. 'Nicely made and played, but all in one key.'—*Variety*

I Start Counting
GB 1969 105m De Luxe
UA / Triumvirate (David Greene)

A young girl thinks her foster-brother may be the sex murderer known to be rampant in the locality. But after a great many red herrings, of course, he is not. Strained psychological suspenser with good moments between the *longueurs*.
w Richard Harris, *novel* Audrey Erskine Lindop d David Greene ph Alex Thomson m Basil Kirchin pd Brian Eatwell

Jenny Agutter, Bryan Marshall, Clare Sutcliffe, Simon Ward, Lana Morris, Billy Russell, Fay Compton, Lally Bowers

I Stole a Million
US 1939 89m bw
Universal (Burt Kelly)

A cab driver cheated by a finance company becomes a criminal to support his family.
Ho-hum star melodrama.
w Nathanael West, *story* Lester Cole d Frank Tuttle ph Milton Krasner

George Raft, Claire Trevor, Dick Foran, Henry Armetta, Victor Jory, Joe Sawyer, Stanley Ridges
'Crime drama neatly packaged . . . topper for key duals at normal b.o.'—*Variety*

I Take This Woman
US 1931 74m bw
Paramount

A reckless society girl falls for a cowhand and agrees to live in his ramshackle house.
Patchy romantic comedy-drama of little remaining interest.
w Vincent Lawrence, *novel* Lost Ecstasy by Mary Roberts Rinehart d Marion Gering, Slavko Vorkapitch ph Victor Milner

Gary Cooper, Carole Lombard, Helen Ware, Lester Vail, Charles Trowbridge, Clara Blandick

I Take This Woman
US 1939 97m bw
MGM (Louis B. Mayer)

A doctor marries a beautiful European and decides too late that he does not love her.
Thin comedy-drama which Louis B. Mayer unaccountably took it into his head to produce personally. The results had to be re-shot so much and so often that Hollywood dubbed the film *I Re-Take This Woman*. It offers little in the way of entertainment.
w James Kevin McGuinness, *story* Charles MacArthur d W. S. Van Dyke ph Harold Rosson m Bronislau Kaper

Spencer Tracy, Hedy Lamarr, Verree Teasdale, Kent Taylor, Laraine Day, Mona Barrie, Jack Carson, Paul Cavanagh, Marjorie Main

I Thank a Fool
GB 1962 100m Metrocolor
Cinemascope
MGM (Anatole de Grunwald)

A woman found guilty of the murder of her

lover is offered a fresh start in the home of the prosecutor's family . . . but another nightmare situation builds up.
Jane Eyre melodrama of the loonier type, with good actors struggling through a wild but unrewarding script.
w Karl Tunberg, *novel* Audrey Erskine Lindop d Robert Stevens ph Harry Waxman m Ron Goodwin

Peter Finch, Susan Hayward, Diane Cilento, Cyril Cusack, Kieron Moore, Athene Seyler

I Thank You
GB 1941 81m bw

Actors seeking a backer become servants to a titled ex-star. Acceptable comedy vehicle. Arthur Askey, Richard Murdoch, Lily Morris, Moore Marriott, Graham Moffatt, Kathleen Harrison. Written by Howard Irving Young, Val Guest and Marriott Edgar; directed by Marcel Varnel; for Gainsborough.

I the Jury
US 1953 87m bw 3-D
Parklane (Victor Saville)

Private eye Mike Hammer avenges the murder of his friend.
Charmless toughie, roughly made and devoid of plot or character interest.
wd Harry Essex ph John Alton m Franz Waxman

Biff Elliott, Peggie Castle, Preston Foster, Elisha Cook Jnr, John Qualen

I the Jury
US 1982 109m colour
American Cinema / Larco / Solofilm (Robert Solo)

An amoral private eye avenges the murder of his Vietnam buddy.
Hard, brutal thriller more in line than the previous version with the tone of the novel.
w Larry Cohen d Richard T. Heffron ph Andrew Laszlo m Bill Conti pd Robert Gundlach

Armand Assante, Barbara Carrera, Luarene London, Alan King, Geoffrey Lewis, Paul Sorvino
'The repellent formula as usual, with the gun and the penis as interchangeable instruments of quick-fire tough-guy virility.'—*Sunday Times*

I Wake Up Screaming**
US 1941 79m bw
TCF (Milton Sperling)
GB and alternative title: *Hot Spot*

A model is murdered and her sister joins forces with the chief suspect to find the real killer.
Moody thriller with plenty going for it including one memorable performance.
w Dwight Taylor, *novel* Steve Fisher d H. Bruce Humberstone ph Edward Cronjager m Cyril Mockridge

Betty Grable, Victor Mature, Carole Landis, *Laird Cregar*, William Gargan, Alan Mowbray, Allyn Joslyn, Elisha Cook Jnr
† Remade as *Vicki* (qv).

I Walk Alone*
US 1947 98m bw
Paramount (Hal B. Wallis)

An ex-smuggler comes out seeking vengeance after fourteen years in prison.
Dreary gangster drama unworthy of its stars.

w Charles Schnee, *play* Beggars Are Coming to Town by Theodore Reeves d Byron Haskin ph Leo Tover m Victor Young

Burt Lancaster, Kirk Douglas, Lizabeth Scott, Wendell Corey, Kristine Miller, George Rigaud, Marc Lawrence, Mike Mazurki
  'The picture deserves, like four out of five other movies, to walk alone, tinkle a little bell, and cry Unclean, unclean.'—*James Agee*

I Walk the Line*
US 1970 97m Eastmancolor
Panavision
Columbia / Frankenheimer / Lewis / Halcyon / Atticus (Harold D. Cohen)

A Tennessee sheriff protects moonshiners for the favours of their daughter; when an investigator arrives, bloodshed results.
Competent but uninteresting hothouse melodrama in which only the plot twists compel attention.

w Alvin Sargent, *novel* An Exile by Madison Jones d John Frankenheimer ph David M. Walsh md Robert Johnson

Gregory Peck, Tuesday Weld, Estelle Parsons, Ralph Meeker

● Video: RCA / Columbia

I Walked with a Zombie*
US 1943 68m bw
RKO (*Val Lewton*)

A nurse is retained by a Caribbean planter to care for his voodoo-sick wife.
Mild horror from the famous Lewton package; some style, but generally thin stuff, the plot having been mirthfully borrowed from *Jane Eyre*.

w Curt Siodmak, Ardel Wray d *Jacques Tourneur* ph J. Roy Hunt m Roy Webb

Frances Dee, James Ellison, Tom Conway, Christine Gordon, Edith Barrett, James Bell, Sir Lancelot

I Wanna Hold Your Hand
US 1978 104m Technicolor
Universal / Steven Spielberg (Tamara Asseyev, Alex Rose)

A day in 1964 finds assorted New Jersey teenagers eagerly awaiting the Beatles' appearance on the Ed Sullivan Show. Modest period comedy utilizing fresh young talent.

w Robert Zemeckis, Bob Gale d Robert Zemeckis ph Donald M. Morgan m Meredith Wilson

Nancy Allen, Bobby diCicco, Marc McClure, Susan Kendall Newman

I Want a Divorce
US 1940 74m bw
Paramount

A young law student marries rashly, but is prevented from doing anything about it by examples of the unhappiness brought by divorce.
Peculiar comedy-drama which never seems to make up its mind to any particular course.

w Frank Butler, *story* Adela Rogers St John d Ralph Murphy ph Ted Tetzlaff m Victor Young

Dick Powell, Joan Blondell, Frank Fay, Gloria Dickson, Jessie Ralph, Conrad Nagel, Harry Davenport, Sidney Blackmer, Louise Beavers

I Want to Live*
US 1958 120m bw
(UA) Walter Wanger

A vagrant prostitute is executed in the gas chamber despite growing doubt as to her guilt.
Sober, harrowing treatment of the Barbara Graham case, uneasily adapted to provide a star role amid the tirade against capital punishment.

w Nelson Gidding, Don Mankiewicz d Robert Wise ph Lionel Lindon m John Mandel

Susan Hayward, Simon Oakland, Virginia Vincent, Theodore Bikel, Wesley Lau, Philip Coolidge
  'An inconclusive amalgam of variously unexplored themes.'—*Peter John Dyer*
AA: Susan Hayward
AAN: Nelson Gidding, Don Mankiewicz; Robert Wise; Lionel Lindon

' Want What I Want
GB 1971 105m Eastmancolor
Marayan (Raymond Stross)

Roy has a sex change operation and becomes Wendy.
Although based on an actual trans-sexual experience, this film confuses more than it informs, and provokes unintentional mirth when its glamorous star is playing a boy.

w Gillian Freeman, *novel* Geoff Brown d John Dexter ph Gerry Turpin m Johnny Harris

Anne Heywood, Paul Rogers, Harry Andrews, Jill Bennett

I Want You
US 1951 101m bw
Samuel Goldwyn

A family reacts to the Korean war.
Glossy small-town flagwaver; no *Best Years of Our Lives*.

w Irwin Shaw d Mark Robson ph Harry Stradling m Leigh Harline ad Richard Day

Dorothy McGuire, Dana Andrews, Farley Granger, Peggy Dow, Robert Keith, Ray Collins, Mildred Dunnock, Martin Milner, Jim Backus
  'A recruiting picture which seems to accept a third world war almost as a present reality.'—*Penelope Houston*
  'Below the entertaining surface it has very little of value to offer.'—*Richard Mallett, Punch*

'Blonde bomber—she flew them into the ground!'
I Wanted Wings*
US 1941 131m bw
Paramount (Arthur Hornblow Jnr)

The fortunes of three recruits to the American Air Force.
Cheerful, overlong recruiting poster with concessions to melodrama.

w Richard Maibaum, Beirne Lay Jnr, Sig Herzig d Mitchell Leisen ph Leo Tover, Elmer Dyer m Victor Young

Ray Milland, William Holden, Brian Donlevy, Wayne Morris, Veronica Lake, Constance Moore, Harry Davenport, Phil Brown
  'Far more a poster than a drama.'—*Howard Barnes, New York Herald Tribune*

'All the life and death moments a man can know!'
I Was a Communist for the FBI
US 1951 83m bw
Warner (Bryan Foy)

Matt Cvetic, a Pittsburgh steel worker, is actually an FBI agent working undercover to trap communists.
Crude and shoddy Red-baiting melodrama, a kind of updating of *Confessions of a Nazi Spy* but using a sadly deteriorated technique.

w Crane Wilbur, Matt Cvetic d Gordon Douglas ph Edwin DuPar m Max Steiner

Frank Lovejoy, Dorothy Hart, Phil Carey, James Millican, Richard Webb, Paul Picerni, Konstantin Shayne
  'It seems that this is a subject which Hollywood is incapable of tackling even at its customary level of journalistic efficiency.'—*Penelope Houston*

I Was a Male War Bride**
US 1949 105m bw
TCF (Sol C. Siegel)
GB title: *You Can't Sleep Here*

A WAC in Europe marries a French officer and can't get him home.
High-spirited farce against realistic backgrounds of war-torn Europe, which scarcely accord with Cary Grant's pretending to be a Frenchman (and later a Frenchwoman). Funny, though.

w Charles Lederer, Hagar Wilde, Leonard Spigelgass d Howard Hawks ph Norbert Brodine, Osmond Borradaile m Cyril Mockridge md Lionel Newman

Cary Grant, *Ann Sheridan*, Marion Marshall, Randy Stuart

I Was a Spy**
GB 1933 89m bw
Gaumont (Michael Balcon)

In Belgium 1914, a nurse is trained as a spy.
Good standard war espionage melodrama.

w W. P. Lipscomb, Ian Hay, *book* Marthe McKenna d Victor Saville ph Charles Van Enger

Madeleine Carroll, Conrad Veidt, Herbert Marshall, Gerald du Maurier, Edmund Gwenn, Donald Calthrop, Nigel Bruce, Anthony Bushell, Martita Hunt

WHO SAID THE DEAD DON'T WALK?

SHE'S ALIVE ...YET DEAD!

SHE'S DEAD ...YET ALIVE!

THE STRANGEST CASE IN ALL MYSTERIA!

SEE IT HAPPEN — right before your startled eyes..in the screen sensation that rips the mask from the darkest secrets of forbidden voodoo!

STRANGE VOODOO SECRETS SENSATIONALLY REVEALED!

I WALKED WITH A ZOMBIE

RKO RADIO PICTURES

JAMES ELLISON • FRANCES DEE • TOM CONWAY

Produced by VAL LEWTON
Directed by JACQUES TOURNEUR
Screen Play by Curt Siodmak and Ardel Wray
Based on an Original Story by Inez Wallace

I WALKED WITH A ZOMBIE.   The curiously familiar plot of this uneasy thriller led some critics to label it 'Jane Eyre in the Tropics'.

'Body of a boy! Mind of a monster! Soul of an unearthly thing!'

I Was a Teenage Frankenstein
US 1957   72m   bw
American International (Herman Cohen)
GB title: *Teenage Frankenstein*

Professor Frankenstein fashions a creature from selected morsels of old corpses, and kills a teenager to give it a more handsome head.
It seemed gruesome enough at the time, but by 1980 standards this is tame, cheap stuff, only notable for its occasional bravura.

w Kenneth Langtry *d* Herbert J. Strock
ph Lothrop Worth *m* Paul Dunlap

Whit Bissell, Phyllis Coates, Gary Conway, Robert Burton

† In-joke: when the professor crates up the monster to send it to London, the address is 113 Wardour Street, which is Hammer House . . .

I Was a Teenage Werewolf
US 1957   76m   bw
AIP / Sunset (Herman Cohen)

A scientist experiments on an aggressive student and turns him into a werewolf.
Hilarious farrago with a title which achieved a splendour of its own.

w Ralph Thornton *d* Gene Fowler Jnr
ph Joseph La Shelle *m* Paul Dunlap

Michael Landon, Whit Bissell, Yvonne Lime

I Was An Adventuress*
US 1940   81m   bw
TCF (Darryl F. Zanuck)

A ballerina works as decoy for a pair of confidence tricksters.
Pleasing comedy drama with striking cast.

w Karl Tunberg, Don Ettlinger, John O'Hare *d* Gregory Ratoff *ph* Leon Shamroy, Edward Cronjager *md* David Buttolph

Vera Zorina, Erich Von Stroheim, Peter Lorre, Richard Greene, Sig Rumann, Fritz Feld, Cora Witherspoon

I Was Happy Here*
GB 1965   91m   bw
Partisan (Roy Millichip)
US title: *Time Lost and Time Remembered*

A girl leaves her husband in London and returns to the little Irish port of her childhood.
Nicely made, over-mannered study in nostalgia and lost illusions.

w Edna O'Brien, Desmond Davis *d* Desmond Davis *ph* Manny Wynn *m* John Addison
Sarah Miles, Cyril Cusack, Julian Glover, Sean Caffrey, Marie Kean

I Was Monty's Double**
GB 1958   100m   bw
ABP / Maxwell Setton
US title: *Hell, Heaven and Hoboken*

To distract the Nazis in Africa, an actor is hired to pose as General Montgomery.
An amusing and intriguing first hour gives way to spy chases, but the overall provides solid entertainment.

w Bryan Forbes, *book* M. E. Clifton-James *d* John Guillermin *ph* Basil Emmott *m* John Addison

John Mills, Cecil Parker, M. E. Clifton-James, Patrick Allen, Leslie Phillips, Michael Hordern, Marius Goring

I Will . . . I Will . . . for Now
US 1975   108m   Technicolor
Brut (C. O. Erickson)

Divorcees with sex problems eventually get together again.
Witless soft core farrago of coy jokes, as clumsy and unappealing as its title.

w Norman Panama, Albert E. Lewin
d Norman Panama *ph* John A. Alonzo
m John Cameron *pd* Fernando Carrere

Elliott Gould, Diane Keaton, Paul Sorvino, Victoria Principal, Warren Berlinger, Candy Clark, Robert Alda

I Wonder Who's Kissing Her Now*
US 1947   104m   Technicolor
TCF (George Jessel)

The career of nineties songwriter Joseph E. Howard.
Routine biopic, quite pleasantly handled.

w Lewis R. Foster *d* Lloyd Bacon *ph* Ernest Palmer *md* Alfred Newman *ad* Richard Day, Boris Leven *ch* Hermes Pan

Mark Stevens, June Haver, Martha Stewart, Reginald Gardiner, Lenore Aubert, William Frawley, Gene Nelson

Ice Castles
US 1978   109m   Metrocolor
Columbia / International Cinemedia Center (John Kemeny)

Nick and Lexie meet and fall in love at the ice rink. He goes into professional ice hockey; she becomes an Olympic champion but an accident leaves her blind.
Slick, empty, three-handkerchief wallow in the modern manner; well made but instantly forgettable.

w Donald Wrye, Gary L. Baim *d* Donald Wrye *ph* Bill Butler *m* Marvin Hamlisch *pd* Joel Schiller

Robby Benson, Lynn-Holly Johnson, Colleen Dewhurst, Tom Skerritt, Jennifer Warren, David Huffman

Ice Cold in Alex**
GB 1958   132m   bw
ABP (W. A. Whittaker)
US title: *Desert Attack*

In 1942 Libya, the commander of a motor ambulance gets his vehicle and passengers to safety despite the hazards of minefields and a German spy.
Engrossing desert adventure with plenty of suspense sequences borrowed from *The Wages of Fear*; long, but very well presented.

w T. J. Morrison, Christopher Landon
d J. Lee-Thompson *ph* Gilbert Taylor
m Leighton Lucas

John Mills, Sylvia Sims, Anthony Quayle, Harry Andrews

● *Video: Thorn EMI*

Ice Follies of 1939
US 1939   82m   bw (Technicolor sequence)
MGM (Harry Rapf)

A Hollywood star goes east to help her old ice-skating friends put on a show.
The downright peculiar sight of these particular stars on ice is backed by good turns and practically no story.

w Florence Ryerson, Edgar Allan Woolf
d Reinhold Schunzel *ph* Joseph Ruttenberg, Oliver T. Marsh *m* Roger Edens

Joan Crawford, James Stewart, Lew Ayres, Lewis Stone, Lionel Stander, Bess Ehrhardt, Charles D. Brown, the International Ice Follies

Ice Palace
US 1960   143m   Warnercolor Cinemascope
Warner (Henry Blanke)

After World War I, two men set up a fishery business in Alaska, and their subsequent lives are tied up with the political development of the state.
Tedious saga from a bestseller, with entertaining incidents but no real grip.

w Harry Kleiner, *novel* Edna Ferber
d Vincent Sherman *ph* Joseph Biroc *m* Max Steiner *ad* Malcolm Bert

Richard Burton, Robert Ryan, Martha Hyer, Carolyn Jones, Jim Backus, Ray Danton, Diane McBain, Karl Swenson

Ice Station Zebra
US 1968   148m   Metrocolor   Super Panavision
MGM / Filmways (James C. Pratt)

Russian and American agents speed towards the North Pole to recover a lost capsule containing vital military information.
Talky and unconvincingly staged spy adventure with a disappointing lack of action and a great many cold war platitudes.

w Douglas Heyes, Harry Julian Fink, *novel* Alistair MacLean *d* John Sturges *ph* Daniel L. Fapp *m* Michel Legrand

Rock Hudson, Patrick McGoohan, Ernest Borgnine, Jim Brown, Tony Bill, Lloyd Nolan, Gerald S. O'Loughlin, Alf Kjellin
  'It's terrible in such a familiar way that at some level it's pleasant. We learn to settle for so little, we moviegoers.'—*Pauline Kael*

AAN: Daniel L. Fapp

● *Video: MGM / UA*

Ichabod and Mr Toad**
US 1949   68m   Technicolor
Walt Disney

Cartoon versions of stories by Washington Irving and Kenneth Grahame.
An uncomfortable double bill; the story of Ichabod, though well narrated by Basil Rathbone, is macabre without being very interesting; *The Wind in the Willows*, however, is charmingly pictured, and Mr Toad is splendidly voiced by Eric Blore.

d Jack Kinney, Clyde Geronimi, James Algar
supervisor Ben Sharpsteen

I'd Climb the Highest Mountain*
US 1951 88m Technicolor
TCF (Lamar Trotti)

A Methodist preacher and his wife face the problems of life in a remote part of North Georgia.

Pleasant, rambling, adequately serious and old-fashioned family entertainment, well presented in Hollywood's medium style.

w Lamar Trotti, *novel* Corra Harris d Henry King ph Edward Cronjager m Sol Kaplan md Lionel Newman

Susan Hayward, William Lundigan, Rory Calhoun, Barbara Bates, Gene Lockhart, Lynn Bari, Ruth Donnelly, Alexander Knox

I'd Rather Be Rich*
US 1964 96m Eastmancolor
U–I / Ross Hunter

To comfort her dying grandfather, an heiress introduces an eligible stranger as her fiancé . . . but the old man recovers and begins matchmaking.

Reasonably zesty remake of It Started with Eve, kept afloat by Chevalier's performance.

w Oscar Brodney, Leo Townsend, Norman Krasna d Jack Smight ph Russell Metty m Percy Faith

Maurice Chevalier, Sandra Dee, Robert Goulet, Andy Williams, Gene Raymond. Hermione Gingold, Charles Ruggles

An Ideal Husband*
GB 1947 96m Technicolor
British Lion / London Films (Alexander Korda)

In the nineties, the career of a London diplomat is threatened by the reappearance of an old flame.

A slight, stiff play is swamped by the cast, the decor, and very garish colour, but there are moments of enjoyment along the way.

w Lajos Biro, *play* Oscar Wilde d Alexander Korda ph Georges Périnal m Arthur Benjamin ad Vincent Korda cost Cecil Beaton

Paulette Goddard, Hugh Williams, Michael Wilding, Diana Wynyard, *C. Aubrey Smith*, *Constance Collier*, Glynis Johns, Christine Norden

'The composing and cutting of this fine raw material is seldom above medium grade.'— *James Agee*

● Video: Polygram

Idiot's Delight*
US 1939 105m bw
MGM (Hunt Stromberg)

At the outbreak of World War II, in a hotel on the Swiss border, a hoofer with an all-girl troupe meets an old flame masquerading as a Russian countess.

Interesting but quite unsuccessful film version of a highly artificial play which had been carried off superbly by the Lunts but was now somewhat less well cast, though it did represent an early Hollywood challenge to Hitler. The flagwaving in fact made it more than a little boring.

w Robert E. Sherwood, from his play d Clarence Brown ph William Daniels m Herbert Stothart

Clark Gable, Norma Shearer, Edward Arnold, Charles Coburn, Burgess Meredith, Joseph Schildkraut, Laura Hope Crews, Skeets Gallagher, Pat Patterson, Fritz Feld

'Exceptionally entertaining comedy, a b.o. sock.'—*Variety*

'The fun and excitement are still there, however filtered it may be.'—*Film Daily*

'The mood of the whole thing is forced and cheap—the coming world war staged by Maurice Chevalier.'—*Otis Ferguson*

'Exactly the same pseudo-qualities as The Petrified Forest: a moral pretentiousness, a kind of cellophaned intellectuality.'—*Graham Greene*

The Idle Class*
US 1922 20m approx bw silent
First National / Charles Chaplin

A tramp dreams of the rich life and is mistaken for the husband of a lady.

Rather slight later Chaplin without the full-blooded farcical elements which made him so popular around 1917.

wd Charles Chaplin ph Rollie Totheroh

Charles Chaplin, Edna Purviance, Mack Swain

The Idol
GB 1966 111m bw
Embassy (Leonard Lightstone)

A divorced woman falls in love with her son's friend.

Stupefyingly boring generation-gap sex drama.

w Millard Lampell d Daniel Petrie ph Ken Higgins m Johnny Dankworth

Jennifer Jones, Michael Parks, John Leyton, Jennifer Hilary, Guy Doleman, Natasha Pyne

Idol of Paris
GB 1948 105m bw
Premier (R. J. Minney)

In old Paris, a ragman's daughter becomes queen of the demi-mondaines.

Unintentionally hilarious copy of the Gainsborough period romances which had been so popular; much criticized because the leading ladies fight a duel with whips, but that's the least of its faults.

w Norman Lee, Stafford Dickens, Henry Ostrer, *novel* Paiva Queen of Love by Alfred Shirkauer d Leslie Arliss ph Jack Cox

Beryl Baxter, Christine Norden, Michael Rennie, Margaretta Scott, Keneth Kent, Henry Oscar, Miles Malleson, Andrew Osborn, Andrew Cruickshank

The Idolmaker
US 1980 119m Technicolor
United Artists / Gene Kirkwood, Howard W. Koch

A songwriter accurately sums up his own limited talent and turns agent and starmaker.

Sharp but padded look behind the scenes of the pop industry; in the end of interest only to initiates.

w Edward Di Lorenzo d Taylor Hackford ph Adam Holender m Jeff Barry

Ray Sharkey, Tovah Feldshuh, Peter Gallagher, Paul Land

If . . .***
GB 1968 111m Eastmancolor
Paramount / Memorial (Lindsay Anderson, Michael Medwin)

Discontent at a boys' public school breaks out into rebellion.

Allegorical treatment of school life with much fashionable emphasis on obscure narrative, clever cutting, variety of pace, even an unaccountable changing from colour to monochrome and vice versa. Intelligence is clearly at work, but it seems to have suffered from undigested gobs of Pinter, and the film as a whole makes no discernible point.

w David Sherwin d Lindsay Anderson ph Miroslav Ondricek m Marc Wilkinson pd Jocelyn Herbert

Malcolm McDowell, David Wood, Richard Warwick, Robert Swann, Christine Noonan, Peter Jeffrey, Arthur Lowe, Anthony Nicholls

'The school . . . is the perfect metaphor for the established system all but a few of us continue to accept.'—*David Wilson*

'It's something like the Writing on the Wall.'—*Lindsay Anderson*

'Combines a cold and queasy view of youth with a romantic view of violence.'—*New Yorker*

If a Man Answers
US 1962 102m Technicolor
Universal / Ross Hunter

A wife decides to make her husband jealous.

Derivative second-team matrimonial comedy, all dressed up but with nowhere to go.

w Richard Morris, *novel* Winifred Wolfe d Henry Levin ph Russell Metty m Hans Salter

Sandra Dee, Bobby Darin, Micheline Presle, John Lund, Cesar Romero, Stephanie Powers

If I Had a Million**
US 1932 88m bw
Paramount (Benjamin Glazer, Louis D. Lighton)

Various people each receive a million dollars from an eccentric who wants to test their reactions.

Interesting, dated multi-part comedy drama remembered chiefly for the brief sequence in which Laughton blows a raspberry to his boss and Fields chases road hogs. As an entertainment it's patchy, lacking an overall style.

w Claude Binyon, Whitney Bolton, Malcolm Stuart Boylan, John Bright, Sidney Buchman, Lester Cole, Isabel Dawn, Boyce DeGaw, Walter de Leon, Oliver H. P. Garrett, Harvey Gates, Grover Jones, Ernst Lubitsch, Lawton Mackaill, Joseph L. Mankiewicz, William Slavens McNutt, Seton I. Miller, Tiffany Thayer, *story* Robert D. Andrews d Ernst Lubitsch, Norman Taurog, Stephen Roberts,

Norman Z. McLeod, James Cruze, William A. Seiter, H. Bruce Humberstone

W. C. Fields, *Charles Laughton, May Robson*, Richard Bennett, Alison Skipworth, Gary Cooper, Wynne Gibson, George Raft, Jack Oakie, Frances Dee, Charles Ruggles, Mary Boland, Roscoe Karns, Gene Raymond, Lucien Littlefield

'Not uninteresting, but spotty in retrospect . . . the cinematic porridge is naturally replete with a diversity of seasonings.'—*Variety*

'It develops an obvious idea in an obvious way.'—*Time*

If I Had My Way*
US 1940   82m   bw
Universal (David Butler)

Two vaudevillians help an orphan girl and open a new night club.
Quite likeable and very typical star vehicle of its period.

w William Conselman, James V. Kern *d* David Butler *ph* George Robinson *m* Frank Skinner

Bing Crosby, Charles Winninger, Gloria Jean, El Brendel, Allyn Joslyn, Donald Woods, Eddie Leonard, Claire Dodd, Blanche Ring

If I Were Free
US 1933   65m   bw

A man and woman, each unhappily married, try to get together. Rather soppy drama which fails to develop. Irene Dunne, Clive Brook, Nils Asther, Henry Stephenson, Laura Hope Crews. Written by Dwight Taylor from the play Behold We Live by John Van Druten; directed by Elliott Nugent; for RKO. 'Thin in texture, it never reaches a pace that really counts.'—*Variety*

'His love-making was as dangerous as his swordplay!'

If I Were King*
US 1938   101m   bw
Paramount

The 14th-century poet and rascal François Villon matches wits with Louis XI and leads an uprising of the people.
A story which we have grown used to seeing with music as The Vagabond King is here well presented but somehow rings hollow, with insufficient derring-do; it is the wrong kind of swashbuckling for its star, who is for once outacted by Rathbone in an unusual wily characterization.

w Preston Sturges *d* Frank Lloyd *m* Richard Hageman *ph* Theodor Sparkuhl

Ronald Colman, *Basil Rathbone*, Frances Dee, Ellen Drew, C. V. France, Heather Thatcher, Henry Wilcoxon, Sidney Toler
'Healthy box office that will hit extended runs right down the line.'—*Variety*

AAN: Richard Hageman; Basil Rathbone

If I'm Lucky
US 1945   79m   bw
TCF (Brian Foy)

A singer runs for state governor and exposes corruption.

Lacklustre remake of *Thanks a Million*, with decidedly dispirited elements.

w Snag Werris, Robert Ellis, Helen Logan, George Bricker *d* Lewis Seiler *ph* Glen MacWilliams *songs* Edgar de Lange, Joseph Myrow *md* Emil Newman

Vivian Blaine, Perry Como, Carmen Miranda, Harry James, Phil Silvers, Edgar Buchanan, Reed Hadley

If It's Tuesday, This Must Be Belgium*
US 1969   98m   De Luxe
UA / Wolper (Stan Margulies)

A group of American tourists have various adventures during a lightning tour of Europe.
Amusing comedy which does pretty well by a good idea.

w David Shaw *d* Mel Stuart *ph* Vilis Lapenieks *m* Walter Scharf

Suzanne Pleshette, Ian McShane, Mildred Natwick, Murray Hamilton, Michael Constantine, Sandy Baron, Norman Fell, Peggy Cass, Marty Ingels, Pamela Britton, Luke Halpin, Aubrey Morris

If Winter Comes
US 1948   97m   bw
MGM (Victor Saville)

A sentimental idealist, unhappily married, finds himself at the mercy of village gossip when he takes in a pregnant girl.
Artificial romantic nonsense, unconvincingly staged and modernized from a very dated bestseller.

w Marguerite Roberts, Arthur Wimperis, *novel* A. S. M. Hutchinson *d* Victor Saville *ph* George Folsey *m* Herbert Stothart

Walter Pidgeon, Deborah Kerr, Janet Leigh, Angela Lansbury, Binnie Barnes, Dame May Whitty, Reginald Owen

If You Could Only Cook
US 1935   72m   bw ,
Columbia

A young millionaire meets a poor girl and they get jobs as cook and butler.
Whimsical comedy-romance; thin but moderately beguiling.

w F. Hugh Herbert, Gertrude Purcell, Howard J. Green *d* William A. Seiter

Jean Arthur, Herbert Marshall, Leo Carrillo, Lionel Stander, Frieda Inescort
'Plenty of chuckles . . . offers particularly strong promise for the nabes.'—*Variety*
† This was the film which enabled Frank Capra to get out of his Columbia contract, because they accidentally promoted it in Europe as being directed by him.

If You Knew Susie*
US 1948   90m   bw
RKO (Eddie Cantor)

A vaudeville couple retire to his ancestral home in New England.
Mild family comedy capitalizing on the team established in *Show Business*.

w Warren Wilson, Oscar Brodney *d* Gordon Douglas *ph* Frank Redman

Eddie Cantor, Joan Davis, Allyn Joslyn, Bobby Driscoll, Charles Dingle

Ikiru*
Japan 1952   143m   bw
Toho
aka: *Living; Doomed*

A clerk learns that he is dying and spends his last months creating a children's playground. A moving and beautifully made personal drama which also gives an interesting background of modern Japan.

w Hideo Oguni, Shinobu Hashimoto, Akira Kurosawa *d* Akira Kurosawa *ph* Asaishi Nakai *m* Fumio Hayasaka

Takashi Shimura, Nobuo Kaneko, Kyoko Seki

'Both living a secret—each afraid to tell!'
I'll Be Seeing You**
US 1944   85m   bw
David O. Selznick (Dore Schary)

A lady convict at home on parole for Christmas meets and falls for a shell-shocked soldier.
Schmaltzy, middle-American romantic drama with some nicely handled moments and plenty of talent on hand. In the Hollywood mainstream.

w Marion Parsonnet, *novel* Charles Martin *d* William Dieterle *ph* Tony Gaudio *m* Daniele Amfitheatrof

Ginger Rogers, Joseph Cotten, Shirley Temple, Spring Byington, Tom Tully, Chill Wills
'A sentimental, improbable picture, but unexpectedly rewarding in detail.'—*Richard Mallett, Punch*
● Video: Guild

I'll Be Your Sweetheart
GB 1945   104m   bw
Gainsborough (Louis Levy)

In 1900, songwriters fight with copyright pirates.
Studio-bound musical romance without the necessary resonance.

w Val Guest, Val Valentine *d* Val Guest *ph* Phil Grindrod *md* Louis Levy

Margaret Lockwood, Michael Rennie, Vic Oliver, Peter Graves, Moore Marriott, Frederick Burtwell, Maudie Edwards, Garry Marsh

I'll Be Yours
US 1947   90m   bw
Universal (Felix Jackson)

A small-town girl tries to make good in the big city.
Slackly handled remake of *The Good Fairy*. A doubtful 'A' production which did nothing for its star's ailing career.

w Preston Sturges (adapted anonymously from his previous screenplay based on the Molnar original) *d* William A. Seiter *ph* Hal Mohr

Deanna Durbin, Tom Drake, William Bendix, Adolphe Menjou, Walter Catlett, Franklin Pangborn

I'll Cry Tomorrow*
US 1955   119m   bw
MGM (Lawrence Weingarten)

Lillian Roth, a Broadway / Hollywood star of
the early thirties, becomes an alcoholic.
Fictionalized biopic, pretty well done of the
True Confessions kind.

w Helen Deutsch, Jay Richard Kennedy, *book*
Lillian Roth, Gerold Frank   d Daniel Mann
ph Arthur E. Arling   m Alex North

Susan Hayward, Richard Conte, Eddie
Albert, Jo Van Fleet, Don Taylor, Ray
Danton, Margo

'By emphasizing physical degradation in
almost every frame, the film makes her less an
object of acutely personal concern than a
street casualty seen remotely from the top of a
bar.'—*Alexander Walker*

AAN: Arthur E. Arling; Susan Hayward

I'll Get By
US 1950   86m   Technicolor
TCF   (William Perlberg)

Two song writers meet success, then join the
marines and are reunited with their former girl
friends.
Fair standard musical, a modernization of *Tin
Pan Alley*.

w Mary Loos, Richard Sale   d Richard Sale
ph Charles G. Clarke   md Lionel Newman

June Haver, Gloria de Haven, William
Lundigan, Dennis Day, Harry James, Thelma
Ritter

AAN: Lionel Newman

I'll Get You for This
GB 1950   83m   bw

An American gambler in Italy goes after the
gangsters who framed him. Second-grade star
thick-ear. George Raft, Coleen Gray, Charles
Goldner, Walter Rilla, Greta Gynt, Enzo
Staiola. Written by George Callahan and
William Rose, from the novel *High Stakes* by
James Hadley Chase; directed by Joseph M.
Newman; for Romulus. (US title: *Lucky Nick
Cain*.)

I'll Give a Million*
US 1938   70m   bw
TCF (Darryl F. Zanuck)

A millionaire becomes a tramp and disappears,
letting it be known that he will give a
fortune for genuine acts of kindness. Tramps
are then royally entertained all over town.
Amusing depression comedy with satirical
touches.

w Boris Ingster, Milton Sperling   d Walter
Lang   ph Lucien Andriot   md Louis Silvers

Warner Baxter, Peter Lorre, Marjorie
Weaver, Jean Hersholt, John Carradine, J.
Edward Bromberg, Lynn Bari, Fritz Feld, Sig
Rumann

'Not worth that much . . . the plot sags at
the halfway mark and the wind-up is
disappointing.'—*Variety*

Ill Met by Moonlight
GB 1956   104m   bw   Vistavision
Rank / Vega (Michael Powell, Emeric
Pressburger)
US title: *Night Ambush*

In Crete during the German occupation,
British agents work with partisans to capture a
German general.
Disappointingly dreary war adventure with too
many night locations, too little suspense and
characterization, and photography which
seems to be deliberately unattractive.

wd Michael Powell, Emeric Pressburger, *book*
W. Stanley Moss   ph Christopher Challis
m Mikis Theodorakis

Dirk Bogarde, Marius Goring, David Oxley,
Cyril Cusack, John Cairney, Laurence Payne,
Wolfe Morris, Michael Gough

I'll Never Forget Whatshisname*
GB 1967   96m   Technicolor
Universal / Scimitar (Michael Winner)

An advertising executive gives up power and
money for integrity on a small literary
magazine, but is won back by a mogul.
Vivid yet muddled tragi-comedy of the sixties,
with splashes of sex and violence in trendy
settings, a hero one really doesn't believe in,
and a title which seems to have no meaning
whatsoever.

w Peter Draper   d Michael Winner   ph Otto
Heller   m Francis Lai

Oliver Reed, Orson Welles, Carol White,
Harry Andrews, Michael Hordern, Wendy
Craig, Marianne Faithfull

I'll See You in My Dreams*
US 1952   112m   bw
Warner (Louis F. Edelman)

The domestic and professional life of
songwriter Gus Kahn.
Quiet-toned, well made, quite forgettable
musical.

w Melville Shavelson, Jack Rose   d Michael
Curtiz   ph Ted McCord   md Ray Heindorf
ch Le Roy Prinz

Doris Day, Danny Thomas, Frank Lovejoy,
Patrice Wymore, James Gleason

I'll Take Romance
US 1937   85m   bw
Columbia (Everett Riskin)

When an opera singer refuses to fulfil a South
American contract, her impresario kidnaps
her.
Moderate star vehicle.

w George Oppenheimer, Jane Murfin
d Edward H. Griffith   ph Lucien Andriot
songs various

Grace Moore, Melvyn Douglas, Helen
Westley, Stuart Erwin, Margaret Hamilton,
Walter Kingsford, Esther Muir

I'll Take Sweden
US 1965   96m   Technicolor
UA / Edward Small

A widowed oil company executive accepts a
Stockholm posting to remove his teenage
daughter from an unsuitable attachment.

Feeble comedy which unwisely attempts to be
with it, but is bogged down by amateurish
handling and wit-wise is sadly without it.

w Nat Perrin, Bob Fisher, Arthur Marx
d Frederick de Cordova   ph Daniel L. Fapp
m Jimmy Haskell

Bob Hope, Tuesday Weld, Frankie Avalon,
Dina Merrill, Jeremy Slate, John Qualen,
Walter Sande

I'll Tell the World
US 1934   76m   bw

A small-town sports announcer starts a lonely
hearts programme. Amiable second feature, a
reworking of the star's earlier *Advice to the
Lovelorn*. Lee Tracy, Brenda Joyce, Raymond
Walburn, June Preisser, Thomas Gomez.
Written by Henry Blankfort; directed by
Leslie Goodwins; for Universal. 'Feasible
b.o., but not a strong drafter where the Tracy
name can't help.'—*Variety*

Illegal*
US 1955   88m   bw
Warner (Frank P. Rosenberg)

A disillusioned District Attorney becomes a
racketeer's lawyer but finally denounces him at
the cost of his own life.
Competent remake of *The Mouthpiece* (qv), a
good star melodrama.

w W. R. Burnett, James R. Webb, *story*
Frank J. Collins   d Lewis Allen   ph Peverell
Marley   m Max Steiner

Edward G. Robinson, Nina Foch, Albert
Dekker, Hugh Marlowe, Jayne Mansfield,
Howard St John, Ellen Corby

'Hard-hitting stuff in the old gangster
tradition.'—*MFB*

Illegal Entry
US 1949   84m   bw

Undercover agents investigate a smuggling
racket. Routine, quite entertaining alleged
exposé. Howard Duff, George Brent, Marta
Toren, Tom Tully, Paul Stewart, Gar Moore.
Written by Joel Malone; directed by Frederick
de Cordova; for Universal-International.

Illegal Traffic
US 1938   67m   bw

The FBI tracks down an organization devoted
to smuggling criminals away from danger.
Smart second feature based on J. Edgar
Hoover's *Persons in Hiding*. J. Carrol Naish,
Mary Carlisle, Robert Preston. Written by
Robert Yost, Lewis Foster and Stuart
Anthony; directed by Louis King; for
Paramount. 'Good racketeer film . . . should
do better than average business.'—*Variety*

Illicit
US 1931   81m   bw

A disillusioned wife walks out on her husband
and seeks solace elsewhere. Undistinguished
weepie, which later became *Ex-Lady*. Barbara
Stanwyck, Ricardo Cortez, Joan Blondell,
Charles Butterworth. Written by Harvey
Thew; directed by Archie Mayo; for Warner.
'Lacks a wallop and action.'—*Variety*

'Don't dare stare at . . .'
The Illustrated Man*
US 1969   103m   Technicolor
Panavision
Warner / SKM (Howard B. Kreitsek, Ted
Mann)

A strange wanderer tells weird stories based
on the tattooed pictures which cover him from
tip to toe.
Oddball compendium based rather insecurely
on Ray Bradbury stories; in this form they
don't amount to much but the presentation is
assured.

w Howard B. Kreitsek d Jack Smight
ph Philip Lathrop m Jerry Goldsmith ad Joel
Schiller

Rod Steiger, Claire Bloom, Robert Drivas,
Don Dubbins, Jason Evers
  'A curiously passionless affair – efficient
enough, meaty enough, but without poetry,
without charm, without beauty.'—*Philip Strick*
  'A pretentious comic strip of maudlin and
muddled fantasies.'—*Judith Crist*

Illustrious Corpses*
Italy / France 1975   120m   Technicolor
PEA / UA (Alberto Grimaldi)
original title: *Cadaveri Eccellenti*

A right-wing conspiracy to arouse feelings
against dissidents is found to be behind the
murders of public figures.
Elegant police melodrama on an unlikely
political thesis.

w Francesco Rosi, Tonino Guerra, Lino
Jannuzzi, *novel* Il Contesto by Leonardo
Sciascia d Francesco Rosi ph Pasqualino de
Santis m Piero Piccioni

Lino Ventura, Alain Cuny, Maolo Bonacelli,
Marcel Bozzuffi, Max Von Sydow, Fernando
Rey, Charles Vanel, Tina Aumont
  'Like watching layer after layer peeled off
some diseased flower until the poisoned root is
reached.'—*Michael Billington, Illustrated
London News*

I'm All Right Jack***
GB 1959   104m   bw
British Lion / Charter (Roy Boulting)

A world-innocent graduate takes a job in
industry; by starting at the bottom he
provokes a national strike.
Satirical farce which manages to hit most of its
widespread targets and finds corruption in
high, low and middle places. A not inaccurate
picture of aspects of British life in the fifties,
and a presage of the satire boom to come with
Beyond the Fringe and *That Was the Week
That Was*.

w Frank Harvey, John Boulting, *novel* Private
Life by *Alan Hackney* d John Boulting
ph Max Greene m Ken Hare

Ian Carmichael, Peter Sellers, Irene Handl,
Richard Attenborough, *Terry-Thomas*, Dennis
Price, Margaret Rutherford, Liz Fraser, *John
Le Mesurier*, Sam Kydd
● Video: Thorn EMI

I'm Dancing as Fast as I Can
US 1982   106m   Movielab
Paramount / Edgar J. Scherick / Scott Rudin

A documentary film-maker is rehabilitated
after dependence on drugs.
Unabsorbing case history more suitable as a
TV movie except that the acting for TV would
not have been so far over the top.

w David Robe, *book* Barbara Gordon d Jack
Hofsiss ph Jan de Bont m Stanley Silverman

Jill Clayburgh, Nicol Williamson, Dianne
Wiest, Joe Pesci, Geraldine Page, James
Sutorius, Richard Masur, Kathleen Widdoes
● Video: CIC

I'm from Missouri
US 1939   77m   bw

The wife of a Missouri farmer and mule
breeder has social aspirations. Rural comedy
patterned after the Will Rogers successes. Bob
Burns, Gladys George, Gene Lockhart, Judith
Barrett, William Henry, Patricia Morrison,
E. E. Clive, Melville Cooper. Written by
John C. Moffitt and Duke Atterbury; directed
by Theodore Reed; for Paramount. 'Moderate
grosser for family trade.'—*Variety*

'Just a sensitive gal who climbed the
    ladder of success . . . wrong by wrong! A
    story about a gal who lost her
    reputation—and never missed it!'
I'm No Angel***
US 1933   88m   bw
Paramount (William Le Baron)

A carnival dancer gets off a murder charge,
moves into society and sues a man for breach
of promise.
The star's most successful vehicle, credited
with saving the fortunes of Paramount,
remains a highly diverting side show with
almost a laugh a minute. Released before the
Legion of Decency was formed, it also
contains some of Mae's fruitiest lines.

w Mae West d Wesley Ruggles ph Leo
Tover songs Harvey Brooks (m), Gladys
Dubois (ly)

Mae West, Edward Arnold, Cary Grant,
Gregory Ratoff, Ralf Harolde, Kent Taylor,
Gertrude Michael
  'The most freewheeling of all Mae's screen
vehicles, and the most satisfying of the lot.'—
James Robert Parish
  'A quality of balance and proportion which
only the finest films attain.'—*Views and
Reviews*

Images
Eire 1972   101m   Technicolor
Panavision
Lions Gate / Hemdale (Tommy Thompson)

A semi-hysterical woman is confronted by the
images of her former lovers.
Pretentious psycho-drama which might have
made a good half-hour.

wd Robert Altman ph Vilmos Zsigismond
m John Williams

Susannah York, René Auberjonois, Marcel
Bozzuffi
AAN: John Williams

Imitation General
US 1958   88m   bw
MGM (William Hawks)

France 1944: when a general is killed, a
sergeant takes his place to preserve morale.
Odd, rather unpalatable war comedy-drama.

w William Bowers d George Marshall
ph George Folsey

Glenn Ford, Red Buttons, Taina Elg, Dean
Jones, Kent Smith

Imitation of Life**
US 1934   109m   bw
Universal

A woman becomes rich through the pancake
recipe of her black servant, but the latter has a
tragic life because her daughter passes for
white.
Monumentally efficient tearjerker, generally
well done.

w William Hurlbut, *novel* Fannie Hurst
d John Stahl ph Merritt Gerstad m Heinz
Roemheld

Claudette Colbert, Warren William, *Louise
Beavers*, Ned Sparks, Rochelle Hudson, Fredi
Washington, Alan Hale, Henry Armetta
  'Grim and harsh stuff . . . its reception in
the south cannot be judged or guessed by a
northerner.'—*Variety*
  'Classic, compulsively watchable rags-to-
riches-and-heartbreak weeper.'—*New Yorker,
1977*

AAN: best picture

Imitation of Life*
US 1959   124m   Eastmancolor
U-I (Ross Hunter)

Glossy remake of the above with its heroine
now an actress; stunningly produced but dully
acted, making its racially sensitive plot seem
insincere.

w Eleanore Griffin, Allan Scott d Douglas
Sirk ph Russell Metty m Frank Skinner

Lana Turner, Juanita Moore, John Gavin,
Susan Kohner, Dan O'Herlihy, Sandra Dee,
Robert Alda

AAN: Juanita Moore; Susan Kohner

The Immigrant**
US 1917   20m approx   bw   silent
Mutual

A penniless immigrant befriends a girl on the
boat and later helps her in a café.
One of the most inventive early Chaplins, with
touches of sentiment and social comment
which for once only strengthen and do not
antagonize.

wd Charles Chaplin ph William C. Foster,
Rollie Totheroh

Charles Chaplin, Edna Purviance, Albert
Austin, Henry Bergman, Eric Campbell
  'In its roughness and apparent simplicity it is
as much a jewel as a story by O. Henry.'—
Photoplay

Immoral Tales

France 1974   103m   Eastmancolor
Argos (Anatole Dauman)

Four bawdy stories, ranging from 1498 to
1970.
The usual sex portmanteau with a little more
strength in the detail and interest in human
behaviour than usual.

wd Walerian Borowczyk *ph* Bernard
Daillencourt, Guy Durban, Michel Zolat,
Noel Véry   *m* Maurice Le Roux

Lise Danvers, Charlotte Alexandra, Paloma
Picasso, Florence Bellamy

'You come out having learned something
about the waywardness of life and love and
having been taken on a mystery tour into the
present, the past, and the enigmatic
strangeness of womanhood.'—*Michael
Billington, Illustrated London News*

● Video: Thorn EMI

The Immortal Sergeant*

US 1943   90m   bw
TCF (Lamar Trotti)

In the North African campaign, a battle-
toughened sergeant is killed after inspiring the
raw recruits under his command.
'Inspirational' war adventure, quite neatly
done but a shade embarrassed by its own
poetic leanings.

w Lamar Trotti, *novel* John Brophy   *d* John
Stahl   *ph* Arthur Miller   *m* David Buttolph

Henry Fonda, Thomas Mitchell, Maureen
O'Hara, Allyn Joslyn, Reginald Gardiner,
Melville Cooper, Branwell Fletcher, Morton
Lowry

'By the time the first soldier has bit the
sand, the film identifies itself: it is none other
than Hollywood's old friend the Foreign
Legion of Beau Geste vintage, jerked from the
shelf and clothed in a new uniform.'—*Time*

The Immortal Story

France 1968   60m   Eastmancolor
Albina / ORTF (Micheline Rozan)

In 19th-century Macao, a rich merchant tries
to make an old seaman's story come true.
Muddled and stiltedly told fable which would
have excited no attention if it had not been
associated with the elusive Mr Welles.

wd Orson Welles, *story* Isak Dinesen
ph Willy Kurant   *m* Erik Satie

Orson Welles, Jeanne Moreau, Roger Coggio,
Norman Eshley

Impact

US 1949   111m   bw
(UA) Harry M. Popkin

A woman and her lover plan the murder of
her rich industrialist husband, but things go
wrong and the husband survives under another
name . . .
Curiously elongated but watchable
melodrama, with the impression of a second
team doing its best.

w Dorothy Reid   *d* Arthur Lubin   *ph* Ernest
Laszlo

Brian Donlevy, Ella Raines, Charles Coburn,
Helen Walker

The Impatient Maiden

US 1932   78m   bw

A romantic maidservant learns the difference
between life and fantasy. Solidly made
comedy-drama which doesn't seem to have
inspired its director. Mae Clarke, Lew Ayres,
Una Merkel, John Halliday, Andy Devine,
Berton Churchill. Written by Richard Schayer
and Winifred Dunn, from the novel *The
Impatient Virgin* by Donald Henderson
Clarke; directed by James Whale; for
Universal. 'Trashy stuff . . . aims at smartness
and sophistication, and achieves but
crudity.'—*Variety*

The Impatient Years

US 1944   91m   bw
Columbia

A soldier finds difficulty in adjusting to his
civilian matrimonial state.
Thin star comedy.

w Virginia Van Upp   *d* Irving Cummings
ph Hal Mohr   *m* Marlin Skiles

Jean Arthur, Lee Bowman, Charles Coburn,
Edgar Buchanan, Harry Davenport, Grant
Mitchell, Jane Darwell

'Scandal seeks her out—even on her
  wedding night!'

The Imperfect Lady

US 1946   97m   bw
Paramount (Karl Tunberg)
GB title: *Mrs Loring's Secret*

In nineties London, an MP marries a lady with
a past.
Dusty melodrama, adequately produced.

w Karl Tunberg, *story* Ladislas Fodor   *d* Lewis
Allen   *ph* John F. Seitz   *m* Victor Young

Ray Milland, Teresa Wright, Cedric
Hardwicke, Virginia Field, Anthony Quinn,
Reginald Owen, Melville Cooper, George
Zucco, Rhys Williams, Charles Coleman,
Miles Mander, Edmund Breon, Frederick
Worlock

The Impersonator*

GB 1961   64m   bw
Bryanston / Herald (Anthony Perry)

Americans at a British air base are suspected
when a murderous prowler strikes.
Well made second-feature thriller with
effective locations, suspense sequences and
village atmosphere.

wd Alfred Shaughnessy   *ph* John Coquillon
m de Wolfe

John Crawford, Jane Griffith, Patricia Burke,
John Salew

The Importance of Being Earnest**

GB 1952   95m   Technicolor
Rank / Javelin / Two Cities (Teddy Baird)

Two wealthy and eligible bachelors of the
nineties have problems with their marriage
prospects.

Disappointingly stagey rendering (when
compared, say, with *Occupe-toi d'Amélie*) of
Britain's most wondrously witty lighter-than-
air comedy of manners. As a record of a
theatrical performance, however, it is
valuable.

w Anthony Asquith, *play* Oscar Wilde
d Anthony Asquith   *ph* Desmond Dickinson
m Benjamin Frankel   *ad* Carmen Dillon

*Michael Redgrave, Michael Denison, Edith
Evans, Margaret Rutherford, Joan
Greenwood, Miles Malleson, Dorothy Tutin,
Walter Hudd*

'A more positive decision on style should
have been taken. A film of this kind must be
either an adaptation or a piece of filmed
theatre. This one, being partially both, is not
wholly either.'—*Gavin Lambert*

● Video: Rank

The Impossible Years

US 1968   98m   Metrocolor   Panavision
MGM / Marten (Lawrence Weingarten)

A university psychiatrist has trouble
controlling his nubile 17-year-old daughter.
Wacky farce which veers between the tasteless
and the ludicrous, and is never more than
momentarily entertaining.

w George Wells, *play* Bob Fisher, Arthur
Marx   *d* Michael Gordon   *ph* William H.
Daniels   *m* Don Costa

David Niven, Lola Albright, Chad Everett,
Ozzie Nelson, Cristina Ferrare, Don Beddoe

'A comedy of the generation gap which
didn't bridge it but fell right into it.'—*Gerald
Garrett*

The Impostor

US 1944   92m   bw

A French convict escapes during a Nazi
bombing raid, and in the guise of a dead man
fights bravely for France. Propagandist
melodrama, more stiffly made than its talent
would suggest. Jean Gabin, Ellen Drew,
Richard Whorf, Allyn Joslyn, Peter Van Eyck,
Ralph Morgan. Written and directed by Julien
Duvivier; for Universal. (TV title: *Strange
Confession.*)

Improper Channels

Canada 1979   91m   colour

A father runs into administrative trouble when
he takes his injured daughter to hospital.
Salutary but not very commanding tale for our
times, with a leading performance that suffers
from overfamiliarity.

w Morrie Rubinsky, Ian Sutherland, Adam
Arkin   *d* Eric Till   *ph* Anthony Richmond
m Maribeth Solomon, Micky Erbe

Alan Arkin, Mariette Hartley, Monica Parker,
Harry Ditson

Impulse

US 1984   88m   De Luxe
TCF / ABC (Tim Zinnemann)

When every inhabitant of a small community

becomes paranoid, the cause is traced to toxic substances in the water from which the cows drink.
Oddball melodrama which might have been more memorable had it been played as comedy.

w Bart Davis, Don Carlos Dunaway d Graham Baker ph Thomas del Ruth m Paul Chihara ed David Holden

Tim Matheson, Meg Tilly, Hume Cronyn, John Karlen, Bill Paxton

In a Lonely Place*
US 1950 93m bw
Columbia / Santana (Robert Lord)

An embittered Hollywood scriptwriter escapes a murder charge but loses his girl friend through his violent temperament.
Curious character melodrama which intrigues without satisfying.

w Andrew Solt, novel Dorothy B. Hughes d Nicholas Ray ph Burnett Guffey m George Antheil

Humphrey Bogart, Gloria Grahame, Frank Lovejoy, Carl Benton Reid, Art Smith, Jeff Donnell
'It remains better than average, but lacks the penetration which would make it really interesting.'—Gavin Lambert

In a Year with 13 Moons
West Germany 1978 129m colour

Ordeals of a man who undergoes a sex change. Unattractive case history with expressionist decoration. Volker Spengler, Ingrid Caven, Gottfried John. Written and directed by Rainer Werner Fassbinder; for Tango / Project / Filverlag der Autoren.

In Caliente
US 1935 85m bw
Warner

In a Mexican horse racing resort, a dancer falls for the magazine editor who criticized her act. Very slim storyline fails to make this a major musical despite attractive numbers including 'The Lady in Red'.

w Jerry Wald, Julius Epstein d Lloyd Bacon ph Sol Polito, George Barnes ch Busby Berkeley songs various

Dolores del Rio, Pat O'Brien, Edward Everett Horton, Leo Carrillo, Glenda Farrell, Judy Canova, Phil Regan, Wini Shaw, Herman Bing

In Celebration
GB 1974 131m Eastmancolor
Ely Landau / Cinevision

Three sons travel north for their miner father's fortieth wedding anniversary.
Sharply observant but fairly predictable dramatics, plainly filmed.

w David Storey, from his play d Lindsay Anderson ph Dick Bush m Christopher Gunning

Alan Bates, James Bolam, Brian Cox, Constance Chapman, Bill Owen

In Cold Blood*
US 1967 134m bw Panavision
Columbia / Richard Brooks

An account of a real life crime in which an entire family was brutally murdered by wandering gunmen.
Unnecessarily complicated as narrative, and uncompromisingly brutal in treatment, this well-meaning film is hard to take in many ways.

wd Richard Brooks, book Truman Capote ph Conrad Hall m Quincy Jones

Robert Blake, Scott Wilson, John Forsythe, Paul Stewart, Gerald S. O'Loughlin, Jeff Corey
'It marks a slight step up for its director, best remembered for reducing Lord Jim to pablum and The Brothers Karamazov to pulp.'—John Simon
AAN: Richard Brooks (as writer); Richard Brooks (as director); Conrad Hall; Quincy Jones

In Enemy Country
US 1968 107m Technicolor
Universal (Harry Keller)

In 1939 Paris, the French secret service evolves an elaborate four-year undercover plan.
Standard, overlong espionage melodrama with no surprises.

w Edward Anhalt, story Sy Bartlett d Harry Keller ph Loyal Griggs m William Lava

Tony Franciosa, Anjanette Comer, Guy Stockwell, Paul Hubschmid, Tom Bell, Harry Townes, Michael Constantine, John Marley

In Gay Madrid
US 1930 78m bw

A Spanish blade is torn between two women. Feeble star vehicle, presumably aimed at the Spanish market. Ramon Novarro, Dorothy Jordan, Lettice Howell, Claude King, Eugenie Besserer. Written by Bess Meredyth, Edwin Justus Mayer and Salisbury Field from a novel by Alejandro Perez Lugin; directed by Robert Z. Leonard; for MGM. 'Unreal story, poor acting, ditto direction and general lack of popular appeal.'—Variety

In God We Trust
US 1980 97m Technicolor

A monk leaves his monastery to raise some ready cash. Dismal and tasteless attempt at religious satire. Marty Feldman, Peter Boyle, Louise Lasser, Richard Pryor, Wilfrid Hyde White. Written by Marty Feldman and Chris Allen; directed by Marty Feldman; for Universal. 'A rare achievement—a comedy with no laughs. Its energy is prodigious. But only rarely is it matched by invention.'—Variety

In Harm's Way*
US 1965 167m bw Panavision
Paramount / Sigma (Otto Preminger)

The American navy retaliates after Pearl Harbor.

Odd mix of all-star action, spectacle (mostly models) and personal romances, with a few interesting scenes; shorn of colour it seems rather half-hearted.

w Wendell Mayes, novel James Bassett d Otto Preminger ph Loyal Griggs , m Jerry Goldsmith titles Saul Bass

John Wayne, Kirk Douglas, Patricia Neal, Tom Tryon, Paula Prentiss, Brandon de Wilde, Stanley Holloway, Burgess Meredith, Henry Fonda, Dana Andrews, Franchot Tone, Jill Haworth, George Kennedy, Hugh O'Brian, Carroll O'Connor, Patrick O'Neal, Slim Pickens, Bruce Cabot, Larry Hagman, James Mitchum
'Lacks even a touch of the touch.'—Stanley Kauffmann
AAN: Loyal Griggs

In Like Flint
US 1967 107m De Luxe Cinemascope
TCF (Saul David)

Top agent Derek Flint unmasks a subversive female spy ring which has kidnapped the President.
This sequel to Our Man Flint (qv) is silly rather than funny, a spy spoof which becomes irritatingly hard to take.

w Hal Fimberg d Gordon Douglas ph William Daniels m Jerry Goldsmith

James Coburn, Lee J. Cobb, Jean Hall, Andrew Duggan, Anna Lee
'It gently founders in yards of flat dialogue, lavishly uninteresting sets, fuzzy colour processing, and a supporting cast in which all the girls look alarmingly mass produced.'—MFB

In Love and War
US 1958 111m Eastmancolor Cinemascope
TCF (Jerry Wald)

Three men from different backgrounds join the US Marines and see service in the Pacific. Self-conscious propaganda concoction of bare routine interest.

w Edward Anhalt, novel Anton Myrer d Philip Dunne ph Leo Tover m Hugo Friedhofer

Jeffrey Hunter, Robert Wagner, Bradford Dillman, Dana Wynter, Hope Lange, Sheree North, France Nuyen

In Name Only*
US 1939 94m bw
RKO (Pandro S. Berman)

A rich man falls in love but his wife refuses a divorce. The stars seem unhappy in this sombre matrimonial drama, but of its kind it's surprisingly well made.

w Richard Sherman, novel Memory of Love by Bessie Brewer d John Cromwell ph J. Roy Hunt m Roy Webb

Cary Grant, Carole Lombard, Kay Francis, Charles Coburn, Helen Vinson
'Sock romantic drama . . . will get maximum playing time and the best dating the country offers.'—Variety

'Shot with a refined taste for interior decoration . . . it is oversweetened with the material for tears.'—*Graham Greene*

'The talking picture reaches perfection!'

In Old Arizona**
US 1929 95m bw
Fox

Adventures of the Cisco Kid.
Primitive sound western, a sensation in its day but now of purely historical interest.

w Tom Barry, *stories* O. Henry *d* Raoul Walsh, Irving Cummings *ph* Arthur Edeson

Warner Baxter, Edmund Lowe, Dorothy Burgess, J. Farrell MacDonald
† See also *The Cisco Kid*.

AA: Warner Baxter
AAN: best picture; Tom Barry; Raoul Walsh, Irving Cummings; Arthur Edeson

In Old California
US 1942 89m bw

A Boston pharmacist heads west towards gold rush California. Moderate star western with parsimonious budget. John Wayne, Binnie Barnes, Albert Dekker, Helen Parrish, Patsy Kelly, Edgar Kennedy, Dick Purcell, Charles Halton. Written by Gertrude Purcell and Frances Hyland; directed by William McGann; for Republic.

In Old Chicago***
US 1937 115m bw
TCF (Kenneth MacGowan)

Events leading up to the great Chicago fire include a torrid romance between a gambler and a café singer.
Spectacular melodrama which with its two-million-dollar budget was a deliberate attempt to outdo *San Francisco*, and only failed because the cast was less interesting. A splendid studio super-production.

w Lamar Trotti, Sonya Levien, *novel* We the O'Learys by Niven Busch *d* Henry King, *ph* Peverell Marley *m* Louis Silvers *sp* H. Bruce Humberstone, Daniel B. Clark, Fred Sersen, Louis J. Witte *ad* William Darling

Tyrone Power, Alice Faye, Don Ameche, *Alice Brady*, Andy Devine, Brian Donlevy, Phyllis Brooks, Tom Brown, Sidney Blackmer, Berton Churchill, Paul Hurst, Rondo Hatton, Eddie Collins

'Sock spectacle film . . . an elaborate and liberally budgeted entertainment.'—*Variety*

AA: Alice Brady
AAN: best picture; Niven Busch (original story); Louis Silvers

In Our Time*
US 1944 110m bw
Warner (Jerry Wald)

English girl marries Polish count and helps defy the Nazis.
Ambitious, would-be meaningful melodrama that doesn't quite come off.

w Ellis St Joseph, Howard Koch *d* Vincent Sherman *ph* Carl Guthrie *m* Franz Waxman

Ida Lupino, Paul Henreid, Nancy Coleman, *Nazimova*, Mary Boland, Victor Francen, Michael Chekhov

'The story starts a good many hares but prudently refrains from following them.'—*Richard Mallett, Punch*

In Person
US 1935 85m bw
RKO (Pandro S. Berman)

A glamorous but exhausted film star tries to escape her public by fleeing incognito to the country.
Mild star comedy.

w Allan Scott, *novel* Samuel Hopkins Adams *d* William A. Seiter *ph* Edward Cronjager *m* Roy Webb *songs* Oscar Levant, Dorothy Fields

Ginger Rogers, George Brent, Alan Mowbray, Grant Mitchell, Samuel S. Hinds, Spencer Charters

'Inept starring debut for Ginger Rogers . . . a very weak affair.'—*Variety*

In Search of Gregory
GB 1969 90m Technicolor
Universal / Vic Films / Vera Films (Joe Janni, Daniele Senatore)

A girl attends her father's wedding to meet a mysterious guest named Gregory, whom she never quite contacts.
Irritatingly pretentious Pinterish puzzle-drama with apparently no hidden depths except the urge to be clever.

w Tonino Guerra, Lucile Laks *d* Peter Wood *ph* Otto Heller, Giorgio Tonti *m* Ron Grainer

Julie Christie, Michael Sarrazin, John Hurt, Adolfo Celi, Roland Culver, Tony Selby

'Moments in a vacuum: however lively the surface, the centre remains depressingly inert.'—*MFB*

In Search of the Castaways***
GB 1961 100m Technicolor
Walt Disney (Hugh Attwooll)

With the aid of an eccentric professor, three children seek their lost explorer father in some geographically fantastic regions of South America.
Engaging Victorian fantasy which starts realistically but builds up to sequences in the manner of *The Wizard of Oz* and concludes in *Treasure Island* vein. Jaunty juvenile fare.

w Lowell S. Hawley, *novel* Captain Grant's Children by Jules Verne *d* Robert Stevenson *ph* Paul Beeson *m* William Alwyn *ad* Michael Stringer

Maurice Chevalier, Hayley Mills, George Sanders, Wilfrid Hyde White, *Wilfrid Brambell*

'A thousand thrills . . . and Hayley Mills!'—*publicity*

In Society*
US 1944 74m bw
Universal (Edmund Hartmann)

Two incompetent plumbers ruin a mansion. One of the better A & C romps, with little padding between the comedy highlights, though the trimmings are fearsomely dated.

w John Grant, Hal Finberg, Edmund L. Hartmann *d* Jean Yarbrough *ph* Jerome Ash *m* Edgar Fairchild

Bud Abbott, Lou Costello, Kirby Grant, Ann Gillis, Arthur Treacher, Steve Geray, George Dolenz, Marion Hutton

In the Cool of the Day
US 1962 91m Metrocolor Panavision
MGM (John Houseman)

The frail wife of a New York publisher dies in Greece after an affair with his colleague. Travelogue with romantic asides; a pretty glum business.

w Meade Roberts, *novel* Susan Ertz *d* Robert Stevens *ph* Peter Newbrook *m* Francis Chagrin *ad* Ken Adam

Jane Fonda, Peter Finch, Arthur Hill, Angela Lansbury, Constance Cummings

In the Doghouse
GB 1961 93m bw
Rank (Hugh Stewart)

Misadventures of a newly qualified vet. Easy-going farce with animal interest and a great many familiar faces.

w Michael Pertwee, *novel* It's a Vet's Life by Alex Duncan *d* Darcy Conyers *ph* Alan Hume *m* Philip Green

Leslie Phillips, Peggy Cummins, Hattie Jacques, James Booth, Dick Bentley, Colin Gordon, Joan Heal, Fenella Fielding, Esma Cannon, Richard Goolden, Joan Hickson, Vida Hope, Harry Locke, Kynaston Reeves

In the French Style*
US / France 1962 105m bw
Columbia / Casanna / Orsay (Robert Parrish, Irwin Shaw)

An American girl in Paris has affairs with a young boy and with a divorced newspaperman.
Smooth, episodic, romantic character study, well made but with no perceptible dramatic point.

w Irwin Shaw *d* Robert Parrish *ph* Michel Kelber *m* Josef Kosma

Jean Seberg, Stanley Baker, Philippe Fouquet

In the Good Old Summertime*
US 1949 102m Technicolor
MGM (Joe Pasternak)

In a Chicago music store in 1906, a salesgirl corresponds through a dating service with a man who turns out to be the manager she detests.
Cheerful remake of *The Shop around the Corner* (qv), with agreeable music, garish colour and not much style.

w Albert Hackett, Frances Goodrich, Ivan Tors, *play* Miklos Laszlo d Robert Z. Leonard *ph* Harry Stradling *md* George Stoll *ad* Randell Duell *ch* Robert Alton

Judy Garland, Van Johnson, S. Z. Sakall, Spring Byington, Clinton Sundberg, Buster Keaton, Lilian Bronson

In the Heat of the Night**
US 1967 109m De Luxe
UA / Mirisch (Walter Mirisch)

In a small southern town, the bigoted and bombastic sheriff on a murder hunt grudgingly accepts the help of a black detective.
Overrated policier in which the personality clash is amusing (and was timely) but the murder puzzle is a complete throwaway.

w Sterling Silliphant *d Norman Jewison*
ph Haskell Wexler *m* Quincy Jones

Sidney Poitier, Rod Steiger, Warren Oates, Quentin Dean, William Schallert

'A very nice film and a very good film and yes, I think it's good to see a black man and a white man working together . . . but it's not going to take the tension out of New York City; it's not going to stop the riots in Chicago.'—*Rod Steiger*
† Poitier subsequently starred in a couple of very inferior sequels, *They Call Me Mister Tibbs* and *The Organization* (both qv).

AA: best picture; Sterling Silliphant; Rod Steiger
AAN: Norman Jewison
● Video: Warner

In the Meantime, Darling
US 1944 72m bw
TCF (Otto Preminger)

A wealthy bride lives in an overcrowded boarding house to be near her husband's army camp.
Unassuming wartime soaper of very little interest.

w Arthur Kober, Michael Uris d Otto Preminger *ph* Joe MacDonald *m* Emil Newman

Jeanne Crain, Frank Latimore, Mary Nash, Eugene Pallette, Stanley Prager, Gale Robbins, Jane Randolph

In the Navy*
US 1941 86m bw
Universal (Alex Gottlieb)

Two incompetents and a singing heart-throb are naval recruits.
A basically feeble follow-up to *Buck Privates* which outgrossed its predecessor and now stands as an interesting pointer to how mass entertainment has changed since 1941.

w John Grant, Arthur T. Horman d Arthur Lubin *ph* Joseph Valentine *songs* Gene de Paul, Don Raye

Bud Abbott, Lou Costello, Dick Powell, The Andrews Sisters, Claire Dodd, Dick Foran, Shemp Howard

In the Soup
GB 1936 72m bw

A solicitor and his wife are forced to pose as their own servants. Undernourished star comedy, and this star's last screen appearance.
Ralph Lynn, Judy Gunn, Morton Selten, Nelson Keyes, Bertha Belmore. Written by H. Fowler Mear, from a play by Ralph Lumley; directed by Henry Edwards; for Twickenham.

'No one is as good as Bette when she's bad!'
In This Our Life**
US 1942 101m bw
Warner (David Lewis)

A neurotic girl steals her sister's husband, leaves him in the lurch, dominates her hapless family and is killed while on the run from the police.
Splendid star melodrama with good supporting acting and background detail.

w Howard Koch, *novel* Ellen Glasgow *d John Huston* *ph* Ernest Haller *m* Max Steiner

Bette Davis, Charles Coburn, Olivia de Havilland, Frank Craven, George Brent, Dennis Morgan, Billie Burke, Hattie McDaniel, Lee Patrick, Walter Huston (uncredited)

In Which We Serve****
GB 1942 114m bw
Rank / Two Cities (Noel Coward)

Survivors from a torpedoed destroyer recall their life at sea and on leave.
Dated but splendid flagwaver; an archetypal British war film of almost limitless propaganda value.

w Noel Coward d Noel Coward, David Lean *ph* Ronald Neame *m* Noel Coward

Noel Coward, Bernard Miles, *John Mills*, Richard Attenborough, *Celia Johnson*, Kay Walsh, Joyce Carey, Michael Wilding, Penelope Dudley Ward, Kathleen Harrison, Philip Friend, George Carney, Geoffrey Hibbert, James Donald

COMMANDER (Noel Coward): 'The *Torrin* has been in one scrap after another, but even when we've had men killed, the majority survived and brought the old ship back. Now she lies in 1500 fathoms and with her more than half our shipmates. If they had to die, what a grand way to go! And now they lie all together with the ship we loved, and they're in very good company. We've lost her, but they're still with her. There may be less than half the *Torrin* left, but I feel that we'll all take up the battle with even stronger heart. Each of us knows twice as much about fighting, and each of us has twice as good a reason to fight. You will all be sent to replace men who've been killed in other ships, and the next time you're in action, remember the *Torrin*! I should like to add that there isn't one of you that I wouldn't be proud and honoured to serve with again.'

'One of the screen's proudest achievements at any time and in any country.'—*Newsweek*
'Never at any time has there been a reconstruction of human experience which could touch the savage grandeur and

compassion of this production.'—*Howard Barnes, New York Herald Tribune*
† The story and the Coward character were based on the experiences of Louis Mountbatten, whose ship, HMS *Kelly*, was sunk under him.

AAN: best picture; Noel Coward (as writer)
● Video: Rank

Inadmissible Evidence**
GB 1968 96m bw
Paramount / Woodfall (Ronald Kinnoch)

A frustrated 40-year-old solicitor is on the verge of a nervous breakdown.
Interesting and surprisingly successful transcription of a difficult play which was virtually an anti-humanity soliloquy.

w John Osborne, from his play d Anthony Page *ph* Kenneth Hodges *m* Dudley Moore *ad* Seamus Flannery

Nicol Williamson, Eleanor Fazan, Jill Bennett, Peter Sallis, Eileen Atkins, Isobel Dean

'A play that was conceived as an increasingly bad dream has been made into a grittily detailed, naturalistic film.'—*Stanley Kauffmann*

'She was the biggest sucker of them all!'
Incendiary Blonde*
US 1945 112m Technicolor
Paramount (Joseph Sistrom)

The life of twenties nightclub queen Texas Guinan.
Laundered biopic with guns, girls and gangsters as well as songs.

w Claude Binyon, Frank Butler d George Marshall *ph* Ray Rennahan *m* Robert Emmett Dolan

Betty Hutton, Arturo de Cordova, Charles Ruggles, Albert Dekker, Barry Fitzgerald, Mary Phillips, Bill Goodwin, Eduardo Ciannelli, Maurice Rocco

'It runs its noisy but high-minded course through steamy emotion, painful misunderstanding and dramatic self-sacrifice, winding up in the snow among the blood of dead gangsters. Have we ever seen gangsters in Technicolor before?'—*Richard Mallett, Punch*
'A brassy synthesis of colour, song and dance, spattered with laughs.'—*Daily Herald*
AAN: Robert Emmett Dolan

Inchon
US 1981 140m colour
One Way Productions (Mitsuharu Ishii)

General MacArthur is affected by divine guidance during a major battle of the Korean war.
A very curious enterprise apparently financed by the Moonies. The religious angle sits oddly with the war scenes, and the result is an unsatisfactory mess.

w Robin Moore, Laird Koenig d Terence Young *ph* Bruce Surtees *m* Jerry Goldsmith

Laurence Olivier (as MacArthur), Jacqueline Bisset, David Janssen, Ben Gazzara, Toshiro Mifune, Richard Roundtree, Gabriele Ferzetti, Rex Reed

'A near total loss as well as a laugh.'—*Bruce Williamson, Playboy*

'The worst movie ever made, a turkey the size of Godzilla.'—*Jack Kroll, Newsweek*

'Quite possibly the worst movie ever made . . . stupefyingly incompetent.'—*Peter Rainer, Los Angeles Herald Examiner*

'As military spectacles go, one of the sorriest in military history.'—*Richard Schickel, Time*

Incident at Owl Creek*

France 1961 27m bw
Marcel Ichac / Films de Centaure / Paul de Roubaix
original title: *La Rivière du Hibou*

During the American Civil War a man is about to be hanged, and imagines how he might escape.

Intriguing but somewhat overpraised short with a rather obvious solution.

wd Robert Enrico, *story* Ambrose Bierce *ph* Jean Boffety *m* Henri Lanoë

Roger Jacquet, Anne Cornaly, Anker Larsen
'A powerful and remarkable film.'—*MFB*

Incident at Phantom Hill

US 1966 88m Technicolor

Two men face desperate odds to reach one million dollars in gold. Full-blooded western programmer with useful performances. Robert Fuller, Dan Duryea, Jocelyn Lane, Claude Akins, Noah Beery Jnr. Written by Frank Nugent; directed by Earl Bellamy; for Universal.

Les Inconnus dans la Maison*

France 1941 94m bw
Continental

An embittered ex-barrister saves his teenage daughter from a murder charge.

Unlikely melodrama remade as *Stranger in the House*; this version has more compelling writing and acting.

w Henri-Georges Clouzot, *novel* Georges Simenon *d* Henri Decoin *ph* Jules Kruger *m* Roland Manuel

Raimu, Juliette Faber, Jacques Baumer, Jean Tissier

The Incredible Journey**

US 1963 80m Technicolor
Walt Disney (James Algar)

Two dogs and a cat, separated from their owners, escape and travel 250 miles home. A novelty attraction which keeps going purely on its animal interest, which is considerable.

w James Algar, *book* Sheila Burnford *d* Fletcher Markle *ph* Kenneth Peach, Jack Couffer, Lloyd Beebe *m* Oliver Wallace

● *Video: Disney*

The Incredible Melting Man

US 1977 84m Movielab
AIP / Quartet (Max J. Rosenberg)

The survivor of a space flight is rushed to hospital with radiation burns and an infection which causes his flesh to melt.

Unpleasant and nonsensical horror film with a few unintentional laughs and a plot borrowed from *The Quatermass Experiment*.

wd William Sachs *ph* Willy Curtis *m* Arlon Ober

Alex Rebar, Burr DeBenning, Myron Healey, Myron Aldredge

The Incredible Mr Limpet

US 1964 102m Technicolor
Warner (John C. Rose)

A meek but patriotic clerk is turned down by the navy and turns into a fish. In this form he becomes a radar assistant to a warship. Sentimental sub-Disney goo, part animated.

w Jameson Bewer, John C. Rose, *novel* Theodore Pratt *d* Arthur Lubin *ph* Harold Stine *m* Frank Perkins

Don Knotts, Andrew Duggan, Larry Keating, Jack Weston

The Incredible Sarah*

GB 1976 105m Technicolor
Readers Digest (Helen M. Strauss)

The career of French actress Sarah Bernhardt up to the age of thirty-five.

Mildly pleasing old-fashioned biopic with remarkably unreliable detail and a regrettably bland approach to its fascinating subject.

w Ruth Wolff *d* Richard Fleischer *ph* Christopher Challis *m* Elmer Bernstein *pd* Elliot Scott

Glenda Jackson, Daniel Massey, Yvonne Mitchell, Douglas Wilmer, David Langton, Simon Williams, John Castle, Edward Judd, Peter Sallis

'An incredibly old-fashioned movie full of the most unforgettable moments you have ever tried to forget.'—*Andrew Sarris, Village Voice*

'A job lot of obligatory Hollywood platitudes strung together with all the skill of Captain Hook trying to thread a needle.'—*Benny Green, Punch*

'In the stupefying tradition of *Song of Norway*.'—*Pauline Kael.*

'So incredible you'll talk about it for years to come!'

The Incredible Shrinking Man*

US 1957 81m bw
U-I (Albert Zugsmith)

After being caught in a radioactive mist, a man shrinks inexorably to micro-size. Horrifyingly inevitable sci-fi with imaginative touches gracing a cheap production.

w Richard Matheson *d* Jack Arnold *ph* Ellis W. Carter *m* Joseph Gershenson *sp* Clifford Stine, Roswell A. Hoffman, Everett H. Bronssard

Grant Williams, Randy Stuart, April Kent, Paul Langton

'It opens up new vistas of cosmic terror.'—*Peter John Dyer*

'One hails a science fiction film which is both inventive and humane.'—*Sunday Times*

'Simple, ingenious, effective.'—*The Times*

The Incredible Shrinking Woman

US 1981 88m Technicolor
Universal / Lija (Hank Moonjean)

A housewife finds herself shrinking after using a new perfume . . .

Hamfisted spoof on *The Incredible Shrinking Man*, with flat jokes and rather poor trick photography.

w Jane Wagner *d* Joel Schumacher *ph* Bruce Logan *m* Suzanne Ciani

Lily Tomlin, Charles Grodin, Ned Beatty, Henry Gibson, Elizabeth Wilson

'Leaden satire on consumerism . . . even the special effects are barely passable.'—*Time Out, 1984*

The Incredible Two-Headed Transplant

US 1970 88m De Luxe
Mutual General / Trident / American International (John Lawrence)

A mad doctor grafts an extra head onto a homicidal maniac.

Full-blooded nonsense on a low budget; utterly repellent to some, but done with sufficient verve to be a minor cult title to others.

w James Gordon White, John Lawrence *d* Anthony M. Lanza *ph* John Steely, Glen Gano, Paul Hipp *m* John Barber

Bruce Dern, Pat Priest, Casey Kasem, Berry Kroeger

Incubus

Canada 1981 92m colour

Women are raped by a rampant demon. Utterly distasteful horror film. John Cassavetes, Kerrie Keane, Helen Hughes, Erin Flannery, John Ireland. Written by George Franklin, from the novel by Ray Russell; directed by John Hough; for Guardian Trust Company.

Indestructible Man

US 1956 70m bw

The dead body of a vicious killer is given new life by a mad doctor. Low-budget horror mayhem with no style at all. Lon Chaney Jnr, Robert Shayne, Casey Adams, Marian Carr. Written by Vy Russell and Sue Bradford; directed by Jack Pollexfen; for Allied Artists.

The Indian Fighter

US 1955 88m Technicolor
Cinemascope
UA / Bryna (William Schorr)

An Indian fighter protects a wagon train from the Sioux.

Simple-minded western with touches of philosophy and not much drive.

w Frank Davis, Ben Hecht *d* André de Toth *ph* Wilfrid M. Cline *m* Franz Waxman

Kirk Douglas, Elsa Martinelli, Walter Abel, Walter Matthau, Diana Douglas, Eduard Franz, Lon Chaney Jnr, Alan Hale Jnr, Elisha Cook Jnr

Indian Scout
US 1949 70m bw

Episodes in the life of Davy Crockett. Minor western which hit the spot with small-town audiences, and in the late fifties, after the success of the Disney film, was reissued as *Davy Crockett, Indian Scout*. George Montgomery, Ellen Drew, Philip Reed, Noah Beery Jnr. Written by Richard Schayes; directed by Ford Beebe; for Edward Small.

'The hero is back!'
Indiana Jones and the Temple of Doom*
US 1984 118m Rank / De Luxe
Panavision
Paramount / Lucasfilm (Robert Watts)

A prequel to *Raiders of the Lost Ark*: Jones in 1935 finds the sacred Sankara stone. Slow-starting adventure romp with much ingenuity and too much brutality and horror. In the US it caused the creation of a new censor certificate: PG(13).

w Willard Huyck, Gloria Katz, *story* George Lucas d Steven Spielberg ph Douglas Slocombe, Allan Daviau m John Williams pd Elliot Scott

Harrison Ford, Kate Capshaw, Ke Huy Kwan, Philip Stone
   'One of the most sheerly pleasurable physical comedies ever made.'—*Pauline Kael, New Yorker*
   'A thin, arch, graceless affair.'—*Observer*
   'A two-hour series of none too carefully linked chase sequences . . . sitting on the edge of your seat gives you a sore bum but also a numb brain.'—*Guardian*

Indianapolis Speedway
US 1939 82m bw

A racetrack driver wants his kid brother to continue in college, but he has the racing fever. Editor's-bench mélange of *The Crowd Roars* (1932) and *Here Comes the Navy*; this doesn't star Cagney. Pat O'Brien, Ann Sheridan, John Payne, Gale Page, Frank McHugh, Regis Toomey. Written by Sig Herzig and Wally Klein; directed by Lloyd Bacon; for Warners. 'It contains just about every cliché such type melodrama can have.'—*Variety*
†Frank McHugh played the same role in the 1932 version.

'Through one indiscretion . . . a woman with a future became a woman with a past!'
Indiscreet
US 1931 92m bw
United Artists

A socialite endangers her own romance when she tries to protect her younger sister. Embarrassing and slow-moving farce which helped to kill its star's career.

w / songs Brown, de Sylva and Henderson d Leo McCarey ph Ray June, Gregg Toland

Gloria Swanson, Ben Lyon, Monroe Owsley, Barbara Kent, Arthur Lake, Maude Eburne, Henry Kolker

'How dare he make love to me—and not be a married man!'
Indiscreet**
GB 1958 100m Technicolor
Grandon (Stanley Donen)

An American diplomat in London falls in love with an actress but protects himself by saying he is married.
Affairs among the ultra rich, amusing when played by these stars but with imperfect production values which the alarmingly thin plot allows one too much time to consider.

w Norman Krasna, from his play Kind Sir d Stanley Donen ph Frederick A. Young m Richard Bennett, Ken Jones

Cary Grant, Ingrid Bergman, Phyllis Calvert, Cecil Parker, David Kossoff, Megs Jenkins
   'One is often on the point of being bored, but one never is, quite.'—*Richard Roud*
   'A film to which you would not hesitate to take your jeweller, your architect, your home decorator, your dressmaker and your domestic staff.'—*Alexander Walker*
● *Video: BBC*

Indiscretion of an American Wife*
Italy / US 1954 75m bw
David O. Selznick (Vittorio de Sica)
Alternative titles: *Terminus Station, Indiscretion*

An American woman and an Italian professor say goodbye in Rome's terminal station. Strained attempt to re-do *Brief Encounter* against the busy background of a great railway station; moments of interest, but artificiality prevails, and the plot never gets up enough steam.

w Cesare Zavattini, Truman Capote, etc d Vittorio de Sica ph G. R. Aldo m Aldo Cicognini

Jennifer Jones, Montgomery Clift, Gino Cervi, Richard Beymer

Inferno**
US 1953 83m Technicolor 3-D
TCF (William Bloom)

When a millionaire breaks his leg in the desert, his wife and her lover leave him to die; but he contrives to catch up with them.
An outdoor melodrama which made better use of 3-D than any other film, suggesting the lone handicapped figure in the vast spaces; but the lovers are dull and the fire climax perfunctory.

w Francis Cockrell d Roy Baker ph Lucien Ballard m Paul Sawtell

Robert Ryan, William Lundigan, Rhonda Fleming

Inferno
Italy 1980 107m Technicolor

A New York apartment house is occupied by satanists who murder those who learn their secret. Absurdly overplotted and mainly incomprehensible shocker with some small pretensions to style. Leigh McCloskey, Irene Miracle, Eleonora Giorgi. Written and directed by Dario Argento; for TCF.

The Informer****
US 1935 91m bw
RKO (Cliff Reid)

An IRA leader is betrayed by a simple-minded hanger-on who wants money to emigrate; he is hounded by fellow rebels and his own conscience.
A tedious plot is turned into brilliant cinema by full-blooded acting and a highly stylized yet brilliantly effective *mise en scène* which never attempts reality.

w Dudley Nichols, *novel* Liam O'Flaherty d John Ford ph Joseph H. August m Max Steiner ad Van Nest Polglase

Victor McLaglen, Heather Angel, Margot Grahame, Una O'Connor, Wallace Ford, Preston Foster, J. M. Kerrigan, Joe Sawyer, Donald Meek
   'A tough subject, a sure critic's picture, but dubious box office.'—*Variety*
   'As impressive as *Scarface*, or anything in the whole powerful literature redolent of fog and grime and dreariness which the Germans gave to the Americans.'—*Bardèche and Brasillach*
† An early British sound version was made in 1929 by Arthur Robison for BIP, with Lars Hansen and Lya de Putti.

AA: Dudley Nichols; John Ford; Max Steiner; Victor McLaglen
AAN: best picture

The Informers
GB 1963 104m bw
Rank (William MacQuitty)
US title: *Underworld Informers*

A police informer is murdered and his brother takes revenge.
Basic police melodrama, with clumsy script and jaded direction.

w Alun Falconer, *novel* Death of a Snout by Douglas Warner d Ken Annakin ph Reg Wyer m Clifton Parker

Nigel Patrick, Colin Blakely, Derren Nesbitt

L'Ingénue Libertine
France 1950 88m approx bw
Codo-Cinéma (Jean Velter)

A romantic girl lives in an imaginary world of affairs, but can't bring herself to consummate her marriage.
Minor period sex comedy which has the distinction of being Britain's first 'X' film, though the naughtiness is more implied than stated.

w P. Laroche, *novel* Colette d Jacqueline Audry ph Grignon m Vincent Scotto

Daniele Delorme, Frank Villard, Jean Tissier

Inherit the Wind**
US 1960 127m bw
UA / Lomitas (Stanley Kramer)

A fictionalized account of the 1925 Scopes 'monkey trial', when a schoolmaster was accused of teaching the theory of evolution. Splendid theatrics with fine performances, marred by boring subplots but enhanced by a realistic portrait of a sweltering southern town.

A
BUDDY ADLER
PRODUCTION · STARRING

INGRID BERGMAN
CURT JURGENS
ROBERT DONAT

LOVE HAD SUDDENLY COME TO HER UNDER THE CHINA SKY... LOVE FOR THIS EURASIAN SOLDIER WHO NOW PRESSED HIS EARTHY, ORIENTAL SKIN AGAINST HER OWN...

20 Century-Fox PRESENTS

THE INN OF THE SIXTH HAPPINESS

CINEMASCOPE

COLOR by DE LUXE

SIG

DIRECTED BY
MARK ROBSON
SCREENPLAY BY
ISOBEL LENNART

THE INN OF THE SIXTH HAPPINESS. It was never made clear what the real Gladys Aylward thought of the love affair grafted onto her life in this movie, but Ingrid Bergman certainly touched all hearts.

w Nathan E. Douglas, Harold Jacob Smith, *play* Jerome Lawrence, Robert E. Lee *d* Stanley Kramer *ph* Ernest Laszlo *m* Ernest Gold

Spencer Tracy, Fredric March, Florence Eldridge, Gene Kelly, Dick York, Donna Anderson, Harry Morgan, Elliott Reid, Claude Akins

AAN: script; Ernest Laszlo; Spencer Tracy

The In-Laws

US 1979   103m   Technicolor
Warner (Alan Arkin)

A timorous dentist and a CIA spy, whose children are to marry, find themselves unwillingly linked together in gunplay in a South American republic.
Two charismatic actors can't fail to get some laughs, but the extended script makes it a bumpy ride.

w Andrew Bergman *d* Arthur Hiller *ph* David M. Walsh *m* John Morris *pd* Pato Guzman

Peter Falk, Alan Arkin, Richard Libertini, Penny Peyser, Nancy Dussault
'It seems incapable either of adhering to the conventions of a comedy-thriller plot or of mustering sufficient invention to abandon plot altogether for a farcical free-for-all.'—*Tim Pulleine, MFB*

The Inn of the Sixth Happiness**

GB 1958   158m   De Luxe   Cinemascope
TCF (Mark Robson)

An English servant girl becomes a missionary and spends many arduous years in China. Romanticized biopic of Gladys Aylward, with lots of children, a happy ending, and everyone sensationally miscast. Somehow it all works, even North Wales standing in for China.

w Isobel Lennart, *book* The Small Woman by Alan Burgess *d* Mark Robson *ph* Frederick A. Young *m* Malcolm Arnold

Ingrid Bergman, Curt Jurgens, Robert Donat, Athene Seyler, Ronald Squire, Richard Wattis, Moultrie Kelsall

AAN: Mark Robson

Inner Sanctum

The title was taken from a radio show featuring mystery stories with a last minute twist. The films were introduced rather oddly by a misshapen head in a crystal ball on the empty table of a boardroom. The head belonged to David Hoffman, and he introduced each film: 'This . . . is the inner sanctum . . .' (The original reference was presumably to the innermost working of the human mind.) The films, made for Universal, all starred Lon Chaney Jnr (who alternated as hero and villain); they were among the most boring and badly made second feature thrillers of the forties.

1943: CALLING DR DEATH
1944: WEIRD WOMAN, DEAD MAN'S EYES
1945: STRANGE CONFESSION (remake of THE MAN WHO RECLAIMED HIS HEAD), THE FROZEN GHOST
1946: PILLOW OF DEATH

Innocent Bystanders*

GB 1972   110m   Eastmancolor
Sagittarius (George H. Brown)

The British secret service sends three agents to trace a Russian traitor.
Confused and violent espionage thriller; rather a waste of good production.

w James Mitchell *d* Peter Collinson *ph* Brian Probyn *m* John Keating

Stanley Baker, Geraldine Chaplin, Dana Andrews, Donald Pleasence

Innocent Sinners**

GB 1957   95m   bw
Rank (Hugh Stewart)

A 13-year-old London girl builds a garden in the rubble of a bombed church, and gets into trouble with the police.
Likeable, slightly unfinished, mildy astringent little human drama full of well-observed character sketches.

w Neil Paterson, *novel* An Episode of Sparrows by Rumer Godden *d* Philip Leacock *ph* Harry Waxman *m* Philip Green

Flora Robson, Catherine Lacey, David Kossoff, Barbara Mullen, June Archer

The Innocents**

GB 1961   99m   bw   Cinemascope
TCF / Achilles (Jack Clayton)

In Victorian times, a spinster governess in a lonely house finds her young charges possessed by evil demons of servants now dead.
Elaborate revamping of Henry James' *The Turn of the Screw*, the ghosts being now (possibly) the figments of a frustrated woman's imagination. The frissons would have worked better on a normal-shaped screen, but the decor, lighting and general handling are exceptional.

w William Archibald, Truman Capote *d* Jack Clayton *ph* Freddie Francis *m* Georges Auric *ad* Wilfrid Shingleton

Deborah Kerr, Megs Jenkins, Pamela Franklin, Martin Stephens, Michael Redgrave, Peter Wyngarde

Innocents in Paris

GB 1953   102m   bw
Romulus (Anatole de Grunwald)

British tourists spend a weekend in the gay city.
Strained compendium of anecdotes which misses an easy target.

w Anatole de Grunwald *d* Gordon Parry *ph* Gordon Lang *m* Josef Kosma

Alastair Sim, Margaret Rutherford, Jimmy Edwards, Claire Bloom, Laurence Harvey, Ronald Shiner

Innocents of Paris

US 1929   69m   bw
Paramount / Jesse L. Lasky

A Parisian junk dealer saves a boy's life and falls for his aunt.
Heavygoing and dated musical comedy which introduced Chevalier to world audiences.

w Ethel Doherty, Ernest Vajda, *play* Flea Market by Charles Andrews *d* Richard Wallace *ph* Charles Lang *songs* Leo Robin, Richard A. Whiting

Maurice Chevalier, Sylvia Beecher, Russell Simpson, George Fawcett

Inquest*

GB 1939   60m   bw
Charter (John Boulting)

A coroner has his suspicions as to who murdered the deceased.
Modest courtroom suspenser which marked the Boultings' first attempt (the second was *Suspect*) to raise the standard of second features.

w Francis Miller, *play* Michael Barringer *d* Roy Boulting

Elizabeth Allan, Herbert Lomas, Hay Petrie, Barbara Everest, Olive Sloane

'A degenerate film with dignity!'

Inserts

GB 1975   117m   De Luxe
UA / Film and General (Davina Belling, Clive Parsons)

In 1930 Hollywood, a fading silent queen and a has-been director take to drugs.
Curious, interesting semi-porno melodrama with Pinterish asides and an inaccurate but stimulating feel of the film city at its height.

wd John Byrum *ph* Denys Coop *md* Jessica Harper

Richard Dreyfuss, Jessica Harper, Veronica Cartwright, Bob Hoskins, Stephen Davies
'The ludicrous plot and the painfully obvious symbolism make it tempting to interpret *Inserts* as a comedy. Yet to assume that a bad movie about the making of a bad movie is somehow good by virtue of its badness is to be guilty of a kind of mimetic fallacy.'—*Robert Asahina, New Leader*

● *Video: Warner*

Inside Daisy Clover*

US 1965   128m   Technicolor
Panavision
Warner / Pakula–Mulligan (Alan J. Pakula)

Tribulations of an adolescent movie star in thirties Hollywood.
Amusing, rather hysterical variant on *A Star Is Born*; agreeably wacky in spots, glum in others. Would have benefited from the greater permissiveness possible a few years later.

w Gavin Lambert, from his novel *d* Robert Mulligan *ph* Charles Lang Jnr *m* André Previn *ch* Herbert Ross *ad* Robert Clatworthy

Natalie Wood, Robert Redford, Ruth Gordon, Christopher Plummer, Roddy MacDowall

'The movie is short on characters, detail, activity, dialogue, even music; it's as if it's so determined to be stylish and sophisticated that rather than risk vulgarity or banality, it eliminates almost everything.'—*Pauline Kael, 1968*

AAN: Ruth Gordon

Inside Detroit

US 1955 82m bw

A racketeer comes out of prison and tries to regain control of the car workers' union.
Tedious support, like a grossly extended *Crime Does Not Pay*. Pat O'Brien, Dennis O'Keefe, Tina Carver, Mark Damon. Written by Robert E. Kent and James B. Gordon; directed by Fred F. Sears; for Sam Katzman / Columbia.

Inside Moves

US 1980 113m colour
Goodmark (Mark M. Tanz, R. W. Goodwin)

A failed suicide makes friends in Max's bar with other handicapped people.
Curious tragi-comedy which generally settles for sentimentality but provides a few funny moments along the way.

w Valerie Curtin, Barry Levinson, *novel* Todd Walton *d* Richard Donner *ph* Laszlo Kovacs *m* John Barry

John Savage, David Morse, Diana Scarwid, Amy Wright, Tony Burton, Harold Russell
'A dismal contribution in the Year of the Disabled Person.'—*John Pym, MFB*
'If you imagine *The Iceman Cometh* rewritten by William Saroyan as a tribute to Frank Capra, that's about it.'—*Sunday Times*

AAN: Diana Scarwid (supporting actress)

● Video: Intervision

Inside Out*

GB / West Germany 1975 97m
Technicolor
Warner / Kettledrum (Judd Bernard)
TV title: *The Golden Heist*
aka: *Hitler's Gold*

A German ex-commandant of a POW camp enlists the aid of Americans in a daring plan to kidnap a Nazi war criminal from East Germany and find buried Nazi loot.
Entertaining but very silly actioner with too many changes of mood, though some sequences please.

w Judd Bernard, Stephen Schneck *d* Peter Duffell *ph* John Coquillon *m* Konrad Elfers

Telly Savalas, James Mason, Robert Culp, Aldo Ray, Gunter Meisner, Adrian Hoven, Charles Korvin, Richard Warner

Inside Straight

US 1951 89m bw
MGM (Richard Goldstone)

The life of a 19th-century tycoon is revealed in flashbacks during a poker game.
Solid melodrama which doesn't quite have the required spark.

w Guy Trosper *d* Gerald Mayer *ph* Ray June *m* Lennie Hayton

David Brian, Arlene Dahl, Barry Sullivan, Mercedes McCambridge, Paula Raymond, Claude Jarman Jnr, Lon Chaney Jnr, John Hoyt

Inside the Walls of Folsom Prison

US 1951 87m bw

A prison riot results in the death of the governor; when a replacement with more humane ideas is appointed, this does not stop violence from breaking out again. Old-fashioned prison movie on highly predictable lines. Steve Cochran, David Brian, Phil Carey, Ted de Corsia, Scott Forbes. Written and directed by Crane Wilbur; for Bryan Foy / Warner.

The Inspector*

GB 1961 111m De Luxe Cinemascope
TCF (Mark Robson)
US title: *Lisa*

In 1946 a Dutch policeman rescues a Jewish girl from an ex-Nazi and helps smuggle her to Palestine.
Peripatetic melodrama with surface suspense and subdued thoughts of ideology and race. Moments of interest, but generally dully developed and acted.

w Nelson Gidding, *novel* Jan de Hartog *d* Philip Dunne *ph* Arthur Ibbetson *m* Malcolm Arnold

Stephen Boyd, Dolores Hart, Leo McKern, *Hugh Griffith*, Donald Pleasence, Harry Andrews, Robert Stephens, Marius Goring
'A sluggish mélange of melodrama, romance, mystery and what the inactive might call action.'—*Judith Crist*

An Inspector Calls**

GB 1954 79m bw
British Lion / Watergate (A. D. Peters)

In 1912 a prosperous Yorkshire family is visited by a mysterious inspector who proves that each of them was partly responsible for the death of a young girl.
Tactful, enjoyable record of a celebrated play in its author's most typical manner.

w Desmond Davis, *play* J. B. Priestley *d* Guy Hamilton *ph* Ted Scaife *m* Francis Chagrin *ad* Joseph Bato

Alastair Sim, Jane Wenham, Arthur Young, Olga Lindo, Brian Worth, Eileen Moore, Bryan Forbes

Inspector Clouseau

GB 1968 105m Eastmancolor
Panavision
UA / Mirisch (Lewis J. Rachmil)

An incompetent French policeman is brought to London to investigate the aftermath of the Great Train Robbery.
Tiresome charade with all the jokes well telegraphed, and a background of swinging London.

w Tom and Frank Waldman *d* Bud Yorkin *ph* Arthur Ibbetson *m* Ken Thorne

Alan Arkin, Delia Boccardo, Frank Finlay, Patrick Cargill, Beryl Reid, Barry Foster

The Inspector General**

US 1949 101m Technicolor
Warner (Jerry Wald)
aka: *Happy Times*

An assistant elixir salesman with a travelling fair is mistaken by villagers for the dreaded inspector general.
Well wrought but basically boring version of a basically boring classic farce full of rhubarbing Old Russians. Nice production and hilarious moments do not quite atone for the dull stretches.

w Philip Rapp, Harry Kurnitz, *play* Nikolai Gogol *d* Henry Koster *ph* Elwood Bredell *songs* Sylvia Fine *m* John Green *ad* Robert Haas

Danny Kaye, Walter Slezak, Barbara Bates, Elsa Lanchester, Gene Lockhart, Alan Hale, Benny Baker, Walter Catlett

● Video: Mountain

Inspector Hornleigh*

GB 1938 87m bw
TCF (Robert T. Kane)

The Chancellor of the Exchequer's bag is stolen.
First of three police comedy-dramas based on a character created for the radio series Monday Night at Eight by Hans Priwin. Not bad, but the thinnest of the trio.

w Bryan Wallace, Gerald Elliott, Richard Llewellyn *d* Eugene Forde *ph* Derrick Williams

Gordon Harker, Alastair Sim, Hugh Williams, Steve Geray, Wally Patch, Edward Underdown, Gibb McLaughlin, Ronald Adam
'The opening shots—the murder in the squalid lodging and the stamp auction with the rows of poker faces and the elaborately mute bids—are not only good cinema, they are good English cinema, as national as a shot, say, from a Feyder, a de Mille or a Pommer.'—*Graham Greene*

Inspector Hornleigh Goes to It*

GB 1940 87m bw
TCF (Edward Black)
US title: *Mail Train*

Hornleigh and Bingham track down a fifth columnist.
Zestful comedy thriller climaxing on an express train: good fun for addicts of the genre.

w Val Guest, J. O. C. Orton, Frank Launder *d* Walter Forde *ph* John Cox *md* Louis Levy

Gordon Harker, Alastair Sim, Phyllis Calvert, Edward Chapman, Charles Oliver, Raymond Huntley, Percy Walsh, David Horne, Peter Gawthorne

Inspector Hornleigh on Holiday*

GB 1939 87m bw
TCF (Edward Black)

The inspector and his sergeant solve the death of a fellow boarder at a seaside hotel.
Lively Hitchcockian comedy-thriller romp with an excellent script and plenty of variety of location.

*w Frank Launder, Sidney Gilliat, J. O. C.
Orton d Walter Forde ph John Cox
md Louis Levy*

Gordon Harker, Alastair Sim, Linden Travers,
Wally Patch, Edward Chapman, Philip
Leaver, Kynaston Reeves

Inspiration
US 1930 74m bw
MGM

A French artists' model renounces her lover in
case she harms his career.
Inane romantic melodrama.

*w Gene Markey d Clarence Brown
ph William Daniels*

Greta Garbo, Robert Montgomery, Lewis
Stone, Marjorie Rambeau, Beryl Mercer,
John Miljan

'As an adult problem it holds and never
offends . . . box office certainly, and a cinch
for women.'—*Variety*

'Camille without the cough.'—*Motion
Picture*

The Intelligence Men
GB 1965 104m Eastmancolor
Rank / Hugh Stewart
US title: *Spylarks*

Two incompetent spies blunder through a
series of adventures.
Inept and rather embarrassing big-screen
debut for two excellent television comedians.

*w S. C. Green, R. M. Hills d Robert Asher
ph Jack Asher m Phillip Green*

Eric Morecambe, Ernie Wise, William
Franklyn, April Olrich, Richard Vernon,
David Lodge, Warren Mitchell, Francis
Matthews

● *Video: Rank*

Intent to Kill°
GB 1958 89m bw Cinemascope
TCF / Zonic (Adrian Worker)

In a Montreal hospital, attempts are made on
the life of a South American dictator
recovering from a brain operation.
Solidly entertaining suspenser.

*w Jimmy Sangster d Jack Cardiff
ph Desmond Dickinson m Kenneth V. Jones*

Richard Todd, Betsy Drake, Herbert Lom,
Warren Stevens, Alexander Knox

Interference
US 1929 75m bw

To prevent his wife from being blackmailed, a
dying man commits murder and turns himself
in. Dreary drama with the distinction of being
Paramount's first talking picture. William
Powell, Evelyn Brent, Clive Brook, Doris
Kenyon. Written by Ernest Pascal and Hope
Loring, from the play by Roland Pertwee and
Harold Dearden; directed by Lothar Mendes
and Roy Pomeroy; for Paramount.

Interiors°
US 1978 95m Technicolor
UA / Jack Rollins-Charles H. Joffe

Everybody in a well-heeled American family
has problems.

Curious attempt by Woody Allen to make his
own version of the Bergmanesque psycho-
dramas he usually satirizes. Apparently this is
the real Woody, and the comedian was a
mask. Oh, well.

wd Woody Allen ph Gordon Willis m none

Kristin Griffith, Marybeth Hurt, Richard
Jordan, Diane Keaton, E. G. Marshall,
Geraldine Page, Maureen Stapleton, Sam
Waterston

AAN: script; direction; Geraldine Page;
Maureen Stapleton
    'As dull as toothache and as predictable as a
metronome.'—*Barry Took, Punch*

● *Video: Warner*

Interlude
US 1957 89m Technicolor
           Cinemascope
U-I (Ross Hunter)

An American girl in Munich falls in love with
an orchestral conductor but leaves him
because of his insane wife.
Dull remake of *When Tomorrow Comes* (qv),
with poor script and performances.

*w Daniel Fuchs, Franklin Coen d Douglas
Sirk ph R. F. Schoengarth m Frank Skinner*

Rossano Brazzi, June Allyson, Françoise
Rosay, Marianne Cook, Keith Andes, Jane
Wyatt

'Contains every cliché known to romantic
fiction.'—*MFB*

Interlude°
GB 1968 113m Technicolor
Columbia / Domino (David Deutsch, Jack
Hanbury)

A girl reporter falls for a celebrated orchestral
conductor; they have an affair but he finally
goes back to his wife.
Intermezzo remade for the swinging London
set, quite agreeable in parts because of the
acting but generally rather soggy.

*w Lee Langley, Hugh Leonard d Kevin
Billington ph Gerry Fisher m Georges
Delerue pd Tony Woolard*

Oskar Werner, Barbara Ferris, *Virginia
Maskell, John Cleese*, Donald Sutherland,
Nora Swinburne, Alan Webb

'If you laughed at *Brief Encounter* you will
roar over this one.'—*Wilfrid Sheed*

'It's got all the schmaltz and none of the
style of the tearjerkers of yesteryear.'—*Judith
Crist, 1973*

'Wild longings . . . fierce desires he could
    not name . . . for an interlude of stolen
    love! To one woman he gave his
    memories—to another he gave his
    dreams!'

Intermezzo°°°
US 1939 69m bw
David O. Selznick
GB title: *Escape to Happiness*

A renowned, married violinist has an affair
with his musical protégée.
Archetypal cinema love story, Hollywoodized
from a Swedish original but quite perfect in its
brief, sentimental way.

*w George O'Neil, original scenario Gosta
Stevens, Gustav Molander d Gregory Ratoff
ph Gregg Toland m Robert Henning, Heinz
Provost m (score) Lou Forbes*

Leslie Howard, Ingrid Bergman, John
Halliday, Edna Best, Cecil Kellaway
† William Wyler is said to have assisted in the
direction.

AAN: Lou Forbes

● *Video: Guild*

    Stars of stage, screen radio and boudoir
    throw a party for your entertainment!'

International House°
US 1933 73m bw
Paramount

A weird variety of travellers are quarantined
in a Shanghai hotel where a local doctor has
perfected television.
Madcap farce which succeeds in hits and
misses.

*w Francis Martin, Walter de Leon, Lou
Heifetz, Neil Brant d Edward Sutherland
ph Ernest Haller*

W. C. Fields, George Burns, Gracie Allen,
Peggy Hopkins Joyce, Stuart Erwin, Sari
Matitza, Bela Lugosi, Edmund Breese,
Lumsden Hare, Rose Marie, Rudy Vallee,
Sterling Holloway, Cab Calloway and his
band, Colonel Stoopnagle and Budd

'Cast includes enough names to offset the
effects of an otherwise second-rate picture.'—
Variety

'Constructed along the lines of a mammoth
vaudeville show, the motivating story often is
sidetracked entirely to permit a lot of
unrelated hokum comedy.'—*Motion Picture
Herald*

'A thousand thrills as two men battle
    across a continent!'

International Lady°
US 1941 102m bw
Edward Small

An FBI man falls for the lady Axis agent he is
chasing.
Cliché-ridden melodrama partially saved by
light comedy touches.

*w Howard Estabrook d Tim Whelan ph Hal
Mohr m Lucien Moraweck*

George Brent, Basil Rathbone, Ilona Massey,
Gene Lockhart, George Zucco, Francis
Pierlot, Martin Kosleck, Marjorie Gateson

International Settlement
US 1938 75m bw
TCF (Darryl F. Zanuck)

An adventurer becomes involved in Shanghai
gun-running during the war between China
and Japan.
Brisk action romance with good technical
credits.

*w Lou Breslow, John Patrick d Eugene
Forde ph Lucien Andriot md Samuel Kaylin*

George Sanders, Dolores del Rio, June Lang,
Dick Baldwin, Ruth Terry, John Carradine,
Keye Luke, Harold Huber, Pedro de Cordoba

'Strong supporting picture for double
bills.'—*Variety*

INTERMEZZO. The young Ingrid Bergman caused a stir in the film world when she innocently lured Leslie Howard from fame and family.

International Squadron*
US 1941 87m bw
Warner (Edmund Grainger)

A playboy becomes a fighting air ace. Standard war story, quite well done; remake of *Ceiling Zero* (qv).

w Barry Trivers, *story* Frank Wead *d* Lewis Seiler *ph* Arthur Edeson

Ronald Reagan, James Stephenson, Julie Bishop, Cliff Edwards, Reginald Denny, Olympe Bradna, William Lundigan, John Ridgely

International Velvet
GB 1978 125m Metrocolor
MGM (Bryan Forbes)

A hostile orphan becomes an international horsewoman. Disappointing attempt to produce a sequel to 1944's *National Velvet*; none of it coheres, one is not clear to whom it is intended to appeal, and some of the dialogue is fearsome.

wd Bryan Forbes *ph* Tony Imi *m* Francis Lai *pd* Keith Wilson

Nanette Newman, Tatum O'Neal, Anthony Hopkins, Christopher Plummer, Peter Barkworth, Dinsdale Landen
● *Video: MGM / UA*

The Internecine Project*
GB 1974 89m Eastmancolor
Maclean and Co / Lion International / Hemisphere (Barry Levinson, Andrew Donally)

A Harvard professor arranges the mutual extermination of four people who could spoil a politician's presidential chances. Coldly murderous romp with plenty of style.

w Barry Levinson, Jonathan Lynn, *novel* Mort W. Elkind *d* Ken Hughes *ph* Geoffrey Unsworth *m* Roy Budd

James Coburn, Lee Grant, Harry Andrews, Ian Hendry, Michael Jayston, Keenan Wynn

'He risked his life to save a rat—and what did he get for it?'
Internes Can't Take Money*
US 1937 75m bw
Paramount (Benjamin Glazer)
GB title: *You Can't Take Money*

A hospital doctor persuades a gangster friend to help a woman find her missing child. Quite interesting minor melodrama, first of the Dr Kildare series which was subsequently recast and restyled by MGM.

w Rian James, Theodore Reed, *story* Max Brand *d* Alfred Santell *ph* Theodor Sparkuhl *m* Gregory Stone

Joel McCrea, Barbara Stanwyck, Lloyd Nolan, Stanley Ridges, Lee Bowman, Irving Bacon

'Satisfactory melodrama with a tear . . . better than average standing at the box office.'—*Variety*

'Their nights are as fast and frantic as their days! Don't miss the wildest party ever filmed!'
The Interns*
US 1962 130m bw
Columbia / Interns Co. / Robert Cohn

In an American hospital, newly qualified doctors have personal and career problems. Birth, abortion, sudden death, drugs and women's lib all figure in this melodramatic compendium which succeeds well enough on its own level and spawned a sequel (*The New Interns*) and an unsuccessful TV series.

w Walter Newman, David Swift, *novel* Richard Frede *d* David Swift *ph* Russell Metty *m* Leith Stevens

Cliff Robertson, Michael Callan, James MacArthur, Nick Adams, Suzy Parker, Buddy Ebsen, Telly Savalas

Interpol
GB 1957 92m bw Cinemascope
Columbia / Warwick (Irving Allen, Albert R. Broccoli)
US title: *Pickup Alley*

The US Anti-Narcotics Squad trails across Europe the insane and ruthless leader of a drug ring.
Drearily routine thick ear electrified by one performance but not helped by wide screen.

w John Paxton *d* John Gilling *ph* Ted Moore *m* Richard Bennett

Victor Mature, Anita Ekberg, *Trevor Howard*, Bonar Colleano, Marne Maitland, Eric Pohlmann, Alec Mango, Peter Illing, Sidney Tafler

The Interrupted Journey
GB 1949 80m bw
Valiant (Anthony Havelock-Allan)

An author leaves his wife for another woman, changes his mind on the journey, pulls the communication cord and causes a train crash. Or does he?
Minor melodrama with expressionist tendencies and a dream explanation. Interesting for its parts rather than its whole.

w Michael Pertwee *d* Daniel Birt *ph* Erwin Hillier

Richard Todd, Valerie Hobson, Christine Norden, Tom Walls, Ralph Truman, Vida Hope

Interrupted Melody
US 1955 106m Eastmancolor
Cinemascope
MGM (Jack Cummings)

The story of Marjorie Lawrence, an Australian opera singer who fell victim to polio.
Standard biopic which jells less well than some.

w William Ludwig, Sonya Levien d Curtis Bernhardt ph Joe Ruttenberg, Paul Vogel music supervisor Saul Chaplin

Eleanor Parker, Glenn Ford, Roger Moore, Cecil Kellaway, Stephen Bekassy.

AA: script
AAN: Eleanor Parker

Intimacy*
US 1965 87m bw
Goldstone (David Heilwell)

A businessman in need of a government contract tries to compromise the official concerned.
Unusual minor melodrama, interesting but not quite successful.

w Eva Wolas d Victor Stoloff ph Ted Saizis m Geordie Hormel

Barry Sullivan, Nancy Malone, Jack Ging, Joan Blackman, Jackie Shannon

Intimate Relations see Les Parents Terribles

The Intimate Stranger*
GB 1956 95m bw
Anglo–Guild (Alec Snowden)
US title: Finger of Guilt

An American film producer in England is plagued by a strange girl who claims to have been his mistress.
Acceptable mystery thriller which holds the interest and has good detail.

w Peter Howard d Joseph Walton (Joseph Losey) m Trevor Duncan ph Gerald Gibbs

Richard Basehart, Mary Murphy, Mervyn Johns, Constance Cummings, Roger Livesey, Faith Brook

Into the Blue
GB 1950 83m bw

A cheerful stowaway on a yacht helps the owners catch smugglers. Emaciated comedy which never gets going. Michael Wilding, Odile Versois, Jack Hulbert, Constance Cummings, Edward Rigby. Written by Pamela Wilcox Bower, Donald Taylor and Nicholas Phipps; directed by Herbert Wilcox; for Imperadio.

Intolerance****
US 1916 115m approx (24 fps) bw silent
D. W. Griffith

Four stories—including Belshazzar's feast and the massacre of St Bartholomew—of intolerance through the ages are intercut and linked by the image of a mother and her baby: 'out of the cradle, endlessly rocking'.
A massive enterprise of which audiences at the time and after were quite intolerant. Hard to take in parts, it rises to a fine climax as all the stories come to a head, including a modern one with a race between a car and train, and has been called 'the only film fugue'. At the time, by far the most expensive film ever made.

wd D. W. Griffith ph Billy Bitzer

Mae Marsh, Lillian Gish, Constance Talmadge, Robert Harron, Elmo Lincoln, Eugene Pallette

'A mad, brilliant, silly extravaganza. Perhaps the greatest movie ever made. In it one can see the source of most of the major traditions of the screen: the methods of Eisenstein and Von Stroheim, the Germans and the Scandinavians, and, when it's bad, de Mille.'—New Yorker, 1980
● Video: Spectrum

Intrigue
US 1947 90m bw
UA / Star

In Shanghai after the war, a civilian pilot becomes unwittingly involved in drug smuggling.
Tedious and flashy pot-boiler.

w Barry Trivers, George Slavin d Edwin L. Marin ph Lucien Andriot m Louis Forbes

George Raft, June Havoc, Tom Tully, Helena Carter

The Intruder*
GB 1953 84m bw
British Lion / Ivan Foxwell

An ex-army officer surprises a burglar and recognizes his old commander who has been ill-served by society.
Watchable but rather mechanical compendium drama in which a series of cameos supposedly sum up the problems of life in post-war Britain.

w Robin Maugham, John Hunter, novel Line on Ginger by Robin Maugham d Guy Hamilton ph Ted Scaife m Francis Chagrin

Jack Hawkins, Michael Medwin, Hugh Williams, George Cole, Dennis Price, Dora Bryan

The Intruder*
US 1961 84m bw
Filmgroup (Roger Corman)
GB title: The Stranger

A mild-mannered stranger arrives in a southern town and stirs up racist trouble.
Cheaply-made social melodrama with many effective moments.

w Charles Beaumont, from his novel d Roger Corman ph Taylor Byars m Herman Stein

William Shatner, Frank Maxwell, Beverly Lunsford, Robert Emhardt, Jeanne Cooper, Leo Gordon, Charles Beaumont

Intruder in the Dust***
US 1949 87m bw
MGM (Clarence Brown)

In a southern town, a boy and an old lady solve a mystery and prevent a black man from being lynched.
Excellent character drama which also offers vivid local colour, a murder puzzle and social comment. A semi-classic.

w Ben Maddow, novel William Faulkner d Clarence Brown ph Robert Surtees m Adolph Deutsch

Juano Hernandez, Elizabeth Patterson, David Brian, Claude Jarman Jnr, Porter Hall, Will Geer

'It is surely the years of range and experience which have given him a control of the medium so calm, sure and—apparently—easy that he can make a complex story seem simple and straightforward.'—Pauline Kael
'A really good movie that is also and incidentally the first honestly worked out "racial" film I have seen.'—Richard Winnington
'An example of gripping film craftsmanship.'—News of the World

'From out of space—came hordes of green monsters!'
Invaders from Mars
US 1953 82m Cinecolor 3D
Edward L. Alperson

Martian invaders use hypnotized humans as saboteurs.
Poverty Row sci-fi partly redeemed by its erratic but talented designer who provides flashes of visual imagination.

w Richard Blake d / pd William Cameron Menzies ph John Seitz m Raoul Kraushaar

Helena Carter, Arthur Franz, Leif Erickson, Hillary Brooke

Invasion**
GB 1966 82m bw
AA / Merton Park (Jack Greenwood)

An English village is beset one night by invaders from outer space.
Understated, effective little suspenser, well done in all departments.

w Roger Marshall d Alan Bridges ph James Wilson m Bernard Ebbinghouse

Edward Judd, Valerie Gearon, Lyndon Brook, Yoko Tani, Tsai Chin, Barrie Ingham, Arthur Sharp

'The world as they knew it was slipping away from them. Time was running out for the human race. And there was nothing to hold on to—except each other!'
Invasion of the Body Snatchers****
US 1956 80m bw Superscope
Allied Artists / Walter Wanger

A small American town is imperceptibly taken over by an alien force.
Persuasive, thoroughly satisfying, low-budget science fiction, put across with subtlety and intelligence in every department.

w Daniel Mainwaring, novel Jack Finney d Don Siegel ph Ellsworth Fredericks m Carmen Dragon

Kevin McCarthy, Dana Wynter, Larry Gates, King Donovan, Carolyn Jones, Virginia Christine, Sam Peckinpah
● Video: BBC

Invasion of the Body Snatchers*
US 1978 115m Technicolor
UA / Robert H. Solo

Flashy updating of the 1956 classic, mistakenly set in a big city (San Francisco) and confusingly unravelled, with nobody for the audience to empathize with. Its nicest effect is to have Kevin McCarthy repeat his old role in a cameo.

w W. D. Richter *d* Philip Kaufman *ph* Michael Chapman *m* Denny Zeitlin *pd* Charles Rosen

Donald Sutherland, Brooke Adams, Leonard Nimoy, Veronica Cartwright, Jeff Goldblum, Art Hindle, Lelia Goldoni, Kevin McCarthy, Don Siegel

Invasion Quartet

GB 1961 87m bw
MGM (Ronald Kinnoch)

An ill-assorted foursome of officers and a boffin take on the dangerous mission of silencing a Nazi gun trained on Dover.
A plot which could have been handled any way is played unsatisfactorily for farce, and all concerned are understandably uneasy.

w Jack Trevor Story, John Briley, *story* Norman Collins *d* Jay Lewis *ph* Geoffrey Faithfull, Gerald Moss *m* Ron Goodwin

Bill Travers, Spike Milligan, Grégoire Aslan, John Le Mesurier, Thorley Walters, Maurice Denham, Millicent Martin, Cyril Luckham

Invasion USA

US 1952 70m bw
Columbia (Albert Zugsmith)

A hypnotist in a New York bar gives a group of people a foretaste of what might happen to them under atomic attack.
Ludicrous, dangerous, hilarious low-budget exploitationer composed mainly of rubber rocks and old newsreels.

w Robert Smith *d* Alfred E. Green *ph* John L. Russell *m* Albert Glasser

Dan O'Herlihy, Gerald Mohr, Peggie Castle

Investigation of a Citizen above Suspicion°

Italy 1970 115m Technicolor
Vera (Daniele Senatore)

A successful police inspector kills his mistress and, paranoically considering himself above suspicion, plants clues leading to himself and even confesses the crime.
Fairly engrossing character study with political undertones; cinematically quite striking, too.

w Ugo Pirro, Elio Petri *d* Elio Petri *ph* Luigi Kuveiller *m* Ennio Morricone

Gian Maria Volonte, Florinda Bolkan, Salvo Randone, Gianni Santuccio

AAN: best foreign film; script

Invisible Agent°

US 1942 84m bw
Universal (George Waggner)

Nazi and Japanese spies seek the secret of invisibility from its inventor.
Lively fantasy thriller with a cast more distinguished than it deserves.

w Curt Siodmak *d* Edwin L. Marin *sp* John P. Fulton *m* Hans Salter

Cedric Hardwicke, Peter Lorre, Ilona Massey, Jon Hall, Albert Basserman, J. Edward Bromberg, John Litel

Invisible Boy

US 1957 89m bw
MGM / Pan (Nicholas Nayfack)

A scientist allows his 10-year-old son to repair a robot, which comes under the control of an alien force.
Minor sci-fi utilizing the robot from *Forbidden Planet*.

w Cyril Hume *d* Herman Hoffman *ph* Harold Wellman *m* Les Baxter

Richard Eyer, Philip Abbott, Harold J. Stone, Diane Brewster

'Even the moon is frightened of me— frightened to death!'

The Invisible Man****

US 1933 71m bw
Universal (Carl Laemmle Jnr)

A scientist discovers a means of making himself invisible, but in the process becomes a megalomaniac.
Superb blend of eccentric character comedy, melodrama and trick photography in a Hollywood English setting; remarkably faithful to the spirit of the book. It made a star of Claude Rains in his first film, even though he is seen for only a couple of seconds.

w R. C. Sheriff, Philip Wylie, novel H. G. Wells *d* James Whale *ph* Arthur Edeson *sp* John P. Fulton

Claude Rains, Gloria Stuart, William Harrigan, Henry Travers, E. E. Clive, Una O'Connor, Forrester Harvey, Dudley Digges, Holmes Herbert

GRIFFIN (Claude Rains): 'We'll start with a few murders. Big men, little men—just to show we make no distinction.'

'Well made and full of intentional and unintentional laughs. Should do well.'— *Variety*

'Taken either as a technical exercise or as a sometimes profoundly moving retelling of the Frankenstein fable, it is one of the most rewarding of recent films.'—*William Troy*

† Sequels, successively less interesting, were (all qv) *The Invisible Man Returns* (1940), *Invisible Woman* (1941), *Invisible Agent* (1942), *The Invisible Man's Revenge* (1944) and *Abbott and Costello Meet the Invisible Man* (1951). A TV series with an anonymous hero was made by ATV in 1955; a Universal one with David McCallum followed in 1975, and was restructured as *The Gemini Man* in 1976.

†† Boris Karloff had been first choice for the role, but he turned it down.

The Invisible Man Returns

US 1940 81m bw
Universal (Ken Goldsmith)

A man convicted of killing his brother uses the secret of invisibility to find the real culprit.
Second in the series takes itself too seriously: a slow starter which works its way to a strong climax.

w Curt Siodmak, Lester Cole, Cedric Belfrage *d* Joe May *ph* Milton Krasner *m* Hans Salter, Frank Skinner *sp* John P. Fulton

Vincent Price, Cedric Hardwicke, John Sutton, Nan Grey, Cecil Kellaway, Alan Napier, Forrester Harvey

'Though the film has its bright moments, and some weird ones too, the first freshness is gone. Even the effects seem repetitive.'— *Pauline Kael, 70s*

The Invisible Man's Revenge

US 1944 77m bw
Universal (Ford Beebe)

A psychopathic killer on the run takes refuge with a doctor who has discovered the secret of invisibility.
Curious reversion to the original story in that the invisible man is now again the villain; but otherwise there's no flavour at all to this horror comic set in a phoney England.

w Bertram Millhauser *d* Ford Beebe *m* Hans Salter *sp* John P. Fulton

Jon Hall, Leon Errol, John Carradine, Alan Curtis, Evelyn Ankers, Gale Sondergaard, Halliwell Hobbes

The Invisible Menace

US 1938 55m bw

Murder at an army base brings strange revelations of the past. Standard mystery in which the star seems misplaced. Boris Karloff, Regis Toomey, Marie Wilson, Henry Kolker. Written by Crane Wilbur, from a play by Ralph S. Zink; directed by John Farrow; for Warner. (NB: Remade in 1943 as *Murder at the Waterfront*.) 'Undistinguished mystery meller, for bottom-lining the duals.'—*Variety*

The Invisible Ray°

US 1935 79m bw
Universal (Edmund Grainger)

A scientist discovers a superpowerful element which makes him homicidal.
Slow-moving science fiction with a touch of horror, and the pattern for its star's many later roles as a sympathetic man who turns into a monster. Interesting rather than stimulating.

w John Colton, *story* Howard Higgin, Douglas Hodges *d* Lambert Hillyer *ph* George Robinson *m* Franz Waxman *sp* John P. Fulton

Boris Karloff, Bela Lugosi, Frances Drake, Frank Lawton, Walter Kingsford, Beulah Bondi, Violet Kemble Cooper, Nydia Westman

'An easy number to sell, it should do pretty good business.'—*Variety*

Invisible Stripes

US 1939 82m bw
Warner (Hal B. Wallis)

An ex-con finds it difficult to go straight.
By 1940 Warners must have been able to make rip-offs of *Angels with Dirty Faces* in their sleep, and this one, despite its cast, suggests that they did.

w Warren Duff, *book* Warden Lewis E. Lawes *d* Lloyd Bacon *ph* Ernest Haller *m* Heinz Roemheld

George Raft, Humphrey Bogart, William Holden, Flora Robson, Jane Bryan, Paul Kelly, Lee Patrick, Henry O'Neill, Moroni Olson

'It's a familiar cinematic yarn but strengthened by a zippy pace, excellent performances and direction.'—*Variety*

The Invisible Woman*
US 1941 72m bw
Universal (Burt Kelly)

A mad scientist turns a model invisible. Screwball comedy with a deteriorating star at his hammiest: generally very laboured, but with some funny moments.

w Robert Lees, Fred Rinaldo, Gertrude Purcell *d* A. Edward Sutherland *ph* Elwood Bredell

John Barrymore, Charles Ruggles, Virginia Bruce, John Howard, Oscar Homolka, Donald MacBride, Edward Brophy, Shemp Howard, Margaret Hamilton, Maria Montez

Invitation
US 1952 81m bw
MGM (Lawrence Weingarten)

When a millionaire's daughter believes she is dying, revelations ensue about her beloved husband's original intentions.
Competently idiotic weepie with a happy ending.

w Paul Osborn, *story* Jerome Weidman *d* Gottfried Reinhardt *ph* Ray June *m* Bronislau Kaper

Dorothy McGuire, Van Johnson, Ruth Roman, Louis Calhern, Ray Collins, Michael Chekhov

'The dialogue is stagey and the treatment indeterminate, with overmuch reliance on the dubious emotional reinforcement of loud background music.'—*Penelope Houston*

Invitation to a Gunfighter*
US 1964 92m De Luxe
UA / Stanley Kramer (Richard Wilson)

A small-town tyrant hires a smooth gunfighter to keep down the farmers he has cheated.
Predictable, rather self-satisfied little western with a studio look. Smart script and performances.

w Elizabeth and Richard Wilson *d* Richard Wilson *ph* Joseph MacDonald *m* David Raksin

Yul Brynner, George Segal, Janice Rule, Pat Hingle

Invitation to Happiness
US 1939 95m bw
Paramount (Wesley Ruggles)

A society girl marries a prizefighter.
Routine star romantic drama.

w Claude Binyon *d* Wesley Ruggles *ph* Leo Tover *m* Frederick Hollander

Irene Dunne, Fred MacMurray, Charles Ruggles, Billy Cook, William Collier Snr, Marion Martin

'Heartthrob drama, geared for good biz.'—*Variety*

Invitation to the Dance**
GB 1954 92m Technicolor
MGM (Arthur Freed)

Three stories in dance and mime.
Unsuccessful ballet film which closed its star's great period and virtually ended the heyday of the Hollywood musical. The simple fact emerged that European ballet styles were not Kelly's forte; yet there was much to enjoy in *Circus, Ring around the Rosy* and *The Magic Lamp*.

w, ch, d Gene Kelly *ph* Frederick A. Young *m* Jacques Ibert, André Previn, Rimsky-Korsakov *ad* Alfred Junge

Gene Kelly, Igor Youskevitch, Tommy Rall, Belita, Tamara Toumanova

The Ipcress File**
GB 1965 109m Techniscope
Rank / Steven / Lowndes (Harry Saltzman)

An intelligence man traces a missing scientist and finds that one of his own superiors is a spy.
The attempt to present a low-key James Bond (glasses, good at cookery, supermarket shopper) is frustrated by flashy direction and a confused plot. It did herald a new genre though the whole ambiance is now sadly dated, like an old copy of *The Sunday Times* Colour Supplement.

w Bill Canaway, James Doran, *novel* Len Deighton *d* Sidney J. Furie *ph* Otto Heller *m* John Barry *ad* Ken Adam

Michael Caine, Nigel Green, Guy Doleman, Sue Lloyd, Gordon Jackson
† Two sequels appeared starring 'Harry Palmer' (never named in the books): *Funeral in Berlin* and *Billion Dollar Brain* (both qv).

● *Video: Rank*

Irene
US 1940 101m bw (colour sequence)
RKO / Imperator (Herbert Wilcox)

A New York Irish shopgirl moves into society.
Fairly dim picturization of the old musical: the cast does its best.

w Alice Duer Miller, *play* James H. Montgomery *d* Herbert Wilcox *ph* Russell Metty *md* Anthony Collins *songs* Harry Tierney, Joseph McCarthy

Anna Neagle, Ray Milland, Roland Young, Alan Marshal, May Robson, Billie Burke, Arthur Treacher, Marsha Hunt, Isabel Jewell, Ethel Griffies

'This pre-camp version tries to be innocuously charming, and the effort is all too evident.'—*New Yorker, 1976*
† Previously filmed in 1926 with Colleen Moore.

AAN: Anthony Collins

Irish Eyes Are Smiling**
US 1944 90m Technicolor
TCF (Damon Runyon)

The life and times of a nineties songwriter, Ernest R. Ball.

Standard musical biopic, handsomely mounted.

w Earl Baldwin, John Tucker Battle *d* Gregory Ratoff *ph* Harry Jackson *md* Alfred Newman, Charles Henderson

Dick Haymes, June Haver, Monty Woolley, Anthony Quinn, Beverly Whitney, Maxie Rosenbloom, Veda Ann Borg, Clarence Kolb

AAN: Alfred Newman, Charles Henderson

The Irish in Us
US 1935 84m bw
Warner (Samuel Bischoff)

Adventures of three New York brothers.
Routine, good-natured star action frolic.

w Earl Baldwin *d* Lloyd Bacon *ph* George Barnes *md* Leo F. Forbstein

James Cagney, Pat O'Brien, Olivia de Havilland, Mary Gordon, Frank McHugh, Allen Jenkins, J. Farrell MacDonald, Thomas Jackson

'A hokey laugh ensemble that will be oke.'—*Variety*

'A story of bloodshed, passion, desire and death . . . everything in fact that makes life worth living!'

Irma La Douce*
US 1963 146m Technicolor
Panavision
UA / Phalanx / Mirisch / Edward L. Alperson (Billy Wilder)

A Paris policeman falls for a prostitute and becomes her pimp.
A saucy yarn originally presented inventively as a small-scale stage musical becomes a tasteless yawn on the big screen, especially when presented at such length and without the songs. Minor compensations abound but are insufficient.

w Billy Wilder, I. A. L. Diamond *d* Billy Wilder *ph* Joseph La Shelle *md* André Previn *musical themes* Marguerite Monnot *ad* Alexander Trauner

Shirley Maclaine, Jack Lemmon, Lou Jacobi, Herschel Bernardi, Joan Shawlee, Bruce Yarnell

AA: André Previn
AAN: Joseph La Shelle; Shirley Maclaine

The Iron Curtain
US 1948 87m bw
TCF (Sol C. Siegel)

A Russian official in Ottawa becomes disillusioned and reveals to the US authorities details of a spy ring.
Cold war biopic of Igor Gouzenko; not badly done in the semi-documentary mould.

w Milton Krims *d* William Wellman *ph* Charles G. Clarke *md* Alfred Newman, using Russian themes

Dana Andrews, Gene Tierney, Berry Kroeger, Edna Best

The Iron Duke*
GB 1934 88m bw
Gaumont (Michael Balcon)

After Waterloo, the Duke of Wellington defeats a French scheme to discredit him.

A popular historical star vehicle of its time and a good example of British pre-war production in the Korda mould.

w Bess Meredith, play H. M. Harwood *d* Victor Saville *ph* Curt Courant

George Arliss, Gladys Cooper, Emlyn Williams, Ellaline Terriss, A. E. Matthews, Edmund Willard, Felix Aylmer

The Iron Glove
US 1954 77m Technicolor

A staunch supporter of the Old Pretender meets friends and enemies in London at the court of George I. Stilted costume piece, unsuitably cast and flatly written. Robert Stack, Ursula Thiess, Richard Stapley, Alan Hale Jnr. Written by Jesse L. Lasky Jnr, De Vallon Scott and Douglas Heyes; directed by William Castle; for Columbia.

The Iron Horse*
US 1924 119m (24 fps) bw silent
Fox

A man seeking to avenge his father's murder works on the first transcontinental railroad. Archetypal western, very slow to start but with an authentic cast of thousands.

w Charles Kenyon, John Russell *d* John Ford *ph* George Schneidermann

George O'Brien, Madge Bellamy, Cyril Chadwick, Fred Kohler

The Iron Maiden
GB 1962 98m Eastmancolor
Anglo Amalgamated / GHW (Peter Rogers)
US title: *The Swinging Maiden*

An aircraft designer gets into trouble because of his affection for traction engines.
Feeble attempt to duplicate the success of *Genevieve*, this time starring a steamroller. Very English.

w Vivian Cox, Leslie Bricusse *d* Gerald Thomas *ph* Alan Hume *m* Eric Rogers

Michael Craig, Alan Hale Jnr, Jeff Donnell, Cecil Parker, Noel Purcell, Roland Culver, the Duke of Bedford, Anne Helm

The Iron Major
US 1943 85m bw

The life of Frank Cavanaugh, football coach and hero of World War I. Sub-standard biopic. Pat O'Brien, Ruth Warrick, Robert Ryan, Leon Ames. Written by Aben Kandel and Warren Duff; directed by Ray Enright; for RKO. 'A respectful, rather dull picture . . . all the talk is in words of less than one syllable.'—*James Agee*.

The Iron Man
US 1931 73m bw
Universal (Carl Laemmle Jnr)

A prizefighter is spurred on by his money-hungry wife.
Competent, routine, ringside melodrama.

w Francis Edward Faragoh, *novel* W. R. Burnett *d* Tod Browning *ph* Percy Hilburn

Lew Ayres, Jean Harlow, Robert Armstrong, John Miljan, Eddie Dillon, Ned Sparks
† Remade in 1937 as *Some Blondes Are Dangerous* and in 1951 under the original title.

Iron Man
US 1951 81m bw

A coal miner is persuaded to become a prizefighter, but success changes his character. A somewhat changed version of the 1931 film; no better. Jeff Chandler, Evelyn Keyes, Stephen McNally, Joyce Holden, Rock Hudson, Jim Backus, James Arness. Written by George Zuckerman and Borden Chase; directed by Joseph Pevney; for Universal-International.

The Iron Mask*
US 1929 97m bw talking sequences, sound and music score
(UA) Douglas Fairbanks

The true prince of France is kidnapped and imprisoned, but the villains reckon without D'Artagnan and the three musketeers. Spirited star rendition of Dumas, the last big silent costume drama of the twenties.

w W. Elton Thomas (Douglas Fairbanks), *novel* Ten Years After by Alexandre Dumas *d* Allan Dwan *ph* Henry Sharp *pd* Maurice Leloir

Douglas Fairbanks, Nigel de Brulier, Belle Bennett, Marguerite de la Motte

The Iron Mistress
US 1952 107m Technicolor
Warner (Henry Blanke)

The life of westerner Jim Bowie and his famous knife.
Stolid actioner with uninspired script and performances.

w James R. Webb, *novel* Paul I. Wellman *d* Gordon Douglas *ph* John Seitz *m* Max Steiner

Alan Ladd, Virginia Mayo, Joseph Calleia, Phyllis Kirk, Alf Kjellin, Douglas Dick, Tony Caruso, George Voskovec

The Iron Petticoat
GB 1956 96m Technicolor Vistavision
Remus / Harry Saltzman (Betty E. Box)

An American air force officer persuades a Russian lady flier of the advantages of the western way of life.
Feeble imitation of *Ninotchka* with a saucy star team which simply doesn't jell.

w Ben Hecht *d* Ralph Thomas *ph* Ernest Steward

Bob Hope, Katharine Hepburn, James Robertson Justice, Robert Helpmann, David Kossoff, Alan Gifford, Paul Carpenter, Noelle Middleton

'They seem amazed to find themselves in a comedy that has no humour, and they go through the motions grimly, like children at dancing school, hoping it will all be over soon.'—*William K. Zinsser*

Is Everybody Happy?
US 1929 80m bw

The life of a clarinettist who rises from poverty. Or, The Ted Lewis Story, a primitive musical. Ted Lewis, Alice Day, Ann Pennington, Lawrence Grant. Written by Joseph Jackson and James A. Starr; directed by Archie Mayo; for Warner.

Is Everybody Happy?
US 1943 73m bw

A virtual remake of the above, with the star fourteen years older; low-budget filler with a few good numbers. Ted Lewis, Larry Parks, Michael Duane, Nan Gwyn. Written by Monte Brice; directed by Charles Barton; for Columbia.

Is Paris Burning?
France / US 1965 165m Panavision bw (colour sequence)
Paramount / Transcontinental / Marianne (Paul Graetz)

A multi-storied account of the 1944 liberation of Paris.
Muddled, scribbled, tedious and confusing attempt at a thinking man's all-star war epic.

w Francis Ford Coppola, Gore Vidal *d* René Clément *ph* Marcel Grignon *m* Maurice Jarre

Leslie Caron, Gert Frobe, Charles Boyer, Yves Montand, Orson Welles, Alain Delon, Jean-Pierre Cassel, Jean-Paul Belmondo, Kirk Douglas, Glenn Ford, Claude Dauphin, Daniel Gélin, Anthony Perkins, Simone Signoret, Robert Stack, George Chakiris

AAN: Marcel Grignon

Isadora*
GB 1968 138m Eastmancolor Panavision
Universal (Robert and Raymond Hakim)
US title: *The Loves of Isadora*

Eccentric character dancer Isadora Duncan reflects on her crowded and unconventional life.
Ambitious and expensive but finally unsatisfactory biopic of a controversial figure of the twenties.

w Melvyn Bragg, Clive Exton *d* Karel Reisz *ph* Larry Pizer *m* Maurice Jarre *pd* Jocelyn Herbert *ad* Michael Seymour, Ralph Brinton

Vanessa Redgrave, Jason Robards Jnr, James Fox, Ivan Tchenko, John Fraser, Bessie Love
'A brave attempt at a daunting task.'—*Tom Milne*

AAN: Vanessa Redgrave

The Island*
Japan 1961 92m bw
Kindai Eiga Kyokai (Kaneto Shindo)
original title: *Hadaka no Shima*

The quiet tenor of life for the only family inhabiting a tiny island is eventually broken by illness and death.
Slow, controlled, beautiful film in which not a single word of dialogue is spoken. The artificiality of this concept eventually diminishes its stature.

wd Kaneto Shindo *ph* Kiyoshi Kuroda *m* Hikaru Hayashi

Nobuko Otowa, Taiji Tonoyama, Shinji Tanaka, Masanori Horimoto
'A visual poem which mirrors tedium without ever inducing it.'—*MFB*

The Island
US 1980 114m Technicolor
Universal (Richard Zanuck and David Brown)

A journalist is in fear of his life on a Caribbean island inhabited by the bloodthirsty descendants of seventeenth-century buccaneers.
Ridiculous shocker from the *Jaws* people; stupidly plotted and gruesome in detail.
w Peter Benchley, from his novel d Michael Ritchie ph Henri Decaë m Ennio Morricone

Michael Caine, David Warner, Angela Punch McGregor, Frank Middlemass, Dudley Sutton, Clyde Jeavons
'Suspense gives way to gut-level sadism aimed at the lowest common audience denominator.'—*Variety*
● Video: CIC

The Island at the Top of the World●●
US 1974 93m Technicolor
Walt Disney (Winston Hibler)

In 1907, a rich Englishman commissions an airship to take him to a mythical arctic Shangri-La in search of his lost son.
Generally brisk and effective adventure fantasy whose trick effects are sufficiently splendid to redeem a sag in the middle and an overplus of Viking chatter which has to be laboriously translated.
w John Whedon, *novel* The Lost Ones by Ian Cameron d Robert Stevenson ph Frank Phillips m Maurice Jarre pd Peter Ellenshaw sp Art Cruickshank, Danny Lee

Donald Sinden, David Hartman, Jacques Marin, Mako
● Video: Rank

Island in the Sky●
US 1953 109m bw
Wayne–Fellows (Robert Fellows)

A transport plane makes a forced landing north of Greenland, and the crew must survive till help comes.
Well made outdoor suspenser shot in the California Sierras.
w Ernest K. Gann, from his novel d William Wellman ph Archie Stout m Emil Newman ad James Basevi

John Wayne, Lloyd Nolan, Walter Abel, Allyn Joslyn, Andy Devine, James Arness

Island in the Sun●
GB 1957 119m Technicolor
Cinemascope
TCF (Darryl F. Zanuck)

Sexual and racial problems erupt on a West Indian island.
Portmanteau romantic melodrama which generally misfires, especially in an attempt to parallel *Crime and Punishment*; but the cast is interesting.
w Alfred Hayes, *novel* Alec Waugh d Robert Rossen ph Frederick A. Young m Malcolm Arnold

James Mason, Joan Fontaine, Harry Belafonte, John Williams, Dorothy Dandridge, Joan Collins, Michael Rennie, Patricia Owens, Stephen Boyd, Basil Sydney, Diana Wynyard, Ronald Squire, John Justin

The Island of Dr Moreau●
US 1977 98m Movielab
AIP / Cinema 77 (Skip Steloff, John Temple-Smith)

In 1911, shipwrecked sailors land on a Pacific island where a mad doctor experiments with animal mutations.
A sprightly version of an old story; unfortunately it lacks any sense of the sinister, and the star is no match for Charles Laughton in *Island of Lost Souls*.
w John Herman Shaner, Al Ramrus, *story* H. G. Wells d Don Taylor ph Gerry Fisher m Laurence Rosenthal

Burt Lancaster, Michael York, Nigel Davenport, Barbara Carrera, Richard Basehart, Nick Cravat
'Cursed with lush colour photography instead of black and white atmospherics, and Lancaster's stolid mania instead of Laughton's manic zeal.'—*Sight and Sound*
● Video: Guild

Island of Lost Men
US 1939 64m bw

An Oriental girl seeks her lost father in waterfront dives and finds him on a prison island. Adequate action programmer. Anna May Wong, Broderick Crawford, Anthony Quinn, J. Carrol Naish. Written by William R. Lipman and Horace McCoy; directed by Kurt Neumann; for Paramount.
† A remake of *White Woman*.

'Out of the dark fantastic madness of his science he created her—the panther woman—throbbing to the hot flush of new-found love!'

Island of Lost Souls●
US 1932 74m bw
Paramount

On a remote South Sea island, mad Dr Moreau transforms animals into humans by vivisection.
Unchilling but interesting thriller with a rolling-eyed star performance.
w Waldemar Young, Philip Wylie, *story* The Island of Dr Moreau by H. G. Wells d Erle C. Kenton ph Karl Struss

Charles Laughton, Bela Lugosi, Richard Arlen, Kathleen Burke, Leila Hyams

Island of Lost Women
US 1958 72m bw

A newspaperman lands on a remote island where a scientist has retired from the world with his daughters. Unexciting hokum with more talk than action. Jeff Richards, Venetia Stevenson, John Smith, Alan Napier. Written by Ray Buffum; directed by Frank Tuttle; for Jaguar / Warner.

Island of Love
US 1963 101m Technicolor
Panavision
Warner / Belgrave (Morton da Costa)

A gangster finances a film providing his girl friend stars, but when it flops he chases the producers to a Greek island.
Dismally unfunny comedy wasting a talented cast.
w David R. Schwarz d Morton da Costa ph Harry Stradling m George Duning

Robert Preston, Tony Randall, Walter Matthau, Giorgia Moll

Island of Terror
GB 1966 89m Eastmancolor
Planet (Tom Blakeley)

On an Irish island, a scientist makes monsters who thrive on bone.
Horror hokum, moderately done.
w Edward Andrew Mann, Alan Ramsen d Terence Fisher ph Reg Wyer m Malcolm Lockyer sp John St John Earl

Peter Cushing, Edward Judd, Carole Gray, Eddie Byrne, Sam Kydd, Niall MacGinnis

Island of the Blue Dolphins
US 1964 93m Eastmancolor
U-I / Robert B. Radnitz

Two orphaned children grow up alone on a Californian island, protected by wild dogs.
Pleasant if unconvincing family film based on a true story.
w Ted Sherdeman, Jane Klove, *novel* Scott O'Dell d James B. Clark ph Leo Tover m Paul Sawtell

Celia Kaye, Larry Dornasin, George Kennedy

Island of the Lost
US 1968 92m colour

An anthropologist sets sail for an uncharted island and is shipwrecked on it. Good-looking but singularly plotless action adventure. Richard Greene, Luke Halpin, Mark Hulswit. Written by Richard Carlson and Ivan Tors; directed by Richard Carlson; for Ivan Tors.

Islands in the Stream
US 1976 105m Metrocolor Panavision
Paramount (Peter Bart, Max Palevsky)

On a Bahamian island in 1940, an expatriate American artist welcomes his three sons and reflects on the futility of life.
Shapeless semi-autobiographical fragments culminating unpersuasively in an action climax of heroic self-sacrifice. A film on which no expense has been spared and which doesn't work at all.
w Denne Bart Petitclerc, *novel* Ernest Hemingway d Franklin Schaffner ph Fred J. Koenekamp m Jerry Goldsmith

George C. Scott, David Hemmings, Gilbert Roland, Susan Tyrell, Richard Evans, Claire Bloom, Hart Bochner, Julius Harris
'It is all too awful for words.'—*Benny Green, Punch*

AAN: photography

Isle of Fury
US 1936 60m bw

A fugitive from justice finds temporary peace on a South Sea island. Limp remake of *The Narrow Corner* (qv); its star later pretended he hadn't made it. Humphrey Bogart, Margaret Lindsay, Donald Woods. Written by Robert Andrews and William Jacobs; directed by Frank McDonald; for Warner.

Isle of Missing Men
US 1942 67m bw

Convicts on a prison island try to make a break. The very poor man's *Papillon*. Gilbert Roland, Helen Gilbert, John Howard. Written by Richard Oswald and Robert Chapin; directed by Richard Oswald; for Monogram.

Isle of the Dead**
US 1945 72m bw
RKO (Val Lewton)

On a Balkan island in 1912 a group of people shelter from the plague and fear that one of their number is a vampire.
Glum, ghoulish melodrama with some neatly handled shocks; quite different from any other horror film.

w Ardel Wray, Josef Mischel *d* Mark Robson *ph* Jack Mackenzie *m* Leigh Harline

Boris Karloff, Ellen Drew, Helene Thimig, Marc Cramer, Katherine Emery, Alan Napier, Jason Robards

● *Video: Kingston*

Isn't It Romantic*
US 1948 87m bw
Paramount (Daniel Dare)

Romance hits the household of an ex-Civil War colonel in Indiana.
Pleasant but forgettable period semi-musical.

w Theodore Strauss, Josef Mischel, Richard Breen *d* Norman Z. McLeod *ph* Lionel Lindon *m* Joseph J. Lilley

Veronica Lake, Mona Freeman, Mary Hatcher, Roland Culver, Billy de Wolfe, Patric Knowles, Richard Webb, Kathryn Givney, Pearl Bailey

Isn't Life Wonderful?*
US 1924 99m (24 fps) bw silent
(UA) David Wark Griffith

The life of a family in post-war Germany.
An unpopular subject, and a grey-looking film, but the director shows a lot of his strength in it.

wd D. W. Griffith, *story* Geoffrey Moss

Carol Dempster, Neil Hamilton, Helen Lowell, Frank Puglia, Marcia Harris, Lupino Lane

Isn't Life Wonderful?*
GB 1952 83m Technicolor
ABP (Warwick Ward)

In 1902, drunken Uncle Willie runs a bicycle shop and manages to reconcile a lovers' quarrel.
Engaging, well cast family comedy.

w Brock Williams *d* Harold French *ph* Erwin Hillier *m* Philip Green *ad* Terence Verity

Donald Wolfit, Eileen Herlie, Cecil Parker, Eleanor Summerfield, Robert Urquhart, Cecil Trouncer

Istanbul
US 1956 84m Technicolor Cinemascope
U-I (Albert J. Cohen)

Various adventurers and an amnesiac girl seek stolen diamonds in Istanbul.
Dim remake of a flat-footed piece of thick ear called *Singapore*.

w Seton I. Miller, Barbara Gray, Richard Alan Simmons *d* Joseph Pevney *ph* William Daniels *m* Joseph Gershenson

Errol Flynn, Cornell Borchers, John Bentley, Torin Thatcher, Leif Erickson, Martin Benson, Vladimir Sokoloff, Werner Klemperer, Nat King Cole, Peggy Knudsen

It*
US 1927 72m (24 fps) bw silent
Famous Players-Lasky / Paramount (B. P. Schulberg)

A shopgirl tries to live by the tenets of Elinor Glyn's book, and finally marries her boss.
In its day a fast and funny spoof, and the years have not dealt too unkindly with it.

w Hope Loring, Louis D. Lighton, *adaptation* Elinor Glyn *d* Clarence Badger *ph* H. Kinley Martin

Clara Bow, Antonio Moreno, William Austin, Jacqueline Gadson, Gary Cooper, Elinor Glyn

It Ain't Hay
US 1943 79m bw
Universal (Alex Gottlieb)
GB title: *Money for Jam*

When a racehorse dies, a New York cabbie and his friend try to find a new one for the impecunious owners.
Formula Abbott and Costello with a small injection of sentiment and Runyonese. Not their best by a mile.

w Allen Boretz, John Grant, *story* Princess O'Hara by Damon Runyon *d* Erle C. Kenton *ph* Charles Von Enger *songs* Harry Revel, Paul Francis Webster

Bud Abbott, Lou Costello, Grace McDonald, Cecil Kellaway, Patsy O'Connor, Eugene Pallette, Shemp Howard, Eddie Quillan

It All Came True*
US 1940 97m bw
Warner (Mark Hellinger)

A gangster hides out in a boarding house and puts it back on its feet.
Competent New York fairy story full of sweetness and light.

w Michael Fessier, Lawrence Kimble, *story* Better Than Life by Louis Bromfield *d* Lewis Seiler *ph* Ernest Haller *m* Heinz Roemheld

Humphrey Bogart, Ann Sheridan, Jeffrey Lynn, Zasu Pitts, Una O'Connor, Jessie Busley, John Litel, Grant Mitchell, Felix Bressart

It Always Rains on Sunday***
GB 1947 92m bw
Ealing (Henry Cornelius)

An escaped convict takes refuge in his married mistress's house in East London.
Influential slumland melodrama, now dated—the stuff of every other television play—but at the time electrifyingly vivid and very well done.

w Angus Macphail, Robert Hamer, Henry Cornelius, *novel* Arthur La Bern *d* Robert Hamer *ph* Douglas Slocombe *m* Georges Auric

Googie Withers, John McCallum, Jack Warner, Edward Chapman, Susan Shaw, Sidney Tafler

It Came from beneath the Sea
US 1955 80m bw
Columbia / Sam Katzman (Charles Schneer)

A giant octopus half destroys San Francisco.
Tepid monster movie; special effects only fair.

w George Worthing Yates, Hal Smith *d* Robert Gordon *ph* Henry Freulich *md* Mischa Bakaleinikoff

Kenneth Tobey, Faith Domergue, Donald Curtis, Ian Keith

It Came from Outer Space**
US 1953 80m bw 3-D
U-I (William Alland)

A young astronomer sees a space ship land in the Arizona desert and tracks down the occupants who can adopt human appearance at will.
Quite bright science fiction, the first to use this theme of borrowing bodies and the first to utilize the western desert locations. 3-D adds a shock moment or two.

w Harry Essex, *story* Ray Bradbury *d* Jack Arnold *ph* Clifford Stine *m* Herman Stein *md* Joseph Gershenson

Richard Carlson, Barbara Rush, Charles Drake, Kathleen Hughes
'Desert was Arnold's favourite location, and he used it consistently to create a sense of strangeness and menace otherwise much restricted by his budgets.'—*Time Out, 1982*

● *Video: CIC*

It Conquered the World
US 1956 68m bw

Something from another planet is sheltered by a well-meaning scientist who discovers too late that its intentions are evil. Tolerable horror comic on a risibly low budget. Peter Graves, Beverly Garland, Lee Van Cleef, Sally Fraser, Charles B. Griffith. Written by Lou Rusoff; directed and produced by Roger Corman; for AIP.

It Could Happen to You
US 1939 73m bw

After a stag party, an advertising man finds a body in his car. Neat second-feature mystery. Stuart Erwin, Gloria Stuart, Raymond Walburn, Douglas Fowley. Written by Allen Rivkin and Lou Breslow; directed by Alfred Werker; for TCF.

ISLE OF THE DEAD. In the forties this was startling enough to get itself banned in Britain. It would rate few shudders these days.

It Grows on Trees
US 1952 84m bw
U-I (Leonard Goldstein)

A housewife finds a money tree in her backyard.
Protracted fantasy comedy.

w Leonard Praskins, Barney Slater d Arthur Lubin ph Maury Gertsman m Frank Skinner

Irene Dunne (her last film), Dean Jagger, Joan Evans, Richard Crenna, Edith Meiser, Dee Pollock

It Had To Be You
US 1947 98m bw
Columbia / Don Hartman

A dizzy dame runs out on three prospective husbands and is pursued by an Indian.
Weak sex farce without the courage of its lack of convictions.

w Norman Panama, Melvin Frank d Don Hartman, Rudolph Maté ph Rudolph Maté m Heinz Roemheld md Morris Stoloff

Ginger Rogers, Cornel Wilde, Percy Waram, Spring Byington, Thurston Hall, Ron Randell

It Had to Happen
US 1936 80m bw

An Italian immigrant becomes the political boss of New York City. Unconvincing melodrama with star appeal. George Raft, Rosalind Russell, Leo Carrillo, Arline Judge, Alan Dinehart, Andrew Tombes. Written by Howard Ellis Smith, Kathryn Scola, Rupert Hughes; directed by Roy del Ruth; for Raymond Griffith / Fox. 'Incredible story precludes its b.o. chances.'—*Variety*

It Happened at the World's Fair
US 1962 104m Metrocolor Panavision
MGM / Ted Richmond

At the Seattle World's Fair, two crop-dusting pilots have romantic intrigues.
Routine star vehicle.

w Si Rose, Seaman Jacobs d Norman Taurog ph Joseph Ruttenberg m Leith Stevens

Elvis Presley, Gary Lockwood, Joan O'Brien, Yvonne Craig, Ginny Tiu

It Happened Here**
GB 1963 99m bw
UA / Kevin Brownlow, Andrew Mollo

What might have happened if the Germans had invaded England in 1940.
A remarkable semi-professional reconstruction which took seven years to film and is totally convincing in detail, but unfortunately rather confused and padded as drama.

wd Kevin Brownlow, Andrew Mollo ph Peter Suschitzky m Jack Beaver

Sebastian Shaw, Pauline Murray, Fiona Lekland, Honor Fehrson
'For a grain of artistic truth, we can forgive even the grainy photography and wavering sound with which part of it is afflicted.'—*John Simon*

It Happened in Athens
US 1961 100m De Luxe Cinemascope
TCF (James S. Elliott)

At the first revival of the Olympic Games in 1896 a publicity-seeking actress announces that she will marry whoever wins the Marathon. Witless extravagant romp, well mounted but adding up to zero.

w Laszlo Vadnay d Andrew Marton ph Curt Courant m Manos Hadjikis

Jayne Mansfield, Trax Colton, Bob Mathias

It Happened in Brooklyn*
US 1947 103m bw
MGM (Jack Cummings)

Young New Yorkers with musical talents find their way to fame.
Well-handled routine musical of its time.

w Isobel Lennart d Richard Whorf ph Robert Planck m Johnny Green songs Jule Styne, Sammy Cahn

Frank Sinatra, Jimmy Durante, Kathryn Grayson, Peter Lawford, Gloria Grahame
'Aside from Sinatra and Durante the show amounts to practically nothing, but there is a general kindliness about it which I enjoyed.'—*James Agee*

It Happened in Hollywood
US 1937 67m bw

A silent cowboy star is washed up when talkies come in. Indifferent studio story. Richard Dix, Fay Wray, Victor Kilian, Franklin Pangborn, Charles Arnt, Granville Bates. Written by Ethel Hill, Harvey Ferguson, Sam Fuller, Myles Connolly; directed by Harry Lachman; for Columbia. 'It will have difficulty fitting in . . . won't particularly satisfy 'em in the duals.'—*Variety*

It Happened on Fifth Avenue*
US 1947 115m bw
Allied Artists (Roy del Ruth)

A child of divorce finds amiable squatters in her millionaire father's house.
Curious, overlong, cheerful Capraesque comedy with the mildest of social pretensions.

w Everett Freeman, Frederick Stephani, Herbert Clyde Lewis d Roy del Ruth ph Henry Sharp

Gale Storm, Ann Harding, Victor Moore, Charles Ruggles, Don Defore

AAN: script

It Happened One Night****
US 1934 105m bw
Columbia (Frank Capra)

A runaway heiress falls in love with the reporter who is chasing her across America. Highly successful and influential romantic comedy, the first to use buses and motels as background and still come up sparkling; it remains superlative in patches, but overall has a faded, dated air.

w Robert Riskin, story Night Bus by Samuel Hopkins Adams d Frank Capra ph Joseph Walker md Louis Silvers

Clark Gable, Claudette Colbert, Walter Connolly, Roscoe Karns, Alan Hale, Ward Bond, Jameson Thomas, Arthur Hoyt
'A laughing hit that will mean important coin.'—*Variety*
'It will be a long day before we see so little made into so much.'—*Otis Ferguson*
'Something to revive your faith in a medium which could belong among the great arts.'—*Robert Forsythe*
'We may look askance at Capra's sententious notions about the miserable rich and the happy poor, but there's no doubting the chord he struck in depression audiences.'—*Time Out, 1980*
'It made audiences happy in a way that only a few films in each era do. In the mid-30s, the Colbert and Gable of this film became Americans' idealized view of themselves— breezy, likeable, sexy, gallant, and maybe just a little harebrained. It was the *Annie Hall* of its day—before the invention of anxiety.'— *Pauline Kael, 70s*
† Remade 1956 (badly) as *You Can't Run away From It*.
†† Robert Montgomery was the first choice for the Gable role, but he refused it because he had been on a bus in *Fugitive Lovers*.

AA: best picture; Robert Riskin; Frank Capra; Clark Gable; Claudette Colbert

It Happened One Sunday
GB 1943 99m bw

In Liverpool, a Canadian seaman falls for an Irish maid. Overlong romantic comedy with nowhere to go. Robert Beatty, Barbara White, Marjorie Rhodes, Ernest Butcher, Judy Kelly, Irene Vanbrugh. Written by Victor Skuzetsky, Friedrich Gotfurt and Stephen Black; directed by Karel Lamac; for ABPC.

It Happened to Jane
US 1959 98m Technicolor Cinemascope
Columbia / Arwin (Richard Quine)

A lady lobster dealer becomes involved in a battle with the railroad whose inefficiency affects her business.
Witless, wholesome farce which promises more than it delivers.

w Norman Karkov d Richard Quine ph Charles Lawton Jnr m George Duning

Doris Day, Jack Lemmon, *Ernie Kovacs*, Steve Forrest

It Happened Tomorrow***
US 1944 84m bw
(UA) Arnold Pressburger

A reporter meets an old man with the power to show him tomorrow's newspaper headlines, so that he always gets scoops—including his own death . . .
Engaging fantasy, flawlessly made and quietly very entertaining.

w Dudley Nichols, René Clair d René Clair ph Archie Stout m Robert Stolz

Dick Powell, Linda Darnell, Jack Oakie, *John Philliber*, Edgar Kennedy, Ed Brophy, George Cleveland, Sig Rumann

'Students of cinematic style will find many shrewdly polished bits to admire and enjoy.'— *James Agee*

AAN: Robert Stolz

It Happens Every Spring

US 1949　80m　bw
TCF (William Perlberg)

A chemistry teacher discovers a formula that makes baseballs repellent to wood.
Smartly produced but rather desperate fantasy comedy.

w Valentine Davies　*d* Lloyd Bacon　*ph* Joe MacDonald　*m* Leigh Harline

Ray Milland, Jean Peters, Paul Douglas, Ed Begley, Ted de Corsia, Ray Collins, Jessie Royce Landis, Alan Hale Jnr

AAN: original story (Shirley W. Smith, Valentine Davies)

It Happens Every Thursday°

US 1953　80m　bw
U-I (Anton Leader)

The new owner of a small-town newspaper becomes unpopular through his attempts to boost the circulation.
Pleasant comedy with amusing scenes.

w Dane Lussier　*d* Joseph Pevney　*ph* Russell Metty　*m* Joseph Gershenson

Loretta Young, John Forsythe, Jimmy Conlin, Frank McHugh, Edgar Buchanan, Jane Darwell

It Pays to Advertise

US 1931　66m　bw

A mild youth is turned by his girl into a business success. Fair film version of a popular stage comedy. Norman Foster, Carole Lombard, Skeets Gallagher, Eugene Pallette, Louise Brooks, Lucien Littlefield. Written by Arthur Kober from the play by Walter Hackett; directed by Frank Tuttle; for Paramount. 'Good enough programme material.'—*Variety*

It Should Happen to You°°

US 1954　87m　bw
Columbia (Fred Kohlmar)

A slightly daffy New York model with an urge to be famous rents a huge billboard and puts her name on it.
Likeable comedy which starts brightly and slowly falls apart, disappointing considering the credentials of the talents involved and the satiric possibilities of the plot.

w Ruth Gordon, Garson Kanin　*d* George Cukor　*ph* Charles Lang　*m* Frederick Hollander

Judy Holliday, Jack Lemmon, Peter Lawford, Michael O'Shea

It Shouldn't Happen to a Dog

US 1946　70m　bw

A lady detective, her dog and a reporter solve a murder case more by good luck than good management. Acceptable comedy support.

Allyn Joslyn, Carole Landis, Margo Woode, Henry Morgan, Reed Hadley, John Alexander. Written by Eugene Ling and Frank Gabrielson; directed by Herbert I. Leeds; for TCF.

It Shouldn't Happen to a Vet

GB 1976　93m　Technicolor
EMI / Talent Associates / Readers Digest

Adventures of a Yorkshire vet just before World War II.
Competent sequel to *All Creatures Great and Small* (qv).

w Alan Plater, *books* James Herriot　*d* Eric Till　*ph* Arthur Ibbetson　*m* Laurie Johnson

John Alderton, Colin Blakely, Lisa Harrow, Bill Maynard, Richard Pearson, Raymond Francis, John Barrett, Paul Shelley

It Started in Naples°

US 1960　100m　Technicolor
　　Vistavision
Paramount / Capri (Jack Rose)

A Philadelphia lawyer goes to Naples to settle his dead brother's affairs, and falls for his nephew's aunt.
Nicely made, formula romantic comedy which started life as a vehicle for Gracie Fields.

w Melville Shavelson, Jack Rose, Susi Cecchi d'Amico　*d* Melville Shavelson　*ph* Robert Surtees　*m* Alessandro Cicognini

Clark Gable, Sophia Loren, Vittorio de Sica, Marietto, Paulo Carlini

It Started in Paradise

GB 1952　94m　Technicolor
GFD / British Film Makers (Leslie Parkyn, Sergei Nolbandov)

The career of an ambitious dress designer.
Stilted and garishly coloured but often amusing backstage melodrama of the fashion world: a Hollywood-style star vehicle which seems faintly surprising as a British product.

w Marghanita Laski　*d* Compton Bennett *ph* Jack Cardiff　*m* Malcolm Arnold *ad* Edward Carrick

Jane Hylton, Ian Hunter, Terence Morgan, Muriel Pavlow, Brian Worth, *Martita Hunt, Ronald Squire, Harold Lang*, Joyce Barbour, Kay Kendall

It Started with a Kiss

US 1959　104m　Metrocolor
　　Cinemascope
MGM / Arcola (Aaron Rosenberg)

An army sergeant posted to Spain is embarrassed when his wife follows him.
Flabby comedy with the emphasis on sex and pratfalls.

w Charles Lederer　*d* George Marshall *ph* Robert Bronner　*m* Jeff Alexander

Glenn Ford, Debbie Reynolds, Fred Clark, Edgar Buchanan, Eva Gabor

It Started with Eve°°

US 1941　93m　bw
Universal (Joe Pasternak)

A dying millionaire wants to see his grandson engaged, so a waitress obliges for an hour . . . but the old man recovers.

Charming comedy which was probably the star's best film; remade as *I'd Rather be Rich* (qv).

w Norman Krasna, Leo Townsend　*d* Henry Koster　*ph* Rudolph Maté　*md* Charles Previn, Hans Salter

Deanna Durbin, Charles Laughton, Robert Cummings, Margaret Tallichet, Guy Kibbee, Walter Catlett, Catherine Doucet

AAN: Charles Previn, Hans Salter

It! The Terror from Beyond Space

US 1958　69m　bw

A space ship returning from Mars is invaded by a worm-like monster. Laughable but lively precursor of *Alien*; rather more fun on the whole. Marshall Thompson, Shawn Smith, Kim Spaulding, Ann Doran, Dabbs Greer. Written by Jerome Bixby; directed by Edward L. Cahn; for Vogue/United Artists.

The Italian Job°°

GB 1969　100m　Eastmancolor
　　Panavision
Paramount / Oakhurst (Michael Deeley)

Crooks stage a traffic jam in Turin in order to pull off a bullion robbery.
Lively caper comedy which provides a good measure of entertainment.

w Troy Kennedy Martin　*d* Peter Collinson *ph* Douglas Slocombe, Norman Warwick *m* Quincy Jones

Michael Caine, Noel Coward, Benny Hill, Raf Vallone, Tony Beckley, Rossano Brazzi, Maggie Blye, Irene Handl, John Le Mesurier, Fred Emney

● *Video: CIC*

An Italian Straw Hat°°°

France 1927　74m (24 fps)　bw　silent
Albatross
original title: *Un Chapeau de Paille d'Italie*

The hero is prevented from getting to a wedding when his horse chews up a lady's straw hat and her escort demands that it be replaced.
Lively but gentle comedy of errors, a stage farce expanded for the screen and filled with visual gags. A very influential and still amusing piece.

wd René Clair, *play* Eugène Labiche *ph* Maurice Desfassiaux, Nicolas Roudakoff *ad* Lazare Meerson

Albert Préjean, Olga Tschekowa, Marise Maia, Alice Tissot

'The very springtime of screen comedy.'— *Tatler*

'One of the funniest films ever made.'— *Tribune, 1945*

'Still one of the funniest films in the world.'—*Sunday Times, 1948*

It's a Big Country

US 1952　89m　bw
MGM (Robert Sisk)

Seven stories show the diversity of the US and the glory of being one of its citizens.

THE ITALIAN JOB.   A frame from the chase sequence which sold so many tickets.

Stultifying flagwaver memorable chiefly as a
waste of good actors.

w William Ludwig, Helen Deutsch, George
Wells, Allen Rivkin, Dorothy Kingsley, Isobel
Lennart *d* Richard Thorpe, Don Weis, John
Sturges, Don Hartman, William Wellman,
Charles Vidor, Clarence Brown *ph* John
Alton, Ray June, William Mellor, Joseph
Ruttenberg *m* Bronislau Kaper, Rudolph G.
Kopp, David Raksin, David Rose

Ethel Barrymore, Keefe Brasselle, Nancy
Davis, Van Johnson, Gene Kelly, Janet Leigh,
Marjorie Main, Fredric March, George
Murphy, William Powell, S. Z. Sakall, Lewis
Stone, James Whitmore

It's a Boy
GB 1933   80m   bw

A blackmailer claims to be a bridegroom's
long-lost illegitimate son. Heavy-footed
version of popular stage farce. Leslie Henson,
Edward Everett Horton, Heather Thatcher,
Alfred Drayton, Albert Burdon, Robertson
Hare, Wendy Barrie. Written by Austin
Melford, John Paddy Carstairs and L. H.
Gordon, from the play by Franz Arnold, Ernst
Bach and Austin Melford; directed by Tim
Whelan; for Gainsborough.

It's a Gift**
US 1934   73m   bw
Paramount (William Le Baron)

A general store proprietor buys an orange
ranch by mail and transports his family to
California.
Roughly assembled comedy of disasters which
happens to show the star more or less at his
best, though the expected climax is lacking.

w Jack Cunningham, *story* W. C. Fields, J. P.
McEvoy *d* Norman Z. McLeod *ph* Henry
Sharp

W. C. Fields, Kathleen Howard, Jean
Rouverol, Julian Madison, Tommy Bupp,
Baby LeRoy
  'An enormously amusing succession of
rough and ready gags.'—*Literary Digest*

It's a Great Feeling*
US 1949 85m Technicolor
Warner (Alex Gottlieb)

No one will direct a Jack Carson movie, so he has to do it himself.
Amiable studio farce with plenty of guest appearances.

w Jack Rose, Mel Shavelson d David Butler ph Wilfrid M. Cline m / ly Jule Styne, Sammy Cahn

Jack Carson, Doris Day, Dennis Morgan, Bill Goodwin, Gary Cooper, Joan Crawford, Errol Flynn, Sidney Greenstreet, Danny Kaye, Patricia Neal, Edward G. Robinson, Jane Wyman, Eleanor Parker, Ronald Reagan

AAN: title song

It's a Mad Mad Mad Mad World**
US 1963 192m Technicolor Ultra Panavision 70
UA / Stanley Kramer

An assortment of people including a frustrated cop are overcome by greed when they hear of buried loot.
Three hours of frantic chasing and violent slapstick is too much even when done on this scale and with this cast, but one must observe that scene for scene it is extremely well done and most of the players are in unusually good form though they all outstay their welcome and are upstaged by the stunt men.

w William and Tania Rose d Stanley Kramer ph Ernest Laszlo m Ernest Gold stunts Carey Loftin titles Saul Bass

Spencer Tracy, Jimmy Durante, Milton Berle, Sid Caesar, Ethel Merman, Buddy Hackett, Mickey Rooney, Dick Shawn, Phil Silvers, Terry-Thomas, Jonathan Winters, Edie Adams, Dorothy Provine, Eddie Anderson, Jim Backus, William Demarest, Peter Falk, Paul Ford, Leo Gorcey, Ben Blue, Edward Everett Horton, Buster Keaton, Joe E. Brown, Carl Reiner, the Three Stooges, Zasu Pitts, Sterling Holloway, Jack Benny, Jerry Lewis

'To watch on a Cinerama screen in full colour a small army of actors inflict mayhem on each other with cars, planes, explosives and other devices for more than three hours with stereophonic sound effects is simply too much for the human eye and ear to respond to, let alone the funny bone.'—Dwight MacDonald

AAN: Ernest Laszlo; Ernest Gold; title song (m Ernest Gold, ly Mack David)

● Video: Warner

It's a Pleasure
US 1945 90m Technicolor

The career of an ice-skating couple is interrupted when he takes to drink.
Unimpressive vehicle from the star's waning years: the numbers are good but the rest very soggy. Sonja Henie, Michael O'Shea, Marie McDonald. Written by Lynn Starling and Eliot Paul; directed by William A. Seiter; for International / RKO.

It's a Small World
US 1935 72m bw

A man and woman fall in love after being stranded by a car crash in a small Louisiana town. Mildly amusing comedy. Spencer Tracy, Wendy Barrie, Raymond Walburn, Virginia Sale, Irving Bacon. Written by Sam Hellman and Gladys Lehman; directed by Irving Cummins; for Fox. 'Very weak entertainment, strictly for double bills.'—Variety

It's a 2'6" above the Ground World
GB 1972 96m Eastmancolor
British Lion / Welbeck / Betty E. Box–Ralph Thomas
Also known as: The Love Ban

A Roman Catholic couple go on the pill. Smutty, not very funny sex comedy.

w Kevin Laffan, from his play d Ralph Thomas ph Tony Imi m Stanley Myers

Nanette Newman, Hywel Bennett, Russell Lewis, Simon Henderson, Milo O'Shea

It's a Wise Child
US 1931 73m bw

When a girl is thought to be pregnant, her family hunts the father. Tasteless comedy with too few laughs. Marion Davies, Sidney Blackmer, James Gleason, Polly Moran. Marie Prevost, Lester Vail. Written by Laurence E. Johnson from his play; directed by Robert Z. Leonard; for Cosmopolitan / MGM. 'No subject matter here for family audiences . . . it must prove embarrassing to young unmarried couples attending the theatre together.'—Variety

It's a Wonderful Life****
US 1946 129m bw
RKO / Liberty Films (Frank Capra)

A man is prevented from committing suicide by an elderly angel, who takes him back through his life to show him what good he has done.
Superbly assembled small-town comedy drama in a fantasy framework; arguably Capra's best and most typical work.

w Frances Goodrich, Albert Hackett, Frank Capra d Frank Capra ph Joseph Walker, Joseph Biroc m Dmitri Tiomkin

James Stewart, Henry Travers, Donna Reed, Lionel Barrymore, Thomas Mitchell, Beulah Bondi, Frank Faylen, Ward Bond, Gloria Grahame, H. B. Warner, Frank Albertson, Samuel S. Hinds, Mary Treen

CLARENCE (Henry Travers): 'Every time you hear a bell ring, it means that some angel's just got his wings.'

'One of the most efficient sentimental pieces since A Christmas Carol.'—James Agee
'The most brilliantly made motion picture of the 1940s, so assured, so dazzling in its use of screen narrative.'—Charles Higham
'In its own icky, bittersweet way, it's terribly effective.'—New Yorker, 1977

AAN: best picture; Frank Capra; James Stewart

It's a Wonderful World**
US 1939 86m bw
MGM (Frank Davis)

Kidnapped by a suspected murderer, a girl helps him track down the real criminal. Madcap comedy mystery which now seems much fresher and funnier than it did at the time. A highlight of the crazy comedy cycle.

w Ben Hecht, Herman J. Mankiewicz d W. S. Van Dyke II ph Oliver Marsh

Claudette Colbert, James Stewart, Guy Kibbee, Nat Pendleton, Frances Drake, Edgar Kennedy, Ernest Truex, Richard Carle, Sidney Blackmer, Andy Clyde, Cliff Clark, Hans Conried

'It's right down the alley for general audiences.'—Variety
'One of the few genuinely comic pictures in a dog's age.'—Otis Ferguson

'Save your screams till you see its face!'
It's Alive
US 1974 91m Technicolor
Warner / Larco (Larry Cohen)

A new-born baby turns out to be a vicious monster.
Exploitation horror flick in the worst of taste, with a good central performance.

wd Larry Cohen ph Fenton Hamilton m Bernard Herrmann

John Ryan, Sharon Farrell, Andrew Duggan, Guy Stockwell, James Dixon, Michael Ansara

It's All Happening
GB 1963 101m Eastmancolor
British Lion / Magna / KNP (Norman Williams)

A talent scout for a recording agency helps to save an orphanage and makes himself a star in the process.
Unassuming, jolly little comedy with music; a better title would have made it more memorable.

w Leigh Vance d Don Sharp ph Ken Hodges m Philip Green

Tommy Steele, Angela Douglas, Michael Medwin, Bernard Bresslaw, Walter Hudd, Jean Harvey, Richard Goolden

It's All Yours
US 1937 80m bw

A millionaire leaves a fortune to his favourite secretary, hoping that it will make his nephew take notice of her. Unpersuasive romantic comedy with slightly crazy touches. Madeleine Carroll, Francis Lederer, Mischa Auer, Grace Bradley. Written by Mary C. McCall Jnr; directed by Elliott Nugent; for Columbia. 'Of the whimsy, gay school currently in vogue . . . too light to figure importantly at solo b.o.'—Variety

It's Always Fair Weather**
US 1955 101m Eastmancolor Cinemascope
MGM (Arthur Freed)

In 1945 three army veterans vow to meet ten years on, but they find each other dull failures until they go on a wild spree.

Rather dejected New Yorkish comedy with musical sequences; some of it works very well, but the colour is crude and the wide screen doesn't help.

w / ly / m Betty Comden, Adolph Green d Gene Kelly, Stanley Donen ph Robert Bronner md André Previn

Gene Kelly, Dan Dailey, Michael Kidd, Dolores Gray, Cyd Charisse

AAN: Betty Comden, Adolph Green (as writers); André Previn

It's Great to Be Young*
GB 1956 93m Technicolor
AB–Pathé / Marble Arch (Victor Skutezky)
A popular teacher falls foul of the new headmaster who tries to disband the school orchestra.
Very acceptable but totally forgettable star comedy.

w Ted Willis d Cyril Frankel ph Gilbert Taylor m Ray Martin, Lester Powell, John Addison

John Mills, Cecil Parker, Jeremy Spenser, Dorothy Bromiley, John Salew, Derek Blomfield, Eleanor Summerfield, Bryan Forbes

It's Hard to Be Good
GB 1948 93m bw
GFD / Two Cities (Jeffrey Dell)
A demobbed war hero determines to spread peace and goodwill, but comes one cropper after another.
Well intended but somehow unprofessional comedy which irritates more than it amuses.

wd Jeffrey Dell ph Laurie Friedman m Antony Hopkins

Jimmy Hanley, Anne Crawford, Raymond Huntley

It's in the Air*
GB 1938 86m bw
ATP (Basil Dean)
Adventures of an accident-prone RAF recruit.
Amiable star comedy with good situations and songs.

wd Anthony Kimmins ph Gordon Dines, Ronald Neame

George Formby, Garry Marsh, Polly Ward, Julien Mitchell, Jack Hobbs, Hal Gordon

It's in the Bag**
US 1945 87m bw
(UA) Manhattan Productions
GB title: The Fifth Chair
The owner of a flea circus seeks a legacy hidden in one of five chairs which have been sold to a variety of people.
Patchily amusing, star-studded comedy which was also filmed as Keep Your Seats Please and The Twelve Chairs. Full enjoyment requires some knowledge of American radio characters.

w Jay Dratler, Alma Reville d Richard Wallace ph Russell Metty m Werner Heymann

Fred Allen, Binnie Barnes, Jack Benny, Robert Benchley, Don Ameche, Victor Moore, Rudy Vallee, William Bendix, Jerry Colonna

'An untidy piece that doesn't make the most of itself but is full of fun.'—Richard Mallett, Punch

It's Love Again*
GB 1936 83m bw
Gaumont (Michael Balcon)
A chorus girl poses as a socialite who has hit the headlines without ever existing.
Delightfully dated comedy musical.

w Lesser Samuels, Marian Dix, Austin Melford d Victor Saville ph Glen MacWilliams

Jessie Matthews, Robert Young, Sonnie Hale, Ernest Milton, Robb Wilton, Sara Allgood, Athene Seyler, Cyril Raymond.

'Mr Saville has directed it with speed, efficiency and a real sense of the absurd.'—Graham Greene

'The tops in topsy-turvy romance!'

It's Love I'm After*
US 1937 90m bw
Warner (Harry Joe Brown)
A beloved stage star couple fight like cat and dog behind the scenes.
Amusing romantic farce which has worn rather less well than might have been expected but does present two stars at their peak.

w Casey Robinson d Archie Mayo ph James Van Trees m Heinz Roemheld

Bette Davis, Leslie Howard, Olivia de Havilland, Patric Knowles, Eric Blore, George Barbier, Spring Byington, Bonita Granville, E. E. Clive

'Smash comedy hit. Arrange extra playing time for this one.'—Variety

'One of the most delightful and diverting comedies the madcap cinema has yet turned out.'—New York World Telegram

'Proceeds like a somewhat deranged Taming of the Shrew . . . [BD and LH] are surrounded by that set of millionaires, valets and heiresses that were at one time as much of a convention in American comedy as the fops of Restoration theatre.'—American Film Institute

It's My Turn
US 1980 90m Metrocolor
Columbia / Rastar / Martin Elfand
A lady mathematics professor decides to seize her chances when she falls for the son of her father's new wife.
Unattractive and rather uninteresting comedy-drama with strong overtones of women's lib.

w Eleanor Bergstein d Claudia Weill ph Bill Butler m Patrick Williams

Jill Clayburgh, Michael Douglas, Charles Grodin, Beverly Garland, Steven Hill

It's Never Too Late
GB 1956 95m Eastmancolor
A mother considered dull by her family starts a new career as a scriptwriter. Acceptable but

quite unexciting matinée comedy. Phyllis Calvert, Guy Rolfe, Susan Stephen, Patrick Barr, Delphi Lawrence, Sarah Lawson, Peter Hammond. Written by Edward Dryhurst, from the play by Felicity Douglas; directed by Michael McCarthy; for Park Lane / ABP.

It's Never Too Late to Mend
GB 1937 67m bw
An evil squire schemes for the hand of the farmer's beautiful daughter. Archetypal melodrama of the 'Fie, Sir Jasper' school, mainly interesting in this version for the antics of its heavy-breathing star. Tod Slaughter, Marjorie Taylor, Jack Livesey, Lawrence Hanray. Written by H. F. Maltby, from the play by Charles Reade and Arthur Shirley; directed by David MacDonald; for George King.

It's Not Cricket
GB 1948 77m bw
GFD / Gainsborough
Bowler-hatted officers catch a Nazi spy.
Over-spoofed comedy which barely allows the stars a real chance.

w Lyn Lockwood, Bernard MacNab d Alfred Roome ph Gordon Lang m Arthur Wilkinson

Basil Radford, Naunton Wayne, Maurice Denham, Susan Shaw, Nigel Buchanan

It's Only Money
US 1962 84m bw
Paramount / York / Jerry Lewis Productions (Paul Jones)
A TV repair mechanic hampers his detective friend in a search for a missing heir, which turns out to be himself.
Patchy mystery spoof with the star in rather better form than usual, and a memorable scene in which he is chased by an army of lawnmowers.

w John Fenton Murray d Frank Tashlin ph W. Wallace Kelley m Walter Scharf

Jerry Lewis, Zachary Scott, Joan O'Brien, Jesse White, Jack Weston

It's That Man Again**
GB 1942 84m bw
GFD / Gainsborough (Edward Black)
The Mayor of Foaming-at-the-Mouth puts on a show to save a bombed theatre.
Smart, fast-moving comedy which no longer seems particularly funny in itself but is an invaluable record of the characters and wisecracks of a radio show which proved a prime morale booster during World War II.

w Howard Irving Young, Ted Kavanagh d Walter Forde

Tommy Handley, Jack Train, Greta Gynt, Dino Galvani, Dorothy Summers, Horace Percival, Sidney Keith, Clarence Wright

It's Tough to be Famous
US 1932 81m bw
A young naval hero finds that fame destroys his private life. Unco-ordinated comedy-

drama. Written by Robert Lord, Mary McCall Jnr; directed by Alfred E. Green; for First National. 'Lightweight feature possessing sufficient entertainment value to give theatres a moderate week.'—*Variety*

Ivan the Terrible**
USSR 1942–6   100m (part one), 88m (part two)   bw. (some Agfacolor in part two)
Mosfilm
original title: *Ivan Groznyi*

The life of a 16th-century tsar.

A heavy-going film overflowing with grim, gloomy and superbly composed images: the plot is by the way, and part two (also known as *The Boyars' Plot*) is not up to the standard of part one, in which the coronation sequence alone is a masterpiece of cinema.

wd, ed Sergei Eisenstein ph Edouard Tissé (exteriors), Andrei Moskvin (interiors) *m Sergei Prokoviev ad Isaac Shpinel, L. Naumova*

Nikolai Cherkassov, Ludmilla Tselikovskaya, Serafima Birman

   'A visual opera, with all of opera's proper disregard of prose-level reality . . . an extraordinarily bold experiment, fascinating and beautiful to look at.'—*James Agee*

Ivanhoe*
GB 1952   106m   Technicolor
MGM (Pandro S. Berman)

Derring-do among the knights of medieval England.

Tolerable, big-budget spectacular based on Sir Walter Scott's novel.

w Noel Langley, Aeneas Mackenzie d Richard Thorpe ph F. A. Young m Miklos Rozsa

Robert Taylor, Joan Fontaine, Elizabeth Taylor, Emlyn Williams, George Sanders, Robert Douglas, Finlay Currie, Felix Aylmer, Francis de Wolff, Guy Rolfe, Norman Wooland, Basil Sydney

AAN: best picture; F. A. Young; Miklos Rozsa
● *Video: MGM / UA*

I've Always Loved You
US 1946   116m   Technicolor
Republic
GB title: *Concerto*

A brilliant pianist becomes jealous of his girl pupil, despite his love for her.

High-flown romantic tosh with music, an unusual departure for this studio; most notable for Artur Rubenstein on the sound track.

w Borden Chase d Frank Borzage ph Tony Gaudio m Walter Scharf

Philip Dorn, Catherine McLeod, Felix Bressart, Maria Ouspenskaya, William Carter

I've Got Your Number
US 1934   68m   bw

Telephone service engineers help prove a girl innocent of burglary. Cheerful, fast-moving programmer typical of its studio at the time. Joan Blondell, Pat O'Brien, Allen Jenkins, Glenda Farrell, Eugene Pallette. Written by Warren Duff and Sidney Sutherland; directed by Ray Enright; for Warner.

I've Lived Before
US 1956   82m   bw
U–I (Howard Christie)

After a plane crash, the pilot recovers but believes himself to be another airman who died in 1918.

Dullish, talky drama which wastes its interesting reincarnation theme.

w Norman Jolley, William Talman d Richard Bartlett ph Maury Gertsman m Herman Stein

Jock Mahoney, Leigh Snowden, Ann Harding, John McIntire, Raymond Bailey, Jerry Paris

Ivy*
US 1947   99m   bw
Universal (William Cameron Menzies)

In Edwardian society England, a lady poisoner gets her come-uppance.

Curiously ineffective period thriller in which the star is the elegant but artificial production design: the script is deadly dull.

w Charles Bennett, novel Mrs Belloc Lowndes d Sam Wood ph Russell Metty m Daniele Amfitheatrof pd William Cameron Menzies

Joan Fontaine, Herbert Marshall, Patric Knowles, Richard Ney, Cedric Hardwicke, Lucile Watson, Sara Allgood, Henry Stephenson, Rosalind Ivan, Lilian Fontaine, Una O'Connor, Isobel Elsom, Alan Napier, Paul Cavanagh, Gavin Muir, Norma Varden

   'The real star is whoever was responsible for the dressing, setting, lighting and shooting, and that, I infer from past performance, is the producer, William Cameron Menzies.'—*James Agee*

J. W. Coop*

US 1971 112m Eastmancolor
Columbia / Robertson and Associates (Cliff Robertson)

After ten years in prison, a rodeo rider returns to his home town.
Well-made but rather inconsequential drama with attractive locations.

w Cliff Robertson, Gary Cartwright, Bud Shrake d Cliff Robertson ph Frank Stanley m Don Randi, Louie Shelton

Cliff Robertson, Cristina Ferrare, Geraldine Page, R. G. Armstrong

Jabberwocky

GB 1977 101m Technicolor
Umbrella (John Goldstone, Sandy Lieberson)

A medieval cooper's apprentice is mistaken for a prince and slays the dragon which is terrorizing the neighbourhood.
An intellectual Carry On film, with very little more taste and a great deal more unpleasant imagery. Despite much re-editing, the laughs are very intermittent.

w Charles Alverson, Terry Gilliam d Terry Gilliam ph Terry Bedford m De Wolfe pd Roy Smith

Michael Palin, Max Wall, Deborah Fallender, Warren Mitchell, John Le Mesurier, Harry H. Corbett, Rodney Bewes, Bernard Bresslaw
'The constant emphasis on blood, excrement, dismemberment and filth ultimately becomes rather wearing.'—Michael Billington, Illustrated London News

Jack Ahoy

GB 1934 82m bw

An accident-prone naval rating routs bandits and wins the girl. Tailor-made star comedy with skilful moments. Jack Hulbert, Nancy O'Neil, Alfred Drayton, Tamara Desni. Written by Jack Hulbert, Leslie Arliss, Gerald Fairlie and Austin Melford; directed by Walter Forde; for Gaumont. 'Mr Hulbert is equal to all his occasions . . . his abounding energy and high spirits are never monotonous or wearisome.'—E. V. Lucas, Punch.

Jack and the Beanstalk

US 1952 78m Supercinecolor
Warner / Alex Gottlieb

A babysitter dreams the story he is reading aloud.

Rather feeble star comedy aimed entirely at the kiddie set, and with none of the familiar routines. The 'bookends', as is customary, are in black and white.

w Nat Curtis d Jean Yarbrough ph George Robinson m Heinz Roemheld

Bud Abbott, Lou Costello, Buddy Baer, Dorothy Ford, William Farnum

Jack McCall Desperado

US 1952 75m Technicolor

A Union officer is forced into outlawry but redeems himself. Tolerable minor western. George Montgomery, Angela Stevens, Douglas Kennedy, James Seay, Jay Silverheels. Written by John O'Dea; directed by Sidney Salkow; for Sam Katzman / Columbia.

Jack of All Trades*

GB 1936 76m bw

A cheerful con man talks his way into a top job in an international firm. Odd amalgam of star comedy, musical numbers of the Astaire / Rogers type, shafts of satire from the original play, and finally some flat-footed farce. Certainly worth a look. Jack Hulbert, Gina Malo, Robertson Hare, Athole Stewart, Felix Aylmer, H. F. Maltby. Written by Jack Hulbert, Austin Melford and J. O. C. Orton, from the play Youth at the Helm by Paul Vulpius; directed by Jack Hulbert and Robert Stevenson; for Gainsborough.

Jack of Diamonds

US / West Germany 1967 105m Metrocolor

A retired jewel thief introduces a brilliant pupil into society. Repetitive and rather glum comedy-drama which perks up occasionally. George Hamilton, Joseph Cotten, Marie Laforet, Maurice Evans, Wolfgang Preiss, Lilli Palmer, Carroll Baker, Zsa Zsa Gabor. Written by Jack de Witt and Sandy Howard; directed by Don Taylor; for Harris / Bavaria Atelier / MGM.

Jack Slade

US 1953 90m bw

A western gunman becomes a psychopathic killer. Cliché-ridden but rather brutish western, thought sensationally violent at the time. Mark Stevens, Dorothy Malone, Barton Maclane, John Litel, Paul Langton, Harry

Shannon. Written by Warren Douglas; directed by Harold Schuster; for Allied Artists. (GB title: Slade.)

Jack the Giant Killer**

US 1961 94m Technicolor
Zenith / Edward Small (Robert E. Kent)

Demon Pendragon kidnaps the princess of Cornwall but she is rescued by a farmer's son. Very creditable fairy tale, with the right style and atmosphere assisted by vigorous acting, good pace and excellent trick effects. Unfortunately it turned out rather scary for a child audience and so fell between two stools.

w Orville Hampton, Nathan Juran d Nathan Juran ph David S. Horsley m Paul Sawtell, Bert Shefter sp Howard Anderson ad Fernando Carere, Frank McCoy

Kerwin Mathews, Judi Meredith, Torin Thatcher, Don Beddoe, Walter Burke, Barry Kelley

'He baffled the great Scotland Yard, the celebrated Arthur Conan Doyle, and Robert Louis Stevenson!'

Jack the Ripper

GB 1958 84m bw
Mid Century (Baker and Berman)

In Victorian London the Ripper murders are finally attributed to a demented surgeon. Flat and rather flabby treatment of a cause célèbre, saved by a reasonably convincing period look.

w Jimmy Sangster d / ph Robert S. Baker, Monty Berman m Stanley Black

Ewen Solon, Lee Patterson, Eddie Byrne, Betty McDowell, John Le Mesurier

Jackass Mail

US 1942 80m bw
MGM (John Considine Jnr)

A horse thief marries the proprietress of a gambling saloon in the hope of hijacking her mail line, but she reforms him.
Boisterously conceived but anaemically scripted western comedy with the stars in full throttle.

w Lawrence Hazard d Norman Z. McLeod ph Clyde de Vinna m David Snell, Earl Brent

Wallace Beery, Marjorie Main, J. Carrol Naish, Darryl Hickman, William Haade, Hobart Cavanaugh
'This time at least they are repeating their

variation on the Min-and-Bill routine among companions whose resemblance to burlesque is as unabashed as their own.'—*Bosley Crowther, New York Times*

Jackboot Mutiny
Germany 1955   77m   bw
Arca-Ariston
original title: *Es Geschah am 20 Juli*
An account of the army officers' plot to assassinate Hitler.
Documentary-like treatment without much attempt at characterization. An important historical document nevertheless.

w W. P. Zibaso, Gustav Machaty   *d* G. W. Pabst   *ph* Kurt Hasse   *m* Johannes Weissenbach

Bernhard Wicki, Karl Ludwig Diehl, Carl Wery

The Jackpot**
US 1950   85m   bw
TCF (Samuel G. Engel)
A suburban husband finds that life becomes complicated when winning the jackpot on a radio quiz makes him a celebrity.
Modest, skilful comedy in Hollywood's best manner.

w Phoebe and Henry Ephron   *d* Walter Lang   *ph* Joseph La Shelle   *md* Lionel Newman

James Stewart, Barbara Hale, James Gleason, Fred Clark, Alan Mowbray, Patricia Medina, Natalie Wood, Tommy Rettig, Robert Gist, Lyle Talbot

Jack's the Boy*
GB 1932   91m   bw
Gainsborough (Michael Balcon)
The police commissioner's son proves his worth in rounding up a smash-and-grab gang.
Dated but lively farce which established its star as a British box office attraction of the thirties.

w W. P. Lipscomb   *d* Walter Forde   *ph* Leslie Rowson

Jack Hulbert, Cicely Courtneidge, Francis Lister, Winifred Shotter, Peter Gawthorne, Ben Field
  'A riotously funny, good, clean, honest British picture.'—*Sydney Carroll, Sunday Times*
† The film in which Hulbert sang 'The Flies Crawled Up the Window' (*m* Vivian Ellis, *ly* Douglas Furber).

Jackson County Jail
US 1976   84m   Metrocolor
(UA) New World (Roger Corman)
A lady driver is hijacked, attacked, disbelieved by the local police, thrown into jail and raped by the jailer, whom she brains with a stool.
An exploitation piece with social pretensions which it in no way justifies: it is however quite competently entertaining in its mindlessly violent way.

w Donald Stewart   *d* Michael Miller   *ph* Bruce Logan   *m* Loren Newkirk

Yvette Mimieux, Tommy Lee Jones, Robert Carradine, Frederic Cook, Severn Darden, Howard Hesseman

Jacqueline*
GB 1956   93m   bw
Rank (George H. Brown)
A Belfast shipyard worker cannot stand heights, takes to drink, and is helped by his small daughter.
Convincing, well-made, realistically set domestic comedy-drama.

w Patric Kirwan, Liam O'Flaherty   *d* Roy Baker   *ph* Geoffrey Unsworth   *m* Cedric Thorpe Davie

John Gregson, Kathleen Ryan, Jacqueline Ryan, Noel Purcell, Cyril Cusack, Marie Kean, Liam Redmond, Maureen Delany

Jaguar Lives
US 1979   90m   Eastmancolor
Exploits of an international secret agent with skill in the martial arts. Flashy, violent, James Bond rip-off, years behind its time. Joe Lewis, Christopher Lee, Donald Pleasence, Capucine, Barbara Bach, Joseph Wiseman, Woody Strode, John Huston. Written by Yabo Yablonsky; directed by Ernest Pintoff; for Sandy Howard / Jaguar.

Jailhouse Rock*
US 1957   96m   bw   Cinemascope
MGM (Pandro S. Berman)
An ex-convict becomes a pop star.
Reasonably competent star vehicle, sourer in tone than most.

w Guy Trosper   *d* Richard Thorpe   *ph* Robert Bronner   *md* Jeff Alexander

Elvis Presley, Judy Tyler, Mickey Shaughnessy, Vaughn Taylor, Dean Jones

● *Video: MGM / UA*

Jalna
US 1935   75m   bw
Episodes in the life of the Whiteoaks family.
Flat adaptation of a Canadian bestseller. Kay Johnson, Ian Hunter, C. Aubrey Smith, Jessie Ralph, Nigel Bruce, David Manners, Peggy Wood, Halliwell Hobbes. Written by Anthony Veiller, Garrett Fort, Larry Bachmann, from the novel by Mazo de la Roche; directed by John Cromwell; for RKO. 'Nice production of a not very good adaptation.'—*Variety*

Jamaica Inn*
GB 1939   107m   bw
Mayflower (Erich Pommer)
In old Cornwall, an orphan girl becomes involved with smugglers.
Stagey, stilted adventure story which never loses its studio feel or takes fire as a Hitchcock picture. The cast keeps it interesting.

w Sidney Gilliat, Joan Harrison, J. B. Priestley, *novel* Daphne du Maurier   *d* Alfred Hitchcock   *ph* Harry Stradling, Bernard Knowles   *m* Eric Fenby

Charles Laughton, Maureen O'Hara, Leslie Banks, Robert Newton, Emlyn Williams, Wylie Watson, Marie Ney, Morland Graham
  'Should get good but not outstanding b.o. Superb direction, excellent casting, expressive playing and fine production offset an uneven screenplay.'—*Variety*
  'I was irresistibly reminded of an all-star charity matinee.'—*Graham Greene*

Jamaica Run
US 1953   92m   Technicolor
Paramount Pine–Thomas
A search for documents, which may apportion a great house to another branch of the family, leads to murder.
Plot-bound romantic mystery in period, with elements of a Caribbean *Rebecca*. Watchable medium-budget hokum.

wd Lewis R. Foster, *novel* Max Murray   *ph* Lionel Lindon   *m* Lucien Cailliet

Ray Milland, Arlene Dahl, Wendell Corey, Patric Knowles

Jane Eyre
US 1934   62m   bw
A Poverty Row transcription of the Charlotte Brontë novel: see below. Virginia Bruce, Colin Clive, Beryl Mercer, Jameson Thomas, Aileen Pringle. Written by Adele Comandini; directed by Christy Cabanne; for Monogram. 'The cast appear to have considered their tasks with considerable melancholy.'—*Variety*

'A love story every woman would die a thousand deaths to live!'
Jane Eyre***
US 1943   96m   bw
TCF (William Goetz)
In Victorian times, a harshly treated orphan girl becomes governess in a mysterious Yorkshire mansion with a brooding master.
Sharply paced, reasonably faithful and superbly staged Hollywood version of Charlotte Brontë's archetypal romantic novel which stimulated so many imitations, including *Rebecca*.

w Aldous Huxley, Robert Stevenson, John Houseman   *d* Robert Stevenson   *ph* George Barnes   *m* Bernard Herrmann   *sp* Fred Sersen   *ad* Wiard B. Ihnen, James Basevi

Joan Fontaine, Orson Welles, Margaret O'Brien, *Henry Daniell*, John Sutton, Agnes Moorehead, Elizabeth Taylor, Peggy Ann Garner, Sara Allgood, Aubrey Mather, Hillary Brooke, Edith Barrett, Ethel Griffies, Barbara Everest, *John Abbott*
  'A careful and tame production, a sadly vanilla-flavoured Joan Fontaine, and Orson Welles treating himself to road operatic sculpturings of body, cloak and diction, his eyes glinting in the Rembrandt gloom, at every chance, like side orders of jelly.'—*James Agee*

'The essentials are still there; and the non-essentials, such as the gloom, the shadows, the ground mist, the rain and the storms, have been expanded and redoubled and magnified to fill up the gaps.'—*Richard Mallett, Punch*

Janice Meredith

US 1924 153m bw silent
Metro-Goldwyn / Cosmopolitan
GB title: *The Beautiful Rebel*

Vicissitudes of the coquettish daughter of a New Jersey family through the War of Independence.
Marathon melodrama not unlike *Gone with the Wind* in subject matter, but of no remaining interest.

w Lilly Hayward, *novel* Paul Leicester Ford
d E. Mason Hopper ad Joseph Urban *music score* Deems Taylor

Marion Davies, Harrison Ford, Macklyn Arbuckle, Joseph Kilgour, George Nash, Tyrone Power Snr, May Vokes, W. C. Fields, Olin Howland

Janie

US 1944 106m bw
Warner (Brock Pemberton)

The teenage daughter of a middle-class American household gets into innocent scrapes with the army.
Deafening tomboy farce.

w Agnes Christine Johnson, Charles Hoffman, *play* Josephine Bentham, Herschel V. Williams Jnr d Michael Curtiz ph Carl Guthrie *songs* Lee David, Sammy Cahn, Jule Styne

Joyce Reynolds, Robert Hutton, Ann Harding, Edward Arnold, Robert Benchley, Claire Foley, Hattie McDaniel
† *Janie Gets Married*, made the following year and running 89m, had almost identical credits except that Joan Leslie replaced Joyce Reynolds and Dorothy Malone joined the cast.

Japanese War Bride°

US 1952 94m bw
TCF / Bernhard (Joseph Bernhard)

An officer wounded in Korea marries his Japanese nurse and takes her home to California.
Predictable domestic drama very similar to the British *Frieda*, marginally interesting for sociological reasons.

w Catherine Turney d King Vidor ph Lionel Lindon m Emil Newman

Shirley Yamaguchi, Don Taylor, Cameron Mitchell, Marie Windsor, James Bell, Louise Lorimer

Jason and the Argonauts°°°

GB 1963 104m Technicolor
Columbia / Charles H. Schneer

With help and hindrance from the gods, Jason voyages in search of the Golden Fleece and meets all kinds of monsters.
Rambling semi-classic mythological fantasy

which keeps its tongue firmly in its cheek and provides a framework for some splendid stop-frame animation.

w Jan Read, Beverly Cross d Don Chaffey
ph Wilkie Cooper m Bernard Herrmann
sp Ray Harryhausen

Todd Armstrong, Honor Blackman, Niall MacGinnis, Andrew Faulds, Nancy Kovack

● Video: RCA / Columbia

Jassy

GB 1947 102m Technicolor
GFD / Gainsborough (Sydney Box)

A gypsy servant girl falls in love with her master but is accused of murder.
Period romantic melodrama of the *Man in Grey* school; poor of its kind despite high production values.

w Dorothy and Campbell Christie, Geoffrey Kerr, *novel* Norah Lofts d Bernard Knowles
ph Geoffrey Unsworth

Margaret Lockwood, Patricia Roc, Dennis Price, Basil Sydney, Dermot Walsh, Nora Swinburne, Linden Travers, Ernest Thesiger, Cathleen Nesbitt, John Laurie, Jean Cadell, Clive Morton
'As a piece of unabashed romantic hokum, I found it more and more diverting as the plot thickened.'—*Evening Standard*

Java Head°

GB 1934 85m bw
ATP (Basil Dean)

In 1850 Bristol, a shipbuilder forsakes his Manchu wife for an English girl.
Rather obvious period melodrama with full-blooded acting.

w Martin Brown, Gordon Wellesley
d J. Walter Ruben ph Bert Glennon

Anna May Wong, John Loder, Ralph Richardson, Elizabeth Allan, Edmund Gwenn, Herbert Lomas, George Curzon, Roy Emerton

Jaws°°

US 1975 125m Technicolor
Panavision
Universal / Zanuck–Brown (William S. Gilmore Jnr)

A man-eating shark causes havoc off the Long Island coast.
In the exploitation-hungry seventies this film took more money than any other. In itself, despite genuinely suspenseful and frightening sequences, it is a slackly narrated and sometimes flatly handled thriller with an over-abundance of dialogue and, when it finally appears, a pretty unconvincing monster.

w Peter Benchley, Carl Gottlieb, *novel* Peter Benchley d Steven Spielberg ph Bill Butler
m John Williams

Robert Shaw, Roy Scheider, Richard Dreyfuss, Lorraine Gary, Murray Hamilton, Carl Gottlieb
'A mind-numbing repast for sense-sated gluttons. Shark stew for the stupefied.'—*William S. Pechter*
'The opening sequences have few parallels in modern cinema; like the shower scene in

Psycho they will haunt a whole generation.'—*Les Keyser, Hollywood in the Seventies*
AA: John Williams
AAN: best picture
● Video: CIC

Jaws 2

US 1978 117m Technicolor
Panavision
Universal / Richard Zanuck, David Brown (Joe Alves)

Another man-eating shark menaces teenagers in the Long Island resort of Amity.
Repetitive and feeble sequel aimed directly at the popcorn market.

w Carl Gottlieb, Howard Sackler, Dorothy Tristan d Jeannot Szwarc ph Michael Butler, David Butler, Michael McGowan m John Williams

Roy Scheider, Lorraine Gary, Murray Hamilton, Joseph Mascolo, Colin Wilcox
'A manipulation of the audience, in the best sense of the term.'—*Jeannot Szwarc, director*

● Video: CIC

Jaws 3-D

US 1983 99m Technicolor Arrivision
3-D

A man-eating shark turns up in a Florida theme park. Noisy final chapter to this string of shocks. Dennis Quaid, Bess Armstrong, Simon MacCorkindale, Louis Gossett Jnr, John Putch, Lea Thompson. Written by Richard Matheson, Carl Gottlieb; directed by Joe Alves; for Alan Landsburg / Universal.

The Jayhawkers

US 1959 110m Technicolor
Vistavision
Paramount / Panama and Frank

Before the Civil War, a farmer defeats a militant posse of private raiders.
Unconvincing but rather unusual western, flat patches alternating with striking ones.

w Melvin Frank, Joseph Petracca, Frank Fenton, A. I. Bezzerides d Melvin Frank
ph Loyal Griggs m Jerome Moross

Fess Parker, Jeff Chandler, Nicole Maurey, Henry Silva, Herbert Rudley

Jazz Comedy°

USSR 1934 93m bw
Mosfilm
original title: *Vesolye Rebyata*

A shepherd is frequently mistaken for a famous conductor.
Peripatetic comedy with many sight gags and western slapstick: Russian comedy being still a rare thing, it seems something of a revelation.

w Grigori Alexandrov, Nikolai Erdman, V. Mass d Grigori Alexandrov ph Vladimir Nilsen m Isaac Dunayevsky

Lubov Orlova, Leonid Utyosov, Maria Strelkova

The Jazz Singer****
US 1927 89m bw
Warner

A cantor's son makes it big in show business.
Archetypal Jewish weepie which became of
absorbing interest as the first talkie film (songs
and a few fragments of speech) and in its way,
surprisingly, is not half bad.

w Alfred A. Cohn, play Samson Raphaelson
d Alan Crosland ph Hal Mohr

Al Jolson, May McAvoy, Warner Oland,
Eugenie Besserer, Otto Lederer
  'A beautiful period piece, extravagantly
sentimental . . . yet entirely compelling in its
own conviction.'—NFT, 1969
  'The Jazz Singer definitely establishes the
fact that talking pictures are imminent.
Everyone in Hollywood can rise up and
declare that they are not, and it will not alter
the fact. If I were an actor with a squeaky
voice I would worry.'—Welford Beaton, The
Film Spectator
AAN: Alfred A. Cohn

The Jazz Singer
US 1953 107m Technicolor
Warner (Louis F. Edelman)

Ill-considered, schmaltzy remake of the above.

w Frank Davis, Leonard Stern, Lewis Meltzer
d Michael Curtiz ph Isidore Mankofsky md Ray
Heindorf m Max Steiner

Danny Thomas, Peggy Lee, Mildred
Dunnock, Eduard Franz
AAN: Ray Heindorf; Max Steiner

The Jazz Singer
US 1980 115m De Luxe
EMI / Jerry Leider

Oddly-timed reprise of the above, with doting
mum replaced by patient wife. A good basis
for a best-selling album, otherwise a pointless
enterprise.

w Herbert Baker, Stephen H. Foreman
d Richard Fleischer ph Isidore Mankofsky
m Leonard Rosenman pd Harry Horner

Neil Diamond, Laurence Olivier, Lucie
Arnaz, Catlin Adams, Sully Boyar
  'What is jazz to Neil Diamond and what is
Neil Diamond to jazz? Old title has nothing to
do with music on display here and would seem
meaningless to modern audiences.'—Variety
  ● Video: Thorn EMI

Jazzboat
GB 1959 96m bw Cinemascope

A jazz musician pretends to be a crook and
leads the police to an important gang. Flimsy
comedy with a background of pop acts. Very
dated. Anthony Newley, Anne Aubrey, David
Lodge, Lionel Jeffries, Bernie Winters, James
Booth, Al Mulock, Joyce Blair, Leo McKern,
Ted Heath and his Music. Written by Ken
Hughes and John Antrobus; directed by Ken
Hughes; for Warwick / Columbia.

Jealousy
US 1929 66m bw

A young artist is jealous of his wife's older
friend, and kills him. Turgid adaptation of a
two-character play; interesting only for its
cast, though the star died before it was
released. Jeanne Eagels, Fredric March,
Halliwell Hobbes, Henry Daniell. Written by
Garrett Fort and John D. Williams, from the
play by Louis Verneuil; directed by Jean De
Limur; for Paramount.

Jealousy
US 1934 66m bw

A boxer is knocked out and dreams that his
jealousy has landed him in the electric chair.
Disagreeable melodrama not saved by its
tricks. Nancy Carroll, George Murphy,
Donald Cook, Raymond Walburn. Written by
Kubec Glasmon, Joseph Moncure March;
directed by Roy William Neill; for Columbia.

Jealousy*
US 1945 70m bw

A failed writer, jealous of his wife's friendship
with another man, is found murdered. Curious
but interesting melodrama with much talent
breaking through. Nils Asther, John Joder,
Jane Randolph, Karen Morley. Written by
Arnold Phillips, Gustav Machaty and Dalton
Trumbo; directed by Gustav Machaty; music
by Hans Eisler; for Republic. 'It is a
sympathetic film, and in spite of its overall
failure, contains enough sincerity and enough
artistry to make most of the other films
mentioned here look sick.'—James Agee.

Jeanne Eagels*
US 1957 114m bw
Columbia (George Sidney)

A sideshow dancer becomes a Broadway star
of the twenties but dies of drugs.
Well-upholstered but basically too
conventional showbiz biopic.

w Daniel Fuchs, Sonya Levien, John Fante
d George Sidney ph Robert Planck m George
Duning

Kim Novak, Jeff Chandler, Agnes
Moorehead, Charles Drake, Larry Gates,
Virginia Grey

Jeannie*
GB 1941 101m bw
GFD / Tansa (Marcel Hellman)
US title: Girl in Distress

A Scots girl comes into money and takes a
European holiday.
Mildly astringent, generally amusing comedy
which overcomes shaky production. Remade
as Let's Be Happy in 1952.

w Anatole de Grunwald, Roland Pertwee,
play Aimée Stuart d Harold French
ph Bernard Knowles

Barbara Mullen, Michael Redgrave, Albert
Lieven, Wilfrid Lawson, Kay Hammond,
Edward Chapman, Googie Withers, Gus
MacNaughton
  'One of the easiest, sweetest of light
comedies.'—James Agee

'The drama of all women who meet the
  demands of love!'
Jennie Gerhardt
US 1933 85m bw
Paramount (B. P. Schulberg)

An unmarried mother is hard done by but gets
the man she loves in the end.
Archetypal weepie, adequately put across.

w Josephine Lovett, Joseph M. March, S. K.
Lauren, Frank Portos, novel Theodore
Dreiser d Marion Gering ph Leon Shamroy

Sylvia Sidney, Donald Cook, Mary Astor,
Edward Arnold, H. B. Warner, Theodor Von
Eltz
  'Doesn't look to become a general b.o.
favourite because it is a story without
action.'—Variety

Jennifer
US 1953 73m bw
AA (Berman Swartz)

The lady housekeeper of a California mansion
broods on the mysterious disappearance of her
predecessor.
Slight, quietly effective suspenser with a let-
down ending.

w Virginia Myers d Joel Newton ph James
Wong Howe m Ernest Gold

Ida Lupino, Howard Duff, Robert Nicholas,
Mary Shipp

Jeopardy
US 1952 69m bw
MGM (Sol Baer Fielding)

A man on a camping holiday falls off a jetty
and gets stuck in the timbers while the water
rises; his wife frantically seeks help from an
escaped convict.
Panic melodrama enjoyable for its clichés.

w Mel Dinelli d John Sturges ph Victor
Milner m Dmitri Tiomkin

Barbara Stanwyck, Barry Sullivan, Ralph
Meeker

Jeremiah Johnson**
US 1972 107m Technicolor
  Panavision
Warner (Joe Wizan)

In the 1850s an ex-soldier becomes a mountain
trapper.
Splendidly made if rather desultorily plotted
adventure story with the feel of raw reality.

w John Milius, Edward Anhalt d Sydney
Pollack ph Andrew Callaghan m John
Rubinstein, Tim McIntire

Robert Redford, Will Geer, Allyn McLerie
  ● Video: Warner

Jeremy
US 1973 90m De Luxe
UA / Kenasset (George Pappas)

A music student falls in love with a ballet
dancer.
Sentimental love story with nothing positive to
commend it, chiefly interesting because for
commercial release it was blown up from
16mm.

wd Arthur Barron *ph* Paul Goldsmith *m* Lee
Holdridge

Robby Benson, Glynnis O'Connor, Len Bari,
Leonardo Cimino

Jericho
GB 1937 77m bw
Buckingham (Walter Futter, Max Schach)
US title: *Dark Sands*

A court-martialled officer pursues a
murderous deserter across Africa.
Lively star vehicle of its day.

w Frances Marion, George Barraud, Peter
Ruric, Robert N. Lee *d* Thornton Freeland
ph John W. Boyle

Paul Robeson, Henry Wilcoxon, Wallace
Ford, John Laurie, James Carew
  'Can't fail to interest audiences throughout
the world.'—*Variety*

The Jerk
US 1979 94m Technicolor
Universal / Aspen (Peter MacGregor-Scott)

An innocent white man brought up by black
sharecroppers goes out into the world and first
makes, then loses a fortune.
Hit-or-miss star vehicle with flashes of satire
and fallen aspirations to be a modern *Candide*.

w Steve Martin, Carl Gottlieb, Michael Elias
d Carl Reiner *ph* Victor J. Kemper *m* Jack
Elliott

Steve Martin, Bernadette Peters, Catlin
Adams, Bill Macy, Maurice Evans
  'Goofy, dumb, innocent, loud,
uncoordinated, bashful and quite dirty.'—
Variety
● Video: CIC

The Jerusalem File
US / Israel 1971 96m Metrocolor
MGM / Sparta (Ram Ben Efraim)

American archaeologists in Jerusalem become
involved in Arab / Israeli espionage.
Muddled mixture of action and politics.

w Troy Kennedy Martin · *d* John Flynn
ph Raoul Coutard *m* John Scott

Bruce Davison, Nicol Williamson, Donald
Pleasence, Ian Hendry

Jesse James**
US 1938 106m Technicolor
TCF (Nunnally Johnson)

After the Civil War, two brothers take to train
robbing when railroad employees harass their
family.
The life of an outlaw turns into family
entertainment when Hollywood bathes it in
sentiment, soft colour, family background and
warm humour. It works dangerously well, and
the action sequences are splendid.

w Nunnally Johnson *d* Henry King
ph George Barnes *md* Louis Silvers
ad William Darling, George Dudley

Tyrone Power, Henry Fonda, Nancy Kelly,
Jane Darwell, Randolph Scott, Henry Hull,
Slim Summerville, Brian Donlevy, J. Edward
Bromberg, John Carradine, Donald Meek
  'Sock outdoors meller, vigorous and
intensely dramatic in its unfolding . . . box
office smacko.'—*Variety*

'An authentic American panorama.'—*New
York Times*
† Sequel 1940: *The Return of Frank James*.
Remake 1957: *The True Story of Jesse James*.

Jessica
France / Italy / US 1962 105m
  Technicolor Panavision
UA / Ariane / Dear Film (Jean Negulesco)

The attractive midwife in a Sicilian village
causes the women to go on a sex strike.
Synthetic rustic naughtiness showing several
influences imperfectly assimilated.

w Edith Sommer, *novel* The Midwife of Pont
Clery by Flora Sundstrom *d* Jean Negulesco
ph Piero Portalupi *m* Mario Nascimbene

Angie Dickinson, Maurice Chevalier, Noel
Noel, Gabriele Ferzetti, Sylva Koscina, Agnes
Moorehead, Marcel Dalio

Jesus Christ Superstar*
US 1973 107m Technicolor Todd-AO
  35
Universal (Norman Jewison, Robert
  Stigwood)

Young tourists in Israel re-enact episodes of
the life of Christ.
Location-set fantasia based on the
phenomenally successful rock opera; some of
it works, but the original concept was a
theatrical one.

w Melvyn Bragg, Norman Jewison, *book* Tim
Rice *d* Norman Jewison *m* Andrew Lloyd
Webber *ph* Douglas Slocombe *md* André
Previn

Ted Neeley, Carl Anderson, Yvonne Elliman,
Barry Dennen
  'One of the true fiascos of modern
cinema.'—*Paul D. Zimmerman*

AAN: André Previn
● Video: CIC

Jet over the Atlantic
US 1958 95m bw
Warner / Inter Continental (Benedict
  Bogeaus)

A noble British passenger on a plane from
Madrid to New York has planted a gas bomb
in the luggage compartment.
Mechanical airborne suspenser with the usual
assortment of unconvincing types making
unconvincing gestures.

w Irving H. Cooper *d* Byron Haskin
ph George Stahl *m* Lou Forbes

Guy Madison, Virginia Mayo, George Raft,
George Macready, Ilona Massey, Anna Lee,
Margaret Lindsay, Venetia Stevenson, Mary
Anderson, Brett Halsey, Frederic Worlock

Jet Pilot
US 1950–57 112m Technicolor
Howard Hughes (Jules Furthman)

A Russian lady spy falls for an American pilot.
Lamentably dull and stupid romantic actioner
of which all concerned should be thoroughly
ashamed, especially as it took seven years to
complete and is not even technically
competent.

w Jules Furthman *d* Josef Von Sternberg (and
others) *ph* Winton C. Hoch *m* Bronislau
Kaper

John Wayne, Janet Leigh, Jay C. Flippen,
Paul Fix, Richard Rober, Roland Winters,
Ivan Triesault, Hans Conried
  'One of the most childish, tedious and futile
cold war spy dramas yet concocted by a
Hollywood screenwriter.'—*John Gillett*

Jet Storm*
GB 1959 99m bw
British Lion / Britannia / Pendennis (Steven
  Pallos)

An airliner in flight from London to New York
is discovered to have a bomb on board.
All-star slice-of-life suspenser with
competently handled dialogue and situations.

w Cy Endfield, Sigmund Miller *d* Cy
Endfield *ph* Jack Hildyard *m* Thomas Rajna

Richard Attenborough, George Rose,
Hermione Baddeley, Mai Zetterling, Diane
Cilento, Stanley Baker, Harry Secombe,
Virginia Maskell, Elizabeth Sellars, Sybil
Thorndike, Bernard Braden, Cec Linder,
David Kossoff

Jeux Interdits***
France 1952 84m bw
Robert Dorfmann (Paul Joly)
aka: *Forbidden Games; The Secret Game*

In 1940, the little daughter of refugee parents
sees her parents killed, and takes refuge with a
peasant family, the small son of which helps
her bury her dead puppy. They make a game
of building a cemetery, which leads to a village
feud . . .
Poignant anti-war tract which seemed a
masterpiece at the time and is full of
marvellous moments, but no longer holds up
as a whole.

w Jean Aurenche, Pierre Bost, *novel* François
Boyer *d* René Clément *ph* Robert Julliard
m Narciso Yepes

*Brigitte Fossey, Georges Poujouly, Amédée,
Laurence Badie, Jacques Marin, Suzanne
Courtal, Lucien Hubert*
  'A truly imposing achievement of blending
several seemingly unrelated elements into a
totally meaningful whole.'—*John Simon, 1967*

AA: best foreign film
AAN: François Boyer (original story)

Les Jeux Sont Faits*
France 1947 91m bw
Films Gibe

Falling in love in Purgatory, two murdered
people get a second chance to return to earth,
but spend their time quarrelling.
Somewhat despondent romantic fantasy with
morsels of wit.

w Jean-Paul Sartre *d* Jean Delannoy
ph Christian Matras *m* Georges Auric

Micheline Presle, Marcel Pagliero, Marguerite
Moreno, Charles Dullin

Jew Suss**
GB 1934 109m bw
Gaumont (Michael Balcon)
US title: *Power*

In old Württemberg, a Jew gains power to
help his people, then finds he is Gentile.
Interesting, heavy-handed historical satire on
the pointlessness of race distinctions, made
partly in answer to Nazi oppression in
Germany.

w Dorothy Farnum, A. R. Rawlinson, *novel*
Leon Feuchtwanger *d* Lothar Mendes

Conrad Veidt, Benita Hume, Frank Vosper,
Cedric Hardwicke, Gerald du Maurier,
Pamela Ostrer
'Powerful as an artistic film achievement
. . . but may have to struggle for commercial
contentment.'—*Variety*

Jew Suss*
Germany 1940 85m bw
Terra

Celebrated travesty of the above, in which the
Jew is wholly evil and rapes Aryan girls.

w Ludwig Metzger, Veit Harlan, Eberhard
Wolfgang Möller *d* Veit Harlan *ph* Bruno
Mondi *m* Wolfgang Zeller

Ferdinand Marian, Werner Krauss, Heinrich
George, Kristina Söderbaum
'The epitome of anti-semitic propaganda
. . . the most notorious film of the Third Reich
and one which brought disgrace on almost
everyone connected with it.'—*Georges Sadoul*
'Highly recommended for its artistic value
and, to serve the politics of the State,
recommended for young people.'—*Josef
Goebbels*

Jewel Robbery*
US 1932 68m bw
Warner

A jewel thief and a millionaire's wife fall in
love in Vienna.
Good sparkling fun in the shadow of *Trouble
in Paradise* (qv).

w Erwin Gelsey, *play* Ladislaus Fodor
d William Dieterle *ph* Robert Kurrle

William Powell, Kay Francis, Hardie Albright,
André Luguet, Henry Kolker, Spencer
Charters, Alan Mowbray, Helen Vinson,
Lawrence Grant

Jezebel***
US 1938 104m bw
Warner (Henry Blanke)

Before the Civil War, a southern belle stirs up
trouble among the menfolk by her wilfulness
and spite, but atones when a plague strikes.
Superb star melodrama, tossed to her in
compensation for losing *Gone with the Wind*,
and dealt with in high style by all concerned.

w Clements Ripley, Abem Finkel, John
Huston, *play* Owen Davis Snr *d* William
Wyler *ph* Ernest Haller *m* Max Steiner

Bette Davis, Henry Fonda, George Brent,
Margaret Lindsay, Fay Bainter, Richard
Cromwell, Donald Crisp, Henry O'Neill, John

Litel, Spring Byington, Eddie Anderson,
Gordon Oliver, Irving Pichel
'Good femme film, assured of okay
results.'—*Variety*
'Its excellences come from many sources—
good plotting and writing, a director and
photographer who know how to make the
thing flow along with dramatic pictorial effect,
and a cast that makes its story a record of
living people.'—*James Shelley Hamilton,
National Board of Review*
'Without the zing Davis gave it, it would
have looked very mossy indeed.'—*Pauline
Kael, 1968*

AA: Bette Davis; Fay Bainter
AAN: best picture; Ernest Haller; Max
Steiner

Jigsaw
US 1949 72m bw
(UA) Tower (The Danzigers)

An assistant District Attorney uncovers a mob
stirring up racial hatred.
Undistinguished piece of do-goodery,
curiously decorated by guest stars doing bit
parts as a gesture of goodwill.

w Fletcher Markle, Vincent McConnor
d Fletcher Markle *ph* Don Malkames
m Robert Stringer

Franchot Tone, Jean Wallace, Myron
McCormick, Marc Lawrence, Marlene
Dietrich, Henry Fonda, John Garfield, Marsha
Hunt, Leonard Lyons, Burgess Meredith

Jigsaw**
GB 1962 107m bw Cinemascope
British Lion / Britannia / Figaro (Val Guest)

Brighton policemen track down the murderer
of a woman found in a lonely house on the
beach.
Absorbing and entertaining little murder
mystery which sustains its considerable length
with interesting detail and plays as fair as can
be with the audience. Excellent unassuming
entertainment.

wd Val Guest, *play* Sleep Long My Love by
Hilary Waugh *ph* Arthur Grant *m* none

Jack Warner, Ronald Lewis, *Michael
Goodliffe*, Yolande Donlan, John Barron

Jim Thorpe, All-American
US 1951 105m bw
Warner (Everett Freeman)
GB title: *Man of Bronze*

A Red Indian becomes a star footballer, but
later succumbs to drink.
Adequate sporting biopic.

w Douglas Morrow, Everett Freeman
d Michael Curtiz *ph* Ernest Haller *m* Max
Steiner

Burt Lancaster, Charles Bickford, Steve
Cochran, Phyllis Thaxter, Dick Wesson

Jimmy the Gent*
US 1934 67m bw
Warner (Robert Lord)

A racketeer supplies heirs for unclaimed
estates.
Adequate star crime comedy.

w Bertram Millhauser *d* Michael Curtiz
ph Ira Morgan *md* Leo F. Forbstein

Jimmy Cagney, Bette Davis, Alice White,
Allen Jenkins, Arthur Hohl, Mayo Methot,
Alan Dinehart, Hobart Cavanaugh, Ralf
Harolde, Philip Reed, Joe Sawyer
'Fast and flip, rough and rowdy.'—*New
York American*

Jitterbugs*
US 1943 75m bw
TCF (Sol M. Wurtzel)

Laurel and Hardy help a nightclub singer to
fight off gangsters.
The last Laurel and Hardy film to contain any
good scenes, and almost the only one of their
TCF films that did.

w Scott Darling *d* Mal St Clair *ph* Lucien
Andriot

Stan Laurel, Oliver Hardy, Vivian Blaine,
Bob Bailey, Douglas Fowley, Noel Madison,
Lee Patrick

Jivaro
US 1953 91m Technicolor 3D
Paramount / William H. Pine, William
   C.Thomas
GB title: *Lost Treasure of the Amazon*

A mixed party of Americans follows a
drunken treasure seeker into the jungle.
Elementary treasure hunt adventure,
hampered by studio foliage, bad script and
half-hearted acting.

w Winston Miller, *story* David Duncan
d Edward Ludwig *ph* Lionel Lindon
m Gregory Stone

Fernando Lamas, Rhonda Fleming, Brian
Keith, Lon Chaney Jnr, Marvin Miller,
Richard Denning

Joan of Arc
US 1948 145m Technicolor
(RKO) Sierra / Walter Wanger

The last campaign of the Maid of Orleans.
Strictly from Dullsville; one studio-set piece
follows another, and a group of talented
people clearly thought that prestige would sell
itself without the hard work that goes into
more commercial productions.

w Maxwell Anderson, Andrew Solt, *play* Joan
of Lorraine by Maxwell Anderson *d* Victor
Fleming *ph* Joe Valentine *m* Hugo
Friedhofer *md* Emil Newman *ad* Richard
Day

Ingrid Bergman, Jose Ferrer, George
Coulouris, Francis L. Sullivan, Gene
Lockhart, Ward Bond, John Ireland, Hurd
Hatfield, Cecil Kellaway, George Zucco, J.
Carrol Naish
'A bad film with one or two good things. It
is childishly oversimplified, its battles *papier
mâché*, its heroine far too worldly, its spiritual
content that of a chromo art calendar.'—
Herman G. Weinberg

AA: Joe Valentine
AAN: Hugo Friedhofer; Ingrid Bergman; Jose
Ferrer

● *Video: Motion Epics*

Joan of Ozark

US 1942 82m bw

A hillbilly sharpshooter becomes a national spy heroine. Scatty comedy of moderate liveliness. Judy Canova, Joe E. Brown, Eddie Foy Jnr, Jerome Cowan, Alexander Granach. Written by Robert Harari, Eve Greene and Jack Townley; directed by Joseph Santley; for Republic. (GB title: *The Queen of Spies*.)

Joan of Paris

US 1942 95m bw

TCF (David Hempstead)

A French resistance leader sacrifices herself so that Allied pilots can escape.

Well-made propaganda adventure dignified by excellent cast.

w Charles Bennett, Ellis St. Joseph, *story* Jacques Thery, Georges Kessel *d* Robert Stevenson *ph* Russell Metty *m* Roy Webb

Michele Morgan, Paul Henreid, Thomas Mitchell, Laird Cregar, May Robson, Alexander Granach, Alan Ladd

AAN: Roy Webb

Joanna

GB 1968 122m De Luxe Panavision

TCF / Laughlin (Michael S. Laughlin)

A girl art student comes to London and quickly finds the road to ruin.

Antediluvian rubbish tarted up with swinging London settings.

wd Michael Sarne *ph* Walter Lassally *m* Rod McKuen

Genevieve Waite, Christian Doermer, Calvin Lockhart, Donald Sutherland

'An unnecessarily protracted punishing of a very dead quadruped.'—*MFB*

The Job**

Italy 1961 90m bw

24 Horses Films (Alberto Soffientini) original title: *Il Posto*

A teenage boy gets his first job, and progresses from office boy to clerk when a senior man dies.

Appealingly observant social comedy, very simple and extremely effective.

wd Ermanno Olmi *ph* Lamberto Caimi

Sandro Panzeri, Loredana Detto

'Rueful and funny and honest . . . the players have been encouraged not so much to act as to behave. Olmi stalks them like a naturalist, and the result is a small, unique and perfect achievement in film-making.'—*Penelope Houston, MFB*

Joe*

US 1970 107m De Luxe

Cannon (David Gil)

A construction worker in a bar meets a businessman who has just killed his daughter's drug addicted lover; they become buddies in their hatred of hippies.

Highly successful in America as a backlash against permissiveness, this rough-hewn opportunistic melodrama is vivid enough but moves in fits and starts.

w Norman Wexler *d / ph* John G. Avildsen *m* Bobby Scott

Peter Boyle, Dennis Patrick, Audrey Caire, Susan Sarandon

'A bad film disfigured by brute strokes of tendentiousness.'—*Penelope Gilliatt*

AAN: Norman Wexler

● *Video: Intervision*

Joe Butterfly

US 1957 90m Technicolor Cinemascope

U-I (Aaron Rosenberg)

Shortly after World War II, American occupying troops are conned by a Japanese interpreter.

Dull comedy intent on healing old wounds.

w Sy Gomberg, Jack Sher, Marion Hargrove *d* Jesse Hibbs *ph* Irving Glassberg *m* Joseph Gershenson

Burgess Meredith, Audie Murphy, George Nader, Keenan Wynn, Fred Clark, John Agar, Charles McGraw

Joe Dakota

US 1957 90m Technicolor Cinemascope

U-I (Howard Christie)

A stranger appears in a western town in search of his Indian friend, who turns out to have been murdered by the townspeople so that they can share the profits from his oil well. Feeble rip-off of *Bad Day at Black Rock*.

w William Talman, Norman Jolley *d* Richard Bartlett *ph* George Robinson *md* Joseph Gershenson

Jock Mahoney, Luana Patten, Charles McGraw, Barbara Lawrence, Claude Akins, Lee Van Cleef

Joe Kidd

US 1972 87m Technicolor Panavision

Universal / Malpaso (Sidney Beckerman)

A disreputable bounty hunter tracks down the leader of a tribe of Mexican bandits.

Rough and tumble star western with untenable moral attitudes.

w Elmore Leonard *d* John Sturges *ph* Bruce Surtees *m* Lalo Schifrin

Clint Eastwood, Robert Duvall, John Saxon, Don Stroud, James Wainwright

● *Video: CIC*

Joe Macbeth

GB 1955 90m bw

Columbia / Frankovich (George Maynard)

A gangster is urged by his wife to rub out his boss.

Almost too bad to be funny, this effort to update Shakespeare has actors behaving as though they were stuck in treacle, and its gimmick quality is quickly dissipated by an indifferent production.

w Philip Yordan *d* Ken Hughes *ph* Basil Emmott *m* Trevor Duncan

Paul Douglas, Ruth Roman, Grégoire Aslan, Bonar Colleano, Sidney James

Joe Smith American*

US 1942 63m bw

MGM (Jack Chertok)

GB title: *Highway to Freedom*

An aircraft factory worker with special knowledge is kidnapped by Nazis but leads the FBI to his captors.

Watchable propaganda thriller credited with easing Americans into a war mood.

w Allen Rivkin, *story* Paul Gallico *d* Richard Thorpe *ph* Charles Lawton Jnr

Robert Young, Marsha Hunt, Darryl Hickman, Harvey Stephens, Jonathan Hale, Noel Madison, Joseph Anthony

'Not a high-powered movie, it is a first rate die for the new propaganda models which Hollywood is readying for mass production.'—*Time*

Joey Boy

GB 1965 91m bw

British Lion / Launder–Gilliat

In 1941, a group of petty crooks join the army. Abysmal service comedy, incredibly cheap and tatty and the nadir of several of the talents involved.

wd Frank Launder *ph* Arthur Lavis *m* Philip Green

Harry H. Corbett, Stanley Baxter, Bill Fraser, Reg Varney, Percy Herbert, Lance Percival

'As visually shoddy as it is unfunny . . . the final shot (Corbett pulling a lavatory chain) is all too crudely apt.'—*MFB*

Johann Mouse***

US 1952 8m Technicolor

Strauss' mouse dances to his master's music; the cat, to lure him out, learns to play the piano. Splendid Tom and Jerry cartoon from the great period of this neglected art.

Produced by Fred Quimby; for MGM. AA: best cartoon.

John and Julie

GB 1955 82m Eastmancolor

Group Three (Herbert Mason)

Two children run away to see the coronation. Genial little family comedy full of stock comic characters.

wd William Fairchild *ph* Arthur Grant *m* Philip Green

Colin Gibson, Leslie Dudley, Peter Sellers, Moira Lister, Wilfrid Hyde White, Sidney James, Andrew Cruickshank

John and Mary*

US 1969 92m De Luxe Panavision

TCF / Debrod (Ben Kadish)

Two New Yorkers have a one-night affair and cannot decide whether to continue.

Slight, disappointing sex comedy vehicle for two stars who were very hot at the time.

w John Mortimer, *novel* Mervyn Jones
d Peter Yates *ph* Gayne Rescher *m* Quincy
Jones *pd* John Robert Lloyd

Dustin Hoffman, Mia Farrow, Michael Tolan,
Sunny Griffin, Tyne Daly

'The emphasis is not on action but on
acting, which although skilful and subtly
nuanced does not in this case amount to the
same thing as character.'—*Ian Dawson*

'Despite all the "now" sets and surfaces, it's
like an old comedy of the thirties—minus the
comedy.'—*Judith Crist*

John Goldfarb Please Come Home

US 1965 96m De Luxe Cinemascope
TCF / Steve Palmer / J. Lee-Thompson

An American spy pilot crashlands near the
palace of a Middle Eastern potentate at the
same time as a girl reporter arrives for an
interview.
Would-be satire on the cold war, anti-
feminism, American football, American /
Arab relations, etc. None of it works for a
minute, and the actors' desperation can be
plainly seen.

w William Peter Blatty d J. Lee-Thompson
ph Leon Shamroy *m* Johnny Williams

Shirley Maclaine, Richard Crenna, Peter
Ustinov, Fred Clark, Wilfrid Hyde White, Jim
Backus

John Loves Mary

US 1948 87m bw
Warner

A GI returns home to get married, but
unfortunately, to help a friend, he has already
entered into a marriage of convenience.
Moderately amusing comedy with an excess of
complications.

w Phoebe and Henry Ephron, *play* Norman
Krasna d David Butler *ph* Peverell Marley
m David Buttolph

Ronald Reagan, Patricia Neal, Jack Carson,
Virginia Field

John Meade's Woman

US 1937 82m bw

A timber industrialist marries a farm girl.
Solemn star drama. Edward Arnold, Francine
Larrimore, Gail Patrick, George Bancroft.
Written by Vincent Lawrence and Herman J.
Mankiewicz; directed by Richard Wallace; for
Paramount. 'One more picture with a
message. Edward Arnold's pictures are
beginning to look alike.'—*Variety*

John Paul Jones

US 1959 126m Technirama
Warner / Samuel Bronston

At the time of the American revolution a
young Scotsman rises to great heights in the
American navy.
Fragmented biopic with a succession of guest
stars which turn it into a charade almost as
silly as *The Story of Mankind*. On that level it
is not unentertaining.

wd John Farrow *ph* Michel Kelber *m* Max
Steiner

Robert Stack, Charles Coburn (as Benjamin
Franklin), Bette Davis (as Catherine the
Great), Marisa Pavan, Jean-Pierre Aumont,
Peter Cushing, Bruce Cabot, Macdonald
Carey

Johnny Allegro*

US 1949 81m bw
Columbia (Irving Starr)
GB title: *Hounded*

A private eye eliminates a counterfeiter and
marries his wife.
Cheeky variation on the plot of *Gilda*, with
Macreedy repeating his role; later stages
borrow from *The Most Dangerous Game*. All
mildly diverting.

w Karen de Wolf, Guy Endore, James
Edward Grant d Ted Tetzlaff *ph* Joseph
Biroc *m* George Duning

George Raft, George Macready, Nina Foch,
Will Geer, Ivan Triesault

'Without any particular distinction, but
certainly not boring.'—*Richard Mallett, Punch*

Johnny Angel*

US 1945 79m bw
RKO (William L. Pereira)

A seaman solves the mystery of his father's
ship, found empty and adrift in the Gulf of
Mexico.
Very watchable mystery with plenty of plot
twists and efficient presentation.

w Steve Fisher d Edwin L. Marin *ph* Harry
J. Wild *m* Leigh Harline

George Raft, Claire Trevor, Signe Hasso,
Lowell Gilmore, Hoagy Carmichael, Marvin
Miller

Johnny Apollo*

US 1940 93m bw
TCF (Harry Joe Brown)

A well-heeled young man turns crook.
Moderate crime melo, impeccably turned out.

w Philip Dunne, Rowland Brown d Henry
Hathaway *ph* Arthur Miller *m* Cyril
Mockridge *md* Alfred Newman

Tyrone Power, Dorothy Lamour, Edward
Arnold, Lloyd Nolan, Charles Grapewin,
Lionel Atwill, Marc Lawrence, Jonathan Hale

'There was temptation in her helpless
    silence—and then torment!'

Johnny Belinda**

US 1948 103m bw
Warner (Jerry Wald)

In a remote fishing community, a deaf mute
girl is raped and the sympathetic local doctor is
suspected of being the father of her baby.
Melodrama of the old school which in 1948
seemed oddly to mark a new permissiveness
and made a big star out of Jane Wyman; the
production and locations were also persuasive.

w Irmgard Von Cube, Allen Vincent, *play*
Elmer Harris d Jean Negulesco *ph* Ted
McCord *m* Max Steiner *md* Leo F. Forbstein

Jane Wyman, Lew Ayres, Charles Bickford,
Agnes Moorehead, Stephen McNally, Jan
Sterling, Rosalind Ivan, Mabel Paige

'An atmosphere in which the hokey,
tearjerking elements are used for more than
mere pathos—an example of technique over
subject matter.'—*Pauline Kael, 70s*

AA: Jane Wyman
AAN: best picture; script; Jean Negulesco;
Ted McCord; Max Steiner; Lew Ayres;
Charles Bickford; Agnes Moorehead

Johnny Come Lately*

US 1943 97m bw
Cagney Productions (William Cagney)
GB title: *Johnny Vagabond*

A travelling newspaperman is jailed for
vagrancy in a small town and stays to expose
corrupt politicians.
A turn-of-the-century folksy drama seemed an
odd choice for a Cagney independent
production, and it was not very persuasively
made, but the star produced moments of his
old charisma.

w John Van Druten, *novel* McLeod's Folly by
Louis Bromfield d William K. Howard
ph Theodor Sparkuhl *m* Leigh Harline

James Cagney, Grace George, Marjorie Main,
Marjorie Lord, Hattie McDaniel, Edward
McNamara, Bill Henry, Robert Barrat,
George Cleveland, Margaret Hamilton,
Lucien Littlefield, Irving Bacon

'The kind of business that might result if
Jimmy Cagney, the immortal Hollywood
movie star, had returned to play the lead in
the annual production of his old high school's
Masque and Film Club.'—*John T. McManus*

'The film does show a fatal commercial
uneasiness and, I half suspect, radical loss or
atrophy of cinematic judgment. But . . . there
is a general ambience of hope and pleasure
about the production which, regrettably, loses
its glow.'—*James Agee*

AAN: Leigh Harline

Johnny Concho

US 1956 84m bw
UA / Kent (Frank Sinatra)

A coward runs Cripple Creek because he has a
gunfighter brother, but when the latter is shot
another gunman takes over.
Unexpected small-scale western, pleasantly
made but no *High Noon*.

w David P. Harmon, Don McGuire d Don
McGuire *ph* William Mellor *m* Nelson
Riddle

Frank Sinatra, *William Conrad*, Phyllis Kirk,
Wallace Ford, John Qualen

Johnny Cool*

US 1963 101m bw
UA / Chrislaw (William Asher)

A Sicilian bandit is sent to the US on a mission
of vengeance.
Chilling gangster thriller, the callousness of
which is apparently meant to be
counterpointed by the humorous cameo
appearances of several well-known faces. This
does not work.

w Joseph Landon, *novel* John McPartland
d William Asher *ph* Sam Leavitt *m* Billy
May

Henry Silva, Elizabeth Montgomery, Jim Backus, Marc Lawrence, John McGiver, Sammy Davis Jnr, Mort Sahl, Telly Savalas, Joseph Calleia, Robert Armstrong, Douglass Dumbrille, Elisha Cook Jnr

Johnny Dangerously
US 1984 90m De Luxe
TCF / Edgewood (Michael Hertzberg)

A boy takes up crime to pay for an operation for his ailing mother.
1930s gangster send-up which fails to register, and is filled with unnecessary excesses.

w Norman Steinberg, Bernie Kukoff, Harry Colomby, Jeff Harris d Amy Heckerling ph David M. Walsh m John Morris pd Joseph R. Jennings ed Pembroke J. Herring

Michael Keaton, Joe Piscopo, Marilu Henner, Maureen Stapleton, Peter Boyle, Griffin Dunne, Richard Dmitri, Glynnis O'Connor, Dom DeLuise, Ray Walston

Johnny Dark
US 1954 85m Technicolor
U-I (William Alland)

A motor company produces a new sports car designed by an employee, who drives it in a race.
Competent, unremarkable action melodrama tailor-made for its star.

w Franklin Coen d George Sherman ph Carl Guthrie m Joseph Gershenson

Tony Curtis, Piper Laurie, Don Taylor, Paul Kelly, Ilka Chase, Sidney Blackmer

Johnny Eager*
US 1942 107m bw
MGM (John W. Considine)

A gangster makes a play for a society girl.
Well-made, rather unattractive gangster melodrama.

w John Lee Mahin, James Edward Grant d Mervyn Le Roy ph Harold Rosson m Bronislau Kaper

Robert Taylor, Van Heflin, Lana Turner, Edward Arnold, Robert Sterling, Patricia Dane, Glenda Farrell, Henry O'Neill
'The flaming drama of a high-born beauty who blindly loved the most icy-hearted big shot gangland ever knew!'—publicity
AA: Van Heflin

Johnny Frenchman
GB 1945 111m bw
Ealing (S. C. Balcon)

Rivalry between the fishermen of Cornwall and Brittany prevents the course of true love from running smooth.
Rhubarbing extras and studio sets make this an unreal and disappointing Ealing melodrama, and all the actors look helpless.

w T. E. B. Clarke d Charles Frend ph Roy Kellino m Clifton Parker

Françoise Rosay, Tom Walls, Patricia Roc, Paul Dupuis, Ralph Michael, Frederick Piper, Arthur Hambling

Johnny Got His Gun
US 1971 111m colour
World Entertainments Ltd (Bruce Campbell)

In 1918 a soldier is so badly wounded as to lose arms, legs, eyes, ears, mouth and nose, and begs his doctors to kill him.
A horrifying and fascinating premise turns out to have nowhere to go, at least not in this talky treatment which the author has nurtured too long.

wd Dalton Trumbo ph Jules Brenner m Jerry Fielding

Timothy Bottoms, Jason Robards Jnr, Marsha Hunt, Donald Sutherland, Kathy Fields, Diane Varsi

Johnny Guitar*
US 1953 110m Trucolor
Republic (Nicholas Ray)

In old Arizona, the proprietress of a gambling saloon stakes a claim to valuable land and incurs the enmity of a lady banker.
Weird Freudian western notable for a running catfight between its lady protagonists; the title character is decidedly secondary. Not exactly a good movie, but memorable because it's almost always over the top.

w Philip Yordan, novel Roy Chanslor d Nicholas Ray ph Harry Stradling m Victor Young

Joan Crawford, Mercedes McCambridge, Sterling Hayden, Ernest Borgnine, Ward Bond, John Carradine, Scott Brady
'A very rum western, with cockeyed feminist attitudes.'—New Yorker, 1975
● Video: BBC

Johnny Holiday
US 1949 92m bw

A reform school boy becomes a goodie through devotion to his sergeant. Sentimental mush. William Bendix, Stanley Clements, Allen Martin Jnr, Herbert Newcomb, Hoagy Carmichael. Written by Jack Andrews, Willis Goldbeck and Frederick Stephani; directed by Willis Goldbeck; for R. W. Alcorn / United Artists.

Johnny Nobody
GB 1960 88m bw Warwickscope
Columbia / Viceroy (Irving Allen, Albert Broccoli)

A drunken Irish author challenges God to strike him dead for blasphemy. When an amnesiac shoots him, a nationwide religious controversy begins, but the deed is found to have a mercenary motive.
A mysterious rigmarole which irritates more than it entertains.

w Patrick Kirwan, story The Trial of Johnny Nobody by Albert Z. Carr d Nigel Patrick ph Ted Moore m Ron Goodwin

Nigel Patrick, Aldo Ray, Yvonne Mitchell, William Bendix, Cyril Cusack, Niall MacGinnis, Bernie Winters, Noel Purcell, Jimmy O'Dea

'The more one thinks of it, the more one is amazed that anyone should have thought a plot and players as uniformly unlikely as these could have worked out satisfactorily.'—Peter John Dyer, MFB

Johnny O'Clock
US 1946 95m bw

A gambler appears to be involved in the death of a crooked policeman, but a girl helps to clear him. Tawdry material made palatable by surface slickness. Dick Powell, Ellen Drew, Lee J. Cobb, Evelyn Keyes. Written and directed by Robert Rossen; photographed by Burnett Guffey; for Columbia.

Johnny One-Eye
US 1950 80m bw

Two gangsters out to get each other are led together by a small girl and a dog. Unpalatable mixture of violence and sentiment. Pat O'Brien, Wayne Morris, Dolores Moran, Gayle Reed. Written by Richard E. Landau, from a story by Damon Runyon; directed by Robert Florey; for Benedict Bogeaus / United Artists.

Johnny Rocco
US 1958 83m bw

The small son of a gangster is affected by his father's notoriety. Awful sentimental melodrama with tear-stained ending; for connoisseurs of cliché. Richard Eyer, Stephen McNally, Coleen Gray, Russ Conway. Written by James O'Hanlon and Samuel F. Roeca; directed by Paul Landres; for Allied Artists.

'Their bullets talked where law stopped!'
Johnny Stool Pigeon
US 1949 75m bw
U-I (Aaron Rosenberg)

A detective releases a convict on condition that he leads him to a drug smuggling gang. Competent low budget addition to the documentary police cycle.

w Robert L. Richards d William Castle ph Maury Gertsman m Milton Schwarzwald

Howard Duff, Shelley Winters, Dan Duryea, Gary Moore, Tony Curtis, John McIntire, Barry Kelley, Leif Erickson

Johnny Tremain
US 1957 81m Technicolor
Walt Disney

In 1773 Boston an apprentice silversmith joins the Sons of Liberty and helps start the War of Independence.
Schoolbook history with little vitality.

w Tom Blackburn, novel Esther Forbes d Robert Stevenson ph Charles B. Boyle m George Bruns

Hal Stalmaster, Luana Patten, Jeff York, Sebastian Cabot, Richard Beymer, Walter Sande

Johnny Trouble
US 1956 88m bw
Clarion (John H. Auer)

An elderly widow becomes involved with a

JOHNNY BELINDA.   Comfort for the blind Jane Wyman is offered by Lew Ayres. The violinist is not credited.

boys' college and thinks she has found her lost grandson.
Sentimental, whimsical star vehicle.

w Charles O'Neal, David Lord d John H. Auer ph Peverell Marley m Frank de Vol

Ethel Barrymore, Stuart Whitman, Cecil Kellaway, Carolyn Jones, Jesse White

The Johnstown Flood*

US 1926 70m approx (24 fps) bw
  silent
Fox

A construction worker is warned by his girl friend of an approaching flood, in which she dies.
Curious melodrama with mild spectacle.

w Efrid Bingham, Robert Lord d Irving Cummings

George O'Brien, Janet Gaynor (her first film), Paul Panzer, George Harris

The Joker Is Wild*

US 1957 126m bw Vistavision
Paramount / Charles Vidor

Joe E. Lewis, a twenties nightclub singer, loses his voice after an attack by gangsters, and becomes a comedian.
Reasonably lively showbiz biopic in jaundiced vein; good atmosphere but far too long.

w Oscar Saul, *book* Art Cohn d Charles Vidor ph Daniel L. Fapp m Walter Scharf

Frank Sinatra, Mitzi Gaynor, Eddie Albert, Jeanne Crain, Beverly Garland, Jackie Coogan, Ted de Corsia

AA: song 'All the Way' (*m* Jimmy Van Heusen, *ly* Sammy Cahn)

The Jokers**

GB 1967 126m Technicolor
Universal / Adastra / Gildor / Scimitar
  (Maurice Foster, Ben Arbeid)

Two young brothers in London society plan to create a sensation by borrowing (and replacing) the crown jewels.
Bright suspense comedy which sums up the swinging London era pretty well and is generally amusing though it finally lacks aplomb.

w Dick Clement, Ian La Frenais d Michael Winner ph Ken Hodges m Johnny Pearson

Michael Crawford, Oliver Reed, Harry Andrews, *James Donald*, Daniel Massey, Michael Hordern, Gabriella Licudi, Frank Finlay, Warren Mitchell, Rachel Kempson, Peter Graves

A Jolly Bad Fellow*

GB 1964 95m bw
British Lion / Pax / Tower / Michael Balcon
  (Donald Taylor)
US title: *They All Died Laughing*

A brash chemistry don tries a new poison on his enemies.
Interesting but finally irritating comedy of murders with a punnish rather than a donnish script and only moments of genuine sub-Ealing hilarity.

w Robert Hamer, Donald Taylor, *novel* Don Among the Dead Men by C. E. Vulliamy d Robert Hamer ph Gerald Gibbs m John Barry

Leo McKern, Janet Munro, Maxine Audley, Duncan Macrae, Dennis Price, Miles Malleson, Leonard Rossiter

Jolson Sings Again**

US 1949 96m Technicolor
Columbia (Sidney Buchman)

Al Jolson's later career and second marriage to a nurse he met while entertaining troops in World War II.
Breezy, routine, rather empty sequel to the following.

w Sidney Buchman d Henry Levin ph William Snyder md Morris Stoloff, George Duning

Larry Parks, Barbara Hale, William Demarest, Ludwig Donath, Bill Goodwin, Tamara Shayne, Myron McCormick

AAN: Sidney Buchman; William Snyder; Morris Stoloff, George Duning

The Jolson Story****

US 1946 129m Technicolor
Columbia (Sidney Skolsky)

Asa Yoelson, son of a cantor, becomes Al Jolson, the great entertainer of the twenties; but showbiz success brings marital difficulties.
Whitewashed biopic in impeccable Hollywood style, with everything working shamelessly right, a new star in the leading role, perfect if unambitious production values, and a deluge of the best songs ever written.

w Stephen Longstreet d Alfred E. Green, Joseph H. Lewis ph Joseph Walker md Morris Stoloff

Larry Parks (using Jolson's own voice), *William Demarest, Evelyn Keyes, Ludwig Donath, Tamara Shayne*, Bill Goodwin, *Scotty Beckett*, John Alexander
  'I have nothing in the world against this picture except that at least half of it seemed to me enormously tiresome.'—*James Agee*

AA: Morris Stoloff
AAN: Joseph Walker; Larry Parks; William Demarest

'Everyone's book is now everyone's
  motion picture!'

Jonathan Livingston Seagull

US 1973 114m De Luxe Panavision
Paramount / JLS Partnership / Hall Bartlett

The life of a seagull who aims to fly faster than any of his peers and eventually arrives in a perfect world.

Weird 'family' fantasy based on a
phenomenally successful book which clearly
could not translate easily to the screen. The
bird photography is much more successful than
the mysticism.

w Richard Bach, from his book d Hall
Bartlett ph Jack Couffer m Neil Diamond,
Lee Holdridge ph Boris Leven

'A parable couched in the form of a nature
film of overpowering beauty and strength in
which, perhaps to our horror, we are forced to
recognize ourselves in a seagull obsessed with
the heights.'—Michael Korda

'It may be that the creature best qualified to
review it is another seagull.'—Benny Green,
Punch

'If one must spend two hours following the
adventures of a bird, far better that the hero
be Donald Duck.'—Jay Cocks, Time

'The sort of garbage that only a seagull
could love.'—Judith Crist

AAN: Jack Couffer

● Video: CIC

The Jones Family

Less human, more farcical than the Hardy
films (qv), this series was TCF's second feature
answer to MGM's money-makers, and pleased
a lot of people at the time. Pop was Jed
Prouty, Mom was Spring Byington, Grandma
was Florence Roberts, and the youngsters
included Kenneth Howell, George Ernest,
Billy Mahan, June Carlson and June Lang.
The first script was from a play by Katharine
Cavanaugh, and the principal director was
Frank Strayer.

1936: EVERY SATURDAY NIGHT,
EDUCATING FATHER, BACK TO
NATURE
1937: OFF TO THE RACES, BORROWING
TROUBLE, HOT WATER
1938: LOVE ON A BUDGET, TRIP TO
PARIS, SAFETY IN NUMBERS, DOWN
ON THE FARM
1939: EVERYBODY'S BABY, QUICK
MILLIONS, THE JONES FAMILY IN
HOLLYWOOD, TOO BUSY TO WORK
1940: ON THEIR OWN

† An earlier series with different actors was
abandoned after two episodes: Young as You
Feel (1931), Business and Pleasure (1932).

Joseph Andrews

GB 1977 104m Eastmancolor
UA / Woodfall (Neil Hartley)

Adventures of a naïve 18th-century footman.
Woebegone attempt to restage Tom Jones.

w Allan Scott, Chris Bryant d Tony
Richardson ph David Watkin m John
Addison pd Michael Annals

Peter Firth, Ann-Margret, Michael Hordern,
Beryl Reid, Jim Dale, Peter Bull, John
Gielgud, Hugh Griffith, Timothy West,
Wendy Craig, Peggy Ashcroft, James Villiers,
Karen Dotrice, Ronald Pickup

'Even the incidental pleasures cannot offset
the sense of déjà vu which pervades this musty
enterprise.'—John Pym, MFB

'The epic love story in which everybody has
a great role and a big part.'—publicity

Josephine and Men

GB 1955 98m Eastmancolor
Charter (John and Roy Boulting)

The three romances of a determined young
woman.
Alarmingly thin, old-fashioned romantic
comedy with all resolved in a country cottage.
Nothing quite works, especially the colour.

w Nigel Balchin, Roy Boulting, Frank Harvey
d Roy Boulting ph Gilbert Taylor m John
Addison

Glynis Johns, Jack Buchanan, Donald Sinden,
Peter Finch, Heather Thatcher, Ronald Squire

Josette

US 1938 73m bw
TCF (Gene Markey)

A New Orleans coquette teases two men.
Very minor musical, well enough presented
but adding up to almost nothing.

w James Edward Grant d Allan Dwan
ph John Mescall songs Harry Revel, Mack
Gordon

Simone Simon, Don Ameche, Robert Young,
Joan Davis, Bert Lahr, Paul Hurst, William
Collier Snr, Lynn Bari, William Demarest

'Rollicking farce with music . . . a corking
good entertainment.'—Variety

Jour de Fête***

France 1948 87m bw
Francinex (Fred Drain)

A village postman sees a film about the
efficiency of the American postal service and
decides to smarten himself up.
First, and some say best, of Tati's comedy
vehicles: two-thirds superb local colour, one-
third hilarious slapstick.

w Jacques Tati, Henri Marquet d Jacques
Tati ph Jacques Mercanton m Jean Yatove

Jacques Tati, Guy Decomble, Paul Fankeur,
Santa Relli

† A reissue version had colour items hand-
painted in each frame, and proved quite
effective.

● Video: Video Media

Le Jour Se Lève***

France 1939 95m bw
Sigma
aka: Daybreak

A murderer is besieged by police in his attic
room, remembers his past through the night,
and shoots himself.
A model of French poetic realism, and a
much-praised film which was almost destroyed
when it was bought for an American remake
(The Long Night).

w Jacques Viot, Jacques Prévert d Marcel
Carné ph Curt Courant, Philippe Agostini,
André Bac m Maurice Jaubert ad Alexander
Trauner

Jean Gabin, Jules Berry, Arletty, Jacqueline
Laurent

'The man walks about his room, moves a
few things, lies on his bed, looks out of the
window, chain-smokes . . . and one is
genuinely interested in him all the time

(remembering afterwards that there exist
directors who contrive to be boring even when
they use fifteen characters in a motor car chase
crackling with revolver shots).'—Richard
Mallett, Punch

● Video: Palace

Journal of a Crime

US 1934 65m bw

A woman shoots her husband's mistress and
gets amnesia before she can confess.
Melodramatic farrago which entertains by its
very excesses. Ruth Chatterton, Adolphe
Menjou, Claire Dodd, Douglass Dumbrille,
George Barbier. Written by F. Hugh Herbert
and Charles Kenyon from the play by Jacques
Deval; directed by William Keighley; for
Warner. 'High in sympathetic interest and
force.'—Variety

The Journey

US 1959 125m Technicolor
MGM / Alby (Anatole Litvak)

During the 1956 Hungarian uprising, a busload
of international passengers is detained
overnight by a Russian major.
Pretentious, predictable and dull multi-
melodrama peopled by uninteresting
characters; different handling might have
made a Casablanca of it.

w George Tabori d Anatole Litvak ph Jack
Hildyard m Georges Auric

Yul Brynner, Deborah Kerr, Jason Robards
Jnr, Anouk Aimée, Robert Morley, E. G.
Marshall, Anne Jackson, David Kossoff, Kurt
Kasznar, Gerard Oury

'Ten minutes of this and we know where we
are: we are back in the 1930s with Alfred
Hitchcock and that glamorous band of
international characters trapped in
Mitteleuropa.'—Steven Marcus

Journey for Margaret*

US 1942 81m bw
MGM (B. P. Fineman)

An American correspondent brings home an
orphan from the London blitz.
Efficient tearful propaganda which
coincidentally made a star of little Margaret
O'Brien.

w David Hertz, William Ludwig, book
William L. White d W. S. Van Dyke ph Ray
June m Franz Waxman

Robert Young, Laraine Day, Margaret
O'Brien, Billy Severn, Fay Bainter, Signe
Hasso, Nigel Bruce, Halliwell Hobbes

Journey into Autumn*

Sweden 1954 86m bw
Sandrews (Rune Waldekrantz)
original title: Kvinnodrom

Two business women visiting Gothenburg
have difficult relationships to settle.
Moody, impressionistic sex drama which
succeeds by fits and starts.

wd Ingmar Bergman ph Hilding Bladh

Eva Dahlbeck, Harriet Andersson, Gunnar
Bjornstrand, Ulf Palme, Inga Landgre, Naima
Wifstrand

'Scenes of austere anti-romanticism and
painful irony.'—*Peter John Dyer, MFB*

Journey into Fear*
US 1942   71m   bw
RKO (Orson Welles)

A munitions expert finds himself in danger
from assassins in Istanbul, and has to be
smuggled home.
Highly enjoyable impressionist melodrama
supervised by Orson Welles and full of his
touches and excesses.

*w Joseph Cotten, Orson Welles, novel Eric
Ambler   d Norman Foster* (and *Orson Welles*)
ph Karl Struss   m Constantin Bakaleinikoff
Joseph Cotten, Dolores del Rio, Jack Moss,
Orson Welles, Ruth Warrick, Agnes
Moorehead
   'Brilliant atmosphere, the nightmare of
pursuit, eccentric encounters on the way, and
when the shock comes it leaps at eye and
ear.'—*William Whitebait*
† A 1976 remake, much heralded, was for
obscure legal reasons hardly seen. Directed by
Daniel Mann for New World, it starred Zero
Mostel, Shelley Winters, Stanley Holloway,
Vincent Price, Donald Pleasence, Sam
Waterston, Joseph Wiseman, Scott Marlowe
and Yvette Mimieux.

Journey into Light
US 1951   87m   bw
TCF / Joseph Bernhard

A minister loses his faith, becomes a derelict,
and is reformed by a blind girl.
An old-fashioned tract in pictures. Has to be
seen to be believed, but quite nicely made.
Sterling Hayden, Viveca Lindfors, Thomas
Mitchell, H. B. Warner, Ludwig Donath, Jane
Darwell, Charles Evans
   'Slow, inept, and often extremely
embarrassing.'—*MFB*

Journey to Shiloh
US 1966   101m   Techniscope

Seven young Texans leave home to fight in the
Civil War. Episodic western which failed in its
ambition to reach epic stature. James Caan,
Michael Sarrazin, Brenda Scott, Paul
Petersen, Don Stroud, Michael Burns,
Michael Vincent, Harrison Ford, John
Doucette, Noah Beery Jnr. Written by Gene
Coon, from the novel *Fields of Honour* by
Will Henry; directed by William Hale; for
Universal.

Journey to the Center of the Earth*
US 1959   132m   De Luxe   Cinemascope
TCF (Charles Brackett)

An Edinburgh professor and assorted
colleagues follow an explorer's trail down an
extinct Icelandic volcano to the earth's centre.
Enjoyable hokum which gets more and more
fantastic but only occasionally misses its
footing; it ends splendidly with the team being
catapulted out of Stromboli on a tide of lava.

w Walter Reisch, Charles Brackett, novel Jules
Verne   *d Henry Levin   ph* Leo Tover
m Bernard Herrmann   ad Lyle R. Wheeler,
Franz Bachelin, Herman A. Blumenthal

JOURNEY INTO FEAR.   One of the most entertaining films that Orson Welles didn't quite
direct.

James Mason, Arlene Dahl, Pat Boone, Peter Ronson, Diane Baker, Thayer David

'The attraction of a Jules Verne fantasy . . . is in the endearing contrast between the wildest adventures and the staidest Victorian propriety on the part of those undergoing them . . . There is about the whole film a good-natured enjoyment of its own excesses.'—*Penelope Houston*

Journey to the Far Side of the Sun*
GB 1969 99m De Luxe Cinemascope
Universal / Century 21 Productions (Gerry Anderson)
Alternative title: *Doppelgänger*

An astronaut on a mission to a hitherto undetected planet discovers it to be an exact duplicate of Earth, and his own double returns in his place.
Intriguing, impeccably produced, but rather dull science fiction.

w Gerry and Sylvia Anderson, Donald James *d* Robert Parrish *ph* John Read *m* Barry Gray *sp* Harry Oakes *models* Derek Meddings

Ian Hendry, Roy Thinnes, Patrick Wymark, Lynn Loring, Herbert Lom, George Sewell, Ed Bishop

Journey Together*
GB 1944 95m bw
RAF Film Unit

Trainee pilots receive instruction in England and America before going on their first bombing mission.
Modest wartime semi-documentary, pleasingly done.

w Terence Rattigan *d* John Boulting *ph* Harry Waxman *m* Gordon Jacob *pd* John Howell

Richard Attenborough, Jack Watling, David Tomlinson, Edward G. Robinson, Hugh Wakefield, Sebastian Shaw, Ronald Adam, Bessie Love

Journey's End*
GB-US 1930 120m bw
Gainsborough / Welsh-Pearson / Tiffany-Stahl (George Pearson)

France 1917: personal tensions mount as men die in the trenches.
Primitive early sound version (made in Hollywood because of better equipment) of a justly celebrated play first performed a year earlier. Cinematically uninteresting, with acting generally over the top, but it kept Whale and Clive in Hollywood where they shortly collaborated on *Frankenstein*.

w Joseph Moncure March, Gareth Gundrey, *play* R. C. Sheriff *d* James Whale *ph* Benjamin Kline

Colin Clive, Ian MacLaren, David Manners, Billy Bevan, Anthony Bushell, Robert Adair
'No crystal gazing required to forecast a big measure of success.'—*Variety*
'It has been transferred to the screen with the greatest possible tact and discretion.'—*James Agate*

'Hollywood has produced its first sex-appeal-less film. Mr George Pearson is to be congratulated on his restraint.'—*Punch*
'Almost painfully English . . . I cannot believe that the strangulated emotions which resulted can have meant much to audiences outside the English-speaking world.'—*Basil Wright, 1972*
† NB: The first Anglo-American co-production.

Joy House
US 1964 98m colour Transcope

The husband of a wealthy American woman in France tries to kill her boy friend. Weird hothouse drama, an unsuccessful attempt to combine French and American styles. Jane Fonda, Alain Delon, Lola Albright. Written by René Clément, Pascal Jardin and Charles Williams; directed by René Clément; for Jacques Bar / MGM. (Aka: *The Love Cage*.)

Joy in the Morning
US 1965 103m Metrocolor
MGM (Henry T. Weinstein)

Early episodes in the marriage of a poor teenage student.
Glutinous romantic drama, quite well made.

w Sally Benson, Alfred Hayes, Norman Lessing, *novel* Betty Smith *d* Alex Segal *ph* Ellsworth Fredericks *m* Bernard Herrmann

Richard Chamberlain, Yvette Mimieux, Arthur Kennedy, Oscar Homolka, Joan Tetzel, Sidney Blackmer

Joy of Living*
US 1938 90m bw
RKO (Felix Young)

A practical-minded Broadway songstress succumbs to the charms of an aristocratic freewheeler.
Zany romantic comedy, not quite zippy enough to make one forget its irritating archness, but socio-historically very interesting, in the mould of *You Can't Take It with You*.

w Gene Towne, Allan Scott, Graham Baker *d* Tay Garnett *ph* Joseph Walker *md* Frank Tours *songs* Jerome Kern, Dorothy Fields

Irene Dunne, Douglas Fairbanks Jnr, Alice Brady, Guy Kibbee, Lucille Ball, Eric Blore, Jean Dixon, Warren Hymer, Billy Gilbert
'Fair farce . . . bereft of sufficient novelty or comedy plot to sustain itself through an hour and a half of gags.'—*Variety*

Joyless Street*
Germany 1925 139m (24 fps) bw silent
Sofar Film
original title: *Die Freudlose Gasse*

Problems of the inhabitants of a street in Vienna after World War I.
Realistic but studio-set melodrama which brought its director and Greta Garbo to international fame. In itself the film begins by stimulating and ends by boring.

w Willy Haas, *novel* Hugo Bettauer *d* G. W. Pabst *ph* Guido Seeber, Curt Oertel, Robert Lach

Asta Nielsen, Werner Krauss, *Greta Garbo*, Valeska Gert, Agnes Esterhazy
'Moments of searing pain, of mental anguish, of sheer unblemished beauty.'—*Paul Rotha, The Film Till Now*

'See it now! Remember it always!'
'A story so momentous it required six Academy Award stars and a cast of 1,186 players!'

Juarez**
US 1939 132m bw
Warner (Hal. B. Wallis, Henry Blanke)

A revolutionary leader causes the downfall of Emperor Maximilian of Mexico.
Spectacular historical drama with many fine moments which do not quite coalesce into a dramatic whole, chiefly owing to the lack of a single viewpoint.

w John Huston, Wolfgang Reinhardt, Aeneas Mackenzie *d* William Dieterle *ph* Tony Gaudio *m* Erich Wolfgang Korngold

Brian Aherne, Bette Davis, Paul Muni, Claude Rains, John Garfield, Donald Crisp, Gale Sondergaard, Joseph Calleia, Gilbert Roland, Henry O'Neill, Pedro de Cordoba, Montagu Love, Harry Davenport
'With such potent box office values, its success at theatres seems assured.'—*Variety*
'A million dollars' worth of ballroom sets, regimentals, gauze shots and whiskers.'—*Otis Ferguson*
'Dramatically by far the most effective of Warners' biographical films of the thirties.'—*Graham Greene*
'Muni's big-star solemn righteousness is like a dose of medicine.'—*New Yorker, 1977*
† Based vaguely on two novels: *The Phantom Crown* by Bertita Harding, and *Maximilian and Carlotta* by Franz Werfel.
†† According to Brian Aherne the film was to have been called *The Phantom Crown*, but Muni's contract enabled him to insist that the name of his character should appear in the title.
AAN: Brian Aherne

Jubal
US 1955 101m Technicolor
Cinemascope
Columbia (William Fadiman)

A rancher's wife causes trouble when she falls in love with a wandering cowhand.
Solid sex western, moderately interestingly done.

w Russell S. Hughes, Delmer Daves, *novel* Jubal Troop by Paul Wellman *d* Delmer Daves *ph* Charles Lawton *m* David Raksin

Glenn Ford, Ernest Borgnine, Felicia Farr, Rod Steiger, Valerie French, Charles Bronson, Noah Beery Jnr

Jubilee*
GB 1978   104m   colour
Whaley-Malin / Megalovision

Queen Elizabeth I is transported by her
astrologer into the latter part of the 20th
century, and is appalled by what she sees.
Outrageous dissection of modern urban life,
full of black jokes: it has the right attitudes but
is not free of a determination to shock at all
costs.

w Derek Jarman and others d Derek Jarman
ph Peter Middleton m Brian Eno

Jenny Runacre, Little Nell, Toyah Willcox,
Jordan, Hermine Demoriane
    'One of the most intelligent and interesting
films to be made in Britain in a long time.'—
Scott Meek, MFB

Jubilee Trail*
US 1954   103m   Trucolor
Republic (Joseph Kane)

Jealousy and murder by covered wagon en
route from New Orleans to the California gold
fields.
Bumpy adventure melodrama, generally quite
entertaining.

w Bruce Manning, novel Gwen Bristow
d Joseph Kane ph Jack Marta m Victor
Young

Vera Hruba Ralston, Forrest Tucker, Joan
Leslie, Pat O'Brien, John Russell, Ray
Middleton

Judex**
France 1916   12 episodes totalling 5 hours
    approx   bw   silent
Gaumont

A Robin Hood type crimefighter destroys the
empire of an evil banker.
Stylishly enjoyable serial from the maker of
Les Vampires and Fantômas.

w Arthur Bernade, Louis Feuillade d Louis
Feuillade

René Creste, Musidora, Yvette Andreyor,
Louis Leubas
† Another Judex serial was made in 1917, and
in 1933 came a feature version directed by
Maurice Champreux, with René Ferte. In 1963
Georges Franju directed another feature
remake with Channing Pollock, and this was
extremely well received.

Judge Priest*
US 1934   79m   bw

A political judge sees fair play through a
criminal case. Mainly effective star vehicle.
Will Rogers, Tom Brown, Anita Louise,
Henry B. Walthall, David Landau, Rochelle
Hudson. Written by Dudley Nichols, Lamar
Trotti, from the stories by Irvin S. Cobb;
directed by John Ford; for Fox. 'A great part
for Will Rogers and a box office bet.'—Variety

The Judge Steps Out*
US 1947   91m   bw
RKO
GB title: Indian Summer

A middle-aged judge leaves his wife and sets
off on an aimless journey in the course of

which he falls in love with a café proprietress.
A pleasing human story, simply told in a
manner which at the time seemed more
French than American.

w Boris Ingster, Alexander Knox d Boris
Ingster ph Robert de Grasse m Constantin
Bakaleinikoff

Alexander Knox, Ann Sothern, George
Tobias, Sharyn Moffett

'The things you'll see and the things you'll
feel are the things that will be part of you
as long as you live!'

Judgment at Nuremberg**
US 1961   190m   bw
UA / Roxlom (Stanley Kramer)

A fictionalized version of the 1948 trial of the
Nazi leaders for crimes against humanity.
Interminable, heavy-going dramatic
documentary expanded from a succinct TV
play into a courtroom marathon with
philosophical asides. All good stuff, but too
much of it.

w Abby Mann, from his play d Stanley
Kramer ph Ernest Laszlo m Ernest Gold
pd Rudolph Sternad

Spencer Tracy, Marlene Dietrich, Burt
Lancaster, Richard Widmark, Maximilian
Schell, Judy Garland, Montgomery Clift,
William Shatner, Edward Binns, Werner
Klemperer, Torben Meyer, Alan Baxter, Ray
Teal
    'Some believe that by tackling such themes
Kramer earns at least partial remission from
criticism. How much? 20 per cent off for
effort?'—Stanley Kauffmann
† Burt Lancaster replaced Laurence Olivier,
who was originally cast.

AA: Abby Mann; Maximilian Schell
AAN: best picture; Stanley Kramer; Ernest
Laszlo; Spencer Tracy; Judy Garland;
Montgomery Clift

Judgment Deferred
GB 1951   88m   bw
Group Three (John Baxter)

A collection of Dorset eccentrics brings to
book the head of a dope smuggling ring who
has framed one of their associates.
An unusual story can't compensate for stagey
handling in this first disappointing production
of a company set up by the National Film
Finance Corporation to make low budget films
with top talent.

w Geoffrey Orme, Barbara Emary, Walter
Meade d John Baxter ph Arthur Grant

Hugh Sinclair, Helen Shingler, Abraham
Sodaer, Leslie Dwyer, Joan Collins, Harry
Locke, Elwyn Brook Jones, Bransby Williams,
Maire O'Neill, Harry Welchman

Judith
US 1965   109m   Technicolor
Panavision
Paramount / Cumulus / Command (Kurt
Unger)

In 1947 Israel, loyalists rescue the wife of an
escaped war criminal and ask her to identify
him, but she takes her own revenge.
Glowering kibbutz adventures, well enough

made but adding up to neither one thing nor
the other, and rather confusing to non-Jews.

w Jon Michael Hayes, story Lawrence Durrell
d Daniel Mann ph John Wilcox m Sol
Kaplan pd Wilfrid Shingleton

Sophia Loren, Peter Finch, Jack Hawkins,
Hans Verner, André Morell

Judith of Bethulia
US 1913   42m (24 fps)   bw   silent
D. W. Griffith for Biograph

A widow in a city attacked by the Assyrians
courts their leader and beheads him.
Semi-biblical melodrama in Griffith's most
Victorian style.

w Frank Woods d D. W. Griffith ph Billy
Bitzer

Blanche Sweet, Henry B. Walthall, Lillian
Gish, Dorothy Gish, Lionel Barrymore, Mae
Marsh, Robert Harron

Juggernaut
GB 1937   64m   bw
Ambassador

A scientist lacking funds for his experiments
agrees to commit murder.
Tedious melodrama which wastes Karloff's
time.

w Cyril Campion, H. Fowler Mear, H.
Fraenkel d Henry Edwards ph Sidney Blythe

Boris Karloff, Mona Goya, Joan Wyndham,
Arthur Margetson, Arthur Ireland, Morton
Selten
    'It gets into motion slowly and reaches the
meat of the plot after numerous
distractions.'—Variety

Juggernaut**
GB 1974   110m   De Luxe   Panavision
United Artists / David E. Picker (Richard
Alan Simmons)

A transatlantic liner is threatened by a mad
bomber.
Elaborate suspense spectacular, most of which
works pretty well.

w Richard Alan Simmons d Richard Lester
ph Gerry Fisher m Ken Thorne pd Terence
Marsh

Richard Harris, David Hemmings, Omar
Sharif, Anthony Hopkins, Ian Holm, Shirley
Knight, Roy Kinnear, Cyril Cusack, Freddie
Jones
    'However unoriginal its basic ingredients, it
hardly ever slackens its pace or diverts
attention from its central premise.'—Jonathan
Rosenbaum
    'Jaunty, cynical slapstick.'—New Yorker

The Juggler
US 1953   88m   bw
Columbia / Stanley Kramer

A Jewish refugee in Palestine has a horror of
being imprisoned, and runs away from a
transit camp with a small wandering boy.
Well-meaning cheapie, a curiously aimless
topical drama which fails to make any of its
several points.

w Michael Blankfort, from his novel
d Edward Dmytryk *ph* Roy Hunt *m* Georges
Antheil

Kirk Douglas, Milly Vitale, Paul Stewart, Joey
Walsh

Juke Girl
US 1942 90m bw
Warner (Jack Saper, Jerry Wald)

Fruit workers in Florida get involved in
murder.
Hokum melodrama with all concerned
treading water.

w A. I. Bezzerides, *novel* Theodore Pratt
d Curtis Bernhardt *ph* Bert Glennon
m Adolph Deutsch

Ann Sheridan, Ronald Reagan, Richard
Whorf, Gene Lockhart, Faye Emerson,
George Tobias, Alan Hale, Howard da Silva,
Donald McBride, Fuzzy Knight, Willie Best

Jules et Jim***
France 1962 105m bw Franscope
Films du Carrosse / SEDIF (Marcel Berbert)

Before World War I, in Paris, a girl alternates
between a French and a German student, and
after the war they meet again to form a
constantly shifting triangle.
The plot bores before the end, but the
treatment is consistently interesting and the
acting almost equally so.

w François Truffaut, Jean Gruault,
novel Henri-Pierre Roche *d* François
Truffaut *ph* Raoul Coutard *m* Georges
Delerue

Oskar Werner, Jeanne Moreau, Henri Serre
'The sense is of a director intoxicated with
the pleasure of making films.'—*Penelope
Houston, MFB*

Julia***
US 1977 117m Technicolor
TCF (Julien Derode)

Lillian Hellman reflects on the fortunes of her
friend Julia, filled with enthusiasm for
European causes and finally killed by the
Nazis.
Thoughtful, elegant patchwork of thirties
memories, a vehicle for actors and a subtle,
self-effacing director.

w Alvin Sargent, *book* Pentimento by Lillian
Hellman *d* Fred Zinnemann *ph* Douglas
Slocombe *m* Georges Delerue *ph* Carmen
Dillon, Gene Callahan, Willy Holt

Jane Fonda, Vanessa Redgrave, Jason
Robards Jnr, Maximilian Schell, Hal
Holbrook, Rosemary Murphy, Cathleen
Nesbitt, Maurice Denham
'After a while it becomes apparent that
Zinnemann and Sargent are trafficking in too
many quotations and flashbacks because they
can't find the core of the material.'—*Pauline
Kael*

AA: script; Vanessa Redgrave; Jason Robards
Jnr
AAN: best picture; Fred Zinnemann; Douglas
Slocombe; Georges Delerue; Jane Fonda;
Maximilian Schell
● *Video: CBS / Fox*

Julia Misbehaves
US 1948 99m bw
MGM (Everett Riskin)

An actress returns to her stuffy husband when
her daughter is about to marry.
Desperate attempt to find a vehicle for a
fading star team.

w William Ludwig, Arthur Wimperis, Harry
Ruskin, *novel* The Nutmeg Tree by Margery
Sharp *d* Jack Conway *ph* Joseph Ruttenberg
m Adolph Deutsch

Greer Garson, Walter Pidgeon, Elizabeth
Taylor, Peter Lawford, Cesar Romero, Lucile
Watson, Nigel Bruce, Mary Boland, Reginald
Owen, Ian Wolfe, Edmund Breon, Fritz Feld,
Aubrey Mather, Henry Stephenson

Julie*
US 1956 97m bw
MGM / Arwin (Marty Melcher)

A concert pianist plans to murder his wife.
Wildly improbable but entertaining suspenser
in which the lady finally has to assume control
of an airplane.

wd Andrew Stone *ph* Fred Jackman Jnr
m Leith Stevens

Doris Day, Louis Jourdan, Barry Sullivan,
Frank Lovejoy, John Gallaudet
'Some of the dialogue reaches a fine pitch of
banality.'—*MFB*

AAN: Andrew Stone (as writer); title song
(*m* Leith Stevens, *ly* Tom Adair)

Juliet of the Spirits*
Italy / France 1965 145m Technicolor
Federiz / Francoriz (Clemente Fracassi)
original title: *Giulietta degli Spiriti*

A bored middle-aged woman finds she can
conjure up spirits who lead her into a life of
sensual gratification.
A fascinating patchwork of autobiographical
flashbacks, the distaff side of *Eight and a Half*.

w Federico Fellini, Tullio Pinnelli, Brunello
Rondi, Ennio Flaiano *d* Federico Fellini
ph Gianni di Venanzo *m* Nino Rota

Giulietta Masina, Mario Pisu, Sandra Milo,
Valentina Cortese, Sylva Koscina
'A kaleidoscope of fantasy, a series of
cerebral inventions, of which only a few are
artistically justified . . . an extravagant
illusion, a huge confidence trick, with little
new to say and an often pedantic way of saying
it.'—*David Wilson, MFB*

'Greater than *Ivanhoe*!'
Julius Caesar***
US 1953 121m bw
MGM (John Houseman)

Cassius and Brutus lead the conspirators who
murder Caesar, but are themselves routed by
Mark Antony.
Straightforward, rather leaden presentation of
Shakespeare's play, lit by effective moments in
the acting, but the sudden change from talk to
battle is not smoothed over.

wd Joseph L. Mankiewicz *ph* Joseph
Ruttenberg *m* Miklos Rozsa *ad* Cedric
Gibbons, Edward Carfagno

John Gielgud, James Mason, Marlon Brando,
Greer Garson, Deborah Kerr, Louis Calhern,
Edmond O'Brien, George Macready, Michael
Pate, John Hoyt, Alan Napier
'Thrill to ruthless men and their goddess-
like women in a sin-swept age!'—*publicity*
'Thrill to traitors and heroes, killings and
conspiracies, passions and violence in Rome's
most exciting age!'—*publicity*

AAN: best picture; Joseph Ruttenberg;
Miklos Rozsa; Marlon Brando

Julius Caesar
GB 1969 116m Technicolor
Panavision
Commonwealth United (Peter Snell)

Elementary production with a surprising
number of faults and very few merits.

w Robert Furnival *d* Stuart Burge *ph* Ken
Higgins *m* Michael Lewis *pd* Julia Trevelyan
Oman

Richard Johnson, Jason Robards Jnr, *John
Gielgud*, Charlton Heston, Robert Vaughn,
Richard Chamberlain, Diana Rigg, Jill
Bennett, Christopher Lee, Alan Browning,
Andrew Crawford

AAN: Michael Lewis

Jumbo*
US 1962 124m Metrocolor Panavision
MGM (Joe Pasternak, Martin Melcher)
aka: *Billy Rose's Jumbo*

In 1910, the daughter of the owner of a shaky
circus prevents a take-over bid.
Hoary circus story with music. General effect
disappointing: the elephant steals the show.

w Sidney Sheldon, *play* Ben Hecht, Charles
MacArthur *d* Charles Walters *ph* William H.
Daniels *m* / *ly* Richard Rodgers, Lorenz
Hart *md* George Stoll *ch* Busby Berkeley

Doris Day, Jimmy Durante, Stephen Boyd,
Martha Raye, Dean Jagger

AAN: George Stoll

Jump for Glory
GB 1937 89m bw
Criterion (Douglas Fairbanks Jnr, Marcel
Hellman)
US title: *When Thief Meets Thief*

Adventures of a cat burglar who accidentally
kills his ex-partner.
Curious star comedy drama with pleasing
scenes.

w John Meehan Jnr, Harold French,
novel Gordon MacDonnell *d* Raoul Walsh
ph Cedric Williams

Douglas Fairbanks Jnr, Valerie Hobson, Alan
Hale, Edward Rigby, Barbara Everest, Jack
Melford, Anthony Ireland
'Starts off at a commendable pace but
doesn't carry through.'—*Variety*

Jump into Hell
US 1955 93m bw
Warner (David Weisbart)

Paratroops relieve a fort in Indo-China.
Mediocre semi-documentary war heroics.

w Irving Wallace *d* David Butler *ph* Peverell Marley *m* David Buttolph

Jacques Sernas, Kurt Kasznar, Arnold Moss, Peter Van Eyck, Pat Blake

Jumping for Joy
GB 1955 88m bw
Rank / Raymond Stross

A track attendant acquires a winning greyhound and exposes a group of crooks.
Totally predictable star comedy which needs livening up.

w Jack Davies, Henry E. Blyth *d* John Paddy Carstairs *ph* Jack Cox *m* Larry Adler

Frankie Howerd, Stanley Holloway, A. E. Matthews, Tony Wright, Alfie Bass, Joan Hickson, Lionel Jeffries

Jumping Jacks*
US 1952 96m bw
Paramount / Hal B. Wallis

Two cabaret comedians join the paratroops.
Standard star farce, one of Martin and Lewis' best.

w Robert Lees, Fred Rinaldo, Herbert Baker *d* Norman Taurog *ph* Daniel L. Fapp *m* Joseph J. Lilley

Dean Martin, *Jerry Lewis*, Mona Freeman, Robert Strauss, Don DeFore

June Bride
US 1948 97m bw
Warner (Henry Blanke)

Two bickering reporters are sent to cover a small-town wedding.
Sloppily structured romantic farce in which nothing ever comes together.

w Ranald MacDougall, *play* Feature for June by Eileen Tighe, Graeme Lorimer *d* Bretaigne Windust *ph* Ted McCord *m* David Buttolph

Bette Davis, Robert Montgomery, Fay Bainter, Tom Tully, Betty Lynn, Barbara Bates, Jerome Cowan, Mary Wickes, Debbie Reynolds

The Jungle Book*
US 1942 109m Technicolor
Alexander Korda (W. Howard Greene)
aka: *Rudyard Kipling's Jungle Book*

Growing up with animals in an Indian forest, a boy forestalls the getaway of three thieves.
High-budgeted but rather boring live action version with stiff-jointed model animals.

w Laurence Stallings, *stories* Rudyard Kipling *d* Zoltan Korda, André de Toth *ph* Lee Garmes, W. Howard Greene *m* Miklos Rozsa

Sabu, Joseph Calleia, John Qualen, Frank Puglia, Rosemary de Camp

'More thrilling than the deeds of man . . . more beautiful than the love of woman . . . more wonderful than the dreams of children!'—*publicity*

AAN: cinematography; Miklos Rozsa

Jungle Book*
US 1967 78m Technicolor
Walt Disney

Cartoon version relying less on action than on songs and voices; patchily successful but no classic.

d Wolfgang Reitherman *m / ly* Richard and Robert Sherman, Terry Gilkyson

voices George Sanders, Phil Harris, Louis Prima, Sebastian Cabot, Sterling Holloway

AAN: song 'The Bare Necessities' (*m / ly* Terry Gilkyson)

Jungle Captive
US 1945 63m bw

A mad doctor steals the body of Paula the ape woman and restores it to life. Arrant rubbish, a sequel to *Captive Wild Woman* and *Jungle Woman*. Otto Kruger, Phil Brown, Rondo Hatton, Jerome Cowan, Amelita Ward. Written by M. Coates Webster and Dwight V. Babcock; directed by Harold Young; for Universal.

Jungle Jim

When Johnny Weissmuller began to show his middle-age spread, Columbia put him in a jacket and more or less redid his Tarzan thing in a series of second features which appeared to be shot in producer Sam Katzman's back garden and gradually indulged in wilder and wilder plots. None of them has more than curiosity value. Main scriptwriters were Carroll Young, Dwight Babcock, Sam Newman; main directors William Berke, Lee Sholem, Spencer G. Bennet.

1948: JUNGLE JIM
1949: THE LOST TRIBE
1950: CAPTIVE GIRL, MARK OF THE GORILLA, PYGMY ISLAND
1951: FURY OF THE CONGO, JUNGLE MANHUNT
1952: JUNGLE JIM IN THE FORBIDDEN LAND, VOODOO TIGER
1953: SAVAGE MUTINY, VALLEY OF THE HEADHUNTERS, KILLER APE
1954: JUNGLE MANEATERS, CANNIBAL ATTACK
1955: JUNGLE MOON MEN, DEVIL GODDESS

'Men staked their lives for just one look at the thrilling beauty of this tiger woman!'

The Jungle Princess*
US 1936 84m bw
Paramount (E. Lloyd Sheldon)

A British hunter is injured on a tropical island and rescued by a native girl and her animal retinue.
Dorothy Lamour's first film role cast her as the female Tarzan she was to play (in a sarong, of course) a dozen times again. This is strictly a programmer, but after its success it was all done again, rather better, as *Her Jungle Love*.

w Cyril Hume, Gerald Geraghty, Gouverneur Morris *d* William Thiele *ph* Harry Fischbeck *md* Boris Morros

Dorothy Lamour, *Ray Milland*, Akim Tamiroff, Lynne Overman, Molly Lamont, Hugh Buckler

'Fairly palatable entertainment most of the way.'—*Variety*

'Poor Mr Lynne Overman is expected to lend humorous relief to a film already richly comic.'—*Graham Greene*

† On this trip the tiger was Liamu and the chimp Bogo.

Jungle Woman
US 1944 54m bw

A mad doctor restores an ape to life. It turns into a beautiful woman. Middle section of a talentless trio of which the first is *Captive Wild Woman* and the third *Jungle Captive*. Written by Bernard Schubert, Henry Sucher and Edward Dein; directed by Reginald LeBorg; for Universal.

Junior Bonner*
US 1972 105m Movielab Todd-AO 35
ABC / Booth–Gardner / Joe Wizan / Solar

An ageing rodeo star returns to his home town and finds his family in trouble.
Well-made, rather downcast and not very interesting drama, remarkably gentle from this director.

w Jeb Rosebrook *d* Sam Peckinpah *ph* Lucien Ballard *m* Jerry Fielding

Steve McQueen, Ida Lupino, Robert Preston, Joe Don Baker, Ben Johnson

● *Video: Rank*

Junior Miss*
US 1945 94m bw
TCF (William Perlberg)

A teenager causes trouble by meddling in the lives of her family.
Amusing family comedy from a hit play.

w George Seaton, *play* Jerome Chodorov and Joseph Fields, *and stories* Sally Benson *d* George Seaton *ph* Charles Clarke *m* David Buttolph

Peggy Ann Garner, Allyn Joslyn, Faye Marlowe, Mona Freeman, Michael Dunne, John Alexander

Juno and the Paycock*
GB 1930 85m bw
British International (John Maxwell)

During the Irish troubles of the early twenties, tragedy comes to a poor Dublin family.
A plainly done film version of a modern classic whose changes of mood would not in any case have worked well on the screen.

w Alfred Hitchcock, Alma Reville, *play* Sean O'Casey *d* Alfred Hitchcock *ph* Jack Cox

Sara Allgood, Edward Chapman, Maire O'Neill, Sidney Morgan, John Laurie

'A film which completely justifies the talkies.'—*James Agate*

'Just a photograph of a stage play.'—*Alfred Hitchcock*

Jupiter's Darling*
US 1954 96m Eastmancolor
    Cinemascope
MGM (George Wells)

Advancing on Rome, Hannibal falls in love with the dictator's fiancée.

A splendid example of the higher lunacy, with coloured elephants decorating an MGM musical about the fall of the Roman Empire. Small elements can be salvaged, and the gall is enough to be divided into three parts.

w Dorothy Kingsley, *play* The Road to Rome by Robert E. Sherwood *d* George Sidney *ph* Paul C. Vogel, Charles Rosher *m* Burton Lane *ly* Harold Adamson *ch* Hermes Pan *ad* Cedric Gibbons, Uric McCleary

Esther Williams, Howard Keel, George Sanders, Marge and Gower Champion, Richard Haydn, William Demarest

Jury's Evidence
GB 1935   71m   bw

The jury in a murder trial disagrees. Courtroom drama with an unsatisfactory finish. Hartley Power, Margaret Lockwood, Nora Swinburne, Sebastian Shaw. Written by Ian Dalrymple, Jack de Leon; directed by Ralph Ince; for British Lion.

The Jury's Secret
US 1937   64m   bw

The guilty man in a murder case is on the jury. Slow-moving courtroom drama with an unsatisfactory twist. Kent Taylor, Fay Wray, Jane Darwell, Nan Grey, Larry Blake, Fritz Leiber. Written by Lester Cole, Newman Levy; directed by Edward Sloman; for Universal. 'Doomed for no honours such as b.o.'—*Variety*

Just a Gigolo
US 1931   71m   bw

A young lord masquerades as a gigolo to avoid being the prey of gold diggers. Slackly handled comedy which doesn't come off. William Haines, Irene Purcell, C. Aubrey Smith, Lillian Bond. Written by Hans Kraly, Richard Schayer, Claudine West; directed by Jack Conway; for MGM. 'Too much talk, too little action.'—*Variety*

Just a Gigolo
West Germany 1978   147m   colour
Leguan (Rolf Thiele)

A young Prussian veteran of World War I intends to succeed, but stumbles through the Berlin underworld and is accidentally shot in a street skirmish.
An international misadventure whose English version is not only interminable and badly dubbed but extremely clumsily made.

w Ennio de Concini, Joshua Sinclair *d* David Hemmings *ph* Charly Steinberger *m* Gunther Fischer *pd* Peter Rothe

David Bowie, Sydne Rome, Kim Novak, Marlene Dietrich, David Hemmings, Maria Schell, Curt Jurgens, Erika Pluhar
'It often goes for laughs it hasn't a hope of getting; sometimes it aspires to tragic dignity and looks truly inept. It would be kinder to yourself and to everybody involved to overlook it.'—*Time Out*

● Video: VCL

Just Across the Street
US 1952   78m   bw

Complications arise when a plumber's secretary pretends to be rich. Silly and pointless comedy which provides its talent with nothing to do. Ann Sheridan, John Lund, Robert Keith, Cecil Kellaway, Harvey Lembeck, Natalie Schaefer, Alan Mowbray. Written by Rosell Rogers and Joel Malone; directed by Joseph Pevney; for Leonard Goldstein / Universal–International.

Just Around the Corner
US 1938   70m   bw
TCF (David Hempstead)

A little girl helps her dad to get on in business. Tedious Little Miss Fixit tale from the period when Shirley's star was sliding.

w Ethel Hill, J. P. McEvoy, Darrel Ware *d* Irving Cummings *ph* Henry Sharp *md* Louis Silvers

Shirley Temple, Charles Farrell, Bert Lahr, Joan Davis, Amanda Duff, Bill Robinson, Franklin Pangborn, Cora Witherspoon
'Top flight for general all-round entertainment.'—*Variety*

Just Before Dawn
US 1980   90m   Movielab

Visitors to a mountain area are terrorized by a cleaver-wielding killer. Teenage shocker with just a little more style than most. George Kennedy, Mike Kellin, Chris Lemmon, Gregg Henry, Deborah Benson. Written by Mark Arywitz and Gregg Irving; directed by Jeff Lieberman; for Oakland.

Just for You
US 1952   104m   Technicolor
Paramount (Pat Duggan)

A successful songwriter finds that his troublesome teenage son is in love with his own fiancée.
Tiresomely scripted, pleasantly played romantic comedy with music.

w Robert Carson, *novel* Famous by Stephen Vincent Benet *d* Elliott Nugent *ph* George Barnes *m* Hugo Friedhofer *md* Emil Newman *songs* Harry Warren, Leo Robin

Bing Crosby, Jane Wyman, Bob Arthur, Ethel Barrymore, Natalie Wood, Cora Witherspoon, Regis Toomey

AAN: song 'Zing a Little Zong'

Just Imagine
US 1930   102m   bw
Fox

A man who dies in 1930 is revived in 1980 and can't get used to the pace of life.
Famous fantasy which doesn't live up to its reputation and can now be seen as hampered by poor sets, script and acting. Futuristic sets are few but choice.

d David Butler *w, songs* De Sylva, Brown, Henderson *ch* Seymour Felix *ph* Ernest Palmer

El Brendel, Maureen O'Sullivan, John Garrick, Frank Albertson, Marjorie White, Hobart Bosworth, Mischa Auer, Wilfred Lucas
'Needs to be sold in advance on its novelty angle . . . it seems essential that something be done to make them say "Go down and take a look at that crazy picture".'—*Variety*

Just Like a Woman
GB 1966   89m   Eastmancolor
Dormar (Bob Kellett)

A TV director's wife leaves him and gets ideas above her station.
Curious comedy which aims at sophistication but starts flagging in the first five minutes. Familiar performers just about keep it afloat.

wd Bob Fuest *ph* Billy Williams *m* Ken Napper

Wendy Craig, Francis Matthews, John Wood, Dennis Price, Miriam Karlin, Peter Jones, Clive Dunn, Ray Barrett

Just My Luck
GB 1957   86m   bw
Rank (Hugh Stewart)

A jeweller's assistant becomes involved in horse racing.
Flat star vehicle.

w Alfred Shaughnessy *d* John Paddy Carstairs *ph* Jack Cox *m* Philip Green

Norman Wisdom, Leslie Phillips, Margaret Rutherford, Delphi Lawrence

Just Tell Me What You Want
US 1980   112m   Technicolor
Warner / Jay Presson Allen, Sidney Lumet

A powerful tycoon starts to weave plots when one of his harem wants to go independent.
Thoroughly silly melodrama with a few incidental humours.

w Jay Presson Allen, from her novel *d* Sidney Lumet *ph* Oswald Morris *m* Charles Strouse *pd* Tony Walton

Ali MacGraw, Alan King, Myrna Loy, Keenan Wynn, Tony Roberts, Dina Merrill, Peter Weller
'Jay Presson Allen has adapted her trashy novel into a trashy picture . . . Myrna Loy looks as if she's constantly amazed at the kinds of films getting made these days, and she's absolutely right.'—*Variety*

Just the Way You Are
US 1984   95m   Metrocolor

A young fluteplayer tries to carve a career for herself while overcoming a physical disability. Odd little comedy-drama with little plot beyond the central character's crippled leg; not likely to make much headway. Kristy McNichol, Michael Ontkean, Kaki Hunter, André Dussolier, Robert Carradine. Written by Allan Burns; directed by Edouard Molinaro; for Leo L. Fuchs / MGM-UA.

Just You and Me, Kid

US 1979   93m   Metrocolor

Columbia / Irving Fein-Jerome M. Zeitman

An elderly comedian reluctantly takes care of a naked teenager on the run from a dope pusher.

Virtually a one-set comedy which quickly tires the eye and ear; not a good idea despite the veteran star.

w Oliver Hailey, Leonard Stern d Leonard Stern ph David Walsh m Jack Elliott

George Burns, Brooke Shields, Burl Ives, Lorraine Gary, John Schuck, Keye Luke, Leon Ames, Ray Bolger, Carl Ballantine

Justice Est Faite*

France 1950   105m   bw

Silver Films

The personal lives of jurors in a mercy killing case affect their verdict.

Absorbing courtroom drama with a message.

w *Charles Spaak, André Cayatte d André Cayatte ph* Jean Bourgoin *m* Raymond Legrand

Valentine Tessier, Claude Nollier, Jacques Castelot, Michel Auclair

Justine

US 1969   116m   De Luxe   Panavision

TCF / Pandro S. Berman

In Alexandria in the thirties, the beautiful wife of a wealthy banker influences the lives of all who meet her.

Disastrous condensed version of a very unusual set of novels whose atmosphere has not translated at all well. The result is like a bad rehearsal for a film, which is not surprising in view of the number of producers variously involved. The author feared 'a sort of *Peyton Place* with camels', and got it.

w Lawrence B. Marcus, *novels* The Alexandria Quartet by Lawrence Durrell *d* George Cukor *ph* Leon Shamroy *m* Jerry Goldsmith

Anouk Aimée, Michael York, Dirk Bogarde, Anna Karina, John Vernon, George Baker, Philippe Noiret, Robert Forster, Jack Albertson, Michael Dunn, Barry Morse, Cliff Gorman, Severn Darden

'Could well stand as a model of what can happen when Hollywood gets to grips with a celebrated literary property.'—*David Wilson*

'Despite leaden forays into homosexuality, transvestitism, incest, and child prostitution, it remains as naively old-fashioned in its emotional and intellectual vocabulary as in its actual verbiage and cinematic technique.'—*John Simon*

Kagemusha**
Japan 1980 179m Eastmancolor
TCF / Toho (Akira Kurosawa)
aka: *The Double; Shadow Warrior*

On the death of a clan chief his place is taken
by the lookalike hired to overlook battlefields
while the chief is really busy elsewhere.
Fascinating Japanese epic centring on stately
ritual and court intrigue, with the occasional
battle for spectacular action; one of the
director's most impressive works.

w Akira Kurosawa, Masato Ide *d* Akira
Kurosawa
ph Kazuo Miyagawa, Asaichi Nakai
m Shinichiro Ikebe

Tatsura Nakadai, Tsutomu Yamazaki, Kenichi
Hagiwara

AAN: best foreign film; art direction
BFA: direction; costume design

● *Video: CBS / Fox*

Kaleidoscope*
GB 1966 103m Technicolor
Warner / Winkast (Elliott Kastner)
Reissue title: *The Bank Breaker*

An American playboy breaks into a playing
card factory and marks the designs so that he
can win in every European casino.
Would-be swinging comedy-thriller which in
fact is entertaining only when it stops trying to
dazzle.

w Robert and Jane Howard-Carrington
d Jack Smight *ph* Christopher Challis
m Stanley Myers *ad* Maurice Carter

Warren Beatty, Susannah York, Clive Revill,
Eric Porter, Murray Melvin

'A "groovie movie" it certainly is, with a
battery of fashionable camera tricks,
kaleidoscopic dissolves, and virtually every
scene introduced from behind an irrelevant
piece of furniture.'—*David Wilson*

Kameradschaft*
Germany 1931 92m bw
Nerofilm
aka: *Comradeship*

On the Franco-German border French miners
are imprisoned below ground and Germans
burrow to free them.
Salutary message film with good dramatic
pointing.

w Laszlo Vajda, Karl Otten, Peter Martin
Lampel *d* G. W. Pabst *ph* Fritz Arno
Wagner, Robert Baberski

Ernst Busch, Alexander Granach, Fritz
Kampers, Gustav Puttjer

Kanal*
Poland 1956 97m bw
Film Polski (Stanislaw Adler)
aka: *They Loved Life*

In 1944, an anti-Nazi resistance group is
trapped in a sewer.
A suffocatingly unpleasant film to watch; its
message and technical excellence are
undoubted.

w Jerzy Stawinski, from his novel Kloakerne
d Andrzej Wajda *ph* Jerzy Lipman *m* Jan
Krenz

Teresa Izewska, Tadeusz Janczar, Emil
Kariewicz, Wienczylaw Glinski

● *Video: Thorn EMI*

Kangaroo
US 1952 84m Technicolor
TCF (Robert Bassler)

In old Australia, a con man pretends to be a
rancher's long lost heir, then complicates
things by falling in love with the rancher's
daughter.
Standard romantic action hokum.

w Harry Kleiner *d* Lewis Milestone
ph Charles G. Clarke *m* Sol Kaplan

Maureen O'Hara, Peter Lawford, Finlay
Currie, Richard Boone, Chips Rafferty,
Charles Tingwell

Kansas City Bomber
US 1972 99m Metrocolor
MGM / Levy–Gardner–Laven / Raquel
Welch (Marty Elfand)

A roller skating star finds time between affairs
to beat her rival in a big match.
Vulgar melodrama with good action scenes.

w Thomas Rickman, Calvin Clements
d Jerrold Freedman *ph* Fred Koenekamp
m Don Ellis

Raquel Welch, Kevin McCarthy, Norman
Alden, Jeanne Cooper

● *Video: MGM / UA*

Kansas City Confidential
US 1952 98m bw
United Artists / Edward Small
GB title: *The Secret Four*

An ex-detective plans a perfect crime, and

recruits three confederates who all remain
unknown to each other by wearing masks.
Moderately lively if violent thriller which gets
less inventive as it goes along but satisfies the
action buffs.

w George Bruce, Harry Essex *d* Phil Karlson
ph George Diskant *m* Paul Sawtell

Preston Foster, John Payne, Coleen Gray, Lee
Van Cleef, Neville Brand, Jack Elam, Dona
Drake

Kansas City Princess
US 1934 64m bw

Gold diggers go to Paris. Light farce comedy,
somewhat lacking in punch. Joan Blondell,
Glenda Farrell, Hugh Herbert, Robert
Armstrong, Osgood Perkins, Hobart
Cavanaugh. Written by Sy Bartlett and
Manuel Seff; directed by William Keighley;
for Warners. 'Just a comedy, good for better
than moderate biz.'—*Variety*

Kansas Raiders
US 1951 80m Technicolor

During the Civil War, Jesse James joins
Quantrill's Raiders. Fast-moving, fairly violent
western only remotely based on fact. Audie
Murphy, Brian Donlevy, Marguerite
Chapman, Scott Brady, Tony Curtis, Richard
Arlen, James Best, Richard Long. Written by
Robert L. Richards; directed by Ray Enright;
for Universal-International.

Kaos**
Italy 1984 188m Eastmancolor
RAI-TV / Filmtre (Giuliano de Negri)

Five stories by Pirandello are combined in
settings near his birthplace.
Generally fascinating mixture of tales which
range from comedy to horror, styled by master
film-makers.

w,d Paolo and Vittorio Taviani *ph* Giuseppe
Lanci *m* Nicola Piovanni *ed* Roberto
Perignani

Margarita Lozano, Claudio Bigagli, Enrica
Maria Modugno, Ciccio Ingrassia, Franco
Franchi, Biagio Barone, Omero Antonutti

Kapo
Italy / France 1960 115m bw
Vides / Zebra / Francinex

A French Jewess survives the horrors of a Nazi
concentration camp and becomes camp guard.

Curious exploitation piece which turns tragedy
into melodrama, and doesn't even do that with
much flair.

w Franco Solinas, Gillo Pontecorvo *d* Gillo
Pontecorvo *ph* Goffredo Bellisario,
Alexander Sekulovic *m* Carlo Rustichelli

Susan Strasberg, Laurent Terzieff,
Emmanuelle Riva

The Karate Kid
US 1984   127m   Metrocolor

A teenage boy, new to California, joins a
karate club and defeats the local bullies.
A kind of amateur *Rocky*, not bad in its way,
but its huge commercial success in the US
remains mystifying.

w Robert Mark Kamen *d* John G. Avildsen
ph James Crabe *m* Bill Conti *pd* William J.
Cassidy *ed* Bud Smith, Walt Mulconery

Ralph Macchio, Noriyuki 'Pat' Morita,
Elizabeth Shue, Martin Kove, Randee Heller,
William Zabka

Kate Plus Ten
GB 1938   81m   bw
Wainwright (Richard Wainwright)

A police inspector falls for the attractive
female leader of a bullion gang.
Curious comedy thriller with insufficient of
either commodity.

w Jack Hulbert, Jeffrey Dell, *novel* Edgar
Wallace *d* Reginald Denham *ph* Roy Kellino

Jack Hulbert, Genevieve Tobin, Noel
Madison, Francis L. Sullivan, Arthur
Wontner, Frank Cellier, Googie Withers,
Peter Haddon, Felix Aylmer, Leo Genn,
Edward Lexy

Kathleen
US 1941   88m   bw
MGM (George Haight)

A neglected daughter finds a new wife for her
widowed father.
One of the reasons for Shirley Temple's early
retirement.

w Mary McCall Jnr, *story* Kay Van Riper
d Harold S. Bucquet *ph* Sidney Wagner
m Franz Waxman

Shirley Temple, Herbert Marshall, Laraine
Day, Gail Patrick, Felix Bressart, Nella
Walker, Lloyd Corrigan

Kathy O
US 1958   99m   Eastmancolor
Cinemascope
U-I (Sy Gomberg)

A temperamental child star befriends a lonely
columnist.
Overlong Hollywood comedy drama with
amusing moments.

w Jack Sher, Sy Gomberg *d* Jack Sher
ph Arthur E. Arling *m* Frank Skinner
songs Charles Tobias, Ray Joseph

Patty McCormack, Dan Duryea, Jan Sterling,
Sam Levene

Katie Did It
US 1951   81m   bw
Universal–International (Leonard
   Goldstein)

A small town is shocked when young Katie
comes back having posed in scanty attire for a
commercial artist.
Feeble comedy which totters to a lame
conclusion.

w Jack Henley *d* Frederick de Cordova
Russell Metty *m* Frank Skinner

Ann Blyth, Mark Stevens, Cecil Kellaway,
Elizabeth Patterson, Jesse White, Harold
Vermilyea, Craig Stevens

Keep 'Em Flying
US 1941   86m   bw
Universal (Glenn Tryon)

Two incompetents in the Army Air Corps get
mixed up with identical twin girls.
A big moneymaker of its day, this comedy
now seems especially resistible.

w True Boardman, Nat Perrin, John Grant
d Arthur Lubin *ph* Joseph Valentine

Bud Abbott, Lou Costello, Martha Raye,
Carol Bruce, William Gargan, Dick Foran,
Charles Lang

Keep Fit°
GB 1937   82m   bw
ATP (Basil Dean)

A barber mistaken for an athlete finally excels
at sport and also catches a thief.
Good star vehicle with snappy songs and fast
comedy scenes.

w Anthony Kimmins, Austin Melford
d Anthony Kimmins *ph* Ronald Neame,
Gordon Dines

George Formby, Kay Walsh, Guy Middleton,
Gus McNaughton, Edmund Breon, George
Benson, C. Denier Warren, Hal Gordon, Hal
Walters, Leo Franklyn

Keep Smiling°
GB 1938   91m   bw
TCF (Robert T. Kane)
US title: *Smiling Along*

Problems of a touring concert party.
Pretty good star vehicle, though with
unfortunate signs of an attempt to glamorize
Our Gracie.

w Val Valentine, Rodney Ackland *d* Monty
Banks *ph* Max Greene

Gracie Fields, Roger Livesey, Mary Maguire,
Peter Coke, Jack Donohue, Tommy Fields,
Eddie Gray, Edward Rigby, Hay Petrie

Keep Smiling
US 1938   77m   bw

The niece of a Hollywood director finds him
on the skids. More than usually substantial
star comedy-drama. Jane Withers, Henry
Wilcoxon, Gloria Stuart, Helen Westley, Jed
Prouty, Pedro de Cordoba, Douglas Fowley.
Written by Frances Hyland, Albert Ray;
directed by Herbert I. Leeds; for John Stone /
TCF. 'A kids' picture with an adult punch.'—
Variety

Keep Your Powder Dry
US 1945   93m   bw
MGM (George Haight)

Three girls from different backgrounds join
the WACS.
Totally uninteresting and unconvincing female
flagwaver.

w Mary C. McCall Jnr, George Bruce
d Edward Buzzell *ph* Ray June *m* David
Snell

Lana Turner, Laraine Day, Susan Peters,
Agnes Moorehead, Bill Johnson, Natalie
Schaefer, June Lockhart, Lee Patrick

Keep Your Seats Please°
GB 1936   82m   bw
ATP (Basil Dean)

A prospective heir seeks a fortune hidden in
one of six chairs.
Good star comedy on a theme later reworked
in *It's in the Bag* (qv) and *The Twelve Chairs*
(qv).

w Tom Geraghty, Ian Hay, Anthony
Kimmins, *play* Twelve Chairs by Elie Ilf,
Eugene Petrov *d* Monty Banks

George Formby, Florence Desmond, Alastair
Sim, Gus McNaughton, Harry Tate

Keeper of the Bees
US 1935   76m   bw

A country boy makes good. Victorian-style
fable for rural audiences. Neil Hamilton, Betty
Furness, Emma Dunn, Edith Fellows, Hobart
Bosworth. Written by Adele Buggington from
the novel by Gene Stratton Porter; directed by
Christy Cabanne; for Trem Carr / Monogram.
'For discriminating patronage, a washout . . .
a calico narrative for the crossroads.'—*Variety*

Keeper of the Flame°
US 1942   100m   bw
MGM (Victor Saville)

A reporter befriends the widow of a politician
and forces her to disclose her husband's guilty
secret.
Well-acted but over-solemn melodrama which
badly needs a sting in the tail.

w Donald Ogden Stewart, *novel* I. A. R.
Wylie *d* George Cukor *ph* William Daniels
m Bronislau Kaper

Spencer Tracy, Katharine Hepburn, Richard
Whorf, Margaret Wycherly, Donald Meek,
Stephen McNally, Audrey Christie, Frank
Craven
   'An expensive testimonial to Hollywood's
inability to face a significant theme.'—*Time*
   'Unorthodox and on the whole absorbing
drama. Ominous portents and overtones take
the place of physical action.'—*Christian
Science Monitor*
   'A gothic wet blanket of a movie.'—*Pauline
Kael, 70s*

Keepers of Youth
GB 1931   70m   bw
BIP

A young schoolmaster finds his fresh ideas
make him unpopular, especially when he is

found in a compromising position with the assistant matron.
Old-fashioned drama with a few lively scenes.

w Frank Launder, *play* Arnold Ridley
d Thomas Bentley *ph* James Wilson, Bert Ford

Garry Marsh, Ann Todd, Robin Irvine, John Turnbull, O. B. Clarence, Mary Clare

Keeping Company
US 1940 80m bw

A young man announces his engagement but has trouble when his ex-girlfriend returns to town. Amiable family comedy which was announced to be the first of a series, but stayed lonely. Frank Morgan, Irene Rich, John Shelton, Ann Rutherford, Virginia Weidler, Dan Dailey, Gene Lockhart, Virginia Grey. Written by James Hill, Harry Ruskin and Adrian Scott; directed by S. Sylvan Simon; for MGM.

Kelly and Me
US 1956 86m Technicolor
Cinemascope
U-I (Robert Arthur)

The ups and downs of a song and dance man and the dog who shares his act.
Mild vaudeville saga with totally predictable twists.

w Everett Freeman d Robert Z. Leonard
ph Maury Gertsman m Joseph Gershenson

Van Johnson, Piper Laurie, Martha Hyer, Onslow Stevens

Kelly's Heroes
US / Yugoslavia 1970 143m
Metrocolor Panavision
MGM / The Warriors / Avala (Irving Leonard)

During World War II, an American platoon abducts a German general and accidentally discovers the whereabouts of a fortune in gold. Crude slam-bang actioner for the obvious market.

w Troy Kennedy Martin d Brian G. Hutton
ph Gabriel Figueroa m Lalo Schifrin *2nd unit* Andrew Marton

Clint Eastwood, Telly Savalas, Don Rickles, Donald Sutherland, Carroll O'Connor, Stuart Margolin, Dick Davalos
'Over two hours of consistently devastating explosions, pyrotechnics and demolition.'—*MFB*
'Made for no possible reason other than a chance to use the Yugoslav army at cut rates.'—*Judith Crist, 1973*
● *Video: MGM / UA*

Kelly the Second
US 1936 71m bw

A determined lady trains a dimwitted prizefighter. Easy-going farce from a studio which knew how to make them; but this wasn't one of the best. Patsy Kelly, Guinn Williams, Charley Chase, Pert Kelton, Harold Huber. Written by Jack Jevne and Gordon Douglas; directed by Hal Roach; for MGM.

The Kennel Murder Case*
US 1933 73m bw
Warner

Philo Vance proves that an apparent suicide is really murder.
Complex murder mystery, very smartly handled and often cited as a classic of the genre; later remade as *Calling Philo Vance.*

w Robert N. Lee, Peter Milner, *novel* S. S. Van Dine d Michael Curtiz ph William Reese

William Powell, Mary Astor, Eugene Pallette, Ralph Morgan, Helen Vinson, Jack La Rue, Paul Cavanagh, Robert Barrat
'Entertaining all the way.'—*Variety*
'Players are cast so inevitably to type that the film is like a demonstration of the principles of running a stock company.'—*New Yorker, 1978*
'Stylistically a little gem.'—*Clive Hirschhorn*
† See also *Philo Vance.*

The Kentuckian
US 1955 104m Technicolor
Cinemascope
UA / Hecht–Lancaster

A Kentucky backwoodsman takes his small son to settle in Texas.
Ambling mid-western with moments of interest.

w A. B. Guthrie Jnr, *novel* The Gabriel Horn by Felix Holt d Burt Lancaster ph Ernest Laszlo m Bernard Herrmann

Burt Lancaster, Dianne Foster, Diana Lynn, Walter Matthau, John McIntire, Una Merkel, John Carradine

Kentucky*
US 1938 95m Technicolor
TCF (Gene Markey)

Horse-breeding rivalry prevents the smooth running of true love.
Harmless family entertainment, more professionally handled than its innumerable later imitations. Remade as *April Love.*

w Lamar Trotti, *novel* The Look of Eagles by John Taintor Foote d David Butler ph Ernest Palmer md Louis Silvers

Loretta Young, Richard Greene, Walter Brennan, Douglass Dumbrille, Karen Morley, Moroni Olsen, Russell Hicks
'An outstanding effort, geared for top money.'—*Variety*
AA: Walter Brennan

Kentucky Kernels
US 1934 74m bw

An orphan left with two musicians proves to be the heir to a fortune, but the way to it is through feuding hillbilly country. Fairly funny Wheeler and Woolsey comedy, in other words one of their better efforts. Bert Wheeler, Robert Woolsey, Mary Carlisle, Spanky McFarland, Noah Beery, Willie Best. Written by Bert Kalmar, Harry Ruby and Fred Guiol; directed by George Stevens; for RKO. (GB title: *Triple Trouble.*)

Kentucky Moonshine*
US 1938 87m bw

In the hope of a radio contract, the Ritz Brothers masquerade as hillbillies and find themselves in the middle of a feud. One of the trio's best solo vehicles. *The Ritz Brothers,* Tony Martin, Marjorie Weaver, Slim Summerville, John Carradine, Wally Vernon, Berton Churchill, Eddie Collins. Written by Art Arthur and M. M. Musselman; directed by David Butler; for TCF. 'It's crazy and it's wild, but it's funny and grand entertainment.'—*Variety*

La Kermesse Héroïque**
France 1935 115m bw
Tobis
aka: *Carnival in Flanders*

When Spaniards invade a Flemish town in 1616, the men make themselves scarce and the women find other ways of conquering.
Sprightly though overlong comedy which seemed risqué at the time and therefore enjoyed international success.

w Charles Spaak, Jacques Feyder, *novel* Charles Spaak d Jacques Feyder ph Harry Stradling m Louis Beydts ad Lazare Meerson

Françoise Rosay, Louis Jouvet, Jean Murat, Alfred Adam, André Alerme
'A mixture of gay absurdity and shrewd comment, selecting its own pitch and holding it—comedy, you might say, self-contained.'—*Otis Ferguson*
'Everything fits perfectly into the pattern of cultured and sophisticated entertainment. Nowhere is there a false touch.'—*The Times, 1952*

Kes*
GB 1969 109m Technicolor
UA / Woodfall (Tony Garnett)

In a northern industrial town, a boy learns about life from the fate of his pet bird.
'Realistic' family drama, full of the kind of merit that does not equate with entertainment: hard to take and harder to hear.

w Barry Hines, Ken Loach, Tony Garnet, *novel* A Kestrel for a Knave by Barry Hines d Ken Loach ph Chris Menges m John Cameron

David Bradley, Lynne Perrie, Colin Welland, Freddie Fletcher, Brian Glover
'There emerges a most discouraging picture of life in the industrial north . . . infinitely sad in its total implications, it is also immensely funny in much of its detail.'—*Brenda Davies*

The Kettles
The rustic couple evolved from characters in *The Egg and I* (qv); Marjorie Main and Percy Kilbride went on to play them in a cheap but very popular series for Universal, variously scripted and directed.

1949: MA AND PA KETTLE
1950: MA AND PA KETTLE GO TO TOWN

1951: MA AND PA KETTLE BACK ON
THE FARM
1952: MA AND PA KETTLE AT THE FAIR
1953: MA AND PA KETTLE ON
VACATION
1954: MA AND PA KETTLE AT HOME
1955: MA AND PA KETTLE AT WAIKIKI
1956: THE KETTLES IN THE OZARKS
(Arthur Hunnicutt instead of Kilbride)
1957: THE KETTLES ON OLD
MACDONALD'S FARM (Parker Fennelly
instead of Kilbride)

The Key*
US 1934 71m bw

In Ireland in the twenties, a British army
captain falls for the wife of an intelligence
officer. Heroics among the black and tans;
interesting but dated drama. William Powell,
Edna Best, Colin Clive, Hobart Cavanaugh,
Halliwell Hobbes, Henry O'Neill, Arthur
Treacher, Donald Crisp. Written by Laird
Doyle, from the play by R. Gore-Brown and
J. L. Hardy; directed by Michael Curtiz; for
Warner.

The Key*
GB 1958 134m bw Cinemascope
Columbia / Open Road (Carl Foreman)

World War II tugboat skippers, about to
embark on dangerous missions, pass on the
key to an apartment and a girl to go with it.
Rather foolish symbolic melodrama which
never makes its purpose clear but along the
way provides fragments of love story, chunks
of the supernatural and dollops of war action,
rather languidly assembled with great technical
competence but little real feeling. The talent
occasionally shows through.

w Carl Foreman, *novel* Stella by Jan de
Hartog *d* Carol Reed *ph* Oswald Morris
m Malcolm Arnold

William Holden, Sophia Loren, *Trevor
Howard*, Oscar Homolka, Kieron Moore

'A storm of fear and fury in the sizzling
    Florida keys!'
Key Largo***
US 1948 101m bw
Warner (Jerry Wald)

A returning war veteran fights gangsters on
the Florida keys.
Moody melodrama on similar lines to *To Have
and Have Not*: it sums up the post-war mood
of despair, allows several good acting
performances, and builds up to a pretty good
action climax.

w Richard Brooks, John Huston, *play* Maxwell
Anderson *d* John Huston *ph* Karl Freund
m Max Steiner

Humphrey Bogart, Lauren Bacall, *Claire
Trevor*, Edward G. Robinson, Lionel
Barrymore, Thomas Gomez, Marc Lawrence
'It's a confidently directed, handsomely shot
movie, and the cast go at it as if the nonsense

about gangsters and human dignity were high
drama.'—*New Yorker, 1977*
'A completely empty, synthetic work.'—
Gavin Lambert
AA: Claire Trevor
● *Video: Warner*

Key to the City
US 1950 101m bw
MGM (Z. Wayne Griffin)

At a San Francisco convention, two mayors
get involved in several escapades and fall in
love.
Routine romantic comedy. .

w Robert Riley Crutcher *d* George Sidney
ph Harold Rosson *m* Bronislau Kaper

Clark Gable, Loretta Young, Frank Morgan,
James Gleason, Marilyn Maxwell, Raymond
Burr, Lewis Stone, Raymond Walburn,
Pamela Britton
'A comedy made to measure . . . the script
concerns itself with wringing every possible
laugh from a number of stock situations.'—
Variety

The Keyhole*
US 1933 70m bw

A divorce investigator falls for the wife he is
commissioned to frame. Unsavoury little
drama, unusual enough to be interesting. Kay
Francis, George Brent, Glenda Farrell, Allen
Jenkins, Monroe Owsley. Written by Robert
Presnell from Adventures by Alice Duer
Miller; directed by Michael Curtiz; for
Warners.

The Keys of the Kingdom*
US 1944 137m bw
TCF (Joseph L. Mankiewicz)

The life of a 19th-century Scottish priest in
China.
Studio-made missionary melodrama, a big hit
for its new star but otherwise an
undistinguished piece of work with a shuffling
pace and not much by way of climax.

w Joseph L. Mankiewicz, Nunnally Johnson,
novel A. J. Cronin *d* John M. Stahl
ph Arthur Miller *m* Alfred Newman
ad James Basevi, William Darling

Gregory Peck, Thomas Mitchell, Vincent
Price, Rose Stradner, Roddy McDowall,
Edmund Gwenn, Cedric Hardwicke, Peggy
Ann Garner, James Gleason, Anne Revere
'Long, earnest, long, worthy, interesting
and long.'—*Richard Mallett, Punch*

AAN: Arthur Miller; Alfred Newman;
Gregory Peck

'Where the Nile divides, their mighty
    conflict begins!'
Khartoum*
GB 1966 134m Technicolor Ultra
Panavision
UA / Julian Blaustein

The last years of General Gordon.

Dullish history book stuff which fails to
explain Gordon the man but occasionally
erupts into glowing action.

w Robert Ardrey *d* Basil Dearden
ph Edward Scaife, Harry Waxman *m* Frank
Cordell

Charlton Heston, Laurence Olivier, Ralph
Richardson, Richard Johnson, Hugh Williams,
Alexander Knox, Johnny Sekka, Nigel Green,
Michael Hordern
'Academic accuracy and spectacular battles
are unhappy partners.'—*MFB*
'Beautifully photographed, lavishly
mounted, intelligently acted, but ultimately
dull.'—*Sight and Sound*

AAN: Robert Ardrey

Kicking the Moon Around
GB 1938 78m bw
Vogue (Howard Welsch)
US titles: *The Playboy; Millionaire Merry
Go Round*

A millionaire goes into show business to
establish a career for his singing protégée.
Mild, frothy comedy, dated but quite fluent.

w Angus McPhail, Roland Pertwee, Michael
Hogan, Harry Fowler Mear *d* Walter Forde
ph Francis Carver

Ambrose and his Orchestra, Evelyn Dall, Hal
Thompson, Florence Desmond, Harry
Richman, C. Denier Warren, Max Bacon

The Kid***
US 1921 52m approx (24 fps) bw
    silent
First National / Charles Chaplin

A tramp brings up an abandoned baby, and
later loses him to his mother; but there is a
happy ending.
Sentimental comedy set in the slums. The
comedy is very sparingly laid on, but the effect
of the whole is much less painful than the
synopsis would suggest, the production is
comparatively smooth, the child actor is
sensational, and the film contains much of the
quintessential Chaplin.

wd Charles Chaplin *ph* Rollie Totheroh

Charles Chaplin, Jackie Coogan, Edna
Purviance

● *Video: Polygram*

Kid Auto Races at Venice
US 1914 6m approx bw silent
Keystone / Mack Sennett

This much mentioned film is no more than a
few candid camera shots of a children's car
race on the California beach. It so happened
that the young Charles Chaplin was called
upon to liven up proceedings by causing a
nuisance, and hastily conceived his tramp
costume to do so. His fragments of comedy,
primitive though they now seem, made him a
star.

wd Henry Lehrman *ph* Frank D. Williams

Kid Blue
US 1973 100m De Luxe Panavision
TCF / Marvin Schwarz Productions

In 1902 Texas a young outlaw tries to go
straight.
Deliberately myth-deflating western with
agreeably rich detail.

w Edwin Shrake d James Frawley ph Billy
Williams m Tim McIntyre, John Rubenstein
pd Joel Schiller

Dennis Hopper, Warren Oates, Peter Boyle,
Ben Johnson, Lee Purcell, Janice Rule,
Clifton James
● Video: CBS / Fox

The Kid Comes Back
US 1937 61m bw

A tenderfoot from Texas is trained by an
ex-champion prizefighter. Not really a sequel
to Kid Galahad, but a second feature in its
wake; as such, fair. Wayne Morris, Barton
MacLane, June Travis, Maxie Rosenbloom.
Written by George Bricker, E. J. Flanagan;
directed by B. Reeves Eason; for Warners.
'Brisk, fast, strong dualler.'—Variety

A Kid for Two Farthings*
GB 1955 96m Eastmancolor
London Films (Carol Reed)

Among the colourful characters of London's
Petticoat Lane market moves a boy whose pet
goat seems to have the magical power of a
unicorn.
Whimsical character comedy-drama made with
some style but too insubstantial and
unconvincing to be affectionately
remembered.

w Wolf Mankowitz d Carol Reed ph Ted
Scaife m Benjamin Frankel

Celia Johnson, Diana Dors, David Kossoff,
Brenda de Banzie, Sidney Tafler, Primo
Carnera, Joe Robinson

The Kid from Brooklyn
US 1946 114m Technicolor
Samuel Goldwyn

A timid milkman becomes a prizefighter.
Yawn-provoking comedy, a remake of Harold
Lloyd's The Milky Way; the first indication
that Danny Kaye could be a bore.

w Grover Jones, Frank Butler, Richard
Connell d Norman Z. McLeod ph Gregg
Toland md Carmen Dragon songs Jule Styne,
Sammy Cahn

Danny Kaye, Virginia Mayo, Vera-Ellen,
Steve Cochran, Eve Arden, Walter Abel,
Lionel Stander, Fay Bainter, Clarence Kolb
† NB: Lionel Stander played the same role in
The Milky Way.

The Kid from Kokomo
US 1939 92m bw

A farm boy's fight manager decides that for
publicity purposes he must acquire a family.

Yet another follow-up to Kid Galahad, this
time on the farcical side. Not bad, but too
long. Pat O'Brien, Wayne Morris, Joan
Blondell, May Robson, Jane Wyman, Stanley
Fields, Maxie Rosenbloom, Sidney Toler, Ed
Brophy. Written by Jerry Wald, Richard
Macauley, Dalton Trumbo; directed by Lewis
Seiler; for Warners. 'Full of laughs, and a very
probable money-getter.'—Variety

The Kid from Left Field
US 1953 80m bw

A big league basketball player is reduced to
selling peanuts at the games, but passes on
advice through his small son, who is appointed
team manager. Half-hearted whimsy for
addicts. Dan Dailey, Billy Chapin, Anne
Bancroft, Lloyd Bridges, Ray Collins, Richard
Egan. Written by Jack Sher; directed by
Harmon Jones; for TCF.

The Kid from Spain**
US 1932 90m bw
Samuel Goldwyn

A simpleton is mistaken for a celebrated
bullfighter.
Charmingly dated star musical which, though
primitive in some respects, is a splendid
reminder of its period.

w William Anthony McGuire, Bert Kalmar,
Harry Ruby d Leo McCarey ph Gregg
Toland ch Busby Berkeley

Eddie Cantor, Lyda Roberti, Robert Young,
Ruth Hall, John Miljan, Noah Beery, J.
Carrol Naish, Stanley Fields, Betty Grable,
Paulette Goddard
'A corking comedy . . . it'll get a lot of
money.'—Variety

The Kid from Texas
US 1950 85m Technicolor

The last rampage of Billy the Kid. Surprisingly
violent western for its time; otherwise
unremarkable. Audie Murphy, Gale Storm,
Albert Dekker, Shepperd Strudwick, Will
Geer, William Talman. Written by Robert
Hardy Andrews and Karl Kamb; directed by
Kurt Neumann; for Universal–International.
(GB title: Texas Kid, Outlaw.)

Kid Galahad*
US 1937 101m bw
Warner (Samuel Bischoff)
TV title: Battling Bellhop

A bellhop is groomed as a prizefighter, and his
trainer grows jealous.
Good standard prizefight melodrama, remade
as The Wagons Roll at Night and later as Kid
Galahad with Elvis Presley (see below).

w Seton I. Miller, novel Francis Wallace
d Michael Curtiz ph Tony Gaudio m Heinz
Roemheld, Max Steiner

Edward G. Robinson, Bette Davis, Wayne
Morris, Jane Bryan, Humphrey Bogart, Harry
Carey

'Good prizefight picture with action,
melodrama and names. Unusual in that
women will like it.'—Variety

Kid Galahad
US 1962 96m De Luxe
UA / Mirisch (David Weisbart)

Tolerable light-hearted musical remake of the
above.

w William Fay d Phil Karlson ph Burnett
Guffey m Jeff Alexander

Elvis Presley, Lola Albright, Gig Young, Joan
Blackman, Charles Bronson, Ned Glass,
David Lewis, Robert Emhardt

Kid Glove Killer*
US 1942 73m bw
MGM (Jack Chertok)

A police laboratory scientist tracks down the
murderer of the mayor and finds his best
friend is the culprit.
Professional police suspenser of the kind now
tackled by television.

w John Higgins, Allen Rivkin d Fred
Zinnemann ph Paul C. Vogel m David Snell

Van Heflin, Lee Bowman, Marsha Hunt,
Samuel S. Hinds, Eddie Quillan

Kid Millions*
US 1935 90m bw (Technicolor
sequence)
Samuel Goldwyn

An East Side kid inherits a fortune and has the
time of his life.
Dated star musical with moments which still
please.

w George Oppenheimer, William Anthony
McGuire d Roy del Ruth ph Gregg Toland
m / ly Bert Kalmar, Harry Ruby ad Richard
Day

Eddie Cantor, Ethel Merman, Ann Sothern,
George Murphy, Warren Hymer
'Goldwyn-Cantor girl-and-gag socko.'—
Variety

Kid Nightingale
US 1939 56m bw

A waiter is promoted into a prizefighter, and
sings as he knocks out each opponent. Self-
spoofing comedy with some laughs. John
Payne, Jane Wyman, Walter Catlett, Ed
Brophy, Charles D. Brown. Written by
Charles Belden, Raymond Schrock, Lee Katz;
directed by George Amy; for Warners. 'It's so
absolutely silly it's almost good.'—Variety

Kidnapped*
US 1938 93m bw
TCF (Kenneth MacGowan)

During the Jacobite rebellion a young boy is
sold by his wicked uncle as a slave, and is
helped by an outlaw.
Much altered version of a classic adventure
story, exciting enough in its own right, and
well made in the thirties tradition.

w Sonya Levien, Richard Sherman, Walter Ferris, *novel* Robert Louis Stevenson *d* Alfred L. Werker *ph* Bert Glennon *m* Arthur Lange

Warner Baxter, Freddie Bartholemew, Arleen Whelan, John Carradine, C. Aubrey Smith, Nigel Bruce, Reginald Owen

'Strange modifications have been wrought . . . ambitious effort which misses top rating.'—*Variety*

Kidnapped*
GB 1959   95m   Technicolor
Walt Disney (Hugh Attwooll)

A remake fairly faithful to the book, which results in a few *longueurs*; but in general the action is spirited.

wd Robert Stevenson *ph* Paul Beeson *m* Cedric Thorpe Davie

Peter Finch, James MacArthur, Bernard Lee, John Laurie, Finlay Currie, Niall MacGinnis, Peter O'Toole, Miles Malleson, Oliver Johnston, Duncan Macrae, Andrew Cruickshank

Kidnapped*
GB 1971   107m   Movielab   Panavision
Omnibus (Frederick H. Brogger)

Remake incorporating sections of *Catriona*. Not particularly exciting, but the acting helps.

w Jack Pulman *d* Delbert Mann *ph* Paul Beeson *m* Roy Budd

Michael Caine, Lawrence Douglas, Trevor Howard, Jack Hawkins, Donald Pleasence, Gordon Jackson, Freddie Jones, Jack Watson
● *Video: Rank*

The Kidnappers*
GB 1953   95m   bw
Rank / Nolbandov–Parkyn
US title: *The Little Kidnappers*

In a Nova Scotian village at the turn of the century a stern old man denies his young grandchildren a pet, so they borrow a baby and hide it in the woods.
Fairly pleasing and popular whimsy for family audiences.

w Neil Paterson *d* Philip Leacock *ph* Eric Cross *m* Bruce Montgomery

Duncan Macrae, Vincent Winter, Jon Whiteley, Theodore Bikel, Jean Anderson

The Kidnapping of the President*
Canada 1980   113m   De Luxe
Sefel (George Menduluk, John Ryan)

Third-world terrorists devise a plot to bring America to its knees by kidnapping the president.
Spirited political thriller which suffers chiefly from overlength.

w Richard Murphy, *novel* Charles Templeton *d* George Mendeluk *ph* Mike Malloy *m* Paul J. Zaza

Hal Holbrook, William Shatner, Van Johnson, Ava Gardner, Miguel Fernandez, Cindy Girling, Elizabeth Shepherd

Kiki
US 1931   96m   bw
UA / Mary Pickford (Joseph M. Schenck)

Long unseen star musical.
A tomboyish chorus girl sets her cap at her divorced producer.

w Sam Taylor, *play* David Belasco *d* Sam Taylor *ph* Karl Struss

Mary Pickford, Reginald Denny, Joseph Cawthorne, Margaret Livingston

'Too long and too light . . . what was to have been a cocktail has turned out to have been a soda.'—*Variety*

Kill Her Gently
GB 1958   75m   bw

A madman hires two convicts to murder his wife. Very mild and unmemorable thriller. Griffith Jones, Maureen Connell, Marc Lawrence, George Mikell. Written by Paul Erickson; directed by Charles Saunders; for Fortress / Columbia.

Kill Me Tomorrow
GB 1957   80m   bw

A down-and-out reporter confesses to murder in order to obtain cash for his son's operation. Tepid melodrama without much chemistry. Pat O'Brien, Lois Maxwell, George Coulouris, Wensley Pithey, Tommy Steele. Written by Robert Falconer and Manning O'Brine; directed by Terence Fisher; for Renown.

Kill or Cure
GB 1962   88m   bw
MGM (George H. Brown)

A series of murders at a nature clinic are solved by a bumbling private detective. Flatfooted and unprofessional murder farce whose only pace is slow.

w David Pursall, Jack Seddon *d* George Pollock *ph* Geoffrey Faithfull *m* Ron Goodwin

Terry-Thomas, Eric Sykes, Dennis Price, Lionel Jeffries, Moira Redmond, David Lodge, Ronnie Barker

Kill the Umpire
US 1950   78m   bw

An over-age baseball player can't get the game out of his mind, and returns as an argumentative umpire. Minor comedy of presumed pleasure to sports addicts. William Bendix, Una Merkel, Ray Collins, Gloria Henry, William Frawley. Written by Frank Tashlin; directed by Lloyd Bacon; for Columbia.

The Killer Elite
US 1975   120m   De Luxe   Panavision
UA / Exeter–Persky Bright (Martin Baum, Arthur Lewis)

A private crime fighting organization handles cases which the CIA prefers not to. Smooth, fashionable violence which seems to proclaim the end of a cycle.

w Marc Norman, Stirling Silliphant, *novel* Monkey in the Middle by Robert Rostand *d* Sam Peckinpah *ph* Philip Lathrop *m* Jerry Fielding

James Caan, Robert Duvall, Arthur Hill, Gig Young, Mako, Bo Hopkins, Burt Young, Tom Clancy

'Merely a commercial chore.'—*Tom Milne*
'A mysterious, elliptical, visually triumphant film about personal survival in a world of mean-minded machination.'—*Michael Billington, Illustrated London News*
● *Video: Warner*

Killer Fish
France / Brazil 1978   101m   colour

The leader of a burglary gang hides their haul in a dammed reservoir which he stocks with piranha fish. Heavy-going underwater shocker, with no fun while the fish are off-screen. Lee Majors, Karen Black, Margaux Hemingway, Marisa Berenson, James Franciscus. Written by Michael Rogers; directed by Antonio Margheriti; for Fawcett-Majors / Victoria / Filmar do Brazil. 'A slapdash actioner which casts its rod in water so overfished of late that it's amazing there's still anything down there biting.'—*Variety*.
● *Video: Precision*

The Killer Is Loose
US 1956   73m   bw

A bank robber swears revenge on a policeman who accidentally killed his wife. Star potboiler, just about tolerable. Joseph Cotten, Wendell Corey, Rhonda Fleming, Alan Hale Jnr, Michael Pate. Written by Harold Medford; directed by Budd Boetticher; for Crown / United Artists.

Killer McCoy
US 1947   104m   bw
MGM (Sam Zimbalist)

A prizefighter becomes involved in a murder. Grade A production applied to a grade B script.

w Frederick Hazlitt Brennan, Thomas Lennon, George Bruce, George Oppenheimer *d* Roy Rowland *ph* Joseph Ruttenberg *m* David Snell

Mickey Rooney, Ann Blyth, Brian Donlevy, James Dunn, Tom Tully, Sam Levene, James Bell, Gloria Holden

The Killer That Stalked New York
US 1950   75m   bw
Columbia (Robert Cohn)
GB title: *Frightened City*

New York is on the alert for a girl smallpox carrier.
Absurdly-titled minor thriller, quite competent but wholly unsurprising.

w Harry Essex *d* Earl McEvoy *ph* Joseph Biroc *m* Hans Salter

Charles Korvin, Evelyn Keyes, William Bishop, Dorothy Malone, Lola Albright, Barry Kelley, Carl Benton Reid, Ludwig Donath

The Killers***
US 1946 105m bw
U-I (Mark Hellinger)
TV title: *A Man Alone*

In a small sleazy town a gangster waits for two assassins to kill him, and we later find out why.
Elaborate tale of cross and double-cross, stunningly executed.

w Anthony Veiller, story Ernest Hemingway d Robert Siodmak ph Elwood Bredell m Miklos Rozsa

Burt Lancaster, Edmond O'Brien, Ava Gardner, Albert Dekker, Sam Levene, John Miljan, Virginia Christine, Vince Barnett, Charles D. Brown, Donald MacBride, Phil Brown, Charles McGraw, William Conrad

'About one tenth is Hemingway's, the rest is Universal-International's.'—*Richard Winnington*

'Seldom does a melodrama maintain the high tension that distinguishes this one.'—*Variety*

'There is nothing unique or even valuable about the picture, but energy combined with attention to form and detail doesn't turn up every day; neither does good entertainment.'—*James Agee*
† John Huston contributed to the script but is not credited.

AAN: Anthony Veiller; Robert Siodmak; Miklos Rozsa

The Killers*
US 1964 95m Pathecolor
U-I (Don Siegel)

Zesty, brutal remake intended for TV, but released theatrically because of its violence.

w Gene L. Coon d Don Siegel ph Richard L. Rawlings m Johnny Williams

John Cassavetes, Lee Marvin, Clu Gulager, Angie Dickinson, Ronald Reagan, Claude Akins

● *Video: CIC*

'Her soft mouth was the road to sin-smeared violence!'

Killer's Kiss
US 1955 64m bw
UA / Stanley Kubrick

A prizefighter rescues a girl from her gangster lover, and is marked for death.
Tedious low-budget indie which first brought its director into notice.

w / d / ph Stanley Kubrick m Gerald Fried

Frank Silvera, Irene Kane, Jamie Smith

The Killers of Kilimanjaro
GB 1959 91m Technicolor
Cinemascope
Columbia / Warwick (John R. Sloan)
US title: *Adamson of Africa*

A railroad engineer helps a girl find her lost father and fiancé.
Old-fashioned safari adventure full of action and animals.

w Richard Maibaum, Cyril Hume d Richard Thorpe ph Ted Moore m William Alwyn

Robert Taylor, Anne Aubrey, Grégoire Aslan, Anthony Newley

The Killing**
US 1956 83m bw
UA / Harris–Kubrick (J. B. Harris)

An ex-convict recruits helpers to steal two million dollars from a racetrack.
Incisive, entertaining, downbeat caper movie clearly influenced by *The Asphalt Jungle* and *Rififi*.

wd Stanley Kubrick, novel Clean Break by Lionel White ph Lucien Ballard m Gerald Fried

Sterling Hayden, Marie Windsor, Jay C. Flippen, Elisha Cook Jnr, Coleen Gray, Vince Edwards, Ted de Corsia, Joe Sawyer, Tim Carey

'The visual authority constantly dominates a flawed script.'—*Arlene Croce*

'The camera watches the whole shoddy show with the keen eye of a terrier stalking a pack of rats.'—*Time*

The Killing Fields***
GB 1984 141m colour
Goldcrest / Enigma (David Puttnam)

An American journalist is engulfed in the horror of Cambodia, and his native adviser disappears and is thought to be dead.
Brilliantly filmed, but probably too strong for a commercial audience to stomach, this true adventure tosses one into the horror of modern war and leaves one reeling despite its comparatively happy ending.

w Bruce Robinson, from the article 'The Death and Life of Dith Pran' by Sidney Schanberg d Roland Joffe ph Chris Menges m Mike Oldfield pd Roy Walker ed Jim Clark

Sam Waterston (as Sidney Schanberg), *Haing S. Ngor* (as Dith Pran), John Malkovitch, Julian Sands, Craig T. Nelson

The Killing of a Chinese Bookie
US 1976 113m colour

A Los Angeles nightclub owner is prevailed upon by gangsters to pay off his debt by eliminating a troublesome Chinese. Another unendurable slab of Cassavetes pretentiousness; why he goes on trying, in the face of twenty years of public indifference, is beyond imagining. Ben Gazzara, Timothy Carey, Seymour Cassel, Morgan Woodward. Written and directed by John Cassavetes, for his own company.

The Killing of Sister George*
US 1969 138m Metrocolor
Associates and Aldrich / Palomar

An ageing lesbian actress is fired from a TV serial and her life collapses around her.
Heavily handled film version of an amusing and moving play; everything is clumsily spelt out, including the love scenes, and the actresses are forced to repeat themselves.

w Lukas Heller, play Frank Marcus d Robert Aldrich ph Joseph Biroc m Gerald Fried

Beryl Reid, Susannah York, *Coral Browne*, Roland Fraser, Patricia Medina, Hugh Paddick, Cyril Delevanti

'The play was second-rate, but with its nice blend of the homely and the chilling, the absurdist and the perverse, it had the quality of a Kraft-Ebbing comic book. Aldrich and Heller have turned this material into a crawling tear-jerker, the lines spoken at a speed adjusted to non-English or non-language-speaking audiences.'—*John Simon*

'A clumpingly archaic piece of film-making.'—*New Yorker, 1982*
● *Video: Rank*

Kim*
US 1950 112m Technicolor
MGM (Leon Gordon)

The orphaned son of a British soldier in India has adventures with his horseman friend who belongs to the British secret service.
Colourful Boys' Own Paper high jinks, quite lively but never convincing.

w Leon Gordon, Helen Deutsch, Richard Schayer, novel Rudyard Kipling d Victor Saville ph William Skall m André Previn

Errol Flynn, Dean Stockwell, Paul Lukas, Robert Douglas, Thomas Gomez, Cecil Kellaway, Arnold Moss, Reginald Owen

'Ornate, lavish, but curiously lacking in genuine atmosphere, vitality or period sense.'—*Penelope Houston*

Kind Hearts and Coronets***
GB 1949 106m bw
Ealing (Michael Relph)

An impecunious heir eliminates eight D'Ascoynes who stand between him and the family fortune.
Witty, genteel black comedy well set in the stately Edwardian era and quite deserving of its reputation for wit and style; yet the effect is curiously muffled and several opportunities missed.

w Robert Hamer, John Dighton, novel Noblesse Oblige by Roy Horniman d Robert Hamer ph Douglas Slocombe

Dennis Price, Alec Guinness (in eight roles), *Valerie Hobson, Joan Greenwood*, Miles Malleson, Arthur Lowe

'A brilliant misfire for the reason that its plentiful wit is literary and practically never pictorial.'—*Richard Winnington*

'Enlivened with cynicism, loaded with dramatic irony and shot through with a suspicion of social satire.'—*Daily Telegraph*

'A film which can be seen and seen again with undiminished pleasure.'—*Basil Wright, 1972*
● *Video: Thorn EMI*

Kind Lady*
US 1935 76m bw
MGM / Lucien Hubbard
aka: *House of Menace*

A confidence trickster insinuates himself and

his criminal friends into the house of an invalid lady.
Unusual but unconvincing melodrama with overwrought leading performances.

w Bernard Schubert, *play* Edward Chodorov, *story* Hugh Walpole *d* George B. Seitz *ph* George Folsey *m* Edward Ward

Basil Rathbone, Aline MacMahon, Mary Carlisle, Frank Albertson, Dudley Digges, Doris Lloyd

'Leisurely pace cramps effectiveness.'— *Variety*

Kind Lady*
US 1951 78m bw
MGM (Armand Deutsch)

Edwardian-set remake of the above, rather more subtly acted but failing to extract all possible frissons.

w Jerry Davis, Edward Chodorov, Charles Bennett *d* John Sturges *ph* Joseph Ruttenberg *m* David Raksin

Maurice Evans, Ethel Barrymore, Angela Lansbury, Keenan Wynn, Betsy Blair, John Williams

'A curiously tame melodrama whose shocks, when they do come, are muffled and ineffectual.'— *Penelope Houston*

A Kind of Loving***
GB 1962 112m bw
Anglo-Amalgamated / Waterhall / Vic Films (Joe Janni)

A young north country draughtsman is forced into marriage, has to live with his dragon-like mother in law, and finally sorts out a relationship with his unhappy wife.
Blunt melodrama with strong kinship to *Saturday Night and Sunday Morning*, strikingly directed and photographed amid urban grime and suburban conformity.

w Keith Waterhouse, Willis Hall, *novel* Stan Barstow *d* John Schlesinger *ph* Denys Coop *m* Ron Grainer

Alan Bates, June Ritchie, Thora Hird, Bert Palmer, Gwen Nelson

● *Video: Thorn EMI*

King and Country*
GB 1964 86m bw
BHE (Norman Priggen, Joseph Losey)

In the trenches during World War I, a private is courtmartialled and shot for desertion.
Neat cinematic treatment of a very downbeat play.

w Evan Jones, *play* Hamp by John Wilson *d* Joseph Losey *ph* Denys Coop *m* Larry Adler *pd* Richard Macdonald

Tom Courtenay, *Dirk Bogarde*, Leo McKern, Barry Foster, James Villiers, Peter Copley

The King and Four Queens
US 1956 86m De Luxe Cinemascope
UA / Russ / Field / Gabco (David Hempstead)

A cowboy braves the wrath of a lady sharpshooter to gain gold and the hand of one of her four daughters.

Tawdry sex western sporadically enlivened by good-humoured playing.

w Margaret Fitts, Richard Alan Simmons *d* Raoul Walsh *ph* Lucien Ballard *m* Alex North

Clark Gable, Eleanor Parker, Jo Van Fleet, Jean Willes, Barbara Nichols, Sara Shane, Roy Roberts

'A superficially cynical exercise in the rival attractions of sex and money.'— *MFB*

The King and I*
US 1956 133m Eastmancolor
Cinemascope 55
TCF (Charles Brackett)

Musical remake of *Anna and the King of Siam* (qv), from the highly successful stage production. The film is opulent in lush detail but quite lacking in style.

w Ernest Lehman *d* Walter Lang *ph* Leon Shamroy *m Richard Rodgers book / ly* Oscar Hammerstein II *md* Alfred Newman, Ken Darby *ad* Lyle Wheeler, John de Cuir

Deborah Kerr, Yul Brynner, Rita Moreno, Martin Benson, Alan Mowbray, Geoffrey Toone, Terry Saunders

'Gaiety has something of a struggle to survive.'— *Penelope Houston*

AA: Yul Brynner; Alfred Newman, Ken Darby
AAN: best picture; Walter Lang; Leon Shamroy; Deborah Kerr

● *Video: CBS / Fox*

The King and the Chorus Girl
US 1937 94m bw
Warner (Mervyn Le Roy)
GB title: *Romance Is Sacred*

A European prince on the spree falls for a New York chorine.
Reasonably lively romantic comedy.

w Norman Krasna, Groucho Marx, from their story Grand Passion *d* Mervyn Le Roy *ph* Tony Gaudio *m* Werner Heymann

Joan Blondell, Fernand Gravet, Edward Everett Horton, Jane Wyman, Alan Mowbray, Mary Nash, Kenny Baker

'Sure word of mouth and a shoo-in for dough.'— *Variety*

King Arthur Was a Gentleman
GB 1942 99m bw
GFD / Gainsborough (Edward Black)

A soldier becomes a hero when he believes he has King Arthur's sword.
Not-too-successful attempt to turn a music hall comedian into a figure of Chaplinesque pathos.

w Val Guest, Marriott Edgar *d* Marcel Varnel

Arthur Askey, Evelyn Dall, Anne Shelton, Max Bacon, Jack Train, Peter Graves, Vera Frances, Ronald Shiner, Brefni O'Rourke

King Creole
US 1958 116m bw Vistavision
(Paramount) Hal B. Wallis

A failed graduate becomes a singer in a New

Orleans night club, and gets involved with gangsters.
Disagreeable crook melodrama turned into a musical star vehicle.

w Herbert Baker, Michael V. Gazzo, *novel* A Stone for Danny Fisher by Harold Robbins *d* Michael Curtiz *ph* Russell Harlan *m* Walter Scharf

Elvis Presley, Carolyn Jones, Dean Jagger, Walter Matthau, Dolores Hart, Paul Stewart

● *Video: CBS / Fox*

King for a Night
US 1933 78m bw

A minister's son becomes a boxer and goes to the electric chair for a murder committed by his sister. Glum and incredible moral saga.
Chester Morris, Helen Twelvetrees, Grant Mitchell, Alice White, John Miljan, George E. Stone. Written by W. A. McGuire and others; directed by Kurt Neumann; for Universal.

A King in New York*
GB 1957 109m bw
Attica (Charles Chaplin)

A penniless European king finds himself at odds with the American way of life.
Feeble Chaplin comedy from his anti-American period; tedious dialogue and poor physical production allow only momentary flashes of the satire intended.

wd / m Charles Chaplin *ph* Georges Périnal

Charles Chaplin, Michael Chaplin, *Oliver Johnson*, Dawn Addams, Jerry Desmonde, Harry Green, Maxine Audley, Sid James

'Unhappily he is a sadder and an older man; the real punch is gone. His dethroned king is an ironically apt image.'— *Marvin Felheim*
'Maybe the worst film ever made by a celebrated film artist.'— *New Yorker, 1977*
'It shows how the coming of sound was a curse to Chaplin; how its freedoms dissipated his strengths; how his attempts to exploit it intellectually and ideologically played to his weaknesses; how, in short, he was much more grievously hurt by history in art than by history in politics.'— *Stanley Kauffmann*
'An overblown, self-piteous excursion into autobiography.'— *Time Out, 1984*

King Kong****
US 1933 100m bw
RKO (Merian C. Cooper)

A film producer on safari brings back a giant ape which terrorizes New York.
The greatest monster movie of all, a miracle of trick work and suspense, with some of the most memorable moments in film history.

w James Creelman, Ruth Rose, *story* Edgar Wallace *d* Merian C. Cooper, Ernest Schoedsack *ph* Edward Linden, Verne Walker, J. O. Taylor *sound effects* Murray Spivak *chief technician* Willis J. O'Brien *m* Max Steiner

Robert Armstrong, Fay Wray, Bruce Cabot, Frank Reicher

KING KONG (1933). An artist's impression of the climactic fight between Kong and tyrannosaurus rex. Fay Wray is matted into the branch of the tree.

CARL DENHAM (Robert Armstrong): 'It wasn't the airplanes. It was beauty killed the beast.'

'If properly handled, should gather good grosses in a walk . . . and may open up a new medium for scaring babies via the screen.'—*Variety*

'Just amusing nonsense punctuated by such reflections as why, if the natives wanted to keep the monster on the other side of the wall, they should have built a door big enough to let him through.'—*James Agate*

AAN: photography

● *Video: Thorn EMI*

'The most exciting motion picture event of all time!'

King Kong

US 1976 135m Metrocolor Panavision
Dino de Laurentiis

Semi-spoof remake with added sexual overtones; though launched on a massive wave of publicity, it lacks both the charm and the technical resources of its predecessor.

w Lorenzo Semple Jnr d John Guillermin
ph Richard H. Kline m John Barry pd Dale Hennesy, Mario Chiari

Jeff Bridges, Charles Grodin, Jessica Lange, John Randolph, René Auberjonois, Julius Harris, Ed Lauter

'The one and original lovable monster is lost amid all the hydraulic manipulations in what now emerges as the story of a dumb blonde who falls for a huge plastic finger.'—*Judith Crist, Saturday Review*

'Even with colour, the settings of Kong II are no match for the rich black-and-white chiaroscuro of Kong I, with its echoes of artists like Gustave Doré and Max Ernst and its sensitivity to the emotional values of tone and texture.'—*Jack Kroll, Newsweek*

AAN: Richard H. Kline

● *Video: Thorn EMI*

King Lear*
GB / Denmark 1970 137m bw
Columbia / Filmways–Laterna (Michael
  Birkett)

Tragedy ensues when an old king prematurely divides his kingdom between his daughters. Miserably photographed in freezing Jutland, this is a deliberately downbeat version which despite its varied points of interest is extremely hard to sit through.

w William Shakespeare (a cut text) *d* Peter Brook *ph* Henning Kristiansen *m* none *pd* Georges Wakhevitch

Paul Scofield, Irene Worth, Alan Webb, Tom Fleming, Susan Engel, Cyril Cusack, Patrick Magee, Jack MacGowran

King of Alcatraz*
US 1938 56m bw
Paramount (William C. Thomas)

Convicts escape on a freighter, but one needs surgery. Pacy programmer with a stalwart cast.

w Irving Reis *d* Robert Florey *ph* Harry Fischbeck *md* Boris Morros

Gail Patrick, J. Carrol Naish, Lloyd Nolan, Harry Carey, Robert Preston, Anthony Quinn, Dennis Morgan, Porter Hall
  'Good gangster actioner . . . will please those liking crime cinematics.'—*Variety*

King of Burlesque*
US 1935 88m bw
TCF (Kenneth MacGowan)

A vaudeville impresario overcomes his troubles.
Well-written musical with plenty of variety talent.

w James Seymour, Gene Markey, Harry Tugend *d* Sidney Lanfield *ph* Peverell Marley *songs* various

Warner Baxter, Alice Faye, Jack Oakie, Mona Barrie, Arline Judge, Dixie Dunbar, Gregory Ratoff, Herbert Mundin, Fats Waller, Kenny Baker

Songs: 'I've Got My Fingers Crossed'; 'Lovely Lady'; 'Spreadin' Rhythm Around'; 'Who's Big Baby Are You?'; 'I'm Shooting High'; 'I Love to Ride the Horses'
  'Big-time musical, with production, material and cast making up for story shortcomings.'—*Variety*

† Remade as *Hello Frisco Hello.*

King of Chinatown
US 1939 56m bw

A top racketeer is double-crossed by his henchman. Smartly paced underworld melodrama. Anna May Wong, Akim Tamiroff, Sidney Toler, J. Carrol Naish, Philip Ahn, Anthony Quinn. Written by Lillie Hayward, Irving Reis, Herbert Biberman; directed by Nick Grinde; for Stuart Walker / Paramount. 'Good support for key duals.'—*Variety*

King of Comedy**
US 1982 109m Technicolor
TCF / Embassy International (Arnon
  Milchan)

Obsessed with becoming a chat show host, an aspiring comedian kidnaps his idol and ransoms him for a spot in the show.
Amusing, underplayed farce with a tragic lining: a very convincing picture of the media today.

w Paul D. Zimmermann *d* Martin Scorsese *ph* Fred Schuler *m* various *pd* Boris Leven

Robert de Niro, Jerry Lewis, Diahnne Abbott, Sandra Bernard
  'This is a very frightening film, and in retrospect nothing about it seems funny at all.'—*Variety*
  'Unquestionably one of the films of the year.'—*Guardian*
  'A most eerie and memorable picture.'—*Spectator*

BFA: best original screenplay

King of Gamblers
US 1937 79m bw
Paramount
aka: *Czar of the Slot Machines*

A ruthless gangster loves a singer who loves a reporter who is out to expose him.
A muddled script mars this pacy lower-birth item.

w Doris Anderson *d* Robert Florey *ph* Harry Fischbeck *md* Boris Morros

Akim Tamiroff, Claire Trevor, Lloyd Nolan, Buster Crabbe, Porter Hall
  'Well enough done to rate okay in the smaller spots solo.'—*Variety*

King of Hearts
France / Italy 1966 110m Eastmancolor
UA / Fildebroc / Montoro (Philippe de
  Broca)
original title: *Le Roi de Coeur*

In World War I, a Scottish soldier finds a war-torn town occupied only by lunatics who have escaped from the asylum and who want to make him their king.
Heavy-handed whimsy which never catches fire despite the talents involved.

w Daniel Boulanger *d* Philippe de Broca *ph* Pierre Lhomme *m* Georges Delerue

Alan Bates, Geneviève Bujold, Jean-Claude Brialy, Françoise Christophe, Pierre Brasseur, Micheline Presle, Adolfo Celi, Julien Guiomar

King of Jazz**
US 1930 101m Technicolor
Universal (Carl Laemmle Jnr)

Musical revue.
Stylish, spectacular, revelatory early musical: a treasure trove.

devised / d John Murray Anderson *w* Harry Ruskin, Charles MacArthur *pd* Hal Mohr, Ray Rennahan, Jerome Ash *ad* Herman Rose

Paul Whiteman and his orchestra, John Boles, Bing Crosby (with the Rhythm Boys), Laura la Plante, Glenn Tryon, Slim Summerville, Walter Brennan

Songs: 'Happy Feet'; 'A Bench in the Park'; 'My Bridal Veil'; 'Song of the Dawn'; 'I Like to Do Things for You'; 'Music Has Charms'; 'My Lover'; 'It Happened in Monterey'; 'Ragamuffin Romeo'; 'So the Bluebirds and the Blackbirds Got Together'
  'A box office picture anywhere for one week.'—*Variety*

'Under a master director and the reverent
  genius of great players, the story of
  Christ has taken human form and greater
  understanding!'
'Dramatic magnificence, spectacular
  splendour, riotous joy, tigerish rage,
  undying love, terrifying tempests,
  appalling earthquakes!'

King of Kings**
US 1927 155m approx (24 fps) (various
  versions) bw silent
(Pathé) Cecil B. de Mille
Famous subtitle: *Harness my zebras, gift of
  the Nubian king!*

The life of Jesus, seen more or less from the viewpoint of Mary Magdalene.
A patchy but frequently moving and pictorially effective work, ranging from the sublime (the first view of Jesus as a blind man regains his sight) to the ridiculous ('Harness my zebras, gift of the Nubian king!' says Mary Magdalene in a sub-title).

w Jeanie Macpherson *d* Cecil B. de Mille *ph* J. Peverell Marley

H. B. Warner, Jacqueline Logan, Joseph Schildkraut (Judas), Ernest Torrence (Peter), Victor Varconi (Pilate), Dorothy Cumming (Mary, mother of Jesus), Rudolph Schildkraut (Caiaphas)
  'The most impressive of all motion pictures.'—*Mordaunt Hall, New York Times*
  'A picture which will tend to standardize the world's conception of the New Testament . . . de Mille has one of the best business minds in pictures and making *King of Kings* was the most brilliant stroke of his successful business career.'—*Welford Beaton, The Film Spectator*

'A story of the Christ! The glory of his
  spoken words!'

King of Kings*
US 1961 161m Super Technirama
MGM / Samuel Bronston

The life of Jesus Christ.
Known in the trade as *I Was a Teenage Jesus*, this good-looking but rather tedious film is neither vulgar nor very interesting; a solemn, decent, bible-in-pictures pageant.

w Philip Yordan *d* Nicholas Ray *ph* Franz Planer, Manuel Berenger *m* Miklos Rozsa *ad* Georges Wakhevitch

Jeffrey Hunter, Robert Ryan, Siobhan McKenna, Frank Thring, Hurd Hatfield, Rip Torn, Harry Guardino, Viveca Lindfors, Rita Gam

The King of Marvin Gardens*
US 1972   104m   Eastmancolor
Columbia / BBS (Bob Rafaelson)

The host of a late night radio talk show gets embroiled in his brother's schemes. Thoughtful tragi-comedy overweighted by talk, but with good performances.

w Jacob Brackman d Bob Rafaelson
ph Laszlo Kovacs

Jack Nicholson, Bruce Dern, Ellen Burstyn, Julia Anne Robinson
   'Indecipherable dark nonsense about brothers and goals and the American dream. An unqualified disaster.'—New Yorker
   'Glum news from the people who made Five Easy Pieces, which had a lot of good work in it along with some pretentious flab. In their new picture the flab has taken over.'—Stanley Kauffmann

King of Paris
GB 1935   75m   bw

The story of a French stage impresario, supposedly based on Sacha Guitry. Interesting try for a minority audience. Cedric Hardwicke, Marie Glory, Ralph Richardson, Phyllis Monkman. Written by John Van Druten from the play La Voie Lactée by Alfred Savoir; directed by Herbert Wilcox; for British and Dominions. 'Nothing much to be desired in this picture, excepting a story.'—Variety

King of the Damned*
GB 1935   76m   bw
Gaumont (Michael Balcon)

On a South Seas convict settlement, harsh treatment leads to mutiny.
A downright peculiar project for a British studio at this time, but technically very competent for those who like this kind of thing.

w Charles Bennett, Sidney Gilliat, Noel Langley, play John Chancellor d Walter Forde ph Bernard Knowles md Louis Levy

Conrad Veidt, Helen Vinson, Noah Beery, Cecil Ramage, Edmund Willard, Raymond Lovell, Allan Jeayes, Percy Parsons
   'Goes so far overboard on gloom that it defeats its own end.'—Variety

King of the Gypsies
US 1978   112m   Technicolor
Paramount / Dino de Laurentiis (Anna Gross)

A gypsy leader is denied the hand in marriage of the daughter of a rival, so he kidnaps her. Ethnic melodrama which despite its vigorous insistence on tradition—or perhaps because of it—plays like a mad musical without any songs.

w Frank Pierson, novel Peter Maas d Frank Pierson ph Sven Nykvist, Edward Lachman m David Grisman pd Gene Callahan

Sterling Hayden, Brooke Shields, Shelley Winters, Susan Sarandon, Judd Hirsch, Eric Roberts

'Body of a Greek god! Strength of a Hercules!'

King of the Jungle
US 1933   73m   bw

A small boy grows up with lions; he is captured with them and sold to an American circus. Sub-Tarzan hokum which cheered up the kids. Buster Crabbe, Frances Dee, Douglass Dumbrille, Robert Adair, Robert Barrat. Written by Philip Wylie, Fred Niblo Jnr, C. T. Stoneham; directed by H. Bruce Humberstone and Max Marcin; for Paramount. 'Minus any help from the marquee it will have to attract on merit alone, and on merit it rates fair business.'—Variety

King of the Khyber Rifles
US 1954   100m   Technicolor
Cinemascope
TCF (Frank Rosenberg)

In 1857 a British garrison in India is threatened by the forces of Kuuram Khan but saved by a half-caste officer.
Standard North-West Frontier adventure, old-fashioned and rather dull.

w Ivan Goff, Ben Roberts d Henry King
ph Leon Shamroy m Bernard Herrmann

Tyrone Power, Terry Moore, Michael Rennie, Guy Rolfe, John Justin

King of the Roaring Twenties
US 1961   106m   bw
Warner / AA / Bischoff–Diamond
GB title: The Big Bankroll

A gambler, Arnold Rothstein, becomes powerful among twenties gangsters. Routine crime drama, shoddily made.

w Jo Swerling d Joseph M. Newman ph Carl Guthrie m Franz Waxman

David Janssen, Dianne Foster, Mickey Rooney, Mickey Shaughnessy, Diana Dors, Dan O'Herlihy, Jack Carson, Keenan Wynn, William Demarest, Joseph Schildkraut, Regis Toomey, Murvyn Vye
   'Superficial, shopworn biography of an infamous bookie.'—MFB

King of the Turf
US 1939   88m   bw

A gambler out of luck befriends a small boy who turns out to be his own son. Hard to take even at the time, this sentimental tarididdle does not bear later scrutiny. Adolphe Menjou, Dolores Costello, Walter Abel, Roger Daniel. Written and directed by George Bruce; for Edward Small.
   'Dandy racetrack yarn . . . it has a refreshing appeal and the dialogue is excellent.'—Variety

King of the Underworld
US 1938   69m   bw

When her husband is killed by gangsters, a doctor takes her own steps to round them up. Sex-change remake of Dr Socrates; certainly no better. Kay Francis, Humphrey Bogart, James Stephenson, John Eldredge. Written by George Bricker, Vincent Sherman; directed by Lewis Seiler; for Warners. 'It will have trouble even in the duals.'—Variety

King, Queen, Knave*
US / West Germany 1972   92m
Eastmancolor
Wolper / Maran (Lutz Hengst)

The wife of a Munich bookseller falls for his adolescent nephew.
Amusing, capriciously directed sex comedy.

w David Shaw, David Seltzer, novel Vladimir Nabokov d Jerzy Skolomowski ph Charly Steinberger m Stanley Myers

Gina Lollobrigida, David Niven, John Moulder-Brown, Mario Adorf, Carl Fox-Duering

'Even Hell had to have a monarch!'

King Rat**
US 1965   134m   bw
Columbia / Coleytown (James Woolf)

In Singapore's Changi Gaol during World War II an American corporal lives more comfortably than the other prisoners by shabby dealings with the camp guards.
Overlong but generally gripping character melodrama—'not a story of escape but a story of survival'.

wd Bryan Forbes, novel James Clavell
ph Burnett Guffey m John Barry

George Segal, Tom Courtenay, John Mills, James Fox, Denholm Elliott, Todd Armstrong, Patrick O'Neal, James Donald, Alan Webb, Leonard Rossiter, Geoffrey Bayldon

AAN: Burnett Guffey

King Richard and the Crusaders
US 1954   113m   Warnercolor
Cinemascope
Warner (Henry Blanke)

During the Crusades, the dreaded Saladin arrives in England in disguise and falls in love with Lady Edith . . .
Crudely confected comic strip version of Sir Walter Scott's The Talisman, ineptly written and cast, with poor production values.

w John Twist d David Butler ph Peverell Marley m Max Steiner

Rex Harrison (as Saladin), Virginia Mayo, George Sanders, Laurence Harvey, Robert Douglas

   LADY EDITH (Virginia Mayo): 'Fight, fight, fight! That's all you think of, Dick Plantagenet!'

   'Do not adjust your set—the sound you hear is Sir Walter Scott turning in his grave.'—Sunday Express

   'It shows why the Crusades never really amounted to much.'—Time

King Solomon of Broadway
US 1935   72m   bw

A night-club owner gambles away money he has borrowed from the mob. Stale underworld melodrama. Edmund Lowe, Dorothy Page, Pinky Tomlin, Louise Henry, Charles Grapewin. Written by Harry Clork, Doris Malloy; directed by Alan Crosland; for Universal. 'Won't go very far; mostly for doubles.'—Variety

King Solomon's Mines*
GB 1937 80m bw
Gainsborough (Geoffrey Barkas)

Explorers in Africa persuade an exiled chief to
help them find a diamond mine.
Rather somnolent though well-cast version of
a favourite adventure novel, with a splendid
final reel.

w Michael Hogan, A. R. Rawlinson, Roland
Pertwee, Ralph Spence, Charles Bennett,
novel H. Rider Haggard d Robert Stevenson
ph Glen MacWilliams m Mischa Spoliansky

Cedric Hardwicke, Paul Robeson, Roland
Young, John Loder, Anna Lee, Sydney
Fairbrother, Robert Adams

'If the pop houses can accept its half-throttle
speed, they'll get all the thrills and
entertainment they want.'—Variety

'They kept the eye of the camera open for
every form of wild and savage life and
crammed it all into the picture, so one gets the
impression that Allan Quartermain is
delivering a lecture with illustrations rather
than taking part in an adventure.'—Richard
Mallett, Punch

King Solomon's Mines*
US 1950 102m Technicolor
MGM (Sam Zimbalist)

A remake which is largely travelogue with the
merest trimmings of story.

w Helen Deutsch d Compton Bennett
ph Robert Surtees

Stewart Granger, Deborah Kerr, Richard
Carlson, Hugo Haas, Lowell Gilmore
† Andrew Marton directed the second unit
sequences.

AA: Robert Surtees
AAN: best picture

The King Steps Out*
US 1936 85m bw
Columbia (William Perlberg)

Emperor Franz Josef falls in love with the
sister of the princess to whom he is betrothed.
Rather heavy-handed romance with music, not
in its director's best style but showing flashes
of his decorative talent.

w Sidney Buchman, operetta Cissy by Herbert
and Ernst Marischka d Josef Von Sternberg
ph Lucien Ballard songs Fritz Kreisler,
Dorothy Fields ad Stephen Goossen

Grace Moore, Franchot Tone, Walter
Connolly, Raymond Walburn, Herman Bing,
Victor Jory, Elizabeth Risdon, Nana Bryant,
Frieda Inescort, Thurston Hall

'Josef Von Sternberg asked that it not be
included in retrospectives of his work, but he
really did make the damned thing.'—New
Yorker, 1977

Kingdom of the Spiders
US 1977 95m colour
Arachnid / Dimension (Henry Fownes)

In an Arizona valley the death rate soars when
tarantulas begin preying in groups on humans
instead of singly on each other.

The spiders is coming, as Hitch might have
remarked, and not even giant-size. Standard
shudders, efficiently presented.

w Richard Robinson, Alan Caillou d John
Cardos ph John Morrill, John Wheeler
md Igo Kantor

William Shatner, Tiffany Bolling, Woody
Strode, David MacLean

Kings Go Forth
US 1958 109m bw
UA / Ross–Eton (Frank Ross)

August 1944: two American soldiers fall out
over a black French woman who is torn
between them.
Heavy-going war melodrama, well enough
done for those who can take it.

w Merle Miller, novel Joe David Brown
d Delmer Daves ph Daniel Fapp m Elmer
Bernstein

Frank Sinatra, Tony Curtis, Natalie Wood,
Leora Dana, Karl Swenson

Kings of the Road
Germany 1975 176m bw

Two men on a bus talk of their past lives, their
problems, their hopes and their fears.
Impossibly tedious two-hander which
doubtless says something about life for those
with the patience to sit it out. Ruediger
Vogler, Hanns Zischler. Written and directed
by Wim Wenders; for Wim Wenders
Productions. (Original title: Im Lauf der Zeit.)

Kings of the Sun
US 1963 108m De Luxe Panavision
UA / Mirisch (Lewis J. Rachmil)

A Mayan tribe emigrates from Mexico to
Texas and makes peace with the local Indian
chief.
Ponderous dark age epic replete with human
sacrifice, high-mindedness and solemn pauses.
The actors and sets carry it as far as it will go.

w Elliot Arnold, James R. Webb d J. Lee-
Thompson ph Joe MacDonald m Elmer
Bernstein ad Alfred Ybarra

Yul Brynner, George Chakiris, Shirley Anne
Field, Richard Basehart, Brad Dexter, Barry
Morse

The King's Pirate
US 1967 100m Technicolor
Universal (Robert Arthur)

An American in the 18th-century British navy
infiltrates a pirate stronghold in Madagascar.
Tatty remake of Against All Flags, rising to a
few minor heights of swashbuckling.

w Paul Wayne d Don Weis ph Clifford Stine
m Ralph Ferraro

Doug McClure, Jill St John, Guy Stockwell,
Kurt Kasznar, Torin Thatcher, Richard
Deacon, Sean McClory

King's Rhapsody
GB 1955 93m Eastmancolor
Cinemascope
Everest (Herbert Wilcox)

An exiled Ruritanian king leaves his mistress
to return home to a political marriage.

Love versus duty in a ludicrously inept film of
Ivor Novello's highly theatrical musical drama,
cheaply made and killed stone dead by casting
and wide screen.

w Pamela Bower, Christopher Hassall, A. P.
Herbert d Herbert Wilcox ph Max Greene

Errol Flynn, Anna Neagle, Patrice Wymore,
Martita Hunt, Finlay Currie

'The town they talk of in whispers!'

King's Row****
US 1941 127m bw
Warner (David Lewis)

In a small American town during the early
years of the century, three children grow up
into a world of cruelty and madness.
Superb Hollywood melodrama, a Peyton Place
with great visual strength, haunting music and
a wholly absorbing if incredible plot.

w Casey Robinson, novel Henry Bellamann
d Sam Wood ph James Wong Howe m Erich
Wolfgang Korngold pd William Cameron
Menzies

Ann Sheridan, Robert Cummings, Ronald
Reagan, Claude Rains, Betty Field, Charles
Coburn, Nancy Coleman, Maria Ouspenskaya,
Harry Davenport, Judith Anderson, Karen
Verne

DRAKE (Ronald Reagan): 'Where's the rest
of me?'

'Half masterpiece and half junk.'—James
Agate

'Out of the hushed strangeness of these
lives, and out of the shadows that hid their
shame, filmdom has fashioned a drama most
unusual, most touching and most
wonderful!'—publicity

'Tranquilly accepting many varieties of
psychopathic behaviour as the simple facts of
life, this film has its own kind of sentimental
glow, yet the melodramatic incidents are
surprisingly compelling.'—New Yorker, 1982

'One of the great melodramas, a veritable
Mount Rushmore of physical and emotional
cripples.'—Time Out, 1981

AAN: best picture; Sam Wood; James Wong
Howe

A King's Story*
GB 1965 102m Technicolor
Le Vien Films (Jack Le Vien)

Interviews with the Duke and Duchess of
Windsor are interspersed with newsreels of the
abdication crisis.
Earnest popular documentary with many
points in its favour, including a resounding
commentary by Orson Welles.

w Glyn Jones d Harry Booth m Ivor Slaney
● Video: Thorn EMI

The King's Thief
US 1955 79m Eastmancolor
Cinemascope
MGM (Edwin H. Knopf)

The Duke of Brampton plots treason against
Charles II but a highwayman robs him of an
incriminating notebook.
Dismal swashbuckler with neither zest nor
style, just a cast of unhappy-looking actors.

w Charles Knopf d Robert Z. Leonard
ph Robert Planck m Miklos Rozsa

David Niven, Edmund Purdom, Ann Blyth,
George Sanders, Roger Moore

The King's Vacation
US 1933 62m bw

A king abdicates to seek the simple life.
Pleasing fable with a few theatrical ironies.
George Arliss, Florence Arliss, Dick Powell,
Marjorie Gateson, Dudley Digges. Written by
Ernest Pascal and Maude T. Howell; directed
by John Adolfi; for Warner.

Kipps***
GB 1941 112m bw
TCF (Edward Black)
US title: The Remarkable Mr Kipps

In 1906, a draper's assistant comes into money
and tries to crash society.
Charming, unassuming film of a well-loved
novel, later musicalized as Half a Sixpence.

w Sidney Gilliat, novel H. G. Wells d Carol
Reed ph Arthur Crabtree m Charles
Williams

Michael Redgrave, Phyllis Calvert, Diana
Wynyard, Arthur Riscoe, Max Adrian, Helen
Haye, Michael Wilding, Lloyd Pearson,
Edward Rigby, Hermione Baddeley, Frank
Pettingell, Beatrice Varley, Kathleen
Harrison, Felix Aylmer.

Kismet
US 1930 90m bw 65mm Vitascope
Warner

An Oriental magician overcomes a wicked
vizier.
Rather tame filming of a spectacular which
belongs on the stage.

w Howard Estabrook, play Edward Knoblock
d John Francis Dillon ph John Seitz

Otis Skinner, Loretta Young, David Manners,
Mary Duncan, Sidney Blackmer, Fred
Sterling, Edmund Breese, Montagu Love

Kismet*
US 1944 100m Technicolor
MGM (Everett Riskin)
TV title: Oriental Dream

Hollow and humourless but striking-looking
remake of the above.

w John Meehan, d William Dieterle
ph Charles Rosher m Herbert Stothart
ad Cedric Gibbons, Daniel B. Cathcart

Ronald Colman, Marlene Dietrich, James
Craig, Edward Arnold, Hugh Herbert, Joy
Ann Page, Florence Bates, Harry Davenport,
Hobart Cavanaugh, Robert Warwick

AAN: Charles Rosher; Herbert Stothart

Kismet
US 1955 113m Eastmancolor
Cinemascope
MGM (Arthur Freed)

Unlucky musical remake from the stage show
with Borodin music.

w Charles Lederer, Luther Davis, from their
musical play d Vincente Minnelli ph Joseph
Ruttenberg ch Jack Cole ad Cedric Gibbons,
Preston Ames

Howard Keel, Ann Blyth, Dolores Gray, Vic
Damone, Monty Woolley, Sebastian Cabot,
Jay C. Flippen, Mike Mazurki, Jack Elam

The Kiss*
US 1929 64m approx (24 fps) bw
silent
MGM (Albert Lewin)

A woman is accused of the murder of her
jealous husband.
A wisp of a melodrama, enlivened by its star;
otherwise only notable as MGM's last silent
picture.

w Hans Kraly d Jacques Feyder ph William
Daniels

Greta Garbo, Lew Ayres, Conrad Nagel,
Holmes Herbert, Anders Randolf

'Women were putty in his hands!'

Kiss and Make Up
US 1934 80m bw
Paramount (B. P. Schulberg)

A Parisian beauty specialist forsakes a rich
client for his loyal secretary.
Forgettable romantic comedy.

w Harlan Thompson, George Marion Jnr, play
Stephen Bekeffi d Harlan Thompson
ph Leon Shamroy

Cary Grant, Genevieve Tobin, Helen Mack,
Edward Everett Horton, Lucien Littlefield,
Mona Maris
  'More gags than romance . . . a nice picture
lacking sufficient strength to wow, but should
do all right.'—Variety

Kiss and Tell*
US 1945 92m bw
Columbia (Sol C. Siegel)

To protect another girl, an irrepressible
teenager pretends to be pregnant.
Good-humoured farcical comedy which at the
time was thought pretty shocking, especially
with the infant darling of the thirties in the
lead.

w F. Hugh Herbert, from his play d Richard
Wallace ph Charles Lawton m Werner
Heymann

Shirley Temple, Robert Benchley, Walter
Abel, Jerome Courtland, Katherine
Alexander, Porter Hall, Tom Tully
  'All brilliantly characteristic of the worst
anyone could think of American life.'—James
Agee

A Kiss before Dying*
US 1956 94m De Luxe Cinemascope
UA / Crown (Robert Jacks)

A college boy kills women who get in his way.
Reasonably absorbing exercise in
psychopathology which would have been more
effective on a smaller screen.

w Lawrence Roman, novel Ira Levin d Gerd
Oswald ph Lucien Ballard m Lionel
Newman

Jeffrey Hunter, Joanne Woodward, Robert
Wagner, Virginia Leith, Mary Astor, George
Macready

The Kiss before the Mirror
US 1933 66m bw

A lawyer defends a man who killed his wife
from jealousy, then finds that the same thing is
happening to him. Stilted drama which was
thought stylish at the time but is now a
disappointment from this director; miscast,
too. Frank Morgan, Nancy Carroll, Gloria
Stuart, Paul Lukas, Charles Grapewin.
Written by William Anthony McGuire, from
the play by Lazslo Fodor; directed by James
Whale; for Universal. (NB: remade in 1938 as
Wives Under Suspicion.) 'Direction and
adaptation lift this one into passable
entertainment.'—Variety

A Kiss for Corliss
US 1949 88m bw
UA / James Nasser
aka: Almost a Bride

A teenager develops a crush on a middle-aged
roué.
Dismal sequel to Kiss and Tell in the shadow
of The Bachelor and the Bobby Soxer.

w Howard Dimsdale d Richard Wallace
ph Robert de Grasse m Werner Heymann

David Niven, Shirley Temple, Tom Tully,
Darryl Hickman, Virginia Welles
  'A disastrous teenage potboiler.'—David
Niven
  'I sometimes think that David Niven
  Should not take all the parts he's given;
  While of the art of Shirley Temple
  I, for the moment, have had ample.'—C. A.
Lejeune

A Kiss in the Dark
US 1949 87m bw
Warner (Harry Kurnitz)

A concert pianist finds romance in a boarding
house peopled with zany characters.
Paper-thin romantic comedy.

w Harry Kurnitz d Delmer Daves ph Robert
Burks m Max Steiner

David Niven, Jane Wyman, Broderick
Crawford, Maria Ouspenskaya, Victor Moore,
Wayne Morris, Joseph Buloff, Curt Bois

Kiss Me Again**
US 1925 77m approx (24 fps) bw
silent
Warner

A bored wife is tempted to stray, but doesn't.
Excellent silent comedy from an old boulevard
farce, remade to less effect in the forties as
That Uncertain Feeling.

w Hans Kraly, play Divorcons by Victorien
Sardou, Emile de Najac d Ernst Lubitsch
ph Charles Von Enger

Marie Prévost, Monte Blue, John Roche,
Willard Louis, Clara Bow
  'Another sex masterpiece from the Attila of
Hollywood . . . Continental high comedy done

in the central European manner with Germanic harshness and irony of attack.'—*Ted Shane, New Yorker*

'Perhaps the most exquisite light screen comedy ever made on the subject of l'amour.'—*Herman G. Weinberg*

Kiss Me Again
US 1931 74m Technicolor

A French lieutenant and a cabaret singer chase each other half across the world. Modest musical from Victor Herbert's *Mademoiselle Modiste*; popular at the time as a vehicle for two-colour Technicolor. Walter Pidgeon, Bernice Claire, Frank McHugh, Edward Everett Horton. Written by Julien Josephson and Paul Perez; directed by William A. Seiter; for Warner. (GB title: *Toast of the Legion*.)
'Doubtful as strong b.o. but clean, deserving, and may get a break.'—*Variety*

'I don't care what you do to me, Mike—just
   do it fast!'
Kiss Me Deadly
US 1955 105m bw
UA / Parklane (Robert Aldrich)

By helping a girl who is nevertheless murdered, Mike Hammer prevents crooks from stealing a case of radio-active material.
Curiously arty and excruciatingly boring private eye thriller, a ripe piece of cinematic cheese full of tilt shots and symbols: even the titles read from down to up.

w A. I. Bezzerides *d* Robert Aldrich *ph* Ernest Laszlo *m* Frank de Vol

Ralph Meeker, Albert Dekker, Cloris Leachman, Paul Stewart, Juano Hernandez, Wesley Addy, Maxene Cooper

Kiss Me Goodbye
US 1982 101m De Luxe
TCF / Boardwalk / Burt Sugarman / Keith Barish (Robert Mulligan)

A widow planning to marry again is harassed by the ghost of her first husband.
It worked in *Blithe Spirit*, but this is on a different level, a toned-down rendering of the heavy-breathing Brazilian farce *Donna Flor and Her Two Husbands*, and it doesn't work on any level.

w Charlie Peters *w* Robert Mulligan *ph* Donald Peterman *m* Ralph Burns *pd* Philip M. Jefferies *ed* Sheldon Kahn

James Caan, Sally Field, Jeff Bridges, Paul Dooley, Claire Trevor, Mildred Natwick, William Prince

Kiss Me Kate**
US 1953 111m Anscocolor 3-D
MGM (Jack Cummings)

The married leading players of a musical version of *The Taming of the Shrew* lead an equally tempestuous life backstage.
Brisk, bright screen version of the Broadway musical hit.

w Dorothy Kingsley, *play* Samuel and Bella Spewack *d* George Sidney *ph* Charles

Rosher *m* / *ly* Cole Porter *md* André Previn, Saul Chaplin *ch* Hermes Pan

Howard Keel, Kathryn Grayson, Ann Miller, Keenan Wynn, Bobby Van, Tommy Rall, James Whitmore, Bob Fosse, Kurt Kasznar

AAN: André Previn, Saul Chaplin

● *Video: MGM / UA*

Kiss Me Stupid*
US 1964 124m bw Panavision
UA / Mirisch / Phalanx / (Billy Wilder)

A womanizing pop singer stops overnight in a small California desert town and shows interest in an unsuccessful songwriter in order to get at his wife.
Draggy, tasteless, surprisingly unamusing smoking room story, with the actors behaving as though driven against their will (apart from Dean Martin, ideally cast as the idol who gets a headache if he doesn't have sex every night). Some good wisecracks, but it should have been much faster and funnier.

w Billy Wilder, I. A. L. Diamond, *play* L'oro della fantasia by Anna Bonacci *d* Billy Wilder *ph* Joseph La Shelle *m* André Previn *pd* Alexander Trauner *songs* George and Ira Gershwin

Dean Martin, Kim Novak, Ray Walston, Cliff Osmond
'A work of ferocious tastelessness . . . Swiftian in its relentless disgust.'—*Peter Barnes*

'You know what I do to squealers? I let
   them have it in the belly. So they can roll
   around for a long time thinking it over!'
Kiss of Death**
US 1947 98m bw
TCF (Fred Kohlmar)

A captured thief informs on his own gang, and a psychopathic killer is sent to extract vengeance.
Gloomy, well-made semi-location thriller which descends into heavy melodrama. Remade as *The Fiend Who Walked the West*.

w Ben Hecht, Charles Lederer *d* Henry Hathaway *ph* Norbert Brodine *m* David Buttolph

Victor Mature, Richard Widmark, Brian Donlevy, Coleen Gray, Karl Malden, Taylor Holmes
'A tense, terrifying crime melodrama with an unusually authentic seamy atmosphere.'—*New Yorker, 1980*
'Economy of narration enhances the compactness and tautness of the whole and achieves that rarity, a picture minus unnecessary footage.'—*National Board of Review*
'It illustrates a new and vigorous trend in US moviemaking. One of the best things that is happening in Hollywood is the tendency to move out of the studio—to base fictional pictures on fact, and to shoot them not in painted studio sets but in actual places.'—*James Agee*

AAN: original story (E. Lipsky); Richard Widmark

Kiss of Fire
US 1955 86m Technicolor
Universal–International (Samuel Marx)

An ex-soldier escorts an exiled princess on a dangerous journey through Mexico.
Slightly unusual but rather clumsy swashbuckler of no especial merit.

w Franklin Coen, Richard Collins, *novel* The Rose and the Flame by Jonreed Luaritzen *d* Joseph M. Newman *ph* Carl Guthrie *md* Joseph Gershenson

Jack Palance, Barbara Rush, Martha Hyer

Kiss of the Vampire*
GB 1962 88m Eastmancolor
U-I / Hammer (Anthony Hinds)
US title: *Kiss of Evil*

In 1910 a Bavarian disciple of Dracula lures a British honeymoon couple.
This unsubtle variation on *Dracula* is handled in lively fashion, with a splendid climax in which assorted white-robed vampires are destroyed by bats.

w John Elder *d* Don Sharp *ph* Alan Hume *m* James Bernard

Noel Willman, Clifford Evans, Edward De Souza, Jennifer Daniel, Isobel Black

   PROF. ZIMMER (Noel Willman): 'You must not expect your Queensberry rules here, Mr Harcourt.'

'They won't stop us—nobody can stop us!'
Kiss the Blood Off My Hands
US 1948 80m bw
Universal / Hecht-Norma (Harold Hecht)
GB title: *Blood on My Hands*

A nurse helps a seaman on the run for murder.
Risible romantic melodrama in never-was London docks setting, with Newton large as life and twice as villainous.

w Leonardo Bercovici, *novel* Gerald Butler *d* Norman Foster *ph* Russell Metty *m* Miklos Rozsa

Joan Fontaine, Burt Lancaster, Robert Newton, Lewis Russell, Aminta Dyne

Kiss the Boys Goodbye*
US 1941 85m bw
Paramount

A Broadway producer falls for one of his chorines.
Moderately smart musical entertainment of its time.

w Harry Tugend, Dwight Taylor, *play* Clare Boothe *d* Victor Schertzinger *m* / *ly* Victor Schertzinger, Frank Loesser *ph* Ted Tetzlaff

Don Ameche, Mary Martin, Oscar Levant, Rochester, Raymond Walburn, Connie Boswell, Virginia Dale, Barbara Jo Allen, Elizabeth Patterson

Kiss the Bride Goodbye
GB 1944 89m bw

A runaway couple are unwittingly abetted by her uncle. Unsubtle family farce. Patricia Medina, Jimmy Hanley, Frederick Leister,

Marie Lohr, Claud Allister, Ellen Pollock, Wylie Watson. Written by Jack Whittingham; directed by Paul Stein; for Butcher.

Kiss the Girls and Make Them Die

Italy 1966 106m Technicolor
Dino de Laurentiis

original title: *Si Tutte le Donne del Mondo . . .*

A rich industrialist has a plan to sterilize the whole male population of the world and restock it with his own mistresses, whom he keeps in suspended animation.
Patchy James Bond spoof.

w Jack Pulman, Dino Maiuri d Henry Levin, Dino Maiuri ph Aldo Tonti m Mario Nascimbene

Michael Connors, Dorothy Provine, Raf Vallone, Terry-Thomas

Kiss Them for Me

US 1957 105m Eastmancolor
Cinemascope
TCF (Jerry Wald)

Three navy pilots spend a weekend's unofficial leave in San Francisco, and get into various kinds of trouble.
Based on a novel which also served as source for the musical *Hit the Deck*, this very heavy-footed comedy with serious asides is most unsuitably cast and generally ill-timed and unattractive.

w Julius Epstein, *novel* Shore Leave by Frederick Wakeman d Stanley Donen ph Milton Krasner m Lionel Newman

Cary Grant, Jayne Mansfield, Suzy Parker, Ray Walston, Larry Blyden, Leif Erickson, Werner Klemperer

Kiss Tomorrow Goodbye

US 1950 102m bw
Cagney Productions (William Cagney)

A violent criminal breaks jail and plans several daring robberies.
Surprisingly brutal star melodrama which failed to repeat the success of *White Heat*.

w Harry Brown, *novel* Horace McCoy d Gordon Douglas ph Peverell Marley m Carmen Dragon

James Cagney, Barbara Payton, Ward Bond, Luther Adler, Helena Carter, Steve Brodie, Rhys Williams, Barton MacLane, Frank Reicher, John Litel
'The mixture as before without an ingredient changed.'—*Otis Guernsey Jnr*

Kisses for My President

US 1964 113m bw
Warner / Pearlayne (Curtis Bernhardt)

America's first woman president causes problems for her husband.
Solidly-carpentered comedy with too few ideas for its length.

w Claude Binyon, Robert G. Kane d Curtis Bernhardt ph Robert Surtees m Bronislau Kaper

Polly Bergen, Fred MacMurray, Arlene Dahl, Eli Wallach, Edward Andrews

Kissin' Cousins

US 1963 96m Metrocolor Panavision
MGM / Four Leaf (Sam Katzman)

The USAF wants to build a missile base on Smokey Mountain, and their PR man discovers that one of the hillbillies is his double.
A feeble production in every sense, even below its star's usual standard.

w Gerald Drayson Adams, Gene Nelson d Gene Nelson ph Ellis W. Carter md Fred Karger

Elvis Presley, Arthur O'Connell, Glenda Farrell, Jack Albertson

The Kissing Bandit

US 1948 102m Technicolor
MGM (Joe Pasternak)

In old California, a young businessman finds he is expected to keep up his bandit father's criminal and romantic reputation.
Silly, witless musical which never settles into gear; mocked by its star as Benny mocked *The Horn Blows at Midnight*.

w Isabel Lennart, John Briard Harding d Laslo Benedek ph Robert Surtees m Georgie Stoll songs Nacio Herb Brown, Earl Brent, Edward Heyman

Frank Sinatra, Kathryn Grayson, J. Carrol Naish, Mildred Natwick, Mikhail Rasumny, Billy Gilbert, Clinton Sundberg

Kitten with a Whip

US 1964 83m bw

A girl escaped from reform school takes refuge with a politician whose wife is away.
Over-the-top melodrama thought bannable at the time. Ann-Margret, John Forsythe, Patricia Barry, Ann Doran, Audrey Dalton. Written and directed by Douglas Heyes, from a book by Wade Miller; for Universal.

Kitty

GB 1928 90m (24 fps) bw silent
BIP / Burlington (Victor Saville)

A shopgirl loves a paralysed amnesiac, but his mother interferes.
Uninteresting romantic melodrama, notable only as Britain's first sound film: a few dialogue sequences were quickly added for a reissue in 1929.

w Violet Powell, Benn W. Levy, *novel* Warwick Deeping d Victor Saville

John Stuart, Estelle Brody, Dorothy Cumming, Marie Ault, Olaf Hytten

'She had all London on a MARRY-go-round!'
Kitty***

US 1945 103m bw
Paramount (Karl Tunberg)

In 18th-century London, an aristocrat makes a duchess of a guttersnipe.
Well-detailed period *Pygmalion* which works much better than one would expect.

w Darrell Ware, Karl Tunberg, *novel* Rosamund Marshall d Mitchell Leisen ph Daniel L. Fapp m Victor Young

Paulette Goddard, Ray Milland, Cecil Kellaway, Constance Collier, Reginald Owen, Patric Knowles, Dennis Hoey, Sara Allgood, Eric Blore, Gordon Richards, Michael Dyne
'Enough sex, wit and urbane cynicism to make one forget a footling ending.'—*Peter John Dyer, MFB*

'The most daring novel every written by a man about a woman!'
Kitty Foyle**

US 1940 108m bw
RKO (Harry E. Edgington, David Hempstead)

A white-collar girl has a troubled love life.
Solid entertainment of its time, especially aimed at ambitious young ladies.

w Dalton Trumbo, Donald Ogden Stewart, *novel* Christopher Morley d Sam Wood ph Robert de Grasse m Roy Webb

Ginger Rogers, Dennis Morgan, James Craig, Eduardo Ciannelli, Ernest Cossart, Gladys Cooper, Mary Treen
AA: Ginger Rogers
AAN: best picture; Dalton Trumbo, Donald Ogden Stewart; Sam Wood

The Klansman

US 1974 112m Technicolor
Paramount / Atlanta (William Alexander)

An Alabama sheriff confronts the Ku Klux Klan.
Violent melodrama, all noise, brutality and bad acting.

w Millard Kaufman, Samuel Fuller, *novel* William Bradford Huie d Terence Young ph Lloyd Ahern, Aldo Tonti m Stax Organisation

Lee Marvin, Richard Burton, Cameron Mitchell, O. J. Simpson, Lola Falana, David Huddleston, Luciana Paluzzi, Linda Evans
'There's not a shred of quality, dignity, relevance or impact in this yahoo-oriented bunk.'—*Variety*
● Video: VCL

'Mae goes north and Alaska goes west!'
Klondike Annie

US 1936 83m bw
Paramount (William Le Baron)

A torch singer on the run disguises herself as a missionary and revivifies a Klondike mission.
Laundered Mae West vehicle, from her fading period but not too bad.

w Mae West, Marion Morgan, George B. Dowell d Raoul Walsh ph George Clemens

Mae West, Victor McLaglen, Philip Reed, Helen Jerome Eddy, Harry Beresford, Harold Huber, Esther Howard

Klute***

US 1971 114m Technicolor
Panavision
Warner (Alan J. Pakula)

A policeman leaves the force to investigate the disappearance of a research scientist, and takes up with a call girl who is involved.

Excellent adult thriller with attention to detail and emphasis on character.

w Andy K. Lewis, Dave Lewis d Alan J. Pakula ph Gordon Willis m Michael Small

Jane Fonda, Donald Sutherland, Charles Cioffi, Roy Scheider, Rita Gam

AA: Jane Fonda
AAN: Andy K. Lewis, Dave Lewis
● Video: Warner

The Knack***
GB 1965 84m bw
UA / Woodfall (Oscar Lewenstein)

A sex-starved young teacher lets one room of his house to a successful womanizer, another to an innocent girl from the north.
An excuse for an anarchic series of visual gags, a kaleidoscope of swinging London in which anything goes. Brilliantly done in the style of A Hard Day's Night.

w Charles Wood, play Ann Jellicoe d Richard Lester ph David Watkin m John Barry

Michael Crawford, Ray Brooks, Rita Tushingham, Donal Donnelly

Knave of Hearts*
GB 1954 103m bw
Transcontinental (Paul Graetz)
aka: Monsieur Ripois et Son Nemesis
US title: Lover Boy

A born philanderer confesses all his affairs to his wife.
Well-observed though strangely flat and disappointing sex comedy, something of a pioneer in its time and therefore perhaps too diffident in its approach.

w René Clément, Hugh Mills d René Clément ph Oswald Morris m Roman Vlad

Gérard Philipe, Margaret Johnston, Joan Greenwood, Natasha Parry, Valerie Hobson

Knickerbocker Holiday
US 1944 84m bw
UA / Harry Joe Brown / PCA

In old New Amsterdam, a one-legged tyrant finally sees the light.
Artificial musical from a famous stage original, with engaging moments including Charles Coburn singing 'September Song'.

w Thomas Lennon, from the 1938 stage musical (m Kurt Weill, ly Maxwell Anderson) based on Father Knickerbocker's History of New York by Washington Irving d Harry Joe Brown ph Phil Tammura m Werner Heymann

Charles Coburn, Nelson Eddy, Constance Dowling, Ernest Cossart, Shelley Winters, Otto Kruger

AAN: Werner Heymann

Knife in the Water*
Poland 1962 94m bw
ZRF Kamera (Stanislaw Zylewicz)
original title: Noz w Wodzie

A young couple ask a hitchhiker to spend a weekend on their yacht, and regret it.
Detached little melodrama in which the sex

and violence hover beneath the surface. All very watchable, but in a minor key.

w Jerzy Skolimowski, Roman Polanski, Jakub Goldberg d Roman Polanski ph Jerzy Lipman m Krzystof Komeda

Leon Niemczyk, Jolanta Umecka, Zygmunt Malanowicz

AAN: best foreign film
● Video: Thorn EMI

Knight without Armour**
GB 1937 107m bw
London Films (Alexander Korda)

During the Russian Revolution of 1917, a widowed countess is helped to safety by a British translator.
Underrated romantic adventure with big production values and some splendid moments.

w Lajos Biro, Arthur Wimperis, Frances Marion, novel James Hilton ph Harry Stradling d Jacques Feyder m Miklos Rozsa

Robert Donat, Marlene Dietrich, Irene Vanbrugh, Herbert Lomas, Austin Trevor, Basil Gill, David Tree, John Clements, Lawrence Hanray

'Another feather in the cap of Alexander Korda for his series of artistic film productions. There is relatively little to find fault with and much to praise.'—Variety

'A first class thriller, beautifully directed, with spare and convincing dialogue and a nearly watertight scenario.'—Graham Greene
● Video: Polygram

Knights of the Round Table*
GB 1953 115m Eastmancolor Cinemascope
MGM (Pandro S. Berman)

Lancelot, banished from King Arthur's court for loving Guinevere, returns to defeat the evil Modred.
Disappointingly flat, pageant-like adaptation of the legends, with a few lively strands insufficiently firmly drawn together.

w Talbot Jennings, Jan Lustig, Noel Langley d Richard Thorpe ph Frederick A. Young, Stephen Dade m Miklos Rozsa ad Alfred Junge, Hans Peters

Robert Taylor, Mel Ferrer, Ava Gardner, Anne Crawford, Stanley Baker, Felix Aylmer, Robert Urquhart, Niall MacGinnis

Knights of the Teutonic Order*
Poland 1960 180m Eastmancolor Dyaliscope
Studio Unit (Zygmunt Krol)

Teutonic knights pillage Poland on the pretext of converting the inhabitants to Christianity; when they kill a noblewoman, her daughter swears revenge.
Medieval epic differing little from those of Hollywood, but splendid to look at.

w Jerzy Stafan Stawinski, Aleksander Ford, novel Henryk Sienkiewicz d Aleksander Ford ph Mieczyslaw Jahoda m Kazimierz Serocki

Urszula Modrzynska, Grazyna Staniszewska, Andrzej Szalawski

Knock on Any Door*
US 1949 100m bw
Columbia / Santana (Robert Lord)

A defence lawyer pleads with the jury for the life of a slum boy on a murder charge.
Smartly-made but empty melodrama making facile social points.

w Daniel Taradash, John Monks Jnr, novel Willard Motley d Nicholas Ray ph Burnett Guffey m George Antheil

Humphrey Bogart, John Derek, George Macready, Allene Roberts

Knock on Wood**
US 1954 103m Technicolor
Paramount (Norman Panama, Melvin Frank)

Stolen plans are hidden inside the dummy of an unsuspecting ventriloquist.
Excellent star comedy with good script and production (but some strange ideas of London's geography).

wd Norman Panama, Melvin Frank ph Daniel Fapp songs Sylvia Fine m Leith Stevens ch Michael Kidd

Danny Kaye, Mai Zetterling, David Burns, Torin Thatcher, Leon Askin, Abner Biberman, Steve Geray

AAN: Norman Panama, Melvin Frank (script)

Knute Rockne, All American
US 1940 98m bw
Warner (Robert Fellows)
GB titles: Knockout; A Modern Hero

The career of a famous Notre Dame football coach.
Standard sporting biopic.

w Robert Buckner d Lloyd Bacon ph Tony Gaudio

Pat O'Brien, Ronald Reagan, Gale Page, Donald Crisp, Albert Basserman, John Qualen, John Sheffield

Koenigsmark
France 1935 114m bw

A princess falls for a commoner. Rather elementary royal romance in a Ruritanian background, filmed simultaneously in French and English by the same principals. Elissa Landi, Pierre Fresnay, John Lodge. From a novel by Pierre Benoit; directed by Maurice Tourneur; for Roger Richebé.

Kongo
US 1932 86m bw
MGM

An embittered African recluse takes revenge on the daughter of his enemy.
No-holds-barred melodrama which never really exerts the right grip; a remake of the Lon Chaney silent West of Zanzibar.

w Leon Gordon, play Chester de Vonde, Kilbourn Gordon d William Cowen ph Harold Rosson

Walter Huston, Lupe Velez, Virginia Bruce, Conrad Nagel, C. Henry Gordon

'Horror and tropical stuff combined . . .
chiefly for the daily grinds.'—*Variety*

Kotch*
US 1971   114m   Metrocolor
ABC / Kotch Company (Richard Carter)

An eccentric 72-year-old widower is at odds
with his family and helps a pregnant
babysitter.
Variously amusing, moving and sentimental,
this generally likeable film about a crotchety
grandpa is sustained by its star performance.

w John Paxton, *novel* Katherine Topkins
d Jack Lemmon ph Richard H. Kline
m Marvin Hamlisch

Walter Matthau, Deborah Winter, Felicia Farr,
Charles Aidman

AAN: Walter Matthau; song 'Life Is What
You Make It' (*m* Marvin Hamlisch, *ly* Johnny
Mercer)

● *Video: Guild*

Koyaanisqatsi*
US 1983   86m   De Luxe

A panoramic view of contemporary America
without commentary or narrative, using time-
lapse photography. The title is an Indian word
meaning 'a state of life that calls for another
way of living'. A rather pointless, very
beautiful, and finally rather boring experience.
Written by Ron Fricke, Godfrey Reggio,
Michael Hoenig, Alton Walpole; directed by
Godfrey Reggio; for the Institute for Regional
Education. 'Arrogant bombast, provoking no
response except "wow".'—*Sight & Sound*

Krakatoa, East of Java
US 1968   136m   Technicolor   Cinerama
ABC / Cinerama (Lester A. Sansom)

In 1883 the SS *Batavia Queen* leaves Singapore
and is engulfed by the Krakatoa eruption.
Mindless spectacular, technically quite
impressive but with no dramatic interest
whatsoever.

w Clifford Newton Gould, Bernard Gordon
d Bernard Kowalski ph Manuel Berenguer
m Frank de Vol pd / sp Eugene Lourié

Maximilian Schell, Diane Baker, Brian Keith,
Rossano Brazzi, Barbara Werle, John Leyton,
Sal Mineo, J. D. Cannon, Marc Lawrence

'Apparently designed to disprove the old
adage, "they don't make them like that any
more". At a conservative count it includes
such sure-fire cinematic ingredients as hidden
treasure, deep-sea divers with shattered lungs
and claustrophobia, mutiny *and* fire on board
ship, nuns, convicts, a lost orphan boy, girl
divers and even a little striptease, climaxing in
the biggest explosion and the greatest tidal
wave known to history.'—*MFB*

'There are three sides to this love story!'

Kramer versus Kramer***
US 1979   105m   Technicolor
Columbia / Stanley Jaffe (Richard C.
   Fischoff)

A divorced advertising executive gets
temporary custody of his seven-year-old son.
New-fashioned tearjerker, as slick as a colour
supplement and catnip to the emotion-starved
masses.

wd Robert Benton, *novel* Avery Corman
ph Nestor Almendros md Erma E. Levin
pd Paul Sylbert

Dustin Hoffman, Justin Henry, Meryl Streep,
Jane Alexander, Howard Duff

'Pastel colours, a cute kid and a good script
made this one of the most undeserved
successes of the year: wall-to-wall
sentiment.'—*Time Out*

AA: best picture; Robert Benton (as
director); Dustin Hoffman; Meryl Streep;
screen play adapted from another medium

'If you miss the first five minutes you miss
   one suicide, two executions, one
   seduction and the key to the plot!'

The Kremlin Letter
US 1970   122m   De Luxe   Panavision
TCF (Carter de Haven, Sam Wiesenthal)

An American intelligence team is sent
undercover to Moscow to retrieve an arms
treaty mistakenly signed.

KNIGHT WITHOUT ARMOUR.   Marlene Dietrich and Robert Donat were an unlikely pair,
but this spy adventure held many pleasures.

Tediously violent cold war mystifier: a few
good performances do not make it worth
unravelling.

w John Huston, Gladys Hill, *novel* Noel Behn
d John Huston ph Ted Scaife m Robert
Drasnin pd Ted Haworth

Richard Boone, Orson Welles, Bibi
Andersson, Max Von Sydow, Patrick O'Neal,
Ronald Radd, George Sanders, Dean Jagger,
Nigel Green, Barbara Parkins, Lila Kedrova,
Michael MacLiammoir, Sandor Eles, Niall
MacGinnis, John Huston

'One of those all-star international spy sagas
that trick out an indecipherably tortuous plot
with a series of vignettes in which the
pleasures of star-spotting are expected to
compensate for any narrative longueurs.'—
Nigel Andrews

Krull
GB 1983   121m   Metrocolor
Columbia / Ted Mann–Ron Silverman

Prince Colwyn's bride-to-be is abducted by the
Beast of the Black Fortress.
Old-fashioned derring-do taking place on a

somewhat unattractive planet; nevertheless fairly lively in its action and trick effects.

w Stanford Sherman *d* Peter Yates *ph* Peter Suschitzky *m* James Horner *pd* Stephen Grimes

Ken Marshall, Lysette Anthony, Freddie Jones, Francesca Annis, Alun Armstrong, David Battley, Bernard Bresslaw, John Welsh, Tony Church, Bernard Archard

'Nearly everything in it has been done before, in some cases rather better, but rarely quite so likeably.'—*Nick Roddick, MFB*

'Not really thrilling enough to be a blockbuster and not light enough to be anything else.'—*Sight and Sound*

Kwaidan*
Japan 1964   164m   Eastmancolor
  Tohoscope
Ninjin Club / Bungei

Four elegant ghost stories by Lafcadio Hearn. Visually a superb production; all the stories have merit, but *en masse* prove a bit much at one sitting.

w Yoko Mizuki *d* Masaki Kobayashi *ph* Yoshio Miyajima *m* Toru Takemitsu *ad* Shigemasa Toda

Rentaro Mikuni, Ganjiro Nakamura, Katsuo Nakamura

● *Video: Palace*

The L-Shaped Room*
GB 1962   142m   bw
British Lion / Romulus (James Woolf, Richard Attenborough)

A girl intending to have an abortion takes a room in a London suburban house which is none too clean but full of characters. Watchable, mildly sensational low-life-melodrama of the pre-swinging London era when well-to-dos thought it amusing to live in garrets. Hellishly overlong but enjoyable in patches because of the professionalism with which it is made.

w Bryan Forbes, *novel* Lynne Reid Banks *d* Bryan Forbes *ph* Douglas Slocombe *m* Brahms, John Barry

Leslie Caron, Tom Bell, Brock Peters, Cicely Courtneidge, Bernard Lee, Avis Bunnage, Patricia Phoenix, Emlyn Williams
'It would be hard to imagine a more unlikely, or commercially more sure-fire group of lodgers living under a single roof than this pregnant French girl, maladjusted negro, lesbian actress, couple of prostitutes, and unpublished writer who finally commits it all to paper—shades of *I Am a Camera* as well as *A Taste of Honey*.'—*MFB*
AAN: Leslie Caron

Laburnum Grove**
GB 1936   73m   bw
ATP (Basil Dean)

A suburban father reveals he is a forger. Agreeable worm-turns comedy melodrama, much copied since.

w Gordon Wellesley, Anthony Kimmins, *play* J. B. Priestley *d* Carol Reed *ph* John W. Boyle

Cedric Hardwicke, Edmund Gwenn, Victoria Hopper, Ethel Coleridge, Katie Johnson, Francis James
'Here at last is an English film one can unreservedly praise.'—*Graham Greene*

The Lacemaker
France / Switzerland / West Germany 1977   107m   Eastmancolor
Action / FR3 / Citel / Janus (Yves Gasser)
original title: *La Dentellière*

An 18-year-old girl becomes ill and withdrawn when her first affair breaks up. Careful social character study, witty and observant but in memory insufficiently differentiated from numerous exploitation pieces with similar plots.

w Pascal Lainé, Claude Goretta, *novel* Pascal Lainé *d* Claude Goretta *ph* Jean Boffety *m* Pierre Jansen

Isabelle Huppert, Yves Beneyton, Florence Giorgetti, Anne Marie Düringer

● *Video: VCL*

Laddie
US 1935   70m   bw

A young farmer loves the squire's daughter, but the squire says no. Rather dim old-fashioned rural romance. John Beal, Gloria Stuart, Virginia Weidler, Charlotte Henry, Donald Crisp. Written by Ray Harris, Dorothy Yost, from novel and play by Gene Stratton Porter; directed by George Stevens; for Pandro S. Berman / RKO.

Ladies Courageous
US 1944   88m   bw
Universal (Walter Wanger)

Girls ferry war planes from base to base for the USAF. Absolutely predictable propaganda potboiler.

w Norman Reilly Raine, Doris Gilbert *d* John Rawlins *ph* Hal Mohr *m* Dmitri Tiomkin

Loretta Young, Geraldine Fitzgerald, Diana Barrymore, Evelyn Ankers, Anne Gwynne, Philip Terry, David Bruce, Lois Collier, Samuel S. Hinds

Ladies in Love*
US 1936   97m   bw
TCF (B. G. De Sylva)

Man-hunting girls in Budapest form a joint plan. Amusing romantic nonsense.

w Melville Baker, *play* Ladislaus Bus-Fekete *d* Edward H. Griffith *ph* Hal Mohr *md* Louis Silvers

Janet Gaynor, Loretta Young, Constance Bennett, Simone Simon, Don Ameche, Paul Lukas, Tyrone Power, Alan Mowbray, Wilfred Lawson, J. Edward Bromberg, Virginia Field

Ladies in Retirement**
US 1941   92m   bw
Columbia

A housekeeper murders her employer for the sake of her two mentally disturbed sisters. Splendidly effective Grand Guignol, from a well-written play but filmically quite interesting. Remade with lots of gore as *The Mad Room* (qv).

w Reginald Denham, Edward Percy, Garrett Fort, *play* Reginald Denham, Edward Percy *d* Charles Vidor *ph* George Barnes *m* Ernst Toch

Ida Lupino, Louis Hayward, Isobel Elsom, Edith Barrett, Elsa Lanchester, Emma Dunn
AAN: Ernst Toch

Ladies Love Brutes
US 1930   83m   bw
Paramount

A gangster tries to improve himself to marry a socialite. Uneasy comedy-drama with good moments.

w Waldemar Young, Herman J. Mankiewicz, *play* Pardon My Glove by Zoe Akins *d* Rowland V. Lee *ph* Harry Fischbeck

George Bancroft, Mary Astor, Fredric March, Margaret Quimby, Stanley Fields

Ladies Love Danger
US 1935   69m   bw

A playwright and amateur sleuth solves a series of murders. Light, bright whodunit. Gilbert Roland, Mona Barrie, Donald Cook, Adrienne Ames, Hardie Albright, Herbert Mundin. Written by Samson Raphaelson from a story by Ilya Zorn; directed by H. Bruce Humberstone; for Fox. 'Stronger marquee strength would have sent it into ace spots. As is, looks best for secondaries.'—*Variety*

Ladies' Man*
US 1931   70m   bw
Paramount

A man of the world preys successfully on rich women until one grows jealous when her daughter falls for him. Vivid, hard melodrama showing the blacker side of early thirties high society living.

w Herman J. Mankiewicz *d* Lothar Mendes *ph* Victor Milner

William Powell, Kay Francis, Carole Lombard, Gilbert Emery, Olive Tell

'He's a hit with the misses, they go for his kisses!'

Ladies' Man
US 1947 90m bw

A poor farmer strikes oil, becomes a millionaire, and finds himself a prize for the ladies. Below-par comedy which wastes an agreeable cast. Eddie Bracken, Cass Daley, Virginia Welles, Spike Jones and his City Slickers. Written by Edmund Beloin, Jack Rose and Lewis Meltzer; directed by William D. Russell; for Paramount.

Ladies' Man
US 1961 106m Technicolor
Paramount / York (Jerry Lewis)

The adventures of an accident-prone houseboy at a Hollywood hotel for aspiring actresses. Hit-or-miss collection of comic scraps which might have benefited from being put together on a less grandiose scale.

w Jerry Lewis, Bill Richmond d Jerry Lewis ph W. Wallace Kelley m Walter Scharf

Jerry Lewis, Helen Traubel, Jack Kruschen, Doodles Weaver, Gloria Jean
   'Regression into infantilism cannot be carried much further than this.'—MFB

Ladies Must Live: see The Home Towners

Ladies of Leisure
US 1930 98m bw

A gold digger gets an attack of conscience and gives up her rich fiancé. Only fitfully interesting early Capra, with little sparkle in any department. Barbara Stanwyck, Lowell Sherman, Ralph Graves, Marie Prevost. Written by Milton Herbert Gropper and Jo Swerling; directed by Frank Capra; for Columbia.

Ladies of the Big House
US 1931 77m bw
Paramount

A married couple are framed on a murder charge and sent to prison.
Melodramatic nonsense in the wake of *The Big House*.

w Louis Weitzenkorn d Marion Gering ph David Abel

Sylvia Sidney, Gene Raymond, Wynne Gibson, Rockliffe Fellows, Earle Foxe
   'Powerful in heart appeal and should do very well.'—Variety

Ladies of the Chorus
US 1949 61m bw

A Broadway burlesque queen falls for a socialite. Threadbare backstage support, notable only for the first leading performance of Marilyn Monroe. Adele Jergens and Rand Brooks. Written by Harry Sauber and Joseph Carole; directed by Phil Karlson; for Columbia.

Ladies of the Jury
US 1932 64m bw

A lady changes the minds of a murder jury to 'not guilty'. Light-hearted early variation on

Twelve Angry Men. *Edna May Oliver*, Ken Murray, Roscoe Ates, Kitty Kelly, Guinn Williams, Cora Witherspoon. From the play by Frederick Ballard; directed by Lowell Sherman; for RKO. 'A highly satisfying B house release.'—Variety

Ladies Should Listen
US 1934 63m bw
Paramount (Douglas MacLean)

A knowledgeable switchboard operator helps a financier with his problems.
Moderately beguiling, instantly forgettable romantic frou-frou.

w Claude Binyon, Frank Butler, Guy Bolton d Frank Tuttle ph Harry Sharp

Cary Grant, Frances Drake, Edward Everett Horton, Rosita Morena, George Barbier, Nydia Westman, Charles Ray
   'Synthetic farce that strains too hard for laughs.'—Variety

Ladies They Talk About*
US 1933 69m bw
Warner

Trouble in a women's prison.
Entertaining comedy-melodrama which had some brushes with the Hays Office because of its frankly man-hungry characters.

w Sidney Sutherland, Brown Holmes, *play* Women in Prison by Dorothy Mackaye, Carlton Miles d Howard Bretherton, William Keighley ph John Seitz

Barbara Stanwyck, Lyle Talbot, Preston Foster, Dorothy Burgess, Lillian Roth, Maude Eburne, Ruth Donnelly, Harold Huber
   'Will get average business if sold to the hilt.'—Variety

Ladies Who Do
GB 1963 85m bw
British Lion / Bryanston / Fanfare (George H. Brown)

Charladies form a successful company from tips they salvage from wastepaper baskets. Mild farce sustained by familiar actors.

w Michael Pertwee d C. M. Pennington-Richards ph Geoffrey Faithfull m Ron Goodwin

Peggy Mount, Miriam Karlin, Robert Morley, Harry H. Corbett, Dandy Nichols

The Lady and the Bandit
US 1951 78m bw

A highwayman sacrifices his own life to avenge his father and protect his wife. Fairly pathetic example of historical whitewashing to provide minor excitements. Louis Hayward, Patricia Medina, Suzanne Dalbert, Tom Tully, John Williams, Alan Mowbray. Written by Robert Libbott and Frank Burt; directed by Ralph Murphy; for Harry Joe Brown / Columbia. (GB title: *Dick Turpin's Ride*.)

The Lady and the Mob
US 1939 65m bw
Columbia (Fred Kohlmar)

A lady bank owner menaced by gangsters forms her own mob.
Weak comedy.

w Richard Maibaum, Gertrude Purcell d Ben Stoloff ph John Stumar

Fay Bainter, Ida Lupino, Lee Bowman, Henry Armetta, Warren Hymer, Harold Huber
   'Neat, entertaining farce; rates exploitation.'—Variety

The Lady and the Monster
US 1944 86m bw
Republic (George Sherman)
aka: *Tiger Man*
GB title: *The Lady and the Doctor*

A scientist keeps alive the brain of a mortally injured financier, and it comes to dominate him.
Fair, over-padded version of a much filmed thriller (see also *Donovan's Brain, Vengeance*).

w Dane Lussier, Frederick Kohner, *novel* Donovan's Brain by Curt Siodmak d George Sherman ph John Alton m Walter Scharf

Erich Von Stroheim, Richard Arlen, Vera Hruba Ralston, Mary Nash, Sidney Blackmer, Helen Vinson

Lady and the Tramp**
US 1955 76m Technicolor
Cinemascope
Walt Disney (Erdmann Penner)

A pedigree spaniel falls foul of two Siamese cats and has a romantic adventure with a mongrel who helps her.
Pleasant cartoon feature in Disney's cutest and most anthropomorphic vein.

d Hamilton Luske, Clyde Geronomi, Wilfred Jackson m Oliver Wallace

Lady Be Good
US 1941 111m bw
MGM (Arthur Freed)

Married songwriters produce a musical. Thin musical with good talent and tunes; very little connection with the 1924 musical show.

w Jack McGowan, Kay Van Riper, John McClain d Norman Z. McLeod ph George J. Folsey, Oliver T. Marsh md George Stoll *songs* various

Eleanor Powell, Robert Young, Ann Sothern, Red Skelton, Dan Dailey, Virginia O'Brien, Reginald Owen, John Carroll, Lionel Barrymore, Jimmy Dorsey and his Orchestra

AA: song 'The Last Time I Saw Paris' (*m* Jerome Kern, *ly* Oscar Hammerstein II)

Other songs: 'Hang on to Me'; 'Fascinating Rhythm'; 'Lady Be Good'; 'You'll Never Know'; 'Your Words and My Music'

Lady By Choice*
US 1934 78m bw
Columbia

A publicity-mad dancer adopts an old rummy as a Mother's Day stunt.

What's he got that gets the gals...
Besides $10,000,000 ????

starring Eddie **Bracken**

"Ladies' Man"

Cass **Daley**

Eddie's a howl as the oil king who comes to the big town, goes on the radio, and becomes the heart-throb of every girl — from six to sixty!

Virginia **Welles**

and Spike **Jones**

and His City Slickers

SEE Spike Jones play "Cocktails for Two" and "Holiday for Strings" in THE FIRST COMEDY RIOT OF 1947!

with
Johnny **Coy** · Virginia **Field**
Produced by Daniel **DARE**
Directed by William D. **RUSSELL**
A Paramount Picture

LADIES' MAN (1947).   A forgotten comedy chiefly notable for its Spike Jones numbers.

Amusing sentimental comedy in the wake of *Lady for A Day.*

w Jo Swerling, Dwight Taylor d David Burton ph Ted Tetzlaff

Carole Lombard, May Robson, Walter Connolly, Roger Pryor, Arthur Hohl, Raymond Walburn, James Burke, Henry Kolker

'Can very well stand on its own outside the deluxers if properly sold.'—*Variety*

Lady Caroline Lamb*
GB 1972 123m Eastmancolor Panavision
EMI / GEC / Pulsar / Video Cinematographica (Fernando Ghia)

In 1805, impulsive Lady Caroline Ponsonby marries William Lamb, later Lord Melbourne, and then disgraces him by her wildness.
Pale, disappointing historical fiction with good spots but no reverence for fact; slackly written and handled, and not helped by the wide screen.

wd Robert Bolt ph Oswald Morris m Richard Rodney Bennett ad Carmen Dillon

Sarah Miles, Jon Finch, Richard Chamberlain (as Byron), Margaret Leighton, John Mills (as Cobbett), *Ralph Richardson* (as George III), *Laurence Olivier* (as Wellington)

● *Video: Thorn EMI*

Lady Chatterley's Lover
France 1955 101m / 84m (English version) bw
Regie du Film / Orsay Film (Gilbert Cohen-Séat)

The wife of a crippled and impotent mine-owner has an affair with a coarse gamekeeper and enjoys it.
Hilariously po-faced transcription of a notorious novel, of no cinematic interest whatever.

w Gaston Bonheur, Philippe de Rothschild, Marc Allégret, *novel* D. H. Lawrence d Marc Allégret ph Georges Périnal m Joseph Kosma

Danielle Darrieux, Leo Genn, Erno Crisa

'The classic of erotic literature!'
Lady Chatterley's Lover
GB / France 1981 104m colour
Cannon / Producteurs Associés

A 'period' remake, lovingly photographed but with some risible soft porn episodes and no great interest in the acting.

w Christopher Wicking, Just Jaeckin d Just Jaeckin ph Robert Fraisse m Stanley Myers, Richard Harvey

Sylvia Kristel, Nicholas Clay, Shane Briant, Ann Mitchell, Elizabeth Spriggs

The Lady Consents
US 1936 76m bw
RKO (Edward Kaufman)

When a doctor's wife sees that he is in love with another woman, she makes it easy for

him to get a divorce; but he finally comes back to her.
Unbelievable matinée drama for star fans.

w P. J. Wolfson, Anthony Veiller, *play* The Indestructible Mrs Talbot by P. J. Wolfson d Stephen Roberts ph J. Roy Hunt

Ann Harding, Herbert Marshall, Margaret Lindsay, Walter Abel, Edward Ellis, Hobart Cavanaugh, Ilka Chase

'Pretty fair entertainment; good woman's picture.'—*Variety*

The Lady Eve***
US 1941 97m bw
Paramount (Paul Jones)

A lady cardsharper and her father are outsmarted on a transatlantic liner by a millionaire simpleton; she plans an elaborate revenge.
Hectic romantic farce, the first to show its director's penchant for mixing up sexual innuendo, funny men and pratfalls. There are moments when the pace drops, but in general it's scintillating entertainment, especially after viewing its weak remake *The Birds and the Bees* (qv).

wd Preston Sturges, *play* Monckton Hoffe ph Victor Milner m Leo Shuken, Charles Bradshaw

Barbara Stanwyck, Henry Fonda, Charles Coburn, Eugène Pallette, William Demarest, Eric Blore, Melville Cooper, Martha O'Driscoll, Janet Beecher, Robert Greig, Luis Alberni, Jimmy Conlin

'The whole theme, with all its variations of keys, is played to one end, to get laughs, and at several different levels it gets them.'—*National Board of Review*

'Preston Sturges, they tell me, is known in Hollywood as "the streamlined Lubitsch". This needn't put you off, because if he goes on producing films as lively as this one he will one day come to be known as Preston Sturges.'—*William Whitebait*

'This time Preston Sturges has wrapped you up another package that is neither very big nor very flashy, but the best fun in months.'—*Otis Ferguson*

'A mixture of visual and verbal slapstick, of high artifice and pratfalls . . . it represents the dizzy high point of Sturges' writing.'—*New Yorker, 1977*

'The brightest sort of nonsense, on which Preston Sturges' signature is written large. The result has a sustained comic flavour and an individual treatment that are rarely found in Hollywood's antic concoctions.'—*New York Herald Tribune*

'A more charming or distinguished gem of nonsense has not occurred since *It Happened One Night*.'—*New York Times*

AAN: Monckton Hoffe (original story)

Lady for a Day***
US 1933 95m bw
Columbia

Gangsters help an old apple seller to pose as a rich woman when her daughter visits.

Splendid sentimental comedy full of cinematic resource; the best translation of Runyon to the screen.

w *Robert Riskin, story* Madame La Gimp by Damon Runyon d Frank Capra ph Joseph Walker

May Robson, Warren William, Guy Kibbee, Glenda Farrell, Ned Sparks, Jean Parker, Walter Connolly, Nat Pendleton

'Exceptionally adroit direction and scenario . . . sell it with plenty of adjectives as it will please everybody.'—*Variety*

AAN: best picture; Robert Riskin; Frank Capra; May Robson

Lady for a Night
US 1941 87m bw
Republic (Albert J. Cohen)

The lady owner of a gambling boat determines to break into society.
Moderate period comedy with a belated murder plot.

w Isabel Dawn, Boyce DeGaw d Leigh Jason ph Norbert Brodine m David Buttolph

Joan Blondell, John Wayne, Ray Middleton, Philip Merivale, Blanche Yurka, Edith Barrett, Leonid Kinskey, Montagu Love

The Lady from Cheyenne
US 1941 87m bw
Universal (Frank Lloyd)

In 1860 Wyoming, a schoolmistress fights for women's rights.
Mild western star romance.

w Kathryn Scola, Warren Duff d Frank Lloyd ph Milton Krasner m Frank Skinner

Loretta Young, Robert Preston, Gladys George, Edward Arnold, Frank Craven, Jessie Ralph, Spencer Charters, Alan Bridge

Lady from Louisiana
US 1941 84m bw
Republic (Bernard Vorhaus)

In old Mississippi, a lottery-owner's daughter falls in love with a lawyer employed to make her father's business illegal.
Curious pot-boiler containing everything but the kitchen stove, including murder and a raging storm.

w Vera Caspary, Guy Endore, Michael Hogan d Bernard Vorhaus ph Jack Marta m Cy Feuer

John Wayne, Ona Munson, Ray Middleton, Henry Stephenson, Helen Westley, Dorothy Dandridge, Jack Pennick

The Lady from Nowhere
US 1936 60m bw

A manicurist tries to lose her identity after witnessing a gangland killing. A silly plot robs this second feature of the interest it might otherwise deserve. Mary Astor, Charles Quigley, Thurston Hall, Victor Kilian, Spencer Charters. Written by Fred Niblo Jnr, Ben G. Kohn, Arthur Strawn, Joseph Krumgold; directed by Gordon Wiles; for Columbia. 'Mild entertainment.'—*Variety*

The Lady from Shanghai**
US 1948 87m bw
Columbia (Richard Wilson, William Castle)

A seaman becomes involved in the maritime
wanderings of a crippled lawyer and his
homicidal frustrated wife.
Absurd, unintelligible, plainly much cut and
rearranged, this thriller was obviously left too
much in Welles' hands and then just as
unfairly taken out of them; but whole
sequences of sheer brilliance remain, notably
the final shoot-out in the hall of mirrors.
wd Orson Welles, novel If I Die Before I
Wake by Sherwood King ph Charles Lawton
Jnr m Heinz Roemheld

Orson Welles, Rita Hayworth, Everett Sloane,
Glenn Anders, Ted de Corsia, Erskine
Sanford, Gus Schilling
'The slurred social conscience of the hero
leads him to some murky philosophizing, all of
which with many individualities of diction clog
the issue and the sound track. Sub-titles, I
fear, would have helped.'—Richard
Winnington

The Lady from Texas
US 1951 78m Technicolor

A Civil War widow is thought to be
committable. Mild comedy of insanity, a pale
shadow of Harvey whose star it borrows.
Josephine Hull, Mona Freeman, Howard
Duff, Gene Lockhart, Craig Stevens, Ed
Begley. Written by Gerald Drayson Adams
and Connie Lee Bennett; directed by Joseph
Pevney; for Universal-International.

The Lady Gambles
US 1949 99m bw
U-I (Michael Kraike)

A happy woman destroys her marriage when
she becomes addicted to gambling.
Boring, overwrought, underplotted fiction for
women.
w Lewis Meltzer, Oscar Saul d Michael
Gordon ph Russell Metty m Frank Skinner

Barbara Stanwyck, Robert Preston, Stephen
McNally, Edith Barrett, John Hoyt
'A kind of Lost Weekend of the gaming
tables.'—Ella Smith
'The relentless drama of a woman driven to
the depths of emotion by a craving beyond
control!'—publicity

Lady Godiva
US 1955 89m Technicolor
U-I (Robert Arthur)
GB title: Lady Godiva of Coventry

Lord Leofric tames a Saxon shrew but she
suspects his motives and rides naked through
the streets of Coventry to prove the loyalty of
the Saxons.
Comic strip historical legend, reliably turned
out for midwestern family audiences.
w Oscar Brodney, Harry Ruskin d Arthur
Lubin ph Carl Guthrie m Joseph Gershenson

George Nader, Maureen O'Hara, Vic
Morrow, Eduard Franz, Torin Thatcher

Lady Godiva Rides Again
GB 1951 90m bw
British Lion / London Films / Sidney Gilliat,
     Frank Launder

A waitress wins a local beauty contest and
becomes a charm school starlet and later a
stripteaser.
Disappointing satirical comedy with good
credentials.
w Frank Launder, Val Valentine d Frank
Launder ph Wilkie Cooper m William
Alwyn

Pauline Stroud, Stanley Holloway, Diana
Dors, Alastair Sim, George Cole, Dennis
Price, John McCallum, Bernadette O'Farrell,
Kay Kendall, Dora Bryan

The Lady Has Plans
US 1942 77m bw
Paramount (Fred Kohlmar)

A lady reporter in Lisbon is mistaken for a
Nazi spy.
Competent fluff which veers between comedy
and melodrama.
w Harry Tugend d Sidney Lanfield
ph Charles Lang

Paulette Goddard, Ray Milland, Albert
Dekker, Roland Young, Margaret Hayes,
Cecil Kellaway, Addison Richards, Edward
Norris

Lady Ice
US 1973 92m Technicolor Panavision
Tomorrow Entertainment (Harrison Starr)

An insurance investigator steals a diamond
and goes into partnership with a gangster's
daughter.
Unamusing Miami-based thriller.
w Alan Trustman, Harold Clemins d Tom
Gries ph Lucien Ballard m Perry Botkin Jnr

Donald Sutherland, Jennifer O'Neil, Robert
Duvall, Patrick Magee

'Because of its frank nature, we urge you—
     do not see it alone!'

Lady in a Cage
US 1964 97m bw
American Entertainments Corp. (Luther
     Davis)

A rich widow is trapped by roving marauders
in her private elevator.
Unpleasant and boring suspenser with nasty
details.
w Luther Davis d Walter Grauman ph Lee
Garmes m Paul Glass pd Rudolf Sternad

Olivia de Havilland, James Caan, Ann
Sothern, Jeff Corey
'The film parades its pretensions on a note
of high-pitched hysteria.'—MFB

Lady in a Jam
US 1942 78m bw
Universal (Gregory La Cava)

A scatterbrained socialite loses her money and
inherits an Arizona farm.
A very thin vehicle for a star who deserved
better.

w Eugene Thackey, Frank Cockrell, Otho
Lovering d Gregory La Cava ph Hal Mohr
m Frank Skinner

Irene Dunne, Patric Knowles, Ralph Bellamy,
Eugene Pallette, Robert Homans, Samuel S.
Hinds

Lady in Cement
US 1968 93m De Luxe Panavision
TCF / Arcola / Millfield (Aaron Rosenberg)

A Florida private eye on his morning swim
finds a dead blonde.
Routine private eye stuff with fashionable sex
and violence added.
w Marvin H. Albert, Jack Guss d Gordon
Douglas ph Joseph Biroc m Hugo
Montenegro

Frank Sinatra, Raquel Welch, Richard Conte,
Martin Gabel, Lainie Kazan, Pat Henry, Steve
Peck
'While Tony Rome seemed to herald a
return to the forties thriller, Lady in Cement
marks nothing more exciting than a return to
Tony Rome.'—MFB

The Lady in Question*
US 1940 81m bw
Columbia

A Parisian shopkeeper on a jury is responsible
for getting a girl acquitted of a murder charge,
but begins to worry when his son falls in love
with her.
Stagey but quite satisfying Hollywood remake
of the French drama Gribouille, with Raimy
and Michele Morgan.
w Lewis Meltzer, story Marcel Achard
d Charles Vidor ph Lucien Andriot
m Lucien Moraweck

Brian Aherne, Rita Hayworth, Glenn Ford,
Irene Rich, George Coulouris, Lloyd
Corrigan, Evelyn Keyes, Edward Norris, Curt
Bois, Frank Reicher

The Lady in Red
US 1979 93m Metrocolor

The story of Dillinger's mistress. Okay but
uninspired gangster drama from a fresh angle.
Pamela Sue Martin, Robert Conrad, Louise
Fletcher, Robert Hogan, Rod Gist. Written by
John Sayles; directed by Lewis Teague; for
New World.

The Lady in the Car with Glasses and a
Gun
France / US 1969 105m Eastmancolor
Panavision
Lira Film / Columbia (Anatole Litvak)

An English secretary in Paris decides to drive
to the coast but has various adventures which
make her believe she is either mad or
amnesiac.
Muddled, tedious suspenser with a totally
implausible 'explanation'.
w Richard Harris, Eleanor Perry,
novel Sebastien Japrisot d Anatole Litvak
ph Claude Renoir m Michel Legrand

Samantha Eggar, Oliver Reed, John
McEnery, Stéphane Audran

THE LADY HAS PLANS.   A good cast deserved a better script.

'The minx in mink with a yen for men!'
Lady in the Dark**
US 1944 100m Technicolor
Paramount (Richard Blumenthal)
The editress of a fashion magazine is torn
between three men, has worrying dreams, and
takes herself to a psychoanalyst.
Lush, stylish and frequently amusing version

of a Broadway musical, lacking most of the
songs; despite its faults, an excellent example
of studio spectacle and a very typical forties
romantic comedy.
w Frances Goodrich, Albert Hackett, *play*
Moss Hart *d* Mitchell Leisen *ph* Ray
Rennahan *m* Kurt Weill *ly* Ira Gershwin
md Robert Emmett Dolan *sp* Gordon
Jennings *ad* Hans Dreier

*Ginger Rogers, Warner Baxter, Ray Milland,
Jon Hall, Mischa Auer, Mary Phillips, Barry
Sullivan*
† The film was completed in 1942 but held up
because of overstock.
†† Paramount chief Buddy de Sylva is credited
with ruining the film by cutting the theme song,
'My Ship', which is the key to the
psychoanalysis.
AAN: Ray Rennahan; Robert Emmett Dolan

Lady in the Iron Mask

US 1952   78m   Natural Colour

Princess Anne's twin sister is kept in an iron mask to prevent dispute about the succession. Naïve twist on a well-worn legend; production values below par. Louis Hayward, Patricia Medina, Alan Hale Jnr, Judd Holden, Steve Brodie, John Sutton. Written by Jack Pollexfen and Aubrey Wisberg; directed by Ralph Murphy; for Wanger–Frenke / TCF.

Lady in the Lake*

US 1946   103m   bw
MGM (George Haight)

A private eye is assigned to find a missing wife . . .

Complex private eye yarn which makes the original Chandler dialogue sound childish by over-reliance on the subjective camera method: we see the hero's face only when he looks in a mirror. An experiment that failed because it was not really understood.

w Steve Fisher, novel Raymond Chandler d Robert Montgomery ph Paul C. Vogel m David Snell

Robert Montgomery, Audrey Totter, Lloyd Nolan, Tom Tully, Leon Ames

Lady in the Morgue*

US 1938   70m   bw
(GB title: The Case of the Missing Blonde)

A private eye investigates a suicide and uncovers three murders. Smart 'B' feature frequently cited as a model of its kind. Preston Foster, Frank Jenks, Patricia Ellis, Thomas Jackson. Written by Eric Taylor and Robertson White from the novel by Jonathan Latimer; directed by Otis Garrett; for Universal. (A previous film with the same characters, actors and director was The Westland Case.)

The Lady Is a Square

GB 1958   99m   bw
ABP / Wilcox–Neagle

An impoverished socialite widow tries to keep her husband's symphony orchestra going and is helped by a pop singer.
Strained attempt to carry on the Spring in Park Lane tradition, with a few inspirations from Joe Pasternak and One Hundred Men and a Girl. Earnest performances, obvious jokes.

w Harold Purcell, Pamela Bower, Nicholas Phipps d Herbert Wilcox ph Gordon Dines md Wally Stott

Anna Neagle, Frankie Vaughan, Anthony Newley, Janette Scott, Wilfrid Hyde White

The Lady is Willing

GB 1933   74m   bw

An ex-officer becomes a detective and takes his revenge on the financier who ruined him. Interesting comedy-melodrama with strong cast. Leslie Howard, Cedric Hardwicke, Binnie Barnes, Nigel Playfair, Nigel Bruce. Written by Guy Bolton, from the play by Louis Verneuil; directed by Gilbert Miller; for Columbia British.

The Lady Is Willing

US 1942   91m   bw
Columbia (Mitchell Leisen)

A musical comedy star adopts a baby and falls in love with its pediatrician.
Dull mixture of light drama and heavy comedy, with all concerned ill at ease.

w James Edward Grant, Albert McCleery d Mitchell Leisen ph Ted Tetzlaff m W. Frank Harling

Marlene Dietrich, Fred MacMurray, Aline MacMahon, Stanley Ridges, Arline Judge, Marietta Canty

Lady Killer***

US 1933   76m   bw
Warner (Henry Blanke)

A cinema usher turns to crime, flees to Hollywood, and becomes a movie star. Hectic slam-bang action comedy with melodramatic moments. Great fun.

w Ben Markson, novel The Finger Man by Rosalind Keating Shaffer d Roy del Ruth ph Tony Gaudio md Leo F. Forbstein

James Cagney, Mae Clarke, Leslie Fenton, Margaret Lindsay, Henry O'Neill, Willard Robertson, Raymond Hatton, Russell Hopton

'An all-time high in roughneck character work even for this rough-and-tumble star.'—Variety

'A kind of résumé of everything he has done to date in the movies.'—New York Evening Post

'Sprightly, more or less daring, thoroughly entertaining.'—New York World Telegram

The Lady Killers: see The Ladykillers

Lady L

France / Italy / US 1965   124m
Eastmancolor   Panavision
Concordia / Champion / MGM (Carlo Ponti)

An 80-year-old lady recalls her romantic life from her youth as a Paris laundress.
Unhappy, lumbering, styleless attempt to recapture several old forms, indifferently though expensively made and acted.

wd Peter Ustinov, novel Romain Gary ph Henri Alekan m Jean Françaix ad Jean D'Eaubonne, Auguste Capelier

Sophia Loren, David Niven, Paul Newman, Peter Ustinov, Claude Dauphin, Philippe Noiret, Michel Piccoli, Marcel Dalio, Cecil Parker, Eugène Deckers

The Lady Lies

US 1929   75m   bw

A wealthy widowed attorney courts a working-class girl and offends his children. Dated melodrama in primitive talkie technique. Walter Huston, Claudette Colbert, Charles Ruggles, Tom Brown. Written by John Meehan and Garrett Fort; directed by Hobart Henley; for Paramount.

Lady Luck

US 1946   97m   bw
RKO (Warren Duff)

The daughter of a long line of ill-fated gamblers marries one and tries to reform him, but the reverse happens.
Tedious comedy drama.

w Lynn Root, Frank Fenton d Edwin L. Marin ph Lucien Andriot m Leigh Harline

Robert Young, Barbara Hale, Frank Morgan, James Gleason, Don Rice, Harry Davenport, Lloyd Corrigan

Lady of Burlesque*

US 1943   91m   bw
Hunt Stromberg
GB title: Striptease Lady

A burlesque dancer solves a number of backstage murders.
Agreeable murder mystery with strong injections of comedy.

w James Gunn, novel The G-String Murders by Gypsy Rose Lee d William A. Wellman ph Robert de Grasse m Arthur Lange

Barbara Stanwyck, Michael O'Shea, J. Edward Bromberg, Iris Adrian, Gloria Dickson, Charles Dingle

AAN: Arthur Lange

Lady of Scandal

US 1930   67m   bw

The son of a noble house wants to marry an actress, but the family is nasty to her. Dated melodrama with sophisticated comedy asides. Ruth Chatterton, Basil Rathbone, Ralph Forbes, Nance O'Neill, Frederick Kerr, Herbert Bunston. Written by Hans Kraly from the play The High Road by Frederick Lonsdale; directed by Sidney Franklin; for MGM. 'Should register well in any but the lowest grind.'—Variety

Lady of Secrets

US 1936   73m   bw

A rich girl's father prevents her marriage without knowing that she is pregnant. Complicated and very boring mother-love yarn with the faint perfume of a bygone age. Ruth Chatterton, Otto Kruger, Lionel Atwill, Lloyd Nolan, Marion Marsh, Elizabeth Risdon. Written by Joseph Anthony, Zoe Akins, Katherine Brush; directed by Marion Gering; for B. P. Schulberg / Columbia. 'Chatterton, back to the screen after a long absence, is still having trouble with her offspring. This time she is also having trouble with the play, the direction, and the photography.'—Variety

Lady of the Tropics

US 1939   92m   bw
MGM (Sam Zimbalist)

An American playboy in Saigon marries a half-caste girl but her former admirer prevents her from getting a passport.
Interminable romantic melodrama with stars apparently straight from the taxidermist.

w Ben Hecht d Jack Conway ph George Folsey m Franz Waxman

Robert Taylor, Hedy Lamarr, Joseph Schildkraut, Gloria Franklin, Ernest Cossart

'Mediocre and stagey romance, but stars should pull it through.'—Variety

Lady on a Train*
US 1945 84m bw
Universal (Felix Jackson)

A girl arriving in New York by train sees a
murder committed and can't make anyone
believe her.
Cheerful mystery which starts in the right
spirit but does not progress too satisfactorily.
w Edmund Beloin, Robert O'Brien, *novel*
Leslie Charteris d Charles David ph Elwood
Bredell m Miklos Rozsa

Deanna Durbin, Ralph Bellamy, David Bruce,
Edward Everett Horton, George Coulouris,
Allen Jenkins, Dan Duryea, Patricia Morison

The Lady Pays Off
US 1951 80m bw

A gambling schoolteacher agrees to pay off
her debts by tutoring the casino owner's
daughter. Flat and unprofitable romantic
comedy-drama. Linda Darnell, Stephen
McNally, Gigi Perreau, Virginia Field, Ann
Codee. Written by Frank Gill Jnr and Albert
J. Cohen; directed by Douglas Sirk; for
Universal-International.

Lady Possessed
US 1952 86m bw
Republic / Portland (James Mason)

An unbalanced woman imagines she is
destined to take the place of a pianist's dead
wife.
Weary melodramatic nonsense dating from
Hollywood's first obsession with psychiatry.
w Pamela Kellino, James Mason, *novel* Del
Palma by Pamela Kellino d William Spier,
Roy Kellino ph Karl Struss m Nathan Scott

James Mason, June Havoc, Stephen Dunne,
Fay Compton, Pamela Kellino, Steven Geray

The Lady Says No
US 1951 83m bw
UA / Stillman (Frank Ross, John Stillman
Jnr)

A magazine photographer tames a female
chauvinist author.
Very silly comedy with neither wit nor style.
w Robert Russell d Frank Ross ph James
Wong Howe m Emil Newman

Joan Caulfield, David Niven, James
Robertson Justice, Lenore Lonergan, Henry
Jones

Lady Scarface
US 1941 69m bw
RKO (Cliff Reid)

A police lieutenant captures a dangerous
female gangster.
Weird gangster second feature with too many
domestic comedy asides; notable only for the
appearance in it of its dignified lead, fresh
from *Rebecca*.
w Armand D'Usseau, Richard Collins
d Frank Woodruff ph Nicholas Musuraca

Judith Anderson, Dennis O'Keefe, Frances
Neal, Mildred Coles, Eric Blore, Marc
Lawrence

Lady Sings the Blues*
US 1972 144m Eastmancolor
    Panavision
Paramount / Motown / Weston / Furie (Jay
Weston, James S. White)

The disastrous private life of blues singer Billie
Holliday.
Old-fashioned showbiz biopic with new-
fashioned drugs, sex and squalor.
w Terence McCloy, Chris Clark, Suzanne de
Passe d Sidney J. Furie ph John Alonzo
m Michel Legrand md Gil Askey

Diana Ross, Billy Dee Williams, Richard
Pryor, James Callahan, Sid Melton

AAN: script; Gil Askey; Diana Ross

A Lady Surrenders
US 1930 95m bw

A misunderstanding turns an innocent
husband into a bigamist after his wife has
supposedly divorced him. Totally effete
romantic drama with no comedy relief.
Conrad Nagel, Genevieve Tobin, Basil
Rathbone, Rose Hobart, Carmel Myers.
Written by Gladys Lehman from the novel
Sincerity by John Erskine; directed by John
Stahl; for Universal. 'It fails from all angles:
too stilted, slow, talky and punchless.'—
Variety

A Lady Takes a Chance
US 1943 86m bw
RKO (Frank Ross)
aka: *The Cowboy and the Girl*

A New York office girl on holiday in Oregon
falls for a rodeo rider.
Slender star action romance.
w Robert Ardrey d William A. Seiter
ph Frank Redman m Roy Webb

Jean Arthur, John Wayne, Charles Winninger,
Phil Silvers, Mary Field, Don Costello, John
Philliber, Grady Sutton, Hans Conried

The Lady Takes a Flyer
US 1958 95m Eastmancolor
    Cinemascope

A pilot's wife finds that life at home is not
easy, especially with a baby. Heavy comedy or
light drama; on either count a bore. Lana
Turner, Jeff Chandler, Richard Denning,
Chuck Connors, Andra Martin. Written by
Danny Arnold; directed by William Alland;
for Universal-International.

The Lady Takes a Sailor*
US 1949 99m bw

A girl devoted to telling the truth insists on
proving her story of a mysterious submarine
which saved her after a sailing accident.
Curious romantic farce with echoes of the old
slapstick tradition. Jane Wyman, Dennis
Morgan, Eve Arden, Allyn Joslyn, Robert
Douglas, William Frawley. Written by Everett
Freeman; directed by Michael Curtiz; for
Warner.

A Lady to Love
US 1930 92m bw
MGM

An ageing grape grower spots an attractive
waitress, sends her a marriage proposal by
mail, but encloses a photo of his handsome
foreman.
Rather primitive but well acted version of a
subject later filmed more fluently under the
title of the original play.
w Sidney Howard, from his play They Knew
What They Wanted d Victor Seastrom
ph Merritt B. Gerstad

Edward G. Robinson, Vilma Banky, Robert
Ames, Richard Carle
  'A hit as a talker: well directed, acted and
treated.'—*Variety*

Lady Tubbs
US 1935 69m bw

An ex-cook crashes society and shows up the
pretenders. Mildly agreeable sentimental
farce. Alice Brady, Douglass Montgomery,
Anita Louise, Alan Mowbray, Minor Watson,
Russell Hicks, Hedda Hopper. Written by
Barry Trivers from the novel by Homer Croy;
directed by Alan Crosland; for Universal.
'Solid laugh fare for the nabes.'—*Variety*

The Lady Vanishes****
GB 1938 97m bw
Gaumont British / Gainsborough (Edward
Black)

En route back to England by train from
Switzerland, an old lady disappears and two
young people investigate.
The disappearing lady trick brilliantly
refurbished by Hitchcock and his
screenwriters, who even get away with a
horrid model shot at the beginning. Superb,
suspenseful, brilliantly funny, meticulously
detailed entertainment.
w Sidney Gilliat, Frank Launder, *novel* The
Wheel Spins by Ethel Lina White d Alfred
Hitchcock ph Jack Cox md Louis Levy

*Margaret Lockwood, Michael Redgrave, Dame
May Whitty, Paul Lukas, Basil Radford,
Naunton Wayne, Catherine Lacey, Cecil
Parker, Linden Travers,* Googie Withers,
Mary Clare, Philip Leaver
  'If it were not so brilliant a melodrama, we
should class it as a brilliant comedy.'—*Frank
S. Nugent*
  'No one can study the deceptive
effortlessness with which one thing leads to
another without learning where the true
beauty of this medium is to be mined.'—*Otis
Ferguson*
  'Directed with such skill and velocity that it
has come to represent the very quintessence of
screen suspense.'—*Pauline Kael, 70s*
  † Hitchcock was actually second choice as
director. The production was ready to roll as
Lost Lady, directed by Roy William Neill,
with Charters and Caldicott already in place,
when Neill became unavailable and Hitch
stepped in.
  ● *Video: Rank*

The Lady Vanishes
GB 1979 97m Eastmancolor
Panavision
Rank / Hammer (Michael Carreras, Tom
Sachs)

A remake of the above in which everything
goes wrong: wrong shape, wrong actors,
wrong style (or lack of it). Reasonable
adherence to the original script can't save it.

w George Axelrod d Anthony Page
ph Douglas Slocombe m Richard Hartley
pd Wilfred Shingleton

Cybill Shepherd, Elliott Gould, Angela
Lansbury, Herbert Lom, Arthur Lowe, Ian
Carmichael, Gerald Harper, Jenny Runacre,
Jean Anderson
● Video: Rank

Lady Windermere's Fan*
US 1925 80m (24 fps) bw silent
Warner

The mysterious Mrs Erlynne almost causes a
scandal in London society.
Oscar Wilde's play transposed to the twenties,
with the Lubitsch touch daringly displacing
Wildean epigrams. Still more amusing than the
sound remake, The Fan.

w Julien Josephson d Ernst Lubitsch
ph Charles Van Enger

Ronald Colman, May McAvoy, Irene Rich,
Bert Lytell, Edward Martindel
  'Lubitsch's best silent film, full of incisive
details, discreet touches, nuances of gestures,
where behaviour betrays the character and
discloses the sentiment of the personages.'—
Georges Sadoul

The Lady with a Lamp*
GB 1951 110m bw
British Lion / Imperadio (Herbert Wilcox)

The life of Florence Nightingale and her work
in reforming the nursing service in 19th-
century England.
Solid biopic, not quite in accord with history.

w Warren Chetham Strode, play Reginald
Berkeley d Herbert Wilcox ph Max Greene
m Anthony Collins ad William C. Andrews

Anna Neagle, Michael Wilding, Gladys
Young, Felix Aylmer, Julian D'Albie, Arthur
Young, Edwin Styles, Barbara Couper, Cecil
Trouncer, Rosalie Crutchley
  'A slow, sedate, refined chronicle . . .
Herbert Wilcox is a good deal more at ease
with the balls and dinners, than with anything
that happens later.'—Penelope Houston
  'It may please fans of Anna Neagle and
Michael Wilding, but not fans of Florence
Nightingale.'—Richard Mallett, Punch

Lady with a Past*
US 1932 80m bw
RKO (Charles R. Rogers)
GB title: Reputation

A wealthy but shy girl almost accidentally
finds herself with a reputation as a scarlet
woman, and the men flock around her.
Moderately enjoyable star comedy drama.

w Horace Jackson, novel Harriet Henry
d Edward H. Griffith ph Hal Mohr m Max
Steiner

Constance Bennett, Ben Lyon, David
Manners, Astrid Allwyn, Merna Kennedy,
Blanche Frederici, Nella Walker
  'Light and satisfying material for the
women.'—Variety

Lady with Red Hair*
US 1940 78m bw
Warner (Edmund Grainger)

The life of actress Mrs Leslie Carter and her
association with impresario David Belasco.
Mildly interesting but unsatisfying biopic of a
lady scarcely remembered.

w Charles Kenyon, Milton Krims, N. Brewster
Morse, Norbert Faulkner d Curtis Bernhardt
ph Arthur Edeson m Heinz Roemheld

Miriam Hopkins, Claude Rains, Richard
Ainley, John Litel, Laura Hope Crews, Helen
Wesley, Mona Barrie, Victor Jory, Cecil
Kellaway, Fritz Leiber, Halliwell Hobbes

The Lady with the Little Dog*
USSR 1959 90m bw
Lenfilm
original title: Dama s Sobachkoi

In Yalta at the turn of the century, an
unhappily married woman and a married man
start an affair which lasts secretly over the
years.
Modestly pleasing, subtly acted anecdote.

wd Josef Heifits, story Anton Chekhov
ph Andrei Moskvin, D. Meschiev m Jiri
Sternwald

Ya Savvina, Alexei Batalov, Ala Chostakova

A Lady without Passport*
US 1950 84m bw
MGM (Samuel Marx)

A secret service undercover man tracks down
aliens being smuggled into the US, and falls in
love with one of them.
Routine material, very well handled.

w Howard Dimsdale d Joseph H. Lewis
ph Paul C. Vogel m David Raksin

Hedy Lamarr, John Hodiak, James Craig,
George Macready, Steve Geray

The Ladykillers*
GB 1955 97m Technicolor
Ealing (Seth Holt)

An old lady takes in a sinister lodger, who
with his four friends commits a robbery. When
she finds out, they plot to kill her, but are
hoist with their own petards.
Overrated comedy in poor colour; those who
made it quite clearly think it funnier than it is.

w William Rose d Alexander Mackendrick
ph Otto Heller m Tristam Cary

Alec Guinness, Katie Johnson, Peter Sellers,
Cecil Parker, Herbert Lom, Danny Green,

Jack Warner, Frankie Howerd, Kenneth
Connor
AAN: William Rose
● Video: Thorn EMI

The Lady's from Kentucky
US 1939 75m bw

A crooked bookie is reformed by a lady horse
breeder. Yawnworthy drama with an
unattractive hero. George Raft, Ellen Drew,
Hugh Herbert, Zasu Pitts, Louise Beavers,
Forrester Harvey. Written by Malcolm Stuart
Boylan; directed by Alexander Hall; for Jeff
Lazarus / Paramount. 'It starts with promise,
stumbles in the middle section, and drags itself
across the line for the finish.'—Variety

A Lady's Morals
US 1930 86m bw
MGM
GB titles: Jenny Lind; The Soul Kiss

The 'Swedish nightingale' learns that love is
more important than a singing career.
Cliché-strewn romance with music.

w Hans Kraly, Claudine West, John Meehan,
Arthur Richman d Sidney Franklin

Grace Moore, Reginald Denny, Wallace
Beery, Jobyna Howland
  'Class production of money potentialities.'—
Variety
† Wallace Beery played P. T. Barnum, a role
he was to repeat four years later in The Mighty
Barnum.

A Lady's Profession
US 1933 65m bw

A British nobleman comes to America to
retrieve his lost fortune, and starts a
speakeasy. Rather silly farce which generally
disappoints. Alison Skipworth, Roland
Young, Sari Maritza, Kent Taylor, Roscoe
Karns. Written by Walter de Leon and
Malcolm Stuart Boylan; directed by Norman
McLeod; for Paramount. 'Slow. Some bright
spots, but too widely spaced.'—Variety

Lafayette
France / Italy 1961 158m Super
Technirama 70
Copernic / Cosmos (Maurice Jacquin)

French officers help America in the
revolutionary war of 1776.
Nerveless international epic, interesting only
for its star cameos.

w Jean-Bernard Luc, Suzanne Arduini,
Jacques Sigurd, François Ponthier, Jean
Dréville, Maurice Jacquin d Jean Dréville
ph Claude Renoir, Roger Hubert m Steve
Laurent, Pierre Duclos

Michel Le Royer, Jack Hawkins, Orson
Welles, Howard St John, Vittorio de Sica,
Edmund Purdom, Jacques Castelot, Folco
Lulli
  'It looks, sounds and smells like nothing so
much as the same old indigestible, ill-dubbed,

co-produced continental spectaculars which have already turned the stomach in a whole range of lesser screen ratios.'—*MFB*

Lafayette Escadrille
US 1957   93m   bw
Warner (William Wellman)
GB title: *Hell Bent for Glory*

Early in World War I, a young American joins the French air force.
The director's valedictory film, on a subject close to his heart, is a curiously disappointing, flat and disjointed affair, partly salvaged by a good period feel.

w A. S. Fleischmann *d* William A. Wellman
ph William Clothier *m* Leonard Rosenman

Tab Hunter, David Janssen, Clint Eastwood, Will Hutchins, Paul Fix

The Lambeth Walk
GB 1939   84m   bw
CAPAD / Pinebrook (Anthony Havelock-Allan)

A cockney bloke inherits a dukedom.
Mild screen version of a popular musical play and a song which became a nationwide hit.

w Clifford Grey, John Paddy Carstairs, Robert Edmunds, *play* Me and My Girl by Louis Rose, Douglas Furber, Noel Gay
d Albert de Courville

Lupino Lane, Sally Gray, Seymour Hicks, Enid Stamp Taylor, Wilfrid Hyde White, Charles Heslop, Norah Howard

The Lamp Still Burns
GB 1943   90m   bw
GFD / Two Cities (Leslie Howard)

Adventures of wartime probationary nurses.
Understated wartime morale-builder, no longer very interesting.

w Elizabeth Baron, Roland Pertwee, *novel* One Pair of Feet by Monica Dickens
d Maurice Elvey *ph* Robert Krasker

Rosamund John, Stewart Granger, Godfrey Tearle, Sophie Stewart, John Laurie, Margaret Vyner, Cathleen Nesbitt, Joyce Grenfell

Lancashire Luck
GB 1937   74m   bw

A poor girl's life is changed when her father wins the pools. Modest comedy which started its star's career. Wendy Hiller, George Carney, Muriel George, Nigel Stock, George Galleon. Written by A. R. Rawlinson, from a story by Ronald Gow; directed by Henry Cass; for Paramount British.

Lancelot and Guinevere*
GB 1962   117m   Eastmancolor
   Panavision
Emblem (Cornel Wilde)
US title: *Sword of Lancelot*

Sir Lancelot covets the wife of his beloved King Arthur, but after Arthur's death she takes the veil.

Decently made, rather tame transcription of the legends, with all concerned doing quite creditably but not brilliantly.

w Richard Schayer, Jefferson Pascal *d* Cornel Wilde *ph* Harry Waxman *m* Ron Goodwin

Cornel Wilde, Jean Wallace, Brian Aherne, George Baker, John Barrie

Lancer Spy*
US 1937   80m   bw
TCF

A German spy is captured and his English double is sent back to replace him.
World War I yarn on the lines of *The Great Impersonation* (qv). Excellent production and a good beginning and end, but a slow middle.

w Philip Dunne, *novel* Marthe McKenna
d Gregory Ratoff *ph* Barney McGill
m Arthur Lange

George Sanders, Dolores del Rio, Peter Lorre, Joseph Schildkraut, Virginia Field, Sig Rumann, Fritz Feld
   'Sometimes exciting, always absorbing, and played with serious intensity.'—*Variety*

Land of Liberty*
US 1939   137m   bw

A compilation of footage from American historical films, amounting hopefully to a history of America as seen by Hollywood. A pretty impressive job of selection and editing, compiled for the New York World's Fair. Written by Jeannie McPherson, Jesse Lasky Jnr; edited by Cecil B. de Mille and others; for Motion Picture Producers and Distributors of America.

'Her treachery stained every stone of the
   pyramid!'
Land of the Pharaohs*
US 1955   105m   Warnercolor
   Cinemascope
Warner / Continental (Howard Hawks)

Pharaoh is obsessed with life after death and builds a great pyramid for himself and his treasures . . . but his wife is ambitious . . .
Unexpected, interesting excursion into Ancient Egypt, distended by Cinemascope; basically a macabre melodrama with a final spectacular twist. The engineering details would make a fascinating documentary.

w William Faulkner, Harry Kurnitz, H. Jack Bloom *d* Howard Hawks *ph* Lee Garmes, Russell Harlan *m* Dmitri Tiomkin
ad Alexander Trauner

Jack Hawkins, Joan Collins, Alexis Minotis, James Robertson Justice, Sidney Chaplin
   '20,000 workers and technicians! 1,600 camels! 104 specially built barges! 9,753 players in one scene alone!'—*publicity*

The Land That Time Forgot*
GB 1974   91m   Technicolor
Amicus (John Dark)

In 1916, survivors from a torpedoed supply ship find themselves on a legendary island full of prehistoric monsters.

Lively old-fashioned adventure fantasy with good technical credits.

w James Cawthorne, Michael Moorcock, *novel* Edgar Rice Burroughs *d* Kevin Connor
ph Alan Hume *m* Douglas Gamley
pd Maurice Carter *sp* Derek Meddings, Roger Dicken

Doug McClure, John McEnery, Susan Penhaligon, Keith Barron, Anthony Ainley
● *Video: Thorn EMI*

The Land Unknown*
US 1957   78m   bw   Cinemascope
U-I (William Alland)

A plane is forced down into a strange Antarctic valley where dinosaurs still roam.
Efficient adventure fantasy on *King Kong* lines but without any of that film's panache.

w Laslo Gorog *d* Virgil Vogel *ph* Ellis Carter *m* Joseph Gershenson *sp* Roswell Hoffman, Fred Knoth, Orien Ernest, Jack Kevan

Jock Mahoney, Shawn Smith, William Reynolds, Henry Brandon

Land without Bread*
Spain 1932   27m   bw
Ramon Acin
aka: *Las Hurdes*

A famous documentary showing the poorest region of northern Spain, notable for some stunningly unpleasant images impeccably staged.

wd, ed Luis Bunuel *ph* Eli Lotar

Land without Music*
GB 1936   80m   bw
Capitol Films (Max Schach)
US title: *Forbidden Music*

The ruler of a Ruritanian country bans music because her subjects are too busy singing to make money. A revolutionary singer however wins the duchess's hand and reverses her decision.

Artless but attractively played operetta with the star in excellent form.

w Marian Dix, L. Du Garde Peach *d* Walter Forde *ph* John Boyle *m* Oscar Straus

Richard Tauber, Jimmy Durante, Diana Napier, June Clyde, Derrick de Marney, Esme Percy, George Hayes, Edward Rigby

Landfall
GB 1949   88m   bw
ABPC (Victor Skuzetzky)

A test pilot mistakenly believes that he accidentally sank a British submarine.
Second rate transcription of a popular novel.

w Talbot Jennings, Gilbert Gunn, Anne Burnaby, *novel* Nevil Shute *d* Ken Annakin

Michael Denison, Patricia Plunkett, Kathleen Harrison, David Tomlinson, Joan Dowling, Maurice Denham, A. E. Matthews, Margaretta Scott, Sebastian Shaw, Laurence Harvey

The Landlord*
US 1970 110m De Luxe
United Artists / Mirisch / Carter (Norman Jewison)

A tycoon's son buys a tenement in Brooklyn's black ghetto, and conscience diverts him into improving the lot of his tenants.
Overlong satirical comedy, good on detail but short on structure.

w Bill Gunn, *novel* Kristin Hunter *d* Hal Ashby *ph* Gordon Willis *m* Al Kooper *pd* Robert Boyle

Beau Bridges, Lee Grant, Pearl Bailey, Diana Sands

'Bad taste from start to finish . . . not an avenue of offensiveness to any race is left unexplored.'—*Judith Crist*

AAN: Lee Grant

Landru
France / Italy 1962 115m Eastmancolor
Rome-Paris / CC Champion (Carlo Ponti, Georges de Beauregard)
aka: *Bluebeard*

The true story of a furniture dealer who murdered women for financial gain, also treated by Chaplin in *Monsieur Verdoux.*
A curious artificial style has been adopted, making a tragi-comedy look like a farce which isn't very funny, and falls on very stony ground indeed despite the all star cast.

w Françoise Sagan *d* Claude Chabrol *ph* Jean Rabier *m* Pierre Jansen

Charles Denner, Michèle Morgan, Danielle Darrieux, Hildegarde Knef, Stéphane Audran, Catherine Rouvel

Larceny
US 1948 89m bw
Universal (Aaron Rosenberg)

A con man fleeces a war widow into paying for a memorial to her husband, but falls in love with her.
Drearily predictable melodrama.

w Herbert F. Margolis, Louis Markein, William Bowers *novel* The Velvet Fleece by Lois Ely, John Fleming *d* George Sherman *ph* Irving Glassberg *m* Leith Stevens

Joan Caulfield, John Payne, Dan Duryea, Shelley Winters, Dorothy Hart, Richard Rober, Dan O'Herlihy

Larceny Inc.
US 1942 95m bw
Warner (Jack Saper, Jerry Wald)

An ex-convict tries to rob a bank but finds that honesty pays best.
Tepid comedy-drama from the period when Warners were taming their gangster image.

w Everett Freeman, Edwin Gilbert, *play* The Night before Christmas by Laura and S. J. Perelman *d* Lloyd Bacon *ph* Tony Gaudio

Edward G. Robinson, Jane Wyman, Broderick Crawford, Anthony Quinn, Jack Carson, Edward Brophy, Harry Davenport, John Qualen, Barbara Jo Allen, Jackie Gleason, Grant Mitchell, Andrew Tombes

The Las Vegas Story
US 1952 88m bw
RKO (Robert Sparks)

When an investment broker and his new wife stop at Las Vegas, her shady past begins to emerge.
So-so programmer with some eccentric talents in average form, capped by a desert helicopter chase.

w Earl Felton, Harry Essex *d* Robert Stevenson *ph* Harry J. Wild *m* Constantin Bakaleinikoff

Jane Russell, Victor Mature, Vincent Price, Hoagy Carmichael, Colleen Miller, Brad Dexter, Jay C. Flippen

The Lash
US 1930 76m bw

Adventures of a Spanish-Californian Robin Hood. Or, *The Mark of Zorro* in all but name: a stalwart early talkie. Richard Barthelmess, Mary Astor, James Rennie, Marian Nixon. Written by Bradley King from the story Adios by Lanier Virginia Bartlett; directed by Frank Lloyd; for First National. 'A good action talker in the western romantic strain.'—*Variety*
NB: Filmed in VitaScope (65mm).

Lassie
The official Lassie series, made by MGM, was as follows:
1943: LASSIE COME HOME (qv)
1945: SON OF LASSIE (*d* S. Sylvan Simon *with* Peter Lawford, Donald Crisp, Nigel Bruce)
1946: COURAGE OF LASSIE (*d* Fred M. Wilcox *with* Elizabeth Taylor, Frank Morgan, Tom Drake)
1948: THE HILLS OF HOME[1] (*d* Fred M. Wilcox *with* Edmund Gwenn, Donald Crisp, Tom Drake)
1949: THE SUN COMES UP (*d* Richard Thorpe *with* Jeanette MacDonald, Lloyd Nolan)
1949: CHALLENGE TO LASSIE (*d* Richard Thorpe *with* Edmund Gwenn, Donald Crisp)
1951: THE PAINTED HILLS (*d* Harold F. Kress *with* Paul Kelly, Bruce Cowling)
† Later 'Lassie' features were taken from episodes of the long-running TV series.
[1](GB title: *Master of Lassie*)

Lassie Come Home*
US 1943 88m Technicolor
MGM (Samuel Marx)

A poor family is forced to sell its beloved dog, but she makes a remarkable journey to return to them.
First of the Lassie films and certainly the best: an old-fashioned heartwarmer.

w Hugo Butler, *novel* Eric Knight *d* Fred M. Wilcox *ph* Leonard Smith *m* Daniele Amfitheatrof

Roddy McDowall, Elizabeth Taylor, Donald Crisp, Edmund Gwenn, Dame May Whitty, Nigel Bruce, Elsa Lanchester, J. Pat O'Malley

'The late Eric Knight wrote this immortal essay in Doggery-Woggery. MGM finished it off.'—*Richard Winnington*

AAN: Leonard Smith

Lassiter
US 1984 100m Technicolor
Pan Pacific / Golden Harvest (Albert S. Ruddy)

An American detective in pre-war London is forced by Scotland Yard to steal papers from the German Embassy.
Flat to the point of stultification, this marks yet another failure to make a big screen star of Tom Selleck.

w David Taylor *d* Roger Young *ph* Gil Taylor *m* Ken Thorne *pd* Peter Mullins *ed* Benjamin Weissman, Richard Hiscott

Tom Selleck, Jane Seymour, Lauren Hutton, Bob Hoskins, Joe Regalbuto, Ed Lauter, Warren Clarke

The Last Adventurers
GB 1937 77m bw

Adventures on board a fishing trawler. Acceptable low-budget outdoor drama. Niall MacGinnis, Linden Travers, Roy Emerton, Kay Walsh, Peter Gawthorne, Katie Johnson. Written by Denison Clift; directed by Roy Kellino; for Conway.

The Last American Hero*
US 1973 95m De Luxe Panavision
TCF / Wizan / Rojo (John Cutts, William Roberts)

The adventures of an illicit whisky distiller with a passion for fast cars.
Observant, amusing hillbilly comedy drama based on the early life of racing driver Junior Johnson.

w William Roberts *d* Lamont Johnson *ph* George Silano *m* Charles Fox

Jeff Bridges, Valerie Perrine, Geraldine Fitzgerald, Ned Beatty, Art Lund, Gary Busey
† Reissue title: *Hard Driver.*

● *Video: CBS / Fox*

The Last Angry Man*
US 1959 100m bw
Columbia (Fred Kohlmar)

An old doctor in a Brooklyn slum is made the subject of a TV documentary.
Self-confidently sentimental wallow which just about works.

w Gerald Green *d* Daniel Mann *ph* James Wong Howe *m* George Duning

Paul Muni, David Wayne, Betsy Palmer, Luther Adler, Dan Tobin, Robert F. Simon

AAN: Paul Muni

The Last Blitzkrieg
US 1959 84m bw
Columbia / Sam Katzman

During the Battle of the Bulge a German leads a squad of American saboteurs.
Weakly pacifist, technically incompetent war adventure.

LARCENY INC.   Broderick Crawford and Edward G. Robinson support a young Jane Wyman.

w Lou Morheim d Arthur Dreifuss ph Ted Scaife m Hugo de Groot

Van Johnson, Kerwin Mathews, Dick York, Larry Storch

The Last Bridge

Austria / Yugoslavia 1953   95m   bw
Cosmopol / UFUS (Carl Szokoll)

During World War II, a German nurse in Yugoslavia is captured by partisans and turns to their point of view.
Message melodrama, very ably put together with a bleakly tragic climax; but nothing at all new.

w Helmut Kautner, Norbert Kunze d Helmut Kautner ph Elio Carniel m Carl de Groof

Maria Schell, Bernhard Wicki, Barbara Rütting, Carl Möhner

The Last Chance*

Switzerland 1945   105m   bw
Praesens Film

In 1943 an Englishman and an American escape from a fascist camp in northern Italy and with the help of refugees cross the mountains into Switzerland.
Earnest propaganda piece which struck the spot at the time: cinematically rather plodding, but with some exciting scenes.

w Richard Schweitzer d Leopold Lindtberg ph Emil Berna m Robert Blum

E. G. Morrison, Ray Reagan, John Hoy, Luisa Rossi

The Last Command**

US 1928   100m approx (24 fps)   bw
silent
Paramount

An exiled Russian general goes berserk when given a role in a movie which virtually involves playing himself.
Fascinating ironic comedy tailored for an international star who was not to survive the talkies.

w John S. Goodrich, story Lajos Biro d Josef Von Sternberg ph Bert Glennon ad Hans Dreier

Emil Jannings, William Powell, Evelyn Brent, Nicholas Soussanin

AA: Emil Jannings
AAN: best picture; Lajos Biro

The Last Command*

US 1955   110m   Trucolor
Republic (Frank Lloyd)

Jim Bowie returns to Texas in the 1830s and dies at the Alamo alongside other famous men.

Reasonably interesting western on a subject which has often figured but seldom worked.

w Warren Duff d Frank Lloyd ph Jack Marta m Max Steiner

Ernest Borgnine, Sterling Hayden, Anna Maria Alberghetti, Arthur Hunnicutt, Richard Carlson, J. Carrol Naish

The Last Days of Dolwyn*

GB 1949   95m   bw
London / BLPA (Anatole de Grunwald)
US title: *Woman of Dolwyn*

A Welsh valley is flooded to make a reservoir and a village has to be evacuated.
Interesting but rather stagey drama based on an actual 19th-century event, with personal melodrama added.

wd Emlyn Williams ph Otto Heller m John Greenwood

Edith Evans, Emlyn Williams, Richard Burton, Hugh Griffith, Barbara Couper, Allan Aynesworth
   'The conventionally picturesque Welsh flavour and mounting probabilities apart, the treatment is stiff and episodic.'—MFB

'Pompeii . . . drunk with wealth and power . . . rotten with pagan pleasures . . . doomed to fiery death from the skies!'

The Last Days of Pompeii*

US 1935   96m   bw
RKO (Merian C. Cooper)

In ancient Pompeii, various personal dramas are submerged in the eruption of Vesuvius.
Starchy melodrama capped by a reel of spectacular disaster.

w Ruth Rose, Boris Ingster, novel Lord Lytton d Merian C. Cooper, Ernest Schoedsack ph Eddie Linden Jnr, J. Roy Hunt m Roy Webb sp Vernon Walker, Harry Redmond

Preston Foster, Basil Rathbone, Alan Hale, Dorothy Cooper
   'Well-done spectacle minus romance and cast names. Should do all right generally.'—Variety

● Video: Kingston

The Last Detail**

US 1973   104m   Metrocolor
Columbia / Acrobat / Persky–Bright (Gerald Ayres)

Two hardened naval petty officers escort a young recruit, sentenced for thieving, from Virginia to a New Hampshire jail, and give him a wild last night.
Foul-mouthed weekend odyssey, with a few well-observed moments for non-prudes.
Technically the epitome of Hollywood's most irritating seventies fashion, with fuzzy sound recording, dim against-the-light photography, and a general determination to show up the ugliness of everything around us.

w Robert Towne, novel Darryl Ponicsan d Hal Ashby ph Michael Chapman m Johnny Mandel

Jack Nicholson, Otis Young, Randy Quaid, Clifton James, Carol Kane

'Visually it is relentlessly lower-depths gloomy, and the material, though often very funny, is programmed to wrench your heart.'—*New Yorker*

AAN: Robert Towne; Jack Nicholson; Randy Quaid

● *Video: RCA / Columbia*

The Last Dinosaur

US 1977   100m   colour
Rankin-Bass Productions

An oil-drilling team discovers a *tyrannosaurus rex* while probing the polar oil-cap.
Inept monster saga with poorish special effects from a Japanese team.

w William Overgard d Alex Grasshof, Tom Kotani ph Shoshi Ueda m Maury Laws

Richard Boone, Joan Van Ark, Steven Keats

'He thinks someone is trying to kill him. He's dead right!'

Last Embrace

US 1979   101m   Technicolor
UA (Michael Taylor, Dan Wigutow)

An investigator survives a number of attacks on his life, though his wife is killed in the first of them.
Hitchcockian mystery without the master's zest or humour, though it leads to a pretty exciting climax at Niagara Falls.

w David Shaber, *novel* The 13th Man by Murray Teigh Bloom d Jonathan Demme ph Tak Fujimoto m Miklos Rozsa

Roy Scheider, Janet Margolin, Sam Levene, John Glover, Charles Napier, Christopher Walken, Jacqueline Brookes

'A case study of late seventies movie-making which does everything in its power to avoid taking risks.'—*John Pym, MFB*

The Last Flight***

US 1931   80m   bw
Warner

In 1919, four veteran American fliers stay on in Paris in the hope of calming their shattered physical and emotional states.
Fascinatingly offhand study on post-war cynicism and the faint hope of a better world, beautifully written and directed in a manner more effective than *The Sun Also Rises*.

w John Monk Saunders, from his novel Single Lady d William Dieterle ph Sid Hickox

Richard Barthelmess, Helen Chandler, David Manners, John Mack Brown, *Elliott Nugent*, Walter Byron

'If the crowd can understand that girl character in this picture the film is an undoubted grosser.'—*Variety*

'A narrative as tight and spare as a Racine tragedy . . . unique in Hollywood of that time in its persistent, calculated understatement.'— *Tom Milne, 1975*

† In magazine form the story was known as 'Nikki and her War Birds'.

The Last Flight of Noah's Ark

US 1980   98m   Technicolor
Walt Disney

An impecunious pilot reluctantly flies an orphanage worker and a cargo of animals across the Pacific, only to be stranded with them on a desert island.
It must have sounded like a good idea, but if it was to work at all it needed much sharper handling.

w Steven W. Carabatsos, Sandy Glass, George Arthur Bloom, *story* The Gremlin's Castle by Ernest K. Gann d Charles Jarrott ph Charles F. Wheeler m Maurice Jarre

Elliott Gould, Geneviève Bujold, Ricky Schroder, Tammy Lauren, Vincent Gardenia

The Last Gangster*

US 1937   81m   bw
MGM (J. J. Cohn)

A gangster is released from Alcatraz and plans vengeance on his wife for deserting him.
Clean-cut star melodrama which suddenly turns sentimental.

w John Lee Mahin d Edward Ludwig ph William Daniels *montage* Slavko Vorkapitch

Edward G. Robinson, Rose Stradner, James Stewart, Lionel Stander, Douglas Scott, John Carradine, Sidney Blackmer, Edward Brophy

'May indeed be the last gangster movie . . . a good film which will blossom at the b.o.'— *Variety*

'A lot of water has flowed under the bridge since *Little Caesar*, but Mr Robinson has breasted the tides to make his impersonation of a 1937 thug as persuasive as was his portrait of a killer in that earlier classic of rats and rackets.'—*Frank Nugent*

The Last Gentleman

US 1934   80m   bw

The career of a New England millionaire. Pleasing star family drama. George Arliss, Edna May Oliver, Ralph Morgan, Janet Beecher, Charlotte Henry. Written by Leonard Praskins; directed by Sidney Lanfield; for Fox. 'A prolonged monologue . . . mediocre film which must depend on the star's rep.'—*Variety*

The Last Grenade

GB 1969   93m   Eastmancolor
Panavision
Cinerama / Dimitri de Grunwald / Josef Shaftel

An army mercenary is betrayed by an ex-friend in the Congo and pursues him to Hong Kong.
Violent action melodrama with few redeeming qualities.

w Kenneth Ware, *novel* The Ordeal of Major Grigsby by John Sherlock d Gordon Flemyng ph Alan Hume m Johnny Dankworth

Stanley Baker, Alex Cord, Honor Blackman, Richard Attenborough, Rafer Johnson, Andrew Keir, Ray Brooks, Julian Glover, John Thaw

The Last Hard Men

US 1976   97m   De Luxe   Panavision
TCF / Belasco–Seltzer–Thatcher

A train robber breaks jail and sets out to revenge himself on the now-retired lawman who committed him.
Tough action adventure without much sense except to paint the end of the golden days of the west.

w Guerdon Trueblood, *novel* Gun Down by Brian Garfield d Andrew V. McLaglen ph Duke Callaghan m Jerry Goldsmith

Charlton Heston, James Coburn, Barbara Hershey, Christopher Mitchum, Michael Parks, Jorge Rivero, Thalmus Rasulala

'Script and direction seem equally tired.'— *Sight and Sound*

'The action proceeds slackly from one setpiece shoot-up to the next, barely providing the voltage for the two leads to expand their stereotyped roles into displays of star power.'—*Richard Combs, MFB*

Last Holiday*

GB 1950   88m   bw
ABPC / Watergate (Stephen Mitchell, A. D. Peters, J. B. Priestley)

A man with a short time to live has a thoroughly enjoyable and useful final fling.
Slight, amusing and moving comedy drama spoiled by an unnecessary double twist.

w J. B. Priestley d Henry Cass ph Ray Elton m Francis Chagrin

Alec Guinness, Kay Walsh, Beatrice Campbell, Grégoire Aslan, Bernard Lee, Wilfrid Hyde White, Helen Cherry, Sidney James, Muriel George

The Last Hunt*

US 1955   103m   Eastmancolor
Cinemascope
MGM (Dore Schary)

Buffalo hunters fall out with each other. Terse, brutish outdoor western with something to say about old western myths and a famous ending in which the bad guy freezes to death while waiting to gun down the hero.

wd Richard Brooks ph Russell Harlan m Daniele Amfitheatrof

Stewart Granger, Robert Taylor, Debra Paget, Lloyd Nolan, Russ Tamblyn, Constance Ford

The Last Hurrah***

US 1958   125m   bw
Columbia (John Ford)

The political boss of a New England town fights his last campaign.
Enjoyable if disjointed melodrama, an old man's film crammed with cameo performances from familiar faces: important as one of Hollywood's great sentimental reunions.

w Frank Nugent, *novel* Edwin O'Connor d John Ford ph Charles Lawton Jnr

Spencer Tracy, Jeffrey Hunter, Dianne Foster, *Pat O'Brien*, Basil Rathbone, Edward Brophy, Donald Crisp, James Gleason, John Carradine, Ricardo Cortez, Wallace Ford,

Frank McHugh, Frank Albertson, Anna Lee, Jane Darwell, Willis Bouchey, Basil Ruysdael
† A TV version was subsequently made with Carroll O'Connor.

The Last Journey*
GB 1935   66m   bw
Twickenham (Julius Hagen)

The driver of an express train, driven mad with jealousy, goes berserk.
Workmanlike little train suspenser with an exciting climax.

w John Soutar, H. Fowler Mear, *story* J. Jefferson Farjeon   d Bernard Vorhaus

Godfrey Tearle, Hugh Williams, Julien Mitchell, Judy Gunn, Nelson Keys, Frank Pettingell, Olga Lindo, Sydney Fairbrother

The Last Laugh***
Germany 1924   73m approx (24 fps)   bw   silent
UFA
original title: *Der Letzte Mann*

The old doorman of a luxury hotel is given the job of lavatory attendant but comes into a fortune and gets his revenge.
Ironic anecdote made important by its virtual abandonment of dialogue and whole-hearted adoption of the camera eye technique which gives some thrilling dramatic effects.

w *Carl Mayer*   d F. W. Murnau   ph Karl Freund

Emil Jannings, Max Hiller, Maly Delschaft, Hans Unterkirchen

'A marvellous picture—marvellous in its simplicity, its economy of effect, its expressiveness, and its dramatic power.'—*Life*
† A German remake of 1955 had Hans Albers in the lead and was of no interest.

The Last Married Couple in America
US 1979   102m   Technicolor
Universal / Cates Brothers

A Los Angeles couple resist the efforts of their friends to involve them in the swinging life.
Tolerable sex comedy of modern mores, a shade too long delayed after *Bob and Carol and Ted and Alice*.

w John Herman Shaner   d Gilbert Cates   ph Ralph Woolsey   m Charles Fox   pd Gene Callahan

Natalie Wood, George Segal, Richard Benjamin, Arlene Golonka, Arlan Arbus, Marilyn Sokol, Dom DeLuise, Valerie Harper

The Last Metro*
France 1980   131m   Fujicolor
Les Films du Carrosse / Andrea / SEDIF / TF1 / SFP (Jean-José Richer)

In occupied Paris, the Jewish manager of a theatre hides in the cellar of the building.
Tightly enclosed symbolic melodrama which doesn't work nearly so well as *Les Visiteurs du Soir*, which had something very similar to say about the spirit of la belle France.

w François Truffaut, Suzanne Schiffman   d François Truffaut   ph Nestor Almendros   m Georges Delerue

Catherine Deneuve, Gérard Depardieu, Jean Poiret, Heinz Bennent

AAN: best foreign film

The Last Mile*
US 1932   84m   bw
World Wide (E. W. Hammons)

Tensions mount in jail as the execution of Killer Mears approaches.
Strident melodrama which works up quite a head of hysteria.

w Seton I. Miller, *play* John Wexley   d Sam Bischoff   ph Arthur Edeson

Preston Foster, Howard Phillips, George E. Stone, Noel Madison

'Subject's lure is confined to the morbid-minded sensation seeker . . . without feminine interest.'—*Variety*

The Last Mile
US 1959   81m   bw
UA / Vanguard (Milton Subotsky)

Even more hysterical remake, retaining the original period. A cheerless, though literally electrifying, entertainment.

w Milton Subotsky, Seton I. Miller   d Howard W. Koch   ph Joseph Brun   m Van Alexander

Mickey Rooney, Clifford David, Frank Conroy, Frank Overton, Leon Janney

The Last Movie
US 1971   108m   Technicolor

Moviemakers go to Peru to film a western. Muddled and pretentious melodrama following the success of *Easy Rider*. Dennis Hopper, Julie Adams, Rod Cameron, Daniel Ades, Michael Anderson Jnr. Written by Stewart Stern; directed by Dennis Hopper; for Universal.

The Last of Mrs Cheyney
US 1929   94m   bw
MGM

A confidence woman in British high society falls in love.
Old theatrical warhorse, much filmed but never quite satisfactorily. (See below.)

w Hans Kraly, Claudine West, *play* Frederick Lonsdale   d Sidney Franklin   ph William Daniels

Norma Shearer, Basil Rathbone, George Barraud, Hedda Hopper, Maude Turner Gordon, Herbert Bunston

The Last of Mrs Cheyney
US 1937   98m   bw
MGM (Lawrence Weingarten)

Adequate, unexciting remake.

w Leon Gordon, Samson Raphaelson, Monckton Hoffe   d Richard Boleslawski   ph George Folsey   m William Axt

Joan Crawford, Robert Montgomery, William Powell, Frank Morgan, Jessie Ralph, Nigel Bruce, Benita Hume, Melville Cooper, Sara Haden

'Good film fodder, although not particularly socko.'—*Variety*
† A further remake was *The Law and the Lady* (qv).

The Last of Sheila*
US 1973   123m   Technicolor
Warner (Herbert Ross)

A Hollywood star is killed by a hit-and-run driver; a year later her husband invites six friends to his yacht, and murders begin.
Confused, in-jokey showbiz whodunnit with flashes of interest.

w Stephen Sondheim, Anthony Perkins   d Herbert Ross   ph Gerry Turpin   m Billy Goldenberg   ad Ken Adam

Richard Benjamin, Dyan Cannon, James Coburn, James Mason, Joan Hackett, Ian MacShane, Raquel Welch

'The most teasing riddles for an audience are likely to be the real identities of the personalities being satirized.'—*MFB*

The Last of the Buccaneers
US 1950   79m   Technicolor

The story of Jean Lafitte, French privateer in the war of 1812. Cheerful low-budget swashbuckler. Paul Henreid, Jack Oakie, Karin Booth, Edgar Barrier, Mary Anderson, John Dehner. Written by Robert E. Kent; directed by Lew Landers; for Columbia.

The Last of the Comanches*
US 1953   85m   Technicolor
Columbia (Buddy Adler)
GB title: *The Sabre and the Arrow*

Survivors of an Indian raid take refuge in an abandoned mission until help arrives.
Competent western remake of *Sahara* (which was a remake of *The Lost Patrol*).

w Kenneth Gamet   d André de Toth   ph Charles Lawton Jnr   m George Duning

Broderick Crawford, Barbara Hale, Lloyd Bridges, Martin Milner

Last of the Fast Guns
US 1959   82m   Eastmancolor   Cinemascope

Rival gunfighters form a friendship but fall out over their mission. Mildly unusual western programmer. Gilbert Roland, Jock Mahoney, Linda Cristal, Eduard Franz, Lorne Greene, Carl Benton Reid. Written by David P. Harmon; directed by George Sherman; for Universal-International.

The Last of the Mohicans
US 1936   91m   bw
Edward Small

Incidents during colonial America's French–Indian war.
Vigorous if rough-and-ready western, later remade (poorly) as *Last of the Redmen* and as a Canadian TV series.

w Philip Dunne, John Balderston, Paul Perez, Daniel Moore, *novel* James Fenimore Cooper   d George B. Seitz   ph Robert Planck   m Roy Webb

Randolph Scott, Binnie Barnes, Bruce Cabot, Henry Wilcoxon, Heather Angel, Hugh Buckler

Last of the Red Hot Lovers*
US 1972 98m Technicolor
Paramount (Howard W. Koch)

A middle-aged fish restaurateur feels the need for an extra-marital spree.
Modest, plainly-filmed sex comedy from a reliable stable.

w Neil Simon, from his play d Gene Saks ph Victor J. Kemper m Neal Hefti

Alan Arkin, Paula Prentiss, Sally Kellerman, Renée Taylor

Last of the Secret Agents
US 1966 90m Technicolor

Two odd job men are recruited as spies. Pratfall comedy featuring a briefly existing comedy double act. Marty Allen, Steve Rossi, John Williams, Nancy Sinatra, Lou Jacobi, Theo Marcuse, Sig Rumann. Written by Mel Tolkin; directed by Norman Abbott; for Paramount.

'Open war between a handful of English and swarming tribesmen! Hidden war between fellow-officers who love the same woman!'

The Last Outpost*
US 1935 75m bw
Paramount (E. Lloyd Sheldon)

A British officer is captured by the Kurds and freed by an adventurer whose wife he covets. Patchy, unusual adventure story with good moments.

w Philip MacDonald, story F. Britten Austin d Charles Barton, Louis Gasnier ph Theodor Sparkuhl

Cary Grant, Claude Rains, Gertrude Michael, Kathleen Burke, Colin Tapley, Akim Tamiroff, Billy Bevan, Jameson Thomas
'Loosely-woven melodramatic mélange.'—Variety
'Half of it is remarkably good and half of it quite abysmally bad. One can even put one's finger on the joins.'—Graham Greene

The Last Outpost
US 1951 89m Technicolor
Paramount / Pine–Thomas

A Civil War colonel finds his brother fighting on the other side.
Routine historical action romance.

w Geoffrey Homes, G. Worthing Yates, Winston Miller d Lewis R. Foster ph Loyal Griggs m Lucien Cailliet

Ronald Reagan, Bruce Bennett, Rhonda Fleming, Noah Beery Jnr

The Last Page
GB 1952 84m bw

A bookseller is framed for the death of a blackmailer. Curious English mystery with American stars. George Brent, Marguerite Chapman, Diana Dors, Raymond Huntley, Peter Reynolds, Eleanor Summerfield.

Written by Frederick Knott, from a play by James Hadley Chase; directed by Terence Fisher; for Hammer-Lippert. (US title: Manbait.)

The Last Parade
US 1931 82m bw

A detective and a racketeer are buddies in the war, but not afterwards. Predictable character melodrama with no remaining interest. Jack Holt, Constance Cummings, Tom Moore, Gaylord Pendleton. Written by Dorothy Howell, Casey Robinson; directed by Erle C. Kenton; for Columbia. 'In for money, but not that strong for a holdover.'—Variety

The Last Picture Show***
US 1971 118m bw
Columbia / LPS / BDS (Stephen J. Friedman)

Teenage affairs in a small Texas town in 1951, ending with the hero's embarkation for Korea and the closing of the tatty cinema.
Penetrating nostalgia with over-emphasis on sex; the detail is the attraction.

w Larry McMurty, Peter Bogdanovich d Peter Bogdanovich ph Robert Surtees m original recordings pd Polly Platt

Timothy Bottoms, Jeff Bridges, Cybill Shepherd, Ben Johnson, Cloris Leachman, Ellen Burstyn
'The most important work by a young American director since Citizen Kane.'—Paul D. Zimmerman
'So many things in it are so good that I wish I liked it more.'—Stanley Kauffmann

AA: Ben Johnson; Cloris Leachman
AAN: best picture; script; Peter Bogdanovich (as director); Robert Surtees; Jeff Bridges; Ellen Burstyn

The Last Posse
US 1953 73m bw

Members of a thief-catching posse fall out on the way and return in disgrace. Stumbling little western, a poor return to the star after All the King's Men. Broderick Crawford, John Derek, Wanda Hendrix, Charles Bickford. Written by Seymour and Connie Lee, Bennett and Kenneth Gamet; directed by Alfred Werker; for Columbia.

'A different kind of love story!'
The Last Remake of Beau Geste
US 1977 85m Technicolor
Universal (William S. Gilmore Jnr)

The Geste brothers find themselves in the Foreign Legion after the theft of the Blue Water sapphire.
Woebegone spoof of a romantic original, with most of the jokes totally irrelevant to the purpose and seldom at all funny.

w Marty Feldman, Chris J. Allen d Marty Feldman ph Gerry Fisher m John Morris

Marty Feldman, Michael York, Ann-Margret, Peter Ustinov, Trevor Howard, James Earl Jones, Henry Gibson, Terry-Thomas, Roy Kinnear, Spike Milligan, Hugh Griffith, Irene Handl

'A ragbag of a film which looks like nothing so much as a Monty Python extravaganza in which inspiration has run dry and the comic timing gone sadly awry.'—Tom Milne, MFB

The Last Run*
US 1971 92m Metrocolor Panavision
MGM (Carter de Haven)

An ex-Chicago gangster retired to a Portuguese fishing village undertakes one last fatal job.
Well-made, rather uninteresting downbeat melodrama.

w Alan Sharp d Richard Fleischer ph Sven Nykvist m Jerry Goldsmith

George C. Scott, Tony Musante, Trish Van Devere

The Last Safari
GB 1967 110m Technicolor
Paramount (Henry Hathaway)

A disillusioned white hunter takes on one last safari.
Dullsville adventure story with good animal photography redeeming some of the clichés.

w John Gay, novel Gilligan's Last Elephant by Gerald Hanley d Henry Hathaway ph Ted Moore m Johnny Dankworth

Stewart Granger, Kaz Garas, Gabriella Licudi, Johnny Sekka, Liam Redmond, Eugene Deckers

The Last Shot You Hear
GB 1970 90m bw

Lovers plot murder, but the scheme backfires. Unassuming mystery programmer from a West End success. Hugh Marlowe, Zena Walker, Patricia Haines, William Dysart, Thorley Walters. Written by Tim Shields, from the play The Sound of Murder by William Fairchild; directed by Gordon Hessler; for Lippert-TCF.

The Last Stage*
Poland 1947 110m bw
Film Polski
original title: Ostatni Etap

Women suffer but one is finally rescued from the Nazi concentration camp at Auschwitz.
A dour, obsessive, horrifying record of human inhumanity, set in the actual camp and made by two former inmates.

w Wanda Jakubowska, Gerda Schneider d Wanda Jakubowska ph Borys Monastyrski m R. Palester

Huguette Faget, W. Bartowna, T. Gorecka

The Last Starfighter*
US 1984 101m Technicolor Panavision
Lorimar / Universal (Gary Adelson, Edward O. Denault)

A teenage whiz at video games is abducted by the survivors of a distant planet who need his skills if they are to outwit their enemies.
A surprisingly pleasant variation on the Star Wars boom, with sharp and witty

performances from two reliable character actors and some elegant gadgetry to offset the teenage mooning.

w *Jonathan Betuel* d Nick Castle *ph* King Baggot *m* Craig Safan *pd* Ron Cobb *ed* C. Timothy O'Meara

Lance Guest, *Robert Preston*, *Dan O'Herlihy*, Catherine Mary Stewart, Barbara Bosson, Norman Snow

Last Summer*

US 1969 97m Eastmancolor
Alsid / Francis (Alfred Crown, Sidney Beckerman)

Well-to-do teenagers have sexual adventures on a summer seaside holiday.
Striking off-beat melodrama with vividly sketched characters.

w *Eleanor Perry*, novel Evan Hunter *d* Frank Perry *ph* Gerald Hirschfeld *m* John Simon

Barbara Hershey, Richard Thomas, Bruce Davison, Cathy Burns, Ernesto Gonzales, Ralph Waite

AAN: Cathy Burns

The Last Sunset

US 1961 112m Eastmancolor
U-I (Brynaprod) (Eugene Frenke, Edward Lewis)

A killer and his hunter learn a lot about each other before the final showdown.
Slow psycho-western with pretensions to tragedy.

w *Dalton Trumbo*, novel Showdown at Crazy Horse by Howard Rigsby *d* Robert Aldrich *ph* Ernest Laszlo *m* Ernest Gold

Rock Hudson, Kirk Douglas, Dorothy Malone, Carol Lynley, Joseph Cotten, Regis Toomey, Neville Brand

Last Tango in Paris*

France / Italy / US 1972 129m Technicolor
Les Artistes Associés / PEA / UA (Alberto Grimaldi)

A middle-aged man and a young French girl have a doomed love affair.
Pretentious sex melodrama mainly notable for being banned.

w *Bernardo Bertolucci*, Franco Arcalli *d* Bernardo Bertolucci *ph* Vittorio Storaro *m* Gato Barbieri

Marlon Brando, Maria Schneider, Jean-Pierre Léaud
'An intense meditation on the realization of mortality.'—*Sight and Sound*

AAN: Bernardo Bertolucci (as director); Marlon Brando

● *Video: Intervision*

The Last Time I Saw Archie

US 1961 98m bw
UA / Mark VII / Manzanita / Talbot (Jack Webb)

Adventures of a con man amid overage civilian pilots at an army / air force base.
Patchy service comedy.

w William Bowers *d* Jack Webb *ph* Joe MacDonald *m* Frank Comstock

Jack Webb, Robert Mitchum, Martha Hyer, France Nuyen, Louis Nye, Jimmy Lydon, Richard Arlen, Don Knotts, Robert Strauss, Joe Flynn

The Last Time I Saw Paris

US 1954 116m Technicolor
MGM (Jack Cummings)

A writer recalls his romance with a wealthy American girl in Paris.
Dull romantic drama which very deadeningly and predictably updates F. Scott Fitzgerald's *Babylon Revisited*.

w Julius J. and Philip G. Epstein, Richard Brooks *d* Richard Brooks *ph* Joseph Ruttenberg *m* Conrad Salinger

Elizabeth Taylor, Van Johnson, Walter Pidgeon, Donna Reed, Eva Gabor

Last Train from Bombay

US 1952 72m bw

A diplomat in Bombay is falsely accused of the murder of an old friend. Stilted melodrama culminating in a hectic train ride. Jon Hall, Christine Larson, Lisa Ferraday, Douglas Kennedy. Written by Robert Yale Libbott; directed by Fred F. Sears; for Sam Katzman / Columbia.

Last Train from Gun Hill*

US 1959 98m Technicolor Vistavision
(Paramount) Hal B. Wallis / Bryna

A marshal tracks down the man who raped and murdered his wife; it turns out to be the son of an old friend.
Good suspense and action western culminating in a *High Noon* situation.

w James Poe *d* John Sturges *ph* Charles Lang Jnr *m* Dmitri Tiomkin

Kirk Douglas, Anthony Quinn, Earl Holliman, Carolyn Jones, Brian Hutton

● *Video: CBS / Fox*

'Flaming love drama set against the background of Spain's Civil War!'

The Last Train from Madrid

US 1937 85m bw
Paramount (George M. Arthur)

A variety of people escape the fighting in the Spanish Civil War.
Tawdry topical melodrama with cliché characters and situations.

w Louis Stevens, Robert Wyler *d* James Hogan *ph* Harry Fischbeck *md* Boris Morros

Dorothy Lamour, Lew Ayres, Gilbert Roland, Karen Morley, Lionel Atwill, Helen Mack, Robert Cummings, Olympe Bradna, Anthony Quinn, Lee Bowman, George Lloyd
'It is probably the worst film of the decade and should have been the funniest.'—*Graham Greene*
'Simply a topical and different background for a glib little fiction.'—*Frank S. Nugent*

The Last Tycoon

US 1976 124m Technicolor
Paramount / Academy / Sam Spiegel

The production head of a Hollywood studio in the thirties has his troubles complicated when he falls in love with a girl who reminds him of his dead wife.
Astonishingly inept and boring big budget all-star melodrama which doesn't even begin promisingly (the scenes from supposed thirties films are woefully inaccurate in style); it then bogs down in interminable dialogue scenes, leaving its famous cast all at sea.

w Harold Pinter, novel F. Scott Fitzgerald *d* Elia Kazan *ph* Victor Kemper *m* Maurice Jarre *pd* Eugene F. Callahan

Robert de Niro, Robert Mitchum, Tony Curtis, Jeanne Moreau, Jack Nicholson, Ingrid Boulting, Donald Pleasence, Ray Milland, Dana Andrews, John Carradine
'So enervated it's like a vampire movie after the vampires have left.'—*New Yorker*
'That the result is incoherent is no surprise; that it is so hollow and visually graceless adds a kind of wonder to the disappointment.'—*Sight and Sound*
'The breathless reverence that informs the movie kills it stone dead.'—*Michael Billington, Illustrated London News*
'It seems to me that Kazan and Pinter have failed disastrously, but then perhaps the task is impossible anyway.'—*Benny Green, Punch*

● *Video: Videoform*

The Last Valley

GB 1970 128m Eastmancolor Todd-AO
ABC / Season / Seamaster (James Clavell)

In 1641 during the Thirty Years War a scholar tries to defend a remote and prosperous Swiss valley against a horde of mercenaries.
Big-scale historical action picture crammed with pillage, torture, rape, death at the stake, throat cutting and general carnage; reasonably literate for all that, and convincingly set.

wd James Clavell, novel J. B. Pick *ph* Norman Warwick *m* John Barry *ad* Peter Mullins

Michael Caine, Omar Sharif, Florinda Bolkan, Nigel Davenport, Per Oscarsson, Arthur O'Connell, Brian Blessed

● *Video: Rank*

The Last Voyage*

US 1960 91m Metrocolor
MGM / Andrew and Virginia Stone

A boiler room explosion causes an old passenger liner to sink.
Spectacular if dramatically deficient actioner for which a genuine liner (awaiting scrapping) was sunk.

wd *Andrew L. Stone* *ph* Hal Mohr *m* Rudy Schrager

Robert Stack, Dorothy Malone, Edmond O'Brien, George Sanders, Woody Strode, Jack Kruschen
'A prolonged nerve stretcher.'—*MFB*

'They pitted the fire of their youth against the flame of the frontier—when America was moving west!'

The Last Wagon
US 1956 99m Eastmancolor
  Cinemascope
TCF (William B. Hawks)

A half breed wanted for murder joins an 1875 wagon train.
Heavy-going big-scale western.

w James Edward Grant, Delmer Daves, Gwen Bagni d Delmer Daves ph Wilfrid Cline m Lionel Newman

Richard Widmark, Felicia Farr, Tommy Rettig, Susan Kohner, Ray Stricklyn, Nick Adams, Carl Benton Reid

The Last Waltz
US 1978 115m De Luxe
UA / Martin Scorsese, Jonathan Taplin

Rock documentary featuring the last concert of The Band.
An occasion for specialists, very adequately packaged.

d Martin Scorsese pd Boris Leven ph Michael Chapman

The Last Warning*
US 1929 88m bw
Universal

Murder backstage.
Shot as a silent film, with sound hurriedly added, this remains a stylish comedy-thriller with all the familiar ingredients of the whodunnit.

w Alfred A. Cohn d Paul Leni ph Hal Mohr

Laura La Plante, Montagu Love, Roy D'Arcy, John Boles, Mack Swain, Slim Summerville, Margaret Livingston
† Remade in 1938 as *The House of Fear*, a William Gargan second feature.

The Last Warning
US 1938 62m bw
Universal

A private eye mystery.
Better-than-average second feature.

w Edmund L. Hartmann, *novel* The Dead Don't Care by Jonathan Latimer d Albert S. Rogell

Preston Foster, Joyce Compton, Frank Jenks

The Last Wave*
Australia 1977 106m Atlab
(UA) Ayer / MacElroy / Derek Power

During a spell of freak weather, a lawyer has recurrent dreams which give him the key to an Aborigine prophecy about the world being destroyed by flood . . .
Curious supernatural drama successfully played as a mystery, with excellent atmosphere and special effects.

w Peter Weir, Tony Morphett, Petru Popescu d Peter Weir ph Russell Boyd m Charles Wain pd Goran Warff

Richard Chamberlain, Olivia Hamnet, Frederick Parslow
'A Hitchcockian sense of minatory dislocation.'—*Tim Pulleine, MFB*

"You lived in it... you fought in it... you loved in it... and sometimes you died in it!"

20th CENTURY-FOX presents

RICHARD WIDMARK in THE LAST WAGON

co-starring FELICIA FARR CINEMASCOPE COLOR by DE LUXE

Produced by WILLIAM HAWKS · Directed by DELMER DAVES · JAMES EDWARD GRANT, DELMER DAVES and GWEN BAGNI GIELGUD Story by GWEN BAGNI GIELGUD

THE LAST WAGON. One of the better films about the pioneering west.

The Last Word
US 1979 105m colour

An Irish inventor by wily stratagems prevents the demolition of the apartment block he occupies. Oddly old-fashioned comedy drama of little obvious appeal. Richard Harris, Karen Black, Martin Landau, Biff McGuire. Written by Michael Varhol, Greg Smith and Kit Carson; directed by Roy Boulting; for Variety International Pictures.

Last Year in Marienbad**
France / Italy 1961 94m bw Dyaliscope
Terra / Tamara / Cormoran / Precitel / Como / Argos / Cinetel / Silver / Cineriz (Raymond Froment)

In a vast old-fashioned hotel, a man meets a woman who may or may not have had an affair with him the previous year in Marienbad—or was it Frederiksbad?
A dreamy, elegant film which presents a puzzle with no solution. It has its attractions for film buffs and cryptogram addicts, but is not for anyone who simply wants to be told a story.

w Alain Robbe-Grillet d Alain Resnais ph Sacha Vierny m Francis Seyrig ad Jacques Saulnier

Delphine Seyrig, Giorgio Albertazzi, Sacha Pitoeff
'Elaborate, ponderous and meaningless.'—*Newsweek*
'Clearly the film's creators know exactly what they want to do and have done it with complete success. Whether one responds to the result is entirely a matter of temperament.'—*John Russell Taylor, MFB*
AAN: Alain Robbe-Grillet

The Late Edwina Black*
GB 1951 78m bw
IFD / Elvey–Gartside
US title: *Obsessed*

When a schoolteacher's wife is found dead, the police have three suspects.
Adequately suspenseful Victorian thriller from a successful play.

w Charles Frank, David Evans, play William Dinner, William Morum d Maurice Elvey ph Stephen Dade m Allan Gray

Geraldine Fitzgerald, David Farrar, Roland Culver, Jean Cadell, Mary Merrall, Harcourt Williams, Charles Heslop, Ronald Adam

The Late George Apley*
US 1946 96m bw
TCF (Fred Kohlmar)

The uneventful family life of a Boston blueblood.
Pleasant but tame family comedy-drama, solidly carpentered.

w Philip Dunne, novel John P. Marquand d Joseph L. Mankiewicz ph Joseph La Shelle m Cyril Mockridge

Ronald Colman, Edna Best, Vanessa Brown, Richard Haydn, Peggy Cummins, Charles Russell

The Late Show*
US 1977 93m Metrocolor
Warner (Robert Altman)

An ageing private eye in Los Angeles finds that his ex-partner's death and a lost cat have a complex connection.
A more-or-less engaging spoof of, or perhaps a valediction to, the private eye genre, with engaging scenes marred by poor colour and occasional excesses of violent action.

wd Robert Benton ph Chuck Rosher m Ken Wannberg

Art Carney, Lily Tomlin, Bill Macy, Ruth Nelson, Howard Duff, Joanna Cassidy, Eugene Roche
'On its own terms, it's perfectly executed. The squalid settings stink of decay; the spare pacing captures the tough style of Hammett prose; and the stylized use of blood puts some sting into murder.'—*Frank Rich, New York Post*
AAN: Robert Benton

Latin Lovers
US 1953 104m Technicolor
MGM (Joe Pasternak)

An heiress on holiday in Brazil looks for a man who will love her for herself alone.
Barren romantic drama, flatfooted and drawn out.

w Isobel Lennart d Mervyn Le Roy ph Joseph Ruttenberg m George Stoll

Lana Turner, Ricardo Montalban, John Lund, Louis Calhern, Jean Hagen

Latin Quarter*
GB 1945 80m bw
British National
US title: *Frenzy*

In nineties Paris a mad sculptor murders his fiancée and hides her inside his latest exhibit.
Artificial-looking but melodramatically effective thriller with a chilling climax and a detailed Dégas-period background.

wd Vernon Sewell ph Gunther Krampf, play l'Angoisse by Pierre Mills, Charles Vylars

Derrick de Marney, Joan Greenwood, Beresford Egan, Frederick Valk, Lily Kann, Martin Miller

Laugh and Get Rich
US 1931 72m bw

A man invests his wife's money in a tyre with a whistling valve. Inconsequential comedy with ancient jokes. Hugh Herbert, Edna May Oliver, Dorothy Lee, Robert Emmett Keane. Written by Ralph Spence, Gregory La Cava; directed by Gregory La Cava; for RKO. 'Entertainment for the willing.'—*Variety*

Laugh with Max Linder**
France 1963 88m bw
Films Max Linder
original title: *En Compagnie de Max Linder*

Excerpts from three of the dapper comedian's most famous American comedies: *Be My Wife* (1921), *The Three Must Get Theres* (1922), *Seven Years' Bad Luck* (1923)

A compilation which must serve as a consensus of this almost forgotten comedian's work. The gag with a broken mirror in particular was borrowed by innumerable other comedians, notably the Marx Brothers in *Duck Soup*. Audiences new to Linder's work will find him not especially sympathetic but capable of many felicities. He wrote, produced and directed all three films.
compiler Maud Max Linder

Laughing Anne
GB 1953 90m Technicolor
Republic / Wilcox–Neagle

French Anne and her boxing lover are characters of the Javanese waterfront; he kills her after she has fallen for a sea captain. Cheap and turgid adaptation of a Joseph Conrad story; the author would not recognize it. Studio settings put the lid on hilariously bad work all round.

w Pamela Bower d Herbert Wilcox ph Max Greene m Anthony Collins

Margaret Lockwood, Forrest Tucker, Ronald Shiner, Wendell Corey, Robert Harris

Laughing Boy
US 1934 80m bw

A young Navajo brave marries an outcast maiden. Misguided and absurd melodrama for unsuitable stars. Ramon Novarro, Lupe Velez, Chief Thunderbird, William Davidson. Written by John Colton and John Lee Mahin, from a novel by Oliver La Farge; directed by W. S. Van Dyke; for MGM. 'Touchy theme and plot . . . below par as entertainment.'—*Variety*

Laughing Gravy***
US 1931 20m bw

Stan and Ollie retrieve their dog when the landlord throws it out into the snow. One of the most endearing comedies of these stars, and one of the simplest. Laurel and Hardy, Charlie Hall. Written by H. M. Walker; directed by James W. Horne; for Hal Roach.

'Eight people know who the killer is—and they're all dead!'
The Laughing Policeman*
US 1973 112m De Luxe
TCF (Stuart Rosenberg)
GB title: *An Investigation of Murder*

A mad machine-gunner eludes the San Francisco police.
Downbeat, semi-documentary police thriller with pretensions. Too complex by half, with an overplus of characterization, but the location work is excellent.

w Thomas Rickman, novel Maj Sjowall, Per Wahloo d Stuart Rosenberg ph David Walsh m Charles Fox

Walter Matthau, Bruce Dern, Lou Gossett, Albert Paulsen, Anthony Zerbe

Laughing Sinners
US 1931 71m bw

A girl with a past joins the Salvation Army.

Glum romance which however started an effective star combination. Joan Crawford, Clark Gable, Neil Hamilton, Marjorie Rambeau, Guy Kibbee. Written by Bess Meredyth and Martin Flavin; directed by Harry Beaumont; for MGM.

Laughter**
US 1930 99m bw
Paramount (Herman J. Mankiewicz)

An ex-Follies girl marries a millionaire but later goes on a spree with the composer she once loved.
Sharply observed, before its time romantic comedy reminiscent now of the later *Philadelphia Story* in its attitudes to wealth and love. A precursor of the smart crazy comedies of the mid-thirties.

w Donald Ogden Stewart d Harry d'Abbadie d'Arrast ph George Folsey

Fredric March, Nancy Carroll, Frank Morgan, Glen Anders, Diane Ellis
'One of the best talking pictures I have ever seen.'—*James Agate*
'A talkie with so fast a pace that it crowds the comprehension of half the customers . . . marked at intervals by superb dialogue and the quick hand of a smart director.'—*Pare Lorentz*
'A lovely sophisticated comedy.'—*New Yorker, 1977*
AAN: Donald Ogden Stewart

Laughter in Paradise*
GB 1951 93m bw
ABPC (*Mario Zampi*)

An eccentric leaves in his will a fortune for each of his relations providing they will perform certain embarrassing or criminal acts. A funny idea gets half-hearted treatment, but the good bits are hilarious.

w Michael Pertwee, Jack Davies d Mario Zampi ph William McLeod m Stanley Black

Alastair Sim, Joyce Grenfell, Hugh Griffith, Fay Compton, John Laurie, George Cole, Guy Middleton, Ronald Adam, Leslie Dwyer, A. E. Matthews, Beatrice Campbell
† Remade 1972 as *Some Will, Some Won't*.

Laughter in the Dark*
GB / France 1969 104m De Luxe
UA / Woodfall / Winkast / Marceau (Neil Hartley)

A wealthy art dealer is taken in by an ambitious usherette and her lover, and after being blinded in a car accident tries to kill them.
Unsatisfactory adaptation of a novel with a very specialized appeal: conventional swinging London and Riviera settings only confuse the spectator. Moments do work, though.

w Edward Bond, *novel* Vladimir Nabokov d Tony Richardson ph Dick Bush m Raymond Leppard ad Julia Trevelyan Oman

Nicol Williamson, Anna Karina, Jean-Claude Drouot, Peter Bowles, Sian Phillips
'It fails to create the slightest interest in its trio of repulsive characters.'—*Philip Strick*

Laughterhouse*
GB 1984 93m colour
Greenpoint / Film Four International

A Norfolk farmer decides to walk his fattened geese to market.
An attempt to revive the tradition of Ealing comedy lands up somewhere on the wrong side of Group Three. Not enough plot, almost no jokes, and the geese are almost the only pleasant creatures.

w Brian Glover d Richard Eyre ph Clive Tickner m Dominic Muldowney

Ian Holm, Penelope Wilton, Bill Owen, Richard Hope, Stephen Moore, Rosemary Martin

Laura***
US 1944 85m bw
TCF (Otto Preminger)

A beautiful girl is murdered . . . or is she? A cynical detective investigates.
A quiet, streamlined little murder mystery that brought a new adult approach to the genre and heralded the mature *film noir* of the later forties. A small cast responds perfectly to a classically spare script, and in Clifton Webb a new star is born.

w Jay Dratler, Samuel Hoffenstein, Betty Reinhardt, *novel* Vera Caspary d Otto Preminger ph Joseph La Shelle m David Raksin

Dana Andrews, Clifton Webb, Gene Tierney, Judith Anderson, *Vincent Price*, Dorothy Adams, James Flavin

WALDO LYDECKER (Clifton Webb): 'It's lavish, but I call it home.'

WALDO: 'I shall never forget the weekend Laura died. A silver sun burned through the sky like a huge magnifying glass. It was the hottest Sunday in my recollection. I felt as if I were the only human being left in New York . . . I had just begun Laura's story when another of those detectives came to see me. I had him wait.'

WALDO: 'In my case, self-absorption is completely justified. I have never discovered any other subject quite so worthy of my attention.'

'Everybody's favourite chic murder mystery.'—*New Yorker, 1977*
† Rouben Mamoulian directed some scenes before handing over to Preminger.
AA: Joseph La Shelle
AAN: script; Otto Preminger; Clifton Webb
● *Video: CBS / Fox*

The Laurel and Hardy Murder Case
US 1930 30m bw

Heirs to a fortune are menaced by a mad murderer. Empty spoof on *The Cat and the Canary* which affords little scope to Laurel and Hardy. Written by H. M. Walker; directed by James Parrott; for Hal Roach.

Laurel and Hardy's Laughing Twenties**
US 1965 90m bw
MGM / Robert Youngson

Excerpts from lesser comedians of the period—Max Davidson, Charlie Chase—are interspersed with highlights from Laurel and Hardy's silent two reelers.
A hilarious and craftsmanlike compilation, perhaps a little too long for its own good.

w, ed Robert Youngson commentator Jay Jackson m Skeets Alquist

† Films extracted include *Putting Pants on Philip, From Soup to Nuts, Wrong Again, The Finishing Touch, Liberty, Double Whoopee, Leave 'Em Laughing, You're Darn Tooting* and the custard pie climax from *The Battle of the Century*.

The Lavender Hill Mob****
GB 1951 78m bw
Ealing (Michael Truman)

A timid bank clerk conceives and executes a bullion robbery.
Superbly characterized and inventively detailed comedy, one of the best ever made at Ealing or in Britain.

w T. E. B. Clarke d Charles Crichton ph Douglas Slocombe m Georges Auric

Alec Guinness, Stanley Holloway, Sidney James, Alfie Bass, Marjorie Fielding, Edie Martin, John Gregson, Gibb McLaughlin
'Amusing situations and dialogue are well paced and sustained throughout: the climax is delightful.'—*MFB*
AA: T. E. B. Clarke
AAN: Alec Guinness
● *Video: Thorn EMI*

Law and Disorder*
GB 1958 76m bw
British Lion / Hotspur (Paul Soskin)

Crooks rally round a confederate about to be arrested, to prevent his son from learning of his father's real career.
Amusing, well-pointed caper on sub-Ealing lines.

w T. E. B. Clarke, *novel* Smuggler's Circuit by Denys Roberts d Charles Crichton ph Ted Scaife m Humphrey Searle

Michael Redgrave, Robert Morley, Joan Hickson, Lionel Jeffries, Ronald Squire, Elizabeth Sellars

Law and Disorder*
US 1975 102m Technicolor Panavision
Memorial / Leroy Street / Ugo Fadsin (William Richert)

New York suburbanites aghast at escalating violence form themselves into a vigilante patrol.
Bewilderingly uneven comedy drama which starts as satirical comedy and ends with one of the heroes dead and the other moralizing. Sporadically interesting, and certainly topical.

w Ivan Passer, William Richert, Kenneth Harris Fishman d Ivan Passer ph Arthur J. Ornitz m Andy Badale

Ernest Borgnine, Carroll O'Connor, Karen Black, Ann Wedgeworth, Leslie Ackerman, David Spielberg

The Law and Jake Wade*
US 1958 86m Metrocolor
Cinemascope
MGM (William Hawks)

A marshal helps an old outlaw friend to escape from jail, and lives to regret it.
Good standard western, enjoyable throughout but with no outstanding merits.

w William Bowers d John Sturges ph Robert Surtees

Robert Taylor, Richard Widmark, Patricia Owens, Robert Middleton, Henry Silva

Law and Order*
US 1932 80m bw

A cowboy becomes marshal and cleans up Tombstone. Drily effective fictionalization of Wyatt Earp's exploits, with a good star performance. *Walter Huston, Harry Carey, Raymond Hatton, Russell Simpson, Russell Hopton. Written by John Huston, from the novel Saint Johnson by W. R. Burnett; directed by Edward L. Cahn; for Universal.*

Law and Order
US 1953 80m Technicolor

Curious belated sequel to the above with Johnson moving on to tame Cottonwood; actual presentation rather dull. Ronald Reagan, Dorothy Malone, Preston Foster, Alex Nicol, Russell Johnson. Written by John and Gwen Bagni and D. D. Beauchamp; directed by Nathan Juran; for Universal-International.

The Law and the Lady
US 1951 104m bw
MGM (Edwin H. Knopf)

A couple of confidence tricksters inveigle themselves into the house of a vulgar millionairess, but one of them has an attack of conscience.
Dreary remake of *The Last of Mrs Cheyney* (qv) with the locale altered, the plot simplified, and the level of wit diluted.

w Leonard Spiegelgass, Karl Tunberg d Edwin H. Knopf ph George Folsey m Carmen Dragon

Greer Garson, Michael Wilding, Fernando Lamas, Marjorie Main, Hayden Rorke, Margalo Gillmore, Ralph Dumke

Law of the Lawless
US 1963 87m Techniscope
Paramount / A. C. Lyles

A judge arrives in a small western town to conduct the murder trial of a former friend. Jaded western of interest only for the producer's custom of packing the bit roles with former stars.

w Steve Fisher d William F. Claxton ph Lester Shorr

Dale Robertson, Yvonne de Carlo, William Bendix, Bruce Cabot, Barton MacLane, John Agar, Richard Arlen, Kent Taylor, Lon Chaney Jnr

Law of the Tropics
US 1941 76m bw
Warner (Ben Stoloff)

A café singer on the run from a murder charge marries a South American rubber plantation owner.
Hackneyed melodrama born from a mating of *Oil for the Lamps of China* and *Tropic Zone*.

w Charles Grayson d Ray Enright ph Sid Hickox m Howard Jackson

Constance Bennett, Jeffrey Lynn, Regis Toomey, Mona Maris, Frank Puglia, Thomas Jackson, Craig Stevens

The Law Versus Billy the Kid
US 1954 73m Technicolor

Billy the Kid is driven into crime to avenge a friend. Technicolor seems wasted on this two-bit western which can't even manage to tell a clear story. Scott Brady, Betta St John, James Griffith, Alan Hale Jnr, Paul Cavanagh. Written by John T. Williams; directed by William Castle; for Sam Katzman / Columbia.

The Lawless
US 1949 83m bw
Paramount / Pine–Thomas
GB title: *The Dividing Line*

The editor of a California small-town newspaper defends a Spanish boy who is being victimized by the racist element.
Well-meaning 'realistic' melodrama, unfortunately among the dullest of the socially conscious movies of this period.

w Geoffrey Homes d Joseph Losey ph Roy Hunt m Mahlon Merrick

Macdonald Carey, Gail Russell, John Sands, John Hoyt, Lee Patrick, Lalo Rios

The Lawless Breed
US 1952 83m Technicolor
U-I (William Alland)

The adventures and repentance of badman John Wesley Hardin.
Standard western programmer with the star in an unlikely role.

w Bernard Gordon d Raoul Walsh ph Irving Glassberg m Joseph Gershenson

Rock Hudson, Julie Adams, John McIntire, Dennis Weaver, Hugh O'Brian

A Lawless Street
US 1955 78m Technicolor
Columbia (Harry Joe Brown)

A marshal marries a dance hall entertainer, and loses interest in his job when she leaves him.
Enjoyable minor western.

w Kenneth Gamet, *novel* Marshal of Medicine Bend by Brad Ward d Joseph H. Lewis ph Ray Rennahan m Paul Sawtell

Randolph Scott, Angela Lansbury, Warner Anderson, Jean Parker, Wallace Ford, John Emery, James Bell, Ruth Donnelly, Michael Pate, Jeanette Nolan, Don Megowan

Lawman*
US 1970 99m Technicolor
UA / Scimitar (Michael Winner)

When a marshal tracks down drunken cowboys who have killed an old man, the townsfolk's resistance leads to a bloodbath. Terse, violent western with a good cast.

w Gerald Wilson d Michael Winner ph Bob Paynter m Jerry Fielding

Burt Lancaster, Robert Ryan, Lee J. Cobb, Sheree North, Robert Duvall, Joseph Wiseman, John McGiver, Albert Salmi, J. D. Cannon

Lawrence of Arabia***
GB 1962 221m Technicolor Super
Panavision 70
Columbia / Horizon (Sam Spiegel)

An adventurer's life with the Arabs, told in flashbacks after his accidental death in the thirties.
Sprawling epic which manages after four hours to give no insight whatever into the complexities of character of this mysterious historic figure, but is often spectacularly beautiful and exciting along the way.

w Robert Bolt d David Lean ph Frederick A. Young m Maurice Jarre pd John Box ad John Stoll

Peter O'Toole, Omar Sharif, Arthur Kennedy, Jack Hawkins, Donald Wolfit, Claude Rains, Anthony Quayle, Alec Guinness, Anthony Quinn, Jose Ferrer, Michel Ray, Zia Mohyeddin

'Grandeur of conception is not up to grandeur of setting.'—*Penelope Houston*
'Lean has managed to market epics as serious entertainment rather than as the spectacles they are.'—*Time Out, 1980*

† Albert Finney turned down the role before O'Toole was offered it.

AA: best picture; David Lean; Frederick A. Young; Maurice Jarre
AAN: Robert Bolt; Peter O'Toole; Omar Sharif

● *Video: RCA / Columbia*

The Lawyer*
US 1970 120m Technicolor
Paramount (Brad Dexter)

An ambitious young Italian-American defence lawyer takes on a murder case.
Smartly-scripted, perfectly ordinary courtroom drama in a well-detailed western setting. The star subsequently played the same character in a TV series, *Petrocelli*.

w Sidney J. Furie, Harold Buchman d Sidney J. Furie ph Ralph Woolsey m Malcolm Dodds

Barry Newman, Harold Gould, Diana Muldaur, Robert Colbert, Kathleen Crowley, Booth Colman

Lawyer Man
US 1932   68m   bw
Warner

An honest lawyer becomes corrupted by
success.
Smart, cynical melodrama, dated but
sufficiently fast-paced to remain interesting.
w Rian James, James Seymour, *novel* Max
Trell d William Dieterle ph Robert Kurrle

William Powell, Joan Blondell, Helen Vinson,
Alan Dinehart, Allen Jenkins, David Landau,
Claire Dodd
'Good picture in the lawyer cycle.'—*Variety*

Laxdale Hall
GB 1952   77m   bw
Group Three (Alfred Shaughnessy)
US title: *Scotch on the Rocks*

MPs are sent to investigate a tiny Hebridean
island which refuses to pay road tax.
Thin rehash of *Whisky Galore* put together
without the Ealing style. Minor compensations
can be found.
w John Eldridge, Alfred Shaughnessy d John
Eldridge ph Arthur Grant m Frank Spencer

Raymond Huntley, Ronald Squire, Sebastian
Shaw, Fulton Mackay, Kathleen Ryan,
Kynaston Reeves

Le Mans*
US 1971   108m   De Luxe   Panavision
Solar / Cinema Center (Jack N. Reddish)

A sullen American enters for the 24-hour race.
Almost no plot and little documentary
examination; what's left is a multitude of
racing shots with Steve McQueen at the wheel.
For some this may be enough.
w Harry Kleiner d Lee H. Katzin ph Robert
B. Hauser, René Gruissart Jnr m Michel
Legrand

Steve McQueen, Siegfried Rauch, Elga
Andersen, Ronald Leigh-Hunt

League of Frightened Men
US 1937   71m   bw

Nero Wolfe solves another murder case from
his armchair. Fair detective story, but a
negation of film. Walter Connolly, Lionel
Stander, Eduardo Ciannelli, Irene Hervey,
Victor Kilian, Nana Bryant. Written by
Eugene Solow, Guy Endore, from the novel
by Rex Stout; directed by Alfred E. Green;
for Columbia. 'Hardly any audience likes to
watch a character who just sits and thinks.'—
Variety

The League of Gentlemen***
GB 1960   112m   bw
Rank / Allied Film Makers (Michael Relph)

An ex-army officer recruits high-class misfits
with guilty secrets to help him in a bank
robbery.
Delightfully handled comedy adventure, from
the days (alas) when crime did not pay; a
lighter ending would have made it a classic.

w Bryan Forbes, *novel* John Boland d Basil
Dearden ph Arthur Ibbetson m Philip Green
Jack Hawkins, Richard Attenborough, *Roger
Livesey*, *Nigel Patrick*, Bryan Forbes, Kieron
Moore, Terence Alexander, *Norman Bird*,
Robert Coote, Melissa Stribling, Nanette
Newman, Gerald Harper, Patrick Wymark,
David Lodge, Doris Hare, Lydia Sherwood

● *Video: Rank*

Lease of Life*
GB 1954   94m   Eastmancolor
Ealing (Jack Rix)

A poor clergyman is given a year to live, and
puts it to good use.
Somewhat depressing but well-acted drama
with excellent village atmosphere.
w Eric Ambler d Charles Frend ph Douglas
Slocombe m Alan Rawsthorne
Robert Donat, Kay Walsh, Adrienne Corri,
Denholm Elliott

The Leather Boys*
GB 1963   108m   bw   Cinemascope
British Lion / Garrick (Raymond Stross)

Two working-class teenagers marry for sex;
she becomes a drudge and he develops a
relationship with a homosexual motorcyclist.
Sharply-observed slice of low life which now
seems quite dated, the central figures no
longer being of the 'heroic' interest given them
at the time. Technically the film is tediously
and fashionably flashy.
w Gillian Freeman, *novel* Elliot George
d Sidney J. Furie ph Gerald Gibbs m Bill
McGuffie

Rita Tushingham, Dudley Sutton, Colin
Campbell, Gladys Henson

The Leather Saint
US 1955   86m   bw   Vistavision
Paramount (Norman Retchin)

To provide his parish hospital with medical
equipment, a Catholic priest becomes a
commercial prizefighter.
Unlikely piece of religiosity, not too badly
done.
w Norman Retchin, Alvin Ganzer d Alvin
Ganzer ph Haskell Boggs md Irvin Talbot

Paul Douglas, John Derek, Cesar Romero,
Ernest Truex, Jody Lawrance

Leathernecking
US 1930   80m   bw (colour sequence)
RKO (Louis Sarecky)
GB title: *Present Arms*

A Honolulu socialite falls for a marine, but
grows cool when she discovers that he is a
private and not an officer as he pretended.
Curiously cast, spasmodically funny non-
musical version of a Rodgers and Hart
Broadway hit.
w Alfred Jackson, Jane Murfin, *play* Present
Arms by Herbert Fields, Rodgers and Hart
d Edward Cline ph J. Roy Hunt m Oscar
Levant

Irene Dunne (her first role), Ken Murray,
Eddie Foy Jnr, Louise Fazenda, Ned Sparks,
Lilyan Tashman
'Weak medley of horseplay and romantic
musical, and both poor.'—*Variety*

Leave 'Em Laughing*
US 1928   20m   bw   silent

Stan has toothache, visits the dentist, and
accidentally causes all concerned to inhale an
overdose of laughing gas. The earlier
sequences are only mildly funny, but the
laughing finale is irresistible. Laurel and
Hardy, Edgar Kennedy, Charlie Hall. Written
by Hal Roach and Reed Heustis; directed by
Clyde Bruckman; for Hal Roach.

Leave Her to Heaven
US 1945   111m   Technicolor
TCF (William A. Bacher)

A selfish, jealous woman causes unhappiness
for those around her, even in her suicide.
No-holds-barred melodrama of the old school;
what seemed lush production at the time now
looks tatty.
w Jo Swerling, *novel* Ben Ames Williams
d John M. Stahl ph Leon Shamroy m Alfred
Newman

Gene Tierney, Cornel Wilde, Jeanne Crain,
Vincent Price, Mary Phillips, Ray Collins,
Gene Lockhart, Reed Hadley, Chill Wills
'The story's central idea might be plausible
enough in a dramatically lighted black and
white picture . . . but in the rich glare of
Technicolor, all its rental library
characteristics are doubly glaring.'—*James
Agee*
'The sum total of all human emotion!'—
publicity
AA: Leon Shamroy
AAN: Gene Tierney

The Leavenworth Case
US 1935   66m   bw

Police investigate the murder of a wealthy
man. Sluggish transcription of what claims to
be the first American detective story. Donald
Cook, Jean Rouverol, Norman Foster, Erin
O'Brien-Moore, Maude Eburne, Warren
Hymer. Written by Albert DeMond, Sidney
Sutherland, from the novel by Anna Katherine
Green; for Republic. 'Just another detective
meller.'—*Variety*

Leaves from Satan's Book*
Denmark 1919   80m approx (24 fps)
  bw   silent
Nordisk

Episodes from the activities of Satan through
the ages: with Christ, the Inquisition, the
French Revolution and the Russian
Revolution.
Vaguely propagandist short-story compilation
with effective moments.
w Edgar Hoyer, Carl Dreyer, *novel* The
Sorrows of Satan by Marie Corelli d Carl
Dreyer ph George Schneevoigt

ONE FALSE STEP LEADS TO BIGGER ONES...

He profaned the cloth he wore!

She fought against a forbidden relationship!

20th Century-Fox presents

HUMPHREY **BOGART** GENE **TIERNEY**

THE **LEFT HAND OF GOD**

The most challenging story of faith ever told on the screen!

COLOR by DE LUXE

CinemaScope

LEE J. COBB · with AGNES MOOREHEAD · BUDDY ADLER · EDWARD DMYTRYK · ALFRED HAYES

In the wonder of High-Fidelity STEREOPHONIC SOUND

S I G N A T U R E

THE LEFT HAND OF GOD.   One of Bogart's last films put him in the sort of equivocal role that doesn't win Oscars.

'You can count the truly daring concepts in the making of motion pictures on the fingers of your right hand. Now add . . .'
The Left Hand of God
US 1955 87m De Luxe Cinemascope
TCF (Buddy Adler)

China, 1947: a Catholic priest newly arrived in a small village proves to be an American flier on the run from a warlord; but he contrives to work a small 'miracle'.
Hollywood religiosity at its most contrived, put together without distinction; the players have a wary look.

w Alfred Hayes, *novel* William E. Barrett
d Edward Dmytryk *ph* Franz Planer
m Victor Young

Humphrey Bogart, Gene Tierney, Lee J. Cobb, E. G. Marshall, Agnes Moorehead

The Left Handed Gun•
US 1958 102m bw
Warner / Haroll (Fred Coe)

Billy the Kid sets out to shoot four men who have killed his friend.
'Method'-oriented western, efficiently made but somewhat downcast.

w Leslie Stevens, *TV play* Gore Vidal
d Arthur Penn *ph* Peverell Marley
m Alexander Courage

Paul Newman, John Dehner, Lita Milan, Hurd Hatfield

'Top of the poll for laughs!'
Left Right and Centre•
GB 1959 95m bw
British Lion / Launder and Gilliat

A TV personality becomes Tory candidate at a by-election.
Scrappy political comedy with the saving grace of a large number of comic talents.

w Sidney Gilliat, Val Valentine *d* Sidney Gilliat *ph* Gerald Gibbs *m* Humphrey Searle

Ian Carmichael, Alastair Sim, Patricia Bredin, Richard Wattis, Eric Barker, Gordon Harker, George Benson, Frederick Leister

The Legacy
GB 1978 102m colour
Columbia / Pethurst / Turman-Foster (David Foster)

An American designer goes to stay with her employer and finds herself in the middle of an occult murder plot.
Cliché-ridden screamer which will please the easily pleased.

w Jimmy Sangster, Patrick Tilley, Paul Wheeler *d* Richard Marquand *ph* Dick Bush, Alan Hume *m* Michael J. Lewis

Katharine Ross, Sam Elliot, John Standing, Ian Hogg, Margaret Tyzack, Charles Gray, Lee Montague, Hildegard Neil

'For the sake of your sanity, pray it isn't true!'
The Legend of Hell House•
GB 1973 94m De Luxe
TCF / Academy (Albert Fennell, Norman T. Herman)

Four people arrive at a haunted house in which several psychic investigators have been killed.
Harrowing thriller, a less solemn but more frightening version of *The Haunting*.

w Richard Matheson, from his novel *d* John Hough *ph* Alan Hume *m* Brian Hodgson, Delia Derbyshire

Pamela Franklin, Roddy McDowall, Clive Revill, Gayle Hunnicutt, Roland Culver, Peter Bowles, Michael Gough
'One of the most absorbing, goose-fleshing and mind-pleasing ghost breaker yarns on film.'—*Judith Crist, 1977*

The Legend of Lobo•
US 1962 67m Technicolor
Walt Disney (James Algar)

The life of a forest wolf.
Anthropomorphic entertainment in which a dreaded animal becomes something of a hero and finally saves his mate from bounty hunters. Impeccably contrived, like a live-action *Bambi*.

w Dwight Hauser, James Algar, *story* Ernest Thompson Seton *d* James Algar *ph* Jack Couffer, Lloyd Beebe *m* Oliver Wallace

The Legend of Lylah Clare*
US 1968 130m Metrocolor Panavision
MGM / Robert Aldrich

A mad director brings an unknown actress to
Hollywood because of her resemblance to a
former star, his creation, who had died
mysteriously.
Unintentionally risible melodrama with echoes
of *Svengali* and *Sunset Boulevard*; not to the
public's taste, or anyone else's, in the late
sixties.

w Hugo Butler, Jean Rouverol, *TV play*
Robert Thom, Edward de Blasio *d* Robert
Aldrich *ph* Joseph Biroc *m* Frank de Vol

Peter Finch, Kim Novak, Ernest Borgnine,
Coral Browne, Milton Seltzer, Rossella Falk,
Gabriele Tinti, Valentina Cortesa, George
Kennedy

'The film where you hiss the villain and
cheer the hero!'

The Legend of the Lone Ranger
US 1981 98m Technicolor Panavision
ITC / Jack Wrather (Walter Conlenz)

A much-betrayed young Texan, almost killed
in an ambush, is nursed back to health by an
Indian and becomes a masked avenger.
Extremely ill-constructed and moody western,
apparently photographed through brown
windsor soup, which doesn't slip into the right
gear until twenty minutes before the end.

w Ivan Goff, Ben Roberts, Michael Kane,
William Roberts *d* William A. Fraker
ph Laszlo Kovacs *m* John Barry

Klinton Spilsbury, Michael Horse, Christopher
Lloyd, Matt Clark

'Wallows in endless sentiment before
switching to what may possibly have been
intended as parody.'—*Sight and Sound*

'Tedious hokum . . . the kind of film that
closes cinemas.'—*Sunday Times*

● *Video: Precision*

Legend of the Lost
US 1957 107m Technirama
UA / Batjac / Robert Haggiag / Dear (Henry
Hathaway)

Two adventurers and a slave girl seek a lost
city in the Sahara.
Tediously vague and underplotted desert
adventure with a few attractive moments.

w Robert Presnell Jnr, Ben Hecht *d* Henry
Hathaway *ph* Jack Cardiff *m* A. F.
Lavagnino

John Wayne, Sophia Loren, Rossano Brazzi

The Legend of the Seven Golden Vampires
GB / Hong Kong 1974 89m
Eastmancolor Panavision
Hammer–Shaw (Don Houghton, Vee King
Shaw)

In 1904 Chungking, Professor Van Helsing
finds his old enemy Dracula behind a Chinese
vampire cult.
Hectic, outlandish mix of Hammer horror and
Kung Fu; plenty of gusto but not much sense.

w Don Houghton *d* Roy Ward Baker
ph John Wilcox, Roy Ford *m* James Bernard

Peter Cushing, David Chiang, Julie Ege,
Robin Stewart, John Forbes Robertson

The Legend of Tom Dooley
US 1959 77m bw
Columbia / Shpetner

At the end of the Civil War, Confederate
youths take the law into their own hands and
attack Unionists.
Youthful rebellion in historical mould,
decently but rather dully delivered, based on a
folk ballad.

w Stan Shpetner *d* Ted Post *ph* Gilbert
Warrenton *m* Ronald Stein

Michael Landon, Richard Rust, Jo Morrow

The Lemon Drop Kid*
US 1951 91m bw
Paramount (Robert A. Welch)

A gangster forces a bookie to find the money
which he has lost on a horse through the
bookie's incompetence.
Amusing Bob Hope / Runyon vehicle despite
heavy sentiment about an old folks' home.
The Santa Claus sequences are memorable.

w Edmund Hartman, Frank Tashlin, Robert
O'Brien, *story* Damon Runyon *d* Sidney
Lanfield *ph* Daniel L. Fapp *m* Victor Young

Bob Hope, Marilyn Maxwell, Lloyd Nolan,
Jane Darwell, Andrea King, Fred Clark, Jay
C. Flippen, William Frawley, Harry Bellaver

Lenin in October*
USSR 1937 111m bw
Mosfilm
original title: *Lenin v Octiabrye*

The activities of Lenin during the revolution.
Stalwart propaganda piece, of solid but not
outstanding cinematic interest.

w Alexei Kapler *d* Mikhail Romm *ph* Boris
Volchok *m* Anatoli Alexandrov

Boris Shchukin

† The success of this film provoked *Lenin in
1918*, made in the following year (132m) by
the same talents, with Cherkassov as Gorky.
Many other Russian films on Lenin have
followed.

Lenny**
US 1974 111m bw
UA (Marvin Worth)

The career of obscene comedian Lenny Bruce
and his struggles with the law.
Old-fashioned rags-to-riches-to-rags story,
rampant with the new permissiveness.
Filmically extremely clever, emotionally
hollow.

w Julian Barry, from his play *d* Bob Fosse
ph Bruce Surtees *md* Ralph Burns *pd* Joel
Schiller

Dustin Hoffman, Valerie Perrine, Jan Miner,
Stanley Beck, Gary Morton

'For audiences who want to believe that
Lenny Bruce was a saintly gadfly who was
martyred for having lived before his time.'—
New Yorker

AAN: best picture; Julian Barry; Bob Fosse;
Bruce Surtees; Dustin Hoffman; Valerie
Perrine

● *Video: Intervision*

Leo the Last
GB 1969 104m De Luxe
UA / Char / Wink / Boor (Irwin Winkler,
Robert Chartoff)

An alienated aristocrat brings his retinue to a
London slum and has an effect on most of the
inhabitants.
Infuriating symbolic fantasy; only the writer-
director (presumably) has any idea what it is
about.

w William Stair, John Boorman *d* John
Boorman *ph* Peter Suschitsky *m* Dred
Myrow *pd* Tony Woollard

Marcello Mastroianni, Billie Whitelaw, Calvin
Lockhart, Glenna Forster Jones, Graham
Crowden, Gwen Ffrangcon Davies, David de
Keyser, Vladek Sheybal, Kenneth J. Warren

Léon Morin, Priest*
France / Italy 1961 117m bw
Rome-Paris Films (Georges de Beauregard)

During the German occupation of France a
young widow finds herself falling in love with
the young priest who is converting her to
religion.
An intellectual romance, sharp and witty for
the most part, with vivid wartime
backgrounds.

wd Jean-Pierre Melville, *novel* Béatrix Beck
ph Henri Decaë *m* Martial Solal, Albert
Raisner

Jean-Paul Belmondo, Emmanuele Riva, Irène
Tunc, Marielle Gozzi

The Leopard***
US / Italy 1963 205m Technirama
TCF / Titanus / SNPC / GPC (Goffredo
Lombardo)
original title: *Il Gattopardo*

The family life of an Italian nobleman at the
time of Garibaldi.
Elaborate, complex family saga, painted like
an old master with great care and attention to
detail, but with not much chance outside Italy
of delivering its original dramatic force.
Visconti had asked for Lancaster, so TCF
picked up the international release but
couldn't make head or tail of it commercially;
they even ruined its high quality by releasing a
dubbed, shortened version in Cinemascope
and De Luxe colour of poor standard.

wd Luchino Visconti, *novel* Giuseppe de
Lampedusa *ph* Giuseppe Rotunno *m* Nino
Rota *ad* Mario Garbuglia

Burt Lancaster, Claudia Cardinale, Alain
Delon, Paolo Stoppa, Serge Reggiani, Leslie
French

Leopard in the Snow
GB / Canada 1977 94m Technicolor
Seastone / Leopard in the Snow
(W. Laurence Heisey)

A girl caught in a Cumberland blizzard is
rescued by a mysterious stranger with a pet

leopard. He turns out to be a disfigured racing
driver, and she falls in love with him.
A deliberate cross between *Jane Eyre* and a
shopgirl's romance, adequately produced for
its intended audience.

w Anne Mather, Jill Hyem, *novel* Anne
Mather *d* Gerry O'Hara *ph* Alfie Hicks
m Kenneth V. Jones

Keir Dullea, Susan Penhaligon, Jeremy Kemp,
Kenneth More, Billie Whitelaw

The Leopard Man**
US 1943 59m bw
RKO (*Val Lewton*)

Murders in a Mexican border town are
attributed to an escaped leopard.
Effective minor piece in the Lewton horror
gallery; poor plot countered by highly effective
suspense sequences.

w Ardel Wray, Edward Dein, *novel* Black
Alibi by Cornell Woolrich *d* Jacques
Tourneur *ph* Robert de Grasse *m* Roy Webb

Dennis O'Keefe, Jean Brooks, Margo, James
Bell, Isabel Jewell

Lepke
US 1974 110m De Luxe Panavision
Warner / AmeriEuro Pictures (Menahem
Golan)

After World War I a small-time crook
becomes head of Murder Incorporated.
Violent but totally uninteresting gangster
melodrama; fidelity to fact is not enough.

w Wesley Hau, Tamor Hoffs *d* Menahem
Golan *ph* Andrew Davis *m* Ken Wannberg
pd Jack Degovia

Tony Curtis, Anjanette Comer, Michael
Callan, Warren Berlinger, Milton Berle,
Gianni Russo
  'A kosher version of *The Godfather*.'—
Verina Glaessner

Les Girls: see under Girls

Les Miserables: see under Miserables

A Lesson in Love
Sweden 1953 95m bw
Svensk Filmindustri

A gynaecologist and his wife grow bored and
turn to other partners, but are reconciled.
Slight comedy, surprisingly unsubtle for its
creator, but passable.

wd Ingmar Bergman *ph* Martin Bodin, Bengt
Nordwal *m* Dag Wiren

Gunnar Bjornstrand, Eva Dahlbeck, Harriet
Andersson, Yvonne Lombard, Ake Grönberg

Let 'Em Have It*
US 1935 90m bw
Edward Small
GB title: *False Faces*

The FBI go after criminals on a terror spree.
Lively cops and robbers with some starkly
effective moments.

w Joseph Moncure March, Elmer Harris
d Sam Wood *ph* J. Peverell Marley, Robert
Planck

Richard Arlen, Virginia Bruce, Alice Brady,
Bruce Cabot, Harvey Stephens, Eric Linden,
Joyce Compton, J. Farrell MacDonald

Let Freedom Ring
US 1939 100m sepia
MGM (Harry Rapf)

A westerner returns to his home town and
clears it of corruption.
Elementary Hollywood actioner with curious
credits, climaxed by Eddy singing *The Star
Spangled Banner*.

w Ben Hecht *d* Jack Conway *ph* Sidney
Wagner *m* Arthur Lange

Nelson Eddy, Victor McLaglen, Virginia
Bruce, Lionel Barrymore, H. B. Warner,
Raymond Walburn, Edward Arnold, Guy
Kibbee, Charles Butterworth, Billy Bevan
  'Big box office . . . lusty patriotic meller.
Cinch for exploitation.'—*Variety*

Let George Do It**
GB 1940 82m bw
Ealing (Basil Dearden)

A ukelele player accidentally goes to Bergen
instead of Blackpool and is mistaken for a spy.
Generally thought to be the best George
Formby vehicle, with plenty of pace, good
situations and catchy tunes.

w John Dighton, Austin Melford, Angus
MacPhail, Basil Dearden *d* Marcel Varnel
ph Gordon Dines, Ronald Neame

George Formby, Phyllis Calvert, Garry Marsh,
Romney Brent, Bernard Lee, Coral Browne,
Torin Thatcher, Hal Gordon

● *Video: Thorn EMI*

Let No Man Write My Epitaph
US 1960 106m bw
Columbia / Boris D. Kaplan

A slum boy wants to become a concert pianist
but falls in with gangsters.
Squalid, predictable melodrama without many
redeeming features.

w Robert Presnell Jnr, *novel* Willard Motley
d Philip Leacock *ph* Burnett Guffey
m George Duning

James Darren, Shelley Winters, Burl Ives,
Jean Seberg, Jeanne Cooper, Ricardo
Montalban, Ella Fitzgerald

Let the People Sing*
GB 1942 105m bw
British National (John Baxter)

An out-of-work comedian persuades a
drunken nobleman to join a protest against the
closing of a village hall.
A development of *The Good Companions*
which compares quite nicely with the Capra
films from across the water: naïve but
entertaining, with good star performances.

w John Baxter, Barbara K. Emery, Geoffrey
Orme, *novel* J. B. Priestley *d* John Baxter

Alastair Sim, Fred Emney, Edward Rigby,
Patricia Roc, Oliver Wakefield, Marian
Spencer, Olive Sloane, Gus McNaughton,
Charles Hawtrey

Let Them Live
US 1937 71m bw

A young man matches wits with a crooked
town boss. Tepid second-feature drama. John
Howard, Nan Grey, Edward Ellis, Judith
Barrett. Written by Bruce Manning and Lionel
House; directed by Harold Young; for
Universal. 'Better than many of its kind . . .
should please in nabes.'—*Variety*

Let Us Be Gay
US 1930 79m bw

Divorcees meet again, many years later, in
Paris. Predictable star romance, now very
dated, like its title. Norma Shearer, Rod La
Rocque, Marie Dressler, Sally Eilers,
Raymond Hackett, Hedda Hopper. Written
by Frances Marion, from the play by Rachel
Crothers; directed by Robert Z. Leonard; for
MGM. 'Strong on all counts, romance,
comedy, human sympathy and gorgeous
clothes against a glamorous setting.'—*Variety*

Let Us Live
US 1937 67m bw

An innocent taxi driver is convicted of
murder. Intense little melodrama which served
its purpose. Maureen O'Sullivan, Henry
Fonda, Ralph Bellamy. Written by Joseph F.
Dineen, Anthony Veiller and Allen Rivkin;
directed by John Brahm; for Columbia.
'Heavy dramatic preachment with limited
appeal.'—*Variety*

Let's Be Famous
GB 1939 83m bw
Ealing (Michael Balcon)

A stage struck Irish lad and Lancashire lass
have various adventures in London.
Easy-going comedy introducing radio
personalities of the day.

w Roger MacDougall, Allan MacKinnon
d Walter Forde *ph* Ronald Neame, Gordon
Dines *md* Ernest Irving

Jimmy O'Dea, Betty Driver, Sonnie Hale,
Patrick Barr, Basil Radford, Milton Rosmer,
Garry Marsh

Let's Be Happy
GB 1957 107m Technicolor
  Cinemascope
ABP / Marcel Hellman

Footling musical remake of *Jeannie* (qv).

w Diana Morgan *d* Henry Levin *ph* Erwin
Hillier *m* Nicholas Brodszky *md* Louis Levy
songs Nicholas Brodszky, Paul Francis
Webster

Vera-Ellen, Tony Martin, Robert Flemyng,
Zena Marshall, Guy Middleton, Katherine
Kath, Jean Cadell, Gordon Jackson
  'Success still eludes the Anglo-American
musical.'—*MFB*

Let's Dance
US 1950 112m Technicolor
Paramount (Robert Fellows)

Show business partners reunite after five years
of private life.

Tediously plotted musical with a couple of good numbers.

w Allan Scott, *story* Maurice Zolotow d Norman Z. McLeod *ph* George Barnes *m* Robert Emmett Dolan *songs* Frank Loesser

Fred Astaire, Betty Hutton, Roland Young, Ruth Warrick, Lucile Watson, Barton MacLane, Shepperd Strudwick, Melville Cooper, Harold Huber, George Zucco

Let's Do It Again
US 1953 95m Technicolor
Columbia (Oscar Saul)

A songwriter and his wife plan a divorce but call it off in the nick of time.
Tame musical remake of *The Awful Truth* (qv), pleasant enough but lacking style and punch.

w Mary Loos, Richard Sale *d* Alexander Hall *ph* Charles Lawton Jnr *m* George Duning *md* Morris Stoloff *songs* Lester Lee, Ned Washington

Jane Wyman, Ray Milland, Aldo Ray, Leon Ames

Let's Do It Again
US 1975 113m Technicolor
Warner / First Artists / Verdon (Melville Tucker, Pembroke J. Herring)

Three Atlanta workers conceive a zany plan to raise money for their church by hypnotizing a boxer into winning a big fight.
Lively but overlong farce reassembling the black talents of *Uptown Saturday Night.*

w Richard Wesley *d* Sidney Poitier *ph* Donald M. Morgan *m* Curtis Mayfield

Sidney Poitier, Bill Cosby, Calvin Lockhart, John Amos, Denise Nicholas, Ossie Davis, Jimmy Walker

Let's Face It
US 1943 76m bw
Paramount (Fred Kohlmar)

A smart-alec soldier has a plot involving a ladies' health camp, but finds himself up to his neck in spies.
Tepid star comedy which unaccountably ditches almost all the numbers from the musical on which it was based.

w Harry Tugend, from the musical play by Dorothy and Herbert Fields and Cole Porter, based on the play Cradle Snatchers by Norma Mitchell and Russell Medcraft *d* Sidney Lanfield *ph* Lionel Lindon *songs* Cole Porter

Bob Hope, Betty Hutton, Eve Arden, Phyllis Povah, Dona Drake, Zasu Pitts, Marjorie Weaver, Raymond Walburn, Joe Sawyer

Let's Fall in Love
US 1934 67m bw

A film director passes off a circus attendant as a glamorous foreign star. Lightweight comedy with music which did okay. Edmund Lowe, Ann Sothern, Miriam Jordan, Gregory Ratoff. Written by Herbert Fields; directed by David Burton; for Columbia. 'No chorus, no legs, no undressing for a change . . . moderately geared for moderate income.'—*Variety*

Let's Get Married
US 1937 68m bw

A politician's daughter falls for the weather bureau chief. Aimless romantic comedy which gets by on its performers. Ida Lupino, Walter Connolly, Ralph Bellamy, Reginald Denny, Raymond Walburn. Written by Ethel Hill from a story by A. H. Z. Carr; directed by Alfred E. Green; for Columbia. 'Mediocre dualler.'—*Variety*

Let's Go Native
US 1930 75m bw

Various people are shipwrecked on a South Sea island. Easy-going farce comedy with music. Jack Oakie, Jeanette MacDonald, Skeets Gallagher, James Hall, Kay Francis. Written by George Marion Jnr, Percy Heath; directed by Leo MacCarey; for Paramount. 'Hokum laughs with songs and dances.'—*Variety*

Let's Go Places
US 1930 70m bw

A young tenor goes to Hollywood, is mistaken for someone more famous and becomes a star. Lightweight comedy with mildly interesting studio scenes. Joseph Wagstaff, Lola Lane, Sharon Lynn, Ilka Chase, Walter Catlett, Dixie Lee. Written by William K. Wells; directed by Frank Strayer; for Fox. 'Plenty of music, no drawing names. Rates moderate for the big houses.'—*Variety*

Let's Kill Uncle
US 1966 92m colour
Universal / William Castle

A boy is threatened by his wicked uncle, and retaliates.
Mildly intriguing black comedy, leadenly handled.

w Mark Rodger, *novel* Rohan O'Grady *d* William Castle *ph* Harold Lipstein *m* Herman Stein

Nigel Green, Mary Badham, Pat Cardi, Robert Pickering

Let's Live a Little
US 1948 85m bw
Eagle-Lion / United California Productions

An advertising agent falls for his lady psychiatrist, and after many vicissitudes they and their former partners make it to the altar. Mild comedy which just about bubbles along despite a rather uncomfortable cast.

w Albert J. Cohen, Jack Harvey *d* Richard Wallace *ph* Ernest Laszlo *m* Werner Heymann

Hedy Lamarr, Robert Cummings, Anna Sten, Robert Shayne, Mary Treen

Let's Live Tonight
US 1935 75m bw

Two millionaire brothers in Monte Carlo love the same girl. Flimsy romantic comedy which gets by on its music. Lilian Harvey, Tullio

Carminati, Hugh Williams, Janet Beecher, Tala Birell, Luis Alberni. Written by Gene Markey, Bradley King; directed by Victor Schertzinger; for Columbia. 'A parrot gets most of the laughs, which tips off the script.'—*Variety*

Let's Make a Night of It
GB 1937 92m bw

In Nice, a husband and wife own rival night clubs. Slim musical with rather too many interpolated turns. Buddy Rogers, June Clyde, Claire Luce, Fred Emney, Iris Hoey, Steve Geray, and Syd Walker, Afrique, Oliver Wakefield, Brian Michie, Joe Loss and his Band, Sidney Lipton and his Band. Written by Hugh Brooke, from the radio play The Silver Spoon by Henrik Ege; directed by Graham Cutts; for Associated British. 'Definitely no appeal for the US.'—*Variety*

Let's Make It Legal
US 1951 77m bw

An attractive grandmother divorces her gambler husband and takes up with an old boy friend. Unremarkable but competent star comedy. Claudette Colbert, Zachary Scott, Macdonald Carey, Barbara Bates, Robert Wagner, Marilyn Monroe. Written by F. Hugh Herbert and I. A. L. Diamond; directed by Richard Sale; for TCF.

Let's Make Love*
US 1960 118m De Luxe Cinemascope
TCF (Jerry Wald)

A multi-millionaire, learning that he is to be burlesqued in a Broadway show, joins the cast as an actor.
Complex, moderately sophisticated, occasionally funny musical inspired by On the Avenue (qv); lively characterizations but poor numbers.

w Norman Krasna *d* George Cukor *ph* Daniel L. Fapp *ch* Jack Cole *md* Lionel Newman, Earl H. Hagen *songs* Sammy Cahn, Jimmy Van Heusen

Yves Montand, Marilyn Monroe, Tony Randall, Wilfrid Hyde White, Frankie Vaughan, David Burns, and guests Bing Crosby, Gene Kelly, Milton Berle

AAN: Lionel Newman, Earl H. Hagen

Let's Scare Jessica to Death
US 1971 89m colour
Paramount / Jessica Co (Charles B. Mars Jnr)

Back home after a nervous breakdown, our heroine is troubled by voices and visions, not to mention an ambulant corpse and a vampire or two.
Competent screamie.

w Norman Jonas, Ralph Rose *d* John Hancock *ph* Bob Baldwin *m* Orville Stoeber

Zohra Lampert, Barton Heyman

Let's Try Again
US 1934 64m bw

A doctor and his wife drift apart, then get back together again. Formula high-life drama without much conviction. Diana Wynyard, Clive Brook, Irene Hervey, Helen Vinson. Written by Worthington Miner and Allen Scott from the play by Vincent Lawrence; directed by Worthington Miner; for RKO.
'Talky, tedious and far from original: where the cast doesn't mean anything the picture will have plenty of worries.'—*Variety*

The Letter°
US 1929 61m bw
Paramount

Early talkie version of a solid piece of theatre. See below.

story and play W. Somerset Maugham *d* Jean de Limur

Jeanne Eagels, O. P. Heggie, Reginald Owen, Herbert Marshall, Irene Browne

AAN: Jeanne Eagels

'With all my heart, I still love the man I killed!'

The Letter°°°°
US 1940 95m bw
Warner (Robert Lord)

A rubber plantation owner's wife kills a man in what seems to have been self-defence; but a letter from her proves it to have been a crime of passion, and becomes an instrument of blackmail.
Excellent performances and presentation make this the closest approximation on film to reading a Maugham story of the Far East, though censorship forced the addition of an infuriating moral ending.

w Howard Koch, story W. Somerset Maugham *d* William Wyler *ph* Tony Gaudio *m* Max Steiner

Bette Davis, Herbert Marshall, James Stephenson, Sen Yung, Frieda Inescort, Gale Sondergaard, Bruce Lester, Tetsu Komai
'The writing is taut and spare throughout . . . the unravelling of Maugham's story is masterly and the presentation visual and cinematic . . . the audience at the trade show did not move a finger.'—*James Agate*
† Herbert Marshall played the lover in the first version and the husband in the second.

AAN: best picture; William Wyler; Tony Gaudio; Max Steiner; Bette Davis; James Stephenson

'The story that will live . . . as long as there is love!'

Letter from an Unknown Woman°°°°
US 1948 89m bw
Universal (John Houseman)

A woman wastes her life in unrequited love for a rakish pianist.
Superior 'woman's picture' which gave its director his best chance in America to recreate his beloved Vienna of long ago. Hollywood production magic at its best.

w Howard Koch, novel Stefan Zweig *d Max Ophuls ph* Franz Planer *m* Daniele Amfitheatrof *ad Alexander Golitzen*

Joan Fontaine, Louis Jourdan, Mady Christians, Art Smith, Marcel Journet
'A film full of snow, sleigh bells, lights gleaming in ornamental gardens and trysts at night.'—*Charles Higham, 1972*
'It is fascinating to watch the sure deft means by which Ophuls sidetracks seemingly inevitable clichés and holds on to a shadowy, tender mood, half buried in the past. Here is a fragile filmic charm that is not often or easily accomplished.'—*Richard Winnington*
'Film narrative of a most skilled order.'— *William Whitebait*
'Probably the toniest "woman's picture" ever made.'—*Pauline Kael, 70s*
● *Video: Intervision*

Letter of Introduction°
US 1938 100m bw
Universal (John M. Stahl)

A young actress is encouraged by an ageing star whom she does not know is her father. Commercial melodrama with luxury trimmings, all very neatly packaged.

w Sheridan Gibney, Leonard Spiegelgass *d* John M. Stahl *ph* Karl Freund *m* Charles Previn

Adolphe Menjou, Andrea Leeds, Edgar Bergen (and Charlie McCarthy), George Murphy, Eve Arden, Rita Johnson, Ernest Cossart, Ann Sheridan
'Headed for big business everywhere.'— *Variety*

'A peek into the other woman's male!'

A Letter to Three Wives°°
US 1949 102m bw
TCF (Sol C. Siegel)

Three wives on a picnic receive word from a friend that she has run off with one of their husbands.
Amusing short-story compendium which seemed more revelatory at the time than it does now, and paved the way for its writer-director's heyday.

wd Joseph L. Mankiewicz, novel John Klempner *ph* Arthur Miller *m* Alfred Newman

Jeanne Crain, Ann Sothern, Linda Darnell, Jeffrey Lynn, Kirk Douglas, *Paul Douglas*, Barbara Lawrence, Connie Gilchrist, Florence Bates, Hobart Cavanaugh, and the voice of Celeste Holm
'A mere shadow of those acid Hollywood comedies of the thirties . . . over-written and under-directed . . . but it has a supply of ironies and makes a certain alkaline comment on present-day American customs and manners.'—*Richard Winnington*
AA: Joseph L. Mankiewicz (as writer); Joseph L. Mankiewicz (as director)
AAN: best picture

Letty Lynton
US 1932 84m bw

When one lover is murdered, Letty turns to another to prove her innocent. Bad girl drama which established the star's box office appeal. Joan Crawford, Robert Montgomery, Nils Asther, May Robson, Lewis Stone. Written by John Meehan and Wanda Tuchock; directed by Clarence Brown; for MGM. 'Big grosses are written all over this one.'—*Variety*

Les Liaisons Dangereuses°
France 1959 106m bw
Films Marceau

Valmont and his wife compare notes on each other's affairs.
Showy modernization of a notorious minor classic.

w Roger Vailland, Roger Vadim, Claude Brûlé, *novel* Choderlos de Laclos *d* Roger Vadim *ph* Marcel Grignon *m* Jack Murray, Thelonius Monk

Gérard Philipe, Jeanne Moreau, Annette Vadim, Jeanne Valerie, Simone Renant, Jean-Louis Trintignant
'A woman's picture par excellence.'—*John Russell Taylor, MFB*

Lianna
US 1983 112m Du Art

A wife and mother becomes a lesbian. That's all there is, folks, not much in the way of plot, and barely enough for a TV movie; but some good observation and acting come through. Linda Griffiths, Jane Hallaren, Jon de Vries, Jo Henderson. Written and directed by John Sayles; for Winwood.

Libel°
GB 1959 100m bw
MGM / Comet (Anatole de Grunwald)

An ex-POW baronet is accused of being an impostor.
Old-fashioned courtroom spellbinder, quite adequately done though occasionally creaky.

w Anatole de Grunwald, Karl Tunberg, *play* Edward Wooll *d* Anthony Asquith *ph* Robert Krasker *m* Benjamin Frankel

Dirk Bogarde, Olivia de Havilland, Paul Massie, Wilfrid Hyde White, Robert Morley, Anthony Dawson, Richard Wattis, Martin Miller, Millicent Martin

Libeled Lady°°
US 1936 98m bw
MGM (Lawrence Weingarten)

An heiress sues a newspaper, and the editor hires a friend to compromise her.
Lively four-star romantic comedy which sums up its era as well as any.

w Maurine Watkins, Howard Emmett Rogers, George Oppenheimer d Jack Conway ph Norbert Brodine

Jean Harlow, Myrna Loy, Spencer Tracy, William Powell, Walter Connolly, Charley Grapewin, Cora Witherspoon, E. E. Clive, Charles Trowbridge

'Handsomely mounted and produced, lavishly costumed, cleverly written and artfully directed, *Libeled Lady* is entirely worthy of the noble comedians who head its cast.'— *Bland Johaneson, New York Daily Mirror*
† Remade as *Easy to Wed* (qv); central situation borrowed for *Man's Favorite Sport* (qv).

AAN: best picture

'All she wanted was her black man's money and her white man's love!'

The Liberation of L. B. Jones*
US 1970   102m   Technicolor
Columbia / Liberation Co (Ronald Lubin)

Racial murder is the result when a black undertaker wants a divorce in a small Tennessee town.
Violent, pointless but well-made melodrama which really does not take matters much further than *Intruder in the Dust.*

w Stirling Silliphant, Jesse Hill Ford, from Ford's novel *d* William Wyler *ph* Robert Surtees *m* Elmer Bernstein

Lee J. Cobb, Anthony Zerbe, Roscoe Lee Browne, Lola Falana, Lee Majors, Barbara Hershey, Yaphet Kotto, Arch Johnson, Chill Wills

'With its genuinely ferocious climax it adds up to probably the most powerful, if not the most sophisticated, race-war film the commercial studios have yet produced.'— *Nigel Andrews*

Liberty**
US 1929   20m   bw   silent

Two convicts escape and have adventures high on a construction site. Amusing gags are succeeded by breathtaking thrills in the Harold Lloyd style. Laurel and Hardy, James Finlayson. Written by Leo McCarey and H. M. Walker; directed by Leo McCary; for Hal Roach.

Licensed to Kill
GB 1965   97m   Eastmancolor
Alistair Films (Estelle E. Richmond)
US title: *The Second Best Secret Agent in the Whole Wide World*

The Foreign Office calls in agent Charles Vine to protect a top international scientist.
Cheap copy of James Bond which wins no laurels but produces a few efficient routine thrills.

w Howard Griffiths, Lindsay Shontoff *d* Lindsay Shonteff *ph* Terry Maher *m* Bertram Chappell

Tom Adams, Veronica Hurst, Karel Stepanek, Felix Felton, Peter Bull

Liebelei*
Austria 1932   85m   bw
Fred Lissa

A young army officer falls in love; but he is killed in a duel and his girl commits suicide.
Semi-classic romantic novelette, like a warm-up for *Letter from an Unknown Woman.*

w Hans Wilhelm, Kurt Alexander, *story* Arthur Schnitzler *d* Max Ophuls *ph* Franz Planer *m* Theo Macheber

Magda Schneider, Wolfgang Liebeneiner, Luise Ullrich, Willy Eichberger, Gustaf Gruendgens, Paul Hoerbiger
† A revised French version played as *Une Histoire d'Amour.* The story had previously been shot under the same title in Germany in 1927; and in the sixties Romy Schneider and Alain Delon appeared in a French remake called *Christine.*

Lies My Father Told Me
Canada 1975   102m   colour
Columbia / Pentimento / Pentacle (Anthony Bedrich, Harry Gulkin)

Adventures of a poor Jewish boy and his grandfather in Montreal in the twenties.
Effectively if rather dishonestly sentimental, this is the kind of family picture for which critics are always clamouring but which few people in the seventies will pay to see.

w Ted Allan, from his book *d* Jan Kadar *ph* Paul Van der Linden *m* Sol Kaplan

Yossi Yadin, Len Birman, Marilyn Lightstone, Jeffrey Lynas

'Sentiment by numbers . . . a lovable child awakening to discovery of the world; a lovable, whimsical old grandfather; a lovable, ne'er-do-well father; a lovable, long-suffering mother; a lovable, broken-down horse; lovable neighbours; a lovable whore across the way. It all strives so hard to be lovable that you want to scream.'—*David Robinson, The Times*
† A British low-budgeter was made from the same story in 1940, changing the venue to Ireland and the race to Irish.

AAN: Ted Allan

Lt Robin Crusoe USN
US 1966   114m   Technicolor
Walt Disney (Bill Walsh, Ron Miller)

A navy pilot parachutes on to a Pacific island and gets involved in the local women's lib movement.
Slow-paced family comedy with very few laughs.

w Bill Walsh, Don da Gradi *d* Byron Paul *ph* William Snyder *m* Bob Brunner

Dick Van Dyke, Nancy Kwan, Akim Tamiroff

The Lieutenant Wore Skirts
US 1955   99m   Eastmancolor
Cinemascope
TCF (Buddy Adler)

When a TV writer joins the service, his wife enlists to be near him; but he is rejected on medical grounds.
Raucous, tasteless farce which tries far too hard to raise laughs.

w Albert Beich, Frank Tashlin *d* Frank Tashlin *ph* Leo Tover *m* Cyril Mockridge

Tom Ewell, Sheree North, Rita Moreno, Rick Jason, Les Tremayne

The Life and Death of a Hollywood Extra*
US 1927   11m (24 fps)   bw   silent

A nonentity arrives in Hollywood and dreams of becoming a star. Avant-garde short, still interesting if less revolutionary than it seemed at the time. Jules Raucort, Georges Voya. Written, produced and directed by *Robert Florey* and *Slavko Vorkapich*; photographed by Slavko Vorkapich and Gregg Toland; editor and art director, *Slavko Vorkapich.*

The Life and Death of Colonel Blimp***
GB 1943   163m   Technicolor
GFD / Archers (Michael Powell, Emeric Pressburger)
US title: *Colonel Blimp*

A British soldier survives three wars and falls in love with three women.
Not the Blimp of the cartoon strip, but a sympathetic figure in a warm, consistently interesting if idiosyncratic love story against a background of war. The Archers as usual provide a sympathetic German lead (friend of the hero); quite a coup in wartime.

wd Michael Powell, Emeric Pressburger *ph* Jack Cardiff *m* Allan Gray *ad* Alfred Junge

Roger Livesey, Anton Walbrook, Deborah Kerr, Roland Culver, James McKechnie, Albert Lieven, Arthur Wontner, A. E. Matthews, David Hutcheson, Ursula Jeans, John Laurie, Harry Welchman

'There is nothing brilliant about the picture, but it is perceptive, witty and sweet-tempered.'—*James Agee*

● Video: Rank

The Life and Times of Judge Roy Bean*
US 1972   124m   Technicolor
Panavision
National General / Famous Artists (John Foreman)

A fantasia on the famous outlaw judge of the old west.
Sporadically entertaining but schematically messy mixture of burlesqued folklore and violent action, not in the same league as *Butch Cassidy.*

w John Milius *d* John Huston *ph* Richard Moore *m* Maurice Jarre

Paul Newman, Ava Gardner, Jacqueline Bisset, Tab Hunter, Stacy Keach, Roddy McDowall, Anthony Perkins, John Huston

AAN: song 'Marmalade, Molasses and Honey' (*m* Maurice Jarre, *ly* A. and M. Byrne)

Life at the Top*
GB 1965   117m   bw
Columbia / Romulus (James Woolf)

Ten years after marrying into money, Joe Lampton is dissatisfied, and he and his wife both have affairs.
Rough-talking but basically predictable and old-fashioned sequel to *Room at the Top*, a bit compromised by having to reflect the sixties London scene; the early Yorkshire sequences are the best.

w Mordecai Richler d Ted Kotcheff
ph Oswald Morris m Richard Addinsell

Laurence Harvey, Jean Simmons, Honor
Blackman, Michael Craig, Donald Wolfit,
Margaret Johnston, Allan Cuthbertson,
Ambrosine Philpotts, Robert Morley, Nigel
Davenport, George A. Cooper
  'Another thoroughly mean-spirited film of a
kind which has been taking root in the British
cinema.'—*Tom Milne*
† The character of Joe Lampton was later used
in a long running TV series called *Man at the
Top*, which sprouted a film of its own under
that title.

Life Begins
US 1932 72m bw
Warner (Ray Griffith)
GB title: *Dream of Life*

A night in a maternity hospital.
Multi-melodrama later remade as *A Child Is
Born*. Passable.

w Earl Baldwin, *play* Mary McDougal
Axelson d James Flood ph James Van Trees

Loretta Young, Eric Linden, Aline
MacMahon, Preston Foster, Glenda Farrell,
Frank McHugh, Clara Blandick, Elizabeth
Patterson, Gilbert Roland
  'Splendid women's picture promising at least
solid matinée business.'—*Variety*

Life Begins at Eight Thirty*
US 1942 85m bw
TCF (Nunnally Johnson)
GB title: *The Light of Heart*

A distinguished actor is reduced through drink
to being a street corner Santa Claus.
Diluted and sentimentalized version of an
agreeable play.

w Nunnally Johnson, *play* The Light of Heart
by Emlyn Williams d Irving Pichel
ph Edward Cronjager m Alfred Newman

Monty Woolley, Ida Lupino, Cornel Wilde,
Sara Allgood, Melville Cooper, J. Edward
Bromberg

Life Begins in College*
US 1937 80m bw

Three zanies save the honour of the college
football team. Another of the myriad college
football stories of the thirties, but this time
enlivened by comedians in the leads. The Ritz
Brothers, Joan Davis, Tony Martin, Gloria
Stuart, Fred Stone, Nat Pendleton. Written by
Karl Tunberg and Don Ettlinger; directed by
William A. Seiter; for TCF. 'The Ritzes soar
to stardom: a box office touchdown.'—*Variety*

Life for Ruth*
GB 1962 91m bw
Rank / Allied Film Makers (Michael Relph,
  Basil Dearden)
US title: *Condemned to Life*

A little girl dies because her parents' religion
forbids blood transfusions.
Dramatized from the headlines, this little case
history is small beer as film-making, and not
exactly entertainment, but absorbing as a
comment on human behaviour.

w Janet Green, John McCormick d Basil
Dearden ph Otto Heller m William Alwyn
md Muir Mathieson

Michael Craig, Patrick McGoohan, Janet
Munro

A Life in the Balance*
US 1954 75m bw
TCF / Panoramic (Leonard Goldstein)

A Mexican widower springs into action when
his young son is kidnapped by a murderer.
Taut little melodrama taking place during one
night in Mexico City; made with vigour on a
low budget.

w Robert Presnell Jnr, Leo Townsend
d *Harry Horner*
ph J. Gomez Urquiza m Raul Lavista

Ricardo Montalban, Anne Bancroft, Lee
Marvin

Life Is a Bed of Roses*
France 1983 111m Eastmancolor
Philippe Dusart / Soprofilms / Films A2 /
  Fideline / Ariane / Filmedis / Ministry of
  Culture (Philippe Dusart)
Original title: *La Vie est un Roman*

A count opens a temple of happiness and
starts to re-educate his friends.
Dense fantasy which never really explains
itself but provides pleasant moments along the
way.

w Jean Gruault d Alain Resnais ph Bruno
Nuytten m M. Philippe-Gerard

Vittorio Gassman, Ruggero Raimondi,
Geraldine Chaplin, Fanny Ardant, Pierre
Arditi

The Life of Adolf Hitler*
West Germany 1961 102m bw

A documentary culled from newsreel material;
somehow less arresting than one would have
hoped, though undoubtedly worthy. Written
by Helga Koppel; directed and edited by Paul
Rotha; for Real Film.

'He plucked from the gutter a faded rose
    and made an immortal masterpiece!'
The Life of Emile Zola***
US 1937 116m bw
Warner (Henry Blanke)

The French writer intervenes in the case of
Alfred Dreyfus, condemned unjustly to
Devil's Island.
The box office success of this solidly-
carpentered piece of Hollywood history was
compounded in equal parts of star power and
the sheer novelty of having such a thing turn
up at the local Odeon.

w Norman Reilly Raine *story* Heinz Herald
and Geza Herczeg d *William Dieterle*
ph Tony Gaudio m Max Steiner ad Anton
Grot

Paul Muni, *Joseph Schildkraut*, Gale
Sondergaard, Gloria Holden, Donald Crisp,
Erin O'Brien Moore, John Litel, Henry
O'Neill, Morris Carnovsky, Ralph Morgan,
Louis Calhern, Robert Barrat, Vladimir
Sokoloff, Harry Davenport, Robert Warwick,
Walter Kingsford

'Destined to box office approval of the most
substantial character. It is finely made and
merits high rating as cinema art and significant
recognition as major showmanship.'—*Variety*
  'Along with *Louis Pasteur*, it ought to start
a new category—the Warner crusading films,
costume division.'—*Otis Ferguson*
  'A grave story told with great dignity and
superbly played and produced.'—*Pare Lorentz*
  'One of the fine ones which begin as a film
and end as an experience.'—*John Grierson*

AA: best picture; script; Joseph Schildkraut
AAN: original story; William Dieterle; Max
Steiner; Paul Muni

A Life of Her Own
US 1950 108m bw
MGM (Voldemar Vetluguin)

An innocent girl from Kansas becomes one of
New York's top models.
Road to ruin, American style, from the pages
of a women's magazine.

w Isabel Lennart d George Cukor
ph George Folsey m Bronislau Kaper

Lana Turner, Ray Milland, Tom Ewell, Louis
Calhern, Ann Dvorak, Barry Sullivan, Jean
Hagen
  'This story belongs to the realms of soap
opera—extremely artificial, highly moral in
tone, and deliberately concocted to combine
luxurious settings with an elementary assault
on the audience's emotions.'—*MFB*

The Life of Jimmy Dolan
US 1933 85m bw
Warner (Hal B. Wallis)
GB title: *The Kid's Last Fight*

An amiable wanderer is mistaken for a prize-
fighter wanted for murder.
Modest character romance, later remade as
They Made Me a Criminal.

w David Boehm, Erwin Gelsey, *play* Bertram
Millhauser, Beulah Marie Dix d Archie
Mayo ph Arthur Edeson

Douglas Fairbanks Jnr, Loretta Young, Aline
MacMahon, Guy Kibbee, Lyle Talbot, Fifi
D'Orsay, Harold Huber, George Meeker

Life of the Party
US 1930 78m Technicolor

Two gold-digging shop girls operate from a
modiste's. Half-hearted vulgar comedy, rather
oddly given colour status. Winnie Lightner,
Irene Delroy, Charles Butterworth, Jack
Whiting. Written by Arthur Caesar from a
story by Melville Crossman (Darryl F.
Zanuck); directed by Roy del Ruth; for
Warners. 'Spotty for laughs and business.'—
Variety

Life of the Party
US 1937 86m bw

A girl tries to evade suitors arranged by her
mother. Very thin comedy with several
second-bracket names; not at all memorable.
Joe Penner, Harriet Hilliard, Gene Raymond,
Parkyakarkus, Victor Moore, Helen
Broderick, Billy Gilbert, Ann Miller. Written

by Bert Kalmar, Harry Ruby, Viola Brothers Shore; directed by William A. Seiter; for RKO. 'Should prove fairish entertainment and do fairly at the b.o.'—*Variety*

The Life of Vergie Winters
US 1934 82m bw
RKO (Pandro S. Berman)

A rising politician marries for position but keeps watch over his mistress and their child. Archetypal soap opera, a cross between *Stella Dallas* and *Back Street*.

w Jane Murfin, *novel* Louis Bromfield d Alfred Santell ph Lucien Andriot m Max Steiner

Ann Harding, John Boles, Helen Vinson, Frank Albertson, Lon Chaney Jnr, Sara Haden, Ben Alexander, Donald Crisp

Life Returns
US 1938 62m bw

A fictional story leads up to the actual experiment performed in 1934 by Dr Robert E. Cornish when he brought a dead dog back to life. Weird mélange of fact and fiction; despite the achievement, the presentation never catches fire. The film was banned in Britain. Onslow Stevens, George Breakston, Valerie Hobson, Lois Wilson. Written by Arthur Horman, John F. Goodrich; directed by Eugen Frenke; for Scienart. 'A picture much longer to the audience than its accredited running time would indicate.'—*Variety*

Life Upside Down*
France 1964 92m bw
A.J. Films
original title: *La Vie à l'Envers*

A pleasant, ordinary young man discovers the joy of being absolutely alone, and begins to detach himself from his surroundings, ending up in a barren flat and a private hospital ward. Engaging semi-comic case history which generates much sympathy for its eccentric hero.

wd Alain Jessua ph Jacques Robin m Jacques Loussier

Charles Denner, Anna Gaylor, Guy Saint-Jean, Nicole Gueden
  'The tone is civilized, quiet, infinitely peaceful and often brilliantly funny.'—*Brenda Davies, MFB*
  'Amusing or disturbing depending on whether it is viewed from the outside or the inside, but perceptive and artistic whichever way one views it.'—*John Simon*

Life with Father*
US 1947 118m Technicolor
Warner (Robert Buckner)

Turn-of-the-century anecdotes of an irascible well-to-do paterfamilias who won't be baptized.
Well-upholstered screen version of a long running play; oddly tedious considering the talent involved.

w Donald Ogden Stewart, *play* Howard Lindsay, Russel Crouse d Michael Curtiz ph Peverell Marley, William V. Skall m Max Steiner ad Robert Hass

William Powell, Irene Dunne, Edmund Gwenn, Zasu Pitts, Elizabeth Taylor, Martin Milner, Jimmy Lydon, Emma Dunn, Moroni Olsen, Elizabeth Risdon
  'Everybody seems to be trying too hard . . . the director is totally out of his element in this careful, deadly version.'—*New Yorker, 1978*
† Censorship of the day absurdly clipped Father's famous last line: 'I'm going to be baptized, damn it!'

AAN: Peverell Marley, William V. Skall; Max Steiner; William Powell

● *Video: European Video*

Lifeboat**
US 1944 96m bw
TCF (Kenneth MacGowan)

Survivors from a torpedoed passenger ship include the U-Boat commander responsible. Propaganda gimmick melodrama interesting for the casting and for Hitchcock's response to the challenge of filming in one cramped set.

w Jo Swerling, *story* John Steinbeck d Alfred Hitchcock ph Glen MacWilliams m Hugo Friedhofer

Tallulah Bankhead, Walter Slezak, Henry Hull, John Hodiak, Canada Lee, William Bendix, Mary Anderson, Heather Angel, Hume Cronyn
  'The initial idea—a derelict boat and its passengers as microcosm—is itself so artificial that . . . it sets the whole pride and brain too sharply to work on a tour de force for its own sake.'—*James Agee*

AAN: John Steinbeck; Alfred Hitchcock; Glen MacWilliams

The Lift
Netherlands 1983 99m Eastmancolor

An office block elevator seems to assume deadly powers. After a murderous car, a murderous lift. Slick but rather empty semi-horror. Huub Stapel, Willeke Van Ammelrooy, Josine Van Dalsum. Written and directed by Dick Maas; for Sigma Films.

Lift to the Scaffold*
France 1957 89m bw
Nouvelles Editions de Films (Jean Thuillier)
original title: *Ascenseur pour l'Echafaud*

An executive murders his employer but is trapped in the building all night; meanwhile his car is stolen and he is arrested for a murder committed by the thief.
Complex, watchable suspenser with pretensions.

w Roger Nimier, Louis Malle, *novel* Noel Calef d Louis Malle ph Henri Decaë m Miles Davis

Maurice Ronet, Jeanne Moreau, Georges Poujouly, Yori Bertin, Lino Ventura
  'Cold, clever and rather elegant.'—*Penelope Houston, MFB*

The Light across the Street
France 1955 99m bw
EGC / Fernand Rivers (Jacques Gauthier)
original title: *La Lumière d'en Face*

A lorry driver, injured in an accident, becomes insanely jealous of his young wife. Low-life melodrama tailored for the sultry attractions of its new star.

w Louis Cahavance, René Masson, René Lefèvre d Georges Lacombe ph Louis Page m Norbert Glanzberg

Brigitte Bardot, Raymond Pellégrin, Roger Pigaut, Claude Romain

The Light at the Edge of the World
US / Spain / Liechtenstein 1971 120m
  Eastmancolor Panavision
Bryna / Jet / Triumfilm (Kirk Douglas, Ilya Salkind)

A lighthouse keeper near Cape Horn resists a band of wreckers.
Pretentious, disaster-prone version of a simple adventure story; one wonders not so much what went wrong as whether anything went right in this international venture.

w Tom Rowe, *novel* Jules Verne d Kevin Billington ph Henri Decaë m Piero Piccioni

Kirk Douglas, Yul Brynner, Samantha Eggar, Jean-Claude Drouot, Fernando Rey, Renato Salvatori

● *Video: Thorn EMI*

The Light in the Forest
US 1958 92m Technicolor
Walt Disney

Kidnapped by Indians as an infant, a teenager is returned to his parents but finds the white man's ways disturbing.
Modest frontier drama with a moral.

w Lawrence Edward Watkin, *novel* Conrad Richter d Herschel Daugherty ph Ellsworth Fredericks m Paul Smith

James MacArthur, Carol Lynley, Jessica Tandy, Wendell Corey, Fess Parker, Joanne Dru, Joseph Calleia

The Light in the Piazza
GB 1962 101m Metrocolor
  Cinemascope
MGM (Arthur Freed)

An American matron in Florence tries to marry off her mentally retarded daughter to a wealthy Italian.
Puzzling romantic drama in which one is never quite sure why the characters behave as they do; in the end all one appreciates is the tour of northern Italy.

w Julius J. Epstein, *novel* Elizabeth Spencer d Guy Green ph Otto Heller m Mario Nascimbene

Olivia de Havilland, Yvette Mimieux, George Hamilton, Rossano Brazzi, Barry Sullivan

Only **RUDYARD KIPLING** could write such a romance!
Only **RONALD COLMAN** could play such a role!

"Laugh, you little fool, laugh...for I'm giving you something you've never had before... A soul...on canvas!"

Rudyard Kipling's great romance of Dick Heldar, artist, adventurer, gentleman unafraid, gloriously re-created by the year's most distinguished cast!

Paramount Presents **RONALD COLMAN**

in *Rudyard Kipling's*

"THE LIGHT THAT FAILED"

with **WALTER HUSTON**

and Ida Lupino • Muriel Angelus • Dudley Digges
Produced and Directed by WILLIAM A. WELLMAN • Screen
Play by Robert Carson • Based on the Novel by Rudyard Kipling

THE LIGHT THAT FAILED. Colman relished the role, but the story was too unhappy for public acceptance.

'Laugh, you little fool, laugh . . . for I'm giving you something you never had before—a soul . . . on canvas!'
The Light that Failed*
US 1939 97m bw
Paramount (William A. Wellman)
A London artist is going blind as the result of a war wound, and must finish the portrait of the little cockney whom he loves.
Nicely-made but rather boring star romance; no surprises in plot or performance.

w Robert Carson, *story* Rudyard Kipling
d William Wellman *ph* Theodor Sparkuhl
m Victor Young

Ronald Colman, Walter Huston, Ida Lupino, Dudley Digges, Muriel Angelus, Fay Helm
'Production fine for moderate b.o. Will catch attention of the carriage trade, the literati crowd and the critics.'—*Variety*
† Previously filmed in 1916 and 1923.

The Light Touch
US 1951 107m bw
MGM (Pandro S. Berman)

An elegant art thief tries to doublecross the gangster who employs him.
Elongated and witless romantic charade on European locations.

wd Richard Brooks, story Jed Harris, Tom Reed ph Robert Surtees m Miklos Rozsa

Stewart Granger, George Sanders, Pier Angeli, Kurt Kasznar, Larry Keating, Rhys Williams, Norman Lloyd, Mike Mazurki
'A comedy thriller which moves far too slowly for its imperfections to be overlooked.'—Penelope Houston, MFB

Light Up the Sky
GB 1960 90m bw
British Lion / Bryanston (Lewis Gilbert)

Life on a searchlight battery during World War II.
Wartime comedy-drama with accent on the laughs but adding dollops of tragedy and sentiment. A very patchy entertainment.

w Vernon Harris, play Touch It Light by Robert Storey d Lewis Gilbert ph John Wilcox m Douglas Gamley

Ian Carmichael, Tommy Steele, Benny Hill, Sydney Tafler, Victor Maddern, Harry Locke, Johnny Briggs, Dick Emery

Lightnin'*
US 1930 94m bw

A country fellow is wiser than he seems, and in between setting other folks' lives right, persuades his own wife not to divorce him.
Archetypal Will Rogers star part which he played on the stage; now his first big talkie hit. Will Rogers, Louise Dresser, Joel McCrea, Sharon Lynn, J. M. Kerrigan. From the play by Frank Bacon and Winchell Smith; directed by Henry King; for Fox. 'A production of the highest quality in all its phases.'—Variety

Lightning Over Water
West Germany / Sweden 1980 91m Movielab

A record of the last months of Nicholas Ray's life, when he was hoping to revive his career while visibly dying from cancer. Unique and uneasy, something for film buffs to chew over.
Written and directed by Nicholas Ray and Wim Wenders; for Road Movies / Viking Film. (Aka: Nick's Movie.)

Lightning Strikes Twice
US 1951 91m bw
Warner (Henry Blanke)

A woman decides to clear her lover of suspicion of murder, but later has her own doubts.
Silly melodrama with no credibility, little suspense, and too much talk.

w Lenore Coffee, novel Margaret Echard d King Vidor ph Sid Hickox m Max Steiner

Richard Todd, Ruth Roman, Mercedes McCambridge, Zachary Scott, Darryl Hickman, Frank Conroy, Kathryn Givney

Lights of New York***
US 1928 57m bw
Warner

A chorus girl becomes involved with gangsters.
The first '100 per cent all-talking' film, dramatically primitive but historically important.

w F. Hugh Herbert, Murray Roth d Bryan Foy ph E. B. DuPar

Helene Costello, Cullen Landis, Wheeler Oakman, Eugene Pallette, Tom Dugan, Gladys Brockwell, Mary Carr
'100 per cent crude.'—Variety

Lights of Old Broadway
US 1925 80m approx at 24 fps bw silent

Twin orphan girls find very different routes to happiness. One of the star's most popular vehicles. Marion Davies, Conrad Nagel, George K. Arthur, Julia Swayne Gordon. Written by Carey Wilson; directed by Monta Bell; for MGM.

Lights of Variety*
Italy 1950 94m bw
Film Capitolium (Alberto Lattuada)

A stage-struck young girl forsakes the manager of the troupe in which she found stardom for the bright lights of the city.
Tragi-comical backstage story in which the bits of detail are more entertaining than the plot.

w Federico Fellini d Alberto Lattuada ph Otello Martelli m Felice Lattuada

Peppino de Filippo, Carla del Poggio, Giulietta Masina, John Kitzmiller, Folco Lulli

The Likely Lads*
GB 1976 90m bw
EMI (Aida Young)

Two Geordie friends, with wife and mistress, go on a touring holiday.
Valuable as a record of an excellent and long-running TV series, this big screen version finds most of the humour regrettably broadened.

w Dick Clement, Ian La Frenais d Michael Tuchner ph Tony Imi m Mike Hugg

Rodney Bewes, James Bolam, Brigit Forsyth, Mary Tamm, Sheila Fearn, Zena Walker
● Video: Thorn EMI

A Likely Story
US 1947 88m bw
RKO (Richard H. Berger)

A man thinks he has only a short time to live, and in trying to do his best for a girl friend gets mixed up with gangsters.
Even a star cast could not have made much of this zany comedy script.

w Bess Taffel d H. C. Potter ph Roy Hunt m Leigh Harline md Constantin Bakaleinikoff

Barbara Hale, Bill Williams, Lanny Rees, Sam Levene, Dan Tobin, Nestor Paiva

Li'l Abner*
US 1959 113m Technicolor Vistavision
Paramount / Panama–Frank (Norman Panama)

The hillbilly town of Dogpatch, tagged the most useless community in America, fights being used as a test site for A-bombs.
Set-bound, intrinsically American, but bright and cheerful film of a stage show about Al Capp's famous comic strip characters.

wd Norman Panama, Melvin Frank from the musical show (ly Johnny Mercer, words Gene de Paul) ph Daniel L. Fapp m Gene de Paul md Joseph Lilley, Nelson Riddle ch Dee Dee Wood, Michael Kidd

Peter Palmer, Leslie Parrish, Billie Hayes, Howard St John, Stubby Kaye, Stella Stevens, Julie Newmar, Robert Strauss
AAN: Joseph Lilley, Nelson Riddle

The Lilac Domino
GB 1937 79m bw

A Hungarian count is attracted at the gambling tables by a masked girl. Surprisingly undercast version of a popular operetta. June Knight, Michael Bartlett, Athene Seyler, Richard Dolman, S. Z. Sakall, Fred Emney, Jane Carr. Written by Basil Mason, Neil Gow, R. Hutter and Derek Neame, from the play by Rudolf Bernauer, E. Gatti and B. Jenbach; directed by Fred Zelnik; for Grafton-Capitol-Cecil.

Lilac Time*
US 1928 90m approx bw silent with sound effects
GB title: Love Never Dies

A French girl promises to wait for an American flyer, but his stern father tells her he is dead.
Popular war romance which retains moments of interest.

w Carey Wilson, play Jane Cowl, Jane Murfin d / p George Fitzmaurice ph Sid Hickox m Nathaniel Shilkret

Colleen Moore, Gary Cooper, Eugenie Besserer, Burr McIntosh, Arthur Lake

Lilacs in the Spring
GB 1954 94m Trucolor
Republic / Everest (Herbert Wilcox)
US title: Let's Make Up

During the London blitz a young actress is knocked unconscious and dreams of herself as Nell Gwyn, Queen Victoria and her own mother before waking up to deal with her personal problems.
Good-humoured theatrical charade deadened by poorish production and colour, strengthened by the star's game run-through of her staple characters. How Mr Flynn came to be involved is anybody's guess.

w Harold Purcell, from his play The Glorious Days d Herbert Wilcox ph Max Greene m Robert Farnon

Anna Neagle, Errol Flynn, Peter Graves, David Farrar, Kathleen Harrison
● Video: Video Media

Lili*
US 1952 81m Technicolor
MGM (Edwin H. Knopf)

A 16-year-old orphan girl joins a carnival and
falls in love with the magician.
Romantic whimsy dependent entirely on
treatment, which is sometimes heavy-handed.
Charm, ballet and puppets are provided, but a
little cheerful song and dance would not have
been amiss.

w Helen Deutsch, *novel* Paul Gallico *d, ch*
Charles Walters *ph* Robert Planck
m Bronislau Kaper *ad* Cedric Gibbons, Paul
Stroesse

Leslie Caron, Jean-Pierre Aumont, Mel
Ferrer, Kurt Kasznar
  'A lovely and beguiling little film, touched
with the magic of romance.'—*Bosley Crowther*

AA: Bronislau Kaper
AAN: Helen Deutsch; Charles Walters;
Robert Planck; Leslie Caron

Lili Marleen*
West Germany 1980 116m colour
Roxy / CIP / Rialto / Bayerische Rundfunk
(Luggi Waldleitner)

A German girl singer becomes famous and
notorious during World War II by her
rendition of an old song.
Curious mixture of melodrama and satire
which doesn't really work but is always lively
to watch.

w Manfred Purzer, Joshua Sinclair, Rainer
Werner Fassbinder, *novel* The Sky Has Many
Colours by Lale Andersen *d* Rainer Werner
Fassbinder *ph* Xaver Schwarzenberger
m Peer Raben

Hanna Schygulla, Giancarlo Giannini, Mel
Ferrer, Karl Heinz
● *Video: Intervision*

Lilies of the Field
US 1930 60m bw

A chorus girl has been robbed of her child by
framed divorce court evidence. Backstage
melodrama with music, very dated now but
with interesting credits. Corinne Griffith,
Ralph Forbes, John Loder, Patsy Paige,
Freeman Wood, Virginia Bruce. Written by
John Goodrich from the play by William
Hurlbut; directed by Alexander Korda; for
First National. 'Big revue sequences in
backstage locale. Better than average
programmer.'—*Variety*

Lilies of the Field*
US 1963 94m bw
UA / Rainbow / Ralph Nelson

An itinerant black workman in New Mexico
helps a group of German nuns to build a
chapel.
Liberal, sentimental, under-dramatized little
comedy with everyone coming to understand
each other's point of view, so that the
audience feels improved if not especially
entertained.

w James Poe, *novel* William E. Barrett
d Ralph Nelson *ph* Ernest Haller *m* Jerry
Goldsmith

Sidney Poitier, Lilia Skala
AA: Sidney Poitier
AAN: best picture; James Poe; Ernest Haller;
Lilia Skala

Liliom*
US 1930 94m bw
Fox

A Budapest carnival man is killed in a fight
but later comes back from heaven to see how
his family is doing.
Ingeniously-staged fantasy, very dated but a
lot more interesting than its musical remake
Carousel (qv).

w S. N. Behrman, *play* Ferenc Molnar
d Frank Borzage *ph* Chester Lyons
m Richard Fall

Charles Farrell, Rose Hobart, Estelle Taylor,
Lee Tracy, Walter Abel, Guinn Williams, H.
B. Warner, Dawn O'Day (Anne Shirley)
  'Beyond the depth of Farrell's dramatic
ability . . . shapes up as passable for a week-
stand in the keys.'—*Variety*

Lilith*
US 1964 126m bw
Columbia / Centaur (Robert Rossen)

A trainee therapist at an asylum falls in love
with a patient.
Strange, wistful, poetic and rather soporific
character melodrama.

wd Robert Rossen, *novel* J. R. Salamanca
ph Eugen Schufftan *m* Kenyon Hopkins
pd Richard Sylbert

Warren Beatty, Jean Seberg, Peter Fonda,
Kim Hunter, Anne Meacham, James
Patterson, Jessica Walter, Gene Hackman
  'A remarkable attempt to dig a little deeper
in an almost untilled field, and to throw some
light on the relationship between madness and
the creative imagination.'—*Tom Milne*

Lillian Russell**
US 1940 130m bw
TCF (Gene Markey)

The life and loves of the famous nineties
entertainer.
Whitewashed biopic, extremely well made of
its kind, and very typical.

w William Anthony McGuire *d* Irving
Cummings *ph* Leon Shamroy *md* Alfred
Newman

Alice Faye, Don Ameche, Edward Arnold,
Warren William, Henry Fonda, Leo Carrillo,
Helen Westley, Dorothy Peterson, Ernest
Truex, Nigel Bruce, Claud Allister, Lynn
Bari, Weber and Fields, Eddie Foy Jnr, Una
O'Connor

Lily Turner
US 1933 65m bw

A girl unwittingly marries a bigamist, then a
drunk who will give her baby a name. Turgid
mother-love saga. Ruth Chatterton, George
Brent, Frank McHugh, Ruth Donnelly, Guy
Kibbee, Robert Barrat. Written by Gene
Markey and Kathryn Scola from the play by
Philip Dunning and George Abbott; directed
by William A. Wellman; for Warners. 'Spotty
returns most probable.'—*Variety*

Limbo*
US 1972 111m Technicolor
Universal (Linda Gottlieb)
aka: *Chained to Yesterday*

Women wait for their husbands to return from
Vietnam.
Worthy but dramatically uninteresting multi-
storied semi-propaganda piece with an untried
cast.

w Joan Silver, James Bridges *d* Mark
Robson *ph* Charles Wheeler *m* Anita Kerr

Kate Jackson, Katherine Justice, Stuart
Margolin, Hazel Medina, Kathleen Nolan

'Romantic ruler of London's half-world!'
Limehouse Blues*
US 1934 65m bw
Paramount
aka: *East End Chant*

In London's shady quarter, an oriental
roustabout tries to leave his jealous mistress
for a girl with a shady past.
Artificial, atmospheric melodrama set in a
never-never Limehouse redolent of *Broken
Blossoms*. Interesting for its very excesses.

w Arthur Phillips, Cyril Hume, Grover Jones
d Alexander Hall *ph* Harry Fischbeck

George Raft, Anna May Wong, Jean Parker,
Kent Taylor, Billy Bevan
  'Weak and slow-moving . . . won't satisfy
the average fan.'—*Variety*

Limelight
GB 1935 80m bw
GFD / Herbert Wilcox

A chorus girl helps a street singer to become a
star.
Highly predictable backstage musical drama
which made a nine days wonder of 'The Street
Singer'.

w Laura Whettier *d* Herbert Wilcox

Anna Neagle, *Arthur Tracy*, Jane Winton,
Ellis Jeffreys, Muriel George
  'A syrupy concatenation to win all British
hearts.'—*James Agate*

Limelight***
US 1952 144m bw
Charles Chaplin

A broken-down music hall comedian is
stimulated by a young ballerina to a final hour
of triumph.
Sentimental drama in a highly theatrical
London East End setting. In other hands it
would be very hokey, but Chaplin's best
qualities, as well as his worst, are in evidence,
and in a way the film sums up his own career.

w,d, m Charles Chaplin *ph* Karl Struss
ad Eugene Lourié *photographic consultant*
Rollie Totheroh

Charles Chaplin, Claire Bloom, Buster Keaton,
Sydney Chaplin, Nigel Bruce, Norman Lloyd
  'From the first reel it is clear that he now
wants to talk, that he *loves* to talk . . . where a
development in the story line might easily be
conveyed by a small visual effect, he prefers to
make a speech about it . . . it is a disturbing
rejection of the nature of the medium itself.'—
Walter Kerr

'Surely the richest hunk of self-gratification since Huck and Tom attended their own funeral.'—*New Yorker, 1982*

'His exhortations about life, courage, consciousness and "truth" are set in a self-pitying, self-glorifying story.'—*Pauline Kael, 70s*

AA: Charles Chaplin (for music)
● Video: Polygram

The Limping Man
GB 1953   74m   bw

An American leaving his plane at Heathrow sees another passenger shot by a limping man.
Initially intriguing thriller which gives up the ghost and tacks on a dream ending. Lloyd Bridges, Moira Lister, Helene Cordet, Bruce Beeby, Alan Wheatley, Leslie Phillips. Written by Ian Stuart and Reginald Long; directed by Charles de Lautour; for Banner / Eros.

Linda*
GB 1960   61m   bw

A teenage girl falls for a member of a street gang. Nicely atmospheric low-life romance; no real content but plenty of raw style. Carol White, Alan Rothwell, Cavan Malone, Lois Dane, Edward Cast. Written by Bill MacIlwraith; directed by Don Sharp; for Independent Artists.

The Lineup*
US 1958   86m   bw
Columbia (Frank Cooper)

San Francisco police trap a gunman who is also a drug contact.
Energetic, polished movie version of a popular TV series, *San Francisco Beat*.
w Stirling Silliphant d *Don Siegel* ph Hal Mohr m Mischa Bakaleinikoff

Warren Anderson, Robert Keith, Eli Wallach

The Lion
GB 1962   96m   De Luxe   Cinemascope
TCF (Samuel G. Engel)

An American lawyer goes to Africa to visit his ex-wife and their child.
Unabsorbing marital drama with child and animal interest.
w Irene and Louis Kamp, *novel* Joseph Kessel d Jack Cardiff ph Ted Scaife m Malcolm Arnold

William Holden, Trevor Howard, Capucine, Pamela Franklin
'The main fault must be attributed to the spiritless direction of Jack Cardiff, whose recent change of métier has resulted in the industry losing a great lighting cameraman.'—*John Gillett*

The Lion Has Wings*
GB 1939   76m   bw
Alexander Korda

A documentary drama tracing the steps leading up to the outbreak of war.

Once-inspiring propaganda piece, now regrettably hilarious. Valuable social history, though.
w Adrian Brunel, E. V. H. Emmett d Michael Powell, Brian Desmond Hurst, Adrian Brunel ph Harry Stradling m Richard Addinsell

Merle Oberon, Ralph Richardson, June Duprez, Robert Douglas, Anthony Bushell, Derrick de Marney, Brian Worth, Austin Trevor
'As a statement of war aims, one feels, this leaves the world beyond Roedean still expectant.'—*Graham Greene*

The Lion in Winter*
GB 1968   134m   Eastmancolor
Panavision
Avco Embassy / Haworth (Martin Poll)

Henry II and Eleanor of Aquitaine celebrate Christmas together and have a family row.
An acting feast for two principals and assorted supports, a talking marathon in which not all the talk is good, a smart comedy with sudden lapses into melodrama; stimulating in parts but all rather tiresome by the end, especially as there is not much medieval splendour.
w James Goldman, from his play d Anthony Harvey ph Douglas Slocombe m John Barry
Katharine Hepburn, *Peter O'Toole*, Jane Merrow, John Castle, Anthony Hopkins, Nigel Terry, Timothy Dalton
'He is not writing a factual movie about the Plantagenets but an interpretation in which he combines their language and ours.'—*Philip T. Hartung*

AA: James Goldman; John Barry; Katharine Hepburn
AAN: best picture; Anthony Harvey; Peter O'Toole
● Video: CBS / Fox

A Lion Is in the Streets*
US 1953   88m   Technicolor
Warner / Cagney Productions (William Cagney)

An itinerant confidence trickster becomes a defender of the people, is nominated for governor, and becomes corrupt.
Busy melodrama which came a bit soon after *All the King's Men*.
w Luther Davis, *novel* Adria Locke Langley d Raoul Walsh ph Harry Stradling m Franz Waxman pd Wiard Ihnen
James Cagney, Barbara Hale, Anne Francis, Warner Anderson, John McIntire, Jeanne Cagney, Lon Chaney Jnr, Frank McHugh, Larry Keating, Onslow Stevens, James Millican, Sara Haden
'A headlong and dynamic drama which offers Mr Cagney one of his most colourful and meaningful roles.'—*Bosley Crowther*

Lion of the Desert
US 1980   163m   Eastmancolor
Panavision
Falcon International (Moustapha Akkad)

In 1929 an Italian general in Libya withstands

the attacks of rebel leader Omar Mukhtar.
Whitewashed account of the activities of a patriarchal partisan who was hanged in 1931.
Of interest primarily to Arab zealots.
w H. A. L. Craig d Moustapha Akkad ph Jack Hildyard m Maurice Jarre pd Mario Garbuglia, Syd Cain

Anthony Quinn, Oliver Reed, Irene Papas, Raf Vallone, Rod Steiger, John Gielgud, Andrew Keir

Lipstick
US 1976   90m   Technicolor
Paramount / Dino de Laurentiis (Freddie Fields)

A girl is raped but gets nowhere in court until her sister lures the man to rape her too.
Franker but not very interesting extension of a fifties co-feature, with all the developments well telegraphed.
w David Rayfiel d Lamont Johnson ph Bill Butler m Michel Polnareff

Margaux Hemingway, Perry King, Anne Bancroft, Chris Sarandon, Mariel Hemingway, Robin Gammell
'One of *Lipstick*'s points is that voyeurism encourages senseless crime, but it unfortunately ignores its own lesson.'—*Marsha McCreadie, Films in Review*
● Video: CIC

The Liquidator*
GB 1965   104m   Metrocolor   Panavision
MGM / Leslie Elliott (Jon Pennington)

An ex-war hero is recruited by the secret service as an eliminator of security risks.
Fairly lively James Bond spoof which is never quite as funny as it imagines.
w Peter Yeldham, *novel* John Gardner d Jack Cardiff ph Ted Scaife m Lalo Schifrin

Rod Taylor, Trevor Howard, *David Tomlinson*, Jill St John, Wilfrid Hyde White, Derek Nimmo, Eric Sykes, Akim Tamiroff

Lisbon
US 1956   90m   Trucolor   Naturama
Republic (Ray Milland)

An international crook negotiates an Iron Curtain prisoner's release, but the man's wife has other ideas.
Glossy international intriguer with smart performances.
w John Tucker Battle d Ray Milland ph Jack Marta m Nelson Riddle

Ray Milland, *Claude Rains*, Maureen O'Hara, Yvonne Furneaux, Francis Lederer, Percy Marmont, Edward Chapman
● Video: BBC

The Lisbon Story
GB 1946   103m   bw

Spies in 1940 Lisbon rescue a French atom scientist. Flat filming of a musical show which kept Britons humming 'Pedro the Fisherman' throughout World War II. Patricia Burke, David Farrar, Walter Rilla, *Richard Tauber*, Austin Trevor, Harry Welchman. Written by Jack Whittingham, from the play by Harold Purcell and Harry Parr-Davies; directed by Paul Stein; for British National.

The List of Adrian Messenger**
US 1963   98m   bw
U-I / Joel (Edward Lewis)

An intelligence officer traps a mass murderer with a penchant for disguise.
Old-fashioned mystery thriller, as though Holmes and Watson were combating a modern Moriarty (and a rough-hewn production). The whole thing is camped up like an end-of-term treat, and as a further gimmick four guest stars allegedly appear under heavy disguise in cameo parts.

w Anthony Veiller, *novel* Philip MacDonald *d* John Huston *ph* Joe MacDonald *m* Jerry Goldsmith

George C. Scott, Kirk Douglas, Clive Brook, Dana Wynter, Jacques Roux, Walter Tony Huston, Herbert Marshall, Bernard Archard, Gladys Cooper; and Robert Mitchum, Frank Sinatra, Burt Lancaster, Tony Curtis
'A leisurely, underplayed thriller with some good performances and a gimmick which turns it into a guessing contest.'—*L.A. Times*

Listen Darling
US 1938   70m   bw
MGM (Jack Cummings)

Children try to find their widowed mother a new husband.
Slight domestic comedy chiefly notable for its young talent.

w Elaine Ryan, Anne Morrison Chapin, *story* Katherine Brush *d* Edwin L. Marin *ph* Charles Lawton Jnr *m* George Axt *md* George Stoll

Mary Astor, Judy Garland, Freddie Bartholomew, Walter Pidgeon, Alan Hale, Scotty Beckett, Charley Grapewin, Barnett Parker, Gene Lockhart
'Inauspicious start for the Garland-Bartholomew team . . . mediocre story hurts.'—*Variety*

Lisztomania
GB 1975   104m   colour   Panavision
Warner / VPS / Goodtimes (Roy Baird, David Puttnam)

The life of Liszt seen in terms of a modern pop performer.
The most excessive and obscene of all this director's controversial works, incapable of criticism on normal terms except that it seems unusually poor in production values.

wd Ken Russell *ph* Peter Suschitzky *md* John Forsyth

Roger Daltrey, Sara Kestelman, Paul Nicholas, Fiona Lewis, John Justin, Ringo Starr
Sample dialogue: 'Piss off, Brahms!'
'Ken Russell's first completely unmitigated catastrophe in several years . . . a welter of arbitrary gags, manic self-references and frantic exploitation-movie clichés.'—*Tony Rayns*
'Oscar Wilde once said "Each man kills the thing he loves", and the remark perfectly suits Ken Russell's film treatments of classical composers . . . he has bludgeoned into pulp some of the finest music civilization has produced.'—*Patrick Snyder*

'This gaudy compendium of camp, second-hand Freud and third-rate pastiche is like a bad song without end.'—*Sight and Sound*

Little Accident
US 1930   82m   bw

A man is about to marry again when he finds that his first wife is having his baby. Stretched-out comedy which fumbles its way along.
Douglas Fairbanks Jnr, Anita Page, Sally Blanc, Zasu Pitts, Joan Marsh, Roscoe Karns, Slim Summerville. Written by Gladys Lehman from the play by Floyd Dell and Thomas Mitchell; directed by William James Craft; for Universal. 'If anybody thinks 82 minutes is the proper time for this film, they should be made to sit through it twice.'—*Variety*

Little Accident
US 1939   65m   bw

A baby is passed from hand to hand after her father abandons her. Simple-minded comedy bearing little relation to the above: it's now a vehicle for the baby. Baby Sandy, Hugh Herbert, Richard Carlson, Florence Rice, Ernest Truex, Fritz Feld, Edgar Kennedy. Written by Paul Yawitz and Eve Greene; directed by Charles Lamont; for Universal. 'Elemental comedy for supporting attraction in nabes.'—*Variety*

Little Annie Rooney*
US 1925   99m (24 fps)   bw   silent
United Artists / Mary Pickford

A gangster's child in a New York slum rounds up the killer of her policeman father. Sentimental melodrama tailored for a 32-year-old star who liked playing kids. Of minor historical interest.

w Hope Loring, Louis D. Lighton *d* William Beaudine *ph* Charles Rosher, Hal Mohr *m* Joseph Plunkett

Mary Pickford, William Haines, Walter James, Gordon Griffith

The Little Ark
US 1971   86m   De Luxe   Panavision
Cinema Center / Robert B. Radnitz

Two war orphans and their pets, trapped in a flood, sail to safety in a houseboat.
Well-meaning, somewhat allegorical family film, too desultory to maintain interest and rather too frightening for children.

w Joanna Crawford, *novel* Jan de Hartog *d* James B. Clark *ph* Austin Dempster, Denys Coop *m* Fred Karlin

Theodore Bikel, Philip Frame, Genevieve Ambas

AAN: song, 'Come Follow Follow Me'

Little Big Horn*
US 1951   86m   bw
Lippert (Carl K. Hittleman)
GB title: *The Fighting Seventh*

A cavalry squad sets out to warn Custer about Little Big Horn, but all the men are massacred before Custer arrives.
Dour, impressive low-budget western.

wd Charles Marquis Warren *ph* Ernest Miller *m* Paul Dunlap

Lloyd Bridges, John Ireland, Marie Windsor, Reed Hadley, Hugh O'Brian, Wally Cassell, King Donovan

Little Big Man*
US 1970   147m   Technicolor   Panavision
Stockbridge / Hiller / Cinema Center (Stuart Millar)

An aged veteran of the old west recounts his life story—with elaborations.
A number of episodes varying from stark tragedy to satirical farce are framed for no good reason by the star in heavy disguise; the intention is hard to guess but there are goodies along the way.

w Calder Willingham, *novel* Thomas Berger *d* Arthur Penn *ph* Harry Stradling *m* John Hammond *pd* Dean Tavoularis

Dustin Hoffman, Martin Balsam, Faye Dunaway, *Chief Dan George*, Richard Mulligan, Jeff Corey
'A hip epic, with an amiable first hour. Then the massacres and messages take over.'—*New Yorker, 1976*
'A tangy and, I think, unique film with American verve, about some of the things American verve has done.'—*Stanley Kauffmann*

Little Big Shot
US 1935   80m   bw

A gangster's child is orphaned and cared for by two con men. Reasonably lively vehicle for a new child star who didn't last. Sybil Jason, Glenda Farrell, Robert Armstrong, Edward Everett Horton, Jack La Rue, J. Carrol Naish, Edgar Kennedy. Written by Jerry Wald, Julius J. Epstein, Robert Andrews; directed by Michael Curtiz; for Warners. 'Should pave the way handily for young Miss Jason's future.'—*Variety*

A Little Bit of Heaven
US 1940   87m   bw
Universal (Joe Pasternak)

A 12-year-old girl becomes a singing sensation but runs into family opposition.
Predictable vehicle for a young star being built up as a stop-gap Deanna Durbin.

w Daniel Taradash, Gertrude Purcell, Harold Goldman, *story* Grover Jones *d* Andrew Marton *ph* John Seitz *m* Charles Previn

Gloria Jean, Robert Stack, Hugh Herbert, C. Aubrey Smith, Stuart Erwin, Nan Grey, Eugene Pallette, Billy Gilbert, Butch and Buddy

Little Boy Lost
US 1953   95m   bw
Paramount (William Perlberg)

An American returns to Paris after the war to find his wife dead and his small son missing.
Rather dull tearjerker.

wd George Seaton, *novel* Marghanita Laski *ph* George Barnes *m* Victor Young

Bing Crosby, Claude Dauphin, Christian Fourcade, Gabrielle Dorziat, Nicole Maurey.

Little Caesar°°°°
US 1930   77m   bw
Warner

The rise and fall of a vicious gangster.
Its central character clearly modelled on Al Capone, this also has historical interest as vanguard of a spate of noisy gangster films. The star was forever identified with his role, and the film, though technically dated, moves fast enough to maintain interest over fifty years later.

w Francis Faragoh, Robert E. Lee, *novel* W. R. Burnett *d* Mervyn Le Roy *ph* Tony Gaudio *m* Erno Rapee

Edward G. Robinson, Douglas Fairbanks Jnr, Glenda Farrell, William Collier Jnr, Ralph Ince, George E. Stone, Thomas Jackson, Stanley Fields, Sidney Blackmer

'It has irony and grim humour and a real sense of excitement and its significance does not get in the way of the melodrama.'—*Richard Dana Skinner*

'One of the best gangster talkers yet turned out . . . a swell picture.'—*Variety*

AAN: Francis Faragoh, Robert E. Lee

● Video: Warner

The Little Colonel°°
US 1935   80m   bw (colour sequence)
TCF (B. G. De Sylva)

In a southern household after the Civil War, a little girl ends a family feud, plays Cupid to her sister, routs a few villains and mollifies her cantankerous grandfather.
First-class Temple vehicle, the first to boast an expensive production.

w William Conselman, *novel* Annie Fellows Johnson *d* David Butler *ph* Arthur Miller *md* Arthur Lange

Shirley Temple, Lionel Barrymore, Evelyn Venable, John Lodge, Bill Robinson, Hattie McDaniel, Sidney Blackmer

The Little Damozel
GB 1933   73m   bw

A gambler marries a young singer for a bribe, but falls in love with her. Lavender-tinted romance with music; notable as its star's first major role. Anna Neagle, James Rennie, Benita Hume, Athole Stewart, Alfred Drayton. Written by Donovan Pedelty, from the play by Monckton Hoffe; directed by Herbert Wilcox; for British and Dominions.

Little Darlings
US 1980   92m   Metrocolor

Teenage girls at a summer camp take bets on who will lose her virginity first. Crass and tasteless comedy with only prurient appeal. Tatum O'Neal, Kristy McNichol, Krista Errickson, Armande Assante. Written by Kimi Peck and Dalene Young; directed by Ronald F. Maxwell; for Stephen J. Friedman / Paramount.

● Video: CIC

The Little Drummer Girl°
US 1984   130m   Technicolor
Warner / Pan Arts (Robert L. Crawford)

An American actress in Britain is persuaded by Israeli agents to lose her Arab sympathies and spy for them.
Tediously protracted and unexciting version of a novel which was generally agreed to have been based on Vanessa Redgrave. Interesting for its quality look and surface style only: the intricate plotting of the Le'Carré manner is surely no longer fashionable.

w Loring Mandel, *novel* John Le Carré *d* George Roy Hill *ph* Wolfgang Treu *m* Dave Grusin *pd* Henry Bumstead *ed* William Reynolds

Diane Keaton, Yorgo Voyagis, Klaus Kinski, Sami Frey, Michael Cristofer, David Suchet, Eli Danker, Thorley Walters, Anna Massey

Little Egypt
US 1951   81m   Technicolor
Universal–International (Jack Gross)
GB title: *Chicago Masquerade*

An American girl poses as an Egyptian princess at the Chicago World's Fair. Sluggish turn-of-the-century romantic melodrama based on a factual swindle involving a phoney Nile reclamation project.

w Oscar Brodney, Doris Gilbert *d* Frederick de Cordova *ph* Russell Metty *md* Joseph Gershenson

Rhonda Fleming, Mark Stevens, Nancy Guild, Charles Drake, Tom D'Andrea, Minor Watson, Steve Geray

Little Fauss and Big Halsy
US 1970   99m   Movielab   Panavision
Paramount / Alfran / Furie (Albert S. Ruddy)

Two motor cycle track racers team up and have violent adventures round the country. Rather pointless capers in the wake of *Easy Rider*, neither interesting nor well done.

w Charles Eastman *d* Sidney J. Furie *ph* Ralph Woolsey

Robert Redford, Michael J. Pollard, *Noah Beery Jnr*, Lauren Hutton

'A sort of *Batman and Robin* on wheels.'—*Rex Reed*

The Little Foxes°°°
US 1941   116m   bw
Samuel Goldwyn

A family of schemers in post-Civil War days will stop at nothing to outwit each other. Superb film of a brilliant play; excellent to look at and listen to, with a compelling narrative line and memorable characters.

w *Lillian Hellman*, from her play *d* William Wyler *ph* Gregg Toland *m* Meredith Willson

Bette Davis, Herbert Marshall, Teresa Wright, Richard Carlson, *Charles Dingle, Dan Duryea, Carl Benton Reid, Patricia Collinge*, Jessica Grayson, Russell Hicks

HORACE GIDDENS (Herbert Marshall): 'Maybe it's easy for the dying to be honest. I'm sick of you, sick of this house, sick of my unhappy life with you. I'm sick of your brothers and their dirty tricks to make a dime. There must be better ways of getting rich than building sweatshops and pounding the bones of the town to make dividends for you to spend. You'll wreck the town, you and your brothers. You'll wreck the country, you and your kind, if they let you. But not me, I'll die my own way, and I'll do it without making the world any worse. I leave that to you.'

'One of the really beautiful jobs in the whole range of movie making.'—*Otis Ferguson*

'No one knows better than Wyler when to shift the camera's point of view, when to cut, or how to relate the characters in one shot to those in the next . . . you never have to wonder where you are in a Wyler picture.'—*Arthur Knight*

AAN: best picture; Lillian Hellman; William Wyler; Meredith Willson; Bette Davis; Teresa Wright; Patricia Collinge

Little Friend
GB 1934   85m   bw

A girl is driven to attempt suicide by her parents' proposed divorce. Fairly well written but rather stilted domestic drama which maintained a small reputation. Nova Pilbeam, Matheson Lang, Lydia Sherwood, Arthur Margetson, Allan Aynesworth, Jean Cadell, Jimmy Hanley. Written by Margaret Kennedy, Christopher Isherwood and Berthold Viertel, from the novel by Ernst Lothar; directed by Berthold Viertel; for Gaumont.

The Little Giant
US 1933   74m   bw
Warner

At the end of Prohibition, a beer baron moves to California and tries to break into society. Disappointingly unfunny gangster comedy which never really gets going.

w Robert Lord, Wilson Mizner *d* Roy del Ruth *ph* Sid Hickox *md* Leo F. Forbstein

Edward G. Robinson, Mary Astor, Helen Vinson, Kenneth Thompson, Russell Hopton, Donald Dillaway

'It makes Robinson a comedy character surrounded by semi-travesty and the fans are likely to resent it.'—*Variety*

Little Giant
US 1946   91m   bw
Universal (Joseph Gershenson)
GB title: *On the Carpet*

Misadventures of a vacuum cleaner salesman. Curious, unsatisfactory Abbott and Costello comedy in which the boys play separate characters instead of working as a team. They should have waited for a better script before experimenting.

w Paul Jarrico, Richard Collins, Walter de Leon *d* William A. Seiter *ph* Charles van Enger *m* Edgar Fairchild

Bud Abbott, Lou Costello, Brenda Joyce, George Cleveland, Elena Verdugo

The Little Girl Who Lives Down the Lane

US / Canada / France 1976   94m   colour
Zev Braun / ICL / Filmedis-Filmel (Zev Braun)

A 13-year-old girl, when her father dies, is discovered to be keeping her mother's corpse in the cellar, and doesn't stop at more murders to keep her secret.
Tasteless piece of grand guignol, badly directed and over-acted.

w Laird Koenig, from his novel d Nicolas Gessner ph Pene Verzier m Christian Gaubert

Jodie Foster, Alexis Smith, Martin Sheen, Scott Jacoby
† Originally intended as a TV movie.

The Little Hut

US 1957   90m   Eastmancolor
MGM / Herbson S A (F. Hugh Herbert, Mark Robson)

A man, his wife and her lover are shipwrecked on a desert island.
Sophisticated French farce which falls resoundingly flat in this bowdlerized Hollywood version in bilious colour, fatally compromising itself at the beginning with a 'realistic' London prologue.

w F. Hugh Herbert, play André Roussin and Nancy Mitford d Mark Robson ph Frederick A. Young m Robert Farnon ad Elliot Scott

Stewart Granger, David Niven, Ava Gardner, Walter Chiari, Finlay Currie, Jean Cadell

Little Johnny Jones

US 1930   73m   bw

An American jockey wins the Derby. Mild comedy with music from the old George M. Cohan play. Eddie Buzzell, Alice Day, Edna Murphy, Robert Edeson. Written by Adelaide Heilbron and Eddie Buzzell; directed by Mervyn Le Roy; for First National. 'Familiar formula but done nicely.'—*Variety*

Little Lord Fauntleroy*

US 1921   11m (24 fps)   bw   silent
United Artists / Mary Pickford

An American boy who lives with his widowed mother discovers he is heir to an English dukedom.
Over-upholstered sentimental extravaganza tailored for a star in her twenties playing both young Cedric and his mother, a curious double. One can now only wonder at the immense appeal this film had in its own time; but that is not to diminish the vitality of its star.

w Bernard McConville, novel Frances Hodgson Burnett d Jack Pickford, Alfred E. Green ph Charles Rosher m Louis F. Gottschalk

Mary Pickford, Claude Gillingwater, Kate Price, James A. Marcus, Emmet King

Little Lord Fauntleroy*

US 1936   98m   bw
David O. Selznick

A sound remake which did surprisingly well at the box office and is still very watchable.

w Richard Schayer, Hugh Walpole, David O. Selznick d John Cromwell m Max Steiner
Freddie Bartholomew, C. Aubrey Smith, Mickey Rooney, Dolores Costello, Jessie Ralph, Guy Kibbee
† A TV movie version appeared in 1980, with Ricky Schroder and Alec Guinness.

Little Man, What Now?*

US 1934   95m   bw
Universal

Problems of Germany in the grip of unemployment.
One of the studio's several 'sequels' to *All Quiet on the Western Front*, poignant at the time but now very dated.

w William Anthony McGuire, novel Hans Fallada d Frank Borzage ph Norbert Brodine

Margaret Sullavan, Douglass Montgomery, Alan Hale, Muriel Kirkland, Alan Mowbray, Mae Marsh
'Human, homely and romantic . . . should get ample b.o. attention.'—*Variety*

Little Men

US 1935   77m   bw

Joe and her professor run a school for boys. Slapdash sequel to *Little Women*; not an ambitious production. Ralph Morgan, Erin O'Brien-Moore, Junior Durkin, Cora Sue Collins, Frankie Darro, Dickie Moore. Written by Gertrude Orr from the novel by Louisa M. Alcott; directed by Phil Rosen; for Mascot. 'Goes overboard on pathos . . . tears flow over the most insignificant matters.'—*Variety*

The Little Minister

US 1934   110m   bw
RKO (Pandro S. Berman)

In 1840 Scotland, the gypsy girl with whom the new pastor falls unsuitably in love is really the local earl's wayward daughter.
Tedious film version of a cloyingly whimsical play.

w Jane Murfin, Sarah Y. Mason, Victor Heerman, play J. M. Barrie d Richard Wallace ph Henry Gerrard m Max Steiner
Katharine Hepburn, John Beal, Alan Hale, Donald Crisp, Lumsden Hare, Andy Clyde, Beryl Mercer, Dorothy Stickney, Frank Conroy, Reginald Denny
'Fine production of an old favourite.'—*Variety*
'Although dear Babbie's elfin whimsies are likely to cause teeth-gnashing among unsympathetic moderns, Miss Hepburn plays the part with likeable sprightliness and charm.'—*André Sennwald, New York Times*

Little Miss Broadway

US 1938   70m   bw
TCF (David Hempstead)

A small girl is adopted by the owner of a hotel for vaudeville artistes.
One of the child star's more casual vehicles, but quite pleasing.

w Harry Tugend, Jack Yellen d Irving Cummings ph Arthur Miller md Louis Silvers

Shirley Temple, George Murphy, Jimmy Durante, Edna May Oliver, Phyllis Brooks, George Barbier, Edward Ellis, Jane Darwell, El Brendel, Donald Meek, Claude Gillingwater, Russell Hicks
'It can't be old age, but it does look like weariness.'—*New York Times*
'Shirley is better than her new vehicle, which in turn is better than her last one.'—*Variety*

Little Miss Marker**

US 1934   80m   bw
Paramount (B. P. Schulberg)
GB title: *The Girl in Pawn*

A cynical racetrack gambler is forced to adopt a little girl, who not only softens him but saves him from his enemies.
The twin appeals of Temple (a new hot property) and Runyon made this a big hit of its time.

w William R. Lipman, Sam Hellman, Gladys Lehman, story Damon Runyon d Alexander Hall ph Alfred Gilks songs Leo Robin, Ralph Rainger

Shirley Temple, Adolphe Menjou, Dorothy Dell, Charles Bickford, Lynne Overman, Frank McGlynn Snr, Willie Best
'A good response to that element which claims there is nothing good in pictures. Clean, funny, with thrills and heart appeal all nicely blended.'—*Variety*
'No one can deny that the infant was a trouper: she delivers her lines with a killer instinct.'—*Pauline Kael, 70s*
† Remade as *Sorrowful Jones* (qv).
● *Video: CIC*

Little Miss Marker

US 1980   103m   Technicolor
Universal (Jennings Lang)

Mainly glutinous remake of the above, with acerbic asides from the star.

wd Walter Bernstein ph Philip Lathrop m Henry Mancini

Walter Matthau, Julie Andrews, Tony Curtis, Bob Newhart, Sara Stimson, Lee Grant, Brian Dennehy

Little Murders

US 1971   108m   De Luxe
TCF / Brodsky–Gould (Jack Brodsky)

A young photographer rises above all the urban horror of New York life, but when his wife is killed by a sniper he takes to violence.
This adaptation of an ultrablack comedy would have worked better as a comic strip, for its characters are satirical puppets, and when played by human beings the whole thing seems violently silly.

w Jules Feiffer, from his play d Alan Arkin ph Gordon Willis m Fred Kaz

Elliot Gould, Marcia Rodd, Elizabeth Wilson, Vincent Gardenia, Alan Arkin

Little Nellie Kelly*
US 1940 100m bw
MGM (Arthur Freed)

The daughter of a New York Irish cop makes good on the stage.
Sentimental nostalgic vehicle for young Judy Garland, who plays both wife and daughter and sings plenty of standard melodies.

w Jack McGowan, *play* George M. Cohan
d Norman Taurog *songs* George M. Cohan, Roger Edens, Lew Brown, Arthur Freed
ph Ray June

Judy Garland, George Murphy, Charles Winninger, Douglas McPhail, Arthur Shields, Forrester Harvey

A Little Night Music*
Austria / West Germany 1977 125m
  Eastmancolor
Sascha Film / S & T (Elliott Kastner)

In Vienna at the turn of the century, a middle-aged lawyer, frustrated by the virginity of his young wife, turns to an old actress flame.
Fumbled version of a rather splendid Broadway musical based on Ingmar Bergman's *Smiles of a Summer Night*. The locale is changed, several of the songs are cut, and the leads are miscast.

m Hugh Wheeler, from his stage play
d Harold Prince ph Arthur Ibbetson
m / ly Stephen Sondheim

Elizabeth Taylor, Diana Rigg, Len Cariou, Lesley-Anne Down, Hermione Gingold, Christopher Guard, Laurence Guittard

● Video: Guild

Little Old New York
US 1940 100m bw
TCF (Raymond Griffith)

The story of Robert Fulton and his invention of the steamboat.
Romantic hokum with a veneer of fact; good production.

w Harry Tugend, *play* Rida Johnson Young
d Henry King ph Leon Shamroy m Alfred Newman

Alice Faye, Richard Greene, Fred MacMurray, Henry Stephenson, Brenda Joyce, Andy Devine, Fritz Feld, Ward Bond

The Little Prince
US 1974 89m Technicolor
Paramount / Stanley Donen

A small boy leaves the asteroid he rules to learn of life on earth.
A whimsical bestseller turns into an arch musical which falls over itself early on and never recovers; in any case it fatally lacks the common touch, though it has pleasing moments.

w Alan Jay Lerner, *novel* Antoine de St-Exupery d Stanley Donen ph Christopher Challis m / ly Frederick Loewe, Alan Jay Lerner pd John Barry

Richard Kiley, Steven Warner, *Bob Fosse*, Gene Wilder, Joss Ackland, Clive Revill, Victor Spinetti, Graham Crowden

'Handsome production cannot obscure limited artistic achievement.'—*Variety*
† Kiley replaced Frank Sinatra, who backed out.

AAN: title song; musical adaptation (Angela Morley, Douglas Gamley)

The Little Princess**
US 1939 93m Technicolor
TCF (Gene Markey)

In Victorian London a little girl is left at a harsh school when her father goes abroad.
One of the child star's plushest vehicles, a charming early colour film complete with dream sequence and happy ending.

w Ethel Hill, Walter Ferris, *novel* Frances Hodgson Burnett d Walter Lang ph Arthur Miller, William Skall md Louis Silvers

Shirley Temple, Richard Greene, Anita Louise, Ian Hunter, Cesar Romero, Arthur Treacher, Mary Nash, Sybil Jason, Miles Mander, Marcia Mae Jones, Beryl Mercer, E. E. Clive

A Little Romance
US 1979 108m Technicolor
Warner / Orion (Patrick Kelley)

A French teenager elopes with an American girl, encouraged by a garrulous old pickpocket.
Treacly juvenile romance enriched by in-jokes and an enjoyably over-the-top star performance.

w Allan Burns, *novel* Patrick Cauvin
d George Roy Hill ph Pierre William Glenn
,m Georges Delerue pd Henry Bumstead

Laurence Olivier, Diane Lane, Thelonious Bernard, Arthur Hill, Sally Kellerman, Broderick Crawford, David Dukes

A Little Sex
US 1982 94m Technicolor
Universal / MTM (Robert de Laurentiis, Bruce Paltrow)

A young husband has a wandering eye.
Very thin comedy drama more suitable for TV if it were a little less outspoken.

w Robert de Laurentiis d Bruce Paltrow
ph Ralf D. Bode m Georges Delerue

Tim Matheson, Kate Capshaw, Edward Herrmann, John Glover

Little Tough Guy
US 1938 83m bw

A New York slum boy gets involved with a gang and is sent to reform school. A development of the Dead End Kids, with attitudes not yet crystallized, the overall tone being heavy. Billy Halop, Helen Parrish, Marjorie Main, Huntz Hall, Gabriel Dell, Bernard Punsley, Frankie Searl, Hally Chester. Written by Gilson Brown and Brenda Weisburg; directed by Harold Young; for Universal.

Little Tough Guys in Society
US 1938 75m bw

A society matron invites slum boys to her mansion as a corrective for her stuffy son. The cast makes it plain that the Dead End Kids / Little Tough Guys are now headed for comedy, the reason being that their 'serious' films were thought to set a bad example. Mary Boland, Mischa Auer, Edward Everett Horton, Helen Parrish, Jackie Searl, Frankie Thomas, Billy Benedict, Hally Chester, David Gorcey. Written by Edward Eliscu and Mortimer Offner; directed by Erle C. Kenton; for Universal.

'They leap from the book and live!'
Little Women***
US 1933 115m bw
RKO (David O. Selznick, Merian C. Cooper, Kenneth MacGowan)

The growing up of four sisters in pre-Civil War America.
Charming 'big picture' of its day, with excellent production and performances.

w Sarah Y. Mason, Victor Heerman, *novel* Louisa May Alcott d George Cukor
ph Henry Gerrard m Max Steiner

Katharine Hepburn, Paul Lukas, Joan Bennett, Frances Dee, Jean Parker, *Spring Byington*, Edna May Oliver, Douglass Montgomery, Henry Stephenson, Samuel S. Hinds, John Lodge, Nydia Westman

  'If to put a book on the screen with all the effectiveness that sympathy and good taste and careful artifice can devise is to make a fine motion picture, then *Little Women* is a fine picture.'—*James Shelley Hamilton*
  'One of the most satisfactory pictures I have ever seen.'—*E. V. Lucas, Punch*
  'A reminder that emotions and vitality and truth can be evoked from lavender and lace as well as from machine guns and precision dances.'—*Thornton Delehanty, New York Post*

AA: script
AAN: best picture; George Cukor

Little Women*
US 1949 122m Technicolor
MGM (Mervyn Le Roy)

Syrupy Christmas-card remake, notably lacking the light touch.

w Andrew Solt, Sarah Y. Mason, Victor Heerman d Mervyn Le Roy ph Robert Planck, Charles Schoenbaum m Adolph Deutsch (after Max Steiner)

June Allyson, Elizabeth Taylor, Peter Lawford, Margaret O'Brien, Janet Leigh, Mary Astor

  'It will raise a smile and draw a tear from the sentimental.'—*MFB*

AAN: cinematography

The Little World of Don Camillo*
France / Italy 1952 106m bw
Rizzoli-Amato-Francinex (Giuseppe Amato)

In a small Italian village the parish priest and the communist mayor are in a constant state of amiable feud.

Slightly lethargic character comedy with a mild message for its times, popular enough to warrant several sequels.

w Julien Duvivier, René Barjavel, *novel* Giovanni Guareschi d Julien Duvivier ph Nicolas Hayer m Alessandro Cicognini

Fernandel, Gino Cervi, Sylvie, Manara, Vera Talqui, Franco Interlenghi

'Cute and cosy.'—*MFB*

The Littlest Rebel*
US 1935 70m bw
TCF (B. G. De Sylva)

A small southern girl persuades President Lincoln to release her father.
Charming, archetypal early Temple vehicle, very well produced.

w Edwin Burke, *play* Edward Peple d David Butler ph John Seitz m Cyril Mockridge

Shirley Temple, John Boles, Jack Holt, Karen Morley, *Bill Robinson*, Guinn Williams, Willie Best, Frank McGlynn Snr

'Shirley Temple as the public likes her . . . which means money.'—*Variety*

Live a Little, Steal a Lot
US 1974 102m CFI
American International (Dominick Galate)

Jewel thieves go from success to success, but the police finally force them to strike a bargain and return the gems.
Elaborate but rather unattractive caper story based on the exploits of two real criminals.

w E. Arthur Kuhn d Marvin Chomsky ph Michael Hugo m Philip Lambro

Robert Conrad, Don Stroud, Donna Mills, Robyn Miller, Luther Adler, Paul Stewart

Live and Let Die*
GB 1973 121m Eastmancolor
UA / Eon (Harry Saltzman)

James Bond chases a black master criminal and becomes involved in West Indian Voodoo.
Standard tongue-in-cheek spy adventure with a new lightweight star and an air of *déjà vu*. Professional standards high.

w Tom Mankiewicz, *novel* Ian Fleming d Guy Hamilton ph Ted Moore m George Martin *titles* Maurice Binder

Roger Moore, Yaphet Kotto, Jane Seymour, Clifton James, David Hedison, Bernard Lee, Lois Maxwell

'Plot lines have descended further to the level of the old Saturday afternoon serial, and the treatment is more than ever like a cartoon.'—*Variety*

'A Bond movie is not made. It is packaged. Like an Almond Joy. So much coconut to this much chocolate and a dash of raisins.'—*Joseph Gelmis*

AAN: title song (m / ly Paul and Linda McCartney)
● *Video:* Warner

Live for Life
France / Italy 1967 130m Eastmancolor
UA / Ariane / Vides
original title: *Vivre pour Vivre*

A news reporter forsakes his wife for a fashion model.
Interminable and unoriginal romantic drama against Sunday supplement backgounds.

w Pierre Uytterhoeven, Claude Lelouch d, ph Claude Lelouch m Francis Lai

Yves Montand, Candice Bergen, Annie Forardot, Irene Tunc

'The overall effect is of *Gone with the Wind* remade by Jacopetti.'—*New Yorker*

The Live Ghost
US 1934 20m bw

Two reluctant sailors think they have murdered one of their mates. Somewhat unyielding material for Stan and Ollie, but still funnier than any of their rivals at the time. Laurel and Hardy, Walter Long, Arthur Housman. Written by H. M. Walker; directed by Charles Rogers; for Hal Roach.

Live, Love and Learn
US 1937 78m bw
MGM (Harry Rapf)

A bohemian painter is tamed by marriage. Tiresome romantic trifle.

w Charles Brackett, Cyril Hume, Richard Maibaum d George Fitzmaurice ph Ray June m Edward Ward

Robert Montgomery, Rosalind Russell, Robert Benchley, Helen Vinson, Mickey Rooney, Monty Woolley, E. E. Clive, Maude Eburne

'Mildly entertaining mixture of slapstick and drama around the theme of art vs material success.'—*Variety*

Live Now, Pay Later
GB 1962 104m bw
(Regal) Woodlands / Jay Lewis (Jack Hanbury)

A credit store salesman is himself heavily in debt, and his private life is in ruins; but even after a chapter of unexpected and tragic events he remains irrepressibly optimistic.
A satirical farce melodrama which lets fly in too many directions at once and has a cumulatively cheerless effect despite funny moments.

w Jack Trevor Story d Jay Lewis ph Jack Hildyard m Ron Grainer

Ian Hendry, John Gregson, June Ritchie, Geoffrey Keen, Liz Fraser

'1750 to 1! Always outnumbered! Never outfought!'

Lives of a Bengal Lancer**
US 1934 119m bw
Paramount (Louis D. Lighton)

Adventures on the North-West Frontier. British army heroics are here taken rather solemnly, but the film is efficient and fondly remembered.

w Waldemar Young, John F. Balderston, Achmed Abdullah, Grover Jones, William Slavens McNut, *book* Francis Yeats-Brown d Henry Hathaway ph Charles Lang m Milan Roder

Gary Cooper, *Franchot Tone, Richard Cromwell, Sir Guy Standing*, C. Aubrey Smith, Monte Blue, Kathleen Burke, Colin Tapley, *Douglass Dumbrille*, Akim Tamiroff, Noble Johnson

'The best army picture ever made.'—*Daily Telegraph*

AAN: best picture; script; Henry Hathaway

The Living Corpse*
Germany / USSR / 1928 108m (24 fps) bw silent
Prometheus / Mezhrabpomfilm
original title: *Zhivoi Trup*

An unhappy husband, whose wife loves another, tries all manner of means to give her a divorce. Refused by both church and state, he kills himself.
Heavy-going dramatic tract, photographed and directed with stirring style.

w B. Gusman, Anatoly Marienhof, *play* Leo Tolstoy d Fedor Ozep ph Anatoly Golovnya

Vsevolod Pudovkin, Maria Jacobini, V. Garden, Gustav Diessl

'One of the really few achievements of the Russian industry: a picture so gripping that it will hold any audience.'—*Variety*

The Living Desert**
US 1953 72m Technicolor
Walt Disney (James Algar)

A light-hearted documentary showing the animals and insects which live in American desert areas. The aim is entertainment and Disney is not above faking, i.e. the famous sequence in which scorpions appear to do a square dance, but on its level the thing is brilliantly done.

w James Algar, Winston Hibler, Ted Sears d James Algar ph N. Paul Kenworthy Jnr, Robert H. Grandall m Paul Smith *special processes* Ub Iwerks

'The film has the same cosy anthropomorphism as a Disney cartoon and its facetious commentary and vulgar music score are typical of others in the series.'—*Georges Sadoul*

† The other 'True Life Adventures' were: *Seal Island* 49 (3 reels), *Beaver Valley* 50 (3 reels), *Nature's Half Acre* 51 (3 reels), *Water Birds* 52 (3 reels), *Prowlers of the Everglades* 53 (3 reels), *The Vanishing Prairie* 54, *The African Lion* 55, *Secrets of Life* 56, *White Wilderness* 58, *Jungle Cat* 60.

Living Free
GB 1972 92m colour
Columbia / Open Road / High Road (Paul Radin)

On the death of Elsa the lioness, George and Joy Adamson capture her three cubs and

1750 to 1!

Always out-numbered!
Never out-fought! These
are the Bengal Lancers . . .
heroes all . . . guarding each
other's lives, sharing each
other's tortures, fighting
each other's battles . . . !

Set in the spectacle of
mystic India with its glittering mosques, oriental
palaces, weird music,
bronzed nautch dancers
Adolph Zukor presents

"The LIVES OF A BENGAL LANCER"

with

**GARY COOPER
FRANCHOT TONE
RICHARD CROMWELL
SIR GUY STANDING**
C. AUBREY SMITH · MONTE BLUE
and KATHLEEN BURKE
A Paramount Picture
Directed by Henry Hathaway

THE LIVES OF A BENGAL LANCER. A film remembered vividly by everybody of a certain age . . . perhaps because the title took a lot of explaining.

transfer them for their own safety to Serengeti.
Sloppy sequel to *Born Free*, depending very heavily on the appeal of the cubs.

w Maurice Kaufman d Jack Couffer
ph Wolfgang Suschitzky m Sol Kaplan

Susan Hampshire, Nigel Davenport, Geoffrey Keen

The Living Idol
Mexico / US 1956   100m   Eastmancolor
Cinemascope
MGM (Albert Lewin)

A Mexican girl becomes possessed by the spirit of the jaguar to whom local maidens were once sacrificed.
Pretentious but rather enjoyable highbrow hokum of the heady kind expected from this producer.

wd Albert Lewin ph Jack Hildyard
m Rodolpho Halffter

James Robertson Justice, Steve Forrest, Liliane Montevecchi

Living in a Big Way
US 1947   103m   bw
MGM (Pandro S. Berman)

A demobbed GI finds he can't get on with his rich selfish wife and opens up a charity home for the families of war casualties.
Odd mixture of comedy, drama and a few songs and dances, not forgetting a message or two. It mostly falls flat on its face.

w Gregory La Cava, Irving Ravetch
d Gregory La Cava ph Harold Rosson
m Lennie Hayton

Gene Kelly, Marie McDonald, Charles Winninger, Phyllis Thaxter, Spring Byington, Clinton Sundberg

Living It Up*
US 1954   95m   Technicolor
Paramount / Hal B. Wallis (Paul Jones)

A suspected victim of radium poisoning is played up by the press into a national hero.
Remake of *Nothing Sacred* with Lewis as Carole Lombard; deserves a mark for cheek.

w Jack Rose, Mel Shavelson d Norman Taurog ph Daniel Fapp

Dean Martin, Jerry Lewis, Janet Leigh, Edward Arnold, Fred Clark, Sheree North, Sig Rumann

Living on Velvet*
US 1935   77m   bw
Warner (Edward Chodorov)

A happy-go-lucky aviator changes his life style when he narrowly escapes death in a crash.
Reasonably interesting 'serious' drama of its period.

w Jerry Wald, Julius Epstein d Frank Borzage ph Sid Hickox md Leo F. Forbstein

George Brent, Kay Francis, Warren William, Helen Lowell, Henry O'Neill, Samuel S. Hinds, Russell Hicks, Edgar Kennedy

'Three good names but doubtful of pulling above ordinary business.'—*Variety*

Lizzie
US 1957 81m bw
MGM / Bryna (Jerry Bresler)

Murder and rape turn a girl into a triple personality.
Preposterous cash-in on *The Three Faces of Eve*, too silly to be even funny.

w Mel Dinelli, *novel* The Bird's Nest by Shirley Jackson d Hugo Haas ph Paul Ivano m Leith Stevens

Eleanor Parker, Richard Boone, Joan Blondell, Hugo Haas
'Ruddy peculiar.'—*MFB*

Lloyd's of London**
US 1936 115m bw
TCF (Kenneth MacGowan)

A young messenger boy in the 18th century grows up to found a great insurance company.
Thoroughly well mounted, if unconvincing and slightly boring, historical charade in which the Prince of Wales, Lord Nelson, Dr Johnson and other personages make guest appearances. An archetypal prestige film of its time which also turned out to be box office.

w Ernest Pascal, Walter Ferris, *book* Curtis Kenyon d Henry King ph Bert Glennon md Louis Silvers

Tyrone Power, Madeleine Carroll, George Sanders, Freddie Bartholomew, C. Aubrey Smith, Guy Standing, Virginia Field, Montagu Love, Gavin Muir, Miles Mander, Una O'Connor, E. E. Clive
'Fictional history with fine production but weak from marquee standpoint . . . basically it's the story of the beginning and rise of an insurance company, and how can average audiences be asked to get excited about that?'—*Variety*
'The name of England is so freely on the characters' lips that we recognize at once an American picture. These people live, make love, bear children all from the most patriotic motives, and it's all rather like London in coronation week.'—*Graham Greene*

Local Hero**
GB 1983 111m colour
Enigma / Goldcrest (David Puttnam)

A young American executive meets various difficulties when he is sent to a Scottish coastal village to arrange for the building of a new refinery.
Reminiscent of various Ealing comedies, especially *Whisky Galore* and *The Maggie*, this ambitious comedy is really not funny enough for its great length.

w,d Bill Forsyth ph Chris Menges m Mark Knopfler

Burt Lancaster, Peter Riegert, *Denis Lawson*, Peter Capaldi, Fulton Mackay, Jenny Seagrove
'Little in the way of obvious commercial hooks . . . dominated by a constantly surprising sense of whimsicality.'—*Variety*

BFA: direction
● *Video: Thorn EMI*

'The restoration comedy about what cannot be restored!'

Lock Up Your Daughters
GB 1969 103m Technicolor
Columbia / Domino (David Deutsch)

In 18th-century London an aristocratic rake and various lower orders are all in search of female companionship and get their wires crossed.
Noisy, vulgar, ill-acted version (without music) of a successful musical based on two old theatrical warhorses.

w Keith Waterhouse, Willis Hall, *play* Bernard Miles based on Rape upon Rape by Henry Fielding and The Relapse by John Vanbrugh d Peter Coe ph Peter Suschitzky m Ron Grainer pd Tony Woollard

Christopher Plummer, Roy Kinnear, Georgia Brown, Susannah York, Glynis Johns, Ian Bannen, Tom Bell, Elaine Taylor, Jim Dale, Kathleen Harrison, Roy Dotrice, Vanessa Howard, Fenella Fielding, Peter Bayliss, *Richard Wordsworth*, Peter Bull, Fred Emney
'Subtlety is neither required nor displayed.'—*Jack Ibberson*

The Locked Door
US 1929 70m bw

Husband and wife try to save each other by assuming guilt for a murder. Rather static filmed play. Barbara Stanwyck, Rod la Rocque, William Boyd, Betty Bronson, Zasu Pitts, Mack Swain. Written by C. Gardner Sullivan from the play The Sign on the Door by Channing Pollock; directed by George Fitzmaurice; for United Artists.

The Locket
US 1946 85m bw
RKO

A *femme fatale* is bent on destroying men, and eventually we discover why.
Dark, confusing melodrama very typical of the immediate post-war years; it has little to say but says it dourly, even achieving flashbacks within flashbacks within flashbacks.

w Sheridan Gibney d John Brahm ph Nicholas Musuraca m Roy Webb

Laraine Day, Robert Mitchum, Brian Aherne, Gene Raymond, Ricardo Cortez

The Lodger***
GB 1926 84m approx (24 fps) bw silent
Gainsborough (Michael Balcon)
Subtitle: *A Story of the London Fog*

A modern version of the novel about a stranger who is (in this case) wrongly thought to be Jack the Ripper.
The first true Hitchcock film, full of his familiar dramatic visual touches. Oddly enough it was followed by three years during which he seemed to forget them.

w Eliot Stannard, Alfred Hitchcock, *novel* Mrs Belloc Lowndes d Alfred Hitchcock ph Baron Ventimiglia ed Ivor Montagu

Ivor Novello, June, Marie Ault, Arthur Chesney, Malcolm Keen
'It was the first time I exercised my style . . . you might almost say it was my first picture.'— *Alfred Hitchcock, 1966*

The Lodger*
GB 1932 85m bw
Twickenham (Julius Hagen)
US title: *The Phantom Fiend*

The upstairs lodger is suspected of being Jack the Ripper.
Modernized version of a story already tackled by Hitchcock as a silent and to be done again in costume in 1944. Not bad, for a minor British film of the time.

w Ivor Novello, Miles Mander, Paul Rotha, H. Fowler Mear, *novel* Mrs Belloc Lowndes d Maurice Elvey ph Stanley Blythe, Basil Emmott

Ivor Novello, Elizabeth Allan, A. W. Baskcomb, Jack Hawkins, Barbara Everest, Peter Gawthorne, Kynaston Reeves
'They can make pictures in England . . . the only point for discussion is why they do not make them oftener.'—*Variety*

The Lodger*
US 1944 84m bw
TCF (Robert Bassler)

1880s version of the above in which the lodger *is* Jack the Ripper.
Nicely mounted apart from some anachronisms, but a little dull.

w Barre Lyndon d John Brahm ph Lucien Ballard m Hugo Friedhofer

Laird Cregar, Merle Oberon, George Sanders, Cedric Hardwicke, Sara Allgood, Aubrey Mather, Queenie Leonard, Helena Pickard, Lumsden Hare, Frederick Worlock

Logan's Run*
US 1976 118m Metrocolor Todd-AO
MGM (Saul David)

In the future, people try to escape from a society which dooms everyone to death at thirty.
Interesting and quite exciting fantasy melodrama which mercifully moves instead of preaching.

w David Zelag Goodman, *novel* William F. Nolan d Michael Anderson ph Ernest Laszlo m Jerry Goldsmith pd Dale Hennesy

Michael York, Richard Jordan, Jenny Agutter, Roscoe Lee Browne, Farrah Fawcett-Majors, Peter Ustinov, Michael Anderson Jnr
'A science fiction film made by people who don't understand science fiction for the amusement of people who don't care one way or the other.'—*S. Frank, L. A. Panorama*
'It puts the future back two thousand years.'—*Benny Green, Punch*

AAN: Ernest Laszlo
● *Video: MGM / UA*

Lola*

France / Italy 1960 91m bw Franscope
Rome-Paris / Euro-International

A cabaret dancer in Nantes chooses between
three men.
A slight romance which was much admired for
its decoration and visual style, which reminded
many of Max Ophuls.

wd Jacques Demy *ph* Raoul Coutard
m Michel Legrand

Anouk Aimée, Jacques Harden, Marc Michel,
Elina Labourdette

'Like an adolescent's dream of romance,
formed from old movies.'—*Pauline Kael, 70s*

Lola Montes*

France / Germany 1955 140m
Eastmancolor Cinemascope
Gamma / Florida / Oska

The life of the famous courtesan and her
romance with the King of Bavaria, told in
diverting fragments by a circus ringmaster.
An elaborate, expensive and trickily presented
historical charade which confused the public
and bankrupted its production company; but
the various shorter versions released didn't
help.

w Max Ophuls, Annette Wademant, Franz
Geiger, *novel* Cécil Saint-Laurent *d* Max
Ophuls *ph* Christian Matras *m* Georges
Auric *ad* Jean d'Aubonne, Willy Schatz

Martine Carol, Anton Walbrook, Peter
Ustinov, Ivan Desny, Oskar Werner, Will
Quadflieg

'If you want to know what form can really
do for content, rush along.'—*Derek Malcolm,
The Guardian, 1978*

Lolita**

GB 1962 152m bw
MGM / Seven Arts / AA / Anya / Transworld
(James B. Harris)

A middle-aged lecturer falls for a 14-year-old
girl and marries her mother to be near her.
Fitfully amusing but slightly plotted and very
lengthy screen version of a sensational novel in
which the heroine is only twelve, which makes
a difference. The flashback introduction and
various comic asides are pretentious and
alienating.

w Vladimir Nabokov, from his novel
d Stanley Kubrick *ph* Oswald Morris
m Nelson Riddle

James Mason, Shelley Winters, Sue Lyon,
Peter Sellers

'The director's heart is apparently
elsewhere. Consequently, we face the problem
without the passion, the badness without the
beauty, the agony without the ecstasy.'—
Andrew Sarris

'A diluted *Blue Angel* with a teenage
temptress instead of a tart.'—*Stanley
Kauffmann*

'So clumsily structured that you begin to
wonder whether what was shot and then cut
out, whether the beginning was intended to be
the end; and it is edited in so dilatory a fashion
that after the first hour, almost every scene
seems to go on too long.'—*Pauline Kael*

† Before Mason was cast, Noel Coward and
Laurence Olivier were sought for the role of
Humbert Humbert.
AAN: Vladimir Nabokov

Lolly Madonna XXX

US 1973 105m Metrocolor
MGM (Rodney Carr-Smith)
GB title: *The Lolly Madonna War*

Tennessee hillbilly farmers fight over a
meadow.
Violent feudin' melodrama, technically
accomplished but of limited interest to non-
hillbillies.

w Rodney Carr-Smith, Sue Grafton, from her
novel *d* Richard C. Sarafian *ph* Philip
Lathrop *m* Fred Myrow

Rod Steiger, Robert Ryan, Scott Wilson, Jeff
Bridges, Season Hubley

London After Midnight*

US 1927 approx 75m bw silent
MGM (Tod Browning)
GB title: *The Hypnotist*

A creepy house murder is solved by
hypnotism, and a grinning monster proves to
be a red herring.
Famous star thriller of which lamentably no
prints survive; remade as *Mark of the
Vampire.*

w Tod Browning, Waldemar Young *d* Tod
Browning *ph* Merritt Gerstad

Lon Chaney, Marceline Day, Conrad Nagel,
Henry B. Walthall, Polly Moran

London Belongs to Me**

GB 1948 112m bw
GFD / Individual (Frank Launder, Sidney
Gilliat)
US title: *Dulcimer Street*

A young boy is arrested on a murder charge
and his boarding-house friends rally to his
defence.
Unconvincing but highly entertaining sub-
Dickensian comedy-drama with a rousing
finish and an abundance of character roles.

w Sidney Gilliat, J. B. Williams, *novel*
Norman Collins *d* Sidney Gilliat *ph* Wilkie
Cooper *m* Benjamin Frankel

Alastair Sim, Stephen Murray, Richard
Attenborough, Fay Compton, Wylie Watson,
Susan Shaw, Ivy St Helier, Joyce Carey,
Andrew Crawford, Eleanor Summerfield,
Hugh Griffith, Gladys Henson

The London Blackout Murders

US 1942 58m bw

A mild tobacconist murders people who are
sabotaging the war effort. Curious, set-bound
little melodrama with an interesting lead
performance. *John Abbott*, Mary McLeod,
Lloyd Corrigan, Lester Matthews, Anita
Bolster, Billy Bevan, Frederick Worlock.
Written by Curt Siodmak; directed by George
Sherman; for Republic. (GB title: *Secret
Motive.*)

London by Night*

US 1937 70m bw

Apparent murders are really part of a
blackmail scheme. Reasonably intriguing
mystery with good cast and atmosphere.
George Murphy, Rita Johnson, Leo G.
Carroll, George Zucco, Virginia Field,
Montagu Love, Eddie Quillan, Leonard
Mudie. Written by George Oppenheimer from
the play The Umbrella Man by Will Scott;
directed by William Thiele; for MGM.
'Quality is there, but drawing power isn't.'—
Variety

London Melody

GB 1937 75m bw
GFD / Herbert Wilcox
US title: *Girls in the Street*

A diplomat falls for a dancer.
Light but rather humourless musical drama.

w Florence Tranter, Monckton Hoffe
d Herbert Wilcox *ph* F. A. Young

Anna Neagle, Tullio Carminati, Robert
Douglas, Horace Hodges

'Excellent compilation of bromidial mush,
beautifully produced and directed, which
should satisfy.'—*Variety*

The London Nobody Knows*

GB 1967 53m Eastmancolor

James Mason wanders round the capital's
by-ways in search of relics from former ages.
Unhurried but generally delightful
documentary. Written by Geoffrey Fletcher,
from his book; directed by Norman Cohen; for
Norcon / British Lion.

London Town*

GB 1946 126m Technicolor
GFD / Wesley Ruggles
US title: *My Heart Goes Crazy*

An understudy finally achieves stardom thanks
to his daughter's schemes.
Disastrous and expensive attempt to make a
major British musical without a single new
idea. Tasteless, tawdry and sluggish, but it
does record for posterity four of the star's
sketches.

w Elliot Paul, Siegfried Herzig, Val Guest
d Wesley Ruggles *ph* Erwin Hiller

Sid Field, Greta Gynt, Kay Kendall, Tessie
O'Shea, Claude Hulbert, Sonnie Hale, Mary
Clare, Petula Clark, Jerry Desmonde

'I can't see the point of importing an
American director and giving him all the time
and money in the world to play with when we
can make bad musicals on our own and
quicker.'—*Richard Winnington*

The Lone Hand

US 1953 80m Technicolor

A quiet western farmer is really a Pinkerton
detective. Slightly unusual western in which
the happy ending is not however in doubt. Joel
McCrea, Barbara Hale, Alex Nicol, Charles
Drake, James Arness. Written by Joseph
Hoffman; directed by George Sherman; for
Universal-International.

The Lone Ranger

This high-minded western character, with his black mask, his horse Silver and his Indian friend Tonto, originated (complete with 'William Tell' overture) as a 1933 radio serial in which he was played by Bruce Bemmer. In 1938 he came to film via a Republic serial in which he was played by Lee Powell. In 1939 there was a sequel with Robert Livingstone. In 1949 Clayton Moore brought him to TV in innumerable half-hour adventures. These eventually encouraged two feature versions; see below. Also, *The Legend of the Lone Ranger* (qv).

The Lone Ranger

US 1955   85m   Warnercolor

The masked do-gooder foils a ranchers' plot to destroy an Indian reservation. Tolerably watchable adventures. Clayton Moore, Jay Silverheels, Lyle Bettger, Bonita Granville, Perry Lopez. Written by Herb Meadow; directed by Stuart Heisler; for Jack Wrather.

The Lone Ranger and the Lost City of Gold

US 1958   81m   bw

The masked rider solves murders which have been committed for a mysterious medallion. Lively western for kids. Clayton Moore, Jay Silverheels, Douglas Kennedy, Charles Watts. Written by Robert Schaefer and Eric Freiwald; directed by Lesley Selander; for Jack Wrather.

Lone Star

US 1952   90m   bw
MGM (Z. Wayne Griffin)

Andrew Jackson enlists the aid of a Texas adventurer to persuade Sam Houston to change his mind about an agreement with Mexico.
Slow-moving semi-western, hard to follow for non-Americans. Production values quite high.

w Borden Chase, Howard Estabrook d Vincent Sherman ph Harold Rosson m David Buttolph

Clark Gable, Ava Gardner, Lionel Barrymore, Broderick Crawford, Ed Begley, Beulah Bondi, James Burke, William Farnum, Lowell Gilmore, Moroni Olsen, Russell Simpson, William Conrad

The Lone Wolf

The jewel thief turned sleuth was created by Louis Joseph Vance and turned up in several silent films. During the talkie period several actors played Michael Lanyard; the role of his valet passed from Raymond Walburn to Eric Blore to Alan Mowbray. All the films were made for Columbia, but only the first was anything like a main feature.
1935: THE LONE WOLF RETURNS (d Roy William Neill with Melvyn Douglas)
1938: THE LONE WOLF IN PARIS (d Albert S. Rogell with Francis Lederer)
1939: THE LONE WOLF SPY HUNT (d Peter Godfrey with Warren William)

1940: THE LONE WOLF STRIKES (d Sidney Salkow with Warren William)
1941: THE LONE WOLF MEETS A LADY, THE LONE WOLF TAKES A CHANCE, THE LONE WOLF KEEPS A DATE (all as above), SECRETS OF THE LONE WOLF (d Edward Dmytryk; WW)
1943: ONE DANGEROUS NIGHT (d Michael Gordon: WW), PASSPORT TO SUEZ (d André de Toth: WW)
1946: THE NOTORIOUS LONE WOLF (d D. Ross Lederman; with Gerald Mohr)
1947: THE LONE WOLF IN LONDON (d Leslie Goodwins: GM), THE LONE WOLF IN MEXICO (d D. Ross Lederman: GM)
1949: THE LONE WOLF AND HIS LADY (d John Hoffman: GM)

Lone Wolf McQuade

US 1983   107m   De Luxe

A tough Texas Ranger takes on horse rustlers and hijackers. Adults-only action rubbish, disarmingly competently made. Chuck Norris, David Carradine, Barbara Carrera, Leon Isaac Kennedy. Written by B. J. Nelson; directed by Steve Carver; for 1818 / Top Kick / Orion. 'A winningly ludicrous mish-mash of mayhem-movie rudiments and action-man reputations.'—*Paul Taylor, MFB*

The Loneliness of the Long Distance Runner*

GB 1962   104m   bw
British Lion / Bryanston / Woodfall (Tony Richardson)

The only thing a Borstal boy does well is run, and as he trains he thinks back to his depressing life.
Rather pale study of a social outcast; interesting scenes do not quite form a compelling whole.

w Alan Sillitoe, from his short story d Tony Richardson ph Walter Lassally m John Addison

Tom Courtenay, Michael Redgrave, James Bolam, Avis Bunnage, Alec McCowen, Joe Robinson, Julia Foster

Lonely Are the Brave*

US 1962   107m   bw   Panavision
U-I / Joel (Edward Lewis)

The last of the cowboy rebels is no match for pursuit by jeep and helicopter.
A strange, sad, rather moving fable, with very good performances and action scenes, but a shade too unrelenting in its downbeat tone to become a popular classic.

w Dalton Trumbo, *novel* Brave Cowboy by Edward Abbey d David Miller ph Philip Lathrop m Jerry Goldsmith

Kirk Douglas, Walter Matthau, Gena Rowlands, Michael Kane, Carroll O'Connor, Karl Swenson, George Kennedy, Bill Raisch

Lonely Hearts*

Australia 1981   95m   Eastmancolor
Adams Packer Films (John B. Murray)

When his mother dies, a 50-year-old attempts to go on a belated romantic spree.

Unexpectedly amusing comedy reminiscent of a New Yorker cartoon.

w Paul Cox, John Clarke d Paul Cox ph Yuri Sokol m Norman Kaye

Wendy Hughes. *Norman Kaye*. John Finlayson, Julia Blake, Jonathan Hardy

The Lonely Lady

US 1982   92m   Technicolor

A girl graduate in Los Angeles suffers various setbacks and assaults on her way to being a film star. Risible concoction designed to show off the non-talents of a non-star in a film financed by her husband. Pia Zadora, Lloyd Bochner, Bibi Besch, Joseph Cali, Anthony Holland, Jared Martin. Written by John Kershaw, Shawn Randall, from the novel by Harold Robbins; directed by Peter Sasdy; for KGA Industries / Harold Robbins International.

The Lonely Man

US 1957   87m   bw   Vistavision
Paramount (Pat Duggan)

An outlaw hopes to regain social recognition and contacts the son who abhors him. Dullish psycho western.

w Harry Essex, Robert Smith d Henry Levin ph Lionel Lindon m Van Cleave

Jack Palance, Anthony Perkins, Elaine Aiken, Neville Brand, Lee Van Cleef, Elisha Cook Jnr, Robert Middleton

Lonelyhearts*

US 1958   103m   bw
UA / Dore Schary

A young journalist finds himself engrossed, appalled and sickened by his work on the agony column.
Episodic, occasionally interesting but generally too vaguely liberal; an intellectual reshaping of a despairing novel. The producer as usual is well meaning but doesn't quite make it.

w Dore Schary, *novel* Nathanael West d Vincent J. Donehue ph John Alton m Conrad Salinger

Montgomery Clift, Robert Ryan, Myrna Loy, Dolores Hart, Maureen Stapleton

AAN: Maureen Stapleton

Lonesome*

US 1928   69m (24 fps)   bw   silent
Universal

Young lovers lose each other at Luna Park but later discover that they are neighbours. Amiable exploration of the life of city workers, comparable with *The Crowd* but showing a lighter touch.

w Edmund T. Lowe d Paul Fejos ph Gilbert Warrenton

Glenn Tryon, Barbara Kent

The Long and the Short and the Tall*

GB 1960   105m   bw
ABP / Michael Balcon
US title: *Jungle Fighters*

In Malaya during World War II a Japanese

scout is captured by a British patrol.
Stark war melodrama with the emphasis on
character. Vivid at the time, it now seems very
routine.

w Wolf Mankowitz, *play* Willis Hall *d* Leslie
Norman *ph* Erwin Hillier *m* Stanley Black

Laurence Harvey, Richard Todd, David
McCallum, Richard Harris, Ronald Fraser,
John Meillon, John Rees, Kenji Takaki

The Long Arm**
GB 1956 96m bw
Ealing (Tom Morahan)
US title: *The Third Key*

A Scotland Yard superintendent solves a
series of robberies.
Good straightforward police thriller with
careful detail.

w Janet Green, Robert Barr *d* Charles Frend
ph Gordon Dines *m* Gerbrand Schurmann

Jack Hawkins, Dorothy Alison, John Stratton,
Michael Brooke, Geoffrey Keen, Sidney
Tafler, Meredith Edwards, Ralph Truman,
Ursula Howells
'A generally efficient example of popular
British film-making.'—*MFB*

The Long Dark Hall
GB 1951 86m bw
British Lion / Five Oceans (Anthony
Bushell)

A chorus girl is murdered and her married
lover is accused.
Miserable mystery with a trick ending, most
inappropriately cast.

w Nunnally Johnson, W. E. C. Fairchild
d Anthony Bushell, Reginald Beck *ph* Wilkie
Cooper *m* Benjamin Frankel

Rex Harrison, Lilli Palmer, Raymond
Huntley, Denis O'Dea, Anthony Bushell,
Henry Longhurst, Patricia Wayne, Meriel
Forbes, Brenda de Banzie, Anthony Dawson

The Long Day's Dying
GB 1968 95m Techniscope
Paramount / Junction Films (Harry Fine)

Three British paratroopers in Europe are cut
off from their unit and die pointlessly.
Violent, irritating anti-war film which
resurrects all the clichés and makes itself
unpleasant into the bargain.

w Charles Wood, *novel* Alan White *d* Peter
Collinson *ph* Brian Probyn *m* Malcolm
Lockyer *pd* Disley Jones

David Hemmings, Tom Bell, Tony Beckley,
Alan Dobie
'It is typical of all that is wrong with the film
that it should end on a frozen frame of a
soldier in the act of dying while heavily ironic
patriotic music swells on the sound track.'—
David Wilson

Long Day's Journey into Night**
US 1961 174m bw
Ely Landau

Connecticut 1912: days in the life of an ageing
actor, his drug addicted wife and their sons,

one of whom is an alcoholic and the other
Eugene O'Neill.
Heavy going, nicely handled, superbly acted
version of a play which can be a player's
triumph and certainly is here; but it still has
more effect in the theatre.

w Eugene O'Neill *d* Sidney Lumet *ph* Boris
Kaufman *m* André Previn *pd* Richard Sylbert

Ralph Richardson, Katharine Hepburn, Jason
Robards Jnr, *Dean Stockwell*
'Letting his players have their head, lighted
miraculously so that every flicker of emotion is
preserved, and pursuing them with Kaufman's
unobtrusive camera, Lumet illuminates the
play, line by line, and gives it all the impact of
a live performance.'—*Brenda Davies*
'A very great play has been not translated to
the screen but reverently put behind glass.'—
John Simon

AAN: Katharine Hepburn

● *Video: Polygram*

The Long Duel
GB 1967 115m Technicolor
Panavision
Rank (Ken Annakin)

On the North-West Frontier in the twenties,
British officers disagree about handling the
natives, and one of them forms a strong regard
for the native leader.
Unconvincing cut-price Indian adventure with
little cohesion and less entertainment value.

w Peter Yeldham *d* Ken Annakin *ph* Jack
Hildyard *m* Patrick John Scott

Trevor Howard, Yul Brynner, Harry
Andrews, Charlotte Rampling, Virginia
North, Andrew Keir, Laurence Naismith,
Maurice Denham
'The dialogue seems to have been written by
a computer fed a programme of execrable
films on the same theme.'—*MFB*

The Long Good Friday*
GB 1980 105m colour
Black Lion / Calendar (Barry Hanson)

A gangland boss faces violent reprisals from
the competition.
Heavily melodramatic stylish updating of
Scarface in a London East End setting. A
critical success despite vicious detail and IRA
plot involvement.

w Barrie Keefe *d* John Mackenzie *ph* Phil
Meheux *m* Francis Monkman

Bob Hoskins, Helen Mirren, Dave King,
Brian Hall, Eddie Constantine, Stephen Davis

● *Video: Thorn EMI*

The Long Goodbye
US 1973 111m Technicolor
Panavision
UA / Lions Gate (Jerry Bick)

Philip Marlowe helps an eccentric friend who
is suspected of murdering his wife.
Ugly, boring travesty of a well-respected
detective novel, the apparent intention being
to reverse the author's attitudes completely

and to substitute dullness and
incomprehensibility.

w Leigh Brackett, *novel* Raymond Chandler
d Robert Altman *ph* Vilmos Zsigmond
m John T. Williams

Elliott Gould, Nina Van Pallandt, Sterling
Hayden, Mark Rydell, Henry Gibson
'Altman's fragmentation bomb blows up
itself rather than the myths he has said he
wants to lay to rest.'—*Sight and Sound*
'The trouble is that this Marlowe is an
untidy, unshaven, semi-literate dimwit slob
who could not locate a missing skyscraper and
who would be refused service at a hot dog
stand.'—*Charles Champlin*
'A spit in the eye to a great writer.'—
Michael Billington, Illustrated London News

The Long Gray Line*
US 1955 138m Technicolor
Cinemascope
Columbia (Robert Arthur)

The career of an athletics trainer at West
Point.
Dim biopic, the kind of true life yarn that
Americans like, produced in the cheerful,
sentimental, sparring way that John Ford
likes.

w Edward Hope, *book* Bring Up the Brass by
Merty Maher *d* John Ford *ph* Charles
Lawton Jnr *m* George Duning *md* Morris
Stoloff

Tyrone Power, Maureen O'Hara, Donald
Crisp, Ward Bond, Robert Francis, Betsy
Palmer, Phil Carey, Harry Carey Jnr, Patrick
Wayne, Sean McClory
'Its celebration of the codes and ideals of
West Point vexatiously combines sentimental
cosiness and a kind of religious awe.'—*Gavin
Lambert*

The Long Hot Summer*
US 1958 118m Eastmancolor
Cinemascope
TCF (Jerry Wald)

Conflict arises between a Mississippi town boss
and a tenant farmer.
Busy Peyton Place-style family brawling saga
with sex on the side, flabby as narrative but
compulsive as character study.

w Irving Ravetch, Harriet Frank,
stories William Faulkner *d* Martin Ritt
ph Joseph La Shelle *m* Alex North

Orson Welles, Paul Newman, Joanne
Woodward, Tony Franciosa, Lee Remick,
Angela Lansbury

Long John Silver
Australia 1953 106m Eastmancolor
Cinemascope
TI Pictures (Joseph Kaufman)

Back from Treasure Island, Silver and
Hawkins plan a return visit with fresh clues to
the treasure.
Cheaply produced, bitsy-piecy adventure
fragments with no one to restrain the star from
eye-rolling.

w Martin Rackin *d* Byron Haskin *ph* Carl Guthrie *m* David Buttolph

Robert Newton, Connie Gilchrist, Kit Taylor, Rod Taylor

The Long Long Trailer*
US 1954 96m Anscocolor
MGM (Pandro S. Berman)

A construction engineer and his bride buy a trailer for their honeymoon, and wish they hadn't.
Disaster comedy with long bright periods and the inevitable saggy bits.

w Frances Goodrich, Albert Hackett, *novel* Clinton Twiss *d* Vincente Minnelli *ph* Robert Surtees *m* Adolph Deutsch

Lucille Ball, Desi Arnaz, Marjorie Main, Keenan Wynn, Moroni Olsen

Long Lost Father
US 1934 63m bw
RKO

A restaurant owner saves his daughter from a theft charge.
Competent minor star drama.

w Dwight Taylor, *novel* G. B. Stern *d* Ernest B. Schoedsack *ph* Nicholas Musuraca *m* Max Steiner

John Barrymore, Helen Chandler, Donald Cook, Alan Mowbray, Claude King
'A mild piece with an unbelievable story ... British background and dialogue, mostly dull.'—*Variety*

The Long Memory
GB 1952 96m bw
Rank / Europa (Hugh Stewart)

An ex-con, framed for a murder he did not commit, plots revenge but instead uncovers a fresh crime.
Slow and dreary melodrama set largely on a barge, never rising to anything like excitement.

w Robert Hamer, Frank Harvey, *novel* Winston Clewes *d* Robert Hamer *ph* Harry Waxman *m* William Alwyn

John Mills, John McCallum, Elizabeth Sellars, Geoffrey Keen

The Long Night*
US 1947 97m bw
(RKO) Anatole Litvak

A young man shoots the seducer of his sweetheart and barricades himself in a room against the police.
Good-looking but empty remake of *Le Jour se Lève*.

w John Wexley, *story* Jacques Viot *d* Anatole Litvak *ph* Sol Polito *m* Dmitri Tiomkin

Henry Fonda, Barbara Bel Geddes, Vincent Price, Ann Dvorak, Queenie Smith
'This film faithfully reproduces the letter while altering the spirit of the original almost beyond recognition.'—*MFB*
'It would be interesting to see it on a double bill with its French original. Both films clearly rate themselves as tragedies; they are merely intelligent trash. But the old one is much more discreet with its self-pity and much more sharply edged.'—*James Agee*

Long Pants*
US 1927 58m (24 fps) bw silent
First National / Harry Langdon

A country bumpkin has trouble in the city.
Far from the best Langdon comedy, but funny in flashes.

w Arthur Ripley *d* Frank Capra *ph* Elgin Lessley

Harry Langdon, Gladys Brockwell, Alan Roscoe, Alma Bennett

'All the world loves an outlaw. For some damn reason they remember 'em!'

The Long Riders
US 1980 99m Technicolor
UA / Huka (Tim Zinnemann)

The story of western outlaw brothers named Younger, Miller and James.
Well-worn territory with new-fangled violent detail. Not much of an attraction despite the gimmick of having the various anti-heroes played by real brothers.

w Bill Bryden, Steven Phillip Smith, Stacy Keach, James Keach *d* Walter Hill *ph* Ric Waite *m* Ry Cooder *pd* Jack T. Collis

Stacy Keach, James Keach, David Carradine, Keith Carradine, Robert Carradine, Dennis Quaid, Randy Quaid

The Long Ships
GB / Yugoslavia 1963 126m Technirama
Columbia / Warwick / Avila (Irving Allen)

A Viking adventurer and a Moorish prince fall out over a golden bell.
Stilted medieval epic with some visual compensations but more chat than action.

w Berkely Mather, Beverly Cross, *novel* Frank G. Bengtsson *d* Jack Cardiff *ph* Christopher Challis *m* Dusan Radic

Richard Widmark, Sidney Poitier, Russ Tamblyn, Rosanna Schiaffino, Oscar Homolka, Colin Blakely

The Long, the Short and the Tall: see
The Long and the Short and the Tall

The Long Voyage Home**
US 1940 104m bw
Walter Wanger

Merchant seamen on shore leave get drunk, philosophize and have adventures.
Stagey-looking but dramatically interesting amalgam of four one-act plays by Eugene O'Neill, with talent abounding.

w Dudley Nichols *d John Ford* *ph* Gregg Toland *m* Richard Hageman

John Wayne, Thomas Mitchell, Ian Hunter, Ward Bond, Barry Fitzgerald, Wilfrid Lawson, *Mildred Natwick*, John Qualen, Arthur Shields, Joe Sawyer
'One of the finest of all movies that deal with life at sea.'—*Pauline Kael, 70s*

AAN: best picture; Dudley Nichols; Gregg Toland; Richard Hageman

The Long Wait
US 1954 93m bw
UA / Parklane (Lesser Samuels)

An amnesia victim returns home to solve a murder in which he was involved.
Flatulent version of a Mickey Spillane novel, over-plotted and inadequately motivated.

w Alan Green, Lesser Samuels *d* Victor Saville *ph* Franz Planer *m* Mario Castelnuovo Tedesco

Anthony Quinn, Charles Coburn, Gene Evans, Peggie Castle, Dolores Donlan

The Longest Day**
US 1962 169m bw Cinemascope
TCF (*Darryl F. Zanuck, Elmo Williams*)

A multi-faceted account of the landings in Normandy in June 1944.
Extraordinarily noisy war spectacular, enjoyable as a violent entertainment once one has caught all the threads, but emotionally unaffecting because every part is played by a star.

w Cornelius Ryan, Romain Gary, James Jones, David Pursall, Jack Seddon, *book* Cornelius Ryan *d* Andrew Marton, Ken Annakin, Bernhard Wicki *ph* Henri Persin, Walter Wottitz, Pierre Levent, Jean Bourgoin *m* Maurice Jarre, Paul Anka

John Wayne, Robert Mitchum, Henry Fonda, Robert Ryan, Rod Steiger, Robert Wagner, Paul Anka, Fabian, Tommy Sands, Richard Beymer, Mel Ferrer, Jeffrey Hunter, Sal Mineo, Roddy McDowall, Stuart Whitman, Steve Forrest, Eddie Albert, Edmond O'Brien, Red Buttons, Tom Tryon, Alexander Knox, Ray Danton, Ron Randell, Richard Burton, Donald Houston, Kenneth More, Peter Lawford, Richard Todd, Leo Genn, John Gregson, Sean Connery, Michael Medwin, Leslie Phillips, Irina Demich, Bourvil, Jean-Louis Barrault, Christian Marquand, Arletty, Curt Jurgens, Paul Hartmann, Gert Frobe, Wolfgang Preiss, Peter Van Eyck, Christopher Lee, Eugene Deckers, Richard Wattis

AA: photography
AAN: best picture
● *Video: CBS / Fox*

The Longest Yard
US 1974 122m Technicolor
Paramount / Long Road (Albert S. Ruddy)
GB title: *The Mean Machine*

Imprisoned for drunkenness and car theft, a football star is blackmailed into training a prison football team of hulking misfits.
Violent, meandering comedy-drama with murderous jokes but no narrative grip.

w Tracy Keenan Wynn *d* Robert Aldrich *ph* Joseph Biroc *m* Frank de Vol

Burt Reynolds, Eddie Albert, Ed Lauter, Michael Conrad, Jim Hampton
● *Video: CIC*

Look Back in Anger*
GB 1959 99m bw
ABP / Woodfall (Gordon L. T. Scott)

A bad-tempered young man with a grudge against life and the government runs a market stall, lives in a squalid flat, and has an affair with his wife's best friend.

Well-made version of a play whose sheer dreariness was theatrically stimulating but in terms of film realism becomes only depressing and stupid despite competence all round. It also set shoddy standards for its many less proficient imitators.

w Nigel Kneale, play John Osborne d Tony Richardson ph Oswald Morris m Chris Barber

Richard Burton, Mary Ure, Claire Bloom, Edith Evans, Gary Raymond, Glen Byam Shaw, Phyllis Neilson-Terry, Donald Pleasence, George Devine

● Video: Thorn EMI

Look Before You Love
GB 1948 96m bw

Romance in Rio for a girl of the embassy staff. Abysmal romantic comedy with little of either commodity in evidence. Margaret Lockwood, Griffith Jones, Norman Wooland, Phyllis Stanley, Michael Medwin, Maurice Denham. Written by Reginald Long; directed by Harold Huth; for Burnham / Rank.

Look for the Silver Lining*
US 1949 106m Technicolor
Warner (William Jacobs)

The life story of twenties stage star Marilyn Miller.

Harmless musical biopic with a sense of humour.

w Phoebe and Henry Ephron, Marian Spitzer, Bert Kalmar, Harry Ruby d David Butler ph Peverell Marley md Ray Heindorf

June Haver, Ray Bolger, Charles Ruggles, Gordon Macrae, Rosemary de Camp, S. Z. Sakall, Walter Catlett

AAN: Ray Heindorf

Look in Any Window
US 1961 87m bw

A rich but psychotic youth despises his friends and relations and is arrested as a peeping tom. Psychiatric case history which also wags a social finger. Not particularly convincing. Paul Anka, Ruth Roman, Alex Nicol, Gigi Perreau, George Dolenz, Jack Cassidy. Written by Laurence E. Mascott; directed by William Alland; for Allied Artists.

Look Up and Laugh*
GB 1935 82m bw
ATP (Basil Dean)

Market stallholders defy a big chain store. Good star comedy with music.

w Gordon Wellesley, story J. B. Priestley d Basil Dean

Gracie Fields, Douglas Wakefield, Harry Tate, Alfred Drayton, Morris Harvey, Vivien Leigh, Robb Wilton

Looking for Love
US 1964 83m Metrocolor Panavision

A talented girl can't decide between show business and marriage. Limp, would-be-cute romantic nonsense with poor musical numbers. Connie Francis, Jim Hutton, Susan Oliver, Joby Davis, Barbara Nicholas, Jay C. Flippen, Jesse White, Charles Lane. Written by Ruth Brooks Flippen; directed by Don Weis; for Joe Pasternak / MGM.

Looking for Mr Goodbar
US 1977 136m Metrocolor
Paramount (Freddie Fields)

A teacher of deaf children leads a sordid secret night life.

Exploitative and very boring sex melodrama which doesn't even make one believe in its central character.

wd Richard Brooks, novel Judith Rossner ph William A. Fraker m Artie Kane ad Edward Carfagno

Diane Keaton, Tuesday Weld, William Atherton, Richard Kiley

'Brooks has laid a windy jeremiad about permissive sex on top of fractured film syntax.'—Judith Crist

AAN: William A. Fraker; Tuesday Weld

● Video: CIC

Looking for Trouble
US 1933 77m bw

Two telephone engineers brawl over a girl. Early star vehicle, quite watchable. Spencer Tracy, Jack Oakie, Constance Cummings, Morgan Conway, Arline Judge. Written by Leonard Praskins and Elmer Harris; directed by William Wellman; for Darryl F. Zanuck / UA. 'Too much of a plug for the phone company . . . plus an overpacked plot and certain dialogue failings.'—Variety

The Looking Glass War
GB 1969 107m Technicolor
Panavision
Columbia / M. J. Frankovich (John Box)

The British secret service sends a young Pole into East Germany to find a top secret film. Jaundiced spy story which aims for irony and tragedy but becomes merely verbose and irritating.

wd Frank R. Pierson, novel John Le Carré ph Austin Dempster m Wally Scott

Christopher Jones, Pia Degermark, Ralph Richardson, Anthony Hopkins, Paul Rogers, Susan George, Ray McAnally, Robert Urquhart, Maxine Audley, Anna Massey

'There are a lot of incidental pleasures, but in the final analysis they only add up to half a film.'—Nigel Andrews

● Video: RCA / Columbia

Looking on the Bright Side*
GB 1931 81m bw
ATP (Basil Dean)

A songwriter gets ideas above his station but eventually returns to the manicurist who loves him.

Dated but lively musical which helped confirm Gracie's stardom.

w Basil Dean, Archie Pitt, Brock Williams d Basil Dean

Gracie Fields, Richard Dolman, Julian Rose, Wyn Richmond

Lookin' to Get Out
US 1982 105m colour
Lorimar / North Star / Voight-Schaffel (Robert Schaffel)

A couple of inveterate gamblers take on the Las Vegas establishment.

Fairly pleasant, mindless, quite forgettable comedy.

w Al Schwartz, Jon Voight d Hal Ashby ph Haskell Wexler m Johnny Mandel pd Robert Boyle

Jon Voight, Ann-Margret, Burt Young, Bert Remsen, Jude Farese, Richard Bradford

● Video: Guild

Loophole
GB 1980 105m colour
Brent Walker (Julian Holloway, David Korda)

A safecracker plans to rob the vault of a London bank.

Dim caper yarn which can't make its mind up how serious it means to be. As it stands, it is all very old hat and has a cop-out finish.

w Jonathan Hales, novel Robert Pollock d John Quested ph Michael Reed m Lalo Schifrin

Albert Finney, Martin Sheen, Susannah York, Colin Blakeley, Jonathan Pryce, Robert Morley, Alfred Lynch

Loose Ankles
US 1930 66m bw

A girl's inheritance will be cancelled if she is involved in scandal. Rival claimants try to ensure that she is. Thin, amiable comedy based on a Broadway success. Loretta Young, Douglas Fairbanks Jnr, Louise Fazenda, Otis Harlan, Daphne Pollard, Inez Courtney. Written by Gene Towne from the play by Sam Janney; directed by Ted Wilde; for First National. 'Will bring a chuckle to the most hard-boiled metropolite.'—Variety

Loose Connections*
GB 1983 96m colour
Umbrella / Greenpoint (Simon Perry)

Adventures on a drive to Munich. Thin, easy-going road comedy. Pleasant enough, but no Genevieve.

w Maggie Brooks d Richard Eyre ph Clive Tickner m Dominic Muldowney

Lindsay Duncan, Stephen Rea, Carole Harrison, Frances Low

Loot*
GB 1970 101m Eastmancolor
Performing Arts Ltd (Arthur Lewis)

A crook hides his mother's body and uses the

coffin to carry the proceeds of a robbery. Breakneck black farce which still can't move quite fast enough to cover up its bad taste, though well done by all concerned.

w Ray Galton, Alan Simpson, *play* Joe Orton d Silvio Narizzano *ph* Austin Dempster m Keith Mansfield, Richard Willing-Denton *ad* Anthony Pratt

Richard Attenborough, Lee Remick, Hywel Bennett, Milo O'Shea, Dick Emery

● Video: *Thorn EMI*

Lord Camber's Ladies
GB 1932 80m bw

A nobleman tries to murder his way out of a romantic tangle. Rather dull suspenser notable only for its stagey cast and the fact that Alfred Hitchcock produced it. Gerald du Maurier, Gertrude Lawrence, Benita Hume, Nigel Bruce, Clare Greet, A. Bromley Davenport. Written by Benn W. Levy, Edwin Greenwood and Gilbert Wakefield, from the novel *The Case of Lady Camber* by Horace Annesley Vachell; directed by Benn W. Levy; for BIP.

Lord Edgware Dies
GB 1934 81m bw

Hercule Poirot proves that an elderly nobleman was not killed by his young wife. Modest whodunnit: the intended series did not catch on. Austin Trevor, Jane Carr, Richard Cooper, John Turnbull, Michael Shepley. Written by H. Fowler Mear, from the novel by Agatha Christie; directed by Henry Edwards; for Twickenham.

Lord Jeff
US 1938 78m bw
MGM (Frank Davis)
GB title: *The Boy from Barnardo's*

A well-brought-up boy gets into trouble and is sent under supervision to a naval school. Adequate family film with absolutely no surprises.

w Bradford Roper, Val Burton, André Boehm d Sam Wood *ph* John Seitz m Edward Ward

Freddie Bartholemew, Mickey Rooney, Charles Coburn, Herbert Mundin, Terry Kilburn, Gale Sondergaard, Peter Lawford

Lord Jim*
GB 1964 154m Technicolor Super Panavision
Columbia / Keep (René Dupont)

Adventures of a sailor who prowls the Far East looking for truth; he helps enslaved natives, is raped by a tribal chief, and finally sacrifices his life.

Lush and very boring farrago of miscellaneous incident, with a central character about whose fate no one can care. However, an expensive production must have its points of interest, and the belated introduction of a gentleman villain gives a little edge.

wd Richard Brooks, *novel* Joseph Conrad *ph* Frederick A. Young *m* Bronislau Kaper pd Geoffrey Drake

Peter O'Toole, *James Mason*, Eli Wallach, Paul Lukas, Jack Hawkins, Daliah Lavi, Curt Jurgens, Akim Tamiroff

Lord Love a Duck*
US 1966 105m bw
UA / Charleston (George Axelrod)

A senior Los Angeles student practises hypnotism on his girl friend. Rather sloppy satire on American culture and fancies, dressed up as crazy comedy; occasional laughs.

w Larry H. Johnson, George Axelrod, *novel* Al Hine d George Axelrod *ph* Daniel Fapp m Neal Hefti

Roddy McDowall, Tuesday Weld, Lola Albright, Ruth Gordon, Harvey Korman, Max Showalter

Lord of the Flies
GB 1963 91m bw
Allen–Hogdon Productions / Two Arts (Lewis M. Allen)

After a plane crash, a party of English schoolboys are stranded on an uncharted tropical island and gradually turn savage. Semi-professional production of a semi-poetic novel which worked well on the printed page but on screen seems crude and unconvincing.

wd Peter Brook, *novel* William Golding *ph* Tom Hollyman, Gerald Feil *m* Raymond Leppard

James Aubrey, Tom Chapin, Hugh Edwards, Roger Elwin, Tom Gaman

Lord of the Rings*
US 1978 133m De Luxe
UA / Fantasy (Saul Zaentz)

In Middle Earth the Dark Lord loses a powerful ring, and a Hobbit tries to prevent him from getting it back.
Disappointingly stolid, overlong and confused cartoon version of a modern classic which may well deserve all those adjectives. Parts of it are charming, and the method of making cartoons from film of actors photographed in the ordinary way is certainly ingenious though it denies the cartoon characters their own full richness.

w Chris Conkling, Peter S. Beagle, *books* J. R. R. Tolkien d Ralph Bakshi *ph* Timothy Galfas m Leonard Rosenman

voices: Christopher Guard, John Hurt, William Squire, Michael Scholes

● Video: *Thorn EMI*

The Lords of Discipline
US 1982 103m Eastmancolor

Murky goings-on at the Carolina Military Institute. Strictly for those interested in army cadets being unpleasant to each other. David Keith, Robert Prosky, G. D. Spradlin, Barbara Babcock, Michael Biehn, Rick Rossovich. Written by Thomas Pope, Lloyd Fonvielle, from the novel by Pat Conroy; directed by Franc Roddam; for Paramount.

● Video: *CIC*

Lorna Doone**
GB 1934 90m bw
ATP (Basil Dean)

In 1625 on Exmoor, a farmer comes to love an outlaw's daughter who proves to be in reality a kidnapped heiress.
Simple, straightforward, effective version of the famous romance, with refreshing use of exteriors.

w Dorothy Farnum, Miles Malleson, Gordon Wellesley, *novel* R. D. Blackmore *d Basil Dean ph* Robert Martin

Victoria Hopper, John Loder, Margaret Lockwood, *Roy Emerton*, Edward Rigby, Mary Clare, Roger Livesey, George Curzon, D. A. Clarke-Smith, Lawrence Hanray, Amy Veness, Eliot Makeham

'It has polish, but it lacks drama and grip.'— *Variety*

Lorna Doone
US 1951 89m Technicolor
Columbia (Edward Small)

Grotesque remake which treats the story like a cheap western.

w Jesse L. Lasky Jnr, Richard Schayer d Phil Karlson *ph* Charles Van Enger *m* George Duning

Barbara Hale, Richard Greene, Anne Howard, William Bishop, Carl Benton Reid, Ron Randell, Sean McClory, Onslow Stevens, Lester Matthews, John Dehner

Loser Takes All
GB 1956 88m Eastmancolor Cinemascope
British Lion / John Stafford

An accountant and his wife are invited to Monte Carlo but the high life estranges them. Tedious taradiddle from an unexpected quarter; not a success by any standard.

w Graham Greene, from his novel d Ken Annakin *ph* Georges Périnal *m* Alessandro Cicognini

Glynis Johns, Rossano Brazzi, Robert Morley, Joyce Carey, A. E. Matthews, Tony Britton, Felix Aylmer, Albert Lieven, Geoffrey Keen

Lost*
GB 1955 89m Technicolor
Rank (Vivian A. Cox)
US title: *Tears for Simon*

The police go on the trail of a stolen child. Mildly effective semi-documentary police story, with good use of locations.

w Janet Green d Guy Green *ph* Harry Waxman m Benjamin Frankel

David Farrar, David Knight, Julia Arnall, Anthony Oliver, Thora Hird, Eleanor Summerfield, Marjorie Rhodes, Joan Sims

Lost and Found
US 1979 105m Technicolor
Columbia / Gordon (Melvin Frank)

A widowed American professor meets an English divorcee on a skiing holiday, but after marriage they prove to be incompatible.

Unattractive romantic comedy-drama which despite capable stars degenerates into a series of wounding slanging matches.

w Melvin Frank, Jack Rose d Melvin Frank ph Douglas Slocombe m John Cameron pd Trevor Williams

Glenda Jackson, George Segal, Maureen Stapleton, Paul Sorvino, John Cunningham, Hollis McLaren

● Video: RCA / Columbia

Lost Angel*
US 1943 91m bw
MGM (Robert Sisk)

A lost little girl is adopted by a reporter.
Good star vehicle for the sentimentally-inclined, with solid production and casting back-up.

w Isabel Lennart d Roy Rowland ph Robert Surtees m Daniele Amfitheatrof

Margaret O'Brien, James Craig, Marsha Hunt, Philip Merivale, Henry O'Neill, Donald Meek, Keenan Wynn

'A beautiful opportunity for true satire is offered and, I regret to say, thrown away. For our little Gulliver is rapidly decivilized by all the familiar bromidic palliatives: love, crooning, fairies and night clubs.'—Richard Winnington

Lost Boundaries*
US 1949 105m bw
Film Classics (Louis de Rochemont)

In a New Hampshire town in the forties, a beloved doctor and his wife are found to have negro blood.
Well-meaning but dramatically ineffective racial drama which meanders along allowing an occasional burst of genuine feeling to come through.

w Virginia Shaler, Eugene Ling d Alfred Werker ph William J. Miller m Louis Applebaum

Mel Ferrer, Beatrice Pearson, Richard Hylton, Susan Douglas, Canada Lee, Grace Coppin

'It cannot be said to betray its subject, but is, rather, unequal to it.'—Gavin Lambert

'Wherever their feet touched ground, a new adventure was born!'
Lost Command
US 1966 128m Technicolor
Panavision
Columbia / Red Lion (Mark Robson)

Adventures of a French paratroop regiment in Indo-China and Algeria.
Anti-war war adventure; noisy but scarcely inspired.

w Nelson Gidding, novel The Centurions by Jean Larteguy d Mark Robson ph Robert Surtees m Franz Waxman

Anthony Quinn, Alain Delon, George Segal, Michèle Morgan, Maurice Ronet, Claudia Cardinale, Grégoire Aslan, Jean Servais

The Lost Continent*
GB 1968 98m Technicolor
Hammer (Michael Carreras)

The captain of a tramp steamer illegally carries dynamite, and he and his passengers are stranded in a weird Sargasso Sea colony run by the Spanish Inquisition.
Hilariously imaginative hokum with splendid art direction and some of the grottiest monsters on film; but memorable moments do not quite add up to a classic of the genre.

w Michael Nash, novel Uncharted Seas by Dennis Wheatley d Michael Carreras ph Paul Beeson m Gerard Schurmann sp Robert A. Mattey, Cliff Richardson ad Arthur Lawson

Eric Porter, Hildegarde Neff, Suzanna Leigh, Tony Beckley, Nigel Stock, Neil McCallum, Jimmy Hanley, James Cossins, Victor Maddern

'One of the most ludicrously enjoyable bad films since Salome Where She Danced.'—MFB

Lost Honeymoon
US 1947 70m bw

An amnesiac GI fails to remember either his wife or his young family. Artificial comedy which the actors can't carry off. Franchot Tone, Ann Richards, Tom Conway. Written by Joseph Fields; directed by Leigh Jason; for Eagle-Lion.

Lost Horizon****
US 1937 130m (released at 118m) bw
Columbia (Frank Capra)

Escaping from an Indian revolution, four people are kidnapped by plane and taken to an idyllic civilization in a Tibetan valley, where the weather is always kind and men are not only gentle to each other but live to a very advanced age.
Much re-cut romantic adventure which leaves out some of the emphasis of a favourite Utopian novel but stands up pretty well on its own, at least as a supreme example of Hollywood moonshine, with perfect casting, direction and music. If the design has a touch of Ziegfeld, that's Hollywood.

w Robert Riskin, novel James Hilton d Frank Capra ph Joseph Walker m Dmitri Tiomkin ad Stephen Goosson

Ronald Colman, H. B. Warner, Thomas Mitchell, Edward Everett Horton, Sam Jaffe, Isabel Jewell, Jane Wyatt, Margo, John Howard

'One of the most impressive of all thirties films, a splendid fantasy which, physically and emotionally, lets out all the stops.'—John Baxter, 1968

'One is reminded of a British critic's comment on Mary of Scotland, "the inaccuracies must have involved tremendous research".'—Robert Stebbins

'The best film I've seen for ages, but will somebody please tell me how they got the grand piano along a footpath on which only one person can walk at a time with rope and pickaxe and with a sheer drop of three thousand feet or so?'—James Agate

'If the long dull ethical sequences had been cut to the bone there would have been plenty of room for the real story: the shock of western crudity and injustice on a man returned from a more gentle and beautiful way of life.'—Graham Greene

† A 1943 reissue trimmed down the negative still further, to 109 minutes; but in 1979 the American Film Institute was busily restoring a print of the original length.

AAN: best picture; Dmitri Tiomkin; H. B. Warner

'The adventure that will live forever has been transformed into spectacular musical drama!'
'Come to Shangri-La and a new world of love!'
Lost Horizon*
US 1972 143m Panavision
Technicolor
Columbia / Ross Hunter

Torpid remake with a good opening followed by slabs of philosophizing dialogue and an unbroken series of tedious songs.

w Larry Kramer d Charles Jarrott ph Robert Surtees m Burt Bacharach songs Burt Bacharach, Hal David ad Preston Ames

Peter Finch, Liv Ullmann, Sally Kellerman, Bobby Van, George Kennedy, Michael York, Olivia Hussey, James Shigeta, John Gielgud, Charles Boyer

'It will never play again outside of Shangri-La.'—Les Keyser, Hollywood in the Seventies

'Only Ross Hunter would remake a 1937 movie into a 1932 one.'—Judith Crist

'It can't even be enjoyed as camp.'—Newsweek

'The narrative has no energy, and the pauses for the pedagogic songs are so awkward that you feel the director's wheelchair needs oiling.'—Pauline Kael

Lost in a Harem**
US 1944 89m bw
MGM (George Haight)

Two travelling entertainers in the Middle East get mixed up with a conniving sultan, who hypnotizes them.
Lively, well-staged romp which shows the comedians at their best and uses astute borrowings from burlesque, pantomime, and Hollywood traditions of fantasy and running jokes.

w Harry Ruskin, John Grant, Harry Crane d Charles Reisner ph Lester White m David Snell

Bud Abbott, Lou Costello, Douglass Dumbrille, Marilyn Maxwell, John Conte, Jimmy Dorsey and his Orchestra

Lost in Alaska: see Abbott and Costello Lost in Alaska

A Lost Lady
US 1934 71m bw

A girl falls in love with a much older man.

Empty-headed and over-familiar romantic melodrama. Barbara Stanwyck, Frank Morgan, Ricardo Cortez, Lyle Talbot, Philip Reed, Hobart Cavanaugh, Henry Kolker. Written by Gene Markey, Kathryn Scola, from the novel by Willa Cather; directed by Alfred E. Green; for Warners. 'Lightweight in story and interesting only as a femme style display.'—*Variety*

'He crowded a lifetime into 37 suspenseful hours!'

The Lost Man
US 1969 113m Technicolor
Panavision
Universal (Ernest B. Wehmeyer)

After a robbery, a crook is pursued by the police and goes into hiding.
Odd Man Out made over as a vehicle for polemics about civil rights for blacks: too shiny, too long, too talky to have any grip.

wd Robert Alan Aurthur *ph* Jerry Finnerman *m* Quincy Jones

Sidney Poitier, Joanna Shimkus, Al Freeman Jnr, Michael Tolan, Leon Bibb, Richard Dysart, David Steinberg, Paul Winfield

'In a strange house of hate—they loved where love had never dared to live before!'

The Lost Moment*
US 1947 89m bw
Universal / Walter Wanger (Martin Gabel)

An American publisher goes to Venice to recover love letters written by a famous poet to a lady now aged 105.
Slightly absurd but memorable period drama with a guilty secret eventually coming to light, all put across with apparently deliberate artificiality.

w Leonardo Bercovici, *novel* The Aspern Papers by Henry James *d* Martin Gabel *ph* Hal Mohr *m* Daniele Amfitheatrof

Robert Cummings, Susan Hayward, *Agnes Moorehead*, Joan Lorring, Eduardo Ciannelli
'A compelling piece, highly stylized and very personal, with a beautifully photographed studio recreation of Venice.'—*NFT, 1973*

'Boiling passions in the burning sands!'

The Lost Patrol*
US 1934 74m bw
RKO (Cliff Reid)

A small British army group is lost in the Mesopotamian desert under Arab attack.
Much-copied adventure story of a small patrol under attack (compare *Sahara, Bataan* and *The Last of the Comanches* for a start). The original now seems pretty starchy but retains moments of power.

w Dudley Nichols, *story* Patrol by Philip MacDonald *d* John Ford *ph* Harold Wenstrom *m* Max Steiner

Victor McLaglen, Boris Karloff, Wallace Ford, Reginald Denny, J. M. Kerrigan, Billy Bevan, Alan Hale
Although the running time is long, there's nothing draggy about it.'—*Variety*

† A silent British version was released in 1929, written and directed by Walter Summers for British Instructional, with Cyril McLaglen, Sam Wilkinson and Terence Collier.
AAN: Max Steiner

The Lost People
GB 1949 89m bw
GFD / Gainsborough (Gordon Wellesley)

Displaced persons gather for comfort in a disused German theatre.
Once again a very flat film has been unsuitably made from an effective piece of theatre, with all possible types present and all views represented. Not on.

w Bridget Boland, from her play Cockpit *d* Bernard Knowles *ph* Jack Asher *m* John Greenwood

Richard Attenborough, Mai Zetterling, Siobhan McKenna, Dennis Price, Maxwell Reed, William Hartnell, Gerard Heinz, Harcourt Williams, Marcel Poncin

The Lost Squadron*
US 1932 79m bw
RKO (David O. Selznick)

World War I pilots find work stunting for a movie studio.
Unusual comedy-drama with several points of interest.

w Herman J. Mankiewicz, Wallace Smith *d* George Archainbaud *ph* Leo Tover, Edward Cronjager *m* Max Steiner

Richard Dix, Mary Astor, Erich Von Stroheim, Joel McCrea, Dorothy Jordan, Hugh Herbert, Robert Armstrong
'A pretty good show . . . whether it will get back what it cost is something else again.'—*Variety*

'From the best-seller that was talked about in whispers!'
'The picture that dares to bare a man's soul!'

The Lost Weekend***
US 1945 101m bw
Paramount *(Charles Brackett)*

Two days in the life of a young dipsomaniac writer.
Startlingly original on its release, this stark little drama keeps its power, especially in the scenes on New York streets and in a dipso ward. It could scarcely have been more effectively filmed.

w Charles Brackett, Billy Wilder, *novel* Charles Jackson *d* Billy Wilder *ph* John F. Seitz *m* Miklos Rozsa
Ray Milland, Jane Wyman, Philip Terry, *Howard da Silva, Frank Faylen*

DON BIRNAM (Ray Milland): 'It shrinks my liver, doesn't it, Nat? It pickles my kidneys, yeah. But what does it do to my mind? It tosses the sandbags overboard so the balloon can soar. Suddenly I'm above the ordinary. I'm competent, supremely competent. I'm walking a tightrope over Niagara Falls. I'm one of the great ones. I'm Michelangelo, moulding the beard of Moses. I'm Van Gogh,

painting pure sunlight. I'm Horowitz, playing the Emperor Concerto. I'm John Barrymore before the movies got him by the throat. I'm Jesse James and his two brothers—all three of 'em. I'm W. Shakespeare. And out there it's not Third Avenue any longer—it's the Nile. Nat, the Nile—and down it moves the barge of Cleopatra.'

'A reminder of what celluloid is capable of achieving when used by a good director.'—*Spectator*

'I undershtand that liquor interesh; innerish; intereshtsh are rather worried about thish film. Thatsh tough.'—*James Agee*

'Most to be admired are its impressions of bare dreadful truth: the real crowds in the real streets as the hero-victim lugs his typewriter to the pawnshop, the trains screaming overhead, the awful night as he makes his escape from the alcoholics' ward.'—*Dilys Powell*

AA: best picture; script; Billy Wilder (as director); Ray Milland
AAN: John F. Seitz; Miklos Rozsa

'In the middle of the twentieth century you fall off the brink of time!'

The Lost World
US 1960 98m De Luxe Cinemascope
TCF / Saratoga (Irwin Allen)

Professor Challenger is financed by a newspaper to confirm the report of prehistoric life on a South African plateau.
Pitiful attempt to continue the success of *Journey to the Center of the Earth*, with the story idiotically modernized, unconvincing monsters, a script which inserts conventional romance and villainy, and fatal miscasting of the central part.

w Irwin Allen, Charles Bennett, *novel* Sir Arthur Conan Doyle *d* Irwin Allen *ph* Winton C. Hoch *m* Bert Shefter, Paul Sawtell

Claude Rains, *Michael Rennie*, David Hedison, *Richard Haydn*, Fernando Lamas, Jill St John, Ray Stricklyn
'Resembles nothing so much as a ride on a rundown fairground Ghost Train.'—*MFB*

The Lottery Bride
US 1930 85m bw

A girl goes on the run when she finds herself first prize in a lottery. Dismal operetta from the period when silent techniques were still giving way to sound. Jeanette MacDonald, Joe E. Brown, John Garrick, Zasu Pitts. Written by Horace Jackson, Howard Emmett Rogers, from a story by Herbert Stothart; directed by Paul Stein; for Arthur Hammerstein / United Artists. 'One of the worst of the really very bad features released since sound.'—*Variety*

Lottery Lover
US 1935 80m bw

A shy sailor wins a lottery prize, an introduction to a Folies Bergère star, but falls in love with the public relations girl organizing the stunt. Faded romantic comedy of little surviving interest. Lew Ayres, Reginald Denny, Pat Paterson, Sterling Holloway. Written by Sig Herzic; directed by William Thiele; for Fox.

LOST HORIZON.   One of the scenes missing from all known prints of the 1937 version. Ronald Colman and Jane Wyatt meet one of Chopin's pupils.

Louisa*
US 1950   90m   bw

A much-married man finds that both his daughter and his mother have boy friend trouble. Friendly generation gap comedy with practised talent. Ronald Reagan, Spring Byington, Charles Coburn, Ruth Hussey, Edmund Gwenn, Piper Laurie, Scotty Beckett. Written by Stanley Roberts; directed by Alexander Hall; for Universal-International.

Louise
France 1939   99m   bw

A seamstress is rescued from a life of shame. Ill-advised venture into film opera for an American star. Grace Moore, Georges Thill, André Pernet. Written by Steve Passeur from the opera by Gustave Charpentier; directed by Abel Gance; for European Film Distributors. 'Tedious and unconvincing.'—*Variety*

Louisiana Purchase*
US 1941   98m   Technicolor
Paramount (Harold Wilson)

Efforts are made to compromise a politician. Quite lively transcription of a Broadway musical success with elements of political satire including a climactic filibuster scene.

w Jerome Chodorov, Joseph Fields, *play* Morrie Ryskind *songs* Irving Berlin *d* Irving Cummings *ph* Harry Hallenberger, Ray Rennahan

Bob Hope, Vera Zorina, *Victor Moore*, Irene Bordoni, Dona Drake, Raymond Walburn, Maxie Rosenbloom, Frank Albertson, Donald MacBride, Andrew Tombes

AAN: Harry Hallenberger, Ray Rennahan

Louisiana Story*
US 1948   77m   bw
Standard Oil Company (Robert Flaherty)

In the Louisiana bayous a young native boy watches as oil drillers make a strike. Quite beautiful but over-extended semi-documentary.

w Robert and Frances Flaherty *d* Robert Flaherty *ph* Richard Leacock *m* Virgil Thompson

Joseph Boudreaux, Lionel Leblanc, Frank Hardy

AAN: original story

Loulou
France 1980   105m   Eastmancolor
Gaumont / Action Films

A smart young business woman sets up an uneasy menage with a working-class layabout. Curious but not particularly interesting character study, watchable mainly for its detail.

w Arlette Langmann *d* Maurice Pialat *ph* Pierre-William Glenn, Jacques Loiseleux *md* Philippe Sarde

LOST HORIZON. A scene that remains: Colman meets H. B. Warner in the high Himalayas . . . by courtesy of a Los Angeles ice house.

Isabelle Huppert, Gérard Depardieu, Guy Marchand, Humbert Balsan

Love*

US 1927 82m (24 fps) bw silent
MGM (Edmund Goulding)

Anna Karenina leaves her husband and child for Count Vronsky.

Marginally interesting first shot at a famous subject by a star who came back to it in 1935.

w Frances Marion, Lorna Moon, *novel* Leo Tolstoy *d* Edmund Goulding *ph* William Daniels *m* Ernst Luz *ad* Cedric Gibbons, Alexander Toluboff

Greta Garbo, John Gilbert, Brandon Hurst, Philippe de Lacy, George Fawcett, Emily Fitzroy

† An alternative happy ending was provided for exhibitors who wanted it.

Love Affair

US 1932 68m bw
Columbia

An heiress falls for a flying instructor.
Mild romantic comedy drama.

w Jo Swerling, *story* Ursula Parrott
d Thornton Freeland *ph* Ted Tetzlaff

Dorothy Mackaill, Humphrey Bogart, Jack Kennedy, Astrid Allwyn, Halliwell Hobbes, Barbara Leonard

'A neighbourhood operation, that's about its worth.'—*Variety*

Love Affair**

US 1939 89m bw
RKO (Leo McCarey)

On a transatlantic crossing, a European man of the world meets a New York girl, but their romance is flawed by misunderstanding and physical accident.

The essence of Hollywood romance, and one of the most fondly remembered films of the thirties, perhaps because of the easy comedy sense of the first half.

w Delmer Daves, Donald Ogden Stewart, *story* Mildred Cram, Leo McCarey *d* Leo McCarey *ph* Rudolph Maté

Charles Boyer, Irene Dunne, Maria Ouspenskaya, Lee Bowman, Astrid Allwyn, Maurice Moscovitch

'Production is of grade A quality . . . its b.o. chances look good.'—*Variety*

'Those excited over the mastery of form already achieved in pictures, will like to follow this demonstration of the qualities of technique and imagination the films must always have and keep on recruiting to their service . . . Clichés of situation and attitude are lifted almost beyond recognition by a morning freshness of eye for each small thing around.'—*Otis Ferguson*

'McCarey brought off one of the most difficult things you can attempt with film. He created a mood, rather than a story; he kept it alive by expert interpolations; he provided comedy when he needed comedy and poignancy when he needed substance; and he did it with the minimum of effort.'—*Pare Lorentz*

† Remade as *An Affair to Remember* (qv).

AAN: best picture; original story; Irene Dunne; Maria Ouspenskaya; song 'Wishing' (*m* / *ly* Buddy de Sylva)

Love among the Millionaires
US 1930 70m bw

A waitress falls for the son of a railroad president. Ho-hum star vehicle without much get-up-and-go. Clara Bow, Stanley Smith, Mitzi Green, Skeets Gallagher, Stuart Erwin. Written by Grover Jones, William Conselman, Joseph L. Mankiewicz; directed by Frank Tuttle; for Paramount. 'It will call for a lot of faith from the Clara Bow admirers to accept her in this kind of a part, the sweet wishy-washy thing, after the bum publicity she's been getting.'—*Variety*

Love and Bullets
US 1978 103m Metrocolor
ITC (Pancho Kohner)

A gangster's mistress is brought back from Switzerland by a revengeful Phoenix cop. Downbeat bang-bang with a high death rate and a glum finale; generally low-grade stuff.

w Wendell Mayes, John Melson *d* Stuart Rosenberg *ph* Fred Koenekamp *m* Lalo Schifrin *pd* John de Cuir

Charles Bronson, Jill Ireland, Rod Steiger, Henry Silva, Strother Martin, Bradford Dillman, Michael V. Gazzo

'A relatively dismaying example of the Lew Grade entertainment formula: as locations, production values and clichéd set-pieces proliferate, scripts increasingly look like shaggy dog stories desperately in search of a point, and actors are left to do their own thing as characters disintegrate.'—*Richard Combs, MFB*

'Love and bullets my eye: embarrassment and tedium would be more like it.'—*Time Out*

Love and Death*
US 1975 85m De Luxe
UA / Jack Rollins, Charles H. Joffe

In 1812 Russia, a man condemned reviews the follies of his life.
Personalized comedy fantasia inspired by *War and Peace*, Ingmar Bergman and S. J. Perelman. Basically only for star fans.

wd Woody Allen *ph* Ghislain Cloquet *m* Prokofiev

Woody Allen, Diane Keaton, Georges Adel, Despo, Frank Adu

'I have a feeling that one of these days Allen will get it most dreadfully together and make a film which is more than a string of funny one-liners and set-pieces. He hasn't quite done it here.'—*Benny Green, Punch*

● *Video: Warner*

Love and Hisses*
US 1937 84m bw
TCF (Kenneth MacGowan)

A gossip columnist and a bandleader continue their feud.
Moderate sequel to *Wake Up and Live* (qv); it got by.

w Art Arthur, Curtis Kenyon *d* Sidney Lanfield *ph* Robert Planck *m* Louis Silvers

Walter Winchell, Ben Bernie and his orchestra, Joan Davis, Bert Lahr, Simone Simon, Ruth Terry

Love and Learn
US 1947 83m bw

Two impoverished songwriters are secretly helped by a rich girl. Tame comedy with few laughs. Jack Carson, Robert Hutton, Martha Vickers, Janis Paige, Otto Kruger. Written by Eugene Conrad, Francis Swann and I. A. L. Diamond; directed by Frederick de Cordova; for Warner.

Love and Money
US 1980 95m Metrocolor

A banker kidnaps a financier's wife, and finds himself in dead trouble. Incoherent light melodrama which barely got released. Ray Sharkey, Ornella Muti, Klaus Kinski, Armand Assante, King Vidor (as the hero's senile grandfather), William Prince. Written and directed by James Toback; for Lorimar.

Love and Pain and the Whole Damn Thing
US 1972 113m Eastmancolor
Columbia / Gus (Alan J. Pakula)

An asthmatic young American on holiday in Spain has an affair with an older woman suffering from an incurable disease.
Dreary doomed romance studiously treated as tourist comedy.

w Alvin Sargent *d* Alan J. Pakula *ph* Geoffrey Unsworth *m* Michael Small

Maggie Smith, Timothy Bottoms

Love at First Bite*
US 1979 96m colour
Simon (Joel Freeman)

Count Dracula flees from the communists and settles in New York.
Energetic spoof, with jokes on the sexy side; good work all round.

w Robert Kaufman *d* Stan Dragoti *ph* Edward Rosson *m* Charles Bernstein *pd* Serge Krizman

George Hamilton, Susan St James, Richard Benjamin, Dick Shawn, Arte Johnson

● *Video: Guild*

Love Before Breakfast
US 1936 90m bw

Two Park Avenue beaux vie for a socialite. Thinly plotted but quite amusing romantic comedy. Carole Lombard, Preston Foster, Cesar Romero, Janet Beecher, Bert Roach. Written by Herbert Fields, from the novel

Spinster Dinner by Faith Baldwin; directed by Walter Lang; for Universal.

The Love Bug**
US 1968 107m Technicolor
Walt Disney (Bill Walsh)

An unsuccessful racing driver finds that his small private Volkswagen has a mind of its own.
Amusing, pacy period fantasy in the best Disney style.

w Bill Walsh, Don da Gradi *d* Robert Stevenson *ph* Edward Colman *m* George Bruns *sp* Eustace Lycett

David Tomlinson, Dean Jones, Michele Lee, Buddy Hackett, Joe Flynn, Benson Fong, Joe E. Ross

● *Video: Rank*

Love Crazy*
US 1941 100m bw
MGM (Pandro S. Berman)

When his wife threatens to divorce him, a businessman hatches all manner of crazy schemes, including disguising himself as his own sister.
Zany romantic comedy, over-stretched but with a fair share of hilarity.

w William Ludwig, Charles Lederer, David Hertz *d* Jack Cummings *ph* Ray June *m* David Snell

William Powell, Myrna Loy, Gail Patrick, Jack Carson, Florence Bates, Sidney Blackmer, Vladimir Sokoloff, Donald MacBride, Sig Rumann, Sara Haden, Elisha Cook Jnr, Kathleen Lockhart

Love Eternal*
France 1943 111m bw
André Paulvé
original title: *L'Eternel Retour*

The love story of Tristan and Isolde.
This modernized version had a Teutonic look and was respected rather than admired.

w Jean Cocteau *d* Jean Delannoy *ph* Roger Hubert *m* Georges Auric *ad* Wakhevitch

Jean Marais, Madeleine Sologne, Jean Murat, Yvonne de Bray

Love from a Stranger*
GB 1936 90m bw
Trafalgar (Max Schach)

A young woman realizes she may have married a maniac.
Stalwart suspenser from a popular novel and play.

w Frances Marion, *play* Frank Vosper, *story* Philomel Cottage by Agatha Christie *d* Rowland V. Lee *ph* Philip Tannura *m* Benjamin Britten

Ann Harding, Basil Rathbone, Binnie Hale, Bruce Seton, Jean Cadell, Bryan Powley, Joan Hickson, Donald Calthrop

'Gorgeously photographed and splendidly cut . . . takes front rank with the long list of gruesome films produced in recent years.'—*Variety*

Love from a Stranger
US 1947   81m   bw
Eagle Lion (James J. Geller)
GB title: *A Stranger Walked In*

Stilted period remake.

w Philip MacDonald   d Richard Whorf
ph Tony Gaudio   m Hans Salter

Sylvia Sidney, John Hodiak, Ann Richards,
John Howard, Isobel Elsom, Frederick
Worlock

The Love God?
US 1969   103m   Techniscope
Universal (Edward J. Montagne)

A meek ornithologist is thought to be the
brains behind a girlie magazine, and becomes
a national sex symbol.
Dispiriting and very talkative star farce which
would have been long at half the time.

wd Nat Hiken   ph William Margulies   m Vic
Mizzy

Don Knotts, Edmond O'Brien, Anne Francis,
James Gregory, Maureen Arthur.
   'Strictly for admirers of Don Knotts. Can
there really be many?'—*MFB*

The Love Goddesses**
US 1965   87m   bw
Paramount / Walter Reade / Sterling

A light-hearted account of female sexuality on
the Hollywood screen.
Sharp-eyed compilation film which is worth a
dozen books on the subject.

pd Saul J. Turell, Graeme Ferguson   m Percy
Faith   narrator Carl King
   'A compilation of shrapnel from old sex-
bomb movies, full of deliciously improbable
moments.'—*Newsweek*
† Clips include *Blonde Venus, Morocco, True
Heart Susie, Cleopatra* (1934), *Intolerance, The
Cheat, The Sheik, Blood and Sand, The
Sorrows of Satan, The Loves of Sunya, Diary
of a Lost Girl, Ecstasy, L'Atlantide, Peter the
Tramp, Cabin in the Cotton, Platinum Blonde,
Gold Diggers of 1933, No Man of Her Own,
Professional Sweetheart, Love Me Tonight, I'm
No Angel, Baby Face, They Won't Forget,
College Swing, Her Jungle Love, Gilda, A
Place in the Sun, Some Like it Hot.*

Love Happy*
US 1949   85m   bw
Lester Cowan / Mary Pickford

A group of impoverished actors accidentally
gets possession of the Romanov diamonds.
The last dismaying Marx Brothers film, with
Harpo taking the limelight and Groucho
loping in for a couple of brief, tired
appearances. A roof chase works, but Harpo
tries too hard for sentiment, and the
production looks shoddy.

w Ben Hecht, Frank Tashlin, Mac Benoff
d David Miller   ph William Mellor

Groucho, Harpo, Chico, Eric Blore, Ilona
Massey, Marilyn Monroe, Vera-Ellen

Love Has Many Faces
US 1964   104m   Eastmancolor
Columbia / Jerry Bresler

A rich woman marries a beach boy and has an
affair with another, who is murdered.
Hilarious but unentertaining sex melodrama
built around an overage star.

w Marguerite Roberts   d Alexander Singer
ph Joseph Ruttenberg   m David Raksin

Lana Turner, Cliff Robertson, Hugh O'Brian,
Stefanie Powers, Ruth Roman, Virginia Grey
   'For connoisseurs of perfectly awful
movies.'—*Judith Crist*

Love in a Goldfish Bowl
US 1961   88m   Technicolor   Panavision

On holiday in Honolulu, two teenagers get
into mischief. Tiresome youth-oriented family
comedy with pleasant backgrounds. Tommy
Sands, Fabian, Jan Sterling, Toby Michaels,
Edward Andrews, John McGiver. Written and
directed by Jack Sher; for Paramount / Jurow-
Shepherd.

Love in Bloom
US 1935   76m   bw

A carnival owner's daughter marries a
songwriter. Lame little romance broken up by
crosstalk from Burns and Allen; an ill-
considered entertainment. George Burns,
Gracie Allen, Dixie Lee, Joe Morrison.
Written by J. P. McEvoy, Keene Thompson;
directed by Elliott Nugent; for Paramount.
'Radio pair may save their latest celluloid
effort, but it won't help their future on the
screen.'—*Variety*

Love in Exile
GB 1936   78m   bw

A Ruritanian king is induced to abdicate but
fights back. Airy comedy with little general
appeal. Clive Brook, Helen Vinson, Mary
Carlisle, Will Fyffe, Ronald Squire, Tamara
Desni, Henry Oscar. Written by Herman
Mankiewicz, Roger Burford and Ernest Betts,
from the novel *His Majesty's Pajamas* by Gene
Markey; directed by Alfred L. Werker; for
Capitol.

Love in the Afternoon
US 1957   126m   bw
AA (Billy Wilder)

The daughter of a private detective warns an
American philanderer in Paris that an enraged
husband is en route to shoot him.
Tired and dreary romantic sex comedy,
miscast and far too long. With the talent
around, there are of course a few
compensations.

w Billy Wilder, I. A. L. Diamond, *novel*
Claude Anet   d Billy Wilder   ph William
Mellor   m Franz Waxman   ad Alexander
Trauner

Gary Cooper, Audrey Hepburn, Maurice
Chevalier, John McGiver

Love Is a Ball
US 1962   112m   Technicolor
   Panavision
UA / Oxford / Gold Medal (Martin H. Poll)
GB title: *All This and Money Too*

A Riviera matchmaker recruits instructors to
train his star pupil, but one of them walks
away with the lady.
Forgettable comedy in which more effort goes
into the glamorous background than the script.

w David Swift, Tom and Frank Waldman,
novel The Grand Duke and Mr Pimm by
Lindsay Hardy   d David Swift   ph Edmond
Séchan   m Michel Legrand

Glenn Ford, Charles Boyer, Hope Lange,
Ricardo Montalban, Telly Savalas, Ruth
McDevitt, Ulla Jacobsson

Love is a Headache
US 1938   73m   bw

An actress on hard times gets a break through
freak publicity. Wholly artificial comedy,
hammed up to little avail. Franchot Tone,
Gladys George, Mickey Rooney, Ralph
Morgan, Jessie Ralph, Ted Healy, Barnett
Parker, Frank Jenks, Virginia Weidler, Fay
Holden. Written by Marion Parsonnet, Harry
Ruskin, William Lipman, Lou Heifetz,
Herbert Klein; directed by Richard Thorpe;
for MGM. 'Dialogue is pungent, but fails to
cover up slap-happy situations.'—*Variety*

'A love that defied five thousand years of
   tradition!'
Love Is a Many Splendored Thing*
US 1955   102m   De Luxe   Cinemascope
TCF (Buddy Adler)

During the Korean War, a Eurasian lady
doctor in Hong Kong falls in love with a war
correspondent.
Self-admittedly sentimental soaper with a
tragic ending; the theme tune kept it popular
for years.

w John Patrick, *novel* Han Suyin   d Henry
King   ph Leon Shamroy   m Alfred Newman

Jennifer Jones, William Holden, Torin
Thatcher, Isobel Elsom, Murray Matheson,
Virginia Gregg, Richard Loo

AA: Alfred Newman; title song (m Sammy
Fain, ly Paul Francis Webster)
AAN: best picture; Leon Shamroy; Jennifer
Jones

Love Is a Racket
US 1932   72m   bw

A newspaperman covers up for a girl
suspected of murder, but she lets him down.
Jaundiced comedy-drama of Broadway night
life; quite effective. Douglas Fairbanks Jnr,
Frances Dee, Ann Dvorak, Lee Tracy, Lyle
Talbot, Warren Hymer. Written by Courtney
Terrett; directed by William Wellman; for
Warner.

Love Is Better Than Ever
US 1951   81m   bw
MGM (William H. Wright)
GB title: *The Light Fantastic*

A small-town girl falls for a New York
theatrical agent.
Only moderate production values are brought
to bear on this wispy plot which shows no signs
of development.

w Ruth Brooks Flippen d Stanley Donen
ph Harold Rosson md Lennie Hayton

Larry Parks, Elizabeth Taylor, Josephine
Hutchinson, Tom Tully, Ann Doran

Love Is News*
US 1937 78m bw
TCF (Earl Carroll, Harold Wilson)

An heiress marries a scoop-hunting reporter
just to show him how embarrassing publicity
can be.
Silly romantic comedy with plenty of laughs.

w Harry Tugend, Jack Yellen d Tay Garnett
ph Ernest Palmer

Tyrone Power, Loretta Young, Don Ameche,
Slim Summerville, Dudley Digges, Walter
Catlett, Jane Darwell, Stepin Fetchit, George
Sanders, Frank Conroy, Elisha Cook Jnr
  'Fast-moving comedy and good star names.
Surefire.'—Variety

† Remade as Sweet Rosie O'Grady and That
Wonderful Urge.

'Blood on her hands . . . love in her heart!'
Love Letters*
US 1945 101m bw
Paramount (Hal B. Wallis)

A girl who has lost her memory through war
shock is threatened by more physical danger.
Oddly unexciting romantic melodrama
directed and designed in heavy but satisfying
style. Typical post-war depressive fare.

w Ayn Rand, novel Pity My Simplicity by
Chris Massie d William Dieterle ph Lee
Garmes m Victor Young ad Hans Dreier,
Roland Anderson

Jennifer Jones, Joseph Cotten, Ann Richards,
Gladys Cooper, Anita Louise, Cecil Kellaway,
Robert Sully, Byron Barr, Reginald Denny,
Lumsden Hare

AAN: Jennifer Jones; title song (m Victor
Young, ly Edward Heyman); Victor Young

Love Letters of a Star
US 1936 66m bw

A blackmailed rich girl takes poison.
Complicated but efficient murder mystery.
Henry Hunter, Polly Rowles, C. Henry
Gordon, Walter Coy, Hobart Cavanaugh,
Mary Alice Rice. Written by Lewis R. Foster,
Milton Carruth, James Mulhauser, from the
novel The Case of the Constant God by Rufus
King; directed by Lewis R. Foster and Milton
Carruth; for Universal. 'Good family
entertainment . . . ought to do all right.'—
Variety

Love, Life and Laughter*
GB 1934 83m bw
ATP (Basil Dean)

A film actress catches the eye of a Ruritanian
prince.
Lively star vehicle ranging from sentiment to
slapstick.

w Robert Edmunds d Maurice Elvey

Gracie Fields, John Loder, Norah Howard,
Allan Aynesworth, Esme Percy, Robb Wilton,
Fred Duprez, Horace Kenney, Veronica
Brady

The Love Lottery
GB 1953 83m Technicolor
Ealing (Monja Danischewsky)

A British film star is persuaded to offer
himself as first prize in a lottery.
Satirical farce which doesn't come off, mainly
owing to paucity of comedy ideas.

w Harry Kurnitz d Charles Crichton
ph Douglas Slocombe m Benjamin Frankel
pd Tom Morahan

David Niven, Herbert Lom, Peggy Cummins,
Anne Vernon, Charles Victor, Gordon
Jackson, Felix Aylmer, Hugh McDermott

The Love Machine
US 1971 110m Eastmancolor
Columbia / Mike Frankovich

Megalomaniac TV reporter progresses to
network programme controller but is finally
undone by his vivid sex life.
Stodgy, silly melodrama from a bestseller
whose inspiration was well known in TV
circles.

w Samuel Taylor, novel Jacqueline Susann
d Jack Haley Jnr ph Charles Lang Jnr
m Artie Butler

John Philip Law, Dyan Cannon, Robert Ryan,
Jackie Cooper, David Hemmings, Shecky
Greene

Love Me Forever
US 1935 92m bw
Columbia
GB title: On Wings of Song

A down and out singer makes good.
Fair vehicle.

w Jo Swerling, Sidney Buchman d Victor
Schertzinger ph Joe Walker md Louis Silvers

Grace Moore, Leo Carillo, Robert Allen,
Spring Byington, Michael Bartlett, Thurston
Hall, Douglass Dumbrille, Luis Alberni
  'Gangsters and grand opera are tough to
mix, but . . . should be all right in major
towns.'—Variety

Love Me or Leave Me**
US 1955 122m Eastmancolor
  Cinemascope
MGM (Joe Pasternak)

Twenties singer Ruth Etting is befriended by a
racketeer who pushes her to the top but drives
her to drink and despair in the process.
Agreeably bitter showbiz biopic which gives
the impression of being not too far from the
truth.

w Daniel Fuchs, Isabel Lennart d Charles
Vidor ph Arthur E. Arling md George Stoll
ad Cedric Gibbons, Urie McCleary

Doris Day, James Cagney, Cameron Mitchell,
Robert Keith, Tom Tully, Harry Bellaver,
Richard Gaines

AA: original story (Daniel Fuchs)
AAN: script; George Stoll; James Cagney;
song 'I'll Never Stop Loving You' (m Nicholas
Brodszky, ly Sammy Cahn)

Love Me Tender
US 1956 95m bw Cinemascope
TCF (David Weisbart)

Three brothers fall out over loot they have
brought home from the Civil War.
Odd western designed (perhaps after shooting
began) as Presley's introductory vehicle; he
sings four songs before getting shot, and
reappears in ghostly form at the end.

w Robert Buckner d Robert D. Webb
ph Leo Tover m Lionel Newman

Richard Egan, Debra Paget, Elvis Presley,
Robert Middleton, William Campbell, Neville
Brand, Mildred Dunnock, Bruce Bennett,
James Drury, Ken Clark, Barry Coe

Love Me Tonight****
US 1932 104m bw
Paramount (Rouben Mamoulian)

A Parisian tailor accidentally moves into the
aristocracy.
The most fluently cinematic comedy musical
ever made, with sounds and words, lyrics and
music, deftly blended into a compulsively and
consistently laughable mosaic of sophisticated
nonsense; one better than the best of Lubitsch
and Clair.

w Samuel Hoffenstein, Waldemar Young,
George Marion Jnr, play Tailor in the Château
by Leopold Marchand and Paul Armont
d Rouben Mamoulian ph Victor Milner
songs Rodgers and Hart

Maurice Chevalier, Jeanette MacDonald,
Charles Butterworth, Charles Ruggles, Myrna
Loy, C. Aubrey Smith, Elizabeth Patterson,
Ethel Griffies, Blanche Frederici, Robert
Greig
  'A musical frolic, whimsical in its aim and
delicately carried out in its pattern.'—Variety
  'Gay, charming, witty, it is everything that
the Lubitsch musicals should have been but
never were.'—John Baxter, 1968
  'With the aid of a pleasant story, a good
musician, a talented cast and about a million
dollars, he has done what someone in
Hollywood should have done long ago—he has
illustrated a musical score.'—Pare Lorentz
  'It has that infectious spontaneity which
distinguishes the American musical at its
best.'—Peter Cowie, 1970
  'A rich amalgam of filmic invention, witty
decoration and wonderful songs.'—NFT, 1974
  'What a picture! First you have Chevalier,
and last you have Chevalier!'—Photoplay

The Love Nest
US 1923 22m (24 fps) bw silent

Buster dreams of a solitary voyage in a small
boat. Long lost but ultimately disappointing
Keaton short. Buster Keaton, Joe Roberts,
Virginia Fox. Written and directed by Buster
Keaton and Eddie Cline; for Buster Keaton
Productions.

Love Nest
US 1951 84m bw

A writer and his wife invest in an apartment
building but find their tenants time-consuming.

Fairly lively comedy with varied talent.
William Lundigan, June Haver, Frank Fay,
Marilyn Monroe, Jack Paar, Leatrice Joy.
Written by I. A. L. Diamond, from a novel by
Scott Corbett; directed by Joseph Newman;
for TCF.

The Love of Jeanne Ney*
Germany 1927   98m (24 fps)   bw   silent
UFA

In the Crimea during the Russian Revolution,
a political observer is accidentally killed by his
daughter's lover.
Inconsistently-styled contemporary
melodrama. The abiding interest is in the
detailed treatment rather than the story or
acting.

w Ladislas Vájda, Rudolph Leonhardt, Ilya
Ehrenberg d G. W. Pabst ph Fritz Arno
Wagner, Walter Robert Lach

Edith Jehane, Uno Henning, Fritz Rasp,
Brigitte Helm

Love on the Dole***
GB 1941   100m   bw
British National (John Baxter)

Life among unemployed cotton workers in
industrial Lancashire between the wars.
Vividly characterized, old-fashioned social
melodrama, well made on a low budget; a rare
problem picture for Britain at this time.

w Walter Greenwood, Barbara K. Emery,
Rollo Gamble, novel Walter Greenwood
d John Baxter

Deborah Kerr, Clifford Evans, George
Carney, Joyce Howard, Frank Cellier,
Geoffrey Hibbert, Mary Merrall, Maire
O'Neill, Marjorie Rhodes, A. Bromley
Davenport, Marie Ault, Iris Vandeleur,
Kenneth Griffith

'Kissing and kidding their way from
    Mayfair to the Mediterranean in a
    transcontinental caravan of jollity!'

Love on the Run*
US 1936   81m   bw
MGM (Joseph L. Mankiewicz)

Rival newspapermen help an heiress to escape
an unwanted wedding and in the process
uncover a ring of spies.
Harebrained star farce, smoothly assembled
and still fairly funny.

w John Lee Mahin, Manuel Seff, Gladys
Hurlbut d W. S. Van Dyke ph Oliver T.
Marsh m Franz Waxman

Clark Gable, Joan Crawford, Franchot Tone,
Reginald Owen, Mona Barrie, Ivan Lebedeff,
William Demarest

'Should collect its share at the gate through
the sheer momentum of the Gable-Crawford
combo.'—Variety

'A slightly daffy cinematic item of absolutely
no importance.'—New York Times

Love on the Run*
France 1978   95m   Eastmancolor

Antoine Doinel, separated from his family, is
still having girl trouble. Amorous adventure of
the character first glimpsed in Les Quatre Cent

LOVE ME TONIGHT.   Maurice Chevalier takes Jeanette MacDonald's measure.

Coups and presumably based on the director;
fair sophisticated fun for those who appreciate
the joke. Jean-Pierre Leaud, Marie-France
Pisier, Claude Jade, Rosy Varte. Written by
François Truffaut and others; directed by
François Truffaut; for Les Films du Carrosse.

Love on Wheels
GB 1932   87m   bw

A department store assistant becomes
publicity-conscious. Zippy little comedy of its
day. Jack Hulbert, Edmund Gwenn, Leonora
Corbett, Gordon Harker, Percy Parsons,
Roland Culver, Miles Malleson. Written by
Victor Saville, Angus Macphail, Robert
Stevenson and Douglas Furber; directed by
Victor Saville; for Gainsborough.

The Love Parade**
US 1929   112m   bw
Paramount (Ernst Lubitsch)

The prince of Sylvania marries.
Primitive sound operetta set among the idle
European rich, with clear but faded instances
of the Lubitsch touch.

w Ernest Vajda, Guy Bolton, play The Prince
Consort by Leon Xanrof and Jules Chancel
d Ernst Lubitsch ph Victor Milner
songs Victor Schertzinger, Clifford Grey

Maurice Chevalier, Jeanette MacDonald,
Lupino Lane, Lillian Roth, Edgar Norton,
Lionel Belmore, Eugene Pallette

'The first truly cinematic screen musical in
America.'—Theodore Huff

AAN: best picture; Ernst Lubitsch; Victor
Milner; Maurice Chevalier

Love, Soldiers and Women
France / Italy 1953   96m   bw
Franco-London / Continental
original title: Destinées; US title:
Daughters of Destiny

Three stories of women in war: Joan of Arc,
Lysistrata, and a modern American war
widow visiting her husband's grave.
Uninteresting patchwork with Lysistrata
predictably stealing the show.

'Jeanne': w Jean Aurenche, Pierre Bost
d Jean Delannoy with Michèle Morgan
'Elizabeth': w Sergio Amedei d Marcel
Pagliero with Claudette Colbert, Eleanora
Rossi Drago
'Lysistrata': w Jean Ferry, Henri Jeanson,
Carlo Rim, play Aristophanes d Christian-
Jaque with Martine Carol, Raf Vallone, Paolo
Stoppa

Love Story
GB 1944   112m   bw
GFD / Gainsborough (Harold Huth)
US title: A Lady Surrenders

In Cornwall during World War II, a half-blind
airman falls for a pianist with a weak heart.

Novelettish love story which became popular because of its Cornish Rhapsody.

w Leslie Arliss, Doreen Montgomery, Rodney Ackland, *novel* J. W. Drawbell *d* Leslie Arliss *ph* Bernard Knowles *m* Hubert Bath

Margaret Lockwood, Stewart Granger, Patricia Roc, Tom Walls, Reginald Purdell, Moira Lister

'A splendid, noble and fatuous piece.'—*C. A. Lejeune*

'In psychology and dialogue this is straight out of *Mabel's Weekly*.'—*Richard Winnington*

Love Story°
US 1970 100m Movielab
Paramount (David Golden)

Two students marry; she dies.
A barrage of ripe old Hollywood clichés spiced with new-fangled bad language. In the circumstances, well enough made, and certainly astonishingly popular.

w Erich Segal, from his novelette *d* Arthur Hiller *ph* Dick Kratina *m* Bach, Mozart, Handel *md* Francis Lai

Ali MacGraw, Ryan O'Neal, Ray Milland, John Marley

'Camille with bullshit.'—*Alexander Walker*

AAN: best picture; Erich Segal; Arthur Hiller; Francis Lai; Ali MacGraw; Ryan O'Neal; John Marley

● Video: CIC

Love Streams
US 1984 141m Metrocolor

A distraught woman whose marriage has gone sour moves in with her philandering brother.
Elongated study of two life styles, not so shapeless as most Cassavetes films, but not exactly dramatic or endearing either. Gene Rowlands, John Cassavetes, Diahnne Abbott, Seymour Cassel, Margaret Abbott. Written by Ted Allan and John Cassavetes, from Allan's play; directed by John Cassavetes; for Cannon.

Love That Brute
US 1950 85m bw
TCF (Fred Kohlmar)

A ruthless Chicago gangleader is actually a softy, leaving his supposedly rubbed-out enemies in a comfortable cellar; a young governess persuades him to reform.
Rickety, dully-scripted gangster farce.

w Darrell Ware, John Lee Mahin, Karl Tunberg *d* Alexander Hall *ph* Lloyd Ahern *m* Cyril Mockridge

Paul Douglas, Jean Peters, Cesar Romero, Joan Davis, Arthur Treacher

Love Thy Neighbour
GB 1973 85m Technicolor
EMI / Hammer (Roy Skeggs)

A prejudiced white worker has coloured neighbours.
Elongated screen version of the popular TV series in which the West Indians smile through all the insults and come out top in the end. It might have been worse, but not much.

w Vince Powell, Harry Driver *d* John Robins *ph* Moray Grant *m* Albert Elms

Jack Smethurst, Kate Williams, Rudolph Walker, Nina Baden-Semper, Bill Fraser, Charles Hyatt, Keith Marsh, Patricia Hayes, Arthur English

Love Time
US 1934 72m bw

Franz Schubert falls for a duke's daughter.
Curious, off-putting costumer with music. Pat Paterson, Nils Asther Herbert Mundin, Harry Green, Henry B. Walthall, Lucien Littlefield. Written by William Conselman, Henry Johnson; directed by James Tinling; for Fox.
'Thin story, and slim chances.'—*Variety*

Love under Fire
US 1937 75m bw
TCF (Nunnally Johnson)

A detective catches up with a lady jewel thief in Madrid during the Spanish Civil War.
Adequately entertaining but rather tasteless adventure comedy.

w Gene Fowler, Allen Rivkin, Ernest Pascal, *play* Walter Hackett *d* George Marshall *ph* Ernest Palmer *m* Arthur Lange

Loretta Young, Don Ameche, Frances Drake, Walter Catlett, John Carradine, Borrah Minevitch and his Rascals, Sig Rumann, Harold Huber, E. E. Clive, Katherine de Mille

'Melodrama with music cooked up for the duals.'—*Variety*

'There is a moment . . . a long moment . . .
when everything is risked with the
proper stranger!'

Love with the Proper Stranger°°
US 1964 100m bw
Paramount / Boardwalk (Alan J. Pakula)

A musician tries to help his pregnant shopgirl friend get an abortion, but they decide to get married instead.
Oddly likeable comedy drama set on New York's Italian East Side, with an excellent location sense.

w Arnold Schulman *d* Robert Mulligan *ph* Milton Krasner *m* Elmer Bernstein

Steve McQueen, Natalie Wood, Tom Bosley, Edie Adams, Herschel Bernardi

AAN: Arnold Schulman; Milton Krasner; Natalie Wood

The Loved One°
US 1965 118m bw
MGM / Filmways (Neil Hartley)

A young English poet in California gets a job at a very select burial ground.
A pointed satire on the American way of death has been allowed to get out of hand, with writer and actors alike laying it on too thick; but there are pleasantly waspish moments in a movie advertised as 'the motion picture with something to offend everybody'.

w Terry Southern, Christopher Isherwood, *novel* Evelyn Waugh *d* Tony Richardson *ph* Haskell Wexler *m* John Addison *pd* Rouben Ter-Arutunian

Robert Morse, John Gielgud, Rod Steiger, *Liberace*, Anjanette Comer, Jonathan Winters, Dana Andrews, Milton Berle, James Coburn, Tab Hunter, Margaret Leighton, Roddy McDowall, Robert Morley, Lionel Stander

'Even a chaotic satire like this is cleansing, and it's embarrassing to pan even a bad movie that comes out against God, mother and country.'—*Pauline Kael, 1968*

'A spineless farrago of collegiate gags.'—*Stanley Kauffmann*

'A sinking ship that makes it to port because everyone on board is too giddy to panic.'—*New Yorker, 1978*

Lovely to Look At°
US 1952 102m Technicolor
MGM (Jack Cummings)

Three Broadway producers inherit a Paris fashion house.
Lavish but dullish remake of *Roberta* (qv), in itself no great shakes as a storyline; again the fashions and the numbers are the thing.

w George Wells, Harry Ruby *d* Mervyn Le Roy *ph* George J. Folsey *m* Jerome Kern *ad* Cedric Gibbons, Gabriel Scognamillo

Howard Keel, Kathryn Grayson, Ann Miller, Red Skelton

A Lovely Way to Die
US 1968 98m Techniscope
Universal (Richard Lewis)
GB title: *A Lovely Way to Go*

An ex-cop becomes bodyguard to a suspected murderess, but proves her innocent.
Offbeat mélange of caper comedy, black farce, private eye detection, courtroom drama, spectacular action and routine thick ear. Doesn't work.

w A. J. Russell *d* David Lowell Rich *ph* Morris Hartzband *m* Kenyon Hopkins

Kirk Douglas, Sylva Koscina, Eli Wallach, *Martyn Green*, Kenneth Haigh, Sharon Farrell

'The net result is rather as though Philip Marlowe had met Doris Day on his not very inspiring way to the forum.'—*MFB*

Lover Come Back°°
US 1961 107m Eastmancolor
U-I / Seven Pictures / Nob Hill / Arwin (Stanley Shapiro, Marty Melcher)

Rival executives find themselves advertising a non-existent product.
Fairly sharp advertising satire disguised as a romantic comedy; the most entertaining of the Day-Hudson charmers.

w Stanley Shapiro, Paul Henning *d* Delbert Mann *ph* Arthur E. Arling *m* Frank de Vol

Doris Day, Rock Hudson, *Tony Randall*, Jack Oakie, Edie Adams

AAN: Stanley Shapiro, Paul Henning

The Lovers
GB 1972 89m Eastmancolor
British Lion / Gildor (Maurice Foster)

A Manchester bank clerk with a prim girl

friend finds it difficult to lose his virginity.
Well-written but rather arch comedy which
seemed much funnier and fresher as a TV
series.

w Jack Rosenthal d Herbert Wise ph Bob
Huke m Carl Davis

Richard Beckinsale, Paula Wilcox, Joan Scott,
Susan Littler, John Comer, Stella Moray,
Nikolas Simmonds

Lovers and Other Strangers•••
US 1969 104m Metrocolor
ABC / David Susskind

After living together for eighteen months,
Susan and Mike decide to get married, and
find their parents have sex problems of their
own.
Wise, witty and well acted sex farce, with
many actors making the most of ample
chances under firm directorial control.

w Renée Taylor, Joseph Bologna, David Zelag
Goodman d Cy Howard ph Andrew Laszlo
m Fred Karlin

Gig Young, Anne Jackson, Richard
Castellano, Bonnie Bedelia, Michael Brandon,
Beatrice Arthur, Robert Dishy, Harry
Guardino, Diane Keaton, Cloris Leachman,
Anne Meara, Marian Hailey
  'An extremely engaging comedy.'—Gillian
Hartnoll

AA: song 'For All We Know' (m Fred Karlin,
ly Robb Wilson, Arthur James)
AAN: script; Richard Castellano

● Video: Rank

Lovers Courageous
US 1932 78m bw

An unsuccessful playwright covets the
admiral's daughter. Heavily-titled comedy
with good performances of the period. Robert
Montgomery, Madge Evans, Roland Young,
Frederick Kerr, Reginald Owen, Halliwell
Hobbes, Alan Mowbray. Written by Frederick
Lonsdale; directed by Robert Z. Leonard; for
MGM.

The Lovers of Lisbon•
France 1954 112m bw
EGC / Hoche / Fides (Jacques Gauthier)
original title: Les Amants du Tage

A man who has killed his unfaithful wife is
acquitted of murder, gets a job as a taxi driver
in Lisbon, and falls for a rich Englishwoman
who has killed her husband and is being
pursued by a police inspector.
Pretentious tosh with a few compensations.

w Marcel Rivet, novel Joseph Kessel d Henri
Verneuil ph Roger Hubert m Lucien
Legrand

Daniel Gélin, Françoise Arnoul, Trevor
Howard, Ginette Leclerc, Marcel Dalio

The Lovers of Toledo
Italy / France / Spain 1952 82m bw
EGE / Lux / Athenea (Raymond Eger)

In 1825 a cruel police chief releases a political
prisoner in return for the hand in marriage of
his mistress.
Curiously unpersuasive period melodrama

with good credits but too many international
cooks.

w Claude Vermorel, story Le Coffre et le
Revenant by Stendhal d Henri Decoin
ph Michel Kelber m Jean-Jacques
Grunenwald

Pedro Armendariz, Alida Valli, Gérard
Landry, Françoise Arnoul

Loves of a Blonde•
Czechoslovakia 1965 82m bw
Barrandov Studios
original title: Lasky Jedne Plavovlasky
aka: A Blonde in Love

A factory girl falls for a visiting musician but
meets suspicion from his family when she
pursues him.
Mild anecdote with excellent humorous detail
which endeared it to international critics.

w Milos Forman, Jaroslav Papousek, Ivan
Passer d Milos Forman ph Miroslav
Ondricek m Evzen Illin

Hanna Brejchova, Vladimir Pucholt
  'It depends on an instinctive sense of timing
and a consistent vision of life and people.'—
Georges Sadoul

AAN: best foreign film

The Loves of Carmen
US 1948 99m Technicolor
Columbia (Charles Vidor)

In 1820s Seville, a dragoon corporal is
enslaved by a gypsy, kills her husband and
becomes an outlaw.
Unrewarding version of the original much-
filmed story, with both stars plainly wishing
they were elsewhere.

w Helen Deutsch, novel Prosper Mérimée
d Charles Vidor ph William Snyder m Mario
Castelnuovo-Tedesco

Rita Hayworth, Glenn Ford, Victor Jory, Ron
Randell, Luther Adler, Arnold Moss,
Margaret Wycherly, Bernard Nedell

AAN: William Snyder

The Loves of Edgar Allan Poe
US 1942 67m bw
TCF (Bryan Foy)

The famous writer marries his childhood
sweetheart but becomes an alcoholic.
A curiosity which fails to bring out the bizarre
truth and emerges as a stilted charade.

w Samuel Hoffenstein, Tom Reed d Harry
Lachman ph Lucien Andriot m Emil
Newman

John Shepperd, Linda Darnell, Virginia
Gilmore, Jane Darwell, Frank Conroy, Henry
Morgan

The Loves of Joanna Godden
GB 1947 89m bw
Ealing (Sidney Cole)

On Romney Marsh at the turn of the century,
a woman farmer has three suitors.
Dullish 'woman's picture'.

w H. E. Bates, Angus Macphail, novel Sheila
Kaye-Smith d Charles Frend ph Douglas
Slocombe m Ralph Vaughan Williams

Googie Withers, John McCallum, Jean Kent,
Derek Bond, Chips Rafferty, Henry Mollison,
Sonia Holm, Edward Rigby, Josephine Stuart
† Robert Hamer directed some scenes.

The Loves of Sunya
US 1927 80m (24 fps) bw silent
Swanson Producing Corporation

A yogi recognizes two young lovers as people
he wronged in a previous existence, and warns
them of impending disaster.
Star vehicle of its period, unthinkable now as a
screen attraction.

w Earle Brown, play The Eyes of Youth by
Max Marcin, Charles Guernon d Albert
Parker ph Dudley Murphy ad Hugo Ballin

Gloria Swanson, John Boles, Anders
Randolph, Hush Miller, Florbelle Fairbanks,
Raymond Hackett
† Previously filmed as Eyes of Youth with
Clara Kimball Young.

Lovesick
US 1983 96m Technicolor
Warner / Ladd (Charles Okun)

A New York psychiatrist in love with a patient
is guided by the ghost of Sigmund Freud.
Depressing comedy with a non-star and
supporting players who must have been
embarrassed.

w,d Marshall Brickman ph Gerry Fisher
m Philippe Sarde pd Philip Rosenberg

Dudley Moore, Elizabeth McGovern, Alec
Guinness (as Freud), John Huston, Larry
Rivers, Gene Saks, Renee Taylor, Alan King
  'Flat, lamebrained and indigestible.'—Geoff
Brown, MFB

Lovin' Molly•
US 1973 98m Movielab
Stephen Friedman (David Golden)

In Texas between 1925 and 1945, two men
friends and an accommodating lady have a
shifting relationship.
Odd little drama compendium, with fragments
told by each in turn; too slight in structure and
substance for complete success, but interesting
most of the way.

w Stephen Friedman, novel Leaving Cheyenne
by Larry McMurtry d Sidney Lumet
ph Edward Brown m Fred Hellerman

Blythe Danner, Anthony Perkins, Beau
Bridges, Edward Binns, Susan Sarandon

Loving••
US 1970 90m Eastmancolor
Columbia / Brooks Ltd (Don Devlin)

A commercial artist reaches crisis point with
both his wife and his mistress.
Smart New Yorkish sex comedy, typical of
many but better than most.

w Don Devlin, novel Brooks Wilson Ltd by J.
M. Ryan d Irvin Kershner ph Gordon Willis
m Bernardo Segall pd Walter Scott Herndon

George Segal, Eva Marie Saint, Sterling
Hayden, Keenan Wynn, Nancie Phillips, Janis
Young, David Doyle

Loving Couples

US 1980 98m Metrocolor
Time Life (Renee Valente)

Man-and-wife doctors decide to liven up their lives by having affairs.

Embarrassingly with-it romantic charade.

w Martin Donovan d Jack Smight ph Philip Lathrop m Fred Karlin

Shirley Maclaine, James Coburn, Susan Sarandon, Stephen Collins, Sally Kellerman

Loving Couples*

Sweden 1964 118m bw
Sandrew (Rune Waldekranz)
original title: Alskande Par

Three expectant mothers think back over their sex lives.

Superbly made, rather hollow diatribe against sex, presented as a series of intricate flashbacks. Along the way, there is much to enjoy, but the result is not really a film of importance.

w Mai Zetterling, David Hughes, novel Froknarna von Pahlen by Agnes von Krusenstjerna d Mai Zetterling ph Sven Nykvist m Rodger Wallis

Harriet Andersson, Gunnel Lindblom, Anita Bjork, Gunnar Bjornstrand, Eva Dahlbeck, Frank Sundstrom, Inga Landgre

'. . . that air of packaged neurosis so peculiar to the Swedish cinema.'—Tom Milne, MFB

Loving You

US 1957 101m Technicolor
Vistavision
Paramount / Hal B. Wallis

A press agent signs a young hillbilly singer to give zest to her husband's band.

Empty-headed, glossy star vehicle.

w Herbert Baker, Hal Kanter d Hal Kanter ph Charles Lang Jnr m Walter Scharf

Elvis Presley, Lizabeth Scott, Wendell Corey, Dolores Hart, James Gleason

● Video: Select

The Luck of Ginger Coffey*

Canada / US 1964 100m bw
Crawley / Roth–Kershner (Leon Roth)

An Irish layabout in Canada finds it difficult to keep a job or protect his family.

Mildly interesting character study with good background detail of Montreal.

w Brian Moore, from his novel d Irvin Kershner ph Manny Wynn m Bernardo Segall

Robert Shaw, Mary Ure, Liam Redmond

The Luck of the Irish*

US 1947 99m bw
TCF (Fred Kohlmar)

A New York newsman's love life is complicated by a helpful leprechaun he meets in Ireland.

Hollywood moonshine, second class: the will and the players are there, but the script is not funny enough.

w Philip Dunne, novel There Was a Little Man by Constance and Guy Jones d Henry Koster ph Joseph La Shelle m Cyril Mockridge

Tyrone Power, Cecil Kellaway, Anne Baxter, Lee J. Cobb, James Todd, Jayne Meadows, J. M. Kerrigan, Phil Brown

AAN: Cecil Kellaway

The Luckiest Girl in the World

US 1936 75m bw

A rich girl bets her father that she can live in New York for a month on 150 dollars.

Lighthearted comedy with farcical trimmings. Jane Wyatt (who really was from the social register), Louis Hayward, Eugene Pallette, Nat Pendleton, Catherine Doucet, Philip Reed. Written by Herbert Fields, Henry Myers, Anne Jordon; directed by Eddie Buzzell; for Charles R. Rogers / Universal. 'Speed and gags offset story absurdity.'—Variety

Lucky Devils

US 1933 63m bw

Hollywood stuntmen rescue an actress from a suicide attempt. Tolerable action special with interesting sidelights. William Boyd, Dorothy Wilson, William Gargan, Robert Rose, Roscoe Ates, Bruce Cabot. Written by Agnes Christine Johnson, Ben Markson, Casey Robinson, Bob Rose; directed by Ralph Ince; for David O. Selznick / RKO.

Lucky Jim**

GB 1957 95m bw
British Lion / Charter (Roy Boulting)

At a provincial university, an accident-prone junior lecturer has a disastrous weekend with his girl friend and his professor.

Quite funny in its own right, this is a vulgarization of a famous comic novel which got its effects more subtly, with more sense of place, time and character.

w Jeffrey Dell, Patrick Campbell, novel Kingsley Amis d John Boulting ph Max Greene

Ian Carmichael, Hugh Griffith, Terry-Thomas, Sharon Acker, Jean Anderson, Maureen Connell, Clive Morton, John Welsh, Reginald Beckwith, Kenneth Griffith

'An almost endless ripple of comfortable laughter.'—News Chronicle

● Video: Thorn EMI

'When he smiles, it's not because he likes you—it's because he likes what he's going to do to you!'

Lucky Jordan

US 1942 83m bw
Paramount (Fred Kohlmar)

A con man is drafted and overcomes Nazi agents.

Forgettable star cheapie.

w Darrell Ware, Karl Tunberg d Frank Tuttle ph John F. Seitz m Adolph Deutsch

Alan Ladd, Helen Walker, Sheldon Leonard, Marie McDonald, Mabel Paige, Lloyd Corrigan, Dave Willock, Miles Mander

'It's still cops and robbers, no matter how you slice it . . . Mr Ware and Mr Tunberg are not above dragging in mother love as the reason the gangster changes from a selfish killer to a patriot.'—Joseph Pihodna, New York Herald Tribune

Lucky Lady

US 1975 118m De Luxe
TCF / Gruskoff / Venture (Michael Gruskoff)

A cabaret girl in 1930 Tijuana joins two adventurers in smuggling liquor into the US by boat.

Whatever can be done wrong with such a story has been done, including irritatingly washed out photography, kinky sex, and sudden switches from farce to gore. None of it holds the interest for a single moment.

w Willard Huyck, Gloria Katz d Stanley Donen ph Geoffrey Unsworth m Ralph Burns pd John Barry

Liza Minnelli, Gene Hackman, Burt Reynolds, Michael Hordern, Geoffrey Lewis, Robby Benson

'A manic mess that tries to be all things to all people and ends up offering nothing to anyone.'—Frank Rich

'It sports its calculations on its sleeve like rhinestones.'—Sight and Sound

'They're all rumrunners in the early 30s, and they're meant to be adorable. This is a big expensive movie for people who don't mind being treated like hicks: the audience is expected to shudder with delight every time it hears an obscenity or sees a big movie star grin.'—Pauline Kael, New Yorker

Lucky Me*

US 1954 100m Warnercolor
Cinemascope
Warner (Henry Blanke)

Theatrical entertainers stranded in Florida get a lucky break.

Watchable, forgettable musical.

w James O'Hanlon, Robert O'Brien, Irving Elinson d Jack Donohue ph Wilfrid M. Cline md Ray Heindorf

Doris Day, Robert Cummings, Phil Silvers, Eddie Foy Jnr, Nancy Walker, Martha Hyer, Bill Goodwin, Marcel Dalio

'The first Cinemascope musical . . . pleasant, light-hearted, frothy entertainment.'—MFB

Lucky Night

US 1939 90m bw
MGM (Louis D. Lighton)

An heiress goes out into the world to make a life for herself, and falls for a man she finds on a park bench.

Tedious pattern romance which did neither of its stars any good.

w Vincent Laurence, Grover Jones d Norman Taurog ph Ray June

Myrna Loy, Robert Taylor, Joseph Allen, Henry O'Neill, Douglas Fowley, Marjorie Main, Charles Lane, Bernard Nedell

'Light romantic comedy, okay for box office . . . but certain sections might object to so much liquor-imbibing.'—*Variety*

Lucky Partners*
US 1940 101m bw
RKO (George Haight)

Two strangers share a sweepstake ticket and fall in love.
A very thin comedy kept afloat by its stars.

w Allan Scott, John Van Druten, *story* Bonne Chance by Sacha Guitry *d* Lewis Milestone *ph* Robert de Grasse *m* Dmitri Tiomkin

Ronald Colman, Ginger Rogers, Jack Carson, Spring Byington, Cecilia Loftus, Harry Davenport

The Lucky Star*
Canada 1980 110m colour
Tele Metropole International / Claude Leger

During World War II a Dutch Jewish boy studies wild west films and captures a German colonel.
Unusual and likeable family adventure story with an unnecessary downbeat ending.

w Max Fischer, Jack Rosenthal *d* Max Fischer *ph* Frank Tody *m* Art Philipps

Rod Steiger, Louise Fletcher, Brett Marx, Lou Jacobi, Helen Hughes

The Lucky Stiff
US 1948 101m bw

A cabaret singer sentenced to death for murder is secretly reprieved but comes back as a 'ghost' to scare the real culprit into confession. Weird comedy-melodrama which seems to embarrass all concerned. Dorothy Lamour, Brian Donlevy, Claire Trevor, Irene Hervey. Written and directed by Lewis R. Foster, from a novel by Craig Rice; for Amusement Enterprises / UA.

Lucretia Borgia
France / Italy 1952 105m approx
   Technicolor
Ariane / Filmsonor / Rizzoli

Cesare Borgia uses his beautiful sister as a political pawn.
Well-mounted but rather boring period barnstormer.

w Cécil Saint-Laurent, Jacques Sigurd, Christian-Jaque *d* Christian-Jaque *ph* Christian Matras *m* Maurice Thiriet

Martine Carol, Pedro Armendariz, Massimo Serato, Ventine Tessier

Lucy Gallant*
US 1955 104m Technicolor
   Vistavision
Paramount / Pine–Thomas

The success story of a dressmaker who comes to run a group of fashion shops but neglects her love life.
Efficient, smartly-handled woman's picture.

w John Lee Mahin, Winston Miller, *novel* The Life of Lucy Gallant by Margaret Cousins *d* Robert Parrish *ph* Lionel Lindon *m* Van Cleave

Jane Wyman, Charlton Heston, Claire Trevor, Thelma Ritter, William Demarest, Wallace Ford, Tom Helmore, Mary Field

Ludwig*
Italy / France / West Germany 1972
   186m Technicolor Panavision
Mega / Cinetel / Dieter Gessler / Divina
   (Robert Gordon Edwards)

The 19th-century King of Bavaria becomes involved in scandal and goes mad.
A stylish but historically questionable and highly coloured view of events; it drags its heels long before history did.

w Luchino Visconti, Enrico Medioli *d* Luchino Visconti *ph* Armando Nannuzzi *md* Franco Nannino

Helmut Berger, Romy Schneider, Trevor Howard, Silvana Mangano, Helmut Griem, Nora Ricci, Gert Frobe, John Moulder Brown

'Happiness is busting out all over!'
Lullaby of Broadway*
US 1951 92m Technicolor
Warner (William Jacobs)

The daughter of a faded Broadway star becomes the new toast of the town.
Reasonably lively musical with solid production values but little style or wit.

w Earl Baldwin *d* David Butler *ph* Wilfrid Cline *md* Ray Heindorf

Doris Day, Billy de Wolfe, Gene Nelson, Gladys George, Florence Bates, S. Z. Sakall

Lulu Belle
US 1948 87m bw

A selfish singer has a bad effect on one man after another. Dreary melodrama with a miscast star. Dorothy Lamour, George Montgomery, Otto Kruger, Albert Dekker, Glenda Farrell. Written by Everett Freeman, from the play by Charles MacArthur and Edward Shelton; directed by Leslie Fenton; for Benedict Bogeaus / Columbia.

Lumière D'Eté*
France 1943 112m bw
Discina (André Paulvé)

The idle and decadent rich in a mountain hotel are affected in various ways by workmen in the valley below.
Unusual and generally interesting character melodrama.

w Jacques Prévert, Pierre Laroche *d* Jean Grémillion *ph* Louis Page *m* Roland Manuel

Madeleine Renaud, Pierre Brasseur, Madeleine Robinson, Paul Bernard, Jane Marken, Georges Marchal

La Luna
Italy 1979 142m Eastmancolor
TCF / Fiction Cinematografica (Giovanni Bertolucci)

A singer has an incestuous relationship with her teenage son.
Interminable catalogue of events few people wanted to experience; the kindest description would be 'pretentious claptrap'.

w Giuseppe and Bernardo Bertolucci, Clare Peploe *d* Bernardo Bertolucci *ph* Vittorio Storaro *m* operatic excerpts

Jill Clayburgh, Matthew Barry, Laura Betti, Renato Salvatori, Fred Gwynne

Lunch on the Grass**
France 1959 91m Eastmancolor
Compagnie Jean Renoir
original title: *Déjeuner sur l'Herbe*

An international scientist hears the pipes of pan, embarks on a country idyll and impregnates a housemaid whom he later marries.
Charming if overlong frolic with ideas, a harking back to earlier Renoir themes such as in *Boudu Sauvé des Eaux*.

wd Jean Renoir *ph* Georges Leclerc *m* Joseph Kosma

Paul Meurisse, Catherine Rouvel, Fernand Sardou, Ingrid Nordine

'A warm, loving, garrulous, undisciplined film.'—*Penelope Houston, MFB*

Lure of the Wilderness
US 1952 92m Technicolor
TCF (Robert L. Jacks)

A man falsely accused of murder hides for eight years in Georgia's Okefenokee swamp. Remake of *Swamp Water*, with Walter Brennan playing the same part. The plot works fairly well still, but colour doesn't suit the scenery.

w Louis Lantz, *story* Vereen Bell *d* Jean Negulesco *ph* Edward Cronjager *m* Franz Waxman

Jeffrey Hunter, Jean Peters, Walter Brennan, Constance Smith, Jack Elam

Lured*
US 1947 102m bw
(UA) Hunt Stromberg (James Nasser)
GB title: *Personal Column*

An American dancer stranded in London helps Scotland Yard catch a killer.
Minor murder mystery with a pleasing cast.

w Leo Rosten, from the French film *Pièges* *d* Douglas Sirk *ph* William Daniels *m* Michel Michelet *pd* Nicolai Remisoff

Lucille Ball, George Sanders, Charles Coburn, Boris Karloff, Cedric Hardwicke, Alan Mowbray, George Zucco, Joseph Calleia, Robert Coote, Alan Napier

Lust for a Vampire
GB 1970 95m Technicolor
Hammer (Harry Fine, Michael Style)

In 1830 an English writer discerns that a pupil

in an exclusive mid-European girls' school is a reincarnated vampire.
Moderate Hammer horror.

w Tudor Gates, based on J. Sheridan Le Fanu's Carmilla d Jimmy Sangster ph David Muir m Harry Robinson

Ralph Bates, Michael Johnson, Barbara Jefford, Suzanna Leigh, Yutte Stensgaard, Mike Raven, Helen Christie

Lust for Gold
US 1949 90m bw
Columbia (S. Sylvan Simon)

A young man goes to Arizona to search for a lost gold mine discovered by his grandfather.
Moderate western drama consisting largely of flashback.

w Ted Sherdeman, Richard English, *novel* Thunder God's Gold by Barry Storm d S. Sylvan Simon ph Archie Stout m George Duning

Ida Lupino, Glenn Ford, Gig Young, William Prince, Edgar Buchanan, Will Geer, Paul Ford

Lust for Life**
US 1956 122m Metrocolor
Cinemascope
MGM (John Houseman)

The life of Vincent Van Gogh.
Fairly absorbing, not inaccurate, but somehow uninspiring biopic, probably marred by poor colour and wide screen; despite good work all round, it simply doesn't fall into a classic category.

w Norman Corwin, *book* Irving Stone d Vincente Minnelli ph F. A. Young, Russell Harlan m Miklos Rozsa ad Cedric Gibbons, Hans Peters, Preston Ames

Kirk Douglas, Anthony Quinn (as Gauguin), James Donald, Pamela Brown, Everett Sloane, Niall MacGinnis, Noel Purcell, Henry Daniell, Lionel Jeffries, Madge Kennedy, Jill Bennett, Laurence Naismith
  'Two hours of quite shattering and exciting entertainment.'—*Alan Dent, Illustrated London News*

AA: Anthony Quinn
AAN: Norman Corwin; Kirk Douglas

Lust in the Dust
US 1984 87m CFI colour
Fox Run (Allan Glaser, Tab Hunter)

In the old west, a strong silent man and a drag queen beat the baddies to the gold.
Fitfully funny spoof for adults.

w Philip Taylor d Paul Bartel ph Paul Lohmann m Peter Matz ed Alan Toomayan

Tab Hunter, Divine, Lainie Kazan, Geoffrey Lewis, Henry Silva, Cesar Romero, Woody Strode

The Lusty Men*
US 1952 113m bw
RKO / Wald–Krasna (Jerry Wald)

Tensions lead to the death of one of a pair of rider friends on a rodeo tour.
Standard melodrama with semi-documentary detail and star performances.

w Horace McCoy, David Dortort d Nicholas Ray ph Lee Garmes m Roy Webb

Robert Mitchum, Arthur Kennedy, Susan Hayward, Arthur Hunnicutt

Luther*
GB 1973 112m Eastmancolor
American Express / Ely Landau / Cinevision

In 1525, the teachings of Luther culminate in the Peasants' Revolt.
Hard-to-watch filming by the American Film Theatre of a singularly theatrical play, and not a very good one at that. Some good acting.

w Edward Anhalt, *play* John Osborne d Guy Green ph Freddie Young m John Addison pd Peter Mullins

Stacy Keach, Patrick Magee, Hugh Griffith, Robert Stephens, Alan Badel, Julian Glover, Judi Dench, Leonard Rossiter, Maurice Denham

Luv
US 1967 95m Technicolor Panavision
Columbia / Jalem (Martin Manulis)

When a man prevents an old friend from jumping off the Brooklyn Bridge and brings him home, a sexual square dance develops.
A modern comedy that should have stayed in the theatre.

w Elliott Baker, *play* Murray Shisgal d Clive Donner ph Ernest Laszlo m Gerry Mulligan

Jack Lemmon, Peter Falk, Elaine May, Nina Wayne, Eddie Mayehoff, Paul Hartman, Severn Darden
  'A light but incisive comedy about the patterns and language of love in a Freud-ridden society has become an inept and lethally unamusing film farce.'—*MFB*

Luxury Liner
US 1933 72m bw
Paramount

Stories of various passengers on a liner bound from New York to Bremerhaven.
Interesting minor multi-drama, like a rough sketch for *Ship of Fools* (qv).

w Gene Markey, Kathryn Scola, *novel*, Gina Kaus d Lothar Mendes ph Victor Milner

George Brent, Zita Johann, Vivienne Osborne, Alice White, Verree Teasdale, C. Aubrey Smith, Frank Morgan, Henry Wadsworth, Billy Bevan
  'Not even the frank hook-up with *Grand Hotel* will help this entry much . . . a loose and thin catch-as-catch-can affair.'—*Variety*

Luxury Liner
US 1948 98m Technicolor
MGM (Joe Pasternak)

The captain of a liner has trouble with his teenage daughter.
Minor shipboard musical with pleasing talents applied.

w Gladys Lehmann, Richard Connell d Richard Whorf ph Ernest Laszlo md George Stoll

George Brent, Jane Powell, Lauritz Melchior, Frances Gifford, Marina Koshetz, Xavier Cugat, Richard Derr, Connie Gilchrist

'The girl who thought she knew all about love!'
Lydia*
US 1941 104m bw
Alexander Korda (Lee Garmes)

An ageing lady recalls her former beaux.
Pleasing remake of *Carnet du Bal*, with excellent production values.

w Ben Hecht, Samuel Hoffenstein, *story* Julien Duvivier, Laszlo Bus-Fekete d Julien Duvivier ph Lee Garmes m Miklos Rozsa pd Vincent Korda

Merle Oberon, Joseph Cotten, Alan Marshal, Edna May Oliver, Hans Yaray, George Reeves, John Halliday, Sara Allgood

AAN: Miklos Rozsa

Lydia Bailey
US 1952 89m Technicolor
TCF (Jules Schermer)

In 1802 a Boston lawyer visits Haiti to obtain the signature of a wayward heiress, and becomes involved in the negro fight against the French.
Standard adventure romance with plenty of excitements.

w Michael Blankfort, Philip Dunne, *novel* Kenneth Roberts d Jean Negulesco ph Harry Jackson m Hugo Friedhofer

Dale Robertson, Anne Francis, Charles Korvin, William Marshall, Adeline de Walt Reynolds

M••••
Germany 1931 118m bw
Nero Film (Symour Nebenzal)

A psychopathic murderer of children evades the police but is caught by the city's criminals who find his activities getting them a bad name.

An unmistakable classic whose oddities are hardly worth criticizing, this is part social melodrama and part satire, but entirely unforgettable, with most of its sequences brilliantly staged.

w *Thea Von Harbou, Paul Falkenberg, Adolf Jansen, Karl Vash* d *Fritz Lang* ph Fritz Arno Wagner m Adolf Jansen ad Karl Vollbrecht, Emil Hasler

Peter Lorre, Otto Wernicke, Gustav Grundgens

  'Visual excitement, pace, brilliance of surface and feeling for detail.'—*New Yorker, 1977*

† Of Lang's later work, *Fury* comes closest to the feeling and style of *M*.

M•
US 1951 82m bw
Columbia (Seymour Nebenzal)

Faithful but fated remake; without the heavy expressionist techniques, the story seems merely silly and the atmosphere is all wrong.

w Norman Reilly Raine, Leo Katcher
d Joseph Losey ph Ernest Laszlo m Michel Michelet

David Wayne, Howard da Silva, Luther Adler, Martin Gabel, Glenn Anders, Karen Morley, Norman Lloyd, Walter Burke

Ma and Pa Kettle•
US 1949 75m bw
U-I (Leonard Goldstein)

Pa Kettle wins a house in a contest and is accused of cheating.

First of a series of low-budget comedies which, based on characters from *The Egg and I* (qv), had astonishing commercial success in America. The standard varied from adequate to painful.

w Herbert Margolis, Louis Morheim, Al Lewis d Charles Lamont ph Maury Gertsman m Milton Schwarzwald

Marjorie Main, Percy Kilbride, Richard Long, Meg Randall

  'Not exactly Noel Coward.'—*Leonard Maltin*

† For others in the series, see under *The Kettles*.

Ma Nuit chez Maud•
France 1969 110m bw
Films du Losange
aka: *My Night at Maud's*

A Catholic clerk in a small town falls in love with an elegant divorcee but can't bring himself to court her openly and marries someone else.

Subdued, literate talk-piece which finally exhausts rather than stimulates.

wd Eric Rohmer ph Nestor Almendros

Jean-Louis Trintignant, Françoise Fabian, Marie-Christine Barault

AAN: best foreign film; Eric Rohmer (as writer)

'So terrifying we have to insure your life!'
Macabre
US 1958 73m bw
AA (William Castle)

When a small-town doctor's daughter is kidnapped, he fears she may have been buried alive in the cemetery.

Genuine but unsuccessful attempt to film a horror comic; incredibly stodgy writing, acting and direction put the lid on it.

w Robb White d William Castle ph Carl Guthrie m Les Baxter

William Prince, Jim Backus, Jacqueline Scott, Philip Tonge, Ellen Corby

  'A ghoulish but totally ineffective horror piece, set mainly in undertakers' offices and an atmosphere of graveyards and swirling fog.'—*MFB*

† When first released, admission carried insurance against death by fright. Some said it should have been death by boredom.

Macao
US 1952 81m bw
RKO (Alex Gottlieb)

A wandering American in the Far East helps a detective catch a gangster.

A few flashy decorative touches show the director's hand, otherwise this is routine, murky thick ear.

w Bernard C. Schoenfeld, Stanley Rubin
d Josef Von Sternberg (and Nicholas Ray)
ph Harry J. Wild m Anthony Collins

Robert Mitchum, Jane Russell, William Bendix, Gloria Grahame, Thomas Gomez

MacArthur the Rebel General•
US 1977 130m Technicolor
Universal / Richard D. Zanuck, David Brown (Frank McCarthy)

The exploits of General MacArthur during the Pacific wars and his strained relationships with two presidents.

Sober, earnest political biography with war sequences; very well done but somehow unsympathetic.

w Hal Barwood, Matthew Robbins d Joseph Sargent ph Mario Tosi m Jerry Goldsmith

Gregory Peck, Dan O'Herlihy (as Roosevelt), Ed Flanders (as Truman), Ward Costello, Marj Dusay, Ivan Bonar

  'A biopic that begins when its subject is sixty lacks roots—and in this case revelation.'—*Judith Crist*

● *Video: CIC*

Macbeth•
US 1948 89m bw
Republic (Orson Welles)

A famous—or infamous—attempt to film Shakespeare in twenty-one days in papier mâché settings running with damp; further hampered by the use of a form of unintelligible bastard Scots. A few striking moments at the beginning remain; the rest should be silence.

d Orson Welles ph John L. Russell
m Jacques Ibert ad Fred Ritter

Orson Welles, Jeanette Nolan, Dan O'Herlihy, Roddy McDowall, Edgar Barrier, Robert Coote

● *Video: Intervision*

Macbeth•
GB 1971 140m Technicolor Todd-AO 35
Playboy / Caliban (Andrew Braunsberg)

A sharpened and brutalized version; the blood swamps most of the cleverness and most of the poetry.

d Roman Polanski ph Gilbert Taylor m the Third Ear Band pd Wilfrid Shingleton

Jon Finch, Francesca Annis, Martin Shaw, Nicholas Selby, John Stride

McCabe and Mrs Miller

US 1971 120m Technicolor
Panavision
Warner (David Foster, Mitchell Brower)

At the turn of the century a gambling
gunfighter comes to a northwest mining town
and uses his money to set up lavish brothels.
Obscurely scripted, muddy-coloured and
harshly recorded western melodrama whose
squalid 'realism' comes as close to fantasy as
does *The Wizard of Oz*.

w Robert Altman, Brian Mackay, *novel*
McCabe by Edmund Naughton d Robert
Altman ph Vilmos Zsigmond pd Leon
Erickson

Warren Beatty, Julie Christie, René
Auberjonois, Shelley Duvall, John Schuck
 'A fleeting, diaphanous vision of what
frontier life might have been.'—*Pauline Kael*
 'Altman directed *M*A*S*H*, which
wandered and was often funny; then *Brewster
McCloud*, which wandered and was not funny;
now this, which wanders and is repulsive. The
thesis seems to be that if you take a corny
story, fuzz up the exposition, vitiate the
action, use a childishly ironic ending, and put
in lots of profanity and nudity, you have
Marched On with Time.'—*Stanley Kauffmann*
AAN: Julie Christie

The McConnell Story

US 1955 107m Warnercolor
Cinemascope
Warner (Henry Blanke)
GB title: *Tiger in the Sky*

The career and accidental death of a jet ace of
the Korean war.
Crude, obvious and saccharine biopic.

w Ted Sherdeman, Sam Rolfe d Gordon
Douglas ph John Seitz, Ted McCord m Max
Steiner

Alan Ladd, June Allyson, James Whitmore,
Frank Faylen, Willis Bouchey

McFadden's Flats

US 1935 65m bw

The quarrel between a bricklayer and a barber
affects their children. Modest working-class
comedy from a well-worn play. Walter C.
Kelly, Andy Clyde, Richard Cromwell, Jane
Darwell, Betty Furness, George Barbier.
Written by Arthur Caesar, Edward Kaufman,
Casey Robinson, Andy Rice, from play by
Gus Hill; directed by Ralph Murphy; for
Paramount. 'Better-than-average family
picture.'—*Variety*

Macho Callahan

US 1970 100m Movielab Panavision
Avco / Felicidad (Bernard Kowalski, Martin
C. Schute)

A vengeful cowboy annihilates all who stand
in his way.
Squalid Mexican-made western with
unremitting emphasis on violence.

w Clifford Newton Gould d Bernard
Kowalski ph Gerry Fisher m Pat Williams

David Janssen, Lee J. Cobb, David Carradine,
James Booth, Jean Seberg

MacKenna's Gold*

US 1969 136m Technicolor Super
Panavision
Columbia / Highroad (Carl Foreman, Dmitri
Tiomkin)

A dying Indian entrusts a sheriff with a map of
the legendary Valley of Gold, and when the
news breaks the map is in demand.
Curious serial-like western melodrama packed
with stars and pretensions above its station.
On a lower level, it is quite enjoyable.

w Carl Foreman, *novel* Will Henry d J. Lee-
Thompson ph Joseph MacDonald, Harold
Wellman m Quincy Jones pd Geoffrey
Drake

Gregory Peck, Omar Sharif, Telly Savalas,
Camilla Sparv, Keenan Wynn, Julie Newmar,
Ted Cassidy, Eduardo Ciannelli, Eli Wallach,
Edward G. Robinson, Raymond Massey,
Burgess Meredith, Anthony Quayle, Lee J.
Cobb
 'Preposterous hotch-potch of every cliché
known to the gold lust book.'—*MFB*
 'Twelve-year-olds of all ages might tolerate
it.'—*Judith Crist*
 'A western of truly stunning absurdity, a
thriving example of the old Hollywood maxim
about how to succeed by failing big.'—*Vincent
Canby*

The McKenzie Break*

GB 1970 106m De Luxe
UA / Levy–Gardner–Laven

During World War II, German prisoners at a
Scottish camp stage an escape.
Effective little action suspenser.

w William Norton d Lamont Johnson
ph Michael Reed m Riz Ortolani

Brian Keith, Helmut Griem, Ian Hendry, Jack
Watson, Patrick O'Connell, Horst Janson

The Mackintosh Man*

GB 1973 99m Technicolor
Warner / Newman–Foreman / John Huston

A government agent is sent to prison to
contact a criminal gang.
Convoluted but entertaining spy thriller with
good performances and action sequences.

w Walter Hill, *novel* The Freedom Trap by
Desmond Bagley d John Huston ph Oswald
Morris m Maurice Jarre

Paul Newman, James Mason, Dominique
Sanda, Nigel Patrick, Harry Andrews, Michael
Hordern, Ian Bannen, Peter Vaughan, Roland
Culver, Percy Herbert, Robert Lang, Leo
Genn

McLintock*

US 1963 127m Technicolor
Panavision
UA / Batjac (Michael Wayne)

A cattle baron can control a whole town but
not his termagant wife.
Sub-Ford western farce borrowed from *The
Taming of the Shrew*, with much fist-fighting
and mud-splattering, and rather too much chat
in between.

w James Edward Grant d Andrew V.
McLaglen ph William H. Clothier m Frank
de Vol

John Wayne, Maureen O'Hara, Yvonne de
Carlo, Patrick Wayne, Stefanie Powers, Chill
Wills, Bruce Cabot, Jack Kruschen

The McMasters

US 1969 90m Technicolor
JayJen (Dimitri de Grunwald)

A black man returning home from the Civil
War gets unexpected help from a tough
landowner.
Racial western with black, white and red
points of view, all very violently expressed.

w Harold Jacob Smith d Alf Kjellin
ph Lester Shorr m Coleridge-Taylor
Parkinson

Brock Peters, Burl Ives, David Carradine,
Nancy Kwan, Jack Palance, Dane Clark, John
Carradine, I. Q. Jones, R. G. Armstrong

The Macomber Affair*

US 1947 89m bw
(UA) Benedict Bogeaus (Casey Robinson)

The wife of a bullying big game hunter falls for
their guide.
Safari melodrama with a plot which has
become a cliché but seemed fresh enough at
the time. Goodish writing and acting.

w Casey Robinson, *story* The Short Happy
Life of Francis Macomber by Ernest
Hemingway d Zoltan Korda ph Karl Struss
m Miklos Rozsa

Gregory Peck, Joan Bennett, Robert Preston,
Reginald Denny, Carl Harbord, Jean Gillie
 'The best movie job on Hemingway to
date.'—*James Agee*

Macon County Line

US 1973 89m Eastmancolor
Sam Arkoff / Max Baer

In mid-fifties Louisiana, a couple of hell-
raisers are harassed by a local sheriff, and
much bloodshed results.
Shapeless melodrama more or less in the wake
of *Easy Rider*; an unattractive film which
unaccountably had great box-office success.

w Max Baer, Richard Compton d Richard
Compton ph Daniel Lacambre m Stu Phillips

Alan Vint, Cheryl Waters, Geoffrey Lewis,
Joan Blackman, Jesse Vint, Max Baer

'He's a busted cop, his gun is unlicensed,
 his methods unlawful, his story
 incredible!'

McQ

US 1974 111m Technicolor
Panavision
Warner / Batjac / Levy–Gardner

A Seattle police detective goes after the
gangster who killed his friend.

Rambling, violent thriller with good sequences but no cohesion.

w Lawrence Roman d John Sturges
ph Harry Stradling Jnr m Elmer Bernstein

John Wayne, Eddie Albert, Diana Muldaur, Colleen Dewhurst, Clu Gulager, David Huddleston, Julie Adams

McVicar
GB 1980   112m   Eastmancolor

The true story of the escapes from prison of a violent criminal who was subsequently reformed and rehabilitated. Some smart sequences don't prevent this from being an exploitation item. Roger Daltrey, Adam Faith, Cheryl Campbell, Billy Murray, Georgina Hale. Written by John McVicar and Tom Clegg; directed by Tom Clegg; for The Who Films.

Mad About Men
GB 1954   90m   Technicolor
GFD / Group Films (Betty Box)

By mutual agreement, a sports mistress and a mermaid change places for a while.
Laborious rehash of *Miranda* with familiar jokes.

w Peter Blackmore d Ralph Thomas
ph Ernest Steward m Benjamin Frankel

Glynis Johns, Donald Sinden, Anne Crawford, Margaret Rutherford, Dora Bryan, Nicholas Phipps, Irene Handl

Mad about Music°
US 1938   98m   bw
Universal (Joe Pasternak)

A girl at a Swiss school adopts a personable visitor as her father.
Pleasing star vehicle with charm and humour; badly remade as *Toy Tiger* (qv).

w Bruce Manning, Felix Jackson d Norman Taurog ph Joseph Valentine m / ly Harold Adamson, Jimmie McHugh m Frank Skinner, Charles Previn

Deanna Durbin, Herbert Marshall, Gail Patrick, Arthur Treacher, Helen Parrish, Marcia Mae Jones, William Frawley
'Another Durbin smash . . . will mop up at the b.o.'—*Variety*

AAN: original story (Marcella Burke, Frank Kohner); Joseph Valentine; Frank Skinner, Charles Previn

'She knew the ecstasy and terror of loving him!'
The Mad Doctor
US 1940   90m   bw
Paramount (George Arthur)
GB title: *A Date with Destiny*

A doctor marries wealthy women and then murders them.
Naïve melodrama of little interest except as a vehicle for its star.

w Howard J. Green d Tim Whelan ph Ted Tetzlaff m Victor Young

Basil Rathbone, Ellen Drew, John Howard, Barbara Allen, Ralph Morgan, Martin Kosleck

The Mad Doctor of Market Street
US 1942   61m   bw

Shipwrecked people on a tropical island find that one of their number is a dangerous paranoiac. Dull and misleadingly titled second-feature melodrama. Lionel Atwill, Nat Pendleton, Una Merkel, Claire Dodd. Written by Al Martin; directed by Joseph H. Lewis; for Universal.

The Mad Game
US 1933   73m   bw

A gangster turns stool pigeon to round up kidnappers. Fairly lively crime melodrama. Spencer Tracy, Claire Trevor, Ralph Morgan, J. Carrol Naish, John Miljan. Written by William Conselman, Henry Johnson; directed by Irving Cummings; for Fox. 'Enough romance and action to satisfy.'—*Variety*

The Mad Genius
US 1931   81m   bw
Warner

A crippled puppeteer adopts a boy and makes him into a great dancer.
Curious variation on *Trilby*, filmed as *Svengali* the previous year with much the same cast. Not a great success: the script is dreadful.

w J. Grubb Alexander, Harvey Thew, *play* The Idol by Martin Brown d Michael Curtiz ph Barney McGill ad Anton Grot

John Barrymore, Marian Marsh, Donald Cook, Luis Alberni, Carmel Myers, Charles Butterworth, Boris Karloff, Frankie Darro
'Magnificent acting, but not the sort of thing that will panic the fans.'—*Variety*
† Many of the sets in this production had ceilings, ten years before the idea was supposed to have been invented for *Citizen Kane*.

The Mad Ghoul
US 1943   65m   bw
Universal (Ben Pivar)

A mad scientist needs fresh hearts to keep alive the victims of his experiments with a poison vapour.
Stagey, tasteless horror melodrama.

w Brenda Weisberg, Paul Gangelin, *story* Hans Kraly d James Higan ph Milton Krasner md Hans Salter

George Zucco, David Bruce, Evelyn Ankers, Turhan Bey, Robert Armstrong, Charles McGraw, Milburn Stone

Mad Holiday
US 1936   72m   bw

A rebellious film actor goes on a cruise and gets involved in a murder. Spotty mystery comedy in which the elements don't really jell. Edmund Lowe, Elissa Landi, Edmund Gwenn, Zasu Pitts, Ted Healy, Edgar Kennedy. Written by Florence Ryerson and Edgar Allen Woolf from the story Murder in a

Chinese Theatre by Joseph Santley; directed by George B. Seitz; for MGM. 'Very draggy . . . largely a bore.'—*Variety*

Mad Love**
US 1935   83m   bw
MGM (John Considine Jnr)
GB title: *The Hands of Orlac*

A pianist loses his hands in an accident; a mad surgeon, in love with the pianist's wife, grafts on the hands of a murderer.
Absurd Grand Guignol done with great style which somehow does not communicate itself in viewer interest, only in cold admiration.

w Guy Endore, P. J. Wolfson, John Balderston, *novel* The Hands of Orlac by Maurice Renard d Karl Freund ph Chester Lyons, Gregg Toland m Dmitri Tiomkin

Colin Clive, Peter Lorre, Frances Drake, Ted Healy, Edward Brophy, Isabel Jewell, Sara Haden
'The results in screen potency are disappointing . . . will probably do fair biz.'—*Variety*

The Mad Magician
US 1954   72m   bw
Columbia (Bryan Foy)

A magician's star-struck inventor murders his employer and several others who stand between him and the big time.
Hokey horror flick set in the eighties and originally shown in 3-D.

w Crane Wilbur d John Brahm ph Bert Glennon m Emil Newman

Vincent Price, Mary Murphy, Eva Gabor, John Emery, Patrick O'Neal

Mad Max
Australia 1979   100m   Eastmancolor
    Todd-AO 35
Mad Max Pty (Byron Kennedy)

In the future, motor cycle gangs combat the police.
Violent extravaganza with no real merit save its enthusiasm for destruction of both bikes and bodies.

w James McCausland, George Miller
d George Miller ph David Eggby m Brian May

Mel Gibson, Joanne Samuel, Hugh Keays-Byrne, Steve Bisley

● *Video: Warner*

Mad Max 2
Australia 1981   96m   colour   Panavision
Kennedy Miller Entertainment (Byron Kennedy)
US title: *The Road Warrior*

A shortage of petrol causes all-out war between police and bikers.
Not much more than a retread of the above, but a more expensive, spectacular and violent one.

w Terry Hayes, George Miller, Brian Hannant d George Miller ph Dean Semler
m Brian May

THE MAD GHOUL.   A tasteless horror of the forties. Evelyn Ankers, Turhan Bey, David Bruce.

Woolly and unattractive farce which proved something of a disaster for all the talents concerned but historically is of considerable interest. It begins with an excerpt from *The Freshman* and continues to comic adventures with a lion.

wd / pd Preston Sturges (re-edited by others) *ph* Robert Pittack *m* Werner Richard Heymann

Harold Lloyd, Jimmy Conlin, Raymond Walburn, Franklin Pangborn, Al Bridge, Margaret Hamilton, Edgar Kennedy

'Whatever it is that French women have—
    Madame Bovary had more of it!'
Madame Bovary
US 1949 114m bw
MGM (Pandro S. Berman)

A passionate girl marries a dull husband, takes a lover, and commits suicide.
Dull, emasculated version of a classic.

w Robert Ardrey, *novel* Gustave Flaubert *d* Vincente Minnelli *ph* Robert Planck *m* Miklos Rozsa

Jennifer Jones, Van Heflin, James Mason, Louis Jourdan, Christopher Kent, Gene Lockhart, Gladys Cooper, John Abbott, George Zucco
    'If you hadn't read the book, you wouldn't guess what it was about from this film.'— *Pauline Kael, 70s*
† Previously filmed in 1932 as *Unholy Love*.

'One of the world's magnificent romances
    of great, unselfish love!'
Madame Butterfly
US 1932 88m bw
Paramount

A Japanese geisha commits hara kiri when an American lieutenant passes her up for a western girl.
Drearily modernized version of the opera without its music; an odd idea to say the least.

w Josephine Lovett, Joseph M. March, *play* David Belasco, John Luther Long *d* Marion Gering *ph* David Abel *md* W. Franke Harling

Sylvia Sidney, Cary Grant, Charlie Ruggles, Sandor Kallay, Irving Pichel, Helen Jerome Eddy
    'The long-drawn tragedy might be bearable if it were expressed in music or poetry, without any such embellishment it is apt to be painfully pathetic.'—*The Times*
    'Travels slow and makes for only fair entertainment.'—*Variety*

'Mr and Mrs Miniver together again!'
Madame Curie*
US 1944 124m bw
MGM (Sidney Franklin)

The life and marriage of the woman who discovered radium.
Dignified and rather dull biopic which well exemplifies MGM's best production style of the forties.

Mel Gibson, Bruce Spence, Vernon Wells, Emil Minty
    'Essentially just another display of vehicles smashing into each other.'—*David McGillivray, MFB*
● Video: Warner

The Mad Miss Manton*
US 1938 80m bw
RKO (Pandro S. Berman)

A zany socialite involves her friends in a murder mystery.
Mildly funny comedy-thriller without too much of either, but a good example of the style of thirties craziness at its zenith.

w Philip G. Epstein *d* Leigh Jason *ph* Nicholas Musuraca *m* Roy Webb

Barbara Stanwyck, Henry Fonda, Sam Levene, Frances Mercer, Stanley Ridges, Whitney Bourne, Hattie McDaniel, Miles Mander
    'Something ground out by people in a desperate mood.'—*Pauline Kael, 70s*

The Mad Parade
US 1931 62m bw

A story told by women about the effect of the war on their sex. Not really strong enough to be taken seriously, this was played as a

novelty. Evelyn Brent, Irene Rich, Louise Fazenda, Lilyan Tashman, Marceline Day. Written by Henry McCarthy and Frank R. Conklin from a story by Gertrude Orr and Doris Malloy; directed by William Beaudine; for Liberty / Paramount. 'Chances for disappointing business greater than the opposite.'—*Variety*

The Mad Room
US 1969 92m Berkey Pathecolor
Columbia / Norman Mauer

A companion kills her wealthy employer so that her mentally retarded brother and sister will have a home.
Tasteless remake of *Ladies in Retirement*, in the brutalized vein which audiences are supposed by producers to want. In modern dress and sharp locations, it succeeds only in being nauseating.

w Bernard Girard, A. Z. Martin *d* Bernard Girard *ph* Harry Stradling Jnr *m* Dave Grusin

Stella Stevens, Shelley Winters, Skip Ward, Carol Cole, Severn Darden

Mad Wednesday*
US 1947 77m bw
Howard Hughes

A middle-aged book-keeper is sacked and goes on the town.

w Paul Osborn, Paul H. Rameau, *book* Eve Curie *d* Mervyn Le Roy *ph* Joseph Ruttenberg *m* Herbert Stothart *ad* Cedric Gibbons, Paul Groesse

Greer Garson, Walter Pidgeon, Henry Travers, Albert Basserman, Robert Walker, C. Aubrey Smith, Dame May Whitty, Victor Francen, Elsa Basserman, Reginald Owen, Van Johnson

'It achieves a notable triumph in making the discovery of a new element seem almost as glamorous as an encounter with Hedy Lamarr.'—*C. A. Lejeune*

AAN: best picture; Joseph Ruttenberg; Herbert Stothart; Greer Garson; Walter Pidgeon

Madame De*

France / Italy 1953   102m   bw
Franco-London / Indus / Rizzoli
US title: *The Earrings of Madame de*

Tragic misunderstandings arise when a society wife sells her earrings and tells her husband she has lost them.

Elegant, rather heavy-handed but superbly glossy extension of a fashionable novelette.

w Marcel Achard, Max Ophuls, Annette Wademant, *novel* Louise de Vilmorin *d* Max Ophuls *ph* Christian Matras *m* Oscar Straus, Georges Van Parys *ad* Jean d'Eaubonne

Charles Boyer, Danielle Darrieux, Vittorio de Sica, Lea di Lea, Jean Debucourt

Madame Dubarry**

Germany 1919   85m (24 fps)   bw   silent
Union-UFA
US title: *Passion*

The life and times of the glamorous courtesan of Louis XV.

Milestone silent film which introduced to the cinemas of America and Britain not only the subtleties of the European cinema but the more adaptable subtleties of a key director, here dealing rather heavy-handedly with material which he should later have re-used.

w Fred Orbing, Hans Kraly *d* Ernst Lubitsch *ph* Theodor Sparkuhl

Pola Negri, Emil Jannings, Harry Liedtke, Reinhold Schunzel

Madame Dubarry

US 1934   77m   bw

The life of the legendary courtesan at Versailles. Utterly unpersuasive but sometimes decorative historical charade. Dolores del Rio, Reginald Owen, Victor Jory, Anita Louise, Osgood Perkins, Verree Teasdale. Written by Edward Chodorov; directed by William Dieterle; for Warner. 'A lavish but not particularly distinguished production.'—*Variety*

Madame Racketeer

US 1932   68m   bw

Tactics of a middle-aged lady larcenist. Light crime comedy drama, not bad but overlookable. Alison Skipworth, Richard

Bennett, Evalyn Knapp, George Raft, Robert McWade. Written by Malcolm Stuart Boylan and Harvey Gates; directed by Alexander Hall and Harry Wagstaff Gribble; for Paramount. 'The subtle high comedy that flows so gently through the script is likely to pass over the hats of the peasantry.'—*Variety*

Madame Rosa

France 1977   120m   Eastmancolor

An elderly Jewish prostitute runs an unofficial nursery school and cares especially for a fourteen-year-old Arab. Splendidly acted but basically dreary fable twisted from a novel which took the child's point of view. *Simone Signoret*, Claude Dauphin, Samy Ben Youb. Written and directed by Moshe Mizrahi, from the novel by Emile Ajar; for Lira Films. (Original title: *La Vie Devant Soi.*)

Madame Sans-Gêne

US 1925   110m (24 fps)   bw   silent

During the French Revolution, Napoleon plays Cupid to a laundry-maid and her lover. The story formed the basis of one of Gloria Swanson's last successes; but it was made in France and did not have the zip of her Hollywood productions. With Charles De Roche, Emile Drain. Written by Forrest Halsey; directed by Leonce Perret; for Paramount.

Madame Sans-Gêne

France / Italy / Spain 1962   100m
Technirama
TCF / Cine Alliance / Gesi / Champion / Agata (Maleno Malenotti)
GB and US title: *Madame*

Historical romp based on an old theatrical warhorse. Pretty stilted in this version, especially when dubbed.

w Henri Jeanson and others, *play* Victorien Sardou *d* Christian-Jaque *ph* Roberto Gerardi *m* Francesco Lavagnino

Sophia Loren, Robert Hossein, Julien Bertheau, Marina Berti

Madame Satan*

US 1930   105m   bw
MGM (C. B. de Mille)

When her husband strays, a socialite disguises herself as a mysterious *femme fatale* and wins him back.

Abysmal comedy in which both director and principals appear frozen until the closing reels present a crazy, spectacular party on a dirigible which crashes but allows a happy ending.

w Jeanie Macpherson *d* C. B. de Mille *ph* Harold Rosson *m* Herbert Stothart

Kay Johnson, Reginald Denny, Lillian Roth, Roland Young

'A strange conglomeration of unreal incidents that are sometimes set forth with no little technical skill.'—*Mordaunt Hall, New York Times*

Madame Spy

US 1934   70m   bw

Russian and Austrian spies are married to each other. Absurd melodrama which never gets a grip. Fay Wray, Nils Asther, Edward Arnold, John Miljan, David Torrence. Written by William Hurlbut from a German film, Under False Flags; directed by Karl Freund; for Universal. 'Story too hopeless to mean money anywhere.'—*Variety*

Madame X*

US 1929   95m   bw
MGM
TV title: *Absinthe*

After an accidental death, a wealthy woman disappears and goes down in the world; at a subsequent murder trial she is defended by her unrecognizing son.

Two silent versions (with Dorothy Donnelly and Pauline Frederick) had been made of this old theatrical warhorse; two sound versions followed this one. The thing defies criticism.

w Willard Mack, *play* Alexandre Bisson *d* Lionel Barrymore

Ruth Chatterton, Raymond Hackett, Mitchell Lewis, Sidney Toler, Carroll Nye, Lewis Stone, Richard Carle

'Works like this confound the reformers, elevate the name of pictures, and tell the world that there is an art in film making.'—*Variety*

AAN: Lionel Barrymore; Ruth Chatterton

Madame X*

US 1937   72m   bw
MGM (James K. McGuinness)

Competent remake with an excellent cast.

w John Meehan *d* Sam Wood *ph* John B. Seitz *m* David Snell

Gladys George, John Beal, Warren William, Reginald Owen, Lynne Carver, Henry Daniell, Emma Dunn, Ruth Hussey, George Zucco

'An upper bracketer when played with a strong companion.'—*Variety*

'A fine old play, dated and outmoded. Audiences will leave the theatre expecting to find the coachman with horse and buggy.'—*Variety*

Madame X

US 1965   100m   Technicolor
Universal / Ross Hunter / Eltee

An elaborately dressed remake which suffered from a wooden lead; the more expensive the production, the more obvious the holes in the plot and the psychology.

w Jean Holloway *d* David Lowell Rich *ph* Russell Metty *m* Frank Skinner

Lana Turner, John Forsythe, Ricardo Montalban, Constance Bennett, Burgess Meredith, Keir Dullea, Virginia Grey, Warren Stevens

'One is free to enjoy a luxurious wallow in emotions that are all the more enjoyable for having no connection whatever with reality.'—*Brenda Davies*

Made for Each Other*
US 1938 90m bw
David O. Selznick

Problems of a lawyer and his new wife culminate in the near-death of their infant son. Smooth star tearjerker.

w Jo Swerling d John Cromwell ph Leon Shamroy m Hugo Friedhofer, David Buttolph, theme Oscar Levant pd William Cameron Menzies

Carole Lombard, James Stewart, Charles Coburn, Lucile Watson, Harry Davenport, Eddie Quillan, Esther Dale, Louise Beavers
'Made to order for strong box office.'—Variety

Made for Each Other*
US 1971 107m De Luxe
TCF / Wylde Films (Roy Townshend)

Romance between two New Yorkers with inferiority complexes.
Elongated cabaret sketch, a Brooklynesque comedy of flashy brilliance but limited general interest.

w Renée Taylor, Joe Bologna d Robert B. Bean ph William Storz

Renée Taylor, Joe Bologna

Made in Heaven
GB 1952 81m Technicolor

Married couples compete for the Dunmow Flitch. Easy-going family comedy which aims to be liked. David Tomlinson, Petula Clark, Sonja Ziemann, A. E. Matthews, Charles Victor, Sophie Stewart, Richard Wattis, Athene Seyler. Written by William Douglas Home; directed by John Paddy Carstairs; for Fanfare / Rank.

Madeleine*
GB 1949 114m bw
GFD / David Lean / Cineguild (Stanley Haynes)

In Victorian Glasgow a well-to-do young woman is accused of murdering her lover, but the verdict is 'not proven'.
Dramatically dead because of its ambiguous ending, this lavish and good-looking treatment of a cause célèbre was a mistake for all concerned, but its incidental pleasures are considerable.

w Nicholas Phipps, Stanley Haynes d David Lean ph Guy Green w William Alwyn pd John Bryan costumes Margaret Furse

Ann Todd, Leslie Banks, Elizabeth Sellars, Ivor Barnard, Ivan Desny, Norman Wooland, Edward Chapman, Barbara Everest, André Morell, Barry Jones, Jean Cadell, John Laurie, Eugene Deckers

Mademoiselle Docteur*
GB 1937 84m bw
Grafton / Trafalgar (Max Schach)

A German lady spy falls for a British agent. War melodrama vaguely based on fact and later remade as Fräulein Doktor.

w Jacques Natanson, Marcel Achard, Ernest Betts d Edmond Greville ph Otto Heller

Dita Parlo, John Loder, Erich Von Stroheim, Claire Luce, Gyles Isham, Clifford Evans, John Abbott

Mademoiselle Fifi*
US 1944 69m bw
RKO (Val Lewton)

During the Franco-Prussian war a stagecoach is held up because a prostitute, despite the urging of her fellow passengers, refuses to sleep with a Prussian officer. When she gives in, they shun her, and she kills him.
Interesting low budget version of a story which inspired many films.

w Josef Mischel, Peter Ruric, stories Boule de Suif / Mademoiselle Fifi by Guy de Maupassant d Robert Wise ph Harry Wild m Werner Heymann

Simone Simon, Kurt Kreuger, John Emery, Alan Napier, Jason Robards Sr, Norma Varden, Helen Freeman, Fay Helm
'There is a gallant, fervent quality about the whole picture, faults and all, which gives it a peculiar kind of life and likeableness, and which signifies that there is one group of men working in Hollywood who have neither lost nor taken care to conceal the purity of their hope and intention.'—James Agee

Madhouse*
GB 1974 92m Eastmancolor
AIP / Amicus (Milton Subotsky)

A reluctant horror actor makes a comeback and finds himself involved in a series of grisly murders.
In-jokey horror piece with clips from old AIP chillers; quite likeable.

w Greg Morrison, novel Devilday by Angus Hall d Jim Clark ph Ray Parslow m Douglas Gamley

Vincent Price, Peter Cushing, Robert Quarry, Adrienne Corri, Natasha Pyne, Linda Hayden, Barry Dennen

Madigan*
US 1968 100m Techniscope
Universal (Frank P. Rosenberg)

A Brooklyn police detective brings in a dangerous escaped criminal at the cost of his own life.
Lively, well-characterized police thriller with excellent locations.

w Henri Simoun, Abraham Polonsky, novel The Commissioner by Richard Dougherty d Don Siegel ph Russell Metty m Don Costa

Richard Widmark, Henry Fonda, Michael Dunn, Inger Stevens, Harry Guardino, James Whitmore, Susan Clark, Steve Ihnat, Don Stroud, Sheree North, Warren Stevens, Raymond St Jacques
† The character was later resurrected for a TV series also starring Richard Widmark.

Madison Avenue
US 1961 94m bw Cinemascope
TCF (Bruce Humberstone)

An advertising executive plans to revenge himself on his treacherous boss.

Predictable melodrama with an adequate plot but dismal acting and presentation.

w Norman Corwin, novel The Build-Up Boys by Jeremy Kirk d Bruce Humberstone ph Charles G. Clarke m Harry Sukman

Dana Andrews, Jeanne Crain, Eleanor Parker, Eddie Albert, Howard St John, Henry Daniell, Kathleen Freeman
'Simply nowhere near grand enough.'—MFB

Madness of the Heart
GB 1949 105m bw
GFD / Two Cities (Richard Wainwright)

A blind girl marries a French aristocrat and has to cope with a jealous neighbour.
Heavily disguised version of the Rebecca theme, with a happy ending after many alarums and excursions, most of them irrelevant. As film-making, very thin.

wd Charles Bennett, novel Flora Sandstrom ph Desmond Dickinson m Allan Gray

Margaret Lockwood, Paul Dupuis, Kathleen Byron, Maxwell Reed

Madonna of the Seven Moons
GB 1944 110m bw
GFD / Gainsborough (R. J. Minney)

Affected by childhood rape, a demure lady has a second life as a daring gypsy.
Novelettish balderdash killed stone dead by stilted presentation; but highly successful in its day.

w Roland Pertwee, Brock Williams, novel Margery Lawrence d Arthur Crabtree

Phyllis Calvert, Stewart Granger, Patricia Roc, Peter Glenville, John Stuart, Jean Kent, Nancy Price, Peter Murray Hill, Reginald Tate
'One of the most diverting British films of the forties.'—Richard Roud

The Madwoman of Chaillot*
GB 1969 142m Technicolor Panavision
Warner / Commonwealth United (Ely Landau)

An eccentric Parisian lady has equally eccentric friends, but her real life is in the past.
A highly theatrical whimsy which somewhat lacks humour, this should never have been considered as a film, certainly not as an all-star extravaganza; but it was, and it falls flat on its face in the first reel of tedious conversation.

w Edward Anhalt, play Jean Giraudoux d Bryan Forbes ph Claude Renoir, Burnett Guffey m Michael J. Lewis pd Ray Simm

Katharine Hepburn, Yul Brynner, Danny Kaye, Edith Evans, Charles Boyer, Claude Dauphin, John Gavin, Paul Henreid, Nanette Newman, Oscar Homolka, Margaret Leighton, Giulietta Masina, Richard Chamberlain, Donald Pleasence, Fernand Gravet
'One finds oneself too often longing for the drop of the curtain.'—Brenda Davies
'The intentions are honourable—defeat is inevitable.'—Rex Reed

When in Southern California visit Universal City Studios

RICHARD WIDMARK · HENRY FONDA
INGER STEVENS
"MADIGAN"

...the
savage
story of
a city
stripped
naked!

CO-STARRING HARRY GUARDINO · JAMES WHITMORE   SUSAN CLARK · MICHAEL DUNN · DON STROUD
Screenplay by HENRI SIMOUN and ABRAHAM POLONSKY
Directed by DON SIEGEL · Produced by FRANK P. ROSENBERG A UNIVERSAL PICTURE · TECHNICOLOR®

MADIGAN.   Police stories were always a dime a dozen, but they didn't all have Henry Fonda in support of the star.

'One of Giraudoux's less good and most fragile plays has been rewritten, bloated with inept contemporary references, drawn out to gigantic proportions of humourless vacuity, and peopled with a barrelful of nonacting stars.'—*John Simon*

'The remnants of Giraudoux' slight, whimsical play can still be perceived in Edward Anhalt's vile modernization, and a lot of famous actors can be recognized even in the performances they give here.'—*Pauline Kael, New Yorker*

Maedchen in Uniform*
Germany 1931 90m bw
Deutsche Film-Gemeinschaft
aka: *Girls in Uniform*

A girl at a strict boarding school falls in love with one of the teachers and commits suicide. Famous early stab at lesbianism, remade in 1958 with Romy Schneider and Lilli Palmer. Interesting for content, not style.

w F. D. Andam, Christa Winsloe, *play* Gestern und Heute by Christa Winsloe *d* Leontine Sagan *ph* Reimar Kuntze *m* Hansen Milde-Meissner

Dorothea Wieck, Ellen Schwannecke, Hertha Thiele, Emilie Lunde

'At once a strident warning against the consequences of Hitler's regime and the first truly radical lesbian film.'—*Time Out, 1981*

The Maggie**
GB 1953 93m bw
Ealing (Michael Truman)
US title: *High and Dry*

An American businessman is tricked into sending his private cargo to a Scottish island on an old puffer in need of repair. Mildly amusing comedy about the wily Scots; not the studio at its best, but pretty fair.

w William Rose *d* Alexander Mackendrick *ph* Gordon Dines *m* John Addison

Paul Douglas, *Alex Mackenzie*, James Copeland, Abe Barker, Dorothy Alison, Hubert Gregg, Geoffrey Keen, Andrew Keir, Tommy Kearins

● Video; Thorn EMI

Magic
US 1978 107m Technicolor
TCF / Joseph E. Levine

A ventriloquist obsessed by his dummy is impelled to murder. Pretentious and occasionally unpleasant version of an oft-told tale.

w William Goldman, from his novel *d* Richard Attenborough *ph* Victor J. Kemper *m* Jerry Goldsmith *pd* Terence Marsh

Anthony Hopkins, Ann-Margret, Burgess Meredith, Ed Lauter, E. J. Andre, David Ogden Stiers

'The gloomily withdrawn Hopkins has no vulgarity in his soul—nothing that suggests any connection with the world of entertainment— and the picture grinds along.'—*New Yorker*

The Magic Bow
GB 1946 106m bw
GFD / Gainsborough

Episodes in the life of the violin virtuoso Paganini.
Poor costumer, dramatically and historically unpersuasive.

w Norman Ginsbury, Roland Pertwee *d* Bernard Knowles *ph* Jack Cox *violin solos* Yehudi Menuhin

Stewart Granger, Jean Kent, Phyllis Calvert, Dennis Price, Cecil Parker, Felix Aylmer, Frank Cellier, Marie Lohr, Henry Edwards

The Magic Box*
GB 1951 118m Technicolor
Festival Films (Ronald Neame)

The life of William Friese-Greene, a British cinema pioneer who died in poverty.
A joint British film industry venture to celebrate the Festival of Britain, this rather downbeat and uneventful story takes on the nature of a pageant or a series of charades, with well-known people appearing to no good purpose. But it means well.

w Eric Ambler *d* John Boulting *ph* Jack Cardiff *m* William Alwyn *pd* John Bryan

Robert Donat, Margaret Johnson, Maria Schell, John Howard Davies, Renée Asherson, Richard Attenborough, Robert Beatty, Michael Denison, Leo Genn, Marius Goring, Joyce Grenfell, Robertson Hare, Kathleen Harrison, Jack Hulbert, Stanley Holloway, Glynis Johns, Mervyn Johns, Barry Jones, Miles Malleson, Muir Mathieson, A. E. Matthews, John McCallum, Bernard Miles, Laurence Olivier, Cecil Parker, Eric Portman, Dennis Price, Michael Redgrave, Margaret Rutherford, Ronald Shiner, Sybil Thorndike, David Tomlinson, Cecil Trouncer, Peter Ustinov, Kay Walsh, Emlyn Williams, Harcourt Williams, Googie Withers

'Patriotic, sentimental, overlong and faintly embarrassing.'—*Time Out, 1984*

The Magic Carpet
US 1951 84m Supercinecolor

The caliph's son returns as the Scarlet Falcon to rout the usurper. Hopeless kid's matinee rubbish, not even performed with verve. Lucille Ball, Raymond Burr, John Agar, Patricia Medina, George Tobias. Written by David Matthews; directed by Lew Landers; for Sam Katzman / Columbia.

The Magic Christian
GB 1970 95m Technicolor
Commonwealth United / Grand Films (Dennis O'Dell)

An eccentric millionaire spends his wealth deflating those who pursue money or power. A series of variably funny but always unpleasant sketches, climaxing with citizens delving for spoils in a vat of blood and manure. In its aim to be satirical, very typical of its time.

w Terry Southern, Joseph McGrath, Peter Sellers, *novel* Terry Southern *d* Joseph

McGrath *ph* Geoffrey Unsworth *m* Ken Thorne *pd* Assheton Gorton

Peter Sellers, Ringo Starr, Richard Attenborough, Laurence Harvey, Christopher Lee, Spike Milligan, Yul Brynner, Roman Polanski, Raquel Welch, Wilfrid Hyde White, Fred Emney, John Le Mesurier, Dennis Price, Patrick Cargill, John Cleese, Graham Chapman

● Video: Video Form

The Magic Face
US 1951 90m bw
Columbia (Mort Briskin, Robert Smith)

A brilliant German impersonator kills Hitler, takes his place, and leads Germany deliberately into defeat.
Hilariously unlikely anecdote 'as told to William Shirer', performed with vigour but handicapped by a shoddy production.

w Mort Briskin, Robert Smith *d* Frank Tuttle *ph* Tony Braun *m* Herschel Burke Gilbert

Luther Adler, Patricia Knight, Ilka Windish, William L. Shirer

'If Shirer believed this story, then he must be the only person in the world to do so.'—*Gavin Lambert*

Magic Fire
US 1954 94m Trucolor
Republic (William Dieterle)

The life and loves of Richard Wagner.
Remarkably boring biopic with much music but little story or characterization. Ugly colour minimizes German locations.

w Bertita Harding, E. A. Dupont, David Chantler *d* William Dieterle *ph* Ernest Haller *md* Erich Wolfgang Korngold

Alan Badel, Yvonne de Carlo, Peter Cushing, Frederick Valk, Carlos Thompson, Valentina Cortesa

The Magic of Lassie
US 1978 99m colour
Jack Wrather (Bonita Granville)

A collie dog is sold but makes its way back home.
Downright peculiar revamp of *Lassie Come Home* with music and an ageing all-star cast.

w Jean Holloway, Richard B. Sherman, Robert M. Sherman *d* Don Chaffey *m / ly* Richard and Robert Sherman

James Stewart, Alice Faye, Mickey Rooney, Pernell Roberts, Stephanie Zimbalist, Gene Evans

AAN: song, 'When You're Loved'

The Magic Sword
US 1962 80m Eastmancolor
UA / Bert I. Gordon

The son of a well-meaning witch rescues a princess from the clutches of an evil sorcerer. Shaky medieval fantasy on too low a budget.

w Bernard Schoenfeld *d* Bert I. Gordon *ph* Paul Vogel *m* Richard Markowitz *sp* Milt Rice

Basil Rathbone, Estelle Winwood, Gary Lockwood, Anne Helm

'The guy with the dynamite heart meets the girl with the firecracker eyes!'

Magic Town
US 1947 103m bw
William A. Wellman (Robert Riskin)

An opinion pollster discovers a small town which exactly mirrors the views of the USA at large.
A bright Capraesque idea is extraordinarily dully scripted, the production looks dim, and all concerned are operating one degree under.

w Robert Riskin d William A. Wellman ph Joseph Biroc m Roy Webb

James Stewart, Jane Wyman, Kent Smith, Regis Toomey, Donald Meek

The Magician*
US 1926 approx 80m bw silent
MGM

A dabbler in the occult comes to grief when he tries to influence a young girl.
A melodrama with interesting credits; unfortunately no prints remain.

from the novel by Somerset Maugham d Rex Ingram

Paul Wegener, Ivan Petrovitch, Alice Terry

The Magician of Lublin
West Germany / Israel 1979 114m colour
Geria-Golan-Globus (Harry N. Blum)

In 1901 an itinerant magician with an active sex life dreams of being able really to fly. Curious muddled fable with apparent correspondences to the Christ story, like Bergman's The Face. In the end it does not confidently address itself to any audience, despite clever moments.

w Irving S. White, Menahem Golan novel Isaac Bashevis Singer d Menahem Golan ph David Gurfinkel m Maurice Jarre pd Jurgen Kiebach

Alan Arkin, Louise Fletcher, Valerie Perrine, Shelley Winters, Lou Jacobi, Warren Berlinger
'California Polish accents grapple with hamfisted direction and a script of surpassing banality.'—Sight and Sound

The Magnet
GB 1950 79m bw
Ealing (Sidney Cole)

A small boy steals a magnet and accidentally becomes a hero.
Very mild Ealing comedy, not really up to snuff.

w T. E. B. Clarke d Charles Frend ph Lionel Banes m William Alwyn

Stephen Murray, Kay Walsh, William Fox, Meredith Edwards, Gladys Henson, Thora Hird, Wylie Watson

The Magnetic Monster*
US 1953 75m bw
UA / Ivan Tors

A new radio-active element causes

'implosions' of increasing size by drawing energy from the area around it.
Well-told low-budget sci-fi with the audience kept abreast of all developments; the undersea lab scenes are borrowed from an old German film, Gold.

w Curt Siodmak, Ivan Tors d Curt Siodmak ph Charles Van Enger pd George Van Marter m Blaine Sanford

Richard Carlson, King Donovan, Jean Byron, Byron Foulger

'Real life screened more daringly than it's ever been before!'

The Magnificent Ambersons****
US 1942 88m bw
RKO (Orson Welles)

A proud family loses its wealth and its control of the neighbourhood, and its youngest male member gets his come-uppance.
Fascinating period drama told in brilliant cinematic snippets; owing to studio interference the last reels are weak, but the whole is a treat for connoisseurs, and a delight in its fast-moving control of cinematic narrative.

wd Orson Welles, novel Booth Tarkington ph Stanley Cortez m Bernard Herrmann ad Mark-Lee Kirr

Joseph Cotten, Dolores Costello, Agnes Moorehead, Tim Holt, Anne Baxter, Ray Collins, Richard Bennett, Erskine Sanford, Donald Dillaway

NARRATOR (Welles): 'And now Major Amberson was engaged in the profoundest thinking of his life, and he realized that everything which had worried him or delighted him during his lifetime—all his buying and building and trading and banking—that it was all a trifle and a waste beside what concerned him now, for the Major knew now that he had to plan how to enter an unknown country where he was not even sure of being recognized as an Amberson.'

NARRATOR: 'Something had happened. A thing which years ago had been the eagerest hope of many, many good citizens of the town. And now it had come at last: George Amberson Minafer had got his come-uppance. He got it three times filled and running over. But those who had so longed for it were not there to see it, and they never knew it. Those who were still living had forgotten all about it and all about him.'
'Rich in ideas that many will want to copy, combined in the service of a story that few will care to imitate.'—C. A. Lejeune
'Nearly every scene is played with a casual perfection which could only come from endless painstaking planning and rehearsals, and from a wonderful sense of timing.'—Basil Wright, 1972
'Even in this truncated form it's amazing and memorable.'—Pauline Kael, 70s
† Previously filmed in 1925 as Pampered Youth.
†† The credits are all at the end and all spoken, ending with: 'I wrote and directed the picture. My name is Orson Welles.'

AAN: best picture; Stanley Cortez; Agnes Moorehead

The Magnificent Brute
US 1936 77m bw

A blast furnace boss becomes involved with stolen money. Star character drama; very predictable. Victor McLaglen, Binnie Barnes, Billy Burrud, William Hall, Jean Dixon. Written by Owen Francis, Lewis J. Foster and Bertram Millhauser; directed by John G. Blystone; for Universal.

'The whisper of every woman—the toast of every man!'

Magnificent Doll
US 1946 95m bw
Universal (Jack H. Skirball, Bruce Manning)

Dolly Madison, wife of the President, finds that traitor Aaron Burr is a memory from her own past.
Uneasy historical semi-fiction, badly cast and rather boring, yet with some sense of period style.

w Irving Stone d Frank Borzage ph Joseph Valentine m Hans Salter

Ginger Rogers, David Niven, Burgess Meredith, Stephen McNally, Peggy Wood, Robert Barrat
'No duller case has ever been made out for liberty.'—Daily Mail
'Some day the moviemakers will discover that they can make history wonderfully believable and exciting by just sticking roughly to the facts.'—The Times

The Magnificent Dope
US 1942 83m bw
TCF (William Perlberg)

As a publicity stunt a success school brings the nation's most complete failure to New York, and he outsmarts them all.
Dim sub-Capra comedy.

w George Seaton d Walter Lang ph Peverell Marley md Emil Newman

Henry Fonda, Lynn Bari, Don Ameche, Edward Everett Horton, George Barbier, Frank Orth, Hobart Cavanaugh

The Magnificent Fraud
US 1939 78m bw

The president of a Latin American republic is murdered, and an impersonator takes his place. Sharply played dramatic hokum. Akim Tamiroff, Lynne Overman, Patricia Morison, Mary Boland. Written by Gilbert Gabriel and Walter Ferris; directed by Robert Florey; for Paramount. 'Dull drama; no marquee names; filler fodder for duals.'—Variety

The Magnificent Matador
US 1955 94m Eastmancolor Cinemascope
Edward L. Alperson
GB title: The Brave and the Beautiful

A matador trains his illegitimate son to follow in his footsteps but has a premonition of his death in the ring.
Dreary bullfighting drama with romantic interludes.

w Charles Lang d Budd Boetticher ph Lucien Ballard m Raoul Kraushaar

Anthony Quinn, Maureen O'Hara, Manuel Rojas, Richard Denning, Thomas Gomez, Lola Albright

Magnificent Obsession**
US 1935 112m bw
Universal (John M. Stahl)

The playboy who is half-responsible for the death of a woman's husband and for her own blindness becomes a surgeon and cures her. Absurd soaper which was phenomenally popular and is certainly well done.

w George O'Neil, Sarah Y. Mason, Victor Heerman, novel *Lloyd C. Douglas* d *John M. Stahl* ph John Mescall m Franz Waxman

Irene Dunne, Robert Taylor, Ralph Morgan, Sara Haden, Charles Butterworth, Betty Furness, Arthur Hoyt, Gilbert Emery, Arthur Treacher
'Capital romance, a cinch for the femme trade.'—*Variety*

Magnificent Obsession**
US 1954 108m Technicolor
Universal (*Ross Hunter*)

Glossy remake which sent Ross Hunter to the commercial heights as a remaker of thirties weepies. This one worked best.

w Robert Blees d *Douglas Sirk* ph Russell Metty m Frank Skinner

Jane Wyman, Rock Hudson, Agnes Moorehead, Barbara Rush, Otto Kruger, Gregg Palmer, Paul Cavanagh, Sara Shane

AAN: Jane Wyman

The Magnificent Rebel
US 1960 94m Technicolor
Walt Disney (Peter V. Herald)

Episodes in the life of the young Beethoven. Solid Disney biopic, shot in Vienna with good period detail.

w Joanne Court d Georg Tressler ph Goran Strindberg md Frederick Stark

Karl Boehm, Ernst Nadhering, Ivan Desny, Gabriele Porks

'They were seven—and they fought like seven hundred!'
The Magnificent Seven**
US 1960 138m De Luxe Panavision
UA / Mirisch–Alpha (John Sturges)

A Mexican village hires seven American gunmen for protection against bandits. Popular western based on the Japanese *Seven Samurai*; good action scenes, but the rest is verbose and often pretentious.

w William Roberts d John Sturges ph Charles Lang Jnr m *Elmer Bernstein*

Yul Brynner, Steve McQueen, Robert Vaughn, *James Coburn, Charles Bronson*, Horst Buchholz, Eli Wallach, Brad Dexter, Vladimir Sokoloff, Rosenda Monteros

AAN: Elmer Bernstein
● *Video: Warner*

The Magnificent Seven Deadly Sins
GB 1971 107m colour
Tigon (Graham Stark)

Compendium of comedy sketches, a very variable ragbag of old jokes.

w Bob Larbey, John Esmonde, Dave Freeman, Barry Cryer, Graham Chapman, Graham Stark, Marty Feldman, Alan Simpson, Ray Galton, Spike Milligan d Graham Stark ph Harvey Harrison Jnr m Roy Budd

Bruce Forsyth, Joan Sims, Roy Hudd, Harry Secombe, Leslie Phillips, Julie Ege, Harry H. Corbett, Ian Carmichael, Alfie Bass, Spike Milligan, Ronald Fraser

The Magnificent Seven Ride
US 1972 100m De Luxe
UA / Mirisch (William A. Calihan)

Tired finale to a patchy series (*Return of the Seven, Guns of the Magnificent Seven*) in which the original leader returns to save a Mexican village once again from bandits. Very modest.

w Arthur Rowe d George McCowan ph Fred Koenekamp m Elmer Bernstein

Lee Van Cleef, Stefanie Powers, Mariette Hartley, Pedro Armendariz Jnr, Luke Askew

The Magnificent Two
GB 1967 100m Eastmancolor
Rank (Hugh Stewart)

One of two incompetent travelling salesmen in a Latin American banana republic is persuaded to pose as a dead rebel leader. More or less a Bob Hope vehicle, adapted for the less realistic Morecambe and Wise with unhappy results: too few sight gags and a curious emphasis on violence. The third and last of their attempts to find film vehicles.

w S. C. Green, R. M. Hills, Michael Pertwee, Peter Blackmore d Cliff Owen ph Ernest Steward m Ron Goodwin

Eric Morecambe, Ernie Wise, Margit Saad, Cecil Parker, Virgilio Teixeira, Isobel Black, Martin Benson
● *Video: Rank*

The Magnificent Yankee*
US 1951 88m bw
MGM (Armand Deutsch)
GB title: *The Man with Thirty Sons*

Episodes in the later life of Judge Oliver Wendell Holmes.
Vaguely well-meaning biopic without much dramatic sense.

w Emmet Lavery, from his play d John Sturges ph Joseph Ruttenberg m David Raksin

Louis Calhern, Ann Harding, Eduard Franz, Philip Ober, Richard Anderson, Edith Evanson

AAN: Louis Calhern

Magnum Force
US 1973 124m Technicolor
Panavision
Warner / Malpaso (Robert Daley)

Inspector Harry Callahan has to track down

his partner who is slaughtering gangsters in cold blood.
Toned-down sequel to *Dirty Harry*; the violence is still there but the hero no longer commits it.

w John Milius d Ted Post ph Frank Stanley m Lalo Schifrin

Clint Eastwood, Hal Holbrook, Mitch Ryan, Felton Perry, David Soul
'A ragbag of western mythology and head-on thuggery.'—*Sight and Sound*
● *Video: Warner*

The Magus
GB 1968 116m De Luxe Panavision
TCF / Blazer (John Kohn, Jud Kinberg)

An English schoolmaster on a Greek island is influenced by the local magician.
Fashionable philosophical nonsense, an elaborate mystery with no solution; the kind of film that all concerned begin to wish they had never thought of, especially as the presentation has nothing like the panache required, so that not even the critics liked it.

w John Fowles, from his novel d Guy Green ph Billy Williams m Johnny Dankworth pd Don Ashton

Michael Caine, Anthony Quinn, Candice Bergen, Anna Karina, Paul Stassino, Julian Glover, George Pastell
'Faintly ludicrous some of the time and painfully unexciting all of the time.'—*MFB*
'This may not be the most misguided movie ever made, but it's in there pitching.'—*Rex Reed*
'There's enough incoherence pretending to be enigma, sex play and chat about existentialism and self-discovery to make teenagers think they're having an experience; for grown-ups it's an ordeal.'—*Judith Crist*
'It has much of the fascination of a Chinese puzzle, but it would have been infinitely more enthralling if it hadn't been quite so flatly acted and directed.'—*Michael Billington, Illustrated London News*
'Probably the only movie in which one will ever see a copy of Empson's *Seven Types of Ambiguity*.'—*Pauline Kael, New Yorker*

Mahler*
GB 1974 115m Technicolor
Goodtimes Enterprises (Roy Baird)

Fantasia on the life and times of the Jewish composer.
Fairly successful Ken Russell musical biopic on the lines of his early BBC specials.

wd Ken Russell ph Dick Bush

Robert Powell, Georgiana Hale, Richard Morant, Lee Montague, Rosalie Crutchley, Benny Lee, David Collings
'A piece of movie making that sets my pulses racing.'—*Michael Billington, Illustrated London News*
'Whether the title of the opus happens to be *Strauss* or *Tchaikovsky* or *Elgar* or *Brubeck*, the real title is always *Russell*.'—*Benny Green, Punch*
● *Video: Guild*

Mahogany
US 1975   109m   colour   Panavision
Paramount / Nikor (Rob Cohen, Jack
Ballard)

The love life of a model and fashion designer.
Virtually a Joan Crawford vehicle redesigned
for a black heroine who creates her own
clothes. Fairly hilarious.

w John Byrum d Berry Gordy ph David
Watkin m Michael Masser

Diana Ross, Billy Dee Williams, Anthony
Perkins, Jean-Pierre Aumont, Nina Foch,
Beah Richards, Marisa Mell
  'The level of silliness rises steadily.'—*Geoff
Brown*
  'Movies as frantically bad as *Mahogany* can
be enjoyed on at least one level; the spectacle
of a lot of people making fools of themselves.'
—*Time*
  'What *Mahogany* does so fascinatingly and
sometimes hilariously is to pilfer certain stock
clichés of 50's Hollywood and adapt them to a
black milieu.'—*Molly Haskell*

AAN: song 'Do You Know Where You're
Going To?' (*m* Michael Masser, *ly* Gerry
Goffin)

'Love so glorious it was denounced as sin!'
Maid of Salem°
US 1937   86m   bw
Paramount (Frank Lloyd)

In 1692 Salem, a young girl is accused of
witchcraft but saved by her lover.
Remarkably solemn period melodrama,
unfortunately betrayed by amiable but miscast
leads.

w Bradley King, Walter Ferris, Durward
Grinstead d Frank Lloyd ph Leo Tover
m Victor Young

Claudette Colbert, Fred MacMurray, Harvey
Stephens, Gale Sondergaard, Louise Dresser,
Edward Ellis, Beulah Bondi, Bonita Granville
  'Weak and slow saga of witchcraft: stars the
only hope.'—*Variety*
  'Once the panic of witchcraft starts you are
carried along on a vicious crescendo of
madness and terror.'—*Stage*

The Maids
GB 1974   95m   Technicolor
Ely Landau / Cinevision

Two Paris maids evolve a sado-masochistic
ritual involving the death of their employer,
but never go through with it.
Unbalanced and dreary film version of an
essentially theatrical play.

w Robert Enders, Christopher Miles,
play Jean Genet d Christopher Miles
ph Douglas Slocombe m Laurie Johnson

Glenda Jackson, Susannah York, Vivien
Merchant, Mark Burns

Maid's Night Out
US 1937   65m   bw

A wealthy girl falls for the milkman, who is
really a rich man who thinks she's the maid.
Skittish second-feature comedy which helped

to build a new star. Joan Fontaine, Allan
Lane, Billy Gilbert, Cecil Kellaway, Hedda
Hopper. Written by Bert Granet; directed by
Ben Holmes; for RKO.

Maigret Sets a Trap°
France / Italy 1957   119m   bw
Intermondia / J. P. Guibert / Jolly Film

Maigret sets a policewoman as decoy for a
knife murderer . . .
Probably the best Maigret film, with excellent
Parisian atmosphere and excellent acting.

w Michel Audiard, *novel* Georges Simenon
d Jean Delannoy ph Louis Page m Paul
Misraki *ad* René Renoux

Jean Gabin, Annie Girardot, Jean Desailly,
Oliver Hussenot, Alfred Adam, Lino Ventura

Mail Order Bride
US 1963   83m   Metrocolor   Panavision
MGM (Richard E. Lyons)
GB title: *West of Montana*

An old westerner tries to find a bride for a
wild young man in his charge.
Mild western comedy drama; quite tolerable.

wd Burt Kennedy ph Paul C. Vogel
m George Bassman

Buddy Ebsen, Lois Nettleton, Keir Dullea,
Warren Oates, Marie Windsor

The Main Attraction
GB 1962   90m   Metrocolor
Seven Arts (John Patrick)

A wandering singer causes emotional
problems backstage at a circus.
Limp melodrama with the star miscast as a
fatal charmer.

w John Patrick d Daniel Petrie ph Geoffrey
Unsworth m Andrew Adorian

Pat Boone, Mai Zetterling, Nancy Kwan,
Yvonne Mitchell, John Le Mesurier

The Main Event
US 1979   112m   Technicolor
Warner / First Artists / Barwood (Jon
Peters, Barbra Streisand)

A lady entrepreneur takes on a prizefighter.
Thin and very patchy comedy for confirmed
addicts of its star.

w Gail Parent, Andrew Smith d Howard
Zieff ph Mario Tosi m Michael Melvoin
pd Charles Rosen

Barbra Streisand, Ryan O'Neal, Paul Sand,
Whitman Mayo, James Gregory

Main Street: see I Married a Doctor

Main Street to Broadway°
US 1953   102m   bw
Lester Cowan Productions

After several reverses a young playwright sees
his work through to a Broadway opening
night; it fails, but he has learned several
lessons.
Curious, flat attempt to show the public how
Broadway works, with big stars playing
themselves in cameo roles.

w Samson Raphaelson d Tay Garnett
ph James Wong Howe

Tom Morton, Mary Murphy, Ethel
Barrymore, Lionel Barrymore, Shirley Booth,
Rex Harrison, Lilli Palmer, Helen Hayes,
Henry Fonda, Tallulah Bankhead, Mary
Martin, Louis Calhern, John Van Druten,
Cornel Wilde, Joshua Logan, Agnes
Moorehead, Gertrude Berg

Les Mains Sales
France 1951   103m   bw
Fernand Rivers
aka: *Dirty Hands*

A young communist intellectual, required to
kill a traitor, finds he can do so only when he
suspects the man of making love to his wife.
Verbose and dull version of a play which had
some international success as *Crime Passionel*.

wd Fernand Rivers, *play* Jean-Paul Sartre
ph Jean Bachelet

Pierre Brasseur, Daniel Gélin, Claude Nollier

Maisie
US 1939   74m   bw
MGM (J. Walter Ruben)

Adventures of a Brooklyn showgirl.
Acceptable programmer which led to a series,
all quite watchable and absolutely forgettable.

w Mary McCall Jnr, *novel* Dark Dame by
Wilson Collinson d Edwin L. Marin
ph Leonard Smith

Ann Sothern, Robert Young, Ian Hunter,
Ruth Hussey, Anthony Allan (John
Hubbard), Cliff Edwards

The succeeding titles, mostly written by Mary
McCall and directed by Marin or Harry
Beaumont or Roy del Ruth, were:
1940: CONGO MAISIE (with John Carroll; a
remake of RED DUST), GOLD RUSH
MAISIE (with Lee Bowman), MAISIE WAS
A LADY (with Lew Ayres, Maureen
O'Sullivan)
1941: RINGSIDE MAISIE (with George
Murphy; GB title CASH AND CARRY)
1942: MAISIE GETS HER MAN (with Red
Skelton; GB title SHE GOT HER MAN)
1943: SWING SHIFT MAISIE (with James
Craig; GB title THE GIRL IN OVERALLS)
1944: MAISIE GOES TO RENO (with John
Hodiak; GB title YOU CAN'T DO THAT
TO ME)
1946: UP GOES MAISIE (with George
Murphy; GB title UP SHE GOES)
1947: UNDERCOVER MAISIE (with Barry
Nelson; GB title UNDERCOVER GIRL)

'Is she a kid—or is she kidding?'
The Major and the Minor°°
US 1942   100m   bw
Paramount (Arthur Hornblow Jnr)

A girl poses as a child in order to travel half
fare on a train, and is helped by an officer who
falls for her.
Moderately smart comedy showing the writer-
director's emergent style. Remade as *You're
Never Too Young* (qv).

w Charles Brackett, Billy Wilder *d Billy Wilder ph* Leo Tover *m* Robert Emmett Dolan

Ginger Rogers, Ray Milland, Rita Johnson, Robert Benchley, Diana Lynn, Edward Fielding, Frankie Thomas, Charles Smith

OSBORNE (Robert Benchley): 'Why don't you get out of that wet coat and into a dry martini?'

'The script seems to have been concocted after the title.'—*New Yorker, 1977*

Major Barbara***
GB 1941 121m bw
Gabriel Pascal

The daughter of an armaments millionaire joins the Salvation Army but resigns when it accepts her father's donation.
Stagey but compulsive version of a play in which the author takes typical side swipes at anything and everything within reach, allowing for some gorgeous acting (and overacting) by an impeccable cast.

w Anatole de Grunwald, Gabriel Pascal, *play Bernard Shaw d* Gabriel Pascal, Harold French, David Lean *ph* Ronald Neame *m* William Walton *ed* Charles Friend *costumes* Cecil Beaton *ad* Vincent Korda, John Bryan

Wendy Hiller, Rex Harrison, Robert Morley, Robert Newton, Marie Lohr, Emlyn Williams, Sybil Thorndike, Deborah Kerr, David Tree, Felix Aylmer, Penelope Dudley Ward, Walter Hudd, Marie Ault, Donald Calthrop

'Shaw's ebullience provides an unslackening fount of energy . . . his all-star cast of characters are outspoken as no one else is in films except the Marx Brothers.'—*William Whitebait*

'To call it a manifest triumph would be an arrant stinginess with words.'—*New York Times*

Major Dundee*
US 1965 134m Eastmancolor
Panavision
Columbia (Jerry Bresler)

A small group of men from a US cavalry post sets out to annihilate marauding Indians.
Large-scale, rough and ready western which rambles along in humourless vein but rises to some spectacularly bloodthirsty climaxes.

w Harry Julian Fink, Oscar Saul, Sam Peckinpah *d* Sam Peckinpah *ph* Sam Leavitt *m* Daniele Amfitheatrof

Charlton Heston, Richard Harris, Jim Hutton, James Coburn, Michael Anderson Jnr, Warren Oates, Senta Berger, Slim Pickens

● *Video: RCA / Columbia*

A Majority of One
US 1961 156m Technicolor
Warner (Mervyn Le Roy)

A Jewish widow has a shipboard romance with a Japanese businessman.
Interminable stage-bound comedy-drama, boringly assembled and fatally compromised by the casting of stars who are neither Jewish nor Japanese.

w Leonard Spiegelgass, from his play *d* Mervyn Le Roy *ph* Harry Stradling *m* Max Steiner

Rosalind Russell, Alec Guinness, Ray Danton, Madlyn Rhue

AAN: Harry Stradling

Make a Wish
US 1937 75m bw
(RKO) Sol Lesser

A composer discovers a boy singer at a summer camp.
Acceptable family entertainment.

w Gertrude Berg, Bernard Schubert, Earle Snell *d* Kurt Neumann *ph* John Mescall *songs* Oscar Strauss *m* Hugo Riesenfeld

Basil Rathbone, Bobby Breen, Marion Claire, Leon Errol, Henry Armetta, Ralph Forbes, Donald Meek

AAN: Hugo Riesenfeld

Make Haste to Live
US 1954 89m bw
Republic (William A. Seiter)

A lady newspaper owner is embarrassed, to say the least, by the reappearance of her murderer husband, long thought dead.
Competent but rather dull programmer.

w Warren Duff, *novel* The Gordons *d* William A. Seiter *ph* John L. Russell *m* Elmer Bernstein

Dorothy McGuire, Stephen McNally, Mary Murphy, Edgar Buchanan, John Howard

Make Me a Star
US 1932 80m bw
Paramount (Lloyd Sheldon)

A grocery clerk goes to Hollywood and becomes a film star.
Modest remake of a silent success; see also *Merton of the Movies.*

w Sam Wintz, Walter de Leon, Arthur Kober, *novel* Merton of the Movies by Harry Leon Wilson *d* William Beaudine *ph* Allen Siegler

Stuart Erwin, Joan Blondell, Zasu Pitts, Ben Turpin, Florence Roberts; and Tallulah Bankhead, Clive Brook, Gary Cooper, Maurice Chevalier, Claudette Colbert, Fredric March, Jack Oakie, Charlie Ruggles, Sylvia Sidney

'Packed with laughs which offsets the longish running time.'—*Variety*

Make Me an Offer*
GB 1954 88m Eastmancolor
Group Three (W. P. Lipscomb)

An antique dealer has an ambition to own a famous vase.
Mildly pleasant Jewish comedy with interesting sidelights on the antique business.

w W. P. Lipscomb, *novel* Wolf Mankowitz *d* Cyril Frankel *ph* Denny Densham *m* John Addison

Peter Finch, Adrienne Corri, *Meier Tzelniker,* Rosalie Crutchley, Finlay Currie, *Ernest Thesiger,* Wilfrid Lawson, Alfie Bass

Make Mine Music**
US 1946 74m Technicolor
Walt Disney (Joe Grant)

A programme of cartoon shorts: JOHNNY FEDORA, ALL THE CATS JOIN IN, WITHOUT YOU, TWO SILHOUETTES, CASEY AT THE BAT, THE MARTINS AND THE COYS, BLUE BAYOU, AFTER YOU'VE GONE, WILLIE THE SINGING WHALE.

An insubstantial banquet, sometimes arty and sometimes chocolate boxy, which occasionally rises to the expected heights.

w various *d* various

'There is enough genuine charm and imagination and humour to make up perhaps one good average Disney short.'—*James Agee*

Make Way for a Lady
US 1936 63m bw

A girl determines to find a mate for her widowed father. Rather irritating comedy of embarrassment. Herbert Marshall, Anne Shirley, Gertrude Michael, Margot Grahame, Clara Blandick, Taylor Holmes, Willie Best. Written by Gertrude Purcell from the novel Daddy and I by Elizabeth Jordan; directed by David Burton; for Zion Myers / RKO. 'It lacks suspense, surprise, and plausibility.'—*Variety*

'Grandpa moves in! Daughter moves out! And the riot starts!'
Make Way for Tomorrow**
US 1937 94m bw
Paramount (Leo McCarey)

An elderly couple are in financial difficulty and have to be parted because their children will not help.
Sentimental drama which had a devastating effect at the time but now seems oversimplified and exaggerated.

w Vina Delmar, *novel* The Years Are So Long by Josephine Lawrence *d* Leo McCarey *ph* William C. Mellor *m* George Antheil

Victor Moore, Beulah Bondi, Thomas Mitchell, Fay Bainter, Porter Hall, Barbara Read, Maurice Moscovitch, Elizabeth Risdon, Gene Lockhart

'Needs special exploitation: even so, business is apt to be spotty where played solo.'—*Variety*

'The most brilliantly directed and acted film of the year.'—*John Grierson*

'A sense of misery and inhumanity is left vibrating in the nerves.'—*Graham Greene*

Make Your Own Bed
US 1944 82m bw

A detective and his girl friend pretend to be servants in order to protect an inventor from Nazis. Mirthless pratfall farce. Jack Carson, Jane Wyman, Irene Manning, Ricardo Cortez, Alan Hale, George Tobias. Written by Francis Swann and Edmund Joseph; directed by Peter Godfrey; for Warner.

Making Love
US 1982   111m   De Luxe
TCF / IndieProd (Allen Adler, Danny Melnick)

A young married doctor declares that he is gay and moves in with a friend.
Would-be daring melodrama whose producers quickly found that nobody was interested.

w Barry Sandler, story A. Scott Berg
d Arthur Hiller ph David M. Walsh
m Leonard Rosenman pd James D. Vance
ed William H. Reynolds

Michael Ontkean, Kate Jackson, Harry Hamlin, Wendy Hiller, Arthur Hill, Nancy Olson

● Video: CBS / Fox

Malachi's Cove
GB 1973   75m   Technicolor
Penrith / Impact Quadrant Films (Andrew Sinclair, Kent Walwin)
aka: The Seaweed Children

In 1880 Cornwall, a 14-year-old girl lives by selling seaweed.
Slimly-plotted film for the family, pleasant without being very interesting.

wd Henry Herbert, story Anthony Trollope
ph Walter Lassally m Brian Gascoigne

Donald Pleasence, Dai Bradley, Veronica Quilligan, Arthur English, David Howe

Malaga
GB 1954   84m   bw

An American woman agent catches drug smugglers in Tangier. Routine international thick ear. Maureen O'Hara, Macdonald Carey, Binnie Barnes, Guy Middleton, Leonard Sachs. Written by Robert Westerby; directed by Richard Sale; for M. J. Frankovich / Film Locations. (US title: Fire Over Africa.)

Malaya*
US 1949   95m   bw
MGM (Pandro S. Berman)
GB title: East of the Rising Sun

An adventurer attempts to smuggle rubber out of Japanese-occupied Malaya.
Dour action melodrama, unworthy of its considerable cast but watchable.

w Frank Fenton d Richard Thorpe
ph George Folsey m Bronislau Kaper

Spencer Tracy, James Stewart, Sidney Greenstreet, John Hodiak, Valentina Cortesa, Lionel Barrymore, Gilbert Roland

The Male Animal*
US 1942   101m   bw
Warner (Wolfgang Reinhardt)

A dry college professor emancipates himself when his wife becomes attracted to a football star.
Stagebound but amusing college comedy with pleasant humour and good performances. Remade as She's Working Her Way through College (qv).

w Julius J. and Philip G. Epstein, Stephen Morehouse Avery, play James Thurber and Elliott Nugent d Elliott Nugent ph Arthur Edeson m Heinz Roemheld

Henry Fonda, Olivia de Havilland, Jack Carson, Joan Leslie, Eugene Pallette, Don Defore, Herbert Anderson, Hattie McDaniel

The Malta Story
GB 1953   103m   bw
GFD / British Film Makers (Peter de Sarigny)

An English flier is involved in the defence of Malta during World War II.
Glib propaganda piece which is not very excitingly written or characterized, and fails to convince on any but the most elementary level.

w William Fairchild, Nigel Balchin d Brian Desmond Hurst ph Robert Krasker
m William Alwyn

Alec Guinness, Anthony Steel, Muriel Pavlow, Jack Hawkins, Flora Robson, Renée Asherson, Ralph Truman, Reginald Tate, Hugh Burden

The Maltese Falcon**
US 1931   80m   bw
Warner
TV title: Dangerous Female

After the death of his partner, private eye Sam Spade is dragged into a quest for a priceless statuette.
Excellent crime melodrama with smart pace and performances. Remade as Satan Met a Lady (1936); and see below.

w Maude Fulton, Lucien Hubbard, Brown Holmes, novel Dashiell Hammett d Roy del Ruth ph William Rees

Ricardo Cortez, Bebe Daniels, Dudley Digges, Dwight Frye, Robert Elliott, Thelma Todd, Oscar Apfel

'Any type of audience will enjoy it.'—Variety
'The best mystery thriller of the year.'—New York Times
'A nice blend of humour, intelligence and suspense.'—Clive Hirschhorn, 1979

'A guy without a conscience! A dame without a heart!'
'He's as fast on the draw as he is in the drawing room!'

The Maltese Falcon****
US 1941   101m   bw
Warner (Henry Blanke)

A remake which shows the difference between excellence and brilliance; here every nuance is subtly stressed, and the cast is perfection.

wd John Huston ph Arthur Edeson
m Adolph Deutsch

Humphrey Bogart, Mary Astor, Sidney Greenstreet, Elisha Cook Jnr, Barton MacLane, Lee Patrick, Peter Lorre, Gladys George, Ward Bond, Jerome Cowan

GUTMAN (Sidney Greenstreet): 'I distrust a close-mouthed man. He generally picks the wrong time to talk and says the wrong things. Talking's something you can't do judiciously, unless you keep in practice. Now, sir, we'll talk if you like. I'll tell you right out, I'm a man who likes talking to a man who likes to talk.'

SPADE (Humphrey Bogart) to Cairo (Peter Lorre): 'When you're slapped, you'll take it and like it!'

SPADE to Brigid (Mary Astor): 'Don't be too sure I'm as crooked as I'm supposed to be.'

GUTMAN: 'I distrust a man who says when. If he's got to be careful not to drink too much, it's because he's not to be trusted when he does.'

'The first crime melodrama with finish, speed and bang to come along in what seems like ages.'—Otis Ferguson
'A work of entertainment that is yet so skilfully constructed that after many years and many viewings, it has the same brittle explosiveness—and some of the same surprise—that it had in 1941.'—Pauline Kael, 1968
'The trick which Mr Huston has pulled is a combination of American ruggedness with the suavity of the English crime school—a blend of mind and muscle—plus a slight touch of pathos.'—Bosley Crowther, New York Times
'Admirable photography of the sort in which black and white gives full value to every detail, every flicker of panic.'—Francis Wyndham

AAN: best picture; John Huston (as writer); Sidney Greenstreet

● Video: Warner

Mama Loves Papa*
US 1933   70m   bw

A middle-class wife decides to do some social climbing. Slight but amusing comedy which put together a useful team. Charles Ruggles, Mary Boland, Lilyan Tashman, George Barbier, Morgan Wallace. Written by Arthur Kober, Nunnally Johnson, Douglas MacLean, Keene Thompson; directed by Norman Z. McLeod; for Paramount. 'Exceptionally funny comedy . . . a cinch builder.'—Variety

Mamba
US 1930   76m   Technicolor

Germans in East Africa go to the bad during World War I. Absurd melodrama climaxing with a Zulu uprising. Jean Hersholt, Eleanor Boardman, Ralph Forbes, Josef Swickard. Written by Tom Miranda, Winifred Dunn, from a story by F. Schumann-Heink and John Reinhardt; directed by Al Rogell; for Tiffany. 'It has its lowlights and highlights; in between it's not a bad programmer.'—Variety

Mambo
Italy / USA 1954   92m (English version), 107m (Italian version)   bw
Paramount / Ponti / De Laurentiis

A Venetian shopgirl loves a worthless gambler, is romanced by a haemophiliac

THE MALTESE FALCON (1941).   Three men weigh each other up: Elisha Cook Jnr, Sidney Greenstreet, Humphrey Bogart.

count, and joins a dance troupe.
Patchy melodrama with plenty going on but no grip.

w Guido Piovene, Ivo Perelli, Ennio de Concini, Robert Rossen d Robert Rossen ph Harold Rosson m Nino Rota, Francesco Lavagnino sets Andrei Andrejew ch Katherine Dunham

Silvana Mangano, Michael Rennie, Shelley Winters, Vittorio Gassman, Eduardo Cianelli, Mary Clare, Katherine Dunham and her troupe

Mame*

US 1974 131m Technicolor
Panavision
Warner / ABC (Robert Fryer, James Cresson)

In 1928, a 10-year-old boy goes to live with his eccentric, sophisticated aunt.

Old-fashioned and rather bad film of a much overrated Broadway musical, inept in most departments but with occasional show-stopping moments.

w Paul Zandel, play Jerome Lawrence, Robert E. Lee, book Patrick Dennis d Gene Saks ph Philip Lathrop m / ly Jerry Herman pd Robert F. Boyle

Lucille Ball, Beatrice Arthur, Robert Preston, Bruce Davison, Jane Connell, Joyce Van Patten, John McGiver

'It makes one realize afresh the parlous state of the Hollywood musical, fighting to survive against misplaced superstars and elephantine budgets matched with minuscule imagination.'—Geoff Brown

'The cast seem to have been handpicked for their tone-deafness, and Lucille Ball's close-ups are shot blatantly out of focus.'—Sight and Sound

'So terrible it isn't boring; you can get fixated staring at it and wondering what Lucille Ball thought she was doing.'—New Yorker, 1977
● Video: Warner

Mammy*

US 1930 84m bw
Warner

Murder backstage at a minstrel show.
One of the star's better musicals.

w L. G. Rigby, Joseph Jackson d Michael Curtiz ph Barney McGill m Irving Berlin

Al Jolson, Lowell Sherman, Hobart Bosworth, Louise Dresser, Lee Moran

'Looks like money . . . a lively picture playing fast.'—Variety

A Man, a Woman and a Bank
Canada 1979 101m CFI color

A civil engineer and a computer expert devise a foolproof way of robbing a bank. We have been here before, except that these days the criminals are allowed to get away with it. Ho-hum. Donald Sutherland, Brooke Adams, Paul Mazursky. Written by Raynold Gideon, Bruce A. Evans and Stuart Margolin; directed by Noel Black; for Bennett / McNichol.

A Man About the House
GB 1947 95m bw
British Lion (Edward Black)

Two English ladies inherit an Italian villa and fall under the spell of the handsome handyman, who marries one of them and proceeds slowly to poison her.
Now clearly dull, at the time this seemed a fairly enterprising rehash of *Gaslight*, *Kind Lady* and *Rebecca*.

w J. B. Williams, Leslie Arliss, *novel* Francis Brett Young and *play* John Perry d Leslie Arliss ph Georges Perinal m Nicholas Brodsky

Margaret Johnston, Dulcie Gray, Kieron Moore, Felix Aylmer, Lilian Braithwaite

A Man About the House
GB 1974 90m colour
EMI / Hammer (Roy Skeggs)

Two young women, their male flatmate and their landlords combine forces to prevent the terrace from being razed for redevelopment. Mild and rather exhausting sex comedy from the TV series, as relentlessly single-minded as a 'Carry On'.

w Johnnie Mortimer, Brian Cooke d John Robins ph Jimmy Allen m Christopher Gunning

Richard O'Sullivan, Paula Wilcox, Sally Thomsett, Yootha Joyce, Brian Murphy, Peter Cellier, Patrick Newell, Spike Milligan, Arthur Lowe

Man about Town
US 1932 75m bw

A society gambler is really a secret service man. Flabby melodrama which practically dislocates the long arm of coincidence. Warner Baxter, Karen Morley, Conway Tearle, Lawrence Grant, Leni Stengel, Alan Mowbray, Lillian Bond, Halliwell Hobbes. Written by Leon Gordon from the novel by Denison Clift; directed by John Francis Dillon; for Fox. 'Plenty of hodge-podge, and doubtful b.o. Will need strong support almost everywhere.'—*Variety*

Man About Town*
US 1939 85m bw
Paramount (Arthur Hornblow Jnr)

A Broadway producer in London makes his girlfriend jealous.
Fairly amusing comedy-musical programmer.

w Morrie Ryskind d Mark Sandrich ph Ted Tetzlaff md Victor Young

Jack Benny, Dorothy Lamour, Edward Arnold, Binnie Barnes, Phil Harris, Eddie Anderson, Monty Woolley, Isabel Jeans, Betty Grable, E. E. Clive
'Good comedy, rates okay biz.'—*Variety*

Man Afraid
US 1957 84m bw Cinemascope

A priest is forced to kill a hoodlum in self-defence, and is then threatened by the dead man's psychopathic father. Heavy-going melodrama not helped at all by the very wide screen. George Nader, Phyllis Thaxter, Harold J. Stone, Tim Hovey, Eduard Franz. Written by Herb Meadow; directed by Harry Keller; for Universal-International.

Man Alive
US 1945 70m bw

A husband thought to be dead comes back as a 'ghost' and frightens away his wife's new suitor. Curious and rather tasteless comedy. Pat O'Brien, Ellen Drew, Adolphe Menjou, Rudy Vallee, Jack Norton. Written by Edwin Harvey Blum; directed by Ray Enright; for RKO.

A Man Alone*
US 1955 96m Trucolor
Republic

A wandering gunman is framed by other badmen.
Solemn, slow-moving but generally interesting western, the star's first attempt at direction.

w John Tucker Battle d Ray Milland ph Lionel Lindon m Victor Young

Ray Milland, Mary Murphy, Ward Bond, Raymond Burr, Arthur Space, Lee Van Cleef, Alan Hale Jnr

A Man and a Woman**
France 1966 102m Eastmancolor
Les Films 13
aka: *Un Homme et une Femme*

A racing driver and a script girl, both of whose spouses are dead, meet while visiting their children, and an affair leads to marriage. Slight romantic drama so tricked out with smart images that it looks like a series of expensive commercials. A great box office success, but its director never again succeeded in this vein which he made his own.

w Claude Lelouch, Pierre Uytterhoven d Claude Lelouch ph Claude Lelouch m Francis Lai

Anouk Aimée, Jean-Louis Trintignant
'When in doubt, Lelouch's motto seems to be, use a colour filter or insert lyrical shots of dogs and horses; when in real doubt, use both.'—*Tom Milne, MFB*
'A slick item with all the Hollywood ingredients.'—*John Simon*
AA: Claude Lelouch, Pierre Uytterhoven
AAN: Claude Lelouch (as director); Anouk Aimée

Man at the Top*
GB 1973 87m Technicolor
Hammer / Dufton (Peter Charlesworth)

A pharmaceutical executive finds that his firm is marketing an unsafe drug.

Further adventures of the belligerent hero of *Room at the Top* (qv), this time following a popular television series. All very fashionable and predictable.

w Hugh Whitemore d Mike Vardy ph Bryan Probyn m Roy Budd

Kenneth Haigh, Nanette Newman, Harry Andrews, John Quentin, Charlie Williams

The Man Behind the Gun
US 1952 82m Technicolor

A cavalry officer is sent to quell a rebellion and helps to found Los Angeles. Cheerful western programmer. Randolph Scott, Patrice Wymore, Dick Wesson, Phil Carey. Written by John Twist; directed by Felix Feist; for Warner.

The Man Behind the Mask
GB 1936 79m bw

A mad scientist kidnaps a nobleman's daughter. Serial-like hokum with interesting credits. Hugh Williams, Maurice Schwarz, Jane Baxter, Donald Calthrop, Henry Oscar. Written by Ian Hay, Syd Courtenay, Jack Byrd and Stanley Haynes; directed by Michael Powell; for Joe Rock.

The Man Between*
GB 1953 101m bw
British Lion / London Films (Carol Reed)

Ivo Kern operates successfully as a West Berlin racketeer; love causes a softening of his attitudes and leads to his death.
Imitation *Third Man* with an uninteresting mystery and a solemn ending. Good acting and production can't save it.

w Harry Kurnitz d Carol Reed ph Desmond Dickinson m John Addison ad André Andreiev

James Mason, Hildegarde Neff, Claire Bloom, Geoffrey Toone, Ernst Schroeder
'Reed's love of photogenic corruption, his technical finesse, and his feeling for atmospheric intrigue almost make something really good out of a synthetic script.'—*Variety*
'A cold-hearted film about people with cold feet.'—*Daily Express*

A Man Called Gannon
US 1969 105m Technicolor

A wandering cowboy helps a widow rancher in her fight against encroaching cattlemen.
Adequate remake of *The Man Without a Star*, which somehow had much more stature. Tony Franciosa, Michael Sarrazin, Judi West, Susan Oliver, John Anderson. Written by Gene Kearney, D. D. Beauchamp and Borden Chase; directed by James Goldstone; for Universal.

A Man Called Horse*
US 1970 114m Technicolor
Panavision
Cinema Center / Sanford Howard

In 1825 an English aristocrat is captured by Indians, lives with them and eventually becomes their leader.

Harrowing account of tribal life and customs, with much bloodshed and torture and most of the dialogue in Indian. Occasionally impressive but not exactly entertaining.

w Jack di Witt, *story* Dorothy M. Johnson *d* Elliot Silverstein *ph* Robert Hauser *m* Leonard Rosenman

Richard Harris, Judith Anderson, Jean Gascon, Manu Tupou

† Sequels 1976: *The Return of a Man Called Horse.* 1984: *Triumphs of a Man Called Horse.*

● Video: CBS / Fox

The Man Called Noon

GB / Spain / Italy 1973 95m Technicolor Frontier / Montana / Finarco (Euan Lloyd)

A western gunslinger loses his memory. Childish western melodrama in the violent manner.

w Scot Finch, *novel* Louis L'Amour *d* Peter Collinson *ph* John Cabrera *m* Luis Bacalov

Richard Crenna, Stephen Boyd, Rosanna Schiaffino, Farley Granger

A Man Called Peter*

US 1955 119m De Luxe Cinemascope TCF (Samuel G. Engel)

The life of Peter Marshall, a Scottish clergyman who became chaplain to the US Senate.
Careful but rather dreary biopic.

w Eleanore Griffin, *book* Catherine Marshall *d* Henry Koster *ph* Harold Lipstein *m* Alfred Newman

Richard Todd, Jean Peters, Marjorie Rambeau, Jill Esmond, Les Tremayne, Robert Burton

AAN: Harold Lipstein

A Man Called Sledge

Italy 1970 92m Techniscope Dino de Laurentiis (Carl Olsen)

A bandit tries in vain to mastermind a bank robbery.
Curious change of pace for a genial star. A spaghetti western without style but with plenty of violence, the result doesn't linger in the memory.

w Vic Morrow, Frank Kowalsky *d* Vic Morrow *ph* Luigi Kuveiller *m* not credited

James Garner, Dennis Weaver, Claude Akins, John Marley

A Man Could Get Killed*

US 1966 98m Technicolor Panavision Universal / Cherokee (Ernest Wehmeyer)

An American businessman in Lisbon is mistaken for a secret agent.
Minor thrill comedy with a confused plot and a willing cast.

w T. E. B. Clarke, Richard Breen, *novel* Diamonds Are Danger by David Walker *d* Ronald Neame, Cliff Owen *ph* Gabor Pogany *m* Bert Kaempfert

James Garner, Melina Mercouri, Sandra Dee, Tony Franciosa, Robert Coote, Roland Culver, Cecil Parker, Grégoire Aslan, Dulcie Gray, Martin Benson, Niall MacGinnis

A Man for All Seasons****

GB 1966 120m Technicolor Columbia / Highland (Fred Zinnemann)

Sir Thomas More opposes Henry VIII's divorce, and events lead inexorably to his execution.
Irreproachable film version of a play which has had its narrative tricks removed but stands up remarkably well. Acting, direction, sets, locations and costumes all have precisely the right touch.

w Robert Bolt, from his play *d* Fred Zinnemann *ph* Ted Moore *m* Georges Delerue *pd* John Box

Paul Scofield, Wendy Hiller, Susannah York, *Robert Shaw,* Orson Welles, Leo McKern, Nigel Davenport, John Hurt, Corin Redgrave, Cyril Luckham, Jack Gwyllim

† Reports indicate that Charlton Heston badly wanted the role of Sir Thomas More.

AA: best picture; Robert Bolt; Fred Zinnemann; Ted Moore; Paul Scofield

AAN: Wendy Hiller; Robert Shaw

● Video: RCA / Columbia

'If you've read the book, forget it!'

Man Friday

GB 1975 115m Eastmancolor Panavision Avco-Embassy / ITC / ABC / Keep Films (Jules Buck)

The story of Robinson Crusoe told so that Friday appears the more intelligent.
A pointless and not very entertaining exercise which wears out its welcome very early.

w Adrian Mitchell *d* Jack Gold *ph* Alex Phillips *m* Carl Davis

Peter O'Toole, Richard Roundtree

'Liberal intentions trail sadly through every sequence and cause absurd fluctuations of tone, since no one seems to have decided whether laborious slapstick, heavy portentousness or method acting is the best vehicle for the message.'—*Jill Forbes*

● Video: Precision

The Man from Bitter Ridge

US 1955 80m Technicolor

A special agent goes undercover to nail stagecoach bandits, but himself comes under suspicion. Adequate western programmer. Lex Barker, Mara Corday, Stephen McNally, Trevor Bardette, John Dehner. Written by Lawrence Roman; directed by Jack Arnold; for Universal-International.

The Man from Blankley's

US 1930 67m bw Warner

A drunken aristocrat goes to the wrong party and teaches those present, and himself, a thing or two.
Amusing star trifle, previously filmed as a silent.

w Harvey Thew, Joseph Jackson, *story* F. Anstey *d* Alfred E. Green *ph* James Van Trees

John Barrymore, Loretta Young, William Austin, Albert Gran, Emily Fitzroy

'Dickens comedy, in the Sennett vein, with the Barrymore finesse.'—*Variety*

The Man from Colorado

US 1949 99m Technicolor Columbia (Jules Schermer)

A maladjusted Civil War veteran becomes a western judge and rules by the gun.
Slightly unusual, watchable star western.

w Robert D. Andrews, Ben Maddow, Borden Chase *d* Henry Levin *ph* William Snyder *m* George Duning

Glenn Ford, William Holden, Ellen Drew, Ray Collins, Edgar Buchanan, Jerome Courtland, James Millican, Jim Bannon

'No more humour than a lawyer's shingle, but it has suspense and some exciting shots of fist fights and burning houses.'—*Time*

The Man from Dakota*

US 1940 75m bw

A Yankee soldier is taken prisoner by the south and becomes a spy. Good period action piece. Wallace Beery, Dolores Del Rio, John Howard, Donald Meek, H. B. Warner, Victor Varconi. Written by Laurence Stallings, from the novel by Mackinlay Kantor; directed by Leslie Fenton; for MGM. (GB title: *Arouse and Beware*.)

Man from Del Rio

US 1956 82m bw UA / Robert L. Jacks

A Mexican hobo becomes sheriff and forces the local badman to leave town.
Modest, efficient, rather brutal little western.

w Richard Carr *d* Harry Horner *ph* Stanley Cortez *m* Fred Steiner

Anthony Quinn, Katy Jurado, Peter Whitney, Douglas Fowley

The Man from Down Under

US 1943 103m bw

A veteran of World War I smuggles two orphans back into Australia. Appallingly indulgent sentimental star vehicle, a mistake for all concerned. Charles Laughton, Binnie Barnes, Donna Reed, Richard Carlson, Horace McNally, Arthur Shields. Written by Wells Root and Thomas Seller; directed by Robert Z. Leonard; for MGM.

The Man from Laramie**

US 1955 104m Technicolor Cinemascope Columbia (William Goetz)

A wandering cowman seeks revenge on those who killed his brother.
Grade A western with new-fangled touches of brutality touching off the wide screen spectacle.

w Philip Yordan, Frank Burt *d Anthony Mann ph* Charles Lang Jnr *m* George Duning *md* Morris Stoloff

James Stewart, Arthur Kennedy, Donald Crisp, Cathy O'Donnell, Alex Nicol, Aline MacMahon, Wallace Ford, Jack Elam

The Man from Morocco
GB 1944 116m bw
ABP

Members of the international brigade are captured and later sent by Vichy to build a Sahara railway for the Germans; one escapes to London with vital information.
Stilted, meandering and extremely unconvincing melodrama with a star ill at ease.

w Warwick Ward, Edward Dryhurst, Marguerite Steen, *story* Rudolph Cartier *d* Max Greene *ph* Basil Emmott

Anton Walbrook, Margaretta Scott, Mary Morris, Reginald Tate, Peter Sinclair, David Horne

The Man from Planet X
US 1951 70m bw

On a remote Scottish island a spacecraft deposits a strange creature with a large head and mesmeric powers. Early, minor, moderately pleasing fragment in the *Close Encounters* cycle. Margaret Field, Raymond Bond, William Schallert. Written and produced by Aubrey Wisberg and Jack Pollexfen; directed by Edgar G. Ulmer; for Sherrill Corwin / United Artists.

The Man from Snowy River
Australia 1982 104m Eastmancolor
  Panavision
Cambridge Films / Michael Edgley
  International (Geoff Burrowes)

In 1888, an orphan boy grows up with an obsession about wild horses.
Essentially no more than an Audie-Murphy-style Western given full down-under treatment. An Australian smash, a programmer elsewhere.

w John Dixon, Fred Cullen, from the poem by A. B. Paterson *d* George Miller *ph* Keith Wagstaff *m* Bruce Rowland

Kirk Douglas, Jack Thompson, Sigrid Thornton, Tom Burlinson, Terence Donovan, Lorraine Bayly

The Man from the Alamo*
US 1953 79m Technicolor
U-I (Aaron Rosenberg)

A survivor of the Alamo is thought to be a deserter but proves his story and exposes a villain.
Satisfying western programmer.

w Steve Fisher, D. D. Beauchamp *d* Budd Boetticher *ph* Russell Metty *m* Frank Skinner

Glenn Ford, Victor Jory, Julia Adams, Hugh O'Brian

The Man from the Diners' Club*
US 1963 96m bw
Columbia / Dena / Ampersand (Bill Bloom)

A clerk accidentally lets a credit card go to a notorious gangster, and makes desperate efforts to retrieve it.
Minor star comedy with funny moments surviving a slapdash script.

w Bill Blatty *d* Frank Tashlin *ph* Hal Mohr *m* Stu Philips

Danny Kaye, Telly Savalas, Martha Hyer, Cara Williams, Everett Sloane, George Kennedy

The Man from Uncle
This long-running one-hour TV series (1964-8) began as a spoof of James Bond, which was itself a spoof. Not much more serious or convincing than *Batman*, they caused a lot of people to suspend their disbelief. Robert Vaughn played Napoleon Solo, David McCallum Ilya Kuryakin, and Leo G. Carroll Mr Waverly. Several feature films were made up from various episodes, and did well in cinemas in some countries. They were: TO TRAP A SPY, THE SPY WITH MY FACE, THE KARATE KILLERS, THE SPY IN THE GREEN HAT, ONE OF OUR SPIES IS MISSING, THE HELICOPTER SPIES, HOW TO STEAL THE WORLD and ONE SPY TOO MANY.

A Man from Wyoming
US 1930 70m bw

A slow-speaking engineer joins the army, serves overseas and marries an ambulance driver. Uncertain star vehicle which helped to mould his screen character. Gary Cooper, June Collyer, Regis Toomey, E. H. Calvert, Morgan Farley. Written by John Weaver and Albert Shelby Le Vino; directed by Rowland V. Lee; for Paramount. 'Bad enough to be good entertainment if taken as farce.'—*New York Evening Post.*

'Her body ached for the man she loved!'
The Man from Yesterday
US 1932 71m bw
Paramount

A man is reported missing in World War I, but years later his wife and her new fiancé find him in Switzerland, dying of gas poisoning.
Enoch Arden rides again, and very boringly.

w Oliver H. P. Garrett *d* Berthold Viertel *ph* Karl Struss

Claudette Colbert, Clive Brook, Charles Boyer, Andy Devine, Alan Mowbray, Christian Rub
  'Rather too late in the day to expect war scenes, and when the war peters out, there is only scenery and conversation.'—*Variety*

Man Hunt
US 1932 65m bw

A cub reporter hunts a bank robber. Standard support action fare of its time. William Gargan, Ricardo Cortez, Marguerite Chapman, Chic Sale, Maude Eburne. Written by Roy Chanslor, Earl Felton; directed by William Clemens; for Warners. 'Script never lives up to the title's promise.'—*Variety*

Man Hunt**
US 1941 98m bw
TCF (Kenneth MacGowan)

A big game hunter misses a shot at Hitler and is chased back to England by the Gestapo. Despite hilariously inaccurate English backgrounds, this is perhaps its director's most vivid Hollywood thriller, though watered down in tone from the original novel.

w Dudley Nichols, *novel* Rogue Male by Geoffrey Household *d* Fritz Lang *ph* Arthur Miller *m* Alfred Newman

Walter Pidgeon, Joan Bennett, *George Sanders*, John Carradine, Roddy McDowall, Ludwig Stossel, Heather Thatcher, Frederick Worlock
  'A tense and intriguing thriller that is both propaganda and exciting entertainment.'— *Paul M. Jensen, 1969*
  'In its manipulation of these dark and intent forces on a checkerboard, it manages to take your breath away.'—*Otis Ferguson*
† Remade for TV in 1976 as *Rogue Male.*

The Man I Love
US 1946 76m bw
Warner (Arnold Albert)

A nightclub singer is involved with a mobster. Dreary little melodrama which never really gets going.

w Catherine Turney *d* Raoul Walsh *ph* Sid Hickox *m* Max Steiner

Ida Lupino, Robert Alda, Andrea King, Martha Vickers, Bruce Bennett, Alan Hale, Dolores Moran, John Ridgely

The Man I Married*
US 1940 79m bw
TCF (Raymond Griffith)
aka: *I Married a Nazi*

When an American couple take a European vacation, the wife is horrified to find her husband, who is of German parentage, agreeing with the Nazis.
Naïve but striking melodrama exploring attitudes of its time.

w Oliver H. P. Garrett, *novel* Swastika by Oscar Shisgall *d* Irving Pichel *ph* Peverell Marley *m* David Buttolph

Joan Bennett, Francis Lederer, Lloyd Nolan, Anna Sten, Otto Kruger, Maria Ouspenskaya, Ludwig Stossel, Johnny Russell

The Man in Grey**
GB 1943 116m bw
GFD / Gainsborough (Edward Black)

In Regency times, an aristocratic girl's love for her less fortunate friend is repaid by jealousy, treachery and murder.
Rather dully performed flashback costume melodrama which caught the public imagination in the middle of a dreary world war, especially as its evil leading characters were played by stars who rapidly went right to the top. The several imitations which followed, including *The Wicked Lady, Jassy* and *Hungry Hill*, became known as the Gainsborough school.

w Margaret Kennedy, Leslie Arliss, Doreen Montgomery, *novel* Lady Eleanor Smith *d* Leslie Arliss *ph* Arthur Crabtree *m* Cedric Mallabey *ad* Walter Murton

James Mason, Margaret Lockwood, Phyllis Calvert, Stewart Granger, Helen Haye, Nora Swinburne, Raymond Lovell, Martita Hunt

'There was not a moment when I would not gladly have dived for my hat.'—*James Agate*

'All the time-tested materials: gypsy fortune-teller; scowling, black-browed villain; gushy diary kept by a doe-eyed girl who munches candied violets; fire-breathing adventuress who dotes on discord and low-cut gowns . . .'—*Time*

'Even the one girl who loved enough to ask no questions—had to face the fearful truth!'

The Man in Half Moon Street
US 1944 91m bw
Paramount (Walter MacEwen)

A mysteriously handsome young scientist is actually a 90-year-old who has discovered a surgical method of preserving youth.
Boring screen version of a play which was conceived in an almost romantic vein; Hollywood has taken it too literally.

w Charles Kenyon, *play* Barre Lyndon *d* Ralph Murphy *ph* Henry Sharp *m* Miklos Rozsa

Nils Asther, Helen Walker, Brandon Hurst, *Reinhold Schunzel*
† Remade in straight horror vein as *The Man Who Could Cheat Death* (qv).

The Man in Possession
US 1931 81m bw

A lady falls in love with the bailiff's man in temporary charge of her establishment. Light comedy subsequently remade as *Personal Property*; quite tolerable. Robert Montgomery, Irene Purcell, Charlotte Greenwood, C. Aubrey Smith, Beryl Mercer, Reginald Owen, Alan Mowbray. Written by Sarah Y. Mason from the play by H. M. Harwood; directed by Sam Wood; for MGM.
'Should have no trouble where the censors don't interfere . . . where it gets by with the dirt, the dirt should let it get over.'—*Variety*

The Man in the Attic
US 1953 82m bw

Remake of the much-remade *The Lodger*, this time with parsimonious production values and no style. Jack Palance, Constance Smith, Byron Palmer, Frances Bavier, Rhys Williams. Written by Robert Presnell Jnr and Barre Lyndon; directed by Hugo Fregonese; for TCF.

The Man in the Back Seat*
GB 1961 57m bw
Independent Artists (Julian Wintle, Leslie Parkyn)

Two robbers fail to separate a bookie from the locked bag chained to his wrist; at first taking him with them they finally kill him and are apparently haunted by him.

Taut, downbeat little crime thriller which won a few critical plaudits.

w Malcolm Hulke, Eric Paice *d* Vernon Sewell *ph* Reg Wyer *m* Stanley Black

Derren Nesbitt, Keith Faulkner, Carol White, Harry Locke

Man in the Dark*
US 1953 70m bw 3-D
Columbia (Wallace Macdonald)

A convict submits to a brain operation which will remove his criminal tendencies. Unfortunately it also removes his memory, and on his release he is bewildered when gangsters expect him to know where the loot is hidden.
Silly low-budgeter which is only notable as the 3-D film which most exploited the short-lived medium. Apart from a roller coaster ride, objects hurled at the audience include scissors, spiders, knives, forceps, fists and falling bodies.

w George Bricker, Jack Leonard *d* Lew Landers *ph* Floyd Crosby *md* Ross de Maggio

Edmond O'Brien, Audrey Totter, Ted de Corsia, Horace MacMahon

The Man in the Gray Flannel Suit*
US 1956 152m Eastmancolor Cinemascope
TCF (Darryl F. Zanuck)

A young New York executive is offered a demanding job but decides that his first loyalty is to his wife and children.
An amusingly accurate novel of Madison Avenue mores becomes a marathon emotional melodrama in which the mordant bits quickly give way to domestic problems and a guilt complex about a wartime affair, shown in lengthy flashback. It's all too much.

w Nunnally Johnson, *novel* Sloan Wilson *d* Nunnally Johnson *ph* Charles G. Clarke *m* Bernard Herrmann

Gregory Peck, Fredric March, Jennifer Jones, Ann Harding, *Arthur O'Connell, Henry Daniell,* Marisa Pavan, Lee J. Cobb, Keenan Wynn, Gene Lockhart, Gigi Perreau, Connie Gilchrist, Joseph Sweeney

The Man in the Iron Mask**
US 1939 110m bw
Edward Small

King Louis XIV keeps his twin brother prisoner.
Exhilarating swashbuckler based on a classic novel, with a complex plot, good acting and the three musketeers in full cry.

w George Bruce, *novel* Alexandre Dumas *d* James Whale *ph* Robert Planck *m* Lucien Moraweck

Louis Hayward, Warren William (as D'Artagnan), Alan Hale, Bert Roach, Miles Mander, Joan Bennett, *Joseph Schildkraut,* Walter Kingsford, Marion Martin, Montagu Love, Albert Dekker

'Substantial entertainment for general appeal and satisfaction.'—*Variety*

'A sort of combination of *The Prisoner of Zenda* and *The Three Musketeers*, with a few wild west chases thrown in . . . not unentertaining.'—*Richard Mallett, Punch*
† Remade 1976 as a TV movie with Richard Chamberlain, and 1978 as *The Fifth Musketeer* (qv).

AAN: Lucien Moraweck

The Man in the Middle*
GB 1964 94m bw Cinemascope
TCF / Pennebaker / Belmont (Walter Seltzer)

In India during World War II, an American lieutenant is indicted for murder and the defence counsel is instructed to lose the case.
Courtroom melodrama with unusual angles; quite intriguing, though the wide screen doesn't help.

w Keith Waterhouse, Willis Hall, *novel* The Winston Affair by Howard Fast *d* Guy Hamilton *ph* Wilkie Cooper *m* John Barry

Robert Mitchum, Trevor Howard, Keenan Wynn, Barry Sullivan, France Nuyen, Alexander Knox

'For once Mitchum seems to have an excuse for keeping his eyes at half mast.'—*Judith Crist*

The Man in the Mirror
GB 1936 82m bw
JH Productions / Wardour (Julius Hagen)

A timid man's reflection steps out of the mirror and organizes him.
Modest comedy with a pleasing star.

w F. McGrew Willis, Hugh Mills, *novel* William Garrett *d* Maurice Elvey *ph* Curt Courant

Edward Everett Horton, Geneviève Tobin, Garry Marsh, Ursula Jeans, Alastair Sim, Aubrey Mather, Felix Aylmer

Man in the Moon
GB 1960 99m bw
Allied Film Makers / Excalibur (Michael Relph)

A man who earns his living as Mr Normal, a human guinea pig for scientific research, is chosen as the first astronaut.
Dated comedy which rather dismayingly turns from mild satire to outright farce and fantasy.

w Michael Relph, Bryan Forbes *d* Basil Dearden *ph* Harry Waxman *m* Philip Green

Kenneth More, Shirley Anne Field, Michael Hordern, John Phillips, John Glyn-Jones, Charles Gray, Norman Bird

The Man in the Net
US 1958 96m bw
UA / Mirisch-Jaguar (Walter Mirisch)

When a painter is accused of murdering his wife, he goes into hiding and is helped by children.
Extremely tedious and inept mystery, doubly disappointing in view of the credits.

w Reginald Rose, *novel* Patrick Quentin *d* Michael Curtiz *ph* John Seitz *m* Hans Salter

Alan Ladd, Carolyn Jones, Diane Brewster,
John Lupton, Charles McGraw, Tom
Helmore, John Alexander

Man in the Saddle
US 1951 87m Technicolor

A small rancher is victimized by his wealthy
neighbour. Fairly lively western which
develops into a series of gunfights. Randolph
Scott, Alexander Knox, Joan Leslie, Ellen
Drew, Richard Rober. Written by Kenneth
Gamet; directed by André de Toth; for Harry
Joe Brown / Columbia. (GB title: *The
Outcast*.)

Man in the Shadow°
US 1957 80m bw Cinemascope
U-I (Albert Zugsmith)
GB title: *Pay the Devil*

The sheriff of a small western town
investigates a murder against the wishes of a
powerful local rancher.
Mini-social drama in which the honest man
wins out at last . . . and who would expect
anything different. A brooding melodrama
which delivers less than it promises.

w Gene L. Coon *d* Jack Arnold *ph* Arthur
E. Arling *m* Hans Salter

Jeff Chandler, Orson Welles, Colleen Miller,
John Larch, Joe Schneider, Leo Gordon

The Man in the Sky°
GB 1956 87m bw
Ealing (Seth Holt)
US title: *Decision against Time*

A test pilot refuses to bale out when an engine
catches fire; his plight is interwoven with
scenes of his family, friends and associates.
Thin suspense drama with some effective
moments but too many irrelevant asides.

w William Rose, John Eldridge *d* Charles
Crichton *ph* Douglas Slocombe *m* Gerbrand
Schurmann

Jack Hawkins, Elizabeth Sellars, Walter
Fitzgerald, Eddie Byrne, John Stratton, Victor
Maddern, Lionel Jeffries, Donald Pleasence

The Man in the Trunk
US 1942 70m bw

The ghost of a murder victim helps a young
attorney to nail the culprit. Slightly uneasy
spook comedy with a good star performance.
Raymond Walburn, Lynne Roberts, George
Holmes, J. Carrol Naish, Dorothy Peterson.
Written by John Larkin; directed by Malcolm
St Clair; for TCF.

The Man in the White Suit°°°°
GB 1951 81m bw
Ealing (Sidney Cole)

A scientist produces a fabric that never gets
dirty and never wears out. Unions and
management are equally aghast.
Brilliant satirical comedy played as farce and
put together with meticulous cinematic
counterpoint, so that every moment counts
and all concerned give of their very best.

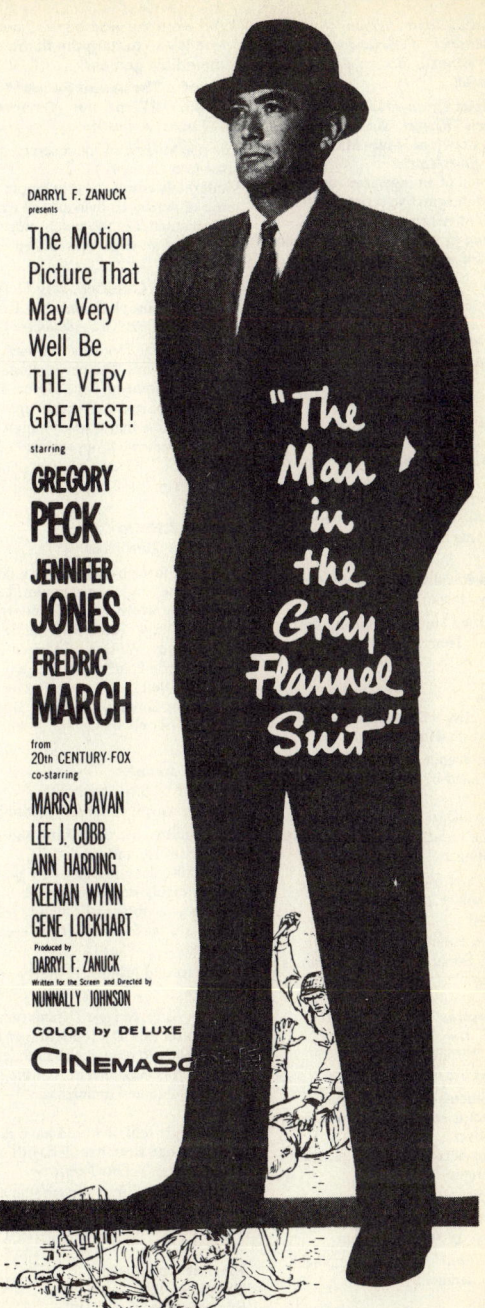

DARRYL F. ZANUCK
presents

The Motion
Picture That
May Very
Well Be
THE VERY
GREATEST!

starring

GREGORY
PECK

JENNIFER
JONES

FREDRIC
MARCH

from
20th CENTURY-FOX
co-starring

MARISA PAVAN
LEE J. COBB
ANN HARDING
KEENAN WYNN
GENE LOCKHART

Produced by
DARRYL F. ZANUCK
Written for the Screen and Directed by
NUNNALLY JOHNSON

COLOR by DE LUXE

CINEMASCOPE

"The
Man
in
the
Gray
Flannel
Suit"

THE MAN IN THE GRAY FLANNEL SUIT. A film rather too aware of its very moderate
importance.

w Roger Macdougall, John Dighton, Alexander Mackendrick d Alexander Mackendrick ph Douglas Slocombe m Benjamin Frankel

Alec Guinness, Joan Greenwood, Cecil Parker, Vida Hope, Ernest Thesiger, Michael Gough, Howard Marion Crawford, Miles Malleson, George Benson, Edie Martin
'The combination of an ingenious idea, a bright, funny and imaginative script, skilful playing and perceptive brisk direction has resulted once more in a really satisfying Ealing comedy.'—*Richard Mallett, Punch*

AAN: script
● *Video: Thorn EMI*

Man in the Wilderness*

US 1971   105m   Technicolor Panavision
Warner / Wilderness (Sanford Howard)

In 1820 in the Canadian northwest, a fur trapper is mauled by a grizzly and left for dead, but he learns to survive and sets out for revenge.
Endurance melodrama modelled after *A Man Called Horse*; a bit stretched and only for the hardened, but taking an agreeably unromantic view of nature.

w Jack di Witt d Richard Sarafian ph Gerry Fisher m Johnny Harris

Richard Harris, John Huston, John Bindon, Prunella Ransome, Henry Wilcoxon, Ben Carruthers

The Man Inside

GB 1958   97m   bw   Cinemascope
Columbia / Warwick (Harold Huth)

A jeweller's book-keeper steals a priceless diamond and is trailed by various factions half across Europe.
Fairly modest and unenterprising British thriller which hadn't much hope of the world market it was aiming at.

w John Gilling, David Shaw, novel M. E. Graber d John Gilling ph Ted Moore m Richard Bennett

Nigel Patrick, Jack Palance, Anita Ekberg, Anthony Newley, Bonar Colleano, Sid James, Donald Pleasence

Man Made Monster*

US 1940   57m   bw
Universal (Jack Bernard)
GB title: *The Electric Man*

A scientist experiments with a man who is impervious to electric shock, and turns him into a walking robot.
A smart little semi-horror originally planned for Karloff and Lugosi.

w Joseph West d George Waggner ph Elwood Bredell m Hans Salter md Charles Previn sp John P. Fulton

Lon Chaney Jnr, Lionel Atwill, Anne Nagel, Frank Albertson, Samuel S. Hinds

'Who were the women who twisted his life and love—gutting the flame of his incredible genius?'

Man of a Thousand Faces**

US 1957   122m   bw   Cinemascope
U-I (Robert Arthur)

The rise to fame of silent screen character actor Lon Chaney.
Moderately commendable biopic with a strong sense of period Hollywood, an excellent star performance, but too much sudsy emoting about deaf mute parents and an ungrateful wife.

w R. Wright Campbell, Ivan Goff, Ben Roberts d Joseph Pevney ph Russell Metty m Frank Skinner ad Alexander Golitzen

James Cagney, Dorothy Malone, Robert Evans (as Irving Thalberg), Roger Smith, Marjorie Rambeau, Jane Greer, Jim Backus
'The script and conception are so maudlin and degrading that Cagney's high dedication becomes somewhat oppressive.'—*Pauline Kael, 70s*

AAN: script

Man of Affairs

GB 1937   70m   bw

When the foreign secretary is kidnapped, his twin brother impersonates him. Lighthearted star vehicle which satisfied. George Arliss, Romilly Lunge, Rene Ray, Jessie Winter, Allan Jeayes. Written by Maude Howell and L. Du Garde Peach from the play The Nelson Touch by Neil Grant; directed by Herbert Mason; for Gaumont British. 'Business possibilities only moderate.'—*Variety*

Man of Aran**

GB 1934   75m   bw
Gainsborough (Michael Balcon)

The primitive life of crofting and fishing folk in the west of Ireland.
A lowering documentary very typical of its maker: highly impressive scene for scene, but tedious as a whole; still, highly remarkable that it was made at all for the commercial cinema.

w Robert and Frances Flaherty d Robert Flaherty

Colman King, Maggie Dirane (amateurs)
'In so far as it is a rendering of the efforts of the Atlantic to overwhelm and demolish a wall of rock, it is magnificent; but the human note is inadequate and unnecessary.'—*E. V. Lucas, Punch*
'However real, it would have made better truth if it had been handled with more of the art of fiction.'—*Otis Ferguson*
'Six thousand feet of such fine and purposeful pictorial composition have seldom been seen on the screen.'—*Observer*

Man of Conquest

US 1939   99m   bw
Republic (Sol C. Siegel)

The life of western hero Sam Houston, who became president of Texas.
Competent action / domestic biopic.

w Wells Root, E. E. Paramore Jnr d George Nicholls Jnr ph Joseph H. August m Victor Young

Richard Dix, Joan Fontaine, Gail Patrick, Edward Ellis, Victor Jory, Robert Barrat, George Hayes, Ralph Morgan, Robert Armstrong, C. Henry Gordon, Janet Beecher
'A grown-up hoss opera, based on authentic and colourful history, with fairly believable characters, ample action and reasonable suspense.'—*Variety*

AAN: Victor Young

Man of Iron

US 1935   62m   bw

A steel works foreman rises to the boardroom, but doesn't like it. Rather obvious moral tale without much excitement. Barton MacLane, Mary Astor, John Eldredge, Dorothy Peterson, Joseph Crehan. Written by William Wister Haines, Dawn Powell; directed by William McGann; for Warners. 'Unimportant programme material.'—*Variety*

Man of Iron*

Poland 1981   152m   colour and bw
PRF / Filowy X

The events of 1980 in Poland are seen through the eyes of a strike leader.
A stirring companion piece to *Man of Marble*; hard tack for the entertainment seeker but as honest a piece of history as one is likely to get from a so-called fiction film.

w Aleksander Scibor-Rylski d Andrzej Wajda ph Edward Klosinski m Andrzej Korzynski

Jerzy Radziwilowicz, Krystyna Janda, Marian Opania

AAN: best foreign film

Man of La Mancha*

US 1972   132m   De Luxe
UA / PEA (Arthur Hiller)

Arrested by the Inquisition and thrown into prison, Miguel de Cervantes relates the story of Don Quixote.
Unimaginative but generally good-looking attempt to recreate on the screen an essentially theatrical experience.

w Dale Wasserman, from his play d Arthur Hiller ph Goffredo Rotunno m Mitch Leigh ly Joe Darion md Laurence Rosenthal ad Luciano Damiani

Peter O'Toole, Sophia Loren, James Coco, Harry Andrews, John Castle, Brian Blessed
'Needful of all the imagination the spectator can muster.'—*Variety*

AAN: Laurence Rosenthal

Man of Marble*

Poland 1978   165m   colour
PRF / Zespol X (Andrzej Wajda)

Young film makers gather material on a political hero of the fifties.
An extended drama on the style of *Citizen Kane* but with much more relevance to

contemporary history. A key film to students of Poland, but too specialized for general entertainment.

w Aleksander Scibor-Rylski *d* Andrzej Wajda *ph* Edward Klosinski *m* Andrzej Korzinski

Jerzy Radziwilowicz, Krystyna Janda, Michael Tarkowski, Tadeusz Lomnicki

Man of the Moment
GB 1935 82m bw

An engaged young man saves a girl from suicide and falls in love with her. Minor romantic comedy of predictable development. Douglas Fairbanks Jnr, Laura La Plante, Claude Hulbert, Margaret Lockwood, Donald Calthrop, Monty Banks. Written by Roland Pertwee, Guy Bolton and A. R. Rawlinson, from a play by Yves Mirande; directed by Monty Banks; for Warner.

Man of the People
US 1937 80m bw

An Italian immigrant works for a law degree but is forced in with crooks. Political power play without much zest despite good acting. Joseph Calleia, Thomas Mitchell, Florence Rice, Ted Healy, Catherine Doucet. Written by Frank Dolan; directed by Edwin L. Marin; for Lucien Hubbard / MGM. 'Patently primed for duals, where it can hold its own.'—*Variety*

Man of the West
US 1958 100m De Luxe Cinemascope
UA / Ashton (Walter M. Mirisch)

In 1874 Arizona, a reformed gunman is cajoled by his old buddies to help them rob a bank.
Talkative, set-bound, cliché-ridden star western with minor compensations.

w Reginald Rose, *novel* Will C. Brown *d* Anthony Mann *ph* Ernest Haller *m* Leigh Harline

Gary Cooper, Lee J. Cobb, Julie London, Arthur O'Connell, Jack Lord, John Dehner, Royal Dano, Robert Wilke

Man of the World
US 1931 71m bw

A gentleman racketeer operates on American playboys in Paris. Predictable but smooth star vehicle. William Powell, Carole Lombard, Wynne Gibson, Guy Kibbee, Lawrence Gray. Written by Herman J. Mankiewicz; directed by Richard Wallace; for Paramount. 'Anything better than moderate for gross must come through the star's personal pull.'—*Variety*

Man of Two Worlds
US 1933 92m bw

An Eskimo is temporarily civilized, but returns to the Arctic wild. Uneventful and somewhat chilly drama which fails to convince. Francis Lederer, Elissa Landi, Henry Stephenson, J. Farrell MacDonald, Walter Byron. Written by Howard and Ainsworth Morgan, from Ainsworth Morgan's novel; directed by J. Walter Ruben; for RKO.

Man on a String
US 1960 92m bw
Columbia / Louis de Rochemont
GB title: *Confessions of a Counterspy*

A Russian-born Hollywood producer is asked by the Russians to work as a spy but becomes a double agent.
Slightly unbelievable biopic about Boris Morros, rather childlike in its simplicity and not too entertaining either.

w John Kafka, Virginia Shaler, *book* Ten Years a Counterspy by Boris Morros *d* André de Toth *ph* Charles Lawton Jnr and others *m* George Duning

Ernest Borgnine, Kerwin Mathews, Colleen Dewhurst, Alexander Scourby, Glenn Corbett, Vladimir Sokoloff

Man on a Swing
US 1975 108m Technicolor
Paramount (Howard B. Jaffe)

Investigations into a murder are helped by a would-be medium.
Overlong and confused psycho-mystery with one stand-out performance.

w David Zelag Goodman *d* Frank Perry *ph* Adam Holender *m* Lalo Schifrin

Cliff Robertson, *Joel Grey*, Dorothy Tristan, Peter Masterson
'Runs out of interest long before it runs out of film.'—*Variety*

Man on a Tightrope*
US 1953 105m bw
TCF (Robert L. Jacks)

A Czech circus owner has trouble with the communist authorities and tries to escape. Adventure story with cold war pretensions which virtually kill it.

w Robert Sherwood *d* Elia Kazan *ph* Georg Krause *m* Franz Waxman

Fredric March, Cameron Mitchell, Adolphe Menjou, Gloria Grahame, Terry Moore, Richard Boone, John Dehner, Dorothea Wieck

Man on Fire
US 1957 95m bw
MGM (Sol C. Siegel)

When his wife divorces him, a middle-aged man refuses to hand over their son.
Low-key personal drama of very moderate interest and modest budget.

wd Ranald MacDougall *ph* Joseph Ruttenberg *m* David Raksin

Bing Crosby, Inger Stevens, Mary Fickett, E. G. Marshall

A Man on the Beach
GB 1956 29m Eastmancolor

A man on the run is cared for and handed over to the police by a blind recluse. Modest featurette which scarcely justifies its credits. Donald Wolfit, Michael Medwin, Michael Ripper. From a story by Victor Canning; directed by Joseph Losey; for Anthony Hinds / Exclusive.

The Man on the Eiffel Tower*
US 1948 82m Anscocolor
A & T (Irving Allen)

A crazy killer defies Inspector Maigret to discover his identity.
Early independent production, an unsatisfactory crime melodrama with international talent and Paris locations. Some quirky acting carries it through.

w Harry Brown, *novel* A Battle of Nerves by Simenon *d* Burgess Meredith *ph* Stanley Cortez

Charles Laughton, Burgess Meredith, Franchot Tone, Robert Hutton, Jean Wallace, Patricia Roc, Wilfrid Hyde White, Belita

The Man on the Flying Trapeze*
US 1935 65m bw
Paramount (William Le Baron)
GB title: *The Memory Expert*

Adventures of an oppressed family man who is useful to his boss because of his prodigious memory.
Plotless rigmarole of shapeless comedy sketches, for star fans.

w Ray Harris, Sam Hardy, Jack Cunningham, Bobby Vernon, *story* Charles Bogle (W. C. Fields) *d* Clyde Bruckman *ph* Al Gilks

W. C. Fields, Kathleen Howard, Mary Brian, Grady Sutton, Vera Lewis, Lucien Littlefield, Oscar Apfel
'A series of gags unrelated to the title. Under average.'—*Variety*

The Man on the Roof*
Sweden 1976 109m Eastmancolor
Svensk Filmindustri (Per Berglund)
original title: *Mannen pa Taket*

A brutal policeman is murdered, and a rooftop sniper turns out to be the culprit.
Alternately vivid and lumbering police thriller with a regrettable tendency to moralize.

wd Bo Widerberg, *novel* The Abominable Man by Max Sjöwall, Max Wahlöös *ph* Odd Geir Saether, Per Kallberg, others *m* Björn Lindh

Carl Gustav Lindstedt, Gunnel Wadner, Hakan Serner, Sven Wollter

Man on the Run
GB 1949 82m bw

A deserter becomes innocently involved in a jewel robbery. Competent crime programmer. Derek Farr, Joan Hopkins, Edward Chapman, Laurence Harvey, John Stuart. Written and directed by Lawrence Huntingdon; for ABPC.

Man Proof
US 1937 74m bw
MGM (Louis D. Lighton)

In trying to win back her man a woman discovers she really loves someone else.
Modest romantic comedy which leaves its stars at sea.

w Vincent Lawrence, Waldemar Young, George Oppenheimer, *novel* The Four Marys by Fanny Heaslip Lea *d* Richard Thorpe *ph* Karl Freund *m* Franz Waxman

Myrna Loy, Franchot Tone, Walter Pidgeon, Rosalind Russell, Nana Bryant, Ruth Hussey

'A smartly produced, well-directed and excellently acted society comedy drama.'— *Variety*

The Man They Could Not Hang
US 1939 65m bw
Columbia

A scientist working on a mechanical heart causes the death of a volunteer student. He is executed, but his assistant restores him to life and he determines to murder those who convicted him.

Predictable horror hokum which set Karloff on his mad doctor cycle.

w Karl Brown d Nick Grinde ph Benjamin Kline md Morris Stoloff

Boris Karloff, Lorna Gray, Robert Wilcox, Roger Pryor, Don Beddoe, Byron Foulger

A Man to Remember*
US 1938 80m bw
RKO (Robert Sisk)

At a small-town doctor's funeral, his life is remembered by mourners.

Modestly effective family film.

w Dalton Trumbo, *novel* Failure by Katharine Haviland-Taylor d Garson Kanin ph J. Roy Hunt m Roy Webb

Edward Ellis, Anne Shirley, Lee Bowman, William Henry, Granville Bates

'No sock for the marquee but a fine, well-made little picture.'—*Variety*

The Man Upstairs*
GB 1958 88m bw
British Lion / ACT (Robert Dunbar)

A mild-mannered lodger becomes violent, injures a policeman, and barricades himself in his room.

Character melodrama reminiscent of both *Fourteen Hours* and *Le Jour se Lève*, but not so interesting as either.

w Alun Falconer d Don Chaffey ph Gerald Gibbs

Richard Attenborough, Bernard Lee, Donald Houston, Dorothy Alison, Maureen Connell, Kenneth Griffith, Virginia Maskell, Patricia Jessel

Man Wanted
US 1932 60m bw

A business woman takes on a male secretary. Yawnworthy comedy drama with no surprises. Kay Francis, David Manners, Andy Devine, Una Merkel, Kenneth Thompson. Written by Robert Lord; directed by William Dieterle; for Warners. 'Threadbare plot weakens this for the big theatres and makes it extremely light and familiar entertainment for the others.'— *Variety*

The Man Who Broke the Bank at Monte Carlo*
US 1935 67m bw
TCF (Nunnally Johnson)

A Russian émigré becomes a taxi driver, wins

a fortune at roulette, loses it all again, and returns happily to his cab.

Very mild, unconvincing and not very entertaining malarkey which rested squarely on its star, who carried it with aplomb.

w Nunnally Johnson d Stephen Roberts ph Ernest Palmer

Ronald Colman, Joan Bennett, Colin Clive, Nigel Bruce, Montagu Love, Frank Reicher, Ferdinand Gottschalk

'Nice production though lacks dash . . . Colman at times seems to be playing under wraps. Should do fairly well.'—*Variety*

'The richest roles of romance and redemption they ever played!'

The Man Who Came Back
US 1930 74m bw
Fox

A reckless young man is reformed when he finds his erstwhile sweetheart now a drug addict in Hong Kong.

Earnest melodrama which not surprisingly damaged the talkie success of a celebrated screen team, and must now seem risible in the extreme.

w Edwin J. Burke, *story and novel* John Fleming Wilson, *play* Jules Eckert Goodman d Raoul Walsh ph Arthur Edeson pd Joseph Urban

Janet Gaynor, Charles Farrell, Kenneth MacKenna, William Holden, Mary Forbes, Peter Gawthorne

'Gripping old melodrama of drugs and degradation tamed down and made into a cheerful sentimental piece. Co-star names make it a strong bid.'—*Variety*

'Sophisticates will give it one big horse laugh.'—*Photoplay*

The Man Who Came to Dinner***
US 1941 112m bw
Warner (Jack Saper, Jerry Wald)

An acid-tongued radio celebrity breaks his hip while on a lecture tour, and terrorizes the inhabitants of the suburban home where he must stay for several weeks.

Delightfully malicious caricature of Alexander Woolcott which, though virtually confined to one set, moves so fast that one barely notices the lack of cinematic variety, and certainly provides more than a laugh a minute, especially for those old enough to understand all the references.

w Julius J. and Philip G. Epstein, *play George S. Kaufman, Moss Hart* d William Keighley ph Tony Gaudio m Frederick Hollander

Monty Woolley, Bette Davis, Ann Sheridan, *Jimmy Durante* (spoofing Harpo Marx), *Reginald Gardiner* (spoofing Noel Coward), Richard Travis, *Billie Burke, Grant Mitchell, Ruth Vivian, Mary Wickes*, George Barbier, Elisabeth Fraser

WHITESIDE (Monty Woolley) to his nurse, who won't let him eat chocolates: 'I had an aunt who ate a box of chocolates every day of her life. She lived to be a hundred and two, and when she had been dead three days, she looked healthier than you do now!'

NURSE (Mary Wickes): 'I am not only walking out on this case, Mr Whiteside, I am leaving the nursing profession. I became a nurse because all my life, ever since I was a little girl, I was filled with the idea of serving a suffering humanity. After one month with you, Mr Whiteside, I am going to work in a munitions factory. From now on, anything I can do to help exterminate the human race will fill me with the greatest of pleasure. If Florence Nightingale had ever nursed YOU, Mr Whiteside, she would have married Jack the Ripper instead of founding the Red Cross!'

WHITESIDE (introducing his secretary): 'This ageing debutante, Mr Jefferson, I retain in my employ only because she is the sole support of her two-headed brother.'

BANJO (Jimmy Durante): 'Did you ever get the feeling that you wanted to stay, and still get the feeling that you wanted to go?'

BEVERLY CARLTON (Reginald Gardiner impersonating Noel Coward): 'Don't tell me how you are, Sherry, I want none of the tiresome details. I've very little time, and so the conversation will be entirely about me, and I shall love it. Shall I tell you how I glittered through the South Seas like a silver scimitar, or would you rather hear how I finished a three-act play with one hand and made love to a maharaja's daughter with the other?'

The Man Who Changed His Mind
GB 1936 66m bw

A scientist dabbles in brain transplants. Mild British-style horror piece; not a success. Boris Karloff, Anna Lee, Donald Calthrop, John Loder, Frank Cellier, Cecil Parker. Written by John L. Balderston, L. DuGarde Peach and Sidney Gilliat; directed by Robert Stevenson; for Gainsborough. (US title: *The Man Who Lived Again*.) 'A spine-freezer of routine construction. The accents are very limey and the way laboratory is pronounced may have American schoolchildren wondering.'—*Variety*

The Man Who Cheated Himself
US 1950 81m bw
TCF (Jack M. Warner)

A woman shoots her husband and her homicide detective lover covers up for her. Efficient crime melodrama.

w Seton I. Miller, Philip MacDonald d Felix Feist ph Russell Harlan m Louis Forbes

Lee J. Cobb, Jane Wyatt, John Dall, Terry Frost

The Man Who Could Cheat Death
GB 1959 83m Technicolor
Paramount / Hammer (Anthony Nelson-Keys)

A surgeon looks 35 but is really 104, having had a series of gland operations performed on himself.

Vulgar, gory, gruesomely coloured Hammer version of a rather attractive play, previously filmed under its original title *The Man in Half Moon Street* (qv). The shocks are routine, and entertainment value is minimal.

w Jimmy Sangster, *play* Barre Lyndon
d Terence Fisher *ph* Jack Asher *m* Richard
Rodney Bennett

Anton Diffring, Hazel Court, Christopher
Lee, Arnold Marle, Delphi Lawrence, Francis
de Wolff

The Man Who Could Work Miracles***
GB 1936 82m bw
London (Alexander Korda)

A city clerk discovers he has the power to
work miracles (given him by sportive gods)
and nearly causes the end of the earth.
Slow-moving but rather pleasing variation on a
simple theme.

w Lajos Biro, *story* H. G. Wells *d* Lothar
Mendes *ph* Harold Rosson *m* Mischa
Spoliansky

Roland Young, Ralph Richardson, Ernest
Thesiger, Edward Chapman, Joan Gardner,
Sophie Stewart, Robert Cochrane, George
Zucco, Lawrence Hanray, George Sanders

'Supposedly a comedy. A weakling: little
draw power on this side.'—*Variety*

'Sometimes fake poetry, sometimes
unsuccessful comedy, sometimes farce,
sometimes sociological discussion, without a
spark of creative talent or a trace of film
ability.'—*Graham Greene*

The Man Who Cried Wolf
US 1937 67m bw

An actor continually confesses to crimes he
didn't commit in the hope that when he does
commit one he won't be believed. An
attractive idea rather poorly handled. Lewis
Stone, Tom Brown, Barbara Read, Marjorie
Main, Forrester Harvey. Written by Charles
Grayson and Sy Bartlett; directed by Lewis R.
Foster; for Universal. 'Will get by as the
number two feature on dual bills.'—*Variety*

The Man Who Dared
US 1933 72m bw

The life of a local politician, based on Mayor
Cermak of Chicago. Episodic but not
unpleasant biopic; it adds up to very little,
though. Preston Foster, Zita Johann, Joan
Marsh, Irene Biller, Leon Waycoff. Written
by Dudley Nichols, Lamar Trotti; directed by
Hamilton McFadden; for Fox. 'The most
flattering account ever written of any man's
life . . . but as a commercial talker it's not
likely to get very far. Even in Chicago they
didn't care for it.'—*Variety*

The Man Who Fell to Earth*
GB 1976 138m colour Panavision
British Lion (Michael Deeley, Barry
Spikings)

A visitor from another planet tries to colonize
Earth, but his powers are destroyed and he
ends an alcoholic cripple.
A weird piece of intellectual science fiction
made weirder by longueurs of all varieties:
obscure narrative, voyeuristic sex, pop music
and metaphysics. Not an easy film or a likeable
one, despite its great technical skill.

w Paul Mayersburg, *novel* Walter Tevis
d Nicolas Roeg *ph* Anthony Richmond
md John Phillips

David Bowie, Rip Torn, Candy Clark, Buck
Henry

'Once you have pierced through its glittering
veneer, you find only another glittering veneer
underneath.'—*Michael Billington, Illustrated
London News*

'There is a punch line, but it takes forever,
and great expectations slump away.'—*Charles
Champlin, L.A. News*

'You feel finally that all that has been
achieved has been to impose an aura of
mystery and enigma where essentially there is
none; to turn a simple tale into the sort of
accumulation of sensations that has become
fashionable.'—*David Robinson, The Times*

● *Video: Thorn EMI*

The Man Who Finally Died
GB 1962 100m bw Cinemascope
British Lion / Magna / White Cross (Norman
Williams)

A German-born Englishman returns to
Bavaria for news of his father, and becomes
involved in a spy plot.
Busy adaptation of a TV serial with a
convoluted plot which might have been more
pacily developed and better explained.

w Lewis Greifer, Louis Marks *d* Quentin
Lawrence *ph* Stephen Dade *m* Philip Green

Stanley Baker, Peter Cushing, Mai Zetterling,
Eric Portman, Niall MacGinnis, Nigel Green,
Barbara Everest, Harold Scott

The Man Who Found Himself
US 1937 67m bw
RKO (Cliff Reid)

A nurse helps a downcast doctor face his
problems and renew his enthusiasm for life.
Simple-minded programmer.

w J. Robert Bren, Edmund Hartman, G. V.
Atwater *d* Lew Landers *ph* Roy Hunt

John Beal, Joan Fontaine, Philip Huston, Jane
Walsh, George Irving

'No names in this hokey B session . . .
flapdoodle with a capital F.'—*Variety*

The Man Who Had His Hair Cut Short*
Belgium 1966 94m bw
Belgian Cultural Ministry

A frustrated law clerk has an aberration after
attending an autopsy and meeting again an old
love.
Pessimistic case history with unpleasant details
often brilliantly recorded.

w Anna de Pagter, André Delvaux *d* André
Delvaux *ph* Ghislain Cloquet *m* Freddy
Devreese

Seene Rouffaer, Beata Tyszkiewicz, Hector
Camerlynck

The Man Who Had Power over Women
GB 1970 89m Eastmancolor

A successful public relations man comes to
hate himself, his job and what it has done to

his marriage. Fashionable wallow in guilt and
luxury, not very convincingly done. Rod
Taylor, Carol White, James Booth, Penelope
Horner, Charles Korvin, Alexandra Stewart,
Keith Barron. Written by Alan Scott and
Chris Bryant, from the novel by Gordon
Williams; directed by John Krish; for
Kettledrum / Avco.

The Man Who Haunted Himself
GB 1970 94m Technicolor
ABP / Excalibur (Michael Relph)

After recovering from a road accident, a staid
businessman finds that he has an evil
doppelganger who steals his wife and his job.
Mildly effective if inexplicable story idea
which served more suitably as a Hitchcock TV
half hour and here, despite adequate
production, outstays its welcome.

w Basil Dearden, Michael Relph, *story* The
Case of Mr Pelham by Anthony Armstrong
d Basil Dearden *ph* Tony Spratling
m Michael Lewis

Roger Moore, Hildegarde Neil, Olga-Georges
Picot, Anton Rodgers, Freddie Jones, Thorley
Walters, John Carson, John Welsh

● *Video: Thorn EMI*

The Man Who Knew Too Much***
GB 1934 84m bw
GFD / Gaumont British (Ivor Montagu)

A chil¹ i⁻ kidnapped by spies to ensure her
father's silence, but he springs into action.
Splendid early Hitchcock which after a faded
start moves into memorable sequences
involving a dentist, an East End mission and
the Albert Hall. All very stagey by today's
standards, but much more fun than the
expensive remake.

w A. R. Rawlinson, Charles Bennett, D. B.
Wyndham Lewis, Edwin Greenwood, Emlyn
Williams *d* Alfred Hitchcock *ph* Curt
Courant *m* Arthur Benjamin

Leslie Banks, Edna Best, *Peter Lorre*, Nova
Pilbeam, Frank Vosper, Hugh Wakefield,
Pierre Fresnay

'A natural and easy production that runs
smoothly and has the hallmark of sincerity.'—
Variety

'The film's mainstay is its refined sense of
the incongruous.'—*Peter John Dyer, 1964*

'A single clash of cymbals that will rock the
lives of an American family!'

The Man Who Knew Too Much*
US 1956 120m Technicolor
Vistavision
(Paramount) Alfred Hitchcock

Flaccid remake of the above, twice as long and
half as entertaining, though it does improve
after a very slow start.

w John Michael Hayes, Angus MacPhail
d Alfred Hitchcock *ph* Robert Burks
m Bernard Herrmann

James Stewart, Doris Day, Bernard Miles,
Brenda de Banzie, Daniel Gelin, Ralph
Truman, Mogens Wieth, Alan Mowbray,
Hillary Brooke

'The balance between character and incident in the earlier film makes a far better thriller.'—*Observer*

'The remake is heavy and oppressive, the suspense often risible, and the moments of comic relief fall flat.'—*Sunday Times*

'Let's say the first version is the work of a talented amateur and the second was made by a professional.'—*Alfred Hitchcock*

AA: song 'Que Sera Sera' (*m / ly* Jay Livingston, Ray Evans)

The Man Who Loved Cat Dancing
US 1973 114m Metrocolor Panavision
MGM (Martin Poll, Eleanor Perry)

A runaway wife is kidnapped by train thieves and comes to love one of them.
Outdoor variation on *No Orchids for Miss Blandish*, remarkably lacking in any kind of entertainment value.

w Eleanor Perry, *novel* Marilyn Durham
d Richard Sarafian *ph* Harry Stradling Jnr
m John Williams

Sarah Miles, Burt Reynolds, Lee J. Cobb, Jack Warden, George Hamilton, Bo Hopkins, Robert Donner, Jay Silverheels
'Any number of things have gone wrong with this peculiarly dreary western.'—*Tom Milne*
'Sarah Miles undergoes more perils than Pauline.'—*Variety*
● *Video: MGM / UA*

The Man Who Loved Redheads
GB 1954 90m Eastmancolor
British Lion / London Films (Josef Somlo)

Throughout his career, a diplomat seeks women who resemble the redhead with whom in youth he had had an idyllic affair.
West End theatrical moonshine, poorly filmed in ugly colour but saved by the cast.

w Terence Rattigan, from his play Who Is Sylvia? *d* Harold French *ph* Georges Périnal *m* Benjamin Frankel

John Justin, Moira Shearer, *Roland Culver*, Gladys Cooper, Denholm Elliott, Harry Andrews, Patricia Cutts, Moira Fraser, *Joan Benham*, Jeremy Spenser

The Man Who Loved Women
France 1977 119m Eastmancolor
Les Films du Carrosse / PAA (Marcel Bebert)

A man spends his life in pursuit of women and dies in the chase.
Sour comedy which doesn't quite come off.

w François Truffaut, Michel Fermaud, Suzanne Schiffman *d* François Truffaut
ph Nestor Almendros *m* Maurice Jaubert

Charles Denner, Brigitte Fossey, Leslie Caron, Nelly Borgeaud, Nathalie Baye

The Man Who Loved Women
US 1983 110m Metrocolor
Columbia / Delphi / Blake Edwards (Blake Edwards, Tony Adams)

An American remake of the above, with even less success.

w Blake Edwards, Milton Wexler, Geoffrey Edwards *d* Blake Edwards *ph* Haskell Wexler *m* Henry Mancini

Burt Reynolds, Julie Andrews, Kim Basinger, Marilu Henner, Cynthia Sikes, Jennifer Edwards

'The strangest story in the annals of naval espionage!'

The Man Who Never Was**
GB 1955 102m De Luxe Cinemascope
TCF / André Hakim

In 1943, the British secret service confuses the Germans by dropping a dead man into the sea with false documents.
Mainly enjoyable true life war story marred by an emotional romantic sub-plot with a double twist but helped by an equally fictitious spy hunt which cheers up the last half hour.

w Nigel Balchin, *book* Ewen Montagu
d Ronald Neame *ph* Oswald Morris *m* Alan Rawsthorne

Clifton Webb, *Robert Flemyng*, Gloria Grahame, *Stephen Boyd*, Laurence Naismith, Josephine Griffin

The Man Who Played God*
US 1932 81m bw
Warner
GB title: *The Silent Voice*

A musician goes deaf but finds satisfaction in helping a young student.
Stagey but effective star vehicle which Arliss also played as a silent film. Remade as *Sincerely Yours* (qv).

w Julian Josephson, Maude Howell, *play* The Silent Voice by Jules Eckert Goodman
d John G. Adolfi *ph* James Van Trees

George Arliss, Violet Heming, Ivan Simpson, *Bette Davis*, Louise Closser Hale, Donald Cook, Ray Milland
'Will need all the Arliss name strength to pull average returns.'—*Variety*

The Man Who Reclaimed His Head*
US 1934 81m bw
Universal (Henry Henigson)

A writer who feels he has been betrayed and his brain sapped by his publisher takes a gruesome revenge.
Oddball period melodrama tailored rather unsuccessfully for a new star. Remade as *Strange Confession* (see *Inner Sanctum*).

w Jean Bart, Samuel Ornitz, *play* Jean Bart
d Edward Ludwig *ph* Merrit Gerstad

Claude Rains, Joan Bennett, Lionel Atwill, Juanita Quigley, Henry O'Neill, Lawrence Grant
'Interesting screen diversion . . . Far from a smash, but good enough to keep to the average level or above.'—*Variety*

The Man Who Shot Liberty Valance*
US 1962 122m bw
Paramount / John Ford (Willis Goldbeck)

A tenderfoot becomes a hero for shooting a

bad man, but the shot was really fired by his friend and protector.
Clumsy, obvious western with the director over-indulging himself but providing some good scenes in comedy vein.

w James Warner Bellah, Willis Goldbeck
d John Ford *ph* William H. Clothier *m* Cyril Mockridge

James Stewart, John Wayne, Vera Miles, Lee Marvin, Edmond O'Brien, Andy Devine, Jeanette Nolan, John Qualen, Ken Murray, Woody Strode, Lee Van Cleef, Strother Martin, John Carradine
'Like Queen Victoria, John Wayne has become lovable because he stayed in the saddle into a new era.'—*Judith Crist*
'A heavy-spirited piece of nostalgia.'—*Pauline Kael, 1975*
'A film whose fascination lies less in what it is itself than in what it reveals about the art of its maker.'—*William S. Pechter*

The Man Who Talked Too Much
US 1940 75m bw
Warner (Edmund Grainger)

A smart defence attorney gets the goods on a gangster and decides to turn him in.
Below-par remake of *The Mouthpiece* (qv), later filmed again as *Illegal* (qv).

w Walter de Leon, Tom Reed, *play* The Mouthpiece by Frank J. Collins *d* Vincent Sherman *ph* Sid Hickox

George Brent, Brenda Marshall, Richard Barthelmess, Virginia Bruce, William Lundigan, John Litel, George Tobias, Henry Armetta, Alan Baxter

The Man Who Turned to Stone
US 1957 71m bw

A girls' reformatory is taken over by a group of zombie scientists born in the eighteenth century. Cheap horror item with a few choice moments for connoisseurs of the absurd.
Victor Jory, Ann Doran, Charlotte Austin, William Hudson, Paul Cavanagh. Written by Raymond T. Marcus; directed by Leslie Kardos; for Clover / Columbia.

The Man Who Understood Women
US 1959 105m Eastmancolor
Cinemascope
TCF (Nunnally Johnson)

An arrogant, exhibitionist film producer finally alienates his long-suffering wife.
Something of an aberration, with good scenes submerged in an unholy mixture of sharp comedy and sentimental melodrama.

wd Nunnally Johnson, *novel* Colours of the Day by Romain Gary *ph* Milton Krasner *m* Robert Emmett Dolan

Henry Fonda, Leslie Caron, Myron McCormick, Cesare Danova, Marcel Dalio, Conrad Nagel, Harry Ellerbe
'A pretentious extravaganza on a romantic theme.'—*MFB*

THE MOST FIENDISH PLOT EVER CONCEIVED! THE MOST AMAZING *"HUMAN BEING"* EVER CREATED! THE MOST DIABOLICAL PHANTOM —

TERRIFYINGLY TRUE! UNBELIEVABLY REAL!

A dead man goes to war!

"THE MAN WHO NEVER WAS"

CINEMASCOPE
COLOR by DE LUXE

starring CLIFTON WEBB · GLORIA GRAHAME

with Robert Flemyng · Josephine Griffin · Stephen Boyd · Produced by ANDRE HAKIM · Directed by RONALD NEAME
Screenplay by NIGEL BALCHIN · From the Book by EWEN MONTAGU · Released by 20th Century-Fox

THE MAN WHO NEVER WAS. A semi-documentary spy thriller which caught the public pulse at the right time.

The Man Who Watched Trains Go By

GB 1952   80m   Technicolor
Raymond Stross
aka: *Paris Express*

A clerk steals money in order to fulfil his wish
of world travel, and this leads to murder.
Miscast minor Simenon, not exactly badly
made but with no spark of excitement or
suspense.

wd Harold French, *novel* Georges Simenon
ph Otto Heller *m* Benjamin Frankel

Claude Rains, Marius Goring, Marta Toren,
Anouk Aimée, Herbert Lom, Ferdy Mayne

The Man Who Would Be King*

US 1975   129m   colour   Panavision
Columbia / Allied Artists / Persky-Bright /
Devon (John Foreman)

In India in the 1880s, two adventurers find
themselves accepted as kings by a remote
tribe, but greed betrays them.
After an ingratiating start this ambitious fable
becomes more predictable, and comedy gives
way to unpleasantness. Despite its sporadic
high quality, one does not remember it with
enthusiasm.

w John Huston, Gladys Hill, *story* Rudyard
Kipling *d* John Huston *ph* Oswald Morris
m Maurice Jarre *pd* Alexander Trauner

Sean Connery, Michael Caine, Christopher
Plummer (as Kipling), Saeed Jaffrey, Jack
May, Shakira Caine

AAN: script

The Man Who Wouldn't Talk

GB 1957   97m   bw
British Lion / Everest (Herbert Wilcox)

A lady QC gets an acquittal for a man who
can't defend himself on a murder charge
because of loyalty to a scientist on the run.
Efficient courtroom melodrama based on a
somewhat incredible and even uninteresting
situation.

w Edgar Lustgarten, *story* Stanley Jackson
d Herbert Wilcox *ph* Gordon Dines
m Stanley Black

Anna Neagle, Anthony Quayle, Zsa Zsa
Gabor, Katherine Kath, Dora Bryan, Patrick
Allen

The Man with a Cloak*

US 1951   81m   bw
MGM (Stephen Ames)

In 1848 New York, a mysterious stranger (who
turns out to be Edgar Allan Poe) helps a
young French girl to keep her inheritance.
Curious domestic melodrama set on MGM's
choicest sets; its playful literary allusion causes
it to fall between suspense thriller and
character drama, but the acting keeps one
watching.

w Frank Fenton, *story* John Dickson Carr
d Fletcher Markle *ph* George Folsey *m* David
Raksin

Joseph Cotten, Barbara Stanwyck, Leslie
Caron, Louis Calhern, Joe de Santis, Jim
Backus, Margaret Wycherly

The Man with Bogart's Face

US 1980   106m   CFI color
TCF / Melvin Simon (Andrew J. Fenady)

An unremarkable private eye gets lots of
assignments because he looks like Humphrey
Bogart.
Amiably nostalgic romp, not too spoofy to be
enjoyable for its own sake, but notably
underproduced.

w Andrew J. Fenady, from his novel
d Robert Day *ph* Richard C. Glouner
m George Duning

Robert Sacchi, Misty Rowe, Michelle Phillips,
Franco Nero, Olivia Hussey, Victor Buono,
Herbert Lom, George Raft, Yvonne de Carlo,
Jay Robinson, Mike Mazurki, Henry
Wilcoxon, Victor Sen Yung

The Man with My Face

US 1951   77m   bw

A successful young man finds a double in his
place at both home and office, and himself
branded as an imposter. Intriguing yarn which
deserved a better production. Barry Nelson,
Lynn Ainley, John Harvey, Carole Matthews,
Jack Warden. Written by Samuel W. Taylor,
Edward J. Montagne, T. J. McGowan and
Vincent Bogart, from a novel by Samuel W.
Taylor; directed by Edward J. Montagne; for
Edward F. Gardner / UA.

The Man with Nine Lives*

US 1940   73m   bw
Columbia
GB title: *Behind the Door*

A scientist believes he can cure cancer by
freezing, but accidentally locks himself and his
patients in an underground ice chamber for
seven years, and goes berserk when thawed
out.
Interesting, rather prophetic science fiction
thriller which rather lacks the style required to
put it over.

w Karl Brown, *story* Harold Shumate *d* Nick
Grinde *ph* Benjamin Kline

Boris Karloff, Byron Foulger, Roger Pryor, Jo
Ann Sayers

The Man with the Golden Arm*

US 1956   119m   bw
Otto Preminger

A Chicago poker dealer finally kicks the drug
habit.
Sensational on its first release, with its cold
turkey scenes, this now seems a muddled
impressionist melodrama with echoes of the
silent German cinema and much over-acting
and miscasting all round. But Sinatra is good;
and it *is* different . . .

w Walter Newman, Lewis Meltzer, *novel*
Nelson Algren *d* Otto Preminger *ph* Sam
Leavitt *m* Elmer Bernstein *pd* Joe Wright
titles Saul Bass

Frank Sinatra, Kim Novak, Eleanor Parker,
Darren McGavin, Arnold Stang, Robert
Strauss, John Conte, Doro Merande, George
E. Stone

'Nothing very surprising or exciting . . . a
pretty plain and unimaginative look-see at a
lower depths character.'—*Bosley Crowther*

'A very inferior film . . . the script is
inexcusably clumsy, the sets are unbelievable
and the casting is ridiculous.'—*Diana Willing,
Films in Review*

'It has the same running time as *Citizen
Kane* but it seems a whole lot longer.'—*Robert
James*

AAN: Elmer Bernstein; Frank Sinatra

The Man with the Golden Gun*

GB 1974   125m   Eastmancolor
UA / Eon (Harry Saltzman, Albert R.
Broccoli)

James Bond goes to the Far East to liquidate a
professional assassin named Scaramanga.
Thin and obvious Bond extravaganza with
conventional expensive excitements.

w Richard Maibaum, Tom Mankiewicz, *novel*
Ian Fleming *d* Guy Hamilton *ph* Ted Moore,
Oswald Morris *m* John Barry *pd* Peter
Murton

Roger Moore, Christopher Lee, Britt Ekland,
Maud Adams, Hervé Villechaize, Clifton
James, Richard Loo, Marc Lawrence

'The script lacks satiric insolence and the
picture grinds on humourlessly.'—*New Yorker*

● *Video: Warner*

'His gun was for sale—and so was his life!'

The Man with the Gun*

US 1955   84m   bw
UA / Formosa (Sam Goldwyn Jnr)
GB title: *The Trouble Shooter*

A gunfighter in search of his estranged wife
becomes lawman of a lawless town.
Modest, watchable western.

w N. B. Stone Jnr, Richard Wilson *d* Richard
Wilson *ph* Lee Garmes *m* Alex North

Robert Mitchum, Jan Sterling, Karen Sharpe,
Henry Hull, Emile Meyer, John Luplon

The Man with the Movie Camera**

USSR 1928   60m approx   bw   silent
VUFKU
original title: *Chelovek s Kinoapparatom*

A 'camera eye' documentary without any plot,
showing, through a succession of street and
interior scenes, all the tricks of which the
instrument is capable; it takes a bow at the
end.
Unique documentary which was
understandably a sensation when it first
appeared but now often seems merely quaint.

wd, ed Dziga Vertov *ph* Mikhail Kaufman

The Man with Two Faces*

US 1934   72m   bw
Warner

An actor takes revenge on a scoundrel who
had preyed on his sister.
Pleasing melodrama hinging on disguise; the
Hays Office surprisingly allowed the hero to
get away with it.

w Tom Reed, Niven Busch, *play* The Dark Tower by George S. Kaufman, Alexander Woolcott *d* Archie Mayo *ph* Tony Gaudio

Edward G. Robinson, Mary Astor, Ricardo Cortez, Louis Calhern, Mae Clarke, John Eldredge

'Fair fodder, but undistinguished in the main, and in spots very confusing.'—*Variety*

The Man Within*
GB 1947 88m Technicolor
GFD / Production Film Service (Muriel and Sydney Box)
US title: *The Smugglers*

An orphan boy discovers that his mysterious new guardian is a smuggler.
Unconvincing period yarn which has managed to drain every vestige of subtlety from the novel, but at least looks good.

w Muriel and Sydney Box, *novel* Graham Greene *d* Bernard Knowles *ph* Geoffrey Unsworth *m* Clifton Parker

Michael Redgrave, Richard Attenborough, Jean Kent, Joan Greenwood

'With more style this might have been rather good. Outside of life more private than I am normally party to I can't recall hearing so many men so often say, to other men, *I hate him!* or *I hate you!*'—James Agee

The Man Without a Body
GB 1957 80m bw

A tycoon with a brain tumour steals the head of Nostradamus and has it kept alive to replace his own. Hilarious horror-comic, inept in every department. George Coulouris, Robert Horton, Nadja Regin, Julia Arnall. Written by William Grote; directed by W. Lee Wilder and Charles Saunders; for Guido Coen / Eros.

The Man without a Star*
US 1955 89m Technicolor
U-I (Aaron Rosenberg)

A wandering cowboy helps settlers to put up barbed wire against an owner of vast cattle herds.
Conventional but entertaining star western.

w Borden Chase, D. D. Beauchamp, *novel* Dee Linford *d* King Vidor *ph* Russell Metty *m* Joseph Gershenson

Kirk Douglas, Jeanne Crain, Claire Trevor, William Campbell, Jay C. Flippen, Mara Corday, Richard Boone
† Remade for TV as *A Man Called Gannon*.

Man, Woman and Child
US 1982 100m De Luxe

A married professor discovers that he has a son by his only infidelity. *Angst* among the well-to-do, from the author of *Love Story*. Martin Sheen, Blythe Danner, Craig T. Nelson, David Hemmings, Nathalie Nell. Written by Erich Segal, David Selag Goodman, from the novel by Erich Segal; directed by Dick Richards; for Gaylord.

Man, Woman and Sin
US 1927 85m approx at 24 fps bw
silent

A reporter has an affair with his boss's mistress. Glossy romantic drama marking the first screen appearance of a sensational stage star; her effect on screen was more muted. Jeanne Eagels, John Gilbert, Marc McDermott. Written by Alice Duer Miller; directed by Monta Bell; for MGM.

The Manchurian Candidate***
US 1962 126m bw
UA / MC (Howard W. Koch)

A Korean war 'hero' comes back a brainwashed zombie triggered to kill a liberal politician, his control being his own monstrously ambitious mother.
Insanely plotted but brilliantly handled spy thriller, a mixture of Hitchcock, Welles and *All the King's Men*.

w George Axelrod, *novel* Richard Condon *d* John Frankenheimer *ph* Lionel Lindon *m* David Amram *pd* Richard Sylbert

Frank Sinatra, Laurence Harvey, Janet Leigh, James Gregory, Angela Lansbury, Henry Silva, John McGiver

'The unAmerican film of the year.'—*Penelope Houston*
'An intelligent, funny, superbly written, beautifully played, and brilliantly directed study of the all-embracing fantasy in everyday social, emotional and political existence.'—*Philip Strick, 1973*
'Although it's a thriller, it may be the most sophisticated political satire ever to come out of Hollywood.'—*Pauline Kael, 70s*

AAN: Angela Lansbury

Mandalay
US 1934 65m bw

A lady of the tropics murders her lover and pushes his body through a porthole. Steamy melodrama which the masses found absorbing. Kay Francis, Ricardo Cortez, Lyle Talbot, Ruth Donnelly, Shirley Temple, Warner Oland, Lucien Littlefield, Reginald Owen. Written by Austin Parker and Charles Kenyon; directed by Michael Curtiz; for Warner.

Mandingo
US 1975 126m Technicolor
Dino de Laurentiis (Peter Herald)

On a slave breeding plantation in 1840 Louisiana, passions ride high.
Like *Gone with the Wind* with all the characters on heat, this exuberant and unpleasant melodrama goes several points over the top from start to finish but proved to have wide appeal for the groundlings, in the *Tobacco Road* tradition of a wallow in other people's depravities.

w Norman Wexler, *play* Jack Kirkland, *novel* Kyle Onstott *d* Richard Fleischer *ph* Richard H. Kline *m* Maurice Jarre *pd* Boris Leven

James Mason, Susan George, Perry King, Richard Ward, Brenda Sykes, Ken Norton
● *Video: CIC*

'She'll find a home in every heart! She'll reach the heart of every home!'

Mandy***
GB 1952 93m bw
Ealing (Leslie Norman)
US title: *The Crash of Silence*

A little girl, born deaf, is sent to a special school.
Carefully wrought and very sympathetic little semi-documentary film in which all the adults underplay in concession to a new child star who alas did not last long at the top.

w Nigel Balchin, Jack Whittingham, *novel* This Day Is Ours by Hilda Lewis *d* Alexander Mackendrick *ph* Douglas Slocombe *m* William Alwyn

Jack Hawkins, Terence Morgan, Phyllis Calvert, *Mandy Miller*, Godfrey Tearle, Dorothy Alison

Manèges*
France 1950 90m bw
Films Modernes-Discina (Emil Natan)
GB title: *The Wanton*

A scheming girl marries the middle-aged owner of a riding school and, with her greedy mother, milks him of his money.
A neat little melodrama with flashbacks so arranged that the girl, paralysed in an accident, seems for the first half to have an angelic character.

w Jacques Sigurd *d* Yves Allégret *ph* Jean Bourgoin

Simone Signoret, Bernard Blier, *Frank Villard*, Jane Marken

Manhandled
US 1949 97m bw
Paramount / Pine–Thomas

The secretary of a bogus psychiatrist becomes involved in a murder and finds herself in danger from all comers.
Modest, overlong suspenser with adequate production values.

w Lewis R. Foster, Whitman Chambers, *novel* The Man Who Stole a Dream by L. S. Goldsmith *d* Lewis R. Foster *ph* Ernest Laszlo *m* David Chudnow

Dorothy Lamour, Dan Duryea, Sterling Hayden, Irene Hervey, Harold Vermilyea, Philip Reed, Alan Napier, Art Smith, Irving Bacon

Manhattan***
US 1979 96m bw Panavision
UA / Jack Rollins / Charles H. Joffe

Episodes in the sex life of a TV comedy writer with an obsession about New York.
As close to a summation of Woody Allen's views and *oeuvre* as anybody needs; some smart jabs about the lives we lead are sometimes bogged down in earnestness and half-comic despair.

w Woody Allen, Marshall Brickman *d* Woody Allen *ph* Gordon Willis *md* Tom Pierson

Woody Allen, Diane Keaton, Meryl Streep, Mariel Hemingway, Michael Murphy

'Given that the identity of his films has increasingly been determined by his compulsion to talk about the things he finds important, but also by his fear of having them come out as anything but a joke, it is not surprising that he has scarcely been able to decide on a form for his "art": from the anything-for-a-laugh skittering of his early films, to the broad parodies and pastiches of his middle period, to the recent confessional / psychoanalytical mode.'—*Richard Combs, MFB*

'A masterpiece that has become a film for the ages by not seeking to be a film of the moment.'—*Andrew Sarris*

Manhattan Melodrama**
US 1934 93m bw
MGM (David O. Selznick)

Two slum boys grow up friends, one as district attorney and the other as a gangster.
Archetypal American situation drama (cf *Angels with Dirty Faces, Cry of the City*, etc), with the bad guy inevitably indulging in self-sacrifice at the end. An all-star cast makes it palatable in this case, though the film is inevitably dated.

w Oliver H. P. Garrett, Joseph L. Mankiewicz, *story* Arthur Caesar d W. S. Van Dyke ph James Wong Howe

William Powell, Clark Gable, Myrna Loy, Leo Carrillo, Nat Pendleton, George Sidney, Isabel Jewell, Thomas E. Jackson

'Action meller of the big town . . . replete with punchy, popularly-appealing ingredients.'—*Variety*
† *Manhattan Melodrama* gained some irrelevant fame as the movie John Dillinger was watching when he was cornered and shot.

AA: Arthur Caesar

Manhattan Merry-go-round*
US 1937 82m bw

A sound recording studio is taken over by a band of racketeers. Sufficient comedy plot to sustain a revue of historical interest. Phil Regan, Leo Carrillo, Ann Dvorak, Tamara Geva, James Gleason, Ted Lewis and his Orchestra, Cab Calloway and his Orchestra, the Kay Thompson Ensemble, Louis Prima and his Band, Gene Autry, Joe Di Maggio. Written by Harry Sauber, Frank Hummert; directed by Charles F. Reisner; for Republic.
'So much talent and novelty has been compressed within the limits of the film that customers dare not sneeze for fear of missing something . . . for the territorial distributors and independent theatres it is something to get excited about.'—*Variety*

Manhattan Parade
US 1931 77m Technicolor

Behind the scenes as a theatrical costumier tries to get into the revue business. Aimless backstage comedy with turns. Smith and Dale, Winnie Lightner, Charles Butterworth, Walter

Miller, Luis Alberni. Written by Robert Lord and Houston Branch from a play by Sam Shipman; directed by Lloyd Bacon; for Warners. 'A few laughs dot the scenery, and they're all this musical possesses in value.'—*Variety*

Maniac
GB 1963 86m bw Hammerscope
Columbia / Hammer (Jimmy Sangster)

Murders by oxyacetylene torch in the Camargue, with the wrong lunatic going to the asylum.
Hammer's mark two plot, the shuddery murder mystery in which someone is not quite what he seems; feebly done in this case, with a fatally slow start.

w Jimmy Sangster d Michael Carreras ph Wilkie Cooper

Kerwin Mathews, Donald Houston, Nadia Gray, Justine Lord

The Manitou
US 1978 104m CFI Color
Herman Weist / Melvin Simon (William Girdler)

A fake spiritualist finds his girl friend is possessed by the demon of a 400-year-old Indian.
Boring retread of *The Exorcist*.

w William Girdler, Jon Cedar, Tom Pope, *novel* Graham Masterton d William Girdler ph Michel Hugo m Lalo Schifrin

Tony Curtis, Susan Strasberg, Michael Ansara, Stella Stevens, Jon Cedar, Ann Sothern, Burgess Meredith, Paul Mantee

Mannequin
US 1937 95m bw
MGM (Joseph L. Mankiewicz)

The wife of a small-time crook gets a modelling job and falls for a shipping magnate.
Competent star melodrama about a working girl's harassments.

w Lawrence Hazard d Frank Borzage ph George Folsey m Edward Ward

Joan Crawford, Spencer Tracy, Alan Curtis, Ralph Morgan, Mary Philips, Elizabeth Risdon, Leo Gorcey

AAN: song 'Always and Always' (m Edward Ward, ly Chet Forrest, Bob Wright)

Manon*
France 1949 96m bw
Alcina (P. E. Decharme)

After the liberation, a girl who has been a collaborator becomes involved in the black market, passes from man to man, and ends up being shot by Arabs in the Sahara desert.
Oddball modernized version of *Manon Lescaut*, with post-war pessimism and the glamour of sin going hand in hand. Worth comparing with *Gilda*.

w H. G. Clouzot, J. Ferry, *novel* L'Abbé Prévost d H. G. Clouzot ph Armand Thirard m Paul Misraki

Michel Auclair, Cécile Aubry, Serge Reggiani, Gabrille Dorziat

'A clever idea, handled cleverly, but without depth of feeling.'—*Penelope Houston*

Manon des Sources
France 1952 190m bw
Films Marcel Pagnol

A Provençal girl who lives in the hills with her goats is thought to be a witch, and takes her revenge on the populace by stopping the water supply.
Insanely long idyll of the countryside with the writer-director unintentionally caricaturing himself.

wd Marcel Pagnol ph Willy m Raymond Legrand

Jacqueline Pagnol, Raymond Péllégrin, Henri Vibert

'Something of an endurance test for all but the most enthusiastic Pagnol admirers.'—*John Gillett, MFB*

Manpower*
US 1941 103m bw
Warner (Mark Hellinger)

Power linesmen fall out over a nightclub hostess.
Yet another variation on *Tiger Shark*, with vivid fisticuff and storm sequences supporting the star performers.

w Richard Macaulay, Jerry Wald d Raoul Walsh ph Ernest Haller m Adolph Deutsch

Edward G. Robinson, George Raft, Marlene Dietrich, Alan Hale, Frank McHugh, Eve Arden, Barton MacLane, Walter Catlett, Joyce Compton, Ward Bond

'The pace and cutting are those of the best gangster films . . . the climax outdoes anything the Lyceum may have known.'—*William Whitebait*

Man's Castle*
US 1933 70m bw
Columbia (Frank Borzage)

Romance blooms among the unemployed who live in a shanty town on the banks of the East River.
Depression moonshine which at the time was taken for realism; sociologically very interesting but very faded as entertainment.

w Jo Swerling, *play* Lawrence Hazard d Frank Borzage ph Joseph August m W. Franke Harling

Spencer Tracy, Loretta Young, Glenda Farrell, Walter Connolly, Arthur Hohl, Marjorie Rambeau, Dickie Moore

'A picture that goes contrary to normal entertainment appetites and tastes, its possibilities of going places look slender at best.'—*Variety*
'Heavily sentimental yet magically romantic.'—*New Yorker, 1977*

Man's Favourite Sport?*
US 1963 120m Technicolor
Universal / Gibraltar / Laurel (Howard Hawks)

A star salesman of fishing tackle finds his bluff

called when he has to enter a fishing competition.

Over-extended romantic farce drawn by the director from memories of older and better films, such as *Libeled Lady* and his own *Bringing Up Baby*.

w John Fenton Murray d Howard Hawks ph Russell Harlan m Henry Mancini

Rock Hudson, Paula Prentiss, Maria Perschy, Charlene Holt, John McGiver, Roscoe Karns

'Hawks' deadpan documentation of a physical gag is as effective as ever, but the overall pace of his direction is curiously contemplative, as though he were savoring all his past jokes for the last time.'—*Andrew Sarris*

Manslaughter*
US 1922 80m approx (24 fps) bw silent
Paramount / Famous Players (Cecil B. de Mille)

An idle rich girl accidentally kills a man while driving, and is sent to prison, but falls for the district attorney who convicted her.
De Mille was here testing out his *Ten Commandments* format, with a long flashback during the DA's speech to the idle rich of ancient Rome. It worked like a charm at the box office.

w Jeanie McPherson, *novel* Alice Duer Miller d Cecil B. de Mille ph Alvin Wyckoff

Leatrice Joy, Thomas Meighan, Lois Wilson, John Miltern

† A 1930 sound remake for Paramount was directed by George Abbott, who also tried in vain to modernize the screenplay (by omitting the flashback). Claudette Colbert and Fredric March starred.

Mantrap
US 1961 93m bw Panavision
Paramount / Tiger (Edmond O'Brien, Stanley Frazen)

An honest man is lured by an old Marine friend into a hi-jack attempt which leads to the death of his wife.
Rather uninteresting melodrama, played and directed for more than it's worth.

w Ed Waters, *novel* Taint of the Tiger by John D. Macdonald d Edmond O'Brien ph Loyal Griggs m Leith Stevens

Jeffrey Hunter, David Janssen, Stella Stevens, Hugh Sanders

Manuela*
GB 1957 95m bw
British Lion / Ivan Foxwell
US title: *Stowaway Girl*

In a South American port, the engineer of a tramp steamer smuggles aboard a half caste girl, but it is the disillusioned captain who falls in love with her.
Downbeat seafaring melodrama, fine for those seeking a mood piece.

w William Woods, from his novel d Guy Hamilton ph Otto Heller m William Alwyn

Trevor Howard, Elsa Martinelli, Pedro Armendariz, Donald Pleasence

The Manxman
GB 1929 90m (24 fps) bw silent
British International (John Maxwell)

A fisherman thought drowned comes back to find that his girl is expecting his best friend's baby.
Stern romantic melodrama of virtually no interest despite its director.

w Eliot Stannard, *novel* Hall Caine d Alfred Hitchcock ph Jack Cox

Carl Brisson, Malcolm Keen, Anny Ondra, Randle Ayrton, Clare Greet

† Previously filmed in 1916 with Henry Ainley and Elizabeth Risdon.

Many Happy Returns
US 1934 62m bw

A scatty girl jinxes her father's department store and a Hollywood studio. Silly comedy with stops for vaudeville. George Burns, Gracie Allen, Guy Lombardo and his Band, Veloz and Yolanda, Ray Milland, George Barbier, Joan Marsh, Franklin Pangborn, William Demarest, Larry Adler. Written by J. P. McEvoy, Claude Binyon, Keene Thompson, Ray Harris, Lady Mary Cameron(!); directed by Norman Z. McLeod; for Paramount. 'Often very funny, at other moments it lags.'—*Variety*

Many Rivers to Cross*
US 1955 94m Eastmancolor Cinemascope
MGM (Jack Cummings)

A trapper bound for Canada is helped by a sharp-shooting girl, and in return he saves her from marauding Indians.
Simple-minded, cheerful, quite refreshing western compounded of equal parts comedy and action.

w Harry Brown, Guy Trosper d Roy Rowland ph John Seitz m Cyril Mockridge

Robert Taylor, Eleanor Parker, Victor McLaglen, Josephine Hutchinson, Jeff Richards, Russ Tamblyn, James Arness, Alan Hale Jnr

Mara Maru
US 1952 98m bw
Warner (David Weisbart)

A Manila salvage expert locates a sunken treasure and defeats crooks who are also in pursuit of it.
Lethargic but pleasant-looking star vehicle with a plot borrowed from *The Maltese Falcon*.

w N. Richard Nash, Philip Yordan, Sidney Harmon, Hollister Noble d Gordon Douglas ph Robert Burks m Max Steiner

Errol Flynn, Ruth Roman, Raymond Burr, Paul Picerni, Richard Webb

Maracaibo
US 1958 88m Technicolor Vistavision
Paramount / Theodora (Cornel Wilde)

A Texan oil fire expert finds himself unexpectedly busy when on holiday in Venezuela.

Meandering action melodrama with too much local colour.

w Ted Sherdeman, *novel* Stirling Silliphant d Cornel Wilde ph Ellsworth Fredericks m Laurindo Almeida

Cornel Wilde, Jean Wallace, Abbe Lane, Francis Lederer, Joe E. Ross, Michael Landor

The Marat / Sade*
GB 1966 116m De Luxe
UA / Marat Sade (Michael Birkett)
aka: *The Persecution and Assassination of Jean-Paul Marat as performed by the inmates of the Asylum of Charenton under the direction of the Marquis de Sade*

The title tells all, except that at the end the inmates go berserk.
Fairly plain filming of an Old Vic *succès d'estime* which it became fashionable to announce that one had seen and understood. The film makes no effort to attract the unbeliever.

w Adrian Mitchell, *play* Peter Weiss d Peter Brook ph David Watkin m Richard Peaslee

Glenda Jackson, Patrick Magee, Ian Richardson, Michael Williams, Robert Lloyd, Clifford Rose, Freddie Jones

Marathon Man**
US 1976 126m Metrocolor
Paramount (Robert Evans, Sidney Beckerman)

A vicious Nazi returns from Uruguay to New York in search of diamonds which had been kept for him by his now-dead brother, and is outwitted by the young brother of an American agent he has killed.
Complex mystery thriller which seems to have things to mutter about freedom and McCarthyism and Nazism, but finally settles down to being a simple shocker with a nick-of-time climax. The presentation is dazzling.

w William Goldman, from his novel d John Schlesinger ph Conrad Hall m Michael Small pd Richard MacDonald

Dustin Hoffman, *Laurence Olivier*, Roy Scheider, William Devane, Marthe Keller, Fritz Weaver, Marc Lawrence

'A film of such rich texture and density in its construction, so fascinatingly complex in its unfolding, so engrossing in its personalities, and so powerful in its performance and pace that the seduction of the senses has physical force.'—*Judith Crist, Saturday Review*

'Fashionably violent . . . distinctly self-conscious . . . conventionally moralistic . . . and absolutely devoid of resonance.'—*Tom Milne, MFB*

'If at the film's end, you have followed the series of double and triple crosses, braved the torture scenes, and still don't know what it was about, you're bound to have company.'—*Paul Coleman, Film Information*

'A Jewish revenge fantasy.'—*Pauline Kael*

'He has made a most elegant, bizarre, rococo melodrama out of material which, when you think about it, makes hardly any sense at all.'—*Vincent Canby, New York Times*

AAN: Laurence Olivier

The Marauders

US 1955 81m Eastmancolor
MGM (Arthur M. Loew Jnr)

A rancher hires gunmen to drive away
squatters, but the gunmen kill him and take
over.
Slightly sinister western with a plot probably
worth trying again.

w Jack Leonard, Earl Fenton, *novel* Alan
Marcus *d* Gerald Mayer *ph* Harold
Marzorati *m* Paul Sawtell

Dan Duryea, Jeff Richards, Keenan Wynn,
Jarma Lewis, Harry Shannon

March or Die

GB 1977 107m Technicolor
ITC / Associated General (Dick Richards,
Jerry Bruckheimer)

In 1918, tensions rise at a Foreign Legion
outpost threatened by Arabs.
Incredibly old-hat romantic melodrama of the
kind that was being spoofed forty years ago.
The considerable talent involved seems
unfortunately under instruction to take it
seriously.

w David Zelag Goodman *d* Dick Richards
ph John Alcott *m* Maurice Jarre

Gene Hackman, Terence Hill, Catherine
Deneuve, Max Von Sydow, Ian Holm, Marcel
Bozzuffi

† The writer and director more successfully
revived a different set of clichés in *Farewell
My Lovely.*

● *Video: Precision*

Mardi Gras

US 1958 107m De Luxe Cinemascope
TCF (Jerry Wald)

In New Orleans at holiday time, a film star
falls for a cadet.
Mindless musical using up available talent.

w Winston Miller, Hal Kanter *d* Edmund
Goulding *ph* Wilfrid M. Cline *md* Lionel
Newman

Pat Boone, Christine Carere, Sheree North,
Tommy Sands, Gary Crosby, Fred Clark,
Richard Sargent, Barrie Chase

AAN: Lionel Newman

Mare Nostrum*

US 1925 approx 110m bw silent
MGM

A Spanish captain loves a German spy.
Tragic romantic melodrama, a major
attraction of its time.

w Willis Goldbeck, *novel* Vicente Blasco
Ibanez *d* Rex Ingram *ph* John Seitz

Antonio Moreno, Alice Terry

Margie***

US 1946 94m Technicolor
TCF (Walter Morosco)

A married woman reminisces about her
college days, when she married the French
teacher despite her tendency to lose her
bloomers at the most embarrassing moments.

Wholly pleasing nostalgia, very smartly and
brightly handled.

w F. Hugh Herbert, *stories* Ruth McKinney,
Richard Bransten *d* Henry King *ph* Charles
Clarke *md* Alfred Newman

Jeanne Crain, Glenn Langan, Alan Young,
Lynn Bari, Barbara Lawrence, Conrad Janis,
Esther Dale

Margin for Error*

US 1943 74m bw
TCF (Ralph Dietrich)

Just before World War II, the Nazi consul in
New York is murdered in his own office.
Mildly intriguing whodunnit with the case
solved by a Jewish cop.

w Lillie Hayward, *play* Clare Boothe Luce
d Otto Preminger *ph* Edward Cronjager
m Leigh Harline

Milton Berle, Joan Bennett, Otto Preminger,
Carl Esmond, Howard Freeman, Poldy Dur,
Hans Von Twardowski

Marguerite de la Nuit*

France / Italy 1955 126m Technicolor
SNEG / Gaumont Actualités / Cino del Duca
(Léon Carré)

An octogenarian signs a pact with the devil in
return for his lost youth; but when he has it he
causes the death of the woman he loves.
Expensive, sporadically interesting, but
unpersuasive updating of *Faust.*

w Ghislaine Autant-Lara, Gabriel Arout
d Claude Autant-Lara *ph* Jacques Natteau
m René Cloërc

Michèle Morgan, Yves Montand, Jean-
François Calvé, Massimo Girotti

Maria Chapdelaine*

France 1935 73m bw

In a hard Quebec winter Maria loses her
mother and her lover, but resists temptation
by a man from the city. Artistically telling
drama, later flatly remade as *The Naked
Heart.* Madeleine Renaud, Jean Gabin,
Suzanne Despres, Jean-Pierre Aumont. From
the novel by Louis Hemon; directed by Julien
Duvivier; for Société Nouvelle. 'A fine
achievement, it gives the feeling of a sort of
epic poem.'—*Variety*

Maria Marten, or The Murder in the
Red Barn

GB 1935 67m bw
George King

A wicked Victorian squire kills his pregnant
mistress and is haunted.
Stilted melodrama, ripely played, from a real-
life case. (The villain's scalp is still exhibited in
a museum at Bury St Edmunds.)

w Randall Faye *d* George King *ph* George
Stretton

Tod Slaughter, Sophie Stewart, Eric Portman,
Clare Greet

† Several versions had been made in silent
days.

Marie Antoinette*

US 1938 160m bw
MGM (Hunt Stromberg)

The last days of the French court before the
revolution.
Too slow by half, and so glamorized and
fictionalized as to lack all interest, this long
delayed production stands only as an example
of MGM's expensive prestige movies of the
thirties.

w Claudine West, Donald Ogden Stewart,
Ernest Vajda *d* W. S. Van Dyke *ph* William
Daniels *montage* Slavko Vorkapitch
m Herbert Stothart *ad* Cedric Gibbons

Norma Shearer, Tyrone Power, John
Barrymore, Robert Morley, Gladys George,
Anita Louise, Joseph Schildkraut, Henry
Stephenson, Reginald Gardiner, Peter Bull,
Albert Dekker, Cora Witherspoon, Barnett
Parker, Joseph Calleia, Henry Kolker, George
Zucco, Henry Daniell, Harry Davenport,
Barry Fitzgerald, Mae Busch, Robert Barrat

'Produced on a scale of incomparable
splendour and extravagance, it approaches
real greatness as cinematic historical
literature.'—*Variety*

'A resplendent bore.'—*New Yorker, 1977*

AAN: Herbert Stothart; Norma Shearer;
Robert Morley

La Marie du Port

France 1949 95m bw
Sacha Gordine

A Cherbourg restaurateur takes his mistress
home for her father's funeral, and falls in love
with her younger sister.
Slight romantic drama, well enough put over
but not very memorable except for its slightly
cynical mood.

w Louis Chavance, Marcel Carné,
novel Georges Simenon *d* Marcel Carné
ph Henri Alekan *m* Joseph Kosma

Jean Gabin, Blanchette Brunoy, Nicole
Courcel, Claude Romain, Louis Cseigner,
Jeanne Marken, Carette

Marie Galante

US 1934 90m bw

A French girl stranded in the Canal Zone
becomes involved in international intrigue.
Slightly unusual spy romance. Spencer Tracy,
Ketti Gallian, Ned Sparks, Helen Morgan, Sig
Rumann, Leslie Fenton, Stepin Fetchit.
Written by Reginald Berkeley, from the novel
by Jacques Deval; directed by Henry King; for
Fox. 'Production and handling should carry it
to moderate grosses.'—*Variety*

Marie Octobre

France 1958 102m bw
Orex / SF / Abbey / Doxa (Lucien Viard)
US title: *Secret Meeting*

At a reunion dinner of a wartime resistance
group, a traitor is exposed and killed.
Stultifying one-set talkfest employing
Hitchcock's long-discarded ten-minute take.

w Julien Duvivier, Jacques Robert,
novel Jacques Robert *d* Julien Duvivier
ph Robert Le Fèbvre *m* Jean Yatove
ad Georges Wakhevitch

Danielle Darrieux, Serge Reggiani, Bernard
Blier, Paul Meurisse, Noel Roquevert, Lino
Ventura, Paul Guers, Paul Frankeur

The Marines Fly High
US 1940   68m   bw

Two leathernecks combat a mysterious South
American villain. Formula action fare,
intended as a Flagg and Quirt adventure but
made with a second team. Richard Dix,
Chester Morris, Lucille Ball, John Eldredge,
Steffi Duna. Written by Jerry Cady and A. J.
Bolton; directed by George Nicholls Jnr and
Ben Stoloff; for Robert Sisk / RKO.

'Up to their necks in fightin' and lovin'!'

Marines Let's Go
US 1961   103m   De Luxe   Cinemascope
TCF (Raoul Walsh)

Marines fighting in Korea are granted leave in
Japan.
Brawling tragi-farce with predictable
characters, a long way after *What Price Glory*.
w John Twist, *story* Raoul Walsh *d* Raoul
Walsh *ph* Lucien Ballard *m* Irving Gertz

Tom Tryon, David Hedison, Tom Reese,
Linda Hutchins, William Tyler
  'A typically noisy, insensitive and maudlin
tribute to the American Marines.'—*MFB*

Marius**
France 1931   125m   bw
Marcel Pagnol / Paramount

The son of a Marseilles waterfront café owner
gives up his sweetheart to go to sea.
Celebrated character drama which succeeds
through the realism and vitality of its people
and their dialogue.
w Marcel Pagnol, from his play *d* Alexander
Korda *ph* Ted Pahle *m* Francis Grammon

Raimu, Pierre Fresnay, Charpin, Orane
Demazis
† Two sequels with the same players and from
the same pen made this a famous trilogy. In
Fanny (1932, 128m, *d* Marc Allégret) the
heroine marries an old widower to give her
baby a father. In *César* (1936, 117m, *d* Marcel
Pagnol) Marius comes back twenty years later
and is reunited with his family.
†† *Port of Seven Seas* (MGM 1938) was a
hammy and stagey Hollywood compression of
the trilogy. See also *Fanny* (1960) a dull
version of the stage musical, with the songs
removed.

Marjorie Morningstar
US 1958   123m   Warnercolor
(Warner) United States Pictures (Milton
  Sperling)

A New York Jewish girl has great ambitions
for herself but ends up a suburban housewife.
Stodgy 'woman's picture' with all talents
somewhat uneasy in their assignments, mainly
because the Jewish quality is imperfectly
conveyed.

w Everett Freeman, *novel* Herman Wouk
d Irving Rapper *ph* Harry Stradling *m* Max
Steiner

Natalie Wood, Gene Kelly, Claire Trevor,
Everett Sloane, Ed Wynn, Martin Milner,
Carolyn Jones, George Tobias, Jesse White,
Martin Balsam
† The first film in which perfume was credited.
AAN: song 'A Very Precious Love'
(*m* Sammy Fain, *ly* Paul Francis Webster)

The Mark*
GB 1961   127m   bw   Cinemascope
TCF / Raymond Stross / Sidney Buchman

A sexual psychopath finds on emerging from
prison that his past still haunts him despite the
help of his psychiatrist.
Worthy but evasive social drama which
outstays its welcome but provides good
performances.
w Sidney Buchman, Stanley Mann *d* Guy
Green *ph* Douglas Slocombe *m* Richard
Rodney Bennett

Stuart Whitman, Maria Schell, *Rod Steiger*,
Brenda de Banzie, Maurice Denham, Donald
Wolfit, Paul Rogers, Donald Houston
  'There is seriousness and care, but neither
boldness nor passion . . . no hint of the truly
sordid is allowed to seep through.'—*MFB*

AAN: Stuart Whitman

The Mark of Cain
GB 1947   88m   bw
GFD / Two Cities (W. P. Lipscomb)

The attractive housekeeper of a Manchester
businessman is blamed when his brother
accidentally poisons him.
Turgid period melodrama in which few
opportunities are offered and none taken.
w Francis Crowdy, Christianna Brand, W. P.
Lipscomb, *novel* Airing in a Closed Carriage
by Joseph Shearing *d* Brian Desmond Hurst
ph Erwin Hillier *m* Bernard Stevens

Sally Gray, Eric Portman, Patrick Holt,
Dermot Walsh, Denis O'Dea, Edward Lexy,
Miles Malleson

The Mark of the Hawk
US 1958   84m   Technicolor   Superscope

An educated African fights for the emergence
of his people by peaceful means. Well-
intentioned but muddled topical drama.
Sidney Poitier, Juano Hernandez, Eartha Kitt,
John McIntire. Marne Maitland, Patrick
Allen. Written by H. Kenn Carmichael;
directed by Michael Audley; for Universal-
International.

Mark of the Renegade
US 1951   81m   Technicolor

In 1824, a Mexican agent in California
pretends to be a rotter in order to unmask
villains. Shakily constructed action piece which
quickly wears out its welcome. Ricardo
Montalban, Gilbert Roland, Cyd Charisse, J.
Carrol Naish, Andrea King, George Tobias,

Antonio Moreno. Written by Louis Solomon
and Robert Hardy Andrews, from a story by
Johnston McCulley; directed by Hugo
Fregonese; for Jack Gross / Universal-
International.

Mark of the Vampire*
US 1935   61m   bw
MGM (E. J. Mannix)

A policeman tries to solve an old murder in an
eerie house by hiring vaudeville performers to
pose as vampires.
Semi-spoof horror which is flawed by lack of
pace and a patchy script, but contains splendid
visual moments. A remake of the Lon Chaney
silent, *London After Midnight*.
w Guy Endore, Bernard Schubert *d* Tod
Browning *ph* James Wong Howe

Lionel Barrymore, Jean Hersholt, Elizabeth
Allan, Bela Lugosi, Carol Borland, Lionel
Atwill, Henry Wadsworth, Donald Meek,
Jessie Ralph, Ivan Simpson, Holmes Herbert
  'Deftly combines murder mystery, chiller
and novelty elements for pretty good
entertainment results.'—*Variety*

The Mark of Zorro?
US 1920   90m (24 fps)   bw   silent
Douglas Fairbanks

A Mexican Robin Hood carves his initial
wherever he turns up to harass the Spanish
invaders.
A little faded now, but this swashbuckler
opened up a whole new career for its star; the
1940 version clearly has more style.
w from the novel The Curse of Capistrano by
Johnston McCulley *d* Fred Niblo *ph* William
McGann *m* William Perry

Douglas Fairbanks, Marguerite de la Motte,
Noah Beery
● *Video: Polygram*

The Mark of Zorro***
US 1940   94m   bw
TCF (Raymond Griffith)

After being educated in Spain, Diego de Vega
returns to California and finds the country
enslaved and his father half-corrupted by
tyrants. Disguising himself as a masked bandit,
he leads the country to expel the usurpers.
Splendid adventure stuff for boys of all ages,
an amalgam of *The Scarlet Pimpernel* and
Robin Hood to which in this version the
director adds an overwhelming pictorial sense
which makes it stand out as the finest of all.
w John Tainton Foote, Garrett Fort, Bess
Meredyth *d* Rouben Mamoulian *ph* Arthur
Miller *m* Alfred Newman *ad* Richard Day,
Joseph C. Wright

*Tyrone Power, Basil Rathbone, J. Edward
Bromberg*, Linda Darnell, Eugene Pallette,
Montagu Love, Janet Beecher, Robert
Lowery
AAN: Alfred Newman

Marked Woman°
US 1937 96m bw
Warner (Lou Edelman)

A nightclub girl is persuaded to testify against an underworld boss.
A twist on the usual run of gangster melodramas, performed with the star's accustomed intensity and presented with the studio's usual panache.

w Robert Rossen, Abem Finkel d Lloyd Bacon ph George Barnes m Heinz Roemheld md Leo F. Forbstein

Bette Davis, Humphrey Bogart, Jane Bryan, Eduardo Ciannelli, Isabel Jewell, Allen Jenkins, Mayo Methot, Lola Lane, Henry O'Neill

'Spotty draw depending on feminine reaction . . . there is nothing that is light, and very little that is funny.'—*Variety*

† Remade as *Lady Gangster*.

†† Humphrey Bogart's character was based on Thomas E. Dewey, and Eduardo Ciannelli's on Lucky Luciano.

Marlowe°
US 1969 95m Metrocolor
MGM / Katzka–Berne–Cherokee / Beckerman (Sergei Petchnikoff)

Private eye Philip Marlowe is hired by a nervous girl to find her missing brother.
The authentic Chandler atmosphere is caught by this busy thriller, but there seems to be a deliberate attempt to make a confusing plot even more obscure, so that the end result is more tiresome than amusing.

w Stirling Silliphant, *novel* The Little Sister by Raymond Chandler d Paul Bogart ph William H. Daniels m Peter Matz

James Garner, Rita Moreno, Sharon Farrell, Bruce Lee, Gayle Hunnicutt, Carroll O'Connor, William Daniels, Jackie Coogan

'One does wonder whether the simple human squalor of the Bogart–Chandler era can ever be recaptured by an increasingly meretricious Hollywood.'—*MFB*

Marnie°
US 1964 130m Technicolor
Universal / Geoffrey Stanley Inc (Alfred Hitchcock)

A rich man marries a kleptomaniac and cures her, but a nightmare in her past makes her still sexually frigid.
Psychodrama with background crime and suspense, lethargically handled by the old master, who alone knows what he saw in it in the first place, as this heroine does not even have fire under her ice. The production is curiously artificial in many ways, from dummy horses to backcloths to back projection.

w Jay Presson Allen, *novel* Winston Graham d Alfred Hitchcock ph Robert Burks m Bernard Herrmann pd Robert Boyle

Tippi Hedren, Sean Connery, Martin Gabel, Diane Baker, Louise Latham

Maroc 7
GB 1967 91m Eastmancolor
Panavision

The lady editor of a top fashion magazine doubles as a jewel thief and becomes involved in Moroccan intrigue. Complex sub-Bond tale of cross and double cross; hardly worth following, really. Gene Barry, Elsa Martinelli, Cyd Charisse, Leslie Phillips, Denholm Elliott, Alexandra Stewart, Eric Barker, Angela Douglas. Written by David Osborn; directed by Gerry O'Hara; for Cyclone / Rank.

Marooned°
US 1969 134m Technicolor
Panavision 70
Columbia / Frankovich–Sturges (Frank Capra Jnr)

Three astronauts are stranded in space, and a rescue mission gets under way.
Very heavy-going space suspenser with all possible technical accomplishment but little life of its own.

w Mayo Simon, *novel* Martin Caidin d John Sturges ph Daniel Fapp pd Lyle R. Wheeler

Gregory Peck, Richard Crenna, David Janssen, James Franciscus, Gene Hackman, Lee Grant, Nancy Kovack, Mariette Hartley, Scott Brady

'In something like the plight of Ironman One, Sturges' work seems on the point of slowing to a standstill as it drifts further into projects of ever-increasing, self-effacing size and anonymous technical dexterity.'—*Richard Combs*

'It has all the zip, zest and zing of a moon walk, and I suspect a computer fed a dictionary could come up with better dialogue.'—*Judith Crist, 1973*

'A space epic with a horse-and-buggy script.'—*Pauline Kael*

AAN: Daniel Fapp

The Marquise of O°
West Germany / France 1976 107m Eastmancolor
Janus / Films du Losange

At the end of the eighteenth century, during the Russian invasion of an Italian town, a noblewoman finds herself pregnant . . .
Careful novella with many ambiguities, more concerned with what might have happened than with what did. Interesting but exasperating.

wd Eric Rohmer, *story* Heinrich von Kleist ph Nestor Almendros m Roger Delmotte

Edith Clever, Bruno Ganz, Peter Luhr, Edda Seippel

'Some may find it slow, sentimental, naïve and old-fashioned; others leisurely, beautiful, controlled and illuminating. I found it both often at the same time.'—*Alan Brien, Sunday Times*

'A bold, funny story becomes a formal, tame film, like a historical work recreated for educational TV.'—*New Yorker, 1980*

The Marriage Circle°°
US 1924 78m (24 fps) bw silent
Warner

A bachelor on the loose becomes amorously involved in two marriages.
Feather-light comedy of manners which began a whole new American school, heavily influenced by various European masters.

w Paul Bern, *play* Only a Dream by Lothar Schmidt d Ernst Lubitsch ph Charles Van Enger

Monte Blue, Florence Vidor, Marie Prevost, Adolphe Menjou, Creighton Hale

'A vanished world of roses, kisses and embraces, of whispers and sighs, of a woman's shadowed arm encased in georgette beckoning across a moonlit garden . . . and hand-kissing all over the place.'—*Herman G. Weinberg*

'At once perfect cinematography and perfect conventional drama.'—*Iris Barry, The Spectator*

'So slim a plot, so hackneyed if you will, is told with gaiety and a wit that lift it into the very first rank of screen comedy.'—*National Board of Review*

† Remade as *One Hour with You*, also by Lubitsch.

'It's the most hilarious proposition a wife ever had!'

The Marriage Go Round
US 1961 98m De Luxe Cinemascope
TCF (Leslie Stevens)

A Swedish girl suggests to a married American professor that she borrow his body for mating purposes, believing they would produce the perfect child.
Silly, unfunny sex comedy.

w Leslie Stevens d Walter Lang ph Leo Tover m Dominic Frontière

James Mason, Susan Hayward, Julie Newmar, Robert Paige, June Clayworth

'As tedious as it is tasteless.'—*Evening Standard*

'It offers James Mason, an actor who couldn't crack a joke if it was a lichee nut, and Susan Hayward, a bargain basement Bette Davis whose lightest touch as a comedienne would stun a horse.'—*Time*

Marriage Is a Private Affair
US 1943 116m bw
MGM (Pandro S. Berman)

A spoilt rich girl becomes a petulant wife.
Abysmally slow, uninvolving and poorly acted star fodder.

w David Hertz, Lenore Coffee, *novel* Judith Kelly d Robert Z. Leonard ph Ray June m Bronislau Kaper

Lana Turner, James Craig, John Hodiak, Frances Gifford, Keenan Wynn, Natalie Schaefer, Hugh Marlowe, Paul Cavanagh

The Marriage of a Young Stockbroker°°
US 1971 95m De Luxe
TCF / Laurence Turman

A stockbroker who finds his life and his

marriage dull tries voyeurism and extra-marital sex.
Sardonic adult comedy of the battle between the sexes, pretty lively from start to finish.

w *Lorenzo Semple Jnr, novel* Charles Webb d Laurence Turman *ph* Laszlo Kovacs m Fred Karlin

Richard Benjamin, Joanna Shimkus, Elizabeth Ashley, Adam West, Patricia Barry

The Marriage of Corbal
GB 1936 93m bw

Before the French revolution, an aristocratic lady tries to escape disaster by the right marriage. Stilted adventure story with too much talk. Nils Asther, Hugh Sinclair, Hazel Terry, Noah Beery, Davy Burnaby. Written by S. Fullman, from the novel *The Nuptials of Corbal* by Rafael Sabatini; directed by Karl Grune; for Capitol.

The Marriage of Maria Braun*
West Germany 1978 119m Fujicolor
Albatros / Trio / WDR / FdA (Michael Fengler)

Vicissitudes of a post-war bride who is eventually blown up in a gas explosion.
A mixture of solemnity and irony which keeps its basic points well concealed but, despite a sometimes flagging pace, more or less consistently entertains the eye.

w Peter Märthesheimer, Pea Fröhloch d Rainer Werner Fassbinder *ph* Michael Ballhaus *m* Peer Raben

Hanna Schygulla, Klaus Lowitsch, Ivan Desny, Gottfried John

● Video: VCL

Marriage on the Rocks
US 1965 109m Technicolor
Panavision
Warner / A-C / Sinatra (William H. Daniels)

An ad man and his wife decide to go to Mexico for a divorce but once there change their minds; she ends up accidentally married to his best friend.
All this talent retreats fearfully from a witless, tasteless script and slow handling. A dismal comedy.

w Cy Howard d Jack Donohue *ph* William H. Daniels *m* Nelson Riddle

Frank Sinatra, Dean Martin, Deborah Kerr, Cesar Romero, Hermione Baddeley, Tony Bill, Nancy Sinatra, John McGiver
'A long, coarse, and nearly always unfunny comedy, hammered together for no apparent reason except to make money.'—*New Yorker*

The Marriage Playground
US 1929 70m bw
Paramount

Children of divorced rich parents wander round Europe in a group.
Slightly unusual drama of its day; sound technique very thin.

w J. Walter Rubin, Doris Anderson, *novel* The Children by Edith Wharton *d* Lothar Mendes *ph* Victor Milner

Fredric March, Kay Francis, Mary Brian, Lilyan Tashman, Huntley Gordon, Anita Louise

Married before Breakfast
US 1937 70m bw

An impecunious inventor has a razorless shaving cream. Scatty comedy which seldom amuses. Robert Young, Florence Rice, June Clayworth, Barnett Parker, Warren Hymer. Written by George Oppenheimer, Everett Freeman, Harry Ruskin; directed by Edwin L. Marin; for MGM. 'It has practically nothing in its favour.'—*Variety*

A Married Woman*
France 1964 98m bw
Anouchka / Orsay (Philippe Dusart)
original title: *Une Femme Mariée*

A pilot's wife has an actor lover.
Fragments of character observation, in various cinematic techniques, build up into an intense personal study if not a plot.

wd *Jean-Luc Godard ph* Raoul Coutard m Claude Nougaro

Macha Meril, Bernard Noel, Roger Leenhardt
'A minefield of paradoxes . . . the essence of cinema 1965.'—*Peter John Dyer, MFB*

Marry Me
GB 1949 97m bw
GFD / Gainsborough (Betty Box)

Four stories of a marriage bureau.
A styleless portmanteau of anecdotes put over by a clear second team.

w Lewis Gilbert, Denis Waldock d Terence Fisher *ph* Ray Elton *d* Clifton Parker

Derek Bond, Susan Shaw, Patrick Holt, Carol Marsh, David Tomlinson, Zena Marshall, Guy Middleton, Nora Swinburne, Jean Cadell, Mary Jerrold

The Marrying Kind*
US 1952 93m bw
Columbia (Bert Granet)

A couple seeking divorce tell their troubles to a judge, and change their minds.
Smart, New Yorkish, tragi-comic star vehicle which works pretty well.

w Ruth Gordon, Garson Kanin d George Cukor *ph* Joseph Walker *m* Hugo Friedhofer
Judy Holliday, Aldo Ray, Madge Kennedy, Mickey Shaughnessy

Marry the Girl
US 1937 66m bw

A crazy family owns a newspaper syndicate.
Fashionable comedy which goes far too far. Mary Boland, Frank McHugh, Hugh Herbert, Mischa Auer, Carol Hughes, Allen Jenkins, Alan Mowbray, Hugh O'Connell. Written by Sig Herzig, Pat C. Flick, Tom Reed, from the novel by Edward Hope; directed by William McGann; for Warners. 'Pic will probably get by on duals in the nabes and should be a panic with juve audiences. But it will probably lay an egg in first runs.'—*Variety*

La Marseillaise*
France 1938 145m bw
Films La Marseillaise (Andre Zwoboda)

The story of the French revolution of 1789.
A rather disconnected epic which, despite a few splendid scenes, never moved its audiences to enthusiasm.

wd *Jean Renoir ph* Jean Bourgoin and others *md* Joseph Kosma

Pierre Renoir, Lise Delemare, Louis Jouvet, Leon Larive, Georges Spanelly, Elisa Ruis, William Aguet
'France's super-super film production is a near flopperoo.'—*Variety*

The Marseilles Contract
GB / France 1974 89m Eastmancolor
Warner / AIP / Kettledrum / PECF (Judd Bernard)
US title: *The Destructors*

An American narcotics agent in Paris hires an assassin to dispose of a drug smuggler.
Routine action melodrama with a jokey atmosphere not sustained by a downbeat script.

w Judd Bernard d Robert Parrish *ph* Douglas Slocombe *m* Roy Budd

Michael Caine, Anthony Quinn, James Mason, Alexandra Stewart, Marcel Bozzufi, Maurice Ronet

Martin Luther*
US / Germany 1953 114m bw
Louis De Rochemont / Lutheran Church Productions (Lothar Wolff)

The career and doubts of Martin Luther.
Frequently vivid, occasionally boring, small-scale account of the first Protestant.

w Allan Sloane, Lothar Wolff, others d Irving Pichel *ph* Joseph C. Brun *m* Mark Lothar

Niall MacGinnis, John Ruddock, Pierre Lefèvre, Guy Verney, David Horne, Philip Leaver, Irving Pichel, Alexander Gauge
AAN: Joseph C. Brun

Martin Roumagnac
France 1946 99m bw
Alcina (Marc Le Pelletier)

The trial, with flashbacks, of a small-town businessman who has murdered his mistress.
Wholly unabsorbing and ordinary story of a *crime passionnel*, totally wasting its stars.

wd *Georges Lacombe ph* Roger Hubert m Marcel Mirouze

Jean Gabin, Marlene Dietrich, Margo Lion, Marcel Hérrand

Marty****
US 1955 91m bw
UA / Hecht–Hill–Lancaster (Harold Hecht)

A 34-year-old Brooklyn butcher fears he will never get a girl because he is unattractive, but at a Saturday night dance he meets a girl with similar fears. Unfortunately she is not Italian . . .
The first of the filmed teleplays which in the mid-fifties seemed like a breath of spring to

Hollywood (they were cheap) and also brought in a new wave of talent. This is one of the best, its new naturalistic dialogue falling happily on the ear; but it has been so frequently imitated since that its revolutionary appearance is hard to imagine.

w Paddy Chayevsky, from his play d Delbert Mann ph Joseph La Shelle m Roy Webb

Ernest Borgnine, Betsy Blair, Esther Minciotti, Joe Mantell, Karen Steele, Jerry Paris

'Something rare in the American cinema today: a subtle, ironic and compassionate study of ordinary human relationships.'—*Gavin Lambert*

AA: best picture; Paddy Chayevsky; Delbert Mann; Ernest Borgnine

AAN: Joseph La Shelle; Betsy Blair; Joe Mantell

Mary Burns Fugitive*
US 1935 84m bw
Paramount (Walter Wanger)

The innocent girl friend of a gangster is convicted through circumstantial evidence, escapes from prison and finds true love. Competent meshing of well-tried thirties elements, a good typical wish-fulfilment melodrama of its time.

w Gene Towne, Graham Baker, Louis Stevens d William K. Howard ph Leon Shamroy

Sylvia Sidney, Melvyn Douglas, Alan Baxter, Pert Kelton, Wallace Ford, Brian Donlevy, Esther Dale

'As a piece of synthetic studio slickness it has enough on the ball to qualify.'—*Variety*

Mary Jane's Pa
US 1935 70m bw

A husband goes wandering for ten years. On his return, his wife has magnified what he left into a newspaper empire. Adequate stagey comedy, well acted. Aline MacMahon, Guy Kibbee, Tom Brown, Robert McWade, Minor Watson, Nan Gray. Written by Tom Reed, Peter Milne, from the play by Edith Ellis Furness and the novel by Norman Way; directed by William Keighley; for Warners. 'Okay for secondary bills.'—*Variety*

Mary Mary
US 1963 126m Technicolor
Warner (Mervyn Le Roy)

A publisher falls in love again with his ex-wife but finds she is being pursued by a film star. Feeble film version of a lighter-than-air Broadway success, with the actors paralysed behind the footlights and the camera asleep in the stalls.

w Richard L. Breen, play Jean Kerr d Mervyn Le Roy ph Harry Stradling m Frank Perkins

Debbie Reynolds, Barry Nelson, Michael Rennie, Diane McBain

Mary of Scotland*
US 1936 123m bw
RKO (Pandro S. Berman)

Mary Stuart refuses to give up her claim to the English throne, and is eventually executed. Sombre historical charade with splendid sets and atmosphere but suffering from script and performances that don't quite make it despite effort all round.

w Dudley Nichols, play Maxwell Anderson d John Ford ph Joseph H. August m Nathaniel Shilkret ad Van Nest Polglase, Carroll Clark

Katharine Hepburn, Fredric March, Donald Crisp, Florence Eldridge, Douglas Walton, John Carradine, Robert Barrat, Monte Blue, Moroni Olsen, Frieda Inescort, Alan Mowbray

'An unpromising and stagey play is fleshed out into a rich and confident exercise in filmcraft.'—*John Baxter, 1968*

'Events are walked through as though they were rooms in a museum, and closing time at three.'—*Otis Ferguson*

Mary Poppins***
US 1964 139m Technicolor
Walt Disney (Bill Walsh)

In Edwardian London a magical nanny teaches two slightly naughty children to make life enjoyable for themselves and others. Sporadically a very pleasant and effective entertainment for children of all ages, with plenty of brightness and charm including magic tricks, the mixing of live with cartoon adventures, and just plain fun. It suffers, however, from a wandering narrative in the second half (when Miss Poppins scarcely appears) and from Mr Van Dyke's really lamentable attempt at Cockney.

w Bill Walsh, Don da Gradi, novel P. L. Travers d Robert Stevenson ph Edward Colman m / ly Richard M. and Robert B. Sherman pd Tony Walton sp Eustace Lycett, Peter Ellenshaw, Robert A. Mattey

Julie Andrews, David Tomlinson, Glynis Johns, Dick Van Dyke, Reginald Owen, Ed Wynn, Matthew Garber, Karen Dotrice, Hermione Baddeley, Elsa Lanchester, Arthur Treacher, Jane Darwell

AA: Richard M. and Robert B. Sherman; Julie Andrews; song 'Chim Chim Cheree'
AAN: best picture; script; Robert Stevenson; Edward Colman
● *Video: Disney*

'They used every passion in their incredible duel, and every man in their savage games of intrigue!'

Mary Queen of Scots
GB 1971 128m Technicolor
Panavision
Universal / Hal B. Wallis

The story of Mary Stuart's opposition to Elizabeth I, her imprisonment and execution. Schoolbook history in which none of the characters comes to life; dramatic movement is almost entirely lacking despite the liberties taken with fact.

w John Hale ph Christopher Challis d Charles Jarrott m John Barry

Vanessa Redgrave, Glenda Jackson, Trevor Howard, Patrick McGoohan, Nigel Davenport

'Without a better script, Hercules couldn't lift this story off the ground.'—*Pauline Kael, New Yorker*

AAN: John Barry; Vanessa Redgrave

Mary Stevens M.D.
US 1933 71m bw

A lady doctor decides to have a baby before getting married. Saucy drama which engrossed audiences in its day. Kay Francis, Lyle Talbot, Glenda Farrell, Thelma Todd, Una O'Connor, Hobart Cavanaugh, Harold Huber. Written by Rian James, from the novel by Virginia Kellogg; directed by Lloyd Bacon; for Warners. 'Exceptionally good adult entertainment, with a pronounced feminine appeal.'—*Variety*

M*A*S*H***
US 1970 116m De Luxe Panavision
TCF / Aspen (Ingo Preminger, Leon Ericksen)

Surgeons at a mobile hospital in Korea spend what spare time they have chasing women and bucking authority.
Savage comedy of man's rebellion in the face of death, alternating sex farce with gory operation scenes; hailed as the great anti-everything film, and certainly very funny for those who can take it. It led to a television series which for once did not disgrace its original.

w Ring Lardner Jnr, novel Richard Hooker d Robert Altman ph Harold E. Stine m Johnny Mandel

Donald Sutherland, Elliott Gould, Tom Skerritt, Sally Kellerman, Robert Duvall, Jo Ann Pflug, René Auberjonois, Gary Burghof

'Bloody funny. A hyper-acute wiretap on mankind's death wish.'—*Joseph Morgenstern*

'The laughter is blood-soaked and the comedy cloaks a bitter and terrible truth.'—*Judith Crist*

'A foul-mouthed, raucous, anti-establishment comedy, combining gallows humour, sexual slapstick and outrageous satire.'—*Les Keyser, Hollywood in the Seventies*

AA: Ring Lardner Jnr
AAN: best picture; Robert Altman; Sally Kellerman
● *Video: CBS / Fox*

The Mask of Dijon
US 1946 73m bw

A conjuror becomes obsessed by hypnotism and takes to murder to prove his superiority. Heavy-going thriller with little discernible point. Erich Von Stroheim, Jeanne Bates, William Wright. Written by Arthur St Claire and Griffin Jay; directed by Lew Landers; for PRC.

The Mask of Dimitrios**
US 1944   99m   bw
Warner (Henry Blanke)

A timid Dutch novelist is drawn into a Middle-Eastern intrigue with money at the centre of it.
Generally successful international intriguer, moodily shot in evocative sets, and remarkable for its time in that the story is not distorted to fit romantic stars: character actors bear the entire burden.

w Frank Gruber, novel Eric Ambler d Jean Negulesco ph Arthur Edeson m Adolph Deutsch

Peter Lorre, Sidney Greenstreet, Zachary Scott, Faye Emerson, Victor Francen, Steven Geray, Florence Bates, Eduardo Ciannelli, Kurt Katch, John Abbott, Monte Blue
    'The picture has more mood than excitement.'—*Pauline Kael, 70s*

The Mask of Fu Manchu**
US 1932   70m   bw
MGM

Nayland Smith and his party are caught and threatened with torture by the yellow terror. Highly satisfactory episode in the nefarious adventures of the master criminal, fast moving, humorous and very good to look at.

w John Willard, Edgar Woolf, Irene Kuhn, *stories* Sax Rohmer d Charles Brabin, Charles Vidor ph Tony Gaudio

Boris Karloff, Myrna Loy, Lewis Stone, Karen Morley, Charles Starrett, Jean Hersholt, Lawrence Grant
    'The diabolical stuff is piled on so thick at the finish, audiences are liable to laugh where they oughtn't.'—*Variety*
    'A tolerable, campy entertainment.'—*Pauline Kael, 70s*

Mask of the Avenger
US 1951   83m   Technicolor

During the Austro-Italian War, a count's son avenges his father's death and exposes a traitor. Very moderate swashbuckler on the lines of *The Mark of Zorro*. John Derek, Anthony Quinn, Jody Lawrence, Arnold Moss, Eugene Iglesias. Written by Jesse Lasky Jnr; directed by Phil Karlson; for Hunt Stromberg / Columbia.

Maskerade*
Austria 1935   87m   bw

An inveterate ladies' man finds himself trapped. Charming romantic comedy. Anton Walbrook, Paula Wessely, Olga Tscheshowa. Written and directed by Willi Forst; for Tobis / Sascha. 'Not a real masterpiece like *Liebelei*, but it has the same b.o. elements.'—*Variety*

The Masque of the Red Death**
GB 1964   89m   Pathecolor 'Scope
AIP / Alta Vista (George Willoughby)

A medieval Italian prince practises devil worship while the plague rages outside, but when he holds a ball, death is an uninvited guest.

Languorous, overstretched, often visually striking horror piece with some extremely effective touches among its longueurs.

w Charles Beaumont, R. Wright Campbell, *story* Edgar Allan Poe d Roger Corman ph Nicolas Roeg m David Lee ad Robert Jones costumes Laura Nightingale

Vincent Price, Hazel Court, Jane Asher, Patrick Magee, John Westbrook

Masquerade*
GB 1965   101m   Eastmancolor
UA / Novus (Michael Relph)

To avert friction between Arab states the young heir to one of them is abducted by a British secret service agent; but one of the plotters has other fish to fry.
Quite a lively spy romp with a spectacular action climax, but the plot is simply too complicated.

w Michael Relph, William Goldman, *novel* Castle Minerva by Victor Canning d Basil Dearden ph Otto Heller m Philip Green pd Don Ashton

Cliff Robertson, Jack Hawkins, Charles Gray, Bill Fraser, Marisa Mell, Michel Piccoli, John Le Mesurier

'A gay and gorgeous whirl of romance, adventure and rhythm . . . in the billion-dollar pan-American postwar playground!'

Masquerade in Mexico
US 1945   96m   bw
Paramount (Karl Tunberg)

A stranded showgirl is hired by a Mexican banker to entice a gigolo away from his wife. Talent-starved remake of *Midnight* (qv), which seems second-hand even if you don't know why.

w Karl Tunberg d Mitchell Leisen ph Lionel Lindon m Victor Young

Dorothy Lamour, Arturo de Cordova, Patric Knowles, Ann Dvorak, George Rigaud, Natalie Schafer, Mikhail Rasumny, Billy Daniels

The Masquerader*
US 1933   75m   bw
Samuel Goldwyn

A drug-addicted politician is replaced by his lookalike cousin.
Pleasing dual role star vehicle with good production and support. Very much of its period.

w Howard Estabrook, Moss Hart, *play* John Hunter Booth, *novel* Katherine Cecil Thurston d Richard Wallace ph Gregg Toland

Ronald Colman, Elissa Landi, Halliwell Hobbes, Juliette Compton, David Torrence
    'A fine production with too much story handicap . . . Colman's best is not enough.'—*Variety*
    'The first amusing and believable tale of English politics and society . . . made of all places in Hollywood.'—*Newsweek*

Mass Appeal*
US 1984   100m   Technicolor
Universal / Turman-Foster

An idealistic student matches wits with a compromising priest.
Amusing, opened-out version of a two-character play: good for minority audiences.

w Bill C. David from his play d Glenn Jordan ph Don Peterman m Bill Conti pd Philip Jeffries

Jack Lemmon, Zeljko Ivanek, Charles Durning, Louise Latham

The Master Gunfighter
US 1975   120m   Metrocolor   Panavision

In gold rush California, a mysterious avenger rights a variety of wrongs. Pretentious western which failed to advance the career of its somewhat over-confident creator. Tom Laughlin, Ron O'Neal, Lincoln Kilpatrick, Barbara Carrera. Written by Harold Lapland, from a Japanese film *Goyokin* written by Kei Tasaka and Hideo Gosha; directed by Tom Laughlin; for Avondale / Warner.

The Master of Ballantrae
GB 1953   89m   Technicolor
Warner

Two brothers toss to decide which shall join Bonnie Prince Charlie's 1745 rebellion.
Half-hearted version of a classic adventure novel.

w Herb Meadow, *novel* R. L. Stevenson d William Keighley ph Jack Cardiff m William Alwyn

Errol Flynn, Anthony Steel, Roger Livesey, Beatrice Campbell, Felix Aylmer, Mervyn Johns, Jacques Berthier, Yvonne Furneaux, Ralph Truman
    'All that can be salvaged from this rather unforgivable Anglo-American junket are some pleasant exteriors.'—*Gavin Lambert*

Master of Bankdam*
GB 1947   105m   bw
GFD / Holbein (Nat Bronsten, Walter Forde, Edward Dryhurst)

19th-century chronicles of a mill-owning Yorkshire family.
Archetypal 'trouble at t'mill' saga with moderate production, good acting and undeniably compulsive story.

w Edward Dryhurst, Moie Charles, *novel* Thomas Armstrong d Walter Forde ph Basil Emmott

Tom Walls, Anne Crawford, Dennis Price, Stephen Murray, Linden Travers, Jimmy Hanley, Nancy Price, David Tomlinson, Herbert Lomas

Master of the World
US 1961   104m   Magnacolor
AIP / Alta Vista (James H. Nicholson, Anthony Carras)

In 1848 a mad inventor takes to the air in his magnificent flying machine in the hope of persuading men to stop war.

Aerial version of *Twenty Thousand Leagues under the Sea*, with cheap sets and much use of stock footage; some scenes however have a certain vigour.

w Richard Matheson, *novels* Jules Verne *d* William Witney *ph* Gil Warrenton *m* Les Baxter

Vincent Price, Charles Bronson, Henry Hull, Mary Webster, David Frankham

The Master Plan
GB 1954 78m bw

An American agent, concealing the fact that he suffers from blackouts, is sent to investigate information leakages in England. Quite lively second feature spylarks. Wayne Morris, Tilda Thamar, Norman Wooland, Mary Mackenzie, Arnold Bell. Written and directed by Hugh Raker; for Grand National.

Masterson of Kansas
US 1955 73m Technicolor

The sheriff of Dodge City prevents an Indian uprising by saving an innocent man from the gallows. Unhistorical two-bit western. George Montgomery, Nancy Gates, James Griffith, Jean Willes. Written by Douglas Heyes; directed by William Castle; for Sam Katzman / Columbia.

'Men worshipped her like a goddess, only to be betrayed by a kiss!'

Mata Hari**
US 1931 92m bw
MGM

The career of the famous lady spy of World War I.

Elaborate melodrama, pictorially satisfying and generally more entertaining than might be supposed, with both star and supporting cast in rich thespian form.

w Benjamin Glazer, Leo Birinski, Doris Anderson, Gilbert Emery *d* George Fitzmaurice *ph* William Daniels

Greta Garbo, Ramon Novarro, Lionel Barrymore, Lewis Stone, C. Henry Gordon, Karen Morley, Blanche Frederici

'Picture's strength is all in the players; an important grosser on that account.'—*Variety*

Mata Hari, Agent H21*
France / Italy 1964 99m bw
Filmel / Les Films du Carrosse / Simar / Fida Cinematografica (Eugene Lepicier)

A rather unnecessary revamp of the same story, with interesting details but not much resonance.

w Jean-Louis Richard, François Truffaut *d* Jean-Louis Richard *ph* Michel Kelber *m* Georges Delerue *ad* Claude Pignot

Jeanne Moreau, Jean-Louis Trintignant, Claude Rich, Frank Villard

'All that we are left with is a generous dollop of period charm, and the fascinating spontaneity of an actress.'—*Peter John Dyer, MFB*

The Match King
US 1932 80m bw

A world-famous match manufacturer gets into spectacular money difficulties. Thinly veiled biopic of Ivar Kreuger; not at all bad. *Warren William*, Lili Damita, Glenda Farrell, Harold Huber. Written by Houston Branch and Sidney Sutherland; directed by Howard Bretherton; for Warner. 'Good entertainment, uncommonly well acted . . . in Swedish-populated sections should be top moneymaker.'—*Variety*

The Matchmaker*
US 1958 101m bw Vistavision
Paramount (Don Hartman)

In New York at the turn of the century, a rich merchant decides to marry again but the matchmaker he consults has her own eye on him.

Cold and lifeless version of an amusing play which also served as the basis for the musical *Hello Dolly* (qv).

w John Michael Hayes, *play* Thornton Wilder *d* Joseph Anthony *ph* Charles Lang *m* Adolph Deutsch

Shirley Booth, Paul Ford, Anthony Perkins, Shirley Maclaine, Wallace Ford, Robert Morse, Perry Wilson

DOLLY LEVI (Shirley Booth) to the audience: 'Life's never quite interesting enough, somehow. You people who come to the movies know that.'

'Long static dialogue exchanges are further extended by frequent confidences expressed directly to the audience . . . but in spite of the general lack of pace, lightness and dimension there is still a great deal to enjoy.'—*Peter John Dyer*

La Maternelle*
France 1932 89m bw
Photosonor

A maid in a nursery school becomes devoted to the children and in particular to one who causes trouble when her friend decides to marry.

A touching drama of its day which now seems rather primitive.

w Jean Benoit-Lévy *d* Jean Benoit-Lévy, Marie Epstein *ph* Georges Asselin *m* Edouard Flament

Madeleine Renaud, Paulette Elambert, Alice Tissot, Mady Berry

'By any standard the finest foreign-language talker shown in the US in a couple of years.'—*Variety*

Matilda
US 1978 105m Movielab
AIP / Albert S. Ruddy

A down-at-heel theatrical agent finds success with a boxing kangaroo.
Damon Runyon meets Walt Disney in an old-fashioned family audience picture for which there may no longer be an audience.

w Albert S. Ruddy, Timothy Galfas, *novel* Paul Gallico *d* Daniel Mann *ph* Jack Woolf *pd* Boris Leven *m* Jerrold Immel

Elliott Gould, Robert Mitchum, Harry Guardino, Clive Revill, Karen Carlson, Lionel Stander, Art Metrano, Roy Clark

The Mating Game
US 1959 96m Metrocolor Cinemascope
MGM (Philip Barry Jnr)

An income-tax inspector becomes involved in the affairs of an unorthodox farming family. Dismally unfunny adaptation for Americans of a very English novel; everyone works hard to no avail.

w William Roberts, *novel* The Darling Buds of May by H. E. Bates *d* George Marshall *ph* Robert Bronner *m* Jeff Alexander

Debbie Reynolds, Tony Randall, Paul Douglas, Fred Clark, Una Merkel, Philip Ober, Charles Lane, Philip Coolidge

'Every joke is driven past the point of exhaustion.'—*MFB*

The Mating of Millie
US 1948 87m bw

A self-confident young woman wants to adopt a small boy and tries to propel a bus driver into a marriage of convenience. Amiable if protracted romantic comedy with dashes of sentiment and an obvious outcome. Glenn Ford, Evelyn Keyes, Willard Parker, Jimmy Hunt, Ron Randell. Written by Louella MacFarlane and St Clair McKelway; directed by Henry Levin; for Columbia.

The Mating Season
US 1950 101m bw
Paramount (Charles Brackett)

A factory draughtsman marries an ambassador's daughter; his mother loses her job and comes incognito to work for them as a cook.

Uninteresting mechanical domestic comedy in which the young folk are dull and the older ones overplay.

w Walter Reisch, Charles Brackett, Richard Breen *d* Mitchell Leisen *ph* Charles Lang

Gene Tierney, John Lund, Miriam Hopkins, Thelma Ritter, Jan Sterling

AAN: Thelma Ritter

A Matter of Dignity*
Greece 1957 104m bw
Finos (Anis Nohra)
original title: *To Telefteo Psemma*

The daughter of a bankrupt family reluctantly agrees to marry a millionaire, and the family's false values lead to tragedy.
Rather offbeat melodrama with the director in good form.

wd Michael Cacoyannis *ph* Walter Lassally *m* Manos Hadjidakis

Ellie Lambetti, Georges Pappas, Athena Michaelidou

A Matter of Life and Death°°°°
GB 1946   104m   Technicolor
GFD / Archers (Michael Powell, Emeric Pressburger)
US title: *Stairway to Heaven*

A pilot with brain damage after bailing out is torn between this world and the next, but an operation puts things to rights.

Outrageous fantasy which seemed more in keeping after the huge death toll of a world war, and in any case learned the Hollywood lesson of eating its cake and still having it, the supernatural elements being capable of explanation. A mammoth technical job in the heavenly sequences, it deserves full marks for its sheer arrogance, wit, style and film flair.

wd Michael Powell, Emeric Pressburger *ph* Jack Cardiff *m* Allan Gray *pd* Hein Heckroth

David Niven, Roger Livesey, Kim Hunter, Marius Goring, Raymond Massey, Abraham Sofaer

'Powell and Pressburger seem to have reached their heaven at last . . . an illimitable Wembley stadium, surrounded by tinkly music and mists, from which all men of insight, if they were ever careless enough to get there, would quickly blaspheme their way out.'— *Richard Winnington*

'A dazzling mesh of visionary satire, post-war politics and the mystical side of English romanticism.'—*Tony Rayns, Time Out, 1979*

'Beautifully written, beautifully acted, beautifully executed . . . you would think such formidable merits would add up to quite a film—and darned if they don't.'—*Time Out*

'This film, whether or not you find its philosophy half-baked, is downright good cinema, doing things that couldn't be done in any other medium'—*Tribune*

'It compelled attention and created emotion.'—*Basil Wright, 1972*

'Some women are born to have a glorious affair with life . . . !'
A Matter of Time
US / Italy 1976   97m (originally 165m) Technicolor
(AIP) Jack H. Skirball, J. Edmund Grainger

An Italian country chambermaid is taught about life by a faded countess.

Interminable even in its abbreviated form, this woebegone fantasy is a tribute to his miscast daughter by a director who never had much sense of plot to begin with. It has to be seen to be believed.

w John Gay, *novel* The Film of Memory by Maurice Druon *d* Vincente Minnelli *ph* Geoffrey Unsworth *m* Nino Oliviero

Liza Minnelli, Ingrid Bergman, Charles Boyer, Tina Aumont, Gabriele Ferzetti, Spiros Andros

'So hackneyed, inept and stupid as to be almost amusing.'—*John Simon, New York*

'So spectacularly crazy that if Minnelli could only persuade Mel Brooks to put his name on it, *A Matter of Time* might yet be the comedy sleeper of the year.'—*Frank Rich, New York Post*

A Matter of Who
GB 1961   92m   bw
MGM / Foray (Walter Shenson, Milton Holmes)

The World Health Organization tracks down a smallpox outbreak.

Curious blend of semi-documentary with suspense and comedy; not really a starter.

w Milton Holmes *d* Don Chaffey *ph* Erwin Hillier *m* Edwin Astley

Terry-Thomas, Sonja Ziemann, Alex Nicol, Guy Deghy, Richard Briers, Clive Morton, Geoffrey Keen, Martin Benson, Honor Blackman, Carol White

The Maverick Queen
US 1955   90m   Trucolor   Naturama

A lady rustler falls for a Pinkerton detective sent to arrest her. Tedious western in bilious colour. Barbara Stanwyck, Barry Sullivan, Scott Brady, Mary Murphy, Wallace Ford, Jim Davis. Written by Kenneth Gamet and DeVallon Scott, from the novel by Zane Grey; directed by Joe Kane; for Republic.

Maya
US 1966   91m   Technicolor   Panavision
MGM / King Brothers (Mary P. Murray, Herman King)

A teenage American boy arrives in India to visit his disillusioned father, who finally comes to understand him only after he has run away. Good-looking but otherwise uninteresting animal drama which served as the pilot for a TV series.

w John Fante *d* John Berry *ph* Gunter Senftleben *m* Riz Ortolani

Clint Walker, Jay North, I. S. Johar, Sajid Khan

Mayerling°°
France 1935   90m   bw

In 1889, imperial lovers are found dead in a country house. Classic French version of a somewhat chilly subject. Charles Boyer, *Danielle Darrieux*, Marthe Regnier, Yolande Laffon, Suzy Prim. Written by Joseph Kessel and V. Cube, from the novel by Claude Anet; directed by *Anatole Litvak*; for Seymour Nebenzal / Nero Film. 'As good a picture as Hollywood could produce, plus some local touches that are inaccessible to Hollywood.'—*Variety*

Mayerling
France / GB 1968   141m   Eastmancolor Panavision
Corona / Winchester (Robert Dorfmann)

In 1888 the heir to the Habsburg Empire is forced into a suicide pact with his mistress. Tedious dramatization of historical events which in 1936 had made a delicate French film but in these hands seems an endless and boring manipulation of doubtful events into turgid romance.

wd Terence Young, *novel* Claude Anet *ph* Henri Alekan *m* Francis Lai *pd* Georges Wakhevitch

Omar Sharif, Catherine Deneuve, James Mason, Ava Gardner, James Robertson Justice, Genevieve Page, Ivan Desny, Maurice Teynac

● Video: *Thorn EMI*

The Mayor of 44th Street
US 1942   86m   bw
RKO (Cliff Reid)

Dance bands are threatened by hooligans demanding protection money.

Boring melodrama with music.

w Lewis R. Foster *d* Alfred E. Green *ph* Robert de Grasse *songs* Mort Greene, Harry Revel

George Murphy, Anne Shirley, Richard Barthelmess, William Gargan, Joan Merrill, Millard Mitchell, Mary Wickes, Freddie Martin and band

AAN: song 'There's a Breeze on Lake Louise'

The Mayor of Hell°
US 1933   90m   bw
Warner

A racketeer becomes superintendent of a reform school, and it changes his life. Moderate star vehicle with a plot that did yeoman service thereafter in Dead End Kids films.

w Edward Chodorov *d* Archie Mayo *ph* Barney McGill *m* Leo F. Forbstein

James Cagney, Madge Evans, Allen Jenkins, Dudley Digges, Frankie Darro

'Has the outline of a junior *Big House.* Offers exploitation easily.'—*Variety*

'Propaganda for nothing: like most of what comes out of Hollywood, it is entertaining trash.'—*Time*

† Remade in 1938 as *Crime School* with Humphrey Bogart, 1939 as *Hell's Kitchen* with Ronald Reagan.

Maytime°°
US 1937   132m   bw (sepia sequence)
MGM (Hunt Stromberg)

An opera star falls in love with a penniless singer but her jealous impresario shoots him. Lush romantic musical which turns gradually into melodrama and ends in a ghostly reunion for the lovers. If that's what you like, it could scarcely be better done.

w Noel Langley, *operetta* Rida Johnson Young *d* Robert Z. Leonard *ph* Oliver T. Marsh *m* Sigmund Romberg *md* Herbert Stothart

Jeanette MacDonald, Nelson Eddy, John Barrymore, Herman Bing, Lynne Carver, Rafaela Ottiano, Paul Porcasi, Sig Rumann

'Click operetta . . . cinch for the foreign market also.'—*Variety*

'Enjoyable for more than camp reasons . . . the atmosphere of thwarted passion is compelling.'—*Pauline Kael, 70s*

† Shooting had begun in colour with Frank Morgan in Bing's part and Paul Lukas in Barrymore's; this footage, directed by

Edmund Goulding, was abandoned on Irving Thalberg's death.

AAN: Herbert Stothart

Maytime in Mayfair

GB 1949   95m   Technicolor
British Lion / Imperadio (Herbert Wilcox)

A playboy inherits a dress salon and falls for the lady manager.
Witless comedy fit to set one's teeth on edge, with over-acting and poor musical numbers. Not in the same street as its predecessor *Spring in Park Lane*.

w Nicholas Phipps d Herbert Wilcox ph Max Greene md Robert Farnon

Anna Neagle, Michael Wilding, Nicholas Phipps, Peter Graves
  'Painstakingly refined.'—*MFB*

The Maze

US 1953   81m   bw   3-D
Allied Artists (Richard Heermance)

The heir to a title also inherits a family curse and turns into a giant frog.
Rather splendidly idiotic horror film which raises plenty of laughs but no frissons.

w Dan Ullman, *story* Maurice Sandoz d William Cameron Menzies ph Harry Neumann m Marlin Skiles

Richard Carlson, Veronica Hurst, Katherin Emery, Michael Pate, Lillian Bond, Hillary Brooke, Owen McGiveney

Me and Marlborough*

GB 1935   84m   bw
GFD / Gainsborough (Michael Balcon)

In Marlborough's army, a woman takes the place of her soldier husband to prove his innocence of spying.
Curious period service farce, not quite a success but an interesting attempt at something different.

w Ian Hay, Marjorie Gaffney, *story* W. P. Lipscomb, Reginald Pound d Victor Saville

Cicely Courtneidge, Tom Walls, Barry McKay, Alfred Drayton
  'In most cases the comedy is totally uncalled for and destroys the period atmosphere.'—*Variety*

Me and My Gal*

US 1932   79m   bw
Fox
GB title: *Pier 13*

A cop on the beat romances a hashslinger and catches a crook.
Pleasant little programmer, very evocative of its period.

w Arthur Kober d Raoul Walsh ph Arthur Miller

Spencer Tracy, Joan Bennett, George Walsh, Marion Burns, J. Farrell MacDonald, Noel Madison, Henry B. Walthall
  'Lacking in nearly everything that makes box office.'—*Variety*

† Remade in 1949 as *Pier 13*.

Me and My Pal*

US 1933   20m   bw

Ollie becomes engrossed in a jigsaw puzzle and forgets to get married. Oddball star comedy which nearly comes off but simply doesn't provide enough jokes. Laurel and Hardy, James Finlayson, Eddie Dunn. Written by Stan Laurel; directed by Charles Rogers and Lloyd French; for Hal Roach.

Me and the Colonel

US 1958   110m   bw
Columbia / Court–Goetz (William Goetz)

In 1940 an anti-semitic Polish colonel is obliged to flee from France in the company of a Jewish refugee.
Rather obvious war comedy with predictable but not very entertaining situations, sentiment, action and pathos. The stars cope well enough but the picture never picks up steam.

w S. N. Behrman, George Froeschel, *play* Franz Werfel d Peter Glenville ph Burnett Guffey m George Duning

Danny Kaye, Curt Jurgens, Nicole Maurey, Françoise Rosay, Akim Tamiroff, Martita Hunt, Alexander Scourby, Liliane Montevecchi, Ludwig Stossel

Me, Natalie*

US 1969   111m   De Luxe
Cinema Center (Stanley Shapiro)

An unattractive 18-year-old girl moves into Greenwich Village and learns to accept herself as she is.
Basically very predictable but rather well done character study with excellent detail.

w A. Martin Zweiback d Fred Coe ph Arthur J. Ornitz m Henry Mancini

Patty Duke, James Farentino, Martin Balsam, Elsa Lanchester, Salome Jens, Nancy Marchand, Al Pacino

Mean Streets**

US 1973   110m   Technicolor
Taplin–Perry–Scorsese (Jonathan T. Taplin)

Four young Italian-Americans use Tony's Bar as a base for drinking, brawling and hustling. Relentlessly sordid melodrama with a good eye for realistic detail.

w Martin Scorsese, Mardik Martin d Martin Scorsese ph Norman Gerard

Harvey Keitel, Robert de Niro, David Proval, Amy Robinson, Richard Romanus
  'Lacks a sense of story and structure . . . unless a film-maker respects the needs of his audience, he can't complain if that audience fails to show up.'—*Variety*
  'A thicker-textured rot than we have ever had in an American movie, and a deeper sense of evil.'—*New Yorker*
  'Extraordinarily rich and distinguished on many levels.'—*Joseph Gelmis*

The Meanest Man in the World

US 1943   57m   bw

An easy-going small-town lawyer finds that business picks up when he becomes tough and

mean. Very minor star comedy with a muddled opening followed by strictly rationed laughs. Jack Benny, Priscilla Lane, Rochester, Edmund Gwenn, Anne Revere. Written by George Seaton and Allan House, from a play by George M. Cohan; directed by Sidney Lanfield; for TCF.

The Mechanic

US 1972   100m   Technicolor
UA / Chartoff / Winkler / Carlino
reissue title: *Killer of Killers*

A professional assassin under contract to the Mafia makes his missions look like accidents. Violent thriller with a few pretensions, but too flashily made to be taken seriously.

w Lewis John Carlino d Michael Winner ph Richard Kline, Robert Paynter m Jerry Fielding

Charles Bronson, Jan-Michael Vincent, Keenan Wynn, Jill Ireland

A Medal for Benny*

US 1945   77m   bw
Paramount (Paul Jones)

An old rustic is the centre of small town celebrations in honour of his dead war hero son.
Satirical-sentimental location drama, effective but not memorable.

w Frank Butler, *original story* John Steinbeck, Jack Wagner d Irving Pichel ph Lionel Lindon m Victor Young

Dorothy Lamour, Arturo de Cordova, J. Carrol Naish, Mikhail Rasumny, Charles Dingle, Frank McHugh, Grant Mitchell

AAN: original story; J. Carrol Naish

Medal for the General

GB 1944   99m   bw

An old general takes in evacuees and finds a new interest in life. Uneventful character drama which seemed mildly pleasing at the time. Godfrey Tearle, Jeanne de Casalis, Morland Graham, Mabel Constanduros, John Laurie, Petula Clark. Written by Elizabeth Baron, from the novel by James Ronald; directed by Maurice Elvey; for British National.

Medea*

Italy / France / West Germany 1970
    118m   Eastmancolor
San Marco / Number One / Janus (Franco Rossellini, Marina Cicogna)

Jason brings back as his wife the high priestess of the Golden Fleece, but her adjustment is to say the least uncomfortable.
In modern terms the case history of a psychopath, this weird production plays like an opera without music, and seems to have been designed as a vehicle for its charismatic star.

wd Pier Paolo Pasolini, *play* Euripides ph Ennio Guarnieri

Maria Callas, Giuseppe Gentile, Laurent Terzieff, Massimo Girotti

The Medium*

Italy 1951   80m   bw
Transfilm (Walter Lowendahl)

A fake medium feels a genuine manifestation, shoots at it and kills her assistant, but is still not sure whether he was responsible.
A filmic but not entirely satisfactory treatment of a modest but popular modern opera.

wd, m Gian-Carlo Menotti, his opera
co-d Alexander Hammid   *ph* Enzo Serafin

Marie Powers, Anna Maria Alberghetti, Leo Coleman

AAN: Gian-Carlo Menotti (for music)

Medium Cool**

US 1969   111m   Technicolor
Paramount / H & J Pictures (Tully Friedman)

A TV news cameraman is made apathetic by the events around him.
Stimulating if overlong comment on the quality of life in the sixties, immaculately made and with a rather effective though obvious twist ending.

wd, ph Haskell Wexler   *m* Mike Bloomfield
ad Leon Ericksen

Robert Forster, Verna Bloom, Peter Bonerz, Marianna Hill, Sid McCoy

'A deeply moving questioning of America's violence and voyeurism.'—*Jan Dawson*
'I can't think of any film that tells one more about the texture of American life today.'—*Michael Billington, Illustrated London News*

'By the time he was eleven he had killed nine people!'

The Medusa Touch*

GB / France 1978   109m   Technicolor
ITC / Bulldog / Citeca (Arnon Milchan, Elliott Kastner)

A novelist is haunted by the belief that he can cause disaster.
And he does, very predictably, while any intellectual excitement in the script is rapidly replaced by mere mayhem.
Different, but not exciting.

w John Briley, *novel* Peter Van Greenway
d Jack Gold   *ph* Arthur Ibbetson   *m* Michael J. Lewis   *sp* Doug Ferris

Richard Burton, Lee Remick, Lino Ventura, Harry Andrews, Alan Badel, Jeremy Brett, Michael Hordern, Gordon Jackson

● *Video: Precision*

Meet Danny Wilson

US 1951   83m   bw
U-I (Leonard Goldstein)

An overbearing crooner gets to the top with the help of gangsters.
Fairly abrasive star vehicle, almost amounting to self-parody.

w Don McGuire   *d* Joseph Pevney   *ph* Maury Gertsman   *md* Joseph Gershenson

Frank Sinatra, Shelley Winters, Alex Nicol, Raymond Burr

Meet Dr Christian

US 1939   68m   bw

A dedicated small-town doctor has no concern for financial reward. Adequate pot-boiler based on a radio character, and following Hersholt's popularity as Dr Dafoe. Jean Hersholt, Dorothy Lovett, Robert Baldwin, Enid Bennett, Paul Harvey, Marcia Mae Jones. Written by Ian McLellan Hunter, Harvey Gates, Ring Lardner Jnr; directed by Bernard Vorhaus; for William Stephens / RKO. 'First of a series . . . profitable programme material for the family trade.'—*Variety*

Meet John Doe***

US 1941   123m   bw
Liberty Films (Frank Capra)

A tramp is hired to embody the common man in a phony political drive, and almost commits suicide.
Vividly staged but over-sentimental Capra extravaganza with high spots outnumbering low.

w Robert Riskin   *d* Frank Capra   *ph* George Barnes   *m* Dmitri Tiomkin

Gary Cooper, *Barbara Stanwyck*, Edward Arnold, Walter Brennan, James Gleason, Spring Byington, Gene Lockhart, Rod la Rocque, Irving Bacon, Regis Toomey, Ann Doran, Warren Hymer, Andrew Tombes

'For the sake of a happy ending that would keep Gary Cooper alive, the meanings were so distorted that the original authors sued.'—*New Yorker, 1978*
'Capra is as skilled as ever in keeping things moving along briskly and dramatically.'—*National Board of Review*
'The meanings were so distorted that the original authors sued . . . It starts out in the confident Capra manner, but with a darker tone; by the end, you feel puzzled and cheated.'—*Pauline Kael, 70s*

AAN: original story (Richard Connell, Robert Presnell)

Meet Me after the Show*

US 1951   88m   Technicolor
TCF (George Jessel)

A musical star thinks she has discovered an affair between her husband and his glamorous backer.
Surprisingly bright routine musical.

w Mary Loos, Richard Sale   *d* Richard Sale
ph Arthur E. Arling   *md* Lionel Newman
songs Jule Styne, Leo Robin

Betty Grable, Macdonald Carey, Rory Calhoun, Eddie Albert, Irene Ryan

Meet Me at Dawn

GB 1946   99m   bw
TCF / Marcel Hellman
US title: *The Gay Duellist*

A professional duellist is commissioned to provoke a duel with a senator, but unwittingly hires the senator's daughter to play the injured party.
A totally laborious and artificial period comedy which never seems even to aspire to the style required.

w Lesley Storm, James Seymour, Maurice Cowan, *story* Le Tueur by Anatole Litvak, Marcel Achard   *d* Thornton Freeland
ph Gunther Krampf   *m* Mischa Spoliansky

Hazel Court, William Eythe, Stanley Holloway, Margaret Rutherford, Basil Sydney, Irene Browne

Meet Me at the Fair

US 1952   87m   Technicolor
U-I (Albert J. Cohen)

In 1900, an orphan joins a travelling medicine show.
Mildly pleasing open-air comedy drama.

w Irving Wallace, *novel* The Great Companions by Gene Markey   *d* Douglas Sirk   *ph* Maury Gertsman   *md* Joseph Gershenson

Diana Lynn, Dan Dailey, Hugh O'Brian, Chet Allen, Rhys Williams

Meet Me in Las Vegas

US 1956   112m   Eastmancolor Cinemascope
MGM (Joe Pasternak)
GB title: *Viva Las Vegas!*

A gambler's luck changes when he grabs the hand of a passing ballerina.
Listless song-and dance extravaganza which wastes a great deal of talent.

w Isabel Lennart   *d* Roy Rowland   *ph* Robert Bronner   *m* Georgie Stoll, Johnny Green
ly Sammy Cahn   *ch* Eugène Loring, Hermes Pan

Dan Dailey, Cyd Charisse, Agnes Moorehead, Lili Darvas, Paul Henreid, Oscar Karlweis, Lena Horne, Jerry Colonna, Frankie Laine

'A large-scale musical of almost stupefying banality.'—*MFB*

AAN: Georgie Stoll, Johnny Green

Meet Me in St Louis***

US 1944   113m   Technicolor
MGM (Arthur Freed)

Scenes in the life of an affectionate family at the turn of the century.
Patchy but generally highly agreeable musical nostalgia with an effective sense of the passing years and seasons.

w Irving Brecher, Fred F. Finklehoffe, *novel* Sally Benson   *d* Vincente Minnelli   *ph* George Folsey   *md* Georgie Stoll

Judy Garland, Margaret O'Brien, Tom Drake, Leon Ames, Mary Astor, Lucille Bremer, June Lockhart, *Harry Davenport*, Marjorie Main, Joan Carroll, Hugh Marlowe, Robert Sully, Chill Wills

'A family group framed in velvet and tinsel . . . it has everything a romantic musical should have.'—*Dilys Powell, 1955*

AAN: script; George Folsey; Georgie Stoll; song 'The Trolley Song' (*m / ly* Ralph Blane, Hugh Martin)

● *Video: MGM / UA*

Meet Me Tonight

GB 1952   85m   Technicolor
Rank / Anthony Havelock Allan

Three short Noel Coward plays: *Red Peppers, Fumed Oak, Ways and Means*.
Regrettably bald treatment of three playlets which have not lasted well. A thoroughly artificial evening.

w / m Noel Coward *d* Anthony Pelissier
ph Desmond Dickinson

Ted Ray, Kay Walsh, Stanley Holloway, Betty Ann Davies, Nigel Patrick, Valerie Vobson

Meet Mr Callaghan

GB 1954   88m   bw

A private detective unmasks a rich man's killer. Routine thick ear on American lines; moderately popular at the time, it spawned no sequels. Derrick de Marney, Harriet Johns, Peter Neil, Adrienne Corri, Delphi Lawrence, Belinda Lee. Written by Brock Williams, from the play by Gerald Verner based on Peter Cheyney's novel *The Urgent Hangman*; directed by Charles Saunders; for Pinnacle.

Meet Mr Lucifer*

GB 1953   81m   bw
Ealing (Monja Danischewsky)

The Demon King in a tatty provincial pantomime dreams he is the devil preventing people from wasting time watching television. Clean and occasionally amusing piece of topical satire on tellymania; but the prologue is funnier than the sketches.

w Monja Danischewsky, *play* Beggar My Neighbour by Arnold Ridley *d* Anthony Pelissier *ph* Desmond Dickinson *m* Eric Rogers

Stanley Holloway, Peggy Cummins, Jack Watling, Barbara Murray, Joseph Tomelty, Gordon Jackson, Jean Cadell, Kay Kendall, Ian Carmichael, Gilbert Harding, Charles Victor, Humphrey Lestocq

Meet Mr Penny

GB 1938   70m   bw

A meek clerk leads a revolt against a speculator who wants to build on allotments. Early Ealing-style social comedy based on a radio character; of no abiding interest. Richard Goolden, Vic Oliver, Fabia Drake, Kay Walsh, Patrick Barr, Hermione Gingold, Wilfrid Hyde-White. Written by Victor Kendall and Doreen Montgomery, from the character created by Maurice Moisiewicz; directed by David MacDonald; for British National.

Meet Nero Wolfe*

US 1936   73m   bw
Columbia

A corpulent stay-at-home sleuth solves a disappearance and a murder.
The film debut of an engaging crime character, who oddly never made it to a series.

w Howard J. Green, Bruce Manning, Joseph Anthony, *novel* Fer de Lance by Rex Stout *d* Herbert Biberman *ph* Henry Freulich

Edward Arnold, Lionel Stander, Joan Perry, Rita Hayworth, Victor Jory, Nana Bryant, Walter Kingsford, John Qualen

Meet Simon Cherry

GB 1949   67m   bw

A clergyman on holiday proves that a rich recluse was not murdered. Elementary programme filler from a radio series. Hugh Moxey, Zena Marshall, John Bailey, Anthony Forwood, Ernest Butcher, Courtney Hope. Written by Gale Pedrick, A. R. Rawlinson and Godfrey Grayson, from Gale Pedrick's radio series *Meet the Rev*; directed by Godfrey Grayson; for Exclusive.

Meet the Baron

US 1933   79m   bw

A nincompoop is fêted as the real Baron Munchhausen. An incoherent script provides an opportunity for several comics to do their stuff. Jack Pearl, Jimmy Durante, Zasu Pitts, Ted Healy and his Stooges, Edna May Oliver, Henry Kolker. Written by Herman J. Mankiewicz, Norman Krasna, Allen Rivkin, P. J. Wolfson, Arthur Kober, William K. Wells; directed by Walter Lang; for MGM. 'Not so forte in the material division, but saved by its capable crew of comics.'—*Variety*

Meet the Mayor

US 1938   63m   bw

A veteran small-town elevator operator becomes involved in politics. Curious semi-comedy in which the star uses up most of his old vaudeville routines. Frank Fay, Ruth Hall, Hale Hamilton, George Meeker, Berton Churchill, Franklin Pangborn. Written by Walter DeLeon, Charles Belden, Frank Fay; directed by Ralph Ceder; for Frank Fay / Times. 'Flimsy meller for secondary duallers.'—*Variety*

Meet the Missus

US 1937   65m   bw

A worm turns when his wife constantly involves him in newspaper contests. Very slight farce for the rurals. Victor Moore, Helen Broderick, Anne Shirley, Alan Bruce, Willie Best. Written by Jack Townley, Bert Granet, Joel Sayre, from the story Lady Average by Jack Goodman and Albert Rice; directed by Joseph Santley; for Albert Lewis / RKO. 'Destined for the lower half of duals.'—*Variety*

Meet the People

US 1944   100m   bw
MGM (E. Y. Harburg)

A Broadway musical star proves she isn't snooty by taking a job in a shipyard.
Thin propaganda musical which wastes a fair amount of talent.

w S. M. Herzig, Fred Saidy, *play* Louis Lantz, Sol and Ben Barzman *d* Charles Reisner *ph* Robert Surtees *songs* various

Lucille Ball, Dick Powell, Virginia O'Brien, Bert Lahr, Rags Ragland, June Allyson, Steve Geray, Phil Regan, Spike Jones and his City Slickers, Vaughn Monroe and his Orchestra

Meet the Stewarts

US 1942   74m   bw

Newlyweds have trouble when he's poor and she's used to rich living. Modest marital comedy with young talent. William Holden, Frances Dee, Grant Mitchell. Written by Elizabeth Dunn and Karen de Wolf; directed by Alfred E. Green; for Columbia.

Mein Kampf*

Sweden 1961   118m   bw

A newsreel compilation tracing the rise and fall of Nazi Germany. A simple but highly effective and reliable selection of actualities leaves conclusions to the viewer, letting the events speak for themselves. A powerful documentary. Written, directed and edited by *Erwin Leiser*; for Töre Sjöberg / Minerva International. (Original title: *Den Blodiga Tiden*.)

Melba

GB 1953   113m   Technicolor
Horizon (Sam Spiegel)

The life of the internationally famous Australian opera singer of Victorian days. Moderately interesting recreation of a woman and an era, though dramatically rather stodgy.

w Harry Kurnitz *d* Lewis Milestone *ph* Ted Scaife *md* Muir Mathieson *ad* André Andreiev

Patrice Munsel, Robert Morley, Alec Clunes, Martita Hunt, Sybil Thorndike, John McCallum

Melody

GB 1971   106m   Eastmancolor
Hemdale / Sagittarius / Goodtimes (David Puttnam)
aka: *S.W.A.L.K.*

Calf love at school causes jealousy between two boys.
Tough-sentimental teenage comedy-drama of little interest to adults.

w Alan Parker *d* Waris Hussein *ph* Peter Suschitzky *m* Richard Hewson

Jack Wild, Mark Lester, Tracy Hyde

Melody Cruise

US 1933   74m   bw

A lady killer gets his come-uppance on board ship, but wins the girl he really wants. Very messy mixture of comedy, romance and music. Phil Harris, Charles Ruggles, Greta Nissen, Helen Mack, Chick Chandler. Written by Mark Sandrich, Ben Holmes; directed by Mark Sandrich; for Merian C. Cooper / RKO. 'Ought to be a moderate grosser . . . the meat just isn't there for the principals, and they seem to feel it in their work.'—*Variety*

Melody for Two
US 1937　60m　bw

A singing bandleader argues with his team and picks up with an all-girl crew. Simple-minded peg for a few songs; rather a yawn. James Melton, Patricia Ellis, Wini Shaw, Marie Wilson, Fred Keating, Dick Purcell. Written by George Bricker, Luci Ward, Joseph K. Watson; directed by Louis King; for Warners.
'Okay twin-bill fodder.'—*Variety*

Melody in Spring
US 1934　75m　bw

An ambitious radio singer follows the sponsor's daughter on a European holiday. Mild vehicle for a tenor who didn't sustain. Lanny Ross, Charles Ruggles, Mary Boland, Ann Sothern, George Meeker, Herman Bing. Written by Benn W. Levy; directed by Norman Z. McLeod; for Douglas MacLean / Paramount. 'Farfetched, somewhat boresome, and generally airy.'—*Variety*

The Melody Lingers On
US 1935　65m　bw

During World War I, an Italian soldier is killed after fathering an illegitimate baby, which grows up with no knowledge of mother, who watches from afar. Old-fashioned tearjerker with musical background. Josephine Hutchinson, George Houston, John Halliday, Mona Barrie, Helen Westley, Laura Hope Crews. Written by Ralph Spence, Philip Dunne, from the novel by Lowell Brentano; directed by David Burton; for Edward Small. 'Will probably wind up topping the duals.'—*Variety*

Melody Time*
US 1948　75m　Technicolor
Walt Disney (Ben Sharpsteen)

An unlinked variety show of cartoon segments.
A mainly mediocre selection with the usual moments of high style: *Once upon a Wintertime, Bumble Boogie, Johnny Appleseed, Little Toot, Trees, Blame it on the Samba, Pecos Bill.*

w various　d various
'There seems to be an obvious connection between the Disney artists' increasing insipidity and their increasing talent for fright, but I will leave it to accredited sado-masochists to make the discovery.'—*James Agee*

Melvin and Howard*
US 1980　95m　Technicolor
Universal (Terry Nelson)

The life of a factory worker is changed when a man he picks up in the Nevada desert claims to be Howard Hughes.
Eccentric comedy which has been compared to the work of Preston Sturges, but has an agreeable style of its own.

w *Bo Goldman* d *Jonathan Demme* ph Tak Fujimoto m Bruce Langhorne

Paul Le Mat, Jason Robards Jnr, Mary Steenburgen, Elizabeth Cheshire, Michael J. Pollard, Gloria Grahame
'An almost flawless act of sympathetic imagination . . . it's what might have happened if Jean Renoir had directed a comedy script by Preston Sturges.'—*New Yorker*
AA: Bo Goldman; Mary Steenburgen
AAN: Jason Robards Jnr (supporting actor)

The Member of the Wedding*
US 1953　91m　bw
Columbia / Stanley Kramer

A 12-year-old girl learns something about life when her sister gets married and a young boy dies.
Boringly contained in a kitchen set, this filmed play has interesting characters but is really not good enough for the talent involved.

w Edna and Edward Anhalt, *play* and *novel* Carson McCullers d Fred Zinnemann ph Hal Mohr m Alex North

Julie Harris, *Ethel Waters*, Brandon de Wilde, Arthur Franz, Nancy Gates, James Edwards
AAN: Julie Harris

Memed My Hawk
GB 1984　110m　colour

In 1923 Turkey, an inept tyrant chases one of his young villagers, who flees to the rebels. Weird but not wonderful mix of comedy and melodrama in an unfamiliar and unattractive setting. Peter Ustinov, Herbert Lom, Denis Quilley, Michael Elphick, Simon Dutton. Written and directed by Peter Ustinov, from the novel by Yashar Kemal; for Fuad Kavur / Peter Ustinov Productions.

Memoirs of a Survivor
GB 1981　115m　Technicolor
EMI / Memorial (Michael Medwin, Penny Clark)

In the future, a single woman finds that urban civilization has decayed, and after many horrors finds refuge in an old Victorian house. Unappetizing mixture of *1984* and *Alice in Wonderland*, too despairing and plotless to find many takers.

w Kerry Crabbe, David Gladwell, *novel* Doris Lessing d David Gladwell ph Walter Lassally m Mike Thorn pd Keith Wilson ed William Shapter

Julie Christie, Christopher Guard, Debbie Hutchings, Leonie Mellinger, Nigel Hawthorne, Pat Keen
'A film of wild ambition, sadly and hopelessly bungled.'—*Geoff Brown, MFB*
● Video: Thorn EMI

The Memphis Belle*
US / GB 1943　43m　Technicolor
The last mission over Germany of a Flying Fortress. Impressive on-the-spot documentary which provided a lot of library footage for later movies. Directed by William Wyler; for the War Activities Commission.

The Men***
US 1950　85m　bw
Stanley Kramer
reissue title: *Battle Stripe*

Paraplegic war veterans are prepared for civilian life; the fiancée of one of them helps overcome his problems.
Vivid semi-documentary melodrama, at the time rather shocking in its no-holds-barred treatment of sexual problems.

w *Carl Foreman* d *Fred Zinnemann* ph Robert de Grasse m Dmitri Tiomkin

Marlon Brando, Teresa Wright, Everett Sloane, Jack Webb, Howard St John
'A completely new experience between men and women!'—*publicity*
'Don't be misled into feeling that to see this film is merely a duty; it is, simply, an experience worth having.'—*Richard Mallett, Punch*
'I was afraid I was gonna die . . . now I'm afraid I'm gonna live!'—*more publicity*
AAN: Carl Foreman

Men Are Not Gods
GB 1936　92m　bw
London (Alexander Korda)

An actor playing Othello nearly strangles his wife.
Tepid melodramatic attempt at a theme later used in
A Double Life.

w G. B. Stern, Iris Wright d Walter Reisch ph Charles Rosher

Miriam Hopkins, Sebastian Shaw, Rex Harrison, Gertrude Lawrence, A. E. Matthews, Val Gielgud, Laura Smithson
'A nearer approximation to box office quality than some recent London productions.'—*Variety*

Men Are Such Fools
US 1938　69m　bw

The worm turns when his wife threatens to leave him for a singing career. Mediocre is the word for this threadbare drama. Wayne Morris, Humphrey Bogart, Priscilla Lane, Hugh Herbert, Penny Singleton. Written by Norman Reilly Raine and Horace Jackson; directed by Busby Berkeley; for Warner.

Men in Her Diary
US 1945　73m　bw

A jealous woman tries to hire an unattractive girl as her husband's secretary. Very mild lower-berth comedy. Peggy Ryan, Jon Hall, Louise Allbritton, William Terry, Virginia Grey, Ernest Truex, Alan Mowbray, Eric Blore, Sig Rumann. Written by F. Hugh Herbert and Elwood Ullman, from a story by Kerry Shaw; directed by Charles Barton; for Universal.

The Men in Her Life
US 1941　90m　bw
Columbia (Gregory Ratoff)

A former circus rider becomes a ballerina.

MEN ARE NOT GODS.   Miriam Hopkins is swept off her feet.

Well-worn rags-to-riches romance of little interest.

w Frederick Kohner, Michael Wilson, Paul Trivers, *novel* Ballerina by Lady Eleanor Smith *d* Gregory Ratoff *ph* Harry Stradling, Arthur Miller *md* David Raksin

Loretta Young, Conrad Veidt, Dean Jagger, Eugenie Leontovich, Shepperd Strudwick, Otto Kruger, Paul Baratoff

Men in War
US 1957   104m   bw
Security (Sidney Harmon)

Korea 1950: an infantry platoon is cut off from HQ and tries to take an enemy-occupied hill. Stereotyped small-scale war heroics; the film makes its points but fails to entertain.

w Philip Yordan *d* Anthony Mann *ph* Ernest Haller *m* Elmer Bernstein

Robert Ryan, Robert Keith, Aldo Ray, Vic Morrow, James Edwardes, Sen Yung

Men in White*
US 1934   80m   bw
MGM (Monta Bell)

An ambitious intern is in love with an attractive socialite who resents his devotion to duty.
Popular but obvious star drama.

w Waldemar Young, *play* Sidney Kingsley *d* Richard Boleslawski *ph* George Folsey

Clark Gable, Myrna Loy, Jean Hersholt, Elizabeth Allan, Otto Kruger, C. Henry Gordon, Wallace Ford

'Belongs in the strictly adult class of pictures . . . show spells money from plenty of angles.'—*Variety*

Men Must Fight
US 1933   73m   bw

War comes to New York in 1940. A forgotten pacifist tract which trod the same paths as did H. G. Wells; of historical interest only apart from a spectacular air raid climax. Robert Young, Diana Wynyard, May Robson, Phillips Holmes, Lewis Stone. Written by S. K. Lauren, Reginald Lawrence and C. Gardner Sullivan; directed by Edgar Selwyn; for MGM.

Men of Boys' Town
US 1941 106m bw
MGM (John W. Considine Jnr)

Further adventures of Father Flanagan.
Mushy sequel to *Boys' Town* (qv).

w James Kevin McGuinness d Norman
Taurog ph Harold Rosson m Herbert
Stothart

Spencer Tracy, Mickey Rooney, Bobs
Watson, Larry Nunn, Lee J. Cobb, Mary
Nash, Henry O'Neill, Darryl Hickman, Anne
Revere

Men of Texas
US 1942 71m bw

After the Civil War, a Yankee reporter is sent
to investigate rumours of a further uprising.
Routine western, not unentertaining in its
modest way. Robert Stack, Anne Gwynne,
Broderick Crawford, Jackie Cooper, Ralph
Bellamy, Jane Darwell, Leo Carrillo, John
Litel. Written by Harold Shumate; directed by
Ray Enright; for Universal.

Men of the Fighting Lady
US 1954 80m Anscocolor
MGM (Henry Berman)

Adventures of an aircraft carrier during the
Korean War.
Tepid war actioner with a few effective semi-
documentary sequences of naval tactics.

w Art Cohn d Andrew Marton ph George
Folsey m Miklos Rozsa

Van Johnson, Walter Pidgeon, Louis Calhern,
Dewey Martin, Keenan Wynn, Frank
Lovejoy, Robert Horton

Men of Tomorrow
GB 1932 88m bw
Paramount (Alexander Korda)

Oxford students have more than academic
work on their minds.
Dim comedy-drama with an interesting cast.

w Arthur Wimperis, Anthony Gibbs, *play*
Young Apollo by Anthony Gibbs d Leontine
Sagan ph Bernard Browne

Maurice Braddell, Joan Gardner, Emlyn
Williams, Merle Oberon, Robert Donat

Men of Two Worlds
GB 1946 109m Technicolor
GFD / Two Cities (John Sutro)
US title: *Witch Doctor*
aka: *Kisenga, Man of Africa*

In Tanganyika, an educated native helps white
men to counter the force of witch doctors and
persuade tribes to leave an infected area.
Earnest but totally unpersuasive semi-
documentary shot in unconvincing sets and
garish colour.

w Thorold Dickinson, Joyce Cary, E. Arnot
Robertson, Herbert Victor d Thorold
Dickinson ph Geoffrey Unsworth, Desmond
Dickinson m Arthur Bliss

Eric Portman, Phyllis Calvert, Robert Adams,
Orlando Martins, Arnold Marle, Cathleen
Nesbitt, David Horne, Cyril Raymond

Men o' War*
US 1929 20m bw

Two sailors and two girls have adventures in a
park. Simple-minded early talkie star comedy
featuring their famous soda fountain routine.
Laurel and Hardy, James Finlayson. Written
by H. M. Walker; directed by Lewis R.
Foster; for Hal Roach.

Men of Yesterday
GB 1936 82m bw

Old army rivalries die down at a reunion.
Dated but interesting drama with interpolated
variety talent. Stewart Rome, Sam Livesey,
Hay Petrie, Cecil Parker, with George Robey,
Ella Shields, Will Fyffe, Dick Henderson.
Written by Gerald Elliott and Jack Francis;
directed by John Baxter; for UK Films.

Men with Wings
US 1938 106m Technicolor
Paramount (William Wellman)

Civil aviation pioneers fall out over a girl.
Disappointing epic from the maker of *Wings*,
with highly predictable story line, modest
acting and ho-hum spectacle.

w Robert Carson d William Wellman ph W.
Howard Greene m W. Franke Harling,
Gerald Carbonara

Fred MacMurray, Ray Milland, Louise
Campbell, Andy Devine, Lynne Overman,
Porter Hall, Walter Abel, Virginia Weidler,
Donald O'Connor

'To all women who love and admire the
fearless heroes of the air, and who, with brave
hearts, encourage them, hope, and pray for
them.'—*director's dedication*
'Lavish air spectacle in Technicolor that
means big business . . . it will triumph through
rain, sleet or snow.'—*Variety*

'Give the rats a taste of their own
medicine!'
Men without Names
US 1935 67m bw

Bank robbers are cornered in a small town and
picked off by the FBI. Routine crime feature,
less exciting than it sounds. Fred MacMurray,
Madge Evans, Lynne Overman, David Holt,
John Wray, Dean Jagger. Written by
Marguerite Roberts, Kubec Glasmon, Dale
Van Every; directed by Ralph Murphy; for
Paramount. 'Another of the new gangster
films, and too flimsy. Grooved for the pops.'—
Variety

Men without Women
US 1930 77m bw
Fox

Men in a submarine are trapped on the ocean
bed.
Early talkie action drama noted more for its
credits than its accomplishment.

w Dudley Nichols d John Ford ph Joseph H.
August

Kenneth MacKenna, Frank Albertson, Paul
Page, Pat Somerset, Stuart Erwin, Warren
Hymer, John Wayne
'Stunning, realistic picture that will make
talk.'—*Variety*

The Menace
US 1932 64m bw

A convict escapes, gets a new face through
plastic surgery, and plans his revenge.
Muddled melodrama from a story by Edgar
Wallace. Walter Byron, H. B. Warner, Bette
Davis, Natalie Moorehead, William Davidson,
Halliwell Hobbes. Written by Dorothy
Howell, Charles Logue, Roy Chanslor;
directed by Roy William Neill; for Columbia.
'A halting and frequently clumsy development
leads to a weak climax.'—*Variety*

Menace
US 1934 58m bw

Murders follow the suicide of a mining
engineer. Compact little dark house thriller
with good stagey performances. Gertrude
Michael, Paul Cavanagh, Henrietta Crosman,
John Lodge, Ray Milland, Berton Churchill,
Halliwell Hobbes. Written by Chandler
Sprague and Anthony Veiller, from a story by
Philip MacDonald; directed by Ralph Murphy;
for Paramount. 'A pat specimen of the
mystery film, expertly manipulated.'—*Variety*

Menilmontant*
France 1924 50m (24 fps) bw silent

Respected but fairly impenetrable piece of
avant-garde which appears to be about two
sisters haunted by memories of the murder of
their parents, for which they may or may not
have been responsible. Written, directed,
edited and produced by *Dimitri Kirsanov*; for
his own company. 'A flurry of hand-held
camera shots, incisive montages and elliptical
progressions.'—*Geoff Brown, MFB, 1981.*

Mephisto**
Hungary 1981 144m Eastmancolor
Mafilm / Manfred Durniok

In Germany in the twenties, an actor
committed to the idea of a workers' theatre
becomes a puppet of the Nazis.
Heavy-going but stylishly made political
melodrama.

w Peter Dobai, Istvan Szabo, *novel* Klaus
Mann d Istvan Szabo ph Lajos Koltai
m Zdenko Tamassy

Klaus Maria Brandauer, Ildiko Bansagi,
Krystyna Janda

AA: best foreign film
● *Video: Palace*

The Mephisto Waltz*
US 1971 109m De Luxe
TCF / QM Productions

A satanic concert pianist on the point of death
wills his soul into the body of a journalist.
Complex diabolical mumbo-jumbo with plenty
of style.

w Ben Maddow, *novel* Fred Mustard Stewart
d Paul Wendkos ph William W. Spencer
m Jerry Goldsmith

Alan Alda, Jacqueline Bisset, Curt Jurgens,
Barbara Parkins

The Mercenaries
GB 1968 100m Metrocolor Panavision
MGM / George Englund
US title: *Dark of the Sun*

In the Belgian Congo in 1960 a mercenary officer is ordered to bring back a fortune in diamonds by armoured train.
Basically an old-fashioned thriller about the hazards of a journey beset by brutish villains and damsels in distress, this unpleasant film is notable for the amount of sadistic action it crams into its running time.

w Quentin Werty, Adrian Spies, *novel* Dark of the Sun by Wilbur Smith *d* Jack Cardiff *ph* Edward Scaife *m* Jacques Loussier

Rod Taylor, Yvette Mimieux, Kenneth More, Jim Brown, Peter Carsten, André Morell, Guy Deghy, Calvin Lockhart, Alan Gifford
'The violence done to the human body is matched by violence done to the intelligence by a stock adventure story given a gloss of topicality and social insult.'—*Judith Crist*

Merely Mary Ann
US 1931 74m bw

The maid of all work falls for the gentleman lodger. Cinderella stuff redesigned for two popular stars, but of no lasting appeal. Janet Gaynor, Charles Farrell, Beryl Mercer, J. M. Kerrigan, G. P. Huntley Jnr. Written by Jules Furthman from the story by Israel Zangwill; directed by Henry King; for Fox. 'Bound to pull after a summer of gang violence, mystery shockers, and much sex urge study.'—*Variety*

Merrill's Marauders
US 1962 98m Technicolor
Cinemascope
Warner / US Pictures (Milton Sperling)

Adventures of a crack US army unit in 1942 Burma.
Physically exhausting war adventure with emphasis on hand-to-hand fighting and much bloodshed.

w Samuel Fuller, Milton Sperling *d* Samuel Fuller *ph* William Clothier *m* Howard Jackson

Jeff Chandler, Ty Hardin, Andrew Duggan, Peter Brown, Will Hutchins, Claude Akins

Merrily We Go to Hell
US 1932 78m bw
Paramount

A socialite marries a dipsomaniac journalist.
Glum problem drama.

w Edwin Justin Mayer, *novel* I Jerry Take Thee Joan by Cleo Lucas *d* Dorothy Arzner *ph* David Abel

Sylvia Sidney, Fredric March, Adrienne Allen, Richard Gallagher, Florence Burton, Esther Howard, Kent Taylor

Merrily We Live*
US 1938 90m bw
Hal Roach

A zany family hires a chauffeur who is actually a famous writer posing as a tramp.

Quite likeable compound of *My Man Godfrey* and *You Can't Take It with You.*

w Eddie Moran, Jack Jevne *d* Norman Z. McLeod *ph* Norbert Brodine *md* Marvin Hatley

Constance Bennett, Brian Aherne, Billie Burke, Alan Mowbray, Patsy Kelly, Ann Dvorak, Tom Brown, Bonita Granville, Marjorie Rambeau, Clarence Kolb
'In the high cost bracket and rates top billing when dualled, with a chance it is strong enough to carry first runs as a single.'—*Variety*

AAN: Norbert Brodine; Billie Burke; title song (*m* Phil Craig, *ly* Arthur Quenzer)

Merry Andrew
US 1958 103m Metrocolor
Cinemascope
MGM / Sol C. Siegel

A stuffy teacher in search of an ancient statue joins a travelling circus.
Deliberately charming star comedy which plumps too firmly for whimsy and, despite its professionalism, provokes barely a smile, let alone a laugh.

w Isabel Lennart, I. A. L. Diamond, *story* Paul Gallico *d / ch* Michael Kidd *ph* Robert Surtees *m* Saul Chaplin *ly* Johnny Mercer

Danny Kaye, Pier Angeli, Baccaloni, Noel Purcell, Robert Coote, Patricia Cutts, Rex Evans, Walter Kingsford, Tommy Rall, Rhys Williams

Merry Christmas, Mr Lawrence*
GB 1982 124m Eastmancolor

In a Japanese prisoner-of-war camp in Java in 1942, an English captive strikes up a strange relationship with the commandant.
Uncomfortably titled and unavoidably downbeat character drama with some unpleasant moments; despite good work all round it seems to head straight for every cliché perpetuated by *The Bridge on the River Kwai.*

w Nagisa Oshima with Paul Mayersberg, *novel* The Seed and the Sower by Laurens van der Post *d* Nagisa Oshima *ph* Toichiro Narushima *m* Ryuichi Sakamoto
'It always seems like a cocktail of saleable ingredients rather than genuine cinema.'—*Sunday Times*

Merry Comes to Town
GB 1937 79m bw

A professor's family is disappointed when a relative visiting from America turns out to be as poor as they are. Thin, predictable comedy with the visitor finally hailed as a saviour. Zasu Pitts, Guy Newall, Betty Ann Davies, Muriel George, Basil Langton. Written by Evadne Price; directed by George King; for Embassy / Sound City. 'A pleasant comedy which will improve with cutting.'—*Variety*

The Merry Frinks
US 1934 68m bw

A sportswriter down on his luck has a crazy family. And didn't everybody in the mid-thirties? But this one is crazy without being

very funny. Aline MacMahon, Guy Kibbee, Allen Jenkins, Hugh Herbert, Frankie Darro. Written by Gene Markey, Kathryn Scola; directed by Alfred E. Green; for First National. (GB title: *Happy Family.*) 'The most disagreeable family group since *Three-Cornered Moon*. Poor comedy and lacks names.'—*Variety*

Merry Go Round of 1938
US 1937 87m bw

Four vaudevillians adopt a small girl, and later head for Hollywood. Sentimental farce with zany moments and an encouraging cast. Jimmy Savo, Bert Lahr, Mischa Auer, Billy House, Alice Brady, Louise Fazenda. Written by Monte Brice and A. Dorian Atvos; directed by Irving Cummings; for Universal. 'First rate filmusical packed with laughs.'—*Variety*

The Merry Monahans
US 1944 90m bw
Universal (Michael Fessier, Ernest Pagano)

Adventures of a family of vaudeville performers.
Acceptable backstage comedy drama with good atmosphere.

w Michael Fessier, Ernest Pagano *d* Charles Lamont *ph* Charles Van Enger *m* Hans Salter

Donald O'Connor, Jack Oakie, Rosemary de Camp, Peggy Ryan, Ann Blyth, Isabel Jewell, John Miljan

AAN: Hans Salter

The Merry Widow*
US 1925 111m (24 fps) bw silent
MGM (Irving Thalberg)

A bankrupt king orders a nobleman to woo a wealthy American widow.
An operetta without music (or dialogue) is usually a poor thing, but the director added a few unpredictable touches.

w Erich Von Stroheim, Benjamin Glazer, *operetta* Victor Leon, Leo Stein *d* Erich Von Stroheim *ph* Oliver Marsh, Ben Reynolds, William Daniels *m* William Axt, D. Mendoza

Mae Murray, John Gilbert, Roy D'Arcy, Tully Marshall
† The story goes that when reproved by Thalberg for wasting film stock on, for instance, endless shots of a wardrobe full of shoes, Von Stroheim remarked: 'The character has a foot fetish.' 'And you,' said Thalberg, 'have a footage fetish!'

'Surrender to the happy seduction of Ernst Lubitsch's most glorious picture holiday!'
The Merry Widow**
US 1934 99m bw
MGM

Patchy, but sometimes sparkling version.

w Samson Raphaelson, Ernest Vajda *d* Ernst Lubitsch *ph* Oliver T. Marsh *m* Franz Lehar

Maurice Chevalier, Jeanette MacDonald,
Edward Everett Horton, Una Merkel, George
Barbier, Donald Meek, Sterling Holloway,
Shirley Ross
  'Fine all-around job and an entertainment
natural.'—*Variety*
  'It is Lubitsch; it is also Hollywood; it is the
cream of the American bourgeois film. It is a
charlotte russe.'—*Peter Ellis, New Masses*

The Merry Widow
US 1952 105m Technicolor
MGM (Joe Pasternak)

Chill, empty remake.

w Sonya Levien, William Ludwig *d* Curtis
Bernhardt *ph* Robert Surtees

Fernando Lamas, Lana Turner, Richard
Haydn, Una Merkel, Thomas Gomez, John
Abbott
  'Nothing has been omitted (except the spirit
of the original).'—*MFB*

The Merry Wives of Reno*
US 1934 61m bw

Three couples go to a Reno hotel to get a
divorce. Amusing but scrappy comedy in the
vein of the successful *Convention City*.
Margaret Lindsay, Donald Woods, Guy
Kibbee, Glenda Farrell, Ruth Donnelly, Hugh
Herbert, Frank McHugh, Roscoe Ates,
Hobart Cavanaugh. Written by Robert Lord;
directed by H. Bruce Humberstone; for
Warners. 'Stylized farce with excellent cast
and considerable humour.'—*Variety*

Merton of the Movies*
US 1947 82m bw
MGM

An innocent young man in Hollywood
becomes a star.
The plot and characterizations of this old
chestnut are resistible, but the Hollywood
background is well managed and convincing.

w George Wells, Lou Breslow, *novel* Henry
Leon Wilson *d* Robert Alton *ph* Paul C.
Vogel *m* David Snell

Red Skelton, Virginia O'Brien, Alan
Mowbray

A Message to Garcia*
US 1936 86m bw
TCF (Raymond Griffith)

During the Spanish–American war a Cuban
girl helps an American agent get through to
the rebel leader with a diplomatic message.
Agreeable embroidery of a historical incident:
good production values and entertaining star
performances.

w W. P. Lipscomb, Gene Fowler, *book*
Andrew S. Rohan *d* George Marshall
ph Rudolph Maté *m* Louis Silvers

Wallace Beery, Barbara Stanwyck, John
Boles, Alan Hale, Herbert Mundin, Mona
Barrie

Meteor
US 1979 107m Movielab Panavision
Palladium (Sandy Howard, Gabriel Katzka)

A huge meteor, preceded by dangerous
fragments, heads relentlessly towards
Earth . . .
Talkative disaster movie with occasional
moments of interest.

w Stanley Mann, Edmund H. North *d* Ronald
Neame *ph* Paul Lohmann *m* Laurence
Rosenthal *visual effects* Margo Anderson,
William Cruse

Sean Connery, Natalie Wood, Karl Malden,
Brian Keith, Martin Landau, Trevor Howard,
Henry Fonda, Joseph Campanella

Metropolis***
Germany 1926 120m approx (24 fps)
  bw silent
UFA (Erich Pommer)

In the year 2000, the workers in a modernistic
city live underground and unrest is quelled by
the persuasion of a saintly girl, Maria; but a
mad inventor creates an evil Maria to incite
them to revolt.
Always somewhat overlong, and certainly
heavy-going in places, this futuristic fantasy
not only has many brilliant sequences which
created genuine excitement and terror, but it
inspired a great many Hollywood clichés to
come, notably the Frankenstein theme. The
BBC's version of the seventies, with an
electronic music sound track, is the most
satisfactory.

w Thea Von Harbou *d* Fritz Lang *ph* Karl
Freund, Günther Rittau *sp* Eugen Schufftan
ad Otto Hunte, Erich Kettelhut, Karl
Vollbrecht

Brigitte Helm, Alfred Abel, Gustav Fröhlich,
Rudolf Klein-Rogge, Fritz Rasp
  'It goes too far and always gets away with
it.'—*New Yorker, 1978*
  'A wonderful, stupefying folly.'—*New
Yorker, 1982*
† In 1984 Giorgio Moroder put out his own
new version, with tinted sequences and a
re-edited running time of 83 minutes. It was
received with a mixture of distaste, respect
and caution.

● *Video: Thorn EMI*

Metropolitan*
US 1935 79m bw
TCF (Darryl F. Zanuck)

A capricious prima donna walks out of the
Metropolitan Opera and forms her own
company.
Earnest and well-made melodrama with song;
it earned critical plaudits but was a
disappointment at the box office.

w Bess Meredyth, George Marion Jnr
d Richard Boleslawski *ph* Rudolph Maté
md Alfred Newman

Lawrence Tibbett, Alice Brady, Virginia
Bruce, Cesar Romero, Thurston Hall, Luis
Alberni
  'Tibbett and exploitation should carry so-so
operatic story into fair money.'—*Variety*

Meurtres*
France 1950 91m bw

A doctor's wife suffering from an incurable
illness begs him to give her an overdose of
morphia; he does so and proposes to give
himself up for murder; his family, afraid of
scandal, try to have him certified. A distinct
change of pace for a star comedian, and not an
unsuccessful one, though the satire is rather
crudely handled. *Fernandel*, Raymond
Souplex, Jacques Varennes, Jeanne Moreau.
Written by Charles Plisnier and Maurice
Barry; directed by Richard Pottier; for Cité
Film / Fides.

Mexican Hayride
US 1948 77m bw
Universal (Robert Arthur)

Various swindlers come together at a Mexican
bullfight.
A Cole Porter Broadway musical without the
music makes an odd sort of vehicle for Abbott
and Costello, but they inject a few good
vaudeville gags.

w Oscar Brodney, John Grant, *play* Herbert
and Dorothy Fields *d* Charles Barton
ph Charles Van Enger

Bud Abbott, Lou Costello, Virginia Grey,
John Hubbard, Pedro de Cordoba, Fritz Feld,
Luba Malina

Mexican Manhunt
US 1953 73m bw

A detective helps solve an old crime. Routine
support which coasts along on the strength of
its star. George Brent, Hillary Brooke, Morris
Ankrum, Karen Sharpe, Marjorie Lord.
Written by George Bricker; directed by Rex
Bailey; for Lindsley Parsons / AA.

Mexican Spitfire

A series of second feature comedies nominally
about a young businessman and his
temperamental Mexican wife (Donald Woods
and Lupe Velez), whose interest shifted firmly
to the young man's accident-prone uncle Matt
and his aristocratic boss Lord Epping, both of
whom were played by the rubber-legged
Ziegfeld comic Leon Errol at something near
the top of his form. The plots made little
sense, but the hectic situations provoked
hearty roars of laughter. The films were all
made by RKO, and all directed by Leslie
Goodwins.

1939: THE GIRL FROM MEXICO,
MEXICAN SPITFIRE
1940: MEXICAN SPITFIRE OUT WEST
1941: MEXICAN SPITFIRE'S BABY,
MEXICAN SPITFIRE AT SEA
1942: MEXICAN SPITFIRE SEES A
GHOST, MEXICAN SPITFIRE'S
ELEPHANT
1943: MEXICAN SPITFIRE'S BLESSED
EVENT

Miami Exposé
US 1956 74m bw

An undercover policeman cracks down on a
vice operation. Routine thick ear with more

suspense than sense. Lee J. Cobb, Patricia Medina, Edward Arnold. Written by James B. Gordon; directed by Fred F. Sears; for Sam Katzman / Columbia.

The Miami Story
US 1954 75m bw

The syndicate is cracked by a reformed gangster. Routine gangster alarms and excursions, like an extended Crime Does Not Pay. Barry Sullivan, Luther Adler, John Baer, Adele Jergens, Beverly Garland. Written by Robert E. Kent; directed by Fred F. Sears; for Sam Katzman / Columbia.

Michael and Mary
GB 1931 85m bw

A husband thought dead for many years returns to disturb his wife's second marriage. Acceptable comedy from a popular stage play; it headed its stars towards Hollywood. Herbert Marshall, Edna Best, Elizabeth Allan, Frank Lawton, D. A. Clarke-Smith. Written by Angus MacPhail, Robert Stevenson and Lajos Biro, from the play by A. A. Milne; directed by Victor Saville; for Gaumont.

Michael Shayne
The private eye created by Brett Halliday was featured in several second features starring Lloyd Nolan, mostly directed by Eugene Forde for Fox. They were adequate time-passers without too much sparkle.
1940: MICHAEL SHAYNE PRIVATE DETECTIVE
1941: DRESSED TO KILL, JUST OFF BROADWAY, THE MAN WHO WOULDN'T DIE
1942: TIME TO KILL (a version of Chandler's FAREWELL MY LOVELY), BLUE WHITE AND PERFECT

The Michigan Kid
US 1947 70m Cinecolor

Several people hunt for treasure stolen from a stagecoach. Lower berth western. Jon Hall, Victor McLaglen, Rita Johnson, Andy Devine, Byron Foulger, Milburn Stone. Written by Roy Chanslor, from a novel by Rex Beach; directed by Ray Taylor; for Universal.

Mickey One*
US 1965 93m bw
Columbia / Florin / Tatira (Arthur Penn, Harrison Starr)

A nightclub entertainer runs away after an orgy to find some meaning in his life. Obscure symbolic melodrama whose flashes of talent and interest needed firmer control.

w Alan Surgal d Arthur Penn ph Ghislain Cloquet m Eddie Sauter pd George Jenkins

Warren Beatty, Hurd Hatfield, Alexandra Stewart, Franchot Tone, Teddy Hart, Jeff Corey

'Arresting at first, it becomes more and more bogged down by its own pretensions, until one's main interest is simply in seeing it through.'—MFB

Mickey's Christmas Carol***
US 1983 26m Technicolor

A cartoon version of Dickens with the parts played by familiar Disney characters; and a supreme re-establishment of the old Disney production values. Produced and directed by Burney Mattinson; for Disney. 'For anyone over 35, this little jewel of a film is truly the Ghost of Christmas Past.'—Gilbert Adair, MFB

Micki and Maude*
US 1984 118m Metrocolor Panavision
Columbia / Delphi III / B.E.E. (Tony Adams)

A TV show host accidentally gets his wife and his mistress pregnant at the same time. Wild and overlong farce with some undeniably funnier scenes than have been noted in the participants' work for some years.

w Jonathan Reynolds d Blake Edwards ph Harry Stradling m Lee Holdridge pd Roger Maus ed Ralph E. Winters

Dudley Moore, Amy Irving, Ann Reinking, Richard Mulligan, George Gaynes, Wallace Shawn, John Pleshette

Midas Run
US 1969 104m Technicolor
Raymond Stross / MPI (Leon Chooluck)
GB title: A Run on Gold

An ageing secret service chief plans to hi-jack a bullion shipment. Incompetently handled caper story with interest unwisely shifted for romantic purposes to the plotter's recruits.

w James D. Buchanan, Ronald Austin, Berne Giler d Alf Kjellin ph Ken Higgins m Elmer Bernstein

Fred Astaire, Richard Crenna, Anne Heywood, Ralph Richardson, Roddy McDowall, Adolfo Celi, Maurice Denham, Cesar Romero

Middle Age Crazy
Canada 1980 91m De Luxe

A 40-year-old husband begins to feel his age. Mildly satirical sex comedy, all too easily forgotten among the rest. Bruce Dern, Ann-Margret, Graham Jarvis, Eric Christmas. Written by Carl Kleinschmitt; directed by John Trent; for Sid and Marty Krofft / Tormont.

Middle of the Night**
US 1959 118m bw
Columbia (George Justin)

An elderly garment manufacturer falls in love with a young girl. Serious and moving examination of a human predicament, shot against beautifully observed New York backgrounds.

w Paddy Chayevsky, from his TV play d Delbert Mann ph Joseph Brun m George Bassman

Fredric March, Kim Novak, Glenda Farrell, Jan Norris, Lee Grant

'A work of greater cogency than his New York play script and of deeper maturity than his Marty.'—Time

'The best of the TV transformations into film.'—Stanley Kauffmann

The Middle Watch
GB 1930 112m bw

Female guests on board ship have to be hidden from the captain. Naval froth in primitive talkie form; absurdly long but popular. Owen Nares, Jacqueline Logan, Jack Raine, Dodo Watts, Reginald Purdell. Written by Norman Walker and Frank Launder, from the play by Ian Hay and Stephen King-Hall; directed by Norman Walker; for BIP. (NB: In 1940 ABPC made a smoother version with Jack Buchanan, Greta Gynt, David Hutcheson, Kay Walsh, Fred Emney and Reginald Purdell [in the same role]; directed by Thomas Bentley.)

Midnight
US 1934 80m bw
Universal / All Star (Chester Erskine)
aka: Call It Murder

A jury foreman in a murder trial tips the scales in favour of guilty, but is haunted when his own daughter kills her lover. Tepid family melodrama, very stagebound.

wd Chester Erskine, play Paul and Claire Sifton ph William Steiner

Sidney Fox, O. P. Heggie, Henry Hull, Humphrey Bogart, Margaret Wycherly, Lynne Overman, Richard Whorf, Cora Witherspoon

'It's pretty strong stuff and will hold audiences once they're in . . . but it's not a good adaptation and is badly dialogued.'—Variety

Midnight***
US 1939 95m bw
Paramount (Arthur Hornblow Jnr)

A girl stranded in Paris is hired by an aristocrat to seduce the gigolo paying unwelcome attention to his wife. Sparkling sophisticated comedy which barely flags until a slightly disappointing ending; all the talents involved are in excellent form.

w Billy Wilder, Charles Brackett, story Edwin Justus Mayer, Franz Schultz d Mitchell Leisen ph Charles Lang m Frederick Hollander

Claudette Colbert, Don Ameche, John Barrymore, Francis Lederer, Mary Astor, Elaine Barrie, Hedda Hopper, Rex O'Malley

'Leisen's masterpiece, one of the best comedies of the thirties.'—John Baxter, 1968

'One of the authentic delights of the thirties.'—New Yorker, 1976

'It has the elements of an American La Règle du Jeu.'—John Gillett

'Just about the best light comedy ever caught by the camera.'—Motion Picture Daily

Midnight Club
US 1933 65m bw

An American detective in London nabs a jewel gang. Very tolerable smart-set crime melodrama. Clive Brook, George Raft, Helen Vinson, Alison Skipworth, Sir Guy Standing, Alan Mowbray. Written by Seton I. Miller and Leslie Charteris, from a story by E. Phillips Oppenheim; directed by Alexander Hall; for

Paramount. 'Its London manners and locale lend it a polish which should renew interest in this school of celluloid melodramatics.'—*Variety*

'To tell you the truth, I ain't a real cowboy. But I'm one helluva stud!'

Midnight Cowboy***
US 1969 113m De Luxe
UA / Jerome Hellman

A slightly dim-witted Texan comes to New York to offer his services as a stud for rich ladies, but spends a hard winter helping a tubercular con man.

Life in the New York gutter, brilliantly if not too accurately observed by a master showman with no heart.

w Waldo Salt, *novel* James Leo Herlihy
d John Schlesinger ph Adam Holender
md John Barry pd John Robert Lloyd

Jon Voight, Dustin Hoffman, Brenda Vaccaro, Sylvia Miles, John McGiver

'If only Schlesinger's directorial self-discipline had matched his luminous sense of scene and his extraordinary skill in handling actors, this would have been a far more considerable film.'—*Arthur Schlesinger Jnr (no relation)*

'A great deal besides cleverness, a great deal of good feeling and perception and purposeful dexterity.'—*Stanley Kauffmann*

AA: best picture; Waldo Salt; John Schlesinger
AAN: Dustin Hoffman; Jon Voight; Sylvia Miles

Midnight Episode
GB 1950 78m bw
Columbia / Triangle (Thomas Lageard)

An old busker stumbles over a dead body and a lot of money.

Tame British version of Raimu's French success *Monsieur La Souris*, saved only by its star performance.

w Rita Barisse, Reeve Taylor, Paul Vincent Carroll, David Evans, William Templeton
d Gordon Parry ph Hone Glendining

Stanley Holloway, Natasha Parry, Leslie Dwyer, Reginald Tate, Meredith Edwards, Wilfrid Hyde White, Joy Shelton

Midnight Express*
GB 1978 121m Eastmancolor
Columbia / Casablanca (Alan Marshall, David Puttnam)

Tribulations of an American student arrested in Turkey for carrying hashish.

Misleadingly-titled wallow in prison atrocities, extremely well made but certainly not entertaining and with little discernible point.

w Oliver Stone, *memoir* Billy Hayes d Alan Parker ph Michael Seresin m Giorgio Moroder

Brad Davis, Randy Quaid, John Hurt, Irene Miracle, Bo Hopkins

'One of the ugliest sado-masochistic trips, with heavy homosexual overtones, that our

thoroughly nasty movie age has yet produced.'—*Richard Schickel, Time*

'The film details all [the horrors] so relentlessly on one screaming note that it is rather like being hit in the gut until you no longer feel a thing.'—*Derek Malcolm, The Guardian*

'Muted squalor with a disco beat in the background, all packaged as social protest.'—*New Yorker, 1982*

AA: script; music
AAN: best picture; Alan Parker; John Hurt

● *Video: RCA / Columbia*

Midnight Lace*
US 1960 108m Eastmancolor
Universal (Ross Hunter, Martin Melcher)

The wife of a rich Londoner is terrorized by threatening phone calls and voices in the fog.

Thoroughly silly rehash of *Gaslight* and *The Boy Who Cried Wolf*; its glamorous accoutrements can't fight a lack of humour or predictable plot development.

w Ivan Goff, Ben Roberts, *play* Matilda Shouted Fire by Janet Green d David Miller ph Russell Metty m Frank Skinner

Doris Day, Rex Harrison, John Gavin, Myrna Loy, Roddy McDowall, Herbert Marshall, Natasha Parry, John Williams, Anthony Dawson, Hermione Baddeley, Richard Ney, Rhys Williams, Doris Lloyd

Midnight Madonna
US 1937 56m bw

There is a legal fight for custody of a child who has inherited a fortune. Efficient programmer built around a new child actress, Kitty Clancy, who didn't take. Warren William, Mady Corell, Edward Ellis, Robert Baldwin, Jonathan Hale. Written by Doris Malloy, Gladys Lehman; directed by James Flood; for Paramount. 'It will be found fairly entertaining by the family trade.'—*Variety*

The Midnight Man
US 1974 117m Technicolor
Universal / Norlan (Roland Kibbee, Burt Lancaster)

An ex-cop, paroled after killing his wife's lover, takes a job as security guard and runs into a murder case.

Muddled mystery with pretentious characterization and bouts of violence.

wd Roland Kibbee, Burt Lancaster, *novel* The Midnight Lady and the Mourning Man by David Anthony ph Jack Priestley m Dave Grusin

Burt Lancaster, Susan Clark, Cameron Mitchell, Morgan Woodward, Harris Yulin, Robert Quarry, Joan Lorring, Lawrence Dobin, Ed Lauter

'A thriller that has the impenetrability of Chandler but none of the flavour.'—*Tom Milne*

'Efficient enough but lifeless, and burdened with portentous sentiments about solitude, violence and the nature of the beast.'—*Sight and Sound*

Midnight Mary
US 1933 76m bw

A gangster's moll on trial for her life thinks back to her past. Intolerable now, but a hit of its year despite star miscasting. Loretta Young, Ricardo Cortez, Franchot Tone, Una Merkel, Andy Devine, Harold Huber. Written by Gene Markey and Anita Loos; directed by William Wellman; for MGM.

Midnight Patrol*
US 1933 20m bw

Incompetent policemen arrest their own chief as a burglar. Good standard star slapstick. Laurel and Hardy, Charlie Hall, Walter Plinge. Writer uncredited; directed by Lloyd French; for Hal Roach.

Midnight Taxi
US 1937 73m bw

A G-man becomes a taxi driver to rout a gang of counterfeiters. Competent, predictable crime programmer. Brian Donlevy, Frances Drake, Alan Dinehart, Sig Rumann, Gilbert Roland, Harold Huber, Lon Chaney Jnr. Written by Lou Breslow and John Patrick; directed by Eugene Forde; for TCF.

The Midshipmaid
GB 1932 84m bw

A naval commander loves the daughter of a politician out to effect navy cuts. Very modest comedy with music, a key step in the star's success story. Jessie Matthews, Frederick Kerr, Basil Sydney, Nigel Bruce, Claud Allister, John Mills, George Zucco. Written by Ian Hay and Stephen King-Hall, from their play; directed by Albert de Courville; for Gaumont.

Midshipman Easy
GB 1935 77m bw
ATP (Basil Dean, Thorold Dickinson)
US title: *Men of the Sea*

In 1790, young naval officers rescue a girl from Spanish bandits.

Stilted adventure story with interesting credits.

w Anthony Kimmins, *novel* Frederick Marryat d Carol Reed ph John W. Boyle

Hughie Green, Margaret Lockwood, Harry Tate, Robert Adams, Roger Livesey, Lewis Casson

'Three centuries in the making!'

A Midsummer Night's Dream***
US 1935 133m bw
Warner (Max Reinhardt)

Two pairs of lovers sort out their problems with fairy help at midnight in the woods of Athens.

Shakespeare's play is treated with remarkable respect in this super-glamorous Hollywood adaptation based on the Broadway production by Max Reinhardt. Much of it comes off, and visually it's a treat.

w Charles Kenyon, Mary McCall Jnr, *play* William Shakespeare d Max Reinhardt, William Dieterle ph Hal Mohr, Fred Jackman,

Byron Haskin, H. F. Koenekamp
m Mendelssohn *md* Erich Wolfgang
Korngold *ch* Bronislawa Nijinska *ad* Anton
Grot

James Cagney, Dick Powell, Jean Muir, Ross
Alexander, Olivia de Havilland, Joe E.
Brown, Hugh Herbert, Arthur Treacher,
Frank McHugh, Otis Harlan, Dewey
Robinson, *Victor Jory*, Verree Teasdale,
Mickey Rooney, Anita Louise, Grant Mitchell,
Ian Hunter, Hobart Cavanaugh
    'General b.o. chances could be improved by
judicious pruning and appreciative selling . . .
a fine prestige picture not only for Warners
but for the industry as a whole.'—*Variety*
    'The publicity push behind the film is
tremendous—it is going to be a success or
everyone at Warner Brothers is going to get
fired.'—*Robert Forsythe*
    'Its assurance as a work of film technique is
undoubted.'—*John Baxter, 1968*
    'Its worst contradiction lies in the way
Warners first ordered up a whole batch of
foreign and high-sounding names to handle
music, dances, general production—and then
turned around and handed them empty vessels
for actors.'—*Otis Ferguson*
AA: photography
AAN: best picture

A Midsummer Night's Sex Comedy*
US 1982 88m Technicolor
Warner / Orion (Robert Greenhut)

Around the turn of the century, a Wall Street
broker expects various weekend guests at his
country retreat.
Subdued, melancholy and rather uninventive
Woody Allen variation on *Smiles of a Summer
Night.*
wd Woody Allen *ph* Gordon Willis *m* from
Mendelssohn *pd* Mel Bourne *ed* Susan E.
Morse

Woody Allen, Mia Farrow, Jose Ferrer, Julie
Hagerty, Tony Roberts, Mary Steenburgen
● *Video: Warner*

Midway*
US 1976 131m Technicolor
Panavision Sensurround
Universal / Mirisch Corporation (Walter
    Mirisch)
GB title: *The Battle of Midway*

The tide turns for the Americans when the
Japanese attack the Pacific island of Midway in
1942.
Noisy flagwaver with confused strategy and
too many stars in small parts.
w Donald S. Sanford *d* Jack Smight
ph Harry Stradling Jnr *m* John Williams

Charlton Heston, Henry Fonda, Robert
Mitchum, Glenn Ford, Edward Albert, James
Coburn, Hal Holbrook, Toshiro Mifune,
Robert Wagner, Robert Webber, Ed Nelson,
James Shigeta, Monte Markham, Chris
George, Glenn Corbett
    'We are over-informed about the
movements of every ship and plane, under-

informed about how the battle was finally
won, and positively swamped with tedious
human interest.'—*Sight and Sound*

The Mighty Barnum*
US 1934 87m bw
Twentieth Century (Darryl F. Zanuck)

A fictionalized biopic of the great showman of
the nineties.
Lively without being very memorable.
w Gene Fowler, Bess Meredyth from their
play *d* Walter Lang *ph* Peverell Marley
m Alfred Newman

Wallace Beery, Virginia Bruce, Adolphe
Menjou, Janet Beecher, Rochelle Hudson

'The ten most terrific thrills ever pictured!'
Mighty Joe Young*
US 1949 94m bw
RKO (Merian C. Cooper)

A little girl brings back from Africa a pet
gorilla which grows to enormous size and
causes a city to panic.
Rather tired comic-sentimental follow-up to
King Kong, with a tedious plot and variable
animation but a few endearing highlights.
w Ruth Rose *d* Ernest Schoedsack *ph* J. Roy
Hunt *m* Roy Webb *sp* Willis O'Brien, Ray
Harryhausen

Terry Moore, Ben Johnson, Robert
Armstrong, Frank McHugh, Douglas Fowley
● *Video: Kingston*

The Mikado*
GB 1939 91m Technicolor
GFD / G and S (Geoffrey Toye, Victor
    Somlo)

In Japan, a timid official is appointed Lord
High Executioner and finds that his first
intended victim is the Emperor's son,
travelling incognito.
Agreeable film version of the classic Gilbert
and Sullivan comic opera, with some of the
D'Oyly Carte Company's most celebrated
members in excellent form.
w Geoffrey Toye, *opera* W. S. Gilbert
m Arthur Sullivan *d* Victor Schertzinger
ph Bernard Knowles

Martyn Green, John Barclay, Sydney
Granville, Kenny Baker, Jean Colin,
Constance Willis
† The 1966 version by British Home
Entertainment featured a later D'Oyly Carte
company including John Reed but suffered
from a frozen camera and flat lighting, so that
little of the original vivacity and charm came
over.

Mikey and Nicky
US 1976 118m colour
Paramount (Michael Hausman)

Two crooks are old friends, but one has been
hired to kill the other . . .
Intolerable improvisatory sentimental
melodrama. Who on earth shells out the
money for pictures like this?
wd Elaine May *ph* Victor Kemper *m* John
Strauss

Peter Falk, John Cassavetes, Ned Beatty,
Sanford Meisner, Rose Arrick, Joyce Van
Patten
    'An impenetrable, ugly and almost
unendurable mess.'—*Frank Rich, New York
Post*
    'A pretext for Falk and Cassavetes to
indulge in one of those long, lugubrious
Actors' Studio exercises that wore out its
welcome with the last frame of *Husbands* and
the first frame of *The Killing of a Chinese
Bookie*.'—*Molly Haskell, Village Voice*

'The kind of woman most men want . . .
    and shouldn't have!'
Mildred Pierce**
US 1945 113m bw
Warner (Jerry Wald)

A dowdy housewife breaks with her husband,
becomes the owner (through hard work) of a
restaurant chain, and survives a murder case
before true love comes her way.
A woman's picture par excellence, glossily and
moodily photographed, with a star suffering in
luxury on behalf of the most ungrateful
daughter of all time.
w Ranald MacDougall, Catherine Turney,
novel James M. Cain *d* Michael Curtiz
ph Ernest Haller *m* Max Steiner *ad* Anton
Grot

Joan Crawford, Jack Carson, Zachary Scott,
Eve Arden, Ann Blyth, Bruce Bennett,
George Tobias, Lee Patrick, Moroni Olsen
    'Constant, lambent, virulent attention to
money and its effects, and more authentic
suggestions of sex than one hopes to see in
American films.'—*James Agee*
AA: Joan Crawford
AAN: best picture; script; Ernest Haller; Eve
Arden; Ann Blyth

The Milkman
US 1950 87m bw
Universal-International (Ted Richmond)

Two milkmen tangle with gangsters.
Odd little comedy which gets the benefit of the
doubt more by bringing its stars together than
by giving them anything to do.
w Albert Beich, James O'Hanlon, Martin
Ragaway, Leonard Stern *d* Charles Barton
ph Clifford Stine *m* Milton Rosen

Donald O'Connor, Jimmy Durante, Joyce
Holden, Piper Laurie, William Conrad, Paul
Harvey, Henry O'Neill

The Milky Way*
US 1936 88m bw
Paramount / Harold Lloyd (Edward
    Sheldon)

A milkman becomes a prizefighter and
overcomes a gang of crooks.
Modest Harold Lloyd comedy towards the end
of his career; remade as *The Kid from
Brooklyn* (qv).

w Grover Jones, Frank Butler, Richard
Connell, *play* Lynn Root, Harry Clark
ph Alfred Gilks *d* Leo McCarey

Harold Lloyd, Adolphe Menjou, Verree
Teasdale, Helen Mack, William Gargan,
George Barbier, Lionel Stander

'The work of many hands, all laid on
expertly.'—*Otis Ferguson*

'One is more amazed than ever at the good
fortune of this youngish man whose chief
talent is not to act at all, to do nothing, to
serve as a blank wall for other people to scrawl
their ideas on.'—*Graham Greene*

The Milky Way*
France / Italy 1968   102m   Eastmancolor
Greenwich / Medusa (Serge Silberman)
original title: *La Voie Lactée*

Two tramps set off on pilgrimage from Paris to
a Spanish shrine, and have various surprising
encounters.
A picaresque examination of Catholic
doctrine, full of surface interest but requiring
special knowledge for full appreciation.

w Luis Bunuel, Jean-Claude Carrière *d* Luis
Bunuel *ph* Christian Matras *m* Luis Bunuel

Laurent Terzieff, Paul Frankeur, Delphine
Seyrig, Edith Scon

'A mere trifle wrapped in a triple cloak of
befuddling obscurantism.'—*John Simon*

The Mill on the Floss
GB 1937   94m   bw

A Victorian mill owner and the lord of the
manor start a family feud which ends in
tragedy. Romeo and Juliet in crinolines; a
stilted and unpersuasive film of the book.
Geraldine Fitzgerald, Frank Lawton, James
Mason, Victoria Hopper, Fay Compton,
Griffith Jones, Mary Clare, Athene Seyler,
Felix Aylmer. Written by John Drinkwater,
Garnett Weston, Austin Melford and Tim
Whelan, from the novel by George Eliot;
directed by Tim Whelan; for Morgan /
National Provincial. 'A series of stiff little
sequences, decorously posed.'—*New York
Times.*

Le Million****
France 1931   89m   bw
Tobis (Frank Clifford)

An artist and an ingratiating crook search
Paris for a lost lottery ticket.
With its delicate touch, perfect sense of
comedy timing and infectious use of recitative
and song, this is superb screen entertainment
using most of the medium's resources.

wd René Clair, *musical comedy* Georges Berr,
M. Guillemaud *ph* Georges Périnal
m Georges Van Parys, Armand Bernard,
Philippe Parès *ad* Lazare Meerson

Annabella, René Lefèvre, *Paul Olivier*, Louis
Allibert, Vanda Gréville, Raymond Cordy

'A good musical farce that ought to do well
everywhere . . . it has speed, laughs, splendid
photography and a good cast.'—*Variety*

'René Clair at his exquisite best; no one else
has ever been able to make a comedy move
with such delicate inevitability.'—*New Yorker,
1978*

† The style of this film was developed and
expanded in Hollywood by Lubitsch in *One
Hour with You* and by Mamoulian in *Love Me
Tonight.*

Million Dollar Baby
US 1941   100m   bw
Warner (Hal B. Wallis, David Lewis)

A girl inherits a fortune and a lot of problems.
Very predictable but sometimes sprightly
comedy with a hard-working cast.

w Richard Macaulay, Jerry Wald, Casey
Robinson, *story* Miss Wheelwright Discovers
America by Leonard Spiegelgass *d* Curtis
Bernhardt *ph* Charles Rosher *m* Max Steiner

Priscilla Lane, Jeffrey Lynn, Ronald Reagan,
May Robson, Lee Patrick, Helen Westley,
George Barbier, John Qualen, Walter Catlett,
Nan Wynn

Million Dollar Duck
US 1971   92m   Technicolor
Walt Disney (Bill Anderson)

A duck lays eggs with solid gold yolks, which
provoke interest from gangsters as well as the
government.
Minor Disney fantasy borrowed without
permission from *Mr Drake's Duck* (qv).

w Roswell Rogers *d* Vincent McEveety
ph William Snyder *m* Buddy Baker

Dean Jones, Sandy Dennis, Joe Flynn

● *Video: Rank*

'Roaring laughs in a story built of goofer
   dust and frog fur!'
Million Dollar Legs*
US 1932   64m   bw
Paramount

A mythical sport-ridden country decides to
enter the Olympic Games.
The good gags in this film are weighted down
by plodding treatment, and the general effect
is more doleful than funny.

w Harry Myers, Nick Barrows, Joseph L.
Mankiewicz *d* Edward Cline *ph* Arthur Todd

W. C. Fields, Jack Oakie, Andy Clyde, Lyda
Roberti, Ben Turpin, Hugh Herbert, Billy
Gilbert, George Barbier, Susan Fleming

'One of the silliest and funniest pictures ever
made.'—*New Yorker, 1977*

Million Dollar Legs
US 1939   59m   bw
Paramount

College students back a favourite horse.
Very modest collegiate comedy.

w Lewis Foster, Richard English *d* Nick
Grinde *ph* Harry Fischbeck

Betty Grable, John Hartley, Donald
O'Connor, Jackie Coogan, Buster Crabbe,
Thurston Hall

Million Dollar Mermaid*
US 1952   115m   Technicolor
MGM (Arthur Hornblow Jnr)
GB title: *The One Piece Bathing Suit*

The story of Australian swimmer Annette
Kellerman.

Inaccurate biopic with a *raison d'être* in its
spectacular aquashow scenes, but nothing at
all new in its script.

w Everett Freeman *d* Mervyn Le Roy
ph George J. Folsey *md* Adolph Deutsch
ch Busby Berkeley

Esther Williams, Victor Mature, Walter
Pidgeon, David Brian, Jesse White, Maria
Tallchief, Howard Freeman

AAN: George J. Folsey

Million Dollar Ransom
US 1934   67m   bw

A racketeer consolidates his family affairs
before being bumped off by his gang. Slightly
odd underworld melodrama, interesting but
not very satisfying. Edward Arnold, Phillips
Holmes, Mary Carlisle, Wini Shaw, Andy
Devine. Written by William R. Lipman, Ben
Ryan, from a story by Damon Runyon;
directed by Murray Roth; for Universal.
'Lacks names but offers fair possibilities.'—
Variety

The Million Pound Note*
GB 1954   91m   Technicolor
GFD / Group Films (John Bryan)
US title: *Man with a Million*

A man inherits a million dollars in the form of
a single banknote and finds it difficult to
spend.
Fairly pleasing period comedy which wears its
one joke pretty thin but is nicely decorated
and acted.

w Jill Craigie, *story* Mark Twain *d* Ronald
Neame *ph* Geoffrey Unsworth *m* William
Alwyn

Gregory Peck, Jane Griffiths, Ronald Squire,
Joyce Grenfell, A. E. Matthews, Reginald
Beckwith, Hartley Power, Wilfrid Hyde White

The Millionaire*
US 1931   80m   bw

A bored millionaire retires and secretly buys a
garage. Fairly deft star comedy which well
satisfied depression audiences. *George Arliss,
Florence Arliss*, Evalyn Knapp, David
Manners, Noah Beery, J. Farrell MacDonald,
James Cagney. Written by Julien Josephson
and Booth Tarkington, from a story by Earl
Derr Biggers; directed by John Adolfi; for
Warner. (NB: Remade in 1947 as *That Way
with Women* [qv].) 'Should bring Arliss within
mental reach of all theatres. . . Should enjoy a
substantial career.'—*Variety*

A Millionaire for Christy
US 1951   91m   bw
TCF (Bert Friedlob)

A lawyer's secretary is sent to Los Angeles to
inform an heir of his good fortune, and
decides to marry him.
Modest romantic comedy with plenty to be
modest about.

w Ken Englund *d* George Marshall *ph* Harry
Stradling *m* Victor Young

Eleanor Parker, Fred MacMurray, Richard
Carlson, Douglass Dumbrille

'From naughty, notorious George Bernard Shaw, the sultry story of the beautiful babe in the Balmain gowns who pants for romance . . . !'

The Millionairess*
GB 1960   90m   De Luxe   Cinemascope
TCF / Dimitri de Grunwald (Pierre Rouve)

The richest woman in the world falls for a poor Indian doctor.
Messy travesty of a Shavian comedy that was never more than a star vehicle to begin with. Hardly any of it works despite the star cast, who are mostly miscast.

w Wolf Mankowitz, *play* Bernard Shaw
d Anthony Asquith ph Jack Hildyard
m Georges Van Parys

Sophia Loren, Peter Sellers, Alastair Sim, Vittorio de Sica, Dennis Price, Gary Raymond, Alfie Bass, Miriam Karlin, Noel Purcell

'The result, lacking any sort of dramatic cohesion or continuity and seemingly planned less as a film than as a series of haphazard effects, is merely tiring.'—*Peter John Dyer*

Millions
GB 1936   70m   bw

A struggling composer is really the son of a millionaire. Fairly lively comedy of rival self-made men. Gordon Harker, Frank Pettingell, Richard Hearne, Jane Carr. Written by Michael Barringer; directed by Leslie Hiscott; for Herbert Wilcox.

Millions in the Air
US 1935   72m   bw

Complications of a radio amateur contest. Scrappy comedy with more historical interest than entertainment value. Willie Howard, John Howard, Robert Cummings, Inez Courtney, Benny Baker, Dave Chasen, Wendy Barrie, Samuel S. Hinds. Written by Sig Herzig, Jane Storm; directed by Ray McCarey; for Harold Hurley / Paramount. 'Without a substantial moniker in the cast, it hasn't much to offer at the box office.'—*Variety*

Millions like Us*
GB 1943   103m   bw
GFD / Gainsborough (Edward Black)

The tribulations of a family in wartime, especially of the meek daughter who goes into war work and marries an airman, who is killed.
Fragmentary but reasonably accurate picture of the Home Front during World War II; a little more humour would not have been out of place, but as propaganda it proved an effective weapon.

wd Frank Launder, Sidney Gilliat ph Jack Cox md Louis Levy

Patricia Roc, Gordon Jackson, Moore Marriott, Eric Portman, Anne Crawford, Basil Radford, Naunton Wayne, Joy Shelton, Megs Jenkins

'There is an unsentimental warmheartedness which I hope we shall cling to and extend in filmed representations of the British scene.'—*Richard Winnington*
† The only picture Launder and Gilliat directed side by side on the floor.

Mills of the Gods
US 1934   66m   bw

An elderly businesswoman, unimpressed by her family, turns her business over to a committee of executives. Interesting plot which would have justified better production. May Robson, Fay Wray, Victor Jory, Raymond Walburn, Mayo Methot. Written by Garrett Fort, John S. Kirkland, Melville Baker; directed by Roy William Neill; for Columbia. 'Stilted story with some good trouping. A double-upper.'—*Variety*

Mimi
GB 1935   94m   bw

In a Paris garret, a poor girl dies after encouraging a playwright. *La Bohème* without the music; not a good idea. Douglas Fairbanks Jnr, Gertrude Lawrence, Diana Napier, Harold Warrender, Carol Goodner, Richard Bird. Written by Clifford Grey, Paul Merzbach, Jack Davies and Denis Waldock, from the novel *La Vie Bohème* by Henri Murger; directed by Paul Stein; for BIP.

Min and Bill**
US 1930   69m   bw
MGM

A boozy old waterfront character and his wife try to keep their daughter from being placed in care.
Well-remembered and much-loved character comedy which led to the even more successful *Tugboat Annie* with the same team.

w Frances Marion, Marion Jackson, *play* Dark Star by Lorna Moon d George Hill
ph Harold Wenstrom

Marie Dressler, Wallace Beery, Dorothy Jordan, Marjorie Rambeau, Donald Dillaway, Russell Hopton

'Comedy-drama of distinction. All ingredients for all theatres, from keys down.'—*Variety*
AA: Marie Dressler

The Mind Benders*
GB 1963   113m   bw
Anglo–Amalgamated / Novus (Michael Relph)

A scientist undergoes an experiment aimed at depriving him of all sensation. It works too well; he becomes a sadist; and his colleagues can't reverse the process.
Matter-of-factly played hocus-pocus with spy asides; quite gripping while it's on, but in no way memorable.

w James Kennaway d Basil Dearden
ph Denys Coop m Georges Auric

Dirk Bogarde, John Clements, Mary Ure, Michael Bryant

The Mind of Mr Reeder*
GB 1939   75m   bw

An elderly government employee unmasks a forger and murderer. Entertaining crime comedy-drama which never quite realizes its potential. Will Fyffe, Kay Walsh, George Curzon, Chili Bouchier, John Warwick. Written by Bryan Edgar Wallace, Marjorie Gaffney and Michael Hogan, from the novel by Edgar Wallace; directed by Jack Raymond; for Grand National.

The Mind of Mr Soames
GB 1970   98m   Technicolor
Columbia / Amicus (Teresa Bolland)

A man who has lived in a coma for thirty years is cured but faces the world as a new-born infant.
Ill-advised attempt at science fiction with meaning; its earnestness becomes a bore.

w John Hale, Edward Simpson, *novel* Charles Eric Maine d Alan Cooke ph Billy Williams
m Michael Dress

Terence Stamp, Robert Vaughn, Nigel Davenport, Donal Donnelly, Christian Roberts, Vickery Turner, Scott Forbes

The Mind Reader*
US 1933   69m   bw

A phoney mind reader tries to go straight for his wife's sake, and ends up in jail.
Reasonably mordant satirical drama with good performances. *Warren William,* Constance Cummings, Allen Jenkins, Donald Dillaway, Mayo Methot, Clarence Muse. Written by Wilson Mizner and Robert Lord, from the play by Vivian Cosby; directed by Roy del Ruth; for Warners. 'Star performance plus laugh dialogue enough to send this into okay programmer class.'—*Variety*

Mind Your Own Business
US 1937   75m   bw

Boy scouts help to capture gangsters. Slightly rocky comedy which finally comes across as unsatisfactory. Charles Ruggles, Alice Brady, Lyle Talbot, Benny Baker, Jack La Rue, William Demarest, Frankie Darro. Written by Dore Schary from a story by John Francis Larkin; directed by Norman Z. McLeod; for Emmanuel Cohen / Paramount. 'It will have a tough time standing alone.'—*Variety*

Mine Own Executioner***
GB 1947   108m   bw
London Films

A lay psychiatrist undertakes the care of a mentally disturbed war veteran, but fails to prevent him from murdering his wife.
When this film first appeared it seemed like the first adult drama featuring sophisticated people to emerge from a British studio. Time and television have blunted its impact, but it remains a well told suspense melodrama with memorable characters.

w Nigel Balchin, from his novel d Anthony Kimmins ph Wilkie Cooper m Benjamin Frankel

Burgess Meredith, Kieron Moore, Dulcie Gray, Barbara White, Christine Norden
'The first psychoanalytical film that a grown-up can sit through without squirming.'—*Richard Winnington*

'His secret meant death to one man if he didn't talk . . . to countless thousands if he did!'

Ministry of Fear**
US 1944   85m   bw
Paramount (Seton I. Miller)

During World War II in England, a man just out of a mental hospital wins a cake at a village fair and finds himself caught up in bewildering intrigues.
Little to do with the novel, but a watchable, well-detailed little thriller on Hitchcock lines, once you forgive the usual phoney Hollywood England.

w Seton I. Miller, *novel* Graham Greene *d* Fritz Lang *ph* Henry Sharp *m* Victor Young

Ray Milland, Marjorie Reynolds, Carl Esmond, Hillary Brooke, Dan Duryea, Percy Waram, Alan Napier, Erskine Sanford
'A crisp and efficiently made thriller with no pretension to intellectual content.'—*Paul Jensen*

The Miniver Story
GB 1950   104m   bw
MGM (Sidney Franklin)

Mrs Miniver faces the tribulations of post-war Britain.
Glum sequel to *Mrs Miniver*, with the dauntless heroine finally succumbing to a glossy but fatal disease. Well enough made, but very hard to take.

w Ronald Millar, George Froeschel *d* H. C. Potter *ph* Joseph Ruttenberg *m* Herbert Stothart

Greer Garson, Walter Pidgeon, Cathy O'Donnell, John Hodiak, Leo Genn, Reginald Owen, Henry Wilcoxon, William Fox, Anthony Bushell

Minnie and Moskowitz*
US 1971   115m   Technicolor
Universal (Al Rubin)

Two lonely Los Angeles misfits have a bumpy courtship.
Enjoyably aimless character comedy.

wd John Cassavetes *ph* Arthur J. Ornitz *m* Bob Harwood

Gena Rowlands, Seymour Cassel

Minstrel Man*
US 1944   70m   bw

A minstrel star seeks his long-lost daughter.
Interesting sidelights on old-time minstrel shows in a production somewhat less tatty than is usual from this company. Benny Fields, Gladys George, Roscoe Karns. Written by Irwin Franklin and Pierre Gendron; directed by Joseph H. Lewis; for PRC.

AAN: song, 'Remember Me to Carolina'.

The Miracle
Italy 1948   40m   bw
Tania Film (Roberto Rossellini)

A simple-minded peasant woman is seduced by a shepherd but believes her baby has been immaculately conceived.
Curious, rather unsatisfactory parable originally intended as part of a two-item tribute to the power of a star actress. (The other section, Cocteau's *The Human Voice*, was withdrawn for copyright reasons.)

w Tullio Pinelli, Roberto Rossellini, Federico Fellini *d* Roberto Rossellini *ph* Aldo Tonti *m* Renzo Rossellini

Anna Magnani, Federico Fellini
'Acting on a plane scarcely known to the cinema.'—*Sunday Times*

'The mightiest story of fame and the flesh known to our time!'

The Miracle
US 1959   121m   Technirama
Warner (Henry Blanke)

In Spain during the Peninsular War, a nun breaks her vows in order to follow a British soldier, and a statue of the Virgin Mary steps down to take her place.
And that's only the beginning in this very tall tale, full of heavy breathing, violent action and religiosity, from the old Max Reinhardt pageant. Quite incredible, and sloppily done.

w Frank Butler, *play* Karl Vollmoeller *d* Irving Rapper *ph* Ernest Haller *m* Elmer Bernstein

Carroll Baker, Roger Moore, Walter Slezak, Vittorio Gassman, Katina Paxinou, Dennis King, Isobel Elsom, Torin Thatcher

Miracle in Milan**
Italy 1951   101m   bw
PDS / ENIC

A foundling goes to live with the poor on the outskirts of Milan, and his erstwhile guardian returns from heaven to help them repel capitalists and fly away on broomsticks to a better land.
An unlikely fable which manages to avoid all the obvious pitfalls and sends one out of the cinema in a warm glow.

w Cesare Zavattini, Vittorio de Sica, *novel* Toto il Buono by Cesare Zavattini *d* Vittorio de Sica *ph* G. R. Aldo *m* Alessandro Cicognini

Francesco Golisano, Brunella Bovo, Emma Gramatica, Paolo Stoppa

Miracle in Soho
GB 1957   93m   Eastmancolor
Rank (Emeric Pressburger)

A Soho roadworker falls for a barmaid.
Rudimentary romantic whimsy in an unconvincing street set, with characters either too voluble or just plain dull.

w Emeric Pressburger *d* Julian Amyes *ph* Christopher Challis *m* Brian Easdale

John Gregson, Belinda Lee, Cyril Cusack

'A street corner pick-up that worked a miracle of love! A picture of very special greatness!'

Miracle in the Rain**
US 1954   107m   bw
Warner (Frank P. Rosenberg)

A plain New York girl falls for a soldier; when he is killed in action, he keeps their appointment on the church steps as a ghost.
Archetypal Hollywood schmaltz, half acute observation of amusing types, half sentimental whimsy, with a final supernatural touch of eating your cake and having it.

w Ben Hecht *d* Rudolph Maté *ph* Russell Metty *m* Franz Waxman

Jane Wyman, Van Johnson, Fred Clark, Eileen Heckart, William Gargan

The Miracle Man
US 1932   85m   bw
Paramount

A gang of crooks is reformed by a faith healer they have exploited.
Adequate remake of the silent Lon Chaney vehicle; no sparks this time.

w Waldemar Young, Samuel Hoffenstein, *play* Frank L. Packard, George M. Cohan *d* Norman Z. McLeod *ph* David Abel

Sylvia Sidney, Chester Morris, Irving Pichel, John Wray, Robert Coogan, Hobart Bosworth, Boris Karloff, Ned Sparks, Virginia Bruce

The Miracle of Morgan's Creek***
US 1943   99m   bw
Paramount (Preston Sturges)

Chaos results when a stuttering hayseed tries to help a girl accidentally pregnant by a soldier she met hazily at a dance.
Weird and wonderful one-man assault on the Hays Office and sundry other American institutions such as motherhood and politics; an indescribable, tasteless, roaringly funny mêlée, as unexpected at the time as it was effective, like a kick in the pants to all other film comedies.

wd Preston Sturges *ph* John Seitz *m* Leo Shuken, Charles Bradshaw

Betty Hutton, Eddie Bracken, William Demarest, Diana Lynn, Porter Hall, Akim Tamiroff, Brian Donlevy, Alan Bridge

OFFICER KOCKENLOCKER (William Demarest): 'Daughters. They're a mess no matter how you look at 'em. A headache till they get married—*if* they get married—and after that they get worse . . . Either they leave their husbands and come back with four kids and move into your guest room or the husband loses his job and the whole caboodle comes back. Or else they're so homely that you can't get rid of them at all and they sit around like Spanish moss and shame you into an early grave.'

EMILY KOCKENLOCKER (Diana Lynn): 'If you don't mind my mentioning it, father, I think you have a mind like a swamp.'

'Like taking a nun on a roller coaster.'—
James Agee

'This film moves in a fantastic and irreverent whirl of slapstick, nonsense, farce, sentiment, satire, romance, melodrama—is there any ingredient of dramatic entertainment except maybe tragedy and grand opera that hasn't been tossed into it?'—*National Board of Review*

'Bad taste or no bad taste, I thoroughly enjoyed it.'—*Richard Mallett, Punch*

AAN: Preston Sturges (as writer)

The Miracle of Our Lady of Fatima
US 1952 102m Warnercolor
Warner (Bryan Foy)
GB title: *The Miracle of Fatima*

An account of the 1917 appearance of the Virgin Mary to three Portuguese peasant children.

Poorly staged religious film which manages to be less pro-Catholic than anti-communist, and was clearly seen by Jack L. Warner as a means of atoning for *Mission to Moscow*. A real cold war piece.

w Crane Wilbur, James O'Hanlon *d* John Brahm *ph* Edwin DuPar *m* Max Steiner *ad* Edward Carrere

Gilbert Roland, Frank Silvera, Angela Clarke, Jay Novello

AAN: Max Steiner

The Miracle of the Bells
US 1948 120m bw
Jesse L. Lasky

The death of a glamorous film star causes a small-town miracle and a nationwide publicity stunt.

One hopes that this oddity was intended as a satire; as a straight entertainment it's more than a little icky, and good production values scarcely help.

w Ben Hecht, *novel* Russell Janney *d* Irving Rapper *ph* Robert de Grasse *m* Leigh Harline

Fred MacMurray, Alida Valli, Frank Sinatra, Lee J. Cobb

'An offensive exhibition of vulgar insensitivity.'—*MFB*

'I hereby declare myself the founding father of the Society for the Prevention of Cruelty to God.'—*James Agee*

● Video: Intervision

The Miracle of the White Stallions*
US 1962 118m Technicolor
Walt Disney (Peter V. Herald)
GB title: *The Flight of the White Stallions*

During World War II the Nazis occupy Vienna and the owner of the Spanish Riding School guides his stallions to safety.

Adequate family adventure fare with a dull hero but interesting backgrounds.

w A. J. Carothers *d* Arthur Hiller *ph* Gunther Anders *m* Paul Smith

Robert Taylor, Lilli Palmer, Eddie Albert, Curt Jurgens

Miracle on Main Street*
US 1940 76m bw
RKO / Jack Skirball

A cabaret dancer finds an abandoned baby but her plans are thwarted by the return of her husband.

Odd, interesting but flatly handled melodrama.

w Sam Ornitz, Boris Ingster, *story* Felix Jackson *d* Steve Sekely *ph* Charles Van Enger

Walter Abel, Margo, William Collier, Jane Darwell, Lyle Talbot, Wynne Gibson

Miracle on 34th Street***
US 1947 94m bw
TCF (William Perlberg)
GB title: *The Big Heart*

A department store Santa Claus claims to be the real thing.

Mainly charming comedy fantasy which quickly became an American classic but does suffer from a few dull romantic stretches.

wd George Seaton, *story* Valentine Davies *ph* Charles Clarke, Lloyd Ahern *m* Cyril Mockridge

Edmund Gwenn, Maureen O'Hara, John Payne, Natalie Wood, Gene Lockhart, Porter Hall, William Frawley, Jerome Cowan, Thelma Ritter

'Altogether wholesome, stimulating and enjoyable.'—*Motion Picture Herald*

AA: George Seaton (as writer); Valentine Davies; Edmund Gwenn
AAN: best picture

'Never give away what you can sell!'

The Miracle Woman*
US 1932 90m bw
Columbia (Harry Cohn)

A lady evangelist turns confidence trickster. Mild satirical drama inspired by the career of Aimée Semple Macpherson.

w Jo Swerling, *play* Bless You Sister by Robert Riskin, John Meehan *d* Frank Capra *ph* Joseph Walker *m* uncredited

Barbara Stanwyck, Sam Hardy, David Manners, Beryl Mercer, Russell Hopton

'Splendid programme leader, a big and strong film opening up numerous channels of publicity.'—*Variety*

'Such a beauty, well staged and handsomely lighted.'—*New Yorker, 1977*

The Miracle Worker*
US 1962 106m bw
UA / Playfilms (Fred Coe)

The childhood of Helen Keller, taught by Annie Sullivan after being left blind, deaf and dumb in an illness.

A moving real-life story is given hysterical treatment and the good scenes have a hard task winning through; in any case a documentary might have been more persuasive.

w William Gibson, from his play *d* Arthur Penn *ph* Ernest Caparros *m* Laurence Rosenthal *ad* George Jenkins

Anne Bancroft, Patty Duke, Victor Jory, Inga Swenson, Andrew Prine, Beah Richards

AA: Anne Bancroft; Patty Duke
AAN: William Gibson; Arthur Penn

Miracles for Sale
US 1939 71m bw

An illusionist catches a murderer. What could have been a smart mystery piece is sabotaged by stilted writing and direction, a muddled narrative style, and illusions which are patently faked by the camera. Robert Young, Florence Rice, Henry Hull, Frank Craven, Lee Bowman, William Demarest. Written by James Edward Grant, Marion Parsonnet and Harry Ruskin, from the novel *Death in a Top Hat* by Clayton Rawson; directed by Tod Browning; for MGM. 'Unexciting whodunit . . . the plot stumbles over itself most of the time.'—*Variety*

Mirage***
US 1965 109m bw
U-I (Harry Keller)

During a New York power blackout, an executive falls to his death from a skyscraper and a cost accountant loses his memory. Striking puzzler, rather slowly developed but generally effective and with a strong sense of place and timing.

w Peter Stone, *novel* Walter Ericson *d* Edward Dmytryk *ph* Joe MacDonald *m* Quincy Jones

Gregory Peck, Diane Baker, Walter Abel, Walter Matthau, Leif Erickson, Kevin McCarthy

Miranda*
GB 1947 80m bw
GFD / Gainsborough / Sydney Box (Betty Box)

A doctor on holiday in Cornwall catches a mermaid and takes her to London disguised as an invalid.

Simple-minded comedy which scores a few easy laughs on obvious targets.

w Peter Blackmore, from his play *d* Ken Annakin *ph* Ray Elton *m* Temple Abady

Glynis Johns, Griffith Jones, Googie Withers, Margaret Rutherford, David Tomlinson, Sonia Holm, John McCallum

† Sequel 1949, *Mad about Men*.

'Mirror, mirror, on the wall, who's the killer among them all?'

The Mirror Crack'd*
GB 1980 105m Technicolor
EMI / John Brabourne, Richard Goodwin

Murders result from the making of an all-star film in an English village.

After adventures on the Orient Express and the Nile, this follow-up in the Agatha Christie stakes seems somewhat subdued, but the production is polished and the murder plot compels attention.

w Jonathan Hales, Barry Sandler *novel* Agatha Christie *d* Guy Hamilton *ph* Christopher Challis *m* John Cameron *pd* Michael Stringer

Angela Lansbury, Geraldine Chaplin,
Elizabeth Taylor, Rock Hudson, Tony Curtis,
Edward Fox, Kim Novak, Marella
Oppenheim, Charles Gray
● *Video: Thorn EMI*

Les Misérables****
US 1935   109m   bw
Twentieth Century (Darryl F. Zanuck)

Unjustly convicted and sentenced to years in
the galleys, Jean Valjean emerges to build up
his life again but is hounded by a cruel and
relentless police officer.
Solid, telling, intelligent version of a much-
filmed classic novel; in adaptation and
performance it is hard to see how this film
could be bettered.

w W. P. Lipscomb, *novel* Victor Hugo
d Richard Boleslawski *ph* Gregg Toland
m Alfred Newman

Fredric March, Charles Laughton, Cedric
Hardwicke, Rochelle Hudson, Frances Drake
John Beal, Jessie Ralph, Florence Eldridge

'Brilliant filmization, sure fire for heavy
money.'—*Variety*
'Unbelievably thrilling in all the
departments of its manufacture . . . a
memorable experience in the cinema.'—*New
York Times*
'A superlative effort, a thrilling, powerful,
poignant picture.'—*New York Evening Post*
'Deserving of rank among the cinema's
finest achievements.'—*New York World
Telegram*
† Other versions of the story: 1909, 1913
(French); 1917 (William Farnum); 1923
(French: Gabriel Gabrio); 1929 as *The
Bishop's Candlesticks* (Walter Huston); 1934
(French: Harry Baur); 1946 (Italian: Gino
Cervi); 1952 (see below); 1956 (French: Jean
Gabin); 1978 (British: Richard Jordan).

AAN: best picture; Gregg Toland

Les Misérables**
US 1952   106m   bw
TCF (Fred Kohlmar)

Solemn remake, well done but lacking the
spark of inspiration.

w Richard Murphy *d* Lewis Milestone
ph Joseph La Shelle *m* Alex North

Michael Rennie, Robert Newton, Edmund
Gwenn, Debra Paget, Cameron Mitchell,
Sylvia Sidney, Elsa Lanchester, James
Robertson Justice, Joseph Wiseman, Rhys
Williams

The Misfits*
US 1961   124m   bw
United Artists / Seven Arts (Frank E. Taylor)

Cowboys gather in the Nevada desert to rope
wild mustangs, and a divorcee becomes
involved with one of them.
Ill-fated melodrama whose stars both died
shortly afterwards; a solemn, unattractive,
pretentious film which seldom stops wallowing
in self-pity.

w Arthur Miller *d* John Huston *ph* Russell
Metty *m* Alex North

LES MISERABLES.   Cedric Hardwicke allows Fredric March to steal the bishop's
candlesticks.

Clark Gable, Marilyn Monroe, Montgomery
Clift, Eli Wallach, Thelma Ritter, James
Barton, Estelle Winwood, Kevin McCarthy
● *Video: Warner*

The Misleading Lady
US 1932   75m   bw

A social butterfly aspires to be an actress.
Ho-hum romantic comedy, quite
unmemorable. Claudette Colbert, Edmund
Lowe, Stuart Erwin, Robert Strange, George
Meeker. Written by Adelaide Heilbron,
Caroline Francke, from the play by Charles
W. Goddard and Paul Dickey; directed by
Stuart Walker; for Paramount. 'Lightweight
stuff of conventional pattern.'—*Variety*

Miss Annie Rooney
US 1942   86m   bw
Edward Small

Poor Irish girl loves rich boy.
A totally routine offering for a teenage star;
no wonder she didn't make it.

w George Bruce *d* Edwin L. Marin
ph Lester White *md* Edward Paul

Shirley Temple, William Gargan, Guy Kibbee,
Dickie Moore, Peggy Ryan, Gloria Holden,
Jonathan Hale, Mary Field

Miss Fane's Baby Is Stolen
US 1933 67m bw

A film star's baby is kidnapped. Fairly straightforward crime yarn with comic asides. Dorothea Wieck, Alice Brady, Baby LeRoy, William Frawley, George Barbier, Alan Hale, Jack La Rue. Written by Adela Rogers St John, Rupert Hughes; directed by Alexander Hall; for Paramount. 'Box office as well as entertainment . . . the first picture of its kind since the Lindbergh kidnapping.'—*Variety* (GB title: *Kidnapped*.)

Miss Grant Takes Richmond*
US 1949 87m bw
Columbia (S. Sylvan Simon)
GB title: *Innocence Is Bliss*

A dumb secretary helps defeat crooks and improve the local housing situation.
Mildly amusing star comedy.

w Nat Perrin, Devery Freeman, Frank Tashlin *d* Lloyd Bacon *ph* Charles Lawton Jnr *m* Heinz Roemheld *md* Morris Stoloff

Lucille Ball, William Holden, Janis Carter, James Gleason, Gloria Henry, Frank McHugh, George Cleveland
'One of the more delightful comedies of the season.'—*Lawrence J. Quirk*

Miss Julie*
Sweden 1950 87m bw
Sandrew (Rene Waldekranz)

In a lonely house, the count's daughter kills herself after being seduced by a valet. Intense melodramatic fragment, just a little long for comfort.

wd Alf Sjoberg, *play* August Strindberg *ph* Goran Strindberg *m* Dag Wiren

Anita Bjork, Ulf Palme, Anders Henrison
'The outstanding achievement of the Swedish cinema in recent years.'—*Gavin Lambert, Sight and Sound*

Miss London Ltd
GB 1943 99m bw
GFD / Gainsborough (Edward Black)

An escort agency is formed to assist soldiers on leave.
Flagwaving light entertainment with popular performers of the time.

w Val Guest, Marriott Edgar *d* Val Guest

Arthur Askey, Anne Shelton, Evelyn Dall, Richard Hearne, Max Bacon, Jack Train, Peter Graves, Jean Kent

Miss Marple
Agatha Christie's inquisitive spinster detective was brought to the screen by director George Pollock and star Margaret Rutherford in four increasingly disappointing films for MGM.

1962: MURDER SHE SAID (qv)
1963: MURDER AT THE GALLOP
1964: MURDER MOST FOUL, MURDER AHOY
See also *The Mirror Crack'd.*

Miss Pacific Fleet
US 1935 76m bw

Two stranded show girls enter a popularity contest to win the fare back home. A comedy with little to laugh at. Glenda Farrell, Joan Blondell, Hugh Herbert, Allen Jenkins, Warren Hull, Guinn Williams. Written by Lucille Newmark, Peter Milne and Patsy Flick; directed by Ray Enright; for Warner. 'Maybe oke for double feature bills, but that's the best it can hope for.'—*Variety*

Miss Pilgrim's Progress
GB 1949 82m bw

An American working girl in Britain helps to save a village from development. Wholly artificial and unendearing comedy. Yolande Donlan, Michael Rennie, Garry Marsh, Emrys Jones, Reginald Beckwith, Helena Pickard, Jon Pertwee. Written and directed by Val Guest; for Daniel M. Angel.

Miss Pinkerton*
US 1932 66m bw
Warner

A private nurse helps a police detective to solve a murder case.
Pleasing little mystery comedy.

w Lilyan Hayward, Niven Busch, *story* Mary Roberts Rinehart *d* Lloyd Bacon *ph* Barney McGill

Joan Blondell, George Brent, Mae Madison, John Wray, Ruth Hall, C. Henry Gordon, Elizabeth Patterson
'Formula mystery story . . . picture is outdated and has nothing to draw.'—*Variety*
† Remade as *The Nurse's Secret* (1946).

Miss Robin Hood
GB 1952 78m bw

A lady author pits her wits against crooks and saves an old lady's fortune. Disappointing star comedy with no build-up. Margaret Rutherford, Richard Hearne, Michael Medwin, Peter Jones, James Robertson Justice, Sidney James, Dora Bryan. Written by Val Valentine, Patrick Campbell and Geoffrey Orme; directed by John Guillermin; for Group 3.

Miss Sadie Thompson*
US 1953 91m Technicolor 3-D
Columbia (Lewis J. Rachmil)

Vigorous semi-musical remake of *Rain* (qv); a good star vehicle, but not otherwise notable.

w Harry Kleiner *d* Curtis Bernhardt *ph* Charles Lawton *md* George Duning

Rita Hayworth, Jose Ferrer, Aldo Ray, Russell Collins, Harry Bellaver

AAN: song 'Blue Pacific Blues' (*m* Lester Lee, *ly* Ned Washington)

'A story for lovers . . . past, present and perfect!'

Miss Susie Slagle's
US 1946 88m bw
Paramount (John Houseman)

Romances of nursing students in 1910 Baltimore.

Modest melodramatic potboiler.

w Anne Froelich, Hugo Butler, *novel* Augusta Tucker *d* John Berry *ph* Charles Lang Jnr *m* Daniele Amfitheatrof

Veronica Lake, Joan Caulfield, Sonny Tufts, Lillian Gish, Ray Collins, Billy de Wolfe, Bill Edwards, Roman Bohnen, Morris Carnovsky, Lloyd Bridges

Miss Tatlock's Millions*
US 1948 101m bw
Paramount (Charles Brackett)

A stunt man impersonates the idiot heir to a fortune.
Tasteless but quite funny comedy with a cast of eccentrics indulging in enjoyable fooling.

w Charles Brackett, Richard L. Breen *d* Richard Haydn *ph* Charles Lang Jnr *m* Victor Young

John Lund, Wanda Hendrix, Monty Woolley, Barry Fitzgerald, Robert Stack, Ilka Chase, Dorothy Stickney

Miss V from Moscow
US 1943 70m bw

A Russian spy impersonates a German spy in Paris. Hilariously inept propaganda piece; since the Cold War it has been retitled *Intrigue in Paris*. Lola Lane, Noel Madison, Howard Banks. Written by Arthur St Claire and Sherman Lowe; directed by Albert Herman; for PRC.

Missing*
US 1982 122m Technicolor
Universal / Polygram / Peter Guber, Jon Peters (Edward and Mildred Lewis)

An American seeks his young son who has disappeared in Chile.
A further link in the chain of political thrillers from this director; well-wrought and compulsive but finally disappointing in its mixture of fact and fiction.

w Costa-Gavras, Donald Stewart, *book* Thomas Hauser *d* Costa-Gavras *ph* Ricardo Aronovich *m* Vangelis *pd* Peter Jamieson *ed* Françoise Bonnot

Jack Lemmon, Sissy Spacek, Melanie Mayron, John Shea, Charles Cioffi, Richard Bradford
'Provocation and entertainment prove to be uneasy allies.'—*Tom Milne, MFB*
AA: Screenplay (adaptation)
AAN: Jack Lemmon; best picture; Sissy Spacek
● *Video: CIC*

The Missing Juror
US 1944 71m bw

Members of a murder jury are killed off one by one. Minor puzzle piece from the *I Love a Mystery* series. Jim Bannon, Janis Carter, George Macready. Written by Charles O'Neal; directed by Budd Boetticher; for Columbia.

The Missing Rembrandt
GB 1932 82m bw

Sherlock Holmes saves a lady's honour and

nails a blackmailer. Not the best of this particular series, but Wontner is a Holmes to relish. Arthur Wontner, Ian Fleming, Jane Welsh, Miles Mander, Francis L. Sullivan. Written by Cyril Twyford and H. Fowler Mear, from the story *Charles Augustus Milverton* by Arthur Conan Doyle; directed by Leslie Hiscott; for Twickenham.

Mission to Moscow••
US 1943 112m bw
Warner (Robert Buckner)

The Russian career of US Ambassador Joseph E. Davies.
Stodgy but fascinating wartime propaganda piece viewing the Russians as warm-hearted allies; in the later days of the McCarthy witch hunt, Jack L. Warner regretted he had ever allowed it to be made.

w Howard Koch, *book* Joseph E. Davies
d Michael Curtiz ph Bert Glennon m Max Steiner

Walter Huston, Ann Harding, Oscar Homolka, George Tobias, Gene Lockhart, Eleanor Parker, Richard Travis, Helmut Dantine, Victor Francen, Henry Daniell, Barbara Everest, Dudley Field Malone, Roman Bohnen, Maria Palmer, Moroni Olsen, Minor Watson

'A mishmash: of Stalinism with New Dealism with Hollywoodism with opportunism with shaky experimentalism with mesmerism with onanism, all mosaicked into a remarkable portrait of what the makers of the film think the Soviet Union is like—a great glad two-million-dollar bowl of canned borscht, eminently approvable by the Institute of Good Housekeeping.'—*James Agee*

The Missionary•
GB 1983 86m colour Panavision
HandMade Films (Michael Palin)

In 1906, a clergyman returns from darkest Africa and sets up a Mission to Fallen Women in the East End of London.
Sporadically amusing comedy of a reformer being tempted; the decoration is funnier than the central theme.

w Michael Palin d Richard Loncraine
ph Peter Hannan m Mike Moran ad Norman Garwood

Michael Palin, Maggie Smith, Michael Hordern, Trevor Howard, Denholm Elliott, Graham Crowden, Phoebe Nichols, Roland Culver

'It leaves one with a half-frozen smile, in anticipation of a comic fulfilment which never quite happens.'—*Nick Roddick, MFB*
● Video: Thorn EMI

Mississippi•
US 1935 75m bw
Paramount (Arthur Hornblow Jnr)

A showboat singer has a cloud on his reputation.
Mild period musical with occasional stops for comedy.

w Herbert Fields, Claude Binyon, *story* Booth Tarkington d Edward A. Sutherland
ph Charles Lang m / ly Rodgers and Hart

Bing Crosby, W. C. Fields, Joan Bennett, Gail Patrick, Claude Gillingwater, John Miljan, Queenie Smith
'A dull film, rambling and hokey.'—*Variety*

Mississippi Gambler
US 1953 98m Technicolor
U-I (Ted Richmond)

A showboat gambler has trouble with a bad loser, but finally marries his sister.
Picturesque star melodrama with period settings and not much meat in the story.

w Seton I. Miller d Rudolph Maté ph Irving Glassberg m Frank Skinner

Tyrone Power, Piper Laurie, John McIntyre, Julia Adams, Dennis Weaver

The Missouri Breaks
US 1976 126m De Luxe
UA / Elliott Kastner / Robert B. Sherman

Montana ranchers and rustlers fight over land and livestock, and a hired killer shoots it out with a horse thief.
Savage, dislikeable western with both stars over the top.

w Thomas McGuane d Arthur Penn
ph Michael Butler m John Williams

Marlon Brando, Jack Nicholson, Randy Quaid, Kathleen Lloyd, Frederic Forrest, Harry Dean Stanton

'It is typical of the film's richness and ambiguity that the title has about five possible punning meanings.'—*Michael Billington, Illustrated London News*

'Although listed as the director, Mr Penn finds himself perched on Brando's knee and manipulated as shamelessly as Edgar Bergen used to waggle Charlie McCarthy.'—*Benny Green, Punch*

'Nothing more than the self-conscious cleverness of some merry prankster with a blanket of scorn for all who don't share his flippancy.'—*William S. Pechter*

'A pair of million dollar babies in a five and ten cent flick.'—*Charles Champlin, Los Angeles Times*

'A picture of which it might be said they shouldn't make 'em like that any more . . . a picture that explains very little, including why anyone thought it a work that demanded to be made.'—*Robert Hatch, Nation*
● Video: Warner

Mr Ace
US 1946 84m bw
Benedict Bogeaus

A rich, spoiled congresswoman is backed by a gangster but gets religion.
Odd star drama, perfunctorily made.

w Fred Finklehoffe d Edwin L. Marin
ph Karl Struss m Heinz Roemheld

Sylvia Sidney, George Raft, Stanley Ridges, Sara Haden, Jerome Cowan

Mr and Mrs Smith•
US 1941 95m bw
RKO (Harry E. Edington)

A much-married couple discover that their marriage wasn't legal.

Smartish matrimonial comedy, surprisingly but not obviously directed by the master of suspense.

w Norman Krasna d Alfred Hitchcock
ph Harry Stradling m Edward Ward

Carole Lombard, Robert Montgomery, Gene Raymond, Jack Carson, Philip Merivale, Lucile Watson, William Tracy

'I doubt that your interest or amusement will last as long as the picture.'—*Otis Ferguson*

Mr Belvedere Goes to College•
US 1949 88m bw
TCF (Samuel G. Engel)

A self-styled genius goes back to school and helps a college widow.
Flat follow up to *Sitting Pretty* (qv), with only a few laughs.

w Richard Sale, Mary Loos, Mary McCall Jnr
d Elliott Nugent ph Lloyd Ahern m Alfred Newman

Clifton Webb, Shirley Temple, Alan Young, Tom Drake, Jessie Royce Landis, Kathleen Hughes, Taylor Holmes

Mr Belvedere Rings the Bell•
US 1951 87m bw
TCF (André Hakim)

Imperturbable Mr Belvedere enters an old folks' home under false pretences to test his theories of ageing.
A not unagreeable star vehicle for those who can stand the sentiment.

w Ranald MacDougall, *play* The Silver Whistle by Robert E. McEnroe d Henry Koster ph Joseph La Shelle m Cyril Mockridge

Clifton Webb, Joanne Dru, Hugh Marlowe, Zero Mostel, Doro Merande

Mr Billion•
US 1977 93m De Luxe
TCF / Pantheon (Gabriel Katzka, Steve Bach, Ken Friedman)

An Italian garage mechanic becomes heir to a vast estate, providing he can get to San Francisco in time for the signing ceremony and outwit the villains trying to stop him.
Moderately engaging old-fashioned comedy-adventure.

w Ken Friedman, Jonathan Kaplan
d Jonathan Kaplan ph Matthew F. Leonetti
m Dave Grusin

Terence Hill, Valerie Perrine, Jackie Gleason, Slim Pickens, William Redfield, Chill Wills

Mr Blandings Builds His Dream House•••
US 1948 84m bw
RKO (Norman Panama, Melvin Frank)

A New York advertising man longs to live in the Connecticut countryside, but finds the way to rural satisfaction is hard.
It hasn't the lightness and brightness of the book, but this is a fun film for the middle-aged who like to watch three agreeable stars doing their thing.

MR AND MRS SMITH. Hitchcock's only comedy . . . and the reason he didn't try again was obvious.

w Norman Panama, Melvin Frank, *novel* Eric Hodgkin *d* H. C. Potter *ph* James Wong Howe *m* Leigh Harline *md* Constantin Bakaleinikoff

Cary Grant, Myrna Loy, Melvyn Douglas, Reginald Denny, Louise Beavers, Ian Wolfe, Harry Shannon, Nestor Paiva, Jason Robards
'A bulls-eye for middle-class middlebrows.' —James Agee
'I loved it. That was really a pleasure to make.'—H. C. Potter, 1973
● Video: Kingston

Mister Buddwing
US 1966 99m bw
MGM / DDD / Cherokee (Douglas Laurence, Delbert Mann)
GB title: *Woman without a Face*

An amnesiac wakes up in Central Park and goes in search of his identity.
Rather muddled melodrama in which the characters are so dull that by the time the flashbacks fall into place we scarcely care.

w Dale Wassermann, *novel* Buddwing by Evan Hunter *d* Delbert Mann *ph* Ellsworth Fredericks *m* Kenyon Hopkins

James Garner, Jean Simmons, Angela Lansbury, Suzanne Pleshette, Katharine Ross, George Voskovec, Jack Gilford, Joe Mantell, Raymond St Jacques

Mr Bug Goes to Town*
US 1941 78m Technicolor
Max Fleischer
aka: *Hoppity Goes to Town*

An urban community of insects is in danger from developers.
A cartoon feature which failed to make its mark despite clever detail; perhaps because insects make poor heroes, or because there simply wasn't enough plot.

d Dave Fleischer

Mister Cinderella
US 1936 75m bw

A meek-and-mild youth aspires to crash high society. Milk-and-water comedy with insufficient get-up-and-go. Jack Haley, Betty Furness, Arthur Treacher, Raymond Walburn, Rosina Lawrence, Monroe Owsley. Written by Arthur Vernon Jones, Richard Flournoy, Jack Jevne; directed by Edward Sedgwick; for Hal Roach / MGM. 'Too crammed with slaptrap hokum to stand alone.'—*Variety*

Mister Cory
US 1957 92m Eastmancolor Cinemascope
U-I (Robert Arthur)

A small-time gangster leaves the Chicago slums to seek fame and fortune among the country-club set.
Modest star comedy drama.

wd Blake Edwards *ph* Russell Metty *m* Joseph Gershenson

Tony Curtis, Martha Hyer, Charles Bickford, Kathryn Grant

Mr Deeds Goes to Town***
US 1936 118m bw
Columbia (Frank Capra)

A small-town poet inherits a vast fortune and sets New York on its heels by his honesty.
What once was fresh and charming now seems rather laboured in spots, and the production is parsimonious indeed, but the courtroom scene still works, and the good intentions conquer all.

w Robert Riskin, story Opera Hat by Clarence Budington Kelland d Frank Capra ph Joseph Walker m Adolph Deutsch md Howard Jackson

Gary Cooper, Jean Arthur, Raymond Walburn, Lionel Stander, Walter Catlett, George Bancroft, Douglass Dumbrille, H. B. Warner, Ruth Donnelly, Margaret Seddon, Margaret McWade

'I have an uneasy feeling he's on his way out. He's started to make pictures about themes instead of people.'—Alistair Cooke
'Everywhere the picture goes, from the endearing to the absurd, the accompanying business is carried through with perfect zip and relish.'—Otis Ferguson
'A comedy quite unmatched on the screen.'—Graham Greene
'The film culminates in a courtroom sequence that introduced the word "pixilated" to just about every American home, and set people to examining each other's casual scribbles or sketches—their "doodles".'—Pauline Kael, 70s

AA: Frank Capra
AAN: best picture; Robert Riskin; Gary Cooper

Mr Denning Drives North
GB 1951 93m bw
London Films (Anthony Kimmins, Stephen Mitchell)

A wealthy man accidentally kills a criminal in love with his daughter; he hides the body, which then disappears.
Initially suspenseful but finally disappointing melodrama which seems to lack a twist or two.

w Alec Coppel d Anthony Kimmins ph John Wilcox m Benjamin Frankel

John Mills, Phyllis Calvert, Sam Wanamaker, Freda Jackson

Mr Dodd Takes the Air
US 1937 78m bw
Warner (Mervyn Le Roy)

A country cousin becomes a hit as a crooner.
Modest comedy for small towns.

w William Wister Haines, Elaine Ryan, story Clarence Budington Kelland d Alfred E. Green ph Arthur Edeson songs Al Dubin, Harry Warren

Kenny Baker, Jane Wyman, Alice Brady, Gertrude Michael, Frank McHugh, Luis Alberni, Henry O'Neill, Harry Davenport

AAN: Al Dubin and Harry Warren for 'Remember Me'

Mr Drake's Duck**
GB 1950 85m bw
Daniel M. Angel / Douglas Fairbanks

A duck lays a uranium egg, and a gentleman farmer finds himself at the centre of international military disagreement.
Brisk and amusing minor comedy deploying British comic types to good purpose.

wd Val Guest, radio play Ian Messiter ph Jack Cox m Philip Martell

Douglas Fairbanks Jnr, Yolande Donlan, Wilfrid Hyde White, A. E. Matthews, Jon Pertwee, Reginald Beckwith, Howard Marion-Crawford, Peter Butterworth, Tom Gill

Mr Dynamite
US 1935 75m bw

An unconventional private detective outsmarts the police. Amusing, wisecracking crime caper. Edmund Lowe, Jean Dixon, Esther Ralston, Victor Varconi, Minor Watson, Robert Gleckler. Written by Doris Malloy, Harry Clork, from a story by Dashiell Hammett; directed by Alan Crosland; for Universal. 'Nice entertainment.'—Variety

Mister 880**
US 1950 90m bw
TCF (Julian Blaustein)

An elderly counterfeiter perplexes the US Secret Service.
Whimsical star comedy which moves along cheerfully enough to be a good example of the Hollywood programmer at its prime.

w Robert Riskin d Edmund Goulding ph Joseph La Shelle m Sol Kaplan

Edmund Gwenn, Burt Lancaster, Dorothy McGuire, Millard Mitchell

AAN: Edmund Gwenn

Mr Emmanuel*
GB 1944 97m bw
Two Cities (William Sistrom)

In 1936 an elderly Jew visits Germany in search of the mother of an orphan boy.
Simply made but quite effective and unusual story giving Aylmer his only star part.

w Gordon Wellesley, Norman Ginsburg, novel Louis Golding d Harold French ph Otto Heller

Felix Aylmer, Greta Gynt, Walter Rilla, Peter Mullins, Ursula Jeans, Elspeth March, Meier Tzelniker

Mr Forbush and the Penguins*
GB 1971 101m Technicolor
EMI / PGI / Henry Trettin

A biologist is sent to the Antarctic to study penguins, and gets a new understanding of life.
Rather broken-backed animal film with a moral; pleasant enough, its two halves don't fit together.

w Anthony Shaffer, novel Graham Billey d Roy Boulting, Arne Sucksdorff ph Harry Waxman, Ted Scaife m John Addison

John Hurt, Hayley Mills, Tony Britton

Mr Hobbs Takes a Vacation*
US 1962 116m De Luxe Cinemascope
TCF (Jerry Wald)

A city dweller takes a seaside house for a family holiday, but it turns out to be a crumbling ruin.
Overlong, sloppy comedy which devotes too much time to teenage romance but manages occasional smiles.

w Nunnally Johnson, novel Edward Streeter d Henry Koster ph W. C. Mellor m Henry Mancini

James Stewart, Maureen O'Hara, Fabian, John Saxon, Marie Wilson, Reginald Gardiner, John McGiver

Mr Imperium
US 1951 87m Technicolor
MGM (Edwin H. Knopf)
GB title: You Belong to My Heart

An exiled king in Hollywood meets a famous film star with whom he once had a romance.
Minor romantic drama with songs.

w Edwin Knopf, Don Hartman d Don Hartman ph George J. Folsey songs Harold Arlen m Bronislau Kaper

Lana Turner, Ezio Pinza, Marjorie Main, Barry Sullivan, Cedric Hardwicke, Debbie Reynolds

Mr Klein*
France / Italy 1976 123m Eastmancolor
Lira / Adel / Nova / Mondial Te-Fi (Raymond Danon, Alain Delon)

In 1942 Paris, a prosperous antique dealer is mistaken for a mysterious Jew of the same name, and despite the danger gradually assumes his identity.
Complex Kafkaesque character study: occasionally arresting but generally rather glum.

w Franco Solinas d Joseph Losey ph Gerry Fisher m Egisto Macchi, Pierre Porte

Alain Delon, Jeanne Moreau, Suzanne Flon, Michael Lonsdale, Louis Seigner, Juliet Berto

Mr Lucky*
US 1943 98m bw
RKO (David Hempstead)

During World War II a gambling ship owner goes straight and instigates Bundles for Britain.
Unconvincing mixture of comedy and drama with the actors looking somewhat bewildered.

w Milton Holmes, Adrian Scott d H. C. Potter ph George Barnes m Roy Webb

Cary Grant, Laraine Day, Charles Bickford, Gladys Cooper, Alan Carney, Henry Stephenson, Paul Stewart, Walter Kingsford

'If it weren't for Cary Grant's persuasive personality the whole thing would melt away to nothing at all.'—Philip G. Hartung
† Remade 1950 as Gambling House.

Mr Majestyk*

US 1974 103m De Luxe
UA / Mirisch (Walter Mirisch)

A Colorado melon grower crosses swords with the local Mafia.
Violent but unexpectedly enjoyable action melodrama.

w Elmore Leonard d Richard Fleischer
ph Richard Kline m Charles Bernstein

Charles Bronson, Al Lettieri, Linda Cristal, Lee Purcell, Paul Keslo

Mr Mom

US 1983 91m Metrocolor

Dad loses his executive job and stays home to mind the kids while his wife works. Obvious farce with too much messy slapstick and no real development. Michael Keaton, Teri Garr, Frederick Koehler, Martin Mull, Ann Jillian. Written by John Hughes; directed by Stan Dragoti; for Aaron Spelling / Sherwood. (GB title: Mr Mum.) 'The jokes almost sink without trace in a hazy domestic setting straight from the hoariest sitcom.'—Geoff Brown, MFB

Mister Moses*

GB 1965 103m Technicolor
Panavision
UA / Frank Ross / Talbot

A quack doctor is the only person who can persuade an African tribe to move before their land is flooded, and he leads them to their promised land.
Adventure spectacle with naïve biblical parallels; quite agreeable.

w Charles Beaumont, Monja Danischewsky, novel Max Catto d Ronald Neame
ph Oswald Morris m John Barry

Robert Mitchum, Carroll Baker, Ian Bannen, Alexander Knox, Reginald Beckwith, Raymond St Jacques

Mr Moto

The Japanese detective created by John P. Marquand and played by Peter Lorre figured in several above-average second features of the late thirties, but the outbreak of war caused him to vanish. The casts were interesting, the TCF production excellent, and the director usually Norman Foster. The 1965 attempt to revive the character with Henry Silva was painfully boring.

1937: THINK FAST MR MOTO (with Virginia Field, Sig Rumann), THANK YOU MR MOTO (with Pauline Frederick, Sidney Blackmer)
1938: MR MOTO'S GAMBLE (with Keye Luke, Lynn Bari), MR MOTO TAKES A CHANCE (with Rochelle Hudson, J. Edward Bromberg), MYSTERIOUS MR MOTO (with Henry Wilcoxon, Erik Rhodes)
1939: MR MOTO'S LAST WARNING (with Ricardo Cortez, George Sanders, Robert Coote, John Carradine), MR MOTO IN DANGER ISLAND (with Jean Hersholt, Warren Hymer), MR MOTO TAKES A VACATION (with Joseph Schildkraut, Lionel Atwill)
1965: THE RETURN OF MR MOTO

Mr Music*

US 1950 113m bw
Paramount (Robert L. Welch)

A college girl is employed to keep an idle middle-aged songwriter's nose to the grindstone.
Bland musical remake of Accent on Youth (qv); pleasant performances, moments of comedy, guest stars.

w Arthur Sheekman d Richard Haydn
ph George Barnes songs Johnny Burke, James Van Heusen ad Hans Dreier, Earl Hedrick

Bing Crosby, Nancy Olson, Charles Coburn, Ruth Hussey, Marge and Gower Champion, Peggy Lee, Groucho Marx

Mr Peabody and the Mermaid

US 1948 89m bw
U-I (Nunnally Johnson)

A middle-aged husband imagines an affair with a mermaid.
Bone-headed quick-cash-in on Miranda (qv); it never begins to work.

w Nunnally Johnson, novel Guy and Constance Jones d Irving Pichel ph Russell Metty m Robert Emmett Dolan

William Powell, Ann Blyth, Irene Hervey, Andrea King, Clinton Sundberg

Mr Perrin and Mr Traill*

GB 1948 92m bw
GFD / Two Cities (Alexander Galperson)

A handsome young master at a boys' school incurs the jealousy of an embittered colleague.
Flat, over-acted but mildly watchable picturization of a well-known story.

w L. A. G. Strong, novel Hugh Walpole
d Lawrence Huntington ph Erwin Hillier
m Alan Gray

Marius Goring, David Farrar, Greta Gynt, Edward Chapman, Raymond Huntley, Mary Jerrold, Finlay Currie, Ralph Truman

Mister Quilp

GB 1975 119m Technicolor
Panavision
Reader's Digest (Helen M. Straus)
aka: The Old Curiosity Shop

In 1840 London, an antique-shop owner is in debt to a hunchback moneylender who has designs on his business.
The novel, with its villainous lead, is a curious choice for musicalizing, and in this treatment falls desperately flat, with no sparkle of imagination visible anywhere.

w Louis Kamp, Irene Kamp, novel The Old Curiosity Shop by Charles Dickens d Michael Tuchner ph Christopher Challis m Anthony Newley pd Elliot Scott md Elmer Bernstein ch Gillian Lynne

Anthony Newley, Michael Hordern, David Hemmings, Sarah-Jane Varley, David Warner, Paul Rogers, Jill Bennett
'Another soggy piece of family entertainment from Reader's Digest, who produced the toothless screen musicals of Tom Sawyer and Huckleberry Finn.'—Philip French

'Dickens shorn of sentiment, melodrama or love . . . Mr Newley's Quilp, a galvanized Quasimodo on a permanent high, is something of a strain to watch.'—Michael Billington, Illustrated London News

Mr Ricco

US 1975 98m Panavision colour
MGM (Douglas Netter)

A defence counsel risks his life to prove his black client innocent.
Complex urban action thriller with a tired, ageing hero and impenetrable plot.

w Robert Hoban d Paul Bogart ph Frank Stanley m Chico Hamilton

Dean Martin, Eugene Roche, Thalmus Rasulala, Denise Nicholas, Cindy Williams, Geraldine Brooks, Frank Puglia

Mister Roberts**

US 1955 123m Warnercolor
Cinemascope
Warner / Leland Hayward

Life aboard a World War II cargo ship yearning for action.
A mixture of comedy and sentimentality which has become an American minor classic as a play; this film version is a shambling affair but gets most of the effects over.

w Frank Nugent, Joshua Logan, play Thomas Heggen and Joshua Logan, novel Thomas Heggen d John Ford, Mervyn Le Roy ph Winton Hoch m Franz Waxman

Henry Fonda, James Cagney, William Powell, Jack Lemmon, Betsy Palmer, Ward Bond, Phil Carey, Ken Curtis, Harry Carey Jnr

AA: Jack Lemmon
AAN: best picture

Mr Robinson Crusoe

US 1932 76m bw
Douglas Fairbanks

A playboy takes a bet that he could live alone on a desert island . . . but a girl turns up.
Mild adventure comedy with the star in subdued form.

w Douglas Fairbanks d Edward Sutherland ph Max Dupont m Alfred Newman

Douglas Fairbanks, William Farnum, Earle Browne, Maria Alba

Mr Sardonicus

US 1961 90m bw
Columbia / William Castle

A surgeon is lured to an ex-girl friend's remote home to cure her sadistic husband's crippled face.
Flatly handled, boring semi-horror.

w Robb White d William Castle ph Burnett Guffey m Von Dexter

Ronald Lewis, Guy Rolfe, Audrey Dalton, Oscar Homolka

Mr Scoutmaster

US 1953 87m bw
TCF

A TV personality wants to understand children and is persuaded to take over a scout troop.

A star vehicle which starts promisingly enough in the *Sitting Pretty* vein but quickly falls headlong into an abyss of sentimentality.

w Leonard Praskins, Barney Slater *d* Henry Levin *ph* Joseph La Shelle *m* Cyril Mockridge, *md* Lionel Newman

Clifton Webb, Edmund Gwenn, George Winslow, Frances Dee, Veda Ann Borg

Mr Skeffington***
US 1944 127m bw
Warner (Julius J. and Philip G. Epstein)

A selfish beauty finally turns to her discarded dull husband; when he is blind, he doesn't mind her faded looks.

Long, patchily made, but thoroughly enjoyable star melodrama.

w Julius J. and Philip G. Epstein, *novel* 'Elizabeth' *d* Vincent Sherman *ph* Ernest Haller *m* Franz Waxman

Bette Davis, Claude Rains, Walter Abel, Richard Waring, George Coulouris, John Alexander, Jerome Cowan

'An endless woman's page dissertation on What To Do When Beauty Fades.'—*James Agee*

'To call the film a good one would be to exaggerate; but entertaining and interesting, I insist, it is.'—*Richard Mallett, Punch*

AAN: Bette Davis; Claude Rains

Mr Skitch
US 1933 70m bw

A Missouri family heads for California. Very passable star family entertainment. Will Rogers, Zasu Pitts, Florence Desmond, Rochelle Hudson. Written by Anne Cameron from her novel *Green Dice*; directed by James Cruze; for TCF. 'Enough laughs to please in general.'—*Variety*

'Stirring—in the seeing! Precious—in the remembering!'
Mr Smith Goes to Washington****
US 1939 130m bw
Columbia (Frank Capra)

Washington's youngest senator exposes corruption in high places, almost at the cost of his own career.

Archetypal high-flying Capra vehicle, with the little man coming out top as he seldom does in life. Supreme gloss hides the corn, helter-skelter direction keeps one watching, and all concerned give memorable performances. A cinema classic.

w Sidney Buchman, *story* Lewis R. Foster *d* Frank Capra *ph* Joseph Walker *m* Dmitri Tiomkin *montage* Slavko Vorkapich

James Stewart, Claude Rains, Jean Arthur, Thomas Mitchell, Edward Arnold, Guy Kibbee, Eugene Pallette, Beulah Bondi, *Harry Carey*, H. B. Warner, Astrid Allwyn, Ruth Donnelly, Charles Lane, Porter Hall

SMITH (James Stewart): 'I wouldn't give you two cents for all your fancy rules if, behind them, they didn't have a little bit of plain, ordinary kindness—and a little looking out for the other fella, too.'

'Timely and absorbing drama presented in best Capra craftsmanship.'—*Variety*

'More fun, even, than the Senate itself . . . not merely a brilliant jest, but a stirring and even inspiring testament to liberty and freedom.'—*Frank S. Nugent, New York Times*

'A totally compelling piece of movie-making, upholding the virtues of traditional American ideals.'—*NFT, 1973*

'Very good, beautifully done and extremely entertaining; long, but worth the time it takes.'—*Richard Mallett, Punch*

'More of the heartfelt than is good for the stomach.'—*New Yorker, 1977*

AA: Lewis R. Foster
AAN: best picture; Sidney Buchman; Frank Capra; Dmitri Tiomkin; James Stewart; Claude Rains; Harry Carey

Mr Soft Touch
US 1949 93m bw

A gangster is reformed at Christmas by a social worker. Dewy-eyed romance with Damon Runyonish asides; only for soft touches. Glenn Ford, Evelyn Keyes, John Ireland, Beulah Bondi, Percy Kilbride, Roman Bohnen. Written by Orin Jannings; directed by Henry Levin and Gordon Douglas; for Columbia. (GB title: *House of Settlement*.)

Mr Topaze
GB 1961 84m Eastmancolor
Cinemascope
TCF / Dimitri de Grunwald (Pierre Rouve)
US title: *I Like Money*

An honest ex-schoolmaster becomes prosperous when he joins some shady businessmen.

Predictable, sluggish character comedy, with a good actor unable to make it as a star. Or as a director.

w Pierre Rouve, *play* Topaze by Marcel Pagnol *d* Peter Sellers *ph* John Wilcox *m* Georges Van Parys

Peter Sellers, Herbert Lom, Leo McKern, Nadia Gray, Martita Hunt, John Neville, Billie Whitelaw, Michael Gough, Joan Sims, John Le Mesurier, Michael Sellers

'A film of minor pleasures and major inadequacies.'—*Penelope Houston, MFB*

† See also *Topaze* (1933).

Mr Winkle Goes to War
US 1944 80m bw
Columbia (Jack Moss)
GB title: *Arms and the Woman*

A middle-aged bank clerk joins the army and becomes a hero.

Agreeable, forgettable propaganda comedy-drama.

w Waldo Salt, George Corey, Louis Solomon, *novel* Theodore Pratt *d* Alfred E. Green *ph* Joseph Walker *m* Carmen Dragon, Paul Sawtell

Edward G. Robinson, Ruth Warrick, Ted Donaldson, Bob Haymes, Richard Lane, Robert Armstrong, Walter Baldwin

Mr Wong
A cheeseparing set of second features from Monogram, based on stories by Hugh Wiley. Boris Karloff was unsuitably cast as a Chinese detective, and in the last film he was replaced by Keye Luke. The films were directed by William Nigh.

1938: MR WONG DETECTIVE
1939: THE MYSTERY OF MR WONG, MR WONG IN CHINATOWN
1940: THE FATAL HOUR, DOOMED TO DIE (GB title: THE MYSTERY OF THE WENTWORTH CASTLE)
1941: PHANTOM OF CHINATOWN

Mr Wu*
US 1927 80m approx (24 fps) bw
silent
MGM

A Chinese villain kills his daughter when she wants to marry an Englishman.

Turgid outmoded melodrama from a stage success: purely a star vehicle.

w Lorna Moon, *play* Maurice Vernon, Harold Owen *d* William Nigh *ph* John Arnold

Lon Chaney, Louise Dresser, Anna May Wong, Ralph Forbes, Renee Adoree, Holmes Herbert

Mrs Fitzherbert
GB 1947 99m bw
British National

The Prince Regent secretly marries a Catholic widow.

Stilted, ill-cast historical charade.

w Montgomery Tully, *novel* Winifred Carter *d* Montgomery Tully *ph* James Wilson *m* Hans May

Peter Graves, Joyce Howard, Leslie Banks, Margaretta Scott

Mrs Gibbons' Boys
GB 1962 82m bw Byronscope

A widow plans to marry respectably for the sake of her three convict sons. Unattractive farce with clodhopping characters and too much slapstick. Kathleen Harrison, Lionel Jeffries, Diana Dors, John Le Mesurier, Frederick Bartman, David Lodge, Dick Emery, Eric Pohlmann, Milo O'Shea. Written by Peter Blackmore and Max Varnel, from the play by Joseph Stein and Will Glickman; directed by Max Varnel; for Byron / British Lion.

Mrs Mike
US 1949 99m bw
Nassour / Huntingdon Hartford (Edward Gross)

A Mountie takes his new wife to live in the frozen northwest.

Predictable sentimental drama, well enough done to keep interest, but only just.

w Lewis Levitt, De'Witt Bodeen *d* Louis King *ph* Joseph Biroc *m* Max Steiner

Dick Powell, Evelyn Keyes, J. M. Kerrigan, Angela Clarke

Mrs Miniver**
US 1942   134m   bw
MGM (Sidney Franklin)

An English housewife survives World War II.
This is the rose-strewn English village,
Hollywood variety, but when released it
proved a beacon of morale despite its false
sentiment, absurd rural types and
melodramatic situations. It is therefore beyond
criticism, except that some of the people
involved should have known better.

w Arthur Wimperis, George Froeschel, James
Hilton, Claudine West, *novel* Jan Struther
d William Wyler *ph* Joseph Ruttenberg
m Herbert Stothart

Greer Garson, Walter Pidgeon, Teresa Wright,
Richard Ney, Dame May Whitty, Henry
Travers, Reginald Owen, Henry Wilcoxon,
Helmut Dantine, Rhys Williams, Aubrey
Mather

VICAR (Henry Wilcoxon) preaching final
sermon in bombed church: 'This is not only a
war of soldiers in uniforms. It is a war of the
people—of all the people—and it must be
fought not only on the battlefield but in the
cities and in the villages, in the factories and
on the farms, in the home and in the heart of
every man, woman and child who loves
freedom. Well, we have buried our dead, but
we shall not forget them. Instead, they will
inspire us with an unbreakable determination
to free ourselves and those who come after us
from the tyranny and terror that threaten to
strike us down. This is the people's war. It is
our war. We are the fighters. Fight it, then.
Fight it with all that is in us. And may God
defend the right.'

'That almost impossible feat, a war picture
that photographs the inner meaning, instead
of the outward realism of World War II.'—
Time

AA: best picture; script; William Wyler;
Joseph Ruttenberg; Greer Garson; Teresa
Wright
AAN: Walter Pidgeon; Dame May Whitty;
Henry Travers

Mrs O'Malley and Mr Malone*
US 1950   69m   bw
MGM (William H. Wright)

On a train to New York, a radio contest
winner and a lawyer help solve a murder.
Lively second feature farce.

w William Bowers *d* Norman Taurog
ph Adolph Deutsch

Marjorie Main, James Whitmore, Ann
Dvorak, Fred Clark, Dorothy Malone, Phyllis
Kirk

Mrs Parkington
US 1944   124m   bw
MGM (Leon Gordon)

A lady's maid marries a miner who becomes
wealthy, and pushes her way into society.
Thoroughly unconvincing three-generation
drama, with a bewigged and powdered star
giving the boot to her conniving relations. It
has production values and nothing else.

w Robert Thoeren, Polly James, *novel* Louis
Bromfield *d* Tay Garnett *ph* Joseph
Ruttenberg *m* Bronislau Kaper

Greer Garson, Walter Pidgeon, Edward
Arnold, Agnes Moorehead, Cecil Kellaway,
Gladys Cooper, Frances Rafferty, Tom
Drake, Peter Lawford, Dan Duryea, Hugh
Marlowe, Selena Royle
† The heroine is shown having a romance with
Edward VII when Prince of Wales; special
scenes were shot for the European version
substituting Cecil Kellaway, who played
Edward, by Hugo Haas who played a
European king of indeterminate origin.
AAN: Greer Garson; Agnes Moorehead

Mrs Pollifax—Spy
US 1970   110m   De Luxe
UA / Mellor (Frederick Brisson)

A respectable American matron offers her
services to the CIA and sees active service in
Albania.
Incredible comedy-dramatic vehicle for a star
who won't give up. An obvious failure from
the word go.

w C. A. McKnight, *novel* Dorothy Gilman
d Leslie Martinson *ph* Joseph Biroc *m* Lalo
Schifrin

Rosalind Russell, Darren McGavin
† C. A. McKnight was Rosalind Russell.

Mrs Pym of Scotland Yard
GB 1939   65m   bw

A lady detective exposes a fake spiritualist. A
would-be series character bites the dust
through plot malnutrition. Mary Clare,
Edward Lexy, Nigel Patrick, Anthony Ireland,
Irene Handl. Written by Fred Elles, Peggy
Barwell and Nigel Morland, from the novel by
Nigel Morland; directed by Fred Elles; for
Hurley / Grand National.

Mrs Wiggs of the Cabbage Patch*
US 1934   80m   bw
Paramount (Douglas MacLean)

Adventures of a poor family who live on the
wrong side of the tracks in a broken down old
shack.
A Depression fantasy of respectability and
optimism, almost incredible to see now,
although it plumbed the same never-never
milieu as did Chaplin. Moments of comedy
still please, but one does long for Mr Fields'
delayed entry.

w William Slavens McNutt, Jane Storm, *novel*
Alice Hegan Rice *d* Norman Taurog
ph Charles Lang

Pauline Lord, *Zasu Pitts, W. C. Fields*, Evelyn
Venable, Kent Taylor, Charles Middleton,
Donald Meek, Edith Fellows, Virginia
Weidler, George Breakston

'A nasty all's-right-with-the-world burlesque
of poverty, with emotions to tug at such
heartstrings as are worn dangling from the
mouth.'—*Otis Ferguson*

Mrs Wiggs of the Cabbage Patch
US 1942   80m   bw
Paramount

Curiously quick remake, almost word for
word, but without the moments of inspiration.

w Doris Anderson, Jane Storm, William
Slavens McNutt *d* Ralph Murphy *ph* Leo
Tover

Fay Bainter, Hugh Herbert, Vera Vague,
Barbara Britton, Carl Switzer, Moroni Olsen,
Billy Lee

Mix Me a Person
GB 1961   116m   bw
Wessex (Sergei Nolbandov)

A barrister's psychiatrist wife takes on one of
his failures, a client condemned to death for
murder.
Once it gets started, a routine suspense thriller
with the wrong man convicted and an espresso
bar background. Not a very good one, though.

w Ian Dalrymple, *novel* Jack Trevor Story
d Leslie Norman *ph* Ted Moore
songs Johnny Worth *md* Muir Mathieson

Anne Baxter, Donald Sinden, Adam Faith,
Walter Brown, Glyn Houston

Mixed Company
US 1974   109m   De Luxe
UA / Cornell (Melville Shavelson)

A basketball coach and his wife adopt several
children of different races.
Room for One More and then some, but not
very interesting.

w Melville Shavelson, Mort Lachman
d Melville Shavelson *ph* Stan Lazan *m* Fred
Karlin *pd* Stan Jolley

Barbara Harris, Joseph Bologna, Lisa
Gerritson, Arianne Heller

M'liss
US 1936   66m   bw

A drunkard's daughter washes dishes in a
western saloon. Laundered and fairly inept
family version of a roistering tale. Anne
Shirley, Guy Kibbee, John Beal, Douglass
Dumbrille, Moroni Olsen, Arthur Hoyt.
Written by Dorothy Yost, from the story by
Bret Harte; directed by George Nicholls Jnr;
for RKO.

The Mob*
US 1951   87m   bw
Columbia (Jerry Bresler)
GB title: *Remember That Face*

A policeman works undercover to catch a
dockside racketeer.
Tough, lively thriller with effectively sustained
mystery and a serial-like finale.

w William Bowers *d* Robert Parrish
ph Joseph Walker *m* George Duning

Broderick Crawford, Richard Kiley, Ernest
Borgnine, Neville Brand, Charles Bronson

Mob Town
US 1941   61m   bw

A policeman tries to rehabilitate the young

brother of an executed gangster. Another
spin-off from the Dead End Kids, quite
unremarkable. Dick Foran, Anne Gwynne,
Billy Halop, Huntz Hall, Bernard Punsley,
Gabriel Dell, Samuel S. Hinds. Written by
Brenda Weisberg; directed by William Nigh;
for Universal.

'America's greatest actor—as you like him!'
Moby Dick*
US 1930   75m   bw
Warner

Captain Ahab returns minus a leg from
fighting the white whale, and finds that his
fiancée is too shocked to love him.
Mangled remake of a fine novel filmed in
silent form as *The Sea Beast*.

w J. Grubb Alexander, *novel* Herman
Melville d Lloyd Bacon ph Robert Kurrie

John Barrymore, Joan Bennett, Lloyd
Hughes, May Boley, Walter Long
    'Money picture, guaranteed by its action
and by Barrymore.'—*Variety*

Moby Dick**
GB 1956   116m   Technicolor
Warner / Moulin (John Huston)

A whaling skipper is determined to harpoon
the white whale which robbed him of a leg.
Pretentious period adventure, rather too
obsessed with symbolism and certainly too
slowly developed, but full of interesting detail
which almost outweighs the central miscasting.

w Ray Bradbury, John Huston, *novel* Herman
Melville d John Huston ph Oswald Morris
m Philip Stainton

Gregory Peck, Richard Basehart, Friedrich
Ledebur, Leo Genn, Orson Welles, James
Robertson Justice, Harry Andrews, Bernard
Miles, Noel Purcell, Edric Connor, Joseph
Tomelty, Mervyn Johns
    'Interesting more often than exciting.'—
Variety

● *Video: Thorn EMI*

Mockery
US 1927   75m approx at 24 fps   bw
    silent

A noble peasant saves a countess from the
Russian revolution. Overly serious vehicle for
a star more at ease in melodrama. Lon
Chaney, Barbara Belford, Ricardo Cortez,
Emily Fitzroy. Written and directed by
Benjamin Christensen; for MGM.

The Model and the Marriage Broker
US 1951   103m   bw
TCF (Charles Brackett)

A broker conceals her profession from a friend
but gets the friend fixed up.
Moderate, unsurprising comedy somewhat
overweighted by talent which can't express
itself.

w Charles Brackett, Walter Reisch, Richard
Breen d George Cukor ph Milton Krasner
m Cyril Mockridge

Thelma Ritter, Jeanne Crain, Scott Brady,
Zero Mostel, Michael O'Shea, Nancy Kulp

Model Wife
US 1941   78m   bw

Young marrieds must pretend to be single in
order to keep their jobs. Tedious comedy.
Joan Blondell, Dick Powell, Charles Ruggles,
Lee Bowman, Lucile Watson. Written by
Charles Kaufman, Horace Jackson and Grant
Garrett; directed by Leigh Jason; for
Universal.

A Modern Hero*
US 1934   70m   bw

A young circus rider becomes an automobile
tycoon but overreaches himself. Unconvincing
moral tale, performed and presented with nice
touches. Richard Barthelmess, Jean Muir,
Marjorie Ranbeau, Verree Teasdale, Florence
Eldredge. Written by Gene Markey and
Kathryn Scola, from the novel by Louis
Bromfield; directed by G. W. Pabst; for
Warners. 'Essentially weak on plot and
characterization.'—*Variety*

'You'll never laugh as long and as loud
again as long as you live! The laughs
come so fast and so furious you'll wish it
would end before you collapse!'
Modern Times***
US 1936   87m   bw
Charles Chaplin

An assembly-line worker goes berserk but
can't get another job.
Silent star comedy produced in the middle of
the sound period; flashes of genius alternate
with sentimental sequences and jokes without
punch.

wd / m Charles Chaplin ph Rollie Totheroh,
Ira Morgan

Charles Chaplin, Paulette Goddard, Henry
Bergman, Chester Conklin, Tiny Sandford
    'A natural for the world market . . . box
office with a capital B.'—*Variety*
    'A feature picture made out of several one-
and two-reel shorts, proposed titles being *The
Shop, The Jailbird, The Singing Waiter*.'—*Otis
Ferguson*

● *Video: Polygram*

Modesty Blaise
GB 1966   119m   Technicolor
TCF / Modesty Blaise Ltd (Joseph Janni)

Female arch-agent Modesty Blaise defends a
shipload of diamonds against a sadistic master
criminal.
Comic-strip adventures made by people with
no sense of humour; Fu Manchu was much
more fun.

w Evan Jones, *comic strip* Peter O'Donnell,
Jim Holdaway d Joseph Losey ph Jack
Hildyard m Johnny Dankworth

Monica Vitti, Dirk Bogarde, Terence Stamp,
Harry Andrews, Michael Craig, Scilla Gabel,
Clive Revill, Rossella Falk, Joe Melia

● *Video: CBS / Fox*

'Flaming love found in the savage heart of
the jungle!'
Mogambo*
GB 1953   116m   Technicolor
MGM (Sam Zimbalist)

The headquarters of a Kenyan white hunter is
invaded by an American showgirl and a British
archaeologist and his wife, and they all go off
on a gorilla hunt.
Amiable, flabby remake of *Red Dust*, with
direction scarcely in evidence and the gorillas
out-acting a genial cast.

w John Lee Mahin d John Ford ph Robert
Surtees, F. A. Young

Clark Gable, Ava Gardner, Grace Kelly,
Donald Sinden, Laurence Naismith, Philip
Stainton

† The story was also made as *Congo Maisie* in
1940.

AAN: Ava Gardner; Grace Kelly

Mohammed, Messenger of God
Lebanon 1976   182m   Eastmancolor
Panavision
Filmco International (Moustapha Akkad)
aka: *The Message*

The life of the seventh-century religious
leader.
Predictably reverential and exceedingly
tedious religious epic, rather like a lesser de
Mille item and fatally handicapped by the
decision never to show Mohammed at all.

w H. A. L. Craig (with Arab advice)
d Moustapha Akkad ph Jack Hildyard
m Maurice Jarre pd Tambi Larsen, Maurice
Fowler

Anthony Quinn, Irene Papas, Michael Ansara,
Johnny Sekka, Michael Forest, André Morell
    'For well over three hours this film
stumbles, staggers, lurches and bumbles
ahead, without any true rhythm, construction,
vision, or even bare minimum of craft.'—*John
Simon, New York*

'Horror crawls from the depths of the
earth!'
The Mole People
US 1956   78m   bw

Archaeologists fall down a shaft and find
themselves in a subterranean civilization
where mole people are ruled by albinos.
Thoroughly boring nonsense which would
insult a Saturday matinee. John Agar, Cynthia
Patrick, Hugh Beaumont, Alan Napier.
Written by Lazlo Gorog; directed by Virgil
Vogel; for Universal–International.

Molly and Me
US 1945   76m   bw
TCF

A cantankerous old man is tamed by his new
housekeeper.
Sentimental little star vehicle.

w Leonard Praskins d Lewis Seiler
ph Charles G. Clarke m Cyril Mockridge

Gracie Fields, Monty Woolley, Reginald
Gardiner, Roddy McDowall, Natalie Schaefer,
Edith Barrett

† This followed the more successful teaming of the stars in *Holy Matrimony*.

The Molly Maguires
US 1970 123m Technicolor
Panavision
Paramount / Tamm (Martin Ritt, Walter Bernstein)

In the Pennsylvania coalmining district in the 1870s, an undercover detective exposes the leaders of a secret society.
Sober-sided and slow-moving account of actual events which also formed the basis for Conan Doyle's rather more entertaining *The Valley of Fear*. Expensive, nicely photographed, but unpersuasive and empty.

w Walter Bernstein *d* Martin Ritt *ph* James Wong Howe *m* Henry Mancini

Richard Harris, Sean Connery, Samantha Eggar, Frank Finlay, Anthony Zerbe, Bethel Leslie, Art Lund
'The film's vague sense of grievance and harrowing circumstances hangs in the air like the smoky pall cast up by the anthracite workings.'—*Richard Combs*
'A cold, dry and rather perfunctory film.'—*Arthur Schlesinger Jnr*

Moment by Moment
US 1979 105m Technicolor
Panavision
Universal (Robert Stigwood)

A bored Beverly Hills wife has an affair with a young drifter.
Tedious proof that even the biggest new stars of the seventies can't carry a no-good picture.

wd Jane Wagner *ph* Philip Lathrop *m* Lee Holdridge *pd* Harry Horner

John Travolta, Lily Tomlin, Andra Akers, Bert Kramer, Debra Feuer
'Little more than an animated snapshot of its leading man, baring body and soul to various effect . . . truly terrible.'—*Gilbert Adair, MFB*

Moment of Danger
GB 1960 87m bw

Thieves fall out and pursue each other to Malaga. Falling between the stools of thriller and character drama, this is a poor effort in either category. Trevor Howard, Dorothy Dandridge, Edmund Purdom, Michael Hordern, Paul Stassino. Written by David Osborn and Donald Ogden Stewart, from a novel by Donald MacKenzie; directed by Laslo Benedek; for ABPC / Douglas Fairbanks Jnr. (US title: *Malaga*.)

Moment to Moment
US 1966 108m Technicolor
Universal (Mervyn Le Roy)

A housewife finds herself with a body on her hands.
Incredibly old-fashioned romantic / melodramatic malarkey set on the French Riviera but scarcely moving a step out of Hollywood. Lush settings made it marketable to women.

w John Lee Mahin, Alec Coppel *d* Mervyn Le Roy *ph* Harry Stradling *m* Henry Mancini

Jean Seberg, *Honor Blackman*, Sean Garrison, Arthur Hill, Grégoire Aslan

Mommie Dearest
US 1981 129m Metrocolor
Paramount / Frank Yablans

An account of the private life of Joan Crawford, from the biography by her adopted daughter Christina, who claimed spectacular ill-treatment.
On the screen it all seemed too silly for words, and nobody cared anyway.

w Frank Yablans, Frank Perry, Tracy Hotchner, Robert Getchell *d* Frank Perry *ph* Paul Lohmann *m* Henry Mancini *pd* Bill Malley

Faye Dunaway, Diana Scarwid, Steve Forrest, Howard da Silva (as Louis B. Mayer)
'The only thing that is not transparent about this film is why it was ever made.'—*Jo Imeson, MFB*

● Video: CIC

Mon Oncle*
France 1956 116m Eastmancolor
Specta / Gray / Alterdel–Centaure (Louis Dolivet)

A small boy has less affection for his parents than for his vague, clumsy uncle.
Tiresomely long star vehicle, with Tati harping on his theory of detachment, ie keeping his comic character on the fringes of the action. It really doesn't work in a film of this length, and the jokes are thin.

w Jacques Tati, Jacques Lagrange *d* Jacques Tati *ph* Jean Bourgoin *m* Alain Romains, Franck Barcellini

Jacques Tati, Jean-Pierre Zola, Adrienne Servatie, Alain Becourt, Yvonne Arnaud
'Deft, elusive, full of heart.'—*Brenda Davies, MFB*

AA: best foreign film

● Video: Video Media

Mondo Cane*
Italy 1961 105m Technicolor
Cineriz
aka: *A Dog's Life*

A documentary of thirty sequences of violently eccentric human behaviour, including cannibalism, pig killing, a dog meal restaurant, etc.
Emetic exploitation piece, quite glibly assembled. Its huge commercial success made one worry for the world.

wd Gualtiero Jacopetti *ph* Antonio Climati, Benito Frattari

AAN: song 'More' (*m* Riz Ortolani, Nino Oliviero, *ly* Norman Newell)

Money from Home
US 1954 100m Technicolor 3-D
Paramount / Hal Wallis

A racing tipster and an assistant veterinary surgeon find themselves in charge of a horse.
A comedy with two strokes against it: the

stars, and that never-never gangster land which was already a terrible cliché in the early fifties.

w Hal Kanter, *story* Damon Runyon *d* George Marshall *ph* Daniel L. Sapp *m* Leigh Harline

Dean Martin, Jerry Lewis, Marjie Millar, Pat Crowley, Richard Haydn, Robert Strauss, Gerald Mohr, Sheldon Leonard

The Money Trap
US 1966 92m bw Panavision
MGM (Max E. Youngstein, David Karr)

A hard-up policeman turns to crime.
A cheap thriller decorated with waning stars; competent at the lowest level.

w Walter Bernstein, *novel* Lionel White *d* Burt Kennedy *ph* Paul C. Vogel *m* Hal Schaefer

Glenn Ford, Rita Hayworth, Elke Sommer, Ricardo Montalban, Joseph Cotten, Tom Reese, James Mitchum

Money, Women and Guns
US 1959 80m Eastmancolor
Cinemascope

A murdered prospector scrawls a will before dying; a detective investigates the beneficiaries. What could have been an effective western whodunnit is jinxed by erratic writing and direction. Jock Mahoney, Kim Hunter, Tim Hovey, Gene Evans, William Campbell, Lon Chaney Jnr, Tom Drake, James Gleason. Written by Montgomery Pittman; directed by Richard H. Bartlett; for Universal-International.

'The 1931 nut crop is ready!'

Monkey Business***
US 1931 81m bw
Paramount (Herman J. Mankiewicz)

Four ship's stowaways crash a society party and catch a few crooks.
The shipboard part of this extravaganza is one of the best stretches of Marxian lunacy, but after the Chevalier impersonations it runs out of steam. Who's grumbling?

w S. J. Perelman, Will B. Johnstone, Arthur Sheekman *d* Norman Z. McLeod *ph* Arthur L. Todd

Groucho, Chico, Harpo, Zeppo, Thelma Todd, Rockcliffe Fellowes, Ruth Hall, Harry Woods
'Surefire for laughs despite working along familiar lines . . . picture has started off by doing sweeping business all over, and no reason why it shouldn't continue to tickle wherever it plays.'—*Variety*

Monkey Business*
US 1952 97m bw
TCF (Sol C. Siegel)
original title: *Darling I Am Growing Younger*

A chimpanzee in a research lab accidentally concocts an elixir of youth.

Remarkably laboured comedy by and with top people; it can't fail to have funny moments, but they are few and far between.

w Ben Hecht, Charles Lederer, I. A. L. Diamond d Howard Hawks ph Milton Krasner m Leigh Harline

Cary Grant, Ginger Rogers, *Charles Coburn*, *Marilyn Monroe*, Hugh Marlowe

CHARLES COBURN to Marilyn Monroe (playing his secretary): 'Find someone to type this.'

A Monkey in Winter*
France 1962   103m   bw   Totalvision
CIPRA / Cité (Jacques Bar)
aka: *Une Singe en Hiver; It's Hot in Hell*

In a small Normandy resort, a hotel owner and a literary guest get drunk together and plan great fantasies, but finally return to their responsibilities.
Amiable, meandering star character comedy.

w François Boyer, *novel* Antoine Blondin d Henri Verneuil ph Louis Page m Michel Magne

Jean Gabin, Jean-Paul Belmondo, Suzanne Flon, Noel Roquevert, Paul Frankeur, Gabrielle Dorziat

Monkey on My Back
US 1957   93m   bw
UA / Imperial / Edward Small

A Guadalcanal hero is given morphine to relieve malaria and becomes addicted.
Dreary case history sold as exploitation.

w Crane Wilbur, Anthony Veiller, Peter Dudley, from the experiences of Barney Ross d André de Toth ph Maury Gertsman m Paul Sawtell, Bert Shafter

Cameron Mitchell, Dianne Foster, Jack Albertson, Paul Richards

Monkeys Go Home
US 1966   101m   Technicolor
Walt Disney (Ron Miller)

An American inherits a French olive farm and trains chimpanzees to harvest the crop.
Footling comedy with not much of an idea, let alone a plot.

w Maurice Tombragel, *novel* The Monkeys by G. K. Wilkinson d Andrew V. McLaglen ph William Snyder m Robert F. Brunner

Maurice Chevalier, Dean Jones, Yvette Mimieux, Bernard Woringer, Jules Munshin, Alan Carney

'Innocuous, extrovertly cheerful and good-humoured—and very dull.'—*MFB*

The Monolith Monsters
US 1957   77m   bw
U–I (Howard Christie)

A meteorite lands in the desert and causes rocks to rise and expand, becoming toppling pillars which threaten a local community.
Dully-written science fiction with moderate special effects.

w Norman Jolley, Robert M. Fresco d John Sherwood ph Ellis Carter md Joseph Gershenson

Lola Albright, Grant Williams, Les Tremayne, Phil Harvey

Monsieur Beaucaire*
US 1946   93m   bw
Paramount (Paul Jones)

King Louis XV's bumbling barber impersonates a court dandy.
What seemed a lively period burlesque has faded somewhat with age, but it still has its moments. Any relation between this and the silent Valentino film is quite accidental.

w Melvin Frank, Norman Panama d George Marshall ph Lionel Lindon md Robert Emmett Dolan

Bob Hope, Joan Caulfield, Patric Knowles, Marjorie Reynolds, Cecil Kellaway, Joseph Schildkraut, Reginald Owen, Constance Collier, Hillary Brooke, Douglass Dumbrille, Mary Nash

'Whether you yawn or rather wearily laugh depends chiefly on your chance state of mind.'—*James Agee*

Monsieur Hulot's Holiday***
France 1953   91m   bw
Cady / Discina (Fred Orain)
original title: *Les Vacances de Monsieur Hulot*

An accident-prone bachelor arrives at a seaside resort and unwittingly causes havoc for himself and everyone else.
Despite lame endings to some of the jokes, this is a film to set the whole world laughing, Hulot himself being an unforgettable character and some of the timing magnificent. One feels that it could very nearly happen.

w Jacques Tati, Henri Marquet d Jacques Tati ph Jacques Mercanton, Jean Mouselle m Alain Romans

Jacques Tati, Nathalie Pascaud, Michèle Rolla, Valentine Camax

'The casual, amateurish air of his films clearly adds to their appeal: it also appears to explain their defects.'—*Penelope Houston, MFB*

'It had me laughing out loud with more enjoyment than any other comedy film this year.'—*Daily Express*

AAN: script
● *Video: Video Media*

Monsieur Verdoux**
US 1947   125m   bw
Charles Chaplin

A bank cashier marries and murders rich women to support his real wife.
Interesting but unsatisfactory redrafting of the Landru case; the star is more dapper than funny, the moral is unconvincing, and the slapstick sequences too often raise yawns.

wd / m Charles Chaplin ph Rollie Totheroh

Charles Chaplin, Martha Raye, Isobel Elsom

'The cleverest and most brilliant film I have yet made.'—*Charles Chaplin*

'Even today it will seem a failure to anyone who has taken half a dozen lessons in film technique.'—*Andrew Sarris, 1970*

AAN: Charles Chaplin (as writer)
● *Video: Polygram*

Monsieur Vincent*
France 1947   113m   bw
EDIC / UGC

The life of 17th-century St Vincent de Paul, who gave up all worldly goods to devote his life to the poor.
Earnest, realistic Catholic biopic.

w Jean-Bernard Luc, Jean Anouilh d Leon Carré ph Claude Renoir m J. J. Grunenwald

Pierre Fresnay, Aimé Clairiond, Jean Debucourt, Lise Delemare

● *Video: Palace*

Monsignor
US 1982   121m   De Luxe
TCF / Frank Yablans (Kurt Neumann)

An Irish cardinal supports the Vatican by doubtful financial means.
A largely boring *roman à clef*, with a sluggish story and uninspired performances.

w Abraham Polonsky, Wendell Mayes, *novel* Jack Alain Leger d Frank Perry ph Billy Williams m John Williams pd John de Cuir

Christopher Reeve, Genevieve Bujold, Fernando Rey, Jason Miller, Joe Cortese, Adolfo Celi, Leonardo Cimino

'Irrevocably grounded in a hash of breastbeating and pious platitudes.'—*Sight and Sound*

The Monster
US 1925   70m approx at 24 fps   bw
silent

A scientist abducts passing motorists and uses them in his experiments at bringing the dead back to life. Typical star grotesquerie without much flair. Lon Chaney, Gertrude Olmstead, Hallam Cooley, Walter James. Written by Willard Mack and Albert Kenyon, from a play by Crane Wilbur; directed by Roland West; for MGM.

The Monster and the Girl
US 1940   64m   bw
Paramount (Jack Moss)

A man is wrongfully executed and his brain is implanted in a gorilla, which goes on the rampage.
Curiously ineffectual considering its plot and cast, this little horror thriller seems to have been the first to use this particular situation, which became very well worn later.

w Stuart Anthony d Stuart Heisler ph Victor Milner m Sigmund Krumgold

Paul Lukas, Ellen Drew, Joseph Calleia, George Zucco, Robert Paige, Rod Cameron, Phillip Terry, Onslow Stevens, Gerald Mohr

The Monster Club
GB 1980   97m   colour
ITC / Chips (Milton Subotsky)

A vampire introduces his victim to a club for ghouls and witches, who tell their stories.
A spoofy but not very entertaining variation on a too-familiar formula.

w Edward and Valerie Abraham, *stories* R. Chetwynd-Hayes d Roy Ward Baker ph Peter Jessop md Graham Walker

Vincent Price, John Carradine, Anthony Steel, Simon Ward, James Laurenson, Geoffrey Bayldon, Donald Pleasence, Richard Johnson, Britt Ekland, Anthony Valentine, Stuart Whitman, Patrick Magee
● Video: Precision

The Monster Walks

US 1932 57m bw

A supposed paralytic plans the death of his rich niece. Spooky house murder mystery, too hammy by half. Sheldon Lewis, Mischa Auer, Martha Mattox, Vera Reynolds, Willie Best. Written by Robert Ellis; directed by Frank Strayer; for Like / Action. 'Not badly done, but lacking utterly in novelty.'—*Variety*

Montana

US 1950 76m Technicolor
Warner (William Jacobs)

An Australian sheepman fights the cattle barons of Montana.
Modest western from the star's declining years at Warner.

w James R. Webb, Borden Chase, Charles O'Neal, *story* Ernest Haycox *d* Ray Enright *ph* Karl Freund *m* David Buttolph

Errol Flynn, Alexis Smith, S. Z. Sakall, Douglas Kennedy, James Brown, Ian MacDonald

Montana Belle

US 1952 82m Trucolor
RKO (Howard Welsch)

The Daltons rescue Belle Starr and insist that she works with them on a dangerous raid.
Warmed-over western melodramatics, quite unmemorable.

w Horace McCoy, Norman S. Hall *d* Allan Dwan *ph* Jack Marta *m* Nathan Scott

Jane Russell, George Brent, Scott Brady, Forrest Tucker, Andy Devine, Jack Lambert, John Litel, Ray Teal
† The film was completed in 1948, but held over.

Montana Moon

US 1930 88m bw

A wealthy rancher's spoiled daughter is about to leave for New York when she falls for a handsome cowboy. A long string of nothings with bursts of song; incompetent early talkie. Joan Crawford, Johnny Mack Brown, Ricardo Cortez, Lloyd Ingraham, Cliff Edwards. Written by Sylvia Thalberg and Frank Butler; directed by Malcolm St Clair; for MGM.

Monte Carlo*

US 1930 94m bw
Paramount (Ernst Lubitsch)

A count passes himself off as a hairdresser to win a gambling lady.
Faded but charming romantic comedy with music, the first to show its director's sound style in full throttle, notably in the final 'Beyond the Blue Horizon' sequence.

w Ernest Vajda, *play* The Blue Coast by Hans Muller, *novel* Monsieur Beaucaire by Booth Tarkington *d* Ernst Lubitsch *ph* Victor Milner *m* W. Franke Harling *songs* Leo Robin, Richard Whiting *ad* Hans Dreier

Jack Buchanan, Jeanette MacDonald, Zasu Pitts, Tyler Brooke, Claud Allister, Lionel Belmore
'Nothing extra beyond usual par programmer.'—*Variety*
'Very stylish and sly, not to be missed.'— *New Yorker, 1978*

The Monte Carlo Story

Italy / US 1956 101m Technirama
Tatanus (Marcello Girosi)

A gambler looks for a rich wife, and finds instead a glamorous woman as penniless as himself: they become confidence tricksters but suffer a change of heart.
Lubitsch might have made something of it, but this is a flavourless pudding of a film and the stars can do nothing with it.

wd Samuel Taylor, *story* Marcello Girosi, Dino Risi *ph* Giuseppe Rotunno *m* Renzo Rossellini

Marlene Dietrich, Vittorio de Sica, Arthur O'Connell, Mischa Auer, Natalie Trundy, Jane Rose, Renato Rascel

Monte Walsh*

US 1970 108m Technicolor
Cinema Center (Hal Landis, Bobby Roberts)

Two ageing cowboys find life increasingly hard and hopeless; an old acquaintance kills one and is shot by the other.
'Realistic' western developed in leisurely style with the emphasis on character and on the real drudgery of frontier life.

w David Z. Goodman, Lukas Heller, *novel* Jack Schaefer *d* William A. Fraker *ph* David M. Walsh *m* John Barry

Lee Marvin, Jack Palance, Jeanne Moreau, Mitch Ryan, Jim Davis
'As boring a western as ever involved a bronco-busting scene that alone cost almost half a million dollars.'—*Judith Crist*

Montenegro*

Sweden / GB 1981 96m Eastmancolor
Viking / Europa / Smart Egg (Bo Jonsson)

A housewife driven mad by boredom takes a lover and murders him.
Another case history in which the creator finds more symbolic meaning than the audience is likely to see. On the surface, a mildly entertaining piece of near-pornography.

w,d Dusan Makavejev *ph* Tomislav Pinter *m* Kornell Kovach

Susan Anspach, Erland Josephson, Bora Todorovic, Per Oscarsson
● Video: Guild

'Makes *Ben-Hur* look like an epic!'

Monty Python and the Holy Grail**

GB 1975 90m Technicolor
EMI / Python (Monty) Pictures / Michael White (Mark Forstater)

King Arthur and his knights seek the Holy Grail.

Hellzapoppin-like series of linked sketches on a medieval theme; some slow bits, but often uproariously funny and with a remarkable visual sense of the middle ages.

w Graham Chapman, John Cleese, Terry Gilliam, Eric Idle, Michael Palin *d* Terry Gilliam, Terry Jones *ph* Terry Bedford *animation* Terry Gilliam *m* Neil Innes *pd* Roy Smith

Graham Chapman, John Cleese, Terry Gilliam, Eric Idle, Michael Palin
'The team's visual buffooneries and verbal rigmaroles are piled on top of each other with no attention to judicious timing or structure, and a form which began as a jaunty assault on the well-made revue sketch and an ingenious misuse of television's fragmented style of presentation, threatens to become as unyielding and unfruitful as the conventions it originally attacked.'—*Geoff Brown*
● Video: Brent Walker

Monty Python's Life of Brian**

GB 1979 93m Eastmancolor
Hand Made Films (John Goldstone)

A contemporary of Jesus is mistaken for him and crucified.
Controversial middle-eastern romp which left its creators battered but extremely wealthy. In the face of such an onslaught of bad taste, criticism seems irrelevant.

written by and starring John Cleese, Graham Chapman, Eric Idle, Michael Palin, Terry Gilliam, Terry Jones *d* Terry Jones *ph* Peter Biziou *m* Geoffrey Burgon
● Video: Thorn EMI

Monty Python's the Meaning of Life

GB 1983 90m Technicolor
Universal / Celandine / The Monty Python Partnership (John Goldstone)

A series of sketches in questionable taste. Subjects include organ transplants, sex, death and the results of overeating.

d Terry Jones *w* and starring Graham Chapman, John Cleese, Terry Gilliam, Eric Idle, Michael Palin, Terry Jones *ph* Peter Hannan *pd* Harry Lange *m* various

The Moon and Sixpence***

US 1943 85m bw (colour sequence)
Albert Lewin / David L. Loew (Stanley Kramer)

A stockbroker leaves his wife and family, spends some selfish years painting in Paris and finally dies of leprosy on a South Sea island.
Pleasantly literary adaptation of an elegant novel based on the life of Gauguin; a little stodgy in presentation now, but much of it still pleases.

w Albert Lewin, *novel* W. Somerset Maugham *d* Albert Lewin *ph* John Seitz *m* Dmitri Tiomkin

George Sanders, Herbert Marshall (as Maugham), *Steve Geray,* Doris Dudley, Elena Verdugo, Florence Bates, Heather Thatcher, Eric Blore, Albert Basserman
'An admirable film until the end, when it

lapses into Technicolor and techni-pathos.'—
James Agate

AAN: Dmitri Tiomkin

The Moon Is Blue*
US 1953   99m   bw
Otto Preminger

A spry young girl balances the attractions of a
middle-aged lover against her young one.
Paper-thin comedy partly set on top of the
Empire State Building (and thereafter in a
dowdy set); mildly amusing in spots, it gained
notoriety, and a Production Code ban, by its
use of such naughty words as 'virgin' and
'mistress'.

w F. Hugh Herbert, from his play *d* Otto
Preminger *ph* Ernest Laszlo *m* Herschel
Burke Gilbert

Maggie McNamara, David Niven, William
Holden, Tom Tully, Dawn Addams

PATTY (Maggie McNamara): Men are
usually bored with virgins. I'm so glad you're
not. . . . Have you a mistress?'

DONALD: 'Don't you think it's better for a
girl to be preoccupied with sex than occupied
with it?'

'It adds nothing to the art of cinema and
certainly does not deserve the attention it will
get for flouting the Production Code.'—*Philip
T. Hartung*

† The film was made simultaneously in
German, as *Die Jungfrau auf dem Dach*, with
Hardy Kruger, Johanna Matz and Johannes
Heesters.

AAN: Maggie McNamara; title song
(*m* Herschel Burke Gilbert, *ly* Sylvia Fine)

● *Video: CBS / Fox*

The Moon Is Down**
US 1943   90m   bw
TCF (Nunnally Johnson)

A Norwegian village resists the Nazis.
Sombre, talkative, intelligent little drama, the
best of the resistance films, shot on the set of
How Green Was My Valley (with snow
covering).

w Nunnally Johnson, *novel* John Steinbeck
d Irving Pichel *ph* Arthur Miller *m* Alfred
Newman

Henry Travers, Cedric Hardwicke, Lee J.
Cobb, Dorris Bowden, Margaret Wycherly,
Peter Van Eyck, John Banner

'This may well be a true picture of Norway
and its people. But it fails to strike fire, to
generate passion. It leaves one feeling rather
proud but also sad.'—*Bosley Crowther*

'Jungle love tease! It's hot!'

Moon over Burma
US 1940   76m   bw
Paramount

Jungle lumbermen fight over a stranded
American entertainer.
Routine adventure romance climaxing in a
forest fire.

w Frank Wead, W. P. Lipscomb, Harry Clark
d Louis King *ph* William Mellor *m* Victor
Young

Dorothy Lamour, Robert Preston, Preston
Foster, Doris Nolan, Albert Basserman,
Frederick Worlock, Addison Richards

Moon over Miami*
US 1941   92m   Technicolor
TCF (Harry Joe Brown)

Two sisters seek rich husbands in Florida.
Musical remake of *Three Blind Mice*, which
was suspiciously similar to *Golddiggers of
Broadway*, *The Greeks Had a Word for Them*,
etc., and the later *How to Marry a Millionaire*
and *Three Little Girls in Blue*. In short, a
Hollywood standard, not too badly done.

w Vincent Lawrence, Brown Holmes
d Walter Lang *ph* Peverell Marley, Leon
Shamroy *md* Alfred Newman *songs* Leo
Robin, Ralph Rainger

Don Ameche, Betty Grable, Carole Landis,
Charlotte Greenwood, Jack Haley, Cobina
Wright Jnr, Robert Greig

Moon Pilot**
US 1961   98m   Technicolor
Walt Disney (Ron Miller)

A reluctant astronaut falls in love with a girl
from outer space, who finally accompanies him
on his mission.
Engaging science-fiction spoof with good
performances.

w Maurice Tombragel, *serial* Robert Buckner
d James Neilson *ph* William Snyder *m* Peter
Smith *sp* Eustace Lycett

Edmond O'Brien, Tom Tryon, Brian Keith

The Moon Spinners*
GB 1964   119m   Technicolor
Walt Disney (Bill Anderson)

A young girl holidaying in Crete becomes
involved with jewel robbers.
Teenage adventure against attractive
locations; quite agreeable but overlong.

w Michael Dyne, *novel* Mary Stewart *d* James
Neilson *ph* Paul Beeson *m* Ron Grainer

Hayley Mills, Peter McEnery, Eli Wallach,
Joan Greenwood, John Le Mesurier, *Pola
Negri*

Moon Zero Two
GB 1969   100m   Technicolor
Hammer (Michael Carreras)

In 2021, the moon is being colonized and
crooks are trying to get control of an asteroid.
A self-acknowledged 'space western' which
has a few bright ideas but suffers from a
childish script.

w Michael Carreras, *story* Gavin Lyall, Frank
Hardman, Martin Davidson *d* Roy Ward
Baker *ph* Paul Beeson *m* Don Ellis

James Olson, Catherina Von Schell, Warren
Mitchell, Ori Levy, Adrienne Corri, Dudley
Foster, Bernard Bresslaw, Neil McCallum

'It's all just about bad enough to fill older
audiences with nostalgia for the inspired
innocence of Flash Gordon, or even the good
old days of Abbott and Costello in outer
space.'—*MFB*

Moonfleet*
US 1955   87m   Eastmancolor
Cinemascope
MGM (John Houseman)

In Dorset in 1770 an orphan boy finds that his
elegant guardian leads a gang of smugglers.
Period gothic melodrama which nearly, but
not quite, comes off; the script simply doesn't
build to the right climax, and too many
characters come to nothing. But there are
splendid moments.

w Margaret Fitts, Jan Lustig, *novel* J. Meade
Faulkner *d* Fritz Lang *ph* Robert Planck
m Miklos Rozsa

Stewart Granger, Jon Whiteley, George
Sanders, Joan Greenwood, Viveca Lindfors,
Liliane Montevecchi, Melville Cooper, Sean
McClory, John Hoyt, Alan Napier

Moonlight Sonata*
GB 1937   90m   bw
Pall Mall (Lothar Mendes)

Stranded victims of a plane crash are affected
by the art of a famous pianist.
Curious, slight, unexpected play-on-film
designed to showcase the talent of Paderewski.

w Edward Knoblock, E. M. Delafield
d Lothar Mendes *ph* Jan Stallich

Ignace Paderewski, Eric Portman, *Marie
Tempest*, Charles Farrell, Barbara Greene,
Binkie Stuart

'Should make good with class audiences.'—
Variety

The Moonlighter
US 1953   77m   bw   3-D
Warner (Joseph Bernhard)

A cattle rustler moves towards reforming.
Ho-hum western which offers its stars little to
work with and was not even very exciting in
3-D.

w Niven Busch *d* Roy Rowland *ph* Bert
Glennon *m* Heinz Roemheld

Fred MacMurray, Barbara Stanwyck, Ward
Bond, William Ching, John Dierkes, Morris
Ankrum

Moonlighting**
GB 1982   97m   colour
Michael White / Channel Four (Mark
Shivas, Jerzy Skolimowski)

In 1981 four Polish building workers arrive in
London to renovate a house for their boss and
make a quick profit. The scheme is somewhat
upset by the news of martial law at home . . .
Very interesting and well-acted anecdote,
virtually constructed out of the headlines.

wd Jerzy Skolimowski *ph* Tony Pierce
Roberts *m* Stanley Myers *pd* Tony Woollard
ed Barrie Vince

Jeremy Irons, Eugene Lipinski, Jiri Stanislaw,
Eugeniusz Haczkiewicz

The Moonraker*
GB 1958   82m   Technicolor
ABPC (Hamilton Inglis)

During the English Civil War, a noble

highwayman smuggles the king's son into
France.
Likeable swashbuckler which confines its
second half to suspense at an inn, a who-is-it
rather than a whodunnit. Good fun.

w Robert Hall, Wilfred Eades, Alistair Bell,
play Arthur Watkyn d David MacDonald
ph Laurie Johnson

George Baker, Sylvia Syms, Marius Goring,
Peter Arne, Richard Leech, Clive Morton,
Paul Whitsun-Jones, Gary Raymond, John Le
Mesurier (as Cromwell), Patrick Troughton,
Michael Anderson Jnr

Moonraker
GB 1979 126m Technicolor
Panavision
UA / Eon (Albert S. Broccoli)
James Bond investigates the disappearance of
a space shuttle during a test flight.
Adventures in Venice, Rio and the upper
Amazon; all very repetitive and no longer
more than faintly amusing.

w Christopher Wood, novel Ian Fleming
d Lewis Gilbert ph Jean Tournier m John
Barry pd Ken Adam

Roger Moore, Lois Chiles, Michael Lonsdale,
Richard Kiel, Geoffrey Keen, Lois Maxwell,
Bernard Lee
'Conspicuously expensive production values
but an unmistakably cut price plot.'—Sight
and Sound

● Video: Warner

Moonrise*
US 1948 90m bw
Republic
A murderer's son is driven into violence by
memories and fears of his childhood.
Broody melodrama set against a remote
village and swamp background; not a very
interesting story, but memorable detail.

w Charles Haas d Frank Borzage ph John L.
Russell m William Lava

Gail Russell, Dane Clark, Ethel Barrymore,
Allyn Joslyn, Rex Ingram

'If the world is sane—then they're
completely mad!'
The Moon's Our Home*
US 1936 80m bw
Paramount (Walter Wanger)
A headstrong actress marries an adventurer on
impulse, and they both try to work it out.
Light, bright romantic comedy with the zany
tinge then in fashion.

w Isabel Dawn, Boyce DeGaw, novel Faith
Baldwin d William A. Seiter ph Joseph
Valentine

Margaret Sullavan, Henry Fonda, Beulah
Bondi, Charles Butterworth, Margaret
Hamilton, Dorothy Stickney, Lucien
Littlefield

The Moonshine War
US 1970 100m Metrocolor Panavision
MGM / Filmways (James C. Pratt, Leonard
Blair)
In Kentucky just before the repeal of

prohibition, a corruptible revenue agent
regrets bringing in a sadistic crook to help
confiscate illegal whisky.
Downright peculiar hillbilly melodrama,
neither straight nor satirical; interesting only
in fits and starts.

w Elmore Leonard, from his novel d Richard
Quine ph Richard H. Kline m Fred Karger

Patrick McGoohan, Richard Widmark, Alan
Alda, Melodie Johnson, Will Geer

The Moonspinners see The Moon
Spinners

Moontide*
US 1942 94m bw
TCF (Mark Hellinger)
A seaman cares for an unhappy waif.
A Hollywood attempt at romantic melodrama
in the French manner. It looks good, and the
cast is fine, but everything is just a bit too
glum.

w John O'Hara, novel Willard Robertson
d Archie Mayo ph Charles G. Clarke
m Cyril Mockridge, David Buttolph

Jean Gabin, Ida Lupino, Claude Rains,
Thomas Mitchell, Jerome Cowan, Sen Yung,
Tully Marshall, Helen Reynolds

AAN: Charles G. Clarke

The Morals of Marcus
GB 1936 75m bw
Gaumont British (W. J. Locke)
A girl escapes from a Middle Eastern harem
by stowing away with a British aristocrat.
Feeble 'naughty' comedy, killed by lack of wit
and pace.

w Guy Bolton, Miles Mander, play W. J.
Locke d Miles Mander ph John W. Boyle

Lupe Velez, Ian Hunter, Adrienne Allen,
Noel Madison, J. H. Roberts, H. F. Maltby
'Acceptable feature for general
consumption.'—Variety

More American Graffiti
US 1979 111m Technicolor
Universal / Lucasfilm (Howard Kazanjian)
In 1964, American small-town teenagers
quarrel over drugs and dragracing.
Tedious sequel to a movie which was more
than enough.

wd B. W. L. Norton ph Caleb Deschanel
m various

Candy Clark, Bo Hopkins, Ron Howard, Paul
Le Mat, Mackenzie Philips, Richard Bradford
'What once was a crate of dynamite has
been cosmetically giftwrapped à la Happy
Days.'—Cynthia Rose, MFB

More Dead Than Alive
US 1968 99m De Luxe
United Artists / Aubrey Schenck
Revenge erupts some years after a violent jail
break.
Eccentric and pretentious western with a
complex story which might have intrigued if
handled better.

w George Schenck d Robert Sparr ph Jack
Marquette m Philip Springer

Clint Walker, Vincent Price, Anne Francis,
Paul Hampton, Mike Henry, Craig Littler

More Than a Secretary
US 1936 80m bw
A dowdy secretary loses her glasses and wins
her boss. That old story, and the treatment
isn't anything to get excited about either. Jean
Arthur, George Brent, Lionel Stander, Ruth
Donnelly, Reginald Denny, Dorothea Kent,
Charles Halton. Written by Dale Van Every,
Lynn Starling; directed by Alfred E. Green;
for Columbia. 'Fair b.o. possibilities, but the
story doesn't belong on the same block as the
production afforded to it.'—Variety

The More the Merrier***
US 1943 104m bw
Columbia (George Stevens)
In crowded Washington during World War II,
a girl allows two men to share her apartment
and falls in love with the younger one.
Thoroughly amusing romantic comedy with
bright lines and situations; remade less
effectively as Walk Don't Run (qv).

w Robert Russell, Frank Ross, Richard
Flournoy, Lewis R. Foster d George Stevens
ph Ted Tetzlaff m Leigh Harline md Morris
Stoloff

Jean Arthur, Joel McCrea, Charles Coburn,
Richard Gaines, Bruce Bennett
'The gayest comedy that has come from
Hollywood in a long time. It has no more
substance than a watermelon, but is equally
delectable.'—Howard Barnes
'Farce, like melodrama, offers very special
chances for accurate observation, but here
accuracy is avoided ten times to one in favour
of the easy burlesque or the easier idealization
which drops the bottom out of farce. Every
good moment frazzles or drowns.'—James
Agee
† Garson Kanin has claimed to have written
virtually all the script.

AA: Charles Coburn
AAN: best picture; script; original story
(Frank Ross, Robert Russell); George
Stevens; Jean Arthur

Morgan—A Suitable Case for
Treatment**
GB 1966 97m bw
British Lion / Quintra (Leon Clore)
A young woman determines to leave her
talented but half-mad artist husband, who has
a fixation on gorillas and behaves in a
generally uncivilized manner.
Archetypal sixties marital fantasy, an
extension of Look Back in Anger in the mood
of swinging London. As tiresome as it is
funny—but it is funny.

w David Mercer, from his play d Karel Reisz
ph Larry Pizer, Gerry Turpin m Johnny
Dankworth

Vanessa Redgrave, David Warner, Robert
Stephens, Irene Handl, Newton Blick, Nan
Munro

'Poor Morgan: victim of a satire that doesn't bite, lost in a technical confusion of means and ends, and emerging like an identikit photograph, all bits and pieces and no recognizable face.'—*Penelope Houston*

'The first underground movie made above ground.'—*John Simon*

'I think *Morgan* is so appealing to college students because it shares their self-view: they accept this mess of cute infantilism and obsessions and aberrations without expecting the writer and director to resolve it and without themselves feeling a necessity to sort it out.'—*Pauline Kael*

AAN: Vanessa Redgrave

● Video: Thorn EMI

Morning Departure*

GB 1950   102m   bw
Rank / Jay Lewis (Leslie Parkyn)
US title: *Operation Disaster*

Twelve men are caught in a trapped submarine, and only eight can escape.
Archetypal stiff-upper-lip service tragedy, which moves from briskness to a slow funereal ending.

w William Fairchild, *play* Kenneth Woolard
d Roy Baker   *ph* Desmond Dickinson

John Mills, Richard Attenborough, Nigel Patrick, Lana Morris, Peter Hammond, Helen Cherry, James Hayter, Andrew Crawford, George Cole, Michael Brennan, Wylie Watson, Bernard Lee, Kenneth More

Morning Glory**

US 1933   74m   bw
RKO (Pandro S. Berman)

A young actress comes to New York determined to succeed.
Marvellously evocative theatrical drama which provided a strong star part for a fresh young actress and surrounded her with accomplished thespians. Remade to much less effect as *Stage Struck* (qv).

w Howard J. Green, *play* Zoe Akins
d Lowell Sherman   *ph* Bert Glennon   *m* Max Steiner

Katharine Hepburn, Douglas Fairbanks Jnr, Adolphe Menjou, Mary Duncan, C. Aubrey Smith, Don Alvarado

'Star vastly superior to this sometimes misdirected arty story.'—*Variety*

AA: Katharine Hepburn

'Revealing the amazing things a woman will do for love!'

Morocco***

US 1930   97m   bw
Paramount (Louis D. Lighton)

A cabaret singer arrives in Morocco and continues her wicked career by enslaving all the men in sight; but true love reaches her at last.
The star's first American film reveals her quintessence, and although wildly dated in subject matter remains a perversely enjoyable entertainment.

w Jules Furthman, *novel* Amy Jolly by Benno Vigny   *d* Josef Von Sternberg   *ph* Lee Garmes   *m* Karl Hajos

Marlene Dietrich, Gary Cooper, Adolphe Menjou, Ullrich Haupt, Juliette Compton, Francis McDonald

'Lightweight story with good direction . . . needs plenty of exploitation to do over average.'—*Variety*

'A definite step forward in the art of motion pictures.'—*National Board of Review*

'A cinematic pattern brilliant, profuse, subtle, and at almost every turn inventive.'—*Wilton A. Barrett*

'Enchantingly silly, full of soulful grand passions, drifting cigarette smoke, and perhaps a few too many pictorial shots of the Foreign Legion marching this way and that.'—*New Yorker, 1979*

AAN: Josef Von Sternberg; Lee Garmes; Marlene Dietrich

The Mortal Storm**

US 1940   100m   bw
MGM (Sidney Franklin)

A German family in the thirties is split by Nazism.
Solid anti-Nazi melodrama typical of the period before America entered the war; good performances outweigh unconvincing studio sets.

w Claudine West, George Froeschel, Andersen Ellis, *novel* Phyllis Bottome   *d* Frank Borzage   *ph* William Daniels   *m* Edward Kane

Margaret Sullavan, Robert Young, James Stewart, Frank Morgan, Robert Stack, Bonita Granville, Irene Rich, Maria Ouspenskaya

'The love story of today with the popular stars of *The Shop Around the Corner*!'—*publicity*

† The film caused Goebbels to ban the showing of MGM pictures in all German territories.

Moscow Distrusts Tears*

USSR 1979   148m   Sovcolor
Mosfilm (V. Kuchinsky)
original title: *Moskva Slezam Ne Verit*

In Moscow in 1958, three working girls have love affairs. Twenty years later they compare notes.
Odd portmanteau drama, most interesting for its picture of life in Russia.

w Valentin Chernykh   *d* Vladimir Menshov   *ph* Igor Slabnevich   *m* Sergei Nikitin

AAN: best foreign film

Moscow Nights

GB 1935   75m   bw

A Russian girl sacrifices her virtue to save her lover from execution. Cardboard melodrama of pre-revolutionary Moscow; not by any means a classic. Laurence Olivier, Penelope Dudley Ward, Harry Baur, Robert Cochran, Morton Selten, Athene Seyler. Written by Erich Seipmann, from the novel by Pierre Benoit; directed by Anthony Asquith; for London Films / Capitol Films. (US title: *I Stand Condemned*.)

† This was based directly on a 1934 French film, *Nuits Moscovites*, with Annabella, Pierre-Richard Willm, and Harry Baur.

Mosquito Squadron

GB 1968   90m   De Luxe

In 1944, the RAF tries out bouncing bombs in a French offensive. Very minor and belated war heroics for double-billing. David McCallum, Suzanne Neve, David Buck, Dinsdale Landen, Charles Gray. Written by Donald Sanford and Joyce Perry; directed by Boris Sagal; for Lewis J. Rachmil / UA.

Moss Rose

US 1947   82m   bw
TCF (Gene Markey)

A Victorian chorus girl suspects her aristocratic admirer of being a murderer.
Absurd, stilted mystery melodrama with a better-looking production than it deserves.

w Jules Furthman, Tom Reed   *d* Gregory Ratoff   *ph* Joe MacDonald   *m* David Buttolph

Peggy Cummins, Victor Mature, Ethel Barrymore, Vincent Price

The Most Dangerous Game***

US 1932   63m   bw
(RKO) Merian C. Cooper
GB title: *The Hounds of Zaroff*

A mad hunter lures guests to his island so that he can hunt them down like animals.
Dated but splendidly shivery melodrama with moments of horror and mystery and a splendidly photographed chase sequence. Much imitated in curious ways, and not only by direct remakes such as *A Game of Death* and *Run for the Sun* (qv).

w James Creelman, *story* Richard Connell   *d* Ernest B. Schoedsack, Irving Pichel   *ph* Henry Gerrard   *m* Max Steiner

Leslie Banks, Joel McCrea, Fay Wray, Robert Armstrong, Noble Johnson

'Futile stab at horror film classification, ineffective as entertainment and minus cast names to compensate.'—*Variety*

The Most Dangerous Man in the World

GB 1969   99m   De Luxe   Panavision
TCF / APJAC (Mort Abrahams)
US title: *The Chairman*

A top scientist is sent by western intelligence on a mission into Red China, with a transmitter and a detonator implanted in his skull.
Wild Boys' Own Paper adventure which regrettably slows down in the middle for political philosophizing.

w Ben Maddow, *novel* The Chairman by Jay Richard Kennedy   *d* J. Lee-Thompson   *ph* Ted Moore   *m* Jerry Goldsmith

Gregory Peck, Anne Heywood, Arthur Hill, Conrad Yama, Francisca Tu, Keye Luke, Alan Dobie, Ori Levy

The Most Precious Thing

US 1934   67m   bw

A college boy marries a waitress; his mother

eases the girl out but keeps the baby.
Unconvincing domestic drama, rather drab.
Anita Louise, Mary Forbes, Jane Darwell,
Ben Alexander, John Wray, Ward Bond.
Written by Ethel Hill, Dore Schary, from a
magazine story by Travis Ingham; directed by
Lambert Hillyer; for Columbia. 'Not enough
strength for the more important spots.'—
Variety

Motel Hell

US 1980 106m Technicolor
United Artists / Camp Hill (Herb Jaffe)

Benign motel owners are famous for their
spiced meat, which is in fact made from their
human guests.
Horror comic intended to amuse, but too
repulsive to do so.

w Robert Jaffe, Steven-Charles Jaffe d Kevin
Connor ph Thomas Del Ruth m Lance
Rubin

Rory Calhoun, Paul Linke, Nancy Parsons,
Nina Axelrod, Wolfman Jack

Mother***

USSR 1926 90m approx (24 fps) bw
  silent
Mezhrabpom–Russ
original title: *Mat*

A mother incriminates her strike-breaking
son, but realizes her error.
Propagandist social melodrama which is also
brilliantly conceived and edited, with
sequences matching those of Eisenstein.

w N. Zarkhi, V. I. Pudovkin, *novel* Maxim
Gorky d V. I. Pudovkin ph A. Golovnia

Vera Baranovskaya, Nikolai Batalov
† Other versions appeared in 1920 and
(d Mark Donskoi) 1955.

Mother Carey's Chickens

US 1938 82m bw
RKO (Pandro S. Berman)

The tribulations of a small-town family in the
nineties.
Modest domestic drama, not totally
unpleasing.

w S. K. Lauren, Gertrude Purcell, *novel* Kate
Douglas Wiggin d Rowland V. Lee ph Roy
Hunt

Anne Shirley, Ruby Keeler, Fay Bainter,
James Ellison, Walter Brennan, Donnie
Dunagan, Frank Albertson, Alma Kruger,
Jackie Moran, Virginia Weidler, Margaret
Hamilton
† Remade 1963 as *Summer Magic*.

Mother Didn't Tell Me

US 1950 88m bw
TCF (Fred Kohlmar)

A working girl marries a doctor and their off
duty hours don't coincide.
Thin comedy.

wd Claude Binyon. *novel* The Doctor Wears
Three Faces by Mary Baird ph Joseph La
Shelle m Cyril Mockridge

Dorothy McGuire, William Lundigan, June
Havoc, Gary Merrill, Jessie Royce Landis

Mother Is a Freshman

US 1948 80m Technicolor

A mother goes to college and falls for the
teacher with whom her daughter is infatuated.
Thin romantic comedy lacking the piquancy at
which it aims. Loretta Young, Van Johnson,
Rudy Vallee, Barbara Lawrence, Betty Lynn,
Robert Arthur. Written by Mary Loos and
Richard Sale; directed by Lloyd Bacon; for
TCF. (GB title: *Mother Knows Best.*)

Mother, Jugs and Speed

US 1976 98m De Luxe Panavision
TCF (Joseph R. Barbera)

Comic and tragic events in the lives of Los
Angeles drivers of private commercial
ambulances.
Black comedy of incidents ranging from
farcical to sentimental, sometimes funny but
basically unacceptable in either vein.

w Tom Mankiewicz d Peter Yates ph Ralph
Woolsey m various md Joel Sill

Bill Cosby, Raquel Welch, Harvey Keitel,
Allen Garfield, Bruce Davison, Larry Hagman

Mother Lode

US 1982 101m colour
Agamemnon / Martin Shafter, Andrew
  Scheinman (Fraser Clarke Heston,
  Andrew Snell)

A villainous miner stops at nothing to protect
his goldfield.
More-or-less old fashioned western with a
change of pace for the star. No world beater,
but not bad.

w Fraser Clarke Heston, Peter Snell
d Charlton Heston ph Richard Leiterman
m Ken Wannberg pd Douglas Higgins

Charlton Heston, Nick Mancuso, Kim
Basinger, John Marley

Mother Riley Meets the Vampire

GB 1952 74m bw
Renown (John Gilling)
US title: *My Son the Vampire*

An old washerwoman accidentally catches a
robot-wielding crook called The Vampire.
Childish farce notable for Lucan's last
appearance in his dame role, and Lugosi's last
substantial appearance of any kind—two pros
at the end of their tether.

w Val Valentine d John Gilling ph Stan
Pavey m Linda Southworth

Arthur Lucan, Bela Lugosi, Dora Bryan,
Richard Wattis
'Stupid, humourless and repulsive.'—*MFB*

Mother Wore Tights*

US 1947 109m Technicolor
TCF (Lamar Trotti)

Recollections of a vaudeville team and their
growing family.
Well-mounted, reasonably charming family
musical, one of the best of the many TCF
examples of this genre.

w Lamar Trotti, *book* Miriam Young
d Walter Lang ph Harry Jackson md Alfred
Newman, Charles Henderson

Betty Grable, Dan Dailey, Mona Freeman,
Connie Marshall, Vanessa Brown, Robert
Arthur, Sara Allgood, William Frawley, Ruth
Nelson

AA: Alfred Newman, Charles Henderson
AAN: Harry Jackson; song 'You Do' (*m* Josef
Myrow, *ly* Mack Gordon)

Moulin Rouge

US 1934 69m bw
Twentieth Century (Darryl F. Zanuck)

The wife of a songwriter impersonates her own
sister in order to revitalize her marriage and
her stage career.
Predictable minor star vehicle, quite
competently done.

w Nunnally Johnson, Henry Lehrman, *play*
Lyon de Bri d Sidney Lanfield ph Charles
Rosher md Alfred Newman *songs* Harry
Warren, Al Dubin

Constance Bennett, Franchot Tone, Tullio
Carminati, Helen Westley, Andrew Tombes,
Hobart Cavanaugh

Moulin Rouge**

GB 1952 119m Technicolor
Romulus (Jack Clayton)

Fictional biopic of Toulouse Lautrec.
The dramatic emphasis is on the love affairs of
the dwarfish artist, but the film's real interest
is in its evocation of 19th-century Montmartre,
and especially in the first twenty-minute can
can sequence. Nothing later can stand up to
the exhilaration of this, and the film slowly
slides into boredom.

w John Huston, Anthony Veiller, *novel* Pierre
La Mure d John Huston ph Oswald Morris
m Georges Auric ad Paul Sheriff

Jose Ferrer, Zsa Zsa Gabor, Katherine Kath,
Colette Marchand

AAN: best picture; John Huston (as director);
Jose Ferrer; Colette Marchand
● Video: CBS / Fox

The Mountain*

US 1956 105m Technicolor
Vistavision
Paramount (Edward Dmytryk)

After an airplane crash the wreck is difficult to
reach. A young man sets off alone to loot it,
and his elder brother follows to stop him.
An indeterminate production in which one
believes neither the setting, the plot nor the
characters, especially not with Vistavision
making everything sharply unreal and the
brothers seeming two generations apart.

w Ranald MacDougall, *novel* Henri Troyat
d Edward Dmytryk ph Franz Planer
m Daniele Amfitheatrof

Spencer Tracy, Robert Wagner, Claire
Trevor, William Demarest, E. G. Marshall

The Mountain Eagle

GB 1926 72m approx (24 fps) bw
  silent
Gainsborough / Emelka (Michael Balcon)
US title: *Fear o'God*

A young schoolmistress resists the attentions

of a businessman, escapes to the mountains, and marries a recluse.

Unremarkable romantic drama; one of the lost Hitchcock films.

w Eliot Stannard *d* Alfred Hitchcock *ph* Baron Ventimiglia

Nita Naldi, Bernard Goetzke, Malcolm Keen

Mountain Justice
US 1937 82m bw

A frightened hillbilly girl kills her brutal father and is protected by a lawyer. Involved backwoods melodrama, not really worth the trouble. Josephine Hutchinson, George Brent, Robert Barrat, Guy Kibbee, Mona Barrie, Margaret Hamilton, Robert McWade. Written by Norman Reilly Raine, Luci Ward; directed by Michael Curtiz; for Warners. 'Too much plot, but okay for duals.'—*Variety*

The Mountain Men
US 1980 102m Metrocolor Panavision

Two nineteenth-century trappers have adventures with Indians. Rumbustious, foul-mouthed and lethargic western of the primitive kind; no possible interest. Charlton Heston, Brian Keith, Victoria Racino, Stephen Macht, John Glover. Written by Fraser Clarke Heston; directed by Richard Lang; for Martin Ransohoff / Columbia. 'It plays like a Sunn Classic four-waller uncomfortably spiced up with violence and profanity.'—*Variety*.

Mountain Music
US 1937 76m bw

A hillbilly runs from a marriage and loses his memory. Tiresome comedy with music. Martha Raye, Bob Burns, John Howard, George Hayes, Rufe Davis, Fuzzy Knight. Written by J. C. Moffitt, Duke Atteberry, Russel Crouse, Charles Lederer, from a story by Mackinlay Kantor; directed by Robert Florey; for Paramount. 'Burns and Raye have trouble topping a cast. Mild and minor.'—*Variety*

The Mountain Road
US 1960 102m bw
Columbia / William Goetz

In 1944 China, an American officer helps peasants against the Japanese.
Confused and rather dreary war adventure with pretensions.

w Alfred Hayes, *novel* Theodore White *d* Delbert Mann *ph* Burnett Guffey *m* Jerome Moross *md* Morris Stoloff

James Stewart, Lisa Lu, Glenn Corbett, Henry Morgan, Frank Silvera, James Best, Mike Kellin, Frank Maxwell, Alan Baxter

'Mother and daughter! Rivals in love!'
Mourning Becomes Electra*
US 1947 170m bw
RKO / Theatre Guild (Dudley Nichols)

Murder, doom and guilt affect a New England family at the end of the Civil War.

A mark for trying is all. This is a clearly fated attempt to film the unfilmable, a long and lugubrious updating of Sophocles with more than its share of risible moments.

wd Dudley Nichols, *play* Eugene O'Neill *m* Richard Hagemann *ph* George Barnes *ad* Albert D'Agostino

Michael Redgrave, Rosalind Russell, Katina Paxinou, Kirk Douglas, Raymond Massey, Nancy Coleman, Leo Genn

'A star cast fumbles with helpless and sometimes touching ineptitude.'—*Gavin Lambert*

'Within its own terms of mistaken reverence, a good, straight, deliberately unimaginative production.'—*James Agee*

'It is apparent from their accents that they have only recently become a family.'—*Pauline Kael, 70s*

AAN: Michael Redgrave; Rosalind Russell

The Mouse on the Moon
GB 1963 85m Eastmancolor
UA / Walter Shenson

The tiny duchy of Grand Fenwick discovers that its home-made wine makes excellent rocket fuel.
Piddling sequel to *The Mouse that Roared*, suffering from a hesitant script, too few jokes, and overacting.

w Michael Pertwee *d* Richard Lester *ph* Wilkie Cooper *m* Ron Grainer

Margaret Rutherford, Ron Moody, Bernard Cribbins, David Kossoff, Terry-Thomas, Michael Crawford

The Mouse that Roared**
GB 1959 85m Technicolor
Columbia / Open Road (Carl Foreman)

The tiny duchy of Grand Fenwick is bankrupt, and its minister decides to declare war on the United States, be defeated, and receive Marshall Aid.
Lively comedy which sounds rather better than it plays, but has bright moments.

w Roger Macdougall, Stanley Mann, *novel* Leonard Wibberley *d* Jack Arnold *ph* John Wilcox *m* Edwin Astley

Peter Sellers (playing three parts), Jean Seberg, David Kossoff, William Hartnell, Leo McKern, Macdonald Parke, Harold Kasket

'The kind of irrepressible topical satire whose artistic flaws become increasingly apparent but whose merits outlast them.'—*Peter John Dyer*

● *Video: RCA / Columbia*

The Mouthpiece**
US 1932 90m bw
Warner (Lucien Hubbard)

A prosecuting counsel successfully turns to defence but becomes corrupt.
A hard-hitting and entertaining melodrama allegedly based on the career of William Fallon, a New York lawyer.

w Joseph Jackson, Earl Baldwin *d* James Flood, Elliott Nugent *ph* Barney McGill

Warren William, Sidney Fox, Aline MacMahon, John Wray, Ralph Ince, Guy Kibbee

'First-grade melodrama, a bet for all grades of houses.'—*Variety*

Move
US 1970 88m De Luxe Panavision

A frustrated playwright writes pornography to make money; he moves to a larger apartment but his mind is full of fantasies. None of which are of much interest to the paying customers, the movie being drenched with self-pity. Elliott Gould, Paula Prentiss, Genevieve Waite, John Larch, Joe Silver. Written by Joel Lieber and Stanley Hart, from a novel by Joel Lieber; directed by Stuart Rosenberg; for TCF.

Move Over Darling**
US 1963 103m De Luxe Cinemascope
TCF / Arcola / Arwin (Aaron Rosenberg, Marty Melcher)

A wife who has spent five years shipwrecked on a desert island returns to find that her husband has just remarried.
Thin but fitfully amusing remake of *My Favorite Wife*; sheer professionalism gets it by.

w Hal Kanter, Jack Sher *d* Michael Gordon *ph* Daniel L. Fapp *m* Lionel Newman

Doris Day, James Garner, Polly Bergen, Thelma Ritter, Chuck Connors, Fred Clark

Movie Crazy**
US 1932 82m bw
Harold Lloyd

A filmstruck young man is mistakenly invited to Hollywood for a film test.
The silent comedian is not quite at his best in this early sound comedy, but it contains his last really superb sequences and its picture of Hollywood is both amusing and nostalgic.

w Harold Lloyd and others *d* Clyde Bruckman *ph* Walter Lundin

Harold Lloyd, Constance Cummings
'A corking comedy, replete with wow belly laughs. Sure-fire.'—*Variety*

Movie Movie**
US 1978 106m part colour
ITC (Stanley Donen)

A pastiche of a thirties double bill, including a boxing yarn (*Dynamite Hands*) and a Busby-Berkeley style girlie show (*Baxter's Beauties of 1933*).
Unfortunately there weren't enough paying customers to appreciate the spoofs, which are pretty patchy anyway; but golden moments stay in the mind.

w Larry Gelbart, Sheldon Keller *d* Stanley Donen *ph* Chuck Rosher Jnr, Bruce Surtees *m* Ralph Burns *ch* Michael Kidd

George C. Scott, Trish Van Devere, Red Buttons, Eli Wallach, Michael Kidd, Barbara Harris, Barry Bostwick, Art Carney, Jocelyn Brando

'*Camp*, which has to do with a switch of vision from one era to another, cannot be created, and where it is, as this and previous attempts testify, it is immediately swallowed in its own idiocy.'—*Richard Combs, MFB*

● *Video: Precision*

Movietone Follies of 1930
US 1930 70m bw

A rich boy courts a chorus girl, and her friends give a show on his estate. Thin, fumbling drama which doesn't remember to become a musical till it's halfway through, and even then has little spark. El Brendel, Marjorie White, William Collier Jnr, Miriam Seegar, Frank Richardson. Written by William K. Wells; directed by Ben Stoloff; for Fox.

Moving Violation*
US 1976 91m De Luxe
TCF / Roger Corman

Small-town teenagers are pursued by the sheriff because they saw him commit a murder.
Old hat suspenser with a smart new line in thrills.

w David R. Osterhout, William Norton d Charles S. Dubin ph Charles Correll m Don Leake

Stephen McHattie, Kay Lenz, Eddie Albert Lonnie Chapman, Will Geer
'Probably the most hair-raising pursuit sequences in the history of film.'—*Cleveland Amory*

Much Too Shy
GB 1942 92m bw
Columbia (Ben Henry)

A gormless handyman gets into trouble when the portraits of his lady clients are sold to an advertising agency with nude bodies added to them.
A slightly vulgar and talkative farce which restricts the star.

w Ronald Frankau d Marcel Varnel

George Formby, Kathleen Harrison, Hylda Bayley, Eileen Bennett, Joss Ambler, Jimmy Clitheroe

The Mudlark**
GB 1950 98m bw
TCF (Nunnally Johnson)

A scruffy boy from the docks breaks into Windsor Castle to see Queen Victoria and ends her fifteen years of seclusion.
A pleasant whimsical legend which could have done without the romantic interest, but which despite an air of unreality provides warm-hearted, well upholstered entertainment for family audiences.

w Nunnally Johnson, novel Theodore Bonnet d Jean Negulesco ph Georges Périnal m William Alwyn ad C. P. Norman

Alec Guinness, Irene Dunne, *Andrew Ray*, Anthony Steel, Constance Smith, *Finlay Currie, Edward Rigby*

Mug Town
US 1943 60m bw

The Little Tough Guys get mixed up with hi-jackers. A failing entry in this series: the ageing teenagers shortly decided to play for laughs. Billy Halop, Huntz Hall, Bernard Punsley, Gabriel Dell, Grace McDonald, Edward Norris, Jed Prouty. Written by Brenda Weisberg, Harold Tarshis, Harry Sucher and Lewis Amster; directed by Ray Taylor; for Universal.

'It comes to life!'
'A love story that lived for three thousand years!'
The Mummy**
US 1932 72m bw
Universal (Stanley Bergerman)

An Egyptian mummy comes back to life and covets a young girl.
Strange dreamlike horror film with only fleeting frissons but plenty of narrative interest despite the silliest of stories and some fairly stilted acting.

w John I. Balderston d Karl Freund ph Charles Stumar

Boris Karloff, Zita Johann, David Manners, Arthur Byron, Edward Van Sloan
'Should show profit despite fairy tale theme.'—*Variety*
'It beggars description . . . one of the most unusual talkies ever produced.'—*New York Times*
'Editing very much in the Germanic style, magnificent lighting and a superb performance from Karloff make this a fantasy almost without equal.'—*John Baxter, 1968*
† The star was billed simply as 'Karloff the uncanny'.

The Mummy*
GB 1959 88m Technicolor
Hammer (Michael Carreras)

A mummy brought back to England by archaeologists wakes up and goes on the rampage.
Typical Hammer vulgarization of a Hollywood legend; starts slowly and unpleasantly, but picks up speed and resource in the last half hour.

w Jimmy Sangster d Terence Fisher ph Jack Asher m Frank Reizenstein

Peter Cushing, Christopher Lee, Yvonne Furneaux, Eddie Byrne, Felix Aylmer, Raymond Huntley, John Stuart
† Hammer sequels, of little interest, were *Curse of the Mummy's Tomb* (1964), *The Mummy's Shroud* (1966) and *Blood from the Mummy's Tomb* (1971).

Mummy's Boys
US 1936 68m bw

Two ditch diggers in Egypt encounter some dirty work by a mad archaeologist. Ho-hum comedy with tired old gags. Bert Wheeler, Robert Woolsey, Barbara Pepper, Moroni Olsen, Willie Best. Written by Jack Townley,

Philip G. Epstein, Charles Roberts; directed by Fred Guiol; for Lee Marcus / RKO. 'Poorly acted, raggedly written . . . net result of the dialogue is about four snickers.'—*Variety*

'Tomb of a thousand terrors!'
The Mummy's Hand**
US 1940 67m bw
Universal (Ben Pivar)

The high priest of an evil sect revivifies an Egyptian mummy and uses it to kill off members of an archaeological expedition. Semi-sequel to 1932's *The Mummy*, economically using the same flashback. It starts off in comedy vein, but the last half hour is among the most scary in horror film history.

w Griffin Jay, Maxwell Shane d Christy Cabanne ph Elwood Bredell

Dick Foran, Wallace Ford, *George Zucco*, Cecil Kellaway, Peggy Moran, *Tom Tyler, Eduardo Ciannelli*
† Sequels, of decreasing merit, were *The Mummy's Tomb* (1942) (in which the heroes of *The Mummy's Hand* are killed off), *The Mummy's Ghost* (1944) and *The Mummy's Curse* (1944). See also *Abbott and Costello Meet the Mummy*.

The Mummy's Shroud
GB 1966 84m Technicolor
Hammer (Anthony Nelson-Keys)

In the twenties, an exhumed mummy brought to England is restored to life and slaughters those who disturbed his rest.
Uninventive rehash of every other mummy movie; too hackneyed to be saved even by a good cast and production values.

wd John Gilling ph Arthur Grant m Don Banks

John Phillips, André Morell, David Buck, Elizabeth Sellars, Catherine Lacey, Maggie Kimberley, Michael Ripper, Tim Barrett, Roger Delgado, Dickie Owen
'Beware the beat of the cloth-wrapped feet!'—*publicity*

Mumsy, Nanny, Sonny and Girly
GB 1959 102m Eastmancolor
CIRO / Brigitte (Ronald J. Kahn)
aka: *Girly*

Two adolescents bring home lonely people as playthings for a homicidal family.
Revolting black comedy for masochists, representing the British cinema at its lowest ebb.

w Brian Comport, play Maisie Mosco d Freddie Francis ph David Muir m Bernard Ebbinghouse

Michael Bryant, Ursula Howells, Pat Heywood, Howard Trevor, Vanessa Howard

'More entertainment than humanly possible!'
The Muppet Movie**
GB 1979 97m Eastmancolor
ITC (Jim Henson)

Kermit the Frog and friends travel across America to Hollywood and are offered a film contract by Lew Lord, the famous impresario. Technically an adroit transfer of the celebrated puppets from their TV backstage milieu to a wider canvas; but the latter tends to dwarf them, the material is very variable, the guest stars look embarrassed and the show goes on too long.

w Jerry Juhl, Jack Burns *d* James Frawley *ph* Isidore Mankofsky *pd* Joel Schiller *m* Paul Williams, Kenny Ascher

Charles Durning, Edgar Bergen, Bob Hope, Milton Berle, Mel Brooks, James Coburn, Dom DeLuise, Elliott Gould, Cloris Leachman, Telly Savalas, Orson Welles

● *Video: Precision*

Murder**
GB 1930   92m   bw
British International (John Maxwell)

A girl is convicted of murder, but one of the jurors sets out to prove her innocent. Interesting early Hitchcock, a rare whodunnit for him.

w Alma Reville, *novel* Enter Sir John by Clemence Dane and Helen Simpson *d* Alfred Hitchcock *ph* Jack Cox

Herbert Marshall, Nora Baring, Phyllis Konstam, Edward Chapman, Miles Mander, Esmé Percy, Donald Calthrop

'If Hitchcock produced in Hollywood and was wise enough to keep his films to six or seven reels, he might be a rave anywhere.'— *Variety*

Murder Ahoy
GB 1964   74m   bw
MGM (Lawrence P. Bachmann)

Miss Marple investigates murders on a naval cadet training ship. Weakest of the Marple mysteries: all chat and no interest.

w David Pursall, Jack Seddon *d* George Pollock *ph* Desmond Dickinson *m* Ron Goodwin

Margaret Rutherford, Lionel Jeffries, Stringer Davis, Charles Tingwell, William Mervyn, Joan Benham, Nicholas Parsons, Miles Malleson, Henry Oscar, Derek Nimmo, Francis Matthews, Gerald Cross

Murder at Monte Carlo
GB 1934   70m   bw
Warner (Irving Asher)

A professor is murdered for his roulette system. Modest second feature notable only as a springboard for the career of its star.

w John Hastings Turner, Michael Barringer, *novel* Tom Van Dyke *d* Ralph Ince *ph* Basil Emmott

Errol Flynn, Eve Gray, Paul Graetz, Molly Lamont, Ellis Irving

Murder at the Gallop*
GB 1963   81m   bw
MGM (Lawrence P. Bachmann)

Miss Marple investigates when an old man is

apparently frightened to death by a cat. Probably the best of the Marples, with a good sense of place and lively performances.

w James P. Cavanagh, *novel* After the Funeral by Agatha Christie *d* George Pollock *ph* Arthur Ibbetson *m* Ron Goodwin

Margaret Rutherford, Flora Robson, Robert Morley, Stringer Davis, Charles Tingwell, Duncan Lamont, James Villiers, Robert Urquhart, Katya Douglas

Murder at the Vanities*
US 1934   95m   bw
Paramount (E. Lloyd Sheldon)

Murder backstage at the first night of Earl Carroll's Vanities. Curious, stylish mixture of musical numbers, broad comedy and mystery. Dated, but fun.

w Carey Wilson, Joseph Gollomb, Sam Hellman *d* Mitchell Leisen *ph* Leo Tover *songs* Arthur Johnston, Sam Coslow

Jack Oakie, Victor McLaglen, Carl Brisson, Kitty Carlisle, Dorothy Stickney, Gertrude Michael, Jessie Ralph, Gail Patrick

'Above average and for the masses . . . long but does not drag.'— *Variety*

Murder at the Windmill
GB 1949   70m   bw

At London's famous girlie show, a front row patron is murdered. Rather rushed-looking whodunnit with interesting detail. Garry Marsh, Jack Livesey, Jon Pertwee, Diana Decker, Jimmy Edwards, Eliot Makeham. Written and directed by Val Guest; for Daniel Angel and Nat Cohen.

Murder by Contract*
US 1958   81m   bw
Columbia / Orbin (Leon Chooluck)

A professional killer makes a fatal mistake and is shot down by police. Low-budgeter which seemed stark and original at the time, but television has familiarized its contents. Moody, contrasty photography and restrained style give it a minor distinction.

w Ben Simcoe *d* Irving Lerner *ph* Lucien Ballard *m* Perry Borkin

Vince Edwards, Philip Pine, Herschel Bernardi, Caprice Toriel

'Ice cold and completely unsentimental.'— *John Gillett*

'A bloody funny movie!'
Murder by Death*
US 1976   94m   Metrocolor
Columbia / Ray Stark

Several (fictional) detectives are invited to stay at the home of a wealthy recluse, and mystery and murder follow. Sometimes thin but generally likeable spoof of a longstanding genre; the stars seize their opportunities avidly, and the film does not outstay its welcome.

w Neil Simon *d* Robert Moore *ph* David M. Walsh *m* Dave Grusin *pd* Stephen Grimes

Peter Falk, Alec Guinness, Peter Sellers, Truman Capote, Estelle Winwood, Elsa Lanchester, Eileen Brennan, James Coco, David Niven, Maggie Smith, Nancy Walker

'Plenty of scene-stealing actors but not many scenes worth stealing.'—*Michael Billington, Illustrated London News*

'Polished performances fail to compensate for a vacuous and frustratingly tortuous plot.'—*Sight and Sound*

'It seems to me that if you haven't watched the real Thin Man and the real Bogie in the real *Maltese Falcon* you won't see the joke; and if you have watched them, the joke is not good enough.'—*Dilys Powell, Sunday Times*

Murder by Decree
GB / Canada 1978   112m   Metrocolor
Avco / Decree Productions / Saucy Jack (Robert A. Goldstone)

Sherlock Holmes investigates the matter of Jack the Ripper and comes upon a Masonic conspiracy. Interminably long and unpardonably muddled variation on this over-familiar theme, with halts for the performances of guest artists and no clear grip on narrative or character.

w John Hopkins *d* Bob Clark *ph* Reginald H. Morris *m* Carl Zittrer, Paul Zaza *pd* Harry Pottle

Christopher Plummer, James Mason, Anthony Quayle, David Hemmings, Susan Clark, John Gielgud, Donald Sutherland, Frank Finlay, Geneviève Bujold

● *Video: CBS / Fox*

Murder by the Clock
US 1931   76m   bw
Paramount

Creepy goings on in an old house after the death of a dowager who has built herself a tomb from which she can escape if buried alive. Tasteless chiller which had the distinction of being withdrawn from British circulation after public protests.

w Henry Myers, Rufus King, Charles Beahan, *play* Charles Beahan, *novel* Rufus King *d* Edward Sloman *ph* Karl Struss

Lilyan Tashman, William 'Stage' Boyd, Regis Toomey, Irving Pichel, Blanche Frederici, Walter McGrail

'Lacking in punch as a strongie for first runs. Below that should do oke.'—*Variety*

Murder Goes to College
US 1937   77m   bw

A reporter on vacation helps solve a campus killing. Reasonably lively comedy mystery which might have started a series, but didn't. Roscoe Karns, Lynne Overman, Marsha Hunt, Astrid Allwyn, Harvey Stephens, Larry Crabbe. Written by Brian Marlow, Eddie Welch, Robert Wyler, from a novel by Kurt Steele; directed by Charles Reisner; for Paramount. 'Dialogue crackles with humour . . . this whodunit will be welcome material on many programmes.'—*Variety*

'You'll die laughing!'
Murder He Says**
US 1945 91m bw
Paramount (E. D. Leshin)

An insurance salesman stays with a homicidal family of hillbillies.
A curious black farce which seems to be compounded of *Cold Comfort Farm* and *The Red Inn*. Very funny, and ahead of its time.

w Lou Breslow d George Marshall
ph Theodor Sparkuhl

Fred MacMurray, Marjorie Main, Helen Walker, Peter Whitney, Jean Heather, Porter Hall, Mabel Paige

Murder in Reverse
GB 1945 88m bw

After long imprisonment for a supposed murder, a convict comes out and hunts down the victim, who isn't really dead. A reasonable crime entertainment of its day which seemed to introduce a new star; but it hasn't worn well. William Hartnell, Jimmy Hanley, Chili Bouchier, John Slater, Dinah Sheridan, Wylie Watson. Written and directed by Montgomery Tully, from a novel by 'Seamark'; for British National.

Murder in the Big House
US 1942 67m bw

Two reporters uncover a murder ring in a prison. Acceptable second feature which catapulted its star to fame—at another studio. Van Johnson, George Meeker, Faye Emerson, Frank Wilcox. Written by Raymond Schrock; directed by B. Reeves Eason; for Warner. (NB: A previous 1936 version was called *Jailbreak* and starred Craig Reynolds. *Murder in the Big House* was reissued in 1945 as *Born for Trouble*.)

Murder in the Cathedral
GB 1951 136m bw
George Hoellering

The 12th-century struggle between Henry II and his archbishop culminates in the assassination of Becket in Canterbury Cathedral.
Plainly filmed, slightly amateur version of the celebrated verse play; scarcely a rewarding cinematic experience.

wd George Hoellering, play T. S. Eliot
ph David Kosky m Laszlo Lajtha ad Peter Pendrey

Father John Grosner, Alexander Gauge, David Ward, George Woodbridge, Basil Burton, Paul Rogers, Niall MacGinnis, Mark Dignam, Leo McKern
'A curious ordeal for the audience . . . a no-man's-land between cinema and drama has been discovered, rather than any extension of either.'—*Gavin Lambert*

Murder in the Family
GB 1938 75m bw

Who killed rich Aunt Octavia? Mild whodunnit with interesting cast. Barry Jones, Jessica Tandy, Evelyn Ankers, Donald Gray, David Markham, Glynis Johns, Roddy McDowall. Written by David Evans, from the novel by James Ronald; directed by Al Parker; for TCF.

Murder in the Fleet
US 1935 70m bw
MGM (Lucien Hubbard)

Sabotage on a navy cruiser turns out to be the work of a mad inventor.
Weak and confused mixture of melodrama and comedy.

wd Edward Sedgwick ph Milton Krasner

Robert Taylor, Jean Parker, Jean Hersholt, Ted Healy, Una Merkel, Nat Pendleton, Raymond Hatton, Donald Cook, Mischa Auer

Murder in the Music Hall
US 1946 84m bw
Republic (Herman Millakowsky)
reissue title: *Midnight Melody*

A former criminal, now Broadway producer, is murdered on opening night.
Humdrum extravaganza built round its star, whose last skating appearance this was.

w Frances Hyland, Laszlo Gorog d John English ph John Alton md Walter Scharf

Vera Hruba Ralston, William Marshall, Helen Walker, Nancy Kelly, William Gargan, Ann Rutherford, Julie Bishop, Jerome Cowan, Edward Norris, Paul Hurst, Jack La Rue

Murder in Times Square
US 1943 72m bw

An actor-playwright is suspected of four theatrical murders. Standard detection work with some slight claim to sophistication. Edmund Lowe, Sidney Blackmer, Marguerite Chapman, John Litel. Written by Stuart Palmer and Paul Gangelin; directed by Lew Landers; for Columbia.

Murder in Trinidad
US 1934 74m bw

A quiet detective solves a murder in the tropics. Modest whodunit with Nigel Bruce for once playing the sleuth instead of the Watson. Nigel Bruce, Heather Angel, Victor Jory, Murray Kinnell, Douglas Walton, J. Carrol Naish. Written by Seton I. Miller from the novel by John W. Vandercook; directed by Louis King; for Fox. 'Amusing, but not particularly intriguing.'—*Variety*

Murder, Incorporated
US 1960 103m bw Cinemascope
TCF (Burt Balaban)

In the thirties, Anastasia and Lepke build up their crime syndicate which spreads terror through New York.
Tedious and poorly made gangster thriller, unforgivable faults considering the many admirable models it has to follow.

w Irve Tunick, Mel Barr d Burt Balaban, Stuart Rosenberg ph Gayne Rescher m Frank de Vol

Stuart Whitman, Mai Britt, Henry Morgan, Peter Falk, David J. Stewart, Simon Oakland, Morey Amsterdam
AAN: Peter Falk

The Murder Man*
US 1935 84m bw
MGM (Harry Rapf)

A reporter commits murder and frames someone else.
Good low-key melodrama with an interesting cast.

w Tim Whelan, John C. Higgins d Tim Whelan ph Lester White m William Axt

Spencer Tracy, Virginia Bruce, Lionel Atwill, James Stewart, Harvey Stephens, William Collier Snr
'It will please in the lesser houses.'—*Variety*

Murder Most Foul
GB 1964 91m bw
MGM / Lawrence P. Bachmann (Ben Arbeid)

Refusing to return a guilty verdict, juror Miss Marple makes her own murder investigation backstage at a third-rate repertory company. Moderate Marple mystery which hasn't quite found the light touch it seeks.

w David Pursall, Jack Seddon, novel Mrs McGinty's Dead by Agatha Christie d George Pollock ph Desmond Dickinson m Ron Goodwin

Margaret Rutherford, Ron Moody, Charles Tingwell, Andrew Cruickshank, Megs Jenkins, Ralph Michael, James Bolam, Stringer Davis, Francesca Annis, Dennis Price, Terry Scott

The Murder of Dr Harrigan
US 1935 67m bw

A hospital founder disappears while on his way to the operating room. Formula murder mystery without much special interest. Kay Linaker, Ricardo Cortez, Mary Astor, John Eldredge, Joseph Crehan, Frank Reicher. Written by Peter Milne and Sy Bartlett from a novel by Mignon G. Eberhart; directed by Frank McDonald; for Warners. 'Will probably do no better than mildly.'—*Variety*

Murder on the Blackboard
US 1934 71m bw

Hildegarde Withers solves a murder in school. Modest mystery with popular leads; it satisfied. Edna May Oliver, James Gleason, Bruce Cabot, Gertrude Michael, Regis Toomey, Edgar Kennedy. Written by Willis Goldbeck, Stuart Palmer; directed by George Archainbaud; for RKO. 'Moderate entertainment in its class.'—*Variety*

Murder on the Orient Express**
GB 1974 131m Technicolor
EMI / GW Films (John Brabourne, Richard Goodwin)

In the early thirties, Hercule Poirot solves a murder on a snowbound train.

HAUNTED BY A LOVELY FACE... HUNTED FOR ANOTHER'S CRIME!

A night of murder the police won't let him forget! The only key to his safety...a woman's face he can't remember!

A Sensational Triumph for the NEW Dick Powell

Dick POWELL
Claire TREVOR
Anne SHIRLEY

in

MURDER, MY SWEET

with

OTTO KRUGER
MIKE MAZURKI
MILES MANDER
DOUGLAS WALTON
DON DOUGLAS

RKO RADIO Pictures

MURDER MY SWEET. Also known as *Farewell My Lovely (qv)*. This is the 1944 version.

Reasonably elegant but disappointingly slackly-handled version of a classic mystery novel. Finney overacts and his all-star support is distracting, while as soon as the train chugs into its snowdrift the film stops moving too, without even a dramatic 'curtain'.

w Paul Dehn, *novel* Agatha Christie *d* Sidney Lumet *ph* Geoffrey Unsworth *m* Richard Rodney Bennett *pd* Tony Walton

Albert Finney, *Ingrid Bergman*, Lauren Bacall, Wendy Hiller, Sean Connery, Vanessa Redgrave, Michael York, Martin Balsam, Richard Widmark, Jacqueline Bisset, Jean-Pierre Cassel, Rachel Roberts, George Coulouris, *John Gielgud*, Anthony Perkins, Colin Blakely, Jeremy Lloyd, Denis Quilley

'Audiences appear to be so hungry for this type of entertainment that maybe it hardly matters that it isn't very good.'—*Judith Crist*

AA: Ingrid Bergman
AAN: Paul Dehn; Geoffrey Unsworth; Richard Rodney Bennett; Albert Finney

● *Video: Thorn EMI*

Murder She Said*
GB 1961 87m bw
MGM (George H. Brown)

An elderly spinster investigates after seeing a woman strangled in a passing train. Frightfully British and disappointingly tame adaptation of an Agatha Christie character, with only the star (who is somewhat miscast) holding one's attention.

w David Pursall, Jack Seddon, *novel* 4.50 from Paddington by Agatha Christie *d* George Pollock *ph* Geoffrey Faithfull *m* Ron Goodwin

Margaret Rutherford, Charles Tingwell, Muriel Pavlow, Arthur Kennedy, James Robertson Justice, Thorley Walters, Gerald Cross, Conrad Phillips

† Thanks to Miss Rutherford's popularity, three increasingly poor sequels were made: *Murder at the Gallop* (1963), *Murder Most Foul* (1964), *Murder Ahoy* (1964).

Murder without Crime
GB 1950 76m bw

A blackmailer extracts money for a crime not yet committed. Thin four-hander from a rather mysterious West End success. Dennis Price, Derek Farr, Joan Dowling, Patricia Plunkett. Written and directed by J. Lee-Thompson, from his play; for ABPC.

The Murderers Are Among Us*
Germany 1947 87m bw
Defa
original title: *Die Mörder Sind Unter Uns*

In the ruins of Berlin several post-war characters indulge in gloomy self-examination. Almost a caricature of what one would expect from a defeated people, this now-curious item has a certain power of its own.

wd Wolfgang Staudte *ph* Friedl Behn-Grund, Eugen Klagemann *m* Ernst Roters

Hildegard Knef, Ernst Fischer, Arno Paulsen

Murderer's Row

US 1966 108m Technicolor
Columbia / Meadway–Claude / Euan Lloyd

Matt Helm tracks down an international villain who has kidnapped an inventor.
Witless and uninventive spy spoof which drags itself wearily along but never attempts an explanation of its own title.

w Herbert Baker, novel Donald Hamilton d Henry Levin ph Sam Leavitt m Lalo Schifrin

Dean Martin, Ann-Margret, Karl Malden, Camilla Sparv, James Gregory, Beverly Adams, Tom Reese

● Video: RCA / Columbia

'The blood will run cold in your veins!'
Murders in the Rue Morgue*
US 1932 62m bw
Universal (Carl Laemmle Jnr)

A series of grisly murders prove to be the work of a trained ape.
A distant relation of the original story, mildly interesting for its obvious Caligari influences, but not very good in any way.

w Tom Reed, Dale Van Avery, John Huston, story Edgar Allan Poe d Robert Florey ph Karl Freund

Bela Lugosi, Sidney Fox, Leon Ames, Bert Roach, Brandon Hurst
    Synthetic studio rewrite . . . Poe wouldn't recognize his story.'—Variety

Murders in the Rue Morgue*
US 1971 86m Foto Film Color
AIP (Louis M. Heyward)

Poe's story is being presented at a Grand Guignol theatre in Paris, and when murders happen within the company Inspector Vidocq comes to investigate.
Playfully plotted chiller which has more to do with The Phantom of the Opera than with Poe. A good time waster for addicts.

w Charles Wicking, Henry Slesar d Gordon Hessler ph Manuel Berengier m Waldo de Los Rios

Jason Robards Jnr, Herbert Lom, Lilli Palmer, Adolfo Celi, Michael Dunn

Murders in the Zoo
US 1933 64m bw

A jealous zoologist finds interesting ways to murder any man who shows interest in his wife. Modest time-passer with a rampant star. Lionel Atwill, Charles Ruggles, Kathleen Burke, John Lodge, Randolph Scott, Gail Patrick. Written by Philip Wylie and Seton I. Miller; directed by Edward Sutherland; for Paramount. 'Has what it takes to chill and entertain.'—Variety

Muriel*
France / Italy 1963 116m Eastmancolor
Argos / Alpha / Eclair / Films de la Pléiade / Dear Films (Anatole Dauman)
aka: Muriel, ou le Temps d'un Retour

A widow and her stepson are both misled by memories of past loves.

Elusive character drama which, though over-generous in length, fails to satisfy.

w Jean Cayrol d Alain Resnais ph Sacha Vierny m Hans Werner Henze

Delphine Seyrig, Jean-Pierre Kérien, Nita Klein, Jean-Baptiste Thierrée
    'One has to watch and listen with every nerve alert.'—Tom Milne, MFB

Murph the Surf*
US 1975 101m colour

Two Miami playboys steal a famous sapphire from a museum. Criminal autobiography based on fact; but it never settles down to being comedy or drama. Robert Conrad, Don Stroud, Donna Mills, Luther Adler. Written by E. Arthur Kean, from a story by Allan Dale Kuhn; directed by Marvin Chomsky; for AIP. (Aka: Live a Little, Steal a Lot.)

Murphy's War*
GB 1971 108m Eastmancolor
    Panavision
Hemdale / Yates–Deeley (Michael Deeley)

A torpedoed British merchantman in Venezuela devotes himself to bombing a U-boat from a home-made plane.
Modest adventure story with the star in better form than the script.

w Stirling Silliphant, novel Max Catto d Peter Yates ph Douglas Slocombe m John Barry

Peter O'Toole, Sian Phillips, Philippe Noiret, Horst Janson

● Video: VCL

The Music Box**
US 1932 30m bw

Two delivery men take a piano to a house at the top of a flight of steps. Quintessential Laurel and Hardy, involving almost all their aspects including a slight song and dance. With Billy Gilbert. Written by H. M. Walker; directed by James Parrott; for Hal Roach. AA: best short.

Music for Madame*
US 1937 81m bw
RKO (Jesse L. Lasky)

An opera singer goes to Hollywood and becomes the dupe of jewel thieves.
Tolerable star musical with rather stale comedy elements.

w Gertrude Purcell, Robert Harari d John G. Blystone

Nino Martini, Joan Fontaine, Alan Mowbray, Erik Rhodes, Alan Hale, Billy Gilbert, Grant Mitchell, Lee Patrick
    'Seems that Nino just can't make the grade as a film star.'—Variety

Music for Millions*
US 1944 117m bw
MGM (Joe Pasternak)

A small girl helps her pregnant sister who is a member of Jose Iturbi's orchestra.
Dewy-eyed wartime musical, full of popular classics, sentiment and child interest, all

smoothly packaged. As an example of what the public wanted in 1944, quite an eye-opener.

w Myles Connelly d Henry Koster ph Robert Surtees md George Stoll

Margaret O'Brien, June Allyson, Jose Iturbi, Jimmy Durante, Marsha Hunt, Hugh Herbert, Henry Davenport, Connie Gilchrist

AAN: Myles Connelly

Music Hath Charms*
GB 1935 70m bw
BIP (Walter C. Mycroft)

A dance band's broadcast has various effects on listeners.
Pleasing, modest portmanteau of sketches with music.

w Jack Davies, Courtney Territt, L. Du Garde Peach d Thomas Bentley, Alexander Esway, Walter Summers, Arthur Woods

Henry Hall and his Orchestra, Carol Goodner, W. H. Berry, Arthur Margetson, Antoinette Cellier, Billy Milton

Music in My Heart*
US 1940 70m bw

An alien singer wins the lead in a Broadway musical, which prevents him from being deported. Forgettable second feature which was its leading lady's last stepping stone before stardom. Rita Hayworth, Tony Martin, Edith Fellows, Alan Mowbray, George Tobias, Eric Blore, Andre Kostelanetz and his orchestra. Written by James Edward Grant; directed by Joseph Santley; for Columbia. AAN: song, 'It's a Blue World'.

Music in the Air*
US 1934 85m bw
Fox (Erich Pommer)

An opera singer is torn between two men. Heavy-going light entertainment.

w Howard Young, Billy Wilder, play Oscar Hammerstein II, Jerome Kern ph Ernest Palmer d Joe May

Gloria Swanson, John Boles, Douglass Montgomery, June Lang, Al Shean, Reginald Owen, Joseph Cawthorn, Hobart Bosworth
    'Mild operetta of class appeal, which limits its b.o. sturdiness.'—Variety

Music Is Magic*
US 1935 67m bw

By a series of unexpected events, a young girl becomes a Hollywood star. Unpretentious and fairly snappy musical which still provides moments to enjoy. Alice Faye, Bebe Daniels, Ray Walker, Frank Mitchell, Jack Durant, Hattie McDaniel. Written by Edward Eliscu and Lou Breslow; directed by George Marshall; for TCF. 'One of those flighty affairs that will have trouble getting past the dual barricade.'—Variety

The Music Lovers*
GB 1970 123m Eastmancolor
    Panavision
UA / Rossfilms (Roy Baird)

Homosexual composer Tchaikovsky is

impelled to marry, loses his sponsor, drives his wife into an asylum and dies of cholera.
Absurd fantasia on the life of a great composer, produced in a manner reminiscent of MGM's sillier musicals; up to a point hysterically (and unintentionally) funny, then rather sickening.

w Melvyn Bragg, *book* Beloved Friend by C. D. Bowen, Barbara Von Meck *d* Ken Russell *ph* Douglas Slocombe *md* André Previn

Richard Chamberlain, *Glenda Jackson*, *Christopher Gable*, Max Adrian, Isabella Telezynska, Maureen Pryor, Andrew Faulds
'Tchaikovsky has been made the excuse for a crude melodrama about sex.'—*Konstantin Bazarov*
'The story of a homosexual who married a nymphomaniac!'—*publicity*

● *Video: Warner*

The Music Man***
US 1962   151m   Technirama
Warner (Morton da Costa)

A confidence trickster persuades a small-town council to start a boys' band, with himself as the agent for all the expenses.
Reasonably cinematic, thoroughly invigorating transference to the screen of a hit Broadway musical. Splendid period 'feel', standout performances, slight sag in second half.

w Marion Hargrove, *book* Meredith Willson *d* Morton da Costa *ph* Robert Burks *md* Ray Heindorf *ch* Onna White *songs* Meredith Willson

Robert Preston, Shirley Jones, Buddy Hackett, *Hermione Gingold*, Pert Kelton, Paul Ford
'This is one of those triumphs that only a veteran performer can have; Preston's years of experience and his love of performing come together joyously.'—*Pauline Kael*

AA: Ray Heindorf
AAN: best picture

Muss 'em Up
US 1936   70m   bw

A cop with a Philo Vance complex routs out gangsters. Competent crime programmer.
Preston Foster, Margaret Callahan, Alan Mowbray, Ralph Morgan, Guinn Williams, Maxie Rosenbloom. Written by Erwin Gelsey, James Edward Grant; for Pandro S. Berman / RKO. 'Enough comedy and other values to make it fairly passable fare.'—*Variety*

Mustang Country
US 1976   79m   Technicolor
Universal (John Champion)

In 1925 Montana, a rancher comes out of retirement to help to round up a wild stallion. Mild outdoor yarn for family audiences.

wd John Champion *ph* J. Barry Herron *m* Lee Holdridge

Joel McCrea, Nika Mina, Robert Fuller, Patrick Wayne

The Mutations
GB 1974   92m   Eastmancolor
Columbia / Getty (Robert D. Weinbach)

A bio-chemist uses circus freaks in his experiments to find the perfect synthesis of plant and animal.
Tasteless horror film with little style of any kind.

w Robert D. Weinbach, Edward Mann *d* Jack Cardiff *ph* Paul Beeson *m* Basil Kirchin

Donald Pleasence, Tom Baker, Brad Harris, Julie Ege, Michael Dunn, Scott Antony, Jill Haworth, Lisa Collings

Mutiny
US 1952   77m   Technicolor

During the war of 1812, an American ship runs the English blockade to collect gold bullion from France. Fairly lively swashbuckler. Mark Stevens, Angela Lansbury, Patric Knowles, Gene Evans, Rhys Williams. Written by Philip Yordan and Sydney Harmon; directed by Edward Dmytryk; for King Brothers / United Artists.

Mutiny in the Big House
US 1939   83m   bw

A chaplain is at the centre of a prison break, and tries to calm the mob. Archetypal cellblock movie, and not the worst of them. Charles Bickford, Barton Maclane. Written by Robert D. Andrews and Martin Mooney; directed by William Nigh; for Monogram. 'Will edge toward the profit side of the ledger for the pop-pricers.'—*Variety*

The Mutiny of the Elsinore
GB 1937   79m   bw

A reporter on a sailing ship for a story finds himself in the middle of a mutiny. Very studio-bound seafaring adventure. Paul Lukas, Lyn Harding, Kathleen Kelly, Clifford Evans. Written by Walter Summers and Beaufoy Milton, from the novel by Jack London; directed by Roy Lockwood; for Argyle British.

'They'll take this town by storm . . .
    fighting, laughing, loving, breaking every
    law of the seven seas!'

Mutiny on the Bounty***
US 1935   135m   bw
MGM (Irving Thalberg, Albert Lewin)

An 18th-century British naval vessel sets off for South America but during a mutiny the captain is cast adrift and the mutineers settle in the Pitcairn Islands.
A still-entertaining adventure film which seemed at the time like the pinnacle of Hollywood's achievement but can now be seen to be slackly told, with wholesale pre-release editing very evident. Individual scenes and performances are however refreshingly well-handled.

w Talbot Jennings, Jules Furthman, Carey Wilson, *book* Charles Nordhoff, James Hall *d* Frank Lloyd *ph* Arthur Edeson *m* Herbert Stothart

Charles Laughton, *Clark Gable*, Franchot Tone, Movita, Dudley Digges, Henry Stephenson, Donald Crisp, Eddie Quillan, Francis Lister, Spring Byington, Ian Wolfe

BLIGH (Charles Laughton): 'Casting me adrift 3,500 miles from a port of call! You're sending me to my doom, eh? Well, you're wrong, Christian. I'll take this boat, as she floats, to England if I must. I'll live to see you—all of you—hanging from the highest yardarm in the British fleet . . .'

'Nothing to stand in the way of a box office dynamite rating.'—*Variety*
'Incidents are made vivid in terms of the medium—the swish and pistol crack of the lash, the sweating lean bodies, the terrible labour, and the ominous judgment from the quarterdeck.'—*Otis Ferguson*

AA: best picture
AAN: script; Frank Lloyd; Herbert Stothart; Charles Laughton; Clark Gable; Franchot Tone (whose role was originally to have been played by Robert Montgomery)

Mutiny on the Bounty
US 1962   185m   Technicolor   Ultra   Panavision 70
MGM / Arcola (Aaron Rosenberg)

Overlong and unattractive remake marred principally by Brando's English accent and various production follies, not to mention his overlong and bloody death scene. The shipboard sadism still works pretty well, but after the landing in Tahiti boredom takes over.

w Charles Lederer *d* Lewis Milestone *ph* Robert Surtees *m* Bronislau Kaper

Trevor Howard, Marlon Brando, Richard Harris, Hugh Griffith, Tarita, Richard Haydn, Percy Herbert, Duncan Lamont, Gordon Jackson, Chips Rafferty, Noel Purcell

AAN: best picture; Robert Surtees; Bronislau Kaper; song 'Follow Me' (*m* Bronislau Kaper, *ly* Paul Francis Webster)

● *Video: MGM / UA*

Mutiny on the Elsinore
GB 1937   74m   bw

A novelist passenger takes command when the captain of a windjammer is murdered. Unconvincingly set action yarn without much action. Paul Lukas, Lyn Harding, Kathleen Kelly, Clifford Evans, Michael Martin-Harvey. Written by Beaufoy Milton from the novel by Jack London; directed by Roy Lockwood; for Argyle. 'More or less tedious.'—*Variety*

My American Uncle*
France 1980   126m   Eastmancolor
Andrea Films / TFI (Philippe Dussart)
Original title: *Mon Oncle Américain*

Professor Henri Laborit explains the lives of two men and a woman in terms of animal behaviour.
Fascinatingly assembled but basically pessimistic dissection of human life, in the

director's most meticulous style. The American uncle is the piece of good luck which may be just around the corner (but probably isn't).

w Jean Gruault, from the works of Henri Laborit d Alain Resnais ph Sacha Vierny m Arié Dzierlatka

Gerard Depardieu, Nicole Garcia, Roger Pierre, Henri Laborit

AAN: screenplay

My Best Girl*
US 1927 84m (24 fps) bw silent
Mary Pickford Corporation

A shopgirl falls for a co-worker, unaware that he is the son of the owner.
The star's last silent film is a charming comedy which tends to fade in the memory.

w Allen McNeil, Tim Whelan d Sam Taylor ph Charles Rosher m Gaylord Carter

Mary Pickford, Charles 'Buddy' Rogers, Sunshine Hart, Lucien Littlefield, Hobart Bosworth

AAN: Charles Rosher

'Perhaps it is not for the living to know the truth about reincarnation!'
'If you give away the ending, may your blood run cold forever!'

My Blood Runs Cold
US 1965 108m bw Panavision
Warner (William Conrad)

A spoilt heiress meets a strange young man who claims she is the reincarnation of a long dead charmer; he turns out to be a madman who has come across an old diary.
Initially intriguing but eventually exhausting melodrama with a weak solution.

w John Mantley d William Conrad ph Sam Leavitt m George Duning

Troy Donahue, Joey Heatherton, Barry Sullivan, Jeanette Nolan
'Not all that bad, but not worth missing I Love Lucy for either.'—Leonard Maltin

My Blue Heaven
US 1950 96m Technicolor
TCF (Sol C. Siegel)

A pair of troupers want a family, by adoption if not otherwise.
Routine musical drenched in sentimentality.

w Lamar Trotti, Claude Binyon d Henry Koster ph Alfred E. Arling m Alfred Newman songs Harold Arlen

Betty Grable, Dan Dailey, Mitzi Gaynor, David Wayne, Jane Wyatt, Una Merkel

My Bodyguard
US 1980 96m CFI Color
Market Street / Melvin Simon

A 15-year-old Chicago boy has trouble at school.
Oddly titled, uncommercial but quite watchable drama of adolescence. Not surprisingly, it failed to find an audience.

w Alan Ormsby d Tony Bill ph Michael D. Margulies m Dave Grusin pd Jackson de Givia

Chris Makepeace, Adam Baldwin, Ruth Gordon, Matt Dillon, Martin Mull, John Houseman

My Brilliant Career*
Australia 1979 100m Eastmancolor
NSW Film Corporation / Margaret Fink

The daughter of an Australian bush farmer at the turn of the century dreams of the world beyond and writes a memoir.
Pleasing but very slow picture of a world gone by.

w Eleanor Witcombe, novel Miles Franklin d Gillian Armstrong ph Don McAlpine m Nathan Waks

Judy Davis, Sam Neill, Wendy Hughes, Robert Grubb, Max Cullen

BFA: Judy Davis

● Video: Guild

My Brother Jonathan
GB 1947 108m bw
ABP

The life of a small-town doctor who wanted to be a great surgeon.
Unobjectionable, unexciting novel-on-film with the typically British artificial studio look of the time.

w Leslie Landau, Adrian Alington, novel Francis Brett Young d Harold French ph Derick Williams m Hans May

Michael Denison, Dulcie Gray, Ronald Howard, Stephen Murray

My Brother Talks to Horses
US 1946 93m bw
MGM (Samuel Marx)

A boy who can talk to horses finds himself in demand by racetrack gamblers.
Well-mounted but uninspired whimsy with a fatal lack of pace.

w Morton Thomson, from his novel Joe the Wounded Tennis Player d Fred Zinnemann ph Joseph Ruttenberg m Rudolph Kopp

Butch Jenkins, Peter Lawford, Charlie Ruggles, Edward Arnold, Beverly Tyler, Spring Byington

My Brother's Keeper
GB 1948 91m bw
GFD / Gainsborough (Anthony Darnborough)

Two convicts escape, handcuffed together; one is violent, the other innocent.
Pre-Defiant Ones social melodrama, quite well made but suffering from miscasting.

w Frank Harvey, story Maurice Wiltshire d Alfred Roome, Roy Rich ph Gordon Lang m Clifton Parker

Jack Warner, George Cole, Jane Hylton, David Tomlinson, Bill Owen, Raymond Lovell, Yvonne Owen, Beatrice Varley

My Cousin Rachel*
US 1952 98m bw
TCF (Nunnally Johnson)

A Cornish gentleman dies in Italy after marrying a mysterious lady; when she comes to England she arouses the hostility, and love, of her husband's foster son.
Well-wrought but dramatically unsatisfactory Victorian melodrama from a bestseller; plenty of suspicion but no solution makes Rachel a dull girl.

w Nunnally Johnson, novel Daphne du Maurier d Henry Koster ph Joseph La Shelle m Franz Waxman

Olivia de Havilland, Richard Burton, John Sutton, Audrey Dalton, Ronald Squire

AAN: Joseph La Shelle; Richard Burton

'She was everything the west was—young, fiery, exciting!'

My Darling Clementine***
US 1946 98m bw
TCF (Samuel G. Engel)

Wyatt Earp cleans up Tombstone and wipes out the Clanton gang at the OK corral.
Archetypal western mood piece, full of nostalgia for times gone by and crackling with memorable scenes and characterizations.

w Samuel G. Engel, Winston Miller, book Wyatt Earp, Frontier Marshal by Stuart N. Lake d John Ford ph Joe MacDonald m Cyril Mockridge

Henry Fonda, Victor Mature, Walter Brennan, Linda Darnell, Cathy Downs, Tim Holt, Ward Bond, Alan Mowbray, John Ireland, Jane Darwell

'Every scene, every shot is the product of a keen and sensitive eye.'—Bosley Crowther
'Considerable care has gone to its period reconstruction, but the view is a poetic one.'—Lindsay Anderson

My Daughter Joy
GB 1950 81m bw
Columbia / Gregory Ratoff
US title: Operation X

In order to cement a new trade pact, an international financier plans to marry his daughter to the son of an African sultan.
Turgid melodrama swamping some good actors.

w Robert Thoeren, William Rose, novel David Golder by Irene Neirowsky d Gregory Ratoff ph Georges Périnal m Raymond Gallois-Montbrun

Edward G. Robinson, Peggy Cummins, Nora Swinburne, Richard Greene, Finlay Currie, Gregory Ratoff, Ronald Adam, Walter Rilla, James Robertson Justice, David Hutcheson

My Dear Miss Aldrich
US 1937 73m bw

The glamorous new owner of a newspaper never agrees with its editor. Skilful light comedy with good work all round. Maureen O'Sullivan, Walter Pidgeon, Edna May

Oliver, Rita Johnson, Janet Beecher. Written by Herman Mankiewicz; directed by George B. Seitz; for MGM.

My Dear Secretary
US 1948 96m bw

A secretary marries her boss and becomes jealous of his new secretary. Slow-paced, frivolous romantic comedy. Kirk Douglas, Laraine Day, Keenan Wynn. Written and directed by Charles Martin; for Cardinal / UA.

My Dinner with Andre*
US 1981 111m Movielab
Andre Company / George W. George / Michael White

Two men start a dinner table conversation which becomes a philosophical argument. Curious two-hander which can please the right audience when it's in the mood; for selling tickets, forget it.

w Wallace Shawn, Andre Gregory d Louis Malle ph Jeri Sopanen m Allen Shawn
Wallace Shawn, Andre Gregory, Jean Lenauer, Roy Butler
'A magical mystery tour of thoughts, dreams, fantasies and emotions.'—Time Out
'An adventure through a magically cracked looking glass.'—San Francisco Chronicle
'A dazzling cerebral comedy of ideas.'—Los Angeles Times

My Dream Is Yours
US 1949 101m Technicolor
Warner (Michael Curtiz)

A Hollywood talent scout discovers a new singer.
Competent, forgettable musical.

w Harry Kurnitz, Dane Lussier d Michael Curtiz ph Ernest Haller m Harry Warren ly Ralph Blane ch Le Roy Prinz
Doris Day, Jack Carson, Lee Bowman, Adolphe Menjou, Eve Arden, S. Z. Sakall
† A remake of Twenty Million Sweethearts.

My Fair Lady***
US 1964 175m Technicolor
Super Panavision 70
CBS / Warner (Jack L. Warner)

Musical version of Pygmalion, about a flower girl trained by an arrogant elocutionist to pass as a lady.
Careful, cold transcription of a stage success; cinematically quite uninventive when compared with Pygmalion itself, but a pretty good entertainment.

w Alan Jay Lerner, play Pygmalion by Bernard Shaw d George Cukor ph Harry Stradling m Frederick Loewe ch Hermes Pan ad Gene Allen costumes Cecil Beaton
Rex Harrison, Audrey Hepburn, Stanley Holloway, Wilfrid Hyde White, Gladys Cooper, Jeremy Brett, Theodore Bikel, Isobel Elsom, Mona Washbourne, Walter Burke
'The property has been not so much adapted as elegantly embalmed.'—Andrew Sarris

AA: best picture; George Cukor; Harry Stradling; Rex Harrison
AAN: Alan Jay Lerner; Stanley Holloway; Gladys Cooper
● Video: MGM / UA

My Favorite Blonde***
US 1942 78m bw
Paramount (Paul Jones)

A burlesque comic travelling by train helps a lady in distress and lives to regret it.
Smartly paced spy comedy thriller, one of its star's best vehicles.

w Don Hartman, Frank Butler, Melvin Frank, Norman Panama d Sidney Lanfield ph William Mellor m David Buttolph
Bob Hope, Madeleine Carroll, Gale Sondergaard, George Zucco, Lionel Royce, Walter Kingsford, Victor Varconi

My Favorite Brunette*
US 1947 87m bw
Paramount / Hope Enterprises (Daniel Dare)

A photographer gets mixed up with mobsters. Pretty fair star vehicle which half-heartedly spoofs Farewell My Lovely.

w Edmund Beloin, Jack Rose d Elliott Nugent ph Lionel Lindon m Robert Emmett Dolan
Bob Hope, Dorothy Lamour, Peter Lorre, Lon Chaney Jnr, John Hoyt, Charles Dingle, Reginald Denny

My Favorite Spy
US 1942 86m bw

The bandleader Kay Kyser has to postpone his honeymoon when he is called up and set to spy-catching. Fairly slick nonsense featuring a band popular at the time. Kay Kyser, Ginny Simms, Ish Kabibble, Ellen Drew, Jane Wyman. Written by Sig Herzig, William Bowers; directed by Tay Garnett; for RKO.

My Favorite Spy*
US 1951 93m bw
Paramount (Paul Jones)

A burlesque comic is asked by the US government to pose as an international spy who happens to be his double.
Moderately funny star vehicle with more willing hands than good ideas. The chase finale however is worth waiting for.

w Edmund Hartmann, Jack Sher d Norman Z. McLeod ph Victor Milner m Victor Young
Bob Hope, Hedy Lamarr, Francis L. Sullivan, Arnold Moss, Mike Mazurki, Luis Van Rooten

'The funniest, fastest honeymoon ever screened!'

My Favorite Wife***
US 1940 88m bw
RKO (Leo McCarey)

A lady explorer returns after several shipwrecked years to find that her husband has married again.

A well-worn situation gets its brightest treatment in this light star vehicle.

w Sam and Bella Spewack, Leo McCarey d Garson Kanin ph Rudolph Maté m Roy Webb
Cary Grant, Irene Dunne, Randolph Scott, Gail Patrick, Ann Shoemaker, Donald MacBride
'One of those comedies with a glow on it.'—Otis Ferguson
† Other variations (qv): Too Many Husbands, Our Wife, Three for the Show, Move Over Darling.
AAN: script; Roy Webb

My Favorite Year**
US 1982 92m Metrocolor
MGM–UA / Brooksfilms / Michael Gruskoff

In 1954, a legendary Hollywood star noted for wine and women is unwisely invited to star in a television series.
A good-humoured and well-researched romp with a central character not too far removed from Errol Flynn.

w Norman Steinberg, Dennis Palumbo d Richard Benjamin ph Gerald Hirschfeld m Ralph Burns pd Charles Rosen ed Richard Chew
Peter O'Toole, Mark Linn-Baker, Jessica Harper, Joseph Bologna, Bill Macy, Lainie Kazan, Lou Jacobi, Cameron Mitchell
'A field day for a wonderful bunch of actors.'—Variety
AAN: Peter O'Toole
● Video: MGM / UA

'I was a good girl—wasn't I?'
My Foolish Heart*
US 1949 98m bw
Samuel Goldwyn

A woman deceives her husband into thinking her forthcoming child is his.
A 'woman's picture' par excellence, and among the first to benefit from commercial plugging of a schmaltzy theme tune.

w Julius J. and Philip G. Epstein, story J. D. Salinger d Mark Robson ph Lee Garmes m Victor Young
Susan Hayward, Dana Andrews, Kent Smith, Robert Keith, Gigi Perreau, Lois Wheeler, Jessie Royce Landis
'Obviously designed to pull the plugs out of the tear glands and cause the ducts to overflow.'—Bosley Crowther, New York Times
AAN: Susan Hayward; title song (m Victor Young, ly Ned Washington)

My Forbidden Past
US 1951 81m bw
RKO (Polan Banks)

A New Orleans beauty seeks vengeance when her cousin prevents her marriage.
Stuffy period melodrama with vigorous performances.

w Marion Parsonnet, novel Polan Banks d Robert Stevenson ph Harry J. Wild m Frederick Hollander ad Albert S. D'Agostino

Ava Gardner, Melvyn Douglas, Robert Mitchum, Janis Carter, Lucile Watson

My Friend Flicka*
US 1943 89m Technicolor
TCF

Adventures of a young boy and his pet colt. Winsome boy-and-horse story, one of the most popular family films of the forties. Sequel 1945 with virtually the same cast: *Thunderhead Son of Flicka*.

w Mary O'Hara from her novel *d* Harold Schuster *m* Alfred Newman

Roddy McDowall, Preston Foster, Rita Johnson, James Bell, Jeff Corey

My Friend Irma*
US 1949 103m bw
Paramount / Hal B. Wallis

Dumb blonde Irma's con-man boy friend lends her apartment to two soda jerks. Comic strip humour responsible for the screen debut of Martin and Lewis. Sequel 1950: *My Friend Irma Goes West*.

w Cy Howard, Parke Levy, *radio show* Cy Howard *d* George Marshall *ph* Leo Tover *m* Roy Webb

Marie Wilson, John Lund, Diana Lynn, Dean Martin, Jerry Lewis, Don Defore, Hans Conried, Kathryn Givney

My Friend Irma Goes West
US 1950 90m bw
Paramount / Hal Wallis

Irma's friends Steve and Seymour are offered a Hollywood contract and have adventures on the train. Witless farce of mild historical interest.

w Cy Howard, Parke Levy *d* Hal Walker *ph* Lee Garmes *m* Leigh Harline

John Lund, Marie Wilson, Dean Martin, Jerry Lewis, Diana Lynn, Corinne Calvet, Lloyd Corrigan

'The general mental level can be judged from the fact that the performance of the chimpanzee seems the most natural thing in the film.'—*MFB*

'It takes a girl like Rita to play a gal like Sal!'
My Gal Sal*
US 1942 103m Technicolor
TCF (Robert Bassler)

The career and romances of songwriter Paul Dreiser.
Conventional nineties musical biopic, more vigorous and likeable than most.

w Seton I. Miller, Darrell Ware, Karl Tunberg, *book* My Brother Paul by Theodore Dreiser *d* Irving Cummings *ph* Ernest Palmer *m* Alfred Newman

Rita Hayworth, Victor Mature, John Sutton, Carole Landis, James Gleason, Phil Silvers, Walter Catlett, Mona Maris, Frank Orth

AAN: Alfred Newman

My Geisha
US 1962 120m Technirama
Paramount / Steve Parker

A director makes a film in Japan; his wife disguises herself as a geisha and gets the leading role.
Silly, overstretched comedy with pretty locations.

w Norman Krasna *d* Jack Cardiff *ph* Shunichuro Nakao *m* Franz Waxman

Shirley Maclaine, Yves Montand, Robert Cummings, Edward G. Robinson, Yoko Tani

My Girl Tisa***
US 1948 95m bw
United States Pictures (Milton Sperling)

An immigrant girl in New York in the nineties falls for an aspiring politician, is threatened with deportation but saved by the intervention of Theodore Roosevelt.
Charming period fairy tale with excellent background detail and attractive performances.

w Allen Boretz, *play* Lucille S. Prumbs, Sara B. Smith *d* Elliott Nugent *ph* Ernest Haller *m* Max Steiner

Lilli Palmer, Sam Wanamaker, Alan Hale, Stella Adler, Akim Tamiroff

My Gun Is Quick
US 1957 90m bw
United Artists / Victor Saville

Mike Hammer investigates the murder of a bar girl and is led to rival gangs of jewel thieves.
Impenetrably plotted but quite violent brew of typical Spillane ingredients.

w Richard Collins, Richard Powell, *novel* Mickey Spillane *d* George A. White, Phil Victor *ph* Harry Neuman *m* Marlin Skiles

Robert Bray, Whitney Blake, Pat Donahue, Pamela Duncan, Booth Colman

My Heart Is Calling
GB 1935 91m bw

An opera singer falls for a stowaway to Monte Carlo. Musical trifle with little to be said for or against it. Jan Kiepura, Marta Eggerth, Sonnie Hale, Hugh Wakefield, Ernest Thesiger, Marie Lohr. Written by Sidney Gilliat from a story by Ernst Marischka; directed by Carmine Gallone; for Gaumont-British.

My Learned Friend***
GB 1943 76m bw
Ealing (Robert Hamer)

A shady lawyer is last on a mad ex-convict's murder list of those who helped get him convicted.
Madcap black farce, plot-packed and generally hilarious; the star's last vehicle, but one of his best, with superbly timed sequences during a pantomime and on the face of Big Ben.

w John Dighton, Angus Macphail *d* Basil Dearden, Will Hay *ph* Wilkie Cooper *m* Ernest Irving

Will Hay, Claude Hulbert, Mervyn Johns, Ernest Thesiger, Charles Victor, Lloyd Pearson, Maudie Edwards, G. H. Mulcaster, Gibb McLaughlin

● *Video: Thorn EMI*

My Life with Caroline*
US 1941 81m bw
RKO (Lewis Milestone)

An understanding husband thinks his high-spirited wife may be having an affair.
Very minor romantic comedy with an agreeable air but no substance whatever.

w John Van Druten, Arnold Belgard *d* Lewis Milestone *ph* Victor Milner *m* Werner Heymann

Ronald Colman, Anna Lee, Reginald Gardiner, Charles Winninger, Gilbert Roland

My Little Chickadee*
US 1939 83m bw
Universal (Lester Cowan)

A shady lady and an incompetent cardsharp unmask a villain in the old west.
A clash of comedy personalities which is affectionately remembered but in truth does not play very well apart from the odd line.

w Mae West, W. C. Fields *d* Edward Cline *ph* Joseph Valentine *m* Frank Skinner *md* Charles Previn

Mae West, W. C. Fields, Joseph Calleia, Dick Foran, Margaret Hamilton

'It obstinately refuses to gather momentum.'—*The Times*
'A classic among bad movies . . . the satire never really gets off the ground. But the ground is such an honest mixture of dirt, manure and corn that at times it is fairly aromatic.'—*Pauline Kael, 1968*

My Love Came Back*
US 1940 85m bw

A millionaire helps the career of a pretty young violinist. Palatable comedy of its day, promptly forgotten. Olivia de Havilland, Jeffrey Lynn, Charles Winninger, Eddie Albert, Spring Byington, S. Z. Sakall, Jane Wyman. Written by Robert Buckner, Ivan Goff and Earl Baldwin; directed by Curtis Bernhardt; for Warner.

My Lucky Star*
US 1938 84m bw
TCF (Harry Joe Brown)

A shopgirl is innocently caught in a compromising situation with the owner's son. Fluffy comedy, acceptable as a background for skating sequences.

w Harry Tugend, Jack Yellen *d* Roy del Ruth *ph* John Mescall *songs* Mack Gordon, Harry Revel *m* Louis Silvers

Sonja Henie, Richard Greene, Joan Davis, Buddy Ebsen, Cesar Romero, Arthur Treacher, George Barbier, Louise Hovick, Billy Gilbert

'The characters act and talk like living people!'

My Man
US 1928 85m approx part talkie bw

A poor girl becomes a Broadway star. Lachrymose and technically primitive debut for the ebullient Fanny Brice; with Guinn Williams, Edna Murphy. Written by Robert Lord and Darryl F. Zanuck; directed by Archie Mayo; for Warner.

My Man and I
US 1952 99m bw
MGM (Stephen Ames)

A Mexican farm labourer, proud of his American citizenship, is drawn into trouble. Eccentric melodrama in which all the native Americans are whores, cheats or murderers; well enough made but not very interesting.

w John Fante, Jack Leonard d William Wellman ph William Mellor m David Buttolph

Ricardo Montalban, Shelley Winters, Claire Trevor, Wendell Corey

My Man Godfrey*
US 1936 90m bw
Universal (Gregory La Cava)

A zany millionaire family invite a tramp to be their butler and find he is richer than they are. Archetypal Depression concept which is also one of the best of the thirties crazy sophisticated comedies, though its pacing today seems somewhat unsure.

w Morrie Ryskind, Eric Hatch, Gregory La Cava d Gregory La Cava ph Ted Tetzlaff m Charles Previn

Carole Lombard, William Powell, Alice Brady, Mischa Auer, Eugene Pallette, Gail Patrick, Alan Mowbray, Jean Dixon

AAN: best picture; script; Gregory La Cava (as director); Carole Lombard; William Powell; Alice Brady; Mischa Auer

'The butler did it! He made every lady in the house oh so very happy!'

My Man Godfrey
US 1957 92m Technicolor
Cinemascope
U-I (Ross Hunter)

Tepid remake which without the period background, and in unsuitable wide screen, raises very few laughs.

w Everett Freeman, Peter Berneis, William Bowers d Henry Koster ph William Daniels m Frank Skinner

June Allyson, David Niven, Jessie Royce Landis, Jay Robinson, Robert Keith, Martha Hyer, Eva Gabor

My Marriage
US 1936 68m bw

A girl finds that her marriage is not accepted by her high society in-laws. Satisfactory woman's picture. Claire Trevor, Kent Taylor,

Pauline Frederick, Paul Kelly, Thomas Beck, Beryl Mercer. Written by Frances Hyland; directed by George Archainbaud; for TCF. 'Will get by with family audiences.'—Variety

My Name Is Julia Ross**
US 1945 65m bw
Columbia

A girl is kidnapped and forced to impersonate an heiress.
A very good second feature which has been culted into a reputation beyond its worth, though it is undeniably slick and entertaining.

w Muriel Roy Bolton, novel The Woman in Red by Anthony Gilbert d Joseph H. Lewis ph Burnett Guffey md Mischa Bakaleinikoff

Nina Foch, Dame May Whitty, George Macready, Roland Varno, Doris Lloyd
'A superior, well-knit thriller.'—Don Miller
'A likeable, unpretentious, generally successful attempt to turn good trash into decently artful entertainment.'—James Agee

My Old Dutch
GB 1934 82m bw

Ageing cockney parents see their son die a hero. Historically interesting sentimental wallow, built around a popular song; very primitive by most standards. Gordon Harker, Betty Balfour, Michael Hogan, Florrie Forde. Written by Bryan Wallace, Marjorie Gaffney, Mary Murillo and Michael Hogan; directed by Sinclair Hill; for Gainsborough. (NB: A 1915 version had starred the original singer, Albert Chevalier, with Florence Turner and Henry Edwards.)

My Outlaw Brother
US 1951 78m bw

A young man is shocked to find that his elder brother is a notorious bandit. Glum little semi-western, unpersuasively cast. Mickey Rooney, Robert Preston, Robert Stack, Wanda Hendrix. Written by Gene Fowler Jnr; directed by Elliott Nugent; for Eagle Lion.

'Desperately loved by two men—father and son!'

My Own True Love
US 1948 84m bw
Paramount

A lonely man home from the war quarrels with his son over a girl twenty years younger than himself.
Minor romantic drama, competently but coldly presented.

w Arthur Kober, novel Yolanda Foldes d Compton Bennett ph Charles Lang m Robert Emmett Dolan

Phyllis Calvert, Melvyn Douglas, Philip Friend, Wanda Hendrix, Binnie Barnes

My Pal Gus
US 1952 84m bw
TCF (Stanley Rubin)

A business man has a five-year-old problem son and in sorting him out falls in love with his schoolteacher.

Unrewarding domestic drama with actors who look as though they would rather be somewhere else.

w Fay and Michael Kanin d Robert Parrish ph Leo Tover m Leigh Harline

Richard Widmark, Joanne Dru, Audrey Totter, George Winslow, Joan Banks, Regis Toomey, Ludwig Donath

My Reputation
US 1946 96m bw
Warner (Henry Blanke)

A widow is talked about for dispensing too soon with her weeds.
Dim drama, hastily shot on familiar sets with a reach-me-down script.

w Catherine Turney, novel Instruct My Sorrows by Clare Jaynes d Curtis Bernhardt ph James Wong Howe m Max Steiner

Barbara Stanwyck, George Brent, Warner Anderson, Lucile Watson, John Ridgely, Eve Arden, Jerome Cowan, Esther Dale, Scotty Beckett

My Sin
US 1931 79m bw

A drunken lawyer helps a woman who has shot her husband. Turgid melodrama which failed to make a screen idol of its star. Tallulah Bankhead, Fredric March. Harry Davenport, Scott Kolk, Anne Sutherland. Written by Owen David and Adelaide Heilbron, from the story by Frederick Jackson; directed by George Abbott; for Paramount. 'Fair returns will be top.'—Variety

My Sister Eileen*
US 1942 96m bw
Columbia (Max Gordon)

Two Ohio girls come to New York and live with some zany friends in a Greenwich Village basement apartment.
Rather strained high jinks which were, not surprisingly, later musicalized.

w Ruth McKinney, Joseph Fields, Jerome Chodorov, book Ruth McKinney d Alexander Hall ph Joseph Walker md Morris Stoloff

Rosalind Russell, Janet Blair, Brian Aherne, Allyn Joslyn, George Tobias, Elizabeth Patterson, June Havoc

AAN: Rosalind Russell

My Sister Eileen*
US 1955 108m Technicolor
Cinemascope
Columbia (Fred Kohlmar)

Musical version of the above, via a Broadway show. Watchable but hardly stimulating.

w Blake Edwards, Richard Quine, play Joseph Fields, Jerome Chodorov d Richard Quine ph Charles Lawton Jnr m George Duning md Morris Stoloff ch Bob Fosse songs Jule Styne, Leo Robin

Betty Garrett, Janet Leigh, Jack Lemmon, Bob Fosse, Kurt Kasznar, Horace MacMahon, Dick York

My Six Convicts*
US 1952 104m bw
Columbia / Stanley Kramer

A psychologist joins the staff of an American prison and gains the trust of six inmates. Moderately interesting semi-documentary melodrama marred by a conventional prison break climax.

w Michael Blankfort, *book* Donald Powell Wilson *d* Hugo Fregonese *ph* Guy Roe *m* Dmitri Tiomkin

John Beal, *Millard Mitchell, Gilbert Roland*, Marshall Thompson, Regis Toomey

My Six Loves
US 1963 101m Technicolor Vistavision
Paramount / Gant Gaither

A musical comedy star goes to the country for a rest and with the help of the local minister adopts six scruffy children.
Icky sentimental comedy for the easily pleased.

w John Fante, Joseph Calvelli, William Wood *d* Gower Champion *ph* Arthur E. Arling *m* Walter Scharf *songs* Jimmy Van Heusen, Sammy Cahn

Debbie Reynolds, David Janssen, Cliff Robertson, Eileen Heckart
'Enough to make you settle for cyclamates—or cyanide.'—*Judith Crist, 1973*

My Son John
US 1952 122m bw
Paramount (Leo McCarey)

An American Catholic family is horrified when its eldest son is revealed as a communist. The lower depths of Hollywood's witch hunt cycle are marked by this Goldwynesque family saga, all sweetness and light, in which the commie son is treated as though he had rabies. Purely as entertainment the plot is pretty choppy and defeats all attempts at acting.

w Myles Connelly, Leo McCarey *d* Leo McCarey *ph* Harry Stradling *m* Robert Emmett Dolan

Helen Hayes, Robert Walker, Dean Jagger, Van Heflin, Minor Watson, Frank McHugh, Richard Jaeckel

AAN: Leo McCarey (original story)

'Their tangled loves wove a web of hate!'

My Son My Son*
US 1940 117m bw
Edward Small

A man who becomes rich spoils his son and lives to regret it.
Solid narrative from a bestseller.

w Lenore Coffee, *novel* Howard Spring *d* Charles Vidor *ph* Harry Stradling *m* Edward Ward

Brian Aherne, Madeleine Carroll, Louis Hayward, Laraine Day, Henry Hull

My Song for You
GB 1934 90m bw

A grand opera tenor tries to help a young girl and falls for her. The story is an excuse for the

songs, and looks it. Jan Kiepura, Aileen Marson, Sonnie Hale, Emlyn Williams, Gina Malo. Written by Austin Melford, Robert Edmunds, Richard Benson, from a German original, *Ein Lied für Dich*, by Ernst Marischka and Irmgard Von Cube; directed by Maurice Elvey; for Gaumont-British.

My Teenage Daughter
GB 1956 100m bw
British Lion / Everest (Herbert Wilcox)
US title: *Teenage Bad Girl*

A widow's seventeen-year-old daughter meets an aggressive young man and ends up in court. Predictable domestic drama, a tame British version of *Rebel without a Cause*.

w Felicity Douglas *d* Herbert Wilcox *ph* Max Greene

Anna Neagle, Sylvia Syms, Kenneth Haigh, Norman Wooland, Wilfrid Hyde White, Julia Lockwood, Helen Haye

My Tutor
US 1982 97m De Luxe

Two teenage boys try to lose their virginity. As woeful as it sounds. Matt Lattanzi, Caren Kaye, Kevin McCarthy, Arlene Golonka. Written by Joe Roberts; directed by George Bowers; for Crown.

My Uncle Antoine
Canada 1971 110m Eastmancolor

In a Quebec village a young boy reluctantly helps his undertaker uncle to deliver a coffin. French-speaking comedy drama with a sour edge, as thoughts of death mar a family Christmas. Jacques Gagnon, Lyne Champagne, Jean Duceppe, Olivette Thibault. Written by Clément Perron; directed by Claude Jutra; for the National Film Board of Canada.

My Weakness*
US 1933 74m bw

As part of a joke, a hotel slavey is disguised as a grand lady, and warms to the part. Tolerable comedy with songs, using some ingenuity of presentation to ingratiate its German star with American audiences. *Lilian Harvey*, Lew Ayres, Charles Butterworth, Harry Langdon, Sid Silvers, Henry Travers. Written by B. G. De Sylva; directed by David Butler; for Fox.
'A highly favourable début.'—*Variety*

My Wife's Best Friend
US 1952 87m bw

A wife learns of her husband's infidelity, and imagines how Cleopatra, Joan of Arc and other historical figures might handle the situation. A sharp little comedy rather similar to *Unfaithfully Yours*. Anne Baxter, Macdonald Carey, Cecil Kellaway, Casey Adams, Catherine McLeod. Written by Isobel Lennart; directed by Richard Sale; for TCF.

My Wife's Family
GB 1931 80m bw

A wife thinks her husband has an illegitimate child. Archetypal British farce. This may be

the best version; it was also made with Charlie Clapham in 1941 and with Ronald Shiner in 1956. Gene Gerrard, Muriel Angelus, Jimmy Godden, Amy Veness. Written by Fred Duprez and Val Valentine, from the play by Fred Duprez, Hal Stephens and Harry B. Linton; directed by Monty Banks; for BIP.

My Wild Irish Rose
US 1947 101m Technicolor
Warner (William Jacobs)

The ups and downs of Irish tenor Chauncey Olcott and his encounters with Lillian Russell. Inoffensive but not very exciting period musical, rather lacking in humour.

w Peter Milne, *book* Rita Ilcott *d* David Butler *ph* Arthur Edeson *m* Ray Heindorf, Max Steiner *ch* Le Roy Prinz

Dennis Morgan, Arlene Dahl, Andrea King, Alan Hale, George Tobias

AAN: Ray Heindorf, Max Steiner

'At last, the book that couldn't be written is now the motion picture that couldn't be made!'

Myra Breckinridge
US 1970 94m De Luxe Panavision
TCF (Robert Fryer)

After a sex change operation a film critic goes to Hollywood to accomplish the deflation of the American male.
A sharply satirical novel has been turned into a sleazy and aimless picture which became a watershed of permissiveness; after international outcry it was shunned even by its own studio. A few good laughs do emerge from the morass, but even the old clips are misused.

w Mike Sarne, David Giler, *novel* Gore Vidal *d* Mike Sarne *ph* Richard Moore *m* Lionel Newman

Mae West, Raquel Welch, John Huston, Rex Reed, Jim Backus, John Carradine, Andy Devine
'Whatever the novel may be like, it surely cannot be this sort of witless, lip-smacking, continuously inept cop-out.'—*John Simon*
'About as funny as a child molester.'—*Time*
'A disjointed patchwork of leers, vulgarity and general ineptness.'—*Cue*
'An incompetent attempt at exploitation by an industry that knew once, at the very least, how to make a dishonest buck.'—*Newsweek*
'I don't want subtlety. I want vulgarity.'—*Michael Sarne*
● *Video: CBS / Fox*

The Mysterious Doctor
US 1942 57m bw

Nazis strike at an English village by staging a headless ghost. Risible propaganda hokum which somehow earned an 'H' certificate. John Loder, Eleanor Parker, Bruce Lester, Lester Matthews, Forrester Harvey. Written by Richard Weil; directed by Ben Stoloff; for Warner.

Mysterious Intruder
US 1946 62m bw

A private detective seeks a missing heiress.

Intriguing minor thriller, part of the *Whistler*
series. Richard Dix, Barton Maclane, Nina
Vale, Regis Toomey. Written by Eric Taylor;
directed by William Castle; for Columbia.

Mysterious Island*
GB 1961   101m   Technicolor
Columbia / Ameran (Charles Schneer)
Confederate officers escape by balloon and
join shipwrecked English ladies on a strange
island where they are menaced by prehistoric
monsters and helped by Captain Nemo.
Rambling, lively juvenile adventure with good
moments and excellent monsters.

w John Prebble, Dan Ullman, Crane Wilbur,
novel Jules Verne *d* Cy Endfield *ph* Wilkie
Cooper *m* Bernard Herrmann *sp* Ray
Harryhausen

Joan Greenwood, Michael Craig, Herbert
Lom, Michael Callan, Gary Merrill
† An early sound version was made by MGM
in 1929, directed by Lucien Hubbard. Despite
Technicolor and a cast which included Lionel
Barrymore it was judged unsatisfactory, and
concentrated less on stop-frame monsters than
on the submarine elements ignored in the
above but remade in *Captain Nemo and the
Underwater City* (qv).

The Mysterious Lady
US 1928   84m (24 fps)   bw   silent
MGM
A glamorous Russian spy has to save her lover
from execution as a traitor.
Threadbare star melodrama.

w Bess Meredyth *d* Fred Niblo *ph* William
Daniels

Greta Garbo, Conrad Nagel, Gustav Von
Seyffertitz

Mysterious Mr Wong
US 1935   60m   bw
A mandarin in New York's Chinatown will
stop at nothing to collect the twelve coins of
Confucius. Tolerable programme filler with
old-fashioned thrills. Bela Lugosi, Wallace
Ford, Arline Judge, Fred Warren. Written by
Nina Howatt from a story by Stephen Keeler;
directed by William Nigh; for Monogram.
'Passably exciting.'—*Variety*

Mystery in Mexico
US 1948   65m   bw
An insurance detective disappears in Mexico;
another is sent to find him and uncovers a
complex plot. Fairly effective time-passer shot
on location. William Lundigan, Ricardo
Cortez, Jacqueline White, Tony Barrett.
Written by Lawrence Kimble; directed by
Robert Wise; for RKO.

Mystery Junction
GB 1951   67m   bw
Passengers stranded in a snowbound railway
station solve a mystery. One of the better
second features of its type. Sidney Tafler,
Barbara Murray, Pat Owens, Martin Benson.
Written and directed by Michael McCarthy;
for Anglo Amalgamated.

THE MYSTERY OF MARIE ROGET. Like most films which acknowledge Edgar Allan Poe
among their authors, this had nothing to do with his story.

Mystery Liner
US 1934 62m bw

Several murders take place at sea on a
passenger liner. Reputedly above-average
whodunit. Noah Beery, Astrid Allwyn,
Cornelius Keefe, Gustav Von Seyffertitz,
Edwin Maxwell. Written by Wellys Totman
from the novel The Ghost of John Holling by
Edgar Wallace; directed by William Nigh; for
Monogram. 'Too good for the lesser grinds:
exceptional indie entertainment.'—*Variety*

'A thing to bewitch your senses for days
    and days! Charming in the thrills!
    Gripping in the suspense!'
The Mystery of Edwin Drood*
US 1935 85m bw
Universal

In a cathedral town, a drug- addicted
choirmaster is his nephew's rival for the hand
of Rosa Bud.
Fairly creditable attempt to deal with a famous
unfinished novel. Slightly stilted, but good
visuals and performances.

w John L. Balderston, Gladys Unger, Bradley
King, Leopold Atlas, *novel* Charles Dickens
d Stuart Walker ph George Robinson
m Edward Ward

Claude Rains, Douglass Montgomery,
Heather Angel, David Manners, E. E. Clive,
Valerie Hobson

The Mystery of Marie Roget
US 1942 61m bw
Universal (Paul Malvern)

A Parisian music hall star plots to kill her
sister but herself disappears.
Ham-fisted, stilted mystery drama relying
hardly at all on its original.

w Michael Jacoby, *story* Edgar Allan Poe
d Phil Rosen *ph* Elwood Bredell *m* Hans
Salter

Maria Montez, Patric Knowles, *Maria
Ouspenskaya*, Lloyd Corrigan, John Litel,
Edward Norris, Frank Reicher

The Mystery of Mr X*
US 1934 84m bw
MGM (Lawrence Weingarten)

In foggy London, a jewel thief protects himself
by finding the murderer of several policemen.

Passable mystery, later remade as *The Hour of
Thirteen*.

w Howard Emmett Rogers, Philip
MacDonald, Monckton Hoffe, *novel* X vs Rex
by Philip MacDonald *d* Edgar Selwyn
ph Oliver T. Marsh

Robert Montgomery, Elizabeth Allan, Lewis
Stone, Ralph Forbes, Henry Stephenson,
Forrester Harvey
'One of the best-made mystery mellers
yet.'—*Variety*

The Mystery of the Mary Celeste
GB 1935 80m bw

A mad sailor kills his fellow crew members
and jumps overboard. Unpersuasive solution
to an unsolved mystery in a production which
sounds more interesting than it is. Bela
Lugosi, Shirley Grey, Arthur Margetson,
Edmund Willard, Dennis Hoey. Written and
directed by Denison Clift; for Hammer. (US
title: *Phantom Ship*.) 'Very strong stuff for
those who like tragic entertainment.'—*Variety*

'Images of wax that throbbed with human
    passion. Almost woman! What did they
    lack?'
Mystery of the Wax Museum****
US 1933 77m Technicolor
Warner (Henry Blanke)

A sculptor disfigured in a fire builds a wax
museum by covering live victims in wax.
Archetypal horror material is augmented by a
sub-plot about drug-running and an
authoritative example of the wisecracking
reporter school of the early thirties. The film is
also notable for its highly satisfactory use of
two-colour Technicolor and for its splendid art
direction. Remade 1953 as *House of Wax* (qv).

w *Don Mullally, Carl Erickson, play* Charles
S. Belden *d Michael Curtiz ph* Ray
Rennahan ad Anton Grot

Lionel Atwill, Fay Wray, *Glenda Farrell,
Frank McHugh*, Gavin Gordon, Allen
Vincent, Edwin Maxwell
'Would have been certain of better gate
support a year ago. Recognizing this, the
Technicolor and hyper-weirdness were
apparently mandatory studio precautions to
offset the element of belated arrival.'—*Variety*
'Marvellously grisly chiller.'—*Judith Crist,
1977*

'Its most telling details are its horrific ones.
The fire at the beginning, with lifelike figures
melting into grisly ooze; night time in the city
morgue, with a dead body suddenly popping
up as a side effect of embalming fluid; chases
through shadows as the ghoulish sculptor
collects bodies for his exhibit; and the shock
when Atwill's homemade wax face crumbles to
the floor and exposes the hidden demon.'—
*Tom Shales, The American Film Heritage,
1972*

Mystery Street*
US 1950 93m bw
MGM (Frank E. Taylor)

Harvard medical scientists help solve a murder
by examining the victim's bones.
Standard semi-documentary police thriller;
well paced and quite entertaining.

w *Sidney Boehm, Richard Brooks d* John
Sturges *ph* John Alton *m* Rudolph Kopp

Ricardo Montalban, Sally Forrest, Elsa
Lanchester, Bruce Bennett, Marshall
Thompson, Jan Sterling

AAN: Leonard Speigelgass (original story)

Mystery Submarine
GB 1962 92m bw
British Lion / Britannia / Bertram Ostrer
US title: *Decoy*

A Nazi submarine is captured and sent out
again with a British crew.
Routine war adventure.

w Hugh Woodhouse, Bertram Ostrer, Jon
Manchip White *d* C. M. Pennington-
Richards *ph* Stan Pavey *m* Clifton Parker

Edward Judd, James Robertson Justice,
Laurence Payne, Albert Lieven

Mystery Woman
US 1934 69m bw

Recovery of a secret document will mean
freedom for a soldier sent to Devil's Island.
Tolerable time-passer, with action mostly on a
liner. Mona Barrie, Gilbert Roland, John
Halliday, Rod La Rocque, Mischa Auer, Billy
Bevan. Written by Philip MacDonald, Dudley
Nichols, E. E. Paramore Jnr; directed by
Eugene Forde; for Fox. 'Entertainment of a
just passable sort.'—*Variety*

N

Nagana
US 1933 73m bw

Doctors in Africa try to cure sleeping sickness. Dreary drama with cut-in animal footage. Tala Birell, Melvyn Dougas, M. Morita, Onslow Stevens. Written by James Light, Dale Van Every, Don Ryan, Lester Cohen; directed by Ernst L. Frank; for Universal.

Naked Alibi
US 1954 85m bw
U-I (Ross Hunter)

The police track a homicidal baker to a Mexican border town.
Modest police thriller which sags after it crosses the border.

w Lawrence Roman *d* Jerry Hopper
ph Russell Metty *m* Joseph Gershenson

Sterling Hayden, Gene Barry, Gloria Grahame, Marcia Henderson, Casey Adams, Chuck Connors

The Naked and the Dead
US 1958 131m Technicolor RKOscope
RKO Teleradio / Gregjac (Paul Gregory)

Adventures of an army platoon in the Pacific war.
Shorn of the four letter words which made the novel notorious, this is a routine war film, neither very good nor very bad.

w Denis and Terry Sanders, *novel* Norman Mailer *d* Raoul Walsh *ph* Joseph La Shelle *m* Bernard Herrmann

Aldo Ray, Cliff Robertson, Raymond Massey, William Campbell, Richard Jaeckel, James Best, Joey Bishop, Robert Gist, Jerry Paris, L. Q. Jones
● Video: Kingston

The Naked City**
US 1948 96m bw
Universal (Mark Hellinger)

New York police track down a killer.
Highly influential documentary thriller which, shot on location in New York's teeming streets, claimed to be giving an impression of city life; actually its real mission was to tell an ordinary murder tale with an impressive accumulation of detail and humour. The narrator's last words became a cliché: 'There are eight million stories in the naked city. This has been one of them.'

w Malvin Wald, Albert Maltz *d* Jules Dassin
ph William Daniels *m* Frank Skinner, Miklos Rozsa *md* Milton Schwarzwald
Barry Fitzgerald, Don Taylor, Howard Duff, Dorothy Hart, Ted de Corsia, Adelaide Klein
AA: William Daniels
AAN: original story (Malvin Wald)

The Naked Dawn
US 1956 82m Technicolor

A hired robber finds that his boss is not to be trusted. Heavy-going Mexican western. Arthur Kennedy, Eugene Iglesias, Betta St John. Written by Nina and Herman Schneider; directed by Edgar G. Ulmer; for Universal-International.

Naked Earth
GB 1958 96m bw Cinemascope
TCF / Foray Films (Adrian Worker)

In 1895 a young Irish farmer goes to Africa to grow tobacco, but moves on to crocodile hunting.
Predictable and uninteresting epic of endurance; not very convincing either.

w Milton Holmes *d* Vincent Sherman
ph Erwin Hillier

Richard Todd, Juliette Greco, John Kitzmiller, Finlay Currie, Laurence Naismith, Christopher Rhodes, Orlando Martins

The Naked Edge
GB 1961 100m bw
US / Pennebaker / Baroda (Walter Seltzer, George Glass)

A successful executive is suspected by his wife of an old murder in which he testified against the man who was convicted.
Dreary thriller which piles up red herrings in shoals, then abandons them all for a razor-and-bathroom finale.

w Joseph Stefano, *novel* First Train to Babylon by Max Ehrlich *d* Michael Anderson *ph* Erwin Hillier *m* William Alwyn

Gary Cooper, Deborah Kerr, Peter Cushing, Eric Portman, Diane Cilento, Hermione Gingold, Michael Wilding, Ronald Howard

The Naked Face
US 1984 106m Metrocolor
Cannon (Rony Yacov)

A Chicago psychiatrist finds himself a potential victim of the Mafia.

Muddled and violent mystery with a rather boring solution.

w,d Bryan Forbes, *novel* Sidney Sheldon
ph David Gurfinkel *m* Michael J. Lewis
pd William Fosser

Roger Moore, Rod Steiger, Elliott Gould, Anne Archer, David Hedison, Art Carney, Ron Parady

The Naked Hills
US 1955 73m Pathecolor
Allied Artists / La Salle (Josef Shaftel)

Starting in 1849, a young prospector spends his life looking for gold.
Curious, mildly interesting saga with an obsession instead of a plot.

wd Josef Shaftel *ph* Frederick Gately
m Herschel Burke Gilbert

David Wayne, Marcia Henderson, Keenan Wynn, James Barton, Jim Backus, Denver Pyle

The Naked Jungle*
US 1954 95m Technicolor
Paramount / George Pal (Frank Freeman Jnr)

In 1901 a young woman is married by proxy to a South American cocoa planter, and when she arrives at his jungle home she has to conquer not only him but an army of soldier ants.
Mixture of *Rebecca* elements with a more unusual kind of thrill; all quite watchable, and the ant scenes very effective.

w Philip Yordan, Ranald MacDougall, *story* Leiningen Versus the Ants by Carl Stephenson *d* Byron Haskin *ph* Ernest Laszlo *m* Daniele Amfitheatrof

Charlton Heston, Eleanor Parker, William Conrad, Abraham Sofaer, John Dierkes, Douglas Fowley

The Naked Maja
Italy / US 1959 112m Technirama
MGM / Titanus (Goffredo Lombardo)

Peasant Francisco Goya becomes a famous painter through the influence of the Duchess of Alba.
Boring and unconvincing biopic.

w Giorgio Prosperi, Norman Corwin, Albert Lewin, Oscar Saul *d* Henry Koster
ph Giuseppe Rotunno *m* Francesco Lavagnino

Anthony Franciosa, Ava Gardner, Amedeo
Nazzari, Gino Cervi, Lea Padovani, Massimo
Serrato

'This travesty of Goya's life, country and
period adds up to nothing more entertaining
than a perfunctory, heavy-handed pageant.'—
MFB

The Naked Prey*
US 1966 94m Technicolor Panavision
Paramount / Theodora / Sven Persson
(Cornel Wilde)

In 1840, a white hunter becomes brutalized
when a tribe hunts him down as though he
were a lion.
Savage adventure story with bloodthirsty
detail; unusual and certainly effective.

w Clint Johnston, Don Peters *d* Cornel Wilde
ph I. A. R. Thompson *md* Andrew Tracy,
from African folk music

Cornel Wilde, Gert Van Den Berg, Ken
Gampu

'Overtones pretentious, but it tries.'—*Sight
and Sound*

AAN: script

The Naked Runner
GB 1967 104m Techniscope
Warner / Artanis (Brad Dexter)

British intelligence conceive a plan to turn an
innocent businessman into a spy killer.
Silly espionage thriller further marred by its
director's penchant for making a zany
composition of every frame.

w Stanley Mann, *novel* Francis Clifford
d Sidney J. Furie *ph* Otto Heller *m* Harry
Sukman

Frank Sinatra, Peter Vaughan, Derren
Nesbitt, Nadia Gray, Toby Robins, Cyril
Luckham, Edward Fox, Inger Stratton

'It might be a good movie to read by if there
were light in the theatre.'—*Pauline Kael*

The Naked Spur*
US 1952 91m Technicolor
MGM (William H. Wright)

A bounty hunter has trouble getting his quarry
back to base.
Standard big studio western shot in Colorado,
with all characters motivated by greed.

w Sam Rolfe, Harold Jack Bloom *d* Anthony
Mann *ph* William Mellor *m* Bronislau Kaper

James Stewart, Robert Ryan, Janet Leigh,
Millard Mitchell

AAN: script

The Naked Street
US 1955 83m bw
Edward Small

A racketeer's daughter marries a worthless
crook: her father saves him from the electric
chair but he murders again.
Semi-documentary exposé melodrama about
unpleasant people; reasonably proficient on its
level.

w Maxwell Shane, Leo Katcher *d* Maxwell
Shane *ph* Floyd Crosby *m* Emil Newman

THE NAKED TRUTH. Peter Sellers and Terry-Thomas led an all-star cast in a jolly jape
which sold a lot of tickets.

Anthony Quinn, Anne Bancroft, Farley
Granger, Peter Graves

The Naked Truth*
GB 1957 92m bw
Rank / Mario Zampi
US title: *Your Past is Showing*

Celebrities band together to kill a blackmailer
who threatens to expose unsavoury aspects of
their lives.
Frenzied black farce, quite a lot of which
comes off.

w Michael Pertwee *d* Mario Zampi *ph* Stan
Pavey *m* Stanley Black

Peter Sellers, Terry-Thomas, Peggy Mount,
Dennis Price, Shirley Eaton, Georgina
Cookson

● *Video: Rank*

Nana*
US 1934 89m bw
Samuel Goldwyn
GB title: *Lady of the Boulevards*

The high life and subsequent degradation of a
Parisian demi-mondaine in the nineties.
Stylish yet stolid slice of *le beau monde*,
intended to create a new star.

w Willard Mack, Harry Wagstaff Gribble,
novel Emile Zola *d* Dorothy Arzner
ph Gregg Toland *m* Alfred Newman

Anna Sten, Lionel Atwill, Phillips Holmes,
Richard Bennett, Mae Clarke, Muriel
Kirkland, Reginald Owen, Jessie Ralph

'The star's resources should be sufficient to
offset some of the lesser script deficiencies.'—
Variety

Nancy Drew
This series of second features starring Bonita
Granville as a teenage small-town detective
was moderately well received but quickly
forgotten. The character was created in novels
by Edward Stratemeyer and his daughter
Harriet Evans; the films were all directed by
William Clemens for Warners.

1938: NANCY DREW, DETECTIVE
1939: NANCY DREW, REPORTER;
NANCY DREW, TROUBLE SHOOTER;
NANCY DREW AND THE HIDDEN
STAIRCASE

Nancy Goes to Rio
US 1950 99m Technicolor
MGM (Joe Pasternak)

Two actresses, mother and daughter, are both
after the same part.
Mild shipboard musical.

w Sidney Sheldon *d* Robert Z. Leonard
ph Ray June *m* George Stoll

Jane Powell, Ann Sothern, Carmen Miranda,
Barry Sullivan, Louis Calhern, Fortunio
Bonanova, Hans Conried

Nancy Steele Is Missing*
US 1937   85m   bw
TCF (Nunnally Johnson)

Crooks try to pass off a girl as the long lost heir to a fortune.
Slightly unusual, well cast melodrama.

w Gene Fowler, Hal Long, *novel* C. F. Coe *d* George Marshall *ph* Barney McGill *m* David Buttolph

Victor McLaglen, Peter Lorre, June Lang, Jane Darwell, John Carradine

The Nanny*
GB 1965   93m   bw
ABP / Hammer (Jimmy Sangster)

A ten-year-old boy hates his nanny, and with good reason, for she is a neurotic murderess. Muted Hammer experiment in psychopathology, with too much equivocation before the dénouement; the star's role allows few fireworks, and the plot is rather unpleasant.

w Jimmy Sangster, *novel* Evelyn Piper *d* Seth Holt *ph* Harry Waxman *m* Richard Rodney Bennett

Bette Davis, Jill Bennett, William Dix, James Villiers, Wendy Craig, Pamela Franklin, Maurice Denham

Nanook of the North*
US 1921   57m (1947 sound version)
    bw   silent
Revillon Freres

The life of an Eskimo and his family. Primitive but trail-blazing documentary, hard to sit through for modern audiences.

w, d, ph, ed Robert Flaherty
  'In a day of emotional and artistic deliquescence on the screen, a picture with the fresh strength and pictorial promise of *Nanook of the North* is in the nature of a revolution.'— *Frances Taylor Patterson*
† Nanook himself died of hunger on the ice shortly after the film was released.

Napoleon****
France 1927   378m approx (24 fps)   bw
    (some colour)   silent
WESTI / Société Générale de Films

The early life of Napoleon.
A cinematic epic which, although brilliant in most particulars, owes its greatest interest to its narrative sweep, its flair for composition and its use of triptych screens which at the end combine to show one giant picture, the clear precursor of Cinerama. In 1934 Gance revised his film and added stereophonic sound.

w, d, ed Abel Gance *ph* various *m* Arthur Honegger

Albert Dieudonné, Antonin Artaud, Pierre Batcheff
† The 1934 version ran 140m and included three-dimensional sound.

Napoleon and Samantha
US 1972   91m   Technicolor
Walt Disney (Winston Hibler)

When his old guardian dies, a small boy and his girl friend run away with their pet lion. Patchy, episodic action drama for older children, with a very sleepy lion.

w Stewart Raffil *d* Bernard McEveety *ph* Monroe Askins *m* Buddy Baker

Michael Douglas, Will Geer

AAN: Buddy Baker

The Narrow Corner
US 1933   71m   bw

On an eastern island, a man on the run for murder finds he can't escape his fate. Mediocre adaptation of a Somerset Maugham novel in which very little happens; the added love interest doesn't help. Douglas Fairbanks Jnr, Ralph Bellamy, Dudley Digges, Arthur Hohl, Patricia Ellis. Written by Robert Presnell; directed by Alfred E. Green; for Warner. (Remade three years later as *Isle of Fury* [qv].) 'Considerably better than fair.'— *Variety*

The Narrow Margin***
US 1950   70m   bw
RKO (Stanley Rubin)

Police try to guard a prosecution witness on a train from Chicago to Los Angeles.
Tight little thriller which takes every advantage of its train setting. What the trade used to call a sleeper, it gave more satisfaction than many a top feature.

w Earl Felton *d* Richard Fleischer *ph* George E. Diskant

Charles McGraw, Marie Windsor, Jacqueline White, Queenie Leonard

AAN: original story (Martin Goldsmith, Jack Leonard)

The Narrowing Circle
GB 1955   66m   bw

Murder on the staff of a magazine. Very tolerable mystery which wastes no time and plays fair. Paul Carpenter, Hazel Court, Ferdy Mayne, Russell Napier, Trevor Reid. Written by Doreen Montgomery, from the novel by Julian Symons; directed by Charles Saunders; for Fortress Films / Eros.

'The damnedest thing you ever saw!'
Nashville**
US 1975   161m   Metrocolor   Panavision
Paramount / ABC (Robert Altman)

A political campaign in Nashville organizes a mammoth pop concert to gain support. Kaleidoscopic, fragmented, multi-storied musical melodrama, a mammoth movie which can be a bore or an inspiration according to taste. Certainly many exciting moments pass by, but the length is self-defeating.

w Joan Tewkesbury *d* Robert Altman *ph* Paul Lohmann *md* Richard Baskin

Geraldine Chaplin, David Arkin, Barbara Baxley, Ned Beatty, Karen Black, Keith Carradine, Henry Gibson, Keenan Wynn, Lily Tomlin, Ronee Blakley
  'A gigantic parody . . . crammed with samples taken from every level of Nashville

society, revealed in affectionate detail bordering on caricature in a manner that would surely delight Norman Rockwell.'— *Philip Strick*
  'Wildly over-praised Altman, with all the defects we once looked on as marks of healthy ambitiousness: terrible construction, messy editing, leering jokes at its own characters, unending pomposity.'—*Time Out, 1980*

AA: song 'I'm Easy' (*m / ly* Keith Carradine)
AAN: best picture; Robert Altman; Lily Tomlin; Ronee Blakley

Nasty Habits*
GB 1976   92m   Technicolor
Brut / Bowden (Robert Enders)

An abbess dies and the nuns vie for succession.
Satirical comedy rather obviously based on the Watergate scandals; initially amusing , but very tiresome by the end.

w Robert Enders, *novel* The Abbess of Crewe by Muriel Spark *d* Michael Lindsay-Hogg *ph* Douglas Slocombe *m* John Cameron

Glenda Jackson, Melina Mercouri, Genevieve Page, Sandy Dennis, Anne Jackson, Anne Meara, Edith Evans, Susan Penhaligon, Rip Torn, Eli Wallach, Jerry Stiller
  'The sort of material just about fit for a half-hour TV sketch.'—*Richard Combs, MFB*

The National Health*
GB 1973   97m   Eastmancolor
Columbia (Ned Sherrin, Terry Glinwood)

Life in the general men's ward of a large antiquated hospital.
Acerbic comedy from a National Theatre play which mixes tragedy and farce into a kind of *Carry on Dying*.

w Peter Nichols, from his play *d* Jack Gold *ph* John Coquillon *m* Carl Davis *pd* Ray Simm

Jim Dale, Lynn Redgrave, Eleanor Bron, Sheila Scott-Wilkinson, Donald Sinden, Colin Blakely, Clive Swift

National Lampoon's Animal House*
US 1978   109m   Technicolor
Universal (Matty Simmons, Ivan Reitman)

On an American campus around 1962, scruffy newcomers challenge the elegant elite.
A ragbag of college gags, of interest only to those who have had the experience; but its success caused much imitation, especially in American television.

w Harold Ramis, Douglas Kenney, Chris Miller *d* John Landis *ph* Charles Correll *m* Elmer Bernstein

John Belushi, Tim Matheson, John Vernon, Donald Sutherland, Verna Bloom, Cesare Danova, Mary Louise Weller
● *Video: CIC*

National Lampoon's Class Reunion
US 1982   85m   Metrocolor

The class of '72 foregathers at Lizzie Borden High, where a murderer is lurking. An entertainment in which the presentation is better than the material, which is a vague spoof of high school and horror films. Gerrit Graham, Michael Lerner, Fred McCarren, Miriam Flynn, Stephen Furst. Written by John Hughes; directed by Michael Miller; for Matty Simmons / ABC Motion Pictures.

National Lampoon's Vacation
US 1983   98m   Technicolor

An inventor drives his family on a holiday starting in Chicago and ending in California, but the journey is fraught with disaster. Episodic, more or less straight black comedy, with detail more often boring or repellent than funny. Chevy Chase, Imogene Coca, Beverly D'Angelo, Randy Quaid, Eddie Bracken. Written by John Hughes; directed by Harold Ramis; for Matty Simmons / Warners.

National Velvet*
US 1945   125m   Technicolor
MGM (Pandro S. Berman)

Children train a horse to win the Grand National.
A big bestseller from another era; its flaws of conception and production quickly became evident.

w Theodore Reeves, Helen Deutsch, *novel* Enid Bagnold d Clarence Brown ph Leonard Smith m Herbert Stothart

Mickey Rooney, Elizabeth Taylor, *Anne Revere*, Donald Crisp, Angela Lansbury, Jackie Jenkins, Reginald Owen, Terry Kilburn, Norma Varden, Alec Craig, Arthur Shields, Dennis Hoey
† Sequel 1978: *International Velvet.*

AA: Anne Revere
AAN: Clarence Brown; Leonard Smith

Naughty But Nice
US 1939   90m   bw
Warner (Sam Bischoff)

A professor of classical music accidentally writes a popular song.
Mildly amusing comedy musical with all the tunes adapted from the classics (cf *That Night with You*).

w Jerry Wald, Richard Macaulay d Ray Enright ph Arthur L. Todd songs Harry Warren, Johnny Mercer

Dick Powell, Ann Sheridan, Ronald Reagan, Gale Page, Zasu Pitts, Jerry Colonna

Naughty Marietta**
US 1935   106m   bw
MGM (Hunt Stromberg)

A French princess goes to America and falls in love with an Indian scout.
Period operetta which set the seal of success on the MacDonald-Eddy team. In itself, dated but quite pleasing for those who like the genre.

w John Lee Mahin, Frances Goodrich, Albert Hackett, *operetta* Rida Johnson Young d W. S. Van Dyke ph William Daniels m Victor Herbert ad Cedric Gibbons

Jeanette MacDonald, Nelson Eddy, Frank Morgan, Elsa Lanchester, Douglass Dumbrille, Joseph Cawthorn, Cecelia Parker, Walter Kingsford
'Slow-moving operetta which singing must sustain.'—*Variety*
'When these two profiles come together to sing Ah Sweet Mystery of Life, it's beyond camp, it's in a realm of its own.'—*Judith Crist, 1977*
AAN: best picture

The Naughty Nineties
US 1945   72m   bw
Universal (Edward L. Hartmann, John Grant)

Two incompetents help an old showboat owner.
Dim star comedy apart from the team's rendition of their most famous routine, 'Who's On First'.

w Edmund L. Hartmann, John Grant, Edmund Joseph, Hal Fimburg d Jean Yarborough ph George Robinson

Bud Abbott, Lou Costello, Henry Travers, Alan Curtis, Rita Johnson, Joe Sawyer

The Navigator***
US 1924   63m approx (24 fps)   bw
silent
Metro-Goldwyn / Buster Keaton (Joseph M. Schenck)

A millionaire and his girl are the only people on a transatlantic liner marooned in mid-ocean.
A succession of hilarious sight gags: the star in top form.

w Jean Havez, Clyde Bruckman, J. A. Mitchell d Buster Keaton, Donald Crisp ph Elgin Lessley, Byron Houck

Buster Keaton, Kathryn McGuire
'Studded with hilarious moments and a hundred and one adroit gags.'—*Photoplay*

'It is not the victory that is important, it is how the game is played!'

Navy Blue and Gold
US 1937   93m   bw

An unpopular naval cadet makes good.
Ingenuous flagwaver, like a wrap-up of umpteen others but with better production. Robert Young, James Stewart, Florence Rice, Billie Burke, Lionel Barrymore, Tom Brown, Samuel S. Hinds, Paul Kelly. Written by George Bruce; directed by Sam Wood; for Sam Zimbalist / MGM. 'Expertly made and sure box office.'—*Variety*

Navy Blues
US 1941   109m   bw
Warner (Jerry Wald)

Naval ratings get into trouble in Honolulu.
Undernourished musical comedy with not too much of either commodity.

w Jerry Wald, Richard Macaulay, Arthur T. Horman d Lloyd Bacon ph Tony Gaudio ch Seymour Felix songs Arthur Schwarz, Johnny Mercer

Ann Sheridan, Jack Oakie, Martha Raye, Jack Haley, Herbert Anderson, Jack Carson, Richard Lane, Jackie Gleason, Howard da Silva

Navy Wife
US 1935   72m   bw

A girl who marries a navy doctor is unhappy with the life. Routine domestic drama with a propaganda angle. Claire Trevor, Ralph Bellamy, Jane Darwell, Ben Lyon, Warren Hymer, Kathleen Burke. Written by Sonya Levien from the novel Beauty's Daughter by Kathleen Norris; directed by Allan Dwan; for Fox. 'Problem play for the duals.'—*Variety*

Navy Wife
US 1956   83m   bw

A commander's wife visits her husband in Japan and learns about Japanese attitudes. Silly hands-across-the-sea comedy which takes a long time to get nowhere. Joan Bennett, Gary Merrill, Shirley Yagamuchi, Judy Nugent. Written by Kay Lenard; directed by Edward Bernds; for Allied Artists. (GB title: *Mother, Sir!*)

Nazarin*
Mexico 1958   94m   bw
Barbachano Ponce

A Catholic priest tries to take the teachings of Christ literally, but is drastically misunderstood.
A black atheistic satire pretty typical of its director, but not among his most enjoyable works.

w Julio Alejandro, Luis Bunuel, *novel* Benito Perez Galdos d Luis Bunuel ph Gabriel Figueroa

Francisco Rabal, Marga Lopez, Rita Macedo, Ignacio Lopez Tarso

Nazi Agent*
US 1942   84m   bw
MGM (Irving Asher)

A German-American is forced by his Nazi twin to help a group of German spies.
Modest suspenser with a plot twist similar to *The Great Impersonation* and *Dead Ringer*.

w Paul Gangelin, John Meehan Jnr d Jules Dassin ph Harry Stradling m Lennie Hayton

Conrad Veidt, Ann Ayars, Frank Reicher, Dorothy Tree, Martin Kosleck

The Neanderthal Man
US 1953   75m   bw

A scientist transforms a cat into a sabre-toothed tiger and himself into a neanderthal man; he is then eaten by the tiger. By no means as amusing as it sounds. Robert Shayne, Richard Crane, Doris Merrick, Joyce Terry. Written by Aubrey Wisberg and Jack Pollexfen; directed by E. A. Dupont; photographed by Stanley Cortez; for Global / United Artists.

Nearly a Nasty Accident
GB 1961 91m bw
British Lion / Britannia / Marlow (Bertram Ostrer)

A mild-mannered aircraftman causes disaster wherever he goes.
Familiar faces just about save from disaster this underscripted comedy for indulgent audiences.

w Jack Davies, Hugh Woodruff, play Touch Wood by David Stringer, David Carr d Don Chaffey ph Paul Beeson m Ken Jones

Kenneth Connor, Jimmy Edwards, Shirley Eaton, Richard Wattis, Ronnie Stevens, Jon Pertwee, Eric Barker, Peter Jones, Jack Watling, Joyce Carey, Terry Scott

The Nebraskan
US 1953 66m Technicolor 3D

An army scout proves the innocence of an Indian supposed to have murdered a Sioux chief. Two-bit western which looked even worse in three dimensions. Phil Carey, Roberta Haynes, Wallace Ford, Richard Webb, Lee Van Cleef. Written by David Lang and Martin Berkeley; directed by Fred F. Sears; for Columbia.

Necromancy
US 1973 83m colour
Cinerama (Bert I. Gordon)

Two young people become involved in small-town witchcraft.
Low-key, low-talent thriller overbalanced by its star.

wd Bert I. Gordon ph Winton C. Hoch m Fred Karger

Orson Welles, Pamela Franklin, Michael Onthean, Lee Purcell

Ned Kelly
GB 1970 103m Technicolor
UA / Woodfall (Neil Hartley)

The career of a 19th-century Australian outlaw.
Obstinately unlikeable action picture with some kind of message which never becomes clear amid all the cleverness.

w Tony Richardson, Ian Jones d Tony Richardson ph Gerry Fisher m Shel Silverstein pd Jocelyn Herbert

Mick Jagger, Allen Bickford, Geoff Gilmour, Mark McManus

Negatives*
GB 1968 98m Eastmancolor
Crispin / Kettledrum (Judd Bernard)

Three people indulge in sexual fantasies involving Dr Crippen and Baron Von Richthofen.
Smoothly done but impenetrable psychological poppycock: what is fact and what is fancy, only the author knows.

w Peter Everett, Roger Lowry, novel Peter Everett d Peter Medak ph Ken Hodges m Basil Kirchin

Glenda Jackson, Peter McEnery, Diane Cilento, Maurice Denham, Steven Lewis, Norman Rossington

Neighbors*
US 1981 94m Technicolor
Columbia / Zanuck–Brown

A staid suburbanite is first irritated, then taken over by his splashy neighbours.
Hit-or-miss but generally quite funny comedy in a style familiar to viewers of American late night television.

w Larry Gelbart, novel Thomas Berger d John G. Avildsen ph Gerald Hirschfeld m Bill Conti pd Peter Larkin ed Jan Kurson

John Belushi, Dan Aykroyd, Kathryn Walker, Cathy Moriarty, Igors Gavon, Dru-Ann Chukron

Nell Gwyn**
GB 1934 85m bw
B and D (Herbert Wilcox)

The affair of Charles II and an orange seller.
Naïve, vivid account of a famous couple; physically cheap and rather faded, but the best film on the subject and one of the best covering this period.

w Miles Malleson d Herbert Wilcox ph F. A. Young

Anna Neagle, Cedric Hardwicke, Jeanne de Casalis, Muriel George, Miles Malleson, Esmé Percy, Moore Marriott
'Slow costumer, also lacking marquee value.'—Variety

'Wherever you've been—this is where you've never been before!'
The Neptune Factor
Canada 1972 98m De Luxe Panavision
TCF / Quadrant / Bellevue–Pathe (Sanford Howard)
Later retitled: The Neptune Disaster

American oceanologists conduct an experiment in underwater living.
Wet 'actioner' in which very little happens except a few porthole views of magnified fish.

w Jack de Witt d Daniel Petrie ph Harry Makin m Lalo Schifrin

Ben Gazzara, Walter Pidgeon, Yvette Mimieux, Ernest Borgnine, Chris Wiggins

Neptune's Daughter*
US 1949 93m Technicolor
MGM (Jack Cummings)

A lady bathing suit designer has a South American romance.
Generally thought one of the better aquatic musicals, and certainly very typical of them and its studio at this time.

w Dorothy Kingsley d Edward Buzzell ph Charles Rosher m George Stoll songs Frank Loesser

Esther Williams, Red Skelton, Ricardo Montalban, Betty Garrett, Keenan Wynn, Xavier Cugat and his Orchestra, Mike Mazurki, Ted de Corsia, Mel Blanc

AA: song, 'Baby, It's Cold Outside'

The Net
GB 1953 86m bw
Rank / Two Cities (Anthony Darnborough)
US title: Project M7

Tension among boffins in an aviation research station leads to murder and the discovery of a spy.
Low-key suspenser, quite adequately presented.

w William Fairchild, novel John Pudney d Anthony Asquith ph Desmond Dickinson m Benjamin Frankel

Phyllis Calvert, Noel Willman, Herbert Lom, James Donald, Robert Beatty, Muriel Pavlow, Walter Fitzgerald, Maurice Denham

'Television will never be the same!'
'Prepare yourself for a perfectly outrageous motion picture!'
Network**
US 1976 121m Metrocolor Panavision
MGM / UA (Howard Gottfried, Fred Caruso)

A network news commentator begins to say what he thinks about the world and becomes a new messiah to the people and an embarrassment to his sponsors.
Overheated satire which in between its undoubted high points becomes noisy and tiresome, not helped by fuzzy photography. Its very existence in a commercial system, however, is as remarkable as its box-office success.

w Paddy Chayevsky d Sidney Lumet ph Owen Roizman m Elliot Lawrence

Peter Finch, William Holden, Faye Dunaway, Robert Duvall, Wesley Addy, Ned Beatty, Beatrice Straight, John Carpenter

HOWARD BEALE (Peter Finch) on live television: 'I don't know what to do about the depression and the inflation and the Russians and the crime in the streets. All I know is that first you've got to get mad. You've got to say: "I'm a human being, god damn it, my life has some value!" So I want you to get up now. I want all of you to get up out of your chairs. I want you to get up right now and go to the window, open it and stick your head out and yell "I'm mad as hell, and I'm not going to take this any more!" '

Ditto: 'Ladies and gentlemen, I would like at this moment to announce that I will be retiring from this programme in two weeks' time because of poor ratings. Since this show was the only thing I had going for me in my life, I have decided to kill myself. I'm going to blow my brains out right on this programme a week from today.'

MAX SCHUMACHER (William Holden): 'You're television incarnate, Diana, indifferent to suffering, insensitive to joy. All of life is reduced to the common rubble of banality. War, murder, death—all the same to you as bottles of beer, and the daily business of life is a corrupt comedy. You even shatter the sensations of time and space into split seconds and instant replays. You're madness, Diana.'

'The cast of this messianic farce take turns yelling at us soulless masses.'—*New Yorker*
'Too much of this film has the hectoring stridency of tabloid headlines.'—*Michael Billington, Illustrated London News*
† The theme was taken up a year later in the shortlived TV series *W.E.B.*

AA: Paddy Chayevsky; Peter Finch; Faye Dunaway; Beatrice Straight
AAN: best picture; Sidney Lumet; Owen Roizman; William Holden; Ned Beatty

● *Video: Intervision*

Neutral Port
GB 1940 92m bw

A merchant navy captain avenges the loss of his ship by sabotaging a German U-boat.
Unconvincing propaganda, rather stagily presented. Will Fyffe, Phyllis Calvert, Leslie Banks, Yvonne Arnaud, Hugh McDermott, Frederick Valk. Written by J. B. Williams and T. J. Morrison; directed by Marcel Varnel; for Gainsborough.

Nevada Smith*
US 1966 131m Eastmancolor Panavision
Avco / Solar (Joe Levine, Henry Hathaway)

A cowboy takes a long revenge on the outlaws who murdered his parents.
Violent, sour, occasionally lively but frequently boring western melodrama on a well worn theme.

w John Michael Hayes, from the 'early life' of a character in The Carpetbaggers by Harold Robbins d Henry Hathaway ph Lucien Ballard m Alfred Newman

Steve McQueen, Karl Malden, Brian Keith, Suzanne Pleshette, Arthur Kennedy, Janet Margolin, Howard da Silva, Raf Vallone, Pat Hingle

The Nevadan
US 1950 81m Cinecolor

A marshal recovers stolen gold. Solid western programmer, compromised by poor colour. Randolph Scott, Dorothy Malone, Forrest Tucker, Frank Faylen, George Macready. Written by George W. George and George F. Slavin; directed by Gordon Douglas; for Harry Joe Brown / Columbia. (GB title: *The Man from Nevada*.)

Never a Dull Moment
US 1943 60m bw

Three comedians prevent a nightclub owner from carrying out a robbery. The last thin vehicle for a famous comedy trio; even here they have their moments. The Ritz Brothers, Frances Langford, Mary Beth Hughes, George Zucco, Franklin Pangborn. Written by Mel Ronson and Stanley Roberts; directed by Edward Lilley; for Universal.

Never a Dull Moment
US 1950 89m bw
RKO (Harriet Parsons)

A lady music critic marries a rodeo cowboy and finds life hard down on the ranch.
Very mild star programmer.

w Lou Breslow, Doris Anderson, *novel* Who Could Ask for Anything More? by Kay Swift d George Marshall ph Joseph Walker m Frederick Hollander md Constantin Bakaleinikoff

Irene Dunne, Fred MacMurray, William Demarest, Andy Devine, Gigi Perreau, Natalie Wood, Philip Ober, Jack Kirkwood

Never a Dull Moment
US 1967 100m Technicolor
Walt Disney (Ron Miller)

An unsuccessful actor is mistaken for a notorious gangster.
Slapstick romp with vigour but not much flair.

w A. J. Carothers, *novel* John Godey d Jerry Paris ph William Snyder m Robert F. Brunner

Dick Van Dyke, Edward G. Robinson, Dorothy Provine, Henry Silva, Joanna Moore, Tony Bill, Slim Pickens, Jack Elam

Never Cry Wolf
US 1983 105m Technicolor

A scientist is dumped alone in the Arctic to collect evidence against wolves. Weird fable whose comic asides diminish its serious intent, and whose leading characterization is so eccentric as to bewilder any audience. Charles Martin Smith, Brian Dennehy, Samson Jorah. Written by Curtis Hanson, Sam Hamm, Richard Kletter, from the book by Farley Mowat; directed by Carroll Ballard; for Walt Disney.

Never Give a Sucker an Even Break*
US 1941 70m bw
Universal
GB title: *What a Man*

W. C. Fields dives off an aeroplane into the lap of a young woman who has never seen a man; she falls in love with him.
Stupefyingly inept in its scripting and pacing, this comedy is often irresistibly funny because of the anti-everything personality of its writer-star. No one else could have got away with it, or would have been likely to try.

w John T. Neville, Prescott Chaplin, *story* Otis Criblecoblis (W. C. Fields) d Edward Cline ph Charles Van Enger m Frank Skinner

W. C. Fields, Gloria Jean, Leon Errol, Butch and Buddy, Franklin Pangborn, Anne Nagel, Mona Barrie, Ann Miller, Margaret Dumont

Never Let Go
GB 1960 91m bw
Rank / Julian Wintle–Leslie Parkin (Peter de Sarigny)

A travelling salesman has his car stolen and stands up to the sadistic gang boss responsible. Brutishly unattractive thriller, apparently designed for the sole purpose of giving Peter Sellers a villainous part.

w Alun Falconer d John Guillermin ph Christopher Challis m John Barry

Richard Todd, Peter Sellers, Elizabeth Sellars, Adam Faith, Carol White, Mervyn Johns, Noel Willman

Never Let Me Go
GB 1953 94m bw
MGM (Clarence Brown)

After World War II an American correspondent marries a Russian ballerina but is later deported by the authorities.
Ho-hum romantic melodrama, quite interestingly cast.

w Roland Millar, George Froeschel, *novel* Came the Dawn by Roger Bax d Delmer Daves ph Robert Krasker m Hans May

Clark Gable, Gene Tierney, Richard Haydn, Belita, Bernard Miles, Kenneth More, Karel Stepanek, Theodore Bikel, Frederick Valk

Never Look Back
GB 1952 73m bw

A lady barrister finds she must defend an old boy friend on a murder charge. Plausible drama which never quite comes to the boil. Rosamund John, Hugh Sinclair, Guy Middleton, Henry Edwards, Terence Longdon. Written by John Hunter, Guy Morgan and Francis Searle; directed by Francis Searle; for Michael Carreras / Exclusive.

Never Love a Stranger
US 1958 93m bw
Harold Robbins / Allied Artists (Peter Gettlinger)

A Catholic boy who has become a gangster helps his Jewish friend who has become assistant district attorney to trap a vicious hoodlum.
The old *Manhattan Melodrama* theme is dusted off once again, this time to very little effect.

w Harold Robbins, Richard Day, *novel* Harold Robbins d Robert Stevens ph Lee Garmes m Raymond Scott

John Drew Barrymore, Steve McQueen, Robert Bray, Lita Milan, R. G. Armstrong, Salem Ludwig

Never on Sunday*
Greece 1959 97m bw
Lopert / Melinafilm (Jules Dassin)
original title: *Pote tin Kyriaki*

An American scholar in Greece is infatuated by a prostitute and sets about improving her. Amiable if rather shoddy variation on *Pygmalion*: the star performance and the music carried it, along with its own naughtiness, to success.

wd Jules Dassin ph Jacques Natteau m Manos Hadjidakis

Melina Mercouri, Jules Dassin, Georges Foundas, Tito Vandis, Despo Diamantidou
'It barely stands scrutiny, but it communicates cheerfulness, and this in itself is no mean achievement.'—*Penelope Houston, MFB*

AA: title song (Manos Hadjidakis)
AAN: direction; script; Melina Mercouri

Never Put it in Writing*
GB 1963 93m bw
MGM / Andrew Stone

A young executive tries to recover from the mails an indiscreet letter he has written to his boss.
Frantic hit-or-miss farcical comedy distinguished by Dublin locations and cast.

wd Andrew Stone *ph* Martin Curtis *m* Frank Cordell

Pat Boone, Fidelma Murphy, Reginald Beckwith, John Le Mesurier, Colin Blakely

Never Say Die*
US 1939 80m bw
Paramount (Paul Jones)

A millionaire hypochondriac is convinced he is dying.
Thin farce with Hope on the very brink of stardom; some bright moments.

w Don Hartman, Frank Butler, Preston Sturges *d* Elliott Nugent *ph* Leo Tover *md* Boris Morros

Martha Raye, Bob Hope, Andy Devine, Alan Mowbray, Gale Sondergaard, Sig Rumann, Ernest Cossart, Monty Woolley, Christian Rub

'Needs strong support for top dual spots.'—*Variety*

'The most enjoyable film for weeks . . . consistently absurd . . . no dignity, no passion, and a magnificent cast.'—*Graham Greene*

Never Say Goodbye
US 1946 97m bw
Warner (William Jacobs)

A seven-year-old girl draws her divorced parents back together.
Highly derivative romantic comedy mishmash which did its star's career no good at all.

w James V. Kern, I. A. L. Diamond, Lewis R. Foster, Ben and Norma Barzman *d* James V. Kern *ph* Arthur Edeson *m* Frederick Hollander

Errol Flynn, Eleanor Parker, Lucile Watson, S. Z. Sakall, Donald Woods, Patti Brady, Forrest Tucker, Hattie McDaniel

Never Say Goodbye
US 1955 96m Technicolor
U-I (Albert J. Cohen)

In 1945 Berlin an American army doctor marries a pianist who is later trapped in the Russian zone; they meet years later in America.
Romantic drama aimed at a female audience, remade from *This Love of Ours* (qv).

w Charles Hoffman *d* Jerry Hopper *ph* Maury Gertsman *m* Frank Skinner

Rock Hudson, George Sanders, Cornell Borchers, Ray Collins, David Janssen

Never Say Never Again*
GB 1983 134m Technicolor
Panavision
Warner / Woodcote / Taliafilm (Jack Schwartzman)

James Bond foils a world domination attempt by Blofeld.

Reasonably enjoyable mishmash of Bondery; the plot is technically a remake of *Thunderball*, not that it matters much until the end, when the underwater stuff becomes tiresome because one hardly knows who is under the masks.

w Lorenzo Semple Jnr *d* Irvin Kershner *ph* Douglas Slocombe *m* Michel Legrand *pd* Philip Harrison, Stephen Grimes

Sean Connery, Klaus Maria Brandauer, Max Von Sydow, Barbara Carrera, Kim Basinger, Bernie Casey, Alec McCowen, Edward Fox, Rowan Atkinson

'Q' (Alec McCowen): 'Good to see you again, Mr Bond. Let's get back to some gratuitous sex and violence, I say.'

● *Video: Warner*

Never So Few
US 1959 124m Metrocolor
Cinemascope
MGM / Canterbury (Edmund Grainger)

Adventures of World War II Americans commanding Burmese guerrillas.
Jungle actioner with pauses for philosophizing; well enough made but not very interesting.

w Millard Kaufman, *novel* Tom Chamales *d* John Sturges *ph* William H. Daniels *m* Hugo Friedhofer

Frank Sinatra, Gina Lollobrigida, Peter Lawford, Steve McQueen, Paul Henreid, Richard Johnson, Brian Donlevy, Charles Bronson, Dean Jones

Never Steal Anything Small
US 1958 94m Eastmancolor
Cinemascope
U-I (Aaron Rosenberg)

The reformation of a corrupt but sympathetic dockers' union boss.
Curious semi-musical which doesn't come off at all despite excellent credentials.

wd Charles Lederer, *play* The Devil's Hornpipe by Rouben Mamoulian, Maxwell Anderson *ph* Harold Lipstein *m* Allie Wrubel *ly* Maxwell Anderson *ch* Hermes Pan

James Cagney, Shirley Jones, Roger Smith, Cara Williams, Nehemiah Persoff, Royal Dano, Anthony Caruso

Never Take No for an Answer*
GB 1951 82m bw
Anthony Havelock-Allan

A small boy goes to Rome to get permission from the Pope to take his sick donkey to be blessed in the church.
Slight, easy-going whimsy with attractive sunlit locations.

w Paul and Pauline Gallico, *novel* The Small Miracle by Paul Gallico *d* Maurice Cloche, Ralph Smart *ph* Otto Heller *m* Nino Rota

Vittorio Manunta, Denis O'Dea, Guido Cellano, Nerio Bernardi

'The main pleasures of this slender film are visual ones.'—*MFB*

† Remade as a TV movie *Small Miracle*.

Never the Twain Shall Meet
US 1931 89m bw

A young lawyer goes native when he falls for a South Sea island girl. Stilted misalliance melodrama, previously made in 1925 as a silent with Bert Lytell and Anita Stewart; its faded notions simply didn't survive sound.
Leslie Howard, Conchita Montenegro, Karen Morley, C. Aubrey Smith. Written by Ruth Cummings and Edwin Justus Mayer, from the novel by Peter B. Kyne; directed by W. S. Van Dyke; for MGM.

Never Too Late
US 1965 104m Technicolor
Panavision
Warner / Lear–Yorkin (Norman Lear)

A well-to-do middle-aged housewife discovers she is pregnant.
Predictable, rather hysterical domestic comedy, flatly developed from a successful play which offered two star parts for old stagers.

w Sumner Arthur Long, from his play *d* Bud Yorkin *ph* Philip Lathrop *m* David Rose

Paul Ford, Maureen O'Sullivan, Connie Stevens, Jim Hutton, Lloyd Nolan, Henry Jones, Jane Wyatt

Never Wave at a WAC
US 1952 87m bw
Independent Artists (Frederick Brisson)
GB title: *The Private Wore Skirts*

A Washington hostess joins the WACs and finds she can't get beyond the rank of private.
Pattern comedy, unconvincing in all respects but with a smattering of funny moments. Flagwaving takes over towards the end.

w Ken Englund *d* Norman Z. McLeod *ph* William Daniels *m* Elmer Bernstein

Rosalind Russell, Paul Douglas, Marie Wilson, William Ching, Leif Erickson, Arleen Whelan, Charles Dingle

The New Adventures of Get-Rich-Quick Wallingford
US 1931 76m bw

Exploits of an attractive go-getter. Reliable comedy of its day. William Haines, Jimmy Durante, Leila Hyams, Guy Kibbee. Written by Charles MacArthur, from the novel by G. R. Chester; directed by Sam Wood; for MGM.

The New Babylon*
USSR 1929 80m approx (24 fps) bw
silent
Sovkino
original title: *Novyi Vavilon*

The rise and fall of the 1871 French commune, seen through the eyes of a girl department store worker.
Propagandist socio-historical melodrama, most interesting now for its sub-Eisenstein technique.

wd Leonid Trauberg, Grigori Kozintsev *ph* Andrei Moskvin, Yevgeni Mikhailov *m* Dmitri Shostakovich *ad* Yevgeni Enei

Yelena Kuzmina, Pyotr Sobelevsky, Sophie Magarill

The New Centurions*
US 1972 103m Eastmancolor
Panavision
Columbia / Chartoff–Winkler
GB title: *Precinct 45: Los Angeles Police*

An old cop teaches a new one.
'Realistic' crime prevention saga which spawned the TV series *Police Story* and *Police Woman*. Well done within its limits.

w Stirling Silliphant, *novel* Joseph Wambaugh *d* Richard Fleischer *ph* Ralph Woolsey *m* Quincy Jones

George C. Scott, Stacy Keach, Jane Alexander, Rosalind Cash, Scott Wilson

New Faces*
US 1954 99m Eastmancolor
Cinemascope
Edward L. Alperson (Leonard Sillman)

A revue goes on despite money problems.
Five minutes of plot, ninety-five minutes of revue from the Broadway stage; mostly quite amusing, and chiefly notable for introducing Eartha Kitt with all her standards.

w various *d* Harry Horner *ph* Lucien Ballard *m* Raoul Kraushaar *revue deviser* John Murray Anderson

Eartha Kitt, Ronny Graham, Alice Ghostley, Robert Clary, Paul Lynde

New Faces of 1937
US 1937 105m bw

Talent auditions for a Broadway show.
Shapeless agglomeration of variety acts with a wisp of story; the level of talent is not outstandingly high. Joe Penner, Milton Berle, Parkyakarkus, Harriet Hilliard, Jerome Cowan, Bert Gordon, Ann Miller, Richard Lane. Written by Nat Perrin, P. G. Epstein, Irving Brecher, Harold Russell, Harry Clork, Howard J. Green, from a story Shoestring by George Bradshaw; directed by Leigh Jason; for RKO. 'A hodgepodge of vaudeville, night club and radio talent, unskilfully blended and rather inanely promulgated.'—*Variety*

The New Gulliver*
USSR 1933 85m approx bw

Gulliver's Travels is retold in puppet form, but the plot has become a satire against capitalism. Interesting both as animation and as propaganda. Written by A. Ptoushko, B. Roshal; directed by A. Ptoushko, A. Vanitchkin.

The New Interns
US 1964 123m bw
Columbia (Robert Cohn)

Young doctors at a city hospital have trouble saving a rapist and his victim.
Unnecessary sequel to *The Interns*, its 'realism' requiring large pinches of salt.

w Wilton Schiller *d* John Rich *ph* Lucien Ballard *m* Earle Hagen

George Segal, Telly Savalas, Michael Callan, Dean Jones, Inger Stevens, Stefanie Powers, Lee Patrick

A New Kind of Love
US 1963 110m Technicolor
Paramount / Llenroc (Melville Shavelson)

An American dress designer in Paris is softened by a boorish newspaper columnist. Very thin sex comedy, dressed to kill but with nowhere to go.

wd Melville Shavelson *ph* Daniel Fapp *m* Leith Stevens

Paul Newman, Joanne Woodward, Maurice Chevalier, Thelma Ritter, George Tobias

AAN: Leith Stevens

The New Land see The Emigrants

A New Leaf*
US 1970 102m Movielab
Paramount / Aries / Elkins (Joe Manduke)

A middle-aged playboy, close to bankruptcy, thinks of acquiring a wealthy wife.
Agreeably mordant comedy which sparkles in patches rather than as a whole.

wd Elaine May, *story* The Green Heart by Jack Ritchie *ph* Gayne Rescher *m* John Mandel, Neal Hefti *pd* Richard Fried

Walter Matthau, Elaine May, Jack Weston, George Rose, William Redfield, James Coco

'Unashamedly a thirties fairy tale in modern, but not fashionable, dress.'—*Jan Dawson*

New Mexico
US 1952 78m Anscocolor

A cavalry officer tries to make peace with the Indians, but when an Indian child is accidentally killed a savage war breaks out. Standard western, not badly made. Lew Ayres, Marilyn Maxwell, Robert Hutton, Andy Devine, Raymond Burr, Jeff Corey. Written by Max Trell; directed by Irving Reis; for Irving Allen / United Artists.

New Moon*
US 1940 105m bw
MGM (Robert Z. Leonard)

Romance in old French Louisiana.
Stalwart adaptation of an operetta previously filmed in 1930 with Lawrence Tibbett and Grace Moore.

w Jacques Deval, Robert Arthur *d* Robert Z. Leonard *ph* William Daniels *m / ly* Sigmund Romberg, Oscar Hammerstein

Jeanette MacDonald, Nelson Eddy, Mary Boland, George Zucco, H. B. Warner, Stanley Fields, Grant Mitchell

New Morals for Old
US 1932 77m bw

John Van Druten's play *After All*, about the generation gap in the London aristocracy, was here rather unwisely translated to the American middle class and emerged as a decided curiosity. Robert Young, Myrna Loy, Jean Hersholt, Lewis Stone, Laura Hope Crews, Elizabeth Patterson. Written by Zelda Sears and Wanda Tuchock; directed by

Charles Brabin; for MGM. 'A weak sister, swathed in gloom, muddled, and without names that will draw.'—*Variety*

New Orleans*
US 1947 89m bw
Jules Levey

How jazz was born, according to the movies. Routine low-budgeter enlivened by a splendid array of guest musicians.

w Elliot Paul, Dick Irving Hyland *d* Arthur Lubin *ph* Lucien Andriot *md* Nathaniel Finston

Louis Armstrong and his All Stars, Arturo de Cordova, Dorothy Patrick, *Billie Holiday*, Meade Lux Lewis, Woody Herman and his Orchestra

New Wine
US 1941 89m bw

Franz Schubert seeks the patronage of Beethoven and sacrifices his love life to music. Weirdly cast romantic drama, rather fumbling in all departments. Alan Curtis (as Schubert!), Ilona Massey, Albert Basserman, Binnie Barnes, Sterling Holloway. Written by Howard Estabrook and Nicholas Jory; directed by Reinhold Schunzel; for Gloria / UA. (GB title: *The Great Awakening*.)

New York Confidential
US 1955 87m bw
Warner / Russel Rouse, Clarence Greene

The head of a crime syndicate is assassinated by his own hired killer.
Unexciting 'realistic' thriller with the gangsters presented as family and businessmen; seventeen years later *The Godfather* did it rather better.

w Clarence Greene, Russel Rouse *d* Russel Rouse *ph* Edward Fitzgerald *m* Joseph Mullendore *pd* Fernando Carrere

Broderick Crawford, Richard Conte, Anne Bancroft, Marilyn Maxwell, Onslow Stevens, J. Carrol Naish, Barry Kelley, Mike Mazurki, Celia Lovsky

The New York Hat*
US 1912 10m approx (24 fps) bw
silent
D. W. Griffith

A small-town minister is gossiped about when he buys a hat for a young girl.
Influential early short story film with good local backgrounds.

w Anita Loos *d* D. W. Griffith *ph* Billy Bitzer

Mary Pickford, Lionel Barrymore, Lillian Gish, Dorothy Gish, Robert Harron, Mack Sennett, Mae Marsh

New York, New York*
US 1977 153m Technicolor
Panavision
UA / Chartoff–Winkler (Gene Kirkwood)

In the late forties in New York, a single-minded saxophonist fails to do right by his girl friend, who becomes a Hollywood star.

A clever recreation of the big band era, hampered by gross overlength, unattractive characters and a pessimistic plot.

w Earl Mac Rauch, Mardik Martin d Martin Scorsese ph Laszlo Kovacs pd Boris Leven md Ralph Burns

Liza Minnelli, Robert de Niro, Lionel Stander, Barry Primus

● Video: Warner

New York Nights
US 1929 81m bw

A musical comedy star has a husband who drinks, and she accepts help from a gangster. The star's sound début was a hit-and-miss affair composed of familiar elements. Norma Talmadge, Gilbert Roland, John Wray, Lilyan Tashman, Roscoe Karns. Written by Jules Furthman from the play Tin Pan Alley by Hugh Stanislaus Stange; directed by Lewis Milestone; for UA / Talmadge. 'Good performance, fair picture.'—Variety

New York Town
US 1941 94m bw
Paramount (Anthony Veiller)

A girl new to the Big Apple befriends a sidewalk photographer.
Flat romantic comedy, a soufflé which doesn't rise despite the talents involved.

w Lewis Seltzer (and, uncredited, Preston Sturges) d Charles Vidor (and Sturges) ph Charles Schoenbaum m Leo Shuken

Fred MacMurray, Mary Martin, Robert Preston, Akim Tamiroff, Lynne Overman, Eric Blore, Cecil Kellaway, Fuzzy Knight

Newman's Law
US 1974 99m Technicolor
Universal (Richard Irving)

A cop uses unconventional methods to trap drug smugglers.
Very routine police actioner, just above TV movie level.

w Anthony Wilson d Richard Heffron ph Vilis Lapenieks m Robert Prince

George Peppard, Roger Robinson, Eugene Roche, Gordon Pinsent, Abe Vegoda

News Is Made at Night
US 1939 72m bw

To boost circulation, a news editor pins a string of murders on a well-known gangster, and soon regrets it. Pacy crime comedy-drama, very acceptable as the lower half of a double bill. Preston Foster, Lynn Bari, Eddie Collins, Russell Gleason, George Barbier, Charles Halton. Written by John Larkin; directed by Alfred Werker; for TCF. 'Above average B; should do all right where properly placed.'—Variety

Newsboys' Home
US 1939 73m bw

A girl inherits a newspaper which sponsors a home for boys. Modest début for the East Side Kids, a spin-off group from the Dead End Kids. Jackie Cooper, Edmund Lowe, Wendy

Barrie, Edward Norris, Samuel S. Hinds; and Elisha Cook Jnr, Hally Chester, Harris Berger, David Gorcey, Billy Benedict, Charles Duncan. Written by Gordon Kahn; directed by Harold Young; for Universal. 'Another in the tough kid cycle. Will easily handle its end of dual depots.'—Variety

The Next Man
US 1976 107m Technicolor
Artists Entertainment Complex (Martin Bregman)

A female assassin is hired to kill the Saudi Arabian Minister of State at the United Nations.
Fractured and uninteresting thriller in which all manner of cinematic styles obscure the storyline but point up the lack of narrative skill.

w Mort Fine, Alan R. Trustman, David M. Wolf, Michael Chapman d Richard C. Sarafian ph Michael Chapman m Michael Kamen pd Gene Callahan

Sean Connery, Cornelia Sharpe, Albert Paulsen, Adolfo Celi, Charles Cioffi

'The director takes forever to set up the film's premise, and then he lingers over interminable street festivals and lush scenery.'—Dave Pomeroy, Film Information

● Video: Rank

The Next of Kin***
GB 1942 102m bw
Ealing (S. C. Balcon)

Careless talk causes loss of life in a commando raid.
A propaganda instructional film which was made so entertainingly that it achieved commercial success and remains an excellent example of how to make a bitter pill palatable.

w Thorold Dickinson, Basil Bartlett, Angus Macphail, John Dighton d Thorold Dickinson ph Ernest Palmer m William Walton

Mervyn Johns, Nova Pilbeam, Stephen Murray, Reginald Tate, Basil Radford, Naunton Wayne, Geoffrey Hibbert, Philip Friend, Mary Clare, Basil Sydney

'The detail everywhere is curious and surprising, with something of the fascination of a Simenon crime being unravelled.'—William Whitebait

Next of Kin
Australia 1982 86m Eastmancolor

A young girl teacher inherits an old people's home, and finds murder lurking. Slow-starting but finally over-the-top melodrama, with elements borrowed from Psycho, Taste of Fear and a score of other creepies. Kacjkie Kerin, John Jarratt, Alex Scott, Gerda Nicolson. Written by Michael Heath, Tony Williams; directed by Tony Williams; for SIS productions / Filmco. 'Genre awareness is one thing; a dreary sense of déjà vu is another matter entirely.'—Paul Taylor, MFB

Next Stop Greenwich Village*
US 1975 111m Movielab
TCF (Paul Mazursky, Tony Ray)

In 1953 in a poor quarter of New York, a young Jew tries to stretch his wings.
A bumper bundle of Jewish clichés dressed up as autobiography, and switching abruptly from comedy to tragedy and back. Vivid, but not exactly entertaining.

wd Paul Mazursky ph Arthur Ornitz m Bill Conti

Lenny Baker, Shelley Winters, Ellen Greene, Lois Smith, Dori Brenner

'Some tartly comic observation, but the fragmented structure keeps the mixture inert.'—Sight and Sound

The Next Time I Marry
US 1938 64m bw

In order to become the richest girl in America, an heiress must marry in haste. Tedious comedy which falls apart halfway. Lucille Ball, James Ellison, Lee Bowman, Granville Bates, Mantan Moreland. Written by John Twist and Helen Meinardi; directed by Garson Kanin; for RKO. 'A very poor entry. The story is banal, production values poor, direction sloppy and most of the performances bad.'—Variety

Next Time We Love
US 1936 87m bw
Universal (Paul Kohner)
GB title: Next Time We Live

The wife of a war-correspondent has plenty of time for romance.
Romantic drama which badly needs an injection of comedy.

w Melville Baker, stories Ursula Parrott d Edward H. Griffith ph Joseph Valentine

Margaret Sullavan, Ray Milland, James Stewart, Grant Mitchell, Robert McWade

'Draggy, complex tale . . . will have to be sold on the star's past performances.'—Variety

Next to No Time
GB 1958 93m Eastmancolor
British Lion / Montpelier (Albert Fennell)

A meek-and-mild engineer crossing the Atlantic gains confidence when told that anything is possible during the hour 'lost' every day.
Whimsical comedy which never gains momentum.

wd Henry Cornelius, story The Enchanted Hour by Paul Gallico ph Freddie Francis m Georges Auric

Kenneth More, Betsy Drake, Bessie Love, Harry Green, Roland Culver, Reginald Beckwith, John Welsh, John Laurie, Howard Marion-Crawford

The Next Voice You Hear*
US 1950 83m bw
MGM (Dore Schary)

God speaks to mankind on the radio, and the life of Joe Smith American is changed.

Soppy parable, the archetypal instance of Schary's reign of do-goodery at MGM. (He wrote a book about it, *Case History of a Movie*.) The idea is handled with deadly reverence, and falls quite flat, while the depiction of the inhabitants of American suburbia is depressing.

w Charles Schnee *d* William Wellman *ph* William Mellor *m* David Raksin

James Whitmore, Nancy Davis, Lillian Bronson, Jeff Corey

'The sins of the American working man are singularly uninteresting and their obliteration seems scarcely to require the very voice of God.'—*Henry Hart*

'A raging torrent of emotion that even nature can't control!'

Niagara***
US 1952 89m Technicolor
TCF (Charles Brackett)

While visiting Niagara Falls, a faithless wife is plotting to murder her husband, but he turns the tables.
Excellent suspenser with breathtaking locations; in the best Hitchcock class though slightly marred by the emphasis on Monroe's wiggly walk (it was her first big part).

w Charles Brackett, Walter Reisch, Richard Breen *d* Henry Hathaway *ph* Joe MacDonald *m* Sol Kaplan

Joseph Cotten, Jean Peters, *Marilyn Monroe*, Don Wilson, Casey Adams

'A masterly example of fluid screen narrative.'—*Charles Higham*

'It would have turned out a much better picture if James Mason had played the husband as I wanted. He has that intensity, that neurotic edge. He was all set to do it, but his daughter Portland said she was sick of seeing him die in his pictures.'—*Henry Hathaway*

'This isn't a good movie but it's compellingly tawdry and nasty . . . the only movie that explored the mean, unsavoury potential of Marilyn Monroe's cuddly, infantile perversity.'—*Pauline Kael, 70s*

Nice Girl?*
US 1941 95m bw
Universal (Joe Pasternak)

A teenager finds herself in demand by two older men.
Amusing romantic trifle supposed to mark the growing up of Universal's great teenage star.
w Richard Connell, Gladys Lehman *d* William A. Seiter *ph* Joseph Valentine *md* Charles Previn

Deanna Durbin, Franchot Tone, Robert Stack, Walter Brennan, Robert Benchley, Helen Broderick, Ann Gillis

A Nice Girl Like Me
GB 1969 91m Eastmancolor
Anglo Embassy / Partisan (Roy Millichip)

A sheltered young lady sets out to see life but keeps getting pregnant.
Insufferable romantic whimsy, made to look

like a marathon TV commercial but never so interesting.
w Anne Piper, Desmond Davis *d* Desmond Davis *ph* Gil Taylor, Manny Wynn *m* Pat Williams

Barbara Ferris, Harry Andrews, Gladys Cooper, Joyce Carey, Bill Hinnant, James Villiers, Christopher Guinee, Fabia Drake

'High-toned woman's magazine nostalgia.'—*MFB*

A Nice Little Bank That Should Be Robbed
US 1958 87m bw Cinemascope
TCF (Anthony Muto)
GB title: *How to Rob a Bank*

Two incompetent crooks rob a bank and buy a racehorse.
Feeble comedy, a sad waste of its stars.
w Sidney Boehm *d* Henry Levin *ph* Leo Tover *m* Lionel Newman

Mickey Rooney, Tom Ewell, Mickey Shaugnessy, Dina Merrill

Nicholas and Alexandra*
GB 1971 189m Eastmancolor
Panavision
Columbia / Horizon (Sam Spiegel)

The life of Tsar Nicholas II from 1904 to the execution of the family in 1918.
Inflated epic of occasional interest, mainly for its sets; generally heavy going.
w James Goldman, *book* Robert K. Massie *d* Franklin Schaffner *ph* Frederick A. Young *m* Richard Rodney Bennett *pd* John Box

Michael Jayston, Janet Suzman, Laurence Olivier, Jack Hawkins, Tom Baker, Harry Andrews, Michael Redgrave, Alexander Knox
† Original preferred casting: Rex Harrison, Vanessa Redgrave.

AAN: best picture; Frederick A. Young; Richard Rodney Bennett; Janet Suzman

● *Video: RCA / Columbia*

Nicholas Nickleby**
GB 1947 108m bw
Ealing (John Croydon)

The adventures of a Victorian schoolmaster, deprived of his rightful fortune, who joins a band of travelling entertainers.
Quite tasteful and expert but too light-handed potted version of Dickens, which suffered by comparison with the David Lean versions.
w John Dighton, *novel* Charles Dickens *d* Alberto Cavalcanti *ph* Gordon Dines *m* Lord Berners

Derek Bond, *Cedric Hardwicke, Alfred Drayton, Sybil Thorndike*, Stanley Holloway, James Hayter, Sally Ann Howes, Jill Balcon, Cyril Fletcher, Fay Compton

● *Video: Thorn EMI*

Nick Carter, Master Detective
US 1939 57m bw

Carter uncovers a spy ring in a plane factory.
Dull, devitalized version of the old dime novel

adventures; generally characterless and unmemorable. Walter Pidgeon, Rita Johnson, Henry Hull, Stanley Ridges, Donald Meek, Addison Richards, Milburn Stone, Martin Kosleck. Written by Bertram Millhauser, directed by Jacques Tourneur; for Lucien Hubbard / MGM. 'Just another screen sleuth.'—*Variety*

The Nickel Ride
US 1975 110m De Luxe

A wheeler dealer in downtown Los Angeles learns that he is marked for elimination. Unpleasant and entirely uninteresting low-life crime melodrama. Jason Miller, Linda Haynes, Victor French, John Hillerman, Bo Hopkins. Written by Eric Roth; directed by Robert Mulligan; for TCF.

Nickelodeon*
US / GB 1976 122m Metrocolor
Columbia / EMI / Chartoff–Winkler (Frank Marshall)

In 1910, various characters come together to make movies, finally attending the 1915 opening in Hollywood of *The Birth of a Nation*.
What should have been a hugely entertaining chunk of comic nostalgia is killed stone dead by embarrassed acting, poor timing, and a general lack of funny ideas, despite having so much to borrow from.
w W. D. Richter, Peter Bogdanovich *d* Peter Bogdanovich *ph* Laszlo Kovacs *md* Richard Hazard

Ryan O'Neal, Burt Reynolds, Tatum O'Neal, Brian Keith, Stella Stevens, John Ritter, Jane Hitchcock

'Ponderous slapstick and a pathetic parody of Harold Lloyd.'—*Sight and Sound*

'Another collection of scenes from other people's films.'—*Howard Kissel, Women's Wear Daily*

'The slightest familiarity with the early works of Hal Roach—not to mention D. W. Griffith, here pretentiously quoted—reveals how little Bogdanovich understands his vastly superior predecessors.'—*Robert Asahina, New Leader*

'The crudest, stupidest, unfunniest farce of this or any other year.'—*John Simon, New York*

● *Video: Thorn EMI*

The Niebelungen***
Germany 1924 bw silent
Decla–Bioscop
Part One: 'Siegfried': 115m approx (24 fps)
Part Two: 'Kriemheld's Revenge': 125m approx (24 fps)

Siegfried kills a dragon and marries a princess of Burgundy but the fierce queen Brunhilde arranges his death. His widow marries Attila the Hun and they massacre the Burgundians. Stately, warlike legends are transformed into a slow, chilling, awe-inspiring sequence of films, the décor being of special interest. The films were conceived as a tribute to the German nation, and were among Hitler's favourites.

w Thea Von Harbou *d* Fritz Lang *ph* Carl Hoffman, Gunther Rittau *ad* Otto Hunte, Karl Vollbrecht, Erich Kettelhut

Paul Richter, Marguerite Schön, Theodor Loos, Hannah Ralph, Rudolph Klein-Rogge

'They all loved him—a schoolteacher, a night club hostess, and a luscious society bud!'

Night after Night*
US 1932   76m   bw
Paramount

An ex-boxer seeking refinement buys a night club and falls for a socialite.
Dim little drama which is remembered for introducing Mae West to the screen with her famous line, 'Goodness had nothing to do with it'.

w Vincent Laurence, *novel* Single Night by Louis Bromfield *d* Archie Mayo *ph* Ernest Haller

George Raft, Constance Cummings, Wynne Gibson, *Mae West,* Alison Skipworth, Roscoe Karns, Louis Calhern

Night and Day*
US 1946   132m   Technicolor
Warner (Arthur Schwarz)

The life of Cole Porter.
Or rather, a fictitious story about a composer who happens to be called Cole Porter. A careful but undistinguished musical with pleasant moments.

w Charles Hoffman, Leo Townsend, William Bowers *d* Michael Curtiz *ph* Peverell Marley, William V. Skall *m / ly* Cole Porter *md* Max Steiner, Ray Heindorf *ch* Le Roy Prinz

Cary Grant, Alexis Smith, Monty Woolley, Mary Martin, Ginny Simms, Jane Wyman, Eve Arden, Victor Francen, Alan Hale, Dorothy Malone

AAN: Max Steiner, Ray Heindorf

Night and Fog*
France 1955   31m   Eastmancolor
Argos / Como
original title: *Nuit et Brouillard*

An account of the concentration camp at Auschwitz, contrasted with the peaceful surroundings ten years after its disbandment. An official film of great dignity.

d, ed Alain Resnais *ph* Ghislain Cloquet, Sacha Vierny

Night and the City
GB 1950   101m   bw
TCF (Samuel G. Engel)

A crooked wrestling promoter is tracked down by an underworld gang.
A fated attempt to extend the success of *Naked City* in a London setting; the surface is accomplished enough, but the plot and characters are just plain dull, especially as little is seen of the police.

w Jo Eisinger, *novel* Gerald Kersh *d* Jules Dassin *ph* Max Greene *m* Benjamin Frankel

Richard Widmark, Gene Tierney, Googie Withers, Hugh Marlowe, Herbert Lom
'Brilliantly photographed, it is an example of neo-expressionist techniques at their most potent.'—*Richard Roud, 1964*

The Night Angel
US 1931   75m   bw

A Prague lawyer falls for the daughter of the brothel keeper he has sent to prison, and after killing a jealous suitor is himself accused of murder. Would-be Dietrichean high-style melodrama which did its stars no good at all and virtually ended Miss Carroll's career.
Fredric March, Nancy Carroll, Alan Hale, Alison Skipworth, Katherine Emmett. Written and directed by Edmund Goulding; for Paramount. 'Mild and frequently boring entertainment of the kind that can just about last a week in most of the de luxers.'—*Variety*

A Night at Earl Carroll's
US 1940   63m   bw

When gangsters kidnap stars of Earl Carroll's nightclub, the restaurant staff put on their own show. Tinseltown time-passer which served a very small purpose. Ken Murray, J. Carrol Naish, Lilian Cornell, Blanche Stewart. Written by Lynn Starling; directed by Kurt Neumann; for Paramount.

A Night at the Opera**
US 1935   96m   bw
MGM (Irving Thalberg)

Three zanies first wreck, then help an opera company.
Certainly among the best of the Marxian extravaganzas, and the first to give them a big production to play with as well as musical interludes by other than themselves for a change of pace. The mix plays beautifully.

w George S. Kaufman, Morrie Ryskind *d* Sam Wood *ph* Merritt Gerstad *md* Herbert Stothart

Groucho, Chico, Harpo (Zeppo absented himself from here on), *Margaret Dumont,* Kitty Carlisle, Allan Jones, Walter Woolf King, *Sig Rumann*
'Corking comedy with the brothers at par and biz chances excellent . . . songs in a Marx picture are generally at a disadvantage because they're more or less interruptions, the customers awaiting the next laugh.'—*Variety*

● Video: MGM / UA

Night Boat
GB 1948   91m   bw

Demobbed, a commando becomes a policeman and his friend becomes a crook.
Manhattan Melodrama, British style; no more than an adequate offering of its type. Anne Crawford, Maxwell Reed, Ronald Howard, Christine Norden, Hector Ross, Sidney James. Written by T. J. Morrison, Roland Pertwee and Robert Westerby; directed by Harold Huth; for BLPA.

Night Boat to Dublin
GB 1945   99m   bw
ABP (Hamilton Inglis)

An MI5 man saves an atom scientist from kidnapping.
Generally watchable low key thriller with familiar British ingredients.

w Lawrence Huntington, Robert Hall *d* Lawrence Huntington

Robert Newton, Raymond Lovell, Muriel Pavlow, Guy Middleton, Herbert Lom, Martin Miller, Marius Goring

Night-Club Lady
US 1932   66m   bw

A police commissioner solves the murder of a night-club hostess. Straightforward cops and killers melodrama with the star in his first non-romantic role. Adolphe Menjou, Mayo Methot, Skeets Gallagher, Blanche Friderici, Nat Pendleton. Written by Robert Riskin from a novel by Anthony Abbott; directed by Irving Cummings; for Columbia.

Night Club Scandal
US 1937   74m   bw
Paramount

A society doctor murders his wife and incriminates her lover.
Smooth second feature remake of *Guilty as Hell,* chiefly notable for its star's last controlled performance.

w Lillie Hayward, *play* Riddle Me This by Daniel Rubin *d* Ralph Murphy *ph* Leo Tover

John Barrymore, Lynne Overman, Charles Bickford, Elizabeth Patterson, Evelyn Brent, Louise Campbell, J. Carrol Naish

Night Court
US 1932   90m   bw

A corrupt judge frames a girl on a prostitution charge. Tough star melodrama. Walter Huston, Lewis Stone, Anita Page, Phillips Holmes, Jean Hersholt. Written by Mark Hellinger, Bayard Veiller, Charles Beehan and Lenore Coffee; directed by W. S. Van Dyke; for MGM. (GB title: *Justice for Sale*). 'Political frame-up of women is made the subject of a vigorous melodrama, though it comes after the New York scandal on the subject is largely forgotten.'—*Variety*

Night Crossing
US 1982   106m   Technicolor
Walt Disney (Tom Leetch)

East Germans escape to the west via air balloon.
Well-meaning melodrama which sadly lacks plot development and suspense, and is also rather miserable to look at.

w John McGreevey *d* Delbert Mann *ph* Tony Imi *m* Jerry Goldsmith

John Hurt, Jane Alexander, Doug McKeon, Frank McKeon, Beau Bridges, Glynnis O'Connor, Ian Bannen

The Night Digger

GB 1971   100m   colour

A frustrated spinster protects a handyman clearly guilty of murder, and runs away with him. How this came to be made at all when the Finney version of *Night Must Fall* had recently flopped is a mystery; it had so little box office appeal that it was barely released. Patricia Neal, Nicholas Clay, Pamela Browne, Jean Sanderson, Yootha Joyce, Peter Sallis, Graham Crowden. Written by Roald Dahl, from a story by Joy Cowley; directed by Alastair Reid; for MGM.

Night Flight*

US 1933   84m   bw

MGM (David O. Selznick)

The president of a civil airline insists that dangerous night flights must continue as a mark of progress.

Spurious, unsatisfactory, multi-star air melodrama lacking both narrative flow and the common touch.

w Oliver H. P. Garrett, *stories* Antoine de St Exupéry *d* Clarence Brown *ph* Oliver T. Marsh, Elmer Dyer, Charles Marshall

John Barrymore, Helen Hayes, Lionel Barrymore, Clark Gable, Robert Montgomery, Myrna Loy, William Gargan, C. Henry Gordon

'Punch aviation film with a flock of potent marquee names.'—*Variety*

'It is in the sense it conveys of human beings caught in the swift machinery of modern living that *Night Flight* soars above other pictures of its kind.'—*James Shelley Hamilton*

Night Games*

Sweden 1966   105m   bw

Sandrews (Lena Malmsjö)

original title: *Nattlek*

A 35-year-old man is sexually inhibited by memories of his dead mother's passions and perversions.

Curious Freudian parable apparently intended as a comment on the state of Europe. Audiences found it merely peculiar.

wd Mai Zetterling, from her novel *ph* Rune Ericson *m* Jan Johansson, George Riedel

Ingrid Thulin, Keve Hjelm, Lena Brundin, Naima Wifstrand

'The best one can say is that it never lets up for a moment.'—*David Wilson, MFB*

Night Games

US 1980   100m   Technicolor

A neurotic Beverly Hills housewife is terrified of men. Crazy mix of case history, eroticism and suspense with insufficient of any to satisfy fans. Cindy Pickett, Joanna Cassidy, Barry Primus. Written by Anton Diether and Clarke Reynolds; directed by Roger Vadim; for Golden Harvest / Avco.

Night Hair Child

GB 1971   89m   Movielab

Leander / Harry Alan Towers (Graham Harris)

A 12-year-old boy makes sexual advances to his stepmother.

Corrupt voyeuristic weirdie which has to be seen to be believed.

w Trevor Preston *d* James Kelly *ph* Harry Waxman *m* Stelvio Cipriani

Mark Lester, Britt Ekland, Hardy Kruger, Harry Andrews, Lilli Palmer

'Was his strange power a blessing or a curse? He was a refugee from love— because he could foretell that their marriage and their kisses would dissolve in a tragedy of tears!'

Night Has a Thousand Eyes

US 1948   80m   bw

Paramount (André Boehm)

A vaudeville mentalist finds that he really does have the power to predict the future. Predictable supernatural melodrama closely modelled on *The Clairvoyant* (qv); quite nicely made but simply not exciting.

w Barre Lyndon, Jonathan Latimer, *novel* Cornell Woolrich *d* John Farrow *ph* John F. Seitz *m* Victor Young

Edward G. Robinson, Gail Russell, John Lund, Virginia Bruce, William Demarest, Richard Webb, Jerome Cowan

The Night Has Eyes*

GB 1942   79m   bw

ABP (John Argyle)

US title: *Terror House*

A young teacher disappears on the Yorkshire moors; her friend goes in search, and comes under the influence of a strange young man and his sinister housekeeper. Stagey but effective little thriller, with oodles of fog and bog to help the suspense.

w Alan Kennington *d* Leslie Arliss *ph* Gunther Krampf *m* Charles Williams

James Mason, Joyce Howard, *Wilfrid Lawson, Mary Clare,* Tucker McGuire, John Fernald

'Some ingenuity and not a little style.'—*The Times*

The Night Holds Terror*

US 1955   86m   bw

Columbia (Andrew Stone)

Three gunmen on the run kidnap a factory worker and hold him to ransom. Effective, detailed, low-budget police melodrama; its plot may be over familiar now, but at the time it was refreshing and the whole film an intelligent exercise in suspense.

wd Andrew Stone *ph* Fred Jackman Jnr *m* Lucien Calliet

Jack Kelly, Hildy Parks, John Cassavetes, David Cross, Edward Marr, Jack Kruschen

A Night in Casablanca**

US 1946   85m   bw

David L. Loew

Three zanies rout Nazi refugees in a North African hotel.

The last authentic Marxian extravaganza; it starts uncertainly, builds to a fine sustained frenzy, then peters out in some overstretched airplane acrobatics.

w Joseph Fields, Roland Kibbee, Frank Tashlin *d* Archie Mayo *ph* James Van Trees *m* Werner Janssen *pd* Duncan Cramer

Groucho, Chico, Harpo, Sig Rumann, Lisette Verea, Charles Drake, Lois Collier, Dan Seymour

KORNBLOW (Groucho Marx): 'I don't mind being killed, but I resent hearing it from a character whose head comes to a point.'

KORNBLOW: 'From now on the essence of this hotel will be speed. If a customer asks you for a three-minute egg, give it to him in two minutes. If he asks you for a two-minute egg, give it to him in one minute. If he asks you for a one-minute egg, give him the chicken and let him work it out for himself.'

BEATRICE (Lisette Verea): 'My name's Beatrice Ryner. I stop at the hotel.'
KORNBLOW: 'My name's Ronald Kornblow. I stop at nothing.'

'It is beside the main point to add that it isn't one of their best movies; for the worst they might ever make would be better worth seeing than most other things I can think of.'—*James Agee*

A Night in Paradise

US 1946   84m   Technicolor

(Universal) Walter Wanger

Aesop falls in love at the court of King Croesus.

Deadly boring, unintentionally funny Arabian Nights farrago without the saving grace of action.

w Ernest Pascal, Emmet Lavery, *novel* Peacock's Feather by George S. Hellman *d* Arthur Lubin *ph* Hal Mohr *m* Frank Skinner

Merle Oberon, Turhan Bey, Thomas Gomez, Gale Sondergaard, Ray Collins, George Dolenz, John Litel, Ernest Truex, Jerome Cowan, Douglass Dumbrille

Night into Morning

US 1951   86m   bw

MGM (Edwin H. Knopf)

A college professor loses his wife and son in an accident; despair drives him to drink and attempted suicide.

Well-made and well meaning melodrama whose virtual absence of plot makes it seem by the end merely maudlin.

w Karl Tunberg, Leonard Spiegelgass *d* Fletcher Markle *ph* George Folsey *m* Carmen Dragon

Ray Milland, Nancy Davis, John Hodiak, Lewis Stone, Jean Hagen, Rosemary de Camp

'Tediously uneventful, as sincere and futile as a note of condolence.'—*Time*

The Night Invader

GB 1942   81m   bw

A Britisher in an occupied country is helped to capture a Nazi count. Propaganda potboiler for double billing. Anne Crawford, David Farrar, Carl Jaffe, Sybilla Binder, Marius Goring. Written by Brock Williams, Edward

Dryhurst and Roland Pertwee, from the novel *Rendezvous with Death* by John Bentley; directed by Herbert Mason; for Warner.

Night Is My Future

Sweden 1947 87m bw
Terra Film (Lorens Marmstedt)
original title: *Musik I Mörker*

A war veteran learns to live with his blindness and finds romance.
Cliché romantic melodrama suffused by Scandinavian gloom. An unmemorable early work from this director.

w Dagmar Edqvist d Ingmar Bergman
ph Göran Strindberg m Erland von Koch

Mai Zetterling, Birger Malmsten, Bengt Eklund, Gunnar Björnstrand, Naima Wifstrand

The Night Is Young

US 1934 82m bw

A European archduke loves a ballerina. High-class musical which failed despite an intriguing cast and a Romberg and Hammerstein score.
Evelyn Laye, Ramon Novarro, Una Merkel, Edward Everett Horton, Rosalind Russell, Charles Butterworth, Herman Bing, Henry Stephenson, Donald Cook. Written by Vicki Baum; directed by Dudley Murphy; for MGM. 'Disappointing entertainment . . . feeble in plot, with a cast struggling to carry assignments and failing to ignite any real romantic fire, film also seems to lack a single strong musical number.'—*Variety*

Night Key

US 1937 67m bw
Universal

An inventor's idea is stolen by his former partner, and he takes an appropriate revenge.
Low-key star melodrama: competent, but no great shakes.

w Tristam Tupper, John C. Moffit d Lloyd Corrigan ph George Robinson m Louis Forbes make up Jack Pierce

Boris Karloff, Jean Rogers, Warren Hull, Samuel S. Hinds, Alan Baxter, Ward Bond, Edwin Maxwell
  'Mildly entertaining dualler . . . one of those impossible gadget yarns with liberal injections of cops and robbers stuff.'—*Variety*

The Night Life of the Gods

US 1935 75m bw

An inventor turns statues into people, and vice versa. Fantasy comedy from a well-known comic novel; interesting despite low level of invention. Alan Mowbray, Florine McKinney, Richard Carle, Peggy Shannon. Written by Barry Trivers, from Thorne Smith's novel; directed by Lowell Sherman; for Universal.
'Universal has managed to keep in the fun and restrain it from getting too rough.'—*Variety*

A Night Like This

GB 1932 74m bw

An Irish policeman breaks up a crooked gambling club. Minor Aldwych farce which

hasn't worn well. Tom Walls, Ralph Lynn, Robertson Hare, Winifred Shotter, Mary Brough, Claude Hulbert. Written by Ben Travers, from his play; directed by Tom Walls; for British and Dominions.

Night Mail***

GB 1936 24m bw
GPO Film Unit (John Grierson)

A 'film poem' showing the journey of the mail train from London to Glasgow.
One of the best and most influential of British documentaries: despite a few absurdities, it remains a pleasure to watch.

wd Basil Wright, Harry Watt ph J. Jones, H. E. Fowle m Benjamin Britten poem W. H. Auden sound arrangements Alberto Cavalcanti

Night Mayor

US 1932 65m bw

The Mayor of New York pays too much attention to night life and not enough to his desk. Thinly veiled account of the Jimmy Walker affair, released after Walker had been discredited. As entertainment, punchy, but in the end only fair. Lee Tracy, Evalyn Knapp, Eugene Pallette, Warren Hymer, Donald Dillaway, Astrid Allwyn. Written by Gertrude Purcell, Sam Marx; directed by Ben Stoloff; for Columbia. 'It is a safe general statement that the screen ought never to exploit a public character who is the centre of debate.'—*Variety*

Night Monster

US 1942 73m bw
Universal
GB title: *House of Mystery*

Murders are committed in a spooky house by a cripple who produces synthetic legs by self-hypnotism.
Stilted, creaky would-be thriller with a good cast and an impertinent plot.

w Clarence Upson Young d Ford Beebe ph Charles Van Enger

Ralph Morgan, Don Porter, Irene Hervey, Bela Lugosi, Lionel Atwill, Nils Asther, Leif Erickson, Frank Reicher

Night Moves*

US 1975 99m Technicolor
Warner / Hillier / Layton (Robert M. Sherman)

A private eye is engaged to find a runaway teenager.
Apparently a Chandlerish mystery, this is really a Pinterish audience-teaser with obsessions about communication and the meaning of life. A smart-ass entertainment for eager trendies.

w Alan Sharp d Arthur Penn ph Bruce Surtees m Michael Small pd George Jenkins

Gene Hackman, Jennifer Warren, Edward Binns, Harris Yulin, Kenneth Mars
  'Beneath the complicated unravelling of a mystery, an anti-mystery, with the hero's

detection registering as an evasion of his own problems; beneath a densely charted intrigue of betrayals and cross purposes, a cryptic void . . .'—*Jonathan Rosenbaum*
  'A suspenseless suspenser . . . there's very little rhyme or reason for the plot's progression.'—*Variety*
  'Rich and dense enough to set up reverberations long after one has left the cinema.'—*Michael Billington, Illustrated London News*
● Video: Warner

Night Must Fall**

US 1937 117m bw
MGM (Hunt Stromberg)

A bland young bellboy who is really a psychopathic murderer attaches himself to the household of a rich old lady.
Unconvincing but memorable Hollywood expansion of an effective British chiller.

w John Van Druten, play Emlyn Williams d Richard Thorpe ph Ray June m Edward Ward

Robert Montgomery, Rosalind Russell, May Whitty, Alan Marshal, Merle Tottenham, Kathleen Harrison, Matthew Boulton, E. E. Clive
  'Too long and not box office . . . tedious, slow, and even dull in spots.'—*Variety*
  'A pretty little murder play has made a long dim film.'—*Graham Greene*
  'The most exhilarating shrouds of horror hang over it. It represents a provocative imagination, a skilled adapter, a sensitive director, a splendid acting job.'—*Bland Johaneson, New York Daily Mirror*
† Louis B. Mayer so disliked this film that at the New York première he ordered the distribution of leaflets disowning it on behalf of MGM.

AAN: Robert Montgomery; May Whitty

Night Must Fall

GB 1964 105m bw
MGM (Albert Finney, Karel Reisz)

Dreary remake with a mannered star performance and the emphasis on axe murders. A mistake from beginning to end.

w Clive Exton d Karel Reisz ph Freddie Francis m Ron Grainer

Albert Finney, Susan Hampshire, Mona Washbourne, Sheila Hancock, Michael Medwin, Joe Gladwin, Martin Wyldeck
  'Not so much a thriller as a typically humourless example of that overworked genre known as psychological drama . . . (Finney) constantly recalls a ventriloquist's dummy.'—*MFB*

The Night My Number Came Up*

GB 1954 94m bw
Ealing (Tom Morahan)

A man dreams that his plane will crash, and the dream begins to come true.
Intriguing little melodrama which badly lacks a twist ending and foxes itself by a flashback construction which leaves very little open to doubt. Production generally good.

w R. C. Sherriff d Leslie Norman ph Lionel Banes m Malcolm Arnold

Michael Redgrave, Alexander Knox, Sheila Sim, Denholm Elliott, Ursula Jeans, George Rose, Nigel Stock, Michael Hordern, Ralph Truman, Victor Maddern, Bill Kerr, Alfie Bass

Night Nurse*
US 1931 72m bw
Warner

A nurse uncovers a plot by other members of the household against her patient's children.
Fast-moving melodrama with solid star performances; just what the public wanted in 1931.

w Oliver H. P. Garrett, *novel* Dora Macy d William Wellman ph Chick McGill

Barbara Stanwyck, Ben Lyon, Joan Blondell, Clark Gable, Charles Winninger, Vera Lewis, Blanche Frederici, Charlotte Merriam
'A conglomeration of exaggerations, often bordering on serial dramatics.'—*Hollywood Reporter*

The Night of January 16th
US 1941 79m bw

A secretary is arrested for her boss's murder; but is he really dead? A stage thriller full of theatrical trickery becomes a very mundane film. Robert Preston, Ellen Drew, Nils Asther, Margaret Hayes. Written by Delmer Daves, Robert Pirosh and Eve Greene from a play by Ayn Rand; directed by William Clemens; for Paramount.

The Night of June 13th
US 1932 76m bw

A suburban street is transformed when one of its residents goes on trial for murder.
Combination courtroom and slice-of-life drama which satisfied most audiences. Clive Brook, Lila Lee, Mary Boland, Adrienne Allen, Gene Raymond, Frances Dee, Charley Grapewin. Written by Agnes Brand Leahy, Brian Marlow, William Slavens McNutt, from a story by Vera Caspary; directed by Stephen Roberts; for Paramount. 'Absorbingly worked out with fascinating character study and a touch of satire.'—*Variety*

'What happens after they turn the lights out on Broadway?'
The Night of Nights
US 1939 86m bw

A once-famous Broadway writer, now a drunk, tries to ensure his daughter's fame.
Curious downbeat melodrama without the courage of its convictions, or the actors to give the right bravura performances. Pat O'Brien, Olympe Bradna, Reginald Gardiner, Roland Young. Written by Donald Ogden Stewart; directed by Lewis Milestone; for Paramount.
'Backstage drama lightened by direction and cast performances. Nominal supporter for key duals.'—*Variety*

The Night of San Lorenzo*
Italy 1981 107m Agfacolor
RAI / Ager (Giuliani G. De Negri)

A Tuscan township suffers under the Nazis and is liberated by the Americans.
One would have to be Italian for full appreciation, but this affectionate memoir of the war years is clearly in the Rossellini tradition and it bursts with energy and memorable moments.

wd Paolo and Vittorio Taviani ph Franco Di Giacomo m Nicola Piovani ed Roberto Perpignani

Omero Antonutti, Margarita Lozano, Claudio Bigagli, Massimo Bonetti, Norma Martelli

Night of the Big Heat
GB 1967 94m Eastmancolor

Invaders from outer space take over a remote Scottish island and make it unbearably hot so that they can survive. Sloppily made and over-prolonged science fiction with far too much irrelevant talk. Christopher Lee, Peter Cushing, Patrick Allen, Sarah Lawson, Jane Merrow, William Lucas, Kenneth Cope. Written by Ronald Liles, from the novel by John Lymington; directed by Terence Fisher; for Tom Blakeley / Planet.

Night of the Demon***
GB 1957 87m bw
Columbia / Sabre (Frank Bevis)
US title: *Curse of the Demon*

An occultist despatches his enemies by raising a giant medieval devil.
Despite dim work from the leads, this supernatural thriller is intelligently scripted and achieves several frightening and memorable sequences in the best Hitchcock manner.

w *Charles Bennett, Hal E. Chester, story* Casting the Runes by *M. R. James* d Jacques Tourneur ph Ted Scaife m Clifton Parker ad Ken Adam

Dana Andrews, Peggy Cummins, *Niall MacGinnis, Athene Seyler*, Brian Wilde, Maurice Denham, Ewan Roberts, Liam Redmond, Reginald Beckwith

Night of the Eagle**
GB 1961 87m bw
Independent Artists (Albert Fennell)
US title: *Burn, Witch, Burn*

At a medical school, a jealous witch sets an evil force on her rival.
Pretty good supernatural thriller, let down by leading performances and sustained by character roles and solid production values in creepy sequences.

w Charles Beaumont, Richard Matheson, George Baxt, *novel* Conjure Wife by Fritz Leiber Jnr d Sidney Hayers ph Reg Wyer m William Alwyn

Margaret Johnston, Janet Blair, Peter Wyngarde, Anthony Nicholls, Reginald Beckwith, Kathleen Byron

The Night of the Following Day*
US 1969 100m Technicolor
Universal / Gina (Hubert Cornfield)

A young girl arriving in Paris to stay with her father is kidnapped and held to ransom by an eccentric gang.
Straightforward suspense thriller with delusions of grandeur; the second half bogs down in pretentious talk and the end suggests that the whole thing was a dream.

w Hubert Cornfield, Robert Phippeny, *novel* The Snatchers by Lionel White d Hubert Cornfield ph Willy Kurant m Stanley Myers

Marlon Brando, Richard Boone, Rita Moreno, Pamela Franklin, Jess Hahn

Night of the Garter
GB 1933 86m bw

A newly married man tries to retrieve an intimate gift from an old flame. One of the best-remembered comedies of Sydney Howard; with Winifred Shotter, Elsie Randolph, Austin Melford. Written by Austin Melford and Marjorie Gaffney, from the play *Getting Gertie's Garter* by Avery Hopwood and Wilson Collison; directed by Jack Raymond; for Herbert Wilcox.

The Night of the Generals**
GB 1967 148m Technicolor Panavision
Columbia / Horizon / Filmsonor (Sam Spiegel)

A German intelligence agent tracks down a psychopathic Nazi general who started killing prostitutes in Warsaw during World War I.
A curiously bumpy narrative which is neither mystery nor character study but does provide a few effective sequences and impressive performances. The big budget seems well spent.

w Joseph Kessel, Paul Dehn, *novel* Hans Helmut Hirst d Anatole Litvak ph Henri Decaë m Maurice Jarre pd Alexander Trauner

Peter O'Toole, *Omar Sharif, Tom Courtenay*, Donald Pleasence, Joanna Pettet, *Philippe Noiret*, Charles Gray, Coral Brown, John Gregson, Harry Andrews, Nigel Stock, Christopher Plummer, Juliette Greco
'The "who" is obvious from the first and the "dunnit" interminable.'—*Judith Crist, 1973*
'Lurid and vivid, if nothing else.'—*Robert Windeler*

● *Video: RCA / Columbia*

The Night of the Grizzly
US 1966 102m Techniscope
Paramount (Burt Dunne)

A Wyoming ex-sheriff kills a marauding bear and earns the respect of his son.
Stout-hearted family film, rather sluggishly made.

w Warren Douglas d Joseph Pevney ph Harold Lipstein, Loyal Griggs m Leith Stevens

Clint Walker, Martha Hyer, Keenan Wynn, Leo Gordon, Kevin Brodie, Nancy Kulp, Ellen Corby, Jack Elam, Ron Ely

..."We have your daughter. You can have her back intact if you do what we say and keep silent. We've made no mistakes. Don't you make any. Just follow our instructions or..."

The story of a girl who is stolen... not just for money!

Marlon Brando

Richard Boone

in a JERRY GERSHWIN—ELLIOTT KASTNER Production

The Night Of The Following DAY

R RESTRICTED — Person under 16 not admitted, unless accompanied by parent or adult guardian.

CO-STARRING

RITA MORENO • PAMELA FRANKLIN AND **JESS HAHN**

Music by STANLEY MYERS • Screenplay by HUBERT CORNFIELD and ROBERT PHIPPENY • Based on the novel 'The Snatchers' by LIONEL WHITE
Produced and Directed by HUBERT CORNFIELD • A Gina Production Universal Pictures Ltd. **A UNIVERSAL RELEASE TECHNICOLOR**

Because of the unusual ending no one will be admitted during the final 14 minutes!

THE NIGHT OF THE FOLLOWING DAY.   Despite Brando, then at his height, this glum thriller drew few takers.

The Night of the Hunter•••
US 1955 93m bw
UA / Paul Gregory

A psychopathic preacher goes on the trail of hidden money, the secret of which is held by two children.
Weird, manic fantasy in which evil finally comes to grief against the forces of sweetness and light (the children, an old lady, water, animals). Although the narrative does not flow smoothly there are splendidly imaginative moments, and no other film has ever quite achieved its texture.

w James Agee, novel Davis Grubb d Charles Laughton ph Stanley Cortez m Walter Schumann

Robert Mitchum, Shelley Winters, Lillian Gish, Don Beddoe, Evelyn Varden, Peter Graves, James Gleason

PREACHER (Robert Mitchum): 'Lord, you sure knew what you was doing when you brung me to this very cell at this very time. A man with ten thousand dollars hid somewhere, and a widder in the makin'.'

'One of the most frightening movies ever made.'—*Pauline Kael, 1968*
'A genuinely sinister work, full of shocks and over-emphatic sound effects, camera angles and shadowy lighting.'—*NFT, 1973*
'One of the most daring, eloquent and personal films to have come from America in a long time.'—*Derek Prouse*

The Night of the Iguana•••
US 1964 125m bw
MGM / Seven Arts (Ray Stark)

A disbarred clergyman becomes a travel courier in Mexico and is sexually desired by a teenage nymphomaniac, a middle-aged hotel owner and a frustrated itinerant artist.
The author is most tolerable when poking fun at his own types, and this is a sharp, funny picture with a touch of poetry.

w Anthony Veiller, *play Tennessee Williams* d John Huston ph Gabriel Figueroa m Benjamin Frankel ad Stephen Grimes

Richard Burton, Deborah Kerr, Ava Gardner, Sue Lyon, *Grayson Hall, Cyril Delevanti*
'One man . . . three women . . . one night!'—*publicity*
'Whatever poetry it had seems to have leaked out.'—*New Yorker, 1982*
AAN: Gabriel Figueroa; Grayson Hall

Night of the Juggler
US 1980 100m Technicolor

A New Yorker relentlessly pursues the kidnapper of his daughter. Average chase thriller with good location staging of car crashes. James Brolin, Cliff Gorman, Richard Castellano, Abby Bluestone. Written by Bill Norton Snr and Rick Natkin; directed by Robert Butler; for Columbia.

Night of the Lepus
US 1972 88m Metrocolor
MGM (A. C. Lyles)

A serum meant to control a surplus of rabbits instead produces monster varieties four feet tall.
Tolerable sci-fi tailored to a very tired formula.

w Don Holiday, Gene R. Kearney, *novel* The Year of the Angry Rabbit by Russell Braddon d William F. Claxton ph Ted Voigtlander m Jimmie Haskell

Stuart Whitman, Rory Calhoun, Janet Leigh, Paul Fix, De Forrest Kelley
'For insomniacs with lax standards.'—*Judith Crist*

The Night of the Living Dead
US 1968 98m bw

Flesh-eating zombies, activated by radiation from a space rocket, ravage the countryside.
Gruesome horror comic with effective moments; the director was still doing the same schtick ten years later. Judith O'Dea, Duane Jones, Karl Hardman, Keith Wayne. Written by John A. Russo; directed by George A. Romero; for Image Ten. 'The best film ever made in Pittsburgh.'—*Anon.*

Night Owls•
US 1930 20m bw

A policeman wanting to record an arrest bribes two tramps to burgle a house. The stars at their most hilariously incompetent, unable even to get through a doorway efficiently. Laurel and Hardy, Edgar Kennedy, James Finlayson. Written by Leo McCarey and H. M. Walker; directed by James Parrott; for Hal Roach.

Night of the Party
GB 1934 60m bw

A game of murder at a dinner party leads to a real one. Solid supporting thriller with interesting credits. Leslie Banks, Jane Baxter, Viola Keats, Ian Hunter, Ernest Thesiger, Malcolm Keen. Written by Roland Pertwee and John Hastings Turner; directed by Michael Powell; for Gaumont-British.
'Nothing original, but good entertainment.'—*Variety*

Night Passage•
US 1957 90m Technirama
U-I (Aaron Rosenberg)

A railroad worker entrusted with a payroll finds that the bandits trying to rob it are led by his own brother.
Obscurely titled and rather empty western providing standard excitements.

w Borden Chase d James Neilson ph William Daniels m Dmitri Tiomkin

James Stewart, Audie Murphy, Dan Duryea, Brandon de Wilde, Dianne Foster, Elaine Stewart

Night People•
US 1954 93m Technicolor
Cinemascope
TCF (Nunnally Johnson)

When a US corporal stationed in Berlin is kidnapped by the Russians, his influential father flies into action.
Curiously titled cold war suspenser which would have been more memorable if not in Cinemascope; the pace and talent are visible, but the wide screen and poor colour dissipate them.

wd Nunnally Johnson ph Charles G. Clarke m Cyril Mockridge

Gregory Peck, Broderick Crawford, Anita Bjork, Walter Abel, Rita Gam, Buddy Ebsen, Jill Esmond, Peter Van Eyck
'You have never really seen Gregory Peck until you see him in Cinemascope!'—*publicity*
'We didn't say nice people, we said *night people*!'—*publicity*
AAN: original story (Jed Harris, Tom Reed)

'Seven in the skies over China—and one of them a dangerous Axis spy!'
Night Plane from Chungking
US 1942 69m bw
Paramount

Assorted international passengers are flown from Chungking to India, but one of their number is a German spy who will kill to get his hands on vital information.
A lower-case 'who is it' based on *Shanghai Express*. Not bad according to its lights.

w Earl Felton, Theodore Reeves, Lester Cole d Ralph Murphy ph Theodor Sparkuhl

Ellen Drew, Robert Preston, Otto Kruger, Steve Geray, Ernest Dorian, Tamara Geva, Sen Yung

'The most controversial film of our time!'
The Night Porter
Italy 1973 118m Technicolor
Lotar Films (Robert Gordon Edwards, Esa De Simone)

The wife of an opera conductor recognizes a hotel porter as the sadistic SS commandant of a concentration camp in which she spent the war years; they now resume a sado-masochistic love affair.
A downright deplorable film, with no cinematic skill or grace to excuse it; the visuals are as loathsome as the sound is indecipherable, and the sheer pointlessness of it is insulting.

w Liliana Cavani, Italo Moscati d Liliana Cavani ph Alfio Contini m Daniele Paris

Dirk Bogarde, Charlotte Rampling, Philippe Leroy, Gabriele Ferzetti, Isa Miranda
'Its claim to be saying something important is offensive, but the picture is too crudely trumped up to be a serious insult.'—*New Yorker*
● Video: Intervision

Night Ride
GB 1937 70m bw

Unemployed lorry drivers start an independent co-operative. Brisk action programmer. Julian Vedey, Wally Patch, Jimmy Hanley, Joan Ponsford. Written by Ralph Bettinson; directed by John Paddy Carstairs; for Paramount.

Night Shift
US 1982   106m   Technicolor
Warner / Ladd (Brian Grazer)

A weary financial analyst becomes a morgue
attendant and finds himself involved with
gangsters and pimps.
Unattractive comedy which outstays its
welcome, which wasn't very enthusiastic in the
first place.

w Lowell Ganz, Babaloo Mandel d Ron
Howard ph James Crabe m Burt Bacharach
pd Jack Collis

Henry Winkler, Michael Keaton, Shelley
Long, Gina Hecht

Night Song
US 1947   101m   bw
RKO (Harriet Parsons)

A wealthy socialite falls for a blind pianist and
pretends to be blind also, and poor to boot.
Silly, pretentious soaper, moodily
photographed.

w Frank Fenton, Irving Hyland, De Witt
Bodeen d John Cromwell ph Lucien Ballard
m Leith Stevens

Dana Andrews, Merle Oberon, Hoagy
Carmichael, Ethel Barrymore, Artur
Rubenstein, Eugene Ormandy

The Night They Raided Minsky's**
US 1968   99m   De Luxe
UA / Tandem (Norman Lear)
GB title: The Night They Invented
    Striptease

Various human problems are posed and solved
during a night at a burlesque theatre.
Marvellous kaleidoscopic ragbag of brilliant
fragments which unfortunately don't cohere in
the mind into a really memorable film, though
it gives detailed pleasure on every viewing.

w Arnold Schulman, Sidney Michaels,
Norman Lear, book Rowland Barber
d William Friedkin ph Andrew Laszlo
m Charles Strouse pd William Eckart, Jean
Eckar ch Danny Daniels narrator Rudy
Vallee

Jason Robards, Britt Ekland, Norman
Wisdom, Forrest Tucker, Joseph Wiseman,
Bert Lahr, Harry Andrews, Denholm Elliott,
Elliot Gould, Jack Burns
  'The Fanny Brice country stunningly
brought to life—every face a snapshot of
yesterday.'—Alexander Walker
  'It's lightweight and disorganized; it's a
shambles; yet a lot of it is charming, and it has
a wonderful seedy chorus line—a row of pudgy
girls with faces like slipped discs.'—Pauline
Kael, New Yorker

Night Tide
US 1961   84m   bw

A sailor falls in love with a fairground freak
show girl who may be a real mermaid.
Cheaply made and very derivative romantic
fantasy which seemed to hold a promise never
fulfilled. Dennis Hopper, Linda Lawson,
Gavin Muir, Luana Anders. Written and
directed by Curtis Harrington; for Virgo
Films.

A Night to Remember*
US 1941   91m   bw
Columbia (Samuel Bischoff)

A Greenwich Village mystery-writing couple
try to solve a murder.
Reasonably sparkling comedy whodunnit with
a zany tinge.

w Richard Flournoy, Jack Henley d Richard
Wallace ph Joseph Walker m Werner
Heymann md Morris Stoloff

Loretta Young, Brian Aherne, Jeff Donnell,
William Wright, Sidney Toler, Gale
Sondergaard, Donald MacBride, Lee Patrick,
Blanche Yurka

A Night to Remember***
GB 1958   123m   bw
Rank (William Macquitty)

The story of the 1912 sea disaster when the
Titanic struck an iceberg.
A major film enterprise featuring hundreds of
cameos, none discernibly more important than
the other. On this account the film seems
alternately stiff and flabby as narrative, but
there is much to enjoy and admire along the
way, though the sense of awe is dissipated by
the final model shots.

w Eric Ambler, book Walter Lord d Roy
Baker ph Geoffrey Unsworth m William
Alwyn

Kenneth More, Honor Blackman, Michael
Goodliffe, David McCallum, George Rose,
Anthony Bushell, Ralph Michael, John
Cairney, Kenneth Griffith, Frank Lawton,
Michael Bryant
  'A worthy, long-drawn-out documentary,
with noticeably more honesty about human
nature than most films, but little shape or
style.'—Kenneth Cavender
● Video: Rank

Night Train to Munich***
GB 1940   93m   bw
TCF (Edward Black)
aka: Gestapo; Night Train

A British agent poses as a Nazi in order to
rescue a Czech inventor.
First-rate comedy suspenser obviously inspired
by the success of The Lady Vanishes and
providing much the same measure of thrills
and laughs.

w Frank Launder, Sidney Gilliat, novel Report
on a Fugitive by Gordon Wellesley d Carol
Reed ph Otto Kanturek m Charles Williams
md Louis Levy

Margaret Lockwood, Rex Harrison, Basil
Radford, Naunton Wayne, Paul Henreid,
Keneth Kent, Felix Aylmer, Roland Culver,
Eliot Makeham, Raymond Huntley, Wyndham
Goldie
  'A very nice triumph of skill and maturity in
films, and thus a pleasure to have.'—Otis
Ferguson

AAN: Gordon Wellesley

Night unto Night*
US 1949   85m   bw
Warner (Owen Crump)

An epileptic scientist falls for a girl
hallucinated by the ghost of her dead husband.
Cheerless nuthouse melodrama, one of the
well-meant aberrations which Hollywood
studios used to produce as a sop to conscience.

w Kathryn Scola, novel Philip Wylie d Don
Siegel ph Peverell Marley m Franz Waxman

Ronald Reagan, Viveca Lindfors, Rosemary
de Camp, Broderick Crawford, Osa Massen,
Craig Stevens, Erskine Sanford

The Night Walker*
US 1964   86m   bw
U-I / William Castle

The widow of a tough executive, killed and
disfigured in an explosion, is haunted in her
dreams not only by him but by a mysterious
lover who turns up in reality.
Stiff and unconvincing but still fairly
frightening low-budget shocker with a plot
twist or two.

w Robert Bloch d William Castle ph Harold
Stine m Vic Mizzy

Robert Taylor, Barbara Stanwyck, Lloyd
Bochner, Rochelle Hudson, Judi Meredith,
Hayden Rorke

Night Watch
GB 1973   98m   Technicolor
Avco / Brut (David White)

A widow recovering from a nervous
breakdown keeps seeing bodies in the night.
Her friends try to help, but things are not
quite what they seem.
Predictable coiled-spring shocker which goes
curiously flat despite a star cast and lashings of
blood. Perhaps we have all been here once too
often.

w Tony Williamson, play Lucille Fletcher
d Brian G. Hutton ph Billie Williams
m John Cameron

Elizabeth Taylor, Laurence Harvey, Billie
Whitelaw, Robert Lang, Tony Britton, Bill
Dean
  'It has all the trappings of a Joan Crawford
vehicle of the forties, with numerous elegant
dresses for Miss Taylor, an appropriately
unbecoming wardrobe for Miss Whitelaw, and
a set which is an art director's dream.'—
Brenda Davies
  'Elizabeth Taylor's gowns are by Valentino,
her jewellery is by Van Cleef and Arpels, even
her kitchen is by Westinghouse. And she is
still going out of her mind.'—Alexander
Walker

The Night We Dropped a Clanger
GB 1959   86m   bw

During World War II, a wing commander's
double is accidentally sent to the front line in
his place. Feeble take-off on I Was Monty's
Double; a few bright gags survive. Brian Rix,
Cecil Parker, William Hartnell, Leslie Phillips,
Leo Franklyn, John Welsh, Liz Fraser.
Written by John Chapman; directed by Darcy
Conyers; for Sidney Box / Four Star / Rank.

The Night We Got the Bird
GB 1960 82m bw

A husband is driven bonkers by a talking parrot which he believes to be the reincarnation of his predecessor. Pretty awful farce with the sole virtue of a frantic pace.
Brian Rix, Dora Bryan, Ronald Shiner, Leo Franklyn, Irene Handl, John Slater, Liz Fraser, Reginald Beckwith, Robertson Hare, John Le Mesurier, Terry Scott. Written by Ray Cooney, Tony Hilton and Darcy Conyers; directed by Darcy Conyers; for Rix–Conyers / British Lion.

Night without Sleep
US 1952 77m bw
TCF (Robert Bassler)

A man reconstructs his drunken actions the night before, and fears he has committed a murder.
Dreary melodrama, all frayed tempers, drunkenness and cigarette smoke.

w Frank Partos, Elick Moll d Roy Baker ph Lucien Ballard m Cyril Mockridge

Gary Merrill, Linda Darnell, Hildegarde Neff, Hugh Beaumont, Mae Marsh

Night Without Stars
GB 1951 86m bw

A blind lawyer solves the death of a traitor. Enervated romantic melodrama. David Farrar, Nadia Gray, Maurice Teynac, Gilles Queyant. Written by Winston Graham, from his novel; directed by Anthony Pelissier; for Hugh Stewart / GFD.

Night World
US 1932 58m bw

Characters with an assortment of problems congregate in a nightclub. Tolerable slice-of-life drama with interesting cast. Lew Ayres, Boris Karloff, Mae Clarke, Russell Hopton, Dorothy Revier, Bert Roach, Hedda Hopper. Written by P. J. Wolfson and Allen Rivkin; directed by Hobart Henley; for Universal.
'Sum total is an impression that this was a two-reeler blown up into five.'—Variety

The Nightcomers*
GB 1971 96m Technicolor
Scimitar / Kastner–Kanter–Ladd (Michael Winner)

How the ghost-ridden children in The Turn of the Screw became evil; they became involved in aberrant sexual activities between the gardener and the housekeeper, and finally murdered the former.
Despite its unexpected literariness this is unpleasant and unconvincing nonsense with a boring script punctuated by shock cuts and very little period feel.

w Michael Hastings d Michael Winner ph Robert Paynter m Jerry Fielding

Stephanie Beacham, Marlon Brando, Thora Hird, Harry Andrews, Verna Harvey, Christopher Ellis

'It leaves the viewer cold—perhaps even repelled. How could anybody think this movie would be entertaining?'—Pauline Kael, New Yorker

● Video: Embassy

Nightfall*
US 1956 78m bw
Columbia (Ted Richmond)

The police and two bank robbers chase an innocent artist who happens to know that the loot is hidden in a Wisconsin snowdrift. Occasionally stylish but obscurely narrated suspenser.

w Stirling Silliphant, novel David Goodis d Jacques Tourneur ph Burnett Guffey m George Duning

Anne Bancroft, Aldo Ray, Brian Keith, James Gregory, Jocelyn Brando, Frank Albertson

Nighthawks
GB 1978 113m Eastmancolor

The life of an actively homosexual schoolteacher. Painful low-life drama with many signs of its amateur status. Ken Robertson and non-professionals. Written and directed by Ron Peck and Paul Hallam; for Nashburgh / Four Corner Films.

Nighthawks
US 1981 99m Technicolor
Universal / Herb Nanas (Martin Poll)

New York cops track an international terrorist.
Kojak-style thriller with a rather glum attitude to its subject.

w David Shaber d Bruce Malmuth ph James A. Contner m Keith Emerson

Sylvester Stallone, Billy Dee Williams, Rutger Hauer, Lindsay Wagner, Persis Khambatta, Nigel Davenport

Nightmare
US 1942 81m bw
Universal

A gambler in wartime London helps a beautiful girl escape from Nazi spies.
Thin espionage thriller with a good sequence or two and a smooth villain.

w Dwight Taylor, novel Escape by Philip MacDonald d Tim Whelan ph George Barnes m Frank Skinner

Brian Donlevy, Diana Barrymore, Gavin Muir, Henry Daniell, Hans Conried, Arthur Shields

Nightmare*
US 1956 89m bw
UA / Pine–Thomas / Shane (Maxwell Shane)

A young musician is hypnotized into committing a murder, and reconstructs his actions with the help of his policeman brother-in-law.
Lethargic remake of the ingenious Fear in the Night (qv). Watchable.

wd Maxwell Shane, novel Cornell Woolrich ph Joseph Biroc m Herschel Burke Gilbert

Edward G. Robinson, Kevin McCarthy, Virginia Christine, Connie Russell
'A chilling, highly suspenseful little item.'—Motion Picture Herald

Nightmare*
GB 1964 82m bw Hammerscope
U-I / Hammer (Jimmy Sangster)

18-year-old Janet still has nightmares after seeing her mad mother kill her father six years ago; brought home, even more frightening visions afflict her.
Genuinely scary Diabolique-type mystery with the usual Hammer borrowings put to good use.

w Jimmy Sangster d Freddie Francis ph John Wilcox m Don Banks

Moira Redmond, David Knight, Brenda Bruce, John Welsh, Jennie Linden

Nightmare Alley**
US 1947 112m bw
TCF (George Jessel)

A fairground barker becomes a successful confidence trickster dealing with the supernatural, but finally sinks to the depths. Unusual road to ruin melodrama, a striking oddity from Hollywood at the time, and still quite interesting and well done.

w Jules Furthman, novel William Lindsay Gresham d Edmund Goulding ph Lee Garmes m Cyril Mockridge

Tyrone Power, Coleen Gray, Joan Blondell, Taylor Holmes, Helen Walker, Mike Mazurki, Ian Keith
'The picture goes just short of all that might have made it very interesting . . . even so, two or three sharply comic and cynical scenes make it worth seeing.'—James Agee

Nightmare in the Sun*
US 1963 81m De Luxe
Afilmco (Marc Lawrence, John Derek)

A rich man kills his wife and blames a hitch-hiker who has had a brief affair with her. Modest independent melodrama, quite interestingly made though not entirely effective.

w Ted Thomas d Marc Lawrence ph Stanley Cortez m Paul Glass

John Derek, Ursula Andress, Arthur O'Connell, Aldo Ray

Nightwing
Netherlands 1979 105m Metrocolor
Columbia / Polyc / Martin Ransohoff

In Arizona, mysterious deaths turn out to be caused by plague-bearing vampire bats. Tedious shocker in the vein of Them but with 'modern' unpleasantness of detail.

w Steve Shagan, Bud Shrake, novel Martin Cruz Smith d Arthur Hiller ph Charles Rosher m Henry Mancini

David Warner, Kathryn Harrold, Steven Macht, Strother Martin, Nick Mancuso, Ben Piazza

Nijinsky**
US 1980 125m Metrocolor
Paramount / Hera (Harry Saltzman)

The rise and fall of a great dancer groomed for stardom in the Ballets Russes by the impresario Diaghilev.
Rather boringly scripted with the emphasis on homosexual love, this film finally survives through its electrifying personalities and its strong sense of period.

w Hugh Wheeler d Herbert Ross ph Douglas Slocombe md John Lanchbery pd John Blezard

Alan Bates, George de la Pena, Leslie Brown, Alan Badel, Colin Blakely, Ronald Pickup, Ronald Lacey, Jeremy Irons, Anton Dolin, Janet Suzman, Sian Phillips, members of the London Festival Ballet

'The impression is left of a fascinating subject which proved too challenging for its makers, who settle eventually for what is uncomfortably near All About Eve with Bette Davis in a dinner jacket and Anne Baxter in a jock strap.'—Alan Brien, Sunday Times

Nikki, Wild Dog of the North*
US 1961 74m Technicolor
Walt Disney (Winston Hibler)

The life of a Canadian trapper's wolf dog.
Pleasing 'true life fiction' which didn't quite reach top feature status.

w Ralph Wright, Winston Hibler, novel James Oliver Curwood d Jack Couffer m Oliver Wallace

Emile Genest, Jean Coutu

Nine Girls
US 1944 78m bw
Columbia (Burt Kelly)

College girls are murdered in a sorority house.
Cheapjack whodunnit with a cardboard look and feel.

w Karen de Wolff, Connie Lee, play Wilfred H. Pettit d Leigh Jason ph James Van Trees m Leo Leopold

Ann Harding, Evelyn Keyes, Jinx Falkenberg, Anita Louise, Leslie Brooks, Lynn Merrick, Jeff Donnell, Nina Foch, Marcia Mae Jones, William Demarest

Nine Hours to Rama
GB 1962 125m De Luxe Cinemascope
TCF / Red Lion (Mark Robson)

Events leading to the assassination of Mahatma Gandhi.
Fictionalized, sensationalized and very dull, this multi-character drama holds interest only for snatches of acting and location backgrounds.

w Nelson Gidding, novel Stanley Wolpert d Mark Robson ph Arthur Ibbetson m Malcolm Arnold

Jose Ferrer, Diane Baker, Robert Morley, J. S. Casshyap, Horst Buchholz, Harry Andrews

'The only interesting line in the movie is the thick brown one visible on the inside of every white collar.'—John Simon

Nine Lives Are Not Enough
US 1941 63m bw

A reporter solves a multi-murder in a boarding house. Lively second feature which moves at a commendable pace. Ronald Reagan, Howard da Silva, James Gleason, Ed Brophy, Faye Emerson, Peter Whitney, Charles Drake. Written by Fred Niblo Jnr; directed by A. Edward Sutherland; for Warner.

Nine Men*
GB 1943 68m bw

A sergeant and a handful of men in an old fort hold off the Italians in the Libyan desert. Sharp semi-documentary of the war which paled against the mightier epics to follow. Jack Lambert, Gordon Jackson, Frederick Piper, Grant Sutherland, Bill Blewett. Written and directed by Harry Watt; for Ealing.

Nine to Five*
US 1980 110m De Luxe
TCF / IPC (Bruce Gilbert)

Three office women plot to get rid of their boss, and nearly make it.
Sporadically agreeable comedy somewhat reminiscent of Sturges' Unfaithfully Yours.

w Colin Higgins, Patricia Resnick d Colin Higgins ph Reynaldo Villalobos m Charles Fox pd Dean Mitzner

Jane Fonda, Dolly Parton, Lily Tomlin, Dabney Coleman, Sterling Hayden, Elizabeth Fraser, Henry Jones

'An effective escapist feast with lotsa funny physical schtick.'—Variety

AAN: best song (Dolly Parton)

● Video: CBS / Fox

1984*
GB 1955 91m bw
Holiday (N. Peter Rathvon)

Europe has become the fascist state of Oceania, ruled by Big Brother; Winston Smith yearns for the old days, and is brainwashed.
The famous prophecy of a dehumanized future is followed with reasonable fidelity apart from the defiant ending, but the novel is too literary for cinematic success and the result is too often both downbeat and boring.

w William P. Templeton, Ralph Bettinson, novel George Orwell d Michael Anderson ph C. Pennington Richards m Malcolm Arnold

Michael Redgrave, Edmond O'Brien, Jan Sterling, David Kossoff, Mervyn Johns, Donald Pleasence

1984*
GB 1984 110m Eastmancolor
Umbrella / Rosenblum / Virgin (Simon Perry)

Winston Smith comes to love Big Brother after being brainwashed and taught Doublethink.
Pointless, perhaps, to make a prophetic film in the year that was supposed to be prophesying, but this version adds a few twists to Orwell's nightmarish original and is well if sometimes confusingly made.

w Michael Radford, novel George Orwell d Michael Radford ph Roger Deakins m Dominic Muldowney pd Allan Cameron ed Tom Priestley

John Hurt, Richard Burton, Suzanna Hamilton, Cyril Cusack, Gregor Fisher, James Walker

1941*
US 1979 118m Metrocolor Panavision
Columbia / Universal / A-Team (John Milius)

Just after Pearl Harbor, a stray Japanese submarine terrorizes Hollywood.
Absurdly over-budgeted manic farce which substitutes noise for wit and slapstick for comedy; it fails on every level.

w Robert Zemeckis, Bob Gale d Steven Spielberg ph William A. Fraker m John Williams pd Dean Edward Mitzner

Dan Aykroyd, Ned Beatty, John Belushi, Lorraine Gary, Murray Hamilton, Christopher Lee, Tim Matheson, Toshiro Mifune, Warren Oates, Robert Stack, Elisha Cook Jnr

'So overloaded with visual humour of rather monstrous nature that the feeling emerges that once you've seen ten explosions, you've seen them all.'—Variety

'Aimed at young audiences, who deserve better fun.'—New Yorker

'Its sheer relentless physicality, its elaborately orchestrated pointlessness on every other level, make it probably the purest demonstration of what it means to have two of the all-time commercial blockbusters to one's record and one's hands firmly on the fantasy machine.'—Richard Combs, MFB

'Spielberg intended it as "a stupidly outrageous celebration of paranoia" . . . audiences found it curiously unfunny and elephantine.'—Les Keyser, Hollywood in the Seventies

● Video: CIC

1900*
Italy / France / West Germany 1976
320m Technicolor
TCF / PEA / Artistes Associés / Artemis (Alberto Grimaldi)
original title: Novecento

The political and personal vicissitudes of a noble Italian family between 1900 and 1945.
Immensely long and heavy-going study of the rise of fascism in the form of a family saga. For specialists only.

w Bernardo Bertolucci, Franco Arcalli, Giuseppe Bertolucci d Bernardo Bertolucci ph Vittorio Storaro m Ennio Morricone ad Enzo Frigiero

Burt Lancaster, Robert de Niro, Gerard Depardieu, Dominique Sanda, Donald Sutherland, Sterling Hayden

'Exasperatingly uneven, but its most powerful moments can't be matched by any movie since Godfather Two.'—Time

'Bertolucci tried to write a 19th-century novel on film: the result is appalling, yet it has the grandeur of a classic visionary folly.'—New Yorker

† The film was normally shown in two separate parts.

99 and 44 / 100 Per Cent Dead
US 1974 98m De Luxe Panavision
TCF / Joe Wizan / Vashon
aka: *Call Harry Crown*

A losing gang boss hires a trouble shooter.
Violent gangster melodrama apparently
intended as a black comedy; if so, as clumsy as
its title.

w Robert Dillon *d* John Frankenheimer
ph Ralph Woolsey *m* Henry Mancini

Richard Harris, Edmond O'Brien, Bradford
Dillman, Ann Turkel, Chuck Connors,
Constance Ford
 'Esthetically, commercially and morally, a
quintessential fiasco.'—*Variety*
† The title in fact spoofs an ad familiar to
Americans for a soap which was said to be '99
and 44 / 100 per cent pure'.

99 River Street°
US 1953 83m bw
UA / Edward Small

A taxi driver becomes involved in a diamond
robbery.
Adequate thick ear with quite good detection
and action sequences.

w Robert Smith *d* Phil Karlson *ph* Franz
Planer

John Payne, Evelyn Keyes, Frank Faylen,
Brad Dexter, Peggie Castle

NINOTCHKA. The Russians are about to disagree. Alexander Granach, Greta Garbo, Felix
Bressart, Sig Rumann.

'The picture that kids the commissars!'
'Garbo laughs!'
'Don't pronounce it—see it!'
Ninotchka°°°
US 1939 110m bw
MGM (Ernst Lubitsch)

A Paris playboy falls for a communist emissary
sent to sell some crown jewels.
Sparkling comedy on a theme which has been
frequently explored; delicate pointing and
hilarious character comedy sustain this version
perfectly until the last half hour, when it
certainly sags; but it remains a favourite
Hollywood example of this genre.

w Charles Brackett, Billy Wilder, Walter
Reisch, story Melchior Lengyel *d* Ernst
Lubitsch *ph* William Daniels *m* Werner
Heymann

*Greta Garbo, Melvyn Douglas, Sig Rumann,
Alexander Granach, Felix Bressart,* Ina Claire,
Bela Lugosi

PROLOGUE: This picture takes place in Paris
in those wonderful days when a siren was a
brunette and not an alarm—and if a
Frenchman turned out the light it was not on
account of an air raid!
 NINOTCHKA (Greta Garbo): 'I must have a
complete report of your negotiations and a
detailed expense account.'
 BULJANOFF (Felix Bressart): 'No, non,
Ninotchka. Don't ask for it. There is an old
Turkish proverb that says, if something smells
bad, why put your nose in it?'
 NINOTCHKA: 'And there is an old Russian
saying, the cat who has cream on his whiskers
had better find good excuses.'

NINOTCHKA: 'The last mass trials were a
great success. There are going to be fewer but
better Russians.'
 'High calibre entertainment for adult
audiences, and a top attraction for the key
de-luxers.'—*Variety*
 'The Lubitsch style, in which much was
made of subtleties—glances, finger
movements, raised eyebrows—has
disappeared. Instead we have a hard, brightly
lit, cynical comedy with the wisecrack
completely in control.'—*John Baxter, 1968*
† William Powell and Robert Montgomery
were formerly considered for the Melvyn
Douglas role.

AAN: best picture; script; story; Greta Garbo

The Ninth Configuration
US 1980 105m Metrocolor

A new psychiatrist in a compound of military
misfits becomes the victim of a terror
campaign. Weirdly obscure would-be thriller
which only mystifies and annoys. Stacy Keach,
Scott Wilson, Jason Miller, Ed Flanders,
Neville Brand, Moses Gunn. Written, directed
and produced by William Peter Blatty; for
Lorimar. 'Quite astonishingly garbled, trailing
yards of portentous religious allegory.'—
Observer. 'The pretensions are enough to raise
the *Titanic*—and sink it again.'—*Guardian*

The Ninth Guest
US 1934 65m bw

Eight people are trapped by a murderer in a
penthouse suite. Whodunit which must have
been seen by Agatha Christie before she wrote
And Then There Were None. This version
however is flatly scripted and characterized,
with no real interest in the (unlikely) outcome.
Donald Cook, Genevieve Tobin, Hardie
Albright, Edward Ellis, Edwin Maxwell,
Vince Barnett, Samuel S. Hinds. Written by
Garnett Weston from the stage play by Owen
Davis and the novel by Gene Bristow; directed
by Roy William Neill; for Columbia. 'It ought
to get a neat return in most spots.'—*Variety*

The Nitwits
US 1935 81m bw

Two cigar-stand assistants solve the murder of
a music publisher. Overlong crime comedy
with a good finale. Bert Wheeler, Robert
Woolsey, Fred Keating, Betty Grable, Evelyn
Brent. Written by Fred Guiol, Al Boasberg,
Stuart Palmer; directed by George Stevens;
for RKO. 'Fair.'—*Variety*

No Blade of Grass
GB 1970 97m Metrocolor Panavision
MGM (Cornel Wilde)

Industrial pollution sets a destructive virus

ruining the crops of the world; anarchy spreads through Britain and one family takes refuge in the Lake District.
Apocalyptic sci-fi, moderately well done though so humourless as to be almost funny.

w Sean Forestal, Jefferson Pascal, *novel* John Christopher *d* Cornel Wilde *ph* H. A. R. Thompson *m* Burnell Whibley

Nigel Davenport, Jean Wallace, Patrick Holt, John Hamill

No Deposit, No Return
US 1976 112m Technicolor
Walt Disney (Ron Miller)

Airport confusion causes crooks to abduct (unwittingly) a millionaire's grandchildren; the millionaire gives chase.
Overlong and tedious action comedy which makes little sense.

w Arthur Alsberg, Don Nelson *d* Norman Tokar *ph* Frank Phillips *m* Buddy Baker

David Niven, Darren McGavin, Don Knotts, Herschel Bernardi, Barbara Feldon, John Williams, Vic Tayback, Kim Richards
'Once again one is left wondering why there should be such an unbridgeable gulf between the brilliant professionalism and sometimes innovative genius of the Disney animated films, and the dull artlessness of the majority of their live-action pictures.'—*Philip French, The Times*

'You can't throw so many young couples together and not expect explosions!'
No Down Payment**
US 1957 105m bw Cinemascope
TCF (Jerry Wald)

Tension among smart suburban couples in a Los Angeles housing development.
Lively domestic melodrama, very useful to sociologists as a mirror of its times.

w *Philip Yordan, novel* John McPartland *d Martin Ritt ph* Joseph La Shelle *m* Leigh Harline

Joanne Woodward, Tony Randall, Sheree North, Jeffrey Hunter, Cameron Mitchell, Patricia Owens, Barbara Rush, Pat Hingle

No Escape
GB 1936 85m bw

A man pretends to be dead as a hoax, and when he is found so, his accomplice is suspected. Twisty thriller from a popular play. Valerie Hobson, Leslie Perrins, Robert Cochran, Billy Milton, Henry Oscar. From the play No Exit by George Goodchild and Frank Witty; directed by Norman Lee; for Pathé Welwyn. 'Good programme picture for almost anywhere.'—*Variety*

No Funny Business
GB 1933 75m bw
John Stafford

Two professional co-respondents are sent to the Riviera; each mistakes the other as his client.

Stagey farce, notable for its unlikely star teaming and its hilariously dated style.

w Victor Hanbury, Frank Vosper, Dorothy Hope *d* John Stafford, Victor Hanbury

Gertrude Lawrence, Laurence Olivier, Jill Esmond, Edmund Breon, Gibb McLaughlin, Muriel Aked

No Greater Glory
US 1934 78m bw

Boys learn through their play that there is no greater glory than to die for one's country.
Glum parable which probably worked better in the original German. George Breakston, Jimmy Butler, Jackie Searl, Frankie Darro, Ralph Morgan, Christian Rub. Written by Jo Swerling from the film script The Paul Street Boys by Ferenc Molnar; directed by Frank Borzage; for Columbia. 'Not for the general trade, but a prospective hit in the arties.'—*Variety*

'Turn back, I tell you! Any minute may be too late!'
No Highway**
GB 1951 98m bw
TCF (Louis D. Lighton)
US title: *No Highway in the Sky*

During a transatlantic flight, a boffin works out that the plane's tail is about to fall off from metal fatigue.'
The central premise of this adaptation from a popular novel is fascinating, but the romantic asides are a distraction and the characters cardboard; the film still entertains through sheer professionalism.

w R. C. Sherriff, Oscar Millard, Alec Coppel, *novel* Nevil Shute *d* Henry Koster *ph* Georges Périnal

James Stewart, Marlene Dietrich, Glynis Johns, Jack Hawkins, Janette Scott, Elizabeth Allan, Kenneth More, Niall MacGinnis, Ronald Squire

No Leave, No Love
US 1946 118m bw
MGM (Joe Pasternak)

Sailors on leave meet an English girl.
Witless, overlong musical extravaganza.

w Charles Martin, Leslie Karkos *d* Charles Martin *ph* Harold Rosson, Robert Surtees *md* Georgie Stoll

Van Johnson, Pat Kirkwood, Keenan Wynn, Guy Lombardo and his Orchestra, Edward Arnold, Marie Wilson, Leon Ames

No Limit*
GB 1935 79m bw
ATP (Basil Dean)

A motor mechanic enters for the TT Races.
Lively star comedy with Isle of Man locations.

w Tom Geraghty, Fred Thompson, *story* Walter Greenwood *d* Monty Banks

George Formby, Florence Desmond, Edward Rigby, Jack Hobbs, Peter Gawthorne, Alf Goddard

No Love for Johnnie*
GB 1960 111m bw Cinemascope
Rank / Five Star (Betty E. Box)

The personal and political problems of a Labour MP.
Predictable but quite lively study of ambition and frustration, with good cameos; Cinemascope all but ruins its impact.

w Nicholas Phipps, Mordecai Richler, *novel* Wilfred Fienburgh *d* Ralph Thomas *ph* Ernest Steward *m* Malcolm Arnold

Peter Finch, Mary Peach, Stanley Holloway, Donald Pleasence, Billie Whitelaw, Hugh Burden, Rosalie Crutchley, Michael Goodliffe, Mervyn Johns, Geoffrey Keen, Paul Rogers, Dennis Price, Peter Barkworth, Fenella Fielding, Gladys Henson

No Man Is an Island
US 1962 114m Eastmancolor
U-I / Gold Coast (John Monks Jnr, Richard Goldstone)
GB title: *Island Escape*

After the Japanese attack on Guam, a radioman finds refuge in a leper colony and sets up his own resistance unit.
Unexceptional war adventure in the jungle.

wd John Monks Jnr, Richard Goldstone *ph* Carl Kayser *m* Restie Umali

Jeffrey Hunter, Marshall Thompson, Barbara Perez, Ronald Remy
'Good clean fun for right-minded teenagers.'—*MFB*

'He was a hit and run lover . . . personally, he preferred a cigarette to any dame!'
No Man of Her Own*
US 1932 98m bw
Paramount

A big-time gambler marries a local girl on a bet and tries to keep her innocent of his activities.
Star romantic comedy drama, quite professionally assembled and played.

w Maurine Watkins, Milton H. Gropper *d* Wesley Ruggles *ph* Leo Tover

Clark Gable, Carole Lombard, Dorothy Mackail, Grant Mitchell, George Barbier, Elizabeth Patterson, J. Farrell MacDonald
'Entertaining film with national appeal.'—*Variety*
'Just about everything that the ordinary picture fan looks for: drama, romance, comedy, strong build-ups, exciting climaxes, a fine line of human interest.'—*Film Daily*

No Man of Her Own*
US 1949 98m bw
Paramount (Richard Maibaum)

A pregnant wanderer is involved in a train crash and assumes the identity of the wife of a dead passenger.
Glossy star melodrama, very watchable.

w Catherine Turney, Sally Benson, Mitchell Leisen *d Mitchell Leisen ph* Daniel L. Fapp *m* Hugo Friedhofer

Barbara Stanwyck, John Lund, Lyle Bettger, *Jane Cowl,* Phyllis Thaxter, Henry O'Neill, Richard Denning

No Minor Vices
US 1948 96m bw
(MGM) Enterprise (Lewis Milestone)

A doctor brings home an artist friend who proceeds to wreck his household.
Interminable thin comedy which gives no clue as to what the talent involved thought it was doing.

w Arnold Manoff d Lewis Milestone
ph George Barnes m Franz Waxman

Dana Andrews, Lilli Palmer, Louis Jourdan, Jane Wyatt, Norman Lloyd

No More Ladies
US 1935 79m bw
MGM

A society girl thinks that by marrying a rake she can reform him.
Breezy sophisticated comedy which doesn't quite maintain its impetus.

w Donald Ogden Stewart, Horace Jackson, play A. E. Thomas d Edward H. Griffith, George Cukor ph Oliver T. Marsh
m Edward Ward

Joan Crawford, Robert Montgomery, Franchot Tone, Charles Ruggles, Edna May Oliver, Gail Patrick, Reginald Denny, Arthur Treacher

'Sophistication plus in society setting and probably too much on the ultra side for sock appreciation. But okay.'—Variety

No More Women
US 1934 73m bw

Deep sea divers compete for jobs and a woman. Flagg and Quirt in all but name, with action melodrama largely substituted for skirt-chasing. Edmund Lowe, Victor McLaglen, Sally Blane, Minna Gombell, Harold Huber. Written by Delmer Daves, Lou Beslow, from a story by John M. Strong; directed by Al Rogell; for Paramount. 'Quirt and Flagg under the Hays morality code, and they can't take it.'—Variety

No, My Darling Daughter
GB 1961 96m bw
Rank / Five Star / Betty E. Box–Ralph Thomas

Chaos ensues when a tycoon's daughter is thought to be eloping with an American boy friend.
Clumsy comedy with moments of brightness provided by the actors.

w Frank Harvey, play A Handful of Tansy by Harold Brooke, Kay Bannerman d Ralph Thomas ph Ernest Steward m Norrie Paramor

Michael Redgrave, Michael Craig, Roger Livesey, Rad Fulton, Juliet Mills, Renee Houston, Joan Sims, Peter Butterworth

No Name on the Bullet
US 1958 77m Eastmancolor
Cinemascope
Universal (Howard Christie, Jack Arnold)

A hired gunman books into the hotel of a small western town, and everybody wonders who he is after.
Tolerable western programmer with more emphasis than usual on characterization.

w Gene L. Coon d Jack Arnold ph Harold Lipstein m Herman Stein

Audie Murphy, Charles Drake, Joan Evans, R. G. Armstrong, Willis Bouchey, Karl Swenson

No No Nanette
US 1930 90m approx bw with
Technicolor sequences

A married bible publisher secretly helps three girls, who all visit him on the same day. Early talkie version of the rather naïve musical hit, with a priceless moment or two among the dross. Bernice Claire, Lucien Littlefield, Lilyan Tashman, Bert Roach, Zasu Pitts. Written by Howard Emmett Rogers, from the play by Otto Harbach and Frank Mandel; directed by Clarence Badger; for Warner.

No No Nanette
US 1940 90m bw
RKO / Suffolk (Herbert Wilcox)

Slightly altered remake with too little attention to the musical numbers.

w Ken Englund d Herbert Wilcox
md Anthony Collins

Anna Neagle, Richard Carlson, Victor Mature, Helen Broderick, Roland Young, Zasu Pitts, Eve Arden, Billy Gilbert

'It's overboard on inaction, with most of the dead wood up front.'—Variety

† A previous version was made in 1929, by First National, partly in colour; it starred Bernice Claire, Alexander Gray and Lucien Littlefield, and was directed by Clarence Badger.

No Orchids for Miss Blandish
GB 1948 102m bw
Renown (A. R. Shipman, Oswald Mitchell)

An heiress is kidnapped by gangsters and falls for their psychopathic leader.
Hilariously awful gangster movie from a bestselling shocker. Everyone concerned is all at sea, and the result is one of the worst films ever made.

wd St John L. Clowes, novel James Hadley Chase ph Gerald Gibbs

Jack La Rue, Linden Travers, Hugh McDermott, Walter Crisham, Lily Molnar, Zoe Gail

'This must be the most sickening exhibition of brutality, perversion, sex and sadism ever to be shown on a cinema screen . . . with pseudo-American accents the actors literally battle their way through a script laden with suggestive dialogue.'—MFB

'A most vicious display of sadism, brutality and suggestiveness.'—Milton Shulman, Evening Standard

'The morals are about level with those of a scavenger dog.'—Daily Express

'It has all the morals of an alley cat and all the sweetness of a sewer.'—Observer

'The worst film I have ever seen.'—Sunday Express

† Remade as The Grissom Gang (qv).

No Parking
GB 1938 72m bw
Herbert Wilcox

A car park attendant is mistaken for an American killer.
Modest, entertaining star comedy.

w Gerald Elliott, story Carol Reed d Jack Raymond

Gordon Harker, Leslie Perrins, Irene Ware, Cyril Smith

No Peace among the Olives
Italy 1950 99m bw
Lux (Domenico Davanzati)

A young shepherd goes home after the war and finds himself at war again—against a local racketeer.
A rather crude melodrama comparable with the American Thieves' Highway and other films noirs of the time.

w Giuseppe de Santis and others d Giuseppe de Santis ph Pietro Portalupi m Goffredo Petrassi

Lucia Bose, Raf Vallone, Folco Lulli, Dante Maggio

No Place for Jennifer
GB 1949 90m bw

Divorcing parents think again when their twelve-year-old daughter runs away. Very predictable tearjerker which kept box offices busy in its day. Leo Genn, Rosamund John, Janette Scott, Beatrice Campbell, Guy Middleton, Anthony Nicholls, Jean Cadell. Written by J. Lee-Thompson, from the novel No Difference to Me by Phyllis Hambledon; directed by Henry Cass; for ABPC.

No Questions Asked
US 1951 80m bw
MGM (Nicholas Nayfack)

A young lawyer undertakes shady business and finds himself framed for murder.
Well made second feature on conventional lines.

w Sidney Sheldon d Harold Kress ph Harold Lipstein m Leith Stevens

Barry Sullivan, George Murphy, Arlene Dahl, Jean Hagen, William Reynolds, Mari Blanchard

No Resting Place
GB 1951 77m bw
Colin Lesslie

A wandering Irish tinker accidentally kills a man and is hounded by a Civil Guard.
Interesting attempt at realistic location drama, suffering from a dejected plot and unsympathetic characters.

w Paul Rotha, Colin Lesslie, Michael Orrom, novel Ian Niall d Paul Rotha ph Wolfgang Suschitzky m William Alwyn

Michael Gough, Noel Purcell, Jack McGowran

No Room at the Inn
GB 1948 82m bw
British National (Ivan Foxwell)

A monstrous woman half-starves evacuees and turns her house into a brothel.
Absurd melodrama from a play which was popular because it offered a full-blooded star performance. The film is less convincing but works pretty well on its level.

w Ivan Foxwell, Dylan Thomas, *play* Joan Temple *d* Dan Birt *ph* James Wilson

Freda Jackson, Joy Shelton, Hermione Baddeley, Joan Dowling, Harcourt Williams, Sydney Tafler, Frank Pettingell, Niall MacGinnis

No Room for the Groom°
US 1952 82m bw
Universal-International (Ted Richmond)

An army veteran returns to his wife, who has moved in with her family without telling them of her marriage.
Amiable comedy which rises to a fair pitch of frenzy.

w Joseph Hoffman, *story* Darwin H. Teilhet *d* Douglas Sirk *ph* Clifford Stine *m* Frank Skinner

Tony Curtis, Piper Laurie, Don Defore, *Spring Byington*, Lee Aaker, Jack Kelly, Lillian Bronson

No Sad Songs for Me
US 1950 89m bw
Columbia (Buddy Adler)

A young wife discovers she has only eight months to live, and spends it planning her husband's future.
Well-meant but rather icky melodrama featuring one of those beautiful illnesses that appear to have no physical effect.

w Howard Koch, *novel* Ruth Southard *d* Rudolph Maté *ph* Joseph Walker *m* George Duning

Margaret Sullavan, Wendell Corey, Viveca Lindfors, Natalie Wood, John McIntire

AAN: George Duning

No Sex Please, We're British°
GB 1973 91m Technicolor
Columbia / BHP (John R. Sloan)

A wrongly addressed parcel of dirty postcards causes chaos when it arrives at a bank.
Archetypal British farce with less plot than one might expect, but quite brightly performed.

w Anthony Marriott, Johnnie Mortimer, Brian Cooke, *play* Anthony Marriott, Alistair Foot *d* Cliff Owen *ph* Ken Hodges *m* Eric Rogers

Ronnie Corbett, Beryl Reid, *Arthur Lowe*, Ian Ogilvy, Susan Penhaligon, David Swift, Michael Bates, Gerald Sim

No Time for Comedy°
US 1940 93m bw
Warner (Robert Lord)

A playwright is depressed by the times and has lost the knack of making people laugh.
Smooth film version of a thoughtful romantic comedy play.

w Julius J. and Philip G. Epstein, *play* S. N. Behrman *d* William Keighley *ph* Ernest Haller *m* Heinz Roemheld

James Stewart, Rosalind Russell, Charles Ruggles, Genevieve Tobin, Allyn Joslyn, Clarence Kolb, Louise Beavers

'Claudette loves the men with muscles!'
No Time for Love°
US 1943 83m bw
Paramount (Mitchell Leisen)

A lady photographer falls for the foreman of a crew digging a tunnel under the Hudson.
Agreeable romantic slapstick farce.

w Claude Binyon *d* Mitchell Leisen *ph* Charles Lang Jnr *m* Victor Young

Claudette Colbert, Fred MacMurray, Ilka Chase, Richard Haydn, June Havoc, Marjorie Gateson, Bill Goodwin

No Time for Sergeants
US 1958 111m bw
Warner (Mervyn Le Roy)

Adventures of a hillbilly army conscript.
Heavy-handed adaptation of the stage success, a real piece of filmed theatre with not much sparkle to it.

w John Lee Mahin, *play* Ira Levin, *novel* Mac Hyman *d* Mervyn Le Roy *ph* Harold Rosson *m* Ray Heindorf

Andy Griffith, William Fawcett, Murray Hamilton, Nick Adams, Myron McCormick, Bartlett Robinson

No Time for Tears
GB 1957 86m Eastmancolor
Cinemascope
ABPC (W. A. Whittaker)

Problems of a children's hospital.
Totally predictable British tearjerker with a happy ending.

w Anne Burnaby *d* Cyril Frankel *ph* Gilbert Taylor *m* Francis Chagrin

Anna Neagle, Anthony Quayle, Sylvia Syms, Flora Robson, George Baker, Alan White, Daphne Anderson, Michael Hordern, Joan Hickson, Sophie Stewart, Rosalie Crutchley

No Trees in the Street
GB 1958 96m bw
ABP / Allegro (Frank Godwin)

Problems of a London slum family in the thirties.
Artificial and unconvincing attempt at a London *Love on the Dole*, dragged up and redigested in a later era when 'realism' was thought to be fashionable.

w Ted Willis, from his play *d* J. Lee-Thompson *ph* Gilbert Taylor *m* Laurie Johnson

Sylvia Syms, Herbert Lom, Joan Miller, Melvyn Hayes, Stanley Holloway, Liam Redmond, Ronald Howard, Carole Lesley, Lana Morris, Lily Kann

'Nothing remains but crude sensationalism and several moments of unconscious humour.'—*MFB*

No Way Out°
US 1950 106m bw
TCF (Darryl F. Zanuck)

A crook stirs up racial feeling against a black doctor in whose hands his brother has died.
Vivid, hard-hitting melodrama with a hospital background and a strong sociological flavour.

w *Joseph L. Mankiewicz, Lesser Samuels d* Joseph L. Mankiewicz *ph* Milton Krasner *m* Alfred Newman

Richard Widmark, Sidney Poitier, Linda Darnell, Stephen McNally, Harry Bellaver, Stanley Ridges, Ossie Davis, Ruby Dee

'A production designed solely for purposes of agitation and propaganda, unworthy of literary or cinematic consideration.'—*Henry Hart, Films in Review*

AAN: script

No Way to Treat a Lady°
US 1968 108m Technicolor
Paramount / Sol C. Siegel

A mass murderer of women who is also a master of disguise has a running battle with a police detective.
Curious mixture of star show-off piece, murder mystery, black farce, suspense melodrama and Jewish comedy. Bits of it come off very well, but it's a bumpy ride.

w John Gay, *novel* William Goldman *d* Jack Smight *ph* Jack Priestley *m* Stanley Myers

Rod Steiger, George Segal, Lee Remick, Eileen Heckart, Murray Hamilton, Michael Dunn

'The sweetest love story ever told! The epic drama of the age! Drama with a world sweep, colossal and sublime!'
Noah's Ark°°
US 1929 135m bw
Warner

The biblical story of Noah is paralleled, rather loosely, with a tragedy of World War I.
Naïve but fascinating Hollywood epic which in patches triumphantly overcomes the problems of the part-talkie period and is always fascinating to look at.

w Anthony Coldeway, Darryl F. Zanuck *d* Michael Curtiz *ph* Hal Mohr, Barney McGill *ph* Anton Grot

Dolores Costello, Noah Beery, Louise Fazenda, Guinn Williams, Paul McAllister, Myrna Loy

'The biggest and best edited picture of the industry . . . mobs, Niagaras, train wrecks, war aplenty, crashes, deluges and everything that goes to give the picture fan a thrill.'—*Variety*

'Staggering . . . the greatest thing the screen has done.'—*The Film Spectator*
† On première it was Warners' longest film, but the release version was cut by nearly half.

Nob Hill*
US 1945 95m Technicolor
TCF (André Daven)

In the gay nineties, a San Francisco saloon owner tries to step into society and win one of its most eligible young ladies.
Engaging period musical drama with all talents working well.

w Wanda Tuchock, Norman Reilly Raine
d Henry Hathaway ph Edward Cronjager
md Emil Newman, Charles Henderson

George Raft, Joan Bennett, Peggy Ann Garner, Vivian Blaine, Alan Reed, B. S. Pully, Edgar Barrier

Nobody Lives Forever
US 1946 100m bw
Warner (Robert Buckner)

A con man fleeces a rich widow, then falls in love with her.
Forgettable romantic melodrama.

w W. R. Burnett d Jean Negulesco
ph Arthur Edeson m Adolph Deutsch

John Garfield, Geraldine Fitzgerald, Walter Brennan, Faye Emerson, George Coulouris, George Tobias

Nobody Runs Forever*
GB 1968 101m Eastmancolor
Rank / Selmur (Betty E. Box)
US title: The High Commissioner

An Australian detective is sent to arrest the high commissioner in London on a charge of murdering his first wife.
Sub-Hitchcock thriller which comes to life in patches but has a plot and dialogue which obviously embarrass the actors.

w Wilfred Greatorex, novel The High Commissioner by Jon Cleary ph Ernest Steward m Georges Delerue

Rod Taylor, Christopher Plummer, Lilli Palmer, Camilla Sparv, Daliah Lavi, Clive Revill, Lee Montague, Calvin Lockhart, Derren Nesbitt, Leo McKern, Franchot Tone

● Video: Rank

Nobody's Baby
US 1937 67m bw

Girls at a training school for nurses find themselves looking after a baby. Lightweight comedy filler. Lyda Roberti, Patsy Kelly, Lynne Overman, Robert Armstrong, Rosina Lawrence, Don Alvarado, Tom Dugan. Written by Harold Law, Hal Yates, Pat C. Flick; directed by Gus Meins; for Hal Roach / MGM. 'Agreeable enough number two feature for duals.'—Variety

Nobody's Perfect
US 1968 103m Techniscope
Universal (Howard Christie)

An ex-naval officer returns to Japan to make amends for stealing a buddha.
Flatfooted comedy adventure.

w John D. F. Black, novel The Crows of Edwina Hill by Allan R. Bosworth d Alan Rafkin ph Robert H. Wyckoff m Irving Gertz

Doug McClure, Nancy Kwan, Steve Carlson, James Whitmore, David Hartman, Gary Vinson, James Shigeta

Nocturne*
US 1946 87m bw
RKO (Joan Harrison)

A police detective investigates the death of a composer.
Amusingly self-mocking crime thriller, quite smoothly done in all departments.

w Jonathan Latimer d Edwin L. Marin
ph Harry J. Wild m Leigh Harline

George Raft, Lynn Bari, Virginia Huston, Joseph Pevney, Myrna Dell, Edward Ashley, Walter Sande, Mabel Paige

Non Stop New York
GB 1937 71m bw
GFD / Gaumont

In 1940, gangsters on a transatlantic airliner try to kill a key witness.
Slightly futuristic thriller of its time, now hilariously dated but quite entertaining as well as giving a rare picture of air travel in the thirties.

w Curt Siodmak, Roland Pertwee, J. O. C. Orton, Derek Twist, novel Sky Steward by Ken Attiwill d Robert Stevenson

John Loder, Anna Lee, Francis L. Sullivan, Frank Cellier, Desmond Tester, Athene Seyler, Jerry Verno

None But the Brave
US 1965 105m Technicolor
Panavision
Warner / Eiga / Toho / Artanis (Frank Sinatra)

During World War II a plane carrying US Marines to the Pacific front crashlands on an island held by Japanese.
Anti-war melodrama in which the action scenes are more memorable than the admirable sentiments.

w John Twist, Katsuya Susaki d Frank Sinatra ph Harold Lipstein m Johnny Williams

Frank Sinatra, Clint Walker, Tommy Sands, Tony Bill, Brad Dexter

'When is the world coming out of its midnight? When is the human race going to get off its knees?'

None But the Lonely Heart*
US 1944 113m bw
RKO (David Hempstead)

In the thirties, a cockney drifter finds himself when he learns that his mother is dying.
Wildly astonishing moodpiece to come from Hollywood during World War II; its picture of East End low life is as rocky as its star performance, but it started Miss Barrymore on the west coast career which sustained her old age.

wd Clifford Odets, novel Richard Llewellyn ph George Barnes m Hanns Eisler
md Constantin Bakaleinikoff

Cary Grant, Ethel Barrymore, June Duprez, Barry Fitzgerald, Jane Wyatt, George Coulouris, Dan Duryea, Konstantin Shayne, Morton Lowry, Helene Thimig

'A perplexing mixture of good and bad, authentic and phony.'—Hermione Rich Isaacs, Theatre Arts

AA: Ethel Barrymore
AAN: Hanns Eisler; Cary Grant

None Shall Escape*
US 1944 85m bw
Columbia (Sam Bischoff)

The career of a Nazi officer shown as flashbacks from his trial as a war criminal.
Taut topical melodrama reflecting the mood of the time.

w Lester Cole d André de Toth ph Lee Garmes m Ernst Toch

Alexander Knox, Marsha Hunt, Henry Travers, Dorothy Morris, Richard Crane

AA: Lester Cole; original story (Alfred Neumann, Joseph Thau)

Noose
GB 1948 98m bw
ABPC / Edward Dryhurst

A Soho black market gang is exposed.
Vivid though rather tatty film version of a West End play success.

w Richard Llewellyn, from his play
d Edmond T. Greville ph Hone Glendining
m Charles Williams

Nigel Patrick, Carole Landis, Derek Farr, Joseph Calleia, Stanley Holloway, Hay Petrie, John Slater

The Noose Hangs High
US 1948 77m bw

Two window washers are hired by a crooked bookie who finds their incompetence hard to tolerate when they lose his winnings. Thin star comedy filled with the team's cornier routines, not too cleverly revived. Bud Abbott, Lou Costello, Leon Errol, Joseph Calleia, Murray Leonard, Cathy Downs, Mike Mazurki, Fritz Feld. Written by John Grant and Howard Harris; directed by Charles Barton; for Eagle-Lion. (A previous film of the same story was made in 1939 under the title For Love or Money, with June Lang, Robert Kent and Ed Brophy.)

Nor the Moon By Night
GB 1958 92m Eastmancolor
Rank (John Stafford)
US title: Elephant Gun

An African game warden marries a longtime penfriend who finds that Africa presents unexpected problems.
Paperback romance with pleasant backgrounds.

w Guy Elmes, novel Joy Packer d Ken Annakin ph Harry Waxman m James Bernard

Belinda Lee, Michael Craig, Patrick McGoohan, Anna Gaylor, Eric Pohlmann

'Neither character nor incident nor theme has any coherence or interest.'—MFB

'A mouth like hers is just for kissing . . . not for telling!'

Nora Prentiss°
US 1946 117m bw
Warner (William Jacobs)

A doctor falls for a café singer who ruins his life.
Standard star melodrama aimed at women, and appreciated by them.

w N. Richard Nash, *story* Paul Webster, Jack Sobell d Vincent Sherman ph James Wong Howe m Franz Waxman

Ann Sheridan, Kent Smith, Bruce Bennett, Robert Alda, Rosemary de Camp, John Ridgely, Wanda Hendrix

Norma Rae°
US 1979 114m De Luxe Panavision
TCF / Martin Ritt / Rose and Asseyev

A southern girl becomes an angry union organizer.
Well-intentioned and well-acted pamphlet of political enlightenment with an inevitably ambivalent attitude.

ı w Irving Ravetch, Harriet Frank Jnr d Martin Ritt ph John A. Alonzo m David Shire pd Walter Scott Herndon

Sally Field, Beau Bridges, Ron Leibman, Pat Hingle, Barbara Baxley

● *Video: CBS / Fox*

Norman, Is That You?
US 1976 92m Metrocolor

Adulterous parents find that their son is a homosexual. Unattractive comedy roughly filmed and given a black ambience. Not worth buying a ticket. Redd Foxx, Pearl Bailey, Dennis Dugan, Michael Warren, Tamara Dobson. From the play by Ron Clark and Sam Bobrick; directed by George Schlatter; for George Schlatter / MGM.

The Norseman
US 1978 90m Movielab
AIP / Charles B. Pierce / Fawcett Majors

A Viking heads across the sea to America in search of his long lost father.
Low grade hokum for the easily pleased.

wd Charles B. Pierce ph Robert Bethard m Jaime Mendoza-Nava

Lee Majors, Cornel Wilde, Mel Ferrer, Jack Elam, Chris Connelly

The North Avenue Irregulars
US 1978 99m Technicolor

A Presbyterian minister becomes an undercover agent for the FBI, helping to expose a crooked gambling syndicate. Very heavy comedy which seems to find itself much funnier than the audience does. Edward Herrmann, Barbara Harris, Susan Clark, Karen Valentine, Michael Constantine, Cloris Leachman, Patsy Kelly, Douglas Fowley, Alan Hale Jnr. Written by Don Tait, from the novel by the Rev. Albert Fay Hill; directed by Bruce Bilson; for Disney. (GB title: *Hill's Angels*.)

North by Northwest°°°°
US 1959 136m Technicolor
Vistavision
MGM (Alfred Hitchcock)

A businessman is mistaken for a spy, and enemy agents then try to kill him because he knows too much.
Delightful chase comedy-thriller with a touch of sex, a kind of compendium of its director's best work, with memories of *The 39 Steps, Saboteur* and *Foreign Correspondent* among others.

w Ernest Lehman d Alfred Hitchcock ph Robert Burks m Bernard Herrmann

Cary Grant, Eva Marie Saint, James Mason, Leo G. Carroll, Martin Landau, Jessie Royce Landis, Adam Williams

'It is only when you adopt the basic premise that Cary Grant could not possibly come to harm that the tongue in Hitchcock's cheek becomes plainly visible.'—*Hollis Alpert, Saturday Review*

AAN: Ernest Lehman

● *Video: MGM / UA*

North Dallas Forty
US 1979 118m Metrocolor
Paramount (Frank Yablans)

The gruelling life of a professional football player, laced with drugs, sex and alcohol.
Well made but generally unattractive, the kind of movie for which one wouldn't expect to find an audience.

w Frank Yablans, Ted Kotcheff, Peter Gent, *novel* Peter Gent d Ted Kotcheff ph Paul Lohmann m John Scott pd Alfred Sweeney

Nick Nolte, Mac Davis, Charles Durning, Dayle Haddon, Bo Swenson

North Sea Hijack
GB 1979 100m Technicolor
Universal / Cinema Seven (Mo Rothman)
US title: *ffoulkes*

A British oil rig in the North Sea is held for ransom.
Asinine *Boy's Own Paper* adventure story with the very minimum of thrills and a totally miscast hero.

w Jack Davies, from his novel Esther, Ruth and Jennifer d Andrew V. McLaglen ph Tony Imi m Michael J. Lewis pd Maurice Carter

Roger Moore, Anthony Perkins, James Mason, Michael Parks, David Hedison, Jack Watson, George Baker, Faith Brook

● *Video: Rank*

North Star°
US 1943 105m bw
Samuel Goldwyn (William Cameron Menzies)
aka: *Armored Attack*

A Russian village defends itself against the Nazi onslaught.
Highly artificial propaganda piece later disowned by its makers and retitled. Good acting can't make its mark when the Russian steppes become a never-never land.

w Lillian Hellman d Lewis Milestone ph James Wong Howe m Aaron Copland

Anne Baxter, Farley Granger, Jane Withers, Dana Andrews, Walter Brennan, Erich Von Stroheim, Dean Jagger, Ann Harding, Carl Benton Reid, Walter Huston

'Putting American villagers into Russian costumes and calling them by Russian names is never going to deceive this old bird.'—*James Agate*

'Its failure is the case history of every Hollywood film that steps out of its scope.'—*Richard Winnington*

'Something to be seen more in sorrow than in anger and more in the attitude of the diagnostician in any emotion at all.'—*James Agee*

AAN: Lillian Hellman; James Wong Howe; Aaron Copland

North to Alaska°
US 1960 122m De Luxe Cinemascope
TCF (Henry Hathaway)

In 1900, two successful gold prospectors have woman trouble.
Good-natured brawling adventure story which could do with cutting but is certainly the type of action movie they don't make 'em like any more.

w John Lee Mahin, Martin Rackin, Claude Binyon, *play* Birthday Gift by Ladislas Fodor d Henry Hathaway ph Leon Shamroy m Lionel Newman

John Wayne, Stewart Granger, Fabian, Capucine, Ernie Kovacs, Mickey Shaughnessy, Karl Swenson, Joe Sawyer, John Qualen

North to the Klondike
US 1942 60m bw

Gold hunters protect the rights of a girl who has made a strike. Typical economy size programme filler with a studio look and a stalwart cast. Broderick Crawford, Lon Chaney Jnr, Andy Devine, Evelyn Ankers, Keye Luke. Written by Clarence Upson Young, Lew Sarecky, George Bricker and William Castle; directed by Erle C. Kenton; for Universal.

Northern Pursuit°
US 1943 94m bw
Warner (Jack Chertok)

A Mountie tracks a stranded Nazi pilot through the Canadian wastes.
Rather unusual star actioner, not badly done.

w Frank Gruber, Alvah Bessie d Raoul Walsh ph Sid Hickox m Adolph Deutsch

Errol Flynn, Helmut Dantine, Julie Bishop, John Ridgely, Gene Lockhart, Tom Tully, Bernard Nedell

Northwest Frontier°°°
GB 1959 129m Eastmancolor
Cinemascope
Rank / Marcel Hellman
US title: *Flame Over India*

In 1905 an English officer during a rebellion

escorts a young Hindu prince on a dangerous train journey.
Thoroughly enjoyable Boys' Own Paper adventure story with excellent set pieces and a spot-the-villain mystery.

w Robin Estridge d J. Lee-Thompson ph Geoffrey Unsworth m Mischa Spoliansky

Kenneth More, Lauren Bacall, Herbert Lom, Ursula Jeans, Wilfrid Hyde White, I. S. Johar, Eugene Deckers, Ian Hunter

'*Northwest Frontier* seems to have borrowed its eccentric engine from *The General*, its hazardous expedition from *Stagecoach* and its background of tribal violence from *The Drum*.'—*Penelope Houston*

● *Video: Rank*

'Ten stars! Two love stories! One thousand thrills!'
Northwest Mounted Police*
US 1940 125m Technicolor
Paramount (Cecil B. de Mille)

A Texas Ranger seeks a fugitive in Canada.
Typical big-scale action concoction by de Mille, but in this case none of it's very memorable and the detail is poor.

w Alan Le May, Jesse Lasky Jnr, C. Gardner Sullivan d Cecil B. de Mille ph Victor Milner, Howard Greene m Victor Young

Gary Cooper, Paulette Goddard, Madeleine Carroll, Preston Foster, Robert Preston, George Bancroft, Lynne Overman, Akim Tamiroff, Walter Hampden, Lon Chaney Jnr, Montagu Love, George E. Stone

'Two hours of colour, killing, kindness and magnificent country.'—*Otis Ferguson*
'A movie in the grand style. God's own biggest trees and mountains for prop and backdrop; staunch courage and lofty aims among the good people; cunning and treachery lurking within the sinister forces; the ominous note of doom finally stifled by the fortitude of noble men.'—*Time*

AAN: Victor Milner, Howard Greene; Victor Young

Northwest Outpost
US 1947 91m bw
Republic (Allan Dwan)
GB title: *End of the Rainbow*

Adventures of California cavalrymen.
Milk-and-water adventures in a forgettable operetta.

w Elizabeth Meehan, Richard Sale d Allan Dwan ph Reggie Lanning m Rudolf Friml

Nelson Eddy, Ilona Massey, Hugo Haas, Elsa Lanchester

Northwest Passage***
(Part One, Rogers' Rangers)
US 1940 126m Technicolor
MGM (Hunt Stromberg)

Colonial rangers fight it out with hostile Indians.
Part Two was never made, but no one seemed to mind that the characters in Part One never got round to seeking the titular sea route. The adventures depicted had the feel of historical actuality, and the star was well cast.

w Lawrence Stallings, Talbot Jennings, novel Kenneth Roberts d King Vidor ph Sidney Wagner, William V. Skall m Herbert Stothart

Spencer Tracy, Robert Young, Ruth Hussey, Walter Brennan, Nat Pendleton, Robert Barrat, Lumsden Hare, Donald MacBride

'Half men, half demons, warriors such as the world has never known . . . they lived with death and danger for the women who hungered for their love!'—*publicity*

AAN: Sidney Wagner, William V. Skall

Norwood
US 1969 95m Technicolor
Paramount / Hal B. Wallis

A Vietnam veteran returns to his Texas home but feels restless and decides to become a radio singer.
A rather ordinary film about an innocent abroad, neither very funny nor very moving.

w Marguerite Roberts d Jack Haley Jnr ph Robert B. Hauser m Al de Lory

Glen Campbell, Kim Darby, Joe Namath, Carol Lynley, Pat Hingle, Tisha Sterling, Dom De Luise, Jack Haley, Cass Daley, Gil Lamb

Nosferatu***
Germany 1921 72m approx (24 fps) bw
Prana

Count Dracula goes to Bremen and is destroyed by sunlight.
An unofficial treatment of the Bram Stoker novel, with a terrifying count and several splendid moments. It took its director to Hollywood.

w Henrik Galeen d F. W. Murnau ph Fritz Arno Wagner ad Albin Grau

Max Schreck, Gustav Von Wangenheim, Greta Schroeder, Alexander Granach

● *Video: Thorn EMI*

Nosferatu the Vampyre*
West Germany / France 1979 107m
Eastmancolor

Excruciatingly slow retread of the German silent film. Despite the star's splendidly loathsome appearance, the overall is no improvement, and the colour in the English prints is quite dreadful. *Klaus Kinski*, Isabelle Adjani, Bruno Ganz, Walter Ladengast. Written and directed by Werner Herzog; for Gaumont / Werner Herzog Filmproduktion. 'Like a dream from which you keep waking with indigestion.'—*Guardian*. (Original title: *Nosferatu, Phantom der Nacht*.)

● *Video: CBS / Fox*

Nostalgia*
Italy 1983 126m Eastmancolor

A Russian writer in Italy meets a social outcast who is expecting the end of the world.
Indescribably doomladen, occasionally beautiful, stylistically interesting and for the most part very boring parable of a kind unique to this director. Oleg Jankovsky, Erland Josephson, Domiziana Giordano. Written by Andrei Tarkovsky, Tonino Guerra; directed by Andrei Tarkovsky; for Opera Film / Sovin Film / RAI.

Not as a Stranger**
US 1955 135m bw
UA / Stanley Kramer

A medical student has professional and personal struggles.
Earnest filming of a bestseller, with all the actors too old for their parts.

w Edna and Edward Anhalt, novel Morton Thompson d Stanley Kramer ph Franz Planer m George Antheil pd Rudolph Sternad

Robert Mitchum, Olivia de Havilland, Broderick Crawford, Frank Sinatra, Gloria Grahame, Charles Bickford, Myron McCormick, Lon Chaney Jnr, Jesse White, Henry Morgan, Lee Marvin, Virginia Christine

Not Now, Darling
GB 1972 97m Eastmancolor

A furrier gets into a complicated situation when he arranges for his mistress to have a cheap mink coat. Interminable film version (in Multivista, a shoot-and-edit equivalent to TV taping which gives a dingy look and can only work in a single set) of a West End farce which wasn't marvellous to begin with. Leslie Phillips, Ray Cooney, Moira Lister, Julie Ege, Joan Sims, Derren Nesbitt, Barbara Windsor, Jack Hulbert, Cicely Courtneidge, Bill Fraser. Written by John Chapman, from the play by Ray Cooney; directed by Ray Cooney and David Croft; for LMG / Sedgemoor / Not Now Films.

Not of This Earth**
US 1957 72m bw
AA (Roger Corman)

An alien comes to earth in human form in search of blood which may save his planet.
Modestly budgeted minor sci-fi; ruthless, original and competent.

w Charles Griffith, Mark Hanna d Roger Corman ph John Mescall m Ronald Stein

Paul Birch, Beverly Garland, Morgan Jones

Not So Dumb
US 1929 80m approx at 24 fps bw
silent

A naïve girl throws a big party in the hope of advancing her boy friend's career. Popular comedy of its time. Marion Davies, Elliott Nugent, Raymond Hackett, Franklin Pangborn, Julia Faye. Written by Wanda Tuchock and Edwin Justus Mayer, from the play *Dulcy* by George S. Kaufman and Marc Connolly; directed by King Vidor; for MGM. (NB: Previously made as *Dulcy* by Warner in 1923, directed by Sidney Franklin, with Constance Talmadge.)

Not with My Wife You Don't
US 1966 119m Technicolor
Warner / Fernwood / Reynard (Norman Panama, Joel Freeman)

A Korean war veteran is furious when an old rival turns up in London and again makes eyes at his wife.
Extraordinarily flat star comedy of cross and double cross among friends.

w Norman Panama, Larry Gelbart, Peter Barnes d Norman Panama ph Charles Lang, Paul Beeson m Johnny Williams

Tony Curtis, George C. Scott, Virna Lisi, Carroll O'Connor, Richard Eastham

'About as frothy as a tin of dehydrated milk.'—MFB

'It has all the verve, subtlety and sophistication of its title.'—Judith Crist

Nothing But the Best**
GB 1964 99m Eastmancolor
Anglo Amalgamated / Domino (David Deutsch)

An ambitious clerk learns to fight his way to the top by cheek and one-upmanship. Hard, skilful, rather unattractive comedy with interesting social comments on its time.

w Frederic Raphael d Clive Donner ph Nicolas Roeg m Ron Grainer ad Reece Pemberton

Alan Bates, Denholm Elliott, Harry Andrews, Millicent Martin, Pauline Delany

'The nightmare has already killed five people. Now it's yours to live!'

Nothing But the Night*
GB 1972 90m Eastmancolor
Rank / Charlemagne (Anthony Nelson Keys)

The trustees of an orphanage die off mysteriously, and it seems that the orphans themselves are responsible.
Convoluted murder mystery with horror elements and a twist hardly worth waiting for; earnest performances help.

w Brian Hayles, novel John Blackburn d Peter Sasdy ph Ken Talbot m Malcolm Williamson

Christopher Lee, Peter Cushing, Diana Dors, Georgia Brown, Keith Barron, John Robinson

Nothin' But the Truth
US 1941 90m bw
Paramount (Arthur Hornblow Jnr)

A stockbroker takes a bet that he can tell the absolute truth for twenty-four hours.
Rather unsurprising version of a stage comedy previously filmed as a silent. It lacks the style one might expect from the team which made The Cat and the Canary.

w Don Hartman, Ken Englund, play James Montgomery, novel Frederic S. Isham d Elliott Nugent ph Charles Lang

Bob Hope, Paulette Goddard, Edward Arnold, Leif Erickson, Glen Anders, Helen Vinson, Grant Mitchell, Willie Best

Nothing But Trouble
US 1945 70m bw
MGM (B. F. Ziedman)

A chef and butler accidentally prevent a poison plot against a young king.
Feebly-devised star comedy, their last for a big studio.

w Russel Rouse, Ray Golden d Sam Taylor ph Charles Salerno Jnr m Nathaniel Shilkret

Stan Laurel, Oliver Hardy, Mary Boland, Henry O'Neill, David Leland

Nothing Personal
US 1980 97m Movielab

A professor and a lady lawyer try to stop seal hunting. The subject is an unsuitable starting point for a thin and zany comedy which gets nowhere and stays there. Donald Sutherland, Suzanne Somers, Larence Dane, Roscoe Lee Browne. Written by Robert Kaufman; directed by George Bloomfield; for David M. Perlmutter / AIP.

Nothing Sacred****
US 1937 77m Technicolor
David O. Selznick

A girl thought to be dying of a rare disease is built up by the press into a national heroine; but the diagnosis was wrong.
Hollywood's most bitter and hilarious satire, with crazy comedy elements and superb wisecracks; a joy.

w Ben Hecht, story Letter to the Editor by James H. Street d William Wellman ph W. Howard Greene m Oscar Levant

Carole Lombard, Fredric March, Walter Connolly, Charles Winninger, Sig Rumann, Frank Fay, Maxie Rosenbloom, Margaret Hamilton, Hedda Hopper, Monty Woolley, Hattie McDaniel, Olin Howland, John Qualen

DOCTOR (Charles Winninger): 'I'll tell you briefly what I think of newspapermen. The hand of God, reaching down into the mire, couldn't elevate one of them to the depths of degradation.'

EDITOR (Walter Connolly): 'I am sitting here, Mr Cook, toying with the idea of cutting out your heart and stuffing it—like an olive!'

'Hit comedy . . . will be one of the big grossers of the year.'—Variety

'Because it does hold up a mirror, even though a distorting mirror, to a very real world of ballyhoo and cheap sensationalism, the pleasure to be obtained from it is something more than the usual mulish guffaw.'—Spectator

† Refashioned in 1953 as a stage musical, Hazel Flagg, with music by Jule Styne; this in turn became a Martin and Lewis comedy Living It Up (Jerry Lewis in the Carole Lombard part).

Notorious***
US 1946 101m bw
RKO (Alfred Hitchcock)

In Rio, a notorious lady marries a Nazi renegade to help the US government but finds herself falling in love with her contact.
Superb romantic suspenser containing some of Hitchcock's best work.

w Ben Hecht d Alfred Hitchcock ph Ted Tetzlaff m Roy Webb

Cary Grant, Ingrid Bergman, Claude Rains, Louis Calhern, Leopoldine Konstantin, Reinhold Schunzel

'Velvet smooth in dramatic action, sharp and sure in its characters, and heavily charged with the intensity of warm emotional appeal.'—Bosley Crowther

'The suspense is terrific.'—New Yorker, 1976

'A film in the supercharged American idiom which made Casablanca popular.'—Hermione Rich Isaacs, Theatre Arts

AAN: Ben Hecht; Claude Rains

● Video: Guild

A Notorious Gentleman
US 1935 73m bw

A man plans murder and incriminates the victim's fiancée. Basically intriguing crime yarn spoiled by over-enthusiastic direction. Charles Bickford, Helen Vinson, Sidney Blackmer, Onslow Stevens, Dudley Digges. Written by Leopold Atlas, Robert Trasker; directed by Edward Laemmle; for Universal. 'Too heavily handled for first consideration.'—Variety

The Notorious Landlady
GB 1962 127m bw
Columbia / Kohlmar / Quine (Fred Kohlmar)

An American diplomat in London takes rooms with a murder suspect; after many mysterious happenings he helps to clear her.
Flatly whimsical goings on in comical old London, complete with fog and eccentrics. The actors all try hard but are deflated by the script.

w Larry Gelbart, Richard Quine d Richard Quine ph Arthur E. Arling m George Duning

Kim Novak, Jack Lemmon, Fred Astaire, Lionel Jeffries, Estelle Winwood, Maxwell Reed

The Notorious Sophie Lang
US 1934 60m bw

A lady jewel thief matches wits with a rival from abroad. Frothy crime comedy which isn't quite smart enough to avoid boredom. Gertrude Michael, Paul Cavanagh, Arthur Byron, Alison Skipworth, Leon Errol. Written by Anthony Veiller; directed by Ralph Murphy; for Paramount. 'No marquee strength, but nice pace and some genuine amusement.'—Variety

La Notte*
Italy / France 1960 121m bw
Nepi / Sofitedip / Silver

A moderately successful novelist and his wife begin to question their marriage and their life. Slow but engaging character drama set during one night in Milan.

w Michelangelo Antonioni, Ennio Flaiano, Antonio Guerra d Michelangelo Antonioni ph Gianni di Venanzo m Giorgio Gaslini

Marcello Mastroianni, Jeanne Moreau, Monica Vitti, Bernhard Wicki

Nous Sommes Tous les Assassins*
France 1952 108m bw
UGC
aka: Are We All Murderers?

An illiterate youth is taught to kill during the war; afterwards he kills again for money and is sent for execution.

A solemn sermon on capital punishment, and a powerful though rather glib one.

w André Cayatte, Charles Spaak d André Cayatte ph Jean Bourgoin

Marcel Mouloudji, Raymond Péllégrin, Antoine Balpêtre, Claude Laydu

Les Nouveaux Messieurs*
France 1928 135m approx (24 fps) bw silent
Albatros / Séquance

A glamorous dancer forsakes a count for a rising trade union official.
Lengthy political satire which caused a few headlines when first released.

w Charles Spaak, Jacques Feyder, play Robert de Flers, Francis de Grosset d Jacques Feyder ph Georges Périnal, Maurice Defassiaux ad Lazare Meerson

Albert Préjean, Gaby Morlay, Henri Roussel

Now About These Women . . .*
Sweden 1964 80m Eastmancolor
Svensk Filmindustri
aka: All These Women

A critic comes to stay with a famous cellist whose biography he is writing, but his efforts are hampered by all the women in the house.
Virtually indescribable black farce comedy which doesn't really work, yet, as always with this director, is continually of interest.

w Erland Josephson, Ingmar Bergman d Ingmar Bergman ph Sven Nykvist m Erik Nordgren

Jarl Kulle, Georg Funkquist, Eva Dahlbeck, Karen Kavli, Harriet Andersson, Bibi Andersson, Gertrud Fridh

Now and Forever*
US 1934 82m bw
Paramount (Louis D. Lighton)

A jewel thief and his mistress are taught a thing or two by his small daughter.
Odd mixture of comedy and drama which was box office at the time but seems pretty dated after nearly fifty years, though technically very smooth.

w Vincent Lawrence, Sylvia Thalberg d Henry Hathaway ph Harry Fischbeck

Gary Cooper, Carole Lombard, Shirley Temple, Guy Standing, Charlotte Granville, Gilbert Emery, Henry Kolker

'Cinch b.o. entertainment.'—Variety
'Expertly contrived to furnish first-rate entertainment.'—Thornton Delehanty, New York Post

Now and Forever
GB 1955 91m Technicolor
ABPC / Mario Zampi

A lonely schoolgirl plans an elopement and is chased across England by two sets of parents.
Teenage romance with elements of both farce and melodrama. It seemed to please at the time.

w R. F. Delderfield, Michael Pertwee, play The Orchard Walls by R. F. Delderfield d Mario Zampi ph Erwin Hillier m Stanley Black

Janette Scott, Vernon Gray, Kay Walsh, Jack Warner, Pamela Brown, Charles Victor, Wilfrid Lawson, Marjorie Rhodes, Sonia Dresdel, Ronald Squire, David Kossoff

Now Barabbas . . .
GB 1949 87m bw
Warner / Anatole de Grunwald
aka: Now Barabbas Was a Robber

Stories of men in prison.
Thinly intercut dramas; from a stage success.

w Anatole de Grunwald, play William Douglas Home d Gordon Parry ph Otto Heller

Richard Greene, Cedric Hardwicke, William Hartnell, Kathleen Harrison, Leslie Dwyer, Richard Burton, Kenneth More, Ronald Howard, Stephen Murray, Beatrice Campbell, Betty Ann Davies, Alec Clunes

Now I'll Tell
US 1934 72m bw
Fox (Winfield Sheehan)
GB title: When New York Sleeps

The story of Arnold Rothstein, gambler-racketeer of the twenties, as told by his widow.
Competent crime / domestic programmer.

wd Edwin Burke ph Ernest Palmer m Hugo Friedhofer

Spencer Tracy, Helen Twelvetrees, Hobart Cavanaugh, Alice Faye, G. P. Huntley Jnr, Shirley Temple, Leon Ames

'In spite of the breezy sequences with which it starts, it quickly gets improbable and goes from bad to maudlin.'—Otis Ferguson

Now Voyager***
US 1942 117m bw
Warner (Hal B. Wallis)

A dowdy frustrated spinster takes the psychiatric cure and embarks on a doomed love affair.
A basically soggy script still gets by, and how, through the romantic magic of its stars, who were all at their best; and suffering in mink went over very big in wartime.

w Casey Robinson, novel Olive Higgins Prouty d Irving Rapper ph Sol Polito m Max Steiner

Bette Davis, Claude Rains, Paul Henreid, Gladys Cooper, John Loder, Bonita Granville, Ilka Chase, Lee Patrick, Charles Drake, Franklin Pangborn

CHARLOTTE (Bette Davis): 'Oh, Jerry, don't let's ask for the moon. We have the stars!'

'If it were better, it might not work at all. This way, it's a crummy classic.'—New Yorker, 1977

AA: Max Steiner
AAN: Bette Davis; Gladys Cooper
● Video: Warner

Now You See Him Now You Don't
US 1972 88m Technicolor
Walt Disney

Two students discover an elixir of invisibility and help prevent a gangster from taking over the college.
Flat Disney frolic with fair trick effects.

w Joseph L. McEveety d Robert Butler ph Frank Phillips m Robert F. Brunner sp Eustace Lycett, Danny Lee

Kurt Russell, Cesar Romero, Joe Flynn, Jim Backus, William Windom, Edward Andrews, Richard Bakalyan

Nowhere to Go
GB 1958 87m bw
Ealing (Eric Williams)

A thief escapes from prison but can get no help from the underworld and is accidentally shot after being sheltered by a socialite.
Glum character melodrama which fails to sustain interest despite the best intentions.

w Seth Holt, Ken Tynan, book Donald MacKenzie d Seth Holt ph Paul Beeson m Dizzy Reece

George Nader, Maggie Smith, Bernard Lee, Geoffrey Keen, Andree Melly, Bessie Love, Howard Marion Crawford

The Nude Bomb
US 1980 94m Technicolor

An incompetent secret agent chases a missile-launching villain. Curious and unsatisfactory attempt to revive a twenty-year-old TV situation comedy minus half its personnel.
Don Adams, Sylvia Kristel, Dana Elcar, Rhonda Fleming, Andrea Howard, Norman Lloyd. Written by Arne Sultan, Bill Dana and Leonard B. Stern; directed by Clive Donner; for Universal. 'Fans of the vidshow will derive much more enjoyment by crowding round their television sets with a bowl of popcorn watching Get Smart re-runs.'—Variety.

Number Seventeen*
GB 1932 63m bw
BIP (John Maxwell)

A girl jewel thief reforms and helps the police track down her former gang.
Minor Hitchcock thriller largely confined to a single interior until the final train chase, which despite obvious models remains exhilarating.

w Alfred Hitchcock, Alma Reville, Rodney Ackland, play J. Jefferson Farjeon d Alfred Hitchcock ph Jack Cox

Leon M. Lion, Anne Grey, John Stuart, Donald Calthrop, Barry Jones, Garry Marsh

'Only spasmodically good photography and usual slow tempo British direction. Wonder why they can't speed up a picture? Maybe it's the tea.'—Variety

† The same play had been filmed as a silent in 1928 by Geza Bolvary, with Guy Newall; it was shot in Germany.

The Nun and the Sergeant
US 1962 74m bw
UA / Springfield

In Korea, a tough sergeant commanding a 'dirty dozen' mission is joined by a schoolgirl and a nun.
Minor war adventure, moderately well done but highly unconvincing.

w Don Cerveris d Franklin Adreon ph Paul Ivano m Jerry Fielding

Anna Sten, Robert Webber, Leo Gordon, Hari Rhodes

The Nun's Story*
US 1959 151m Technicolor
Warner (Henry Blanke)

A Belgian girl joins a strict order, endures hardship in the Congo, and finally returns to ordinary life.
The fascinating early sequences of convent routine are more interesting than the African adventures, but this is a careful, composed and impressive film with little Hollywood exaggeration.

w Robert Anderson, book Kathryn C. Hulme d Fred Zinnemann ph Franz Planer m Franz Waxman

Audrey Hepburn, Peter Finch, Edith Evans, Peggy Ashcroft, Dean Jagger, Mildred Dunnock, Patricia Collinge, Beatrice Straight
  'A major directorial achievement . . . the best study of the religious life ever made in the American cinema.'—Albert Johnson, Film Quarterly

AAN: best picture; Robert Anderson; Fred Zinnemann; Franz Planer; Franz Waxman; Audrey Hepburn

Nurse Edith Cavell
US 1939 98m bw

The story of a British nurse executed as a spy during World War I; previously filmed in 1930 as Dawn with Sybil Thorndike. This is a moderately touching but uninspired treatment. Anna Neagle, George Sanders, May Robson, Edna May Oliver, Alan Marshal. Written by Michael Hogan from the novel Dawn by Reginald Berkeley; directed by Herbert Wilcox; for Imperator / RKO. AAN: music by Anthony Collins. 'Excellently produced documentary film, but not for general audience appeal . . . no light moments to relieve the tragic aspects.'—Variety

Nurse on Wheels
GB 1963 86m bw
Anglo Amalgamated / GHW (Peter Rogers)

Adventures of a young District Nurse.
Part sentimental, part Carry On; watchable of its curious kind.

w Norman Hudis, novel Nurse Is a Neighbour by Joanna Jones d Gerald Thomas ph Alan Hume m Eric Rogers

Juliet Mills, Ronald Lewis, Joan Sims, Raymond Huntley, Athene Seyler

The Nursemaid Who Disappeared
GB 1939 86m bw

A domestic agency hides a gang of kidnappers.
Fairly pleasing mystery of the old school.
Arthur Margetson, Peter Coke, Lesley Brook,

Edward Chapman, Coral Browne, Martita Hunt. Written by Paul Gangelin and Connery Chappell, from the novel by Philip MacDonald; directed by Arthur Woods; for Warner.

Nutcracker
GB 1982 101m Eastmancolor
Rank / Ezshaw (Panos Nicolaou)

A Russian ballerina defects in London but finds that she is being used for business / political purposes.
Weird, dated and utterly mediocre melodrama with pauses for sexual revels. Not a goer.

w Raymond Christodoulou d Anwar Kawadri ph Peter Jessop m Simon Park

Joan Collins, Carol White, Paul Nicholas, Finola Hughes, William Franklyn, Murray Melvin

The Nutty Professor
US 1963 107m Technicolor
Paramount / Jerry Lewis (Ernest D. Glucksman)

An eccentric chemistry professor discovers an elixir which turns him into a pop idol.
Long dreary comedy which contains patches of its star at somewhere near his best; but even Dr Jekyll and Mr Hyde is funnier.

w Jerry Lewis, Bill Richmond d Jerry Lewis ph W. Wallace Kelley m Walter Scharf

Jerry Lewis, Stella Stevens, Howard Morris, Kathleen Freeman

O. Henry's Full House**
US 1952 117m bw
TCF (André Hakim)
GB title: *Full House*

John Steinbeck introduces five stories by O. Henry.
Modelled on the success of *Quartet* (qv), this compendium was less successful because these turn-of-the century tales of New York depend less on character than on the sting in the tail; but the cast and production were lavish.

m Alfred Newman

THE COP AND THE ANTHEM *w* Lamar Trotti *d* Henry Koster *ph* Lloyd Ahern
Charles Laughton, David Wayne, Marilyn Monroe
THE CLARION CALL *w* Richard Breen *d* Henry Hathaway *ph* Lucien Ballard
Dale Robertson, Richard Widmark
THE LAST LEAF *w* Ivan Goff, Ben Roberts *d* Jean Negulesco *ph* Joe MacDonald
Anne Baxter, Jean Peters, Gregory Ratoff
THE RANSOM OF RED CHIEF
w Nunnally Johnson *d* Howard Hawks *ph* Milton Krasner
Fred Allen, Oscar Levant
THE GIFT OF THE MAGI *w* Walter Bullock *d* Henry King *ph* Joe MacDonald
Jeanne Crain, Farley Granger

O.H.M.S.
GB 1936 86m bw
Gaumont (Geoffrey Barkas)
US title: *You're in the Army Now*

British forces fighting in China are joined by an American gangster on the run, who dies a hero.
Stiff-upper-lip adventure of no particular interest.

w Bryan Edgar Wallace, Austin Melford, A. R. Rawlinson, Lesser Samuels, Ralph Bettinson *d* Raoul Walsh *ph* Roy Kellino

John Mills, Wallace Ford, Anna Lee, Frank Cellier, Grace Bradley, Frederick Leister
'As near 100% entertainment value as can reasonably be hoped for without the employment of a superstar, super-cast, super-director and super-production.'—*Variety*

O Lucky Man**
GB 1973 174m Eastmancolor
Warner / Memorial / Sam (Michael Medwin, Lindsay Anderson)

The odyssey of a trainee salesman who after a while as an international financier settles down to be a do-gooder.
Modern revue-style version of *Candide / Decline and Fall*; very hit or miss in style and effect, and hellishly overlong, but with good things along the way.

w David Sherwin *d* Lindsay Anderson *ph* Miroslav Ondricek *m* Alan Price *pd* Jocelyn Herbert

Malcolm McDowell, Arthur Lowe, Ralph Richardson, Rachel Roberts, Helen Mirren, Mona Washbourne, Dandy Nichols
'A sort of mod *Pilgrim's Progress*.'—*New Yorker*

● *Video: Warner*

'He's deep in danger, deeper in love!'
O.S.S.*
US 1946 107m bw
Paramount (Richard Maibaum)

American spies are parachuted into France in 1943.
Espionage heroics with an unhappy ending and a slight documentary flavour. Not bad of its kind.

w Richard Maibaum *d* Irving Pichel *ph* Lionel Lindon *m* Daniele Amfitheatrof, Heinz Roemheld

Alan Ladd, Geraldine Fitzgerald, Patric Knowles, John Hoyt, Don Beddoe

Oasis
France / Germany 1956 100m approx
Eastmancolor Cinemascope
TCF / Roxy / Criterion (Gerd Oswald, Luggi Waldleitner)

An ex-pilot gets involved with two attractive women who are smuggling gold across the Sahara.
Glum romantic adventure.

w Joseph and Georges Kessel *d* Yves Allégret *ph* Roger Hubert *m* Paul Misraki

Pierre Brasseur, Michèle Morgan, Cornell Borchers, Grégoire Aslan

Objective Burma*
US 1944 142m bw
Warner (Jerry Wald)

Exploits of an American platoon in the Burma campaign.
Overlong but vivid war actioner which caused a diplomatic incident by failing to mention the British contribution.

w Ranald MacDougall, Lester Cole, Alvah Bessie *d* Raoul Walsh *ph* James Wong Howe *m* Franz Waxman

Errol Flynn, James Brown, William Prince, George Tobias, Henry Hull, Warner Anderson, John Alwin
'At the rate Errol Flynn and co. knock off the Japanese, it may make you wonder why the war need outlast next weekend.'—*Time*
'I am amazed that Warner Brothers ever made it, or having made it failed to think again and smother it.'—*Reynolds News*
† The film was not released in Britain until 1982, and then with an apologetic prologue.

AAN: original story (Alvah Bessie); Franz Waxman

The Obliging Young Lady
US 1941 80m bw

A secretary escorts a wealthy child out of town while her parents wrangle over custody.
Tedious comedy with interest occasionally provided by the supporting cast. Joan Carroll, Ruth Warrick, Edmond O'Brien, Eve Arden, Franklin Pangborn, Marjorie Gateson, John Miljan, George Cleveland. Luis Alberni, Charles Lane. Written by Frank Ryan and Bert Granet; directed by Richard Wallace; for RKO.

The Oblong Box
GB 1969 95m Eastmancolor
AIP (Gordon Hessler)

One of two 19th-century brothers is mysteriously disfigured and buried alive; he recovers and runs amok.
Nastily effective horror film with a frail story but good background detail.

w Lawrence Huntington *d* Gordon Hessler *ph* John Coquillon *m* Harry Robinson

Vincent Price, Christopher Lee, Alastair Williamson, Hilary Dwyer, Peter Arne, Maxwell Shaw, Rupert Davies
'A pervasive aura of evil.'—*MFB*

Obsession*
GB 1948 98m bw
GFD / Independent Sovereign (Nat Bronsten)
US title: *The Hidden Room*

A doctor decides to kill his wife's lover by imprisoning him in a lonely cellar while he accumulates enough acid to destroy all traces of his body.

Implausible, overstretched thriller, carefully enough done to be bearable.

w Alec Coppel, from his play A Man About a Dog d Edward Dmytryk ph C. Pennington Richards m Nino Rota

Robert Newton, Sally Gray, Phil Brown, Naunton Wayne

Obsession*
US 1976 98m Technicolor Panavision
Columbia (Robert S. Bremson)

A widower with guilt feelings meets the double of his dead wife and is drawn into a strange plot.
Hitchcockian adventure with a few unwise attempts at seriousness, à la Don't Look Now. Generally entertaining, skilled and quite rewarding.

w Paul Schrader d Brian de Palma
ph Vilmos Zsigmond m Bernard Herrmann

Cliff Robertson, Geneviève Bujold, John Lithgow, Sylvia Williams, Wanda Blackman, Patrick McNamara

'An unholy mess. Intended as an hommage to Hitchcock . . . it attitudinizes [also] towards the old-fashioned tearjerker and towards the sophisticated European film, with cultural references strewn like breadcrumbs along the way of Hansel and Gretel . . .'—John Simon, New York

'Merely a mannered cerebral exercise without any emotional underpinning or unconscious feeling of its own.'—Andrew Sarris, Village Voice

AAN: Bernard Herrmann

Occupe-Toi d'Amélie***
France 1949 95m bw
Lux (Louis Wipf)
aka: Keep an Eye on Amelia

A Parisian cocotte agrees to go through a mock marriage ceremony with her lover's best friend to fool his uncle: but the ceremony turns out to be real.
Hilarious and superbly stylized adaptation of a period boulevard farce: the play starts in a theatre, showing the audience, but gradually cinema technique takes over. Acting, timing and editing are all impeccable, and the production stands as a model of how such things should be done.

w Jean Aurenche, Pierre Bost, play Georges Feydeau d Claude Autant-Lara ph André Bac m René Cloërc

Danielle Darrieux, Jean Desailly, Bourvil, Carette, Grégoire Aslan

'Even those who do not respond to the artificialities of French vaudeville will admire the ingenuity and elegance of treatment.'— Gavin Lambert, MFB

'Most people, I think, could see it with considerable enjoyment even twice on the same evening.'—Richard Mallett, Punch

Ocean's Eleven*
US 1960 128m Technicolor
Panavision
Warner / Dorchester (Lewis Milestone)

A gang of friends plan to rob a Las Vegas casino.

Self-indulgent and overlong caper comedy which marked Hollywood's entry into a subsequently much overworked field. In this case the plot stops all too frequently for guest spots and in-jokes.

w Harry Brown, Charles Lederer d Lewis Milestone ph William H. Daniels m Nelson Riddle

Frank Sinatra, Peter Lawford, Sammy Davis Jnr, Richard Conte, Dean Martin, Angie Dickinson, Cesar Romero, Joey Bishop, Patrice Wymore, Akim Tamiroff, Henry Silva, Ilka Chase

● Video: Warner

The October Man**
GB 1947 98m bw
GFD / Two Cities (Eric Ambler)

After an accident which causes a head injury and subsequent depression, a lonely man staying at a small hotel is suspected of a local murder.
Nice blend of character study, mystery and suspense, with excellent attention to suburban detail.

w Eric Ambler d Roy Baker ph Erwin Hillier

John Mills, Joan Greenwood, Edward Chapman, Kay Walsh, Catherine Lacey, Joyce Carey, Adrianne Allen, Felix Aylmer

'This film of psychological suspense tells its complicated story with complete clarity, but it is mainly to be noted for its settings.'—Basil Wright, 1972

October Moth
GB 1959 54m bw

A mentally retarded farmhand goes berserk after causing a fatal car crash. Unattractive and singularly pointless little melodrama which neither edifies nor entertains. Lana Morris, Lee Patterson, Peter Dynely, Robert Cawdron. Written and directed by John Kruse; for Independent Artists.

Octopussy
GB 1983 131m Technicolor
Panavision
Eon / Danjaq (Albert R. Broccoli)

James Bond takes on an evil Afghan prince and a glamorous woman who plan between them to plunder Tsarist treasures.
Bond at the end of his tether: such far-stretched adventures have become merely a tedious way of passing the time.

w George MacDonald Fraser, Richard Maibaum, Michael G. Wilson d John Glen ph Alan Hume m John Barry pd Peter Lamont

Roger Moore, Maud Adams, Louis Jourdan, Kristina Wayborn, Kabir Bedi, Desmond Llewellyn, Lois Maxwell

'As the films drift further and further into self-parody, no one seems to notice and no one (at any rate in box office terms) seems to mind.'—Nick Roddick, MFB

● Video: Warner

The Odd Couple**
US 1968 105m Technicolor
Panavision
Paramount (Howard W. Koch)

A fussy divorce-shocked newswriter moves in with his sloppy sportscaster friend, and they get on each other's nerves.
Straight filming of a funny play which sometimes seems lost on the wide screen, but the performances are fine.

w Neil Simon, from his play d Gene Saks
ph Robert B. Hauser m Neal Hefti

Jack Lemmon, Walter Matthau, John Fiedler, Herb Edelman, David Sheiner, Larry Haines, Monica Evans, Carole Sheely, Iris Adrian

OSCAR (Walter Matthau): 'I can't take it anymore, Felix. I'm crackin' up. Everything you do irritates me. And when you're not here, the things I know you're gonna do when you come in irritate me. You leave me little notes on my pillow. I told you 158 times I cannot stand little notes on my pillow. "We are all out of cornflakes, F.U." It took me three hours to figure out that F.U. was Felix Ungar. It's not your fault, Felix. It's a rotten combination, that's all.'

AAN: Neil Simon

Odd Man Out***
GB 1946 115m bw
GFD / Two Cities (Carol Reed)
US title: Gang War

An IRA gunman, wounded and on the run in Belfast, is helped and hindered by a variety of people.
Superbly crafted but rather empty dramatic charade, visually and emotionally memorable but with nothing whatever to say.

w F. L. Green, R. C. Sherriff, novel F. L. Green d Carol Reed ph Robert Krasker
m William Alwyn

James Mason, Robert Newton, Kathleen Ryan, F. J. McCormick, Cyril Cusack, Robert Beatty, Fay Compton, Dan O'Herlihy, Denis O'Dea, Maureen Delany, Joseph Tomelty, William Hartnell

'The story seems to ramify too much, to go on too long, and at its unluckiest to go arty. Yet detail by detail Odd Man Out is made with great skill and imaginativeness and with a depth of ardour that is very rare.'—James Agee

'Quite simply the most imaginative film yet produced in England, comparable with Quai des Brumes and Le Jour se Lève.'—William Whitebait, New Statesman

● Video: Rank

Odds against Tomorrow*
US 1959 96m bw
UA / Harbel (Robert Wise)

Three crooks plan to rob a bank, but two of them cause the enterprise to fail because of their own racist hatreds.
Sour, glossy crime thriller with elementary social significance.

ALAN LADD
GERALDINE
FITZGERALD
"O.S.S."

He's deep in danger...
deeper in love...
in the Top
Thrill Show
of the Year!

with
PATRIC KNOWLES
JOHN HOYT
Written and Produced by RICHARD MAIBAUM
Directed by IRVING PICHEL
A Paramount Picture

O.S.S. Alan Ladd in one of his more serious wartime exploits. It wasn't popular because of an unhappy ending.

w John O. Killens, Nelson Gidding, *novel* John P. McGivern d Robert Wise ph Joseph Brun m John Lewis

Robert Ryan, Harry Belafonte, *Ed Begley*, Shelley Winters, Gloria Grahame, Will Kuluva, Kim Hamilton
  'An efficient but unnecessarily portentous thriller.'—*Penelope Houston*

The Odessa File**
GB 1974 129m Eastmancolor
  Panavision
Columbia / Domino / Oceanic (John Woolf)

In 1963, a young German reporter tracks down a gang of neo-Nazis.

Elaborate but uninvolving suspenser with several excellent cliffhanging sequences and a let-down climax.

w Kenneth Ross, George Markstein, *novel* Frederick Forsyth d Ronald Neame ph Oswald Morris m Andrew Lloyd Webber pd Rolf Zeherbauer

Jon Voight, Maria Schell, Maximilian Schell, Mary Tamm, Derek Jacobi, Peter Jeffrey, *Noel Willman*
  'As resistible a parcel of sedative entertainment as ever induced narcolepsy in a healthy man.'—*Benny Green, Punch*

Odette°
GB 1950 123m bw
Herbert Wilcox

A Frenchwoman with an English husband spies for the French resistance, is caught and tortured.
Deglamorized true life spy story with emotional moments let down by generally uninspired handling, also by the too well-known image of its star, who however gives a remarkable performance.

w Warren Chetham Strode, *book* Jerrard Tickell d Herbert Wilcox ph Max Greene m Anthony Collins

Anna Neagle, Trevor Howard, Peter Ustinov, Marius Goring
  'As a work of art, pretty flat . . . though innumerable people will find it moving and impressive, they will have done the work themselves.'—*Richard Mallett, Punch*

Odongo
GB 1956 85m Technicolor
  Cinemascope

A collector of animals for zoos runs into various kinds of trouble during an African safari. Elementary jungle adventure centring on a small Sabu-like jungle boy. For the now extinct family audience. Macdonald Carey, Rhonda Fleming, Juma, Eleanor Summerfield, Francis de Wolff, Earl Cameron. Written and directed by John Gilling; for Warwick / Columbia.

Of Human Bondage**
US 1934 83m bw
(RKO) Pandro S. Berman

A well-to-do Englishman is brought down by his infatuation with a sluttish waitress.
This version of the famous novel brought Bette Davis to prominence but is not otherwise any better than the others.

w Lester Cohen, *novel* W. Somerset Maugham d John Cromwell ph Henry W. Gerrard m Max Steiner

Leslie Howard, Bette Davis, Frances Dee, Reginald Owen, Reginald Denny, Kay Johnson, Alan Hale
  'Stars and the novel rep will have to carry a lethargic romance.'—*Variety*
  'A totally obtuse concoction, serving only to demonstrate how untalented an actress Bette Davis was before she perfected those camp mannerisms.'—*John Simon, 1967*

Of Human Bondage°
US 1946 105m bw
Warner (Henry Blanke)

Good-looking but thoroughly dull remake.

w Catherine Turney d Edmund Goulding ph Peverell Marley m Erich Wolfgang Korngold

Paul Henreid, Eleanor Parker, Alexis Smith, Edmund Gwenn, Patric Knowles, Janis Paige, Henry Stephenson

Of Human Bondage
GB 1964 99m bw
MGM / Seven Arts (James Woolf)

Disastrous remake with both star roles miscast.

w Bryan Forbes *d* Henry Hathaway, Ken Hughes *ph* Oswald Morris *m* Ron Goodwin *pd* John Box

Laurence Harvey, Kim Novak, Nanette Newman, Roger Livesey, Jack Hedley, Robert Morley, Siobhan McKenna, Ronald Lacey

Of Human Hearts*
US 1938   100m   bw
MGM (John Considine Jnr)

A 19th-century idyll of middle America and especially of a preacher and his wayward son.
Curious all-American moral fable, splendidly made and acted.

w Bradbury Foote, *novel* Benefits Forgot by Honoré Morrow *d* Clarence Brown *ph* Clyde de Vinna *m* Herbert Stothart

Walter Huston, James Stewart, Beulah Bondi, Gene Reynolds, Charles Coburn, Guy Kibbee, John Carradine, Gene Lockhart, Ann Rutherford

'Long on narrative and short on romance . . . the box office reaction is likely to dampen the enthusiasm of those who believe the film possesses any wide public appeal.'—*Variety*
† The title was chosen via a radio contest, the winner being a high-school student.

AAN: Beulah Bondi

Of Love and Desire
US 1963   97m   De Luxe
New World (Victor Stoloff)

An engineer in Mexico takes up with the boss's nymphomaniac sister.
Unwise sensationalist vehicle for an ageing leading lady who is past such carryings on.

w Laslo Gorag, Richard Rush *d* Richard Rush *ph* Alex Phillips *m* Ronald Stein

Merle Oberon, Steve Cochran, John Agar, Curt Jurgens

'I'm decent, I tell ya! Nobody's got the right to call me names!'
'The picture Hollywood said could never be made!'

Of Mice and Men***
US 1939   107m   bw
Hal Roach (Lewis Milestone)

An itinerant worker looks after his mentally retarded cousin, a giant who doesn't know his own strength.
A strange and unexpected tragedy which has strength and is very persuasively made but seems somehow unnecessary.

w Eugene Solow, *novel* John Steinbeck *d* Lewis Milestone *ph* Norbert Brodine *m* Aaron Copland

Burgess Meredith, Lon Chaney Jnr, Betty Field, Charles Bickford, Roman Bohnen, Bob Steele, Noah Beery Jnr

AAN: best picture; Aaron Copland

Off Limits
US 1953   89m   bw
Paramount (Harry Tugend)
GB title: *Military Policemen*

A boxing manager trains a young fighter in the military police.
Flat star comedy.

w Hal Kanter, Jack Sher *d* George Marshall *ph* Peverell Marley *m* Van Cleave

Bob Hope, Mickey Rooney, Marilyn Maxwell, Marvin Miller

Off the Dole
GB 1935   89m   bw

An amateur detective catches burglars. Artless comedy shot on a minuscule budget; it helped to make George Formby a star. With Beryl Formby, Constance Shotter, Dan Young. Written and directed by Arthur Mertz; for Mancunian.

Off the Record
US 1939   71m   bw

A star reporter exposes the mob's use of youngsters as spotters in the gambling racket.
Predictable crime support. Pat O'Brien, Joan Blondell, Bobby Jordan, Alan Baxter, Morgan Conway. Written by Niven Busch, Lawrence Kimble, Earl Baldwin; directed by James Flood; for Warners. 'Stereotype dualler.'—*Variety*

Offbeat*
GB 1960   72m   bw
British Lion / Northiam (M. Smedley Aston)

An MI5 undercover man finds himself sympathizing with a gang of robbers and falling in love with one of them.
Sharply observed thriller which gets a bit glum in dealing with its rather contrived 'switch'.

w Peter Barnes *d* Cliff Owen *ph* Geoffrey Faithfull *m* Ken Jones

William Sylvester, Mai Zetterling, Anthony Dawson, John Meillon, John Phillips, Victor Brooks, Joseph Furst, Neil McCarthy, Harry Baird

The Offence*
GB 1972   113m   De Luxe
United Artists / Tantallon (Denis O'Dell)

A tough police inspector bullies a suspected child molester.
Tortuous psychological study on the fringe of hysteria; good performances.

w John Hopkins, from his play This Story of Yours *d* Sidney Lumet *ph* Gerry Fisher *m* Harrison Birtwhistle

Sean Connery, Trevor Howard, Ian Bannen, Vivien Merchant

An Officer and a Gentleman*
US 1982   126m   Metrocolor
Paramount / Lorimar (Martin Elfand)

A potential officer suffers thirteen weeks of agony at the Naval Aviation Officer Candidate School.

Old-hat stuff given a fresh look and some smart acting.

w Douglas Day Stewart *d* Taylor Hackford *ph* Donald Thorin *m* Jack Nitzsche *pd* Philip M. Jefferies

Richard Gere, Debra Winger, *Louis Gossett Jnr*, David Keith, Lisa Blount, Lisa Eilbacher

'Shamelessly manipulative, but whether the manipulations are funny, dramatic or tear-jerking, it knows exactly what and how to deliver.'—*Sunday Telegraph*

AA: Louis Gossett Jnr (as supporting actor); *song* 'Up Where We Belong'
AAN: Debra Winger; original screenplay; editing (Peter Zinner); music
● *Video: CIC*

Oh Dad, Poor Dad, Mamma's Hung You in the Closet and I'm Feelin' So Sad
US 1966   86m   Technicolor
Paramount / Seven Arts (Ray Stark, Stanley Rubin)

A dead father helps his son to get married despite his mother's influence to the contrary.
Zany black comedy which never really worked on the stage, let alone the screen.

w Ian Bernard, *play* Arthur Kopit *d* Richard Quine *ph* Geoffrey Unsworth *m* Neal Hefti

Rosalind Russell, Jonathan Winters, Robert Morse, Hugh Griffith, Barbara Harris, Lionel Jeffries, Cyril Delevanti, Hiram Sherman

Oh Doctor
US 1937   67m   bw

A rich hypochondriac is the target of confidence tricksters. Moderate star comedy.
Edward Everett Horton, Donrue Leighton, Eve Arden, Thurston Hall, William Demarest. 'Smooth dialogue keeps this hokey picture from going completely corkscrew.'—*Variety*

'It's an almighty laugh!'
Oh, God*
US 1977   104m   Technicolor
Warner (Jerry Weintraub)

A bewildered supermarket manager is enlisted by God to prove to the world that it can only work if people try.
Overlong but generally amiable reversion to the supernatural farces of the forties: its success seems to show that people again need this kind of comfort.

w Larry Gelbart, *novel* Avery Corman *d* Carl Reiner *ph* Victor Kemper *m* Jack Elliott

George Burns, John Denver, Ralph Bellamy, Donald Pleasence, Teri Garr, William Daniels, Barnard Hughes, Paul Sorvino, Barry Sullivan, Dinah Shore, Jeff Corey, David Ogden Stiers

'Undeniably funny and almost impossible to dislike.'—*Tom Milne, MFB*
'Basically a single-joke movie: George Burns is God in a football cap.'—*Pauline Kael, New Yorker*

AAN: Larry Gelbart
● *Video: Warner*

Oh God Book Two
US 1980 94m Technicolor

God enlists a child to remind people that he is still around. Crass sequel with sentiment replacing jokes. George Burns, Suzanne Pleshette, David Birney, Louanne, Howard Duff, Hans Conried, Wilfrid Hyde White. Written by Josh Greenfield, Hal Goldman, Fred S. Fox, Seaman Jacobs and Melissa Miller; directed by Gilbert Cates; for Warner.

Oh God, You Devil
US 1984 96m Technicolor
Warner (Robert M. Sherman)

A struggling musician sells his soul to the devil in exchange for success.
A comic version of Faust, appended to the two films in which George Burns played God; he now puts on the other hat to fairly, but not very, comic effect.

w Andrew Bergman d Paul Bogart ph King Baggot m David Shire pd Peter Wooley ed Andy Zall

George Burns, Ted Wass, Ron Silver, Roxanne Hart, Eugene Roche

Oh Heavenly Dog
US 1980 103m De Luxe

A private eye is reincarnated as a dog and solves his own murder. Witless fantasy comedy, an uncredited remake of You Never Can Tell which also rates as a Benji movie with curious additions of sex and profanity. A total muddle. Chevy Chase, Jane Seymour, Omar Sharif, Robert Morley, Alan Sues. Written by Rod Browning and Joe Camp; directed by Joe Camp; for Mulberry Square / TCF.

Oh Men! Oh Women!
US 1957 90m Eastmancolor
Cinemascope
TCF (Nunnally Johnson)

A psychoanalyst discovers that his wife is involved with two of his patients.
Scatty Broadway comedy which strains the patience.

wd Nunnally Johnson, play Edward Chodorov ph Charles G. Clarke m Cyril Mockridge

David Niven, Ginger Rogers, Dan Dailey, Barbara Rush, Tony Randall
'The ugliest sort of fun.'—Observer
'Cinemascope discovers a solution to the problem of filling its wide screen; the characters spend most of their time full length on the psychoanalyst's couch.'—Sunday Times

Oh Mr Porter°°°°
GB 1937 84m bw
GFD / Gainsborough (Edward Black)

The stationmaster of an Irish halt catches gun-runners posing as ghosts.
Marvellous star comedy showing this trio of comedians at their best, and especially Hay as the seedy incompetent. The plot is borrowed from The Ghost Train, but each line and gag brings its own inventiveness. A delight of character comedy and cinematic narrative.

w Marriott Edgar, Val Guest, J. O. C. Orton, story Frank Launder d Marcel Varnel ph Arthur Crabtree md Louis Levy
Will Hay, Moore Marriott, Graham Moffatt, Dave O'Toole, Dennis Wyndham
'That rare phenomenon: a film comedy without a dud scene.'—Peter Barnes, 1964
'Behind it lie the gusty uplands of the British music hall tradition, whose rich soil the British film industry is at last beginning to exploit.'—Basil Wright

Oh Rosalinda!
GB 1955 105m Technicolor
Cinemascope
ABP / Powell and Pressburger

A playboy in four-power Vienna plays a practical joke on four officers and the flirtatious wife of one of them.
Lumbering attempt to modernize Die Fledermaus, unsuitably wide-screened and totally lacking the desired Lubitsch touch. A monumental step in the decline of these producers, and a sad stranding of a brilliant cast.

wd Michael Powell, Emeric Pressburger ph Christopher Challis m Johann Strauss ad Hein Heckroth

Anton Walbrook, Michael Redgrave, Anthony Quayle, Mel Ferrer, Dennis Price, Ludmilla Tcherina

Oh What a Lovely War°°
GB 1969 144m Technicolor
Panavision
Paramount / Accord (Brian Duffy, Richard Attenborough)

A fantasia with music on World War I.
A brave all-star attempt which comes off only in patches; the pier apparatus from the stage show really doesn't translate, the piece only works well when it becomes cinematic, as in the recruiting song and the final track-back from the graves. But there are many pleasures, as well as yawns, along the way.

w Len Deighton, stage show Joan Littlewood, Charles Chilton d Richard Attenborough ph Gerry Turpin m various md Alfred Ralston pd Don Ashton

Ralph Richardson, Meriel Forbes, John Gielgud, Kenneth More, John Clements, Paul Daneman, Joe Melia, Jack Hawkins, John Mills, Maggie Smith, Michael Redgrave, Laurence Olivier, Susannah York, Dirk Bogarde, Phyllis Calvert, Vanessa Redgrave
'This musical lampoon is meant to stir your sentiments, evoke nostalgia, and make you react to the obscenity of battles and bloodshed, and apparently it does all that for some people.'—New Yorker, 1977
'A naïve, sentimental, populist affair, using many (too many) clever devices yet making the same old simplistic statements.'—John Simon
'An overlong and rarely cinematic musical satire that ladles its anti-war message on by the bucketload.'—Time Out, 1984

Oh You Beautiful Doll°
US 1949 93m Technicolor
TCF (George Jessel)

Fred Fisher wants to write opera but is more successful with pop songs.
Standard turn of the century biopic, very pleasantly handled and performed.

w Albert and George Lewis d John M. Stahl ph Harry Jackson md Alfred Newman

S. Z. Sakall, Mark Stevens, June Haver, Charlotte Greenwood, Jay C. Flippen, Gale Robbins

Oil for the Lamps of China°
US 1935 98m bw
Warner (Robert Lord)

The career in China of an American oil company representative.
Adequate general audience picture from a bestseller.

w Laird Doyle, novel Alice Tisdale Hobart d Mervyn Le Roy ph Tony Gaudio m Heinz Roemheld md Leo F. Forbstein

Pat O'Brien, Josephine Hutchinson, Jean Muir, Lyle Talbot, Arthur Byron, John Eldredge, Henry O'Neill, Donald Crisp
'Long and choppy version of a best-seller novel. Little marquee strength will probably mean light returns.'—Variety
'Far above average in performance, direction and content.'—John Baxter, 1968
† Remade 1941 as Law of the Tropics.

Okay America
US 1932 80m bw

A brash reporter saves a politician's daughter from kidnapping. Okay melodrama remade in 1939 as Risky Business. Lew Ayres, Maureen O'Sullivan, Louis Calhern, Walter Catlett, Edward Arnold. Written by William Anthony McGuire; directed by Tay Garnett; for Universal. (GB title: Penalty of Fame.)

Okay for Sound°
GB 1937 85m bw
GFD / Gainsborough (Edward Black)

The Crazy Gang runs amok in a film studio. Patchy farce with music hall talents of the time.

w Marriott Edgar, Val Guest, R. P. Weston, Bert Lee d Marcel Varnel ph Jack Cox md Louis Levy

Bud Flanagan, Chesney Allen, Jimmy Nervo, Teddy Knox, Charlie Naughton, Jimmy Gold, Fred Duprez, Enid Stamp-Taylor, Graham Moffatt, Meinhart Maur, H. F. Maltby, Peter Dawson, The Radio Three, The Sherman Fisher Girls
'A picture straight from the heart of America!'

Oklahoma!°°
US 1955 143m Technicolor Todd-AO
Magna / Rodgers and Hammerstein (Arthur Hornblow Jnr)

A cowboy wins his girl despite the intervention of a sinister hired hand.

Much of the appeal of the musical was in its
simple timeworn story and stylized sets; the
film makes the first merely boring and the
latter are replaced by standard scenery, not
even of Oklahoma. The result is efficient
rather than startling or memorable.

w Sonya Levien, William Ludwig, *'book'*
Oscar Hammerstein, *play* Green Grow the
Rushes by Lynn Riggs *d* Fred Zinnemann
ph Robert Surtees *songs* Richard Rodgers,
Oscar Hammerstein II *m* Robert Russell
Bennett, Jay Blackton, Adolph Deutsch
pd Oliver Smith

Gordon Macrae, Shirley Jones, Rod Steiger,
Gloria Grahame, Charlotte Greenwood, Gene
Nelson, Eddie Albert

AA: music score
AAN: Robert Surtees; Robert Russell
Bennett, Jay Blackton, Adolph Deutsch

● *Video: MGM / UA*

Oklahoma Crude°
US 1973   111m   Technicolor
Columbia / Stanley Kramer

In 1913, a drifting oil man stops to help a girl
develop her rig.
Dour, downbeat melodrama with restricted
action and much bad language; within its lights
quite entertaining, but odd.

w Marc Norman *d* Stanley Kramer
ph Robert Surtees *m* Henry Mancini
pd Alfred Sweeney

Faye Dunaway, George C. Scott, John Mills,
Jack Palance, Woodrow Parfrey

The Oklahoma Kid°°
US 1939   80m   bw
Warner (Samuel Bischoff)

During the settlement of the Cherokee Strip a
cowboy avenges the unjust lynching of his
father.
Competent but slightly disappointing star
western memorable for the clash in this guise
of its protagonists, more usually seen as
gangsters.

w Warren Duff, Robert Buckner, Edward E.
Paramore *d* Lloyd Bacon *ph* James Wong
Howe *m* Max Steiner

James Cagney, Humphrey Bogart, Rosemary
Lane, Donald Crisp, Harvey Stephens,
Charles Middleton, Edward Pawley, Ward
Bond

'Its b.o. potency will depend on Cagney's
name and draw, rather than story or
production, neither of which is
commendable.'—*Variety*

'There's something entirely disarming about
the way he has tackled horse opera, not
pretending for a minute to be anything but
New York's Jimmy Cagney all dressed up as a
Robin Hood of the old west.'—*Frank Nugent*

The Oklahoman
US 1956   78m   De Luxe   Cinemascope

A widowed doctor becomes the subject of
gossip when he takes an Indian girl for his
housekeeper. Rather curious domestic western

THE OKLAHOMA KID.   James Cagney looks ill at ease in western gear, but he was game
for anything.

which erupts into action sequences but devotes
too much time to talk and romance. Joel
McCrea, Barbara Hale, Brad Dexter, Gloria
Talbott, Michael Pate. Written by Daniel B.
Ullman; directed by Francis D. Lyon; for
Walter Mirisch / Allied Artists.

Old Acquaintance°°
US 1943   110m   bw
Warner (Henry Blanke)

Two jealous lady novelists interfere in each
other's love lives.

A dated but rather splendid battle of the wild
cats, with two stars fighting their way through
a plush production and a rather overlong
script.

w John Van Druten, Lenore Coffee, *play* John
Van Druten *d* Vincent Sherman *ph* Sol
Polito *m* Franz Waxman

Bette Davis, Miriam Hopkins, Gig Young,
John Loder, Dolores Moran, Philip Reed,
Roscoe Karns, Anne Revere

'The odd thing is that the two ladies and the director can make the whole business look fairly intelligent, detailed and plausible; and that on the screen such trash can seem, even, mature and adventurous.'—*James Agee*

'Trashy fun, on an unusually literate level.'—*New Yorker, 1978*

Old Bill and Son

GB 1940 96m bw

Too old for active duty, a veteran follows his son to Flanders. Ineffective screen version of a popular newspaper strip. Morland Graham, John Mills, Mary Clare, Renée Houston, Rene Ray, Roland Culver. Written by Bruce Bairnsfather and Ian Dalrymple, from Bairnsfather's cartoons; directed by Ian Dalrymple; for Legeran Films.

Old Bones of the River*

GB 1938 90m bw

GFD / Gainsborough (Edward Black)

A teacher in Africa accidentally quells a native rising.

Tediously funny star comedy; enough said.

w Marriott Edgar, Val Guest, J. O. C. Orton *character* Edgar Wallace *d* Marcel Varnel *ph* Arthur Crabtree *m* Louis Levy *ad* Vetchinsky

Will Hay, Moore Marriott, Graham Moffatt, Robert Adams, Jack Livesey

Old Boyfriends*

US 1978 103m Technicolor

Edward R. Pressman Productions (Paul Schrader)

A divorcee survives a nervous breakdown and goes on a journey of her past life to find out where she went wrong.

Low-key and somehow rather flat romantic odyssey, with interesting sequences and characters muted by the director's jaundiced eye.

w Paul and Leonard Schrader *d* Joan Tewkesbury *ph* William A. Fraker *m* David Shire

Talia Shire, Richard Jordan, John Belushi, Keith Carradine, John Houseman, Buck Henry, Bethel Leslie

● Video: Precision

The Old Curiosity Shop*

GB 1934 95m bw

BIP / Wardour

The lives of a gambler and his granddaughter are affected by a miserly dwarf.

Heavy-going Dickens novel given reasonably rich production and well enough acted; sentimentality prevented a remake until the unsuccessful *Mister Quilp* (qv) in 1975.

w Margaret Kennedy, Ralph Neale, *novel* Charles Dickens *d* Thomas Bentley

Hay Petrie, Ben Webster, Elaine Benson, Beatrice Thompson, Gibb McLaughlin, Reginald Purdell, Polly Ward

The Old Dark House****

US 1932 71m bw

Universal (Carl Laemmle Jnr)

Stranded travellers take refuge in the house of a family of eccentrics.

Marvellous horror comedy filled with superb grotesques and memorable lines, closely based on a Priestley novel but omitting the more thoughtful moments. A stylist's and connoisseur's treat.

w Benn W. Levy, R. C. Sherriff, *novel* Benighted by *J. B. Priestley d James Whale ph Arthur Edeson ad Charles D. Hall*

Melvyn Douglas, Charles Laughton, Raymond Massey, Boris Karloff, Ernest Thesiger, Eva Moore, Gloria Stuart, Lilian Bond, Brember Wills, John Dudgeon (Elspeth Dudgeon)

'Somewhat inane, it's a cinch for trick ballyhooing. Better for the nabes than the big keys.'—*Variety*

'An unbridled camp fantasy directed with great wit.'—*Charles Higham*

'Each threat as it appears is revealed to be burlap and poster paint . . . despite storm, attempted rape and a remarkable final chase, the film is basically a confidence trick worked with cynical humour by a brilliant technician.'—*John Baxter, 1968*

'Basically a *jeu d'esprit* in which comedy of manners is edged into tragedy of horrors, the film never puts a foot wrong.'—*Tom Milne, MFB, 1978*

'The ghost doesn't walk in this family—it runs riot!'

The Old Dark House

GB 1962 86m Eastmancolor

Columbia / Hammer / William Castle

An American accepts an invitation to visit Femm Manor and finds the inhabitants either mad or homicidal.

A travesty which has nothing to do with the 1932 film and possesses no merit of its own. The cast is left floundering.

w Robert Dillon *d* William Castle *ph* Arthur Grant *m* Benjamin Frankel

Tom Poston, Janette Scott, Robert Morley, Joyce Grenfell, Mervyn Johns, Fenella Fielding, Peter Bull

'Come and meet a grand old sinner!'

Old English

US 1930 87m bw

In order to provide for his grandchildren, a financier makes certain illegal arrangements which involve his prearranged death.

Satisfying pattern play arranged for its star. *George Arliss*, Leon Janney, Doris Lloyd, Betty Lawford, Ivan Simpson. Written by Walter Anthony and Maude Howell, from the play by John Galsworthy; directed by Alfred E. Green; for Warner. 'Will call for most careful placement by chains and indies to draw the class trade it will only appeal to.'—*Variety*

'You dastard! Get thee hence or I shall smite thee in the puss!'

The Old-Fashioned Way*

US 1934 74m bw

Paramount / (William Le Baron)

Adventures of The Great McGonigle and his troupe of travelling players.

Period comedy tailored for its star and incorporating fragments of *The Drunkard*. Not so funny as it might be, but essential for students.

w Garnett Weston, Jack Cunningham, Charles Bogle (W. C. Fields) *d* William Beaudine *ph* Benjamin Reynolds *m* Harry Revel

W. C. Fields, Joe Morrison, Judith Allen, Jan Duggan, Jack Mulhall, Baby Leroy

Old Hutch

US 1936 80m bw

An idler finds a fortune but can't spend it because everybody knows he hasn't worked for years. Satisfactory star comedy. Wallace Beery, Elizabeth Patterson, Eric Linden, Cecilia Parker, Donald Meek, Virginia Grey. Written by George Kelly; directed by J. Walter Ruben; for MGM. 'Hasn't the backbone usually associated with Wallace Beery's vehicles. A nice light comedy which will doubtless garner fair box office.'—*Variety*

Old Iron

GB 1938 80m bw

A shipping magnate disowns his son for marrying against his will, but a car accident reconciles them. Very boring drama, an odd choice for this star, who can't cope with it. Tom Walls, Eva Moore, Cecil Parker, Richard Ainley, David Tree, Enid Stamp-Taylor. Written by Ben Travers; directed by Tom Walls; for TW Productions / British Lion.

The Old Maid**

US, 1939 95m bw

Warner (Henry Blanke)

When her suitor is killed in the Civil War, an unmarried mother lets her childless cousin bring up her daughter as her own.

A 'woman's picture' par excellence, given no-holds-barred treatment by all concerned but a little lacking in surprise.

w Casey Robinson, *play* Zoe Akins, *novel* Edith Wharton *d* Edmund Goulding *ph* Tony Gaudio *m* Max Steiner *md* Leo F. Forbstein

Bette Davis, Miriam Hopkins, George Brent, Jane Bryan, Donald Crisp, Louise Fazenda, Henry Stephenson, Jerome Cowan, William Lundigan, Rand Brooks

'Stagey, sombre and generally confusing fare. Must aim for the femme trade chiefly.'—*Variety*

'It is better than average and sticks heroically to its problem, forsaking all delights and filling a whole laundry bag with wet and twisted handkerchiefs.'—*Otis Ferguson*

'The picture isn't bad, but it trudges along and never becomes exciting.'—*New Yorker, 1977*

THE OLD DARK HOUSE (1932). Three undeniable eccentrics get together. Charles Laughton, Boris Karloff, Ernest Thesiger.

The Old Man and the Sea*
US 1958 89m Technicolor
Warner / Leland Hayward

An old fisherman dreams of hooking a great fish.
Expensive but poor-looking and stultifyingly dull one-character drama with variable production effects, a low key *Moby Dick*. Interesting but not effective.

w Ernest Hemingway, from his novel *d* John Sturges *ph* James Wong Howe, Floyd Crosby, Tom Tutweiler, Lamar Boren *m* Dmitri Tiomkin

Spencer Tracy, Felipe Pazos, Harry Bellaver
  'A literary property about as suited for the movie medium as *The Love Song of J. Alfred Prufrock.'*—Time*

'A strange amalgam of practically unassisted acting, good camerawork and editing, and a lot of special effects.'—*Ernest Callenbach, Film Quarterly*
  'Tracy struggles valiantly with the endless monologues . . . misguided in the extreme.'—*Time Out, 1984*
  'This is not a picture audiences are going to tear down the doors to see.'—*Motion Picture Herald*

AA: Dmitri Tiomkin
AAN: James Wong Howe; Spencer Tracy

Old Mother Riley

This Irish washerwoman with flailing arms and a nice line in invective was a music hall creation of Arthur Lucan, a variation of a pantomime dame. His wife Kitty Macshane

played Mother Riley's daughter, and despite personal difficulties they were top of the bill for nearly 30 years. The films were very cheaply made and the padding is difficult to sit through, but Lucan at his best is a superb comedian: they were made for small independent companies such as Butcher's and usually directed by Maclean Rogers.

1937: OLD MOTHER RILEY
1938: OLD MOTHER RILEY IN PARIS
1939: OLD MOTHER RILEY MP, OLD MOTHER RILEY JOINS UP
1940: OLD MOTHER RILEY IN BUSINESS, OLD MOTHER RILEY'S GHOSTS
1941: OLD MOTHER RILEY'S CIRCUS
1942: OLD MOTHER RILEY IN SOCIETY
1943: OLD MOTHER RILEY DETECTIVE
1944: OLD MOTHER RILEY AT HOME

1945: OLD MOTHER RILEY
HEADMISTRESS
1947: OLD MOTHER RILEY'S NEW
VENTURE
1949: OLD MOTHER RILEY'S JUNGLE
TREASURE
1952: MOTHER RILEY MEETS THE
VAMPIRE

Old Yeller*
US 1957 83m Technicolor
Walt Disney

The love of a boy for his dog.
Archetypal family movie set in a remote rural
area.

w Fred Gipson, William Tubberg, novel Fred
Gipson d Robert Stevenson ph Charles P.
Boyle m Oliver Wallace

Dorothy McGuire, Fess Parker, Tommy Kirk,
Kevin Corcoran, Jeff York, Chuck Connors

● Video: Disney

The Oldest Profession
France / West Germany / Italy 1967
115m Eastmancolor

Six sketches about prostitution. Very variable
portmanteau, with moments of interest
towards the end. Michele Mercier, Elsa
Martinelli, Jeanne Moreau, Jean-Claude
Brialy, Raquel Welch, Nadia Gray, Anna
Karina. Written by Ennio Flaiano, Daniel
Boulanger, Georges and André Tabet, Jean
Aurenche, Jean-Luc Godard; directed by
Franco Indovina, Mauro Bolognini, Philippe
de Broca, Michel Pfleghar, Claude Autant-
Lara, Jean-Luc Godard; for Gibe / Francoriz /
Rialto / Rizzoli.

'Much much more than a musical!'
Oliver!***
GB 1968 146m Technicolor
Panavision 70
Columbia / Warwick / Romulus (John
Woolf)

A musical version of Oliver Twist.
The last, perhaps, of the splendid film musicals
which have priced themselves out of existence;
it drags a little in spots but on the whole it
does credit both to the show and the original
novel, though eclipsed in style by David
Lean's straight version.

w Vernon Harris, play Lionel Bart, novel
Charles Dickens d Carol Reed ph Oswald
Morris m Lionel Bart md John Green
pd John Box ch Onna White

Ron Moody, Oliver Reed, Harry Secombe,
Mark Lester, Shani Wallis, Jack Wild, Hugh
Griffith, Joseph O'Conor, Leonard Rossiter,
Hylda Baker, Peggy Mount, Megs Jenkins
'Only time will tell if it is a great film but it
is certainly a great experience.'—Joseph
Morgenstern
'There is a heightened discrepancy between
the romping jollity with which everyone goes
about his business and the actual business
being gone about . . . such narrative elements
as the exploitation of child labour, pimping,
abduction, prostitution and murder combine

to make Oliver! the most non-U subject ever
to receive a U certificate.'—Jan Dawson
AA: best picture; Carol Reed; John Green
AAN: Vernon Harris; Oswald Morris; Ron
Moody; Jack Wild

● Video: RCA / Columbia

Oliver the Eighth
US 1933 20m bw

Ollie goes on a blind date, and the lady turns
out to be homicidal. Star farce which never
quite rises to the occasion; pleasant fooling but
no more. Laurel and Hardy, Mae Busch, Jack
Barty. Written by anon; directed by Lloyd
French; for Hal Roach.

Oliver Twist****
GB 1948 116m bw
GFD / Cineguild (Ronald Neame)

A foundling falls among thieves but is rescued
by a benevolent old gentleman.
Simplified, brilliantly cinematic version of a
voluminous Victorian novel, beautiful to look
at and memorably played, with every scene
achieving the perfect maximum impact.

w David Lean, Stanley Haynes, novel Charles
Dickens d David Lean ph Guy Green
m Arnold Bax pd John Bryan

Alec Guinness, Robert Newton, Francis L.
Sullivan, John Howard Davies, Kay Walsh,
Anthony Newley, Henry Stephenson, Mary
Clare, Gibb McLaughlin, Diana Dors
'A thoroughly expert piece of movie
entertainment.'—Richard Winnington

● Video: Rank

Oliver's Story
US 1978 92m Technicolor
Paramount (David V. Picker)

A sequel to Love Story, showing how Oliver
succumbed to depression but finally found
another girl friend.
Love means never having to watch this trendy
rubbish.

w Erich Segal, John Korty d John Korty
ph Arthur Ornitz m Francis Lai, Lee
Holdridge

Ryan O'Neal, Candice Bergen, Nicola Pagett,
Edward Binns, Ray Milland

Olly Olly Oxen Free
US 1978 93m Metrocolor
Rico Lion (Richard A. Colla)

A junkyard proprietress helps two young
children to launch a decrepit hot-air balloon.
Simpleminded children's adventure with a
surprising star.

w Eugene Poinc d Richard A. Colla
ph Gayne Rescher m Bob Alcivar pd Peter
Wooley

Katharine Hepburn, Kevin McKenzie, Dennis
Dimster

Los Olvidados*
Mexico 1951 88m bw
Utramar / Oscar Dancigers
aka: The Young and the Damned

A good boy is contaminated by the young

thugs in Mexico City's slums, and both he and
his tormentor die violently.
Sober but penetrating analysis of social
conditions leading to violence. The film was
widely acclaimed, yet its very proficiency and
excellent photography tend to glamorize its
subject. Compare, however, the Hollywood
resolutions of Dead End, on a similar subject.

w Luis Bunuel, Luis Alcoriza, Oscar
Dancigers d Luis Bunuel ph Gabriel
Figueroa m Gustavo Pitaluga

Alfonso Mejia, Miguel Inclan, Estela Inda,
Roberto Cobo

Olympische Spiele***
Germany 1936 Part 1, 118m; Part 2,
107m bw
Leni Riefenstahl

An account of the Berlin Olympic Games.
This magnificent film is in no sense a mere
reporting of an event. Camera movement,
photography and editing combine with music
to make it an experience truly olympian,
especially in the introductory symbolic
sequence suggesting the birth of the games. It
was also, dangerously, a hymn to Nazi
strength.

d, ed Leni Riefenstahl assistant Walter
Ruttman ph Hans Ertl, Walter Franz and 42
others m Herbert Windt
'Here is the camera doing superbly what
only the camera can do: refashioning the
rhythms of the visible; of the moment seen.'—
Dilys Powell

The Omaha Trail
US 1942 62m bw

The laying of train track across the west causes
Indian wars. Brisk second feature western with
good production values. James Craig, Dean
Jagger, Edward Ellis, Chill Wills, Donald
Meek, Pamela Blake, Howard da Silva.
Written by Jesse Lasky Jnr and Hugo Butler;
directed by Edward Buzzell; for MGM.

'One thousand years ago, Omar Khayyam
was a poet, a scientist and military leader
so great that an army of Assassins
dedicated to world domination fell
before his genius!'
Omar Khayyam
US 1956 101m Technicolor
Vistavision
Paramount (Frank Freeman Jnr)

The Persian poet and philosopher defends his
Shah against the Assassins.
Clean but dull Arabian Nights fantasy with
pantomime sets and no humour.

w Barre Lyndon d William Dieterle
ph Ernest Laszlo m Victor Young

Cornel Wilde, Michael Rennie, Raymond
Massey, John Derek, Yma Sumac, Sebastian
Cabot, Debra Paget

The Omega Man*
US 1971 98m Technicolor Panavision
Warner / Walter Seltzer

In 1977 a plague resulting from germ warfare
has decimated the world's population; in Los

Angeles, one man wages war against loathsome carriers of the disease.
'Realistic' version of a novel which was about vampires taking over, and was previously filmed unsatisfactorily as *The Last Man on Earth*. This nasty version rises to a few good action sequences but is bogged down by talk in between.

w John William Corrington and Joyce M. Corrington, *novel* I am Legend by Richard Matheson *d* Boris Sagal *ph* Russell Metty *m* Ron Grainer

Charlton Heston, Rosalind Cash, Anthony Zerbe

'Good morning. You are one day closer to the end of the world!'

The Omen••
US 1976 111m De Luxe Panavision
TCF (Harvey Bernhard)

The adopted child of an ambassador to Great Britain shows unnerving signs of being diabolically inspired.
Commercially successful variation on *The Exorcist*, quite professionally assembled and more enjoyable as entertainment than its predecessor.

w David Seltzer *d* Richard Donner *ph* Gil Taylor *m* Jerry Goldsmith

Gregory Peck, Lee Remick, David Warner, Billie Whitelaw, Leo McKern, Harvey Stevens, Patrick Troughton, Anthony Nicholls, Martin Benson
'A cut above the rest in that it has an ingenious premise, a teasingly labyrinthine development, a neat sting in its tail, and enough confidence in its own absurdities to carry them off.'—*David Robinson, The Times*
'Dreadfully silly . . . its horrors are not horrible, its terrors are not terrifying, its violence is ludicrous.'—*New York Times*
'More laughs than an average comedy.'—*Judith Crist*
'I did it strictly for the money.'—*David Seltzer*
† See *Damien: Omen II* and *The Final Conflict*.
†† Gregory Peck inherited his role from Charlton Heston, who turned it down.
AA: Jerry Goldsmith
AAN: song '*Ave Satani*'
● *Video: CBS / Fox*

On a Clear Day You Can See For Ever•
US 1970 129m Technicolor
Panavision
Paramount (Howard Koch)

A psychiatric hypnotist helps a girl to stop smoking, and finds that in trances she remembers previous incarnations.
Romantic musical which tries, and fails, to substitute wispy charm for its original Broadway vitality. There are compensations.

w Alan Jay Lerner, from his play *d* Vincente Minnelli *ph* Harry Stradling *m* Burton Lane

Barbra Streisand, Yves Montand, Bob Newhart, Larry Blyden, Jack Nicholson, Simon Oakland

On an Island with You
US 1948 104m Technicolor
MGM (Joe Pasternak)

A film actress on location in the South Seas is chased by a naval officer.
Below par musical which far outstays its welcome.

w Dorothy Kingsley, Dorothy Cooper, Charles Martin, Hans Wilhelm *d* Richard Thorpe *ph* Charles Rosher *md* George Stoll

Esther Williams, Peter Lawford, Jimmy Durante, Ricardo Montalban, Cyd Charisse, Xavier Cugat and his Orchestra

On Approval•••
GB 1943 80m bw
(GFD) Clive Brook

An Edwardian duke and an American heiress plan a chaperoned trial marriage in a remote Scottish castle.
Sparkling comedy of manners made even more piquant by careful casting and mounting; a minor delight.

w Clive Brook, Terence Young, play Frederick Lonsdale *d* Clive Brook

Clive Brook, Beatrice Lillie, Googie Withers, Roland Culver, O. B. Clarence, Lawrence Hanray, Hay Petrie
'Totally diverting, highly cinematic.'—*NFT, 1974*
'There has probably never been a richer, funnier anthology of late-Victorian mannerisms.'—*Time*
'I enjoyed it so thoroughly that I have to fight off superlatives.'—*James Agee*
† Also filmed in 1930 by Tom Walls for Herbert Wilcox, with Walls, Yvonne Arnaud, Winifred Shotter and Edmund Breon.

On Borrowed Time•
US 1939 98m bw
MGM (Sidney Franklin)

An old man refuses to die and chases Death up the apple tree.
Amiable, very American fantasy with much sentiment and several effective moments.

w Alice Duer Miller, Frank O'Neill, Claudine West, *novel* Lawrence Edward Watkin *d* Harold S. Bucquet *ph* Joseph Ruttenberg *m* Franz Waxman

Lionel Barrymore, Bobs Watson, Beulah Bondi, Cedric Hardwicke (as Mr Brink), Una Merkel, Ian Wolfe, Philip Terry, Eily Malyon
'General audiences may cotton to the novelty . . . artistically fine prestige production.'—*Variety*
'A weird, wild, totally unpredictable fantasy with dream sequences more like Bunuel than anything in the cinema.'—*John Russell Taylor, 1965*

On Dangerous Ground
US 1951 82m bw
RKO (John Houseman)

A tough cop falls in love with the blind sister of a mentally defective murderer.
Pretentious Hollywood *film noir* in the Gabin manner, partly redeemed by its glossy surface.

w A. I. Bezzerides, *novel* George Butler *d* Nicholas Ray *ph* George E. Diskant *m* Bernard Herrmann

Robert Ryan, Ida Lupino, Ward Bond, Ed Begley, Cleo Moore, Charles Kemper

On Dress Parade
US 1939 62m bw

The Dead End Kids go to military school. Cleaned-up comedy-drama, the last for the Kids before they split up. Billy Halop, Leo Gorcey, Huntz Hall, Bobby Jordan, Gabriel Dell, Bernard Punsley, John Litel, Frankie Thomas. Written by Tom Reed, Charles Balden; directed by William Clemens; for Warners. 'It just doesn't ring true. Dualler.'—*Variety*

On Friday at Eleven
West Germany / France / Italy 1960 93m bw
Corona / Criterion / Erredi (Alexander Gruter)
aka: *The World in My Pocket*

A cold-hearted gang plans to rob a heavily armoured American army truck.
Unsurprising but vaguely unpleasant thriller with nary a character left alive at the end.

w Frank Harvey, *novel* James Hadley Chase *d* Alvin Rakoff *ph* Vaclav Vich *m* Claude Bolling

Rod Steiger, Nadja Tiller, Peter Van Eyck, Jean Servais, Ian Bannen

'Growing up isn't easy at any age.'

On Golden Pond•••
US 1981 109m colour
ITC / IPC (Bruce Gilbert)

An 80-year-old, his wife and his daughter spend a holiday at their New England lakeside cottage.
A film remarkable not so much for what it is—a well-acted, decent screen presentation of a rather waffling and sentimental play—as for the fact that in the sophisticated eighties enough people paid to see it to make it a box office record breaker. This was mainly due to affection for its star, whose last film it was, but also to an American desire for a reversion to the old values of warmth and humanity after the sex and violence which the screen had lately been offering.

w Ernest Thompson, from his play *d* Mark Rydell *ph* Peter R. Norman *m* Dave Grusin

Henry Fonda, Katharine Hepburn, Jane Fonda, Doug McKeon, Dabney Coleman
'Moments of truth survive some cloying contrivance; Rydell directs on bended knees.'—*Sight and Sound*
'Two of Hollywood's best-loved veterans deserve a far better swansong than this sticky confection.'—*Time Out*
'The kind of uplifting twaddle that traffics heavily in rather basic symbols: the gold light on the pond stands for the sunset of life, and so on.'—*Pauline Kael, New Yorker*

ON GOLDEN POND.   Katharine Hepburn and Henry Fonda blow out the birthday cake, with help from Jane.

AA: Ernest Thompson; Henry Fonda;
Katharine Hepburn
AAN: Mark Rydell; editing (Robert L.
Wolfe); Dave Grusin; Jane Fonda
BFA: best actress (Katharine Hepburn)
● *Video: Precision*

On Her Majesty's Secret Service**
GB 1969   140m   Technicolor
   Panavision
UA / Eon / Danilaq (Harry Saltzman, Albert
   R. Broccoli)
James Bond tracks down master criminal
Blofeld in Switzerland.

Perhaps to compensate for no Sean Connery
and a tragic ending, the producers of this sixth
Bond opus shower largesse upon us in the
shape of no fewer than four protracted and
spectacular climaxes. Splendid stuff, but too
much of it, and the lack of a happy centre does
show.

w Richard Maibaum, *novel* Ian Fleming
d Peter Hunt   *ph* Michael Reed, Egil
Woxholt, Roy Ford, John Jordan   *m* John
Barry   *pd* Syd Cain

George Lazenby, Diana Rigg, Telly Savalas,
Ilse Steppat, Gabriele Ferzetti, Yuri
Borienko, Bernard Lee, Lois Maxwell
● *Video: Warner*

On Moonlight Bay**
US 1951   95m   Technicolor
Warner (William Jacobs)

Family crises, to do with growing up and
young love, in a 1917 Indiana town.
Pleasant musical, competently made, from the
Penrod stories, with the emphasis switched to
big sister.

w Melville Shavelson, Jack Rose, *stories*
Booth Tarkington   *d* Roy del Ruth   *ph* Ernest
Haller   *md* Ray Heindorf

Doris Day, Gordon Macrae, Leon Ames,
Rosemary de Camp, Billy Gray
† See also *By the Light of the Silvery Moon*, a
companion piece.

On Our Merry Way*
US 1948 107m bw
Benedict Bogeaus, Burgess Meredith
aka: A Miracle Can Happen

A reporter is urged by his wife to dig up some human interest stories.
Frail compendium of anecdotes which barely work.

w Laurence Stallings, story Arch Oboler d King Vidor, Leslie Fenton ph Joseph August, Gordon Avil, John Seitz, Edward Cronjager m Heinz Roemheld md David Chudnow, Skitch Henderson

Burgess Meredith, Paulette Goddard, Fred MacMurray, Hugh Herbert, James Stewart, Dorothy Lamour, Victor Moore, Henry Fonda, William Demarest

On Stage Everybody
US 1945 65m bw

A vaudevillian helps youngsters put on a radio show. Tired musical support. Jack Oakie, Peggy Ryan, Johnny Coy, Julie London, Otto Kruger. Written by Warren Wilson and Oscar Brodney; directed by Jean Yarbrough; for Universal.

On Such a Night
US 1937 71m bw

Gangsters get caught in a Mississippi flood. Confusing action yarn which fizzles out before it gets going. Grant Richards, Roscoe Karns, Karen Morley, Eduardo Ciannelli, Alan Mowbray, Robert McWade. Written by Doris Malloy, William Lipman, and various hands; directed by E. A. Dupont; for Emmanuel Cohen / Paramount. 'So many baffling twists that the thread of the narrative is soon lost.'—Variety

On Such a Night*
GB 1955 37m Eastmancolor

An American is initiated into the splendours of Glyndebourne Opera. Modestly pleasing documentary with fictionalized bookends. David Knight, Josephine Griffin, Marie Lohr. Written by Paul Dehn; directed by Anthony Asquith; for Screen Audiences / Rank.

On the Avenue**
US 1937 89m bw
TCF (Gene Markey)

An heiress rages because she is being satirized in a revue, but later falls in love with the star. Bright musical which keeps moving and uses its talents wisely.

w Gene Markey, William Conselman d Roy del Ruth ph Lucien Andriot m / ly Irving Berlin ch Seymour Felix

Dick Powell, Madeleine Carroll, The Ritz Brothers, George Barbier, Alice Faye, Walter Catlett, Joan Davis, E. E. Clive
Songs include 'He Ain't Got Rhythm'; 'The Girl on the Police Gazette'; 'This Year's Kisses'; 'I've Got My Love to Keep Me Warm'. The title song was dropped before release

'An amusing revue, with a pleasant score and a disarming informality in its production to lure us into liking it.'—New York Times
† Revamped as Let's Make Love (qv).

On the Beach**
US 1959 134m bw
United Artists / Stanley Kramer

When most of the world has been devastated by atomic waste, an American atomic submarine sets out to investigate.
Gloomy prophecy which works well in spasms but is generally too content to chat rather than imagine. A solid prestige job nevertheless.

w John Paxton, James Lee Barrett, novel Nevil Shute d Stanley Kramer ph Giuseppe Rotunno, Daniel Fapp m Ernest Gold pd Rudolph Sternad

Gregory Peck, Ava Gardner, Fred Astaire, Anthony Perkins, Donna Anderson, John Tate, Lola Brooks
'Its humanism is clearly of the order that seeks the support of a clamorous music score. The characters remain little more than spokesmen for timid ideas and Salvation Army slogans, their emotions hired from a Hollywood prop room; which is all pretty disturbing in a film about nothing less than the end of the world.'—Robert Vas

AAN: Ernest Gold

On the Beat
GB 1962 105m bw
Rank (Hugh Stewart)

A Scotland Yard car park attendant manages to capture some crooks and become a policeman.
Busy but flat comedy vehicle, never very likeable.

w Jack Davies d Robert Asher ph Geoffrey Faithfull m Philip Green

Norman Wisdom, Jennifer Jayne, Raymond Huntley, David Lodge

On the Buses
GB 1971 88m Technicolor
EMI / Hammer (Ronald Woolfe, Ronald Chesney)

Women drivers cause trouble at a bus depot. Grotesque, ham-handed farce from a TV series which was sometimes funny; this is merely vulgar.

w Ronald Woolfe, Ronald Chesney d Harry Booth ph Mark MacDonald m Max Harris

Reg Varney, Doris Hare, Anna Karen, Michael Robbins, Stephen Lewis
† Mutiny on the Buses followed in 1972 and Holiday on the Buses in 1973. Both were deplorably witless.

On the Double*
US 1961 92m Technicolor Panavision
Paramount / Dena–Capri (Jack Rose)

During World War II, an American private is asked to impersonate a British intelligence officer.
From the plot and the talents it seems one might start laughing at this while still in the queue, but in fact most of it goes sadly awry and it never quite comes to the boil.

w Jack Rose, Melville Shavelson d Melville Shavelson ph Harry Stradling, Geoffrey Unsworth m Leith Stevens

Danny Kaye, Dana Wynter, Wilfrid Hyde White, Diana Dors, Margaret Rutherford, Allan Cuthbertson, Jesse White

On the Fiddle*
GB 1961 97m bw
Anglo-Amalgamated / S. Benjamin Fisz
US title: Operation Snafu

A wide boy and a slow-witted gypsy have comic and other adventures in the RAF.
Curious mixture of farce and action, more on American lines than British, but quite entertainingly presented.

w Harold Buchman, novel Stop at a Winner by R. F. Delderfield d Cyril Frankel ph Ted Scaife m Malcolm Arnold

Alfred Lynch, Sean Connery, Cecil Parker, Wilfrid Hyde White, Kathleen Harrison, Alan King, Eleanor Summerfield, Eric Barker, Terence Longdon, John Le Mesurier, Harry Locke

On the Night of the Fire*
GB 1939 94m bw
GFD / G & S (Josef Somlo)
US title: The Fugitive

A barber kills the blackmailer of his wife. Dour little drama, rather unusual for pre-war British studios.

w Brian Desmond Hurst, Terence Young, novel F. L. Green d Brian Desmond Hurst ph Gunther Krampf

Ralph Richardson, Diana Wynyard, Romney Brent, Mary Clare, Henry Oscar, Frederick Leister
'The kind of film either liked very much or very little . . . absorbingly entertaining, and b.o. should profit considerably by word of mouth.'—Variety

On the Riviera**
US 1951 90m Technicolor
TCF (Sol C. Siegel)

A cabaret artist is persuaded to pose as a philandering businessman.
Remake of Folies Bergère and That Night in Rio (see also On the Double); disliked at the time and accused of tastelessness, it now seems smarter and funnier than comparable films of its era.

w Valentine Davies, Phoebe and Henry Ephron d Walter Lang ph Leon Shamroy m Alfred Newman

Danny Kaye, Corinne Calvet, Gene Tierney, Marcel Dalio, Jean Murat

AAN: Alfred Newman

On the Threshold of Space
US 1956 96m Eastmancolor
  Cinemascope
TCF (William Bloom)

The USAF medical corps explores human reactions at high altitudes.
Semi-documentary flagwaver with dreary domestic asides; very dated now, and of no particular nostalgic interest.

w Simon Wincelberg, Francis Cockrill
d Robert D. Webb ph Joe MacDonald
m Lyn Murray

Guy Madison, Virginia Leith, John Hodiak,
Dean Jagger, Warren Stevens

On the Town****

US 1949 98m Technicolor
MGM (Arthur Freed)

Three sailors enjoy twenty-four hours' leave in
New York.
Most of this brash location musical counts as
among the best things ever to come out of
Hollywood; the serious ballet towards the end
tends to kill it, but it contains much to be
grateful for.

w Betty Comden, Adolph Green, ballet Fancy
Free by Leonard Bernstein d / ch Gene Kelly,
Stanley Donen ph Harold Rosson md Lennie
Hayton, Roger Edens songs various

Gene Kelly, Frank Sinatra, Jules Munshin,
Vera-Ellen, Betty Garrett, Ann Miller, Tom
Dugan, Florence Bates, Alice Pearce
 'A film that will be enjoyed more than
twice.'—Lindsay Anderson
 'So exuberant that it threatens at moments
to bounce right off the screen.'—Time
 'The speed, the vitality, the flashing colour
and design, the tricks of timing by which
motion is fitted to music, the wit and invention
and superlative technical accomplishment
make it a really exhilarating experience.'—
Richard Mallett, Punch

AA: Lennie Hayton, Roger Edens
● Video: MGM / UA

On the Twelfth Day*

GB 1956 23m Eastmancolor

A balletic presentation of the song about the
twelve days of Christmas, with plenty of maids
a'milking and lords a'leaping. A refreshing
and extravagant novelty. Wendy Toye,
Franklin Bennett, David O'Brien. Written by
James Matthews and Val Valentine; directed
by Wendy Toye; for George K. Arthur /
Bahamian.

On the Waterfront***

US 1954 108m bw
Columbia / Sam Spiegel

After the death of his brother, a young
stevedore breaks the hold of a waterfront gang
boss.
Intense, broody dockside thriller with
'method' performances; very powerful of its
kind, and much imitated.

w Budd Schulberg, from his novel d Elia
Kazan ph Boris Kaufman 'm Leonard
Bernstein ad Richard Day

Marlon Brando, Eva Marie Saint, Lee J.
Cobb, Rod Steiger, Karl Malden, Pat
Henning, Leif Erickson, James Westerfield,
John Hamilton
 'An uncommonly powerful, exciting and
imaginative use of the screen by gifted
professionals.'—New York Times

 'A medley of items from the Warner
gangland pictures of the thirties, brought up to
date.'—Steven Sondheim, Films in Review
† Sample dialogue: 'Charlie, oh Charlie, you
don't understand. I coulda had class. I coulda
been a contender.'

AA: best picture; Budd Schulberg; Elia
Kazan; Boris Kaufman; Richard Day; Marlon
Brando; Eva Marie Saint
AAN: Leonard Bernstein; Lee J. Cobb; Rod
Steiger; Karl Malden
● Video: RCA / Columbia

On Trial

US 1939 60m bw

A man kills his wife's lover and is put on trial
for murder. Dozy film version of a once
sensational play. John Litel, Margaret
Lindsay, Edward Norris, James Stephenson.
Written by Don Ryan from the play by Elmer
Rice; directed by Terry Morse; for Warners.
'Strictly dual fodder, talking along for an hour
without going anywhere.'—Variety

On with the Show

US 1929 98m Technicolor (two-colour)
Warner

Crude early talkie musical revue with
historical interest.

w Robert Lord, play Shoestring by Humphrey
Pearson d Alan Crosland ph Tony Gaudio
ch Larry Ceballos songs Grant Clarke, Harry
Akst

Betty Compson, Louise Fazenda, Sally
O'Neil, Joe E. Brown, Ethel Waters, Arthur
Lake

On Your Toes*

US 1939 94m bw
Warner (Robert Lord)

Backstage jealousies at the ballet.
Smooth film version of a top Broadway show
of its time.

w Jerry Wald, Richard Macaulay, play George
Abbott d Ray Enright ph James Wong
Howe, Sol Polito m / ly Richard Rodgers,
Lorenz Hart

Vera Zorina, Eddie Albert, Alan Hale, Frank
McHugh, James Gleason, Donald O'Connor,
Gloria Dickson
 'Box office prospects appear to be pretty
good, but more than the average campaigning
should be indulged.'—Variety

Once a Crook

GB 1941 81m bw

A publican with a shady past helps his son who
is in trouble with the law. Low-key character
comedy for two stars who would benefit from
a greater tendency to farce. Gordon Harker,
Sydney Howard, Frank Pettingell, Carla
Lehmann, Bernard Lee, Kathleen Harrison,
Cyril Cusack. Written by Roger Burford, from
the play by Evadne Price and Ken Attiwill;
directed by Herbert Mason; for TCF.

Once a Jolly Swagman*

GB 1948 100m bw
GFD / Wessex (Ian Dalrymple)
US title: Maniacs on Wheels

A factory worker becomes a speedway rider.
Competent sporting drama of no particular
interest.

w William Rose, Jack Lee d Jack Lee ph H.
E. Fowle m Bernard Stevens

Dirk Bogarde, Renée Asherson, Bonar
Colleano, Bill Owen

Once a Lady

US 1931 65m bw

An illegitimate baby grows up to meet her
mother without recognizing her. A plot that
was often tried out during the early thirties,
seldom more boringly than on this occasion.
Ruth Chatterton, Ivor Novello, Jill Esmond,
Geoffrey Kerr, Doris Lloyd. Written by Zoe
Akins and Samuel Hoffenstein from the play
The Second Life by Rudolf Bernauer and
Rudolf Oesterreicher; directed by Guthrie
McClintic; for Paramount. 'Another crying
towel special.'—Variety

Once a Sinner

US 1930 71m bw

A girl criminal reforms but almost loses the
love of her new boy friend when he finds out
about her past. Transparent melodrama,
strictly for indulgent ladies. Dorothy Mackail,
Joel McCrea, John Halliday, C. Henry
Gordon, Ilka Chase, Clara Blandick, George
Brent. 'Slow drama that needs plenty of
support.'—Variety

Once a Sinner

GB 1950 80m bw

A girl with a shady past finds her husband is
being threatened by her ex-partner.
Uninteresting character melodrama which
defeats its lightweight stars. Pat Kirkwood,
Jack Watling, Joy Shelton, Sidney Tafler,
Thora Hird. Written by David Evans, from
the novel Irene by Ronald Marsh; directed by
Lewis Gilbert; for John Argyle / Butcher.

Once a Thief

US 1965 107m bw Panavision
MGM / Cipra / RN / Fred Engel (Jacques
Bar)

An ex-convict is hounded by a vengeful cop.
Glum crime melodrama gleamingly
photographed but otherwise quite routine.

w Zekial Marko d Ralph Nelson ph Robert
Burks m Lalo Schifrin

Alain Delon, Ann-Margret, Van Heflin, Jack
Palance, John David Chandler

Once Before I Die

US 1966 97m Eastmancolor
F.8 Productions (John Derek)

In the Philippines, after a Jap aerial attack, a
cavalry major's girl friend causes
complications in her bids to escape.

Mildly hilarious action melodrama in which the star's superstructure is made the focus of the action.

w Vance Skarstedt d John Derek ph Arthur Arling m Emmanuel Vardi

Ursula Andress, John Derek, Richard Jaeckel, Rod Lauren

Once in a Blue Moon
US 1936 (produced 1934) 65m bw

Adventures of an innocent abroad in contemporary Russia. Would-be satire which was seen by very few people indeed. Jimmy Savo, Nikita Balieff, Whitney Bourne, Cecilia Loftus. Written and directed by Ben Hecht and Charles MacArthur; for Paramount. 'A dud. The exhibitors who are kidded into playing it won't be very happy afterwards.'—Variety

Once in a Lifetime**
US 1933 80m approx bw
Universal

How a script was sold in old-time Hollywood. Half good-humoured, half-scathing satire on Hollywood; technique dated, content still amusing.

w Seton I. Miller, play Moss Hart, George S. Kaufman d Russell Mack ph George Robinson

Jack Oakie, Sidney Fox, Aline MacMahon, Russell Hopton, Zasu Pitts, Louise Fazenda, Gregory Ratoff, Onslow Stevens
'Idol-smashing satire, strictly for the initiated.'—Variety

Once in Paris
US 1978 100m TVC color

A naïve American writer is introduced to the delights of Paris by a worldly chauffeur and an amorous British noblewoman. A movie that adds up to very little, but pleases along the way. Wayne Rogers, Gayle Hunnicutt, Jack Lenoir, Philippe Hart, Tanya Lopert. Written and directed by Frank D. Gilroy, for his own company.

'The darkest alleys of love among the international set!'

Once Is Not Enough
US 1975 122m Movielab Panavision
Paramount / Sujac / Aries (Howard W. Koch)
aka: Jacqueline Susann's Once Is Not Enough

The daughter of a movie producer is corrupted by his circle.
Old-fashioned jet-set melodrama with new-fashioned sexual novelties.

w Julius J. Epstein, novel Jacqueline Susann d Guy Green ph John A. Alonzo m Henry Mancini pd John de Cuir

Kirk Douglas, Alexis Smith, David Janssen, George Hamilton, Melina Mercouri, Gary Conway, Brenda Vaccaro, Deborah Raffin

AAN: Brenda Vaccaro

Once More My Darling
US 1949 92m bw
Universal (Joan Harrison)

A young girl is romantically pursued by an older man.
Tame comedy.

w Robert Carson d Robert Montgomery ph Franz Planer m Elizabeth Firestone

Robert Montgomery, Ann Blyth, Jane Cowl, Taylor Holmes, Charles McGraw

Once More with Feeling
GB 1960 92m Technicolor
Columbia / Stanley Donen

The volatile private life of an orchestral conductor.
Thin comedy from a West End play, something between a shouting match and a fashion show.

w Harry Kurnitz, from his play d Stanley Donen ph Georges Périnal md Muir Mathieson pd Alexander Trauner

Yul Brynner, Kay Kendall, Geoffrey Toone, Maxwell Shaw, Mervyn Johns, Martin Benson, Gregory Ratoff

Once to Every Woman
US 1934 70m bw

A young doctor saves a patient's life by pushing his ailing chief aside during an operation. Tedious, routine hospital stuff. Walter Connolly, Ralph Bellamy, Fay Wray, Mary Carlisle, Walter Byron. Written by Jo Swerling from a story by A. J. Cronin; directed by Lambert Hillyer; for Columbia. 'A programmer which won't make the grade in key houses.'—Variety

Once Upon a Dream
GB 1948 84m bw

An officer's wife has a romantic dream about her husband's batman, and comes to believe it true. Very wispy comedy which does none of its principals any good. Googie Withers, Griffith Jones, Guy Middleton, Raymond Lovell, Hubert Gregg. Written by Patrick Kirwan and Victor Katona; directed by Ralph Thomas; for Triton / Rank.

Once Upon a Honeymoon*
US 1942 116m bw
RKO (Leo McCarey)

An American radio correspondent and an ex-burlesque queen cheat the Nazis—and her husband—in Europe during World War II. Smooth but curious mixture of comedy and drama, a satisfactory but unmemorable star vehicle.

w Sheridan Gibney, Leo McCarey d Leo McCarey ph George Barnes m Robert Emmett Dolan

Cary Grant, Ginger Rogers, Walter Slezak, Albert Dekker, Albert Bassermann, Ferike Boros, Harry Shannon
'The attempt to play for both laughs and significance against a terrifying background of Nazi aggression is on the whole a little disappointing.'—Newsweek

Once Upon a Horse
US 1958 85m bw Cinemascope

Two cowboys steal a herd of cattle but can't afford to feed them. Unprepossessing comedy vehicle for a team which found success only on television. Dan Rowan, Dick Martin, Martha Hyer, Leif Erickson, Nita Talbot, James Gleason. Written, directed and produced by Hal Kanter; for Universal.

Once Upon a Time*
US 1944 89m bw
Columbia (Louis Edelman)

A luckless producer makes a sensation out of a boy and his dancing caterpillar.
Thin whimsical comedy, too slight to come off given such standard treatment, but with nice touches along the way.

w Lewis Meltzer, Oscar Saul, radio play My Client Curley by Norman Corwin, Lucille F. Herrmann d Alexander Hall ph Franz Planer m Frederick Hollander

Cary Grant, Janet Blair, James Gleason, Ted Donaldson, Howard Freeman, William Demarest, Art Baker, John Abbott
'There just isn't enough material here for a full-length feature.'—Philip T. Hartung
'It would be nice to see some screen fantasy if it were done by anyone with half a heart, mind and hand for it. But when the studios try to make it, duck and stay hid till the mood has passed.'—James Agee

Once Upon a Time in America**
US 1984 228m (also in 147m version) Technicolor
Warner / Embassy / Ladd / PSO (Arnon Milchan)

The lives of four gangsters between 1922 and 1968.
Vast, sprawling, violent crime saga with a pretentious approach and a confusing time scheme. Some scenes have great power but the total effect is overwhelming in the wrong way.

w Leonardo Benvenuti, Piero de Bernardi, Enrico Medioli, Franco Arcalli, Franco Ferrini, Sergio Leone, from The Hoods by David Aaronson ('Harry Grey') d Sergio Leone ph Tonino Delli Colli m Ennio Morricone ed Nino Baragli

Robert de Niro, James Woods, Elizabeth McGovern, Treat Williams, Tuesday Weld, Burt Young, Danny Aiello, William Forsythe
'It is, finally, a heart-breaking story of mutual need. By matching that need with his own need to come to terms with his own cultural memories, Leone has made his most oneiric and extraordinary film.'—Tony Rayns, MFB

Once Upon a Time in the West*
Italy / US 1969 165m Techniscope
Paramount / Rafran / San Marco (Fulvio Morsella)

A lonely woman in the old west is in danger from a band of gunmen.
Immensely long and convoluted epic western marking its director's collaboration with an American studio and his desire to make

serious statements about something or other. Beautifully made, empty, and very violent.

w Sergio Leone, Sergio Donati *d* Sergio Leone *ph* Tonino Delli Colli *m* Ennio Morricone

Henry Fonda, Claudia Cardinale, Jason Robards, Charles Bronson, Gabriele Ferzetti, Keenan Wynn, Paolo Stoppa, Lionel Stander, Jack Elam, Woody Strode
† This film has the longest credits of all: they sprawl through the first twelve minutes.
● Video: CIC

The One and Only
US 1978 98m Movielab
Paramount / First Artists (Steve Gordon, David V. Picker)

A stage-struck egomaniac finds success at the expense of happiness with his wife.
Uneasy mixture of farce and sentiment intended as a star vehicle, but not a very successful one.

w Steve Gordon *d* Carl Reiner *ph* Victor J. Kemper *m* Patrick Williams

Henry Winkler, Kim Darby, Gene Saks, William Daniels, Polly Holiday, Herve Villechaize, Harold Gould, Richard Lane

One Day in the Life of Ivan Denisovich*
GB 1971 105m Eastmancolor
Group W / Leontes / Norsk (Caspar Wrede)

Life in a Siberian labour camp in 1950.
A fairly successful book adaptation, as far as mere pictures can cope with the harrowing detail.

w Ronald Harwood, *novel* Alexander Solzhenitsyn *d* Caspar Wrede *ph* Sven Nykvist *m* Arne Nordheim

Tom Courtenay, Espen Skjonberg, James Maxwell, Alfred Burke, Eric Thompson, Matthew Guinness
'The film's general air of earnestness deflects rather than stimulates involvement.'—*David Wilson*

One Deadly Summer*
France 1983 133m Eastmancolor

In a Provençal village, a girl's strange behaviour turns out to have a revenge motive. Complex and overlong thriller which loses most of its interest once one knows what it is about. Written by Sébastien Japrisot, from his novel; directed by Jean Becker; for SNC / CAPAC / TFI. 'That the film could have been worse does not make it any better.'—*Gilbert Adair, MFB*. (Original title: *L'Eté Meurtrier*.)

One Desire
US 1955 94m Technicolor
U-I (Ross Hunter)

The romantic career of the lady owner of a gambling saloon.
Tawdry nineties drama which never really gets going.

w Lawrence Roman, Robert Blees, *novel* Tacey Cromwell by Conrad Richter *d* Jerry

Hopper *ph* Maury Gertsman *m* Frank Skinner *md* Joseph Gershenson

Anne Baxter, Rock Hudson, Julia Adams, Natalie Wood, Barry Curtis, William Hopper, Carl Benton Reid
'The standards of writing and characterization belong to a Victorian servant girl's paper-covered romance.'—*MFB*

One Brief Summer
GB 1969 86m Eastmancolor
TCF / Twickenham (Guido Coen)

A wealthy man loses interest in his mistress and begins courting his daughter's friend. Odd, downbeat melodrama with hints of incest; a sophisticated time-passer.

w Wendy Marshall, *play* Valkyrie's Armour by Harry Tierney *d* John Mackenzie *ph* David MacDonald *m* Roger Webb

Clifford Evans, Felicity Gibson, Jennifer Hilary, Jan Holden, Peter Egan, Fanny Carby, Richard Vernon, Brian Wilde
● Video: Precision

One Exciting Night
GB 1944 89m bw

A singing welfare worker averts a plan to steal a Rembrandt. Very ho-hum stuff for a very popular but histrionically untried star. Vera Lynn, Donald Stewart, Mary Clare, Frederick Leister, Richard Murdoch. Written by Howard Irving Young, Peter Fraser, Margaret Kennedy and Emery Bonnet; directed by Walter Forde; for Columbia British.

One Eyed Jacks
US 1961 141m Technicolor Vistavision
Paramount / Pennebaker (Frank P. Rosenberg)

An outlaw has a running battle with an old friend.
Grossly self-indulgent western controlled (unwisely) by its star, full of solemn pauses and bouts of violence.

w Guy Trosper, Calder Willingham, *novel* The Authentic Death of Hendry Jones by Charles Neider *d* Marlon Brando *ph* Charles Lang Jnr *m* Hugo Friedhofer

Marlon Brando, Karl Malden, Pina Pellicier, Katy Jurado, Slim Pickens, Ben Johnson, Timothy Carey, Elisha Cook Jnr

AAN: Charles Lang Jnr

One Flew over the Cuckoo's Nest***
US 1975 134m De Luxe
UA / Fantasy Films (Paul Zaentz, Michael Douglas)

A cheerful immoralist imprisoned for rape is transferred for observation to a state mental hospital.
Wildly and unexpectedly commercial film of a project which had lain dormant for fourteen years, this amusing and horrifying film conveniently sums up anti-government attitudes as well as make love not war and all that. It's certainly impossible to ignore.

w Laurence Hauben, Bo Goldman, *novel* Ken Kesey *d* Milos Forman *ph* Haskell Wexler *m* Jack Nitzche *pd* Paul Sylbert

Jack Nicholson, Louise Fletcher, William Redfield, Will Sampson, Brad Dourif, Christopher Lloyd
'Lacks the excitement of movie art, but the story and the acting make the film emotionally powerful.'—*New Yorker*

AA: best picture; script; Milos Forman; Jack Nicholson; Louise Fletcher
AAN: Haskell Wexler; Jack Nitzche; Brad Dourif
● Video: Thorn EMI

One Foot in Heaven*
US 1941 108m bw
Warner (Robert Lord, Irving Rapper)

The small-town doings of a methodist minister.
Slow but pleasing chronicle, nicely assembled.

w Casey Robinson, *biography* (of his father) Hartzell Spence *d* Irving Rapper *ph* Charles Rosher *m* Max Steiner

Fredric March, Martha Scott, Beulah Bondi, Gene Lockhart, Elizabeth Fraser, Harry Davenport, Laura Hope Crews, Grant Mitchell, Moroni Olsen, Ernest Cossart, Jerome Cowan
'A clean, sweet, decent picture.'—*Cecilia Ager*
AAN: best picture

One Foot in Hell
US 1960 89m De Luxe Cinemascope
TCF (Sydney Boehm)

The sheriff of a small western town is secretly plotting revenge on the townsfolk for their long-ago treatment of his wife.
Unusual western suspenser with plenty of violent action and an extremely equivocal hero.

w Aaron Spelling, Sydney Boehm *d* James B. Clark *ph* William C. Mellor *m* Dominic Frontière

Alan Ladd, Dan O'Herlihy, Don Murray, Dolores Michaels, Barry Coe, Larry Gates, John Alexander

One Frightened Night
US 1935 67m bw

Relatives assemble in a spooky house in the hope of inheriting an old man's wealth. Low-budget thriller that sometimes seems like a spoof of *The Cat and the Canary*. Charles Grapewin, Mary Carlisle, Arthur Hohl, Evalyn Knapp, Wallace Ford, Hedda Hopper, Lucien Littlefield, Regis Toomey, Rafaela Ottiano. Written by Wellyn Totman; directed by Christy Cabanne; for Mascot.

One from the Heart*
US 1982 101m Metrocolor
Zoetrope Studios (Gray Frederickson, Fred Roos, Armyan Bernstein)

On Independence Day in Las Vegas, a pair of lovers quarrel and make up.
Extraordinarily slim (for its cost) romantic

fantasy which makes one wonder why, of all stories in the world, its creator chose this one. It does however boast attractive visuals.

w Armyan Bernstein, Francis Coppola *d* Francis Coppola *ph* Vittorio Storaro *m* Tom Waits *pd* Dean Tavoularis

Frederic Forrest, Teri Garr, Raul Julia, Nastassja Kinski, Lainie Kazan, Harry Dean Stanton

'Giddy heights of visual imagination and technical brilliance are lavished on a wafer-thin story.'—*Guardian*
'If this is the essence of cinema, then Salvador Dali is the essence of painting.'—*Sunday Times*
'A very beautiful film, the background of which totally drowns a wafer-thin plot. A musical non-musical, a spectacular non-spectacular, a fantasy with realist aspirations.'—*Guardian*
'Escapism running away with itself.'—*Standard*

AAN: original song score
● *Video: CBS / Fox*

One Good Turn
US 1931 20m bw

Two odd job men see their benefactress rehearsing a play, and think she is really being evicted. Moderate star comedy with nice moments. Laurel and Hardy, Mary Carr, Billy Gilbert. Written by H. M. Walker; directed by James W. Horne; for Hal Roach.

One Good Turn
GB 1954 90m bw
GFD / Two Cities (Maurice Cowan)

An orphan stays on to become an odd job man, and tries to raise money to buy an old car.
The star's second comedy is an almost unmitigated disaster, disjointed and depending too much on pathos.

w Maurice Cowan, John Paddy Carstairs, Ted Willis *d* John Paddy Carstairs *ph* Jack Cox *m* John Addison

Norman Wisdom, Joan Rice, Shirley Abicair, Thora Hird, William Russell, Richard Caldicot

One Heavenly Night
US 1930 82m bw

A flower girl in a Budapest music hall finds herself imitating the absent star. Would-be-Lubitsch-like musical comedy which doesn't quite succeed in its pleasant aims. Evelyn Laye, John Boles, Leon Errol, Lilyan Tashman, Hugh Cameron, Lionel Belmore. Written by Sidney Howard from a story by Louis Bromfield; directed by George Fitzmaurice; for Samuel Goldwyn. 'It will satisfy the customers, but lacks the intrinsic quality that makes 'em talk and recommends it as an entertainment for big grosses.'—*Variety*

'Gayest screen event of the year!'
One Hour with You***
US 1932 84m bw
Paramount (*Ernst Lubitsch*)

The affairs of a philandering Parisian doctor. Superbly handled comedy of manners in Lubitsch's most inventive form, handled by a most capable cast. Unique entertainment of a kind which is, alas, no more.

w Samson Raphaelson, *play* Only a Dream by Lothar Schmidt *d* George Cukor, Ernst Lubitsch *ph* Victor Milner *m* Oscar Straus, Richard Whiting *ly* Leo Robin *ad* Hans Dreier

Maurice Chevalier, Jeanette MacDonald, Genevieve Tobin, Roland Young, Charles Ruggles, George Barbier

'Sure fire if frothy screen fare, cinch b.o. at all times.'—*Variety*
'A brand new form of musical entertainment . . . he has mixed verse, spoken and sung, a smart and satiric musical background, asides to the audience, and sophisticated dialogue, as well as lilting and delightful songs . . . The result is something so delightful that it places the circle of golden leaves jauntily upon the knowing head of Hollywood's most original director.'—*Philadelphia Inquirer*
† A remake of Lubitsch's silent success *The Marriage Circle.*
AAN: best picture

One Hundred and One Dalmatians***
US 1961 79m Technicolor
Walt Disney

The dogs of London help save puppies which are being stolen for their skins by a cruel villainess.
Disney's last really splendid feature cartoon, with the old flexible style cleverly modernized and plenty of invention and detail in the story line. The London backgrounds are especially nicely judged.

w Bill Peet, *novel* Dodie Smith *d* Wolfgang Reitherman, Hamilton S. Luske, Clyde Geronimi

120 Days of Sodom
Italy / France 1975 117m Technicolor

After the Italian campaign of 1944, four local dignitaries marry each other's daughters, withdraw with a bevy of nubile girls to a mountain retreat, and tell each other sado-masochistic sexual adventures. Thoroughly revolting and much banned piece with no perceptible point but a good deal of emetic detail. Paolo Bonacelli, Giorgio Cataldi, Uberto P. Quintavalle, Aldo Valetti. Written and directed by Pier Paolo Pasolini, from the novel by the Marquis de Sade; for PEA / PAA.

One Hundred Men and a Girl***
US 1937 84m bw
Universal (*Joe Pasternak*)

A young girl persuades a great conductor to form an orchestra of unemployed musicians.
Delightful and funny musical fable, an instance of the Pasternak formula of sweetness and light at its richest and best.

w Bruce Manning, Charles Kenyon, Hans Kraly *d* Henry Koster *ph* Joseph Valentine *m* Charles Previn *songs* various

Deanna Durbin, Adolphe Menjou, Leopold Stokowski, Alice Brady, Mischa Auer, Eugene Pallette, Billy Gilbert, Alma Kruger, Jed Prouty, Frank Jenks, Christian Rub
'Smash hit for all the family . . . something new in entertainment.'—*Variety*
AA: Charles Previn
AAN: best picture; original story (Hans Kraly)

100 Rifles*
US 1969 109m De Luxe
TCF / Marvin Schwartz

In war-torn Mexico, a black American sheriff and his prisoner become involved in a girl's fight for vengeance after her father's death. Blood-soaked adventure with plenty of tough action and tight pace. A little too purposeful in its unpleasantness to be very entertaining.

w Clair Huffaker, Tom Gries, *novel* Robert MacLeod *d* Tom Gries *ph* Cecilio Paniagua *m* Jerry Goldsmith

Jim Brown, Raquel Welch, Burt Reynolds, Fernando Lamas, Dan O'Herlihy, Hans Gudegast
● *Video: CBS / Fox*

One in a Million**
US 1936 94m bw
TCF (Raymond Griffith)

The daughter of a Swiss innkeeper becomes an Olympic ice-skating champion.
Sonja Henie's film debut shows Hollywood at its most professional, making entertainment out of the purest moonshine with considerable injections of novelty talent.

w Lenore Praskins, Mark Kelly *d* Sidney Lanfield *ph* Edward Cronjager *md* Louis Silvers *songs* Sidney Mitchell, Lew Pollack

Sonja Henie, Don Ameche, *The Ritz Brothers*, Jean Hersholt, Ned Sparks, Arline Judge, Dixie Dunbar, Borrah Minnevitch and his Rascals, Montagu Love
'A very entertaining, adroitly mixed concoction of romance, music, comedy and skating. . . Miss Henie is a screen find.'—*Variety*

One Is a Lonely Number*
US 1972 97m Metrocolor
MGM (Stan Margulies)

When her husband leaves her, a woman tries to develop new interests.
Satirical sentimental view of American divorce, with interesting moments.

w David Seltzer, *novel* Rebecca Morris *d* Mel Stuart *ph* Michel Hugo *m* Michel Legrand

Trish Van Devere, Monte Markham, Melvyn Douglas, Janet Leigh

One Little Indian
US 1973 91m Technicolor
Walt Disney (Winston Hibler)

A cavalry corporal escapes from jail and falls in with a ten-year-old Indian.

Sentimental semi-western, a bit dull for Disney apart from a camel.

w Harry Spalding *d* Bernard McEveety *ph* Charles F. Wheeler *m* Jerry Goldsmith

James Garner, Vera Miles, Pat Hingle, Morgan Woodward, John Doucette

One Man's Journey

US 1933 72m bw

The career of a rural doctor for whom fame arrives too late. Pleasant, predictable, rather downbeat small-town drama. Lionel Barrymore, May Robson, Dorothy Jordan, Joel McCrea, Frances Dee, David Landau, Samuel S. Hinds. Written by Lester Cohen and Sam Ornitz from a story Failure by Katherine Haviland Taylor; directed by John Robertson; for RKO. 'Carries sympathetic interest and appeal.'—*Variety*

One Man's Way

US 1964 105m bw

A crime reporter becomes a priest. Rather self-conscious biography of Norman Vincent Peale, adequately assembled but containing no surprises. Don Murray, Diana Hyland, William Windom, Virginia Christine, Carol Ohmart. Written by Eleanore Griffin and John W. Bloch, from the book *Minister to Millions* by Arthur Gordon; directed by Denis Sanders; for UA.

One Mile from Heaven

US 1937 68m bw

A girl reporter makes hay with the story of a black woman who is raising a white child. Curious mixture of melodrama and wisecracking farce, with tap dancing from Bill Robinson thrown in. Claire Trevor, Sally Blane, Douglas Fowley, Fredi Washington, Ralf Harolde. Written by Lou Breslow and John Patrick; directed by Allan Dwan; for TCF. 'Whether the theme fits into the popular groove is something to think about.'—*Variety*

One Million BC*

US 1940 80m bw
Hal Roach
GB title: *Man and His Mate*
aka: *The Cave Dwellers*

Life between warring tribes of primitive man in the stone age.
Impressive-looking but slow-moving grunt-and-groan epic originally based on D. W. Griffith's *Man's Genesis* and on which Griffith did some work. The totally unhistoric dinosaurs (which had disappeared long before man arrived) are impressively concocted by magnifying lizards.

w Mickell Novak, George Baker, Joseph Frickert *d* Hal Roach, Hal Roach Jnr, D. W. Griffith *ph* Norbert Brodine *m* Werner R. Heymann

Victor Mature, Carole Landis, Lon Chaney Jnr, John Hubbard, Nigel de Brulier, Conrad Nagel

AAN: Werner R. Heymann

'This is the way it was!'

One Million Years BC*

GB 1966 100m Technicolor
Hammer (Michael Carreras)

A vague remake of the above, with animated monsters. Not badly done, with some lively action.

w Michael Carreras *d* Don Chaffey *ph* Wilkie Cooper *m* Mario Nascimbene

John Richardson, Raquel Welch, Robert Brown, Percy Herbert, Martine Beswick

'Very easy to dismiss the film as a silly spectacle; but Hammer production finesse is much in evidence and Don Chaffey has done a competent job of direction. And it is all hugely enjoyable.'—*David Wilson*

● *Video: Thorn EMI*

One Minute to Zero

US 1952 105m bw
RKO (Edmund Grainger)

In Korea a US colonel is evacuating American civilians but is forced to bomb refugees.
Flat war film with Something To Say and the star at his most humourless.

w Milton Krims, William Haines *d* Tay Garnett *ph* William E. Snyder *m* Constantin Bakaleinikoff

Robert Mitchum, Ann Blyth, William Talman, Charles McGraw, Richard Egan

One More River*

US 1934 88m bw
Universal (James Whale)
GB title: *Over the River*

A wife runs away from her husband, and he sets detectives on her and her lover.
Old-fashioned, well made picturization of a novel.

w R. C. Sherriff, *novel* John Galsworthy *d* James Whale *ph* John Mescalle *m* W. Franke Harling

Colin Clive, Diana Wynyard, C. Aubrey Smith, Jane Wyatt, Lionel Atwill, Mrs Patrick Campbell, Frank Lawton, Reginald Denny, Henry Stephenson, Alan Mowbray, E. E. Clive

'Galsworthy beautifully transmuted to the screen . . . Very British and ultra, but should prove nice enough b.o.'—*Variety*

'Taste, elegance, narrative drive and a deliberate nostalgia for the Galsworthy period.'—*Peter John Dyer, 1966*

'One of the finest courtroom episodes ever projected on a screen.'—*Motion Picture Herald*

One More Spring*

US 1935 87m bw
Fox (Winfield Sheehan)

Three strangers, in reduced circumstances due to the Depression, meet in Central Park and pool their resources.
Topical serio-comedy which looks pretty dated but still serves as a summation of American mid-thirties attitudes.

w Edwin Burke, *novel* Robert Nathan *d* Henry King *ph* John Seitz *md* Arthur Lange

Janet Gaynor, Warner Baxter, Walter Woolf King, Grant Mitchell, Jane Darwell, Roger Imhof, John Qualen, Dick Foran, Stepin Fetchit

'Whimsical comedy with plenty of laughs. Should do well.'—*Variety*

One More Time

GB 1969 93m De Luxe
UA / Chrislaw–Tracemark (Milton Ebbins)

More crime-solving adventures of Salt and Pepper.
Even less funny than before; see *Salt and Pepper*.

w Michael Pertwee *d* Jerry Lewis *ph* Ernest Steward *m* Les Reed

Peter Lawford, Sammy Davis Jnr, Esther Anderson, Maggie Wright

One More Tomorrow*

US 1946 89m bw
Warner (Henry Blanke)

A wealthy playboy marries a left-wing photographer and buys up her magazine.
An interesting but dated play fails to come to life because neither cast nor director seem to understand what it's about.

w Charles Hoffman, Catherine Turney, Julius J. and Philip G. Epstein, *play* The Animal Kingdom by Philip Barry *d* Peter Godfrey *ph* Bert Glennon *d* Max Steiner

Ann Sheridan, Dennis Morgan, Jack Carson, Alexis Smith, Jane Wyman, Reginald Gardiner, John Loder, Marjorie Gateson

One More Train to Rob

US 1971 108m Technicolor
Universal (Robert Arthur)

A train robber comes out of prison and warily takes up with his old partners.
Undistinguished western which tries to be funny and serious at the same time.

w Don Tait, Dick Nelson *d* Andrew V. McLaglen *ph* Alric Edens *m* David Shire

George Peppard, Diana Muldaur, John Vernon, France Nuyen, Steve Sandor

One New York Night*

US 1935 80m bw
MGM (Bernard Hyman)
GB title: *The Trunk Mystery*

A young farmer in Manhattan on a visit finds a body in the hotel room next to his.
Slick comedy thriller very typical of its date and studio.

w Frank Davis *play* Edward Childs Carpenter *d* Jack Conway

Franchot Tone, Una Merkel, Steffi Duna, Conrad Nagel, Charles Starrett, Harold Huber

'Sprightly devised murder mystery accounting for plenty of laughs . . . studded with multiple touches of production value.'—*Variety*

'A comedy of astonishing intelligence and finish . . . it ought to take its place immediately with the classics.'—*Graham Greene*

One Night in Lisbon
US 1941 97m bw
Paramount (Edward H. Griffith)

During World War II an American flier falls for a British socialite who is being used by the government as a decoy for spies.
Flabby romantic comedy-drama which mostly wastes a good cast.
w Virginia Van Upp, *play* There's Always Juliet by John Van Druten *d* Edward H. Griffith *ph* Bert Glennon *m* Sigmund Krumgold

Madeleine Carroll, Fred MacMurray, Edmund Gwenn, Patricia Morison, Billie Burke, John Loder, Dame May Whitty, Reginald Denny, Billy Gilbert

One Night in the Tropics
US 1940 69m bw
Universal (Leonard Spiegelgass)

Holidays on a Caribbean island lead to a double wedding.
Very lightweight comedy-musical notable only for introducing Abbott and Costello.
w Gertrude Purcell, Charles Grayson, *play* Love Insurance by Earl Derr Biggers *d* A. Edward Sutherland *ph* Joseph Valentine *md* Charles Previn *songs* Oscar Hammerstein II, Jerome Kern, Otto Harbach, Dorothy Fields

Allan Jones, Nancy Kelly, Bud Abbott, Lou Costello, Robert Cummings, Leo Carillo, Peggy Moran, Mary Boland

One Night of Love**
US 1934 95m bw
Columbia (Harry Cohn)

An opera star rebels against her demanding teacher.
Light classical musical which was a surprising box office success and brought Hollywood careers for Lily Pons, Gladys Swarthout, Miliza Korjus, etc.
w Dorothy Speare, Charles Beahan, S. K. Lauren, James Gow, Edmund North *d* Victor Schertzinger *ph* Joseph Walker *songs* Victor Schertzinger, Gus Kahn *m* Louis Silvers *md* Pietro Cimini

Grace Moore, Tullio Carminati, Lyle Talbot, Mona Barrie, Nydia Westman, Jessie Ralph, Luis Alberni, Jane Darwell

AA: Victor Schertzinger, Gus Kahn (as songwriters)
AAN: best picture; direction; Louis Silvers; Grace Moore

One Night With You
GB 1948 92m bw

An English girl and an Italian tenor, stranded by a train failure, are taken for forgers.
Rather frantic but occasionally amusing Italian-set comedy. Nino Martini, Patricia Roc, Hugh Wakefield, Bonar Colleano, Guy

Middleton, Stanley Holloway, Irene Worth, Charles Goldner. Written by Caryl Brahms and S. J. Simon; directed by Terence Young; for Two Cities / Rank.

One of Our Aircraft Is Missing*
GB 1941 102m bw
British National (Michael Powell, Emeric Pressburger)

A bomber is grounded after a raid and its crew is helped by the Dutch resistance.
Efficient propaganda piece which starts vigorously but gets bogged down in talk.
wd Michael Powell, Emeric Pressburger *ph* Ronald Neame

Godfrey Tearle, Eric Portman, Hugh Williams, Bernard Miles, Hugh Burden, Emrys Jones, Googie Withers, Pamela Brown, Peter Ustinov, Joyce Redman, Hay Petrie, Robert Helpmann, Alec Clunes

AAN: script
● Video: BBC

One of Our Dinosaurs Is Missing*
US 1975 94m Technicolor
Walt Disney (Bill Walsh)

In the 1920s a strip of secret microfilm is smuggled out of China and hidden in a dinosaur's skeleton in the Natural History Museum.
Unexceptional family comedy with everyone trying hard; somehow it just misses, perhaps because it is told through talk rather than cinematic narrative.
w Bill Walsh, *novel* The Great Dinosaur Robbery by David Forrest *d* Robert Stevenson *ph* Paul Beeson *m* Ron Goodwin

Helen Hayes, Peter Ustinov, Derek Nimmo, Clive Revill, Joan Sims, Bernard Bresslaw, Roy Kinnear, Deryck Guyler, Richard Pearson
● Video: Disney

One Rainy Afternoon*
US 1935 79m bw

In a cinema one afternoon, a gigolo kisses the wrong girl. Rather heavy-handed light comedy with interesting credentials. Francis Lederer, Ida Lupino. Written by Stephen Morehouse Avery and Maurice Hanline from a play by Emeric Pressburger and René Pujal ; directed by Rowland V. Lee; for Pickford-Lasky.

One Summer Love
US 1976 97m colour Panavision

A young man leaves mental hospital for his Connecticut home, only to find everyone there nuttier than he is. Over-the-top melodrama. Beau Bridges, Susan Sarandon, Mildred Dunnock, Michael B. Miller. Written by N. Richard Nash; directed by Gilbert Cates; for AIP. (Aka: *Dragonfly*.)

One Sunday Afternoon**
US 1933 93m bw
Paramount (Louis D. Lighton)

In 1910, a Brooklyn dentist feels he has

married the wrong girl, but discovers that his choice was the right one.
Pleasant period comedy drama which was twice remade; as The Strawberry Blonde (qv) and see below.
w William Slavens McNutt, Grover Jones, *play* James Hagan *d* Stephen Roberts *ph* Victor Milner

Gary Cooper, Frances Fuller, Fay Wray, Neil Hamilton, Roscoe Karns
'Still pitched in stage tempo and unfolds haltingly.'—*Variety*

One Sunday Afternoon
US 1948 90m Technicolor
Warner (Jerry Wald)

Pleasant but undistinguished musical remake of the above.
w Robert L. Richards *d* Raoul Walsh *ph* Sid Hickox, Wilfrid M. Cline *md* Ray Heindorf *ad* Anton Grot

Dennis Morgan, Dorothy Malone, Janis Paige, Don Defore, Ben Blue
'A lackadaisical and uninspired jaunt down memory lane.'—*New Yorker, 1978*

The One That Got Away**
GB 1957 111m bw
Rank (Julian Wintle)

A German flier, Franz Von Werra, is captured and sent to various British prisoner-of-war camps, from all of which he escapes.
True-life biopic, developed in a number of suspense and action sequences, all very well done.
w Howard Clewes, book Kendal Burt, James Leasor *d* Roy Baker *ph* Eric Cross *m* Hubert Clifford

Hardy Kruger, Michael Goodliffe, Colin Gordon, *Alec McCowen*

One Third of a Nation*
US 1939 79m bw
Federal Theatre (Dudley Murphy)

A shopgirl persuades a landlord to tear down his dangerous slums and put up good buildings.
Naïve do-goodery, not too persuasively managed.
w Dudley Murphy, Oliver H. P. Garrett, *play* Arthur Arent *d* Dudley Murphy *ph* William Mellor

Sylvia Sidney, Leif Erickson, Myron McCormick, Hiram Sherman, Sidney Lumet, Percy Waram
'No worse and rather better than a commensurate modest-budgeter essayed on the coast . . . the cinematic transition however seems to have almost wholly ditched the Federal Housing "living newspaper" purpose of the stage version, emphasizing the boy-meets-girl premise against the shocking slum background.'—*Variety*

One Touch of Venus*
US 1948 82m bw
Universal / Lester Cowan

In a fashionable department store, a statue of Venus comes to life and falls for a window dresser.

Pleasant satirical comedy, watered down from the Broadway original.

w Harry Kurnitz, Frank Tashlin, *play* S. J. Perelman, Ogden Nash *d* William A. Seiter *ph* Franz Planer *songs* Kurt Weill *ad* Bernard Herzbrun, Emrich Nicholson

Ava Gardner, Robert Walker, Eve Arden, Dick Haymes, Olga San Juan, Tom Conway

● Video: Intervision

One, Two, Three***
US 1961 115m bw Panavision
United Artists / Mirisch / Pyramid (Billy Wilder)

An executive in West Berlin is trying to sell Coca Cola to the Russians while preventing his boss's daughter from marrying a communist.

Back to *Ninotchka* territory, but this time the tone is that of a wild farce which achieves fine momentum in stretches but also flags a lot in between, teetering the while on the edge of taste.

w Billy Wilder, I. A. L. Diamond, *play* Ferenc Molnar *d* Billy Wilder *ph* Daniel Fapp *m* André Previn

James Cagney, Horst Buchholz, Arlene Francis, Pamela Tiffin, Lilo Pulver, Howard St John, Leon Askin

'A sometimes bewildered, often wonderfully funny exercise in nonstop nuttiness.'—*Time*

'This first-class featherweight farce is a serious achievement.'—*Stanley Kauffmann*

AAN: Daniel Fapp

One Way Passage*
US 1932 69m bw
Warner (Robert Lord)

On an ocean voyage, a dying girl falls in love with a crook going home to face a life sentence.

Pattern melodrama which stood Hollywood in good stead.

w Wilson Mizner, Joseph Jackson, Robert Lord *d* Tay Garnett *ph* Robert Kurrie

William Powell, Kay Francis, Frank McHugh, Aline MacMahon, Warren Hymer, Herbert Mundin, Roscoe Karns, Stanley Fields

'Will reach house averages for this time of year.'—*Variety*

† Remade as *'Til We Meet Again* (qv).

AA: original story (Robert Lord)

One Way Pendulum
GB 1964 85m bw
UA / Woodfall (Michael Deeley)

A suburban clerk leads a dream existence; his son teaches speak-your-weight machines to sing, while he sets an imaginary murder trial in motion.

A nonsense play (which has many adherents) resists the literalness of the camera eye.

w N. F. Simpson, from his play *d* Peter Yates *ph* Denys Coop *m* Richard Rodney Bennett

Eric Sykes, George Cole, Peggy Mount, Alison Leggatt, Mona Washbourne

One Way Street
US 1950 79m bw
U-I / Leonard Goldstein (Sam Goldwyn Jnr)

A disillusioned doctor steals a fortune and hides out in a Mexican village, where he regains his self-respect.

Thin and pointless melodrama.

w Lawrence Kimble *d* Hugo Fregonese *ph* Maury Gertsman *m* Frank Skinner

James Mason, Marta Toren, Dan Duryea, William Conrad, King Donovan, Jack Elam

'It is reported that James Mason chooses his own parts, and if this is true I have to report that he is a glutton for punishment.'—*Daily Herald*

'One of the dullest, most stupid films of the year.'—*Sunday Pictorial*

One-Way Ticket
US 1935 66m bw

A convicted bank robber falls in love with the warden's daughter. Prison break drama which seems to be trying to make a point but is not sure what. Lloyd Nolan, Walter Connolly, Peggy Conklin, Edith Fellows, Nana Bryant, Thurston Hall. Written by Vincent Lawrence, Joseph Anthony, Oliver H. P. Garrett, Grover Jones, from a novel by Ethel Turner; directed by Herbert Biberman; for Columbia. 'It is "different" at the cost of credulity.'—*Variety*

One Wild Oat
GB 1951 78m bw

An old flame tries to blackmail a highly respectable solicitor. Modest film version of a popular West End farce. Robertson Hare, Stanley Holloway, Sam Costa, Andrew Crawford, Vera Pearce, Robert Moreton, Irene Handl. Written by Vernon Sylvaine and Lawrence Huntingdon, from the play by Vernon Sylvaine; directed by Charles Saunders; for Coronet / Eros.

Onibaba*
Japan 1964 104m bw Tohoscope
Kindai Eiga Kyokai / Tokyo Eiga
aka: The Hole

In medieval times on a remote marshy plain, mother and daughter live by killing stray soldiers and selling their armour, until daughter takes one for a lover and mother becomes jealous.

A kind of original horror legend is told by this strange, compelling piece with its frequent moments of nastiness. It remains, perhaps mercifully, unique.

wd Kaneto Shindo *ph* Kiyomi Juroda *m* Hikaru Hayashi

Nobuko Otowa, Jitsuko Yoshimura, Kei Sato

● Video: Intervision

The Onion Field
US 1979 126m Eastmancolor
Black Marble (Walter Coblenz)

Two policemen are shot at by a manic killer, and the one who survives finds that he is suspected of cowardice and has to resign from the force.

Well meaning but lumbering case history. The author must carry the blame, as for once the picture was made exactly on his terms.

w Joseph Wambaugh, from his novel *d* Harold Becker *ph* Charles Rosher *m* Eumir Depdato *pd* Brian Eatwell

John Savage, James Woods, Franklyn Seales, Ted Danson, Ronny Cox, David Huffman

● Video: Embassy

Onionhead
US 1958 110m bw
Warner (Jules Schermer)

Adventures of a ship's cook in the US Coastguard.

Service comedy that must have seemed funnier in the US than in Britain.

w Nelson Gidding, *novel* Weldon Hill *d* Norman Taurog *ph* Harold Rosson *md* Ray Heindorf

Andy Griffith, Felicia Farr, Walter Matthau, Erin O'Brien, Joe Mantell, Ray Danton, Roscoe Karns, James Gregory, Tige Andrews

† An attempt to cash in on the success of *No Time for Sergeants*.

'Romance as glorious as the towering Andes!'

Only Angels Have Wings**
US 1939 121m bw
Columbia (Howard Hawks)

Tension creeps into the relationships of the men who fly cargo planes over the Andes when a stranded showgirl sets her cap at the boss.

For an action film this is really too restricted by talk and cramped studio sets, and its theme was more entertainingly explored in *Red Dust*. Still, it couldn't be more typical of the Howard Hawks film world, where men are men and women have to be as tough as they are.

w Jules Furthman, *story* Howard Hawks *d* Howard Hawks *ph* Joseph Walker, Elmer Dyer *m* Dmitri Tiomkin *md* Morris Stoloff

Cary Grant, Jean Arthur, Rita Hayworth, Richard Barthelmess, Thomas Mitchell, Sig Rumann, Victor Kilian, John Carroll, Allyn Joslyn

'All these people did the best they could with what they were given—but look at it.'—*Otis Ferguson*

The Only Game in Town
US 1969 113m De Luxe
TCF (Fred Kohlmar)

A Las Vegas chorus girl and a piano player have an unhappy life because of his gambling fever.

Uninteresting two-header from a play that didn't make it; no light relief, no action, and not even very good acting.

w Frank D. Gilroy, from his play *d* George Stevens *ph* Henri Decaë *m* Maurice Jarre

Elizabeth Taylor, Warren Beatty, Charles Braswell, Hank Henry

'It epitomizes the disaster the studio and star systems foist on films . . . the only two-character tale around to cost $11 million.'— *Judith Crist*

† Frank Sinatra was originally cast but walked out after production started; Warren Beatty astonishingly chose to do this rather than *Butch Cassidy and the Sundance Kid*.

'They were six and they fought like six hundred!'

Only the Valiant
US 1950   105m   bw
William Cagney

A tough cavalry officer in a lonely fort wins a battle against Indians.
Standard top-of-the-bill western; competent but not very gripping.

w Edmund H. North, Harry Brown   *d* Gordon Douglas   *ph* Lionel Lindon   *m* Franz Waxman

Gregory Peck, Ward Bond, Gig Young, Lon Chaney Jnr, Barbara Payton, Neville Brand

Only Two Can Play°°°
GB 1962   106m   bw
British Lion / Vale (Launder and Gilliat)

A much married assistant librarian in a Welsh town has an abortive affair with a councillor's wife.
Well characterized and generally diverting 'realistic' comedy which slows up a bit towards the end but contains many memorable sequences and provides its star's last good character performance.

w Bryan Forbes, *novel* That Uncertain Feeling by *Kingsley Amis d Sidney Gilliat ph* John Wilcox *m* Richard Rodney Bennett *ad* Albert Witherick

Peter Sellers, Mai Zetterling, Virginia Maskell, Richard Attenborough, Raymond Huntley, John Le Mesurier, *Kenneth Griffith*

● *Video: Thorn EMI*

Only When I Larf°
GB 1968   103m   Eastmancolor
Paramount / Beecord (Len Deighton, Brian Duffy, Hugh Attwooll)

The adventures of three confidence tricksters. Quite likeable but unmemorable 'with it' comedy of the sixties; the tricks are more amusing than the characterization.

w John Salmon, *novel* Len Deighton *d* Basil Dearden *ph* Anthony Richmond *m* Ron Grainer

Richard Attenborough, David Hemmings, Alexandra Stewart, Nicholas Pennell, Melissa Stribling, Terence Alexander, Edric Connor, Calvin Lockhart, Clifton Jones

Only When I Laugh
US 1981   120m   Metrocolor
Columbia (Roger M. Rothstein, Neil Simon)
GB title: *It Hurts Only When I Laugh*

An alcoholic actress tries to rebuild her life. Last desperate fling (one hopes) of the Neil Simon industry, dispensing in this case more bitter tears than laughs, and generally failing to stay the course.

w Neil Simon, from his play The Gingerbread Lady *d* Glenn Jordan *ph* David M. Walsh *m* David Shire

Marsha Mason, Kristy McNichol, James Coco, Joan Hackett, David Dukes, John Bennett Perry

'One can almost hear the click of typewriter keys.'—*Geoff Brown, MFB*

AAN: Marsha Mason; James Coco (supporting actor); Joan Hackett (supporting actress)

Only Yesterday°
US 1933   105m   bw

An unmarried mother is seduced twice by the same man. One that Ross Hunter didn't get around to remaking . . . and a good job too.
Margaret Sullavan, John Boles, Billie Burke, Reginald Denny, Edna May Oliver, Benita Hume. Written by William Hurlbut, George O'Neill and Arthur Richman; directed by John M. Stahl; for Universal. 'The film needs little more praise than that it warrants its unusual length.'—*Variety*

† The original intention seems to have been to mirror recent history as in Frederick Lewis Allen's book of the same title.

Ooh, You Are Awful°
GB 1972   97m   Eastmancolor
British Lion / Quintain (E. M. Smedley Aston)
US title: *Get Charlie Tully*

A London con man seeks a fortune, the clue to which is tattooed on the behind of one of several girls.
Amusing star vehicle with plenty of room for impersonations and outrageous jokes.

w John Warren, John Singer *d* Cliff Owen *ph* Ernest Stewart *m* Christopher Gunning

Dick Emery, Derren Nesbitt, Ronald Fraser, Pat Coombs, William Franklyn, Brian Oulton, Norman Bird

● *Video: Thorn EMI*

Open City°°
Italy 1945   101m   bw
Minerva
original title: *Roma, Città Aperta*

Italian underground workers defy the Nazis in Rome towards the end of the war.
A vivid newsreel quality is achieved by this nerve-stretching melodrama in which all the background detail is as real as care could make it.

w Sergio Amidei, Federico Fellini *d* Roberto Rossellini *ph* Ubaldo Arata *m* Renzo Rossellini

Aldo Fabrizzi, *Anna Magnani*, Marcello Pagliero, Maria Michi

AAN: script

Open Season
US / Spain / Switzerland 1974   104m
Eastmancolor   Panavision
Impala / Arpa (George H. Brown, Jose S. Vicuna)

Three young criminals hunt human prey, but one of their victims takes his own revenge. Rough, flashy, violent melodrama which pretends to have something to say but in fact is merely sensationalist.

w David Osborn, Liz Charles Williams *d* Peter Collinson *ph* Fernando Arribas *m* Ruggero Cini

Peter Fonda, Cornelia Sharp, John Phillip Law, Richard Lynch, Albert Mendoza, William Holden

'An offensive, gamy potboiler.'—*Variety*
'Both patience and the plot line are severely strained by the artiness Collinson frequently indulges, with frozen shots to mark the moments of truth and a meaningless punctuation throughout of long shots, angles and flashes.'—*Tom Milne*

Opening Night
US 1978   144m   Metrocolor
Faces Distribution (Al Ruban)

A Broadway actress is on the point of a nervous breakdown.
Interminable addition to the director's list of unwatchable personal films.

wd John Cassavetes *ph* Al Ruban *m* Bo Horwood

Gena Rowlands, Ben Gazzara, John Cassavetes, Joan Blondell, Paul Stewart, Zohra Lampert, Laura Johnson

'Shrill, puzzling, depressing and overlong.'—*Variety*

L'Opéra de Quat' Sous see Die Dreigroschenoper

Operation Amsterdam°
GB 1958   104m   bw
Rank / Maurice Cowan

In 1940 spies are sent into Holland to prevent the invading Germans from finding Amsterdam's stock of industrial diamonds. Semi-documentary war adventure, well mounted and played.

w Michael McCarthy, John Eldridge, *book* Adventure in Diamonds by David Walker *d* Michael McCarthy *ph* Reg Wyer, *m* Philip Green

Peter Finch, Tony Britton, Eva Bartok, Alexander Knox, Malcolm Keen, Tim Turner, John Horsley, Melvyn Hayes, Christopher Rhodes

● *Video: Rank*

Operation Bullshine
GB 1959   84m   Technicolor

In 1942, complications ensue when an ATS private suspects her husband of infidelity. Flabby army comedy with a few laughs. Donald Sinden, Barbara Murray, Carole Lesley, Ronald Shiner, Naunton Wayne, Daniel Massey, Dora Bryan. Written by Anne Burnaby, Rupert Lang and Gilbert Gunn; directed by Gilbert Gunn; for ABPC.

Operation CIA

US 1965 90m bw

An agent is rushed to Saigon to find a secret message which was never delivered. Crude thick-ear with a few suspenseful moments.
Burt Reynolds, John Hoyt, Daniele Aubry, Kieu Chinh, Cyril Collick. Written by Bill S. Ballinger and Peer J. Oppenheimer; directed by Christian Nyby; for Allied Artists.

Operation Crossbow*

GB 1965 116m Metrocolor Panavision
MGM / Carlo Ponti
aka: *The Great Spy Mission*

In World War II, trained scientists are parachuted into Europe to destroy the Nazi rocket-making plant at Peenemunde.
Unlikely, star-packed war yarn with more passing tragedy than most, all obliterated by a shoot-em-up James Bond finale.

w Robert Imrie (Emeric Pressburger), Derry Quinn, Ray Rigby d Michael Anderson ph Erwin Hillier m Ron Goodwin

George Peppard, Tom Courtenay, John Mills, Sophia Loren, Lilli Palmer, Anthony Quayle, Patrick Wymark, Jeremy Kemp, Paul Henreid, Trevor Howard, Sylvia Sims, Richard Todd

Operation Daybreak

US 1975 119m Technicolor
Warner / Howard R. Schuster / American Allied (Carter de Haven)

In 1941, Czech patriots kill the hated Nazi Heydrich and are hunted down.
Curiously-timed evocation of wartime resistance adventures, too realistic for the squeamish and certainly not very entertaining despite a fair level of professionalism.

w Ronald Harwood, *novel* Seven Men at Daybreak by Alan Burgess d Lewis Gilbert ph Henri Decaë m David Hentschel

Timothy Bottoms, Martin Shaw, Joss Ackland, Nicola Pagett, Anthony Andrews, Anton Diffring, Carl Duering, Diana Coupland

Operation Eichmann

US 1961 94m bw

After the war, the Nazi who exterminated six million Jews escapes from Europe but is eventually recaptured. Crude exploitation item designed to cash in on Eichmann's trial, a documentary on which would have been much more interesting. Werner Klemperer (as Eichmann), Ruta Lee, Donald Buka, John Banner. Written by Lewis Copley; directed by R. G. Springsteen; for Allied Artists.

Operation Kid Brother

Italy 1967 105m Techniscope

007's brother defeats an international mastermind with the help of a Scottish archery team. Very elementary James Bond spoof, with a confusing array of old and new elements but less than the required minimum of style. Neil Connery (Sean's kid brother), Daniela Bianchi, Adolfo Celi, Bernard Lee,

Lois Maxwell, Agata Flori. Written by Paolo Levi, Vincenzo Mannino and Carlo Tritto; directed by Alberto de Martino; for Dario Sabatello. (Aka: *OK Connery*.) 'A grotesque parody of a parody . . . bad enough to be hysterically funny.'—*MFB*.

Operation Mad Ball*

US 1957 105m bw
Columbia (Jed Harris)

American troops in Normandy are forbidden to fraternize with nurses, but a clandestine dance is arranged.
Madcap army farce which keeps promising to be funnier than it is.

w Arthur Carter, Jed Harris, Blake Edwards, *play* Arthur Carter d Richard Quine ph Charles Lawton Jnr m George Duning

Jack Lemmon, Ernie Kovacs, Kathryn Grant, Mickey Rooney, James Darren, Arthur O'Connell

Operation Pacific

US 1950 109m bw
Warner (Louis F. Edelmann)

Adventures of a submarine commander in the Pacific war.
Routine war heroics, tolerably done but overstretched.

wd George Waggner ph Bert Glennon m Max Steiner

John Wayne, Patricia Neal, Ward Bond, Scott Forbes, Phil Carey, Paul Picerni, William Campbell, Martin Milner

Operation Petticoat*

US 1959 124m Eastmancolor
Universal / Granart (Robert Arthur)

During World War II, a crippled submarine is refloated by fair means and foul, and a party of nurses is taken aboard.
Flabby comedy with good moments, but not many.

w Stanley Shapiro, Maurice Richlin d Blake Edwards ph Russell Harlan m David Rose

Cary Grant, Tony Curtis, Joan O'Brien, Dina Merrill, Gene Evans, Arthur O'Connell, Richard Sargent

'Grant is a living lesson in getting laughs without lines.'—*Variety*

AAN: script

Operation St Peter's

Italy 1968 100m colour

Three thieves steal Michelangelo's Pietà and sell it for forty dollars to an American gangster. Rather surprisingly watchable comedy chase, with the star parodying his past roles. Edward G. Robinson, Lando Buzzanca, Heinz Ruhmann, Jean-Claude Brialy. Written by Ennio de Concini, Adriano Baracco, Roberto Gianviti and Lucio Fulci; directed by Lucio Fulci; for Turi Vasile / Paramount.

Operation Secret

US 1952 108m bw
Warner (Henry Blanke)

A traitor in the French resistance movement

shoots a colleague, and the wrong man is accused.
Belated World War II adventure which gives the impression of having been discarded by Errol Flynn.

w James R. Webb, Harold Medford d Lewis Seiler ph Ted McCord m Roy Webb

Cornel Wilde, Steve Cochran, Paul Picerni, Karl Malden

Operation Thunderbolt*

Israel 1977 117m Eastmancolor Panavision
GS Films (Menahem Golan, Yoram Globus)
aka: *Entebbe: Operation Thunderbolt*

An account of the rescue of Israeli hostages from terrorists who have hijacked their plane to Entebbe.
Victory at Entebbe and *Raid on Entebbe* were made with all-star casts for American television. This home-grown account of a famous deed is more modest yet more authoritative.

w Clarke Reynolds d Menahem Golan ph Adam Greenberg m Dov Seltzer

Klaus Kinski, Assaf Dayan, Ori Levy, Yehoram Geon, Mark Heath

Operator 13

US 1934 86m bw
MGM / Cosmopolitan (Lucien Hubbard)
GB title: *Spy 13*

During the Civil War an actress becomes a Union spy.
Elaborate period romance with action highlights.

w Harry Thew, Zelda Sears, Eve Greene d Richard Boleslawski ph George Folsey m William Axt

Marion Davies, Gary Cooper, Jean Parker, Katherine Alexander, Ted Healy, Russell Hardie, Henry Wadsworth, Douglass Dumbrille

'Will please generally . . . one of Davies' best.'—*Variety*

AAN: George Folsey

The Opposite Sex

US 1956 116m Metrocolor Cinemascope
MGM (Joe Pasternak)

A New York socialite divorces her unfaithful husband but finally takes him back.
Softened, musicalized version of *The Women* (qv); very patchy, shapeless, and not nearly sharp enough.

w Fay and Michael Kanin, *play* Clare Boothe d David Miller ph Robert Bronner m Nicholas Brodszky songs Nicholas Brodszky, Sammy Cahn

June Allyson, Dolores Gray, Joan Collins, Ann Sheridan, Agnes Moorehead, Joan Blondell, Barbara Jo Allen, Charlotte Greenwood

The Optimists of Nine Elms*
GB 1973   110m   Eastmancolor
Cheetah / Sagittarius (Adrian Gaye, Victor Lyndon)

Children of a London slum make friends with an old busker.
Gentle, sentimental, quite well-observed piece of wistful melancholia, falsified by its star performance.

wd Anthony Simmons, from his novel
co-w Tudor Gates ph Larry Pizer m George Martin

Peter Sellers, Donna Mullane, John Chaffey, David Daker, Marjorie Yates

The Oracle
GB 1952   83m   bw
Group Three (Colin Lesslie)

A reporter discovers that a village well in Ireland contains an oracle which can predict the future.
Weak sub-Ealing comedy which aims to please and gets a few laughs. All very British.

w Patrick Campbell d C. M. Pennington-Richards ph Wolfgang Suschitzky m Temple Abady

Robert Beatty, Virginia McKenna, Mervyn Johns, Gilbert Harding

Orca—Killer Whale
US 1977   92m   Technicolor   Panavision
Famous Films / Dino de Laurentiis (Luciano Vincenzoni)

Off Newfoundland, a killer whale takes revenge for its mate's death.
A rather unpleasant attempt to mix horror and thrills with ecology: not very entertaining, and not for the squeamish.

w Luciano Vincenzoni, Sergio Donati d Michael Anderson ph Ted Moore, J. Barry Herron m Ennio Morricone

Richard Harris, Charlotte Rampling, Will Sampson, Keenan Wynn
'The biggest load of cod imaginable.'—Philip Bergson, Sunday Times
'There are more thrills to be had in the average dolphinarium.'—Sight and Sound
● Video: Thorn EMI

Orchestra Wives**
US 1942   97m   bw
TCF (William Le Baron)

A small town girl marries the trumpet player of a travelling swing band.
Fresh and lively musical of its period, full of first-class music and amusing backstage backbiting.

w Karl Tunberg, Darrell Ware d Archie Mayo ph Lucien Ballard md Alfred Newman

Ann Rutherford, George Montgomery, Lynn Bari, Glenn Miller and his Orchestra, Carole Landis, Jackie Gleason, Cesar Romero
'A natural for any theatre that hasn't got an ironclad rule against jive.'—Hollywood Reporter

AAN: song 'I've Got a Girl in Kalamazoo' (m Harry Warren, ly Mack Gordon)

Orchids to You*
US 1935   74m   bw

A florist pulls several strokes to prevent an attorney from taking over her lease. Amusing comedy drama which failed through lack of strong names. John Boles, Jean Muir, Charles Butterworth, Ruthelma Stevens, Arthur Lake, Spring Byington. Written by William Hurlbut, Bartlett Cormack, Glenn Tryon, Howard Estabrook; directed by William A. Seiter; for Robert T. Kane / Fox. 'One of those productions that just misses the top rung.'—Variety

Orders Are Orders
GB 1954   78m   bw
Group 3 (Donald Taylor)

Flabby update of Orders Is Orders with an interesting cast below par.

w Donald Taylor, Geoffrey Orme d David Paltenghi ph Arthur Grant m Stanley Black

Peter Sellers, Brian Reece, Sid James, Tony Hancock, Margot Grahame, Raymond Huntley, Maureen Johnson, June Thorburn, Bill Fraser

Orders is Orders*
GB 1933   88m   bw
Gaumont British (Michael Balcon)

An army barracks is disrupted when an American film company gets permission to work there.
Breezy farce which pleased at the time.

w Leslie Arliss, Sidney Gilliat, play Ian Hay, Anthony Armstrong d Walter Forde ph Glen MacWilliams

Charlotte Greenwood, James Gleason, Cedric Hardwicke, Cyril Maude, Ian Hunter, Ray Milland, Jane Carr, Donald Calthrop, Eliot Makeham, Wally Patch, Finlay Currie
'A wow from start to finish.'—Variety

Orders to Kill*
GB 1958   111m   bw
British Lion / Lynx (Anthony Asquith, Anthony Havelock-Allan)

During World War II a bomber pilot undertakes a mission to parachute into occupied France and kill a double agent, who turns out afterwards to have been innocent.
Strong, hard-to-take but well made war story about the effect of war on conscience.

w Paul Dehn d Anthony Asquith ph Desmond Dickinson m Benjamin Frankel

Paul Massie, Irene Worth, James Robertson Justice, Leslie French, Eddie Albert, Lillian Gish, John Crawford, Jacques Brunius, Lionel Jeffries

Ordinary People**
US 1980   124m   Technicolor
Paramount / Wildwood (Ronald L. Schwary)

The eldest son of a well-heeled American family is drowned, and the survivors take stock and indulge in recriminations.

An actor's piece which on that level succeeds very well, and accurately pins down a certain species of modern American family.

w Alvin Sargent, novel Judith Guest d Robert Redford ph John Bailey m Marvin Hamlisch

Donald Sutherland, Mary Tyler Moore, Timothy Hutton, Judd Hirsch, Elizabeth McGovern, M. Emmet Walsh
'This is an academic exercise in catharsis: it's earnest, it means to improve people, and it lasts a lifetime.'—New Yorker

AA: best film; Alvin Sargent; Robert Redford; Timothy Hutton
AAN: Mary Tyler Moore; Judd Hirsch (supporting actor)
● Video: CIC

The Oregon Trail
US 1959   86m   De Luxe   Cinemascope

A New York reporter in 1846 is sent to cover a westward trek. Prototype settlers vs Indians western with all the expected incident. Fred MacMurray, William Bishop, Nina Shipman, Gloria Talbot, Henry Hull, John Carradine, Elizabeth Patterson. Written by Louis Vittes and Gene Fowler Jnr; directed by Gene Fowler Jnr; for TCF.

The Organization
US 1971   108m   De Luxe
UA / Mirisch (Walter Mirisch)

San Francisco policemen combat an international drug smuggling organization.
The third and weakest adventure of Virgil Tibbs, black policeman of In the Heat of the Night. Absolutely routine.

w James R. Webb d Don Medford ph Joseph Biroc m Gile Melle

Sidney Poitier, Barbara McNair, Sheree North, Gerald S. O'Loughlin

Orient Express*
US 1934   71m   bw

Various stories conflict on the Orient Express. Moderately successful multi-drama in the wake of Grand Hotel. Heather Angel, Ralph Morgan, Norman Foster, Herbert Mundin, Una O'Connor, Irene Ware, Dorothy Burgess. Written by Paul Martin, Carl Hovey, Oscar Levant, William Conselman, from the novel by Graham Greene; directed by Paul Martin; for Fox. 'Rather too much story all of a sudden; auditors may be lulled to quiet by the easy, non-exciting early action.'—Variety

'Can a woman love more than one man?'
Orphans of the Storm*
US 1921   124m (24 fps)   bw   silent
D. W. Griffith

Two sisters are caught up in the French revolution of 1789.
Half melodrama, half epic, this celebrated film survives chiefly by its careful attention to historical detail and by the excitement of its crowd scenes.

w D. W. Griffith, play Adolph Ennery d D. W. Griffith ph Henrick Sartov

ORDINARY PEOPLE. Mary Tyler Moore and Timothy Hutton triumph over adversity.

Lillian Gish, Dorothy Gish, Joseph
Schildkraut, Lucille La Verne, Morgan
Wallace, Frank Puglia, Creighton Hale
'There is scarcely a scene or an effect in the
entire production that is not beautiful to look
upon, and there is scarcely a moment that is
not charged with intense dramatic power.'—
Robert E. Sherwood, Life

Orphée***
France 1949 112m bw
André Paulvé 1 / Films du Palais Royal

Death, represented by a princess, falls in love
with Orpheus, a poet, and helps him when he
goes into hell in pursuit of his dead love.
Fascinating poetic fantasy which may have
been finally unintelligible but was filled to
overflowing with memorable scenes and
cinematic tricks, from the entry to the
hereafter through a mirror to intercepted code
messages such as 'L'oiseau compte avec ses
doigts'. The closest the cinema has got to
poetry.
w d Jean Cocteau, from his play ph Nicolas
Hayer m Georges Auric ad Jean d'Eaubonne
Jean Marais, François Périer, Maria Casarès,
Marie Déa, Edouard Dermithe, Juliette Greco
'It is a drama of the visible and the invisible
. . . I interwove many myths. Death condemns
herself in order to help the man she is duty
bound to destroy. The man is saved but Death
dies: it is the myth of immortality.'—Jean
Cocteau
† See the sequel Le Testament d'Orphée.

†† The film was dedicated to its designer
Christian Bérard (1902–49).
● Video: Thorn EMI

The Oscar*
US 1966 118m Pathecolor
Paramount / Greene-Rouse (Russel Rouse)
On the night of the Academy Awards his
friend recalls a heel's rise to stardom.
Squalid, sensationalist account of Hollywood
mores; one hopes it isn't quite true.
w Harlan Ellison, Russel Rouse, Clarence
Greene, novel Richard Sale d Russel Rouse
ph Joseph Ruttenberg m Percy Faith
Stephen Boyd, Elke Sommer, Tony Bennett,
Eleanor Parker, Milton Berle, Joseph Cotten,
Jill St John, Edie Adams, Ernest Borgnine,
Ed Begley, Walter Brennan, Broderick
Crawford, James Dunn, Peter Lawford, Edith
Head, Hedda Hopper, Merle Oberon, Bob
Hope, Frank Sinatra
'This is the sort of film that only Hollywood
could make, and on that level it is
preposterously enjoyable.'—David Wilson
'That true movie rarity—a picture that
attains a perfection of ineptitude quite beyond
the power of words to describe.'—Richard
Schickel

Oscar Wilde**
GB 1959 96m bw
Vantage (William Kirby)
Scandal strikes Oscar Wilde through his

involvement with Lord Alfred Douglas.
Competent, well acted version of well-known
events of the nineties, with Morley in his
original stage role; generally more satisfactory
than The Trials of Oscar Wilde which was shot
simultaneously.
w Jo Eisinger d Gregory Ratoff ph Georges
Périnal m Kenneth V. Jones
Robert Morley, John Neville, Phyllis Calvert,
Ralph Richardson, Dennis Price, Alexander
Knox, Edward Chapman, Martin Benson,
Robert Harris, Henry Oscar, William Devlin

O'Shaughnessy's Boy
US 1935 88m bw

A circus performer is reunited with the son his
wife took away in childhood. Shameless
sentiment which failed to repeat for its stars
the success of The Champ. Wallace Beery,
Jackie Cooper, Leona Maricle, Sara Haden,
Henry Stephenson, Spanky MacFarland.
Written by Leonard Praskins and Otis Garrett;
directed by Richard Boleslawski; for MGM.
'Far too much crying. Good production will
help.'—Variety

Ossessione*
Italy 1942 135m bw
ICI
A wanderer falls for the wife of an innkeeper
and they murder him, but fate takes a hand.
Unofficial remake of The Postman Always
Rings Twice, barely released outside Italy. A
powerful melodrama credited with starting the
neo-realist school.
w Antonio Pietrangeli, Giuseppe de Santis,
Gianni Puccini, Luchino Visconti, Mario
Alicata d Luchino Visconti ph Aldo Tonti,
Domenico Scala m Giuseppe Rosati
Massimo Girotti, Clara Calamai, Elio
Marcuzzo
† Other versions: Le Dernier Tournant
(France 1939); The Postman Always Rings
Twice (US 1945).

The Osterman Weekend
US 1983 102m De Luxe
A CIA chief tries to convince a powerful TV
journalist that several of his trusted informants
are Soviet agents. Convoluted bloodbath with
absolutely nothing new in its locker. Rutger
Hauer, John Hurt, Burt Lancaster, Craig T.
Nelson, Dennis Hopper, Chris Sarandon, Meg
Foster, Helen Shaver. Written by Alan Sharp,
Ian Masters, from the novel by Robert
Ludlum; directed by Sam Peckinpah; for
Davis-Panzer / Fox. 'A competent,
professional, but thoroughly impersonal
meller.'—Variety

Othello*
US / France 1951 91m bw
Mercury / Films Marceau (Orson Welles)
Shakespeare's play as rearranged by Orson
Welles at the start of his European
wanderings; modest budget, flashes of
brilliance, poor technical quality, variable
acting. Not really the best way to film
Shakespeare.

w Orson Welles, *play* William Shakespeare
d Orson Welles *ad* Alexander Trauner
ph Anchise Brizzi, George Fanto, Obadan
Troania, Roberto Fusi, G. Araldo
m Francesco Lavagnino, Alberto Barberis

Orson Welles, Micheal MacLiammoir, Fay
Compton, Robert Cook, Suzanne Cloutier,
Michael Laurence, Hilton Edwards, Doris
Dowling

Othello*
GB 1965   166m   Technicolor
  Panavision
BHE (Richard Godwin)

A record of the National Theatre production,
disappointing in terms of cinema but a
valuable record of a famous performance.

d Stuart Burge *ph* Geoffrey Unsworth
md Richard Hampton

Laurence Olivier, Frank Finlay, Joyce
Redman, Maggie Smith, Derek Jacobi, Robert
Lang, Anthony Nicholls

AAN: Laurence Olivier; Frank Finlay; Joyce
Redman; Maggie Smith

● *Video: Rank*

The Other*
US 1972   100m   De Luxe
TCF / Rex-Benchmark (Tom Tryon)

A boy insists that his dead twin is responsible
for several unexplained deaths.
Subtle family ghost story for intellectuals; a bit
pretentious and restrained for popular success.

w Tom Tryon, from his novel *d* Robert
Mulligan *ph* Robert Surtees *m* Jerry
Goldsmith *pd* Albert Brenner

Uta Hagen, Diana Muldaur, Chris Connelly,
Victor French

'Her every exciting moment was an
unforgettable experience!'
The Other Love
US 1947   96m   bw
Enterprise (David Lewis)

At a Swiss sanatorium, a lady concert pianist
who is dying falls in love with her doctor.
Fairly icky 'woman's picture' with
uncomfortable performances.

w Ladislas Fodor, Harry Brown, *story* Erich
Maria Remarque *d* André de Toth *ph* Victor
Milner *m* Miklos Rozsa

Barbara Stanwyck, David Niven, Richard
Conte, Gilbert Roland, Joan Lorring, Lenore
Aubert

Other Men's Women
US 1931   70m   bw

A train driver falls for his partner's wife.
Stilted heavy-breathing melodrama. Grant
Withers, James Cagney, Mary Astor, Joan
Blondell, Regis Toomey. Written by William
K. Wells; directed by William A. Wellman;
for Warner. 'Good railroad melo for the lesser
run theatres.'—*Variety*

'The romance of passion and power!'
The Other Side of Midnight
US 1977   166m   De Luxe   Panavision
TCF / Frank Yablans, Martin Ransohoff
  (Howard W. Koch Jnr)

Before and after World War II a young
Parisienne courts an American flyer, but her
tycoon husband eventually exacts a grim
revenge on both of them.
Turgid and interminable adaptation of a bestseller, with no likeable characters and several
unpleasant sequences.

w Herman Raucher, Daniel Taradash,
novel Sidney Sheldon *d* Charles Jarrott
ph Fred J. Koenekamp *m* Michel Legrand
pd John De Cuir

Marie-France Pisier, John Beck, Susan
Sarandon, Raf Vallone, Clu Gulager,
Christian Marquand

  'After 166 minutes the feeling that one has
actually lived through it all is a little too real
for comfort.'—*David Badder, MFB*
  'A fatuous, money-spinning film from the
fatuous, money-spinning book.'—*New Yorker*
  'Right down to the nonsense title, this epic
of schlock restores the era of *Now Voyager*
. . . the movie equivalent of a good bad
read.'—*Time Out*

● *Video: CBS / Fox*

'Once in your life—may someone love you
like this!'
The Other Side of the Mountain
US 1975   102m   Technicolor
Universal / Filmways / Larry Peerce
  (Edward S. Feldman)
GB title: *A Window to the Sky*

A girl skiing champion is paralysed by polio.
Maudlin tearjerker based on a real case;
altogether too much of a good thing.

w David Seltzer, *book* A Long Way Up by E.
G. Valens *d* Larry Peerce *ph* David M.
Walsh *m* Charles Fox

Marilyn Hassett, Beau Bridges, Belinda
Montgomery, Nan Martin, William Bryant,
Dabney Coleman

AAN: song 'Richard's Window' (*m* Charles
Fox, *ly* Norman Gimbel)

'For everyone who believes in happy
endings!'
**The Other Side of the Mountain Part
Two**
US 1977   99m   Technicolor
Universal / Filmways (Edward S. Feldman)

Crippled skier Jill Kinmont becomes a teacher
and falls in love again.
More true-life weepie material spun out from
the first successful film; the sequel is quickly
forgettable.

w Douglas Day Stewart *d* Larry Peerce
ph Ric Waite *m* Lee Holdridge

Marilyn Hassett, Timothy Bottoms, Nan
Martin, Belinda J. Montgomery

Otley**
GB 1968   91m   Technicolor
Columbia / Open Road (Bruce Cohn Curtis)

An inoffensive Londoner falls in with spies
and murderers.

Semi-spoof comedy thriller taking in James
Bondery and the swinging London set.
Generally pretty funny, but not entirely
certain of its own motives.

w Ian La Frenais, Dick Clement, *novel* Martin
Waddell *d* Dick Clement *ph* Austin
Dempster *m* Stanley Myers

Tom Courtenay, Romy Schneider, Alan
Badel, James Villiers, Leonard Rossiter,
Freddie Jones, James Bolam, Fiona Lewis

Our Betters*
US 1933   83m   bw
RKO (David O. Selznick)

An American woman in London finds her
titled husband is unfaithful and sets about
causing society scandals.
Dimly adapted West End success makes an
interesting but unamusing film.

w Jane Murfin, Harry Wagstaff Gribble, *play*
W. Somerset Maugham *d* George Cukor
ph Charles Rosher *md* Max Steiner

Constance Bennett, Violet Kemble Cooper,
Alan Mowbray, Gilbert Roland, Phoebe
Foster, Charles Starrett, Grant Mitchell, Anita
Louise, Minor Watson, Hugh Sinclair

  'It's all very English and so sophisticated
. . . they will really have to go for Constance
Bennett to go for this picture.'—*Variety*
  'One of those familiar dreams of high life in
which we are asked to admire even while we
condemn the superb immorality of our almost
godlike betters.'—*The Times*

Our Blushing Brides see Our Dancing
Daughters

Our Daily Bread*
US 1934   80m   bw
(UA) Viking / King Vidor

A young couple in the Depression inherit a
broken-down farm and make it work.
A rather drab sequel to *The Crowd*, with an
irrigation ditch finale in clear imitation of
Eisenstein.

w Elizabeth Hill, *story* King Vidor *d* King
Vidor *ph* Robert Planck *m* Alfred Newman

Karen Morley, Tom Keene, John Qualen,
Barbara Pepper, Addison Richards

  'Regardless of the scepticism on the matter
of box office, and its chances seem thin, it
ranks as a fine effort.'—*Variety*
  'With the arrival of the ditchdigging
sequence, all that has gone before seems but
buildup for this compelling climax.'—*Eileen
Bowser, Film Notes, 1969*
† Vidor so desperately wanted to make the
film that, discovering its theme to be
unpopular with sponsors, he pawned
everything he owned to finance it.

Our Dancing Daughters*
US 1928   86m approx (24 fps)   bw
  silent
MGM / Cosmopolitan (Hunt Stromberg)

A wild young socialite knows when to stop,
and makes a good marriage; her friend doesn't
and falls to her death while drunk.

Mild exploitation piece of its time which swept Joan Crawford to stardom after her dance in her underwear.

w Josephine Lovett d Harry Beaumont
ph George Barnes

Joan Crawford, Johnny Mack Brown, Dorothy Sebastian, Anita Page, Nils Asther
† Sequels: *Our Modern Maidens* (silent, 1929) with JC, Rod La Rocque, Douglas Fairbanks Jnr, Anita Page, w Josephine Lovett; *Our Blushing Brides* (sound, 1930) with JC, Robert Montgomery, Anita Page, Dorothy Sebastian, Raymond Hackett, w Bess Meredyth and John Howard Lawson. Neither was remarkable.
AAN: Josephine Lovett; George Barnes.

Our Fighting Navy
GB 1937 75m bw

In South America, a British naval captain saves the consul's daughter from a revolutionary. Tuppenny blood heroics, unconvincingly staged. Robert Douglas, H. B. Warner, Noah Beery, Richard Cromwell, Hazel Terry, Esme Percy. Written by 'Bartimeus', Guy Pollock, H. T. Bishop, Gerald Elliott and Harrison Owens; directed by Norman Walker; for Herbert Wilcox. (US title: *Torpedoed*.)

Our Girl Friday
GB 1953 87m Eastmancolor

Four shipwrecked survivors are washed up on a desert island. Coy sex comedy for the family; pretty unbearable. Kenneth More, Joan Collins, George Cole, Robertson Hare, Hermione Gingold, Walter Fitzgerald. Written and directed by Noel Langley; for Renown.

Our Hearts Were Young and Gay*
US 1944 81m bw
Paramount (Sheridan Gibney)

Two well-to-do flappers of the twenties find fun and romance in Paris.
A pleasant, undemanding piece of nostalgia based on a popular biography; in 1946 a less successful sequel, *Our Hearts Were Growing Up*, involved the young ladies with bootleggers at Princeton.

w Sheridan Gibney, *book* Cornelia Otis Skinner, Emily Kimbrough d Lewis Allen
ph Theodor Sparkuhl m Werner Heymann

Gail Russell, Diana Lynn, Charles Ruggles, Dorothy Gish, Beulah Bondi, James Brown, Bill Edwards, Jean Heather

Our Hospitality**
US 1923 70m approx (24 fps) bw
silent
Metro / Buster Keaton (Joseph M. Schenck)

Around 1850, a southerner returns home to claim his bride and finds himself in the middle of a blood feud.
Charming rather than hilarious star comedy with a splendid ancient train and at least one incredible stunt by the star.

w Jean Havez, Joseph Mitchell, Clyde Bruckman d Buster Keaton, Jack Blystone
ph Elgin Lessley, Gordon Jennings

Buster Keaton, Natalie Talmadge, Joe Keaton, Buster Keaton Jnr

Our Leading Citizen
US 1939 87m bw

A philosophical lawman tries to deal with labour unrest in his community. Another attempt to make a star out of a character who appealed only in rural districts. Bob Burns, Susan Hayward, Joseph Allen, Charles Bickford, Elizabeth Patterson, Clarence Kolb, Paul Guilfoyle. Written by John C. Moffitt from stories by Irvin S. Cobb; directed by Alfred Santell; for George Arthur / Paramount. 'Confusing and burdensome script . . . programme supporter.'—*Variety*

Our Little Girl
US 1935 63m bw
TCF (Edward Butcher)

A doctor's daughter brings her parents together.
One of the child star's thinner and more sentimental vehicles.

w Stephen Morehouse Avery, Allen Rivkin, Jack Yellen, *story* Heaven's Gate by Florence Leighton Pfalzgraf d John Robertson
ph John Seitz md Oscar Bradley

Shirley Temple, Joel McCrea, Rosemary Ames, Lyle Talbot, Erin O'Brien-Moore
  'She should easily satisfy her following and assure business.'—*Variety*

Our Man Flint*
US 1965 108m De Luxe Cinemascope
TCF (Saul David)

An American secret agent and super stud fights an organization bent on controlling the world through its weather.
Comic strip imitation of James Bond; in its wild way the first instalment scored a good many laughs, but the sequel, *In Like Flint* (qv), quickly ended the series.

w Hal Fimberg, Ben Starr d Daniel Mann
ph Daniel L. Fapp m Jerry Goldsmith

James Coburn, Lee J. Cobb, Gila Golan, Edward Mulhare, Benson Fong, Sigrid Valdis
  'Despite the fact that everyone from designers to actors seems to be having a ball, the film somehow goes over the edge of parody—ultimately it looks suspiciously like a case of wish-fulfilment.'—*John Gillett*

● *Video: CBS / Fox*

Our Man in Havana*
GB 1959 112m bw Cinemascope
Columbia / Kingsmead (Carol Reed)

A British vacuum cleaner salesman in Havana allows himself to be recruited as a spy, and wishes he hadn't.
The wry flavour of the novel does not really translate to the screen, and especially not to the wide screen, but a few lines and characters offer compensation.

w Graham Greene, from his novel d Carol Reed ph Oswald Morris m Hermanos Deniz Cuban Rhythm Band

Alec Guinness, *Noel Coward*, Burl Ives, Maureen O'Hara, Ernie Kovacs, *Ralph Richardson*, Jo Morrow, Paul Rogers, Grégoire Aslan, Duncan Macrae
  'The main weakness is the absence of economic, expressive cutting and visual flow. As a result . . . stretches of dialogue become tedious to watch; and the essential awareness of the writer's shifting tensions yields disappointingly to the easier mannerisms of any conventional comedy-thriller.'—*Peter John Dyer*

Our Miss Brooks
US 1955 85m bw

A lady teacher finds that the professor to whom she is engaged is tied to mother's apron strings. Verbose comedy considerably less funny than the TV series from which it was spun off. Eve Arden, Gale Gordon, Robert Rockwell, Don Porter, Jane Morgan, Richard Crenna, Nick Adams. Written by Al Lewis and Joseph Quillan; directed by Al Lewis; for Warner.

Our Miss Fred*
GB 1972 96m Technicolor
EMI / Willis World Wide (Josephine Douglas)

In World War II France, an actor escapes in women's clothes when his troupe is captured by the Nazis.
A carefully nurtured vehicle for Britain's top female impersonator somehow doesn't come off; celluloid both constrains his range and reveals his inadequacies.

w Hugh Leonard d Bob Kellett ph Dick Bush m Peter Greenwell

Danny La Rue, Alfred Marks, Lance Percival, Lally Bowers, Frances de la Tour, Walter Gotell

Our Modern Maidens see Our Dancing Daughters

Our Mother's House*
GB 1967 105m Metrocolor
MGM / Filmways (Jack Clayton)

When mother dies, seven children, who don't want to go to an orphanage, bury her in the garden. Then their ne'er-do-well father turns up.
Unpleasant and rather boring melodrama, too silly to have much dramatic impact.

w Jeremy Brooks, Haya Harareet, *novel* Julian Gloag d Jack Clayton ph Larry Pizer
m Georges Delerue

Dirk Bogarde, Margaret Brooks, Pamela Franklin, Mark Lester, Yootha Joyce, Anthony Nicholls
  'The children begin to display an alarming variety of accents . . . and when Dirk Bogarde enters, doing a rich Bill Sykes act as the long lost wicked father to a predominantly genteel family, the whole structure collapses.'—*Tom Milne*

Our Neighbours the Carters
US 1939   85m   bw

A small-town pharmacist is so poor that he
considers an offer from a wealthy friend to
adopt one of his children. A small-town saga
of smiles and tears, much appreciated at the
time. Frank Craven, Genevieve Tobin,
Edmund Lowe. Written by S. K. Lauren and
Renaud Hoffman; directed by Ralph Murphy;
for Paramount. 'Neatly set up as a
programmer for the family trade.'—*Variety*

Our Relations***
US 1936   65m   bw
Hal Roach / Stan Laurel Productions

Two sailors entrusted with a diamond ring get
mixed up with their long lost and happily
married twin brothers.
A fast-moving comedy which contains some of
Laurel and Hardy's most polished work as well
as being their most satisfying production.

w Richard Connell, Felix Adler, Charles
Roger, Jack Jevne, *story* The Money Box by
W. W. Jacobs *d* Harry Lachman *ph* Rudolph
Maté

Stan Laurel, Oliver Hardy, James Finlayson,
Alan Hale, Sidney Toler, Daphne Pollard, Iris
Adrian, Noel Madison, Ralf Harolde, *Arthur
Housman*

'The story of a love affair that lasted a
    lifetime!'
Our Town**
US 1940   90m   bw
Principal Artists / Sol Lesser

Birth, life and death in a small New
Hampshire community.
One of the main points of the play, the
absence of scenery, is abandoned in this screen
version, and the graveyard scene has to be
presented as a dream, but the film retains the
narrator and manages to make points of its
own while absorbing the endearing qualities
which made the play a classic.

w Thornton Wilder, Frank Craven, Harry
Chantlee, *play* Thornton Wilder *d* Sam
Wood *ph* Bert Glennon *m* Aaron Copland
pd William Cameron Menzies

*Frank Craven, William Holden, Martha Scott,
Thomas Mitchell, Fay Bainter, Guy Kibbee,
Beulah Bondi,* Stuart Erwin
    'You can nearly smell things cooking, and
feel the night air.'—*Otis Ferguson*

AAN: best picture; Aaron Copland; Martha
Scott

Our Very Own
US 1950   93m   bw
Samuel Goldwyn

A girl is shocked to discover that she is
adopted.
Another Goldwyn foray into chintzy, middle-
class, small-town America, but not a winning
example.

w F. Hugh Herbert *d* David Miller *ph* Lee
Garmes *m* Victor Young *ad* Richard Day

Ann Blyth, Farley Granger, Joan Evans, Jane
Wyatt, Ann Dvorak, Donald Cook, Natalie
Wood, Gus Schilling, Phyllis Kirk

Our Vines Have Tender Grapes*
US 1945   105m   bw
MGM (Robert Sisk)

Life in a Norwegian farm community in
southern Wisconsin.
Unexceptional family picture produced in
MGM's best manner.

w Dalton Trumbo, *novel* George Victor
Martin *d* Roy Rowland *ph* Robert Surtees
m Bronislau Kaper

Edward G. Robinson, Margaret O'Brien,
James Craig, Agnes Moorehead, Jackie
'Butch' Jenkins, Morris Carnovsky, Frances
Gifford, Sara Haden

Our Wife*
US 1931   20m   bw

Stan helps Ollie to elope. Good standard star
comedy with a rather disappointing third
sequence as three people try to get into a car
designed for one. Laurel and Hardy, James
Finlayson, Jean London. Written by H. M.
Walker; directed by James W. Horne; for Hal
Roach.

Our Wife
US 1941   95m   bw
Columbia (John M. Stahl)

A composer is romantically torn between a
lady scientist and his own ex-wife.
Middling romantic comedy of a kind very
familiar at the time.

w P. J. Wolfson, *play* Lillian Day by Lyon
Mearson *d* John M. Stahl *ph* Franz Planer
m Leo Shuken

Melvyn Douglas, Ruth Hussey, Ellen Drew,
Charles Coburn, John Hubbard, Harvey
Stephens

Ourselves Alone
GB 1936   87m   bw

An Irish colleen has a brother in the IRA and
a lover in the British Army. Rather tired
hawking of a theme already treated in *Beloved
Enemy*. Written by Dudley Leslie, Marjorie
Jeans, Dennis Johnston from the play by
Dudley Sturrock and Noel Scott; directed by
Brian Desmond Hurst; for British
International. 'Will find tough sledding
because of the subject matter.'—*Variety*

Out of Season*
GB 1975   90m   Technicolor
EMI / Lorimar (Robert Enders, Merv
    Adelson)

One winter in an English seaside resort, an old
love is rekindled.
Restrained sexual fireworks in the old French
manner, well enough done with excellent
atmosphere but a shade overlong and marred
by the need to indulge in modern tricks such
as a deliberately ambiguous ending.

w Reuben Bercovitch, Eric Bercovici *d* Alan
Bridges *ph* Arthur Ibbetson *m* John
Cameron

Cliff Robertson, Vanessa Redgrave, Susan
George, Edward Evans

● *Video: RCA / Columbia*

Out of the Blue
GB 1931   88m   bw

An aristocrat's daughter loves the radio singer
who is engaged to her sister. Dated frou-frou
with interesting talent. Jessie Matthews, Gene
Gerrard, Kay Hammond, Kenneth Kove,
Binnie Barnes. Written by R. P. Weston,
Frank Miller and Bert Lee, from the play
Little Tommy Tucker by Caswell Garth and
Desmond Carter; directed by Gene Gerrard
and John Orton; for BIP.

Out of the Blue
US 1947   86m   bw

A Greenwich village artist thinks a girl who
has passed out in his apartment is dead, and
tries to hide the body. Tasteless and very
unfunny farce. George Brent, Carole Landis,
Ann Dvorak, Turhan Bey, Virginia Mayo,
Elizabeth Patterson, Julia Dean, Richard
Lane. Written by Vera Caspary, Walter
Bullock and Edward Eliscu; directed by Leigh
Jason; for Eagle Lion.

Out of the Clouds*
GB 1954   88m   Eastmancolor
Ealing (Michael Relph, Basil Dearden)

Several personal stories mesh against a
background of London airport during a fog.
A dull compendium of stories with a
background of documentary detail which is
now fascinating because it's so dated.

w John Eldridge, Michael Relph *d* Michael
Relph, Basil Dearden *ph* Paul Beeson
m Richard Addinsell

Anthony Steel, Robert Beatty, David Knight,
Margo Lorenz, James Robertson Justice,
Eunice Gayson, Isabel Dean, Gordon Harker,
Bernard Lee, Michael Howard, Marie Lohr,
Esme Cannon, Abraham Sofaer
    'The film relies considerably on small-time
players and marginal incidents; the detail,
however, never looks like adding up to a
satisfactory whole.'—*Penelope Houston*

Out of the Fog*
US 1941   86m   bw
Warner (Henry Blanke)

Gangsters move in to terrorize an innocent
Brooklyn family.
Standard exploration of a situation which
became routine.

w Robert Rossen, Jerry Wald, Richard
Macaulay, *play* The Gentle People by Irwin
Shaw *d* Anatole Litvak *ph* James Wong
Howe

Ida Lupino, John Garfield, Thomas Mitchell,
Eddie Albert, George Tobias, Aline
MacMahon, Jerome Cowan, John Qualen,
Leo Gorcey

'You're no good and neither am I. We deserve each other!'

Out of the Past••
US 1947 97m bw
RKO (Warren Duff)
GB title: *Build My Gallows High*

A private detective is hired by a hoodlum to find his homicidal girl friend; he does, and falls in love with her.
Moody *film noir* with Hollywood imitating French models; plenty of snarling and a death-strewn climax.

w Geoffrey Homes, from his novel Build My Gallows High *d* Jacques Tourneur *ph* Nicholas Musuraca *m* Roy Webb

Robert Mitchum, Jane Greer, Kirk Douglas, Rhonda Fleming, Richard Webb, Steve Brodie, Virginia Huston, Dickie Moore
'Is this not an outcrop of the national masochism induced by a quite aimless, newly industrialized society proceeding rapidly on its way to nowhere?'—*Richard Winnington*
'Mitchum is so sleepily self-confident with the women that when he slopes into clinches you expect him to snore in their faces.'—*James Agee*

● Video: Kingston

'The laugh-a-minute lowdown on the birth of swoon!'
Out of this World
US 1945 96m bw
Paramount (Sam Coslow)

A Western Union messenger becomes a hit crooner and a national phenomenon.
Very mild comedy with the gimmick that Bing Crosby dubbed the singing.

w Walter de Leon, Arthur Phillips *d* Hal Walker *ph* Stuart Thompson *m* Victor Young

Eddie Bracken, Veronica Lake, Diana Lynn, Cass Daley, Parkyakarkus, Donald MacBride, Florence Bates, Carmen Cavallero

The Out of Towners•
US 1970 98m Movielab
Paramount / Jalem (Paul Nathan)

An executive and his wife fly into New York for an interview, but their encounter with the city is a mounting series of traumatic disasters.
A love-hate relationship with a city demonstrated by a resident is something of an in-joke and becomes increasingly hysterical and unsympathetic, but there are bright moments in this company.

w Neil Simon *d* Arthur Hiller *ph* Andrew Laszlo *m* Quincy Jones

Jack Lemmon, Sandy Dennis

Outback•
Australia 1970 109m Technicolor
NIT / Group W (George Willoughby)

A young teacher becomes involved in the rougher side of life in a remote Australian village.
A convincingly brutal picture of a community whose interests range from homosexuality to a bloody kangaroo hunt.

w Evan Jones, *novel* Wake in Fright by Kenneth Cook *d* Ted Kotcheff *ph* Brian West *m* John Scott

Gary Bond, Donald Pleasence, Chips Rafferty

Outcast Lady
US 1934 79m bw

A spoilt rich girl goes from man to man but helps her drunken brother. Modest remake of the Garbo vehicle *A Woman of Affairs*.
Constance Bennett, Hugh Williams, Mrs Patrick Campbell, Elizabeth Allan, Henry Stephenson, Leo G. Carroll. Written by Zoe Akins, from the novel *The Green Hat* by Michael Arlen; directed by Robert Z. Leonard; for MGM. (GB title: *A Woman of the World*.)

'Even her love was primitive!'
An Outcast of the Islands••
GB 1951 102m bw
London Films (Carol Reed)

A shiftless trader finds a secret Far Eastern trading post where he can be happy – but even here he becomes an outcast.
An interesting but not wholly successful attempt to dramatize a complex character study. It looks great and is well acted.

w William Fairchild, *novel* Joseph Conrad *d* Carol Reed *ph* John Wilcox *m* Brian Easdale

Trevor Howard, Ralph Richardson, Kerima, Robert Morley, Wendy Hiller, George Coulouris, Frederick Valk, Wilfrid Hyde White, Betty Ann Davies
'The script is so overwhelmed by the narrative itself that the characters and relationships fail to crystallize . . . while the handling is often intelligent, ingenious, and has its effective moments, no real conception emerges.'—*Gavin Lambert*
'Its sordidness is not veneered by the usual lyricism of Hollywood.'—*London Evening News*
'The most powerful film ever made in this country.'—*Observer*

The Outcasts of Poker Flat
US 1937 68m bw
RKO (Robert Sisk)

Four undesirables are run out of town and stuck in a mountain cabin during a snowstorm.
Overstretched anecdote with a predictably downbeat finale and not much action.

w John Twist, Harry Segall, *story* Bret Harte *d* Christy Cabanne *ph* Robert de Grasse

Preston Foster, Jean Muir, Van Heflin

The Outcasts of Poker Flat
US 1952 80m bw
TCF (Julian Blaustein)

Good-looking but equally undramatic remake of the above.

w Edmund H. North *d* Joseph M. Newman *ph* Joseph La Shelle *m* Hugo Friedhofer

Dale Robertson, Anne Baxter, Cameron Mitchell, Miriam Hopkins

'Fails badly either as dramatic or as western fare . . . best where two features prevail.'—*Variety*

The Outfit
US 1973 103m Metrocolor
MGM (Carter de Haven)

A criminal just out of prison finds himself in danger from the Syndicate.
Unattractive rehash of *Point Blank* with much gratuitous violence.

wd John Flynn, *novel* Richard Stark *ph* Bruce Surtees *m* Jerry Fielding

Robert Duvall, Karen Black, Robert Ryan, Joe Don Baker, Timothy Carey, Richard Jaeckel, Sheree North, Marie Windsor, Jane Greer, Elisha Cook Jnr
'A nice profusion of Hollywood character actors makes up for the overall lack of drive.'—*Sight and Sound*

'Even in space, the ultimate enemy is man!'
'On Jupiter's moon, something deadly is happening!'
Outland
GB 1981 109m Technicolor
Panavision

The marshal of a mining base on the third moon of Jupiter waits for hired killers to arrive from Earth and try to assassinate him.
Ludicrous, over-plotted outer-space version of *High Noon*, in such thick colour that the action is hard to follow.

w,d Peter Hyams *ph* Stephen Goldblatt *m* Jerry Goldsmith *pd* Philip Harrison

Sean Connery, Peter Boyle, Francis Sternhagen, James B. Sikking, Kika Markham, Clarke Peters
'Acres of footage are expended on the same old dreary electronic gadgetry and the same old hollowly echoing metalwork sets.'—*Tom Milne, MFB*

'Action! Thrills! Sensations! Primitive Love!'
The Outlaw•
US 1943 126m bw
Howard Hughes

Billy the Kid, Doc Holliday and Pat Garrett meet up at a way station and quarrel over a half-breed girl.
Half-baked western with much pretentious chat and the main interest squarely focused on the bosom of the producer's new discovery. This aspect kept censorship ballyhoo going for six years before the film was finally released in truncated form, and audiences found it not worth the wait, though it does look good.

w Jules Furthman *d* Howard Hughes *ph* Gregg Toland *md* Victor Young

Jack Beutel, Jane Russell, Thomas Mitchell, Walter Huston

● Video: Kingston

Outlaw Blues
US 1977   101m   Technicolor
Warner / Fred Weintraub–Paul Heller
(Steve Tisch)

An ex-con finds that a singing star has stolen
his song.
Fashionable comedy-melodrama with no great
entertainment value despite action scenes
towards the end.

w B. W. L. Norton d Richard T. Heffron
ph Jules Brenner m Charles Bernstein

Peter Fonda, Susan Saint James, John
Crawford, James Callahan, Michael Lerner

The Outlaw Josey Wales*
US 1976   135m   De Luxe   Panavision
Warner / Malpaso (Robert Daley)

A westerner gradually avenges the death of his
wife at the hands of bandits.
Bloodthirsty actioner in the star's usual mould;
likely to prove unintentionally funny for
hardened addicts.

w Phil Kaufman, Sonia Chernus, novel Gone
to Texas by Forrest Carter d Clint Eastwood
ph Bruce Surtees m Jerry Fielding

Clint Eastwood, Chief Dan George, Sondra
Locke, John Vernon, Bill McKinney
'If only the actors hadn't got in the way of
the scenery, it would have been a very
beautiful film indeed.'—Benny Green, Punch

AAN: Jerry Fielding

● Video: Warner

Outpost in Morocco
US 1949   92m   bw
Joseph N. Ermolieff

A romantic Foreign Legion officer falls for the
daughter of an enemy Arab.
Despite authentic locations and the co-
operation of the Legion this is a stolid piece of
work, too dull even for children's matinees.

w Charles Grayson, Paul de St Columbe
d Robert Florey ph Lucien Andriot

George Raft, Akim Tamiroff, Marie Windsor,
John Litel, Eduard Franz

Outrage
US 1950   75m   bw
Filmmakers (Collier Young)

A girl who has been raped is almost unhinged
by the experience.
Well-meaning low-budgeter, thin in
entertainment value.

w Ida Lupino, Collier Young, Marvin Wald
d Ida Lupino ph Archie Stout m Paul
Sawtell md Constantin Bakaleinikoff
pd Harry Horner

Mala Powers, Tod Andrews, Robert Clarke,
Raymond Bond, Lilian Hamilton
'An unconvincing mixture of sensationalism,
sentiment and half-baked sociology.'—MFB

The Outrage*
US 1964   97m   bw   Panavision
MGM / Harvest / February / Ritt / Kayos (A.
Ronald Lubin)

Conflicting views of a western murder.

Wildly ineffective remake of Rashomon, with
everyone strangely overacting and little sense
of the west as it is normally depicted.

w Michael Kanin d Martin Ritt ph James
Wong Howe m Alex North

Paul Newman, Edward G. Robinson,
Laurence Harvey, Claire Bloom, William
Shatner, Albert Salmi

The Outriders
US 1950   93m   Technicolor
MGM (Richard Goldstone)

Three Confederate soldiers escape from a
yankee prison camp.
Competent star western with solid production
values.

w Irving Ravetch d Roy Rowland ph Charles
Schoenbaum m André Previn

Joel McCrea, Arlene Dahl, Barry Sullivan,
Claude Jarman Jnr, Ramon Novarro

Outside the Law
US 1930   76m   bw

A girl becomes involved between two crooks
planning a bank robbery. Incompetent early
talkie with some familiar talents all at sea.
Mary Nolan, Edward G. Robinson, Owen
Moore, Edwin Sturgis. Written by Tod
Browning, Garrett Fort; directed by Tod
Browning; for Universal. 'One of the worst
examples of claptrap since sound came in . . .
no continuity and the director lets the cast run
wild.'—Variety

The Outsider
GB 1931   93m   bw

A 'quack' osteopath is finally able to make a
surgeon's crippled daughter walk. Cast-iron
theatre and a fairly successful quota quickie
which was also released in America. Harold
Huth, Joan Barry, Norman McKinnel, Frank
Lawton, Mary Clare. Written by Harry
Lachman and Alma Reville, from the play by
Dorothy Brandon; directed by Harry
Lachman; for Cinema House / MGM.

The Outsider
GB 1939   90m   bw

Sturdy remake of the above. George Sanders,
Mary Maguire, Frederick Leister, Peter
Murray Hill, Kathleen Harrison. Written by
Dudley Leslie; directed by Paul Stein; for
ABPC. 'Up-to-date and should appeal to
popular-priced audiences.'—Variety

The Outsider
US 1961   108m   bw
U-I (Sy Bartlett)

Ira Hayes, a simple Red Indian, becomes a
war hero but cannot reconcile himself to living
in a white society.
Prolonged biopic which proves a shade too
much for an eager star; it's all earnest and
mildly interesting but not cinematically
compulsive.

w Stewart Stern d Delbert Mann ph Joseph
La Shelle m Leonard Rosenman

Tony Curtis, James Franciscus, Bruce
Bennett, Gregory Walcott, Vivian Nathan,
Edmund Hashim, Stanley Adams

Outward Bound*
US 1930   82m   bw
Warner

Passengers on a strange liner discover that
they are all dead and heading for purgatory.
Early sound version of a popular twenties play
which does not translate too well to cinematic
forms and now seems very dated apart from a
couple of performances; remade as Between
Two Worlds (qv).

w J. Grubb Alexander, play Sutton Vane
d Robert Milton ph Hal Mohr

Leslie Howard, Douglas Fairbanks Jnr, Alec
B. Francis, Helen Chandler, Beryl Mercer,
Alison Skipworth, Montagu Love, Dudley
Digges
'Intelligentsia subject that must be spotted
carefully . . . seems to lack the essentials of
mass entertainment.'—Variety

Over She Goes*
GB 1937   74m   bw

An old friend helps a nobleman to thwart a
blackmailer. Lively comedy vehicle for a
forgotten star. Stanley Lupino, Laddie Cliff,
Gina Malo, Clare Luce, Max Baer, Sally
Gray, Syd Walker. Written by Elizabeth
Meehan and Hugh Brooke, from the play by
Stanley Lupino; directed by Graham Cutts; for
ABPC.

Over the Brooklyn Bridge
US 1983   106m   Metrocolor

Misadventures of a family-ridden Jewish
restaurant owner in New York. Frantic ethnic
comedy with an unsympathetic hero. Elliott
Gould, Margaux Hemingway, Sid Caesar,
Shelley Winters, Burt Young, Carol Kane.
Written by Arnold Somkin; directed by
Menahem Golan; for Golan-Globus. 'The
film's lip service to liberalism is offset by a
blatantly sexist storyline.'—Ruth Baumgarten,
MFB

Over the Hill
US 1931   87m   bw

An ageing mother is sent to the poorhouse by
her hard-hearted older son, but rescued by her
ne'er-do-well younger one. Sound remake of a
silent success which in 1920 made a star of
Mary Carr, who thereafter specialized in
playing dear old ladies. James Dunn, Sally
Eilers, Mae Marsh, Edward Crandall, James
Kirkwood. Written by Tom Barry and Jules
Furthman from poems by Will Carleton;
directed by Henry King; for Fox. 'There isn't a
single overacted scene and there isn't a
sequence that doesn't reach straight to the
heart.'—Variety

Over the Moon
GB 1937   78m   Technicolor
London Films (Alexander Korda)

A poor girl comes into a fortune but this does

not help her romance with a proud young
doctor.
Insubstantial comedy which turns itself into a
European travelogue before petering out.

w Anthony Pelissier, Arthur Wimperis, Alec
Coppel d Thornton Freeland ph Harry
Stradling m Mischa Spoliansky

Merle Oberon, Rex Harrison, Ursula Jeans,
Robert Douglas, Louis Borell, Zena Dare,
Peter Haddon, David Tree

Over the Wall
US 1938 72m bw

A man wrongly convicted of murder fights the
prison system. Predictable semi-documentary
thriller from the prolific pen of Warden Lewis
E. Lawes; just an efficient second feature.
Dick Foran, John Litel, June Travis, Dick
Purcell, Veda Ann Borg, George E. Stone.
Written by Crane Wilbur, George Bricker;
directed by Frank MacDonald; for Warners.
'Authentic melodrama, headed for nice biz.'—
Variety

Over Twenty-One
US 1945 102m bw
Columbia (Sidney Buchman)

A famous lady screenwriter copes with
wartime domestic problems while her husband
is off at the war.
Thin star comedy based on Ruth Gordon's
play about her own predicament; not for the
wider audience, and not very good anyway.

w Sidney Buchman, *play* Ruth Gordon
d Alexander Hall ph Rudolph Maté
m Marlin Skiles

Irene Dunne, Alexander Knox, Charles
Coburn, Jeff Donnell, Lee Patrick, Phil
Brown, Cora Witherspoon

The Overlanders**
Australia 1946 91m bw
Ealing (Ralph Smart)

In 1943 a drover saves a thousand head of

cattle from the Japanese by taking them two
thousand miles across country.
Attractive, easy-going semi-western, the first
and best of several films made by Ealing
Studios in Australia.

wd Harry Watt ph Osmond Borradaile
m John Ireland

Chips Rafferty, John Heyward, Daphne
Campbell

Overlord*
GB 1975 83m bw
EMI / Jowsend (James Quinn)

An eighteen-year-old is called up in early 1944
and killed in the D-Day landings.
Semi-documentary recreating a time in history
(with much aid from newsreels) but making no
discernible point. Interesting, though.

w Stuart Cooper, Christopher Hudson
d Stuart Cooper ph John Alcott m Paul
Glass

Brian Stirner, Davyd Harries, Nicholas Ball,
Julie Neesam

● Video: Thorn EMI

Owd Bob*
GB 1938 78m bw
GFD / Gainsborough (Edward Black)
US title: *To the Victor*

A Cumberland farmer's faithful dog is accused
of killing sheep.
Sentimental yarn with good location
backgrounds; the plot was later reused as
Thunder in the Valley.

w Michael Hogan, J. B. Williams,
novel Alfred Olivant d Robert Stevenson
ph Jack Cox md Louis Levy

Will Fyffe, John Loder, Margaret Lockwood,
Moore Marriott, Graham Moffatt, Wilfred
Walter, Elliot Mason

The Owl and the Pussycat*
US 1970 96m Eastmancolor
Panavision
Columbia / Rastar (Ray Stark)

A bookstore assistant reports a fellow tenant
for prostitution, and when she is evicted she
moves in with him.
Wacky, bawdy double act which starts
promisingly but outstays its welcome. A solid
step forward in permissiveness, with kinky
behaviour as well as four-letter words.

w Buck Henry, *play* Bill Manhoff d Herbert
Ross ph Harry Stradling, Andrew Laszlo
m Richard Halligan

Barbra Streisand, George Segal, Robert Klein.
Allen Garfield
'If computers ever turn out romantic
comedies, the results will look like this.'—
Stanley Kauffmann

● Video: RCA / Columbia

The Ox-Bow Incident**
US 1943 75m bw
TCF (Lamar Trotti)
GB title: *Strange Incident*

A cowboy is unable to prevent three
wandering travellers being unjustly lynched for
murder.
Stark lynch law parable, beautifully made but
very depressing.

w Lamar Trotti, *novel* Walter Van Tilburg
Clark d William Wellman ph Arthur Miller
m Cyril Mockridge

Henry Fonda, Henry Morgan, Jane Darwell,
Anthony Quinn, Dana Andrews, Mary Beth
Hughes, William Eythe, Harry Davenport,
Frank Conroy
'Realism that is as sharp and cold as a
knife.'—*Frank S. Nugent, New York Times*
'Very firm, respectable, and sympathetic;
but I still think it suffers from *rigor artis*.'—
James Agee

AAN: best picture

P.J.
US 1967 109m Techniscope
Universal (Edward J. Montagne)
GB title: *New Face in Hell*

A down-at-heel private eye takes a job as
bodyguard to a boorish businessman.
Routine thick-ear with a predictable turnabout
plot.

w Philip Reisman Jnr *d* John Guillermin
ph Loyal Griggs *m* Neal Hefti

George Peppard, Gayle Hunnicutt, Raymond
Burr, Susan St James, Coleen Gray, Jason
Evers, Wilfrid Hyde White, Severn Darden
  'Enough action to keep you from noticing
that the plot doesn't make any sense.'—*Judith
Crist*

'A killer and a girl—trapped in America's
first air raid!'

Pacific Blackout
US 1942 76m bw
Paramount (Sol C. Siegel)

An inventor escapes from jail and proves his
innocence during a practice air raid blackout.
Minor melo which proved profitably topical,
being released shortly after the Japanese
attack on Pearl Harbor.

w Lester Cole, W. P. Lipscomb *d* Ralph
Murphy *ph* Theodor Sparkuhl

Robert Preston, Martha O'Driscoll, Philip
Merivale, Eva Gabor, Louis Jean Heydt,
Thurston Hall

Pacific Destiny
GB 1956 97m Eastmancolor
Cinemascope
James Lawrie

Experiences of a British colonial servant in the
South Seas.
Pleasant episodic drama which needed a firmer
hand all round.

w Richard Mason, *autobiography* A Pattern
of Islands by Sir Arthur Grimble *d* Wolf
Rilla *ph* Martin Curtis *m* James Bernard

Denholm Elliott, Susan Stephen, Michael
Hordern

Pacific Liner
US 1938 73m bw

Cholera breaks out on a ship bound from
Shanghai to San Francisco. Rather a
depressing melodrama with all the action
below decks, and very slow at that. Victor
McLaglen, Chester Morris, Wendy Barrie,
Alan Hale, Barry Fitzgerald, Halliwell
Hobbes, Cy Kendall. Written by John Twist,
Anthony Coldeway, Henry Roberts Symonds;
directed by Lew Landers; for RKO. 'Drab
melodrama with little of interest to hold
attention.'—*Variety*
AAN: music (Robert Russell Bennett)

Pacific Rendezvous
US 1942 76m bw

A coding expert breaks up an enemy spy ring.
Competent propaganda potboiler, rehashed
from the rather smarter *Rendezvous*, which
was set one war earlier. Lee Bowman, Jean
Rogers, Mona Maris, Carl Esmond, Paul
Cavanagh, Blanche Yurka. Written by Harry
Kurnitz, P. J. Wolfson, George Oppenheimer;
directed by George Sidney; for MGM.

The Pack
US 1977 99m colour

Abandoned dogs on a remote island turn on
holidaymakers. *The Birds* becomes *The Dogs*;
competently made but unsurprising thriller.
Joe Don Baker, Hope Alexander Willis,
Richard B. Shull, R. G. Armstrong. Written
and directed by Robert Clouse, from the novel
by Dave Fisher; for Warner.

Pack Up Your Troubles*
US 1931 68m bw
Hal Roach

Two World War I veterans try to look after
their late pal's orphan daughter.
Patchy comedy vehicle in which too many gags
are not fully thought out or timed.

w H. M. Walker *d* George Marshall, Ray
McCarey *ph* Art Lloyd

Stan Laurel, Oliver Hardy, Donald Dillaway,
Mary Carr, Charles Middleton, Dick Cramer,
James Finlayson, Tom Kennedy, Billy Gilbert

Pack Up Your Troubles*
US 1939 75m bw
GB title: *We're In the Army Now*

Exploits in Flanders of three zany soldiers.
Good slapstick antics in an unfamiliar venue.
The Ritz Brothers, Jane Withers, Joseph
Schildkraut, Lynn Bari, Stanley Fields.
Written by Lou Breslow and Owen Francis;
directed by H. Bruce Humberstone; for TCF.
'A pretty good programmer in the B
division.'—*Variety*

The Pad, and How to Use It*
US 1966 86m Technicolor
Universal (Ross Hunter)

A shy young man has his first date.
Pleasant, odd little comedy apparently made
in emulation of *The Knack*.

w Thomas C. Ryan, Benn Starr, *play* The
Private Ear by Peter Shaffer *d* Brian C.
Hutton *ph* Ellsworth Fredericks *m* Russ
Garcia

Brian Bedford, James Farentino, Julie
Sommars, Edy Williams, Nick Navarro

Paddy O'Day
US 1935 73m bw

An Irish child emigrates to America to find
that her mother has died. One of the more
satisfactory vehicles for a child star maintained
by the studio as an antidote to the cuter antics
of Shirley Temple. *Jane Withers,* Pinky
Tomlin, Rita Hayworth, Jane Darwell, Francis
Ford. Written by Lou Breslow and Edward
Eliscu; directed by Lewis Seiler; for TCF.

Paddy the Next Best Thing
US 1933 75m bw
Fox

Adventures of an Irish tomboy in New York.
Modest star comedy from a popular play.

w Edwin Burke, *play* Gertrude Page *d* Harry
Lachman *ph* John Seitz

Janet Gaynor, Warner Baxter, Walter
Connolly, Harvey Stephens, Margaret Lindsay
  'Easy entertainment: excellent, wholesome
and amusing.'—*Variety*

Padre Padrone**
Italy 1977 113m Eastmancolor
Radiotelevisione Italia (Tonino Paoletti)
aka: *Father and Master*

The author recounts how he grew up with a
violent and tyrannical father.
A vivid chunk of autobiography with food for
thought on several levels, and a clever piece of
film-making to boot.

wd Paolo Taviani, Vittorio Taviani,
book Gavino Ledda *ph* Mario Masini
md Egisto Macchi

Omero Antonutti, Saverio Marconi, Marcella
Michelangeli

The Pagan
US 1929   85m approx   bw

A South Sea islander falls for the daughter of
a white trader. Highly commercial star vehicle
apparently made as an afterthought to *White
Shadows in the South Seas*. Ramon Novarro,
Renee Adoree, Dorothy Janis, Donald Crisp.
Written by Dorothy Farnum; directed by W.
S. Van Dyke; for MGM.

Pagan Lady
US 1931   70m   bw

A nice American boy in Havana falls for a girl
who is no better than she should be. Sultry
melodrama reminiscent of *Rain* but of no
intrinsic merit. Evelyn Brent, Conrad Nagel,
Charles Bickford, Roland Young, William
Farnum. Written by Ben Glazer from the play
by William Dubois; directed by John Francis
Dillon; for Columbia. 'Something of a
lightweight; the storm is quite the best thing in
the picture.'—*Variety*

Pagan Love Song
US 1950   76m   Technicolor
MGM (Arthur Freed)

An American schoolteacher marries a Tahitian
girl.
Very mild musical potboiler using familiar
talents.

w Robert Nathan, Jerry Davis d Robert
Alton ph Charles Rosher m Harry Warren
ly Arthur Freed

Esther Williams, Howard Keel, Rita Moreno,
Minna Gombell

Page Miss Glory*
US 1935   90m   bw
Warner / Cosmopolitan

A con man wins a beauty contest with a
composite photograph of a non-existent girl.
Amusing comedy-musical, unjustly forgotten.

w Delmer Daves, Robert Lord, play Joseph
Schrank, Philip Dunning d Mervyn Le Roy
ph George Folsey m / ly Harry Warren, Al
Dubin

Dick Powell, Marion Davies, Frank McHugh,
Pat O'Brien, Mary Astor, Lyle Talbot, Patsy
Kelly, Allen Jenkins, Barton MacLane

Pagliacci*
GB 1936   92m   colour

A jealous clown kills his wife and her lover. A
surprising British enterprise of the time which
did fairly well at the box office, presumably
because of the colour. Richard Tauber, Steffi
Duna, Diana Napier, Arthur Margetson,
Esmond Knight, Jerry Verno. Written by
Monckton Hoffe, John Drinkwater, Roger
Burford and Ernest Betts, from the opera by
Ruggiero Leoncavallo; directed by Karl
Grune; for Trafalgar. (US title: *A Clown Must
Laugh*.)

Paid*
US 1930   80m   bw
MGM
GB title: *Within the Law*

A woman sent to prison unjustly plots revenge
on those responsible.
Reliable melodrama with the heroine
eventually forgiving and forgetting.

w Charles MacArthur, Lucien Hubbard,
play Within the Law by Bayard Veiller d Sam
Wood ph Charles Rosher

Joan Crawford, Kent Douglass, Robert
Armstrong, Marie Prévost, John Miljan, Polly
Moran

Paid in Full
US 1949   105m   bw
Paramount / Hal B. Wallis

A woman is responsible for the death of her
sister's child, and becomes pregnant herself in
the knowledge that giving birth will be fatal to
her.
Stolid, contrived tearjerker.

w Robert Blees, Charles Schnee d William
Dieterle ph Leo Tover m Victor Young

Lizabeth Scott, Diana Lynn, Robert
Cummings, Eve Arden, Ray Collins, Frank
McHugh, Stanley Ridges, Louis Jean Heydt

'Ben and pardner shared everything—even
  their wife!'
Paint Your Wagon*
US 1969   164m   Technicolor
  Panavision 70
Paramount / Alan Jay Lerner (Tom Shaw)

During the California Gold Rush, two
prospectors set up a Mormon menage with the
same wife.
Good-looking but uncinematic and
monumentally long version of an old musical
with a new plot and not much dancing. There
are minor pleasures, but it really shouldn't
have been allowed.

w Paddy Chayevsky, musical play Alan Jay
Lerner, Frederick Loewe d Joshua Logan
ph William A. Fraker md Nelson Riddle
pd John Truscott

Lee Marvin, Clint Eastwood, Jean Seberg,
Harve Presnell, Ray Walston

'One of those big movies in which the
themes are undersized and the elements are
juggled around until nothing fits together right
and even the good bits of the original show
you started with are shot to hell.'—*Pauline
Kael*

AAN: Nelson Riddle

Painted Boats
GB 1945   63m   bw

Romance among the bargees. Excessively thin
location drama, which nevertheless has an
early place in the Ealing tradition. Jenny
Laird, Bill Blewett, Robert Griffith, May
Hallatt. Written by Louis MacNeice and
Michael McCarthy; directed by Charles
Crichton; for Ealing. (US title: *The Girl on the
Canal*.)

The Painted Veil*
US 1934   84m   bw
MGM (Hunt Stromberg)

In China, a doctor's wife gives up her lover to
join her husband fighting an epidemic.
Soulful melodrama which seemed much more
acceptable in this version than in the summer
stock style remake *The Seventh Sin*.

w John Meehan, Salka Viertel, Edith
Fitzgerald, novel W. Somerset Maugham
d Richard Boleslawski ph William Daniels
m Herbert Stothart

Greta Garbo, George Brent, Herbert
Marshall, Warner Oland, Jean Hersholt
'Confused and slow, but extra heavy name
cast should get it by.'—*Variety*

Painted Woman
US 1932   73m   bw

A floozie stranded on a South Sea island
resists offers of help from several men.
Another variation on *Rain*, and not the best.
Spencer Tracy, Peggy Shannon, William Stage
Boyd, Irving Pichel, Raul Roulien. Written by
Guy Bolton, Leon Gordon, from A. C.
Kennedy's After the Rain; directed by John
Blystone; for Fox. 'It's hard to see how the
studio figured a good picture would result
from the material at hand.'—*Variety*

Painting the Clouds with Sunshine
US 1951   86m   Technicolor
Warner (William Jacobs)

Three singing sisters go to Las Vegas in search
of rich husbands.
Yet another revamp of the original *Gold
Diggers* (qv), and not a very lively one.

w Henry Clark, Roland Kibbee, Peter Milne
d David Butler ph Wilfred Cline

Virginia Mayo, Gene Nelson, Dennis Morgan,
S. Z. Sakall, Lucille Norman, Tom Conway

A Pair of Briefs
GB 1961   90m   bw
Rank / Betty E. Box–Ralph Thomas

Barristers Tony and Frances fall in love while
opposing each other in court.
Adam's Rib need have no fears; this is the
palest of imitations.

w Nicholas Phipps, play How Say You by
Harold Brooke, Kay Bannerman d Ralph
Thomas ph Ernest Steward m Norrie
Paramor

Michael Craig, Mary Peach, Brenda de
Banzie, James Robertson Justice, Roland
Culver, Liz Fraser, Ron Moody, Jameson
Clark, Charles Heslop

Paisà*
Italy 1946   115m   bw
Foreign Film Productions / OFI

Six episodes in the Battle of Italy between
1943 and 1945.
More important historically than dramatically,
Paisà was always a somewhat disappointing
experience, especially as the earlier episodes

are stronger than the later ones. Like *Open City*, it was partly improvised and had a gritty documentary quality.

w Federico Fellini, Roberto Rossellini
d Roberto Rossellini *ph* Otello Martelli
m Renzo Rossellini

William Tubbs, Gar Moore, Maria Michi and non-professionals

AAN: script

The Pajama Game•••
US 1957   101m   Warnercolor
Warner / George Abbott

Workers in a pajama factory demand a pay rise, but their lady negotiator falls for the new boss.
Brilliantly conceived musical on an unlikely subject, effectively concealing its Broadway origins and becoming an expert, fast-moving, hard-hitting piece of modern musical cinema.

w George Abbott, Richard Bissell, *book* Seven and a Half Cents by Richard Bissell
d Stanley Donen, *ph* Harry Stradling *songs* Richard Adler, Jerry Ross *ch* Bob Fosse

Doris Day, John Raitt, *Eddie Foy Jnr*, Reta Shaw, Carol Haney

Pal Joey••
US 1957   109m   Technicolor
Columbia / Essex–Sidney (Fred Kohlmar)

The rise of a nightclub entertainer who is also a heel.
Smart musical which begins very brightly indeed but slides off alarmingly into conventional sentiment.

w Dorothy Kingsley, *play* John O'Hara, *stories* John O'Hara *d* George Sidney
ph Harold Lipstein *songs* Richard Rodgers, Lorenz Hart

Frank Sinatra, Rita Hayworth, Kim Novak, Bobby Sherwood, Hank Henry, Elizabeth Patterson, Barbara Nichols

The Paleface•••
US 1948   91m   Technicolor
Paramount (Robert L. Welch)

Calamity Jane undertakes an undercover mission against desperadoes, and marries a timid dentist as a cover.
Splendid wagon train comedy western with the stars in excellent form. Sequel, *Son of Paleface* (qv); remake, *The Shakiest Gun in the West* (1968).

w Edmund Hartman, Frank Tashlin
d Norman Z. McLeod *ph* Ray Rennahan
m Victor Young

Bob Hope, Jane Russell, Robert Armstrong, Iris Adrian, Robert Watson, Jack Searle, Joe Vitale, Clem Bevans, Charles Trowbridge

AA: song 'Buttons and Bows' (*m* Jay Livingston, *ly* Ray Evans)

The Palm Beach Story•••
US 1942   88m   bw
Paramount (Paul Jones)

The wife of a penurious engineer takes off for Florida to set her sights on a millionaire.

Flighty comedy, inconsequential in itself, but decorated with scenes, characters and zany touches typical of its creator, here at his most brilliant if uncontrolled.

wd Preston Sturges *ph* Victor Milner
m Victor Young

Claudette Colbert, Joel McCrea, Rudy Vallee, Mary Astor, Sig Arno, Robert Warwick, Torben Meyer, Jimmy Conlin, William Demarest, Jack Norton, Robert Greig, Roscoe Ates, Chester Conklin, Franklin Pangborn, Alan Bridge, *Robert Dudley*

HACKENSACKER (Rudy Vallee): 'That's one of the tragedies of this life, that the men most in need of a beating up are always enormous.'

WEENIE KING (Robert Dudley): 'Anyway, I'd be too old for you. Cold are the hands of time that creep along relentlessly, destroying slowly but without pity that which yesterday was young. Alone, our memories resist this disintegration and grow more lovely with the passing years. That's hard to say with false teeth.'

'Surprises and delights as though nothing of the kind had been known before . . . farce and tenderness are combined without a fault.'—*William Whitebait*

Palm Springs
US 1936   74m   bw

An elderly Englishman becomes a gambler in order to give his daughter the appropriate upbringing. Slight romantic comedy which gave a young Englishman a foothold in Hollywood. David Niven, Sir Guy Standing, Frances Langford, Ernest Cossart, Spring Byington. Written by Joseph Fields; directed by Aubrey Scotto; for Paramount. (GB title: *Palm Springs Affair*.)

Palm Springs Weekend
US 1963   100m   Technicolor
Warner (Michael Hoey)

Various holidaymakers at Palm Springs get romantically involved.
Youth-oriented farce, better produced than most but basically a depressing experience.

w Earl Hanmer Jnr *d* Norman Taurog
ph Harold Lipstein *m* Frank Perkins

Troy Donahue, Ty Hardin, Connie Stevens, Stefanie Powers, Robert Conrad, Jack Weston, Andrew Duggan

Palmy Days
US 1932   77m   bw
Samuel Goldwyn

Shady fortune tellers find a willing stooge.
Dated star comedy.

w Eddie Cantor, Mornie Ryskind, David Greenman *d* A. Edward Sutherland
ph Gregg Toland *ch* Busby Berkeley

Eddie Cantor, Charlotte Greenwood, Charles Middleton, George Raft, Walter Catlett
'Heavily hoked but funny throughout.'—*Variety*

Palooka
US 1934   80m   bw

An eccentric manager makes a prizefighter of a country cousin. Fairly amusing first-feature version of the strip cartoon hero Joe Palooka. Jimmy Durante (as Knobby Walsh), Stuart Erwin, Lupe Velez, Marjorie Rambeau, Robert Armstrong, Mary Carlisle, William Cagney, Thelma Todd. Written by Jack Jevne, Arthur Kober, Gertrude Purcell, from Ham Fisher's strip; directed by Ben Stoloff; for Reliance (Edward Small). 'A laugh riot, the nearest approach to a Marx picture that's been around.'—*Variety*

Pan-Americana•
US 1945   85m   bw
RKO (Sid Rogell)

A New York magazine sends editors around South America to choose the prettiest girl of each nation.
Slick, mindless musical with good numbers.

w Laurence Kimble *d* John H. Auer
ph Frank Redman *md* Constantin Bakaleinikoff *ch* Charles O'Curran

Audrey Long, Philip Terry, Robert Benchley, Eve Arden, Ernest Truex, Marc Cramer

Panama Hattie
US 1942   79m   bw
MGM (Arthur Freed)

A showgirl in Panama helps to capture Nazis.
Dim film version of a Broadway musical, stripped of most of its music and more like a *Maisie* comedy.

w Jack McGowan, Wilkie Mahoney, *musical play* Herbert Fields, B. G. De Sylva, Cole Porter *d* Norman Z. McLeod *ph* George Folsey *md* George Stoll

Ann Sothern, Dan Dailey, Red Skelton, Marsha Hunt, Rags Ragland, Virginia O'Brien, Alan Mowbray, Ben Blue, Carl Esmond

Pancho Villa
Spain 1972   93m   Technicolor
Granada Films (Bernard Gordon)

In 1916 Villa is rescued from execution and starts a reign of terror.
Mexican banditry played half for laughs and half for real; not a successful compromise.

w Julian Halevy *d* Eugenio Martin
ph Allejandro Ulloa *m* Anton Garcia-Abril

Telly Savalas, Clint Walker, Chuck Connors

Pandora and the Flying Dutchman•
GB 1950   122m   Technicolor
Romulus (Albert Lewin)

A cold but beautiful American woman in Spain falls for a mystery man who turns out to be a ghostly sea captain; she dies so as to be with him.
Pretentious, humourless, totally unpersuasive fantasy of the kind much better done in *Portrait of Jennie*. The writer-director wears Omar Khayyam's moving finger to the bone, and the actors look thoroughly unhappy; even the colour is a bit thick.

wd Albert Lewin ph Jack Cardiff *m* Alan Rawsthorne *ad* John Bryan

James Mason, Ava Gardner, Harold Warrender, Nigel Patrick, Sheila Sim, Mario Cabre, John Laurie, Pamela Kellino, Marius Goring

'Conspicuous in its confident assumption of scholarship and its utter poverty of imagination and taste.'—*C. A. Lejeune*

'It might have been enjoyably silly but for Lewin's striving to be classy and an air of third-rate decadence that hangs about it. This is an Anglo-American co-production and one of the occasions, I think, when we might be generous and let Hollywood have all the credit.'—*Richard Winnington*

Pandora's Box*

Germany 1929   97m approx (24 fps)
   bw   silent
Nero Film
original title: *Die Büchse der Pandora*
aka: *Lulu*

A woman murders her lover, becomes a prostitute, and is murdered in London by Jack the Ripper.
Oddball fantasy on a few favourite German themes: very watchable, and benefiting from its star performance.

w G. W. Pabst, Laszlo Wajda, *plays* Erdgeist and Pandora's Box by Franz Wedekind *d* G. W. Pabst *ph* Günther Krampf

Louise Brooks, Fritz Kortner, Franz Lederer, Gustav Diessl

† Remade in Austria in 1962 as *No Orchids for Lulu*, with Nadja Tiller.

Panic Button

US 1963   98m   bw

A hasbeen film star is hired by gangsters to star in a film which must lose money; but it wins the Venice Festival award. Artless and padded comedy with good moments provided by an intriguing cast. Maurice Chevalier, Akim Tamiroff, Jayne Mansfield, Eleanor Parker, Michael Connors. Written by Hal Biller; directed by George Sherman; for Gorton Associates.

The Panic in Needle Park

US 1971   110m   De Luxe
Gadd Productions (Dominick Dunne)

Drug addiction problems in a New York ghetto.
Vivid, intimate but overlong and unsympathetic account of a junkie and his mistress.

w Joan Didion, John Gregory Dunne, *novel* James Mills *d* Jerry Schatzberg *ph* Adam Holender *m* none

Al Pacino, Kitty Winn, Adam Vint, Richard Bright, Kiel Martin

Panic in the Streets***

US 1950   96m   bw
TCF (Sol C. Siegel)

On the New Orleans waterfront, public health officials seek a carrier of bubonic plague.

Semi-documentary suspenser in the *Naked City* manner; location Hollywood at its best.

w Richard Murphy, Edward and Edna Anhalt *d* Elia Kazan *ph* Joe MacDonald *m* Alfred Newman

Richard Widmark, Jack Palance, Paul Douglas, Barbara Bel Geddes, Zero Mostel

'A model of what an action story should be . . . every department is admirably handled.'—*Richard Mallett, Punch*

AA: original story (Edward and Edna Anhalt)

Panic in Year Zero*

US 1962   93m   bw   Cinemascope
AIP (Lou Rusoff, Arnold Houghland)

Adventures of a family on a fishing trip in the mountains when Los Angeles is blasted by a nuclear attack.
Mildly interesting catalogue of predictable events—thugs, looting, fear of fall-out—in a simple-minded script finishing with a hopeful meeting of the UN.

w Jay Simms, John Morton *d* Ray Milland *ph* Gil Warrenton *m* Les Baxter

Ray Milland, Jean Hagen, Frankie Avalon, Joan Freeman

Panique*

France 1946   98m   bw
Filmsonor

A respectable man knows who committed a murder, and the murderer cunningly swings the blame onto him.
Careful suspenser with a twist ending.

w Charles Spaak, Julien Duvivier, *novel* Georges Simenon *d* Julien Duvivier *ph* Nicolas Hayer

Michel Simon, Viviane Romance, Paul Bernard

'Whether you like it or not, you may be forced to agree that it's a near-perfect movie.'—*Pauline Kael, 1972*

The Panther's Claw

US 1942   73m   bw

Thatcher Colt solves a blackmail case which ends in murder. Unassuming but efficient second-feature mystery. Sidney Blackmer, Byron Foulger, Rick Vallin. Written by Martin Mooney and Athony Abbott; directed by William Beaudine; for PRC.

Papa's Delicate Condition

US 1963   98m   Technicolor
Paramount / Amro (Jack Rose)

At the turn of the century in a small Texas town an amiable family man gets into scrapes when he drinks too much.
Basically pleasing period comedy which suffers from slow, stiff treatment.

w Jack Rose, *book* Corinne Griffith *d* George Marshall *ph* Loyal Griggs *m* Joseph J. Lilley

Jackie Gleason, Glynis Johns, Charles Ruggles, Charles Lane, Laurel Goodwin, Juanita Moore, Elisha Cook Jnr, Murray Hamilton

AA: song 'Call Me Irresponsible' (*m* James Van Heusen, *ly* Sammy Cahn)

The Paper Chase**

US 1973   111m   De Luxe   Panavision
TCF (Robert C. Thompson, Rodrick Paul)

A Harvard law graduate falls in love with the divorced daughter of his tetchiest professor.
A thoughtful analysis of attitudes to learning turns into just another youth movie.

wd James Bridges, *novel* John Jay Osborn Jnr *ph* Gordon Willis *m* John Williams

Timothy Bottoms, Lindsay Wagner, *John Houseman*, Graham Bickel

'A slightly unfocused account of conformism and milk-mild rebellion on the campus.'—*Sight and Sound*

'A worthy film which engages the eye and the brain.'—*Benny Green, Punch*

AA: John Houseman
AAN: James Bridges (as writer)

● *Video:* CBS / Fox

Paper Lion

US 1968   105m   colour

The training of a professional football player. Rather single-minded sporting biography from a book by George Plimpton. Alan Alda, Lauren Hutton, David Doyle, Sugar Ray Robinson. Written by Lawrence Roman; directed by Alex March; for United Artists.

Paper Moon**

US 1973   103m   bw
Paramount / Saticoy (Peter Bogdanovich)

In the American midwest in the thirties, a bible salesman and a plain little girl make a great con team.
Unusual but overrated comedy, imperfectly adapted from a very funny book, with careful but disappointing period sense and photography. A lot more style and gloss was required.

w Alvin Sargent, *novel* Addie Pray by *Joe David Brown* *d* Peter Bogdanovich *ph* Laszlo Kovacs *m* popular songs and recordings

Ryan O'Neal, Tatum O'Neal, Madeleine Kahn, John Hillerman

'I've rarely seen a film that looked so unlike what it was about.'—*Stanley Kauffmann*

'At its best the film is only mildly amusing, and I'm not sure I could recall a few undeniable highlights if pressed to the point.'—*Gary Arnold*

Bogdanovich once again deploys the armoury of nostalgia with relentless cunning to evoke the threadbare side of American life forty years ago . . . one of those rare movies which engages at least two of the senses.'—*Benny Green, Punch*

AA: Tatum O'Neal
AAN: Alvin Sargent; Madeleine Kahn

Paper Orchid

GB 1949   86m   bw

A girl reporter is suspected of murdering an actor. Mystery programmer which did not displease. Hugh Williams, Hy Hazell, Sidney

James, Garry Marsh, Andrew Cruickshank, Ivor Barnard, Walter Hudd. Written by Val Guest, from the novel by Arthur La Bern; directed by Roy Baker; for Ganesh / Columbia.

Paper Tiger
GB 1975 99m Technicolor
Maclean and Co (Euan Lloyd)

An ageing Englishman becomes tutor to the son of the Japanese ambassador in a Pacific state, and finds he has to live his heroic fantasies in reality.
Uneasy adventure comedy drama which might, given more skilled handling, have been much better than it is.

w Jack Davies d Ken Annakin ph John Cabrera m Roy Budd

David Niven, Toshiro Mifune, Hardy Kruger, Ando, Ivan Desny, Irene Tsu, Miiko Taka, Ronald Fraser, Jeff Corey
'Makes no demands, except on 99 minutes of our time.'—Michael Billington, Illustrated London News
● Video: Rank

Papillon*
US 1973 150m Technicolor
Panavision
Papillon Partnership / Corona / General Production Co (Robert Dorfmann)

Filmed autobiography of life on Devil's Island. Overlong and rather dreary film of a bestseller; it determinedly rubs the audience's nose in ordure from the start, and the final successful escape is one try too many.

w Dalton Trumbo, Lorenzo Semple Jnr, book Henri Charrière d Franklin Schaffner ph Fred Koenekamp m Jerry Goldsmith

Steve McQueen, Dustin Hoffman, Don Gordon, Anthony Zerbe, George Coulouris, Woodrow Parfrey
'A 2½-hour epic trampling the corn growing round the theme of man's inhumanity to man.'—Sight and Sound
'Papillon offers torture as entertainment but winds up making entertainment a form of torture . . . a tournament of brutality unrelieved by imagination.'—Paul D. Zimmermann
'So overloaded with details that the stars are almost lost in exposition, repetition and unfocused drama.'—Judith Crist, 1977
'So solemn one would think it the story of a pope at the very least.'—New Yorker, 1980
AAN: Jerry Goldsmith

Parachute Jumper
US 1932 70m bw

Ex-flying Marines out of a job fall in with gangsters. Easy-going adventure yarn with agreeable players. Douglas Fairbanks Jnr, Bette Davis, Leo Carrillo, Claire Dodd, Frank McHugh, Harold Huber. Written by Rian James, John Francis Larkin; directed by Alfred E. Green; for Warners. 'Breezy treatment of a not very brilliant yarn.'—Variety

Parade*
France / Sweden 1974 85m Technicolor

Jacques Tati introduces a series of acts in a small-scale circus. Pleasant, sometimes boring variety show, to be included in the Tati canon for completeness; it does include some of his unique pieces of mime. Written and directed by Jacques Tati; for Gray Film / Sveriges Radio. 'A curious, unresolved envoi.'—John Pym, MFB. 'Moments of great good humour and flashes of incomparable magic.'—Sight and Sound

The Paradine Case**
US 1947 115m bw
Selznick

A barrister falls in love with his client, a murder suspect who, it turns out, is actually guilty.
A stodgy and old-fashioned script is given gleaming treatment; this and the acting make it seem better thirty years later than it did on release.

w David O. Selznick, novel Robert Hichens d Alfred Hitchcock ph Lee Garmes m Franz Waxman

Gregory Peck, Alida Valli, Ann Todd, Louis Jourdan, Charles Laughton, Charles Coburn, Ethel Barrymore, Leo G. Carroll
'This is the wordiest script since the death of Edmund Burke.'—James Agee
'The characters and their problems don't make much imprint on a viewer; if you can't remember whether you've seen the picture or not, chances are you did and forgot it.'—New Yorker, 1976
† Original choices were Olivier instead of Peck, Garbo instead of Valli, and Robert Newton instead of Jourdan.

AAN: Ethel Barrymore
● Video: Guild

Paradise Alley
US 1978 107m Technicolor
Universal / Force Ten (John F. Roach, Ronald A. Suppa)

The adventures of three wrestling brothers in New York's Hell's Kitchen during the forties. Fashionable update of the City for Conquest school, not in itself very interesting despite amusing bits.

wd Sylvester Stallone ph Laszlo Kovacs m Bill Conti pd John W. Corso

Sylvester Stallone, Kevin Conway, Anne Archer, Joe Spinell, Armand Assante, Lee Canalito

Paradise for Three
US 1937 78m bw

A businessman goes to Germany to find out how the workers live. An interesting premise leads inevitably into a flimsy romantic comedy. Robert Young, Frank Morgan, Mary Astor, Edna May Oliver, Florence Rice, Reginald Owen, Henry Hull, Sig Rumann, Herman Bing. Written by George Oppenheimer and Harry Ruskin; directed by Edward Buzzell; for MGM. (GB title: Romance for Three.)

Paradise for Two
GB 1937 77m bw
US title: Gaiety Girls

A millionaire posing as a reporter is asked to pose as a millionaire. Cheerful comedy-romance. Jack Hulbert, Patricia Ellis, Arthur Riscoe, Googie Withers, Sidney Fairbrother, Wylie Watson, David Tree. Written by Robert Stevenson and Arthur Macrae; directed by Thornton Freeland; for Korda / Denham.

Paradise Hawaiian Style
US 1965 91m Technicolor
(Paramount) Hal Wallis / Joseph H. Hazen

An amorous airline pilot returns to Hawaii and sets up a helicopter service.
Mindless musical vehicle for an increasingly resistible star.

w Allan Weiss, Anthony Lawrence d Michael Moore ph W. Wallace Kelley md Joseph J. Lilley

Elvis Presley, Suzanna Leigh, James Shigeta, Irene Tsu
● Video: CBS / Fox

The Parallax View*
US 1974 102m Technicolor
Panavision
Paramount / Gus / Harbour / Doubleday (Alan J. Pakula)

Witnesses to a political assassination are systematically killed, despite the efforts of a crusading journalist.
Stylish, persuasive political thriller with a downbeat ending; the villains win.

w David Giler, Lorenzo Semple Jnr, novel Loren Singer d Alan J. Pakula ph Gordon Willis m Michael Small

Warren Beatty, Paula Prentiss, William Daniels, Hume Cronyn, Walter McGinn
'Pakula at his best . . . the test sequence is one of the most celebrated, manipulating the audience as it bombards Beatty's psyche.'—Les Keyser, Hollywood in the Seventies
'It is terribly important to give an audience a lot of things they may not get as well as those they will, so that finally the film does take on a texture and is not just simplistic communication.'—Alan J. Pakula

Paramount on Parade*
US 1930 102m bw (Technicolor sequence)
Paramount (Elsie Janis)

A revue featuring Paramount contract stars. A ragged affair by any standard, but worth a look for a couple of Chevalier's numbers.

w various d Dorothy Arzner, Otto Brower, Edmund Goulding, Victor Heerman, Edwin H. Knopf, Rowland V. Lee, Ernst Lubitsch, Lothar Mendes, Victor Schertzinger, Edward Sutherland, Frank Tuttle ph Harry Fischbeck Victor Milner m various

Richard Arlen, Jean Arthur, George Bancroft, Clara Bow, Nancy Carroll, Ruth Chatterton, Maurice Chevalier, Gary Cooper, Leon Errol, Kay Francis, Harry Green, Mitzi

Green, Dennis King, Fredric March, Nino
Martini, Jack Oakie, Charles 'Buddy' Rogers,
Lillian Roth, Fay Wray, Clive Brook, Warner
Oland, Eugene Pallette, William Powell

'Pip revue packed with laughs and talent.'—
Variety

Paranoiac*
GB 1963 80m bw Cinemascope
U-I / Hammer (Anthony Hinds)

An heiress is saved from a suicide attempt by a
young man claiming to be her dead brother.
A complex maze of disguise, mistaken
identity, family curses and revelations of
something nasty in the woodshed, out of
Psycho by *Taste of Fear*. Not very good in
itself, but interesting in its borrowings.

w Jimmy Sangster d Freddie Francis
ph Arthur Grant m Elisabeth Lutyens

Oliver Reed, Janette Scott, Alexander
Davion, Sheila Burrell, Liliane Brousse,
Maurice Denham, John Bonney

Les Parapluies de Cherbourg**
France / West Germany 1964 92m
  Eastmancolor
Parc / Madeleine / Beta
aka: *The Umbrellas of Cherbourg*

PARANOIAC.   The mystery killer revealed! (It turns out to be Oliver Reed.)

A shopgirl loves a gas station attendant. He
goes on military service; she finds she is
pregnant and marries for security. Years later
they meet briefly by accident.
Unexpected, charming, pretty successful
screen operetta with only sung dialogue.
Careful acting and exquisite use of colour and
camera movement paste over the thinner
sections of the plot.

wd Jacques Demy ph Jean Rabier m Michel
Legrand ad Bernard Evein

Catherine Deneuve, *Anne Vernon*, Nino
Castelnuovo

'Poetic neo-realism.'—*Georges Sadoul*
'We are told that in Paris the opening night
audience wept and the critics were ecstatic. It
would have made a little more sense the other
way round.'—*John Simon*

AAN: script; Michel Legrand; song, 'I Will
Wait for You'

Pardners
US 1956 88m Technicolor Vistavision
Paramount (Paul Jones)

An incompetent idiot goes west and
accidentally cleans up the town.
Stiff western star burlesque, a remake of
Rhythm on the Range.

w Sidney Sheldon d Norman Taurog
ph Daniel Fapp songs Sammy Cahn, Jimmy
Van Heusen

Dean Martin, Jerry Lewis, Agnes Moorehead,
Lori Nelson, John Baragrey, Jeff Morrow,
Lon Chaney Jnr

Pardon My Past*
US 1945 88m bw
Columbia

A man unwittingly takes on the problems of
his double, a shady playboy.
Amusing mistaken identity comedy.

w Earl Felton, Karl Kamb d Leslie Fenton
ph Russell Metty m Dmitri Tiomkin

Fred MacMurray, Marguerite Chapman,
Akim Tamiroff, Rita Johnson, William
Demarest, Harry Davenport

Pardon Us*
US 1931 55m bw
Hal Roach
aka: *Jailbirds*

Two zany bootleggers find themselves in and
out of prison.
Patchy star comedy which finds the boys on
the whole not in quite their best form.

w H. M. Walker d James Parrott ph Jack
Stevens

Stan Laurel, Oliver Hardy, Wilfred Lucas,
Walter Long, James Finlayson

'Their first full-length, with not over two
reels of value.'—*Variety*

The Parent Trap*
US 1961 129m Technicolor
Walt Disney (George Golitzen)

Twin daughters of separated parents
determine to bring the family together again.
Quite bright but awesomely extended juvenile
romp.

wd David Swift, *novel Das Doppelte
Lottchen* by Erich Kastner ph Lucien Ballard
m Paul Smith

Hayley Mills, Maureen O'Hara, Brian Keith,
Charles Ruggles, Leo G. Carroll, Una Merkel,
Joanna Barnes, Cathleen Nesbitt, Ruth
McDevitt, Nancy Kulp

Les Parents Terribles**
France 1948 98m bw
Sirius

Life with a family in which the children are as
neurotic as the parents.
Alternately hilarious and tragic, this is a
fascinating two-set piece of filmed theatre,
with every performance a pleasure.

wd Jean Cocteau, from his play ph Michel
Kelber m Georges Auric ad Christian
Bérard, Guy de Gastyne

Jean Marais, Yvonne de Bray, Gabrielle
Dorziat, Marcel André, Josette Day
† In 1953 a curious and unsatisfactory British
version was made by Charles Frank under the
title *Intimate Relations*, with Marian Spencer,
Russell Enoch, Ruth Dunning, Harold
Warrender and Elsy Albiin.

Paris
US 1929 88m part colour

An American stage star, her fiancé, her
partner and her mother-in-law-to-be converge
on the Champs Elysées. Shaky musical with
interesting talent, but bereft of its original
Cole Porter score. Irene Bordoni, Jack

Buchanan, Louise Closser Hale, Jason Robards. Written by Hope Loring; directed by Clarence Badger; for Warner.

Paris after Dark
US 1943   85m   bw

In wartime Paris a doctor leads the resistance forces. Propaganda potboiler, quite neatly made and cast. George Sanders, Philip Dorn, Brenda Marshall, Marcel Dalio, Madeleine LeBeau. Written by Howard Buchman; directed by Leonide Moguy; for TCF. (GB title: *The Night Is Ending*.)

Paris Blues*
US 1961   98m   Technicolor
UA / Pennebaker / Diane / Jason / Monica / Monmouth (Sam Shaw)

Two jazz musicians have romantic problems in Paris.
Semi-serious mini-drama with emphasis on the music; one is not quite sure what the actors thought they were up to.
w Jack Sher, Irene Kamp, Walter Bernstein, *novel* Harold Flender d Martin Ritt
ph Christian Matras m Duke Ellington
Paul Newman, Joanne Woodward, Sidney Poitier, Louis Armstrong, Diahann Carroll, Serge Reggiani, Barbara Laage
AAN: Duke Ellington

Paris Calling
US 1941   95m   bw
Universal / Charles K. Feldman

When the Nazis invade Paris, a woman discovers that her husband is a traitor.
Totally predictable flagwaver.
w Benjamin Glazer, Charles Kaufmann
d Edwin L. Marin ph Milton Krasner
m Richard Hageman
Elisabeth Bergner, Basil Rathbone, Randolph Scott, Gale Sondergaard, Lee J. Cobb, Eduardo Ciannelli, Charles Arnt

Paris Holiday*
US 1957   101m   Technirama
UA / Tolda (Bob Hope)

An American comedian meets a French one in Paris, and both have narrow escapes because their script contains the clue to a gang of counterfeiters.
Amiable location romp with the stars in pretty good form.
w Edmund Beloin, Dean Riesner d Gerd Oswald ph Roger Hubert m Joseph J. Lilley
Bob Hope, Fernandel, Anita Ekberg, Martha Hyer, André Morell, Maurice Teynac, Jean Murat, Preston Sturges

Paris Honeymoon
US 1938   85m   bw

An American in Paris persuades his fiancée to forget a French nobleman. Candy floss musical for star fans. Bing Crosby, Franciska Gaal, Akim Tamiroff. Written by Frank Butler and Don Hartman; directed by Frank Tuttle; for Paramount. 'Entertaining offering that will click substantially at the box office.'—*Variety*

Paris in Spring
US 1935   81m   bw
GB title: *Paris Love Song*

Four visitors change partners in the romantic city. Predictable romance with good ingredients. Mary Ellis, Tullio Carminati, Lynne Overman, Ida Lupino. Written by Samuel Hoffenstein, Franz Schulz and Keene Thompson, from the play by Dwight Taylor; directed by Lewis Milestone; for Paramount.
'In everything except the unhappy choice of narrative it comes close to being an ideal production.'—*Variety*

Paris Interlude
US 1934   72m   bw

American newspapermen hang out in a Paris bar. Aimless comedy-drama which fails to achieve the intended mood of world-weariness. Madge Evans, Otto Kruger, Robert Young, Una Merkel, Ted Healy, Louis Henry, Edward Brophy. Written by Wells Root from the play All Good Americans by S. J. and Laura Perelman; directed by Edwin L. Marin; for MGM. '60 minutes instead of 72 would still have left something to be desired—further cutting.'—*Variety*

Paris Model
US 1953   88m   bw

Stories involving four copies of the same Paris gown. Depressing dramatic package with production values at a low ebb and some pleasant talents going awry. Paulette Goddard, Eva Gabor, Marilyn Maxwell, Barbara Lawrence, Tom Conway, Leif Erickson, Florence Bates, Cecil Kellaway, Robert Hutton. Written by Robert Smith; directed by Alfred E. Green; for Albert Zugsmith / Columbia.

Paris Qui Dort*
France 1923   40m approx (24 fps)   bw silent
Films Diamant (Maurice Diamant-Berger)
aka: *The Crazy Ray*

A mad scientist invents a ray which brings everyone but six people in Paris to a halt. Mildly entertaining semi-professional comedy showing several of its director's most engaging traits.
wd, ed René Clair ph Maurice Défassiaux, Paul Guichard
Henri Rollan, Albert Préjean, Marcel Vallée, Madeleine Rodrigue

Paris, Texas**
West Germany / France 1984   148m colour
Road Movies / Argos (Don Guest, Anatole Dauman)

After separating from his wife a man goes missing and is later found in the small town where he was born.
Long, enigmatic but generally fascinating puzzle-without-a-solution, about people who never find what they want.

w Sam Shepard d Wim Wenders ph Robby Müller m Ry Cooder
Harry Dean Stanton, Dean Stockwell, Aurore Clement, Hunter Carson, Nastassja Kinski, Bernhard Wicki
† NB: Filmed in English.

Paris Underground
US 1945   97m   bw
(UA) Constance Bennett
GB title: *Madame Pimpernel*

Two women caught in Paris when the Nazis invade continue their resistance activities. Artificial and not very exciting flagwaver.
w Boris Ingster, Gertrude Purcell, *novel* Etta Shiber d Gregory Ratoff ph Lee Garmes
m Alexander Tansman
Constance Bennett, Gracie Fields, George Rigaud, Kurt Kreuger, Leslie Vincent
'Mainly trash, involving enough handsome young men, in various poses of gallant gratitude, to satisfy Mae West in her prime.'—*James Agee*
AAN: Alexander Tansman

Paris When It Sizzles
US 1963   110m   Technicolor
Paramount (Richard Quine, George Axelrod)

A film writer tries out several script ideas with his secretary as heroine and himself as hero or villain.
As a French film called *La Fête à Henriette* this was a charming whimsy, but Hollywood made it heavy-handed and boring, especially as no one in it seems to be having much fun.
w George Axelrod, *screenplay* Julien Duvivier, Henri Jeanson d Richard Quine
ph Charles Lang Jnr m Nelson Riddle
William Holden, Audrey Hepburn, Grégoire Aslan, Noel Coward, Raymond Bussières
'The new script embalms the original instead of reviving it.'—*Stanley Kauffmann, New Republic*

Park Row
US 1952   83m   bw
UA / Samuel Fuller

Conflict breaks out between two newspapers in 1886 New York.
Earnest but flat low-budgeter of a rather unusual kind.
wd Samuel Fuller ph Jack Russell ad Ray Robinson
Gene Evans, Mary Welch, Herbert Hayes, Forrest Taylor

Parlor, Bedroom and Bath
US 1931   72m   bw

A mild-mannered husband has trouble when he becomes a landlord. Rather flatfooted farce, on a par with the star's other talkies. Buster Keaton, Charlotte Greenwood, Reginald Denny, Cliff Edwards. Written by Richard Schayer, Robert Hopkins, from the farce by Charles W. Bell and Mark Swan;

directed by Edward Sedgwick; for MGM. NB: The film was largely shot on location in Keaton's own house. 'Funny, clean enough for kids, and generally well made.'—*Variety*. (GB title: *Romeo in Pyjamas*.)

'As though torn from life's pages!'
Parnell*
US 1937   115m   bw
MGM (John M. Stahl)

A 19th-century Irish politician comes to grief through his love for a married woman.
Well made but miscast biopic, a resounding thud at the box office.

w John Van Druten, S. N. Behrman, *play* Elsie T. Schauffler *d* John M. Stahl *ph* Karl Freund *m* William Axt

Clark Gable, Myrna Loy, Edmund Gwenn, Edna May Oliver, Alan Marshal, Donald Crisp, Billie Burke, Berton Churchill, Donald Meek, Montagu Love, George Zucco

'Dull and overlong historical drama . . . word of mouth is likely to be poor.'—*Variety*
'A singularly pallid, tedious and unconvincing drama.'—*Frank Nugent*
'Poor though the picture may be, it is pleasing to think how clean a film magnate's wish-fulfilments are, how virginal and high-minded the tawdry pathetic human past becomes when the Mayers and Goldwyns turn the magic ring.'—*Graham Greene*

Parrish
US 1961   137m   Technicolor
Warner (Delmer Daves)

A young tobacco plantation worker has an ample sex life and the luck to become boss.
Predictable trudge through scenes from a bestselling novel, less offensive than most such adaptations.

wd Delmer Daves, *novel* Mildred Savage *ph* Harry Stradling *m* Max Steiner

Troy Donahue, Claudette Colbert, Karl Malden, Dean Jagger, Connie Stevens, Diane McBain, Sharon Hugueny

The Parson of Panamint
US 1941   84m   bw
Paramount (Harry Sherman)

A gold rush mountain town is corrupted by success until a two-fisted parson puts things right.
Middling western morality play.

w Harold Shumate, Adrian Scott, *novel* Peter B. Kyne *d* William McGann *ph* Russell Harlan *m* Irwin Talbot

Charles Ruggles, Ellen Drew, Philip Terry, Joseph Schildkraut, Henry Kolker, Janet Beecher, Paul Hurst

Une Partie de Campagne***
France 1936   40m   bw
Pantheon / Pierre Braunberger
aka: *A Day in the Country*

Around 1880, a Parisian tradesman and his family picnic one Sunday in the country, and one of the daughters falls in love.

An unfinished film which was much admired for its local colour, like an impressionist picture come to life.

wd Jean Renoir, *story* Guy de Maupassant *ph* Claude Renoir, Jean Bourgoin *m* Joseph Kosma

Sylvie Bataille, Georges Darnoul, Jane Marken, Paul Temps

Une Partie de Plaisir*
France 1975   100m   colour
La Boétie / Sunchild / Gerico (André Genoves)

The analysis of a divorce.
Bitter comedy drama, with the director's usual scriptwriter playing out his own life story. A little too incestuous for its own good, but with striking moments.

w Paul Gegauff *d* Claude Chabrol *ph* Jean Rabier

Paul Gegauff, Danielle Gegauff, Paula Moore, Michel Valette

Partners
US 1982   98m   Movielab
Titan (Aaron Russo)

Two Los Angeles police officers, one straight and one gay, investigate the murder of a homosexual.
Uneasy comedy-melodrama of somewhat mysterious purpose.

w Francis Veber *d* James Burrows *ph* Victor J. Kemper *m* Georges Delerue

John Hurt, Ryan O'Neal, Kenneth McMillan, Robyn Douglass, Jay Robinson

Partners in Crime
US 1937   66m   bw

A private eye stumbles on a plot to victimize the reform candidate in a local election.
Reliable second feature with few surprises.
Lynne Overman, Roscoe Karns, Muriel Hutchinson, Anthony Quinn, Inez Courtney, Charles Halton, Lucien Littlefield. Written by Garnett Weston from the novel by Kurt Steel; directed by Ralph Murphy; for Paramount. 'A cockeyed affair, perforated with surprises.'—*Variety*

The Party*
US 1968   98m   De Luxe   Panavision
UA / Mirisch / Geoffrey (Blake Edwards)

An accident-prone Indian actor is accidentally invited to a swank Hollywood party and wrecks it.
Would-be Tatiesque comedy of disaster, occasionally well-timed but far too long for all its gloss.

w Blake Edwards, Tom and Frank Waldman *d* Blake Edwards *ph* Lucien Ballard *m* Henry Mancini *pd* Fernando Carrere

Peter Sellers, Claudine Longet, Marge Champion, Fay McKenzie, Steve Franken, Buddy Lester

'One thing the old movie makers did know is that two reels is more than enough of this stuff.'—*Wilfred Sheed*

'It is only rarely that one laughs or even smiles; mostly one just chalks up another point for ingenuity.'—*Tom Milne*

Party Girl
US 1958   98m   Metrocolor   Cinemascope
MGM / Euterpe (Joe Pasternak)

In twenties Chicago, a lawyer wins a girl from a gangster.
Heavy-handed Scarface-style saga which at one time won a curious reputation for being a satire.

w George Wells *d* Nicholas Ray *ph* Robert Bronner *m* Jeff Alexander

Robert Taylor, Cyd Charisse, Lee J. Cobb, John Ireland, Kent Smith, Claire Kelly, Corey Allen

Party, Party
GB 1983   98m   colour

A teenager throws a drunken party while his parents are out. Ghastly British rubbish: no plot and nothing to laugh at at all, just young people making asses of themselves. Daniel Peacock, Karl Howman, Perry Fenwick, Sean Chapman, Phoebe Nicholls, Caroline Quentin. Written by Daniel Peacock, Terry Winsor; directed by Terry Winsor; for A & M Records.

Party Wire
US 1935   70m   bw

Small-town gossipers listen in on party wires and draw the wrong conclusions. Multi-stranded comedy-drama; not important but quite pleasant. Jean Arthur, Victor Jory, Helen Lowell, Charley Grapewin, Clara Blandick, Maude Eburne. Written by Ethel Hill, John Howard Lawson, Bruce Manning; directed by Erle C. Kenton; for Columbia. 'Entertaining for the family trade.'—*Variety*

The Party's Over
GB 1963   94m   bw
Tricastle (Anthony Perry)

An American girl joins a group of Chelsea beatniks and dies in a fall from a balcony; her father investigates.
Tasteless and boring swinging London trash which became notorious when its producers (Rank) disowned it because it features a party at which a man makes love to a dead girl. An unattractive display of moral squalor.

w Marc Behm *d* Guy Hamilton *ph* Larry Pizer *m* John Barry

Oliver Reed, Eddie Albert, Ann Lynn, Louise Sorel

The Passage
GB 1978   98m   Eastmancolor   Technovision
Hemdale / Passage / Lester Goldsmith-Maurice Binder (John Quested)

A Basque shepherd guides a scientist and his family from occupied France over the mountains into Spain.

Routine war suspenser given an unnecessary taint of sadism. Only those addicted to unpleasant detail will enjoy it.

w Bruce Micolaysen from his novel The Perilous Passage d J. Lee Thompson ph Michael Reed m Michael J. Lewis

Anthony Quinn, James Mason, Malcolm McDowell, Patricia Neal, Kay Lenz, Paul Clemens, Christopher Lee
● Video: VCL

Passage Home
GB 1955 102m bw
GFD / Group Films (Julian Wintle)

In 1931, tensions run high on a merchant ship when the captain accepts an attractive girl as passenger from South America.
Obvious melodrama complete with drunken captain and storm at sea; not badly done if it must be done at all.

w William Fairchild, novel Richard Armstrong d Roy Baker ph Geoffrey Unsworth m Clifton Parker

Peter Finch, Anthony Steel, Diane Cilento, Cyril Cusack, Geoffrey Keen, Hugh Griffith, Duncan Lamont, Bryan Forbes, Gordon Jackson, Michael Craig

A Passage to India**
GB 1984 163m Technicolor
EMI / John Brabourne-Richard Goodwin / HBO / John Heyman / Edward Sands

An English girl in India accuses a native of rape.
Another film about India under the Raj seems somewhat redundant after The Jewel in the Crown, Gandhi and The Far Pavilions, but at least under David Lean's direction this is intelligent and good to look at.

w,d,ed David Lean from the novel by E. M. Forster ph Ernest Day m Maurice Jarre pd John Box

Judy Davis, Alec Guinness, Victor Bannerjee, Peggy Ashcroft, James Fox, Nigel Havers, Richard Wilson, Antonia Pemberton, Michael Culver, Art Malik

Passage to Marseilles*
US 1944 110m bw
Warner (Hal B. Wallis)

Convicts escape from Devil's Island and join the Free French.
A rare example of a film boasting flashbacks within flashbacks within flashbacks, this confusing if sometimes entertaining all-star saga is done to death by its unconvincing flagwaving endpapers which prevent it from being at all comparable with Casablanca, as was clearly intended.

w Casey Robinson, Jack Moffitt, story Charles Nordhoff, James Hall ph James Wong Howe d Michael Curtiz m Max Steiner

Humphrey Bogart, Michèle Morgan, Claude Rains, Philip Dorn, Sidney Greenstreet, Peter

Lorre, Helmut Dantine, George Tobias, John Loder, Victor Francen, Eduardo Ciannelli
'Invincibly second rate.'—Richard Mallet, Punch

Passage West
US 1951 81m Technicolor

Religious pioneers headed west are menaced by escaped convicts. Entertaining minor western. John Payne, Dennis O'Keefe, Arleen Whelan, Peter Hanson. Written by Lewis R. Foster and Nedrick Young; directed by Lewis R. Foster; for Pine-Thomas / Paramount.

Passenger*
Poland 1963 63m bw Dyaliscope
Kadr
original title: Pasazerka

A German woman on a liner sees a woman she thinks she recognizes, and realizes that it is one of her charges when she was an official in a concentration camp.
Minor but effective character drama, in essence an investigation of guilt. The director died during its making, so some scenes are replaced by still photographs.

wd Andrzej Munk, play Zofia Posmysz-Piasecka ph Krzysztof Winiewicz

Aleksandra Slaska, Anna Ciepielewska

'I used to be somebody else; but I traded myself in . . .'

The Passenger*
Italy / France / Spain 1975 119m
Metrocolor
MGM / CCC / Concordia / CIPI (Carlo Ponti)
aka: Profession: Reporter

A TV reporter in a desert hotel changes identities with a dead man and finds he is now an African gun runner being drawn irresistibly towards his own death.
Pretty much in the style of Blow Up, but this time with no frills of fashion or nudity to bring the public in. After this, Antonioni was given up by the commercial cinema.

w Mark Peploe, Peter Wollen, Michelangelo Antonioni d Michelangelo Antonioni ph Luciano Tovoli md Ivan Vandor

Jack Nicholson, Maria Schneider, Jenny Runacre, Ian Hendry
'A film of real romance, depth and power . . . the very quintessence of cinema.'—Michael Billington, Illustrated London News

The Passing of the Third Floor Back*
GB 1935 90m bw
Gaumont (Ivor Montagu)

A Christ-like visitor stays at a London boarding house and changes the lives of the inmates.
Competent film version of a famous, sentimental, dated play.

w Michael Hogan, Alma Reville, play Jerome K. Jerome d Berthold Viertel ph Curt Courant

Conrad Veidt, René Ray, Anna Lee, Frank Cellier, Mary Clare, Beatrix Lehmann, Cathleen Nesbitt, Sara Allgood

'Drawing power of the book, the play, the picturization and the star should, on form, be invincible.'—Variety
'The pious note has been toned down, the milk of human kindness has been agreeably watered, and the types in the small London private hotel are observed with malicious realism.'—Graham Greene

Passion
US 1954 84m Technicolor

Jealousy erupts between ranchers in Spanish California. Peculiarly titled western of no merit whatsoever. Yvonne de Carlo, Cornel Wilde, Raymond Burr, Lon Chaney Jnr, Rodolfo Acosta, John Qualen. Written by Beatrice A. Dresher and Joseph Leytes; directed by Allan Dwan; for Benedict Bogeaus / RKO.

Passion Flower
US 1930 78m bw

Two rich girls marry beneath them. Tedious romantic drama about class and true love. Kay Francis, Kay Johnson, Charles Bickford, Lewis Stone, Zasu Pitts, Dickie Moore, Winter Hall. Written by Martin Flavin, L. E. Johnson, Edith Fitzgerald, from the novel by Kathleen Norris; directed by William de Mille; for MGM. 'A flock of talent, but talent doesn't always count on a marquee.'—Variety

The Passionate Friends**
GB 1948 91m bw
GFD / Cineguild (Eric Ambler)
US title: One Woman's Story

A woman marries an older man, then meets again her young lover.
A simple and obvious dramatic situation is tricked out with flashbacks and the inimitable high style of its director to make a satisfying entertainment.

w Eric Ambler, novel H. G. Wells d David Lean ph Guy Green m Richard Addinsell

Ann Todd, Trevor Howard, Claude Rains, Betty Ann Davies, Isabel Dean, Arthur Howard, Wilfrid Hyde White

The Passionate Plumber
US 1932 73m bw

A woman hires a professional lover to fend off the man she really loves but thinks she shouldn't have. Much revamped farce version of a comedy made straight in 1927 and 1942. All flopped, but this is the worst. Buster Keaton, Jimmy Durante, Irene Purcell, Polly Moran, Gilbert Roland, Mona Maris, Maude Eburne. Written by Laurence E. Johnson from the play Her Cardboard Lover by Frederick Lonsdale; directed by Edgar Sedgwick; for MGM. 'Another lay-me-down-to-sleeper for box offices.'—Variety

The Passionate Stranger
GB 1956 97m part bw, part Eastmancolor
British Lion / Beaconsfield (Peter Rogers, Gerald Thomas)
US title: A Novel Affair

A lady novelist bases a character on her virile

chauffeur; he reads the book and thinks she fancies him.
Feeble comedy, half of it consisting of a dramatization of the heroine's very dull novel.

w Muriel and Sydney Box d Muriel Box
ph Otto Heller m Humphrey Searle

Ralph Richardson, Margaret Leighton, Carlo Justini, Patricia Dainton, Marjorie Rhodes, Thorley Walters, Frederick Piper

Passionate Summer
GB 1958 104m Eastmancolor
Rank / Kenneth Harper

A divorced headmaster at a Jamaican school is loved by three women.
Silly melodrama with splendid backgrounds ruined by poor colour.

w Joan Henry, novel The Shadow and the Peak by Richard Mason d Rudolph Cartier
ph Ernest Steward m Angelo Lavagnino

Virginia McKenna, Bill Travers, Yvonne Mitchell, Alexander Knox, Ellen Barrie, Carl Mohner.

'The climactic hurricane does little to dispel the overall feeling of emotional suffocation.'—MFB

Passport to Hell
US 1932 72m bw

A woman tainted by scandal moved from country to country and marries a German commandant in the Cameroons to avoid internment. Reasonably lively drama which ends less well than it began. Elissa Landi, Paul Lukas, Warner Oland, Alexander Kirkland, Donald Crisp. Written by Bradley King, Leon Gordon, Harry Hervey; directed by Frank Lloyd; for Fox. 'Not a de luxer; Broadway spotted because of the product shortage.'—Variety

Passport to Pimlico****
GB 1949 84m bw
Ealing (E. V. H. Emmett)

Part of a London district is discovered to belong to Burgundy, and the inhabitants find themselves free of rationing restrictions.
A cleverly detailed little comedy which inaugurated the best period of Ealing, its preoccupation with suburban man and his foibles. Not exactly satire, but great fun, and kindly with it.

w T. E. B. Clarke d Henry Cornelius
ph Lionel Banes m Georges Auric

Stanley Holloway, Margaret Rutherford, Basil Radford, Naunton Wayne, Hermione Baddeley, John Slater, Paul Dupuis, Jane Hylton, Raymond Huntley, Betty Warren, Barbara Murray, Sidney Tafler

† The film was based on a genuine news item. The Canadian government presented to the Netherlands the room in which Princess Juliana was to bear a child.

AAN: T. E. B. Clarke

Passport to Treason
GB 1956 80m bw

A detective traces the death of his colleague to fascists working within an alleged peace group. Stock melodramatic situations straightforwardly presented make this a watchable support. Rod Cameron, Lois Maxwell, Clifford Evans, John Colicos, Ballard Berkeley. Written by Kenneth Hayles and Norman Hudis; directed by Robert S. Baker; for Mid Century / Eros.

The Password Is Courage*
GB 1962 116m bw
MGM / Andrew and Virginia Stone

In Europe during World War II, Sgt-Major Charles Coward has a career of escapes and audacious anti-Nazi exploits.
Lively, slightly over-humorous account of one man's war, well mounted and shot entirely on location.

wd Andrew L. Stone, biography John Castle
ph David Boulton

Dirk Bogarde, Maria Perschy, Alfred Lynch, Nigel Stock, Reginald Beckwith
'The experiences are, it seems, mainly true but they do not seem so.'—Guardian

Pastor Hall*
GB 1940 97m bw
Charter (John Boulting)

The story of German village pastor Niemoller, who in 1934 was shot for denouncing the Nazis.
A courageous film of its time, not very interesting dramatically or cinematically.

w Leslie Arliss, Haworth Bromley, Anna Reiner, play Ernst Toller d Roy Boulting
ph Max Greene

Wilfrid Lawson, Nova Pilbeam, Seymour Hicks, Marius Goring, Percy Walsh, Brian Worth, Peter Cotes, Hay Petrie

'Not much meat on her, but what there is is cherce!'

Pat and Mike**
US 1952 95m bw
MGM (Lawrence Weingarten)

A small-time sports promoter takes on a female intellectual multi-champion.
A comedy which amuses because of its star playing, but doesn't really develop. All very easy going, with guest appearances from sporting personalities.

w Ruth Gordon, Garson Kanin d George Cukor ph William Daniels m David Raksin

Spencer Tracy, Katharine Hepburn, Aldo Ray, William Ching, Sammy White, Jim Backus, Phyllis Povah

AAN: script

Pat Garrett and Billy the Kid
US 1973 106m Metrocolor Panavision
MGM (Gordon Carroll)

Blood-spattered version of a western legend, with violence always to the fore, accentuated by the impossibility of listening to the dialogue because of poor direction and recording.

w Rudolph Wurlitzer d Sam Peckinpah
ph John Coquillon m Bob Dylan

James Coburn, Kris Kristofferson, Bob Dylan, Richard Jaeckel, Katy Jurado, Slim Pickens, Chill Wills, Jason Robards Jnr

'A sombre, intense, downbeat essay on the truth behind the legend and the legend behind the truth.'—Sight and Sound
'Shows what Peckinpah can do when he doesn't put his mind to it.'—Stanley Kauffmann
'A rash adventure in inadvertent self-parody.'—William S. Pechter
'Ambitious, erotic, peculiarly unrealized . . .'—Pauline Kael, New Yorker

● Video: MGM / UA

A Patch of Blue*
US 1965 105m bw Panavision
MGM / Pandro S. Berman

A blind girl who lives in a slum is helped by a negro with whom she falls in love without realizing his colour.
Polished tearjerker with racial overtones; nicely done for those who can take it.

wd Guy Green, novel Be Ready with Bells and Drums by Elizabeth Kata ph Robert Burks m Jerry Goldsmith

Sidney Poitier, Elizabeth Hartman, Shelley Winters, Wallace Ford, Ivan Dixon, Elizabeth Fraser, John Qualen

AA: Shelley Winters
AAN: Robert Burks; Jerry Goldsmith; Elizabeth Hartman

Paternity
US 1981 93m Movielab
Paramount (Jerry Tokofsky)

A middle-aged bachelor decides to father a son via a hired mother, who will then return the child to him.
Tastelessly up-dated Hollywood romance with predictable complications. Not worth sitting through.

w Charlie Peters d David Steinberg
ph Bobby Byrne m David Shire

Burt Reynolds, Beverly D'Angelo, Norman Fell, Paul Dooley, Elizabeth Ashley, Lauren Hutton, Juanita Moore

Pather Panchali**
India 1955 115m bw
Government of West Bengal

In a small Bengal village, the son of a would-be writer grows up in poverty and tragedy before setting off with what remains of the family to seek a living in Benares.
A remarkable first film of a director now famous, showing that people are much the same though the details of their daily lives may be different. The pace may be slow but the content is mainly absorbing.

wd Satyajit Ray, novels Bhibuti Bashan Bannerjee ph Subrata Mitra m Ravi Shankar

Kanu Bannerjee, Karuna Bannerjee, Uma Das Gupta, Subir Bannerjee, Chunibala

Paths of Glory****
US 1957 86m bw
UA / Bryna (James B. Harris)

In 1916 in the French trenches, three soldiers
are courtmartialled for cowardice.
Incisive melodrama chiefly depicting the
corruption and incompetence of the high
command; the plight of the soldiers is less
interesting. The trench scenes are the most
vivid ever made, and the rest is shot in
genuine castles, with resultant difficulties of
lighting and recording; the overall result is an
overpowering piece of cinema.

w Stanley Kubrick, Calder Willingham, Jim
Thompson, *novel* Humphrey Cobb *d Stanley
Kubrick ph* Georg Krause *m* Gerald Fried

*Kirk Douglas, Adolphe Menjou, George
Macready, Wayne Morris, Richard Anderson,
Ralph Meeker, Timothy Carey*
  'A bitter and biting tale, told with stunning
point and nerve-racking intensity.'—*Judith
Crist*
  'Beautifully performed, staged,
photographed, cut and scored.'—*Colin Young*

Patrick the Great*
US 1944 88m bw
Universal (Howard Benedict)

An actor whose career is waning is jealous of
his young son.
Slick teenage family comedy, virtually a one-
man show for O'Connor.

w Jane Hall, Bertram Millhauser, Dorothy
Bennett, Frederick and Ralph Block *d* Frank
Ryan *ph* Frank Redman *m* Hans Salter

*Donald O'Connor, Donald Cook, Peggy
Ryan, Frances Dee, Eve Arden, Thomas
Gomez, Gavin Muir, Andrew Tombes*

The Patriot**
US 1928 110m approx (24 fps) bw
  silent
Paramount

Mad Czar Paul I is assassinated by his chief
adviser for the good of the state.
Historical melodrama with a good many
comedy touches: the director makes the most
of both aspects, but they don't in the end hang
together despite bravura acting.

w Hans Kraly, *novel* Alfred Neumann
d Ernst Lubitsch *ph* Bert Glennon *ad* Hans
Dreier

*Emil Jannings, Lewis Stone, Florence Vidor,
Neil Hamilton*
  'I believe this picture the most suggestive we
ever ran. Just another reason why we need
censorship. Small-town exhibitors need clean
pictures.'—*Ohio exhibitor's report in Motion
Picture Herald*

AA: Hans Kraly
AAN: best picture; Ernst Lubitsch; Lewis
Stone

The Patsy*
US 1927 80m approx (24 fps) bw
  silent
MGM
GB title: *The Politic Flapper*

Tired of being taken for granted, a girl puts on
a surprising show for her family.
Amusing comedy which, in sound, might have
made Miss Davies a bigger star than she ever
became.

w Agnes Christine Johnson, *play* Barry
Connors *d* King Vidor

Marion Davies, Marie Dressler, Lawrence
Gray, Del Henderson, Jane Winton
  'Marion Davies is in my opinion Filmland's
Funniest Female, the only one I would
mention in the same breath as Charlie
Chaplin.'—*A. P. Herbert, Punch*

The Patsy
US 1964 101m Technicolor
Paramount / Jerry Lewis (E. J. Glicksman)

Hollywood executives try to mould a bellboy
to replace a deceased comedian.
A few mildly funny scenes scarcely atone for a
long raucous comedy in which the star
upstages his betters.

wd Jerry Lewis *ph* Wallace Kelley *m* David
Raksin

*Jerry Lewis, Everett Sloane, Peter Lorre,
John Carradine, Phil Harris, Hans Conried*

'Inside the skyscraper jungle! Ruthless men
  and ambitious women clawing for
  control of a billion-dollar empire!'

Patterns***
US 1956 88m bw
UA / Jed Harris, Michael Myerberg
GB title: *Patterns of Power*

The tough boss of a New York corporation
forces a showdown between a young executive
and the older ineffectual man who he hopes
will resign.
Tense little boardroom melodrama with
domestic asides, one of the best of the filmed
TV plays of the mid-fifties.

w Rod Serling, from his play *d* Fielder Cook
ph Boris Kaufman

*Van Heflin, Everett Sloane, Ed Begley,
Beatrice Straight, Elizabeth Wilson*

Patton***
US 1970 171m De Luxe Dimension
  150
TCF (Frank McCarthy)
GB title: *Patton—Lust for Glory*

World War II adventures of an aggressive
American general.
Brilliantly handled wartime character study
which is also a spectacle and tries too hard to
have it both ways, but as a piece of film-
making is hard to beat.

w Francis Ford Coppola, Edmund H. North
d Franklin Schaffner *ph* Fred Koenekamp
m Jerry Goldsmith

George C. Scott, Karl Malden, Michael Bates,
Stephen Young, Michael Strong, Frank
Latimore

  'Here is an actor so totally immersed in his
part that he almost makes you believe he is
the man himself.'—*John Gillett*

AA: best picture; script; Franklin Schaffner;
George C. Scott
AAN: Fred Koenekamp; Jerry Goldsmith
● *Video: CBS / Fox*

Paula
US 1952 80m bw
Columbia (Buddy Adler)
GB title: *The Silent Voice*

A barren wife causes a boy's deafness in an
accident; she cures and adopts him.
Adequate woman's picture, a vehicle for a star
and a luxuriant wardrobe.

w James Poe, William Sackheim *d* Rudolph
Maté *ph* Charles Lawton Jnr *m* George
Duning

*Loretta Young, Kent Smith, Alexander Knox,
Tommy Rettig*

The Pawnbroker**
US 1965 114m bw
Landau–Unger (Worthington Miner)

A Jew in slummy New York is haunted by his
experiences in Nazi prison camps.
Engrossing, somewhat over-melodramatic
character study, generally well done.

w David Friedkin, Morton Fine, *novel* Edward
Lewis Wallant *d* Sidney Lumet *ph* Boris
Kaufman *m* Quincy Jones

Rod Steiger, Brock Peters, Geraldine
Fitzgerald, Jaime Sanchez, Thelma Oliver,
Juano Hernandez

AAN: Rod Steiger
● *Video: Polygram*

Pay or Die!*
US 1960 109m bw
Allied Artists (Richard Wilson)

In 1906, a New York Italian police detective
forms a special squad to combat the Black
Hand.
Tough, convincing period melodrama.

w Richard Wilson, Bertram Millhauser
d Richard Wilson *ph* Lucien Ballard
m David Raksin *ad* Fernando Carrere

Ernest Borgnine, Alan Austin, Zohra
Lampert, Robert F. Simon, Renata Vanni

Payday
US 1972 103m colour
Cinerama / Pumice / Fantasy (Ralph J.
  Gleason)

An over-age pop singer has personal problems
which erupt into violence.
Well made, dislikeable melodrama.

w Don Carpenter *d* Daryl Duke *ph* Richard
C. Glouner *md* Ed Bogas

*Rip Torn, Ahna Capri, Elayne Heilveil,
Michael C. Gwynn*

Payment Deferred*
US 1932 75m bw
MGM

A man desperate for money poisons his
wealthy nephew.
Watchable photographed play.

w Ernest Vajda, Claudine West, *play* Jeffrey
Dell *d* Lothar Mendes *ph* Merritt Gerstad

Charles Laughton, Maureen O'Sullivan, Ray
Milland, Dorothy Peterson, Veree Teasdale,
Billy Bevan, Halliwell Hobbes
  'In spite of its excellence, it will probably
prove indifferent box office.'—*Variety*

Payment on Demand*
US 1951 90m bw
RKO / Jack H. Skirball

A happy wife and mother is appalled when her
husband asks for a divorce.
A star suffers her way through luxury to a
happy ending; good enough stuff for its
intended audience.

w Bruce Manning, Curtis Bernhardt *d* Curtis
Bernhardt *ph* Leo Tover *m* Victor Young

Bette Davis, Barry Sullivan, Jane Cowl, Kent
Taylor, Betty Lynn, John Sutton, Frances
Dee, Otto Kruger
  'An absolutely typical Joan Crawford
picture except that Bette Davis happens to be
in the Joan Crawford part.'—*Richard Mallett,
Punch*

Payroll*
GB 1961 105m bw
Anglo Amalgamated / Lynx (Norman
  Priggen)

Small-time crooks snatch £100,000, but after
the getaway things begin to go wrong.
Tense, vivid, thoroughly predictable *Rififi*-
style thriller, handled with solid
professionalism.

w George Baxt, *novel* Derek Bickerton
d Sidney Hayers *ph* Ernest Steward *m* Reg
Owen

Michael Craig, Billie Whitelaw, Françoise
Prévost, Kenneth Griffith, William Lucas,
Tom Bell, Barry Keegan, Joan Rice, Glyn
Houston

Peach O'Reno
US 1931 66m bw

Two incompetent lawyers work on a divorce
case. Burlesque-style comedy with cabaret
asides. Thin stuff. Bert Wheeler, Robert
Woolsey, Dorothy Lee, Joseph Cawthorn,
Cora Witherspoon, Zelma O'Neal. Written by
Ralph Spence, Tim Whelan; directed by
William Seiter; for RKO-Pathé. 'Less than
average; low comedy laughs for the minor
spots.'—*Variety*

The Pearl of Death*
US 1944 67m bw
Universal (Howard S. Benedict)

When a valuable pearl is stolen, Sherlock
Holmes has only his own cleverness to blame;

THE PEARL OF DEATH.   Basil Rathbone as Sherlock Holmes lays a trap for villainess-in-
disguise Evelyn Ankers. Nigel Bruce and Ian Wolfe are mere pawns.

but he redeems himself by trapping 'The
Creeper'.
An amusing picturization of Doyle's *The Six
Napoleons*, with the addition of a horror
figure; it plays very well and is certainly among
the best of this series.

w Bertram Millhauser *d* Roy William Neill
ph Virgil Miller *m* Paul Sawtell

Basil Rathbone, *Nigel Bruce*, Dennis Hoey,
Miles Mander, Rondo Hatton, Evelyn Ankers

Peck's Bad Boy
US 1934 70m bw

Adventures of a well-intentioned but accident-
prone boy in a midwestern town. Old-
fashioned American juvenile classic, modestly
well done. Jackie Cooper, Jackie Searle,
Dorothy Peterson, Thomas Meighan. Written
by Bernard Schubert and Marguerite Roberts
from the story by G. W. Peck; directed by
Edward Cline; for Sol Lesser / Fox.
(Previously made in 1921 with Jackie Coogan.)

Peeper
US 1975 87m De Luxe Panavision
TCF / Chartoff–Winkler (Ron Buck)

In 1947 Los Angeles, a poor British private
eye gets into trouble when he seeks a man's
lost daughter.
Semi-spoofing Chandleresque caper which is
never quite funny or quite thrilling enough.

w W. D. Richter, *novel* Deadfall by Keith
Laumer *d* Peter Hyams *ph* Earl Rath
m Richard Clements

Michael Caine, Natalie Wood, Kitty Winn,
Thayer David, Liam Dunn
  'Flimsy whimsy.'—*Variety*

Peeping Tom
GB 1959 109m Eastmancolor
Anglo Amalgamated / Michael Powell

A film studio focus puller is obsessed by the
lust to murder beautiful women and
photograph the fear on their faces.
Thoroughly disagreeable suspenser, a kind of
compendium of the bad taste the director
showed in flashes during his career.

w Leo Marks *d* Michael Powell *ph* Otto
Heller *m* Brian Easdale

Carl Boehm, Moira Shearer, Anna Massey,
Maxine Audley, Esmond Knight, Michael
Goodliffe, Shirley Ann Field, Jack Watson
  'Of enormous and deserved reputation.'—
Time Out, 1982

Peg of Old Drury*
GB 1935 76m bw
Herbert Wilcox / B & D

The romance of 18th-century actress Peg
Woffington with David Garrick.

Primitive but vivacious historical romp with adequate star performances.

w Miles Malleson, *play* Masks and Faces by Charles Reade, Tom Taylor *d* Herbert Wilcox *ph* F. A. Young

Anna Neagle, Cedric Hardwicke, Jack Hawkins, Margaretta Scott, Hay Petrie

Peg o' My Heart
US 1933 86m bw

To the concern of his family, an English nobleman falls for an Irish colleen. Half-hearted version of a famous lavender-tinted stage hit previously filmed in the twenties with its original star Laurette Taylor; but by 1933 its time was past. Marion Davies, Onslow Stevens, Alan Mowbray, Robert Greig, Irene Browne, J. Farrell MacDonald, Juliette Compton. Written by Frances Marion, from the play by J. Hartley Manners; directed by Robert Z. Leonard; for MGM. 'Just an 86-minute Irish monologue . . . undeservedly flattered by an almost perfect production.'— *Variety*

Peking Express
US 1951 90m bw
Paramount / Hal B. Wallis

In communist China, an assortment of people are aboard a train which is diverted by outlaws.
Pot-boiling remake of *Shanghai Express* (qv); an adequate time-passer.

w John Meredyth Lucas *d* William Dieterle *ph* Charles Lang *m* Dmitri Tiomkin

Joseph Cotten, Corinne Calvet, Edmund Gwenn, Marvin Miller
'Lacks flavour or distinction.'—*Leonard Maltin*

The Penalty
US 1941 81m bw
MGM (Jack Chertok)

The son of a gangster is regenerated by farm life and turns against his father.
Antediluvian sweetness and light which wastes a good cast.

w Harry Ruskin, John C. Higgins *d* Harold S. Bucquet *ph* Harold Rosson

Edward Arnold, Lionel Barrymore, Marsha Hunt, Robert Sterling, Gene Reynolds

Pendulum*
US 1969 102m Technicolor
Columbia / Pendulum (Stanley Niss)

A convicted murderer and rapist is freed on appeal and kills the wife of the detective who arrested him.
Heavy-going police melodrama, efficient but not very interesting.

w Stanley Niss *d* George Schaefer *ph* Lionel Lindon *m* Walter Scharf

George Peppard, Jean Seberg, Richard Kiley, Charles McGraw, Robert F. Lyons, Madeleine Sherwood

Penelope
US 1966 98m Metrocolor Panavision
MGM / Euterpe (Joe Pasternak, Arthur Loew Jnr)

The wife of a bank vice-president is a bank robber and kleptomaniac.
Would be cute comedy which only sickens one for wasting its talent.

w George Wells, *novel* E. V. Cunningham *d* Arthur Hiller *ph* Harry Stradling *m* Johnny Williams

Natalie Wood, Ian Bannen, Dick Shawn, Peter Falk, Jonathan Winters, Lila Kedrova, Lou Jacobi, Norma Crane, Arthur Malet, Jerome Cowan

The Penguin Pool Murder*
US 1932 69m bw

Inspector Piper on a murder case is outsmarted by schoolmarm Hildegarde Withers. Mystery comedy which started a short series: plot smothered by wisecracks. *Edna May Oliver*, *James Gleason*, Mae Clarke, Robert Armstrong, Donald Cook, Edgar Kennedy. Written by Willis Goldbeck from the novel by Stuart Palmer; directed by George Archainbaud; for RKO. 'An odd blend of illogical happenings, but basically broad comedy.'—*Variety*

Penitentiary
US 1938 78m bw

A district attorney becomes prison warden, and his daughter falls for a convict. Scene-for-scene remake of *The Criminal Code* (qv) but considerably less dynamic. Walter Connolly, John Howard, Jean Parker, Robert Barrat, Marc Lawrence, Arthur Hohl, Paul Fix. Written by Fred Niblo Jnr and Seton I. Miller from a play by Martin Flavin; directed by John Brahm; for Columbia.

Penn of Pennsylvania
GB 1941 79m bw
British National (Richard Vernon)
US title: *The Courageous Mr Penn*

Persecuted Quakers leave England for America.
Stodgily fictionalized history.

w Anatole de Grunwald, *book* William Penn by C. E. Vulliamy *d* Lance Comfort

Clifford Evans, Deborah Kerr, Denis Arundell, Aubrey Mallalieu, Henry Oscar, Max Adrian

Pennies from Heaven
US 1936 81m bw

A wanderer protects a homeless little girl from the truant officer. Mild star musical, lucky enough to have a hit title song. Bing Crosby, Edith Fellows, Madge Evans, Louis Armstrong and his band. Written by Katherine Leslie Moore, William Rankin and Jo Swerling; directed by Norman Z. McLeod; for Columbia.

Pennies from Heaven*
US 1982 108m Metrocolor
MGM / Hera (Nora Kaye, Herbert Ross)

In 1934 Chicago, a sheet music salesman consoles himself for his drab and tragic life by fantasies induced by his songs.
The essence of Dennis Potter's British TV serial was hard enough to get at; transposed to America it becomes unattractive nonsense, and the song sequences are not even well staged despite the enormous expense.

w Dennis Potter *d* Herbert Ross *ph* Gordon Willis *md* Marvin Hamlisch, Billy May *pd* Ken Adam

Steve Martin, Bernadette Peters, Christopher Walken, Jessica Harper, John McMartin

AAN: Dennis Potter

Penny Paradise
GB 1938 72m bw

A tugboat captain thinks he has won the football pools; but the coupon wasn't posted.
An old, old story, put over with modest effectiveness. Edmund Gwenn, Betty Driver, Jimmy O'Dea, Marie O'Neill, Jack Livesey. Written by Tommy Thompson, W. L. Meade and Thomas Browne; directed by Carol Reed; for ATP.

Penny Points to Paradise
GB 1951 77m bw

A pools winner takes cash but nearly loses it to a forger. Abysmally made comedy, only interesting as an early teaming of the Goons. Harry Secombe, Peter Sellers, Spike Milligan, Alfred Marks, Bill Kerr, Freddie Frinton, Paddy O'Neil. Written by John Ormonde; directed by Tony Young; for Advance / Adelphi.

Penny Princess
GB 1952 94m Technicolor
Rank / Conquest (Frank Godwin)

A New York shopgirl inherits a tiny European state and boosts its economy by marketing a mixture of cheese and schnapps.
Thin, spoofy comedy with mild moments of fun.

wd Val Guest *ph* Geoffrey Unsworth *m* Ronald Hamner

Dirk Bogarde, Yolande Donlan, A. E. Matthews, Anthony Oliver, Edwin Styles, Reginald Beckwith, Kynaston Reeves, Peter Butterworth, Laurence Naismith, Mary Clare, Desmond Walter-Ellis

Penny Serenade*
US 1941 120m bw
Columbia (Fred Guiol)

Courtship, marriage and the death of two children are recollected by a woman contemplating divorce.
Well-played but uneasy film which veers suddenly and disconcertingly from light comedy into tragedy.

w Morrie Ryskind *d* George Stevens *ph* Joseph Walker *m* W. Franke Harling

Cary Grant, Irene Dunne, Beulah Bondi, Edgar Buchanan, Ann Doran

'To make something out of very little, and that so near at hand, is one of the tests of artistry.'—*Otis Ferguson*

'A tear compeller showing how Cary Grant and Irene Dunne lose first their own baby and then the one they adopt. Which, as Lady Bracknell would certainly have observed, looks like carelessness.'—*James Agate*

AAN: Cary Grant

Penrod and Sam
US 1937 68m bw

Exploits of a club for juvenile sleuths. Start of a second feature series which had little to do with the original period characters but was generally well received. Later the same year came *Penrod and his Twin Brother*. Billy Mauch, Frank Craven, Spring Byington, Craig Reynolds, Charles Halton. Written by Lillie Hayward and Hugh Cummings from the characters created by Booth Tarkington; directed by William McGann; for Warners. 'Should serve as a nucleus for swell exploitation tie-ups.'—*Variety*

† There had been an earlier version in 1931, starring Leon Janney; and the family turned up again in the Doris Day musicals *On Moonlight Bay* and *By the Light of the Silvery Moon*.

Penthouse*
US 1933 90m bw
GB title: *Crooks in Clover*

When he outlives his usefulness to the underworld, a lawyer is framed for murder. Sprightly murder comedy-drama which plays like a try-out for *The Thin Man*. Warner Baxter, Myrna Loy, C. Henry Gordon, Nat Pendleton, Charles Butterworth, George E. Stone. Written by Frances Goodrich and Albert Hackett; directed by W. S. Van Dyke; for Hunt Stromberg / MGM. 'Well-sustained crime solution with smashing climax and arresting title.'—*Variety*

The Penthouse
GB 1967 96m Eastmancolor
Paramount / Tahiti (Harry Fine)

Illicit lovers in an unfinished block of flats are terrorized by intruders.
Thoroughly objectionable and unpleasant melodrama with no attractive characters and no attempt to explain itself.

wd Peter Collinson, *play* The Meter Man by J. Scott Forbes *ph* Arthur Lavis *m* John Hawkesworth

Suzy Kendall, Terence Morgan, Tony Beckley, Norman Rodway, Martine Beswick
'Pornography in Pinter's clothing.'—*MFB*

The People against O'Hara*
US 1951 102m bw
MGM (William H. Wright)

An ex-alcoholic defence lawyer sacrifices himself to prove his client's innocence.

Formula drama, well made and entertainingly performed, with snatches of bright dialogue.

w John Monks Jnr, *novel* Eleanor Lipsky *d* John Sturges *ph* John Alton *m* Carmen Dragon

Spencer Tracy, Diana Lynn, Pat O'Brien, John Hodiak, James Arness, Arthur Shields, Eduardo Ciannelli, Louise Lorimer

The People Next Door
US 1970 93m De Luxe
Avco Embassy (Herb Brodkin)

Suburban parents have trouble with their drug-addicted teenage daughter.
Hysterical melodrama with good credentials.

w J. P. Miller, from his TV play *d* David Greene *ph* Gordon Willis *m* Don Sebesky

Eli Wallach, Julie Harris, Hal Holbrook, Cloris Leachman, Stephen McHattie, Nehemiah Persoff

'As unlovely a picture of suburban living as one is likely to see.'—*Judith Crist*

People on Sunday*
Germany 1929 72m approx (24 fps) bw silent
Filmstudio 1929
original title: *Menschen am Sonntag*

Two couples spend a day in Berlin's countryside.
Influential semi-documentary with fascinating credits.

w Billy Wilder, Curt Siodmak *d* Robert Siodmak, Fred Zinnemann, Edgar G. Ulmer *ph* Eugen Schüfftan

Brigitte Borchert, Christl Ehlers, Annie Schreyer

The People That Time Forgot
GB 1977 90m Technicolor
AIP / Amicus (John Dark)

Major McBride tries to rescue his old friend from a prehistoric island on which he disappeared in 1916.
Tepid sequel to *The Land That Time Forgot*: even the dinosaurs don't rise to the occasion.

w Patrick Tilley *d* Kevin Connor *ph* Alan Hume *m* John Scott *pd* Maurice Carter

Patrick Wayne, Sarah Douglas, Dana Gillespie, Doug McClure, Thorley Walters, Shane Rimmer, Tony Britton

People Will Talk
US 1935 60m bw

Mr and Mrs Wilton try to patch up their daughter's failing marriage. Slight domestic comedy with popular leads. Charles Ruggles, Mary Boland, Leila Hyams, Dean Jagger, Edward Brophy. Written by Herbert Fields, Sophie Kerr, F. Hugh Herbert; directed by Al Santell; for Paramount. 'Strictly light summer fare and not solid enough to stand alone.'—*Variety*

People Will Talk**
US 1951 110m bw
TCF (Darryl F. Zanuck)

A surgeon's unorthodox psychological

methods cause jealousy among his colleagues, especially when he falls in love with a pregnant patient.
Oddly entertaining jumble of melodrama, comedy, romance, speeches and a little mystery, all quite typical of its director.

wd Joseph L. Mankiewicz, *play* Dr Praetorius by Curt Goetz *ph* Milton Krasner *md* Alfred Newman

Cary Grant, Jeanne Crain, Finlay Currie, Hume Cronyn, Walter Slezak, Sidney Blackmer, Basil Ruysdael

'A picture so mature and refreshingly frank as to hold that an erring young woman might be rewarded with a wise and loving mate is most certainly a significant milestone in the moral emancipation of American films.'—*New York Times*

Pepe
US 1960 195m Eastmancolor
Cinemascope
Columbia / George Sidney (Jacques Gelman)

A Mexican peasant in Hollywood gets help from the stars.
Feeble and seemingly endless extravaganza in which the boring stretches far outnumber the rest, and few of the guests have anything worthwhile to do.

w Dorothy Kingsley, Claude Binyon *d* George Sidney *ph* Joe MacDonald *md* Johnny Green

Cantinflas, Dan Dailey, Shirley Jones, Ernie Kovacs, Jay North, William Demarest, Michael Callan, Maurice Chevalier, Bing Crosby, Richard Conte, Bobby Darin, Sammy Davis Jnr, Jimmy Durante, Zsa Zsa Gabor, Judy Garland, Hedda Hopper, Joey Bishop, Peter Lawford, Janet Leigh, Jack Lemmon, Kim Novak, André Previn, Donna Reed, Debbie Reynolds, Greer Garson, Edward G. Robinson, Cesar Romero, Frank Sinatra, Billie Burke, Tony Curtis, Dean Martin, Charles Coburn

AAN: Joe MacDonald; Johnny Green; song, 'Faraway Part of Town' (*m* André Previn, *ly* Dory Langdon)

Pépé le Moko**
France 1936 90m bw
Paris Film

A Parisian gangster lives in the Algerian casbah where the police can't get at him; but love causes him to emerge and be shot.
Romantic melodrama modelled on the American gangster film but with a decided poetic quality of its own: the Americans promptly paid it the compliment of remaking it as the not-too-bad *Algiers*.

w Henri Jeanson, Roger d'Ashelbe, *novel* Roger d'Ashelbe (Henri La Barthe) *d* Julien Duvivier *ph* Jules Kruger *m* Vincent Scotto *ad* Jacques Krauss

Jean Gabin, Mireille Ballin, Gabriel Gabrio, Lucas Gridoux

'One of the most compelling of all French films.'—*New Yorker, 1977*

'Perhaps there have been pictures as exciting on the thriller level . . . but I cannot remember one which has succeeded so admirably in raising the thriller to a poetic level.'—*Graham Greene*

Percy
GB 1971 103m Eastmancolor
Anglo EMI / Welbeck (Betty E. Box)

After an unfortunate accident, a young man undergoes a successful penis transplant, and sets out to discover who the donor was.
Barrage of phallic jokes, some quite funny, but mostly as witless as the whole idea.

w Hugh Leonard, *novel* Raymond Hitchcock d Ralph Thomas ph Ernest Steward m Ray Davies

Hywel Bennett, Elke Sommer, *Denholm Elliott*, Britt Ekland, Cyd Hayman

● *Video: Thorn EMI*

Percy's Progress
GB 1974 101m Eastmancolor
EMI (Betty E. Box)

A chemical causes impotence in all males except the owner of the first transplanted penis.
Percy dug deep, but this is really the bottom of the barrel.

w Sid Colin d Ralph Thomas ph Tony Imi m Tony Macauley

Leigh Lawson, Elke Sommer, Denholm Elliott, Judy Geeson, Harry H. Corbett, Vincent Price, Adrienne Posta, Julie Ege, James Booth

● *Video: Thorn EMI*

A Perfect Couple°
US 1979 112m De Luxe
TCF / Lions Gate (Robert Altman)

A middle-aged Greek much dependent on his family meets a jazz singer through a dating service.
A free-speaking update of *Marty*, featuring the Altman repertory company; intelligent sequences are muffled by the familiar Altman messiness of approach.

w Robert Altman, Allan Nicholls d Robert Altman ph Edmond L. Koons md Tom Pierson, Tony Berg

Paul Dooley, Marta Heflin, Titos Vandis, Belita Moreno, Henry Gibson, Dimitra Arliss

Perfect Day°
US 1929 20m bw

Various problems delay a family's departure for a picnic. Technically a most adept star comedy but its repetition can annoy. Laurel and Hardy, Edgar Kennedy. Written by Hal Roach, Leo McCarey and H. M. Walker; directed by James Parrott; for Hal Roach. (NB: The picnic was originally to have occupied the second reel, but the departure gags swelled to occupy the entire footage.)

Perfect Friday°
GB 1970 95m Eastmancolor
London Screenplays / Sunnymede (Dimitri de Grunwald)

A bank manager engages aristocratic help to rob his own bank.
Middling comedy caper.

w Anthony Greville-Bell, J. Scott Forbes d Peter Hall ph Alan Hume m Johnny Dankworth pd Terence Marsh

Stanley Baker, Ursula Andress, David Warner, Patience Collier, T. P. McKenna, David Waller, Joan Benham, Julian Orchard

● *Video: VCL*

The Perfect Furlough
US 1958 93m Eastmancolor
Cinemascope
U-I (Robert Arthur)
GB title: *Strictly for Pleasure*

To help morale at a remote Arctic army unit, one of the men is selected to enjoy the perfect leave in Paris on behalf of the others.
Amiable farce which entertains while it's on but is quickly forgotten.

w Stanley Shapiro d Blake Edwards ph Philip Lathrop m Frank Skinner

Tony Curtis, Janet Leigh, Elaine Stritch, Keenan Wynn, Troy Donahue, King Donovan, Linda Cristal

The Perfect Gentleman
US 1935 73m bw

A retired officer helps an actress make a comeback. Genial comedy which didn't quite work well enough to make an English variety star popular on both sides of the Atlantic. Cicely Courtneidge, Frank Morgan, Heather Angel, Herbert Mundin, Henry Stephenson. Written by Edward Childs Carpenter; directed by Tim Whelan; for MGM. (GB title: *The Imperfect Lady*.)

The Perfect Marriage
US 1946 88m bw
Paramount / Hal B. Wallis

On their tenth wedding anniversary, a happy couple have a row and start divorce proceedings.
Wispy comedy, unmemorable and rather tiresome.

w Leonard Spiegelgass, *play* Samson Raphaelson d Lewis Allen ph Russell Metty m Frederick Hollander

David Niven, Loretta Young, Eddie Albert, Nona Griffith, Virginia Field, Jerome Cowan, Rita Johnson, Charles Ruggles, Nana Bryant, Zasu Pitts

'Another film about disillusionment and reconciliation in a mansion with constant evening dress.'—*Sunday Times*

The Perfect Specimen
US 1937 82m bw
Warner (Harry Joe Brown)

The grandmother of a rich young man brings him up uncontaminated by the world, but

when a girl crashes her car into his fence he proves fitted to deal with the situation. Fantasticated comedy a long way after *Mr Deeds* and too slow by half.

w Norman Reilly Raine, Lawrence Riley, Brewster Morse, Fritz Falkenstein, Samuel Hopkins Adams d Michael Curtiz ph Charles Rosher

Errol Flynn, Joan Blondell, Hugh Herbert, Edward Everett Horton, May Robson, Dick Foran, Beverly Roberts, Allen Jenkins

'Upper bracket comedy for the family trade.'—*Variety*

Perfect Strangers°°
GB 1945 102m bw
MGM / London Films (Alexander Korda)
US title: *Vacation from Marriage*

A downtrodden clerk and his dowdy wife go to war, and come back unrecognizably improved. Pleasant comedy with good actors; but the turnabout of two such caricatures really strains credibility.

w Clemence Dane, Anthony Pelissier d Alexander Korda ph Georges Périnal m Clifton Parker

Robert Donat, Deborah Kerr, Glynis Johns, Ann Todd, Roland Culver, Elliot Mason, Eliot Makeham, Brefni O'Rourke, Edward Rigby

'War is supposed to be the catalyst, the sportsman's bracer; and the film's chief weakness is its failure to show the briefly exalted couple sinking back, uncontrollably, under their peacetime stone.'—*James Agee*

AA: original story (Clemence Dane)

'They met by chance, and once they kissed, they knew they never should have!'

Perfect Strangers
US 1950 87m bw
Warner (Jerry Wald)
GB title: *Too Dangerous to Love*

Two jurors on a murder case fall in love. Talkative, unlikely, and rather boring potboiler.

w Edith Sommer, *play* Ladies and Gentlemen by Charles MacArthur, Ben Hecht d Bretaigne Windust ph Peverell Marley m Leigh Harline

Ginger Rogers, Dennis Morgan, Thelma Ritter, Margalo Gillmore, Howard Freeman, Alan Reed, Paul Ford, George Chandler

Perfect Understanding°
GB 1933 80m bw
Gloria Swanson British Pictures Ltd

A couple agree to marry on condition that they will never disagree with each other. Silly comedy with a unique star combination looking acutely uncomfortable.

w Miles Malleson, Michael Powell d Cyril Gardner ph Curt Courant

Gloria Swanson, Laurence Olivier, John Halliday, Nigel Playfair, Michael Farmer, Genevieve Tobin, Nora Swinburne

'Dull and talky picture, done in the uninspiring British style.'—*Variety*

The Perfect Woman°
GB 1949 89m bw
GFD / Two Cities (George and Alfred Black)

A girl changes places with her inventor uncle's robot woman.

Described as a romp, this is in fact a pretty good farce, very fast moving and well played after the usual expository start.

w George Black, Bernard Knowles, J. B. Boothroyd, play Wallace Geoffrey, Basil Mitchell d Bernard Knowles ph Jack Hildyard m Arthur Wilkinson

Patricia Roc, Nigel Patrick, Stanley Holloway, David Hurst, Miles Malleson, Irene Handl

Performance°
GB 1970 105m Technicolor
Warner / Goodtimes (Donald Cammell)

A vicious gangster moves in with an ex-pop star.

Dense, Pinterish melodrama about alter egos; not really worth the trouble it takes, but superficially very flashily done.

w Donald Cammell d Nicolas Roeg, Donald Cammell ph Nicolas Roeg m Jack Nitzche md Randy Newman

James Fox, Mick Jagger, Anita Pallenberg, Michèle Breton, Stanley Meadows, Allan Cuthbertson

'A humourless, messy mixture of crime and decadence and drug-induced hallucination.'—New Yorker, 1980

'You don't have to be a drug addict, pederast, sado-masochist or nitwit to enjoy it, but being one or more of these things would help.'—John Simon

● Video: Warner

Perilous Holiday
US 1946 89m bw

A newly acquainted couple become involved with counterfeiters in Mexico City. Passable comedy-crime programme filler. Pat O'Brien, Ruth Warrick, Alan Hale, Minna Gombell. Written by Robert Carson and Roy Chanslor; directed by Edward H. Griffith; for Columbia.

A Perilous Journey
US 1953 87m bw
Republic (W. J. O'Sullivan)

A party of women sail to the California goldfields to sell themselves into marriage. Reasonably lively action drama.

w Richard Wormser, novel The Golden Tide by Virgie Roe d R. G. Springsteen ph Jack Marta m Victor Young

Vera Ralston, David Brian, Charles Winninger, Scott Brady, Virginia Grey, Ben Cooper

The Perils of Pauline°
US 1947 96m Technicolor
Paramount (Sol C. Siegel)

The career of silent serial queen Pearl White. An agreeable recreation of old time Hollywood, with plenty of slapstick chases but a shade too much sentiment also.

w P. J. Wolfson d George Marshall ph Ray Rennahan md Robert Emmett Dolan

Betty Hutton, John Lund, Billy de Wolfe, William Demarest, Constance Collier, Frank Faylen, William Farnum, Paul Panzer, Snub Pollard, Creighton Hale, Chester Conklin, James Finlayson, Hank Mann, Bert Roach, Francis McDonald, Chester Clute

'People who can accept such stuff as solid gold have either forgotten a lot, or never knew first-rate slapstick when they saw it, twenty or thirty years ago, when it was one of the wonders of the world.'—James Agee

AAN: song 'I Wish I Didn't Love You So' (m / ly Frank Loesser)

● Video: European

Period of Adjustment
US 1962 122m bw Panavision
MGM / Marton (Lawrence Weingarten)

A Korean War veteran has the shakes and his sexual adequacy is effected, as his wife furiously discovers.

Comedy of maladjustment, tolerably witty but unsuitably widescreened.

w Isabel Lennart, play Tennessee Williams d George Roy Hill ph Paul bc. Vogel m Lyn Murray

Tony Franciosa, Jane Fonda, Jim Hutton, Lois Nettleton

Les Perles de la Couronne°
France 1937 118m bw

The history over four centuries of seven pearls given by Pope Clement VII to Catherine de Medici. Generally amusing series of historical sketches in Guitry's inimitable style. Sacha Guitry, Renée Saint-Cyr, Lyn Harding, Percy Marmont, Arletty, Claude Dauphin, Raimu, Jean-Louis Barrault, Jacqueline Delubac. Written by Sacha Guitry; directed by Sacha Guitry and Christian-Jaque; for Serge Sandburg / Tobis. 'Headed to bring in returns both at home and abroad.'—Variety.
† The picture tried, but failed, to be intelligible without sub-titles to all language-speakers.

Permission to Kill
US / Austria 1975 97m Technicolor Panavision
Warner / Sascha (Paul Mills)

British agents try to stop a communist returning home from the west.

Prolonged, confusing and boring spy melodrama in which everyone looks understandably glum.

w Robin Estridge, from his novel d Cyril Frankel ph Freddie Young m Richard Rodney Bennett

Bekim Fehmiu, Dirk Bogarde, Ava Gardner, Timothy Dalton, Frederic Forrest

'Pretentious political mishmash.'—MFB

Perri°°
US 1957 75m Technicolor
Walt Disney (Winston Hibler)

The life of a squirrel.

Disney's first True Life Fantasy, in which live footage of animals is manipulated against artificial backgrounds to produce an effect as charming and unreal as a cartoon.

w Ralph Wright, Winston Hibler, novel Felix Salten d Ralph Wright ph various m Paul Smith

AAN: Paul Smith

Persecution
GB 1974 96m Eastmancolor
Fanfare / Tyburn (Kevin Francis)

A rich American woman in England is hated by her son and fearful that her murky past will be revealed.

Rich but not engrossing nonsense, somewhat à la Baby Jane, with hazy script and stolid production.

w Robert B. Hutton, Rosemary Wootten d Don Chaffey ph Ken Talbot m Paul Ferris

Lana Turner, Ralph Bates, Olga Georges-Picot, Trevor Howard, Suzan Farmer, Ronald Howard, Patrick Allen

'Gives off the unmistakable odour of damp mothballs.'—Michael Billington, Illustrated London News

Persona°°
Sweden 1966 81m bw
Svensk Filmindustri (Lars-Owe Carlberg)

A nurse begins to identify with her mentally ill patient, and herself has a nervous breakdown. Intense clinical study presented in a very complex cinematic manner which tends to obscure the main theme while providing endless fascination for cinéastes.

wd Ingmar Bergman ph Sven Nykvist m Lars Johan Werle, Liv Ullmann, Bibi Andersson, Gunnar Bjornstrand

'Reactions have ranged from incomprehension to irritation with what is dismissed as a characteristic piece of self-indulgence on Bergman's part—Bergman talking to himself again.'—David Wilson, MFB

'A puzzling, obsessive film that Bergman seems not so much to have worked out as to have torn from himself.'—New Yorker, 1977

Personal Affair
GB 1953 83m bw
Rank / Two Cities (Anthony Darnborough)

A schoolmaster and his neurotic wife run into trouble when a girl pupil develops a crush on him.

Preposterous domestic drama making much ado about nothing.

w Lesley Storm, from her play d Anthony Pelissier ph Reg Wyer m William Alwyn

Leo Genn, Gene Tierney, Glynis Johns, Pamela Brown

Personal Best

US 1982 122m Technicolor
Warner (Robert Towne)

A female Olympic track star has a lesbian
relationship.
So what, is the response to two numbing hours
of tedium.

wd Robert Towne *ph* Michael Chapman
m Jack Nitzsche

Mariel Hemingway, Scott Glenn, Patrice
Donnelly, Kenny Moore, Jim Moody
  'There's an undercurrent of flabbergasted
awe in this celebration of women's bodies, and
everything in the movie is physically
charged.'—*Pauline Kael, New Yorker*

Personal Property*

US 1937 84m bw
MGM (John W. Considine Jnr)
GB title: *The Man in Possession*

An American widow in England, in financial
straits, falls for the bailiff sent to keep an eye
on her.
Moderate star comedy which still amuses.

w Hugh Mills, Ernest Vajda, *play* The Man
in Possession by H. M. Harwood *d* W. S. Van
Dyke II *ph* William Daniels *m* Franz
Waxman

Jean Harlow, Robert Taylor, Reginald Owen,
Una O'Connor, Henrietta Crosman,
E. E. Clive, Cora Witherspoon, Barnett
Parker
  'Harmless boudoir farce, for the
undergraduates.'—*Variety*

The Personality Kid

US 1934 70m bw

A prizefighter becomes intoxicated by his own
success and ignores his faithful wife. Mediocre
filler wasting reliable stars. Pat O'Brien,
Glenda Farrell, Claire Dodd, Henry O'Neill,
Robert Gleckler, Thomas Jackson. Written by
F. Hugh Herbert, Erwin Gelsey, Gene
Towne, Graham Baker; directed by Alan
Crosland; for Warners. 'Rates poorly: strictly
cuffo yarn.'—*Variety*

'She's the woman behind the killer behind
the gun!'

Persons in Hiding*

US 1939 71m bw
Paramount

A bored girl absconds with gangsters and
becomes a public enemy.
Interesting programmer which led to several
sequels using the same book as source; this
one was vaguely inspired by the story of
Bonnie and Clyde.

w William R. Lipman, Horace McCoy,
book J. Edgar Hoover *d* Louis King
ph Harry Fischbeck *m* Boris Morros

Patricia Morison, J. Carrol Naish, Lynne
Overman, William Henry, Helen Twelvetrees,
William Frawley
  'Strong supporter for the duals . . . will
depend entirely on rep of J. Edgar Hoover to
attract.'—*Variety*

'A little on the tame side, but distinguished
by the presence of a crooked and merciless
heroine.'—*Graham Greene*

Persons Unknown*

Italy 1958 105m bw
Lux / Vides / Cinecittà (Franco Cristaldi)
original title: *I Soliti Ignoti;* US title: *Big
Deal on Madonna Street*

Adventures of a gang of incompetent thieves,
who get arrested more often than they get
away, and finally, elaborately drill through a
wall into the bank . . . only to find it's the
wrong wall and they are in another room of
the same flat.
Spoof black comedy working up to an
elaborate take-off of *Rififi*; a great success in
Italy and the USA, mildly received elsewhere.

w Age Scarpelli, Suso Cecchi d'Amico, Mario
Monicelli *d* Mario Monicelli *ph* Gianni di
Venanzo *m* Piero Umiliani

Vittorio Gassman, Renato Salvatori, Toto,
Marcello Mastroianni, Memmo Carotenuto,
Carla Gravina, Rosanna Rory

'Honeymoon's over—time to get married!'

Pete 'n Tillie*

US 1972 100m Technicolor
  Panavision
Universal (Julius J. Epstein)

The tragi-comic marriage of two eccentrics.
Curious: plain drama treated as comedy, with
surprisingly satisfactory results, but not an
example to be followed.

w Julius J. Epstein, *novel* Witch's Milk by
Peter de Vries *d* Martin Ritt *ph* John
Alonzo *m* John T. Williams

Walter Matthau, Carol Burnett, Geraldine
Page, René Auberjonois, Barry Nelson,
Henry Jones
  'For the most part an amusing, moving,
sentimental comedy. The wisecracks stay on
this side of human possibility – that is, we
don't feel, as we do so often with Neil Simon,
that the characters have private gag writers in
their homes.'—*Stanley Kauffmann*

AAN: Julius J. Epstein; Geraldine Page

Pete Kelly's Blues*

US 1955 95m Warnercolor
  Cinemascope
Warner (Jack Webb)

Jazz musicians in the twenties get involved
with gangsters.
Minor cult film, mainly for the score;
dramatically it is not exactly compelling.

w Richard L. Breen *d* Jack Webb *ph* Hal
Rosson *ph* Harper Goff *m* Sammy Cahn,
Ray Heindorf, Arthur Hamilton, Matty
Matlock

Jack Webb, Edmond O'Brien, Janet Leigh,
Peggy Lee, Andy Devine, *Ella Fitzgerald,* Lee
Marvin, Martin Milner
  'Concerned with striking attitudes and
establishing an atmosphere rather than
developing anything very coherent in the way

of narrative . . . one remains aware of an
over-deliberate straining after effect.'—
Penelope Houston

AAN: Peggy Lee

'The most beautiful romance in all modern
  literature!'

Peter Ibbetson*

US 1935 85m bw
Paramount (Louis D. Lighton)

Childhood sweethearts meet again as adults,
are separated when he is imprisoned for her
husband's murder, but are reunited in heaven.
Downright peculiar romantic fantasy, even
more oddly cast, but extremely well produced.

w Vincent Lawrence, Waldemar Young,
Constance Collier, *novel* George du Maurier
d Henry Hathaway *ph* Charles Lang *m* Ernst
Toch

Gary Cooper, Ann Harding, Ida Lupino, John
Halliday, Douglass Dumbrille, Virginia
Weidler, Dickie Moore, Doris Lloyd
  'In a day and a world hard-boiled and
realistic Paramount hopes to sell a picture
about dreams and beauty and love. It just isn't
in the cards.'—*Variety*
  'A triumph of surrealist thought.'—*André
Breton*
  'One of the world's ten best films.'—*Luis
Bunuel*

AAN: Ernst Toch

Peter Pan***

US 1953 76m Technicolor
Walt Disney

Three London children are taken into
fairyland by a magic flying boy who cannot
grow up.
Solidly crafted cartoon version of a famous
children's play; not Disney's best work, but
still miles ahead of the competition.

supervisor Ben Sharpsteen *d* Wilfred Jackson,
Clyde Geronomi, Hamilton Luske

Peter the Great*

USSR 1937 96m bw

The rise to power of the famous autocrat.
Standard Russian first feature with plenty of
action and striking composition, but not really
memorable. Nikolai Simonov, Nikolai
Cherkassov, Alla Tarasova, M. Zharov.
Written by Alexei Tolstoy and Vladimir
Petrov; directed by Vladimir Petrov; for
Lenfilm. 'Surprisingly strong: a cinch in
Russian-languagers.'—*Variety*

The Peterville Diamond

GB 1942 85m bw
Warner (A. H. Salomon)

A bored wife revives her husband's interest by
cultivating the advances of a jewel thief.
Modest comedy-drama, smoothly presented:
the same play formed the basis of Dieterle's
Jewel Robbery.

w Brock Williams, Gordon Wellesley,
play Jewel Robbery by Ladislas Fodor
d Walter Forde *ph* Basil Emmott *md* Jack
Beaver

Anne Crawford, Donald Stewart, Renee
Houston, Oliver Wakefield, Charles Heslop,
William Hartnell, Felix Aylmer, Charles
Victor

Pete's Dragon
US 1977   127m   Technicolor
Walt Disney (Ron Miller, Jerome
    Courtland)

In Maine in 1900, a nine-year-old boy escapes
from grasping foster-parents with his pet
dragon, which no one but himself can see.
A kind of juvenile rewrite of *Harvey*. The
dragon is drawn (rather poorly) and the
human characters are not exactly three-
dimensional. A long way from *Mary Poppins*.

w Malcolm Marmorstein, *story* Seton
I. Miller, S. S. Field d Don Chaffey
ph Frank Phillips *anim* Ken Anderson
md Irwin Kostal *songs* Al Kasha, Joel
Hirschhorn ch Onna White

Sean Marshall, Mickey Rooney, Jim Dale,
Helen Reddy, Red Buttons, Shelley Winters,
Jim Backus, Joe E. Ross, Ben Wrigley
    'For a Disney film it's terribly badly made,
in parts so clumsy that it looks like the work of
the Burbank Amateur Camera Club.'—*Barry
Took, Punch*

AAN: music; song, 'Candle on the Water'
● Video: Rank

The Petrified Forest**
US 1936   83m   bw
Warner (Henry Blanke)

Travellers at a way station in the Arizona
desert are held up by gangsters.
Rather faded melodrama (it always was),
which is important to Hollywood for
introducing such well used figures as the poet
idealist hero and the gangster anti-hero, and
for giving Bogart his first meaty role.
Otherwise, the settings are artificial, the acting
theatrical, the development predictable and
the dialogue pretentious.

w Charles Kenyon, Delmer Daves,
play Robert E. Sherwood d Archie Mayo
ph Sol Polito md Leo F. Forbstein

Leslie Howard, Bette Davis, *Humphrey
Bogart,* Genevieve Tobin, Dick Foran, Joe
Sawyer, Porter Hall, Charley Grapewin

    ALAN SQUIER (Leslie Howard): 'Let there
be killing. All this evening I've had a feeling of
destiny closing in.'

    JACKIE (Joe Sawyer): 'Now, just behave
yourself and nobody'll get hurt. This is Duke
Mantee, the world-famous killer, and he's
hungry.'

    'Marquee draft should offset the philosophic
meanderings which minimize appeal.'—*Variety*
    'Drama slackens under the weight of Mr
Sherwood's rather half-baked philosophy.'—
Alistair Cooke
    'There is good dramatic material here, but
Mr Sherwood doesn't see his play as certain
things happening, but as ideas being
expressed, "significant" cosmic ideas. . . . Life
itself, which crept in during the opening scene,

embarrassed perhaps at hearing itself so
explicitly discussed, crept out again, leaving us
only with the symbols, the too pasteboard
desert, the stunted cardboard studio trees.'—
Graham Greene
† Remade as *Escape in the Desert* (qv).

Petticoat Fever
US 1936   80m   bw
MGM (Frank Davis)

A girl and her stuffy fiancé crash land their
plane in sub-Arctic Labrador and are helped
by a wireless operator who has not seen a
woman for two years.
Pert, slightly unusual comedy which comes off
pretty well.

w Harold Goldman, *play* Mark Reed
d George Fitzmaurice ph Ernest Haller
m William Axt

Robert Montgomery, Myrna Loy, Reginald
Owen, Winifred Shotter

The Petty Girl
US 1950   88m   Technicolor
Columbia (Nat Perrin)
GB title: *Girl of the Year*

A calendar artist takes a staid college
professor as his model, and causes a scandal.
Witless comedy musical which barely lingers in
the memory.

w Nat Perrin, *story* Mary McCarthy d Henry
Levin ph William Snyder m George Duning
songs Harold Arlen, Johnny Mercer

Robert Cummings, Joan Caulfield, Melville
Cooper, Elsa Lanchester, Audrey Long, Mary
Wickes, Frank Orth

Petulia*
US 1968   105m   Technicolor
Warner / Petersham (Raymond Wagner)

A doctor's life is disrupted by his meeting and
loving a kooky girl who has family problems.
Swinging London melodrama which happens
to be set in San Francisco. All very flashy, and
occasionally arresting or well acted, but adding
up to nothing.

w Lawrence B. Marcus, *novel* Me and the
Arch Kook Petulia by John Haase d Richard
Lester ph Nicolas Roeg m John Barry

George C. Scott, Julie Christie, Richard
Chamberlain, Joseph Cotten, Arthur Hill,
Shirley Knight, Kathleen Widdoes, Pippa
Scott

    'A sad and savage comment on the ways we
waste our time and ourselves in upper-middle-
class America.'—*Richard Schickel*
    'A soulless, arbitrary, attitudinizing piece of
claptrap.'—*John Simon*

'Everybody in this town hides behind plain
    wrappers!'

Peyton Place**
US 1957   157m   De Luxe   Cinemascope
TCF (Jerry Wald)

Sex, frustration and violence ferment under
the placid surface of a small New England
town.

Well-made film of what was at the time a
scandalous bestseller, one of the first to reveal
those nasty secrets of 'ordinary people'.

w John Michael Hayes, *novel* Grace
Metalious d Mark Robson ph William
Mellor m Franz Waxman

Lana Turner, Arthur Kennedy, Hope Lange,
Lee Philips, Lloyd Nolan, Diane Varsi, Russ
Tamblyn, Terry Moore, Barry Coe, David
Nelson, Betty Field, Mildred Dunnock, Leon
Ames, Lorne Greene

AAN: best picture; John Michael Hayes;
Mark Robson; William Mellor; Lana Turner;
Arthur Kennedy; Hope Lange; Diane Varsi;
Russ Tamblyn

Phaedra*
US / Greece 1961   116m   bw
UA / Melinafilm (Jules Dassin)

A tycoon's wife falls in love with her stepson.
Ludicrous, awesomely folly-filled attempt to
modernize and sex up Greek tragedy.

wd Jules Dassin ph Jacques Natteau m Mikis
Theodorakis

Melina Mercouri, Anthony Perkins, Raf
Vallone, Elizabeth Ercy
    'Unfortunately unforgettable.'—*John Simon*

Phantom Lady**
US 1944   87m   bw
Universal (Joan Harrison)

A man is accused of murder and his only alibi
is a mysterious lady he met in a bar.
Odd little thriller which doesn't really hold
together but is made for the most part with
great style.

w Bernard C. Schoenfeld, *novel* William Irish
d Robert Siodmak ph Woody Bredell
m Hans Salter

Franchot Tone, Alan Baxter, Ella Raines,
Elisha Cook Jnr, Fay Helm, Andrew Tombes

The Phantom Light
GB 1934   75m   bw

Wreckers try to scare off a new lighthouse
keeper. Effective minor comedy-thriller with
good credentials. Gordon Harker, Binnie
Hale, Ian Hunter, Donald Calthrop, Milton
Rosmer, Herbert Lomas. Written by Austin
Melford and Ralph Smart, from the play *The
Haunted Light* by Evadne Price and Joan Roy
Byford; directed by Michael Powell; for
Gainsborough. 'A very strong melodrama,
atmospheric to a marked degree.'—*Variety*

Phantom of Crestwood*
US 1932   77m   bw
RKO (David O. Selznick)

Murder strikes when a blackmailer assembles
her victims.
Lively mystery with spoof elements.

w Bartlett Cormack, J. Walter Ruben
d J. Walter Ruben ph Henry Gerrard m Max
Steiner

Ricardo Cortez, H. B. Warner, Anita Louise, Karen Morley, Pauline Frederick, Robert McWade, Skeets Gallagher
'Below the deluxe classification it should give a good account of itself.'—*Variety*

Phantom of Paris
US 1931   73m   bw

A magician proves by a complex plan that he did not kill his fiancée's father. Unusual but tortuous thriller which fails to thrill. John Gilbert, Leila Hyams, Ian Keith, C. Aubrey Smith, Lewis Stone, Jean Hersholt. Written by Bess Meredyth, John Meehan and Edwin Justus Mayer; directed by John S. Robertson; for MGM. 'It isn't Gilbert that makes the picture, it makes itself. Merits above-average gross.'—*Variety*

Phantom of the Opera***
US 1925   94m (24 fps)   bw (Technicolor sequence)   silent
Universal

A disfigured man in a mask abducts the prima donna of the Paris Opera House to his lair in the sewers below.
Patchy but often splendid piece of Grand Guignol which not only provided its star with a famous role but was notable for its magnificent visual style.
w Raymond Shrock, Elliot Clawson, *novel* Gaston Leroux *d* Rupert Julian *ph* Charles Van Enger, Virgil Miller *ad* Dan Hall
Lon Chaney, Mary Philbin, Norman Kerry, Gibson Gowland
† In 1930 an 89m talkie version was issued, with approximately 35% dialogue which had been recorded by the surviving actors, and some new footage.
● *Video: Polygram*

The Phantom of the Opera*
US 1943   92m   Technicolor
Universal (George Waggner)

This version is more decorous and gentlemanly, with much attention paid to the music, but it certainly has its moments.
w Erich Taylor, Samuel Hoffenstein, *d* Arthur Lubin *ph* Hal Mohr, W. Howard Greene *m* Edward Ward *ad* John B. Goodman, Alexander Golitzen
Claude Rains, Nelson Eddy, Susanna Foster, Edgar Barrier, Leo Carrillo, J. Edward Bromberg, Jane Farrar, Hume Cronyn
AA: Hal Mohr, W. Howard Greene; John B. Goodman, Alexander Golitzen

Phantom of the Opera
GB 1962   90m   Technicolor
U-I / Hammer (Anthony Hinds)

Stodgy remake with the accent on shock.
w John Elder *d* Terence Fisher *ph* Arthur Grant *m* Edwin Astley
Herbert Lom, Edward de Souza, Heather Sears, Thorley Walters, Michael Gough, Ian Wilson, Martin Miller, John Harvey, Miriam Karlin

'The only shock is that the British, who could have had a field day with this antique, have simply wafted it back with a lick and a promise.'—*New York Times*

Phantom of the Paradise*
US 1974   91m   Movielab
TCF / Pressman Williams (Edward R. Pressman)

A modern satirical remake of *Phantom of the Opera* in rock opera terms, set in a pop music palace. Not bad in spots, but it doesn't really know where it's going.
wd Brian de Palma *ph* Larry Pizer *m* Paul Williams *pd* Jack Fisk
Paul Williams, William Finley, Jessica Harper, George Memmoli, Gerrit Graham
'Too broad in its effects and too bloated in style to cut very deeply as a parody . . . closer to the anything goes mode of a *Mad* magazine lampoon.'—*Richard Combs*
AAN: Paul Williams

Phantom of the Rue Morgue
US 1954   84m   Warnercolor   3-D
Warner (Henry Blanke)

In old Paris, a killer of pretty girls turns out to be an ape.
Dull revamping of a rather dull story, with boring characters and little horror.
w Harold Medford, James R. Webb, *story* Murders in the Rue Morgue by Edgar Allan Poe *d* Roy del Ruth *ph* Peverell Marley *m* David Buttolph
Karl Malden, Claude Dauphin, Steve Forrest, Patricia Medina, Allyn McLerie, Dolores Dorn

The Phantom President*
US 1932   78m   bw
Paramount

A fast-talking quack doubles for a lacklustre presidential candidate.
A likely but in fact unsuccessful film debut for a famous Broadway star: many points of interest.
w Walter de Leon, Harlan Thompson *d* Norman Taurog *ph* David Abel *songs* Richard Rodgers, Lorenz Hart
George M. Cohan, Claudette Colbert, Jimmy Durante, George Barbier, Sidney Toler, Jameson Thomas, Paul Hurst, Alan Mowbray
'A lot of smart stuff is packed into the footage . . . should do well without threatening to rate itself a smash.'—*Variety*
'For anyone who cares about American theatrical history, it's an indispensable record of Cohan's style.'—*New Yorker, 1978*

The Phantom Tollbooth**
US 1969   90m   Metrocolor
MGM / Animation Visual Arts

A bored boy goes through a magic tollbooth to land beyond his wildest imagination, rescues Rhyme and Reason, and defeats the Demons of Ignorance.

Ambitious and well-devised, though rather slow-starting, cartoon feature which falls in style somewhere between *Alice in Wonderland* and *The Wizard of Oz* but is more intellectual than either and would be beyond the reach of most children. Discerning adults may have a ball.
w Chuck Jones, Sam Rosen, *novel* Norton Juster *d* Chuck Jones, Abe Levitow *ph* Maurice Noble
Butch Patrick

'The day the earth was turned into a cemetery!'
Phase IV
GB 1973   84m   Technicolor
Paramount / Alced (Paul B. Radin)

In the Arizona desert, ants attack a scientific installation.
Oddly effective if repulsive science fiction; the ants are all the more unpleasant because they stay the normal size.
w Mayo Simon *d* Saul Bass *ph* Dick Bush *m* Brian Gascoyne
Nigel Davenport, Lynne Frederick, Michael Murphy, Alan Gifford

The Phenix City Story*
US 1955   100m   bw
Allied Artists (Sam Bischoff, David Diamond)

A young lawyer fights the racketeers who control his town.
Goodish example of the semi-documentary melodramas of small-town corruption which swarmed out of Hollywood following the Kefauver investigations.
w Crane Wilbur, Dan Mainwaring *d* Phil Karlson *ph* Harry Neumann *m* Harry Sukman
Richard Kiley, *Edward Andrews*, John McIntire, Kathryn Grant

Phffft
US 1954   91m   bw
Columbia (Fred Kohlmar)

The title refers to the sound of an expiring match; the story tells of a couple who get divorced and try to find out what they have been missing.
Champagne comedy with no bubbles.
w George Axelrod *d* Mark Robson *ph* Charles Lang *m* Frederick Hollander
Jack Lemmon, Judy Holliday, Kim Novak, Jack Carson, Luella Gear, Donald Randolph, Donald Curtis, Merry Anders

The Philadelphia Experiment*
US 1984   101m   CFI colour
New World / Cinema Group (Joel B. Michaels, Douglas Curtis)

Seamen on a 1943 destroyer fall through a time warp into 1984, and have one hell of a job getting back.
Science fiction, *Outer Limits / Final Countdown* style; quite watchable, and technically proficient, but the claim that it was based on an actual incident seems a bit tall.

w William Gray, Michael Janover,
book William I. Moore, Charles Berlitz
d Stewart Raffill

Michael Paré, Nancy Allen, Eric Christmas,
Bobby di Cicco, Louise Latham

'Uncle Leo's bedtime story for you older
tots! The things they do among the
playful rich—oh, boy!'

The Philadelphia Story****
US 1940 112m bw
MGM (Joseph L. Mankiewicz)

A stuffy heiress, about to be married for the
second time, turns human and returns
gratefully to number one.
Hollywood's most wise and sparkling comedy,
with a script which is even an improvement on
the original play. Cukor's direction is so
discreet you can hardly sense it, and all the
performances are just perfect.

*w Donald Ogden Stewart, play Philip Barry
d George Cukor ph Joseph Ruttenberg
m Franz Waxman ad Cedric Gibbons*

*Katharine Hepburn, Cary Grant, James
Stewart, Ruth Hussey, Roland Young, John
Halliday, Mary Nash, Virginia Weidler, John
Howard, Henry Daniell*

'There are just not enough superlatives
sufficiently to appreciate this show.'—
Hollywood Reporter
'An exceptionally bright job of screenplay
writing . . . though films like this do little to
advance the art of motion pictures, they may
help to convince some of the more discerning
among cultural slugabeds that when movies
want to turn their hand to anything, they can
turn it.'—*Otis Ferguson*
† Cary Grant donated his salary to war relief.

AA: Donald Ogden Stewart; James Stewart
AAN: best picture; George Cukor; Katharine
Hepburn; Ruth Hussey

Philo Vance

The smooth sleuth created by S. S. Van Dine
was a popular film hero of the thirties, for
several different companies and with several
different actors. As a series it was very
variable indeed.
1929: THE CANARY MURDER CASE
(Paramount: William Powell); THE GREENE
MURDER CASE (Paramount: William
Powell)
1930: THE BISHOP MURDER CASE
(MGM: Basil Rathbone); THE BENSON
MURDER CASE (Paramount: William
Powell)
1933: THE KENNEL MURDER CASE (qv)
(Warner: William Powell)
1934: THE DRAGON MURDER CASE
(Warner: Warren William)
1935: THE CASINO MURDER CASE
(MGM: Paul Lukas)
1936: THE GARDEN MURDER CASE
(MGM: Edmund Lowe)
1937: NIGHT OF MYSTERY (Paramount:
Grant Richards)
1937: THE SCARAB MURDER CASE
(British: Wilfrid Hyde White)

THE PHILADELPHIA STORY.   John Howard (centre) isn't in the same league for wit as
Katharine Hepburn and Cary Grant.

1939: THE GRACIE ALLEN MURDER
CASE (Paramount: Warren William);
CALLING PHILO VANCE (Warner: James
Stephenson)
1947: PHILO VANCE RETURNS (PRC:
William Wright); PHILO VANCE'S
GAMBLE (PRC: Alan Curtis); PHILO
VANCE'S SECRET MISSION (PRC: Alan
Curtis)

Phobia
Canada 1980 90m colour
Borough Park (Zale Magder)

Five volunteer phobics, released from jail for
experiments, are killed one by one.
Unprepossessing whodunit with horror
touches but none of the style one might expect
from its director.

*w Lew Lehman, Jimmy Sangster, Peter
Bellwood d John Huston ph Reginald H.
Morris m Andre Gagnon*

Paul Michael Glaser, John Colicos, Susan
Hogan, Alexandra Stewart, David Bolt

● *Video: Thorn EMI*

Phone Call from a Stranger
US 1952 96m bw
TCF (Nunnally Johnson)

Of four airplane acquaintances, only one

survives a crash; he visits the families of the
others.
Four stories with an unlikely link. (The
compendium craze, which had started in 1948
with *Quartet*, was now straining itself.)
Nothing to remember except Miss Davis.

*w Nunnally Johnson d Jean Negulesco
ph Milton Krasner m Franz Waxman*

Bette Davis, Gary Merrill, Michael Rennie,
Shelley Winters, Keenan Wynn, Evelyn
Varden, Warren Stevens, Craig Stevens

'A cinematic party line on which several
conversations are going at once, none of them
coming across very distinctly.'—*Time*

Piccadilly*
GB 1929 105m (24 fps) bw silent
BIP (E. A. Dupont)

A club owner's fiancée is accused of killing his
Chinese mistress.
Sub-Edgar Wallace melodrama, no longer
watchable with a straight face.

*w Arnold Bennett d E. A. Dupont
ph Werner Brandes*

Gilda Gray, Anna May Wong, Jameson
Thomas, Cyril Ritchard, Ellen Pollock,
Charles Laughton, Debroy Somers and his
Band

Piccadilly Incident*
GB 1946 102m bw
ABP (Herbert Wilcox)

During World War II, a girl believed drowned
returns from the front to find her husband
remarried.
The Enoch Arden theme again, and the first of
the Wilcox-Neagle 'London' films, though
untypically a melodrama with a sad ending.
Efficient enough for its chosen audience.

w Nicholas Phipps d Herbert Wilcox ph Max
Greene

Anna Neagle, Michael Wilding, Michael
Laurence, Frances Mercer, Coral Browne, A.
E. Matthews, Edward Rigby, Brenda Bruce
† Michael Wilding was cast only after Rex
Harrison and John Mills had proved
unavailable.

Piccadilly Jim*
US 1936 100m bw
MGM (Harry Rapf)

A cartoonist helps his father to marry by
making the bride's stuffy family objects of
ridicule.
Amiable comedy with a diverting London
setting.

w Charles Brackett, Edwin Knopf, novel P.
G. Wodehouse d Robert Z. Leonard
ph Joseph Ruttenberg m William Axt

Robert Montgomery, Madge Evans, Frank
Morgan, Billie Burke, Eric Blore, Robert
Benchley, Ralph Forbes, Cora Witherspoon,
E. E. Clive

Piccadilly Third Stop
GB 1960 90m bw
Rank / Sydney Box / Ethiro (Norman
Williams)

A smooth crook seduces the daughter of an
eastern ambassador in London to gain entry to
the embassy and rob it.
Boring and rather unpleasant thriller partly
redeemed by a final chase through the
Underground.

w Leigh Vance d Wolf Rilla ph Ernest
Steward m Philip Green

Terence Morgan, Yoko Tani, John Crawford,
William Hartnell, Mai Zetterling, Dennis
Price, Ann Lynn

Pick a Star
US 1937 76m bw
Hal Roach / MGM

An innocent girl in Hollywood achieves
stardom with the help of a publicity man.
Perfectly awful Cinderella story with
interesting glimpses behind the studio scenes
and (if you can wait that long) a couple of
good Laurel and Hardy sequences.

w Richard Flournoy, Arthur Vernon Jones,
Thomas J. Dugan d Edward Sedgwick
ph Norbert Brodine

Rosina Lawrence, Jack Haley, Patsy Kelly,
Mischa Auer, Stan Laurel, Oliver Hardy,
Charles Halton, Lyda Roberti
'Part farce, part comedy, part musical and
three parts dull.'—Variety

Pick Up
US 1933 80m bw

A girl released from jail picks up with a truck
driver, but her crooked husband reappears.
Sob story of the Peg's Paper type; a yawn.
Sylvia Sidney, George Raft, William Harrigan,
Lillian Bond. Written by S. K. Lauren, Agnes
Leahy, Vina Delmar; directed by Marion
Gering; for B. P. Schulberg / Paramount.
'Good title and cast, weakish film.'—Variety

Pick Up
US 1951 78m bw
Columbia (Hugo Haas)

A lonely middle-aged man falls for a tart who
is interested only in his money.
Modest variation on The Blue Angel, the first
of several second features made by Haas to
feature himself as a second Emil Jannings.
They got progressively more maudlin.

wd Hugo Haas ph Paul Ivano

Hugo Haas, Beverly Michaels, Allan Nixon,
Howard Chamberlin

Pickup on South Street*
US 1953 80m bw
TCF (Jules Schermer)

A pickpocket steals a girl's wallet and finds
himself up to his neck in espionage.
Over-rich mixture of crime, violence and anti-
communism, smartly made without being very
interesting.

wd Samuel Fuller ph Joe MacDonald
m Leigh Harline

Richard Widmark, Jean Peters, Thelma Ritter,
Richard Kiley
† Remade 1968 as Capetown Affair.
AAN: Thelma Ritter

The Pickwick Papers*
GB 1952 115m bw
George Minter (Bob McNaught)

Various adventures of the Pickwick Club
culminate in Mrs Bardell's suit for breach of
promise.
Flatly conceived and loosely constructed
Dickensian comedy; good humour and lots of
well-known faces do not entirely atone for lack
of artifice.

wd Noel Langley ph Wilkie Cooper
m Antony Hopkins ad Fred Pusey

James Hayter, James Donald, Donald Wolfit,
Hermione Baddeley, Hermione Gingold,
Kathleen Harrison, Nigel Patrick, Alexander
Gauge, Lionel Murton

'A town—a stranger—and the things he
  does to its people! Especially its
  women!'
Picnic***
US 1956 113m Technicolor
  Cinemascope
Columbia (Fred Kohlmar)

A brawny wanderer causes sexual havoc one
summer in a small American town.

Seminal melodrama setting new directions for
Hollywood and illustrating the side of life the
Hardy family never showed. Generally quite
compulsive despite some overacting.

w Daniel Taradash, play William Inge
d Joshua Logan ph James Wong Howe
m George Duning pd Jo Mielziner
ad William Flannery

William Holden, Kim Novak, Rosalind
Russell, Susan Strasberg, Arthur O'Connell,
Cliff Robertson, Betty Field, Verna Felton,
Reta Shaw

'Mr Logan's idea of an outing in the corn
country includes a choir of at least a hundred
voices, a camera so alert that it can pick up the
significance of the reflection of a Japanese
lantern in a pool (futility, wistfulness, the
general transience of life, as I get it) and a
sound track let loose in the most formidable
music I've heard in my time at the movies.'—
New Yorker
AAN: best picture; Joshua Logan; George
Duning; Arthur O'Connell

Picnic at Hanging Rock*
Australia 1975 115m Eastmancolor
Picnic Productions / Australia Film
  Corporation (Hal and Jim McElroy)

In 1900, schoolgirls set out for a picnic; some
disappear and are never found.
An intriguing but finally irritating puzzle with
no answer; the atmosphere is nicely
calculated, but as in L'Avventura the whole
thing outstays its welcome.

w Cliff Green, novel Joan Lindsay d Peter
Weir ph Russell Boyd m Bruce Smeaton

Rachel Roberts, Dominic Guard, Helen
Morse, Jacki Weaver, Vivean Gray, Kirsty
Child
'Atmospherically vivid, beautifully shot, and
palpably haunting.'—Michael Billington,
Illustrated London News
● Video: Home Video

Picture Mommy Dead
US 1966 88m Pathecolor
Embassy / Berkeley (Bert I. Gordon)

A girl who has been hospitalized following the
death of her mother in a fire returns home to
find, apparently, that her father's new wife is
trying to kill her.
Twist-ending shocker with tired stars, from the
tag end of the Baby Jane cycle.

w Robert Sherman d Bert I. Gordon
ph Ellsworth Fredericks m Robert Drasnin

Don Ameche, Martha Hyer, Zsa Zsa Gabor,
Susan Gordon, Maxwell Reed, Signe Hasso,
Wendell Corey

The Picture of Dorian Gray***
US 1945 110m bw (Technicolor
  inserts)
MGM (Pandro S. Berman)

A Victorian gentleman keeps in the attic a
picture of himself, which shows his age and
depravity while he stays eternally young.

Elegant variation on *Dr Jekyll and Mr Hyde*, presented in portentous style which suits the subject admirably.

wd Albert Lewin, *novel* Oscar Wilde *ph* Harry Stradling *m* Herbert Stothart

George Sanders, Hurd Hatfield, Donna Reed, Angela Lansbury, Peter Lawford

SIR HENRY (George Sanders): 'If I could get back my youth, I'd do anything in the world—except get up early, take exercise or be respectable.'

SIR HENRY: 'I apologize for the intelligence of my remarks, Sir Thomas, I had forgotten that you were a Member of Parliament.'

DORIAN (Hurd Hatfield): 'If only the picture could change and I could be always what I am now. For that, I would give anything. Yes, there's nothing in the whole world I wouldn't give. I'd give my soul for that.'

'Respectful, earnest, and, I'm afraid, dead.'—*James Agee*

'Loving and practised hands have really improved Wilde's original, cutting down the epigrammatic flow . . . and rooting out all the preciousness which gets in the way of the melodrama.'—*Richard Winnington*

AA: Harry Stradling
AAN: Angela Lansbury

The Picture Show Man*
Australia 1977 98m Eastmancolor
Limelight (Joan Long)

Adventures of a travelling picture show troupe in the 1920s.
Agreeably nostalgic incidents, not very dramatically connected.

w Joan Long *d* John Power *ph* Geoffrey Burton *m* Peter Best

Rod Taylor, John Meillon, John Ewart, Harold Hopkins, Judy Morris, Patrick Cargill

The Picture Snatcher**
US 1933 77m bw
Warner

An ex-racketeer just out of prison becomes a scandal photographer.
Lively star vehicle, interesting for period detail.

w Allen Rivkin, P. J. Wolfson *d* Lloyd Bacon *ph* Sol Polito *md* Leo F. Forbstein

James Cagney, Ralph Bellamy, Patricia Ellis, Alice White, Ralf Harolde, Robert Emmett O'Connor, Robert Barrat

'A vulgar but generally funny collection of blackouts.'—*Time*

'Fast, snappy, tough and packed with action.'—*New York Herald Tribune*

† Remade 1947 as *Escape from Crime*, with Richard Travis.

A Piece of the Action
US 1977 135m Metrocolor
Warner / First Artists / Verdon (Melville Tucker)

Crooks are blackmailed into helping rebellious adolescents.

A black version, at immense length, of the hoodlum comedies in which the Dead End Kids so often featured. Not badly made, but out of date without being nostalgic.

w Charles Blackwell, *story* Timothy March *d* Sidney Poitier *ph* Don Morgan *m* Curtis Mayfield

Sidney Poitier, James Earl Jones, Bill Cosby, Denise Nicholas, Hope Clarke, Tracy Reed, Jason Evers, Marc Lawrence

The Pied Piper**
US 1942 86m bw
TCF (Nunnally Johnson)

An elderly man who hates children finds himself smuggling several of them out of occupied France.
Smart, sentimental, occasionally funny war adventure.

w Nunnally Johnson, *novel* Nevil Shute *d* Irving Pichel *ph* Edward Cronjager *m* Alfred Newman

Monty Woolley, Anne Baxter, Roddy McDowall, Otto Preminger, J. Carrol Naish, Lester Matthews, Jill Esmond, Peggy Ann Garner

AAN: best picture; Edward Cronjager; Monty Woolley

The Pied Piper
GB 1971 90m Eastmancolor Panavision
Sagittarius / Goodtimes (David Puttnam, Sanford Lieberson)

In 1349 a strolling minstrel rids Hamelin of a plague of rats.
Paceless, slightly too horrific, and generally disappointing fantasy, especially from this director; poor sets and restricted action.

w Jacques Demy, Mark Peploe, Andrew Birkin *d* Jacques Demy *ph* Peter Suschitsky *m* Donovan *pd* Assheton Gorton

Donovan, Donald Pleasence, Michael Hordern, Jack Wild, Diana Dors, John Hurt

Pierre of the Plains
US 1942 66m bw

Adventures of a cheerful trapper in Canada's northwest territory. Unashamed second-feature version of a play which its producer, Edgar Selwyn, had written in 1907 and which had been filmed in 1918 (as *Hearts of the Wild*) and in 1922 (as *Over the Border*). (Selwyn was the man who once merged with Goldfish to form Goldwyn, a name which Goldfish then kept.) John Carroll, Ruth Hussey, Bruce Cabot, Reginald Owen, Henry Travers, Evelyn Ankers. Written by Bertram Millhauser and Laurence Kimble; directed by George B. Seitz; for MGM.

The Pigeon That Took Rome
US 1962 101m bw Panavision
Paramount / Llenroc (Melville Shavelson)

American undercover agents are smuggled into Rome during the German occupation.
Heavy-going war comedy-drama with bright sequences countered by too little wit and too many voluble Italians.

wd Melville Shavelson, *novel* The Easter Dinner by Donald Downes *ph* Daniel Fapp *m* Alessandro Cicognini

Charlton Heston, Elsa Martinelli, Brian Donlevy, Harry Guardino, Baccaloni

Pigskin Parade
US 1936 93m bw
TCF (Bogart Rogers)
GB title: *Harmony Parade*

A country farmer becomes a college football hero.
Livelier-than-average college comedy.

w Harry Tugend, Jack Yellen, William Conselman *d* David Butler *ph* Arthur Miller *md* David Buttolph *songs* Sidney Mitchell, Lew Pollack

Stuart Erwin, Patsy Kelly, Jack Haley, Johnny Downs, Betty Grable, Arline Judge, Dixie Dunbar, Judy Garland, Tony Martin, Elisha Cook Jnr

AAN: Stuart Erwin

The Pilgrim*
US 1923 38m approx (24 fps) bw silent
First National / Charles Chaplin

An escaped convict disguises himself as a minister and does a few good deeds.
Star comedy with more sentiment than laughter.

wd Charles Chaplin *ph* Rollie Totheroh

Charles Chaplin, Edna Purviance, Kitty Bradbury, Mack Swain

Pilgrimage*
US 1933 95m bw

A selfish mother sees the error of her ways when she makes a post-war journey to her son's grave. Strong character study, put across with style. Henrietta Crosman, Heather Angel, Norman Foster, Marian Nixon, Maurice Murphy, Charley Grapewin, Hedda Hopper. Written by Dudley Nichols, Philip Klein, Barry Conners, from the story by I. A. R. Wylie; directed by John Ford; for Fox. 'A natural for residential clienteles: mother love from a new angle.'—*Variety*

Pillars of the Sky
US 1956 95m Technicolor Cinemascope
U-I (Robert Arthur)
GB title: *The Tomahawk and the Cross*

An indian scout and a missionary help bring peace between cavalry and indians.
Modest western, adequately done.

w Sam Rolfe *d* George Marshall *ph* Harold Lipstein *m* Joseph Gershenson

Jeff Chandler, Dorothy Malone, Ward Bond, Keith Andes, Lee Marvin, Sydney Chaplin, Michael Ansara, Willis Bouchey

Pillow of Death
US 1945 66m bw

A lawyer is suspected when his wife is murdered. First fumbling story in the Inner

PILLOW OF DEATH. Another Inner Sanctum mystery for the bottom of the bill.

Sanctum series, of which the title sequence was always the most entertaining portion. Lon Chaney Jnr, Brenda Joyce, J. Edward Bromberg, Rosalind Ivan, Clara Blandick. Written by George Bricker; directed by Wallace Fox; for Universal.

Pillow Talk°°
US 1959   110m   Eastmancolor
   Cinemascope
Universal / Arwin (Ross Hunter, Martin Melcher)

Two people who can't stand each other fall in love via a party line.
Slightly elephantine romantic comedy which nevertheless contains a number of funny scenes and was notable for starting off the Hudson-Day partnership and a run of similar comedies which survived the sixties.

w Stanley Shapiro, Maurice Richlin
d Michael Gordon   ph Arthur E. Arling
m Frank de Vol

Doris Day, Rock Hudson, Tony Randall, Thelma Ritter, Nick Adams, Julia Meade, Allen Jenkins, Marcel Dalio, Lee Patrick

AA: Stanley Shapiro, Maurice Richlin
AAN: Frank de Vol; Doris Day; Thelma Ritter

Pillow to Post
US 1945   96m   bw
Warner (Alex Gottlieb)

A girl poses as a soldier's wife to get a hotel room.
World War II comedy on a familiar theme (The More the Merrier, Standing Room Only, The Doughgirls, etc). Uninspired.

w Charles Hoffman, play Pillar to Post by Rose Simon Kohn   d Vincent Sherman   ph Wesley Anderson   m Frederick Hollander

Ida Lupino, Sidney Greenstreet, William Prince, Stuart Erwin, Ruth Donnelly, Barbara Brown, Frank Orth

Pilot Number Five
US 1943   71m   bw
MGM (B. P. Fineman)

A pilot in the South Pacific volunteers for a desperate mission because—we learn in flashback—he hates fascists.
Rather unpalatable propaganda encased in dim drama.

w David Hertz   d George Sidney   ph Paul C. Vogel   m Lennie Hayton

Franchot Tone, Gene Kelly, Marsha Hunt, Van Johnson, Alan Baxter, Dick Simmons, Steve Geray

Pimpernel Smith°°
GB 1941   121m   bw
British National (Leslie Howard)
US titles: Mister V; The Fighting Pimpernel

A professor of archaeology goes into war-torn Europe to rescue refugees.
The Scarlet Pimpernel unassumingly and quite effectively brought up to date, with memorable scenes after a slow start.

w Anatole de Grunwald, Roland Pertwee, Ian Dalrymple   d Leslie Howard   ph Max Greene   m John Greenwood

Leslie Howard, Mary Morris, Francis L. Sullivan, Hugh McDermott, Raymond Huntley, Manning Whiley, Peter Gawthorne, David Tomlinson
● Video: BBC

Pin Up Girl
US 1944   83m   Technicolor
TCF (William Le Baron)

A Washington secretary becomes a national celebrity when she meets a navy hero.
Adequate star flagwaver, mildly interesting for its new streamlined set designs.

w Robert Ells, Helen Logan, Earl Baldwin   d Bruce Humberstone   ph Ernest Palmer   md Emil Newman, Charles Henderson   songs James V. Monaco, Mack Gordon   ch Hermes Pan   ad James Basevi, Joseph C. Wright

Betty Grable, John Harvey, Martha Raye, Joe E. Brown, Eugene Pallette, Dave Willcock, Charles Spivak and his Orchestra
   'A spiritless blob of a musical, and a desecration of a most inviting theme.'—Bosley Crowther

Pink Floyd The Wall°
GB 1982   95m   Metrocolor
MGM / Tin Blue / Goldcrest (Alan Marshall)

A washed-up pop star finds his life a mixture of fact and fiction, of reality and animation.
Dislikeable self-pitying dirge, accompanied by animation which will not be to everybody's taste but is sometimes brilliantly arranged.

w Roger Waters   d Alan Parker   ph Peter Biziou   m Roger Waters   animation designer Gerald Scarfe

Bob Geldof, Christine Hargreaves, James Laurenson, Eleanor David, Kevin McKeon, Bob Hoskins
   'A vacuous, bombastic and humourless piece of self-indulgence.'—Steve Jenkins, MFB
   'Roger Waters flounders in woman-hating self-pity; Gerald Scarfe turns up particularly weedy examples of his animated savagery; and Alan Parker revels in the chance to make a feature-length TV commercial.'—Sight and Sound

The Pink Jungle
US 1968   104m   Techniscope
Universal / Cherokee (Stan Margulies)

A photographer and his model are stranded in a South American village and become involved in a diamond hunt.
Curious mixture of adventure and light comedy that works only in patches.

w Charles Williams, novel Snake Water by Alan Williams   d Delbert Mann   ph Russell Metty   m Ernie Freeman

James Garner, Eva Renzi, George Kennedy, Nigel Green, Michael Ansara, George Rose
   'Another backlot cheapie.'—Robert Windeler

The Pink Panther°°
US 1963   113m   Technirama
UA / Mirisch (Martin Jurow)

An incompetent surêté inspector is in Switzerland on the trail of a jewel thief called The Phantom.
Sporadically engaging mixture of pratfalls, Raffles, and Monsieur Hulot, all dressed to kill and quite palatable for the uncritical. Inspector Clouseau later became a cartoon character and also provoked five sequels: A Shot in the Dark, Inspector Clouseau, The Return of the Pink Panther, The Pink Panther Strikes Again and The Revenge of the Pink Panther.

w Maurice Richlin, Blake Edwards   d Blake Edwards   ph Philip Lathrop   m Henry Mancini   ad Fernando Carrere   animation De Patie-Freleng

David Niven, Peter Sellers, Capucine, Claudia Cardinale, Robert Wagner, Brenda de Banzie, Colin Gordon

AAN: Henry Mancini
● Video: Warner

The Pink Panther Strikes Again°
GB 1976   103m   De Luxe   Panavision
United Artists / Amjo (Blake Edwards)

After a nervous breakdown, Chief Inspector Dreyfus builds up a vast criminal organization devoted to the extermination of Inspector Clouseau.
Zany pratfall farce with signs of overconfidence since the success of The Return of the Pink Panther. But some gags are funny, despite a rather boring star.

w Frank Waldman, Blake Edwards   d Blake Edwards   ph Harry Waxman   m Henry Mancini

Peter Sellers, Herbert Lom, Colin Blakely, Leonard Rossiter, Lesley-Anne Down, Burt Kwouk

AAN: song, 'Come To Me' (ly Don Black, m Henry Mancini)
● Video: Intervision

Pink String and Sealing Wax°
GB 1945   89m   bw
Ealing (S. C. Balcon)

In 1880 Brighton, a publican's wife plans to have her husband poisoned.
Unusual, carefully handled period crime melodrama which needed a slightly firmer grip.

w Diana Morgan, Robert Hamer, play Roland Pertwee   d Robert Hamer   ph Stanley Pavey   m Norman Demuth

Googie Withers, Mervyn Johns, Gordon Jackson, Sally Ann Howes, Mary Merrall, John Carol, Catherine Lacey, Gary Marsh

   'She passed for white!'
Pinky°°
US 1949   102m   bw
TCF (Darryl F. Zanuck)

In the American south, a negro girl who passes for white has romantic problems.

Rather blah problem picture which seemed brave at the time; a highly professional piece of work nevertheless.

w Philip Dunne, Dudley Nichols, *novel* Quality by Cid Ricketts Summer *d* Elia Kazan *ph* Joe MacDonald *m* Alfred Newman

Jeanne Crain, Ethel Barrymore, Ethel Waters, William Lundigan, Basil Ruysdael, Nina Mae McKinney, Frederick O'Neal, Evelyn Varden

AAN: Jeanne Crain; Ethel Barrymore; Ethel Waters

'Out of a dream world into yours!'
Pinocchio**
US 1940   77m   Technicolor
Walt Disney

The blue fairy breathes life into a puppet, which has to prove itself before it can turn into a real boy.
Charming, fascinating, superbly organized and streamlined cartoon feature without a single second of boredom.

supervisors Ben Sharpsteen, Hamilton Luske *m / ly* Leigh Harline, Ned Washington, Paul J. Smith

 'A film of amazing detail and brilliant conception.'—*Leonard Maltin*
 'A work that gives you almost every possible kind of pleasure to be got from a motion picture.'—*Richard Mallett, Punch*
 'The limits of the animated cartoon have been blown so wide open that some of the original wonder of pictures has been restored.'—*Otis Ferguson*

AA: Leigh Harline (*m*); song 'When You Wish Upon a Star' (*m* Leigh Harline, *ly* Ned Washington)

Piranha*
US 1978   92m   Metrocolor
New World (Roger Corman, Jeff Schechtman, Jon Davison)

A mad doctor's stock of man-eating fish is accidentally released into the local rivers.
Slightly spoofy thriller with a high death rate and a better than usual script. On the whole, an improvement on *Jaws*.

w John Sayles *d* Joe Dante *ph* Jamie Anderson *m* Pino Danaggio *sp* Jon Berg

Bradford Dillman, Heather Menzies, Kevin McCarthy, Bruce Gordon, Barbara Steele, Keenan Wynn, Dick Miller

The Pirate**
US 1948   102m   Technicolor
MGM (Arthur Freed)

In a West Indian port, a girl imagines that a wandering player is a famous pirate, who in fact is her despised and elderly suitor.
Minor MGM musical with vivid moments and some intimation of the greatness shortly to come; all very set-bound, but the star quality is infectious.

w Albert Hackett, Frances Goodrich, *play* S. N. Behrman *d* Vincente Minnelli *ph* Harry Stradling *m / ly* Cole Porter *md* Lennie Hayton

Gene Kelly, Judy Garland, Walter Slezak, Gladys Cooper, Reginald Owen, George Zucco, *the Nicholas Brothers*

AAN: Lennie Hayton

The Pirate Movie
Australia 1982   105m   Colorfilm

A girl dreams herself back into *The Pirates of Penzance* but changes some of the details.
Galumphing fantasy which suggests that Australian film-makers had better stick to *Botany Bay, Gallipoli* and sheep shearing.

Kristy McNichol, Christopher Atkins, Ted Hamilton, Bill Kerr, Maggie Kirkpatrick, Garry Macdonald. Written by Trevor Farrant; directed by Ken Annakin; for Joseph Hamilton International. 'The slapstick and the swordplay are as ineptly choreographed as the production numbers.'—*Kim Newman, MFB*

Pirates of Blood River*
GB 1961   84m   Technicolor
Hammerscope
Hammer (Anthony Nelson Keys)

Pirates in search of gold terrorize a Huguenot settlement.
Land-locked blood and thunder for tough schoolboys.

w John Hunter, John Gilling *d* John Gilling *ph* Arthur Grant

Christopher Lee, Andrew Keir, Kerwin Mathews, Glenn Corbett, Peter Arne, Oliver Reed, Marla Landi, Michael Ripper

Pirates of Monterey
US 1947   72m   Technicolor

A Spanish girl goes to California to marry a soldier but is romanced by an outlaw.
Predictable action hokum. Maria Montez, Rod Cameron, Mikhail Rasumny, Philip Reed, Gilbert Roland, Gale Sondergaard, Tamara Shayne, Robert Warwick. Written by Sam Hellman and Margaret Buell Wilder; directed by Alfred Werker; for Paul Malvern / Universal-International.

The Pirates of Penzance
GB 1982   112m   Technicolor Panavision

An adaptation of the Gilbert and Sullivan operetta in the form of the Joseph Papp Broadway revival. What was tolerably pretty and witty on the stage is a great bore on wide film. Kevin Kline, Angela Lansbury, Linda Ronstadt, George Rose, Tony Azito, Rex Smith. Written and directed by Wilford Leach; for Universal. 'Not the slightest trace of imagination.'—*MFB*. 'Anyone who thinks Gilbert and Sullivan indestructible should see this.'—*Observer*

Pirates of Tortuga
US 1961   97m   De Luxe   Cinemascope
In the 17th-century Caribbean, a privateer is

ordered by the king to go undercover and rout Sir Henry Morgan. Listless swashbuckler with inferior talent. Ken Scott, Dave King, Letitia Roman, John Richardson, Robert Stephens, Edgar Barrier. Written by Melvin Levy, Jesse L. Lasky Jnr and Pat Silver; directed by Robert D. Webb; for Sam Katzman / TCF.

Pirates of Tripoli
US 1955   72m   Technicolor

A pirate captain comes to the aid of an oriental princess. More akin to the Arabian Knights than Blackbeard, but not bad for a double-biller. Paul Henreid, Patricia Medina, Paul Newland, John Miljan, Lillian Bond. Written by Allen March; directed by Felix Feist; for Sam Katzman / Columbia.

The Pit and the Pendulum*
US 1961   85m   Pathecolor Panavision
AIP / Alta Vista (Roger Corman)

Lovers plan to drive her brother mad; he responds by locking them in his torture chamber.
The centrepiece only is borrowed from Poe; the rest is lurid but mostly ineffective. Still, its commercial success started the Poe cycle of the sixties.

w Richard Matheson *d* Roger Corman *ph* Floyd Crosby *m* Les Baxter

Vincent Price, Barbara Steele, John Kerr
 'As in *House of Usher*, the quality of the film is its full-blooded feeling for Gothic horror—storms and lightning, mouldering castles and cobwebbed torture chambers, bleeding brides trying to tear the lids from their untimely tombs.'—*David Robinson*

● *Video: Guild*

Pitfall
US 1948   85m   bw
Samuel Bischoff

An insurance investigator proves easy prey for a grasping woman.
Modest suspenser, quite efficiently made.

w Jay Dratler, from his novel *d* André de Toth *ph* Harry Wild *md* Louis Forbes

Dick Powell, Lizabeth Scott, Jane Wyatt, Raymond Burr, John Litel, Byron Barr, Ann Doran

Pittsburgh
US 1942   91m   bw
Universal (Charles K. Feldman)

A coal miner's daughter has two loves, all of them trying to improve their social status as Pittsburgh becomes a world centre of steel production.
Routine melodrama ending as a flagwaver, and allowing none of its stars any opportunity.

w Kenneth Gamet, Tom Reed *d* Lewis Seiler *ph* Robert de Grasse *m* Hans Salter

Marlene Dietrich, Randolph Scott, John Wayne, Frank Craven, Louise Allbritton, Shemp Howard, Ludwig Stossel, Thomas Gomez

'They do it in the name of love!'
A Place for Lovers
US 1969 102m colour

A dying American fashion designer retires to
her Italian villa and has a high old time with
an Italian engineer. Incomparably crass
tearjerker which seems eager to offer too
many morals about life and love and art. Faye
Dunaway, Marcello Mastroianni, Caroline
Mortimer, Karin Engh. Written by Peter
Baldwin, Ennio de Concini, Tonino Guerra,
Julian Halevy, Cesare Zavattini; directed by
Vittorio de Sica; for MGM. 'The most God-
awful piece of pseudo-romantic slop I've ever
seen.'—*Roger Ebert, Chicago Sun Times*. 'The
worst movie I have seen all year and possibly
since 1926.'—*Charles Champlin, L.A. Times*.
'The five scriptwriters who supposedly worked
on the film must have spent time enough at the
watercooler to flood a camel.'—*Time*

A Place in the Sun**
US 1951 122m bw
Paramount / George Stevens

A poor young man, offered the chance of a
rich wife, allows himself to be convicted and
executed for the accidental death of his former
fiancée.
Overblown, overlong and over-praised
melodrama from a monumental novel of social
guilt; sometimes visually striking, this version
alters the stresses of the plot and leaves no
time for sociological detail. A film so clearly
intended as a masterpiece could hardly fail to
be boring.

w Michael Wilson, Harry Brown, *novel* An
American Tragedy by Theodore Dreiser
d George Stevens *ph* William C. Mellor
m Franz Waxman *ad* Hans Dreier, Walter
Tyler

Montgomery Clift, Elizabeth Taylor, Shelley
Winters, Anne Revere, Keefe Brasselle, Fred
Clark, Raymond Burr, Frieda Inescort,
Shepperd Strudwick, Kathryn Givney, Walter
Sande
  'An almost incredibly painstaking work . . .
mannered enough for a very fancy Gothic
murder mystery. This version gives the story a
modern setting, but the town is an
arrangement of symbols of wealth, glamour
and power versus symbols of poor, drab
helplessness—an arrangement far more
suitable to the thirties than to the fifties.'—
Pauline Kael

AA: script; George Stevens; William C.
Mellor; Franz Waxman
AAN: best picture; Montgomery Clift; Shelley
Winters

A Place of One's Own**
GB 1944 92m bw
GFD / Gainsborough (R. J. Minney)

In Edwardian times, an old house is taken
over by an elderly couple, and their young
companion is possessed by the spirit of a
murdered girl.
Charming little ghost story, not quite detailed
enough to be totally effective.

w Brock Williams, *novel* Osbert Sitwell
d Bernard Knowles *ph* Stephen Dade
m Hubert Bath *md* Louis Levy
James Mason, Barbara Mullen, Margaret
Lockwood, Dennis Price, Helen Haye,
Michael Shepley, Dulcie Gray, Moore
Marriott
  'A fine piece of work . . . gripping,
marvellous, outstanding, eerie, perky,
beautiful, lovely and different.'—*C. A.
Lejeune*
  'One comes away with an impression of
elegance which has not so far been frequent in
the British cinema.'—*Dilys Powell*

A Place to Go
GB 1963 86m bw
British Lion / Excalibur (Michael Relph,
  Basil Dearden)

A young man depressed by his urban
environment turns to crime.
Panorama of London low life, efficiently
varied and well made but not in any way
memorable. *It Always Rains on Sunday*,
fifteen years earlier, wears better.

w Michael Relph, Clive Exton, *novel* Bethnal
Green by Michael Fisher *d* Basil Dearden
ph Reg Wyer *m* Charles Blackwell
Rita Tushingham, Mike Sarne, Doris Hare,
John Slater, Bernard Lee, Barbara Ferris, Roy
Kinnear

The Plague Dogs
GB / US 1982 103m Technicolor

Two dogs escape from a research laboratory
and are in danger of infecting the country with
a deadly virus. Misguided and woefully
overlong attempt to preach a message through
a cartoon. Like *Watership Down*, it needs the
printed word and is deflected by the inevitably
cuddly look of the animated animals. Written
and directed by Martin Rosen, from the book
by Richard Adams; for Nepenthe Productions.

The Plague of the Zombies*
GB 1965 91m Technicolor
Hammer (Anthony Nelson Keys)

A voodoo-practising Cornish squire raises
zombies from the dead and uses them to work
his tin mine.
They don't explain why he didn't simply hire
the living; apart from that this is Hammer on
its better side, with a charming elderly hero
and good suspense sequences.

w Peter Bryan *d* John Gilling *ph* Arthur
Grant *m* James Bernard
André Morell, John Carson, Diane Clare,
Brook Williams, Jacqueline Pearce, Alex
Davion, Michael Ripper
  'Visually the film is splendid . . . the script
manages several offbeat strokes.'—*MFB*

'Grandest love story ever told!'
The Plainsman**
US 1936 113m bw
Paramount / Cecil B. de Mille

The life of Wild Bill Hickok and his friends
Buffalo Bill and Calamity Jane.

Standard big-scale thirties western; narrative
lumpy, characters idealized, spectacle
impressive, technical credits high.

w Waldemar Young, Lynn Riggs, Harold
Lamb *d* Cecil B. de Mille *ph* Victor Milner,
George Robinson *m* George Antheil
md Boris Morros
Gary Cooper, James Ellison, Jean Arthur,
Charles Bickford, Helen Burgess, Porter Hall,
Paul Harvey, Victor Varconi
  'It should do all right for business, ranging
from big to good, possibly irregular in
spots.'—*Variety*
  'Certainly the finest western since *The
Virginian*; perhaps the finest western in the
history of the film.'—*Graham Greene*
† The story was remade as a TV movie in
1966, with Don Murray.

The Plainsman and the Lady
US 1946 84m bw

In 1847, the Pony Express is threatened by
stagecoach owners. Moderate western for
family consumption. William Elliott, Gail
Patrick, Vera Ralston, Joseph Schildkraut.
Written by Richard Wormser; directed by
Joseph Kane; for Republic.

Le Plaisir*
France 1952 97m bw
Stera / CCFC

Three stories by Guy de Maupassant, about
the search for pleasure: 'Le Masque', 'La
Maison Tellier', 'Le Modèle'.
Stylish but rather subdued compendium, with
no highlights to stay in the memory.

w Jacques Natanson, Max Ophuls *d* Max
Ophuls *ph* Christian Matras, Philippe
Agostini *m* Joe Hajos
Claude Dauphin, Gaby Morlay; Madeleine
Renaud, Danielle Darrieux, Ginette Leclerc,
Jean Gabin, Pierre Brasseur; Simone Simon,
Daniel Gélin
  'An attractive theme tune, good
performances, and the pleasure itself of
virtuosity.'—*Gavin Lambert, MFB*

Plan 9 from Outer Space
US 1959 79m bw

Space people try to resurrect the Earth's dead
and turn them against the world. Inept mini-
budgeter often hailed as the worst film ever
made. It is certainly among the most boring.
Bela Lugosi (who died after four days of
shooting and is mostly represented by a
double), Tor Johnson, Gregory Walcott,
Mona McKinnon, Vampira, Lyle Talbot.
Written and directed by Edward D. Wood Jnr;
for William J. Reynolds.

● *Video: Palace*

'Somewhere in the universe, there must be
  something better than man!'
Planet of the Apes***
US 1968 119m De Luxe Panavision
TCF / Apjac (Mort Abrahams)

Astronauts caught in a time warp land on a
planet which turns out to be Earth in the

distant future, when men have become beasts and the apes have taken over.
Stylish, thoughtful science fiction which starts and finishes splendidly but suffers from a sag in the middle. The ape make-up is great.

w Michael Wilson, Rod Serling, novel Monkey Planet by Pierre Boulle d Franklin Schaffner ph Leon Shamroy m Jerry Goldsmith

Charlton Heston, Roddy McDowall, Kim Hunter, Maurice Evans, James Whitmore, James Daly, Linda Harrison
'One of the most telling science fiction films to date.'—Tom Milne
† Sequels, in roughly descending order of interest, were BENEATH THE PLANET OF THE APES (1969), ESCAPE FROM THE PLANET OF THE APES (1970), CONQUEST OF THE PLANET OF THE APES (1972) and BATTLE FOR THE PLANET OF THE APES (1973). A TV series followed in 1974, and a cartoon series in 1975.
AAN: Jerry Goldsmith
● Video: CBS / Fox

The Planter's Wife
GB 1952 91m bw
Rank / Pinnacle (John Stafford)
US title: Outpost in Malaya; original title: White Blood

Malaya under the terrorists. A wife is planning to leave but changes her mind after she and her husband defend their home in a siege.
Superficial studio-bound melodrama unworthy of its subject but a good star vehicle.

w Peter Proud, Guy Elmes d Ken Annakin ph Geoffrey Unsworth m Allan Gray

Claudette Colbert, Jack Hawkins, Ram Gopal, Jeremy Spenser, Tom Macauley, Helen Goss

Platinum Blonde*
US 1931 92m bw
Columbia

A newspaper reporter falls for an heiress. Limp romantic comedy with interesting performances: the film which established Jean Harlow.

w Robert Riskin, Jo Swerling, story Harry E. Chandler, Doug Churchill d Frank Capra ph Joseph Walker

Robert Williams, Loretta Young, Jean Harlow, Halliwell Hobbes, Reginald Owen
'A programmer that fully entertains, is laughy and represents what cast, dialogue and direction can do with a lean story.'—Variety

Platinum High School
US 1960 96m bw

A father investigates his son's death at a military academy for rich juvenile delinquents. Hilarious serial-like melodrama with the worm turning to some effect. Mickey Rooney, Dan Duryea, Terry Moore, Warren Berlinger, Yvette Mimieux, Conway Twitty, Elisha Cook Jnr, Richard Jaeckel. Written by Robert Smith; directed by Charles Haas; for Albert Zugsmith / MGM. (GB title: Rich, Young and Deadly.)

Play Dirty*
GB 1969 118m Technicolor Panavision
UA / Lowndes (Harry Saltzman)

During World War II, a squad of ex-criminals is given the job of destroying an enemy oil depot in North Africa.
Small-scale Dirty Dozen with would-be ironic twists; well made entertainment for the stout-hearted.

w Lotte Colin, Melvyn Bragg d André de Toth ph Edward Scaife m Michel Legrand

Michael Caine, Nigel Davenport, Nigel Green, Harry Andrews, Bernard Archard, Daniel Pilon

Play It Again Sam*
US 1972 86m Technicolor Panavision
Paramount / APJAC / Rollins–Joffe (Arthur P. Jacobs)

A neurotic film critic is abandoned by his wife and seeks fresh companionship, with help from the shade of Humphrey Bogart.
Random comedy for star fans, mainly quite lively and painless.

w Woody Allen, from his play d Herbert Ross ph Owen Roizman m Billy Goldenberg

Woody Allen, Diane Keaton, Jerry Lacy, Susan Anspach
● Video: CIC

Play It as It Lays
US 1972 94m Technicolor Panavision

An unsuccessful actress takes stock of her wrecked life. With-it melodrama which audiences preferred to be without. Anthony Perkins, Tuesday Weld, Tammy Grimes, Adam Roarke, Ruth Ford. Written by Joan Didion and John Gregory Dunne, from the novel by Joan Didion; directed by Frank Perry; for Universal.

'The scream you hear may be your own!'
Play Misty for Me*
US 1971 102m Technicolor
Universal / Malpaso (Robert Daley)

A radio disc jockey is pestered by a girl who turns out to be homicidally jealous.
Smartly made if over-extended psycho melodrama with good suspense sequences and a fair quota of shocks.

w Jo Heims, Dean Reisner d Clint Eastwood ph Bruce Surtees m Dee Barton

Clint Eastwood, Jessica Walter, Donna Mills, John Larch

'Maurice brings a new kind of love to you!'
Playboy of Paris
US 1930 82m bw

A waiter inherits a million but finds he can't leave his job, so he becomes a playboy by night only. Rather rickety star vehicle which demands attention only when he is on screen.
Maurice Chevalier, Frances Dee, O. P. Heggie, Stuart Erwin, Eugene Pallette. Written by Percy Heath from the play The Little Café by Tristan Bernard; directed by

Ludwig Berger; for Paramount. 'Light, amusing farce story doesn't help and may hurt . . . Chevalier's the only draw.'—Variety

Players
US 1979 120m Metrocolor
Paramount (Robert Evans)

A pro tennis player is trained for top stardom by a sculptress with a mysterious past.
Entirely uninvolving romantic drama stretched around a Wimbledon match; slickness does not compensate for a gaping hole at the centre.

w Arnold Schulman d Anthony Harvey ph James Crabe m Jerry Goldsmith pd Richard Sylbert

Ali MacGraw, Dean-Paul Martin, Maximilian Schell, Pancho Gonzalez

Playgirl
US 1954 85m bw

A small-town girl becomes a good-time girl in the big city. Totally unsurprising melodrama. Shelley Winters, Barry Sullivan, Colleen Miller, Gregg Palmer, Richard Long, Kent Taylor. Written by Robert Blees; directed by Joseph Pevney; for Universal-International.

Playmates*
US 1941 96m bw
RKO (Cliff Reid)

For the sake of a lucrative radio contract, John Barrymore agrees to turn bandleader Kay Kyser into a Shakespearian actor.
Barrymore's last film is a weird comedy concoction, awesome in its waste of his talents but fairly funny in a high school kind of way.

w James V. Kern d David Butler ph Frank Redman songs James Van Heusen, Johnny Burke

Kay Kyser and his Band, John Barrymore, Ginny Simms, Lupe Velez, May Robson, Patsy Kelly, Peter Lind Hayes, George Cleveland

Playtime*
France 1968 152m Eastmancolor 70mm
Specta Films (René Silvera)

Hulot and a group of American tourists are bewildered by life in an airport, a business block and a restaurant.
Incredibly extended series of sketches, none of which is devastatingly funny. The irritation is that the talent is clearly there but needs control.

w Jacques Tati, Jacques Lagrange d Jacques Tati ph Jean Badal, Andreas Winding m Francis Lemarque pd Eugene Roman

Jacques Tati, Barbara Dennek, Jacqueline Lecomte, Henri Piccoli
'Tati still seems the wrong distance from his audience: not so far that we cannot see his gifts, not close enough so that they really touch.'—Stanley Kauffmann
'How sad that the result of all this, though it includes a great deal of intermittent pleasure, comes at times so dangerously close to boredom.'—Brenda Davies, MFB

'A series of brilliant doodles by an artist who has earned the right to indulge himself on such a scale.'—*Alexander Walker*

● *Video: Video Media*

Plaza Suite*
US 1971   114m   Technicolor
Paramount (Howard B. Koch)

Three sketches set in the same suite at New York's Plaza Hotel, with Walter Matthau appearing in all three but in different character.
A highly theatrical entertainment which was bound to seem flattened on the screen, but emerges with at least some of its laughs intact.
w Neil Simon, from his play *d* Arthur Hiller *ph* Jack Marta *m* Maurice Jarre

Walter Matthau, Maureen Stapleton, Barbara Harris, Lee Grant, Louise Sorel

Please Believe Me
US 1950   87m   bw
MGM (Val Lewton)

An English girl inherits an American ranch and is chased by a millionaire, a con man and a lawyer.
Dullsville comedy which failed to establish its star in America.
w Nathaniel Curtis *d* Norman Taurog *ph* Robert Planck *m* Hans Salter

Deborah Kerr, Robert Walker, Mark Stevens, Peter Lawford, James Whitmore, Spring Byington

Please Don't Eat the Daisies
US 1960   111m   Metrocolor   Panavision
MGM (Joe Pasternak)

The family of a drama critic move to the country.
Thin, obvious comedy, all dressed up but with nowhere to go.
w Isobel Lennart, *book* Jean Kerr *d* Charles Walters *ph* Robert Bronner *m* David Rose

Doris Day, David Niven, Janis Paige, Spring Byington, Patsy Kelly, Richard Haydn, Jack Weston, John Harding, Margaret Lindsay

Please Murder Me
US 1956   78m   bw
DCA (Donald Hyde)

An attorney defends an accused murderess, at great cost to himself.
Adequate Poverty Row suspenser with a foreseeable trick ending.
w Al C. Ward, Donald Hyde *d* Peter Godfrey *ph* Allen Stensvold

Angela Lansbury, Raymond Burr, Dick Foran, John Dehner, Lamont Johnson, Denver Pyle

Please Sir
GB 1971   101m   Eastmancolor
Rank / LWL / Leslie Grade (Andrew Mitchell)

The masters and pupils of Fenn Street school go on an annual camp.

Grossly inflated, occasionally funny big-screen version of the TV series.
w John Esmonde, Bob Larbey *d* Mark Stuart *ph* Wilkie Cooper *m* Mike Vickers

John Alderton, Deryck Guyler, Joan Sanderson, Noel Howlett, Eric Chitty, Richard Davies

● *Video: Rank*

Please Teacher
GB 1937   75m   bw

An heir tries to find his bequest in the country house he has sold as a girls' school. Cheerful star farce with songs. Bobby Howes, René Ray, Vera Pearce, Wylie Watson, Bertha Belmore, Lyn Harding. Written by Stafford Dickens from the musical by K. R. G. Browne and R. P. Weston; directed by Stafford Dickens; for Associated British. 'Plenty of laughs.'—*Variety*

Please Turn Over
GB 1959   87m   bw

A teenager writes a sexy best-seller clearly featuring her family and friends. Acceptable but uninspired comedy from a West End success. Ted Ray, Jean Kent, Leslie Phillips, Joan Sims, Julia Lockwood, Charles Hawtrey, Lionel Jeffries. Written by Norman Hudis, from the play *Book of the Month* by Basil Thomas; directed by Gerald Thomas; for Beaconsfield / Anglo Amalgamated.

The Pleasure Garden
GB / Germany 1925   74m approx (24 fps)
bw   silent
Gainsborough / Emelka (Michael Balcon, Erich Pommer)

A chorus girl marries a rich colonial who goes native.
Boring melodrama with a few touches typical of its director, whose first film it is.
w Eliot Stannard, *novel* Oliver Sandys *d* Alfred Hitchcock *ph* Baron Ventimiglia

Virginia Valli, John Stuart, Miles Mander, Carmelita Gerghty

The Pleasure Girls
GB 1965   88m   bw
Compton Tekli (Harry Fine)

Girl flatmates in London have trouble with their boy friends.
The road to ruin sixties style, hackneyed but quite well observed.
wd Gerry O'Hara *ph* Michael Reed *m* Malcolm Lockyer

Ian McShane, Francesca Annis, Tony Tanner, Klaus Kinski, Mark Eden, Suzanna Leigh

The Pleasure of His Company
US 1961   114m   Technicolor
Paramount / Perlberg–Seaton

An ageing playboy arrives unexpectedly in San Francisco for his daughter's wedding.
Tame family comedy, very flatly adapted from the stage; dressed to kill, but with no narrative or cinematic drive.

w Samuel Taylor, *play* Samuel Taylor, Cornelia Otis Skinner *d* George Seaton *ph* Robert Burks *m* Alfred Newman

Fred Astaire, Lilli Palmer, Debbie Reynolds, Charles Ruggles, Tab Hunter, Gary Merrill, Harold Fong
'Smart comedy in its most diluted form.'—*MFB*

The Pleasure Seekers
US 1964   107m   De Luxe   Cinemascope
TCF (David Weisbart)

Three girls in Madrid find boy friends.
Dim remake of *Three Coins in the Fountain*, adequate but unstimulating on all levels.
w Edith Sommer *d* Jean Negulesco *ph* Daniel L. Fapp *m* Lionel Newman, Alexander Courage

Ann-Margret, Tony Franciosa, Carol Lynley, Gene Tierney, Brian Keith, Gardner McKay, Isobel Elsom

AAN: Lionel Newman, Alexander Courage

The Plough and the Stars*
US 1936   72m   bw
RKO (Cliff Reid, Robert Sisk)

In 1916, a Dublin marriage is threatened by the husband's appointment as commander of the citizen army.
Rather elementary film version of the play about the Troubles; interesting for effort rather than performance, and for the talent involved.
w Dudley Nichols, *play* Sean O'Casey *d* John Ford *ph* Joseph August *m* Roy Webb

Barbara Stanwyck, Preston Foster, Barry Fitzgerald, Denis O'Dea, Eileen Crowe, F. J. McCormick, Arthur Shields, Una O'Connor, Moroni Olsen, J. M. Kerrigan, Bonita Granville
'Skilfully made but not impressive as a money entry.'—*Variety*

The Plow That Broke the Plains**
US 1936   28m   bw

The story of how overcultivation of America's Great Plains resulted in the Dust Bowl. Classic documentary which inevitably means less now than it did at the time but is still an impressive counterpoint to *The Grapes of Wrath*. Written and directed by Pare Lorenz; for Resettlement Administration Film Unit.

Plunder*
GB 1930   98m   bw

Two society friends turn jewel thieves to help an heiress. Primitive talkie version of a Ben Travers farce which veered towards melodrama but had a successful stage revival at the National Theatre in 1978; valuable as a record of the original performances. Tom Walls, Ralph Lynn, Robertson Hare, Winifred Shotter, Sydney Lynn, Ethel Coleridge. Written by W. P. Lipscomb; directed by Tom Walls; for Herbert Wilcox / British and Dominions. 'Just a photographic record of the stage success.'—*Variety*

Plunder of the Sun*
US 1953 81m bw
Warner (Robert Fellows)

Various criminal elements seek buried
treasure among the Mexican Aztec ruins.
Interestingly located, well made,
unconvincingly scripted melodrama, yet
another borrowing from *The Maltese Falcon*.

w Jonathan Latimer, *novel* David Dodge
d John Farrow ph Jack Draper m Antonio
D. Conde

Glenn Ford, Diana Lynn, Francis L. Sullivan,
Patricia Medina, Sean McClory, Douglass
Dumbrille, Eduardo Noriega

The Plunderers
US 1947 87m bw

An undercover cavalry officer becomes friends
with an outlaw who saves his life. Routine
western, just about watchable. Rod Cameron,
Ilona Massey, Adrian Booth. Written by
Gerald Geraghty and Gerald Drayson Adams;
directed by Joseph Kane; for Republic.

The Plunderers
US 1960 94m bw
Allied Artists / August (Joseph Pevney)

In the old west, four juvenile delinquents take
over a town.
The Wild One in period dress. Nothing in
particular.

w Bob Barbash d Joseph Pevney ph Eugene
Polito m Leonard Rosenman

Jeff Chandler, John Saxon, Ray Sticklyn,
Roger Torrey, Dee Pollock, Marsha Hunt,
Dolores Hart, Jay C. Flippen, James
Westerfield

Plymouth Adventure*
US 1952 105m Technicolor
MGM (Dore Schary)

The Pilgrim Fathers sail from Plymouth on the
Mayflower and spend their first months ashore
on the coast of America.
Well-meaning schoolbook history, totally
unconvincing and very dull despite obvious
effort all round. One or two of the actors have
their moments.

w Helen Deutsch, *novel* Ernest Gebler
d Clarence Brown ph William Daniels
m Miklos Rozsa

Spencer Tracy, Gene Tierney, Van Johnson,
Leo Genn, Dawn Addams
  'It demonstrates how Hollywood can dull
down as well as jazz up history.'—*Judith Crist,
1973*

Pocket Money*
US 1972 100m Technicolor
First Artists / Coleytown (John Foreman)

Two slow-thinking Arizona cowboys try to
make money herding cattle.
Peculiar modern western comedy drama which
doesn't work.

w Terry Malick, *novel* Jim Kane by
J. K. S. Brown d Stuart Rosenberg
ph Laszlo Kovacs m Alex North

Paul Newman, Lee Marvin, Strother Martin,
Kelly Jean Peters, Wayne Rogers
● *Video: Guild*

Pocketful of Miracles
US 1961 136m Technicolor
Panavision
UA / Franton (Frank Capra)

Kindly gangsters help an old apple seller to
persuade her long lost daughter that she is a
lady of means.
Boring, overlong remake of *Lady for a Day*,
showing that Capra's touch simply doesn't
work on the wide screen, that his themes are
dated anyway, and that all the fine character
actors in Hollywood are a liability unless you
find them something to do.

w Hal Kanter, Harry Tugend,
scenario Robert Riskin, *story* Damon
Runyon d Frank Capra ph Robert Bronner
m Walter Scharf

Bette Davis, Glenn Ford, Hope Lange,
Arthur O'Connell, Peter Falk, Thomas
Mitchell, Edward Everett Horton, Sheldon
Leonard, Barton MacLane, Jerome Cowan,
Fritz Feld, Snub Pollard, David Brian, Ann-
Margret, John Litel, Jay Novello, Willis
Bouchey, George E. Stone, Mike Mazurki,
Jack Elam, Mickey Shaughnessy, Peter Mann,
Frank Ferguson
  'The effect is less one of whimsy than of
being bludgeoned to death with a toffee
apple.'—*Peter John Dyer*
  'The story has enough cracks in it for the
syrup to leak through.'—*Playboy*

AAN: title song (m James Van Heusen,
ly Sammy Cahn); Peter Falk

Poet's Pub
GB 1949 79m bw
GFD / Aquila

A rowing blue takes over a Tudor inn and
discovers a priceless jewelled gauntlet, the
wearer of which is kidnapped during the
performance of a pageant.
Very thin, naive treatment of a whimsical
novel. The last film to use the Independent
Frame process.

w Diana Morgan, *novel* Eric Linklater
d Frederick Wilson ph George Stretton
m Clifton Parker

Derek Bond, Rona Anderson, Barbara
Murray, Leslie Dwyer, Joyce Grenfell

Poil de Carotte*
France 1932 94m bw

A small boy is picked on by his ageing mother
to the point where he attempts suicide.
Country melodrama which made its director's
name but seems a little faded now despite
bravura sequences.

w Jules Renard d Julien Duvivier ph Thirard
Monniot

Harry Baur, Robert Lynen, Catherine
Fontenoy
  'Looks like the best chance ever for a
French film to get American distribution on
the grand scale.'—*Variety*

Point Blank*
US 1967 92m Metrocolor Panavision
MGM / Judd Bernard, Irwin Winkler

A gangster takes an elaborate revenge on his
cheating partner.
Extremely violent gangster thriller, well shot
on location and something of a cult, but with
irritating pretentiousness and obscure plot
points.

w Alexander Jacobs, David Newhouse, Rafe
Newhouse, *novel* The Hunter by Richard
Stark d John Boorman ph Philip Lathrop
m Johnny Mandel

Lee Marvin, Angie Dickinson, Keenan Wynn,
Carroll O'Connor, Lloyd Bochner, Michael
Strong, John Vernon, Sharon Acker
†*The Outfit* (qv) is a kind of sequel / reprise.

● *Video: MGM / UA*

Pointed Heels
US 1929 61m bw (colour sequence)

A theatrical producer loves a musical comedy
star but loses her to a young composer.
Predictable backstage drama. William Powell,
Fay Wray, Helen Kane, Phillips Holmes,
Richard 'Skeets' Gallagher, Eugene Pallette.
Written by Florence Ryerson and John V. A.
Weaver, from a story by Charles Brackett;
directed by A. Edward Sutherland; for
Paramount. 'Moderate business likely for a
light comedy that choked on too big a
mouthful.'—*Variety*

Poison Pen*
GB 1939 79m bw
ABP (Walter C. Mycroft)

A village community is set at odds by a writer
of vindictive anonymous letters.
Effective minor drama, with good location
atmosphere.

w Doreen Montgomery, William Freshman,
N. C. Hunter, Esther McCracken,
play Richard Llewellyn d Paul Stein

Flora Robson, Reginald Tate, Robert Newton,
Ann Todd, Geoffrey Toone, Belle Chrystal,
Edward Chapman, Edward Rigby
  'Sordid theme makes it doubtful film
fare.'—*Variety*
  'A lamentably artificial piece.'—*Richard
Mallett, Punch*

'Call them what you like. Just don't call
  them when you're in trouble!'
Police Academy
US 1984 96m Technicolor

The mayor of an American city lifts all
restrictions on entry to the police force.
Appallingly unfunny series of snippets about
police training, like an American Carry On
with few jokes leading to a punch line and
occasional resorting to dirty bits. Steve
Guttenberg, Kim Cattrall, G. W. Bailey,
Bubba Smith, Donovan Scott, George
Gaynes. Written by Neal Israel, Pat Proft,
Hugh Wilson; directed by Hugh Wilson; for
Paul Maslansky / Ladd Company / Warner

Brothers. 'Hit or miss comic juvenilia . . .
pure popcorn fantasy fodder.'—*Paul Taylor,
MFB*

Politics
US 1931   71m   bw

Two small-town women get into politics to
fight racketeers. Scrappy star comedy which
probably seemed funnier at the time. Marie
Dressler, Polly Moran, Roscoe Ates, Karen
Morley, William Bakewell, John Miljan.
Written by Robert E. Hopkins, Wells Root,
Zelda Sears, Malcolm Stuart Boylan; directed
by Charles F. Reisner; for MGM. 'Loaded
with technical faults, but it has too many laugh
moments to fail to sock the b.o.'—*Variety*

Polly of the Circus
US 1932   72m   bw
MGM

A trapeze artiste falls for the local minister,
but incurs disapproval from his bishop.
Elementary romance reminiscent of silent
drama.

w Carey Wilson, *play* Margaret Mayo
d Alfred Santell *ph* George Barnes

Marion Davies, Clark Gable, C. Aubrey
Smith, Raymond Hatton, David Landau,
Maude Eburne, Guinn Williams, Ray Milland
   'Frail entertainment with both leads
miscast.'—*Variety*

Pollyanna*
US 1960   134m   Technicolor
Walt Disney (George Golitzen)

A 12-year-old orphan girl cheers up the
grumps of the small town where she comes to
live.
Well cast but overlong and rather humourless
remake of a children's classic from an earlier
age.

wd David Swift, *novel* Eleanor Porter
ph Russell Harlan *m* Paul Smith *ad* Carroll
Clark, Robert Clatworthy

Hayley Mills, Jane Wyman, Karl Malden,
Nancy Olson, Adolphe Menjou, Donald
Crisp, Agnes Moorehead, Richard Egan,
Kevin Corcoran, James Drury, Reta Shaw,
Leora Dana
   'Even Hayley Mills can neither prevent one
from sympathizing with the crusty aunts,
hermits, vicars and hypochondriacs who get so
forcibly cheered up, nor from feverishly
speculating whether films like this don't run
the risk of inciting normally kind and gentle
people into certain excesses of violent crime –
child murder, for instance.'—*MFB*

Poltergeist**
US 1982   114m   Metrocolor   Panavision
MGM / SLM (Steven Spielberg)

Suburban life is disrupted when through her
TV set a young girl releases unpleasant forces
from the cemetery over which the modern
estate was built.
Skilful but dramatically thin and sometimes
rather nasty horror movie in which the
producer's hand seems often to have

controlled the director's. Misjudgment must
be the reason that it was not the huge success
intended.

w Steven Spielberg, Michael Grais, Mark
Victor *d* Tobe Hooper *ph* Matthew F.
Leonetti *m* Jerry Goldsmith *ed* Michael
Kahn

Jobeth Williams, Craig T. Nelson, Beatrice
Straight, Dominique Dunne, Oliver Robbins

AAN: music, visual effects (Richard Edlund,
Michael Wood, Bruce Nicholson)

Pony Express*
US 1953   101m   Technicolor
Paramount (Nat Holt)

In 1860 Buffalo Bill Cody and Wild Bill
Hickok are sent to establish pony express
stations across California.
Standard western which tells a factual tale
adequately if rather slowly.

w Charles Marquis Warren *d* Jerry Hopper
ph Ray Rennahan *m* Paul Sawtell

Charlton Heston, Forrest Tucker, Rhonda
Fleming, Jan Sterling

Pony Soldier
US 1952   82m   Technicolor
TCF (Samuel G. Engel)
GB title: *MacDonald of the Canadian
Mounties*

The mounties settle the hash of Canadian
Indian renegades who have been causing
trouble on the American border.
Mediocre outdoor adventure.

w John C. Higgins *d* Joseph M. Newman
ph Harry Jackson *m* Alex North

Tyrone Power, Cameron Mitchell, Robert
Horton, Thomas Gomez, Penny Edwards,
Adeline de Walt Reynolds

Pool of London
GB 1950   85m   bw
Ealing (Michael Relph)

A smuggling sailor gets involved in murder.
Routine semi-documentary police thriller with
locations in London docks decorating a
standard piece of thick ear.

w Jack Whittingham, John Eldridge *d* Basil
Dearden *ph* Gordon Dines *m* John Addison

Bonar Colleano, Susan Shaw, Earl Cameron,
Renée Asherson, Moira Lister, Max Adrian,
James Robertson Justice, Joan Dowling
   'Done with such imagination, humour and
visual attractiveness as to hold the pleased
attention of all who like to use their eyes and
their ears.'—*Richard Mallett, Punch*

Poor Cow*
GB 1967   101m   Eastmancolor
Anglo Amalgamated / Vic / Fenchurch (Joe
Janni)

The dismal life of a young London mother
who lives in squalor with her criminal
husband.
Television-style fictional documentary
determined to rub one's nose in the mire.
Innovative and occasionally striking but not
very likeable.

w Nell Dunn, Ken Loach, *novel* Nell Dunn
d Ken Loach *ph* Brian Probyn *m* Donovan

Carol White, Terence Stamp, John Bindon,
Kate Williams, Queenie Watts
   'A superficial, slightly patronizing excursion
into the nether realms of social realism.'—*Jan
Dawson*

Poor Little Rich Girl*
US 1936   79m   bw
TCF (Darryl F. Zanuck)

A child is separated from her father and joins
a radio singing act.
Pleasing star vehicle with all the expected
elements, adapted from a Mary Pickford
vehicle of 1917.

w Sam Hellman, Gladys Lehman, Harry
Tugend *d* Irving Cummings *ph* John Seitz
songs Mack Gordon, Harry Revel

Shirley Temple, Jack Haley, Alice Faye,
Gloria Stuart, Michael Whalen, Sara Haden,
Jane Darwell, Claude Gillingwater, Henry
Armetta

Pope Joan
GB 1972   132m   Eastmancolor
   Panavision
Big City Productions / Kurt Unger
aka: *The Devil's Imposter*

The legend of a 9th-century German semi-
prostitute who discovered a vocation to preach
and was made Pope.
Uninspiring pageant, brutish and rather silly,
full of would-be medieval sensationalism.

w John Briley *d* Michael Anderson *ph* Billy
Williams *m* Maurice Jarre *pd* Elliott Scott

Liv Ullmann, Trevor Howard, Olivia de
Havilland, Maximilian Schell, Keir Dullea,
Robert Beatty, Franco Nero, Patrick Magee

● *Video: Guild*

The Pope of Greenwich Village
US 1984   120m   Metrocolor
MGM-UA / Koch-Kirkwood (Benjy
Rosenberg)

In New York, Charlie and his cousin Paulie
become thieves and fall foul of the Mafia.
Back again to the mean streets of the east
side, but with nothing at all new to add to the
scores of indistinguishable real-life
melodramas of this kind.

w Vincent Patrick, from his novel *d* Stuart
Rosenberg *ph* John Bailey *m* Dave Grusin
pd Paul Sylbert

Eric Roberts, Mickey Rourke, Daryl Hannah,
Geraldine Page, Kenneth McMillan, Tony
Musante, M. Emmet Walsh, Burt Young

Popeye
US 1980   114m   colour
Paramount / Disney (Robert Evans)

Popeye returns to Sweethaven in search of the
father who abandoned him.
Lamentable attempt by an ill-chosen director
to humanize and sentimentalize a celebrated
cartoon character who doesn't get into the

expected physical action until the film is nearly over.

w Jules Feiffer, from characters created by E. C. Segar *d* Robert Altman *ph* Giuseppe Rotunno *m / ly* Harry Nilsson *pd* Wolf Kroeger

Robin Williams, Shelley Duvall, Ray Walston, Paul Dooley

'The picture doesn't come together, and much of it is cluttered, squawky, and eerily unfunny.'—*Pauline Kael, New Yorker*

● Video: Rank

Popi°
US 1969   113m   De Luxe
UA / Leonard Films (Herbert B. Leonard)

Adventures of a cheerful inhabitant of New York's Puerto Rican ghetto.
Ethnic comedy-drama of the kind that has since found its way in abundance into American TV series. Very competently done for those who like it, e.g. Puerto Ricans.

w Tina and Lester Pine *d* Arthur Hiller
ph Ross Lowell *m* Dominic Frontière

Alan Arkin, Rita Moreno, Miguel Alejandro, Ruben Figuero

'An appropriately disenchanted view of an immigrant's struggling ambitions in the Promised Land.'—*Richard Combs*

Poppy°
US 1936   74m   bw
Paramount (Paul Jones)

An itinerant medicine-seller sets up his stall in a small town where his daughter falls in love with the mayor's son.
Clumsily but heavily plotted vehicle for W. C. Fields, who as usual has great moments but seems to rob the show of its proper pace.

w Waldemar Young, Virginia Van Upp, *play* Dorothy Donnelly *d* A. Edward Sutherland
ph William Mellor *m* Frederick Hollander

W. C. Fields, Rochelle Hudson, Richard Cromwell, Granville Bates, Catherine Doucet, Lynne Overman, Maude Eburne

'Antique hokum trussed up for a Fields vehicle.'—*Literary Digest*

Porgy and Bess°
US 1959   138m   Technicolor   Todd-AO
Samuel Goldwyn

A slum girl falls in love with a crippled beggar.
Negro opera about the inhabitants of Catfish Row; full of interest for music lovers, but not lending itself very readily to screen treatment.

w N. Richard Nash, *libretto* Du Bose Heyward, *play* Porgy by Du Bose and Dorothy Heyward *d* Otto Preminger
ph Leon Shamroy *m* George Gershwin
m André Previn, Ken Darby *ch* Hermes Pan

Sidney Poitier, Dorothy Dandridge, Sammy Davis Jnr, Pearl Bailey, Brock Peters, Diahann Carroll, Clarence Muse

AA: André Previn, Ken Darby
AAN: Leon Shamroy

PONY SOLDIER. The advertising is of a higher standard than the photoplay.

'Bold! blunt! blustering! the battle picture without equal!'

Pork Chop Hill*
US 1959 97m bw
United Artists / Melville / Lewis Milestone

The Americans in Korea take a vital hill but the colonel in command finds it difficult to hold.
Ironic war film with vivid spectacle separated by much talk.

w James R. Webb d Lewis Milestone ph Sam Leavitt m Leonard Rosenman pd Nicolai Remisoff

Gregory Peck, Harry Guardino, George Shibata, Woody Strode, James Edwards, Rip Torn, George Peppard, Barry Atwater, Robert Blake

Porky's
Canada 1982 98m colour
Melvin Simon / Astral Bellevue Pathe / Porky's Productions / (Don Carmody, Bob Clark)

In Florida in the early fifties, high school boys try to get into a local brothel.
Ghastly teenage goings-on taking cinema bad taste just about as far as it will get.

wd Bob Clark ph Reginald H. Morris m Carl Zittrer, Paul Zaza pd Reuben Freed

Dan Monahan, Mark Herrier, Wyatt Knight, Roger Wilson, Kim Cattrall, Art Hindle, Wayne Maunder, Alex Karras, Nancy Parsons
  'It is difficult to say which is the more depressing: the technical expertise with which this mind-numbing tripe has been put together, or its great success at the US box office.'—Jo Imeson, MFB
  'One of those movies that makes you weep for the state of the contemporary commercial cinema—and, even more, for the gullibility of the public that pays to see it.'—Margaret Hinxman, Daily Mail
† Porky's 2 followed in 1983 and was even worse.

Porridge*
GB 1979 93m Eastmancolor
Black Lion / Witzend

Old lags at Slade Prison try to arrange an escape for a first offender.
Genial expansion of a successful TV series to the big screen; alas, as usual the material is stretched to snapping point, and the welcome irony of the original becomes sentimentality. Still, the film is a valuable record of memorable characters.

w Dick Clement, Ian La Frenais d Dick Clement ph Bob Huke md Terry Oates

Ronnie Barker, Richard Beckinsale, Fulton Mackay, Brian Wilde, Peter Vaughan, Geoffrey Baydon, Julian Holloway

Port Afrique
GB 1956 92m Technicolor

In Morocco, an American pilot solves the shooting of his wife. Tropical variation on The

Maltese Falcon and *The Blue Dahlia*; not much cop on its own account. Phil Carey, Pier Angeli, Dennis Price, Eugene Deckers, James Hayter, Rachel Gurney, Anthony Newley. Written by Frank Partos and John Cresswell, from a novel by Bernard Victor Dyer; directed by Rudolph Maté; for David E. Rose / Columbia.

Port of New York*
US 1949 82m bw
Eagle Lion (Aubrey Schenck)

A woman narcotics smuggler determines to betray her colleagues to the authorities.
Good routine semi-documentary thick ear, notable for an early appearance by Yul Brynner as villain-in-chief.

w Eugene Ling d Laslo Benedek ph George E. Diskant w Sol Kaplan

Scott Brady, Richard Rober, K. T. Stevens, Yul Brynner

Port of Seven Seas*
US 1938 81m bw
MGM (Henry Henigson)

Love on the Marseilles waterfront.
Stagey Hollywoodization of Pagnol's *Marius* trilogy: some vigour shows through.

w Preston Sturges d James Whale ph Karl Freund m Franz Waxman

Wallace Beery, Frank Morgan, Maureen O'Sullivan, John Beal, Jessie Ralph, Cora Witherspoon
  'Genuine and touching drama . . . strong solo biller.'—Variety

Porte des Lilas*
France / Italy 1957 95m bw
Filmsonor / Rizzoli (Jacques Plante)
aka: Gate of Lilacs

A gangster on the run shelters in a poor quarter of Paris, but his treachery is his undoing.
Atmospheric comedy-drama put across with the expected style but providing very little to smile at.

w René Clair, Jean Aurel, novel La Grande Ceinture by René Fallet d René Clair ph Robert Le Fèbvre m Georges Brassens

Pierre Brasseur, Georges Brassens, Henri Vidal, Dany Carrel, Raymond Bussières, Amédée, Alain Bouvette

Les Portes de la Nuit*
France 1946 106m bw
Pathé Cinema
aka: Gates of Night

Various people in post-war Paris are drawn into a pattern woven by Destiny—who appears as a melancholy tramp.
A polished piece of post-war gloom, and the archetype of all *films noirs* of the period. The beginning, also, of its director's decline.

w Jacques Prévert d Marcel Carné ph Philippe Agostini m Joseph Kosma ad Alexander Trauner

Pierre Brasseur, Yves Montand, Nathalie Nattier, Serge Reggiani, Jean Vilar, Saturnin Fabre, Mady Berry, Dany Robin
† One of the few films to have been based on a ballet—Le Rendezvous by Prévert. Oddly enough its realistic scenes of daily life are among its most successful elements.

● Video: Thorn EMI

Portia on Trial*
US 1937 83m bw

A lady lawyer uses her skills in the courtroom to right the personal wrongs done to her years before. Efficient tearjerker, *Madame X* style, and one of the comparatively big productions Republic occasionally tried. Frieda Inescort, Walter Abel, Neil Hamilton, Heather Angel, Ruth Donnelly, Barbara Pepper, Clarence Kolb. Written by Sam Ornitz, E. E. Paramore Jnr, from the novel by Faith Baldwin; directed by George Nicholls Jnr; for Republic. 'A distinguished production: exploitation required to overcome title and no-name handicap.'—Variety

Portnoy's Complaint
US 1972 101m Technicolor
Panavision
Warner / Chenault (Ernest Lehman)

A young New York Jewish boy has mother and masturbation problems.
Foolhardy attempt to film a fashionably sensational literary exercise; one of Hollywood's last attempts – thank goodness – to be 'with it'.

wd Ernest Lehman, novel Philip Roth ph Philip Lathrop m Michel Legrand

Richard Benjamin, Karen Black, Lee Black, Jack Somack, Jill Clayburgh, Jeannie Berlin
  'The spectator is forced into the doubly uncomfortable position of a voyeur who can't actually see anything.'—Jan Dawson

Portrait from Life
GB 1948 90m bw
GFD / Gainsborough (Antony Darnborough)
US title: The Girl in the Painting

In an art gallery, a German professor recognizes a portrait as that of his daughter, lost during the war in Germany, and after a search discovers her to have been an amnesiac under the protection of a leading Nazi.
Tolerable melodrama with similarities to The Seventh Veil (the girl has to choose between four men).

w Frank Harvey Jnr, Muriel and Sydney Box d Terence Fisher ph Jack Asher m Benjamin Frankel

Mai Zetterling, Robert Beatty, Guy Rolfe, Herbert Lom, Patrick Holt

Portrait in Black*
US 1960 113m Eastmancolor
U-I / Ross Hunter

An elderly shipping tycoon is murdered by his wife and doctor, but they are blackmailed.
Absurd old-fashioned melodrama of dark doings among the idle rich. Quite entertaining for addicts.

w Ivan Goff, Ben Roberts *d* Michael Gordon
ph Russell Metty *m* Frank Skinner

Lana Turner, Anthony Quinn, Richard
Basehart, Anna May Wong, Lloyd Nolan,
Sandra Dee, John Saxon, Ray Walston,
Virginia Grey

'Connoisseurs of the higher tosh should find
it irresistible.'—*Penelope Houston*

Portrait of a Mobster
US 1961 108m bw
Warner

The career of twenties gangster Dutch Schultz.
Over-familiar, warmed over racketeering stuff
with no particular edge or style.

w Howard Browne *d* Joseph Pevney
ph Eugene Polito *m* Max Steiner

Vic Morrow, Leslie Parrish, Peter Breck, Ray
Danton (repeating as Legs Diamond),
Norman Alden, Ken Lynch

Portrait of Alison*
GB 1955 84m bw
Anglo-Amalgamated / Insignia (Frank
Godwin)
aka: *Postmark for Danger*

A journalist dies while investigating an
international smuggling ring, and his brother
takes up the case.
Solidly carpentered mystery with all the twists
expected from this source.

w Guy Green, Ken Hughes, *radio
serial* Francis Durbridge *d* Guy Green
ph Wilkie Cooper *m* John Veale

Robert Beatty, Terry Moore, William
Sylvester, Josephine Griffin, Geoffrey Keen,
Allan Cuthbertson, Henry Oscar

Portrait of Clare
GB 1950 98m bw
ABPC (Leslie Landau)

In 1900, a woman looks back on her three
marriages.
High school novelette for easily pleased
female audiences.

w Leslie Landau, Adrian Arlington,
novel Francis Brett Young *d* Lance Comfort
ph Gunther Krampf *ad* Don Ashton

Margaret Johnston, Richard Todd, Robin
Bailey, Ronald Howard, Mary Clare, Marjorie
Fielding, Anthony Nicholls, Lloyd Pearson

Portrait of Jennie***
US 1948 86m bw (tinted sequence)
David O. Selznick
GB title: *Jennie*

A penniless artist meets a strange girl who
seems to age each time he sees her; they fall in
love and he discovers that she has long been
dead, though she finally comes to life once
more during a sea storm like the one in which
she perished.
A splendid example of the higher Hollywood
lunacy: a silly story with pretensions about life
and death and time and art, presented with
superb persuasiveness by a first-class team of
actors and technicians.

w Peter Berneis, Paul Osborn, Leonard
Bernovici, *novel* Robert Nathan *d* William
Dieterle *ph* Joseph August *m* Dmitri
Tiomkin, after Debussy

*Jennifer Jones, Joseph Cotten, Ethel
Barrymore*, David Wayne, Lillian Gish, Henry
Hull, Florence Bates

PROLOGUE: Since time began man has
looked into the awesome reaches of infinity
and asked the eternal questions: What is time?
What is life? What is space? What is death?
Through a hundred civilizations, philosophers
and scientists have come together with
answers, but the bewilderment remains. . . .
Science tells us that nothing ever dies but only
changes, that time itself does not pass but
curves around us, and that the past and the
future are together at our side for ever. Out of
the shadows of knowledge, and out of a
painting that hung on a museum wall, comes
our story, the truth of which lies not on our
screen but in your hearts.

JENNIE'S SONG: 'Where I come from, nobody
knows . . .
And where I'm going,
everything goes . . .
The wind blows,
The sea flows . . .
And nobody knows . . .'

EBEN (Joseph Cotten): 'I want you, not
dreams of you.'

JENNIE (Jennifer Jones): 'There is no life,
my darling, until you love and have been
loved. And then there is no death.'

'Easily the Selznick masterpiece, rich in
superb performances, tasteful direction and
superb photography.'—*Motion Picture Herald*
'One of the most exquisite fantasy films
ever made . . . a milieu rich in visual and
aural imagery . . . a sensuous evocation of
time and timelessness.'—*Cinefantastique*
'Though the story may not make sense, the
pyrotechnics, joined to the dumbfounded
silliness, keep one watching.'—*New Yorker
1976*

AAN: Joseph August
● *Video: Guild*

The Poseidon Adventure**
US 1972 117m De Luxe Panavision
TCF / Kent (Irwin Allen)

A luxury liner is capsized, and trapped
passengers have to find their way to freedom
via an upside down world.
Tedious disaster movie which caught the
public fancy and started a cycle. Spectacular
moments, cardboard characters, flashes of
imagination.

w Stirling Silliphant, Wendell Mayes,
novel Paul Gallico *ph* Harold Stine *d* Ronald
Neame *m* John Williams *pd* William Creber

Gene Hackman, Ernest Borgnine, Shelley
Winters, Red Buttons, Carol Lynley, Leslie
Nielson, Arthur O'Connell, Pamela Sue
Martin, Roddy McDowall, Eric Shea, Jack
Albertson, Stella Stevens

'The script is the only cataclysm in this
waterlogged *Grand Hotel*.'—*New Yorker*
† See also: *Beyond the Poseidon Adventure*.

AA: song 'The Morning After' (*m* / *ly* Al
Kasha, Joel Hirschhorn)
AAN: Harold Stine; John Williams; Shelley
Winters
● *Video: CBS / Fox*

Posse**
US 1975 93m Technicolor Panavision
Paramount / Bryna (Kirk Douglas)

A US marshal seeking higher office vows to
capture a railroad bandit, but the tables are
smartly turned.
Unusual minor western, quite pleasing in all
departments and neither mindless nor violent.

w William Roberts, Christopher Knopf *d* Kirk
Douglas *ph* Fred Koenekamp *m* Maurice
Jarre

Kirk Douglas, Bruce Dern, Bo Hopkins,
James Stacy, Luke Askey, David Canary

Posse from Hell
US 1961 89m Technicolor

Four killers escape from jail and take over a
town. Moderate western programmer with
more violence than usual. Audie Murphy,
John Saxon, Zohra Lampert, Vic Morrow,
Robert Keith. Written by Clair Huffaker;
directed by Herbert Coleman; for Universal /
International.

Possessed*
US 1931 76m bw
MGM

A factory girl goes to New York in search of
riches.
Reasonably gutsy Depression melodrama
which moves at a fair pace.

w Lenore Coffee, *play* The Mirage by Edgar
Selwyn *d* Clarence Brown *ph* Oliver T.
Marsh

Joan Crawford, Clark Gable, Wallace Ford,
Skeets Gallagher, Frank Conroy, Marjorie
White, John Miljan

'Lots of luxury; lots of charm; lots of
smooth talk about courage and marriage and
what women want.'—*James R. Quirk*

'You'll be possessed by its love madness!'
Possessed*
US 1947 108m bw
Warner (Jerry Wald)

An emotionally unstable nurse marries her
employer but retains a passionate love for an
engineer whom she kills when he does not
respond.
Extremely heavy, almost Germanic, flashback
melodrama with everyone tearing hammer and
tongs at the rather ailing script. Fun if you're
in that mood, and an interesting example of
the American *film noir* of the forties.

w Silvia Richards, Ranald MacDougall,
novel One Man's Secret by Rita Weiman
d Curtis Bernhardt *ph* Joseph Valentine
m Franz Waxman

Joan Crawford, Raymond Massey, Van
Heflin, Geraldine Brooks, Stanley Ridges,
John Ridgely, Moroni Olsen
  'Acting with bells on.'—*Richard Winningtor*
  'Miss Crawford performs with the passion
and intelligence of an actress who is not
content with just one Oscar.'—*James Agee*
AAN: Joan Crawford

The Possession of Joel Delaney*
US 1971 108m Eastmancolor
ITC / Haworth (George Justin)

A wealthy New York divorcee tries to save he
brother from death at the hands of a Puerto
Rican occult group who believe in ritual
murder and demonic possession.
Unpleasant, frightening and overlong horror
film with some kind of message struggling to
get out but precious little entertainment value.

w Matt Robinson, Grimes Grice,
novel Ramona Stewart *d* Waris Hussein
ph Arthur J. Ornitz *m* Joe Ragoso

Shirley Maclaine, Perry King, Lisa Kohane,
David Ellacott
  'Some see the film as a political allegory; I
see it as a piece of political tosh.'—*Michael
Billington, Illustrated London News*

● *Video: Precision*

The Postman Always Rings Twice*
US 1946 113m bw
MGM (Carey Wilson)

A guilty couple murder her husband but get
their come-uppance.
Pale shadow of *Double Indemnity*, efficient
but not interesting or very suspenseful.

w Harry Ruskin, Niven Busch, *novel* James
M. Cain *d* Tay Garnett *ph* Sidney Wagner
m George Bassman

Lana Turner, John Garfield, Cecil Kellaway,
Hume Cronyn, Leon Ames, Audrey Totter,
Alan Reed
  'It was a real chore to do *Postman* under the
Hays Office, but I think I managed to get the
sex across.'—*Tay Garnett*

'You will feel the heat!'
'Their love was a war that destroyed!'
The Postman Always Rings Twice*
US 1981 121m Metrocolor

A remake of the above with more heavy
breathing and some table-ending. Not
otherwise any better, but an interesting
measure of the times. Jack Nicholson, Jessica
Lange, John Colicos, Michael Lerner, John P.
Ryan, Anjelica Huston. Written by David
Mamet; directed by Bob Rafelson; for
Northstar International / Lorimar. 'Too
cheerless to be erotic, too charmless to be
titillating.'—*Margaret Hinxman, Daily Mail*

● *Video: Guild*

Postman's Knock*
GB 1961 88m bw
MGM (Ronald Kinnoch)

A village postman is transferred to London,
finds life and work bewildering, but captures
some crooks and ends up a hero.

THE POSTMAN ALWAYS RINGS TWICE (1981).   Not till the 1980s version did the sex really
show.

Mildly amusing star vehicle rising to good
comic climaxes.

w John Briley, Jack Trevor Story *d* Robert
Lynn *ph* Gerald Moss *m* Ron Goodwin

Spike Milligan, Barbara Shelley, Wilfrid
Lawson

Pot Luck*
GB 1936 71m bw

A Scotland Yard inspector enlists the aid of
department store staff to recover a stolen
Chinese vase. Surprisingly not from a stage
original, this action farce gets better as it goes
along and finds time for a quick spoof of *The
Old Dark House*. Tom Walls, Ralph Lynn,
Robertson Hare, Diana Churchill, Gordon
James, Martita Hunt. Written by Ben Travers;
directed by Tom Walls; for Gainsborough.

Pot o' Gold
US 1941 87m bw
(UA) James Roosevelt
GB title: *The Golden Hour*

A radio giveaway show finds work for idle
musicians.
Thin Capraesque comedy which needed more
determined handling.

w Walter de Leon *d* George Marshall *ph* Hal
Mohr *md* Lou Forbes

James Stewart, Paulette Goddard, Horace
Heidt, Charles Winninger, Mary Gordon,
Frank Melton, Jed Prouty

Potemkin: see The Battleship Potemkin

Powder River
US 1953 77m Technicolor

A marshal finds that an embittered doctor is
the killer he is seeking. Satisfactory
programmer, more of a suspense drama than a
western. Rory Calhoun, Cameron Mitchell,
Corinne Calvet, Penny Edwards, Carl Betz,
John Dehner. Written by Geoffrey Holmes,
from a novel by Stuart Lake; directed by Louis
King; for TCF.

Powder Town
US 1942 79m bw

A scientist in a munitions plant comes into
conflict with a tough foreman. Propaganda
action programmer. Victor McLaglen,
Edmond O'Brien, June Havoc. Written by
David Boehm and Vicki Baum from a novel
by Max Brand; directed by Rowland V. Lee;
for RKO.

The Power*

US 1967 109m Metrocolor
Cinemascope
MGM / George Pal

Scientists researching into human endurance are menaced by one of their number who has developed the ability to kill by will power. Interesting but finally unexciting and exasperating science fiction which badly lacks a gimmick one can actually see.

w John Gay, *novel* Frank M. Robinson
d Byron Haskin ph Ellsworth Fredericks
m Miklos Rozsa

Michael Rennie, George Hamilton, Suzanne Pleshette, Nehemiah Persoff, Earl Holliman, Arthur O'Connell, Aldo Ray, Barbara Nichols, Yvonne de Carlo, Richard Carlson, Gary Merrill, Ken Murray, Miiko Taka, Celia Lovsky

'The movie takes itself very seriously. We don't have to.'—*Robert Windeler*

The Power and the Glory*

US 1933 76m bw
Fox (Jesse L. Lasky)

The flashback story of a tycoon who rose from nothing and was corrupted by power.
Often noted as a forerunner of *Citizen Kane,* this is in fact a disappointing film with a very thin script and a general sense of aimlessness. 'Presented in narratage' meant that the characters voice their unspoken thoughts. Most interesting for its credits.

w Preston Sturges d William K. Howard
ph James Wong Howe m Louis de Francesco

Spencer Tracy, Colleen Moore, Ralph Morgan, Helen Vinson

'Débuting at two dollars on Broadway. Not two dollars but decidedly above-average film fare. Packs plenty of appeal, even with a not too punch marquee cast.'—*Variety*

The Power and the Prize*

US 1956 98m bw Cinemascope
MGM (Nicholas Nayfack)

An ambitious company executive is criticized by his president for wanting to marry a European refugee, but the other executives support him.
Unconvincing big business fairy tale which passes the time competently enough, though Taylor is a humourless hero.

w Robert Ardrey, *novel* Howard Swiggett
d Henry Koster ph George Folsey
m Bronislau Kaper

Robert Taylor, Elizabeth Mueller, Mary Astor, Burl Ives, Charles Coburn, Cedric Hardwicke

Power of the Press

US 1943 63m bw

The owner of a New York paper kills to maintain its isolationist line. Hard-hitting melodrama which overdoes the propaganda. Lee Tracy, Guy Kibbee, Otto Kruger, Gloria Dickson. Written by Samuel Fuller and Robert D. Andrews; directed by Lew Landers; for Columbia.

Power Play

GB / Canada 1978 109m colour
Robert Cooper / Canada United Kingdom (Christopher Dalton)

In a mythical country, a tank commander joins the leaders of a coup d' ètat only to doublecross them.
Uninteresting mixture of violent action and verbosity.

wd Martyn Burke ph Ousama Rawi m Ken Thorne

Peter O'Toole, David Hemmings, Donald Pleasence, Barry Morse

The Powers Girl

US 1942 92m bw
UA / Charles R. Rogers
GB title: *Hello Beautiful*

Girls come to New York to become models for John Robert Powers.
Extremely thin and forgettable musical.

w Edwin Moran, Harry Segall, *book* John Robert Powers d Norman Z. McLeod
ph Stanley Cortez md Louis Silvers

George Murphy, Anne Shirley, Carole Landis, Alan Mowbray (as Powers), Dennis Day, Benny Goodman and his Orchestra, Mary Treen

Practically Yours

US 1944 89m bw
Paramount (Mitchell Leisen)

A war hero comes back after being supposed dead, and finds himself with a fiancée he never met.
Silly romantic comedy which never gets going.

w Norman Krasna d Mitchell Leisen
ph Charles Lang Jnr m Victor Young

Claudette Colbert, Fred MacMurray, Gil Lamb, Cecil Kellaway, Robert Benchley, Rosemary de Camp, Tom Powers, Jane Frazee

Prelude to Fame

GB 1950 88m bw
Rank / Two Cities (Donald B. Wilson)

The health of a child musical prodigy is endangered by an ambitious woman who pushes him to the top.
Banal drama with classical music, generally overacted by the adults.

w Robert Westerby, *story* Young Archimedes by Aldous Huxley d Fergus McDonell
ph George Stretton

Jeremy Spenser, Guy Rolfe, Kathleen Ryan, Kathleen Byron, James Robertson Justice, Henry Oscar, Rosalie Crutchley

The Premature Burial

US 1961 81m Eastmancolor
Panavision
AIP (Roger Corman)

A man afraid of being buried alive suffers just that fate, but later comes to and wreaks revenge on his tormentors.
Gloomy Gothic horror based vaguely on Edgar Allan Poe: the ultimate in graveyard ghoulishness.

w Charles Beaumont, Ray Russell d Roger Corman ph Floyd Crosby m Ronald Stein
ad Daniel Haller

Ray Milland, Heather Angel, Hazel Court, Richard Ney, Alan Napier, John Dierkes

Premiere

GB 1938 71m bw

The principal backer of a stage show is shot during the first performance. Slightly unusual mystery drama. John Lodge, Judy Kelly, Joan Marion, Hugh Williams, Edmund Breon, Steven Geray, Edward Chapman. Written by F. McGrew Willis; directed by Walter Summers; for ABPC.

Presenting Lily Mars*

US 1943 104m bw
MGM (Joe Pasternak)

A girl from the sticks hits it big on Broadway. No, the plot wasn't new, but some of the numbers were nice.

w Richard Connell, Gladys Lehman, *novel* Booth Tarkington d Norman Taurog
ph Joseph Ruttenberg md George Stoll

Judy Garland, Van Heflin, Fay Bainter, Richard Carlson, Martha Eggerth, Spring Byington, Bob Crosby and his band, Tommy Dorsey and his band

The President Vanishes

US 1934 80m bw

The president of the US agrees to drop out of sight for a few days, pretending to have been kidnapped, so that his country will not be drawn into a European war. Reasonably intriguing political fantasy with good production and performances. Arthur Byron, Janet Beecher, Paul Kelly, Peggy Conklin, Rosalind Russell, Sidney Blackmer, Walter Kingsford, Charley Grapewin, Edward Arnold. Written by Lynn Starling, Carey Wilson, Cedric Worth, from the anonymous novel; directed by William A. Wellman; for Walter Wanger (Paramount). 'Provocative topical meller, but likely to be spotty.'—*Variety* (GB title: *Strange Conspiracy*.)

The President's Analyst*

US 1967 104m Technicolor
Panavision
Paramount / Panpiper (Stanley Rubin)

A psychiatrist who has been asked to treat the President is pursued by spies of every nationality.
Wild political satirical farce which finally unmasks as its chief villain the telephone company. Laughs along the way, but it's all rather too much.

wd Theodore J. Flicker ph William A. Fraker m Lalo Schifrin ph Pato Guzman

James Coburn, Godfrey Cambridge, Severn Darden, Joan Delaney, Pat Harrington, Eduard Franz, Will Geer

The President's Lady*

US 1953 96m bw
TCF (Sol C. Siegel)

An account of the early career of Andrew

Jackson, a lawyer whose frail wife died shortly after he became president.
Well-produced political historical romance.

w John Patrick, *novel* Irving Stone d Henry Levin ph Leo Tover m Alfred Newman

Charlton Heston, Susan Hayward, John McIntire, Fay Bainter, Carl Betz
'History plays a curious second fiddle to love's old sweet song.'—*New York Times*

Pressure Point*
US 1962 89m bw
UA / Larcas / Stanley Kramer

A black prison psychiatrist has longstanding trouble with a violent racist inmate.
Curious, quite compelling case history, told in pointless and confusing flashback; sharply made and photographed, melodramatically acted.

w Hubert Cornfield, S. Lee Pogostin d Hubert Cornfield ph Ernest Haller m Ernest Gold

Sidney Poitier, Bobby Darin, Peter Falk, Carl Benton Reid

Prestige
US 1932 71m bw

A woman follows her fiancé to a Malayan prison colony where he is on the staff, and finds he has become an alcoholic. Tediously stilted romantic melodrama which seems at least twice as long as its actual running time.
Ann Harding, Melvyn Douglas, Adolphe Menjou, Guy Bates Post, Clarence Muse. Written by Francis Edwards Faragoh, from the novel *Lips of Steel* by Harry Hervey; directed by Tay Garnett; for RKO.

Pretty Baby*
US 1950 92m bw
Warner (Harry Kurnitz)

A girl finds it easier to get a seat on the subway if she is carrying a (dummy) baby, but gets into complications when she meets a baby food king.
Silly but quite pleasant comedy variation on *Bachelor Mother*.

w Everett Freeman, Harry Kurnitz d Bretaigne Windust ph Peverell Marley m David Buttolph

Betsy Drake, Edmund Gwenn, Dennis Morgan, Zachary Scott, William Frawley

Pretty Baby
US 1978 109m Metrocolor
Paramount (Louis Malle)

A 12-year-old girl grows up in a New Orleans brothel.
Tedious elaboration of a sensational subject; neither good art nor good commerce.

w Polly Platt, Louis Malle d Louis Malle ph Sven Nykvist md Jerry Wexler

Keith Carradine, Susan Sarandon, Brooke Shields, Francis Faye, Antonio Fargas

AAN: Jerry Wexler
● Video: CIC

Pretty Ladies
US 1925 70m at 24 fps bw silent

The husband of a Broadway actress leaves her for a chorus girl. Heavy-going melodrama with a star who later turned comedienne and a couple of stars-to-be playing bits. Zasu Pitts, Tom Moore, Norma Shearer, Lilyan Tashman, Conrad Nagel, George K. Arthur, Myrna Loy, Joan Crawford. Written by Adela Rogers St John; directed by Monta Bell; for MGM.

Pretty Maids All in a Row*
US 1971 95m Metrocolor
MGM (Gene Roddenberry)

High school girl students are being murdered by their guidance counsellor.
Uneasy murder comedy with few laughs, casting its star as a most unlikely villain. An interesting if unsuccessful attempt to be different.

w Gene Roddenberry, *novel* Francis Pollini d Roger Vadim ph Charles Rosher m Lalo Schifrin

Rock Hudson, Angie Dickinson, Telly Savalas, Roddy McDowall, Keenan Wynn

Pretty Poison**
US 1968 89m De Luxe
TCF / Lawrence Turman / Mollino (Marshal Backlar, Noel Black)

A psychotic arsonist enlists the aid of a teenager but soon discovers she is kinkier than he and has murder in mind.
Bizarre black comedy-melodrama, quite successfully mixed and served.

w Lorenzo Semple Jnr, *novel* She Let Him Continue by Stephen Geller d Noel Black ph David Quaid m Johnny Mandel

Anthony Perkins, Tuesday Weld, Beverly Garland, John Randolph, Dick O'Neill, Clarice Blackburn

Pretty Polly
GB 1967 102m Techniscope
Universal / George W. George, Frank Granat
US title: *A Matter of Innocence*

On a world tour with her vulgar aunt, a timid maiden finds romance in Singapore.
Slight romantic fable decked out with travel guide backgrounds and at odds with the cynicism of the short story from which it originates.

w Keith Waterhouse, Willis Hall, *story* Noel Coward d Guy Green ph Arthur Ibbetson m Michel Legrand

Hayley Mills, Trevor Howard, Shashi Kapoor, Brenda de Banzie, Dick Patterson, Peter Bayliss, Patricia Routledge, Dorothy Alison
'It came and went this winter, leaving a slight trace of camphor and old knitting needles.'—*Wilfrid Sheed*

The Price of Fear
US 1956 79m bw
Universal-International (Howard Christie)

A lady hit-and-run driver falls for a man on the run from racketeers but plans to give him away in order to save herself.
Vaguely unpleasing programmer in which nobody is sympathetic.

w Robert Tallman d Abner Biberman ph Irving Glassberg md Joseph Gershenson

Merle Oberon, Lex Barker, Charles Drake, Gia Scala, Warren Stevens

'Five charming sisters on the gayest, merriest manhunt that ever snared a bewildered bachelor! Girls! take a lesson from these husband hunters!'

Pride and Prejudice***
US 1940 116m bw
MGM (Hunt Stromberg)

An opinionated young lady of the early 19th-century wins herself a rich husband she had at first despised for his pride.
A pretty respectable version of Jane Austen's splendid romantic comedy, with a generally excellent cast; full of pleasurable moments.

w Aldous Huxley, Jane Murfin, *play* Helen Jerome, *novel* Jane Austen d Robert Z. Leonard ph Karl Freund m Herbert Stothart

Laurence Olivier, Greer Garson, Edmund Gwenn, Mary Boland, Melville Cooper, Edna May Oliver, Karen Morley, Frieda Inescort, Bruce Lester, Edward Ashley, Ann Rutherford, Maureen O'Sullivan, E. E. Clive, Heather Angel, Marsha Hunt
'The most deliciously pert comedy of old manners, the most crisp and crackling satire in costume that we can remember ever having seen on the screen.'—*Bosley Crowther*
'Animated and bouncing, the movie is more Dickens than Austen; once one adjusts to this, it's a happy and carefree viewing experience.'—*New Yorker, 1980*

The Pride and the Passion*
US 1957 131m Technicolor Vistavision
UA / Stanley Kramer

In 1810 Spain a British naval officer helps Spanish guerrillas, by reactivating an old cannon, to win their fight against Napoleon. Stolid, miscast adventure spectacle, its main interest being the deployment of the gun across country by surging throngs of peasants.

w Edna and Edward Anhalt, *novel* The Gun by C. S. Forester d Stanley Kramer ph Franz Planer m Georges Antheil

Cary Grant, Sophia Loren, Frank Sinatra, Theodore Bikel, John Wengraf, Jay Novello, Philip Van Zandt
'The whirr of the cameras often seems as loud as the thunderous cannonades. It evidently takes more than dedication, co-operative multitudes and four million dollars to shoot history in the face.'—*Time*

The Pride of St Louis
US 1952 93m bw
TCF (Jules Schermer)

The life of baseball star Dizzy Dean, who injured himself and became a commentator.

Sporting biopic of clearly restricted interest; modestly well done.

w Herman J. Mankiewicz · d Harmon Jones ph Leo Tover m Arthur Lange

Dan Dailey, Joanne Dru, Richard Haydn, Richard Crenna, Hugh Sanders

AAN: original story (Guy Trosper)

Pride of the Marines*
US 1945   120m   bw
Warner (Jerry Wald)
GB title: *Forever in Love*

The story of Marine Al Schmid, blinded while fighting the Japanese.
Over-dramatic, sudsy biopic which is well enough mounted to carry quite an impact in the flagwaving Hollywood style.

w Albert Maltz d Delmer Daves ph Peverell Marley m Franz Waxman

John Garfield, Eleanor Parker, Dane Clark, John Ridgely, Rosemary de Camp, Ann Doran, Warren Douglas, Tom D'Andrea
'Long drawn out and never inspired, but very respectably honest and dogged.'—*James Agee*

AAN: Albert Maltz

'The most wonderful story America ever took to its heart!'
The Pride of the Yankees*
US 1942   128m   bw
Samuel Goldwyn

The story of baseball star Lou Gehrig, who died of amytropic lateral sclerosis at the height of his powers.
Standard sporting biopic ending on Gehrig's famous speech to the crowd; emotion covers the film's other deficiencies.

w Jo Swerling, Herman J. Mankiewicz, *story* Paul Gallico d Sam Wood ph Rudolph Maté m Leigh Harline pd William Cameron Menzies ed Daniel Mandell

Gary Cooper, Teresa Wright, Babe Ruth, Walter Brennan, Dan Duryea, Elsa Janssen, Ludwig Stossel, Virginia Gilmore
'A simple, tender, meticulous and explicitly narrative film . . . a real saga of American life, homey, humorous, sentimental, and composed in patient detail.'—*New York Times*

AA: Daniel Mandell
AAN: best picture; script; Paul Gallico; Rudolph Maté; Leigh Harline; Gary Cooper; Teresa Wright

'Their extravagant romance was more tempestuous than anything he wrote!'
Priest of Love
GB 1981   125m   colour
Ronceval / Milesian (Stanley J. Seeger)

The last years of D. H. Lawrence, when his books were banned and he was seeking warmer climes to help his TB.
An extremely disappointing film, seeming to consist of aimless travelling by fractious people who never have anything interesting to say. Stilted in all departments.

w Alan Plater d Christopher Miles ph Ted Moore m Joseph James

Ian McKellen, Janet Suzman, Helen Mirren, Penelope Keith, Jorge Rivero, John Gielgud
'Miles has assigned himself a missionary role but he is just not up to the task.'—*Jill Forbes, MFB*

Prime Cut
US 1972   91m   Technicolor   Panavision
Cinema Center (Joe Wizan)

A Kansas gangster incurs the wrath of his Chicago bosses, and a hired killer is sent to eliminate him.
Gory cat-and-mouse chase melodrama with no interest save its excesses.

w Robert Dillon d Michael Ritchie ph Gene Polito m Lalo Schifrin

Gene Hackman, Lee Marvin, Angel Tompkins, Sissy Spacek

The Prime Minister*
GB 1940   109m   bw
Warner (Max Milder)

Episodes in the life of Disraeli.
Modestly budgeted historical pageant notable only for performances.

w Brock Williams, Michael Hogan d Thorold Dickinson

John Gielgud, Diana Wynyard, Will Fyffe, Stephen Murray, Owen Nares, Fay Compton (as Queen Victoria), Lyn Harding, Leslie Perrins

The Prime of Miss Jean Brodie*
GB 1969   116m   De Luxe
TCF (Robert Fryer)

A sharp-minded Edinburgh schoolmistress of the thirties is a bad influence on her more easily-swayed pupils.
Interesting but slackly handled and maddeningly played character drama.

w Jay Presson Allen, *novel* Muriel Spark d Ronald Neame ph Ted Moore m Rod McKuen pd John Howell

Maggie Smith, Robert Stephens, Pamela Franklin, Celia Johnson, Gordon Jackson, Jane Carr
'The novel lost a good deal in its stage simplification, and loses still more in its movie reduction of that stage version.'—*John Simon*

AA: Maggie Smith
AAN: song 'Jean' (m / ly Rod McKuen)

The Primrose Path
US 1940   92m   bw
RKO (Gregory La Cava)

The youngest of a family of shanty-town prostitutes falls in love with an honest hamburger stand proprietor.
Downright peculiar melodrama for its day and age, and not very entertaining either, spending most of its time being evasive.

w Allan Scott, Gregory La Cava, *play* Robert Buckner, Walter Hart, *novel* February Hill by Victoria Lincoln d Gregory La Cava ph Joseph H. August m Werner Heymann

Ginger Rogers, Joel McCrea, Marjorie Rambeau, Henry Travers, Miles Mander, Queenie Vassar, Joan Carroll
'The story isn't good enough, the direction isn't sincere enough, to give any pain to the lumps in the throat which its designers obviously had in mind.'—*Richard Mallett, Punch*

AAN: Marjorie Rambeau

The Prince and the Pauper*
US 1937   118m   bw
Warner (Robert Lord)

In Tudor London, young Edward VI changes places with a street urchin who happens to be his double.
Well-produced version of a famous story; it never quite seems to hit the right style or pace, but is satisfying in patches.

w Laird Doyle, *novel* Mark Twain d William Keighley ph Sol Polito m Erich Wolfgang Korngold

Errol Flynn, Claude Rains, Billy and Bobby Mauch, Henry Stephenson, Barton MacLane, Alan Hale, Eric Portman, Montagu Love (as Henry VIII), Lionel Pape, Halliwell Hobbes, Fritz Leiber
'Lavish but not convincing. Doubtful box office: the commercial aspect seems wholly concerned in the timeliness of a Coronation sequence and the name of Errol Flynn. It is not enough.'—*Variety*

The Prince and the Pauper*
Panama 1977   121m   Technicolor   Panavision
International Film Production / Ilya and Alexander Salkind (Pierre Spengler)
US title: *Crossed Swords*

Young Edward VI changes place with a beggar, who helps to expose a traitor.
Moderately well-made swashbuckler with an old-fashioned air, not really helped by stars in cameo roles or by the poor playing of the title roles.

w George MacDonald Fraser, *novel* Mark Twain d Richard Fleischer ph Jack Cardiff m Maurice Jarre pd Anthony Pratt

Mark Lester, Oliver Reed, Raquel Welch, Ernest Borgnine, George C. Scott, Rex Harrison, David Hemmings, Charlton Heston (as Henry VIII), Harry Andrews, Murray Melvin, Julian Orchard

The Prince and the Showgirl*
GB 1957   117m   Technicolor
Warner / Marilyn Monroe Productions (Laurence Olivier)

In London for the 1911 coronation, a Ruritanian prince picks up a chorus girl and they come to understand and respect each other.
Heavy-going comedy, rich in production values but weak in dramatic style and impact.

w Terence Rattigan, from his play The Sleeping Prince d Laurence Olivier ph Jack Cardiff m Richard Addinsell pd Roger Furse ad Carmen Dillon

Laurence Olivier, Marilyn Monroe, Sybil Thorndike, Richard Wattis, Jeremy Spenser, Esmond Knight, Rosamund Greenwood, Maxine Audley

● Video: Warner

'A saga of scoundrels in a century of infamy!'
Prince of Foxes*
US 1949 107m bw
TCF (Sol. C. Siegel)

A wandering adventurer in medieval Italy gets mixed up with the Borgias.
Good-looking historical fiction with a slight edge to it.

w Milton Krims, novel Samuel Shellabarger d Henry King ph Leon Shamroy m Alfred Newman

Tyrone Power, Orson Welles, Wanda Hendrix, Felix Aylmer, Everett Sloane, Katina Paxinou, Marina Berti
'Plot, counterplot, action and vengeance.'— MFB
'This pretentious chapter of pseudo-history never rises above the merely spectacular, hovers mostly around the conventionally banal, and descends once to the unpardonably crude.'—Richard Mallett, Punch

AAN: Leon Shamroy

Prince of Pirates
US 1953 80m Technicolor

A young prince of the Netherlands turns pirate when his brother allies with the Spanish invader. Fast-moving costume potboiler with lavish use of action scenes from Joan of Arc. John Derek, Barbara Rush, Carla Balenda, Whitfield Connor, Edgar Barrier. Written by John O'Dea and Samuel Newman; directed by Sidney Salkow; for Columbia.

Prince of Players*
US 1955 102m De Luxe Cinemascope
TCF (Philip Dunne)

Episodes in the life of actor Edwin Booth, brother of the man who killed Abraham Lincoln.
Earnest but ham-fisted biopic more notable, as a Hollywood entertainment, for its dollops of straight Shakespeare than for any dramatic interest.

w Moss Hart, book Eleanor Ruggles d Philip Dunne ph Charles G. Clarke m Bernard Herrmann

Richard Burton, Eva Le Gallienne, Maggie McNamara, John Derek, Raymond Massey, Charles Bickford, Elizabeth Sellars, Ian Keith

Prince of the City*
US 1981 167m Technicolor
Warner / Orion (Jay Presson Allen)

A New York policeman on the drug beat is induced to inform on his corrupt colleagues.
Punishingly long police semi-documentary based on real events and apparently filmed with a political motive. Excellent acting and production detail do not prevent the enterprise

from seeming like a half-speed version of Serpico.

w Jay Presson Allen, Sidney Lumet, book Robert Daley d Sidney Lumet

Treat Williams, Jerry Orbach, Don Billett, Richard Foronjy, Carmine Caridi, Kenny Marino

AAN: screenplay

Prince of Thieves
US 1948 72m bw

Robin Hood saves a nobleman's intended from Baron Tristram. Tatty second-feature version of a legendary figure. Jon Hall, Patricia Morison, Alan Mowbray, Michael Duane, Adele Jergens. Written by Maurice Tombragel; directed by Howard Bretherton; for Sam Katzman / Columbia.

Prince Valiant*
US 1954 100m Technicolor
         Cinemascope
TCF (Robert L. Jacks)

The son of the exiled king of Scandia seeks King Arthur's help against the usurper, and becomes involved in a court plot.
Agreeable historical nonsense for teenagers, admittedly and sometimes hilariously from a comic strip.

w Dudley Nichols, comic strip Harold Foster d Henry Hathaway ph Lucien Ballard m Franz Waxman

Robert Wagner, James Mason, Debra Paget, Janet Leigh, Sterling Hayden, Victor McLaglen, Donald Crisp, Brian Aherne, Barry Jones, Primo Carnera

The Prince Who Was a Thief
US 1951 88m Technicolor
U-I (Leonard Goldstein)

An Arabian Nights prince is lost as a baby and brought up by thieves, but finally fights back to his rightful throne.
Given the synopsis, any viewer can write the script himself. Standard eastern western romp.

w Gerald Drayson Adams, Aeneas Mackenzie, story Theodore Dreiser d Rudolph Maté ph Irving Glassberg m Hans Salter

Tony Curtis, Piper Laurie, Everett Sloane, Jeff Corey

The Princess and the Pirate*
US 1944 94m Technicolor
Samuel Goldwyn (Don Hartman)

An impostor is on the run from a vicious pirate.
Typical star costume extravaganza with fewer laughs than you'd expect.

w Don Hartman, Melville Shavelson, Everett Freeman d David Butler ph William Snyder, Victor Milner m David Rose

Bob Hope, Virginia Mayo, Victor McLaglen, Walter Slezak, Walter Brennan, Marc Lawrence, Hugo Haas, Maude Eburne

'From start to finish, Hope dominates the action with well-timed colloquial nifties.'— Variety
AAN: David Rose

Princess Charming
GB 1934 78m bw

A Ruritanian revolution forces a princess to escape in disguise. Light operetta with an intriguing cast. Evelyn Laye, Yvonne Arnaud, George Grossmith, Max Miller, Henry Wilcoxon, Ivor Barnard, Francis L. Sullivan. Written by L. DuGarde Peach, Arthur Wimperis and Lauri Wylie, from the play Alexandra by F. Martos; directed by Maurice Elvey; for Gainsborough. 'Still just below the peak of excellence for which Hollywood is noted.'—Variety

The Princess Comes Across*
US 1936 76m bw
Paramount (Arthur Hornblow Jnr)

A starstruck Brooklyn girl makes a transatlantic liner voyage disguised as a princess, and finds herself involved in a murder mystery.
Zany comedy thriller with plenty of jokes.

w Walter de Leon, Frances Martin, Frank Butler, Don Hartman, Philip MacDonald, novel Louis Lucien Rogger d William K. Howard ph Ted Tetzlaff m Phil Boutelje

Carole Lombard, Fred MacMurray, Alison Skipworth, Douglass Dumbrille, William Frawley, Porter Hall, George Barbier, Lumsden Hare, Sig Rumann, Mischa Auer, Tetsu Komai

Princess of the Nile
US 1954 71m Technicolor

An Egyptian princess of the middle ages leads her country against the invasion of a bedouin prince. Lethargic costume piece with hopelessly miscast actors. Debra Paget, Michael Rennie, Jeffrey Hunter, Dona Drake, Edgar Barrier, Jack Elam, Lee Van Cleef. Written by Gerald Drayson Adams; directed by Harmon Jones; for TCF.

Princess O'Hara
US 1935 79m bw

In her father's memory a girl steals the racehorse he loved. Sentimental comedy from Damon Runyon, later remade for Abbott and Costello as Money from Home. Not up to much in either version. Jean Parker, Chester Morris, Leon Errol, Vince Barnett, Henry Armetta, Ralph Remley, Clara Blandick. Written by Doris Malloy, Harry Clork; directed by David Burton; for Universal. 'Poor construction limits this one's chances . . . not likely to go above average grosses.'— Variety

Princess O'Rourke
US 1943 94m bw
Warner (Hal B. Wallis)

An ace pilot falls for a princess and causes diplomatic complications.

Very thin wartime comedy with a propaganda ending involving Franklin Roosevelt.

wd Norman Krasna ph Ernest Haller
m Frederick Hollander

Olivia de Havilland, Robert Cummings, Charles Coburn, Jack Carson, Jane Wyman, Harry Davenport, Gladys Cooper, Minor Watson, Curt Bois

AA: Norman Krasna (as writer)

Prison Farm
US 1938   69m   bw

A girl denounces her boy friend when he is wanted for robbery and murder. Good example of this studio's tour of criminals and penal institutions. Lloyd Nolan, Shirley Ross, John Howard, J. Carrol Naish, Porter Hall, Anna Q. Nilsson, Esther Dale, May Boley. Written by Eddie Welch, Robert Yost, Stuart Anthony; directed by Louis King; for Paramount. 'First-rate entertainment despite lightweight star names.'—Variety

Prison without Bars
GB 1938   80m   bw

The newest inmate of a reform school for girls vies with the superintendent for the love of the doctor. Basically paperback trash, this film of a notorious original was shot in three languages, but the English version at least omitted the lesbianism, except by implication. Cinematically it was without style. Edna Best, Corinne Luchaire, Barry K. Barnes, Mary Morris, Lorraine Clewes, Martita Hunt, Glynis Johns. Written by Hans Wilhelm, Margaret Kennedy and Arthur Wimperis, from the play by Kaus, Eis and Koveloff; directed by Brian Desmond Hurst; for Alexander Korda / Irving Asher.

The Prisoner*
GB 1955   91m   bw
(Columbia) Facet / London Independent   Producers (Vivian A. Cox)

In a European totalitarian state, a Cardinal is tortured and brainwashed.
Virtually a two-character talkpiece from an offbeat play which should have stayed in the theatre.

w Bridget Boland, from her play d Peter Glenville ph Reg Wyer m Benjamin Frankel

Alec Guinness, Jack Hawkins, Wilfrid Lawson, Kenneth Griffith, Ronald Lewis, Raymond Huntley

The Prisoner of Second Avenue*
US 1975   98m   Technicolor   Panavision
Warner (Melvin Frank)

A New York clerk and his wife are driven to distraction by the problems of urban living. Gloomier-than-usual (from this author) collection of one-liners which almost turns into a psychopathic melodrama and causes its amiable leading players to overact horrendously.

w Neil Simon, from his play d Melvin Frank ph Philip Lathrop m Marvin Hamlisch

Jack Lemmon, Anne Bancroft, Gene Saks, Elizabeth Wilson

● Video: Warner

The Prisoner of Shark Island**
US 1936   95m   bw
TCF (Darryl F. Zanuck)

The story of the doctor who treated the assassin of President Lincoln.
Well-mounted historical semi-fiction with excellent detail.

w Nunnally Johnson d John Ford ph Bert Glennon md Louis Silvers

Warner Baxter, Gloria Stuart, Joyce Kay, Claude Gillingwater, Douglas Wood, Harry Carey, Paul Fix, John Carradine

'Strong film fare for men; will have to be sold for femme appeal.'—Variety

'A powerful film, rarely false or slow, maintaining the relentless cumulative pressure, the logical falling of one thing into another, until the audience is included in the movement and carried along with it in some definite emotional life that is peculiar to the art of motion pictures at its best.'—Otis Ferguson

Prisoner of War
US 1954   81m   bw
MGM (Henry Berman)

Life in a communist prison camp in Korea. Sensational propaganda, reduced to comic strip level.

w Allen Rivkin d Andrew Marton ph Robert Planck m Jeff Alexander

Ronald Reagan, Steve Forrest, Dewey Martin, Oscar Homolka, Steve Horton, Paul Stewart, Henry Morgan, Stephen Bekassy

'It presents its catalogue of horrors in a manner unworthy of the cause it attempts to uphold.'—John Gillett

The Prisoner of Zenda****
US 1937   101m   bw
David O. Selznick

An Englishman on holiday in Ruritania finds himself helping to defeat a rebel plot by impersonating the kidnapped king at his coronation.
A splendid schoolboy adventure story is perfectly transferred to the screen in this exhilarating swashbuckler, one of the most entertaining films to come out of Hollywood.

w John Balderston, Wills Root, Donald Ogden Stewart, novel Anthony Hope d John Cromwell ph James Wong Howe m Alfred Newman

Ronald Colman, Douglas Fairbanks Jnr, Madeleine Carroll, David Niven, Raymond Massey, Mary Astor, C. Aubrey Smith, Byron Foulger, Montagu Love

'The most pleasing film that has come along in ages.'—New York Times

'One of those rare movies that seem, by some magic trick, to become more fascinating and beguiling with each passing year.'—John Cutts, 1971

† Previously filmed in 1913 and 1922.

AAN: Alfred Newman

The Prisoner of Zenda*
US 1952   100m   Technicolor
MGM (Pandro S. Berman)

A costly scene-for-scene remake which only goes to show that care and discretion are no match for the happy inspiration of the original.

w John Balderston, Noel Langley d Richard Thorpe ph Joseph Ruttenberg m Alfred Newman

Stewart Granger, James Mason, Deborah Kerr, Robert Coote, Robert Douglas, Jane Greer, Louis Calhern, Francis Pierlot, Lewis Stone

The Prisoner of Zenda
US 1979   108m   Technicolor
Universal (Walter Mirisch)

Palpably uneasy version of the above which teeters between comedy and straight romance, with barely a moment of real zest creeping in. The star is way off form in both roles.

w Dick Clement, Ian La Frenais d Richard Quine ph Arthur Ibbetson m Henry Mancini pd John J. Lloyd

Peter Sellers, Lynne Frederick, Lionel Jeffries, Elke Sommer, Gregory Sierra, Stuart Wilson, Jeremy Kemp, Catherine Schell, Simon Williams, Norman Rossington, John Laurie

'Flatly directed, leadenly unfunny.'—Paul Taylor, MFB

Prisoners of the Casbah
US 1953   78m   Technicolor

An Eastern princess and her lover take refuge from the evil Grand Vizier in the Casbah, a haven for outcasts. Inept sword and sandal actioner; you can almost smell the Turkish delight. Gloria Grahame, Cesar Romero, Turhan Bey, Nestor Paiva. Written by DeVallon Scott; directed by Richard Bare; for Sam Katzman / Columbia.

Private Affairs
US 1940   74m   bw

A girl with problems seeks out the father she has never met. Thin comedy with a pleasant cast. Nancy Kelly, Robert Cummings, Roland Young, Hugh Herbert, Montagu Love, Jonathan Hale. Written by Charles Grayson, Leonard Spiegelgass and Peter Milne, from a story by Walter Green; directed by Albert S. Rogell; for Universal.

'All women take to men who have the   appearance of wickedness!'
The Private Affairs of Bel Ami*
US 1947   119m   bw
UA / David L. Loew (Ray Heinz)

In nineties Paris, a career journalist climbs to fame over the ruined lives of his friends. Tame and stuffy adaptation of an incisive novel, rather poorly produced.

wd Albert Lewin, novel Guy de Maupassant ph Russell Metty m Darius Milhaud

George Sanders, Angela Lansbury, Ann
Dvorak, Frances Dee, John Carradine, Hugo
Haas, Marie Wilson, Albert Basserman,
Warren William

Private Angelo
GB 1949 106m bw
Pilgrim (Peter Ustinov)

An Italian soldier hates war and spends World
War II on the run from both sides.

Listless satirical comedy that just isn't funny
enough.

w Peter Ustinov, Michael Anderson, *novel*
Eric Linklater d Peter Ustinov ph Erwin
Hillier

Peter Ustinov, Godfrey Tearle, Robin Bailey,
Maria Denis, Marjorie Rhodes, James
Robertson Justice, Moyna McGill

Private Benjamin
US 1980 110m Technicolor
Warner / Hawn–Myers–Shyer–Miller

A well-heeled Jewish widow, at a crossroads in
her life, joins the army.

Half-assed attempt at combining slapstick,
character study, sentiment, sex and a
recruiting poster. Some funny moments don't
really make it worth sitting through.

w Nancy Meyers, Charles Shyer, Harvey
Miller d Howard Zieff ph David M. Walsh
m Bill Conti

Goldie Hawn, Eileen Brennan, Armand
Assante, Robert Webber, Sam Wanamaker,
Barbara Barrie, Harry Dean Stanton

AAN: screenplay; Goldie Hawn; Eileen
Brennan (supporting actress)

● *Video: Warner*

Private Buckaroo
US 1942 68m bw

The difficulties of putting on shows for
soldiers. Slaphappy second feature worth
preserving for the talent. The Andrews Sisters,
Harry James and his Orchestra, Joe E. Lewis,
Donald O'Connor, Peggy Ryan, Huntz Hall,
Ernest Truex, Shemp Howard. Written by
Edmund Kelso and Edmund James; directed
by Edward Cline; for Universal.

The Private Files of J. Edgar Hoover*
US 1978 112m Movielab
AIP / Larco (Larry Cohen)

The supposedly true facts of the career of the
longtime head of the FBI.

Unreliable exposé with some interesting bits.

wd Larry Cohen ph Paul Glickman m Miklos
Rosza

Broderick Crawford, Jose Ferrer, Michael
Parks, Ronee Blakely, Rip Torn, Celeste
Holm, Dan Dailey, Raymond St Jacques,
Howard Da Silva, June Havoc, John Marley,
Andrew Duggan, Lloyd Nolan

A Private Function**
GB 1984 94m colour
Handmade (Mark Shivas)

In 1947 Yorkshire, a doctor and his family
secretly fatten an unlicensed pig.

Sharply-detailed comedy typical of its author,
but less likeable than many.

w Alan Bennett d Malcolm Mowbray
ph Tony Pierce-Roberts m John Du Prez
pd Stuart Walker ed Barrie Vince

Michael Palin, Maggie Smith, Denholm
Elliott, Richard Griffiths, Tony Haygarth, *Liz
Smith*, John Normington

Private Izzy Murphy
US 1926 80m approx at 24 fps bw
silent

A Jewish boy loves a Catholic girl. Dreary
variant on *Abie's Irish Rose*, popular enough
for a 1927 sequel called *Sailor Izzy Murphy*.
George Jessel, Patsy Ruth Miller, Vera
Gordon. Written by Philip Lonergan; directed
by Lloyd Bacon; for Warner.

The Private Life of Don Juan
GB 1934 90m bw
London Films (Alexander Korda)

In 17th-century Spain, the famous lover fakes
death and makes a comeback in disguise.

Lacklustre frolic by an overage star through
dismal sets. The production was meant to
extend the success of *The Private Life of
Henry VIII*, but totally failed to do so.

w Lajos Biro, Frederick Lonsdale, *play* Henri
Bataille d Alexander Korda ph Georges
Périnal m Ernst Toch

Douglas Fairbanks, Merle Oberon, Binnie
Barnes, Benita Hume, Joan Gardner, Melville
Cooper, Athene Seyler, Owen Nares

'Technically it has so much in its favour that
it's too bad it doesn't promise solid b.o.
attraction.'—*Variety*

'One of those ideas that never really take
off.'—*New Yorker, 1977*

'The things I do for England!'
The Private Life of Henry VIII***
GB 1933 97m bw
London Films (*Alexander Korda*)

How Henry beheaded his second wife and
acquired four more.

This never was a perfect film, but certain
scenes are very funny and its sheer sauciness
established the possibility of British films
making money abroad, as well as starting
several star careers. It now looks very dated
and even amateurish in parts.

w Lajos Biro, Arthur Wimperis d Alexander
Korda ph Georges Périnal m Kurt Schroeder

Charles Laughton, Elsa Lanchester, Robert
Donat, Merle Oberon, Binnie Barnes,
Franklin Dyall, Miles Mander, Wendy Barrie,
Claud Allister, Everly Gregg

'Among the best anywhere and by far the
top British picture . . . figures a sock entry,
especially for the best houses.'—*Variety*

AA: Charles Laughton
AAN: best picture

The Private Life of Sherlock Holmes***
GB 1970 125m De Luxe Panavision
UA / Phalanx / Mirisch / Sir Nigel (Billy
Wilder)

A secret Watson manuscript reveals cases in
which Sherlock Holmes became involved with
women.

What started as four stories is reduced to two,
one brightly satirical and the other no more
than a careful and discreet recreation, with the
occasional jocular aside, of the flavour of the
stories themselves. A very civilized and
pleasing entertainment except for the hurried
rounding-off which is a let-down.

w Billy Wilder, I. A. L. Diamond d Billy
Wilder ph Christopher Challis m Miklos
Rozsa ad Alexander Trauner

Robert Stephens, Colin Blakely, Genevieve
Page, Clive Revill, Christopher Lee,
Catherine Lacey, Stanley Holloway

'Affectionately conceived and flawlessly
executed.'—*NFT, 1974*

'Wilder's least embittered film, and by far
his most moving. Great.'—*Time Out, 1984*

Private Lives*
US 1931 82m bw
MGM (Albert Lewin)

Ex-marrieds desert their intended new spouses
to try each other again.

An essentially theatrical comedy, and a great
one, seems somewhat slow-motion on film.

w Hans Kraly, Richard Schayer, *play* Noel
Coward d Sidney Franklin ph Ray Binger

Norma Shearer, Robert Montgomery,
Reginald Denny, Una Merkel, Jean Hersholt

'Stars are a big asset to this parlour comedy
which will amuse the women more than the
men.'—*Variety*

'For polish, few comedies of the thirties can
equal this early alliance of cinema and
stage.'—*John Baxter, 1968*

The Private Lives of Elizabeth and Essex**
US 1939 106m Technicolor
Warner (Robert Lord)
reissue title: *Elizabeth the Queen*

Elizabeth I falls in love with the Earl of Essex,
but events turn him into a rebel and she has to
order his execution.

Unhistorical history given the grand
treatment; a Hollywood picture book, not
quite satisfying dramatically despite all the
effort.

w Norman Reilly Raine, Aeneas Mackenzie,
play Elizabeth the Queen by Maxwell
Anderson d Michael Curtiz ph Sol Polito
m Erich Wolfgang Korngold

Bette Davis, Errol Flynn, Olivia de Havilland,
Donald Crisp, Vincent Price, Alan Hale,
Henry Stephenson, Henry Daniell, Leo G.
Carroll, Nanette Fabray, Robert Warwick,
John Sutton

'Solid box office material, with fine grosses
and holdovers indicated . . . in all technical
departments, picture has received topnotch
investiture.'—*Variety*

'A rather stately, rigorously posed and artistically technicolored production.'—*Frank S. Nugent*

AAN: Sol Polito; Erich Wolfgang Korngold

The Private Navy of Sergeant O'Farrell
US 1968   92m   Technicolor
Hope Enterprises (John Beck)

After World War II, military personnel congregate on an island which has been by-passed by hostilities.
Nothing much wrong with the plot, but at this time in his career Hope seemed unable to do anything right, and the film was barely released.

wd Frank Tashlin *ph* Alan Stensvold *m* Harry Stikman

Bob Hope, Gina Lollobrigida, Phyllis Diller, Jeffrey Hunter, Mylene Demongeot, Henry Wilcoxon

Private Number
US 1936   80m   bw
TCF (Raymond Griffith)
GB title: *Secret Interlude*

A wealthy young man keeps a secret of his marriage to a housemaid.
Warmed-over class melodrama previously filmed in 1930 as *Common Clay*. Adequate within its lights.

w Gene Markey, William Conselman, *play* Common Clay by Cleves Kinkead *d* Roy del Ruth *ph* Peverell Marley *m* Louis Silvers

Loretta Young, Robert Taylor, Basil Rathbone, Patsy Kelly, Marjorie Gateson, Paul Harvey, Monroe Owsley, John Miljan

Private Potter
GB 1962   89m   bw
MGM / Ben Arbeid

A young soldier is court-martialled for cowardice but claims he had a vision of god. Stilted morality play, unpersuasively made and acted.

w Ronald Harwood, from his TV play *d* Caspar Wrede *ph* Arthur Lavis *m* George Hall

Tom Courtenay, Mogens Wieth, Ronald Fraser, James Maxwell, Ralph Michael, Brewster Mason

The Private Secretary
GB 1935   70m   bw

A clerical gentleman is duped into protecting a rich young idler from his creditors. Moderately effective filming of a popular stage farce from a German original. Edward Everett Horton, Barry Mackay, Judy Gunn, Oscar Asche, Sydney Fairbrother, Alastair Sim, Michael Shepley. Written by Arthur Macrae, George Broadhurst and H. Fowler Mear, from the play by Van Moser; directed by Henry Edwards; for Twickenham.

The Private War of Major Benson
US 1955   105m   Technicolor
Cinemascope
U-I (Howard Pine)

A soldier with outspoken views is sent to cool

off as commander of a military academy run by an order of nuns.
Cute and sentimental nonsense with unlikely situations, a martinet becoming soft-centred and a happy-ever-after finale.

w William Roberts, Richard Alan Simmons *d* Jerry Hopper *ph* Harold Lipstein *m* Joseph Gershenson

Charlton Heston, Julie Adams, Tim Hovey, William Demarest, Tim Considine, Sal Mineo, Nana Bryant, Milburn Stone, Mary Field

AAN: original story (Bob Mosher, Joe Connelly)

Private Worlds*
US 1935   84m   bw
Paramount (Walter Wanger)

Romance among the doctors at a mental hospital.
Melodrama treated with what was at the time unexpected seriousness.

w Lynn Starling, *novel* Phyllis Bottome *d* Gregory La Cava *ph* Leon Shamroy *m* Heinz Roemheld

Claudette Colbert, Charles Boyer, Joel McCrea, Joan Bennett, Helen Vinson, Esther Dale, Samuel S. Hinds
  'Fine but not too artistic production . . . woman's picture of fair b.o. potentialities.'— *Variety*

AAN: Claudette Colbert

A Private's Affair
US 1959   92m   De Luxe   Cinemascope
TCF (David Weisbart)

Three army recruits form a close harmony trio and get into various scrapes.
Thin service comedy for the 'new' youth audience.

w Winston Miller *d* Raoul Walsh *ph* Charles G. Clarke *m* Cyril Mockridge

Sal Mineo, Christine Carere, Barry Coe, Barbara Eden, Gary Crosby, Terry Moore, Jim Backus, Jessie Royce Landis

Privates on Parade*
GB 1982   113m   colour
Handmade (Simon Relph)

Farcical and serious incidents in the lives of an army concert party in 1948 Singapore.
Rather heavy-going comedy with much bad language and an overdose of effeminacy; on the whole no funnier than *It Ain't Half Hot, Mum.*

w Peter Nichols from his play   *d* Michael Blakemore *ph* Ian Wilson *m* Denis King
John Cleese, *Denis Quilley*, Michael Elphick, Nicola Pagett, Bruce Payne, Joe Melia
● Video: Thorn EMI

Private's Progress***
GB 1956   97m   bw
British Lion / Charter (Roy Boulting)

An extremely innocent young national serviceman is taught a few army dodges and becomes a dupe for jewel thieves.

Celebrated army farce with satirical pretensions; when released it had something to make everyone in Britain laugh.

w Frank Harvey, John Boulting, *novel* Alan Hackney *d* John Boulting *ph* Eric Cross *m* John Addison

Ian Carmichael, Terry-Thomas, Richard Attenborough, *Dennis Price,* Peter Jones, William Hartnell, Thorley Walters, Ian Bannen, Jill Adams, Victor Maddern, Kenneth Griffith, Miles Malleson, *John Le Mesurier*

Privilege*
GB 1967   103m   Technicolor
Universal / Worldfilm / Memorial (John Heyman)

The publicity campaign for a pop star turns him into a religious messiah.
Rather hysterical fable for our time, undeniably forceful in spots and yawnful in others.

w Norman Bogner, *story* Johnny Speight *d* Peter Watkins *ph* Peter Suschitsky *m* Mike Leander

Paul Jones, Jean Shrimpton, Mark London, Max Bacon, Jeremy Child, James Cossins, Victor Henry
  'Everything in it goes wrong, and one can do little but catalogue the failures.'—*MFB*

Privileged*
GB 1982   96m   Technicolor

Oxford undergraduates rehearsing *The Duchess of Malfi* become involved in sexual intrigues which result in suicide. Highly unusual because made and funded by the students themselves, this melodrama has vivid patches but generally lacks a professional eye. Robert Woolley, Diana Katis, Hughie Grant, Victoria Studd, James Wilby. Written by Michael Hoffman, David Woollcombe and Rupert Walters; directed by Michael Hoffman; for The Oxford Film Company.

The Prize***
US 1963   135m   Metrocolor   Panavision
MGM / Roxbury (Pandro S. Berman)

In Stockholm during the Nobel Prize awards, a drunken American author stumbles on a spy plot.
Whatever the original novel is like, the film is a Hitchcock pastiche which works better than most Hitchcocks: suspenseful, well characterized, fast moving and funny from beginning to end.

w Ernest Lehman, *novel* Irving Wallace *d* Mark Robson *ph* William Daniels *m* Jerry Goldsmith

Paul Newman, Elke Sommer, *Edward G. Robinson,* Diane Baker, Kevin McCarthy, *Leo G. Carroll,* Micheline Presle

A Prize of Arms
GB 1961   105m   bw
British Lion / Interstate (George Maynard)

An ex-army officer and an explosives expert plan to steal an army payroll.

These are **Night Faces** ...living on the edge of evil and violence ...making their own

PRIVATE HELL 36

A FILMAKERS Presentation
Starring

IDA LUPINO · STEVE COCHRAN
HOWARD DUFF · DEAN JAGGER
DOROTHY MALONE

Written for the screen by
COLLIER YOUNG
and IDA LUPINO
Produced by COLLIER YOUNG
Directed by DON SIEGEL
Distributed by Filmakers Releasing Organization

PRIVATE HELL 36. The Filmakers were people with talent, but it didn't come together in this case.

Standard, pacy caper melodrama offering nothing at all new.

w Paul Ryder *d* Cliff Owen *ph* Gilbert Taylor *m* Robert Sharples

Stanley Baker, Tom Bell, Helmut Schmid, John Phillips

A Prize of Gold

GB 1955   100m   Technicolor
Columbia / Warwick (Phil C. Samuel)

An American army sergeant in Berlin decides to steal a cargo of Nazi loot.
Routine caper thriller with sentimental leanings.

w Robert Buckner, John Paxton, *novel* Max Catto *d* Mark Robson *ph* Ted Moore *m* Malcolm Arnold

Richard Widmark, Mai Zetterling, Nigel Patrick, George Cole, Donald Wolfit, Andrew Ray, Joseph Tomelty, Karel Stepanek

The Prizefighter and the Lady

US 1933   102m   bw
MGM (Hunt Stromberg)
GB title: *Every Woman's Man*

A boxer falls for a high class gangster's girl.
Plodding romantic melodrama, popular because it starred a real boxer.

w John Meehan, John Lee Mahin *d* W. S. Van Dyke *ph* Lester White *m* David Snell

Myrna Loy, Max Baer, Otto Kruger, Walter Huston, Jack Dempsey, Primo Carnera
'Freak Max Baer starrer, a picture that entertains in high-pressure manner.'—*Variety*

AAN: original story (Frances Marion)

The Prodigal

US 1931   76m   bw

The scion of a southern plantation becomes a tramp. Pleasant minor musical with a star who never really caught on. Laurence Tibbett, Esther Ralston, Roland Young, Cliff Edwards, Purnell Pratt, Hedda Hopper, Stepin Fetchit. Written by Bess Meredyth, Wells Root; directed by Harry Pollard; for MGM. 'Between average and good . . . should top the normal gross.'—*Variety*

'The story of woman's beauty and man's temptation!'

The Prodigal

US 1955   115m   Eastmancolor
Cinemascope
MGM (Charles Schnee)

The son of a Hebrew farmer falls for the high priestess of a pagan cult.
Wildly apocryphal 'biblical' story of obvious expensiveness but no merit.

w Maurice Zimm *d* Richard Thorpe *ph* Joseph Ruttenberg *m* Bronislau Kaper

Lana Turner, Edmund Purdom, Louis Calhern, James Mitchell, Walter Hampden, Francis L. Sullivan, Joseph Wiseman, Audrey Dalton, Taina Elg, Neville Brand, Cecil Kellaway
'A few lines of dialogue derive from the Bible; the rest is pure Hollywood, but

Hollywood in its mood of sham solemnity when even the unintentional jokes are not funny.'—*MFB*
'A costume stinker . . . it should have played Disneyland!'—*Lana Turner*

The Producers*

US 1967   88m   Pathecolor
Avco / Springtime / MGM / Crossbow (Sidney Glazier)

A Broadway producer seduces elderly widows to obtain finance for his new play, sells 25000 per cent in the expectation that it will flop, and is horrified when it succeeds.
Dismally unfunny satire except for the play itself, *Springtime for Hitler*, which is neatly put down. This has, however, become a cult film, so that criticism is pointless.

wd Mel Brooks *ph* Joseph Coffey *m* John Morris

Zero Mostel, Gene Wilder, Kenneth Mars, Estelle Winwood, Renee Taylor, Dick Shawn
'Over and over again promising ideas are killed off, either by over-exposure or bad timing.'—*Tom Milne*
'An almost flawless triumph of bad taste, unredeemed by wit or style.'—*Arthur Schlesinger Jnr*

AA: Mel Brooks (as writer)
AAN: Gene Wilder
● *Video: CBS / Fox*

Professional Soldier

US 1936   75m   bw
TCF (Darryl F. Zanuck)

A kidnapper befriends the young prince who is his victim.
Predictable, polished family film.

w Gene Fowler, Howard Willis Smith, *story* Damon Runyon *d* Tay Garnett *ph* Rudolph Maté *m* Louis Silvers

Victor McLaglen, Freddie Bartholemew, Constance Collier, Gloria Stuart, Michael Whalen
'Some of the sequences are amusing; some of the action is very fast. But fundamentally the story is not believable.'—*Variety*

Professional Sweetheart

US 1933   70m   bw
RKO (Merian C. Cooper)
GB title: *Imaginary Sweetheart*

A radio 'purity girl' seeks some real life romance.
Modestly smart comedy of no lasting merit.

w Maurine Watkins *d* William Seiter *ph* Edward Cronjager *m* Max Steiner

Ginger Rogers, Betty Furness, Gregory Ratoff, Sterling Holloway, Frank McHugh, Zasu Pitts, Allen Jenkins, Norman Foster, Edgar Kennedy, Franklin Pangborn
'After a fast start this radio satire loses a lot of ground . . . but comedy's there all the way.'—*Variety*

The Professionals**

US 1966   123m   Technicolor
Panavision
Columbia / Pax (Richard Brooks)

Skilled soldiers of fortune are hired by a millionaire rancher to get back his kidnapped wife.
Strong-flavoured star western with good suspense sequences.

wd Richard Brooks, *novel* A Mule for the Marquesa by Frank O'Rourke *ph* Conrad Hall *m* Maurice Jarre

Burt Lancaster, Lee Marvin, Robert Ryan, Jack Palance, Ralph Bellamy, Claudia Cardinale, Woody Strode
'After the *Lord Jim* excursion, it is good to see Brooks back on his own professional form, filming the tight, laconic sort of adventure which usually seems to bring out the best in Hollywood veterans.'—*Penelope Houston*
'It has the expertise of a cold old whore with practised hands and no thoughts of love.'—*Pauline Kael, 1968*

AAN: Richard Brooks (as writer and as director); Conrad Hall

Professor Beware*

US 1938   93m   bw
Paramount

A staid professor finds himself on the run across America in pursuit of an Egyptian artefact.
Slow-starting comedy with only moments of the comedian at his best.

w Delmer Daves, Jack Cunningham, *story* Crampton Harris, Francis M. and Marian B. Cockrell *d* Elliott Nugent *ph* Archie Stout

Harold Lloyd, Phyllis Welch, Raymond Walburn, Lionel Stander, William Frawley, Thurston Hall, Cora Witherspoon, Sterling Holloway
'Both Lloyd and the audience are out of breath after 3000 miles cross country, but most of it is exhaustion from laughing.'—*Variety*

Professor Mamlock**

USSR 1938   100m   bw

The leading surgeon of a Berlin hospital is driven to attempt suicide because he is a Jew. Ironic in all kinds of ways, this quite devastating film was a unique attack by one government on a neighbouring one. S. Mezhinski, E. Nikitina, O. Zhakov. Written by Friedrich Wolf, Adolph Minkin, Herbert Rappaport; directed by Adolph Minkin and Herbert Rappaport; for Lenfilm. 'An arresting picture which is sure to arouse strenuous comment.'—*Variety*

Project X*

US 1968   97m   Technicolor
Paramount / William Castle

In the year 2118, a man is scientifically induced to think he lives in the 1960s so that he can recover a lost secret.
Fearsomely complex science fiction, cheaply made but on the whole intriguingly imagined.

w Edmund Morris, *novels* Leslie P. Davies
d William Castle *ph* Harold Stine *m* Van
Cleave

Christopher George, Greta Baldwin, Henry
Jones, Monte Markham, Harold Gould

The Promise

GB 1969 98m Eastmancolor
Commonwealth United / Howard and
Wyndham

Two young men and a girl share a flat after the
1942 siege of Leningrad; thirteen years later,
their dreams of life considerably modified,
they meet again and change partners.
Talky and too carefully budgeted screen
version of a somewhat pretentious play.

w Michael Hayes, *play* Aleksei Arbuzov
d Michael Hayes *ph* Brendan Stafford
m Iwan Williams *pd* William McCrow

Ian McKellen, John Castle, Susan Macready,
Mary Jones, David Mettheim

The Promise

US 1978 97m Technicolor Panavision
Universal (Fred Weintraub, Paul Heller)
GB TV title: *Face of a Stranger*

A young man fails to recognize his lost love
when her face has been rebuilt after an
accident.
Rambling teenage variation on *Random
Harvest*, not very well done and about forty
years behind its proper times.

w Garry Michael White *d* Gilbert Cates
ph Ralph Woolsey *m* David Shire

Kathleen Quinlan, Stephen Collins, Beatrice
Straight, Larry Luckinbill, William Prince
  'Appalling romantic tushery by any
standards.'—*Tom Milne, MFB*

Promise at Dawn

US / France 1970 102m De Luxe
Avco / Nathalie (Jules Dassin)

The boyhood of novelist Romain Gary and the
last years of his fearsome Russian Jewish
actress mother with whom he traipses around
Europe.
Scrappy star vehicle and unnecessary biopic in
a variety of indulgent styles.

w Jules Dassin, *play* First Love by Samuel
Taylor *d* Jules Dassin *ph* Jean Badal
m Georges Delerue

Melina Mercouri, Assef Dayan

Promise Her Anything

GB 1966 97m Technicolor
Seven Arts (Stanley Rubin)

A mail order movie maker falls for a young
French widow in the next flat.
Scatty comedy set in Greenwich Village and
aiming in vain for a kind of frantic bohemian
charm, with a baby as deus ex machina.

w William Peter Blatty *d* Arthur Hiller
ph Douglas Slocombe *m* Lynn Murray

Warren Beatty, Leslie Caron, Hermione
Gingold, Lionel Stander, Robert Cummings,
Keenan Wynn, Cathleen Nesbitt

Promises in the Dark

US 1979 115m Metrocolor
Warner / Orion (Jerome Hellman)

A young girl dies of cancer.
Depressing and not particularly well done case
history, a curious enterprise in view of the
hundreds of television movies relentlessly
exploring the same field.

w Loring Mandel *d* Jerome Hellman
ph Adam Holender *m* Leonard Rosenman

Marsha Mason, Ned Beatty, Susan Clark,
Michael Brandon, Kathleen Beller, Paul
Clemens

Prophecy

US 1979 102m Movielab Panavision
Paramount (Robert L. Rosen)

In rural Maine, mercury poisoning produces
huge animal mutants.
Unpleasant ecological shocker with no
particular talent in evidence.

w David Seltzer *d* John Frankenheimer
ph Harry Stradling Jnr *m* Leonard
Rosenman *pd* William Craig Smith

Talia Shire, Robert Foxworth, Armand
Assante, Richard Dysart

● *Video: CIC*

Prosperity

US 1932 90m bw

Mothers-in-law disagree about the marriage of
their children. Reliable comedy of the
depression, marking the last teaming of its
popular stars. *Marie Dressler, Polly Moran*,
Anita Page, Norman Foster, Henry Armetta.
Written by Eve Greene and Zelda Sears;
directed by Sam Wood; for MGM. 'Sure-fire
money picture . . . could stand a little cutting
but on the whole it's a workmanlike
production.'—*Variety*

Prostitute

GB 1980 96m colour
Kestrel (Tony Garnett)

A provincial tart moves into the West End.
Downbeat, supposedly realistic documentary
drama which ends up being depressing but not
in the least titillating.

w Tony Garnett *ph* Charles Stewart *m* The
Gangsters

Eleanor Forsythe, Kate Crutchley, Kim
Lockett, Nancy Samuels

Protocol

US 1984 96m Technicolor
Warner (Anthea Sylbert)

A cocktail waitress thwarts an assassination
and becomes a career diplomat.
Star comedy with Something to Say and not
much to laugh at; a step down even from
Private Benjamin.

w Buck Henry *d* Herbert Ross *ph* William
A. Fraker *m* Basil Poledouris *pd* Bill Malley
ed Paul Hirsch

Goldie Hawn, Chris Sarandon, Gail
Strickland, Richard Romanus, André
Gregory, Cliff de Young

The Proud and Profane

US 1956 112m bw Vistavision
Paramount (William Perlberg)

In the Pacific War a Roman Catholic widow
falls for a tough Lieutenant Colonel. ('My
pleasure is physical; my men call me The
Beast.')
Unlikely romantic melodrama with a certain
amount of plain speaking, otherwise routine.

wd George Seaton, *novel* The Magnificent
Bastards by Lucy Herndon Crockett *ph* John
F. Warren *m* Victor Young

William Holden, Deborah Kerr, Thelma
Ritter, Dewey Martin, William Redfield

The Proud Ones

US 1956 94m Eastmancolor
Cinemascope
TCF (Robert L. Jacks)

A marshal cleans up a crooked town despite
the hazards of his own physical disability and a
deputy who hates him.
Entertaining though rather foolishly scripted
western.

w Edmund North, Joseph Patracca *d* Robert
D. Webb *ph* Lucien Ballard *m* Lionel
Newman

Robert Ryan, Jeffrey Hunter, Virginia Mayo,
Robert Middleton

The Proud Rebel

US 1958 103m Technicolor
MGM / Sam Goldwyn Jnr

After the Civil War, a southerner wanders the
Yankee states in search of a doctor to cure his
mute son; he falls for a lady farmer and his
son finds his voice at a crucial moment.
Pretty dim family western for pretty dim
families; everything happens precisely
according to plan.

w Joseph Patracca, Lillie Hayward *d* Michael
Curtiz *ph* Ted McCord *m* Jerome Moross

Alan Ladd, Olivia de Havilland, David Ladd,
Dean Jagger, Cecil Kellaway, Dean Stanton,
Henry Hull, John Carradine, James
Westerfield

The Proud Valley*

GB 1939 76m bw
Ealing (Sergei Nolbandov)

A black stoker helps unemployed Welsh
miners reopen their pits.
Neat little propaganda drama.

w Roland Pertwee, Louis Golding, Jack
Jones *d* Pen Tennyson *ph* Roy Kellino, Glen
MacWilliams *m* Ernest Irving

Paul Robeson, Edward Chapman, Edward
Rigby, *Rachel Thomas*, Simon Lack, Clifford
Evans, Allan Jeayes

Providence*

France / Switzerland 1977 107m
Eastmancolor
Action Film / Société Française de
Production / FR3 / Citel (Philippe Dussart)

A famous writer, dying, spends a painful night
in unpleasant and sometimes fantastic

recollections of his sons and their women; but the reality, when they come to lunch next day, is somewhat different.

Despite its cast and other credits, this is a repellent and not too well acted study in the lack of communication, told at undue length and in turgid colour.

w David Mercer d Alain Resnais ph Ricardo Aronovitch m Miklos Rozsa ad Jacques Saulnier

John Gielgud, Dirk Bogarde, Ellen Burstyn, David Warner, Elaine Stritch

'The movie is peculiarly fastidious and static: you feel as if it were going to dry up and blow away.'—*New Yorker*

The Prowler*
US 1951 92m bw
Horizon (Sam Spiegel)

A discontented wife thinks she sees a prowler and calls a cop; they have an affair and murder her husband.

Another variant on *Double Indemnity* and *The Postman Always Rings Twice*; the script is terse and the actors well-handled.

w Hugo Butler d Joseph Losey ph Arthur Miller m Lyn Murray

Van Heflin, Evelyn Keyes, John Maxwell, Katharine Warren

'A rivetingly cool, clean thriller.'—*NFT, 1973*

Prudence and the Pill*
GB 1968 92m De Luxe
TCF / Kenneth Harper, Ronald Kahn

A girl borrows her mother's contraceptive pills and replaces them with aspirin, causing no end of complications.

Self-consciously naughty sex comedy with a long dénouement and some stiff patches to affect one's enjoyment of the brighter moments.

w Hugh Mills, from his play d Fielder Cook ph Ted Moore m Bernard Ebbinghouse

David Niven, Deborah Kerr, Edith Evans, Keith Michell, Robert Coote, Irina Demick, Joyce Redman, Judy Geeson

'Everybody winds up arrogant to clutter the earth, apparently, with people as obnoxious as their progenitors.'—*Judith Crist*

Psyche 59
GB 1964 94m bw
Columbia / Troy / Schenck (Philip Hazelton)

A wife recovers from blindness after realizing that her husband is in love with her sister. Pretentious melodrama with stuffy dialogue, pompous direction and irritating characters.

w Julian Halevy, *novel* Françoise de Ligneris d Alexander Singer ph Walter Lassally m Kenneth V. Jones

Patricia Neal, Curt Jurgens, Samantha Eggar, Ian Bannen, Beatrix Lehmann

'The screen's master of suspense moves his camera into the icy blackness of the unexplained!'

'Don't give away the ending—it's the only one we have!'

Psycho•••
US 1960 109m bw
Shamley / Alfred Hitchcock

At a lonely motel vicious murders take place and are attributed to the manic mother of the young owner.

Curious shocker devised by Hitchcock as a tease and received by most critics as an unpleasant horror piece in which the main scene, the shower stabbing, was allegedly directed not by Hitchcock but by Saul Bass. After enormous commercial success it achieved classic status over the years; despite effective moments of fright, it has a childish plot and script, and its interest is that of a tremendously successful confidence trick, made for very little money by a TV crew.

w Joseph Stefano, *novel* Robert Bloch d Alfred Hitchcock *(and Saul Bass)* ph John L. Russell m Bernard Herrmann

Anthony Perkins, Vera Miles, John Gavin, Janet Leigh, John McIntire, Martin Balsam, Simon Oakland

'Probably the most visual, most cinematic picture he has ever made.'—*Peter Bogdanovich*

'I think the film is a reflection of a most unpleasant mind, a mean, sly, sadistic little mind.'—*Dwight MacDonald*

† When asked by the press what he used for the blood in the bath, Mr Hitchcock said: 'Chocolate sauce'.

AAN: Alfred Hitchcock; John L. Russell; Janet Leigh

● *Video: CIC*

Psycho 2*
US 1983 113m Technicolor
Universal / Oak (Hilton A. Green)

Despite protests from the sister of one of his victims, Norman Bates is released after 22 years in a mental institution . . . and the murders begin again.

A reasonably inventive sequel, if on the gory side. It probably holds the record for the longest delayed follow-up.

w Tom Holland d Richard Franklin ph Dean Cundey m Jerry Goldsmith pd John W. Corso

Anthony Perkins, Vera Miles, Meg Tilly, Robert Loggia, Dennis Franz

'It's all very well having your tongue in your cheek, but it helps to have a brain in your head.'—*Sunday Times*

Psychomania
GB 1972 91m Technicolor
Benmar (Andrew Donally)

A Hells Angels motor cyclist commits suicide and returns from the dead an invulnerable monster.

Arrant nonsense of the macabre sort, sometimes irresistibly amusing.

w Armand d'Usseau d Don Sharp ph Ted Moore m David Whitaker

George Sanders, Nicky Henson, Beryl Reid, Robert Hardy

The Psychopath
GB 1966 83m Techniscope
Paramount / Amicus (Milton Subotsky)

Men are found dead in London, each with a doll beside him.

Complicated horror thriller in which the actors go further over the top the more the plot winds down.

w Robert Bloch d Freddie Francis ph John Wilcox m Philip Martell

Patrick Wymark, Margaret Johnston, John Standing, Alexander Knox, Judy Huxtable, Don Borisenko, Thorley Walters, Colin Gordon

PT 109
US 1963 140m Technicolor
Panavision
Warner (Brian Foy)

Adventures of president-to-be John F. Kennedy when he was a naval lieutenant in the Pacific during World War II.
Extraordinarily protracted and very dull action story which seems to have been overawed by its subject.

w Richard L. Breen d Leslie H. Martinson ph Robert Surtees m William Lava, David Buttolph

Cliff Robertson, Ty Hardin, James Gregory, Robert Blake

Puberty Blues
Australia 1982 81m Eastmancolor
Panavision

Teenage girls aim to become beach groupies. Both repellent and boring, this mindless sex movie has little more to offer than the beach extravaganzas of the sixties. Nell Schofield, Jad Capelja, Geoff Rhoe, Tony Hughes, Sandy Paul. Written by Margaret Kelly, from the novel by Kathy Lette and Gabrielle Carey; directed by Bruce Beresford; for Limelight.

Public Deb Number One
US 1940 80m bw

A waiter spanks a spoiled society girl at a communist rally, and accepts a job which makes him a capitalist. Lively comedy packed with familiar faces. Brenda Joyce, George Murphy, Ralph Bellamy, Elsa Maxwell, Mischa Auer, Charles Ruggles, Maxie Rosenbloom, Berton Churchill, Franklin Pangborn, Hobart Cavanaugh, Lloyd Corrigan, Elisha Cook Jnr. Written by Karl Tunberg and Darrell Ware; directed by Gregory Ratoff; for TCF.

'Drama that hurls a mighty challenge to all
humanity!'

The Public Enemy***
US 1931 84m bw
Warner
GB title: *Enemies of the Public*

Two slum boys begin as bootleggers, get too
big for their boots, and wind up dead.
Although it doesn't flow as a narrative, this
early gangster film has most vivid and startling
scenes and was most influential in the
development of the urban American crime
film.

w Harvey Thew, Kubec Glasmon, John
Bright *d William Wellman ph Dev Jennings
m* David Mendoza

James Cagney, Edward Woods, Jean Harlow,
Joan Blondell, Beryl Mercer, Donald Cook,
Mae Clarke, Leslie Fenton

'Roughest, most powerful and best gang
picture to date. So strong as to be repulsive in
some aspects, plus a revolting climax. No
strong cast names but a lot of merit.'—*Variety*

'The real power of *The Public Enemy* lies in
its vigorous and brutal assault on the nerves
and in the stunning acting of James Cagney.'—
James Shelley Hamilton

'A postscript said that the producers wanted
to "depict honestly an environment that exists
today in certain strata of American life, rather
than glorify the hoodlum or the criminal". The
film had a different effect: Cagney was playful
and dynamic, and so much more appealing
than the characters opposed to him that
audiences rooted for him in spite of
themselves.'—*Martin Quigley Jnr, 1970*

AAN: Kubec Glasmon, John Bright

Public Enemy's Wife
US 1936 78m bw
Warner (Sam Bischoff)
GB title: *G-Man's Wife*

A girl agrees to marry an escaped convict so
that the FBI can track him down.
Lower-berth gangster thrills culminating in a
chase climax; neatly enough done.

w Abem Finkel, Harold Buckley, *story* David
O. Selznick, P. J. Wolfson *ph* Ernest Haller
d Nick Grinde

Pat O'Brien, Margaret Lindsay, Robert
Armstrong, Cesar Romero, Dick Foran, Dick
Purcell

† Remade as *Bullets for O'Hara* (1942).

Public Hero Number One
US 1935 89m bw
MGM (Lucien Hubbard)

A G-man goes undercover to track down the
Purple Gang.
Moderate thick ear dating from the time when
studios tried to smother public outcry against
gangster films by presenting the cop as the
hero.

w Wells Root *d* J. Walter Ruben *ph* Gregg
Toland

Chester Morris, Jean Arthur, Joseph Calleia,
Lionel Barrymore, Paul Kelly, Lewis Stone,
Paul Hurst

'Rates with the best of the G-men
pictures.'—*Variety*

'The best picture on criminal life I've
seen.'—*Otis Ferguson*

Pufnstuf
US 1970 98m Technicolor
Universal / Krofft Enterprises

A dejected boy is led by his talking flute on a
talking boat to Living Island, full of strange
but friendly animals in fear of an incompetent
witch.
Amalgam of a TV series using life-size puppets
to project a mildly pleasing variation on *The
Wizard of Oz*, without quite achieving the
right blend of wit and charm.

w John Fenton Murray, Si Rose
d Hollingsworth Morse *ph* Kenneth Peach
m Charles Fox *ad* Alexander Golitzen

Jack Wild, Billie Hayes, Martha Raye, Mama
Cass

Pulp*
GB 1972 95m colour
UA / Klinger–Caine–Hodges (Michael
Klinger)

An ex-funeral director now living in the
Mediterranean as a successful pulp fiction
writer gets involved with gangsters and
weirdos.
Occasionally funny pastiche which sorely lacks
shape and is sustained by guest appearances
and zany ideas.

wd Mike Hodges *ph* Ousama Rawi
m George Martin

Michael Caine, *Mickey Rooney*, Lizabeth
Scott, Lionel Stander, Nadia Cassini, Al
Lettieri, Dennis Price

'Various eccentrics act out their "turns", but
never quite lift a light comedy-thriller through
the more playful and productive inversions of
parody.'—*Richard Combs*

The Pumpkin Eater***
GB 1964 118m bw
Columbia / Romulus (James Woolf)

A compulsive mother (of eight children) finds
her third marriage rocking when she gets
evidence of her husband's affairs.
Brilliantly made if basically rather irritating
kaleidoscope of vivid scenes about silly
people, all quite recognizable as sixties
Londoners; very well acted.

w Harold Pinter, *novel* Penelope Mortimer
d Jack Clayton *ph* Oswald Morris *m* Georges
Delerue

Anne Bancroft, Peter Finch, James Mason,
Maggie Smith, Cedric Hardwicke, Richard
Johnson, Eric Porter

'There never was a film so rawly
memorable.'—*Evening Standard*

'It is solid, serious, intelligent, stylish. It is
also, for the most part, quite dead.'—*The
Times*

AAN: Anne Bancroft

The Punch and Judy Man*
GB 1962 96m bw
(ABP) Macconkey (Gordon L. T. Scott)

A seaside children's entertainer tries and
fails to establish himself as an important
citizen.
Melancholy comedy of failure which did not
please its star's adherents and indeed just
missed the style it was seeking.

w Philip Oakes, Tony Hancock *d* Jeremy
Summers *ph* Gilbert Taylor *m* Derek Scott,
Don Banks

Tony Hancock, Sylvia Syms, Ronald Fraser,
Barbara Murray, John Le Mesurier, Hugh
Lloyd

Puppet on a Chain*
GB 1970 98m Technicolor
Big City (Kurt Unger)

An American Interpol agent hunts down drug
smugglers in Amsterdam.
Sadistic adventure thriller, a toughened
version of James Bond, climaxing in a splendid
boat chase through Amsterdam.

w Alistair MacLean, Don Sharp, Paul
Wheeler, *novel* Alistair MacLean *d* Geoffrey
Reeve, *Don Sharp ph* Jack Hildyard, Skeets
Kelly *m* Piero Piccioni

Sven Bertil Taube, Barbara Parkins, Patrick
Allen, Alexander Knox, Vladek Sheybal

'One suspects that a marionette also sat in
for Alistair MacLean.'—*Judith Crist*

● Video: Guild

The Purple Gang
US 1960 85m bw

In Detroit during prohibition a gang of
juvenile delinquents become as powerful as
the gangsters. Unpleasant detail mars this
cops-and-robbers subject; twenty years later it
would have been even more of a shocker, but
it's bad enough as it is. Robert Blake, Barry
Sullivan, Elaine Edwards, Marc Cavell, Jody
Lawrance, Susie Marquette, Paul Dubov.
Written by Jack DeWitt; directed by Frank
McDonald; for Allied Artists.

The Purple Heart*
US 1944 99m bw
TCF (Darryl F. Zanuck)

American prisoners of war in Japan are tried
and executed.
Relentlessly sombre flagwaver, extremely
persuasively presented.

w Jerome Cady, Darryl F. Zanuck *d* Lewis
Milestone *ph* Arthur Miller *m* Alfred
Newman

Dana Andrews, Richard Conte, Farley
Granger, Kevin O'Shea, Sam Levene, Don
Barry, Richard Loo

'It is unusually edged, well organized and
solidly acted. But I feel extremely queasy
watching fiction—especially persuasive
fiction—which pretends to clarify facts that are
not clear, and may never become so.'—*James
Agee*

The Purple Mask
US 1955 82m Technicolor
Cinemascope
U-I (Howard Christie)

In 1802 Paris the Royalist resistance to
Napoleon is led by the mysterious Purple
Mask, who also disguises himself as a foppish
dandy.
Cheeky rewrite of *The Scarlet Pimpernel*, with
plenty of gusto but not much style.

w Oscar Brodney d Bruce Humberstone
ph Irving Glassberg m Joseph Gershenson

Tony Curtis, Dan O'Herlihy, Colleen Miller,
Gene Barry, Angela Lansbury, George
Dolenz, John Hoyt

'Sir Percy, one feels, would have personally
conducted this lot to the guillotine.'—*MFB*

The Purple Plain*
GB 1954 100m Technicolor
GFD / Two Cities (John Bryan)

During the Burma campaign, a Canadian
squadronleader regains his shattered nerves
during an arduous trek across country.
Psychological study and eastern adventure
combined; not the best of either, but a potent
crowd-puller.

w Eric Ambler, *novel* H. E. Bates d Robert
Parrish ph Geoffrey Unsworth m John Veale

Gregory Peck, Maurice Denham, Win Min
Than, Lyndon Brook, Brenda de Banzie,
Bernard Lee, Anthony Bushell, Ram Gopal

● Video: Rank

Pursued*
US 1947 101m bw
(Warner) United States (Milton Sperling)

A revenge-seeking cowboy accidentally causes
a tragedy in his adopted family.
Glum, good-looking revenge western.

w Niven Busch d Raoul Walsh ph *James
Wong Howe* m Max Steiner

Robert Mitchum, Teresa Wright, Judith
Anderson, Dean Jagger, Alan Hale, Harry
Carey Jnr

Pursuit
US 1935 73m bw

A child is kidnapped, and several people want
the reward for restoring him. Rather frantic
chase thriller with insufficient variety. Chester
Morris, Sally Eilers, Scotty Beckett, Henry
Travers, C. Henry Gordon, Dorothy Peterson,
Harold Huber. Written by Wells Root,
Lawrence G. Blochman; directed by Edwin L.
Marin; for Lucien Hubbard-Ned Marin /
MGM.

The Pursuit of D. B. Cooper
US 1981 100m Metrocolor
Polygram (Daniel Wigutow, Michael
Taylor)

A skyjacker bails out with his loot and is
chased by various people after the reward.
Fantasy variation on a real case which was
never solved; of no interest whatever despite
the talent involved.

w Jeffrey Alan Fiskin, *book* Free Fall by J. D.
Reed d Roger Spottiswoode (also John
Frankenheimer, Buzz Kulik) ph Harry
Stradling m James Horner pd Preston Ames

Robert Duvall, Treat Williams, Kathryn
Harrod, Ed Flanders, Paul Gleason, R. G.
Armstrong

'Doubtless a law-enforcement ploy to lure
the skyjacker out of hiding: surely after seeing
this mess he will want to surface and sue
somebody.'—*Variety*

The Pursuit of Happiness
US 1934 75m bw
Paramount (Arthur Hornblow Jnr)

In 1776 Connecticut a Puritan maid falls for a
Hessian soldier.
Mildly pleasing romantic comedy centring on
the ancient practice of 'bundling' in which
betrothed couples might sleep together fully
clothed.

w Stephen Morehouse Avery, Jack
Cunningham, J. P. McEvoy, Virginia Van
Upp, *play* Lawrence Langner, Armina
Marshall d Alexander Hall ph Karl Struss

Francis Lederer, Joan Bennett, Charles
Ruggles, Mary Boland, Walter Kingsford,
Minor Watson

'A comedy that will entertain and merits
business.'—*Variety*

The Pursuit of Happiness*
US 1970 98m Eastmancolor
Columbia / TA Films / Norton–Simon
(David Susskind)

A New York college dropout is sent to prison
after a hit and run accident.
Smooth, watchable but empty youth movie.

w Sidney Carroll, George L. Sherman
d Robert Mulligan ph Dick Kratina m Dave
Grusin

Michael Sarrazin, Barbara Hershey, Robert
Klein, Ruth White, E. G. Marshall, Arthur
Hill

Pursuit to Algiers
US 1945 65m bw
Universal (Roy William Neill)

Sherlock Holmes guards the young king of
Ruritania on a sea voyage.
After an amiably lunatic first reel, this settles
down as one of the dullest of the series, but it
never entirely taxes the patience.

w Leonard Lee d Roy William Neill ph Paul
Ivano md Edgar Fairchild

Basil Rathbone, Nigel Bruce, Martin Kosleck,
Marjorie Riordan, Rosalind Ivan, John
Abbott, Frederic Worlock, Morton Lowry

Pushover*
US 1954 91m bw
Columbia (Jules Schermer)

An honest policeman involves himself in
murder for loot.
Another variation on *Double Indemnity*,
smoothly carpentered as the first appearance
of newly-groomed star Kim Novak. The events
of a night were familiar and watchable.

w Roy Huggins, *novels* The Night Watch by
Thomas Walsh, Rafferty by William S.
Ballinger d Richard Quine ph Lester B.
White m Arthur Morton

Fred MacMurray, Kim Novak, Phil Carey,
Dorothy Malone, E. G. Marshall

Puttin' on the Ritz
US 1930 88m bw (colour sequence)
(UA) Joseph M. Schenck

A has-been vaudevillian gets a second chance
but succumbs to the demon rum.
Primitive early musical melodrama valuable
only as an example of the work of its star.

w, p John W. Considine Jnr d Edward
Sloman ph Ray June ad William Cameron
Menzies

Harry Richman, Joan Bennett, James
Gleason, Aileen Pringle, Lilyan Tashman,
Purnell Pratt

'Entertaining backstage story with ultra
production values.'—*Variety*

Putting Pants on Philip*
US 1927 20m bw silent

A respectable man meets his randy Scottish
nephew who wears nothing under his kilt.
Early star comedy, allegedly their first as a
team but before their more recognizable
characteristics had developed. Not at all bad in
its way, though developing into one long
chase. Laurel and Hardy, Sam Lufkin, Harvey
Clark. Written by H. M. Walker; directed by
Clyde Bruckman; for Hal Roach.

Puzzle of a Downfall Child
US 1970 104m Technicolor
Universal / Newman–Foreman

Fantasy reminiscences of a top fashion model.
Pretentious, fashionable, seemingly
interminable collage of sex and high living.

w Adrien Joyce (Carol Eastman) d Jerry
Schatzberg ph Adam Holender m Michael
Small

Faye Dunaway, Barry Primus, Viveca
Lindfors, Barry Morse, Roy Scheider

Pygmalion****
GB 1938 96m bw
Gabriel Pascal

A professor of phonetics takes a bet that he
can turn a cockney flower seller in six months
into a lady who can pass as a duchess.
Perfectly splendid Shavian comedy of bad
manners, extremely well filmed and containing
memorable lines and performances;
subsequently turned into the musical *My Fair
Lady* (qv). One of the most heartening and
adult British films of the thirties.

w Anatole de Grunwald, W. P. Lipscomb,
Cecil Lewis, Ian Dalrymple, *play Bernard
Shaw* d Anthony Asquith, Leslie Howard
ph Harry Stradling m Arthur Honegger

Leslie Howard, Wendy Hiller, Wilfrid Lawson,
Scott Sunderland, Marie Lohr, David Tree,
Esmé Percy, Everley Gregg, Jean Cadell

PYGMALION. Eliza Dolittle is about to drop her famous clanger. Sitting round the table: David Tree, Wendy Hiller, Everley Gregg.

HIGGINS (Leslie Howard): 'Yes, you squashed cabbage leaf, you disgrace to the noble architecture of these columns, you incarnate insult to the English language, I can pass you off as the Queen of Sheba.'

HIGGINS: 'Where the devil are my slippers, Eliza?'

'Ought to have big potentialities in the US, with some cutting. . . . An introductory title briefly gives the source of the play, which was Shakespeare's *Pygmalion*.' (!)—*Variety*

'An exhibition of real movie-making – of a sound score woven in and out of tense scenes, creating mood and tempo and characterization.'—*Pare Lorentz*

'Every possible care has been taken in the presentation of what may well prove to have a significant effect on future British film production, for it is live, human entertainment, flawlessly presented and making an obvious appeal to all kinds of audiences.'—*The Cinema*

AAN: best picture; script; Bernard Shaw; Leslie Howard; Wendy Hiller

Q Planes**
GB 1939 82m bw
Harefield / London Films (Irving Asher,
Alexander Korda)
US title: *Clouds over Europe*

A secret ray helps spies to steal test aircraft
during proving flights.
Lively comedy thriller distinguished by a droll
leading performance.

w Ian Dalrymple, Brock Williams, Jack
Whittingham, Arthur Wimperis *d* Tim
Whelan *ph* Harry Stradling *md* Muir
Mathieson

Ralph Richardson, Laurence Olivier, Valerie
Hobson, George Merritt, George Curzon, Gus
McNaughton, David Tree

**Quackser Fortune Has a Cousin in the
Bronx***
US 1970 90m Eastmancolor
UMC (John H. Cushingham)

An Irish layabout strikes up an acquaintance
with an American student.
Likeable if plotless Dublin comedy, pleasantly
photographed.

w Gabriel Walsh *d* Waris Hussein *ph* Gil
Taylor *m* Michael Dress

Gene Wilder, Margot Kidder, Eileen Colgen,
Seamus Ford

● *Video: Videoform*

Quadrophenia
GB 1979 120m Eastmancolor

A drama of bitter rivalry between Mods and
Rockers on the Brighton beaches in 1964.
What passes for a successful musical at the end
of the seventies is typified by this violent,
screaming and wholly unattractive amalgam of
noise, violence, sex and profanity. The Who,
Kate Williams, Michael Elphick. Written by
Dave Humphries, Martin Stellman and Franc
Roddam; directed by Franc Roddam; for
Polytel.

● *Video: Polygram*

Quai des Brumes***
France 1938 89m bw
Rabinovitch
US title: *Port of Shadows*

An army deserter rescues a girl from crooks
but is killed before they can escape.

Artificial, set-bound, but at the time wholly
persuasive melodrama which became one of
the archetypal French films of the thirties, its
doomed lovers syndrome not being picked up
by Hollywood until after World War II.

w Jacques Prévert, novel Pierre MacOrlan
d Marcel Carné *ph* Eugen Schüfftan
m Maurice Jaubert *ad* Alexander Trauner

Jean Gabin, Michèle Morgan, Michel Simon,
Pierre Brasseur

'Unity of space, time and action give the
film a classical finish.'—*Georges Sadoul*
† The plot was in fact almost identical with
that of *Pépé le Moko*. The romantic pessimism
of these films, plus *Le Jour Se Lève*, so suited
the mood of France that Vichy officials later
said: 'If we have lost the war it is because of
Quai des Brumes.'

Quai des Orfèvres*
France 1947 105m bw
Majestic

A music hall artiste is accused of murdering
the man he took to be seducing his mistress.
The equivalent of many a British Scotland
Yard thriller, but a good one, with excellent
acting, atmosphere and suspense.

w Henri-Georges Clouzot, Jean Ferry,
novel Legitime Défense by Stanislas-André
Steeman *d* Henri-Georges Clouzot
ph Armand Thirard *m* Francis Lopez

Louis Jouvet, Bernard Blier, Suzy Delair,
Pierre Larquey, Simone Rennant

'The wonder of *Quai des Orfèvres* is the way
Clouzot has pricked it with life.'—*Guardian*
'A stunningly well made entertainment.'—
New Yorker, 1982

'Two love experts in a daring game of
hearts!'
Quality Street*
US 1937 84m bw
RKO (Pandro S. Berman)

When an officer returns from the Napoleonic
wars, he does not recognize his sweetheart,
whose beauty has faded, so she masquerades
as her own capricious niece.
Fairly successful attempt to capture on screen
the essence of Barrie whimsy; everyone tries
hard, anyway.

w Mortimer Offner, Allan Scott, *play* J. M.
Barrie *d* George Stevens *ph* Robert de
Grasse *m* Roy Webb

Katharine Hepburn, Franchot Tone, Fay
Bainter, Eric Blore, Cora Witherspoon,
Estelle Winwood, Florence Lake, Joan
Fontaine

'Hepburn and Tone unable to instil any life,
and little entertainment, into this old-timer
from legit . . . one for the bonnet and shawl
trade.'—*Variety*
'It is strictly a self-propelled picture, tearing
breathlessly, even hysterically, through
Barrie's quizzical account of a man-hunt. . . .
But we were exhausted by the intensity of
Miss Hepburn's concentration on it. Her
Phoebe needs a neurologist far more than a
husband. Such flutterings and jitterings and
twitchings, such hand-wringings and mouth-
quiverings, such runnings-about and eyebrow-
raisings have not been on the screen in many a
moon.'—*Frank Nugent, New York Times*
† Previously made by MGM in 1927 (silent),
with Marion Davies and Conrad Nagel;
directed by Sidney Franklin.

AAN: Roy Webb

Quantez
US 1957 80m Eastmancolor
Cinemascope

Robbers hiding for the night in a frontier town
become involved in an Indian attack. Curious,
slow-paced attempt to redo *The Gunfight* with
inferior materials; not a profitable experience.
Fred MacMurray, Dorothy Malone, James
Barton, Sydney Chaplin, John Gavin, John
Larch, Michael Ansara. Written by R. Wright
Campbell; directed by Harry Keller; for
Universal-International.

The Quare Fellow
GB 1962 90m bw
BLC / Bryanston (Anthony Havelock-Allan)

Life in a Dublin prison when two men are to
be hanged, as experienced by a new young
warder.
Watered-down version of a rumbustious stage
tragi-comedy, with not much but the gloom
left.

wd Arthur Dreifuss, *play* Brendan Behan
ph Peter Hennessey *m* Alexander Faris

Patrick McGoohan, Sylvia Syms, Walter
Macken, Dermot Kelly, Hilton Edwards

Quartet***
GB 1948 120m bw
GFD / Gainsborough (Anthony Darnborough)

Four stories introduced by the author. This entertaining production began the compendium fashion (*Full House, Phone Call from a Stranger*, etc) and is fondly remembered, though all the stories had softened endings and the middle two did not work very well as drama. Subsequent Maugham compilations were *Trio* and *Encore* (both qv).

w R. C. Sherriff, stories W. Somerset Maugham m John Greenwood

THE FACTS OF LIFE d Ralph Smart ph Ray Elton

Basil Radford, Naunton Wayne, Mai Zetterling, Jack Watling, James Robertson Justice

THE ALIEN CORN d Harold French ph Ray Elton

Dirk Bogarde, Françoise Rosay, Raymond Lovell, Honor Blackman, Irene Browne

THE KITE d Arthur Crabtree ph Ray Elton

George Cole, Hermione Baddeley, Susan Shaw, Mervyn Johns, Bernard Lee

THE COLONEL'S LADY d Ken Annakin ph Reg Wyer

Cecil Parker, Linden Travers, Nora Swinburne, Ernest Thesiger, Felix Aylmer, Henry Edwards, Wilfrid Hyde White

Quartet*
GB / France 1981 101m GTC colour
TCF / Merchant Ivory (Ismail Merchant, Jean Pierre Mahot de la Querantonnais)

In 1927 Paris, a convict's wife finds herself part of a *ménage à trois*.
Slow-moving, good-looking study of characters in a milieu; as usual with films from this stable, it has nothing to please the majority.

w Ruth Prawer Jhabvala, novel Jean Rhys d James Ivory ph Pierre Lhomme m Richard Robbins

Isabelle Adjani, Maggie Smith, Alan Bates, Anthony Higgins
● Video: CBS / Fox

Quatermass and the Pit**
GB 1967 97m Technicolor
Hammer / Anthony Nelson Keys
US title: *Five Million Years to Earth*

Prehistoric skulls are unearthed during London Underground excavations, and a weird and deadly force makes itself felt.
The third film of a Quatermass serial is the most ambitious, and in many ways inventive and enjoyable, yet spoiled by the very fertility of the author's imagination: the concepts are simply too intellectual to be easily followed in what should be a visual thriller. The climax, in which the devil rears over London and is 'earthed', is satisfactorily harrowing.

w Nigel Kneale, from his TV serial d Roy Ward Baker ph Arthur Grant m Tristam Cary

Andrew Keir, James Donald, Barbara Shelley, Julian Glover, Duncan Lamont, Edwin Richfield, Peter Copley

The Quatermass Experiment**
GB 1955 82m bw
Exclusive / Hammer (Anthony Hinds)
US title: *The Creeping Unknown*

When a rocketship returns from space, two of its three crew members have disappeared and the third is slowly taken over by a fungus which thrives on blood.
Intelligent science fiction based on a highly successful BBC TV serial; the film version is generally workmanlike despite its obvious low budget.

w Richard Landau, Val Guest, serial Nigel Kneale d Val Guest ph Jimmy Harvey

Brian Donlevy, Jack Warner, Margia Dean, *Richard Wordsworth,* David King Wood, Thora Hird, Gordon Jackson

Quatermass II**
GB 1957 85m bw
Hammer (Anthony Hinds)
US title: *Enemy from Space*

A research station operating under military secrecy is supposed to be making synthetic foods, but is in fact an acclimatization centre for invaders from outer space.
Simplified version of a TV serial, a bit stodgy in the talk scenes, but building into sequences of genuine alarm and based on an idea of lingering persuasiveness.

w Nigel Kneale, Val Guest, serial Nigel Kneale d Val Guest ph Gerald Gibbs m James Bernard

Brian Donlevy, John Longden, Sidney James, Bryan Forbes, William Franklyn, Charles Lloyd Pack, Percy Herbert, Tom Chatto

Quebec
US 1951 85m Technicolor

The wife of the loyalist governor of Quebec is in love with the leader of the rebels. Ho-hum period actioner with some pretty backgrounds and not much personality. Corinne Calvet, John Barrymore Jnr, Barbara Rush, Patric Knowles, John Hoyt, Arnold Moss. Written by Alan Le May; directed by George Templeton; for Paramount.

'She's so excitingly good when she's so wonderfully bad!'
Queen Bee*
US 1955 95m bw
Columbia (Jerry Wald)

A wealthy woman has a compulsion to dominate everyone around her. Claustrophobic southern-set melodrama obviously created for its star.

wd Ranald MacDougall, novel Edna Lee ph Charles Lang m George Duning md Morris Stoloff

Joan Crawford, Barry Sullivan, Betsy Palmer, John Ireland, Lucy Marlow, William Leslie, Fay Wray
AAN: Charles Lang

Queen Christina***
US 1933 101m bw
MGM (Walter Wanger)

The queen of 17th-century Sweden, distressed at the thought of a political marriage, goes wandering through her country in men's clothes and falls in love with the new Spanish ambassador.
The star vehicle par excellence, superb to look at and one of its star's most fondly remembered films. Historically it's nonsense, but put across with great style.

w Salka Viertel, H. M. Harwood, S. N. Behrman d Rouben Mamoulian ph William Daniels m Herbert Stothart

Greta Garbo, John Gilbert, Ian Keith, Lewis Stone, C. Aubrey Smith, Reginald Owen, Elizabeth Young

ANTONIO (John Gilbert): 'It's all a question of climate. You cannot serenade a woman in a snowstorm. All the graces in the art of love— elaborate approaches that will make the game of love amusing—can only be practised in those countries that quiver in the heat of the sun.'

CHRISTINA (Greta Garbo): 'I have been memorizing this room. In the future, in my memory, I shall live a great deal in this room.'

'The shortcomings, such as they are, are so far overshadowed by the potency of the premier satellite, the sterling support, the Mamoulian montage and the Behrman crisp dialogue that they're relatively unimportant; for *Christina* is cinch b.o.'—Variety

'Garbo, as enchanting as ever, is still enveloped by her unfathomable mystery.'—Photoplay

'An unending series of exceptional scenes.'—Modern Screen

† The leading male role was announced in turn for Leslie Howard, Franchot Tone, Nils Asther, Bruce Cabot and Laurence Olivier: Garbo turned them all down.

Queen Elizabeth*
France 1912 35m approx (24 fps) bw silent
Histrionic Film
original title: *Les Amours de la Reine Elisabeth*

Scenes from the life of the queen.
Abysmally boring now, this film is important in several ways. It is our best record of Sarah Bernhardt. It was immensely successful throughout the world. It made cinema interesting to all classes, not just the hoi polloi. It made the fortunes of Adolph Zukor, who bought it cheaply and went on to found Paramount Pictures. (Bernhardt is said to have remarked to him: 'You have put me in pickle for all time!')

w Eugene Moreau d Henri Desfontaines, Louis Mercanton

Sarah Bernhardt, Lou Tellegen

Queen Kelly**
US 1928   100m approx (24 fps)
(unfinished version)   bw   silent
United Artists / Gloria Productions / Joseph
Kennedy

A convent girl goes to the bad, is ill-used by a
prince, becomes a white slave in Africa but
finally inherits a fortune.
Sexually-oriented extravaganza, the last great
folly of its director but never finished by him.
Various versions exist: in all of them
individual scenes are more entertaining than
the whole. Extracts were shown in *Sunset
Boulevard*.
wd Erich Von Stroheim *ph* Gordon Pollock,
Paul Ivano, Ben Reynolds *m* Adolf Tandler
ad Harry Miles

Gloria Swanson, Walter Byron, Seena Owen

Queen of Atlantis see L'Atlantide

Queen of Hearts*
GB 1936   80m   bw
ATP (Basil Dean)

A working girl poses as a socialite and wins a
matinee idol.
Stalwart romantic comedy with its star slightly
more glamorized than usual.
w Clifford Grey, H. F. Maltby, Douglas
Furber, Anthony Kimmins, Gordon
Wellesley *d* Monty Banks

Gracie Fields, John Loder, Enid Stamp
Taylor, Fred Duprez, Edward Rigby, Hal
Gordon

The Queen of Spades**
GB 1948   96m   bw
ABP / World Screen Plays (Anatole de
Grunwald)

A Russian officer tries to wrest from an
ancient countess the secret of winning at cards,
in return for which he has sold his soul to the
devil; but she dies of fright and haunts him.
Disappointingly slow-moving but splendidly
atmospheric recreation of an old Russian story
with all the decorative stops out; the chills
when they come are quite frightening, the
style is impressionist and the acting suitably
extravagant.
w Rodney Ackland, Arthur Boys,
novel Alexander Pushkin *d* Thorold
Dickinson *ph* Otto Heller *m* Georges Auric
ad Oliver Messel

Anton Walbrook, Edith Evans, Ronald
Howard, Yvonne Mitchell, Mary Jerrold
'The photography is adventurous, the
cutting imaginative and the sets startling.'—
Evening Standard
'It is fine to come across such distinguished
filmcraft.'—*Evening News*
● *Video: Thorn EMI*

Queen of the Mob*
US 1940   61m   bw
Paramount

A murderess and her three sons are captured
by the FBI.

Pacy crime melodrama from the *Persons in
Hiding* series, based on the exploits of Ma
Barker.
w Horace McCoy, William R. Lippmann
d James Hogan *ph* Theodor Sparkuhl

Blanche Yurka, Ralph Bellamy, Jack Carson,
Richard Denning, Paul Kelly, J. Carrol Naish,
Jeanne Cagney, William Henry, James Seay,
Hedda Hopper

The Queen's Guards
GB 1960   112m   Technicolor
Cinemascope
TCF / Imperial (Michael Powell)

Reminiscences during trooping the colour of
father and son guardsmen.
Incredibly old-fashioned family melodrama
complete with skeleton in family closet;
despite its date it has a decidedly pre-war air,
except that it might have been more smartly
done then.
w Roger Milner *d* Michael Powell *ph* Gerald
Turpin *m* Brian Easdale

Raymond Massey, Daniel Massey, Robert
Stephens, Ursula Jeans, Judith Stott,
Elizabeth Shepherd, Duncan Lamont, Ian
Hunter, Jack Watling
'This flagwaving museum piece would be
distressing if it weren't so inept . . . [the
actors] battle manfully with dialogue and
characters as dated as a Crimean cavalry
charge. The film could scarcely be taken as a
tribute to the Guards except, just possibly, by
elderly aunts in Cheltenham.'—*MFB*

Queimada!
France / Italy 1968   132m   De Luxe
PEA / PPA (Alberto Grimaldi)
aka: *Burn!*

A diplomat is sent to a Caribbean island to
break the Portuguese sugar monopoly and
becomes involved with revolutionaries.
An indigestible attempt to combine adventure
with the film of ideas; very tedious.
w Franco Solinas, Giorgio Arlorio *d* Gillo
Pontecorvo *ph* Marcello Gatti *m* Ennio
Morricone

Marlon Brando, Renato Salvatori, Norman
Hill, Evaristo Marquez

Quentin Durward*
GB 1955   101m   Eastmancolor
Cinemascope
MGM (Pandro S. Berman)
aka: *The Adventures of Quentin Durward*

An elderly English lord sends his nephew to
woo a French lady on his behalf; but the boy
falls in love with her himself.
Haphazardly constructed and produced, but
quite enjoyable, period romp, with a bold
black villain and several rousing set pieces
including a final set-to on bell ropes.
w Robert Ardrey, *novel* Sir Walter Scott
d Richard Thorpe *ph* Christopher Challis
m Bronislau Kaper

Robert Taylor, Kay Kendall, Robert Morley,
Alec Clunes, Marius Goring, Wilfrid Hyde
White, Ernest Thesiger, Duncan Lamont,
Harcourt Williams, Laya Raki, George Cole

Querelle
West Germany / France 1982   108m
Eastmancolor
Planet / Albatross / Gaumont

A homosexual sailor has a mystical quest
which involves murder.
Overheated fantasy which may have
something to say to gays, but not much to
other audiences.
wd Rainer Werner Fassbinder, *book* Jean
Genet *ph* Xaver Schwarzenberger *m* Peer
Raben

Brad Davis, Franco Nero, Jeanne Moreau,
Laurent Malet
● *Video: Palace*

Quest for Fire
Canada / France 1981   100m   Bellevue-
Pathecolor Panavision
ICC / Cine Trail / Belstar / Stephan (Michael
Gruskoff)

Eighty thousand years ago, a primitive tribe
uses the discovery of fire to defeat its enemies.
Scientifically cosseted but sometimes
unintentionally funny attempt to make us care
about the problems of primitive man. Lively
sequences are separated by longueurs.
w Gérard Brach, *novel* La Guerre du Feu by
J. H. Rosny *d* Jean-Jacques Annaud
ph Claude Agostini *m* Philippe Sarde
pd Guy Comtois, Brian Morris *special
language* Anthony Burgess *body
movement* Desmond Morris

Everett McGill, Ron Perlman, Rae Dawn,
Nameer El-Kadi

Quest for Love*
GB 1971   90m   Eastmancolor
Rank / Peter Rogers Productions (Peter
Eton)

After an explosion during an experiment, a
young physicist finds himself living a different
life, in love with a dying girl; returning to
normal, he finds the girl and saves her.
Pleasing variation on *Berkeley Square*, quite
well staged and played.
w Terence Feely, *story* Random Quest by
John Wyndham *d* Ralph Thomas *ph* Ernest
Steward *m* Eric Rogers

Tom Bell, Joan Collins, Denholm Elliott,
Laurence Naismith, Lyn Ashley
● *Video: Rank*

A Question of Adultery
GB 1958   84m   bw
Eros / Connaught Place / Raymond Stross

When a husband is discovered to be sterile, his
wife suggests artificial insemination, but when
she seems to have a lover he institutes divorce
proceedings.
Opportunist melodrama from the headlines.
Not even interesting *then*.
w Anne Edwards, *play* Breach of Marriage by
Dan Sutherland *d* Don Chaffey *ph* Stephen
Dale *m* Philip Green

Julie London, Anthony Steel, Basil Sidney, Donald Houston, Anton Diffring, Andrew Cruickshank, Conrad Philips, Kynaston Reeves

Quick before It Melts

US 1964 97m Metrocolor Panavision
MGM / Biography (Douglas Lawrence, Delbert Mann)

A journalist is sent to cover a naval enterprise in the Antarctic, and gets a scoop despite his shyness.
Noisy service comedy with precious little plot.

w Dale Wasserman, novel Philip Benjamin d Delbert Mann ph Russell Harlan m David Rose

George Maharis, Robert Morse, Anjanette Comer, James Gregory, Howard St John, Janine Gray, Michael Constantine
'The combination of romantic dalliance, service high jinks and hectic journalism remains uniformly flat all through.'—MFB

The Quick Gun

US 1964 88m Techniscope

A gunfighter gets an icy welcome when he returns home to claim his father's farm. Standard western with the hero redeemed and elected sheriff at the end. Audie Murphy, Merry Anders, James Best, Ted de Corsia, Walter Sande, Frank Ferguson. Written by Robert E. Kent; directed by Sidney Salkow; for Admiral / Columbia.

Quick Let's Get Married

US 1965 100m colour
Golden Eagle (William Marshall)
aka: The Confession, Seven Different Ways

The voice of a sneak thief in a ruined church is taken by an unwed mother as a miracle. Downright peculiar mishmash wasting intesting stars; an independent production by Rogers and husband in Jamaica.

w Allen Scott d William Dieterle ph Robert Bronner m Michael Colicchio

Ginger Rogers, Ray Milland, Barbara Eden, Walter Abel, Cecil Kellaway, Elliott Gould, Michael Ansara, David Hurst

Quick Millions**

US 1931 69m bw
Fox

An ambitious truck driver becomes a ruthless racketeer.
Fast-moving, otherwise naïve early gangster melodrama notable for Tracy's first star performance.

w Courtney Terrett, Rowland Brown, John Wray d Rowland Brown ph Joseph August

Spencer Tracy, Marguerite Churchill, Sally Eilers, Robert Burns, John Wray, George Raft
'This film is in the money. Ranks with the best of the gangster items.'—Variety

Quicksand

US 1950 79m bw

A garage mechanic gets involved in crime for the sake of an unworthy girl. Lower-case melodrama of no notable merit. Mickey

Rooney, Jeanne Cagney, Barbara Bates, Peter Lorre. Written by Robert Smith; directed by Irving Pichel; for Mort Briskin / UA.

The Quiet American**

US 1957 122m bw
UA / Figaro (Joseph L. Mankiewicz)

An American in Saigon has naïve ideas for ending the war; he saves the life of a journalist who for various reasons becomes jealous and is duped into betraying the American to the communists.
Semi-successful excursion into the territory of Graham Greene, who as in Brighton Rock has allowed his ironic ending to be totally re-emphasized, here making the film anti-communist instead of anti-American.

wd Joseph L. Mankiewicz, novel Graham Greene ph Robert Krasker m Mario Nascimbene

Michael Redgrave, Audie Murphy, Claude Dauphin, Giorgia Moll, Bruce Cabot, Fred Sadoff, Richard Loo

The Quiet Man***

US 1952 129m Technicolor
Republic / Argosy (John Ford, Merian C. Cooper)

An Irish village version of The Taming of the Shrew, the tamer being an ex-boxer retired to the land of his fathers and in need of a wife. Archetypal John Ford comedy, as Irish as can be, with everything but leprechauns and the Blarney Stone on hand. Despite some poor sets the film has a gay swing to it, much brawling vigour and broad comedy, while the actors all give their roistering best.

w Frank Nugent, story Maurice Walsh d John Ford ph Winton C. Hoch, Archie Stout m Victor Young

John Wayne, Maureen O'Hara, Barry Fitzgerald, Victor McLaglen, Ward Bond, Mildred Natwick, Francis Ford, Arthur Shields, Eileen Crowe, Sean McClory, Jack McGowran
'Ford's art and artifice . . . are employed to reveal a way of life—stable, rooted, honourable, purposeful in nature's way, and thereby rhythmic. Everyone is an individual, yet everyone and everything has a place.'—Henry Hart, Films in Review

AA: John Ford; Winton C. Hoch, Archie Stout
AAN: best picture; Frank Nugent; Victor McLaglen
.

Quiet Please, Murder*

US 1943 70m bw
TCF (Ralph Dietrich)

Nazis and art thieves cause a high death rate in a public library.
Unusual, stylish second feature.

wd John Larkin ph Joe MacDonald m Emil Newman

George Sanders, Kurt Katch, Gail Patrick, Richard Denning, Lynne Roberts, Sidney Blackmer, Byron Foulger

Quiet Wedding***

GB 1940 80m bw
Paramount / Conqueror (Paul Soskin)

Middle-class wedding preparations are complicated by family guests.
A semi-classic British stage comedy is admirably filmed with a splendid cast.

w Terence Rattigan, Anatole de Grunwald, play Esther McCracken d Anthony Asquith

Margaret Lockwood, Derek Farr, A. E. Matthews, Marjorie Fielding, Athene Seyler, Peggy Ashcroft, Margaretta Scott, Frank Cellier, Roland Culver, Jean Cadell, David Tomlinson, Bernard Miles
† Remade as Happy is The Bride (qv).

Quiet Weekend

GB 1946 92m bw
Associated British

The Royds spend a weekend at their country cottage and get involved with poachers.
Trivial and poorly-made sequel, not up to the standard of Quiet Wedding as a comic study of British types.

w Victor Skuzetsky, play Esther McCracken d Harold French ph Eric Cross

Derek Farr, Marjorie Fielding, George Thorpe, Frank Cellier

The Quiller Memorandum*

GB 1966 105m Eastmancolor Panavision
Rank / Ivan Foxwell / Carthay

A British secret service man is sent to Berlin to combat a neo-Nazi organization.
Disappointingly thin but smooth and watchable spy story.

w Harold Pinter, novel The Berlin Memorandum by Adam Hall (Elleston Trevor) d Michael Anderson ph Erwin Hillier m John Barry

George Segal, Max Von Sydow, Alec Guinness, Senta Berger, George Sanders, Robert Helpmann, Robert Flemyng
'In disposing of most of the storyline Pinter has virtually thrown out the baby with the bathwater; all that remains is a skeleton plot which barely makes sense and is totally lacking in excitement.'—Brenda Davies
'Harold Pinter wrote the screenplay and for each word of dialogue there has to be a separate scene involving several different camera angles, which is perhaps why they asked him to do it as the story is pretty thin.'—J. A., Illustrated London News
● Video: Rank

Quintet

US 1979 118m De Luxe
TCF / Lions Gate (Robert Altman)

In an icebound city of the future, citizens play a death game and a survivor hunts down a killer who plays for real.
Dismayingly pretentious claptrap which did its star's career no good at all.

w Frank Barhydt, Robert Altman, Patricia Resnick d Robert Altman ph Jean Boffety m Tom Pierson pd Leon Ericksen

Paul Newman, Vittorio Gassman, Fernando Rey, Bibi Andersson, Brigitte Fossey, Nina Van Pallandt

Quo Vadis**
US 1951   171m   Technicolor
MGM (Sam Zimbalist)

A Roman commander under Nero falls in love with a Christian girl and jealous Poppea has them both thrown to the lions.
Spectacular but stagey and heavy-handed Hollywood version of a much-filmed colossus which shares much of its plot line with *The*
Sign of the Cross. Three hours of solemn tedium with flashes of vigorous acting and a few set pieces to take the eye; but the sermonizing does not take away the bad taste of the emphasis on physical brutality.

w John Lee Mahin, S. N. Behrman, Sonya Levien *d* Mervyn Le Roy *ph* Robert Surtees, William V. Skall *m* Miklos Rozsa *ad* Cedric Gibbons, Edward Carfagno, William Horning

Robert Taylor, Deborah Kerr, *Peter Ustinov, Leo Genn, Patricia Laffan,* Finlay Currie, Abraham Sofaer, Marina Berti, Buddy Baer, Felix Aylmer, Nora Swinburne, Ralph Truman, Norman Wooland

'In making this film, MGM feel privileged to add something of permanent value to the cultural treasure house of mankind . . .'— *publicity*

'Ancient Rome is going to the dogs, Robert Taylor is going to the lions, and Peter Ustinov is going crazy!'—*publicity*

AAN: best picture; Robert Surtees, William V. Skall; Miklos Rozsa; Peter Ustinov; Leo Genn

RPM (Revolutions Per Minute)
US 1970 97m colour
Columbia / Stanley Kramer

At an American college, a middle-aged professor teaches liberal ideas.
Dim, thankfully forgotten addition to the *Strawberry Statement* cycle.

w Erich Segal d Stanley Kramer ph Michel Hugo, Perry Botkin Jnr m Barry de Vorzon

Anthony Quinn, Ann-Margret, Gary Lockwood, Paul Winfield, Alan Hewitt

Rabbit, Run
US 1970 94m Technicolor Panavision
Warner (Howard Kreitsek)

A man leaves his pregnant wife for a prostitute.
Uninteresting sex melodrama without any of the wit which distinguishes the book; hard to sit through.

w Howard B. Kreitsek, *novel* John Updike d Jack Smight ph Philip Lathrop m Ray Burton, Brian King

James Caan, Anjanette Comer, Arthur Hill, Jack Albertson, Carrie Snodgress

The Rabbit Trap*
US 1959 76m bw
UA / Canon (Harry Kleiner)

A hardworking draughtsman finally defies his boss and completes his holiday with his family.
Watchable minor drama just about marking the end of Hollywood's infatuation with TV plays which had begun with *Marty*; the moral and family problems of ordinary people were beginning to prove a shade lacking in excitement.

w J. P. Miller, from his TV play d Philip Leacock ph Irving Glassberg m Jack Marshall

Ernest Borgnine, Bethel Leslie, David Brian, Kevin Corcoran

Race for the Yankee Zephyr
New Zealand / Australia 1981 108m
  Eastmancolor Panavision

Adventurers discover an American aircraft wrecked in 1944, and argue over the loot without knowing that it contains a 50-million-dollar payroll.
Very moderate adventure story distinguished only by good locations.

w Everett de Roche d David Hemmings ph Vincent Monton m Brian May

Kan Wahl, Lesley Ann Warren, Donald Pleasence, George Peppard, Bruno Lawrence, Robert Bruce

Race Street
US 1948 79m bw
RKO (Nat Holt)

A bookie vows revenge when his pal is killed by an extortionist gang, but discovers that his girl friend is married to the leader.
Routine thick-ear, quite adequately handled.

w Martin Rackin, *story* Maurice Davis d Edwin L. Marin ph J. Roy Hunt m Roy Webb

George Raft, Marilyn Maxwell, William Bendix, Frank Faylen, Henry Morgan, Gale Robbins

Race with the Devil
US 1975 88m De Luxe
TCF / Saber / Maslansky (Wes Bishop)

Holidaymakers witness a black mass and are pursued by the diabolists.
Silly melodrama which resolves into a wild car chase and much violence.

w Lee Frost, Wes Bishop d Jack Starrett ph Robert Jessup m Leonard Rosenman

Peter Fonda, Warren Oates, Loretta Swit, Lara Parker, R. G. Armstrong

'Why do you need a woman when death is your mistress every afternoon?'
'A love story that hurtles full speed across the barriers of convention!'

The Racers
US 1955 112m De Luxe Cinemascope
TCF (Julian Blaustein)
GB title: *Such Men Are Dangerous*

A Monte Carlo Rally contestant is financed by an attractive lady gambler.
Routine racing car melodrama, totally unmemorable but impersonally efficient.

w Charles Kaufman, *novel* Hans Ruesch d Henry Hathaway ph Joe MacDonald m Alex North

Kirk Douglas, Bella Darvi, Gilbert Roland, Cesar Romero, Lee J. Cobb, Katy Jurado, Charles Goldner, George Dolenz

Rachel and the Stranger*
US 1948 92m bw
RKO (Richard H. Berger)

A western farmer feels real love for his wife for the first time when an attractive stranger seems likely to take her away from him.
Modestly appealing romantic drama in a western setting.

w Martin Rackin, *novel* Howard Fast d Norman Foster ph Maury Gertsman m Roy Webb md Constantin Bakaleinikoff

Loretta Young, Robert Mitchum, William Holden, Gary Gray, Tom Tully, Sara Haden, Frank Ferguson

Rachel, Rachel**
US 1968 101m Eastmancolor
Warner / Kayos (Paul Newman)

Events in the life of a middle-aged schoolmistress in a small New England town.
Appealing and freshly observed study of a limited personality in a small community.

w Stewart Stern, *novel* A Jest of God by Margaret Laurence d Paul Newman ph Gayne Rescher m Jerome Moross

Joanne Woodward, Estelle Parsons, James Olson, Kate Harrington, Donald Moffat, Geraldine Fitzgerald, Bernard Barrow

'It could all very easily degenerate into a woman's weepy; and the fact that it doesn't is due largely to Newman's refusal to treat Manawaka as another Peyton Place.'—Jan Dawson

'It tends to verge on dullness, but something always saves it.'—John Simon

AAN: best picture; Stewart Stern; Joanne Woodward; Estelle Parsons

Racing with the Moon
US 1984 108m Movielab
Paramount / Jaffe-Lansing (Alain Bernheim, John Kohn)

In 1942 California, two young men await induction into the Marines and say goodbye to their girl friends.
Disappointing flashback by people who fail to capture the spirit of the time, and replace it by conventional boy-girl teenage antics.

w Steven Kloves d Richard Benjamin ph John Bailey m Dave Grusin pd David L. Snyder

Sean Penn, Elizabeth McGovern, Nicolas Cage, John Karlen, Max Showalter

The Rack
US 1956 100m bw
MGM (Arthur M. Loew Jnr)

A veteran of the Korean War is

courtmartialled for collaborating with the enemy under torture.
Dullish courtroom melodrama overstretched from a TV play.

w Stewart Stern TV play Rod Serling d Arnold Laven ph Paul Vogel m Adolph Deutsch

Paul Newman, Walter Pidgeon, Edmond O'Brien, Lee Marvin, Cloris Leachman, Wendell Corey

The Racket°
US 1951 88m bw
RKO / Edmund Grainger

Police break up the empire of a powerful gangster.
Oddly timed and rather weak remake of the 1928 film; glossy but very old-fashioned in treatment.

w William Wister Haines, play Bartlett Cormack d John Cromwell ph George E. Diskant m Constantin Bakaleinikoff

Robert Ryan, Robert Mitchum, Ray Collins, Lizabeth Scott, William Talman

Racket Busters
US 1938 71m bw
Warner (Samuel Bischoff)

A gangster aiming to take over a trucking enterprise is opposed by the special prosecutor's office.
Routine cops and robbers, still very watchable but also forgettable.

w Robert Rossen, Leonardo Bercovici d Lloyd Bacon ph Arthur Edeson m Adolph Deutsch

George Brent, Humphrey Bogart, Gloria Dickson, Allen Jenkins, Walter Abel, Penny Singleton, Henry O'Neill

Rackety Rax
US 1932 65m bw

Gangster methods are applied to collegiate football. Muddled transfer of a light satirical book. Victor McLaglen, Greta Nissen, Neil O'Day, Alan Dinehart, Allen Jenkins, Vince Barnett. Written by Ben Markson, Lou Breslow, story Joel Sayre; directed by Alfred Werker; for Fox. 'Doubtful b.o. entertainment . . . it looks and sounds silly.'—Variety

Radio City Revels
US 1938 90m bw

A songwriter can work only in his sleep. A wisp of plot is the peg for a very moderate revue. Bob Burns, Jack Oakie, Kenny Baker, Victor Moore, Ann Miller, Milton Berle, Helen Broderick, Jane Froman, Buster West, Richard Lane. Written by Matt Brooks, Eddie Davis, Anthony Veiller, Mortimer Offner; directed by Ben Stoloff; for RKO. 'Should do well at b.o., but no smash.'—Variety

Radio Parade of 1935
GB 1934 96m bw with colour sequence

Amateur talent makes it big for a radio station. Historically interesting revue which

unfortunately requires its comic lead to play straight. Will Hay, Helen Chandler, Clifford Mollison, Davy Burnaby, The Western Brothers, Alfred Drayton, Lily Morris, Nellie Wallace, Clapham and Dwyer, Claude Dampier, Ronald Frankau, Ted Ray, Beryl Orde, Stanelli. Written by Jack Davies, Paul Perez, Arthur Woods and James Bunting; directed by Arthur Woods; for BIP.

Rafferty and the Gold Dust Twins
US 1975 92m Technicolor Panavision
Warner / Gruskoff-Venture-Linson

A drifter encounters two female vagrants who force him at gunpoint to drive them to New Orleans and get him into various adventures.
Indulgent and unattractive 'road' movie which despite occasional amusing incident gets nowhere very slowly.

w John Kaye d Dick Richards ph Ralph Woolsey m Artie Butler

Alan Arkin, Sally Kellerman, MacKenzie Phillips, Alex Rocco, Charlie Martin Smith, Harry Dean Stanton, John McLiam

Raffles°
US 1939 72m bw
Samuel Goldwyn

Raffles the famous cricketer is also a compulsive and daring amateur thief.
Slight, modernized version of the turn-of-the-century stories; very palatable, but it could have been better.

w John Van Druten, Sydney Howard, novel Raffles the Amateur Cracksman by E. W. Hornung d Sam Wood ph Gregg Toland m Victor Young

David Niven, Olivia de Havilland, Dudley Digges, May Whitty, Douglas Walton, Lionel Pape, E. E. Clive, Peter Godfrey
'Fair remake . . . moderate b.o. potential.'—Variety
† This was virtually a scene-for-scene remake of the 1930 Goldwyn version starring Ronald Colman, Kay Francis and Alison Skipworth. It was written by Sidney Howard and directed by George Fitzmaurice.

Rage
US 1966 103m Technicolor
Columbia / Joseph M. Schenck / Cinematografico Jalisco (Gilberto Gazcon)

A drunken doctor finds a new will to live during a difficult journey to avert a rabies epidemic.
Pattern melodrama with no surprises, but gripping most of the way.

w Teddi Sherman, Gilberto Gazcon, Fernando Mendez d Gilberto Gazcon ph Rosalio Solano m Gustavo Cesar Carreon

Glenn Ford, Stella Stevens, David Reynoso, Armando Silvestre

Rage
US 1972 99m De Luxe Panavision
Warner (Fred Weintraub)

A father takes revenge when his son dies after a chemical warfare accident.

Well-meaning but turgid and boring melodrama.

w Philip Friedman, Dan Kleinman d George C. Scott ph Fred Koenekamp m Lalo Schifrin

George C. Scott, Richard Basehart, Martin Sheen, Barnard Hughes, Stephen Young
'Sluggish, tired and tiring.'—Variety

Rage at Dawn
US 1955 86m Technicolor

Detectives stage a fake train robbery to attract the evil Reno brothers. Very moderate western programmer. Randolph Scott, Forrest Tucker, J. Carrol Naish, Mala Powers, Edgar Buchanan, Ray Teal. Written by Horace McCoy; directed by Tim Whelan; for Nat Holt / RKO.

Rage in Heaven
US 1941 82m bw
MGM (Gottfried Reinhardt)

An unstable millionaire becomes jealous of his wife and arranges his own death so that her supposed lover will be suspected.
Stilted melodrama with the stars more or less at sea.

w Christopher Isherwood, Robert Thoeren, novel James Hilton d W. S. Van Dyke II ph Oliver T. Marsh m Bronislau Kaper

Robert Montgomery, Ingrid Bergman, George Sanders, Lucile Watson, Oscar Homolka, Philip Merivale, Matthew Boulton, Aubrey Mather
'Nothing happens but the obvious, and that only after a long and confused struggle.'—Otis Ferguson

The Rage of Paris°
US 1938 78m bw
Universal (B. G. De Sylva)

Confidence tricksters invest their money in a French girl who is out to nail a millionaire.
If memory serves right, an amusingly amoral trifle in the best style of its year.

w Bruce Manning, Felix Jackson d Henry Koster

Danielle Darrieux, Douglas Fairbanks Jnr, Louis Hayward, Mischa Auer, Helen Broderick, Harry Davenport, Samuel S. Hinds, Mary Martin (in a bit part)
'Smart comedy of first-run calibre . . . a finished and polished job.'—Variety

A Rage to Live
US 1965 101m bw Panavision
UA / Mirisch (Lewis J. Rachmil)

The unhappy college and married life of a nymphomaniac.
Well made but deliberately 'daring' case history which becomes too obvious and silly.

w John T. Kelley, novel John O'Hara d Walter Grauman ph Charles Lawton m Nelson Riddle

Suzanne Pleshette, Bradford Dillman, Ben Gazzara, Peter Graves, Bethel Leslie, James Gregory, Ruth White

RAFFLES. David Niven in the 1940 remake. Since then, gentlemen thieves seem to have been out of fashion.

'Stuff like this needs the exuberance of grand opera; sadly, all it gets here is a blue note.'—*MFB*

Raggedy Ann and Andy*
US 1977 85m Movielab Panavision
Lester Osterman (Richard Horner)

Toys come to life and have their own adventures while their owner is absent.
Attractive fully animated cartoon feature in which only the central story is lacking in pace and humour.

w Patricia Thackray, Max Wilk, *stories* Johnny Gruelle *d* Richard Williams

Raggedy Man
US 1981 94m Technicolor
Universal / William D. Wittliff, Burt Weissbourd

In 1944, a small-town switchboard operator and her two children are protected by a mysterious stranger.
Curious and quite unnecessary melodrama of some skill but very dubious appeal.

w William D. Wittliff *d* Jack Fisk *ph* Ralf Bode *m* Jerry Goldsmith *ed* Edward Warschilka

Sissy Spacek, Eric Roberts, Sam Shepard, William Sanderson, Tracey Walter, R. G. Armstrong

'Despite the casual, unhurried pace of the film, it doesn't seem to observe much.'—*Richard Combs, MFB*
● *Video: CIC*

Raging Bull*
US 1980 119m colour
UA / Chartoff-Winkler

The rise to fame of an unlikeable middleweight boxer, based on the autobiography of Jake La Motta.
Powerfully made but very violent and alienating ringside melodrama.
w Paul Schrader, Mardik Martin *d* Martin Scorsese *ph* Michael Chapman *m* from library sources *pd* Gene Rudolf

Robert De Niro, Cathy Moriarty, Joe Pesci, Frank Vincent, Nicholas Colasanto
'Scorsese makes pictures about the kind of people you wouldn't want to know.'—*Variety*

AA: editing (Thelma Schoonmaker); Robert De Niro
AAN: best film; best direction; Cathy Moriarty; Joe Pesci
BFA: editing

The Raging Moon*
GB 1970 111m Technicolor
EMI (Bruce Cohn Curtis)
aka: *Long Ago Tomorrow*

A love affair develops between two inmates of a home for the physically handicapped.
Appealing romantic drama which nearly became a big commercial success.
wd Bryan Forbes, *novel* Peter Marshall *ph* Tony Imi *m* Stanley Myers

Malcolm McDowell, Nanette Newman, Georgia Brown, Bernard Lee, Gerald Sim, Michael Flanders
● *Video: Thorn EMI*

The Raging Tide
US 1951 93m bw
U-I (Aaron Rosenberg)

A San Francisco gangster stows away on a fishing trawler and redeems himself when he perishes saving the life of a fisherman.
Fearfully old-fashioned seafaring melodrama, rather well made.
w Ernest K. Gann, from his novel Fiddler's Green *d* George Sherman *ph* Russell Metty *m* Frank Skinner

Richard Conte, Charles Bickford, Shelley Winters, Stephen McNally, Alex Nicol, Jesse White, John McIntire

The Ragman's Daughter
GB 1972 94m Technicolor
TCF / Penelope (Harold Becker)

A Nottingham layabout falls in love with an exciting middle-class girl; they fail to overcome parental opposition and she is killed in a road accident.
Wispy drama framed in pointless flashbacks; done on the cheap, it never seems to get anywhere and even fails to use its locations to advantage.
w Alan Sillitoe, from his short story *d* Harold Becker *ph* Michael Seresin *m* Kenny Clayton

Simon Rouse, Victoria Tennant, Patrick O'Connell, Leslie Sands

'What a time it was, an incredible time, a good time, a bad time . . .'

Ragtime*
US 1981 155m Technicolor Todd-AO
Ragtime / Sunley (Dino de Laurentiis)

Just before World War I, various Americans are affected by world events, and a chapter of accidents turns a placid negro into a revolutionary.
The fascinating patchwork of the novel has been virtually abandoned in favour of its least interesting episode, which is even further drawn out by the decision to bring on the aged James Cagney as a comic turn not in the novel. The early sequences show what might have been.
w Michael Weller, *novel* E. L. Doctorow *d* Milos Forman *ph* Miroslav Ondricek *m* Randy Newman

James Olson, Mary Steenburgen, James Cagney, Pat O'Brien, Elizabeth McGovern,

Howard E. Rollins Jnr, Brad Dourif, Moses Gunn, Kenneth McMillan, Donald O'Connor

'It's limp . . . it always seems to be aiming about halfway toward the effects that Doctorow achieved in his literary extravaganza.'—*New Yorker*

'The book, despite its defects, was funny, radical and angry. The film, despite its virtues, is solemn, liberal and passive.'—*Sunday Times*

AAN: screenplay; Miroslav Ondricek; Randy Newman; Elizabeth McGovern (supporting actress); Howard E. Rollins Jnr

● *Video: Thorn EMI*

The Raid*
US 1954   83m   Technicolor
TCF (Robert L. Jacks)

In 1864 six confederate soldiers escape from a union prison, and from a Canadian refuge carry out a revenge raid on a small Vermont town.
Interesting little action drama, crisply characterized and plotted, and based on a historical incident.

w Sidney Boehm, *story* Affair at St Albans by Herbert Ravenal Sass   *d* Hugo Fregonese   *ph* Lucien Ballard   *m* Roy Webb

Van Heflin, Anne Bancroft, Richard Boone, Lee Marvin, Tommy Rettig, Peter Graves, Douglas Spencer, Will Wright, John Dierkes

Raid on Rommel
US 1971   99m   Technicolor
Universal (Harry Tatelman)

In North Africa during World War II, a British officer releases prisoners of war and leads them in an assault on Tobruk.
Dispirited low-budget actioner apparently first intended for television.

w Richard Bluel   *d* Henry Hathaway   *ph* Earl Rath   *m* Hal Mooney

Richard Burton, John Colicos, Clinton Greyn, Wolfgang Preiss

The Raiders
US 1964   75m   Technicolor

Cattle drovers enlist the aid of famous western characters to persuade the railroad company to extend its line through dangerous country.
Slightly oddball western with endearing moments amid the miscalculations. Robert Culp (as Wild Bill Hickok), Judi Meredith (as Calamity Jane), James McMullan (as Buffalo Bill Cody). Brian Keith, Alfred Ryder, Simon Oakland. Written by Gene L. Coon; directed by Herschel Daugherty; for Revue / Universal.

Raiders of the Lost Ark**
US 1981   115m   Metrocolor   Panavision
Paramount / Lucasfilm (Frank Marshall)

In the thirties, an American archaeologist and explorer beats the Nazis to a priceless artifact, the magical box containing fragments of the stones on which God wrote his laws.
Commercially very successful, this attempted wrap-up of the Saturday morning serials of two generations ago spends a great deal of

money and expertise on frightening us rather than exciting us; in Dolby sound the experience is horrendous. Second time round, one can better enjoy the ingenious detail of the hero's exploits and ignore the insistence on unpleasantness; still, there are boring bits in between, and the story doesn't make a lot of sense.

w Lawrence Kasdan   *d* Steven Spielberg   *ph* Douglas Slocombe   *pd* Norman Reynolds   *m* John Williams

Harrison Ford, Karen Allen, Ronald Lacey, Paul Freeman, John Rhys-Davies, Denholm Elliott

'Both de trop and not enough.'—*Sight and Sound*

'Children may well enjoy its simple-mindedness, untroubled by the fact that it looks so shoddy and so uninventive.'—*Observer*

'Kinesthetically, the film gets to you, but there's no exhilaration, and no surge of feeling at the end.'—*Pauline Kael, New Yorker*

† Tom Selleck was the first choice for the lead, but was tied up with his TV series *Magnum*.

AA: editing (Michael Kahn); visual effects
AAN: best picture; Steven Spielberg; Douglas Slocombe; John Williams
BFA: Norman Reynolds

● *Video: CIC*

Rails into Laramie
US 1954   81m   Technicolor

Railway construction is hampered in Laramie by a saloon keeper who keeps the workers too happy. Solid co-feature western, quite enjoyable. John Payne, Dan Duryea, Mari Blanchard, Barton Maclane, Harry Shannon, Lee Van Cleef. Written by D. D. Beauchamp and Joseph Hoffman; directed by Jesse Hibbs; for Universal-International.

The Railway Children***
GB 1970   108m   Technicolor
EMI (Robert Lynn)

Three Edwardian children and their mother move into Yorkshire when their father is imprisoned as a spy, and have adventures on the railway line while helping to prove his innocence.
Fresh and agreeable family film with many pleasing touches to compensate for its meandering plot.

wd Lionel Jeffries, *novel* E. Nesbit   *ph* Arthur Ibbetson   *m* Johnny Douglas

Dinah Sheridan, William Mervyn, Jenny Agutter, Bernard Cribbins, Iain Cuthbertson, Gary Warren, Sally Thomsett

● *Video: Thorn EMI*

Rain*
US 1932   92m   bw
(UA)

Stranded passengers in Pago Pago during an epidemic include a prostitute and a missionary who lusts after her.

Early talkie version of a much filmed story; interesting but not very entertaining now that the sensational aspects have worn off.

w Maxwell Anderson, *play* John Colton, Clemence Randolph, *story* W. Somerset Maugham   *d* Lewis Milestone   *ph* Oliver T. Marsh   *m* Alfred Newman

Joan Crawford, Walter Huston, William Gargan, Beulah Bondi, Matt Moore, Guy Kibbee, Walter Catlett

'A b.o. disappointer. Only the play's rep and Joan Crawford's personal pull will save it.'—*Variety*

† Other versions: *Sadie Thompson* (1928) with Gloria Swanson; *Miss Sadie Thompson* (1953) (qv).

The Rain People
US 1969   101m   Technicolor
Warner / American Zoetrope (Bart Patton, Ronald Colby)

A depressed housewife leaves home, drives across country, and picks up a mentally retarded hitch-hiker who tries to protect her.
Slow, pretentious character drama which strains after art but only presents an unedifying study of failure.

wd Francis Ford Coppola   *ph* Wilmer Butler   *m* Ronald Stein

Shirley Knight, James Caan, Robert Duvall, Tom Aldredge, Marya Zimmet

'The rain people are people made of rain and when they cry they disappear because they cry themselves away.'—*sample dialogue*

'The siren of the sarongs is calling you!'
Rainbow Island
US 1944   95m   Technicolor
Paramount (I. D. Leshin)

A white girl brought up by her doctor father on a Pacific island is pursued by three sailors escaping from the Japanese.
Cheerful spoof of the sarong cycle with the star seeing the joke; otherwise a silly service farce with South Sea trimmings.

w Walter de Leon, Seena Owen, Arthur Phillips   *d* Ralph Murphy   *ph* Karl Struss   *m* Roy Webb   *songs* Burton Lane, Ted Koehler

Dorothy Lamour, Eddie Bracken, Gil Lamb, Barry Sullivan, Forrest Orr, Anne Revere, Reed Hadley, Marc Lawrence

The Rainbow Jacket
GB 1954   99m   Technicolor
Ealing (Michael Relph)

A boy jockey is blackmailed into losing a big race.
Disappointing racecourse drama which packs in all the expected ingredients.

w T. E. B. Clarke   *d* Basil Dearden   *ph* Otto Heller   *m* William Alwyn

Kay Walsh, Bill Owen, Edward Underdown, Robert Morley, Wilfrid Hyde White, Charles Victor, Honor Blackman, Sidney James

Rainbow on the River
US 1936 83m bw

After the Civil War, an orphan is brought up by a Black mammy and later discovered to be rich. Sentimental drama with songs from its boy star; not much, but popular. Bobby Breen, May Robson, Charles Butterworth, Louise Beavers, Alan Mowbray, Benita Hume, Henry O'Neill. Written by Earle Snell, William Hurlbut, from a story by Mrs C. V. Jamison; directed by Kurt Neumann; for Sol Lesser (RKO). 'Phoney and over-sugared sentimentality.'—*Variety*

The Rainmaker
US 1956 121m Technicolor Vistavision
Paramount / Hal B. Wallis (Paul Nathan)

In 1913 Kansas, a fake rainmaker has more success melting the heart of a confirmed spinster.
Such a whimsical play is too talky to make a good movie, especially as the actors are over-age, their performances are mannered, the dialogue seems interminable and the production is too stagey.

w N. Richard Nash, from his play *d* Joseph Anthony *ph* Charles Lang Jnr *m* Alex North

Katharine Hepburn, Burt Lancaster, Wendell Corey, Lloyd Bridges, Earl Holliman, Cameron Prud'homme, Wallace Ford

AAN: Alex North; Katharine Hepburn

The Rainmakers
US 1935 79m bw

Fake rainmakers are chased by midwestern farmers to California, where they get involved in an irrigation scheme. Slow-paced comedy with a train chase finale which comes too late. Bert Wheeler, Robert Woolsey, Dorothy Lee, Berton Churchill, George Meeker. Written by Grant Garrett, Leslie Goodwins; directed by Fred Guiol; for RKO. 'May appeal mildly to their fans, but won't make new business.'—*Variety*

The Rains Came***
US 1939 103m bw
TCF (Harry Joe Brown)

High-class parasites in India during the Raj redeem themselves when a flood disaster strikes.
Wholly absorbing disaster spectacular in which the characterization and personal plot development are at least as interesting as the spectacle, and all are encased in a glowingly professional production.

w Philip Dunne, Julien Josephson, *novel* Louis Bromfield *d* Clarence Brown *ph* Arthur Miller *m* Alfred Newman *sp* Fred Sersen

Myrna Loy, *George Brent*, Tyrone Power, Brenda Joyce, *Maria Ouspenskaya, Joseph Schildkraut*, H. B. Warner, Nigel Bruce, Mary Nash, Jane Darwell, Marjorie Rambeau, Henry Travers

'A big box-office picture with the advantage of a new locale.'—*Variety*

'It would be difficult to improve on the direction, the outbreak of the monsoon, a curtain billowing in the breeze, a lamp casting the shadow of lattice work against white silk, servants scattering for cover . . .'—*Charles Higham, 1972*

'Slick Hollywood film-making at its professional best.'—*Channel 4, 1982*

† Myrna Loy was third choice after Dietrich and Lamarr; Brent second choice after Ronald Colman.

AAN: Alfred Newman

The Rains of Ranchipur
US 1955 104m Eastmancolor Cinemascope
TCF (Frank Ross)

Dismal remake of *The Rains Came*, with bored actors and inferior production, all the character of the original being wiped out by badly processed wide-screen spectacle.

w Merle Miller *d* Jean Negulesco *ph* Milton Krasner *m* Hugo Friedhofer

Lana Turner, Fred MacMurray, Richard Burton, Joan Caulfield, Eugenie Leontovich, Michael Rennie

Raintree County
US 1958 166m Technicolor Panavision (Camera 65)
MGM (David Lewis)

During the Civil War a southern belle gets the man she thinks she wants, but subsequently finds life as a schoolmaster's wife boring. Dreary attempt by MGM to out-do *Gone with the Wind*, with neither characters nor plot one third as interesting and the production values merely expensive.

w Millard Kaufman, *novel* Ross Lockridge *d* Edward Dmytryk *ph* Robert Surtees *m* Johnny Green

Montgomery Clift, Elizabeth Taylor, Eva Marie Saint, Nigel Patrick, Lee Marvin, Rod Taylor, Agnes Moorehead, Walter Abel, Jarma Lewis, Tom Drake, Gardner McKay, Rhys Williams

AAN: Johnny Green; Elizabeth Taylor

Raise the Roof
GB 1930 77m bw

An actress is bribed to sabotage a touring show. Early talkie which retains surprising freshness. Betty Balfour, Maurice Evans, Jack Raine, Sam Livesey, Ellis Jeffreys. Writer uncredited; directed by Walter Summers; for BIP.

† Credited as the first British musical.

Raise the Titanic!
US 1980 122m De Luxe
Lord Grade / Martin Starger (William Frye)

Assorted Americans try to recover rare minerals from the wreck of the ship which sank in the North Atlantic in 1912.
Heavy-going exploiter with little action and even less plot.

w Adam Kennedy, Eric Hughes, *novel* Clive Cussler *d* Jerry Jameson *ph* Matthew F. Leonetti *second unit ph* Rex Metz *underwater ph* Bob Steadman *m* John Barry *pd* John F. DeCuir

Jason Robards, Richard Jordan, Alec Guinness, David Selby, Anne Archer, J. D. Cannon

'Hits new depths hitherto unexplored by the worst of Lew Grade's overloaded ark melodramas. This one wastes a potentially intriguing premise with dull scripting, a lacklustre cast, laughably phony trick work and clunky direction that makes *Voyage of the Damned* seem inspired by comparison.'—*Variety*

'The longer it all goes on, the more one hopes that, if they ever do raise the *Titanic*, they'll heave the film overboard to replace it.'—*Guardian*

● *Video: Precision*

A Raisin in the Sun*
US 1961 128m bw
Columbia / Paman–Doris (David Susskind, Philip Rose)

The life of a struggling black family in a cramped Chicago flat.
Earnest but claustrophobic play-on-film which long outstays its welcome but contains good performances.

w Lorraine Hansberry, from her play *d* Daniel Petrie *ph* Charles Lawton Jnr *m* Laurence Rosenthal

Sidney Poitier, Ruby Dee, Claudia McNeil, Diana Sands, Ivan Dixon, John Fielder, Lou Gossett

Raising the Wind
GB 1961 91m colour

Misadventures of students at a music academy. A Carry On in all but name, from the same stable; good moments among the dross. James Robertson Justice, Leslie Phillips, Kenneth Williams, Sidney James, Paul Massie, Liz Fraser, Eric Barker, Jennifer Jayne, Geoffrey Keen, Esma Cannon. Written by Bruce Montgomery; directed by Gerald Thomas; for GHW / Anglo Amalgamated.

The Rake's Progress*
GB 1945 123m bw
GFD / Individual (Frank Launder, Sidney Gilliat)
US title: *Notorious Gentleman*

The career of a cheerful ne'er-do-well playboy of the thirties.
The road to ruin played for light comedy, with silly endpapers in which, quite out of character, the rake becomes a war hero. Generally good production, witty script.

w Frank Launder, Sidney Gilliat, *story* Val Valentine *d* Sidney Gilliat *ph* Wilkie Cooper *m* William Alwyn *pd* David Rawnsley

Rex Harrison, Lilli Palmer, Margaret Johnston, Godfrey Tearle, Griffith Jones, Guy Middleton, Jean Kent, Marie Lohr, Garry Marsh, David Horne, Alan Wheatley

† In the American version Harrison crowned the Martyrs' Memorial not with a chamber pot but with a top hat.

Rally Round the Flag Boys

US 1958 106m De Luxe Cinemascope
TCF (Leo McCarey)

A small community protests at the siting nearby of a missile base.

Raucous service and sex comedy which becomes frenetic without ever being very funny.

w Claude Binyon, Leo McCarey, novel Max Shulman d Leo McCarey ph Leon Shamroy m Cyril Mockridge

Paul Newman, Joanne Woodward, Joan Collins, Jack Carson, Dwayne Hickman, Tuesday Weld, Gale Gordon, Murvyn Vye

Ramona

US 1936 90m Technicolor
TCF (Sol M. Wurtzel)

A half-breed girl and an Indian chief's son combat the greed of white pioneers.

Old-fashioned, stuffy adventure romance, much filmed in silent days.

w Lamar Trotti, novel Helen Hunt Jackson d Henry King ph William Skall, Chester Lyons m Alfred Newman

Loretta Young, Don Ameche, Kent Taylor, Pauline Frederick, Jane Darwell, Katherine de Mille, Victor Kilian, John Carradine

Rampage

US 1963 98m Technicolor
Warner Seven Arts / Talbot (William Fadiman)

Two white hunters love the same girl; one releases a tiger to harm the other, but it escapes.

Silly, unconvincing, old-style melodrama in which even the animals seem to overact.

w Robert Holt, Marguerite Roberts, novel Alan Caillou d Phil Karlson ph Harold Lipstein m Elmer Bernstein

Robert Mitchum, Jack Hawkins, Elsa Martinelli, Sabu, Emile Genest

'A woman is soft and warm . . . and deadlier than steel!'

Ramrod

US 1947 94m bw
(MGM) Enterprise

A predatory lady ranch owner hires a tough foreman and her ruthlessness causes several deaths and a stampede.

Ho-hum minor western with fading stars.

w Jack Moffit, Graham Baker, Cecile Kramer, story Luke Short d André de Toth ph Russell Harlan m Adolph Deutsch

Veronica Lake, Joel McCrea, Preston Foster, Charles Ruggles, Donald Crisp, Arleen Whelan, Lloyd Bridges

Rancho De Luxe

US 1974 95m De Luxe
UA / EK (Anthony Ray)

Cheerful cattle rustlers go on a binge and end up in prison.

Modern anti-everything western; it's anti-entertainment as well.

w Thomas McGuane d Frank Perry ph William A. Fraker m Jimmy Buffett

Sam Waterston, Jeff Bridges, Elizabeth Ashley, Charlene Dallas, Clifton James, Slim Pickens

'Where anything goes . . . for a price!'

Rancho Notorious

US 1952 89m Technicolor
RKO / Fidelity (Howard Welsch)

A cowboy seeking revenge for his girl friend's murder follows a clue to a lonely ranch run by a saloon singer.

Curious western which seems to have been intended as another Destry Rides Again but is made in a hard inflexible style which prevents it from appealing.

w Daniel Taradash d Fritz Lang ph Hal Mohr m Emil Newman

Marlene Dietrich, Arthur Kennedy, Mel Ferrer, Gloria Henry, William Frawley, Jack Elam

'Every quality you might ask of a western is in lavish supply—except entertainment value.'—Alton Cook

Random Harvest***

US 1942 126m bw
MGM (Sidney Franklin)

A shell-shocked officer in the 1914–18 war escapes from an asylum, marries a music hall singer and is idyllically happy until a shock makes him remember that he is the head of a noble family. His wife, whom he does not now remember, dutifully becomes his secretary and years later another shock brings memory and happiness back.

A silly enough story works remarkably well in this rather splendid, no holds barred, roses round the door romance in Hollywood's best style with incomparable stars. A triumph of the Peg's Paper syndrome, and hugely enjoyable because it is done so enthusiastically.

w Claudine West, George Froeschel, Arthur Wimperis, novel James Hilton d Mervyn Le Roy ph Joseph Ruttenberg m Herbert Stothart

Ronald Colman, Greer Garson, Susan Peters, Philip Dorn, Reginald Owen, Henry Travers, Margaret Wycherly, Bramwell Fletcher, Arthur Margetson

'I would like to recommend this film to those who can stay interested in Ronald Colman's amnesia for two hours and who could with pleasure eat a bowl of Yardley's shaving soap for breakfast.'—James Agee

'A strangely empty film . . . its characters are creatures of fortune, not partisans in determining their own fates.'—Bosley Crowther, New York Times

'It is cast with pearly players in every part. Its pedigreed plot is savoured with just the right mixture of ups and downs, ecstasy and well-bred anguish, implausibility and psyche. And it moves towards its climax with the measured tread and nicely timed emotional bumps of a Hearst Cosmopolitan serial. It is

perhaps the clearest example of the year of how a studio possessing lion's shares of movie-making capital and ingratiating talent can mate these two to synthesize a magnificent neuter, which will predictably bring in vast box office returns with which to produce more neuters.'—John McManus, PM

AAN: best picture; script; Mervyn Le Roy; Herbert Stothart; Ronald Colman; Susan Peters

Ransom*

US 1955 104m bw
MGM (Nicholas Nayfack)

A rich man takes desperate measures to rescue his son from a kidnapper.

Solid but overlong suspenser, virtually a vehicle for a star at his twitchiest and most dogged.

w Cyril Hume, Richard Maibaum d Alex Segal ph Arthur E. Arling m Jeff Alexander

Glenn Ford, Donna Reed, Leslie Nielsen, Juano Hernandez, Robert Keith

'He faced a decision that someday may be yours to make!'—publicity

Ransom*

GB 1975 98m Eastmancolor
Lion International (Peter Rawley)
aka: The Terrorists

A British ambassador to Scandinavia is kidnapped by terrorists and a Norwegian security chief gives chase.

Topical but unconvincing action thriller with unfamiliar detail; builds up to exciting sequences but is quickly forgotten.

w Paul Wheeler d Caspar Wrede ph Sven Nykvist m Jerry Goldsmith

Sean Connery, Ian McShane, Norman Bristow, John Cording, Isabel Dean, William Fox, Robert Harris

Rapture

US / France 1965 104m bw
International Classics / TCF (Christian Ferry)

A mentally unstable girl has a tragic romance with a fugitive murderer.

Gloomy all the way, and if it's art it needs explaining.

w Stanley Mann, novel Rapture in My Rags by Phyllis Hastings d John Guillermin ph Marcel Grignon

Patricia Gozzi, Dean Stockwell, Melvyn Douglas, Gunnel Lindblom

The Rare Breed

US 1966 97m Technicolor Panavision
Universal (William Alland)

An English bull is taken by its woman owner to St Louis to breed with American longhorns, and various frictions are caused among the ranchers.

Amusing western idea which misses fire by not coming down firmly as either drama or comedy; it does however pass the time amiably enough.

w Ric Hardman *d* Andrew V. McLaglen
ph William H. Clothier *m* Johnny Williams

James Stewart, Maureen O'Hara, Brian Keith, Juliet Mills, Don Galloway, David Brian, Jack Elam, Ben Johnson

Rascals
US 1938 77m bw

A rich young man and a girl suffering from amnesia join a gypsy troupe. Absurdly cast and plotted semi-musical with a certain liveliness to keep it going. Jane Withers, Borrah Minevitch and his Rascals, Robert Wilcox, Rochelle Hudson, Steffi Duna. Written by Robert Ellis, Helen Logan; directed by H. Bruce Humberstone; for TCF.
'In the main amusing and entertaining.'— *Variety*

Rashomon***
Japan 1951 83m bw
Daiei
aka: *In the Woods*

In medieval Japan, four people have different versions of a violent incident when a bandit attacks a nobleman in the forest. Indescribably vivid in itself, and genuinely strange (one of the versions is told by a ghost), *Rashomon* reintroduced Japanese films to the world market and was remade (badly) in Hollywood as *The Outrage*.

wd Akira Kurosawa, *story* Inside a Bush by Ryunosuke Akutagawa *ph* Kazuo Matsuyama *m* Takashi Matsuyama

Toshiro Mifune, Machiko Kyo, Masayuki Mori, Takashi Shimura
'A masterpiece, and a revelation.'—*Gavin Lambert, MFB*
AA: best foreign film

Raskolnikov*
Germany 1923 80m approx (at 24 fps)
  bw silent
Neumann (Robert Wiene)

A student kills a pawnbroker and is hounded by a police inspector until he confesses. Interesting adaptation of *Crime and Punishment* with some of the expressionist aspects of the same director's *The Cabinet of Dr Caligari*.

wd Robert Wiene *ph* Willy Godberger
ad Andre Andreyev

Gregory Khmara, Michael Tarkhanov, Pavel Pavlov, Vera Toma

Rasputin and the Empress*
US 1932 133m bw
MGM (Irving Thalberg)
GB title: *Rasputin the Mad Monk*

 The story of the last years of the Russian court, when a sinister monk gained influence over the empress.
An unhappy film which was besieged by lawsuits and never generated much drama of its own despite starring the three Barrymores, who all seemed to be acting in separate rooms. Production values are the most impressive thing about it.

w Charles MacArthur *d* Richard Boleslawski
ph William Daniels *m* Herbert Stothart

John Barrymore, Ethel Barrymore, Lionel Barrymore, Diana Wynyard, Ralph Morgan, C. Henry Gordon, Edward Arnold, Jean Parker, Gustav Von Seyffertitz, Anne Shirley (Dawn O'Day)
† The lawsuit was by Prince Youssoupoff (portrayed as Chegodieff), who claimed that although he did kill Rasputin his wife was never raped. He was awarded one million dollars.
AAN: Charles MacArthur

The Rat*
GB 1937 72m bw

A Parisian thief takes the blame for murder, but is saved by the socialite who loves him. Rather smart talkie version of a well-worn theatrical hit, previously filmed in 1925 as a silent, with Ivor Novello as star. Anton Walbrook, Ruth Chatterton, Rene Ray, Beatrix Lehmann, Felix Aylmer, Mary Clare. Written by Hans Rameau, Marjorie Gaffney, Miles Malleson and Romney Brent, from the play by Ivor Novello and Constance Collier; directed by Jack Raymond; for Herbert Wilcox.

The Rat Race*
US 1960 105m Technicolor
Paramount / Perlberg–Seaton

A young jazz musician and a dance hall hostess share a flat and face the adversities of New York.
A kind of sour fairy tale of the big city which has neither enough jokes nor enough incident but purveys the kind of charm that grows on one despite oneself.

w Garson Kanin, from his play *d* Robert Mulligan *ph* Robert Burks *m* Elmer Bernstein

Tony Curtis, Debbie Reynolds, Jack Oakie, Kay Medford, Don Rickles
'The New Yorkers of *The Rat Race* – noisy soft-hearted landlady, philosophical bartender, backchatting taxi driver – are as familiar as the settings of shabby apartment house and quiet little bar across the street. Film makers no longer need to invent here – they simply move in for a few weeks.'—*Penelope Houston*

Rationing
US 1943 93m bw

A small-town shopkeeper is frustrated by wartime restrictions. Amiable comedy for established stars. Wallace Beery, Majorie Main, Donald Meek, Howard Freeman, Connie Gilchrist. Written by William Lipman, Grant Garrett and Harry Ruskin; directed by Willis Goldbeck; for MGM.

Raton Pass
US 1951 84m bw

A greedy wife swindles her husband out of his share in their ranch. Unusual western melodrama; quite entertaining. Dennis Morgan, Patricia Neal, Steve Cochran, Scott

Forbes, Dorothy Hart. Written by Tom Blackburn and James Webb; directed by Edwin L. Marin; for Warner. (GB title: *Canyon Pass*.)

Rattle of a Simple Man
GB 1964 95m bw
Sydney Box (William Gell)

A shy football supporter in London spends the night with a tart for a bet.
Archetypal farcical situation with sentiment added to string it out to twice its proper length. Production values modest but adequate.

w Charles Dyer, from his play *d* Muriel Box
ph Reg Wyer *m* Stanley Black

Harry H. Corbett, *Diane Cilento*, Thora Hird, Charles Dyer
● *Video: Thorn EMI*

The Raven*
US 1935 61m bw
Universal

A doctor obsessed by Poe-inspired torture devices transforms a gangster on the run into a hideous mutant.
Silly but quite effective horror film with memorable sequences.

w David Boehm *d* Lew Landers *ph* Charles Stumar *md* Gilbert Kurland

Bela Lugosi, Boris Karloff, Samuel S. Hinds, Irene Ware, Lester Matthews
'Maintains Universal's high batting average with the shockers . . . should come through with nice grosses.'—*Variety*

The Raven*
US 1963 86m Pathecolor Panavision
AIP / Alta Vista (Roger Corman)

Two 15th-century conjurors fight a deadly duel of magic.
The rather splendid duel is a long time coming; the preliminaries are largely confined to chat in a single set, and the random jokes do not quite atone for the boredom.

w Richard Matheson *d* Roger Corman
ph Floyd Crosby *m* Les Baxter

Vincent Price, Peter Lorre, Boris Karloff, Hazel Court, Jack Nicholson

Raw Deal
US 1948 78m bw

A convict is helped by his girl friend to escape, and the police chase them across country. Fairly violent crime melodrama which holds the attention. Dennis O'Keefe, Claire Trevor, Marsha Hunt, John Ireland, Raymond Burr. Written by Leopold Atlas and John C. Higgins; directed by Anthony Mann; for Reliance / Eagle Lion.

Raw Edge
US 1956 76m Technicolor

A convict escapes and seeks revenge on the gang that sent him up. Tense, fairly adult western. Rory Calhoun, Yvonne de Carlo,

Mara Corday, Rex Reason, Neville Brand.
Written by Harry Essex and Robert Hill;
directed by John Sherwood; for Universal-
International.

Raw Wind in Eden

US 1958 93m Eastmancolor
Cinemascope
U-I (William Alland)

A model is stranded on a Sardinian island, and
fails in love with a mysterious American who
turns out to be a disillusioned millionaire.
Wish-fulfilment woman's picture with the
occasional relief of a smart line.

w Elizabeth and Richard Wilson d Richard
Wilson ph Enzo Serafin m Hans Salter

Esther Williams, Jeff Chandler, Carlos
Thompson, Rossana Podesta, Eduardo de
Filippo, Rik Battaglia

Rawhide**

US 1950 86m bw
TCF (Samuel G. Engel)
TV title: *Desperate Siege*

Four escaped convicts terrorize a stagecoach
stop.
Good suspense western with excellent
technical credits.

w Dudley Nichols d Henry Hathaway
ph Milton Krasner m Sol Kaplan

Tyrone Power, Susan Hayward, Hugh
Marlowe, Jack Elam, Dean Jagger, George
Tobias, Edgar Buchanan, Jeff Corey

'Between love and hatred there is a line as
sharp as a razor's edge!'
The Razor's Edge*

US 1946 146m bw
TCF (Darryl F. Zanuck)

A well-to-do young man spends the years
between the wars first idling, then looking for
essential truth.
The novel was an empty parable with amusing
trimmings. In the film the trimmings seem less
amusing, but the presentation is glossy.

w Lamar Trotti, *novel* W. Somerset
Maugham d Edmund Goulding ph Arthur
Miller m Alfred Newman ad Richard Day,
Nathan Juran

Tyrone Power, Gene Tierney, *Clifton Webb,
Herbert Marshall,* John Payne, Anne Baxter,
Lucile Watson, Frank Latimore, Elsa
Lanchester, Fritz Kortner
  'I like Somerset Maugham when he's
looking through keyholes or down cracks, not
at vistas.'—*Richard Winnington*
  'Almost as irresistibly funny and terrible as
The Fountainhead.'—*Pauline Kael, 70s*
† Maugham has a different source for his title,
in the shape of an Oriental proverb, probably
invented: 'The sharp edge of a razor is difficult
to pass over; thus the wise say that the path to
salvation is hard.'
AA: Anne Baxter
AAN: best picture; Clifton Webb

The Razor's Edge

US 1984 128m colour
Columbia (Robert P. Marucci, Harry Benn)

An unlikely remake which came into being
because the star persuaded the studio to
do it, then failed in his attempt to convey
the necessary spirituality. As for the rest, the
time is out of joint (except for Denholm
Elliott).

w John Byrum, Bill Murray d John Byrum
ph Peter Hannan m Jack Nietzche pd Philip
Harrison ed Peter Boyle

Bill Murray, Denholm Elliott, Theresa Russel,
Catherine Hicks, James Keach, Peter
Vaughan, Faith Brook

Reach for Glory*

GB 1962 86m bw
Columbia / Blazer (John Kohn, Jud
Kinberg)

During World War II, evacuee boys play war
games and a German refugee is accidentally
killed.
Grim and unpalatable parable, competently
rather than excitingly made.

w John Rae, from his novel The Custard
Boys d Philip Leacock ph Bob Huke m Bob
Russell

Kay Walsh, Harry Andrews, Michael
Anderson Jnr, Oliver Grimm, Alexis Kanner,
Martin Stephenson, Richard Vernon

Reach for the Sky*

GB 1956 135m bw
Rank / Pinnacle (Daniel M. Angel)

Douglas Bader loses both legs in a 1931 air
crash, learns to walk on artificial limbs and
flies again in World War II.
Box office exploitation of one man's personal
heroism, adequately but not inspiringly put
together with many stiff upper lips and much
jocular humour.

wd Lewis Gilbert, book Paul Brickhill
ph Jack Asher m John Addison

Kenneth More, Muriel Pavlow, Lyndon
Brook, Lee Patterson, Alexander Knox,
Dorothy Alison, Sydney Tafler, Howard
Marion Crawford

● *Video:* Rank

Reaching for the Moon

US 1931 90m bw
United Artists (Douglas Fairbanks)

On a transatlantic liner, a new cocktail has a
sensational effect on a mild-mannered hero.
Very flimsy comedy with songs and some
athletic stunts for its hero.

wd Edmund Goulding ph Ray June
song Irving Berlin

Douglas Fairbanks, Bebe Daniels, Edward
Everett Horton, Claud Allister, Jack Mulhall,
Bing Crosby
  'Not a smash entry, but should do
moderately and perhaps a little better than
that.'—*Variety*

'You'll love them as much as they love
  each other!'
Reaching for the Sun

US 1941 90m bw

A clam digger who needs an outboard motor
goes to work in a Detroit car plant. Easygoing
comedy, too muted to recommend itself
widely. Joel McCrea, Ellen Drew, Eddie
Bracken, Albert Dekker. Written by W. L.
River from a novel by Wessel Smitter;
directed by William Wellman; for Paramount.

Ready Willing and Able

US 1937 93m bw
Warner (Samuel Bischoff)

Two songwriters import an English leading
lady for their new show.
Lightweight star musical with no outstanding
qualities except a number in which girls dance
on the keys of a huge typewriter.

w Sig Herzig, Jerry Wald, Warren Duff
d Ray Enright ph Sol Polito ch Bobby
Connelly songs Johnny Mercer, Richard
Whiting

Ruby Keeler, Ross Alexander, Lee Dixon,
Wini Shaw, Jane Wyman, Allen Jenkins
  'Too many numbers and a slow script.'—
Variety

'Always outnumbered! Never outfought!'
'One of the most stunning dramas of love
  and courage ever brought to the screen!'
The Real Glory*

US 1939 96m bw
Samuel Goldwyn

Soldiers of fortune help the American
Army to quell a terrorist uprising in the
Philippines just after the Spanish-American
War.
Well made Gunga Dinnery.

w Jo Swerling, Robert R. Presnell d Henry
Hathaway ph Rudolph Maté m Alfred
Newman ad James Basevi

Gary Cooper, David Niven, Broderick
Crawford, Andrea Leeds, Reginald Owen,
Kay Johnson, Russell Hicks, Vladimir
Sokoloff
  'Moro uprisings, guerrilla warfare, cholera
epidemics, and fancy exhibitions of inhuman
cruelty are the frame against which an
innocuous melodramatic yarn is told.'—
Variety
  'The same sort of picture as *Gunga Din*.'—
Richard Mallett, Punch
  'Recommended to adolescents of all
ages.'—*New Statesman*
  'In times like these, we question the wisdom
of rattling the bones in Yankee imperialism's
closet.'—*Daily Worker*

Real Life

GB 1983 93m colour

An estate agent's assistant with a vivid
imagination becomes involved in thefts.
Clumsy, witless comedy which quickly bores.

Rupert Everett, Cristina Raines, Norman Beaton, Warren Clarke, Isla Blair, James Faulkner. Written by Francis Megahy, Bernie Cooper; directed by Francis Megahy; for The Real Life Partnership. 'Try as one may to look sympathetically on this brand of independent British venture, the resolute lack of wit or style wipes the indulgent smile from one's lips early on, and it never returns.'—*Guardian*

'Man against terrifying monster—in the most spectacular underwater scenes ever filmed!'

Reap the Wild Wind**
US 1942 124m Technicolor
Paramount / Cecil B. de Mille

Seafaring salvage engineers fight over a southern belle.
Georgia-set period adventure; intended as another *Gone with the Wind*, it simply doesn't have the necessary, but on its level it entertains solidly, climaxing with the famous giant squid fight.

w Alan le May, Jesse Lasky Jnr *d* Cecil B. de Mille *ph* Victor Milner, Dewey Wrigley, William V. Skall *m* Victor Young *ad* Hans Dreier, Roland Anderson

Ray Milland, John Wayne, *Paulette Goddard*, Raymond Massey, Robert Preston, Lynne Overman, Susan Hayward, Charles Bickford, Walter Hampden, Louise Beavers, Martha O'Driscoll, Hedda Hopper

'The essence of all his experience, the apogee of all his art, and as jamfull a motion picture as has ever played two hours upon a screen.'—*Howard Barnes, New York Herald Tribune*
† The underwater scenes were filmed in the Santa Monica Pan Pacific Marine Museum, which had a pool 100 feet long and 50 feet wide. The 50-foot giant squid was operated by a 24-button electronic keyboard.

AAN: photography

Rear Window***
US 1954 112m Technicolor
Alfred Hitchcock

A news photographer, confined to his room by a broken leg, sees a murder committed in a room on the other side of the court.
Artificial but fairly gripping suspenser of an unusual kind; with such restricted settings, all depends on the script and the acting, and they generally come up trumps.

w John Michael Hayes, *novel* Cornell Woolrich *d* Alfred Hitchcock *ph* Robert Burks *m* Franz Waxman

James Stewart, Grace Kelly, Raymond Burr, Judith Evelyn, Wendell Corey, Thelma Ritter

AAN: John Michael Hayes; Alfred Hitchcock; Robert Burks

Rebecca****
US 1940 130m bw
David O. Selznick

The naïve young second wife of a Cornish landowner is haunted by the image of his glamorous first wife Rebecca.

The supreme Hollywood entertainment package, set in Monte Carlo and Cornwall, with generous helpings of romance, comedy, suspense, melodrama and mystery, all indulged in by strongly-drawn characters, and directed by the new English wizard for the glossiest producer in town, from a novel which sold millions of copies. It really couldn't miss, and it didn't.

w Robert E. Sherwood, Joan Harrison, *novel* Daphne du Maurier *d* Alfred Hitchcock *ph* George Barnes *m* Franz Waxman

Laurence Olivier, Joan Fontaine, George Sanders, Judith Anderson, Nigel Bruce, Gladys Cooper, Florence Bates, Reginald Denny, C. Aubrey Smith, Melville Cooper, Leo G. Carroll, Leonard Carey

NARRATOR: 'Last night I dreamed I went to Manderley again . . .'

FAVELL (George Sanders) to Mrs De Winter: 'I say, marriage with Max is not exactly a bed of roses, is it?'

MRS DANVERS (Judith Anderson): 'You're overwrought, madam. I've opened a window for you. A little air will do you good. Why don't you go? Why don't you leave Manderley? He doesn't need you. He's got his memories. He doesn't love you—he wants to be alone again with *her*. You've nothing to stay for. You've nothing to live for, have you, really? Look down there. It's easy, isn't it? Why don't you? Go on, go on. Don't be afraid . . .'

MAXIM (Laurence Olivier): 'You thought I loved Rebecca? You thought that? I hated her. Oh, I was carried away by her—enchanted by her, as everyone was—and when I was married, I was told I was the luckiest man in the world. She was so lovely, so accomplished, so amusing. "She's got the three things that really matter in a wife," everyone said, "breeding, brains and beauty." And I believed them completely. But I never had a moment's happiness with her. She was incapable of love, or tenderness, or decency.'

'A carefully considered trying out of the superior technical resources now at Hitchcock's disposal.'—*George Perry, 1965*
'Hitchcock fans will have to put up with a surprising lack of the characteristic Hitchcock improvisations in the way of salty minor personages and humorous interludes, and satisfy themselves with a masterly exhibition of the Hitchcock skill in creating suspense and shock with his action and his camera.'—*National Board of Review*

AA: best picture; George Barnes
AAN: script; Alfred Hitchcock; Franz Waxman; Laurence Olivier; Joan Fontaine; Judith Anderson

● *Video: Guild*

Rebecca of Sunnybrook Farm
US 1932 75m bw

A rural glad girl wins over her dour aunt and reforms an atheist. Routine sound remake of the children's classic in a 1921 silent version of which Mary Pickford starred. Marian Nixon, Ralph Bellamy, Mae Marsh, Louise Closser Hale, Alan Hale, Charlotte Henry. Written by S. N. Behrman, Sonya Levien, from the novel

by Kate Douglas Wiggin and Charlotte Thompson; directed by Alfred Santell; for Fox.

Rebecca of Sunnybrook Farm
US 1938 80m bw
TCF (Raymond Griffith)

A child performer becomes a pawn in the fight to exploit her talents on radio.
Unrecognizable revamping of a famous story makes a very thin star vehicle.

w Karl Tunberg, Don Ettlinger, *novel* Kate Douglas Wiggin *d* Allan Dwan *ph* Arthur Miller *m* Arthur Lange *songs* various

Shirley Temple, Randolph Scott, Jack Haley, Gloria Stuart, Phyllis Brooks, Helen Westley, Slim Summerville, Bill Robinson

'More fitting title would be *Rebecca of Radio City* . . . a weak story, indifferently directed and acted.'—*Variety*

● *Video: CBS / Fox*

The Rebel*
GB 1960 105m Technicolor
Associated British (W. A. Whitaker)
US title: *Call Me Genius*

A suburban businessman goes to Paris to become an artist.
A kind of farcical *The Moon and Sixpence*, insufficiently well tailored to the requirements of a very specialized comic, but occasionally diverting none the less.

w Alan Simpson, Ray Galton *d* Robert Day *ph* Gilbert Taylor *m* Frank Cordell

Tony Hancock, George Sanders, Paul Massie, Margit Saad, Grégoire Aslan, Dennis Price, Irene Handl, Mervyn Johns, Peter Bull, John Le Mesurier, Nanette Newman, Oliver Reed, John Wood

'The more prosaic the setting, the funnier Hancock seems; transplanted into a conventionally silly screen art world, he is submerged among the other grotesques.'—*Penelope Houston*

Rebel in Town
US 1956 78m bw

A bank robber accidentally kills a small boy and is hunted down by the father. Surprisingly stark western with no particular merit. John Payne, John Smith, Ruth Roman, J. Carrol Naish, Ben Cooper. Written by Danny Arnold; directed by Alfred Werker; for Bel Air / UA.

The Rebel Son
GB 1939 90m bw
London Films Omnia (E. C. Molinier, Charles David)

A Tartar leader's son falls in love with the daughter of the opposing leader.
Resistible grafting of the Romeo and Juliet story into the barbarians of the Steppes, with much carousing and threatened violence surrounding a good central performance. It includes much footage from a 1936 French film, *Taras Bulba*.

w Adrian Brunel, *story* Gogol *d* Alexis Granowsky and Adrian Brunel *ph* Franz Planer and Bernard Browne

Harry Baur, Patricia Roc, Roger Livesey, Anthony Bushell, Joan Gardner

'The bad boy from a good family!'
Rebel without a Cause••
US 1955   111m   Warnercolor
Cinemascope
Warner (David Weisbart)

The adolescent son of a well-to-do family gets
into trouble with other kids and the police.
The first film to suggest that juvenile violence
is not necessarily bred in the slums, this
somewhat dreary melodrama also catapulted
James Dean to stardom as the prototype fifties
rebel.

w Stewart Stern *d* Nicholas Ray *ph* Ernest
Haller *m* Leonard Rosenman

James Dean, Natalie Wood, Jim Backus, Sal
Mineo, Ann Doran, Dennis Hopper

AAN: original story (Nicholas Ray); Natalie
Wood; Sal Mineo

Rebound
US 1931   88m   bw

A woman tries to forgive her husband when he
is jilted by a girl friend. A sophisticated stage
comedy presented with the minimum of
alteration. Ina Claire, Robert Williams,
Robert Ames, Myrna Loy, Hedda Hopper,
Louise Closser Hale. Written by Horace
Jackson from the play by Donald Ogden
Stuart; directed by E. H. Griffith; for RKO-
Pathé. 'A splendidly made picture which will
delight smart audiences.'—*Variety*

'The biggest musical show of the century,
with a throbbing love story as exciting as
its title!'
Reckless
US 1935   96m   bw
MGM (David O. Selznick)

A theatrical agent loves the glamorous star he
represents, but she marries a drunken
millionaire.
Remarkably flat backstage melodrama with
music, based on the life of Libby Holman.

w P. J. Wolfson *d* Victor Fleming *ph* George
Folsey *songs* various

Jean Harlow, William Powell, Franchot Tone,
May Robson, Ted Healy, Nat Pendleton,
Rosalind Russell, Henry Stephenson

'Several sets of dramatic premises are
established and then permitted to wander
aimlessly, making the 93 minutes seem much
longer than that.'—*Variety*

The Reckless Moment•
US 1949   82m   bw
Columbia (Walter Wanger)

A woman accidentally kills her daughter's
would-be seducer, and is then trailed by a
blackmailer.
Uninteresting melodrama electrified by
Ophuls' direction, which might have been
applied to something more worthwhile.

w Henry Garson, R. W. Soderborg, *novel* The
Blank Wall by Elizabeth Sanxay Holding
d Max Ophuls *ph* Burnett Guffey *m* Hans
Salter *md* Morris Stoloff

Joan Bennett, James Mason, Geraldine
Brooks, Henry O'Neill, Shepperd Strudwick
  'Swift, sure narrative and solidly pleasurable
detail.'—*Richard Winnington*

The Reckoning••
GB 1969   108m   Technicolor
Columbia / Ronald Shedlo (Hugh Perceval)

A tough London executive with a Liverpool-
Irish background has a brutal streak and a
self-destructive urge, but goes on narrowly
averting misfortune.
Interesting melodrama of a man disgusted with
both bourgeois and working-class values;
slickly made and fast-moving.

w John McGrath, *novel* The Harp That Once
by Patrick Hall *d* Jack Gold *ph* Geoffrey
Unsworth *m* Malcolm Arnold

Nicol Williamson, Rachel Roberts, Paul
Rogers, Zena Walker, Ann Bell, Gwen
Nelson, J. G. Devlin

The Red Badge of Courage••
US 1951   69m   bw
MGM (Gottfried Reinhardt)

A youth called up during the Civil War gets
his first taste of battle.
Fresh, poetic, but dramatically unsatisfactory
filming of a classic American novel. The story
of its production is fascinatingly told in
Picture, a book by Lillian Ross.

wd John Huston, *novel* Stephen Crane
ph Harold Rosson *m* Bronislau Kaper

Audie Murphy, Bill Mauldin, Douglas Dick,
Royal Dano, John Dierkes, Andy Devine,
Arthur Hunnicutt

Red Ball Express
US 1952   83m   bw
U-I (Aaron Rosenberg)

A supply column runs from the Normandy
beachhead to Patton's army on the outskirts of
Paris.
Standard war adventure, not too convincingly
mounted but providing the usual excitements.

w John Michael Hayes *d* Budd Boetticher
ph Maury Gertsman

Jeff Chandler, Sidney Poitier, Alex Nicol,
Judith Braun, Hugh O'Brian, Jack Kelly, Jack
Warden

The Red Balloon••••
France 1955   34m   Technicolor

A lonely boy finds a balloon which becomes
his constant companion and finally lifts him to
the skies. Absorbing and quite perfectly timed
fantasy, one of the great film shorts. With
Pascal Lamorisse; written and directed by
Albert Lamorisse; photographed by *Edmond
Sechan*; music by *Maurice Le Roux*; for Films
Montsouris.

The Red Beret
GB 1953   88m   Technicolor
Warwick (Irving Allen, Albert R. Broccoli)
US title: *Paratrooper*

In 1940, an American with a guilt complex
joins the British paratroopers.

Routine war action flagwaver; good battle
scenes, rubbish in between.

w Richard Maibaum, Frank Nugent,
book Hilary St George Saunders *d* Terence
Young *ph* John Wilcox *m* John Addison

Alan Ladd, Susan Stephen, Leo Genn, Harry
Andrews, Donald Houston, Anthony Bushell,
Patric Doonan, Stanley Baker, Lana Morris

The Red Danube
US 1950   119m   bw
MGM (Carey Wilson)

In occupied Vienna, citizens are being
returned to Russia against their will.
Tedious and silly Red-baiting cold war
charade.

w Gina Kaus, Arthur Wimperis,
novel Vespers in Vienna by Bryan Marshall
d George Sidney *ph* Charles Rosher
m Miklos Rozsa

Ethel Barrymore, Walter Pidgeon, Janet
Leigh, Peter Lawford, Francis L. Sullivan,
Angela Lansbury, Louis Calhern, Melville
Cooper

Red Dawn
US 1984   114m   Metrocolor
MGM-UA / Valkyrie (Buzz Feitshans, Barry
Beckerman)

Russians lead a violent invasion into Colorado
and are wiped out by the locals.
Ludicrous and somewhat dangerous Cold War
throwback with little entertainment value to
commend it. Violent teenage nonsense.

w Kevin Reynolds, John Milius *d* John
Milius *ph* Ric Waite *m* Basil Poledouris
pd Jackson de Govia *ed* Thom Noble

Patrick Swayze, C. Thomas Howell, Lea
Thompson, Charlie Sheen, Darren Dalton,
Jennifer Grey, Ben Johnson, Harry Dean
Stanton, Ron O'Neal, Vladek Sheybal,
Powers Boothe

The Red Desert•
Italy / France 1964   116m   Eastmancolor
Duemila / Federiz (Angelo Rizzoli)
original title: *Il Deserto Rosso*

A wife suffers from depression, and a brief
affair with her husband's friend doesn't help.
Elongated character study, very talkative but
rather decoratively designed with the same
subtle use of colour in an urban landscape as
was seen later in *Blow Up*.

w Michelangelo Antonioni, Tonino Guerra
d Michelangelo Antonioni *ph* Carlo di Palma
m Giovanni Chionetti

Monica Vitti, Richard Harris, Carlos Chionetti
  'The beauty is stationary, painterly; and the
arresting image precisely arrests and retards
the already moribund thrust of the film.'—
John Simon

  'Boredom in Ravenna, and it seeps into the
viewer's bones.'—*Pauline Kael, New Yorker,
1984*

'He treated her rough—and she loved it!'
Red Dust***
US 1932 86m bw
MGM (Hunt Stromberg)

On a rubber plantation in Indo-China, the overseer is pursued by his engineer's bride but himself falls for a stranded prostitute.
Vigorous romantic melodrama with echoes of *Rain;* remade as *Congo Maisie* (1940) and *Mogambo* (1954).

w John Lee Mahin, *play* Wilson Collison d Victor Fleming *ph* Harold Rosson

Clark Gable, Jean Harlow, Mary Astor, Gene Raymond, Donald Crisp, Tully Marshall, Forrester Harvey

'Lots of pash, sex and undress . . . an exhib's delight and a cinch for fancy takings. Done so expertly it almost overcomes the basic script shortcomings.'— *Variety*

'Gable and Harlow have full play for their curiously similar sort of good-natured toughness.'— *Time*

† The Gable role was first announced for John Gilbert.
†† Scenes showing the shooting of *Red Dust* are included in *Bombshell.*

Red Garters**
US 1954 91m Technicolor
Paramount (Pat Duggan)

Various familiar types congregate in the western town of Paradise Lost, and settle matters by the Code of the West.
Amusing western musical spoof slightly deadened by its pretty but finally boring theatrically stylized scenery. Songs are catchy, performances good natured.

w *Michael Fessier* d George Marshall *ph* Arthur E. Arling *m* Joseph J. Lilley *songs* Jay Livingston, Ray Evans

Rosemary Clooney, Guy Mitchell, Gene Barry, Jack Carson, Pat Crowley, Cass Daley, Frank Faylen, Reginald Owen

'A musical of considerable freshness and gaiety.'— *MFB*

Red Headed Woman*
US 1932 74m bw
MGM (Albert Lewin)

A shopgirl marries the boss but is rejected in his social circles.
Unconvincing but occasionally entertaining melodrama.

w Anita Loos, *novel* Katharine Brush d Jack Conway *ph* Harold Rosson

Jean Harlow, Chester Morris, Lewis Stone, Leila Hyams, Una Merkel, Henry Stephenson, Charles Boyer, May Robson

'Gingery treatment of a controversial subject that is bound to engage femme interest.'— *Variety*

The Red House*
US 1947 100m bw
(UA) Thalia (Sol Lesser)

A moody farmer's guilty obsession with an old

REBECCA. David O. Selznick and Alfred Hitchcock have fun on the set . . .

house in the woods is that he murdered his parents in it.
Psycho-like suspense melodrama, too extended for comfort and too restricting for the actors, but effective in spurts.

wd Delmer Daves, *novel* George Agnew Chamberlain *ph* Bert Glennon *m* Miklos Rozsa

Edward G. Robinson, Judith Anderson, Lon McCallister, Allene Roberts, Rory Calhoun, Julie London, Ona Munson

The Red Inn*
France 1951 95m bw
Memnon
original title: *L'Auberge Rouge*

In 1833, stagecoach travellers stay at a remote inn, where the owners intend to rob and murder them.
Extreme black farce which manages to be pretty funny for those who can take this kind of thing: even the survivors of the night's massacre fall down a ravine.

w *Jean Aurenche, Pierre Bost* d Claude Autant-Lara *ph* André Bac *m* René Cloërc *ad* Max Douy

Fernandel, Françoise Rosay, Carette, Grégoire Aslan

The Red Light
US 1949 83m bw
UA / Pioneer (Roy Del Ruth)

An industrialist tracks down his brother's murderer.
Competent routine detection piece with engaging clues.

w George Callahan d Roy Del Ruth *ph* Bert Glennon *m* Dmitri Tiomkin

George Raft, Virginia Mayo, Raymond Burr, Gene Lockhart, Henry Morgan, Arthur Franz

Red Line 7000
US 1965 110m Technicolor
Paramount / Laurel (Howard Hawks)

The career and loves of a stock car racer.
Very routine romantic actioner full of the director's favourite situations but failing to find any fresh slant.

w George Kirgo d Howard Hawks *ph* Milton Krasner *m* Nelson Riddle

James Caan, Laura Devon, Gail Hire, Charlene Holt, John Robert Crawford

Red Mountain
US 1951 84m Technicolor
Paramount / Hal B. Wallis

A Confederate captain joins Quantrell's Raiders but is horrified by their brutality.
Fast-moving action western.

. . . but there was no fun for the audience when Judith Anderson tried to persuade Joan Fontaine to jump.

w John Meredyth Lucas, George W. George, George F. Slavin d William Dieterle ph Charles Lang Jnr m Franz Waxman

Alan Ladd, Lizabeth Scott, Arthur Kennedy, John Ireland, Jeff Corey, James Bell

Red Planet Mars
US 1952 87m bw
UA / Donald Hyde, Anthony Veiller

Americans and Russians both tune in to Mars and learn that it is a powerful Christian planet; the news causes first panic, then a religious revival and a determination to live more harmoniously on earth.
Lunatic farrago that has to be seen to be believed.

w Anthony Veiller, John L. Balderston d Harry Horner ph Joseph Biroc m Mahlon Merrick md David Chudnow ad Charles D. Hall

Herbert Berghof, Peter Graves, Andrea King, Marvin Miller

The Red Pony
US 1949 88m Technicolor
Republic (Lewis Milestone)

When his pet pony dies after an illness, a farmer's son loses faith in his father.
Sincere but rather obvious little fable which although capably made does not make inspiring film drama.

w John Steinbeck d Lewis Milestone ph Tony Gaudio m Aaron Copland pd Nicolai Remisoff

Myrna Loy, Robert Mitchum, Peter Miles, Louis Calhern, Shepperd Strudwick, Margaret Hamilton
● Video: BBC

Red River**
US 1948 133m bw
UA / Monterey (Howard Hawks)

How the Chisholm Trail was developed as a cattle drive.
Brawling western, a bit serious and long drawn out but with splendid action sequences.

w Borden Chase, Charles Schnee d Howard Hawks ph Russell Harlan m Dmitri Tiomkin

John Wayne, Montgomery Clift, Joanne Dru, Walter Brennan, Colleen Gray, John Ireland, Noah Beery Jnr, Harry Carey Jnr

AAN: original story (Borden Chase)

Red Salute*
US 1935 78m bw
Edward Small
aka: Runaway Daughter; GB title: Arms and the Girl

A college girl with communist leanings takes a cross country trip with an American soldier.
Odd little romantic comedy modelled on It

Happened One Night; it was picketed for its inconsequential attitude to politics.

w Humphrey Pearson, Manuel Seff d Sidney Lanfield ph Robert Planck

Barbara Stanwyck, Robert Young, Hardie Albright, Cliff Edwards, Ruth Donnelly, Gordon Jones, Henry Kolker
'Tepid comedy romance wrapped up in a preachment against campus agitators who oppose militarism.'—Variety

The Red Shoes****
GB 1948 136m Technicolor
GFD / The Archers (Michael Powell, Emeric Pressburger)

A girl student becomes a great ballet star but commits suicide when torn between love and her career.
Never was a better film made from such a penny plain story so unpersuasively written and performed; the splendour of the production is in the intimate view it gives of life backstage in the ballet world with its larger-than-life characters. The ballet excerpts are very fine, and the colour discreet; the whole film is charged with excitement.

wd Michael Powell, Emeric Pressburger ph Jack Cardiff m Brian Easdale pd Hein Heckroth

Anton Walbrook, Moira Shearer, Marius Goring, Robert Helpmann, Albert Basserman, Frederick Ashton, Leonide Massine, Ludmilla Tcherina, Esmond Knight
'In texture, like nothing the British cinema has ever seen.'—Time Out, 1981

AA: Brian Easdale
AAN: best picture; original story (Michael Powell, Emeric Pressburger)
● Video: Rank

Red Skies of Montana
US 1952 99m Technicolor
TCF (Samuel G. Engel)
aka: Smoke Jumpers

Tension among firefighting crews in the mountains of Montana.
Adequate, routine action melodrama with semi-documentary touches.

w Harry Kleiner d Joseph M. Newman ph Charles G. Clarke m Sol Kaplan

Richard Widmark, Jeffrey Hunter, Constance Smith, Richard Boone, Richard Crenna

Red Sky at Morning
US 1970 113m Technicolor
Universal / Hal Wallis

During World War II the family of an officer on active service find life in New Mexico not what they've been used to.
Peyton Place by any other name, well produced but of little real interest.

w Marguerite Roberts, novel Richard Bradford d James Goldstone ph Vilmos Zsigismond m Billy Goldenberg

Claire Bloom, Richard Thomas, Richard Crenna, Catherine Burns, Desi Arnaz Jnr, John Colicos, Harry Guardino

THE RED SHOES. Moira Shearer and Leonide Massine in the title ballet.

Red Sun

France / Italy / Spain 1971   108m
Eastmancolor
Corona / Oceania / Balcazar (Robert
Dorfman)

In 1870 Arizona, an outlaw is forced to
accompany a Japanese samurai to recover a
ceremonial sword which his partner has stolen.
Unusual but generally ineffective western with
a fashionable international cast.

w Lair Koenig, D. B. Petitclerc, W. Roberts,
L. Roman d Terence Young ph Henri
Alekan m Maurice Jarre

Charles Bronson, Toshiro Mifune, Alain
Delon, Ursula Andress, Capucine
  'A nice exotic item ruined by suburban
direction.'—Sight and Sound

● Video: Polygram

Red Sundown

US 1956   81m   Technicolor

A gunslinger becomes a deputy and tames a
lawless town. Elementary western action
piece, not unentertaining. Rory Calhoun,
Martha Hyer, Dean Jagger, Robert

Middleton, James Millican, Grant Williams.
Written by Martin Berkeley; directed by Jack
Arnold; for Universal-International.

The Red Tent*

Italy / USSR 1970   121m   Technicolor
Paramount / Vides / Mosfilm (Franco
Cristaldi)

The story of General Nobile's ill-fated 1928
expedition by dirigible to the Arctic.
Stiffly-conceived international spectacular with
one striking sequence but not much good
cheer.

w Ennio de Concini, Richard Adams
d Mikhail Kalatozov ph Leonid Kalashnikov
m Ennio Morricone

Peter Finch, Sean Connery, Hardy Kruger,
Claudia Cardinale, Mario Adorf, Massimo
Girotti

Red Tomahawk

US 1967   80m   Technicolor

The small town of Deadwood is caught up in
the aftermath of Little Big Horn. Talkative
western filled with old faces, as is this

producer's wont. Howard Keel, Joan
Caulfield, Broderick Crawford, Scott Brady,
Wendell Corey, Richard Arlen, Tom Drake.
Written by Steve Fisher; directed by R. G.
Springsteen; for A. C. Lyles / Paramount.

Red Wagon

GB 1933   107m   bw

Passions mount in a travelling circus. Gypsies
and jealousies are the ingredients of a
melodrama aimed at the international market.
It failed. Charles Bickford, Raquel Torres,
Greta Nissen, Don Alvarado, Anthony
Bushell, Paul Graetz, Jimmy Hanley, Frank
Pettingell. Written by Roger Burford, Edward
Knoblock and Arthur Woods, from the novel
by Lady Eleanor Smith; directed by Paul
Stein; for BIP.

Redbeard*

Japan 1965   165   bw   Tohoscope
Toho-Kurosawa
original title: Akahige

Problems of a 19th-century doctor.
Almost a Japanese version of The Citadel:

Kurosawa himself called it 'a monument to goodness in man'. Rather heavy-going, but sporadically compelling.

w Masato Ide, Hideo Oguni, Akira Kurosawa, *novel* Shugoro Yamamoto *d* Akira Kurosawa *ph* A. Nakai, T. Saito *m* M. Sato

Toshiro Mifune, Yuzo Kayama

'A three-hour excursion into nineteenth-century hospital soap opera; a mediocre enough script, but beautifully directed and flawlessly acted.'—*John Simon*

Redemption
US 1930 82m bw

A man thought dead commits suicide rather than interrupt his wife's new life. Elaborate but unsuccessful talkie debut of a waning star; very hard going. John Gilbert, Renee Adoree, Eleanor Boardman, Conrad Nagel. Written by Dorothy Farnum and Edwin Justus Mayer, from *The Living Corpse* by Leo Tolstoy; directed by Fred Niblo; for MGM.

Reds**
US 1981 196m Technicolor
Paramount (Warren Beatty)

The last years of John Reed, an American writer who after stormy romantic vicissitudes goes with his wife to Russia and writes *Ten Days That Shook the World*.
Interminably long but full of quality, this immensely detailed work was a most unlikely project to succeed in the eighties, but its very strangeness enabled it to break even.

w Warren Beatty, Trevor Griffiths *d* Warren Beatty *ph* Vittorio Storaro *m* Stephen Sondheim *pd* Richard Sylbert

Warren Beatty, Diane Keaton, Edward Herrman, Jerzy Kosincki, Jack Nicholson, Maureen Stapleton, Paul Sorvino

AA: Warren Beatty (as director); Vittorio Storaro; Maureen Stapleton (supporting actress)
AAN: best picture; screenplay; editing (Dede Allen, Craig McKay); Warren Beatty (as actor); Diane Keaton; Jack Nicholson
BFA: best supporting actor (Jack Nicholson); best supporting actress (Maureen Stapleton)

● *Video: CIC*

Reducing
US 1931 73m bw

The proprietress of a beauty parlour sends for an old family servant to help her. Loosely plotted comedy consisting largely of slapstick in a Turkish bath. Marie Dressler, Polly Moran, Anita Page, Lucien Littlefield, Sally Eilers. Written by Willard Mack, Beatrice Banyard; directed by Charles F. Reisner; for MGM. 'Rough and tumble hoke comedy addressed to the banana peel sense of humour.'—*Variety*

Reflection of Fear
US 1971 90m Eastmancolor
Columbia (Howard B. Jaffe)

A retarded teenage girl kills her mother and her grandmother.
Psycho thriller of little interest or suspense.

w Edward Hume, Lewis John Carlino, *novel* Go to Thy Deathbed by Stanton Forbes *d* William A. Fraker *ph* Laszlo Kovacs *m* Fred Myrow

Robert Shaw, Mary Ure, Signe Hasso, Sondra Locke, Mitch Ryan

● *Video: RCA / Columbia*

Reflections in a Golden Eye*
US 1967 108m Technicolor
Warner Seven Arts (Ray Stark)

Repressions at a peacetime army camp in Georgia. A private soldier rides nude on horseback, a major has the hots for him, the major's wife has an affair with their neighbour, whose wife has cut off her nipples with garden shears.
A film as idiotic as its story line, but smoothly marshalled so that at least it's more amusing than boring.

w Chapman Mortimer, Gladys Hill, *novel* Carson McCullers *d* John Huston *ph* Aldo Tonti *pd* Stephen Grimes *m* Toshiro Mayuzumi

Marlon Brando, Elizabeth Taylor, Brian Keith, Julie Harris, Robert Forster, Zorro David

'One feels trapped in a huge overheated hothouse containing nothing but common snapdragons. Pedestrian, crass, and uninvolving to the point of repellence.'—*John Simon*
'Nothing more than nutty people and pseudo porn.'—*Judith Crist*

The Reformer and the Redhead*
US 1950 90m bw
MGM (Norman Panama, Melvin Frank)

A small-town reform candidate abandons his crooked protector and wins under his own steam, helped by the daughter of the zoo superintendent.
Scatty sub-Capra comedy with a lightweight script but good production and playing.

wd Norman Panama, Melvin Frank *ph* Ray June *m* David Raksin

Dick Powell, June Allyson, Cecil Kellaway, David Wayne, Ray Collins, Robert Keith, Marvin Kaplan

La Règle du Jeu***
France 1939 113m bw
La Nouvelle Edition Française
aka: *The Rules of the Game*

A count organizes a weekend shooting party which results in complex love intrigues among servants as well as masters.
Celebrated satirical comedy with a uniquely bleak outlook.

w Jean Renoir, Carl Koch *d* Jean Renoir *ph* Jean Bachelet, Alain Renoir *m* Joseph Kosma, Roger Desormières *ad* Eugène Lourié, Max Douy

Marcel Dalio, Nora Gregor, Jean Renoir, Mila Parély, Julien Carette, Gaston Modot, Roland Toutain

'It is a question of panache, of preserving a casual indifference to the workings of fate.'—*The Times*
'How brilliantly Renoir focuses the confusion! The rather fusty luxury of the chateau, the constant mindless slaughter of wild animals, the minuets of adultery and seduction, the gavottes of mutual hatred or mistrust. . .'—*Basil Wright, 1972*
† The film was originally banned as indicting the corruption of France, and during the war the negative was destroyed during an air raid; but eventually a full version was pieced together from various materials.

● *Video: Longman*

The Reincarnation of Peter Proud
US 1974 104m Technicolor
Avco Embassy / Bing Crosby (Frank P. Rosenberg)

A history professor is troubled by recurring dreams of his former existence.
Hysterical psychic melodrama which pretty well ruins its own chances by failing to explain its plot.

w Max Ehrlich, from his novel *d* J. Lee-Thompson *ph* Victor J. Kemper *m* Jerry Goldsmith

Michael Sarrazin, Jennifer O'Neill, Margot Kidder, Cornelia Sharpe, Paul Hecht

'It may well be the silliest approach to the subject in any medium . . . all flashbacks trampling the action with the finesse of a rogue elephant.'—*Tom Milne*

The Reivers*
US 1970 111m Technicolor
Panavision
Cinema Center / Duo / Solar (Irving Ravetch)

In Mississippi at the turn of the century a hired hand borrows the new family auto for a trip into Memphis with the grandson of the family and a black stablehand.
Pleasant but insubstantial yarn of more gracious days; most attractive to look at, it entertains gently without ever reaching a point.

w Irving Ravetch, Harriet Frank Jnr, *novel* William Faulkner *d* Mark Rydell *ph* Richard Moore *m* John Williams

Steve McQueen, Sharon Farrell, Will Geer, Rupert Crosse, Mitch Vogel, Michael Constantine, Juano Hernandez, Clifton James

AAN: John Williams; Rupert Crosse

Relentless
US 1948 93m Technicolor

A cowboy framed for murder must clear himself before the posse catches up with him.
Brisk western copy of *The 39 Steps*. Robert Young, Marguerite Chapman, Willard Parker, Barton Maclane, Will Wright. Written by Winston Miller; directed by George Sherman; for Columbia.

The Reluctant Debutante*
US 1958   96m   Metrocolor
  Cinemascope
MGM / Avon (Pandro S. Berman)

A noble couple have difficulty in steering their American-educated daughter through the intricacies of the London season.
A slight but pleasing British comedy has become a rather strident example of lend-lease, but still affords minor pleasures.

w William Douglas Home, from his play
d Vincente Minnelli ph Joseph Ruttenberg
md Eddie Warner ad Jean d'Aubonne

Rex Harrison, Kay Kendall, Sandra Dee, Peter Myers, Angela Lansbury, John Saxon, Diane Clare

The Reluctant Dragon**
US 1941   72m   Technicolor
Walt Disney

A tour of the Disney Studios affords some glimpses of how cartoons are made.
Amiable pot-pourri of cartoon shorts (Baby Weems, How to Ride a Horse and the title story) linked by a studio tour of absorbing interest.

w various d Alfred Werker (live action), various
Robert Benchley, Frances Gifford, Nana Bryant

Reluctant Heroes*
GB 1951   80m   bw
Byron (Henry Halstead)

Comedy of national servicemen and their misdemeanours.
Simple-minded army farce which was popular for years as play and film.

w Colin Morris, from his play d Jack Raymond
Brian Rix, Ronald Shiner, Derek Farr, Christine Norden, Larry Noble

The Reluctant Widow
GB 1950   91m   bw
Rank / Two Cities (Gordon Wellesley)

During the Napoleonic wars a governess is co-opted as a spy.
Thin romantic drama which despite nice art direction never really sparks into life.

w Gordon Wellesley, J. B. Boothroyd, novel Georgette Heyer d Bernard Knowles
ph Jack Hildyard ad Carmen Dillon

Jean Kent, Guy Rolfe, Kathleen Byron, Paul Dupuis, Lana Morris, Julian Dallas, Peter Hammond, Andrew Cruickshank

Remains to be Seen
US 1953   88m   bw
MGM (Arthur Hornblow Jnr)

The manager of an apartment house finds a dead body, and before the police arrive someone sticks a knife into it.
Flabby comedy-thriller giving the cast little to work on.

w Sidney Sheldon, play Howard Lindsay, Russel Crouse d Don Weis ph Robert Planck md Jeff Alexander

June Allyson, Van Johnson, Angela Lansbury, Louis Calhern, John Beal, Dorothy Dandridge

'By thunderation, I'll show America how to get tough!'

The Remarkable Andrew*
US 1942   80m   bw
Paramount (Richard Blumenthal)

A young municipal bookkeeper is framed by local politicians but helped by the ghost of Andrew Jackson and friends.
Pleasant, rather faded, whimsical comedy which also managed to be propaganda for the war effort.

w Dalton Trumbo d Stuart Heisler
ph Theodor Sparkuhl m Victor Young

William Holden, Ellen Drew, Brian Donlevy, Rod Cameron, Richard Webb, Porter Hall, Frances Gifford, Nydia Westman, Montagu Love

'About all that comes through in the juxtaposition of these lithograph characters over modern Shale City is Franklin's delight over the electric light and Jackson's alarm over the radio.'—John McManus, PM

The Remarkable Mr Pennypacker
US 1958   87m   Technicolor
  Cinemascope
TCF (Charles Brackett)

A Pennsylvania businessman leads two lives with two separate families.
Feeble and obvious period comedy of bigamy; very few laughs.

w Walter Reisch, play Liam O'Brien d Henry Levin ph Milton Krasner m Leigh Harline

Clifton Webb, Dorothy McGuire, Charles Coburn, Ray Stricklyn, Jill St John, Ron Ely, David Nelson

Rembrandt****
GB 1936   85m   bw
London Films (Alexander Korda)

Episodes in the life of the 17th-century painter.
Austerely comic, gently tragic character piece, superbly staged and photographed, with a great performance at its centre.

w Lajos Biro, June Head, Carl Zuckmayer
d Alexander Korda ph Georges Perinal, Richard Angst m Geoffrey Toye

Charles Laughton, Elsa Lanchester, Gertrude Lawrence, Edward Chapman, Walter Hudd, Roger Livesey, Herbert Lomas, Allan Jeayes, Sam Livesey, Raymond Huntley, John Clements

'Never exciting, and only partly believable . . . a feature film without a story plot.'—Variety

'Amazingly full of that light which the great master of painting subdued to his supreme purpose.'—James Agate

'The film is ruined by lack of story and continuity: it has no drive. Like The Private Life of Henry the Eighth it is a series of unrelated tableaux.'—Graham Greene

Remember?
US 1939   83m   bw
MGM (Milton Bren)

A newly married couple do not get on, so a friend gives them a potion which makes them lose their memories and fall in love all over again.
Silly, witless comedy which did no good for anyone concerned.

w Corey Ford, Norman Z. McLeod
d Norman Z. McLeod ph George Folsey
m Edward Ward

Robert Taylor, Greer Garson, Lew Ayres, Billie Burke, Reginald Owen, George Barbier, Henry Travers, Richard Carle, Laura Hope Crews, Halliwell Hobbes, Sig Rumann

'Many bright episodes contrast with some bumpy and over-dialogued stretches.'—Variety

Remember Last Night?**
US 1936   80m   bw
Universal

Socialites with hangovers find that murder was committed during their party.
Ingenious but overlong mixture of styles: farce, Thin Man comedy, murder mystery, satire, fantasy. Very well worth looking at.

w Harry Clark, Dan Totheroh, Doris Malloy, novel The Hangover Murders by Adam Hobhouse d James Whale ph Joseph Valentine m Franz Waxman

Robert Young, Edward Arnold, Arthur Treacher, Constance Cummings, Robert Armstrong, Sally Eilers, Reginald Denny, Ed Brophy, Jack La Rue, Gustav Von Seyffertitz, Gregory Ratoff

'It will be hard to sell because it is hard to understand . . . the basic story can scarcely be followed, while the superficial gloss of phoney sophistication neither fits a narrative in which four murders and two suicides are recorded, nor carries conviction of itself.'—Variety

'Parodying the detective thriller in a dazzling cascade of gags, this brilliant divertissement eventually takes off into pure surrealism.'—Tom Milne, MFB, 1974

Remember My Name*
US 1978   94m   De Luxe
Lion's Gate (Robert Altman)

After twelve years in prison, a woman takes calm revenge on the man who allowed her to take the blame for his crime.
Basically reminiscent of a Barbara Stanwyck vehicle of the forties, this interesting film is finally too concerned to strike on all levels, including satire, social awareness and fashionable pessimism.

wd Alan Rudolph ph Tak Fujimoto

Geraldine Chaplin, Anthony Perkins, Moses Gunn, Berry Berenson, Jeff Goldblum

Remember the Day*
US 1941   86m   bw
TCF (William Perlberg)

An elderly schoolteacher recollects her past life.

Pleasant sentimental drama, very well
mounted.

w Tess Schlesinger, Frank Davis, Allan Scott,
play Philo Higley d Henry King ph George
Barnes m Alfred Newman

Claudette Colbert, John Payne, Shepperd
Strudwick, Jane Seymour, Anne Revere,
Frieda Inescort

Remember the Night*
US 1940 94m bw
Paramount (Mitchell Leisen)

An assistant district attorney takes a lady
shoplifter home with him for Christmas.
Eccentric but winning blend of comedy,
romance and drama, deftly mixed by master
chefs.

w Preston Sturges d Mitchell Leisen ph Ted
Tetzlaff m Frederick Hollander

Barbara Stanwyck, Fred MacMurray, Beulah
Bondi, Elizabeth Patterson, Sterling
Holloway, Paul Guilfoyle, Willard Robertson

Remembrance
GB 1982 117m Eastmancolor
Colin Gregg / Channel Four

Young sailors in Plymouth enjoy a last night's
leave before a six-month tour of duty with the
NATO forces.
A few slices of what in the eyes of film-makers
passes for realism these days; boozing,
violence and bad language. The film seems to
make no point and certainly doesn't entertain,
though the components are slickly enough
assembled.

w Hugh Stoddart d Colin Gregg ph John
Metcalfe m various pop performances
ed Peter Delfgou

John Altman, Al Ashton, Martin Barrass,
Nick Dunning, Sally Jane Jackson, David
John, Peter Lee-Wilson, Kenneth Griffith
  'A clear and disheartening case of ambition
exceeding grasp.'—Geoff Brown, MFB

Remorques*
France 1941 80m bw
MAIC
US title: Stormy Waters

A tugboat captain falls in love with a
mysterious woman but remains faithful to his
invalid wife.
Effective, minor, romantic melodrama.

w Jacques Prévert, André Cayatte,
novel Roger Vercel d Jean Grémillon
ph Armand Thirard, Louis Née m Roland
Manuel

Jean Gabin, Michèle Morgan, Madeleine
Renaud, Fernand Ledoux

Rendezvous
US 1935 106m bw
MGM (Lawrence Weingarten)

A decoding expert breaks an enemy spy ring.
Agreeable light romantic comedy drama with
an espionage plot.

w Bella and Samuel Spewack, novel Black
Chamber by Herbert Yardley d William K.
Howard ph William Daniels m William Axt

William Powell, Rosalind Russell, Binnie
Barnes, Lionel Atwill, Cesar Romero, Samuel
S. Hinds, Henry Stephenson, Frank Reicher
  'Another chill-and-chuckle play aiming at
the Thin Man trade and scoring a
bull's-eye.'—Variety

Rendezvous at Midnight
US 1935 60m bw

A police commissioner investigates the murder
of his predecessor. Modest mystery co-feature
which wastes time up front on a fashion show.
Ralph Bellamy, Valerie Hobson, Catherine
Doucet, Irene Ware, Helen Jerome Eddy.
Written by Gladys Unger from the play The
Silver Fox by Gaetano Sazlo; directed by
Christy Cabanne; for Universal. 'The woeful
lack of action drags it down.'—Variety

Rendezvous de Juillet**
France 1949 110m bw
UGC–SNEG (René G. Vuattoux)

A group of young people in post-war St
Germain-des-Pres plan an expedition to the
Congo.
Highly likeable series of impressions of
interesting people, a little indeterminate and
possibly dated now, but in its time extremely
fresh and vital.

wd Jacques Becker ph Claude Renoir m Jean
Wiener, Mezzmezzrow

Daniel Gelin, Maurice Ronet, Brigitte Auber,
Pierre Trabaud, Nicole Courcel

Les Rendezvous du Diable**
France 1958 80m colour
Union Générale Cinématographique /
  Jacques Constant / Haroun Tazieff
aka: Volcano

Adventures of a Belgian volcanologist.
Daring exploits on the rims of the world's
most active volcanoes, including Etna and
Stromboli in eruption. Fascinating footage is
urbanely presented.

w, d, ph Haroun Tazieff m Marius-François
Gaillard
  'Beauty blends with horror, romantic
grandeur with fear.'—MFB

Rendezvous with Annie
US 1946 89m bw

An American soldier in England goes absent
without leave to see his wife in New York, an
exploit which later nearly loses him a fortune.
An engaging comedy idea filmed with
insufficient wit, this gets by on charm. Eddie
Albert, Faye Marlowe, C. Aubrey Smith.
Written by Mary Loos and Richard Sale;
directed by Allan Dwan; for Republic.

Renegades
US 1930 84m bw

A disgraced French officer becomes a hero of
the Foreign Legion. Satisfying romantic
melodrama of its period. Warner Baxter,
Myrna Loy, Bela Lugosi, Noah Beery, C.
Henry Gordon, Gregory Gaye. Written by

Jules Furthman from a novel by André
Armandy; directed by Victor Fleming; for
Fox. 'Everyone in the picture dies in the last
few feet.'—Variety

Renegades
US 1946 88m Technicolor

An outlaw's son tries in vain to go straight.
Unsurprising but efficient bill-topping western
of its day. Evelyn Keyes, Larry Parks, Willard
Parker, Edgar Buchanan. Written by Melvin
Levey and Francis Faragoh; directed by
George Sherman; for Columbia.

Reno
US 1939 72m bw

As Reno becomes a great city for gambling
and divorce, a lawyer becomes a gambling hall
proprietor. Mildly interesting romantic drama
in a flashback format. Richard Dix, Gail
Patrick, Anita Louise, Paul Cavanagh, Laura
Hope Crews, Louis Jean Heydt, Hobart
Cavanaugh, Charles Halton. Written by John
Twist, Ellis St Joseph; directed by John
Farrow; for RKO. 'Capable handling of an
interesting story against a colourful
background.'—Variety

Rentadick
GB 1972 94m Eastmancolor
Rank / Paradine / Virgin (Ned Sherrin)

Incompetent private eyes become involved in
the battle for a deadly nerve gas.
Ineffective crazy comedy which never takes
shape, preferring to aim barbs of satire in all
directions.

w John Cleese, Graham Chapman d Jim
Clark ph John Coquillon m Carl Davis

James Booth, Richard Briers, Julie Ege,
Donald Sinden, Roy Kinnear

Repeat Performance*
US 1947 93m bw
Eagle Lion / Aubrey Schenck

People in trouble find they can repeat the
previous year.
Adequate flashback fantasy, very dated now.

w Walter Bullock d Alfred L. Werker
ph Lew O'Connell m George Antheil

Louis Hayward, Joan Leslie, Tom Conway,
Richard Basehart, Virginia Field

Report to the Commissioner
US 1974 112m Metrocolor
UA / M. J. Frankovich
GB title: Operation Undercover

A policeman's son follows in father's footsteps
but finds life around Times Square dismaying.
Realistic, concerned crime melodrama with
nothing very new to say.

w Abby Mann, Ernest Tidyman, novel James
Mills d Milton Katselas ph Mario Tosi
m Elmer Bernstein

Michael Moriarty, Yaphet Kotto, Susan
Blakely, Hector Elizondo, Tony King,
Michael McGuire

'A clear also-ran in the police thriller stakes.'—*Verina Glaessner*

'A bit too full of sweat and frenzy.'—*Michael Billington, Illustrated London News*

The Reptile*
GB 1966 90m Technicolor
Hammer (Anthony Nelson Keys)

A Cornish village is terrified by several mysterious and unpleasant deaths; it turns out that the daughter of the local doctor, victim of a Malayan sect, periodically turns into a deadly snake.
Silly horror story most effectively filmed as a mixture of chills, detection and good characterization.

w John Elder d John Gilling ph Arthur Grant m Don Banks

Noel Willman, Jennifer Daniel, Ray Barrett, Jaqueline Pearce, Michael Ripper, John Laurie, Marne Maitland

Repulsion**
GB 1965 105m bw
Compton / Tekli (Gene Gutowski)

A Belgian manicurist in London is driven by pressures into neurotic withdrawal; terrified above all by sex, she locks herself up in her gloomy flat and murders her boy friend and landlord when they try to approach her.
Weird, unmotivated but undeniably effective Grand Guignol in the form of a case history; little dialogue, which is just as well as the director at that time clearly had no ear for the language.

w Roman Polanski, Gerard Brach d Roman Polanski ph Gilbert Taylor m Chico Hamilton

Catherine Deneuve, Ian Hendry, John Fraser, Patrick Wymark, Yvonne Furneaux
'An unashamedly ugly film, but as a lynx-eyed view of a crumbling mind it is a masterpiece of the macabre.'—*Daily Mail*
● *Video: Video Media*

Requiem for a Heavyweight*
US 1962 87m bw
Columbia (David Susskind)
GB title: *Blood Money*

The last bouts of a prizefighter who will not realize his career is over.
Tough, effective melodrama, extremely well acted.

w Rod Serling, from his TV play *d Ralph Nelson ph Arthur J. Ornitz m Laurence Rosenthal*

Anthony Quinn, *Jackie Gleason, Mickey Rooney*, Julie Harris, Stan Adams, Madame Spivy, Jack Dempsey, Cassius Clay

The Rescuers*
US 1977 77m Technicolor
Walt Disney (Ron Miller)

The Mouse Rescue Aid Society volunteer to bring back a girl lost in a swamp.
Feature-length cartoon which, while by no means as bad as some of Disney's very routine seventies product, still seems light years away from his classics of the thirties.

w various, from stories by Margery Sharp *d* Wolfgang Reitherman, John Lounsbery, Art Stevens
'The people who really need rescuing are the Disney animators and cameramen.'—*Time Out*
'It's no *Snow White* but there are long moments when its inventiveness and skill are entirely captivating. I have only this one lingering doubt: if you are going to put this amount of effort into a movie shouldn't you have more at the end than a snappy collection of 330,000 drawings and a bill for six million dollars?'—*Barry Took, Punch*
AAN: song, 'Someone's Waiting for You'

'Torn from the blazing pages of Texas history!'
The Restless Breed
US 1957 81m Eastmancolor by Pathé

The son of a secret service agent arrives in a frontier town to avenge his father's death.
Standard star western full of expected elements. Scott Brady, Anne Bancroft, Jay C. Flippen, Jim Davis, Rhys Williams. Written by Steve Fisher; directed by Allan Dwan; for Edward L. Alperson.

The Restless Years
US 1959 86m bw Cinemascope

A small-town dressmaker tries to prevent her daughter from discovering that she is illegitimate. Antediluvian sudser with second-string talent. John Saxon, Sandra Dee, Margaret Lindsay, Luana Patten, Virginia Grey. Written by Edward Anhalt, from the play *Teach Me How to Cry* by Patricia Joudry; directed by Helmut Kautner; for Universal-International.

Resurrection
US 1931 81m bw
Universal

In 1870s Russia, a peasant girl is seduced by a prince and bears his child.
Unremarkable version of a much-filmed melodrama.

w Finis Fox, novel Leo Tolstoy d Edwin Carewe ph Robert B. Kurrle, Al Green m Dmitri Tiomkin

Lupe Velez, John Boles, Nance O'Neil, William Keighley, Rose Tapley
† See also: *We Live Again.*

Resurrection
US 1981 103m Technicolor
Universal (Renee Missel, Howard Rosenman)

A woman who has escaped death in a car crash finds herself miraculously able to heal others.
Curious modern parable with nowhere to go; even religious reactionaries may find it rather boring.

w Lewis John Carlino d Daniel Petrie ph Mario Tosi m Maurice Jarre

Ellen Burstyn, Sam Shepard, Richard Farnsworth, Eva LeGallienne, Roberts Blossom, Clifford David
AAN: Ellen Burstyn; Eva LeGallienne (supporting actress)

Retreat, Hell!
US 1952 95m bw
(Warner) United States (Milton Sperling)

Adventures of a Marine unit in the Korean War.
Standard war film.

w Milton Sperling, Ted Sherdeman d Joseph H. Lewis ph Warren Lynch m William Lava

Frank Lovejoy, Richard Carlson, Anita Louise, Russ Tamblyn

Return from the Ashes*
GB 1965 104m bw Panavision
UA / Mirisch (J. Lee-Thompson)

A woman returns from Dachau to find that her husband is living with her step-daughter and that they plan to murder her.
Broken-backed thriller melodrama, the first half of which is quite irrelevant to the second. The whole is modestly inventive for those who don't mind a mixture of *Enoch Arden, Psycho* and *Dial M for Murder* with a touch of concentration camps and a background of post-war misery.

w Julius J. Epstein, novel Hubert Monteilhet d J. Lee-Thompson ph Christopher Challis m Johnny Dankworth

Ingrid Thulin, Maximilian Schell, Samantha Eggar, Herbert Lom

Return from Witch Mountain
US 1978 93m Technicolor
Walt Disney (Ron Miller, Jerome Courtland)

A brother and sister from outer space come back to earth for a vacation and are used by crooks for their own purposes.
Acceptable sequel to *Escape from Witch Mountain*, with improved special effects.

w Malcolm Marmorstein d John Hough ph Frank Phillips m Lalo Schifrin sp Eustace Lycett, Art Cruickshank, Danny Lee

Bette Davis, Christopher Lee, Ike Eisenmann, Kim Richards, Jack Soo

The Return of a Man Called Horse*
US 1976 125m De Luxe Panavision
UA / Sandy Howard / Richard Harris

The English nobleman of *A Man Called Horse* goes back to the west to save his adopted Indian tribe from extinction.
Another 'realistic' action adventure with torture highlights; nicely made, but not for the squeamish.

w Jack de Witt d Irvin Kershner ph Owen Roizman m Laurence Rosenthal

Richard Harris, Gale Sondergaard, Geoffrey Lewis, Bill Lucking, Jorge Luke
'Maintains a tidy balance between nausea and boredom.'—*Judith Crist*
† At 17 minutes, this pre-title sequence must be the longest so far.

The Return of Bulldog Drummond
GB 1934 71m bw

Drummond forms a society to oust crooked foreigners from Britain. Good Drummond exploit with traces of the original Fascism. Ralph Richardson, Ann Todd, Francis L. Sullivan, Claud Allister, Joyce Kennedy. Written and directed by Walter Summers, from the novel *The Black Gang* by 'Sapper'; for BIP.

The Return of Dr X*
US 1939 62 bw
Warner (Bryan Foy)

A modern vampire terrorizes the city. Minor thriller which doesn't get going till the last reel; only notable for Bogart's appearance as the monster. Nothing to do with *Dr X*.

w Lee Katz, *novel* The Doctor's Secret by William J. Makin *d* Vincent Sherman *ph* Sid Hickox *m* Bernhard Kaun

Dennis Morgan, Rosemary Lane, Wayne Morris, Humphrey Bogart, Olin Howland, John Litel

The Return of Dracula*
US 1958 77m bw
UA / Gramercy (Jules V. Levy, Arthur Gardner)
GB title: *The Fantastic Disappearing Man*

A European vampire makes his way to an American small town in the guise of a refugee Iron Curtain painter.
Quite nicely made low-budget horror film with a good balance of the supernatural and the ordinary.

w Pat Fielder *d* Paul Landres *ph* Jack McKenzie *m* Gerald Fried

Francis Lederer, Norman Eberhardt, Ray Stricklyn, Jimmie Baird, John Wengraf

The Return of Frank James*
US 1940 92m Technicolor
TCF (Darry F. Zanuck)

A sequel to *Jesse James* (qv).
Moody, nicely photographed western in which Jesse's brother avenges his murder.

w Sam Hellman *d* Fritz Lang *ph* George Barnes, William V. Skall *m* David Buttolph

Henry Fonda, Gene Tierney, Jackie Cooper, Henry Hull, John Carradine, J. Edward Bromberg, Donald Meek, Eddie Collins, George Barbier
'I doubt if any character was ever as lily white as that of Frank James here, but that is a present from the Hays Office to you, and anyway the part is played by Henry Fonda. Durn if I don't like that boy.'—*Otis Ferguson*

The Return of Martin Guerre*
France 1982 123m Fujicolor

In the sixteenth century, a man comes to a French village claiming to be the one who left his wife and child eight years before.
Complaints are laid that he is an impostor . . . Mildly intriguing story which falls apart because one is never sure where the film's sympathies lie. Gérard Depardieu, Nathalie Baye, Sylvie Meda, Maurice Barrier. Written by Jean-Claude Carrière, Daniel Vigne; directed by Daniel Vigne; for Marcel Dassault / SFP. 'By far the most enigmatic film

seen in London this year.'—*Sunday Times*. 'A plodding, confusing narrative that neither does proper justice to the story nor really teases out the complex historical, moral and psychological issues which it raises.'—*Observer* (Original title: *Le Retour de Martin Guerre*.)

The Return of October
US 1948 89m Technicolor

A girl's inheritance is contested on the grounds that she thinks a horse is the reincarnation of her Uncle Willie. Thin whimsy which leaves its stars with egg on their faces. Glenn Ford, Terry Moore, Dame May Whitty, James Gleason, Albert Sharpe. Written by Norman Panama and Melvin Frank; directed by Joseph H. Lewis; for Columbia. (GB title: *A Date with Destiny*.)

The Return of Peter Grimm
US 1935 82m bw

A strong-minded family man returns as a ghost to see how his family is getting on without him. Fairly satisfying fantasy with good performances. Lionel Barrymore, Helen Mack, Edward Ellis, Donald Meek. Written by Francis Edwards Faragoh from the play by David Belasco; directed by George Nicholls Jnr; for RKO. (Previously filmed in 1925 with Alec B. Francis and Janet Gaynor.) 'Sombre fantasy . . . pretty dull and boresome.'—*Variety*

Return of the Ape Man: see The Ape Man

The Return of the Bad Men
US 1948 90m bw
RKO (Nat Holt)

A farmer tries to reform the female leader of a terrorist outlaw gang, but she is killed in a bank raid.
Standard, well shot western which contrives to introduce a number of well-known historical bandits.

w Charles O'Neal, Jack Netteford, Luci Ward *d* Ray Enright *ph* J. Roy Hunt *m* Roy Webb *md* Constantin Bakaleinikoff

Randolph Scott, Robert Ryan, Anne Jeffreys, Jacqueline White, Steve Brodie

'Riding to greater glory as the gay O. Henry hero!'
The Return of the Cisco Kid
US 1939 70m bw

The Kid escapes a Mexican firing squad into Arizona and defeats swindlers. Modest western with plenty of zip. Warner Baxter, Lynn Bari, Cesar Romero, Henry Hull, Kane Richmond, C. Henry Gordon, Robert Barrat. Written by Milton Sperling; directed by Herbert I. Leeds; for Kenneth MacGowan / TCF. 'Substantial fare for adventure audiences.'—*Variety*

Return of the Frontiersman
US 1950 74m Technicolor

A man escapes from prison to prove himself innocent of the bank robbery for which he was

convicted. Goodish double-bill western with no surprises. Gordon Macrae, Julie London, Rory Calhoun, Fred Clark, Edwin Rand. Written by Edna Anhalt; directed by Richard Bare; for Warner.

Return of the Jedi*
US 1983 132m De Luxe Panavision
TCF / Lucasfilm (Howard Kazanjian)

'Episode 6' of the *Star Wars* serial: our heroes combat Darth Vader and Jabba the Hutt.
More expensive fantasy for the world's children of all ages, especially the undemanding ones.

w Lawrence Kasdan, George Lucas *d* Richard Marquand *ph* Alan Hume *pd* Norman Reynolds *m* John Williams

Mark Hamill, Harrison Ford, Carrie Fisher, Billy Dee Williams, Anthony Daniels, Peter Mayhew, Kenny Baker
'I admire the exquisite skill and talent which have been poured into these films, while finding the concepts behind these gigantic video games in the sky mindlessly tedious.'—*Margaret Hinxman, Daily Mail*
'An impersonal and rather junky piece of moviemaking.'—*Pauline Kael, New Yorker*
'Only the effects are special.'—*Sight and Sound*
AAN: John Williams; art direction

The Return of the Pink Panther*
GB 1974 113m De Luxe Panavision
UA / Jewel / Pimlico / Mirisch / Geoffrey (Blake Edwards)

When the Pink Panther diamond – national treasure of the Eastern state of Lugash – is once again stolen, bungling Inspector Clouseau is called in.
Rehash of jokes from *The Pink Panther* (qv), not bad in parts but a rather tedious whole.

w Frank Waldman, Blake Edwards *d* Blake Edwards *ph* Geoffrey Unsworth *m* Henry Mancini

Peter Sellers, Christopher Plummer, Herbert Lom, Catherine Schell, Peter Arne, Peter Jeffrey, Grégoire Aslan, David Lodge, Graham Stark
'The film never comes fully to the boil, but simmers in a series of self-contained, self-destructing little set pieces.'—*Richard Combs*
'The first film in history to be upstaged by its own credit titles.'—*Benny Green, Punch*
● Video: Precision

The Return of the Scarlet Pimpernel*
GB 1937 94m bw
London Films (Alexander Korda, Arnold Pressburger)

Sir Percy Blakeney saves his wife and other French aristos from the guillotine.
Predictable, stylish revolutionary romance, much thinner in plot and performance than its predecessor.

w Lajos Biro, Arthur Wimperis, Adrian Brunel *d* Hans Schwarz *ph* Mutz Greenbaum *m* Arthur Benjamin

Barry K. Barnes, Sophie Stewart, Margaretta
Scott, James Mason, *Henry Oscar,* Francis
Lister, Anthony Bushell

The Return of the Seven

US 1966   95m   Technicolor   Panavision
UA / Mirisch / CB (Ted Richmond)

The seven gunmen, slightly reconstituted, fight
again to rescue some kidnapped farmers.
The mixture as before (see *The Magnificent
Seven*); adequate but scarcely inspired.

w Larry Cohen   *d* Burt Kennedy   *ph* Paul
Vogel   *m* Elmer Bernstein

Yul Brynner, Robert Fuller, Julian Mateos,
Warren Oates, Claude Akins, Virgilio
Texeira, Emilio Fernandez, Jordan
Christopher

AAN: Elmer Bernstein

The Return of the Soldier*

GB 1982   102m   Technicolor
Brent Walker / Barry R. Cooper (Ann
Skinner, Simon Relph)

In 1916, a shellshocked soldier returns home,
able to remember his old sweetheart but not
his wife.
Overcast and heavy-handed treatment of a
classy novella.

w Hugh Whitemore, *novel* Rebecca West
d Alan Bridges   *ph* Stephen Goldblatt
m Richard Rodney Bennett   *pd* Luciana
Arrighi

Alan Bates, Ann-Margret, Julie Christie,
Glenda Jackson, Jeremy Kemp, Edward de
Souza, Frank Finlay, Jack May, Ian Holm
  'The film has nowhere to go except into
rhetorical bluster about class distinctions.'—
Tom Milne, MFB
● *Video: Guild*

The Return of the Terror

US 1934   65m   bw

A scientist feigns insanity to avoid prosecution
for murder, and escapes to his old sanatorium,
where murder strikes again. Barnstorming
murder mystery borrowing its title and nothing
else from Edgar Wallace. John Halliday, Mary
Astor, Lyle Talbot, Frank McHugh, Irving
Pichel, J. Carrol Naish. Written by Eugene
Solow and Peter Milne; directed by Howard
Bretherton; for Warner. 'Formula mystery,
but speedy.'—*Variety*

The Return of the Vampire*

US 1943   69m   bw
Columbia (Sam White)

Dracula reappears amid the London blitz.
Surprisingly well made and complexly plotted
horror film; it looks good and only lacks
humour. The wolf man, however, is a
regrettable intrusion.

w Griffin Jay   *d* Lew Landers   *ph* John
Stumar, L. J. O'Connell   *m* Mario
Castelnuovo-Tedesco   *md* Morris Stoloff

Bela Lugosi, Nina Foch, Frieda Inescort,
Miles Mander, Matt Willis, Roland Varno,
Ottola Nesmith

Return to Glennascaul*

Eire 1951   23m   bw
Dublin Gate Theatre

Orson Welles gives a man a lift and is told a
gentle ghost story.
Neither very satisfying nor very well done, this
little film deserves a niche in history because
of the talents involved. It was apparently
made during one of the many intervals in the
filming of *Othello*.

wd Hilton Edwards   *narrator* Orson Welles

Return to Macon County

US 1975   89m   Movielab
AIP / Macon Service Company (Eliot
Schick)

In the fifties, two wandering youths pick up a
waitress and have serious trouble with a manic
policeman in America's unfriendliest area.
Slam-bang sequel to *Macon County Line,*
rather unintentionally comic.

wd Richard Compton   *ph* Jacques Marquette
m Robert O. Ragland

Nick Nolte, Don Johnson, Robin Mattson,
Robert Viharo

Return to Paradise*

US 1953   109m   Technicolor
UA / Aspen (Theron Warth)

A peace seeker settles on a tiny South Sea
island and leaves when his wife dies; he
returns after World War II with his daughter.
Curious idyll, slow but not displeasing.

w Charles Kaufman, *novel* James Michener
d Mark Robson   *ph* Winton Hoch   *m* Dmitri
Tiomkin

Gary Cooper, Barry Jones, Roberta Haynes,
Moira MacDonald

Return to Peyton Place*

US 1961   122m   De Luxe   Cinemascope
TCF / API (Jerry Wald)

Constance Mackenzie's daughter writes a
novel about Peyton Place and falls in love with
the publisher.
More closets are unlocked, more skeletons fall
out; for addicts, the sequel does not
disappoint, and it's all very glossy.

w Ronald Alexander   *d* Jose Ferrer
ph Charles G. Clarke   *m* Franz Waxman

Jeff Chandler, Carol Lynley, Eleanor Parker,
Mary Astor, Robert Sterling, Luciana Paluzzi,
Brett Halsey, Tuesday Weld
  'Enough soap suds to pollute the Mississippi
along with the mind.'—*Judith Crist, 1973*

Return to Yesterday

GB 1940   68m   bw

A bored Hollywood star seeks anonymity in a
seaside repertory company. Mild comedy, not
without interest. Clive Brook, Anna Lee,
Dame May Whitty, Hartley Power, Milton
Rosmer, David Tree, Olga Lindo. Written by
Robert Stevenson, Margaret Kennedy, Roland
Pertwee and Angus MacPhail, from the play
Goodness How Sad by Robert Morley;
directed by Robert Stevenson; for Ealing.

Reuben, Reuben*

US 1982   101m   CFI colour
Saltair / Taft (Walter Shenson)

A drunken British poet upsets a New England
community.
Oddball comedy at which one laughs without
much enthusiasm.

w Julius J. Epstein, *novel* Peter de Vries and
play Spofford by Herman Shumlin   *d* Robert
Ellis Miller   *ph* Peter Stein   *m* Billy
Goldenberg   *pd* Peter Larkin

Tom Conti, Kelly McGillis, Roberts Blossom,
Cynthia Harris, Joel Fabiani

AAN: Tom Conti; adaptation

Reunion

US 1936   83m   bw

When a doctor retires, the townsfolk reunite
him with many of the children he has brought
into the world. Tiresome second attempt to
cash in on the Dionne Quintuplets, who make
several appearances. Jean Hersholt, Rochelle
Hudson, Helen Vinson, Slim Summerville, J.
Edward Bromberg, Sara Haden. Written by
Sam Hellman, Gladys Lehman, Sonya Levien;
directed by Norman Taurog; for Darryl
Zanuck / TCF. 'Too episodic to command
interest or supply suspense.'—*Variety*
† NB: a sequel to *The Country Doctor*.

Reunion in France

US 1943   104m   bw
MGM (Joseph L. Mankiewicz)
GB title: *Mademoiselle France*

A selfish Parisian dress designer gradually
realizes that her world has changed when the
Nazis invade and she is asked to help an
American flier.
Action flagwaver which tries also to be a
woman's picture and goes pretty soppily about
it.

w Jan Lustig, Marvin Borowsky, Marc
Connelly, *story* Ladislas Bus-Fekete   *d* Jules
Dassin   *ph* Robert Planck   *m* Franz Waxman

Joan Crawford, John Wayne, Philip Dorn,
Reginald Owen, Albert Basserman, John
Carradine, Ann Ayars, J. Edward Bromberg,
Henry Daniell, Moroni Olsen, Howard da
Silva
  'Miss Crawford isn't making all the sacrifices
implied in the script . . . Dressing like a
refugee is certainly not in her contract.'—*New
York Herald Tribune*

Reunion in Vienna*

US 1933   100m   bw
MGM

A long-exiled nobleman tries to take up an old
romance even though the lady is married.
Lacklustre adaptation of a play which must
have style; the performances remain
interesting.

w Ernest Vajda, Claudine West, *play* Robert
E. Sherwood   *d* Sidney Franklin   *ph* George
Folsey

John Barrymore, Diana Wynyard, Frank Morgan, May Robson, Eduardo Ciannelli, Una Merkel, Henry Travers
'Unlikely money film outside a few of the larger cities.'—*Variety*

AAN: George Folsey

Revenge
GB 1971   89m   Eastmancolor
Rank / Peter Rogers Productions (George H. Brown)

When children are raped and murdered in a north country town, two men take the law into their own hands.
Crude melodrama set in Cold Comfort Farm country; efficient but unrewarding.

w John Kruse *d* Sidney Hayers *ph* Ken Hodges *m* Eric Rodgers

Joan Collins, Sinead Cusack, James Booth, Ray Barrett, Kenneth Griffith

The Revenge of Frankenstein
GB 1958   89m   Technicolor
Columbia / Hammer (Anthony Hinds)

Baron Frankenstein evades the guillotine and makes a new creature with the brain of a homicidal dwarf.
Dullish horror farrago with a few indications of quirkish humour.

w Jimmy Sangster, Hurford Janes *d* Terence Fisher *ph* Jack Asher *m* Leonard Salzedo

Peter Cushing, Michael Gwynn, Oscar Quitak, Francis Matthews, Eunice Gayson, John Welsh, Lionel Jeffries, Richard Wordsworth, Charles Lloyd Pack, John Stuart, Arnold Diamond
† This second Hammer Frankenstein set the tone for the rest; see *The Curse of Frankenstein.*

The Revenge of the Pink Panther
US 1978   98m   Technicolor   Panavision
UA / Blake Edwards

Inspector Clouseau tracks down a drug-smuggling industrialist.
Feeble addition to a series which was always too pleased with itself.

w Frank Waldman, Ron Clarke, Blake Edwards *d* Blake Edwards *ph* Ernie Day *m* Henry Mancini

Peter Sellers, Herbert Lom, Robert Webber, Dyan Cannon, Burt Kwouk, Paul Stewart, Robert Loggia, Graham Stark

● *Video: Intervision*

The Revengers
US 1972   108m   De Luxe   Panavision
Cinema Center / Martin Rackin

A rancher gathers a posse to hunt down the Indians who have allegedly murdered his wife and family.
Standard major western with a dismal script which echoes *The Dirty Dozen* and *The Wild Bunch:* sometimes repulsive, seldom exciting.

w Wendell Mayes *d* Daniel Mann *ph* Gabriel Torres *m* Pino Calvi

William Holden, Ernest Borgnine, Susan Hayward, Woody Strode, Roger Hanin

The Revolt of Mamie Stover
US 1956   93m   Eastmancolor
   Cinemascope
TCF (Buddy Adler)

A dance hall girl leaves San Francisco for Honolulu, makes money there but reforms for love of a rich novelist.
Absurdly bowdlerized and boring film version of a novel about a sleazy prostitute; hardly worth making at all in this form, especially as the cast seems well capable of a raunchier version.

w Sidney Boehm, *novel* William Bradford Huie *d* Raoul Walsh *ph* Leo Tover *m* Hugo Friedhofer

Jane Russell, Agnes Moorehead, Richard Egan, Joan Leslie

The Revolutionary
US 1970   101m   Technicolor
(UA) Pressman—Williams (Edward R. Pressman)

Episodes in the life of a revolutionary, from distributing leaflets to attempted assassination. A rather casual study of one man's radicalism, in no particular time or place; no doubt of great interest to other revolutionaries.

w Hans Konigsberger *d* Paul Williams *ph* Brian Probyn *m* Michael Small

Jon Voight, Jennifer Salt, Robert Duvall

The Reward
US 1965   92m   De Luxe   Cinemascope
TCF / Aaron Rosenberg

A mixed group of adventurers set out across the desert to capture a murderer; but thieves fall out.
Pretentious and talky melodrama which quickly scuttled its director's chances in Hollywood. Little action, obvious outcome, attractive Death Valley locations.

w Serge Bourgignon, Oscar Mullard, *novel* Michael Barrett *d* Serge Bourgignon *ph* Joe MacDonald *m* Elmer Bernstein

Max Von Sydow, Efrem Zimbalist Jnr, Yvette Mimieux, Gilbert Roland, Emilio Fernandez, Henry Silva

'Emotions clash in a crescendo of drama!'

Rhapsody
US 1954   116m   Technicolor
MGM (Lawrence Weingarten)

A wealthy woman affects the lives of two quite different musicians, each of whom has his weakness.
Tedious romantic drama which vainly attempted a smart veneer but boasted a splendid musical sound track.

w Fay and Michael Kanin, *novel* Maurice Guest by Henry Handel Richardson *d* Charles Vidor *ph* Robert Planck *md* Johnny Green, Bronislau Kaper *pianist* Claudio Arrau *violinist* Michael Rabin

Elizabeth Taylor, Vittorio Gassman, John Ericson, Louis Calhern, Michael Chekhov, Barbara Bates, Celia Lovsky, Richard Hageman

Rhapsody in Blue**
US 1945   139m   bw
Warner (Jesse L. Lasky)

The life story of composer George Gershwin. No more trustworthy on factual matters than other Hollywood biopics of its era, this rather glum saga at least presented the music and the performers to excellent advantage.

w Howard Koch, Elliot Paul *d* Irving Rapper *ph* Sol Polito *md* Ray Heindorf, Max Steiner *ch* Le Roy Prinz *ad* Anton Grot, John Hughes

Robert Alda, Joan Leslie, Alexis Smith, Charles Coburn, Julie Bishop, *Albert Basserman, Oscar Levant, Herbert Rudley,* Rosemary de Camp, Morris Carnovsky, Al Jolson, Paul Whiteman, George White, Hazel Scott
'With no story at all, this two-hour concert of Gershwin music would be well worth the price of admission '—*Daily Mail*

AAN: Ray Heindorf, Max Steiner

Rhino
US 1964   91m   Metrocolor
MGM / Ivan Tors (Ben Chapman)

A scientist working with white rhinos is joined by an unscrupulous big game hunter.
Inoffensive African adventure.

w Art Arthur, Arthur Weiss *d* Ivan Tors *ph* Sven Persson, Lamar Boren *m* Lalo Schifrin

Harry Guardino, Robert Culp, Shirley Eaton

Rhodes of Africa*
GB 1936   91m   bw
Gaumont (Geoffrey Barkas)
US title: *Rhodes*

A rough-hewn diamond miner becomes Prime Minister of Cape Colony.
Heavy-going but generally interesting historical drama shot on location.

w Michael Barringer, Leslie Arliss, Miles Malleson, *book* Sarah Millin *d* Berthold Viertel

Walter Huston, Oscar Homolka, Basil Sydney, Peggy Ashcroft, Frank Cellier, Bernard Lee, Lewis Casson
'One of the better English-made pictures . . . should do all right even if it doesn't get the women.'—*Variety*
'Solid, worthy, humourless, it unrolls its eleven well-bred reels with all the technical advantages of 1936.'—*Graham Greene*

Rhubarb
US 1951   94m   bw
Paramount (Perlberg—Seaton)

A millionaire leaves his fortune, including a baseball team, to a wild ginger cat, which means problems for his publicity agent.
Typical scatty farce of the early fifties, held together by the splendid performance of the disdainful feline in the title role rather than by any special merit in the handling.

w Dorothy Reid, Francis Cockrill, *novel*
H. Allen Smith *d* Arthur Lubin *ph* Lionel
Lindon *m* Van Cleave

Ray Milland, Jan Sterling, Gene Lockhart,
William Frawley

Rhubarb
GB 1969 37m Technicolor

Various village notables congregate on the golf
course. Virtually silent comedy (nobody says
anything but 'rhubarb') which could have been
very funny with better jokes. A TV remake in
1979 was however much worse. Harry
Secombe, Eric Sykes, Jimmy Edwards, Hattie
Jacques, Gordon Rollins, Graham Stark,
Kenneth Connor. Written and directed by Eric
Sykes; for Avalon / ABPC.

Rhythm on the Range*
US 1936 87m bw
Paramount (Benjamin Glazer)

A hired hand saves the boss's daughter when
she is kidnapped by local badmen.
Easy-going musical comedy with a western
background, later remade as *Pardners* (qv).

w John C. Moffett, Sidney Salkow, Walter de
Leon, Francis Martin *d* Norman Taurog
ph Karl Struss *songs* various

Bing Crosby, Martha Raye, Frances Farmer,
Bob Burns, Lucile Watson, Samuel S. Hinds,
George E. Stone, Warren Hymer

  'Bing Crosby as a cowboy; Bing Crosby
crooning a prize bull to sleep on a freight car;
Bing Crosby more than ever like Walt
Disney's Cock Robin; it needs some stamina
to be a film reviewer.'—*Graham Greene*

Rhythm on the River*
US 1940 92m bw
Paramount (William Le Baron)

A song writer employs 'ghosts' to produce his
music and lyrics; they discover this fact and go
into business for themselves.
Cheerful musical with strong billing.

w Dwight Taylor, Billy Wilder, Jacques Théry
d Victor Schertzinger *ph* Ted Tetzlaff
m Johnny Burke, James V. Monaco

*Bing Crosby, Mary Martin, Basil Rathbone,
Oscar Levant*, Oscar Shaw, Charley
Grapewin, William Frawley

AAN: song 'Only Forever'

'From the very beginning, they knew they'd
   be friends to the end. What they didn't
   count on was everything in between!'

Rich and Famous
US 1981 117m Metrocolor
MGM / Jaquet / William Allyn

Two girl friends meet again years after
college; one has become a famous highbrow
novelist, and with her help the other becomes
a lowbrow one.
Unattractively sexed-up remake of *Old
Acquaintance*, with even more talk than the
original, and much less style.

w Gerald Ayres *d* George Cukor *ph* Don
Peterman, Peter Eco *m* Georges Delerue
pd Jan Scott *ed* John F. Burnett

A whirlwind round-up of romance, songs
and gags, with BING singin' and BOB BURNS
tootin' on the old   Bazooka!

Adolph Zukor presents

"RHYTHM ON THE RANGE"

Hear the 7 song hits!
"I Can't Escape From You",
"The House Jack Built for
Jill", "You'll Have to Swing
It", "I'm an Old Cowhand",
"Empty Saddles", "Round-
up Lullaby", "Drink It Down"

A Paramount Picture with

BING CROSBY
FRANCES FARMER
BOB BURNS
MARTHA RAYE

Directed by NORMAN TAUROG

RHYTHM ON THE RANGE. Frances Farmer, whose life later turned to tragedy, looks
singularly untroubled here.

Candice Bergen, Jacqueline Bisset, David
Selby, Hart Bochner, Steven Hill, Meg Ryan
  'A sadly dispiriting occasion . . . a jumbled
conflation of *The Group* and a female version
of *Carnal Knowledge.*'—*Tim Pulleine, MFB*
† The director was 82 when the film was shot,
which must be some kind of record.
● *Video: MGM / UA*

Rich and Strange*
GB 1931   83m   bw
BIP (John Maxwell)
US title: *East of Shanghai*

A young couple come into money and take a
trip around the world.
Slight, agreeable early talkie with a few
Hitchcock touches.

w Alma Reville, Val Valentine, Alfred
Hitchcock, *novel* Dale Collins *d Alfred
Hitchcock ph* Jack Cox, Charles Martin
m Hal Dolphe

Henry Kendall, Joan Barry, Percy Marmont,
Betty Amann, Elsie Randolph
  'Hitchcock, being Britain's D. W. Griffith,
according to the press agents around here,
usually gets a rave as his pictures take the
screen. Here's one where the admirers will
have difficulty knowing what to say.'—*Variety*
  'Perhaps his bravest failure.'—*George
Perry, 1965*

The Rich Are Always with Us
US 1932   73m   bw
Warner (Sam Bischoff)

A socialite determines on a divorce but her
new love is annoyed by her concern for her
ex-husband.
Cocktail drama of a kind which totally
disappeared from the screen.

w Austin Parker, *novel* E. Pettit *d* Alfred E.
Green *ph* Ernest Haller *m* W. Franke
Harling

Ruth Chatterton, George Brent, John Miljan,
Bette Davis, Adrienne Dore, Mae Madison,
Robert Warwick
  'Chiefly a femme picture . . . the title's
appropriateness is as obscure as the wisdom of
so metaphoric a label for a flicker.'—*Variety*

Rich Kids
US 1979   96m   Technicolor

An adolescent boy and girl are mildly
corrupted by the behaviour of their parents.
Spasmodically interesting comedy-drama
which seems ill at ease among the rich and
alternates between exploitation, satire and
whimsy. Trini Alvarado, Jeremy Levy,
Kathryn Walker, John Lithgow, Terry Kiser,
David Selby. Written by Judith Ross; directed
by Robert M. Young; for Robert Altman /
Lion's Gate / UA.

Rich Man, Poor Girl
US 1938   72m   bw

Consternation takes a white-collar family
when a millionaire takes a fancy to one of its
daughters. Unexciting comedy-drama vaguely
modelled on *You Can't Take It With You.* Lew

Ayres, Ruth Hussey, Robert Young, Don
Castle, Guy Kibbee, Lana Turner, Rita
Johnson. Written by Joseph Fields and Jerome
Chodorov, from a play by Edith Ellis; directed
by Reinhold Schunzel; for MGM. 'Lightweight
in marquee strength but should build through
word of mouth.'—*Variety*

Rich Man's Folly
US 1931   80m   bw
Paramount

A rich man has no time for his children.
Curious updating of Dickens' *Dombey and
Son;* not really a success.

w Grover Jones, Edward Paramore Jnr
d John Cromwell *ph* David Abel

George Bancroft, Frances Dee, Robert Ames,
Juliette Compton, Dorothy Peterson
  'Splendid cast and serviceable product
anywhere.'—*Variety*

Rich, Young and Pretty
US 1951   95m   Technicolor
MGM (Joe Pasternak)

A Texas rancher takes his young daughter to
Paris, where she meets her real mother.
Moderate musical.

w Dorothy Cooper, Sidney Sheldon
d Norman Taurog *ph* Robert Planck
m Nicholas Brodszky *ly* Sammy Cahn
ch Nick Castle

Danielle Darrieux, Wendell Corey, Jane
Powell, Fernando Lamas, Vic Damone
  AAN: song 'Wonder Why' (*m* Nicholas
Brodszky, *ly* Sammy Cahn)

Richard III***
GB 1955   161m   Technicolor
  Vistavision
London Films (Laurence Olivier)

Shakespeare's play about Richard Crookback,
his seizure of the throne and his defeat at
Bosworth.
Theatrical but highly satisfying filming of a
splendidly melodramatic view of history.
Interesting but not fussy camera movement,
delightful sets (followed by a disappointingly
'realistic' battle) and superb performances.

w *William Shakespeare* (adapted by Laurence
Olivier, Alan Dent, with additions)
d Laurence Olivier ph Otto Heller *ph* Roger
Furse *m* William Walton *ad* Carmen Dillon

Laurence Olivier, Claire Bloom, *Ralph
Richardson, Cedric Hardwicke*, Stanley Baker,
Alec Clunes, John Gielgud, Mary Kerridge,
Pamela Brown, Michael Gough, Norman
Wooland, Helen Haye, Patrick Troughton,
Clive Morton, Andrew Cruickshank
  'Wherever the play was loose-jointed or
ill-fitting. Sir Laurence has been its tinker and
its tailor, but never once its butcher.'—*Paul
Dehn, News Chronicle*
  AAN: Laurence Olivier

The Richest Girl in the World
US 1934   80m   bw

A millionairess changes places with her
secretary to find a man who will love her for

herself. Rose-coloured romance, remade in
1944 as *Bride by Mistake.* Miriam Hopkins,
Joel McCrea, Fay Wray, Henry Stephenson,
Reginald Denny, Beryl Mercer. Written by
Norman Krasna; directed by William A.
Seiter; for RKO. AAN: Norman Krasna.
  'Eighty minutes of unerring entertainment
. . . a pip picture for Miriam Hopkins.'—
Variety

The Riddle of the Sands*
GB 1978   102m   Eastmancolor
  Panavision
Rank / Worldmark (Drummond Challis)

In 1901 a British yachtsman in the North Sea
hits upon a German trial invasion.
Rather too placid adaptation of a semi-classic
adventure story in which too little happens to
make a rousing action film; points of interest
along the way, though.

w Tony Maylam, John Bailey, *novel* Erskine
Childers *d* Tony Maylam *ph* Christopher
Challis *m* Howard Blake *ph* Hazel Peiser

Michael York, Simon MacCorkindale, Jenny
Agutter, Alan Badel, Jurgen Andersen
● *Video: Rank*

Ride a Crooked Mile*
US 1938   70m   bw

An ex-Cossack cattle hijacker is disappointed
when jailed to find that his son will not help
him escape. Lively crime melodrama with an
unusual twist. Akim Tamiroff, Leif Erickson,
Frances Farmer, Lynne Overman, John
Miljan, Vladimir Sokoloff. Written by
Ferdinand Reyher, John C. Moffitt; directed
by Alfred E. Green; for Jeff Lazarus /
Paramount. 'Fine melodrama, handicapped by
lack of cast strength and so-so title.'—*Variety*

Ride a Crooked Trail
US 1958   88m   Eastmancolor
  Cinemascope

A crook takes refuge in a small town and
becomes its honest marshal. One we've heard
before, and seen better done. Audie Murphy,
Walter Matthau, Gia Scala, Henry Silva.
Written by Borden Chase; directed by Jesse
Hibbs; for Universal-International.

The Ride Back*
US 1957   79m   bw
UA / Associates and Aldrich (William
Conrad)

A lawman arrests an outlaw wanted for
murder, but has the problem of getting him
back to base.
Slightly offbeat low-budget western, well
enough done if it had to be done at all.

w Anthony Ellis *d* Allen H. Miner *ph* Joseph
Biroc *m* Frank de Vol

Anthony Quinn, William Conrad, George
Trevino, Lita Milan

Ride beyond Vengeance
US 1966   100m   Technicolor
Columbia / Tiger / Goodson / Todman /
  Sentinel / Fenady

A young westerner, accused of cattle rustling
and branded, vows revenge.

Dourly brutal but studio-bound and very padded western; if there is any entertainment value it doesn't emerge for more than a few moments.

w Andrew J. Fenady, *novel* The Night of the Tiger by Al Dewlen *d* Bernard McEveety *ph* Lester Shorr *m* Richard Markowitz

Chuck Connors, Michael Rennie, Kathryn Hays, Claude Akins, Bill Bixby, Paul Fix, Gary Merrill, Joan Blondell, Gloria Grahame, Ruth Warrick, Arthur O'Connell, Frank Gorshin, James MacArthur
† Probably intended as a TV movie and found too violent.

Ride Clear of Diablo
US 1954 80m Technicolor

A young man seeking vengeance on his father's murderer becomes deputy to a sheriff hired to kill him too. Lively enough star western. Audie Murphy, Dan Duryea, Susan Cabot, Abbe Lane, Russell Johnson, Paul Birch, Jack Elam. Written by George Zuckerman; directed by Jesse Hibbs; for Universal-International.

Ride 'Em Cowboy
US 1941 82m bw
Universal (Alex Gottlieb)

Two hot dog vendors find themselves working on an Arizona dude ranch.
Slick but routine comedy star vehicle with no outstanding sequences.

w True Boardman, John Grant *d* Arthur Lubin *pn* John W. Boyle *m* Frank Skinner *songs* Don Raye, Gene de Paul

Bud Abbott, Lou Costello, Dick Foran, Anne Gwynne, Samuel S. Hinds, Richard Lane, Johnny Mack Brown, Ella Fitzgerald

Ride Lonesome
US 1959 73m Eastmancolor
Cinemascope

A bounty hunter catches a killer as bait to trap the criminal's brother against whom he plots vengeance. Mildly suspenseful western, rather lost on the wide screen. Randolph Scott, Karen Steele, Pernell Roberts, James Best, James Coburn, Lee Van Cleef. Written by Burt Kennedy; directed by Budd Boetticher; for Columbia.

Ride the High Country**
US 1962 94m Metrocolor
Cinemascope
MGM (Richard E. Lyons)
GB title: Guns in the Afternoon

Two retired lawmen help transport gold from a mining camp to the bank, but one has ideas of his own.
Thoughtful western graced by ageing star presences; generally well done.

w N. B. Stone Jnr *d* Sam Peckinpah *ph* Lucien Ballard *m* George Bassman

Joel McCrea, Randolph Scott, Edgar Buchanan, Mariette Hartley, James Drury
'A nice little conventional unconventional western.'—*Stanley Kauffmann*

Ride the High Iron
US 1957 74m bw

A war veteran gets into the seamier side of public relations. Curious little urban melodrama with a high moral tone, like a cut-price *Sweet Smell of Success*. Don Taylor, Raymond Burr, Sally Forrest. Written by Milton Gelman; directed by Don Weis; for Columbia.

Ride the Man Down
US 1952 90m Trucolor

The death of a rancher sets off a bitter fight for his lands. Flat and uninteresting western melodrama. Brian Donlevy, Ella Raines, Rod Cameron, Forrest Tucker, Barbara Britton, James Bell, Chill Wills, J. Carrol Naish, Jim Davis. Written by Mary McCall Jnr; directed by Joe Kane; for Republic.

Ride the Pink Horse*
US 1947 101m bw
U-I (Joan Harrison)

An ex-serviceman visits a New Mexican town in search of the gangster who killed his buddy. Dour, complex melodrama with a certain amount of style but not enough substance.

w Charles Lederer, *novel* Dorothy B. Hughes *d* Robert Montgomery *ph* Russell Metty *m* Frank Skinner

Robert Montgomery, Wanda Hendrix, Andrea King, Thomas Gomez, Fred Clark, Art Smith
'One of a kind: no one in his right mind would imitate it.'—*Pauline Kael, 70s*

AAN: Thomas Gomez

Ride the Wild Surf
US 1964 101m Eastmancolor
Columbia / Jana (Jo and Art Napoleon)

Surf riders go to Hawaii and find romance. Pleasant, overlong, open air fun and games.

w Jo and Art Napoleon *d* Don Taylor *ph* Joseph Biroc *m* Stu Phillips

Fabian, Shelley Fabares, Tab Hunter, Barbara Eden

The Ride to Hangman's Tree
US 1967 90m Technicolor

Three bandits never quite manage to reform. Easy-going western, played on the light side in a vein later developed in *Butch Cassidy and the Sundance Kid*. Jack Lord, James Farentino, Don Galloway, Melody Johnson, Richard Anderson. Written by Luci Ward, Jack Natteford and William Bowers; directed by Alan Rafkin; for Universal.

Ride, Vaquero
US 1953 90m Anscocolor
MGM (Stephen Ames)

Ranchers settling in New Mexico after the Civil War cause some natives to turn bandit; one of them has a mysterious American associate called Rio.
Very mildly interesting western with the stars rather swamping a humourless script.

w Frank Fenton *d* John Farrow *ph* Robert Surtees *m* Bronislau Kaper

Robert Taylor, Ava Gardner, Howard Keel, Anthony Quinn, Charlita

Rider on a Dead Horse
US 1962 72m bw

A prospector murders one partner for his gold and tries to pin the blame on the other. Watchable minor western with good use of location. John Vyvyan, Bruce Gordon, Kevin Hagen, Lisa Lu. Written by Stephen Longstreet; directed by Herbert L. Strock; for Allied Artists.

Riders of the Purple Sage
US 1931 58m bw

A rootin', tootin' cowboy traps a villain and 'veathers a stampede and an avalanche. Good standard western previously filmed in 1918 with William Farnum and in 1925 with Tom Mix. This version was premièred on the wide screens of the period. George O'Brien, Marguerite Churchill, Noah Beery, Yvonne Pelletier, Stanley Fields. From the novel by Zane Grey; directed by Hamilton McFadden; for Fox. 'Still a good western and okay outside the de luxers.'—*Variety*

Riders of Vengeance
US 1952 80m Technicolor

During the California gold rush, a prospector takes revenge on a local dictator. Standard western themes against a colourful background. Richard Conte, Barbara Britton, Viveca Lindfors, Hugh O'Brian, Morris Ankrum, William Reynolds, Dennis Weaver. Written by Polly James and Lillie Hayward; directed by Lesley Selander; for Universal-International. (GB title: *The Raiders*.)

Riders to the Stars*
US 1954 81m Color Corporation
UA / Ivan Tors

Rocket scientists investigate the problems of cosmic bombardment.
Enjoyably straightforward science fiction with no monsters or political problems; it has decided historic interest as a record of what scientists in 1954 thought rocket travel would be like.

w Curt Siodmak *d* Richard Carlson *ph* Stanley Cortez *m* Harry Sukman

Richard Carlson, Herbert Marshall, William Lundigan, Dawn Addams, Martha Hyer, Robert Karnes, Lawrence Dobkin

'It's a rootin', tootin', six-gun shootin' musicalallapalooza!'
Riding High
US 1943 88m Technicolor
Paramount (Fred Kohlmar)
GB title: Melody Inn

A burlesque queen goes home to Arizona and helps ranchers by performing at a dude ranch. Dim formula musical with exuberance but neither wit nor style.

w Walter de Leon, Arthur Phillips, Art Arthur, play Ready Money by James Montgomery d George Marshall ph Karl Struss, Harry Hallenberger md Victor Young

Dorothy Lamour, Dick Powell, Victor Moore, Gil Lamb, Cass Daley, Bill Goodwin, Rod Cameron, Glenn Langan, Andrew Tombes, Tim Ryan, Douglas Fowley, Milt Britton and his Band

Riding High*
US 1950 112m bw
Paramount (Frank Capra)

An easygoing racing man forsakes the chance of wealth to train his beloved horse for the Imperial Derby.
The director's familiar ingredients—farce, sentimentality, fast cutting, nice people and a lot of noise—seem a shade too tried and tested in this remake of his 1934 success Broadway Bill. Despite the cast, the result is only moderately entertaining.

w Robert Riskin d Frank Capra ph George Barnes, Ernest Laszlo m James Van Heusen ly Johnny Burke

Bing Crosby, Coleen Gray, Charles Bickford, Raymond Walburn, James Gleason, Oliver Hardy, Frances Gifford, William Demarest, Ward Bond, Clarence Muse, Percy Kilbride, Harry Davenport, Margaret Hamilton, Douglass Dumbrille, Gene Lockhart

Riding Shotgun
US 1954 75m Warnercolor

A shotgun stagecoach guard carries on a long vendetta against an outlaw. Routine western excitements, played mainly indoors. Randolph Scott, Wayne Morris, Joan Weldon, Joe Sawyer, James Millican, Charles Bronson, James Bell. Written by Tom Blackburn; directed by André de Toth; for Warner.

Riff Raff*
US 1935 90m bw
MGM (Irving Thalberg)

A con man and his wife end up on the wrong side of the law.
Modest comedy drama that never quite sparks.

w Frances Marion, H. W. Haneman, Anita Loos d Robert Z. Leonard m Edward Ward

Jean Harlow, Spencer Tracy, Joseph Calleia, Una Merkel, Mickey Rooney, Victor Kilian, J. Farrell MacDonald
'It ain't art, but it's box office.'—Variety

Riff Raff*
US 1947 80m bw
RKO (Nat Holt)

A dying man hands a Panama City con man a map to valuable oil deposits, and various shady people are after it.
Rather heavy but well made comedy-drama with some striking scenes.

w Martin Rackin d Ted Tetzlaff ph George E. Diskant m Roy Webb

Pat O'Brien, Walter Slezak, Anne Jeffreys, Percy Kilbride, Jerome Cowan

Rififi**
France 1955 116m bw
Indus / Pathé / Prima
original title: Du Rififi chez les Hommes

After an elaborate raid on a jewellery store, thieves fall out and the caper ends in bloodshed.
A film with much to answer for, in the form of hundreds of imitations showing either detailed accounts of robberies (Topkapi, Gambit) or gloomy looks at the private lives of criminals. At the time it seemed crisp and exciting, and the 25-minute silent robbery sequence is quite something.

w René Wheeler, Jules Dassin, Auguste le Breton, novel Auguste le Breton d Jules Dassin ph Philippe Agostini m Georges Auric

Jean Servais, Carl Mohner, Robert Manuel, Marie Sabouret, Perlo Vita (Jules Dassin)
† Several 'sequels' were made using the word rififi (criminal argot for 'trouble') in the title, but in plot terms they were entirely unrelated.

The Right Approach
US 1961 92m bw Cinemascope
TCF (Oscar Brodney)

A Hollywood opportunist tries to make it as a star.
A potentially witty Hollywood story is sabotaged by a style which is as naïve as it is dismal; and Mr Vaughan's hopes of stardom unfairly ended right here.

w Fay and Michael Kanin, play Garson Kanin d David Butler ph Sam Leavitt m Dominic Frontière

Frankie Vaughan, Martha Hyer, Juliet Prowse, Gary Crosby, David MacLean, Jesse White, Jane Withers

Right Cross
US 1950 90m bw
MGM (Armand Deutsch)

A boxing champion injures his hand and has to abandon his career.
Rather dull sporting melodrama with a Mexican background, saved by good production values.

w Charles Schnee d John Sturges ph Norbert Brodine m David Raksin

Dick Powell, June Allyson, Lionel Barrymore, Ricardo Montalban

The Right Stuff*
US 1983 193m Technicolor
Warner / Ladd (Irwin Winkler, Robert Chartoff)

Test pilots are recruited and trained as astronauts.
A reasonably factual account of the Mercury programme: extremely well made but somehow too brash and inhuman to provide much entertainment. An unexpected commercial flop.

w,d Philip Kaufman, book Tom Wolfe ph Caleb Deschanel m Bill Conti pd Geoffrey Kirkland

Sam Shepard, Scott Glenn, Ed Harris, Dennis Quaid, Fred Ward, Barbara Hershey, Kim Stanley, Veronica Cartwright
AA: Bill Conti; editing; art direction
AAN: best picture; Sam Shepard; Caleb Deschanel

The Right to Live
US 1935 75m bw

Someone in the family mercifully kills a crippled war hero. Uninspired rendering of Somerset Maugham's play The Sacred Flame, previously filmed under its own title in 1929 (with Pauline Frederick, Henrietta Crosman, George Brent). Colin Clive, Josephine Hutchinson, Peggy Wood, C. Aubrey Smith, Leo G. Carroll, Halliwell Hobbes. Written by Ralph Block; directed by William Keighley; for Warner. (GB title: The Sacred Flame.)

The Right to Love*
US 1930 79m bw

A mother has a strong affinity with her illegitimate daughter who is a missionary on the other side of the world. Curious mystic melodrama which adds a twist to the popular mother-love devices. Technically it introduced the Bell light valve which improved sound reproduction, and also the Dunning process which improved the presentation of dual roles. (The star played mother and daughter.) Charles Lang, the cinematographer, was nominated for an Academy Award. Ruth Chatterton, Paul Lukas, David Manners, Irving Pichel, George Baxter. Written by Zoe Akins from the novel Brook Adams by Susan Glaspell; directed by Richard Wallace; for Paramount. 'A profound and thoughtful romantic drama treated with utmost refinement of sophistication and still possessing elements which will appeal to the broadest kind of screen audience.'—Variety

The Ring
US 1952 79m bw
King Brothers

A young Mexican becomes a prizefighter in the hope of winning greater respect for Mexican-Americans.
Well-meant low-budget programmer.

w Irving Shulman d Kurt Neumann ph Russell Harlan m Herschel Burke Gilbert

Gerald Mohr, Lalo Rios, Rita Moreno, Robert Arthur

Ring of Bright Water*
GB 1969 107m Technicolor
Palomar / Brightwater (Joseph Strick)

A civil servant buys a pet otter and moves to a remote cottage in the western Highlands. Disneyesque fable for animal lovers, from a bestselling book.

w Jack Couffer, Bill Travers, book Gavin Maxwell d Jack Couffer ph Wolfgang Suschitsky m Frank Cordell

Bill Travers, Virginia McKenna, Peter Jeffrey, Roddy McMillan, Jameson Clark

● Video: Guild

Ring of Fear

US 1954 88m Warnercolor
Cinemascope
Warner / Wayne–Fellows (Robert M. Fellows)

A homicidal maniac returns to the circus where he used to work and causes various 'accidents'.
Tediously predictable circus melodrama with a curious but not very likeable cast.

w Paul Fix, Philip MacDonald, James Edward Grant d James Edward Grant ph Edwin DuPar m Emil Newman, Arthur Lange

Clyde Beatty, Pat O'Brien, Mickey Spillane, Sean McClory, Marion Carr, John Bromfield, Pedro Gonzalez Gonzalez, Emett Lynn

Ring of Fire

US 1961 90m Metrocolor
MGM / Andrew and Virginia Stone

An Oregon sheriff is kidnapped by teenage delinquents but manages to lead them into both a police trap and a forest fire.
Outdoor action thriller with a plot which is ludicrously unconvincing in detail, though the fire scenes impress.

wd Andrew L. Stone ph William H. Clothier m Duane Eddy

David Janssen, Joyce Taylor, Frank Gorshin, Joel Marston

Ring of Spies*

GB 1963 90m bw
British Lion (Leslie Gilliatt)
US title: Ring of Treason

How the Portland spy ring was tracked down. Documentary drama, rather less intriguing, somehow, than the actual facts; but the sheer thought of spies in the suburbs keeps interest going.

w Frank Launder, Peter Barnes d Robert Tronson ph Arthur Lavis

Bernard Lee, Margaret Tyzack, David Kossoff, Nancy Nevinson, William Sylvester

The Ringer*

GB 1952 78m bw
BL / London (Hugh Perceval)

A dangerous criminal known only as The Ringer threatens to kill the crooked lawyer responsible for his sister's death.
Artful old-fashioned mystery, quite well restaged, and in fact the best extant example of filmed Wallace.

w Val Valentine, novel and play Edgar Wallace d Guy Hamilton ph Ted Scaife m Malcolm Arnold

Donald Wolfit, Mai Zetterling, Herbert Lom, Greta Gynt, William Hartnell, Norman Wooland

† The play was also filmed in 1931 with Patrick Curwen, Franklin Dyall and Gordon Harker; and in 1938 as The Gaunt Stranger (qv).

Rings on Her Fingers*

US 1942 85m bw
TCF (Milton Sperling)

The front girl for a couple of confidence tricksters falls in love with their first victim. Lively comedy which drags into drama in its second half.

w Ken Englund d Rouben Mamoulian ph George Barnes m Cyril Mockridge

Gene Tierney, Henry Fonda, Laird Cregar, Spring Byington, Shepperd Strudwick, Frank Orth, Henry Stephenson, Marjorie Gateson

Rio

US 1939 78m bw
Universal

A crooked financier escapes from Devil's Island to join his wife in Rio, only to find she has been unfaithful.
Modest but well made melodrama.

w Stephen Morehouse Avery, Frank Partos, Edwin Justus Mayer, Abem Kandel, Jean Negulesco d John Brahm ph Hal Mohr m Frank Skinner md Charles Previn

Basil Rathbone, Victor McLaglen, Sigrid Gurie, Robert Cummings, Leo Carrillo, Billy Gilbert, Irving Bacon, Irving Pichel

'A fair programmer with a blend of romance and adventure . . . should stand up satisfactorily as a top dualler in most situations.'—Variety

Rio Bravo**

US 1959 141m Technicolor
Warner / Armada (Howard Hawks)

A wandering cowboy and a drunken sheriff hold a town against outlaws.
Cheerfully overlong and slow-moving western in which everybody, including the director, does his thing. All very watchable for those with time to spare, but more a series of revue sketches than an epic.

w Jules Furthman, Leigh Brackett d Howard Hawks ph Russell Harlan m Dmitri Tiomkin

John Wayne, Dean Martin, Ricky Nelson, Angie Dickinson, Walter Brennan, Ward Bond, John Russell, Pedro Gonzalez Gonzalez, Claude Akins, Harry Carey Jnr, Bob Steele

† More or less remade in 1966 as El Dorado and in 1970 as Rio Lobo.

● Video: Warner

Rio Conchos*

US 1964 107m De Luxe Cinemascope
TCF (David Weisbart)

Two thousand rifles are stolen from an army command port and traced to the hide-out of a former Confederate colonel who wants to continue the Civil War.
Good standard western which shares much of its story line with The Comancheros.

w Clair Huffaker, Joseph Landon d Gordon Douglas ph Joe MacDonald m Jerry Goldsmith

Richard Boone, Edmond O'Brien, Stuart Whitman, Tony Franciosa

Rio Grande*

US 1950 105m bw
Republic / Argosy (John Ford, Merian C. Cooper)

A Cavalry unit on the Mexican border in the 1880s conducts a vain campaign against marauding Indians.
Thin Ford western on his favourite theme, with too many pauses for song, too many studio sets, and too little plot. Aficionados, however, will find much to admire.

w James Kevin McGuinness, story James Warner Bellah d John Ford ph Bert Glennon, Archie Stout m Victor Young

John Wayne, Maureen O'Hara, Ben Johnson, Claude Jarman Jnr, Harry Carey Jnr, Chill Wills, J. Carrol Naish, Victor McLaglen

Rio Lobo*

US 1970 114m Technicolor
Cinema Center (Howard Hawks)

A union colonel near the end of the Civil War recovers a gold shipment and exposes a traitor.
Rambling western with traces of former glory, enjoyable at least for its sense of humour.

w Leigh Brackett, Burton Wohl d Howard Hawks ph William Clothier m Jerry Goldsmith

John Wayne, Jorge Rivero, Jennifer O'Neill, Jack Elam, Victor French, Chris Mitchum, Mike Henry

● Video: MGM / UA

Rio Rita

US 1929 135m bw and Technicolor
RKO (William Le Baron)

Romance on a ranch near the Mexican border. Very early talkie version of a popular Broadway operetta of the twenties; historical interest only.

w Luther Reed, Russell Mack, book Guy Bolton, Fred Thomson, as produced by Florenz Ziegfeld d Luther Reed ph Robert Kurle, Lloyd Knetchel md Victor Baravalle songs Harry Tierney, Joe McCarthy

Bebe Daniels, John Boles, Bert Wheeler, Robert Woolsey, Dorothy Lee, Don Alvarado, George Renavent

Rio Rita

US 1942 91m bw
MGM (Pandro S. Berman)

Flat-footed remake bringing in Nazi spies; poor comedy even by Abbott and Costello standards.

w Richard Connell, Gladys Lehman d S. Sylvan Simon ph George J. Folsey m Herbert Stothart

Bud Abbott, Lou Costello, John Carroll, Kathryn Grayson, Tom Conway, Barry Nelson

Riot

US 1968 98m Technicolor
Paramount / William Castle

While the warden is away, thirty-five convicts take over a state penitentiary and are violently subdued.
Strikingly bloody melodrama set in an actual prison in Arizona; well made, but less entertaining than Cagney and Raft used to be.

w James Poe, *novel* Frank Elli *d* Buzz Kulik
ph Robert B. Hauser *m* Christopher Komeda

Gene Hackman, Jim Brown, Ben Carruthers,
Mike Kellin, Gerald O'Loughlin, Clifford
David

Riot in Cell Block Eleven*
US 1954 80m bw
Allied Artists / Walter Wanger

In a big American prison three convicts seize
their guards, free the other prisoners and
barricade themselves in their block.
Socially concerned low-budgeter, quite nicely
made and persuasive of the need for prison
reform.

w *Richard Collins d Don Siegel ph* Russell
Harlan *m* Herschel Burke Gilbert

Neville Brand, *Emile Meyer*, Frank Faylen,
Leo Gordon, Robert Osterloh, Paul Frees,
Don Keefer

'As a compassionate, angry, unsensational
account of an episode of violence it makes
considerably more impact than many of the
overblown melodramas currently in
fashion.'—*Penelope Houston*

Riptide*
US 1934 90m bw
MGM (Irving Thalberg)

A British diplomat weds a Manhattan chorus
girl, but she later falls for an old flame.
Elegantly set, star-packed drawing-room
drama which somehow didn't click.

wd *Edmund Goulding ph* Ray June
m Herbert Stothart

Norma Shearer, Robert Montgomery, Herbert
Marshall, Mrs Patrick Campbell, Skeets
Gallagher, Ralph Forbes, Lilyan Tashman,
Helen Jerome Eddy, George K. Arthur,
Halliwell Hobbes

'Has all the earmarks of box office . . . a
commendable job all round.'—*Variety*

The Rise and Fall of Legs Diamond
US 1960 101m bw
Warner / United States (Milton Sperling)

The career of a New York hoodlum of the
twenties.
Inspired, like *King of the Roaring Twenties*, by
the TV success of *The Untouchables*, this was
part of a brief attempt by Warners to
recapture its pre-war gangster image. Alas,
stars and style were equally lacking.

w Joseph Landon *d* Budd Boetticher
ph Lucien Ballard *m* Leonard Rosenman

Ray Danton, Karen Steele, Elaine Stewart,
Jesse White, Simon Oakland, Robert Lowery,
Warren Oates, Judson Pratt

The Rise and Rise of Michael Rimmer
GB 1970 101m Technicolor
Warner / David Frost (Harry Fine)

An efficiency expert takes over an advertising
agency and is soon an MP, a cabinet minister,
and PM.
Satirical comedy which quickly goes overboard
and is only occasionally funny; it does,

however, mark the final death throes of the
swinging sixties, and the changeover to *Monty
Python*.

w Peter Cook, John Cleese, Kevin Billington,
Graham Chapman *d* Kevin Billington
ph Alex Thompson *m* John Cameron

Peter Cook, John Cleese, Arthur Lowe,
Denholm Elliott, Ronald Fraser, Vanessa
Howard, George A. Cooper, Harold Pinter,
James Cossins, Roland Culver, Dudley Foster,
Julian Glover, Dennis Price, Ronnie Corbett

Rise and Shine
US 1941 93m bw
TCF (Mark Hellinger)

A dumb but brilliant football player is
kidnapped by the other side.
Drab collegiate comedy, disappointing
considering the credits.

w Herman J. Mankiewicz, *novel* My Life and
Hard Times by James Thurber *d* Allan Dwan
ph Edward Cronjager *m* Emil Newman
songs Leo Robin, Ralph Rainger

Linda Darnell, Jack Oakie, George Murphy,
Walter Brennan, Milton Berle, Sheldon
Leonard, Donald Meek, Ruth Donnelly,
Donald MacBride, Raymond Walburn, Emma
Dunn

Rising Damp
GB 1980 98m colour
ITC / Black Lion (Roy Skeggs)

The amorous and conniving landlord of a slum
boarding house develops a passion for one of
his tenants.
A useful reminder of a TV sitcom worth
remembering, but handicapped by restriction
of action, paucity of plot and the overlength
usual in film versions of such things, not to
mention the premature death of its original
co-star Richard Beckinsale.

w Eric Chappell *d* Joe McGrath *ph* Frank
Watts *m* David Lindup

Leonard Rossiter, Frances de la Tour, Don
Warrington, Denholm Elliott, Christopher
Strauli

'Unforgettably John Ford's finest film!'
The Rising of the Moon
Eire 1957 81m bw
Warner / Four Provinces (Lord Killanin)

Three Irish short stories.
Curiously dull John Ford portmanteau with
the Abbey players.

w Frank Nugent, *stories* Frank O'Connor,
Malcolm J. McHugh, Lady Gregory *d* John
Ford *ph* Robert Krasker *m* Eamonn
O'Gallagher *narrator* Tyrone Power

Maureen Connell, Eileen Crowe, Cyril
Cusack, Maureen Delany, Donald Donelly,
Frank Lawton, Edward Lexy, Jack
MacGowran, Denis O'Dea, Jimmy O'Dea,
Noel Purcell

Risky Business
US 1939 67m bw

A crusading radio columnist tracks down a
kidnapper. Tolerable crime programmer.

George Murphy, Dorothea Kent, Eduardo
Ciannelli, Leon Ames, El Brendel, John
Wray. Written by Charles Grayson from a
previous script by William Anthony McGuire;
directed by Arthur Lubin; for Universal. 'It
will garner nice business in city spots, where
they like their melodrama realistic.'—*Variety*

Risky Business
US 1983 99m Technicolor

A 17-year-old is left in charge of his parents'
house and fills it with pimps and prostitutes
. . . a lucrative business. Would-be outrageous
teenage comedy which is pretty well made but
soon wears out its welcome. Tom Cruise,
Rebecca de Mornay, Joe Pantoliano, Richard
Masur, Bronson Pinchot, Curtis Armstrong,
Nicholas Pryor. Written and directed by Paul
Brickman; for Tisch-Avnet / Geffen.

The Ritz*
US 1976 90m Technicolor
Warner / Courtyard (Denis O'Dell)

A comedy of mistaken identities in a gay New
York turkish bath.
An adaptation of a stage success which doesn't
seem nearly as funny as it thinks it is; but
some of it does work.

w Terrance McNally, from his play *d* Richard
Lester *ph* Paul Wilson *m* Ken Thorne
pd Phillip Harrison

Jack Weston, Rita Moreno, Jerry Stiller, Kaye
Ballard, Bessie Love, George Coulouris, F.
Murray Abrahams, Treat Williams

The River*
India 1951 87m Technicolor
Oriental / International / Theatre Guild
  (Kenneth McEldowney)

Episodes in the life of a small English
community living on the banks of the Ganges.
A slight and surprising work from this
director, superbly observed and a pleasure to
watch but dramatically very thin.

w Rumer Godden; Jean Renoir, *novel* Rumer
Godden *d* Jean Renoir *ph* Claude Renoir
m M. A. Partha Sarathy *pd* Eugene Lourié

Nora Swinburne, Esmond Knight, Arthur
Shields, Adrienne Corri

† Renoir's assistant was Satyajit Ray.

The River
US 1984 122m Technicolor
Universal / Edward Lewis

The Garveys battle flood waters to save the
family farm.
Old-fashioned rural drama, at times
reminiscent of *Way Down East* plus a dash of
symbolism. A surprise in 1984, and not a very
pleasant one, despite or because of its political
awareness.

w Robert Dillon, Julian Barry *d* Mark
Rydell *ph* Vilmos Zsigmond *m* John
Williams *pd* Charles Rosen *ed* Sidney Levin

Mel Gibson, Sissy Spacek, Shane Bailey,
Becky Jo Lynch, Scott Glenn, Billy Green
Bush

River Lady

US 1948 78m Technicolor

The beautiful owner of a Mississippi gambling boat tries to buy up all her rivals. Routine romantic drama. Yvonne de Carlo, Rod Cameron, Dan Duryea, Helena Carter, Lloyd Gough, Florence Bates, John McIntire. Written by D. D. Beauchamp and William Bowers; directed by George Sherman; for Universal-International.

River of No Return°

US 1954 91m Technicolor
Cinemascope
TCF (Stanley Rubin)

During the California gold rush a widower and his 10-year-old son encounter a saloon singer with a gold claim.
Cheerful, clichéd star western designed to exploit the splendours of early Cinemascope, and very adequate for this purpose.

w Frank Fenton d Otto Preminger ph Joseph La Shelle m Cyril Mockridge md Lionel Newman

Robert Mitchum, Marilyn Monroe, Tommy Rettig, Rory Calhoun, Murvyn Vye

The River's Edge

US 1956 87m Eastmancolor
Cinemascope
TCF (Benedict Bogeaus)

A fugitive bank robber forces a farmer to guide him over the mountains into Mexico. Sluggish open-air character melodrama.

w Harold J. Smith d Allan Dwan ph Harold Lipstein m Lou Forbes

Ray Milland, Anthony Quinn, Debra Paget, Byron Foulger

River's End

US 1930 74m bw

A Mountie dies chasing his man, who then impersonates him. Popular, contrived, outdoor thriller, previously filmed in 1922 with Lewis Stone, and subsequently in 1940 with Dennis Morgan (this version became known as *Double Identity*). Charles Bickford, Evalyn Knapp, J. Farrell MacDonald, Zasu Pitts, David Torrence. Written by Charles Kenyon, from the story by James Oliver Curwood; directed by Michael Curtiz; for Warner.

The Road Back°°

US 1937 105m bw
Universal (James Whale)

After World War I, German soldiers go home to problems and disillusion.
A major work, intended as a sequel to *All Quiet on the Western Front*. Despite impressive sequences, it doesn't quite reach inspiring heights.

w R. C. Sherriff, Charles Kenyon, *novel* Erich Maria Remarque d James Whale ph John Mescall, George Robinson m Dmitri Tiomkin ad Charles D. Hall

Richard Cromwell, John King, Slim Summerville, Andy Devine, Barbara Read, Louise Fazenda, Noah Beery Jnr, Lionel Atwill, John Emery, Etienne Girardot, Spring Byington, Laura Hope Crews

'Big and frequently effective, but a let-down in toto . . . does not compare with *All Quiet* in quality or power.'—*Variety*

'They call it an all-star cast and that means there isn't a single player of any distinction to be picked out of the herd. . . . It might be funny if it wasn't horrifying. This is America seeing the world in its own image.'—*Graham Greene*

† The film is said to have been extensively reshot after protests from the German consul in Los Angeles. No 35mm negative now exists, as it reverted to Remarque and was lost.

Road Gang

US 1936 60m bw

Penal corruption and brutality in a southern state is exposed by the *Chicago Sun*. A rough ride over familiar ground. Donald Woods, Carlyle Moore Jnr, Kay Linaker, Harry Cording, Marc Lawrence. Written by Abem Finkel, Dalton Trumbo, Harold Buckley; directed by Louis King; for First National.

Road House

GB 1934 76m bw

A girl on a murder charge is helped by a famous actress who is really her mother. Stock melodrama with a good script and popular players. Violet Loraine, Gordon Harker, Emlyn Williams, Hartley Power, Stanley Holloway, Marie Lohr, Geraldo and his band. Written by Austin Melford and Leslie Arliss, from the play by Walter Hackett; directed by Maurice Elvey; for Gaumont.

Road House°

US 1948 95m bw
TCF (Edward Chodorov)

A road house owner is jealous of his manager and frames him for murder.
Dated but watchable *film noir* of its era, with all characters cynical or homicidal.

w Edward Chodorov d Jean Negulesco ph Joseph La Shelle m Cyril Mockridge

Richard Widmark, Ida Lupino, Cornel Wilde, Celeste Holm

Road Show°

US 1941 86m bw
Hal Roach

A young man wrongly committed to an insane asylum escapes with another inmate and joins a travelling circus.
Engaging scatty comedy on familiar Roach lines which suffers from lame pacing but manages some likeable moments.

w Arnold Beldard, Harry Langdon, Mickell Novak, *novel* Eric Hatch d Gordon Douglas ph Norbert Brodine m George Stoll

John Hubbard, Adolphe Menjou, Carole Landis, Patsy Kelly, George E. Stone

Road to Denver

US 1955 90m Trucolor

An honest ranch hand gets into trouble when he tries to help his lawless brother. Uninspired western which just about passes the time. John Payne, Lee J. Cobb, Skip Homeier, Mona Freeman, Ray Middleton, Andy Clyde, Lee Van Cleef. Written by Horace McCoy and Allen Rivkin; directed by Joe Kane; for Republic.

The Road to Glory°

US 1936 103m bw
TCF (Darryl F. Zanuck)

Adventures of a French regiment in World War I.
Meticulously produced war movie which bears comparison with *All Quiet on the Western Front*.

w Joel Sayre, William Faulkner d Howard Hawks ph Gregg Toland m Louis Silvers

Fredric March, Warner Baxter, Lionel Barrymore, June Lang, Gregory Ratoff, Victor Kilian, John Qualen, Julius Tannen, Leonid Kinskey

The Road to Life°

USSR 1930 100m bw

Moscow street children are rounded up and reformed. A kind of Russian prequel to the *Dead End Kids*, presented with much style. Mikhail Zharov, Maria Gonfa, Tsifan Kyrla. Written and directed by Nikolai Ekk; for Mejrabpom. 'Judged purely as entertainment the film recedes quickly, as do most Russian films.'—*Variety*

Road to Mandalay

US 1926 77m at 24 fps bw silent

Two eastern planters quarrel over a girl. Potboiling star vehicle. Lon Chaney, Lois Moran, Owen Moore, Henry B. Walthall. Written by Elliott Clawson and Herman Mankiewicz; directed by Tod Browning; for MGM.

The Road to Reno

US 1938 69m bw

A rancher won't give his wife the divorce she thinks she wants. Combination comedy, drama, romance and horse opera which doesn't gel. Randolph Scott, Hope Hampton, Glenda Farrell, Helen Broderick, Alan Marshal, Samuel S. Hinds. Written by Roy Chanslor, Adele Comandini, Brian Marlowe, from the novel by I. A. R. Wylie; directed by S. Sylvan Simon; for Universal.

The Road to Salina

France / Italy 1971 96m colour
Panavision

The proprietress of a roadside café recognizes a drifter as her long-lost son. Boring emotional drama stymied by the multi-language problem. Rita Hayworth, Mimsy Farmer, Robert Walker Jnr, Ed Begley, Sophie Hardy. Written by Georges Lautner, Pascal Jardin and Jack Miller; directed by Georges Lautner; for Robert Dorfmann.

Road to Singapore
US 1931 70m bw

A doctor's wife is caught with her lover, and her life falls to pieces. Tensions among the oriental upper crust: very dated and not very convincing. William Powell, Louis Calhern, Doris Kenyon, Marian Marsh, Alison Skipworth. Written by J. Grubb Alexander, from a play by Roland Pertwee; directed by Alfred E. Green; for Warner.

THE 'ROAD' SERIES:

Road to Singapore*
US 1940 84m bw
Paramount (Harlan Thompson)

Two rich playboys swear off women until they quarrel over a Singapore maiden.
The first Hope–Crosby–Lamour 'road' picture is basically a light romantic comedy and quite forgettable; the series got zanier as it progressed.

w Don Hartman, Frank Butler, story Harry Hervey d Victor Schertzinger ph William C. Mellor m Victor Young

Bing Crosby, Bob Hope, Dorothy Lamour, Charles Coburn, Judith Barrett, Anthony Quinn, Jerry Colonna

Road to Zanzibar**
US 1941 92m bw
Paramount (Paul Jones)

The trio on safari in Africa, with Hellzapoppin gags breaking in and an anything-goes atmosphere.

w Frank Butler, Don Hartman d Victor Schertzinger ph Ted Tetzlaff m Victor Young songs Johnny Burke, Jimmy Van Heusen

Hope, Crosby, Lamour, Una Merkel, Eric Blore, Luis Alberni, Douglass Dumbrille
'The funniest thing I've seen on the screen in years. Years.'—Otis Ferguson

Road to Morocco**
US 1942 83m bw
Paramount (Paul Jones)

Hollywood Arab palaces, a captive princess, topical gags and talking camels.

w Frank Butler, Don Hartman d David Butler ph William C. Mellor md Victor Young songs Johnny Burke, Jimmy Van Heusen

Hope, Crosby, Lamour, Anthony Quinn, Dona Drake

AAN: script

Road to Utopia**
US 1945 89m bw
Paramount (Paul Jones)

The California gold rush, with all the previous gag styles in good order, capped by a cheeky epilogue and constant explanatory narration by Robert Benchley.

w Norman Panama, Melvin Frank d Hal Walker ph Lionel Lindon m Leigh Harline songs Johnny Burke, Jimmy Van Heusen

Hope, Crosby, Lamour, Douglass Dumbrille, Hillary Brooke, Jack La Rue

AAN: script
● Video: CIC

Road to Rio**
US 1947 100m bw
Paramount (Daniel Dare)

Guest stars are given their head, plot intrudes again in the shape of a hypnotized heiress, and the style is more constrained (but still funny).

w Edmund Beloin, Jack Rose d Norman Z. McLeod ph Ernest Laszlo md Robert Emmett Dolan songs Johnny Burke, Jimmy Van Heusen

Hope, Crosby, Lamour, Gale Sondergaard, Frank Faylen, the Wiere Brothers, the Andrews Sisters
'Enough laughs to pass the time easily and to remind you how completely, since sound came in, the American genius for movie comedy has disintegrated.'—James Agee

AAN: Robert Emmett Dolan

Road to Bali*
US 1952 91m Technicolor
Paramount (Harry Tugend)

In and around the South Seas, with colour making the sets obvious and the gags only tediously funny. The team's zest was also flagging.

w Frank Butler, Hal Kanter, William Morrow d Hal Walker ph George Barnes md Joseph J. Lilley songs Johnny Burke, Jimmy Van Heusen

Hope, Crosby, Lamour, Murvyn Vye, Peter Coe

Road to Hong Kong
GB 1962 91m bw
UA / Melnor (Norman Panama)

Curious, slightly dismal-looking attempt to continue the series in a British studio and on a low budget. A few good gags, but it's all very tired by now, and the space fiction plot makes it seem more so.

w Norman Panama, Melvin Frank d Melvin Frank ph Jack Hildyard m Robert Farnon pd Roger Furse

Hope, Crosby, Lamour, Joan Collins, Robert Morley, Walter Gotell, Felix Aylmer and guests Peter Sellers, David Niven, Frank Sinatra, Dean Martin, Jerry Colonna

Roadhouse Nights*
US 1930 71m bw
Paramount

A reporter exposes a gangster operating from a country nightclub.
Experimental mingling of elements which later become very familiar.

w Garrett Fort, story Ben Hecht d Hobart Henley ph William Steiner

Helen Morgan, Charles Ruggles, Fred Kohler, Jimmy Durante, Fuller Mellish Jnr

Roar*
US 1981 102m colour Panavision
Noel Marshall / Banjiro Uemura

A research biologist lives in the African bush with assorted wild animals. He is expecting his family, but they arrive a day early when he is out . . .
A rather silly story takes in some of the most remarkable animal photography on record, and there is a sub-plot involving villainous game hunters.

wd Noel Marshall ph Jan de Bont m Dominic Frontière

Noel Marshall, Tippi Hedren, and family
† The Marshalls live with their 150 lions and other wild animals in a ranch near Los Angeles. During production the film, which eventually cost 17 million dollars, was halted by flood, fire, epidemic and injury.

'The land of the free gone wild! The heyday of the hotcha! The shock-crammed days G-men took ten whole years to lick!'

The Roaring Twenties***
US 1939 106m bw
Warner (Hal B. Wallis)

A World War I veteran returns to New York, innocently becomes involved in bootlegging, builds up an empire and dies in a gang war. Among the last of the Warner gangster cycle, this was perhaps the best production of them all, despite the familiar plot line: stars and studio were in cracking form.

w Jerry Wald, Richard Macaulay, Robert Rossen, story Mark Hellinger d Raoul Walsh, Anatole Litvak ph Ernest Haller m Heinz Roemheld

James Cagney, Humphrey Bogart, Priscilla Lane, Jeffrey Lynn, Gladys George, Frank McHugh, Paul Kelly, Elizabeth Risdon
† The James Cagney character was based on Larry Fay, who was Texas Guinan's partner, and Gladys George is clearly Guinan herself.

Rob Roy the Highland Rogue
GB 1953 81m Technicolor
Walt Disney (Perce Pearce)

After the defeat of the clans in the 1715 rebellion, their leader escapes and after several adventures is granted a royal pardon.
A kind of Scottish Robin Hood, so stiffly acted and made that it might as well—or better—be a cartoon.

w Lawrence E. Watkin d Harold French ph Guy Green m Cedric Thorpe Davie

Richard Todd, Glynis Johns, James Robertson Justice, Michael Gough, Finlay Currie, Geoffrey Keen, Archie Duncan

Robbers' Roost
US 1955 82m De Luxe

An honest cowboy is employed by cattle rustlers and strives to clear his name. Fair western programmer. George Montgomery,

Richard Boone, Sylvia Findley, Bruce Bennett, Peter Graves, Warren Stevens, William Hopper. Written by John O'Dea, Sidney Salkow and Maurice Geraghty, from a novel by Zane Grey; directed by Sidney Salkow; for Leonard Goldstein / UA.

Robbery*
GB 1967 113m Eastmancolor
Joseph E. Levine / Oakhurst (Michael Deeley, Stanley Baker)

Criminals conspire to rob the night mail train from Glasgow.
Heavy-going fictionalized account of the famous train robbery of 1963; best seen as standard cops and robbers, with some good chase sequences.

w Edward Boyd, Peter Yates, George Markstein d Peter Yates ph Douglas Slocombe m Johnny Keating

Stanley Baker, James Booth, Frank Finlay, Joanna Pettet, Barry Foster, William Marlowe, Clinton Greyn, George Sewell

● Video: CBS / Fox

Robbery under Arms
GB 1957 99m Eastmancolor
Rank (Joe Janni)

In 19th-century Australia, two farming brothers join the notorious outlaw Captain Starlight.
Howlingly dull film version of a semi-classic adventure novel; a rambling story with no unity of viewpoint is saved only by excellent photography.

w Alexander Baron, W. P. Lipscomb, novel Rolf Boldrewood d Jack Lee ph Harry Waxman m Matyas Seiber

Peter Finch, David McCallum, Ronald Lewis, Maureen Swanson, Jill Ireland, Laurence Naismith, Jean Anderson

'The miracle story of all time!'
The Robe**
US 1953 135m Technicolor Cinemascope
TCF (Frank Ross)

Followers and opponents of Jesus are affected by the robe handed down by him at his crucifixion.
The first film in Cinemascope was, surprisingly, a biblical bestseller, but the crowded Roman sets hid most of the flaws in the process. The film itself was competent and unsurprising in the well-tried Sign of the Cross manner.

w Philip Dunne, novel Lloyd C. Douglas d Henry Koster ph Leon Shamroy m Alfred Newman

Richard Burton, Jean Simmons, Michael Rennie, Victor Mature, Jay Robinson, Torin Thatcher, Dean Jagger, Richard Boone, Betta St John, Jeff Morrow, Ernest Thesiger, Dawn Addams
† Power was originally cast in the Burton role, and Burt Lancaster in Mature's.

THE ROARING TWENTIES.   Cagney meets Bogart head on. And the guy with the gun is going to win.

AAN: best picture; Leon Shamroy; Richard Burton
● Video: CBS / Fox

Roberta*
US 1935 105m bw (Technicolor sequence)
RKO (Pandro S. Berman)

An American inherits a Parisian fashion house.
Thin and remarkably flatly-handled musical romance of the old school, charged only by the occasional appearances in supporting roles of Astaire and Rogers, then on the brink of stardom.

w Jane Murfin, Sam Mintz, Allan Scott, play Otto Harbach, book Gowns by Roberta by Alice Duer Miller d William A. Seiter ph Edward Cronjager m Jerome Kern md Max Steiner ch Fred Astaire ad Van Nest Polglase

Irene Dunne, Fred Astaire, Ginger Rogers, Randolph Scott, Helen Westley, Claire Dodd, Victor Varconi, Torben Meyer
'Musical picture-making at its best—fast, smart, good-looking and tuneful.'—Variety
† Remade as Lovely to Look At (qv).

AAN: song 'Lovely to Look At'

Robin and Marian*
US 1976 107m Technicolor
Columbia / Rastar (Dennis O'Dell)

Robin Hood returns from the Crusades and finds conditions in Britain depressing; he finally conquers the evil Sheriff but dies in the attempt.
A kind of serious parody of medieval life, after the fashion of The Lion in Winter but much glummer; in fact, nothing to laugh at at all.

w James Goldman d Richard Lester ph David Watkin m John Barry pd Michael Stringer

Sean Connery, Audrey Hepburn, Robert Shaw, Ronnie Barker, Nicol Williamson, Richard Harris, Denholm Elliott, Kenneth Haigh, Ian Holm, Bill Maynard, Esmond Knight, Peter Butterworth
'Surface realism only hides a core of mush, suddenly revealed when the hero and heroine settle down for love-making in a field of corn.'—Geoff Brown
'Whimsical jokiness is a bit hard to reconcile with the final plunge into sacrificial romance.'—Michael Billington, Illustrated London News

Robin and the Seven Hoods*
US 1964   123m   Technicolor
Panavision
Warner / PC (Howard W. Koch, William H.
Daniels)

A spoof of the Robin Hood legend set in
gangland Chicago of the twenties.
Too flabby by far to be as funny as it thinks it
is, this farrago of cheerful jokes has effective
moments and lively routines, but most of them
are nearly swamped by flat treatment and the
wide screen.

w David Schwartz d Gordon Douglas
ph William H. Daniels m Nelson Riddle
songs Sammy Cahn, James Van Heusen

Frank Sinatra, Dean Martin, Bing Crosby,
Sammy Davis Jnr, Peter Falk, Barbara Rush,
Edward G. Robinson, Victor Buono, Barry
Kelley, Jack La Rue, Allen Jenkins, Sig
Rumann, Hans Conried

AAN: Nelson Riddle; song 'My Kind of
Town' (m James Van Heusen, ly Sammy
Cahn)

Robin Hood**
US 1922   127m approx (24 fps) bw
silent
Douglas Fairbanks

Robin Hood combats Prince John and the
Sheriff of Nottingham.
An elaborate version of the legend which
featured some of Hollywood's most celebrated
sets and allowed the star to perform a
selection of exhilarating stunts.

w Douglas Fairbanks d Allan Dwan
ph Arthur Edeson ad Wilfrid Buckland, Irvin
J. Martin

Douglas Fairbanks, Wallace Beery, Alan
Hale, Enid Bennett

'The high water mark of film production. It
did not grow from the bankroll, it grew from
the mind.'—R. E. Sherwood
'A story book picture, as gorgeous and
glamorous a thing in innumerable scenes as
the screen has yet shown . . . thrilling
entertainment for the whole family group.'—
National Board of Review
† See also The Adventures of Robin Hood and
The Story of Robin Hood and his Merrie Men.

Robin Hood
US 1973   83m   Technicolor
Walt Disney (Wolfgang Reitherman)

Alarmingly poor cartoon feature with all the
characters 'played' by animals; songs
especially dim and treatment quite lifeless.

w Larry Clemmons, Ken Anderson, others
d Wolfgang Reitherman voices Brian
Bedford, Peter Ustinov, Terry-Thomas, Phil
Harris, Andy Devine, Pat Buttram

AAN: song 'Love' (m George Bruns, ly Floyd
Huddleston)

Robin Hood of El Dorado*
US 1936   86m   bw

Joaquin Murieta turns bandit to avenge
himself on the men who killed his wife.
Whitewashed biopic of a notorious western
desperado, played mainly for action and light

relief. Warner Baxter, Bruce Cabot, Margo,
Eric Linden, J. Carrol Naish, Ann Loring.
Written by William Wellman, Melvin Levy
and Joseph Calleia; directed by William
Wellman; for MGM.

Robinson Crusoe: see The Adventures of
Robinson Crusoe

Robinson Crusoe and the Tiger
Mexico 1969   110m   Eastmancolor

Simple but extremely handsome version of the
famous story, with the addition of a tiger
which Crusoe takes as a pet. Hugo Stieglitz,
Ahui. Written by Mario Marzac and Rene
Cardona Jnr, from the novel by Daniel Defoe;
directed by Rene Cardona Jnr; for Avant /
Avco Embassy.

Robinson Crusoe on Mars**
US 1964   110m   Techniscope
Paramount / Devonshire (Aubrey Schenck)

An astronaut lands on Mars and learns to
survive until rescue comes.
Remarkably close to Defoe (Man Friday being
a refugee in an interplanetary war) this is an
absorbing, entertaining and well-staged piece
of science fiction, strikingly shot in Death
Valley.

w Ib Melchior, John C. Higgins d Byron
Haskin ph Winton C. Hoch m Van Cleave
sp Lawrence Butler ad Hal Pereira, Arthur
Lonergan

Paul Mantee, Adam West, Vic Lundin

Robinson Crusoeland
France / Italy 1950   98m   bw
Sirius / Franco-London / Fortezza
aka: Atoll K; Escapade; Utopia

Stan and Ollie inherit an island in the Pacific,
but uranium is discovered on it.
Laurel and Hardy's last film is a dispiriting
mess, and the less said about it the better.

w unknown, d Leo Joannon, John Berry
ph Armand Thirard, Louis Née m Paul
Misraki

Stan Laurel, Oliver Hardy, Suzy Delair

Rocco and his Brothers**
Italy / France 1960   180m   bw
Titanus / Les Films Marceau (Goffredo
Lombardo)

A peasant family moves into Milan, and each
of its five brothers has his problems.
Massive portmanteau of realistic stories, a bit
hard to take despite its undoubted brilliance.

w Luchino Visconti, Suso Cecchi d'Amico,
Vasco Pratolini d Luchino Visconti
ph Giuseppe Rotunno m Nino Rota

Alain Delon, Renato Salvatori, Annie
Girardot, Katina Paxinou, Roger Hanin,
Paolo Stoppa, Suzy Delair, Claudia Cardinale

Rock a Bye Baby
US 1958   107m   Technicolor
Vistavision
Paramount (Jerry Lewis)

A film star asks her devoted schoolday

admirer to look after her triplets by a secret
marriage.
Tasteless jazzing-up of The Miracle of
Morgan's Creek by talents distinctly
unsympathetic.

wd Frank Tashlin ph Haskell Boggs
m Walter Scharf

Jerry Lewis, Marilyn Maxwell, Reginald
Gardiner, Salvatore Baccaloni, Hans Conried,
Isobel Elsom, James Gleason, Isa Moore,
Connie Stevens

Rock around the Clock*
US 1956   74m   bw
Columbia (Sam Katzman)

A band playing a new form of jive—rock 'n
roll—becomes a nationwide sensation.
A cheap second feature with guest artists, this
cheerful little movie deserved at least a
footnote in the histories because it spotlights
the origins and the leading purveyors of rock
'n roll. It also caused serious riots in several
countries. A sequel in 1957, Don't Knock the
Rock, was merely cheap.

w Robert E. Kent, James B. Gordon d Fred
F. Sears ph Benjamin H. Kline

Bill Haley and the Comets, the Platters, Little
Richard, Tony Martinez and his Band,
Freddie Bell and the Bellboys, Johnny
Johnson, Alan Freed, Lisa Gaye, Alix Talton

Rockabye
US 1932   70m   bw

A great actress who has scratched her way up
is unhappy because of frustrated mother love.
One of many tearjerkers of its type produced
in the first three years of the thirties: it doesn't
travel well across the decades. Constance
Bennett, Joel McCrea, Paul Lukas, Walter
Pidgeon, Jobyna Howland, Walter Catlett.
Written by Jane Murfin and Kubec Glasmon
from the play by Lucia Bronder; directed by
George Cukor; for Radio. 'Moderate grosser,
best for the neighbourhood mats.'—Variety

The Rocket Man
US 1954   79m   bw

A visitor from outer space gives a magic ray
gun to an orphan boy and tells him to use it
only for good. Elementary fantasy with
amusing moments. Charles Coburn, George
'Foghorn' Winslow, Spring Byington, Anne
Francis, John Agar. Written by Lenny Bruce
and Jack Henley; directed by Oscar Rudolph;
for TCF.

Rockets Galore
GB 1958   94m   Technicolor
Rank / Relph and Dearden
US title: Mad Little Island

The Scottish island of Todday resists the
installation of a rocket-launching site.
Amiable but disappointingly listless sequel to
Whisky Galore.

w Monja Danischewsky d Michael Relph
ph Reg Wyer m Cedric Thorpe Davie

Jeannie Carson, Donald Sinden, Roland Culver, Noel Purcell, Ian Hunter, Duncan Macrae, Jean Cadell, Carl Jaffe, Gordon Jackson, Catherine Lacey

Rocketship XM*
US 1950 79m bw
Lippert (Kurt Neumann)

An expedition to the moon lands by accident on Mars.

The first post-war space adventure is sheer hokum, quite likeable for its cheek though not for its cheap sets.

wd Kurt Neumann *ph* Karl Struss *m* Ferde Grofe

Lloyd Bridges, Osa Massen, John Emery, Hugh O'Brian

The Rocking Horse Winner*
GB 1949 90m bw
Rank / Two Cities (John Mills)

A boy discovers he can predict winners while riding an old rocking horse; his mother's greed has fatal results.

A very short story is fatally over-extended and becomes bathetic; but the production is solid and the film deserves a mark for trying.

wd Anthony Pelissier, *story* D. H. Lawrence *ph* Desmond Dickinson *m* William Alwyn *ad* Carmen Dillon

John Mills, Valerie Hobson, John Howard Davies, Ronald Squire, Hugh Sinclair, Cyril Smith

'His whole life was a million-to-one shot!'
Rocky**
US 1976 119m Technicolor
UA / Chartoff-Winkler (Gene Kirkwood)

A slightly dimwitted Philadelphia boxer makes good.

Pleasantly old-fashioned comedy-drama with rather unattractive characters in the modern manner. Despite the freshness, on the whole *Marty* is still preferable.

w Sylvester Stallone *d* John G. Avildsen *ph* James Crabe *m* Bill Conti

Sylvester Stallone, Burgess Meredith, Talia Shire, Burt Young, Carl Weathers, Thayer David

AA: best picture; John G. Avildsen
AAN: Sylvester Stallone (as writer); song 'Gotta Fly Now' (*m* Bill Conti, *ly* Carol Connors, Ayn Robbins); Sylvester Stallone (as actor); Burgess Meredith; Talia Shire; Burt Young

● *Video: Intervision*

Rocky II
US 1979 119m Technicolor
UA / Irwin Winkler, Robert Chartoff

After success comes failure; then Rocky marries his sweetheart and works for another big fight.

Over-inflated but under-nourished sequel with absolutely nothing new to offer.

wd Sylvester Stallone *ph* Bill Butler *m* Bill Conti

Sylvester Stallone, Talia Shire, Burt Young, Carl Weathers, Burgess Meredith

● *Video: Intervision*

Rocky III
US 1982 99m Technicolor
United Artists / Chartoff–Winkler (James D. Brubaker)

Rocky is challenged by a brutal slugger who beats him at the first match . . .

Unnecessary regurgitation of bits and pieces from the first two Rocky movies.

wd Sylvester Stallone *ph* Bill Butler *m* Bill Conti *pd* William J. Cassidy *ed* Don Zimmerman, Mark Warner

Sylvester Stallone, Talia Shire, Burt Young, Burgess Meredith, Carl Weathers, Tony Burton, Mr T, Hulk Hogan

'The time has surely come for Rocky Balboa to take the final count.'—*Tom Milne, MFB*

'The first *Rocky* was primitive in a relatively innocent way. This picture is primitive too, but it's also shrewd and empty and inept.'—*New Yorker*

AAN: original song, 'Eye of the Tiger' by Jim Peterik and Frankie Sullivan III

Rocky Mountain
US 1950 83m bw
Warner (William Jacobs)

A Confederate horseman gets involved in an Indian war.

Routine star western with unusual tragic ending.

w Winston Miller, Alan le May *d* William Keighley *ph* Ted McCord *m* Max Steiner

Errol Flynn, Patrice Wymore, Scott Forbes, Guinn Williams, Slim Pickens

Rocky Mountain Mystery
US 1935 64m bw

An engineer solves a number of murders at a radium mine. Routine whodunit in an unfamiliar setting. Randolph Scott, Charles Chic Sale, Mrs Leslie Carter (a rare screen appearance, and just as well to judge from her performance), Kathleen Burke, Ann Sheridan. Written by Edward E. Paramore Jnr, from the novel Golden Dreams by Zane Grey; directed by Charles Barton; for Paramount. 'Good entertainment in spite of minor shortcomings.'—*Variety*

Roger Touhy, Gangster
US 1944 73m bw

An associate of Al Capone is finally cornered by the FBI. Unsurprising, competent cops-and-robbers melodrama, based more or less on fact. Preston Foster, Victor McLaglen, Lois Andrews, Kent Taylor, Anthony Quinn, Henry Morgan. Written by Crane Wilbur and Jerry Cady; directed by Robert Florey; for TCF. (GB title: *The Last Gangster.*)

Rogue Cop
US 1954 92m bw
MGM (Nicholas Nayfack)

A police detective is on the payroll of a crime syndicate.

Uncompelling star melodrama.

w Sidney Boehm, *novel* William P. McGivern *d* Roy Rowland *ph* John Seitz *m* Jeff Alexander

Robert Taylor, George Raft, Janet Leigh, Steve Forrest, Anne Francis

'Another of the sour, disillusioned crime stories which have recently been coming into fashion.'—*Penelope Houston*

AAN: John Seitz

The Rogue Song*
US 1930 115m Technicolor
MGM (Lionel Barrymore)

A bandit wins the hand of a Russian princess. Primitive early sound operetta, not salvaged by a few Laurel and Hardy scenes added as an afterthought.

w Frances Marion, John Colton, *operetta* Gypsy Love by Franz Lehar, Robert Bodansky *d* Lionel Barrymore, Hal Roach *ph* Percy Hilburn, C. Edgar Schoenbaum *m* Dmitri Tiomkin

Laurence Tibbett, Catherine Dale Owen, Florence Lake, Judith Voselli, Nance O'Neill, Stan Laurel, Oliver Hardy

'Slow unto dullness outside of Tibbett's singing; Laurel and Hardy names draw but their comedy is very weak.'—*Variety*

† No print is known to exist, but in 1980 the sound track was issued on record.

AAN: Laurence Tibbett

Rogue's March
US 1953 84m bw
MGM (Leon Gordon)

A British army officer is unjustly accused of espionage but becomes a hero in India. Victorian comedy adventure set on a never-never frontier. Not much.

w Leon Gordon *d* Allan Davis *ph* Paul C. Vogel *m* Alberto Columbo

Peter Lawford, Richard Greene, Janice Rule, Leo G. Carroll, John Abbott, Patrick Aherne

Rogues of Sherwood Forest*
US 1950 80m Technicolor
Columbia (Fred M. Packard)

Robin Hood's son helps the barons to force the signing of Magna Carta.
Satisfactory action adventure.

w George Bruce *d* Gordon Douglas *ph* Charles Lawton Jnr *m* Heinz Roemheld, Arthur Morton

John Derek, Diana Lynn, George Macready, Alan Hale, Paul Cavanagh, Lowell Gilmore, Billy House

Rogues' Regiment
US 1948 86m bw
U-I

An intelligence man joins the French Foreign

Legion in Saigon to track down an ex-Nazi. Keen but rather muddled actioner.

w Robert Buckner d Robert Florey
ph Maury Gertsman m Daniele Amfitheatrof

Dick Powell, Marta Toren, Vincent Price, Stephen McNally

Rollerball*
US 1975 129m Technicolor Scope
UA / Norman Jewison

In the 21st century an ultra-violent game is used to release the anti-social feelings of the masses.

A one-point parable, and an obvious point at that, is stretched out over more than two hours of violence in which the rules of the game are not even explained. A distinctly unlikeable film.

w William Harrison d Norman Jewison
ph Douglas Slocombe md André Previn
pd John Box

James Caan, John Houseman, Ralph Richardson, Maud Adams, John Beck, Moses Gunn

'A classic demonstration of how several millions of dollars can be unenjoyably wasted.'—*Jonathan Rosenbaum*

● Video: Intervision

Rollercoaster
US 1977 118m Technicolor
Panavision Sensurround
Universal (Jennings Lang)

A saboteur blows up rollercoasters if his blackmail demands are not met.

Limp, unsuspenseful, would-be spectacular in which a stalwart cast struggles with inane dialogue and situations.

w Richard Levinson, William Link d James Goldstone ph David M. Walsh m Lalo Schifrin

George Segal, Timothy Bottoms, Richard Widmark, Susan Strasberg, Harry Guardino, Henry Fonda

Rollover
US 1981 115m Technicolor
Panavision
Orion / IPC (Bruce Gilbert)

The widow of a murdered bank president exposes various kinds of financial chicanery on an international scale.

So complexly plotted as to be virtually unintelligible, this slick romantic melodrama was caviare to the general despite its stars.

w David Shaber d Alan J. Pakula
ph Giuseppe Rotunno, William Garroni
m Michael Small

Jane Fonda, Kris Kristofferson, Hume Cronyn, Josef Sommer, Bob Gunton

Le Roman d'un Tricheur*
France 1936 83m bw
Cinéas
aka: The Story of a Cheat

A reformed elderly cardsharp writes his memoirs.

First person singular comedy, a *tour de force* in which only the narrator speaks, the rest use pantomime only.

wd Sacha Guitry ph Marcel Lucien

Sacha Guitry, Marguerite Moreno, Serge Grave

Roman Holiday**
US 1953 118m bw
Paramount (William Wyler)

A princess on an official visit to Rome slips away incognito and falls in love with a newspaperman.

Wispy, charming, old-fashioned romantic comedy shot in Rome and a little obsessed by the locations; one feels that a studio base would have resulted in firmer control of the elements. The stars, however, made it memorable.

w Ian McLellan Hunter, John Dighton
d William Wyler ph Franz Planer, Henri Alekan m Georges Auric

Gregory Peck, Audrey Hepburn, Eddie Albert, Hartley Power, Harcourt Williams

'While Capra, or in a different way Lubitsch, could have made something wholly enjoyable from it, it would seem that Wyler's technique is now too ponderously inflexible for such lightweight material.'—*MFB*

AA: original story (Ian McLellan Hunter); Audrey Hepburn
AAN: best picture; script; William Wyler; photography; Eddie Albert

Roman Scandals**
US 1933 93m bw
Samuel Goldwyn

A troubled young man dreams himself back in ancient Rome.

Musical farce which is not only pretty entertaining on its own account but remains interesting for a number of reasons; as its star's best vehicle, for its Depression bookends, as a spoof on *The Sign of the Cross* and the inspiration of scores of other comedies in which the heroes dreamed themselves back into other times. Note also the musical numbers, the chariot race finale, and the rare appearance of Ruth Etting.

w William Anthony McGuire, George Oppenheimer, Arthur Sheekman, Nat Perrin, story George S. Kaufman, Robert E. Sherwood d Frank Tuttle chariot sequence Ralph Cedar ph Gregg Toland
m Alfred Newman ch Busby Berkeley
songs various

Eddie Cantor, Gloria Stuart, Ruth Etting, Edward Arnold, Alan Mowbray, Verree Teasdale

The Roman Spring of Mrs Stone*
GB 1961 104m Technicolor
Warner Seven Arts / AA (Louis de Rochemont)

A widowed American actress in Rome begins to drift into lassitude and moral decay. Vivien Leigh gets degraded again in this rambling novella complete with mysterious

dark stranger waiting at the end. Nice to look at, and occasionally compelling, but unsuccessful as a whole.

w Gavin Lambert, novel Tennessee Williams
d José Quintero ph Harry Waxman
m Richard Addinsell pd Roger Furse
ad Herbert Smith

Vivien Leigh, Warren Beatty, Lotte Lenya, Jeremy Spenser, Coral Browne, Ernest Thesiger

AAN: Lotte Lenya

Romance*
US 1930 76m bw
MGM

A clergyman falls in love with the opera singer mistress of an industrialist.

Simple-minded romantic drama with the star not at her best; but an interesting example of 'high class' romance of the time.

w Bess Meredyth, Edwin Justus Mayer, play Edward Sheldon d Clarence Brown
ph William Daniels

Greta Garbo, Lewis Stone, Gavin Gordon, Elliott Nugent, Clara Blandick, Florence Lake, Henry Armetta

'A first-run hit of the sort that won't miss.'—*Variety*

AAN: Clarence Brown; Greta Garbo

Romance in Manhattan
US 1934 78m bw

A New York girl helps a Czech immigrant to find work in the metropolis. Slim, sentimental movie novelette without a touch of sophistication. Ginger Rogers, Francis Lederer, Arthur Hohl, J. Farrell MacDonald, Eily Malyon, Donald Meek. Written by Jane Murfin and Edward Kaufmann; directed by Stephen Roberts; for RKO.

Romance in the Dark
US 1938 78m bw

A famous baritone helps a singing servant to get famous. Musical romance for the carriage trade, with apparently more comedy asides than were originally intended. Gladys Swarthout, John Boles, John Barrymore, Claire Dodd, Fritz Field, Curt Bois. Written by Frank Partos and Anne Morrison Chapin; directed by H. C. Potter; for Paramount.

'Biz will be good, if no wow. Boles and Barrymore will give some tug to the tide against the turnstiles.'—*Variety*

Romance of a Horse Thief
US / Yugoslavia 1971 100m Technicolor
Allied Artists / Jadran / Emmanuel L. Wolf (Gene Gutowski)

In a Polish village in 1904 there is dismay when horses are commandeered by Cossacks for service in the Russo-Japanese war. Nostalgic Jewish drama which ends up rather like *Fiddler on the Roof* without the music.

w David Opatoshu, based on his father's novel d Abraham Polonsky ph Piero Portalupisisic m Mort Shuman

Yul Brynner, Eli Wallach, Jane Birkin, Oliver Tobias, Lainie Kazan, David Opatoshu

The Romance of Rosy Ridge
US 1947 103m bw
MGM (Jack Cummings)

After the Civil War, farmers make their own peace.

Mild period romance with everything settled by a betrothal.

w Lester Cole, novel Mackinlay Kantor
d Roy Rowland ph Sidney Wagner
m George Bassman

Van Johnson, Thomas Mitchell, Janet Leigh, Selena Royle, Marshall Thompson, Dean Stockwell

'Rustic charm spread through it like molasses.'—Douglas Eames

Romance on the High Seas*
US 1948 99m Technicolor
Warner (Alex Gottlieb, George Amy)
GB title: It's Magic

Various romances mesh on an ocean voyage.

Lightweight musical which introduces Doris Day and generally manages to keep afloat.

w Julius J. and Philip G. Epstein, I. A. L. Diamond d Michael Curtiz ph Elwood Bredell m Ray Heindorf songs Jule Styne, Sammy Cahn

Jack Carson, Janis Paige, Don Defore, Doris Day, Oscar Levant, S. Z. Sakall, Eric Blore, Franklin Pangborn, Fortunio Bonanova

AAN: Ray Heindorf; song 'It's Magic' (m Jule Styne, ly Sammy Cahn)

Romancing the Stone*
US 1984 106m De Luxe Panavision
TCF / El Corazon (Michael Douglas)

A best-selling lady romance novelist gets more than she bargained for when she tries to find her kidnapped sister in Colombia.

Spoof adventure thriller which takes too long to get going and then finds it has nowhere to go. But commercial . . .

w Diane Thomas d Robert Zemeckis
ph Dean Cundey m Alan Silvestri
pd Lawrence G. Paull

Michael Douglas, Kathleen Turner, Danny DeVito, Zack Norman, Alfonso Arau

'The picture has a bravura opening and a jolly kind of movement, but it becomes too slambang.'—Pauline Kael, New Yorker

Romanoff and Juliet*
US 1961 103m Technicolor
U-I / Pavla (Peter Ustinov)

Both Americans and Russians woo the tiny country of Concordia, and war threatens while the ambassadors' children fall in love.

Despite the author's wit this pattern comedy became something of a bore as a stylized stage piece, and the film is not smartly enough handled to be anything but a yawn; the humour never becomes cinematic.

wd Peter Ustinov, from his play ph Robert Krasker m Mario Nascimbene ad Alexander Trauner

Peter Ustinov, Sandra Dee, John Gavin, Akim Tamiroff, Tamara Shayne, John Phillips, Alix Talton, Peter Jones

The Romantic Age
GB 1949 86m bw

A precocious French student sets her cap at the art teacher. Fluffy farce in which all the adults behave like children; not well regarded. Mai Zetterling, Hugh Williams, Margot Grahame, Petula Clark, Carol Marsh, Raymond Lovell, Paul Dupuis. Written by Edward Dryhurst and Peggy Barwell, from a novel by Serge Weber; directed by Edmond T. Greville; for Pinnacle - Rank. (US title: Naughty Arlette.)

Romantic Comedy
US 1983 102m Metrocolor
MGM-UA / Taft Entertainment / The Mirisch Corporation (Walter Mirisch, Morton Gottlieb)

A Broadway playwright and a New England schoolteacher have a creative partnership that is more personal than professional.

Tedious film version of a play which wallows in autobiography.

w Bernard Slade, from his play d Arthur Hiller ph David M. Walsh m Marvin Hamlisch pd Alfred Sweeney

Dudley Moore, Mary Steenburgen, Frances Sternhagen, Janet Eilber, Robyn Douglass, Ron Leibman

'When a movie's production notes wax lyrical about the pile of the living room carpet, one senses that they're in trouble.'—Nick Roddick, MFB

The Romantic Englishwoman*
GB 1975 116m Eastmancolor
Dial / Meric–Matalon (Daniel M. Angel)

A discontented woman, holidaying at Baden Baden, falls in love with a stranger while her husband completes a novel on the same theme.

Almost as ambiguous as Last Year in Marienbad, this annoying film wastes good actors in a script which hovers uncertainly between fantasy, melodrama and reality, intending one supposes to make humourless and obvious comparisons between romance and life.

w Tom Stoppard, Thomas Wiseman, novel Thomas Wiseman d Joseph Losey ph Gerry Fisher m Richard Hartley

Glenda Jackson, Michael Caine, Helmut Berger, Marcus Richardson, Kate Nelligan, René Kolldehoff, Michel Lonsdale

'The central trio bite off their lines, play deviously with hypocrisies and humiliations, and seem slightly aware that they're creations by artifice out of artificiality.'—Penelope Houston

'An itsy-bitsy, fragmented film that seems less than the sum of its parts.'—Michael Billington, Illustrated London News

Rome Adventure
US 1962 119m Warnercolor

A pretty American librarian goes to Rome to learn about love, and does. Sluggish and overstretched travelogue with dollops of arch romance; hard to take. Suzanne Pleshette,

Troy Donahue, Angie Dickinson, Rossano Brazzi, Constance Ford, Chad Everett. Written and directed by Delmer Daves; for Warner. (GB title: Lovers Must Learn.)

Rome Express*
GB 1932 94m bw
Gaumont (Michael Balcon)

Thieves and blackmail victims are among the passengers on an express train.

Just a little faded now as sheer entertainment, this remains the prototype train thriller from which The Lady Vanishes, Murder on the Orient Express and a hundred others are all borrowed; it also spawned a myriad movies in which strangers are thrown together in dangerous situations. Technically it still works very well, though the script needs modernizing.

w Clifford Grey, Sidney Gilliat, Frank Vosper, Ralph Stock d Walter Forde ph Gunther Krampf

Conrad Veidt, Gordon Harker, Esther Ralston, Joan Barry, Harold Huth, Cedric Hardwicke, Donald Calthrop, Hugh Williams, Finlay Currie, Frank Vosper, Muriel Aked, Eliot Makeham

'A first class craftsman's job.'—Basil Wright
† Remade 1948 as Sleeping Car to Trieste (qv).

Romeo and Juliet*
US 1936 127m bw
MGM (Irving Thalberg)

Hollywood Shakespeare with a super production and a rather elderly cast. Not entertaining in the strict sense, but full of interest.

w Talbot Jennings d George Cukor ph William Daniels m Herbert Stothart ad Cedric Gibbons

Leslie Howard, Norma Shearer, John Barrymore, Basil Rathbone, Edna May Oliver, Henry Kolker, C. Aubrey Smith, Violet Kemble-Cooper, Robert Warwick, Virginia Hammond, Reginald Denny, Ralph Forbes, Andy Devine, Conway Tearle

'Unimaginative, coarse-grained, a little banal, it is frequently saved—by Shakespeare—from being a bad film.'—Graham Greene

'It is impossible to realize how bad this film was unless you reflect on how good it might have been.'—Alberto Cavalcanti
† Fredric March, Robert Donat and Robert Montgomery all refused the lead before Leslie Howard accepted.

AAN: best picture; Norma Shearer; Basil Rathbone

Romeo and Juliet
GB 1954 138m Technicolor
Rank / Verona (Joe Janni, Sandro Ghenzi)

Good-looking but extremely boring version shot on Italian locations with quite unacceptable leads.

wd Renato Castellani ph Robert Krasker m Roman Vlad

Laurence Harvey, Susan Shentall, Aldo Zollo, Enzo Fiermonte, Flora Robson, Mervyn Johns, Sebastian Cabot, Lydia Sherwood, Giulio Garbinetti, Nietta Zocchi, Bill Travers, Norman Wooland, John Gielgud as prologue speaker

Romeo and Juliet*
GB 1968   152m   Technicolor
Paramount / BHE / Verona / Dino de Laurentiis (Anthony Havelock-Allan, John Brabourne, Richard Goodwin)

The with-it version for modern youngsters; unfortunately the admirably rapid style does not suit the verse, and long before the much-deferred end the thing becomes just as tiresome as the other versions.

w Franco Brusati, Masolino D'Amico d Franco Zeffirelli ph Pasquale de Santis m Nino Rota

Leonard Whiting, Olivia Hussey, John McEnery, Michael York, Pat Heywood, Milo O'Shea, Paul Hardwick, Natasha Parry, Antonio Pierfederici, Esmeralda Ruspoli, Bruce Robinson, Roberto Bisacco, Laurence Olivier as prologue speaker
'A large gold watch should be tossed to Zeffirelli for his part in reversing the movies' reputation for emasculating the classics.'—Newsweek
AA: Pasquale de Santis
AAN: best picture; Franco Zeffirelli

La Ronde***
France 1950   100m   bw
Sacha Gordine

In 1900 Vienna, an elegant compère shows that love is a merry-go-round: prostitute meets soldier meets housemaid meets master meets married woman meets husband meets midinette meets poet meets actress meets officer meets prostitute meets soldier . . . Superb stylized comedy with a fine cast, subtle jokes, rich decor and fluent direction; not to mention a haunting theme tune.

w Jacques Natanson, Max Ophuls, novel Arthur Schnitzler d Max Ophuls ph Christian Matras m Oscar Straus

Anton Walbrook, Simone Signoret, Serge Reggiani, Simone Simon, Daniel Gélin, Danielle Darrieux, Fernand Gravey, Odette Joyeux, Jean-Louis Barrault, Isa Miranda, Gérard Philipe
'One of the most civilized films to have come from Europe in a long time.'—Gavin Lambert, MFB
'A film that drags on and on by what seems like geometric progression.'—John Simon, 1968
AAN: script
● Video: Longman

La Ronde
France 1964   110m   Eastmancolor
Franscope
Robert and Raymond Hakim
Vulgarization of the above, reset in Paris in

1913. The lack of a compère vastly reduces the number of jokes.

w Jean Anouilh d Roger Vadim ph Henri Decaë m Michel Magne

Marie Dubois, Claude Giraud, Anna Karina, Jean-Claude Brialy, Jane Fonda, Maurice Ronet, Catherine Spaak, Bernard Noel, Francine Bergé, Jean Sorel

Rookery Nook**
GB 1930   107m   bw
British and Dominions (Herbert Wilcox)

A nervous husband on holiday tries to hide a runaway girl who has asked for protection against her stepfather.
Primitive talkie technique cannot entirely conceal the brilliance of the original Aldwych farce team in their most enduring vehicle.

w Ben Travers, from his play d Tom Walls

Ralph Lynn, Tom Walls, Robertson Hare, Winifred Shotter, Mary Brough, Ethel Coleridge, Griffith Humphreys, Margot Grahame
'As a talker it is the best specimen so far made on this side.'—Variety

Rookies
US 1927   75m at 24 fps   bw   silent

Army adventures of a tough sergeant and a bumbling recruit. Popular comedy of its day which established the new team of Karl Dane and George K. Arthur; also with Marceline Day, Louise Lorraine, Tom O'Brien. Written by Byron Morgan; directed by Sam Wood; for MGM.

Room at the Top***
GB 1958   117m   bw
Remus (John and James Woolf)

An ambitious young clerk causes the death of his real love but manages to marry into a rich family.
Claimed as the first British film to take sex seriously, and the first to show the industrial north as it really was, this melodrama actually cheats on both counts but scene for scene is vivid and entertaining despite a weak central performance.

w Neil Paterson, novel John Braine d Jack Clayton ph Freddie Francis m Mario Nascimbene

Laurence Harvey, Simone Signoret, Heather Sears, Donald Wolfit, Ambrosine Philpotts, Donald Houston, Raymond Huntley, John Westbrook, Allan Cuthbertson, Hermione Baddeley, Mary Peach
'A drama of human drives and torments told with maturity and precision.'—Stanley Kauffmann
AA: Neil Paterson; Simone Signoret
AAN: best picture; Jack Clayton; Laurence Harvey; Hermione Baddeley
● Video: CBS / Fox

Room for One More
US 1952   95m   bw
Warner (Henry Blanke)

A married couple adopt several underprivileged children.
Slightly mawkish family movie redeemed by star performances.

w Jack Rose, Melville Shavelson d Norman Taurog ph Robert Burks m Max Steiner

Cary Grant, Betsy Drake, Lurene Tuttle, Randy Stuart, George Winslow

Room Service*
US 1938   78m   bw
RKO (Pandro S. Berman)

Penniless theatricals find ways of staying in a hotel until they can find a backer.
Claustrophobic Broadway farce unsuitably adapted for the Marx Brothers, who are constrained by having to play characters with a passing resemblance to human beings.

w Morrie Ryskind, play John Murray, Allen Boretz d William A. Seiter ph Russell Metty m Roy Webb

Groucho, Chico, Harpo, Lucille Ball, Donald MacBride, Frank Albertson, Ann Miller, Philip Loeb
'A natural for the box office . . . the change of pace is a good idea.'—Variety
'It should also be noted . . . that there is a scene in which a turkey is chased around a room. Not everybody will care for this.'—MFB
† Remade as Step Lively (qv).

Rooney*
GB 1958   88m   bw
Rank (George H. Brown)

Adventures of a bachelor Irish dustman. Moderately charming, though unconvincing, Dublin comedy.

w Patrick Kirwan, novel Catherine Cookson d George Pollock ph Christopher Challis m Philip Green

John Gregson, Barry Fitzgerald, Muriel Pavlow, June Thorburn, Noel Purcell, Marie Kean, Liam Redmond, Jack MacGowan, Eddie Byrne

Rooster Cogburn*
US 1975   108m   Technicolor
Panavision
Universal (Paul Nathan)

An elderly marshal after a gang of outlaws is helped by the Bible-thumping daughter of a priest.
Disappointing western too obviously patterned after True Grit and The African Queen. Having had the idea for outrageous star casting, the producers obviously decided erroneously that the film would make itself.

w Martin Julien d Stuart Millar ph Harry Stradling Jnr m Laurence Rosenthal

John Wayne, Katharine Hepburn, Anthony Zerbe, Richard Jordan, John McIntyre, Strother Martin

'Like one of those infuriating exhibition bouts in which two resilient old pros bob, weave and spar without ever landing any punches.'—*Michael Billington, Illustrated London News*
† 'Martin Julien' allegedly covers the writing talents of Hal Wallis, his wife Martha Hyer, and some friends.

The Root of All Evil
GB 1946   110m   bw

A jilted woman becomes unscrupulous in business in order to get even with her ex-boyfriend. Incredible farrago with a star ill at ease. Phyllis Calvert, Michael Rennie, John McCallum, Moore Marriott, Brefni O'Rourke, Hazel Court, Edward Rigby. Written and directed by Brock Williams, from the novel by J. S. Fletcher; for Gainsborough.

The Roots of Heaven*
US 1958   125m   Eastmancolor
    Cinemascope
TCF / Darryl F. Zanuck

A white man in central Africa dedicates himself to prevent the slaughtering of elephants.
Curiously patchy version of a novel which was a strange choice for filming; so many side issues are introduced that at times it takes on the look of another jolly safari adventure.

w Romain Gary, Patrick Leigh-Fermor, *novel* Romain Gary *d* John Huston *ph* Oswald Morris *m* Malcolm Arnold

Trevor Howard, Juliette Greco, Errol Flynn, Eddie Albert, Orson Welles, Paul Lukas, Herbert Lom, Grégoire Aslan, Friedrich Ledebur, Edric Connor
   'The Huston who did *Sierra Madre* would have lighted his cigar with this script.'—*Stanley Kauffmann*

Rope**
US 1948   80m   Technicolor
Transatlantic (Sidney Bernstein, Alfred Hitchcock)

Two homosexuals murder a friend for the thrill of it and conceal his body in a trunk from which they serve cocktails to a party including his father and girl friend.
An effective piece of Grand Guignol on the stage, this seemed rather tasteless when set in a New York skyscraper, especially when the leading role of the investigator was miscast and Hitch had saddled himself with the ten-minute take, a short-lived technique which made the entire action (set in one room) cinematically continuous (and dizzy-making). Of considerable historic interest, nevertheless.

w Arthur Laurents, *play* Patrick Hamilton *d* Alfred Hitchcock *ph* Joseph Valentine, William V. Skall *md* Leo F. Forbstein *theme* François Poulenc

James Stewart, John Dall, Farley Granger, Joan Chandler, Cedric Hardwicke, Constance Collier, Edith Evanson, Douglas Dick
   'It was a limiting use of the medium, and parts of the film are unbearably tedious.'—*George Perry, 1965*

'A mighty story of savage greed and sultry love!'
Rope of Sand*
US 1949   105m   bw
Paramount (Hal B. Wallis)

Various factions seek hidden diamonds in a prohibited South African area.
Ham-fisted adventure story which suggests at times that a violent parody of *Casablanca* was intended. The stars carry it through.

w Walter Doniger *d* William Dieterle *ph* Charles Lang *m* Franz Waxman

Burt Lancaster, Paul Henreid, Claude Rains, Peter Lorre, Corinne Calvet, Sam Jaffe

'The entertainment world is ablaze!'
Rosalie*
US 1937   118m   bw
MGM (William Anthony McGuire)

A college football hero falls for an incognito Balkan princess.
Ambitious light musical with a wispy plot but satisfying numbers.

w William Anthony McGuire, *play* William Anthony McGuire, Guy Bolton *d* W. S. Van Dyke *ph* Oliver T. Marsh *m* Herbert Stothart *songs* Cole Porter

Nelson Eddy, Eleanor Powell, Frank Morgan, Ray Bolger, Ilona Massey, Reginald Owen, Edna May Oliver, Jerry Colonna
   'The most lavish, ornate, tinselled and glittering production which has come from Hollywood.'—*Variety*

'She gave . . . and gave . . . and gave . . . until there was nothing left to give!'
The Rose
US 1979   134m   De Luxe
TCF (Tony Ray)

Drink and drugs cause the decline and death of a famous rock singer.
An unattractive, hysterical, foul-mouthed show business biopic roughly based on Janis Joplin, this does afford an undisciplined nightclub talent a role to get her teeth into.

w Bill Kerby, Bo Goodman *d* Mark Rydell *ph* Vilmos Zsigmond *md* Paul A. Rothchild *pd* Richard MacDonald

Bette Midler, Alan Bates, Frederic Forrest, Harry Dean Stanton, Barry Primus

● *Video: CBS / Fox*

Rose Marie
US 1936   113m   bw
MGM (Hunt Stromberg)

A Canadian Mountie gets his man—and a lady.
Backwoods romance from a stage success, filmed mostly on location and quite successfully.

w Frances Goodrich, Albert Hackett, Alice Duer Miller, *play* Otto Harbach, Oscar Hammerstein II *d* W. S. Van Dyke *ph* William Daniels *md* Herbert Stothart *songs* various

Nelson Eddy, Jeanette MacDonald, James Stewart, Reginald Owen, Allan Jones, Gilda

Gray, George Regas, Alan Mowbray, Robert Greig, Una O'Connor, David Niven, Herman Bing
   'An operatic honey with MacDonald and Eddy for the tungstens.'—*Variety*
† Previously filmed in 1928—and see below.

Rose Marie
US 1954   115m   Technicolor
    Cinemascope
MGM (Mervyn Le Roy)

Dull remake with stodgy handling and poor sets.

w Ronald Millar *d* Mervyn Le Roy *ph* Paul C. Vogel *md* Georgie Stoll *ch* Busby Berkeley

Howard Keel, Ann Blyth, Fernando Lamas, Bert Lahr, Marjorie Main, Ray Collins

'Song by song . . . scene by scene . . . the thrill grows greater!'
Rose of Washington Square**
US 1939   86m   bw
TCF (Nunnally Johnson)

Tribulations of a Broadway singer in love with a worthless husband.
Revamping of the Fanny Brice story; smartly done, but the material interpolated for Jolson is what makes the film notable.

w Nunnally Johnson *d* Gregory Ratoff *ph* Karl Freund *m* Louis Silvers *songs* various

Alice Faye, Tyrone Power, *Al Jolson, Hobart Cavanaugh*, William Frawley, Joyce Compton, Louis Prima and his band
   'This is Jolson's picture . . . the rest is also-ran.'—*Variety*

'The boldest story of love you have ever been permitted to see!'
The Rose Tattoo
US 1955   117m   bw   Vistavision
Paramount / Hal B. Wallis

A Sicilian woman on the gulf coast is tormented by the infidelity of her dead husband, but a brawny truckdriver makes her forget him.
Heavily theatrical material, unsuited to the big screen for all the powerful acting (or perhaps because of it).

w John Michael Hayes, *play* Tennessee Williams *d* Daniel Mann *ph* James Wong Howe *m* Alex North

Anna Magnani, Burt Lancaster, Marisa Pavan, Ben Cooper, Virginia Grey, Jo Van Fleet
AA: James Wong Howe; Anna Magnani
AAN: best picture; Alex North; Marisa Pavan

Roseanna McCoy
US 1949   89m   bw
Samuel Goldwyn

In old Virginia the Hatfields and the McCoys continue their feud with tragic results.
Hillbilly Romeo and Juliet saga, a shade too cornfed despite the credits.

w John Collier *d* Irving Reis *ph* Lee Garmes
m David Buttolph

Joan Evans, Farley Granger, Charles
Bickford, Raymond Massey, Richard
Basehart, Aline MacMahon

Rosebud
US 1975   126m   Eastmancolor
   Panavision
UA / Otto Preminger

Five girls of wealthy families are kidnapped by
the Palestine Liberation Army.
Overlong topical suspenser which goes awry
by not being very suspenseful, and by packing
in too many irrelevant satirical jibes.

w Erik Lee Preminger, *novel* Joan
Hemingway, Paul Bonnecarrere *d* Otto
Preminger *ph* Denys Coop *m* Laurent
Petitgerard *titles* Saul Bass

Peter O'Toole, Richard Attenborough, Cliff
Gorman, Claude Dauphin, John V. Lindsay,
Peter Lawford, Raf Vallone, Adrienne Corri

Roseland*
US 1977   103m   color
Cinema Shares / Merchant Ivory (Ismail
   Merchant)

Generation after generation, the lonely and
the loving come to a New York ballroom.
Pleasantly intentioned slice-of-life drama
which is rather slackly written and handled,
with unprofessionalism showing through at
several points.

w Ruth Prawer Jhabvala *d* James Ivory
ph Ernest Vincze *m* Michael Gibson

Geraldine Chaplin, Teresa Wright, Lou
Jacobi, Don de Natale, Louise Kirkland,
Helen Gallagher, Joan Copeland, Conrad
Janis, Lilia Skala, Christopher Walken
   'Typically discreet and dull film from
Merchant-Ivory . . . what one might call over-
decorous.'—*Time Out, 1984*
● *Video: Home Video*

Rosemary's Baby**
US 1968   137m   Technicolor
Paramount / William Castle

After unwittingly becoming friendly with
diabolists, an actor's wife is impregnated by
the Devil.
Seminal gothic melodrama which led in due
course to the excesses of *The Exorcist*; in itself
well done in a heavy-handed way, the book
being much more subtle.

wd Roman Polanski, *novel* Ira Levin
ph William Fraker *m* Krzysztof Komeda
pd Richard Sylbert

Mia Farrow, John Cassavetes, Ruth Gordon,
Sidney Blackmer, Patsy Kelly, Ralph Bellamy,
Maurice Evans, Angela Dorian, Elisha Cook,
Charles Grodin
   'It may not be for the very young, and
perhaps pregnant women should see it at their
own risk.'—*Motion Picture Herald*
   'Tension is sustained to a degree surpassing
Alfred Hitchcock at his best.'—*Daily
Telegraph*

ROSEMARY'S BABY.   Ruth Gordon, John Cassavetes, Sidney Blackmer and Mia Farrow
drink a toast, which Mia at least may live to regret.

† William Castle, the producer, is glimpsed
outside a phone booth.
†† A TV sequel followed: *Look What
Happened to Rosemary's Baby.*
AA: Ruth Gordon
AAN: Roman Polanski (as writer)

Rosie
US 1967   98m   Techniscope
Universal / Ross Hunter (Jacque Mapes)

A rich woman spends wildly and her daughters
try to have her committed to safeguard their
inheritance.
Hopelessly muddled comedy drama which flits
from one mood to the other without making a
success of either.

w Samuel Taylor, *play* Ruth Gordon, *French
original* Les Joies de la Famille by Philippe
Heriat *d* David Lowell Rich *ph* Clifford
Stine *m* Lyn Murray

Rosalind Russell, Brian Aherne, Sandra Dee,
Vanessa Brown, Audrey Meadows, James
Farentino, Leslie Nielsen, Margaret Hamilton,
Reginald Owen, Juanita Moore, Virginia Grey
   'A mawkish mixture of *Auntie Mame* and
King Lear.'—*MFB*

Rotten to the Core
GB 1965   88m   bw
   Panavision
BL / Tudor (The Boulting Brothers)

Ex-convicts plan an army payroll robbery.

Routine caper comedy, unsuitably
widescreened, with a few good jokes along the
way.

w Jeffrey Dell, Roy Boulting, John Warren,
Len Heath *d* John Boulting *ph* Freddie
Young *m* Michael Dress

Anton Rodgers, *Thorley Walters,* Eric Sykes,
Kenneth Griffith, Charlotte Rampling, Ian
Bannen, Avis Bunnage, Raymond Huntley
† The original title, *Rotten to the Corps,* was
more apt but plainly seemed too subtle.

Le Rouge et le Noir*
France / Italy 1954   170m approx
   Eastmancolor
Franco London / Documento
aka: *Scarlet and Black*

A carpenter's son becomes a private tutor,
seduces his master's wife and is sent to study
for the priesthood . . .
Massive attempt to conquer an unfilmable
novel. Some enjoyable scenes and decor are
the best it can offer.

w Jean Aurenche, Pierre Bost, Claude
Autant-Lara, *novel* Stendhal *d* Claude
Autant-Lara *ph* Michel Kelber *m* René
Cloërc *ad* Max Douy

Gérard Philipe, Danielle Darrieux, Antonella
Lualdi, Jean Martinelli

The Rough and the Smooth
GB 1959 99m bw
Renown (George Minter)
US title: *Portrait of a Sinner*

An archaeologist about to marry the niece of a press lord falls for a mysterious nymphomaniac.
Preposterous melodrama about unreal people; its very excesses become enjoyable for those who can stay the course.

w Audrey Erskine-Lindop, Dudley Leslie, *novel* Robin Maugham d Robert Siodmak ph Otto Heller md Muir Mathieson

Tony Britton, Nadja Tiller, William Bendix, Natasha Parry, Norman Wooland, Donald Wolfit, Tony Wright, Adrienne Corri, Joyce Carey

'The script is never even on nodding terms with life, and tries to make up for this deficiency by a candidly explosive vocabulary which gives the production a weirdly old-fashioned air.'—*MFB*

Rough Cut
US 1980 112m Movielab
Paramount / David Merrick

A retiring Scotland Yard inspector spars with a jewel thief and finally changes sides.
Dated comedy which required a much lighter touch in all departments.

w Francis Burns, *novel* Touch the Lion's Paw by Derek Lambert d Don Siegel ph Frederick Young m Nelson Riddle, from Duke Ellington themes pd Ted Haworth

Burt Reynolds, Lesley Anne Down, David Niven, Timothy West, Patrick Magee, Joss Ackland

'All surface smartness without a single structural idea.'—*Richard Combs, MFB*

Rough Night in Jericho
US 1967 97m Techniscope
Universal (Martin Rackin)

A stagecoach man rids a cattle town of a villain.
Totally uninteresting star western with glum performances.

w Sidney Boehm, Marvin H. Albert, *novel* The Man in Black by Marvin H. Albert d Arnold Laven ph Russell Metty m Don Costa

George Peppard, Dean Martin, Jean Simmons, John McIntire, Slim Pickens, Don Galloway, Brad Weston

Rough Shoot*
GB 1952 86m bw
Raymond Stross
US title: *Shoot First*

A retired US officer in Dorset thinks he has shot a poacher—but the dead man is a spy, and someone else shot him.
Minor Hitchcock-style thriller with a climax in Madame Tussaud's. Generally efficient and entertaining.

w Eric Ambler, *novel* Geoffrey Household d Robert Parrish ph Stan Pavey m Hans May

Joel McCrea, Evelyn Keyes, Marius Goring, Roland Culver, Frank Lawton, Herbert Lom

Roughly Speaking*
US 1945 117m bw
Warner (Henry Blanke)

Oddball, overlong domestic comedy drama about father's wild and impractical schemes.

w Louise Randall Pierson, from her book d Michael Curtiz ph Joseph Walker m Max Steiner

Rosalind Russell, Jack Carson, Robert Hutton, Jean Sullivan, Alan Hale, Donald Woods, Andrea King, Ray Collins, Kathleen Lockhart

Roughshod
US 1949 88m bw
RKO (Richard H. Berger)

Two cowboys journeying to California with a herd of horses come up against villains intent on revenge.
Likeable old-fashioned western.

w Geoffrey Homes, Hugo Butler d Mark Robson ph Joseph F. Biroc m Roy Webb

Robert Sterling, Gloria Grahame, Claude Jarman Jnr, John Ireland, Jeff Donnell, Martha Hyer

The Rounders
US 1965 85m Metrocolor Panavision
MGM (Richard E. Lyons)

Two modern cowboys mean to settle down but never get around to it.
Pale comedy western which never gets going.

wd Burt Kennedy, *novel* Max Evans ph Paul C. Vogel m Jeff Alexander

Henry Fonda, Glenn Ford, Chill Wills, Sue Anne Langdon, Edgar Buchanan

Roustabout
US 1964 101m Techniscope
Hal B. Wallis

A wandering tough guy joins a travelling carnival.
Dreary star vehicle momentarily salvaged by its co-star.

w Allan Weiss, Anthony Lawrence d John Rich ph Lucien Ballard m Joseph L. Lilley

Elvis Presley, Barbara Stanwyck, Sue Ann Langdon, Joan Freeman, Leif Erickson

● *Video: CBS / Fox*

'The low down story of a high class gal!'
Roxie Hart**
US 1942 72m bw
TCF (Nunnally Johnson)

A twenties showgirl confesses for the sake of publicity to a murder of which she is innocent.
Crowded Chicago burlesque which now seems less funny than it did but is full of smart moments.

w Nunnally Johnson, *play* Chicago by Maurine Watkins d William Wellman ph Leon Shamroy m Alfred Newman

Ginger Rogers, George Montgomery, *Adolphe Menjou*, Lynne Overman, Nigel Bruce, Spring Byington, Sara Allgood, William Frawley

DEDICATION: To all the beautiful women in the world who have shot their husbands full of holes out of pique.

'A masterpiece of form, of ensemble acting, of powerhouse comedy and scripting.'—*NFT, 1974*

† The play was also filmed in 1927 under its original title, with Phyllis Haver.

Royal African Rifles
US 1954 75m Cinecolor

In British East Africa in 1914, a lieutenant tracks down a consignment of stolen guns.
Mini-budget *Boys Own Paper* heroics; quite enjoyable on its level. Louis Hayward, Veronica Hurst, Michael Pate, Angela Greene, Steve Geray, Bruce Lester. Written by Dan Ullman; directed by Lesley Selander; for Allied Artists. (GB title: *Storm over Africa.*)

The Royal Bed
US 1931 74m bw

The king and queen of a European country lead their own private lives. Insufficient wit graces this would-be daring romantic drama from a Broadway hit. Mary Astor, Lowell Sherman, Nance O'Neill, Anthony Bushell, Robert Warwick. Written by J. Walter Ruben, from the play *The Queen's Husband* by Robert E. Sherwood; directed by Lowell Sherman; for RKO. (GB title: *The Queen's Husband.*)

Royal Cavalcade
GB 1935 104m bw

A chronicle of the events of the reign of King George V. Thoroughly embarrassing jubilee tribute, of historical interest only. Marie Lohr, Hermione Baddeley, Esme Percy, John Mills, Reginald Gardiner, Syd Walker, Seymour Hicks, Owen Nares, Matheson Lang, George Robey, Florrie Forde, many others. Written by Marjorie Deans; directed by Marcel Varnel, Thomas Bentley, Herbert Brenon, Norman Lee, Walter Summers and Will Kellino; for BIP.

A Royal Divorce
GB 1938 85m bw

Napoleon Bonaparte in 1809 marries a widow whose reputation isn't exactly spotless. Heavy comedy or light drama, take your pick; not exactly riveting as either. Pierre Blanchar, Ruth Chatterton, Frank Cellier, Carol Goodner, George Curzon, John Laurie, Jack Hawkins. Written by Miles Malleson, from the novel *Josephine* by Jacques Thery; directed by Jack Raymond; for Herbert Wilcox.

The Royal Family of Broadway*
US 1930 82m bw
Paramount
GB title: *Theatre Royal*

The off-stage escapades of a famous family of actors.
Fairly funny lampoon of the Barrymores, primitively staged and very talky but still entertaining for those in the joke.

w Herman J. Mankiewicz, Gertrude Purcell, *play* George S. Kaufman, Edna Ferber *d* George Cukor, Cyril Gardner *ph* George Folsey

Fredric March, Henrietta Crosman, Ina Claire, Mary Brian, Charles Starrett, Frank Conroy

'Lionel does not come into the burlesque at all, and I can quite believe that he is the most damaged of the entire family.'—*James Agate*

'Stagebound and awkward, but great fun anyway.'—*New Yorker, 1977*

AAN: Fredric March

Royal Flash
GB 1975   118m   Technicolor
TCF / Two Roads (David V. Picker, Denis O'Dell)

A Victorian bully and braggart has various adventures in Europe and Ruritania.
A rather unsatisfactory romp which takes pot shots at every 19th-century person and object in the encyclopaedia, but is never as funny as it intends to be.

w George Macdonald Fraser, from his novel *d* Richard Lester *ph* Geoffrey Unsworth *m* Ken Thorpe *ph* Terence Marsh

Malcolm McDowall, Oliver Reed, Alan Bates, Florinda Bolkan, Britt Ekland, Lionel Jeffries, Tom Bell, Joss Ackland, Leon Greene, Richard Hurndall, Alastair Sim, Michael Hordern

● *Video: CBS / Fox*

The Royal Hunt of the Sun
GB 1969   121m   Technicolor
Security Pictures (Eugene Frenke, Philip Yordan)

How the Spanish soldier Pizarro on his South American trek overcame the Inca god-king Atahualpa.
Deadly literal rendering with nothing to replace the play's theatrical splendour, resembling nothing so much as an opera without the music.

w Philip Yordan, *play* Peter Shaffer *d* Irving Lerner *ph* Roger Barlow, Marc Wilkinson

Robert Shaw, Christopher Plummer, Nigel Davenport, Michael Craig, Leonard Whiting, Andrew Keir, James Donald, Percy Herbert, Alexander Davion

A Royal Scandal
US 1945   94m   bw
TCF (Ernst Lubitsch)
GB title: *Czarina*

The illicit loves of Catherine the Great.
Censored romps around some chilly court sets; very few moments of interest, and none of the style of the silent version *Forbidden Paradise*.

w Edwin Justus Mayer, *play* Lajos Biro, Melchior Lengyel *d* Otto Preminger *ph* Arthur Miller *m* Alfred Newman

Tallulah Bankhead, Charles Coburn, Anne Baxter, William Eythe, Vincent Price, Mischa Auer, Sig Rumann, Vladimir Sokoloff

'Nothing is one-tenth well enough done, and all the laughs are played for at their cheapest, far down the ramp.'—*James Agee*

Royal Wedding
US 1951   93m   Technicolor
MGM (Arthur Freed)
GB title: *Wedding Bells*

Journalists congregate in London for the royal wedding.
Thin musical with acceptable numbers.

w Alan Jay Lerner *d* Stanley Donen *ph* Robert Planck *md* Johnny Green *songs* Alan Jay Lerner, Burton Lane

Fred Astaire, Jane Powell, Sarah Churchill, Peter Lawford, Keenan Wynn

AAN: song 'Too Late Now' (*m* Burton Lane, *ly* Alan Jay Lerner)

'Dangerous . . . destructive . . . deadly to love!'
Ruby Gentry
US 1952   82m   bw
Joseph Bernhard / King Vidor

A tempestuous girl, brought up as a boy in the Carolina swamps, has a love-hate relationship with a local aristocrat, revenges herself on the people who scorn her, loses her lover in a swamp shooting, and becomes a sea captain.
Richly absurd sex melodrama typical of its director and star yet not very entertaining.

w Sylvia Richards *d* King Vidor *ph* Russell Harlan *m* Heinz Roemheld *ad* Dan Hall

Jennifer Jones, Charlton Heston, Karl Malden, Josephine Hutchinson

● *Video: Guild*

Rue de l'Estrapade*
France 1953   95m   bw
Cinephonic / SGGC / Filmsonor
aka: *Françoise Steps Out*

A young Parisienne suspects her husband of having an affair.
Lightly likeable domestic comedy in the vein of *Edouard et Caroline*, but not quite up to its standard.

w Annette Wademant *d* Jacques Becker *ph* Marcel Grignon *m* Georges Van Parys, Marguerite Monnot

Louis Jourdan, Anne Vernon, Daniel Gelin, Jean Servais, Micheline Dax

'Five comedy stars in a five-star comedy!'
Ruggles of Red Gap**
US 1935   90m   bw
Paramount (Arthur Hornblow Jnr)

A British butler has a startling effect on the family of an American rancher who takes him out west.
A famous comedy which seemed hilarious at the time but can now be seen as mostly composed of flat spots; the performances however are worth remembering.

w Walter de Leon, Harlan Thompson, Humphrey Pearson, *novel* Harry Leon Wilson *d* Leo McCarey *ph* Alfred Gilks

Charles Laughton, Mary Boland, Charles Ruggles, Zasu Pitts, Roland Young, Leila Hyams, James Burke, Maude Eburne, Lucien Littlefield

'Plenty of marquee strength, and dynamite on the inside. An A1 comedy.'—*Variety*

'A sane, witty, moving and quite unusual picture of Anglo-American relations.'—*C. A. Lejeune*

'The most heart-warming comedy of the season . . . there is about it a sympathetic and even a patriotic quality which is touching.'—*Literary Digest*

'The archetypal film they don't make any more, partly because comedy has now grown too raucous to favour the quiet drollery of players like Charlie Ruggles and Mary Boland, partly because even McCarey himself had trouble after the thirties separating sentiment from sentimentality.'—*Time Out, 1980*

† Remade as *Fancy Pants* (qv).

AAN: best picture

Rulers of the Sea*
US 1939   96m   bw
Paramount (Frank Lloyd)

Problems surround the first steamship voyage across the Atlantic.
Well-made period action drama.

w Talbot Jennings, Frank Cavett, Richard Collins *d* Frank Lloyd *ph* Theodor Sparkuhl, Archie Stout *m* Richard Hageman

Douglas Fairbanks Jnr, Margaret Lockwood, Will Fyffe, Montagu Love, George Bancroft, Mary Gordon, Alan Ladd

'Timely in content and grand for exploitation. In the British Empire it will be greeted as inspirational entertainment.'—*Variety*

The Ruling Class*
GB 1971   155m   De Luxe
Keep Films (Jules Buck, Jack Hawkins)

The fetishistic Earl of Gurney is succeeded by his mad son Jack who believes he is God.
An overlong satirical play with brilliant patches is hamfistedly filmed but boasts some bright performances. The hits are as random as the misses, however.

w Peter Barnes, from his play *d* Peter Medak *ph* Ken Hodges *m* John Cameron

Peter O'Toole, Harry Andrews, *Arthur Lowe, Alastair Sim*, Coral Browne, Michael Bryant

'This irritating and unsatisfying film is worth being irritated and unsatisfied by.'—*Stanley Kauffmann*

AAN: Peter O'Toole

'This is the dance of love!'
Rumba*
US 1935   71m   bw
Paramount (William Le Baron)

A society girl has a yen for a Broadway hoofer.
Streamlined star vehicle which attempts to recapture the success of *Bolero* (qv).

w Howard J. Green *d* Marion Gering *ph* Ted Tetzlaff

Carole Lombard, George Raft, Margo, Lynn Overman, Monroe Owsley, Iris Adrian, Gail Patrick, Samuel S. Hinds, Jameson Thomas

Rumble Fish

US 1983　94m　bw (with colour inserts)

A Tulsa teenager survives local gang violence and while working in a petshop sees himself in the rumble fish, which fights even its own image in a glass. Glum piece of self-absorption by a director going rapidly downhill. Matt Dillon, Mickey Rourke, Diane Lane, Dennis Hopper, Diana Scarwid. Written and directed by Francis Ford Coppola from the novel by S. E. Hinton; for Zoetrope.

Run for Cover*

US 1955　92m　Technicolor　Vistavision
Paramount (William H. Pine)

An ex-convict becomes innocently involved in a train robbery.
Adequate star western.

w William C. Thomas, *story* Harriet Frank Jnr, Irving Ravetch　*d* Nicholas Ray　*ph* Daniel Fapp　*md* Howard Jackson

James Cagney, Viveca Lindfors, John Derek, Jean Hersholt, Grant Withers, Ernest Borgnine, Jack Lambert

Run for the Sun

US 1956　99m　Technicolor　Superscope
UA / Russ–Field (Harry Tatelman)

Crashlanding in the Mexican jungle, a disillusioned author and a lady journalist find themselves at the mercy of renegade Nazis. Tame remake of *The Most Dangerous Game* with Count Zaroff replaced by Lord Haw-Haw. Sluggish plot development mars the action.

w Dudley Nichols, Roy Boulting　*d* Roy Boulting　*ph* Joseph La Shelle　*m* Fred Steiner

Richard Widmark, Jane Greer, Trevor Howard, Peter Van Eyck

A Run for Your Money*

GB 1949　83m　bw
Ealing (Leslie Norman)

Welsh Rugby supporters have various adventures on their one day in London. Slight, bright, British chase comedy with characterizations as excellent as they are expected.

w Richard Hughes, Charles Frend, Leslie Norman　*d* Charles Frend　*ph* Douglas Slocombe　*m* Ernest Irving

Alec Guinness, Meredith Edwards, Moira Lister, Donald Houston, Hugh Griffith, Clive Morton, Joyce Grenfell

Run of the Arrow

US 1956　85m　Technicolor　RKOscope
Global (Samuel Fuller)

An ex-Civil War soldier is captured by Indians and accepted by them, but sickened by their violence.
Bloody little western in the accustomed Fuller vein of unpleasantness.

wd Samuel Fuller　*ph* Joseph Biroc　*m* Victor Young

Rod Steiger, Sarita Montiel, Charles Bronson, Tim McCoy, Ralph Meeker

Run Silent Run Deep*

US 1958　93m　bw
UA / Hecht–Hill–Lancaster (William Schorr)

Antagonisms flare up between the officers of a US submarine in Tokyo Bay during World War II.
Competent, unsurprising war actioner trading on its stars.

w John Gay　*d* Robert Wise　*ph* Russell Harlan　*m* Franz Waxman

Clark Gable, Burt Lancaster, Jack Warden, Brad Dexter, Nick Cravat, Joe Maross, H. M. Wynant

'Mostly good sea fights. Otherwise it's damn the torpedoes, half speed ahead.'—*Time*

Run Wild, Run Free*

GB 1969　98m　Technicolor
Columbia / Irving Allen (John Danischewsky)

A mute boy living on Dartmoor gains self-confidence through the love of animals. Rather vaguely developed family film with agreeable sequences.

w David Rook, from his novel The White Colt, *d* Richard C. Sarafian　*ph* Wilkie Cooper　*m* David Whitaker

John Mills, Sylvia Syms, Mark Lester, Bernard Miles, Gordon Jackson, Fiona Fullerton

The Runaround*

US 1946　100m　bw
Universal (Joseph Gershenson)

Two rival detectives are hired to find a missing heiress.
Peripatetic comedy on the lines of *It Happened One Night*; unexpectedly enjoyable.

w Arthur T. Horman, Sam Hellman　*d* Charles Lamont　*ph* George Robinson　*m* Frank Skinner

Rod Cameron, Broderick Crawford, Ella Raines, Samuel S. Hinds, Frank McHugh, George Cleveland

Runaway

US 1984　100m　Metrocolor
Tri-Star / Michael Crichton (Michael Rachmil)

An electronics wizard sets a half-perfected robot on the rampage.
Simple-minded comedy-melodrama which feels as though it ought to have been played entirely for laughs.

w,d Michael Crichton　*ph* John A. Alonzo　*m* Jerry Goldsmith　*pd* Douglas Higgins　*ed* Glenn Farr

Tom Selleck, Cynthia Rhodes, Gene L. Simmons, Kirstie Alley, Stan Shaw

The Runaway Bus*

GB 1954　78m　bw
Eros / Conquest–Guest (Val Guest)

Passengers at London Airport are fogbound, and a relief bus driver takes some of them to Blackbushe. Incognito among them are robbers and detectives . . .

Vaguely plotted variation on *The Ghost Train*, with fair production, a good smattering of jokes, and a hilarious view of a great airport in its earlier days.

wd Val Guest　*ph* Stan Pabey　*m* Ronald Binge

Frankie Howerd, Margaret Rutherford, George Coulouris, Petula Clark, Terence Alexander, Toke Townley, Belinda Lee

The Runner Stumbles

US 1979　110m　CFI color
Melvin Simon Productions (Stanley Kramer)

In the mid-twenties, a Catholic priest is accused of the murder of a nun for whom he had felt a strong romantic attraction. Musty exhumation of a genuine case which has little dramatic interest and even less wider significance. Good acting does not atone.

w Milan Stiff, from his play　*d* Stanley Kramer　*ph* Laszlo Kovacs　*m* Ernest Gold　*pd* Alfred Sweency Jnr

Dick Van Dyke, Kathleen Quinlan, Maureen Stapleton, Ray Bolger, Tammy Grimes, Beau Bridges

'The reanimated corpse of middlebrow Hollywood pretension . . . funereal pacing, portentous low angles and symbolic overkill.'—*Paul Taylor, MFB*

● *Video: Guild*

Runners

GB 1983　106m　colour
Goldcrest (Barry Hanson)

Distraught parents try to trace their missing children in London.
Heavy-going realistic drama with apparent inner meanings which are not brought to the surface.

w Stephen Poliakoff　*d* Charles Sturridge　*ph* Howard Atherton　*m* George Fenton　*pd* Arnold Chapkis

James Fox, Kate Hardie, Jane Asher, Eileen O'Brien, Ruti Simon

● *Video: VCL*

Running Brave

US 1983　106m　colour

A young Sioux from the reservation faces the pressures of the white world and becomes an Olympic runner. The terrible punning title is the best thing in this very predictable piece of do-goodery, which would just about have passed muster as a TV movie. Robby Benson, Pat Hingle, Claudia Cron, Jeff McCracken. Written by Henry Bean, Shirl Hendrix; directed by D. S. Everett; for Englander Productions. 'This is in essence a propaganda film for the American way, masked as a piece of liberal sentiment, and I distrust it thoroughly.'—*Observer*

The Running Man*

GB 1963　103m　Technicolor　Panavision
Columbia / Peet (Carol Reed, John R. Sloan)

A private airline pilot fakes an accident and

disappears, leaving his wife to collect the insurance and meet him in Spain.
Flabby, expensive suspenser; both plot and character take a back seat to scenic views.

w John Mortimer, *novel* The Ballad of the Running Man by Shelley Smith *d* Carol Reed *ph* Robert Krasker *m* William Alwyn

Laurence Harvey, Alan Bates, Lee Remick, Felix Aylmer, Eleanor Summerfield, Allan Cuthbertson

'There seems to be something about the panoramic screen that seduces film-makers into filling it with irrelevant local colour and drawing the whole proceedings out to a length that matches its width.'—*Brenda Davies*

Running Scared
GB 1972 98m Technicolor Panavision
Paramount / Wigan / Hemmings / O'Toole (Gareth Wigan)

A university student is generally condemned for allowing his friend to commit suicide; eventually he takes his own life.
Depressing and rather pointless exercise in death wish complicated by a doomed love affair.

w Clive Exton, David Hemmings, *novel* Gregory MacDonald *d* David Hemmings *ph* Ernest Day *m* Michael J. Lewis

Robert Powell, Gayle Hunnicutt, Barry Morse, Stephanie Bidmead, Edward Underdown, Maxine Audley, Georgia Brown

Russian Roulette
US 1975 90m Eastmancolor
ITC / Elliott Kastner / Bulldog

Real and fake secret agents shoot it out when the Russian premier is about to visit Vancouver.
Fast-moving but impossible to follow location thriller which resolves itself into a series of chases.

w Tom Ardies, Stanley Mann, Arnold Margolin, *novel* Kosygin is Coming by Tom Ardies *d* Lou Lombardo *ph* Brian West *m* Michael J. Lewis

George Segal, Gordon Jackson, Denholm Elliott, Cristina Raines, Richard Romanus, Louise Fletcher, Nigel Stock
'A stale, mechanical espionage caper that wastes its star.'—*Kevin Thomas*

● *Video: Precision*

The Russians Are Coming, The Russians Are Coming*
US 1966 126m De Luxe Panavision
UA / Mirisch (Norman Jewison)

Russian submariners make a forced landing on a Connecticut holiday island and cause panic.
'Daring' cold war comedy which turns out to be of the most elementary and protracted nature, saved from boredom only by a few cameos.

w William Rose, *novel* The Off-Islanders by Nathaniel Benchley *d* Norman Jewison *ph* Joseph Biroc *m* Johnny Mandel

Carl Reiner, Eva Marie Saint, Alan Arkin, John Philip Law, Paul Ford, Tessie O'Shea, Brian Keith, Jonathan Winters, Theodore Bikel, Ben Blue
'Rather amiable, though the film, like its title, seems to repeat most things twice.'—*Sight and Sound*
'Why the crazy title? If we told you, you'd only laugh!'—*publicity*

AAN: best picture; William Rose; Alan Arkin

'Love betrayed them—power destroyed them!'

Ruthless*
US 1948 104m bw
Eagle Lion / Arthur S. Lyons

A conniver breaks several lives on his way to the top.
Rich melodrama with some entertaining moments.

w S. K. Lauren, Gordon Kahn, *novel* Prelude to Night by Dayton Stoddert *d* Edgar G. Ulmer *ph* Bert Glennon *m* Werner Janssen

Zachary Scott, Sidney Greenstreet, Diana Lynn, Louis Hayward, Martha Vickers, Lucille Bremer, Edith Barrett, Raymond Burr, Dennis Hoey

'Beginning pictures at the end
Is, I'm afraid, the modern trend.
But I'd find *Ruthless* much more winning
If it could end at the beginning.'
                              —*C. A. Lejeune*

RX Murder
GB 1958 85m bw Cinemascope

The doctor of a small seaside resort has had four wives die on him. Could it be murder?
Modest mystery with an obvious outcome.
Marius Goring, Rick Jason, Lisa Gastoni, Mary Merrall, Vida Hope, Phyllis Neilson-Terry, Frederick Leister, Nicholas Hannen.
Written and directed by Derek Twist, from the novel The Deeds of Dr Deadcert by Joan Fleming; for TCF. (GB release title: *Family Doctor*.)

Ryan's Daughter**
GB 1970 206m Metrocolor
      Panavision 70
MGM / Faraway (Anthony Havelock-Allan)

1916 Ireland: a village schoolmaster's wife falls for a British officer.
A modestly effective pastoral romantic melodrama, stretched on the rack of its director's meticulous film-making technique and unnecessarily big budget. A beautiful, impressive, well-staged and well-acted film, but not really four hours' worth of drama.

w Robert Bolt *d* David Lean *ph* Frederick A. Young *m* Maurice Jarre *pd* Stephen Grimes (who created an entire village)

Sarah Miles, Robert Mitchum, Chris Jones, John Mills, Trevor Howard, Leo McKern
'Instead of looking like the money it cost to make, the film feels like the time it took to shoot.'—*Alexander Walker*
'Gush made respectable by millions of dollars tastefully wasted.'—*Pauline Kael*

AA: Frederick A. Young; John Mills
AAN: Sarah Miles

● *Video: MGM / UA*

S.O.B.
US 1981   121m   colour   Panavision
Lorimar / Geoffrey (Blake Edwards, Tony
    Adams)

A Hollywood director goes bananas when his
much-touted epic is a fiasco, and decides to
remake it as a sex picture.
Tasteless, vulgar and unfunny comedy, with
everybody shouting at once and most of the
jokes about vomiting, farting and funerals.
Julie Andrews, who is made to bare her
breasts, could surely use it as grounds for
divorce.

wd Blake Edwards *ph* Harry Stradling
m Henry Mancini

Julie Andrews, Richard Mulligan, *Robert
Preston*, William Holden, Robert Vaughn,
Robert Webber, Larry Hagman, Shelley
Winters, Marisa Berenson, Loretta Swit, Craig
Stevens, Robert Loggia
    'One feels that this in-house comedy was in
some way intended as a purge and not an
entertainment.'—*John Pym, MFB*
    'At best the humour is cheap and at worst
unnecessarily vulgar.'—*Margaret Hinxman,
Daily Mail*
† S.O.B., it seems, stands no longer for Son
Of a Bitch but for Standard Operational
Bullshit.
● *Video: Guild*

SOS Iceberg*
US 1933   117m (at first showings)   bw

A young scientist seeks to recover the records
of the lost Wegener expedition to the Arctic.
At the time this was a spectacular semi-
documentary, but it did no business. Rod la
Rocque, Leni Riefenstahl, Sepp Rist, Gibson
Gowland. Written by Tom Reed, Edwin H.
Knopf; directed by Tay Garnett, for
Universal.
† The production was begun in Berlin and
taken over by Universal when the producers
ran out of money.

SOS Pacific*
GB 1959   91m   bw
Rank / Sydney Box (John Nasht, Patrick
    Filmer-Sankey)

Survivors of a Pacific plane crash await rescue
on a small island which is the site of an
imminent H-bomb test.
Satisfactory open-air thick ear with strongly
deployed types and a suspense climax.

w Robert Westerby *d* Guy Green *ph* Wilkie
Cooper

Eddie Constantine, Pier Angeli, John
Gregson, Richard Attenborough, Eva Bartok,
Clifford Evans, Jean Anderson, Cec Linder

Saadia
US 1953   87m   Technicolor
MGM (Albert Lewin)

A young French doctor in the Sahara has
trouble with the local witch doctor.
Pretentious and ill-considered multi-national
romance from the champion of Omar's
Rubaiyat.

wd Albert Lewin, *novel* Echec au Destin by
Francis D'Autheville *ph* Christopher Challis
m Bronislau Kaper

Cornel Wilde, Mel Ferrer, Rita Gam, Michel
Simon, Wanda Rotha, Cyril Cusack, Marcel
Poncin, Peter Bull

Sabotage***
GB 1936   76m   bw
Gaumont British (Michael Balcon, Ivor
    Montagu)
US title: *A Woman Alone*

The proprietor of a small London cinema is a
dangerous foreign agent.
Unattractively plotted but fascinatingly
detailed Hitchcock suspenser with famous
sequences and a splendidly brooding
melodramatic atmosphere.

w Charles Bennett, Ian Hay, Helen Simpson,
E. V. H. Emmett, *novel* The Secret Agent by
Joseph Conrad *d Alfred Hitchcock*
ph Bernard Knowles *md* Louis Levy
Oscar Homolka, Sylvia Sidney, John Loder,
Desmond Tester, Joyce Barbour, Matthew
Boulton
    'Tightly packed, economical, full of
invention and detail.'—*NFT, 1961*

● *Video: Rank*

Saboteur***
US 1942   108m   bw
Universal (Frank Lloyd, Jack H. Skirball)

A war worker unjustly suspected of sabotage
flees across the country and unmasks a spy
ring.
Flawed Hitchcock action thriller, generally
unsatisfactory in plot and pace but with
splendid sequences at a ball, in Radio City
Music Hall, and atop the Statue of Liberty.

w Peter Viertel, Joan Harrison, Dorothy
Parker, *story* Alfred Hitchcock *d Alfred
Hitchcock ph* Joseph Valentine *m* Frank
Skinner *md* Charles Previn

Robert Cummings, Priscilla Lane, Otto
Kruger, Alan Baxter, Alma Kruger, *Norman
Lloyd*
    'It throws itself forward so rapidly that it
allows slight opportunity for looking back.'—
New York Times
    'The drama of a nation stirred to action, of a
people's growing realization of themselves and
their responsibilities.'—*Motion Picture Herald*
† Hitchcock wanted for the three leading roles
Gary Cooper, Barbara Stanwyck and Harry
Carey, but all refused or were unavailable.

'World War II espionage adventure and
    human lives have never before been
    combined so explosively!'

The Saboteur, Code Name Morituri*
US 1965   122m   bw
TCF / Arcola / Colony (Aaron Rosenberg)
aka: *Morituri; The Saboteur*

In 1942 a German pacifist working for the
allies is actually a German spy.
Dreary as a whole, suspenseful in snatches,
this shipboard melodrama is full of
irrelevancies and is in any case played much
more seriously than the matter demands.

w Daniel Taradash, *novel* Werner Jeorg
Kosa *d* Bernhard Wicki *ph* Conrad Hall
m Jerry Goldsmith

Yul Brynner, Marlon Brando, Trevor
Howard, Janet Margolin

AAN: Conrad Hall

Sabre Jet
US 1953   96m   Cinecolor

A US Air Force colonel in Korea has trouble
with his career-hunting wife as well as with the
enemy. Propaganda cheapie with a few stirring
aerial moments. Robert Stack, Coleen Gray,
Richard Arlen, Julie Bishop, and Leon Ames,
Amanda Blake. Written by Dale Eunson and
Katherine Albert; directed by Louis King; for
Krueger Productions / UA.

Sabrina*
US 1954   113m   bw
Paramount (Billy Wilder)
GB title: *Sabrina Fair*

The chauffeur's daughter is wooed by both her
brother employers.

Superior comedy, rather uneasily cast.

w Billy Wilder, *play* Samuel Taylor *d* Billy Wilder *ph* Charles Lang Jnr *m* Frederick Hollander

Humphrey Bogart, William Holden, Audrey Hepburn, Walter Hampden, John Williams, Martha Hyer, Joan Vohs, Marcel Dalio

'This is never less than a glittering entertainment, but somehow a certain measure of lead has found its way into the formula.'—*Time*

† Cary Grant was sought for the role played by Bogart.

AAN: Billy Wilder (as writer and director); Charles Lang Jnr; Audrey Hepburn

The Sad Sack

US 1957   98m   bw   Vistavision
Paramount (Paul Nathan)

Adventures of an army misfit.
Resistible star comedy.

w Edmund Beloin, Nate Monaster, *cartoon* George Baker *d* George Marshall *ph* Loyal Griggs *m* Walter Scharf

Jerry Lewis, David Wayne, Phyllis Kirk, Peter Lorre, Joe Mantell, Gene Evans, George Dolenz, Liliane Montvecchi, Shepperd Strudwick

Saddle the Wind*

US 1958   84m   Metrocolor
Cinemascope
MGM (Armand Deutsch)

A reformed gunman's young brother gets into bad company.
Modestly effective, humourless western drama.

w Rod Serling *d* Robert Parrish *ph* George J. Folsey *m* Jeff Alexander

Robert Taylor, John Cassavetes, Julie London, Donald Crisp, Charles McGraw, Royal Dano, Richard Erdman

Saddle Tramp

US 1950   76m   Technicolor

A wandering cowboy adopts four orphan children and after various adventures marries the eldest of them. Mild family western for star fanciers. Joel McCrea, Wanda Hendrix, John Russell, John McIntire, Jeanette Nolan, Russell Simpson. Written by Harold Shumate; directed by Hugo Fregonese; for Universal-International.

Sadie McKee*

US 1934   88m   bw
MGM (Lawrence Weingarten)

A maid at various times loves her master, a young ne'er-do-well, and a middle-aged millionaire.
Solidly carpentered millgirl's romance of the period.

w John Meehan, *story* Vina Delmar *d* Clarence Brown *ph* Oliver T. Marsh

Joan Crawford, Franchot Tone, Gene Raymond, Edward Arnold, Esther Ralston, Jean Dixon, Leo Carrillo, Akim Tamiroff

'The stuff the fans cry for.'—*Hollywood Reporter*

Sadie Thompson*

US 1928   95m (24 fps)   bw   silent
Gloria Swanson

In the South Seas, a fire-and-brimstone missionary is attracted to a prostitute.
Steamy, much-filmed melodrama (see *Rain, Miss Sadie Thompson*). This version has long been unavailable for revaluation.

w G. Gardner Sullivan, *story* Rain by W. Somerset Maugham *d* Raoul Walsh *ph* George Barnes, Robert Kurrle *ad* William Cameron Menzies

Gloria Swanson, Lionel Barrymore, Blanche Frederici, Charles Lane, Florence Midgley, Raoul Walsh

'It's stirring and ironic and funny. You couldn't ask more.'—*Photoplay*

AAN: George Barnes; Gloria Swanson

Safari

GB 1956   91m   Technicolor
Cinemascope
Warwick (Adrian Worker)

A white hunter falls in love with the wife of his employer and luckily the latter is killed by the Mau Mau.
Feeble adventure story exploiting political tensions.

w Anthony Veiller *d* Terence Young *ph* John Wilcox, Fred Ford, Ted Moore *m* William Alwyn

Victor Mature, Janet Leigh, Roland Culver, John Justin, Earl Cameron, Liam Redmond, Orlando Martins

The Safecracker

GB 1958   96m   bw
MGM / Coronado (David E. Rose)

A safecracker is released to help in a commando raid during World War II.
One-twelfth of a dirty dozen, with a long indecisive lead-up and not much pull as drama or comedy.

w Paul Monash, *story* Rhys Davies *d* Ray Milland *ph* Gerald Gibbs *m* Richard Rodney Bennett

Ray Milland, Barry Jones, Jeanette Sterke, Victor Maddern, Ernest Clark, Cyril Raymond, Melissa Stribling

Safety Last***

US 1923   70m (24 fps)   bw   silent
Harold Lloyd

A small-town boy goes to the big city and to impress his girl friend enters a contest to climb a skyscraper.
Marvellous star comedy which set a new standard not only in sight gags but in the comedy-thrill stunts which became Lloyd's stock-in-trade.

w Harold Lloyd, Sam Taylor, Tim Whelan, Hal Roach *d* Sam Taylor, Fred Newmeyer *ph* Walter Lundin

Harold Lloyd, Mildred Davis, Noah Young

The Saga of Anatahan

Japan 1953   90m   bw

During the Pacific war, castaways on a remote island kill each other for the sake of one woman. A curious footnote to its director's career, this mannered film is entirely in Japanese with English commentary, and does not recommend itself to western audiences. Written and directed by Josef Von Sternberg; for Daiwa productions.

Sahara**

US 1943   97m   bw
Columbia (Harry Joe Brown)

During the retreat from Tobruk a group of men of mixed nationality find water for themselves and harass the Nazis.
Good, simple war actioner with a realistic feel and strong characters deployed in melodramatic situations.

w John Howard Lawson, Zoltan Korda *d* Zoltan Korda *ph* Rudolph Maté *m* Miklos Rozsa

Humphrey Bogart, Bruce Bennett, Lloyd Bridges, Rex Ingram, J. Carrol Naish, Dan Duryea, Kurt Kreuger

'It borrows, chiefly from the English, a sort of light-alloy modification of realism which makes the traditional Hollywood idiom seem as obsolete as a minuet.'—*James Agee*

'The tank keeps rolling, picking up strays along the way until it has a full Hollywood ethnic complement.'—*Pauline Kael, 70s*

AAN: Rudolph Maté; J. Carrol Naish

'It's dynamite—when these two come together in the powderkeg city of the Far East!'
Saigon
US 1947   93m   bw
Paramount (P. J. Wolfson)

Veteran airmen in Saigon are offered half a million to help in a robbery.
Tired studio-set star actioner.

w P. J. Wolfson, Arthur Sheekman *d* Leslie Fenton *ph* John Seitz *m* Robert Emmett Dolan

Alan Ladd, Veronica Lake, Douglas Dick, Wally Cassell, Luther Adler, Morris Carnovsky, Mikhail Rasumny

Sail a Crooked Ship

US 1961   88m   bw
Columbia / Philip Barry Jnr

A shipowner unwittingly takes on a crew of crooks intending to use the boat as a getaway after a bank robbery.
Flimsy comedy sustained by a star comedian.

w Ruth Brooks Flippen, Bruce Geller, *novel* Nathaniel Benchley *d* Irving Brecher *ph* Joseph Biroc *m* George Duning

Robert Wagner, *Ernie Kovacs,* Dolores Hart, Carolyn Jones, Frank Gorshin

Sailing Along

GB 1938   90m   bw
Gaumont-British

A girl barge hand meets an impresario and becomes a dancing star.

Rather deadly British musical romance with the star not at her best, the supporting talents wasted, and a generally heavy hand in evidence.

wd Sonnie Hale *ph* Glen MacWilliams *m / ly* Arthur Johnston, Maurice Sigler *ad* Alfred Junge

Jessie Matthews, Roland Young, Barry Mackay, Jack Whiting, Noel Madison, Alastair Sim, Athene Seyler, Frank Pettingell

Sailor Beware
US 1952 103m bw
Paramount / Hal B. Wallis

Martin and Lewis in the navy.
Unlovable star antics.

w James Allardice, Martin Rackin, *play* Kenyon Nicholson, Charles Robinson *d* Hal Walker *ph* Daniel L. Fapp *m* Joseph J. Lilley

Dean Martin, Jerry Lewis, Corinne Calvet, Marion Marshall, Robert Strauss, Leif Erickson

Sailor Beware*
GB 1956 80m bw
Romulus (Jack Clayton)
US title: *Panic in the Parlor*

A young sailor has trouble with his mother-in-law-to-be.
Plain but adequate film version of a successful lowbrow stage farce about an archetypal female dragon.

w Philip King and Falkland L. Cary, from their play *d* Gordon Parry *ph* Douglas Slocombe *m* Peter Akister

Peggy Mount, Esma Cannon, Cyril Smith, Shirley Eaton, Ronald Lewis

The Sailor Takes a Wife
US 1945 91m bw

A sailor on leave gets married and finds he has acquired a few problems. Rather self-consciously cute sentimental comedy, proficiently staged. June Allyson, Robert Walker, Reginald Owen, Hume Cronyn, Eddie Anderson, Audrey Totter, Gerald Oliver Smith. Written by Anne Chapin and Whitfield Cook, from a play by Chester Erskine; directed by Richard Whorf; for MGM.

'He gave his soul to the sea and his heart to a woman! Their love will arouse you— their story will disturb you—the ending will startle you!'

The Sailor Who Fell from Grace with the Sea
GB 1976 105m Technicolor
AVCO / Sailor Company (Martin Poll)

A precocious boy interferes with his widowed mother's affair with a sailor by castrating the latter.
Weird and unattractive sex fantasy set in Dartmouth of all places and not helped by tiresome sex scenes.

wd Lewis John Carlino, *novel* Gogo No Eiko by Mishima Yukio *ph* Douglas Slocombe *m* John Mandel

Sarah Miles, Kris Kristofferson, Jonathan Kahn, Margo Cunningham, Earl Rhodes

'Like the act of love, this film must be experienced from beginning to end!'—
publicity

'This everyday tale of torture, scopophilia, copulation, masturbation, dismemberment and antique dealing deserves to be traded back to the Japs and made required viewing for timorous kamikaze pilots.'—*Benny Green, Punch*

● *Video: CBS / Fox*

The Sailor's Return
GB 1978 100m colour

A Victorian seaman returns to his native village with a black bride, and opens a pub. Lame-paced and highly predictable yarn of prejudice and doomed love, assembled with almost no cinematic flair. Tom Bell, Shope Sodeinde, Elton Charles, Mick Ford, Clive Swift. Written by James Saunders from the novel by David Garnett; directed by Jack Gold; for Euston Films. (As a theatrical film it found no takers, and in GB was first shown on television in 1980.)

Sailors Three**
GB 1940 86m bw
Ealing (Culley Forde)
US title: *Three Cockeyed Sailors*

Drunken sailors capture a German battleship by mistake.
Low service comedy which keeps moving, is brightly played and reaches a good standard. Sequel: *Fiddlers Three* (qv).

w Angus Macphail, John Dighton, Austin Melford *d* Walter Forde *ph* Gunther Krampf *md* Ernest Irving

Tommy Trinder, Claude Hulbert, Michael Wilding, Carla Lehmann, Jeanne de Casalis, James Hayter, John Laurie

The Saint
Leslie Charteris' famous character, the reformed British gentleman crook who becomes a Robin Hood of crime, has been most popular in the long-running sixties TV series starring Roger Moore. The films which featured him never seemed to hit quite the right note, and now seem slow. All but one were made for RKO, who later switched allegiance to THE FALCON (qv).
1938: THE SAINT IN NEW YORK
1939: THE SAINT STRIKES BACK, THE SAINT IN LONDON
1940: THE SAINT'S DOUBLE TROUBLE, THE SAINT TAKES OVER
1941: THE SAINT IN PALM SPRINGS, THE SAINT'S VACATION
1943 (Republic): THE SAINT MEETS THE TIGER
1954: THE SAINT'S GIRL FRIDAY
Louis Hayward played the role in the first and last; Hugh Sinclair in VACATION and TIGER; George Sanders in the rest.

St Benny the Dip
US 1951 79m bw
Danzigers
GB title: *Escape If You Can*

Gamblers learn to escape the law by dressing as priests, but circumstance converts them to good works.
Unfunny comedy notable only for its cast.

w John Roeburt *d* Edgar G. Ulmer *ph* Don Malkames *m* Robert Stringer

Freddie Bartholemew, Roland Young, Dick Haymes, Lionel Stander, Nina Foch

'He's clean! He's mean! He's the go-between!'

St Ives
US 1976 93m Technicolor
Warner (Pancho Kohner, Stanley Kanter)

An ex-police reporter gets involved in a complex murder puzzle.
Soporific suspenser with every tired situation in the book.

w Barry Beckerman, *novel* The Procane Chronicle by Oliver Bleeck *d* J. Lee-Thompson *ph* Lucien Ballard *m* Lalo Schifrin

Charles Bronson, Harry Guardino, John Houseman, Jacqueline Bisset, Maximilian Schell, Harris Yulin, Dana Elcar, Elisha Cook Jnr

'Much cross-cutting of the sort where the only events you care less about than the ones you cut from are the ones you cut to.'—*John Simon*

'People make love for so many crazy reasons—why shouldn't money be one of them?'

Saint Jack
US 1979 115m colour
New World / Shoals Creek / Playboy / Copa de Oro (Roger Corman)

An American wanderer in Singapore finds his metier as a pimp.
Whimsical, loquacious black comedy which failed to set its wavering director back on the firm ground he needed.

w Peter Bogdanovich, Howard Sackler, Paul Theroux, *novel* Paul Theroux *d* Peter Bogdanovich *ph* Robby Muller *m* various

Ben Gazzara, Denholm Elliott, James Villiers, Joss Ackland, Rodney Bewes, Mark Kingston, Lisa Lu, George Lazenby, Peter Bogdanovich

Saint Joan
GB 1957 110m bw
Otto Preminger

Glumly assembled screen version of the brilliantly argumentative play about the Maid of Orleans. Plenty of talent, but neither wit nor style.

w Graham Greene, *play* Bernard Shaw *d* Otto Preminger *ph* Georges Périnal *m* Mischa Spoliansky *pd* Roger Furse

Jean Seberg, Anton Walbrook, Richard Widmark, John Gielgud, Felix Aylmer, Harry Andrews, Richard Todd

TRAP THAT MURDERER!

He's at it again! Fiction's fighting man of mystery! Chasing down the most dramatic crime in London legend! Shock-charged drama—with a peppery bit of love on the side! You'll laugh—shiver—THRILL!

THE SAINT

READY! - AIM! - FIRE!

HE DID IT ALL WITH HIS LITTLE HALO!

THE SAINT IN LONDON

with
GEORGE SANDERS • SALLY GRAY
DAVID BURNS • GORDON McLEOD
ATHENE SEYLER • HENRY OSCAR

£1,000,000 missing ... girl lost ... diplomat murdered ... No wonder Scotland Yard called "The Saint!"

RKO RADIO Picture

Produced by WILLIAM SISTROM. Directed by JOHN PADDY CARSTAIRS. Screen Play by Lynn Root and Frank Fenton. From the Story "The Million Pound Day" by Leslie Charteris.

THE SAINT IN LONDON.   Before he was the Falcon, George Sanders was the Saint. Few could tell the difference.

St Louis Blues*
US 1939 92m bw
Paramount (Jeff Lazarus)

A Broadway musical star finds new fame down south.

Moderate star entertainment with good guest artists.

w John C. Moffitt, Malcolm Stuart Boylan, Frederick Hazlitt Brennan d Raoul Walsh ph Theodor Sparkuhl songs Frank Loesser, Burton Lane

Dorothy Lamour, Lloyd Nolan, Tito Guizar, Jerome Cowan, Jessie Ralph, William Frawley, the King's Men, Matty Melneck and his Orchestra

'It doesn't quite jell but will suffice as passable divertissement.'—Variety

St Louis Blues
US 1958 93m bw VistaVision
Paramount (Robert Smith)

W. C. Handy, son of a black Memphis preacher, becomes a blues composer.
Unsurprising biopic with some good music and the usual strained plot about father's disapproval of the new music.

w Robert Smith, Ted Sherdeman d Allen Reisner ph Haskell Boggs md Nelson Riddle

Nat King Cole, Eartha Kitt, Pearl Bailey, Cab Calloway, Mahalia Jackson, Ruby Dee, Juano Hernandez, Ella Fitzgerald

The St Louis Kid
US 1934 67m bw
Warner (Sam Bischoff)
GB title: A Perfect Weekend

A hot-headed truck driver takes the side of milk farmers in a trade dispute.
Modest star action comedy with a fair amount to amuse.

w Seton I. Miller, Warren Duff d Ray Enright ph Sid Hickox

James Cagney, Patricia Ellis, Hobart Cavanaugh, Spencer Charters, Addison Richards

'Jimmy in another slugger role, with results this time not so satisfactory.'—Variety

St Martin's Lane*
GB 1938 85m bw
Mayflower (Erich Pommer)
US title: Sidewalks of London

A middle-aged busker falls in love with a brilliant girl dancer who becomes a star.
Well-made romantic drama with star performances and interesting theatrical background.

w Clemence Dane d Tim Whelan ph Jules Kruger m Arthur Johnson

Charles Laughton, Vivien Leigh, Rex Harrison, Tyrone Guthrie, Larry Adler, Gus MacNaughton

'In its choice of subject, its overwhelming interest in character and its introspective, uncompromising treatment, it is experimental in a courageous fashion.'—Film Weekly

The St Valentine's Day Massacre

US 1967 99m De Luxe Panavision
TCF / Los Altos (Roger Corman)

The twenties gang war between Al Capone
and Bugs Moran.
The director's first big studio film is
disappointing; stagey, poorly developed,
unconvincing-looking and overacted.

w Howard Browne d Roger Corman
ph Milton Krasner m Fred Steiner md Lionel
Newman

Jason Robards Jnr, George Segal, Ralph
Meeker, Jean Hale, Clint Ritchie, Joseph
Campanella, Richard Bakalyan, David
Canary, Bruce Dern, Harold J. Stone, Kurt
Kreuger, John Agar, Alex D'Arcy

'You'll love every illegal inch of 'em!'

The Sainted Sisters

US 1948 89m bw
Paramount (Richard Maibaum)

Two New York con girls find themselves taken
in by the inhabitants of the small town in
which they are hiding out.
Unfunny period comedy which misses on all
cylinders.

w Harry Clark d William D. Russell
ph Lionel Lindon m Van Cleave

Veronica Lake, Joan Caulfield, Barry
Fitzgerald, William Demarest, George
Reeves, Beulah Bondi, Chill Wills, Darryl
Hickman

'Lake, Caulfield, and a swarm of clichés,
pleasantly kidded in a manner derived from
Preston Sturges.'—James Agee

Saints and Sinners

GB 1948 85m bw

An ex-convict comes back to his home town to
prove that those who condemned him were
fools or knaves. Curious slice of Irish whimsy
mixed with Ealing comedy; not very
satisfactory. Kieron Moore, Christine Norden,
Sheila Manahan, Michael Dolan, Maire
O'Neill, Noel Purcell. Written by Paul Vincent
Carroll and Leslie Arliss; directed by Leslie
Arliss; for London Films / BLPA.

Sally

US 1930 c. 90m Technicolor
Warner

A waitress makes it to the lights of Broadway.
Lightweight musical play, previously filmed in
1925 with Colleen Moore and Leon Errol,
here the basis of an elaborate colour
production with its original star, who however
did not take too kindly to the camera.

w Waldemar Young, play Guy Bolton and
Jerome Kern d John Francis Dillon ph Dev
Jennings, E. E. Schoenbaum ch Larry
Ceballos

Marilyn Miller, Joe E. Brown, Alexander
Grey, T. Roy Barnes, Pert Kelton, Ford
Sterling

Sally and St Anne

US 1952 90m bw
U-I (Leonard Goldstein)

When an Irish-American family is threatened
with eviction, the daughter appeals to St Anne
for help.
Whimsical comedy, quite nimbly performed.

w James O'Hanlon, Herb Meadow
d Rudolph Maté ph Irving Glassberg
m Frank Skinner

Ann Blyth, Edmund Gwenn, Hugh O'Brian,
John McIntire, Jack Kelly

Sally in Our Alley*

GB 1931 77m bw
ATP / Basil Dean

Poor girl loves wounded soldier.
Early talkie drama with music which made
Gracie Fields a star and gave her a theme
song.

w Miles Malleson, Archie Pitt, Alma Reville,
play The Likes of 'Er by Charles McEvoy
d Maurice Elvey

Gracie Fields, Ian Hunter, Florence
Desmond, Ivor Barnard
'The songs are just numbers, the general
standard nothing to shout about.'—Variety

Sally, Irene and Mary

US 1938 86m bw
TCF (Gene Markey)

Three girls try to break into show business.
Simple-minded romantic comedy-musical, well
enough done.

w Harry Tugend, Jack Yellen d William A.
Seiter ph Peverell Marley md Arthur Lange

Alice Faye, Tony Martin, Fred Allen, Jimmy
Durante, Gregory Ratoff, Joan Davis,
Marjorie Weaver, Gypsy Rose Lee
'Palatable light entertainment that is no
Pulitzer prizer but prize b.o.'—Variety

Sally of the Sawdust

US 1925 78m at 24 fps bw silent

A circus juggler and faker tries to prevent his
daughter from discovering that she is adopted.
Silent version of the stage hit Poppy, remade
under its own title in 1936 (qv). In both
versions W. C. Fields takes over the whole
show (not to one's entire satisfaction) and the
director's name in this case should not lead
one to expect a film of significance, as he
seems to have been glad of the work. With
Carol Dempster, Alfred Lunt, Effie Shannon,
Erville Anderson. Written by Forrest Halsey,
from the play by Dorothy Donnelly; directed
by D. W. Griffith; for Paramount / United
Artists.

● Video: Polygram

Salome

US 1923 80m at 24 fps bw silent

Almost unendurable as an entertainment, this
stylized silent provided a famous role for its
star against backgrounds in Aubrey Beardsley
style, and is much illustrated in film histories.
The New Yorker commented on a 1980
revival: 'The movie looks better in stills than
when one actually sees it, but a folly like this
should probably be experienced.' Nazimova,
Mitchell Lewis, Nigel de Brulier, Based on
Aubrey Beardsley's drawings and Oscar
Wilde's play; sets and costumes by Natacha
Rambova; directed by Charles Bryant; for
Nazimova.

Salome

US 1953 103m Technicolor
Columbia / Beckworth (Buddy Adler)

Princess Salome of Galilee eludes her
licentious stepfather, falls in love with a secret
Christian, and leaves home when her dancing
fails to save the life of John the Baptist.
Distorted biblical hokum with an interesting
cast frozen into unconvincing attitudes.

w Harry Kleiner, Jesse Lasky Jnr d William
Dieterle ph Charles Lang m George Duning
md Daniele Amfitheatrof ad John Meehan

Rita Hayworth, Charles Laughton, Stewart
Granger, Judith Anderson, Cedric Hardwicke,
Alan Badel, Basil Sydney, Maurice Schwartz,
Rex Reason, Arnold Moss
'The supreme screen achievement of our
time!'—publicity

Salome Where She Danced*

US 1945 90m Technicolor
Universal (Walter Wanger, Alexander
Golitzen)

During the Austro-Prussian war a dancer is
suspected of being a spy and flees to Arizona,
where she affects the lives of the citizenry.
Absurdly plotted and stiffly played romantic
actioner whose sheer creakiness made it a
minor cult film.

w Laurence Stallings, story Michael J. Phillips
d Charles Lamont ph Hal Mohr, W. Howard
Green m Edward Ward

Yvonne de Carlo, Rod Cameron, Albert
Dekker, David Bruce, Walter Slezak,
Marjorie Rambeau, J. Edward Bromberg,
Abner Biberman, John Litel, Kurt Katch
'I gratefully salute it as the funniest dead-
pan parody I have ever seen.'—James Agee

● Video: Fletcher

Saloon Bar*

GB 1940 76m bw
Ealing (Michael Balcon)

A murder is solved during an evening in a
pub.
Amusing, well-made little suspenser from a
West End success.

w Angus MacPhail, John Dighton, play Frank
Harvey d Walter Forde ph Ronald Neame
md Ernest Irving

Gordon Harker, Elizabeth Allen, Mervyn
Johns, Joyce Barbour, Anna Konstam, Judy
Campbell, Norman Pierce, Alec Clunes, Felix
Aylmer, Mavis Villiers, Torin Thatcher,
O. B. Clarence

Salt and Pepper

GB 1968 101m De Luxe
UA / Chrislaw / Tracemark (Milton Ebbins)

Soho nightclub proprietors solve a murder.
Infuriating throwaway star vehicle set in the
dregs of swinging London. The sequel, One
More Time (1970), was quite unnecessary.

843

You'll love every illegal inch of 'em!

Meet those not-so-sainted sisters! Just a couple of innocent kids ... who are guilty of *everything*! The hi-jinks are grand ... the hilarity's terrific ... and when they go straight —they'll go straight into your heart!

VERONICA LAKE
JOAN CAULFIELD
BARRY FITZGERALD
in
"The *Sainted* Sisters"

with WILLIAM DEMAREST

George Reeves · Beulah Bondi · Produced by Richard Maibaum · Directed by William D. Russell
Screenplay by Harry Clork and N. Richard Nash · Adapted by Mindret Lord · A Paramount Picture
Based on a Story by Elisa Bialk and a Play by Elisa Bialk and Alden Nash

THE SAINTED SISTERS.   A minor star vehicle from the days when Hollywood made a lot of period pictures and publicists tried to conceal the fact.

w Michael Pertwee d Richard Donner
ph Ken Higgins m Johnny Dankworth

Sammy Davis Jnr, Peter Lawford, Michael
Bates, Ilona Rodgers, John Le Mesurier,
Graham Stark, Ernest Clark

Saludos Amigos*
US 1943 43m Technicolor
Walt Disney

Donald Duck has various South American
adventures with a parrot named Joe Carioca.
Basically a naïve implementation of the good
neighbour policy, but with flashes of brilliant
animation and some mingling of live-action
with cartoon.

Production supervisor Norman Ferguson
  'Self-interested, belated ingratiation
embarrasses me, and Disney's famous
cuteness, however richly it may mirror
national infantilism, is hard on my stomach.'—
James Agee

AAN: music (Edward J. Plumb, Paul J.
Smith, Charles Wolcott); title song (m Charles
Wolcott, ly Ned Washington)

● Video: Rank

Salute for Three
US 1943 75m bw

An all-girl orchestra opens a canteen for
servicemen. Modest, middling propaganda
musical with minimum talents. Betty Jane
Rhodes, Macdonald Carey, Dona Drake and
her orchestra, Marty May, Lorraine and
Rognan. Written by Davis Anderson, Curtis
Kenyon, Hugh Wedlock Jnr and Howard
Snyder; directed by Ralph Murphy; for
Paramount.

Salute John Citizen
GB 1942 98m bw
British National (Wallace Orton)

A clerk and his family suffer cheerfully
through the blitz.
Modest, competent propaganda piece.

w Clemence Dane, Elizabeth Baron, novel
Mr Bunting at War by Robert Greenwood
d Maurice Elvey

Edward Rigby, Stanley Holloway, George
Robey, Mabel Constanduros, Jimmy Hanley,
Dinah Sheridan, Peggy Cummins, Stewart
Rome

Salute to the Marines
US 1943 101m Technicolor
MGM (John Considine Jnr)

A sergeant-major struggles to get his family
out of the Philippines when the Japs attack.
Recruiting poster heroics with comedy
interludes.

w Wells Root, George Bruce, story Robert
Andrews d S. Sylvan Simon ph Charles
Schoenbaum, W. Howard Green m Lennie
Hayton

Wallace Beery, Fay Bainter, Marilyn
Maxwell, William Ludigan, Keye Luke,
Reginald Owen, Ray Collins, Noah Beery,
Russell Gleason

The Salvation Hunters**
US 1925 65m (24 fps) bw silent
Academy Photoplays (Josef Von
  Sternberg, George K. Arthur)

Among the mud flats of San Pedro, a boy wins
his girl from a brute.
Mini-budgeted minor classic whose very
artiness and pretentiousness were keys to its
director's later development.

wd Josef Von Sternberg ph Josef Von
Sternberg, Edward Gheller

George K. Arthur, Georgia Hale, Bruce
Guerin

  'Audience reaction was: even our lives are
not so drab as this, and if they are we don't
want to know about it. Asked to comment on
the failure of a film he had praised so highly,
Chaplin said, "Well, you know I was only
kidding. They all take everything I say so
seriously. I thought I'd praise a bad picture
and see what happened." '—Richard Griffith
and Arthur Mayer, The Movies

Salvation Nell
US 1931 83m bw

A wronged girl sinks lower and lower until she
joins the Salvation Army. One thinks it must
have been meant as a spoof, but apparently
not. Helen Chandler, Ralph Graves, Sally
O'Neill, Jason Robards, Dewitt Jennings.
Written by Selma Stein, Walter Woods, from
the play by Edward Sheldon; directed by
James Cruze; for Tiffany. 'It probably will be
livelier in the states, where the Mme
Cloquette scene is not cut out.'—Variety

Salvatore Giuliano*
Italy 1961 125m bw
Lux / Vides / Galatea (Franco Cristaldi)

The bullet-ridden body of key Sicilian Mafia
leader Giuliano triggers flashbacks to his
complex and brutal career.
Vivid, sometimes obscure, politically oriented
melodrama based on fact. Undoubtedly a local
classic, but not an easy film to appreciate.

w Francesco Rosi, Suso Cecchi d'Amico, Enzo
Provenzale, Franco Solinas d Francesco Rosi
ph Gianni di Venanzo m Piero Piccioni

Frank Wolff, Salvo Randone, Federico Zardi
  'Epic reportage in the twentieth-century
manner of a society reminiscent of some
backward corner of the nineteenth century.'—
Peter John Dyer, MFB

The Salzburg Connection
US 1972 93m De Luxe Panavision
TCF (Ingo Preminger)

An American lawyer on holiday in Salzburg
finds himself suspected by spies of both sides.
Turgid, routine action thriller with attractive
locations.

w Oscar Millard, novel Helen MacInnes
d Lee H. Katzin ph Wolfgang Treu
md Lionel Newman

Barry Newman, Anna Karina, Maria
Brandauer, Karen Jensen, Wolfgang Preiss

  'So dull you can't tell the CIA agents from
the neo-Nazis or double agents—or the inept
actors from the blocks and stones in the
handsome Austrian locales.'—Judith Crist

Sam Whiskey
US 1969 96m De Luxe
UA / Brighton (Jules Levy, Arthur Gardner,
  Arnold Laven)

An itinerant gambler is paid to recover a
fortune in gold bars from the bottom of a
Colorado river.
Easy-going but rather slackly-handled western.

w William W. Norton d Arnold Laven
ph Robert Moreno m Herschel Burke Gilbert

Burt Reynolds, Clint Walker, Ossie Davis,
Angie Dickinson, Rick Davis, William
Schallert

'The story of the longest-run date in the
  history of non-marriage!'

Same Time, Next Year*
US 1978 119m colour
Universal / Walter Mirisch, Robert Mulligan

An illicit affair is carried on for twenty-five
years, the couple confining themselves to one
annual meeting in a hotel.
Careful film version of a smash Broadway
comedy; the flimsiness of the premise is well
concealed, but it remains a one-set play.

w Bernard Slade, from his play d Robert
Mulligan ph Robert Surtees m Marvin
Hamlisch pd Henry Bumstead

Ellen Burstyn, Alan Alda

AAN: Bernard Slade; Robert Surtees; Ellen
Burstyn; song, 'The Last Time I Felt Like
This'

● Video: CIC

Sammy Going South*
GB 1963 128m Eastmancolor
  Cinemascope
Bryanston (Hal Mason)
US title: A Boy Ten Feet Tall

A 10-year-old boy is orphaned in Port Said
and hitch-hikes to his aunt in Durban.
Disappointing family-fodder epic in which the
mini-adventures follow each other too
predictably.

w Denis Cannan, novel W. H. Canaway
d Alexander Mackendrick ph Erwin Hillier
m Tristam Cary

Fergus McClelland, Edward G. Robinson,
Constance Cummings, Harry H. Corbett

'A story as timeless and tumultuous as the
  violent age it spreads before you!'

Samson and Delilah
US 1949 128m Technicolor
Paramount / Cecil B. de Mille

Delilah, rejected by religious strong man
Samson, cuts his hair and delivers him to his
enemies.
Absurd biblical hokum, stodgily narrated and
directed, monotonously photographed and
edited, and notable only for the 30-second
destruction of the temple at the end.

w Jesse L. Lasky Jnr, Fredric M. Frank
d Cecil B. de Mille *ph* George Barnes
m Victor Young *ad* Hans Dreier, Walter
Tyler

Hedy Lamarr, Victor Mature, Angela
Lansbury, George Sanders, Henry Wilcoxon,
Olive Deering, Fay Holden, Russ Tamblyn

'To ignore so enormous, over-coloured,
over-stuffed, flamboyant an "epic" would be
almost as absurd as taking it seriously.'—
Richard Mallett, Punch

'Perhaps de Mille's survival is due to the fact
that he decided in his movie nonage to ally
himself with God as his co-maker and get his
major scripts from the Bible, which he has
always handled with the proprietary air of a
gentleman fondling old love letters.'—*New
Yorker*

AAN: George Barnes; Victor Young

San Antone

US 1952   90m   bw

During the Civil War a Texas rancher
antagonizes an army lieutenant. Very routine,
competent western without any moment of
inspiration. Rod Cameron, Forrest Tucker,
Arleen Whelan, Katy Jurado, Rodolfo
Acosta. Written by Steve Fisher, from the
novel *Golden Herd* by Curt Carroll; directed
by Joe Kane; for Republic.

San Antonio°

US 1945   109m   Technicolor
Warner (Robert Buckner)

A cowboy incurs the jealousy of a saloon
owner.

Typically thinly-plotted Warner star western
which works well enough sequence by
sequence, climaxing with a fight in the
deserted Alamo.

w Alan le May, W. R. Burnett *d* David
Butler *ph* Bert Glennon *m* Max Steiner

Errol Flynn, Alexis Smith, Paul Kelly, Victor
Francen, S. Z. Sakall, John Litel, Florence
Bates, Robert Shayne, Monte Blue, Robert
Barrat

AAN: song 'Some Sunday Morning' (*m* Ray
Heindorf, M. K. Jerome, *ly* Ted Koehler)

San Demetrio London°

GB 1943   105m   bw
Ealing (Robert Hamer)

In 1940, the survivors of a crippled tanker
bring it back home.

Rather flat and dated propaganda piece which
seemed much more vivid at the time.

w Robert Hamer, Charles Frend, *story*
F. Tennyson Jesse *d* Charles Frend
ph Ernest Palmer, Roy Kellino *m* John
Greenwood

Walter Fitzgerald, Mervyn Johns, Ralph
Michael, Robert Beatty, Charles Victor,
Frederick Piper, Gordon Jackson

San Diego I Love You°

US 1944   83m   bw
Universal (Michael Fessier, Ernest Pagano)

A family travels to San Diego to promote
father's inventions.

Pleasing, easy-come-easy-go comedy full of
memorable incident and characterization.

w Michael Fessier, Ernest Pagano *d* Reginald
Le Borg *ph* Hal Mohr *m* Hans Salter

Louise Allbritton, Edward Everett Horton,
Jon Hall, Eric Blore, *Buster Keaton*, Irene
Ryan

'She fell in love with the toughest guy on
  the toughest street in the world!'

San Francisco°°°°

US 1936   117m   bw
MGM (John Emerson, Bernard Hyman)

The loves and career problems of a Barbary
Coast saloon proprietor climax in the 1906
earthquake.

Incisive, star-packed, superbly-handled
melodrama which weaves in every kind of
appeal and for a finale has some of the best
special effects ever conceived.

w Anita Loos, *story* Robert Hopkins *d* W. S.
Van Dyke *ph* Oliver T. Marsh *m* Edward
Ward *md* Herbert Stothart *montage* John
Hoffman *title song* Bronislau Kaper

*Clark Gable, Spencer Tracy, Jeanette
MacDonald, Jack Holt, Jessie Ralph*, Ted
Healy, Shirley Ross, Al Shean, Harold
Huber

'Prodigally generous and completely
satisfying.'—*Frank S. Nugent*

AAN: best picture; Robert Hopkins;
W. S. Van Dyke; Spencer Tracy

'Between the sea and the Sierras stood the
  brawling gateway to gold!'

The San Francisco Story°

US 1952   90m   bw
Warner / Fidelity–Vogue (Howard Welsch)

In 1856, a wanderer bound for China stops in
San Francisco to get involved in politics.
Lively melodrama with good period feel.

w D. D. Beauchamp, *novel* Richard Summers
d Robert Parrish *ph* John Seitz *m* Emil
Newman

Joel McCrea, Yvonne de Carlo, Sidney
Blackmer, Florence Bates

San Quentin°

US 1937   70m   bw
Warner (Sam Bischoff)

A convict's sister loves the warden.
Standard tough prison melodrama,
competently done.

w Peter Milne, Humphrey Cobb, *story* John
Bright, Robert Tasker *d* Lloyd Bacon *ph* Sid
Hickox *m* Heinz Roemheld, David Raksin

Pat O'Brien, Ann Sheridan, Humphrey
Bogart, Barton MacLane, Joseph Sawyer,
Veda Ann Borg

'Fairly good appeal but will need
pushing.'—*Variety*

San Quentin

US 1946   66m   bw

A convict starts a movement for the
rehabilitation of prisoners after release, but
despite himself is caught up in a prison break.

Tolerable support of a familiar kind. Lawrence
Tierney, Barton Maclane, Marian Carr,
Raymond Burr, Joe Devlin. Written by
Lawrence Kimble, Arthur A. Ross and
Howard J. Green; directed by Gordon
Douglas; for RKO.

Sanctuary

US 1960   90m   bw   Cinemascope
TCF (Richard D. Zanuck)

The governor's daughter is seduced by a
bootlegger, and her life goes from one tragedy
to another.

Confused adaptation of unadaptable material,
full of pussyfoot daring but little sense.

w James Poe, *novel* William Faulkner *d* Tony
Richardson *ph* Ellsworth Fredericks *m* Alex
North

Lee Remick, Bradford Dillman, Yves
Montand, Odetta, Harry Townes, Howard St
John, Reta Shaw, Strother Martin

The Sand Pebbles°

US 1966   193m   De Luxe   Panavision
TCF / Argyle / Solar (Robert Wise)

In 1926 an American gunboat patrolling the
Yangtze river gets involved with Chinese
warlords.

Confused action blockbuster with Vietnam
parallels for those who care to pick them up;
pretty thinly stretched entertainment despite
the tons of explosive.

w Robert Anderson, *novel* Richard
McKenna *d* Robert Wise *ph* Joseph
MacDonald *m* Jerry Goldsmith

Steve McQueen, Candice Bergen, Richard
Attenborough, Richard Crenna, Marayat
Andriane, Mako, Larry Gates. Simon
Oakland

'If it had been done twenty years ago, it
would have been fast and unpretentious, with
some ingeniously faked background shots . . .
and we would never have asked for larger
historical meanings.'—*Pauline Kael*

AAN: best picture; Joseph MacDonald; Jerry
Goldsmith; Steve McQueen; Mako

● *Video: CBS / Fox*

Sanders of the River°

GB 1935   98m   bw
London (Alexander Korda)
US title: *Bosambo*

Problems of a British colonial servant in
keeping peace among the tribes.
Much-caricatured African adventure of the
very old school, helped by Robeson's
personality.

w Lajos Biro, Jeffrey Dell, Arthur Wimperis
stories Edgar Wallace *d* Zoltan Korda
ph Georges Perinal *m* Mischa Spoliansky

Leslie Banks, Paul Robeson, Nina Mae
McKinney, Robert Cochran

'It will interest those who are sincerely
interested in the cinema as an art form, but it
will suffer the hazards of all pioneers.'—
Variety

Sandokan the Great

Italy / France / Spain 1963   114m
Techniscope

The son of the Sultan of Borneo wages jungle war against the oppressive British. A curious mixture of Tarzan and Robin Hood, this character appeared in several adventures before expiring; the first chapter is the best, or least worst. Steve Reeves, Genevieve Grad, Rik Battaglia, Andrea Bosic. Written by Fulvio Gicca and Umberto Lenzi, from the novel by Emilio Salgari; directed by Umberto Lenzi; for Filmes / CCF / Ocean.

The Sandpiper

US 1965   116m   Metrocolor   Panavision
MGM / Filmways (John Calley)

An artist lives with her illegitimate son in a Monterey beach shack; when she is forced to send the boy to school he attracts the attention of the minister in charge.
Absurd novelettish love story basically copied from *The Garden of Allah;* pretty seascapes are the most rewarding aspect.

w Dalton Trumbo, Michael Wilson
d Vincente Minnelli ph Milton Krasner
m Johnny Mandel

Elizabeth Taylor, Richard Burton, Eva Marie Saint, Charles Bronson, Robert Webber
'Straight Louisa May Alcott interlarded with discreet pornographic allusions.'—*John Simon*
'Sex-on-the-sand soap opera.'—*Robert Windeler*

AA: song 'The Shadow of Your Smile' (m Johnny Mandel, ly Paul Francis Webster)

'My name is Stryker. Sgt John M. Stryker. You're gonna be my squad!'
Sands of Iwo Jima*

US 1949   109m   bw
Republic (Edmund Grainger)

During World War II in the Pacific, a tough sergeant of marines moulds raw recruits into fighting men but is himself shot by a sniper. Celebrated star war comic, still quite hypnotic in its flagwaving way.

w Harry Brown, James Edward Grant
d Allan Dwan ph Reggie Lanning m Victor Young

John Wayne, John Agar, Adele Mara, Forrest Tucker, Arthur Franz, Julie Bishop, Richard Jaeckel
'The battle sequences are terrifyingly real . . . but the personal dramatics make up a compendium of war-picture clichés.'—*Variety*
'Say what you like about the sentimental flavour of war pictures such as this, there's no denying they keep you in your seat.'—*Richard Mallett, Punch*

AAN: Harry Brown (original story); John Wayne

Sands of the Desert

GB 1960   92m   Technicolor

A diminutive travel agent goes out to investigate a desert holiday camp which has suffered from sabotage. Limp star comedy with poor studio work and meandering script.

Charlie Drake, Peter Arne, Sarah Branch, Raymond Huntley, Peter Illing, Harold Kasket. Written and directed by John Paddy Carstairs; for Associated British.

Sands of the Kalahari

GB 1965   119m   Technicolor
Panavision
Pendennis (Cy Endfield, Stanley Baker)

Survivors of a plane crash trek across the desert and are menaced by baboons and each other.
Hysterical melodrama with predictable heebie-jeebies by all concerned and the baddie finally left to the mercy of the monkeys. For hardened sensationalists.

wd Cy Endfield, *novel* William Mulvihill
ph Erwin Hillier m Johnny Dankworth

Stanley Baker, Stuart Whitman, Harry Andrews, Susannah York, Theodore Bikel, Nigel Davenport, Barry Lowe

The Sandwich Man*

GB 1966   95m   Eastmancolor
Rank / Titan (Peter Newbrook)

In the course of a walking day around London a sandwich man encounters many of his eccentric acquaintances.
Spurned when it was first released, this comedy variety show, mostly in mime, can now be seen to be of a kind popularized by TV, and may have been simply ahead of its time. It certainly seems funnier than it did.

w Michael Bentine, Robert Hartford-Davis
d Robert Hartford-Davis ph Peter Newbrook m Mike Vickers

Michael Bentine, Dora Bryan, Suzy Kendall, Norman Wisdom, Harry H. Corbett, Bernard Cribbins, Ian Hendry, Stanley Holloway, Alfie Bass, Diana Dors, Ron Moody, Wilfrid Hyde White, Donald Wolfit, Max Bacon, Fred Emney, Frank Finlay, Peter Jones, Michael Medwin, Ronnie Stevens, John Le Mesurier, Sidney Tafler, John Junkin, Warren Mitchell

Sangaree

US 1953   95m   Technicolor   3-D
Paramount / Pine—Thomas

Trouble ensues when a plantation owner wills his wealth to the son of a slave.
Period skullduggery rather hammily presented.

w David Duncan, *novel* Frank G. Slaughter
d Edward Ludwig ph Lionel Lindon, W. Wallace Kelley m Lucien Caillet

Fernando Lamas, Arlene Dahl, Patricia Medina, Francis L. Sullivan, Charles Korvin, Tom Drake, John Sutton, Willard Parker, Lester Matthews

Santa Fe

US 1951   89m   Technicolor

After the Civil War, the eldest of four westbound brothers tries to prevent the others from becoming outlaws.
Regulation star western, with action sequences a litte under par. Randolph Scott, Jerome

Courtland, Janis Carter, Peter Thompson, John Archer, Warner Anderson, Roy Roberts. Written by Kenneth Gamet; directed by Irving Pichel; for Harry Joe Brown / Columbia.

Santa Fe Passage

US 1954   89m   Trucolor

An Indian-hating scout with a bad record is hired to transport arms to Santa Fe. Rough-and-ready brawling western with very little going for it. John Payne, Rod Cameron, Faith Domergue, Slim Pickens, Leo Gordon. Written by Lillie Hayward; directed by William Witney; for Republic.

'The thundering story that challenges all filmdom to match its excitement!'
Santa Fe Trail**

US 1940   110m   bw
Warner (Robert Fellows)

A cavalry officer is responsible for the final capture of John Brown.
The most solemn western from star or studio has impressive patches amid routine excitements.

w Robert Buckner d Michael Curtiz ph Sol Polito m Max Steiner

Errol Flynn, Olivia de Havilland, Raymond Massey, Ronald Reagan, Alan Hale, Van Heflin, Gene Reynolds, Henry O'Neill

Santee

US 1972   93m   colour
Vagabond (Deno Paoli, Edward Platt)

A boy goes west to find his father and befriends the bounty hunter who has killed him.
Personable, violent western with adequate style and performances.

w Brand Bell d Gary Nelson ph Donald Morgan m Don Randi

Glenn Ford, Michael Burns, Dana Wynter, Jay Silverheels, Harry Townes, John Larch

Santiago

US 1956   92m   Warnercolor
Cinemascope
Warner (Martin Rackin)
GB title: *The Gun Runner*

A Mississippi paddle-boat sets out for Cuba with a consignment of guns for the rebels. Stiff period actioner of no particular merit.

w Martin Rackin, John Twist d Gordon Douglas ph John Seitz m David Buttolph

Alan Ladd, Rossana Podesta, Lloyd Nolan, Chill Wills, Paul Fix, L. Q. Jones, Frank de Kova

The Saphead*

US 1920   70m (24 fps)   bw   silent
Metro / Buster Keaton

A shy young man reads a manual on how to win the modern girl.
Interesting early star comedy: quite winning in its way, but without the spectacular moments which were a feature of his later films.

w June Mathis, *play* The New Henrietta by Winchell Smith, Victor Mapes *d* Herbert Blache *ph* Harold Wenstrom

Buster Keaton, Beula Booker, William H. Crane, Irving Cummings

Sapphire**
GB 1959 92m Eastmancolor
Rank / Artna (Michael Relph)
Scotland Yard solves the murder of a coloured music student.
Efficient police thriller with a strong race angle.

w Janet Green *d* Basil Dearden *ph* Harry Waxman *m* Philip Green

Nigel Patrick, Michael Craig, Yvonne Mitchell, Paul Massie, Bernard Miles, Olga Lindo, Earl Cameron, Gordon Heath, Robert Adams
  'A dandy murder mystery—taut, tantalizing and beautifully done.'—*Judith Crist, 1980*
● *Video: Rank*

Saps at Sea
US 1940 60m bw
Hal Roach
Olly needs a rest after working in a horn factory, so he and Stan take a boating holiday but are kidnapped by a gangster.
Disappointing star comedy with gags too few and too long drawn out.

w Charles Rogers, Harry Langdon, Gil Pratt, Felix Adler *d* Gordon Douglas *ph* Art Lloyd *m* Marvin Hatley

Stan Laurel, Oliver Hardy, James Finlayson, Dick Cramer, Ben Turpin

Saraband for Dead Lovers*
GB 1948 96m Technicolor
Ealing (Michael Relph)
US title: *Saraband*
The tragic love affair of Konigsmark and Sophie Dorothea, wife of the Elector of Hanover who later became George I of England.
Gloomy but superb-looking historical love story; it just misses being a memorable film.

w John Dighton, Alexander Mackendrick, *novel* Helen Simpson *d* Basil Dearden, Michael Relph *ph* Douglas Slocombe *m* Alan Rawsthorne

Stewart Granger, Joan Greenwood, Françoise Rosay, Flora Robson, Peter Bull
  'Suspense, romance, interest and excitement in full measure.'—*MFB*

The Saracen Blade
US 1954 76m Technicolor
In the thirteenth century a young Italian crusader devotes himself to avenging the murder of his father. Cut-price swashbuckler full of unintentional laughs and therefore quite watchable. Ricardo Montalban, Betta St John, Rick Jason, Carolyn Jones, Michael Ansara. Written by DeVallon Scott and Worthing Yates, from the novel by Frank Yerby; directed by William Castle; for Sam Katzman / Columbia.

SANTA FE TRAIL.   Olivia de Havilland and Errol Flynn have eyes only for each other: Ronald Reagan's mind is perhaps fixed on the 1980 election.

Sarah and Son
US 1930 85m bw
Paramount (David O. Selznick)
A widow seeks the baby her husband took away from her.
Mother love saga; soppy but with good credits.

w Zoe Akins, *novel* Timothy Shea *d* Dorothy Arzner *ph* Charles Lang

Ruth Chatterton, Fredric March, Fuller Mellish Jnr, Gilbert Emery, Doris Lloyd
  '*Madame X* with a slightly varied theme. Photography and recording par.'—*Variety*
AAN: Ruth Chatterton

Saratoga*
US 1937 102m bw
MGM (Bernard H. Hyman)
A bookmaker helps the daughter of a horse breeder.
Forgettable racetrack drama notable chiefly as the last film of Jean Harlow who died before it was completed.

w Anita Loos, Robert Hopkins *d* Jack Conway *ph* Ray June *m* Edward Ward

Clark Gable, Jean Harlow, Lionel Barrymore, Frank Morgan, Walter Pidgeon, Una Merkel, Cliff Edwards, George Zucco, Jonathan Hale

  'Glib, forthright, knowing and adroit.'—*Time*
  'Surefire box office, and tastefully produced.'—*Variety*

Saratoga Trunk*
US 1943 135m bw
Warner (Hal B. Wallis)
A notorious woman comes back to New Orleans and falls for a cowboy helping a railroad combine against their rivals.
Curious, unsatisfactory, miscast and overlong film version of a bestseller; there are enjoyable sequences, but it simply fails to come alive.

w Casey Robinson, *novel* Edna Ferber *d* Sam Wood *ph* Ernest Haller *m* Max Steiner *ph* Joseph St Amaad

Ingrid Bergman, Gary Cooper, Flora Robson, Jerry Austin, Florence Bates, John Warburton, John Abbott, Curt Bois, Ethel Griffies
  'It lacks a logical pattern of drama and character . . . a piece of baggage labelled solely for the stars.'—*Bosley Crowther*
AAN: Flora Robson

Saskatchewan
US 1954   87m   Technicolor
U-I (Aaron Rosenberg)
GB title: *O'Rourke of the Royal Mounted*

A mountie helps the lady survivor of an Indian attack.
Standard star actioner.

w Gil Doud   *d* Raoul Walsh   *ph* John Seitz   *m* Joseph Gershenson

Alan Ladd, Shelley Winters, J. Carrol Naish, Hugh O'Brian, Robert Douglas, Richard Long, Jay Silverheels

The Satan Bug°
US 1965   114m   De Luxe   Panavision
UA / Mirisch / Kappa (John Sturges)

At a top-secret desert research station, one scientist is a traitor, and a deadly virus has been stolen for use by a mad millionaire.
Slow-moving, portentous, gadget-filled actioner which looks good but seldom stimulates.

w James Clavell, Edward Anhalt, *novel* Alistair MacLean   *d* John Sturges   *ph* Robert Surtees   *m* Jerry Goldsmith

George Maharis, Richard Basehart, Anne Francis, Dana Andrews, Ed Asner

Satan Met a Lady°
US 1936   74m   bw
Warner (Henry Blanke)

Various crooks and a private detective pursue a rare artifact.
Perversely rewritten version of *The Maltese Falcon* (qv). Fascinating but not really successful

w Brown Holmes   *w* William Dieterle   *ph* Arthur Edeson   *m* Leo F. Forbstein

Bette Davis, Warren William, Alison Skipworth, Arthur Treacher, Wini Shaw, Marie Wilson, Porter Hall
  'One lives through it in constant expectation of seeing a group of uniformed individuals appear suddenly from behind the furniture and take the entire cast into protective custody.'—*Bosley Crowther*

Satan Never Sleeps
US / GB 1962   126m   De Luxe
Cinemascope
TCF / Leo McCarey
GB title: *The Devil Never Sleeps*

In the late forties in China, Catholic missionaries defy the communists.
Failed anti-Red imitation of *Inn of the Sixth Happiness* with the priests from *Going My Way*. Has to be seen to be believed.

w Claude Binyon, Leo McCarey   *d* Leo McCarey   *ph* Oswald Morris   *m* Richard Rodney Bennett

Clifton Webb, William Holden, France Nuyen, Weaver Lee, Athene Seyler, Martin Benson
  'For all its superficial smirk of piety, this is just a prurient, soft-soapy and holy water version of the spicy story about the lonely missionary and the beautiful native girl.'—*Time*

The Satanic Rites of Dracula
GB 1973   88m   Technicolor
Hammer (Roy Skeggs)
US title: *Dracula is Alive and Well and Living in London*

When vampires infest London, a property speculator proves to be Dracula himself.
Intriguingly plotted screamer with more mystery than horror.

w Don Houghton   *d* Alan Gibson   *ph* Brian Probyn   *m* John Cacavas

Peter Cushing, Christopher Lee, Michael Coles, William Franklyn, Freddie Jones, Richard Vernon, Patrick Barr

'Never told till now! The world's most guarded secret!'
Satellite in the Sky
GB 1956   85m   Warnercolor
Cinemascope
Warner / Tridelta / Danziger

A rocketship is ordered to lose a tritonium bomb in space, but the device attaches itself to the side of the ship.
Boringly talkative low-budget science fiction with ideas beyond its station but not enough talent to put them over.

w John Mather, J. T. McIntosh, Edith Dell   *d* Paul Dickson   *ph* Georges Périnal   *m* Albert Elms

Kieron Moore, Lois Maxwell, Donald Wolfit, Bryan Forbes, Jimmy Hanley, Alan Gifford

Saturday Island
GB 1951   102m   Technicolor
Coronado (David E. Rose)
US title: *Island of Desire*

In 1943 a supply boat is torpedoed and a Canadian nurse finds romance on a desert island with a US marine and a one-armed RAF pilot.
Unlikely, conversational, old-fashioned love story.

wd Stuart Heisler, *novel* Hugh Brooke   *ph* Oswald Morris   *m* William Alwyn

Linda Darnell, Tab Hunter, Donald Gray

Saturday Night and Sunday Morning**
GB 1960   89m   bw
Bryanston / Woodfall (Harry Salzman, Tony Richardson)

A Nottingham factory worker is dissatisfied with his lot, gets into trouble through an affair with a married woman, but finally settles for convention.
Startling when it emerged, this raw working-class melodrama, with its sharp detail and strong comedy asides, delighted the mass audience chiefly because of its strong central character thumbing his nose at authority.
Matching the mood of the times, and displaying a new attitude to sex, it transformed British cinema and was much imitated.

w Alan Sillitoe, from his novel   *d* Karel Reisz   *ph* Freddie Francis   *m* Johnny Dankworth

Albert Finney, Shirley Anne Field, *Rachel Roberts,* Bryan Pringle, Norman Rossington, Hylda Baker

Saturday Night Fever°
US 1978   119m   Movielab
Paramount / Robert Stigwood (Milt Felsen)

Italian roughnecks in Brooklyn live for their Saturday night disco dancing, and one of them falls in love with a girl who makes him realize there are better things in life.
Foul-mouthed, fast-paced slice of life which plays like an updated version of *Marty* except that all the characters seem to have crawled from under stones. The slick direction, fast editing and exciting dance numbers do something to take away the sour taste.

w Norman Wexler, *story* Nik Cohn   *d* John Badham   *ph* Ralf D. Bode   *songs* Barry, Robin and Maurice Gibb (and others), performed by the Bee Gees   *ed* David Rawlins   *pd* Charles Bailey

John Travolta, Karen Lynn Gorney, Barry Miller, Joseph Cali, Paul Pape, Bruce Ornstein
  'A stylish piece of contemporary anthropology, an urban safari into darkest America, a field study of the mystery cults among the young braves and squaws growing up in North Brooklyn.'—*Alan Brien, Sunday Times*

AAN: John Travolta
● *Video: CIC*

Saturday Night Out
GB 1963   96m   bw

Five sailors spend an overnight leave in London. Portmanteau drama in which all elements are equally uninteresting. Bernard Lee, Heather Sears, John Bonney, Francesca Annis, Erika Remberg, Colin Campbell, David Lodge. Written by Donald and Derek Ford; directed by Robert Hartford-Davis; for Compton-Tekli.

Saturday's Children
US 1940   101m   bw
Warner (Henry Blanke)

An impractical young inventor marries an ambitious young woman, but depressed finances lead to discord.
Glum, dated rehash of a 1929 silent; watchable but not compelling.

w Julius J. and Philip G. Epstein, *play* Maxwell Anderson   *d* Vincent Sherman   *ph* James Wong Howe

John Garfield, Claude Rains, Anne Shirley, Lee Patrick, George Tobias, Roscoe Karns, Elizabeth Risdon, Berton Churchill
† The story was also made in 1935 as *Maybe It's Love,* with Ross Alexander, Henry Travers and Gloria Stuart; William McGann directed without flair.

Saturday's Hero
US 1951   110m   bw
Columbia (Sidney Buchman)
GB title: *Idols in the Dust*

A poor boy wins a football scholarship but finds his value to the college is purely commercial and he isn't given time to learn anything.
A spirited attack on the American sporting system, but a dull and overlong film.

w Millard Lampell, Sidney Buchman, *novel* The Hero by Millard Lampell *d* David Miller *ph* Lee Garmes *m* Elmer Bernstein

John Derek, Donna Reed, Sidney Blackmer, Alexander Knox, Elliott Lewis, Howard St John

Saturn Three

GB 1980 87m colour
ITC / Transcontinental (Stanley Donen)

A maniac builds a robot on a remote space station, and they both go berserk.
Rather unpleasant blend of space fiction, horror and suspense, with some nasty detail and a general feeling that the actors wish they were elsewhere.

w Martin Amis, *story* John Barry *d* Stanley Donen *ph* Billy Williams *m* Elmer Bernstein *pd* Stuart Craig

Kirk Douglas, Farrah Fawcett, Harvey Keitel, Ed Bishop

● *Video: Precision*

Satyricon*

Italy / France 1969 129m De Luxe Panavision
UA / PAA / PEA (Alberto Grimaldi)
aka: *Fellini Satyricon*

Sexual adventures of a Roman student.
Garish, sporadically enjoyable sketches on a very thin thread of plot: a more benevolent version of the usual Fellini nightmare.

w Federico Fellini, Bernardino Zapponi *d* Federico Fellini *ph* Giuseppe Rotunno *m* Nino Rota, Ilhan Mimaroglu, Tod Dockstader, Andrew Rudin *pd* Danilo Donati

Martin Potter, Hiram Keller, Salvo Randone, Max Born

'A picaresque satire in fragments . . . a series of tableaux which carry the poetry visually at the price of coherence.'—*Mike Wallington, MFB*

'Part of the gradual decomposition of what once was one of the greatest talents in film history . . . a gimcrack, shopworn nightmare.'—*John Simon*

AAN: Federico Fellini (as director)

Le Sauvage

France / Italy 1978 107m Eastmancolor
Lira / PAI (Raymond Danon)

A business executive has opted out of life to be alone on a desert island, but on his last night in the city he accidentally helps a runaway heiress who follows him.
A promising and amusing start is squandered in the tedious island sequences of this patchy romantic comedy, which does however leave one with a sense of freshness and optimism rare in the cinema of the seventies.

w Jean-Paul Rappeneau, Elizabeth Rappeneau, Jean-Loup Dabadie *d* Jean-Paul Rappeneau *ph* Pierre Lhomme *m* Michel Legrand

Yves Montand, Catherine Deneuve, Luigi Vannucchi, Dana Wynter

The Savage

US 1952 95m Technicolor
Paramount (Mel Epstein)

A white boy grows up with Indians and later suffers from divided loyalties.
Solemn, rather tedious but well produced western.

w Sidney Boehm, *novel* L. L. Foreman *d* George Marshall *ph* John F. Seitz *m* Paul Sawtell

Charlton Heston, Susan Morrow, Peter Hanson, Joan Taylor, Richard Rober, Don Porter

The Savage Eye*

US 1959 68m bw
City Film Corporation (Ben Maddow, Joseph Strick, Sidney Meyers)

An unhappily married young woman takes a jaundiced view of life around her in Los Angeles.
The wisp of plot is merely an excuse to present a documentary exposé of the seamier side of life in America's most eccentric city, with its faith healers and revellers. Much of it is fascinating, though the film is not a cohesive whole and the would-be poetic commentary falls on its face.

wd, ed Ben Maddow, Joseph Strick, Sidney Meyers *m* Leonard Rosenman

Barbara Baxley, Gary Merrill, Herschel Bernardi

The Savage Guns

US / Spain 1961 83m Metrocolor Cinemascope

After the Civil War, an American rancher settles in Mexico but finds his pacifist principles tested by bandits. Unappealing, stodgy western with the Hammer horror team rather curiously cast as co-producers. Richard Basehart, Don Taylor, Alex Nicol, Jose Nieto, Fernando Rey. Written by Edmund Morris (?Jimmy Sangster); directed by Michael Carreras; for Capricorn / Tecisa / MGM.

The Savage Innocents

GB / France / Italy 1960 107m Super Technirama 70
Joseph Janni / Magic Film / Playart / Gray Films (Maleno Malenotti)

Trials of an Eskimo and his wife in Canada's frozen north.
Conscientious, determined and very boring account of Eskimo life played by actors talking pidgin English. Not a success despite the magnificent photography.

w Nicholas Ray, *novel* Top of the World by Hans Ruesch *d* Nicholas Ray, Baccio Bandini *ph* Aldo Tonti, Peter Hennessy *m* Angelo Lavagnino

Anthony Quinn, Yoko Tani, Marie Yang, Peter O'Toole, Carlo Justini, Anna May Wong, Lee Montague, Ed Devereaux

● *Video: Rank*

Savage Messiah*

GB 1972 103m Metrocolor
MGM / Russ–Arts (Ken Russell)

The life together (1910–14) of the 18-year-old painter Gaudier and 38-year-old Sophie Brzeska.
Intense, fragmentary art film about two eccentrics; would have better suited TV.

w Christopher Logue, *book* H. S. Ede *d* Ken Russell *ph* Dick Bush *m* Michael Garrett *pd* Derek Jarman

Dorothy Tutin, Scott Anthony, Helen Mirren, Lindsay Kemp, Michael Gough, John Justin

Savage Pampas

Spain / Argentina / US 1967 108m
Eastmancolor Superpanorama
Jaime Prados–Dasa–Sam Bronston

In 19th-century Argentina the commander of an isolated fort finds that a bandit is bribing his men to desert.
Densely plotted semi-western, sometimes good to look at but slow and lugubrious.

w Hugo Fregonese, John Melson *d* Hugo Fregonese *ph* Marcel Berenguer *m* Waldo de los Rios

Robert Taylor, Ron Randell, Ty Hardin, Rosenda Monteros, Marc Lawrence

Savage Sam*

US 1962 104m Technicolor
Walt Disney (Bill Anderson)

The youngest son of a homesteading family has a troublesome dog which redeems itself by tracking down Apaches.
Folksy boy-and-dog western, good of its kind, with adequate suspense and scenery.

w Fred Gipson, William Tunberg *d* Norman Tokar *ph* Edward Colman *m* Oliver Wallace

Brian Keith, Tommy Kirk, Kevin Corcoran, Dewey Martin, Jeff York
'A cadet edition of the best of Ford.'—*MFB*

Savage Wilderness

US 1956 98m Technicolor Cinemascope
Columbia (William Fadiman)
GB title: *The Last Frontier*

An Indian-hating fort commander puts himself and his charges in jeopardy.
Standard western with good performances and excellent action scenes.

w Philip Yordan, Russell S. Hughes, *novel* The Gilded Rooster by Richard Emery Roberts *d* Anthony Mann *ph* William Mellor *m* Leigh Harline

Victor Mature, *Robert Preston*, Guy Madison, Anne Bancroft, James Whitmore, Peter Whitney

Savages

US 1972 106m colour
Angelika / Merchant–Ivory (Joseph Saleh)

Forest wanderers take over a deserted mansion and begin to feel its civilizing influence.
Mild fable which needed a Bunuel to do it justice; a few lively moments.

w George Swift Trow, Michael O'Donoghue *d* James Ivory *ph* Walter Lassally *m* Joe Raposo

Louis Stadlen, Anne Francine, Thayer David, Salome Jens, Neil Fitzgerald

Save the Tiger°
US 1973 100m Movielab
Paramount / Jalem / Filmways / Cirandinha (Steve Shagan)

A middle-aged businessman regrets the slack morality of modern America.
Self-adulatory drama which really has little point but gets a few marks for meaning well and for vivid scenes.

w Steve Shagan *d* John G. Avildsen *ph* Jim Crabe *m* Marvin Hamlisch

Jack Lemmon, Jack Gilford, Laurie Heineman, Norman Burton, Thayer David
   'A scathing indictment of the US, of materialism, war, marriage—the works. Wordy, literate and deeply felt.'—*NFT, 1974*

AA: Jack Lemmon
AAN: Steve Shagan; Jack Gilford

Sawdust and Tinsel°
Sweden 1953 95m bw
Svensk Filmindustri
aka: *The Naked Night;* original title: *Gycklarnas Afton*

The owner of a travelling circus leaves his mistress for his separated wife, and is challenged to fight by the mistress's new lover.
Powerfully-made yet rather pointless melodrama about unpleasant people.

wd Ingmar Bergman *ph* Sven Nykvist *m* Karl-Birger Blomdahl

Harriet Andersson, Ake Grönberg, Hasse Ekman, Annika Tretow
   'One of the extremely rare instances of a film's elements all blending perfectly.'—*John Simon*

The Saxon Charm
US 1948 88m bw
Universal (Joseph Sistrom)

A Broadway impresario dominates the lives of those around him.
Rather heavy-going comedy drama which could have done with more malicious wit; allegedly based on Jed Harris.

wd Claude Binyon, *novel* Frederick Wakeman *ph* Milton Krasner *m* Walter Scharf

Robert Montgomery, Susan Hayward, John Payne, Audrey Totter, Henry Morgan, Harry Von Zell, Cara Williams, Chill Wills, Heather Angel

Say Hello to Yesterday
GB 1970 92m Eastmancolor
Josef Shaftel (William Hill)

A middle-aged married woman goes to London for shopping and is pursued by a strange young man whom she allows to seduce her.
Unattractive 'with it' romantic drama with a swinging London setting, a long way after *Brief Encounter*.

w Alvin Rakoff, Peter King *d* Alvin Rakoff *ph* Geoffrey Unsworth *m* Riz Ortolani

Jean Simmons, Leonard Whiting, *Evelyn Laye*, John Lee, Jack Woolgar

Say It in French
US 1938 67m bw

A golf champion marries a French girl, but on his return, in order to help his father's finances, has to pretend to be marrying a rich girl, so his wife pretends to be a maid. Thin comedy which has a job to sustain its short running time. Ray Milland, Olympe Bradna, Irene Hervey, Janet Beecher, Mary Carlisle, Holmes Herbert, Erik Rhodes. Written by Frederick Jackson, from a play by Jacques Deval; directed by Andrew L. Stone; for Paramount. 'The harder it strives for hare-brained badinage, the more laboured it becomes.'—*Variety*

Say It with Songs
US 1929 89m bw
Warner

A radio singer accidentally kills a man and is jailed for manslaughter.
Miscalculated star vehicle with a few good moments among the sentiment and melodrama.

w Darryl F. Zanuck, Joseph Jackson, Harvey Gates *d* Lloyd Bacon *ph* Lee Garmes

Al Jolson, Davey Lee, Marian Nixon, Fred Kohler, Holmes Herbert
† Though Jolson was paid half a million dollars to do it, the film was a tremendous flop. The songs were again by De Sylva, Brown and Henderson, but 'Little Pal' was not another 'Sonny Boy'.

Say One for Me
US 1959 117m De Luxe Cinemascope
TCF / Bing Crosby (Frank Tashlin)

Adventures of a parish priest in New York's theatrical quarter.
Unconvincing, unattractive imitation of *Going My Way* which counters bad taste with religiosity.

w Robert O'Brien *d* Frank Tashlin *ph* Leo Tover *songs* Sammy Cahn, James Van Heusen *md* Lionel Newman

Bing Crosby, Robert Wagner, Debbie Reynolds, Ray Walston, Les Tremayne, Connie Gilchrist, Frank McHugh, Joe Besser, Sebastian Cabot
   'Tasteless and disturbing.'—*Variety*

AAN: Lionel Newman

'I am not allowed to love. But I will love you if that is your desire!'
Sayonara°°
US 1957 147m Technirama
Goetz Pictures—Pennebaker (William Goetz)

An American air force major in Tokyo after the war falls in love with a Japanese actress. A lush travelogue interrupted by two romances, one tragic and one happy. A great success at the time, though mainly of interest to Americans; now vaguely dated.

w Paul Osborn, *novel* James A. Michener *d* Joshua Logan *ph* Ellsworth Fredericks *m* Franz Waxman *ad* Ted Haworth

Marlon Brando, Miyoshi Umeki, Miiko Taka, Red Buttons, Ricardo Montalban, Patricia Owens, Kent Smith, Martha Scott, James Garner

AA: Miyoshi Umeki; Red Buttons
AAN: best picture; Paul Osborn; Joshua Logan; Ellsworth Fredericks; Marlon Brando

Says O'Reilly to MacNab
GB 1937 83m bw

A rich Scot is afflicted by an Irish conman. Lively ethnic comedy, a good vehicle for two stars. Will Mahoney, Will Fyffe, Ellis Drake, Sandy McDougal. Written by Leslie Arliss, Howard Irving Young; directed by William Beaudine; for Gaumont-British. 'Most hinterland exhibs have the quakes and headaches when it comes time on their sked to play a British film, but here's one, if sold along American lines, which may be found acceptable to the patrons in most places.'—*Variety*

Scalawag
US / Italy 1973 93m Technicolor
Bryna / Inex–Oceania (Anne Douglas)

Mexico 1840: a one-legged pirate and a boy try to trace a hidden treasure.
Flagrant reworking of *Treasure Island*, heavily overdone by stars and rhubarbing extras alike.

w Albert Maltz, Sid Fleischman *d* Kirk Douglas *ph* Jack Cardiff *m* John Cameron

Kirk Douglas, Mark Lester, Neville Brand, David Stroud, Lesley-Anne Down, Phil Brown

The Scalphunters°
US 1968 102m De Luxe Panavision
UA / Bristol / Norlan (Levy–Gardner–Laven)

An old cowboy and a black ex-slave track down a gang who kill Indians for their scalps.
Vigorous, aimless, likeable comedy western with the emphasis on brawling.

w William Norton *d* Sydney Pollack *ph* Duke Callaghan, Richard Moore *m* Elmer Bernstein

Burt Lancaster, Ossie Davis, Telly Savalas, Shelley Winters, Nick Cravat, Paul Picerni
   'It is the sort of frolic where bodies litter the ground, but you know they'll get up and draw their pay. And where even a villain can crack a joke without losing face.'—*Robert Ottaway*

Scandal at Scourie
US 1953 90m Metrocolor
MGM (Edwin H. Knopf)

The wife of the Protestant reeve of a Scottish-Canadian Protestant community adopts a Catholic child.
Sentimental whimsy with no holds barred, but with rather jaded acting and production.

w Norman Corwin, Leonard Spiegelgass, Karl Tunberg *d* Jean Negulesco *ph* Robert Planck *m* Daniele Amfitheatrof

Greer Garson, Walter Pidgeon, Agnes Moorehead, Arthur Shields, Philip Ober, Donna Corcoran

A Scandal in Paris*
US 1946 100m bw
UA / Arnold Pressburger
aka: *Thieves' Holiday*

Adventures of Vidocq, a 19th-century rogue who became Paris chief of police.
The actors look uneasy in their costumes, and the sets are cardboard, but there is fun to be had from this light comedy-drama.

w Ellis St Joseph d Douglas Sirk ph Guy Roe m Hans Eisler

George Sanders, Signe Hasso, Carole Landis, Akim Tamiroff, Gene Lockhart

Scandal Sheet
US 1931 77m bw

A newspaper editor with principles prints scandal involving his wife. Dated star drama.
George Bancroft, Kay Francis, Regis Toomey, Clive Brook. Written by Vincent Lawrence and Max Marcin; directed by John Cromwell; for Paramount.

Scandal Sheet
US 1939 67m bw

A ruthless publisher sacrifices himself to save his son. Uninteresting star quickie. Otto Kruger, Ona Munson, Edward Norris. Written by Joseph Carole; directed by Nick Grinde; for Columbia.

Scandal Sheet
US 1952 81m bw
Columbia (Edward Small)
GB title: *The Dark Page*

An editor has to allow his star reporter to expose a murderer—himself.
Obvious, reasonably holding melodrama with familiar characters.

w Ted Sherdeman, Eugene Ling, James Poe, *novel* Samuel Fuller d Phil Karlson ph Burnett Guffey m George Duning

Broderick Crawford, John Derek, Donna Reed, Rosemary de Camp, Henry O'Neill, Henry Morgan

Scandal Street
US 1937 63m bw

The arrival in a small town of an innocent young girl causes gossip which leads to murder. Satisfactory mini-drama for the easily pleased. Lew Ayres, Louise Campbell, Roscoe Karns, Porter Hall, Virginia Weidler, Edgar Kennedy, Elizabeth Patterson. Written by Bertram Millhauser and Eddie Welch, from a story by James Hogan; for Paramount. 'A curiously beguiling little hodge-podge.'—*Variety*

Scandalous!
GB 1984 92m Technicolor
Hemdale / Raleigh / Angeles Cinema Investors (Arlene Sellers, Alex Winitsky)

A TV reporter becomes involved with two con artists, who seem to have some connection with the murder of his wife.

Frantic black comedy which never even begins to be funny.

w Rob Cohen, John Byrum d Rob Cohen ph Jack Cardiff m Dave Grusin pd Peter Mullins

Robert Hays, John Gielgud, Pamela Stephenson, M. Emmet Walsh, Nancy Wood, Jim Dale

Scandalous John
US 1971 117m Technicolor
Walt Disney (Bill Walsh)

The elderly owner of a derelict ranch resists all efforts to close him up.
Unsatisfactory Disney attempt to capture a more adult audience than usual; overlong, repetitious and dreary.

w Bill Walsh, Don da Gradi, *novel* Richard Gardner d Robert Butler ph Frank Phillips m Rod McKuen

Brian Keith, Alfonso Arau, Michele Carey, Rick Lenz, Henry Morgan, Simon Oakland

Scanners
Canada 1980 103m Eastmancolor
Filmplan International (Claude Heroux)

Certain people are found to be telepathic 'scanners' able to lock at will into other people's nervous systems. This has the occasional result of blowing apart the other people's heads.
Overlong science fiction which concentrates on the nastier elements.

wd David Cronenberg ph Mark Irwin m Howard Shore

Jennifer O'Neill, Patrick McGoohan, Stephen Lack, Lawrence Dane, Michael Ironside

The Scapegoat*
GB 1959 92m bw
MGM / Du Maurier–Guinness (Dennis Van Thal)

A quiet bachelor on a French holiday is tricked into assuming the identity of a lookalike aristocrat who wants to commit a murder.
Disappointing adaptation of a good story, with much evidence of re-cutting and an especially slack middle section.

w Gore Vidal, Robert Hamer, *novel* Daphne du Maurier d Robert Hamer ph Paul Beeson m Bronislau Kaper

Alec Guinness, Bette Davis, Irene Worth, Nicole Maurey, Pamela Brown, Geoffrey Keen

The Scar
US 1948 83m bw
Eagle–Lion (Bryan Foy, Paul Henreid)
aka: *Hollow Triumph*

A fugitive kills his psychoanalyst double and takes his place, but is caught for the double's crimes.
Cheap suspense thriller with no suspense and no surprises.

w Daniel Fuchs, *novel* Murray Forbes d Steve Sekely ph John Alton m Sol Kaplan

Joan Bennett, Paul Henreid, Eduard Franz, Leslie Brooks, John Qualen, Mabel Paige, Herbert Rudley

Scaramouche**
US 1952 115m Technicolor
MGM (Carey Wilson)

A young man disguises himself as an actor to avenge the death of his friend at the hands of a wicked marquis.
Cheerful swashbuckler set in French revolutionary times, first filmed in the twenties with Ramon Novarro. MGM costume production at somewhere near its best.

w Ronald Millar, George Froeschel, *novel* Rafael Sabatini d George Sidney ph Charles Rosher m Victor Young ad Cedric Gibbons, Hans Peters

Stewart Granger, Mel Ferrer, Eleanor Parker, Janet Leigh, Henry Wilcoxon, Nina Foch, Lewis Stone, Robert Coote, Richard Anderson

† The sword fight, at 6½ minutes, is credited with being the longest in cinema history.

Scarecrow*
US 1973 112m Technicolor
Panavision
Warner (Robert M. Sherman)

Two of the world's losers hitch-hike across America.
Well-shot but eventually dreary parable of friendship, a pedestrian *Easy Rider*.

w Garry Michael White d Jerry Schatzberg ph Vilmos Zsigmond m Fred Myrow

Gene Hackman, Al Pacino
'Here's a picture that manages to abuse two American myths at once—the Road and the Male Pair.'—*Stanley Kauffmann*

The Scarecrow*
New Zealand 1981 88m colour
Oasis / New Zealand National Film Unit (Rob Whitehouse)

In a small town in the early fifties, a strange chain of events is set in motion by the disappearance of six chickens.
A curious mix of sinister atmosphere which seems mystical and sinister events which are all too real. Interesting but unsatisfying, both as a murder mystery and as a study in evil.

w Michael Heath, Sam Pilsbury, *novel* Ronald Hugh Morrieson d Sam Pilsbury ph James Bartle m Schtung

John Carradine, Tracy Mann, Jonathan Smith, Daniel McLaren, Denise O'Connell, Anne Flannery

'They're making a spook-tacle of themselves!'
Scared Stiff
US 1953 108m bw
Paramount (Hal B. Wallis)

Nightclub entertainers get involved with a girl who has inherited a spooky castle off the Cuban coast.
Stretched-out remake of *The Ghost Breakers*; the last half hour, being closest to the original, is the most nearly funny.

w Herbert Baker, Walter de Leon d George
Marshall, Ed Simmons, Norman Lear
ph Ernest Laszlo md Joseph J. Lilley

Dean Martin, Jerry Lewis, Lizabeth Scott,
Carmen Miranda, George Dolenz, Dorothy
Malone, William Ching, Jack Lambert

The Scarf
US 1951 86m bw
UA / Gloria (I. G. Goldsmith)

A man escapes from a lunatic asylum and
proves himself innocent of the crime for which
he was committed.
Glum and pretentious murder mystery with a
pictorial style to match its flowery dialogue.

wd E. A. Dupont ph Franz Planer
m Herschel Burke Gilbert

John Ireland, Mercedes McCambridge, Emlyn
Williams, James Barton, Lloyd Gough, Basil
Ruysdael

'I'm going to run the whole works. There's
  only one law: do it first, do it yourself,
  and keep doing it!'

Scarface****
US 1932 99m bw
Howard Hughes
aka: The Shame of a Nation

The life and death of a Chicago gangster of the
twenties.
Obviously modelled on Al Capone, with an
incestuous sister thrown in, this was perhaps
the most vivid film of the gangster cycle, and
its revelling in its own sins was not obscured
by the subtitle, The Shame of a Nation.

w Ben Hecht, Seton I. Miller, John Lee
Mahin, W. R. Burnett, Fred Pasley, novel
Armitage Traill d Howard Hawks ph Lee
Garmes, L. W. O'Connell m Adolph Tandler,
Gus Arnheim

Paul Muni, Ann Dvorak, George Raft, Boris
Karloff, Osgood Perkins, Karen Morley, C.
Henry Gordon, Vince Barnett, Henry
Armetta, Edwin Maxwell
  'Presumably the last of the gangster films,
on a promise, it is going to make people sorry
that there won't be any more. Should draw
wherever it can play.'—Variety
  'More brutal, more cruel, more wholesale
than any of its predecessors.'—James Shelley
Hamilton
  'Because it was so close to the actual events,
it possesses a kind of newsreel quality which
cannot be recaptured or imitated. It vibrates
with the impact of things that were real and
deeply felt.'—National Film Theatre
programme, 1961
† On original release added scenes showed
Tony tried, convicted and hanged, though since
Muni is never seen, it appears that they were
an afterthought made when he was not
available.

Scarface
US 1983 170m Technicolor
Panavision
Universal (Martin Bregman)

Absurdly brutalized version of the above, with
detailed violence and a superabundance of

foul language. Scarface has now become an
emigré Cuban, and the film seems to want to
make a political statement.

w Oliver Stone d Brian de Palma ph John A.
Alonzo m Giorgio Moroder

Al Pacino, Steven Bauer, Michelle Pfeiffer,
Mary Elizabeth Mastrantonio, Robert Loggia,
Paul Shenar, Harris Yulin
● Video: CIC

The Scarface Mob*
US 1958 96m bw
Desilu (Quinn Martin)

Al Capone's empire thrives while he is in
Alcatraz, and prohibition agent Eliot Ness
recruits a tough squad to fight the gangsters.
Though released theatrically, this was in effect
a pilot film for the successful TV series The
Untouchables, well enough done within its
limits.

w Paul Monash, novel The Untouchables by
Eliot Ness d Phil Karlson ph Charles
Straumer m Wilbur Hatch

Robert Stack, Neville Brand, Keenan Wynn,
Barbara Nichols, Joe Mantell, Pat Crowley,
Bruce Gordon, Paul Picerni, Abel Fernandez

Scarlet Angel
US 1952 81m Technicolor
U-I (Leonard Goldstein)

A saloon hostess presents herself to a wealthy
family as their dead son's wife.
Modest, satisfactorily plotted woman's picture
with action interludes.

w Oscar Brodney d Sidney Salkow
ph Russell Metty m Joseph Gershenson

Yvonne de Carlo, Rock Hudson, Richard
Denning, Henry O'Neill, Amanda Blake

The Scarlet Blade*
GB 1963 82m Technicolor
  Hammerscope
Hammer (Anthony Nelson Keys)
US title: The Crimson Blade

In 1648, a Cromwellian colonel plans to hang
every royalist rebel.
Adequate swashbuckler.

wd John Gilling ph Jack Asher m Gary
Hughes

Lionel Jeffries, Oliver Reed, Jack Hedley,
June Thorburn, Duncan Lamont

The Scarlet Claw**
US 1944 74m bw
Universal (Roy William Neill)

Grisly revenge murders take place in the
fog-bound Canadian village of Le Mort
Rouge.
Possibly the best of the modernized Sherlock
Holmes series, with a plot hastily borrowed
from The Hound of the Baskervilles.

w Edmund L. Hartmann, Roy William Neill
d Roy William Neill ph George Robinson
md Paul Sawtell

Basil Rathbone, Nigel Bruce, Miles Mander,
Gerald Hamer, Paul Cavanagh, Kay Harding,
Arthur Hohl

The Scarlet Coat
US 1955 99m Eastmancolor
  Cinemascope
MGM (Nicholas Nayfack)

During the American War of Independence,
an American officer deserts to the British in
order to unmask a traitor.
Rather talky historical actioner with too much
time spent on friendship and romance.

w Karl Tunberg d John Sturges ph Paul C.
Vogel m Conrad Salinger

Cornel Wilde, Michael Wilding, George
Sanders, Anne Francis, Robert Douglas,
Bobby Driscoll, John McIntire

Scarlet Dawn*
US 1932 76m bw
Warner (Hal Wallis)

During the Russian revolution, an exiled
aristocrat loves a serving maid.
Heavy-going romantic drama distinguished by
stylish direction and sets.

w Niven Busch, Erwin Gelsey, Douglas
Fairbanks Jnr, novel Revolt by Mary McCall
Jnr d William Dieterle ph Ernest Haller
ad Anton Grot

Douglas Fairbanks Jnr, Nancy Carroll, Lilyan
Tashman, Guy Kibbee, Sheila Terry, Frank
Reicher
  'The story starts off to get somewhere but
fails to arrive.'—Variety

'Based on a private diary of Catherine the
  Great!'
'The screen's reigning beauty in a wild
  pageant of barbaric splendour!'
'A cavalcade of fury led by a woman of
  fire!'

The Scarlet Empress***
US 1934 109m bw
Paramount

A fantasia on the love life of Catherine the
Great.
A marvellous, overwhelming, dramatically
insubstantial but pictorially brilliant homage to
a star; not to everyone's taste, but a film to
remember.

w Manuel Komroff d Josef Von Sternberg
ph Bert Glennon md W. Franke Harling,
John M. Leipold, Milan Roder ad Hans
Dreier, Peter Ballbusch, Richard Kollorsz
costumes Travis Banton

Marlene Dietrich, John Lodge, Sam Jaffe,
Louise Dresser, C. Aubrey Smith, Gavin
Gordon, Jameson Thomas
  'She's photographed behind veils and
fishnets, while dwarfs slither about and bells
ring and everybody tries to look
degenerate.'—New Yorker, 1975
  'A ponderous, strangely beautiful, lengthy
and frequently wearying production.'—
Mordaunt Hall, New York Times

The Scarlet Hour
US 1955 93m bw Vistavision
Paramount (Michael Curtiz)

A bored wife persuades her lover to turn thief;
her husband misconstrues the situation and is
accidentally killed.

SCARFACE.   Paul Muni shows Osgood Perkins (father of Anthony) how to use a tommy gun; Vince Barnett, Karen Morley and George Raft are among the onlookers.

Complex suspenser designed to introduce new talent; rather too smooth, and pretty boring.

w Rip van Ronkel, Frank Tashlin, Meredyth Lucas *d* Michael Curtiz *ph* Lionel Lindon *m* Leith Stevens

Carol Ohmart, Tom Tryon, James Gregory, Jody Lawrance, E. G. Marshall, *Elaine Stritch*

The Scarlet Letter*
US 1926   90m (24 fps)   bw   silent
MGM / Jury

In Puritan New England, the mother of an illegitimate child wears the scarlet A (for adulteress) for years rather than reveal that her lover was the village priest.

Celebrated 17th-century melodrama, quite powerfully made in the best silent tradition, but of little intrinsic interest for modern audiences.

w Frances Marion, *novel* Nathaniel Hawthorne *d* Victor Sjostrom *ph* Henrik Sartov *ad* Cedric Gibbons

Lillian Gish, Lars Hanson, Karl Dane, Henry B. Walthall

† Other versions include the following: US 1910, US 1911, US 1913, US 1917, US 1920, GB 1922, US 1934, Germany 1971, US (TV) 1979

The Scarlet Letter
US 1934   70m   bw

A lightened version with an attempt at comedy relief. Not in any way remarkable. Colleen Moore, Hardie Albright, Henry B. Walthall, William Farnum, Alan Hale. Written by Leonard Fields, David Silverstein; directed by Robert G. Vignola; for Darmour / Majestic.

The Scarlet Pimpernel***
GB 1934   98m   bw
London Films (Alexander Korda)

In the early days of the French revolution, an apparently foppish Englishman leads a daring

band in rescuing aristocrats from the guillotine.
First-class period adventure with a splendid and much imitated plot, strong characters, humour and a richly detailed historical background.

w Robert E. Sherwood, Sam Berman, Arthur Wimperis, Lajos Biro, *novel* Baroness Orczy d Harold Young ph Harold Rosson m Arthur Benjamin

Leslie Howard, Merle Oberon, Raymond Massey, Nigel Bruce, Bramwell Fletcher, Anthony Bushell, Joan Gardner, Walter Rilla
'Excellent British import that will do business.'—*Variety*
'One of the most romantic and durable of all swashbucklers.'—*New Yorker, 1976*
'A triumph for the British film world.'—*Sunday Times*
† The story was remade as *The Elusive Pimpernel (qv)* and in 1982 in a TV version starring Anthony Andrews. See also *The Return of the Scarlet Pimpernel.*

'I've been wanting to laugh in your face ever since I met you. You're old and ugly and I'm sick of you—sick, sick, sick!'
Scarlet Street**
US 1945 103m bw
(Universal) Walter Wanger (Fritz Lang)

A prostitute is murdered by her client and her pimp is executed for the crime.
Daring but rather gloomy Hollywood melodrama, the first in which a crime went unpunished (though the culprit was shown suffering remorse). Interesting and heavily Teutonic, but as entertainment not a patch on the similar but lighter *The Woman in the Window*, which the same team had made a year previously.

w Dudley Nichols, *play* La Chienne by George de la Fouchardière (filmed by Jean Renoir in 1932) d Fritz Lang ph Milton Krasner m Hans Salter ad Alexander Golitzen

Edward G. Robinson, Joan Bennett, Dan Duryea, Jess Barker, Margaret Lindsay, Rosalind Ivan, Samuel S. Hinds, Arthur Loft
'The director unerringly chooses the right sound and image to assault the spectator's sensibilities.'—*C. A. Lejeune*

The Scarlet Thread
GB 1950 84m bw

Jewel thieves take refuge in a Cambridge college. Flabby melodrama featuring emergent young talent. Kathleen Byron, Laurence Harvey, Sidney Tafler, Arthur Hill, Dora Bryan. Written by A. R. Rawlinson, from a play by A. R. Rawlinson and Moie Charles; directed by Lewis Gilbert; for Nettlefold / Butcher.

Scars of Dracula
GB 1970 96m Technicolor
Hammer / EMI (Aida Young)

A young man on the run finds himself an unwitting guest of Count Dracula.
Overpadded vampire saga, its few effective moments stemming directly from the original novel.

w John Elder d Roy Ward Baker ph Moray Grant m James Bernard

Christopher Lee, Dennis Waterman, Christopher Matthews, Jenny Hanley, Patrick Troughton, Michael Gwynn, Bob Todd

Scattergood Baines
US 1941 69m bw

The new owner of a small-town hardware store takes an interest in his fellow men. First of several second features featuring the exploits of a likeable busybody. *Guy Kibbee,* Carol Hughes, John Archer, Emma Dunn. Written by Michael L. Simmons and Edward T. Lowe, from the stories by Clarence Budington Kelland; directed by Christy Cabanne; for RKO. (The succeeding episodes were as follows: *Scattergood Pulls the Strings,* 1941; *Scattergood Meets Broadway,* 1941; *Scattergood Rides High,* 1942; *Scattergood Survives a Murder,* 1942; *Cinderella Swings It,* 1943.)

Scavenger Hunt
US 1979 116m De Luxe
TCF / Melvin Simon

A rich man leaves a fortune to the member of his family who can collect most of the useless objects in a list provided.
Depressing cheapjack imitation of Kramer's *It's a Mad Mad Mad Mad World,* which itself was not free from fault.

w Steven A. Vail, Henry Harper d Michael Schultz ph Ken Lamkin m Billy Goldenberg

Richard Benjamin, James Coco, Scatman Crothers, Cloris Leachman, Cleavon Little, Roddy McDowall, Robert Morley, Richard Mulligan, Tony Randall, Dirk Benedict, Vincent Price
'Loud, obnoxious, and above all unfunny.'—*Variety*

● Video: Guild

'First they moved (1895)! Then they talked (1927)! Now they smell!'
Scent of Mystery*
US 1959 125m Technicolor Cinerama (70mm)
Cinerama / Mike Todd Jnr
aka: *Holiday in Spain*

An Englishman on holiday in Spain protects a mysterious girl.
More of a travelogue than a thriller, but worth a note as the cinema's first 'smellie'. A process called Smell-o-Vision released appropriate odours throughout the auditorium . . .

w William Rose d Jack Cardiff ph John Von Kotze m Mario Nascimbene

Denholm Elliott, Peter Lorre, Beverly Bentley, Paul Lukas, Liam Redmond, Leo McKern, Peter Arne, Mary Laura Wood, Elizabeth Taylor
† The first film to credit its providers of shoe polish.

School for Husbands
GB 1937 71m bw
Wainwright (Richard Wainwright)

A romantic novelist annoys the husbands of his adoring fans.

Would-be champagne comedy which bubbles pretty well for most of its length.

w Frederick Jackson, Gordon Aherry, Austin Melford, *play* Frederick Jackson d Andrew Marton ph Phil Tannura

Rex Harrison, Henry Kendall, Romney Brent, Diana Churchill, June Clyde

School for Scoundrels*
GB 1960 94m bw
ABP / Guardsman (Hal E. Chester)

A failure reports to the College of One-Upmanship and his life is transformed.
Amusing trifle, basically a series of sketches by familiar comic actors.

w Patricia Mayes, Hal E. Chester, *books* Stephen Potter d Robert Hamer ph Erwin Hillier m John Addison

Ian Carmichael, Alastair Sim, Terry-Thomas, Janette Scott, Dennis Price, Peter Jones, Edward Chapman, John Le Mesurier

School for Secrets
GB 1946 108m bw
Rank / Two Cities (George H. Brown, Peter Ustinov)
US title: *Secret Flight*

The boffins who invented radar find themselves in a little war action of their own.
An unsatisfactory entertainment which, with the best intentions, shuffles between arch comedy, character drama, war action and documentary, doing less than justice to any of these aspects.

wd Peter Ustinov

Ralph Richardson, Raymond Huntley, Richard Attenborough, Marjorie Rhodes, John Laurie, Ernest Jay, David Tomlinson, Finlay Currie

Schweik's New Adventures
GB 1943 84m bw

An unassuming Czechoslovakian writer gently kids the Nazi occupiers and manages to save some of his friends from the concentration camp. Curious English attempt to film a popular Czechoslovakian character; it made mildly effective wartime propaganda, though few went to see it. Lloyd Pearson, George Carney, Julien Mitchell, Richard Attenborough, Margaret McGrath. Written by Karel Lamac and Con West, from the novel by Jaroslav Hasek; directed by Karel Lamac; for Eden Films.

'When Scorpio wants you, there is nowhere to hide!'
Scorpio
US 1972 114m Technicolor
UA / Scimitar (Walter Mirisch)

CIA agents doublecross each other.
Incredibly complex spy thriller in which it's difficult to know, or care, who's following whom. The brutalities, however, are capably staged.

w David W. Rintels, Gerald Wilson d Michael Winner ph Robert Paynter m Jerry Fielding

Burt Lancaster, Alain Delon, Paul Scofield, John Colicos, Gayle Hunnicutt, J. D. Cannon

'Strictly zoom and thump.'—*Sight and Sound*

'Relying on moments of violence for effect, Winner directs with typically crass abandon.'—*Time Out, 1984*

Scotland Yard

US 1941   68m   bw
TCF (Sol M. Wurtzel)

The Nazis capture a London banker and use his double to turn funds over to them. Outlandish spy melodrama which certainly keeps the interest.

w Samuel G. Engel, John Balderston, *play* Deniston Clift *d* Norman Foster *ph* Virgil Miller *m* Emil Newman

Nancy Kelly, Edmund Gwenn, Henry Wilcoxon, John Loder, Melville Cooper, Gilbert Emery, Norma Varden

Scott of the Antarctic••

GB 1948   111m   Technicolor
Ealing (Sidney Cole)

After long preparation, Captain Scott sets off on his ill-fated 1912 expedition to the South Pole.

The stiff-upper-lip saga par excellence; inevitable knowledge of the end makes it pretty downbeat, and the actors can only be sincere; but the snowscapes, most of them artificial, are fine.

w Ivor Montagu, Walter Meade, Mary Hayley Bell *d* Charles Frend *ph* Geoffrey Unsworth, Jack Cardiff, Osmond Borradaile *m* Ralph Vaughan Williams

John Mills, James Robertson Justice, Derek Bond, Harold Warrender, Reginald Beckwith, Kenneth More, James McKechnie, John Gregson

● *Video: Thorn EMI*

The Scoundrel••

US 1935   74m   bw
Paramount (Ben Hecht, Charles MacArthur)

A famous writer dies; his ghost comes back to find the meaning of love.

Unique thirties supernatural melodrama with barbs of dated wit despatched by a splendid cast. Nonsense, but great nonsense.

wd Ben Hecht, Charles MacArthur *ph* Lee Garmes *m* George Antheil

Noel Coward, Alexander Woolcott, Julie Haydon, Stanley Ridges, Eduardo Ciannelli

'Good Hotel Algonquin literati stuff, but not for the Automat trade.'—*Variety*

'An unmistakeable whiff from a gossip column world which tries hard to split the difference between an epigram and a wisecrack.'—*William Whitebait*

'Practically flawless drama. It's arty, but if this is art, let us have more of it.'—*Photoplay*

'An impudent work . . . but there are brains in it, and observation, and even a kind of stunted poetry.'—*Observer*

† Helen Hayes and Edna Ferber made cameo appearances.

AA: original story
AAN: script

THE SCARLET PIMPERNEL. Leslie Howard and Merle Oberon in a still stressing the romance which was the film's principal ingredient.

Scram!•

US 1932   20m   bw

Two vagrants are ordered out of town but by a series of misadventures are found drunk with the judge's wife. Generally sprightly star comedy culminating in a marathon laughing session. Laurel and Hardy, Arthur Housman, Rychard Cramer, Vivien Oakland. Written by H. M. Walker; directed by Ray McCarey; for Hal Roach.

Scream and Scream Again•

GB 1969   94m   Eastmancolor
AIP / Amicus (Milton Subotsky)

Murders are traced to superhuman composite beings created by a mad scientist.

Energetic and well-staged though rather humourless shocker.

w Christopher Wicking, *novel* The Disorientated Man by Peter Saxon *d* Gordon Hessler *ph* John Coquillon *m* David Whittaker *ad* Don Mingaye

Vincent Price, Christopher Lee, Peter Cushing, Alfred Marks, Anthony Newlands, David Lodge

Screaming Mimi

US 1958   79m   bw

After being sexually assaulted a dancer comes to believe she has committed murder . . . and later we learn that she has. Sub-Freudian

melodrama on the comic strip level. Anita
Ekberg, Phil Carey, Harry Townes, Gypsy
Rose Lee, Romney Brent, Alan Gifford.
Written by Robert Blees, from the book by
Frederic Brown; directed by Gerd Oswald; for
Sage / Columbia.

Scrooge*
GB 1935 78m bw
Twickenham (Julius Hagen, Hans Brahm)
A miser reforms after ghosts haunt him on
Christmas Eve.
Acceptable unambitious version with
interesting performances.
w Seymour Hicks, H. Fowler Mear,
novel Charles Dickens *d* Henry Edwards
ph Sidney Blythe, William Luff

Seymour Hicks, Donald Calthrop (Cratchit),
Athene Seyler, Oscar Asche, Barbara Everest,
Maurice Evans, C. V. France, Marie Ney

Scrooge***
GB 1951 86m bw
Renown (Brian Desmond Hurst)
By far the best available version of the classic
parable; casting, art direction, pace and
general handling are as good as can be.
w Noel Langley *d* Brian Desmond Hurst
ph C. Pennington-Richards *m* Richard
Addinsell

Alastair Sim, Mervyn Johns, Kathleen
Harrison, Jack Warner, Michael Hordern,
Hermione Baddeley, George Cole, Miles
Malleson

Scrooge*
GB 1970 113m Technicolor
  Panavision
Cinema Center / Waterbury (Richard H.
  Solo)
Dim musical version, darkly coloured and
quite lost on the wide screen; but it has its
macabre moments of trick photography.
w / m / ly Leslie Bricusse *d* Ronald Neame
ph Oswald Morris *pd* Terry Marsh

Albert Finney, Michael Medwin, Alec
Guinness, Edith Evans, Kenneth More, David
Collings, Laurence Naismith, Kay Walsh
† Richard Harris and Rex Harrison were both
sought before Finney was signed.

AAN: song 'Thank You Very Much' (*m / ly*
Leslie Bricusse); music

Scrubbers
GB 1982 93m Eastmancolor
Handmade (Don Boyd)
Sensational events in a girls' borstal.
Wild-eyed melodrama which seems to serve no
sort of purpose and is certainly not
entertaining.
w Roy Minton, Jeremy Watt, Mai Zetterling
d Mai Zetterling *ph* Ernest Vincze
m Michael Hurd

Amanda York, Chrissie Cotterill, Elizabeth
Edmonds, Kate Ingram, Honey Bane, Eva
Motley
● *Video: Thorn EMI*

Scudda Hoo, Scudda Hay
US 1948 98m Technicolor
TCF (Walter Morosco)
GB title: *Summer Lightning*
A farmer's son is less interested in girls than in
the welfare of his two mules.
Antediluvian rural romance for the simple-
minded.
wd F. Hugh Herbert, *novel* George Agnew
Chamberlain *ph* Ernest Palmer *m* Cyril
Mockridge

June Haver, Lon McCallister, Walter
Brennan, Anne Revere, Natalie Wood,
Robert Karnes, Henry Hull, Tom Tully,
Marilyn Monroe

Scum
GB 1979 97m Eastmancolor
Injustices in a Borstal institution lead to a riot.
Gorily overstated view of boys' prison life
from the inside, with the camera gloating over
each violent close-up. (The original TV play
had been made, then banned, by the BBC.)
Ray Winstone, Mick Ford, Julian Firth, John
Blundell. Written by Roy Minton; directed by
Alan Clarke; for Berwick Street Films.

The Sea Bat
US 1930 69m bw
Mexican fishermen compete to kill a deadly
sting-ray. The *Jaws* of its time; box office
hokum. Charles Bickford, Raquel Torres, Nils
Asther, John Miljan, Gibson Gowland, Boris
Karloff. Written by Bess Meredyth and John
Howard Lawson; directed by Wesley Ruggles;
for MGM.

The Sea Chase*
US 1955 117m Warnercolor
  Cinemascope
Warner (John Farrow)
In 1939 a German freighter tries to make it
from Sydney harbour back to Germany.
Unusual but not very compelling naval
melodrama, chiefly because the leads are
miscast.
w James Warner Bellah, John Twist, *novel*
Andrew Geer *d* John Farrow *ph* William
Clothier *m* Roy Webb

John Wayne, Lana Turner, David Farrar, Lyle
Bettger, Tab Hunter, James Arness, Dick
Davalos, John Qualen
  'A film compounded of monotonously
familiar ingredients.'—*Penelope Houston*

Sea Devils
US 1937 88m bw
Exploits of the ice patrols of the US Coast
Guard. Flagwaving action hokum for popular
stars. Victor McLaglen, Preston Foster, Ida
Lupino, Donald Woods. Written by Frank
Wead, John Twist and P. J. Wolfson; directed
by Ben Stoloff; for RKO.

Sea Devils
GB 1953 90m Technicolor
Coronado (David E. Rose)
Spies prevent Napoleon's invasion of England.
Cheerful, forgettable swashbuckler.

w Borden Chase *d* Raoul Walsh *ph* Wilkie
Cooper *m* Richard Addinsell

Yvonne de Carlo, Rock Hudson, Maxwell
Reed, Denis O'Dea, Michael Goodliffe,
Bryan Forbes, Ivor Barnard, Arthur Wontner

Sea Fury
GB 1958 97m bw
Rank (Benjamin Fisz)
Rivalry strikes up between an old and a young
sailor on tugboats plying between Spain and
England.
Shapeless, leery melodrama with strong
performances and an exciting storm-at-sea
climax.
w John Kruse, Cy Endfield *d* Cy Endfield
ph Reg Wyer *m* Philip Green

Stanley Baker, Victor McLaglen, Luciana
Paluzzi, Grégoire Aslan, Francis de Wolff,
David Oxley, Rupert Davies, Robert Shaw

'They stand side by side. Young and old.
  Rich and poor. They gather together for a
  single purpose. Survival.'
The Sea Gull*
GB 1968 141m Technicolor
Warner / Sidney Lumet
Loves and hates on a 19th-century Russian
estate.
Rather heavily star-studded, but certainly
proficient film version of a Chekhov favourite.
w Moura Budberg, *play* Anton Chekhov
d Sidney Lumet *ph* Gerry Fisher *m* none
pd Tony Walton

James Mason, Simone Signoret, Vanessa
Redgrave, David Warner, Harry Andrews,
Ronald Radd, Eileen Herlie, Kathleen
Widdoes, Denholm Elliott, Alfred Lynch
  'The camera cannot capture the hollowness
of space, the oppressive immoveableness of a
seemingly harmless enclosure, stasis settling
on everything like a fine, corrosive dust.'—
John Simon

The Sea Hawk***
US 1940 122m bw
Warner (Hal B. Wallis, Henry Blanke)
Elizabeth I encourages one of her most able
captains to acts of piracy against the Spanish.
Wobbly-plotted but stirring and exciting
seafaring actioner, with splendid battle and
duel scenes.
w Seton I. Miller, Howard Koch *d* Michael
Curtiz *ph* Sol Polito *m* Erich Wolfgang
Korngold *ad* Anton Grot

Errol Flynn, Flora Robson, Brenda Marshall,
Henry Daniell, Claude Rains, Donald Crisp,
Alan Hale, Una O'Connor, James
Stephenson, Gilbert Roland, William
Lundigan
  'Endless episodes of court intrigue tend to
diminish the effect of the epic sweep of the
high seas dramatics.'—*Variety*
AAN: Erich Wolfgang Korngold
● *Video: MGM / UA*

A man who loved as ruthlessly as he
ruled. A woman whose indiscretions cost
a lifetime of happiness!'

The Sea of Grass
US 1947 131m bw
MGM (Pandro S. Berman)

A cattle tycoon is so obsessed by his work that
he alienates his family.
Brooding, overlong semi-western with an
unexpected cast.

w Marguerite Roberts, Vincent Lawrence,
novel Conrad Richter d Elia Kazan *ph* Harry
Stradling *m* Herbert Stothart

Spencer Tracy, Katharine Hepburn, Melvyn
Douglas, Phyllis Thaxter, Robert Walker,
Edgar Buchanan, Harry Carey, Ruth Nelson,
James Bell
 'In spite of all the sincerity and talent
involved,' an epically dreary film.'—*Time*

Sea of Lost Ships
US 1953 85m bw

The US Coast Guard saves a passenger ship
from an iceberg. Scrappy, semi-documentary
account punctuated by rough action highlights.
Walter Brennan, John Derek, Wanda
Hendrix, Richard Jaeckel, Barton Maclane,
Darryl Hickman. Written by Steve Fisher;
directed by Joe Kane; for Republic.

Sea of Sand*
GB 1958 98m bw
Rank / Tempean (Robert Baker, Monty
 Berman)
US title: *Desert Patrol*

Just before Alamein an Eighth Army desert
group plans to destroy one of Rommel's last
petrol dumps.
Good standard war suspenser.

w Robert Westerby d Guy Green *ph* Wilkie
Cooper *m* Clifton Parker

Richard Attenborough, John Gregson,
Vincent Ball, Percy Herbert, Michael Craig,
Barry Foster, Andrew Faulds, Dermot Walsh

The Sea Shall Not Have Them
GB 1954 93m bw
Eros / Daniel M. Angel

Survivors of a seaplane crash await rescue in a
dinghy.
Rather dim computerized compendium of
flashback mini-dramas.

w Lewis Gilbert, Vernon Harris d Lewis
Gilbert *ph* Stephen Dade *m* Malcolm Arnold

Dirk Bogarde, Michael Redgrave, Bonar
Colleano, Jack Watling, Anthony Steel, Nigel
Patrick, James Kenney, Sidney Tafler, George
Rose

'One of the most challenging stories of
faith ever told! What happened out there
. . . in the surging vastness of the Indian
Ocean?'

Sea Wife
GB 1957 82m De Luxe Cinemascope
TCF / Sumar (André Hakim)

Survivors of a shipwreck near Singapore in
1942 are rescued, not before the bosun has

fallen in love with the only lady, not knowing
she is a nun.
Flashbacked, uncertain, intermittently
effective film of a popular minor novel.

w George K. Burke, *novel* Sea Wyf by J. M.
Scott d Bob McNaught *ph* Ted Scaife
m Kenneth V. Jones, Leonard Salzedo

Richard Burton, Joan Collins, Basil Sydney,
Cy Grant

The Sea Wolf**
US 1941 90m bw
Warner (Henry Blanke)

Survivors of a ferry crash in San Francisco Bay
are picked up by a psychopathic freighter
captain who keeps them captive.
Much filmed action suspenser which in this
version looks great but overdoes the talk.

w Robert Rossen, *novel* Jack London
d Michael Curtiz *ph* Sol Polito *m* Erich
Wolfgang Korngold

Edward G. Robinson, Alexander Knox, Ida
Lupino, John Garfield, Gene Lockhart, Barry
Fitzgerald, Stanley Ridges, David Bruce,
Howard da Silva
 'A Germanic, powerful work almost devoid
of compromise.'—*Charles Higham, 1972*
† Other versions appeared in 1913, with
Hobart Bosworth; in 1920, with Noah Beery;
in 1925, with Ralph Ince; in 1930, with Milton
Sills; in 1950 (as *Barricade*, turned into a
western), with Raymond Massey; in 1958 (as
Wolf Larsen), with Barry Sullivan; and in 1975
(Italian), as *Wolf of the Seven Seas*, with
Chuck Connors.

The Sea Wolves*
GB-US-Switzerland 1980 122m
 Eastmancolor
Richmond-Lorimar-Varius (Euan Lloyd)

In 1943, elderly British territorials living in
India dispose of a Nazi transmitter in neutral
Goa.
Mildly larkish *Boy's Own Paper* adventure
with a somewhat geriatric air; an interesting
1980 throwback to the films of 1950.

w Reginald Rose *novel* Boarding Party by
James Leasor d Andrew McLaglen *ph* Tony
Imi *m* Roy Budd

Gregory Peck, Roger Moore, Trevor Howard,
David Niven, Barbara Kellerman, Patrick
MacNee, Patrick Allen, Bernard Archard,
Faith Brook, Martin Benson, Allan
Cuthbertson, Kenneth Griffith, Donald
Houston, Glyn Houston, Percy Herbert,
Patrick Holt, Terence Longdon, John
Standing, Michael Medwin
 'As a genre—the arterio-sclerotic war
movie—it'll never catch on.'—*Time Out*
† The film was dedicated to Earl Mountbatten
after his assassination.
● *Video: Rank*

Seagulls over Sorrento
GB 1954 92m bw
MGM (John and Roy Boulting)
US title: *Crest of the Wave*

Life on a naval research station on a small
Scottish island.

A long-running British service comedy has
been Americanized to little effect, but it
remains just about watchable.

w Frank Harvey, Roy Boulting, *play* Hugh
Hastings d John and Roy Boulting
ph Gilbert Taylor *m* Miklos Rozsa

Gene Kelly, John Justin, Bernard Lee, Sidney
James, Jeff Richards, Patric Doonan, Patrick
Barr

Seal Island see The Living Desert

'What is the truth about fraternization?'
Sealed Verdict
US 1948 83m bw
Paramount (Robert Fellows)

An American officer in Germany falls in love
with the ex-girl friend of a Nazi war criminal.
Routine melodrama, as boring as it sounds.

w Jonathan Latimer, *novel* Lionel Shapiro
d Lewis Allen *ph* Leo Tover *m* Hugo
Friedhofer

Ray Milland, Florence Marly, Broderick
Crawford, John Hoyt, John Ridgely, Ludwig
Donath

Seance on a Wet Afternoon*
GB 1964 121m bw
Rank / Allied Film Makers (Richard
 Attenborough, Bryan Forbes, Jack Rix)

A fake medium persuades her husband to
kidnap a child so that she can become famous
by revealing its whereabouts in a trance.
Overlong character melodrama in which the
suspense is better than the psychopathology.
A mannered performance from the lady, a
false nose from the gentleman, and a general
air of gloom.

wd Bryan Forbes *ph* Gerry Turpin *m* John
Barry

Kim Stanley, Richard Attenborough, Nanette
Newman, Patrick Magee

AAN: Kim Stanley

The Search*
US / Switzerland 1948 105m bw
MGM / Praesens Film (Lazar Wechsler)

An American soldier in Germany cares for a
war orphan.
Vivid semi-documentary post-war drama
which falls down in its elementary dramatics
but sent audiences home wiping away tears.

w Richard Schweizer, David Wechsler, Paul
Jarrico d Fred Zinnemann *ph* Emil Berna
m Robert Blum

Montgomery Clift, Aline MacMahon, Ivan
Jandl, Wendell Corey

AA: original story (Richard Schweizer, David
Wechsler)
AAN: script; Fred Zinnemann; Montgomery
Clift

'You never saw so many skins you'd like to
 touch!'
Search for Beauty
US 1934 77m bw

A physical culture magazine sponsors an
international contest for beauties of both

WHAT HAPPENED OUT THERE...

IN THE SURGING VASTNESS OF THE INDIAN OCEAN

?

20th Century-Fox presents

One of the Most Challenging Stories of Faith Ever Told!

"No one ever looks at the face of a nun!"

Released by 20th Century Fox

CINEMASCOPE
COLOR by DE LUXE

starring
JOAN COLLINS · RICHARD BURTON · BASIL SYDNEY · CY GRANT *and introducing*
Produced by ANDRE HAKIM · Directed by BOB McNAUGHT · From the Novel "SEA-WYF" by J. M. SCOTT

SEA WIFE. Joan Collins: a Hollywood star almost thirty years before *Dynasty.*

sexes. Mildly amusing extravaganza staking its popularity on girls in bathing dress. Larry Buster Crabbe, Ida Lupino, Toby Wing, James Gleason, Robert Armstrong, Gertrude Michael, Roscoe Karns. Written by Claude Binyon, Sam Hellman, Frank Butler and others from a play by Schuyler E. Gray and Paul R. Milton; directed by Erle C. Kenton; for Paramount. 'A couple of years ago so many girls in abbreviated dress would have been enough for one picture . . . but they've seen massed pulchritude quite often lately, so the girls here are just trimmings.'—*Variety*

The Search for Bridey Murphy*
US 1956 84m bw Vistavision
Paramount (Pat Duggan)

A Colorado businessman and amateur hypnotist finds a lady neighbour so good a subject that he is able to delve into her previous incarnation as a long-dead Irish peasant.
Adequately presented with alienation effects, but mainly consisting of two-shots and fuzzy flashbacks, this treatment of an actual case (subsequently discredited) works up to a fine pitch of frenzy when the subject seems unable to come back from her previous life.

wd Noel Langley, *book* Morey Bernstein *ph* John F. Warren *m* Irving Talbot

Teresa Wright, Louis Hayward, Kenneth Tobey, Nancy Gates, Richard Anderson

The Searchers**
US 1956 119m Technicolor Vistavision
Warner / C. V. Whitney (Merian C. Cooper)

A Confederate war veteran tracks down the Indians who have slaughtered his brother and sister-in-law and carried off their daughter.
Desultory, easy-going, good-looking western in typical Ford style; a bit more solemn than usual.

w Frank S. Nugent, *novel* Alan le May *d* John Ford *ph* Winton C. Hoch *m* Max Steiner

John Wayne, Jeffrey Hunter, Natalie Wood, Vera Miles, Ward Bond, John Qualen, Henry Brandon, Antonio Moreno
  'You can read a lot into it, but it isn't very enjoyable.'—*Pauline Kael, 70s*

'What strange power could drive this man from the lips of the woman he married to the arms of the woman he loved?'

The Searching Wind*
US 1946 107m bw
Paramount (Hal B. Wallis)

Affairs of an American diplomat in Europe during the thirties.
Earnest melodrama which would have been better timed six years earlier. Excellent production, though.

w Lillian Hellman, from her play *d* William Dieterle *ph* Lee Garmes *m* Victor Young *ad* Hans Drier, Franz Bachelin

Robert Young, Sylvia Sidney, Ann Richards, Douglas Dick, Dudley Digges, Albert Basserman, Dan Seymour

The Seashell and the Clergyman*
France 1928 30m approx (24 fps) bw silent
(Producer unknown)

A clergyman is afflicted by sexual torments. Celebrated surrealist short with memorable images and a great deal of confusion.

w Antonin Artaud *d* Germaine Dulac *ph* Paul Guichard

Alix Allin

† In GB the film was banned by the censor with the famous comment: 'It is so cryptic as to have no apparent meaning. If there is a meaning, it is doubtless objectionable.'

Sebastian
GB 1968 100m Eastmancolor
Paramount / Maccius (Herb Brodkin, Michael Powell)

An Oxford professor and code expert is appointed to the secret service.
Mildly spoofy spy yarn: style but not much substance.

w Gerald Vaughan-Hughes *d* David Greene *ph* Gerry Fisher *m* Jerry Goldsmith *pd* Wilfred Shingleton

Dirk Bogarde, *John Gielgud*, Lilli Palmer, Susannah York, Janet Munro, Margaret Johnston, Nigel Davenport, Ronald Fraser
  'One of the problems with this kind of movie is the enormous pressure put on the audience to have a good time over practically nothing.'—*Renata Adler*

Second Best Bed
GB 1938 74m bw

A magistrate is suspected of adultery. Cheerful star comedy with a touch of sophistication. Tom Walls, Jane Baxter, Veronica Rose, Carl Jaffe, Greta Gynt. Written by Ben Travers; directed by Tom Walls; for Capitol.

Second Chance
US 1953 82m Technicolor 3-D
RKO (Edmund Grainger)

In South America, a professional killer stalks a gangster's moll.
Comic strip antics with a climax on a stalled cable car.

w Oscar Millard, Sidney Boehm, *story* D. M. Marshman jnr *d* Rudolph Maté *ph* William Snyder *m* Roy Webb

Robert Mitchum, Linda Darnell, Jack Palance, Reginald Sheffield, Roy Roberts

Second Chorus
US 1940 84m bw
Paramount (Boris Morros)

Two trumpeters and their lady manager hit Broadway.
Mild musical.

w Elaine Ryan, Ian McClellan Hunter, Frank Cavett *d* H. C. Potter *ph* Theodor Sparkuhl *songs* various *m* Artie Shaw

Fred Astaire, Burgess Meredith, Paulette Goddard, Charles Butterworth, Artie Shaw and his Band, Frank Melton, Jimmy Conlon

AAN: Artie Shaw; song 'Love of my Life' (*m* Artie Shaw, *ly* Johnny Mercer)

● *Video: VCL*

Second Fiddle
US 1939 86m bw
TCF (Gene Markey)

A Minnesota skating schoolteacher goes to Hollywood and becomes a star.
Routine star vehicle.

w Harry Tugend *d* Sidney Lanfield *ph* Leon Shamroy *md* Louis Silvers *songs* Irving Berlin

Sonja Henie, Tyrone Power, Edna May Oliver, Rudy Vallee, Mary Healy, Lyle Talbot, Alan Dinehart

AAN: song 'I Poured My Heart into a Song' (*m* / *ly* Irving Berlin)

The Second-Floor Mystery
US 1930 56m bw

Correspondents through an agony column find themselves enmeshed in mystery and murder. Burlesque whodunit which seemed a smart trick at the time. Loretta Young, Grant Withers, H. B. Warner, Clare McDowell, John Loder. Written by Joseph Jackson from the novel The Agony Column by Earl Derr Biggers; directed by Roy del Ruth; for Warners.

The Second Greatest Sex
US 1955 87m Technicolor
Cinemascope
U-I (Albert J. Cohen)

Western women emulate Lysistrata to stop their men from feuding.
Flat attempt to cash in on *Seven Brides for Seven Brothers*; some good acrobatic dancing but no style.

w Charles Hoffman *d* George Marshall *ph* Wilfrid M. Cline *md* Joseph Gershenson *ch* Lee Scott

Jeanne Crain, George Nader, Bert Lahr, Kitty Kallen, Paul Gilbert, Keith Andes, Mamie Van Doren, Tommy Rall

Second Honeymoon
US 1937 79m bw
TCF (Raymond Griffith)

A man tries to win back his ex-wife.
Moderate star romantic comedy.

w Kathryn Scola, Darrell Ware, *story* Philip Wylie *d* Walter Lang *ph* Ernest Palmer *m* David Buttolph

Tyrone Power, Loretta Young, Stuart Erwin, Claire Trevor, Marjorie Weaver, Lyle Talbot, J. Edward Bromberg

The Second Mrs Tanqueray
GB 1952 75m bw
Vandyke (Roger Proudlock)

A Victorian society widower marries a notorious lady.

Stiff-backed penny-pinching version of an interestingly antiquated play.

play Arthur Wing Pinero *d* Dallas Bower

Pamela Brown, Hugh Sinclair, Ronald Ward, Virginia McKenna, Andrew Osborn

Second Thoughts

US 1982 98m Movielab

A lady lawyer gets into complex trouble when she bails out her inconsiderate lover from a Santa Fe jail. An absurd series of situations is played for drama rather than comedy, and the feminist flag is frequently waved. The result is an unlikeable muddle. Lucie Arnaz, Craig Wasson, Ken Howard, Anne Schedeen. Written by Steve Brown; directed by Lawrence Turman; for Turman-Foster / EMI. 'Alternately dull and risible.'—*Chris Auty, MFB*

The Second Time Around

US 1961 99m De Luxe Cinemascope
TCF / Cummings / Harman (Jack Cummings)

In 1912 Arizona, a widow stands for sheriff and has plenty of choice for a husband. Light-hearted western fun mixed with family sentimentality.

w Oscar Saul, Cecil Van Heusen, *novel* Richard Emery Roberts *d* Vincent Sherman *ph* Ellis W. Carter *m* Gerald Fried

Debbie Reynolds, Steve Forrest, Andy Griffith, Juliet Prowse, Thelma Ritter, Ken Scott, Isobel Elsom
'Keep a lemon handy for sucking to ward off an attack of the terminal cutesies.'—*Judith Crist, 1973*

The Second Woman

US 1950 91m bw
United Artists / Cardinal (Mort Briskin)
GB title: *Ellen*

An architect, apparently paranoic, is proved to be the victim of a revenge plot.
Tolerable semi-star melodrama with a deliberate 'film noir' look.

w Robert Smith *d* James V. Kern *ph* Hal Mohr *md* Nat Finston

Robert Young, Betsy Drake, John Sutton, Florence Bates, Morris Carnovsky, Henry O'Neill

Seconds**

US 1966 106m bw
Paramount / Joel / Gibraltar (Edward Lewis)

A secret organization sells a special service to the jaded rich; apparent death followed by physical rejuvenation.
An intriguing half-hour is followed by a glum new life for our hero, capped by a horrifying finale in which, dissatisfied, he learns he is to become one of the corpses necessary to the organization's continuance.

w Lewis John Carlino, *novel* David Ely *d* John Frankenheimer *ph* James Wong Howe *m* Jerry Goldsmith *titles* Saul Bass

Rock Hudson, *John Randolph, Will Geer*, Salome Jens, Jeff Corey, Richard Anderson, Murray Hamilton, Wesley Addy
'A really horrifying piece of science fiction that burns its way into your mind like a gnawing headache.'—*Sunday Express*
'An ending that is one of the most terrifying episodes I have ever seen on the screen.'—*Daily Express*

AAN: James Wong Howe

The Secret Agent**

GB 1936 83m bw
Gaumont British (Michael Balcon, Ivor Montagu)

A reluctantly recruited spy is ordered to kill a man.
Unsatisfactory in casting and writing, this Hitchcock suspenser nevertheless has many typically amusing moments.

w Charles Bennett, *play* Campbell Dixon, *story* Ashenden by Somerset Maugham *d* Alfred Hitchcock *ph* Bernard Knowles *md* Louis Levy

John Gielgud, Robert Young, *Peter Lorre*, Madeleine Carroll, Percy Marmont, Lilli Palmer, Florence Kahn
'As uncommon as it is unsentimentally cruel.'—*Peter John Dyer, 1964*
'Many sequences which show Hitchcock at his very best: the fake funeral, the murder on the mountainside, the riverside café, and the climax in a chocolate factory.'—*NFT, 1961*
'How unfortunate it is that Mr Hitchcock, a clever director, is allowed to produce and even to write his own films, though as a producer he has no sense of continuity and as a writer he has no sense of life. His films consist of a series of small "amusing" melodramatic situations: the murderer's button dropped on the baccarat board; the strangled organist's hands prolonging the notes in the empty church; the fugitives hiding in the bell tower when the bell begins to swing. Very perfunctorily he builds up to these tricky situations . . . and then drops them.'—*Graham Greene*

'Behind a locked door—the relentless evil of his past!'

The Secret beyond the Door

US 1948 98m bw
Universal / Walter Wanger (Fritz Lang)

An heiress marries a moody millionaire with a death fixation, and comes to think of herself as his next potential victim.
Silly melodrama with much chat and little suspense.

w Sylvia Richards, *story* Rufus King *d* Fritz Lang *ph* Stanley Cortez *m* Miklos Rozsa

Joan Bennett, Michael Redgrave, Anne Revere, Barbara O'Neil, Natalie Schaefer, Paul Cavanagh
'A dog-wagon *Rebecca* with a seasoning of psychiatrics.'—*Otis L. Guernsey Jnr*
'Lang gets a few wood-silky highlights out of this sow's ear, but it is a hopeless job and a worthless movie.'—*James Agee*

● *Video: Intervision*

The Secret Bride

US 1935 63m bw
Warner
GB title: *Concealment*

A District Attorney is secretly married to the daughter of the politician he is trying to convict.
Dismal melodrama, tritely scripted.

w Tom Buckingham, F. Hugh Herbert, Mary McCall Jnr, *play* Concealment by Leonard Ide *d* William Dieterle *ph* Ernest Haller

Barbara Stanwyck, Warren William, Glenda Farrell, Grant Mitchell, Arthur Byron, Henry O'Neill, Douglass Dumbrille
'Fast moving melodrama, well above average.'—*Variety*

Secret Ceremony

GB 1969 109m Eastmancolor
Universal / World Films / Paul M. Heller (John Heyman, Norman Priggen)

A prostitute mothers a young girl with a strange past.
Nuthouse melodrama for devotees of the director.

w George Tabori, *short story* Marco Denevi *d* Joseph Losey *ph* Gerry Fisher *m* Richard Rodney Bennett

Elizabeth Taylor, Robert Mitchum, Mia Farrow, Pamela Brown, Peggy Ashcroft
'This piece of garbage is so totally ridiculous that I can't imagine why anyone would want to be in it, let alone see it.'—*Rex Reed*

Secret Command

US 1944 92m bw
Columbia (Phil L. Ryan)

An ex-foreign correspondent goes undercover at a shipyard to track down saboteurs.
Routine wartime thick ear.

w Roy Chanslor, *story* The Saboteurs by John and Ward Hawkins *d* Eddie Sutherland *ph* Franz Planer *m* Paul Sawtell

Pat O'Brien, Carole Landis, Chester Morris, Ruth Warrick, Barton MacLane, Tom Tully, Wallace Ford, Howard Freeman

The Secret Fury

US 1950 86m bw
RKO (Jack H. Skirball, Bruce Manning)

A successful pianist is deliberately driven insane by her fiancé.
Derivative melodrama of no great interest.

w Lionel House *d* Mel Ferrer *ph* Leo Tover *m* Roy Webb *md* Constantin Bakaleinikoff

Claudette Colbert, Robert Ryan, Jane Cowl, Paul Kelly, Philip Ober, Elizabeth Risdon, Doris Dudley

The Secret Garden*

US 1949 92m bw (Technicolor sequence)
MGM (Clarence Brown)

An orphan girl goes to stay with her moody uncle and brightens up the lives of those around her.

Subdued, richly produced, rather likeable Victorian fable with the same moral as *The Bluebird* and *The Wizard of Oz*: happiness is in your own back yard.

w Robert Ardrey, *novel* Frances Hodgson Burnett d Fred M. Wilcox ph Ray June m Bronislau Kaper

Margaret O'Brien, Herbert Marshall, Gladys Cooper, Elsa Lanchester, Dean Stockwell, Brian Roper

'Uneven, but oddly and unexpectedly interesting.'—*Richard Mallett, Punch*

The Secret Heart

US 1946 97m bw
MGM (Edwin H. Knopf)

A widow has problems with her emotionally disturbed daughter.
Old-fashioned woman's picture.

w Rose Franken, William Brown Meloney d Robert Z. Leonard ph George Folsey m Bronislau Kaper

Claudette Colbert, Walter Pidgeon, June Allyson, Robert Sterling, Marshall Thompson, Elizabeth Patterson, Richard Derr, Patricia Medina

' "There are three things you can't hide," says Walter Pidgeon in one of his bantering moments; "love, smoke, and a man riding a camel." I would add a fourth—that old MGM touch.'—*Richard Winnington*

The Secret Invasion

US 1964 98m De Luxe Panavision
UA / San Carlos (Gene Corman)

During World War II five convicted criminals become commandos.
Cut price *Dirty Dozen*, quite well made and exciting.

w R. Wright Campbell d Roger Corman ph Arthur E. Arling m Hugo Friedhofer

Stewart Granger, Raf Vallone, Henry Silva, Mickey Rooney, Edd Byrnes, William Campbell, Peter Coe

The Secret Life of an American Wife**

US 1968 92m De Luxe
TCF / Charlton (George Axelrod)

A bored suburban housewife sets out to seduce a movie star.
Sympathetic comedy of sixties suburban manners.

wd George Axelrod ph Leon Shamroy m Billy May

Walter Matthau, Anne Jackson, Patrick O'Neal, Edy Williams

'Both a first-class satire on American mores and a compassionate study of wish-fulfilment.'—*NFT, 1970*

The Secret Life of Walter Mitty**

US 1947 110m Technicolor
Samuel Goldwyn

A mother's boy dreams of derring-do, and eventually life catches up with fiction.
This pleasantly remembered star comedy, though it never had much to do with Thurber,

can now be seen to have missed most of its opportunities, though the nice moments do tend to compensate.

w Ken Englund, Everett Freeman, *story* James Thurber d Norman Z. McLeod ph Lee Garmes m David Raksin

Danny Kaye, Virginia Mayo, Boris Karloff, Florence Bates, Fay Bainter, *Thurston Hall*, Ann Rutherford, Gordon Jones, Reginald Denny

Secret Mission

GB 1942 94m bw
GFD / Marcel Hellman / Excelsior

During World War II four British Intelligence officers are landed in occupied France to discover the truth about German defences.
Stilted war suspenser.

w Anatole de Grunwald, Basil Bartlett, Terence Young d Harold French ph Bernard Knowles m Mischa Spoliansky

Hugh Williams, Carla Lehmann, James Mason, Roland Culver, Nancy Price, Michael Wilding, Percy Walsh

The Secret of Blood Island

GB 1964 84m Technicolor
U-I / Hammer (Anthony Nelson Keys)

A girl parachutist secret agent is smuggled into a Japanese POW camp and out again.
Absurd blood and thunder, almost perversely enjoyable—but not quite.

w John Gilling d Quentin Lawrence ph Jack Asher m James Bernard

Barbara Shelley, Jack Hedley, Charles Tingwell, Bill Owen, Lee Montague

The Secret of Convict Lake*

US 1951 83m bw
TCF (Frank P. Rosenberg)

In the 1870s, escaped convicts take over a California town.
Brooding, snowy, set-bound western melodrama; predictable but watchable.

w Oscar Saul d Michael Gordon ph Leo Tover m Sol Kaplan md Lionel Newman

Glenn Ford, Gene Tierney, Ann Dvorak, Ethel Barrymore, Zachary Scott, Barbara Bates, Cyril Cusack, Jeanette Nolan, Ruth Donnelly

The Secret of Madame Blanche

US 1933 85m bw

The woman who takes the blame for murder committed by a young man is the mother he never knew. Or, *Madame X* unofficially revisited: all-stops-out melodrama very typical of its time. Irene Dunne, Phillips Holmes, Lionel Atwill, Douglas Walton, Jean Parker, Una Merkel. Written by Frances Goodrich and Albert Hackett; directed by Charles Brabin; for MGM.

The Secret of My Success

GB 1965 105m Metrocolor Panavision
MGM / Andrew and Virginia Stone

A village policeman follows his mother's dictum that he should not think ill of others,

and accidentally goes from success to success.
Flabby portmanteau comedy full of in-jokes and flat-footed farce; satire is not evident.

wd Andrew L. Stone ph David Boulton m Lucien Caillet and others md Roland Shaw

James Booth, Lionel Jeffries, *Amy Dalby*, Stella Stevens, Honor Blackman, Shirley Jones, Joan Hickson

The Secret of Nimh*

US 1982 82m Technicolor
Aurora / Don Bluth

Forced out of her cosy field, a widowed mouse seeks the help of Nicodemus, king of the rat pack.
Animated cartoon by Disney artists who rejected that company's declining standards and set up their own factory. Alas, though they have the skills, the narrative they have chosen needed refining.

w Don Bluth, John Pomeroy, Gary Foldman, Will Finn, *novel* Mrs Frisby and the Rats of Nimh by Robert C. O'Brien d Don Bluth m Jerry Goldsmith

The Secret of St Ives

US 1949 76m bw

During the Napoleonic War, a French prisoner-of-war escapes from Edinburgh Castle, only to be accused of murder. Modest swashbuckler with a somewhat lacklustre atmosphere. Richard Ney, Vanessa Brown, Henry Daniell, Aubrey Mather. Written by Eric Taylor, from the story by Robert Louis Stevenson; directed by Phil Rosen; for Columbia.

The Secret of Santa Vittoria*

US 1969 140m Technicolor
Panavision
UA / Stanley Kramer

In 1945 an Italian village hides its wine from the occupying Germans.
Expected, exhausting epic comedy with everyone talking at once.

w William Rose, Ben Maddow, *novel* Robert Crichton d Stanley Kramer ph Giuseppe Rotunno m Ernest Gold

Anthony Quinn, Anna Magnani, Virna Lisi, Hardy Kruger, Sergio Franchi, Renato Rascel

'A brainless farrago of flying rolling pins and rotten vegetables, filled with the kind of screaming, belching, eye-rolling lingual Italians only Stanley Kramer could invent.'—*Rex Reed*

AAN: Ernest Gold

The Secret of Stamboul

GB 1936 93m bw

An English adventurer foils a Turkish revolution. Pale rendering of a full-blooded best-seller. Valerie Hobson, Frank Vosper, James Mason, Kay Walsh, Peter Haddon. Written by Richard Wainwright, Howard Irving Young and Noel Langley, from the novel *The Eunuch of Stamboul* by Dennis Wheatley; directed by Andrew Marton; for Wainwright. (NB: Reissue title: *The Spy in White*.)

The Secret of the Blue Room
US 1933 66m bw

An heiress's three suitors all volunteer to
spend the night in the haunted room of her
mansion. Murderous malarkey without the
courage of its convictions. Lionel Atwill,
Gloria Stuart, Paul Lukas, Edward Arnold,
Onslow Stevens, Robert Barrat, Elizabeth
Patterson. Written by William Hurlbut;
directed by Kurt Neumann; for Universal.
(NB: Remade in 1938 as *The Missing Guest*
and in 1944 as *Murder in the Blue Room*.)
'Americanization of a German mystery yarn
which ought to do well in the smaller spots.'—
Variety

The Secret of the Incas
US 1954 101m Technicolor
Paramount (Mel Epstein)

Various adventurers seek a priceless Inca
jewel.
Boys' Own Paper yarn which sounds a good
deal more exciting than it is: too much talk
and a few choice studio backcloths drop the
tension alarmingly, and the script lacks
humour and conciseness.
w Ranald MacDougall, Sidney Boehm
d Jerry Hopper ph Lionel Lindon m David
Buttolph

Charlton Heston, Robert Young, Thomas
Mitchell, Nicole Maurey, Yma Sumac, Glenda
Farrell, Michael Pate

The Secret of the Loch
GB 1934 80m bw
ABFD / Bray Wyndham

A diver thinks he finds a prehistoric monster
in Loch Ness.
Mildly amusing exploitation item following the
1934 rebirth of interest in the old legend.
w Charles Bennett, Billie Bristow d Milton
Rosmer

Seymour Hicks, Nancy O'Neil, Gibson
Gowland, Frederick Peisley, Rosamund John,
Ben Field

'Run for your life! You must find the secret
   before it finds you!'
The Secret Partner*
GB 1961 91m bw
MGM (Michael Relph)

A blackmailing dentist is visited by a
mysterious hooded stranger who forces him to
rob one of his businessman victims.
Complex puzzle thriller, neatly made in sub-
Hitchcock style.
w David Pursall, Jack Seddon d Basil
Dearden ph Harry Waxman m Philip Green

Stewart Granger, Haya Harareet, Bernard
Lee, Hugh Burden, Melissa Stribling, Norman
Bird, Conrad Philips

The Secret People*
GB 1951 96m bw
Ealing (Sidney Cole)

European refugees in London during the
thirties become members of a ring of
anarchists.

Downbeat political melodrama which pleased
neither the masses nor the highbrows, despite
plaudits for sensitive direction and
performances.
w Thorold Dickinson, Wolfgang Wilhelm
d Thorold Dickinson ph Gordon Dines
m Roberto Gerhard

Valentina Cortese, Serge Reggiani, Audrey
Hepburn, Charles Goldner, Megs Jenkins,
Irene Worth, Athene Seyler, Reginald Tate
'The tension and power of the film make it
one of the most remarkable British
productions for some time.'—*Penelope
Houston*
'That *Secret People*, despite the creative
agonies recorded by Mr Lindsay Anderson [in
a book on the making of the film] should turn
out to be a confused, unco-ordinated spy
thriller concealing a tentative message deep
down below some strained effects of style is
another tragedy of British film hopes.'—
Richard Winnington

Secret Service
US 1931 67m bw

During the Civil War a Yankee officer goes
behind enemy lines and falls in love with a
southern girl. Sluggish romantic adventure.
Richard Dix, Shirley Grey, William Post Jnr,
Gavin Gordon. Written by Bernard Schubert
from a play by William Gillette; directed by
J. Walter Ruben; for RKO. 'Dix does a good
character. It's all the picture has.'—*Variety*

Secret Service of the Air
US 1939 61m bw

A government agent tracks down smugglers.
Serial-like thrills and comedy, adequately
presented. Ronald Reagan, Eddie Foy Jnr,
John Litel, Ila Rhodes, James Stephenson.
Written by Raymond Shrock; directed by Noel
Smith; for Warners. 'No marquee names, but
a better than average story of its kind.'—
Variety

The Secret Six*
US 1931 83m bw
MGM

A syndicate of businessmen finance two
reporters to get evidence against a gang of
bootleggers.
Solidly carpentered gangster thriller.
w Frances Marion d George Hill ph Harold
Wenstrom

Wallace Beery, Lewis Stone, Clark Gable,
John Mack Brown, Jean Harlow, Marjorie
Rambeau, Paul Hurst, Ralph Bellamy, John
Miljan
'A gangster talker too rough, crude and
familiar. In big cities it may pull the roughneck
trade . . . but the vocalized expression for it
will be adverse.'—*Variety*

The Secret War of Harry Frigg
US 1967 109m Techniscope
Universal / Albion (Hal E. Chester)

In 1943 a private engineers the escape of five
captured generals.

Unattractive war comedy; slow, uninventive
and overlong.
w Peter Stone, Frank Tarloff d Jack Smight
ph Russell Metty m Carlo Rustichelli

Paul Newman, *John Williams*, Sylva Koscina,
Andrew Duggan, Tom Bosley, Charles D.
Gray, Vito Scotti, James Gregory

The Secret Ways*
US 1961 112m bw
U-I / Heath (Richard Widmark)

An American reporter is recruited to rescue a
scholar from communist Hungary.
Pretentious Iron Curtain melodrama, quite
good to look at but overlong and no *Third
Man*.
w Jean Hazelwood, *novel* Alistair MacLean
d Phil Karlson ph Max Greene m Johnny
Williams

Richard Widmark, Sonja Ziemann, Charles
Regnier, Walter Rilla, Howard Vernon, Senta
Berger

Secrets*
US 1933 85m bw

A pioneering couple stick together despite the
husband's infidelities. Curiously mixed-up star
vehicle, part romantic comedy, part western,
part sob-stuff. Interesting rather than
entertaining. Mary Pickford, Leslie Howard,
C. Aubrey Smith, Blanche Friderici, Doris
Lloyd, Ned Sparks. Written by Frances
Marion from the play by Rudolf Besier and
May Edgington; for Mary Pickford / UA.
'Singularly uneven . . . but at least the story is
given fine production and interesting
playing.'—*Variety*. 'You can be sure you won't
make any mistake by taking the family to see
it.'—*Photoplay*. NB: Norma Talmadge starred
in a 1923 silent version.

Secrets of an Actress
US 1938 70m bw

A star actress falls for one of her backers, a
married architect. High-life suffering of a
familiar kind: it satisfied the Peg's Paper
audience. Kay Francis, George Brent, Ian
Hunter, Gloria Dickson, Isabel Jeans, Peggy
Singleton. Written by Milton Krims, Rowland
Leigh, Julius J. Epstein; directed by William
Keighley; for Warners. 'Miss Francis may be
able to live up to all requirements except an
acrobatic dance on the toes, but it's no use
hitching race horses to milk wagons.'—*Variety*

Secrets of a Secretary
US 1931 76m bw

A social secretary discovers that her ex-
husband is blackmailing her employer's
daughter. *Peg's Paper* romance of a heroine
who rises above her many problems. Claudette
Colbert, Herbert Marshall, George Metaxas,
Mary Boland, Berton Churchill. Written by
Dwight Taylor and Charles Brackett; directed
by George Abbott; for Paramount.

Secrets of a Soul**
Germany 1926   95m (24 fps)   bw   silent
UFA / Hans Neumann

A chemist develops a knife phobia, has
hallucinations, and tries to cut his wife's
throat.
A lesson in elementary psychology which was
innovatory at the time and survives as cinema
for its stylish and impressionist use of visual
techniques.

w Colin Ross, Hans Neumann, G. W. Pabst
d G. W. Pabst ph Guido Seeber, Curt Oertel,
Robert Lach

Werner Krauss, Jack Trevor, Ruth Weyher,
Pawel Pawlow

Secrets of the French Police
US 1932   55m   bw

The Sûreté tracks down a hypnotist and
murderer. Rather wildly-imagined suspenser
with points of interest. Gwili André, Frank
Morgan, Gregory Ratoff, Murray Kinnell,
John Warburton. Written by Samuel Ornitz,
Robert Tasker; directed by Edward
Sutherland; for RKO. 'Hodge-podge of
melodramatics . . . hardly enough for the de
luxers.'—Variety

The Seduction of Joe Tynan*
US 1979   107m   Technicolor
Universal (Martin Bregman)

A young senator alienates his wife when he
sacrifices his principles for advancement.
Fairly arresting political character drama with
strong narrative and acting

w Alan Alda d Jerry Schatzberg ph Adam
Holender m Bill Conti

Alan Alda, Barbara Harris, Meryl Streep,
Melvyn Douglas, Rip Torn, Carrie Nye,
Charles Kimbrough
● Video: CIC

See America Thirst
US 1930   71m   bw

Two hoboes become involved with rum
runners. Poorly constructed talkie début for a
silent comedian who never made it. Harry
Langdon, Slim Summerville, Bessie Love,
Mitchell Lewis, Stanley Fields. Written by
Edward Luddy, Vin Moore, C. J. Horwin;
directed by W. J. Craft; for Universal.
'Direction shows silent technique throughout,
and is unmindful of the talkie advent. Rub is
that this system got reversed in the important
sequences.'—Variety

See Here Private Hargrove*
US 1944   102m   bw
MGM (George Haight)

Adventures of a raw recruit in the US army.
Standard transcription of a humorous
bestseller which did its best to make the war
painless for Americans.

w Harry Kurnitz, book Marion Hargrove
d Wesley Ruggles ph Charles Lawton
m David Snell

Robert Walker, Donna Reed, Robert
Benchley, Keenan Wynn, Bob Crosby, Ray
Collins, Chill Wills, Grant Mitchell
† Sequel 1945: What Next, Corporal
Hargrove?

See My Lawyer
US 1945   67m   bw

Comedians try to get out of a nightclub
commitment by insulting the customers. Thin
vehicle for a team that wasn't going anywhere:
too many variety acts got in their way. Ole
Olsen, Chic Johnson, Grace McDonald,
Franklin Pangborn, Alan Curtis, Noah Beery
Jnr, Ed Brophy. Written by Edmund L.
Hartmann and Stanley Davis; directed by
Edward Cline; for Universal.

Seed
US 1931   96m   bw

A husband leaves his family to become a
novelist, but returns ten years later. Long-
drawn-out domestic drama whose few virtues
have not weathered the years. John Boles,
Genevieve Tobin, Lois Wilson, Raymond
Hackett, Bette Davis, Zasu Pitts. Written by
Gladys Lehman from the novel by Charles G.
Norris; directed by John Stahl; for Universal.
'Good woman's picture that will strike
generous b.o. anywhere.'—Variety

The Seekers
GB 1954   90m   Eastmancolor
GFD / Fanfare (George H. Brown)
US title: Land of Fury

In 1820 a British sailor and his family emigrate
to New Zealand.
Stilted epic which never gains the viewer's
sympathy or interest.

w William Fairchild d Ken Annakin
ph Geoffrey Unsworth m William Alwyn

Jack Hawkins, Glynis Johns, Inia Te Wiata,
Noel Purcell, Kenneth Williams, Laya Raki

Seems Like Old Times*
US 1980   102m   Metrocolor
Columbia / Ray Stark

An innocently involved bank robber takes
refuge with his ex-wife, a lady lawyer married
to the district attorney.
Nostalgic farce which doesn't quite live up to
the old skills and often bogs down in talk.
Funny moments, though.

w Neil Simon d Jay Sandrich ph David M.
Walsh m Marvin Hamlisch pd Gene
Callahan

Goldie Hawn, Chevy Chase, Charles Grodin,
Robert Guillaume, Harold Gould, George
Grizzard
● Video: RCA / Columbia

The Sellout
US 1951   82m   bw
MGM (Nicholas Nayfack)

A newspaper editor exposes a corrupt
administration.
Competent melodrama with no surprises.

w Charles Palmer d Gerald Mayer ph Paul
Vogel m David Buttolph

Walter Pidgeon, John Hodiak, Audrey Totter,
Thomas Gomez, Everett Sloane, Cameron
Mitchell, Karl Malden, Paula Raymond

The Sellout
GB / Italy 1975   102m   colour
Warner / Oceanglade / Amerifilm (Josef
Shaftel)

Russians and Americans lure a double agent
to Jerusalem in order to eliminate him.
Unsmiling spy melodrama with a complex
plot, a bagful of clichés and some
unnecessarily unpleasant violence.

w Judson Kinberg, Murray Smith d Peter
Collinson ph Arthur Ibbetson m Mike
Green, Colin Frechter

Richard Widmark, Oliver Reed, Gayle
Hunnicutt, Sam Wanamaker, Vladek Sheybal,
Ori Levy, Assef Dayan

Seminole
US 1953   86m   Technicolor

A West Point graduate goes to Florida to
make peace with the Indians. Slightly unusual
but not very interesting semi-western with the
usual clichés. Rock Hudson, Anthony Quinn,
Barbara Hale, Richard Carlson, Hugh
O'Brian, Russell Johnson, Lee Marvin, James
Best. Written by Charles K. Peck Jnr; directed
by Budd Boetticher; for Universal-
International.

Semi-Tough*
US 1977   107m   De Luxe
UA / David Merrick

The manager's daughter decides between two
star members of a football team.
Rambling satiric comedy which takes jabs at
various states of mind in America today,
notably the fashionable forms of self-help
therapy. Much of it comes off quite well.

w Walter Bernstein, novel Dan Jenkins
d Michael Ritchie ph Charles Rosher Jnr
m Jerry Fielding

Burt Reynolds, Kris Kristofferson, Jill
Clayburgh, Bert Convy, Robert Preston, Lotte
Lenya, Roger E. Mosley
● Video: Intervision

The Senator Was Indiscreet*
US 1947   95m   bw
U-I (Nunnally Johnson)
GB title: Mr Ashton Was Indiscreet

A foolish politician determines to become
president and hires a press agent.
Satirical political farce which hurls its shafts
wide and doesn't seem to mind how few of
them hit.

w Charles MacArthur, story Edwin Lanham
d George S. Kaufman ph William Mellor
m Daniele Amfitheatrof

William Powell, Ella Raines, Peter Lind
Hayes, Ray Collins, Arleen Whelan, Allen
Jenkins, Hans Conried, Charles D. Brown

Send Me No Flowers*
US 1964   100m   Technicolor
U–I / Martin Melcher (Harry Keller)

A hypochondriac mistakenly thinks he is dying
and tries to provide another spouse for his
wife.
A timeworn farcical situation is handled in the
glossy Doris Day manner; it all starts quite
brightly but gradually fizzles out.

w Julius Epstein, *play* Norman Barrasch,
Carroll Moore *d* Norman Jewison *ph* Daniel
Fapp *m* Frank de Vol *ad* Alexander
Golitzen, Robert Clatworthy

Doris Day, Rock Hudson, Tony Randall, Paul
Lynde, Clint Walker, Hal March, Edward
Andrews

Sensation
GB 1936   67m   bw

A village barmaid is murdered and only our
reporter hero sees the wider implications.
Presentable murder mystery. John Lodge,
Diana Churchill, Francis Lister, Joan Marion,
Margaret Vyner, Athene Seyler, Richard
Bird. Written by Dudley Leslie, Marjorie
Deans and William Freshman, from the play
Murder Gang by Basil Dean and George
Munro; directed by Brian Desmond Hurst; for
BIP. 'The genuine situation is lost in false
trials, in an absurd love story, in humour
based on American films, and in the complete
unreality of the "murder gang".'—*Graham
Greene.*

Sensations of 1945
US 1944   87m   bw
Andrew L. Stone

Father and son disagree over the handling of
their publicity agency.
Slim plot holds together a ragbag of variety
acts, some quite choice.

w Dorothy Bennett *d* Andrew L. Stone
ph Peverell Marley, John Mescall *md* Mahlon
Merrick

Eleanor Powell, W. C. Fields, Sophie Tucker,
Dennis O'Keefe, Eugene Pallette, C. Aubrey
Smith, Lyle Talbot, Dorothy Donegan, Cab
Calloway and his band, Woody Herman and
his band

AAN: Mahlon Merrick

Senso*
Italy 1953   115m   Technicolor
Lux
aka: *The Wanton Countess* (cut version)

In 1866 Venice a noblewoman falls in love
with an officer of the invading Austrian army,
but finally denounces him.
The melodramatic plot is less important than
the portrait of a period, for this is an
expensive film in the grand style, often
breathtaking to look at.

w Luchino Visconti, Suso Cecchi d'Amico and
others *story* Camilla Botto *d* Luchino Visconti
ph G. R. Aldo, Robert Krasker *m* Anton
Bruckner *ad* Ottavio Scotti

Alida Valli, Farley Granger, Massimo Girotti,
Christian Marquand

Sentimental Journey
US 1946   94m   bw
TCF (Walter Morosco)

An actress who knows she is dying arranges
for a little orphan girl to take her place in her
husband's affections.
Hollywood's most incredible three-
handkerchief picture; nicely made, but who
dared to write it?

w Samuel Hoffenstein, Elizabeth Reinhardt,
story Nelia Gardner White *d* Walter Lang
ph Norbert Brodine *m* Cyril Mockridge

Maureen O'Hara, John Payne, William
Bendix, Cedric Hardwicke, Glenn Langan,
Mischa Auer, Connie Marshall, Kurt Kreuger
   'In twenty years of filmgoing I can't
remember being so slobbered at: the
apotheosis of the weepie.'—*Richard
Winnington*
† Remade as *The Gift of Love* (qv).

The Sentinel
US 1976   92m   Technicolor
Universal / Jeffrey Konvitz

A disturbed girl in an old apartment house is
haunted by walking corpses: the house turns
out to be the gateway to hell and her boy
friend its appointed sentinel.
Vulgarly modish rip-off of several fashionable
themes, notably *Rosemary's Baby* and *The
Exorcist.*

w Michael Winner, Jeffrey Konvitz,
novel Jeffrey Konvitz *d* Michael Winner
ph Dick Kratina *m* Gil Melle

Chris Sarandon, Cristina Raines, Martin
Balsam, John Carradine, Jose Ferrer, Ava
Gardner, Arthur Kennedy, Burgess Meredith,
Sylvia Miles, Deborah Raffin, Eli Wallach,
Jerry Orbach
   'Moral or ironic points are hard to discern in
the eye-wrenching flux of a Michael Winner
movie, which drifts and zooms across its
polished people and places in a continual
caressing motion, as crudely excitatory as any
sex movie when the climaxes are
approaching.'—*Richard Combs, MFB*
   'A man with a face that looks like chicken
giblets, a naked whore with a mouse on her
thigh, a cat devouring a canary and Sylvia
Miles in a tight leotard—these are some of the
highlights of *The Sentinel*, a perfect film for
those who like to slow down and look at traffic
accidents.'—*Janet Maslin, Newsweek*
● *Video: CIC*

Separate Tables**
US 1958   98m   bw
UA / Hecht–Hill–Lancaster (Harold Hecht)

Emotional tensions among the boarders at a
British seaside guest house.
The genteel melodramas seem less convincing
on the Hollywood screen than they did on the
London stage, but the handling is thoroughly
professional.

w Terence Rattigan, John Gay, *play* Terence
Rattigan *d* Delbert Mann *m* David Raksin
ph Charles Lang

Burt Lancaster, Rita Hayworth, *David Niven*,
Deborah Kerr, *Wendy Hiller, Gladys Cooper,
Cathleen Nesbitt, Felix Aylmer*, Rod Taylor,
Audrey Dalton, *May Hallatt*

AA: David Niven; Wendy Hiller
AAN: best picture; script; Charles Lang;
David Raksin; Deborah Kerr
● *Video: MGM / UA*

September Affair
US 1950   104m   bw
Paramount (Hal B. Wallis)

Two married people fall in love and a plane
crash in which they are reported dead gives
them their chance.
Turgid romantic melodrama, not very well
made despite the background tour of Capri;
what made it a hit was the playing of the old
Walter Huston record of the title song.

w Robert Thoeren *d* William Dieterle
ph Charles B. Lang *m* Victor Young

Joseph Cotten, Joan Fontaine, Françoise
Rosay, Jessica Tandy, Robert Arthur, Jimmy
Lydon
   'A smooth surface mirrors the film's
essential superficiality.'—*Penelope Houston*

September Storm
US 1960   110m   De Luxe
   Cinemascope   3-D
TCF / Alco (Edward L. Alperson)

A New York model and two adventurers
search for sunken treasure off an uncharted
Mediterranean island.
Thin actioner originally intended to marry 3-D
and Cinemascope, but failed to do so.

w W. R. Burnett, *novel* The Girl in the Red
Bikini by Steve Fisher *d* Byron Haskin
ph Jorge Stahl Jnr, Lamar Boren *m* Edward
L. Alperson Jnr

Joanne Dru, Mark Stevens, Robert Strauss

Sequoia
US 1934   73m   bw

A girl living in the High Sierras defends wild
animals from hunters. Refreshingly unusual
outdoor drama with good location
photography. Jean Parker, Russell Hardie,
Samuel S. Hinds, Paul Hurst. Written by Ann
Cunningham, Sam Arnstrong and Carey
Wilson; directed by Chester Franklin;
photographed by Chester Lyons; for MGM. 'It
was unlikely that either Miss Parker or the
deer would eat the puma, but I hung on
hoping that the puma would eat the deer or
Miss Parker.'—*James Agate.*

Serenade
US 1956   121m   Warnercolor
Warner (Henry Blanke)

A vineyard worker becomes a successful opera
singer and is desired by two women.
Cliché success story with plot taking second
place to singing.

w Ivan Goff, Ben Roberts, John Twist, *novel*
James M. Cain *d* Anthony Mann *ph* Peverell
Marley *md* Ray Heindorf *songs* Nicholas
Brodszky

Mario Lanza, Joan Fontaine, Sarita Montiel,
Vincent Price, Joseph Calleia, Harry Bellaver,
Vince Edwards, Silvio Minciotti

The Sergeant

US 1968   108m   Technicolor
Warner / Robert Wise (Richard Goldstone)

France, 1952. In a dreary army camp, a tough army sergeant with a guilt complex is brought face to face with his own homosexuality.
Well-made but very ponderous and limited melodrama which could have been told in half the time.

w Dennis Murphy, from his novel d John Flynn ph Henri Persin m Michel Mayne

Rod Steiger, John Philip Law, Frank Latimore, Ludmila Mikael

'The funniest foul-up of the space age!'

Sergeant Deadhead

US 1965   89m   CFI colour

An army sergeant is accidentally sent into orbit and undergoes a personality change.
Clumsy comedy partially redeemed by its supporting players. Frankie Avalon, Deborah Walley, Fred Clark, Cesar Romero, Eve Arden, Gale Gordon, Buster Keaton, Harvey Lembeck, John Ashley. Written by Louis M. Heyward; directed by Norman Taurog; for AIP.

Sergeant Madden

US 1939   78m   bw
MGM (J. Walter Ruben)

A policeman's son becomes a gangster.
Routine crime melodrama with sentimental trimmings, quite untypical of its director.

w Wells Root, story A Gun in His Hand by William A. Ulman d Josef Von Sternberg ph John Seitz m William Axt

Wallace Beery, Tom Brown, Alan Curtis, Laraine Day, Fay Holden, Marc Lawrence, Marion Martin

'Good programme drama, geared to supply strong support in the key duals.'—Variety

Sgt Pepper's Lonely Hearts Club Band

US 1978   111m   Technicolor
Panavision
Universal / Robert Stigwood (Dee Anthony)

A family band finds a new sound despite the activities of villains.
Oddball hotch-potch of middle-aged comedy and youth nostalgia with an American small-town setting. Some moments please, but most of it simply doesn't gell.

w Henry Edwards d Michael Schultz
ph Owen Roizman m various (mostly the Beatles) pd Brian Eatwell

Peter Frampton, Barry Gibb, Robin Gibb, Maurice Gibb, George Burns, Frankie Howerd, Donald Pleasence, Paul Nicholas, Sandy Farina, Alice Cooper, Steve Martin, Earth Wind and Fire

'Another of those films which serve as feature-length screen advertising for an album.'—Variety

Sergeant Rutledge*

US 1960   111m   Technicolor
Warner / John Ford (Willis Goldbeck, Patrick Ford)

In 1881 a black army sergeant is on trial for rape and murder, but his defence counsel reveals the real culprit.
Flashback western; not the director's best, but generally of some interest.

w James Warner Bellah, Willis Goldbeck d John Ford ph Bert Glennon m Howard Jackson

Woody Strode, Jeffrey Hunter, Constance Towers, Willis Bouchey, Billie Burke, Carleton Young, Juano Hernandez, Mae Marsh

Sergeant Steiner

West Germany 1979   115m
Eastmancolor   Panavision
Palladium / Rapidfilm (Arlene Sellers, Alex Winitsky)

The German sergeant hero of Cross of Iron survives the Western Front and involvement in an anti-Hitler conspiracy.
Somewhat bloodless though interesting sequel to an exceptionally nasty war film, with an international cast aiming at better box office.

w Tony Williamson d Andrew McLaglen ph Tony Imi m Peter Thomas

Richard Burton, Robert Mitchum, Curt Jurgens, Rod Steiger, Helmut Griem, Michael Parks

Sergeant York**

US 1941   134m   bw
Warner (Jesse L. Lasky)

The story of a gentle hillbilly farmer who became a hero of World War I.
Standard real-life fiction given the big treatment; a key Hollywood film of its time in several ways.

w Abem Finkel, Harry Chandler, Howard Koch, John Huston d Howard Hawks ph Arthur Edeson m Max Steiner

Gary Cooper, Joan Leslie, Walter Brennan, George Tobias, David Bruce, Stanley Ridges, Margaret Wycherly, Dickie Moore, Ward Bond

'I hardly think the effect is any different from that of a parade, with colours and a band; it is stirring and it is too long; there are too many holdups and too many people out of step, and your residue of opinion on the matter is that it will be nice to get home and get your shoes off.'—Otis Ferguson

'It has all the flavour of true Americana, the blunt and homely humour of backwoodsmen and the raw integrity peculiar to simple folk.'—Bosley Crowther, New York Times

AA: Gary Cooper
AAN: best picture; script; Howard Hawks; Sol Polito; Max Steiner; Walter Brennan; Margaret Wycherly

Sergeants Three

US 1961   112m   Technicolor
Panavision
(UA) Essex–Claude (Frank Sinatra)

Just after the Civil War three cavalry sergeants, with the help of an ex-slave bugler, dispose of some hostile Indians.

High-spirited but exhausting parody of Gunga Din, with bouts of unfunny bloodthirstiness separated by tedious slabs of dialogue.

w W. R. Burnett d John Sturges ph Winton Hock, Carl Guthrie m Billy May

Frank Sinatra, Dean Martin, Peter Lawford, Sammy Davis Jnr, Joey Bishop, Henry Silva, Ruta Lee

'The participants have a better time than the onlookers.'—Judith Crist, 1973

Serial*

US 1980   91m   Movielab
Paramount / Sidney Beckerman

Well-heeled Californians in a high suburban community go in for various cults and fashions.
Amusing satire on everything from Peyton Place to Bob and Carol and Ted and Alice.
Just a little late in coming, that's all.

w Rich Eustis, Michael Elias, novel Cyra McFadden d Bill Persky ph Rexford Metz m Lalo Schifrin

Martin Mull, Tuesday Weld, Jennifer McAllister, Sam Chew Jnr, Sally Kellerman, Nita Talbot, Bill Macy, Christopher Lee, Pamela Bellwood, Peter Bonerz, Tom Smothers

Serious Charge

GB 1959   99m   bw
Alva (Mickey Delamar)

A small-town troublemaker, accused by his priest of being responsible for the death of a young girl, amuses himself by accusing the priest of making homosexual advances.
A sensational play of its time makes a dull film despite earnest performances.

w Guy Elmes, Mickey Delamar, play Philip King d Terence Young ph Georges Périnal m Leighton Lucas

Anthony Quayle, Andrew Ray, Sarah Churchill, Irene Browne, Percy Herbert, Cliff Richard

The Serpent

France / Italy / Germany 1974   124m
colour
Films La Boetie (Henri Verneuil)

A top KGB official defects to the west.
Complicated, humourless, multi-lingual spy capers.

w Henri Verneuil, Gilles Perrault, novel Pierre Nord d Henri Verneuil ph Claude Renoir m Ennio Morricone

Yul Brynner, Henry Fonda, Dirk Bogarde, Philippe Noiret, Farley Granger, Virna Lisi

The Serpent's Egg*

West Germany / US 1977   120m
Eastmancolor
Rialto-Dino de Laurentiis

An American trapeze artist has a hard time in Berlin at the time of Hitler's rise to power.
More of a curate's egg, really, with a poor leading performance and too many lapses into nastiness, but much incidental interest of the kind one associates with the director.

wd Ingmar Bergman *ph* Sven Nykvist *m* Rolf Wilhelm *pd* Rolf Zehetbauer

David Carradine, Liv Ullmann, Gert Frobe, James Whitmore, Heinz Bennent
'A crackpot tragedy: everything is strained, insufficient, underfelt.'—*New Yorker*

Serpico*
US 1973 130m Technicolor
Paramount / Artists Entertainment Complex / Dino de Laurentiis (Martin Bregman)

A New York cop reveals police corruption and is eventually forced to leave the country.
A harrowing true story played with authentic gloom and violence.

w Waldo Salt, Norman Wexler, *book* Peter Maas *d* Sidney Lumet *ph* Arthur J. Ornitz *m* Mikis Theodorakis

Al Pacino, John Randolph, Jack Kehoe, Biff McGuire
'There's nothing seriously wrong with *Serpico* except that it's unmemorable, and not even terribly interesting while it's going on.'—*Stanley Kauffmann*

AAN: script; Al Pacino

● Video: CIC

The Servant**
GB 1963 116m bw
Elstree / Springbok (Joseph Losey, Norman Priggen)

A rich, ineffectual young man is gradually debased and overruled by his sinister manservant and his sexy 'sister'.
Acclaimed in many quarters on its first release, this downbeat melodrama now seems rather naïve and long drawn out; its surface gloss is undeniable, but the final orgy is more risible than satanic.

w Harold Pinter, *novel* Robin Maugham *d* Joseph Losey *ph* Douglas Slocombe *m* Johnny Dankworth

Dirk Bogarde, James Fox, Sarah Miles, Wendy Craig, Catherine Lacey, Richard Vernon
'Moodily suggestive, well acted, but petering out into a trickle of repetitious unmeaningful nastiness.'—*John Simon*

● Video: Thorn EMI

Servants' Entrance
US 1934 88m bw
Fox

A maid falls in love with a chauffeur.
Upstairs downstairs style comedy drama; passable.

w Samson Raphaelson, *novel* Sigrid Boo *d* Frank Lloyd *ph* Hal Mohr *m* Arthur Lange

Janet Gaynor, Lew Ayres, Walter Connolly, G. P. Huntley Jnr, Sig Rumann, Louise Dresser, Astrid Allwyn, Ned Sparks
'Capable production, directing and casting manages to make it fair entertainment.'—*Variety*

Service De Luxe*
US 1938 85m bw

Adventures of the members of a super-secretarial agency. Very tolerable but uninspired comedy which doesn't really allow its acting talent full rein. Constance Bennett, Vincent Price, Charles Ruggles, Helen Broderick, Mischa Auer, Halliwell Hobbes. Written by Gertrude Purcell and Leonard Spiegelgass; directed by Rowland V Lee; for Universal. 'A speedy comedy-drama . . . will hold its own as a leadoff attraction in the keys.'—*Variety*

Service for Ladies
GB 1932 93m bw
Paramount (Alexander Korda)
US title: *Reserved for Ladies*

A waiter has a way with his rich lady clients.
Tenuous satirical comedy, a variation on the American silent *The Grand Duchess and the Waiter.*

w Eliot Crawshay-Williams, Lajos Biro, *novel* The Head Waiter by Ernst Vajda *d* Alexander Korda

Leslie Howard, George Grossmith, Benita Hume, Elizabeth Allan, Morton Selten, Cyril Ritchard, Martita Hunt, Merle Oberon
'Too talky and English for general American consumption.'—*Variety*

The Set Up***
US 1949 72m bw
RKO (Richard Goldstone)

An ageing boxer refuses to pull his last fight, and is beaten up by gangsters.
One of the most brilliant little *films noirs* of the late forties; thoroughly studio-bound, yet evoking a brilliant feeling for time and place. Photography, direction, editing, acting are all of a piece.

w Art Cohn, *poem* Joseph Moncure March *d* Robert Wise *ph* Milton Krasner *md* Constantin Bakaleinikoff

Robert Ryan, Audrey Totter, George Tobias, Alan Baxter, Wallace Ford

Seven Angry Men*
US 1954 90m bw
Allied Artists (Vincent M. Fennelly)

In Kansas, John Brown determines to abolish slavery by violence.
Low-budget, intensely felt little biopic of the celebrated 19th-century fanatic and his sons.

w Daniel B. Ullman *d* Charles Marquis Warren *ph* Ellsworth Fredericks *m* Carl Brandt

Raymond Massey, Jeffrey Hunter, Larry Pennell, Debra Paget, Leo Gordon, John Smith, James Best, Dennis Weaver

Seven Beauties*
Italy 1975 115m Technicolor
Medusa (Lina Wertmuller, Giancarlo Giannini, Arrigo Colombo)
original title: *Pasqualino Settebellezze*

An incorrigible survivor manages to get through the rigours of World War II and scarcely notices the damage to his honour.

Candide-like mixture of farce and satire with the addition of a good deal of unpleasantness. Less meaningful abroad than on its home ground.

wd Lina Wertmuller *ph* Tonino delli Colli *m* Enzo Jannacci

Giancarlo Giannini, Fernando Rey, Shirley Stoler, Piero di Iorio

AAN: Lina Wertmuller (as writer and as director); Giancarlo Giannini

'I now pronounce you—men and wives!'
Seven Brides for Seven Brothers**
US 1954 104m Anscocolor Cinemascope
MGM (Jack Cummings)

In the old west, seven hard-working brothers decide they need wives, and carry off young women from the villages around.
Disappointingly studio-bound western musical, distinguished by an excellent score and some brilliant dancing, notably the barn-raising sequence.

w Frances Goodrich, Albert Hackett, *story* Sobbin' Women by Stephen Vincent Benet *d* Stanley Donen *ph* George Folsey *ch* Michael Kidd *songs* Johnny Mercer, Gene de Paul *m* Adolph Deutsch, Saul Chaplin

Howard Keel, Jane Powell, Jeff Richards, Russ Tamblyn, Tommy Rall, Howard Petrie, Marc Platt, Jacques d'Amboise, Matt Mattox

AA: Adolph Deutsch, Saul Chaplin
AAN: best picture; script; George Folsey

● Video: MGM / UA

Seven Chances**
US 1925 69m (24 fps) bw silent
Buster Keaton / Joseph M. Schenck

A meek young man finds that he is to inherit seven million dollars if he is married within a few hours.
Slim and rather slow comedy which builds to a fine climax as the hero is pursued first by hordes of women and then by rolling boulders.

w Clyde Bruckman, Jean Havez, Joseph A. Mitchell, *play* Roi Cooper Megrue *d* Buster Keaton *ph* Elgin Lessley, Byron Houck

Buster Keaton, Ruth Dwyer, Ray Barnes, Snitz Edwards
† The rocks sequence, which makes the film, was added only after a disappointing sneak preview.

'The sword and the cross battle for California's soul!'
Seven Cities of Gold*
US 1955 103m De Luxe Cinemascope
TCF (Robert D. Webb, Barbara McLean)

In 1796, a Spanish expedition sets out from Mexico to annex California, but with it goes Father Junipero Serra . . .
A semi-historical, semi-religious western which ends up not being much of anything but has interesting sequences.

w Richard L. Breen, John C. Higgins, *novel*
Isabelle Gibson Ziegler *d* Robert D. Webb
ph Lucien Ballard *m* Hugo Friedhofer

Michael Rennie, Richard Egan, Anthony
Quinn, Rita Moreno, Jeffrey Hunter, Eduardo
Noriega, John Doucette

Seven Days in May***
US 1964 120m bw
Seven Arts / Joel / John Frankenheimer
(Edward Lewis)

An American general's aide discovers that his
boss intends a military takeover because he
considers the President's pacifism traitorous.
Absorbing political mystery drama marred
only by the unnecessary introduction of a
female character. Stimulating entertainment.

w Rod Serling, *novel* Fletcher Knebel, Charles
W. Bailey II *d* John Frankenheimer
ph Ellsworth Fredericks *m* Jerry Goldsmith

Kirk Douglas, Burt Lancaster, *Fredric March*,
Ava Gardner, Martin Balsam, *Edmond
O'Brien*, George Macready, John Houseman
 'A political thriller which grips from start to
finish.'—*Penelope Houston*
 'It is to be enjoyed without feelings of guilt,
there should be more movies like it, and there
is nothing first class about it.'—*John Simon*
 'In the best tradition of the suspense thriller,
with the ultimate thrill our awareness of its
actual potential.'—*Judith Crist*

AAN: Edmond O'Brien

Seven Days Leave
US 1929 83m bw
Paramount (Louis D. Lighton)
GB title: *Medals*

A London charlady 'adopts' a soldier, and
both their lives are changed.
Sentimental melodrama which suited the times
and confirmed Cooper's stardom.

w John Farrow, Dan Totheroh, *play* The Old
Lady Shows Her Medals by J. M. Barrie
d Richard Wallace *ph* Charles Lang

Gary Cooper, Beryl Mercer, Daisy Belmore,
Nora Cecil, Tempe Piggott, Arthur Hoyt,
Basil Radford

Seven Days Leave
US 1942 87m bw
RKO (Tim Whelan)

In order to inherit a hundred thousand dollars,
a soldier must marry within a week.
Cheerful frivolity featuring radio stars of the
time.

w William Bowers, Ralph Spence, Curtis
Kenyon, Kenneth Earl *d* Tim Whelan
ph Robert de Grasse *md* Roy Webb
songs Frank Loesser, Jimmy McHugh

Lucille Ball, Victor Mature, Harold Peary,
Mary Cortes, Ginny Simms, Ralph Edwards,
Peter Lind Hayes, Marcy McGuire, Wallace
Ford

Seven Days to Noon**
GB 1950 94m bw
London Films (The Boulting Brothers)

A professor engaged on atomic research
threatens to blow up London unless his work
is brought to an end.

THIS IS THE STORY
OF THE MAKING...
AND THE FORGING
...OF CALIFORNIA

...when men chose
gold or God...
the sword
or the Cross!

CINEMASCOPE
revives the glorious
days when Father
Junipero Serra stopped
the Conquistadors from
looting Seven Cities of
Gold...turned them to
raising the wondrous
seven mission cities of
God!

20th Century-Fox presents

SEVEN CITIES OF GOLD

CINEMASCOPE
COLOR by
DE LUXE

Additional Dialogue by Joseph Petracca • From a Novel by Isabelle Gibson Ziegler
In the wonder of STEREOPHONIC SOUND

RICHARD ANTHONY MICHAEL
EGAN · QUINN · RENNIE

JEFFREY RITA
HUNTER · MORENO

PRODUCED BY
ROBERT D. WEBB and BARBARA McLEAN
DIRECTED BY
ROBERT D. WEBB
SCREEN PLAY BY
RICHARD L. BREEN and JOHN C. HIGGINS

SEVEN CITIES OF GOLD.   A well-intentioned movie which tended to make the waters of
history even muddier than they were before.

Persuasively understated suspense piece which was subsequently much copied, so that it now seems rather obvious.

w *Frank Harvey, Roy Boulting, Paul Dehn, James Bernard* d *John Boulting* ph *Gilbert Taylor* m *John Addison*

Barry Jones, Olive Sloane, André Morell, Joan Hickson, Sheila Manahan, Hugh Cross, Ronald Adam, Marie Ney

'A first rate thriller that does not pretend to a serious message, but yet will leave a query in the mind.'—*Richard Winnington*

AA: script

The Seven Deadly Sins*
France / Italy 1952 150m bw
Franco London / Costellazione

The master of ceremonies introduces seven stories and an epilogue.
Among the most successful compendiums of its kind, partly because of cast and credits and partly because it came when French naughtiness was appealing to a wide international audience.

w *Jean Aurenche, Pierre Bost, Roberto Rossellini, Leo Joannon, Carlo Rim, Diego Fabbri, Liana Ferri, Eduardo de Filippo, Charles Spaak, Turi Vaselle, René Wheeler* d *Eduardo de Filippo, Jean Dréville, Yves Allégret, Roberto Rossellini, Carlo Rim, Claude Autant-Lara, Georges Lacombe*

Gérard Philipe, Isa Miranda, Eduardo de Filippo, Noel-Noel, Louis de Funès, Viviane Romance, Frank Villard, Henri Vidal, Michèle Morgan, Françoise Rosay

711 Ocean Drive*
US 1950 102m bw
Columbia (Frank N. Seltzer)

A wireless expert is drawn into the bookie racket.
Overlong but vigorous crime exposé melodrama with excellent location sequences, notably a climax on Hoover Dam.

w *Richard English, Francis Swann* d *Joseph H. Newman* ph *Franz Planer* m *Sol Kaplan*

Edmond O'Brien, Joanne Dru, Otto Kruger, Don Porter, Sammy White, Dorothy Patrick, Barry Kelley, Howard St John

Seven Faces of Dr Lao*
US 1964 100m Metrocolor
MGM / George Pal

An elderly Chinaman with a penchant for spectacular disguise solves the problems of a western desert town.
A pleasant idea and excellent production are submerged in a sloppily sentimental and verbose script.

w *Charles G. Finney, from his novel* d *George Pal* ph *Robert Bronner* m *Leigh Harline* make up *William Tuttle*

Tony Randall, Arthur O'Connell, John Ericson, Barbara Eden, Noah Beery Jnr, Lee Patrick, Minerva Urecal, John Qualen

Seven Footsteps to Satan
US 1929 70m bw

A rich recluse plays an elaborate and macabre joke on his niece and nephew. Richly-designed but dramatically disappointing haunted house spoof. Thelma Todd, Creighton Hale, Sheldon Lewis, Ivan Christie, Sojin. Written by Richard Bee; directed by Benjamin Christensen; for Warner.

Seven Golden Men*
Italy / France / Spain 1965 91m
  Eastmancolor

Seven master criminals plot to rob a bank of its gold. Simple-minded but slickly handled caper story with many visual pleasures. Rossana Podesta, Philippe Leroy, Gastone Moschin, Gabriele Tinti. Written and directed by Marco Vicario; for Atlantica / PUF / Asfilm / Warner. (A sequel, *Seven Golden Men Strike Again*, was less successful.)

Seven Hills of Rome
US / Italy 1957 104m Technirama
MGM / Titanus (Lester Welch)

An American singer in Italy is pursued by the fiancée with whom he has quarrelled.
Thin travelogue with several halts for the star to sing; production very patchy.

w *Art Cohn, Giorgio Prosperi* d *Roy Rowland* ph *Tonino Delli Colli* md *George Stoll*

Mario Lanza, Renato Rascel, Marisa Allasio, Peggie Castle

Seven Keys to Baldpate*
US 1935 69m bw
RKO

A novelist retiring to a lonely inn for inspiration finds it full of criminals and damsels in distress.
An old theatrical warhorse with a trick ending, also filmed in 1929 (with Richard Dix; *Variety* said 'it all happens like a synopsis of what might have occurred') and in 1947 with Philip Terry. There was also a horror variation in 1982, *House of the Long Shadows* (qv). None was as satisfying as a good stage production.

play *George M. Cohan*, story *Earl Derr Biggers* d *William Hamilton, Edward Killy* ph *Robert de Grasse*

Gene Raymond, Margaret Callahan, Eric Blore, Grant Mitchell, Moroni Olsen, Henry Travers

'Too much conversation and too little action.'—*Variety*

The Seven Little Foys*
US 1955 95m Technicolor Vistavision
Paramount (Jack Rose)

The story of a family vaudeville act.
Routine showbiz biopic, a little heavy on the syrup.

w *Melville Shavelson, Jack Rose* d *Melville Shavelson* ph *John F. Warren* md *Joseph J. Lilley*

Bob Hope, Milly Vitale, George Tobias, Angela Clarke, Herbert Heyes, *James Cagney* as George M. Cohan

AAN: script

Seven Men from Now
US 1956 78m Warnercolor
Batjac (Andrew V. McLaglen, Robert E. Morrison)

A sheriff seeks revenge when his wife is killed by bandits.
Good western programmer.

w *Burt Kennedy* d *Budd Boetticher* ph *William H. Clothier* m *Henry Vars*

Randolph Scott, Gail Russell, Lee Marvin, Walter Reed, Don Barry, John Larch

The Seven Minutes
US 1971 102m De Luxe
TCF (Russ Meyer)

A bookseller is arrested for distributing an obscene novel, and many people are unexpectedly involved in the court case.
A fascinating piece of old-fashioned hokum, full of 'daring' words and cameo performances.

w *Richard Warren Lewis*, novel *Irving Wallace* d *Russ Meyer* ph *Fred Mandl* m *Stu Philips*

Wayne Maunder, Marianne MacAndrew, Yvonne de Carlo, Phil Carey, Jay C. Flippen, Edy Williams, Lyle Bettger, Ron Randell, David Brian, Charles Drake, John Carradine, Harold J. Stone

Seven Nights in Japan
GB / France 1976 104m Eastmancolor
EMI–Marianne (Lewis Gilbert)

The heir to the British throne has shore leave in Tokyo and falls in love with a geisha. Tediously daring romance with a banal script which seems over impressed by its own barely-existent controversial qualities.

w *Christopher Wood* d *Lewis Gilbert* ph *Henri Decaë* m *David Hentschel*

Michael York, Hidemi Aoki, James Villiers, Peter Jones, Charles Gray

● *Video: Thorn EMI*

The Seven Per Cent Solution
US 1976 114m Technicolor
Universal (Herbert Ross)

Dr Watson lures Sherlock Holmes to Vienna so that Professor Freud can cure him of persecution complex and cocaine addiction. Drearily serious spoof with only a glimmer of the required style and a totally miscast Holmes.

w *Nicholas Meyer, from his novel* d *Herbert Ross* ph *Oswald Morris* m *John Addison* pd *Ken Adam*

Nicol Williamson, Robert Duvall, Alan Arkin, Vanessa Redgrave, Laurence Olivier, Jeremy Kemp, Samantha Eggar, Joel Grey, Charles Gray, Georgia Brown, Regine

'Sorrily botched all-star extravaganza.'—*Sight and Sound*

'Comes into the category of hit and myth . . . A heavyweight sport in which Sherlock Holmes is placed under hypnosis by Sigmund Freud. The audience is then placed under hypnosis by director Herbert Ross.'—*Michael Billington, Illustrated London News*

AAN: script

Seven Samurai•••
Japan 1954 155m bw
Toho (Shojiro Motoki)
original title: *Shichi-nin no Samurai*

16th-century villagers hire samurai to defend their property against an annual raid by bandits.
Superbly strange, vivid and violent medieval adventure which later served as the basis for the western *The Magnificent Seven*.

w Akira Kurosawa, Shinobu Hashimoto, Hideo Oguni d Akira Kurosawa ph Asaichi Nakai m Fumio Hayasaka

Toshiro Mifune, Takashi Shimura, Kuninori Kodo

'It is as sheer narrative, rich in imagery, incisiveness and sharp observation, that it makes its strongest impact . . . It provides a fascinating display of talent, and places its director in the forefront of creative film-makers of his generation.'—*Gavin Lambert, Sight and Sound*

'This, on the surface, is a work of relentless, unmitigated action, as epic as any film ever made, and, again on the surface, sheer entertainment. Yet it is also an unquestionable triumph of art.'—*John Simon*

Seven Seas to Calais
US / Italy 1962 103m Eastmancolor
Cinemascope
MGM / Adelphia (Paolo Moffa)

In 1577, Sir Francis Drake follows the Spanish treasure route.
Ho-hum swashbuckler with a background of schoolboy history.

w Filippo Sanjust d Rudolph Maté ph Giulio Gianini m Franco Mannino

Rod Taylor, Keith Michell, Irene Worth, Anthony Dawson, Basil Dignam

Seven Sinners•
GB 1936 70m bw
Gaumont (Michael Balcon)
US title: *Doomed Cargo*

Gunrunners wreck trains to cover traces of murder.
Fascinatingly dated comedy suspenser with excellent sub-Hitchcock sequences, the whole thing having a strong flavour of *The 39 Steps*.

w Frank Launder, Sidney Gilliat, L. DuGarde Peach, Austin Melford, *play* The Wrecker by Arnold Ridley, Bernard Merivale d Albert de Courville

Edmund Lowe, Constance Cummings, Thomy Bourdelle, Henry Oscar, Felix Aylmer, Allan Jeayes, O. B. Clarence

Seven Sinners•
US 1940 86m bw
Universal (Joe Pasternak)
GB title: *Café of Seven Sinners*

A cabaret singer is deported from several South Sea islands for causing too many fights among the naval officers.
Ho-hum hokum with an amiable cast and a good-natured final free-for-all.

w John Meehan, Harry Tugend d Tay Garnett ph Rudolph Maté m Frank Skinner

Marlene Dietrich, John Wayne, Albert Dekker, Broderick Crawford, Mischa Auer, Billy Gilbert, Oscar Homolka, Anne Lee, Samuel S. Hinds

'Nothing to worry about, unless you happen to be in the theatre, watching it go from fairly good to worse than worse.'—*Otis Ferguson*

Seven Sweethearts
US 1942 98m bw
MGM (Joe Pasternak)

Seven daughters must marry in sequence, eldest first.
Period musical frou-frou inspired by *Pride and Prejudice*. So light it almost floats.

w Walter Reisch, Leo Townsend d Frank Borzage ph George Folsey m Franz Waxman

Kathryn Grayson, Marsha Hunt, Van Heflin, Cecelia Parker, S. Z. Sakall, Peggy Moran, Isobel Elsom, Diana Lewis, Donald Meek, Louise Beavers

Seven Thieves•
US 1960 102m bw Cinemascope
TCF (Sidney Boehm)

An elderly crook conceives a last plan to rob the Monte Carlo casino.
Routine caper story, efficiently presented with some humour.

w Sidney Boehm, *novel* Lions at the Kill by Max Catto d Henry Hathaway ph Sam Leavitt m Dominic Frontière

Edward G. Robinson, Rod Steiger, Joan Collins, Eli Wallach, Michael Dante, Alexander Scourby, Berry Kroeger, Sebastian Cabot

'Christ, it was supposed to be a fun film, and Steiger is far, far from having a sense of humour.'—*Henry Hathaway*

'They take the third degree one step further!'

The Seven-Ups
US 1973 103m De Luxe
TCF / Philip D'Antoni

Gangsters are hunted down by a secret force of the New York police.
Formulary realistic rough stuff in the wake of *The French Connection*.

w Albert Ruben, Alexander Jacobs d Philip D'Antoni ph Urs Furrer m Don Ellis

Roy Scheider, Victor Arnold, Jerry Leon, Tony Lo Bianco, *Richard Lynch*

Seven Waves Away
GB 1956 95m bw
Columbia / Copa (John R. Sloan)
US title: *Abandon Ship*

After the sinking of a luxury liner, the officer in charge of a lifeboat has to make life or death decisions.
Initially gripping but finally depressing open sea melodrama derived from *Souls at Sea* and later remade for TV as *The Last Survivors*.

wd Richard Sale ph Wilkie Cooper m Arthur Bliss

Tyrone Power, Mai Zetterling, Lloyd Nolan, Stephen Boyd, Moira Lister, James Hayter, Marie Lohr, Moultrie Kelsall, Noel Willman, Gordon Jackson, Clive Morton, John Stratton

'Eventually one is bludgeoned into a grudging admiration for the film's staying power.'—*Peter John Dyer*

Seven Ways from Sundown
US 1960 87m Eastmancolor

A Texas Ranger befriends an outlaw, but has twinges of conscience. Straightforward character western with the inevitable shootout finale. Audie Murphy, Barry Sullivan, Venetia Stevenson, John McIntire, Kenneth Tobey. Written by Clair Huffaker; directed by Harry Keller; for Universal-International.

Seven Women•
US 1966 100m Metrocolor Panavision
MGM / John Ford / Bernard Smith

In 1935, an isolated Chinese mission staffed by American women is overrun by bandits.
Dusty melodrama which might have appealed in the thirties but was quite out of tune with the sixties. Well enough made and acted, but a strange choice for Ford's last film.

w Janet Green, John McCormick, *story* Chinese Finale by Norah Lofts d John Ford ph Joseph La Shelle m Elmer Bernstein

Anne Bancroft, Flora Robson, Margaret Leighton, Sue Lyon, Mildred Dunnock, Betty Field, Anna Lee, Eddie Albert, Mike Mazurki, Woody Strode, Irene Tsu

The Seven Year Itch•
US 1955 105m De Luxe Cinemascope
TCF (Charles K. Feldman, Billy Wilder)

A married man has a fling with the girl upstairs.
An amusing theatrical joke, with dream sequences like revue sketches, is really all at sea on the big screen, especially as the affair remains unconsummated, but direction and performances keep the party going more or less.

w Billy Wilder, George Axelrod, *play* George Axelrod d Billy Wilder ph Milton Krasner m Alfred Newman

Tom Ewell, Marilyn Monroe, Sonny Tufts, Evelyn Keyes, Robert Strauss, Oscar Homolka, Marguerite Chapman, Victor Moore

● *Video: CBS / Fox*

1776•
US 1972 141m Eastmancolor
Panavision
Columbia / Jack L. Warner

The thirteen American colonies prepare to declare their independence of Great Britain.
Plain, low-key filming of the successful Broadway musical showing the domestic lives of the historical figures concerned. Splendid moments alternate with stretches of tedium.

w Peter Stone, from his play *d* Peter Hunt
ph Harry Stradling Jnr *m* / *ly* Sherman
Edwards *ad* George Jenkins

William Daniels, Howard da Silva, Ken
Howard, Donald Madden, Blythe Danner

AAN: Harry Stradling Jnr

Seventh Cavalry

US 1956 75m Technicolor
Columbia / Scott–Brown

An officer accused of cowardice volunteers to
bring back General Custer's body after Little
Big Horn.
Lively co-feature with a good traditional
action climax.

w Peter Packer *d* Joseph H. Lewis *ph* Ray
Rennahan *m* Mischa Bakaleinikoff

Randolph Scott, Barbara Hale, Jay C.
Flippen, Jeanette Nolan, Frank Faylen

The Seventh Cross**

US 1944 112m bw
MGM (Pandro S. Berman)

Seven Germans escape from a concentration
camp, and the Nazis threaten to execute them
all. Just one escapes.
Impressive melodrama, brilliantly limiting its
escape / suspense story to studio sets. Old-
style Hollywood production at its best; but a
rather obviously contrived story.

w Helen Deutsch, *novel* Anna Seghers *d* Fred
Zinnemann *ph* Karl Freund *m* Roy Webb
ad Cedric Gibbons, Leonid Vasian

Spencer Tracy, Signe Hasso, Hume Cronyn,
Jessica Tandy, Agnes Moorehead, Felix
Bressart, George Macready, George Zucco

AAN: Hume Cronyn

The Seventh Dawn

GB 1964 123m Technicolor
UA / Holden / Charles K. Feldman (Karl
Tunberg)

In the early fifties a Malayan rubber planter
finds that his best friend is a leading terrorist.
Doom-laden romantic adventure drama with a
lot of suffering and too little entertainment
value.

w Karl Tunberg, *novel* The Durian Tree by
Michael Keon *d* Lewis Gilbert *ph* Freddie
Young *m* Riz Ortolani

William Holden, Tetsuro Tamba, Capucine,
Susannah York, Michael Goodliffe, Allan
Cuthbertson, Maurice Denham

'Echoes of *The Ugly American, Love Is a
Many-Splendored Thing*, and many another
adventure East of Sumatra, with every
character running absolutely true to form.'—
MFB

'An interminable melange of political, racial
and romantic clichés, with performances and
dialogue as overripe as the jungle setting.'—
Judith Crist, 1973

Seventh Heaven**

US 1927 93m approx (24 fps) bw
silent
Fox

A Paris sewer worker shelters a street waif,
marries her and after idyllic happiness goes off
to war, returning blinded.
All softness, sweetness and light, a very
typical—and attractive—film of its director
and a big influence on Hollywood's European
period.

w Benjamin Glazer, *play* Austin Strong
d Frank Borzage *ph* Ernest Palmer, J A.
Valentine

Janet Gaynor, Charles Farrell, Gladys
Brockwell, David Butler

AA: Benjamin Glazer; Frank Borzage; Janet
Gaynor
AAN: best picture

Seventh Heaven*

US 1937 102m bw
TCF (Raymond Griffith)

Dewy-eyed remake; the mood is antediluvian
but the production impresses.

w Melville Baker *d* Henry King *ph* Merritt
Gerstad *m* Louis Silvers *ad* William Darling

James Stewart, Simone Simon, Jean Hersholt,
Gale Sondergaard, J. Edward Bromberg,
Gregory Ratoff, John Qualen, Victor Kilian,
Sig Rumann, Mady Christians

'A romance that can stand another telling
. . . the older element will join in making it a
bracer for the box office.'—*Variety*

The Seventh Seal***

Sweden 1957 95m bw
Svensk Filmindustri (Allan Ekelund)
original title: *Det Sjunde Inseglet*

Death comes for a knight, who challenges him
to a game of chess while he tries to show
illustrations of goodness in mankind: but
Death takes them all away in the end.
A modestly budgeted minor classic which,
because of its international success and its
famous shots, is seldom analysed in detail. In
fact its storyline is meandering and apparently
pointless, and it is kept going by its splendid
cinematic feel and its atmosphere is that of a
dark world irrationally sustained by religion.

wd Ingmar Bergman *ph* Gunnar Fischer
m Erik Nordgren

Max Von Sydow, Bengt Ekerot, Gunnar
Bjornstrand, Nils Poppe, Bibi Andersson,
Gunnel Lindblom

'The most extraordinary mixture of beauty
and lust and cruelty, Odin-worship and
Christian faith, darkness and light.'—*Alan
Dent, Illustrated London News*

The Seventh Sin

US 1957 94m bw Cinemascope
MGM (David Lewis)

A faithless wife accompanies her bacteriologist
husband to fight a Chinese cholera epidemic,
and regains her self-respect.
Tatty remake of a Garbo vehicle which was
dated even in 1934. (See *The Painted Veil*.)

w Karl Tunberg, *novel* The Painted Veil by
Somerset Maugham *d* Ronald Neame *ph* Ray June *m* Miklos Rozsa

Eleanor Parker, Bill Travers, George Sanders,
Jean-Pierre Aumont, Françoise Rosay

The Seventh Survivor

GB 1941 75m bw

Survivors of a shipwreck gather in a lighthouse
and discover that one of them is a Nazi agent.
Adequate mystery potboiler, comparable with
Hitchcock's talkier *Lifeboat*. Linden Travers,
Austin Trevor, John Stuart, Martita Hunt,
Frank Pettingell, Jane Carr, Felix Aylmer,
Wally Patch, Henry Oscar. Written by
Michael Barringer; directed by Leslie Hiscott;
for British National.

The Seventh Veil***

GB 1945 94m bw
Theatrecraft / Sydney Box / Ortus

A concert pianist is romantically torn between
her psychiatrist, her guardian, and two other
fellows.
A splendid modern melodrama in the tradition
of *Jane Eyre* and *Rebecca*; it set the seal of
moviegoing approval on psychiatry, classical
music, and James Mason, and it is the most
utter tosh.

w Muriel and Sydney Box *d* Compton
Bennett *ph* Reg Wyer *m* Benjamin Frankel

James Mason, Ann Todd, Herbert Lom,
Albert Lieven, Hugh McDermott, Yvonne
Owen, David Horne, Manning Whiley

'An example of the intelligent, medium-
priced picture made with great technical polish
which has represented for Hollywood the
middle path between the vulgar and the
highbrow.'—*Spectator*
'A popular film that does not discard taste
and atmosphere.'—*Daily Mail*
'A rich, portentous mixture of Beethoven,
Chopin, Kitsch and Freud.'—*Pauline Kael,
1968*
'An odd, artificial, best sellerish kind of
story, with reminiscences of *Trilby* and *Jane
Eyre* and all their imitations down to
Rebecca.'—*Richard Mallett, Punch*
'A popular film that does not discard taste
and atmosphere.'—*Daily Mail*
'Maybe, with a few veils stripped away, all
of us have a fantasist inside who gobbles up
this sadomasochistic sundae.'—*Pauline Kael,
70s*

AA: script

● *Video: Precision*

The Seventh Victim*

US 1943 71m bw
RKO (*Val Lewton*)

A girl goes to New York in search of her
sister, who is under the influence of Satanists.
Much praised but in effect rather boring little
thriller, with rather stately acting and
ponderous direction and dialogue. Censorship
made the plot so obscure that it's difficult to
follow.

w Charles O'Neal, De Witt Bodeen *d* Mark
Robson *ph* Nicholas Musuraca *m* Constantin
Bakaleinikoff

Kim Hunter, Tom Conway, Jean Brooks,
Hugh Beaumont, Erford Gage, Isabel Jewell,
Evelyn Brent

'It is the almost oppressive mood, the romantic obsession with death-in-life, which dominates the film.'—*NFT, 1973*
† Note the use in the first scene of the staircase from *The Magnificent Ambersons*.

The Seventh Voyage of Sinbad*
US 1958 89m Technicolor
Columbia / Morningside (Charles Schneer)

Sinbad seeks a roc's egg which will restore his fiancée from the midget size to which an evil magician has reduced her.
Lively fantasy with narrative drive and excellent effects.

w Kenneth Kolb d Nathan Juran ph Wilkie Cooper m Bernard Herrmann sp Ray Harryhausen

Kerwin Mathews, Kathryn Grant, Torin Thatcher, Richard Eyer, Alec Mango

70,000 Witnesses
US 1932 69m bw

A football star is murdered in the middle of a game. Okay for sports fans, but not much of a murder mystery. Phillips Holmes, Johnny Mack Brown, Charles Ruggles, Dorothy Jordan, J. Farrell MacDonald, Lew Cody. Written by Garrett Fort, P. J. Wolfson, Allen Rivkin, from the novel by Cortland Fitzsimmons; directed by Ralph Murphy; for Harry Joe Brown / Paramount. 'Will make money and please . . . enough comedy interwoven to satisfy on laughs alone.'—*Variety*

A Severed Head*
GB 1970 98m Technicolor
Columbia / Winkast (Alan Ladd Jnr)

A wine merchant has a long-standing affair which he thinks is secret, but is annoyed when his wife tries the same game.
Unwisely boisterous screen version of a slyly academic novel; tolerably sophisticated for those who don't know the original.

w Frederic Raphael, *novel* Iris Murdoch
d Dick Clement ph Austin Dempster
m Stanley Myers pd Richard Macdonald

Lee Remick, Richard Attenborough, Ian Holm, Claire Bloom, Jennie Linden, Clive Revill

Sex and the Single Girl
US 1964 114m Technicolor
Warner / Richard Quine / Reynard (William T. Orr)

A journalist worms his way into the life of a lady sexologist in order to unmask her—but guess what.
Coy sex comedy with noise substituting for wit and style, all pretence being abandoned in a wild chase climax.

w Joseph Heller, David R. Schwarz, *book* Helen Gurley Brown d Richard Quine
ph Charles Lang Jnr m Neal Hefti

Natalie Wood, Tony Curtis, Henry Fonda, Lauren Bacall, Mel Ferrer, Fran Jeffries, Edward Everett Horton, Otto Kruger
  'For those willing to devote two hours of their lives to a consideration of Natalie Wood's virginity.'—*Judith Crist, 1973*

Sextette*
US 1978 91m Metrocolor
Briggs and Sullivan (Warren G. Toub)

The honeymoon of a Hollywood film star is interrupted by her previous husbands.
An amazing last stab at her old métier by an 86-year-old ex-star. It doesn't work, of course, and most of it is embarrassing, but the attempt is in itself remarkable.

w Herbert Baker, *play* Mae West d Ken Hughes ph James Crabe m Artie Butler

Mae West, Tony Curtis, Ringo Starr, Dom de Luise, Timothy Dalton, George Hamilton, Alice Cooper, Rona Barrett, Walter Pidgeon, George Raft

Sexton Blake and the Hooded Terror
GB 1938 70m bw

A millionaire is unmasked as the head of a criminal gang. Rather unyielding series melodrama, chiefly interesting for the casting of Tod Slaughter as Blake's Moriarty. George Curzon, Tod Slaughter, Greta Gynt, Charles Oliver, David Farrar. Written by A. R. Rawlinson; directed by George King; for George King. (NB: Other Sexton Blake movies, all cheaply made by British independents, include six 1928 two-reelers starring Langhorne Burton; *Sexton Blake and the Bearded Doctor* and *Sexton Blake and the Mademoiselle*, both 1935, both with Curzon; *Meet Sexton Blake* and *The Echo Murders*, both 1943, both with David Farrar; and *Murder on Site Three*, 1963, with Geoffrey Toone.)

Sh! The Octopus
US 1937 54m bw

Lamebrain detectives fight a giant octopus in a lighthouse. Footling remake of *The Gorilla*, (*qv*). Hugh Herbert, Allen Jenkins, Marcia Ralston, John Eldredge, George Rosener. Written by George Bricker; directed by William McGann; for First National. 'This bit of grist for the double-feature mills is so feeble even the actors seem embarrassed.'—*Variety*

Shack Out on 101*
US 1955 80m bw
AA / William F. Broidy

A waitress at a café near a research establishment unmasks two spies.
Modest suspenser which seemed at the time to have some fresh and realistic attitudes.

w Ed and Mildred Dein d Ed Dein ph Floyd Crosby m Paul Dunlap

Frank Lovejoy, Lee Marvin, Keenan Wynn, Terry Moore, Whit Bissell

Shadow in the Sky
US 1951 78m bw
MGM (William H. Wright)

A shell-shocked marine moves from a psychiatric hospital to live with his sister.
Low-key drama, plainly but quite well done, though of little continuing interest.

w Ben Maddow d Fred M. Wilcox
ph George Folsey m Bronislau Kaper

Ralph Meeker, Nancy Davis, James Whitmore, Jean Hagen

Shadow of a Doubt***
US 1943 108m bw
Universal (Jack H. Skirball)

A favourite uncle comes to visit his family in a small Californian town. He is actually on the run from police, who know him as the Merry Widow murderer.
Hitchcock's quietest film is memorable chiefly for its depiction of small-town life; but the script is well written and keeps the suspense moving slowly but surely.

w Thornton Wilder, Sally Benson, Alma Reville, *story* Gordon McDonell d Alfred Hitchcock ph Joe Valentine m Dmitri Tiomkin

Joseph Cotten, Teresa Wright, Hume Cronyn, Macdonald Carey, Patricia Collinge, Henry Travers, Wallace Ford
  'Some clever observation of rabbity white-collar life which, in spite of a specious sweetness, is the best since *It's a Gift*.'—*James Agee*
† Remade in 1959 as *Step Down to Terror*, with Charles Drake.

AAN: original story

Shadow of a Woman
US 1946 78m bw

A woman suspects her husband of trying to murder his son by a former marriage. Poor melodrama on *Love from a Stranger* lines. Andrea King, Helmut Dantine, Don McGuire, Richard Erdman, William Prince. Written by Whitman Chambers and C. Graham Baker; directed by Joseph Santley; for Warner.

Shadow of Doubt
US 1935 71m bw

An actress suspected of murder is cleared by the efforts of her fiancé's aunt. Routine mystery with a strong part for a new character actress from England. Ricardo Cortez, Virginia Bruce, *Constance Collier*, Arthur Byron, Isabel Jewell, Regis Toomey, Edward Brophy. Written by Wells Root, Arthur Somers Roche; directed by George B. Seitz; for MGM. 'Passable murder mystery.'—*Variety*

Shadow of the Cat
GB 1961 79m bw
U-I / BHP

A cat appears to wreak vengeance on those who murdered its mistress.
Tolerable old dark house shocker with an amusing theme not too well sustained.

w George Baxt d John Gilling ph Alec Grant m Mikis Theodorakis

André Morell, William Lucas, Barbara Shelley, Conrad Phillips, Alan Wheatley, Vanda Godsell, Richard Warner, Freda Jackson

Shadow of the Eagle
GB 1950 92m bw

In 1770, a Russian envoy to Venice falls for the princess he is supposed to kidnap. Limp swashbuckler based on a deservedly shadowy corner of European history. Richard Greene, Valentina Cortese, Greta Gynt, Binnie Barnes, Charles Goldner, Walter Rilla. Written by Doreen Montgomery and Hagar Wilde; directed by Sidney Salkow; for Anthony Havelock-Allan / Valiant.

Shadow on the Wall
US 1949 84m bw
MGM (Robert Sisk)

A child is traumatized by the accidental witnessing of the murder of her unpleasant stepmother.
Forgettable melodramatic suspenser.

w William Ludwig d Pat Jackson ph Ray June m André Previn

Ann Sothern, Zachary Scott, Gigi Perreau, Nancy Davis, Kristine Miller, John McIntire

The Shadow on the Window
US 1957 73m bw
Columbia (Jonie Taps)

Three teenage thugs break into a lonely house, murder its owner and hold a girl hostage.
Routine crime programmer, rather boringly unravelled.

w Leo Townsend, David Harmon d William Asher ph Kit Carson m George Duning

Betty Garrett, Phil Carey, John Barrymore Jnr, Corey Allen, Gerald Saracini

Shadows*
US 1959 81m bw
Cassavetes / Cassel / Maurice McEndree

Two blacks and their sister find their identities in Manhattan.
16mm realistic drama which began a new and essentially dreary trend of grainily true-life pictures with improvised dialogue and little dramatic compression.

w the cast d John Cassavetes ph Erich Kollmar m Charles Mingus

Ben Carruthers, Leila Goldoni, Hugh Hurd, Rupert Crosse, Anthony Ray
'I don't so much object to its mindlessness as to its formlessness, regardless of the practical excuses that may be advanced for its rambling incoherence.'—William S. Pechter
'A picture of startling immediacy and shocking power.'—Robert Hatch, Nation

Shady Lady
US 1945 90m bw

An elderly cardsharp is persuaded to help the district attorney nab others of his kind.
Poorish comedy which offers its star little support. Charles Coburn, Ginny Simms, Robert Paige, Martha O'Driscoll, Alan Curtis. Written by Curt Siodmak, Gerald Geraghty and M. M. Musselman; directed by George Waggner; for Universal.

Shaft*
US 1971 100m Metrocolor
MGM / Shaft Productions (Joel Freeman)

A black private eye finds himself at odds with a powerful racketeer.

Violent, commercial action thriller which spawned two sequels and a tele-series as well as stimulating innumerable even more violent imitations.

w Ernest Tidyman, John D. F. Black d Gordon Parks ph Urs Furrer m Isaac Hayes

Richard Roundtree, Moses Gunn, Charles Cioffi, Christopher St John
'Relentlessly supercool dialogue, all throwaway colloquialisms and tough Chandlerian wisecracks.'—MFB

AA: title song (m / ly Isaac Hayes)
AAN: Isaac Hayes (musical score)

● Video: MGM / UA

Shaft in Africa
US 1973 112m Metrocolor Panavision (MGM) Shaft Productions (Roger Lewis)

Shaft is kidnapped by an Ethiopian emir who wants him to track down a gang of slavers.
More miscellaneous violence, rather shoddily assembled, with a few good jokes.

w Stirling Silliphant d John Guillermin ph Marcel Grignon m Johnny Pate

Richard Roundtree, Frank Finlay, Vonetta McGee

Shaft's Big Score
US 1972 105m Metrocolor Panavision
MGM / Shaft Productions (Richard Lewis, Ernest Tidyman)

Shaft avenges the death of a friend and comes up against the numbers racket.
Violent footage and an incomprehensible plot.

w Ernest Tidyman d Gordon Parks ph Urs Furrer m Gordon Parks

Richard Roundtree, Moses Gunn, Drew Bundini Brown, Joseph Mascolo

The Shaggy DA
US 1976 92m Technicolor
Walt Disney (Ron Miller)

A magic ring enables a young lawyer to become a talking dog and thus expose corruption.
Rather feeble sequel to The Shaggy Dog, with overtones of Watergate.

w Don Tait d Robert Stevenson ph Frank Phillips m Buddy Baker sp Eustace Lycett, Art Cruickshank, Danne Lee

Dean Jones, Tim Conway, Suzanne Pleshette, Jo Anne Worley, Vic Tayback, Keenan Wynn, Dick Van Patten

The Shaggy Dog*
US 1959 101m bw
Walt Disney (Bill Walsh)

A small boy turns into a big shaggy dog and catches some crooks.
Simple-minded, overlong Disney comedy for kids and their indulgent parents; good laughs in the chase scenes.

w Bill Walsh, Lillie Hayward, novel The Hound of Florence by Felix Salten d Charles Barton ph Edward Colman m Paul Sawtell

Fred MacMurray, Jean Hagen, Tommy Kirk, Cecil Kellaway, Annette Funicello, Tim Considine, Kevin Corcoran, Alexander Scourby

Shake Hands with the Devil*
Eire 1959 110m bw
UA / Troy / Pennebaker (Michael Anderson)

In 1921 Dublin a surgeon is the secret leader of the IRA, and comes to cherish violence as an end rather than a means.
Downbeat action melodrama, politically very questionable but well made.

w Ivan Goff, Ben Roberts, novel Rearden Connor d Michael Anderson ph Erwin Hillier m William Alwyn

James Cagney, Glynis Johns, Don Murray, Dana Wynter, Michael Redgrave, Sybil Thorndike, Cyril Cusack, Niall MacGinnis, Richard Harris, Ray McAnally, Noel Purcell

Shakedown
US 1950 80m bw
U-I (Ted Richmond)

A ruthless press photographer becomes a blackmailer.
Routine crime melodrama, adequately done.

w Alfred Lewis, Martin Goldsmith d Joseph Pevney ph Irving Glassberg m Joseph Gershenson

Howard Duff, Brian Donlevy, Anne Vernon, Peggy Dow, Lawrence Tierney, Bruce Bennett

The Shakedown
GB 1959 92m bw
Rank / Alliance / Ethiro (Norman Williams)

A Soho vice boss photographs prominent people in compromising situations and blackmails them.
A semi-remake set in the squalid London so beloved of film makers at the time, before it became 'swinging'. Of no interest or entertainment value.

w Leigh Vance d John Lemont ph Brendan J. Stafford m Philip Green

Terence Morgan, Hazel Court, Donald Pleasence, Bill Owen, Robert Beatty, Harry H. Corbett, Gene Anderson, Eddie Byrne

Shakespeare Wallah*
India 1965 125m bw
Merchant Ivory (Ismail Merchant)

A troupe of English actors find their Indian tour interrupted by romance.
Interesting but sluggish drama on an unusual subject. Not by any means a classic, but it set off this partnership on an enduring wave of critical acclaim and public indifference.

w Ruth Prawer Jhabvala, James Ivory d James Ivory ph Subrata Mitra m Satyajit Ray

Felicity Kendal, Shashi Kapoor, Laura Liddell, Geoffrey Kendal, Madhur Jaffrey, Utpal Dutt

● Video: Home Video

The Shakiest Gun in the West
US 1967 101m Techniscope
Universal (Edward J. Montagne)

A cowardly dentist becomes a western hero.
Dreary farce, an unsubtle remake of *The Paleface.*

w Jim Fritzell, Everett Greenbaum d Alan Rafkin ph Andrew Jackson m Vic Mizzy

Don Knotts, Barbara Rhoades, Jackie Coogan, Don Barry

Shalako
GB 1968 118m Technicolor Franscope
Kingston / Dimitri de Grunwald (Euan Lloyd)

New Mexico, 1880: a cowboy acts as guide to European aristocratic big game hunters, but the Indians become annoyed and attack.
A cute idea is given routine treatment; though packed with stars, the action never becomes very exciting despite incidental brutalities.

w J. J. Griffith, Hal Hopper, Scot Finch, *novel* Louis L'Amour d Edward Dmytryk ph Ted Moore m Robert Farnon

Sean Connery, Brigitte Bardot, Jack Hawkins, Stephen Boyd, Peter Van Eyck, Honor Blackman, Eric Sykes, Alexander Knox, Woody Strode, Valerie French
● *Video: JVC*

Shall We Dance?**
US 1937 116m bw
RKO (Pandro S. Berman)

Dancing partners pretend to be married but are not; until they both get the same idea.
A light musical which was full of good things but nevertheless began the decline of Astaire-Rogers films; repetition was obvious, as was ostentation for its own sake, and the audience was expecting too much.

w Allan Scott, Ernest Pagano d Mark Sandrich ph David Abel m / ly George and Ira Gershwin md Nathaniel Shilkret ad Van Nest Polglase

Fred Astaire, Ginger Rogers, Edward Everett Horton, Eric Blore, Harriet Hoctor, Jerome Cowan, Ketti Gallian, Ann Shoemaker
'Another holdover musical in the Astaire-Rogers string . . . it has everything it needs on production.'—*Variety*

AAN: song 'They Can't Take That Away From Me'
● *Video: Thorn EMI*

Shampoo*
US 1975 110m Technicolor
Columbia / Persky–Bright / Vista (Warren Beatty)

A Beverly Hills hairdresser seduces his most glamorous clients.
Ugly little sex farce with few laughs but much dashing about and bad language. Its setting on election eve 1968 has made some people think it a political satire.

w Robert Towne, Warren Beatty d Hal Ashby ph Laszlo Kovacs m Paul Simon

Warren Beatty, Julie Christie, Lee Grant, Goldie Hawn, Jack Warden, Tony Bill, Jay Robinson
'It has the bursting-with-talent but fuzziness-of-effect aspect of a movie made by a group of friends for their own amusement.'—*Richard Combs*

AA: Lee Grant
AAN: script; Jack Warden

Shamus
US 1972 98m Eastmancolor
Columbia / Robert M. Weitman

A private eye is hired by a wealthy man to recover stolen jewels and find a murderer.
A forties retread with seventies violence; junky stuff, with a few laughs for buffs who can spot the in-jokes.

w Barry Beckerman d Buzz Kulik ph Victor J. Kemper m Jerry Goldsmith

Burt Reynolds, Dyan Cannon, John Ryan, Joe Santos, Giorgio Tozzi, Ron Weyland
'Very hectic, very vividly New York and as idiotic as Reynolds' physical resiliency.'—*Judith Crist*

Shane***
US 1953 118m Technicolor
Paramount (George Stevens, Ivan Moffat)

A mysterious stranger helps a family of homesteaders.
Archetypal family western, but much slower and statelier than most, as though to emphasize its own quality, which is evident anyway.

w A. B. Guthrie Jnr, *novel* Jack Schaefer d George Stevens ph Loyal Griggs m Victor Young

Alan Ladd, Jean Arthur, Van Heflin, *Jack Palance*, Brandon de Wilde, Ben Johnson, Edgar Buchanan, Emile Meyer, Elisha Cook Jnr, John Dierkes
'A kind of dramatic documentary of the pioneer days of the west.'—*MFB*
'Westerns are better when they're not too self-importantly self-conscious.'—*New Yorker, 1975*
'Stevens managed to infuse a new vitality, a new sense of realism into the time-worn story through the strength and freshness of his visuals.'—*Arthur Knight*

AA: Loyal Griggs
AAN: best picture; A. B. Guthrie Jnr; George Stevens; Jack Palance; Brandon de Wilde
● *Video: CIC*

Shanghai
US 1935 77m bw
(Paramount) Walter Wanger

A visiting American lady falls in love with a half caste.
Romantic drama programmer.

w Gene Towne, Graham Baker, Lynn Starling d James Flood ph James Van Trees

Loretta Young, Charles Boyer, Warner Oland, Alison Skipworth, Fred Keating, Charles Grapewin, Walter Kingsford

Shanghai Express***
US 1932 84m bw
Paramount

A British officer and his old flame meet on a train which is waylaid by Chinese bandits.
Superbly pictorial melodrama which set the pattern for innumerable train movies to come, though none matched its deft visual quality and few sketched in their characters so neatly. Plot and dialogue are silent style, but refreshingly so.

w Jules Furthman d Josef Von Sternberg ph Lee Garmes m W. Franke Harling ad Hans Dreier

Marlene Dietrich, Clive Brook, Warner Oland, Anna May Wong, Eugene Pallette, Lawrence Grant, Louise Closser Hale, Gustav Von Seyffertitz

LILY (Marlene Dietrich): 'It took more than one man to change my name to Shanghai Lily.'

'Good programme picture bolstered by the Dietrich name . . . Excellent camerawork overcomes really hoke melodramatic story.'—*Variety*
'A limited number of characters, all meticulously etched, highly atmospheric sets and innumerable striking photographic compositions.'—*Curtis Harrington, 1964*

AA: Lee Garmes
AAN: best picture; Josef Von Sternberg

The Shanghai Gesture*
US 1941 90m bw
Arnold Pressburger (Albert de Courville)

The proprietress of a Shanghai gambling casino taunts her ex-husband by showing him his daughter in a state of degradation; but he proves that the girl is her daughter also.
An ancient theatrical shocker was completely bowdlerized and chopped into nonsense for the screen; but the director's hand showed in the handling of the vast casino set.

w Josef Von Sternberg, Geza Herczeg, Karl Vollmoeller, Jules Furthman, *play* John Colton d Josef Von Sternberg ph Paul Ivano m Richard Hageman ad Boris Leven

Ona Munson, Victor Mature, Walter Huston, Gene Tierney, Albert Basserman, Phyllis Brooks, Maria Ouspenskaya, Eric Blore, Ivan Lebedeff, Mike Mazurki
'The effect of a descent into a maelstrom of iniquity.'—*Curtis Harrington, 1962*
'In spite of all the changes necessitated by the Hays Office, seldom have decadence and sexual depravity been better suggested on the screen.'—*Richard Roud, 1966*
'Hilariously, awesomely terrible.'—*New Yorker, 1977*

AAN: Richard Hageman

Shanghai Madness
US 1933 63m bw

A naval officer is cashiered in Shanghai and gets mixed up with Communists. Weakish melodrama which goes the long way round to

SHALL WE DANCE? Astaire and Rogers at the very top of their box office form, though script and songs had been better.

a happy ending. Spencer Tracy, Fay Wray, Ralph Morgan, Eugene Pallette, Herbert Mundin. Written by Frederick Hazlitt Brennan, Austin Parker, Gordon Wellesley; directed by John G. Blystone; for Fox. 'Okay generally but in big spots will need stage support.'—*Variety*

Shark

US / Mexico 1969   88m   Eastmancolor
Heritage / Cinematografica Calderon

A gunrunner in the Sudan becomes involved with unscrupulous divers after wrecks.
Tepid adventure yarn allegedly damaged by recutting but showing very little sign of original talent.

w Samuel Fuller, John Kingsbridge, *novel* His Bones Are Coral by Victor Canning d Samuel Fuller ph Raul Martinez Solares m Rafael Moroyoqui

Burt Reynolds, Arthur Kennedy, Barry Sullivan, Silvia Pinal, Enrique Lucero

The Sharkfighters

US 1956   72m   Technicolor
Cinemascope
(UA) Formosa (Samuel Goldwyn Jnr)

To save the lives of fliers forced down into the sea, navy scientists experiment with a shark repellent.
Straightforward semi-documentary with suspenseful action sequences.

w Lawrence Roman, John Robinson d Jerry Hopper ph Lee Garmes m Jerome Moross

Victor Mature, Karen Steele, James Olson, Claude Akins

Shark's Treasure*

US 1974   95m   De Luxe
UA / Symbol (Cornel Wilde)

Treasure hunters seek buried gold in the Caribbean where sharks abound.
Fairly thrilling action hokum.

wd Cornel Wilde ph Jack Atcheler, Al Giddings
m Robert O. Ragland

Cornel Wilde, Yaphet Kotto, John Neilson, David Canary, Cliff Osmond
'Wilde maintains his reputation for making the most likeable bad movies around.'—*Tom Milne*

Sharky's Machine

US 1981   120m   Technicolor
Warner / Orion / Deliverance (Hank Moonjean)

A vice squad policeman builds up a new team.
Exceptionally violent cop thriller on the lines of *Dirty Harry*

w Gerald Di Pego, *novel* William Diehl d Burt Reynolds ph William A. Fraker md Al Capps

Burt Reynolds, Vittorio Gassman, Brian Keith, Charles Durning, Earl Holliman, Bernie Casey, Henry Silva

Sharpshooters

US 1938   63m   bw

Adventures of a newsreel cameraman who saves a young prince from kidnapping. Serial-like action and comedy very palatably blended: the first of a short series. Brian Donlevy, Lynn Bari, Wally Vernon, John King, Douglass Dumbrille, C. Henry Gordon, Sidney Blackmer. Written by Robert Ellis, Helen Logan; directed by James Tinling; for TCF . 'A standard programmer to entertain, and a natural for the juve trade.'—*Variety*

She*

US 1935   89m   bw
RKO (Merian C. Cooper)

Ancient papers lead a Cambridge professor and his friends to the lost city where dwells a queen who cannot die—until she falls in love. The producers have the right spirit for this Victorian fantasy, but tried too hard to emulate the mood of their own *King Kong*, and it was a mistake to transfer the setting from Africa to the Arctic. One for connoisseurs, though.

w Ruth Rose, Dudley Nichols, *novel* H. Rider Haggard d Irving Pichel, Lansing G. Holden ph J. Roy Hunt m Alfred Newman

Randolph Scott, Nigel Bruce, Helen Gahagan
'Beautiful production, but story dubious for discriminating adults.'—*Variety*
'To an unrepentant Haggard fan it does sometimes seem to catch the thrill as well as the childishness of his invention.'—*Graham Greene*
'The stagey décor of Kor is in the art deco style of Radio City Music Hall, and you keep expecting the Rockettes to turn up.'—*Pauline Kael, 70s*

She

GB 1965   105m   Technicolor
Hammerscope
ABP / Hammer (Aida Young)

Flat, uninventive and tedious remake which reverts to Africa but does nothing else right; it ignores the essential Cambridge prologue and ignores all suggestions of fantasy.

w David T. Chantler d Robert Day ph Harry Waxman m James Bernard

Peter Cushing, Ursula Andress, Christopher Lee, John Richardson, Bernard Cribbins, André Morell, Rosenda Monteros

She Couldn't Say No

US 1952   89m   bw
RKO (Robert Sparks)
GB title: *Beautiful But Dangerous*

An heiress returns to the town of her childhood to distribute anonymous gifts to those who had helped her.
Moderate Capraesque comedy which doesn't quite come off.

w D. D. Beauchamp, William Bowers, Richard Flournoy d Lloyd Bacon ph Harold J. Wild m Roy Webb

Jean Simmons, Robert Mitchum, Arthur Hunnicutt, Edgar Buchanan, Wallace Ford, Raymond Walburn

She Couldn't Take It*

US 1935   89m   bw
Columbia (B. P. Schulberg)

A rich old reprobate meets a gangster in prison and puts him in charge of his rebellious family.
Little-known crazy comedy with touches of melodrama; not a success, but with interesting elements.

w Gene Towne, Oliver H. P. Garrett, *story* Graham Baker d Tay Garnett ph Leon Shamroy

George Raft, Joan Bennett, Walter Connelly, Billie Burke, Lloyd Nolan, Wallace Ford, Alan Mowbray, Donald Meek

She Didn't Say No!

GB 1958   97m   Technicolor
ABP (Sergei Nolbandov)

A young Irish widow has five illegitimate children, each by a different father.
Coyly daring comedy full of stage Oirishisms and obvious jokes, a few of which work.

w T. J. Morison, Una Troy, from her novel We Are Seven d Cyril Frankel ph Gilbert Taylor m Tristam Cary

Eileen Herlie, Jack MacGowran, Perlita Neilson, Niall MacGinnis, Ian Bannen

She Done Him Wrong***

US 1933   68m   bw
Paramount (William Le Baron)

A lady saloon keeper of the Gay Nineties falls for the undercover cop who is after her.
As near undiluted Mae West as Hollywood ever came: fast, funny, melodramatic and pretty sexy; also a very atmospheric and well-made movie.

w Mae West, from her play Diamond Lil (with help on the scenario from Harry Thew, John Bright) d Lowell Sherman ph Charles Lang songs Ralph Rainger

Mae West, Cary Grant, Owen Moore, Gilbert Roland, Noah Beery, David Landau, Rafaela Ottiano, Rochelle Hudson, Dewey Robinson
'Only alternative to a strong drawing cast, nowadays if a picture wants business, is strong entertainment. This one has neither.'—*Variety*

AAN: best picture

She Gets Her Man*

US 1945   73m   bw
Universal (Warren Wilson)

A country girl in New York tracks down a blowgun murderer.
Disarming mystery farce which tries every slapstick situation known to gag writers, and gets away with it.

w Warren Wilson, Clyde Bruckman d Erle C. Kenton ph Jerry Ash

Joan Davis, William Gargan, Leon Errol, Milburn Stone, Russell Hicks

She Knew All the Answers

US 1935   84m   bw
Columbia (Charles R. Rogers)

A Wall Street tycoon forbids his son to marry a chorine and falls for her himself.

SHANE.   Jean Arthur, Van Heflin and Alan Ladd face the rigours of the pioneer west.

Thin romantic comedy with a generally uneasy cast.

w Harry Segall, Kenneth Earl, Curtis Kenyon d Richard Wallace ph Henry Freulich md Morris Stoloff

Franchot Tone, Joan Bennett, John Hubbard, Eve Arden, William Tracy, Pierre Watkin, Thurston Hall

She Learned about Sailors
US 1934   82m   bw
For complex reasons a night-club singer in Shanghai goes through a form of marriage with a sailor, and afterwards falls in love with him. Overplotted comedy which becomes tedious after a while. Alice Faye, Lew Ayres,

Harry Green, Frank Mitchell, Jack Durant. Written by William Conselman and Henry Johnson; directed by George Marshall; for John Stone / Fox. 'No wow, but it won't bore. Besides, it's clean (MPPDA certificate ensures that, via the lead title) and it has sufficient romance to take care of the heart interest.'— Variety

'The hi-de-hi of higher education!'
She Loves Me Not*
US 1934   85m   bw
Paramount (Benjamin Glazer)
A showgirl murder witness takes refuge in a men's college.

Larky musical farce later remade as True to the Army and How to be Very Very Popular; this first version is perhaps the most nearly amusing.

w Ben Glazer, novel Edward Hope, play Howard Lindsay d Elliott Nugent ph Charles Lang songs various

Bing Crosby, Miriam Hopkins, Kitty Carlisle, Edward Nugent, Lynne Overman, Henry Stephenson, Warren Hymer, George Barbier

AAN: song 'Love in Bloom'

She Married an Artist
US 1938   78m   bw
A wife becomes jealous of her husband's models. Very mild romantic comedy. John

Boles, Francis Drake, Albert Dekker. Written by Avery Strakosch, Delmer Daves and Gladys Lehman; directed by Marion Gering; for Columbia.

She Married Her Boss

US 1935 90m bw

A secretary marries her boss and finds herself taken for granted. Pleasant but rather thin romantic comedy with amiable stars.
Claudette Colbert, Melvyn Douglas, Raymond Walburn, Edith Fellows, Jean Dixon, Katherine Alexander. Written by Sidney Buchman; directed by Gregory La Cava; for Columbia.

She Shall Have Murder

GB 1950 90m bw

A law clerk helps to solve the murder of an elderly client. Old-fashioned light comedy whodunnit, the equivalent of reading a Crime Club thriller. Rosamund John, Derrick de Marney, Mary Jerrold, Felix Aylmer, Joyce Heron, Beatrice Varley. Written by Allan Mackinnon, from a novel by Delano Ames; directed by Daniel Birt; for Concanen / IFD.

She Wolf of London

US 1946 61m bw

A girl thinks she must be the family werewolf.
Risibly inept semi-horror melodrama with a highly implausible solution and poor production. June Lockhart, Don Porter, Sara Haden, Lloyd Corrigan, Dennis Hoey, Martin Kosleck. Written by George Bricker; directed by Jean Yarbrough; for Universal. (GB title: *The Curse of the Allenbys*.)

She Wore a Yellow Ribbon**

US 1949 103m Technicolor
RKO / Argosy (John Ford, Meridan C. Cooper)

Problems of a cavalry officer about to retire.
Fragmentary but very enjoyable western with all Ford ingredients served piping hot.
w Frank Nugent, Laurence Stallings, *story* James Warner Bellah *d* John Ford
ph Winton C. Hoch *m* Richard Hageman
John Wayne, Joanne Dru, John Agar, Ben Johnson, Harry Carey Jnr, Victor McLaglen, Mildred Natwick, George O'Brien, Arthur Shields

AA: Winton C. Hoch

She Wouldn't Say Yes

US 1945 87m bw

A lady psychiatrist falls for the subject of an experiment. Star comedy vehicle which falls rather flat. Rosalind Russell, Lee Bowman, Charles Winninger, Adele Jergens. Written by Laslo Gorog, William Thiele, Virginia Van Upp, John Jacoby and Sarett Tobias; directed by Alexander Hall; for Columbia.

She Wrote the Book

US 1946 72m bw

A lady professor imagines herself to be the glamorous femme fatale heroine of a lurid

novel. Adventures of a female Walter Mitty; one of the star's better comedies. Joan Davis, Mischa Auer, Jack Oakie, Kirby Grant, John Litel, Gloria Stuart, Thurston Hall. Written by Warren Wilson and Oscar Brodney; directed by Charles Lamont; for Universal.

The Sheep Has Five Legs*

France 1954 96m bw
Raoul Ploquin
original title: *Le Mouton a Cinq Pattes*

A town seeking publicity tries to bring together the five quintuplet grandsons of its oldest inhabitant.
Mildly saucy star vehicle which was in fact most notable for introducing Fernandel to an international audience.
w Albert Valentin *d* Henri Verneuil
ph Armand Thirard *m* Georges Van Parys
Fernandel, Françoise Arnoul, Delmont, Paulette Dubost, Louis de Funès

AAN: original story

The Sheepman*

US 1958 91m Metrocolor
Cinemascope
MGM (Edmund Grainger)

A tough sheep farmer determines to settle in a cattle town.
Easy-going western with humorous moments.
w William Bowers, James Edward Grant
d George Marshall *ph* Robert Bronner
m Jeff Alexander
Glenn Ford, Shirley Maclaine, Leslie Nielsen, Mickey Shaughnessy, Edgar Buchanan

AAN: script

The Sheik*

US 1921 73m (24 fps) bw silent
Famous Players-Lasky / George Melford

An English heiress falls for a desert chieftain.
Archetypal romantic tosh which set the seal on Valentino's superstardom.
w Monte M. Katterjohn, *novel* E. M. Hull
d George Melford *ph* William Marshall
Rudolph Valentino, Agnes Ayres, Adolphe Menjou, Walter Long, Lucien Littlefield
'A photoplay of tempestuous love between a madcap English beauty and a bronzed Arab chief!'—*publicity*
† *Son of the Sheik*, released in 1926, was even more popular.

The Sheik Steps Out

US 1937 68m bw
Republic (Herman Schlom)

A modern sheik has a riotous time in the big city.
Uninventive spoof of the Valentino myth.
w Adele Buffington, Gordon Kahn *d* Irving Pichel *ph* Jack Marta *md* Alberto Columbo
Ramon Novarro, Lola Lane, Gene Lockhart, Kathleen Burke, Stanley Fields
'Novarro in a comeback start. An action picture of the desert for the lower half of the duals.'—*Variety*

Shenandoah**

US 1965 105m Technicolor
Universal (Robert Arthur)

How the American Civil War affected the lives of a Virginia family.
Surprisingly hard-centred and moving semi-western for the family; excellent performances and well-controlled mood.
w James Lee Barrett *d* Andrew V. McLaglen
ph William Clothier *m* Frank Skinner
md Joseph Gershenson
James Stewart, Rosemary Forsyth, Doug McClure, Glenn Corbett, Katharine Ross, Philip Alford

The Sheriff of Fractured Jaw

GB 1958 103m Eastmancolor
Cinemascope
TCF / Daniel M. Angel

A London gunsmith in the old west accidentally becomes a hero.
Tame, predictable comedy with a clear lack of invention.
w Arthur Dales *d* Raoul Walsh *ph* Otto Heller
m Robert Farnon
Kenneth More, Jayne Mansfield, Robert Morley, Ronald Squire, David Horne, Henry Hull, Eynon Evans, Bruce Cabot, William Campbell

Sherlock Holmes

The innumerable Sherlock Holmes films are noted in *Filmgoer's Companion*, and in this volume the appropriate films are listed under their own titles including the modernized dozen made in the forties by Universal, starring Basil Rathbone as Holmes and Nigel Bruce as Watson. These followed on from Fox's two period pieces, THE HOUND OF THE BASKERVILLES and THE ADVENTURES OF SHERLOCK HOLMES (qv). The series started and ended somewhat lamely but several of the episodes remain highly enjoyable, for performances and dialogue rather than plot or pacing. All but the first were directed by Roy William Neill.
1942: SHERLOCK HOLMES AND THE VOICE OF TERROR (*d* John Rawlins *with* Reginald Denny, Thomas Gomez);
SHERLOCK HOLMES AND THE SECRET WEAPON* (with Lionel Atwill as Moriarty)
1943: SHERLOCK HOLMES IN WASHINGTON* (*with* Henry Daniell, George Zucco); SHERLOCK HOLMES FACES DEATH** (*with* Halliwell Hobbes, Dennis Hoey)
1944: SHERLOCK HOLMES AND THE SPIDER WOMAN** (*with* Gale Sondergaard, Dennis Hoey); THE SCARLET CLAW** (*with* Gerald Hamer); THE PEARL OF DEATH** (*with* Miles Mander, Dennis Hoey, Rondo Hatton)
1945: THE HOUSE OF FEAR* (*with* Aubrey Mather, Dennis Hoey); THE WOMAN IN GREEN* (*with* Henry Daniell as Moriarty); PURSUIT TO ALGIERS (with Martin Kosleck)

1946: TERROR BY NIGHT* (with Alan Mowbray), DRESSED TO KILL (GB title: SHERLOCK HOLMES AND THE SECRET CODE; with Patricia Morison)

Sherlock Holmes*
US 1932 68m bw
Fox

Moriarty brings Chicago gangsters into London.
Interesting but rather unsatisfactory Holmes adventure.

w Bertram Milhauser d William K. Howard ph George Barnes

Clive Brook, Reginald Owen, Ernest Torrence, Miriam Jordan, Alan Mowbray, Herbert Mundin

'Old-fashioned artificial stage play with modern trimmings that only muddle it. The interpolated modern gangster angle will mystify the mugs who go for underworld and it's a late day to offer the Conan Doyle thing straight to educated clienteles.'—Variety

Sherlock Holmes and the Secret Weapon*
US 1942 68m bw
Universal (Howard Benedict)

Sherlock Holmes saves a stolen bombsight from Nazi agents.
Slightly stiff modernized Holmes story with amusing ingredients.

w Edward T. Lowe, W. Scott Darling, Edmund L. Hartmann, vaguely based on The Dancing Men by Sir Arthur Conan Doyle d Roy William Neill ph Les White m Frank Skinner

Basil Rathbone, Nigel Bruce, Lionel Atwill (as Moriarty), Dennis Hoey, Karen Verne, William Post Jnr, Mary Gordon

Sherlock Holmes and the Voice of Terror
US 1942 65m bw
Universal (Howard Benedict)

Sherlock Holmes unmasks a Lord Haw Haw in the war cabinet.
Fairly risible first entry in the modernized series, with a Hollywood view of London and a singular haircut for the star.

w Lynn Riggs, from His Last Bow by Sir Arthur Conan Doyle d John Rawlins ph Woody Bredell m Frank Skinner

Basil Rathbone, Nigel Bruce, Hillary Brooke, Reginald Denny, Evelyn Ankers, Montagu Love, Thomas Gomez, Mary Gordon

Sherlock Holmes Faces Death**
US 1943 68m bw
Universal (Roy William Neill)

Weird murders occur in a convalescent home for retired officers.
One of the better entries in this rather likeable modernized series; fairly close to the original story except that the events don't make a lot of sense.

w Bertram Millhauser, from The Musgrave Ritual by Sir Arthur Conan Doyle d Roy William Neill ph Charles Van Enger m Hans Salter

Basil Rathbone, Nigel Bruce, Hillary Brooke, Milburn Stone, Halliwell Hobbes, Arthur Margetson, Dennis Hoey, Gavin Muir, Frederic Worlock, Olaf Hytten, Gerald Hamer, Mary Gordon, Vernon Downing

Sherlock Holmes in Washington*
US 1943 70m bw
Universal (Howard Benedict)

Sherlock Holmes flies west and prevents Nazi spies from grabbing a microfilmed document concealed in a match folder.
Moderate adventure in the modernized series, with a good beginning and end but a sag in the middle.

w Bertram Millhauser, Lynn Riggs d Roy William Neill ph Lester White m Frank Skinner

Basil Rathbone, Nigel Bruce, Henry Daniell, George Zucco, Marjorie Lord, John Archer, Gavin Muir

Sherlock Junior**
US 1924 45m (24 fps) bw silent
Metro / Buster Keaton (Joseph M. Schenck)

A film projectionist, unjustly accused of stealing a watch, has dreams of being a great detective.
Fast-moving, gag-filled comedy which ranks among its star's best.

w Clyde Bruckman, Jean Haves, Joseph Mitchell d, ed Buster Keaton ph Elgin Lessley, Bryon Houck

Buster Keaton, Kathryn McGuire, Ward Crane, Joseph Keaton

'She shakes the student body like it's never been shook before!'

She's Working Her Way through College
US 1952 101m Technicolor
Warner (William Jacobs)

A burlesque queen goes to college and brings out the beast in an English professor.
Limp and vulgar musical remake of a well-liked play and film; just about gets by as a lowbrow timekiller.

w Peter Milne, play The Male Animal by James Thurber, Elliott Nugent d Bruce Humberstone ph Wilfrid Cline md Ray Heindorf ch Le Roy Prinz songs Sammy Cahn, Vernon Duke

Virginia Mayo, Ronald Reagan, Don Defore, Gene Nelson, Phyllis Thaxter, Patrice Wymore

† Sequel 1953: She's Back on Broadway.

Shine on Harvest Moon*
US 1944 112m bw (Technicolor sequence)
Warner (William Jacobs)

The life and times of vaudeville singer Nora Bayes.
Standard ragtime biopic, very adequately made.

w Sam Hellman, Richard Weil, Francis Swan, James Kern d David Butler ph Arthur Edeson md Heinz Roemheld

Ann Sheridan, Dennis Morgan, Jack Carson, Irene Manning, S. Z. Sakall, Marie Wilson, Robert Shayne

The Shining*
GB 1980 119m (general release; cut from première length of 146m) colour
Warner / Stanley Kubrick

Under the influence of a desolate hotel where murders had occurred, a caretaker goes berserk and threatens his family.
Uninteresting ghost story sparked by meticulous detail and sets but finally vitiated by overlength and an absurdly over-the-top star performance.

w Stanley Kubrick, Diane Johnson novel Stephen King d Stanley Kubrick ph John Alcott m Bela Bartok (on record) pd Roy Walker

Jack Nicholson, Shelley Duvall, Danny Lloyd, Barry Nelson, Scatman Crothers, Philip Stone

'The truly amazing question is why a director of Kubrick's stature would spend his time and effort on a novel that he changes so much it's barely recognizable, taking away whatever originality it possessed while emphasizing its banality. The answer presumably is that Kubrick was looking for a "commercial" property he could impose his own vision on, and Warners, not having learned its lesson with Barry Lyndon, was silly enough to let him do it.'—Variety

'A grandiose horror tale which consumes itself, snake-like, swallowing its own tail in a series of narrowing spirals.'—Sunday Times

● Video: Warner

The Shining Hour
US 1938 76m bw

A nightclub dancer marries a gentleman farmer, but has trouble with his family.
Overcast melodrama with insufficient basic interest in the characters. Joan Crawford, Melvyn Douglas, Margaret Sullavan, Robert Young, Fay Bainter, Allyn Joslyn, Hattie McDaniel. Written by Ogden Nash and Jane Murfin, from the play by Keith Winter; directed by Frank Borzage; for MGM.
'A confused jumble of cross-purpose motivations and situations that fail entirely to arouse interest.'—Variety

Shining Victory
US 1941 80m bw
Warner (Robert Lord)

A psychiatrist is torn between love and duty.
Adequate romantic programmer.

w Howard Koch, Ann Froelick, play Jupiter Laughs by A. J. Cronin d Irving Rapper ph James Wong Howe m Max Steiner

James Stephenson, Geraldine Fitzgerald, Donald Crisp, Barbara O'Neil, Montagu Love, Sig Rumann

Ship Ahoy
US 1942   95m   bw
MGM (Jack Cummings)

On a trip to Puerto Rico, a tap dancer is enlisted as a spy.
Tepid musi-comedy.

w Harry Clark   d Eddie Buzzell   ph Leonard Smith   md George Stoll   ad Merrill Pye

Eleanor Powell, Red Skelton, Bert Lahr, Virginia O'Brien, William Post Jnr, James Cross

Ship of Fools°°°
US 1965   150m   bw
Columbia / Stanley Kramer

In 1933 a German liner leaves Vera Cruz for Bremerhaven with a mixed bag of passengers. Ambitious, serious, quite fascinating slice-of-life shipboard multi-melodrama. Capable mounting, memorable performances and a bravura finale erase memories of padding and symbolic pretensions.

w Abby Mann, novel Katherine Anne Porter d Stanley Kramer ph Ernest Laszlo m Ernest Gold

Vivien Leigh, Simone Signoret, Oskar Werner, Heinz Ruhmann, Jose Ferrer, Lee Marvin, Elizabeth Ashley, Michael Dunn, George Segal, Jose Greco, Charles Korvin, Alf Kjellin, Werner Klemperer, John Wengraf, Lilia Skala, Karen Verne

GLOCKEN (Michael Dunn): 'My name is Karl Glocken, and this is a ship of fools. I'm a fool. You'll meet more fools as we go along. This tub is packed with them. Emancipated ladies and ballplayers. Lovers. Dog lovers. Ladies of joy. Tolerant Jews, Dwarfs. All kinds. And who knows—if you look closely enough, you may even find yourself on board!'

'When you're not being hit over the head with the symbolism, you're being punched in the stomach by would-be inventive camera work while the music score unremittingly fills your nostrils with acrid exhalations.'—John Simon

AA: Ernest Laszlo
AAN: best picture; Abby Mann; Simone Signoret; Oskar Werner; Michael Dunn

The Ship That Died of Shame
GB 1955   91m   bw
Ealing (Michael Relph, Basil Dearden)

The wartime crew of a motor gunboat buy the vessel and go into postwar business as smugglers.
Thin and rather obvious melodramatic fable.

w John Whiting, Michael Relph, Basil Dearden, novel Nicholas Monsarrat d Michael Relph, Basil Dearden ph Gordon Dines m William Alwyn

Richard Attenborough, George Baker, Bill Owen, Virginia McKenna, Roland Culver, Bernard Lee, Ralph Truman, John Chandos
'A sentimental fantasy tacked on to a basically conventional thriller.'—Penelope Houston

Shipbuilders
GB 1943   89m   bw

A cavalcade of the problems of a Clydeside tycoon in the thirties. Plodding propaganda piece ending with masters and unions working for Britain. Clive Brook, Morland Graham, Finlay Currie, Maudie Edwards. Written by Gordon Wellesley, Stephen Potter and Reginald Pound; directed by John Baxter; for British National.

Shipmates Forever
US 1935   124m   bw

An admiral's son disappoints his dad by preferring song and dance to the navy. Very stretched light musical without any overpowering talents. Dick Powell, Ruby Keeler, Lewis Stone, Ross Alexander, Eddie Acuff, Dick Foran. Written by Delmer Daves; directed by Frank Borzage; for Warner.

Ships with Wings°
GB 1941   103m   bw
Ealing (S. C. Balcon)

Aircraft carriers prepare for World War II.
Historically interesting, dramatically insubstantial flagwaver.

w Sergei Nolbandov, Patrick Kirwan, Austin Melford, Diana Morgan d Sergei Nolbandov ph Max Greene, Eric Cross, Roy Kellino m Geoffrey Wright

John Clements, Leslie Banks, Jane Baxter, Ann Todd, Basil Sydney, Edward Chapman, Hugh Williams, Frank Pettingell, Michael Wilding

Shipyard Sally
GB 1939   79m   bw

A barmaid persuades a shipyard owner to reopen. Sub-Ealing style comedy with music which manages to bring in management and man as well as waving a flag or two. Gracie Fields, Sydney Howard, Morton Selten, Norma Varden, Oliver Wakefield. Written by Karl Tunberg and Don Ettlinger; directed by Monty Banks; for TCF.

The Shiralee°
GB 1957   99m   bw
Ealing (Jack Rix)

An Australian swagman leaves his wife and takes to the road with his small daughter.
Episodic character comedy-drama throwing a fairly sharp light on the Australian scene.

w Neil Paterson, Leslie Norman, novel D'Arcy Niland d Leslie Norman ph Paul Beeson m John Addison

Peter Finch, Dana Wilson, Elizabeth Sellars, George Rose, Russell Napier, Nial MacGinnis, Tessie O'Shea

Shock
US 1946   70m   bw
TCF

A girl in a hotel sees a murder committed, and an elaborate plan is concocted to silence her.
Flat treatment ruins a good suspense situation.

w Eugene Ling d Alfred Werker ph Glen MacWilliams, Joe MacDonald m David Buttolph

Vincent Price, Lynn Bari, Frank Latimore, Annabel Shaw
'Extreme improbabilities and a general lack of finish.'—MFB

Shock Corridor
US 1963   101m   bw (colour sequence)
Leon Fromkess / Sam Firks (Samuel Fuller)

A journalist gets himself admitted to a mental asylum to solve the murder of an inmate. Sensational melodrama, a cinematic equivalent of the yellow press, and on that level quite lively.

wd Samuel Fuller ph Stanley Cortez m Paul Dunlap

Peter Breck, Constance Towers, Gene Evans, James Best, Hari Rhodes, Philip Ahn

Shock Treatment
US 1964   94m   bw
Warner (Aaron Rosenberg)

Murders are committed in a mental institution.
Tasteless thriller, not even very arresting as a yarn.

w Sidney Boehm d Denis Sanders ph Sam Leavitt m Jerry Goldsmith

Lauren Bacall, Roddy MacDowall, Carol Lynley, Ossie Davis, Stuart Whitman, Douglass Dumbrille

The Shocking Miss Pilgrim
US 1946   85m   Technicolor
TCF (William Perlberg)

In 1894 Boston, a lady typist (stenographer) fights for women's rights.
Period comedy with music; not nearly as sharp as it thinks it is.

wd George Seaton ph Leon Shamroy ad James Basevi, Boris Leven songs George and Ira Gershwin

Betty Grable, Dick Haymes, Anne Revere, Allyn Joslyn, Gene Lockhart, Elizabeth Patterson, Arthur Shields, Elizabeth Risdon

Shockproof
US 1949   79m   bw
Columbia (S. Sylvan Simon)

A parole officer falls in love with his protégée and becomes corrupted.
Predictable programmer with a few pleasant touches.

w Helen Deutsch, Samuel Fuller d Douglas Sirk ph Charles Lawton Jnr m George Duning

Cornel Wilde, Patricia Knight, John Baragrey, Esther Minciotti, Howard St John, Russell Collins

The Shoes of the Fisherman°°
US 1968   157m   Metrocolor   Panavision
MGM (George Englund)

After twenty years as a political prisoner, a Russian bishop becomes Pope.
Predigested but heavy-going picturization of a bestseller; big budget, big stars, big hopes. In

fact a commercial dud, with plenty of superficial interest but more dramatic contrivance than religious feeling.

w John Patrick, James Kennaway, *novel* Morris West *d* Michael Anderson *ph* Erwin Hiller *m* Alex North *ad* Edward Carfagno, George W. Davis

Anthony Quinn, David Janssen, Laurence Olivier, Oskar Werner, John Gielgud, Barbara Jefford, Leo McKern, Vittorio de Sica, Clive Revill, Paul Rogers
'A splendidly decorated curate's egg.'—*MFB*

AAN: Alex North

Shoeshine**
Italy 1946 90m bw
Paolo W. Tamburella
original title: *Sciuscià*

In Nazi-occupied Rome two shoeshine boys become involved in black marketeering, with tragic consequences.
Not especially rewarding to watch now, this was a key film in the development of Italian neo-realism.

w Cesare Zavattini, Sergio Amidei, Adolfe Franci, C. G. Viola *d* Vittorio de Sica *ph* Anchise Brizzi, Elio Paccara

Franco Interlenghi, Rinaldo Smordoni
'It is filled in every scene with an awareness of the painful complexity of even simple evil.'—*James Agee*

AAN: script

Shoot the Moon*
US 1981 123m Metrocolor
MGM (Alan Marshall)

The family is affected when well-heeled parents decide to split up.
A halfway decent actors' piece which doesn't really justify its time or leave affectionate memories behind. In essence it adds nothing except noise to what was being done in this field forty years ago.

w Bo Goldman *d* Alan Parker *ph* Michael Seresin *m* no credit *pd* Geoffrey Kirkland

Albert Finney, Diane Keaton, Karen Allen, Peter Weller, Dana Hill, Leora Dana
'Despite their superficial sophistication, these are immature creatures playing grown-up games which would be thought childish in *Bugsy Malone*.'—*Sunday Times*

● Video: MGM / UA

Shoot the Pianist*
France 1960 80m bw Dyaliscope
Films de la Pléiade (Pierre Braunberger)
original title: *Tirez sur le Pianiste*

A bar-room piano player becomes involved with gangsters and his girl friend is killed.
Fair copy of an American *film noir*, not especially interesting except for its sharp observation.

w Marcel Moussy, François Truffaut, *novel* Down There by David Goodis *d* François Truffaut *ph* Raoul Coutard *m* Jean Constantin, Georges Delerue

Charles Aznavour, Nicole Berger, Marie Dubois, Michèle Mercier, Albert Rémy
'Pictorially it is magnificent, revealing Truffaut's brilliant control over his images; emotionally, it is all a little jejeune.'—*John Gillett, MFB*

The Shooting
US 1966 82m De Luxe
Santa Clara (Jack Nicholson, Monte Hellman)

An ex-bounty hunter is trailed by a hired killer.
Simplistic semi-professional western which achieves some power despite poor technical quality and a deliberately obscure ending.

w Adrien Joyce *d* Monte Hellman *ph* Gregory Sandor *m* Richard Markowitz

Warren Oates, Will Hutchins, Jack Nicholson, Millie Perkins

Shooting Stars*
GB 1928 80m (24 fps) bw silent
British Instructional (H. Bruce Woolf)

The wife of a film star puts real bullets in a prop gun but her lover is killed by mistake.
Late silent drama with comedy touches: its main interest lies in its behind-the-scenes background and in the emergence of a new director.

w John Orton, Anthony Asquith *d* Anthony Asquith, A. V. Bramble

Annette Benson, Brian Aherne, Donald Calthrop, Wally Patch, Chili Bouchier

The Shootist**
US 1976 100m Technicolor
Panavision
Paramount / Frankovich-Self

In 1901, a dying ex-gunfighter arrives in a small town to set his affairs in order.
Impressive semi-western melodrama, very well written and acted all round; the kind of solidly entertaining and thoughtful movie one imagined they didn't make any more.

w Miles Hood Swarthout, Scott Hale, *novel* Glendon Swarthout *d* Don Siegel *ph* Bruce Surtees *m* Elmer Bernstein

John Wayne, Lauren Bacall, James Stewart, Ron Howard, Bill McKinney, Richard Boone, John Carradine, Scatman Crothers, Harry Morgan, Hugh O'Brian, Sheree North
'Just when it seemed that the western was an endangered species, due for extinction because it had repeated itself too many times, Wayne and Siegel have managed to validate it once more.'—*Arthur Knight*
'Watching this film is like taking a tour of Hollywood legends.'—*Frank Rich*

Shootout
US 1971 94m Technicolor
Universal (Hal B. Wallis)

After seven years in prison, a bank robber seeks out his betrayer.
Routine, flatly-handled revenge western.

w Marguerite Roberts, *novel* The Lone Cowboy by Will James *d* Henry Hathaway *ph* Earl Rath *m* Dave Grusin

Gregory Peck, Pat Quinn, Robert F. Lyons, Susan Tyrell, Jeff Corey, James Gregory, Rita Gam

Shootout at Medicine Bend
US 1957 87m bw

Three ex-soldiers clean up a corrupt community. Entertaining western programmer. Randolph Scott, James Craig, Angie Dickinson, James Garner, Gordon Jones. Written by John Tucker Battle and D. D. Beauchamp; directed by Richard Bare; for Warner.

The Shop around the Corner**
US 1940 97m bw
MGM (Ernst Lubitsch)

In a Budapest shop, the new floorwalker and a girl who dislikes him find they are pen pals.
Pleasant period romantic comedy which holds no surprises but is presented with great style.

w Samson Raphaelson, *play* Nikolaus Laszlo *d* Ernst Lubitsch *ph* William Daniels *m* Werner Heymann

James Stewart, Margaret Sullavan, *Frank Morgan*, Joseph Schildkraut, Sara Haden, *Felix Bressart*, William Tracy
'It's not pretentious but it's a beautiful job of picture-making, and the people who did it seem to have enjoyed doing it just as much as their audiences will enjoy seeing it.'—*James Shelley Hamilton*
'An agreeably bittersweet example of light entertainment.'—*Charles Higham, 1972*
'One of the most beautifully acted and paced romantic comedies ever made in this country.'—*New Yorker, 1978*
† Remade as *In The Good Old Summertime* (qv).

The Shop at Sly Corner
GB 1946 92m bw
Pennant (George King)
US title: *Code of Scotland Yard*

An antique dealer who is also a fence kills a blackmailer in order to shield his daughter.
Competent but stagey version of a West End success, giving full rein to a bravura star performance.

w Katherine Strueby, *play* Edward Percy *d* George King *ph* Hone Glendinning *m* George Melachrino

Oscar Homolka, Muriel Pavlow, Derek Farr, Manning Whiley, Kenneth Griffith, Kathleen Harrison, Garry Marsh, Irene Handl

The Shop on Main Street*
Czechoslovakia 1965 128m bw
Ceskoslovensky Film
original title: *Obchod na Korze*; aka: *The Shop on the High Street*

During the German invasion of Czechoslovakia, a well-meaning carpenter tries to shield an old Jewish lady, but his own rough treatment kills her.

A rather obvious sentimental fable, developed at too great length, but with bravura acting.

w Ladislav Grosman, Jan Kadar, Einar Klos d Jan Kadar, Einar Klos ph Vladimir Novotny m Zdenek Liska

Ida Kaminska, Jozef Kroner, Hana Slivkova, Martin Holly

'Overlong, derivative, ploddingly directed.'—John Simon

AA: best foreign film
AAN: Ida Kaminska

Shopworn Angel•
US 1928 90m approx bw part-talkie
Paramount (Louis D. Lighton)

A showgirl meets a naïve young soldier off to war and forsakes her man about town.
Hard-boiled, soft-centred romantic drama remade as below and later as That Kind of Woman (qv).

w Howard Estabrook, Albert Shelby Le Vino, play Private Pettigrew's Girl by Dana Burnet d Richard Wallace ph Charles Lang

Nancy Carroll, Gary Cooper, Paul Lukas, Emmett King

Shopworn Angel•
US 1938 85m bw
MGM (Joseph L. Mankiewicz)

Smooth, close remake of the above.

w Waldo Salt d H. C. Potter ph Joseph Ruttenberg m Edward Ward montage Slavko Vorkapitch

Margaret Sullavan, James Stewart, Walter Pidgeon, Hattie McDaniel, Sam Levene

Short Cut to Hell
US 1957 89m bw Vistavision
Paramount (A. C. Lyles)

A racketeer hires a gunman to commit a double murder, then doublecrosses him.
Rough and ready remake of This Gun for Hire (qv), less arresting than the original.

w Ted Berkeman, Raphael Blau, W. R. Burnett, novel A Gun for Sale by Graham Greene d James Cagney ph Haskell Boggs md Irvin Talbot

Robert Ivers, Georgeann Johnson, William Bishop, Murvyn Vye

A Shot in the Dark•
US 1964 101m De Luxe Panavision
UA / Mirisch / Geoffrey (Blake Edwards)

A woman is accused of shooting her lover; accident-prone Inspector Clouseau investigates.
Further adventures of the oafish, Tatiesque clodhopper from The Pink Panther; mildly funny for those in the mood for pratfalls.

w Blake Edwards, William Peter Blatty d Blake Edwards ph Christopher Challis m Henry Mancini pd Michael Stringer

Peter Sellers, Elke Sommer, George Sanders, Herbert Lom, Tracy Reed, Graham Stark

Shotgun
US 1954 81m Technicolor print

A deputy marshal avenges the death of his boss. Rather violent western with a few

unusual angles. Sterling Hayden, Zachary Scott, Yvonne de Carlo, Guy Prescott, Robert Wilke. Written by Clark E. Reynolds and Rory Calhoun; directed by Lesley Selander; for Allied Artists.

Should Ladies Behave?
US 1933 90m bw

A young girl falls for her aunt's lover. Brittle comedy of manners which transferred poorly from Broadway with a star well over the top. Alice Brady, Lionel Barrymore, Conway Tearle, Katherine Alexander, Halliwell Hobbes, Mary Carlisle. Written by Sam and Bella Spewack, from the play The Vinegar Tree by Paul Osborn; directed by Harry Beaumont; for MGM.

Should Married Men Go Home?
US 1928 20m bw silent

Tribulations on the golf course end in a mud-slinging contest. Goodish star slapstick, but the preliminary domestic scene is the funniest. Laurel and Hardy, Edgar Kennedy. Written by Leo McCarey, James Parrott and H. M. Walker, directed by d James Parrott; for Hal Roach.

Shoulder Arms•
US 1918 24m (24 fps) bw silent
Charles Chaplin / First National

A soldier in the trenches dreams of winning the war single-handedly.
A comedy which meant a great deal at the time of its release but now provides precious little to laugh at.

wd Charles Chaplin ph Rollie Totheroh

Charles Chaplin, Edna Purviance, Sydney Chaplin, Henry Bergman, Albert Austin

The Shout•
GB 1978 87m colour
Rank / Recorded Picture (Jeremy Thomas)

A man who may be mad claims that, like the old aborigine magicians, he can kill by shouting.
Curiously gripping but ultimately pointless fable, very well done to little purpose.

w Michael Austin, Jerzy Skolimovsky, story Robert Graves d Jerzy Skolimovsky ph Mike Molloy m Rupert Hine, Anthony Banks, Michael Rutherford

Alan Bates, Susannah York, John Hurt, Robert Stephens, Tim Curry

'Poorly acted, incoherent and unendurably loud.'—Pauline Kael, New Yorker

● Video: Rank

Shout at the Devil•
GB 1976 147m Technicolor
Panavision
Tonav (Michael Klinger)

In 1913 Zanzibar, a hard-drinking American and an old Etonian Englishman join forces to rout a brutal German commissioner who resents their poaching ivory in his territory. The main characters are respectively repellent, effete, and just plain nasty, but the action

scenes are vivid and the production is mainly notable as an expensive old-fashioned British film made at a time when there were few British films of any kind.

w Wilbur Smith, Stanley Price, Alastair Reid, novel Wilbur Smith d Peter Hunt ph Mike Reed m Maurice Jarre

Lee Marvin, Roger Moore, Barbara Parkins, René Kolldehoff, Ian Holm, Karl Michael Vogler, Maurice Denham, Jean Kent, Robert Lang, Murray Melvin, George Coulouris

'Elephantine plod through the action highlights of a best seller.'—Sight and Sound

● Video: Video Media

Show Business•••
US 1944 92m bw
RKO (Eddie Cantor)

The careers of four friends in vaudeville. Lively low-budget period musical which probably presents the best picture of what old-time vaudeville was really like; a lot of fun when the plot doesn't get in the way.

w Joseph Quillan, Dorothy Bennett d Edwin L. Marin ph Robert de Grasse, Vernon L. Walker m George Duning md Constantin Bakaleinikoff ch Nick Castle

Eddie Cantor, Joan Davis, George Murphy, Constance Moore, Don Douglas, Nancy Kelly

'Bits of archaic vaudeville which give off a moderately pleasant smell of peanuts and cigar smoke.'—James Agee

Show Girl in Hollywood
US 1930 77m bw (colour sequence)

Adventures of a New York girl on the west coast. Comedy with music; it seems content to wallow in supposed Hollywood glamour without contributing much by way of wit or storyline. Alice White, Jack Mulhall, Blanche Sweet, Ford Sterling, John Miljan, Herman Bing. Written by Harvey Thew, James A. Starr, J. P. McEvoy; directed by Mervyn Le Roy; for First National.

The Show Goes On
GB 1937 93m bw
ABFD (Basil Dean)

A mill girl becomes a star singer with the help of a dying composer.
An attempt to turn Gracie Fields into a serious performer, this was not much enjoyed by her fans.

w Austin Melford, Anthony Kimmins, E. G. Valentine d Basil Dean

Gracie Fields, Owen Nares, Edward Rigby, John Stuart, Horace Hodges, Amy Veness, Cyril Rutchard

The Show-Off
US 1934 80m bw

A girl's blundering new husband alienates his in-laws and nearly wrecks his brother-in-law's career. Surefire satirical comedy-drama from a Broadway staple, this low-budget item gave MGM a new star. Spencer Tracy, Madge Evans, Clara Blandick, Henry Wadsworth, Grant Mitchell, Lois Wilson. Written by

Herman Mankiewicz from the play by George Kelly; directed by Charles Riesner; for MGM. (NB: The play had been filmed twice in silent days by Paramount, and turned up again in 1946 as a Red Skelton vehicle.)

'In Vitaphone, it eclipses the sun in splendour!'

Show of Shows**
US 1929   128m   Technicolor
Warner (Darryl F. Zanuck)

A big musical show put on by Warner contract artists.
Primitive early talkie, of vital historical interest but mostly photographed from a seat in the stalls.

w / m various d John G. Adolfi ph Barney McGill

Frank Fay, H. B. Warner, Monte Blue, Lupino Lane, Ben Turpin, Chester Morris, Ted Lewis and his band, Georges Carpentier, Patsy Ruth Miller, Beatrice Lillie, Winnie Lightner, Irene Bordoni, Myrna Loy, Douglas Fairbanks Jnr, John Barrymore, Betty Compson
  'Colour photography of the crudest, most garish kind, the resulting impression being that a child of seven has been let loose with a shilling box of paints.'—James Agate

Show People
US 1928   80m at 24 fps   bw   silent

A naïve young actress makes it in Hollywood.
Historically important comedy with cameo appearances by many stars of the time. Marion Davies, William Haines. Written by Wanda Tuchock, Agnes Christine Johnson and Lawrence Stallings; directed by King Vidor; for MGM.

Show Them No Mercy*
US 1935   76m   bw
TCF (Raymond Griffith)
GB title: Tainted Money

Kidnappers are rounded up by G-men.
Lively crime thriller typical of its time.

w Kubec Glasmon, Henry Lehrman d George Marshall ph Bert Glennon m David Buttolph

Rochelle Hudson, Cesar Romero, Bruce Cabot, Edward Norris, Edward Brophy, Warren Hymer
  'Direct, surely dramatic, inevitable and full of terror.'—Otis Ferguson

Showboat***
US 1936   110m   bw
Universal (Carl Laemmle Jnr)

Lives and loves of the personnel on an old-time Mississippi showboat.
Great style and excellent performances mark this version, which still suffers from longueurs in the middle followed by the rapid passage of many years to provide a happy ending.

w Oscar Hammerstein II, from his book for the Broadway musical from Edna Ferber's novel d James Whale ph John Mescall m Jerome Kern ly Oscar Hammerstein II

Irene Dunne, Allan Jones, Helen Morgan, Paul Robeson, Charles Winninger, Hattie McDaniel, Donald Cook, Sammy White
  'For three quarters of its length good entertainment: sentimental, literary, but oddly appealing.'—Graham Greene
† A primitive talkie version of Showboat, now lost, was made in 1929.
†† Before Allan Jones was cast, Walter Pidgeon, Robert Taylor, John Boles, Fredric March and Nelson Eddy were all considered.

Showboat**
US 1951   108m   Technicolor
MGM (Arthur Freed)

Vigorous remake with good ensemble dancing; otherwise inferior to the 1936 version.

w John Lee Mahin d George Sidney ph Charles Rosher md Conrad Salinger, Adolph Deutsch ch Robert Alton

Kathryn Grayson, Howard Keel, Ava Gardner, William Warfield, Joe E. Brown, Robert Sterling, Marge and Gower Champion, Agnes Moorehead

AAN: Charles Rosher; Conrad Salinger, Adolph Deutsch
● Video: MGM / UA

The Showdown
US 1950   86m   bw

A trail boss seeks revenge on his brother's killer. Routine western with a touch of mystery. Wild Bill Elliott, Marie Windsor, Walter Brennan, Henry Morgan, William Ching, Rhys Williams. Written by Richard Wormser and Dan Gordon; directed by Darrell and Stuart McGowan; for Republic.

Showdown
US 1963   79m   Technicolor

Two wandering cowboys become involved with a criminal. Below-par western with little action and rather boring characters. Audie Murphy, Charles Drake, Harold J. Stone, Kathleen Crowley, Skip Homeier, L. Q. Jones, Strother Martin. Written by Bronson Howitzer; directed by R. G. Springsteen; for Universal.

Showdown
US 1972   99m   Technicolor   Todd-AO 35
Universal (George Seaton)

A sheriff finds that his old friend is leader of an outlaw gang.
Routine star western adequately done.

w Theodore Taylor d George Seaton ph Ernest Laszlo m David Shire

Rock Hudson, Dean Martin, Susan Clark, Donald Moffat, Don McLiam

Showdown at Abilene
US 1956   80m   Technicolor

A shellshocked Civil War veteran, returning home to find his girl married, reluctantly takes a job as sheriff. Fairly lively western remade eleven years later as Gunfight in Abilene. Jock Mahoney, David Janssen, Martha Hyer, Lyle Bettger, Grant Williams. Written by Bernie

Giler, from the novel Gun Shy by Clarence Upson Young; directed by Charles Haas; for Universal-International.

Showgirl in Hollywood
US 1930   80m   bw and Technicolor

A girl singer is spotted and trained for movie stardom. Naïve look behind the studio scenes, historically fascinating but dramatically dull. Alice White, Jack Mulhall, Blanche Sweet, Ford Sterling, John Miljan, Herman Bing. Written by Harvey Thew and James A. Starr, from the novel Hollywood Girl by J. P. McEvoy; directed by Mervyn LeRoy; for Warner.

The Shrike
US 1955   88m   bw
U-I (Aaron Rosenberg)

A brilliant theatre man has a nervous breakdown because his wife is a vindictive harpy.
Theatrical two-hander, aridly filmed, of little interest except to show that both stars are capable of sustained emotional acting.

w Ketti Frings, play Joseph Kramm d Jose Ferrer ph William Daniels m Frank Skinner titles Saul Bass

Jose Ferrer, June Allyson, Joy Page, Jacqueline de Wit, Kendall Clark
  'The film is unvaryingly paced, the result, one feels, of a respectable but far from invigorating honesty of purpose.'—MFB

The Shuttered Room
GB 1967   110m   Technicolor
Warner / Troy–Schenck (Philip Hazelton)

Returning to her childhood home on an island off the New England coast, a girl and her husband are subjected to terror and violence.
Stretched out suspenser which looks good and is carefully made but fails in its effort to combine the menace of teenage yobboes with that of the monster lurking upstairs.

w D. B. Ledrov, Nathaniel Tanchuck, story H. P. Lovecraft, August Derleth d David Greene ph Ken Hodges m Basil Kirchin

Gig Young, Carol Lynley, Flora Robson, Oliver Reed, William Devlin

Une Si Jolie Petite Plage*
France 1948   91m   bw
CICC (Emile Darbon)
aka: Such a Pretty Little Beach

A murderer returns to the small seaside town where he spent his childhood, befriends the maid at the hotel, and after a few days kills himself.
A melancholy anecdote which works both as a character study and pictorially.

w Jacques Sigurd d Yves Allégret ph Henri Alekan m Maurice Thiriet

Gérard Philipe, Jean Servais, Madeleine Robinson, Jane Marken, Carette
  'Shows fine craftsmanship and is beautifully sensitive to place and atmosphere.'—Gavin Lambert, MFB

Side Street
US 1950 83m bw
MGM (Sam Zimbalist)

A petty thief finds himself involved with big-time crooks.

Well-made but rather boring crime melodrama with an excellent car chase finale.

w Sidney Boehm d Anthony Mann
ph Joseph Ruttenberg m Lennie Hayton

Farley Granger, Cathy O'Donnell, James Craig, Paul Kelly, Jean Hagen, Edmon Ryan, Paul Harvey

Side Streets
US 1934 63m bw

A lady furrier takes pity on a sailor, and finally marries him, only to find that he has a past.

Strange, rather tedious, and quite unconvincing character drama. Aline MacMahon, Paul Kelly, Ann Dvorak, Helen Lowell, Henry O'Neill, Marjorie Gateson. Written by Manuel Seff from a story by Ann Garrick and Ethel Hill; directed by Alfred E. Green; for First National. (GB title: *A Woman in her Thirties*.)

Sidewalks of New York*
US 1931 73m bw
MGM (Lawrence Weingarten)

The playboy owner of some tenement apartments falls in love with the daughter of one of the tenants.

Interesting rather than wholly successful early sound comedy which marked the beginning of Keaton's decline; he was not allowed full control and the comedy scenes are thinly spaced.

w George Landy, Paul Gerard Smith, Eric Hatch, Robert E. Hopkins d Jules White, Zion Myers ph Leonard Smith

Buster Keaton, Anita Page, Cliff Edwards, Frank Rowan

The Siege at Red River
US 1954 86m Technicolor
TCF / Panoramic (Leonard Goldstein)

During the American Civil War a Confederate agent behind northern lines defeats a treacherous helper and escapes to the south.

Modest, generally watchable, and quite forgettable western.

w Sidney Boehm d Rudolph Maté
ph Edward Cronjager m Lionel Newman

Van Johnson, Joanne Dru, Richard Boone, Milburn Stone, Jeff Morrow, Craig Hill

The Siege of Pinchgut
GB 1959 104m bw
Ealing (Eric Williams)
US title: *Four Desperate Men*

Escaped convicts take over a small island in Sydney harbour.

Disappointingly obvious location melodrama with routine excitements.

w Harry Watt, Jon Cleary d Harry Watt
ph Gordon Dines m Kenneth V. Jones

Aldo Ray, Heather Sears, Neil McCallum, Victor Maddern, Carlo Justini

The Siege of Sidney Street*
GB 1960 92m bw Dyaliscope
Midcentury (Robert S. Baker, Monty Berman)

An account of the anarchists who infiltrated London in 1912.

Detailed but not dramatically absorbing historical reconstruction with unsatisfactory fictional trimmings.

w Jimmy Sangster, Alexander Baron d /
ph Robert S. Baker, Monty Berman
m Stanley Black

Peter Wyngarde, Donald Sinden, Nicole Berger, Kieron Moore, Leonard Sachs, Tutte Lemkow

The Siege of the Saxons
GB 1963 85m Technicolor
Columbia / Ameran (Jud Kinberg)

When King Arthur is ill, the Saxons plot his overthrow but are foiled by a handsome outlaw.

Comic strip adventure with action highlights borrowed from older and better films.

w John Kohn, Jud Kinberg d Nathan Juran
ph Wilkie Cooper, Jack Willis m Laurie Johnson

Ronald Lewis, Janette Scott, Ronald Howard, Mark Dignam, John Laurie, Richard Clarke, Jerome Willis

The Sign of Four
GB 1932 75m bw

Sherlock Holmes clears up a mystery including a hidden fortune, a secret pact, revenge from the east, and a pygmy who blows poison darts through a pipe. Very acceptable version of the famous story, previously filmed as a silent. Arthur Wontner, Ian Hunter, Isla Bevan, Miles Malleson, Herbert Lomas, Roy Emerton. Written by W. P. Lipscomb, from the novel by Sir Arthur Conan Doyle; directed by Rowland V. Lee and Graham Cutts; for ATP.

'A picture which will proudly lead all the
  entertainments the world has ever seen!'
'Like a shining light—the simple faith that
  was mightier than a pagan empire!'

The Sign of the Cross***
US 1932 123m bw
Paramount (Cecil B. de Mille)

In the days of Nero, a Roman officer is converted to Christianity.

A heavily theatrical play becomes one of de Mille's most impressive films, the genuine horror of the arena mingling with the debauched humour of the court. A wartime prologue added in 1943 prolongs the film without improving it.

w Waldemar Young, Sidney Buchman, *play* Wilson Barrett d Cecil B. de Mille ph Karl Struss m Rudolph Kopp

Fredric March, Elissa Landi, *Charles Laughton, Claudette Colbert*, Ian Keith, Harry Beresford, Arthur Hohl, Nat Pendleton
  'A beautiful film to watch . . . a triumph of popular art.'—*Charles Higham, 1972*

'However contemptible one may find de Mille's moralizing, it is impossible not to be impressed by *The Sign of the Cross*.'—*John Baxter, 1968*
  'De Mille's bang-them-on-the-head-with-wild-orgies-and-imperilled-virginity style is at its ripest.'—*New Yorker, 1976*
  'Preposterous, but the laughter dies on the lips.'—*NFT, 1974*
  'This slice of "history" has it all: Laughton's implicitly gay Nero fiddling away while an impressive miniature set burns, Colbert bathing up to her nipples in asses' milk, Christians and other unfortunates thrown to a fearsome menagerie, much suggestive slinking about in Mitchell Leisen's costumes, much general debauchery teetering between the sadistic and the erotic. Not for people with scruples.'—*Geoff Brown, Time Out, 1980*

AAN: Karl Struss

'Against his ruthless pagan lusts—the
  power of a woman's love!'
The Sign of the Pagan
US 1954 92m Technicolor
  Cinemascope
U-I (Albert J. Cohen)

Attila the Hun is defeated by the Romans.
Historic horse opera, rather cheaply done.

w Oscar Brodney, Barre Lyndon d Douglas Sirk ph Russell Metty m Frank Skinner, Hans Salter

Jeff Chandler, Jack Palance, Rita Gam, Ludmilla Tcherina, Jeff Morrow, George Dolenz, Eduard Franz, Alexander Scourby

The Sign of the Ram
US 1948 84m bw
Columbia (Irving Cummings Jnr)

A selfish invalid interferes in her family's affairs.

Stultifying melodrama in the wake of *Guest in the House*, devised for the unfortunate Miss Peters who was crippled after an accident. Poor production values don't help.

w Charles Bennett d John Sturges
ph Burnett Guffey m Hans Salter

Susan Peters, Alexander Knox, Peggy Ann Garner, May Whitty

Signpost to Murder
US 1964 74m bw Panavision
MGM / Martin (Lawrence Weingarten)

A convicted murderer escapes after ten years and a lonely wife promises to help him.

Tricksy mystery set in a never-never English village.

w Sally Benson, *play* Monte Doyle d George Englund ph Paul C. Vogel m Lyn Murray

Joanne Woodward, Stuart Whitman, Edward Mulhare, Alan Napier, Murray Matheson

The Silence*
Sweden 1963 96m bw
Svensk Filmindustri
original title: *Tystnaden*

Of two women in a large hotel in a foreign city where the military are dominant, one masturbates while the other sleeps with a barman.

Bergman may know what this was all about, but it's a certainty that no one else did: so everyone thought it must be very clever and went to see it. Superficially, as usual, it is careful and fascinating.

wd Ingmar Bergman *ph* Sven Nykvist *m* from Bach

Ingrid Thulin, Gunnel Lindblom

'There is not enough forward thrust, not enough momentum to unite the specific points, the complementary but discrete images. The pearls are there, but the string is too weak to hold them.'—*John Simon*

Le Silence est d'Or°
France 1947 99m bw
Pathé / RKO Radio (René Clair)

In 1906 a comedian becomes a film producer and as a result falls into an affair with a young girl.

Somehow not an important film, but quite a delightful one, especially for its local colour and for the combination of Clair and Chevalier up to their old tricks.

wd René Clair *ph* Armand Thirard *m* Georges Van Parys

Maurice Chevalier, François Périer, Marcelle Derrien

The Silence of Dean Maitland°
Australia 1934 95m bw

A girl is seduced by the local minister, who then kills the girl's father in a fight; another man is blamed. Hoary melodrama, well enough put together in what was considered Australia's best film of the thirties. John Longden, George Lloyd, John Garrick, Charlotte Francis. Written by Gayne Dexter; directed by Ken G. Hall; for Cinesound. 'Will do smashing business in Australia, and maybe will break into the overseas market.'—*Variety*

Silence of the North
Canada 1981 94m colour
Universal (Canada) (Murray Shostak)

In 1919 a city girl is courted by a trapper and joins him in the north country.

Nicely filmed but utterly predictable romantic melodrama, based on a biography but not carrying much conviction. D. W. Griffith would have liked it.

w Patricia Louisiana Knop, *book* Olive Fredrickson, Ben East *d* Allan Winton King *ph* Richard Leiterman *m* Allan MacMillan

Ellen Burstyn, Tom Skerritt, Gordon Pinsent, Jennifer McKinney

'Follow his secret from bedroom to bedlam, with guns, girls and dynamite!'

The Silencers°
US 1966 103m Technicolor
Columbia / Irving Allen (Jim Schmerer)

Adventures of a sexy secret agent.

Or, James Bond sent up rotten. Plenty of fun along the way, with in-jokes and characters like Lovey Kravezit, but the plot could have

done with more attention, and the sequels (*Murderers Row, The Ambushers, Wrecking Crew*) were uncontrolled disaster areas.

w Oscar Saul, *novel* Donald Hamilton *d* Phil Karlson *ph* Burnett Guffey *m* Elmer Bernstein

Dean Martin, Stella Stevens, Victor Buono, Daliah Lavi, Cyd Charisse, Robert Webber, James Gregory, Nancy Kovack

The Silent Battle
GB 1939 84m bw

A French agent battles revolutionaries in the Balkans. Unconvincing spy stuff with an uncertain tone. Rex Harrison, Valerie Hobson, John Loder, Muriel Aked, John Salew, George Devine. Written by Wolfgang Wilhelm and Rodney Ackland, from the novel by Jean Bommart; directed by Herbert Mason; for Anthony Havelock-Allan / Pinebrook.

Silent Dust°
GB 1947 82m bw
ABP / Independent Sovereign (Nat Bronsten)

A baronet builds a memorial to his son who has apparently been killed in action, but the son turns up and proves to be an absolute bounder.

Effective stage melodrama, quite neatly filmed.

w Michael Pertwee, *play* The Paragon by Roland and Michael Pertwee *d* Lance Comfort *ph* Wilkie Cooper *m* Georges Auric

Sally Gray, Derek Farr, Stephen Murray, Nigel Patrick, Seymour Hicks

The Silent Enemy
GB 1958 112m bw
Romulus (Bertram Ostrer)

The World War II exploits of a naval frogman in the Mediterranean.

Stereotyped naval underwater adventures, adequately presented.

wd William Fairchild *ph* Egil Woxholt, Otto Heller *m* William Alwyn

Laurence Harvey, John Clements, Michael Craig, Dawn Addams, Sidney James, Alec McCowen, Nigel Stock

The Silent Flute
US 1978 95m colour
Volare (Richard St Johns)

In a martial arts tournament, a hero is chosen to challenge the wizard Zetan.

Curiously mystical adventure allegory with an unhelpful title. Not too bad for those in the mood.

w Stirling Silliphant, Stanley Mann *d* Richard Moore *ph* Ronnie Taylor *m* Bruce Smeaton

Jeff Cooper, David Carradine, Roddy McDowall, Christopher Lee, Eli Wallach

Silent Movie°
US 1976 87m De Luxe
TCF / Crossbow (Michael Hertzberg)

An alcoholic producer gets the idea that a

silent movie would be a great novelty, and tries to get stars to take part.

Fairly lively spoof with the talents concerned in variable form. The shortage of laughter made it a hit in the seventies, but at no time does it approach the Keaton or Laurel and Hardy level.

w Mel Brooks, Ron Clark, Rudy de Luca, Barry Levinson *d* Mel Brooks *ph* Paul Lohmann *m* John Morris

Mel Brooks, Marty Feldman, Dom De Luise, Bernadette Peters, Sid Caesar, Harold Gould, Fritz Feld, Harry Ritz, Henny Youngman *guest stars* Anne Bancroft, Paul Newman, Burt Reynolds, James Caan, Liza Minnelli, Marcel Marceau

† Marcel Marceau utters the only word in the movie, which is *'Non'*.

The Silent Partner
US 1978 105m colour
Carolco (Garth H. Drabinsky)

A bank teller foils an attempted raid and steals the money himself.

A suspense thriller of a familiar kind; it might have been entertaining but elects instead to be unpleasant.

w Curtis Hanson, *novel* Think of a Number by Anders Bodelson *d* Daryl Duke *ph* Stephen Katz *m* Oscar Peterson

Christopher Plummer, Elliott Gould, Susannah York, Celine Lomez, Michael Kirby

The Silent Passenger
GB 1935 75m bw

Lord Peter Wimsey clears a man of a murder charge. Not an unappealing presentation of Dorothy Sayers' famous detective, though he is presented as too much the silly ass and the story is weak. Peter Haddon, John Loder, Mary Newland, Austin Trevor, Donald Wolfit, Leslie Perrins, Robb Wilton. Written by Basil Mason; directed by Reginald Denham; for Phoenix.

Silent Running°
US 1971 90m Technicolor
Universal / Michel Gruskoff / Douglas Trumbull

Members of a space station crew in 2001 are space gardening to replenish nuclear-devasted earth.

Sombre futuristic fantasy, well made but slow and muddled in development.

w Deric Washburn, Mike Cimino, Steve Bocho *d* Douglas Trumbull *ph* Charles F. Wheeler *m* Peter Schickele

Bruce Dern, Cliff Potts, Ron Rifkin, Jesse Vint

● Video: CIC

The Silent Witness
US 1932 73m bw

A man confesses to murder in order to protect his son. Solid courtroom stuff of its day, built for a new star who never quite made it. Lionel Atwill, Helen Mack, Greta Nissen, Bramwell

Fletcher, Alan Mowbray. From the play by Jack de Leon and Jack Celestin; directed by Marcel Varnel; for Fox. 'A gripping talker that rates well above most of the creep releases.'—*Variety*

The Silk Hat Kid
US 1935 70m bw

A settlement housekeeper accepts help from a racketeer. Thin little drama, perfunctorily played. Lew Ayres, Mae Clarke, Paul Kelly, Ralf Harolde, William Harrigan. Written by Edward Eliscu, Lou Breslow, Dore Schary, from a story by Gerald Beaumont; directed by H. Bruce Humberstone; for Joseph Engel / Fox. 'It hasn't the story nor the entertainment weight to lift it out of the double feature classification.'—*Variety*

Silk Stockings*
US 1957 116m Metrocolor
Cinemascope
MGM (Arthur Freed)

A Russian composer in Paris agrees to write music for a Hollywood film; a lady commissar is sent to get him back.
Musical rewrite of *Ninotchka* via a Broadway show; good moments but generally very stretched.

w Leonard Gershe, Leonard Spiegelgass, *play* George S. Kaufman, Leueen McGrath, Abe Burrows, *original play* Melchior Lengyel d Rouben Mamoulian *ph* Robert Bronner *m / ly* Cole Porter *md* André Previn

Fred Astaire, Cyd Charisse, Peter Lorre, Janis Paige, George Tobias, Jules Munshin, Joseph Buloff

● Video: MGM / UA

The Silken Affair
GB 1956 96m bw
Dragon (Fred Feldkamp)

An accountant decides to live it up, and finds himself on trial for manipulating the firm's books.
Unsatisfactory mix of comedy and fantasy, with a dim plot and virtually no comic ideas.

w Robert Lewis Taylor d Roy Kellino *ph* Gilbert Taylor *m* Peggy Stuart

David Niven, Genevieve Page, Wilfrid Hyde White, Ronald Squire, Beatrice Straight, Howard Marion Crawford, Dorothy Alison

Silken Skin*
France 1964 118m bw
Films du Carrosse / SEDIF
original title: *La Peau Douce*

A middle-aged married man leaves his wife for an attractive young girl, but the latter leaves him and his wife shoots him.
Carefully balanced mixture of comedy and melodrama which rings almost every possible change on the theme of adultery and does so with wit.

w François Truffaut, Jean-Louis Richard d François Truffaut *ph* Raoul Coutard *m* Georges Delerue

Jean Desailly, Françoise Dorléac, Nelly Benedetti

Silkwood*
US 1983 131m Technicolor
ABC (Mike Nichols, Michael Hausman)

The true story, more or less, of a girl worker in a nuclear processing plant who mysteriously dies in an accident just before she is going to talk to a reporter about a safety problem. Despite the historical interest of the case, it is too simple to merit a film of this length, which is filled with pregnant pauses and romantic asides. Nor are the actors quite so charismatic as they think they are.

w Nora Ephron, Alice Arlen d Mike Nichols *ph* Miroslav Ondricek *m* Georges Delerue *pd* Patrizia Von Brandenstein

Meryl Streep, Cher, Kurt Russell, Craig T. Nelson, Diana Scarwid, Fred Ward
   'A movie with a preordained conclusion but nowhere to go . . . it submerges what could have been its most telling points in a kind of concentrated soap opera.'—*Richard Combs, MFB*

AAN: Meryl Streep; Cher; direction; screenplay; editing (Sam O'Steen)

Silver Bears
GB 1977 113m Technicolor
EMI / Raleigh (Martin Schute)

A Las Vegas money man invests money in various European outlets and makes a killing.
Extraordinarily complex financial jape which tries the patience of all but financiers.

w Peter Stone, *novel* Paul Erdman d Ivan Passer *ph* Anthony Richmond *m* Claude Bolling

Michael Caine, Louis Jourdan, Cybill Shepherd, Stephane Audran, David Warner, Tom Smothers, Martin Balsam, Charles Gray

● Video: Thorn EMI

Silver Blaze
GB 1937 70m bw

Sherlock Holmes clears a racehorse of having killed its trainer. Not the best of the Holmes series, but this is a very satisfying Holmes. Arthur Wontner, Ian Fleming, Lyn Harding, Judy Gunn, Lawrence Grossmith, Arthur Macrae. Written by Arthur Macrae and H. Fowler Mear, from the story by Sir Arthur Conan Doyle; directed by Thomas Bentley; for Twickenham. (US title: *Murder at the Baskervilles*.)

'I bid you seek the lost silver cup . . . for sin is rising like the swollen rivers!'
'Against the broad canvas of history's mad era of splendour and seduction—here is the story of the sacred cup of silver that challenged the iron sword of tyranny—the mighty struggle to possess it—and the loves and the faith that triumphed in humanity's darkest hour!'

The Silver Chalice
US 1955 142m Warnercolor
Cinemascope
Warner (Victor Saville)

Adventures of a slave freed by Luke the apostle to fashion a chalice to hold the cup used at the Last Supper.

Po-faced biblical hokum, slower and deadlier than most, with howlingly bad casting and direction. On reflection, interesting things are being attempted with limbo set design, but in this sea of boredom the attempt only raises an eyebrow.

w Lesser Samuels, *novel* Thomas B. Costain d Victor Saville *ph* William V. Skall *m* Franz Waxman *pd* Rolf Gerard

Paul Newman, Pier Angeli, Jack Palance, Virginia Mayo, Walter Hampden, Joseph Wiseman, Alexander Scourby, Lorne Greene, Michael Pate, E. G. Marshall

AAN: William V. Skall; Franz Waxman

Silver City
US 1951 90m Technicolor

A mining assayer helps a farmer and his daughter protect the ore found on their land. Standard western programmer with plenty of action. Yvonne de Carlo, Edmond O'Brien, Barry Fitzgerald, Richard Arlen, Gladys George, Laura Elliot, Edgar Buchanan, John Dierkes. Written by Frank Gruber, from a story by Luke Short; directed by Byron Haskin; for Nat Holt / Paramount. (GB title: *High Vermilion*.)

The Silver Cord
US 1933 74m bw
RKO (Pandro S. Berman)

A young wife threatens to leave her husband because of his excessive devotion to his mother.
Stilted version of an old theatrical warhorse.

w Jane Murfin, *play* Sidney Howard d John Cromwell *ph* Charles Rosher

Irene Dunne, Joel McCrea, Laura Hope Crews, Frances Dee, Eric Linden, Helen Cromwell

The Silver Darlings
GB 1947 84m bw

Hebridean islanders take to herring fishing as a last chance to avoid emigration. Uneventful island mood piece which lacks the poetic quality which might have made it memorable. Clifford Evans, Helen Shingler, Carl Bernard, Norman Shelley, Simon Lack, Hugh Griffith. Written by Clarence Elder, from the novel by Neil Gunn; directed by Clarence Elder and Clifford Evans; for Holyrood.

Silver Dollar*
US 1932 84m bw
Warner

A poor farmer goes to Colorado for the gold rush, strikes it rich, and learns that money doesn't bring happiness.
Packed biopic of one H. A. W. Tabor, an excellent star vehicle.

w Carl Erickson, Harvey Thew d Alfred E. Green *ph* James Van Trees

Edward G. Robinson, Bebe Daniels, Aline MacMahon, Jobyna Howland, Robert Warwick, Russell Simpson
   'Historical subject admirably done as to its variety but not so strong on its commercial side.'—*Variety*

Silver Dream Racer

GB 1980 111m Eastmancolor
Panavision
Rank / David Wickes (Rene Dupont)

A garage mechanic becomes a racing
motorcyclist and is killed at the peak of
success.

One wonders who can have thought there was
any box office appeal in this cliché-ridden,
derivative, flashily made update of the Road
to Ruin.

wd David Wickes ph Paul Beeson m David
Essex

David Essex, Beau Bridges, Cristina Raines,
Harry H. Corbett, Lee Montague, Clark
Peters.

'Watching this grotesque hotch-potch of
implausible characters being shunted through
improbable situations is uncannily akin to
being assaulted by a non-stop stream of TV
commercials.'—Tom Milne, MFB

● Video: Rank

The Silver Fleet*

GB 1943 87m bw
GFD / Archers (Michael Powell, Emeric
Pressburger, Ralph Richardson)

In occupied Holland, a shipping magnate
destroys his new U-boat and himself and his
Nazi mentors with it.

Slow-starting, rather stilted melodrama which
when it gets into its stride provides good acting
and gripping propaganda.

wd Vernon Sewell, Gordon Wellesley

Ralph Richardson, Esmond Knight, Googie
Withers, Beresford Egan, Frederick Burtwell,
Kathleen Byron

Silver Lode

US 1954 80m Technicolor print

A respected citizen of Silver Lode proves that
the marshal who rides into town on his
wedding day to accuse him of murder is a
civilian bent on revenge. Broody little western
melodrama, not half bad. John Payne, Dan
Duryea, Lizabeth Scott, Dolores Moran,
Emile Meyer, Robert Warwick. Written by
Karen de Wolf; directed by Allan Dwan; for
Benedict Bogeaus / RKO.

Silver Queen

US 1942 80m bw
UA / Harry Sherman

A chivalrous western gambler rescues a girl
from the wiles of a villain.

Standard romantic melodrama mainly set in
saloons.

w Bernard Schubert, Cecile Kramer d Lloyd
Bacon ph Russell Harlan m Victor Young

George Brent, Priscilla Lane, Bruce Cabot,
Lynne Overman, Eugene Pallette, Janet
Beecher, Guinn Williams, Roy Barcroft

AAN: Victor Young

Silver River

US 1948 110m bw
Warner (Owen Crump)

A ruthless gambler becomes powerful but
loses everything because of his character
defects.

Meandering western drama with a few good
highlights dissipated by long chunks of
character building and a rehash of the David
and Bathsheba story.

w Stephen Longstreet, Harriet Frank Jnr
d Raoul Walsh ph Sid Hickox m Max Steiner

Errol Flynn, Ann Sheridan, Thomas Mitchell,
Bruce Bennett, Tom D'Andrea, Barton
Maclane, Monte Blue, Alan Bridge

The Silver Streak*

US 1934 85m bw

A streamlined train makes its first run from
Chicago to Boulder Dam, where a victim of
infantile paralysis must be got into an iron
lung. Historically interesting melodrama which
seldom pauses for breath. Sally Blane, Charles
Starrett, Hardie Albright, William Farnum,
Irving Pichel, Arthur Lake, Edgar Kennedy.
Written by H. W. Hanemann, Jack
O'Donnell, Roger Whately; directed by
Tommy Atkins; for RKO. 'Pretty absurd, yet
exciting and fast . . . there's scarcely a stunt
known to the railroad picture formula that
hasn't been employed.'—Variety

Silver Streak*

US 1976 113m De Luxe
TCF / Martin Ransohoff, Frank Yablans

On a trans-continental train, a young publisher
discovers a murder and is at the mercy of the
culprits.

Rather like an update of a Bob Hope comedy-
thriller with a whiff of sex, this amiable spoof
goes on too long, brings in a second comic too
late, and ends with fashionable but irrelevant
violence.

w Colin Higgins d Arthur Hiller ph David
M. Walsh m Henry Mancini pd Alfred
Sweeney

Gene Wilder, Jill Clayburgh, Richard Pryor,
Patrick McGoohan, Ned Beatty, Clifton
James, Ray Walston, Richard Kiel

'Nineteen-seventies performers are trapped
in this fake thirties mystery comedy, which is
so inept you can't even get angry.'—New
Yorker

● Video: CBS / Fox

Simba

GB 1955 99m Eastmancolor
GFD / Group Film (Peter de Sarigny)

An English farmer in Kenya fights the Mau
Mau.

Savagely topical melodrama which tends to
cheapen a tragic situation.

w John Baines d Brian Desmond Hurst
ph Geoffrey Unsworth m Francis Chagrin

Dirk Bogarde, Donald Sinden, Virginia
McKenna, Basil Sydney, Marie Ney, Joseph
Tomelty, Earl Cameron, Orlando Martins

● Video: Rank

Simon*

US 1980 97m Technicolor
Warner / Orion (Louis A. Stroller, Martin
Bregman)

Corrupt scientists brainwash a psychology
professor into thinking he's from another
planet.

Solemn comic fantasy which doesn't seem to
make much of a point and only superficially
entertains, but is well made and well acted.

wd Marshall Brickman ph Adam Holender
m Stanley Silverman pd Stuart Wurtzel

Alan Arkin, Madeleine Kahn, Austin
Pendleton, Judy Graubert, William Finley,
Fred Gwynne

Simon and Laura*

GB 1955 91m Technicolor Vistavision
GFD / Group Films (Teddy Baird)

The actors who play husband and wife in a TV
series are married in reality and hate each
other, a fact that shows in the live Christmas
episode.

Adequate film of a reasonably sophisticated
West End comedy; good lines and
performances.

w Peter Blackmore, play Alan Melville
d Muriel Box ph Ernest Steward
m Benjamin Frankel

Peter Finch, Kay Kendall, Ian Carmichael,
Alan Wheatley, Richard Wattis, Muriel
Pavlow, Maurice Denham, Hubert Gregg

The Sin of Madelon Claudet

US 1931 74m bw
MGM (Harry Rapf)
GB title: The Lullaby

A mother is separated from her illegitimate
baby.

Sob stuff for a rising star: hilarious now.

w Charles MacArthur, play Eward Knoblock
d Edgar Selwyn

Helen Hayes, Robert Young, Neil Hamilton,
Lewis Stone, Marie Prevost, Cliff Edwards,
Jean Hersholt, Karen Morley

'Natural sobber for women and grosses . . .
but you don't have to go back as far as
Madame X to find a parallel for the plot.'—
Variety

AA: Helen Hayes

Sin Town

US 1942 74m bw
Universal (George Waggner)

Two confidence tricksters arrive in a western
town and solve a murder.

Members of the studio repertory company in a
passable western discarded by Marlene
Dietrich.

w Gerald Geraghty, W. Scott Darling,
Richard Brooks d Ray Enright m Hans
Salter

Constance Bennett, Broderick Crawford, Leo
Carrillo, Anne Gwynne, Patric Knowles,
Andy Devine, Ward Bond, Ralf Harolde

SILVER STREAK. Did they really drive a train through a wall? Only the producer knows.

Sinbad and the Eye of the Tiger
GB 1977   113m   Metrocolor
Columbia / Andor (Charles H. Schneer, Ray
  Harryhausen)

Sinbad frees a city from a wicked woman's
spell.
Lumpish sequel to a sequel: even the animated
monsters raise a yawn this time.

w Beverly Cross d Sam Wanamaker ph Ted
Moore m Roy Budd sp Ray Harryhausen

Patrick Wayne, Taryn Power, Jane Seymour,
Margaret Whiting, Patrick Troughton

Sinbad the Sailor
US 1947   117m   Technicolor
RKO (Stephen Ames)

Sinbad sets off on his eighth voyage to find the
lost treasure of Alexander.

Well-staged but humourless Arabian Nights
swashbuckler.

w John Twist d Richard Wallace ph George
Barnes m Roy Webb

Douglas Fairbanks Jnr, Walter Slezak,
Maureen O'Hara, Anthony Quinn, George
Tobias, Jane Greer, Mike Mazurki, Sheldon
Leonard

Since You Went Away*
US 1944   172m   bw
David O. Selznick

When hubby is away at the war, his wife and
family adopt stiff upper lips.
Elaborate flagwaving investigation of the well-
heeled American home front in World War II,
with everyone brimming with goodwill and not

a dry eye in the place. Absolutely superbly
done, if it must be done at all, and a
symposium of Hollywood values and
techniques of the time.

w David O. Selznick, *book* Margaret Buell
Wilder d John Cromwell ph Stanley Cortez,
Lee Garmes m Max Steiner pd William L.
Pereira

Claudette Colbert, Joseph Cotten, Jennifer
Jones, Shirley Temple, Agnes Moorehead,
Monty Woolley, Lionel Barrymore, Guy
Madison, Robert Walker, Hattie McDaniel,
Craig Stevens, Keenan Wynn, Albert
Basserman, Nazimova, Lloyd Corrigan

PREFACE: 'This is the story of the
unconquerable fortress—the American home,
1943.'

'A deft, valid blend of showmanship, humour, and yard-wide Americanism.'—*James Agee*

'The whole litany of that middle-class synthetic emotionalism, meticulously annotated over a decade by tough and sentimental experts, has been procured for us.'—*Richard Winnington*

'A rather large dose of choking sentiment.'—*Bosley Crowther*

'It is not an average US reality. It is an average US dream.'—*Time*

'Selznick wrote the script himself, intending his story to be moving and simple, along epic lines; the result is pedestrian in a peculiarly grandiose manner.'—*Pauline Kael, 70s*

AA: Max Steiner
AAN: best picture; Stanley Cortez; Claudette Colbert; Jennifer Jones; Monty Woolley

● *Video: Guild*

Sincerely Yours
US 1955   115m   Warnercolor
Warner (Henry Blanke)

A concert pianist goes deaf and retires to his penthouse, but with the help of binoculars lipreads the humble folk below. Helping them anonymously gives him courage to have an operation.
Absurd updating for a modern non-star of a creaky old George Arliss vehicle *The Man Who Played God*.

w Irving Wallace *d* Gordon Douglas
ph William H. Clothier *m adviser* George Liberace

Liberace, Joanne Dru, Dorothy Malone, Alex Nicol, William Demarest

'Drenched in coy bathos to the point of embarrassment.'—*Films and Filming*

'Given sufficient intoxication, you could find this movie amusing.'—*Saturday Review*

Sinful Davey
GB 1968   95m   Eastmancolor
Panavision
UA / Mirisch / Webb (William N. Graf)

In 1821 a young Scotsman determines to become a criminal like his father, but falls in love.
Thin imitation of *Tom Jones*, highly implausible but played with some zest.

w James R. Webb, based on the autobiography of David Haggart *d* John Huston *ph* Ted Scaife, Freddie Young *m* Ken Thorne *pd* Stephen Grimes

John Hurt, Pamela Franklin, Nigel Davenport, Ronald Fraser, Robert Morley, Maxine Audley, Noel Purcell

Sing and Be Happy
US 1937   67m   bw

A young man is too irresponsible to work in his father's advertising agency. A wisp of a plot with some wisps of music attached; nothing to remember next day. Tony Martin, Leah Ray, Joan Davis, Chick Chandler, Helen

SINBAD THE SAILOR.   Douglas Fairbanks Jnr is at the mercy of Walter Slezak and Anthony Quinn – until the next shot.

Westley, Allan Lane, Berton Churchill.
Written by Ben Markson, Lou Breslow, John Patrick; directed by James Tinling; for Milton H. Feld / Fox. 'This musical will require plenty of exploitative pressure by exhibs.'—*Variety*

Sing As We Go***
GB 1934   80m   bw
ATP (Basil Dean)

An unemployed millgirl gets various holiday jobs in Blackpool.
A splendid, pawky star vehicle which is also the best picture we have of industrial Lancashire in the thirties. Great fun.

w J. B. Priestley, Gordon Wellesley *d* Basil Dean

Gracie Fields, John Loder, *Frank Pettingell*, Dorothy Hyson, Stanley Holloway

'We have an industrial north that is bigger than Gracie Fields running around a Blackpool fun fair.'—*C. A. Lejeune*

Sing Baby Sing*
US 1936   87m   bw
TCF (Darryl F. Zanuck)

A drunken Shakespearian actor sets his sights on a night club singer.
Reasonably hilarious take-off on the John Barrymore-Elaine Barrie affair, with several Fox contractees fooling to the top of their bent with the help of good musical numbers.

w Milton Sperling, Jack Yellen, Harry Tugend *d* Sidney Lanfield *ph* Peverell Marley *songs* various *md* Louis Silvers

Alice Faye, Adolphe Menjou, Gregory Ratoff, Patsy Kelly, Ted Healy, The Ritz Brothers, Montagu Love, Dixie Dunbar

AAN: song 'When Did You Leave Heaven?' (*ly* Walter Bullock, *m* Richard Whiting)

Sing, Boy, Sing
US 1958   91m   bw   Cinemascope
TCF (Henry Ephron)

A rock and roll star comes close to a nervous breakdown because of an unscrupulous manager and a revivalist grandfather.
Fairly painless vehicle for a singing star.

w Claude Binyon *d* Henry Ephron
ph William C. Mellor *m* Lionel Newman

Tommy Sands, Edmond O'Brien, John McIntire, Lili Gentle, Nick Adams, Josephine Hutchinson

Sing Me a Love Song
US 1936   78m   bw

A reformed playboy starts at the bottom as a clerk in his father's department store. Thin but mildly pleasing musical with good comedy support. James Melton, Patricia Ellis, *Hugh Herbert*, Zasu Pitts, Allen Jenkins, Nat

Pendleton. Ann Sheridan. Walter Catlett. Hobart Cavanaugh, Charles Halton. Written by Sig Herzig, Jerry Wald. Harry Sauber; directed by Ray Enright; for Cosmopolitan / First National. 'Story isn't much and the dialogue fails to sparkle, yet there's a constant stream of laughs.'—*Variety*

'The gol-darnedest family in the whole USA!'
Sing You Sinners**
US 1938   88m   bw
Paramount (Wesley Ruggles)

The adventures of a happy-go-lucky family and their racehorse.
Cheerful family musical with amiable cast and good tunes.

w Claude Binyon *d* Wesley Ruggles *ph* Karl Struss *md* Boris Morros *songs* James V. Monaco, Johnny Burke

Bing Crosby, Donald O'Connor, Fred MacMurray, Elizabeth Patterson, Ellen Drew, John Gallaudet
  'Homespun, down to earth, and as natural as eggs for breakfast.'—*Variety*

The Singer Not the Song
GB 1960   132m   colour   Cinemascope
Rank (Roy Baker)

In an isolated Mexican town a priest defies an outlaw who oddly respects him.
Lengthy character drama with little action or humour but a great deal of moody introspection and a suggestion of homosexuality.

w Nigel Balchin, *novel* Audrey Erskine Lindop *d* Roy Baker *ph* Otto Heller *m* Philip Green

John Mills, Dirk Bogarde, Mylene Demongeot, John Bentley, Laurence Naismith, Eric Pohlmann
  'A rewarding film, as startling as a muffled scream from the subconscious.'—*Peter John Dyer*

● *Video: Rank*

The Singing Fool**
US 1928   110m   bw
Warner

A successful singer goes on the skids when his small son dies.
Early talkie musical, a sensation because of its star's personality, but a pretty maudlin piece of drama.

w C. Graham Baker, *play* Leslie S. Barrows *d* Lloyd Bacon *ph* Byron Haskin *songs* Lew Brown, Ray Henderson, B. G. De Sylva

Al Jolson, Davey Lee, Betty Bronson, Josephine Dunn, Arthur Housman
  'Obvious and tedious as the climax is, when the black-faced comedian stands before the camera and sings "Sonny Boy" you know the man is greater, somehow, than the situation, the story or the movie.'—*Pare Lorentz*

Singin' in the Rain****
US 1952   102m   Technicolor
MGM (Arthur Freed)

When talkies are invented, the reputation of

SING AS WE GO.   Gracie Fields, on her way to the top, is a match for John Loder, ex-Hollywood star on his way down.

one female star shrivels while another grows. Brilliant comic musical, the best picture by far of Hollywood in transition, with the catchiest tunes, the liveliest choreography, the most engaging performances and the most hilarious jokes of any musical.

w Adolph Green, Betty Comden *d / ch* Gene Kelly, Stanley Donen *ph* Harold Rosson *m* Nacio Herb Brown *md* Lennie Hayton *ly* Arthur Freed

Gene Kelly, Donald O'Connor, Debbie Reynolds, Millard Mitchell, Jean Hagen, Rita Moreno, Cyd Charisse, Douglas Fowley
  'Perhaps the most enjoyable of all movie musicals.'—*New Yorker, 1975*

AAN: Lennie Hayton; Jean Hagen

● *Video: MGM / UA*

The Singing Kid
US 1936   83m   bw
Warner (Robert Lord)

A cocky night club singer takes a talented juvenile under his wing.
Routine star vehicle most notable for a string of standards sung by him right after the credits.

w Warren Duff, Pat C. Flick *d* William Keighley *ph* George Barnes *md* Leo F. Forbstein *songs* E. Y. Harburg, Harold Arlen

Al Jolson, Sybil Jason, Allen Jenkins, Lyle Talbot, Edward Everett Horton, Beverly Roberts, Claire Dodd

The Singing Marine
US 1937   107m   bw

A marine singer wins a talent contest and success goes to his head. Light musical of very little interest save two dance sequences by Busby Berkeley. Dick Powell, Doris Weston, Jane Darwell, Hugh Herbert, Lee Dixon, Dick Wesson, Allen Jenkins, Jane Wyman, Larry Adler. Written by Delmer Daves; directed by Ray Enright; for Warner.

The Singing Nun
US 1966   98m   Metrocolor   Panavision
MGM (Jon Beck)

Adventures of a nun who takes her music to the outside world.
Icky musical drama based on a true character.

w Sally Benson, John Furia *d* Henry Koster *ph* Milton Krasner *md* Harry Sukman *songs* Soeur Sourire

Debbie Reynolds, Greer Garson, Ricardo Montalban, Agnes Moorehead, Chad Everett, Katharine Ross, Ed Sullivan, Juanita Moore

AAN: Harry Sukman

The Sinister Man*
GB 1961 60m bw
Anglo Amalgamated / Merton Park (Jim O'Connelly)

The murder of an Oxford scholar is linked to the archaeological relics which are coveted for political purposes.
Very tolerable minor thriller in the Edgar Wallace series: short, sharp and snappy.

w Robert Banks Stewart d Clive Donner
ph Bert Mason m Charles Blackwell

Patrick Allen, John Bentley, Jacqueline Ellis, Eric Young, Arnold Lee, John Glyn-Jones, William Gaunt, Wilfrid Brambell

'Personal! Powerful! Human! Heroic!'
Sink the Bismarck**
GB 1960 97m bw Cinemascope
TCF / John Brabourne

In 1941, Britain's director of naval operations arranges the trapping and sinking of Germany's greatest battleship.
Tight little personal drama which would have been better on a standard screen, as its ships are plainly models and much of the footage stretched-out newsreel. Nevertheless, a good example of the stiff-upper-lip school.

w Edmund H. North d Lewis Gilbert
ph Christopher Challis m Clifton Parker
md Muir Mathieson

Kenneth More, Dana Wynter, Karel Stepanek, Carl Mohner, Laurence Naismith, Geoffrey Keen, Michael Hordern, Maurice Denham, Esmond Knight

Sinner Take All
US 1937 74m bw

Members of a family are murdered one by one. Moderate puzzler with a reporter sharing solving honours with the police. Bruce Cabot, Margaret Lindsay, Joseph Calleia, Stanley Ridges, Vivienne Osborne, Charley Grapewin, Edward Pawley, George Zucco. Written by Leonard Lee, Walter Wise, from the novel Murder of a Wanton by Whitman Chambers; directed by Errol Taggart; for Lucien Hubbard / Sam Marx / MGM. 'Above the usual whodunit average . . . able to make its way alone in the less exacting spots.'— Variety

Sinner's Holiday
US 1930 55m bw
Warner

A fairground barker loves the daughter of a penny arcade owner, but is framed by her brother.
Early talkie quickie using Bradway talent, and introducing James Cagney to the screen. It still has vigour if little else.

w Harvey Thew, George Rosener,
play Penny Arcade by Marie Baumer d John G. Adolfi ph Ira Morgan

Grant Withers, Evalyn Knapp, James Cagney, Joan Blondell, Lucille La Verne, Warren Hymer, Noel Madison

Sinners in Paradise
US 1938 65m bw

Air travellers are wrecked on a South Sea island. Much ado about very little, and a grave disappointment from its director. Madge Evans, John Boles, Bruce Cabot, Marion Martin, Gene Lockhart, Charlotte Wynters, Nana Bryant. Written by Lester Cole, Harold Buckley, Louis Stevens; directed by James Whale; for Ken Goldsmith / Universal. 'Melodrama sufficiently lurid to be cut into several parts and released as a serial.'—Variety

Sinners in the Sun
US 1932 69m bw

A young couple break up; each has romantic adventures, but eventually they come together again. Blah comedy-drama with the defects of its period. Carole Lombard, Chester Morris, Adrienne Allen, Alison Skipworth, Walter Byron, Cary Grant. Written by Vincent Lawrence, Waldemar Young, Samuel Hoffenstein, Mildred Cram; directed by Alexander Hall; for Paramount. 'Only high-powered selling will aid a dull and poorly-handled story.'—Variety

The Sins of Rachel Cade
US 1960 123m Technicolor
Warner (Henry Blanke)

An American missionary nurse in the Belgian Congo falls in love with a crashed flier and has a baby.
Romantic melodrama which starts like The Nun's Story and ends like Peg's Paper; competent on its level.

w Edward Anhalt, novel Charles Mercer
d Gordon Douglas ph Peverell Marley
m Max Steiner

Angie Dickinson, Roger Moore, Peter Finch, Errol John, Woody Strode, Juano Hernandez, Frederick O'Neal, Mary Wickes

Sir Henry at Rawlinson's End
GB 1980 71m bw

A grossly eccentric English aristocrat lays a family ghost. Weirdly isolated, semi-professional comedy with elements of everything from Ealing to Monty Python. Trevor Howard, Patrick Magee, Denise Coffey, J. G. Devlin. Written by Vivien Stanshall and Steve Roberts from Stanshall's radio play; directed by Steve Roberts; for Charisma.

Siren of Atlantis see L'Atlantide

Siren of Bagdad
US 1953 72m Technicolor

A travelling magician helps reinstate a deposed sultan. Flippant oriental extravaganza aiming at the Hope–Crosby style but falling sadly short of it. Paul Henreid, Patricia Medina, Hans Conried, Charlie Lung. Written by Robert E. Kent; directed by Richard Quine; for Same Katzman / Columbia.

Sirocco
US 1951 98m bw
Columbia / Santana (Robert Lord)

In 1925 Damascus, an American runs guns for the rebels.

Tedious romantic drama in the Casablanca vein but with none of the magic.

w A. I. Bezzerides, Hans Jacoby, novel Coup de Grâce by Joseph Kessel d Curtis Bernhardt ph Burnett Guffey m George Antheil

Humphrey Bogart, Marta Toren, Lee J. Cobb, Everett Sloane, Gerald Mohr, Zero Mostel, Onslow Stevens

Sister Kenny*
US 1946 116m bw
RKO (Dudley Nichols)

The career of a nurse who instigated treatment for polio.
Standard, well-done biopic.

w Dudley Nichols, Alexander Knox, Mary McCarthy d Dudley Nichols ph George Barnes m Alexander Tansman

Rosalind Russell, Alexander Knox, Dean Jagger, Philip Merivale, Beulah Bondi, Dorothy Peterson
† From the autobiography of Australian nurse Mary Kenny: And They Shall Walk.

AAN: Rosalind Russell

The Sisters*
US 1938 98m bw
Warner (Hal B. Wallis)

The marriages of three sisters from a small Montana town.
Well-made potboiler for women; it even brings in the San Francisco earthquake, and the star teaming is piquant to say the least.

w Milton Krims, novel Myron Brinig
d Anatole Litvak ph Tony Gaudio m Max Steiner

Bette Davis, Errol Flynn, Anita Louise, Ian Hunter, Donald Crisp, Beulah Bondi, Jane Bryan, Alan Hale, Dick Foran, Henry Travers, Patric Knowles, Lee Patrick, Harry Davenport

Sisters under the Skin
US 1934 65m bw

An older man loses his mistress to a bohemian composer. Surprise, surprise: and the screenplay does not enliven the situation. Frank Morgan, Elissa Landi, Joseph Schildkraut, Doris Lloyd, Clara Blandick, Samuel S. Hinds. Written by Jo Swerling, S. K. Lauren; directed by David Burton; for Columbia. 'Mild flicker of obvious triangle story texture.'—Variety

Sitting Bull
US 1954 106m Eastmancolor Cinemascope
United Artists / W. R. Frank / Televoz of Mexico

Despite the massacre of Custer's men, a cavalry officer strives to establish a relationship with Sitting Bull.
Sloppy and undernourished western epic in abysmal colour, not helped by Mexicans pretending to be Indians.

w Jack De Witt, Sidney Salkow d Sidney Salkow ph Charles Van Enger, Victor Herrara m Raoul Kraushaar

Dale Robertson, Mary Murphy, J. Carrol Naish, Iron Eyes Cody, John Litel, William Hopper, Douglas Kennedy (as Custer)

Sitting Ducks
US 1978 88m De Luxe
Sunny Side Up (Meira Atta Dor)

Two men steal a fortune and abscond to Miami with two women who turn out to have a contract on them.
Endlessly talkative sex comedy from a practitioner who scorns built-up gags. The kind of movie that puts people off movies.

wd Henry Jaglom *ph* Paul Glickman *m* Richard Romanus

Michael E. Jaglom, Zack Norman, Patrice Townsend, Irene Forrest, Richard Romanus, Henry Jaglom

Sitting Pretty*
US 1933 85m bw
Paramount (Charles R. Rogers)

Two songwriters strike it rich in Hollywood. Cheerful comedy musical, interesting for its backgrounds.

w Jack McGowan, S. J. Perelman, Lou Breslow *d* Harry Joe Brown *ph* Milton Krasner *songs* Mack Gordon, Harry Revel

Jack Oakie, Jack Haley, Ginger Rogers, Thelma Todd, Gregory Ratoff, Lew Cody, Harry Revel, Mack Gordon
'Should please all over.'—*Variety*

Sitting Pretty***
US 1948 84m bw
TCF (Samuel G. Engel)

A young couple acquire a most unusual male baby sitter, a self-styled genius who sets the neighbourhood on its ears by writing a novel about it.
Out of the blue, a very funny comedy which entrenched Clifton Webb as one of Hollywood's great characters and led to two sequels, *Mr Belvedere Goes to College* and *Mr Belvedere Rings the Bell* (qv).

w F. Hugh Herbert, *novel* Belvedere by Gwen Davenport *d* Walter Lang *ph* Norbert Brodine *m* Alfred Newman

Clifton Webb, Robert Young, Maureen O'Hara, *Richard Haydn*, Louise Allbritton, Ed Begley, Randy Stuart, Larry Olsen
AAN: Clifton Webb

Sitting Target
GB 1972 92m Metrocolor
MGM (Barry Kulick)

A violent killer escapes from jail and seeks revenge on those who 'shopped' him.
Rough, tough action thriller; passes the time for hardened addicts.

w Alexander Jacobs, *novel* Lawrence Henderson *d* Douglas Hickox *ph* Ted Scaife *m* Stanley Myers *pd* Jonathan Barry

Oliver Reed, Jill St John, Edward Woodward, Frank Finlay, Ian McShane, Freddie Jones, Robert Beatty

THE SISTERS.   Bette Davis at her most demure eyes Errol Flynn at his most gentlemanly.

Situation Hopeless But Not Serious
US 1965 97m bw
Paramount / Castle (Gottfried Reinhardt)

In 1944, two American fliers are captured by a friendly, lonely mild-mannered German, who keeps them in his cellar and hasn't the heart to tell them when the war is over . . .
Flat little comedy which leaves a talented cast no room for manoeuvre.

w Silvia Reinhardt, *novel* The Hiding Place by Robert Shaw *d* Gottfried Reinhardt *ph* Kurt Hasse *m* Harold Byrne

Alec Guinness, Robert Redford, Mike Connors, Anita Hoefer

Six Black Horses
US 1962 80m Eastmancolor

A girl hires a gunslinger and a horse thief to escort her across Indian territory. Rather glum western programmer. Audie Murphy, Dan Duryea, Joan O'Brien, George Wallace, Roy Barcroft. Written by Burt Kennedy; directed by Harry Keller; for Universal-International.

Six Bridges to Cross
US 1955 96m bw
U-I (Aaron Rosenberg)

The criminal career of a young hoodlum in Boston in the thirties.
Public Enemy reprise with a sentimental veneer, smooth but uninteresting.

w Sidney Boehm, *novel* They Stole Two and a Half Million Dollars and Got Away with It by Joseph F. Dineen *d* Joseph Pevney *ph* William Daniels *m* Joseph Gershenson

Tony Curtis, George Nader, Julie Adams, Jay C. Flippen, Sal Mineo, Jan Merlin

Six Day Bike Rider
US 1934 69m bw
Warner (Sam Bischoff)

One of life's failures impresses his girl by entering a cycling contest.
One of the star's stronger comedy vehicles.

w Earl Baldwin *d* Lloyd Bacon *ph* Warren Lynch

Joe E. Brown, Maxine Doyle, Frank McHugh, Gordon Westcott

Six Hours to Live*
US 1932 78m bw

A scientist revives a diplomat for six hours so that his murderer can be traced. Fanciful hokum set at a Geneva peace conference. Warner Baxter, John Boles, Miriam Jordan, Irene Ware, George Marion. From the story by Gordon Morris and Morton Barteaux; directed by William Dieterle; for Fox.
'A strong box office title which together with an aggressive sales campaign should bring picture into the money.'—*Variety*

Six Lessons from Madame La Zonga
US 1941 62m bw

A Cuban nightclub proprietress causes mix-ups on a pleasure boat. Witless vehicle for two stars popular at another studio in the *Mexican Spitfire* series. Lupe Velez, Leon Errol, William Frawley, Helen Parrish, Charles Lang, Eddie Quillan, Quinn Williams. Written by Stanley Rubin, Marion Orth, Larry Rhine and Ben Chapman; directed by John Rawlins; for Universal.

'Their first honeymoon was so much fun
They're off to have another one!'
Six of a Kind*
US 1934 69m bw
Paramount

Comic adventures of six people driving across America.
Minor comedy which doesn't come off as a whole but adequately displays the talents of its stars.

w Walter de Leon, Harry Ruskin *d* Leo McCarey *ph* Henry Sharp *m* Ralph Rainger

Charles Ruggles, Mary Boland, W. C. Fields, Alison Skipworth, George Burns, Gracie Allen
'Another pleasing film . . . it reminds the Englishman of *Three Men in a Boat*.'—*E. V. Lucas, Punch*
'Old-fashioned farce that gets a lot of laughs. Better for duals than de luxers.'—*Variety*

Six Pack
US 1982 110m De Luxe
TCF / Lion Share (Michael Trikilis)

A loner stock car driver finds himself fathering six orphan kids.
Old-fashioned family picture built around a country singer.

w Mike Marvin, Alex Matter *d* Daniel Petrie *ph* Mario Tosi *m* Charles Fox

Kenny Rogers, Diane Lane, Erin Gray, Barry Corbin

6,000 Enemies
US 1939 61m bw

A district attorney is framed for a prison stretch and finds himself hated by every convict inside. Formula support climaxing in a prison break: well enough done. Walter Pidgeon, Rita Johnson, Paul Kelly, Nat Pendleton, Harold Huber, Grant Mitchell. Written by Bertram Millhauser; directed by George B. Seitz; for Lucien Hubbard / MGM.
'Prison meller with action aplenty.'—*Variety*

633 Squadron*
GB 1964 94m Technicolor Panavision
UA / Mirisch (Cecil F. Ford)

In 1944 Mosquito aircraft try to collapse a cliff overhanging a munitions factory in a Norwegian fjord.
Standard war heroics with enough noise and disorder to keep most audiences hypnotized.

w James Clavell, Howard Koch, *novel* Frederick E. Smith *d* Walter Grauman *ph* Ted Scaife, John Wilcox *m* Ron Goodwin

Cliff Robertson, George Chakiris, Maria Perschy, Harry Andrews, Donald Houston, Michael Goodliffe

Six Weeks
US 1982 107m Metrocolor
Polygram (Peter Guber, Jon Peters)

A lady cosmetics tycoon whose ten-year-old daughter is dying of leukaemia enlists the aid of a politician to make what's left of her life a triumph.
Icky tearjerker on the lines of *The Christmas Tree*. Everything is done to make it palatable, but it won't be many people's cup of bromide.

w David Seltzer, *novel* Fred Mustard Stewart *d* Tony Bill *ph* Michael D. Margulies *m* Dudley Moore *ad* Hilyard Brown *ed* Stu Linder

Dudley Moore, Mary Tyler Moore, Katherine Healy, Shannon Wilcox, Bill Calvert
'Very sleek and very sickmaking.'—*Observer*

Sixty Glorious Years**
GB 1938 95m Technicolor
Imperator (Herbert Wilcox)
US title: *Queen of Destiny*

Scenes from the life of Queen Victoria.
A stately pageant apparently composed of material which couldn't be fitted into the previous year's black-and-white success *Victoria the Great*. Fascinating, though the camerawork is not very nimble.

w Robert Vansittart, Miles Malleson, Charles de Grandcourt *d* Herbert Wilcox *ph* Frederick A. Young

Anna Neagle, Anton Walbrook, C. Aubrey Smith, Walter Rilla, Charles Carson, Felix Aylmer, Lewis Casson
'One of the most artistic and expensive films made in England.'—*Variety*
† The two films were edited together in 1943 to make a new selection called *Queen Victoria*, and in the process the original negatives were accidentally destroyed, so that both films now have to be printed from unattractive dupes.

Skateboard
US 1977 95m Technicolor

A small-time theatrical agent in trouble builds up a professional skateboard team.
Unsatisfactory exploitation item which devotes more time to its plot than to its sport. Allen Garfield, Kathleen Lloyd, Leif Garrett, Richard Van Der Wyk. Written by Richard A. Wolf, George Gage; directed by George Gage; for Universal.

The Ski Raiders
US 1972 90m Technicolor Panavision
Warner (Edward L. Rissien)
aka: *Snow Job*

An alpine ski instructor devises a scheme to rob a bank.
Very medium caper thriller with a breathtaking opening sequence.

w Ken Kolb, Jeffrey Bloom *d* George Englund *ph* Gabor Pogany, Willy Bogner *m* Jacques Loussier

Jean Claude Killy, Cliff Potts, Vittorio de Sica, Daniele Gaubert

Skidoo
US 1968 98m Technicolor Panavision
Paramount / Sigma (Otto Preminger)

Active and reformed gangsters get involved with hippies and preach universal love.
Abysmal mishmash with top talent abused; clearly intended as satirical farce, but in fact one of the most woebegone movies ever made.

w Doran William Cannon *d* Otto Preminger *ph* Leon Shamroy *m* Harry Nilsson

Jackie Gleason, Carol Channing, Groucho Marx, Frankie Avalon, Fred Clark, Michael Constantine, Frank Gorshin, John Philip Law, Peter Lawford, Burgess Meredith, George Raft, Cesar Romero, Mickey Rooney
'Unspeakable.'—*Michael Billington, Illustrated London News*

The Skin Game
GB 1932 85m bw
BIP (John Maxwell)

A landowner hates his self-made neighbour.
Stiff picturization of a well-known stage play.

w Alfred Hitchcock, Alma Reville, *play* John Galsworthy *d* Alfred Hitchcock *ph* Jack Cox

Edmund Gwenn, John Longden, Jill Esmond, C. V. France, Helen Haye, Phyllis Konstam, Frank Lawton

The Skin Game*
US 1971 102m Technicolor Panavision
Warner / Cherokee (Harry Keller)

A white and a black con man have near escapes in many a western town.
Amusing comedy western with good pace and a few shafts of wit.

w Peter Stone, Richard Alan Simmons *d* Paul Bogart *ph* Fred Koenekamp *m* David Shire

James Garner, Lou Gossett, Susan Clark, Brenda Sykes, Ed Asner, Andrew Duggan, Henry Jones, Neva Patterson

Skippy*
US 1931 88m bw
Paramount

The young son of a local health inspector makes friends in the slums.
Standard, blameless family entertainment.

w Joseph L. Mankiewicz, Norman McLeod, *comic strip* Percy Crosby *d* Norman Taurog *ph* Karl Struss

Jackie Cooper, Robert Coogan, Mitzi Green, Jackie Searl, Willard Robertson
'A great kid talker, but not for kids only . . . if there is such a thing as being 100% inhuman, only then is it possible for anyone to dislike *Skippy* as entertainment.'—*Variety*

AA: Norman Taurog
AAN: best picture; script; Jackie Cooper

Skirts Ahoy
US 1952   105m   Technicolor
MGM (Joe Pasternak)

Three girls join the navy and get their men.
Musical recruiting poster, quite devoid of
interest.

w Isobel Lennart *d* Sidney Lanfield
ph William Mellor *m* Harry Warren *ly* Ralph
Blane *ch* Nick Castle

Esther Williams, Vivian Blaine, Joan Evans,
Barry Sullivan, Keefe Brasselle, Dean Miller,
Debbie Reynolds, Bobby Van, Billy Eckstine

The Skull
GB 1965   83m   Techniscope
Paramount / Amicus (Milton Subotsky)

The skull of the Marquis de Sade haunts two
antiquarians.
Clodhopping horror with very visible wires.

w Milton Subotsky, *story* Robert Bloch
d Freddie Francis *ph* John Wilcox
m Elisabeth Lutyens

Peter Cushing, Christopher Lee, Patrick
Wymark, Jill Bennett, Nigel Green, Michael
Gough, George Coulouris

Skullduggery
US 1969   105m   Technicolor
   Panavision
Universal (Saul David)

Archaeologists and adventurers clash on a trek
in New Guinea.
Fashionable oddball adventure about the
discovery of an unspoiled primitive tribe; the
elements don't jell.

w Nelson Gidding *d* Gordon Douglas
ph Robert Moreno *m* Oliver Nelson

Burt Reynolds, Susan Clark, Roger C.
Carmel, Paul Hubschmid, Chips Rafferty,
Alexander Knox, Edward Fox, Wilfrid Hyde
White, Rhys Williams

Sky Bride
US 1932   75m   bw

An aerial barnstormer loses his nerve after an
accident. Formula melodrama with aerobatics.
Richard Arlen, Jack Oakie, Virginia Bruce,
Robert Coogan, Charles Starrett. Written by
Joseph L. Mankiewicz, Agnes Brand Leahy
and Grover Jones; directed by Stephen
Roberts; for Paramount. 'Lack of romantic
interest is somewhat of a handicap to a
conventional air plot with a suspensive
finish.'—*Variety*

Sky Devils
US 1931   89m   bw
Caddo / Howard Hughes

Two draft dodgers find themselves heroes of
the Army Air Corps in World War I France.
Little-seen but unremarkable adventure
comedy in the Flagg and Quirt tradition.

w Joseph Moncure March, Edward
Sutherland *d* Edward Sutherland *ph* Tony
Guadio *md* Alfred Newman *ch* Busby
Berkeley

Spencer Tracy, William Boyd, Ann Dvorak,
George Cooper, Billy Bevan, Forrester
Harvey

'A hodge-podge of all the laugh war stuff
. . . and how they want something to laugh
about right now. Psychologically and in a
material way, it should do nicely.'—*Variety*

Sky Full of Moon
US 1952   73m   bw
MGM (Sidney Franklin Jnr)

A rodeo cowboy wins money and a showgirl in
Las Vegas.
Ambling comedy with an agreeable air of
innocence.

wd Norman Foster *ph* Ray June *m* Paul
Sawtell

Carleton Carpenter, Jan Sterling, Keenan
Wynn

Sky Giant
US 1938   80m   bw

Romance and adventure at a flying school.
Unremarkable melodrama with expected
heroics. Richard Dix, Joan Fontaine, Chester
Morris, Harry Carey, Paul Guilfoyle. Written
by Lionel Houser; directed by Ken Landers;
for Robert Sisk / RKO. 'Good for the lighter
weight first run houses and the upper berth of
double deckers.'—*Variety*

Sky Riders*
US 1976   91m   De Luxe   Todd-AO 35
TCF (Terry Morse Jnr)

In Athens, the family of an American
businessman is kidnapped by terrorists and
rescued by hang gliders led by a soldier of
fortune.
Old-fashioned actioner with new-fashioned
political concern.

w Jack de Witt, Stanley Mann, Gary Michael
White, Hall T. Sprague, Bill McGaw
d Douglas Hickox *ph* Ousama Rawi *m* Lalo
Schifrin

James Coburn, Susannah York, Robert Culp,
Charles Aznavour, Werner Pochath, Kenneth
Griffith, Harry Andrews

● *Video: CBS / Fox*

Sky West and Crooked
GB 1965   102m   Eastmancolor
Rank / John Mills (Jack Hanbury)
US title: *Gypsy Girl*

A mentally retarded girl falls in love with a
gypsy.
Eccentric rural melodrama with echoes of
Cold Comfort Farm and *Les Jeux Interdits*.
Interesting, but scarcely a runaway success.

w Mary Hayley Bell, John Prebble *d* John
Mills *ph* Arthur Ibbetson *m* Malcolm Arnold

Hayley Mills, Ian McShane, Laurence
Naismith, *Geoffrey Bayldon*, Annette Crosbie,
Norman Bird

'Behind the overwhelming feyness of it all
lurk assumptions which in cold blood look
almost sinister.'—*MFB*

● *Video: Rank*

Skyjacked*
US 1972   101m   Metrocolor   Panavision
MGM / Walter Seltzer

A Boeing 707 on a flight from Los Angeles to
Minneapolis is forced by a mad bomber to fly
to Moscow.
Shamelessly hackneyed aeroplane adventure
with quite enjoyable elements.

w Stanley R. Greenberg, *novel* Hijacked by
David Harper *d* John Guillermin *ph* Harry
Stradling Jnr *m* Perry Botkin Jnr

Charlton Heston, Yvette Mimieux, James
Brolin, Claude Akins, Jeanne Crain, Rosey
Grier, Walter Pidgeon, Leslie Uggams

Skylark
US 1941   94m   bw
Paramount (Mark Sandrich)

A wife decides on her fifth anniversary that
she is tired of being secondary to her
husband's career, and needs a fling.
Formula matrimonial comedy; plenty of talent
but no sparkle.

w Z. Myers, *play* Samson Raphaelson *d* Mark
Sandrich *ph* Charles Lang *m* Victor Young

Claudette Colbert, Ray Milland, Brian
Aherne, Binnie Barnes, Walter Abel, Grant
Mitchell, Mona Barrie, Ernest Cossart

The Sky's the Limit
GB 1937   79m   bw

A sacked aircraft designer suddenly finds
himself in demand. Amiable star musical. Jack
Buchanan, Mara Loseff, William Kendall,
David Hutcheson, H. F. Maltby, Athene
Seyler, Sara Allgood. Written by Jack
Buchanan and Douglas Furber; directed by
Lee Garmes and Jack Buchanan; for Jack
Buchanan.

The Sky's the Limit*
US 1943   89m   bw
RKO (David Hempstead)

A flier on leave meets and falls for a news
photographer.
Thin musical with incidental compensations.

w Frank Fenton, Lynn Root *d* Edward H.
Griffith *ph* Russell Metty *m* Leigh Harline
md Leo F. Forbstein

Fred Astaire, Joan Leslie, *Robert Benchley*,
Robert Ryan, Elizabeth Patterson

AAN: Leigh Harline; song 'My Shining Hour'
(*m* Harold Arlen, *ly* Johnny Mercer)

● *Video: Kingston*

Skyscraper Souls
US 1932   100m   bw

In an office building, several personal
dilemmas interlock. Portmanteau drama in the
Grand Hotel mould, and quite comparable.
Warren William, Maureen O'Sullivan, Verree
Teasdale, Gregory, Ratoff, Jean Hersholt,
Norman Foster, Anita Page, George Barbier,
Wallace Ford, Hedda Hopper. Written by C.
G. Sullivan and Elmer Harris, from the book
by Faith Baldwin; directed by Edgar Selwyn;
for MGM.

Slander
US 1956 81m bw
MGM (Armand Deutsch)

Revelations about a film star in a scandal
magazine lead to blackmail and murder.
Unlikely melodrama, routinely assembled,
based on the Confidential Magazine lawsuits.

w Jerome Weidman d Roy Rowland
ph Harold J. Marzerati m Jeff Alexander

Van Johnson, Ann Blyth, Steve Cochran,
Marjorie Rambeau, Harold J. Stone

Slap Shot*
US 1977 124m Technicolor
Universal / Robert J. Wunsch, Stephen
  Friedman

The wily player-coach of a fading ice hockey
team finds ways, including dirty play, of
keeping it going.
Violent, foul-mouthed comedy which works as
it goes but leaves a bad taste in the mouth.

w Nancy Dowd d George Roy Hill ph Victor
Kemper, Wallace Worsley md Elmer
Bernstein

Paul Newman, Michael Ontkean, Lindsay
Crouse, Jennifer Warren, Strother Martin

  'Fast, noisy, profane . . . gets you laughing,
all right, but you don't necessarily enjoy
yourself.'—*New Yorker*
  'Both indulgent and moralizing, the self-
consciously racy script ends up looking merely
opportunistic.'—*Time Out*

Slattery's Hurricane
US 1949 87m bw
TCF (William Perlberg)

Loves of a storm-spotting pilot with the US
Weather Bureau in Florida.
Forgettable programmer with good storm
sequences.

w Herman Wouk, Richard Murphy, *novel*
Herman Wouk d André de Toth ph Charles
G. Clarke m Cyril Mockridge

Richard Widmark, Linda Darnell, Veronica
Lake, John Russell, Gary Merrill, Walter
Kingsford

Slaughter
US 1972 90m De Luxe Todd-AO 35
AIP / Slaughter United (Monroe Sachson)

A black Vietnam veteran hunts down the
underworld syndicate which killed his mother
and father.
Hectic crime yarn with a pitilessly violent hero
and not enough style to relieve the
unappetizing monotony.

w Mark Hanna, Don Williams d Jack
Starrett ph Rosanio Solano m Luchi de Jesus

Jim Brown, Rip Torn, Don Gordon, Cameron
Mitchell

  'The cast perform their trigger-happy tasks
with all the passionate conviction of a team of
well-oiled robots.'—*Jan Dawson*

Slaughter on Tenth Avenue
US 1957 103m bw
U-I (Albert Zugsmith)

The New York DA's office investigates union
murders on the docks.
Uninteresting imitation of *On the Waterfront*.

w Lawrence Roman, *novel* The Man Who
Rocked the Boat by William J. Keating,
Richard Carter d Arnold Laven ph Fred
Jackman m Richard Rodgers

Richard Egan, Jan Sterling, Dan Duryea, Julie
Adams, Walter Matthau, Charles McGraw,
Sam Levene, Mickey Shaughnessy, Harry
Bellaver

Slaughter Trail
US 1952 78m Cinecolor

Three outlaws cause trouble between white
man and Indian. Rough-hewn western strung
together by verses of a ballad. Brian Donlevy,
Gig Young, Virginia Grey, Andy Devine,
Robert Hutton. Written by Sid Kuller;
directed by Irving Allen; for RKO.

Slaughterhouse Five*
US 1972 104m Technicolor
Universal / Vanadas (Paul Monash)

A suburban optometrist has nightmare space /
time fantasies involving Nazi POW camps and
a strange futuristic planet.
Interesting but infuriating anti-war fantasy for
intellectuals.

w Stephen Geller, *novel* Kurt Vonnegut Jnr
d George Roy Hill ph Miroslav Ondricek
m J. S. Bach, performed by Glen Gould
pd Henry Bumstead

Michael Sacks, Ron Leibman, Eugène Roche,
Sharon Gans, Valerie Perrine, Sorrell Booke,
John Dehner

  'A lot of good makings in this picture; but
very little is made.'—*Stanley Kauffmann*

Slaughter's Big Rip-Off
US 1973 93m Movielab Todd-AO 35
AIP (Monroe Sachson)

Still on the run from gangsters who have killed
his best friend, Slaughter violently disposes of
a number of adversaries.
More routine black violence, a rampage of
senseless brutality against sunny Los Angeles
backgrounds.

w Charles Johnson d Gordon Douglas
ph Charles Wheeler m Jim Brown, Fred
Wesley

Jim Brown, Ed MacMahon, Brock Peters,
Don Stroud

Slave Girl
US 1947 79m Technicolor
U-I (Michael Fessier, Ernest Pagano)

In the early 1800s, a diplomat is sent to Tripoli
to ransom sailors held by the power-mad
potentate.
Criticism would be superfluous: when the film
was finished it was obviously so bad that
executives ordered the addition of a talking
camel and other *Hellzapoppin*-type jokes in
order to turn it into a comedy.

w Michael Fessier, Ernest Pagano d Charles
Lamont ph George Robinson, W. Howard
Greene m Milton Rosen

George Brent, Yvonne de Carlo, Albert
Dekker, Broderick Crawford, Lois Collier,
Andy Devine, Carl Esmond, Arthur Treacher

Slave Girls
GB 1966 95m Technicolor
  Cinemascope
Hammer (Aida Young)
US title: *Prehistoric Women*

A hunter seeking white rhinoceros finds
himself in a lost valley ruled by a tribe of
women.
Feebly preposterous comic strip farrago
without the saving grace of humour.

wd Michael Carreras ph Michael Reed
m Carlo Mantelli

Michael Latimer, Martine Beswick, Edina
Ronay

Slave Ship**
US 1937 100m bw
TCF (Darryl F. Zanuck)

An American slave captain decides to become
respectable but finds a mutiny on his hands.
Well-made adventure movie in the old
tradition, a model of studio production.

w Sam Hellman, Lamar Trotti, Gladys
Lehman, *story* William Faulkner, based on a
novel by George S. King d Tay Garnett
ph Ernest Palmer m Alfred Newman

Wallace Beery, Warner Baxter, Elizabeth
Allen, Mickey Rooney, George Sanders, Jane
Darwell, Joseph Schildkraut, Arthur Hohl,
Minna Gombell, Billy Bevan, Francis Ford,
Edwin Maxwell, J. Farrell MacDonald, Paul
Hurst, Holmes Herbert

  'Plenty of action and de luxe scenic
trimmings . . . good box office blood and
thunder.'—*Variety*

Slaves
US 1969 110m Eastmancolor
Slaves Company / Theatre Guild / Walter
  Reade (Philip Langner)

In 1850 Kentucky a slave stands up for his
rights and plans escape.
Well-meaning but muddled and old-fashioned
melodrama, hardly well enough done to raise
comparison with *Gone with the Wind*.

wd Herbert J. Biberman ph Joseph Brun
m Bobby Scott

Stephen Boyd, Ossie Davis, Dionne Warwick,
Shepperd Strudwick, Nancy Coleman, David
Huddleston, Gale Sondergaard

Slayground
GB 1983 89m Technicolor
EMI / Jennie and Co. (John Dark, Gower
  Frost)

A rich man hires an assassin to track down a
criminal who accidentally killed his daughter.
One of those tedious and violent films in which
the criminal wins out; slickness seems to make
it worse.

w Trevor Preston, *novel* Richard Stark
d Terry Bedford ph Stephen Smith, Herb
Wagreich m Colin Towns pd Keith Wilson

Peter Coyote, Mel Smith, Billie Whitelaw, Philip Sayer, Bill Luhrs
'A disappointingly lame front runner for the new EMI stable.'—*Philip Strick, MFB*

Sleep My Love*
US 1948 96m bw
(UA) Mary Pickford (Charles 'Buddy' Rogers)

A man plots to murder his wife, but is foiled.
Thin suspenser, rather splendidly photographed in the expressionist manner.

w St Clair McKelway, *novel* Leo Rosten *d* Douglas Sirk *ph* Joseph Valentine *m* Rudy Schrager

Claudette Colbert, Don Ameche, Robert Cummings, Rita Johnson, George Coulouris, Hazel Brooks, Keye Luke

'A love story about two people who hate each other!'

Sleeper*
US 1973 88m De Luxe
UA / Charles Rollins, Charles Joffe (Jack Greenberg)

A health food store owner is deep frozen after an operation and wakes two hundred years in the future.
Predictable star vehicle with an agreeable string of bright gags.

w Woody Allen, Marshall Brickman *d* Woody Allen *ph* David M. Walsh *m* Woody Allen *pd* Dale Hennesy

Woody Allen, Diane Keaton, John Beck, Mary Gregory
'Verbal and visual gags rain down like hailstones.'—*Michael Billington, Illustrated London News*

The Sleeping Beauty*
US 1959 75m Technirama 70
Walt Disney (Ken Peterson)

Rather stodgy, unwisely Cinemascoped feature cartoon of the old legend; very fashionable and detailed, but somehow lifeless.

d Clyde Geronomi *md* George Bruns *pd* Don da Gradi, Ken Anderson

AAN: George Bruns

Sleeping Car
GB 1933 82m bw

A woman on the run pretends to marry a sleeping car attendant, then finds they really are married. Artificial comedy with interesting cast from London stage. Madeleine Carroll, Ivor Novello, Laddie Cliff, Kay Hammond, Claud Allister, Stanley Holloway. Written by Franz Schultz; directed by Anatole Litvak; for Gaumont.

The Sleeping Car Murders*
France 1965 95m bw Cinemascope
PECF (Julien Derode)
original title: *Compartiment Tueurs*

When the overnight express from Marseilles reaches Paris, a girl is found dead in the sleeping car.

Rather long-winded whodunnit with an unlikely solution: a good pace helps, however, as do skilful borrowings from American police films of the forties.

wd Costa-Gavras, *novel* Sebastien Japrisot *ph* Jean Tournier *m* Michel Magne

Yves Montand, Simone Signoret, Pierre Mondy, Catherine Allégret, Jacques Pérrin, Jean-Louis Trintignant, Michel Piccoli

Sleeping Car to Trieste*
GB 1948 95m bw
GFD / Two Cities (George H. Brown)

Spy melodrama, a slow-starting but generally entertaining remake of *Rome Express* (qv).

w Allan Mackinnon *d* John Paddy Carstairs *ph* Jack Hildyard *m* Benjamin Frankel

Albert Lieven, Jean Kent, David Tomlinson, David Hutcheson, Rona Anderson, Paul Dupuis, Finlay Currie, *Alan Wheatley*, Derrick de Marney, Grégoire Aslan, Hugh Burden

The Sleeping Cardinal
GB 1931 84m bw

Sherlock Holmes exposes a smuggling ring. Slow-paced but interesting adaptation, vaguely based on *The Empty House*. Arthur Wontner, Ian Fleming, Norman McKinnel, Jane Welsh, Louis Goodrich. Written by Cyril Twyford and H. Fowler Mear, from stories by Sir Arthur Conan Doyle; directed by Leslie Hiscott; for Twickenham.

The Sleeping City**
US 1950 85m bw
U-I (Leonard Goldstein)

A policeman disguises himself as a medical student to learn more about a murder in a general hospital.
A location melodrama of modest excellence.

w Jo Eisinger *d* George Sherman *ph* William Miller *m* Frank Skinner

Richard Conte, Richard Taber, Coleen Gray, John Alexander, Peggy Dow, Alex Nicol

The Sleeping Tiger
GB 1954 89m bw
Anglo-Amalgamated / Insignia (Victor Hanbury)

A psychiatrist overpowers a criminal and takes him home as a guinea pig; the criminal then falls in love with the psychiatrist's wife.
Turgid and unconvincing melodrama, a thoroughgoing bore.

w Harold Buchman, Carl Foreman, *novel* Maurice Moiseiwitch *d* Joseph Losey *ph* Harry Waxman *m* Malcolm Arnold

Dirk Bogarde, Alexander Knox, Alexis Smith, Hugh Griffith, Maxine Audley, Glyn Houston, Billie Whitelaw
'There is a splendour about this film, which has one of the most absurdly extravagant plots on record, and never flinches from it.'—*Gavin Lambert*

The Slender Thread*
US 1966 98m bw
Paramount / Athene (Stephen Alexander)

A volunteer social worker tries to prevent a woman from committing suicide while police track her down from their phone conversations.
Acceptable star melodrama, curiously artificially styled.

w Stirling Silliphant *d* Sydney Pollack *ph* Loyal Griggs *m* Quincy Jones

Anne Bancroft, Sidney Poitier, Steven Hill, Telly Savalas

'Think of the crime . . . then go one step further . . . If it was murder, where's the body? If it was for a woman, which woman? If it's only a game, why the blood?'

Sleuth**
GB 1972 139m colour
Palomar (Morton Gottlieb)

A successful thriller writer invents a murder plot which rebounds on himself.
Well-acted version of a highly successful piece of stage trickery; despite hard work all round it seems much less clever and arresting on the screen, and the tricks do show.

w Anthony Shaffer, from his play *d* Joseph L. Mankiewicz *ph* Oswald Morris *m* John Addison

Laurence Olivier, Michael Caine

AAN: Joseph L. Mankiewicz; John Addison; Laurence Olivier; Michael Caine

● Video: CBS / Fox

A Slight Case of Larceny
US 1952 71m bw

Garage proprietors find a way of tapping their rivals' supply of petrol. Laboured comedy for two rather tiresome stars. Mickey Rooney, Eddie Bracken, Elaine Stewart, Marilyn Erskine, Douglas Fowley. Written by Jerry Davis; directed by Don Weis; for MGM.

A Slight Case of Murder***
US 1938 85m bw
Warner (Sam Bischoff)

When a beer baron tries to go legitimate his colleagues attempt to kill him, but end up shooting each other.
Amusing black farce, remade to less effect as *Stop, You're Killing Me* (qv).

w Earl Baldwin, Joseph Schrank, *play* Damon Runyon, Howard Lindsay *d* Lloyd Bacon *ph* Sid Hickox

m M. K. Jerome, Jack Scholl

Edward G. Robinson, Jane Bryan, Willard Parker, *Ruth Donnelly*, Allen Jenkins, John Litel, Harold Huber, Edward Brophy, Bobby Jordan
'Nothing funnier has been produced by Hollywood for a long time . . . a mirthful and hilarious whimsy.'—*Variety*
'The complications crazily mount, sentiment never raises its ugly head, a long nose is made at violence and death.'—*Graham Greene*

Slightly French
US 1948 81m bw

A film director in trouble passes off a Bowery-born carnival dancer as an exotic French star. Rather tedious comedy which lively performances can't sustain. Dorothy Lamour, Don Ameche, Janis Carter, Jeanne Manet, Willard Parker. Written by Karen de Wolf; directed by Douglas Sirk; for Columbia.

Slightly Honorable
US 1940 85m bw
(UA) Walter Wanger (Tay Garnett)

Lawyer partners set out to break a crime syndicate.
Fair crime thriller which can't decide whether it's comedy or drama.

w John Hunter Lay, Robert Tallman, Ken Englund, *novel* Send Another Coffin by F. G. Presnell *d* Tay Garnett *ph* Merritt Gerstad *m* Werner Janssen

Pat O'Brien, Broderick Crawford, Edward Arnold, Eve Arden, Claire Dodd, Ruth Terry, Bernard Nedell, Alan Dinehart, Douglass Dumbrille, Ernest Truex

Slightly Scarlet
US 1930 72m bw

Two jewel thieves outwit a malicious mastermind. Somewhat effete comedy-drama in a long bygone style. Clive Brook, Evelyn Brent, Paul Lukas, Eugene Pallette, Helen Ware, Virginia Bruce, Henry Wadsworth, Claud Allister. Written by Howard Estabrook, Joseph L. Mankiewicz, Percy Heath; directed by Louis Gasnier, Edwin H. Knopf; for Paramount. 'Fair general programme feature.'—*Variety*

Slightly Scarlet
US 1956 92m Technicolor Superscope
(RKO) Benedict Bogeaus

The mayor's secretary loves the leader of a criminal gang.
Competent but uninteresting crime romance.

w Robert Blees, *novel* James A. Cain *d* Allan Dwan *ph* John Alton *m* Louis Forbes

Arlene Dahl, John Payne, Rhonda Fleming, Kent Taylor, Ted de Corsia
'So complicated that it is difficult to sort out which characters are supposed to be sympathetic.'—*MFB*

Slim
US 1937 85m bw

Electric linesmen argue about their work and their women. A reworking of *Tiger Shark* which itself later became *Manpower*; competent action stuff. Pat O'Brien, Margaret Lindsay, Henry Fonda, Stuart Erwin, J. Farrell MacDonald, Jane Wyman. Written by William Wister Haines; directed by Ray Enright; for Warner. 'A comedy drama which will do all right without setting off fireworks.'—*Variety*

Slim Carter
US 1957 82m Eastmancolor

A playboy is signed up by a Hollywood studio and required to change his image. Curious sentimental comedy which might have worked with stronger casting. Jock Mahoney, Julie Adams, Tim Hovey, William Hopper, Ben Johnson, Barbara Hale. Written by Montgomery Pitman; directed by Richard H. Bartlett; for Universal-International.

'You'll forget every love story you ever saw—or sang to!'

The Slipper and the Rose*
GB 1976 146m Technicolor
Panavision
Paradine Co-Productions (David Frost, Stuart Lyons)

The story of Cinderella.
The elements are charming, but the treatment is fussy yet uninventive and the film is immensely overlong and lacking in magic and wit. Alas, not the renaissance of the family film that was hoped for.

w Bryan Forbes, Robert and Richard Sherman *d* Bryan Forbes *ph* Tony Imi *songs* Robert and Richard Sherman *pd* Ray Simm

Richard Chamberlain, Gemma Craven, Kenneth More, Michael Hordern, Edith Evans, Annette Crosbie, Margaret Lockwood, *Christopher Gable*, Julian Orchard, Lally Bowers, John Turner
'The tunes, I'm afraid, go in one ear and out the other; and, as Dr Johnson said of *Paradise Lost*, no man wished it a minute longer.'—*Michael Billington, Illustrated London News*

AAN: music; song, 'He Danced with Me'

● *Video: Iver*

Slither*
US 1972 96m Metrocolor
MGM / Talent Associates / Jack Sher

An ex-con, some gangsters, and a few mobile homes are involved in a chase across California for some hidden loot.
Wackily with-it comedy-thriller ranging from violence to slapstick, the former always undercut into the latter. Pretty funny, once you get the idea.

w W. D. Richter *d* Howard Zieff *ph* Laszlo Kovacs *m* Tom McIntosh

James Caan, Peter Boyle, Sally Kellerman, Louise Lasser

Slow Dancing in the Big City
US 1978 110m Technicolor
UA / CIP (Michael Levee, John G. Avildsen)

A New York newspaper columnist is affected by a dying eight-year-old drug addict and an ailing girl ballet dancer.
Warners in the thirties might have got away with this corn, but in 1978, played against a realistic backdrop, it seems merely silly and indigestible, its title as pretentious as its use of four-letter words.

w Barra Grant *d* John G. Avildsen *ph* Ralf D. Bode *m* Bill Conti

Paul Sorvino, Anne Ditchburn, Nicholas Coster, Anita Dangler

'The earnestness and shamelessness of the director are so awesome that if the picture fails as romance, it succeeds as camp.'—*New Yorker*

The Small Back Room**
GB 1949 106m bw
London Films / The Archers
US title: *Hour of Glory*

A bomb expert with a lame foot and a drink problem risks his life dismantling a booby bomb and returns to his long-suffering girl friend.
Rather gloomy suspense thriller with ineffective personal aspects but well-made location sequences and a fascinating background of boffins at work in post-war London.

wd Michael Powell, Emeric Pressburger, *novel* Nigel Balchin *ph* Christopher Challis *m* Brian Easdale

David Farrar, Kathleen Byron, Jack Hawkins, Leslie Banks, Robert Morley, Cyril Cusack

Small Change*
France 1976 105m Eastmancolor
Films du Carosse / Artistes Associés (Marcel Berbert, Roland Thenot)
original title: *L'Argent de Poche*

Linked incidents affecting a class of small boys in provincial France.
Competent if rather ordinary little portmanteau which one can't imagine adults actually paying to see.

w François Truffaut, Susan Schiffman *d* François Truffaut *ph* Pierre-William Glenn *m* Maurice Jaubert

Geory Desmouceaux, Philippe Goldman, Claudio Deluca

A Small Circle of Friends
US 1980 112m Technicolor

Adventures of Harvard men at the end of the sixties. Comedy, sex, politics and melodrama are all ploughed into this tiresome and predictable mixture. Brad Davis, Karen Allen, Jameson Parker, Shelley Long, John Friedrich. Written by Ezra Sacks; directed by Rob Cohen; for United Artists. 'Sacks' recreation of his college days relies on a mistaken belief that an audience will love his characters as much as they love each other.'—*John Pym, MFB*

Small Town Girl*
US 1936 90m bw
MGM (Hunt Stromberg)

A girl traps a handsome stranger into offering marriage when he's drunk, then sets out to win him when he's sober.
Thin but adequate romantic comedy, a good example of MGM's production line of the mid-thirties, with established star and character players helping upcoming talents.

w John Lee Mahin, Edith Fitzgerald, *novel* Ben Ames Williams *d* William A. Wellman *ph* Oliver Marsh, Charles Rosher *m* Edward Ward

Janet Gaynor, Robert Taylor, James Stewart, Binnie Barnes, Frank Craven, Elizabeth Patterson, Lewis Stone, Andy Devine, Isabel Jewell, Charley Grapewin, Robert Greig, Agnes Ayres

Small Town Girl*
US 1953 93m Technicolor
MGM (Joe Pasternak)

Musical remake of the above.
Willing hands make the most of it, but the songs are not the best.

w Dorothy Cooper, Dorothy Kingsley
d Leslie Kardos ph Joseph Ruttenberg
songs Leo Robin, Nicholas Brodszky
md André Previn ch Busby Berkeley

Jane Powell, Farley Granger, *Bobby Van,* Ann Miller, Robert Keith, Billie Burke, S. Z. Sakall, Fay Wray, Nat King Cole

AAN: song, 'My Flaming Heart'

A Small Town in Texas
US 1976 96m colour

An ex-convict returns to his hometown seeking revenge on those who framed him.
Unpleasant shock thriller with much violence.
Susan George, Timothy Bottoms, Bo Hopkins, Art Hindle. Written by William Norton; directed by Jack Starrett; for AIP.

The Small Voice*
GB 1948 83m bw
British Lion / Constellation (Anthony Havelock-Allan)
US title: *Hideout*

Escaped convicts hold up a playwright and his wife in their country cottage.
Gripping, well-characterized version of a very well worn plot.

w Derek Neame, Julian Orde, *novel* Robert Westerby d Fergus McDonell

James Donald, Valerie Hobson, Howard Keel, David Greene, Michael Balfour, Joan Young

The Small World of Sammy Lee
GB 1962 107m bw
Bryanston / Seven Arts / Ken Hughes (Frank Godwin)

A small-time Soho crook tries desperately to raise money to pay off threatening bookies.
Overlong 'realist' comedy-melodrama based on a TV play and filled with low-life 'characters'; vivid but cursed with a tedious hero.

wd Ken Hughes, from his TV play
ph Wolfgang Suschitzky m Kenny Graham
ad Seamus Flannery

Anthony Newley, Julia Foster, Robert Stephens, Wilfrid Brambell, Warren Mitchell, Miriam Karlin, Kenneth J. Warren

The Smallest Show on Earth*
GB 1957 81m bw
British Lion / Launder and Gilliat (Michael Relph)
US title: *Big Time Operators*

Two young marrieds inherit a decayed cinema and make it pay.

Amiable caricature comedy with plenty of obvious jokes and a sentimental attachment to old cinemas but absolutely no conviction, little plot, and a very muddled sense of the line between farce and reality.

w William Rose, John Eldridge d Basil Dearden ph Douglas Slocombe m William Alwyn

Bill Travers, Virginia McKenna, Margaret Rutherford, Bernard Miles, Peter Sellers, Leslie Phillips, Francis de Wolff

Smart Blonde*
US 1936 57m bw

A female reporter beats the cops to the solution of a murder. Slick second feature, first in the Torchy Blane series. Glenda Farrell, Barton MacLane, Wini Shaw, Craig Reynolds, Addison Richards, Jane Wyman. Written by Don Ryan, Kenneth Gamet, Frederick Nebel; directed by Frank McDonald; for Warners. 'Fairly well paced with gunplay, an amount of smart talk, but no mountings to mention.'—*Variety*

Smart Girls Don't Talk
US 1948 81m bw

A society girl rats on her gangster boy friend after her brother has been killed. Flatly handled underworld melodrama, as uninteresting as its cast. Virginia Mayo, Bruce Bennett, Robert Hutton, Richard Rober, Tom D'Andrea. Written by William Sackheim; directed by Richard Bare; for Warner.

Smart Money
US 1931 67m bw
Warner

A gambler hits the big time but finally goes to jail.
Rather ordinary crime drama, a distinct letdown for its star after *Little Caesar.*

w Kubec Glasmon, John Bright, Lucien Hubbard, Joseph Jackson d Alfred E. Green
ph Robert Kurrie

Edward G. Robinson, James Cagney, Evalyn Knapp, Ralf Harolde, Noel Francis, Margaret Livingstone, Boris Karloff, Billy House
'It will have no trouble upholding its title at the box office.'—*Variety*

† This film marks the only teaming of Robinson and Cagney.

AAN: script

Smart Woman
US 1948 93m bw
Monogram (Hal E. Chester)

A crafty lady lawyer becomes romantically involved with a crusading district attorney.
What to Monogram was a high-class production would have been a very routine programmer from anyone else.

w Alvah Bessie, Louise Morheim, Herbert Margolis d Edward A. Blatt ph Stanley Cortez m Louis Gruenberg md Constantin Bakaleinikoff

Constance Bennett, Brian Aherne, Barry Sullivan, Michael O'Shea, James Gleason, Otto Kruger, Isobel Elsom, Taylor Holmes, John Litel

Smash and Grab
GB 1937 76m bw

A detective's wife helps him track down a criminal mastermind. Agreeable star comedy.
Jack Buchanan, Elsie Randolph, Arthur Margetson, Antony Holles, Zoe Wynn, Edmund Willard, David Burns. Written by Ralph Spence; directed by Tim Whelan; for Jack Buchanan / GFD.

Smash Palace*
New Zealand 1981 108m colour

The owner of a car-wrecking business goes to pieces when his wife leaves him. Downbeat character study of the kind of psychopath who doesn't arouse much sympathy; but the film is well mounted. Bruno Lawrence, Anna Jemison, Keith Aberdein, Greer Robson. Written and directed by Roger Donaldson; for Aardvark Films.

Smash-up, The Story of a Woman
US 1947 113m bw
Universal-International (Walter Wanger)
GB title: *A Woman Destroyed*

The story of a lady alcoholic.
Tedious distaff side of *The Lost Weekend.*

w John Howard Lawson d Stuart Heisler
ph Stanley Cortez m Daniele Amfitheatrof

Susan Hayward, Lee Bowman, Eddie Albert, Marsha Hunt, Carl Esmond, Carleton Young, Charles D. Brown

AAN: original story (Dorothy Parker, Frank Cavett); Susan Hayward

Smashing Time
GB 1967 96m Eastmancolor
Paramount / Partisan / Carlo Ponti (Ray Millichip)

Two north country girls have farcical adventures in swinging London, including paint squirting and pie throwing.
Horrendous attempt to turn two unsuitable actresses into a female Laurel and Hardy; plenty of coarse vigour but no style or sympathy.

w George Melly d Desmond Davis
ph Manny Wynn m John Addison

Rita Tushingham, Lynn Redgrave, Ian Carmichael, Anna Quayle, Michael York, Irene Handl, Jeremy Lloyd

Smile*
US 1975 113m De Luxe
UA (Michael Ritchie)

A bird's eye view of the Young Miss America pageant in a small California town.
A witty series of sketches in the form of a drama-documentary or satirical mosaic. Highly polished fun for those who can stay the course.

w Jerry Belson d Michael Ritchie ph Conrad Hall m various

Bruce Dern, Barbara Feldon, Michael Kidd, Geoffrey Lewis, Nicholas Pryor
'A beady, precise, technically skilful movie.'—*Michael Billington, Illustrated London News*

Smiles of a Summer Night••
Sweden 1955   105m   bw
Svensk Filmindustri
original title: *Sommarnattens Leende*

A country lawyer meets again a touring actress who was once his mistress, and accepts an invitation to him and his young wife to stay at her mother's country home for a weekend. Comedy of high period manners with an admirable detached viewpoint and elegant trappings. It later formed the basis of Stephen Sondheim's *A Little Night Music*, a stage musical which was later filmed.

wd Ingmar Bergman *ph* Gunnar Fischer *m* Erik Nordgren

Gunnar Björnstrand, Eva Dahlbeck, Ulla Jacobsson, Harriet Andersson, Margit Carlquist, Naima Wifstrand, Jarl Kulle

Smiley•
GB 1956   97m   Technicolor
Cinemascope
TCF / London Films (Anthony Kimmins)

An adventurous Australian boy has various adventures and finally gets the bicycle he wants.
An open-air 'William'-type story for children, quite nicely made and generally refreshing. *Smiley Gets a Gun* was a less effective sequel.

w Moore Raymond, Anthony Kimmin *d* Anthony Kimmins *ph* Ted Scaife, Russ Wood *m* William Alwyn

Colin Petersen, Ralph Richardson, Chips Rafferty, John McCallum

The Smiling Ghost
US 1941   71m   bw

A girl reporter solves a haunted house mystery. Moderate comedy chiller with plenty going on. Alexis Smith, Wayne Morris, Brenda Marshall, Alan Hale, Willie Best, David Bruce, Helen Westley, Richard Ainley. Written by Kenneth Gamet; directed by Lewis Seiler; for Warner.

Smilin' Through•
US 1932   97m   bw
MGM (Irving Thalberg)

Three generations of complications follow when a Victorian lady is accidentally killed by a jealous lover on her wedding day. Archetypal sentimental romantic drama, wholly absorbing to the mass audience and extremely well done; originally a 1922 Norma Talmadge vehicle.

w Ernest Vajda, Claudine West, Donald Ogden Stewart, J. B. Fagan, *play* Jane Cowl, Jane Murfin *d* Sidney Franklin *ph* Lee Garmes

Norma Shearer, Leslie Howard, Fredric March, O. P. Heggie, Ralph Forbes, Beryl Mercer

'A big women's picture of tear-drawing power, done with satisfying sincerity by a cast which spells money.'—*Variety*
'A sensitive and beautiful production distinguished by excellent settings and rich photography.'—*New York Mirror*
AAN: best picture

Smilin' Through•
US 1941   100m   Technicolor
MGM (Victor Saville)

Flat but adequate remake of the above.

w Donald Ogden Stewart, John Balderston *d* Frank Borzage *ph* Leonard Smith *m* Herbert Stothart

Jeanette MacDonald, Gene Raymond, Brian Aherne, Ian Hunter, Frances Robinson, Patrick O'Moore

'His intimate and roguish romance will break your heart—with love and laughter!'

The Smiling Lieutenant••
US 1931   88m   bw
Paramount (Ernst Lubitsch)

A Viennese guards officer leaves his mistress to become consort to a visiting princess. A sophisticated soufflé in Lubitsch's best style, naughty but quite nice, with visual effects largely replacing dialogue.

w Ernest Vajda, Samson Raphaelson, *operetta* A Waltz Dream *d* Ernst Lubitsch *ph* George Folsey *m* Oscar Straus *md* Adolph Deutsch

Maurice Chevalier, Miriam Hopkins, Claudette Colbert, Charles Ruggles, George Barbier, Elizabeth Patterson

'Will delight smart audiences and figures to be liked well enough by the average fan. A good but not a smash picture.'—*Variety*
'All the shrewd delights that were promised in *The Love Parade* all realized with an economy and sureness that give it a luster which no other American-made comedy satire has achieved. One must look to *Le Million* to find its peer.'—*Richard Watts, New York Post*
AAN: best picture

Smokey and the Bandit•
US 1977   97m   Technicolor
Universal / Rastar (Robert L. Levy)

A Georgia bootlegger on a mission picks up a girl in distress and is chased by her irate sheriff fiancé.
Frantic chase comedy full of car crashes and low lines: a surprise box office smash.

w James Lee Barrett, Charles Shyer, Alan Mandel *d* Hal Needham *ph* Bobby Byrne *m* Bill Justis, Jerry Reed, Art Feller

Burt Reynolds, Jackie Gleason, Sally Field, Jerry Reed, Mike Henry, Pat McCormick, Paul Williams
● Video: CIC

Smokey and the Bandit II
US 1980   101m   Technicolor
Universal / Rastar / Mort Engelberg
GB title: *Smokey and the Bandit Ride Again*

A trucker is hired to take a pregnant elephant to the Republican convention.
More mindless chasing and crashing, with even less wit than before and rather more wholesale destruction.

w Jerry Belson, Brock Yates *d* Hal Needham *ph* Michael Butler *md* Snuff Garrett

Burt Reynolds, Jackie Gleason, Sally Field, Jerry Reed, Dom DeLuise, Paul Williams

Smokey and the Bandit III
US 1983   88m   Technicolor

Sheriff Justice mistakes an innocent driver for his old enemy. A rather random car chase movie, obviously the last of a short line. Jackie Gleason, Jerry Reed, Mike Henry, Pat McCormick, Burt Reynolds (for a cameo). Written by Stuart Birnbaum, David Dashev; directed by Dick Lowry; for Mort Engelberg / Universal. 'A patchwork of arbitrary mayhem.'—*Variety*

Smoky
US 1946   87m   Technicolor
TCF (Robert Bassler)

An especially independent horse virtually runs the ranch on which he lives.
Family saga of the great outdoors, well enough assembled.

w Dwight Cummings, Lillie Hayward, Dorothy Yost, *novel* Will James *d* Louis King *ph* Charles Clarke *m* David Raksin *md* Emil Newman

Fred MacMurray, Anne Baxter, Burl Ives, Bruce Cabot, Esther Dale
† The story was also made by Fox in 1933 with Victor Jory, and in 1966 with Fess Parker.

SNAFU
US 1945   85m   bw
Columbia
GB title: *Welcome Home*

Middle-class parents rescue their difficult 15-year-old son from the army, then wish they hadn't.
Predictable, well-greased comedy of a rebellious teenager.

w Louis Solomon, Harold Buchman, from their play *d* Jack Moss *ph* Franz Planer *m* Paul Sawtell

Robert Benchley, Vera Vague, Conrad Janis, Nanetta Parks
† The title can be bowdlerized as 'Situation Normal, All Fouled Up'.

The Snake Pit••
US 1948   108m   bw
TCF (Anatole Litvak, Robert Bassler)

A girl becomes mentally deranged and has horrifying experiences in an institution. A headline-hitting film which made a stirring plea for more sympathetic treatment of mental illness. Very well made, and arrestingly acted, but somehow nobody's favourite movie.

w Frank Partos, Millen Brand, *novel* Mary Jane Ward *d* Anatole Litvak *ph* Leo Tover *m* Alfred Newman

Olivia de Havilland, Leo Genn, Mark Stevens, Celeste Holm, Glenn Langan, Leif Erickson, Beulah Bondi, Lee Patrick, Natalie Schaefer

'A film of superficial veracity that requires a bigger man than Litvak; a good film with bad things.'—*Herman G. Weinberg*

AAN: best picture; script; Anatole Litvak; Alfred Newman; Olivia de Havilland

The Sniper••
US 1952 87m bw
Columbia / Stanley Kramer (Edna and
Edward Anhalt)

A psychopath kills a succession of blondes
with a high-powered rifle.
Semi-documentary police drama which was
quite startling and influential when released
but seems quite routine now.

w Harry Brown d Edward Dmytryk
ph Burnett Guffey m George Antheil

Adolphe Menjou, Arthur Franz, Gerald Mohr,
Richard Kiley, Frank Faylen, Marie Windsor

AAN: original story (Edna and Edward
Annalt)

The Snorkel
GB 1958 80m bw
Columbia / Hammer (Michael Carreras)

A man murders his wife and is given away by
his observant young stepdaughter.
Tenuous suspenser which outstays its
welcome.

w Peter Myers, Jimmy Sangster, Anthony
Dawson d Guy Green ph Jack Asher

Peter Van Eyck, Mandy Miller, William
Franklyn, Grégoire Aslan

Snow Treasure
US 1968 95m Eastmancolor
Sagittarius (Irving Jacoby)

In Nazi-occupied Norway a teenage boy finds
gold hidden in the snow; an underground
agent helps him get it to safety.
Curiously undernourished but attractively
made adventure film.

w Irving Jacoby, Peter Hansen, *novel* Marie
McSwigan d Irving Jacoby ph Sverre Bergli
m Egil Monn-Iversen

James Franciscus, Paul Anstad, Paoul Oyen,
Randi Borch

Snow White and the Seven Dwarfs••••
US 1937 82m Technicolor
Walt Disney

Disney's first feature cartoon, a mammoth
enterprise which no one in the business
thought would work. The romantic leads were
wishy-washy but the splendid songs and the
marvellous comic and villainous characters
turned the film into a world-wide box office
bombshell which is almost as fresh today as
when it was made.

w Ted Sears, Otto Englander, Earl Hurd,
Dorothy Ann Blank, Richard Creedon, Dick
Richard, Merrill de Maris, Webb Smith, from
the fairy tale by the brothers Grimm
supervising director David Hand m Frank
Churchill, Leigh Harline, Paul Smith
songs Larry Morey, Frank Churchill

'The first full-length animated feature, the
turning point in Disney's career, a milestone in
film history, and a great film.'—*Leonard
Maltin*

'Sustained fantasy, the animated cartoon
grown up.'—*Otis Ferguson*

AAN: Frank Churchill, Leigh Harline, Paul
Smith

Snow White and the Three Stooges•
US 1961 107m De Luxe Cinemascope
(TCF) Chanford (Charles Wick)
GB title: *Snow White and the Three Clowns*

The old story retold as a vehicle for a
champion skater and three veteran clowns.
Surprisingly tolerable as a holiday attraction,
once you get over the shock.

w Noel Langley, Elwood Ullman d Walter
Lang ph Leon Shamroy m Lyn Murray
ad Jack Martin Smith, Maurice Ransford

Carol Heiss, Moe Howard, Larry Fine, Joe de
Rita, Edson Stroll, Patricia Medina, Guy
Rolfe, Buddy Baer, Edgar Barrier

Snowball Express
US 1972 99m Technicolor
Walt Disney (Ron Miller)

An insurance accountant inherits a dilapidated
skiing hotel in the Colorado Rockies.
Uninspired family comedy with slapstick on
the snow slopes.

w Don Tait, Jim Parker, Arnold Margolin,
novel Château Bon Vivant by Frankie and
John O'Rear d Norman Tokar ph Frank
Phillips m Robert F. Brunner

Dean Jones, Nancy Olson, Henry Morgan,
Keenan Wynn, Mary Wickes, Johnny
Whittaker

'As wholesome and bland as that old
American favourite the peanut butter and jelly
sandwich.'—*MFB*

Snowbound
GB 1948 87m bw
Gainsborough

Various people congregate at a ski hut in the
Swiss Alps; all are after buried Nazi loot.
A rather foolish story which provides little in
the way of action but at least assembles a fine
crop of character actors.

w David Evans, Keith Campbell, *novel* The
Lonely Skier by Hammond Innes d David
MacDonald ph Stephen Dade

Robert Newton, Dennis Price, Herbert Lom,
Stanley Holloway, Marcel Dalio, Mila Parely,
Guy Middleton

'Out of one masterpiece, another has been
created!'
The Snows of Kilimanjaro••
US 1952 117m Technicolor
TCF (Darryl F. Zanuck)

A hunter lies wounded in Africa and while
waiting for help looks back over his life and
loves.
Hollywood version of a portable Hemingway,
with reminiscences of several novels stirred
into a lush and sprawling mix of action and
romance, open spaces and smart salons. A big
popular star film of its time, despite
constricted and unconvincing characters.

w Casey Robinson, *story* Ernest Hemingway
d Henry King ph Leon Shamroy m Bernard
Herrmann

Gregory Peck, Susan Hayward, Ava Gardner,
Hildegard Neff, Leo G. Carroll, Torin
Thatcher, Marcel Dalio

'A naïve kind of success story with a
conventional boy-meets-lots-of-girls plot.'—
Karel Reisz

'The succinct and vivid qualities associated
with Hemingway are rarely evoked, and what
has been substituted is for the most part
meandering, pretentious and more or less
maudlin romance.'—*Newsweek*

AAN: Leon Shamroy

So Big•
US 1932 80m bw
Warner (Lucien Hubbard)

A schoolteacher marries a farmer, has trouble
with her son, falls in love with a sculptor.
Watchable, superficial, top-talented
adaptation of a best-seller, first filmed in 1925
with Colleen Moore.

w J. Grubb Alexander, Robert Lord, *novel*
Edna Ferber d William Wellman ph Sid
Hickox m W. Franke Harling

Barbara Stanwyck, George Brent, Dickie
Moore, Guy Kibbee, Bette Davis, Hardie
Albright

'Too long getting started, and only has
moments towards the end . . . somewhat of a
bore for the major part of its footage.'—
Variety

So Big
US 1953 101m bw
Warner (Henry Blanke)

By the time this inflated remake came along,
the story was just too corny despite careful
production.

w John Twist d Robert Wise ph Ellsworth
Fredericks m Max Steiner

Jane Wyman, Sterling Hayden, Richard
Beymer, Nancy Olson, Steve Forrest,
Elizabeth Fraser, Martha Hyer

So Dark the Night•
US 1946 71m bw
Columbia

A detective tracks down a murderer whom he
finds to be himself.
Smart second feature with a likeable leading
performance.

w Aubrey Wisberg, Martin Berkeley, Dwight
Babcock d Joseph H. Lewis m Hugo
Friedhofer

Steven Geray, Ann Codee, Micheleine Cheirel

So Dear to My Heart•
US 1948 84m Technicolor
Walt Disney

Life on a country farm in 1903.
Live action nostalgia with a few cartoon
segments; well enough done, but mainly
appealing to well brought up children.

w John Tucker Battle, *novel* Midnight and
Jeremiah by Sterling North d Harold
Schuster ph Winton C. Hoch m Paul Smith

Burl Ives, Beulah Bondi, Harry Carey, Luana Patten, Bobby Driscoll

AAN: song 'Lavender Blue' (*m* Eliot Daniel, *ly* Larry Morey)

So Ends Our Night*
US 1941 120m bw
(UA) David L. Loew, Albert Lewin

Refugees from Nazi Germany are driven from country to country and meet persecution everywhere.
Worthy but rather drab and unfocused melodrama from the headlines.

w Talbot Jennings, *novel* Flotsam by Erich Maria Remarque *d* John Cromwell
ph William Daniels *m* Louis Gruenberg

Fredric March, Margaret Sullavan, Glenn Ford, Frances Dee, Anna Sten, Erich Von Stroheim, Joseph Cawthorn, Leonid Kinskey, Alexander Granach, Sig Rumann

'It ought to be a great picture but it isn't.'—*Archer Winsten, New York Post*

AAN: Louis Gruenberg

So Evil My Love*
US 1948 100m bw
Paramount (Hal B. Wallis)

A missionary's widow is enticed into a life of crime and immorality by a scoundrelly artist.
Curious Victorian melodrama with a Wildean flavour; doesn't quite come off.

w Leonard Spiegelgass, Ronald Miller, *novel* Joseph Shearing *d* Lewis Allen *ph* Max Greene *m* Victor Young, William Alwyn

Ray Milland, Ann Todd, Geraldine Fitzgerald, Leo G. Carroll, Raymond Huntley, Martita Hunt, Moira Lister, Raymond Lovell, Muriel Aked, Finlay Currie, Hugh Griffith

'There's only one thing that can keep them apart—the seven-foot thing she's married to!'

So Fine
US 1981 91m Technicolor
Warner / Lobell–Bergman (Mike Lobell)

A professor of literature trying to save his father from gangsters becomes involved in strange adventures.
Weirdly titled action comedy which tries to be far too clever for its own good.

wd Andrew Bergman *ph* James A. Contner *m* Ennio Morricone

Ryan O'Neal, Jack Warden, Mariangela Melato, Richard Kiel, Fred Gwynne, Mike Kellin

'A visual insult, crudely lighted and framed, and jumping out at you.'—*Pauline Kael, New Yorker*

So Goes My Love
US 1946 88m bw
(U-I) Jack H. Skirball / Bruce Manning
GB title: *A Genius in the Family*

The domestic life of inventor Hiram Maxim.
Formula period family film with pleasant moments.

w Bruce Manning, James Clifden *d* Frank Ryan *ph* Joseph Valentine *m* Hans Salter

Myrna Loy, Don Ameche, Rhys Williams, Bobby Driscoll, Richard Gaines

So Little Time
GB 1952 88m bw
ABP / Mayflower (Aubrey Baring, Maxwell Setton)

In occupied Belgium an aristocratic lady falls in love with a Nazi colonel.
Doomed love story with musical accompaniment; tolerable but slow.

w John Cresswell *d* Compton Bennett *ph* Oswald Morris *m* Robert Gill

Marius Goring, Maria Schell, Gabrielle Dorziat, Barbara Mullen

So Long at the Fair*
GB 1950 86m bw
Rank / Gainsborough / Sydney Box (Betty E. Box)

During the 1889 Paris Exposition a girl books into a hotel with her brother, and next day finds that he has totally disappeared and his existence is denied by all concerned.
Straightforward version of an old yarn which has turned up in such varied forms as *The Lady Vanishes* and *Bunny Lake is Missing*.
This modest production is pleasant enough but badly lacks drive.

w Hugh Mills, Anthony Thorne *d* Terence Fisher, Anthony Darnborough *ph* Reginald Wyer *m* Benjamin Frankel *ad* Cedric Dawe

Jean Simmons, Dirk Bogarde, David Tomlinson, Marcel Poncin, Cathleen Nesbitt, Honor Blackman, Betty Warren, Felix Aylmer, André Morell

'A foxhole was her honeymoon hotel!'
'The first great story of our women at the fighting front!'

So Proudly We Hail*
US 1943 125m bw
Paramount (Mark Sandrich)

The self-sacrifice of war nurses in the Pacific.
Fairly harrowing and well-meant but studio-bound and unconvincing flagwaver.

w Allan Scott *d* Mark Sandrich *ph* Charles Lang *m* Miklos Rozsa

Claudette Colbert, Paulette Goddard, Veronica Lake, George Reeves, Barbara Britton, Walter Abel, Sonny Tufts, John Litel

'Probably the most deadly accurate picture ever made of what war looks like through the lenses of a housewives' magazine romance.'—*James Agee*
'The stars are devotedly, almost gallantly, deglamorized and dishevelled but they cannot escape the smell of studio varnish.'—*Richard Winnington*

AAN: Allan Scott; Charles Lang; Paulette Goddard

'The flower of southern chivalry dewed with the shining glory of a woman's tears!'

So Red the Rose*
US 1935 82m bw
Paramount (Douglas MacLean)

The life of a southern family during the Civil War.
Quiet, pleasing historical romance.

w Laurence Stallings, Maxwell Anderson, Edwin Justus Mayer, *novel* Stark Young *d* King Vidor *ph* Victor Milner *m* W. Franke Harling

Margaret Sullavan, Randolph Scott, Walter Connolly, Elizabeth Patterson, Janet Beecher, Robert Cummings

'Certain to go better in the Dixie belt than north, but okay on average.'—*Variety*

So This Is London
GB 1939 89m bw

An American magnate visits his English rival, and romance springs up between their children. Brightish comedy with a fair scattering of funny lines. Robertson Hare, Alfred Drayton, George Sanders, Berton Churchill, Fay Compton, Carla Lehmann, Stewart Granger, Ethel Revnell, Gracie West. Written by William Conselman, Ben Travers, Tom Phipps and Douglas Furber; directed by Thornton Freeland; for TCF.

So This Is Love
US 1953 101m Technicolor
Warner (Henry Blanke)
GB title: *The Grace Moore Story*

Events leading up to Grace Moore's debut at the Metropolitan Opera in 1928.
Acceptable musical biopic full of the usual Hollywood contrivances.

w John Monks Jnr, from Grace Moore's autobiography *d* Gordon Douglas *ph* Robert Burks *md* Ray Heindorf, Max Steiner *ch* Le Roy Prinz *ad* Edward Carrere

Kathryn Grayson, Merv Griffin, Joan Weldon, Walter Abel, Rosemary de Camp, Jeff Donnell, Douglas Dick, Mabel Albertson, Fortunio Bonanova

So This Is New York*
US 1948 78m bw
Stanley Kramer / Enterprise

In 1919 some country cousins who have come into money have a big time in the gay city.
Curious, sporadically effective, silent-style comedy which doesn't quite come off.

w Carl Foreman, Herbert Baker, *novel* The Big Town by Ring Lardner *d* Richard Fleischer *ph* Jack Russell *m* Dmitri Tiomkin

Henry Morgan, Rudy Vallee, Hugh Herbert, Bill Goodwin, Virginia Grey, Dona Drake, Leo Gorcey

So This Is Paris
US 1955 96m Technicolor
U-I (Albert J. Cohen)

Three American sailors on leave in Paris meet girls and help war orphans.
Very thin imitation of *On the Town*, bogged down by sentimentality and lack of sparkle. The musical numbers, however, are not bad.

w Charles Hoffman *d* Richard Quine *ph* Maury Gertsman *md* Joseph Gershenson *ch* Gene Nelson, Lee Scott

Tony Curtis, Gloria de Haven, Gene Nelson, *Corinne Calvet*, Paul Gilbert, Mara Corday, Allison Hayes

901

The old homestead destroyed

Stark Young's novel brought to thrilling life.

SO RED THE ROSE. An epic of southern gallantry which flopped so resoundingly that one wonders why Selznick dared to make *Gone with the Wind.*

So Well Remembered°
GB 1947   114m   bw
(RKO) Alliance (Adrian Scott)

The ambitious daughter of a mill-owner marries a rising politician but almost ruins his life.
Rather routine treatment of a three-decker north country novel; humdrum incident and unsympathetic characters, but full of minor British virtues.

w John Paxton, novel James Hilton d Edward Dmytryk ph Frederick A. Young

John Mills, Martha Scott, Trevor Howard, Patricia Roc, Richard Carlson

Soak the Rich°
US 1935   74m   bw
Paramount (Ben Hecht, Charles MacArthur)

A rebellious rich girl is cured when she is rescued from kidnapping.
Smartly written social comedy-melodrama.

wd Ben Hecht, Charles MacArthur ph Leon Shamroy

Walter Connolly, John Howard, Mary Taylor, Lionel Stander, Ilka Chase
'Hecht and MacArthur have not been very successful in their attempts to gauge public opinion . . . inadequate entertainment.'—Variety

Social Register
US 1934   71m   bw

A chorus girl fights the prejudices of her in-laws to be. Dull and obvious romantic drama mainly notable for its cast, and for the star who failed to make a comeback. Colleen Moore, Charles Winninger, Pauline Frederick, Alexander Kirkland, Robert Benchley, Ross Alexander. Written by Clara Beranger, Anita Loos, John Emerson; directed by Marshall Neilan; for William de Mille / Columbia.
'Good players lost in a trite story.'—Variety

Society Doctor
US 1935   63m   bw
MGM (Lucien Hubbard)
GB title: After Eight Hours

A doctor's modern ideas incur hostility: he goes into private practice, but returning to the hospital is wounded by a gangster and supervises his own operation under spinal anaesthetic.
Melodramatic hokum with most attention going to the second male lead, the young and rising Robert Taylor.

w Sam Marx, Michael Fessier, novel The Harbor by Theodore Reeves d George B. Seitz ph Lester White m Oscar Radin

Chester Morris, Virginia Bruce, Robert Taylor, Billie Burke, Raymond Walburn, Henry Kolker, William Henry

Society Girl
US 1932   72m   bw

A prizefighter falls for a society girl. Weak melodrama whose best scenes are in the ring.
James Dunn, Spencer Tracy, Peggy Shannon,
Walter Byron, Marjorie Gateson. Written by Charles Benhan, Elmer Harris, from the play by John Larkin Jnr; directed by Sidney Lanfield; for Fox. 'Falls short of first-rate classification.'—Variety

Society Lawyer
US 1939   77m   bw

A lawyer is embarrassed by the gratitude of a racketeer. Tolerable co-feature with class production. Walter Pidgeon, Virginia Bruce, Leo Carrillo, Eduardo Ciannelli, Lee Bowman, Herbert Mundin. Written by Frances Goodrich, Albert Hackett, Leon Gordon, Hugo Butler; directed by Edwin L. Marin; for John W. Considine Jnr / MGM. 'Fairish murder mystery with sophisticated background. For duals.'—Variety

Sodom and Gomorrah
Italy / France 1962   154m   colour
Titanus / S. N. Pathe (Gottfredo Lombardo)

Lot and the Hebrews become involved in a Helamite plan to take over the rich sinful cities of Sodom and Gomorrah.
Dreary biblical blood-and-thunder; an international muddle, tedious in the extreme outside a few hilariously misjudged moments.

w Hugo Butler, Giorgio Prosperi d Robert Aldrich ph Silvano Ippoliti, Cyril Knowles m Miklos Rozsa ad Ken Adam

Stewart Granger, Stanley Baker, Pier Angeli, Anouk Aimée, Rossana Podesta

Soft Beds, Hard Battles
GB 1973   107m   colour
Rank / Charter (John Boulting)
US title: Undercovers Hero

Inhabitants of a Paris brothel help to win World War II.
Ragbag of poor sketches and dirty jokes, with the star in several ineffective roles including Hitler.

w Leo Marks, Roy Boulting d Roy Boulting ph Gil Taylor m Neil Rhoden

Peter Sellers, Lila Kedrova, Curt Jurgens, Gabriella Licudi, Jenny Hanley

● Video: Rank

Sol Madrid
US 1968   90m   Metrocolor   Panavision
MGM / Gershwin–Kastner (Hall Bartlett)
GB title: The Heroin Gang

An undercover narcotics agent is assigned to track down an elusive Mafia executive.
Humdrum, predictable, brutishly violent international crime caper.

w David Karp, novel Fruit of the Poppy by Robert Wilder d Brian G. Hutton ph Fred Koenekamp m Lalo Schifrin

David McCallum, Telly Savalas, Stella Stevens, Ricardo Montalban, Rip Torn, Pat Hingle, Paul Lukas, Perry Lopez, Michael Ansara.

Solaris°°
USSR 1972   165m   Sovcolor   'Scope
Mosfilm

A psychologist is sent to investigate the many deaths in a space station orbiting a remote planet.
Heavy-going but highly imaginative space fiction in which the menaces are ghosts materialized from the subjects' guilty pasts. The technology is superbly managed, but the whole thing is rather humourless.

w Andrei Tarkovsky, Friedrich Gorenstein, novel Stanislaw Lem d Andrei Tarkovsky ph Vadim Yusov m Eduard Artemyev

Natalya Bondarchuk, Donatas Banionis, Yuri Yarvet

The Soldier and the Lady°
US 1937   85m   bw
RKO (Pandro S. Berman)
GB title: Michael Strogoff

In Napoleonic times, a messenger from the Czar sees more trouble than he expected.
Mildly ambitious swashbuckler from a story much remade in Europe; the elements jelled quite well in the Hollywood fashion.

w Mortimer Offner, Anthony Veiller and Anne Morrison Chapin from the novel by Jules Verne d George Nicholls Jnr ph Joseph H. August

Anton Walbrook, Elizabeth Allan, Akim Tamiroff
'Spectacle film lacking strength and names. Will have its troubles.'—Variety

† Exteriors were taken from a German / French film of 1936, Courier to the Star

'Stained with the blood of the innocent!'
Soldier Blue°
US 1970   114m   Technicolor   Panavision
Avco (Gabriel Katzka, Harold Loeb)

A paymaster's detachment of the US cavalry is attacked by Indians seeking gold, and two white survivors trek through the desert.
Extremely violent 'anti-violence' western with a particularly nauseating climax following clichés all the way. From a director with pretensions.

w John Gay, novel Arrow in the Sun by Theodore V. Olsen d Ralph Nelson ph Robert Hauser m Roy Budd

Candice Bergen, Peter Strauss, Donald Pleasence
'One is more likely to be sickened by the film itself than by the wrongs it tries to right.'—Tom Milne

● Video: CBS / Fox

Soldier in the Rain
US 1963   87m   bw
AA / Cedar / Solar (Martin Jurow)

Two army sergeants have wild plans for their demob, but one dies.
Curious sentimental tragi-comedy which misfires on all cylinders.

w Blake Edwards, Maurice Richlin, *novel* William Goldman *d* Ralph Nelson *ph* Philip Lathrop *m* Henry Mancini

Steve McQueen, Jackie Gleason, Tuesday Weld, Tony Bill, Tom Poston, Ed Nelson, John Hubbard

Soldier of Fortune*
US 1955 96m De Luxe Cinemascope TCF (Buddy Adler)

When a photographer disappears in Red China, his wife comes to Hong Kong to institute a search, enlists the aid of an amiable smuggler.
Cheerful Boys' Own Paper adventure romance with attractive locations and some silly anti-Red dialogue.

w Ernest K. Gann, from his novel *d* Edward Dmytryk *ph* Leo Tover *m* Hugo Friedhofer

Clark Gable, Susan Hayward, Gene Barry, Alex D'Arcy, Michael Rennie, Tom Tully, Anna Sten, Russell Collins, Leo Gordon
'A very good adventure film but not one of the Gable smashes.'—*Hollywood Reporter*

Soldiers of the King
GB 1933 80m bw

A guards lieutenant causes trouble when he wants to marry a music hall star. Sprightly star vehicle with all talents in good form. Cicely Courtneidge, Edward Everett Horton, Anthony Bushell, Frank Cellier, Dorothy Hyson, Leslie Sarony. Written by J. O. C. Orton, Jack Hulbert and W. P. Lipscomb; directed by Maurice Elvey; for Gainsborough.

Soldiers Three
US 1951 87m bw
MGM (Pandro S. Berman)

Adventures of three roistering British officers on the North-West Frontier.
A kind of unofficial remake of *Gunga Din* without the title character; one suspects it was meant seriously and found to be so bad that the only way out was strenuously to play it for laughs.

w Marguerite Roberts, Tom Reed, Malcolm Stuart Boylan *d* Tay Garnett *ph* William Mellor *m* Adolph Deutsch

Stewart Granger, David Niven, Robert Newton, Walter Pidgeon, Cyril Cusack, Greta Gynt, Frank Allenby, Robert Coote, Dan O'Herlihy
'Kipling fans will probably have a fit but my guess is that it will have most people in fits of laughter.'—*Daily Mail*

The Solid Gold Cadillac**
US 1956 99m bw
Columbia (Fred Kohlmar)

A very minor stockholder upsets the crooked board of a large corporation.
Vaguely Capraesque comedy which begins brightly but peters out; performances sustain passing interest.

w Abe Burrows, *play* George S. Kaufman, Howard Teichmann *d* Richard Quine *ph* Charles Lang *m* Cyril Mockridge

Judy Holliday, Paul Douglas, *John Williams, Fred Clark*, Hiram Sherman, Neva Patterson, Ralph Dumke, Ray Collins, Arthur O'Connell

The Solitaire Man*
US 1933 68m bw

Crooks doublecross each other on a Paris–London aeroplane. Smart little comedy with top talent. Herbert Marshall, Elizabeth Allan, Mary Boland, Lionel Atwill, May Robson, Ralph Forbes. Written by James Kevin McGuinness, from the play by Bella and Samuel Spewack; directed by Jack Conway; for MGM. 'Diverting crook melodrama in the drawing room manner . . . a lot better than the grosses it will probably get.'—*Variety*

'Only once in 3000 years—anything like it!'
Solomon and Sheba
US 1959 142m Super Technirama 70
UA / Edward Small (Ted Richmond)

When David names his younger son as heir, his older son plots revenge.
Dullish biblical spectacle, alternating between pretentiousness and cowboys and Indians.

w Anthony Veiller, Paul Dudley, George Bruce *d* King Vidor *ph* Frederick A. Young *m* Mario Nascimbene *ad* Richard Day, Alfred Sweeney

Yul Brynner, Gina Lollobrigida, George Sanders, Marisa Pavan, David Farrar, John Crawford, Laurence Naismith, Alejandro Rey, Harry Andrews
'Penance is due.'—*Hollis Alpert*
'Watch out it doesn't put you to sleep.'—*New York Times*

Sombrero
US 1953 103m Technicolor
MGM (Jack Cummings)

Two Mexican villages feud over the burial place of a famous poet.
Rather self-consciously unusual musical which never catches fire but certainly keeps one watching its incredible mixture of music and melodrama.

w Norman Foster, Josefina Niggli, from her novel *A Mexican Village d* Norman Foster *ph* Ray June *m* Leo Arnaud

Ricardo Montalban, Pier Angeli, Yvonne de Carlo, Nina Foch, Cyd Charisse, Rick Jason, Jose Greco, Thomas Gomez, Kurt Kasznar, Walter Hampden, John Abbott
'Staggering is the only word for the hokum of this extraordinary film.'—*Gavin Lambert*

Some Call It Loving
US 1973 103m Technicolor
Pleasant Pastures / James B. Harris

A young man buys a 'sleeping beauty' at a fair but is sorry when he wakes her up.
Fashionable fantasy, amplified from a slender, winning short story.

wd James B. Harris, *story Sleeping Beauty* by John Collier *ph* Mario Tosi *m* Richard Hazard

Zalman King, Carol White, Tisa Farrow, Richard Pryor, Veronica Anderson

Some Came Running
US 1959 136m Metrocolor Cinemascope
MGM / Sol C. Siegel

A disillusioned writer returns after service to his home town and takes up with a gambler and a prostitute.
Strident and rather pointless melodrama with solid acting and production values.

w John Patrick, Arthur Sheekman, *novel* James Jones *d* Vincente Minnelli *ph* William H. Daniels *m* Elmer Bernstein

Frank Sinatra, Dean Martin, Shirley Maclaine, Martha Hyer, Arthur Kennedy, Nancy Gates, Leora Dana

AAN: song 'To Love and Be Loved' (*m* James Van Heusen, *ly* Sammy Cahn); Shirley Maclaine; Martha Hyer; Arthur Kennedy

Some Girls Do
GB 1969 93m Eastmancolor
Rank / Ashdown (Betty E. Box)

Bulldog Drummond traces the sabotage of a supersonic airliner to a gang of murderous women.
Abysmal spoof melodrama in the swinging sixties mould; a travesty of a famous character.

w David Osborn, Liz Charles-Williams *d* Ralph Thomas *ph* Ernest Steward *m* Charles Blackwell

Richard Johnson, Daliah Lavi, Bebi Loncar, James Villiers, Sydne Rome, Robert Morley, Maurice Denham, Florence Desmond, Ronnie Stevens

● Video: Rank

Some Kind of a Nut
US 1969 89m De Luxe
UA / Mirisch / TFT / DFI (Walter Mirisch)

When a bank teller grows a beard because of an unsightly bee sting, he is thought to be flouting authority and his whole life changes.
Laboured, cliché-ridden anti-establishment comedy, a waste of the talent involved.

wd Garson Kanin *ph* Burnett Guffey, Gerald Hirschfeld *m* Johnny Mandel

Dick Van Dyke, Angie Dickinson, Rosemary Forsyth, Zohra Lampert, Elliot Reid, Dennis King

Some Kind of Hero
US 1981 97m Movielab
Paramount (Howard W. Koch)

After six years as a prisoner of the Vietcong, an army veteran returns home to find his life no bed of roses.
Weird mixture of comedy and melodrama which simply doesn't jell, especially when it tries to get earnest.

d James Kirkwood, Robert Boris, *novel* James Kirkwood *d* Michael Pressman *ph* King Battot *m* Patrick Williams

Richard Pryor, Margot Kidder, Ray Sharkey, Ronny Cox, Lynne Moody, Olivia Cole

'The killer-diller of all swing shows!'

Some Like It Hot
US 1939 65m bw
Paramount (William C. Thomas)
TV reissue title: *Rhythm Romance*

A sideshow owner runs out of money.
Very mild comedy, one of several which
helped to establish Hope's star potential.

w Lewis R. Foster, *play* Wilkie C. Mahoney,
Ben Hecht, Gene Fowler *d* George
Archainbaud *ph* Karl Struss

Bob Hope, Shirley Ross, Una Merkel, Gene
Krupa, Richard Denning
'Turned out deliberately to catch the
jitterbug devotees . . . will satisfy
moderately.'—*Variety*
† The play, *The Great Magoo*, was previously
filmed in 1934 as *Shoot the Works*.

Some Like It Hot•••
US 1959 122m bw
UA / Mirisch (Billy Wilder)

Two unemployed musicians accidentally
witness the St Valentine's Day Massacre and
flee to Miami disguised as girl musicians.
Overstretched but sporadically very funny
comedy which constantly flogs its central idea
to death and then recovers with a smart line or
situation. It has in any case become a
milestone of film comedy.

w Billy Wilder, I. A. L. Diamond *d* Billy
Wilder *ph* Charles Lang Jnr *m* Adolph
Deutsch

*Jack Lemmon, Tony Curtis, Marilyn Monroe,
Joe E. Brown*, George Raft, Pat O'Brien,
Nehemiah Persoff, George E. Stone, Joan
Shawlee
'Hectic slapstick, smartass movie pardies,
sexist stereotyping, crass one-liners, and bad
taste galore.'—*Time Out, 1984*

AAN: script; Billy Wilder (as director);
Charles Lang Jnr; Jack Lemmon

Some People
GB 1962 93m Eastmancolor
Vic Films (James Archibald)

Troublesome teenage factory workers are
helped by a church organist and become
model·citizens.
Bland propaganda for the Duke of
Edinburgh's Award scheme for young people,
quite acceptably presented, with pop music ad
lib.

w John Eldridge *d* Clive Donner *ph* John
Wilcox *m* Ron Grainer

Kenneth More, Ray Brooks, Annika Wells,
David Andrews, Angela Douglas, David
Hemmings, Harry H. Corbett

Some Will, Some Won't
GB 1969 90m Technicolor
ABP / Transocean (Giulio Zampi)

In order to inherit under an eccentric will, four
people have to perform tasks out of character.
Thin remake of *Laughter in Paradise* (qv);
funny moments extremely few.

w Lew Schwarz *d* Duncan Wood *ph* Harry
Waxman *m* Howard Blake

Ronnie Corbett, Thora Hird, Michael
Hordern, Leslie Phillips, Barbara Murray,
James Robertson Justice, Dennis Price,
Wilfrid Brambell, Eleanor Summerfield,
Arthur Lowe

Somebody Killed Her Husband
US 1978 96m Movielab
Columbia / Melvin Simon (Martin Poll)

The title tells what happened when an
unhappily married young mother falls in love.
Very thin suspense comedy which starts as it
ends, uncertainly.

w Reginald Rose *d* Lamont Johnson
ph Andrew Laszlo, Ralf D. Bode *m* Alex
North *ph* Ted Haworth

Farrah Fawcett-Majors, Jeff Bridges, John
Wood, Tammy Grimes, John Glover, Patricia
Elliott

● Video: Guild

Somebody Loves Me
US 1952 97m Technicolor
Paramount / Perlberg–Seaton

First successful in San Francisco at earthquake
time, Blossom Seeley climbs to Broadway
success with her partner Benny Fields, then
retires to become his wife.
Adequate, unsurprising star musical of the
second or third rank.

wd Irving Brecher *ph* George Barnes
songs Jay Livingston, Ray Evans

Betty Hutton, Ralph Meeker, Robert Keith,
Adele Jergens, Billie Bird, Sid Tomack,
Ludwig Stossel

Somebody Up There Likes Me•
US 1956 112m bw
MGM (Charles Schnee)

An East Side kid with reform school
experience becomes middleweight boxing
champion of the world.
A sentimental fantasia on the life of Rocky
Graziano, expertly blending violence,
depression, prizefight sequences and fake
uplift.

w Ernest Lehman *d* Robert Wise *ph* Joseph
Ruttenberg *m* Bronislau Kaper

Paul Newman, Pier Angeli, Everett Sloane,
Eileen Heckart, Sal Mineo, Joseph Buloff,
Harold J. Stone, Robert Loggia

AA: Joseph Ruttenberg

Someone at the Door
GB 1936 74m bw

The new owner of a spooky house invents a
murder which seems to come true. Derivative
but quite amusing comedy thriller. Billy
Milton, Aileen Marson, Noah Beery, Edward
Chapman, Hermione Gingold, John Irwin.
Written by Jack Davies and Marjorie Deans,
from the play by Dorothy and Campbell
Christie; directed by Herbert Brenon; for BIP.
(NB: Remade in 1950 with Michael Medwin,
Yvonne Owen and Garry Marsh; directed by
Francis Searle; for Hammer.)

Someone behind the Door
France 1971 97m colour

A brain surgeon takes a psychopathic patient
home and tries to make him commit murder.
Adequate but somehow unexciting suspenser.
Charles Bronson, Anthony Perkins, Jill
Ireland. Written by Mark Boehm and Jacques
Robert; directed by Nicolas Gessner; for Lira
Film. (Aka: *Two Minds for Murder*.)

Something Big
US 1971 108m Technicolor
Cinema Center / Stanmore and Penbar
(Andrew V. McLaglen)

A retiring cavalry colonel has a last battle with
his old enemy.
Wry serio-comic western in the Ford tradition.

w James Lee Barrett *d* Andrew V. McLaglen
ph Harry Stradling Jnr *m* Marvin Hamlisch

Dean Martin, Brian Keith, Honor Blackman,
Carol White, Ben Johnson, Albert Salmi,
Denver Pyle

Something for Everyone•
US 1970 110m colour
National General (John Flaxman)
GB title: *Black Flowers for the Bride*

A young con man insinuates himself into the
household of a widowed Austrian countess.
Unusual black comedy which doesn't quite
come off.

w Hugh Wheeler, *novel* The Cook by Harry
Kressing *d* Harold Prince *ph* Walter
Lassally *m* John Kander

Angela Lansbury, Michael York, Anthony
Corlan, Heidelinde Weis
'Nothing much for anyone, actually.'—*New
Yorker*

Something for the Birds
US 1952 81m bw
TCF (Samuel G. Engel)

An elderly fraud is of help to a Washington
girl trying to save a bird sanctuary.
Derivative, competent but slightly boring
political whimsy on Capra lines.

w I. A. L. Diamond, Boris Ingster *d* Robert
Wise *ph* Joseph La Shelle *m* Sol Kaplan

Edmund Gwenn, Victor Mature, Patricia
Neal, Larry Keating, Christian Rub

Something for the Boys
US 1944 87m Technicolor
TCF (Irving Starr)

A southern plantation is turned into a retreat
for army wives.
Modest musical, vaguely based on a Broadway
success.

w Robert Ellis, Helen Logan, Frank
Gabrielson, *musical comedy* Cole Porter,
Herbert and Dorothy Fields *d* Lewis Seiler
ph Ernest Palmer *title song* Cole Porter *other
songs* Harold Adamson, Jimmy McHugh

Carmen Miranda, Michael O'Shea, Vivian Blaine, Phil Silvers, Sheila Ryan, Perry Como, Glenn Langan, Cara Williams

Something in the Wind
US 1947 89m bw
U-I (Joseph Sistrom)

A lady disc jockey is mistaken for her aunt, who has been seeing too much for the heirs' liking of a wealthy old man.
Poorish star musical comedy.

w Harry Kurnitz, William Bowers *d* Irving Pichel

Deanna Durbin, Donald O'Connor, John Dall, Charles Winninger, Helena Carter

Something Money Can't Buy
GB 1952 82m bw
Rank / Vic (Joe Janni)

After World War II a young couple find civilian life difficult and dreary, but finally start a catering and secretarial business.
Weakly contrived comedy which makes nothing of its possibilities and is limply handled all round.

w Pat Jackson, James Lansdale Hodson *d* Pat Jackson *ph* C. Pennington-Richards *m* Nino Rota

Patricia Roc, Anthony Steel, A. E. Matthews, Moira Lister, David Hutcheson, Michael Trubshawe, Diane Hart, Charles Victor, Henry Edwards

Something of Value
US 1957 113m bw
MGM (Pandro S. Berman)

A young African with many English friends is initiated into the Kikuyu.
An attempt to see all sides in the case of the African ritual murders of the fifties; bloodthirsty and unconvincing as well as dull.

wd Richard Brooks, *novel* Robert Ruark *ph* Russell Harlan *m* Miklos Rozsa

Rock Hudson, Sidney Poitier, Dana Wynter, Wendy Hiller, Robert Beatty, Juano Hernandez, William Marshall, Walter Fitzgerald, Michael Pate

Something to Hide
GB 1971 99m Eastmancolor
Avton (Michael Kinger)

A civil servant has a row with his wife, kills her and buries her body on the Isle of Wight.
Unpleasant and uninteresting melodrama demanding a hysterical performance from its star. Pleasant photography is its only asset.

w,d Alastair Reid, *novel* Nicholas Monsarrat *ph* Wolfgang Suschitzky *m* Roy Budd, Jack Fishman

Peter Finch, Colin Blakely, John Stride, Shelley Winters, Linda Hayden, Harold Goldblatt

● *Video: VCL*

Something to Live For
US 1952 (completed 1950) 89m bw
Paramount (George Stevens)

A commercial artist member of Alcoholics

Anonymous falls for a dipsomaniac actress but refuses to break up his marriage.
Glossy romantic melodrama with some style but no depth; the casting makes it seem like a sequel to *The Lost Weekend*.

w Dwight Taylor *d* George Stevens *ph* George Barnes *m* Victor Young

Ray Milland, Joan Fontaine, Teresa Wright, Richard Derr, Douglas Dick
   'The victory over alcohol becomes a somewhat woebegone business.'—*Penelope Houston*

Something to Shout About
US 1943 93m bw
Columbia

A press agent tries to get rid of an untalented star.
Tolerable musical comedy.

w Fred Shiller, Lou Breslow, Edward Eliscu, George Owen *d* Gregory Ratoff *m* Victor Schertzinger *songs* Cole Porter *md* Morris Stoloff

Don Ameche, Janet Blair, William Gaxton, Perry Como

AAN: Victor Schertzinger; Morris Stoloff; song, 'You'd Be So Nice to Come Home To'

Something to Sing About*
US 1937 90m bw
Grand National (Zion Myers)

A New York bandleader decides to take a fling at Hollywood.
Lightweight but reasonably pleasing musical, made by the star as an independent during a rift with his studio, Warners.

w Austin Parker *d, songs* Victor Schertzinger *ph* John Stumar *md* Constantin Bakaleinikoff

James Cagney, Evelyn Daw, Mona Barrie, William Frawley, Gene Lockhart
   'A first-class comedy with music; will please everywhere.'—*Variety*

● *Video: VCL*

Something Wicked This Way Comes*
US 1983 95m Technicolor
Walt Disney / Bryna (Peter Vincent Douglas)

A sinister carnival with a power over time and age visits a small town in Illinois.
A curious departure for the Disney studio is this grim fairy tale from a novel which was probably intractable. In the cinema, this is the sort of film very lucky to find an audience despite its good qualities.

w Ray Bradbury, from his novel *d* Jack Clayton *ph* Stephen H. Burum *m* James Horner *pd* Richard MacDonald

Jason Robards, Jonathan Pryce, Diane Ladd, Pam Grier, Royal Dano, Vidal Peterson, Shawn Carson

Something Wild
US 1961 112m bw
(UA) Prometheus (George Justin)

A girl's life and attitudes change after she is raped, and she moves in with a garage mechanic.

A bit of a wallow, with much method acting but no clear analysis of the central relationship.

w Jack Garfein, Alex Karmel, *novel* Mary Ann by Alex Karmel *d* Jack Garfein *ph* Eugene Schufftan *m* Aaron Copland *ad* Richard Day

Carroll Baker, Ralph Meeker, Mildred Dunnock, Charles Watts, Martin Kosleck, Jean Stapleton

Sometimes a Great Notion*
US 1971 114m Technicolor
   Panavision
Universal / Newman–Foreman
GB title: *Never Give an Inch*

In a small Oregon township, trouble is caused by an independent family of lumberjacks.
Freewheeling but unsatisfactorily eccentric comedy-melodrama which never quite jells but has flashes of individuality.

w John Gay, *novel* Ken Kesey *d* Paul Newman *ph* Richard Moore *m* Henry Mancini

Paul Newman, Henry Fonda, Lee Remick, Michael Sarrazin, Richard Jaeckel, Linda Lawson, Cliff Potts

AAN: song 'All His Children' (*m* Henry Mancini, *ly* Alan and Marilyn Bergman); Richard Jaeckel

Somewhere I'll Find You*
US 1942 108m bw
MGM (Pandro S. Berman)

Brother war correspondents quarrel over a girl and later find her in Indo-China smuggling Chinese babies to safety.
Absurd but satisfactory star vehicle of the second rank, with the theme designed to prepare America for war.

w Marguerite Roberts, *story* Charles Hoffman *d* Wesley Ruggles *ph* Harold Rosson *m* Bronislau Kaper

Clark Gable, Lana Turner, Robert Sterling, Patricia Dane, Reginald Owen, Lee Patrick, Charles Dingle, Rags Ragland, William Henry

Somewhere in England
GB 1940 79m bw
Mancunian (John E. Blakeley)

High jinks among army recruits staging a show.
One of a series of misshapen and badly made regional comedies which afflicted British cinemas in the forties and should be mentioned for their immense popularity, their new-style vulgarity (later to be refined by the Carry On series) and their highly popular stars.

w Arthur Mertz, Rodney Parsons *d* John E. Blakeley

Frank Randle, Harry Korris, Robbie Vincent, Winki Turner, Dan Young
† Subsequently released, or allowed to escape, between 1941 and 1949 were *Somewhere in Camp, Somewhere on Leave, Somewhere in Civvies* and *Somewhere in Politics*.

Somewhere in the Night*
US 1946 111m bw
TCF (Anderson Lawler)

An amnesiac war veteran tries to discover his
true identity and discovers he is a crook with
much-wanted information.
Overlong suspenser with a tentative *film noir*
atmosphere. A few nice touches partly atone
for a tediously conversational plot.

w Howard Dimsdale, Joseph L. Mankiewicz,
story The Lonely Journey by Marvin
Borowsky *d* Joseph L. Mankiewicz
ph Norbert Brodine *m* David Buttolph

John Hodiak, Nancy Guild, Lloyd Nolan,
Richard Conte, Josephine Hutchinson, *Fritz
Kortner*

Somewhere in Time*
US 1980 104m Technicolor
Universal / Rastar (Stephen Deutsch)

A playwright finds a way back in time for
another encounter with the girl he loved and
lost in a previous incarnation.
Rather a charming variation on *Berkeley
Square*, but hardly a theme to do well in the
hardnosed eighties.

w *Richard Matheson*, from his novel Bid Time
Return *d* Jeannot Szwarc *ph* Isidore
Mankofsky *m* John Barry

Christopher Reeve, Christopher Plummer,
Jane Seymour, Teresa Wright, Bill Erwin,
George Voskovec

The Son-Daughter
US 1932 79m bw

True love among the San Francisco Chinese is
affected by warring Tongs. Ill-advised oriental
romance which failed to please. Ramon
Novarro, Helen Hayes, Lewis Stone, Warner
Oland, Ralph Morgan, H. B. Warner, Louise
Closser Hale. Written by Claudine West, Leon
Gordon and John Goodrich, from a play by
David Belasco and George Scarborough;
directed by Clarence Brown; for MGM.
'Old-time stuff, moving slowly and laboriously
towards a sad climax.'—*Variety*

Son of a Gunfighter
US / Spain 1964 90m Metrocolor
Cinemascope

A young westerner stalks the outlaw
responsible for his mother's death. Tolerable
international western. Russ Tamblyn, Kieron
Moore, James Philbrook, Fernando Rey.
Written by Clarke Reynolds; directed by Paul
Landres; for Lester Welch / Zurbano / MGM.

Son of Ali Baba
US 1952 75m Technicolor
U-I (Leonard Goldstein)

A cadet of the military academy outwits a
wicked caliph.
Routine Arabian Nights hokum.

w Gerald Drayson Adams *d* Kurt Neumann
ph Maury Gertsman *m* Joseph Gershenson

Tony Curtis, Piper Laurie, Susan Cabot,
Victor Jory

Son of Captain Blood
Italy / Spain 1962 95m Eastmancolor
Dyaliscope

Captain Blood's son routs his father's enemies.
Lively swashbuckler with the original star's son
rather unhappily cast. Sean Flynn, Ann Todd,
Jose Nieto, John Kitzmiller. Written by Mario
Caiano; directed by Tullio Demichelli; for
Harry Joe Brown / CCM / BP.

Son of Dr Jekyll
US 1951 77m bw

Dr Jekyll's son worries about developing a
split personality, but discovers that his father's
supposed friend Dr Lanyon is the nigger in the
woodpile. Irresistibly silly elaboration of a
famous story; no thrills but several good
unintentional laughs. Louis Hayward,
Alexander Knox, Jody Lawrance, Lester
Matthews, Paul Cavanagh, Gavin Muir, Rhys
Williams. Written by Mortimer Braus and
Jack Pollexfen; directed by Seymour
Friedman; for Columbia.

Son of Dracula*
US 1943 80m bw
Universal (Ford Beebe)

A mysterious stranger named Alucard, with a
penchant for disappearing in puffs of smoke,
turns up on a southern plantation.
Stolid series entry with a miscast lead; nicely
handled moments.

w Eric Taylor *d Robert Siodmak ph George
Robinson m* Hans Salter

Lon Chaney Jnr, Louise Allbritton, Robert
Paige, Samuel S. Hinds, Evelyn Ankers,
Frank Craven, J. Edward Bromberg
† The title cheats: he isn't the son of, but the
old man himself . . .

'The black shadows of the past bred this
half-man, half-demon!'

Son of Frankenstein***
US 1939 99m bw
Universal (Rowland V. Lee)

The old baron's son comes home and starts to
dabble, with the help of a broken-necked and
vindictive shepherd.
Handsomely mounted sequel to *Bride of
Frankenstein* and the last of the classic trio.
The monster is less interesting, but there are
plenty of other diversions, including the
splendid if impractical sets.

w Willis Cooper *d Rowland V. Lee
ph George Robinson m* Frank Skinner
ad Jack Otterson

*Basil Rathbone, Boris Karloff, Bela Lugosi,
Lionel Atwill*, Josephine Hutchinson, Donnie
Dunagan, Emma Dunn, *Edgar Norton*,
Lawrence Grant
'Rather strong material for the top keys,
picture will still garner plenty of bookings in
the secondary first runs along the main
stem.'—*Variety*

Son of Fury*
US 1942 102m bw
TCF (William Perlberg)

An 18th-century Englishman is deprived of his

inheritance, flees to a South Sea island but
comes back seeking restitution.
Elaborate costumer which suffers from loss of
suspense during the central idyll. Much to
enjoy along the way.

w Philip Dunne, *novel* Benjamin Blake by
Edison Marshall *d John Cromwell ph* Arthur
Miller *m* Alfred Newman

Tyrone Power, Gene Tierney, George
Sanders, Frances Farmer, Roddy McDowall,
John Carradine, Elsa Lanchester, *Dudley
Digges*, Harry Davenport, Halliwell Hobbes
† Remade as *Treasure of the Golden Condor*
(qv).

Son of Kong*
US 1933 69m bw
RKO (Merian C. Cooper)

After Kong has wrecked New York, producer
Carl Denham flees from his creditors and finds
more monsters on the old island.
Hasty sequel to the splendid *King Kong*; the
results were so tame and unconvincing that the
film was sold as a comedy, but it does have a
few lively moments after four reels of padding.

w Ruth Rose *d* Ernest B. Schoedsack
ph Eddie Linden, Vernon Walker, J. O.
Taylor *m* Max Steiner *sp Willis O'Brien*

Robert Armstrong, Helen Mack, Frank
Reicher, John Marston, Victor Wong
'The sequel to and wash-up of the *King
Kong* theme, consisting of salvaged remnants
from the original production . . . the punch is
no longer there.'—*Variety*
● *Video: Kingston*

Son of Monte Cristo*
US 1940 102m bw
(UA) Edward Small

The masked avenger who quashes a
dictatorship in 1865 Lichtenstein is none other
than the son of Edmond Dantes.
Cheerful swashbuckler of the second class.

w George Bruce *d Rowland V. Lee
ph* George Robinson *m* Edward Ward

Louis Hayward, Joan Bennett, George
Sanders, Florence Bates, Lionel Royce,
Montagu Love, Clayton Moore, Ralph Byrd

Son of Paleface*
US 1952 95m Technicolor
(Paramount) Bob Hope (Robe t L. Welch)

A tenderfoot and a government agent compete
for the attentions of a lady bandit.
Gagged-up sequel to *The Paleface*; much of
the humour now seems self-conscious and
dated in the *Road* tradition which it apes, but
there are still moments of delight.

w Frank Tashlin, Joseph Quillan, Robert L.
Welch *d* Frank Tashlin *ph* Harry J. Wild
m Lyn Murray

Bob Hope, Roy Rogers, Jane Russell,
Trigger, Douglass Dumbrille, Harry Von Zell,
Bill Williams, Lloyd Corrigan

AAN: song 'Am I in Love' (*m / ly* Jack
Brooks)

Son of Robin Hood
GB 1958   77m   Eastmancolor
Cinemascope
TCF / Argo (George Sherman)

Robin's daughter joins with the Regent's
brother to overthrow the Black Duke.
Empty-headed romp, more or less in the
accepted tradition.

w George George, George Slavin d George
Sherman ph Arthur Grant m Leighton Lucas

David Hedison, June Laverick, David Farrar,
Marius Goring, Philip Friend, Delphi
Lawrence, George Coulouris, George
Woodbridge

Son of Sinbad°
US 1955   88m   Technicolor   Superscope
RKO (Robert Sparks)

Sinbad and Omar Khayyam are imprisoned by
the Caliph but escape with the secret of green
fire.
Arabian Nights burlesque, mainly quite bright,
with the forty thieves played by harem girls.

w Aubrey Wisberg, Jack Pollexfen d Ted
Tetzlaff ph William Snyder m Victor Young

Dale Robertson, Vincent Price, Sally Forrest,
Lili St Cyr, Mari Blanchard, Leon Askin, Jay
Novello

● Video: Kingston

Son of the Gods
US 1930   90m   bw

A Chinaman falls in love with a white girl . . .
but turns out not to be a Chinaman after all.
Antediluvian miscegenation melodrama with
an unconvincing twist. Richard Barthelmess,
Constance Bennett, Geneva Mitchell, E. Alyn
Warren. Written by Bradley King from a
novel by Rex Beach; directed by Frank Lloyd;
for First National. 'High-class general
programme release.'—Variety

The Son of the Sheik°
US 1926   74m at 24 fps   bw   silent

Ahmed protects a dancing girl from a band of
renegades.
Tongue-in-cheek desert romp which was
probably its star's best film. He plays a dual
role of father and son.

w Frances Marion, George Marion Jnr,
Frederick Gresac d George Fitzmaurice
m (1934 sound version) Jack Ward

Rudolph Valentino, Vilma Banky, Agnes
Ayres

● Video: Polygram

The Song and Dance Man
US 1936   72m   bw

A vaudeville dancer goes on the skids but
turns up when his former partner needs him.
Hokey backstage drama with interesting
detail.
Paul Kelly, Claire Trevor, Michael Whalen,
Ruth Donelly, James Burke. Written by
Maude Fulton, from a play by George M.
Cohan; directed by Allan Dwan; for TCF

A Song Is Born°
US 1948   113m   Technicolor
Samuel Goldwyn

Flat remake of Ball of Fire (qv), graced by an
array of top-flight musical talent.

w Harry Tugend d Howard Hawks ph Gregg
Toland m Hugo Friedhofer md Emil
Newman songs Don Raye, Gene de Paul

Danny Kaye, Virginia Mayo, Hugh Herbert,
Steve Cochran, Felix Bressart, J. Edward
Bromberg, Mary Field, Ludwig Stossel, Louis
Armstrong, Charlie Barnet, Benny Goodman,
Lionel Hampton, Tommy Dorsey, Mel Powell

'We're going to see Jennifer Jones again
in . . .'

The Song of Bernadette°°
US 1943   156m   bw
TCF (William Perlberg)

A peasant girl has a vision of the Virgin Mary
at what becomes the shrine of Lourdes.
Hollywood religiosity at its most commercial;
but behind the lapses of taste and truth is an
excellent production which was phenomenally
popular and created a new star.

w George Seaton, novel Franz Werfel
d Henry King ph Arthur Miller m Alfred
Newman ad James Basevi, William Darling

Jennifer Jones, William Eythe, Charles
Bickford, Vincent Price, Lee J. Cobb, Gladys
Cooper, Anne Revere, Roman Bohnen,
Patricia Morison, Aubrey Mather, Charles
Dingle, Mary Anderson, Edith Barrett, Sig
Rumann

PROLOGUE: 'For those who believe in God,
no explanation is necessary. For those who do
not believe in God, no explanation is
possible.'

'A tamed and pretty image, highly
varnished, sensitively lighted, and exhibited
behind immaculate glass, the window at once
of a shrine and of a box office.'—James Agee

'It contains much to conciliate even the
crustiest and most prejudiced objector.'—
Richard Mallett, Punch

AA: Arthur Miller; Alfred Newman; Jennifer
Jones

AAN: best picture; George Seaton; Henry
King; Charles Bickford; Gladys Cooper; Anne
Revere

Song of Ceylon°°
GB 1934   40m   bw
Ceylon Tea Board (John Grierson)

A pictorial, almost sensuous, but not very
informative documentary in four sections:
'The Buddha', 'The Virgin Island', 'The
Voices of Commerce', 'The Apparel of a
God'. Its influence was immense.

wd, ph Basil Wright m Walter Leigh

Song of Freedom°
GB 1936   80m   bw
Hammer (J. Fraser Passmore)

A black London docker becomes an opera
singer, then goes to Africa to free the tribe of
which he has discovered himself to be the
head.

A weird fable but a good star vehicle and a
surprisingly smart production for the time.

w Fenn Sherie, Ingram d'Abbes, Michael
Barringer, Philip Lindsay d J. Elder Wills

Paul Robeson, Elizabeth Welch, George
Mosart, Esmé Percy

Song of Love°
US 1947   118m   bw
MGM (Clarence Brown)

The story of Clara and Robert Schumann and
their friend Johannes Brahms.
Dignified musical biopic which unfortunately
falls into most of the pitfall clichés of the
genre. Dull it may be, but it looks good and
the music is fine.

w Ivan Tors, Irmgard Von Cube, Allen
Vincent, Robert Ardrey d Clarence Brown
ph Harry Stradling md Bronislau Kaper
ad Cedric Gibbons piano Artur Rubenstein

Katharine Hepburn, Paul Henreid, Robert
Walker, Henry Daniell, Leo G. Carroll, Else
Janssen, Gigi Perreau

'This is how Brahms and the Schumanns
might very possibly have acted if they had
realized that later on they would break into
the movies.'—Time

Song o' My Heart
US 1930   85m   bw

A professional singer looks after the orphaned
children of his former love. A thin story is the
excuse for a great tenor to sing eleven songs.
John McCormack, Maureen O'Sullivan, John
Garrick, J. M. Kerrigan, Alice Joyce. Written
by Tom Barry, J. J. McCarthy; directed by
Frank Borzage; for Fox. 'A simple tale
charmingly told . . . sitting through it is no
hardship.'—Variety

Song of Norway°
US 1970   141m   De Luxe
Super Panavision 70
ABC / Andrew and Virginia Stone

A fantasia on the life of Grieg.
Multinational hodgepodge, mostly in the
Sound of Music style but with everything from
cartoons to Christmas cracker backgrounds.
Quite watchable, and the landscapes are
certainly splendid.

wd Andrew Stone ph Davis Boulton stage
musical Milton Lazarus (book) Robert
Wright, George Forrest (m / ly)

Toralv Maurstad, Florence Henderson,
Christina Schollin, Frank Poretta, Harry
Secombe, Edward G. Robinson, Robert
Morley, Elizabeth Larner, Bernard Archard,
Oscar Homolka, Richard Wordsworth

● Video: Rank

Song of Russia
US 1944   107m   bw
MGM (Joe Pasternak)

An American symphony conductor is in
Russia when hostilities begin, and watches the
citizens' war effort with admiration.

A terrible big-budget film which followed the wartime propaganda line but five years later was heavily criticized by the Unamerican Activities Committee (for the wrong reasons).

w Paul Jarrico, Richard Collins d Gregory Ratoff ph Harry Stradling m Herbert Stothart

Robert Taylor, Susan Peters, John Hodiak, Robert Benchley, Felix Bressart, Michael Chekhov, Darryl Hickman

'Film makers have evolved a new tongue—the broken accent deriving from no known language to be used by foreigners on all occasions.'—Richard Winnington

'MGM performs the neatest trick of the week by leaning over backward in Russia's favour without once swaying from right to left.'—Newsweek

Song of Scheherezade
US 1947 107m Technicolor
Universal (Edward Kaufman)

In 1865 naval cadet Rimsky-Korsakov falls in love with a dancer.
Yet another composer takes a drubbing in this dull and unconvincing hodgepodge.

wd Walter Reisch ph Hal Mohr, William V. Skall md Miklos Rozsa ch Tilly Losch ad Jack Otterson

Yvonne de Carlo, Jean-Pierre Aumont, Brian Donlevy, Eve Arden, Charles Kullman, John Qualen, Richard Lane, Terry Kilburn

'One of the world's great love stories comes to the star who can make it live!'
Song of Songs*
US 1933 89m bw
Paramount (Rouben Mamoulian)

A German peasant girl falls for a sculptor but marries a lecherous baron.
Pretentious romantic nonsense, made fairly palatable by the director's steady hand.

w Leo Birinsky, Samuel Hoffenstein, play Edward Sheldon, novel Das hohe Lied by Herman Sudermann w Rouben Mamoulian ph Victor Milner m Karl Hajos, Milien Rodern ad Hans Dreier

Marlene Dietrich, Brian Aherne, Lionel Atwill, Alison Skipworth, Hardie Albright
'An ornate and irresistible slice of outright hokum.'—Peter John Dyer, 1966

'From the moment she heard this strange, compelling music of love—she was lost!'
Song of Surrender
US 1949 93m bw
Paramount (Richard Maibaum)

In turn-of-the-century New England, a sophisticated visitor from New York falls for the wife of the museum curator.
Ho-hum romantic drama, well enough presented.

w Richard Maibaum d Mitchell Leisen ph Daniel L. Fapp m Victor Young

Wanda Hendrix, Claude Rains, Macdonald Carey, Andrea King, Henry Hull, Elizabeth Patterson, Art Smith

Song of the City
US 1937 73m bw

Italian fisherfolk in San Francisco pull a socialite out of the bay and make a man of him. Unlikely and unlovable moral tale, full of warm-hearted simple people. Margaret Lindsay, Jeffrey Dean, J. Carrol Naish, Nat Pendleton, Stanley Morner, Edward Norris. Written by Michael Fessier; directed by Errol Taggart; for Lucien Hubbard / MGM. 'Elemental stuff with some nice photography but needs bolstering for b.o. allure.'—Variety

Song of the Eagle
US 1933 65m bw

Racketeers try to control the supply of beer both after and during prohibition. Tolerable crime / family saga which becomes sentimental. Charles Bickford, Richard Arlen, Jean Hersholt, Mary Brian, Louise Dresser, George E. Stone, Andy Devine. Written by Casey Robinson, Willard Mack, Gene Towne, Graham Baker; directed by Ralph Murphy; for Charles R. Rogers / Paramount. 'Fairly good programmer and timely. What hurts is the title. Remember Animal Kingdom.'—Variety

Song of the Islands*
US 1942 75m Technicolor
TCF (William Le Baron)

On a South Sea island, the daughter of an Irish beachcomber falls for the son of an American cattle king.
Wispy musical with agreeable settings and lively songs.

w Joseph Schrank, Robert Pirosh, Robert Ellis, Helen Logan d Walter Lang ph Ernest Palmer md Alfred Newman songs various

Betty Grable, Victor Mature, Jack Oakie, Thomas Mitchell, Hilo Hattie, Billy Gilbert, George Barbier

Song of the South*
US 1946 94m Technicolor
Walt Disney (Perce Pearce)

On a long-ago southern plantation, small boys listen to the Brer Rabbit stories from an elderly black servant.
Too much Uncle Remus and not enough Brer Rabbit, we fear, but children liked it. The cartoons were actually very good.

w Dalton Raymond d Harve Foster ph Gregg Toland m Daniele Amfitheatrof, Paul J. Scott, Charles Wolcott cartoon credits various

Ruth Warrick, Bobby Driscoll, James Baskett, Luana Patten, Lucile Watson, Hattie McDaniel
'The ratio of live to cartoon action is approximately two to one, and that is the ratio of the film's mediocrity to its charm.'—Bosley Crowther

AA: song 'Zip a Dee Do Dah' (m Allie Wrubel, ly Ray Gilbert)
AAN: Daniele Amfitheatrof, Paul J. Scott, Charles Wolcott

A Song to Remember**
US 1944 113m Technicolor
Columbia (Louis F. Edelman)

The life and death of Chopin and his liaison with George Sand.
Hilarious classical musical biopic which was unexpectedly popular and provoked a flood of similar pieces. As a production, not at all bad, but the script . . .

w Sidney Buchman d Charles Vidor ph Tony Gaudio md Miklos Rozsa, Morris Stoloff piano José Iturbi ad Lionel Banks, Van Nest Polglase

Cornel Wilde, Merle Oberon, Paul Muni, Stephen Bekassy, Nina Foch, George Coulouris, Sig Arno, Howard Freeman, George Macready
'It is the business of Hollywood to shape the truth into box-office contours.'—Richard Winnington
'As infuriating and funny a misrepresentation of an artist's life and work as I have seen.'—James Agee

AAN: original story (Ernest Marischka); Tony Gaudio; Miklos Rozsa, Morris Stoloff; Cornel Wilde

Song without End
US 1960 142m Eastmancolor
Cinemascope
Columbia (William Goetz)

The life and loves of Franz Liszt.
What worked at the box office for Chopin failed disastrously for Liszt; famous people are turned into papier mâché dullards. Again, the production is elegance itself.

w Oscar Millard d Charles Vidor, George Cukor ph James Wong Howe md Morris Stoloff, Henry Sukman piano Jorge Bolet ad Walter Holscher

Dirk Bogarde, Capucine, Genevieve Page, Patricia Morison, Ivan Desny, Martita Hunt, Lyndon Brook, Alex Davion (as Chopin)

AA: Morris Stoloff, Henry Sukman

Songwriter
US 1984 94m Metrocolor
Tri-Star (Sydney Pollack)

Adventures of a country-music duo.
Very moderate entertainment which gives the impression of stars doing their own thing.

w Bud Shrake d Alan Rudolph ph Matthew Leonetti m Larry Cansler pd Joel Schiller ed Stuart Pappe

Willie Nelson, Kris Kristofferson, Melinda Dillon, Rip Torn, Lesley Ann Warren, Richard C. Sarafian

'The first experiences of a young man in the mysteries of woman!'
Sons and Lovers***
GB 1960 103m bw Cinemascope
TCF / Company of Artists / Jerry Wald

A Nottingham miner's son learns about life and love.
Well-produced and generally absorbing, if unsurprising, treatment of a famous novel.

w Gavin Lambert, T. E. B. Clarke, *novel*
D. H. Lawrence *d* Jack Cardiff *ph* Freddie
Francis m Mario Nascimbene

*Dean Stockwell, Trevor Howard, Wendy
Hiller, Heather Sears, William
Lucas, Donald Pleasence, Ernest Thesiger*
  'An album of decent Edwardian
snapshots.'—*Peter John Dyer*
  'A rare, remarkable and courageous film.'—
Daily Herald

AA: Freddie Francis
AAN: best picture; script; Jack Cardiff;
Trevor Howard; Mary Ure

Sons o' Guns

US 1936 79m bw

A Broadway dancer in uniform finds himself
accidentally enlisted and sent to France.
Among the better comedies of this star. Joe E.
Brown, Joan Blondell, Eric Blore, Wini Shaw,
Robert Barrat. Written by Julius J. Epstein
and Jerry Wald; directed by Lloyd Bacon; for
Warner.

The Sons of Katie Elder*

US 1965 122m Technicolor
  Panavision
Paramount / Hal B. Wallis (Paul Nathan)

At Katie Elder's funeral, her four troublesome
wandering sons find themselves on the verge
of further trouble.
Sluggish all-star western with predictable
highlights.

w Allan Weiss, William H. Wright, Harry
Essex *d* Henry Hathaway *ph* Lucien Ballard
m Elmer Bernstein

John Wayne, Dean Martin, Michael Anderson
Jnr, Earl Holliman, Martha Hyer, Jeremy
Slate, James Gregory, George Kennedy, Paul
Fix

Sons of the Desert****

US 1934 68m bw
Hal Roach
GB title: *Fraternally Yours*

Stan and Ollie want to go to a Chicago
convention, but kid their wives that they are
going on a cruise for health reasons.
Archetypal Laurel and Hardy comedy,
unsurpassed for gags, pacing and sympathetic
characterization.

w Frank Craven, Byron Morgan *d* William A.
Seiter *ph* Kenneth Peach

Stan Laurel, Oliver Hardy, Charlie Chase,
Mae Busch, Dorothy Christie

Sons of the Sea

GB 1939 82m Dufaycolor

Life at the Royal Naval College in Dartmouth.
Simple-minded recruiter with a top dressing of
spy stuff: naive but well liked at the time.
Leslie Banks, Mackenzie Ward, Kay Walsh,
Simon Lack, Cecil Parker, Ellen Pollock,
Nigel Stock. Written by Gerald Elliott,
Maurice Elvey, D. William Woolf, George
Barraud; directed by Maurice Elvey; for
British Consolidated.

Sophie's Choice*

US 1982 157m Technicolor
Universal / AFD / ITC / Keith Barish

In 1947, a Polish girl who has been in a
concentration camp finds that her past still
haunts her in New York.
Glum romantic drama about guilt and
retribution, long and uncinematic as well as
rather poorly done; but its intentions are
doubtless honourable.

wd Alan J. Pakula, *novel* William Styron
ph Nestor Almendros *m* Marvin Hamlisch
pd George Jenkins *ed* Evan Lottman

Meryl Streep, Kevin Kline, Peter MacNicol,
Rita Karin, Stephen D. Newman, Josh Mostel
  'Handsome, doggedly faithful and
astoundingly tedious.'—*Variety*
  'Not boring, simply unilluminating. By the
end, only one question remains: why did
Pakula have to make this movie?'—*Sight and
Sound*

AA: Meryl Streep
AAN: screenplay (adaptation);
cinematography; costume design; music

● *Video: Precision*

Sorcerer

US 1977 121m Technicolor
Universal / Film Properties International
  (William Friedkin)
GB title: *Wages of Fear*

Volunteers are needed to drive nitro-glycerine
to an outpost in the South American jungle.
Why anyone should have wanted to spend
twenty million dollars on a remake of *The
Wages of Fear*, do it badly, and give it a
misleading title is anybody's guess. The result
is dire.

w Walon Green, *novel* Georges Arnaud (and
the film by Henri-Georges Clouzot) *d* William
Friedkin *ph* John M. Stephens, Dick Bush
m various *pd* John Box

Roy Scheider, Bruno Cremer, Francisco
Rabal, Amidou, Ramon Bieri

The Sorcerers

GB 1967 85m Eastmancolor
Tigon / Curtwel / Global (Patrick Curtis,
  Tony Tenser)

An old couple find a way of regaining their
youth through hypnotizing a young man to do
their bidding.
Rather slight but oddly memorable horror
film, with an elegant old lady becoming the
real monster.

w Michael Reeves, Tom Baker, John Burke
d Michael Reeves *ph* Stanley Long *m* Paul
Ferris

Boris Karloff, *Catherine Lacey,* Ian Ogilvy,
Elizabeth Ercy, Victor Henry, Susan George,
Meier Tzelniker

Sorrell and Son

GB 1933 97m bw

When his wife leaves them, a man devotes his
life to his worthless son. Fair picturization of a
popular novel. H. B. Warner, Hugh Williams,
Winifred Shotter, Margot Grahame, Donald

Calthrop, Louis Hayward. Written by Lydia
Hayward, from the novel by Warwick
Deeping; directed by Jack Raymond; for
Herbert Wilcox / B and D. 'Insufficient in
action for the average American screen
devotee.'—*Variety*
† H. B. Warner played the same role in the
silent version of 1927.

Sorrowful Jones

US 1949 88m bw
Paramount (Robert L. Welch)

A racetrack tout unofficially adopts an orphan
girl.
Heavy-going sentimental comedy peopled by
comic gangsters, a remake of *Little Miss
Marker* with the emphasis changed.

w Melville Shavelson, Edmund Hartmann,
Jack Rose, *story* Damon Runyon *d* Sidney
Lanfield *ph* Daniel L. Fapp *m* Robert
Emmett Dolan

Bob Hope, Lucille Ball, William Demarest,
Bruce Cabot, Thomas Gomez, Tom Pedi,
Houseley Stevenson, Mary Jane Saunders

Sorry Wrong Number**

US 1948 89m bw
Paramount (Hal B. Wallis, Anatole Litvak)

A bedridden neurotic woman discovers she is
marked for murder and tries to summon help.
Artificial but effective suspenser, extended
from a radio play.

w Lucille Fletcher, from her play *d* Anatole
Litvak *ph* Sol Polito *m* Franz Waxman

Barbara Stanwyck, Burt Lancaster, Ann
Richards, Wendell Corey, Ed Begley, Harold
Vermilyea, Leif Erickson, William Conrad

AAN: Barbara Stanwyck

'Out of the secret annals of the sea comes
  the strangest story ever told!'

Souls at Sea*

US 1937 93m bw
Paramount (Henry Hathaway)

In a 19th-century shipwreck an intelligence
officer must save himself, and his mission, at
the cost of other lives, and is courtmartialled.
A lively seafaring melodrama produced on a
fairly impressive scale.

w Grover Jones, Dale Van Every *d* Henry
Hathaway *ph* Charles Lang Jnr *m* Milan
Roder, W. Franke Harling *md* Boris Morros

Gary Cooper, George Raft, Frances Dee,
Henry Wilcoxon, Harry Carey, Olympe
Bradna, Robert Cummings, Porter Hall,
George Zucco, Virginia Weidler, Joseph
Schildkraut, Gilbert Emery
  'First rate slave ship adventure.'—*Variety*

AAN: Milan Roder, W. Franke Harling

The Sound and the Fury

US 1959 117m Eastmancolor
  Cinemascope
TCF / Jerry Wald

A once proud southern family has sunk low in
finance and moral stature, and a stern elder
son tries to do something about it.
Heavy melodrama with performances to
match.

w Irving Ravetch, Harriet Frank Jnr, *novel*
William Faulkner *d* Martin Ritt *ph* Charles
G. Clarke *m* Alex North

Yul Brynner, Joanne Woodward, Margaret
Leighton, Stuart Whitman, Ethel Waters, Jack
Warden, Françoise Rosay, John Beal, Albert
Dekker
'A fourth carbon copy of Chekhov in
Dixie.'—*Stanley Kauffmann*

The Sound Barrier**
GB 1952 118m bw
London Films (David Lean)
US title: *Breaking the Sound Barrier*

An aircraft manufacturer takes risks with the
lives of his family and friends to prove that the
sound barrier can be broken.
Riveting, then topical, melodrama with
splendid air sequences; a bit upper crust, but
with well-drawn characters.

w Terence Rattigan *d* David Lean *ph* Jack
Hildyard *m* Malcolm Arnold

Ralph Richardson, Nigel Patrick, Ann Todd,
John Justin, Dinah Sheridan, Joseph Tomelty,
Denholm Elliott
'The most exciting film about the air that
has ever been produced anywhere.'—*Daily
Express*
'A peacetime film as exciting as any wartime
one.'—*Sunday Dispatch*

AAN: Terence Rattigan

The Sound of Music***
US 1965 172m De Luxe Todd-AO
TCF / Argyle (Robert Wise)

In 1938 Austria, a trainee nun becomes
governess to the Trapp family, falls in love
with the widower father, and helps them all
escape from the Nazis.
Slightly muted, very handsome version of an
enjoyably old-fashioned stage musical with
splendid tunes.

w Ernest Lehman, *book* Howard Lindsay,
Russel Crouse *d* Robert Wise *ph* Ted
McCord *m / ly* Richard Rodgers, Oscar
Hammerstein II *md* Irwin Kostal *pd* Boris
Leven

Julie Andrews, Christopher Plummer, Richard
Haydn, Eleanor Parker, *Peggy Wood*, Anna
Lee, Marni Nixon
'. . . sufficient warning to those allergic to
singing nuns and sweetly innocent children.'—
John Gillett

AA: best picture; Robert Wise; Irwin Kostal
AAN: Ted McCord; Julie Andrews; Peggy
Wood

● *Video: CBS / Fox*

Sound Off
US 1952 83m Supercinecolor
Columbia (Jonie Taps)

An entertainer is recruited into the army and
has predictable difficulties.
Dishevelled service farce with funny moments.

w Blake Edwards, Richard Quine *d* Richard
Quine *ph* Ellis Carter *m* Morris Stoloff

Mickey Rooney, Anne James, Sammy White,
John Asher, Gordon Jones

Sounder*
US 1972 105m De Luxe Panavision
TCF / Radnitz–Mattel (Robert B. Radnitz)

During the thirties Depression, black
sharecroppers in the deep south endure
various tribulations.
Well made liberated family movie . . . but not
very exciting.

w Lonnie Elder III, *novel* William H.
Armstrong *d* Martin Ritt *ph* John Alonzo
m Taj Mahal

Paul Winfield, Cicely Tyson, Kevin Hooks,
Carmen Mathews, James Best, Taj Mahal

AAN: best picture; Lonnie Elder III; Paul
Winfield; Cicely Tyson

● *Video: Polygram*

Sous le Ciel de Paris Coule la Seine
France 1951 111m bw
Regina Filmsonor (Pierre O'Connell and
Arys Nisotti)

The adventures of a variety of characters
during a day in Paris.
The director is back on his multi-story band
wagon, but in this case the stories are
undeveloped and the handling less than
interesting.

w René Lefèvre, Julien Duvivier *d* Julien
Duvivier *ph* Nicholas Hayer *m* Jean Winer

Brigitte Auber, Jean Brochard, René
Blancard, Paul Frankeur, Sylvie
'A hotchpotch of familiar story devices,
camera and picturesque
characterizations and settings, bundled
together with an old hand's facility.'—*MFB*

Sous les Toits de Paris*
France 1930 92m bw
Tobis (Frank Clifford)

A Parisian street singer falls in love with a girl,
fights her lover, and proves himself innocent
of theft.
Surprisingly serious and darkly lit little
comedy-drama which, while well enough
directed, hardly seems to merit its classic
status.

wd René Clair *ph* Georges Périnal
m Armand Bernard *pd* Lazare Meerson

Albert Préjean, Pola Illery, Gaston Modot,
Edmond Gréville
'Real film fare of quality . . . a talker which
is intelligible to any country.'—*Variety*
'It is far more movie than talkie, which
exercises the imagination and rests the ear.'—
National Board of Review

South American George
GB 1941 93m bw

An unsuccessful singer poses as a South
American opera star. Not among the star's
best. George Formby, Linden Travers, Enid
Stamp-Taylor, Jacques Brown, Felix Aylmer.
Written by Leslie Arliss, Norman Lee and
Austin Melford; directed by Marcel Varnel;
for Ben Henry / Columbia.

South of Algiers
GB 1952 95m Technicolor
ABP / Mayflower (Aubrey Baring, Maxwell
Setton)
US title: *The Golden Mask*

Archaeologists and thieves search the Sahara
for a priceless mask.
Schoolboy adventure story with a
straightforward plot and plenty of local colour.

w Robert Westerby *d* Jack Lee *ph* Oswald
Morris *m* Robert Gill

Van Heflin, Wanda Hendrix, Eric Portman,
Charles Goldner, Jacques François, Jacques
Brunius, Alec Mango, Marne Maitland

South of St Louis
US 1948 88m Technicolor

Before the Civil War starts, southern farmers
are plagued by Union guerrillas. Pretty good
western with plenty of action. Joel McCrea,
Zachary Scott, Victor Jory, Douglas Kennedy,
Dorothy Malone, Alexis Smith, Alan Hale.
Written by Zachary Gold and James R. Webb;
directed by Ray Enright; for Milton Sperling /
Warner.

South of Suez
US 1940 85m bw

A diamond miner falls for the daughter of a
man he is accused of murdering. Watchable
melodrama with pleasing actors, George
Brent, Brenda Marshall, George Tobias,
James Stephenson, Lee Patrick, Eric Blore,
Cecil Kellaway. Written by Barry Triver;
directed by Lewis Seiler; for Warner.

South of Tahiti
US 1941 75m bw

Four adventurers drift ashore on a tropical
island. Penny-pinching hokum without even
the colour to make it watchable. Brian
Donlevy, Maria Montez, Broderick Crawford,
Andy Devine, Henry Wilcoxon, H. B.
Warner. Written by Gerald Geraghty; directed
by George Waggner; for Universal. (GB title:
White Savage.)

South Pacific**
US 1958 170m Technicolor Todd-AO
Magna / S. P. Enterprises (Buddy Adler)

In 1943 an American navy nurse on a South
Pacific island falls in love with a middle-aged
French planter who becomes a war hero.
Overlong, solidly produced film of the musical
stage hit, with great locations, action climaxes
and lush photography (also a regrettable
tendency to use alarming colour filters for
dramatic emphasis).

w Paul Osborn, Richard Rodgers, Oscar
Hammerstein II, Joshua Logan, *stories* Tales
of the South Pacific by James A. Michener
d Joshua Logan *ph* Leon Shamroy
m / ly Richard Rodgers, Oscar Hammerstein II
md Alfred Newman, Ken Darby *ch* Le Roy
Prinz

Mitzi Gaynor, Rossano Brazzi, Ray Walston,
John Kerr, France Nuyen, Juanita Hall

AAN: Leon Shamroy; Alfred Newman, Ken
Darby

South Riding**
GB 1937 91m bw
London Films (Alexander Korda, Victor
  Saville)

A schoolmistress in a quiet Yorkshire dale
exposes crooked councillors and falls for the
depressed local squire.
Dated but engrossing multi-drama from a
famous novel; a good compact piece of film-
making.

w *Ian Dalrymple, Donald Bull, novel Winifred
Holtby d Victor Saville ph* Harry Stradling
m Richard Addinsell

Ralph Richardson, Edna Best, Edmund
Gwenn, Ann Todd, Glynis Johns, John
Clements, Marie Lohr, Milton Rosmer,
Edward Lexy
  'Another artistic Korda film . . . lacking in a
story of popular appeal.'—*Variety*

South Sea Sinner
US 1949 88m bw

On a South Sea island, a fugitive from justice
is blackmailed by a café owner. Hackneyed
elements are strung together without much
flair in this routine melodrama. Macdonald
Carey, Shelley Winters, Luther Adler, Helena
Carter, Frank Lovejoy, Art Smith, Liberace.
Written by Joel Malone and Oscar Brodney;
directed by Bruce Humberstone; for
Universal-International. (GB title: *East of
Java.*)

South Sea Woman
US 1953 99m bw
Warner (Sam Bischoff)
aka: *Pearl of the South Pacific*

Adventures of a fight-loving marine in the
Pacific war.
Unlovable mixture of brawling, romancing and
war-winning.

w *Edwin Blum, play* William M. Rankin
d Arthur Lubin *ph* Ted McCord *m* David
Buttolph

Burt Lancaster, Virginia Mayo, Chuck
Connors, Arthur Shields, Barry Kelley, Leon
Askin

Southern Comfort
US 1981 106m De Luxe
EMI / Phoenix / Cinema Group Venture
  (David Giler)

National Guardsmen go on a routine exercise
into swampland, and after a brush with
Louisiana Indians succumb to violence.
Brutish retread of *Deliverance* with a few nods
to Vietnam.

w *Michael Kane, Walter Hill, David Giler
d* Walter Hill *ph* Andrew Laszlo *m* Ry
Cooder

Keith Carradine, Powers Boothe, Fred Ward,
Franklyn Seales, T. K. Carter, Lewis Smith

● *Video: Thorn EMI*

'Africa explodes with a thousand
  surprises!'
The Southern Star*
GB / France 1968 105m Techniscope
Columbia / Eurofrance / Capitole (Roger
  Duchet)

In French West Africa in 1912, a penniless
American finds a huge diamond which several
crooks are after.
Quite a likeable adventure romp, with good
suspense sequences and convincing jungle
settings.

w *David Pursall, Jack Seddon, novel* Jules
Verne *d* Sidney Hayers *ph* Raoul Coutard
m Georges Garvarentz

George Segal, Ursula Andress, Orson Welles,
Ian Hendry, Michael Constantine, Johnny
Sekka, Harry Andrews

A Southern Yankee*
US 1948 90m bw
MGM (Paul Jones)
GB title: *My Hero*

During the Civil War a southern bellboy
masquerades as a spy and finds himself behind
enemy lines.
A rather feeble reworking of Buster Keaton's
The General, with some excellent gags
supervised by the master himself.

w *Harry Tugend d* Edward Sedgwick *ph* Ray
June *m* David Snell

Red Skelton, Brian-Donlevy, Arlene Dahl,
George Coulouris, Lloyd Gough, John
Ireland, Minor Watson, Charles Dingle

'She was his woman! And he was her
  man! That's all they had to fight with—
  against the world, the flesh, and the
  devil!'
The Southerner***
US 1945 91m bw
(UA) David Loew, Robert Hakim

Problems of penniless farmers in the deep
south.
Impressive, highly pictorial outdoor drama,
more poetic than *The Grapes of Wrath* and
lacking the acting strength.

wd Jean Renoir, novel Hold Autumn in Your
Hand by George Sessions Perry *ph* Lucien
Andriot *m* Werner Janssen

Zachary Scott, Betty Field, *Beulah Bondi*, J.
Carrol Naish, Percy Kilbride, Blanche Yurka,
Norman Lloyd
  'I cannot imagine anybody failing to be
spellbound by this first successful essay in
Franco-American screen collaboration.'—
Richard Winnington
  'You can smell the earth as the plough turns
it up; you can sense the winter and the rain
and the sunshine.'—*C. A. Lejeune*
† Some sources state that the script was by
William Faulkner.

AAN: Jean Renoir (as director); Werner
Janssen

Soylent Green*
US 1973 97m Metrocolor Panavision
MGM (Walter Seltzer, Russell Thatcher)

In 2022, the population of New York exists in

perpetual heat on synthetic foods; a policeman
hears from his elderly friend about an earlier
time when things were better.
Lively futuristic yarn with a splendid climax
revealing the nature of the artificial food;
marred by narrative incoherence and by
direction which fails to put plot points clearly
across.

w *Stanley R. Greenberg, novel* Make Room,
Make Room by Harry Harrison *d* Richard
Fleischer *ph* Richard H. Kline *m* Fred
Myrow

Charlton Heston, *Edward G. Robinson*, Leigh
Taylor-Young, Chuck Connors, Brock Peters,
Joseph Cotten

● *Video: MGM / UA*

The Space Children
US 1958 71m bw VistaVision

Children at a rocket testing site sabotage
equipment on the instructions of a strange
pulsating object. Naïve moral fable, not badly
done on its level. Adam Williams, Peggy
Webber, Michel Ray, Jackie Coogan. Written
by Bernard Schoenfeld; directed by Jack
Arnold; for William Alland / Paramount.

Spacehunter: Adventures in the
       Forbidden Zone
US 1983 90m Metrocolor 3-D
Columbia / Delphi (Don Carmody, Andre
  Link, John Dunning)

In the 22nd century, a spaceship salvage
expert lands on a long-forgotten planet to
rescue three earthwomen from the tyrants of
Graveyard City.
Mindless and rather unattractive space
fantasy, far less likeable than *Flash Gordon*.

w *David Preston, Edith Rey, Dan Goldbert,
Len Blum d* Lamont Johnson *ph* Frank Tidy
m Elmer Bernstein *pd* Jackson de Govia

Peter Strauss, Molly Ringwald, Ernie Hudson,
Andrea Marcovicci, Michael Ironside

The Spaceman and King Arthur
GB 1979 93m Technicolor

An astronaut and his robot accidentally
land themselves back at the court of King
Arthur. Mindless but occasionally funny
rewrite of Mark Twain's *A Connecticut
Yankee*. Dennis Dugan, Jim Dale, Ron
Moody, Kenneth More, John Le Mesurier,
Rodney Bewes, Robert Beatty. Written by
Don Tait; directed by Russ Mayberry; for
Walt Disney. (US title: *Unidentified Flying
Oddball.*)

Spanish Affair
US 1958 92m Technicolor Vistavision
Paramount / Nomad (Bruce Odlum)

An American architect in Madrid falls in love
with his interpreter and is pursued by her
lover.
Curiously plotless excuse for a travelogue,
lushly photographed but not exactly gripping.

w *Richard Collins d* Don Siegel *ph* Sam
Leavitt *m* Daniele Amfitheatrof

Richard Kiley, Carmen Sevilla, Jose
Guardiola

Spanish Fly
GB 1975   86m   Technicolor

An Englishman in Majorca tries to improve a purchase of local wine by putting an aphrodisiac in it, with predictable results.
Crude, tatty comedy by people who should know better. Terry-Thomas, Leslie Phillips, Graham Armitage, Frank Thornton, Sue Lloyd. Written by Robert Ryerson; directed by Bob Kellett; for Winkle / EMI.

The Spanish Gardener
GB 1956   97m   Technicolor   Vistavision
Rank (John Bryan)

The British consul in Spain is annoyed when his young son develops a strong friendship with the gardener.
Slow, understated study in human relationships which doesn't come off; any sexual relevance is well concealed.
w Lesley Storm, John Bryan, *novel* A. J. Cronin d Philip Leacock ph Christopher Challis m John Veale

Dirk Bogarde, Michael Hordern, Jon Whiteley, Cyril Cusack, Geoffrey Keen, Maureen Swanson, Lyndon Brook, Josephine Griffin, Bernard Lee, Rosalie Crutchley

The Spanish Main*
US 1945   101m   Technicolor
RKO (Robert Fellows)

In the Caribbean, the fiancée of the Spanish viceroy is kidnapped by a pirate who determines to tame her before marrying her.
Slightly tongue-in-cheek pirate hokum; generally good value for the easily amused.
w George Worthing Yates, Herman J. Mankiewicz d Frank Borzage ph George Barnes m Hanns Eisler md Constantin Bakaleinikoff

Paul Henreid, Maureen O'Hara, Binnie Barnes, Walter Slezak, John Emery, Barton MacLane, J. M. Kerrigan, Nancy Gates, Fritz Leiber, Jack La Rue, Mike Mazurki, Victor Kilian

AAN: George Barnes

● *Video: Kingston*

Spare a Copper*
GB 1940   77m   bw

A police war reservist catches saboteurs. One of the last good Formby comedies, with everything percolating as it should. George Formby, Dorothy Hyson, Bernard Lee, John Warwick, John Turnbull, George Merritt. Written by Roger MacDougall, Austin Melford and Basil Dearden; directed by John Paddy Carstairs; for Ealing.

Spare the Rod
GB 1961   93m   bw
British Lion / Bryanston / Weyland (Victor Lyndon)

At an East End school, a novice master wins the confidence of tough pupils.
A British *Blackboard Jungle*, paving the way for *To Sir with Love*; not exciting on its own account.

w John Cresswell, *novel* Michael Croft d Leslie Norman ph Paul Beeson m Laurie Johnson

Max Bygraves, Geoffrey Keen, Donald Pleasence, Richard O'Sullivan, Betty McDowall, Eleanor Summerfield, Mary Merrall

Sparrows Can't Sing
GB 1962   94m   bw
Elstree / Carthage (Donald Taylor)

Returning after two years at sea, a sailor searches for his wife and threatens vengeance on her lover.
Relentlessly caricatured cockney comedy melodrama, too self-conscious to be effective, and not at all likeable anyway.
w Stephen Lewis, Joan Littlewood d Joan Littlewood ph Mac Greene m James Stevens

James Booth, Barbara Windsor, Roy Kinnear, Avis Bunnage, George Sewell, Barbara Ferris, Murray Melvin, Arthur Mullard

Spartacus**
US 1960   196m   Super Technirama 70
U-I / Bryna (Edward Lewis)

The slaves of ancient Rome revolt and are quashed.
Long, well-made, downbeat epic with deeper than usual characterization and several bravura sequences.
w Dalton Trumbo, *novel* Howard Fast d Stanley Kubrick ph Russell Metty m Alex North pd Alexander Golitzen

Kirk Douglas, Laurence Olivier, Charles Laughton, Tony Curtis, Jean Simmons, Peter Ustinov, John Gavin, Nina Foch, Herbert Lom, John Ireland, John Dall, Charles McGraw, Woody Strode

'Everything is depicted with a lack of imagination that is truly Marxian.'—*Anne Grayson*
'A lot of first-rate professionals have pooled their abilities to make a first-rate circus.'—*Stanley Kauffmann*
'One comes away feeling rather revolted and not at all ennobled.'—*Alan Dent, Illustrated London News*

AA: Russell Metty; Peter Ustinov
AAN: Alex North

● *Video: CIC*

Spartacus the Gladiator
Italy 1953   103m   bw
Consorzio Spartacus

Action-oriented remake of a familiar story.
w Jean Ferry, Mario Bori d Riccardo Freda ph Gabor Pigany m Renzo Rossellini

Massimo Girotti, Ludmilla Tcherina, Maria Canala

Spawn of the North**
US 1938   110m   bw
Paramount (Albert Lewin)

In 1890s Alaska, American fishermen combat Russian poachers.
Solidly carpentered all-star action melodrama, a sizzler of its day. Remade 1953 as *Alaska Seas*.

w Talbot Jennings, Jules Furthman d Henry Hathaway ph Charles Lang m Dmitri Tiomkin

George Raft, Henry Fonda, Dorothy Lamour, *John Barrymore*, Akim Tamiroff, Louise Platt, Lynne Overman, Fuzzy Knight, Vladimir Sokoloff, Duncan Renaldo, John Wray

'The visual features are so realistic and terrifying that audiences will find complete satisfaction in the production.'—*Variety*
'This film has something which the cinema of bygone days used to supply as a matter of course—action and thrills, the quickened pulse and the lump in the throat.'—*Basil Wright*

Speak Easily*
US 1932   83m   bw
MGM (Lawrence Weingarten)

A professor inherits a Broadway musical and falls for the lure of the bright lights.
Interesting Keaton talkie at the point of his decline.
w Ralph Spence, Lawrence E. Johnson, *novel* Footlights by Clarence Budington Kelland d Edward Sedgwick ph Harold Wentstrom

Buster Keaton, Jimmy Durante, Hedda Hopper

Special Agent
US 1935   74m   bw

A special investigator pretends to be a newspaperman. Routine rough stuff, quite watchable. Bette Davis, George Brent, Ricardo Cortez, Jack La Rue, Henry O'Neill, J. Carrol Naish. Written by Laird Doyle, Abem Finkel; directed by William Keighley; for Cosmopolitan / Warners. 'Indifferent entertainment but Bette Davis may help.'—*Variety*

Special Delivery
US 1976   99m   De Luxe
TCF / Bing Crosby Productions (Richard Berg)

Three disabled Vietnam veterans rob a bank, and the consequences are complicated.
Unremarkable suspenser which takes itself too seriously.
w Don Gazzaniga d Paul Wendkos ph Harry Stradling Jnr m Lalo Schifrin

Bo Svenson, Cybill Shepherd, Michael C. Gwynne, Vic Tayback, Sorrell Booke

The Speckled Band
GB 1931   80m   bw

Sherlock Holmes saves an heiress from a horrible death. Limp and overstretched version of Conan Doyle's story, interesting only for the actors. Raymond Massey, Athole Stewart (as Watson), Lyn Harding (as Rylott), Angela Baddeley, Nancy Price. Written by W. P. Lipscomb; directed by Jack Raymond; for Herbert Wilcox / B and D.

The Specter of the Rose*
US 1946   90m   bw
Republic

A schizophrenic ballet dancer lives his role and nearly murders his wife.

A rather hilarious bid for culture: hard to sit through without laughing, but unique.

wd Ben Hecht *ph* Lee Garmes *m* Georges Antheil

Viola Essen, Ivan Kirov, Michael Chekhov

The Spellbinder
US 1939 68m bw

A criminal lawyer full of tricks finds himself on trial for murder. Contrived courtroom drama tailored to its star. Lee Tracy, Barbara Read, Patric Knowles, Allan Lane, Morgan Conway. Written by Thomas Lennon and Joseph A. Fields; directed by Jack Hively; for RKO. 'Average supporter for duals.'—*Variety*

Spellbound
GB 1940 82m bw
Pyramid Amalgamated (R. Murray Leslie)
aka: *Passing Clouds*; US title: *The Spell of Amy Nugent*

A young man is in despair when his fiancée dies, and nearly goes mad when a medium materializes her from the dead.
Very odd, very naïve, but somehow rather winning.

w Miles Malleson, *novel* The Necromancers by Robert Benson *d* John Harlow

Derek Farr, Vera Lindsay, Frederick Leister, Hay Petrie, Diana King, Felix Aylmer

Spellbound**
US 1945 111m bw
David O. Selznick

The new head of a mental institution is an impostor and an amnesiac; a staff member falls in love with him and helps him recall the fate of the real Dr Edwardes.
Enthralling and rather infuriating psychological mystery; the Hitchcock touches are splendid, and the stars shine magically, but the plot could have stood a little more attention.

w Ben Hecht, Angus MacPhail, *novel* The House of Dr Edwardes by Francis Beeding *d* Alfred Hitchcock *ph* George Barnes *dream sequence* Salvador Dali *m* Miklos Rozsa *ad* James Basevi

Ingrid Bergman, Gregory Peck, Leo G. Carroll, Michael Chekhov, Rhonda Fleming, John Emery, Norman Lloyd, Steve Geray

'Just about as much of the id as could be safely displayed in a Bergdorf Goodman window.'—*James Agee*

'Glossily produced and wildly improbable.'—*George Perry, 1965*

'Bergman's apple-cheeked sincerity has rarely been so out of place as in this confection whipped up by jaded chefs.'—*New Yorker, 1976*

AA: Miklos Rozsa
AAN: best picture; Alfred Hitchcock; George Barnes; Michael Chekhov

● *Video: Guild*

Spencer's Mountain*
US 1963 121m Technicolor
Panavision
Warner (Delmer Daves)

Life in rural America in the thirties with a poor quarry worker and his family of nine. Sentimental rose-tinted hokum which later became TV's *The Waltons*. Expertly concocted, Hollywood style.

wd Delmer Daves, *novel* Earl Hanmer Jnr *ph* Charles Lawton, H. F. Koenekamp *m* Max Steiner

Henry Fonda, Maureen O'Hara, James MacArthur, Donald Crisp, Wally Cox, Mimsy Farmer, Lilian Bronson

Spendthrift
US 1936 80m bw

A millionaire playboy runs out of cash. Mild romantic comedy. Henry Fonda, Pat Paterson, Mary Brian, George Barbier, Ed Brophy. Written by Raoul Walsh and Bert Hanlon; directed by Raoul Walsh; for Paramount.

The Sphinx
US 1933 63m bw

A murderer uses his deaf mute brother as an alibi. Mildly ingenious low-budget thriller. Lionel Atwill, Sheila Terry, Theodore Newton, Paul Hurst, Luis Alberni. Written by Albert DeMond; directed by Phil Rosen; for Monogram. 'Fair returns are probable if dated properly.'—*Variety*

Sphinx
US 1980 118m Technicolor
Panavision
Warner / Orion (Stanley O'Toole)

Archaeologists in modern Cairo find clues to an ancient treasure.
Expensive penny dreadful which lurches about from comedy to horror but is often well worth looking at.

w John Byrum, *novel* Robin Cook *d* Franklin J. Schaffner *ph* Ernest Day *m* Michael J. Lewis *pd* Terence Marsh

Lesley-Anne Down, Frank Langella, Maurice Ronet, John Gielgud, Vic Tablian, Martin Benson, John Rhys-Davies

'A glossily-packaged exercise in random-selection box-office formulae.'—*Jo Imeson, MFB*

The Spider and the Fly
GB 1949 95m bw
GFD / Maxwell Setton, Aubrey Baring

In 1913 a Parisian safecracker constantly outwits an inspector of the Sûreté, but war brings changes.
Coldly ironic comedy drama which really, regrettably, doesn't work.

w Robert Westerby *d* Robert Hamer *ph* Geoffrey Unsworth *m* Georges Auric

Eric Portman, Guy Rolfe, Nadia Gray, George Cole, Edward Chapman, John Carol, Maurice Denham

'Not sufficiently exciting for a thriller, not quite sharp enough for a real drama of character.'—*Gavin Lambert, MFB*

Spider Woman**
US 1944 62m bw
Universal (Roy William Neill)

A female Moriarty kills her victims with spiders so that she can collect on their insurance policies.
Lively episode in the modernized series, which packs in several suspenseful episodes borrowed from a variety of Conan Doyle originals.

w Bertram Millhauser *d* Roy William Neill *ph* Charles Van Enger *m* Hans Salter

Basil Rathbone, Nigel Bruce, Gale Sondergaard, Dennis Hoey, Vernon Downing, Alec Craig, Mary Gordon

The Spider's Stratagem*
Italy 1970 97m Eastmancolor
Radiotelevisione Italiana / Red Film
(Giovanni Bertolucci)

Revisiting the village in the Po valley where his father was murdered by fascists in 1936, our gradually disillusioned hero learns that his father was really a traitor executed by his own men.
Elaborately mysterious puzzle play for intellectuals, with infinite shades of meaning which few will bother to explore. The atmosphere, however, is superbly caught.

w Bernardo Bertolucci, Eduardo de Gregorio, Marilu Parolini, *story* The Theme of the Traitor and the Hero by Jorge Luis Borges *d* Bernardo Bertolucci *ph* Vittorio Storaro, Franco di Giacomo

Giulio Brogi, Alida Valli, Tino Scotti, Pino Campanini

Spies of the Air
GB 1939 73m bw
British Consolidated (K. C. Alexander)
reissue title: *Law and Disorder*

A solicitor unmasks saboteurs using portable radios to direct bombers.
Thin, tolerable comedy thriller using most of the talents of *This Man is News*.

w Roger MacDonald *d* David MacDonald

Barry K. Barnes, Roger Livesey, Joan Marion, Basil Radford, Felix Aylmer, Henry Oscar

The Spikes Gang
US 1974 96m De Luxe
UA / Mirisch / Duo / Sanford (Walter Mirisch)

Three boys shelter a bank robber and join his gang.
Doom-laden, violent western with a few comic lines.

w Irving Ravetch, Harriet Frank Jnr, *novel* The Bank Robber by Giles Tippette *d* Richard Fleischer *ph* Brian West *m* Fred Karlin

Lee Marvin, Gary Grimes, Ron Howard, Charles Martin Smith, Arthur Hunnicutt, Noah Beery Jnr

Spinout

US 1966 93m Metrocolor Panavision
MGM / Euterpe (Joe Pasternak)
GB title: *California Holiday*

A carefree touring singer agrees to drive an experimental car in a road race.
Mild star musical which at least stays in the open air.

w Theodore J. Flicker, George Kirgo *d* Norman Taurog *ph* Daniel L. Fapp *md* Georgie Stoll

Elvis Presley, Shelley Fabares, Carl Betz, Cecil Kellaway, Diane McBain, Deborah Walley, Jack Mullaney, Will Hutchins, Una Merkel

The Spiral Road

US 1962 145m Eastmancolor
U-I (Robert Arthur)

In 1936 Java, an atheist medical man fights a leprosy epidemic and eventually becomes a missionary.
A long slog through jungle / religious clichés, with a hilariously miscast star and an almost Victorian script.

w John Lee Mahin, Neil Paterson, *novel* Jan de Hartog *d* Robert Mulligan *ph* Russell Harlan *m* Jerry Goldsmith

Rock Hudson, Burl Ives, Geoffrey Keen, Gena Rowlands, Will Kuluva, Neva Patterson, Philip Abbott

The Spiral Staircase***

US 1945 83m bw
RKO (Dore Schary)

A small town in 1906 New England is terrorized by a psychopathic killer of deformed girls.
Archetypal old dark house thriller, superbly detailed and set during a most convincing thunderstorm. Even though the identity of the villain is pretty obvious, this is a superior Hollywood product.

w Mel Dinelli, *novel* Some Must Watch by Ethel Lina White *d* Robert Siodmak *ph* Nicholas Musuraca *m* Roy Webb *ad* Albert S. D'Agostino, Jack Okey

Dorothy McGuire, George Brent, Kent Smith, Ethel Barrymore, Rhys Williams, Rhonda Fleming, Gordon Oliver, Sara Allgood, James Bell
'A nice, cosy and well-sustained atmosphere of horror.'—*C. A. Lejeune*

AAN: Ethel Barrymore

● Video: Guild

The Spiral Staircase

GB 1975 89m Technicolor
Warner / Raven (Peter Shaw)

Modernized remake of the above using virtually the same script, and apparently determined to prove how badly it can be presented.

w Allan Scott, Chris Bryant *d* Peter Collinson *ph* Ken Hodges *m* David Lindup

Jacqueline Bisset, Christopher Plummer, Sam Wanamaker, Mildred Dunnock, Gayle Hunnicutt, Sheila Brennan, Elaine Stritch, John Ronane, Ronald Radd, John Phillip Law
'I don't think this needless remake is going to set anyone's flesh creeping, except at the vulgar flashiness of the whole enterprise.'—*Michael Billington, Illustrated London News*

The Spirit Is Willing

US 1966 100m Technicolor
Paramount / William Castle

A family finds that its holiday home is haunted by the ghosts of a *crime passionel*.
Overlong, overlayed and witless farce with virtually no opportunity well taken.

w Ben Starr, *novel* The Visitors by Nathaniel Benchley *d* William Castle *ph* Hal Stine *m* Vic Mizzy

Sid Caesar, Vera Miles, John McGiver, Cass Daley, John Astin, Mary Wickes, Jesse White

Spirit of Culver

US 1939 89m bw

A boy grows up at Culver Military Academy.
Very humdrum flagwaver combined with a last attempt to maintain stardom for two child performers. Jackie Cooper, Freddie Bartholomew, Tim Holt, Henry Hull, Andy Devine, Gene Reynolds. Written by Nathaniel West, Whitney Bolton; directed by Joseph Santley; for Universal. 'Mild entertainment for duals and kids.'—*Variety*

The Spirit of St Louis*

US 1957 135m Warnercolor
Cinemascope
Warner (Leyland Hayward)

In 1927 Charles Lindbergh flies a specially constructed plane 3,600 miles nonstop New York to Paris in 33½ hours.
Impeccably in its period, this needlessly Cinemascoped reconstruction can scarcely avoid dull patches since for long stretches its hero is on screen solo apart from a fly, and his monologues become soporific.

w Billy Wilder, Wendell Mayes, *book* Charles Lindbergh *d* Billy Wilder *ph* Robert Burks, Peverell Marley *m* Franz Waxman

James Stewart, Murray Hamilton, Marc Connelly

The Spirit of the Beehive*

Spain 1973 98m Eastmancolor
Elias Querejeta

In 1940 in a remote village, two children see a travelling film show of Frankenstein, and their imaginations run riot; or do they?
Sensitive story of childish imagination, reminiscent of *Jeux Interdits* and yet very much its own vision.

w Francisco J. Querejeta *d* Victor Erice *ph* Luis Cuadrado *m* Luis de Pablo

Fernando Fernan Gomez, Teresa Gimpera, Ana Torrent, Isabel Telleria

Spite Marriage*

US 1929 77m (24 fps) bw silent
MGM / Buster Keaton (Lawrence Weingarten)

A tailor's assistant loves an actress, who marries him to spite someone else.

For a Keaton comedy from his great period, this is remarkably thin on invention, and its pleasures, though undeniable, are minor.

w Richard Schayer, Lew Lipton *d* Edward Sedgwick *ph* Reggie Lanning

Buster Keaton, Dorothy Sebastian, Edward Earle, Leila Hyams

Spitfire*

US 1934 88m bw
RKO (Pandro S. Berman)

An Ozark mountain girl believes herself to be a faith healer and is driven from the community.
Curious star melodrama with effective moments.

w Jane Murfin, *play* Trigger by Lula Vollmer *d* John Cromwell *ph* Edward Cronjager *m* Max Steiner

Katharine Hepburn, Robert Young, Ralph Bellamy, Martha Sleeper, Louis Mason
'The veins of the story carry thin milk rather than heavy corpuscles.'—*Variety*
'The picture would suggest that Katharine Hepburn is condemned to elegance, doomed to be a lady for the rest of her natural life, and that her artistry does not extend to the interpretation of the primitive or the uncouth. That her producers have not bothered to give her a scenario of any interest or quality is another aspect of the situation.'—*The New Yorker*

Splash!*

US 1984 110m Technicolor
Touchstone / Buena Vista (Brian Grazer)

A New York wholesaler on holiday off Cape Cod falls in love with a mermaid.
A kind of updated and mildly sexed-up *Miranda*: occasionally funny but far too long.

w Lowell Ganz, Babaloo Mandel, Bruce Jay Friedman, Brian Grazer *d* Ron Howard *ph* Don Peterman *m* Lee Holdridge

Tom Hanks, Daryl Hannah, Eugene Levy, John Candy, Dody Goodman, Shecky Greene, Richard B. Shull, Howard Morris
'A typically Disney subject trying to be grown up.'—*Kim Newman, MFB*
'The picture is frequently on the verge of being more wonderful than it is . . . more lyrical, a little wilder.'—*Pauline Kael, New Yorker*

Splendor

US 1935 77m bw
Samuel Goldwyn

The son of a once-wealthy Park Avenue family marries a poor girl.
Dated romantic drama.

w Rachel Crothers, from her play *d* Elliott Nugent *ph* Gregg Toland *md* Alfred Newman

Joel McCrea, Miriam Hopkins, Helen Westley, Katherine Alexander, David Niven, Paul Cavanagh, Billie Burke, Arthur Treacher
'An unusually good production, but probably too quiet for the lesser spots.'—*Variety*

'A model of dramatic exposition, but it suffers from inaction and its theme is too commonplace.'—*New York Times*

Splendor in the Grass*
US 1961 124m Technicolor
Warner / NBI (Elia Kazan)

Adolescent love in a small Kansas town in the twenties.
Impressive though curiously unmemorable addition to a nostalgic young sex cycle which was already played out; production and performances well up to scratch.

w William Inge *d* Elia Kazan *ph* Boris Kaufman *m* David Amram

Natalie Wood, Warren Beatty, Pat Hingle, Audrey Christie, Barbara Loden, Zohra Lampert, Sandy Dennis
'Less like a high-school version of *Summer and Smoke* than [like] an Andy Hardy story with glands.'—*Stanley Kauffmann*
AA: William Inge
AAN: Natalie Wood

Splinters
GB 1929 82m bw

Soldiers at the front in 1915 form a concert party. Easy-going crowd-pleaser of its time.
Nelson Keys, Sidney Howard, Lew Lake, Hal Jones. Written by W. P. Lipscomb; directed by Jack Raymond; for Herbert Wilcox / B and D. (NB: Sequels, of roughly the same standard, included *Splinters in the Navy*, 1931, and *Splinters in the Air*, 1937; both with Sidney Howard.)

The Split
US 1968 90m Metrocolor Panavision
MGM / Spectrum (Robert Chartoff, Irwin Winkler)

A black criminal plans to rob the Los Angeles Coliseum during a football match.
Busy, brutal crime thriller, well enough done but totally unsympathetic.

w Robert Sabaroff, *novel* The Seventh by Richard Stark *d* Gordon Flemyng *ph* Burnett Guffey *m* Quincy Jones

Jim Brown, Diahann Carroll, Ernest Borgnine, Julie Harris, Gene Hackman, Jack Klugman, Warren Oates, James Whitmore, Donald Sutherland

Split Second
US 1953 85m bw
RKO (Edmund Grainger)

An escaped convict hides out with four hostages in an Arizona ghost town which has been cleared in preparation for an atom bomb test.
Routine suspenser.

w William Bowers, Irving Wallace *d* Dick Powell *ph* Nicholas Musuraca *m* Roy Webb

Stephen McNally, Alexis Smith, Jan Sterling, Keith Andes, Arthur Hunnicutt, Paul Kelly, Richard Egan, Robert Paige

The Spoilers*
US 1930 86m bw
Paramount (Lloyd Sheldon)

In Alaska during the gold rush, crooked government officials begin despoiling the richest claims.
Early talkie version of a famous brawling saga.

w Bartlett Cormack, Agnes Brand Leahy, *novel* Rex Beach *d* Edward Carewe *ph* Harry Fischbeck

Gary Cooper, William 'Stage' Boyd, Betty Compson, Kay Johnson, Harry Green, Slim Summerville
'Fair for a week in the de luxers, but made to order for the neighbourhoods and grinds everywhere.'—*Variety*

The Spoilers**
US 1942 87m bw
Universal (Frank Lloyd)

Two adventurers in the Yukon quarrel over land rights and a saloon entertainer.
Well-packaged mixture of saloon brawls, romance and adventure, much filmed as a silent.

w Lawrence Hazard, Tom Reed *d* Ray Enright *ph* Milton Krasner *m* Hans Salter *ad* Jack Otterson

Marlene Dietrich, Randolph Scott, John Wayne, Margaret Lindsay, Harry Carey, Richard Barthelmess, George Cleveland, Samuel S. Hinds

The Spoilers*
US 1955 82m Technicolor
U-I (Ross Hunter)

Adequate, unmemorable remake of the above.

w Oscar Brodney, Charles Hoffman *d* Jesse Hibbs *ph* Maury Gertsman *m* Joseph Gershenson

Anne Baxter, Jeff Chandler, Rory Calhoun, Barbara Britton, Carl Benton Reid, Ray Danton, John McIntire, Raymond Walburn, Wallace Ford

The Sport of Kings
GB 1931 98m bw

A strict JP inherits a bookie business. Heavy-going adaptation of a stage comedy warhorse, which nevertheless paved the way for many screen farces of the thirties. Leslie Henson, Gordon Harker, Hugh Wakefield, Dorothy Boyd. Written by Angus MacPhail, from the play by Ian Hay; directed by Victor Saville; for Gainsborough.

Sporting Blood
US 1931 80m bw

A horse passes through various hands and finally wins the Kentucky Derby.
Unremarkable programme fodder. Clark Gable, Ernest Torrence, Madge Evans, Lew Cody, Marie Prevost. Written by Charles Brabin, Wanda Tuchock, Willard Mack, from the story Horseflesh by Frederick Hazlitt Brennan; directed by Charles Brabin; for MGM. 'Racetrack romance with a different twist and only name Clark Gable.'—*Variety*

Spring and Port Wine
GB 1970 101m Technicolor
EMI / Memorial (Michael Medwin)

A Lancashire family runs into trouble when stern father insists that teenage daughter should eat a meal she refuses.
A popular old-fashioned stage comedy which simply doesn't work on film, partly from being set in a too-real town (Bolton) and partly because of a miscast lead.

w Bill Naughton, from his play *d* Peter Hammond *ph* Norman Warwick *m* Douglas Gamley *pd* Reece Pemberton

James Mason, Diana Coupland, Susan George, Rodney Bewes, Hannah Gordon, Adrienne Posta, Arthur Lowe

Spring in Park Lane**
GB 1948 92m bw
British Lion / Herbert Wilcox

A diamond merchant's niece falls for a footman who just happens to be an impoverished lord in disguise.
Flimsy but highly successful romantic comedy which managed to get its balance right and is still pretty entertaining, much more so than its sequel *Maytime in Mayfair*.

w Nicholas Phipps, *play* Come Out of the Kitchen by Alice Duer Miller *d* Herbert Wilcox *ph* Max Greene *m* Robert Farnon

Anna Neagle, Michael Wilding, Tom Walls, *Nicholas Phipps*, Peter Graves, Marjorie Fielding, *Nigel Patrick*, Lana Morris
'A never-failing dream of Olde Mayfaire and its eternally funny butlers and maids, its disguised lords and ladies.'—*Richard Winnington*
'A gag comedy which absolutely sparkles.'—*Picture Show*
'The best comedy any British studio has produced for more years than I care to remember.'—*News of the World*

Spring Meeting
GB 1940 93m bw

In Ireland, an impecunious widow wants her son to marry the daughter of an old flame.
Staid film version of a comedy whose characters turned up again in *Treasure Hunt*.
Nova Pilbeam, Basil Sydney, Henry Edwards, Sarah Churchill, Michael Wilding, *Margaret Rutherford*, Enid Stamp Taylor, Hugh McDermott. Written by Walter C. Mycroft and Norman Lee, from the play by M. J. Farrell and John Perry; directed by Walter C. Mycroft; for ABPC.

Spring Parade*
US 1940 89m bw
Universal (Joe Pasternak)

A single baker's assistant falls for a prince.
Pleasing, artificial Austrian frou-frou with star and support in good escapist form.

w Bruce Manning, Felix Jackson, *story* Ernst Marischka *d* Henry Koster *ph* Joseph Valentine *m* Robert Stolz *md* Charles Previn

Deanna Durbin, Robert Cummings, S. Z. Sakall, Mischa Auer, Henry Stephenson, Anne Gwynne, Butch and Buddy

AAN: Joseph Valentine; Charles Previn; song
'Waltzing in the Clouds' (*m* Robert Stolz,
ly Gus Kahn)

Spring Reunion
US 1956 79m bw
UA / Bryna (Jerry Bresler)

College classmates fall in love all over again at
a reunion fifteen years later.
Romantic fiction for the middle-aged,
performed with bare competence.

wd Robert Pirosh *ph* Harold Lipstein
m Herbert Spencer, Earle Hagen

Betty Hutton, Dana Andrews, Jean Hagen,
Robert Simon, James Gleason, Laura La
Plante, Irene Ryan

Spring Tonic
US 1935 55m bw

An escaped tigress causes various farcical
episodes. Comedy extravaganza on modest
lines, like a stretched-out two-reeler. Lew
Ayres, Claire Trevor, Walter Woolf King,
Zasu Pitts, Jack Haley, Tala Birell, Sig
Rumann. Written by Patterson McNutt and
H. W. Hanemann from the play Man Eating
Tiger by Ben Hecht and Rose Caylor; directed
by S. Sylvan Simon; for Fox. 'Hodge-podge of
hokum that offers no hope to distraught
exhibitors.'—*Variety*

'The gun . . . the girl . . . they made one
man the equal of five!'
Springfield Rifle
US 1952 93m Warnercolor
Warner (Louis E. Edelman)

A Union officer gets himself cashiered, joins
the Confederates as a spy, and unmasks a
traitor.
Stolid Civil War western with Grade A
production but not much individuality.

w Charles Marquis Warren, Frank Davis
d André de Toth *ph* Edwin DuPar *m* Max
Steiner

Gary Cooper, Phyllis Thaxter, David Brian,
Lon Chaney Jnr, Paul Kelly, Phil Carey,
James Millican, Guinn Williams

Springtime for Henry
US 1935 73m bw

A rich man makes a vocation of woman
chasing. Modest version of a play which was
toured for many years with Edward Everett
Horton in the lead. Otto Kruger, Nancy
Carroll, Nigel Bruce, Heather Angel, Herbert
Mundin. Written by Keene Thompson, Frank
Tuttle, from the play by Benn W. Levy;
directed by Frank Tuttle; for Jesse L. Lasky /
Fox. 'Farcical intent, but only a few
snickers.'—*Variety*

Springtime in the Rockies
US 1942 91m Technicolor
TCF (Darryl F. Zanuck)

Romances blossom on a mountain holiday.
Flimsily-plotted, studio-bound, absolutely
routine musical.

w Walter Bullock, Ken Englund *d* Irving
Cummings *ph* Ernest Palmer *m* Alfred
Newman *songs* Mack Gordon, Harry Warren

Betty Grable, John Payne, Carmen Miranda,
Edward Everett Horton, Cesar Romero,
Charlotte Greenwood, Frank Orth, Harry
James and his Music Makers

Spy for a Day
GB 1939 71m bw

A farm hand is discovered to be the exact
double of a spy. The only screen vehicle for
this 'gormless' comedian, and not a bad one.
Duggie Wakefield, Paddy Browne, Jack Allen,
Albert Lieven, Nicholas Hannen, Gibb
McLaughlin. Written by Anatole de
Grunwald, Hans Wilhelm, Emeric
Pressburger, Ralph Block and Tommy
Thompson, from a story by Stacy Aumonier;
directed by Mario Zampi; for Two Cities.

Spy Hunt°
US 1950 74m bw
Universal (Ralph Dietrich)
GB title: *Panther's Moon*

Secret microfilm is stowed in the collar of one
of two panthers being transported out of
Europe by train for circus use.
Slick minor espionage thriller.

w George Zuckerman, Leonard Lee, *novel*
Panther's Moon by Victor Canning *d* George
Sherman, *ph* Irving Glassberg *m* Walter
Scharf *md* Joseph Gershenson

Howard Duff, Marta Toren, Philip Friend,
Robert Douglas, Philip Dorn, Walter Slezak,
Kurt Kreuger

The Spy in Black°°
GB 1938 82m bw
Harefield / Alexander Korda (Irving Asher)
US title: *U-Boat 29*

In the Orkneys in 1917, German spies don't
trust each other.
Unusual romantic melodrama which provided
an unexpectedly interesting romantic team.

w Emeric Pressburger, Roland Pertwee, *novel*
J. Storer Clouston *d* Michael Powell
ph Bernard Browne *m* Miklos Rosza

Conrad Veidt, Valerie Hobson, Hay Petrie,
Helen Haye, Sebastian Shaw, Marius Goring,
June Duprez, Athole Stewart, Cyril Raymond

Spy of Napoleon
GB 1936 101m bw

A dancer saves Louis Napoleon from
assassination. Solidly mounted period piece
without much sense of humour. Richard
Barthelmess, Dolly Haas, Frank Vosper,
Francis L. Sullivan, Lyn Harding, Henry
Oscar. Written by L. DuGarde Peach,
Frederick Merrick and Harold Simpson;
directed by Maurice Elvey; for Twickenham.

The Spy Who Came in from the Cold°°
GB 1966 112m bw
Paramount / Salem (Martin Ritt)

A British master spy is offered a chance to get
even with his East German opponent by being

apparently sacked, disillusioned, and open for
recruitment.
The old undercover yarn with trimmings of
such sixties malaises as death wish, anti-
establishmentism and racial problems. As a
yarn, quite gripping till it gets too downbeat,
but very harshly photographed.

w Paul Dehn, Guy Trosper, *novel* John Le
Carré *d* Martin Ritt *ph* Oswald Morris
m Sol Kaplan *pd* Tambi Larsen

Richard Burton, Claire Bloom, *Oskar Werner*,
Peter Van Eyck, Sam Wanamaker, Rupert
Davies, George Voskovec, Cyril Cusack,
Michael Hordern, Robert Hardy, Bernard
Lee, Beatrix Lehmann

AAN: Richard Burton

The Spy Who Loved Me
GB 1977 125m Eastmancolor
 Panavision
UA / Eon (Albert R. Broccoli)

James Bond and a glamorous Russian spy
combine forces to track down and eliminate a
megalomaniac shipping magnate with an
undersea missile base.
Witless spy extravaganza in muddy colour,
with the usual tired chases and pussyfoot
violence but no new gimmicks except a seven-
foot villain with steel teeth.

w Christopher Wood, Richard Maibaum,
novel Ian Fleming *d* Lewis Gilbert
ph Claude Renoir *m* Marvin Hamlisch
pd Ken Adam

Roger Moore, Barbara Bach, Curt Jurgens,
Richard Kiel, Caroline Munro, Walter Gotell,
Bernard Lee, Lois Maxwell, George Baker,
Desmond Llewellyn, Edward De Souza,
Sydney Tafler

 'The film, bearing no relation to its nominal
source, seems to do nothing more than
anthologize its forerunners.'—*Tim Pulleine*,
MFB

AAN: Marvin Hamlisch; song, 'Nobody Does
It Better'

● *Video: Warner*

The Spy with a Cold Nose
GB 1966 93m Eastmancolor
Paramount / Associated London / Embassy
 (Robert Porter)

A fashionable vet is blackmailed by MI5 into
inserting a radio transmitter into a bulldog.
Rather painful, overacted and overwritten
farce full of obvious jokes masquerading as
satire.

w Ray Galton, Alan Simpson *d* Daniel
Petrie *ph* Kenneth Higgins *m* Riz Ortolani

Lionel Jeffries, Laurence Harvey, Daliah Lavi,
Eric Sykes, Eric Portman, Colin Blakely,
Denholm Elliott, Robert Flemyng, Paul Ford,
Bernard Lee, June Whitfield, Bernard
Archard

S°P°Y°S
GB 1974 100m Technicolor
Dymphana / C-W / American Film
 Properties (Irwin Winkler, Robert
 Chartoff)

Clumsy CIA agents in Paris come across a list
of KGB agents in China.

Surprisingly dull and unfashionable parade of
comic spy clichés; the talents involved
obviously intended something closer to
M*A*S*H.

w Malcolm Marmorstein, Lawrence J. Cohen,
Fred Freeman *d* Irwin Kershner *ph* Gerry
Fisher *m* John Scott

Elliott Gould, Donald Sutherland, Zouzou,
Joss Ackland, Kenneth Griffith, Vladek
Sheybal
 'Seems to have arrived several years too late
to find its true niche.'—*Sight and Sound*

Squadron Leader X
GB 1942   100m   bw
RKO (Victor Hanbury)

A Nazi hero poses as a British pilot but has
difficulty getting back home.
Tall war story with dreary romantic trimmings.

w Wolfgang Wilhelm, Miles Malleson
d Lance Comfort

Eric Portman, Ann Dvorak, Walter
Fitzgerald, Barry Jones, Henry Oscar,
Beatrice Varley

The Squall
US 1929   105m   bw

A Hungarian gypsy girl attracts all the male
members of a farming family, and causes
trouble. Perfectly awful melodrama made
worse by early sound techniques. Myrna Loy,
Alice Joyce, Loretta Young, Richard Ticker,
Carroll Nye, Zasu Pitts, Harry Cording.
Written by Bradley King, from the play by
Jean Bart; directed by Alexander Korda; for
Warner.

The Square Jungle
US 1955   85m   bw
U-I (Albert Zugsmith)

A conceited boxer gets his come-uppance.
Tailor-made studio co-feature.

w George Zuckerman *d* Jerry Hopper
ph George Robinson *m* Heinz Roemheld

Tony Curtis, Ernest Borgnine, Pat Crowley,
Jim Backus, Paul Kelly

The Square Peg*
GB 1958   89m · bw
Rank (Hugh Stewart)

An army recruit finds he is the double of a
German general.
Slam-bang star slapstick, shorter than usual
and with a few jokes that can't fail.

w Jack Davies *d* John Paddy Carstairs
ph Jack Cox *m* Philip Green

Norman Wisdom, Edward Chapman,
Campbell Singer, Hattie Jacques, Brian
Worth, Terence Alexander

The Squaw Man
US 1931   106m   bw
MGM (Cecil B. de Mille)
GB title: *The White Man*

An Indian maiden saves the life of a British
aristocrat, bears his child and commits suicide.

THE SQUEAKER.   Robert Newton gives Edmund Lowe the eye, and vice versa. After all,
one of them might be the villain.

Third outing for a hoary miscegenation drama
filmed in 1914 with Dustin Farnum and Red
Wing, and in 1918 with Elliott Dexter and
Ann Little. This talkie version sank without
trace.

w Lucien Hubbard, Lenore Coffee, *play*
Edwin Milton Royle *d* Cecil B. de Mille
ph Harold Rosson *m* Herbert Stothart

Warner Baxter, Lupe Velez, Charles
Bickford, Eleanor Boardman, Roland Young,
Paul Cavanagh, Raymond Hatton
 'Should be generally fair b.o. in the smaller
localities and perhaps not so hot for the
diffident big-town show shoppers.'—*Variety*

The Squeaker*
GB 1937   77m   bw
London Films (Alexander Korda)
US title: *Murder on Diamond Row*

A dangerous diamond fence is unmasked by a
discredited policeman.
Typical Edgar Wallace who-is-it, performed
with old-fashioned bravura.

w Edward O. Berkman, Bryan Wallace, *novel*
Edgar Wallace *d* William K. Howard

Edmund Lowe, Sebastian Shaw, Ann Todd,
Tamara Desni, Alastair Sim, Robert Newton,
Allan Jeayes, Stewart Rome
† Previously filmed in 1930, directed by Edgar
Wallace for British Lion; with Percy Marmont,
Eric Maturin, Anne Grey and Nigel Bruce.

The Squeeze
GB 1977   107m   Technicolor
Warner / Martinat (Stanley O'Toole)

An alcoholic ex-cop rescues his ex-wife from
kidnappers.
Sleazy action thriller which despite efficient
production goes over the top in its search for
unpleasant detail.

w Leon Griffiths, *novel* David Craig
d Michael Apted *ph* Dennis Lewiston
m David Hentschel

Stacy Keach, David Hemmings, Stephen
Boyd, Edward Fox, Carol White, Freddie
Starr

Squibs*
GB 1935   77m   bw

A cockney flowergirl wins a sweepstake.
Acceptable sound version of a series of rather
naïve silents which pleased the crowds in the
early twenties with the same star: they were
Squibs, Squibs MP, Squibs' Honeymoon and
Squibs Wins the Calcutta Sweep. Betty Balfour,
Gordon Harker, Stanley Holloway, Margaret
Yarde, Michael Shepley. Written by Michael
Hogan and H. Fowler Mear, from the play by
Clifford Seyler and George Pearson; directed
by Henry Edwards; for Twickenham.

Squirm
US 1976 92m Movielab
AIP / The Squirm Company (Edgar Lansbury, Joseph Beruh)

A power cable cut in a storm turns worms into maneaters.

Revolting shocker with a few funny moments for those who can take it.

wd Jeff Lieberman *ph* Joseph Mangine *m* Robert Prince

John Scardino, Patricia Pearcy, R. A. Dow, Jean Sullivan

Stablemates
US 1938 89m bw

A broken-down vet saves a stableboy's racehorse. Sentimental comedy vehicle for two masters of the surreptitious tear. Wallace Beery, Mickey Rooney, Margaret Hamilton, Minor Watson, Marjorie Gateson. Written by Reginald Owen and William Thiele; directed by Sam Wood; for MGM.

Stage Door***
US 1937 93m bw
RKO (Pandro S. Berman)

Life in a New York theatrical boarding house for girls.

Melodramatic, sharply comedic, always fascinating slice of stagey life from a Broadway hit; the performances alone make it worth preserving.

w Morrie Ryskind, Anthony Veiller, *play* Edna Ferber, George S. Kaufman *d* Gregory La Cava *ph* Robert de Grasse *m* Roy Webb *ad* Van Nest Polglase

Katharine Hepburn, Ginger Rogers, Adolphe Menjou, Gail Patrick, Constance Collier, Andrea Leeds, Lucille Ball, Samuel S. Hinds, Jack Carson, Franklin Pangborn, Eve Arden

'It is a long time since we have seen so much feminine talent so deftly handled.'—*Otis Ferguson*

'Zest and pace and photographic eloquence.'—*Frank S. Nugent, New York Times*

'A rare example of a film substantially improving on a stage original and a remarkably satisfying film on all levels.'—*NFT, 1973*

'One of the flashiest, most entertaining comedies of the 30s, even with its tremolos and touches of heartbreak.'—*Pauline Kael, 70s*

AAN: best picture; script; Gregory La Cava; Andrea Leeds

Stage Door Canteen*
US 1943 132m bw
Sol Lesser (Barnett Briskin)

How the stars in New York entertained the armed forces during World War II.

Nothing as a film, mildly interesting as sociology and for some rarish appearances.

w Delmer Daves *d* Frank Borzage *ph* Harry Wild *m* Freddie Rich *pd* Harry Horner

Cheryl Walker, Lon McCallister, Judith Anderson, Tallulah Bankhead, Ray Bolger, Katherine Cornell, Helen Hayes, George Jessel, Alfred Lunt, Harpo Marx, Yehudi Menuhin, Elliott Nugent, Cornelia Otis Skinner, Ethel Waters, May Whitty, William Demarest, Gracie Fields, Katharine Hepburn, Gertrude Lawrence, Ethel Merman, Merle Oberon, Johnny Weissmuller, Edgar Bergen, Jane Cowl, Lynn Fontanne, Paul Muni, Gypsy Rose Lee, George Raft, etc; Count Basie, Benny Goodman, Xavier Cugat, Guy Lombardo, Kay Kyser and their bands

'A nice harmless picture for the whole family, and a goldmine for those who are willing to go to it in the wrong spirit.'—*James Agee*

AAN: Freddie Rich; song 'We Mustn't Say Goodbye' (*m* Johnny Monaco, *ly* Al Dubin)

Stage Fright*
GB 1950 110m bw
Warner / ABPC (Alfred Hitchcock)

A man is on the run for a backstage murder, and his girl friend takes a job as maid to the great star he says is responsible.

Creaky Hitchcock thriller in which you can see all the joins and the stars seem stuck in treacle; but a few of the set pieces work well enough.

w Whitfield Cook, *novel* Man Running by Selwyn Jepson *d* Alfred Hitchcock *ph* Wilkie Cooper *m* Leighton Lucas

Marlene Dietrich, Jane Wyman, Richard Todd, Alastair Sim, Michael Wilding, Sybil Thorndike, Kay Walsh, Miles Malleson

Stage Mother
US 1933 85m bw

The mother of a young actress is not above sacrificing her daughter for financial gain. Wisecracking comedy-romance, rather similar to the later *Gypsy*. Alice Brady, Maureen O'Sullivan, Franchot Tone, Phillips Holmes, Ted Healy, C. Henry Gordon. Written by John Meehan, Bradford Ropes, from the latter's novel; directed by Charles Brabin; for MGM. 'Packed with colour, not a little s.a., and certain of adequate b.o. attention.'—*Variety*

Stage Struck
US 1936 95m bw
Warner (Robert Lord)

Young people put on a show and become instant hits.

Dim musical oddly shorn of production numbers.

w Tom Buckinham, Pat C. Flick, Robert Lord *d* / *ch* Busby Berkeley *ph* Byron Haskin *m* Leo F. Forbstein *songs* Harold Arlen, E. Y. Harburg

Dick Powell, Joan Blondell, Jeanne Madden, the Yacht Club Boys, Warren William, Frank McHugh

Stage Struck**
US 1957 95m Technicolor
RKO (Stuart Millar)

A young actress comes to New York intent on stardom . . .

Careful, slightly arid remake of *Morning Glory* marred by a tiresome central performance; good theatrical detail.

w Ruth and Augustus Goetz, *play* Zoe Akins *d* Sidney Lumet *ph* Franz Planer *m* Alex North *ad* Kim Edgar Swados

Susan Strasberg, Henry Fonda, Herbert Marshall, *Joan Greenwood*, Christopher Plummer

● *Video: Kingston*

Stage to Thunder Rock
US 1964 89m Techniscope
Paramount / A. C. Lyles

An ageing sheriff takes a bank robber back to jail by stagecoach.

Acceptable lower-berth western with the producer's usual roster of half-forgotten character actors.

w Charles Wallace *d* William F. Claxton *ph* W. Wallace Kelley *m* Paul Dunlap

Barry Sullivan, Marilyn Maxwell, Scott Brady, Keenan Wynn, Allan Jones, Lon Chaney Jnr, John Agar, Wanda Hendrix, Anne Seymour, Robert Lowery

Stagecoach****
US 1939 99m bw
(UA) Walter Wanger

Various western characters board a stagecoach in danger from an Indian war party.

What looked like a minor western with a plot borrowed from Maupassant's *Boule de suif*, became a classic by virtue of the firm characterization, restrained writing, exciting climax and the scenery of Monument Valley. Whatever the reasons, it damn well works.

w Dudley Nichols, *story* Stage to Lordsburg by Ernest Haycox *d* John Ford *ph* Bert Glennon, Ray Binger *m* Richard Hageman, W. Frank Harling, John Leopold, Leo Shuken, Louis Gruenberg *md* Boris Morros

Claire Trevor, John Wayne, Thomas Mitchell, George Bancroft, Andy Devine, *Berton Churchill*, Louise Platt, *John Carradine, Donald Meek*, Tim Holt, Chris-Pin Martin

'It displays potentialities that can easily drive it through as one of the surprise big grossers of the year.'—*Variety*

'The basic western, a template for everything that followed.'—*John Baxter, 1968*

'Grand Hotel on wheels.'—*New Yorker, 1975*

'A motion picture that sings a song of camera.'—*Frank S. Nugent, New York Times*

AA: music; Thomas Mitchell

AAN: best picture; John Ford; Bert Glennon; Ray Binger

● *Video: Kingston*

Stagecoach
US 1966 114m De Luxe Cinemascope
TCF / Martin Rackin

Absolutely awful remake of the above; costly but totally spiritless, miscast and uninteresting.

w Joseph Landon *d* Gordon Douglas *ph* William H. Clothier *m* Jerry Goldsmith

Ann-Margret, Alex Cord, Bing Crosby, Van
Heflin, Slim Pickens, Robert Cummings,
Stefanie Powers, Michael Connors, Red
Buttons, Keenan Wynn

Staircase*
US / France 1969   101m   De Luxe
    Panavision
TCF / Stanely Donen

The problems of two ageing homosexual
hairdressers.
Unsatisfactorily opened-out and over-acted
version of an effective two-handler play.
Oddly made in France, so that the London
detail seems all wrong.

w Charles Dyer, from his play d Stanley
Donen ph Christopher Challis m Dudley
Moore

Richard Burton, Rex Harrison, Cathleen
Nesbitt, Beatrix Lehmann

'The shape is smashed . . . no longer a
graceful duet, it becomes a waddling tale,
spattered with ugliness, that falls into the
biggest sentimental trap for homosexual
material: it pleads for pity.'—*Stanley
Kauffmann*

Stakeout on Dope Street*
US 1958   83m   bw
Warner (Andrew J. Fenady)

Three young men find a briefcase containing
heroin and are attacked by the gangsters who
lost it.
Lively little crime morality, uneven but worth
a look.

w Irwin Schwartz, Irvin Kershner, Andrew J.
Fenady d Irvin Kershner ph Mark Jeffrey
m Richard Markowitz

Yale Wexler, Jonathon Haze, Morris Miller,
Abby Dalton

Stalag 17**
US 1953   120m   bw
Paramount (Billy Wilder)

Comedy and tragedy for American servicemen
in a Nazi prisoner-of-war camp.
High jinks, violence and mystery in a sharply
calculated mixture; an atmosphere quite
different from the understated British films on
the subject.

w Billy Wilder, Edwin Blum, play Donald
Bevan, Edmund Trzinski d Billy Wilder
ph Ernest Laszlo m Franz Waxman

William Holden, Don Taylor, Otto Preminger,
Robert Strauss, Harvey Lembeck, Richard
Erdman, Peter Graves, Neville Grand, Sig
Rumann

'A facility for continuous rapid-fire action
which alternately brings forth the laughs and
tingles the spine.'—*Otis L. Guernsey Jnr*

'Raucous and tense, heartless and
sentimental, always fast-paced, it has already
been assigned by critics to places on their lists
of the year's ten best movies.'—*Life*

AA: William Holden
AAN: Billy Wilder (as director), Robert
Strauss

Stalker*
USSR 1979   161m   colour
Mosfilm Unit 2

In the centre of an industrial wasteland there
appears a mysterious zone where all normal
laws of life are suspended.
Part political allegory, part personal fantasy,
all very fascinating but rather hard tack for
anybody in search of entertainment.

w Arkady Strugatsky, Boris Strugatsky, from
their story d / pd Andrei Tarkovsky
m Eduard Artemyev

Aleksandr Kaidanovsky, Anatoly Solonitsin,
Nikolai Grinko, Alisa Freindlikh

The Stalking Moon*
US 1968   109m   Technicolor
    Panavision
National General / Stalking Moon Company
    (Alan J. Pakula)

An ageing scout escorts home a white woman
who has escaped from the Indians, and kills a
murderous Apache.
Slow, thoughtful western with effective
moments.

w Alvin Sargent, novel Theodore V. Olsen
d Robert Mulligan ph Charles Lang m Fred
Karlin

Gregory Peck, Eva Marie Saint, Robert
Forster, Frank Silvera

Stallion Road
US 1947   97m   bw
Warner (Alex Gottlieb)

An outbreak of anthrax threatens a racing
stable.
Routine romantic drama with sporting
background.

w Stephen Longstreed d James V. Kern
ph Arthur Edeson m Frederick Hollander

Ronald Reagan, Alexis Smith, Zachary Scott,
Peggy Knudsen, Patti Brady, Harry
Davenport, Frank Puglia

Stamboul Quest
US 1934   88m   bw
MGM (Walter Wanger)

During World War I, Germany's most
notorious lady spy falls for an American
medical student.
Modest variation on the true story twice
filmed as *Fraülein Doktor*; standard
Hollywood values.

w Herman J. Mankiewicz d Sam Wood
ph James Wong Howe m Herbert Stothart

Myrna Loy, George Brent, Lionel Atwill,
C. Henry Gordon, Douglass Dumbrille,
Mischa Auer.

The Stand at Apache River
US 1953   77m   Technicolor

Apaches attack a reservation when the army
won't listen to reason. Conventional western
with sympathy for the Indians. Stephen
McNally, Julie Adams, Hugh Marlowe, Hugh
O'Brian, Jack Kelly. Written by Arthur Ross;
directed by Lee Sholem; for Universal-
International.

Stand by for Action
US 1943   109m   bw
MGM (Robert Z. Leonard, Orville O. Dull)
GB title: *Cargo of Innocents*

A Harvard graduate learns the realities of war
on an old destroyer.
Studio-bound war heroics slurping into
sentiment.

w George Bruce, Herman J. Mankiewicz,
John L. Balderston d Robert Z. Leonard
ph Charles Rosher m Lennie Hayton

Robert Taylor, Charles Laughton, Brian
Donlevy, Walter Brennan, Marilyn Maxwell,
Henry O'Neill

Stand In*
US 1937   90m   bw
Walter Wanger

An efficiency expert is sent to save a
Hollywood studio from bankruptcy.
Amusing satire which could have done with
sharper scripting and firmer control but is
pleasantly remembered.

w Gene Towne, Graham Baker, serial
Clarence Budington Kelland d Tay Garnett
ph Charles G. Clarke m Heinz Roemheld

Leslie Howard, Joan Blondell, Humphrey
Bogart, Alan Mowbray, Marla Shelton, C.
Henry Gordon, Jack Carson, Tully Marshall

Stand Up and Be Counted*
US 1971   99m   Eastmancolor
Columbia / Mike Frankovich

An international woman journalist returns to
Denver and becomes involved in women's lib.
A glamoured-up flirtation with a fashionable
theme, quite nicely done but instantly dated—
and sociologically interesting.

w Bernard Slade d Jackie Cooper ph Fred
Koenekamp m Ernie Wilkins

Jacqueline Bisset, Stella Stevens, Steve
Lawrence, Gary Lockwood, Loretta Swit, Lee
Purcell, Madlyn Rhue

Stand Up and Cheer*
US 1934   80m   bw
Fox (Winfield Sheehan)

The new US Secretary of Amusement
attempts to shake the country's Depression
blues by staging a mammoth revue.
Naïve propaganda, but the whole world was
swept away to cloud nine—by Shirley Temple.

w Ralph Spence, Will Rogers, Philip Klein
d Hamilton McFadden ph Ernest Palmer
md Arthur Lange

Warner Baxter, Madge Evans, Nigel Bruce,
Stepin Fetchit, Frank Melton, Lila Lee, Ralph
Morgan, James Dunn, Shirley Temple, John
Boles, George K. Arthur

'Its intrinsic merits do not quite match its
pretentiousness.'—*Variety*

'Impossible to file it away in an ordinary
drawer marked 'Stinkers'. This one is extra, it
is super, and it butters itself very thickly with
the most obvious sort of topical
significance.'—*Otis Ferguson*
† The original title was Fox Follies.

Stand Up and Fight*
US 1938   99m   bw
MGM (Mervyn Le Roy)

A southern aristocrat comes into conflict with a stagecoach operator used as transportation for stolen slaves.
Superior star action piece with plenty of vigorous brawls.

w James M. Cain, Jane Murfin, Harvey Ferguson d W. S. Van Dyke II ph Leonard Smith m William Axt

Wallace Beery, Robert Taylor, Florence Rice, Helen Broderick, Charles Bickford, Barton MacLane, Charley Grapewin, John Qualen

'An action thriller that will please the muggs more than the dames . . . should prove strong at the b.o.'—*Variety*

Stand Up Virgin Soldiers
GB 1977   90m   Technicolor
Warner / Greg Smith / Maidenhead

More sexual adventures of National Servicemen in Singapore in 1950.
The Virgin Soldiers had a certain authenticity behind the fooling; this is a bawdy romp, and not a very efficient one.

w Leslie Thomas, from his novel d Norman Cohen ph Ken Hodges m Ed Welch

Nigel Davenport, Robin Askwith, George Layton, Robin Nedwell, Warren Mitchell, John Le Mesurier, Edward Woodward, Irene Handl

'The hilarious story of what a girl will do to get her boss a bed in Washington!'

Standing Room Only*
US 1944   83m   bw
Paramount (Paul Jones)

Hotel rooms being hard to find in wartime Washington, a resourceful secretary hires out herself and her boss as a servant couple.
Moderate romantic farce with a few good laughs.

w Darrell Ware, Karl Tunberg d Sidney Lanfield ph Charles Lang m Robert Emmett Dolan

Paulette Goddard, Fred MacMurray, Edward Arnold, Roland Young, Hillary Brooke, Porter Hall, Clarence Kolb, Anne Revere

Stanley and Livingstone***
US 1939   101m   bw
TCF (Kenneth MacGowan)

An American journalist goes to Africa to find a lost Victorian explorer.
A prestige picture which played reasonably fair with history and still managed to please the masses.

w Philip Dunne, Julien Josephson d Henry King ph George Barnes m Alfred Newman ad Thomas Little

Spencer Tracy, Cedric Hardwicke, Richard Greene, Nancy Kelly, Walter Brennan, Charles Coburn, Henry Hull, Henry Travers, Miles Mander, Holmes Herbert

'Sound, worthy, interesting.'—*Richard Mallett, Punch*

'Most of the film consists of long shots of stand-ins moving across undistinguished scenery. . . . Mr Tracy is always a human being, but Sir Cedric is an elocution lesson, a handclasp.'—*Graham Greene*

'Holds box office promise for socko biz . . . it's absorbing and adventurous drama.'—*Variety*

'When the star fades, the woman is born!'
'The story of every woman who ever climbed the stairway to the stars—and found herself at the bottom looking up!'

The Star*
US 1952   91m   bw
TCF / Bert E. Friedlob

A once famous Hollywood star is financially and psychologically on her uppers.
A movie apparently tailor-made for its star turns out to be a disappointingly plotless wallow.

w Katherine Albert, Dale Eunson d Stuart Heisler ph Ernest Laszlo m Victor Young

Bette Davis, Sterling Hayden, Natalie Wood, Warner Anderson, Minor Watson
† The role was originally designed for Joan Crawford.

AAN: Bette Davis

Star!**
US 1968   194m   De Luxe   Todd-AO
TCF / Robert Wise (Saul Chaplin)

Revue artist Gertrude Lawrence rises from poverty to international stardom and a measure of happiness.
Elephantiasis finally ruins this patient, detached, generally likeable recreation of a past theatrical era. In the old Hollywood style, it would probably have been even better on a smaller budget; but alas the star would still have been ill at ease with the drunken termagant scenes.

w William Fairchild d Robert Wise ph Ernest Laszlo md Lennie Hayton ch Michael Kidd pd Boris Leven

Julie Andrews, Richard Crenna, Michael Craig, *Daniel Massey* (as Noel Coward), John Collin, Robert Reed, Bruce Forsyth, Beryl Reid, Jenny Agutter
† Short version: *Those Were the Happy Days*.

AAN: Ernest Laszlo; Lennie Hayton; title song (m James Van Heusen, ly Sammy Cahn); Daniel Massey

The Star Chamber
US 1983   109m   De Luxe   Panavision
TCF / Frank Yablans

Judges get together to retry defendants who have been unjustly freed, and then have them executed by hired assassins.
A bit hard to swallow; also overlong and rather unpleasant.

w Roderick Taylor, Peter Hyams d Peter Hyams ph Richard Hannah m Michael Small pd Bill Malley

Michael Douglas, Hal Holbrook, Yaphet Kotto, Sharon Gless, James B. Sikking, Joe Regalbuto

'Michael Winner territory with a veneer of conscience.'—*Sight and Sound*
'Small-screen material suffering from crippling inflation.'—*Steve Jenkins, MFB*

Star Dust*
US 1940   85m   bw
TCF (Kenneth MacGowan)

A talent scout discovers a new Hollywood star.
Light, amusing studio comedy, a pleasing addition to Hollywood mythology.

w Robert Ellis, Helen Logan d Walter Lang ph Peverell Marley m David Buttolph

Linda Darnell, John Payne, Roland Young, Charlotte Greenwood, William Gargan, Mary Beth Hughes, Donald Meek, Jessie Ralph

Star 80
US 1983   103m   Technicolor
Warner / Ladd (Wolfgang Glattes, Kenneth Utt)

The murder by her husband of Dorothy Stratten, the playboy centrefold model.
Unappetizing recounting, made less palatable by flashy direction, of a story with no possible moral.

w,d Bob Fosse ph Sven Nykvist m Ralph Burns pd Tony Walton

Mariel Hemingway, Eric Roberts, Cliff Robertson (as Hugh Hefner), Carroll Baker, Roger Rees

'A mishmash of embarrassments.'—*Tom Milne, MFB*
'Obviously intended as a cautionary tale for our times, with the beautiful dreamers and ruthless schemers peopling a colour supplement world of success.'—*Sight and Sound*

A Star Is Born***
US 1937   111m   Technicolor
David O. Selznick

A young actress meets Hollywood success and marries a famous leading man, whose star wanes as hers shines brighter.
Abrasive romantic melodrama which is also the most accurate study of Hollywood ever put on film.

w Dorothy Parker, Alan Campbell, Robert Carson, story William A. Wellman, based partly on *What Price Hollywood* (1932) (qv) d William A. Wellman ph W. Howard Greene m Max Steiner

Janet Gaynor, Fredric March, Adolphe Menjou, Lionel Stander, Andy Devine, May Robson, Owen Moore, Franklin Pangborn

'One of those rare ones which everyone will want to see and talk about . . . disproves the tradition that good pictures can't be made with a Hollywood background.'—*Variety*
'Good entertainment by any standards.'—*Frank S. Nugent, New York Times*
'A peculiar sort of masochistic self-congratulatory Hollywood orgy.'—*New Yorker, 1975*

'The first colour job that gets close to what colour must eventually come to: it keeps the thing in its place, underlining the mood and situation of the story rather than dimming everything else out in an iridescent razzle-dazzle.'—*Otis Ferguson*

AA: original story; W. Howard Greene
AAN: best picture; script; William A. Wellman; Janet Gaynor; Fredric March

● *Video: European*

'Fate raised her to fame—and killed the man she loved!'

A Star Is Born**
US 1954 181m Technicolor
Cinemascope
Warner / Transcona (Sidney Luft)

Musical version of the above which begins very strongly and has two splendid performances, but suffers in the second half from a lack of writing strength and heavy post-production cutting. The numbers add very little except length.

w Moss Hart *d* George Cukor *ph* Sam Leavitt *md* Ray Heindorf

Judy Garland, James Mason, Charles Bickford, Jack Carson, Tommy Noonan, Amanda Blake, Lucy Marlow
'Maintains a skilful balance between the musical and the tear jerker.'—*Penelope Houston*
† Cary Grant and Humphrey Bogart were both sought before James Mason was signed.
AAN: Ray Heindorf; song 'The Man that Got Away' (*m* Harold Arlen, *ly* Ira Gershwin); Judy Garland; James Mason

A Star Is Born*
US 1976 140m Metrocolor
Warner / Barwood / First Artists (Barbra Streisand, Jon Peters)

Interminable remake set in the pop world amid screaming crowds and songs at high decibel level; also an insufferable piece of showing off by the star. But some of the handling has style.

w John Gregory Dunne, Joan Didion, Frank Pierson *d* Frank Pierson *ph* Robert Surtees *md* Paul Williams *pd* Polly Platt

Barbra Streisand, Kris Kristofferson, Paul Mazursky, Gary Busey
'A clear case for the monopolies commission.'—*Michael Billington, Illustrated London News*
'A bore is starred.'—*Village Voice*
AA: song 'Evergreen' (*m* Barbra Streisand, *ly* Paul Williams)
AAN: Robert Surtees; Roger Kellaway (music underscoring)

● *Video: Warner*

The Star Maker*
US 1939 94m bw
Paramount (Charles R. Rodgers)

A songwriter makes the big time by organizing kid acts.
Pleasant minor musical based on the career of Gus Edwards.

w Frank Butler, Don Hartman, Arthur Caesar *d* Roy del Ruth *ph* Karl Struss

Bing Crosby, Louise Campbell, Linda Ware, Ned Sparks, Laura Hope Crews, Janet Waldo, Walter Damrosch
'A rollicking filmusical, first-class entertainment.'—*Variety*

Star of Midnight*
US 1935 90m bw
RKO (Pandro S. Berman)

A New York attorney solves the disappearance of a leading lady.
Wisecracking, debonair murder mystery modelled on *The Thin Man*.

w Howard J. Green, Anthony Veiller, Edward Kaufman *d* Stephen Roberts *ph* J. Roy Hunt *m* Max Steiner

William Powell, Ginger Rogers, Paul Kelly, Gene Lockhart, Ralph Morgan, Leslie Fenton, J. Farrell MacDonald
'Too bad the title isn't more attractive, but the picture is excellent otherwise and should be a snappy grosser.'—*Variety*
'It is all suavity and amusement, pistol shots and cocktails.'—*Graham Greene*
'One of the best sophisticated comedy-mysteries in a period full of such films.'—*NFT, 1973*

The Star Spangled Girl
US 1971 92m colour
Paramount (Howard W. Koch)

A sweet old-fashioned girl is fought for by two young radicals.
Unamusingly 'with it' comedy from an unsuccessful play.

w Arnold Margolin, Jim Parker, *play* Neil Simon & Jerry Paris *ph* Sam Leavitt *m* Charles Fox

Sandy Duncan, Tony Roberts, Todd Susman, Elizabeth Allen

Star Spangled Rhythm***
US 1942 99m bw
Paramount (Joseph Sistrom)

The doorman of Paramount Studios pretends to his sailor son that he is a big producer.
Frenetic farce involving most of the talent on Paramount's payroll and culminating in an 'impromptu' show staged for the navy. A good lighthearted glimpse of wartime Hollywood.

w Harry Tugend *d* George Marshall *ph* Leo Tover, Theodor Sparkuhl *md* Robert Emmett Dolan *songs* Johnny Mercer, Harold Arlen

Betty Hutton, Eddie Bracken, *Victor Moore, Walter Abel*, Anne Revere, Cass Daley, Gil Lamb, Macdonald Carey, Bob Hope, Bing Crosby, Paulette Goddard, Veronica Lake, Dorothy Lamour, Vera Zorina, Fred MacMurray, Ray Milland, Lynne Overman, Franchot Tone, Dick Powell, *Walter Dare Wahl and Co, Cecil B. de Mille, Preston Sturges,* Alan Ladd, Rochester, Katherine Dunham, Susan Hayward
AAN: Robert Emmett Dolan; song 'Black Magic' (*m* Harold Arlen, *ly* Johnny Mercer)

'The human adventure is just beginning!'
Star Trek: The Motion Picture
US 1979 132m Metrocolor Panavision
Paramount (Gene Roddenberry)

In the twenty-third century, Admiral Kirk resumes command of the *Enterprise* to combat an alien force.
And a surprisingly boring one. Vast sets and big-screen solemnity hardly make this more enjoyable than some of the TV episodes which got more tricks and philosophical fun into one-third of the length.

w Harold Livingstone, Alan Dean Foster *d* Robert Wise *ph* Richard H. Kline, Richard Yuricich *m* Jerry Goldsmith *pd* Harold Michelson

William Shatner, Leonard Nimoy, DeForest Kelley, Stephen Collins, Persis Khambatta

● *Video: CIC*

Star Trek: The Wrath of Khan
US 1982 114m Movielab Panavision
Paramount (Harve Bennett)

The crew of the starship *Enterprise* counter the wiles of an evil genius on a distant planet.
Comic strip capers a long way from the controlled intelligence of some episodes of the TV series; but more entertaining than the first movie.

w Jack B. Sowards *d* Nicholas Meyer *ph* Gayne Rescher *m* James Horner *pd* Joseph R. Jennings

William Shatner, Leonard Nimoy, Ricardo Montalban, DeForest Kelley, Ike Eisenmann
'A pitiful snack for the eyes with some unappetizing crumbs left over for the mind to chew on.'—*Philip Strick, MFB*

● *Video: CIC*

Star Trek 3: The Search for Spock
US 1984 105m Metrocolor Panavision
Paramount / Cinema Group Venture (Harve Bennett)

Admiral Kirk discovers that Spock is not dead but has been reborn as a Vulcan child . . .
Very silly, empty and unamusing follow-up. Let us hope fervently that the adventure does not continue.

w Harve Bennett *d* Leonard Nimoy *ph* Charles Correll *m* James Horner

William Shatner, De Forrest Kelley, James Doohan, Walter Koenig, Michelle Nichols, Robert Hooks, Leonard Nimoy

Star Wars***
US 1977 121m Technicolor
Panavision
TCF / Lucasfilm (Gary Kurtz)

A rebel princess in a distant galaxy escapes, and with the help of her robots and a young farmer overcomes the threatening forces of evil.
Flash Gordon rides again, but with timing so impeccably right that the movie became a phenomenon and one of the top grossers of all time. In view of the hullaballoo, some

STAR WARS. Some of the friendly folk from outer space who made themselves at home in millions of parlours.

disappointment may be felt with the actual experience of watching it . . . but it's certainly good harmless fun, put together with style and imagination.

wd George Lucas *ph* Gilbert Taylor *m* John Williams *pd* John Barry *sp* many and various

Mark Hamill, Harrison Ford, Carrie Fisher, Peter Cushing, Alec Guinness, Anthony Daniels (See Threepio), Kenny Baker (Artoo Detoo), Dave Prowse (Darth Vader)

'A great work of popular art, fully deserving the riches it has reaped.'—*Time*

'Acting in this movie I felt like a raisin in a giant fruit salad. And I didn't even know who the coconuts or the canteloups were.'—*Mark Hamill*

'He intended his film, Lucas confesses, for a generation growing up without fairy tales. His target audience was fourteen years and younger. . . . It was a celebration, a social affair, a collective dream, and people came again and again, dragging their friends and families with them.'—*Les Keyser, Hollywood in the Seventies*

'The loudness, the smash and grab editing and the relentless pacing drive every idea from your head, and even if you've been entertained you may feel cheated of some dimension—a sense of wonder, perhaps.'—*New Yorker, 1982*

'Heartless fireworks ignited by a permanently retarded director with too much clout and cash.'—*Time Out, 1984*

AA: John Williams
AAN: best picture; script; direction; Alec Guinness

● *Video: CBS / Fox*

The Star Witness*
US 1931 68m bw
Warner

An old man witnesses a crime and threatened by gangsters.
Pacy melodrama with good performances.

w Lucien Hubbard *d* William Wellman *ph* James Van Trees

Walter Huston, Chic Sale, Grant Mitchell, Frances Starr, Sally Blane

'Plenty of action, laughs, and a tear.'—*Variety*

AAN: Lucien Hubbard

Stardust
GB 1974 111m Technicolor
EMI / Goodtimes (David Puttnam, Sandy Lieberson)

The rise and fall of a pop singer.
Unappetizing rehash of the road to ruin, pop music style.

w Ray Connolly d Michael Apted ph Tony Richmond md Dave Edmunds, David Puttnam

David Essex, Adam Faith, Larry Hagman, Marty Wilde, Rosalind Ayres

● Video: Thorn EMI

Stardust Memories*
US 1980 88m bw
UA / Jack Rollinson, Charles H. Joffe

An increasingly melancholy comedian attends a retrospective of his work and is plagued by real and imaginary fears.
A plainly autobiographical work which, while amusing and moving in spots, makes it doubtful that the writer / director / star can even now shake off his obsessions.

wd Woody Allen ph Gordon Willis m Dick Hyman

Woody Allen, Charlotte Rampling, Jessica Harper, Marie-Christine Barrault, Tony Roberts, Helen Hanft

'Its posturing pyrotechnics seem more the symptom of a crisis than its controlled expression.'—Gilbert Adair, MFB

● Video: Warner

Starlift
US 1951 102m bw
Warner (Robert Arthur)

Movie stars entertain at Travis Air Base, where the boys are constantly leaving for Korea.
Insipid musical with even more insipid romantic interludes.

w John Klorer, Karl Kamb d Roy del Ruth ph Ted McCord md Ray Heindorf

Janice Rule, Dick Wesson, Richard Webb, Howard St John; and guest stars Doris Day, Gordon MacRae, Virginia Mayo, Gene Nelson, Ruth Roman, James Cagney, Gary Cooper, Phil Harris, Louella Parsons, Randolph Scott, Jane Wyman

Starman
US 1984 115m MGM color
Columbia / Delphi (Larry J. Franco)

An alien arrives in Wisconsin and takes human form, falling in love with the widow of the man he impersonates.
Derivative but eccentric science-fiction fantasy with lapses of narrative and a general attempt to make the love story predominant over the hardware.

w Bruce A. Evans, Raynold Gideon d John Carpenter ph Donald M. Morgan m Jack Nitzche pd Daniel Lomino ed Marion Rothman

Jeff Bridges, Karen Allen, Charles Martin Smith, Richard Jaeckel, Robert Phalen, Tony Edwards

Stars and Stripes Forever*
US 1952 89m Technicolor
TCF (Lamar Trotti)
GB title: *Marching Along*

In the 1890s John Philip Sousa, a bandmaster who wants to write ballads, finds success as a writer of marches.
Low-key musical biopic with predictably noisy numbers.

w Lamar Trotti, from Sousa's autobiography d Henry Koster ph Charles G. Clarke md Alfred Newman

Clifton Webb, Debra Paget, Robert Wagner, Ruth Hussey, Finlay Currie, Roy Roberts, Lester Matthews

The Stars Are Singing
US 1952 99m Technicolor
Paramount (Irving Asher)

A Polish refugee girl illegally enters the US and becomes an opera star.
Painless Cinderella fantasy in which everybody sings.

w Liam O'Brien d Norman Taurog ph Lionel Lindon md Victor Young

Anna Maria Alberghetti, Lauritz Melchior, Rosemary Clooney, Fred Clark, Mikhail Rasumny

Stars in My Crown*
US 1950 89m bw
MGM (William H. Wright)

A two-gun parson brings peace to a Tennessee town after the Civil War.
Sentimental family western, quite pleasantly made and performed.

w Margaret Fitts, novel Joe David Brown d Jacques Tourneur ph Charles Schoenbaum m Adolph Deutsch

Joel McCrea, Ellen Drew, Dean Stockwell, Juano Hernandez, James Mitchell, Lewis Stone, Alan Hale, Amanda Blake

The Stars Look Down**
GB 1939 110m bw
Grafton (Isadore Goldschmidt)

The son of a coal miner struggles to become an MP.
Economically but well made social drama from a popular novel, with good pace and backgrounds.

w J. B. Williams, A. J. Cronin, novel A. J. Cronin d Carol Reed ph Max Greene m Hans May

Michael Redgrave, Margaret Lockwood, Edward Rigby, Emlyn Williams, Nancy Price, Allan Jeayes, Cecil Parker, Linden Travers

'Dr Cronin's mining novel has produced a very good film—I doubt whether in England we have ever produced a better.'—Graham Greene

Stars over Broadway
US 1935 89m bw
Warner (Sam Bischoff)

Agent turns hotel porter into radio star.
Unremarkable musical, with unusual talent.

w Jerry Wald, Julius J. Epstein, Pat C. Flick d William Keighley ph George Barnes md Leo F. Forbstein ch Busby Berkeley, Bobby Connolly songs Harry Warren, Al Dubin

James Melton, Jane Froman, Pat O'Brien, Jean Muir, Frank McHugh, Marie Wilson, Frank Fay

'A far from inspired backstage yarn with pleasant dialogue and fancy trimmings.'—Variety

Start Cheering
US 1938 78m bw

An actor's agent has problems when his potential star decides to go to college. Fairly amusing low-budget musical with some surprises. Jimmy Durante, Walter Connolly, Joan Perry, Charles Starrett, the Three Stooges, Hal Leroy, Ernest Truex, Gertrude Niesen, Raymond Walburn, Broderick Crawford. Written by Eugene Solow, Richard E. Wormser, Philip Rapp, Corey Ford; directed by Albert S. Rogell; for Columbia. 'Longer on entertainment satisfaction than many of the more formidable pricers.'—Variety

Start the Revolution without Me*
US 1969 90m Technicolor
Warner / Norbud (Norman Lear)

Two sets of twins get mixed up at the court of Louis XVI.
Historical spoof of the kind subsequently made familiar by Mel Brooks; the script might have suited Abbott and Costello better than these two actors.

w Fred Freeman, Lawrence J. Cohen d Bud Yorkin ph Jean Tournier m John Addison

Donald Sutherland, Gene Wilder, Hugh Griffith, Jack McGowran, Billie Whitelaw, Victor Spinetti, Ewa Aulin

Starting Over*
US 1979 106m Movielab
Paramount / Century Associates (Alan J. Pakula, James L. Brooks)

A divorced man nearly goes back to his wife but finally plumps for a nursery school teacher.
Plain-speaking sex comedy-drama with accomplished stars giving rather more than the script is worth.

w James L. Brooks, novel Dan Wakefield d Alan J. Pakula ph Sven Nykvist m Marvin Hamlisch pd George Jenkins

Burt Reynolds, Jill Clayburgh, Candice Bergen, Charles Durning, Austin Pendleton

● Video: CIC

State Fair**
US 1933 98m bw
Fox (Winfield Sheehan)

Dad wants his prize pig to win at the fair, but the younger members of his family have romance in mind.
Archetypal family film, much remade but never quite so pleasantly performed.

w Paul Green, Sonya Levien, *novel* Phil
Stong *d* Henry King *ph* Hal Mohr *md* Louis
de Francesco

*Will Rogers, Janet Gaynor, Lew Ayres, Sally
Eilers, Norman Foster, Louise Dresser, Frank
Craven, Victor Jory, Hobart Cavanaugh*
'A pungent, good-humoured motion
picture.'—*Pare Lorentz*
'Vigour, freshness and sympathy abound in
its admittedly idealized fantasy treatment of
small-town life.'—*Charles Higham, 1972*
AAN: best picture; script

State Fair**
US 1945   100m   Technicolor
TCF (William Perlberg)
TV title: *It Happened One Summer*

Musical remake with an amiable cast and a
rousing score.

w / ly Oscar Hammerstein II *d* Walter Lang
ph Leon Shamroy *m* Richard Rodgers
md Alfred Newman

*Charles Winninger, Jeanne Crain, Dana
Andrews, Vivian Blaine, Dick Haymes, Fay
Bainter, Frank McHugh, Percy Kilbride,
Donald Meek*
'Surely the sort of theme that clamours for
movie treatment. But no, say Twentieth
Century Fox: let's make the fair look like a
night club. Let's look around for stars of
pristine nonentity. Let's screw the camera
down to the studio floor. The result, "an epic
that sings to the skies . . . with glorious,
glamorous new songs".'—*Richard Winnington*
AA: song 'It Might As Well Be Spring'
AAN: Alfred Newman

State Fair
US 1962   118m   De Luxe   Cinemascope
TCF (Charles Brackett)

Dullsville modernized version, condescending
towards the rurals and peopled by unattractive
youngsters.

w Richard Breen *d* Jose Ferrer *ph* William
C. Mellor *md* Alfred Newman

Pat Boone, Alice Faye, Tom Ewell, Pamela
Tiffin, Ann-Margret, Bobby Darin, Wally Cox

State of the Union***
US 1948   110m   bw
(MGM) Liberty Films (Frank Capra)
GB title: *The World and His Wife*

An estranged wife rejoins her husband when
he is running for president.
Brilliantly scripted political comedy which
unfortunately goes soft at the end but offers
stimulating entertainment most of the way.

w Anthony Veiller, Myles Connelly, *play*
Howard Lindsay, Russel Crouse d Frank
Capra *ph* George J. Folsey *m* Victor Young

*Spencer Tracy, Katharine Hepburn, Adolphe
Menjou, Van Johnson*, Angela Lansbury,
Lewis Stone, Howard Smith, Raymond
Walburn, Charles Dingle
'A triumphant film, marked all over by
Frank Capra's artistry.'—*Howard Barnes*

State Secret**
GB 1950   104m   bw
British Lion / London (Frank Launder,
Sidney Gilliat)
US title: *The Great Manhunt*

In a Ruritanian country, spies pursue a
surgeon, the only man who knows that the
dictator is dead.
Hitchcockian chase comedy-thriller which is
well detailed and rises to the heights on
occasion.

wd Sidney Gilliat, *novel* Appointment with
Fear by Roy Huggins *ph* Robert Krasker
m William Alwyn

*Douglas Fairbanks Jnr, Glynis Johns, Herbert
Lom, Jack Hawkins,* Walter Rilla, Karel
Stepanek, Carl Jaffe
'An admirably fast-moving diversion in the
Hitchcock tradition.'—*Richard Mallett, Punch*

State's Attorney*
US 1932   79m   bw
GB title: *Cardigan's Last Case*

A prosecuting counsel nearly pays the penalty
for arrogance. Good star melodrama. John
Barrymore, Jill Esmond, William Boyd, Helen
Twelvetrees. Written by Rowland Brown and
Gene Fowler; directed by George
Archainbaud; for RKO. 'Good programme
box office stuff if not particularly smashing.'—
Variety

Station Six Sahara
GB 1962   101m   bw
British Lion / CCC / Artur Brauner (Victor
Lyndon)

Five men working on a remote Saharan
pipeline quarrel over the favours of an
American girl whose car crashes nearby.
Raging old-fashioned melodrama with the
courage of its lack of convictions.

w Bryan Forbes, Brian Clemens *d* Seth Holt
ph Gerald Gibbs *m* Ron Grainer

Carroll Baker, Ian Bannen, Peter Van Eyck,
Denholm Elliott, Mario Adorf, Jorg Felmy,
Biff McGuire

Station West
US 1948   91m   bw
RKO (Robert Sparks)

A saloon queen is the secret head of a gang of
gold robbers.
Predictable but well made western patterned
after *Destry Rides Again*.

w Frank Fenton, Winston Miller, *novel* Luke
Short *d* Sidney Lanfield *ph* Harry J. Wild
m Heinz Roemheld

Dick Powell, Jane Greer, Agnes Moorehead,
Burl Ives, Tom Powers, Gordon Oliver, Steve
Brodie, Guinn Williams, Raymond Burr,
Regis Toomey

'The face was his . . . the body was his . . .
but suddenly, Hello, Charlie!'

The Statue
US 1970   89m   Eastmancolor
Cinerama / Josef Shaftel (Anis Nohra)

A languages professor is embarrassed when his
sculptress wife makes an immense nude statue
of him—with someone else's private parts.
Strained phallic comedy which doesn't even
make the most of its one joke.

w Alec Coppel, Denis Norden *d* Rod
Amateau *ph* Piero Portalupi *m* Riz Ortolani

David Niven, Virna Lisi, Robert Vaughn, Ann
Bell, John Cleese, Hugh Burden

Stay Away Joe
US 1968   102m   Metrocolor   Panavision
MGM (Douglas Lawrence)

An Indian rodeo rider returns to his
reservation, makes several romantic
conquests, and helps a government
rehabilitation scheme.
Thin if surprising vehicle for a singing star; all
rather tedious.

w Michael A. Hoey, *novel* Dan Cushman
d Peter Tewkesbury *ph* Fred Koenekamp
m Jack Marshall

Elvis Presley, Burgess Meredith, Joan
Blondell, Katy Jurado, Thomas Gomez,
Henry Jones, L. Q. Jones

Stay Hungry
US 1976   102m   De Luxe
UA / Outov (Harold Schneider, Bob
Rafaelson)

The heir to an Alabama estate annoys the
locality by assembling a curious bunch of
friends and making unexpected use of his
money.
Rather obvious and pointless fable; well made
but not very stimulating.

w Charles Gaines, Bob Rafaelson, *novel*
Charles Gaines *d* Bob Rafaelson *ph* Victor
Kemper *m* Bruce Langhorne, Byron Berline

Jeff Bridges, Sally Field, Arnold
Schwarzenegger, R. G. Armstrong, Robert
Englund, Roger E. Mosley

Staying Alive
US 1983   96m   Metrocolor
Paramount / Robert Stigwood / Cinema
Group Venture (Sylvester Stallone)

Tony Manero becomes a Broadway dancer.
Fragile sequel to *Saturday Night Fever*, with
some of its frenetic quality but none of its
impact.

w Sylvester Stallone, Norman Wexler
d Sylvester Stallone *ph* Nick McLean
m Johnny Mandel, Robin Garb, others
pd Robert Boyle

John Travolta, Cynthia Rhodes, Finola
Hughes, Steve Inwood, Julie Bovasso
'By turns exhilarating and absurd.'—*Nick
Roddick, MFB*
'Stallone doesn't bother much with
character, scenes or dialogue. He just puts the
newly muscle-plated Travolta in front of the
camera, covers him with what looks like oil
slick, and goes for the whambams.'—*Pauline
Kael, New Yorker*

Steamboat Bill Jnr*
US 1928   71m (24 fps)   bw   silent
UA / Buster Keaton / Joseph Schenck

A student takes over his father's old

Mississippi steamboat, and wins the daughter of his rival.
Rather flat comedy redeemed by a magnificent cyclone climax.

w Carl Harbaugh, Buster Keaton d Charles Riesner ph J. Devereaux Jennings, Bert Haines

Buster Keaton, Ernest Torrence, Marion Byron

Steamboat Round the Bend*
US 1935 80m bw
TCF (Sol M. Wurtzel)

A Mississippi steamboat captain defeats his rival and finds evidence to clear his nephew of a murder charge.
Rather heavily-scripted star vehicle which sacrifices fun for atmosphere but is often good to look at.

w Dudley Nichols, Lamar Trotti, *novel* Ben Lucien Berman d John Ford ph George Schneiderman m Samuel Kaylin

Will Rogers, Anne Shirley, Eugene Pallette, John McGuire, Irvin S. Cobb, Berton Churchill, Stepin Fetchit, Roger Imhof, Raymond Hatton

'Will Rogers' final picture . . . in the money despite a drab theme.'—*Variety*

Steel
US 1979 101m Movielab
Columbia / Panzer / Davis / Fawcett-Majors (Lee Majors)

When a construction boss is killed, his daughter vows to complete his last project.
Flashy, foul-mouthed, but basically old-fashioned hokum climaxing in a race to complete before foreclosure.

w Leigh Chapman d Steve Carver ph Roger Shearman m Michael Colombier pd Ward Preston

Lee Majors, Jennifer O'Neill, Art Carney, George Kennedy, Harris Yulin, Terry Kiser, Richard Lynch, Albert Salmi

The Steel Bayonet
GB 1957 85m bw Hammerscope
(UA) Hammer (Michael Carreras)

During the assault on Tunis a battle-weary platoon holds a farm against enemy attack.
Dreary cliché-ridden war melodrama peopled by all the usual types.

w Howard Clewes d Michael Carreras ph Jack Asher m Leonard Salzedo

Leo Genn, Kieron Moore, Michael Medwin, Robert Brown, Michael Ripper, John Paul, Bernard Horsfall

Steel Town
US 1952 84m Technicolor
U-I (Leonard Goldstein)

A steel president's nephew joins the company as a furnace hand.
Routine drama with an unusual background.

w Gerald Drayson Adams, Lou Breslow d George Sherman ph Charles P. Boyle m Joseph Gershenson

Ann Sheridan, John Lund, Howard Duff, James Best, Nancy Kulp

The Steel Trap*
US 1952 85m bw
TCF / Thor (Bert E. Friedlob)

An assistant bank manager steals half a million dollars from the vault but is troubled by conscience and manages to put it back before the loss is discovered.
Solidly competent little suspenser with plenty of movement.

wd Andrew Stone ph Ernest Laszlo m Dmitri Tiomkin

Joseph Cotten, Teresa Wright, Jonathan Hale, Walter Sande

Steelyard Blues
US 1972 92m Technicolor
Warner / S. B. Productions (Tony Bill, Michael and Julia Phillips)

An ex-con and his call-girl friend are an embarrassment to his DA brother.
Bits and pieces of anti-establishment comedy are tacked on to a thin plot; a few of them work.

w David S. Ward d Alan Myerson ph Laszlo Kovacs, Steven Larner m Nick Gravenites

Donald Sutherland, Jane Fonda, Peter Boyle, Howard Hesseman

● *Video: Warner*

Stella Dallas*
US 1925 110m approx (24 fps) bw silent
Samuel Goldwyn

An uncouth woman loses both husband and daughter.
Standard weepie complete with 'out into the cold cold snow' ending, but handled here with tact and discretion. A seminal film of its time.

w Frances Marion, *novel* Olive Higgins Prouty d Henry King ph Arthur Edeson

Belle Bennett, Ronald Colman, Lois Moran, Jean Hersholt, Douglas Fairbanks Jnr, Alice Joyce

Stella Dallas*
US 1937 106m bw
Samuel Goldwyn

Fashionable remake with excellent talent; 1937 audiences came to sneer and stayed to weep.

w Victor Heerman, Sara Y. Mason d King Vidor ph Rudolph Maté m Alfred Newman

Barbara Stanwyck, John Boles, Anne Shirley, Barbara O'Neil, Alan Hale, Marjorie Main, Tim Holt

'A tear-jerker of A ranking. There are things about the story that will not appeal to some men, but no one will be annoyed or offended by it. And the wallop is inescapably there for femmes.'—*Variety*

† Goldwyn's premier choices for the lead were Ruth Chatterton and Gladys George.

AAN: Barbara Stanwyck; Anne Shirley

Step Down to Terror
US 1959 76m bw
U-I (Joseph Gershenson)
GB title: *The Silent Stranger*

A man returns to his home town and is

discovered to be a psychopathic killer on the run.
Dismal reworking of *Shadow of a Doubt*; strictly second feature stuff.

w Mel Dinelli, Czenzi Ormonde, Chris Cooper d Harry Keller ph Russell Metty m Joseph Gershenson

Charles Drake, Coleen Miller, Rod Taylor, Josephine Hutchinson, Jocelyn Brando

Step Lively*
US 1944 88m bw
RKO (Robert Fellows)

Gleaming musical remake of *Room Service* (qv); all very efficient if witless.

w Warren Duff, Peter Milne d Tim Whelan ph Robert de Grasse md Constantin Bakaleinikoff songs Jule Styne, Sammy Cahn

Frank Sinatra, George Murphy, Adolphe Menjou, Gloria de Haven, Anne Jeffreys, Walter Slezak, Eugene Pallette

The Stepford Wives*
US 1974 115m TVC
Fadsin / Palomar (Edgar J. Sherick)

A new wife in a commuter village outside New York finds all her female friends too good to be true . . . because their husbands have had them replaced by computerized models.
An attractive idea which needs a much lighter and pacier touch but entertains in patches and shows agreeable sophistication.

w William Goldman, *novel* Ira Levin d Bryan Forbes ph Owen Roizman m Michael Small pd Gene Callahan

Katharine Ross, Paula Prentiss, Nanette Newman, Peter Masterson, Patrick O'Neal, Tina Louise, William Prince

'It was hard to tell Katharine Ross playing a robot from Katharine Ross playing a normal housewife.'—*Les Keyser, Hollywood in the Seventies*

'The first women's lib gothic—hardly the landmark the world had been waiting for.'—*Pauline Kael, New Yorker*

● *Video: VCL*

Steptoe and Son
GB 1972 98m Technicolor
EMI / Associated London Films (Aida Young)

Harold gets married, mislays his wife but thinks he is a father.
Strained attempt to transfer the TV rag-and-bone comedy (which in the US became *Sanford and Son*) to the big screen. Not the same thing at all.

w Ray Galton, Alan Simpson d Cliff Owen ph John Wilcox m Roy Budd, Jack Fishman

Wilfrid Brambell, Harry H. Corbett, Carolyn Seymour, Arthur Howard, Victor Maddern

† *Steptoe and Son Ride Again*, which followed in 1973, was even more crude and out of character.

The Sterile Cuckoo
US 1969 107m Technicolor
Paramount / Boardwalk (Alan J. Pakula)
GB title: *Pookie*

A talkative but insecure college girl has her
first sexual adventures.
Rather tiresome comedy drama with good
scenes; general handling far too restrained.

w Alvin Sargent, *novel* John Nicholson
d Alan J. Pakula *ph* Milton Krasner *m* Fred
Karlin

Liza Minnelli, Tim McIntire, Wendell Burton,
Austin Green, Sandra Faison

AAN: song 'Come Saturday Morning'
(*m* Fred Karlin, *ly* Dory Previn); Liza
Minnelli

Stevie°
US / GB 1978 102m Technicolor
First Artists / Grand Metropolitan (Robert
Enders)

An account of the uneventful life of poetess
Stevie Smith, lived out mainly in a London
suburb under the fear of death.
Claustrophobic showcase for a whimsical lady;
interesting for some specialized audiences.

w Hugh Whitemore, from his play *d* Robert
Enders *ph* Freddie Young *m* Marcus Gowers

Glenda Jackson, Mona Washbourne, Trevor
Howard, Alec McCowen

● Video: *Home Video*

The Stick Up
GB 1977 101m colour
Backstage (Elliott Kastner, Danny
O'Donovan)

In Devon in 1935, an American gives a lift to a
café waitress and finds she is a thief on the
run.
Numbingly peculiar comedy melodrama which
tries too hard to have any chance of
succeeding.

wd Jeffrey Bloom *ph* Michael Reed
m Michael J. Lewis

David Soul, Pamela McMyler, Johnny Wade,
Michael Balfour

'The worst film of this or possibly any
year.'—*Barry Took, Punch*

Stiletto
US 1969 99m Berkey–Pathe
Avco / Harold Robbins (Norman Rosemont)

A wealthy playboy racing driver is in fact a
Mafia executioner.
Dreary, violent, fashionable Mafioso
melodrama with international jet set
trimmings.

w A. J. Russsell, *novel* Harold Robbins
d Bernard Kowalski *ph* Jack Priestly *m* Sid
Ramin

Alex Cord, Britt Ekland, Barbara McNair,
Patrick O'Neal, Joseph Wiseman, John
Dehner, Eduardo Ciannelli, Roy Scheider

Still of the Night°
US 1982 91m Technicolor
MGM / UA (Arlene Donovan)

A psychiatrist finds himself in danger when
one of his patients is murdered.

Hitchcock-style mystery melodrama with the
villain fairly well concealed . . . but somehow
not very entertaining. The actors all take their
characters too seriously.

w Robert Benton, David Newman *d* Robert
Benton *ph* Nestor Almendros *m* John
Gibson *pd* Mel Bourne

Roy Scheider, Meryl Streep, Jessica Tandy,
Sara Botsford, Josef Somner, Joe Grifasi

'A lifeless and frustrating muddle.'—*Steve
Jenkins, MFB*

'All it takes is a little confidence!'
The Sting°°
US 1973 129m Technicolor
Universal / Richard Zanuck, David Brown
(Tony Bill, Michael S. Phillips)

In twenties Chicago, two con men stage an
elaborate revenge on a big time gangster who
caused the death of a friend.
Bright, likeable, but overlong, unconvincingly
studio-set and casually developed comedy
suspenser cashing in on star charisma but
riding to enormous success chiefly on its tinkly
music and the general lack of simple
entertainment.

w David S. Ward *d* George Roy Hill
ph Robert Surtees *m* Scott Joplin (arranged
by Marvin Hamlisch) *ad* Henry Bumstead

Paul Newman, *Robert Redford*, Robert Shaw,
Charles Durning, Ray Walston, Eileen
Brennan

'A visually claustrophobic, mechanically
plotted movie that's meant to be a roguishly
charming entertainment.'—*New Yorker*

'It demonstrates what can happen when a
gifted young screenwriter has the good fortune
to fall among professionals his second time
out.'—*Judith Crist*

'A testament to the value of blue eyes and
bright smiles.'—*Les Keyser, Hollywood in the
Seventies*

AA: best picture; David S. Ward; George Roy
Hill; Marvin Hamlisch

AAN: Robert Surtees; Robert Redford

● Video: *CIC*

The Sting 2
US 1983 102m Technicolor
Universal (Jennings Lang)

Lonnegan plots his revenge on the two who
stung him in twenties Chicago.
Boring reprise of an overrated movie: though
efficiently made, it never catches fire, and the
cast is indisputably a second team.

w David S. Ward *d* Jeremy Paul Kagan
ph Bill Butler *m* Lalo Schifrin *pd* Edward C.
Carfagno

Jackie Gleason, Mac Davis, Karl Malden,
Oliver Reed, Bert Remsen, Teri Garr

'The vivid minor characters have been
squeezed into lifelessness by the python-like
plot.'—*Tom Milne, MFB*

Stingaree
US 1934 76m bw (colour sequence)
RKO (Pandro S. Berman)

An Australian outlaw of the eighties falls for a
rancher's daughter.

Unexciting but unobjectionable piece of Robin
Hoodery.

w Becky Gardiner, *stories* E. W. Hornung
d William A. Wellman *ph* James Van Trees
m Max Steiner

Irene Dunne, Richard Dix, Mary Boland,
Conway Tearle, Andy Devine, Henry
Stephenson, Una O'Connor, Reginald Owen,
Snub Pollard, George Barraud

'Should bring medium results. It does not
promise to rise to greater heights.'—*Variety*

Stir Crazy
US 1980 111m Metrocolor
Columbia / Hannah Weinstein

Two New Yorkers heading for California to
try their luck are wrongly convicted of a bank
robbery but plan escape from prison.
Extended farce giving rather too free rein to
its stars' potential for mugging, and polishing
up every prison gag in the book.

w Bruce Jay Friedman *d* Sidney Poitier
ph Fred Schuler *m* Tom Scott *pd* Alfred
Sweeney

Gene Wilder, Richard Pryor, George Stanford
Brown, Jobeth Williams

● Video: *RCA / Columbia*

A Stitch in Time
GB 1963 94m bw
Rank (Hugh Stewart)

A butcher's boy goes into hospital and falls for
a nurse.
Thin star slapstick; all one can say is that it's
marginally preferable to Jerry Lewis.

w Jack Davies *d* Robert Asher *ph* Jack
Asher *m* Philip Green

Norman Wisdom, Edward Chapman, Jerry
Desmonde, Jeanette Sterke, Jill Melford

Stolen Face
GB 1952 72m bw

Via plastic surgery a girl criminal is given
another face, which produces a different kind
of trouble. Quickie melodrama which proved
fairly popular because of its Hollywood stars.
Paul Henreid, Lizabeth Scott, André Morell,
Susan Stephen, Mary Mackenzie, Arnold
Ridley. Written by Martin Berkeley and
Richard Landau; directed by Terence Fisher;
for Hammer-Lippert.

Stolen Harmony
US 1935 79m bw

An ex-con becomes a saxophonist with a band
and is suspected of a robbery. Tedious mix-up
of mayhem and music. George Raft, Ben
Bernie, Grace Bradley, Iris Adrian, Lloyd
Nolan, Ralf Harolde. Written by Leon
Gordon, Harry Ruskin, Claude Binyon, Lewis
Foster; directed by Alfred Werker; for
Paramount. 'Once under way it provides some
exciting entertainment; but the poor beginning
isn't easily tossed off.'—*Variety*

'Its surprise finish will lift you to amazing
emotional peaks!'
Stolen Heaven
US 1931 72m bw

A boy and girl decide to commit suicide after

spending the twenty thousand dollars they've stolen, but neither can go through with it. A very silly idea, ineptly presented. Nancy Carroll, Phillips Holmes, Louis Calhern, Edward Keane. Written by Dana Burnet; directed by George Abbott; for Paramount. 'It will range down from moderate figures.'— *Variety*

Stolen Heaven
US 1938 88m bw

Two jewel thieves in love are harboured on the run by an old concert pianist. Sentimental melodrama which almost works, with its backing of classical piano pieces. Gene Raymond, Olympe Bradna, Lewis Stone, Glenda Farrell, Porter Hall, Douglass Dumbrille. Written by Eve Greene, Frederick Jackson, Andrew L. Stone; directed by Andrew L. Stone; for Paramount. 'Pleasing entertainment all the way.'—*Variety*

Stolen Holiday
US 1937 82m bw

A model marries a fortune hunter to protect him from the law. Slightly unusual romantic drama based on the career of Alexander Stavisky. *Claude Rains*, Kay Francis, Ian Hunter, Alison Skipworth, Charles Halton, Alex D'Arcy. Written by Casey Robinson; directed by Michael Curtiz; for Warner.

Stolen Hours
GB 1963 97m De Luxe
UA / Mirisch / Barbican (Denis Holt)

An American divorcee with only a year to live falls in love with her surgeon.
Tired remake of *Dark Victory*; pleasant Cornish backgrounds.

w Jessamyn West d Daniel Petrie ph Harry Waxman m Mort Lindsey

Susan Hayward, Michael Craig, Diane Baker, Edward Judd, Paul Rogers

Stolen Kisses*
France 1968 91m Eastmancolor
Films du Carrosse / Artistes Associés (Marcel Berbert)
original title: *Baisers Volés*

An ineffective young man can find neither work nor love.
A pleasing, rather sad little comedy which has almost the feel of a Keaton; but one is not quite sure at the end what its creator intended.

w François Truffaut, Claude de Givray, Bernard Revon d François Truffaut ph Denys Clerval m Antoine Duhamel

Jean-Pierre Léaud, Delphine Seyrig, Michel Lonsdale, Claude Jade

AAN: best foreign film

A Stolen Life*
GB 1939 91m bw
(Paramount) Orion (Anthony Havelock-Allan)

In Brittany, a woman deceives her husband by exchanging identities with her dead twin. An actress's showcase, quite satisfactorily mounted.

w Margaret Kennedy, George Barraud, *novel* Karel J. Benes d Paul Czinner ph Philip Tannura m William Walton

Elisabeth Bergner, Michael Redgrave, Wilfrid Lawson, Richard Ainley, Mabel Terry-Lewis, Clement McCallin

A Stolen Life*
US 1946 107m bw
Warner (Bette Davis)

Enjoyable if slightly disappointing remake with New England backgrounds.

w Catherine Turney d Curtis Bernhardt ph Sol Polito, Sid Hickox m Max Steiner

Bette Davis, Glenn Ford, Dane Clark, Walter Brennan, Charles Ruggles, Bruce Bennett, Peggy Knudsen, Esther Dale
   'A distressingly empty piece of show-off.'— *Bosley Crowther*
   'What I'm waiting for is a film about beautiful identical quintuplets who all love the same man.'—*Richard Winnington*

The Stone Killer*
US 1973 96m Technicolor
Columbia / Dino de Laurentiis (Michael Winner)

A brutal Los Angeles police detective takes on the Mafia.
Fast-moving amalgam of chases and violence with a downbeat hero.

w Gerald Wilson, *novel* A Complete State of Death by John Gardner d Michael Winner ph Richard Moore m Roy Budd

Charles Bronson, Martin Balsam, Ralph Waite, David Sheiner, Norman Fell
   'Film-making as painting by numbers.'— *Sight and Sound*

● Video: RCA / Columbia

The Stooge
US 1951 100m bw
Paramount / Hal B. Wallis

In 1930 a conceited song and dance man fails to realize that his moronic stooge is the act's real attraction.
Typical, and particularly resistible, Martin and Lewis concoction: whenever one thinks of laughing, a dollop of sentimentality comes along and promptly quashes the idea.

w Fred Finkelhoffe, Martin Rackin d Norman Taurog ph Daniel L. Fapp m Joseph J. Lilley

Dean Martin, Jerry Lewis, Polly Bergen, Marie McDonald, Eddie Mayehoff, Marion Marshall, Richard Erdman

Stop Press Girl
GB 1949 78m bw

A girl finds she has the unconscious power to bring all machinery to a halt. Weary comedy which has nowhere to go after its first silly idea. Sally Ann Howes, Gordon Jackson, Basil Radford, Naunton Wayne, James Robertson Justice, Sonia Holm, Nigel Buchanan, Kenneth More. Written by Basil Thomas and T. J. Morrison; directed by Michael Barry; for Aquila / Rank.

Stop You're Killing Me
US 1953 86m Warnercolor
Warner (Louis F. Edelman)

At the end of prohibition a beer baron decides to go straight, but finds his house filled with the corpses of rival gangsters.
Frantic remake of *A Slight Case of Murder* with a few musical numbers added; all rather messy.

w James O'Hanlon d Roy del Ruth ph Ted McCord md Ray Heindorf

Broderick Crawford, Claire Trevor, Virginia Gibson, Bill Hayes, Sheldon Leonard, Joe Vitale, Howard St John, Henry Morgan, Margaret Dumont

Stopover Tokyo
US 1957 100m Eastmancolor
   Cinemascope
TCF (Walter Reisch)

An American spy in Tokyo seeks to capture a communist undercover man.
Sprawling espionage stuff with frequent halts for scenic tours.

w Richard L. Breen, Walter Reisch, *novel* John P. Marquand d Richard L. Breen ph Charles G. Clarke m Paul Sawtell

Robert Wagner, Joan Collins, Edmond O'Brien, Ken Scott, Larry Keating

Stories from a Flying Trunk
GB 1979 88m Technicolor
EMI / Sands (John Brabourne, Richard Goodwin)

Three Hans Andersen stories are performed by stop frame animation and by ballet dancers dressed as vegetables.
Lugubrious attempt to repeat the success of *Tales of Beatrix Potter;* moments to make one smile, but on the whole a depressing experience.

wd Christine Edzard m Gioacchino Rossini ph Robin Browne, Brian West

Murray Melvin, Ann Firbank, Johanna Sonnex, Tasneem Maqsood

The Stork Club
US 1945 98m bw
Paramount (B. G. De Sylva)

A nightclub hat-check girl saves an elderly millionaire from drowning.
Very light comedy with music, a great ad for a once famous night haunt.

w B. G. De Sylva, John McGowan d Hal Walker ph Charles Lang Jnr md Robert Emmett Dolan

Betty Hutton, Barry Fitzgerald, Don Defore, Robert Benchley, Bill Goodwin, Iris Adrian, Mary Young, Mikhail Rasumny

The Storm
US 1930 76m bw

An orphan girl left with a trapper becomes an object of jealousy between him and his partner. Old-fashioned outdoor melodrama, previously filmed in 1916 and 1922. Not really talkie material. Lupe Velez, Paul Cavanagh.

William Boyd, Alphonse Ethier. Written by Wells Root from the play by Langdon McCormick; directed by William Wyler; for Universal. 'A fairly good programmer . . . the fight is a pip.'—*Variety*

The Storm
US 1938 79m bw

Tensions lead to violence among shipboard radio operators. Lively action melodrama culminating in a storm at sea. Charles Bickford, Barton MacLane, Preston Foster, Tom Brown, Nan Grey, Andy Devine, Frank Jenks. Written by Daniel Moore, Hugh King, Theodore Reeves; directed by Harold Young; for Ken Goldsmith / Universal. 'Good enough for the duals, but too weak for solo billing.'—*Variety*

Storm at Daybreak
US 1932 80m bw

A fanciful reconstruction of events leading up to the Sarajevo assassination which precipitated World War I. Unlikely melodrama with stars forced to overact; still, a rich and historically interesting slice of ham. Walter Huston, Kay Francis, Nils Asther, Phillips Holmes, Eugene Pallette, C. Henry Gordon, Jean Parker. Written by Bertram Millhauser, from a play by Sandor Hunyady; directed by Richard Boleslawski; for MGM. 'A good cast unwisely spent on weak material: doubtful as a grosser.'—*Variety*

'Who really set the town aflame?'
Storm Center
US 1956 87m bw
Columbia / Phoenix (Julian Blaustein)

A small-town librarian is dismissed when she refuses to remove a communist book from the shelves.
Formula anti-McCarthy melodrama originally designed for Mary Pickford's comeback; not very absorbing and rather dingily produced.
w Daniel Taradash, Elick Moll d Daniel Taradash ph Burnett Guffey m George Duning

Bette Davis, Brian Keith, Kim Hunter, Paul Kelly, Joe Mantell

Storm Fear
US 1955 88m bw
(UA) Theodora (Cornel Wilde)

Three fugitives from justice hide in a mountain cabin, but all meet violent deaths.
Gloomy, strenuous melodrama, partly shot outdoors.
w Horton Foote, *novel* Clinton Seeley d Cornel Wilde ph Joseph La Shelle m Elmer Bernstein

Cornel Wilde, Jean Wallace, Dan Duryea, Lee Grant, Steven Hill, Dennis Weaver

Storm in a Teacup*
GB 1937 87m bw
Alexander Korda / Victor Saville

A national sensation ensues when a Scottish provost fines an old lady for not licensing her dog, and she refuses to pay.

Early Ealing-type comedy, a bit emaciated by later standards.
w Ian Dalrymple, Donald Bull, *play* Sturm in Wasserglass by Bruno Frank d Ian Dalrymple, Victor Saville ph Max Greene m Frederic Lewis

Vivien Leigh, Rex Harrison, Cecil Parker, Sara Allgood, Ursula Jeans, Gus McNaughton, Arthur Wontner

Storm over Asia*
USSR 1928 93m approx (24 fps) bw silent
Mezhrabpomfilm
original title: *Potomok Chingis-Khana*; aka: *The Heir to Genghis Khan*

A Mongolian trapper is discovered to be descended from Genghis Khan and made puppet emperor of a Soviet province.
Curious yarn without much discernible point though with the usual patches of propagandizing. It certainly looks good.
w Osip Brik d V. I. Pudovkin ph A. L. Golovnya

I. Inkizhinov, Valeri Inkizhinov, A. Dedintsev
'Fetid with propaganda and thematically ridiculous to any semi-intelligent audience. The more illiterate a man is in these Russian blurbs, the better his chances to make a name for himself in the Red World.'—*Variety*

Storm over Lisbon
US 1944 86m bw
Republic (George Sherman)

An international spy mastermind runs a Lisbon night club and sells documents to the highest bidder.
Feeble copy of *Casablanca*.
w Doris Gilbert, Dane Lussier d George Sherman ph John Alton m Walter Scharf

Vera Hruba Ralston, Erich Von Stroheim, Richard Arlen, Eduardo Ciannelli, Otto Kruger, Robert Livingston, Mona Barrie, Frank Orth

Storm over the Andes
US 1935 82m bw

An aeroplane pilot in South America gets into trouble with the authorities and with his superior officer when he falls for his wife. Tolerable action melodrama. Jack Holt, Antonio Moreno, Mona Barrie, Gene Lockhart, Grant Withers. Written by Al De Mond, Frank Wead, Eva Greene, Eliot Gibbons, Laclede Christy; directed by Christy Cabanne; for Maurice Pivar / Columbia. 'Pretty good general entertainment for the masses.'—*Variety*

Storm over the Nile
GB 1955 107m Technicolor Cinemascope
Independent / London (Zoltan Korda)

Feeble remake of *The Four Feathers* (qv), using most of that film's action highlights stretched out to fit the wide screen.
w R. C. Sherriff d Terence Young ph Ted Scaife, Osmond Borradaile m Benjamin Frankel

Anthony Steel, Laurence Harvey, Ronald Lewis, Ian Carmichael, James Robertson Justice, Mary Ure, Geoffrey Keen, Jack Lambert, Ferdy Mayne, Michael Hordern
'The material appears not so much dated as fossilized within its period.'—*Penelope Houston*
● Video: CBS / Fox

Storm over Tibet
US 1951 87m bw
Columbia / Summit (Ivan Tors, Laslo Benedek)

An explorer steals a holy mask which brings bad luck.
Slight adventure yarn ingeniously built around an old German documentary.
w Ivan Tors, Sam Mayer d Andrew Marton ph George E. Diskant, Richard Angst m Arthur Honegger

Rex Reason, Diana Douglas, Myron Healey

Storm Warning*
US 1950 93m bw
Warner (Jerry Wald)

A New York model goes south to visit her sister, and finds that her brother-in-law is an oversexed brute and a Ku Klux Klan killer.
Heavy melodrama disguised as a social document; sufficiently arresting for its purposes.
w Daniel Fuchs, Richard Brooks d Stuart Heisler ph Carl Guthrie m Daniele Amfitheatrof

Ginger Rogers, Doris Day, *Steve Cochran*, Ronald Reagan, Hugh Sanders, Raymond Greenleaf, Ned Glass

Stormy Weather
GB 1935 74m bw

A top executive foils a blackmail racket in Chinatown. Very presentable vehicle for the Aldwych team of farceurs. Tom Walls, Ralph Lynn, Robertson Hare, Yvonne Arnaud, Gordon James, Graham Moffatt. Written by Ben Travers, from his play; directed by Tom Walls; for Gainsborough.

Stormy Weather***
US 1943 77m bw
TCF (Irving Mills)

A backstage success story lightly based on the career of Bill Robinson.
Virtually a high-speed revue with all-black talent, and what talent! The production is pretty slick too.
w Frederick Jackson, Ted Koehler d Andrew Stone ph Leon Shamroy, Fred Sersen md Benny Carter ch Clarence Robinson

Bill Robinson, Lena Horne, Fats Waller, Ada Brown, Cab Calloway, Katherine Dunham and her Dancers, Eddie Anderson, Flournoy Miller, *The Nicholas Brothers*, Dooley Wilson
'A first-rate show, a spirited divertissement . . . a joy to the ear.'—*New York Times*

The Story of a Woman

US / Italy 1969 101m Technicolor
Universal / Westward (Leonardo Bercovici)

A Swedish girl pianist in Rome falls in love
with a fashionable doctor, then back in
Sweden meets an American diplomat.
Intermezzo-type romantic drama with colour
supplement trappings. Tolerable of its kind.

wd Leonardo Bercovici *ph* Piero Portalupi
m John Williams

Robert Stack, Bibi Andersson, James
Farentino, Annie Girardot, Frank Sundstrom

The Story of Adèle H*

France 1975 98m Eastmancolor
Films du Carrosse / Artistes Associés
(Marcel Berbert, Claude Miller)

In 1863, the daughter of Victor Hugo follows
her lover to Nova Scotia.
Surprisingly slow and stilted version of a true
story, though with a few of the expected
subtleties.

w François Truffaut, Jean Gruault, Suzanne
Schiffman *d* François Truffaut *ph* Nestor
Almendros *m* Maurice Jaubert

Isabelle Adjani, Bruce Robinson, Sylvia
Marriott

AAN: Isabelle Adjani

'America's most thrilling story! Of love so
    great and faith so strong that it inspired
    this man to endure ridicule, privation and
    hunger—to achieve the miracle of wings
    for the human voice!'

The Story of Alexander Graham Bell**

US 1939 97m bw
TCF (Kenneth MacGowan)
GB title: *The Modern Miracle*

The inventor of the telephone marries a deaf
girl.
Acceptable history lesson with dullish
principals but excellent production.

w Lamar Trotti *d* Irving Cummings *ph* Leon
Shamroy *m* Louis Silvers

Don Ameche, Henry Fonda, Loretta Young,
Charles Coburn, Gene Lockhart, Spring
Byington, Bobs Watson
    'Production will need teasing to get the
women.'—*Variety*

The Story of Dr Wassell*

US 1944 140m Technicolor
Paramount / Cecil B. de Mille

The adventures of a naval doctor who
heroically saved men during the Pacific war.
Long, slogging, glamorized account of real
events which is typical de Mille and very
unconvincing physically, but keeps one
watching simply as a story.

w Alan le May, Charles Bennett, *book* James
Hilton *d* Cecil B. de Mille *ph* Victor Milner,
William Snyder *m* Victor Young

Gary Cooper, Laraine Day, Signe Hasso,
Dennis O'Keefe, Carol Thurston, Carl
Esmond, Paul Kelly, Stanley Ridges
    'The director has taken a true story of
heroism . . . and jangled it into a cacophony

of dancing girls, phoney self-sacrifice and
melodramatic romance.'—*Howard Barnes*
    'To be regretted beyond qualification. It
whips the story into a nacreous foam of lies
whose speciousness is only the more painful
because Mr de Mille is so obviously free from
any desire to alter the truth except for what he
considers to be its own advantage.'—*James
Agee*

The Story of Esther Costello*

GB 1957 103m bw
Columbia / Romulus (James Woolf)
US title: *The Golden Virgin*

A blind Irish deaf mute girl is adopted by an
American socialite and her plight becomes an
international cause.
Rich melodrama develops from this unlikely
premise and the star enjoys it hugely.

w Charles Kaufman, *novel* Nicholas
Monsarrat *d* David Miller *ph* Robert
Krasker *m* Georges Auric

Joan Crawford, Heather Sears, Rossano
Brazzi, Ron Randell, Lee Patrick, Fay
Compton, John Loder, Denis O'Dea, Sidney
James, Maureen Delany

The Story of GI Joe**

US 1945 108m bw
(UA) Lester Cowan (David Hall)
aka: *War Correspondent*

Journalist Ernie Pyle follows fighting men into
the Italian campaign.
Slow, convincing, sympathetic war film with
good script and performances; not by any
means the usual action saga.

w Leopold Atlas, Guy Endore, Philip
Stevenson, *book* Ernie Pyle *d* William A.
Wellman *ph* Russell Metty *m* Ann Ronell,
Louis Applebaum

Burgess Meredith, Robert Mitchum, Freddie
Steele, Wally Cassell, Jimmy Lloyd, Jack
Reilly
    'It is humorous, poignant and tragic, an
earnestly human reflection of a stern life and
the dignity of man.'—*Thomas M. Pryor*
    'A tragic and eternal work of art.'—*James
Agee*
    'One of the best films of the war.'—*Richard
Mallett, Punch*

AAN: script; music score; song 'Linda' (*m /
ly* Ann Ronell); Robert Mitchum

The Story of Gilbert and Sullivan*

GB 1953 109m Technicolor
British Lion / London Films (Frank Launder,
Sidney Gilliat)

In 1875 a young composer named Arthur
Sullivan and a librettist named William Gilbert
come together under the auspices of Rupert
D'Oyly Carte and write the Savoy Operas.
Light, accurate, well-cast and well-produced
Victorian musical which somehow fails to
ignite despite the immense talent at hand.

w Sidney Gilliat, Leslie Baily *d* Sidney
Gilliat *ph* Christopher Challis *md* Sir
Malcolm Sargent *pd* Hein Heckroth

Robert Morley, Maurice Evans, Peter Finch,
Eileen Herlie, Dinah Sheridan, Isabel Dean,
Wilfrid Hyde White, Muriel Aked

The Story of Louis Pasteur***

US 1936 85m bw
Warner (Henry Blanke)

How the eminent 19th-century French scientist
overcomes obstacles in finding cures for
various diseases.
Adequate biopic which caused a sensation and
started a trend; some of the others were better
but this was the first example of Hollywood
bringing schoolbook history to box office life.

w Sheridan Gibney, Pierre Collins *d* William
Dieterle *ph* Tony Gaudio *m* Bernhard Kaun,
Heinz Roemheld

Paul Muni, Josephine Hutchinson, Anita
Louise, Donald Woods, Fritz Leiber, Henry
O'Neill, Porter Hall, Akim Tamiroff, Walter
Kingsford
    'Probably limited b.o. but a creditable
prestige picture.'—*Variety*
    'What should be vital and arresting has been
made hollow and dull . . . we are tendered
something that is bright and stagey for
something out of life.'—*Otis Ferguson*
    'More exciting than any gangster
melodrama.'—*C. A. Lejeune*

AA: script; Paul Muni
AAN: best picture

'Men and their women from the beginning
    of creation! Never so vast an
    undertaking!'

The Story of Mankind

US 1957 100m Technicolor
Warner / Cambridge (Irwin Allen)

A heavenly tribunal debates whether to allow
man to destroy himself, and both the Devil
and the Spirit of Man cite instances from
history.
Hilarious charade, one of the worst films ever
made, but full of surprises, bad performances,
and a wide range of stock shots.

w Irwin Allen, Charles Bennett, *book* Henrik
Van Loon *d* Irwin Allen *ph* Nicholas
Musuraca *m* Paul Sawtell

Ronald Colman, Vincent Price, Cedric
Hardwicke, the Marx Brothers, Hedy Lamarr,
Agnes Moorehead, Reginald Gardiner, Peter
Lorre, Virginia Mayo, Charles Coburn,
Francis X. Bushman
    'A poor excuse to use a batch of available
actors in some of the weirdest casting ever
committed.'—*Newsweek*

The Story of Molly X

US 1949 82m bw

When a criminal is killed, his wife
masterminds the gang to find out who killed
him. Silly melodrama, generally ineptly
presented. June Havoc, John Russell, Dorothy
Hart, Elliott Lewis, Connie Gilchrist. Written
and directed by Crane Wilbur; for Universal /
International.

The Story of Robin Hood and his Merrie Men

GB 1952 84m Technicolor
Walt Disney (Perce Pearce)

When Prince John starts a ruthless taxation

campaign, Robert Fitzooth turns outlaw.
Fairly competent but quite forgettable version
of the legend, softened for children.

w Laurence E. Watkin *d* Ken Annakin
ph Guy Green *m* Clifton Parker

Richard Todd, Joan Rice, James Hayter,
Hubert Gregg, James Robertson Justice,
Martita Hunt, Peter Finch

The Story of Ruth
US 1960 132m De Luxe Cinemascope
TCF (Samuel G. Engel)

Ruth becomes the favourite of a pagan king
but eventually flees to Israel.
Tedious, portentous bible-in-pictures, of
virtually no interest or entertainment value.

w Norman Corwin *d* Henry Koster
ph Arthur E. Arling *m* Franz Waxman

Elana Eden, Peggy Wood, Viveca Lindfors,
Stuart Whitman, Tom Tryon, Jeff Morrow,
Thayer David, Eduard Franz

The Story of Seabiscuit
US 1949 98m Technicolor
Warner (William Jacobs)
GB title: *Pride of Kentucky*

The success story of a racehorse.
Blue grass vapidities, the kind of family
entertainment that drove the families away.

w John Taintor Foote *d* David Butler
ph Wilfrid Cline *md* David Buttolph

Shirley Temple, Barry Fitzgerald, Lon
McCallister, Rosemary de Camp, Donald
McBride, Pierre Watkin

The Story of Shirley Yorke
GB 1948 92m bw

A nobleman tries to blame his wife's nurse for
her death by poison. Lethargic version of a
play previously filmed as *Lord Camber's
Ladies* (qv). Derek Farr, Dinah Sheridan,
Margaretta Scott, John Robinson, Barbara
Couper, Valentine Dyall. Written by A. R.
Rawlinson, Maclean Rogers and Kathleen
Butler, from the play *The Case of Lady
Camber* by H. A. Vachell; directed by
Maclean Rogers; for Butcher's.

The Story of Temple Drake*
US 1933 71m bw
Paramount (Ben Glazer)

A neurotic southern flapper is abducted by
gangsters, and likes it.
Deliberately shocking melodrama of its time,
restructured from a notorious book later
filmed under its own title. Very dated, but
interesting.

w Oliver H. P. Garrett, *novel* Sanctuary by
William Faulkner *d* Stephen Roberts *ph* Karl
Struss

Miriam Hopkins, Jack La Rue, William
Gargan, William Collier Jnr, Irving Pichel,
Guy Standing, Elizabeth Patterson, Florence
Eldridge

'Under Haysian ban the title of the novel
can't be ballyhooed, but any whispering
campaign about this is the picture's best b.o.
asset. It has little else to commend it.'—
Variety

The Story of Three Loves
US 1953 122m Technicolor
MGM (Sidney Franklin)

Three love stories concerning the passengers
on a transatlantic liner.
Three bits of old-fashioned kitsch, one tragic,
one whimsical, one melodramatic, all rather
slow and dull though well produced.

w John Collier, Jan Lustig, George Froeschel
d Gottfried Reinhardt, Vincente Minnelli
ph Charles Rosher, Harold Rosson *m* Miklos
Rozsa

Ethel Barrymore, James Mason, Moira
Shearer, Pier Angeli, Leslie Caron, Kirk
Douglas, Farley Granger, Agnes Moorehead,
Zsa Zsa Gabor

The Story of Vernon and Irene Castle**
US 1939 93m bw
RKO (George Haight, Pandro S. Berman)

The story of a husband and wife dance team
who had their first success in Paris and became
influential international celebrities before he
was killed as a flier in World War I.
Pleasant understated musical with very
agreeable dance sequences and a firm overall
style. The last of the main stream of Astaire-
Rogers musicals.

w Richard Sherman, Oscar Hammerstein II,
Dorothy Yost, *books* Irene Castle *d* H. C.
Potter *ph* Robert de Grasse *md* Victor
Baravalle *ch* Hermes Pan *ad* Van Nest
Polglase

*Fred Astaire, Ginger Rogers, Edna May
Oliver*, Walter Brennan, Lew Fields, Etienne
Girardot, Donald MacBride

'One of the best Astaire-Rogers musicals
. . . a wealth of nostalgic appeal.'—*Variety*
† The title was devised and insisted on by Mrs
Castle.

The Story of Will Rogers
US 1950 109m Technicolor
Warner (Robert Arthur)

A wild west performer becomes a Ziegfeld
star and pop philosopher.
Bland, unshaped biopic of one of American
show business's best loved figures, who died in
an air crash in 1935.

w Frank Davis, Stanley Roberts *d* Michael
Curtiz *ph* Wilfrid M. Cline *md* Victor Young

Will Rogers Jnr, Jane Wyman, James
Gleason, Eddie Cantor (as himself), Carl
Benton Reid

The Story on Page One
US 1960 123m bw Cinemascope
TCF / Company of Artists (Jerry Wald)

A lawyer undertakes the defence of a woman
who with her lover is charged with the murder
of her husband.
Long drawn out and not very interesting
courtroom drama, performed and presented
with some style.

wd Clifford Odets *ph* James Wong Howe
m Elmer Bernstein

Rita Hayworth, Tony Franciosa, Gig Young,
Mildred Dunnock, Hugh Griffith, Sanford
Meisner, Alfred Ryder

Stowaway*
US 1936 86m bw
TCF (Earl Carroll, Harold Wilson)

The orphan daughter of a Shanghai missionary
stows away on an American pleasure ship.
Very good star vehicle in which Shirley
performs some of her best musical numbers.

w William Conselman, Arthur Sheekman, Nat
Perrin *d* William A. Seiter *ph* Arthur Miller
md Louis Silvers *songs* Mack Gordon,
Harry Revel

Shirley Temple, Robert Young, Alice Faye,
Eugene Pallette, Helen Westley, Arthur
Treacher, J. Edward Bromberg, Astrid
Allwyn

'No exhib worrying necessary for this
one.'—*Variety*

La Strada*
Italy 1954 94m bw
Ponti / de Laurentiis
aka: *The Road*

A half-witted peasant girl is sold to an
itinerant strong man and ill-used by him.
Curious attempt at a kind of poetic neo-
realism, saved by style and performances.

w Federico Fellini, Ennio Flaiano, Tullio
Pinelli *d* Federico Fellini *ph* Otello Martelli
m Nino Rota

Giulietta Masina, Anthony Quinn, Richard
Basehart

AA: best foreign film
AAN: script

Straight on Till Morning
GB 1972 96m Technicolor
EMI / Hammer (Roy Skeggs)

A Liverpool girl in London meets a dangerous
psychotic.
Unattractive suspenser, wildly directed.

w Michael Peacock *d* Peter Collinson
ph Brian Probyn *m* Roland Shaw

Rita Tushingham, Shane Briant, Tom Bell,
Annie Ross, James Bolam

Straight, Place and Show*
US 1938 66m bw

Three pony-ride proprietors impersonate
Russian jockeys to save a race. Lively,
unpretentious vehicle for three zanies, with a
further bonus in its lead singer. The Ritz
Brothers, Ethel Merman, Richard Arlen,
Phyllis Brooks, George Barbier, Sidney
Blackmer. Written by M. M. Musselman and
Allen Rivkin, from a play by Damon Runyon
and Irving Caesar; directed by David Butler;
for TCF. (GB title: *They're Off*.)

Straight Time
US 1978 114m Technicolor
Warner / First Artist / Sweetwall (Stanley
Beck, Tim Zinnemann)

A psychotic parolee fails to go straight.
Unappetizing social melodrama with an
irresolute leading performance.

w Alvin Sargent, Edward Bunker, Jeffrey Boam, *novel* No Beast So Fierce by Edward Bunker *d* Ulu Grosbard *ph* Owen Roizman *m* David Shire

Dustin Hoffman, Theresa Russell, Gary Busey, Harry Dean Stanton

'One leaves the theatre hoping the character will die painfully and slowly in a hail of bullets.'—*Variety*

● *Video: Warner*

'Just keep saying to yourself—it's only a film, it's only a film!'

Strait Jacket

US 1963 92m bw
Columbia / William Castle

A woman who murdered her faithless husband with an axe is released twenty years later, and more axe murders occur.

Dull and unattractive shocker in which all concerned lean over backwards to conceal the trick ending.

w Robert Bloch *d* William Castle *ph* Arthur E. Arling *m* Van Alexander

Joan Crawford, Diane Baker, Leif Erickson, Howard St John, Rochelle Hudson, George Kennedy

Stranded

US 1936 73m bw

A woman working for Traveller's Aid meets an old school beau. Much ado about nothing, the kind of movie that loses stars their reputations. Kay Francis, George Brent, Patricia Ellis, Donald Woods, Robert Barrat, Barton MacLane. Written by Delmer Daves, Carl Erickson, Frank Wead, Ferdinand Reyher; directed by Frank Borzage; for Warners. 'Limited chances.'—*Variety*

The Strange Affair

GB 1968 106m Techniscope
Paramount (Howard Harrison, Stanley Mann)

A young London policeman finds that his superiors are almost as corrupt as the villains.
Stylishly made melodrama of despair, with a sexy nymphet heroine straight from swinging London. It all leaves a sour taste in the mouth.

w Stanley Mann, *novel* Bernard Toms *d David Greene ph* Max Thompson *m* Basil Kirchin

Michael York, Jeremy Kemp, Susan George, Jack Watson, George A. Cooper

The Strange Affair of Uncle Harry

US 1945 82m bw
Universal (Joan Harrison)
aka: *Uncle Harry*

A man henpecked by his two sisters plans to murder one of them.
Stilted melodrama from an uninspired stage original, with a cop-out dream ending tacked on.

w Stephen Longstreet, Keith Winter, *play* Thomas Job *d* Robert Siodmak *ph* Woody Bredell *m* Hans Salter

George Sanders, Geraldine Fitzgerald, Ella Raines, Sara Allgood, Moyna MacGill, Samuel S. Hinds, Harry Von Zell, Ethel Griffies

Strange Bedfellows

US 1965 99m Technicolor
U-I / Panama–Frank (Melvin Frank)

An American executive in London nearly divorces his fiery Italian wife.
Frantic sex comedy with picture postcard background; fatiguing rather than funny, but with minor compensations.

w Melvin Frank, Michael Pertwee *d* Melvin Frank *ph* Leo Tover *m* Leigh Harline

Rock Hudson, Gina Lollobrigida, Gig Young, Edward Judd, Howard St John, Arthur Haynes, Dave King, Terry-Thomas

'The grind of predictable situations is further afflicted by considerable lapses in taste.'—*MFB*

Strange Boarders*

GB 1938 79m bw
GFD / Gainsborough (Edward Black)

A police detective postpones his honeymoon to book into a boarding house and discover which of the guests is a spy.
Quite engaging comedy-thriller in the Hitchcock mould, with entertaining performances and incidents.

w A. R. Rawlinson, Sidney Gilliatt, *novel* The Strange Boarders of Paradise Crescent by E. Phillips Oppenheim *d* Herbert Mason *ph* Jack Cox

Tom Walls, Renee Saint-Cyr, Leon M. Lion, Googie Withers, C. V. France, Ronald Adam, Irene Handl, George Curzon, Martita Hunt

Strange Cargo*

US 1940 105m bw
MGM (Joseph L. Mankiewicz)

Eight convicts escape from Devil's Island and are influenced by a Christ-like fugitive.
One of Hollywood's occasional lunacies; one doubts whether even the author knew the point of this cockamamy parable, but it was well produced and acted.

w Lawrence Hazard, *novel* Not Too Narrow, Not Too Deep by Richard Sale *d* Frank Borzage *ph* Robert Planck *m* Franz Waxman

Clark Gable, Joan Crawford, Ian Hunter, Peter Lorrè, Paul Lukas, Albert Dekker, J. Edward Bromberg, Eduardo Ciannelli, Frederick Worlock

'Even the most hardened mystics may blush.'—*New Yorker, 1978*

The Strange Case of Clara Deane

US 1932 60m bw

A young mother is unjustly convicted of a crime which she didn't commit and bids a tearful farewell to her child . . . Hilariously inept and theatrical rendering of a very outmoded play. Wynne Gibson, Pat O'Brien, Frances Dee, Dudley Digges. Written by Max Marcin from the play by Arthur M. Brillant; directed by Louis Gasnier and Max Marcin; for Paramount. 'Strictly for the minors where the clientele is elderly and naive.'—*Variety*

The Strange Case of Doctor RX

US 1942 66m bw

A mysterious murderer eliminates criminals whom the law can't touch. Inept semi-horror which wastes a good cast, as did the same author's *Night Monster*. Lionel Atwill, Patric Knowles, Anne Gwynne, Samuel S. Hinds, Shemp Howard, Mona Barrie, Paul Cavanagh, Mantan Moreland. Written by Clarence Upson Young; directed by William Nigh; for Universal.

Strange Conquest: see The Crime of Dr Hallet

The Strange Death of Adolf Hitler*

US 1943 74m bw
Universal

A stage impressionist murders the Führer and takes his place, steering Germany deliberately into losing the war.
One of the more eccentric curios of World War II, especially from a mundane studio like Universal. Once one recovers from the shock of its existence, the thing is moderately well done. See also *The Magic Face*.

w Fritz Kortner *d* James Hogan *m* Hans Salter

Ludwig Donath, Gale Sondergaard, Fritz Kortner, George Dolenz

The Strange Door*

US 1951 81m bw
U-I (Ted Richmond)

A young nobleman, passing through the one-way door of a castle, finds himself the prisoner of a madman.
Torture-chamber suspenser, adequately if rather tediously developed, with most of its interest reposing in the cast.

w Jerry Sackheim, *story* The Sire de Maletroit's Door by Robert Louis Stevenson *d* Joseph Pevney *ph* Irving Glassberg *m* Joseph Gershenson

Charles Laughton, Boris Karloff, Michael Pate, Sally Forrest, Richard Stapley, Alan Napier

Strange Evidence

GB 1932 71m bw

When an invalid dies, his adulterous wife is suspected. Mildly interesting quickie whodunnit. Leslie Banks, Carol Goodner, George Curzon, Frank Vosper, Norah Baring, Diana Napier. Written by Miles Malleson, from a story by Lajos Biro; directed by Robert Milton; for Alexander Korda / Paramount.

'A woman suspected! A woman desired! A woman possessed!'
'The film in which you hear the characters think!'

Strange Interlude**

US 1932 110m bw
MGM (Irving Thalberg)
GB title: *Strange Interval*

Problems of an unfulfilled wife and her lover.
Surprising film version of a very heavy modern

classic, complete with asides to the audience; very dated now, but a small milestone in Hollywood's development.

w Bess Meredyth, C. Gardner Sullivan, *play* Eugene O'Neill *d* Robert Z. Leonard *ph* Lee Garmes

Norma Shearer, Clark Gable, May Robson, Alexander Kirkland, Ralph Morgan, Robert Young, Maureen O'Sullivan, Henry B. Walthall

'Chiefly a reserved seat attraction, dubious for general release appeal.'—*Variety*

'A cinematic novelty to be seen by discerning audiences.'—*Film Weekly*

'More exciting than a thousand "action" movies.'—*Pare Lorentz*

Strange Intruder
US 1957 78m bw
AA (Lindsley Parsons)

A psychopathic ex-POW menaces the children of his dead friend's wife.
Gloomy second feature melodrama, rather well presented.

w David Evans, Warren Douglas, *novel* Helen Fowler *d* Irving Rapper *ph* Ernest Haller *m* Paul Dunlap

Edmund Purdom, Ida Lupino, Ann Harding, Jacques Bergerac, Carl Benton Reid

Strange Invaders*
US 1983 93m De Luxe
EMI / Orion / Michael Laughlin (Walter Coblenz)

An Illinois town is taken over by beings from outer space.
Patchy but often amusing take-off of the *Invasion of the Body Snatchers* genre.

w William Condon, Michael Laughlin *d* Michael Laughlin *ph* Louis Horvath, Zoltan Vidor *m* John Addison *pd* Susanna Moore

Paul Le Mat, Nancy Allen, Diana Scarwid, Michael Lerner, Louise Fletcher, Fiona Lewis, Kenneth Tobey

Strange Lady in Town
US 1955 118m Warnercolor
Cinemascope
Warner (Mervyn Le Roy)

Adventures of a woman doctor in 1880 Santa Fe.
Quaint western drama which is never any more convincing than its star.

w Frank Butler *d* Mervyn Le Roy *ph* Harold Rosson *m* Dmitri Tiomkin

Greer Garson, Dana Andrews, Cameron Mitchell, Lois Smith, Walter Hampden

'Fate drew them together and only murder can part them!'
'Whisper her name!'

The Strange Love of Martha Ivers**
US 1946 116m bw
Paramount / Hal B. Wallis

A murderous child becomes a wealthy woman with a spineless lawyer husband; the

melodrama starts when an ex-boy friend returns to town.
Irresistible star melodrama which leaves no stone unturned; compulsive entertainment of the old school.

w Robert Rossen *d* Lewis Milestone *ph* Victor Milner *m* Miklos Rozsa

Barbara Stanwyck, Van Heflin, Kirk Douglas, Lizabeth Scott, Judith Anderson, Roman Bohnen

AAN: original story (Jack Patrick)

The Strange Love of Molly Louvain
US 1932 72m bw

A young mother has gone to the bad through men. Hoary melodrama which the cast seem forever on the point of sending up. Lee Tracy, Ann Dvorak, Richard Cromwell, Guy Kibbee, Leslie Fenton, Frank McHugh. Written by Maurine Watkins and Erwin Gelsey from the play The Tinsel Girl by Maurine Watkins; directed by Michael Curtiz; for Warners. 'A lightweight yarn which never takes a toehold to deliver a sock.'—*Variety*

The Strange One*
US 1957 99m bw
Columbia / Sam Spiegel
GB title: *End as a Man*

A sadistic cadet causes trouble at a southern military college.
A weird and unsavoury but rather compelling melodrama which unreels like a senior version of *Tom Brown's Schooldays*.

w Calder Willingham, from his novel End as a Man *d* Jack Garfein *ph* Burnett Guffey *m* Kenyon Hopkins

Ben Gazzara, George Peppard, Mark Richman, Pat Hingle, Arthur Storch, Paul Richards, Geoffrey Horne, James Olson

'The film's brilliance is in its persuasive depiction of a highly controversial, artificially organized world; its failure is to make any dramatic statement about it.'—*MFB*

The Strange Woman
US 1946 100m bw
(UA) Hunt Stromberg (Jack Chertok)

A scheming woman plays with the lives of three men.
Star wish-fulfilment; otherwise a hammy costume piece.

w Herb Meadows, *novel* Ben Ames Williams *d* Edgar G. Ulmer *ph* Lucien Andriot *m* Carmen Dragon

Hedy Lamarr, George Sanders, Louis Hayward, Gene Lockhart, Hillary Brooke

The Stranger*
US 1946 95m bw
(RKO) Sam Spiegel

An escaped Nazi criminal marries an American woman and settles in a Connecticut village.
Highly unconvincing and artificial melodrama enhanced by directorial touches, splendid photography and no-holds-barred climax involving a church clock.

w Anthony Veiller, *story* Victor Trivas, Decla Dunning *d* Orson Welles *ph* Russell Metty *m* Bronislau Kaper

Edward G. Robinson, Orson Welles, Loretta Young, Philip Merivale, Richard Long, Konstantin Shayne

'Some striking effects, with lighting and interesting angles much relied on.'—*Bosley Crowther*

'A film of confused motivations and clumsy effects.'—*Basil Wright, 1972*

AAN: original story

Stranger at My Door
US 1956 85m bw
Republic (Sidney Picker)

A gunman takes refuge in the house of a preacher who tries to convert him.
Odd, sentimental little western morality play, not badly presented.

w Barry Shipman *d* William Witney *ph* Bud Thackery *m* Dale Butts

Macdonald Carey, Skip Homeier, Patricia Medina, Louis Jean Heydt

The Stranger Came Home
GB 1954 80m bw

After being assaulted in the Far East, a financier loses his memory and does not return home until three years later, when murder ensues. Muddled mystery quickie, only notable as the film which persuaded its star to retire. Paulette Goddard, William Sylvester, Patrick Holt, Paul Carpenter, Russell Napier, Alvys Maben. Written by Michael Carreras, from the novel *Stranger at Home* by George Sanders; directed by Terence Fisher; for Exclusive. (US title: *The Unholy Four*.)

A Stranger in My Arms
US 1958 88m bw Cinemascope
U-I (Ross Hunter)

A test pilot falls in love with his dead friend's widow and helps her face up to her in-laws.
Dreary romantic drama.

w Peter Berneis, *novel* And Ride a Tiger by Robert Wilder *d* Helmut Kautner *ph* William Daniels *m* Joseph Gershenson

June Allyson, Jeff Chandler, *Mary Astor*, Sandra Dee, Charles Coburn, Conrad Nagel, Peter Graves

A Stranger Is Watching
US 1981 92m Metrocolor

A small girl is terrified by the psychopath who raped and murdered her mother. Unpleasant thriller in the modern manner. Kate Mulgrew, Rip Torn, James Naughton, Shawn Van Schreiber. Written by Earl MacRaugh and Victor Miller, from the novel by Mary Higgins Clark; directed by Sean S. Cunningham; for Sidney Beckerman / MGM-UA.

The Stranger Left no Card**
GB 1952 23m bw

A weirdly dressed eccentric comes to a small town and is accepted by the townspeople; but his real purpose is murder. Smart little trick film which as a novelty has not been surpassed. *Alan Badel*, Cameron Hall, Eileen Way. Written by *Sidney Carroll*; directed by *Wendy Toye*; for George K. Arthur / Meteor / British Lion.

Stranger on the Prowl
Italy / US 1952 83m bw
UA / CPCT (Noel Calef)

In an Italian port, a stranger helps a boy but is shot by the police.
Ineffective melodrama, a sad comedown for its star.

wd Andrea Forzano *ph* Henri Alekan *m* C. G. Sonzogno

Paul Muni, Joan Lorring, Vittorio Manunta, Aldo Silvani

Stranger on the Third Floor*
US 1940 64m bw
RKO (Lee Marcus)

A reporter finds that he was wrong in the well-intentioned testimony which helps convict an innocent man for murder.
Stylish B feature with a striking dream scene and a curious fleeting performance by Lorre as the real murderer.

w Frank Partos *d* Boris Ingster *ph* Nicholas Musuraca *m* Roy Webb

Margaret Tallichet, Peter Lorre, John McGuire, Charles Waldron, Elisha Cook Jnr, Charles Halton, Ethel Griffies

The Stranger Wore a Gun
US 1953 83m Technicolor 3-D

An honest adventurer finds that the man who once saved his life has become a stagecoach robber. Routine western with many objects hurled at the audience to show off the 3-D process. Randolph Scott, George Macready, Claire Trevor, Joan Weldon, Lee Marvin, Ernest Borgnine, Alfonso Bedoya. Written by Kenneth Gamet; directed by André de Toth; for Columbia.

The Stranger's Hand
GB 1953 85m bw
British Lion / John Stafford, Peter Moore
aka: *Mano della Straniero*

A schoolboy is due to meet his father in Venice, but the father is kidnapped by enemy agents.
Rather tentative suspense thriller with a vague plot which seems to defeat an excellent cast.

w Guy Elmes, Giorgio Bassani, *story* Graham Greene *d* Mario Soldati *ph* Enzo Serafin *m* Nino Rota

Trevor Howard, Richard O'Sullivan, Francis L. Sullivan, Alida Valli, Eduardo Ciannelli, Richard Basehart, Stephen Murray

809
Strangers in Love
US 1932 68m bw

A ne'er-do-well has some difficulties when he tries to step into his dead twin's shoes.
Predictable comedy-melodrama, quite well acted. Fredric March, Kay Francis, Stuart Erwin, Juliette Compton, George Barbier,

Sidney Toler. Written by Grover Jones and William Slavens McNutt from the play The Shorn Lamb by William J. Locke; directed by Lothar Mendes; for Paramount. 'All the qualities that bespeak wide appeal.'—*Variety*

Strangers May Kiss
US 1931 82m bw
MGM

A sophisticated wife takes love and fidelity lightly.
Dated romantic drama.

w John Meehan, *novel* Ursula Parrott *d* George Fitzmaurice *ph* William Daniels

Norma Shearer, Robert Montgomery, Neil Hamilton, Marjorie Rambeau, Irene Rich
'Outstanding money picture. It'll sell itself.'—*Variety*

'It begins with the scream of a train whistle—and ends with screaming excitement!'
Strangers on a Train***
US 1951 101m bw
Warner (Alfred Hitchcock)

A tennis star is pestered on a train by a psychotic who wants to swap murders, and proceeds to carry out his part of the bargain. This quirky melodrama has the director at his best, sequence by sequence, but the story is basically unsatisfactory. It makes superior suspense entertainment, however.

w Raymond Chandler, Czenzi Ormonde, *novel* Patricia Highsmith *d* Alfred Hitchcock *ph* Robert Burks *m* Dmitri Tionkin *md* Ray Heindorf

Farley Granger, *Robert Walker*, Ruth Roman, Leo G. Carroll, Patricia Hitchcock, *Marion Lorne*, Howard St John, Jonathan Hale, Laura Elliott

BRUNO (Robert Walker): 'Some people are better off dead—like your wife and my father, for instance.'
'You may not take it seriously, but you certainly don't have time to think about anything else.'—*Richard Mallett, Punch*
† Remade 1970 as *Once You Kiss A Stranger*.
AAN: Robert Burks
● Video: Warner

The Stranger's Return
US 1933 89m bw

An old farmer disapproves of his granddaughter's affair with a married man. An American view of Cold Comfort Farm country, too heavy to click at the box office. Lionel Barrymore, Miriam Hopkins, Franchot Tone, Beulah Bondi, Stuart Erwin, Irene Hervey. Written by Brown Holmes and Phil Stong; directed by King Vidor; for MGM.

Strangers When We Meet*
US 1960 117m Technicolor
Cinemascope
Columbia / Bryna (Richard Quine)

A successful architect starts an affair with a beautiful married neighbour.
Beverly Hills soap opera with lots of romantic suffering in luxury. Lumpy but generally palatable.

w Evan Hunter, from his novel *d* Richard Quine *ph* Charles Lang Jnr *m* George Duning

Kirk Douglas, Kim Novak, *Ernie Kovacs, Walter Matthau*, Barbara Rush, Virginia Bruce, Helen Gallagher, Kent Smith

The Strangler
US 1963 80m bw
AA

An obese lab technician murders nurses who help his hated mother.
Modest, lively shocker.

w Bill S. Ballinger *d* Burt Topper *ph* Jacques Marquette *m* Marlin Skiles

Victor Buono, David McLean, Ellen Corby, Diane Sayer

The Stranglers of Bombay
GB 1959 81m bw Megascope
Columbia / Hammer (Anthony Hinds)

In 1826 travellers are waylaid and sacrificially killed by a cult of stranglers.
Semi-historical parade of atrocities, repellent but scarcely exciting.

w David Z. Goodman *d* Terence Fisher *ph* Arthur Grant *m* James Bernard

Guy Rolfe, Allan Cuthbertson, Andrew Cruickshank, Marne Maitland, Jan Holden, George Pastell, Paul Stassino

Strategic Air Command
US 1955 114m Technicolor
Vistavision
Paramount (Samuel J. Briskin)

A baseball player is recalled to air force duty. Sentimental flagwaver featuring the newest jets of the fifties.

w Valentine Davies, Beirne Lay Jnr *d* Anthony Mann *ph* William Daniels *m* Victor Young

James Stewart, June Allyson, Frank Lovejoy, Barry Sullivan, Alex Nicol, Bruce Bennett, Jay C. Flippen, James Millican, James Bell
AAN: original story (Beirne Lay Jnr)

The Stratton Story
US 1949 106m bw
MGM (Sam Wood)

An amateur baseball enthusiast becomes a famous professional, but suffers an accident which involves the amputation of a leg.
Mild sentimental biopic, well made but not very interesting.

w Douglas Morrow, Guy Trosper *d* Sam Wood *ph* Harold Rosson *m* Adolph Deutsch

James Stewart, June Allyson, Frank Morgan, Agnes Moorehead, Bill Williams
AA: original story (Douglas Morrow)

'The knock at the door meant the birth of one man and the death of seven others!'
Straw Dogs
GB 1971 118m Eastmancolor
Talent Associates / Amerbroco (Daniel Melnick)

In a Cornish village, a mild American

university researcher erupts into violence when taunted by drunken villagers who commit sustained assaults on himself and his wife.

Totally absurd, poorly contrived, hilariously overwritten Cold Comfort Farm melodrama with farcical violence.

w David Zelag Goodman, Sam Peckinpah, *novel* The Siege of Trencher's Farm by Gordon M. Williams *d* Sam Peckinpah *ph* John Coquillon, *m* Jerry Fielding

Dustin Hoffman, Susan George, Peter Vaughan, David Warner, T. P. McKenna, Colin Welland

AAN: Jerry Fielding

● *Video:* Guild

The Strawberry Blonde**
US 1941 97m bw
Warner (William Cagney)

A dentist in turn-of-the-century Brooklyn wonders whether he married the right woman. Pleasant period comedy drama, a remake of *One Sunday Afternoon* (qv).

w Julius J. and Philip G. Epstein *d* Raoul Walsh *ph* James Wong Howe *m* Heinz Roemheld

James Cagney, Olivia de Havilland, *Rita Hayworth, Alan Hale*, George Tobias, Jack Carson, Una O'Connor, George Reeves

'It not only tells a very human story, it also creates an atmosphere, recreates a period.'— *New York Sun*

AAN: Heinz Roemheld

Strawberry Roan
GB 1944 84m bw

A farmer weds a showgirl who ruins his life. Rather glum rural drama with some style but little entertainment value. William Hartnell, Carol Raye, Walter Fitzgerald, Sophie Stewart, John Ruddock, Wylie Watson, Petula Clark. Written by Elizabeth Baron, from the novel by A. G. Street; directed by Maurice Elvey; for British National.

The Strawberry Statement
US 1970 109m Metrocolor
MGM / Robert Chartoff, Irwin Winkler

Student rebels occupy a university administration building.

One of a short-lived group of student anti-discipline films of the early seventies, and about the most boring.

w Israel Horowitz, *novel* James Simon Kunen *d* Stuart Hagmann *ph* Ralph Woolsey *m* Ian Freebairn Smith

Bruce Davison, Kim Darby, Bud Cort, Murray MacLeod

Streamers
US 1983 118m Movielab

Tensions mount at a training camp for the 83rd Airborne Division. Claustrophobic photographed play about generally worthless people. Matthew Modine, Michael Wright,

Mitchell Lichtenstein, David Alan Grier, Guy Boyd, George Dzundza. Written by David Rabe from his play; directed by Robert Altman; for Streamers International Distributors.

'A thing of beauty is a joy for ever . . .
Street Angel*
US 1928 101m bw part-talkie
Fox

An unwilling prostitute becomes a circus artiste.

A sentimental and tawdry tale becomes a vehicle for good typical work by director and stars.

w Marion Orth *play* Lady Cristallinda by Monckton Hoffe *d* Frank Borzage *ph* Ernest Palmer, Paul Ivano *ad* Harry Oliver

Janet Gaynor, Charles Farrell, Henry Armetta, Guido Trento

AAN: Ernest Palmer; Janet Gaynor

Street Corner
GB 1953 94m bw
Rank / LIP / Sydney Box (William MacQuitty)
US title: *Both Sides of the Law*

Days in the lives of the women police of Chelsea.

Patter-plotted female *Blue Lamp*; just about watchable.

w Muriel and Sydney Box *d* Muriel Box *ph* Reg Wyer *m* Temple Abady

Rosamund John, Anne Crawford, Peggy Cummins, Terence Morgan, Barbara Murray, Sarah Lawson, Ronald Howard, Eleanor Summerfield, Michael Medwin

Street of Chance
US 1930 78m bw
Paramount (David O. Selznick)

A New York gambler gets his come-uppance. Dullish family melodrama with gangsters as *dei ex machina*.

w Howard Estabrook, Lenore Coffee *d* John Cromwell *ph* Charles Lang

William Powell, Kay Francis, Regis Toomey, Jean Arthur

'Strong exploitation can cinch this one. Strongly hints at recent murder of well-known gambler.'—*Variety*

AAN: script

Street of Shame*
Japan 1956 85m bw
Daiei (Masaichi Nagata)
original title: *Akasen Chitai*

Stories of women in a Tokyo brothel. Unremarkable material executed with the style expected of the director.

w Masashige Narusawa *d* Kenji Mizoguchi *ph* Kazuo Miyagawa *m* Toshiro Mayazumi

Machiko Kyo, Ayako Wakao, Aiko Mimasu

Street of Women
US 1932 59m bw

A property developer is torn between his wife

and his mistress. Choppily developed drama which starts haltingly and gets nowhere. Kay Francis, Alan Dinehart, Roland Young, Marjorie Gateson, Gloria Stuart. Written by Mary McCall Jnr from the novel by Polan Banks; directed by Archie Mayo; for Warners. 'Just a programme picture.'—*Variety*

Street Scene*
US 1931 80m bw
Samuel Goldwyn

In a New York slum street on a hot summer night, an adulterous woman is shot by her husband.

Slice-of-life drama from an influential play; never much of a film, and very dated.

w Elmer Rice, from his play *d* King Vidor *ph* George Barnes *m* Alfred Newman

Sylvia Sidney, William Collier Jnr, Max Mantor, David Landau, Estelle Taylor, Russell Hopton

'Whenever the camera starts to focus on two or three characters, the plot thickens and *Street Scene* flies out the window; petty domestic tragedy supplants the original slice-of-life conception.'—*National Board of Review*

'As a commercial proposition it will cause talk and reap honours, but whether it will prove an exceptional box office attraction remains to be seen.'—*Variety*

The Street Singer
GB 1937 85m bw

A musical comedy star is mistaken for a beggar by a girl with whom he falls in love. Rather tiresome star vehicle. Arthur Tracy, Margaret Lockwood, Arthur Riscoe, Hugh Wakefield. Written by Reginald Arkell; directed by Jean de Marguenat; for British National.

The Street with No Name*
US 1948 93m bw
TCF (Samuel G. Engel)

An FBI man goes undercover to unmask a criminal gang.

The oldest crime plot in the world, applied with vigour to the documentary realism of *The House on 92nd Street* and built around the *Kiss of Death* psychopathic character created by Richard Widmark.

w Harry Kleiner *d* William Keighley *ph* Joe MacDonald *m* Lionel Newman

Richard Widmark, Mark Stevens, Lloyd Nolan, Barbara Lawrence, Ed Begley

† Remade 1955 as *House of Bamboo*.

A Streetcar Named Desire**
US 1951 122m bw
Charles K. Feldman / Elia Kazan

A repressed southern widow is raped and driven mad by her brutal brother-in-law. Reasonably successful, decorative picture from a highly theatrical but influential play; unreal sets and atmospheric photography vaguely Sternbergian.

w Tennessee Williams, from his play *d* Elia Kazan *ph* Harry Stradling *m* Alex North *ad* Richard Day

Vivien Leigh, Marlon Brando, Kim Hunter, Karl Malden

AA: Vivien Leigh; Kim Hunter; Karl Malden
AAN: best picture; Tennessee Williams; Elia Kazan; Harry Stradling; Alex North; Marlon Brando
● *Video: Embassy*

Streets of Fire

US 1984 94m Technicolor
Universal / RKO / Hill-Gordon-Silver
  (Lawrence Gordon, Joel Silver)

A rock singer is kidnapped and a professional trouble shooter takes on the job of recovery.
Violent melodrama with an unsuccessful comic strip approach which fails to raise the material into the realm of myth.

w Walter Hill, Larry Gross *d* Walter Hill
ph Andrew Laszlo *pd* John Vallone *m* Ry Cooder *ed* Freeman Davies, Michael Ripps

Michael Paré, Diane Lane, Rick Moranis, Andy Madigan, Willem Dafoe

Streets of Laredo

US 1949 92m Technicolor
Paramount (Robert Fellows)

Two of three bandit friends become Texas Rangers.
Adequate star western, a remake of *The Texas Rangers*.

w Charles Marquis Warren *d* Leslie Fenton
ph Ray Rennahan *m* Victor Young

William Holden, William Bendix, Macdonald Carey, Mona Freeman

Streets of New York

US 1939 72m bw

The teenage owner of a newsstand studies law at night school. Unconvincing street-life drama, an obvious vehicle for a boy star.
Jackie Cooper, Martin Spellman, George Cleveland, Dick Purcell. Written by Robert Andrews; directed by William Nigh; for Monogram. 'Should do all right if not pointed too high.'—*Variety*

Strictly Dishonourable

US 1951 94m bw
MGM (Melvin Frank, Norman Panama)

A young girl falls in love with a rakish Italian opera star; he is such a sentimentalist that he marries her.
Emasculated sentimental version of the sharp Preston Sturges comedy.

wd Norman Panama, Melvin Frank *ph* Ray June *m* Lennie Hayton

Ezio Pinza, Janet Leigh, Millard Mitchell, Maria Palmer
† Previously filmed in 1931 by Universal, with Paul Lukas, Sidney Fox and Lewis Stone.

Strictly Unconventional: see The Circle

Strike***

USSR 1924 70m approx (24 fps) bw
  silent
Goskino / Proletkult

A 1912 strike of factory workers is brutally put down by the authorities.
Brilliant propaganda piece with superbly cinematic sequences.

wd Sergei M. Eisenstein *ph* Edouard Tissé, Vassili Khvatov

Grigori Alexandrov, Maxim Strauch, Mikhail Gomarov

Strike Me Pink*

US 1935 104m bw
Samuel Goldwyn

A timid amusement park owner is threatened by crooks.
Acceptable star comedy with music.

w Frank Butler, Walter de Leon, Francis Martin *d* Norman Taurog *ph* Gregg Toland, Merritt Gerstad *m* Alfred Newman *songs* Harold Arlen, Lew Brown

Eddie Cantor, Sally Eilers, Ethel Merman, William Frawley, Parkyakarkus
'At the box office both here and abroad the take will be big.'—*Variety*

Strike Up the Band*

US 1940 120m bw
MGM (Arthur Freed)

A high-school band takes part in a nationwide radio contest.
Rather tiresomely high-spirited musical with the stars at the top of their young form.

w Fred Finklehoffe, John Monks Jnr
d / ch Busby Berkeley *ph* Ray June
m Roger Edens, *ly* Arthur Freed
Judy Garland, Mickey Rooney, Paul Whiteman and his Orchestra, June Preisser, William Tracy, Larry Nunn

AAN: Georgie Stoll, Roger Edens; song 'Our Love Affair' (*m / ly* Roger Edens, Georgie Stoll)

The Strip*

US 1951 85m bw
MGM (Joe Pasternak)

A band drummer is accused of the murder of a racketeer.
Minor mystery melodrama intriguingly set on Sunset Strip, with jazz accompaniment.

w Allen Rivkin *d* Leslie Kardos *ph* Robert Surtees *m* George Stoll

Mickey Rooney, Sally Forrest, William Demarest, James Craig, Kay Brown; and Louis Armstrong, Earl Hines, Jack Teagarden

AAN: song 'A Kiss To Build a Dream On (*m / ly* Bert Kalmar, Harry Ruby, Oscar Hammerstein II)

Stripes

US 1981 106m Metrocolor
Columbia (Ivan Reitman, Dan Goldberg)

Sergeant Hulka tries to train a platoon of misfit volunteers.

Ancient army wheezes dressed up with fashionable black comedy and sex, but no funnier than *Carry On Sergeant*.

w Len Blum, Dan Goldberg, Harold Ramis *d* Ivan Reitman *ph* Bill Butler *m* Elmer Bernstein

Bill Murray, Harold Ramis, Warren Oates, P. J. Soles, John Larroquette, Sean Young
● *Video: RCA / Columbia*

The Stripper*

US 1963 95m bw Cinemascope
TCF (Jerry Wald)
GB title: *Woman of Summer*

An ageing beauty queen returns to her Kansas hometown and has an affair with a 19-year-old garage hand.
Downbeat character melodrama typical of its time and its author; competent but sterile and rather tedious.

w Meade Roberts, *play* A Loss of Roses by William Inge *d* Franklin Schaffner *ph* Ellsworth Fredericks *m* Jerry Goldsmith
Joanne Woodward, Richard Beymer, *Claire Trevor*, Carol Lynley, Robert Webber, Louis Nye, Gypsy Rose Lee, Michael J. Pollard

Stromboli

Italy 1949 107m bw
RKO / Be-Ro (Roberto Rossellini)

A Lithuanian refugee accepts the protection of marriage to an Italian fisherman, but resents the barrenness and hostility of her life, especially when the local volcano erupts.
Sloppy melodrama with pretensions, interesting but not even attractive to the eye.

w Roberto Rossellini and others *d* Roberto Rossellini *ph* Otello Martelli *m* Renzo Rossellini

Ingrid Bergman, Mario Vitale, Renzo Cesana
† The international version was cut to 81m.

The Strong Man*

US 1926 75m approx (24 fps) bw
  (colour sequence) silent
First National / Harry Langdon

A war veteran returns and searches the city for his female penfriend.
Quite charming star comedy, probably Langdon's best.

w Frank Capra, Arthur Ripley, Hal Conklin, Robert Eddy *d* Frank Capra *ph* Elgin Lessley, Glenn Kershner

Harry Langdon, Gertrude Astor, Tay Garnett

Stronger than Desire

US 1939 82m bw

A lawyer's wife gets into trouble and lets him try an innocent man for her crime. Fast remake of *Evelyn Prentice*; a good half-bill.
Walter Pidgeon, Virginia Bruce, Ann Dvorak, Lee Bowman, Rita Johnson, Ilka Chase. Written by David Hertz and William Ludwig; directed by Leslie Fenton; for MGM.

The Strongest Man in the World
US 1976 92m Technicolor
Walt Disney (Bill Anderson)

An accident in a science lab gives a student superhuman strength.
Formula comedy for older children.

w Joseph L. McEveety, Herman Groves
d Vincent McEveety ph Andrew Jackson
m Robert F. Brunner

Kurt Russell, Joe Flynn, Eve Arden, Cesar Romero, Phil Silvers, Dick Van Patten, Harold Gould, William Schallert, James Gregory, Roy Roberts, Fritz Feld, Raymond Bailey, Eddie Quillan, Burt Mustin

Strongroom°
GB 1961 80m bw
Bryanston / Theatrecraft (Guido Coen)

Two car breakers plan a once-for-all bank robbery but get involved with potential murder when their hostages get locked in.
Suspenseful second feature with gloss and pace.

w Max Marquis, René Harris d Vernon Sewell ph Basil Emmott m Johnny Gregory

Colin Gordon, Ann Lynn, Derren Nesbitt, Keith Faulkner

The Struggle°
US 1931 88m bw
UA / D. W. Griffith

A New Yorker goes to the bad on bootleg liquor.
The director's last film reveals many of his old skills allied to a Victorian tract.

w Anita Loos, John Emerson d D. W. Griffith ph Joseph Ruttenberg

Hal Skelly, Zita Johann, Charlotte Wynters, Jackson Halliday

'A dull and sodden rendering with old-time ranting and little drama . . . just dull when it isn't in the highest degree maudlin.'—Dwight MacDonald

† The picture failed and was re-released as Ten Nights in a Bar-room.

The Stud
GB 1978 90m colour
Brent Walker / Artoc (Edward D. Simons)

A millionaire's wife installs her lover as manager of a discotheque, but he becomes bored and wants a place of his own.
Life among the unpleasant rich. A surprise box office success, richly undeserved.

w Jackie Collins, from her novel d Quentin Masters ph Peter Hannan m Biddu

Joan Collins, Oliver Tobias, Sue Lloyd, Mark Burns, Doug Fisher, Walter Gotell

'Watching it is rather like being buried alive in a coffin stuffed with back numbers of Men Only.'—Alan Brien

● Video: Brent Walker

The Student Prince
US 1954 107m Anscocolor
Cinemascope
MGM (Joe Pasternak)

A prince studies in Heidelberg and falls for a barmaid.

Ruritanian operetta, lumpishly filmed, with Mario Lanza providing only the voice of the hero as he got too fat to play the part.

w William Ludwig, Sonya Levien, play Old Heidelberg by Wilhelm Meyer-Foerster operetta Dorothy Donnelly d Richard Thorpe ph Paul C. Vogel m Sigmund Romberg md George Stoll

Edmund Purdom, Ann Blyth, John Williams, Edmund Gwenn, S. Z. Sakall, John Ericson, Louis Calhern, Betta St John, Evelyn Varden
† Without the music, the play had been filmed at MGM in 1926, with Ramon Novarro and Norma Shearer under Ernst Lubitsch's direction.

Student Tour
US 1934 80m bw

A professor of philosophy chaperones a world tour by collegiates. Very thin comedy yarn with songs. Jimmy Durante, Charles Butterworth, Maxine Doyle, Phil Regan, Douglas Fowley, Betty Grable, Nelson Eddy. Written by Ralph Spence, Philip Dunne; directed by Charles F. Reisner; for MGM. 'Long, slow, and of mild entertainment appeal.'—Variety

The Studio Murder Mystery
US 1929 62m bw

An actor is murdered on a film set. Primitive talkie comedy mystery now interesting only for its studio backgrounds. Neil Hamilton, Florence Eldridge, Warner Oland, Eugene Pallette, Fredric March, Doris Hill, Chester Conklin. Written by Frank Tuttle, from a magazine serial by the Edingtons; directed by Frank Tuttle; for Paramount.

Studs Lonigan
US 1960 95m bw

The growing up of an unlettered Chicago Irishman in the twenties. Rough-and-ready version of a celebrated novel, not a bad try but insufficiently detailed to be any kind of classic. Christopher Knight, Jack Nicholson, Frank Gorshin. Written by Philip Yordan, from the novel by James T. Farrell; directed by Irving Lerner; for Philip Yordan.

A Study in Scarlet
US 1933 71m bw

Sherlock Holmes solves a mysterious murder. Rather emaciated version of a spirited yarn. Reginald Owen, Warburton Gamble, Anna May Wong, June Clyde, Alan Dinehart, Alan Mowbray. Written by Robert Florey from the story by Sir Arthur Conan Doyle; directed by Edwin L. Marin; for KBS. 'Okay for secondary houses.'—Variety

A Study in Terror°
GB 1965 95m Eastmancolor
Compton–Tekli / Sir Nigel (Henry E. Lester)

Sherlock Holmes discovers the identity of Jack the Ripper.
A reasonably good Holmes pastiche marred by a surfeit of horror and over-riotous local colour; quite literate, but schizophrenic.

w Donald and Derek Ford, novel Ellery Queen d James Hill ph Desmond Dickinson m John Scott ad Alex Vetchinsky

John Neville, Donald Houston, John Fraser, Robert Morley, Cecil Parker, Anthony Quayle, Barbara Windsor, Adrienne Corri, Judi Dench, Frank Finlay, Barry Jones, Kay Walsh, Georgia Brown

● Video: Video Media

The Stunt Man°
US 1978 129m Metrocolor
Melvin Simon (Richard Rush)

A Vietnam veteran on the run from the police finds refuge as a star stunt man for a sinister film director.
Overlong, curious, but sometimes compelling melodrama which entertains on the surface while its actual aims are harder to fathom.

w Lawrence B. Marcus novel Paul Brodeur d Richard Rush ph Mario Tosi m Dominic Frontière

Peter O'Toole, Steve Railsback, Barbara Hershey, Allen Goorwitz, Alex Rocco, Sharon Farrell

AAN: screenplay; Richard Rush; Peter O'Toole

● Video: Guild

The Subject Was Roses°
US 1968 107m Metrocolor
MGM (Edgar Lansbury)

A young war veteran finds he can't communicate with his parents, and vice versa.
Photographed play notable for its performances.

w Frank D. Gilroy, from his play d Ulu Grosbard ph Jack Priestley

Patricia Neal, Jack Albertson, Martin Sheen, Don Saxon, Elaine Williams

AA: Jack Albertson
AAN: Patricia Neal

Submarine Command
US 1951 87m bw
Paramount (John Farrow, Joseph Sistrom)

A submarine officer who considers himself a coward becomes a hero in Korea.
Very routine soul-searching actioner.

w Jonathan Latimer d John Farrow ph Lionel Lindon m David Buttolph

William Holden, Don Taylor, Nancy Olsen, William Bendix, Moroni Olsen, Peggy Webber

Submarine D1
US 1937 93m bw

Adventures of recruits to the naval submarine service. Standard flagwaver of no intrinsic interest. Pat O'Brien, George Brent, Wayne Morris, Frank McHugh, Doris Weston, Ronald Reagan, Henry O'Neill, Regis Toomey, Broderick Crawford. Written by Frank Wead, Warren Duff, Lawrence Kimble; directed by Lloyd Bacon; for Cosmopolitan / Warners. 'An instructive and illuminating document . . . film waves its own flag, the best on earth, and with some exhibitor push it should do business.'—Variety

Submarine Patrol
US 1938 93m bw

Recruits learn to handle sub-chasing boats at Annapolis. Cheerful propaganda comedy-drama with familiar faces on hand and some good thrill sequences. Richard Greene, Nancy Kelly, Preston Foster, George Bancroft, Slim Summerville, John Carradine, Henry Armetta, Warren Hymer, Elisha Cook Jnr, E. E. Clive, Ward Bond, George E. Stone. Written by Rian James, Darrell Ware, Jack Yellen, from a book by Ray Milholland; directed by John Ford; for Gene Markey / TCF. 'Surefire film entertainment directed by a veteran who knows all the tricks.'—*Variety*

Submarine X-I
GB 1967 90m Eastmancolor
UA / Mirisch (John C. Champion)

A submarine commander in World War II trains men to attack the *Lindendorf* in midget submarines.
Belated quota quickie, routine in every department.
w Donald S. Sanford, Guy Elmes *d* William Graham *ph* Paul Beeson

James Caan, Norman Bowler, David Sumner

The Subterraneans
US 1960 89m Metrocolor
Cinemascope
MGM (Arthur Freed)

The love affairs of San Francisco bohemians. A boring oddity with lashings of eccentric behaviour and sexual hang-ups; MGM venturing very timidly outside its field.
w Robert Thom, *novel* Jack Kerouac
d Ranald MacDougall *ph* Joseph Ruttenberg
m André Previn

George Peppard, Leslie Caron, Janice Rule, Roddy McDowall, Anne Seymour, Jim Hutton

Subway in the Sky
GB 1958 87m bw
Sydney Box (John Temple-Smith, Patrick Filmer-Sankey)

A Berlin cabaret star finds her landlady's ex-husband, a deserter, hiding in her apartment and sets out to prove his innocence of drug smuggling.
Tedious photographed play with precious few points of dramatic interest.
w Jack Andrews, *play* Ian Main *d* Muriel Box *ph* Wilkie Cooper *m* Mario Nascimbene

Hildegarde Neff, Van Johnson, Katherine Kath, Cec Linder, Albert Lieven, Edward Judd

Success at Any Price
US 1934 74m bw

A young man climbs to great business heights by crushing those around him, then attempts suicide when the crash comes. Slackly handled drama with an unsympathetic hero. Douglas Fairbanks Jnr, Genevieve Tobin, Frank Morgan, Colleen Moore, Edward Everett

Horton, Nydia Westman, Henry Kolker. Written by John Howard Lawson, Howard J. Green; directed by J. Walter Ruben; for RKO. 'Episodic, unreasonable and anything but audience proof.'—*Variety*

820A
Success Is the Best Revenge
GB / France 1984 91m Technicolor
De Vere / Gaumont (Jerzy Skolimowski)

A Polish theatre director in London stages a symbolic show but alienates his son.
Another study of Polish exiles to follow *Moonlighting*, but this time with surrealist elements.
w Jerzy Skolimowski, Michael Lyndon *d* Jerzy Skolimowski *ph* Mike Fash *m* Stanley Myers, Hans Zimmer

Michael York, Joanna Szczerbic, Michael Lyndon, Jerry Skol, Michel Piccoli, John Hurt, Anouk Aimée, Jane Asher

A Successful Calamity
US 1931 75m bw

A millionaire discovers the true worth of his family when he pretends to be poor. Good star vehicle which pleases despite its predictability. George Arliss, Mary Astor, Evalyn Knapp, Grant Mitchell, William Janney. Written by Maude Howell, Julien Josephson and Austin Parker, from the play by Clare Kummer; directed by John G. Adolfi; for Warner.

Such Good Friends*
US 1971 102m Movielab
Paramount / Sigma (Otto Preminger)

A successful man has a mysterious illness and his wife enlists help from his friends.
Satirical parable which alternates between sex comedy and medical exposé; generally heavy-going but with good moments.
w Elaine May, *novel* Lois Gould *d* Otto Preminger *ph* Gayne Rescher *m* Thomas Z. Shepherd

Dyan Cannon, James Coco, Jennifer O'Neil, Nina Foch, Laurence Luckinbill, Ken Howard, Burgess Meredith, Louise Lasser, Sam Levene, Rita Gam, Nancy Guild

Such Men Are Dangerous
US 1930 83m bw

A crooked financier undergoes plastic surgery and leads a new life. Phoney melodrama with slow pace and unconvincing details. Warner Baxter, Catherine Dale Owen, Albert Conti, Hedda Hopper, Claud Allister, Bela Lugosi. Written by Ernest Vajda, Elinor Glyn; directed by Kenneth Hawks; for Fox. 'Will bore intelligent fans and impress even the gullible with its implausibilities.'—*Variety*

Such Women Are Dangerous
US 1934 81m bw

Through circumstances an innocent man about town is accused of murder. Mild drama which fails through slack handling. Warner Baxter, Rosemary Ames, Rochelle Hudson, Mona Barrie, Herbert Mundin, Henrietta Crosman.

Written by Jane Storm, Oscar M. Sheridan, from the story Odd Thursday by Vera Caspary; directed by James Flood; for Fox. 'Just fair screen amusement.'—*Variety*

Sudden Fear**
US 1952 111m bw
RKO / Joseph Kaufman

A playwright heiress finds that her husband is plotting to kill her.
Archetypal star suspenser, glossy and effectively climaxed.
w Lenore Coffee, Robert Smith *d* David Miller *ph* Charles Lang Jnr *m* Elmer Bernstein

Joan Crawford, Jack Palance, Gloria Grahame, Bruce Bennett, Mike Connors

AAN: Charles Lang Jnr; Joan Crawford; Jack Palance

'Go on—make his day!'
Sudden Impact
US 1983 117m Technicolor
Warner / Malpaso (Clint Eastwood)

San Francisco detective Harry Callahan goes after a lady killer of men who raped her.
Unattractive and overlong cop show featuring an increasingly tired Dirty Harry.
w Joseph C. Stinson *d* Clint Eastwood *ph* Bruce Surtees *m* Lalo Schifrin *pd* Edward Carfagno

Clint Eastwood, Sondra Locke, Pat Hingle, Bradford Dillman, Paul Drake
'Eastwood presumably takes credit for such gems of authorial self-awareness as replacing the orang-outang of the *Which Way* films, with a farting dog.'—*Paul Taylor, MFB*

Suddenly*
US 1954 75m bw
UA / Robert Bassler

Gunmen take over a suburban house and plan to assassinate the President who is due to pass by.
Moderately effective minor suspenser with rather too much psychological chat.
w Richard Sale *d* Lewis Allen *ph* Charles G. Clarke *m* David Raksin

Frank Sinatra, Sterling Hayden, James Gleason, Nancy Gates, Kim Charney

'What she doesn't know about spring—neither does Cupid!'
Suddenly It's Spring
US 1947 87m bw
Paramount (Claude Binyon)

A WAC captain comes home to find that her husband wants a divorce.
Tired romantic comedy with no fizz at all.
w Claude Binyon *d* Mitchell Leisen *ph* Daniel L. Fapp *m* Victor Young

Paulette Goddard, Macdonald Carey, Fred MacMurray, Arleen Whelan, Lillian Fontaine, Frank Faylen, Victoria Horne

Suddenly Last Summer*
GB 1959 114m bw
Columbia / Horizon (Sam Spiegel)

A homosexual poet's young cousin goes mad
when she sees him raped and murdered by
beach boys.
Arty flashback talk-piece from a one-act play,
padded out with much sub-poetic mumbo
jumbo; it takes too long to get to the
revelation, which is ambiguously presented
anyway.

w Gore Vidal, play Tennessee Williams
d Joseph L. Mankiewicz ph Jack Hildyard
m Buxton Orr, Malcolm Arnold pd Oliver
Messel

Katharine Hepburn, Elizabeth Taylor,
Montgomery Clift, Albert Dekker, Mercedes
McCambridge, Gary Raymond
'A short play turns into a ludicrous,
lumbering horror movie.'—New Yorker, 1978
'I loathe this film, I say so candidly. To my
mind it is a decadent piece of work,
sensational, barbarous and ridiculous.'—C. A.
Lejeune, Observer
'A wholly admirable rendering into film of a
work at once fascinating and nauseating,
brilliant and immoral.'—Arthur Knight
AAN: Katharine Hepburn; Elizabeth Taylor

Suez*
US 1938 104m bw
TCF (Gene Markey)

The career of French engineer Ferdinand de
Lesseps, who built the Suez Canal.
Superbly mounted but rather undramatic
fictionalized biopic.

w Philip Dunne, Julien Josephson d Allan
Dwan ph Peverell Marley md Louis Silvers

Tyrone Power, Annabella, Loretta Young, J.
Edward Bromberg, Joseph Schildkraut, Henry
Stephenson, Sidney Blackmer, Maurice
Moscovitch, Sig Rumann, Nigel Bruce, Miles
Mander, George Zucco, Leon Ames, Rafaela
Ottiano
'It's a big film in its attempt, but it misses
out on its epic aims.'—Variety

AAN: Peverell Marley; Louis Silvers

Sugarfoot
US 1951 80m Technicolor

Two men meet on a train for Prescott,
Arizona, and each determines to make the
town his own. Unusual but fatally sluggish
western. Randolph Scott, Raymond Massey,
Adele Jergens, S. Z. Sakall, Robert Warwick,
Arthur Hunnicutt. Written by Russell Hughes,
from a novel by Clarence Budington Kelland;
directed by Edwin L. Marin; for Warner. (TV
title: Swirl of Glory.)

Sugarland Express*
US 1974 110m Technicolor
Panavision
Universal (Richard Zanuck, David Brown)

A convict's wife persuades him to escape
because their baby is being adopted, and they
inadvertently leave behind them a trail of
destruction, ending in tragedy.
Mainly comic adventures with a bitter
aftertaste, very stylishly handled.

w Hal Barwood, Matthew Robbins d Steven
Spielberg ph Vilmos Zsigmond m John
Williams

Goldie Hawn, Ben Johnson, Michael Sacks,
William Atherton
'Ace in the Hole meets Vanishing Point.'—
Sight and Sound

The Suitor*
France 1962 85m bw
CAPAC
original title: Le Soupirant

A nervous young man makes several attempts
to get married.
The most successful feature of Pierre Etaix, a
student of Tati: his jokes are more polished
but in the end his own personality seems
rather lacking.

w Pierre Etaix, Jean-Claude Carrière d Pierre
Etaix m Pierre Levant

Pierre Etaix, Laurence Lignères, France
Arnell

The Sullivans*
US 1944 111m bw
TCF (Sam Jaffe)
Reissue title: The Fighting Sullivans

Five sons of the same family are killed in
World War II.
Inspirational true story which had a wide
appeal.

w Mary C. McCall Jnr d Lloyd Bacon
ph Lucien Andriot m Alfred Newman

Anne Baxter, Thomas Mitchell, Selena Royle,
Edward Ryan, Trudy Marshall, John
Campbell, James Cardwell, John Alvin,
George Offerman Jnr, Roy Roberts
AAN: original story (Jules Schermer, Edward
Doherty)

'There's no speed limit and no brake
When Sullivan travels with Veronica Lake!'
Sullivan's Travels**
US 1941 90m bw
Paramount (Paul Jones)

A Hollywood director tires of comedy and
goes out to find real life.
Marvellously sustained tragi-comedy which
ranges from pratfalls to the chain gang and
never loses its grip or balance.

wd Preston Sturges ph John Seitz m Leo
Shuken

Joel McCrea, Veronica Lake, Robert Warwick,
William Demarest, Franklin Pangborn, Porter
Hall, Byron Foulger, Eric Blore, Robert
Greig, Torben Meyer, Jimmy Conlin,
Margaret Hayes
DEDICATION: 'To all the funny men and
clowns who have made people laugh.'
'A brilliant fantasy in two keys—slapstick
farce and the tragedy of human misery.'—
James Agee
'The most witty and knowing spoof of
Hollywood movie-making of all time.'—Film
Society Review
'Reflecting to perfection the mood of
wartime Hollywood, it danced on the grave of
thirties social cinema.'—Eileen Bowser, 1969

'Bold ideas . . . bolder people!'
Summer and Smoke
US 1961 118m Technicolor
Vistavision
Paramount / Hal B. Wallis

In a small Mississippi town in 1916, the
minister's spinster daughter nurses an
unrequited love for the local rebel.
Wearisome screen version, in hothouse
settings, of a pattern play about earthly and
spiritual love.

w James Poe, Meade Roberts, play Tennessee
Williams d Peter Glenville ph Charles Lang
Jnr m Elmer Bernstein ad Walter Tyler

Geraldine Page, Laurence Harvey, Una
Merkel, John McIntire, Pamela Tiffin, Rita
Moreno, Thomas Gomez, Casey Adams, Earl
Holliman, Lee Patrick, Malcolm Atterbury
AAN: Elmer Bernstein; Geraldine Page; Una
Merkel

Summer Holiday**
US 1948 92m Technicolor
MGM (Arthur Freed)

Life for a small-town family at the turn of the
century.
Musical version of a famous play: excellent
individual numbers, warm playing and
sympathetic scenes, but a surprising lack of
overall style.

w Frances Goodrich, Albert Hackett, Ralph
Blane, play Ah Wilderness by Eugene O'Neill
d Rouben Mamoulian ph Charles
Schoenbaum md Lennie Hayton songs Harry
Warren, Ralph Blane ch Charles Walters

Walter Huston, Mickey Rooney, Frank
Morgan, Agnes Moorehead, Butch Jenkins,
Selena Royle, Marilyn Maxwell, Gloria de
Haven, Anne Francis
† The film was finished in 1946 and held back
because it seemed unlikely to succeed.

Summer Holiday*
GB 1962 109m Technicolor
Cinemascope
ABP / Ivy (Kenneth Harper)

Four young London Transport mechanics
borrow a double decker bus for a continental
holiday.
Pacy, location-filmed youth musical with
plenty of general appeal.

w Peter Myers, Ronnie Cass d Peter Yates
ph John Wilcox md Stanley Black

Cliff Richard, Lauri Peters, Melvyn Hayes,
Una Stubbs, Teddy Green, Ron Moody,
Lionel Murton, David Kossoff
● Video: Thorn EMI

Summer Interlude*
Sweden 1950 97m bw
Svensk Filmindustri (Alan Ekelund)
original title: Sommarlek

A prima ballerina remembers a happy summer
she spent with a boy who was tragically killed.
Melancholy romance quite typical of its
creator but with less density of meaning than
usual.

w Ingmar Bergman, Herbert Grevenius
d Ingmar Bergman ph Gunnar Fischer, Bengt
Jarnmark m Erik Nordgren

Maj-Britt Nilsson, Birger Malmsten, Alf
Kjellin

Summer Magic*
US 1963 104m Technicolor
Walt Disney (Ron Miller)

Children help their widowed mother in 1912
Boston.
Amiable remake of *Mother Carey's Chickens*,
irreproachably presented.

w Sally Benson d James Neilson ph William
Snyder m Buddy Baker songs the Sherman
Brothers

Hayley Mills, Burl Ives, Dorothy McGuire,
Darren McGavin, Deborah Walley, Una
Merkel, Eddie Hodges, Michael J. Pollard

AAN: William Snyder

Summer of '42*
US 1971 103m Technicolor
Warner / Mulligan-Roth (Richard Alan Roth)

Adolescents make sexual explorations on a
New England island in 1942.
Well-observed indulgence in the new
permissiveness.

w Herman Raucher d Robert Mulligan
ph Robert Surtees m Michel Legrand

Jennifer O'Neill, Gary Grimes, Jerry Houser,
Oliver Conant, Lou Frizell

AA: Michel Legrand
AAN: Herman Raucher; Robert Surtees
● Video: Warner

Summer of the Seventeenth Doll
US / Australia 1959 94m bw
UA / Hecht–Hill–Lancaster (Leslie Norman)
US title: *Season of Passion*

Two cane-cutters on their annual city lay-off
have woman trouble.
Miscast and unsatisfactory rendering of a good
play; the humour has evaporated.

w John Dighton, play Ray Lawler d Leslie
Norman ph Paul Beeson m Benjamin
Frankel

Ernest Borgnine, John Mills, Angela
Lansbury, Anne Baxter, Vincent Ball

A Summer Place
US 1959 130m Technicolor
Warner (Delmer Daves)

Romantic summer adventures of teenagers
and their elders on an island off the coast of
Maine.
Sex among the idle rich: a routine piece of
Hollywood gloss, bowdlerized from a
bestseller.

wd Delmer Daves, novel Sloan Wilson
ph Harry Stradling m Max Steiner

Richard Egan, Dorothy McGuire, Sandra
Dee, Arthur Kennedy, Troy Donahue,
Constance Ford, Beulah Bondi

Summer Stock*
US 1950 109m Technicolor
MGM (Joe Pasternak)
GB title: *If You Feel Like Singing*

A theatre troupe takes over a farm for
rehearsals, and the lady owner gets the bug.
Likeable but halting musical with the star's
weight problems very obvious.

w George Wells, Sy Gomberg d Charles
Walters ph Robert Planck md Johnny
Green ch Nick Castle

Judy Garland, Gene Kelly, Gloria de Haven,
Carleton Carpenter, Eddie Bracken, Phil
Silvers, Hans Conried

† June Allyson was to have starred, but
became pregnant.

Summer Storm*
US 1944 106m bw
UA (Seymour Nebenzal)

In 1912 Russia, a provincial judge falls for a
local mancatcher.
One of Hollywood's occasional aberrations, an
attempt to do something very European in
typical west coast style. An interesting failure.

w Rowland Leigh, story The Shooting Party
by Anton Chekhov d Douglas Sirk
ph Archie Stout md Karl Hajos

George Sanders, Linda Darnell, *Edward
Everett Horton,* Anna Lee, Hugo Haas, John
Philiber, Sig Rumann, André Charlot

'There are bits of acting and photography
which put it as far outside the run of American
movies as it laudably tries to be. But most of it
had for me the sporty speciousness of an
illustrated drugstore classic.'—*James Agee*

AAN: Karl Hajos

Summer Wishes, Winter Dreams*
US 1973 88m Technicolor
Columbia / Rastar (Jack Brodsky)

A neurotic New York housewife goes to pieces
when her mother dies but finds a new
understanding of her husband when she
accompanies him on a trip to the World War
II battlefields.
Menopausal melodrama, well observed but
disappointingly wispy and underdeveloped.

w Stewart Stern d Gilbert Cates ph Gerald
Hirschfeld m Johnny Mandel

Joanne Woodward, Martin Balsam, Sylvia
Sidney, Dori Brenner, Win Forman

AAN: Joanne Woodward; Sylvia Sidney

Summer with Monika*
Sweden 1952 97m bw
Svensk Filmindustri (Allan Ekelund)

A wild, restless girl defies her parents and goes
off with her boy friend for an island holiday.
Her subsequent pregnancy and motherhood
don't in the least suit her, and the father is left
alone with the baby.
Probably truthful but rather glum and
unsophisticated drama of young love; not
among Bergman's most interesting films.

w Ingmar Bergman, novel Per Anders
Fogelstrom ph Gunnar Fischer m Erik
Nordgren

Harriet Andersson, Lars Ekborg

● Video: Longman

Summertime***
US 1955 99m Eastmancolor
Ilya Lopert / Alexander Korda
GB title: *Summer Madness*

An American spinster has a holiday in Venice
and becomes romantically involved.
Delightful, sympathetic travelogue with
dramatic asides, great to look at and hinging
on a single superb performance.

w David Lean, H. E. Bates, play The Time of
the Cuckoo by Arthur Laurents d David
Lean ph Jack Hildyard m Sandro Cicognini

Katharine Hepburn, Rossano Brazzi, Isa
Miranda, Darren McGavin, Mari Aldon,
André Morell

'The eye is endlessly ravished.'—*Dilys
Powell*

AAN: David Lean; Katharine Hepburn

Summertree
US 1971 88m Eastmancolor
Warner / Bryna (Kirk Douglas)

A bored student learns about life and becomes
a Vietnam casualty.
Well-made, rather tedious character study;
good social observation.

w Edward Hume, Stephen Yafa, play Ron
Cowen d Anthony Newley ph Richard C.
Glouner m David Shire

Michael Douglas, Brenda Vaccaro, Jack
Warden, Barbara Bel Geddes

The Sun Also Rises**
US 1957 129m Eastmancolor
Cinemascope
TCF (Darryl F. Zanuck)

In Paris after World War I an impotent
journalist meets a nymphomaniac lady of title,
and they and their odd group of friends have
various saddening adventures around Europe.
Not a bad attempt to film a difficult novel,
though Cinemascope doesn't help and the last
half hour becomes turgid. *The Last Flight* (qv)
conveyed the same atmosphere rather more
sharply.

w Peter Viertel, novel Ernest Hemingway
d Henry King ph Leo Tover m Hugo
Friedhofer

Tyrone Power, Ava Gardner, *Errol Flynn,*
Eddie Albert, Mel Ferrer, Robert Evans,
Juliette Greco, Gregory Ratoff, Marcel Dalio,
Henry Daniell

The Sun Never Sets
US 1939 98m bw
Universal (Rowland V. Lee)

Two brothers in the African colonial service
prevent a munitions baron from plunging the
world into war.
Stiff upper lip melodrama, very dated.

w W. P. Lipscomb d Rowland V. Lee
ph George Robinson m Frank Skinner
md Charles Previn

Basil Rathbone, Douglas Fairbanks Jnr,
Virginia Field, Lionel Atwill, Barbara O'Neil,
C. Aubrey Smith, Melville Cooper

'Confusing script and poor direction relegate
this to lower duals . . .'. brightest thing is the
title.'—*Variety*

The Sun Shines Bright**
US 1953 92m bw
Republic / Argosy (John Ford, Merian C. Cooper)

Forty years after the Civil War, the judge of a Kentucky town still has trouble quelling the Confederate spirit.

Mellow anecdotes of time gone by, scrappily linked but lovingly polished; a remake of a Will Rogers vehicle *Judge Priest*.

w Lawrence Stallings, *stories* Irwin S. Cobb *d* John Ford *ph* Archie Stout *m* Victor Young

Charles Winninger, Arleen Whelan, John Russell, Stepin Fetchit, Milburn Stone, Grant Withers, Russell Simpson

'Passages of quite remarkable poetic feeling . . . alive with affection and truthful observation.'—*Lindsay Anderson*

Sun Valley Serenade*
US 1941 86m bw
TCF (Milton Sperling)

The band manager at an Idaho ice resort takes care of a Norwegian refugee.

Simple-minded musical which still pleases because of the talent involved.

w Robert Ellis, Helen Logan *d* H. Bruce Humberstone *ph* Edward Cronjager *songs* Mack Gordon, Harry Warren *m* Emil Newman

Sonja Henie, *Glenn Miller and his Orchestra*, John Payne, *Milton Berle*, Lynn Bari, Joan Davis, *The Nicholas Brothers*, Dorothy Dandridge

AAN: Edward Cronjager; Emil Newman; song 'Chattanooga' (*m* Harry Warren, *ly* Mack Gordon)

Sunburn
GB / US 1979 98m Technicolor
Hemdale / Bind Films (David Korda)

An insurance investigator hires a model to act as his wife while he trails a suspected murderer in Acapulco.

All sun and skin and swirling cameras, this entire movie is a seventies cliché, but it provides some fitful amusement.

w John Daly, Stephen Oliver, James Booth, *novel* The Bind by Stanley Ellin *d* Richard C. Sarafian *ph* Alex Phillips Jnr *m* John Cameron

Farrah Fawcett, Charles Grodin, Art Carney, Joan Collins, William Daniels, John Hillerman, Eleanor Parker, Keenan Wynn

● *Video: VCL*

'It's about three decent people. They will break your heart!'

Sunday, Bloody Sunday***
GB 1971 110m De Luxe
UA / Vectia (Joseph Janni)

A young designer shares his sexual favours equally between two loves of different sexes, a Jewish doctor and a lady executive.

Stylishly made character study with melodramatic leanings, rather self-conscious about its risky subject but, scene by scene, both adult and absorbing, with an overpowering mass of sociological detail about the way we live.

w Penelope Gilliatt *d* John Schlesinger *ph* Billy Williams *m* Ron Geesin *pd* Luciana Arrighi

Glenda Jackson, Peter Finch, Murray Head, Peggy Ashcroft, Maurice Denham, Vivian Pickles, Frank Windsor, Tony Britton, Harold Goldblatt

AAN: Penelope Gilliatt; John Schlesinger; Glenda Jackson; Peter Finch

Sunday Dinner for a Soldier*
US 1944 86m bw
TCF (Walter Morosco)

A poor family living on a derelict Florida houseboat scrape together enough money to invite a soldier for a meal.

Sentimental little flagwaving romance, quite sympathetically presented and agreeably underacted.

w Wanda Tuchock, Melvin Levy *d* Lloyd Bacon *ph* Joe MacDonald *m* Alfred Newman

Anne Baxter, John Hodiak, Charles Winninger, Anne Revere, Connie Marshall, Chill Wills, Bobby Driscoll, Jane Darwell

'Simple, true and tender, the best propaganda America has put out in the current year.'—*Richard Winnington*

'Their eyes met! Their lips questioned! Their arms answered!'—*publicity*

Sunday in New York*
US 1963 105m Metrocolor
MGM / Seven Arts (Everett Freeman)

Complications in the love life of a brother and sister, each of whom thinks the other is very moral.

Fresh, fairly adult sex comedy with New York backgrounds.

w Norman Krasna, from his play *d* Peter Tewkesbury *ph* Leo Tover *m* Peter Nero

Cliff Robertson, Rod Taylor, Jane Fonda, Robert Culp, Jo Morrow, Jim Backus

Sunday in the Country**
France 1984 94m Eastmancolor
Sara Films / Films A2 / Little Bear (Alain Sarde)
Original title: *Un Dimanche à la Campagne*

An elderly artist enjoys a Sunday visit from his family.

Delightful, slight and moving sketch for a drama, which gives nothing but pleasure yet is hard to recapture.

w Bertrand and Colo Tavernier from a novella by Pierre Bost *d* Bertrand Tavernier *ph* Bruno de Keyzer *m* Gabriel Fauré

Louis Ducreux, Sabine Azema, Michel Aumont, Geneviève Mnich, Monique Chaumette, Claude Winter

Sundays and Cybèle*
France 1962 110m bw Franscope
Terra / Fides / Orsa / Trocadéro (Romain Pinès)
original title: *Cybèle ou les Dimanches de Ville d'Avray*

An amnesiac ex-pilot strikes up a friendship

with an abandoned 12-year-old girl, but the relationship is misunderstood and ends in tragedy.

A fashionable film of its time which now has little to offer: its director's reputation sagged alarmingly when he went to Hollywood.

w Serge Bourguignon, Antoine Tudal, *novel* Bernard Echasseriaux *d* Serge Bourguignon *ph* Henri Decaë *m* Maurice Jarre

Hardy Kruger, Nicole Courcel, Patricia Gozzi, Daniel Ivernel

'Studied charm and a creakingly melodramatic dénouement take the place of any serious attempt to probe the characters or situation . . . the film is so busily preoccupied with being as attractive, visually and sentimentally, as it possibly can, that it never has time to consider what it is being attractive about.''—*Tom Milne, MFB*

'Uneven but highly meritorious . . . a near-triumph of the intelligently mobile camera.'—*John Simon*

AA: best foreign film
AAN: script; Maurice Jarre

Sundown
US 1941 91m bw
Walter Wanger

The adopted daughter of an Arab trader assists British troops in Africa during World War II.

Artificial-looking romantic actioner with good cast.

w Barre Lyndon *d* Henry Hathaway *ph* Charles Lang *m* Miklos Rozsa

Gene Tierney, Bruce Cabot, George Sanders, Harry Carey, Joseph Calleia, Cedric Hardwicke, Carl Esmond, Reginald Gardiner

AAN: Charles Lang; Miklos Rozsa

The Sundowners**
GB / Australia 1960 133m Technicolor
Warner (Gerry Blatner)

In the twenties an Irish sheepdrover and his family travel from job to job in the Australian bush.

Easygoing, often amusing but lethargically developed family film with major stars somewhat ill at ease. Memorable sequences.

w Isabel Lennart, *novel* Jon Cleary *d* Fred Zinnemann *ph* Jack Hildyard *m* Dmitri Tiomkin

Robert Mitchum, Deborah Kerr, *Glynis Johns, Peter Ustinov*, Michael Anderson Jnr, Dina Merrill, *Wylie Watson*, Chips Rafferty

'For all Zinnemann's generous attention to character, the hints of longing, despair and indomitable spirit, the overall impression remains one of sheer length and repetition and synthetic naturalism.'—*Richard Winnington*

AAN: best picture; Isabel Lennart; Fred Zinnemann; Deborah Kerr; Glynis Johns

Sunny*
US 1930 81m bw
Warner

A showgirl falls for a rich young man.
Tinny early musical notable for its star.

w Humphrey Pearson, Henry McCarthy, *musical play* Otto Harbach, Oscar Hammerstein II, Jerome Kern *ph* Ernest Haller *d* William A. Seiter

Marilyn Miller, Lawrence Grey, Jack Donahue, Mackenzie Ward, O. P. Heggie

Sunny•
US 1941   97m   bw
RKO / Imperator (Herbert Wilcox)

Adequate remake of the above.

w Sig Herzig *d* Herbert Wilcox *ph* Russell Metty *m* Anthony Collins

Anna Neagle, Ray Bolger, John Carroll, Edward Everett Horton, Frieda Inescort, Grace and Paul Hartman

AAN: Anthony Collins

Sunny Side Up•
US 1929   80m   bw
Fox

A slum girl falls for the son of a rich Southampton family.
Typical early musical of the softer kind; rewarding for those who can project themselves back.

w / m / ly B. G. De Sylva, Lew Brown, Ray Henderson *d* David Butler *ph* Ernest Palmer

Janet Gaynor, Charles Farrell, El Brendel, Marjorie White, Sharon Lynn

Sunnyside•
US 1919   27m approx (24 fps)   bw
   silent
First National / Charles Chaplin

The overworked odd job man at a country hotel has a pastoral dream.
Very mildly funny star comedy which was intended as a satire on the D. W. Griffith / Charles Ray type of rural drama then popular. It doesn't work in this vein either.

wd Charles Chaplin *ph* Rollie Totheroh

Charles Chaplin, Edna Purviance, Tom Wilson, Albert Austin, Henry Bergman

Sunrise••
US 1927   97m (24 fps)   bw   silent
Fox

A villager in love with a city woman tries to kill his wife but then repents and spends a happy day with her.
Lyrical melodrama, superbly handled: generally considered among the finest Hollywood productions of the twenties.

w Carl Meyer, *novel* A Trip to Tilsit by Hermann Sudermann *d* F. W. Murnau *ph* Karl Struss, Charles Rosher *m* (sound version) Hugo Riesenfeld

Janet Gaynor, George O'Brien, Margaret Livingston

OPENING TITLE: 'This story of a man and his wife is of nowhere and everywhere, you might hear it anywhere and at any time.'

'It is filled with intense feeling and in it is embodied an underlying subtlety . . . exotic in many ways for it is a mixture of Russian gloom and Berlin brightness.'—*Mordaunt Hall, New York Times*

'Not since the earliest, simplest moving pictures, when locomotives, fire engines and crowds in streets were transposed to the screen artlessly and endearingly, when the entranced eye was rushed through tunnels and over precipices on runaway trains, has there been such joy in motion as under Murnau's direction.'—*Louise Bogan, The New Republic*

'The story is told in a flowing, lyrical German manner that is extraordinarily sensual, yet perhaps too self-conscious, too fable-like, for American audiences.'—*Pauline Kael, 70s*

AA: Karl Struss, Charles Rosher; Janet Gaynor

Sunrise at Campobello•
US 1960   143m   Technicolor
Warner / Dore Schary

The early life of Franklin Roosevelt, including his battle against polio and return to politics.
Static filming of a rather interesting Broadway success and of a memorable performance.

w Dore Schary, from his play *d* Vincent J. Donehue *ph* Russell Harlan *m* Franz Waxman

Ralph Bellamy, Greer Garson, Ann Shoemaker, Hume Cronyn, Jean Hagen

AAN: Greer Garson

'It happened in Hollywood . . . a love story . . . a drama real and ruthless, tender and terrifying!'

Sunset Boulevard•••
US 1950   110m   bw
Paramount (Charles Brackett)

A luckless Hollywood scriptwriter goes to live with a wealthy older woman, a slightly dotty and extremely possessive relic of the silent screen.
Incisive melodrama with marvellous moments but a tendency to overstay its welcome; the first reels are certainly the best, though the last scene is worth waiting for and the malicious observation throughout is a treat.

w Charles Brackett, Billy Wilder, D. M. Marshman Jnr *d* Billy Wilder *ph* John F. Seitz *m* Franz Waxman

Gloria Swanson, William Holden, Erich Von Stroheim, Fred Clark, Nancy Olson, Jack Webb, Lloyd Gough, Cecil B. de Mille, H. B. Warner, Anna Q. Nilsson, Buster Keaton, Hedda Hopper

'That rare blend of pungent writing, expert acting, masterly direction and unobtrusively artistic photography which quickly casts a spell over an audience and holds it enthralled to a shattering climax.'—*New York Times (T.M.P.)*

'Miss Swanson's performance takes her at one bound into the class of Boris Karloff and Tod Slaughter.'—*Richard Mallett, Punch*

'A weird, fascinating motion picture about an art form which, new as it is, is already haunted by ghosts.'—*Otis L. Guernsey Jnr, New York Herald Tribune*

AA: script; Franz Waxman
AAN: best picture; Billy Wilder (as director); John F. Seitz; Gloria Swanson; William Holden; Erich Von Stroheim; Nancy Olson

'For the price of a movie, you'll feel like a million!'

The Sunshine Boys•
US 1975   111m   Metrocolor
MGM / Rastar (Ray Stark)

Two feuding old vaudeville comedians come together for a television spot, and ruin it.
Over-extended sketch in which one main role is beautifully underplayed, the other hammed up, and the production lacks any kind of style. The one-liners are good, though.

w Neil Simon, from his play *d* Herbert Ross *ph* David M. Walsh *md* Harry V. Lojewski

Walter Matthau, *George Burns*, Richard Benjamin, Carol Arthur

'It's just shouting, when it needs to be beautifully timed routines.'—*New Yorker*

'They feud with ill-matched resources, and the movie's visual delights vanish with the title sequence.'—*Sight and Sound*

† George Burns stepped in when Jack Benny became ill and died.

AA: George Burns
AAN: Neil Simon; Walter Matthau

● *Video: MGM / UA*

Sunshine Susie
GB 1931   87m   bw

A banker pretends to be a clerk in order to court a typist. Viennese-set comedy which worked at the time but quickly dated. Renate Muller, Jack Hulbert, Owen Nares, Morris Harvey, Sybil Grove. Written by Angus MacPhail, Robert Stevenson, Victor Saville and Noel Wood-Smith, from the play *The Private Secretary* by Franz Schultz; directed by Victor Saville; for Gainsborough.

Sunstruck
Australia 1972   92m   Eastmancolor
Immigrant (Jack Neary, James Grafton)

A shy Welsh schoolmaster emigrates to the Australian outback.
Simple-minded, uninspired, predictable family comedy for star fans.

w Stan Mars *d* James Gilbert *ph* Brian West *m* Peter Knight

Harry Secombe, Maggie Fitzgibbon, John Meillon, Dawn Lake

The Super Cops
US 1974   94m   Metrocolor

Two New York cops are suspended for breaking too many rules, but wage their private war on crime. Low-life crime melodrama which plays effectively enough as a lighter-hearted *Serpico*. Ron Leibman, David Selby, Sheila Frazier, Pat Hingle, Dan Frazer. Written by Lorenzo Semple Jnr, from the book by L. H. Whittemore; directed by Gordon Parks Jnr; for St Regis Films / UA.

Superfly
US 1972   98m   Technicolor
Warner (Sig Shore)

The New York adventures of black cocaine peddlers.

'Sensational' comedy with violence in which the pushers exit laughing. Tedious and deplorable.

w Philip Fenty d Gordon Parks ph James Signorelli m Curtis Mayfield

Ron O'Neal, Carl Lee, Sheila Frazier

'It suggests that New York is now nothing more than a concrete junkieyard.'—*Philip Strick*

Supergirl*
GB 1984 124m colour Panavision
Cantharus / Ilya Salkind (Pierre Spengler, Timothy Burrill)

A Krypton power source falls into the hands of a power-hungry witch, and Supergirl is sent to retrieve it.
Playful comic strip spectacular which entertains in *Wizard of Oz* style for most of its way but was savaged by the critics.

w David Odell d Jeannot Szwarc ph Alan Hume m Jerry Goldsmith pd Richard MacDonald

Helen Slater, Faye Dunaway, Peter O'Toole, Mia Farrow, Brenda Vaccaro, Peter Cook, Simon Ward, Marc McClure, Hart Bochner, David Healy

'You'll believe a man can fly!'
Superman
US / GB 1978 142m colour Panavision
Warner / Alexander Salkind (Pierre Spengler)

A baby saved from the planet Krypton when it explodes grows up as a newspaperman and uses his tremendous powers to fight evil and support the American way.
Long, lugubrious and only patchily entertaining version of the famous comic strip, with far too many irrelevant preliminaries and a misguided sense of its own importance.

w Mario Puzo, David Newman, Robert Benton, Leslie Newman d Richard Donner ph Geoffrey Unsworth m John Williams pd John Barry sp various

Christopher Reeve, Marlon Brando, Margot Kidder, Jackie Cooper, Glenn Ford, Phyllis Thaxter, Trevor Howard, Gene Hackman, Ned Beatty, Susannah York, Valerie Perrine

'Though one of the two or three most expensive movies made to date, it's cheesy-looking, and the plotting is so hit or miss that the story never seems to get started; the special effects are far from wizardly and the editing often seems hurried and jerky just at the crucial points.'—*New Yorker*

'It gives the impression of having been made in panic—in fear that style or too much imagination might endanger its approach to the literal-minded.'—*Pauline Kael, New Yorker*

'The epitome of supersell.'—*Les Keyser, Hollywood in the Seventies*

† Reprehensible records were set by Brando getting three million dollars for a ten-minute performance (and then suing for a share of the gross); and by the incredible 7½-minute credit roll at the end.

†† Tiny roles were played by Noel Neill, who was Lois Lane in the TV series, and by Kirk Alyn, who was Superman in two serials.

AAN: John Williams
● *Video: Warner*

Superman 2
US 1980 127m Technicolor
Warner / Alexander Salkind (Pierre Spengler)

Three renegade Kryptonians threaten Earth with a space bomb.
Half the first episode was devoted to a creaky and unnecessary setting up of plot and characters. This sequel is all the better for diving straight into action, but a classic it isn't, even of the comic strip kind.

w Mario Puzo, David Newman, Leslie Newman d Richard Lester ph Geoffrey Unsworth, Robert Paynter m Ken Thorne

Christopher Reeve, Gene Hackman, Ned Beatty, Jackie Cooper, Sarah Douglas, Margot Kidder, Valerie Perrine, Susannah York, Terence Stamp, Jack O'Halloran, E. G. Marshall

● *Video: Warner*

Superman 3
GB 1983 125m colour Panavision
Dovemead / Cantharus (Pierre Spengler)

Synthetic Kryptonite warps Superman's character, but his conscience is reawakened by a plea from a small boy.
Sometimes humorous but overwritten and overacted variation on a tired theme. The special effects are the thing, but there's too much padding in between.

w David Newman, Leslie Newman d Richard Lester ph Robert Paynter m Ken Thorne pd Peter Murton

Christopher Reeve, Richard Pryor, Jackie Cooper, Marc McClure, Annette O'Toole, Annie Ross, Pamela Stephenson, Robert Vaughn, Margot Kidder

● *Video: Thorn EMI*

'Her heart cried out for love—yet her hands reached out to destroy!'
Supernatural*
US 1933 67m bw
Paramount (Victor and Edward Halperin)

A girl is possessed by the soul of a dead murderess.
Mad doctor nonsense, interestingly but not very successfully styled.

w Harvey Thew, Brian Marlow d Victor Halperin ph Arthur Martinelli

Carole Lombard, H. B. Warner, Randolph Scott, Vivienne Osborne, Alan Dinehart

'A 65-minute ghost story that dies after the first half-hour.'—*Variety*

Support Your Local Gunfighter*
US 1971 92m De Luxe
UA / Cherokee / Brigade (Burt Kennedy)

A con man jumps a train at a small mining town and is mistaken for a dreaded gunfighter.

Disappointing sequel to the following; just a couple of good jokes.

w James Edward Grant d Burt Kennedy ph Harry Stradling Jnr m Jack Elliott, Allyn Ferguson

James Garner, Suzanne Pleshette, Joan Blondell, Jack Elam, Chuck Connors, Harry Morgan, Marie Windsor, Henry Jones, John Dehner

Support Your Local Sheriff**
US 1968 92m Technicolor
UA / Cherokee (William Bowers)

Gold is found near a western village, and the resulting influx of desperate characters causes problems for the sheriff.
Amusing comedy, drawing on many western clichés.

w William Bowers d Burt Kennedy ph Harry Stradling Jnr m Jeff Alexander

James Garner, Joan Hackett, Walter Brennan, Jack Elam, Henry Morgan, Bruce Dern, Henry Jones

'It rejuvenates a stagnating genre by combining just the right doses of parody and affectionate nostalgia.'—*Jan Dawson*

Suppose They Gave a War and Nobody Came
US 1969 114m De Luxe
Engel–Auerbach / ABC (Fred Engel)

Three accident-prone PROs try to give the army a good name in a town which wishes it would go away; they eventually cause panic by arriving at a dance in a tank.
Muddled farce which may have hoped to be satire.

w Don McGuire, Hal Captain d Hy Averback ph Burnett Guffey m Jerry Fielding

Tony Curtis, Brian Keith, Ernest Borgnine, Ivan Dixon, Suzanne Pleshette, *Tom Ewell*, Bradford Dillman, Arthur O'Connell, Robert Emhardt, John Fiedler, Don Ameche

Surprise Package
GB 1960 100m bw
Columbia / Stanley Donen

An American gangster is deported to the same Mediterranean island as an exiled European king, whose crown gets stolen.
Flat and feeble comedy which defeats its stars.

w Harry Kurnitz, *novel* Art Buchwald d Stanley Donen ph Christopher Challis m Benjamin Frankel

Yul Brynner, Noel Coward, Mitzi Gaynor, Bill Nagy, Eric Pohlmann, George Coulouris, Warren Mitchell

Surrender
US 1931 69m bw

A French soldier in a German prison camp falls in love with a German girl at the nearby castle. Flabby drama which seems constantly about to make symbolic points. Warner Baxter, Leila Hyams, Ralph Bellamy, C. Aubrey Smith, William Pawley, Alexander

Kirkland. Written by S. N. Behrman, Sonya Levien, from the play Axelle by Pierre Benoit; directed by William K. Howard; for Fox. 'Anaemic picture product, not for A houses in big towns.'—Variety

The Survivors
US 1983 102m Metrocolor
Columbia-Delphi-Rastar-William Sackheim

An executive and a gas station attendant, both potential victims of a hit man, take refuge in the snowy mountains of Vermont.
Bewilderingly unfocused black comedy with some pleasant barbs along the way.

w Michael Leeson d Michael Ritchie ph Billy Williams m Paul Chihara pd Gene Callahan ed Richard A. Harris

Walter Matthau, Robin Williams, Jerry Reed, James Wainwright, Kristen Vigard, Annie McEnroe

Susan and God*
US 1940 117m bw
MGM (Hunt Stromberg)
GB title: The Gay Mrs Trexel

A flighty society woman gets religion but fails to practise what she preaches.
Unusual comedy-drama for MGM to tackle, but a fairly successful one for high class audiences.

w Anita Loos, play Rachel Crothers d George Cukor ph Robert Planck m Herbert Stothart

Joan Crawford, Fredric March, Ruth Hussey, John Carroll, Rita Hayworth, Nigel Bruce, Bruce Cabot, Rita Quigley, Rose Hobart, Constance Collier, Gloria de Haven, Marjorie Main

'It's not a good comedy, but it has a certain fascination, because the theme is such an odd one for Hollywood to have attempted at all.'—Pauline Kael, 70s

'Thrill to them together!'
Susan Lenox, Her Fall and Rise*
US 1931 76m bw
MGM (Paul Bern)
GB title: The Rise of Helga

A farm girl flees to the city when her father tries to marry her off to a brute.
Moderate star melodrama with the star somewhat miscast.

w Wanda Tuchock, novel David Graham Phillips d Robert Z. Leonard ph William Daniels

Greta Garbo, Clark Gable, Jean Hersholt, John Miljan, Alan Hale
'A torrid romance that will fascinate the femmes.'—Variety

Susan Slade
US 1961 116m Technicolor
Warner (Delmer Daves)

An engineer brings his family back to San Francisco from Chile, and his teenage daughter runs into problems of the heart.
Stilted, busy sudser.

w Delmer Daves, novel Doris Hume d Delmer Daves ph Lucien Ballard m Max Steiner

Connie Stevens, Troy Donahue, Dorothy McGuire, Lloyd Nolan, Brian Aherne, Natalie Schaefer, Grant Williams, Bert Convy, Kent Smith

Susan Slept Here
US 1954 98m Technicolor
RKO (Harriet Parsons)

The Hollywood scriptwriter of a film about youth problems agrees to look after a delinquent teenage girl.
Skittish, would-be piquant comedy; quite unattractive.

w Alex Gottlieb d Frank Tashlin ph Nicholas Musuraca md Leigh Harline songs Jack Lawrence, Richard Myers

Dick Powell, Debbie Reynolds, Anne Francis, Glenda Farrell, Alvy Moore, Horace MacMahon

AAN: song 'Hold My Hand'

Susannah of the Mounties*
US 1939 78m bw
TCF (Kenneth MacGowan)

A little girl who is the only survivor of a wagon train massacre is looked after by the Canadian Mounties.
Adequate star action romance, Shirley's last real success.

w John Taintor Foote, Philip Dunne d William A. Seiter ph Bert Glennon m Louis Silvers

Shirley Temple, Randolph Scott, Margaret Lockwood, J. Farrell MacDonald, Maurice Moscovitch, Moroni Olsen, Victor Jory
'Strictly for the juvenile trade . . . illogical situations make it no more than a moderate fairy tale.'—Variety

'His was a strange secret! Hers was a strange love!'
The Suspect*
US 1944 84m bw
Universal

A henpecked husband kills his wife and is blackmailed.
Efficient studio-bound suspenser with theatrically effective acting.

w Bertram Millhauser, novel James Ronald d Robert Siodmak ph Paul Ivano m Frank Skinner

Charles Laughton, Henry Daniell, Rosalind Ivan, Ella Raines, Molly Lamont, Dean Harens
'High marks for tension, local colour, story.'—William Whitebait

Suspect*
GB 1960 81m bw
The Boulting Brothers / British Lion

Government research chemists find a traitor in their midst.
Entertaining but fairly routine spy melodrama, shot on an experimental low budget but confined to lower berth bookings.

w Nigel Balchin, from his novel Sort of Traitors d Roy and John Boulting ph Max Greene m John Wilkes

Tony Britton, Virginia Maskell, Peter Cushing, Ian Bannen, Raymond Huntley, Donald Pleasence, Thorley Walters, Spike Milligan, Kenneth Griffith
'A better standard of second feature film is badly needed, but the way to do it is not by making pictures which look as though they have strayed from TV.'—Penelope Houston

Suspicion**
US 1941 99m bw
RKO (Alfred Hitchcock)

A sedate young girl marries a playboy, and comes to suspect that he is trying to murder her.
Rather artificial and stiff Hitchcock suspenser, further marred by an ending suddenly switched to please the front office. Full of the interesting touches one would expect.

w Samson Raphaelson, Alma Reville, Joan Harrison, novel Before the Fact by Francis Iles d Alfred Hitchcock ph Harry Stradling m Franz Waxman

Joan Fontaine, Cary Grant, Nigel Bruce, Cedric Hardwicke, May Whitty, Isabel Jeans, Heather Angel, Leo G. Carroll
'The fact that Hitchcock throws in a happy end during the last five minutes, like a conjuror explaining his tricks, seems to me a pity; but it spoils the film only in retrospect, and we have already had our thrills.'—William Whitebait, New Statesman

AA: Joan Fontaine
AAN: best picture; Franz Waxman

'The only thing more terrifying than the last twelve minutes of this film is the first eighty!'
'Once you've seen it you will never again feel safe in the dark!'
Suspiria*
Italy 1976 97m Eastmancolor Technovision
Seda Spettacoli (Claudio Argento)

A young American dance student arrives at dead of night at a continental academy where murder is the order of the day.
Psycho meets The Exorcist, with no holds barred: a genuinely scary thriller with gaudy visuals and a screaming sound track. A pyrotechnic display for those who can take it.

w Dario Argento, Dario Nicolodi d Dario Argento ph Luciano Tovoli m Dario Argento

Jessica Harper, Alida Valli, Joan Bennett, Stefania Casini, Udo Kier
'Thunderstorms and explicitly grotesque murders pile up as Argento happily abandons plot mechanics to provide a bravura display of his technical skill.'—Time Out

Sutter's Gold
US 1936 75m bw

During the California gold rush an immigrant has to fight for his rights when a strike starts

THRILL TO THEM TOGETHER *in the greatest emotional hit ever directed by that master of suspenseful drama — ALFRED HITCHCOCK!*

In his arms she felt safety . . . in his absence, haunting dread!

Cary Grant in his most powerful role as a wastrel husband intent on riches *at any cost* . . . Joan Fontaine in her first since "Rebecca", as the bride whose love turned to terror! Completely compelling mystery romance!

Alfred Hitchcock, who gave you "Foreign Correspondent" and "Rebecca", creates his most *romantic* mystery hit!

CARY GRANT JOAN FONTAINE
in
Suspicion
with
SIR CEDRIC HARDWICKE
NIGEL BRUCE
DAME MAY WHITTY
Directed by
ALFRED HITCHCOCK

R K O RADIO PICTURES

SUSPICION. One of Hitch's less satisfactory melodramas, and probably his least eventful; but it won Joan Fontaine an Academy Award.

on his land. Patchily arresting western which by costing much more than it should started the exit of Carl Laemmle from the chairman's office. Edward Arnold, Lee Tracy, Binnie Barnes, Katherine Alexander, Addison Richards, Montagu Love, John Miljan. Written by Jack Kirkland, Walter Woods and George O'Neil; directed by James Cruze; for Universal. (Most of the action footage was reused in a 1939 quickie, *Mutiny on the Blackhawk*.)

Suzy*
US 1936 95m bw
MGM (Maurice Revnes)

A French air ace of World War I marries an American showgirl; they then find that her former husband, thought dead, is still alive. Proficient star comedy-drama with romance, action, comedy and a complex plot. A showcase for its stars.

w Dorothy Parker, Alan Campbell, Horace Jackson, Lenore Coffee, *novel* Herbert Gorman d George Fitzmaurice ph Ray June m William Axt

Jean Harlow, Cary Grant, Franchot Tone, Benita Hume, Lewis Stone

AAN: song 'Did I Remember' (*m* Walter Donaldson, *ly* Harold Adamson)

Svengali**
US 1931 81m bw
Warner

In nineties Paris, a hypnotist turns a girl into a great opera singer but she does not reciprocate his love. Victorian fantasy melodrama with a great grotesque part for the star and interesting artwork.

w J. Grubb Alexander, *novel* Trilby by George du Maurier d Archie Mayo ph Barney McGill

John Barrymore, Marian Marsh, Luis Alberni, Lumsden Hare, Donald Crisp, Paul Porcasi
'A slow and old-fashioned melodrama.'—*Variety*
'Barrymore never needed occult powers to be magnetic, but interest flags when he's offscreen.'—*New Yorker, 1978*

AAN: Barney McGill

Svengali
GB 1954 82m Eastmancolor
Renown / Alderdale (Douglas Pierce)

Flatulent remake which does have the virtue of following the original book illustrations but is otherwise unpersuasive.

wd Noel Langley ph Wilkie Cooper m William Alwyn ad Fred Pusey

Donald Wolfit, Hildegarde Neff, Terence Morgan, Derek Bond, Paul Rogers, David Kossoff, Hubert Gregg, Noel Purcell, Alfie Bass, Harry Secombe

Swallows and Amazons
GB 1974 92m Eastmancolor
EMI / Theatre Projects (Richard Pilbrow)

In the twenties four children have adventures in the Lake District.

Mild family film, great to look at but lacking in real excitement or style.

w David Wood, *novel* Arthur Ransome d Claude Whatham ph Denis Lewiston m Wilfred Josephs

Virginia McKenna, Ronald Fraser, Simon West, Sophie Neville, Zanna Hamilton, Stephen Grenville

● *Video: Thorn EMI*

Swamp Water**
US 1941 90m bw
TCF (Irving Pichel)
GB title: *The Man Who Came Back*

A fugitive holds out for years in the Okefenokee swamp, and affects the lives of the local township.

A strange little story, not very compelling as drama but with striking photography and atmosphere. Remade more straightforwardly as *Lure of the Wilderness* (qv).

w Dudley Nichols, *story* Vereen Bell d Jean Renoir ph Peverell Marley m David Buttolph

Walter Huston, Walter Brennan, Anne Baxter, Dana Andrews, Virginia Gilmore, John Carradine, Eugene Pallette, Ward Bond, Guinn Williams
'So bad it's terrific.'—*Otis Ferguson*

The Swan*
US 1956 108m Eastmancolor
Cinemascope
MGM (Dore Schary)

In 1910 Hungary, a girl of noble stock is groomed to marry the crown prince. Interesting chiefly for a typical Hollywood reaction to a news event; about to lose their top star to a real life prince, MGM dusted off this old and creaky property for her last film. The star cast can't make much of it and the treatment is very heavy.

w John Dighton, *play* Ferenc Molnar d Charles Vidor ph Robert Surtees m Bronislau Kaper ad Cedric Gibbons, Randall Duell

Grace Kelly, Alec Guinness, Louis Jourdan, Agnes Moorehead, Jessie Royce Landis, Brian Aherne, Leo G. Carroll, *Estelle Winwood*, Robert Coote
'Balancing between artificial comedy and a no less artificial romantic theme, the film ultimately requires considerably greater finesse and subtlety in the handling.'—*Penelope Houston*

Swanee River**
US 1939 84m Technicolor
TCF (Darryl F. Zanuck)

The life and loves of Stephen Foster. Attractive, unsurprising family film in rich early colour, sparked by Jolson as E. P. Christy.

w John Taintor Foote, Philip Dunne d Sidney Lanfield ph Bert Glennon md Louis Silvers

Don Ameche, *Al Jolson*, Andrea Leeds, Felix Bressart, Russell Hicks
'An unimpressive story: will hit profitable but not big b.o.'—*Variety*

AAN: Louis Silvers

Swann in Love**
France 1983 111m colour
Gaumont / FR3 / SFPC / Bioskop / Films du Losange (Margaret Menegoz)
Original title: *Un Amour de Swann*

An elegant Jew in 19th-century Paris society becomes obsessed by a beautiful demi-mondaine.

Reasonably successful attempt to film part of an unfilmable book. Comparisons with *Letter from an Unknown Woman* are inevitable.

w Peter Brook, Jean-Claude Carrière, Marie-Hélène Estienne, from the works of Marcel Proust d Volker Schlöndorff ph Sven Nykvist m Hans Werner Henze

Jeremy Irons, Ornella Muti, Alain Delon, Fanny Ardant, Marie-Christine Barrault, Anne Bennent
'A film of more taste than vision.'—*Gilbert Adair, MFB*
'If you've read the original, forget it.'—*Volker Schlöndorff*
'A failure, maybe, but one that deserves to be seen.'—*Observer*

The Swarm
US 1978 116m Technicolor
Panavision
Warner (Irwin Allen)

African killer bees menace the US. Very obvious all-star disaster movie with risible dialogue. A box office flop, probably because several TV movies had already tackled the same subject.

w Stirling Silliphant, *novel* Arthur Herzog d Irwin Allen ph Fred J. Koenekamp m Jerry Goldsmith sp L. B. Abbott, Van Der Veer, Howard Jensen

Michael Caine, Katharine Ross, Richard Widmark, Richard Chamberlain, Olivia de Havilland, Fred MacMurray, Ben Johnson, Lee Grant, Jose Ferrer, Patty Duke Astin, Slim Pickens, Bradford Dillman, Henry Fonda, Cameron Mitchell
'You could pass it all off as a sick joke, except that it cost twelve million dollars, twenty-two million bees, and several years of someone's life.'—*Guardian*
'The story is of a banality matched only by the woodenness of the acting.'—*Barry Took, Punch*

● *Video: Warner*

Swashbuckler*
US 1976 101m Technicolor
Panavision
Universal / Elliott Kastner (Jennings Lang)
GB title: *The Scarlet Buccaneer*

Rival pirates help a wronged lady. Uninspired reworking of some old Errol Flynn ideas; the idea was pleasant, but the old style is sadly lacking.

w Jeffrey Bloom d James Goldstone ph Philip Lathrop m John Addison pd John Lloyd

Robert Shaw, James Earl Jones, Peter Boyle, Geneviève Bujold, Beau Bridges, Geoffrey Holder

'This tacky pastepot job can't make up its mind whether it's serious, tongue-in-cheek, satirical, slapstick, burlesque, parody or travesty; but be assured it is all of the above.'—*Variety*

'The talented cast is left to play living statues, immobilized by dumb dialogue and awkward action.'—*Judith Crist*

Sweeney!*
GB 1976 89m Technicolor
EMI / Euston (Ted Childs)

Scotland Yard's Flying Squad investigates a suicide and uncovers an elaborate political blackmail scheme.
Enjoyable big screen version of a pacy, violent TV cop show.

w Ranald Graham d David Wickes ph Dusty Miller m Denis King

John Thaw, Dennis Waterman, Barry Foster, Ian Bannen, Colin Welland, Michael Coles, Joe Melia
● Video: Thorn EMI

Sweeney 2
GB 1978 108m Technicolor
Euston Films (Ted Childs)

The flying squad discovers that a series of armed bank robberies is being committed by a gang of expatriates who return from a luxurious Malta development for each caper.
Silly, sluggish and violent extension of thin material which would scarcely have made a good one-hour TV episode. There isn't even an exciting climax.

w Troy Kennedy Martin d Tom Clegg ph Dusty Miller m Tony Hatch

John Thaw, Dennis Waterman, Barry Stanton, Denholm Elliott, Nigel Hawthorne, John Flanagan, David Casey
● Video: Thorn EMI

Sweeney Todd, the Demon Barber of Fleet Street*
GB 1936 68m bw
George King

A barber kills his customers and makes them into 'mutton pies' for sale at the shop next door.
Decent version of a famous old melodrama; stilted as film-making, but preserving a swaggering star performance.

w Frederick Hayward, H. F. Maltby, play George Dibdin-Pitt

Tod Slaughter, Bruce Seton, Eve Lister, Stella Rho, Ben Soutten

Sweepings*
US 1933 77m bw

An ambitious Chicago merchant finds that his sons do not wish to emulate him. Curious family melodrama based on fact; interesting but not exactly inspiring. Lionel Barrymore, Alan Dinehart, Eric Linden, William Gargan,

Gloria Stuart, Gregory Ratoff. Written by Lester Cohen from his novel; directed by John Cromwell; for RKO. 'Nothing to interest the women and a subject too sombre to interest the men.'—*Variety*

Sweet Adeline
US 1934 85m bw
Warner (Edward Chodorov)

In the nineties, the daughter of a beer garden owner attracts the attention of a composer and becomes a Broadway star.
Unexceptionable, and quite forgotten, adaptation of a pleasant, old-fashioned Broadway musical.

w Erwin S. Gelsey, play Jerome Kern, Oscar Hammerstein II, Harry Armstrong, Dick Gerard d Mervyn Le Roy m / ly Jerome Kern, Oscar Hammerstein II ph Sol Polito ch Bobby Connolly ad Robert Haas

Irene Dunne, Donald Woods, Ned Sparks, Hugh Herbert, Wini Shaw, Louis Calhern, Nydia Westman, Joseph Cawthorn

'As a production in the bigtime musical class, but strictly on merit it rates no better than fair.'—*Variety*

'He used love like most men use money!'
Sweet Bird of Youth*
US 1962 120m Metrocolor
Cinemascope
MGM / Roxbury (Pandro S. Berman)

A Hollywood drifter brings an ageing glamour star back to his home town, but runs into revenge from the father of a girl he had seduced.
Emasculated version of an overwrought play with the author's usual poetic squalor; comatose patches alternate with flashes of good acting and diverting dialogue, but the wide screen and heavy colour don't direct the attention.

wd Richard Brooks, play Tennessee Williams ph Milton Krasner m Harold Gellman md Robert Armbruster

Paul Newman, Geraldine Page, *Ed Begley*, Mildred Dunnock, Rip Torn, Shirley Knight, Madeleine Sherwood

AA: Ed Begley
AAN: Geraldine Page; Shirley Knight

'Love is what it's all about!'
Sweet Charity*
US 1969 149m Technicolor
Panavision 70
Universal (Robert Arthur)

A New York taxi dancer dreams of love.
A revue-type musical bowdlerized from Fellini's *Le notti di Cabiria* accords ill with real New York locations, especially as its threads of plot come to nothing; but behind the camera are sufficient stylists to ensure striking success with individual numbers.

w Peter Stone, play Neil Simon d Robert Fosse ph Robert Surtees m Cy Coleman ly Dorothy Fields md Joseph Gershenson

Shirley Maclaine, Ricardo Montalban, John McMartin, *Chita Rivera*, Paula Kelly, Stubby Kaye, Sammy Davis Jnr

'The kind of platinum clinker designed to send audiences flying towards the safety of their television sets.'—*Rex Reed*

AAN: Cy Coleman (as music director)

Sweet Kitty Bellairs
US 1930 60m Technicolor

A romance of stagecoach days set in an English seaside resort. A decided curiosity to come from this studio in *Little Caesar* days, and not a successful one. Claudia Dell, Ernest Torrence, Walter Pidgeon, June Collyer, Perry Askam, Lionel Belmore, Flora Finch. Written by Hermann Harrison, from the stage production of David Belasco; directed by Alfred E. Green; for Warners. 'Artistic achievement, but weak on fan pull.'—*Variety*

Sweet Music
US 1934 100m bw

An orchestra leader and a girl singer spar a lot but finally make it up. The slimmest of stories stretches over a few good numbers and some snappy dialogue; but it's all too long. Rudy Vallee, Ann Dvorak, Ned Sparks, Helen Morgan, Allen Jenkins, Alice White, Robert Armstrong. Written by Jerry Wald, Carl Erickson and Warren Duff; directed by Alfred E. Green; for Warner.

Sweet November
US 1968 113m Technicolor
Warner Seven Arts / Jerry Gershwin, Elliott Kastner

An English tycoon in New York meets a girl who takes a new lover every month because she hasn't long to live.
Irritating exercise in eccentric sentimentality, not helped by twitchy stars.

w Herman Raucher d Robert Ellis Miller ph Daniel L. Fapp m Michel Legrand

Anthony Newley, Sandy Dennis, Theodore Bikel, Burr de Benning

The Sweet Ride
US 1967 110m De Luxe Panavision
TCF (Joe Pasternak)

Surfers and drop-outs on a California beach have woman trouble.
Teenage melodrama, well produced but abysmal of content.

w Tom Mankiewicz, novel William Murray d Harvey Hart ph Robert B. Hauser m Pete Rugolo

Jacqueline Bisset, Tony Franciosa, Michael Sarrazin, Bob Denver, Michael Wilding

Sweet Rosie O'Grady*
US 1943 79m Technicolor
TCF (William Perlberg)

A Police Gazette reporter tries to uncover the past of a musical comedy star.
Pleasant nineties musical with plenty of zest but a lack of good numbers. A typical success of the war years.

w Ken Englund d Irving Cummings ph Ernest Palmer ch Hermes Pan songs Mack Gordon, Harry Warren ad James Basevi, Joseph C. Wright

Betty Grable, Robert Young, Adolphe Menjou, Reginald Gardiner, Virginia Grey, Phil Regan, Sig Rumann, Hobart Cavanaugh, Alan Dinehart
† Remake of Love Is News; remade as That Wonderful Urge.

'This is the story of J.J.—but not the way he wants it told!'

Sweet Smell of Success***
US 1957 96m bw
UA / Norma / Curtleigh (James Hill)

A crooked press agent helps a megalomaniac New York columnist break up his sister's marriage.
Moody, brilliant, Wellesian melodrama put together with great artificial style; the plot matters less than the photographic detail and the skilful manipulation of decadent characters, bigger than life-size.

w Clifford Odets, Ernest Lehman
d Alexander Mackendrick ph James Wong Howe m Elmer Bernstein ad Edward Carrere

Burt Lancaster, Tony Curtis, Martin Milner, Sam Levene, Susan Harrison, Barbara Nichols, Emile Meyer
'A sweet slice of perversity, a study of dollar and power worship.'—Pauline Kael

Sweet William
GB 1980 90m Eastmancolor

A London girl discovers that her American lover is constantly unfaithful. A situation in search of a story makes this slight piece with its wry observations rather less memorable than the average TV play. Sam Waterston, Jenny Agutter, Anna Massey, Daphne Oxenford, Arthur Lowe, Geraldine James. Written by Beryl Bainbridge, from her novel; directed by Claude Whatham; for Kendon.

Sweethearts**
US 1938 120m Technicolor
MGM (Hunt Stromberg)

Two stars of the musical stage never stop fighting each other.
The lightest and most successful of the MacDonald / Eddy musicals, with an excellent script, production and cast.

w Dorothy Parker, Alan Campbell
d W. S. Van Dyke ph Oliver Marsh m Victor Herbert md Herbert Stothart

Jeanette MacDonald, Nelson Eddy, Frank Morgan, Ray Bolger, Florence Rice, Mischa Auer, Fay Holden, Reginald Gardiner, Herman Bing, Allyn Joslyn, Raymond Walburn, Lucile Watson, Gene Lockhart
'It will disappoint because of length, and general lethargy and sameness of production values.'—Variety

AA: Oliver Marsh
AAN: Herbert Stothart

'They had the pools—but he had their wives!'

The Swimmer**
US 1968 94m Technicolor
Columbia / Horizon / Dover (Frank Perry, Roger Lewis)

A man clad only in trunks swims his way home via the pools of his rich friends, and arrives home to find that his success is a fantasy.
Strange but compelling fable, too mystifying for popular success, about the failure of the American dream. Annoyingly inexplicit, but well made and sumptuously photographed in a variety of Connecticut estates.

w Eleanor Perry, short story John Cheever
d Frank Perry, Sydney Pollack ph David L. Quaid m Marvin Hamlisch

Burt Lancaster, Janice Rule, Kim Hunter, Diana Muldaur, Cornelia Otis Skinner, Marge Champion

Swing Fever
US 1943 80m bw

A bandleader uses hypnotism to train a boxer. Witless farrago with sprightly musical numbers. Kay Kyser and his band, Marilyn Maxwell, Nat Pendleton, William Gargan, Lena Horne. Written by Nat Perrin and Warren Wilson; directed by Tim Whelan; for MGM.

Swing High Swing Low**
US 1937 97m bw
Paramount (Arthur Hornblow Jnr)

A talented trumpeter goes on a bender but is rescued by his wife.
Backstage comedy-drama, a beautifully cinematic version of a very tedious story also filmed as Dance of Life (1929) and When My Baby Smiles at Me (1948).

w Virginia Van Upp, Oscar Hammerstein II, play Burlesque by George Manker Walters, Arthur Hopkins d Mitchell Leisen ph Ted Tetzlaff m Victor Young md Boris Morros

Carole Lombard, Fred MacMurray, Charles Butterworth, Jean Dixon, Dorothy Lamour, Harvey Stephens, Franklin Pangborn, Anthony Quinn
'No reason to believe it won't jam 'em at the gate . . . it's a cinch for the younger trade, and will satisfy general audience standards.'—Variety
'Enough concentrated filmcraft to fit out half a dozen of those gentlemen who are always dashing around in an independent capacity making just the greatest piece of cinema ever.'—Otis Ferguson

● Video: VCL

Swing Time**
US 1936 103m bw
RKO (Pandro S. Berman)

A dance team can't get together romantically because he has a commitment to a girl back home.
Satisfactory but unexciting musical vehicle for two stars at the top of their professional and box-office form.

w Howard Lindsay, Allan Scott d George Stevens ph David Abel md Nathaniel Shilkret songs Jerome Kern, Dorothy Fields

Fred Astaire, Ginger Rogers, Victor Moore, Helen Broderick, Eric Blore, Betty Furness, Georges Metaxa

AA: song 'The Way You Look Tonight'

Swing Your Lady*
US 1937 77m bw
Warner (Sam Bischoff)

A promoter gets involved in the problems of a hillbilly wrestler.
Minor comedy with some laughs.

w Joseph Schrank, Maurice Leo, story Toehold on Artemus by H. R. Marsh d Ray Enright ph Arthur Edeson m Adolph Deutsch

Humphrey Bogart, Louise Fazenda, Nat Pendleton, Frank McHugh, Penny Singleton, Allen Jenkins, Ronald Reagan, The Weaver Brothers and Elviry
'A comedy of not immense proportions, it is nevertheless a rollicking, considerably different laugh-piece which should do from average to good business everywhere.'—Variety

The Swinger
US 1966 81m Technicolor
Paramount / George Sidney

When a girl writer's wholesome stories are rejected, she pretends to have a naughty past. With-it comedy which audiences preferred to be without.

w Lawrence Roman d George Sidney ph Joseph Biroc m Marty Paich

Ann-Margret, Tony Franciosa, Robert Coote, Yvonne Romain, Horace MacMahon, Nydia Westman
'A hectically saucy mixture of lechery, depravity, perversion, voyeurism and girlie magazines . . . a heavy, witless pudding.'—MFB

The Swiss Family Robinson
US 1940 93m bw
(RKO) Gene Towne, Graham Baker

A shipwrecked family builds a new home on a desert island.
Pleasing low-budgeter.

w Gene Towne, Graham Baker, Walter Ferris, novel Johann Wyss d Edward Ludwig ph Nicholas Musuraca

Thomas Mitchell, Edna Best, Freddie Bartholemew, Tim Holt, Terry Kilburn
'In outlook, dialogue and manner it is frankly old-fashioned.'—MFB

The Swiss Family Robinson*
GB 1960 126m Technicolor Panavision
Walt Disney (Bill Anderson, Basil Keys)

Quite pleasing comedy adventure from the children's classic.

w Lowell S. Hawley d Ken Annakin ph Harry Waxman m William Alwyn

John Mills, Dorothy McGuire, James MacArthur, Tommy Kirk, Kevin Corcoran, Janet Munro, Sessue Hayakawa, Cecil Parker

● Video: Rank

Swiss Miss*
US 1938 73m bw
(MGM) Hal Roach

Two mousetrap salesmen in Switzerland run into trouble with a cook, a gorilla and two opera singers.

Operetta style vehicle which constrains its stars, since their material is somewhat below vintage anyway. Not painful to watch, but disappointing.

w James Parrott, Felix Adler, Charles Nelson d John G. Blystone ph Norbert Brodine

Stan Laurel, Oliver Hardy, Walter Woolf King, Della Lind, Eric Blore

'Story, production, acting and direction suggest a revival of early sound filmusicals presented with stage technique.'—*Variety*

The Swissmakers
Switzerland 1978 108m Eastmancolor

Cases of a department investigating applicants for naturalization. Amusing satirical comedy which presumably has more bite in its home territory. Walo Luond, Emil Steinberger, Beatrice Kessler. Written by Rolf Lyssy and Christa Maerker; directed by Rolf Lyssy; for Lyssy / Rex / Willora / Schoch / Ecco.

The Sword and the Rose
GB 1952 91m Technicolor
Walt Disney (Perce Pearce)

The romantic problems of young Mary Tudor. Unhistorical charade not quite in the usual Disney vein, and not very good.

w Laurence E. Watkin, *novel* When Knighthood Was in Flower by Charles Major d Ken Annakin ph Geoffrey Unsworth m Clifton Parker

Richard Todd, Glynis Johns, James Robertson Justice, Michael Gough, Jane Barrett, Peter Copley, Rosalie Crutchley, Jean Mercure, D. A. Clarke-Smith

The Sword and the Sorcerer
US 1982 99m De Luxe
Sorcerer Productions / Group One / Brandon Chase

A tyrant wins an idyllic kingdom with the help of an evil sorcerer; young Prince Talon gets it back.
Medieval magic and violence, laid on with a shovel; hopefully the last attempt to start an ill-fated cycle.

w Tom Karnowski, Albert Pyun, John Stuckmeyer d Albert Pyun ph Joseph Mangine m David Whitaker

Lee Horsley, Kathleen Beller, Simon MacCorkindale, George Maharis, Richard Lynch

Sword in the Desert
US 1949 100m bw

During World War II, Jewish refugees are smuggled to the Palestine coast. Dim topical melodrama with an anti-British slant which caused international embarrassment. Dana Andrews, Marta Toren, Jeff Chandler, Stephen McNally, Philip Friend. Written by Robert Buckner; directed by George Sherman; for Robert Arthur / Universal.

The Sword in the Stone**
US 1963 80m Technicolor
Walt Disney (Ken Peterson)

In the Dark Ages, a young forest boy named Wart becomes King Arthur.
Feature cartoon with goodish sequences but disappointingly showing a flatness and economy of draughtsmanship.

w Bill Peet, *novel* The Once and Future King by T. H. White d Wolfgang Reitherman m George Bruns *songs* The Sherman Brothers

AAN: George Bruns

Sword of Ali Baba
US 1965 81m Technicolor

Ali Baba is forced from the royal court to become a king of thieves. Cut-rate programme filler utilizing great chunks of *Ali Baba and the Forty Thieves* (twenty-one years older), with one actor, Frank Puglia, playing the same role in both films. Peter Mann, Jocelyn Lane, Peter Whitney, Gavin McLeod. Written by Edmund Hartmann and Oscar Brodney; directed by Virgil Vogel; for Universal.

Sword of Monte Cristo
US 1951 80m Supercinecolor

Virtuous rebels and a villainous minister all seek the fabulous treasure of Monte Cristo. Rubbishy sequel apparently shot in somebody's back garden by people only recently acquainted with film techniques. George Montgomery, Paula Corday, Berry Kroeger, Robert Warwick, William Conrad. Written and directed by Maurice Geraghty; for Edward L. Alperson.

Sword of Sherwood Forest
GB 1960 80m Technicolor Megascope
Columbia / Hammer / Yeoman (Richard Greene, Sidney Cole)

Robin Hood reveals the villainy of the Sheriff of Nottingham and the Earl of Newark.
This big-screen version of a popular TV series makes a rather feeble addition to the legend, but the actors try hard.

w Alan Hackney d Terence Fisher ph Ken Hodges m Alan Hoddinott

Richard Greene, Peter Cushing, Richard Pasco, Niall MacGinnis, Jack Gwyllim, Sarah Branch, Nigel Green

Sword of the Valiant
GB 1984 101m Fujicolor JDC Wide Screen
Cannon (Michael Kagan, Philip M. Breen)

In the mythical middle ages, squire Gawain takes on a challenge from the magical Green Knight.
An unsatisfactory mixture of realism, fantasy and deadly seriousness. Spoofing might have worked better.

w Stephen Weeks, Philip M. Breen, Howard C. Pen d Stephen Weeks ph Freddie Young, Peter Hurst m Ron Geesin pd Maurice Fowler, Derek Nice ed Richard Marden, Barry Peters

Miles O'Keeffe, Sean Connery, Trevor Howard, Leigh Lawson, Cyrielle Claire, Peter Cushing, Ronald Lacey, Lila Kedrova, John Rhys Davies, Douglas Wilmer, Wilfred Brambell

The Swordsman
US 1947 80m Technicolor
Columbia

A young 18th-century Scot tries to end a family feud so that he can marry the girl of his choice.
Amiable costume programmer, quite forgettable but mostly enjoyable while it's on.

w Wilfred Petitt d Joseph H. Lewis ph William Snyder m Hugo Friedlander

Larry Parks, Ellen Drew, George Macready

Sylvia
US 1964 115m bw
Paramount / Joseph E. Levine (Martin H. Poll)

A millionaire with a mysterious fiancée hires a detective to discover the truth about her past. Improbable story of a high-minded prostitute, sluggishly narrated and variably acted.

w Sidney Boehm, *novel* E. V. Cunningham d Gordon Douglas ph Joseph Ruttenberg m David Raksin

Carroll Baker, George Maharis, Peter Lawford, Joanne Dru, Ann Sothern, Viveca Lindfors, Edmond O'Brien, Aldo Ray

Sylvia and the Ghost*
France 1944 93m bw
Ecran Français / André Paulvé
Original title: *Sylvie et la Fantôme*

A sixteen-year-old girl lives in her father's castle and is friendly with the ghost of a man killed in a duel fought for love of her grandmother.
Melancholy comedy which despite some charming moments somehow misses the expected style which would have made it a minor classic.

w Jean Aurenche, *play* Alfred Adam d Claude Autant-Lara ph Philippe Agostini m René Cloerc

Odette Joyeux, François Périer, Jacques Tati, Louis Salou, Jean Desailly

'A charming film, written, handled and acted with wit, feeling and a beautiful lightness of touch.'—*Gavin Lambert*

'She's a boy! It's Mr Hepburn to you!'
Sylvia Scarlett*
US 1935 94m bw
RKO (Pandro S. Berman)

A girl masquerades as a boy in order to escape to France with her crooked father.
Strange, peripatetic English comedy-adventure which failed to ring any bells but preserves aspects of interest.

w Gladys Unger, John Collier, Mortimer Offner, *novel* Compton Mackenzie d George Cukor ph Joseph August m Roy Webb

Katharine Hepburn, Cary Grant, Edmund Gwenn, Brian Aherne, Lennox Pawle

'A story that's hard to believe. Dubious entertainment for the public.'—*Variety*

'It seems to go wrong in a million directions, but it has unusually affecting qualities.'—*New Yorker, 1978*

'A sprawling and ineffective essay in dramatic chaos.'—*Richard Watts Jnr, New York Herald Tribune*

'A tragic waste of time and screen talent.'—*Eileen Creelman, New York Sun*

'A much more polished comedy than most, and consistently engaging.'—*Winston Burdett, Brooklyn Daily Eagle*

La Symphonie Pastorale*
France 1946 105m bw
Les Films Gibe

A Swiss pastor takes in an orphan child who grows up to be a beautiful girl and causes jealousy between himself and his son.
Curious mountain tragedy, a great visual pleasure with its symbolic use of snow and water.

w Jean Delannoy, Jean Aurenche, *novel* André Gide d Jean Delannoy ph Armand Thirard m Georges Auric

Pierre Blanchar, Michèle Morgan

Symphony of Six Million
US 1932 94m bw
RKO (Pandro S. Berman)
GB title: *Melody of Life*

A doctor drags himself from New York's slums to Park Avenue, but feels guilty and demoralized when he can't save the life of his own father.
Monumental tearjerker, not badly done.

w Bernard Schubert, J. Walter Ruben, *novel* Fannie Hurst d Gregory La Cava ph Leo Tover m Max Steiner

Irene Dunne, Ricardo Cortez, Gregory Ratoff, Anna Appel, Noel Madison, Julie Haydon

'Picture of Jewish home life in the familiar Hurst style . . . a good-looking picture without strongly marked cast names.'—*Variety*

Synanon
US 1965 106m bw
Columbia / Richard Quine
GB title: *Get Off My Back*

Stories of the inmates of a voluntary Californian institution for the rehabilitation of drug addicts.
Well-intentioned but rather dreary case histories, unconvincingly dramatized. The house and its leader subsequently came in for much press criticism.

w Ian Bernard, S. Lee Pogostin d Richard Quine ph Harry Stradling m Neal Hefti

Edmond O'Brien (as Chuck Dederich), Chuck Connors, Stella Stevens, Alex Cord, Eartha Kitt, Richard Conte, Barbara Luna

'The real drug addicts who appear in the background are plumpish, greyish and utterly ordinary; but the fictional ones are glamorously handsome, and lead lives which are full of throbbing emotion and upset.'—*Tom Milne, MFB*

The System
US 1953 90m bw
Warner (Sam Bischoff)

A crime leader is softened by love, and allows himself to be convicted.
Strange nonsense inspired by the Kefauver investigations into American society; neither edifying nor entertaining.

w Jo Eisinger d Lewis Seiler ph Edwin DuPar m David Buttolph

Frank Lovejoy, Joan Weldon, Bob Arthur, Paul Picerni, Don Beddoe

The System
GB 1964 90m bw
British Lion / Bryanston / Kenneth Shipman
US title: *The Girl-Getters*

Seaside layabouts have a system for collecting and sharing rich girl visitors, but one of the latter traps the leader at his own game.
Adequate sexy showcase for some looming talents; all very unattractive, but smoothly directed in a number of imitated styles.

w Peter Draper d Michael Winner ph Nicolas Roeg m Stanley Black

Oliver Reed, Jane Merrow, Barbara Ferris, Julia Foster, Ann Lynn, Guy Doleman, Andrew Ray, David Hemmings, John Alderton, Derek Nimmo, Harry Andrews

'A modest, skilful, charming, inconsequential, and fairly dishonest little picture, to be enjoyed and deprecated in roughly equal measure.'—*John Simon*

T. R. Baskin
US 1971 89m Technicolor
Paramount (Peter Hyams)
GB title: *A Date with a Lonely Girl*

A businessman in Chicago meets an unhappy
girl who tells him her story of loneliness and
lack of communication.
Intolerable self-pitying mishmash with no
place to go.

w Peter Hyams *d* Herbert Ross *ph* Gerald
Hirschfeld *m* Jack Elliott

Candice Bergen, Peter Boyle, James Caan,
Marcia Rodd, Erin O'Reilly

Table for Five
US 1983 124m De Luxe
CBS / Voight-Schaffel (Robert Schaffel)

A divorced husband takes his children on a
European holiday and has to tell them that
their mother has been killed.
Slow, sentimental domestic drama with
attractive travel backgrounds, like a TV movie
writ large.

w David Seltzer *d* Robert Lieberman
ph Vilmos Zsigmond *m* John Morris
pd Robert F. Boyle

Jon Voight, Richard Crenna, Marie-Christine
Barrault, Millie Perkins, Roxana Zal, Robby
Kiger, Son Hoang Bui, Maria O'Brien
  'A family problem picture resolutely
updated for the eighties.'—*Robert Brown,
MFB*

Tabu*
US 1931 80m bw
Colorart Synchrotone

The life of a young Tahitian pearl fisherman.
The plot is used only to bring together the
elements of a superb travelogue, but the
conflicts between the aims of the two directors
are clearly seen.

wd F. W. Murnau, Robert Flaherty *ph* Floyd
Crosby, Robert Flaherty *m* Hugo Riesenfeld
  'Never more than interesting . . . it is not
going to set anything on fire.'—*Variety*
AA: Floyd Crosby

Taggart
US 1965 85m Technicolor print

A young western squatter avenges his parents'
murder but finds himself pursued by three
professional gunslingers. Tough adult western,
quite well made. Tony Young, Dan Duryea,
Dick Foran, Emile Meyer, Elsa Cardenas,
Jean Hale, David Carradine. Written by
Robert Creighton Williams, from the novel by
Louis L'Amour; directed by R. G.
Springsteen; for Universal.

Tail Spin
US 1938 83m bw
TCF (Harry Joe Brown)

The interwoven private lives of lady civilian air
pilots.
Predictable romantic goings on; a tear, a
smile, a song, etc.

w Frank Wead *d* Roy del Ruth *ph* Karl
Freund *m* Louis Silvers

Alice Faye, Constance Bennett, Joan Davis,
Nancy Kelly, Charles Farrell, Jane Wyman,
Kane Richmond, Wally Vernon, Harry
Davenport
  'Story zooms and flutters to create many
slow spots in between the spectacular flying
sequences.'—*Variety*

Take a Giant Step
US 1958 100m bw
UA / Sheila / Hecht–Hill–Lancaster
(Julius J. Epstein)

A young black person brought up in a white
town feels ill at ease and runs into adolescent
troubles.
Well-meaning racial drama with good detail
but no real feeling.

w Louis S. Peterson, Julius J. Epstein
d Philip Leacock *ph* Arthur Arling *m* Jack
Marshall

Johnny Nash, Estelle Hemsley, Ruby Dee,
Frederick O'Neal

Take a Girl Like You
GB 1970 101m Eastmancolor
Columbia / Albion (Hal E. Chester)

A north country girl comes to teach in London
and has man trouble.
Old-fashioned novelette with sex trimmings
and neither zest nor humour.

w George Melly, *novel* Kingsley Amis
d Jonathan Miller *ph* Dick Bush *m* Stanley
Myers

Hayley Mills, Oliver Reed, Noel Harrison,
Sheila Hancock, John Bird, Aimi MacDonald

Take a Letter, Darling**
US 1942 94m bw
Paramount (Fred Kohlmar)
GB title: *Green-Eyed Woman*

A woman executive hires a male secretary.
Smartish romantic comedy.

w Claude Binyon *d* Mitchell Leisen *ph* John
Mescall *m* Victor Young

Rosalind Russell, Fred MacMurray,
Macdonald Carey, Constance Moore, Cecil
Kellaway, Charles Arnt, Kathleen Howard,
Dooley Wilson

AAN: John Mescall; Victor Young

Take Care of My Little Girl
US 1951 93m Technicolor
TCF (Julian Blaustein)

A university freshwoman gets into trouble
with her sorority.
Ho-hum exposé of college conventions, of
routine interest at best.

w Julius J. and Philip G. Epstein, *novel* Peggy
Goodwin *d* Jean Negulesco *ph* Harry
Jackson *m* Alfred Newman

Jeanne Crain, Mitzi Gaynor, Dale Robertson,
Jean Peters, Jeffrey Hunter
  'As is customary in college pictures, it
appears that Tri U recruits most of its strength
from the chorus.'—*Penelope Houston*

Take Her, She's Mine*
US 1963 98m De Luxe Cinemascope
TCF (Henry Koster)

A lawyer protects his teenage daughter from
boys and causes.
Routine Hollywood family comedy with some
laughs and an agreeable cast.

w Nunnally Johnson, *play* Phoebe and Henry
Ephron *d* Henry Koster *ph* Lucien Ballard
m Jerry Goldsmith

Take It or Leave It
US 1944 68m bw

A sailor enters a quiz show to raise money for
his expectant wife. Thin link for a string of old
movie clips which form the questions; all from
Fox films of course. Phil Baker, Phil Silvers,
Edward Ryan, Marjorie Massow; with clips of
Shirley Temple, the Ritz Brothers, Betty
Grable, Alice Faye, Sonja Henie, Al Jolson,
etc. Written by Harold Buchman, Snag Werris
and Mac Benoff; directed by Ben Stoloff; for
TCF.

James Stewart, Sandra Dee, Robert Morley, Audrey Meadows, Philippe Forquet, John McGiver

Take Me High
GB 1973 90m Technicolor
EMI (Kenneth Harper)

A bank manager helps an unsuccessful restaurant to launch a new hamburger.
Jaded youth musical with no dancing but some zip and bounce to commend it to mums and dads if not to its intended young audience.

w Christopher Penfold d David Askey
ph Norman Warwick m / songs Tony Cole

Cliff Richard, Debbie Watling, Hugh Griffith, George Cole, Anthony Andrews, Richard Wattis

Take Me Out to the Ball Game•••
US 1949 93m Technicolor
MGM (Arthur Freed)
GB title: Everybody's Cheering

A woman takes over a baseball team and the players are antagonistic.
Lively, likeable nineties comedy musical which served as a trial run for On the Town and in its own right is a fast-moving, funny, tuneful delight with no pretensions.

w Harry Tugend, George Wells d Busby Berkeley ph George Folsey md Adolph Deutsch songs Betty Comden, Adolph Green, Roger Edens

Gene Kelly, Frank Sinatra, Esther Williams, Betty Garrett, Jules Munshin, Edward Arnold, Richard Lane, Tom Dugan

Take Me to Town
US 1953 81m Technicolor
U-I (Ross Hunter)

The three sons of a backwoods widower import a vaudeville artiste as their new mother.
Old-fashioned family schmaltz containing every known cliché professionally stitched into the plot.

w Richard Morris d Douglas Sirk ph Russell Metty m Joseph Gershenson

Ann Sheridan, Sterling Hayden, Philip Reed, Lee Patrick, Lee Aaker, Harvey Grant, Dusty Henley

Take My Life••
GB 1947 79m bw
GFD / Cineguild (Anthony Havelock-Allan)

A man is suspected of murdering an ex-girl friend, and his wife journeys to Scotland to prove him innocent.
Hitchcock-style thriller with excellent detail and performances.

w Winston Graham, Valerie Taylor d Ronald Neame ph Guy Green m William Alwyn

Hugh Williams, Greta Gynt, Marius Goring, Francis L. Sullivan, Rosalie Crutchley, Henry Edwards, Ronald Adam

Take My Tip
GB 1937 74m bw
Gaumont-British

Lord Pilkington gets his revenge on a confidence trickster when they meet at a Dalmatian hotel.
Reasonably lively comedy musical adapted for the stars.

w Sidney Gilliat, Michael Hogan, Jack Hulbert d Herbert Mason ph Bernard Knowles songs Sam Lerner, Al Goodheart, Al Hoffman

Jack Hulbert, Cicely Courtneidge, Frank Cellier, Harold Huth, Frank Pettingell, Robb Wilton, H. F. Maltby

Take One False Step•
US 1949 94m bw
U-I (Chester Erskine)

An innocent middle-aged man who has befriended a girl is hunted by the police when she is murdered.
Fairly absorbing and well-cast chase thriller in a minor key.

w Irwin Shaw, Chester Erskine, story Night Call by Irwin and David Shaw d Chester Erskine ph Franz Planer m Walter Scharf

William Powell, Shelley Winters, Marsha Hunt, Dorothy Hart, James Gleason, Felix Bressart, Art Baker, Sheldon Leonard

Take the High Ground
US 1953 101m Anscocolor
MGM (Dore Schary)

A tough sergeant trains army conscripts for action in Korea.
Very routine flagwaver.

w Millard Kaufman d Richard Brooks
ph John Alton m Dmitri Tiomkin

Richard Widmark, Karl Malden, Carleton Carpenter, Elaine Stewart, Russ Tamblyn, Jerome Courtland, Steve Forrest, Robert Arthur

AAN: Millard Kaufman

Take the Money and Run
US 1968 85m Technicolor
Palomar (Charles H. Joffe)

A social misfit becomes a bungling crook.
A torrent of middling visual gags, not the star's best vehicle.

wd Woody Allen ph Lester Shorr m Marvin Hamlisch

Woody Allen, Janet Margolin, Marcel Hillaire
● Video: Rank

The Taking of Pelham 123•
US 1974 104m Technicolor
Panavision
UA / Palomar / Palladium (Gabriel Katzka)

Four ruthless gunmen hold a New York subway train to ransom and have an ingenious plan for escape.
Entertaining crime caper made less enjoyable by all the fashionable faults the script is deliberately hard to follow and full of four

letter words, the sound track hard to hear, and the visuals ugly.

w Peter Stone, novel John Godey d Joseph Sargent ph Owen Roizman m David Shire

Walter Matthau, Robert Shaw, Martin Balsam, Hector Elizondo, Earl Hindman, James Broderick
'Full of noise and squalling and dirty words used for giggly shock effects.'—New Yorker

Taking Off••
US 1971 92m Movielab
Universal (Alfred W. Crown, Michael Hausman)

Suburban parents seek their errant daughter among the hippies, and gradually lose their own inhibitions.
Slight, formless, but amusing revue-style comment by a Czech director on the American scene.

w Milos Forman, John Guare, Jean-Claude Carrière, John Klein d Milos Forman
ph Miroslav Ondricek

Lynn Carlin, Buck Henry, Linnea Heacock

A Tale of Five Cities
GB 1951 99m bw
Grand National (Alexander Paal)
US title: A Tale of Five Women

An amnesiac American seeks clues to his past in Rome, Vienna, Paris, Berlin and London.
Tedious pattern drama remarkable only for its then untried cast.

w Patrick Kirwan, Maurice J. Wilson
d Montgomery Tully ph Gordon Lang
m Hans May

Bonar Colleano, Gina Lollobrigida, Barbara Kelly, Lana Morris, Anne Vernon, Eva Bartok

'His love challenged the flames of revolution!'
A Tale of Two Cities••
US 1935 121m bw
MGM (David O. Selznick)

A British lawyer sacrifices himself to save another man from the guillotine.
Richly detailed version of the classic melodrama, with production values counting more than the acting.

w W. P. Lipscomb, S. N. Behrman, novel Charles Dickens d Jack Conway ph Oliver T. Marsh m Herbert Stothart

Ronald Colman, Elizabeth Allan, Basil Rathbone, Edna May Oliver, Blanche Yurka, Reginald Owen, Henry B. Walthall, Donald Woods, Walter Catlett, H. B. Warner, Claude Gillingwater, Fritz Leiber
'A screen classic . . . technically it is about as flawless as possible . . . it has been made with respectful and loving care.'—Variety
† Originally prepared at Warners for Leslie Howard.

AAN: best picture

A Tale of Two Cities*
GB 1958 117m bw
Rank (Betty E. Box)

Modest but still costly remake with good moments but a rather slow pace.

w T. E. B. Clarke d Ralph Thomas
ph Ernest Steward m Richard Addinsell

Dirk Bogarde, Dorothy Tutin, Christopher Lee, Athene Seyler, Rosalie Crutchley, Ernest Clark, Stephen Murray, Paul Guers, Donald Pleasence, Ian Bannen, Cecil Parker, Alfie Bass

'Serviceable rather than imaginative.'—MFB

● Video: Rank

A Talent for Loving
US 1969 101m colour

Two generations of an international jet-setting family have woman trouble. Little-seen melodrama apparently disowned by those who made it. Richard Widmark, Cesar Romero, Topol, Genevieve Page. From the novel by Richard Condon; directed by Richard Quine; for Walter Shenson / Paramount.

Tales from the Crypt*
GB 1972 92m Eastmancolor
Metromedia / Amicus (Milton Subotsky)

Five people get lost in catacombs and are shown the future by a sinister monk who turns out to be Satan.
Fair ghoulish fun; a quintet of stories with a recognizable Amicus link.

w Milton Subotsky, from comic strips by William Gaines d Freddie Francis
ph Norman Warwick m Douglas Gamley

Ralph Richardson, Geoffrey Bayldon, Peter Cushing, Joan Collins, Ian Hendry, Robin Phillips, Richard Greene, Barbara Murray, Roy Dotrice, Nigel Patrick, Patrick Magee

Tales of Beatrix Potter**
GB 1971 90m Technicolor
EMI (Richard Goodwin)
US title: Peter Rabbit and the Tales of Beatrix Potter

Children's stories danced by the Royal Ballet in animal masks.
A charming entertainment for those who can appreciate it, though hardly the most direct way to tell these stories.

w Richard Goodwin, Christine Edward
d Reginald Mills ph Austin Dempster
m John Lanchbery ch Frederick Ashton
masks Rotislav Doboujinsky pd Christine Edward

● Video: Thorn EMI

The Tales of Hoffman**
GB 1951 127m Technicolor
British Lion / London / Michael Powell, Emeric Pressburger

The poet Hoffman, in three adventures, seeks the eternal woman and is beset by eternal evil.
Overwhelming combination of opera, ballet, and rich production design, an indigestible hodgepodge with flashes of superior talent.

wd Michael Powell, Emeric Pressburger
ph Christopher Challis m Jacques Offenbach
pd Hein Heckroth

Robert Rounseville, Robert Helpmann, Pamela Brown, Moira Shearer, Frederick Ashton, Leonide Massine, Ludmilla Tcherina, Ann Ayars, Mogens Wieth; music conducted by Sir Thomas Beecham with the Royal Philharmonic Orchestra

'The most spectacular failure yet achieved by Powell and Pressburger, who seem increasingly to dissipate their gifts in a welter of aimless ingenuity.'—Gavin Lambert

'An art director's picnic: I marvelled without being enthralled.'—Richard Mallett, Punch

Tales of Manhattan**
US 1942 118m bw
TCF (Boris Morros, Sam Spiegel)

Separate stories of a tail coat, which passes from owner to owner.
The stories are all rather disappointing in their different veins, but production standards are high and a few of the stars shine. A sequence starring W. C. Fields was deleted before release.

w Ben Hecht, Ferenc Molnar, Donald Ogden Stewart, Samuel Hoffenstein, Alan Campbell, Ladislas Fodor, Laslo Vadnay, Laszlo Gorog, Lamar Trotti, Henry Blankfort d Julien Duvivier ph Joseph Walker m Sol Kaplan

Charles Boyer, Rita Hayworth, Thomas Mitchell, Eugene Pallette; Ginger Rogers, Henry Fonda, Cesar Romero, Gail Patrick, Roland Young; Charles Laughton, Elsa Lanchester, Victor Francen, Christian Rub; Edward G. Robinson, George Sanders, James Gleason, Harry Davenport; Paul Robeson, Ethel Waters, Eddie Anderson

† Duvivier was clearly chosen to make this film because of his success with the similar Carnet de Bal; and he and Boyer went on to make the less successful Flesh and Fantasy on similar lines.

Tales of Ordinary Madness
Italy / France 1981 108m
Eastmancolor English version
23 Giugno / Ginis (Jacqueline Ferreri)

A drunken poet is obsessed by sex but can't find a happy relationship with his women. Outlandish, episodic wallow, mostly on Venice beach in California. Not for maiden aunts, and probably not for anyone else either.

w Marco Ferreri and others, from the book Erections, Ejaculations, Exhibitions and Tales of Ordinary Madness by Charles Bukowski d Marco Ferreri ph Tonino Delli Colli m Philippe Sarde

Ben Gazzara, Ornella Muti, Susan Tyrrell, Tanya Lopert, Katia Berger

'By turns repellent, naive and risible.'—Sight and Sound

● Video: VCL

Tales of Terror*
US 1962 90m Pathecolor Panavision
AIP (Roger Corman)

'Morella': a dying girl discovers the mummified body of her mother. 'The Black Cat': a henpecked husband kills his wife and walls up the body. 'The Facts in the Case of M Valdemar': an old man is hypnotized at the moment of death.
Tolerable short story compendium, rather short on subtlety and style.

w Richard Matheson, stories Edgar Allan Poe
d Roger Corman ph Floyd Crosby m Les Baxter

Vincent Price, Peter Lorre, Basil Rathbone, Debra Paget

● Video: Guild

'An orgy of the damned!'

Tales That Witness Madness
GB 1973 90m colour
Paramount / Amicus (Milton Subotsky, Norman Priggen)

Five ghostly tales linked by an old bookshop. Extreme example of the Amicus compendiums.

w Jay Fairbank d Freddie Francis
ph Norman Warwick m Bernard Ebbinghouse

Jack Hawkins, Donald Pleasence, Georgia Brown, Donald Houston, Suzy Kendall, Peter McEnery, Joan Collins, Michael Jayston, Kim Novak, Michael Petrovitch, Mary Tamm

Talk About a Stranger*
US 1952 65m bw
MGM (Richard Goldstone)

In a small town, gossip is unjustly aroused over a mysterious stranger who is suspected of various crimes.
Unusual though rather naïve second feature, directed for more than its worth.

w Margaret Fitts, novel Charlotte Armstrong
d David Bradley ph John Alton m David Buttolph

George Murphy, Nancy Davis, Lewis Stone, Billy Gray, Kurt Kasznar

Talk About Jacqueline
GB 1942 84m bw

A girl is mistaken for her naughtier sister. Thin, very British comedy with nowhere to go. Hugh Williams, Carla Lehmann, Joyce Howard, Roland Culver, John Warwick, Mary Jerrold, Guy Middleton, Max Adrian. Written by Roland Pertwee and Marjorie Deans, from a novel by Katherine Holland; directed by Harold French; for Excelsior / Marcel Hellman.

Talk of the Devil
GB 1936 78m bw

An impersonator pins a crooked deal on a magnate, who kills himself. Glum drama chiefly notable as the first film to be shot at Pinewood Studios. Ricardo Cortez, Sally Eilers, Basil Sydney, Randle Ayrton, Charles Carson. Written by Carol Reed, George Barraud and Anthony Kimmins; directed by Carol Reed; for B and D.

TAKE MY LIFE. Hugh Williams and Greta Gynt defy the law for a comforting cuddle.

The Talk of the Town°°°
US 1942 118m bw
Columbia (George Stevens, Fred Guiol)

A girl loves both a suspected murderer and the lawyer who defends him.

Unusual mixture of comedy and drama, delightfully handled by three sympathetic stars.

w *Irwin Shaw, Sidney Buchman* d *George Stevens* ph *Ted Tetzlaff* m *Frederick Hollander*

Roland Colman, Cary Grant, Jean Arthur, Edgar Buchanan, Glenda Farrell, Charles Dingle, Emma Dunn, Rex Ingram

'A rip-roaring, knock-down-and-drag-out comedy about civil liberties.'—*John T. McManus*

'Well tuned and witty, at its best when it sticks to the middle ground between farce and melodrama. The chief fault of the script is its excessive length and the fact that a standard lynching mob climax is followed by a prolonged anti-climax.'—*Newsweek*

'I can't take my lynching so lightly, even in a screwball. Still, I am all for this kind of comedy and for players like Arthur and Grant, who can mug more amusingly than most scriptwriters can write.'—*Manny Farber*

'Did the authors think they were writing a Shavian comedy of ideas? The ideas are garbled and silly, but the people are so

pleasant that the picture manages to be quite amiable and high-spirited.'—*Pauline Kael, 70s*

AAN: best picture; original story (Sidney Harmon); script; Ted Tetzlaff; Frederick Hollander

Tall, Dark and Handsome
US 1941 78m bw

In 1929 Chicago, a gangster aspires to be a gentleman. Moderate crime comedy. Cesar Romero, Virginia Gilmore, Charlotte Greenwood, Milton Berle, Sheldon Leonard. Written by Karl Tunberg and Darrell Ware; directed by H. Bruce Humberstone; for TCF.

The Tall Headlines
GB 1952 100m bw
Grand National / Raymond Stross
aka: *The Frightened Bride*

A family is affected when the eldest son is executed for murder.

Glum, boring, badly cast, badly written and generally inept melodrama.

w *Audrey Erskine Lindop* (from her novel), *Dudley Leslie* d *Terence Young* ph *C. M. Pennington-Richards* m *Hans May*

Flora Robson, Michael Denison, Mai Zetterling, Jane Hylton, André Morell, Dennis Price, Mervyn Johns, Naunton Wayne

'A falsity which will surely surprise even those familiar with the conventions of British middle-class cinema.'—*Lindsay Anderson*

Tall in the Saddle
US 1944 87m bw
RKO (Robert Fellows)

The newly-arrived ranch foreman finds that his boss has been murdered.

Quite a watchable, and forgettable, mystery western.

w *Michael Hogan, Paul J. Fix* d *Edwin L. Marin* ph *Robert de Grasse* m *Roy Webb* md *Constantin Bakaleinikoff*

John Wayne, Ella Raines, Ward Bond, George 'Gabby' Hayes, Audrey Long, Elizabeth Risdon, Don Douglas, Paul Fix, Russell Wade

Tall Man Riding
US 1955 83m Warnercolor

An adventurer feuds with a rancher but in the end marries his daughter. Unremarkable star western. Randolph Scott, Robert Barrat, Dorothy Malone, Peggie Castle, John Dehner. Written by Joseph Hoffman; directed by Lesley Selander; for Warner.

The Tall Men°
US 1955 122m De Luxe Cinemascope
TCF (William A. Bacher, William B. Hawks)

After the Civil War, two Texans head north for the Montana goldfields.

Solid star western.

w *Sidney Boehm, Frank Nugent, novel* Clay Fisher d *Raoul Walsh* ph *Leo Tover* m *Victor Young*

Clark Gable, Jane Russell, Robert Ryan, Cameron Mitchell, Juan Garcia, Harry Shannon, Emile Meyer

'A big action feast and value for anyone's money.'—*Newsweek*

Tall Story
US 1960 91m bw
Warner / Mansfield (Joshua Logan)

A college basketball player faces various kinds of trouble when he marries.

Dislikeable campus comedy with leading players miscast.

w *Julius J. Epstein, novel* The Homecoming Game by Howard Nemoor d *Joshua Logan* ph *Ellsworth Fredericks* m *Cyril Mockridge*

Anthony Perkins, Jane Fonda, Ray Walston, Anne Jackson, Marc Connelly, Murray Hamilton, Elizabeth Patterson

The Tall Stranger
US 1957 83m De Luxe Cinemascope

Cared for by wagon train pioneers after being mysteriously shot, a rancher tries to help them settle. Fair star western with some tough action. Joel McCrea, Virginia Mayo, Barry Kelley, Michael Ansara, Whit Bissell. Written by Christopher Knopf, from a story by Louis L'Amour; directed by Thomas Carr; for Allied Artists.

The Tall T°
US 1957 78m Technicolor
Columbia / Scott–Brown (Harry Joe Brown)

Three bandits hold up a stagecoach and take a hostage, but are outwitted by a rancher.

Good small-scale suspense western with plenty of action and a blood-spattered finale.

w *Burt Kennedy* d *Budd Boetticher*
ph Charles Lawton Jnr m Heinz Roemheld

Randolph Scott, Richard Boone, Maureen O'Sullivan, Arthur Hunnicutt, Skip Homeier, John Hubbard, Henry Silva

The Tall Target**
US 1951 78m bw
MGM (Richard Goldstone)

A discredited police officer tries to stop the assassination of Abraham Lincoln on a train to Washington.
Lively period suspenser with excellent attention to detail and much of the attraction of *The Lady Vanishes*. The plot slightly relaxes its hold before the end.

w *George Worthing Yates, Art Cohn*
d *Anthony Mann* ph Paul C. Vogel ad Cedric Gibbons, Eddie Imazu

Dick Powell, Adolphe Menjou, Paula Raymond, Marshall Thompson, *Ruby Dee*, Richard Rober, Will Geer, Florence Bates
'An intelligent minor picture which makes good use of its material.'—*MFB*

Tamahine
GB 1962 95m Technicolor
Cinemascope
ABP (John Bryan)

The headmaster of a boys' school is visited by his glamorous half-caste Polynesian cousin.
Simple-minded school comedy with predictable situations.

w *Denis Cannan*, novel Thelma Niklaus
d *Philip Leacock* ph Geoffrey Unsworth
m Malcolm Arnold

John Fraser, Nancy Kwan, Dennis Price, Derek Nimmo, Justine Lord, James Fox, Coral Browne, Michael Gough, Allan Cuthbertson

The Tamarind Seed*
GB 1974 125m Eastmancolor
Panavision
Jewel / Lorimar / Pimlico (Ken Wales)

While holidaying in Barbados, a British widow falls for a Russian military attaché.
Old-fashioned romance which turns into a mild spy caper. A well-heeled time-passer.

w *Blake Edwards*, novel Evelyn Anthony
d *Blake Edwards* ph Frederick A. Young
m John Barry

Julie Andrews, Omar Sharif, Sylvia Syms, Dan O'Herlihy, Anthony Quayle, Oscar Homolka
'A painless timekiller, but one wishes Miss Andrews didn't always give the impression that she had just left her horse in the hallway.'—*Michael Billington, Illustrated London News*

The Taming of the Shrew*
US 1929 68m bw
United Artists / Pickford / Elton

A condensed version of the play which did not do much in its day for its stars' then declining reputations, but can now be watched with a fair measure of enjoyment.

w *William Shakespeare*, 'with additional dialogue by Sam Taylor' d *Sam Taylor*
ph Karl Struss pd William Cameron Menzies, Laurence Irving

Douglas Fairbanks, Mary Pickford, Edwin Maxwell, Joseph Cawthorn, Clyde Cook, Dorothy Jordan

† A 'widescreen' version was issued in 1976.

'In the war between the sexes, there always comes a time to surrender unconditionally!'
The Taming of the Shrew*
US 1967 122m Technicolor
Panavision
Columbia / Royal / FAI (Richard McWhorter)

Petruchio violently tames his shrewish wife.
Busy version of one of Shakespeare's more proletarian comedies; the words in this case take second place to violent action and rioting colour.

w *Suso Cecchi d'Amico, Paul Dehn, Franco Zeffirelli* d *Franco Zeffirelli* ph Oswald Morris, Luciano Trasatti m Nino Rota

Richard Burton, Elizabeth Taylor, Michael York, Michael Hordern, Cyril Cusack, Alfred Lynch, Natasha Pyne, Alan Webb, Victor Spinetti
'As entertainment *Kiss Me Kate* is infinitely better but then Cole Porter was a real artist and Burton is a culture vulture.'—*Wilfrid Sheed*
'The old warhorse of a comedy has been spanked into uproarious life.'—*Hollis Alpert*

Tam-Lin
GB 1971 106m Technicolor
Panavision
Winkast (Jerry Gershwin, Elliott Kastner) / Commonwealth United
aka: *The Devil's Widow; The Ballad of Tam-Lin*

A sinister, beautiful, middle-aged widow has a diabolic influence on the bright young people she gathers around her.
Self-indulgent melodrama which might have worked with a shorter running time and a tighter script; as it was, it sank almost without trace.

w *William Spier*, poem Robert Burns
d *Roddy McDowall* ph Willy Williams
m Stanley Myers

Ava Gardner, Ian MacShane, Richard Wattis, Cyril Cusack, Stephanie Beacham, David Whitman, Fabia Drake, Sinead Cusack, Joanna Lumley, Jenny Hanley

Tammy and the Bachelor*
US 1957 89m Technicolor
Cinemascope
U-I (Ross Hunter)
GB title: *Tammy*

A backwoods tomboy falls for a stranded flier.
Whimsical romance for middle America, which started Hollywood's last series of proletarian family appeal before the family was entirely forsaken for four letter words.

w *Oscar Brodney*, from stories by Cid Ricketts Summer d *Joseph Pevney* ph Arthur E. Arling m Frank Skinner md Joseph Gershenson

Debbie Reynolds, Walter Brennan, Leslie Nielsen, Mala Powers, Fay Wray, Sidney Blackmer, Mildred Natwick

Tammy and the Doctor
US 1963 88m Eastmancolor
U-I / Ross Hunter

Tammy leaves her riverboat to accompany an old lady who needs an operation in the big city.
More artless family fodder.

w *Oscar Brodney* d *Harry Keller* ph Russell Metty m Frank Skinner

Sandra Dee, Peter Fonda, Macdonald Carey, Beulah Bondi, Margaret Lindsay, Reginald Owen, Adam West
'The aura of simple religion and naïve philosophy remains singularly charmless.'—*MFB*

Tammy and the Millionaire
US 1967 88m Technicolor

Tammy becomes a private secretary in the big city. A re-edit from four half-hour TV shows; not at all watchable. Debbie Watson, Donald Woods, Dorothy Green, Denver Pyle, Frank McGrath. Written by George Tibbles; directed by Sidney Miller, Leslie Goodwins and Ezra Stone; for Universal.

Tammy Tell Me True
US 1961 97m Eastmancolor
U-I (Ross Hunter)

Tammy gets a college education and charms all comers.
Sugar-coated sequel to the original.

w *Oscar Brodney* d *Harry Keller* ph Clifford Stine m Percy Faith

Sandra Dee, John Gavin, Charles Drake, Virginia Grey, *Beulah Bondi*, Julia Meade, Cecil Kellaway, Edgar Buchanan
'The heroine appears to be not so much old-fashioned as positively retarded.'—*MFB*

Tampico
US 1944 75m bw
TCF (Robert Bassler)

A tanker captain picks up survivors from a torpedoed ship and finds himself involved with spies.
Very minor action melodrama, efficiently made.

w *Kenneth Gamet, Fred Niblo Jnr, Richard Macauly* d *Lothar Mendes* ph Charles G. Clarke m David Raksin

Edward G. Robinson, Lynn Bari, Victor McLaglen, Marc Lawrence, E. J. Ballentine, Mona Maris

Tanganyika
US 1954 81m Technicolor

A 1900 settler finds that the African colony of his choice is terrorized by a murderer. Curious blend of outdoor action and who-is-it; not at all bad. Van Heflin, Howard Duff, Ruth Roman, Jeff Morrow, Joe Comadaore. Written by Richard Alan Simmons and William Sackheim; directed by André de Toth; for Universal-International.

Tangier
US 1946 74m bw

A dancer hunts for the Nazi war criminal responsible for her father's death. You can tell returns had been bad from the fact that the queen of Technicolor was sentenced to monochrome, and in a two-bit *Casablanca*. Maria Montez, Kent Taylor, Robert Paige, Sabu, Preston Foster, Louise Allbritton, Reginald Denny, J. Edward Bromberg. Written by M. M. Musselman and Monty Collins; directed by George Waggner; for Universal-International.

Tank
US 1984 113m Metrocolor
Lorimar / Universal (Irwin Yablands)

A retired army sergeant lovingly restores an old tank and uses it to secure justice for his wrongly imprisoned son.
Fairly lively if predictable American fantasy in which one just man stands up against the uncaring and / or corrupt mob.

w Dan Gordon d Marvin Chomsky ph Don Birnkrant m Lalo Schifrin pd Bill Kenney

James Garner, Shirley Jones, C. Thomas Howell, Mark Herrier, Dorian Harewood, G. D. Spradlin

'Further dispiriting evidence of the new reactionary spirit of Reagan's America.'— *Tom Milne, MFB*

The Tanks Are Coming
US 1951 90m bw

A tough sergeant learns humility during the race to Berlin. Tedious war drama which tries in vain to interest us in non-characters. Steve Cochran, Paul Picerni, Mari Aldon, Harry Bellaver, Philip Carey. Written by Robert Hardy Andrews; directed by D. Ross Lederman and Lewis Seiler; for Warner.

Tap Roots
US 1948 109m Technicolor
Universal-International (Walter Wanger)

A southern family tries to remain neutral in the Civil War.
Minor *Gone with the Wind* saga, quite expensively produced but not very exciting.
w Alan le May, *novel* James Street d George Marshall ph Winton C. Hoch, Lionel Lindon m Frank Skinner

Susan Hayward, Van Heflin, Boris Karloff, Julie London, Whitfield Connor

Taps
US 1981 126m De Luxe
TCF / Stanley Jaffe

Cadets at a military academy go on strike when the site is sold for development, and violence ensues.
Rather uninteresting moral fable, comparable with the British *If*. The moral attitudes are worked out on entirely predictable lines.

w Darryl Ponicsan, Robert Mark Kamen, *novel* Father Sky by Devery Freeman d Harold Becker ph Owen Roizman m Maurice Jarre

Timothy Hutton, George C. Scott, Ronny Cox, Sean Penn, Tom Cruise, Brendan Ward

Tarantula
US 1955 80m bw
U-I (William Alland)

Scientists working on an artificial food become grossly misshapen, and an infected spider escapes and grows to giant size.
Moderate monster hokum with the desert setting which became a cliché; the grotesque faces are more horrific than the spider, which seldom seems to touch the ground.

w Robert M. Fresco, Martin Berkeley d Jack Arnold ph George Robinson md Joseph Gershenson

Leo G. Carroll, John Agar, Mara Corday, Nestor Paiva

Taras Bulba*
US 1962 124m Eastmancolor
Panavision
UA / H-H / Avala (Harold Hecht)

A cossack leader has bitter disagreements with his rebellious son.
Violent action epic based on a well-worn story; plenty of spectacular highlights.

w Waldo Salt, Karl Tunberg, *novel* Nicolai Gogol d J. Lee-Thompson ph Joe MacDonald m Franz Waxman pd Edward Carrere

Yul Brynner, Tony Curtis, Christine Kaufmann, Sam Wanamaker, Guy Rolfe, George Macready, Vladimir Sokoloff, Abraham Sofaer

'Now! Add a motion picture to the wonders of the world!'—*publicity*
AAN: Franz Waxman

Target Zero
US 1955 93m bw
Warner (David Weisbart)

An infantry patrol in Korea is cut off behind enemy lines.
Routine battle exploits with a highly unlikely superimposed romance.

w Sam Rolfe d Harmon Jones ph Edwin DuPar m David Buttolph

Richard Conte, Charles Bronson, Richard Stapley, Chuck Connors, L. Q. Jones, Peggie Castle

Targets*
US 1967 90m Pathecolor
(Paramount) Peter Bogdanovich

An elderly horror film star confronts and

disarms a mad sniper at a drive-in movie.
Oddball melodrama apparently meant to contrast real and fantasy violence; it doesn't quite work despite effective moments, and the low budget shows.

wd Peter Bogdanovich ph Laszlo Kovacs

Boris Karloff, Tim O'Kelly, James Brown, Sandy Baron

The Tarnished Angels
US 1957 91m bw Cinemascope
U-I (Albert Zugsmith)

A reporter falls in with a self-torturing family of circus air aces.
Unsatisfactory attempt to reunite the talents of *Written on the Wind*; a dull story, very boringly presented.

w George Zuckerman, *novel* Pylon by William Faulkner d Douglas Sirk ph Irving Glassberg m Frank Skinner md Joseph Gershenson

Rock Hudson, Robert Stack, Dorothy Malone, Jack Carson, Robert Middleton

Tarnished Lady
US 1931 80m bw
Paramount

Two society women and their lovers cross each other's paths. Exaggerated melodrama which failed to justify the London stage reputation of its American star. Tallulah Bankhead, Clive Brook, Phoebe Foster, Alexander Kirkland, Osgood Perkins, Elizabeth Patterson. Written by Donald Ogden Stewart; directed by George Cukor; for Paramount. 'A poor picture that fits the straight grinds best. Heavy production but too ponderous to mean anything.'— *Variety*

The Tartars
Italy 1960 105m Technicolor
Totalscope
Lux (Riccardo Gualino)

Viking settlers on the Russian steppes fight Tartar invaders.
Action-packed comic strip.

d Richard Thorpe ph Amerigo Genarelli m Renzo Rossellini

Orson Welles, Victor Mature, Folco Lulli, Arnoldo Foa

Tarzan
The talkie *Tarzans* began with Johnny Weissmuller and tailed off from there. (See *Filmgoer's Companion* for the silents.) The 1932 version more or less followed the original Edgar Rice Burroughs novel, and all the MGM entries had a special vivid quality about them, but subsequently the productions, usually produced under the aegis of Sol Lesser, tailed off towards the standard of the TV series of the sixties starring Ron Ely.
1932: TARZAN THE APE MAN** (MGM: Weissmuller with Maureen O'Sullivan: d W. S. Van Dyke: 99m)
1933: TARZAN THE FEARLESS (Principal: Buster Crabbe: d Robert Hill: 73m)
1934: TARZAN AND HIS MATE*** (MGM: Weissmuller with Maureen O'Sullivan: d Cedric Gibbons: 105m)

'Certainly one of the funniest things you'll ever see.'—*Otis Ferguson*

1935: THE NEW ADVENTURES OF TARZAN (Burroughs: Herman Brix: *d* Edward Kull: 75m)

1936: TARZAN ESCAPES** (MGM: Weissmuller with Maureen O'Sullivan: *d* Richard Thorpe: 95m)

1938: TARZAN'S REVENGE (Sol Lesser: Glenn Morris: *d* D. Ross Lederman: 70m); TARZAN AND THE GREEN GODDESS (Principal: Herman Brix: *d* Edward Kull: 72m: largely a re-edit of NEW ADVENTURES)

1939: TARZAN FINDS A SON (MGM: Weissmuller with O'Sullivan: Richard Thorpe: 90m)

1941: TARZAN'S SECRET TREASURE (MGM: Weissmuller with O'Sullivan: *d* Richard Thorpe: 81m)

1942: TARZAN'S NEW YORK ADVENTURE (MGM: Weissmuller with O'Sullivan: *d* Richard Thorpe: 71m)

1943: TARZAN TRIUMPHS (RKO: Weissmuller: *d* William Thiele: 78m); TARZAN'S DESERT MYSTERY (RKO: Weissmuller: *d* William Thiele: 70m)

1945: TARZAN AND THE AMAZONS (RKO: Weissmuller: *d* Kurt Neumann: 76m)

1946: TARZAN AND THE LEOPARD WOMAN (RKO: Weissmuller: *d* Kurt Neumann: 72m)

1947: TARZAN AND THE HUNTRESS (RKO: Weissmuller: *d* Kurt Neumann: 72m)

1948: TARZAN AND THE MERMAIDS (RKO: *d* Robert Florey: Weissmuller: 68m)

1949: TARZAN'S MAGIC FOUNTAIN (RKO: Lex Barker: *d* Lee Sholem: 73m)

1950: TARZAN AND THE SLAVE GIRL (RKO: Lex Barker: *d* Lee Sholem: 74m)

1951: TARZAN'S PERIL (RKO: Lex Barker: *d* Byron Haskin: 79m)

1952: TARZAN'S SAVAGE FURY (RKO: Lex Barker: *d* Cy Endfield: 80m)

1953: TARZAN AND THE SHE-DEVIL (RKO: Lex Barker: *d* Kurt Neumann: 76m)

1955: TARZAN'S HIDDEN JUNGLE (RKO: Gordon Scott: *d* Harold Schuster: 73m)

1957: TARZAN AND THE LOST SAFARI (colour) (MGM: Gordon Scott: *d* Bruce Humberstone: 84m)

1958: TARZAN'S FIGHT FOR LIFE (colour) (MGM: Gordon Scott: *d* Bruce Humberstone: 86m)

1959: TARZAN'S GREATEST ADVENTURE (colour) (Paramount: Gordon Scott: *d* John Guillermin: 90m)

1959: TARZAN THE APE MAN (colour: remake of the original story) (MGM: Denny Miller: *d* Joseph Newman: 82m)

1960: TARZAN THE MAGNIFICENT (colour) (Paramount: Gordon Scott: *d* Robert Day: 88m)

1962: TARZAN GOES TO INDIA (colour) (MGM: Jock Mahoney: *d* John Guillermin: 86m)

1963: TARZAN'S THREE CHALLENGES (colour) (MGM: Jock Mahoney: *d* Robert Day: 92m)

1966: TARZAN AND THE VALLEY OF GOLD (colour) (NatGen: Mike Henry: Robert Day: 90m)

1967: TARZAN AND THE GREAT RIVER (colour) (Paramount: Mike Henry: *d* Robert Day: 88m)

1968: TARZAN AND THE JUNGLE BOY (colour) (Paramount: Mike Henry: *d* Robert Day: 90m)

1981: TARZAN THE APE MAN (colour)

1983: GREYSTOKE (*qv*) (MGM: Miles O'Keefe; *d* John Derek; 112m). A debased version with the emphasis on the undressed Jane played by Bo Derek. Because of the star the film had an amusing tagline: 'The most exciting pair in the jungle!'

● *Video: MGM / UA*

Task Force

US 1949   116m   bw (Technicolor sequences)
Warner (Jerry Wald)

An admiral about to retire recalls his struggle to promote the cause of aircraft carriers.
Stilted and long-drawn-out flagwaver with too much chat and action highlights borrowed from wartime newsreel.

wd Delmer Daves   *ph* Robert Burks, Wilfrid M. Cline   *m* Franz Waxman

Gary Cooper, Walter Brennan, Jane Wyatt, Wayne Morris, Julie London, Bruce Bennett, Stanley Ridges, Jack Holt

A Taste of Excitement

GB 1968   99m   Eastmancolor
Trio Films (George Willoughby)

An English girl holidaying on the Riviera suspects that someone is trying to kill her.
Standard frightened lady / 'they won't believe me' mystery with enough twists to satisfy addicts.

w Brian Carton, Don Sharp, *novel* Waiting for a Tiger by Ben Healey   *d* Don Sharp   *ph* Paul Beeson   *m* Keith Mansfield

Eva Renzi, David Buck, Peter Vaughan, Sophie Hardy, Paul Hubschmid, Kay Walsh

Taste of Fear**

GB 1961   82m   bw
Columbia / Hammer (Jimmy Sangster)
US title: *Scream of Fear*

A crippled heiress visits her long-lost father and is haunted by his corpse.
Smartly tricked-out sub-Hitchcock screamer with sudden shocks among the Riviera settings and a plot which Hammer borrowed from *Les Diaboliques* and used again and again.

w Jimmy Sangster   *d* Seth Holt   *ph* Douglas Slocombe   *m* Clifton Parker

Susan Strasberg, Ann Todd, Ronald Lewis, Christopher Lee, Leonard Sachs
'All those creaking shutters, flickering candles, wavering shadows and pianos playing in empty rooms still yield a tiny frisson.'—*Penelope Houston*

A Taste of Honey***

GB 1961   100m   bw
British Lion / Bryanston / Woodfall (Tony Richardson)

Adventures of a pregnant Salford teenager, her sluttish mother, black lover and homosexual friend.
Fascinating offbeat comedy drama with memorable characters and sharply etched backgrounds.

w Shelagh Delaney, Tony Richardson, *play* Shelagh Delaney   *d* Tony Richardson   *ph* Walter Lassally   *m* John Addison

Rita Tushingham, Dora Bryan, Murray Melvin, Robert Stephens, Paul Danquah
'Tart and lively around the edges and bitter at the core.'—*Peter John Dyer*

Taste the Blood of Dracula

GB 1969   95m   Technicolor
Hammer (Aida Young)

A depraved peer involves three Victorian businessmen in the reactivation of Dracula.
Latterday vampire saga, initially lively but mainly dreary.

w John Elder   *d* Peter Sasdy   *ph* Arthur Grant   *m* James Bernard

Christopher Lee, Geoffrey Keen, Gwen Watford, Linda Hayden, Peter Sallis, Anthony Corlan, John Carson, Ralph Bates

The Tattered Dress

US 1957   93m   bw   Cinemascope
U-I (Albert Zugsmith)

While conducting a murder defence, a criminal lawyer annoys a vindictive small-town sheriff, who plots revenge.
Silly melodrama which rapidly loses interest after a promising start.

w George Zuckerman   *d* Jack Arnold   *ph* Carl Guthrie   *m* Frank Skinner

Jeff Chandler, Jack Carson, Jeanne Crain, Gail Russell, George Tobias, Edward Andrews, Philip Reed

'Every great love leaves its mark!'

Tattoo

US 1980   103m   Technicolor
Joseph E. Levine (Robert F. Colesberry)

A mad tattooist kidnaps a cover girl and tattoos her all over before forcing her to have sex. She kills him.
And not before time.

w Joyce Bunuel   *d* Bob Brooks   *ph* Arthur Ornitz   *m* Barry de Vorzon   *pd* Stuart Wurtzel

Bruce Dern, Maud Adams, Leonard Frey, Rikke Borge
'*The Collector* crossed with *Ai No Corrida* . . . a sensational package for the eighties confected from ideas half remembered from other films.'—*Mark Lefanu, MFB*

● *Video: Thorn EMI*

Tawny Pipit*

GB 1944   85m   bw
GFD / Two Cities (Bernard Miles)

The life of a village in wartime is disrupted when two rare birds nest in a local meadow.

Pleasant, thin little comedy, a precursor of the
Ealing school.

w Bernard Miles d Bernard Miles, Charles
Saunders

Bernard Miles, Rosamund John, Niall
MacGinnis, Jean Gillie, Christopher Steele,
Lucie Mannheim, Brefni O'Rourke, Marjorie
Rhodes

'Almost unimaginably genteel.'—*James
Agee*

'Not quite dry enough for the epicures nor
sweet enough for the addicts.'—*C. A. Lejeune*

Taxi!
US 1931 68m bw
Warner (Robert Lord)

Independent cab drivers defy a powerful trust.
Sassy comedy drama with plenty going on.

w Kubec Glasmon, John Bright, *play* The
Blind Spot by Kenyon Nicholson d Roy del
Ruth ph James Van Trees md Leo Forbstein

James Cagney, Loretta Young, George E.
Stone, Guy Kibbee, David Landau, Leila
Bennett, Matt McHugh

'As a deese, dem and dose, chip-on-the-
shoulder, on-the-make example of young
America the audience knows no better
interpretation on the screen than that which
Cagney gives it. The populace are now
expectant of this player socking all and sundry
including all the women in the cast.'—*Variety*

'A sordid but amusing observation on minor
metropolitan endeavours.'—*Time*

Taxi
US 1952 77m bw
TCF (Samuel G. Engel)

A taxi driver helps a young mother find her
husband, and falls for her himself.
Practised sentimental guff, Hollywoodized
from the French film *Sans Laisser d'Adresse*.

w D. M. Marshman Jnr, Daniel Fuchs
d Gregory Ratoff ph Milton Krasner
m Leigh Harline

Dan Dailey, Constance Smith, Neva
Patterson, Blanche Yurka, Walter Woolf King

The Taxi Dancer
US 1926 64m at 24 fps bw silent

A Virginia girl in the big city rises from
dime-a-dance joints to the big time. Mildly
suggestive star melodrama which promises
more than it gives. Joan Crawford, Owen
Moore, Douglas Gilmore, Marc McDermott,
Gertrude Astor. Written by A. P. Younger
and Robert Terry Shannon; directed by Harry
Millarde; for MGM.

Taxi Driver***
US 1976 114m Metrocolor
Columbia / Italo–Judeo (Michael and Julia
   Philips)

A lonely Vietnam veteran becomes a New
York taxi driver and allows the violence and
squalor around him to explode in his mind.
The epitome of the sordid realism of the
seventies, this unlovely but brilliantly made
film haunts the mind and paints a most vivid

picture of a hell on earth. Unfortunately the
plot in the latter stages makes no sense.

w Paul Schraeder d Martin Scorsese
ph Michael Chapman m Bernard Herrmann
Robert de Niro, Jodie Foster, Cybill Shepherd,
Peter Boyle, Leonard Harris, Harvey Keitel

'I don't question the truth of this material. I
question Scorsese's ability to lift it out of the
movie gutters into which less truthful directors
have trampled it.'—*Stanley Kauffmann*
† Schraeder says the story was modelled after
the diaries of would-be assassin Arthur
Bremer.

AAN: best picture; Bernard Herrmann;
Robert de Niro; Jodie Foster

Taza, Son of Cochise
US 1954 79m Technicolor

Peace-loving Taza succeeds his dad and tries
not to be influenced by Geronimo. Routine
pro-Indian western. Rock Hudson (as Taza),
Barbara Rush, Gregg Palmer, Bart Roberts,
Morris Ankrum. Written by George
Zuckerman and Gerald Drayson Adams;
directed by Douglas Sirk; for Universal-
International.

'Years from now, when you talk about
   this—and you will—be kind!'
Tea and Sympathy
US 1956 122m Metrocolor
   Cinemascope
MGM (Pandro S. Berman)

A sensitive teenage schoolboy is scorned by
his tougher classmates, but his housemaster's
wife takes him in hand . . .
Overblown and bowdlerized version of a quiet
little Broadway play; impeccable production
values, but no spark.

w Robert Anderson (and the Hays office),
from his play d Vincente Minnelli ph John
Alton m Adolph Deutsch

Deborah Kerr, *John Kerr*, Leif Erickson,
Edward Andrews, Darryl Hickman

'Even the most daring story can be brought
onto the screen when done with courage,
honesty and good taste.'—*publicity*
'. . . mounted for the screen as if it were a
precious *objet d'art* in danger from rioting but
miraculously saved. Besides being archaic, the
film is a prodigiously silly fable, pulling the
realities with which it deals dishonestly,
systematically out of whack.'—*Parker Tyler*

Tea for Two*
US 1950 97m Technicolor
Warner (William Jacobs)

A nearly bankrupt financier promises his niece
25,000 dollars for her new musical show if she
can say no to every question for twenty-four
hours.
Tinkly, quite amusing light musical which has
little to do with *No No Nanette* on which it is
allegedly based.

w Henry Clark d David Butler ph Wilfrid
Cline md Ray Heindorf ch Le Roy Prinz

Doris Day, Gordon Macrae, Gene Nelson,
Eve Arden, Billy de Wolfe, S. Z. Sakall, Bill
Goodwin, Patrice Wymore

Teachers
US 1984 106m Metrocolor
MGM-UA (Aaron Russo)

A burnt-out teacher is drawn back to his ideas
despite, or because of, apparent lunacy in the
administration.
Wildly unconsidered black comedy which
takes stabs at everything and hits nothing.

w W. R. McKinney d Arthur Hiller
ph David M. Walsh m Sandy Gibson
pd Richard MacDonald ed Don Zimmermann

Nick Nolte, JoBeth Williams, Judd Hirsch,
Ralph Macchio, Richard Mulligan, Allen
Garfield, Royal Dano

Teacher's Pet*
US 1957 120m bw Vistavision
Paramount / Perlberg–Seaton (William
   Perlberg)

A tough city editor falls for a lady professor of
journalism and enrols as a student.
Overlong one-joke comedy which quickly
reneges on its early promise; but the principals
play up divertingly.

w Fay and Michael Kanin d George Seaton
ph Haskell Boggs m Roy Webb

Clark Gable, Doris Day, Gig Young, Mamie
Van Doren, Nick Adams

AAN: Fay and Michael Kanin; Gig Young

The Teahouse of the August Moon*
US 1956 123m Metrocolor
   Cinemascope
MGM (Jack Cummings)

Okinawa 1944: a wily interpreter helps
American troops succumb to the oriental way
of life.
Adequate, well-acted screen version of a
Broadway comedy which succeeded largely
because of its theatricality. A few good jokes
remain.

w John Patrick, from his play d Daniel Mann
ph John Alton m Saul Chaplin

Marlon Brando, Glenn Ford, Eddie Albert,
Paul Ford, Michiko Kyo, Henry Morgan

The Teckman Mystery
GB 1954 90m bw
British Lion / London Films / Corona (Josef
   Somlo)

An author commissioned to write the
biography of a dead airman finds him very
much alive and his own life in danger.
Peripatetic spy story with the twists expected
of this author; all quite enjoyable.

w Francis Durbridge, James Matthews, *BBC
serial* Francis Durbridge d Wendy Toye
ph Jack Hilyard m Clifton Parker

Margaret Leighton, John Justin, Michael
Medwin, Meier Tzelniker, Roland Culver,
George Coulouris, Raymond Huntley,
Duncan Lamont

Teenage Rebel
US 1956 94m bw Cinemascope
TCF (Charles Brackett)

A wealthy California woman is visited by her

teenage daughter from a former marriage; the girl proceeds to make difficulties for everyone. The first film in black-and-white Cinemascope is a tedious drama of unreal people.

w Walter Reisch, Charles Brackett, *play* Edith Sommer *d* Edmund Goulding *ph* Joe MacDonald *m* Leigh Harline

Ginger Rogers, Michael Rennie, Mildred Natwick, Betty Lou Keim, Warren Berlinger, Louise Beavers, Irene Hervey

Teheran
GB 1947 86m bw

A correspondent in Iran foils an assassination plot. Low-key blood and thunder; passable time-filler. Derek Farr, Marta Labarr, Manning Whiley, John Slater, John Warwick. Written by Akos Tolnay and William Freshman; directed by William Freshman and Giacomo Gentilomo; for Pendennis. (US title: *The Plot to Kill Roosevelt*.)

'Your next phone call may be your last!'
Telefon°
US 1977 103m Metrocolor
MGM (James B. Harris)

A Russian agent is instructed to seek out and destroy a ring of hard liners who are opposing detente with the west.
Moderately watchable espionage capers with a slightly new twist.

w Peter Hyams, Stirling Silliphant, *novel* Walter Wager *d* Don Siegel *ph* Michael Butler *m* Lalo Schifrin

Charles Bronson, Lee Remick, Donald Pleasence, Tyne Daly, Alan Badel, Patrick Magee, Sheree North

Television Spy
US 1939 58m bw

Enemy agents compete for the secret of long-range television transmission. Watchable pocket thriller, with the hero and heroine getting acquainted only by television from a 3000-mile distance. William Henry, Judith Barrett, William Collier Snr, Anthony Quinn, Richard Denning, John Eldredge. Written by Horace McCoy, William R. Lipman, Lillie Hayward; directed by Edward Dmytryk; for Paramount. 'It may move slowly, but it does avoid the absurdity that goes with the average film crack at television.'—*Variety*

Tell England
GB 1931 88m bw
US title: *The Battle of Gallipoli*

In 1914, school chums join up and mostly die at Gallipoli. Even the most patriotic audiences ended up roaring with laughter at this stiff-upper-lip charade. Carl Harbord, Fay Compton, Tony Bruce, Dennis Hoey, Gerald Rawlinson, Wally Patch. Written by Anthony Asquith, from the novel by Ernest Raymond; directed by Anthony Asquith and Gerald Barkas; for British Instructional. 'Not likely to bring in any money.'—*Variety*

Tell It to the Judge
US 1949 87m bw
Columbia (Buddy Adler)

A female candidate for judicial honours is suddenly re-attracted to her divorced husband. Leaden farce, relying entirely on its stars.

w Nat Perrin, Devery Freeman, Roland Kibbee *d* Norman Foster *ph* Joseph Walker *m* Werner Heyman

Rosalind Russell, Robert Cummings, Gig Young, Marie McDonald, Harry Davenport

Tell It to the Marines
US 1926 75m at 24 fps bw silent

A marine sergeant has an eventful time during training and in the Philippines. Lively war action piece with a more or less straight role for its star. Lon Chaney, William Haines, Eleanor Boardman, Carmel Myers, Warner Oland. Written by Richard Schayer; directed by George Hill; for MGM.

Tell Me a Riddle
US 1980 90m CFI color

A dying old woman, long a recluse, is reconciled with her family. Adequate if not exciting treatment of a very downbeat subject. Lila Kedrova, Melvyn Douglas, Brooke Adams, Dolores Dorn, Lili Valenty, Zalman King. Written by Joyce Eliason and Alev Lytle, from the novel by Tillie Olsen; directed by Lee Grant; for Godmother / Filmways.

Tell Me That You Love Me, Junie Moon
US 1969 113m Technicolor
Paramount / Sigma (Otto Preminger)

A disfigured girl, a homosexual paraplegic and an introvert epileptic set up house together. Absurd tragicomedy which remains disturbingly icky in conception and execution.

w Marjorie Kellogg, from her novel *d* Otto Preminger *ph* Boris Kaufman *m* Philip Springer

Liza Minnelli, Ken Howard, Robert Moore, Kay Thompson, Leonard Frey, James Coco, Fred Williamson

'Like seeing a venerated senior citizen desperately trying to show he's in love with today by donning see-through clothes.'—*Michael Billington, Illustrated London News*

'It slushes us with sentimentality to the point past compassion.'—*Judith Crist*

Tell No Tales°°
US 1939 68m bw
MGM (Edward Chodorov)

A managing editor seeks a big scoop to save his newspaper, and solves a kidnap-murder case.
Intriguingly written and handled second feature, with excellent pace, performance and entertainment value.

w Lionel Houser *d* Leslie Fenton *ph* Joseph Ruttenberg *m* William Axt

Melvyn Douglas, Louise Platt, Gene Lockhart, Douglass Dumbrille, Zeffie Tilbury, Halliwell Hobbes

'Full of excellent detail, and the smallest part is a genuine character. Add these qualities to its pace and excitement and you have something well worth seeing.'—*Richard Mallett, Punch*

Tell Them Willie Boy is Here°
US 1969 97m Technicolor
Universal (Philip A. Waxman)

In 1909 an Indian turned cowboy comes up against old prejudices and is pursued into the desert after an accidental death.
Boringly predictable story of white man's guilt, very professionally made.

wd Abraham Polonsky, *novel* Willie Boy by Harry Lawton *ph* Conrad Hall *m* Dave Grusin

Robert Redford, Robert Blake, Katharine Ross, Susan Clark, Barry Sullivan, Charles McGraw, Charles Aidman, John Vernon

The Tempest
GB 1980 95m Eastmancolor

A punk version of Shakespeare's play; less horrendous than might have been supposed, but far from interesting in its own right. Heathcote Williams, Karl Johnson, Toyah Willcox, Peter Bull, Richard Warwick, Elisabeth Welch. Written and directed by Derek Jarman; photographed by Peter Middleton; music by Wavemaker; for Boyd's Company.

● *Video: Guild*

Tempest
Italy / France / Yugoslavia 1958 123m Technirama
(Paramount) Dino de Laurentiis / Gray / S. N Pathe / Bosnia

Adventures of a Russian ensign banished by Catherine the Great.
Expensive but sloppy epic which fails to generate much interest.

w Louis Peterson, Alberto Lattuada, Ivo Perelli, *novel* The Captain's Daughter by Alexander Pushkin *d* Alberto Lattuada *ph* Aldo Tonti *m* Piero Piccioni

Van Heflin, Geoffrey Horne, Silvana Mangano, Oscar Homolka, Viveca Lindfors, Robert Keith, Vittorio Gassman, Finlay Currie, Agnes Moorehead, Helmut Dantine, Laurence Naismith

'Most men dream their fantasies. Philip decided to live his!'
Tempest
US 1982 142m De Luxe
Columbia (Paul Mazursky)

An architect leaves his unfaithful wife and takes his daughter to live on a Greek island attended only by a half-witted shepherd. Absurd attempt to update Shakespeare; any initial amusement quickly gives way to abject boredom.

w Paul Mazursky, Leon Capetanos *d* Paul Mazursky *ph* Don McAlpine *m* Stomu Yamashta *pd* Pato Guzman

John Cassavetes, Gena Rowlands, Susan
Sarandon, Vittorio Gassman, Raul Julia, Jerry
Hardin, Molly Ringwald, Paul Stewart

'An aura of dottiness hangs over it . . . the
fact remains that it is handsomely visualized
and, within the limits of the material,
excellently played.'—*Tim Pulleine, MFB*

Temptation
US 1946 92m bw
Universal (Edward Small)

An archaeologist's wife takes to poisoning
both her husband and her blackmailing lover.
Hoary Edwardian melodrama, unpersuasively
restaged.

w Robert Thoeren, *novel* Bella Donna by
Robert Hichens d Irving Pichel ph Lucien
Ballard m Daniele Amfitheatrof

Merle Oberon, George Brent, Charles Korvin,
Paul Lukas, Lenore Ulric, Arnold Moss,
Ludwig Stossel, Gavin Muir, Ilka Gruning,
André Charlot

Temptation Harbour
GB 1946 104m bw
ABP (Victor Skutezky)

A railway signalman finds and keeps stolen
money.
Well-presented but boringly predictable
melodrama with an overwrought leading
performance set against yards of studio fog.

w Victor Skutezky, Frederic Gotfurt, Rodney
Ackland, *novel* Newhaven/Dieppe by Georges
Simenon d Lance Comfort

Robert Newton, Simone Simon, William
Hartnell, Marcel Dalio, Margaret Barton,
Edward Rigby, Joan Hopkins, Charles Victor,
Kathleen Harrison

The Temptress*
US 1927 80m (24 fps) bw silent
MGM

An immoral woman drives men to disgrace,
murder and suicide.
No-holds-barred melodrama which, being
Garbo's second American film, fully confirmed
her stardom.

w Dorothy Farnum d Mauritz Stiller, Fred
Niblo

Greta Garbo, Antonio Moreno, Lionel
Barrymore, Roy D'Arcy, Marc McDermott

'10'
US 1979 122m Metrocolor Panavision
Warner / Orion / Geoffrey (Blake Edwards,
Tony Adams)

A sex-mad middle-aged composer marks his
girls from one to ten according to their
performance.
Randy farce which struck some, but not all,
audiences as the funniest thing since sliced
bread.

wd Blake Edwards ph Frank Stanley
m Henry Mancini pd Rodger Maus

Dudley Moore, Julie Andrews, Bo Derek,
Robert Webber, Dee Wallace, Sam Jones

● *Video: Guild*

Ten Cents a Dance
US 1931 75m bw

A dance hostess is desired by a rich man but
marries a ne'er-do-well. Rubbishy story
inspired by a then-popular song. Barbara
Stanwyck, Monroe Owsley, Ricardo Cortez,
Sally Blane, Blanche Friderici. Written by Jo
Swerling; directed by Lionel Barrymore; for
Columbia. 'It lacks the magic of fancy that
makes for universal entertainment.'—*Variety*

'The mightiest dramatic spectacle of all the
ages!'
The Ten Commandments**
US 1923 150m approx (24 fps)
   part Technicolor silent
Paramount / Famous Players–Lasky (Cecil
B. de Mille)

Moses leads the Israelites into the promised
land in modern San Francisco; a story of two
brothers shows the power of prayer and truth.
The two halves in fact are totally
disconnected; but this is a de Mille spectacular
and therefore beyond reproach, while as a
Hollywood milestone it cannot be denied a
place in the Hall of Fame.

w Jeanie MacPherson d Cecil B. de Mille
ph Bert Glennon and others (*colour*, Ray
Renahan)

Theodore Roberts, Richard Dix, Rod la
Rocque, Edythe Chapman, Leatrice Joy, Nita
Naldi

'It will last as long as the film on which it is
recorded.'—*James R. Quirk, Photoplay*

The Ten Commandments*
US 1956 219m Technicolor
Vistavision
Paramount / Cecil B. de Mille (Henry
Wilcoxon)

The life of Moses and his leading of the
Israelites to the Promised Land.
Popular but incredibly stilted and verbose
bible-in-pictures spectacle. A very long haul
along a monotonous route, with the director at
his pedestrian worst.

w Aeneas Mackenzie, Jesse L. Lasky Jnr, Jack
Gariss, Frederic M. Frank d Cecil B. de
Mille ph Loyal Griggs m Elmer Bernstein

Charlton Heston, Yul Brynner, Edward G.
Robinson, Anne Baxter, Nina Foch, Yvonne
de Carlo, John Derek, H. B. Warner, Henry
Wilcoxon, Judith Anderson, John Carradine,
Douglass Dumbrille, Cedric Hardwicke,
Martha Scott, Vincent Price, Debra Paget

'De Mille not only moulds religion into a set
pattern of Hollywood conventions; he has also
become an expert at making entertainment out
of it.'—*Gordon Gow, Films and Filming*

'The result of all these stupendous efforts?
Something roughly comparable to an eight-
foot chorus girl—pretty well put together, but
much too big and much too flashy. . . . What
de Mille has really done is to throw sex and
sand into the moviegoers' eyes for almost
twice as long as anyone else has ever dared
to.'—*Time*

'What a story it tells! What majesty it

encompasses! What loves it unveils! What
drama it unfolds!'—*publicity*

AAN: best picture; Loyal Griggs

● *Video: CIC*

Ten Days in Paris
GB 1939 82m bw
Columbia (Jerome J. Jackson)
US titles: *Missing Ten Days / Spy in the
Pantry*

An amnesiac wakes up in Paris and finds he
has been involved in espionage activities.
Modest, quite likeable little comedy
suspenser.

w John Meehan Jnr, James Curtis, *novel* The
Disappearance of Roger Tremayne by Bruce
Graeme d Tim Whelan ph Otto Kanturek
m Miklos Rozsa

Rex Harrison, Karen Verne, Leo Genn, Joan
Marion, Anthony Holles, John Abbott, Hay
Petrie

Ten Gentlemen from West Point**
US 1942 104m bw
TCF (William Perlberg)

Adventures in Indian territory, and back at
West Point, of the first recruits to that military
academy in the early 1800s.
Likeable mixture of comedy and flagwaving
adventure, with excellent production values
and a dominating performance.

w Richard Maibaum, George Seaton d Henry
Hathaway ph Leon Shamroy m Alfred
Newman

Laird Cregar, George Montgomery, Maureen
O'Hara, John Sutton, Shepperd Strudwick,
Victor Francen, Harry Davenport, Ward
Bond, Douglass Dumbrille, Ralph Byrd, Louis
Jean Heydt

AAN: Leon Shamroy

Ten Little Indians*
GB 1966 91m bw
Tenlit (Harry Alan Towers)

Ten people, including two servants invited to a
remote house in the Austrian Alps are
murdered one by one.
Fair copy of a classic whodunnit.

w Peter Yeldham, Harry Alan Towers, *novel*
Agatha Christie d George Pollock ph Ernest
Steward m Malcolm Lockyer

Wilfrid Hyde White, Dennis Price, Stanley
Holloway, Leo Genn, Shirley Eaton, Hugh
O'Brian, Daliah Lavi, Fabian, Mario Adorf,
Marianne Hoppe
† Made also in 1945 and 1975, as *And Then
There Were None* (qv).

Ten North Frederick*
US 1958 102m bw Cinemascope
TCF (Charles Brackett)

At the funeral of a local politico, his family
and friends think back to the events of his life.
Small beer, but a generally adult and
entertaining family drama despite a miscast
lead.

wd Philip Dunne, *novel* John O'Hara *ph* Joe MacDonald *m* Leigh Harline

Gary Cooper, Geraldine Fitzgerald, Diane Varsi, Stuart Whitman, Suzy Parker, Tom Tully, Ray Stricklyn, John Emery

Ten Rillington Place*
GB 1970 111m Eastmancolor
Columbia / Filmways (Basil Appleby)

An account of London's sordid Christie murders of the forties.
Agreeably seedy reconstruction of a *cause célèbre*, carefully built around the star part of a murderous aberrant landlord. Too long, however, and finally too lacking in detail.

w Clive Exton, *book* Ludovic Kennedy *d* Richard Fleischer *ph* Denys Coop *m* Johnny Dankworth

Richard Attenborough, *John Hurt*, Judy Geeson, Pat Heywood, Isobel Black, Geoffrey Chater, André Morell, Robert Hardy

Ten Seconds to Hell
US 1959 93m bw
Hammer / Seven Arts (Michael Carreras)

Bomb disposal experts in post-war Berlin quarrel over a girl.
Boring, harsh, hollow melodrama, so artificially constructed that no one can possibly care who gets exploded.

w Robert Aldrich, Teddi Sherman, *novel* The Phoenix by Lawrence Bachmann *d* Robert Aldrich *ph* Ernest Laszlo *m* Kenneth V. Jones

Jack Palance, Jeff Chandler, Martine Carol, Robert Cornthwaite, Dave Willock, Wesley Addy

Ten Tall Men
US 1951 97m Technicolor
Columbia / Norma (Harold Hecht)

A Foreign Legion patrol prevents a Riff attack.
Comic strip adventures, efficiently handled.

w Roland Kibbee, Frank Davis *d* Willis Goldbeck *ph* William Snyder *m* David Buttolph

Burt Lancaster, Gilbert Roland, Kieron Moore, John Dehner, Jody Lawrance, George Tobias, Mike Mazurki

10.30 pm Summer
US / Spain 1966 85m Technicolor
UA / Jorill / Argos (Jules Dassin, Anatole Litvak)

The neurotic Greek wife of an Englishman travelling in Spain becomes obsessed with a murderer on the run.
Preposterously overwrought romantic melodrama.

w Jules Dassin, Marguerite Duras, *novel* Marguerite Duras *d* Jules Dassin *ph* Gabor Pogany *m* Christobel Hallfter

Peter Finch, Melina Mercouri, Romy Schneider, Julian Mateos

Ten Thousand Bedrooms
US 1956 114m Metrocolor
Cinemascope
MGM (Joe Pasternak)

An American millionaire finds romance when he buys a Rome hotel.
Old-fashioned, unfunny comedy sadly lacking pace and style.

w Laslo Vadnay, Art Cohn, William Ludwig, Leonard Spiegelgass *d* Richard Thorpe *ph* Robert Bronner *m* George Stoll *songs* Nicholas Brodszky, Sammy Cahn

Dean Martin, Eva Bartok, Anna Maria Alberghetti, Walter Slezak, Paul Henreid, Jules Munchin, Marcel Dalio

Ten to Midnight
US 1983 102m Metrocolor

A sexual deficient kills girls who reject him, but is tracked down and shot by a cop who is the father of one of the threatened girls.
Crude and rather nasty vigilante melodrama. Charles Bronson, Lisa Eilbacher, Andrew Stevens, Gene Davis, Geoffrey Lewis. Written by William Roberts; directed by J. Lee Thompson; for Golan-Globus. 'Too slow, slick and semi-respectable to live down to its inspirations.'—*Kim Newman, MFB*

Ten Wanted Men
US 1955 80m Technicolor

A rancher and his family are besieged by bandits in a lady's house. Rather elementary but efficient and good-looking western programmer. Randolph Scott, Jocelyn Brando, Richard Boone, Alfonso Bedoya, Donna Martell, Skip Homeier. Written by Kenneth Gamet, from a story by Irving Ravetch and Harriet Frank Jnr; directed by Bruce Humberstone; for Harry Joe Brown / Columbia.

Ten Who Dared
US 1960 92m Technicolor
Walt Disney (James Algar)

In 1869 a scientific expedition sets out to chart the Colorado River.
Tedious and unconvincing adventures.

w Lawrence E. Watkin, from the journal of Major John Wesley Powell *d* William Beaudine *ph* Gordon Avil *m* Oliver Wallace

Brian Keith, John Beal, James Drury, R. G. Armstrong, Ben Johnson, L. Q. Jones

The Tenant
France 1976 126m Eastmancolor
Paramount / Marianne (Andrew Braunsberg)
Original title: *Le Locataire*

A displaced person becomes convinced that his fellow lodgers are out to murder him. Rather like a male version of the same director's *Repulsion*, this wearisome case history shows the total dissipation of whatever talent he once had.

w Gerard Brach, Roman Polanski, *novel* Roland Topor *d* Roman Polanski *ph* Sven Nykvist *m* Philippe Sarde

Roman Polanski, Melvyn Douglas, Isabelle Adjani, Shelley Winters, Jo Van Fleet, Lila Kedrova, Claude Dauphin

'It does not seem to have been designed as self-parody, but it certainly comes across that way.'—*Janet Maslin, Newsweek*
'A long-winded exercise in tedium and morbidity.'—*Kevin Thomas, LA Times*

Tender Comrade
US 1943 101m bw
RKO (David Hempstead)

Lady welders whose husbands are fighting men keep their chins up during World War II.
Dim tearjerker.

w Dalton Trumbo *d* Edward Dmytryk *ph* Russell Metty *m* Leigh Harline

Ginger Rogers, Robert Ryan, Ruth Hussey, Patricia Collinge, Mady Christians, Kim Hunter, Jane Darwell

Tender Is the Night*
US 1961 146m De Luxe Cinemascope
TCF (Henry T. Weinstein)

Adventures around Europe between the wars of a rich American psychiatrist who has married his patient.
Patchy, fairly literal transcription of a patently unfilmable novel about defiantly unreal people in what would now be the jet set. About half the result is superficially entertaining.

w Ivan Moffat, *novel* F. Scott Fitzgerald *d* Henry King *ph* Leon Shamroy *m* Bernard Herrmann

Jennifer Jones, Jason Robards Jnr, *Joan Fontaine, Tom Ewell*, Cesare Danova, Jill St John, Paul Lukas

AAN: title song (*m* Sammy Fain, *ly* Paul Francis Webster)

Tender Mercies*
US 1982 92m Movielab
EMI / Antron Media (Horton Foote, Robert Duvall)

An ex-alcoholic resumes his former career as a country and western singer.
Quiet, downbeat character study with scenic Texas backgrounds. Mildly impressive, but no real reason to go to the cinema.

w Horton Foote *d* Bruce Beresford *ph* Russell Boyd *m* George Dreyfus

Robert Duvall (who sang his own songs), Tess Harper, Betty Buckley, Wilford Brimley, Ellen Barkin

'It conceals its deficiencies behind heartfelt performances . . . the construction is so rickety that it seems at times entirely to lack a plot.'—*Kim Newman, MFB*

AA: Robert Duvall; Horton Foote
AAN: best picture; Bruce Beresford; song ('Over You')

● *Video: VCL*

The Tender Trap*
US 1955 111m Eastmancolor
Cinemascope
MGM (Lawrence Weingarten)

A smart New York agent has a way with

women which annoys his friend; but Casanova gets his come-uppance when he sets his sights on an apparently naïve young actress.
Thin comedy with agreeable moments, not helped by the wide screen.

w Julius J. Epstein, *play* Max Shulman, Robert Paul Smith *d* Charles Walters *ph* Paul Vogel *m* Jeff Alexander

Frank Sinatra, Debbie Reynolds, David Wayne, Celeste Holm, Lola Albright, Carolyn Jones

AAN: title song (*m* James Van Heusen, *ly* Sammy Cahn)

The Tenderfoot
US 1931 73m bw

Adventures of a cowboy in New York. Slapstick version of George Kaufman's often-remade comedy *The Butter and Egg Man*; not remarkable in any way. Joe E. Brown, Ginger Rogers, Lew Cody, Vivian Oakland, Robert Greig. Written by Arthur Caesar, Monty Banks, Earl Baldwin; directed by Ray Enright; for Warners. 'It ought to do well where they like lowdown comedy.'—*Variety*

Tenderloin
US 1928 88m bw

A dancer is accused of stealing a fortune and finds gangsters suddenly interested in her. Primitive part-talkie (15 minutes of dialogue), unspeakably hammy to listen to though visually it had some inventiveness. Dolores Costello, Conrad Nagel, Mitchell Lewis, George E. Stone, Dan Wolheim. Written by Edward T. Lowe, from a story by Darryl Zanuck; directed by Michael Curtiz; for Warner.

Tendre Ennemie*
France 1938 66m bw

A woman's three dead lovers return to prevent her daughter from making a romantic mistake. Decorative whimsy which is not among its director's best, but mildly amusing none the less. Simone Berriau, Jacqueline Daix, Georges Vitray, Marc Valbel, Lucien Nat. Written by Max Ophuls, Kurt Alexander, from the play L'Ennemie by A. P. Antoine; directed by Max Ophuls; for World Pictures. 'Story is sacrificed for camera angles . . . weak even for the arties.'—*Variety*

Tennessee Champ
US 1954 75m Anscocolor

The Lord helps a religious boxer to win a few fights. Tedious sentimental square ring melodrama. Earl Holliman, Dewey Martin, Keenan Wynn, Shelley Winters, Yvette Dugay. Written by Art Cohn; directed by Fred M. Wilcox; for MGM.

Tennessee Johnson*
US 1943 102m bw
MGM (J. Walter Ruben)
GB title: *The Man on America's Conscience*

The rise and the problems of President Andrew Johnson.

Sincere, straightforward, well-produced historical drama which failed to set the Thames—or the Hudson—on fire.

w John Balderston, Wells Root *d* William Dieterle *ph* Harold Rosson *m* Herbert Stothart

Van Heflin, Ruth Hussey, Lionel Barrymore, Marjorie Main, Regis Toomey, Montagu Love, Porter Hall, Charles Dingle, J. Edward Bromberg

'Dieterle's customary high-minded, high-polished mélange of heavy touches and intelligent performances.'—*James Agee*

Tennessee's Partner
US 1955 87m Technicolor

A gambling queen and a tenderfoot are involved in a double cross which leads to murder. Predictable western from a story by Bret Harte. Ronald Reagan, John Payne, Rhonda Fleming, Coleen Gray. Written by Milton Krims, D. D. Beauchamp, Graham Baker and Teddi Sherman; directed by Allan Dwan; for RKO.

Tension
US 1950 91m bw
MGM (Robert Sisk)

A chemist plans the perfect murder of his wife's lover, loses his nerve, then finds himself suspected when the man is murdered after all. Disappointing suspenser which starts well but outstays its welcome.

w Allen Rivkin *d* John Berry *ph* Harry Stradling *m* André Previn

Richard Basehart, Audrey Totter, Barry Sullivan, Cyd Charisse, Lloyd Gough, Tom d'Andrea

Tension at Table Rock
US 1956 93m Technicolor

When a stagecoach station owner is killed, a gunman takes care of his small son and at the same time rids a town of outlaws. All the clichés are in this one, fairly neatly amassed in corners labelled *High Noon, Hondo* and *Shane*. Written by Winston Miller, from a novel by Frank Gruber; directed by Charles Marquis Warren; for RKO.

Tentacles
Italy 1976 102m Technicolor Technovision
Esse Cinematografica (E. F. Doria)

A deadly menace which leaves its victims as skeletons washed up on the California beach turns out to be a giant octopus . . .
Dreary *Jaws* rehash. Sadly there is no element of spoofing, it's all deadly serious.

w Jerome Max, Tito Carpi, Steve Carabatsos, Sonia Molteni *d* Oliver Hellman (Sonia Assonitis) *ph* Roberto d'Ettore Piazzoli *m* S. W. Cipriani

Shelley Winters, John Huston, Bo Hopkins, Henry Fonda, Claude Akins, Cesare Danova, Delia Boccardo

Tenth Avenue Angel
US 1948 74m bw
MGM (Ralph Wheelwright)

The little daughter of poor parents loses her faith in life.
Icky sentimental piece for a waning child star.

w Angna Enters, Craig Rice, Harry Ruskin, Eleanore Griffin *d* Roy Rowland *ph* Robert Surtees *m* Rudolph G. Kopp

Margaret O'Brien, Angela Lansbury, George Murphy, Phyllis Thaxter, Rhys Williams, Warner Anderson, Audrey Totter, Connie Gilchrist

The Tenth Man
GB 1936 68m bw

A wife shows faith in her husband even though she knows him to be a crook. Stock film version of one of Somerset Maugham's less pungent plays. John Lodge, Antoinette Cellier, Aileen Marson, Clifford Evans, George Graves. Written by Geoffrey Kerr, Dudley Leslie, Marjorie Deans and Jack Davies; directed by Brian Desmond Hurst; for BIP.

The Tenth Victim
Italy / France 1965 92m Technicolor
Avco / CC Champion / Concordia (Carlo Ponti)

In the 21st century murder is legalized to avoid birth control and war, and ten killings bring a fabulous prize.
Science fiction satire which just about gets by.

w Tonina Guerra, Giorgio Salvioni, Ennio Flaiano, Elio Petri, *story* The Seventh Victim by Robert Sheckley *d* Elio Petri *ph* Gianni di Venanzo *m* Piero Piccioni

Ursula Andress, Marcello Mastroianni, Elsa Martinelli, Massimo Serato

Teresa**
US 1951 101m bw
MGM (Arthur M. Loew)

A soldier with mother problems brings home an Italian bride.
Careful, sensitive, intelligent variation on a problem frequently considered by films of this period (*Frieda, Fräulein, Japanese War Bride*).

w Stewart Stern *d* Fred Zinnemann *ph* William J. Miller *m* Louis Applebaum

Pier Angeli, John Ericson, Patricia Collinge, Richard Bishop, Peggy Ann Garner, Ralph Meeker, Bill Mauldin

AAN: original story (Arthur Hayes, Stewart Stern)

Term of Trial*
GB 1962 130m bw
Romulus (James Woolf)

An unsuccessful schoolmaster is accused of rape by a nymphomaniac schoolgirl he has scorned.
Rather flabby 'adult' drama, too schematic to be really interesting despite the best that acting can do.

wd Peter Glenville, *novel* The Burden of Proof by James Barlow *ph* Oswald Morris *m* Jean-Michel Demase *ad* Antony Woolard

Laurence Olivier, Sarah Miles, Simone Signoret, Hugh Griffith, Terence Stamp, Roland Culver, Frank Pettingell, Thora Hird, Dudley Foster, Norman Bird

The Terminator°
US 1984 108m CFI colour
Orion / Hemdale / Pacific Western (Gale Anne Hurd)

A man from the future is sent back on a mission of extermination.
Slick rather nasty but undeniably compelling comic book adventures.

w James Cameron, Gale Anne Hurd *d* James Cameron *ph* Adam Greenberg *m* Brad Fiedel *ed* Mark Goldblatt

Arnold Schwarzenegger, Michael Biehn, Linda Hamilton, Paul Winfield, Rick Rossovich, Lance Henriksen

Terminus°°°
GB 1961 30m bw
British Transport Films

Twenty-four hours in the life of Waterloo Station.
An excellent 'fly-on-the-wall' document which launched the feature film career of its director and is still both funny and moving.
wd John Schlesinger *ph* Ken Phipps, Robert Paynter *m* Ron Grainer

Terms of Endearment°°
US 1983 132m Metrocolor
Paramount (James L. Brooks)

An eccentric widow fends off suitors while interfering with her daughter's marriage; but all is forgiven when the daughter dies.
This shapeless film is little more than an excuse for actors and writer to show off, which they do to great excess; but parts of it are entertaining enough and it certainly impressed the Academy Award committee.

w,d James L. Brooks, *novel* Larry McMurtry *ph* Andrzej Bartkowiak *m* Michael Gore *pd* Polly Platt

Shirley Maclaine, Jack Nicholson, Debra Winger, Danny DeVito, Jeff Daniels, John Lithgow

'An outsize sitcom and a crassly constructed slice of anti-feminism that contrives to rub liberal amounts of soap in the viewer's eyes.'—*Sight and Sound*

AA: best picture; Shirley Maclaine; Jack Nicholson; direction; adaptation
AAN: John Lithgow; editing (Richard Marks); Michael Gore; art direction; Debra Winger

La Terra Trema°
Italy 1948 160m bw
Universalia

The life of a Sicilian fisherman and his family. Seriously intended, carefully composed semi-documentary stressing the economic problems of the simple life. A commercial disaster: even the Italians couldn't understand the accents of the local actors.
wd Luchino Visconti *ph* G. R. Aldo *m* Luchino Visconti, Willy Ferrero
† The cast was drawn from the inhabitants of Aci Trezza, Sicily.

A Terrible Beauty
GB 1960 90m bw
UA / Raymond Stross
US title: *Night Fighters*

In a north Irish village, the IRA revive their activities on the outbreak of World War II. Heavily Oirish melodrama with a muddled message.

w Robert Wright Campbell, *novel* Arthur Roth *d* Tay Garnett *ph* Stephen Dade *m* Cedric Thorpe Davie

Robert Mitchum, Anne Heywood, Dan O'Herlihy, Cyril Cusack, Richard Harris, Marianne Benet

The Terror
US 1928 82m approx bw
Warner

A mysterious killer lurks in the cellars of a country house.
Primitive talkie which attempted a few new styles but showed that more were needed, also that some silent actors could not make the transfer.

w Harvey Gates, *novel* and *play* Edgar Wallace *d* Roy del Ruth *ph* Barney McGill

May McAvoy, Edward Everett Horton, Louise Fazenda, Alec B. Francis, John Miljan, Frank Austin

'The only terrible thing about this talkie Terror is its unnatural slowness . . . the characters speak as if they were dictating important letters.'—*A. P. Herbert, Punch*
† The first film without a single subtitle: all the credits were spoken.
†† *Return of the Terror* (US 1934) has little to do with it.

The Terror
GB 1938 73m bw

Stilted remake of the above. Wilfrid Lawson, Arthur Wontner, Alastair Sim, Linden Travers, Bernard Lee, Henry Oscar. Written by William Freshman; directed by Richard Bird; for BIP.

The Terror
US 1963 81m Pathecolor
AIP / Filmgroup (Roger Corman, Francis Ford Coppola)

A baron lives for twenty years in a creepy castle, mourning the death of his wife . . . Shoddy horror improvised over a weekend on the set of *The Raven*. It looks it.

w Leo Gordon, Jack Hill *d* Roger Corman *ph* John Nickolaus *m* Ronald Stein

Boris Karloff, Jack Nicholson, Sandra Knight, Dorothy Neumann

Terror Aboard
US 1933 70m bw

Gruesome murders occur during a pleasure cruise. Fair murder mystery. Charles Ruggles, John Halliday, Shirley Grey, Neil Hamilton, Verree Teasdale, Jack La Rue. Written by Harvey Thew and Manuel Seff; directed by Paul Sloane; for Paramount.

Terror by Night°
US 1946 60m bw
Universal (Howard Benedict)

Sherlock Holmes recovers a stolen jewel and solves a murder or two aboard a speeding train.
An amusing entry in the modernized series despite some bad support acting and hilarious interposed shots of the supposed scenery between London and Edinburgh.

w Frank Gruber *d* Roy William Neill *ph* Maury Gertsman

Basil Rathbone, Nigel Bruce, Dennis Hoey, Alan Mowbray, Renee Godfrey, Bill Bevan, Mary Forbes, Frederic Worlock

Terror in a Texas Town°
US 1958 81m bw
UA / Frank N. Seltzer

A Swedish seaman arrives in a small western town and avenges the death of his brother. Stylish second feature western, a genuine sleeper which holds the interest throughout.

w Ben L. Perry *d* Joseph H. Lewis *ph* Ray Rennahan *m* Gerald Fried

Sterling Hayden, Sebastian Cabot, Carol Kelly, Eugene Martin, Ned Young

Terror in the Aisles
US 1984 82m CFI color

A compilation of fragments from mainly shock films, of no great interest even to film buffs because in most cases the scenes are wrenched out of context to fit a fatuous commentary. Written by Margery Doppelt; directed by Andrew Kuehn; for TEM / Kaleidoscope / Universal.

Terror in the Haunted House
US 1958 81m bw

A bride finds that her honeymoon mansion is one about which she has been having recurring nightmares. The plot has everything, even an axe murderer, but the treatment is soporific. Gerald Mohr, Cathy O'Donnell, William Ching, John Qualen, Barry Bernard. Written by Robert C. Dennis; directed by Harold Daniels; for Howco. (Alternative title: *My World Dies Screaming*.)

Terror in the Wax Museum
US 1973 94m De Luxe
Bing Crosby Productions / Fenady Associates (Andrew J. Fenady)

In Victorian London a waxworks owner is murdered . . .
Cheaply produced murder mystery (even the waxworks can't stand still) with horror asides and a cast of elderly hams.

w Jameson Brewer *d* George Fenady *ph* William Jurgensen *m* George Duning

Ray Milland, Broderick Crawford, Elsa Lanchester, Louis Hayward, John Carradine, Shani Wallis, Maurice Evans, Patric Knowles

'Drug-crazed assassins carrying out their hate-filled ritual murders!'

The Terror of the Tongs
GB 1960   79m   Technicolor
Hammer / Merlin (Kenneth Hyman)

In 1910 Hong Kong a merchant avenges the death of his daughter at the hands of a villainous secret society.
Gory melodrama with dollops of screams, torture and vaguely orgiastic goings-on.

w Jimmy Sangster d Anthony Bushell ph Arthur Grant m James Bernard

Geoffrey Toone, Christopher Lee, Yvonne Monlaur, Brian Worth, Richard Leech

Terror Train
Canada 1980   97m   De Luxe

Participants in a wild party aboard a train are decimated by a mysterious psychotic. Shocks and blood in the Carpenter tradition, adequately mounted. Ben Johnson, Jamie Lee Curtis, David Copperfield, Hart Bochner. Written by T. Y. Drake; directed by Roger Spottiswoode; for Astral.

The Terry Fox Story
Canada 1983   97m   colour

A young man dying of cancer has a leg amputated, but still runs across Canada in aid of research. True it may be, but dramatically this is a one-note film with endless pretty pictures of countryside and in the foreground signs of failing health. Eric Fryer, Robert Duvall, Christopher Makepeace, Rosalind Chao. Written by Edward Hume; directed by Ralph L. Thomas; for Robert Cooper / CTV.

Tess*
France-GB 1979   180m   colour
Renn-Burrill (Claude Berri)

A peasant girl tries to prove her noble heritage but finds herself with an illegitimate child. Solid, unexciting version of a classic Wessex novel; a hard sell for 1980 audiences.

w Roman Polanski, Gerard Brach, John Brownjohn novel Tess of the D'Urbervilles by Thomas Hardy d Roman Polanski ph Geoffrey Unsworth, Ghislain Cloquet m Philippe Sarde pd Pierre Guffroy

Nastassja Kinski, Leigh Lawson, Peter Firth, John Collin, David Markham, Richard Pearson
'It emerges without a hint of what might have drawn Polanski to the material.'—Sight and Sound

AA: Geoffrey Unsworth, Ghislain Cloquet; art direction (Pierre Guffroy, Jack Stevens); costume design (Anthony Powell)
AAN: best film; Roman Polanski; Philippe Sarde
BFA: best photography

Tess of the Storm Country
US 1932   80m   bw
Fox

A retired sea captain's daughter loves the lord of the manor.
Antiquated tushery first filmed as a Mary Pickford silent.

w S. N. Behrman, Sonya Levien, Rupert Hughes, novel Grace Miller White d Alfred Santell ph Hal Mohr

Janet Gaynor, Charles Farrell, Dudley Digges, June Clyde, George Meeker

Test Pilot**
US 1938   118m   bw
MGM (Louis D. Lighton)

A brilliant but unpredictable test pilot is helped by his wife and his self-sacrificing friend.
A big box-office star vehicle of its time, still interesting as a highly efficient product.

w Waldemar Young, Vincent Lawrence, story Frank Wead d Victor Fleming ph Ray June m Franz Waxman

Clark Gable, Myrna Loy, Spencer Tracy, Lionel Barrymore, Samuel S. Hinds, Marjorie Main, Gloria Holden
'B.o. potential of above-average calibre . . . could have been cut 10–15 minutes without spoiling.'—Variety

'The picture is so noisy with sure-fire elements—box office cast, violent excitement, glycerine tears and such—that it may be hard to keep the ear attuned to the quieter, more authentically human things in it.'—James Shelley Hamilton

AAN: best picture; Frank Wead

Testament*
US 1983   90m   CFI

A small California town is hit by a nuclear attack. Probably better than the TV movie The Day After, this was less well publicized and therefore lost out. Jane Alexander, William Devane, Ross Harris, Roxana Zal, Lukas Haas, Lilia Skala, Leon Ames. Written by John Sacret Young from a story by Carol Amen; directed by Lynne Littman; for Entertainment Events / American Playhouse.
'After thirty years of learning to live with the Bomb, we still lack ways of conceiving the Unthinkable.'—Sheila Johnston, MFB

AAN: Jane Alexander

Le Testament d'Orphée*
France 1959   83m   bw
Editions Cinégraphiques (Jean Thullier)
aka: The Testament of Orpheus

The poet, as an 18th-century man, dies, enters space time, is revived, and seeks his identity. Rather like a melancholy madman's Alice in Wonderland, this bizarre jumble has its fascinations but misses by a mile the arresting qualities of Orphée.

wd Jean Cocteau ph Roland Pointoizeau m Georges Auric and others

Jean Cocteau, Edouard Dermithe, Maria Casarès, François Périer, Henri Crémieux, Yul Brynner, Jean-Pierre Léaud, Daniel Gélin, Jean Marais, Pablo Picasso, Charles Aznavour
● Video: Palace

The Testament of Dr Mabuse**
Germany 1933   122m   bw
Nero (Fritz Lang)

A sequel to Dr Mabuse the Gambler: the criminal mastermind dies in an asylum, and his assistant takes over his identity.
Fast-moving penny dreadful, alleged by its director to be a denouncing of the doctrines of Hitler, but showing little evidence of being more than a very slick entertainment.

w Thea Von Harbou, Fritz Lang d Fritz Lang ph Fritz Arno Wagner m Hans Erdmann ad Karl Vollbrecht, Emil Hassler

Rudolf Klein-Rogge, Otto Wernicke, Gustav Diesl
† On arrival in America Lang claimed that 'slogans of the Third Reich have been put into the mouths of criminals in the film'. Yet his wife, who co-scripted it, stayed behind as a confirmed Nazi.

Tevya the Milkman*
US 1939   93m   bw

A Russian village milkman watches with awe as the pogroms begin to affect his people. One of the best Yiddish films with the best Yiddish actor, this pleasing comedy-drama was the basis for the musical Fiddler on the Roof. Maurice Schwarz, Miriam Riselle, Rebecca Weintraub, Paula Lubelska. Written and directed by Maurice Schwarz, from a story by Sholem Aleichem; for Henry Ziskin.

The Texan
US 1930   79m   bw
Paramount (Hector Turnbull)

The Llano Kid absolves his bandit past.
Early sound western, an interesting curiosity.

w Daniel Nathan Rufin, story The Double-Dyed Deceiver by O. Henry d John Cromwell ph Victor Milner

Gary Cooper, Fay Wray, Emma Dunn, Oscar Apfel
'Few westerns are as well made and rate as high in every particular.'—Variety

'Love and glory on America's last frontier!'
The Texans
US 1938   92m   bw
Paramount (Lucien Hubbard)

Problems of the post-Civil War years include new railroads, the Ku Klux Klan, and the new cattle drive routes.
Formula western with fairly well staged excitements backing a routine romantic triangle.

w Bertram Millhauser, Paul Sloane, William Wister Haines d James Hogan ph Theodor Sparkuhl m Gerard Carbonara

Joan Bennett, Randolph Scott, May Robson, Walter Brennan, Robert Cummings, Raymond Halton, Robert Barrat, Francis Ford
'Enough sweep and thrills to justify generally good business.'—Variety

Texas

US 1941 94m bw (released in sepia)
Columbia (Sam Bischoff)

Two veteran Civil War southerners head for
Texas to set up a cattle business.
Western vehicle for two young stars, now very
ordinary-looking.

w Horace McCoy, Lewis Meltzer, Michael
Blankfort d George Marshall ph George
Meehan

William Holden, Glenn Ford, Claire Trevor,
George Bancroft, Edgar Buchanan, Don
Beddoe, Andrew Tombes, Addison Richards

'While spoofing a little along the way, it
observes the etiquette and tradition of an
accepted cinema form. It has rough riding,
cattle rustling, shooting and a story that leaves
out only the Indian raid and the rescue by the
US Cavalry.'—*Christian Science Monitor*

Texas across the River

US 1966 101m Techniscope
Universal (Harry Keller)

A Texan, an Indian and a Spanish nobleman
on the run from jealous rivals have various
adventures.
Sloppy western which seems to have had jokes
added when someone realized it wasn't good
enough to be taken seriously.

w Wells Root, Harold Greene, Ben Starr
d Michael Gordon ph Russell Metty
m Frank de Vol md Joseph Gershenson

Dean Martin, Alain Delon, Joey Bishop,
Rosemary Forsyth, Tina Marquand, Peter
Graves, Andrew Prine, Michael Ansara

Texas Carnival

US 1951 77m Technicolor
MGM (Jack Cummins)

A fairground showman is mistaken for a
millionaire and runs up debts.
Very thin comedy musical relying entirely on
its stars.

w Dorothy Kingsley d Charles Walters
ph Robert Planck m Harry Warren
ly Dorothy Fields ch Hermes Pan

Esther Williams, Red Skelton, Howard Keel,
Ann Miller, Paula Raymond, Keenan Wynn,
Tom Tully

The Texas Chainsaw Massacre

US 1974 81m CFI Color
Vortex (Tobe Hooper)

Visitors to a cemetery in rural Texas find their
house occupied by a homicidal maniac.
Cheapjack horror thriller adapted from real
events which also inspired *Psycho*. Nothing
but shocks and gore, but the beginning of the
wave of such deplorable movies which flooded
the world's screens towards the end of the
decade.

w Kim Henkel, Tobe Hooper d Tobe
Hooper ph Daniel Pearl m Tobe Hooper,
Wayne Bell

Marilyn Burns, Allen Danziger, Paul A.
Partain, William Vail

'An absolute must for all maniacs and blood
drinkers in need of a few tips.'—*Benny Green,
Punch*

Texas Lady

US 1955 85m Technicolor Superscope
RKO (Nat Holt)

A lady newspaper owner runs an anti-
corruption campaign.
Mild family western.

w Horace McCoy d Tim Whelan ph Ray
Rennahan m Paul Sawtell

Claudette Colbert, Barry Sullivan, Grey
Walcott, James Bell, Horace MacMahon, Ray
Collins, Walter Sande, Douglas Fowley

'They wrote their story in words of fire!'
The Texas Rangers*

US 1936 95m bw
Paramount (King Vidor)

Three wandering ne'er-do-wells break up; two
join the Texas Rangers and hunt down the
third, who is an outlaw.
Pleasantly remembered star western, later
remade as *The Streets of Laredo* (qv).

w Louis Stevens d King Vidor ph Edward
Cronjager

Fred MacMurray, Jack Oakie, Lloyd Nolan,
Jean Parker, Edward Ellis

† *The Texas Rangers Ride Again* was released
in 1940, with the rangers going undercover to
catch outlaws; it was only a second feature,
with John Howard and Jack Oakie. Another
film called *The Texas Rangers* came from
Columbia in 1952 and had a similar plot to the
original; otherwise it was a shoddy piece of
work in Supercinecolor, with George
Montgomery and Jerome Courtland.

Thank God It's Friday

US 1978 89m Metrocolor
Columbia / Motown / Casablanca (Rob
Cohen)

Problems of a disc jockey in a Hollywood
disco.
Routine youth programmer, rather like *Rock
Around the Clock* twenty years after.

w Barry Armyan Bernstein d Robert Klane
ph James Crabe pd Tom H. John m various

Valerie Landsburg, Terri Nunn, Chick
Vennera, Donna Summer, The Commodores

AA: song, 'Last Dance'

Thank You, Jeeves*

US 1936 57m bw
TCF (Sol M. Wurtzel)

A valet helps prevent his master from
becoming involved in gun-running.
Competent second feature notable as Niven's
first leading role; also one of the very few
attempts to film Wodehouse.

w Joseph Hoffman, Stephen Gross, *story*
P. G. Wodehouse d Arthur Greville Collins
ph Barney McGill m Samuel Kaylin

David Niven, Arthur Treacher, Virginia Field,
Lester Matthews, Colin Tapley

Thank Your Lucky Stars***

US 1943 127m bw
Warner (Mark Hellinger)

Eddie Cantor and his double get involved in
planning a patriotic show.

All-star wartime musical with some
unexpected turns and a generally funny script.

w Norman Panama, Melvin Frank, James V.
Kern d David Butler ph Arthur Edeson
md Leo F. Forbstein ch Le Roy Prinz
songs Frank Loesser, Arthur Schwartz

*Eddie Cantor, Dennis Morgan, Joan Leslie,
Edward Everett Horton*, S. Z. Sakall,
Humphrey Bogart, Jack Carson, *Bette Davis*,
Olivia de Havilland, *Errol Flynn*, John
Garfield, Alan Hale, Ida Lupino, *Ann
Sheridan*, Dinah Shore, George Tobias, Spike
Jones and his City Slickers, Willie Best, Hattie
McDaniel

'The loudest and most vulgar of the current
musicals, it is also the most fun, if you are
amused when show people kid their own
idiom.'—*James Agee*

'An all-star show with the conspicuous
flavour of amateur night at the studio.'—*New
York Times*

'Everyone had a good time making it.'—
Motion Picture Herald

AAN: song 'They're Either Too Young or
Too Old'

Thanks a Million**

US 1935 87m bw
TCF (Darryl F. Zanuck)

A crooner runs for governor.
Smart, amusing political musical.

w Nunnally Johnson d Roy del Ruth
ph Peverell Marley songs Arthur Johnston,
Gus Kahn m Arthur Lange

Dick Powell, Fred Allen, Ann Dvorak, Patsy
Kelly, Phil Baker, Paul Whiteman and his
band, the Yacht Club Boys, Benny Baker,
Raymond Walburn, Alan Dinehart

'Socko filmusical for big grosses . . . an
example of canny showmanship and
presentation.'—*Variety*

Thanks for Everything*

US 1938 70m bw
TCF (Darryl F. Zanuck)

Mr Average American is discovered,
promoted and merchandised.
Very acceptable satirical comedy of the
advertising world.

w Harry Tugend d William A. Seiter
ph George Meehan m Abe Meyer

Adolphe Menjou, Jack Haley, Jack Oakie,
Arleen Whelan, Tony Martin, Binnie Barnes,
George Barbier

'Light and breezy, a cinch for popular
audience appeal.'—*Variety*

'The funniest film I can remember seeing for
many months, with something of the old
Kaufman touch.'—*Graham Greene*

Thanks for the Memory*

US 1938 75m bw
Paramount (Mel Shaver)

A smart novelist has trouble with his marriage.
Light, agreeable domestic comedy on familiar
lines.

w Lynn Starling, *play* Up Pops the Devil by Frances Goodrich, Albert Hackett *d* George Archainbaud *ph* Karl Struss *m* Boris Morros

Bob Hope, Shirley Ross
'Although lightweight, it will please if not exactly boff them.'—*Variety*

Thark*
GB 1932 79m bw
British and Dominion (Herbert Wilcox)

The heir to an old mansion spends a night in it to prove it is not haunted.
Very funny Aldwych farce, plainly transferred to the screen with the original stage team intact. One's only regret is that it peters out at the end.

w *Ben Travers*, from his play *d* Tom Walls *ph* F. A. Young

Ralph Lynn, Tom Walls, Robertson Hare, Mary Brough, Claude Hulbert, Gordon James
'Scream after scream of laughter of the wobbling midriff variety.'—*Variety*

That Brennan Girl
US 1946 97m bw

A young mother neglects her baby for the sake of a good time. Absurdly padded-out moral tract. Mona Freeman, James Dunn, William Marshall, June Duprez. Written by Doris Anderson; directed by Alfred Santell; for Republic.

That Certain Age*
US 1938 100m bw
Universal (Joe Pasternak)

A girl gets a crush on an older man.
Pleasant, well-cast star musical for the family.

w *Bruce Manning* *d* Edward Ludwig *ph* Joseph Valentine *songs* Jimmy McHugh, Harold Adamson

Deanna Durbin, Melvyn Douglas, Jackie Cooper, Irene Rich, Nancy Carroll, John Halliday, Juanita Quigley, Jackie Searl, Charles Coleman
'Certain for top grosses and extended runs.'—*Variety*

AAN: song 'My Own'

That Certain Feeling
US 1956 102m Technicolor
Vistavision
Paramount (Melvin Frank, Norman Panama)

An arrogant comic strip artist loses his touch and hires a 'ghost'—the ex-husband of his secretary / fiancée.
Arid comedy from a mild Broadway play, totally miscast and lacking any kind of interest.

w Norman Panama, Melvin Frank, I. A. L. Diamond, William Altman, *play* King of Hearts by Jean Kerr, Eleanor Brooke *d* Norman Panama, Melvin Frank *ph* Loyal Griggs *m* Joseph J. Lilley

Bob Hope, George Sanders, Eva Marie Saint, Pearl Bailey, Al Capp

'She got all the breaks—in her heart!'
That Certain Woman*
US 1937 91m bw
Warner (Hal B. Wallis)

A gangster's widow goes straight but runs into complex marriage trouble.
Self-sacrifice and mother love are rewarded by two convenient deaths and a happy ending in this routine romantic melodrama remade from a silent success.

wd Edmund Goulding, from his original screen play The Trespasser *ph* Ernest Haller *m* Max Steiner

Bette Davis, Henry Fonda, Ian Hunter, Anita Louise, Donald Crisp, Katherine Alexander, Mary Philips, Minor Watson
'Big-time cast in a well-made first run film.'—*Variety*

That Championship Season*
US 1982 108m Metrocolor
Cannon—Golan—Globus (Menahem Golan)

Five rather unlikeable middle-aged men live by recreating the glory of a team basketball victory 25 years ago.
Unimaginative film version of a play which had dramatic strength but very limited general appeal. Rather less can be said of the film, as the acting shows a lack of team spirit.

wd Jason Miller, from his play *ph* John Bailey *m* Bill Conti *pd* Ward Preston *ed* Richard Halsey

Bruce Dern, Stacy Keach, Robert Mitchum, Martin Sheen, Paul Sorvino, Arthur Franz
● *Video: Palace*

That Cold Day in the Park
Canada 1969 115m Eastmancolor
(Commonwealth United) Donald Factor / Robert Altman / Leon Mirrell

A spinster invites a lonely wandering boy into her home, makes him a prisoner and becomes possessively jealous.
A companion piece to *The Collector*, rather better done for those who like morbid psychology.

w Gillian Freeman, *novel* Richard Miles *d* Robert Altman *ph* Laszlo Kovacs *m* Johnny Mandel

Sandy Dennis, Michael Burns, Suzanne Benton, Luana Anders, John Garfield Jnr
'About as pretentious, loathsome and stupid as a film can get.'—*John Simon*

That Dangerous Age
GB 1949 98m bw
London Films (Gregory Ratoff)
US title: If This Be Sin

Recovering from a breakdown, a KC discovers that his daughter wants to marry a man with whom his wife once had an affair.
Purple patch melodrama which sympathetic actors can't quite freshen up.

w Gene Markey, *play* Autumn by Margaret Kennedy and Ilya Surgutchoff *d* Gregory Ratoff *ph* Georges Périnal *m* Mischa Spoliansky

Roger Livesey, Myrna Loy, Peggy Cummins, Richard Greene, Elizabeth Allan, Gerard Heinz, Jean Cadell, G. H. Mulcaster

That Darn Cat!*
US 1965 116m Technicolor
Walt Disney (Bill Walsh, Ron Miller)

A troublesome cat inadvertently helps to trail bank robbers.
Overlong but generally pleasing small-town comedy with well-paced sequences and a fascinating feline hero.

w The Gordons, Bill Walsh, *novel* Undercover Cat by the Gordons *d* Robert Stevenson *ph* Edward Colman *m* Bob Brunner

Hayley Mills, Dean Jones, Dorothy Provine, Roddy McDowall, Neville Brand, Elsa Lanchester, William Demarest, Frank Gorshin, Grayson Hall, Ed Wynn
● *Video: Rank*

That Forsyte Woman*
US 1949 114m Technicolor
MGM (Leon Gordon)
GB title: The Forsyte Saga

The wife of an Edwardian man of property falls in love with her niece's fiancé.
Moderately successful American attempt to film the first part of a very British novel sequence; so genteel, however, that it becomes dull.

w Jan Lustig, Ivan Tors, James B. Williams, *novel* A Man of Property by John Galsworthy *d* Compton Bennett *ph* Joseph Ruttenberg *m* Bronislau Kaper

Greer Garson, *Errol Flynn*, Robert Young, Janet Leigh, Walter Pidgeon, Harry Davenport, Aubrey Mather

That Funny Feeling
US 1965 92m Technicolor
U-I (Harry Keller)

A maid pretends she lives in her boss's apartment.
Makeshift romantic comedy which barely takes the attention even while it's on.

w David R. Schwarz *d* Richard Thorpe *ph* Clifford Stine *m* Joseph Gershenson

Sandra Dee, Bobby Darin, Donald O'Connor, Nita Talbot, Larry Storch, Leo G. Carroll, James Westerfield

That Girl from Paris
US 1936 105m bw
RKO (Pandro S. Berman)

A Paris opera singer falls for a swing band leader and stows away on a transatlantic liner to be near him.
Comedy-accented musical romance: not bad but not memorable.

w P. J. Wolfson, Dorothy Yost, Jane Murfin *d* Leigh Jason *ph* J. Roy Hunt *m* Edward Heyman *md* Nathaniel Shilkret

Lily Pons, Gene Raymond, Jack Oakie, Herman Bing, Lucille Ball, Mischa Auer, Frank Jenks
'When it's good it's very very good, and when it's bad it's pretty awful.'—*Variety*

'Around her young heart she wore the scarlet letter of another woman's shame!'

That Hagen Girl

US 1947 83m bw
Warner (Alex Gottlieb)

A girl is convinced she is the illegitimate daughter of her teacher.
Stale teenage drama with odd anti-establishment overtones.

w Charles Hoffman, *novel* Edith Kneipple Roberts *d* Peter Godfrey *ph* Karl Freund *m* Franz Waxman

Shirley Temple, Ronald Reagan, Rory Calhoun, Lois Maxwell, Dorothy Peterson, Charles Kemper, Conrad Janis, Harry Davenport

'Less a film than a series of false situations.'—*MFB*

'They shouldn't do such things to Shirley.'—*Bosley Crowther, New York Times*

That Hamilton Woman**

US 1941 128m bw
London Films (Alexander Korda)
GB title: *Lady Hamilton*

The affair of Lord Nelson and Emma Hamilton.
Bowdlerized version of a famous misalliance; coldly made but quite effective scene by scene, with notable performances.

w Walter Reisch, R. C. Sherriff *d* Alexander Korda *ph* Rudolph Maté *m* Miklos Rozsa

Laurence Olivier, Vivien Leigh, Gladys Cooper, Alan Mowbray, Sara Allgood, Henry Wilcoxon, Halliwell Hobbes

AAN: Rudolph Maté

That Kind of Woman

US 1959 92m bw
Paramount / Ponti–Girosi

World War II remake of *Shopworn Angel* (qv); rather well made but basically dated and dull.

w Walter Bernstein *d* Sidney Lumet *ph* Boris Kaufman *m* Daniele Amfitheatrof

Sophia Loren, Tab Hunter, George Sanders, Jack Warden, Barbara Nicholas, Keenan Wynn

'The romantic reunion of Tab Hunter and Sophia Loren resembles nothing so much as a sea scout given a luxury liner for Christmas.'—*Peter John Dyer*

That Lady

GB 1955 100m Eastmancolor Cinemascope
TCF / Atlanta (Sy Bartlett)

A noble widow at the court of Philip II of Spain loves a minister but incurs the king's jealous hatred.
Tepid historical romance which never flows as a film should.

w Anthony Veiller, Sy Bartlett, *novel* Kate O'Brien *d* Terence Young *ph* Robert Krasker *m* John Addison

Olivia de Havilland, Gilbert Roland, *Paul Scofield,* Françoise Rosay, Dennis Price,

Anthony Dawson, Robert Harris, Peter Illing, Christopher Lee

'Somehow, somewhere, one feels, something went very wrong.'—*MFB*

That Lady in Ermine

US 1948 89m Technicolor
TCF (Ernst Lubitsch)

Two generations of European noblewomen learn to repel invaders.
Cheerless musical comedy which never gets started, what with the director dying during production and unsuitable stars lost in tinselly sets; the result can have appealed to no one.

w Samson Raphaelson *d* Ernst Lubitsch, Otto Preminger *ph* Leon Shamroy *songs* Leo Robin, Frederick Hollander

Betty Grable, Douglas Fairbanks Jnr, Cesar Romero, Walter Abel, Reginald Gardiner, Harry Davenport

AAN: song 'This Seems to be the Moment' (*m* Frederick Hollander, *ly* Leo Robin)

That Lucky Touch

GB 1975 93m Technicolor
Rank / Gloria (Dimitri de Grunwald)

During NATO war games in Brussels, a lady correspondent falls for an arms dealer.
Dim romantic farce which gives the impression of emanating from a dog-eared script written for the kind of stars who no longer shine.

w John Briley, *story* Moss Hart *d* Christopher Miles *ph* Douglas Slocombe *m* John Scott

Roger Moore, Susannah York, Lee J. Cobb, Shelley Winters, Jean-Pierre Cassel, Raf Vallone, Sydne Rome, Donald Sinden

● Video: VCL

That Man Bolt

US 1973 103m Technicolor
Universal (Bernard Schwarz)

Adventures of a professional black courier skilled in the martial arts.
Black Kung Fu hokum from a major company; tolerable of its debased kind.

w Quentin Werty, Charles Johnson *d* Henry Levin, David Lowell Rich *ph* Gerald Perry Finnerman *m* Charles Bernstein

Fred Williamson, Bryon Webster, Miko Mayama, Teresa Graves

'Gives every indication of having been devised by a computer fed with a variety of ingredients currently thought to guarantee box office success.'—*John Raisbeck, MFB*

That Man from Rio

France / Italy 1964 120m Eastmancolor
Ariane / Artistes Associés / Dear Film / Vides (Alexander Mnouchkine, Georges Danciger)
original title: *L'Homme de Rio*

An airforce pilot finds himself helping his girl friend in a worldwide search for stolen statuettes.
Elaborate mock thriller which is never quite as much fun as those involved seem to think. It provoked several inferior sequels.

w J. P. Rappeneau, Ariane Mnouchkine, Daniel Boulanger, Philippe de Broca *d* Philippe de Broca *ph* Edmond Séchan *m* Georges Delerue

Jean-Paul Belmondo, Jean Servais, Françoise Dorléac, Adolfo Celi, Simone Renant

'Fantasy takes over, with Belmondo outdoing Fairbanks in agility, Lloyd in cliffhanging, and Bond in indestructibility.'—*Brenda Davies, MFB*

AAN: script

That Midnight Kiss

US 1949 98m Technicolor
MGM (Joe Pasternak)

An unknown becomes a great singing star.
Simple-minded vehicle for the first appearance of Mario Lanza.

w Bruce Manning, Tamara Hovey *d* Norman Taurog *ph* Robert Surtees *m* Bronislau Kaper

Kathryn Grayson, Ethel Barrymore, Jose Iturbi, Mario Lanza, Keenan Wynn, J. Carrol Naish, Jules Munshin, Thomas Gomez, Marjorie Reynolds

That Night*

US 1957 88m bw
Galahad (Himan Brown)

An overwhelmed TV writer has a heart attack, and recovers after a series of medical setbacks.
Impressive minor case history, hardly entertainment but quite arresting.

w Robert Wallace, Burton J. Rowles *d* John Newland *ph* Maurice Hartzband *m* Mario Nascimbene

John Beal, Augusta Dabney, Shepperd Strudwick, Ralph Murphy

That Night in Rio*

US 1941 90m Technicolor
TCF (Fred Kohlmar)

A nightclub entertainer is paid to impersonate a lookalike count, but this causes complications with the countess.
Zippy musical based on a story first used in *Folies Bergère* (qv) and later in *On the Riviera* (qv).

w George Seaton, Bess Meredyth, Hal Long, *play* Rudolph Lothar, Hans Adler *d* Irving Cummings *ph* Leon Shamroy *songs* Mack Gordon, Harry Warren

Don Ameche, Alice Faye, Carmen Miranda, S. Z. Sakall, J. Carrol Naish, Curt Bois, Leonid Kinskey, Maria Montez

That Night with You

US 1945 84m bw
Universal (Michael Fessier, Ernest Pagano)

A girl singer anxious to get on tells a producer that she is his illegitimate daughter.
Mindless farce with music, its gimmick being that all the songs are set to Tchaikovsky's music. Otherwise very dull.

w Michael Fessier, Ernest Pagano *d* William A. Seiter *ph* Woody Bredell

Franchot Tone, Susanna Foster, David Bruce, Louise Allbritton, Buster Keaton, Irene Ryan, Jacqueline de Wit

That Obscure Object of Desire*
France / Spain 1978   103m   Eastmancolor
Greenwich / Galaxie / In Cine (Serge
  Silberman)

A middle-aged gentleman suffers continual
humiliations from the girl he loves.
Unrecognizable remake of a novel previously
filmed as a vehicle for Dietrich and Bardot.
Despite the tricking out with surrealist touches
(the girl is played by two different actresses) it
is not one of Bunuel's best, and amuses only
on the surface.

w Luis Bunuel, Jean-Claude Carrière,
novel La Femme et le Pantin by Pierre Louys
d Luis Bunuel ph Edmond Richard m from
Richard Wagner

Fernando Rey, Carole Bouquet, Angela
Molina, Julien Bertheau

AAN: script

That Riviera Touch
GB 1966   98m   Eastmancolor
Rank (Hugh Stewart)

Two tourists in the south of France get mixed
up with jewel thieves.
Disappointing star comedy ending in a
surfboard chase.

w S. C. Green, R. M. Hills, Peter Blackmore
d Cliff Owen ph Otto Heller m Ron
Goodwin

Eric Morecambe, Ernie Wise, Suzanne Lloyd,
Paul Stassino, Armand Mestral

● Video: Rank

That Touch of Mink**
US 1962   99m   Eastmancolor
Panavision
U-I / Granley / Arwin / Nob Hill (Stanley
  Shapiro, Martin Melcher)

Bachelor tycoon pursues virginal secretary.
Jaded sex comedy (or what passed for it in
nudge-nudge 1962) enlivened by practised star
performances and smart timing.

w Stanley Shapiro, Nate Monaster d Delbert
Mann ph Russell Metty m George Duning

Cary Grant, Doris Day, Gig Young, Audrey
Meadows, Dick Sargent, John Astin

  'Too often there's a hampering second-hand
air about situation and joke. Throughout, the
determination is to keep faith with the
American sex mythology at all costs.'—Jack
Pitman, Variety

AAN: script

● Video: BBC

That Uncertain Feeling*
US 1941   84m   bw
(UA) Sol Lesser (Ernst Lubitsch)

A wife with insomnia and hiccups befriends a
wacky concert pianist who proceeds to move
into her home.
Although Lubitsch had made this story before,
as the silent Kiss Me Again, the elements
didn't really jell in this version, which seemed
silly rather than funny.

w Donald Ogden Stewart, Walter Reisch, play
Divorçons by Victorien Sardou, Emile de
Najac d Ernst Lubitsch ph George Barnes
m Werner Heymann pd Alexander Golitzen

Merle Oberon, Melvyn Douglas, Burgess
Meredith, Alan Mowbray, Olive Blakeney,
Harry Davenport, Eve Arden, Sig Rumann

AAN: Werner Heymann

That Way With Women
US 1947   84m   bw
Warner (Charles Hoffman)

A millionaire amuses himself by playing Cupid
to a young couple.
Routine remake of The Millionaire: just about
watchable.

w Leo Townsend d Frederick de Cordova
ph Ted McCord m Frederick Hollander

Sidney Greenstreet, Dane Clark, Martha
Vickers, Alan Hale, Craig Stevens, Barbara
Brown

That Woman Opposite
GB 1957   83m   bw
Monarch (William Gell)
US title: City after Midnight

In a small French town, a killer returns to
silence a witness.
Slow-paced semi-mystery, reasonably well
done.

wd Compton Bennett, story The Emperor's
Snuff Box by John Dickson Carr ph Lionel
Banes m Stanley Black

Phyllis Kirk, Dan O'Herlihy, Wilfrid Hyde
White, Petula Clark, Jack Watling, William
Franklyn, Margaret Withers

That Wonderful Urge
US 1948   82m   bw
TCF (Fred Kohlmar)

A newspaperman is forced into marriage with
a publicity-shy heiress.
Tepid romantic comedy, a remake of Love Is
News (qv).

w Jay Dratler d Robert B. Sinclair
ph Charles Clarke m Cyril Mockridge

Gene Tierney, Tyrone Power, Reginald
Gardiner, Arleen Whelan, Lucile Watson,
Gene Lockhart, Porter Hall, Taylor Holmes

That'll Be the Day*
GB 1973   91m   Technicolor
EMI / Goodtimes (David Puttnam, Sanford
  Lieberson)

In 1958, a young drifter becomes a fairground
worker, and eventually walks out on his wife
and family to become a pop star.
Spirited return to British realism, with well-
sketched cameos, a likeable dour viewpoint,
and a cheerful pop music background.

w Ray Connolly d Claude Whatham
ph Peter Suschitzky md Neil Aspinall, Keith
Moon

David Essex, Ringo Starr, Rosemary Leach,
James Booth, Billy Fury, Keith Moon,
Rosalind Ayres

  'As insubstantial as one of its own attempts
at a statement.'—Tony Rayns

● Video: Thorn EMI

That's a Good Girl*
GB 1933   83m   bw

A man about town seeks ways of making
money. Archetypal vehicle for a debonair song
and dance man. Jack Buchanan, Elsie
Randolph, Dorothy Hyson, Garry Marsh,
Vera Pearce, William Kendall. Written by
Douglas Furber, Donovan Pedelty and Jack
Buchanan; directed by Jack Buchanan; for
Herbert Wilcox.

'Boy! do we need it now!'
That's Entertainment**
US 1974   137m   Metrocolor   70mm
  (blown up) / scope
MGM (Daniel Melnick, Jack Haley Jnr)

Fred Astaire, Gene Kelly, Elizabeth Taylor,
James Stewart, Bing Crosby, Liza Minnelli,
Donald O'Connor, Debbie Reynolds, Mickey
Rooney and Frank Sinatra introduce highlights
from MGM's musical past.
A slapdash compilation which was generally
very big at the box office and obviously has
fascinating sequences, though the narration is
sloppily sentimental and the later wide-screen
sequences let down the rest.

wd Jack Haley Jnr ph various m various

principal stars as above plus Judy Garland,
Esther Williams, Eleanor Powell, Clark
Gable, Ray Bolger

  'While many ponder the future of MGM,
none can deny that it has one hell of a
past.'—Variety
  'It is particularly gratifying to get the key
sequences from certain movies without having
to sit through a fatuous storyline.'—Michael
Billington, Illustrated London News
  'No other film in town offers such a harvest
of undiluted joy.'—Sunday Express

● Video: MGM / UA

That's Entertainment Part Two**
US 1976   133m   Metrocolor   70mm
  (blown up) / scope
MGM (Saul Chaplin, Daniel Melnick)

More of the above, introduced by Fred
Astaire and Gene Kelly, with comedy and
drama sequences as well as musical.

d Gene Kelly titles Saul Bass ph various

principal stars as above plus Jeanette
MacDonald, Nelson Eddy, the Marx Brothers,
Laurel and Hardy, Jack Buchanan, Judy
Garland, Ann Miller, Mickey Rooney, Oscar
Levant, Louis Armstrong, etc.

● Video: MGM / UA

That's My Boy
US 1951   98m   bw
Paramount / Hal B. Wallis (Cy Howard)

An athletic father tries to press his
hypochondriac teenage son into the same
mould.
American college comedy of no international
interest.

w Cy Howard d Hal Walker ph Lee Garmes
m Leigh Harline

Dean Martin, Jerry Lewis, Eddie Mayehoff,
Ruth Hussey, Polly Bergen, John McIntire

That's My Man

US 1946 98m bw
Republic (Frank Borzage)
GB title: *Will Tomorrow Ever Come?*

A racing man is reunited with his wife when their son has pneumonia.
A compendium of clichés, with everything but a title card reading *Came the Dawn.* Of no real interest.

w Steve Fisher, Bradley King *d* Frank Borzage *ph* Tony Gaudio *m* Cy Feuer

Don Ameche, Catherine McLeod, Roscoe Karns, John Ridgely

That's My Wife°

US 1929 20m bw silent

Stan dresses up as Ollie's wife to impress his rich uncle. Lesser-known star comedy which well sustains its basic joke and includes some splendidly timed farce in a restaurant. Laurel and Hardy, Vivien Oakland, William Courtright. Written by Leo McCarey and H. M. Walker; directed by Lloyd French; for Hal Roach.

That's Right, You're Wrong°

US 1939 91m bw
RKO (David Butler)

A band leader gets a Hollywood contract but is hated by the studio head.
Typical of the nonsense musicals featuring Kay Kyser and his radio Kollege of Musical Knowledge. The movie background and self-spoofing made this first attempt one of the best.

w William Conselman, James V. Kern *d* David Butler *ph* Russell Metty *m* George Duning *songs* various

Kay Kyser, Adolphe Menjou, Lucille Ball, Dennis O'Keefe, May Robson, Edward Everett Horton, Ish Kabibble, Ginny Simms, Roscoe Karns, Moroni Olsen, Hobart Cavanaugh, Sheilah Graham, Hedda Hopper
'Moderate entertainment which will satisfy as a bill-topper.'—*Variety*

That's the Spirit

US 1943 87m bw

A ghost comes back to tell his actress wife he didn't desert her as she thought. Rather heavy comedy of the *Here Comes Mr Jordan* school. Jack Oakie, Peggy Ryan, June Vincent, Gene Lockhart, Andy Devine, Arthur Treacher, Irene Ryan, Buster Keaton. Written by Michael Fessier and Ernest Pagano; directed by Charles Lamont; for Universal.

Theatre of Blood°

GB 1973 102m De Luxe
UA / Cineman (John Kohn, Stanley Mann)

A Shakespearean actor uses appropriate murder methods on the various critics who have ridiculed his performances.
Spoof horror picture which goes too far with some sick visuals; the idea and some of the performances are fine.

w Anthony Greville-Bell *d* Douglas Hickox *ph* Wolfgang Suschitzky *m* Michael J. Lewis *pd* Michael Seymour

Vincent Price, Diana Rigg, Ian Hendry, Harry Andrews, Coral Browne, Robert Coote, Jack Hawkins, Michael Hordern, Arthur Lowe, Robert Morley, Dennis Price, Diana Dors, Joan Hickson, Renée Asherson, Milo O'Shea, Eric Sykes

Theatre of Death

GB 1966 91m Techniscope

Vampire-like murders in Paris are eventually connected with a Grand Guignol theatre. Dreary backstage shocker with inadequate production values. Christopher Lee, Jenny Till, Lelia Goldoni, Julian Glover, Ivor Dean, Evelyn Laye. Written by Roger Marshall and Ellis Kadison; directed by Sam Gallu; for Michael Smedley–Aston / Pennea.

Theatre Royal

GB 1943 92m bw

A revue and a theatre are saved by a sentimental prop man. Shapeless star comedy with music; not their best. Bud Flanagan and Chesney Allen, Peggy Dexter, Lydia Sherwood, Horace Kenney, Marjorie Rhodes, Finlay Currie. Written by Bud Flanagan, Austin Melford and Geoffrey Orme; directed by John Baxter; for British National.

Their Big Moment

US 1934 68m bw

Phoney mindreaders solve a murder mystery in a spooky house. Quite good, well-organized fun of its type. Zasu Pitts, Slim Summerville, William Gaxton, Ralph Morgan, Bruce Cabot, Julie Haydon, Kay Johnson. Written by Arthur Caesar, Marian Dix, Walter Hackett; directed by James Cruze; for RKO. 'Should have fairly good audience strength.'—*Variety*

Their First Mistake°°

US 1932 20m bw

Ollie decides to improve his marriage by adopting a baby, only to find that his wife has left him. Sublimely silly but endearing star comedy with brilliant passages of imbecilic conversation followed by well-timed farce. Laurel and Hardy, Mae Busch. Written by H. M. Walker; directed by George Marshall (who also plays a bit); for Hal Roach.

Their Purple Moment

US 1928 20m bw silent

Stan and Ollie go out on the town, only to discover that Stan's wife has replaced his money with grocery coupons. Minor star comedy with efficient but predictable restaurant scenes ending in a pie fight. Laurel and Hardy, Anita Garvin, Kay Deslys. Written by H. M. Walker; directed by James Parrott; for Hal Roach.

'Kill one and two others take its place!
   Don't turn your back or you're doomed!
   And don't tell anyone what Them are!'

Them!°°°

US 1954 94m bw
Warner (David Weisbart)

Atomic bomb radiation causes giant ants to breed in the New Mexico desert.

Among the first, and certainly the best, of the post-atomic monster animal cycle, this durable thriller starts with several eerie desert sequences and builds up to a shattering climax in the Los Angeles sewers. A general air of understatement helps a lot.

w Ted Sherdeman, *story* George Worthing Yates *d* Gordon Douglas *ph* Sid Hickox *m* Bronislau Kaper

Edmund Gwenn, James Whitmore, Joan Weldon, James Arness, Onslow Stevens
'I asked the editor: How does it look? And he said: Fine. I said: Does it look honest? He said: As honest as twelve foot ants can look.'—*Gordon Douglas*

Them Thar Hills°°

US 1934 20m bw

Stan and Ollie go camping, drink from a well full of moonshine whisky, and get drunk with another camper's wife. Consistently funny star comedy culminating in a tit-for-tat routine which was reprised in *Tit for Tat* the following year. Laurel and Hardy, Charlie Hall, Mae Busch, Billy Gilbert. Written by Stan Laurel and H. M. Walker; directed by Charles Rogers; for Hal Roach.

Theodora Goes Wild°

US 1936 94m bw
Columbia (Everett Riskin)

A small-town girl writes a titillating bestseller. Mildly crazy comedy which helped develop the trend for stars performing undignified antics but today seems rather slow and dated.

w Sidney Buchman, *story* Mary McCarthy *d* Richard Boleslawski *ph* Joseph Walker *m* Morris Stoloff

Irene Dunne, Melvyn Douglas, Thomas Mitchell, Thurston Hall, Rosalind Keith, Spring Byington, Elizabeth Risdon, Nana Bryant

AAN: Irene Dunne

Theorem°

Italy 1968 98m Eastmancolor
Aetos Film

A handsome young man arrives unexpectedly to stay with a Milan industrialist and his family, gratifying their desires but leaving them tragically unhappy.
Moderately amusing fable with the presumed intent of decrying all universal panaceas, including Christianity.

wd Pier Paolo Pasolini, from his novel *ph* Giuseppe Ruzzolini *m* Ennio Morricone

Terence Stamp, Silvana Mangano, Massimo Girotti, Anne Wiazemsky, Laura Betti

There Ain't No Justice

GB 1939 83m bw

A young boxer refuses to throw a fight. Minor sporting drama, well praised at the time but later forgotten. Jimmy Hanley, Edward Rigby, Mary Clare, Edward Chapman, Phyllis Stanley, Michael Wilding. Written by Pen Tennyson, James Curtis and Sergei Nolbandov; directed by Pen Tennyson; for Ealing.

There Goes My Heart
US 1938 81m bw
Hal Roach

A reporter is assigned to track down a runaway heiress.
Very pale imitation of *It Happened One Night*.

w Jack Jevne, Eddie Moran d Norman Z. McLeod ph Norbert Brodine m Marvin Hatley

Fredric March, Virginia Bruce, Patsy Kelly, Nancy Carroll, Eugene Pallette, Claude Gillingwater, Arthur Lake, Harry Langdon, Etienne Girardot

'A comedy clicko . . . plenty of zip and zing.'—*Variety*

AAN: Marvin Hatley

There Goes the Bride
GB 1980 91m Eastmancolor
Lonsdale (Martin Schute, Ray Cooney)

A harassed advertising executive suffers hallucinations about a lifesize cardboard cut-out of a twenties flapper.
Embarrassingly witless and plotless revamp of innumerable better comedies in the *Topper* tradition; it has to be seen to be believed.

w Terence Marcel, Ray Cooney play Ray Cooney and John Chapman d Terence Marcel ph James Devis m Harry Robinson pd Peter Mullins

Tom Smothers, Twiggy, Sylvia Syms, Martin Balsam, Michael Whitney, Geoffrey Sumner, Hermione Baddeley, Phil Silvers, Broderick Crawford, Jim Backus

'The whole thing would be laughable if it weren't so unfunny.'—*Gilbert Adair, MFB*

There Is Another Sun
GB 1951 95m bw

A fairground wall of death rider turns to crime. Glum quickie which was oddly popular.
Maxwell Reed, Susan Shaw, Laurence Harvey, Hermione Baddeley, Leslie Dwyer. Written by Guy Morgan; directed by Lewis Gilbert; for Butcher's.

There Was a Crooked Man*
GB 1960 107m bw
UA / Knightsbridge (John Bryan)

An ex-safecracker outwits the crooked mayor of an industrial town.
Semi-happy attempt to humanize a knockabout clown; good supporting performances and production.

w Reuben Ship d Stuart Burge ph Arthur Ibbetson m Kenneth V. Jones

Norman Wisdom, Andrew Cruickshank, Alfred Marks, Susannah York, Reginald Beckwith

There Was a Crooked Man*
US 1970 126m Technicolor
   Panavision
Warner Seven Arts (Joseph L. Mankiewicz)

In 1883 Arizona a murderer tries to escape from jail and recover hidden loot but is constantly thwarted by the sheriff who arrested him, now a warden.
Curious black comedy melodrama with lots of talent going nowhere in particular; hard to endure as a whole but with entertaining scenes.

w David Newman, Robert Benton d Joseph L. Mankiewicz ph Harry Stradling Jnr m Charles Strouse ad Edward Carrere

Kirk Douglas, Henry Fonda, Hume Cronyn, Warren Oates, Burgess Meredith, John Randolph, Arthur O'Connell, Martin Gabel, Alan Hale

'This example of commercialized black comedy nihilism seems to have been written by an evil two-year-old, and it has been directed in the Grand Rapids style of moviemaking.'—*Pauline Kael, New Yorker*

There's a Girl in My Soup*
GB 1970 96m Eastmancolor
Columbia / Ascot (John Boulting)

A randy TV personality finds himself outplotted by a waif he picks up.
Flimsy screen version of a long-running sex comedy; some laughs, but the star is uncomfortably miscast.

w Terence Frisby, from his play d Roy Boulting ph Harry Waxman m Mike D'Abo

Peter Sellers, Goldie Hawn, Tony Britton, Nicky Henson, John Comer, Diana Dors, Judy Campbell

There's Always a Woman*
US 1938 81m bw

A private detective's wife beats him to the solution of a murder. Amiably scatty crime comedy in the *Thin Man* tradition. Joan Blondell, Melvyn Douglas, Mary Astor, Frances Drake, Jerome Cowan, Robert Paige, Thurston Hall, Pierre Watkin. Written by Gladys Lehman, Wilson Collison; directed by Alexander Hall; for Columbia. 'Will provide general satisfaction as entertainment and as a grosser.'—*Variety*

There's Always Tomorrow
US 1934 86m bw

A depressed family man is cheered up by a former sweetheart. Basically rather a dull drama, but with sincere performances which lift it. Frank Morgan, Binnie Barnes, Lois Wilson, Louise Latimer, Alan Hale, Robert Taylor. Written by William Hurlbut from the novel by Ursula Parrott; directed by Edward Sloman; for MGM. 'Attractive screen material, it weighs in for what looks like a favourable sprint for coin.'—*Variety*. (NB: Remade 1956 as *These Wilder Years*, with James Cagney and Barbara Stanwyck.)

There's Always Tomorrow
US 1956 84m bw
Universal (Ross Hunter)

A married man falls for another woman.
Very flat variation on *Brief Encounter*, with stars going through mechanical paces.

w Bernard Schoenfeld, story Ursula Parrott d Douglas Sirk ph Russell Metty m Herman Stein, Heinz Roemheld

Barbara Stanwyck, Fred MacMurray, Joan Bennett, Pat Crowley, William Reynolds, Gigi Perreau, Jane Darwell

† Previously made by Universal in 1934 with Frank Morgan and Binnie Barnes.

There's Magic in Music
US 1941 80m bw

An ex-burlesque girl gets her break entertaining at a summer camp. Fair exhibition ground for young musical talent. Allan Jones, Susanna Foster, Diana Lynn, Margaret Lindsay, Lynne Overman, Grace Bradley, William Collier Snr. Written and directed by Andrew L. Stone; for Paramount.

There's No Business like Show Business**
US 1954 117m De Luxe Cinemascope
TCF (Sol C. Siegel)

The life and times of a family of vaudevillians.
Mainly entertaining events and marvellous tunes make up this very Cinemascoped musical, in which the screen is usually filled with six people side by side.

w Phoebe and Henry Ephron d Walter Lang ph Leon Shamroy m / ly Irving Berlin ad John de Cuir, Lyle Wheeler m Lionel Newman, Alfred Newman

Ethel Merman, Dan Dailey, Marilyn Monroe, Donald O'Connor, Johnny Ray, Mitzi Gaynor, Hugh O'Brian, Frank McHugh

AAN: original story (Lamar Trotti); Lionel Newman, Alfred Newman

● *Video: CBS / Fox*

There's That Woman Again
US 1938 75m bw

A district attorney is hampered by his meddlesome spouse. Half-hearted follow-up to *There's Always a Woman*; the *McMillan and Wife* of its day. Melvyn Douglas, Virginia Bruce, Margaret Lindsay, Stanley Ridges, Gordon Oliver, Tom Dugan, Don Beddoe. Written by Philip G. Epstein, James Edward Grant and Ken Englund; directed by Alexander Hall; for Columbia.

These Dangerous Years
GB 1957 92m bw
British Lion / Anna Neagle
US title: *Dangerous Youth*

A Liverpool teenage gang leader is called up and becomes a better guy.
Dim drama with music marking the debut of a singing star.

w John Trevor Story d Herbert Wilcox ph Gordon Dines m Stanley Black

Frankie Vaughan, George Baker, Carole Lesley, Jackie Lane, Katherine Kath, Eddie Byrne, Kenneth Cope

These Glamour Girls
US 1939 78m bw

A drunken college student invites a dime-a-dance girl for a festive weekend with his snobbish friends. Wincingly predictable romantic comedy-drama with no outstanding talent displayed from any quarter. Lew Ayres, Lana Turner, Tom Brown, Richard Carlson, Jane Bryan, Anita Louise, Ann Rutherford, Marsha Hunt. Written by Marion Parsonnet and Jane Hall; directed by S. Sylvan Simon; for MGM. 'Silly situations and mawkish lines. A dualler.'—*Variety*

These Thousand Hills
US 1958 96m Eastmancolor
Cinemascope
TCF (David Weisbart)

A successful cattle rancher finds that his best friend is a rustler.
Large-scale but somehow unimpressive western variant on *The Virginian*, cluttered with sub-plots.

w Alfred Hayes, *novel* A. B. Guthrie Jnr
d Richard Fleischer ph Charles G. Clarke
m Leigh Harline

Richard Egan, Stuart Whitman, Don Murray, Lee Remick, Albert Dekker, Harold J. Stone, Patricia Owens

These Three**
US 1936 93m bw
Samuel Goldwyn

A lying schoolgirl accuses two schoolmistresses of scandalous behaviour.
Bowdlerized version of a famous play (instead of lesbianism we have extra-marital affairs). It worked well enough at the time but now seems dated; oddly enough when the play was filmed full strength in 1962 it didn't work at all.

w Lillian Hellman, from her play *The Children's Hour* d William Wyler ph Gregg Toland m Alfred Newman

Merle Oberon, Miriam Hopkins, Joel McCrea, *Bonita Granville*, Catherine Doucet, Alma Kruger, Marcia Mae Jones, Margaret Hamilton, Walter Brennan

AAN: Bonita Granville

These Wilder Years
US 1956 91m bw
MGM (Jules Schermer)

A wealthy industrialist returns to his home town to trace his illegitimate son.
Modest sentimental drama with practised stars.

w Frank Fenton d Roy Rowland ph George Folsey m Jeff Alexander

James Cagney, Barbara Stanwyck, Walter Pidgeon, Betty Lou Keim, Don Dubbins, Edward Andrews

They All Kissed the Bride
US 1942 86m bw
Columbia (Edward Kaufman)

A woman executive falls in love with the crusading writer who is out to expose working conditions in her company.
No surprises are expected or provided in this very ho-hum romantic comedy.

w P. J. Wolfson d Alexander Hall ph Joseph Walker m Werner Heyman md Morris Stoloff

Joan Crawford, Melvyn Douglas, Roland Young, Billie Burke, Allen Jenkins, Andrew Tombes, Helen Parrish, Mary Treen

AAN: Joan Crawford

They All Laughed*
US 1982 115m Movielab
Time-Life / Moon (George Morfogen, Blaine Novak)

Three agency detectives fall in and out of love in the course of their duties.
It has the air of a somewhat misshapen and Americanized *La Ronde*, with added suggestions of *On the Town*, but it adds up to very little and provides only a few laughs on the way.

w,d Peter Bogdanovich ph Robby Muller
m various

Audrey Hepburn, Ben Gazzara, John Ritter, Dorothy Stratten, Colleen Camp, Patti Hansen, George Morfogen, Blaine Novak
'One tires of long looks that speak volumes, of endless successions of meeting cute.'—*John Pym, MFB*

They Call It Sin
US 1932 68m bw

A Kansas girl joins a New York chorus and needs to be rescued from a villainous producer. Ho-hum romantic drama without much substance. Loretta Young, George Brent, Louis Calhern, David Manners, Una Merkel. Written by Lillie Hayward and Howard Green from the novel by Alberta Steadman Eagan; directed by Thornton Freeland; for First National. 'It needs the sexy title to bolster a just so-so flicker.'—*Variety*

They Call Me Mister Tibbs!
US 1970 108m De Luxe
UA / Mirisch (Herbert Hirshman)

A San Francisco police lieutenant suspects a crusading local minister of murder.
Flat, dispirited police melodrama with irrelevant domestic asides, a long way after *In the Heat of the Night* which introduced the main character. (*The Organization* was the third and last in the so-called series.)

w Alan R. Trustman, James R. Webb
d Gordon Douglas ph Gerald Finnerman
m Quincy Jones

Sidney Poitier, Martin Landau, Barbara McNair, Anthony Zerbe, Jeff Corey, Juano Hernandez, Ed Asner

They Came by Night
GB 1939 72m bw

A jeweller pretends to be a crook in order to lure the men who killed his brother. Smart little suspense yarn. Will Fyffe, Phyllis Calvert, Anthony Hulme, George Merritt, Athole Stewart, John Glyn Jones. Written by Frank Launder, Sidney Gilliatt, Michael Hogan and Roland Pertwee; directed by Harry Lachman; for TCF.

They Came to a City*
GB 1944 77m bw
Ealing (Sidney Cole)

Assorted people find themselves outside the gates of a mysterious city.
The *Outward Bound* format applied to post-war reconstruction, with characters deciding what kind of a world they want. Good talk and good acting, but not quite cinema.

w Basil Dearden, Sidney Cole, *play* J. B. Priestley d Basil Dearden ph Stan Pavey

Googie Withers, John Clements, Raymond Huntley, Renée Gadd, A. E. Matthews, Mabel Terry-Lewis, *Ada Reeve*, Norman Shelley, Frances Rowe

They Came to Blow Up America
US 1973 73m bw

An FBI man of German parentage goes to Nazi Germany and trains with a group of saboteurs, who are arrested when they set foot in the US. Tolerable propaganda potboiler. George Sanders, Anna Sten, Ward Bond, Dennis Hoey, Sig Rumann, Ludwig Stossel. Written by Aubrey Wisberg; directed by Edward Ludwig; for TCF.

They Came to Cordura*
US 1959 123m Technicolor
Cinemascope
Columbia / Goetz–Baroda (William Goetz)

In 1916 Mexico, six American military heroes are recalled to base, but the hardships of the journey reveal their true colours.
Watchable adventure epic, not so arresting as was intended but quite professional.

w Ivan Moffat, Robert Rossen, *novel* Glendon Swarthout d Robert Rossen ph Burnett Guffey m Elie Siegmeister

Gary Cooper, Rita Hayworth, Van Heflin, Richard Conte, Tab Hunter, Michael Callan, Dick York, Robert Keith

They Came to Rob Las Vegas*
Spain / France / Germany / Italy 1969
128m Techniscope
Warner / Isasi / Capitoli / Eichberg / Franca

Criminals ambush a security truck in the Nevada desert.
Long-winded, flashily directed, gleamingly photographed, occasionally lively, frequently violent, finally tedious caper melodrama with a multi-lingual cast.

w Antonio Isasi, Jo Eisinger d Antonio Isasi ph Juan Gelpi m Georges Gavarentz

Jack Palance, Lee J. Cobb, Elke Sommer, Gary Lockwood, Georges Geret, Jean Servais

They Dare Not Love
US 1941 76m bw
Columbia (Sam Bischoff)

An Austrian prince flees the Nazis, but they force him to return and he has to leave his fiancée in America.
Curiously naïve romantic propaganda from this director; not at all memorable.

w Charles Bennett, Ernest Vajda d James Whale ph Franz Planer m Morris Stoloff

George Brent, Martha Scott, Paul Lukas,
Egon Brecher, Roman Bohnen, Edgar
Barrier, Frank Reicher

They Died with Their Boots On••
US 1941 140m bw
Warner (Robert Fellows)

The life of General Custer and his death at
Little Big Horn.
It seems it all happened because of an evil
cadet who finished up selling guns to the
Indians. Oh, well! The first half is romantic
comedy, the second steels itself for the
inevitable tragic outcome, but it's all expertly
mounted and played in the best old Hollywood
style.

w Wally Kline, Aeneas Mackenzie d Raoul
Walsh ph Bert Glennon m Max Steiner

Errol Flynn, Olivia de Havilland, Arthur
Kennedy, Charles Grapewin, Anthony Quinn,
Sidney Greenstreet, Gene Lockhart, Stanley
Ridges, John Litel, Walter Hampden, Regis
Toomey, Hattie McDaniel

They Drive by Night••
GB 1938 84m bw
Warner (Jerome Jackson)

An ex-convict is helped by lorry drivers to
solve the silk stocking murders of which he is
suspected.
Excellent, little-seen British suspenser of the
Hitchcock school.

w Derek Twist, novel James Curtis d Arthur
Woods ph Basil Emmott

Emlyn Williams, Ernest Thesiger, Anna
Konstam, Allan Jeayes, Antony Holles,
Ronald Shiner
  'Dialogue, acting and direction put this
picture on a level with the French cinema.'—
Graham Greene

They Drive by Night••
US 1940 97m bw
Warner (Mark Hellinger)
GB title: The Road to Frisco

A truck driver loses his brother in an accident,
and in an attempt to improve his lot becomes
involved with a scheming murderess.
Solid melodramatic entertainment which
borrows the second half of its plot from
Bordertown.

w Jerry Wald, Richard Macaulay, novel Long
Haul by A. I. Bezzerides d Raoul Walsh
ph Arthur Edeson md Adolph Deutsch

George Raft, Humphrey Bogart, Ann
Sheridan, Ida Lupino, Gale Page, Alan Hale,
Roscoe Karns, John Litel, Henry O'Neill,
George Tobias

They Flew Alone•
GB 1941 103m bw
RKO / Imperator (Herbert Wilcox)
US title: Wings and the Woman

The story of Amy Johnson and Jim Mollison,
married flying pioneers of the thirties.
Adequate fictionalized history with interesting
historical detail.

w Miles Malleson d Herbert Wilcox

THEY CAME TO ROB LAS VEGAS. Cops and robbers were old hat, but in the sixties the audience always seemed to be on the side of the robbers.

Anna Neagle, Robert Newton, Edward Chapman, Nora Swinburne, Joan Kemp-Welch, Charles Carson, Brefni O'Rourke

They Gave Him a Gun
US 1937   94m   bw
MGM (Harry Rapf)

Despite the efforts of his friend, a war-hardened veteran turns to crime and comes to a sticky end.
Dullish moral melodrama with its stars looking as though stuck in glue.

w Cyril Hume, Richard Maibaum, Maurice Rapf, *novel* William Joyce Cowan
d W. S. Van Dyke II ph Harold Rosson

Spencer Tracy, Franchot Tone, Gladys George, Edgar Dearing, Mary Treen, Cliff Edwards
'Meller overboard on grief. Does not sum up as having b.o. punch.'—*Variety*

They Go Boom
US 1929   20m   bw

Stan's nocturnal efforts to cure Ollie's cold nearly bring down the house about their ears.
Average, rather protracted star comedy.
Laurel and Hardy, Charlie Hall. Written by Leo McCarey and H. M. Walker; directed by James Parrott; for Hal Roach.

They Got Me Covered*
US 1943   93m   bw
Samuel Goldwyn

An incompetent foreign correspondent inadvertently breaks up a spy ring in Washington.
One of Hope's better and most typical comedy-thriller vehicles.

w Harry Kurnitz d David Butler ph Rudolph Maté m Leigh Harline

Bob Hope, Dorothy Lamour, Otto Preminger, Lenore Aubert, Eduardo Ciannelli, Marion Martin, Donald Meek, Donald MacBride, Walter Catlett, John Abbott, Florence Bates, Philip Ahn

They Just Had to Get Married
US 1933   69m   bw

A butler and maid come into money and rise in the social scale. Rather muddled comedy for star fans. Zasu Pitts, Slim Summerville, C. Aubrey Smith, Roland Young, Verree Teasdale, Fifi D'Orsay, Robert Greig, David Landau, Elizabeth Patterson. Written by Gladys Lehman and H. M. Walker from the play by Syril Harcourt; directed by Edward Ludwig; for Universal. 'Not for big town first runs, but a booker's selection for B houses or less.'—*Variety*

They Knew Mr Knight
GB 1945   93m   bw

A clerk and his family become rich, then poor, through listening to a speculator. Slightly oddball domestic drama reminiscent of Priestley's *Angel Pavement*. Mervyn Johns,

Alfred Drayton, Nora Swinburne, Joyce Howard, Joan Greenwood, Olive Sloane, Peter Hammond. Written by Norman Walker and Victor MacClure, from the novel by Dorothy Whipple; directed by Norman Walker; for IP / GHW.

They Knew What They Wanted**
US 1940   96m   bw
RKO (Erich Pommer)

A waitress agrees by mail to marry a California-Italian vineyard owner, but is aghast when she arrives to discover that he sent his handsome foreman's photograph.
First-rate minor drama, expertly handled by stars and production team alike.

w Robert Ardrey, *play* Sidney Howard
d Garson Kanin ph Harry Stradling
m Alfred Newman

Charles Laughton, Carole Lombard, William Gargan, Harry Carey, Frank Fay
'For dialogue, acting, background and film creation it's a honey.'—*Otis Ferguson*
† Previous versions include *The Secret Love* (1928) with Pola Negri and *A Lady to Love* (1930) with Vilma Banky (and Edward G. Robinson).
AAN: William Gargan

They Live by Night*
US 1948   96m   bw
RKO

A young man imprisoned for an accidental killing escapes with two hardened criminals and is forced to take part in their crimes.
Well-made if basically uninteresting melodrama with a draggy romantic interest; its 'realistic' yet impressionist style drew attention on its first release, and it was remade in the seventies as *Thieves like Us* (qv).

w Charles Schnee d Nicholas Ray ph George E. Diskant m Leigh Harline

Farley Granger, Cathy O'Donnell, Howard da Silva

They Made Me a Criminal*
US 1939   92m   bw
Warner (Benjamin Glazer)

When he thinks he has killed a boxing opponent, a young man flees to the west and settles on a farm.
Competent remake of *The Life of Jimmy Dolan*, a tribute to the American way.

w Sig Herzig d Busby Berkeley ph James Wong Howe m Max Steiner

John Garfield, Claude Rains, Gloria Dickson, May Robson, Billy Halop, Bobby Jordan, Leo Gorcey, Huntz Hall, Gabriel Dell, Ann Sheridan
'Handsomely mounted and printed on sepia stock—all of which helps.'—*Variety*
● Video: VCL

They Made Me a Fugitive*
GB 1947   104m   bw
Warner / Alliance (Nat Bransten, James Carter)
US title: *I Became a Criminal*

An ex-RAF pilot is drawn into black marketeering. Framed for a killing, he escapes

from Dartmoor and takes revenge on the gang leader.
Deliberately squalid thriller which began a fashion for British realism, but now seems only momentarily entertaining.

w Noel Langley, *novel* A Convict Has Escaped by Jackson Budd d Alberto Cavalcanti ph Otto Heller

Trevor Howard, Sally Gray, *Griffith Jones*, René Ray, Mary Merrall, Vida Hope, Ballard Berkeley, Phyllis Robins

They Met in Bombay*
US 1941   86m   bw
MGM (Hunt Stromberg)

Jewel thieves on the run in the East fall in love.
A rather unusual romantic comedy chase which provides pretty satisfactory star entertainment.

w Edwin Justus Mayer, Anita Loos, Leon Gordon d Clarence Brown ph William Daniels m Herbert Stothart

Clark Gable, Rosalind Russell, Peter Lorre, Reginald Owen, Jessie Ralph, Matthew Boulton, Eduardo Ciannelli, Luis Alberni

They Met in the Dark
GB 1943   104m   bw

A Blackpool theatrical agent is really a master spy. Elementary spy romance with a richly villainous performance from *Tom Walls*. Joyce Howard, James Mason, Phyllis Stanley, Edward Rigby, Ronald Ward, David Farrar. Written by Anatole de Grunwald, Miles Malleson, Basil Bartlett, Victor MacClure and James Seymour, from the novel *The Vanishing Corpse* by Anthony Gilbert; directed by Karel Lamac; for Marcel Hellman / Rank.

They Might be Giants*
US 1972   88m   Technicolor
Universal / Paul Newman, John Foreman

A lawyer imagines he is Sherlock Holmes, and is taken in hand by Dr Mildred Watson.
Curious fantasy comedy which rather tentatively satirizes modern life and the need to retreat into unreality. Mildly pleasing entertainment for intellectuals.

w James Goldman, from his play d Anthony Harvey ph Victor Kemper m John Barry

George C. Scott, Joanne Woodward, Jack Gilford, Lester Rawlins

They Only Kill Their Masters*
US 1972   98m   Metrocolor
MGM (William Belasco)

A village police chief doggedly solves a series of murders.
Atmospheric, serio-comic murder mystery with a cast of old hands.

w Lane Slate d James Goldstone ph Michel Hugo m Perry Botkin Jnr

James Garner, Katharine Ross, Hal Holbrook, June Allyson, Harry Guardino, Tom Ewell, Peter Lawford, Ann Rutherford, Chris Connelly, Edmond O'Brien, Art Metrano, Arthur O'Connell

THEY DRIVE BY NIGHT (1940).   George Raft, Ann Sheridan and Humphrey Bogart don't enjoy being ribbed by John Litel, so anything may happen in the next shot.

'The lovers of *The Caine Mutiny* have a picture all their own!'

They Rode West

US 1954   84m   Technicolor

A cavalry doctor at a frontier fort gets into trouble by trying to help the Indians. Western programmer whose sights are higher than its achievement. Robert Francis, Donna Reed, May Wynn, Phil Carey, Onslow Stevens, Jack Kelly. Written by De Vallon Scott and Frank Nugent; directed by Phil Karlson; for Columbia.

They Shall Have Music

US 1939   105m   bw

Samuel Goldwyn

GB title: *Melody of Youth*

Jascha Heifetz conducts a charity concert to help a music school for slum children.

Formula family film given the best possible production.

w *John Howard Lawson, Irmgard Von Cube* d Archie Mayo ph Gregg Toland md Alfred Newman

Joel McCrea, Jascha Heifetz, Andrea Leeds, Gene Reynolds, Walter Brennan, Porter Hall, Terry Kilburn, Diana Lynn (Dolly Loehr)

   'A natural for the musically minded . . . elemental and surefire audience appeal.'— *Variety*

AAN: Alfred Newman

They Shoot Horses, Don't They?*

US 1969   129m   De Luxe   Panavision

Palomar / Chartoff–Winkler–Pollack

Tragedy during a six-day marathon dance contest in the early thirties.

An unrelievedly harrowing melodrama about dreary people, confused by 'flashforwards' but full of skilled technique, entertaining detail, and one brilliant performance.

w James Poe, Robert E. Thompson, *novel* Horace McCoy d Sydney Pollack ph Philip Lathrop m John Green md John Green, Albert Woodbury pd Harry Horner

Gig Young, Jane Fonda, Susannah York, Michael Sarrazin, Red Buttons, Bonnie Bedelia, Bruce Dern

   COMPÈRE (Gig Young): 'There can only be one winner, folks, but isn't that the American way?'

AA: Gig Young

AAN: script; John Green, Albert Woodbury; Sydney Pollack; Jane Fonda; Susannah York

● *Video:*

They Were Expendable*
US 1945 135m bw
MGM (John Ford, Cliff Reid)

Life in and around motor torpedo boats in the Pacific War.

Long drawn out flagwaver with some nice moments.

w Frank Wead, *book* William L. White
d John Ford *ph* Joseph H. August
m Herbert Stothart

John Wayne, Robert Montgomery, Donna Reed, Jack Holt, Ward Bond, Marshall Thompson, Leon Ames, Cameron Mitchell, Jeff York

'For what seems at least half its dogged, devoted length all you have to watch is men getting on or off PT boats and other men watching them do so. But this is made so beautiful and so real that I could not feel one foot of the film was wasted.'—*James Agee*

They Were Not Divided*
GB 1950 102m bw
Rank / Two Cities (Earl St John)

The life of a Guards officer is paralleled with that of his American friend; they both die on a reconnaissance during the advance on Berlin.

Odd mixture of barrack room comedy, semi-documentary action, propaganda and the most appalling sentimentality. No one questioned it at the box office, though.

wd Terence Young *ph* Harry Waxman
m Lambert Williamson

Edward Underdown, Ralph Clanton, Helen Cherry, Stella Andrews, Michael Brennan, Michael Trubshaw, R.S.M. Brittain

'It is a rather curious experience to see a film made with all the best trappings of realism containing so many of the clichés of the studio.'—*Gavin Lambert*

They Were Sisters
GB 1945 115m bw
GFD / Gainsborough (Harold Huth)

The problems of three married sisters.

Flatly handled multi-melodrama, the chief attraction being 'wicked' James Mason as a sadist.

w Roland Pertwee, *novel* Dorothy Whipple
d Arthur Crabtree *ph* Jack Cox *m* Louis Levy

James Mason, Phyllis Calvert, Dulcie Gray, Hugh Sinclair, Anne Crawford, Peter Murray Hill, Pamela Kellino

They Who Dare
GB 1953 107m Technicolor
British Lion / Mayflower (Aubrey Baring, Maxwell Setton)

During World War II a group of British soldiers are sent on a raiding expedition to Rhodes.

Grimmish war actioner with plenty of noise but not much holding power.

w Robert Westerby *d* Lewis Milestone
ph Wilkie Cooper *m* Robert Gill

Dirk Bogarde, Denholm Elliott, Akim Tamiroff, Gérard Oury, Eric Pohlmann, Alec Mango

They Won't Believe Me*
US 1947 95m bw
RKO (Joan Harrison)

A playboy finds himself on trial for murder because of his philandering with three women.

Unusual suspenser with Hitchcock touches; quite neatly packaged, complete with twist ending.

w Jonathan Latimer *d* Irving Pichel *ph* Harry J. Wild *m* Roy Webb

Robert Young, Susan Hayward, Rita Johnson, Jane Greer, Tom Powers, Don Beddoe, Frank Ferguson

'Talk and die! Until now their lips were frozen with fear!'

They Won't Forget*
US 1937 94m bw
Warner (Mervyn Le Roy)

The murder of a girl in a southern town leads to a lynching.

Finely detailed social drama, a classic of American realism; harrowing to watch.

w Robert Rossen, Aben Kandel, *novel* Death in the Deep South by Ward Greene *d* Mervyn Le Roy *ph* Arthur Edeson, Warren Lynch m Adolph Deutsch *md* Leo F. Forbstein

Claude Rains, Gloria Dickson, Edward Norris, Otto Kruger, Allyn Joslyn, Linda Perry, Elisha Cook Jnr, Lana Turner, Cy Kendall, Elizabeth Risdon

'Not only an honest picture, but an example of real movie-making.'—*Pare Lorenz*

Thicker than Water
US 1924 20m bw silent

Ollie spends his savings on a grandfather clock which is promptly destroyed by a passing truck. Well made but slightly tiresome star comedy, the last short ever made featuring Stan and Ollie. Laurel and Hardy, Daphne Pollard, James Finlayson. Written by Stan Laurel; directed by James W. Horne; for Hal Roach.

The Thief*
US 1952 86m bw
Harry M. Popkin (Clarence Greene)

A nuclear physicist is on the run from the FBI, who suspect him of being a spy.

Curious attempt to produce a thriller with no dialogue whatever; parts are well done, but the strain eventually shows, as the makers are not quite clever enough to flesh out the trickery with human interest.

w Clarence Greene, Russel Rouse *d* Russel Rouse *ph* Sam Leavitt *m* Herschel Gilbert

Ray Milland, Martin Gabel, Rita Gam, Harry Bronson, John McKutcheon

AAN: Herschel Gilbert

Thief
US 1981 123m Astrocolor
United Artists / Michael Mann / Caan Productions
GB title: *Violent Streets*

A high class thief's professional life is contrasted with his personal problems.

And at far too great a length, with the additional problem that few people are really interested. A slick but empty melodrama.

wd Michael Mann, *novel* The Home Invaders by Frank Hohimer *ph* Donald Thorin m Tangerine Dream *pd* Mel Bourne

James Caan, Tuesday Weld, Willie Nelson, James Belushi

'It promises too much and delivers too little.'—*Richard Combs, MFB*

The Thief of Bagdad*
US 1924 approx 135m (24fps) bw silent
Douglas Fairbanks

In old Bagdad, a thief uses magic to outwit the evil Caliph.

Celebrated silent version of the old fable, its camera tricks a little timeworn now but nevertheless maintaining the air of a true classic by virtue of its leading performance and driving narrative energy.

w Lotta Woods, Douglas Fairbanks *d* Raoul Walsh *ph* Arthur Edeson *m* Mortimer Wilson *ad* William Cameron Menzies

Douglas Fairbanks, Snitz Edwards, Charles Belcher, Anna May Wong, Julanne Johnston, Etta Lee, Brandon Hurst, Sojin

'An entrancing picture, wholesome and compelling, deliberate and beautiful, a feat of motion picture art which has never been equalled.'—*New York Times*

'Here is magic. Here is beauty. Here is the answer to cynics who give the motion picture no place in the family of the arts . . . a work of rare genius.'—*James Quirk, Photoplay*

● *Video: Polygram*

The Thief of Bagdad**
GB 1940 109m Technicolor
London Films (Alexander Korda)

A boy thief helps a deposed king thwart an evil usurper.

Marvellous blend of magic, action and music, the only film to catch on celluloid the overpowering atmosphere of the Arabian Nights.

w Miles Malleson, Lajos Biro *d* Michael Powell, Ludwig Berger, Tim Whelan ph Georges Périnal, Osmond Borradaile m Miklos Rozsa *sp* Lawrence Butler

Conrad Veidt, *Sabu*, John Justin, June Duprez, Morton Selten, Miles Malleson, *Rex Ingram*, Mary Morris

ABU (Sabu): 'I'm Abu the thief, son of Abu the thief, grandson of Abu the thief, most unfortunate of ten sons with a hunger that yearns day and night . . .'

AGED KING (Morton Selten): 'This is the Land of Legend, where everything is possible when seen through the eyes of youth.'

'The true stuff of fairy tale.'—*Basil Wright*

'Both spectacular and highly inventive.'—*NFT, 1969*

'Magical, highly entertaining, and now revalued by Hollywood moguls Lucas and Coppola.'—*Time Out, 1980*

AA: Georges Périnal, Osmond Borradaile
AAN: Miklos Rozsa

● *Video: Polygram*

The Thief of Baghdad
Italy / France 1960   100m   Eastmancolor /
  Cinemascope

A very moderate remake in the form of an
action star vehicle. Steve Reeves, Georgia
Moll, Arturo Dominici. Written by Augusto
Frassinetti, Filippo Sanjust and Bruno Vailati;
directed by Arthur Lubin; for Titanus / Lux.

Thief of Damascus
US 1952   78m   Technicolor
Columbia / Sam Katzman

The wicked ruler of Damascus is deposed by
his own general, in league with Sinbad,
Aladdin, and Scheherezade.
Mindless bosh, interesting only for its liberal
use of scenes from *Joan of Arc*; the mind
boggles at the costume compromise.

w Robert E. Kent d Will Jason ph Ellis W.
Carter m Mischa Bakaleinikoff

Paul Henreid, Lon Chaney Jnr, Jeff Donnell,
John Sutton, Elena Verdugo

The Thief Who Came to Dinner
US 1973   105m   De Luxe
Warner / Tandem (Bud Yorkin)

A computer analyst determines to become a
jewel thief.
Tedious comedy aping the *Raffles* school but
saddled with a complex plot and listless script.

w Walter Hill, *novel* Terence L. Smith d Bud
Yorkin ph Philip Lathrop m Henry Mancini

Ryan O'Neal, Jacqueline Bisset, Warren
Oates, Jill Clayburgh, Charles Cioffi

● *Video: Warner*

Thieves' Highway●●
US 1949   94m   bw
TCF (Robert Bassler)

A truck driver tracks down the racketeers who
cheated and maimed his father.
Glossy, highly professional thick ear shedding
a convincing light into one of America's less
salubrious corners.

w A. I. Bezzerides, from his novel Thieves'
Market d Jules Dassin ph Norbert Brodine
m Alfred Newman

Richard Conte, Valentina Cortesa, Lee J.
Cobb, Jack Oakie, Millard Mitchell, Joseph
Pevney, Barbara Lawrence, Hope Emerson
  'You will never be able to eat an apple again
without calling up visions of trickery, mayhem,
vandalism and violent death.'—*New York
Times*
  'The action sequences are brilliantly
done.'—*Daily Mail*

Thieves Like Us●
US 1974   123m   De Luxe
United Artists / Jerry Bick–George Litto
  (Robert Eggenweiler)

Three convicts break jail, and the youngest is
attracted to the daughter of the farmer who
helps them escape.
Gloomy romantic melodrama, agreeably set in
the thirties and feelingly acted, but otherwise
inferior to the much shorter version released
in the forties as *They Live by Night*.

w Calder Willingham, Joan Tewkesbury,
Robert Altman, *novel* Edward Anderson
d Robert Altman ph Jean Boffety m various
songs ed Lou Lombardo

Keith Carradine, Shelley Duvall, John Schuck,
Bert Remsen, Louise Fletcher, Tom Skerritt

Thin Ice●
US 1937   78m   bw
TCF (Raymond Griffith)
GB title: *Lovely to Look At*

A skating instructress at an Alpine resort falls
in love with a visiting prince.
Light-hearted musical vehicle for Hollywood's
newest novelty—a skating star.

w Boris Ingster, Milton Sperling, *novel* Der
Komet by Attilla Orbok d Sidney Lanfield
ph Robert Planck, Edward Cronjager
md Louis Silvers songs Lew Pollack, Sidney
Mitchell

Sonja Henie, Tyrone Power, Arthur Treacher,
Raymond Walburn, Joan Davis, Sig Rumann,
Alan Hale, Melville Cooper
  'She's a flash of winter lightning, a great
combination of muscle and music, a Pavlova
on ice . . . production wallop is the staging of
three elaborate ice ballets.'—*Variety*

'A laugh tops every thrilling moment!'
The Thin Man●●●●
US 1934   93m   bw
MGM (Hunt Stromberg)

In New York over Christmas, a tipsy detective
with his wife and dog solves the murder of an
eccentric inventor.
Fast-moving, alternately comic and
suspenseful mystery drama developed in brief
scenes and fast wipes. It set a sparkling
comedy career for two stars previously known
for heavy drama, it was frequently imitated,
and it showed a wisecracking, affectionate
married relationship almost for the first time.

w Frances Goodrich, Albert Hackett, novel
Dashiell Hammett d W. S. Van Dyke
ph James Wong Howe m William Axt

William Powell, Myrna Loy, Maureen
O'Sullivan, Nat Pendleton, Minna Gombell,
Edward Ellis, Porter Hall, Henry Wadsworth,
William Henry, Harold Huber, Cesar
Romero, Edward Brophy
  'A strange mixture of excitement, quips and
hard-boiled sentiment . . . full of the special
touches that can come from nowhere but the
studio, that really make the feet a movie walks
on.'—*Otis Ferguson*
† Sequels, on the whole of descending merit,
included the following, all made at MGM with
the same star duo: 1936: *After the Thin Man*
(110m). 1939: *Another Thin Man* (102m).
1941: *Shadow of the Thin Man* (97m). 1944:
The Thin Man Goes Home (100m). 1947: *Song
of the Thin Man* (86m).

AAN: best picture; script; W. S. Van Dyke;
William Powell

The Thin Red Line
US 1964   99m   bw   Cinemascope
Security / ACE (Sidney Harmon)

Raw recruits land on Guadalcanal and most of
them are killed.
Weary, routine, realistic war drama.

w Bernard Gordon, *novel* James Jones
d Andrew Marton ph Manuel Berenguer
m Malcolm Arnold

Keir Dullea, Jack Warden, James Philbrook,
Kieron Moore

The Thing●●
US 1951   87m   bw
RKO / Winchester (Howard Hawks)
GB title: *The Thing from Another World*

A US scientific expedition in the Arctic is
menaced by a ferocious being thaw
inadvertently thaw out from a spaceship.
Curiously drab suspense shocker mainly set in
corridors, with insufficient surprises to sustain
its length. It does, however, contain the first
space monster on film, and is quite nimbly
made, though it fails to use the central
gimmick from its original story.

w Charles Lederer, *story* Who Goes There by
J. W. Campbell Jnr d Christian Nyby (with
mysterious help, either Hawks or Orson
Welles) ph Russell Harlan m Dmitri
Tiomkin

Robert Cornthwaite, Kenneth Tobey,
Margaret Sheridan, Bill Self, Dewey Martin,
James Arness (as the thing)
  'There seems little point in creating a
monster of such original characteristics if he is
to be allowed only to prowl about the North
Pole, waiting to be destroyed by the superior
ingenuity of the US Air Force.'—*Penelope
Houston*
  'A monster movie with pace, humour and a
collection of beautifully timed jabs of pure
horror.'—*NFT, 1967*

● *Video: Kingston*

The Thing
US 1982   109m   Technicolor
  Panavision
Universal / Lawrence Turman, David Foster

A remake using the basis of the original story
(the thing conceals itself within each of the
characters in turn) but filled with revolting
detail which alienated many audiences.

w Bill Lancaster d John Carpenter ph Dean
Cundey m Ennio Morricone sp Albert
Whitlock

Kurt Russell, A. Wilford Brimley, T. K.
Carter, David Clennon, Richard Dysart,
Richard Masur

● *Video: CIC*

Things Are Looking Up
GB 1935   78m   bw

A circus horsewoman has to pose as her
schoolmistress sister. Lively star vehicle for an
oddly matched team. Cicely Courtneidge, Max
Miller, Mary Lawson, Dick Henderson, Dick
Henderson Jnr, Judy Kelly. Written by
Stafford Davies and Con West; directed by
Albert de Courville; for Gaumont.

Things to Come●●●●
GB 1936   113m   bw
London Films (Alexander Korda)

War in 1940 is followed by plague, rebellion, a

new glass-based society, and the first
rocketship to the moon.
Fascinating, chilling and dynamically well-
staged vignettes tracing mankind's future. Bits
of the script and acting may be wobbly, but
the sets and music are magnificent, the first
part of the prophecy chillingly accurate, and
the whole mammoth undertaking almost
unique in film history.

w H. G. Wells, from his book The Shape of
Things to Come *d / pd William Cameron
Menzies ph Georges Périnal m Arthur Bliss
sp Harry Zech, Ned Mann ad Vincent Korda*

Raymond Massey, Edward Chapman, Ralph
Richardson, Margaretta Scott, Cedric
Hardwicke, Sophie Stewart, Derrick de
Marney, John Clements

CABAL (Raymond Massey): 'It is this or
that—all the universe or nothing. Which shall
it be, Passworthy? Which shall it be?'

THEOTOCOPULOS (Cedric Hardwicke):
'What is this progress? What is the good of all
this progress onward and onward? We demand
a halt. We demand a rest . . . an end to
progress! Make an end to this progress now!
Let this be the last day of the scientific age!'

'Successful in every department except
emotionally. For heart interest Mr Wells
hands you an electric switch . . . It's too bad
present-day film distribution isn't on a Wells
2040 basis, when the negative cost could be
retrieved by button pushing. It's going to be
harder than that. It's going to be almost
impossible.'—*Variety*

'An amazingly ingenious technical
accomplishment, even if it does hold out small
hope for our race . . . the existence pictured is
as joyless as a squeezed grapefruit.'—*Don
Herold*

'A leviathan among films . . . a stupendous
spectacle, an overwhelming, Dorean, Jules
Vernesque, elaborated *Metropolis,* staggering
to eye, mind and spirit, the like of which has
never been seen and never will be seen
again.'—*The Sunday Times*

The Third Day

US 1965 119m Technicolor
Panavision
Warner (Jack Smight)

An amnesiac learns that he is a rich unpopular
tycoon facing a major crisis.
Glum melodrama which suggests domestic
mystery but provides only interminable chat.

w Burton Wohl, Robert Presnell Jnr, *novel*
Joseph Hayes *d* Jack Smight *ph* Robert
Surtees *m* Percy Faith

George Peppard, Elizabeth Ashley, Roddy
McDowall, Herbert Marshall, Mona
Washbourne, Robert Webber, Charles Drake,
Sally Kellerman, Arte Johnson, Vincent
Gardenia

Third Finger Left Hand

US 1940 96m bw
MGM (John W. Considine Jnr)

A lady fashion editor fends off unwanted
suitors by saying she is already married, but a

THE THIEF OF BAGHDAD. Two shots showing some of the marvellous staging of the 1940
version of this perennial fairy tale. Sabu is nearly crushed by a giant foot . . .

commercial artist trumps this card by claiming
to be the long lost husband of her invention.
Cheerful but overstretched romantic comedy.

w Lionel Houser *d* Robert Z. Leonard
ph George Folsey *m* David Snell

Myrna Loy, Melvyn Douglas, Lee Bowman,
Bonita Granville, Raymond Walburn, Felix
Bressart, Sidney Blackmer

The Third Generation

West Germany 1979 111m colour

A Berlin executive becomes the victim of a
gang of terrorists. Realistic melodrama,
curiously muted in its satire and its anger,
watchable more as an entertainment than as a
polemic. Volker Spengler, Bulle Ogier, Harry
Baer, Eddie Constantine. Written, directed,
photographed and produced by Rainer
Werner Fassbinder; for Tango / Project /
FDA.

The Third Man****

GB 1949 100m bw
British Lion / London Films / David O.
Selznick / Alexander Korda (Carol Reed)

An unintelligent but tenacious writer of
westerns arrives in post-war Vienna to join his
old friend Harry Lime, who seems to have met
with an accident . . . or has he?
Totally memorable and irresistible romantic
thriller. Stylish from the first to the last, with
inimitable backgrounds of zither music and
war-torn buildings pointing up a then-topical
black market story full of cynical characters
but not without humour. Hitchcock with
feeling, if you like.

w Graham Greene *d* Carol Reed *ph* Robert
Krasker *m* Anton Karas

*Joseph Cotten, Trevor Howard, Alida Valli,
Orson Welles, Bernard Lee, Wilfrid Hyde
White,* Ernst Deutsch, Siegfried Breuer, Erich
Ponto, Paul Hoerbiger

HARRY LIME (Orson Welles): 'Look down
there. Would you really feel any pity if one of
those dots stopped moving for ever? If I
offered you twenty thousand pounds for every
dot that stopped, would you really, old man,
tell me to keep my money, or would you
calculate how many dots you could afford to
spare? Free of income tax, old man, free of
income tax. It's the only way to save money
nowadays.'

LIME: 'In Italy for thirty years under the
Borgias they had warfare, terror, murder and

. . . and trapped in the web of a giant spider.

bloodshed, but they produced Michelangelo, Leonardo da Vinci and the Renaissance. In Switzerland, they had brotherly love; they had five hundred years of democracy and peace— and what did that produce? The cuckoo clock.'

'Sensitive and humane and dedicated, [Reed] would seem to be enclosed from life with no specially strong feelings about the stories that come his way other than that they should be something he can perfect and polish with a craftsman's love.'—*Richard Winnington*

'Crammed with cinematic plums which could do the early Hitchcock proud.'—*Time*

AA: Robert Krasker
AAN: Carol Reed

● Video: Thorn EMI

Third Man on the Mountain
GB 1959   103m   Technicolor
Walt Disney (Bill Anderson)

In 1865 a Swiss dishwasher dreams of conquering the local mountain, and befriends a distinguished mountaineer.
Handsomely photographed boys' adventure story.

w Eleanore Griffin, *novel* Banner in the Sky by James Ramsay Ullman   *d* Ken Annakin

ph Harry Waxman, *George Tairraz*
m William Alwyn

James MacArthur, Michael Rennie, Janet Munro, James Donald, Herbert Lom, Laurence Naismith, Walter Fitzgerald, Nora Swinburne

'The story of a man searching for a killer— who might even be himself!'

The Third Secret
GB 1964   103m   bw   Cinemascope
TCF / Hubris (Robert L. Joseph)

A psychiatrist apparently commits suicide; a patient who has relied on his strength finds the truth by interviewing other patients.
Pretentious package of short stories, only one of which is relevant to the frame (yet another one featuring Patricia Neal was shot but discarded); full of philosophical conversations on a Thames mudbank and other absurdities, but well enough put together.

w Robert L. Joseph   *d* Charles Crichton
ph Douglas Slocombe   *m* Richard Arnell

Stephen Boyd, *Pamela Franklin*, Jack Hawkins, Richard Attenborough, Rachel

Kempson, Diane Cilento, Paul Rogers, Freda Jackson

'An unappealing and irritatingly muddled scribble of a film, thoroughly lacking in suspense, veracity and justification.'—*MFB*

The Third Voice**
US 1959   80m   bw   Cinemascope
TCF (Maury Dexter, Hubert Cornfield)

A woman kills her wealthy lover and an accomplice impersonates him through a series of complex negotiations.
Superstylish minor thriller, with a plot fascinating as it unfolds and a climax which is only a slight letdown.

wd Hubert Cornfield, *novel* All the Way by Charles Williams   *ph* Ernest Haller   *m* Johnny Mandel

Edmond O'Brien, Laraine Day, Julie London

Thirteen*
USSR 1937   90m approx   bw

Red Army soldiers are trekking from well to well through the desert. When help arrives only one is left. Russian adventure film which was supposedly copied from *The Lost Patrol* but itself inspired *Sahara*. Good stuff, anyway. Written by L. Prout, M. Romm; directed by M. Romm; for Mosfilm.

Thirteen Ghosts
US 1960   88m   bw (colour sequence)
Columbia / William Castle

A penniless scholar inherits a haunted house. Childish thriller for which the audience was issued with a 'ghost viewer' (anaglyph spectacles) so that they could see the 'spirits'. The gimmick was called Illusion-O.

w Robb White   *d* William Castle   *ph* Joseph Biroc   *m* Von Dexter

Charles Herbert, Jo Morrow, Martin Milner, Rosemary de Camp, Donald Woods, Margaret Hamilton

'Hurtling through space, eight people live fifteen dangerous, unforgettable hours!'

Thirteen Hours by Air*
US 1936   80m   bw
Paramount (E. Lloyd Sheldon)

A transcontinental plane is hijacked by an ex-convict.
Solidly carpentered minor thriller which is also an interesting record of the early days of commercial aviation.

w Bogart Rogers, Kenyon Nicholson
d Mitchell Leisen   *ph* Theodor Sparkhul

Fred MacMurray, Joan Bennett, Zasu Pitts, Alan Baxter, Fred Keating, Brian Donlevy, John Howard, Ruth Donnelly, Dean Jagger

13 Rue Madeleine*
US 1946   95m   bw
TCF (Louis de Rochemont)

Four trained American espionage agents locate a Nazi rocket site in France.
Semi-documentary spy stuff in the tradition of *The House on 92nd Street* but rather less satisfactory despite excellent technique.

w John Monks Jnr, Sy Bartlett *d* Henry Hathaway *ph* Norbert Brodine *m* David Buttolph *md* Alfred Newman

James Cagney, Annabella, Richard Conte, Frank Latimore, Walter Abel, Melville Cooper, Sam Jaffe, Blanche Yurka

'Far and away the roughest, toughest spy chase yet gleaned from the bulging files of the OSS.'—*Time*

'I stole the plot of *The Virginian* and used it. I'd always wanted to make that story anyway.'—*Henry Hathaway*

† Rex Harrison rejected the role taken by Cagney.

'This is where evil lurks!'
13 West Street*
US 1962 80m bw
Columbia / Ladd Enterprises (William Bloom)

An engineer is attacked on the street by teenage hoodlums and becomes obsessed by revenge.
Competent, darkly photographed, rather dislikeable little thriller, a kind of trial run for *Death Wish*.

w Bernard Schoenfeld, Robert Presnell Jnr *d* Philip Leacock *ph* Charles Lawton Jnr *m* George Duning

Alan Ladd, Rod Steiger, Dolores Dorn, Michael Callan, Kenneth MacKenna, Margaret Hayes

Thirteen Women
US 1932 73m bw

One of thirteen boarding school graduates is trying to murder the others. Thin mystery which wastes its cast. Ricardo Cortez, Irene Dunne, Myrna Loy, Jill Esmond, Florence Eldridge, Julie Haydon, Marjorie Gateson, C. Henry Gordon. Written by Bartlett Cormack, from a novel by Tiffany Thayer; directed by George Archainbaud; for RKO.

The Thirteenth Chair
US 1929 85m bw

A medium holds a seance to unmask a murderer. Effective though now very dated chiller from a Broadway hit. Margaret Wycherly, Bela Lugosi, Holmes Herbert, Conrad Nagel, Leila Hyams. Written by Elliott Clawson, from the play by Bayard Veiller; directed by Tod Browning; for MGM. (NB: The same studio remade the vehicle in 1936 with Dame May Whitty, Henry Daniell, Holmes Herbert—again—Elissa Landi and Lewis Stone; the director was George B. Seitz.) 'Playgoer type will get more enjoyment from it than the moviegoer.'—*Variety*

The Thirteenth Guest
US 1932 70m bw
Monogram (M. H. Hoffman)

A haunted house, a will at midnight, and a frightened lady.
Archetypal comedy thriller, shot on Poverty Row but still watchable.

w Francis Hyland, Arthur Hoerl, *novel* Armitage Traill *d* Albert Ray *ph* Harry Neumann, Tom Galligan

Ginger Rogers, Lyle Talbot, J. Farrell MacDonald, James Eagles, Eddie Phillips, Erville Alderson

'For all classes of houses a positive money maker.'—*Variety*

The Thirteenth Letter*
US 1951 85m bw
TCF (Otto Preminger)

A small French-Canadian town suffers from an outbreak of poison pen letters.
Moderate transcription of a memorable French film, *Le Corbeau*; in this version the events seem all too predictable and the performances dull.

w Howard Koch *d* Otto Preminger *ph* Joseph La Shelle *m* Alex North

Charles Boyer, Linda Darnell, Constance Smith, Michael Rennie, Françoise Rosay, Judith Evelyn

–30–
US 1959 96m bw
Warner / Mark VII (Jack Webb)
GB title: *Deadline Midnight*

A night in the newsroom of a paper preoccupied with scoops.
Not very dramatic, oddly titled and rather pretentious newspaper melodrama confined largely to one set.

w William Bowers *d* Jack Webb *ph* Edward Colman *m* Ray Heindorf

Jack Webb, William Conrad, David Nelson, Whitney Blake, James Bell, Nancy Valentine

Thirty Day Princess*
US 1934 74m bw
Paramount (B. P. Schulberg)

An actress is hired to impersonate a princess who gets mumps while visiting New York in hope of a loan.
Modest comedy which needed a wittier script but is stylishly played.

w Preston Sturges, Frank Partos, *novel* Clarence Budington Kelland *d* Marion Gering *ph* Leon Shamroy

Sylvia Sidney, Cary Grant, Edward Arnold, Henry Stephenson, Vince Barnett, Edgar Norton, Lucien Littlewood

'A compact little picture which will entertain generally.'—*Variety*

Thirty Is a Dangerous Age, Cynthia
GB 1967 84m Technicolor
Columbia / Walter Shenson

A timid nightclub pianist has trouble with women but sells his first musical.
Mild star vehicle for a very mild star, basically a few thin sketches, frantically overdirected.

w Dudley Moore, Joe McGrath, John Wells *d* Joe McGrath *ph* Billy Williams *m* Dudley Moore *titles* Richard Williams

Dudley Moore, Eddie Foy Jnr, Suzy Kendall, John Bird, Duncan Macrae, Patricia Routledge, John Wells

The Thirty-Nine Steps***
GB 1935 81m bw
Gaumont British (Ivor Montagu)

A spy is murdered; the man who has befriended her is suspected, but eludes the

police until a chase across Scotland produces the real villains.
Marvellous comedy thriller with most of the gimmicks found not only in Hitchcock's later work but in anyone else's who has tried the same vein. It has little to do with the original novel, and barely sets foot outside the studio, but it makes every second count, and is unparalleled in its use of timing, atmosphere and comedy relief.

w Charles Bennett, Alma Reville, *novel* John Buchan *d* Alfred Hitchcock *ph* Bernard Knowles *m* Hubert Bath, Jack Beaver *md* Louis Levy

Robert Donat, Madeleine Carroll, Godfrey Tearle, Lucie Mannheim, Peggy Ashcroft, John Laurie, *Wylie Watson, Helen Haye*, Frank Cellier

'A narrative of the unexpected—a humorous, exciting, dramatic, entertaining, pictorial, vivid and novel tale told with a fine sense of character and a keen grasp of the cinematic idea.'—*Sydney W. Carroll*

'A miracle of speed and light.'—*Otis Ferguson*

'Such is the zest of the Hitchcock plot that the original point of the title was totally forgotten, and half a line had to be added at the end by way of explanation.'—*George Perry, 1965*

● Video: Rank

The Thirty-Nine Steps
GB 1959 93m Eastmancolor
Rank (Betty E. Box)

Just to show that stars and story aren't everything, this scene-for-scene remake muffs every opportunity for suspense or general effectiveness, and is practically a manual on how not to make a thriller.

w Frank Harvey *d* Ralph Thomas *ph* Ernest Steward *m* Clifton Parker

Kenneth More, Taina Elg, Barry Jones, Faith Brook, Brenda de Banzie, Duncan Lamont, James Hayter, Michael Goodliffe, Reginald Beckwith

The Thirty-Nine Steps*
GB 1978 102m Eastmancolor
Rank / Norfolk International (James Kenelm Clarke)

Eager-to-please remake which goes back to the original period and more or less the original story, but rather spoils itself by a cliffhanger climax on the face of Big Ben, absurdly borrowed from Will Hay's *My Learned Friend*.

w Michael Robson, *d* Don Sharp *ph* John Coquillon *m* Ed Welch *ph* Harry Pottle

Robert Powell, Karen Dotrice, John Mills, Eric Porter, David Warner, George Baker, Ronald Pickup, Timothy West, Donald Pickering, Andrew Keir, Robert Flemyng, Miles Anderson

● Video: Rank

Thirty Seconds over Tokyo**
US 1944 138m bw
MGM (Sam Zimbalist)

How the first American attack on Japan was planned.

Sturdy World War II action flagwaver, with Tracy guesting as Colonel Dolittle.

w Dalton Trumbo *d* Mervyn Le Roy *ph* Harold Rosson, Robert Surtees *m* Herbert Stothart

Spencer Tracy, Van Johnson, Robert Walker, Phyllis Thaxter, Tim Murdock, Don Defore, Robert Mitchum

'All of the production involving planes and technical action is so fine that the film has the tough and literal quality of an air force documentary.'—*Bosley Crowther, New York Times*

'A big studio, big scale film, free of artistic pretensions, it is transformed by its not very imaginative but very dogged sincerity into something forceful, simple and thoroughly sympathetic.'—*James Agee*

AAN: Harold Rosson, Robert Surtees

Thirty-Six Hours*
US 1964   115m   bw   Panavision
MGM / Perlberg–Seaton / Cherokee (William Perlberg)

In 1944 an American major is kidnapped by the Nazis and after drugging is made to think that the war is over.
Well-detailed spy suspenser.

wd George Seaton, *stories* Roald Dahl, Carl K. Hittleman *ph* Philip Lathrop *m* Dmitri Tiomkin

James Garner, Rod Taylor, Eva Marie Saint, Werner Peters, John Banner

Thirty Years of Fun**
US 1962   85m   bw
Robert Youngson Productions

A compilation of silent comedy, including Chaplin's *The Floorwalker, Easy Street, The Pawnshop* and *The Rink*; Keaton's *The Balloonatic* and *Daydreams*; Langdon's *Smile Please*; and Laurel and Hardy's first meeting in *Lucky Dog.*

Not the most hilarious of the compilations, but historically important, with the usual high quality prints which Youngson alone seemed able to provide.

wd Robert Youngson *film quality control* Paul Guffanti

'What we're fighting for is bigger than you or me!'
This above All*
US 1942   110m   bw
TCF (Darryl F. Zanuck)

A surgeon's daughter on active service during World War II falls in love with a conscientious objector who is also an army deserter: he proves his bravery during an air raid.
Superior studio-set war romance.

w R. C. Sheriff, *novel* Eric Knight *d* Anatole Litvak *ph* Arthur Miller *m* Alfred Newman

Tyrone Power, Joan Fontaine, Thomas Mitchell, Henry Stephenson, Nigel Bruce, Gladys Cooper, Philip Merivale, Alexander Knox, Melville Cooper

'Beautiful, stimulating and occasionally powerful.'—*New York Herald Tribune*
'One of the truly great pictures to come out of this war.'—*Motion Picture Herald*
AAN: Arthur Miller

This Angry Age
Italy 1957   104m   Technirama

A French widow in Indo-China struggles to keep her rice fields going despite her family's waning interest. Curious international production which suffers from the audience's lack of interest in the central situation. Moments of interest and even beauty, though. Silvana Mangano, Jo Van Fleet, Anthony Perkins, Alida Valli, Richard Conte, Nehemiah Persoff. Written by Irwin Shaw, René Clément, Ivo Perelli and Diego Fabbri, from the novel *Barrage Contre Le Pacifique* by Marguerite Duras; directed by René Clément; for Dino de Laurentiis. (Alternative title: *The Sea Wall*. Original title: *La Diga sul Pacifico*.)

This Could Be the Night
US 1957   104m   bw   Cinemascope
MGM (Joe Pasternak)

A schoolteacher becomes secretary to a gangster in his Broadway night club.
Unlikely romantic melodrama with music, like a more solemn *Guys and Dolls.*

w Isabel Lennart, *story* Cornelia Baird Gross *d* Robert Wise *ph* Russell Harlan *m* George Stoll

Jean Simmons, Paul Douglas, Tony Franciosa, Julie Wilson, Joan Blondell, J. Carrol Naish, Zasu Pitts

'The master of inspiring spectacle makes his first great spectacle of modern times!'
This Day and Age*
US 1933   98m   bw
Paramount / Cecil B. de Mille

During a youth week, boys put a gangster on trial and by his own methods force him to confess to murder.
A curious aberration for de Mille, this fairly powerful movie was condemned in some quarters as an incitement to fascism.

w Bartlett Cormack *d* Cecil B. de Mille *ph* Peverell Marley *m* Howard Jackson, L. W. Gilbert, Abel Baer

Charles Bickford, Richard Cromwell, Judith Allen, Harry Green, Ben Alexander
'A highly improbable and fantastic story but, as done by de Mille, carries more than average audience appeal.'—*Variety*
'Loaded with that power which excites emotional hysteria . . . should stimulate audiences to the same pitch of enthusiasm as it did the preview crowd.'—*Motion Picture Herald*
'A strange tale from the Hollywood hills . . . the technical work is beyond reproach, but the story is excessively melodramatic.'—*Mordaunt Hall, New York Times*

This Earth Is Mine
US 1959   124m   Technicolor
Cinemascope
U-I / Vintage (Casey Robinson, Claude Heilman)

A French-American vineyard owner in California brings out his granddaughter from England in the hope that she will consolidate his dynasty.
Solidly efficient film of a solidly efficient novel.

w Casey Robinson, *novel* The Cup and the Sword by Alice Tisdale Hobart *d* Henry King *ph* Winton Hoch, Russell Metty *m* Hugo Friedhofer

Jean Simmons, *Claude Rains*, Rock Hudson, Dorothy McGuire, Kent Smith, Anna Lee, Ken Scott

This England
GB 1941   84m   bw

Landowner and labourer express contrary views through five periods of English history. Unintentionally hilarious charade with all concerned left with egg on their faces. With propaganda like this, it's a wonder we still won the war. John Clements, Emlyn Williams, Constance Cummings, Frank Pettingell, Roland Culver, Esmond Knight, Morland Graham, Leslie French. Written by Emlyn Williams, A. R. Rawlinson and Bridget Boland; directed by David MacDonald; for British National.
† In Scotland the film was known as *Our Heritage.*

This Gun for Hire***
US 1942   81m   bw
Paramount (Richard M. Blumenthal)

A professional killer becomes involved in a fifth columnist plot.
Efficient Americanization of one of its author's more sombre entertainments. The melodrama has an authentic edge and strangeness to it, and it established the star images of both Ladd and Lake, as well as being oddly downbeat for a Hollywood product of this jingoistic time.

w Albert Maltz, W. R. Burnett, *novel* A Gun for Sale by *Graham Greene d* Frank Tuttle *ph* John Seitz *m* David Buttolph

Alan Ladd, Veronica Lake, Robert Preston, *Laird Cregar*, Tully Marshall, Mikhail Rasumny, Marc Lawrence

This Happy Breed**
GB 1944   114m   Technicolor
GFD / Two Cities / Cineguild (Noel Coward, Anthony Havelock-Allan)

Life between the wars for a London suburban family.
Coward's domestic epic is unconvincingly written and largely miscast, but sheer professionalism gets it through, and the decor is historically interesting.

w David Lean, Ronald Neame, Anthony Havelock-Allan, *play* Noel Coward *d* David Lean *ph* Ronald Neame

THE THIRTY-NINE STEPS.   The law closes in on the master spy, on stage at the London Palladium.

Robert Newton, Celia Johnson, Stanley Holloway, John Mills, Kay Walsh, Amy Veness, Alison Leggatt

'Nearly two hours of the pleasure of recognition, which does not come very far up the scale of aesthetic values.'—*Richard Mallett, Punch*

This Happy Feeling
US 1958   92m   Eastmancolor
Cinemascope
U-I (Ross Hunter)

An ageing actor is invigorated by a mild affair with his secretary.
Flat romantic comedy: the bubbles obstinately refuse to rise.

wd Blake Edwards, *play* For Love or Money by F. Hugh Herbert *ph* Arthur E. Arling *m* Frank Skinner

Curt Jurgens, Debbie Reynolds, John Saxon, Alexis Smith, *Mary Astor, Estelle Winwood*

This Is My Affair**
US 1937   102m   bw
TCF (Kenneth MacGowan)
GB title: *His Affair*

When President McKinley is assassinated, one of his top undercover agents is suspected of being a criminal, and threatened with execution.
Jolly good romantic melodrama with excellent period trappings; Hollywood of the thirties at its routine best.

w Allen Rivkin, Lamar Trotti d William A. Seiter ph Robert Planck md Arthur Lange

Robert Taylor, Barbara Stanwyck, Victor McLaglen, Brian Donlevy, Sidney Blackmer, John Carradine, Sig Rumann, Alan Dinehart, Douglas Fowley

'Something of a G-man story in a costume setting.'—*Variety*

'The best American melodrama of the year . . . admirable acting, quick and cunning direction . . . a sense of doom, of almost classic suspense.'—*Graham Greene*

This Is My Love
US 1954   91m   Technicolor

A sensitive young writer gives up everything to help her sister and crippled husband run a restaurant. Weird, miscast melodrama which ends with Cinderella murdering the ugly sister.
Linda Darnell, Faith Domergue, Dan Duryea, Rick Jason. Written by Hagar Wilde and Hugh Brooke; directed by Stuart Heisler; for RKO.

This Is My Street
GB 1963   94m   bw
Anglo-Amalgamated / Adder (Jack Hanbury)

A Battersea wife has a fling with her mother's lodger.
Unremarkable low-life drama.

THE THIRTY-NINE STEPS. Robert Donat and Madeleine Carroll conduct the oddest romance that Hitchcock ever dreamed up.

w Bill MacIlwraith, *novel* Nan Maynard
d Sidney Hayers *ph* Alan Hume *m* Eric
Rogers

June Ritchie, Ian Hendry, Avice Landon,
Meredith Edwards, Madge Ryan, John Hurt,
Mike Pratt, Tom Adams

This Is the Army**
US 1943   121m   Technicolor
Warner (Jack L. Warner, Hal B. Wallis)

Army recruits put on a musical revue.
Mammoth musical flagwaver.

w Casey Robinson, Claude Binyon *d* Michael
Curtiz *ph* Bert Glennon, Sol Polito
songs Irving Berlin *m* Ray Heindorf

George Murphy, Joan Leslie, Irving Berlin,
George Tobias, Alan Hale, Charles

Butterworth, Rosemary de Camp, Dolores
Costello, Una Merkel, Stanley Ridges, Ruth
Donnelly, Kate Smith, Frances Langford,
Gertrude Niesen, Ronald Reagan, Joe Louis
AA: Ray Heindorf

This Is the Life
US 1943   87m   bw

A young girl singer gets a crush on an older
man. Lively youth musical from better-
mannered days. Donald O'Connor, Susanna
Foster, Peggy Ryan, Patric Knowles, Louise
Allbritton, Dorothy Peterson, Jonathan Hale.
Written by Wanda Tuchock, from the play
Angela Is 22 by Fay Wray and Sinclair Lewis;
directed by Felix Feist; for Universal.

This Island Earth**
US 1955   86m   Technicolor
U-I (William Alland)

Scientists at a mysterious research station are
really visitors from a planet in outer space, to
which they kidnap brilliant minds who they
hope can help them.

Absorbing science fiction mystery with
splendid special effects and only one mutant
monster to liven the last reels.

w Franklin Coen, Edward G. O'Callaghan,
novel Raymond F. Jones *d* Joseph Newman
ph / sp Clifford Stine, David S. Horsley
m Joseph Gershenson *ad* Alexander
Golitzen, Richard H. Riedel

Jeff Morrow, Faith Domergue, Rex Reason,
Lance Fuller, Russell Johnson, Robert
Nicholas, Karl Lindt

'We women who have known love—have learned how to hate!'

This Land Is Mine*
US 1943   103m   bw
RKO (Jean Renoir, Dudley Nichols)

A European village fights for freedom under occupying Nazis, and a schoolmaster becomes a hero.
Rather superfluous flagwaver with good performances wasted in a totally predictable and rather uninspiring script which gives the director little scope.

w Dudley Nichols d Jean Renoir ph Frank Redman m Lothar Perl

Charles Laughton, Maureen O'Hara, George Sanders, Walter Slezak, Una O'Connor, Kent Smith, Philip Merivale, Thurston Hall, George Coulouris
'Directed with the same Zolaesque intensity, the same excited obsession with locomotives, the same exquisite pictorial sense, that informed La Bête Humaine.'—Guardian
'Dull, prolix and unamusing.'—James Agate
'You cannot afford to dislocate or internationalize your occupied country; or to try to sell it to Americans by making your citizens as well fed, well dressed and comfortably idiomatic as Americans; or to treat the show to the corrupted virtuosities of studio lighting and heavy ballet composition.'—James Agee

This Love of Ours
US 1945   90m   bw
U-I (Edward Dodds)

A jealous doctor leaves his wife but years later saves her from an unhappy second marriage. Stupid romantic melodrama with characters in whose idiotic behaviour one can take no interest. Remade as Never Say Goodbye (qv).

w Bruce Manning, John Klorer, Leonard Lee, play Comè Prima Meglio di Prima by Luigi Pirandello d William Dieterle ph Lucien Ballard m Hans Salter

Merle Oberon, Charles Korvin, Claude Rains, Carl Esmond, Jess Barker, Harry Davenport, Ralph Morgan, Fritz Leiber
'About as captivating as a funeral dirge.'—Thomas M. Pryor, New York Times
'A juicy example of masochistic team work . . . my favourite bad film in two years.'—Richard Winnington

AAN: Hans Salter

This Man in Paris
GB 1939   86m   bw

A London reporter in Paris exposes a counterfeiting gang. Slightly disappointing sequel to the spruce This Man Is News; no more were made. Barry K. Barnes, Valerie Hobson, Alastair Sim, Edward Lexy, Garry Marsh. Written by Allan McKinnon and Roger MacDougall; directed by David MacDonald; for Pinebrook. 'Five years have passed since The Thin Man, and this particular luxurious relationship of loving insults, hygienic sex, and raillery from twin beds is period enough for Punch.'—Graham Greene.

This Man Is Dangerous
GB 1941   82m   bw

A police inspector's son solves the case of a fake doctor and a mysterious nursing home. Nostalgically innocent crime caper; still quite entertaining. James Mason, Mary Clare, Margaret Vyner, Gordon McLeod, Frederick Valk. Written by John Argyle and Edward Dryhurst, from the novel They Called Him Death by David Hume; directed by Lawrence Huntington; for Rialto. (Aka: The Patient Vanishes.)

This Man Is Mine
US 1934   76m   bw

A woman wins back her wandering playboy husband. Tedious marital drama which might have fared better as farce. Irene Dunne, Ralph Bellamy, Constance Cummings, Kay Johnson, Sidney Blackmer, Charles Starrett. Written by Jane Murfin, from the play Love Flies in the Window by Anne Morrison Chapin; directed by John Cromwell; for RKO.

This Man Is Mine
GB 1946   103m   bw

A family invites a Canadian soldier for Christmas. Moderate heartwarmer which still exudes a patriotic sentimental glow. Tom Walls, Glynis Johns, Jeanne de Casalis, Hugh McDermott, Nova Pilbeam, Barry Morse. Written by Doreen Montgomery, Nicholas Phipps, Reginald Beckwith, Mabel Constanduros, Val Valentine and David Evans, from the play A Soldier for Christmas by Reginald Beckwith; directed by Marcel Varnel; for Columbia.

This Man Is News**
GB 1938   77m   bw
(Paramount) Pinebrook (Anthony Havelock-Allan)

A reporter tracks down jewel thieves. Thoroughly brisk and lively comedy-thriller on Thin Man lines. (See This Man in Paris.)

w Allan MacKinnon, Roger Macdougall, Basil Dearden d David MacDonald

Barry K. Barnes, Valerie Hobson, Alastair Sim, John Warwick, Garry Marsh

This Man's Navy
US 1945   100m   bw

Two old navy men compare their sons' exploits, especially in the matter of how many submarines destroyed. Easy-going star flagwaver. Wallace Beery, James Gleason, Tom Drake, Noah Beery, Selena Royle. Written by Borden Chase; directed by William Wellman; for MGM.

This Modern Age
US 1931   68m   bw
MGM

The socialite child of divorced parents goes to Paris to stay with her sophisticated mother. Mildly daring melodrama typical of its star and year.

w Sylvia Thalberg, Frank Butler, story Mildred Cram d Nick Grinde ph Charles Rosher

Joan Crawford, Pauline Frederick, Monroe Owsley, Neil Hamilton, Hobart Bosworth, Emma Dunn

This Property Is Condemned*
US 1966   110m   Technicolor
Paramount / Seven Arts / Ray Stark (John Houseman)

Sexual adventures of a tubercular but beautiful girl in her mother's boarding house in a Mississippi town.
The Tennessee Williams mixture as before, quite well done but almost entirely resistible.

w Francis Ford Coppola, Fred Coe, Edith Sommer, play Tennessee Williams d Sydney Pollack ph James Wong Howe m Kenyon Hopkins

Natalie Wood, Robert Redford, Mary Badham, Kate Reid, Charles Bronson, Jon Provost, John Harding, Alan Baxter, Robert Blake

This Side of Heaven
US 1934   78m   bw

A slightly whacky family gets together when father is accused of embezzlement. Unmemorable but enjoyable domestic comedy drama. Lionel Barrymore, Fay Bainter, Mae Clarke, Tom Brown, Una Merkel, Mary Carlisle, Onslow Stevens. Written by Zelda Sears and Eve Greene from a novel by Marjorie Paradis; directed by William K. Howard; for MGM. 'The type of clean picture Will Hays has been telling Hollywood about.'—Variety

This Sporting Life**
GB 1963   134m   bw
Rank / Independent Artists (Karel Reisz)

A tough miner becomes a successful rugby player, but his inner crudeness and violence keep contentment at bay.
Skilful movie-making around an unattractive hero in dismal settings; for all the excellent detail, we do not care sufficiently for the film to become any kind of classic.

w David Storey d Lindsay Anderson ph Denys Coop m Roberto Gerhard

Richard Harris, Rachel Roberts, Alan Badel, William Hartnell, Colin Blakely, Vanda Godsell, Arthur Lowe

AAN: Richard Harris; Rachel Roberts
● Video: Rank

This Thing Called Love*
US 1941   98m   bw ·
Columbia (William Perlberg)
GB title: Married But Single

A lady executive insists on proving that marriage is best if the partners start out just good friends.
Amusing comedy which at the time seemed a little saucy, and got itself banned by the Legion of Decency.

w George Seaton, Ken Englund, P. J. Wolfson d Alexander Hall ph Joseph Walker m Werner Heyman md Morris Stoloff

Rosalind Russell, Melvyn Douglas, Binnie Barnes, Allyn Joslyn, Gloria Dickson, Lee J. Cobb, Gloria Holden, Don Beddoe

'One of those laborious forties comedies in which the independent-minded woman has no common sense.'—*New Yorker, 1979*

This Time for Keeps
US 1947   105m   Technicolor
MGM (Joe Pasternak)

The son of a famous singer falls in love with a swimming star.
Dim star musical with no outstanding sequences.

w Gladys Lehman   d Richard Thorpe   ph Karl Freund   *songs* various

Esther Williams, Jimmy Durante, Lauritz Melchior, Johnnie Johnston, Xavier Cugat and his Orchestra

'The money spent on this production might easily have kept Mozart and Schubert alive and busy to the age of sixty, with enough left over to finance five of the best movies ever made. It might even have been invested in a good movie musical.'—*James Agee*

This Was a Woman
GB 1948   104m   bw

A paranoid wife, prevented from running the lives of her offspring, tries to poison her husband. Intolerable, interminable melodrama; a stage event makes a very stagey film. Sonia Dresdel, Barbara White, Walter Fitzgerald, Cyril Raymond, Marjorie Rhodes, Emrys Jones. Written by Val Valentine, from the play by Joan Morgan; directed by Tim Whelan; for Excelsior.

This Was Paris
GB 1941   88m   bw

Spies suspect each other in Paris just before the Nazi occupation. Unpersuasive studio-bound potboiler. Ben Lyon, Ann Dvorak, Griffith Jones, Robert Morley, Harold Huth, Mary Maguire. Written by Brock Williams and Edward Dryhurst; directed by John Harlow; for Warner.

This Week of Grace
GB 1933   92m   bw

An unemployed factory girl goes into service. Very typical but underproduced star vehicle. Gracie Fields, Frank Pettingell, Henry Kendall, John Stuart, Douglas Wakefield, Minnie Rayner. Written by H. Fowler Mear and Jack Marks; directed by Maurice Elvey; for Real Art.

'Every inch a lady—till you look at the record!'
This Woman Is Dangerous
US 1952   97m   bw
Warner (Robert Sisk)

A woman gangster goes blind and falls in love with her doctor.
Glossy hokum without much dramatic movement; strictly for star fans.

w Geoffrey Homes, George Worthing Yates   d Felix Feist   ph Ted McCord   m David Buttolph

Joan Crawford, David Brian, Dennis Morgan, Mari Aldon, Phil Carey

This Woman Is Mine
US 1941   92m   bw

Fur traders fall out over a beautiful stowaway. Fairly well-produced but unexciting period drama. Franchot Tone, John Carroll, Walter Brennan, Carol Bruce, Nigel Bruce, Leo G. Carroll, Sig Rumann. Written by Seton I. Miller, from the novel *I, James Lewis* by Gilbert Wolff Gabriel; directed by Frank Lloyd; for Universal.

This'll Make You Whistle*
GB 1936   78m   bw

A playboy pretends to be a crook so as to shock his unwanted fiancée's guardian. Rather flat comedy from a stage musical; all depends on the star. *Jack Buchanan,* Elsie Randolph, Jean Gillie, William Kendall, David Hutcheson, Anthony Holles. Written by Guy Bolton, Fred Thompson; directed by Herbert Wilcox; for Herbert Wilcox Productions.

The Thomas Crown Affair**
US 1968   102m   De Luxe   Panavision
UA / Mirisch / Simkoe / Solar (Norman Jewison)

A bored property tycoon masterminds a bank robbery and is chased by a glamorous insurance investigator.
Not so much a movie as an animated colour supplement, this glossy entertainment makes style its prime virtue, plays cute tricks with multiple images and has a famous sexy chess game, but is not above being boring for the rest of the way.

w Alan R. Trustman   *d Norman Jewison*   *ph Haskell Wexler*   m Michel Legrand   *ad Robert Boyle*

Steve McQueen, Faye Dunaway, Paul Burke, Jack Weston, Yaphet Kotto

'Jewison and Wexler seem to have gone slightly berserk, piling up tricks and mannerisms until the film itself sinks out of sight, forlorn and forgotten.'—*Tom Milne*

'A glimmering, empty film reminiscent of an *haute couture* model—stunning on the surface, concave and undernourished beneath.'—*Stefan Kanter*

AA: song 'The Windmills of Your Mind' (*m* Michel Legrand, *ly* Alan and Marilyn Bergman)
AAN: Michel Legrand
● *Video: Warner*

Thoroughbreds Don't Cry
US 1937   80m   bw

Jockeys fight for the chance to ride a valuable English horse. Ho-hum racetrack yarn significant as the first teaming of two young stars. Mickey Rooney, Judy Garland, Ronald Sinclair, Sophie Tucker, C. Aubrey Smith. Written by Lawrence Hazard, J. Walter Ruben and Eleanor Griffin; directed by Alfred E. Green; for MGM.

Thoroughly Modern Millie*
US 1967   138m   Technicolor
Universal (Ross Hunter)

In the twenties, a young girl comes to New York, becomes thoroughly modern, falls for her boss, and has various adventures unmasking a white slave racket centring on a Chinese laundry.
Initially most agreeable but subsequently very patchy spoof of twenties fads and films, including a Harold Lloyd thrill sequence which just doesn't work and a comedy performance from Beatrice Lillie which does. Tunes and performances are alike variable.

w Richard Morris   d George Roy Hill   *ph Russell Metty   ad* Alexander Golitzen, George Webb   m Elmer Bernstein   *md* André Previn, Joseph Gershenson   *ch* Joe Layton   *songs* various

Julie Andrews, Mary Tyler Moore, *John Gavin,* James Fox, Carol Channing, *Beatrice Lillie,* Jack Soo, Pat Morita, Anthony Dexter

'What a nice 65-minute movie is buried therein!'—*Judith Crist*

AA: Elmer Bernstein
AAN: André Previn, Joseph Gershenson; title song (*m* James Van Heusen, *ly* Sammy Cahn); Carol Channing

Those Calloways
US 1964   131m   Technicolor
Walt Disney (Winston Hibler)

Adventures of a marsh trapper and his family who live near a Maine village and try to protect wild geese from hunters.
Predictable family saga with pleasant backgrounds.

w Louis Pelletier, *novel* Swift Water by Paul Annixter   d Norman Tokar   ph Edward Colman   m Max Steiner

Brian Keith, Vera Miles, Brandon de Wilde, Walter Brennan, Ed Wynn, Linda Evans, Philip Abbott, John Larkin, John Qualen

Those Daring Young Men in Their Jaunty Jalopies
US / Italy / France 1969   125m   Technicolor   Panavision
Paramount / Dino de Laurentiis / Marianne (Ken Annakin, Basil Keys)
GB title: *Monte Carlo or Bust*

Accidents befall various competitors in the Monte Carlo Rally.
Rough-edged imitation of *The Great Race* and *Those Magnificent Men in Their Flying Machines*, much feebler than either but with the waste of a big budget well in evidence.

w Jack Davies, Ken Annakin   d Ken Annakin   ph Gabor Pogany   m Ron Goodwin

Peter Cook, Dudley Moore, Tony Curtis, Bourvil, Walter Chiari, Terry-Thomas, Gert Frobe, Susan Hampshire, Jack Hawkins, Eric Sykes

Those Endearing Young Charms
US 1945   81m   bw

An air corps mechanic loves a shopgirl. Nothing to remember about this light star time-passer. Robert Young, Laraine Day, Bill Williams, Ann Harding, Marc Cramer, Anne Jeffries. Written by Jerome Chodorov, from the play by Edward Chodorov; directed by Lewis Allen; for RKO. 'Well played, well directed, and not quite interesting enough to be worth the time it takes.'—*James Agee*.

Those High Grey Walls

US 1939 80m bw

A doctor is convicted for aiding a criminal. Modest variation on a plot used for *Prisoner of Shark Island*, *Devil's Island*, and so on. Walter Connolly, Onslow Stevens, Iris Meredith, Paul Fix, Bernard Nedell, Don Beddoe. Written by William A. Ullman, Lewis Meltzer; directed by Charles Vidor; for Columbia. 'Effective prison melodrama . . . will do all right where properly booked.'—*Variety*

Those Kids from Town

GB 1941 82m bw

An earl takes in a group of noisy cockney kids evacuated from the city. Sentimental wartime crowdpleaser, not especially good but a fairly rare record of one aspect of the war. Shirley Lenner, Jeanne de Casalis, Percy Marmont, Maire O'Neill, George Cole, Charles Victor. Written by Adrian Arlington, from his novel *These Our Strangers*; directed by Lance Comfort; for British National.

Those Magnificent Men in Their Flying Machines, or How I Flew from London to Paris in 25 hours and 11 Minutes**

GB 1965 133m Technicolor Todd-AO
TCF (Stan Margulies, Jack Davies)

In 1910, a newspaper owner sponsors a London to Paris air race.
Long-winded, generally agreeable knockabout comedy with plenty to look at but far too few jokes to sustain it.

w Jack Davies, Ken Annakin d Ken Annakin
ph Christopher Challis m Ron Goodwin
pd Tom Morahan

Sarah Miles, Stuart Whitman, Robert Morley, Eric Sykes, Terry-Thomas, James Fox, Alberto Sordi, Gert Frobe, Jean-Pierre Cassel, Karl Michael Vogler, Irina Demich, Benny Hill, Flora Robson, Sam Wanamaker, Red Skelton, Fred Emney, Cicely Courtneidge, Gordon Jackson, John Le Mesurier, Tony Hancock, William Rushton
'There is many a likely gag, but none that survives the second or third reprise. It could have been a good bit funnier by being shorter: the winning time is 25 hours 11 minutes, and by observing some kind of neo-Aristotelian unity the film seems to last exactly as long.'—*John Simon*

AAN: script

● *Video: CBS / Fox*

Those Marvellous Benchley Shorts: see Benchley

Those Were the Days*

GB 1934 80m bw
BIP (Walter C. Mycroft)

In the nineties, a magistrate seeks out his teenage stepson in a music hall.
Lively comedy which is valuable as giving the screen's best recreation of an old-time music hall.

w Fred Thompson, Frank Miller, Frank Launder, Jack Jordan, play The Magistrate by Arthur Wing Pinero d Thomas Bentley
ph Otto Kanturek md Idris Lewis

Will Hay, John Mills, Iris Hoey, Angela Baddeley, Claud Allister, George Graves, Jane Carr, H. F. Maltby
† Music hall acts include Gaston and Andrée, Lily Morris, G. H. Elliott, Sam Curtis, Frank Boston and Betty.

Those Were the Days

US 1940 74m bw
Paramount (J. Theodore Reed)
GB title: *Good Old Schooldays*

During their 40th anniversary celebrations, a married couple look back to their courtship days at college.
Pleasant, light, nostalgic escapades.

w Don Hartman, stories George Fitch
d J. Theodore Reed ph Victor Milner

William Holden, Bonita Granville, Ezra Stone, Judith Barrett, Vaughan Glazer, Lucien Littlefield, Richard Denning

Those Wonderful Movie Cranks*

Czechoslovakia 1978 88m colour
Barrandov (Jan Suster)

A travelling conjuror at the turn of the century introduces short cinema films into his act, and solves his woman trouble meanwhile.
Charming melancholy comedy which adds a little to art as well as to history.

w Oldrich Vlcek, Jiri Menzel d Jiri Menzel
ph Jaromir Sofr m Jiri Sust

Rudolf Hrusinsky, Vlasta Fabianova, Blazena Holisova

A Thousand Clowns*

US 1965 115m bw
UA / Harell (Fred Coe)

A New Yorker who has abdicated from work leads a cheerful, useless life with his young nephew, but the school board have their doubts.
Imitative nonconformist comedy with frequent reminiscences of older, better plays such as *You Can't Take It with You*. Good lines occasionally make themselves felt, but the overall effect is patchy, the lead is miscast, and the location montages only emphasize the basic one-room set.

w Herb Gardner, from his play d Fred Coe
ph Arthur J. Ornitz m Don Walker

Jason Robards, Martin Balsam, Barry Gordon, Barbara Harris, *William Daniels*, Gene Saks

AA: Martin Balsam
AAN: best picture; Herb Gardner; Don Walker

Thousands Cheer*

US 1943 126m Technicolor
MGM (Joe Pasternak)

An army base stages an all-star variety show.
Ho-hum studio extravaganza with some good numbers.

w Paul Jarrico, Richard Collins d George Sidney ph George Folsey md Herbert Stothart songs various

Kathryn Grayson, Gene Kelly, John Boles, Mary Astor, Jose Iturbi, Kay Kyser and his Orchestra, Lionel Barrymore, Margaret O'Brien, June Allyson, Mickey Rooney, Judy Garland, Red Skelton, Eleanor Powell, Bob Crosby and his Orchestra, Lena Horne, Frank Morgan
'A thoroughly routine musical distinguished only by Gene Kelly with nothing to use his talents on, a terrible piece of trash by Shostakovich, and the unpleasant sight of Jose Iturbi proving he is a real guy by playing the sort of boogie woogie anyone ought to be able to learn through a correspondence course.'—*James Agee*

AAN: George Folsey; Herbert Stothart

Three Bites of the Apple

US 1966 98m Metrocolor Panavision
MGM (Alvin Ganzer)

An English travel courier wins a lot of money in a Rome casino, and nearly loses it all.
Very dull comedy perked up by attractive locations.

w George Wells d Alvin Ganzer ph Gabor Pogany m Eddy Manson

David McCallum, Sylva Koscina, Tammy Grimes, Harvey Korman, Aldo Fabrizi

Three Blind Mice*

US 1938 75m bw
TCF (Raymond Griffith)

Three Kansas girls in the big city seek rich husbands.
Mild comedy remade as *Three Little Girls in Blue* and *How to Marry a Millionaire*, and not all that different from any of the *Gold Diggers* comedy musicals.

w Brown Holmes, Lynn Starling d William A. Seiter ph Ernest Palmer

Loretta Young, Joel McCrea, David Niven, Stuart Erwin, Marjorie Weaver, Pauline Moore, Binnie Barnes, Jane Darwell, Leonid Kinskey
'More names than can be handled on the marquee . . . good summer entertainment.'—*Variety*

Three Brave Men*

US 1956 88m bw Cinemascope
TCF (Herbert B. Swope Jnr)

A civilian employee in the US Navy is suspended as a security risk and it takes a lawsuit to set things straight.
Semi-factual anti-McCarthy drama proving that America is a great place to live—when you're working. Good courtroom scenes.

wd Philip Dunne, articles Anthony Lewis
ph Charles G. Clarke m Hans Salter

Ray Milland, Ernest Borgnine, Nina Foch,
Dean Jagger, Frank Lovejoy, Edward
Andrews, Frank Faylen, James Westerfield,
Joseph Wiseman

The Three Caballeros•••
US 1945 70m Technicolor
Walt Disney (Norman Ferguson)

A programme of shorts about South America,
linked by Donald Duck as a tourist.
Rapid-fire mélange of fragments supporting
the good neighbour policy, following the
shorter *Saludos Amigos* of 1943. The
kaleidoscopic sequences and the combination
of live action with cartoon remain of absorbing
interest.

w various *d* various *m* Edward Plumb, Paul
J. Smith, Charles Wolcott
† Stories include Pablo the Penguin, Little
Gauchito, a Mexican sequence and some
adventures with Joe Carioca.

AAN: Edward Plumb, Paul J. Smith, Charles
Wolcott

Three Came Home••
US 1950 106m bw
TCF (Nunnally Johnson)

In 1941 writer Agnes Newton Keith tries to
escape from Borneo but is interned and ill-
used by the Japanese.
Well-made, harrowing war adventure.

w Nunnally Johnson, *book* Agnes Newton
Keith *d* Jean Negulesco *ph* Milton Krasner
m Hugo Friedhofer *md* Lionel Newman

Claudette Colbert, Patric Knowles, Sessue
Hayakawa, Florence Desmond, Sylvia
Andrew, Phyllis Morris

Three Cases of Murder•
GB 1954 99m bw
British Lion / Wessex / London Films (Ian
Dalrymple, Hugh Perceval)

'In the Picture': a painting comes to life. 'You
Killed Elizabeth': a man suspects himself of
his faithless fiancée's murder. 'Lord
Mountdrago': the foreign secretary dreams of
killing an MP he hates.
Unlinked compendium, in which the first and
third stories are quite interesting and well
done, the second very commonplace.

w Donald Wilson, Sidney Caroll, Ian
Dalrymple (original stories Roderick
Wilkinson, Brett Halliday, W. Somerset
Maugham) *d* Wendy Toye, David Eady,
George More O'Ferrall *ph* Georges Périnal
m Doreen Carwithen

Alan Badel, Hugh Pryse, Leueen MacGrath,
Elizabeth Sellars, John Gregson, Emrys Jones,
Orson Welles, André Morell

Three Cheers for the Irish
US 1940 100m bw
Warner (Sam Bischoff)

An Irishman's daughter causes family trouble
when she falls for a Scot.
Pleasant, unpretentious but overlong romantic
comedy.

w Richard Macaulay, Jerry Wald *d* Lloyd
Bacon *ph* Charles Rosher

Thomas Mitchell, Priscilla Lane, Dennis
Morgan, Alan Hale, Virginia Grey, Irene
Hervey, William Lundigan

Three Coins in the Fountain••
US 1954 102m De Luxe Cinemascope
TCF (Sol C. Siegel)

Three American girls find romance in Rome.
An enormous box office hit, the pattern of
which was frequently repeated against various
backgrounds; it was actually remade in Madrid
as *The Pleasure Seekers*. In itself a thin
entertainment, but the title song carried it.

w John Patrick, *novel* John H. Secondari
d Jean Negulesco *ph* Milton Krasner
m Victor Young *song Jule Styne, Sammy
Cahn*

Clifton Webb, Dorothy McGuire, Louis
Jourdan, Jean Peters, Rossano Brazzi, Maggie
McNamara, Howard St John, Kathryn
Givney, Cathleen Nesbitt

AA: Milton Krasner; title song
AAN: best picture

'Out of the inferno of war came three men
     and a woman—to live their lives, to
     strive for happiness, to seek love!'
Three Comrades••
US 1938 98m bw
MGM (Joseph L. Mankiewicz)

In twenties Germany, three friends find life
hard but derive some joy from their love for a
high-spirited girl who is dying of tuberculosis.
Despairing romance becomes a sentimental
tearjerker with all the stops out; immaculately
produced and very appealing to the masses,
but prevented by censorship from being the
intended indictment of Nazi Germany. The
final scene in which the two surviving
comrades are joined in the churchyard by their
ghostly friends still packs a wallop.

w F. Scott Fitzgerald, Edward A. Paramore,
novel Erich Maria Remarque *d* Frank
Borzage *ph* Joseph Ruttenberg *m* Franx
Waxman

Margaret Sullavan, Robert Taylor, Robert
Young, Franchot Tone, Guy Kibbee, Lionel
Atwill, Henry Hull, Charley Grapewin
    'Just what Frank Borzage is trying to prove
is very difficult to fathom . . . there must have
been some reason for making this picture, but
it certainly isn't in the name of
entertainment.'—*Variety*
    'A remarkably high combination of talents
has made it all very impressive and moving—
good writing, a good man at the camera, good
actors, and presiding over them a good
director . . . such unforgettable bits as the
pursuit of the boy who shot Gottfried, a
glimpse from under the muffling blanket of the
girl's stricken face, the startling downswoop of
the camera's eye upon the girl getting up from
bed to remove the burden of her illness from
those who love her. These are high moments
in a film full of beauty.'—*National Board of
Review*

'A love story, beautifully told and
consummately acted, but so drenched in
hopelessness and heavy with the aroma of
death, of wasted youth in a world of foggy
shapes and nameless menaces, that its beauty
and strength are often clouded and
betrayed.'—*Time*
AAN: Margaret Sullavan

'They might be the family next door—but if
    they were, you'd move!'
Three Cornered Moon•
US 1933 72m bw
Paramount

A newly-poor Depression family has trouble
finding work.
Slightly screwball romantic comedy, a
predecessor of *You Can't Take It with You*;
the humour now seems very faded, but it was
a signpost of its day.

w S. K. Lauren, Ray Harris, *play* Gertrude
Tonkonogy *d* Elliott Nugent *ph* Leon
Shamroy

Claudette Colbert, Mary Boland, Richard
Arlen, Wallace Ford, Lyda Roberti, Tom
Brown, Hardie Albright

Three Daring Daughters
US 1948 115m Technicolor
MGM (Joe Pasternak)
GB title: *The Birds and the Bees*

Three girls are dismayed to hear that their
mother is remarrying.
Cheerful comedy with music, but nothing to
write home about.

w Albert Mannheimer, Frederick Kohner,
Sonya Levien, John Meehan *d* Fred M.
Wilcox *ph* Ray June *md* Georgie Stoll

Jeanette MacDonald, Jose Iturbi, Jane Powell,
Anne Todd, Mary Elinor Donahue, Larry
Adler, Edward Arnold, Harry Davenport,
Moyna MacGill

Three Days of the Condor••
US 1975 118m Technicolor
Panavision
Paramount/ Dino de Laurentiis / Wildwood
(Stanley Schneider)

An innocent researcher for a branch of the
CIA finds himself marked for death by
assassins employed by another branch.
Entertaining New York-based thriller which
shamelessly follows most of the twists of *The
39 Steps.* It is just possible to follow its
complexities, and the dialogue is smart.

w Lorenzo Semple Jnr, David Rayfiel, *novel*
Six Days of the Condor by James Grady
d Sydney Pollack *ph* Owen Roizman *m* Dave
Grusin

Robert Redford, Faye Dunaway, Cliff
Robertson, Max Von Sydow, John Houseman,
Walter McGinn

Three Faces East*
US 1930 71m bw
Warner (Darryl F. Zanuck)

The butler to the British war minister is a
German spy, and the German nurse sent to
help him is really a British agent . . .
Slow , melodramatic remake of 1926 silent,
later turned into a Karloff vehicle, *British
Intelligence* (qv).

w Oliver H. P. Garrett, Arthur Caesar, *play*
Anthony Paul Kelly d Roy del Ruth *ph*
Chick McGill

Constance Bennett, Erich Von Stroheim,
Anthony Bushell, William Holden
'Bennett and Von Stroheim guarantee a
better than average week.'—*Variety*

The Three Faces of Eve**
US 1957 95m bw Cinemascope
TCF (Nunnally Johnson)

A psychiatrist discovers that a female patient
has three distinct personalities: a drab
housewife, a good time girl and a mature
sophisticated woman.
Alistair Cooke introduces this tall tale as if he
believed it; as presented, it is entertaining but
not very convincing. Its box office success was
sufficient to start a schizophrenia cycle.

w Nunnally Johnson, *book* Corbett H.
Thigpen MD, Hervey M. Cleckley MD
d *Nunnally Johnson ph* Stanley Cortez
m Robert Emmett Dolan

Joanne Woodward, Lee J. Cobb, David
Wayne, Nancy Kulp, Edwin Jerome
AA: Joanne Woodward

Three Faces West
US 1940 79m bw
Republic (Sol C. Siegel)

A dust bowl community is helped by an
Austrian doctor fleeing from the Nazis, but his
daughter is followed by a Nazi suitor.
Unusual modern western, blandly told.

w F. Hugh Herbert, Joseph Moncure March,
Samuel Ornitz d Bernard Vorhaus *ph* John
Alton m Victor Young

John Wayne, Charles Coburn, Sigrid Gurie,
Roland Varno, Spencer Charters, Sonny Bupp

Three for Bedroom C
US 1952 74m Natural Color
Brenco (Edward L. Alperson Jnr)

Confusion reigns on a train when a film star
takes a compartment booked for a Harvard
scientist.
Inept farce which never rises above mediocrity
and coasts along well below it.

wd Milton H. Bren *ph* Ernest Laszlo
m Heinz Roemheld

Gloria Swanson, Fred Clark, James Warren,
Hans Conried, Steve Brodie, Margaret
Dumont

Three for Jamie Dawn
US 1956 81m bw
AA (Hayes Goetz)

A crooked lawyer bribes three members of a
murder jury.

Minor courtroom melodrama, limply
developed.

w John Klempner d Thomas Carr *ph* Duke
Green m Walter Scharf

Laraine Day, Ricardo Montalban, Richard
Carlson, June Havoc

Three for the Show*
US 1955 93m Technicolor
       Cinemascope
Columbia (Jonie Taps)

A married Broadway star finds that her first
husband is still alive.
Adequate musical remake of *Too Many
Husbands* (qv); not bad, not good.

w Edward Hope, Leonard Stern, *play* Too
Many Husbands by W. Somerset Maugham
d H. C. Potter *ph* Arthur E. Arling *ch* Jack
Cole *songs* various

Betty Grable, Jack Lemmon, Marge
Champion, Gower Champion, Myron
McCormick, Paul Harvey

Three Girls about Town*
US 1942 71m bw
Columbia

Three sisters in New York find a corpse in
their hotel bedroom.
A funny 'B' picture: fast paced and lively from
start to finish.

w Richard Carroll d Leigh Jason *ph* Franz
Planer

Joan Blondell, Binnie Barnes, Janet Blair,
John Howard, Robert Benchley, Eric Blore,
Una O'Connor

Three Godfathers*
US 1948 106m Technicolor
MGM / Argosy (John Ford)

Three outlaws escaping across the desert take
charge of an orphan baby.
'Orrible sentimental parable partly redeemed
by splendid scenery.

w Laurence Stallings, Frank S. Nugent, *story*
Frank B. Kyne d *John Ford ph* Winton
Hoch m Richard Hageman

John Wayne, Pedro Armendariz, Harry Carey
Jnr, Ward Bond
† The story also appeared in 1909 as *Bronco
Billy and the Baby*; in 1916 as *Three
Godfathers*, with Harry Carey; in 1920 as
Marked Men, with Harry Carey; in 1929 as
Hell's Heroes, with Charles Bickford; in 1936
as *Three Godfathers*, with Chester Morris; and
in 1975 as a TV movie, *The Godchild*, with
Jack Palance.
†† The film is dedicated 'to the memory of
Harry Carey, bright star of the early western
sky'.

Three Guys Named Mike
US 1951 90m bw
MGM (Armand Deutsch)

An accident-prone air hostess has three
suitors.
Inconsequential romantic comedy which shows
the effort of stretching its thin material to
feature length.

w Sidney Sheldon, *story* Ruth Brooks
Flippen d Charles Walters *ph* Paul Vogel
m Bronislau Kaper

Jane Wyman, Barry Sullivan, Van Johnson,
Howard Keel, Phyllis Kirk, Jeff Donnell

Three Hearts for Julia
US 1943 90m bw

A reporter courts his wife all over again when
she threatens to divorce him. One of those
thin romantic comedies which sent its male
lead back to the theatre. Melvyn Douglas,
Ann Sothern, Lee Bowman, Felix Bressart,
Reginald Owen, Richard Ainley. Written by
Lionel Houser; directed by Richard Thorpe;
for MGM.

365 Nights in Hollywood
US 1934 77m bw

A down-and-out becomes a director of a fake
school of acting. Slight and casually developed
comedy-romance, with comedy interludes by
Mitchell and Durant. James Dunn, Alice
Faye, John Bradford, Grant Mitchell. Written
by William Conselman, Henry Johnson;
directed by George Marshall; for Sol M.
Wurtzel / Fox. 'A picture with no punch and
little appeal.'—*Variety*

The 300 Spartans*
US 1962 114m De Luxe Cinemascope
TCF (Rudolph Maté, George St George)

Sparta leads the ancient Greek states against
Persia's attack at Thermopylae.
Quite a lively epic with some dignity.

w George St George d Rudolph Maté
ph Geoffrey Unsworth m Manos Hadjikakis

Richard Egan, Ralph Richardson, David
Farrar, Diane Baker, Barry Coe, Donald
Houston, Kieron Moore, John Crawford,
Robert Brown

Three Husbands
US 1950 76m bw
UA / Gloria (I. G. Goldsmith)

Three husbands receive letters from a dead
friend claiming that he had affairs with each of
their wives.
Silly copy of *A Letter to Three Wives*, with
neither style nor sophistication.

w Vera Caspary, Edward Eliscu d Irving
Reis *ph* Franz Planer m Herschel Burke
Gilbert

Emlyn Williams, Eve Arden, Howard da
Silva, Ruth Warrick, Shepperd Strudwick,
Vanessa Brown, Billie Burke, Jonathan Hale

Three in the Attic
US 1968 90m Pathecolor
AIP - Hermes (Richard Wilson)

A college Casanova is locked in an attic by
three girls who seduce him by rota until he
cries for mercy.
One of the first outspoken comedies of the
sexual revolution, but not a particularly funny
one.

w Stephen Yafa, from his novel Paxton Quigley's Had the Course d Richard Wilson ph J. Burgi Contner m Chad Stuart

Chris Jones, Yvette Mimieux, Judy Pace, Maggie Turett, Nan Martin

'Hello, Mrs Howard, I'm a friend of Mr Howard!'

Three into Two Won't Go*
GB 1969 100m Technicolor
Universal (Julian Blaustein)

An executive has an affair with a girl hitch-hiker who later moves into his house to his wife's astonishment.

Palatable sex drama with good performances, rather flabbily written and directed.

w Edna O'Brien, novel Andrea Newman d Peter Hall ph Walter Lassally m Francis Lai

Rod Steiger, Claire Bloom, Judy Geeson, Peggy Ashcroft, Paul Rogers

Three Kids and a Queen
US 1935 85m bw

Three boys decide to kidnap a rich old lady, but are dismayed to find that she enjoys the experience. Sentimental comedy which seemed to hit the right note. May Robson, Frankie Darro, Billy Burrud, Billy Benedict, Charlotte Henry, Herman Bing, Henry Armetta, John Miljan, Hedda Hopper. Written by Barry Trivers, Samuel Ornitz, Harry Poppe, Chester Beecroft; directed by Edward Ludwig; for Universal. 'A cinch for box office satisfaction.'—Variety

Three Little Girls in Blue
US 1946 90m Technicolor
TCF (Mack Gordon)

Musical remake of Three Blind Mice (qv); adequate and quite forgettable.

w Valentine Davies d Bruce Humberstone ph Ernest Palmer songs Mack Gordon, Joseph Myrow

June Haver, George Montgomery, Vivian Blaine, Celeste Holm, Vera-Ellen, Frank Latimore, Charles Smith, Charles Halton

Three Little Words*
US 1950 102m Technicolor
MGM (Jack Cummings)

The careers of songwriters Bert Kalmar and Harry Ruby.

Disappointingly ordinary musical in which two witty people are made to seem dull, and the plot allows Fred Astaire only one dance.

w George Wells d Richard Thorpe ph Harry Jackson md André Previn ch Hermes Pan songs Bert Kalmar, Harry Ruby and various collaborators

Fred Astaire, Red Skelton, Vera-Ellen, Arlene Dahl, Keenan Wynn, Gale Robbins, Gloria de Haven, Phil Regan, Debbie Reynolds

AAN: André Previn

The Three Lives of Thomasina
GB 1963 97m Technicolor
Walt Disney

In a Scottish village in 1912, a vet finds that his methods are no match for a local girl who treats animals by giving them love.

Syrupy film for children: the animals are the main interest and one of them narrates . . .

w Robert Westerby, novel Thomasina by Paul Gallico d Don Chaffey ph Paul Beeson m Paul Smith

Susan Hampshire, Patrick McGoohan, Karen Dotrice, Vincent Winter, Laurence Naismith, Finlay Currie, Wilfrid Brambell

Three Loves Has Nancy
US 1938 69m bw
MGM (Norman Krasna)

A jilted bride takes her time about her next selection.

Adequate star comedy.

w Bella and Sam Spewack, George Oppenheimer, David Hertz d Richard Thorpe ph William Daniels

Janet Gaynor, Robert Montgomery, Franchot Tone, Guy Kibbee, Claire Dodd, Reginald Owen, Charley Grapewin, Emma Dunn, Cora Witherspoon

'This may not be the funniest picture of the season, but it's certainly one of the wackiest.'—Variety

The Three Maxims
GB 1937 87m bw
GFD / Pathé Consortium (Herbert Wilcox)

Two trapezists love the girl member of the team, and the situation leads to attempted murder.

Effective Paris-set treatment of a well worn theme (see Trapeze).

w Herman Mankiewicz d Herbert Wilcox

Anna Neagle, Tullio Carminati, Leslie Banks, Horace Hodges

Three Men in a Boat
GB 1956 94m Eastmancolor
Cinemascope
Romulus (Jack Clayton)

In the 1890s, misadventures befall three men holidaying on the Thames.

Flabby burlesque of a celebrated comic novel whose style is never even approached.

w Hubert Gregg, Vernon Harris, novel Jerome K. Jerome d Ken Annakin ph Eric Cross m John Addison ad John Howell

David Tomlinson, Jimmy Edwards, Laurence Harvey, Shirley Eaton, Robertson Hare, Jill Ireland, Lisa Gastoni, Martita Hunt, A. E. Matthews, Ernest Thesiger, Adrienne Corri

† A previous version in 1933 starred William Austin, Edmond Breon and Billy Milton; directed by Graham Cutts for ATP.

Three Men on a Horse*
US 1936 85m bw
Warner (Sam Bischoff)

A timid Brooklynite finds he can always pick winners, and gangsters get interested.

Smooth New Yorkish comedy which pleased at the time.

w Laird Doyle, play John Cecil Holm, George Abbott d Mervyn Le Roy ph Sol Polito

Frank McHugh, Sam Levene, Joan Blondell, Guy Kibbee, Carol Hughes, Allen Jenkins, Edgar Kennedy, Eddie Anderson, Harry Davenport

The Three Mesquiteers
A three-man cowboy team who operated in popular B features at the Hopalong Cassidy level. The make-up of the team varied: the actors most often found in it were John Wayne, Max Terhune, Bob Livingston, Ray Corrigan, Bob Steele, Rufe Davis, Tom Tyler, Raymond Hatton, Duncan Renaldo and Jimmy Dodd. The first film was made for RKO, all the rest for Republic: most frequent directors were George Sherman, Mack V. Wright, Joseph Kane, John English and Lester Orlebeck.

1935: POWDERSMOKE RANGE, THE THREE MESQUITEERS
1936: GHOST TOWN, GOLD, ROARIN' LEAD
1937: RIDERS OF THE WHISTLING SKULL, HIT THE SADDLE, GUNSMOKE RANCH, COME ON COWBOYS, RANGE DEFENDERS, HEART OF THE ROCKIES, THE TRIGGER TRIO, WILD HORSE RODEO
1938: THE PURPLE VIGILANTES, CALL THE MESQUITEERS, CALL OF THE MESQUITEERS, OUTLAWS OF SONORA, RIDERS OF THE BLACK HILLS, HEROES OF THE HILLS, PALS OF THE SADDLE, OVERLAND STAGE RAIDERS, SANTA FE STAMPEDE, RED RIVER RANGE
1939: THE NIGHT RIDERS, THREE TEXAS STEERS, WYOMING OUTLAW, NEW FRONTIER, THE KANSAS TERRORS, COWBOYS FROM TEXAS
1940: HEROES OF THE SADDLE, PIONEERS OF THE WEST, COVERED WAGON DAYS, ROCKY MOUNTAIN RANGERS, OKLAHOMA RENEGADES, UNDER TEXAS SKIES, THE TRAIL BLAZERS, LONE STAR RAIDERS
1941: PRAIRIE PIONEERS, PALS OF THE PECOS, SADDLEMATES, GANGS OF SONORA, OUTLAWS OF THE CHEROKEE TRAIL, GAUCHOS OF EL DORADO, WEST OF CIMARRON
1942: CODE OF THE OUTLAW, RIDERS OF THE RANGE, WESTWARD HO, THE PHANTOM PLAINSMAN, SHADOWS ON THE SAGE, VALLEY OF HUNTED MEN
1943: THUNDERING TRAILS, THE BLOCKED TRAIL, SANTA FE SCOUTS, RIDERS OF THE RIO GRANDE

The Three Musketeers
US 1935 97m bw

See below for synopsis. A thin and poorly handled version. Walter Abel (D'Artagnan), Paul Lukas (Athos), Moroni Olson (Porthos), Onslow Stevens (Aramis), Margot Grahame

(Milady), Heather Angel (Constance), Ian Keith (de Rochefort), Miles Mander (King), Nigel de Brulier (Richelieu). Written by Dudley Nichols, Rowland V. Lee; directed by Rowland V. Lee; for RKO. 'Ineffective and disappointing adaptation . . . dull entertainment.'—*Variety*

The Three Musketeers**
US 1939 73m bw
TCF (Raymond Griffith)
GB title: *The Singing Musketeer*

A burlesque of the familiar story with pauses for song.
A very satisfactory entertainment with all concerned in top form.

w M. M. Musselman, William A. Drake, Sam Hellman d Allan Dwan ph Peverell Marley *songs* Samuel Pokrass, Walter Bullock

Don Ameche, the Ritz Brothers, Binnie Barnes, *Joseph Schildkraut*, Lionel Atwill, Miles Mander, Gloria Stuart, Pauline Moore, John Carradine

'Whenever the action lags, the trio take the rostrum for a slapstick specialty . . . moderate b.o., a topper for the key duals.'—*Variety*

The Three Musketeers***
US 1948 125m Technicolor
MGM (Pandro S. Berman)

High-spirited version of the famous story, with duels and fights presented like musical numbers. Its vigour and inventiveness is a pleasure to behold.

w Robert Ardrey d George Sidney ph Robert Planck m Herbert Stothart

Gene Kelly, Lana Turner, June Allyson, Frank Morgan, Van Heflin, Angela Lansbury, Vincent Price, Keenan Wynn, John Sutton, Gig Young, Robert Coote, Reginald Owen, Ian Keith, Patricia Medina

'A heavy, rough-housing mess. As Lady de Winter, Lana Turner sounds like a drive-in waitress exchanging quips with hotrodders, and as Richelieu, Vincent Price might be an especially crooked used car dealer. Angela Lansbury wears the crown of France as though she had won it at a county fair.'—*New Yorker, 1980*

AAN: Robert Planck

The Three Musketeers (The Queen's Diamonds)**
Panama 1973 107m Technicolor
Film Trust (Alex Salkind)

Jokey version with realistic blood; despite very lively highlights it wastes most of its high production cost by not giving its plot a chance; but money was saved by issuing the second half separately as *The Four Musketeers (The Revenge of Milady)*. The latter section was less attractive.

w George MacDonald Fraser d Richard Lester ph David Watkin m Michel Legrand pd Brian Eatwell

Michael York, Oliver Reed, Richard Chamberlain, Frank Finlay, Raquel Welch,

Geraldine Chaplin, Spike Milligan, Faye Dunaway, Charlton Heston, Christopher Lee, Jean-Pierre Cassel

'It's one dragged-out forced laugh. No sweep, no romance, no convincing chivalric tradition to mock.'—*Stanley Kauffmann*

● *Video: Thorn EMI*

'Move over, Casanova!'
Three on a Couch
US 1966 109m Technicolor

An artist tries to cure the sexual hang-ups of his psychiatrist fiancée's three female patients.
Intolerably lengthy and witless comedy. Jerry Lewis, Janet Leigh, James Best, Mary Ann Mobley, Gila Golan, Leslie Parrish, Kathleen Freeman, Fritz Feld. Written by Bob Ross, Samuel A. Taylor, Arne Sultan, Marvin Worth; directed and produced by Jerry Lewis; for Jerry Lewis Productions / Columbia. 'A long drag through stock situations.'—*MFB.* 'Unintentionally unfunny.'—*Leonard Maltin.* 'Stay on your own couch and don't bother with Jerry's.'—*Steven Scheuer*

Three on a Match*
US 1932 63m bw
Warner (Sam Bischoff)

Three schoolgirl friends meet again in the big city, after which their paths cross melodramatically.
Predictable, watchable multi-story dramatics with an ironic twist: remade in 1938 as *Broadway Musketeers.*

w Lucien Hubbard d Mervyn Le Roy ph Sol Polito

Joan Blondell, Bette Davis, Ann Dvorak, Warren William, Grant Mitchell, Lyle Talbot, Humphrey Bogart, Glenda Farrell, Clara Blandick

'A nice picture descending to mediocrity in its final two reels.'—*Variety*

Three Ring Circus
US 1954 103m Technicolor
Vistavision
Paramount / Hal B. Wallis

Ex-army veterans join a circus.
The mixture as before from Martin and Lewis: variety acts interspersed with sentiment and heavy mugging.

w Don McGuire, Joseph Pevney ph Loyal Griggs d Joseph Pevney m Walter Scharf

Dean Martin, Jerry Lewis, Joanne Dru, Zsa Zsa Gabor, Wallace Ford, Sig Rumann, Gene Sheldon, Nick Cravat, Elsa Lanchester

Three Sailors and a Girl
US 1953 95m Technicolor
Warner (Sammy Cahn)

A ship's funds are unofficially invested in a musical show.
Undernourished comedy musical.

w Roland Kibbee, Devery Freeman, *play* The Butter and Egg Man by George S. Kaufman d Roy del Ruth ph Carl Guthrie *songs* Sammy Fain, Sammy Cahn

Jane Powell, Gordon Macrae, Gene Nelson, Sam Levene, George Givot, Veda Ann Borg

Three Secrets*
US 1949 98m bw
(Warner) US Pictures (Milton Sperling)

Three women wait anxiously to find out whose child survived a plane crash.
Well-made, formula woman's picture.

w Martin Rackin, Gina Kaus d Robert Wise ph Sid Hickox m Davis Buttolph

Eleanor Parker, Patricia Neal, Ruth Roman, Frank Lovejoy, Leif Erickson, Ted de Corsia, Edmon Ryan, Larry Keating

The Three Sisters*
GB 1970 165m Eastmancolor
Alan Clore Films

At the turn of the century, three fatherless sisters dream of abandoning Russian provincial life for the big city.
Filmed Chekhov, better than most but still lacking cinematic vigour.

translator Moura Budberg d Laurence Olivier ph Geoffrey Unsworth m William Walton

Laurence Olivier, Joan Plowright, Jeanne Watts, Louise Purnell, Derek Jacobi, Alan Bates, Ronald Pickup

● *Video: Thorn EMI*

Three Smart Girls**
US 1936 86m bw
Universal (Joe Pasternak)

Three sisters bring their parents back together.
Pleasant, efficient family film which made a world star of Deanna Durbin.

w Adele Comandini, Austin Parker d Henry Koster ph Joseph Valentine md Charles Previn

Deanna Durbin, Barbara Read, Nan Grey, Charles Winninger, Binnie Barnes, Ray Milland, Alice Brady, Mischa Auer, Ernest Cossart, Hobart Cavanaugh

'Surefire entertainment for any and all types of audiences. It also has that rare quality of making an audience feel better for having seen it.'—*Variety*

'Idiotically tuned in to happiness, but it isn't boring.'—*New Yorker, 1978*

AAN: best picture; script

Three Smart Girls Grow Up*
US 1939 87m bw
Universal (Joe Pasternak)

A girl helps her sisters to find beaus.
More of the above, quite palatable but inevitably warmed over.

w Bruce Manning, Felix Jackson d Henry Koster ph Joe Valentine

Deanna Durbin, Helen Parrish, Nan Grey, Charles Winninger, Robert Cummings, William Lundigan, Ernest Cossart, Nella Walker

'The white feminine room which the three sisters share, the quilted beds, the little furry jackets over the pajamas—the whole upholstery is so virginal that it evokes little twitters of nostalgia from the stalls. Pillow fights and first love and being sent to bed

THREE SMART GIRLS.   Deanna Durbin, the new teenage superstar, is flanked by Barbara Read and Nan Grey.

without any dinner—the awkward age has never been so laundered and lavendered and laid away.'—*Graham Greene*

Three Strangers*
US 1946   92m   bw
Warner (Wolfgang Reinhardt)

A sweepstake ticket brings fortune and tragedy to three ill-assorted people.
Humdrum pattern play: the stars work hard to bring a little magic to it.

w John Huston, Howard Koch   *d* Jean Negulesco   *ph* Arthur Edeson   *m* Adolph Deutsch

Sidney Greenstreet, Peter Lorre, Geraldine Fitzgerald, Joan Lorring, Robert Shayne, Marjorie Riordan, Arthur Shields

Three Stripes in the Sun
US 1955   93m   bw
Columbia (Fred Kohlmar)
GB title: *The Gentle Sergeant*

After World War II, a Japanese-hating sergeant in the US occupation forces helps a poverty-stricken orphanage.
Predictable sentimentality based on fact, with good background detail.

wd Richard Murphy, *articles* E. J. Kelly *ph* Burnett Guffey   *m* George Duning

Aldo Ray, Phil Carey, Dick York, Chuck Connors, Mitsuko Kimura

3.10 to Yuma**
US 1957   92m   bw
Columbia (David Heilwell)

A sheriff has to get his prisoner on to a train despite the threatening presence of the prisoner's outlaw friends.
Tense, well-directed but rather talky low-budget western: excellent performances and atmosphere flesh out an unconvincing physical situation.

w Halsted Welles   *d* Delmer Daves *ph* Charles Lawton Jnr   *m* George Duning

Glenn Ford, Van Heflin, Felicia Farr, Leora Dana, Henry Jones, Richard Jaeckel, Robert Emhardt
  'A vivid, tense and intelligent story about probable people, enhanced by economical writing and supremely efficient direction and playing.'—*Guardian*

Three Violent People
US 1956   100m   Eastmancolor
  Vistavision
Paramount (Hugh Brown)

Brother ranchers quarrel over the wife of one of them, an ex-saloon hostess.
Characterless 'character' western, a long way after *Duel in the Sun*.

w James Edward Grant   *d* Rudolph Maté *ph* Loyal Griggs   *m* Walter Scharf

Charlton Heston, Anne Baxter, *Gilbert Roland*, Tom Tryon, Bruce Bennett, Forrest Tucker, Elaine Stritch, Barton MacLane

The Three Weird Sisters
GB 1948   82m   bw
British National (Louis H. Jackson)

Three old maids in a Welsh village plot to kill their rich half-brother but are swept away by a flood.
All-stops-out melodrama which doesn't quite work and is generally remembered, if at all, for the last third of its writing team.

w Louise Birt, David Evans, Dylan Thomas, *novel* Charlotte Armstrong   *d* Dan Birt

Nancy Price, Mary Clare, Mary Merrall, Nova Pilbeam, Raymond Lovell, Anthony Hulme

Three Wise Fools
US 1946   90m   bw
MGM (William Wright)

Three crusty old gents adopt an orphan, who softens them.
Antediluvian whimsy without the expected fun, remade from a silent.

w John McDermott, James O'Hanlon, *play* Austin Strong   *d* Edward Buzzell

Margaret O'Brien, Lionel Barrymore, Thomas Mitchell, Edward Arnold, Lewis Stone, Jane Darwell, Harry Davenport, Cyd Charisse

Three Wise Girls
US 1932   80m approx   bw
Columbia

Three small-town girls gain wisdom in New York.
Three millgirls' romances for the price of one. Adequate, predictable romantic fodder of its time.

w Robert Riskin, Agnes C. Johnson *d* William Beaudine   *ph* Ted Tetzlaff

Jean Harlow, Mae Clarke, Walter Byron, Marie Prevost, Andy Devine, Natalie Moorhead, Jameson Thomas
  'Should turn in a respectable score . . . Miss Harlow fails to be convincing.'—*Variety*

Three Women*
US 1924   60m approx (24 fps)   bw
  silent
Warner

A rake charms three women, each for a different purpose.
Subtle satirical comedy; not one of the director's masterpieces, but with enough barbs to keep one watching.

w Ernst Lubitsch, Hans Kraly, from The Lilie by Yolanthe Marees   *d* Ernst Lubitsch *ph* Charles Van Enger

Lew Cody, Pauline Frederick, May McAvoy, Marie Prevost

Three Women
US 1977   123m   De Luxe   Panavision
TCF / Lion's Gate (Robert Altman)

Three women come to California for different

reasons; when their problems become insurmountable they rely on each other. Tiresomely somnambulistic multi-character . drama, half a satire, half a wallow, and never an entertainment.

wd Robert Altman *ph* Charles Rosher *m* Gerald Busby

Sissy Spacek, Janice Rule, Shelley Duvall, Robert Fortier, Ruth Nelson, John Cromwell, Sierra Pecheur

The Three Worlds of Gulliver
US / Spain 1959 100m Technicolor
Columbia / Morningside (Charles Schneer)

Gulliver's adventures in Lilliput and Brobdingnag.
Flat treatment of marvellous material, with all the excitement squeezed out of it and not even much pizazz in the trick photography.

w Arthur Ross, Jack Sher *d* Jack Sher *ph* Wilkie Cooper *m* Bernard Herrmann *sp* Ray Harryhausen

Kerwin Mathews, Basil Sydney, Mary Ellis, Jo Morrow, June Thorburn, Grégoire Aslan, Charles Lloyd Pack, Martin Benson

Thrill of a Lifetime
US 1937 72m bw

Summer campers put on a show which goes to Broadway. Stereotyped lower-case musical with agreeable acts. Judy Canova, Ben Blue, the Yacht Club Boys, Eleanore Whitney, Betty Grable, Johnny Downs, Dorothy Lamour (guest), Larry Crabbe. Written by Seena Owen, Grant Garrett, Paul Gerard Smith; directed by George Archainbaud; for Paramount. 'Lightweight but pleasant.'—*Variety*

Thrill of a Romance
US 1945 105m Technicolor
MGM (Joe Pasternak)

A lady swimmer falls for a returning serviceman.
Empty musical vehicle with nothing memorable about it except the waste of time and money.

w Richard Connell, Gladys Lehmann *d* Richard Thorpe *ph* Harry Stradling *md* George Stoll

Esther Williams, Van Johnson, Lauritz Melchior, Frances Gifford, Henry Travers, Spring Byington, Tommy Dorsey

The Thrill of it All*
US 1963 104m Eastmancolor
U-I / Ross Hunter / Arwin (Ross Hunter, Marty Melcher)

The wife of a gynaecologist becomes an advertising model, and work pressures disrupt her marriage.
Glossy matrimonial farce which starts brightly but eventually flags and becomes exhausting. Its better jokes linger in the memory.

w Carl Reiner *d* Norman Jewison *ph* Russell Metty *m* Frank de Vol

Doris Day, James Garner, Arlene Francis, Edward Andrews, Reginald Owen, Zasu Pitts, Elliot Reid
'Pleasantly reminiscent of some of the screwball comedies of the thirties.'—*MFB*

Throne of Blood*
Japan 1957 105m bw
Toho (Akira Kurosawa, Sojiro Motoki)
original title: *Kumonosu-Jo*

A samurai, spurred on by his wife and an old witch, murders his lord at Cobweb Castle.
A Japanese version of *Macbeth* with a savage and horrifying final sequence. The whole film is a treat to look at.

w Hideo Oguni, Shinobu Hashimoto, Ryuzo Kikushima, Akira Kurosawa, from Shakespeare's play *d* Akira Kurosawa *ph* Asaichi Nakai *m* Masaru Sato

Toshiro Mifune, Isuzu Yamada
'Its final impression is of a man who storms into a room with an impassioned speech to deliver and then discovers that he has forgotten what he came to say.'—*Kenneth Cavander, MFB*

Through a Glass Darkly*
Sweden 1961 91m bw
Svensk Filmindustri

Four unfulfilled people on a remote island fail to communicate with each other or to understand what God is.
It sounds like a parody Bergman film, and it almost is. The same themes were carried through in *Winter Light* and *The Silence*.

wd Ingmar Bergman *ph* Sven Nykvist *m* Bach

Harriet Andersson, Gunnar Bjornstrand, Max Von Sydow, Lars Passgard

AA: best foreign film
AAN: Ingmar Bergman (as writer)

Through Different Eyes
US 1943 65m bw

A veteran DA cites an old murder case to illustrate the dangers of circumstantial evidence. Neat and peppy crime programme filler. Frank Craven, Donald Woods, Vivian Blaine, Mary Howard, Jerome Cowan. Written by Samuel G. Engel; directed by Thomas Z. Loring; for TCF.

Thumb Tripping*
US 1972 94m De Luxe
Avco (Robert Chartoff, Irwin Winkler)

A boy and a girl hitch-hiker in California have a variety of violent adventures.
Tail end of the *Easy Rider* fashion, with odd moments of interesting detail.

w Don Mitchell, from his novel *d* Quentin Masters *ph* Harry Stradling Jnr *m* Bob Thompson

Michael Burns, Meg Foster, Marianna Hill, Bruce Dern

Thunder
US 1929 90m at 24 fps bw silent
A train driver has trouble with his sons.

Almost forgotten star melodrama, his last silent one, made when his health was already failing. Lon Chaney, James Murray, George Duryea, Phyllis Haver. Written by Byron Morgan and Ann Price; directed by William Nigh; for MGM.

Thunder Afloat
US 1939 95m bw

Rival boat owners vie for a 1918 navy contract, and the winner finds he has been trapped into enlisting. Rumbustious Flagg-and-Quirt style comedy, good enough value for the undemanding. Wallace Beery, Chester Morris, Virginia Grey, Douglass Dumbrille, Regis Toomey, Henry Victor, Jonathan Hale. Written by Ralph Wheelwright, Wells Root and Harvey Haislip; directed by George B. Seitz; for MGM. 'Timely actioner, cinch for exploitation.'—*Variety*

Thunder Bay*
US 1953 102m Technicolor
U-I (Aaron Rosenberg)

An engineer is convinced that oil can be raised from the Louisiana sea-bed.
Well-produced outdoor actioner.

w Gil Doud, John Michael Hayes *d* Anthony Mann *ph* William Daniels *m* Frank Skinner

James Stewart, Joanne Dru, Dan Duryea, Jay C. Flippen, Anthony Moreno, Gilbert Roland, Marcia Henderson

Thunder Below
US 1932 71m bw

A wife loves her husband's best friend. Dreary melodrama with a star already seen to be box office poison. Tallulah Bankhead, Charles Bickford, Paul Lukas. From a novel by Thomas Rourke; directed by Richard Wallace; for Paramount. 'Star as weak as story . . . dull and uneventful.'—*Variety*

Thunder in the City
GB 1937 88m bw
Atlantic (Akos Tolnay, Alexander Esway)

An American salesman in London helps a penniless duke promote a non-existent metal. Mild satire on British and American idiosyncrasies, now very faded.

w Robert Sherwood, Abem Kandel, Akos Tolnay *d* Marion Gering *ph* Al Gilks *m* Miklos Rozsa

Edward G. Robinson, Lulu Deste, Ralph Richardson, Nigel Bruce, Constance Collier, Arthur Wontner
'Cinch to be an important feature and satisfactory booking.'—*Variety*

Thunder in the East
US 1951 98m bw
Paramount (Everett Riskin)

When India becomes independent in 1947, an American wanting to sell arms clashes with the peace-loving chief of a principality, but the arms are needed when rebels attack.
Artificial and boring action melodrama with platitudinous conversations.

w Jo Swerling, *novel* Rage of the Vulture by Alan Moorehead *d* Charles Vidor *ph* Lee Garmes *m* Hugo Friedhofer

Alan Ladd, Charles Boyer, Deborah Kerr, Corinne Calvet, Cecil Kellaway

Thunder in the Night
US 1935   69m   bw

A police captain solves the murder of a blackmailer. Reasonably snappy mystery set in Budapest. Edmund Lowe, Karen Morley, Paul Cavanagh, Una O'Connor, Gene Lockhart, John Qualen, Russell Hicks. Written by Frances Hyland, Eugene Solow, from the play A Woman Lies by Ladislas Fodor; directed by George Archainbaud; for Fox. 'Tops average: deserves to do fairly well.'—*Variety*

Thunder in the Sun
US 1958   81m   Technicolor
Seven Arts / Carollton (Clarence Greene)

In 1847 an Indian scout guides a group of Basques to California with their vines. Overwritten and melodramatic wagon train story.
wd Russel Rouse *ph* Stanley Cortez *m* Cyril Mockridge

Susan Hayward, Jeff Chandler, Jacques Bergerac, Blanche Yurka, Carl Esmond

'I'll make a soldier of you, Mr McQuade—if you don't break first!'
A Thunder of Drums*
US 1961   97m   Metrocolor
Cinemascope
MGM (Robert J. Enders)

Trouble with Apaches at a frontier post in 1870.
Solid, unexciting first feature western, some way after Ford.
w James Warner Bellah *d* Joseph Newman *ph* William Spencer *m* Harry Sukman

Richard Boone, George Hamilton, Arthur O'Connell, Luana Patten, Richard Chamberlain, Charles Bronson

Thunder on the Hill
US 1951   84m   bw
U-I (Michael Kraike)
GB title: *Bonaventure*

In Norfolk, a nun solves a murder mystery during a flood.
Modest whodunnit with an unusual background but not much suspense.
w Oscar Saul, André Solt, *play* Bonaventure by Charlotte Hastings *d* Douglas Sirk *ph* William Daniels *m* Hans Salter

Claudette Colbert, Ann Blyth, Robert Douglas, Anne Crawford, Philip Friend, Gladys Cooper, John Abbott, Connie Gilchrist, Gavin Muir

Thunder over Mexico**
US 1933   60m   bw   silent (with music score)

The Upton Sinclair version of the troubled Eisenstein travelogue. Packed with moments

of genius, but not really a finished film in any sense. Music by Hugo Reisenfeld; for Principal Pictures. See also *Time in the Sun*. 'It will not get to first base either as a critic's picture, or in straight box office parlance . . . beautiful, slow and dull.'—*Variety*

Thunder over the Plains
US 1953   82m   Warnercolor

After the Civil War, a Union officer is posted with his family to the southwest territory, and finds tension. Busy but uninvolving western programmer with a reliable star. Randolph Scott, Phyllis Kirk, Lex Barker, Charles McGraw, Elisha Cook Jnr, Fess Parker. Written by Russell Hughes; directed by André de Toth; for Warner.

Thunder Road*
US 1958   92m   bw
UA / DRM

Hillbilly bootleggers defy a Chicago gangster. Downbeat but actionful crime melodrama with an unusual background and plenty of car chases.
w James Arlee Philips, Walter Wise *d* Arthur Ripley *ph* Alan Stensvold *m* Jack Marshall

Robert Mitchum, Gene Barry, Jacques Aubuchon, Keely Smith

Thunder Rock***
GB 1942   112m   bw
Charter Films (John Boulting)

A journalist disgusted with the world of the thirties retires to a lighthouse on Lake Michigan and is haunted by the ghosts of immigrants drowned a century before. Subtle adaptation of an impressive and topical anti-isolationist play, very well acted and presented.
w Jeffrey Dell, Bernard Miles, *play* Robert Ardrey *d* Roy Boulting *ph* Mutz Greenbaum (Max Greene) *m* Hans May

Michael Redgrave, Lilli Palmer, Barbara Mullen, James Mason, Frederick Valk, Frederick Cooper, Finlay Currie, Sybilla Binder
'Boldly imaginative in theme and treatment.'—*Sunday Express*
'More interesting technically than anything since *Citizen Kane*.'—*Manchester Guardian*
'If I thought it wouldn't keep too many people away, I'd call it a work of art.'—*Daily Express*

Thunderball**
GB 1965   132m   Technicolor
Panavision
UA / Eon / Kevin McClory

James Bond goes underwater.
Commercially the most successful Bond, but certainly not the best despite a plethora of action sequences.
w Richard Maibaum, John Hopkins, *novel* Ian Fleming *d* Terence Young *ph* Ted Moore *m* John Barry

Sean Connery, Adolfo Celi, Claudine Auger, Luciana Paluzzi, Rik Van Nutter, Bernard Lee, Lois Maxwell, Martine Beswick

'The screenplay stands on tiptoe at the outermost edge of the suggestive and gazes yearningly down into the obscene.'—*John Simon*
● *Video: Warner*

Thunderbird Six
GB 1968   90m   Techniscope
UA / AP / Century 21 (Gerry and Sylvia Anderson)

International Rescue combats the Black Phantom.
Bright, suspenseful puppetoon based on the TV series.
w Gerry and Sylvia Anderson *d* David Lane *ph* Harry Oakes *m* Barry Gray *ad* Bob Bell
'Holds some charm for adults, or at least for those who enjoy playing with miniature trains.'—*MFB*

Thunderbirds
US 1942   79m   Technicolor
TCF (Lamar Trotti)

Problems of Arizona flight instructors during World War II.
Very minor flagwaver.
w Lamar Trotti *d* William A. Wellman *ph* Ernest Palmer *m* David Buttolph

Gene Tierney, Preston Foster, John Sutton, Jack Holt, May Whitty, George Barbier, Richard Haydn, Reginald Denny, Ted North

Thunderbirds
US 1952   99m   bw
Republic (John H. Auer)

An Oklahoma unit covers itself in glory during World War II.
Scrappy, noisy war actioner with much newsreel footage.
w Mary McCall Jnr *d* John H. Auer *ph* Reggie Lanning *m* Victor Young

John Derek, John Barrymore Jnr, Mona Freeman, Ward Bond, Gene Evans

Thunderbolt**
US 1929   94m   bw
Paramount

A gangster is caught, tried, and repents. Gloomy melodrama with interesting style and credits.
w Jules Furthman, Herman J. Mankiewicz *d* Josef Von Sternberg *ph* Henry Gerrard

George Bancroft, Fay Wray, Richard Arlen, Tully Marshall, Eugénie Besserer

AAN: George Bancroft

Thunderbolt and Lightfoot*
US 1974   115m   De Luxe   Panavision
UA / Malpaso (Robert Daley)

A bank robber escapes prison, disguises himself as a preacher, befriends a young drifter, and discovers that a new building stands on the spot where the loot is hidden. Violent melodrama reworking an ancient comedy situation; well made on its level.

wd Michael Cimino *ph* Frank Stanley *m* Dee Barton

Clint Eastwood, Jeff Bridges, George Kennedy, Geoffrey Lewis, Catherine Bach

AAN: Jeff Bridges

Thunderhead, Son of Flicka*
US 1945 78m Technicolor
TCF (Robert Bassler)

More where *My Friend Flicka* came from. Unexceptional family film with excellent outdoor photography.

w Dwight Cummins, Dorothy Yost, *novel* Mary O'Hara *d* Louis King *ph* Charles Clarke *m* Cyril Mockridge

Roddy McDowall, Preston Foster, Rita Johnson, James Bell, Carleton Young

Thunderstorm
GB 1955 88m bw
Hemisphere / Binnie Barnes

A Spanish fisherman rescues a mysterious girl from a derelict yacht and falls in love with her although the villagers regard her as a witch. Heady stuff on a low budget, quite smoothly done for lovers of peasant drama.

w George St George, Geoffrey Holmes *d* John Guillermin *ph* Manuel Berenguer *m* Paul Misraki

Linda Christian, Carlos Thompson, Charles Korvin

Thursday's Child
GB 1942 81m bw

A child from an ordinary family has success in films and it goes to her head. Predictable domestic drama with some good moments, but rather overpraised at the time. Sally Ann Howes, Wilfrid Lawson, Kathleen O'Regan, Eileen Bennett, Stewart Granger, Felix Aylmer. Written by Donald Macardle and Rodney Ackland, from the novel by Donald Macardle; directed by Rodney Ackland; for ABPC.

THX 1138*
US 1970 95m Technicolor / scope
Warner / American Zoetrope (Francis Ford Coppola,
  Lawrence Sturhahn)

In a future society, computer programmed and emotionless, an automated human begins to break the rules.
Orwellian science fiction; a thoughtful, rather cold affair which is always good to look at.

w George Lucas, Walter Murch *d* George Lucas *ph* Dave Meyers, Albert Kihn *m* Lalo Schifrin

Robert Duvall, Donald Pleasence, Pedro Colley, Maggie McOmie, Ian Wolfe

Thy Soul Shall Bear Witness*
Sweden 1920 70m approx (24 fps) bw
  silent Svensk Filmindustri
original title: *Korkarlen;* aka: *The Phantom Carriage*

A drunkard is knocked senseless, retraces his misspent life, hears the carriage of death approaching and returns to his family.
Old-fashioned moralistic saga which hit the right note at the time and has scenes which still impress.

wd Victor Sjostrom, *novel* Selma Lagerlöf *ph* J. Julius Jaenzon

Victor Sjostrom, Hilda Borgstrom, Astrid Holm

† Remade in France in 1939 by Julien Duvivier, as *La Charette Fantôme*, with Pierre Fresnay and Louis Jouvet; and again in Sweden in 1958 as *Korkarlen*, by Arne Mattson.

Tiara Tahiti*
GB 1962 100m Eastmancolor
Rank / Ivan Foxwell

An up-from-the-ranks colonel and an aristocratic smoothie captain continue their antipathy in peacetime Tahiti, where one is nearly murdered and the other gets his come-uppance.
Uneasy mixture of light comedy and character drama; enjoyable in parts, but flabbily assembled and muddily photographed.

w Geoffrey Cotterell, Ivan Foxwell, *novel* Geoffrey Cotterell *d* William T. Kotcheff *ph* Otto Heller *m* Philip Green

John Mills, James Mason, Herbert Lom, Claude Dauphin, Rosenda Monteros

Tick, Tick, Tick . . .*
US 1969 100m Metrocolor Panavision
MGM / Nelson-Barrett (Ralph Nelson,
  James Lee Barrett)

The first black sheriff in a southern community has trouble with murder and rape cases.
Socially conscious suspenser, well enough made from predictable elements and leading surprisingly to an upbeat ending.

w James Lee Barrett *d* Ralph Nelson *ph* Loyal Griggs *m* Jerry Stynes

Jim Brown, George Kennedy, Fredric March, Lynn Carlin, Don Stroud, Clifton James

Ticket to Heaven*
Canada 1981 108m colour

A rootless young man is taken over by a religious co-operative. Thinly veiled attack on the Moonies, quite well handled but perhaps better as a straight documentary. Nick Mancuso, Saul Rubinek, Meg Foster, Kim Cattrall. Written by Ralph L. Thomas and Anne Cameron from the book *Moonwebs* by Josh Freed; directed by Ralph L. Thomas; for Ronald Cohen Productions.

A Ticket to Tomahawk*
US 1950 90m Technicolor
TCF (Robert Bassler)

A stagecoach line defies the new western railroad.
Would-be satirical western which doesn't quite have the stamina and after some pleasing touches settles for dullness.

w Mary Loos *d* Richard Sale *ph* Harry Jackson *m* Cyril Mockridge

Anne Baxter, Dan Dailey, Rory Calhoun, Walter Brennan, Charles Kemper, Connie Gilchrist, Arthur Hunnicutt, Sen Yung

Tickle Me
US 1965 90m De Luxe Panavision
AA (Ben Schwalb)

An unemployed rodeo star accepts a job at a health ranch and helps a girl escape from villains after hidden treasure.
Wispy star vehicle with an unexpected haunted ghost town climax.

w Elwood Ullman, Edward Bernds *d* Norman Taurog *ph* Loyal Griggs *m* Walter Scharf

Elvis Presley, Julia Adams, Jocelyn Lane, Jack Mullaney, Merry Anders, Connie Gilchrist

A Ticklish Affair
US 1963 95m Metrocolor Panavision
MGM / Euterpe (Joe Pasternak)

A naval commander in San Diego falls for a widow with several children.
Thin romantic comedy with too many juvenile antics.

w Ruth Brooks Flippen *d* George Sidney *ph* Milton Krasner *m* George Stoll, Robert Van Eyps

Shirley Jones, Gig Young, Red Buttons, Carolyn Jones, Edgar Buchanan

Tiger Bay**
GB 1959 105m bw
Rank / Wintle–Parkyn (John Hawkesworth)

A Polish seaman in Cardiff kills his faithless girl friend and kidnaps a child who proves more than a match for him.
Generally very proficient police chase melodrama with strong characterizations: a considerable box office success of its time.

w John Hawkesworth, Shelley Smith *d* J. Lee-Thompson *ph* Eric Cross *m* Laurie Johnson

Hayley Mills, John Mills, Horst Buchholz, Megs Jenkins, Anthony Dawson, Yvonne Mitchell

Tiger in the Smoke*
GB 1956 94m bw
Rank (Leslie Parkyn)

Ex-commando criminals comb London for hidden loot and threaten a young girl.
Odd little melodrama with a complex plot and a different, Graham Greene-like atmosphere.

w Anthony Pelissier, *novel* Marjorie Allingham *d* Roy Baker *ph* Geoffrey Unsworth *m* Malcolm Arnold

Tony Wright, Muriel Pavlow, Donald Sinden, Bernard Miles, Alec Clunes, Laurence Naismith, Christopher Rhodes, Kenneth Griffith, Beatrice Varley

The Tiger Makes Out*
US 1967 94m Technicolor
Columbia / Elan (George Justin)

A middle-aged New York postman takes revenge on society by kidnapping a young girl—who rather enjoys the experience.
Semi-surrealist comedy misguidedly extended from a two-character play; frantic pace prevents more than a few effective moments.

w Murray Shisgal, from his play *d* Arthur Hiller *ph* Arthur J. Ornitz *m* Milton Rogers

Eli Wallach, Anne Jackson, Bob Dishy, David Burns, Charles Nelson Reilly

Tiger Shark*
US 1932   80m   bw
Warner

A tuna fisherman who has lost a hand to a shark marries the daughter of an old friend, finds she loves someone else, and is conveniently killed by another shark.
Vivid melodrama with a plot partly borrowed from *Moby Dick* and itself partly borrowed from innumerable other Warner films including *Kid Galahad, The Wagons Roll at Night, Slim* and *Manpower*.

w Wells Root, *story* Tuna by Houston Branch *d* Howard Hawks *ph* Tony Gaudio

Edward G. Robinson, J. Carrol Naish, Zita Johann
    'Strong and exceedingly well played and directed sea drama.'—*Variety*

A Tiger Walks*
US 1963   91m   Technicolor
Walt Disney (Ron Miller)

In a small western town, a tiger escapes from the circus.
A splendid animal and a happy ending help to make this a pretty good film for children.

w Lowell S. Hawley, *novel* Ian Niall *d* Norman Tokar *ph* William Snyder *m* Buddy Baker

Sabu, Brian Keith, Vera Miles, Pamela Franklin, Kevin Corcoran, Edward Andrews, Una Merkel, Frank McHugh
    'The Disney message runs true to form—grown-ups should practise what they preach and children are right about animals.'—*MFB*

Tight Spot
US 1955   97m   bw
Columbia (Lewis J. Rachmil)

A material witness in the trial of a gangster is released from prison in the custody of an attorney.
Fairly routine crime melodrama with unexciting star performances.

w William Bowers, *play* Dead Pigeon by Leonard Kantor *d* Phil Karlson *ph* Burnett Guffey *m* Morris Stoloff

Edward G. Robinson, Ginger Rogers, Brian Keith, Lorne Greene, Lucy Marlow, Katherine Anderson

'Til We Meet Again
US 1940   99m   bw
Warner (David Lewis)

On a ship bound from Hong Kong to San Francisco, a dying woman falls for a crook about to be executed.
Stolid remake of *One Way Passage* (qv).

w Warren Duff, *story* Robert Lord *d* Edmund Goulding *ph* Tony Gaudio *m* Ray Heindorf

Merle Oberon, George Brent, Frank McHugh, Pat O'Brien, Geraldine Fitzgerald, Eric Blore, Binnie Barnes, Henry O'Neill, George Reeves
† Marlene Dietrich was originally scheduled for the lead.

Till Death Us Do Part*
GB 1968   100m   Eastmancolor
British Lion / Associated London Films (Jon Pennington)

From the thirties to the sixties with loud-mouthed, bigoted Londoner Alf Garnett.
Unremarkable and frequently misguided opening-up of a phenomenally successful TV series, adapted for the US as *All in the Family* The original cast wades cheerfully enough through a bitty script; the sequel, *The Alf Garnett Saga*, defeated them.

w Johnny Speight *d* Norman Cohen *ph* Harry Waxman *m* Wilfrid Burns

Warren Mitchell, Dandy Nichols, Anthony Booth, Una Stubbs, Liam Redmond, Bill Maynard, Sam Kydd, Brian Blessed

● *Video: Thorn EMI*

Till the Clouds Roll By**
US 1946   137m   Technicolor
MGM (Arthur Freed)

The life and times of composer Jerome Kern.
Better-than-average biopic with better-than-average tunes and stars.

w Myles Connolly, Jean Holloway *d* Richard Whorf *ph* Harry Stradling, George J. Folsey *md* Lennie Hayton

Robert Walker, Judy Garland, Lucille Bremer, Van Heflin, Mary Nash, Dinah Shore, Van Johnson, *June Allyson*, Tony Martin, Kathryn Grayson, *Lena Horne, Frank Sinatra, Virginia O'Brien*
    'A little like sitting down to a soda fountain de luxe atomic special of maple walnut on vanilla on burnt almond on strawberry on butter pecan on coffee on raspberry sherbert on tutti frutti with hot fudge, butterscotch, marshmallow, filberts, pistachios, shredded pineapple, and rainbow sprills on top, go double on the whipped cream.'—*James Agee*

● *Video: Mountain*

Till the End of Time*
US 1946   105m   bw
RKO

Three returning GIs find romance and problems in their small town.
Downbeat variation on *The Best Years of Our Lives* with a theme tune which puts words to a Chopin Polonaise.

w Allen Rivkin *d* Edward Dmytryk *ph* Harry J. Wild *m* Leigh Harline

Dorothy McGuire, Guy Madison, Robert Mitchum

Till We Meet Again
US 1936   87m   bw

Former sweethearts find themselves both spies, but on opposing sides. Unconvincing but climactically suspenseful romantic drama.

Herbert Marshall, Gertrude Michael, Lionel Atwill. Written by Edwin Justus Mayer, Franklin Coen and Brian Marlow from a play by Alfred Davis; directed by Robert Florey; for Paramount.

'She came from a woman's world—into his world of men—and danger!'

Till We Meet Again
US 1944   88m   bw
Paramount (David Lewis)

A French nun helps an American aviator escape from the Nazis.
Very moderate, nicely photographed, romantic war actioner.

w Lenore Coffee, *play* Alfred Maury *d* Frank Borzage *ph* Theodor Sparkuhl *m* David Buttolph

Ray Milland, Barbara Britton, Walter Slezak, Lucile Watson, Konstantin Shayne, Vladimir Sokoloff, Mona Freeman

Tillie and Gus*
US 1933   61m   bw
Paramount (Douglas MacLean)

Two middle-aged cardsharps return home, help their niece and nephew win an inheritance, and come first in a paddleboat race.
Jumbled comedy with good moments and a rousing climax.

w Walter de Leon, Francis Martin *d* Francis Martin *ph* Benjamin Reynolds

W. C. Fields, Alison Skipworth, Baby Le Roy, Jacqueline Wells, Clifford Jones, Clarence Wilson, Edgar Kennedy, Barton MacLane
    'Very funny in spots, but not enough spots.'—*Variety*

Tillie's Punctured Romance*
US 1914   60m approx (24 fps)   bw
silent
Keystone / Mack Sennett

A country maid falls for a con man who steals her money; but she finally gets her revenge.
Museum piece comedy which no longer irritates the funny bone but has clear historical interest.

w Hampton Del Ruth, *play* Tillie's Nightmare by Edgar Smith *d* Mack Sennett *ph* Frank D. Williams

Marie Dressler, Charles Chaplin, Mabel Normand, Mack Swain

Tilly of Bloomsbury
GB 1940   83m   bw

The daughter of a boarding house keeper falls for a rich young man. Basically a millgirl's romance, remembered for one final drunk scene for the star comedian. Sydney Howard, Jean Gillie, Henry Oscar, Athene Seyler, Michael Wilding, Kathleen Harrison, Michael Denison, Martita Hunt, Athole Stewart. Written by Nils Hostius and Jack Marks, from the play by Ian Hay; directed by Leslie Hiscott; for Hammersmith. (Previous versions:

1921, with Tom Reynolds and Edna Best, for Samuelson; 1931, with Sydney Howard and Phyllis Konstam, for Sterling.)

Timberjack
US 1954 94m Trucolor

A young man seeks his father's killer among forest lumberjacks. Resiliently cast action story of no great interest. Sterling Hayden, Vera Ralston, Adolphe Menjou, David Brian, Hoagy Carmichael, Chill Wills, Jim Davis, Elisha Cook Jnr. Written by Allen Rivkin, from the novel by Dan Cushman; directed by Joe Kane, for Republic.

Timbuktu
US 1958 92m bw

A gun runner quells a desert revolt in the French Sudan during World War II. Leaden-footed melodrama full of stock characters despite its complex plot. Yvonne de Carlo, Victor Mature, George Dolenz, John Dehner, Marcia Henderson. Written by Anthony Veiller; directed by Jacques Tourneur; for Edward Small.

Time after Time*
US 1980 112m Metrocolor Panavision
Warner / Orion (Charles Jaffe)

Jack the Ripper escapes via H. G. Wells' time machine from Victorian London to modern San Francisco; Wells gives chase and eventually projects him into limbo. Amusing fantasy for those with light literary inclinations, marred by too much gore and a wandering middle section.

_wd_ Nicholas Meyer, _story_ Karl Alexander and Steve Hayes _ph_ Paul Lohmann _m_ Miklos Rozsa _pd_ Edward Carfagno

Malcolm McDowell, David Warner, Mary Steenburgen, Charles Cioffi, Kent Williams

● Video: Warner

Time Bandits*
GB 1981 113m Technicolor
HandMade Films (Terry Gilliam)

A schoolboy is taken through time by a group of demonic dwarfs. Curious tall tale in which schoolboy fantasy alternates with violence and black comedy. In general, much less funny than it intended to be, but with some hilarious moments.

_w_ Michael Palin, Terry Gilliam _d_ Terry Gilliam _ph_ Peter Biziou _m_ Mike Moran _pd_ Millie Burns

John Cleese (as Robin Hood), Sean Connery (as Agamemnon), Ian Holm (as Napoleon), Ralph Richardson (as God), David Warner (as Satan), Shelley Duvall, Katherine Helmond, Michael Palin, Peter Vaughan, David Rappaport

● Video: Thorn EMI

Time Bomb*
GB 1952 72m bw
MGM (Richard Goldstone)
US title: _Terror on a Train_

A saboteur places a bomb on a goods train

travelling from the north of England to Portsmouth. Tolerable suspenser padded out with domestic asides.

_w_ Ken Bennett _d_ Ted Tetzlaff _ph_ Frederick A. Young _m_ John Addison

Glenn Ford, Anne Vernon, Maurice Denham, Harcourt Williams, Harold Warrender, Bill Fraser, John Horsley, Victor Maddern

Time Flies*
GB 1944 88m bw
GFD / Gainsborough (Edward Black)

A professor invents a time machine and takes his friends back to the court of Good Queen Bess. Very passable star farce.

_w_ J. O. C. Orton, Ted Kavanaugh, Howard Irving Young _d_ Walter Forde _ph_ Basil Emmott _md_ Louis Levy

Tommy Handley, Felix Aylmer, Evelyn Dall, George Moon, Moore Marriott, Graham Moffatt, John Salew, Olga Lindo. Stephane Grappelly

A Time for Killing
US 1967 83m Pathecolor Panavision
Columbia / Sage Western (Harry Joe Brown)
GB title: _The Long Ride Home_

Confederate prisoners escape from a Union fort and the commander sets off in pursuit. Fairly savage western with Something to Say about the corruption of war.

_w_ Halsted Welles, _novel_ Southern Blade by Nelson and Shirley Wolford _d_ Phil Karlson _ph_ Kenneth Peach _m_ Mundell Lowe

Glenn Ford, George Hamilton, Inger Stevens, Max Baer, Paul Petersen, Timothy Carey, Todd Armstrong

A Time for Loving
GB 1971 104m colour
London Screen Plays / Mel Ferrer

Short romantic comedies set at different times in the same Paris flat. Portmanteau ooh-la-la, quite neat but pitifully undernourished; certainly no _Plaza Suite_.

_w_ Jean Anouilh _d_ Christopher Miles _ph_ Andreas Winding _m_ Michel Legrand _pd_ Theo Meurisse

Joanna Shimkus, Mel Ferrer, Britt Ekland, Philippe Noiret, Lila Kedrova, Robert Dhery, Michael Burns

Time Gentlemen Please
GB 1952 83m bw
Group Three (Herbert Mason)

A lazy tramp is the one blot on a prize-winning English village. Artificial, thinly scripted and overlit sub-Ealing comedy with familiar characters and situations.

_w_ Peter Blackmore, _novel_ Nothing to Lose by R. J. Minney _d_ Lewis Gilbert _ph_ Wilkie Cooper _m_ Antony Hopkins

Eddie Byrne, Hermione Baddeley, Jane Barrett, Robert Brown, Raymond Lovell, Marjorie Rhodes, Dora Bryan, Thora Hird, Sidney James, Edie Martin, Ivor Barnard, Sidney Tafler

'Quite a nice little picture.'—_Karel Reisz_

Time in the Sun***
Mexico 1933 60m bw
Marie Seton

Unfinished fragments of Eisenstein's incomplete _Que Viva Mexico_, snippets from which were later released in various forms. This is the longest and presumably best version, with splendidly pictorial sequences of peasant and Indian life culminating with _Death Day_, all skulls and fireworks. Clearly the work of a master, though if completed the film might well have been a bore.

_w_ Marie Seton, Paul Burnford _d_ Sergei Eisenstein _ph_ Edouard Tissé

Time Limit*
US 1957 95m bw
UA / Richard Widmark, William Reynolds

During the Korean war an officer is courtmartialled for suspected collaboration. Suspenseful talk piece from a somewhat intellectualized play.

_w_ Henry Denker, _play_ Henry Denker, Ralph Berkey _d_ Karl Malden _ph_ Sam Leavitt _m_ Fred Steiner

Richard Widmark, Richard Basehart, Dolores Michaels, June Lockhart, Carl Benton Reid, Martin Balsam, Rip Torn

'The tightly constructed story leads logically and unfalteringly to a tense climax.'—_Lindsay Anderson_

Time Lock*
GB 1957 73m bw
Romulus (Peter Rogers)

A small boy is trapped in a bank vault just as it is being locked for the weekend. Acceptable expansion of a Canadian TV suspenser.

_w_ Peter Rogers, _play_ Arthur Hailey _d_ Gerald Thomas _ph_ Peter Hennessy _m_ Stanley Black

Robert Beatty, Betty McDowall, Vincent Winter, Lee Patterson, Alan Gifford, Robert Ayres

The Time Machine*
US 1960 103m Metrocolor
MGM / Galaxy (George Pal)

A Victorian scientist builds a machine which after some trial and error transports him into the year 802701. Surprisingly careful recreation of a period, and an undeniably charming machine, go for little when the future, including the villainous Morlocks, is so dull.

_w_ David Duncan, _novel_ H. G. Wells _d_ George Pal _ph_ Paul C. Vogel _m_ Russell Garcia _ad_ George W. Davis, William Ferrari

Rod Taylor, Yvette Mimieux, Alan Young, Sebastian Cabot, Tom Helmore, Whit Bissell, Doris Lloyd

The Time of Their Lives°
US 1946 82m bw
Universal (Val Burton)

Revolutionary ghosts haunt a country estate.
Unusual, quite effective Abbott and Costello
vehicle with the comedians not playing as a
team.

w Val Burton, Walter de Leon, Bradford
Ropes, John Grant d Charles Barton
ph Charles Van Enger m Milton Rosen

Bud Abbott, Lou Costello, Marjorie
Reynolds, Binnie Barnes, Gale Sondergaard,
John Shelton

The Time of Your Life°
US 1948 109m bw
William Cagney

A group of lovable eccentrics spend much of
their time philosophizing in a San Francisco
bar.
Not really a film at all, this essence of Saroyan
contains much to enjoy or to annoy. The
performances are pretty good.

w Nathaniel Curtis, play William Saroyan
d H. C. Potter ph James Wong Howe
m Carmen Dragon

James Cagney, William Bendix, Wayne
Morris, Jeanne Cagney, Gale Page, Broderick
Crawford, James Barton, Ward Bond, Paul
Draper, James Lydon, Richard Erdman,
Natalie Schaefer
   'They have done so handsomely by Saroyan
that in the long run everything depends on
how much of Saroyan you can take.'—Time

Time out of Mind
US 1947 88m bw
Universal-International (Robert Siodmak)

The housekeeper's daughter finances music
studies for the master's ungrateful son.
Silly romantic melodrama with few visible
compensations.

w Abem Finkel, Arnold Phillips, novel Rachel
Field d Robert Siodmak ph Maury
Gertsman m Miklos Rozsa

Phyllis Calvert, Robert Hutton, Ella Raines,
Eddie Albert, Leo G. Carroll

Time Out for Romance
US 1937 75m bw

A millionairess runs from the altar and teams
up with a car factory driver. Weakish rehash
of It Happened One Night, but the script isn't
up to the intention. Claire Trevor, Michael
Whalen, Joan Davis, Chick Chandler, Douglas
Fowley, William Demarest, Andrew Tombes.
Written by Lou Breslow, John Patrick,
Eleanore Griffin, William Rankin; directed by
Malcolm St Clair; for TCF. 'Just misses being
able to stand on its own legs as a solo
performer.'—Variety

The Time, the Place and the Girl
US 1946 105m Technicolor
Warner (Alex Gottlieb)

Two nightclub owners have problems.
Lightweight musical, indistinguishable from a
dozen others.

w Francis Swann, Agnes Christine Johnson,
Lynn Starling d David Butler ph William V.
Skall m Arthur Schwartz

Dennis Morgan, Jack Carson, Janis Paige,
Martha Vickers, S. Z. Sakall, Alan Hale,
Donald Woods, Angela Greene, Florence
Bates

AAN: song 'A Girl in Calico' (m Arthur
Schwartz, ly Leo Robin)

A Time to Love and a Time to Die°
US 1958 132m Eastmancolor
   Cinemascope
U-I (Robert Arthur)

During World War II, a German officer on his
last leave solves problems at home but is killed
on his return to the front.
Interesting but preachy and generally
misguided attempt, by the studio which made
All Quiet on the Western Front and The Road
Back, to repeat the dose in colour and wide
screen.

w Orin Jannings, novel Erich Maria
Remarque d Douglas Sirk ph Russell Metty
m Miklos Rozsa

John Gavin, Lilo Pulver, Keenan Wynn, Jock
Mahoney, Thayer David, Agnes Windeck,
Erich Maria Remarque

The Time Travelers°
US 1964 84m Pathecolor
AIP / Dobie (William Redlin)

Scientists venture 107 years into the future,
and on escaping find themselves in a time trap.
Ingenious and lively low-budget science fiction
with a sobering ending.

wd Ib Melchior ph William Zsigismond
m Richard La Salle

Preston Foster, Phil Carey, Merry Anders,
John Hoyt, Joan Woodbury

Time without Pity°
GB 1957 88m bw
Harlequin (John Arnold, Anthony
   Simmons)

An alcoholic arrives in London to seek new
evidence which will prevent his son from being
executed for murder.
Heavy-going, introspective, hysterical,
downbeat melodrama which takes itself with a
seriousness which is almost deadly.

w Ben Barzman play Someone Waiting by
Emlyn Williams d Joseph Losey ph Freddie
Francis m Tristam Cary

Michael Redgrave, Alec McCowen, Leo
McKern, Renée Houston, Ann Todd, Peter
Cushing, Paul Daneman, Lois Maxwell,
George Devine, Richard Wordsworth, Joan
Plowright
   'It hammers home its effects with the
concentration of a heavyweight out for the
kill.'—Philip Oakes

Times Square
US 1980 113m Technicolor
EMI / Robert Stigwood

Two ill-matched teenage girls form a shabby
nightclub act and soon have New York by its
ears.

Sometimes sharply made but generally
unpleasant urban fairy story with suicide as the
end, like a cross between Saturday Night Fever
and Midnight Cowboy. Among a number of
forgettable songs is one called 'Pissing in the
River'.

w Jacob Brackman story Alan Moyle and
Leanne Unger
d Alan Moyle ph James A. Contner m Blue
Weaver

Tim Curry, Trini Alvarado, Robin Johnson,
Peter Coffield, Herbert Berghof, David
Margulies

● Video: Thorn EMI

Times Square Lady
US 1935 69m bw

The daughter of a Broadway hustler, being
chiselled by her father's attorney, is helped by
one of his employees. Flat romantic drama
designed as a test for young stars. Robert
Taylor, Virginia Bruce, Pinky Tomlin, Helen
Twelvetrees, Isabel Jewell, Nat Pendleton,
Henry Kolker, Jack La Rue. Written by
Albert Cohen, Robert Shannon; directed by
George B. Seitz; for MGM. 'Not sufficient
heft to be important.'—Variety

Times Square Playboy: see The Home
Towners

Timetable°
US 1955 79m bw
(UA) Mark Stevens

An insurance investigator is assigned to a train
robbery which he actually committed himself.
Concise suspenser with good script and
treatment.

w Aben Kandel d Mark Stevens ph Charles
Van Enger m Walter Scharf

Mark Stevens, Felicia Farr, King Calder,
Wesley Addy

The Tin Drum°
West Germany / France 1979 142m
   Eastmancolor
UA / Franz Seitz / Bioskop / GGB 14 KG /
   Hallelujah / Artemis / Argos / Jadran /
   Film PolskiOriginal title: Die
   Blechtrommel

Not caring for the world he is growing up in, a
small boy determines to remain a child.
Fairly brilliantly made version of a
labyrinthine satire; the emphasis on sex and
scatological detail, however, eventually
defeats its own objects.

w Jean-Claude Carrière, Franz Seitz, Volker
Schlöndorff, novel Gunter Grass d Volker
Schlöndorff ph Igor Luther m Maurice Jarre
pd Nicos Perakis

David Bennent, Mario Adorf, Angela
Winkler, Daniel Olbrychski

Tin Pan Alley***
US 1940 95m bw
TCF (Kenneth MacGowan)

During World War I and after, two dancing girls love the same composer.
Archetypal musical, full of Broadway clichés, razzmatazz and zip. Remade 1950 as *I'll Get By*, not to such peppy effect.

w Robert Ellis, Helen Logan *d* Walter Lang *ph* Leon Shamroy *ch* Seymour Felix *songs* Mack Gordon, Harry Warren *m* Alfred Newman

Alice Faye, Betty Grable, John Payne, Jack Oakie, Allen Jenkins, Esther Ralston, The Nicholas Brothers, John Loder, Elisha Cook Jnr

AA: Alfred Newman

The Tin Star*
US 1957 93m bw Vistavision
Paramount / Perlberg–Seaton

An ex-sheriff turned bounty hunter helps a new young sheriff to catch bandits.
Dignified and well-characterized western with customary pleasures.

w Dudley Nichols *d* Anthony Mann *ph* Loyal Griggs *m* Elmer Bernstein

Henry Fonda, Anthony Perkins, Betsy Palmer, Michel Ray, Neville Brand, John McIntire

AAN: original story (Barney Slater, Joel Kane); script

The Tingler*
US 1959 82m bw
Columbia / William Castle

Fear (it says here) can create on the spinal column a parasite removable only by screaming. A scientist isolates it and it runs amok in a silent cinema.
Ridiculous shocker with generally dull handling but effective moments.

w Robb White *d* William Castle *ph* Wilfrid Cline *m* Von Dexter

Vincent Price, Judith Evelyn, Darryl Hickman, Patricia Cutts
  'The sheer effrontery of this piece of hokum is enjoyable in itself.'—*MFB*

Tip-off Girls*
US 1938 61m bw

Gangsters use girl employees to get tips on merchandise shipments. Routine but watchable G-man second. Lloyd Nolan, Mary Carlisle, J. Carrol Naish, Harvey Stephens, Roscoe Karns, Larry Crabbe, Anthony Quinn. Written by Maxwell Shane, Robert Yost, Stuart Anthony; directed by Louis King; for Paramount. 'Excellent meller . . . bristles with action, tensity and suspense.'—*Variety*

Tip on a Dead Jockey
US 1957 99m bw
MGM (Edwin H. Knopf)
GB title: *Time for Action*

A flier loses his nerve and turns international smuggler, but reforms.
Gloomy, pedestrian star melodrama, dully cast.

w Charles Lederer, *novel* Irwin Shaw *d* Richard Thorpe *ph* George J. Folsey *m* Miklos Rozsa

Robert Taylor, Dorothy Malone, Gia Scala, Martin Gabel, Marcel Dalio, Jack Lord

Titanic*
US 1953 98m bw
TCF (Charles Brackett)

Personal dramas aboard the *Titanic* in 1912 come to a head as the ship hits an iceberg.
An excellent example of studio production is squandered on a dim script which arouses no excitement.

w Charles Brackett, Walter Reisch, Richard Breen *d* Jean Negulesco *ph* Joe MacDonald *m* Sol Kaplan *ad* Lyle Wheeler, Maurice Ransford

Clifton Webb, Barbara Stanwyck, Robert Wagner, Audrey Dalton, Thelma Ritter, Brian Aherne, Richard Basehart, Allyn Joslyn

AA: script

The Titfield Thunderbolt***
GB 1952 84m Technicolor
Ealing (Michael Truman)

When a branch railway line is threatened with closure, the villagers take it over as a private concern.
Undervalued on its release in the wake of other Ealing comedies, this now seems among the best of them as well as an immaculate colour production showing the England that is no more; the script has pace, the whole thing is brightly polished and the action works up to a fine climactic frenzy.

w T. E. B. Clarke *d* Charles Crichton *ph* Douglas Slocombe *m* Georges Auric

Stanley Holloway, George Relph, John Gregson, Godfrey Tearle, *Edie Martin,* Naunton Wayne, Gabrielle Brune, Hugh Griffith, Sidney James, Jack McGowran, Ewan Roberts, Reginald Beckwith

● *Video: Thorn EMI*

Tit for Tat*
US 1934 20m bw

Adjoining shopkeepers violently settle an old difference. Archetypal late star comedy: brilliant timing, but the warmth and sympathy have begun to ebb. Laurel and Hardy, Charlie Hall, Mae Busch. Written by Stan Laurel; directed by Charles Rogers; for Hal Roach.
AAN: best short.

T-Men*
US 1947 96m bw
Eagle Lion (Aubrey Schenck)

Treasury Department detectives trail a gang of counterfeiters.
Tough, well-made crime melodrama which still packs a punch in the traditional vein.

w John C. Higgins *d* Anthony Mann *ph* John Alton *m* Paul Sawtell

Dennis O'Keefe, Alfred Ryder, Mary Meade, Wallace Ford, June Lockhart, Charles McGraw, Jane Randolph, Art Smith

To Be or Not to Be****
US 1942 99m bw
(Alexander Korda) Ernst Lubitsch

Warsaw actors get involved in an underground plot and an impersonation of invading Nazis, including Hitler.
Marvellous free-wheeling entertainment which starts as drama and descends through romantic comedy and suspense into farce; accused of bad taste at the time, but now seen as an outstanding example of Hollywood moonshine, kept alight through sheer talent and expertise.

w Edwin Justus Mayer, *story* Ernst Lubitsch, Melchior Lengyel *d* Ernst Lubitsch *ph* Rudolph Maté *m* Werner Heymann *ad* Vincent Korda

Jack Benny, Carole Lombard, Robert Stack, Stanley Ridges, Felix Bressart, Lionel Atwill, Sig Rumann, Tom Dugan, Charles Halton

  TURA in disguise (Jack Benny): 'That great, great Polish actor Joseph Tura—you must have heard of him.'
  ERHARDT (Sig Rumann): 'Ah, yes . . . what he did to Shakespeare, we are now doing to Poland!'
  ERHARDT (and others): 'So they call me Concentration Camp Erhardt!'
  'The comedy is hilarious, even when it is hysterically thrilling.'—*Commonweal*
  'As effective an example of comic propaganda as *The Great Dictator* and far better directed.'—*Charles Higham, 1972*
  'Based on an indiscretion, but undoubtedly a work of art.'—*James Agee*
  'In any other medium it would be acknowledged as a classic to rank with *The Alchemist* or *A Modest Proposal*.'—*Peter Barnes*
  'Lubitsch's comic genius and corrosive wit are displayed at every turn.'—*John Baxter*
  'The actual business at hand . . . is nothing less than providing a good time at the expense of Nazi myth . . . Lubitsch distinguishes the film's zanier moments with his customary mastery of sly humour and innuendo, and when the story calls for outright melodrama he is more than equal to the occasion.'—*Newsweek*

AAN: Werner Heymann

To Be or Not to Be
US 1983 107m De Luxe
TCF / Brooksfilms (Mel Brooks)

Flat-footed remake of the above, with stagey sets, unconvincing acting (including the unnecessary addition of a gay dresser) and a leading comedian who won't stay still in case his lack of style should be noticed.

w Thomas Meehan, Ronnie Graham *d* Alan Johnson *ph* Gerald Hirschfeld *m* John Morris *pd* Terence Marsh

Mel Brooks, Anne Bancroft, Tim Matheson, Charles Durning, Jose Ferrer, George Gaynes, Christopher Lloyd, James Haake

AAN: Charles Durning

To Catch a Thief°

US 1955 97m Technicolor Vistavision
Paramount / Alfred Hitchcock

A famous cat burglar who has retired to the
Riviera catches a thief who is imitating his old
style.
Very slow, floppy and rather boring
entertainment enlivened by the scenery and
the odd Hitchcock touch.

w John Michael Hayes, *novel* David Dodge
d Alfred Hitchcock *ph* Robert Burks *m* Lyn
Murray

Cary Grant, Grace Kelly, *Jessie Royce Landis,
John Williams*, Charles Vanel, Brigitte Auber

'Why should I steal? I'm rich.'
—'How did you get rich?'
'By stealing.'

'Billed as a comedy-mystery, it stacks up as
a drawn-out pretentious piece that seldom hits
the comedy level.'—*Variety*

AA: Robert Burks

'As long as there are lovers—this picture
will live!'

To Each His Own°°

US 1946 100m bw
Paramount (Charles Brackett)

During World War II, a middle-aged woman
in London meets the soldier who is her own
illegitimate and long-since-adopted-son.
The woman's picture par excellence, put
together with tremendous Hollywood flair and
extremely enjoyable to watch.

w *Charles Brackett, Jacques Théry* d Mitchell
Leisen *ph* Daniel L. Fapp *m Victor Young*
ad Hans Dreier, Roland Anderson

Olivia de Havilland, John Lund, Roland
Culver, Mary Anderson, Philip Terry, Bill
Goodwin, Virginia Welles, Virginia Horne

'Paramount proudly brings to the screens of
America one of the three great love stories of
all time!'—*publicity*

AA: Olivia de Havilland
AAN: original story (Charles Brackett)

To Find a Man°

US 1971 93m Eastmancolor
Columbia / Rastar (Irving Pincus)

The spoiled daughter of a rich family becomes
pregnant and is helped by a young chemist.
Quiet, well-made minor drama about
maturity, with good small-town atmosphere.

w *Arnold Schulman, novel* S. J. Wilson
d Buzz Kulik *ph* Andy Laszlo *m* David Shire

Pamela Martin, Darrell O'Connor, *Lloyd
Bridges*, Phyllis Newman, Tom Ewell, Tom
Bosley

To Have and Have Not°°

US 1945 100m bw
Warner (Howard Hawks)

An American charter boat captain in
Martinique gets involved with Nazis.
Fairly routinely made studio adventure
notable for first pairing of Bogart and Bacall,
as an imitation of *Casablanca*, and for its
consistent though not outstanding
entertainment value. Remade later as *The*

Breaking Point (qv) and *The Gun Runners*
(qv), and not dissimilar from *Key Largo* (qv).

w *Jules Furthman, William Faulkner, novel*
Ernest Hemingway *d Howard Hawks ph* Sid
Hickox *m* Franz Waxman (uncredited)
md Leo F. Forbstein

Humphrey Bogart, Lauren Bacall, Walter
Brennan, Hoagy Carmichael, Dolores Moran,
Sheldon Leonard, Dan Seymour, Marcel
Dalio

'Remarkable for the ingenuity and industry
with which the original story and the
individualities of Ernest Hemingway have
been rendered down into Hollywood basic.'—
Richard Winnington

'Sunlight on the lattice, sex in the corridors,
a new pianist at the café, pistol shots, the fat
sureté man coming round after dark.'—
William Whitebait

To Hell and Back

US 1955 106m Technicolor
     Cinemascope
U-I (Aaron Rosenberg)

The war career of America's most decorated
infantryman.
Routine war story which happens to be about
a fellow who later became a film star.

w Gil Doud, *book* Audie Murphy *d* Jesse
Hibbs *ph* Maury Gertsman *m* Joseph
Gershenson

Audie Murphy, Marshall Thompson, Charles
Drake, Gregg Palmer, Jack Kelly, Paul
Picerni, Susan Kohner

'The emotion is congealed and there is no
real personal response to the anguish of
war.'—*John Gillett*

To Kill a Clown

GB 1971 104m De Luxe
Palomar (Theodore Sills)

A painter and his wife move to a New England
isle and are menaced by a crippled Vietnam
veteran and his vicious dogs.
Pretentious, politically oriented rehash of *The
Most Dangerous Game* (qv), carefully made
but too slow for suspense.

w George Bloomfield, I. C. Rapoport, *novel*
Master of the Hounds by Algis Budrys
d George Bloomfield *ph* Walter Lassally
m Richard Hill, John Hawkins

Alan Alda, Blythe Danner, Heath Lamberts,
Eric Clavering

To Kill a Mockingbird°°

US 1962 129m bw
U-I (Alan Pakula)

A lawyer in a small southern town defends a
black man accused of rape.
Familiar dollops of social conscience, very well
presented with a child interest and excellent
atmosphere, but a mite overlong.

w Horton Foote, *novel* Harper Lee *d* Robert
Mulligan *ph* Russell Harlan *m* Elmer
Bernstein

Gregory Peck, Mary Badham, Philip Alford,
John Megna, Frank Overton, Rosemary
Murphy, Ruth White, Brock Peters

† The narrator is Kim Stanley.

AA: script; Gregory Peck
AAN: best picture; Robert Mulligan; Russell
Harlan; Elmer Bernstein; Mary Badham

To Mary with Love

US 1936 87m bw

A businessman thinks back affectionately over
ten years of married life. Harmless romantic
comedy-drama. Warner Baxter, Myrna Loy,
Ian Hunter, Claire Trevor, Jean Dixon.
Written by Richard Sherman and Howard
Ellis Smith; directed by John Cromwell; for
TCF.

To Paris with Love

GB 1954 78m Technicolor
GFD / Two Cities (Anthony Darnborough)

A middle-aged widower and his son go to
Paris on holiday and devise matrimonial plans
for each other.
Thin, disappointing taradiddle which is short
but seems long.

w Robert Buckner *d* Robert Hamer *ph* Reg
Wyer *m* Edwin Astley

Alec Guinness, Vernon Gray, Odile Versois,
Jacques François, Elina Labourdette, Austin
Trevor

'The general impression is somehow too
aimless, too muted.'—*Gavin Lambert*

To Please a Lady°

US 1950 91m bw
MGM (Clarence Brown)

A ruthless midget-car racer falls for the lady
journalist who is hounding him.
Good action programmer with no frills.

w Barre Lyndon, Marge Decker *d* Clarence
Brown *ph* Harold Rosson *m* Bronislau
Kaper

Clark Gable, Barbara Stanwyck, Adolphe
Menjou, Will Geer, Roland Winters, Emory
Parnell, Frank Jenks

To Sir with Love

GB 1967 105m Technicolor
Columbia (James Clavell)

A West Indian teacher comes to a tough East
End school.
Sentimental non-realism patterned after *The
Blackboard Jungle* but much softer; its
influence led to a TV situation comedy, *Please
Sir*.

w James Clavell, *novel* E. R. Braithwaite
d James Clavell *ph* Paul Beeson *m* Ron
Grainer

Sidney Poitier, Christian Roberts, Judy
Geeson, Suzy Kendall, Lulu, Faith Brook,
Geoffrey Bayldon, Patricia Routledge

'The sententious script sounds as if it has
been written by a zealous Sunday school
teacher after a particularly exhilarating
boycott of South African oranges.'—*MFB*

THE TITFIELD THUNDERBOLT.   The vicar and the bishop win the day with a train stolen from the museum.

To the Devil a Daughter
GB / Germany 1975   93m   Technicolor
EMI / Hammer–Terra Filmkunst (Roy
  Skeggs)

An occult novelist is asked to take care of a
girl who has been 'promised' to a group of
Satanists.
Confusingly told, high camp diabolic thriller.

w Chris Wicking, *novel* Dennis Wheatley
d Peter Sykes ph David Watkin m Paul
Glass

Richard Widmark, Christopher Lee, Denholm
Elliott, Honor Blackman, Michael Goodliffe,
Anthony Valentine, Derek Francis, Nastassja
Kinski

● *Video: Thorn EMI*

To the Ends of the Earth**
US 1948   107m   bw
Columbia (Sidney Buchman)

A government agent follows a world-wide trail
after a narcotics gang.
Thoroughly riveting conventional thriller,
nicely made and photographed.

w Jay Richard Kennedy d Robert Stevenson
ph Burnett Guffey m George Duning

Dick Powell, Signe Hasso, Ludwig Donath,
Vladimir Sokoloff, Edgar Barrier

To the Shores of Tripoli
US 1942   82m   Technicolor
TCF (Milton Sperling)

A cocky playboy becomes a tough marine.
Despite the title, this modest flagwaver with
romantic trimmings never moves out of the
San Diego training grounds.

w Lamar Trotti d Bruce Humberstone
ph Edward Cronjager m Alfred Newman

Maureen O'Hara, John Payne, Randolph
Scott, Nancy Kelly, William Tracy, Maxie
Rosenbloom, Henry Morgan, Russell Hicks,
Minor Watson

AAN: cinematography

To the Victor
US 1948   100m   bw
Warner (Jerry Wald)

French collaborators stand trial for war
crimes.
Glum melodrama with inadequate cast.

w Richard Brooks *d* Delmer Daves
ph Robert Burks *m* David Buttolph

Dennis Morgan, Viveca Lindfors, Bruce Bennett, Victor Francen, Dorothy Malone, Tom d'Andrea, Eduardo Ciannelli, Joseph Buloff, Luis Van Rooten, William Conrad

To What Red Hell
GB 1929 100m bw

A young epileptic kills a prostitute and is protected by his mother. Unpalatable melodrama which failed to be as significant as it wished. Sybil Thorndike, John Hamilton, Bramwell Fletcher, Janice Adair. Written by Leslie Hiscott, from the play by Percy Robinson; directed by Edwin Greenwood; for Strand / Twickenham.

The Toast of New Orleans
US 1950 97m Technicolor
MGM (Joe Pasternak)

A Bayou villager becomes a star of the New Orleans opera.
Very ordinary setting for a new singing star.

w Sy Gomberg, George Wells *d* Norman Taurog *ph* William Snyder *md* George Stoll *ch* Eugene Loring

Kathryn Grayson, David Niven, Mario Lanza, J. Carrol Naish, James Mitchell, Richard Hageman, Clinton Sundberg, Sig Arno
  'Sheer excruciation.'—*Pauline Kael, New Yorker*
AAN: song 'Be My Love' (*m* Nicholas Brodszky, *ly* Sammy Cahn)

'The screen sensation of a decade, played by a galaxy of stars in a hell-bent world of wine and women!'

The Toast of New York**
US 1937 109m bw
RKO (Edward Small)

A 19th-century medicine showman becomes a notorious Wall Street financier.
Smart biopic of Jim Fisk; good entertainment with accomplished production.

w Dudley Nichols, John Twist, Joel Sayre *d* Rowland V. Lee *ph* Peverell Marley *m* Nathaniel Shilkret

Edward Arnold, Cary Grant, Frances Farmer, Jack Oakie, Donald Meek, Clarence Kolb, Thelma Leeds
  'Making no pretence for serious consideration as a faithful and accurate reflection of life and manners in the period it depicts, it rates as a piece of hokum aimed at the box office. It will do business.'—*Variety*

Tobacco Road***
US 1941 84m bw
TCF (Jack Kirkland, Harry H. Oshrin)

Poor whites in Georgia are turned off their land.
This bowdlerized version of a sensational book and play has superbly orchestrated farcical scenes separated by delightfully pictorial quieter moments: it isn't what was intended, but in its own way it's quite marvellous.

w Nunnally Johnson, novel Erskine Caldwell, play Jack Kirkland *d* John Ford *ph* Arthur Miller *m* David Buttolph

Charley Grapewin, Elizabeth Patterson, Dana Andrews, Gene Tierney, *Marjorie Rambeau*, Ward Bond, William Tracy, Zeffie Tilbury, Slim Summerville, Grant Mitchell, Russell Simpson, Spencer Charters

Tobruk
US 1967 110m Techniscope
Universal / Corman / Gibraltar (Gene Corman)

During the North African war, a British major and some German Jews try to blow up the Nazi fuel bunkers.
Routine war adventure, quite tough and spectacular but undistinguished.

w Leo V. Gordon *d* Arthur Hiller *ph* Russell Harlan *m* Bronislau Kaper

Rock Hudson, George Peppard, Nigel Green, Guy Stockwell, Jack Watson, Liam Redmond, Leo Gordon, Norman Rossington, Percy Herbert
● *Video: CIC*

Toby Tyler*
US 1959 96m Technicolor
Walt Disney (Bill Walsh)

In 1910, a young orphan runs away to join a travelling circus in the midwest, and with the help of a chimp becomes a famous star.
Acceptable, predictable family fare.

w Bill Walsh, Lillie Hayward, *novel* James Otis Kaler *d* Charles Barton *ph* William Snyder *m* Buddy Baker

Kevin Corcoran, Henry Calvin, Gene Sheldon, Bob Sweeney, James Drury

Today We Live*
US 1933 113m bw
MGM (Howard Hawks)

During World War I, an aristocratic English girl and her three lovers all find themselves at the front, and two fail to return.
Stilted romantic melodrama with imposing credentials.

w Edith Fitzgerald, Dwight Taylor, William Faulkner, *story* Turnabout by William Faulkner *d* Howard Hawks *ph* Oliver T. Marsh

Joan Crawford, Gary Cooper, Robert Young, Franchot Tone, Roscoe Karns, Louise Closser Hale, Rollo Lloyd
  'One of those overly long features which would serve the purpose better in 2000 or more less feet . . . but the action, the men and the Crawford name should translate into satisfying figures.'—*Variety*
† Much of the flying footage was taken from the *Hell's Angels* stock.

The Todd Killings*
US 1970 93m Technicolor Panavision
National General (Barry Shear)

In a small American town, a 23-year-old boy starts out on a rampage of rape and murder.
Violent psychological melodrama, based on fact, with inventive direction.

w Dennis Murphy, Joe L. Oliansky *d* Barry Shear *ph* Harold E. Stine *m* Leonard Rosenman

Robert F. Lyons, Richard Thomas, Belinda Montgomery, Barbara Bel Geddes, Gloria Grahame
  'The most striking of the many recent film versions of the souring of the American dream.'—*Tony Rayns*

Together Again
US 1944 93m bw
Columbia (Virginia Van Upp)

The widow of a New England mayor commissions a statue in his honour.
The title refers to the reteaming of the stars who were so popular in *Love Affair* and *When Tomorrow Comes*, which is a sign of the lack of invention elsewhere. A comedy without laughs.

w Virgina Van Upp, F. Hugh Herbert *d* Charles Vidor *ph* Joseph Walker *m* Werner Heymann

Charles Boyer, Irene Dunne, Charles Coburn, Mona Freeman, Jerome Courtland, Elizabeth Patterson, Charles Dingle, Walter Baldwin

Tokyo Joe
US 1949 88m bw
Columbia / Santana (Robert Lord)

A former nightclub owner returns to postwar Japan to reclaim his fortune and his ex-wife.
Dispirited star melodrama.

w Cyril Hume, Bertram Millhauser *d* Stuart Heisler *ph* Charles Lawton Jnr *m* George Antheil

Humphrey Bogart, Florence Marly, Alexander Knox, Sessue Hayakawa, Lora Lee Michel, Jerome Courtland

Tol'able David*
US 1921 80m approx (24 fps) bw silent
First National / Inspiration

A quiet farming community is disrupted by three marauding convicts, who are finally despatched by the peace-loving youngest son.
Fresh, sympathetic David-and-Goliath story which was a huge popular success on its release.

w Edmund Goulding, Henry King, *novel* Joseph Hergesheimer *d* Henry King *ph* Henry Cronjager

Richard Barthelmess, Gladys Hulette, Ernest Torrence, Warner Richmond
  'It is sentimental in places, but not sloppy. It is bucolic, but its rusticity is not rubbed in . . . it is restrained, imaginatively suggestive when not briefly literal. For all these reasons it is stimulating.'—*New York Times*
† Columbia remade the story in 1930 with Richard Cromwell, but its time had passed.

Tom Brown of Culver
US 1932 79m bw

Life at a military cadet school. Idealized propaganda, with the hero a boy subsidized by the local legion because his dead father was a war hero. Tom Brown, H. B. Warner, Slim Summerville, Richard Cromwell, Ben Alexander, Sidney Toler, Betty Blythe. Written by Tom Beckingham; directed by William Wyler; for Universal. 'It will probably make acceptable film fare to other than irritated cadets.'—*Variety*

Tom Brown's Schooldays*
US 1940 86m bw
(RKO) The Play's the Thing (Gene Towne, Graham Baker)

Tom Brown finds life at Rugby brutal, but helps to become a civilizing influence.
Pretty lively Hollywood version of a rather unattractive semi-classic.

w Walter Ferris, Frank Cavell, *novel* Thomas Hughes *d* Robert Stevenson *ph* Nicholas Musuraca *m* Anthony Collins

Jimmy Lydon, Cedric Hardwicke, Billy Halop, Freddie Bartholemew, Gale Storm, Josephine Hutchinson

Tom Brown's Schooldays
GB 1951 96m bw
Renown (George Minter)

Unexciting remake featuring one surprisingly strong performance.

w Noel Langley *d* Gordon Parry *ph* C. Pennington-Richards *m* Richard Addinsell

Robert Newton, John Howard Davies, Diana Wynyard, Francis de Wolff, Kathleen Byron, Hermione Baddeley, James Hayter, Rachel Gurney, Amy Veness, Max Bygraves, Michael Hordern, John Charlesworth, John Forrest
'An odd mixture of the brutal and the solemnly improving.'—*Richard Mallett, Punch*

Tom, Dick and Harry**
US 1940 86m bw
RKO (Robert Sisk)

A girl daydreams about her three boy friends, but can't make up her mind.
Brightly-handled comedy which became a minor classic but does seem to have faded a little. Remade as *The Girl Most Likely* (qv).

w Paul Jarrico *d* Garson Kanin *ph* Merritt Gerstad *m* Roy Webb

Ginger Rogers, Burgess Meredith, Alan Marshal, George Murphy, *Phil Silvers*, Joe Cunningham, Jane Seymour, Lenore Lonergan
'Foot by foot the best made picture of this year.'—*Otis Ferguson*
AAN: Paul Jarrico

Tom Horn
US 1979 97m Technicolor Panavision
Warner / Solar / First Artists (Fred Weintraub)

An ex-cavalry scout gets a job as a stock detective, is framed for murder, and allows himself to be hanged.
Curious pessimistic and unsatisfactory semi-western in which the star was found to have lost his old charisma after being too long away.

w Thomas McGuane, Bid Shrake, from the alleged autobiography of Tom Horn
d William Wiard *ph* John Alonzo *m* Ernest Gold

Steve McQueen, Linda Evans, Richard Farnsworth, Billy Green Bush, Slim Pickens, Elisha Cook Jnr.

'Imagine a film that opens up with dialogue that can't be heard at all, then proceeds to build up to a fist fight that's never seen, that cuts away to sunsets to fill in other scenes that have no dramatic point, that presents a meal where the sound of knives and forks drowns out what's being said, and you have just the beginning of what's wrong with *Tom Horn*.'—*Variety*

● Video: Warner

'The whole world loves him!'
Tom Jones***
GB 1963 129m Eastmancolor
UA / Woodfall (Tony Richardson)

In 18th-century England a foundling is brought up by the squire and marries his daughter after many adventures.
Fantasia on Old England, at some distance from the original novel, with the director trying every possible jokey approach against a meticulously realistic physical background. Despite trade fears, the *Hellzapoppin* style made it an astonishing box office success (the sex helped), though it quickly lost its freshness and was much imitated.

w John Osborne, *novel* Henry Fielding *d* Tony Richardson *ph* Walter Lassally, Manny Wynn *m* John Addison *pd* Ralph Brinton

Albert Finney, Susannah York, Hugh Griffith, Edith Evans, Joan Greenwood, Diane Cilento, George Devine, Joyce Redman, David Warner, Wilfrid Lawson, Freda Jackson, Rachel Kempson
'Uncertainty, nervousness, muddled method . . . desperation is writ large over it.'—*Stanley Kauffmann*
'Much of the time it looks like a home movie, made with sporadic talent by a group with more enthusiasm than discipline.'—*Tom Milne*
'It is as though the camera had become a method actor: there are times when you wish you could buy, as on certain juke boxes, five minutes' silence . . . Obviously a film which elicits such lyric ejaculations from the reviewers cannot be all good.'—*John Simon*
† The narrator was Micheal MacLiammoir.

AA: best picture; John Osborne; Tony Richardson; John Addison
AAN: Albert Finney; Hugh Griffith; Edith Evans; Diane Cilento; Joyce Redman

● Video: Thorn EMI

Tom Sawyer
US 1973 103m De Luxe Panavision
UA / Readers Digest (Arthur P. Jacobs)

Reverential, rather tediously over-produced version for family audiences of the seventies, with brief songs and real Mississippi locations.

w / *m* / *ly* Richard and Robert Sherman *d* Don Taylor *ph* Frank Stanley *md* John Williams *pd* Philip Jefferies

Johnnie Whitaker, Celeste Holm, Warren Oates, Jeff East, Jodie Foster
† There had been a version with Jackie Coogan in 1930. Selznick's *The Adventures of Tom Sawyer* followed in 1937. In 1939 Donald O'Connor was Tom Sawyer, Detective.

AAN: Richard and Robert Sherman; John Williams

Tom Thumb*
GB 1958 98m Eastmancolor
MGM / Galaxy (George Pal)

A tiny forest boy outwits a couple of thieves.
Slight musical built round the legend of a two-inch boy; good trickwork and songs make it a delightful film for children.

w Ladislas Fodor *d* George Pal *ph* Georges Périnal *m* Douglas Gamley, Kenneth V. Jones *sp* Tom Howard

Russ Tamblyn, Jessie Matthews, Peter Sellers, Terry-Thomas, Alan Young, June Thorburn, Ian Wallace
† Donald O'Connor badly wanted the role, but it went to the MGM contractee.

Tomahawk
US 1951 82m Technicolor

An Indian scout helps the Sioux to get their territory rights. Competent small-scale western. Van Heflin, Yvonne De Carlo, Alex Nicol, Preston Foster, Jack Oakie, Tom Tully, Rock Hudson. Written by Silvia Richards and Maurice Geraghty; directed by George Sherman; for Universal-International. (GB title: *Battle of Powder River*.)

The Tomb of Ligeia**
GB 1964 81m Eastmancolor Cinemascope
American International (Roger Corman)

A brooding Victorian metamorphoses his dead wife into a cat, then into the beautiful Lady Rowena.
Complex but rather fascinating horror suspenser which rejogs familiar elements into something new; the best of the Corman Poes.

w Robert Towne, *story* Edgar Allan Poe *d* Roger Corman *ph* Arthur Grant *m* Kenneth V. Jones

Vincent Price, Elizabeth Shepherd, John Westbrook, Oliver Johnson, Richard Johnson, Derek Francis

'Good men (and women) live in Tombstone—but not for long!'
Tombstone (The Town Too Tough to Die)
US 1942 80m bw

How Wyatt Earp cleaned up the town.
Lacklustre low-budget version of a famous story. Richard Dix, Frances Gifford, Kent Taylor, Edgar Buchanan, Don Castle, Victor Jory. Written by Albert Shelby Le Vino and Edward E. Paramore; directed by William McGann; for Paramount.

Tommy*
GB 1975   108m   colour
Hemdale / Robert Stigwood

A deaf, dumb and blind child is eventually
cured and becomes a rock celebrity.
Mystical rock opera screened with the
director's usual barrage of effects and an
ear-splitting score. Of occasional interest.

w Ken Russell, from the opera by Pete
Townshend and the Who d Ken Russell
ph Dick Bush, Ronnie Taylor m Pete
Townshend and the Who

Roger Daltrey, Ann-Margret, Oliver Reed,
Elton John, Eric Clapton, Keith Moon

AAN: Ann-Margret
● Video: Thorn EMI

Tomorrow and Tomorrow
US 1932   73m   bw

A happily married woman suddenly falls for a
foreign scientist. Sturdy woman's picture of its
day. Ruth Chatterton, Paul Lukas, Robert
Ames, Harold Minjir, Tad Alexander. Written
by Josephine Lovett from the play by Philip
Barry; directed by Richard Wallace; for
Paramount. 'A screen play of the first grade
. . . reflects credit on everybody concerned in
its making.'—Variety

Tomorrow at Ten*
GB 1962   80m   bw
Mancunian (Tom Blakeley)

A crook kidnaps a small boy and locks him up
with a time bomb while he makes his demands
in person. When the kidnapper is killed, the
police have to hunt against time.
Tense second feature, well acted and
efficiently done.

w Peter Millar, James Kelly d Lance
Comfort ph Basil Emmott m Bernie Fenton

Robert Shaw, John Gregson, Alec Clunes,
Alan Wheatley, Ernest Clark, Kenneth Cope

Tomorrow Is Another Day
US 1951   90m   bw

An ex-convict is soon on the run for a crime
he didn't commit. Miserable melodrama
apparently left over from John Garfield days.
Steve Cochran, Ruth Roman, Lurene Tuttle,
Bobby Hyatt, Ray Teal. Written by Guy
Endore and Art Cohn; directed by Felix Feist;
for Warner.

Tomorrow Is Forever*
US 1945   105m   bw
RKO–International (David Lewis)

A man supposed dead in the war returns with
an altered face to find his wife has remarried.
Enoch Arden rides again in a rampant
woman's picture which is well enough made to
be generally entertaining.

w Lenore Coffee d Irving Pichel ph Joe
Valentine m Max Steiner

Orson Welles, Claudette Colbert, George
Brent, Lucile Watson, Richard Long, Natalie
Wood

Tomorrow Never Comes
Canada / GB 1977   109m   colour
Rank / Classic / Montreal Trust / Neffbourne
(Michael Klinger, Julian Melzack)

A jealous lover shoots a caller at his girl's
beach cabana and a police siege begins.
Far from the class of Le Jour Se Lève, this is
an exploitative and violent melodrama which
need never have been made.

w David Pursall, Jack Seddon, Sydney Banks
d Peter Collinson ph François Protat m Roy
Budd

Oliver Reed, Susan George, Raymond Burr,
Stephen McHattie, John Ireland, Donald
Pleasence, John Osborne, Cec Linder

Tomorrow the World*
US 1944   86m   bw
UA / Lester Cowan

A college professor adopts his orphaned
German nephew, who turns out to be an
ardent 12-year-old Nazi.
Adequate, predictable screen version of a
once-topical play.

w Ring Lardner Jnr, Leopold Atlas, play
James Gow, Armand D'Usseau d Leslie
Fenton ph Henry Sharp m Louis Applebaum

Fredric March, Betty Field, Skip Homeier,
Agnes Moorehead, Joan Carroll

Tomorrow We Live
GB 1942   85m   bw
British Aviation (George King)
US title: At Dawn We Die

French villagers help a spy escape to Britain.
Minor flagwaver marred by cheap sets.

w Anatole de Grunwald, Katherine Strueby
d George King

John Clements, Greta Gynt, Hugh Sinclair,
Judy Kelly, Godfrey Tearle, Yvonne Arnaud,
Bransby Williams

Tonight and Every Night
US 1945   92m   Technicolor
Columbia (Victor Saville)

The lives and loves of London showgirls
during the blitz.
Ludicrous concoction looking nothing like
London and certainly nothing like the
Windmill, the theatre to which it allegedly
pays tribute. There are some tolerable
numbers along the way.

w Lesser Samuels, Abem Finkel, play Heart
of a City by Lesley Storm d Victor Saville
ph Rudolph Maté md Morris Stoloff, Marlin
Skiles

Rita Hayworth, Lee Bowman, Janet Blair,
Marc Platt, Leslie Brooks, Dusty Anderson,
Florence Bates, Ernest Cossart

AAN: Morris Stoloff, Marlin Skiles; song
'Anywhere' (m Jule Styne, ly Sammy Cahn)

Tonight Is Ours
US 1932   76m   bw

A Balkan princess falls for a commoner in
Paris. One of the master's less sparkling plays
gets the heavy Hollywood treatment. Fredric
March, Claudette Colbert, Alison Skipworth,

Paul Cavanagh, Arthur Byron, Ethel Griffies.
Written by Edwin Justus Mayer, from the play
by Noel Coward; directed by Stuart Walker;
for Paramount. 'Slow and talky flicker, better
for the class houses.'—Variety

Tonight or Never
US 1931   80m   bw
Samuel Goldwyn

A prima donna falls for a man she thinks is a
Venetian gigolo, but he turns out to be an
impresario from New York.
Flimsy comedy which turned out to be its
star's last vehicle of any consequence for
twenty years.

w Ernest Vajda, play Lily Hatvany d Mervyn
Le Roy ph Gregg Toland md Alfred
Newman

Gloria Swanson, Melvyn Douglas (debut),
Ferdinand Gottschalk, Robert Greig, Alison
Skipworth, Boris Karloff

Tonight We Raid Calais
US 1943   70m   bw

A British agent lands in occupied France to
pave the way for a bombing raid. Adequate
low-budget morale booster. John Sutton,
Annabella, Lee J. Cobb, Beulah Bondi,
Blanche Yurka, Howard Da Silva, Marcel
Dalio. Written by Waldo Salt; directed by
John Brahm; for TCF.

Tonight We Sing*
US 1953   109m   Technicolor
TCF (George Jessel)

Sol Hurok stifles his own talent to become a
great musical impresario.
Blameless uppercrust biopic, with plenty of
well-staged guest talent.

w Harry Kurnitz, George Oppenheimer
d Mitchell Leisen ph Leon Shamroy
md Alfred Newman ch David Lichine

David Wayne, Anne Bancroft, Ezio Pinza
(Chaliapin), Roberta Peters, Tamara
Toumanova (Pavlova), Isaac Stern (Eugene
Ysaye), Jan Peerce

Tonka
US 1958   97m   Technicolor
Walt Disney

A Sioux Indian tames a magnificent white
horse, and after many adventures is reunited
with him at Little Big Horn.
Unremarkable and overlong adventure story.

w Lewis R. Foster, Lillie Hayward, novel
Comanche by David Appel d Lewis R.
Foster ph Loyal Griggs

Sal Mineo, Phil Carey, Jerome Courtland,
Rafael Campos, H. M. Wynant

Tons of Money
GB 1930   97m   bw

An inventor poses as his own cousin, and in
this guise achieves instant success. A long-
running stage farce makes a grimly overlong
movie. Ralph Lynn, Yvonne Arnaud, Mary
Brough, Robertson Hare, Gordon James,
Madge Saunders. Written by Herbert

TOMORROW IS FOREVER. Orson Welles and Claudette Colbert in a variation on the Enoch Arden theme.

Wilcox and Ralph Lynn, from the play by Will Evans and Arthur Valentine; directed by Tom Walls; for Herbert Wilcox / B and D.

Tony Draws a Horse
GB 1950   91m   bw

How to deal with a naughty boy causes mounting disagreement in the family. Very theatrical farce which on screen seems merely silly. Cecil Parker, Anne Crawford, Derek Bond, Barbara Murray, Mervyn Johns, Edward Rigby. Written by Brock Williams, from the play by Lesley Storm; directed by John Paddy Carstairs; for Pinnacle / GFD.

Tony Rome*
US 1967   111m   De Luxe   Panavision
TCF / Arcola / Millfield (Aaron Rosenberg)

A seedy Miami private eye runs into murder when he guards a millionaire's daughter. Complex old-fashioned murder mystery decorated with the new amorality and fashionable violence. Tolerable for its backgrounds and professional expertise. Sequel: *Lady in Cement* (qv).

w Richard L. Breen, *novel* Miami Mayhem by Marvin H. Albert *d* Gordon Douglas *ph* Joe Biroc *m* Billy May

Frank Sinatra, Jill St John, Richard Conte, Gena Rowlands, Simon Oakland, Jeffrey Lynn, Lloyd Bochner, Sue Lyon

Too Busy to Work
US 1932   76m   bw

A tramp goes looking for his long lost wife. Amiable remake of one of the star's most successful silents. *Will Rogers*, Marian Nixon, Dick Powell, Frederick Burton, Louise Beavers. Written by Barry Conners, Philip Klein, from the story Jubilo by Ben Ames Williams; directed by John Blystone; for Fox. 'A homey story of programmer weight . . . better than average business should be figured on.'—*Variety*

Too Hot to Handle*
US 1938   105m   bw
MGM (Lawrence Weingarten)

Adventures of a scoop-seeking newsreel cameraman.
Boisterous comedy-melodrama with as many sags as highlights but generally making a cheerful star entertainment.

w Laurence Stallings, John Lee Mahin *d* Jack Conway *ph* Harold Rosson *m* Franz Waxman

Clark Gable, Myrna Loy, Walter Connolly, Walter Pidgeon, Leo Carrillo, Johnny Hines, Virginia Weidler
'Even more than *Test Pilot* it's hoked beyond the level of credibility. But it has a driving excitement, crackling dialogue, glittering performances and inescapable romantic pull. So it's a socko audience picture and should make a parachuteful of money.'—*Variety*
'It's like an old-fashioned serial . . . no one can call it dull.'—*Howard Barnes*
'Breathlessly paced, witty, and violent, this is one of the more acid comedies to have been produced by the Thirties.'—*John Baxter*

Too Hot to Handle
GB 1960   100m   Eastmancolor
ABP / Wigmore (Selim Cattan)

Two Soho strip club owners join forces to hunt down a blackmailer.
Rotten, hilarious British gangster film set in a totally unreal underworld and very uncomfortably cast.

w Herbert Kretzmer *d* Terence Young *ph* Otto Heller *m* Eric Spear

Leo Genn, Jayne Mansfield, Karl Boehm, Danik Patisson, Christopher Lee, Patrick Holt

Too Late Blues
US 1961   100m   bw
Paramount (John Cassavetes)

A jazz musician falls for a neurotic girl and has fears of going commercial.
Uninteresting professional feature from a director whose reputation was made with the amateur *Shadows*.

w John Cassavetes, Richard Carr *d* John Cassavetes *ph* Lionel Lindon *m* David Raksin

John Cassavetes, Stella Stevens, Bobby Darin, Everett Chambers, Nick Dennis, Rupert Crosse, Vince Edwards

Too Late for Tears
US 1949   99m   bw
(UA) Hunt Stromberg

A lady bluebeard disposes of both husbands and boyfriends.
Silly melodrama, poorly cast.

w Roy Huggins *d* Byron Haskin *ph* William Mellor *m* Dale Butts

Lizabeth Scott, Don Defore, Arthur Kennedy, Dan Duryea, Kristine Miller, Barry Kelley

Too Late the Hero*
US 1969   144m   Technicolor   70mm
Associates and Aldrich / Palomar

In World War II the Japanese hold one end of a small Pacific island, British and Americans the other.
Semi-cynical, long and bloody war adventure of competence but no great merit.

w Robert Aldrich, Lukas Heller *d* Robert Aldrich *ph* Joseph Biroc *m* Gerald Fried

Michael Caine, Cliff Robertson, Ian Bannen, Henry Fonda, Harry Andrews, Denholm Elliott, Ronald Fraser, Percy Herbert

● *Video: Guild*

Too Many Crooks°
GB 1958 87m bw
Rank / Mario Zampi

Incompetent crooks plot a kidnapping.
Agreeable farce with black edges and an
excellent chase sequence.

w Michael Pertwee d Mario Zampi ph Stan
Pavey m Stanley Black

Terry-Thomas, George Cole, Brenda de
Banzie, Bernard Bresslaw, Sidney James, Joe
Melia, Vera Day, John Le Mesurier

Too Many Girls
US 1940 85m bw
RKO (Harry Edgington, George Abbott)

The father of a wealthy co-ed hires four
football heroes to protect her.
Witless nonsense, flabbily derived from a
Broadway show.

w John Twist, play George Marion Jnr,
Richard Rodgers, Lorenz Hart d George
Abbott ph Frank Redman songs Rodgers
and Hart

Lucille Ball, Desi Arnaz, Richard Carlson,
Ann Miller, Eddie Bracken, Frances
Langford, Harry Shannon
† The film on which Ball and Arnaz first met.

Too Many Husbands°
US 1940 84m bw
Columbia (Wesley Ruggles)
GB title: My Two Husbands

Allegedly drowned on a boat cruise, a man
turns up again after his wife has remarried.
Modest variation on a familiar theme,
professional but unexciting; later remade as
Three for the Show (qv).

w Claude Binyon, play Home and Beauty by
W. Somerset Maugham d Wesley Ruggles
ph Joseph Walker m Frederick Hollander

Jean Arthur, Melvyn Douglas, Fred
MacMurray, Harry Davenport, Dorothy
Peterson, Melville Cooper, Edgar Buchanan

Too Much Harmony
US 1933 76m bw

A star singer helps a promising girl to the top.
Routine light musical which filled a need. Bing
Crosby, Jack Oakie, Judith Allen, Skeets
Gallagher, Lilyan Tashman, Harry Green,
Ned Sparks. Written by Harry Ruskin, Joseph
L. Mankiewicz; directed by Eddie Sutherland;
for Paramount. 'Should be an easy pleaser.'—
Variety

'Always a man! Almost any man!'
Too Much Too Soon°
US 1958 121m bw
Warner (Henry Blanke)

Young actress Diana Barrymore goes to
Hollywood to look after her alcoholic father
John, but mild success goes to her head and
she too turns to drink.
Rather dismal and murkily photographed
account of an absorbing real-life situation; one
performance holds the first half together.

wd Art Napoleon, memoirs Diana Barrymore
ph Nicholas Musuraca, Carl Guthrie
m Ernest Gold ad George James Hopkins

Dorothy Malone, Errol Flynn, Efrem
Zimbalist Jnr, Neva Patterson, Martin Milner,
Ray Danton, Murray Hamilton

Too Young to Kiss
US 1951 89m bw
MGM (Sam Zimbalist)

A girl pianist poses as an infant prodigy, and
falls for the impresario who wants to adopt
her.
Dull conveyor belt comedy.

w Frances Goodrich, Albert Hackett
d Robert Z. Leonard ph Joseph Ruttenberg
m Johnny Green

June Allyson, Van Johnson, Gig Young, Paula
Corday, Larry Keating, Hans Conried

'If this happened to your daughter, would
you be to blame?'
Too Young to Love
GB 1959 89m bw
Rank / Welbeck (Herbert Smith)

A 15-year-old prostitute is brought before a
Brooklyn juvenile court.
Tepid filming of a popular exploitation play of
the fifties, mysteriously made in England.

w Sydney and Muriel Box, play Pick Up Girl
by Elsa Shelley d Muriel Box ph Gerald
Gibbs m Bruce Montgomery

Thomas Mitchell, Pauline Hahn, Joan Miller,
Austin Willis, Jess Conrad, Bessie Love, Alan
Gifford

Tootsie°°
US 1982 116m colour
Columbia / Mirage / Punch (Sydney
Pollack)

An out-of-work actor pretends to be a woman
in order to get a job in a soap opera.
As with Genevieve and Whisky Galore, an
unlikely comedy subject makes an instant
classic. It's all in the handling.

w Larry Gelbart, Murray Shisgal, story Don
McGuire d Sydney Pollack ph Owen
Roizman m Dave Grusin pd Peter Larkin
ed Frederick and William Steinkamp

Dustin Hoffman, Jessica Lange, Teri Garr,
Dabney Coleman, Charles Durning, Sydney
Pollack, George Gaynes

AA: Jessica Lange
AAN: best picture; Dustin Hoffman; Teri
Garr; Sydney Pollack as director; original
screenplay; cinematography; editing; song, 'It
Might Be You'; sound
BFA: Dustin Hoffman

Top Banana°
US 1953 100m Color Corporation
Roadshow / Harry M. Popkin

A TV comedian invites an attractive salesgirl
to join his show.
A wisp of plot is the excuse for a revue, and
the interest is in the old-time burlesque acts,
some of which survive the generally shoddy
treatment.

w Gene Towne d Alfred E. Green
ph William Bradford m / ly Johnny Mercer

Phil Silvers, Rose Marie, Danny Scholl, Jack
Albertson

Top Hat°°°°
US 1935 100m bw
RKO (Pandro S. Berman)

The path of true love is roughened by
mistaken identities.
Marvellous Astaire-Rogers musical, with a
more or less realistic London supplanted by a
totally artificial Venice, and show stopping
numbers in a style which is no more separated
by amusing plot complications lightly handled
by a team of deft farceurs.

w Dwight Taylor, Allan Scott d Mark
Sandrich ph David Abel, Vernon Walker
m / ly Irving Berlin ch Hermes Pan ad Van
Nest Polglase, Carroll Clark

Fred Astaire, Ginger Rogers, Edward Everett
Horton, Helen Broderick, Eric Blore, Erik
Rhodes

'The theatres will hold their own world
series with this one. It can't miss.'—Variety

'In 25 years Top Hat has lost nothing of its
gaiety and charm.'—Dilys Powell, 1960

AAN: best picture; song 'Cheek to Cheek'
● Video: Thorn EMI

Top Man
US 1943 74m bw

When an officer is recalled to active duty his
teenage son becomes head of the family.
Lively little putting-on-a-show comedy musical
which established a new young star. Donald
O'Connor, Richard Dix, Peggy Ryan, Lillian
Gish, Susanna Foster, Anne Gwynne. Written
by Zachary Gold; directed by Charles
Lamont; for Universal.

Top o' the Morning
US 1949 100m bw
Paramount (Robert L. Welch)

Investigations follow the theft of the Blarney
Stone.
More Irish whimsy from the Going My Way
stars.

w Edmund Beloin, Richard Breen d David
Miller ph Lionel Lindon m James Van
Heusen

Bing Crosby, Barry Fitzgerald, Ann Blyth,
Hume Cronyn, Eileen Crowe, John McIntire

Top of the Town
US 1937 86m bw

The daughter of the owner of the Moonbeam
Room wants to oust the swing band and stage
a symbolic ballet. A wisp of plot supports
some expensive but not especially attractive
numbers in a musical variety show that was
supposed to be Universal's answer to other
studios' biggies. George Murphy, Doris
Nolan, Hugh Herbert, Gregory Ratoff, Ella
Logan, Gertrude Niesen, Henry Armetta,
Mischa Auer, Samuel S. Hinds, Peggy Ryan.
Written by Brown Holmes, Charles Grayson,
Lou Brock; directed by Ralph Murphy; for
Universal. 'A bundle of mediocrity . . . it
neither goes nor gets anywhere.'—Variety

Top Secret*
GB 1952 94m bw
ABP (Mario Zampi)
US title: *Mr Potts Goes to Moscow*

A sanitary engineer, mistaken for a spy, is kidnapped to Moscow when his blueprints are taken for atomic secrets.
Farcical satire full of chases and lavatory humour; much of it comes off nicely.

w Jack Davies, Michael Pertwee *d* Mario Zampi *ph* Stan Pavey *m* Stanley Black

George Cole, Oscar Homolka, Nadia Gray, Frederick Valk, Wilfrid Hyde White, Geoffrey Sumner, Ronald Adam

Top Secret!
US 1984 90m Metrocolor
Paramount / Kingsmere (Jon Davison, Hunt Lowry)

An American rock star in Germany gets involved with spies of both sides.
Dull spoof from the folks who gave us *Airplane!* A very few sight gags stand out among the dross.

w Jim Abrahams, David Zucker, Jerry Zucker, Martyn Burke *d* Jim Abrahams, David Zucker, Jerry Zucker *ph* Christopher Challis *m* Maurice Jarre *pd* Peter Lamont

Val Kilmer, Lucy Gutteridge, Peter Cushing, Jeremy Kemp, Warren Clarke, Michael Gough, Omar Sharif, Christopher Villiers

'Too far over the top to retain any comic sense of the targets it sets out to lampoon. The overwhelming impression is of a *Mad* magazine strip in a particularly poor week.'—*Martyn Auty. MFB*

Top Secret Affair*
US 1956 100m bw
Warner / United States (Martin Rackin)
GB title: *Their Secret Affair*

A female news publisher tries to discredit a military diplomat but falls in love with him.
Curious comedy adaptation of a rather heavy novel, moderately skilled in all departments.

w Roland Kibbee, Allan Scott, *novel* Melville Goodwin USA by John P. Marquand *d* H. C. Potter *ph* Stanley Cortez *m* Roy Webb

Kirk Douglas, Susan Hayward, Jim Backus, Paul Stewart, John Cromwell, Roland Winters

Topaz*
US 1969 124m Technicolor
Universal / Alfred Hitchcock

In 1962 the CIA enlists a French agent to break up a Russian spy ring.
Oddly halting, desultory and unconvincing spy thriller shot mainly in flat TV style, with just a few short sequences in its director's better manner. A measure of its unsatisfactoriness is that three different endings were shot and actually used at various points of release.

w Samuel Taylor, *novel* Leon Uris *d* Alfred Hitchcock *ph* Jack Hildyard *m* Maurice Jarre

Frederick Stafford, John Forsythe, John Vernon, *Roscoe Lee Browne*, Dany Robin, Karin Dor, Michel Piccoli, Philippe Noiret

'A larger, slower, duller version of the spy thrillers he used to make in the thirties.'—*New Yorker, 1975*

Topaze*
US 1933 78m bw
(RKO) David O. Selznick

A simple schoolmaster allows himself to be exploited.
Interesting little comedy with the star playing against type: remade as *Mr Topaze* (qv).

w Benn W. Levy, *play* Marcel Pagnol *d* Harry d'Abbadie d'Arrast *ph* Lucien Andriot *m* Max Steiner

John Barrymore, Myrna Loy, Jobyna Howland, Jackie Searl

'Okay, for metropolitan spots, but scarcely for the subsequents . . . there haven't been half a dozen foreign dramas that have clicked on the screen.'—*Variety*
† In 1952 Howard Hughes announced a remake with Vincent Price, but it never happened.

Topkapi*
US 1964 119m Technicolor
UA / Filmways (Jules Dassin)

International thieves try to rob the Istanbul museum.
Light-hearted caper story which gets out of control because of the variety of styles and accents, the director's impression that his wife can do no wrong, and the general slowness and lack of wit; but there are bright moments, colourful backgrounds, and a final suspense sequence in the *Rififi* manner.

w Monja Danischewsky, *novel* The Light of Day by Eric Ambler *d* Jules Dassin *ph* Henri Alekan *m* Manos Hadjidakis

Melina Mercouri, Maximilian Schell, Peter Ustinov, Robert Morley, Akim Tamiroff, Gilles Segal, Jess Hahn

AA: Peter Ustinov

Topper**
US 1937 96m bw
(MGM) Hal Roach (Milton H. Bren)

A stuffy banker is haunted by the ghosts of his sophisticated friends the Kirbys, who are visible only to him.
Influential supernatural farce, still pretty funny and deftly acted though a shade slow to get going.

w Jack Jevne, Eric Hatch, Eddie Moran, *novel* The Jovial Ghosts by Thorne Smith *d* Norman Z. McLeod *ph* Norbert Brodine *md* Arthur Morton

Cary Grant, Constance Bennett, Roland Young, Billie Burke, Alan Mowbray, Eugene Pallette, Arthur Lake, Hedda Hopper

'How substantial the fan support will be is difficult to anticipate . . . None of the other films of similar theme aroused more than mild enthusiasm among a small group who patronize the arty theatres and talk about pictures in terms of art expression . . . Effort to excuse the story's absurdities on the theory that the intent is farce comedy does not entirely excuse the production from severe rebuke. Fact also that the living dead are always facetious may be shocking to

sensibilities. Some of the situations and dialogue offend conventional good taste.'—*Variety*

AAN: Roland Young

Topper Returns***
US 1941 87m bw
Hal Roach

A girl ghost helps Topper solve her own murder.
Spirited supernatural farce which spoofs murder mysteries, spooky houses, frightened servants, dumb cops, etc, in a pacy, accomplished and generally delightful manner.

w Jonathan Latimer, Gordon Douglas, with additional dialogue by Paul Gerard Smith *d* Roy del Ruth *ph* Norbert Brodine *m* Werner Heyman

Roland Young, Joan Blondell, Eddie Anderson, Carole Landis, Dennis O'Keefe, *H. B. Warner*, Billie Burke, *Donald McBride*, Rafaela Ottiano

'Ectoplasm runs riot and blazes a trial of hilarity from 5th Avenue to the French Riviera!'

Topper Takes a Trip*
US 1938 85m bw
Hal Roach

Ghostly Mrs Kirby helps Topper to save his wife from a Riviera philanderer.
Mildly pleasant follow-up, with a dog replacing Cary Grant who had become too expensive.

w Eddie Moran, Jack Jevne, Corey Ford *d* Norman Z. McLeod *ph* Norbert Brodine

Constance Bennett, Roland Young, Billie Burke, Alan Mowbray, Verree Teasdale, Franklin Pangborn, Alexander D'Arcy

'Dandy comedy sequel . . . can't miss at the b.o. . . . the original ended up a fine money-maker . . . no doubt one a year about Topper would be welcomed by exhibitors.'—*Variety*

Tora! Tora! Tora!*
US 1970 144m De Luxe Panavision
TCF (Elmo Williams)

A reconstruction from both sides of the events leading up to Pearl Harbor.
Immense, largely studio-bound, calcified war spectacle with much fidelity to the record but no villains and no hero, therefore no drama and no suspense.

w Larry Forrester, Hideo Oguni, Ryuzo Kikushima, *d* Richard Fleischer, Ray Kellogg, Toshio Masuda, Kinji Fukasaku *ph* Charles F. Wheeler and Japanese crews *m* Jerry Goldsmith *sp* L. B. Abbott, Art Cruickshank

Martin Balsam, Joseph Cotten, James Whitmore, Jason Robards, Edward Andrews, Leon Ames, George Macready, Soh Yamamura, Takahiro Tamura

'One of the least stirring and least photogenic historical epics ever perpetrated on the screen.'—*Gary Arnold*

AAN: Charles F. Wheeler

● *Video: CBS / Fox*

TOPPER TAKES A TRIP. Franklin Pangborn looks astonished as Roland Young's hat is raised by invisible hands.

'She sings torch songs to daddies and
lullabies to babies!'
Torch Singer
US 1933 72m bw
Paramount (Albert Lewis)
aka: *Broadway Singer*

An unwed mother supports her child by singing in night clubs.
Banal melodrama.

w Lenore Coffee, Lynn Starling, *play* Mike by Grace Perkins *d* Alexander Hall *ph* Karl Struss

Claudette Colbert, Ricardo Cortez, David Manners, Lyda Roberti, Baby LeRoy, Florence Roberts, Ethel Griffies, Helen Jerome Eddy
'Unwed mother film not so forte.'—*Variety*

Torch Song
US 1953 90m Technicolor
MGM (Henry Berman, Sidney Franklin Jnr)

A temperamental musical comedy star falls for a blind pianist.
Ossified star vehicle which looks great but is too often unintentionally funny.

w John Michael Hayes, Jan Lustig, *story* Why Should I Cry? by I. A. R. Wylie *d* Charles Walters *ph* Robert Planck *m* Adolph Deutsch

Joan Crawford, Michael Wilding, Gig Young, Marjorie Rambeau, Henry Morgan, Dorothy Patrick

'Here is Joan Crawford all over the screen, in command, in love and in color.'—*Otis L. Guernsey Jnr*
AAN: Marjorie Rambeau

Torchy Blane
Glenda Farrell played the hard-boiled girl reporter and Barton MacLane the tough police inspector who puts up with her in seven out of the nine second features made by Warners in the late thirties. The characters were created in short stories by Frederick Nebel, and the films were mostly directed by William Beaudine or Frank McDonald.
1936: SMART BLONDE
1937: FLY AWAY BABY, THE ADVENTUROUS BLONDE
1938: BLONDES AT WORK, TORCHY BLANE IN PANAMA (with Lola Lane, Paul Kelly), TORCHY GETS HER MAN
1939: TORCHY BLANE IN CHINATOWN, TORCHY RUNS FOR MAYOR, TORCHY PLAYS WITH DYNAMITE (with Jane Wyman, Allen Jenkins)

Torn Curtain**
US 1966 119m Technicolor
Universal / Alfred Hitchcock

A defector who is really a double agent is embarrassed when his girl friend follows him into East Germany.

Patchy Hitchcock with some mechanically effective suspense sequences, a couple of efforts at something new, a few miscalculations, some evidence of carelessness, and a little enjoyable repetition of old situations.

w Brian Moore *d Alfred Hitchcock ph* John F. Warren *m* John Addison

Paul Newman, Julie Andrews, *Wolfgang Kieling*, Ludwig Donath, Lila Kedrova, Hans-Joerg Felmy, Tamara Toumanova
'The pace is plodding, the political background trite, and the actors stranded by their director's customary lack of concern with performance.'—*Time Out, 1984*

Torpedo Run*
US 1958 98m Metrocolor Cinemascope
MGM (Edmund S. Grainger)

A US submarine in World War II destroys a Japanese aircraft carrier in Tokyo Bay.
Well-staged potboiler with excellent action sequences marred slightly by excessive platitudinizing.

w Richard Sale, William Wister Haines *d* Joseph Pevney *ph* George J. Folsey

Glenn Ford, Ernest Borgnine, Diane Brewster, Dean Jones

The Torrent*
US 1925 75m (24 fps) bw silent
MGM (Hunt Stromberg)

Spanish sweethearts are parted by a domineering mother, and the girl consoles herself by becoming a Paris prima donna.
Adequate emotional vehicle of its day which happened to be Garbo's first American film.

w Dorothy Farnum, *novel* Vicente Blasco Ibanez *d* Monta Bell *ph* William Daniels

Ricardo Cortez, Greta Garbo, Gertrude Olmsted, Edward Connelly, Lucien Littlefield

Torrid Zone**
US 1940 88m bw
Warner (Mark Hellinger)

In Central America, a banana plantation manager is tricked by his boss into staying on, and helps a wandering showgirl as well as foiling bandits.
Enjoyable, fast-paced hokum with a plot borrowed from both *The Front Page* and *Red Dust*.

w Richard Macaulay, Jerry Wald *d* William Keighley *ph* James Wong Howe *m* Adolph Deutsch

James Cagney, Pat O'Brien, Ann Sheridan, Helen Vinson, Andy Devine, Jerome Cowan, George Tobias, George Reeves

Tortilla Flat*
US 1942 106m bw
MGM (Sam Zimbalist)

The problems of poor Mexican half-breeds in California.
Expensive but unappealing variation on *The Grapes of Wrath*, with none of the cast quite getting under the skin of their parts, and no sense of reality, rather that of a musical without music.

w John Lee Mahin, Benjamin Glazier, *novel* John Steinbeck *d* Victor Fleming *ph* Sidney Wagner *m* Franz Waxman

Spencer Tracy, Hedy Lamarr, John Garfield. Frank Morgan, Akim Tamiroff, Connie Gilchrist, John Qualen, Sheldon Leonard, Donald Meek, Allen Jenkins, Henry O'Neill

AAN: Frank Morgan

Torture Garden°
GB 1967 93m Technicolor
Columbia / Amicus (Milton Subotsky)

Five fairground visitors are told their future by the mysterious Dr Diablo.
Crude but effective horror portmanteau including one story about the resurrection of Edgar Allan Poe.

w Robert Bloch *d* Freddie Francis *ph* Norman Warwick *m* Don Banks, James Bernard

Burgess Meredith, Jack Palance, Peter Cushing, Beverly Adams, Michael Bryant, John Standing

The Touch°
Sweden / US 1970 112m Eastmancolor
ABC / Cinematograph AB (Lars/Owe Carlburg)

The wife of a provincial surgeon falls in love with an archaeologist.
Freedom versus security: the Bergman treatment is given to a familiar love story, but the expected finesse is lacking.

wd Ingmar Bergman *ph* Sven Nykvist *m* Jan Johansson

Bibi Andersson, Elliott Gould, Max Von Sydow

Touch and Go
GB 1955 85m Technicolor
Ealing (Seth Holt)
US title: *The Light Touch*

A family has doubts about its decision to emigrate to Australia.
Very mild comedy which fails to engage sympathy because the characters don't seem real.

w William Rose *d* Michael Truman *ph* Douglas Slocombe *m* John Addison

Jack Hawkins, Margaret Johnston, June Thorburn, John Fraser, Roland Culver, Alison Leggatt, James Hayter

'They had the perfect love affair. Until they fell in love!'
A Touch of Class°°
GB 1973 106m Technicolor
Panavision
Avco / Brut / Gordon Films (Melvin Frank)

A married American businessman in London has a hectic affair with a dress designer.
Amiable and very physical sex farce with hilarious highlights and a few longueurs between; the playing keeps it above water.

w Melvin Frank, Jack Rose *d* Melvin Frank *ph* Austin Dempster *m* John Cameron

A TOUCH OF CLASS. George Segal and Glenda Jackson make unlikely romantic partners, but the film was a box office smash hit.

Glenda Jackson, George Segal, Paul Sorvino, Hildegarde Neil
'Machine-tooled junk.'—*William S. Pechter*
'Brightly performed and quite engaging until it fades into vapid variations on a one-joke theme.'—*Sight and Sound*
AA: Glenda Jackson
AAN: best picture; script; John Cameron; song, 'All That Love Went to Waste' (*m* George Barrie, *ly* Sammy Cahn)

Touch of Evil°°
US 1958 95m or 114m bw
U-I (Albert Zugsmith)

A Mexican narcotics investigator honeymooning in a border town clashes with the local police chief over a murder.
Overpoweringly atmospheric melodrama crammed with Wellesian touches, but very cold and unsympathetic, with rather restrained performances (especially his) and a plot which takes some following. Hardly the most auspicious return to Hollywood for a wanderer, but now becoming a cult classic.

wd Orson Welles, *novel* Badge of Evil by Whit Masterson *ph* Russell Metty *m* Henry Mancini

Charlton Heston, Orson Welles, Janet Leigh, Marlene Dietrich, Akim Tamiroff, Joseph Calleia, Ray Collins, Dennis Weaver
'Pure Orson Welles and impure balderdash, which may be the same thing.'—*Gerald Weales, Reporter*

A Touch of Larceny°
GB 1959 92m bw
Paramount / Ivan Foxwell

A naval commander mysteriously disappears in the hope that he will be branded a traitor and can sue for libel.
Fairly amusing light comedy with lively performances.

w Roger MacDougall, Guy Hamilton, Ivan Foxwell, *novel* The Megstone Plot by Andrew Garve *d* Guy Hamilton *ph* John Wilcox *m* Philip Green

James Mason, Vera Miles, George Sanders, Robert Flemyng, Ernest Clark, Duncan Lamont, Peter Barkworth
'A beguilingly polished comedy, reminiscent in its style, urbanity and sheen of the sort of thing Lubitsch was doing in the 30s.'—*Daily Mail*

A Touch of Love
GB 1969   107m   Eastmancolor
Amicus / Palomar (Milton Subotsky)
US title: *Thank You All Very Much*

A pregnant London student tries to get an
abortion but later decides against it.
Curious bid for serious drama by horror
producers; all very conscientiously but rather
dreary.

w Margaret Drabble, from her novel The
Millstone   *d* Waris Hussein   *ph* Peter
Suschitsky   *m* Michael Dress

Sandy Dennis, Ian McKellen, Michael Coles,
John Standing, Eleanor Bron

A Touch of the Sun
GB 1956   80m   bw
Eros / Raystro (Raymond Stross)

A hall porter is left a fortune but after living it
up for a while returns to his old hotel which is
on the rocks.
Limp comedy vehicle.

w Alfred Shaughnessy   *d* Gordon Parry
ph Arthur Grant   *m* Eric Spear

Frankie Howerd, Ruby Murray, Dorothy
Bromiley, Gordon Harker, Reginald
Beckwith, Richard Wattis, Dennis Price,
Alfie Bass, Willoughby Goddard

Touchez pas au Grisbi*
France / Italy 1953   90m approx   bw
Del Duca / Antares
aka: *Honour among Thieves; Hands Off
the Loot*

Two crooks succeed in stealing a consignment
of gold, but that's only the start of their
worries.
Smooth underworld hokum, with a slightly
comic attitude implied if not stated.

w Jacques Becker, Maurice Griffe,
novel Albert Simonin   *d* Jacques Becker
ph Pierre Montazel   *m* Jean Wiener

Jean Gabin, Jeanne Moreau, Gaby Basset,
Daniel Cauchy, Marilyn Buferd, Lino
Ventura, René Dary

Toughest Man in Arizona
US 1952   90m   Trucolor
Republic (Sidney Picker)

In 1861 a US marshal falls in love with the
wife of an outlaw.
Easy-going, pleasant western aimed at the top
half of a double bill.

w John K. Butler   *d* R. G. Springsteen
ph Reggie Lanning   *m* Dale Butts

Vaughn Monroe, Joan Leslie, Edgar
Buchanan, Victor Jory, Jean Parker, Henry
Morgan

'The most exciting screen event of all
time!'
Tovarich**
US 1937   98m   bw
Warner (Robert Lord)

A royal Russian husband and wife flee the
revolution to Paris and take jobs as servants in
an eccentric household.

A lively comedy of its time; though many of
the jokes now seem obvious, the playing
preserves its essential quality.

w Casey Robinson, *play adaptation Robert E.
Sherwood, original* Jacques Deval   *d* Anatole
Litvak   *ph* Charles Lang   *m* Max Steiner

*Claudette Colbert, Charles Boyer, Basil
Rathbone*, Anita Louise, Melville Cooper,
Isabel Jeans, Maurice Murphy, Morris
Carnovsky, Gregory Gaye, Montagu Love,
Fritz Feld
   'A yarn of charming and finely shaded
characterizations. Both humour and heart
appeal spring from intimate acquaintance with
the background and motives of each player.
Class production, magnet for first runs.'—
Variety

Toward the Unknown
US 1956   115m   Warnercolor
   Warnerscope
Warner / Toluca (Mervyn Le Roy)
GB title: *Brink of Hell*

An over-age officer takes part in the X2
experiments with rocket-firing aircraft.
Humourless flagwaver, very forgettable.

w Beirne Lay Jnr   *d* Mervyn Le Roy
ph Harold Rosson   *m* Paul Baron

William Holden, Lloyd Nolan, Virginia Leith,
Charles McGraw, Murray Hamilton, L. Q.
Jones, James Garner, Paul Fix, Karen Steele

Towed in a Hole**
US 1932   20m   bw

Two would-be fishermen wreck the boat they
have just bought. Brilliant star farce, filled
with wonderfully lunatic dialogues and freshly
conceived slapstick. Laurel and Hardy.
Written by Stan Laurel; directed by George
Marshall; for Hal Roach.

Tower of London**
US 1939   92m   bw
Universal (Rowland V. Lee)

With the help of Mord the executioner,
Richard Crookback kills his way to the throne
but is destroyed at Bosworth.
The Shakespearean view of history played as a
horror comic: despite an overall lack of pace,
spirited scenes and good performances win the
day.

w Robert N. Lee   *d* Rowland V. Lee
ph George Robinson   *m* Charles Previn

Basil Rathbone, Boris Karloff, Barbara
O'Neil, Ian Hunter, Vincent Price, Nan Grey,
John Sutton, Leo G. Carroll, Miles Mander
   'Spine-tingling horror picture . . . so strong
that it may provide disturbing nightmares as
aftermath.'—*Variety*

Tower of London*
US 1962   79m   bw
AIP / Admiral (Gene Corman)

A variation on the same events, with Price
graduating from Clarence to Crookback, and
the addition of ghostly visions. All very cheap,
but occasionally vivid melodrama, despite
intrusive American accents.

w Leo V. Gordon, Amos Powell, James B.
Gordon   *d* Roger Corman   *ph* Arch Dalzell
m Michael Anderson

Vincent Price, Michael Pate, Joan Freeman,
Robert Brown, Justice Eatson, Sara Salby,
Richard McCauly, Bruce Gordon

The Tower of Terror
GB 1941   78m   bw

British and German agents clash in a
lighthouse tended by a mad keeper. Lurid
penny-dreadful, quite amusing in its way.
Wilfrid Lawson, Movita, Michael Rennie,
Morland Graham, George Woodbridge.
Written by John Argyle and John Reinhart;
directed by Lawrence Huntington; for ABPC.

'One tiny spark becomes a night of
   towering suspense!'
The Towering Inferno**
US 1974   165m   De Luxe   Panavision
TCF / Warner (Irwin Allen)

The world's tallest building is destroyed by fire
on the night of its inauguration.
Showmanlike but relentlessly padded disaster
spectacular, worth seeing for its cast of stars,
its sheer old-fashioned expertise, and its
special effects.

w Stirling Silliphant, *novels* The Tower by
Richard Martin Stern, The Glass Inferno by
Thomas M. Scortia, Frank M. Robinson
d John Guillermin, Irwin Allen   *ph* Fred
Koenekamp, Joseph Biroc   *m* John Williams
sp Bill Abbott   *pd* William Creber

Paul Newman, Steve McQueen, William
Holden, Faye Dunaway, Fred Astaire, Susan
Blakely, Richard Chamberlain, Robert
Vaughn, Jennifer Jones, O. J. Simpson,
Robert Wagner
   'Several generations of blue-eyed charmers
act their roles as if each were under a separate
bell jar.'—*Verina Glaessner*
   'Each scene of someone horribly in flames is
presented as a feat for the audience's
delectation.'—*New Yorker*
   'The combination of Grade A spectacle and
B-picture characters induces a feeling of
sideline detachment.'—*Michael Billington,
Illustrated London News*

AA: photography; song 'We May Never Love
Like This Again' (*m / ly* Al Kasha, Joel
Hirschhorn)
AAN: best picture; John Williams; Fred
Astaire

A Town Called Bastard
GB 1971   97m   Technicolor   Franscope
Benmar / Zurbano (Ben Fisz)
aka: *A Town Like Hell*

Mexican revolutionaries massacre a priest and
his congregation and take over the town. Ten
years later a widow arrives seeking vengeance.
Sadistic western with an opening massacre
followed by twenty-two killings (count 'em).
Pretty dull otherwise.

w Richard Aubrey   *d* Robert Parrish
ph Manuel Berenguer   *m* Waldo de Los Rios

Robert Shaw, Stella Stevens, Telly Savalas, Martin Landau, Michael Craig, Fernando Rey, Dudley Sutton

A Town like Alice**
GB 1956 117m bw
Rank / Vic Films (Joseph Janni)
US title: *The Rape of Malaya*

Life among women prisoners of the Japanese in Malaya, especially one who is finally reunited with her Australian lover.
Genteelly harrowing war film, formlessly adapted from the first part of a popular novel; a big commercial success of its day.

w W. P. Lipscomb, Richard Mason, *novel* Nevil Shute d Jack Lee ph Geoffrey Unsworth m Matyas Seiber

Virginia McKenna, Peter Finch, Takagi, Marie Lohr, Maureen Swanson, Jean Anderson, Renée Houston, Nora Nicholson

● *Video: Rank*

'There she lay, wearing her nylons—right around her neck!'

Town on Trial*
GB 1956 96m bw
Columbia / Marksman (Maxwell Setton)

A police inspector solves the murder of a girl after a tennis club dance in a British country town.
Straightforward murder mystery shot in Weybridge, with a wide variety of suspects having something to hide; settings and characters are quite realistic and also a little dreary.

w Ken Hughes, Robert Westerby d John Guillermin ph Basil Emmott m Tristam Cary

John Mills, Charles Coburn, Derek Farr, Barbara Bates, Alec McCowen, Geoffrey Keen, Elizabeth Seal, Margaretta Scott, Fay Compton

Town without Pity*
US / Switzerland / Germany 1961 103m bw
UA / Mirisch / Osweg / Gloria (Gottfried Reinhardt)

A German girl is raped and four American soldiers are accused; the defence counsel's wiles lead to the girl's suicide.
Dour drama with overpowering expressionist technique but not much real sympathy, interest or surprise.

w Silvia Reinhardt, George Hurdalek, *novel* The Verdict by Manfred Gregor d Gottfried Reinhardt ph Kurt Hasse m Dmitri Tiomkin

Kirk Douglas, E. G. Marshall, Christine Kaufmann, Barbara Rutting, Robert Blake, Richard Jaeckel

AAN: title song (*m* Dmitri Tiomkin, *ly* Ned Washington)

The Toy
US 1983 102m colour
Columbia / Rastar (Phil Feldman)

A black janitor is hired as a toy for a millionaire's nine-year-old son.

Feeble attempt to translate a 1976 French film by Francis Veber. The few laughs are laughs of embarrassment.

w Carol Sobieski d Richard Donner ph Laszlo Kovacs m Patrick Williams pd Charles Rosen

Richard Pryor, Jackie Gleason, Ned Beatty, Scott Schwarz, Teresa Ganzel, Wilfrid Hyde-White, Tony King
    'Tasteless in implication, flavourless in execution.'—*Sight and Sound*

Toy Tiger
US 1956 88m Technicolor Cinemascope
U-I (Howard Christie)

The imaginative small son of a widow 'adopts' her business friend as his father.
Flat sentimental comedy off the studio's conveyor belt, a remake of *Mad about Music*.

w Ted Sherdeman d Jerry Hopper ph George Robinson m Joseph Gershenson

Jeff Chandler, Laraine Day, Tim Hovey, Cecil Kellaway, Richard Haydn, David Janssen

The Toy Wife*
US 1938 95m bw
MGM (Merian C. Cooper)
GB title: *Frou Frou*

In the early 19th century in Louisiana, a flirtatious girl causes jealousy and tragedy.
Another bid in the *Jezebel / Gone with the Wind* stakes, this handsome production proved a commercial misfire and hastened the end of its star's career.

w Zoe Akins d Richard Thorpe ph Oliver T. Marsh m Edward Ward

Luise Rainer, Melvyn Douglas, Robert Young, Barbara O'Neil, H. B. Warner, Alma Kruger, Walter Kingsford
    'Old-fashioned melodrama, beautifully produced but creaky.'—*Variety*

Toys in the Attic*
US 1963 90m bw Panavision
UA / Claude / Mirisch

In a shabby New Orleans home, two ageing spinsters struggle to look after their ne'er-do-well brother.
Play which film doesn't go in this case, but the script and acting are interesting.

w James Poe, play Lillian Hellman d George Roy Hill ph Joseph Biroc m George Duning ad Cary Odell

Geraldine Page, Wendy Hiller, Dean Martin, Yvette Mimieux, Gene Tierney, Larry Gates

'A story of how men and women act when they think nobody is looking!'

Track of the Cat*
US 1954 102m Warnercolor Cinemascope
Warner / Wayne–Fellows / Batjac (Robert Fellows)

In the northern California backwoods one winter in the 1880s a farming family is menaced by a marauding mountain lion.
With the lion a symbol of evil, this is real Cold

Comfort Farm country and despite good intentions all round becomes irresistibly funny before the end, largely because everyone moves and speaks so s-l-o-w-l-y. The bleached colour is interesting but would suit only snowy settings.

w A. I. Bezzerides, *novel* Walter Van Tilburg Clark d William A. Wellman ph William H. Clothier m Roy Webb

Robert Mitchum, Diana Lynn, Beulah Bondi, Teresa Wright, Tab Hunter, Philip Tonge, William Hopper, Carl Switzer
    'Cinemascope's first genuine weirdie . . . the script is redolent of Eugene O'Neill, and to its presentation the director brings a touch of Poe . . . Despair hangs in the air like a curse . . . unfortunately ambition overreaches itself, and the film topples over into barnstorming melodrama.'—*MFB*

Trackdown
US 1976 98m De Luxe
UA / Essaness (Bernard Schwarz)

A Montana rancher follows his sister to Los Angeles and avenges her ill-treatment there by gangsters.
Routine action thriller with fashionable realism and violence.

w Paul Edwards d Richard T. Heffron ph Gene Polito m Charles Bernstein

Jim Mitchum, Karen Lamm, Anne Archer, Erik Estrada, Cathy Lee Crosby, Vince Cannon

Trade Winds
US 1939 93m bw
Walter Wanger

A girl who thinks she has committed murder flees to the Far East, and a cynical detective is sent to bring her back. Guess what happens.
Smartly written mixture of comedy, drama, mystery and travelogue which comes off only in spots; it needed a firmer hand.

w Dorothy Parker, Alan Campbell, Frank R. Adams d Tay Garnett ph Rudolph Maté m Alfred Newman

Fredric March, Joan Bennett, Ralph Bellamy, Ann Sothern, Sidney Blackmer, Thomas Mitchell, Robert Elliott
    'All the elements that provide broad entertainment are present in this picture, and it should reap healthy grosses.'—*Variety*

Trader Horn*
US 1930 120m bw
MGM

An experienced African trader overcomes tribal hostility.
Primitive talkie for which second units were sent to Africa amid much publicity hoo-ha. After fifty years, nothing of interest remains to be seen.

w Richard Schayer, Dale Van Every, Thomas Neville, *novel* Alfred Aloysius Horn, Etheldreda Lewis d W. S. Van Dyke ph Clyde de Vinna

Harry Carey, Edwina Booth, Duncan Renaldo, Mutia Omoolu, C. Aubrey Smith

'Sure money-getter. Outstanding animal stuff, great sound effects, and thin story, which has good-looking white girl romping around scantily clad.'—*Variety*

'A movie that contains all the best features of a zoo, a cannibal dance, and a big yarn by Rider Haggard.'—*National Board of Review*

AAN: best picture

Trader Horn
US 1973 105m Metrocolor
MGM (Lewis J. Rachmil)

Pitiful remake patched together largely from stock footage.

w William Norton, Edward Harper *d* Reza Badiyi *ph* Ronald W. Browne *m* Shelly Manne

Rod Taylor, Anne Heywood, Jean Sorel
'Laughably inept . . . it cannot face word of mouth for long.'—*Variety*

Trading Places**
US 1983 116m Technicolor
Paramount / Landis-Folsey (Aaron Russo)

Two rich men arrange a wager on the effects of environment over heredity, and arrange for a con man and a stockbroker to change places. Surprisingly witty comedy, which while not aspiring to great heights, and marred by a few excesses, brought a refreshing breath of air to a declining genre.

w Timothy Harris, Herschel Weingrod *d* John Landis *ph* Robert Paynter *m* Elmer Bernstein *pd* Gene Rudolf

Dan Aykroyd, Eddie Murphy, *Ralph Bellamy*, *Don Ameche*, *Denholm Elliott*, Jamie Lee Curtis, Kristin Holby
'Proof positive that the genuine American populist comedy can still attract attention.'—*John Pym, MFB*

BFA: Jamie Lee Curtis, Denholm Elliott
● *Video: CIC*

Traffic
France / Italy 1970 96m Eastmancolor
Corona / Gibe / Selenia (Robert Dorfman)

The designer of a camping car has various little accidents on the way from the works to a show.
Rambling comedy with understated jokes and an almost invisible star.

w Jacques Tati, Jacques Legrange *d* Jacques Tati (with Bert Haanstra) *ph* Edouard Van Den Enden, Marcel Weiss *m* Charles Dumont

Jacques Tati

● *Video: Polygram*

The Trail of '98*
US 1928 90m at 24 fps bw silent

San Franciscans leave their homes for the Klondike gold rush. Impressive spectacular while it stays outdoors; not so good when the plot takes over. Dolores Del Rio, Ralph Forbes, Harry Carey, Karl Dane, Tully Marshall. Written by Waldmar Young and Ben Glazer, from the novel by Robert W. Service; directed by Clarence Brown; for MGM.

'The surging drama of love in the Kentucky hills springs to thrilling life as the first outdoor action romance filmed in colour!'

The Trail of the Lonesome Pine*
US 1936 102m Technicolor
Paramount (Walter Wanger)

A hillbilly girl goes back home when her brother is killed in a family feud.
Antediluvian Ozarkian melodrama, notable as the first outdoor film to be shot in three-colour Technicolor.

w Grover Jones, Horace McCoy, Harvey Thew, *novel* John Fox Jnr *d* Henry Hathaway *ph* Howard Greene *m* Hugo Friedhofer, Gerrard Carbonara

Sylvia Sidney, Fred MacMurray, Henry Fonda, Fred Stone, Nigel Bruce, Beulah Bondi, Robert Barrat, Spanky McFarland, Fuzzy Knight
'A good show saleable for big grosses, a flicker the ballyhoo boys can and will do tricks with.'—*Variety*
'Unnatural as it is, the colour does no serious damage to the picture. This moldy bit of hokum . . . takes movies back to the days of their childhood.'—*Newsweek*
† The story was first filmed in 1915 by Cecil B. de Mille.

AAN: song 'A Melody from the Sky' (*m* Louis Alter, *ly* Sidney Mitchell)

Trail of the Pink Panther
GB 1982 97m Technicolor Panavision
MGM–UA / Titan (Blake Edwards, Tony Adams)

Inspector Clouseau is reported missing at sea and a television reporter interviews those who had known him.
Flimsy, necrophiliac excuse for a movie, with a star cast clearly failing to make bricks without straw two years after the nominal star's death.

w Frank and Tom Waldman, Blake Edwards, Geoffrey Edwards *d* Blake Edwards *ph* Dick Bush *m* Henry Mancini *pd* Peter Mullins *ed* Alan Jones

Peter Sellers, Joanna Lumley, Herbert Lom, David Niven, Richard Mulligan, Capucine, Robert Loggia, Harvey Korman, Burt Kwouk, Graham Stark, Leonard Rossiter, Peter Arne, Ronald Fraser

Trail of the Vigilantes*
US 1940 78m bw

In the old west, a reporter sets out to break up a band of outlaws. A mild western which at the time had some reputation as a wild comedy; the fact was that it turned out badly and the editors did the best they could. Franchot Tone, Warren William, Broderick Crawford, Andy Devine, Mischa Auer, Porter Hall, Peggy Moran. Written by Harold Shumate; directed by Allan Dwan; for Universal. 'As light amusement it does all right, but it is amusement in confusion.'—*Otis Ferguson*.

Trail Street
US 1947 84m bw

Wheat is planted in Kansas by the early settlers. Pretty good, unpretentious western. Randolph Scott, Robert Ryan, Anne Jeffreys, Billy House, George 'Gabby' Hayes. Written by Norman Houston and Gene Lewis; directed by Ray Enright; for Nat Holt / RKO.

The Train**
US 1964 140m bw
UA / Ariane / Dear (Jules Bricken)

In 1944, the French resistance tries to prevent the Nazis from taking art treasures back to Germany on a special train.
Proficient but longwinded suspense actioner with spectacular sequences; a safe bet for train enthusiasts.

w Franklin Coen, Frank Davis, Walter Bernstein *d* John Frankenheimer *ph* Jean Tournier, Walter Wottitz *m* Maurice Jarre

Burt Lancaster, *Paul Scofield*, Jeanne Moreau, Michael Simon, Wolfgang Preiss, Suzanne Flon
'Extraordinarily good in many of its parts but rather disappointing as a whole . . . its greatest virtue is an almost overpowering physical realism.'—*Moira Walsh, America*
AAN: script

Train of Events
GB 1949 89m bw
Ealing (Michael Relph)

Portmanteau of stories à la Friday the 13th or Dead of Night, linked by a train disaster. A rather mechanical entertainment, proficiently made.

w Basil Dearden, T. E. B. Clarke, Ronald Millar, Angus MacPhail *d* Basil Dearden, Charles Crichton, Sidney Cole *ph* Lionel Banes, Gordon Dines *m* Leslie Bridgewater

Valerie Hobson, John Clements, Jack Warner, Gladys Henson, Peter Finch, Irina Baronova, Susan Shaw, Patric Doonan, Joan Dowling, Laurence Payne, Mary Morris

The Train Robbers
US 1973 92m Technicolor Panavision
Warner / Batjac (Michael Wayne)

A widow asks three gunmen to help her clear her husband's name by retrieving gold he had stolen.
Shaggy dog western, sadly lacking in comic situation and detail.

wd Burt Kennedy *ph* William Clothier *m* Dominic Frontière

John Wayne, Ann-Margret, Rod Taylor, Ben Johnson, Bobby Vinton, Christopher George

● *Video: Warner*

The Traitor*
GB 1957 88m bw
New Realm (E. J. Fancey)

At the annual reunion of a resistance group, the host announces that one of their number was a traitor.

Heavy-handed theatrical melodrama, helped by a stout plot and some directional flair.

wd Michael McCarthy ph Bert Mason m Jackie Brown

Donald Wolfit, Robert Bray, Jane Griffiths, Carl Jaffe, Anton Diffring, Oscar Quitak, Rupert Davies, John Van Eyssen

The Traitors*
GB 1962 69m bw
Ello (Jim O'Connelly)

A top scientist is killed and MI5 springs into action.
Commendable second feature with narrative virtues absent in most big films.

w Jim O'Connelly d Robert Tronson ph Michael Reed m Johnny Douglas

Patrick Allen, James Maxwell, Ewan Roberts, Zena Walker

Traitor's Gate
GB 1965 80m bw
Columbia / Summit (Ted Lloyd)

A London businessman organizes a gang to steal the Crown Jewels.
Modest caper melodrama, routine but watchable.

w John Sansom, novel Edgar Wallace d Freddie Francis ph Denys Coop

Albert Lieven, Gary Raymond, Margot Trooger, Klaus Kinski, Catherina Von Schell, Edward Underdown

The Tramp*
US 1915 20m approx (24 fps) bw silent
Mutual

A tramp saves a girl from crooks, is wounded and cared for by her, deliriously happy—until her lover arrives.
Fairly funny star comedy, the first with sentimental touches and the origin of the into-the-sunset fade-out.

wd Charles Chaplin ph Rollie Totheroh

Charles Chaplin, Edna Purviance, Bud Jamison, Leo White, Lloyd Bacon

Tramp Tramp Tramp*
US 1926 65m approx (24 fps) bw silent
Harry Langdon

Harry enters a cross-country walking contest in order to impress his girl.
Well-staged peripatetic comedy, the star's first feature.

w Frank Capra, Tim Whelan, Hal Conklin, Gerald Duffy, Murray Roth, J. Frank Holliday d Harry Edwards

Harry Langdon, Joan Crawford, Alec B. Francis

Transatlantic*
US 1931 74m bw

Various personal stories come to a climax aboard a transatlantic liner. Early attempt at what has now become a very worn format; quite lively it must have seemed then.

Edmund Lowe, Lois Moran, John Halliday, Greta Nissen, Jean Hersholt, Myrna Loy, Earle Foxe, Billy Bevan. Written by Guy Bolton, Lynn Starling; directed by William K. Howard; for Fox. 'An aquatic *Grand Hotel*; should prosper.'—*Variety*

Transatlantic Merry Go Round
US 1934 92m bw

Romantic misunderstandings on an ocean liner. Patchy comedy with some good scenes. Jack Benny, Nancy Carroll, Gene Raymond, Sydney Howard. Written by Joseph Moncure March, Harry W. Conn and Leon Gordon; directed by Ben Stoloff; for United Artists. 'Good, popular screen entertainment; certain box office fodder.'—*Variety*

Trans-Europe Express*
France 1966 90m bw
Como Film (Samy Halfon)

Film-makers on a train invent a violent plot and then find life aping it.
A theme beloved of Hollywood is treated intellectually, and almost succeeds in attracting all classes.

wd Alain Robbe-Grillet ph Willy Kurant m Verdi

Jean-Louis Trintignant, Marie-France Pisier, Nadine Verdier, Christian Barbier, Charles Millot, Alain Robbe-Grillet

Transgression
US 1931 70m bw

During a Paris vacation, a man forgives his wife for her affair with a Spanish gigolo. Very routine, matinée drama. Kay Francis, Ricardo Cortez, Paul Cavanagh, Nance O'Neil. Written by Elizabeth Meehan from the novel by Kate Jordan; directed by Herbert Brenon; for RKO. 'Doubtful de luxe subject, principally because its story lacks conviction.'—*Variety*

The Trap*
US 1958 84m Technicolor
Paramount / Parkwood–Heath (Melvin Frank, Norman Panama)
GB title: *The Baited Trap*

A lawyer helps a vicious killer to escape into Mexico, but the plan backfires.
Reasonably tense action thriller with desert backgrounds.

w Richard Alan Simmons, Norman Panama d Norman Panama ph Daniel L. Fapp m Irvin Talbot

Richard Widmark, Lee J. Cobb, Earl Holliman, Tina Louise, Carl Benton Reid, Lorne Green

The Trap
GB / Canada 1966 106m Eastmancolor Panavision
Parallel (George H. Brown)

In nineteenth-century British Columbia a rough trapper takes a wife, who at first is terrified of him but nurses him when he is hurt . . .

Primitive open air melodrama with good action sequences; well made but hardly endearing.

w David Osborn d Sidney Hayers ph Robert Krasker m Ron Goodwin

Oliver Reed, Rita Tushingham, Rex Sevenoaks, Barbara Chilcott

Trapeze**
US 1956 105m De Luxe Cinemascope
UA / Hecht–Lancaster (James Hill)

A circus partnership almost breaks up when a voluptuous third member is engaged.
Concentrated, intense melodrama filmed almost entirely within a French winter circus and giving a very effective feel, almost a smell, of the life therein. Despite great skill in the making, however, the length is too great for a wisp of plot that goes back to *The Three Maxims* and doubtless beyond.

w James R. Webb d Carol Reed ph Robert Krasker m Malcolm Arnold

Burt Lancaster, Tony Curtis, Gina Lollobrigida, Thomas Gomez, Johnny Puleo, Katy Jurado, Sidney James

† This version was supposedly adapted from a Max Catto novel, *The Killing Frost*, but in 1932 Harmonie of Germany issued a film with the title *Trapeze* and a remarkably similar story. It had a scenario by Alfred Machard and was directed by E. A. Dupont. The Anna Neagle film *The Three Maxims* (*qv*) was also very similar, but that was supposedly an original by Herman Mankiewicz.

Traveller's Joy
GB 1949 78m bw

A divorced couple, stranded in Sweden by lack of funds, have to take joint action. Mild topical comedy from a popular play. Googie Withers, John McCallum, Yolande Donlan, Maurice Denham, Geoffrey Sumner, Colin Gordon, Dora Bryan. Written by Allan MacKinnon and Bernard Quayle, from the play by Arthur Macrae; directed by Ralph Thomas; for Gainsborough / Rank.

The Travelling Executioner*
US 1970 95m Metrocolor Panavision
MGM (Jack Smight)

In 1918 an ex-carnival showman travels the American south with his portable electric chair and charges a hundred dollars per execution, but falls for one of his proposed victims. Oddball fable without apparent moral; neither fantastic nor funny enough.

w Garrie Bateson d Jack Smight ph Philip Lathrop m Jerry Goldsmith

Stacy Keach, Mariana Hill, Bud Cort, Graham Jarvis

Travelling Saleslady
US 1935 75m bw

A toothpaste manufacturer's daughter shows her father the value of advertising. Warner stock company comedy which hits no heights but provided reliable entertainment. Joan

Blondell, Hugh Herbert, Glenda Farrell, William Gargan, Al Shean, Grant Mitchell, Ruth Donnelly, Bert Roach. Written by Hugh Herbert, Manuel Seff, Benny Rubin, Frank Howard Clark; directed by Ray Enright; for Warners. 'It will please and should do all right at the wicket.'—*Variety*

Travels with My Aunt*
US 1972 109m Metrocolor Panavision
MGM (Robert Fryer, James Cresson)

A staid bank accountant is landed in a series of continental adventures by his eccentric life-loving aunt.
Busy but fairly disastrous adaptation of a delightful novel, ruined by ceaseless chatter, lack of characterization, shapeless incident and an absurdly caricatured central performance.

w Jay Presson Allen, Hugh Wheeler, *novel* Graham Greene *d* George Cukor *ph* Douglas Slocombe *m* Tony Hatch *pd* John Box

Maggie Smith, *Alec McCowen*, Lou Gossett, Robert Stephens, Cindy Williams
'It seems to run down before it gets started.'—*New Yorker, 1977*
AAN: Douglas Slocombe; Maggie Smith

La Traviata**
Italy 1982 109m colour

A much-acclaimed version of an opera which has previously defied transcription to the screen. Placido Domingo, Teresa Stratas, Cornell MacNeil, Allan Monk, Axell Gall. Written by Francesco Maria Piave from the opera by Verdi; designed and directed by *Franco Zeffirelli*; for Accent Films / RAI.
'Décors so opulent as on occasion to resemble a three-ring circus.'—*Sight and Sound*
AAN: costume design; art direction

Tread Softly Stranger*
GB 1958 91m bw
Alderdale (George Minter)

In a north country town, two brothers in love with the same girl rob a safe.
Hilarious murky melodrama full of glum faces, with a well-worn trick ending; rather well photographed.

w George Minter, Denis O'Dell, *play* Jack Popplewell *d* Gordon Parry *ph* Douglas Slocombe *m* Tristam Cary

George Baker, Terence Morgan, Diana Dors, Wilfrid Lawson, Patrick Allen, Jane Griffith, Joseph Tomelty, Norman Macowan

Treasure Hunt
GB 1952 79m bw
Romulus (Anatole de Grunwald)

The eccentric middle-aged members of an Irish family find their father's fortune is missing.
Theatrical comedy with some charm and humour, but very much a photographed play.

w Anatole de Grunwald, *play* M. J. Perry *d* John Paddy Carstairs *ph* C. Pennington-Richards *m* Mischa Spoliansky

Jimmy Edwards, *Martita Hunt, Athene Seyler*, Naunton Wayne, June Clyde, Susan Stephen, Brian Worth

Treasure Island**
US 1934 105m bw
MGM (Hunt Stromberg)

An old pirate map leads to a long sea voyage, a mutiny, and buried treasure.
Nicely mounted Hollywood version of a classic adventure story, a little slow in development but meticulously produced.

w John Lee Mahin, *novel* Robert Louis Stevenson *d* Victor Fleming *ph* Ray June, Clyde de Vinna, Harold Rosson *m* Herbert Stothart

Wallace Beery, Jackie Cooper, Lewis Stone, *Lionel Barrymore*, Otto Kruger, Douglass Dumbrille, Nigel Bruce, Chic Sale
'While much of it entrances, the whole is somewhat tiring.'—*Variety*
'The first three-quarters is so lively and well established in its mood as to make the whole quite worth going to.'—*Otis Ferguson*

Treasure Island*
GB 1950 96m Technicolor
Walt Disney (Perce Pearce)

Cheerful Disney remake, poor on detail but transfixed by a swaggeringly overplayed and unforgettable leading performance.

w Lawrence Edward Watkin *d* Byron Haskin *ph* F. A. Young *m* Clifton Parker *pd* Thomas Morahan

Robert Newton, Bobby Driscoll, Walter Fitzgerald, Basil Sydney, Denis O'Dea, Geoffrey Wilkinson, Ralph Truman
'Serviceable rather than imaginative.'—*Lindsay Anderson*
● *Video: Disney*

Treasure Island
GB / France / Germany / Spain 1971
95m colour
Massfilms / FDL / CCC / Eguiluz (Harry Alan Towers)

Spiritless and characterless international remake with poor acting, production and dubbing.

w Wolf Mankowitz, O. W. Jeeves (Welles) *d* John Hough *ph* Cicilio Paniagua *m* Natal Massara

Orson Welles, Kim Burfield, Lionel Stander, Walter Slezak, Rik Battaglia

The Treasure of Lost Canyon
US 1952 82m Technicolor
U-I (Leonard Goldstein)

A small boy robbed of his inheritance finds it with the help of a country doctor who turns out to be his uncle.
Modest juvenile adventure, rather boringly narrated.

w Brainerd Duffield, Emerson Crocker, *story* by Robert Louis Stevenson *d* Ted Tetzlaff *ph* Russell Metty *m* Joseph Gershenson

William Powell, Julia Adams, Charles Drake, Rosemary de Camp, Henry Hull, Tommy Ivo

Treasure of Matecumbe
US 1976 116m Technicolor
Walt Disney (Bill Anderson)

Two boys seek buried gold in the Florida keys.

Cheerful adventure tale with a few nods to *Treasure Island*; all very competent in the Disney fashion.

w Don Tait *d* Vincent McEveety *ph* Frank Phillips *m* Buddy Baker

Robert Foxworth, Joan Hackett, Peter Ustinov, Vic Morrow, Jane Wyatt, Johnny Duran, Billy Attmore

The Treasure of Pancho Villa
US 1955 96m Technicolor Superscope
RKO / Edmund Grainger

Mexico 1915: an American adventurer becomes involved with the revolutionary Pancho Villa; both seek a gold consignment but it is buried in an avalanche.
Modestly well made, routine action drama.

w Niven Busch *d* George Sherman *ph* William Snyder *m* Leith Stevens

Rory Calhoun, Shelley Winters, *Gilbert Roland*, Joseph Calleia

Treasure of San Teresa
GB 1959 81m bw
Orbit (John Nasht, Patrick Filmer-Sankey)

An American secret service agent finds Nazi loot in a Czech convent.
Roughly-made, watchable actioner.

w Jack Andrews, Jeffrey Dell *d* Alvin Rakoff *ph* Wilkie Cooper *m* Philip Martell

Eddie Constantine, Dawn Addams, Marius Goring, Christopher Lee, Walter Gotell

Treasure of the Golden Condor
US 1952 93m Technicolor
TCF (Jules Buck)

A young Frenchman flees to the South Seas but returns to discredit his wicked uncle.
Ineffectual remake of *Son of Fury* (qv) with Guatemalan backgrounds and no punch at all.

wd Delmer Daves *ph* Edward Cronjager *m* Sol Kaplan

Cornel Wilde, Finlay Currie, Constance Smith, George Macready, Walter Hampden, Anne Bancroft, Fay Wray, Leo G. Carroll

'Greed, gold and gunplay on a Mexican mountain of malice!'
'The nearer they got to their treasure the further they got from the law!'

The Treasure of the Sierra Madre**
US 1948 126m bw
Warner (Henry Blanke)

Three gold prospectors come to grief through greed.
Well-acted but partly miscast action fable on the oldest theme in the world; rather tedious and studio-bound for a film with such a high reputation.

wd John Huston, *novel* B. Traven *ph* Ted McCord *m* Max Steiner *md* Leo F. Forbstein

Humphrey Bogart, *Walter Huston*, Tim Holt, Alfonso Bedoya, John Huston, Bruce Bennett, Barton MacLane
'This bitter fable is told with cinematic integrity and considerable skill.'—*Henry Hart*

'The faces of the men, in close-up or in a group, achieve a kind of formal pattern and always dominate the screen.'—*Peter Ericsson*

'One of the very few movies made since 1927 which I am sure will stand up in the memory and esteem of qualified people alongside the best of the silent movies.'—*James Agee*

AA: John Huston (as writer and director); Walter Huston
AAN: best picture

A Tree Grows in Brooklyn••••
US 1945 128m bw
TCF (Louis D. Lighton)

Life for an Irish family with a drunken father in New York's teeming slums at the turn of the century.
A superbly-detailed studio production of the type they don't make any more: a family drama with interest for everybody.

w Tess Slesinger, Frank Davis, novel Betty Smith d Elia Kazan ph Leon Shamroy m Alfred Newman

Peggy Ann Garner, James Dunn, Dorothy McGuire, Joan Blondell, Lloyd Nolan, Ted Donaldson, James Gleason, Ruth Nelson, John Alexander, Adeline de Walt Reynolds, Charles Halton

'He tells a maximum amount of story with a minimum of film. Little touches of humour and human understanding crop up throughout.'—*Frank Ward, NBR*

AA: James Dunn
AAN: script

The Tree of Wooden Clogs•
Italy 1978 186m Gevacolor
RAI / GPC

In nineteenth-century Lombardy the lives of four peasant families are interwined.
Sensitive, novel-like investigation of times gone by; never very exciting but certainly never dull, despite the limits of 16mm and a non-professional cast.

w, d, ph Ermanno Olmi m from Bach

Trent's Last Case
GB 1952 90m bw
Wilcox–Neagle (Herbert Wilcox)

A journalist suspects that the death of a tycoon was murder.
Desultory version of a famous novel, with none of the original style and a few naïveties of its own.

w Pamela Bower, novel E. C. Bentley d Herbert Wilcox ph Max Greene m Anthony Collins

Michael Wilding, Margaret Lockwood, Orson Welles, John McCallum, Miles Malleson

Trial•
US 1955 109m bw
MGM (Charles Schnee)

A young lawyer defends a Mexican boy accused of rape and murder.
Stereotyped but pacy and watchable racial drama with political overtones, Our Hero having to resist bigots, Commies *and* McCarthyites.

w Don M. Mankiewicz, from his novel d Mark Robson ph Robert Surtees m Daniele Amfitheatrof

Glenn Ford, Dorothy McGuire, Arthur Kennedy, John Hodiak, Katy Jurado, Rafael Campos, Juano Hernandez, Robert Middleton, John Hoyt

AAN: Arthur Kennedy

The Trial•
France / Italy / West Germany 1962
120m bw
Paris Europe / Ficit / Hisa (Alexander Salkind)
original title: *Le Procès*

Joseph K is tried and condemned for an unspecified crime.
Kafka's nightmares tend to go on too long, and this film of one of them is no exception, despite its pin-screen prologue by Alexeieff and its inventive setting in the old Gare d'Orsay. Once again Welles the magician badly needs a Hollywood studio behind him.

wd, ed Orson Welles ph Edmond Richard m Jean Ledrut pd Jean Mandarut

Orson Welles, Jeanne Moreau, Anthony Perkins, Madeleine Robinson, Elsa Martinelli, Suzanne Flon, Akim Tamiroff, Romy Schneider

'The elaboration of scale and decor is as boring as in any biblical spectacular and for the same reason: because it is used without mind or feeling, not to bring out meaning but to distract us from asking for it.'—*Dwight MacDonald*

Trial by Combat
GB 1976 90m Technicolor
Warner / Combat (Fred Weintraub, Paul Heller)
aka: *Choice of Weapons*

An apparently harmless secret society of 'medieval knights' rededicates itself to the ritual execution of criminals who have escaped the law.
A rare specimen of comic macabre apparently inspired by the TV series *The Avengers*. Sadly, not much of it really works.

w Julian Bond, Steven Rossen, Mitchell Smith d Kevin Conner ph Alan Hume m Frank Cordell pd Edward Marshall

John Mills, Donald Pleasence, Peter Cushing, Barbara Hershey, David Birney, Margaret Leighton, Brian Glover

The Trial of Mary Dugan
US 1929 120m bw

Prosecution and defence counsel both change their feelings towards the girl on trial for murder. A cast-iron audience pleaser, this adapted stage play was the studio's first all-talking picture. It wouldn't stand the test of time. Norma Shearer, H. B. Warner, Raymond Hackett, Lewis Stone, Lilyan Tashman. Written by Bayard Veiller (and Becky Gardner) from his play; directed by Bayard Veiller; for MGM. (A 1940 remake directed by Norman Z. McLeod starred Laraine Day, Tom Conway, Robert Young, John Litel and Frieda Inescort, but was not a particular success.)

The Trial of Vivienne Ware
US 1932 56m bw

An attempt is made to kill a woman witness during a murder trial. Fast, complex courtroom murder mystery which even finds time for frequent bouts of comic relief. Joan Bennett, Donald Cook, Skeets Gallagher, Zasu Pitts, Lillian Bond, Alan Dinehart, Herbert Mundin, Noel Madison. Written by Philip Klein, Barry Connors, from the novel by Kenneth M. Ellis; directed by William K. Howard; for Fox. 'A skilful bit of claptrap melodrama.'—*Variety*

The Trials of Oscar Wilde••
GB 1960 123m Super Technirama 70
Warwick / Viceroy (Harold Huth)
US title: *The Man with the Green Carnation*

Oscar Wilde fatally sues the Marquis of Queensberry for libel, and loses; he is then prosecuted for sodomy.
Plush account of a fascinating event; narrative drive is unfortunately lacking, but one is left with interesting performances.

wd Ken Hughes ph Ted Moore m Ron Goodwin ad Ken Adam, Bill Constable

Peter Finch, Yvonne Mitchell, John Fraser, Lionel Jeffries, Nigel Patrick, James Mason, Emrys Jones, Maxine Audley, Paul Rogers, James Booth

Tribute•
Canada 1980 122m colour
TCF / Joel B. Michaels, Garth B. Drabinsky

A Broadway press agent comes to know his son by his divorced wife just as he comes to know of his own fatal illness.
Satisfactory screen treatment of a play which is really a vehicle for a charismatic star.

w Bernard Slade, from his play d Bob Clark ph Reginald H. Morris m various

Jack Lemmon, Lee Remick, Robby Benson, Colleen Dewhurst, Kim Cattrall, John Marley

AAN: Jack Lemmon
● Video: VTC

Tribute to a Bad Man
US 1956 95m Eastmancolor
Cinemascope
MGM (Sam Zimbalist)

A Wyoming horse breeder is callous in his treatment of rustlers, and wins the woman he wants when he becomes more understanding. Somewhere behind an unsympathetic story and hesitant development lies a convincing picture of life in the old west.

w Michael Blankfort, story Jack Schaefer d Robert Wise ph Robert Surtees m Miklos Rozsa

James Cagney, Irene Papas, Don Dubbins, Stephen McNally, Vic Morrow, Royal Dano, Lee Van Cleef

Trio*
GB 1950 91m bw
Rank / Gainsborough (Antony
  Darnborough)

Following *Quartet* (qv), three more stories
from Somerset Maugham: 'The Verger', 'Mr
Knowall', and 'Sanatorium'.
An enjoyable package, unpretentiously
handled but with full weight to the content.

w W. Somerset Maugham, R. C. Sherriff,
Noel Langley, *stories* W. Somerset Maugham
d Ken Annakin, Harold French *ph* Reg
Wyer, Geoffrey Unsworth *m* John
Greenwood *ad* Maurice Carter

James Hayter, Kathleen Harrison, Michael
Hordern, Felix Aylmer; *Nigel Patrick*, Anne
Crawford, Naunton Wayne, Wilfrid Hyde
White; *Michael Rennie, Jean Simmons, John
Laurie, Finlay Currie*, Roland Culver, Betty
Ann Davies, Raymond Huntley, André
Morell

The Trip*
US 1967 85m Pathecolor
AIP (Roger Corman)

A director of TV commercials tries LSD and
has hallucinations.
Much-banned plotless wallow, the ultimate
opt-out movie; well done for those who can
take it.

w Jack Nicholson *d* Roger Corman *ph* Arch
Dalzell *psychedelic effects* Peter Gardiner
montage Dennis Jakob

Peter Fonda, Susan Strasberg, Bruce Dern,
Salli Sachse, Dennis Hopper

Triple Cross
GB 1967 140m colour
Warner / Cineurop (Fred Feldkamp)

A small-time crook imprisoned on Jersey at
the start of World War II offers to spy for the
Nazis but reports to the English.
Ho-hum biopic of double agent Eddie
Chapman; effective scenes merely interrupt
the general incoherence.

w René Hardy, *book* The Eddie Chapman
Story by Frank Owen *d* Terence Young
ph Henri Alekan *m* Georges Garvarentz

Christopher Plummer, Yul Brynner, Trevor
Howard, Romy Schneider, Gert Frobe,
Claudine Auger

● *Video: VCL*

Triple Echo*
GB 1972 94m colour
Hemdale / Senta (Graham Cottle)

In 1942, a soldier's wife welcomes another
soldier to her farm for tea; he deserts and
poses as her sister.
Foolish story which would possibly have
worked as a TV play but hardly justifies a film
despite the talent on hand.

w Robin Chapman, *novel* H. E. Bates
d Michael Apted *ph* John Coquillon *m* Marc
Wilkinson

Glenda Jackson, Brian Deacon, Oliver Reed

● *Video: VCL*

The Triumph of Sherlock Holmes*
GB 1935 84m bw

Sherlock Holmes solves a murder stemming
from enmity between Pennsylvania coal
miners. Solidly satisfying adaptation of Conan
Doyle's *The Valley of Fear*, with more of
Moriarty added. Arthur Wontner, Ian
Fleming, Lyn Harding, Jane Carr, Leslie
Perrins, Michael Shepley. Written by H.
Fowler Mear; directed by Leslie Hiscott; for
Twickenham.

Triumph of the Will**
Germany 1936 120m bw
Leni Riefenstahl / Nazi Party

The official record of the Nazi party congress
held at Nuremberg in 1934.
A devastatingly brilliant piece of film-
making—right from the opening sequence of
Hitler descending from the skies, his plane
shadowed against the clouds. The rally scenes
are a terrifying example of the camera's power
of propaganda. After World War II it was
banned for many years because of general
fears that it might inspire a new Nazi party.

d, ed Leni Riefenstahl *ph* Sepp Allgeier and
36 assistants *m* Herbert Windt

Triumphs of a Man Called Horse
Spain 1982 89m CFI

Third in a dispensable series (*A Man Called
Horse*, *Return of a Man Called Horse*) of dour
westerns. In this scrappy item the man dies
early on, but his son upholds the tradition.
Richard Harris, Michael Beck, Ana De Sade,
Vaughn Armstrong, Buck Taylor. Written by
Ken Blackwell, Carlos Aured, Jack De Witt;
directed by John Hough; for Sandy Howard /
Redwing / Transpacific / Hesperia.

Tripoli
US 1950 95m Technicolor

In 1805 the United States sends marines to
rout the Barbary pirates. Not a superior
actioner, but it passed the time. John Payne,
Maureen O'Hara, Howard Da Silva, Philip
Reed, Grant Withers, Lowell Gilmore.
Written by Winston Miller; directed by Will
Price; for Pine-Thomas / Paramount.

Trog
GB 1970 91m Technicolor
Warner / Herman Cohen

A man-ape is discovered in a pothole and
trained by a lady scientist.
Ridiculous semi-horror film which degrades its
star.

w Aben Kandel *d* Freddie Francis
ph Desmond Dickinson *m* John Scott

Joan Crawford, Michael Gough, Bernard Kay,
David Griffin

The Trojan Women*
US 1971 111m Eastmancolor
Josef Shaftel (Michael Cacoyannis, Anis
  Nohra)

Troy has fallen to the Greeks and its women
bemoan their fate.

And oh, how they bemoan! Even with this
cast, Greek tragedy does not fill the big
screen.

w Michael Cacoyannis, *play* Euripides
d Michael Cacoyannis *ph* Alfio Contini
m Mikis Theodorakis

Katharine Hepburn, Vanessa Redgrave,
Geneviève Bujold, Irene Papas, Patrick
Magee, Brian Blessed, Pauline Letts

Tron*
US 1982 96m Technicolor Super
  Panavision 70mm
Walt Disney / Lisberger–Kushner

A computer games designer gets his revenge
on an enemy by fighting things out in the
computer world he has created.
Complicated science fantasy chiefly interesting
for its computerized blend of live action and
animation, which isn't always successful.

wd Steven Lisberger *ph* Bruce Logan
m Michael Femer *associate producer
(animation)* Harrison Ellenshaw *pd* Dean
Edward Mitzner

Bruce Boxleitner, Jeff Bridges, David Warner,
Barnard Hughes

  'Loaded with the expected visual delights,
but falls way short of the mark in story and
viewer involvement.'—*Variety*

AAN: costume design; sound

● *Video: Disney*

Trooper Hook
US 1957 92m bw
UA / Sol Baer Fielding

A woman prisoner of the Indians has a half-
breed son and becomes an outcast when
returned to her people.
Peculiar western with good moments, but
generally very slow and downbeat.

w Charles Marquis Warren, David Victor,
Herbert Little Jnr, *story* Jack Schaefer
d Charles Marquis Warren *ph* Ellsworth
Fredericks *m* Gerald Fried

Barbara Stanwyck, Joel McCrea, Earl
Holliman, Edward Andrews, John Dehner,
Susan Kohner, Royal Dano

'Estupendo! Magnifico! Esplendido!'
Tropic Holiday
US 1938 78m bw

A Hollywood scriptwriter finds romance in
Mexico. Musical time-filler with a bit of
everything and not much of anything. Ray
Milland, Dorothy Lamour, Bob Burns,
Martha Raye, Binnie Barnes, Tito Guizar.
Written by Don Hartman, Frank Butler, John
C. Moffett and Duke Atteberry; directed by
Theodore Reed; for Paramount. 'Will need
strong selling to top average business.'—
Variety

AAN: Boris Morros (music direction)

Tropic Zone
US 1953 94m Technicolor

In a banana port a man wanted by the police
saves a plantation from being taken over by

crooks. Tropical thick-ear, not entirely
unendurable. Written and directed by Lewis
R. Foster, from a novel by Tom Gill; for
Pine-Thomas / Paramount.

Trottie True*
GB 1949   98m   Technicolor
GFD / Two Cities (Hugh Stewart)
US title: *The Gay Lady*

Adventures of a Gaiety girl who married a
lord.
Self-conscious period comedy which could
have been highly diverting but manages only
to be sporadically charming in a whimsically
amateurish way.

w C. Denis Freeman, *novel* Caryl Brahms, S.
J. Simon d Brian Desmond Hurst ph Harry
Waxman m Benjamin Frankel ad Ralph
Brinton

Jean Kent, James Donald, Hugh Sinclair, Bill
Owen, Andrew Crawford, Lana Morris

Trouble along the Way
US 1953   110m   bw
Warner (Melville Shavelson)

A famous football coach is co-opted to help a
bankrupt college but some of his methods are
not quite above board.
American college comedy with dollops of
religiosity—a double threat.

w Melville Shavelson, Jack Rose d Michael
Curtiz ph Archie Stout m Max Steiner

John Wayne, Donna Reed, Charles Coburn,
Tom Tully, Sherry Jackson, Marie Windsor

'No opportunites for a laugh or a tear are
missed by the entire cast.'—*MFB*

Trouble Brewing*
GB 1939   87m   bw

A newspaper printer catches counterfeiters.
Lively star comedy. George Formby, Googie
Withers, Gus MacNaughton, Joss Ambler,
Martita Hunt, Garry Marsh, Ronald Shiner,
C. Denier Warren, Basil Radford. Written by
Anthony Kimmins, Angus MacPhail and
Michael Hogan; directed by Anthony
Kimmins; for ATP.

Trouble for Two*
US 1936   75m   bw
MGM (Louis D. Lighton)
GB title: *The Suicide Club*

A European prince in London for an arranged
wedding gets involved with an ingenious
organization for murder.
Light-hearted, black-edged Victorian literary
spoof which starts nicely but can't quite keep
up the pace.

w Manuel Seff, Edward Paramore Jnr, *stories*
New Arabian Nights by Robert Louis
Stevenson d J. Walter Rubin ph Charles G.
Clarke m Franz Waxman

Robert Montgomery, Rosalind Russell,
Reginald Owen, Frank Morgan, *Louis
Hayward*, E. E. Clive, Walter Kingsford

TROUBLE IN PARADISE.   Miriam Hopkins (centre) suspects her lover Herbert Marshall of
finding Kay Francis a new light in his life.

Trouble in Paradise***
US 1932   86m   bw
Paramount (Ernst Lubitsch)

Jewel thieves insinuate themselves into the
household of a rich Parisienne, and one falls in
love with her.
A masterpiece of light comedy, with sparkling
dialogue, innuendo, great performances and
masterly cinematic narrative. For
connoisseurs, it can't be faulted, and is the
masterpiece of American sophisticated
cinema.

w Samson Raphaelson, Grover Jones, *play*
The Honest Finder by Laszlo Aladar d Ernst
Lubitsch ph Victor Milner m W. Franke
Harling

*Herbert Marshall, Miriam Hopkins, Kay
Francis, Edward Everett Horton, Charles
Ruggles*, C. Aubrey Smith, Robert Greig,
Leonid Kinskey

'Swell title, poor picture. Better for the class
houses than the subsequents.'—*Variety*

'One of the gossamer creations of Lubitsch's
narrative art . . . it would be impossible in this
brief notice to describe the innumerable
touches of wit and of narrative skill with which
it is unfolded.'—*Alexander Bakshy*

'A shimmering, engaging piece of work . . .
in virtually every scene a lively imagination
shines forth.'—*New York Times*

'An almost continuous musical background
pointed up and commented on the action. The
settings were the last word in modernistic
design.'—*Theodor Huff, 1948*

Trouble in Store*
GB 1953   85m   bw
GFD / Two Cities (Maurice Cowan)

A stock assistant causes chaos in a department
store.
First, simplest and best of the Wisdom farces.

w John Paddy Carstairs, Maurice Cowan, Ted
Willis d John Paddy Carstairs ph Ernest
Steward m Mischa Spoliansky

Norman Wisdom, Jerry Desmonde, Margaret
Rutherford, Moira Lister, Derek Bond, Lana
Morris, Megs Jenkins, Joan Sims

● *Video:* Rank

Trouble in the Glen
GB 1954   91m   Trucolor
Republic / Wilcox–Neagle (Stuart
Robertson)

An Argentinian laird in a Scottish glen causes
ill-feeling.
Heavy-handed Celtic comedy whose
predictability and sentimentality could have
been forgiven were it not for the most garish
colour ever seen.

w Frank S. Nugent, *novel* Maurice Walsh
d Herbert Wilcox *ph* Max Greene *m* Victor
Young

Margaret Lockwood, Orson Welles, Forrest
Tucker, Victor McLaglen, John McCallum,
Eddie Byrne, Archie Duncan, Moultrie
Kelsall

The Trouble with Angels
US 1966 112m Pathecolor
Columbia / William Frye

Two mischievous new pupils cause trouble at a
convent school.
Fun with the nuns, for addicts only.

w Blanche Hanalis, *novel* Life with Mother
Superior by Jane Trahey *d* Ida Lupino
ph Lionel Lindon *m* Jerry Goldsmith

Rosalind Russell, Hayley Mills, June Harding,
Marge Redmond, Binnie Barnes, Gypsy Rose
Lee, Camilla Sparv, Mary Wickes, Margalo
Gillmore
  'A relentless series of prankish
escapades.'—*MFB*

The Trouble with Girls
US 1969 105m Metrocolor Panavision
MGM (Lester Welch)

In the twenties the manager of a travelling
chautauqua (educational medicine show) gets
involved in a small-town murder.
Curious vehicle for a very bored singing star,
with some interesting background detail.

w Arnold and Lois Peyser, *novel* The
Chautauqua by Day Keene, Dwight Babcock
d Peter Tewksbury *ph* Jacques Marquette
m Billy Strange

Elvis Presley, Marlyn Mason, Nicole Jaffe,
Sheree North, Edward Andrews, John
Carradine, Vincent Price, Joyce Van Patten

The Trouble with Harry**
US 1955 99m Technicolor Vistavision
(Paramount) Alfred Hitchcock

In the New England woods, various reasons
cause various people to find and bury the same
body.
Black comedy which never quite, despite
bright moments, catches the style of the book;
however, it is finely performed and the
autumnal backgrounds are splendid.

w John Michael Hayes, *novel* Jack Trevor
Story *d* Alfred Hitchcock *ph* Robert Burks
m Bernard Herrmann

Edmund Gwenn, Mildred Natwick, John
Forsythe, Shirley Maclaine, Mildred Dunnock

The Trouble with Women
US 1947 80m bw

A psychology professor thinks women enjoy
being treated rough; a lady reporter tests his
theories. Silly romantic comedy. Ray Milland,
Brian Donlevy, Teresa Wright, Rose Hobart,
Charles Smith, Iris Adrian, Lloyd Bridges.
Written by Arthur Sheekman, from a story by
Ruth McKenney; directed by Sidney Lanfield;
for Paramount.
† The film was completed in 1945, but held
from release for two years because of
overstock.

True as a Turtle
GB 1956 96m Eastmancolor
Rank (Peter de Sarigny)

Honeymooners join a variety of friends on a
yacht crossing the Channel, and get involved
in smuggling.
Artless, undemanding comedy for those who
like messing about in boats.

w Jack Davies, John Coates, Nicholas Phipps
d Wendy Toye *ph* Reg Wyer *m* Robert
Farnon

John Gregson, June Thorburn, Cecil Parker,
Elvi Hale, Keith Michell, Avice Landone

True Confession**
US 1937 85m bw
Paramount (Albert Lewin)

A fantasy-prone girl confesses to a murder she
didn't commit, and her upright lawyer
husband defends her.
Archetypal crazy comedy with fine moments
despite longueurs and a lack of cinematic
inventiveness. Remade as *Cross My Heart*
(qv).

w Claude Binyon, *play* Mon Crime by Louis
Verneuil, George Berr *d* Wesley Ruggles
ph Ted Tetzlaff *m* Frederick Hollander

Carole Lombard, Fred MacMurray, *John
Barrymore*, Una Merkel, Porter Hall, Edgar
Kennedy, Lynne Overman, Fritz Feld, *Irving
Bacon*
  'Not a big bet but a favourable enough one
. . . it just falls short of being a smash.'—
Variety
  'The best comedy of the year.'—*Graham
Greene*

True Confessions*
US 1981 108m colour
United Artists / Chartoff–Winkler (James D.
Brubaker)

A policeman working on a murder case finds
that his brother, a priest, is involved.
Unnecessary fictional elaboration on a real
Los Angeles murder case of the forties (the
'Black Dahlia'); chiefly notable for
performances.

w John Gregory Dunne, Joan Didion,
novel John Gregory Dunne *d* Ulu Grosbard
ph Owen Roizman *m* Georges Delerue
pd Stephen S. Grimes

Robert Duvall, Robert De Niro, Charles
Durning, Kenneth McMillan, Ed Flanders,
Cyril Cusack, Burgess Meredith

The True Glory****
GB / US 1945 90m bw
Ministry of Information / Office of War
Information

The last year of the war, retold by edited
newsreels: D-Day to the Fall of Berlin.
A magnificent piece of reportage, worth a
dozen fiction films in its exhilarating
Shakespearean fervour, though the poetic
commentary does occasionally go over the top.
One of the finest of all compilations.

w Eric Maschwitz, Arthur Macrae, Jenny
Nicholson, Gerald Kersh, Guy Trosper
d Carol Reed, Garson Kanin research Peter
Cusick w William Alwyn
  'Dwarfs all the fiction pictures of the
year.'—*Richard Mallett, Punch*
  'Bold, welcome but inadequate use of blank
verse; much more successful use of many bits
of individualized vernacular narration,
unusually free of falseness. Very jab-paced,
energetic cutting; intelligent selection of shots,
of which several hundred are magnificent.'—
James Agee
  'An inspiring recital of human endeavour
which all the world will want to see.'—*The
Cinema*

True Grit*
US 1969 128m Technicolor
Paramount / Hal B. Wallis (Paul Nathan)

In the old west, a young girl wanting to avenge
her murdered father seeks the aid of a hard-
drinking old marshal.
Disappointingly slow-moving and uninventive
semi-spoof western with a roistering
performance from a veteran star, who won a
sentimental Oscar for daring to look fat and
old.

w Marguerite Roberts, *novel* Charles Portis
d Henry Hathaway *ph* Lucien Ballard
m Elmer Bernstein

John Wayne, Kim Darby, Glen Campbell,
Dennis Hopper, Jeremy Slate, Robert Duvall,
Strother Martin, Jeff Corey
  'Readers may remember it as a book about
a girl, but it's a film about John Wayne.'—
Stanley Kauffmann
  'There is a slight consistent heightening or
lowering into absurdity, but there is also a
strong feeling for the unvarnished
preposterousness of everyday existence.'—
John Simon
† *Rooster Cogburn* featured more adventures
of the Wayne character, who also showed up
on TV in 1978 in the guise of Warren Oates
AA: John Wayne
AAN: title song (*m* Elmer Bernstein, *ly* Don
Black)

● *Video: CIC*

True Heart Susie*
US 1919 62m approx (24 fps) bw
silent
D. W. Griffith / Artcraft

A country girl sells her cow to send her boy
friend to college, but he is ungrateful.
Lavender-flavoured rustic romance, with the
director at his most sentimental. But of its
kind it is carefully done.

wd D. W. Griffith, *story* Marion Fremont
ph Billy Bitzer

Lillian Gish, Robert Harron, Clarine Seymour

The True Story of Jesse James
US 1956 92m Eastmancolor
Cinemascope
TCF (Herbert Swope Jnr)
GB title: *The James Brothers*

After the Civil War, Jesse and Frank James
become outlaws and train robbers.

Fairly slavish remake of *Jesse James*, without the style.

w Walter Newman *d* Nicholas Ray *ph* Joe MacDonald *m* Leigh Harline

Robert Wagner, Jeffrey Hunter, Hope Lange, Agnes Moorehead, John Carradine, Alan Hale Jnr, Alan Baxter

True to Life°
US 1943 93m Technicolor
Paramount (Paul Jones)

The writer of a radio soap opera moves in with an average family to get the right atmosphere. Quite a percipient comedy of its day, though it does not forgo the customary romantic entanglements.

w Don Hartman, Harry Tugend *d* George Marshall *ph* Charles Lang *m* Victor Young

Mary Martin, Dick Powell, Franchot Tone, Victor Moore, Mabel Paige, William Demarest, Clarence Kolb, Ernest Truex

True to the Navy
US 1930 70m bw

A drug store girl has too many sailor sweethearts for comfort. Very ordinary star vehicle, with little about it worth remembering next day. Clara Bow, Fredric March, Harry Green, Rex Bell, Eddie Fetherston. Written by Keene Thompson, Doris Anderson, Herman Mankiewicz; directed by Frank Tuttle; for Paramount. 'Hardly better than fair. Slow in tempo, sappy in story, and bearing the stamp of perfunctory production.'—*Variety*

The Trumpet Blows
US 1934 68m bw

A matador comes home to Mexico and quarrels with his bandit brother. Tedious melodrama with bullring scenes. George Raft, Adolphe Menjou, Frances Drake, Sidney Toler, Edward Ellis, Nydia Westman. Written by Bartlett Cormack, Wallace Smith, Porter Emerson Browne, J. Parker Read Jnr; directed by Stephen Roberts; for Paramount. 'Story weak, dialogue bad, casting hopeless.'—*Variety*

Trunk Crime
GB 1939 51m bw

A student goes mad and tries to bury his enemy alive. Now dated, but at the time a smart little programme-filler by an enterprising young producer-director team. Manning Whiley, Barbara Everest, Hay Petrie, Thorley Walters. Written by Francis Miller, from the play by Edward Percy and Reginald Denham; directed by Roy Boulting; produced by John Boulting; for Charter.

The Truth about Spring°
GB 1964 102m Technicolor
U-I / Quota Rentals (Alan Brown)

The bored nephew of a millionaire cruising in the Caribbean jumps at the chance to join friends on a scruffy yacht, but they all get involved with pirates.

Pleasing family film with good scenery and a friendly cast.

w James Lee Barrett, *novel* H. de Vere Stacpoole *d* Richard Thorpe *ph* Ted Scaife *m* Robert Farnon

Hayley Mills, James MacArthur, David Tomlinson, Lionel Jeffries, John Mills, Harry Andrews, Niall MacGinnis

The Truth about Women
GB 1957 107m Eastmancolor
British Lion / Beaconsfield (Sydney Box)

An old roué recounts to his son-in-law his early amorous adventures.
Tedious charade with neither wit nor grace.

w Muriel and Sydney Box *d* Muriel Box *ph* Otto Heller *m* Bruce Montgomery

Laurence Harvey, Julie Harris, Diane Cilento, Mai Zetterling, Eva Gabor, Michael Denison, Derek Farr, Roland Culver, Wilfrid Hyde White, Christopher Lee, Marius Goring, Thorley Walters, Ernest Thesiger, Griffith Jones
'It's amazing that with all those talented people nothing happens on the screen.'—*Pauline Kael, 70s.*

Try and Get Me°
US 1951 92m bw
(UA) Robert Stillman
GB title: *The Sound of Fury*

Two men are arrested for kidnapping and murder, and a journalist stirs the small town to lynch fury.
Harrowing, relentless melodrama, possibly the best on this subject.

w Jo Pagano, from his novel The Condemned *d* Cyril Endfield *ph* Guy Roe *m* Hugo Friedhofer

Frank Lovejoy, Lloyd Bridges, Kathleen Ryan, Richard Carlson, Katherine Locke, Adele Jergens, Art Smith
'The characterization and the handling of the drama are remarkable, at times reaching a complexity rare in films of this type.'—*Gavin Lambert*
'A strange, uncomfortable, sometimes brutal and depressing picture.'—*Richard Mallett, Punch*

The Trygon Factor°
GB 1966 88m Technicolor
Rank / Rialto Film / Preben Phillipsen (Ian Warren)

Bogus nuns plan a million pound bank raid. When you get used to its mixture of styles, this Anglo-German production is pretty good imitation Edgar Wallace, with bags of mystery and melodramatic goings-on involving larger than life characters most of whom come to sticky ends.

w Derry Quinn, Stanley Munro, Kingsley Amis *d* Cyril Frankel *ph* Harry Waxman *m* Peter Thomas

Stewart Granger, Susan Hampshire, Cathleen Nesbitt, Robert Morley, James Culliford, Brigitte Horney, Sophie Hardy, James Robertson Justice

Tudor Rose°
GB 1936 78m bw
GFD / Gainsborough (Michael Balcon)
US title: *Nine Days a Queen*

The brief life and reign of Lady Jane Grey. Modestly well made historical textbook.

w Robert Stevenson, Miles Malleson *d* Robert Stevenson *ph* Max Greene *m* Louis Levy

Cedric Hardwicke, Nova Pilbeam, John Mills, Felix Aylmer, Leslie Perrins, Frank Cellier, Desmond Tester, Gwen Frangcon Davies, Sybil Thorndike, Martita Hunt, Miles Malleson, John Laurie
'There is not a character, not an incident in which history has not been altered for the cheapest of reasons.'—*Graham Greene*

Tugboat Annie°°
US 1933 88m bw
MGM (Harry Rapf)

An elderly waterfront lady and her boozy friend smooth out the path of young love. Hilarious and well-loved comedy vehicle for two great stars of the period.

w Zelda Sears, Eve Greene, *stories* Norman Reilly Raine *d* Mervyn Le Roy *ph* Gregg Toland

Marie Dressler, Wallace Beery, Robert Young, Maureen O'Sullivan, Willard Robertson, Paul Hurst
'One of those rare naturals in the picture business—a flicker that sells itself immediately the stars' names go into the lights.'—*Variety*

Tulsa°
US 1949 88m Technicolor
Eagle–Lion (Walter Wanger)

The daughter of a cattle owner builds an oil empire.
Splendid Hollywood hokum of the second grade, very predictable but well-oiled.

w Frank Nugent, Curtis Kenyon *d* Stuart Heisler *ph* Winton Hoch *m* Frank Skinner

Susan Hayward, Robert Preston, Pedro Armendariz, Lloyd Gough, Chill Wills, Ed Begley
'Like a damp fuse, it produces a loud bang at the end of a long splutter.'—*Time*
'Meet Cherokee Lansing . . . half wildcat . . . half angel . . . all woman!'—*publicity*

Tumbleweeds°°
US 1925 80m (24 fps) bw silent
United Artists / William S. Hart

A wandering cowboy helps a family of settlers. The same plot as *Shane* works wonders in the last film of William S. Hart, which has the apparently authentic flavour of the old west.

w C. Gardner Sullivan, *story* Hal G. Evarts *d* King Baggott *ph* Joseph August

William S. Hart, Barbara Bedford, Lucien Littlefield, Monte Collins
† Reissued in 1939 with an added eight-minute introduction by Hart, showing how the west has changed.

Tunes of Glory**
GB 1960   107m   Technicolor
UA / Knightsbridge (Albert Fennell)

The new disciplinarian CO of a highland
regiment crosses swords with his lax, hard-
drinking predecessor.
Wintry barracks melodrama, finely acted and
well made with memorable confrontation
scenes compensating for a somewhat
underdeveloped script.

w James Kennaway, from his novel   d Ronald
Neame   ph Arthur Ibbetson

Alec Guinness, John Mills, Susannah York,
Dennis Price, Kay Walsh, *Duncan Macrae,*
Gordon Jackson, John Fraser, Allan
Cuthbertson

AAN: James Kennaway

The Tunnel*
GB 1935   94m   bw
Gaumont (Michael Balcon)
US title: *Transatlantic Tunnel*

Crooked finances mar the completion of an
undersea tunnel to America.
A rare example of British science fiction from
this period, though the film was in fact first
made in German and French versions, the
latter with Jean Gabin.

w Curt Siodmak, L. DuGarde Peach,
Clemence Dane, *novel* Bernard Kellerman
d Maurice Elvey   ph Gunther Krampf
m Louis Levy

Richard Dix, Leslie Banks, Madge Evans,
Helen Vinson, C. Aubrey Smith, George
Arliss, Walter Huston, Basil Sydney, Jimmy
Hanley

The Tunnel of Love
US 1958   98m   bw   Cinemascope
MGM / Joseph Fields

A husband applying to adopt an orphan thinks
he may, while drunk, have seduced the
glamorous orphan agency official.
Tasteless and not very funny comedy,
somewhat miscast.

w Joseph Fields,   *play* Joseph Fields, Peter de
Vries,   *novel* Peter de Vries   d Gene Kelly
ph Robert Bronner

Richard Widmark, Doris Day, Gig Young,
Gia Scala, Elizabeth Fraser, Elizabeth Wilson

Turkey Time
GB 1933   73m   bw

Family indiscretions come out at Christmas
time. Vehicle for fruity characterizations by
the popular Aldwych team, but not very
strong as a farce. Tom Walls, Ralph Lynn,
Robertson Hare, Dorothy Hyson, Mary
Brough, Norma Varden. Written by Ben
Travers, from his play; directed by Tom Walls;
for Gaumont.

Turksib*
USSR 1929   60m approx (24 fps)   bw
silent
Vostok Kino

The making of the Turkestan–Siberia railway.
A highly fluent and pictorial documentary with

an especially famous climax as the men
struggle to lay the last rails and meet a
deadline.

w Victor Turin and others   d Victor Turin
ph Yevgeni Slavinsky, Boris Frantzisson

Turn Back the Clock*
US 1933   80m   bw

A man dreams of changing places with his rich
friend. Unusual, quite pleasing comedy-
drama. Lee Tracy, Otto Kruger, Mae Clarke,
C. Henry Gordon, George Barbier. Written
by Edgar Selwyn and Ben Hecht; directed by
Edgar Selwyn; for MGM. 'Neatly turned
domestic comedy with a dramatic touch that
will please all round.'—*Variety*

Turn of the Tide*
GB 1935   80m   bw
British National (John Corfield)

A feud between two fishing families ends in
marriage.
Low-key, location-set action drama with a
moral. The film which brought J. Arthur Rank
into the business, which he saw had religious
possibilities.

w L. DuGarde Peach, J. O. C. Orton,
novel Three Fevers by Leo Walmsley
d Norman Walker

Geraldine Fitzgerald, John Garrick, Niall
MacGinnis, J. Fisher White, Joan Maude,
Sam Livesey, Wilfrid Lawson, Moore Marriott
'Cut to an hour, it should make an
acceptable second feature.'—*Variety*

Turn Off the Moon
US 1937   79m   bw

The proprietor of a department store is
persuaded by an astrologer to stage a big show
in celebration of his 25th anniversary. Thinly
structured musical with some acceptable gags
and turns. Charles Ruggles, Eleanore
Whitney, Johnny Downs, Kenny Baker, Phil
Harris and his Orchestra, Ben Blue, Andrew
Tombes, Marjorie Gateson, Grady Sutton,
Franklin Pangborn. Written by Marguerite
Roberts, Harlan Ware, Paul Gerard Smith,
Mildred Harrington; directed by Lewis Seiler;
for Fanchon / Paramount. 'B from title to
climax.'—*Variety*

Turn the Key Softly
GB 1953   81m   bw
GFD / Chiltern (Maurice Cowan)

The problems of three women released from
prison.
Soppy formula multi-drama with contrived and
uninteresting plots and characters.

w Jack Lee, Maurice Cowan,   *novel* John
Brophy   d Jack Lee   ph Geoffrey Unsworth
m Mischa Spoliansky

Yvonne Mitchell, Terence Morgan, Joan
Collins, Kathleen Harrison, Thora Hird,
Dorothy Alison, Glyn Houston, Geoffrey
Keen, Clive Morton

'Pardon my error, the stork meekly smiled,
I've overlooked wifey, gave hubby the
child!'

Turnabout*
US 1940   83m   bw
Hal Roach

A benevolent god enables a quarrelsome
couple to change bodies and see how they like
it.
'The man's had a baby instead of the lady',
said the ads. Well, not quite, but it did seem
pretty daring at the time, and it still provides a
hilarious moment or two.

w Mickell Novak, Berne Giler, John McLain,
novel Thorne Smith   d Hal Roach   ph Norbert
Brodine   m Arthur Morton

Adolphe Menjou, John Hubbard, Carole
Landis, Mary Astor, Verree Teasdale, Donald
Meek, William Gargan, Joyce Compton

Turned Out Nice Again
GB 1941   81m   bw

An employee teaches an underwear firm to
move with the times. Tolerable star comedy
from his late period. George Formby, Peggy
Bryan, Edward Chapman, Elliot Mason,
Mackenzie Ward, O. B. Clarence. Written by
Austin Melford, John Dighton and Basil
Dearden, from the play *As You Are* by Hugh
Mills and Wells Root; directed by Marcel
Varnel; for ATP.

The Turners of Prospect Road
GB 1947   88m   bw

A taxi driver's family greyhound wins a big
race. Uneasily cast domestic comedy drama.
Wilfrid Lawson, Jeanne de Casalis, Maureen
Glynne, Helena Pickard, Leslie Perrins, Peter
Bull. Written by Victor Katona and Patrick
Kirwan; directed by Maurice J. Wilson; for
Grand National.

The Turning Point*
US 1952   85m   bw
Paramount (Irving Asher)
Original title: *This is Dynamite!*

A young lawyer is appointed by the state
governor to smash a crime syndicate.
Familiar exposé drama of its time, quite crisply
done.

w Warren Duff   w William Dieterle
ph Lionel Lindon   md Irwin Talbot

William Holden, Alexis Smith, Edmond
O'Brien, Tom Tully, Ray Teal

'A story of envy, hatred, friendship,
triumph and love!'

The Turning Point*
US 1977   119m   De Luxe
TCF / Hera (Nora Kaye)

The American Ballet Theatre visits Oklahoma
City, and its ageing star revisits an ex-
colleague, now a housewife.
Posh person's soap opera, rather boringly
made and interesting only for its
performances, which are certainly vivid.

w Arthur Laurents   d Herbert Ross
ph Robert Surtees   m John Lanchbery
pd Albert Brenner

Anne Bancroft, Shirley Maclaine, Mikhail Baryshnikov, Leslie Browne, Tom Skerritt, Martha Scott, Marshall Thompson

'A backstage musical dressed up with smart cultural trimmings.'—*Alan Brien*

'We get a glimpse of something great in the movie—Mikhail Baryshnikov dancing—and these two harpies out of the soaps block the view.'—*New Yorker, 1978*

AAN: best picture; Herbert Ross; Robert Surtees; Anne Bancroft; Shirley Maclaine; Mikhail Baryshnikov; Leslie Browne

● *Video: CBS / Fox*

Twelve Angry Men**
US 1957 95m bw
(UA) Orion–Nova (Henry Fonda, Reginald Rose)

A murder case jury about to vote guilty is convinced otherwise by one doubting member. Though unconvincing in detail, this is a brilliantly tight character melodrama which is never less than absorbing to experience. Acting and direction are superlatively right, and the film was important in helping to establish television talents in Hollywood.

w Reginald Rose, from his play *d Sidney Lumet ph Boris Kaufman m Kenyon Hopkins*

Henry Fonda, Lee J. Cobb, E. G. Marshall, Jack Warden, Ed Begley, Martin Balsam, John Fiedler, Jack Klugman, George Voskovec, Robert Webber, Edward Binns, Joseph Sweeney

AAN: best picture; Reginald Rose; Sidney Lumet

The Twelve Chairs
US 1970 93m Movielab
UMC / Crossbow (Michael Hertzberg)

A Russian bureaucrat chases twelve dining chairs, in one of which is hidden the family jewels.

Tedious Mel Brooks romp with not too many laughs, from a yarn better handled in *Keep Your Seats Please* and *It's in the Bag*, from both of which he might have learned something about comedy timing.

w Mel Brooks, novel Ilf and Petrov d Mel Brooks ph Dorde Nikolic m John Morris

Ron Moody, Frank Langella, Dom De Luise, Bridget Brice, Diana Coupland, Mel Brooks

'In the end it runs out of both steam and jokes.'—*Michael Billington, Illustrated London News*

Twelve Good Men
GB 1936 64m bw

A convict escapes to murder the jury who convicted him. Solidly carpentered suspenser.
Henry Kendall, Nancy O'Neill, Percy Parsons, Morland Graham, Bernard Miles. Written by *Sidney Gilliat* and *Frank Launder* from the novel *Murders in Praed Street* by John Rhode; directed by Ralph Ince; for Warner.

TWENTIETH CENTURY. On a crowded train John Barrymore and Walter Connolly find two bearded intruders only one of the crazy problems they have to cope with.

'A story of twelve men as their women never knew them!'

Twelve O'Clock High*
US 1949 132m bw
TCF (Darryl F. Zanuck)

During World War II, the commander of a US bomber unit in Britain begins to crack under the strain.

Absorbing character drama, justifiably a big box office success of its day, later revived as a TV series. All production values are excellent.

w Sy Bartlett, Beirne Lay Jnr d Henry King ph Leon Shamroy m Alfred Newman

Gregory Peck, Hugh Marlowe, Gary Merrill, Millard Mitchell, Dean Jagger, Robert Arthur, Paul Stewart, John Kellogg

AA: Dean Jagger
AAN: best picture; Gregory Peck

● *Video: CBS / Fox*

Twentieth Century*
US 1934 91m bw
Columbia (Howard Hawks)

A temperamental Broadway producer trains an untutored actress, but when a star she proves a match for him.

Though slightly lacking in pace, this is a marvellously sharp and memorable theatrical burlesque, and the second half, set on the train of the title, reaches highly agreeable peaks of insanity.

w Ben Hecht, Charles MacArthur, play Napoleon of Broadway by Charles Bruce Millholland d Howard Hawks ph Joseph August

John Barrymore, Carole Lombard, Roscoe Karns, Walter Connolly, Ralph Forbes, *Etienne Girardot,* Charles Lane, Edgar Kennedy

'Probably too smart for general consumption . . . a long shot for grosses outside the large cities that boast a cosmopolitan clientele.'—*Variety*

'Notable as the first comedy in which sexually attractive, sophisticated stars indulged in their own slapstick instead of delegating it to their inferiors.'—*Andrew Sarris, 1963*

'In the role of Jaffe John Barrymore fits as wholly and smoothly as a banana in a skin.'—*Otis Ferguson*

The Twenty-Fifth Hour
France / Italy / Yugoslavia 1967 133m
Eastmancolor Franscope
Concordia / CCC / Avala / Carlo Ponti

When the Nazis deport Rumanian Jews, a simple-minded farmer is sent with them because the officer desires his wife. Peripatetic adventure with the storm-tossed hero flitting from one symbolic situation to another. All a bit much.

w Henri Verneuil, Wolf Mankowitz, François Boyer, *novel* C. Virgil Gheorghiu *d* Henri Verneuil *ph* Andreas Winding *m* Georges Delerue

Anthony Quinn, Virna Lisi, Grégoire Aslan, Michael Redgrave, Serge Reggiani, Marcel Dalio, Marius Goring, Alexander Knox, Liam Redmond, Meier Tzelniker, John Le Mesurier, Françoise Rosay

Twenty-Four Hours of a Woman's Life
GB 1952   90m   Technicolor
ABPC (Ivan Foxwell)
US title: *Affair in Monte Carlo*

A young widow tries to reform an inveterate gambler, but he kills himself.
Stilted, over-literary romantic melodrama with philosophical dialogue, flashback framing and Riviera settings.

w Warren Chetham Strode, *novel* Stefan Zweig *d* Victor Saville *ph* Christopher Challis *m* Robert Gill, Philip Green

Merle Oberon, Leo Genn, Richard Todd, Stephen Murray, Peter Illing, Isabel Dean

24 Hours
US 1931   65m   bw

A day in the life of an ultra-rich couple whose marriage has gone sour. Fairly slick matrimonial drama with an attempt at filmic treatment. Written by Louis Witzenkorn, from the novel by Louis Bromfield; directed by Marion Gering; for Paramount. Clive Brook, Kay Francis, Miriam Hopkins, Regis Toomey, George Barbier, Adrienne Ames. 'An absorbing bit of fiction that should engage the attention of the fan regulars and register abundantly at the box office.'—*Variety*

Twenty Million Miles to Earth
US 1957   82m   bw
Columbia / Morningside (Charles Schneer)

An American rocket ship returning from Venus breaks open and a scaly monster escapes into the Mediterranean and is cornered in the Roman coliseum.
Cheeseparing monster fiction which doesn't wake up till the last five minutes, and looks pretty silly even then.

w Bob Williams, Chris Knopf *d* Nathan Juran *ph* Irving Lippmann *m* Mischa Bakaleinikoff *sp* Ray Harryhausen

William Hopper, Joan Taylor, Frank Puglia, John Zaremba

Twenty Million Sweethearts
US 1934   89m   bw
Warner

Singing radio sweethearts are kept apart because of their images.
Thin musical with moderate numbers, remade as *My Dream Is Yours*.

w Warren Duff, Harry Sauber *d* Ray Enright *ph* Sid Hickox *songs* Harry Warren, Al Dubin

Dick Powell, Ginger Rogers, Pat O'Brien, the Mills Brothers, Ted Fio Rito and his band, the Radio Rogues, Allen Jenkins, Grant Mitchell
   'An entry the theatre boys won't have to worry about.'—*Variety*

Twenty Mule Team*
US 1940   84m   bw
MGM (J. Walter Ruben)

Rivalry among the borax miners in Death Valley.
Adequate semi-western with an unusual theme and setting.

w Robert C. DuSoe, Owen Atkinson *d* Richard Thorpe *ph* Clyde De Vinna *m* David Snell

Wallace Beery, Leo Carrillo, Marjorie Rambeau, Anne Baxter, Douglas Fowley, Berton Churchill, Noah Beery Jnr, Arthur Hohl, Clem Bevans, Charles Halton, Minor Watson

29 Acacia Avenue
GB 1945   83m   bw

Young people are having a good time when their parents return unexpectedly from holiday. Popular domestic comedy of its day. Gordon Harker, Betty Balfour, Carla Lehmann, Jimmy Hanley, Jill Evans, Hubert Gregg, Dinah Sheridan, Henry Kendall, Guy Middleton. Written by Muriel and Sydney Box, from the play by Mabel and Denis Constanduros; directed by Henry Cass; for Boca / Columbia.

Twenty-One Days*
GB 1937   75m   bw
London Films (Alexander Korda)
aka: *The First and the Last*

A barrister's brother accidentally kills a man and lets an old eccentric take the blame.
Watchable but very stilted melodrama with interesting early performances by Olivier and Leigh and a few good moments.

w Graham Greene, *play* The First and the Last by John Galsworthy *d* Basil Dean *ph* Jan Stallich *m* John Greenwood

Laurence Olivier, Vivien Leigh, Leslie Banks, Hay Petrie, Francis L. Sullivan, Esmé Percy, Robert Newton, Victor Rietti
   'I wish I could tell the extraordinary story that lies behind this shelved and resurrected picture, a story involving a theme song, and a bottle of whisky, and camels in Wales. Meanwhile let one guilty man, at any rate, stand in the dock, swearing never to do it again. . .'—*Graham Greene*
† The film was not shown until 1940.

The Twenty Questions Murder Mystery
GB 1949   95m   bw

A killer taunts the police with clues sent to a radio quiz show. Somewhat heavy comedy mystery with interest arising from the broadcasting background. Robert Beatty, Rona Anderson, Clifford Evans, Edward Lexy, Olga Lindo, Richard Dimbleby, Jack Train, Stewart MacPherson, Daphne Padel, Norman Hackforth, Jeanne de Casalis. Written by Patrick Kirwan and Victor Katona; directed by Paul Stein; for Pax-Pendennis.

Twenty Thousand Leagues under the Sea**
US 1954   122m   Technicolor
   Cinemascope
Walt Disney

Victorian scientists at sea are wrecked and captured by the mysterious captain of a futuristic submarine.
Pretty full-blooded adaptation of a famous yarn, with strong performances and convincing art and trick work.

w Earl Felton, *novel* Jules Verne *d* Richard Fleischer *ph* Franz Planer, Franz Lehy, Ralph Hammeras, Till Gabbani *m* Paul Smith *ad* John Meehan

Kirk Douglas, James Mason, Paul Lukas, Peter Lorre, Robert J. Wilke, Carlton Young, Ted de Corsia
● *Video: Rank*

Twenty Thousand Men a Year
US 1939   83m   bw

Experiences of recruits to college student aviation training. Very threadbare flagwaver. Randolph Scott, Preston Foster, Margaret Lindsay, Robert Shaw, Mary Healy, Kane Richmond, Maxie Rosenbloom, Sen Yung. Written by Lou Breslow, Owen Francis, Frank Wead; directed by Alfred E. Green; for Sol M. Wurtzel / Cosmopolitan / TCF. 'Needs exploitation as upper-bracket attraction.'—*Variety*

Twenty Thousand Years in Sing Sing**
US 1932   77m   bw
Warner (Robert Lord)

A tough criminal escapes from prison but his girl kills a man during the attempt, and he takes the blame.
Dated but fast-moving and still-powerful crime melodrama, remade to less effect as *Castle on the Hudson* (qv).

w Wilson Mizner, Brown Holmes, *book* Lewis E. Lawes *d* Michael Curtiz *ph* Barney McGill *m* Bernhard Kaun

Spencer Tracy, Bette Davis, Arthur Byron, Lyle Talbot, Louis Calhern, Warren Hymer, Sheila Terry, Edward McNamara
   'Good entertainment and good box office with that inside prison routine touch . . . Finally, it begins to appear Sing Sing wouldn't be a bad place at all to spend a vacation during the depression.'—*Variety*

'Somewhere in the fog there is a voice, a perfume, a glove, a knife—and a victim!'
Twenty-Three Paces to Baker Street*
US 1956   103m   Eastmancolor
   Cinemascope
TCF (Henry Ephron)

A blind playwright in a pub overhears a murder plot and follows the trail to the bitter end despite attacks on his life.
Sufficiently engrossing murder mystery with a weird idea of London's geography: the hero's Portman Square apartment has a balcony overlooking the Thames two miles away. Perhaps this is part of the script's light touch.

w Nigel Balchin, *novel* Philip MacDonald *d* Henry Hathaway *ph* Milton Krasner *m* Leigh Harline

Van Johnson, Vera Miles, *Cecil Parker,* Patricia Laffan, Maurice Denham, *Estelle Winwood,* Liam Redmond

Twice round the Daffodils
GB 1962 89m bw
Anglo Amalgamated / GHW (Peter Rogers)

Comic and serious episodes in the lives of male patients at a TB sanatorium.
Acceptable broadening, almost in *Carry On* style, of a modestly successful play.

w Norman Hudis, *play* Ring for Catty by Patrick Cargill, Jack Beale *d* Gerald Thomas *ph* Alan Hume *m* Bruce Montgomery

Juliet Mills, Donald Sinden, Donald Houston, Kenneth Williams, Ronald Lewis, Joan Sims, Andrew Ray, Lance Percival, Jill Ireland, Sheila Hancock, Nanette Newman

Twice Two
US 1933 20m bw

Stan and Ollie have each married the other's twin sister. . . . Strained and laboured trick comedy in which neither the double exposures nor the gags quite come off. Laurel and Hardy. Written by Stan Laurel; directed by James Parrott; for Hal Roach.

Twilight for the Gods
US 1958 120m Eastmancolor
U-I (Gordon Kay)

The captain of an old sailing ship takes her for a last voyage from Mexico to Tahiti.
Dull and miscast adventure story lacking the spark of the original novel; watchable only for the travelogue elements.

w Ernest K. Gann, from his novel *d* Joseph Pevney *ph* Irving Glassberg *m* David Raskin *md* Joseph Gershenson

Rock Hudson, Cyd Charisse, Arthur Kennedy, Leif Erickson, Charles McGraw, Ernest Truex, Richard Haydn, Wallace Ford, Celia Lovsky, Vladimir Sokoloff
  'Rock Hudson has difficulty in suggesting a dedicated seaman who has served under sail for thirty years.'—*MFB*

The Twilight Hour
GB 1944 85m bw

A nobleman's gardener turns out to be the amnesiac father of the girl about to marry into the family. Plodding and very predictable drama with popular cast. Mervyn Johns, Basil Radford, Marie Lohr, A. E. Matthews, Lesley Brook, Grey Blake. Written by Jack Whittingham, from a novel by Arthur Valentine; directed by Paul Stein; for British National.

Twilight of Honor
US 1963 115m bw Panavision
MGM / Perlsea
GB title: *The Charge Is Murder*

A young small-town lawyer defends a neurotic no-good on a murder charge.
Modest courtroom melodrama in which the detail is better than the main plot.

w Henry Denker, *novel* Al Dewlen *d* Boris Sagal *ph* Philip Lathrop *m* John Green
Richard Chamberlain, *Claude Rains,* Joey Heatherton, Nick Adams, Joan Blackman, James Gregory, Pat Buttram, Jeanette Nolan
AAN: Nick Adams

Twilight's Last Gleaming
US / West Germany 1977 146m Technicolor
Lorimar / Bavaria Studios (Helmut Jedele)

An ex-general commandeers an atomic missile plant and blackmails the president into telling some political truths.
Suspense thriller, fairly incompetent on its level and with ideas above its station. A distinctly overlong and unlikeable entertainment.

w Ronald M. Cohen, Edward Huebsch, *novel* Viper Three by Walter Wager *d* Robert Aldrich *ph* Robert Hauser *m* Jerry Goldsmith

Burt Lancaster, Richard Widmark, Charles Durning, Melvyn Douglas, Paul Winfield, Burt Young, Joseph Cotten, Roscoe Lee Brown, Gerald S. O'Loughlin, Charles Aidman

Twilight Zone: The Movie*
US 1983 101m Technicolor
Warner (Steven Spielberg, John Landis)

Four supernatural stories in the tradition of Rod Serling's long-running TV series of the fifties.
A disappointing collection on the whole, though with these talents what's on the screen is never quite boring.

w John Landis, George Clayton Johnson, Richard Matheson, Josh Rogan, Rod Serling *d* John Landis, Steven Spielberg, Joe Dante, George Miller *ph* Stevan Larner, Allen Daviau, John Hora *m* Jerry Goldsmith

Dan Aykroyd, Vic Morrow, Scatman Crothers, Bill Quinn, Kathleen Quinlan, Kevin McCarthy, John Lithgow
  'If there is an overriding irony to this catalogue of misfortunes, it is that the desire of four up-and-coming directors to honour TV as an imaginative source should have rebounded so disastrously on their cinematic reputations.'—*Richard Combs, MFB*

Twin Beds*
US 1942 84m bw
Edward Small

A married couple are embarrassed by the antics of a drunken neighbour.
Slight pretext for a pretty funny old-fashioned farce.

w Curtis Kenyon, Kenneth Earl, E. Edwin Moran, *play* Margaret Mayo, Edward Salisbury Field *d* Tim Whelan *ph* Hal Mohr *m* Dmitri Tiomkin

George Brent, Joan Bennett, *Mischa Auer,* Una Merkel, Glenda Farrell, Ernest Truex, Margaret Hamilton, Charles Coleman

The Twinkle in God's Eye
US 1955 73m bw
Republic (Mickey Rooney)

A parson rebuilds a church in a western town where his father was killed by Indians.
Amiable if unlikely western drama with the star more convincing than one might expect.

w P. J. Wolfson *d* George Blair *ph* Bud Thackery *m* Van Alexander

Mickey Rooney, Hugh O'Brian, Colleen Gray, Michael Connors, Don Barry

Twinky
GB 1969 98m Technicolor
Rank / World Film Services (Clive Sharp)
US title: *Lola*

A 16-year-old London schoolgirl marries a dissolute 40-year-old American author.
Dreary sex comedy drama, the fag end of London's swinging sixties.

w Norman Thaddeus Vane *d* Richard Donner *ph* Walter Lassally *m* John Scott

Charles Bronson, Susan George, Trevor Howard, Michael Craig, Honor Blackman, Robert Morley, Jack Hawkins
● *Video: Rank*

'They use the satanic power of their bodies to turn men and women into their blood slaves!'

Twins of Evil
GB 1971 87m Eastmancolor
Rank / Hammer (Harry Fine, Michael Style)

Identical Austrian twins become devotees of a vampire cult.
Vampire-chasing Puritans add a little flavour to a routine Hammer horror.

w Tudor Gates *d* John Hough *ph* Dick Bush *m* Harry Robinson

Madeleine and Mary Collinson, Peter Cushing, Kathleen Byron, Dennis Price, Isobel Black
● *Video: Rank*

Twist around the Clock
US 1961 83m bw
Columbia / Sam Katzman

An astute manager discovers a small-town dance called the twist and promotes it nationally.
Rock around the Clock revisited, with an even lower budget and fewer shreds of talent.

w James B. Gordon *d* Oscar Rudolph *ph* Gordon Avil *md* Fred Karger

Chubby Checker, the Marcels, Dion, John Cronin, Mary Mitchell

A Twist of Sand
GB 1968 91m De Luxe
UA / Christina (Fred Engel)

An ill-matched set of criminals seek hidden diamonds on Africa's skeleton coast.
Pattern melodrama of thieves falling out, quite nicely put together but with performances too high pitched.

m Marvin H. Albert, *novel* Geoffrey Jenkins *d* Don Chaffey *ph* John Wilcox *m* Tristam Cary

Richard Johnson, Honor Blackman, Roy Dotrice, Peter Vaughan, Jeremy Kemp

'Enough to make even Hitchcock jump!'

Twisted Nerve
GB 1968　118m　Eastmancolor
British Lion / Charter (John Boulting)

A rich, disturbed young man disguises himself as a retarded teenager in order to kill his hated stepfather.

Absurd, unpleasant, longwinded and naïvely scripted shocker, rightly attacked because it asserted that brothers of mongoloids are apt to become murderers. A long way behind the worst Hitchcock.

w Leo Marks, Roy Boulting d Roy Boulting ph Harry Waxman m Bernard Herrmann

Hayley Mills, Hywel Bennett, Phyllis Calvert, Billie Whitelaw, Frank Finlay, Barry Foster, Salmaan Peer

'Curious and in some respects disagreeable . . . never thrilling enough to reach the Hitchcock level and without sufficient medical credibility to be taken seriously as a case history.'—Michael Billington, Illustrated London News

● Video: Thorn EMI

Two a Penny
GB 1967　98m　Eastmancolor
World Wide (Frank R. Jacobson)

An idle art student becomes involved in the drug racket but finally sees the light. Naïve religious propaganda sponsored by the Billy Graham movement and featuring the evangelist in a cameo. A curiosity.

w Stella Linden d James F. Collier ph Michael Reed m Mike Leander

Cliff Richard, Dora Bryan, Ann Holloway, Avril Angers, Geoffrey Bayldon, Peter Barkworth

Two against the World
US 1936　64m　bw
Warner (Bryan Foy)
GB title: The Case of Mrs Pembroke

A gutter newspaper unnecessarily digs up a sordid murder case and causes the suicide of two people involved.
Remake of Five Star Final with the interest boringly shifted to the do-gooders who don't want to publish the story.

w Michel Jacoby, play Louis Weitzenkorn d William McGann ph Sid Hickox m Heinz Roemheld

Humphrey Bogart, Beverly Roberts, Helen MacKellar, Henry O'Neill, Linda Perry, Virginia Brissac

Two Alone
US 1934　72m　bw

The orphanage drudge on a remote farm gets herself pregnant. Heavy-going Cold Comfort Farm melodrama, with virtually no light relief in sight. Jean Parker, Tom Brown, Arthur Byron, Zasu Pitts, Beulah Bondi, Nydia Westman. Written by Josephine Lovett, Joseph Moncure March, from the play Wild Birds by Dan Totheroh; directed by Elliott Nugent; for RKO.

Two and Two Make Six
GB 1961　89m　bw
Bryanston / Prometheus (Monja Danischewsky)

Two motor cycling couples almost accidentally swap partners.
Reasonably fresh little romantic comedy.

w Monja Danischewsky d Freddie Francis ph Desmond Dickinson, Ronnie Taylor m Norrie Paramor

George Chakiris, Janette Scott, Alfred Lynch, Jackie Lynch, Malcolm Keen, Ambrosine Philpotts, Bernard Braden

Two Bright Boys
US 1939　69m　bw

A British boy and his father help an American boy save his oil ranch from a foreclosing villain. Traditional action stuff, quite pleasantly done for undemanding audiences. Jackie Cooper, Freddie Bartholomew, Melville Cooper, Dorothy Peterson, Alan Dinehart, Willard Robertson. Written by Val Burton, Edmund L. Hartman; directed by Joseph Santley; for Burt Kelly / Universal. 'Adequate support for the duals.'—Variety

The Two Faces of Dr Jekyll
GB 1960　88m　Technicolor　Megascope
Hammer (Anthony Nelson-Keys)
US title: House of Fright

A variation on the much-filmed story: the schizo's evil half is the more handsome. Surprisingly flat and tedious remake.

w Wolf Mankowitz, novel Robert Louis Stevenson d Terence Fisher ph Jack Asher m David Heneker, Monty Norman

Paul Massie, Dawn Addams, Christopher Lee, David Kossoff, Francis de Wolff

Two-Faced Woman*
US 1941　90m　bw
MGM (Gottfried Reinhardt)

A ski instructress who fears she may be losing her publisher husband to another woman poses as her own more vivacious twin sister. The failure of this scatterbrained comedy is alleged to be the reason for Garbo's premature retirement. Looked at half a century later, it is no great shakes but harmless and eager to please; what sabotages it is a shoddy production and flagging pace.

w S. N. Behrman, Salka Viertel, George Oppenheimer, play Ludwig Fulda d George Cukor ph Joseph Ruttenberg m Bronislau Kaper

Greta Garbo, Melvyn Douglas, Constance Bennett, Roland Young, Robert Sterling, Ruth Gordon, George Cleveland
'It is almost as shocking as seeing your mother drunk.'—Time

Two Fisted
US 1935　60m　bw

A prizefighter and his manager join a socialite's household as bodyguards. Flat comedy which doesn't get very far in any direction; a remake of the silent Is Zat So? Lee Tracy, Roscoe Karns, Grace Bradley,

Kent Taylor, Gail Patrick. Written by Sam Hellman, Francis Martin, Eddie Moran, from the play by James Gleason and Richard Taber; directed by James Cruze; for Harold Hurley / Paramount. 'Some periods of hilarity.'—Variety

Two Flags West*
US 1950　92m　bw
TCF (Casey Robinson)

Sixty Confederate prisoners of war are granted an amnesty and go west to fight the Indians. Laboured but good-looking Civil War western.

w Casey Robinson d Robert Wise ph Leon Shamroy m Hugo Friedhofer

Joseph Cotten, Jeff Chandler, Linda Darnell, Cornel Wilde, Dale Robertson, Jay C. Flippen, Noah Beery Jnr, Harry Von Zell
'Its period reconstruction is remarkable.'—Gavin Lambert

Two for the Road*
GB 1966　113m　De Luxe　Panavision
TCF / Stanley Donen

An architect and his wife motoring through France recall the first twelve years of their relationship.
Fractured, fashionable light romantic comedy dressed up to seem of more significance than the gossamer thing it really is; and some of the gossamer has a Woolworth look.

w Frederic Raphael d Stanley Donen ph Christopher Challis m Henry Mancini

Albert Finney, Audrey Hepburn, Eleanor Bron, William Daniels, Claude Dauphin

AAN: Frederic Raphael

Two for the Seesaw
US 1962　120m　bw　Panavision
UA / Seesaw / Mirisch / Argyle / Talbot (Robert Wise)

A New York dance instructress has a tempestuous affair with an Omaha attorney on the verge of divorce.
Serious comedy or light drama, meticulously detailed but immensely long for its content and too revealing of its stage origins.

w Isabel Lennart, play William Gibson d Robert Wise ph Ted McCord m André Previn ad Boris Leven

Robert Mitchum, Shirley Maclaine

AAN: Ted McCord; song 'Second Chance' (m André Previn, ly Dory Langdon)

Two for Tonight
US 1935　60m　bw

Three half-brothers write a play for a temperamental star. Much ado about nothing, but not an unpleasant way of passing an hour. Bing Crosby, Joan Bennett, Mary Boland, Lynne Overman, Thelma Todd, Ernest Cossart. Written by George Marion Jnr, Jane Storm, from the play by Max and J. O. Lief; directed by Frank Tuttle; for Douglas MacLean / Paramount. 'No wow . . . the songs, the fetching title, the competent cast and mostly Crosby will have to offset the other deficiencies.'—Variety

TWO-FACED WOMAN.   Greta Garbo and Melvyn Douglas are instantly attracted in a ski
lodge . . . but they're a long way from a happy ending.

Two Girls and a Sailor**
US 1944 124m bw
MGM (Joe Pasternak)

The title says it all.
Loosely-linked wartime musical jamboree with
first-class talent; a lively entertainment of its
type.

w Richard Connell, Gladys Lehman
d Richard Thorpe ph Robert Surtees
m George Stoll songs various

June Allyson, Gloria de Haven, Van Johnson,
Xavier Cugat and his Orchestra, *Jimmy
Durante*, Tom Drake, Lena Horne, Carlos
Ramirez, Harry James and his Orchestra, Jose
Iturbi, *Gracie Allen*, Virginia O'Brien, Albert
Coates

AAN: script

Two Girls on Broadway
US 1940 73m bw

A song and dance man breaks up a sister act.
Acceptable lower-case vaudeville musical

which rewrites the already wispy plot of
Broadway Melody. George Murphy, Joan
Blondell, Lana Turner, Kent Taylor, Wallace
Ford, Lloyd Corrigan. Written by Joseph
Fields and Jerome Chodorov; directed by S.
Sylvan Simon; for MGM. (GB title: *Choose
Your Partner*.)

Two Guys from Milwaukee
US 1946 90m bw

A young Balkan prince goes incognito in
Brooklyn and befriends a cab driver.
Rumbustious comedy with an amiable cast and
gag guest appearances. Dennis Morgan, Jack
Carson, Joan Leslie, Janis Paige, S. Z. Sakall,
Franklin Pangborn. Written by I. A. L.
Diamond and Charles Hoffman; directed by
David Butler; for Warner. (GB title: *Royal
Flush*.)

Two Guys from Texas
US 1948 86m Technicolor

Two vaudevillians find themselves on the run
from crooks. Little more than a peg on which
to hang some clowning and a few musical
numbers. Dennis Morgan, Jack Carson,
Dorothy Malone, Penny Edwards, Fred Clark,
Gerald Mohr, Forrest Tucker. Written by I.
A. L. Diamond and Allen Boretz; directed by
David Butler; for Warner. (GB title: *Two
Texas Knights*.)

The Two-Headed Spy*
GB 1958 93m bw
Columbia (Hal E. Chester)

A bogus Nazi worms his way into the Gestapo
hierarchy.
Adequate, not too exciting biopic of Colonel
Alex Schottland; standard production values.

w James O'Donnell d André de Toth ph Ted
Scaife m Bernard Schurmann

Jack Hawkins, Gia Scala, Alexander Knox,
Erik Schumann, Felix Aylmer, Laurence
Naismith, Donald Pleasence, Kenneth Griffith

Two in the Dark
US 1936 72m bw

An amnesiac tries to find out whether he was
involved in the murder of a theatrical
producer. Mildly intriguing mystery. Walter
Abel, Margot Grahame, Wallace Ford, Gail
Patrick, Alan Hale, Leslie Fenton, Eric Blore.
Written by Seton I. Miller from the novel by
Gelett Burgess; directed by Ben Stoloff; for
RKO. 'A programmer that'll suit both
audiences and b.o. outside of larger first
runs.'—*Variety*

Two Lane Blacktop
US 1971 103m Technicolor scope
Universal / Michael S. Laughlin

In the American southwest, the aimless
owners of two souped-up cars have an
interminable race.
Occasionally arresting, generally boring
eccentricity by a big studio looking for another
Easy Rider.

w Rudolph Wurlitzer, Will Corry d Monte
Hellman ph Jack Deerson m Billy James

James Taylor, Warren Oates, Laurie Bird,
Dennis Wilson

Two Left Feet
GB 1963   93m   bw
British Lion / Roy Baker (Leslie Gilliat)

A callow 19-year-old has girl trouble.
Ponderous sex comedy with no apparent
purpose but some well observed scenes.

w Roy Baker, John Hopkins, *novel* In My
Solitude by David Stuart Leslie   d Roy Baker
ph Wilkie Cooper   m Philip Green

Michael Crawford, Nyree Dawn Porter, Julia
Foster, David Hemmings, Dilys Watling,
David Lodge, Bernard Lee

Two Loves
US 1961   100m   Metrocolor
   Cinemascope
MGM / Julian Blaustein
GB title: *Spinster*

An American teacher in New Zealand teaches
Maoris and whites and falls for two men.
Pretentious romantic drama with unspeakable
dialogue and eccentric characters.

w Ben Maddow, *novel* Sylvia Ashton Warner
d Charles Walters   ph Joseph Ruttenberg
m Bronislau Kaper

Shirley Maclaine, Jack Hawkins, Laurence
Harvey, Nobu McCarthy

'91,000 people . . . 33 exit gates . . . one
   sniper!'
Two Minute Warning
US 1976   115m   Technicolor
   Panavision
Universal / Filmways (Edward S. Feldman)

A sniper terrifies the crowd at a championship
football game.
Smartly directed but weakly plotted and
scripted disaster movie: the mystery gunman
remains a mystery at the end.

w Edward Hume, *novel* George LaFountaine
d Larry Peerce   ph Gerald Hirschfeld
m Charles Fox

Charlton Heston, John Cassavetes, Martin
Balsam, Beau Bridges, David Janssen,
Marilyn Hassett, Jack Klugman, Gena
Rowlands, Walter Pidgeon, Brock Peters,
Mitch Ryan
   'Even by the standards of exploitation
movies, this film is an unusually dehumanizing
experience. Not only does it exist solely for its
gore, but it reduces the victims to the
dimensions of plastic ducks at a shooting
gallery.'—*Frank Rich, New York Post*

The Two Mrs Carrolls
US 1945 (released 1947)   99m   bw
Warner (Mark Hellinger)

A psychopathic artist paints his wives as the
Angel of Death, then murders them with
poisoned milk.
Stilted film of an old warhorse of a play,
unhappily cast but working up some last-
minute tension.

w Thomas Job, *play* Martin Vale   d Peter
Godfrey   ph Peverell Marley   m Franz
Waxman

Barbara Stanwyck, Humphrey Bogart, Alexis
Smith, Nigel Bruce, Isobel Elsom, Pat
O'Moore, Peter Godfrey

Two Mules for Sister Sara
US 1969   116m   Technicolor
   Panavision
Universal / Malpaso (Martin Rackin)

A wandering cowboy kills three men trying to
rape a nun, but she is not what she seems.
Vaguely unsatisfactory western with patches of
nasty brutality leading to an action-packed
climax.

w Albert Maltz, Budd Boetticher   d Don
Siegel   ph Gabriel Figueroa, Gabriel Torres
m Ennio Morricone

Clint Eastwood, Shirley Maclaine, Manolo
Fabregas, Alberto Morin

Two O'Clock Courage
US 1945   66m   bw

An amnesia victim is suspected of killing a
Broadway producer. Tepid murder mystery.
Tom Conway, Ann Rutherford, Richard
Lane, Roland Drew, Emory Parnell, Jane
Greer. Written by Robert E. Kent, from a
story by Gelett Burgess; directed by Anthony
Mann; for Ben Stoloff / RKO.

Two of a Kind
US 1951   75m   bw
Columbia (William Dozier)

A man is picked up by a glamorous girl who
involves him in an elaborate scheme to
defraud an elderly couple.
Modest suspenser.

w Lawrence Kimble, James Grunn   d Henry
Levin   ph Burnett Guffey   m George Duning

Edmond O'Brien, Lizabeth Scott, Terry
Moore, Alexander Knox, Griff Barnett,
Virginia Brissac

Two of a Kind
US 1983   87m   De Luxe
TCF (Roger M. Rothstein, Joe Wizan)

Four angels propose that Earth be spared from
a second flood if two arbitrarily chosen human
beings can be seen to perform a great sacrifice
for each other.
Curious reversion to angelic comedies of the
thirties and forties. Lacking the right measures
of wit and whimsy, it is totally unsuccessful.

w John Herzfeld   d John Herzfeld   ph Fred
Koenekamp, Warren Rothenberger
md Patrick Williams   pd Albert Brenner

John Travolta, Olivia Newton-John, Charles
Durning, Oliver Reed, Beatrice Straight,
Scatman Crothers
   'It feels as if it must be a remake of
something . . .'—*Sheila Johnston, MFB*

Two on a Guillotine°
US 1965   107m   bw   Panavision
Warner (William Conrad)

An illusionist arranges to be chained into his
coffin at his funeral but promises to return
from the dead.
Longwinded and unconvincing shocker with
some effectively scary sequences.

w Henry Slesar, John Kneubuhl   d William
Conrad   ph Sam Leavitt   m Max Steiner

Connie Stevens, Dean Jones, Cesar Romero,
Parley Baer, Virginia Gregg, Connie Gilchrist,
John Hoyt

'They had just 36 hours to share the love of
   a lifetime!'
Two People
US 1973   100m   Technicolor
Universal (Robert Wise)

An army deserter returns home and falls for a
fashion photographer.
Solemn, inconsequential topical drama which
made no impact whatever.

w Richard de Roy   d Robert Wise   ph Gerald
Hirschfeld   m David Shire

Peter Fonda, Lindsay Wagner, Estelle
Parsons, Alan Fudge
   'Sluggish pacing, lifeless looping and
terminally ludicrous dialogue eventually turn
the film into a travesty of its own form.'—
Variety

Two Rode Together
US 1961   109m   Technicolor
Columbia / John Ford / Shpetner

An army commander and a tough marshal
negotiate with Comanches for the return of
prisoners.
Substandard Ford, moderately good-looking
but uninteresting of plot and dreary of
development.

w Frank Nugent, *novel* Will Cook   d John
Ford   ph Charles Lawton Jnr   m George
Duning

James Stewart, Richard Widmark, Shirley
Jones, Linda Cristal, Andy Devine, John
McIntire

Two Seconds°
US 1932   68m   bw
Warner

In the last two seconds of his life a criminal
reviews the events leading up to his execution.
Competent, pacy crime melodrama.

w Harvey Thew, *play* Elliott Lester   d Mervyn
Le Roy   ph Sol Polito

Edward G. Robinson, Preston Foster,
Vivienne Osborne, J. Carrol Naish, Guy
Kibbee, Adrienne Dare
   'General slowness and stodgy overdramatics
won't draw the flaps, nor will a tragic finale
help.'—*Variety*
   'A film that compels attention.'—*Mordaunt
Hall, New York Times*

Two Sisters from Boston°
US 1946   112m   bw
MGM (Joe Pasternak)

Two girls visiting New York find work in a
Bowery saloon.
Nicely-detailed turn-of-the-century musical
with pleasant talent.

w Myles Connolly   d Henry Koster
ph Robert Surtees   md Charles Previn
songs Sammy Fain, Ralph Freed

June Allyson, Kathryn Grayson, Lauritz
Melchior, Jimmy Durante, Peter Lawford,
Ben Blue

Two Smart People
US 1946 93m bw
MGM (Ralph Wheelwright)

A con man on parole in New Orleans is chased by a lady crook in search of his hidden loot. Dog-eared comedy drama.

w Ethel Hill, Leslie Charteris *d* Jules Dassin *ph* Karl Freund *m* George Bassman

Lucille Ball, John Hodiak, Lloyd Nolan, Hugo Haas, Lenore Ulric, Elisha Cook Jnr, Lloyd Corrigan, Vladimir Sokoloff

Two Tars****
US 1928 20m bw silent

Two sailors in an old banger cause a traffic jam and a consequent escalation of violence. Marvellous elaboration of a tit-for-tat situation, with the stars already at their technical best. Laurel and Hardy, Edgar Kennedy, Charley Rogers. Written by Leo McCarey and H. M. Walker; directed by James Parrott; for Hal Roach.

2001: A Space Odyssey***
GB 1968 141m Metrocolor Panavision
MGM / Stanley Kubrick (Victor Lyndon)

From ape to modern space scientist, mankind has striven to reach the unattainable.
A lengthy montage of brilliant model work and obscure symbolism, this curiosity slowly gathered commercial momentum and came to be cherished by longhairs who used it as a trip without LSD.

w Stanley Kubrick, Arthur C. Clarke, *story* The Sentinel by Arthur C. Clarke *d* Stanley Kubrick *ph* Geoffrey Unsworth, John Alcott *m* various classics *pd* Tony Masters, Harry Lange, Ernie Archer *ad* John Hoesli

Gary Lockwood, Keir Dullea, William Sylvester, Leonard Rossiter, Robert Beaty, Daniel Richter

'Somewhere between hypnotic and immensely boring.'—*Renata Adler*
'Morally pretentious, intellectually obscure and inordinately long . . . intensely exciting visually, with that peculiar artistic power which comes from obsession . . . a film out of control, an infuriating combination of exactitude on small points and incoherence on large ones.'—*Arthur Schlesinger Jnr*
'The satire throughout is tepid and half-hearted, and tends to look like unintended stupidity.'—*John Simon*

AAN: script; Stanley Kubrick

● *Video: MGM / UA*

2010
US 1984 114m Metrocolor Panavision
MGM-UA (Peter Hyams)

With Earth on the brink of war, scientists return to Jupiter to decide on the fate of *Discovery* and the meaning of the black monolith.
Tame, almost flatfooted sequel to *2001: A Space Odyssey*, with none of the supposed significance and not much else to offer.

w,d Peter Hyams, *novel* Arthur C. Clarke *m* David Shire *pd* Albert Brenner *ed* James Mitchell

Roy Scheider, John Lithgow, Helen Mirren, Bob Balaban, Keir Dullea, Dana Elcar, Madolyn Smith

Two Thousand Women
GB 1944 97m bw
GFD / Gainsborough (Edward Black)

Two pilots try to rescue British women from a French concentration camp.
Routine mix of laughter and tears; hardly an outstanding film of its time, but mildly entertaining.

wd Frank Launder *ph* Jack Cox *md* Louis Levy

Phyllis Calvert, Flora Robson, Patricia Roc, Renée Houston, Anne Crawford, Jean Kent, James McKechnie, Reginald Purdell, Robert Arden, Thora Hird, Dulcie Gray, Carl Jaffe, Muriel Aked

Two Tickets to Broadway
US 1951 106m Technicolor
RKO (Jerry Wald)

Small-town college girl finds romance and success in the big city.
Very mild musical with TV studio backdrop.

w Sid Silvers, Hal Kanter *d* James V. Kern *ph* Edward Cronjager, Harry J. Wild *m* Walter Scharf

Janet Leigh, Eddie Bracken, Gloria de Haven, Tony Martin, Barbara Lawrence, *Joe Smith and Charlie Dale*

Two Tickets to London
US 1943 78m bw

A sailor accused of aiding an enemy submarine escapes and finds the true villain.
Routine wartime thick-ear. Alan Curtis, Michele Morgan, C. Aubrey Smith, Barry Fitzgerald, Dooley Wilson, Mary Gordon. Written by Tom Reed; directed by Edwin L. Marin; for Universal.

Two Way Stretch**
GB 1960 87m bw
British Lion / Shepperton (M. Smedley Aston)

Three convicts break jail to rob a maharajah.
Amusing comedy with good performances and situations, unofficially borrowed in part from *Convict 99*.

w John Warren, Len Heath *d* Robert Day *ph* Geoffrey Faithfull *m* Ken Jones

Peter Sellers, *Lionel Jeffries*, Wilfrid Hyde White, Bernard Cribbins, David Lodge, Maurice Denham, Beryl Reid, Liz Fraser, Irene Handl, George Woodbridge

● *Video: Thorn EMI*

Two Weeks in Another Town*
US 1962 107m Metrocolor
   Cinemascope
MGM (John Houseman)

An ex-alcoholic film director gets his comeback chance in Rome but is plagued by old memories.
Self-indulgent melodrama with entertaining patches for *cinéastes*, especially those who saw *The Bad and the Beautiful*.

w Charles Schnee, *novel* Irwin Shaw *d* Vincente Minnelli *ph* Milton Krasner *m* David Raksin

Kirk Douglas, Edward G. Robinson, Cyd Charisse, Daliah Lavi, George Hamilton, Claire Trevor, Rosanna Schiaffino, James Gregory, George Macready

Two Weeks with Love*
US 1950 92m Technicolor
MGM (Jack Cummings)

Adventures on a family summer holiday at the turn of the century.
Pleasant family musical.

w John Larkin, Dorothy Kingsley *d* Roy Rowland *ph* Al Gilks *m* Georgie Stoll

Jane Powell, Ricardo Montalban, Louis Calhern, Ann Harding, Phyllis Kirk, Debbie Reynolds, Carleton Carpenter, Clinton Sundberg

Two Who Dared
GB 1937 75m bw

A Russian officer finds that the nurse of his child is the girl he once loved. Turgid romance with nothing to lighten it, certainly not the heavy-handed stars. Anna Sten, Henry Wilcoxon, John Garrick, Viola Keats, Guy Middleton, Francis L. Sullivan, Esme Percy, Peter Gawthorne. Written by Warren Chetham Strode; directed by Fedor Ozep; for Eugene Frenke / Grand National. 'Not of the timber that will rate attention in first-class houses . . . everybody broods.'—*Variety*

Two Women*
Italy / France 1960 110m bw
Champion / Marceau / Cocinor / SGC (Carlo Ponti)
original title: *La Ciociara*

During the Allied bombing of Rome a woman and her daughter travel arduously south and have a hard time at the hands of invading soldiers.
Rather hysterical character drama allowing for a splendid top-note performance from its star.

w Cesare Zavattini, Vittorio de Sica, *novel* Alberto Moravia *d* Vittorio de Sica *ph* Gabor Pogany *m* Armando Trovaioli

Sophia Loren, Eleonora Brown, Jean-Paul Belmondo, Raf Vallone

AA: Sophia Loren

Two Years before the Mast*
US 1946 98m bw
Paramount

In the mid-19th century, a writer becomes a sailor to expose bad conditions.
Well-made but unconvincing-looking picturization of a famous book.

w Seton I. Miller, George Bruce, *book*
Richard Henry Dana *d* John Farrow
ph Ernest Laszlo *m* Victor Young

Alan Ladd, Brian Donlevy, William Bendix,
Barry Fitzgerald, Howard da Silva, Albert
Dekker, Luis Van Rooten, Darryl Hickman

Two's Company
GB 1936 74m bw

An earl's son loves the daughter of an
American millionaire. Not particularly
successful hands-across-the-sea comedy.
Gordon Harker, Ned Sparks, Mary Brian,
Patric Knowles, Robb Wilton, Morton Selten.
Written by Tom Geraghty. Roland Pertwee,
J. B. Morton, John Paddy Carstairs and Tim

Whelan, from the novel *Romeo and Julia* by
Sidney Horler; directed by Tim Whelan; for
Paul Soskin / B and D.

Tycoon
US 1947 129m Technicolor
RKO

An engineer is hired to drive a tunnel through
the Andes, and starts a feud with his boss
when he falls in love with his daughter.
Boring, studio-set action saga with too many
stops for romance.

w Borden Chase, John Twist *d* Richard
Wallace *ph* Harry J. Wild *m* Leigh Harline

John Wayne, Cedric Hardwicke, Laraine Day,
James Gleason, Judith Anderson, Anthony
Quinn, Grant Withers

● *Video: Kingston*

Typhoon
US 1940 70m Technicolor
Paramount (Anthony Veiller)

On a Dutch Guianan island, two sailors find a
girl who has been a castaway since childhood.
One of Lamour's several sarongers, quite
entertaining in its way and commendably
brisk.

w Allen Rivkin *d* Louis King *ph* William
Mellor *m* Frederick Hollander

Dorothy Lamour, Robert Preston, Lynne
Overman, J. Carrol Naish, Frank Reicher
  'One of the most emphatically silly pictures
I ever saw in my life.'—*Richard Mallet, Punch*
  'The gem of pure, pellucid silliness.'—*James
Agate*

Ugetsu Monogatari*
Japan 1953 94m bw
Daiei (Masaichi Nagata)

During a 16th century civil war two potters find a way of profiteering, but their ambitions bring disaster on their families.
Unique mixture of action, comedy and the supernatural, with strong, believable characters participating and a delightfully delicate touch in script and direction. On its first release it began to figure in many best ten lists, but quickly seemed to fade from public approbation.

w Matsutaro Kawaguchi, from 17th-century collection by Akinara Ueda, Tales of a Pale and Mysterious Moon after the Rain d Kenji Mizoguchi ph Kazuo Miyagawa m Fumio Hayasaka

Masayuki Mori, Machiko Kyo, Sakae Ozawa, Mitsuko Mito

The Ugly American
US 1962 120m Eastmancolor
U-I / George Englund

A publisher is made ambassador to a south-east Asian state.
Self-dating anti-communist drama which was muddled and boring when new.

w Stewart Stern, novel William J. Lederer, Eugene Burdick d George Englund ph Clifford Stine m Frank Skinner

Marlon Brando, Eiji Okada, Sandra Church, Pat Hingle, Arthur Hill, Jocelyn Brando, Kukrit Pramoj

The Ugly Dachshund*
US 1965 93m Technicolor
Walt Disney (Winston Hibler)

A dachshund bitch fosters among its puppies an orphan Great Dane.
Cheerful, fast-moving animal farce.

w Albert Aley, novel G. B. Stern d Norman Tokar ph Edward Colman m George Bruns

Dean Jones, Suzanne Pleshette, Charles Ruggles, Kelly Thordsen, Parley Baer, Mako, Charles Lane

● Video: Rank

The Ultimate Warrior
US 1975 94m Technicolor
Warner (Fred Weintraub, Paul Heller)

In AD 2012 New York is ruled by a gangster, the atmosphere is poisoned, and the only hope is a new community on an island off North Carolina.

Curious pretentious fantasy without the courage of its convictions or much entertainment value.

wd Robert Clouse ph Gerald Hirschfeld m Gil Melle

Yul Brynner, Max Von Sydow, Joanna Miles, William Smith, Richard Kelton, Stephen McHattie
'Less a prophetic vision than a kind of thick-ear West Side Story.'—Richard Combs

'Actually filmed along the route he travelled 3000 years ago!'

Ulysses*
Italy 1954 103m Technicolor
Lux Film / Ponti—de Laurentiis (Fernando Cinquini)

Ulysses and his crew sail under the curse of Cassandra, and encounter Circe, the sirens and the cyclops.
Peripatetic adventure yarn not too far after Homer; narrative style uncertain but highlights good.

w Franco Brusati, Mario Camerini, Ennio de Concini, Hugh Gray, Ben Hecht, Ivo Perelli, Irwin Shaw, poem The Odyssey by Homer d Mario Camerini ph Harold Rosson m Alessandro Cicognini

Kirk Douglas, Silvana Mangano, Anthony Quinn, Rosanna Podesta

● Video: Video Media

Ulysses*
GB 1967 132m bw Panavision
Walter Reade (Joseph Strick)

Twenty-four hours in Dublin with a young poet and a Jewish newspaper man.
A pleasant enough literary exercise, a decent précis of an unmanageably prolix classic novel, this specialized offering would have passed unnoticed were it not for its language, which got it banned in many places but now seems mild indeed.

w Joseph Strick, Fred Haines, novel James Joyce d Joseph Strick ph Wolfgang Suschitzky m Stanley Myers

Maurice Roeves, Milo O'Shea, Barbara Jefford, T. P. McKenna, Anna Manahan, Maureen Potter
'No amount of pious invoking of Joyce's name can disguise the fact that a cheaply produced film is being sold at exorbitant prices so that someone can make his boodle off "culture".'—John Simon

'An act of homage in the form of readings from the book plus illustrated slides.'—Pauline Kael
'A facile and ludicrous reduction.'—Stanley Kauffmann

AAN: script

'Only one man understood the savagery of the early American west!'

Ulzana's Raid
US 1972 103m Technicolor
Universal / Carter de Haven / Robert Aldrich

An ageing Indian fighter and a tenderfoot officer lead a platoon sent out to counter a murderous Apache attack.
Bloodthirsty, reactionary western with unpleasant shock moments.

w Alan Sharp d Robert Aldrich ph Joseph Biroc m Frank de Vol

Burt Lancaster, Bruce Davison, Jorge Luke, Richard Jaeckel, Lloyd Bochner

Umberto D**
Italy 1952 89m bw
Dear Films

A retired civil servant can barely afford his rent but won't part with his dog.
Downbeat, immensely moving study of old age in a society which fails to provide for it.

w Cesare Zavattini, Vittorio de Sica d Vittorio de Sica ph G. R. Aldo m Alessandro Cicognini

Carlo Battista

AAN: Cesare Zavattini (original story)

Unaccustomed As We Are
US 1929 20m bw silent

Ollie takes a friend home to dinner, but his wife walks out, leaving him to get into all kinds of trouble. The team's first sound comedy, rather hesitant in its use of the new medium. The story was later reworked as the last half hour of Blockheads. Laurel and Hardy, Edgar Kennedy, Mae Busch, Thelma Todd. Written by Leo McCarey and H. M. Walker; directed by Lewis R. Foster; for Hal Roach.

The Uncanny
Canada / GB 1977 85m colour
Rank / Cinevideo / Tor (Claude Héroux, Milton Subotsky)

An author tells his publisher three stories about evil cats.

UNCLE SILAS. In the title role, Derrick de Marney is a puzzle to his young niece Jean Simmons.

Below-par horror compendium with crude effects failing to bolster a sagging script.

w Michael Parry *d* Denis Héroux *ph* Harry Waxman, James Bawden *m* Wilfred Josephs

Peter Cushing, Ray Milland, Susan Penhaligon, Joan Greenwood, Simon Williams, Roland Culver, Alexandra Stewart, Donald Pleasence, Samantha Eggar, John Vernon

● *Video: Rank*

Uncensored

GB 1942 108m bw

GFD / Gainsborough (Edward Black)

In Brussels during the Nazi occupation, the leader of a toe-the-line paper secretly leads the patriots.

Unconvincing underground melodrama with stilted presentation and performances.

w Wolfgang Wilhelm, Terence Rattigan, Rodney Ackland, *novel* Oscar Millard *d* Anthony Asquith *ph* Arthur Crabtree *m* Hans May

Eric Portman, Phyllis Calvert, Griffith Jones, Raymond Lovell, Peter Glenville, Irene Handl, Carl Jaffe, Felix Aylmer

Uncertain Glory

US 1944 102m bw

Warner (Robert Buckner)

During World War II, a French playboy sacrifices himself for his country.

Tame star vehicle needing more action and less philosophy.

w Laszlo Vadnay, Max Brand *d* Raoul Walsh *ph* Sid Hickox *m* Adolph Deutsch

Errol Flynn, Paul Lukas, Jean Sullivan, Lucile Watson, Faye Emerson, James Flavin, Douglass Dumbrille, Dennis Hoey

Unchained

US 1955 75m bw

Warner / Hall Bartlett

A new governor experiments with a prison without bars.

Decent documentary drama which reaches no great heights.

wd Hall Bartlett, *book* Prisoners Are People by Kenyon J. Scudder *ph* Virgil Miller *m* Alex North

Chester Morris, Elroy Hirsch, Barbara Hale, Todd Duncan, Johnny Johnston, Peggy Knudsen, Jerry Paris, John Qualen

AAN: title song (*m* Alex North, *ly* Hy Zarek)

Uncle Silas*

GB 1947   103m   bw
GFD / Two Cities (Josef Somlo, Laurence Irving)
US title: *The Inheritance*

A young Victorian heiress finds herself menaced by her uncle and his housekeeper.
Slow-starting but superbly made period suspenser; unfortunately the characters are all sticks.

w Ben Travers, *novel* Sheridan Le Fanu *d* Charles Frank

Jean Simmons, Derrick de Marney, Katina Paxinou, Derek Bond, Esmond Knight, Sophie Stewart, Manning Whiley, Reginald Tate, Marjorie Rhodes

Uncommon Valor

US 1983   105m   Movielab
Paramount / Ted Kotcheff (John Milius, Buzz Feitshans)

A retired colonel goes looking for his son, declared missing in action in Vietnam, and is helped by a similarly placed industrialist who backs a rescue raid.
Slam-bang action piece with the customary patriotic and personal sentiment.

w Joe Gayton *d* Ted Kotcheff *ph* Stephen H. Burum *m* James Horner *pd* James L. Schoppe

Gene Hackman, Robert Stack, Fred Ward, Reb Brown, Randall Cobb, Patrick Swayze

'Plunging over the falls—lashed at the stake—trapped by savages in the mightiest love-spectacle de Mille ever filmed!'

Unconquered

US 1947   146m   Technicolor
Paramount / Cecil B. de Mille

An 18th-century English convict girl is deported to the American colonies and suffers various adventures before marrying a Virginia militiaman.
Cardboard epic, expensive and noisy but totally unpersuasive despite cannon, arrows, fire and dynamite.

w Charles Bennett, Frederic M. Frank, Jesse Lasky Jnr, *novel* Neil H. Swanson *d* Cecil B. de Mille *ph* Ray Rennahan *m* Victor Young

Paulette Goddard, Gary Cooper, Boris Karloff, Howard da Silva, Cecil Kellaway, Ward Bond, Katherine de Mille, Henry Wilcoxon, C. Aubrey Smith, Victor Varconi, Virginia Grey, Porter Hall, Mike Mazurki

'De Mille bangs the drum as loudly as ever but his sideshow has gone cold on us.'—*Richard Winnington*

'A five-million dollar celebration of Gary Cooper's virility, Paulette Goddard's femininity, and the American frontier spirit.'—*Time*

'I bought this woman for my own . . . and I'll kill the man who touches her!'—*publicity*

The Undefeated

US 1969   119m   De Luxe   Panavision
TCF (Robert L. Jacks)

After the Civil War, two colonels from opposite sides meet on the Rio Grande.
Sprawling, lethargic star western with moments of glory.

w James Lee Barrett *d* Andrew V. McLaglen *ph* William H. Clothier *m* Hugo Montenegro

John Wayne, Rock Hudson, Lee Meriwether, Tony Aguilar, Roman Gabriel

● *Video: CBS / Fox*

Under a Texas Moon

US 1930   70m   Technicolor
Warner

A rancher of the Don Juan type makes hay with the ladies but also rounds up cattle rustlers.
Lightweight early talkie outdoor spectacle with music, not at all memorable.

w Gordon Rigby, Stewart Edward White *d* Michael Curtiz *ph* Bill Rees *songs* Ray Perkins

Frank Fay, Myrna Loy, Raquel Torres, Armida, Noah Beery, George E. Stone, Fred Kohler

'Unusually pleasing western . . . de luxe programmer of its kind.'—*Variety*

Under Capricorn

GB 1949   117m   Technicolor
Transatlantic (Sidney Bernstein, Alfred Hitchcock)

In Australia in 1830 an English immigrant stays with his cousin Henrietta, who has become a dipsomaniac because of her husband's cruelty.
Cardboard 'woman's picture' with elements of *Rebecca*, shot with vestiges of Hitch's ten-minute take. A pretty fair disaster.

w James Bridie, *novel* Helen Simpson *d* Alfred Hitchcock *ph* Jack Cardiff, Paul Beeson, Ian Craig *m* Richard Addinsell

Ingrid Bergman, Joseph Cotten, Michael Wilding, Margaret Leighton, Jack Watling, Cecil Parker, Denis O'Dea

● *Video: Motion Epics*

Under Fire*

US 1983   127m   Technicolor
Orion / Lion's Gate / Greenberg Brothers (Jonathan Taplin)

War correspondents in Nicaragua become involved in the dirty politics on both sides.
A thinking man's action piece, but no help to anybody in finding the true facts.

w Ron Shelton, Clayton Frohman *d* Roger Spottiswoode *ph* John Alcott *m* Jerry Goldsmith

Gene Hackman, Nick Nolte, Joanna Cassidy, Jean-Louis Trintignant, Ed Harris, Richard Masur, Rene Enriquez

'A complex, genuinely thrilling drama of commitment, the mercenary mentality and the tortuous ironies of history.'—*Sight and Sound*

AAN: Jerry Goldsmith

Under Milk Wood*

GB 1971   88m   Technicolor
Timon (Hugo French, Jules Buck)

Life in the Welsh village of Llareggub, as seen by the poet's eye.
Attractive but vaguely unsatisfactory screen rendering of an essentially theatrical event (originally a radio play); everything is much too literal, a real place instead of a fantasy.

wd Andrew Sinclair, *play* Dylan Thomas *ph* Bob Huke *m* Brian Gascoigne

Richard Burton, Elizabeth Taylor, Peter O'Toole, Glynis Johns, Vivien Merchant, Sian Phillips, Victor Spinetti, Rachel Thomas, Angharad Rees, Ann Beach

● *Video: CBS / Fox*

Under My Skin

US 1949   86m   bw
TCF (Casey Robinson)

A crooked jockey is idolized by his son and finally reforms rather than disillusion the boy.
Hokey sentimental melodrama with racetrack backgrounds.

w Casey Robinson, *short story* My Old Man by Ernest Hemingway *d* Jean Negulesco *ph* Joseph La Shelle *m* Daniele Amfitheatrof

John Garfield, Micheline Presle, Luther Adler, Orley Lindgren, Ann Codee

Under Ten Flags

US 1960   92m   bw
Paramount / Dino de Laurentiis

In World War II, a German surface raider in disguise menaces British shipping.
Muddled naval epic with too many allegiances.

w Vittorio Petrilli, Duilio Coletti, Ulrich Mohr, William Douglas Home *d* Duilio Coletti, Silvio Narizzano *ph* Aldo Tonti *m* Nino Rota

Van Heflin, Charles Laughton, John Ericson, Mylène Demongeot, Cecil Parker, Folco Lulli, Alex Nicol, Liam Redmond

Under the Gun

US 1950   83m   bw

A racketeer is jailed and tries to escape.
Lower-case prison adventure without much conviction. Richard Conte, Audrey Totter, John McIntire, Sam Jaffe, Shepperd Strudwick, Written by George Zuckerman; directed by Ted Tatzlaff; for Universal-International.

Under the Pampas Moon

US 1935   78m   bw

A gaucho leader recovers his stolen horse.
Amiable modern adventure set in Argentina.
Warner Baxter, Ketti Gallian, Rita Hayworth, Jack La Rue, J. Carrol Naish. Written by Ernest Pascal and Bradley King; directed by James Tinling; for Fox.

Under the Red Robe*

GB 1937   82m   bw
(TCF) Robert T. Kane

A hell-raising nobleman is persuaded by

Cardinal Richelieu to unmask the ringleader of an anti-monarchist conspiracy.
Smart, unusual swashbuckler on the lines of *The Prisoner of Zenda,* modestly but quite effectively made.

w Lajos Biro, Philip Lindsay, J. L. Hodson, *novel* Stanley J. Weyman *d* Victor Sjostrom *ph* Georges Périnal

Conrad Veidt, Raymond Massey, Annabella, Romney Brent, Sophie Stewart, Wyndham Goldie, Lawrence Grant

'Gripping meller of swashbuckling era . . . surprisingly fine entertainment.'—*Variety*

Under the Volcano*
US 1984   111m   Technicolor
TCF / Ithaca / Michael and Kathy Fitzgerald (Moritz Borman, Wieland Schulz-Keil)

Mexico 1938: the ex-British consul, drinking himself to death, is surprised by a visit from his ex-wife.
A subtle novel has on film become a drunken monologue, fascinating as a *tour de force* but scarcely tolerable after the first half-hour.

w Guy Gallo, *novel* Malcolm Lowry *d* John Huston *ph* Gabriel Figueroa *m* Alex North *pd* Gunther Gerzso

Albert Finney, Jacqueline Bisset, Anthony Andrews, Katy Jurado, James Villiers
'Ultimately one is left not, as in the novel, with a man destroyed by the apocalypse of his own imagination, but with little more than another world-weary cuckold following in the wake of Greene's whisky priest and all those other drunkards who have mooned in Mexico.'—*Tom Milne, MFB*

Under the Yum Yum Tree
US 1963   110m   Eastmancolor
Columbia / Sonnis / Swift (Frederick Brisson)

Two college students have a trial marriage in an apartment block with a lecherous landlord.
Coy, non-erotic and extremely tedious comedy which runs out of jokes after reel one.

w Lawrence Roman, David Swift *d* David Swift *ph* Joseph Biroc *m* Frank de Vol

Jack Lemmon, Carol Lynley, Dean Jones, Imogene Coca, Edie Adams, Paul Lynde, Robert Lansing

'Love as burning as Sahara's sands!'
Under Two Flags*
US 1936   111m   bw
TCF (Raymond Griffith)

A dashing French Foreign Legionnaire is helped by a café girl.
Despite a highly predictable plot (of *Destry Rides Again*) this was a solidly-produced epic with a nice deployment of star talent.

w W. P. Lipscomb, Walter Ferris, *novel* 'Ouida' *d* Frank Lloyd *ph* Ernest Palmer *m* Louis Silvers

Ronald Colman, Claudette Colbert, Rosalind Russell, Victor McLaglen, J. Edward Bromberg, Nigel Bruce, Herbert Mundin, Gregory Ratoff, C. Henry Gordon, John Carradine, Onslow Stevens

'How Ouida would have loved the abandon of this picture, the thirty-two thousand rounds of ammunition shot off into the Arizona desert, the cast of more than ten thousand, the five thousand pounds which insured the stars against camel bites . . . and, in the words of the programme, a fort two hundred feet square, an Arabian oasis with eight full-sized buildings, a forest of transplanted date palms, two Arabian cities, a horse market and a smaller fort.'—*Graham Greene*

Under Your Hat*
GB 1940   79m   bw
Grand National (Jack Hulbert)

Film stars chase spies and recover a stolen carburettor.
Light-hearted adaptation of a stage musical, showing the stars in their best film form.

w Rodney Ackland, Anthony Kimmins, *play* Jack Hulbert, Archie Menzies, Geoffrey Kerr, Arthur Macrae *d* Maurice Elvey

Jack Hulbert, Cicely Courtneidge, Austin Trevor, Leonora Corbett, Cecil Parker, H. F. Maltby, Glynis Johns, Charles Oliver

Undercover
GB 1943   80m   bw

Yugoslavian partisans fight the Nazis. A rather obviously English cast doesn't help to make this flagwaver convincing. Tom Walls, Michael Wilding, Mary Morris, John Clements, Godfrey Tearle, Robert Harris, Rachel Thomas. Written by John Dighton, Monja Danischewsky, Sergei Nolbandov and Sergei Sokulich; directed by Sergei Nolbandov; for Ealing.

Undercover Girl
US 1950   80m   bw

A New York policewoman goes undercover to avenge her father's murder. Rather tedious crime programmer. Alexis Smith, Scott Brady, Richard Egan, Gladys George, Edmon Ryan, Gerald Mohr. Written by Harry Essex; directed by Joseph Pevney; for Universal-International.

Undercover Man
US 1942   74m   bw

A man avenges his father's death by going undercover for the FBI and nabbing a bond-stealing gang. Routine gangster thriller with situations well worn even in 1932. George Raft, Nancy Carroll, Roscoe Karns, Gregory Ratoff, Lew Cody. Written by Garrett Fort, Francis Faragoh; directed by James Flood; for Paramount.

Undercover Man*
US 1949   89m   bw
Columbia (Robert Rossen)

US treasury agents indict a gang leader for tax evasion.
Good semi-documentary crime melodrama based on the Al Capone case.

w Sidney Boehm, Malvin Wald *d* Joseph H. Lewis *ph* Burnett Guffey *m* George Duning

Glenn Ford, Nina Foch, Barry Kelley, James Whitmore, David Wolf, Esther Minciotti

Undercurrent*
US 1946   116m   bw
MGM (Pandro S. Berman)

A professor's daughter marries an industrialist and is frightened and finally endangered by the mystery surrounding his brother.
Overlong suspenser with solid performances and production values; a variation on *Gaslight.*

w Edward Chodorov, *story* Thelma Strabel *d* Vincente Minnelli *ph* Karl Freund *m* Herbert Stothart

Katharine Hepburn, Robert Taylor, Robert Mitchum, Edmund Gwenn, Marjorie Main, Jayne Meadows, Clinton Sundberg, Dan Tobin

'The indigestible plot, full of false leads and unkept promises, is like a woman's magazine serial consumed at one gulp.'—*Time*

Underground
US 1941   95m   bw
Warner (William Jacobs)

Underground leaders in Germany during World War II send out radio messages under the noses of the Nazis.
Forgotten actioner, quite solidly made.

w Charles Grayson *d* Vincent Sherman *ph* Sid Hickox *m* Adolph Deutsch

Jeffrey Lynn, Philip Dorn, Karen Verne, Mona Maris, Frank Reicher, Martin Kosleck, Ilka Gruning

Underground
US 1970   100m   De Luxe
UA / Levy–Gardner–Laven

An American paratrooper joins a French resistance group to kidnap a Nazi general.
Routine war actioner.

w Ron Bishop, Andy Lewis *d* Arthur H. Nader *ph* Ken Talbot *m* Stanley Myers

Robert Goulet, Danièle Gaubert, Laurence Dobkin, Carl Duering

The Underpup
US 1939   81m   bw

A slum girl wins a country holiday among rich folk who ignore her. Light comedy-drama with music which seemed about to launch a rival to Deanna Durbin. Gloria Jean, Robert Cummings, Nan Grey, C. Aubrey Smith, Beulah Bondi, Virginia Weidler, Raymond Walburn, Margaret Lindsay. Written by Grover Jones; directed by Richard Wallace; for Joe Pasternak / Universal.

Undertow
US 1949   70m   bw

An ex-racketeer proves his innocence when a big-time gambler is murdered. Stock suspense crime story, not at all memorable. Scott Brady, John Russell, Dorothy Hart, Peggy Dow, Bruce Bennett. Written by Arthur T. Horman and Lee Loeb; directed by William Castle; for Universal-International.

Underwater

US 1955 99m Technicolor
SuperScope
RKO / Howard Hughes

Treasure hunters dive in the Caribbean for
sunken pirate treasure.
Flabby adventure yarn, badly designed for the
purpose of showing off its star in a variety of
dress and undress.

w Walter Newman, Hugh King, Robert B.
Bailey d John Sturges ph Harry J. Wild,
Lamar Boren m Roy Webb

Jane Russell, Gilbert Roland, Richard Egan,
Lori Nelson, Robert Keith, Joseph Calleia
'This presentation of Miss Russell is like one
of those fountain pens guaranteed to write
under water—novel, but impractical.'—Bosley
Crowther, New York Times

● Video: Kingston

Underwater Warrior

US 1958 91m bw Cinemascope

A naval reserve commander trains frogmen.
Dry semi-documentary drama, unlikely to win
any recruits. Dan Dailey, Ross Martin, James
Gregory, Claire Kelly. Written by Gene
Levitt; directed by Andrew Marton; for Ivan
Tors / MGM.

'Revolvers bark! Figures steal slowly
among the shadows of the night! Then
all is still . . . That's just a bit of the
underworld!'

Underworld°

US 1927 82m (24 fps) bw silent
Paramount
GB title: Paying the Penalty

A gangster is rescued from prison by his moll
and his lieutenant, and when he realizes they
are in love he allows them to escape when the
law closes in.
An innovative film in its time, this melodrama
was the first to look at crime from the
gangsters' point of view. Its main appeal now
lies in its lush direction.

w Ben Hecht, Robert N. Lee, Josef Von
Sternberg d Josef Von Sternberg ph Bert
Glennon ad Hans Dreier

George Bancroft, Evelyn Brent, Clive Brook,
Larry Semon
† The film was a great international success
and had an influence on the pessimistic French
school of the thirties.

AA: Ben Hecht

Underworld USA°

US 1960 99m bw
Columbia / Globe (Samuel Fuller)

A young gangster takes elaborate revenge for
the killing of his father.
Violent syndicate melodrama with a semi-
documentary veneer and some brutal scenes.
Well done but heavy going.

wd Samuel Fuller ph Hal Mohr m Harry
Sukman

Cliff Robertson, Beatrice Kay, Larry Gates,
Dolores Dorn, Robert Emhardt, Paul Dubov,
Richard Rust

'Savage! Sinister! Supernatural! The black
fury of a werewolf—sacrificing life and
love to the maddening evil that drove
him to the most monstrous murders man
ever committed!'

The Undying Monster°

US 1943 63m bw
TCF
GB title: The Hammond Mystery

A curse hangs over the English ancestral home
of the Hammonds.
Silly but well-photographed and directed
minor horror on wolf man lines.

w Lillie Hayward, Michel Jacoby,
novel Jessie D. Kerruish d John Brahm
ph Lucien Ballard m Emil Newman, David
Raksin

James Ellison, John Howard, Heather Angel,
Bramwell Fletcher, Heather Thatcher, Eily
Malyon, Halliwell Hobbes, Aubrey Mather

Unearthly Stranger°

GB 1963 75m bw
Independent Artists (Julian Wintle, Leslie
Parkyn, Albert Fennell)

Scientists working on a time-space formula
find that the bride of one of them is an alien in
search of their secret.
Surprisingly effective minor science fiction, in
some ways all the better for its modest,
TV-style production values.

w Rex Carlton d John Krish ph Reg Wyer
m Edward Williams

John Neville, Gabriella Licudi, Philip Stone,
Jean Marsh, Patrick Newell, Warren Mitchell

Uneasy Terms

GB 1948 91m bw

Detective Slim Callaghan proves that a
blackmail victim is not a murderer. The film
which proved that the British simply can't
make crime movies on the American model.
Michael Rennie, Moira Lister, Faith Brook,
Joy Shelton, Nigel Patrick, Paul Carpenter,
Barry Jones. Written by Peter Cheyney, from
his novel; directed by Vernon Sewell; for
British National.

Unexpected Father

US 1939 78m bw

A dancer looks after his late partner's baby.
Genial comedy introducing a baby star who
was popular until she got out of diapers. Baby
Sandy, Mischa Auer, Dennis O'Keefe, Shirley
Ross, Mayo Methot. Written by Leonard
Spiegelgass and Charles Grayson; directed by
Charles Lamont; for Universal. (GB title:
Sandy Takes a Bow.)

Unexpected Uncle

US 1941 67m bw

An elderly steel tycoon gives everything up to
become a tramp and play Cupid. Money-is-
not-everything fable, entirely dependent on
amiable performances. Charles Coburn, Anne
Shirley, James Craig, Ernest Truex, Russell
Gleason, Jed Prouty. Written by Delmer
Daves and Noel Langley, from the novel by
Eric Hatch; directed by Peter Godfrey; for
RKO.

The Unfaithful°

US 1947 109m bw
Warner (Jerry Wald)

A wife gets involved in a murder while her
husband is out of town.
Glossy romantic melodrama, an unofficial
remake of The Letter.

w David Goodis, James Gunn d Vincent
Sherman ph Ernest Haller m Max Steiner

Ann Sheridan, Zachary Scott, Lew Ayres, Eve
Arden, Steve Geray, Jerome Cowan, John
Hoyt
'If she were yours, would you forgive?'—
publicity

Unfaithfully Yours°°

US 1948 105m bw
TCF (Preston Sturges)

An orchestral conductor believes his wife is
unfaithful, and while conducting a concert
thinks of three different ways of dealing with
the situation.
A not entirely happy mixture of romance,
farce, melodrama and wit, but in general a
pretty entertaining concoction and the last
major film of its talented writer-director.

wd Preston Sturges ph Victor Milner
m Alfred Newman

Rex Harrison, Linda Darnell, Barbara
Lawrence, Rudy Vallee, Kurt Kreuger, Lionel
Stander, Edgar Kennedy, Al Bridge, Julius
Tannen, Torben Meyer, Robert Greig
'Harrison discovers more ways of tripping
over a telephone cable than one can count,
and his efforts to falsify evidence through a
recalcitrant tape recorder are as funny as
anything thought up by Clair in A Nous La
Liberté or by Chaplin in Modern Times.'—
Basil Wright, 1972
† The Rex Harrison character is named Sir
Alfred de Carter and is meant to be Sir
Thomas Beecham. (In America the equivalent
of Beecham's Pills is Carter's Little Liver
Pills.)
†† The pieces of music played are as follows:
For murder: the Semiramide Overture by
Rossini
For surrender: the Venusberg music from
Tannhäuser, by Wagner
For Russian roulette: Francesca da Rimini by
Tchaikovsky

Unfaithfully Yours°

US 1983 96m De Luxe
TCF (Marvin Worth, Joe Wizan)

Modernized and simplified version of the
above, with only one plot instead of three.
This proves to be an advantage, and the film
does deliver some laughs.

w Valerie Curtin, Barry Levinson, Robert
Klane d Howard Zieff ph David M. Walsh
m Bill Conti pd Albert Brenner

Dudley Moore, Nastassia Kinski, Armand
Assante, Albert Brooks, Cassie Yates,
Richard Libertini, Richard B. Shull

Unfinished Business
US 1941 95m bw
Universal (Gregory La Cava)

A wife has thoughts that she should have
married her husband's brother.
Smooth but disappointing romantic comedy;
the detail is good enough, but it sadly lacks
drive.

w Eugene Thackery d Gregory La Cava
ph Joseph Valentine m Franz Waxman

Irene Dunne, Robert Montgomery, Eugene
Pallette, Preston Foster, Walter Catlett, June
Clyde, Phyllis Barry, Esther Dale, Samuel S.
Hinds
    'Once sentiment gets the upper hand, reach
for the exit.'—Otis Ferguson

The Unfinished Dance
US 1947 101m Technicolor
MGM (Joe Pasternak)

The young star of a ballet school becomes
jealous of a talented newcomer, and causes
her injury in an accident.
The delicacies of the French original, La Mort
du Cygne, give way to standard Hollywood
hokum and produce an accomplished but
totally uninteresting film.

w Myles Connolly, story Paul Morand
d Henry Koster ph Robert Surtees
md Herbert Stothart

Margaret O'Brien, Cyd Charisse, Karin
Booth, Danny Thomas, Esther Dale
    'The same old story, with pathos, humour
and ballet substituted for pathos, humour and
chorus girls.'—MFB

The Unforgiven*
US 1960 125m Technicolor
Panavision
UA / James Productions / Hecht–Hill–
Lancaster (James Hill)

A rancher's daughter is suspected of being an
Indian orphan, and violence results.
Good-looking, expensive but muddled racist
western, hard to enjoy.

w Ben Maddow, novel Alan le May d John
Huston ph Franz Planer m Dmitri Tiomkin

Burt Lancaster, Audrey Hepburn, Audie
Murphy, Lillian Gish, Charles Bickford, Doug
McClure, John Saxon, Joseph Wiseman,
Albert Salmi
    'How much strain can a director's reputation
take? Of late, John Huston seems to have
been trying to find out. I think he has carried
the experiment too far with The Unforgiven
. . . a work of profound phoniness, part adult
western, part that Oklahoma! kind of folksy
Americana.'—Dwight MacDonald
    'Ludicrous . . . a hodgepodge of crudely
stitched sententiousness and lame story-
conference inspirations.'—Stanley Kauffmann

The Unguarded Hour*
US 1936 87m bw

A blackmailed woman has evidence to free a
man accused of murder, but dare not reveal it.
Twisty suspense thriller with a rather splendid

cast. Franchot Tone, Loretta Young, Roland
Young, Henry Daniell, Jessie Ralph, Lewis
Stone, Dudley Digges, E. E. Clive, Robert
Greig, Aileen Pringle. Written by Howard
Emmett Rogers and Leon Gordon, from the
play by Ladislas Fodor / Bernard Merivale;
directed by Sam Wood; for MGM.

The Unguarded Moment
US 1956 85m Technicolor
U-I (Gordon Kay)

A schoolmistress who receives anonymous
love notes from a psychotic pupil is discredited
by his even more unbalanced father.
Well-meaning but boring melodrama with the
star attractively out of her usual element.

w Herb Meadow, Larry Marcus, story
Rosalind Russell d Harry Keller ph William
Daniels m Herman Stein

Esther Williams, George Nader, John Saxon,
Edward Andrews, Jack Albertson

The Unholy Garden
US 1931 75m bw
Samuel Goldwyn

A gentleman thief hides out in a North
African den of misfits.
Would-be romantic nonsense, much less
interesting than its credits.

w Ben Hecht, Charles MacArthur d George
Fitzmaurice ph Gregg Toland, George
Barnes m Alfred Newman

Ronald Colman, Fay Wray, Estelle Taylor,
Tully Marshall, Warren Hymer, Mischa Auer,
Henry Armetta, Lawrence Grant
    'Splendid presentation of an ordinary
story.'—Variety

The Unholy Night
US 1929 94m bw

A strangler is caught in the London fog.
Clumsy and talkative early talkie, chiefly
interesting for its cast. Lionel Barrymore,
Roland Young, Boris Karloff, John Loder,
Natalie Moorhead, Ernest Torrence, Polly
Moran, John Miljan. Written by Ben Hecht;
directed by Lionel Barrymore; for MGM.

Unholy Partners*
US 1941 95m bw
MGM (Samuel Marx)

The editor of a sensational newspaper has to
accept finance from a gangster, but friction
results when the newspaper exposes some of
the gangster's activities.
Agreeable twenties melodrama with two solid
stars battling it out.

w Earl Baldwin, Lesser Samuels, Bartlett
Cormack d Mervyn Le Roy ph George
Barnes m David Snell

Edward G. Robinson, Edward Arnold,
Laraine Day, Marsha Hunt, William T. Orr,
Don Beddoe, Charles Dingle, Walter
Kingsford, Marcel Dalio

The Unholy Three*
US 1925 76m approx (24 fps) bw
    silent
MGM

A ventriloquist, a dwarf and a strong man
carry out a series of crimes which end in
murder.
Curious melodrama which set its star and
director off on a series of seven more and even
weirder eccentricities.

w Waldemar Young, story Clarence Robbins
d Tod Browning ph David Kesson

Lon Chaney, Harry Earles, Victor McLaglen,
Mae Busch, Matt Moore

The Unholy Three*
US 1930 74m bw

Remake of the above. The star's only
talkie—he died before it was released—is less
effective than the silent version. Lon Chaney,
Lila Lee, Harry Earles, Ivan Linow, Elliott
Nugent, John Miljan. Written by J. C. and
Elliott Nugent from the novel by Clarence
Robbins; directed by Jack Conway; for MGM.

The Unholy Wife
US 1957 94m Technicolor RKOscope
RKO (John Farrow)

A bored wife shoots a friend in mistake for her
husband but is sentenced for the accidental
death of her mother-in-law.
Totally uninteresting melodrama in the
Double Indemnity style, professionally made
but turgid.

w Jonathan Latimer d John Farrow
ph Lucien Ballard m Daniele Amfitheatrof

Diana Dors, Rod Steiger, Tom Tully, Beulah
Bondi, Marie Windsor, Arthur Franz, Luis
Van Rooten

'A love haunted by nameless evil which
    fought to live in their hearts!'
The Uninvited**
US 1944 98m bw
Paramount (Charles Brackett)

A girl returns to her family house and is
haunted by her mother's spirit, which seems to
be evil.
One of the cinema's few genuine ghost stories,
and a good one, though encased in a rather
stiff production; it works up to a fine pitch of
frenzy.

w Dodie Smith, novel Uneasy Freehold by
Dorothy Macardle d Lewis Allen ph Charles
Lang m Victor Young

Ray Milland, Ruth Hussey, Gail Russell,
Donald Crisp, Cornelia Otis Skinner, Dorothy
Stickney, Barbara Everest, Alan Napier

THE UNINVITED.   Donald Crisp sees something that Gail Russell doesn't.

'Thirty-five first-class jolts, not to mention a well-calculated texture of minor frissons.'—*James Agee*

'Still manages to ice the blood with its implied horrors . . . you can almost smell the ghostly mimosa.'—*Peter John Dyer, 1966*

'A superior and satisfying shocker.'—*Newsweek*

† British critics of the time congratulated the director on not showing the ghosts: in fact the visible manifestations had been cut by the British censor.

AAN: Charles Lang

Union Depot
US 1932   68m   bw

The fortunes of several people clash in a railway station. Pale but moderately interesting imitation of *Grand Hotel*. Douglas Fairbanks Jnr, Joan Blondell, Alan Hale, Frank McHugh, George Rosener, Guy Kibbee, David Landau. Written by Kenyon Nicholson and Walter De Leon, from the play by Gene Fowler, Douglas Durkin and Joe Laurie; directed by Alfred E. Green; for Warner. (GB title: *Gentleman for a Day*.)

Union Pacific**
US 1939   133m   bw
Paramount / Cecil B. de Mille

Indians and others cause problems for the railroad builders.
Standard big-scale western climaxing in a spectacular wreck; not exactly exciting, but very watchable.

w Walter de Leon, C. Gardner Sullivan, Jesse Lasky Jnr *d* Cecil B. de Mille *ph* Victor Milner, Dewey Wrigley *m* John Leipold, Sigmund Krumgold *ad* Hans Dreier, Roland Anderson

Barbara Stanwyck, Joel McCrea, Akim Tamiroff, Robert Preston, Lynne Overman, Brian Donlevy, Robert Barrat, Anthony Quinn, Stanley Ridges, Henry Kolker, Evelyn Keyes, Regis Toomey

'A socko spectacular, surefire for big grosses right down the line.'—*Variety*

'This latest de Mille epic contains all the excelsior qualities we expect of his work—that sense of a Salvationist drum beating round the next corner—but it is never as funny as *The Crusades* and he has lost his touch with crowds.'—*Graham Greene*

'Excitement is the dominant emotion, with swift succession of contrasting materials and episodes, grim and gay, often furious, sometimes funny. The narrative and action take hold at the start and never let go.'—*Motion Picture Herald*

'The largest conglomeration of thrills and cold-blooded murder since Pauline was in peril.'—*Brooklyn Daily Eagle*

'A movie in the old tradition, melodramatic and breathtaking and altogether wonderful.'—*Photoplay*

† De Mille's last picture in black and white.

Union Station°°
US 1950 80m bw
Paramount (Jules Schermer)

Kidnappers nominate a crowded railroad station as their ransom collection point.
Compelling little thriller modelled after *Naked City*, with real locations and plenty of excitement.

w Sidney Boehm, *novel* Thomas Walsh *d* Rudolph Maté *ph* Daniel L. Fapp *m* David Buttolph, Heinz Roemheld *md* Irvin Talbot

William Holden, *Barry Fitzgerald*, Nancy Olson, *Lyle Bettger*, Jan Sterling, Allene Roberts

Universal Soldier
GB 1971 96m colour
Appaloosa / Ionian (Frank J. Schwarz, Donald L. Factor)

A mercenary returns to London but can't escape his past.
Solemnly meaningful melodrama on a tight budget.

wd Cy Endfield *ph* Tony Imi *m* Philip Goodhand-Tait

George Lazenby, Edward Judd, Benito Carruthers, Germaine Greer, Rudolph Walker

The Unknown
US 1927 65m bw silent

A fake armless wonder has his arms amputated to please a girl who can't stand the touch of a man's hand. (She then changes her mind.) Weird melodrama which even this contortionist star can't save. Lon Chaney, Joan Crawford, Norman Kerry. Written by Waldemar Young; directed by Tod Browning; for MGM.

The Unknown
US 1946 70m bw

An amnesiac heiress returns to her family mansion. Twisty creeper in the *I Love a Mystery* series; not bad for a second feature. Karen Morley, Jeff Donnell, Jim Bannon. Written by Malcolm Stuart Boylan and Julian Harmon; directed by Henry Levin; for Columbia.

The Unknown Man
US 1951 86m bw
MGM (Robert Thomsen)

A civil court lawyer of high principles successfully undertakes a criminal case, finds his client was really guilty, and sets matters straight.
Contrived but entertaining morality with standard production and performances.

w Ronald Millar, George Froeschel *d* Richard Thorpe *ph* William Mellor *m* Conrad Salinger

Walter Pidgeon, Ann Harding, Lewis Stone, Barry Sullivan, Keefe Brasselle, Eduard Franz, Richard Anderson, Dawn Addams

Unman, Wittering and Zigo
GB 1971 102m colour
Paramount / Mediarts (Gareth Wigan)

A nervous schoolmaster discovers that his predecessor was murdered by the boys.
Macabre school story which overreaches itself and peters out.

w Simon Raven, *TV play* Giles Cooper *d* John Mackenzie *ph* Geoffrey Unsworth *m* Michael J. Lewis

David Hemmings, Douglas Wilmer, Hamilton Dyce, Carolyn Seymour

Unmarried
US 1939 66m bw

An ex-boxer, shy of marriage, raises an orphan boy. Modest domestic drama notable as one of the rare non-western appearances of its star. Buck Jones, Donald O'Connor, Helen Twelvetrees. Written by Lillie Hayward, Brian Marlow and Grover Jones; directed by Kurt Nuemann; for Paramount. (GB title: *Night Club Hostess*.)

An Unmarried Woman°
US 1977 124m Movielab
TCF (Paul Mazursky, Tony Ray)

A sophisticated New York woman is deserted by her husband, fights with her daughter, and takes up with two men.
Frank, well observed depiction of one woman in New York's new society; as modern as all get out but not very attractive.

wd Paul Mazursky *ph* Arthur J. Ornitz *m* Bill Conti *ph* Pato Guzman

Jill Clayburgh, Alan Bates, Michael Murphy, Cliff Gorman, Pat Quinn, Kelly Bishop

AAN: best picture; script; Jill Clayburgh

● *Video: CBS / Fox*

Unpublished Story
GB 1942 91m bw
Columbia / Two Cities (Anthony Havelock-Allan)

A reporter exposes the Nazis behind a pacifist organization.
Ho-hum formula flagwaver with generally stilted production.

w Anatole de Grunwald, Patrick Kirwan *d* Harold French *ph* Bernard Knowles *m* Nicholas Brodzky

Valerie Hobson, Richard Greene, Basil Radford, Roland Culver, Brefni O'Rourke, Miles Malleson, George Carney, André Morell

The Unseen
US 1945 82m bw
Paramount

A London governess comes to suspect that dark deeds have taken place in the empty house next door.
Period suspenser with good atmosphere but an insubstantial plot.

w Hagar Wilde, Raymond Chandler *d* Lewis Allen *ph* John Seitz *m* Ernst Toch

Joel McCrea, Gail Russell, Herbert Marshall, Richard Lyon, Nona Griffith

† The film seems to have been a hurried attempt to repeat and combine the previous year's success, *Gaslight* and *The Uninvited*.

The Unsinkable Molly Brown°
US 1964 128m Metrocolor Panavision
MGM / Marten (Lawrence Weingarten)

Western orphan Molly Brown grows up determined to become a member of Denver society.
Semi-western comedy-musical about a real lady who wound up surviving the *Titanic*.
Bouncy and likeable but not at all memorable.

w Helen Deutsch, *musical play* Richard Morris *d* Charles Walters *ph* Daniel L. Fapp *md* Robert Armbruster *ad* George W. Davis, Preston Ames

Debbie Reynolds, Harve Presnell, *Ed Begley*, Jack Krischen, Hermione Baddeley, Martita Hunt

AAN: Daniel L. Fapp; Robert Armbruster; Debbie Reynolds

The Unsuspected°
US 1947 103m bw
Warner (Charles Hoffman)

A writer-producer of radio crime shows commits a murder and is forced to follow the clues on air.
Sleek, new look mystery thriller with a disappointing plot which gives its interesting cast little to do, and allows itself to peter out in chases.

w Ranald MacDougall, *novel* Charlotte Armstrong *d* Michael Curtiz *ph* Woody Bredell *m* Franz Waxman *ad* Anton Grot

Claude Rains, Joan Caulfield, Audrey Totter, Constance Bennett, Michael North, Hurd Hatfield, Fred Clark

Untamed
US 1940 83m Technicolor
Paramount (Paul Jones)

A doctor in the frozen north is beset by an epidemic as well as natural hazards.
Old-fashioned melodrama which found an eager audience.

w Frederick Hazlitt Brennan, Frank Butler, *novel* Mantrap by Sinclair Lewis *d* George Archainbaud *ph* Leo Tover, W. Howard Greene *m* Victor Young

Ray Milland, Patricia Morison, Akim Tamiroff, William Frawley, Jane Darwell, Esther Dale, J. M. Kerrigan, Eily Malyon

† A remake of Clara Bow's 1926 film *Mantrap*.

Untamed
US 1955 109m Technicolor Cinemascope
TCF (Bert E. Friedlob, William A. Bacher)

A Dutchman and an Irish girl meet again on a Boer trek to South Africa, and survive Zulu attacks.

A long and involved epic-style plot provides standard excitements and predictable romantic complications.

w Talbot Jennings, Michael Blankfort, Frank Fenton, *novel* Helga Moray *d* Henry King *ph* Leo Tover *m* Franz Waxman

Tyrone Power, Susan Hayward, Richard Egan, John Justin, Agnes Moorehead, Rita Moreno, Hope Emerson, Brad Dexter, Henry O'Neill

'A not unenjoyable essay in hokum.'—*MFB*

Untamed Frontier
US 1952 78m Technicolor
U-I (Leonard Goldstein)

The son of an unpopular Texan landowner commits murder.
Stolid minor western.

w Gerald Drayson Adams, Gwen and John Bagni *d* Hugo Fregonese *ph* Charles P. Boyle *m* Hans Salter

Joseph Cotten, Shelley Winters, Scott Brady, Suzan Ball, Minor Watson

Until They Sail
US 1957 95m bw Cinemascope
MGM (Charles Schnee)

Four New Zealand sisters have wartime romances.
Solid 'woman's picture', well enough presented.

w Robert Anderson, *novel* James A. Michener *d* Robert Wise *ph* Joseph Ruttenberg *m* David Raksin

Jean Simmons, Joan Fontaine, Paul Newman, Piper Laurie, Charles Drake, Wally Cassell, Sandra Dee

Up for the Cup
GB 1931 76m bw

A Yorkshireman gets into trouble when he comes to London for the Cup Final. Slap-happy star farce which pleased the public. Sydney Howard, Joan Wyndham, Stanley Kirk, Sam Livesey, Moore Marriott. Written by Con West, R. P. Weston and Bert Lee; directed by Jack Raymond; for Herbert Wilcox / B and D. (The same star appeared in *Up for the Derby* in the following year; and in 1950 the original, with much the same script, was refashioned for Albert Modley; it was also directed by Jack Raymond.)

Up from the Beach*
US 1965 98m bw Cinemascope
TCF / Panoramic (Christian Ferry)

Just after D-Day, GIs have trouble in a Normandy village.
A kind of subdued sequel to *The Longest Day*, well made for war action addicts, but barely memorable.

w Stanley Mann, Claude Brule, *novel* Epitaph for an Enemy by George Barr *d* Robert Parrish *ph* Walter Wottitz *m* Edgar Cosma

Cliff Robertson, Red Buttons, Françoise Rosay, Marius Goring, Irina Demick, Broderick Crawford, James Robertson Justice, Slim Pickens

Up in Arms**
US 1944 106m Technicolor
Samuel Goldwyn

A hypochondriac joins the army.
Loose, generally pleasant introductory vehicle for Danny Kaye.

w Don Hartman, Robert Pirosh, Allen Boretz *d* Elliott Nugent *ph* Ray Rennahan *md* Ray Heindorf, Louis Forbes

Danny Kaye, Dinah Shore, Constance Dowling, Dana Andrews, Louis Calhern, Lyle Talbot

'Not since Greta Garbo made her bow has there been anything so terrific as the inimitable Danny, one of the most exhilarating and spontaneous personalities in film history.'—*New York Daily Mirror*

AAN: song 'Now I Know' (*m* Harold Arlen, *ly* Ted Koehler); Ray Heindorf, Louis Forbes

Up in Central Park
US 1948 88m bw
U-I (Karl Tunberg)

In turn-of-the-century New York, an Irish girl becomes involved in a crooked political set up.
Stiff and unyielding star musical.

w Karl Tunberg *d* William A. Seiter *ph* Milton Krasner *songs* Sigmund Romberg

Deanna Durbin, Vincent Price, Dick Haymes, Albert Sharpe, Tom Powers

Up in Mabel's Room
US 1944 77m bw

A flustered professor has to retrieve incriminating evidence from an old flame's room. Antediluvian bedroom farce which keeps several ardent practitioners working happily. Dennis O'Keefe, Mischa Auer, Marjorie Reynolds, Gail Patrick. Written by Tom Reed from the play by Wilson Collinson and Otto Harbach; directed by Allan Dwan; for Edward Small. 'As horrible, and wonderful, as watching a Gopher Prairie dramatic club play a mail order farce (6m, 6f).'—*James Agee.*

AAN: editing (Edward Paul)

Up in the Cellar
US 1970 94m Movielab
AIP (William J. Immerman)

A dejected freshman tries various schemes to revenge himself on the college president.
Youth satire aimed at a number of targets which quickly became obsolete; mildly interesting sociologically.

wd Theodore J. Flicker, *novel* The Late Boy Wonder by Angus Hall *ph* Earl Roth *m* Don Randi

Wes Stern, Joan Collins, Larry Hagman, Judy Pace

Up in the World
GB 1956 91m bw
Rank (Hugh Stewart)

A window cleaner becomes friendly with a boy millionaire.
Slow and unattractive comedy star vehicle.

w Jack Davies, Henry Blyth, Peter Blackmore *d* John Paddy Carstairs *ph* Jack Cox *m* Philip Green

Norman Wisdom, Martin Carida, Jerry Desmonde, Maureen Swanson, Ambrosine Philpotts, Colin Gordon

Up Periscope
US 1959 111m Technicolor
Warnerscope
Warner / Lakeside (Aubrey Schenck)

During World War II a submarine frogman is landed on a Pacific island to steal a Japanese code book.
Stock adventure story given stock presentation.

w Richard Landau, *novel* Robb White *d* Gordon Douglas *ph* Carl Guthrie *m* Ray Heindorf

James Garner, Edmond O'Brien, Alan Hale Jnr, Carleton Carpenter

Up Pompeii
GB 1971 90m Technicolor

A wily slave outwits Nero and escapes the eruption of Vesuvius.
Yawnmaking spinoff of a lively TV comedy series: the jokes just lie there, and die there.

w Sid Colin *d* Bob Kellett *ph* Ian Wilson *m* Carl Davis

Frankie Howerd, Patrick Cargill, Michael Hordern, Barbara Murray, Lance Percival, Bill Fraser, Adrienne Posta
† Sequels: *Up the Front, Up the Chastity Belt* (qv).
● *Video: Thorn EMI*

Up Pops the Devil
US 1931 74m bw

A wife supports her husband so that he can write novels. Odd little comedy-drama which struck most people as rather half-hearted. Carole Lombard, Norman Foster, Skeets Gallagher, Stuart Erwin, Lilyan Tashman. Written by Arthur Kober, Eve Unsell, from the play by Frances Goodrich and Albert Hackett; directed by A. Edward Sutherland; for Paramount. 'Here's a plenty satisfying strip of celluloid but it won't do any drawing unless it's by word-of-mouth advertising.'—*Variety*

Up the Chastity Belt*
GB 1971 94m Technicolor
EMI / Associated London Films (Ned Sherrin)

Medieval adventures of the serf Lurkalot and his master Sir Coward de Custard.
Patchy pantomime which doesn't always have the courage of its own slapdash vulgarity.

w Sid Colin, Ray Galton, Alan Simpson *d* Bob Kellett *ph* Ian Wilson *m* Carl Davis

Frankie Howerd, Graham Crowden, Bill Fraser, Roy Hudd, Hugh Paddick, Anna Quayle, Eartha Kitt, Dave King, Fred Emney

THE UPTURNED GLASS.   James Mason and his then wife Pamela Kellino are about to disagree.

Up the Creek*
GB 1958   83m   bw   Hammerscope
Byron (Henry Halsted)

A none-too-bright naval lieutenant is assigned command of a broken-down shore establishment.
Cheeky remake of *Oh Mr Porter*. Jokes fair, atmosphere cheerful and easy-going.

wd Val Guest   *ph* Arthur Grant

David Tomlinson, Peter Sellers, Wilfrid Hyde White, Vera Day, Tom Gill, Michael Goodliffe, Reginald Beckwith, Lionel Jeffries
† Sequel: *Further Up the Creek*.

Up the Down Staircase*
US 1967   124m   Technicolor
Warner / Pakula–Mulligan

Problems of a schoolteacher in one of New York's tough sections.
Earnest, well-acted, not very likeable melodrama.

w Tad Mosel, *novel* Bel Kaufman   *d* Robert Mulligan   *ph* Joseph Coffey   *m* Fred Karlin

Sandy Dennis, Patrick Bedford, Eileen Heckart, Ruth White, Jean Stapleton, Sorrel Booke, Roy Poole

'Sandy Dennis, blinking as if she'd taken pills and been awakened in the middle of the night. She reacts confusedly before the situations even develop, but the audience is ahead of her anyway.'—*Pauline Kael, New Yorker*

Up the Front
GB 1972   89m   Technicolor
EMI / Associated London Films (Ned Sherrin)

A footman is hypnotized into enlisting in World War I and has an enemy 'plan' tattooed on his buttocks.
Threadbare end-of-the-pier romp.

w Sid Colin, Eddie Braben   *d* Bob Kellett   *ph* Tony Spratling   *m* Patrick Greenwell   *ad* Seamus Flannery

Frankie Howerd, Bill Fraser, Zsa Zsa Gabor, Stanley Holloway, Hermione Baddeley, Robert Coote, Lance Percival, Dora Bryan

'Don't get caught is what she wasn't taught!'

Up the Junction
GB 1967   119m   Techniscope
Paramount / BHE (Anthony Havelock–Allan, John Brabourne)

A well-off girl crosses London's river to live among the workers of Clapham.
Socially obsolete sensationalism based on a television semi-documentary. An irritating heroine moves hygienically among motorbikes

w Roger Smith, *book* Nell Dunn   *d* Peter Collinson   *ph* Arthur Lavis   *m* Mike Hugg, Manfred Mann

Suzy Kendall, Dennis Waterman, Adrienne Posta, Maureen Lipman, Michael Gothard, Liz Fraser, Hylda Baker, Alfie Bass

Up the River
US 1930   80m   bw
Fox

An ex-convict is threatened with exposure, but his two pals escape to help him.
Very minor comedy with interesting credits.

w Maurine Watkins   *d* John Ford   *ph* Joseph August

Spencer Tracy, Warren Hymer, Claire Luce, Humphrey Bogart, William Collier Snr
'No cast names to draw, but if the exploitation can make 'em attend, the film will meet its entertainment obligations.'—*Variety*
† In 1938 TCF released a remake directed by Alfred Werker, with Preston Foster, Tony Martin, Slim Summerville and Arthur Treacher.

Up the Sandbox
US 1972   98m   Technicolor
Barwood / First Artists (Robert Chartoff, Irwin Winkler)

A professor's wife finds she is pregnant again and fantasizes about her future life.
Muddled comedy-drama with little point and less entertainment value.

w Paul Zindel, *novel* Anne Richardson Roiphe   *d* Irwin Kershner   *ph* Gordon Willis, Andy Marton   *m* Billy Goldenberg   *ad* Harry Horner

Barbra Streisand, David Selby, Ariane Heller, Jane Hoffman
'A magical mystery tour through the picture book mind of one Manhattan housewife.'—*Richard Combs*

Up Tight
US 1968   104m   Technicolor
Paramount / Marlukin (Jules Dassin)

A black street cleaner betrays his criminal pals for money and is hunted down by them.
Ponderous black remake of *The Informer*, too schematic to make any dramatic or human impression.

w Jules Dassin, Ruby Dee, Julian Mayfield   *d* Jules Dassin   *ph* Boris Kaufman   *m* Booker T. Jones   *pd* Alexander Trauner

Raymond St Jacques, Ruby Dee, Julian Mayfield, Frank Silvera, Roscoe Lee Browne, Juanita Moore

Upperworld
US 1934   75m   bw

A society-conscious wife drives her husband into the arms of a girl from the Bronx. Smooth romantic melodrama with a murder angle; dated but enjoyable. Warren William, Mary Astor, Ginger Rogers, Andy Devine, J. Carrol Naish, Henry O'Neill. Written by Ben Markson, from a story by Ben Hecht; directed by Roy del Ruth; for Warner.

Upstairs and Downstairs
GB 1959 101m Eastmancolor
Rank (Betty E. Box)

Newlyweds have trouble with maids and au pair girls.

Glossy, cheerful, empty-headed domestic comedy.

w Frank Harvey, *novel* Ronald Scott Thorn
d Ralph Thomas *ph* Ernest Steward

Michael Craig, Anne Heywood, Mylène Demongeot, James Robertson Justice, Sidney James, Daniel Massey, Claudia Cardinale, Joan Hickson, Joan Sims

Uptown Saturday Night*
US 1974 104m Technicolor
Warner / Verdon / First Artists (Melville Tucker)

Three friends pursue crooks who have inadvertently stolen a winning lottery ticket.

Witless but high-spirited star comedy for blacks, with a variety of sordid backgrounds.

w Richard Wesley *d* Sidney Poitier *ph* Fred J. Koenekamp *m* Tom Scott

Sidney Poitier, Bill Cosby, Harry Belafonte, Flip Wilson, Roscoe Lee Browne, Richard Pryor, Rosalind Cash, Paula Kelly

'If it had been filmed with a white cast this collection of atrophied comedy routines would have been indistinguishable from a Monogram farce of the forties.'—*David McGillivray*

● *Video: Warner*

The Upturned Glass*
GB 1947 86m bw
GFD / Triton (Sydney Box, James Mason)

A Harley Street surgeon murders the woman responsible for the death of the girl he loved.

Rather pointless psychopathology with an ill-explained title; an interesting example of a top star not knowing what's best for him.

w Jon P. Monaghan, Pamela Kellino
d Lawrence Huntington *ph* Reg Wyer
m Bernard Stevens

James Mason, Pamela Kellino, Rosamund John, Ann Stephens, Henry Oscar, Morland Graham, Brefni O'Rourke

'The psychology is genuine; so too is the tension; the camera plays some good quiet tricks.'—*William Whitebait*

Urban Cowboy
US 1980 135m Movielab Panavision
Paramount (Robert Evans, Irving Azoff)

A rural Texan finds it difficult to succeed in the big city.

Unpleasant and uninteresting star melodrama with a plot vaguely reminiscent of the first part of *An American Tragedy*.

w James Bridges, *novel* Aaron Latham
d James Bridges *ph* Ray Villalobos
m various songs *pd* Stephen Grimes

John Travolta, Debra Winger, Scott Glenn, Madolyn Smith

'A fatuous vehicle for John Travolta, requiring him to stride (stiffly and expressionlessly) through various macho torments . . . the two-hour-plus running time, incorporating a wealth of cliché characters, is excruciatingly protracted.'—*Tom Milne, MFB*

● *Video: CIC*

The Vagabond King

US 1956 88m Technicolor Vistavision
Paramount (Pat Duggan)

The life and loves of French medieval poet
and rebel François Villon.
Shiny, antiseptic studio-set remake of an old
musical warhorse.

w Ken Englund, Noel Langley, *operetta*
Rudolf Friml *d* Michael Curtiz *ph* Robert
Burks *md* Victor Young, *songs* Rudolf Friml

Oreste, Kathryn Grayson, Rita Moreno,
Walter Hampden, Leslie Nielsen, Cedric
Hardwicke, William Prince

† A 1930 version with Dennis King is lost.
Non-musical versions of the story include
1928's *The Beloved Rogue* with John
Barrymore, and 1938's *If I Were King* with
Ronald Colman.

Vagabond Lady

US 1935 72m bw

The two sons of a department store owner fall
for their father's secretary. Medium romantic
comedy which didn't seem to stick in anyone's
memory. Robert Young, Reginald Denny,
Evelyn Venable, Frank Craven, Berton
Churchill. Written by Frank Butler; directed
by Sam Taylor; for MGM. 'This just misses
being a charm picture, the kind they hold over
or bring back for repeat dates.'—*Variety*

The Valachi Papers

France / Italy 1972 127m Technicolor
Euro France / de Laurentiis Intermarco
  (Dino de Laurentiis)

A convicted gangster talks to an FBI agent
about his life in the Mafia.
Rough, violent gangster melodrama, none the
better for being based on actual events.

w Stephen Geller, *book* Peter Maas
d Terence Young *ph* Aldo Tonti *m* Riz
Ortolani

Charles Bronson, Fred Valleca, Gerald S.
O'Loughlin, Lino Ventura, Walter Chiari,
Amedeo Nazzari, Joseph Wiseman

● *Video: Thorn EMI*

Valdez Is Coming

US 1970 90m De Luxe
UA / Norlan / Ira Steiner

A Mexican confronts a rancher who has
double-crossed him.
Simply-conceived western which doesn't quite
manage to be the classic intended.

w Roland Kibbee, David Rayfiel *d* Edwin
Sherin *ph* Gabor Pogany *m* Charles Gross

Burt Lancaster, Susan Clark, Jon Cypher,
Barton Heyman, Frank Silvera

Valentino

US 1951 105m Technicolor
Columbia (Edward Small)

An Italian immigrant to the US becomes a
world-famous romantic film star but dies
young.
Disastrously flat attempt to recapture the feel
of Hollywood in the twenties as a background
to a flatulent romance.

w George Bruce *d* Lewis Allen *ph* Harry
Stradling *m* Heinz Roemheld

Anthony Dexter, Eleanor Parker, Richard
Carlson, Patricia Medina, Joseph Calleia,
Dona Drake, Lloyd Gough, Otto Kruger

'One can almost see the decorated border
round the words . . . it mixes fact, speculation,
needless inaccuracy and bathos.'—*Gavin
Lambert*

'The dialogue is unbelievably ham, the
"entirely imaginary" story commonplace; the
players deserve sympathy.'—*Richard Mallett,
Punch*

Valentino*

GB 1977 127m De Luxe
UA / Aperture / Chartoff–Winkler (Harry
Benn)

Reporters quiz celebrities at a star's funeral,
and his eccentric life unfolds.
Sensationalist 'exposé' of Valentino's rise to
fame, with excellent period detail but no
sympathy for its subject.

w Ken Russell, Mardik Martin, *book* Brad
Steiger, Chaw Mank *d* Ken Russell *ph* Peter
Suschitzky *m* Ferde Grofe, Stanley Black
ad Philip Harrison

Rudolf Nureyev, Leslie Caron, Michelle
Phillips, Carol Kane, Felicity Kendal, Huntz
Hall, David de Keyser, Alfred Marks, Anton
Diffring, Jennie Linden, John Justin

Valerie

US 1957 80m bw
UA / Hal R. Makelim

A western rancher is accused of wounding his
wife and murdering her parents.
Curious little *Rashomon*-like courtroom
melodrama, quite well made and acted.

w Leonard Heidemann, Emmett Murphy
d Gerd Oswald *ph* Ernest Laszlo *m* Albert
Glasser

Anita Ekberg, Sterling Hayden, Anthony
Steel, John Wengraf

The Valiant

GB / Italy 1961 89m bw
(UA) BHP / Euro International (Jon
  Penington)

During World War II, a battleship in
Alexandria harbour is mined, and the captain
tries desperately to avert disaster.
Ill-made war fodder, of no interest at any
level.

w Keith Waterhouse, Willis Hall *d* Roy
Baker *ph* Wilkie Cooper, Egil Woxholt
m Christopher Whelen

John Mills, Ettore Manni, Robert Shaw, Liam
Redmond, Ralph Michael, Colin Douglas,
Dinsdale Landen

'I, who have laughed at love, have fallen in
  love at last!'

Valiant Is the Word for Carrie

US 1936 110m bw
RKO (Wesley Ruggles)

A childless woman devotes her life to orphan
children.
Tedious soap opera.

w Claude Binyon, *novel* Barry Benefield
d Wesley Ruggles *ph* Leo Tover

Gladys George, John Howard, Dudley
Digges, Arline Judge, Harry Carey, Isabel
Jewell

AAN: Gladys George

The Valley of Decision*

US 1945 119m bw
MGM (Edwin H. Knopf)

In old Pittsburgh, an Irish housemaid marries
the master's son.
Trouble at t' mill epic romance, American
style; starrily cast but not excitingly made.

w John Meehan, Sonya Levien, *novel* Marcia
Davenport *d* Tay Garnett *ph* Joseph
Ruttenberg *m* Herbert Stothart

Greer Garson, Gregory Peck, Lionel
Barrymore, Donald Crisp, Preston Foster,
Gladys Cooper, Marsha Hunt, Reginald
Owen, Dan Duryea, Jessica Tandy, Barbara
Everest, Marshall Thompson

AAN: Herbert Stothart; Greer Garson

Valley of Eagles
GB 1951 86m bw

A Swedish scientist chases into Lapland after his wife and her lover who have stolen an important formula. Unconvincing scenery mars what might have been an unusual adventure drama. Jack Warner, John McCallum, Nadia Gray, Anthony Dawson, Mary Laura Wood, Christopher Lee. Written by Paul Tabori, Nat Bronsten and Terence Young; directed by Terence Young; for Independent Sovereign / GFD.

The Valley of Gwangi
US 1968 95m Technicolor
Warner / Morningside (Charles H. Schneer)

Cowboys and scientists discover prehistoric monsters in a 'forbidden' Mexican valley. Tedious adventure yarn enhanced by good special effects.

w William E. Bast d James O'Connelly ph Erwin Hillier m Jerome Moross sp Ray Harryhausen

Richard Carlson, Laurence Naismith, James Franciscus, Gila Golan, Freda Jackson

Valley of Song
GB 1953 74m bw

Members of a Welsh valley choir nearly come to blows over the interpretation of The Messiah. Neat, Ealing-style comedy from a well-known radio play. Mervyn Johns, Clifford Evans, Maureen Swanson, John Fraser, Rachel Thomas, Rachel Roberts, Kenneth Williams. Written by Cliff Morgan and Phil Park, from the play Choir Practice by Cliff Morgan; directed by Gilbert Gunn; for ABPC.

Valley of the Dolls*
US 1967 123m De Luxe Panavision
TCF / Red Lion (David Weisbart)

An innocent young actress is corrupted by Broadway and Hollywood, and takes to drugs. Cliché-ridden but good-looking road-to-ruin melodrama from a bitchy bestseller; production values high, but the whole thing goes over the top at the end.

w Helen Deutsch, Dorothy Kingsley, novel Jacqueline Susann d Mark Robson ph William H. Daniels m André Previn md John Williams ad Jack Martin Smith, Richard Day

Barbara Parkins, Patty Duke, Susan Hayward, Paul Burke, Sharon Tate, Martin Milner, Tony Scotti, Charles Drake, Alex Davion, Lee Grant, Robert H. Harris

'What kind of pills do you take to sit through a film like this?'—The Golden Turkey Awards

'A skilfully deceptive imitation of a real drama . . . on a closer look the characters turn out to be images that have almost nothing to do with people.'—Christian Science Monitor

'One of the most stupefyingly clumsy films ever made by alleged professionals.'—Joseph Morgenstern, Newsweek

† Judy Garland was originally slated to play the Susan Hayward part.

AAN: John Williams
● Video: CBS / Fox

Valley of the Giants
US 1938 79m Technicolor

A lumberman fights pirates to preserve his beloved redwoods. Routine outdoor thick-ear to which colour lent the semblance of freshness. Wayne Morris, Claire Trevor, Frank McHugh, Alan Hale, Donald Crisp, Charles Bickford. Written by Seton I. Miller and Michael Fessier, from the novel by Peter B. Kyne; directed by William Keighley; for Warner. 'A yarn which contains nearly all the proven surefire elements of the successful outdoor picture.'—Variety
† This was the third version of the story; the first, in 1919, starred Wallace Reid; the second, in 1927, starred Milton Sills. The 1952 movie The Big Trees, with Kirk Douglas, had a suspiciously similar storyline.

Valley of the Kings
US 1954 86m Eastmancolor
MGM

Archaeologists fight looters in the tomb of a Pharaoh.
Thin as drama, with little action or suspense and dispirited acting, this hokum piece nevertheless benefits from splendid locations.

w Robert Pirosh, Karl Tunberg d Robert Pirosh ph Robert Surtees m Miklos Rozsa

Robert Taylor, Eleanor Parker, Carlos Thompson, Kurt Kasznar, Victor Jory

Valley of the Sun
US 1942 79m bw
RKO (Graham Baker)

A government spy in old Arizona outwits a crooked Indian agent.
Cheapjack western with nothing to commend it.

w Horace McCoy, story Clarence Budington Kelland d George Marshall ph Harry J. Wild m Paul Sawtell

James Craig, Lucille Ball, Dean Jagger, Billy Gilbert, Cedric Hardwicke, Peter Whitney, Tom Tyler, Antonio Moreno, George Cleveland

Value for Money
GB 1955 93m Technicolor Vistavision
Rank / Group Films (Sergei Nolbandov)

A Yorkshire businessman determines to broaden his outlook, and falls in love with a London showgirl.
Highly undistinguished north country romantic farce which wastes a good production and cast.

w R. F. Delderfield, William Fairchild, novel Derick Boothroyd d Ken Annakin ph Geoffrey Unsworth m Malcolm Arnold

John Gregson, Diana Dors, Susan Stephen, Derek Farr, Frank Pettingell, Jill Adams, Ernest Thesiger, Charles Victor, Joan Hickson

Vampira
GB 1974 88m colour
Columbia / World Film Services (Jack H. Wiener)
US title: Old Dracula

A vampire count lures beauty-contest winners to his castle and uses their blood to revive his dead wife.
Would-be spoof which falls flat on its fangs.

w Jeremy Lloyd d Clive Donner ph Tony Richmond m David Whitaker

David Niven, Teresa Graves, Peter Bayliss, Jennie Linden, Linda Hayden, Nicky Henson, Bernard Bresslaw, Veronica Carlson
● Video: Rank

The Vampire
US 1957 74m bw
UA / Gardner–Levy

A research scientist takes bat essence and becomes a vampire.
Silly attempt to turn a legend into science fiction: more risible than sinister.

w Pat Fielder d Paul Landres ph Jack Mackenzie m Gerald Fried

John Beal, Coleen Gray, Kenneth Tobey, Lydia Reed

The Vampire Bat
US 1932 71m bw
Majestic (Phil Goldstone)

A mad doctor kills townsfolk in search of 'blood substitute'.
Primitive but vigorous low budget chiller.

w Edward Lowe d Frank Strayer ph Ira Morgan

Lionel Atwill, Fay Wray, Melvyn Douglas, Maude Eburne, George E. Stone, Dwight Frye, Lionel Belmore

'Shiver picture, well enough done but coming too late in the cycle to take any money.'—Variety

Vampire Circus
GB 1971 87m colour
Hammer (Wilbur Stark)

In 1825 a plague-ridden village is visited by a circus of animal vampires.
Silly but quite inventive horror thriller.

w Judson Kinberg d Robert Young ph Moray Grant m Philip Martell ad Scott MacGregor

Adrienne Corri, Laurence Payne, Thorley Walters, John Moulder Brown, Elizabeth Seal, Lynne Frederick, Robert Tayman, Robin Hunter

The Vampire Lovers
GB 1970 91m Technicolor
Hammer / AIP (Harry Fine, Michael Style)

A lady vampire worms her way into several noble households.
Reasonably close retelling of Sheridan Le Fanu's Carmilla, complete with lesbian love scenes. Adequate production but not much spirit.

w Tudor Gates, Harry Fine, Michael Styles story 'Carmilla' by Sheridan Le Fanu d Roy Ward Baker ph Moray Grant m Harry Robinson

Ingrid Pitt, Peter Cushing, Pippa Steele, Madeleine Smith, George Cole, Dawn Addams, Douglas Wilmer, Kate O'Mara

"They say I'm not the kind of woman to look after two children who aren't even my own!"

"They came to me lonely, unwanted and they believed in me!"

"Now I know I'd die for these two kids ... I'd die to save them from loneliness, to get them happiness."

Adolph Zukor presents

"VALIANT IS THE WORD FOR CARRIE"

From SARY BENEFIELD's dear better
A PARAMOUNT PICTURE with **GLADYS GEORGE**
ARLINE JUDGE · JOHN HOWARD
DUDLEY DIGGES · HARRY CAREY · ISABEL JEWELL
Produced and Directed by WESLEY RUGGLES

GLADYS GEORGE

You're going to fall in love with *Carrie* ... a woman without money, reputation or friends, who fought for the happiness of two youngsters in as stirring a fight as you will witness on stage or screen or read about.

VALIANT IS THE WORD FOR CARRIE.   A tearjerker of a kind very familiar in the mid-thirties.

Vampyr
Germany / France 1931   83m   bw
Tobis Klangfilm / Carl Dreyer
aka: *The Strange Adventure of David Gray*

A young man staying in a remote inn suspects that he is surrounded by vampires and has a dream of his own death.
Vague, misty, virtually plotless but occasionally frightening and always interesting to look at, this semi-professional film long since joined the list of minor classics for two scenes: the hero dreaming of his own death and the villain finally buried by flour in a mill.

w Christen Jul, Carl Dreyer, *story* 'Carmilla' by Sheridan Le Fanu   d Carl Dreyer
ph Rudolph Maté, Louis Née   m Wolfgang Zeller

Julian West, Sybille Schmitz, Maurice Schutz, Jan Hieronimko

Vanessa, Her Love Story
US 1935   76m   bw
MGM (David O. Selznick)

When her husband becomes insane, a Victorian lady falls for a gypsy.
Very dated romance which finished Helen Hayes's star career, for thirty years at least.

w Lenore Coffee, *novel* Hugh Walpole
d William K. Howard   ph Ray June

Helen Hayes, Robert Montgomery, May Robson, Otto Kruger, Lewis Stone, Henry Stephenson, Violet Kemble-Cooper, Jessie Ralph

'It drips with agony and dullness.'—*Variety*

The Vanishing American
US 1925   110m at 24 fps   bw   silent

A history of the American Indian. Solid western epic, now of historical interest only.
Richard Dix, Lois Wilson, Noah Beery, Malcolm McGregor, Charles Stevens. From a story by Zane Grey; directed by George B. Seitz; for Paramount.

The Vanishing Corporal
France 1962   106m   bw
Films du Cyclope (J. W. Beyer)
original title: *Le Caporal Epinglé*

After several attempts, three Frenchmen succeed in escaping from a detention camp.
Symbolic World War II drama told in mainly comic terms. Not one of its director's great films, but a warm and assured one.

w Jean Renoir, Guy Lefranc   d Jean Renoir
ph Georges Leclerc   m Joseph Kosma

Jean-Pierre Cassel, Claude Brasseur, Claude Rich, O. E. Hasse

Vanishing Point
US 1971   107m   De Luxe
TCF / Cupid (Norman Spencer)

An ex-racing driver who delivers cars for a living becomes hepped up on benzedrine and leads police a rare chase through the Nevada desert.
Strange, fashionable action suspenser which is better to look at than to understand.

w Guillermo Cain d Richard Sarafin
ph John A. Alonzo md Jimmy Brown

Barry Newman, Cleavon Little, Dean Jagger, Victoria Medlin, Paul Koslo, Bob Donner

'Uncomfortably reminiscent of *Easy Rider* as an odyssey through an unknown America in its discovery of strange alliances and unpredictable hostilities.'—*Tom Milne*

● *Video: CBS / Fox*

The Vanishing Virginian
US 1941 97m bw
MGM (Edwin H. Knopf)

A conservative Virginian finds that he harbours suffragettes in his household.
Life with Father in another setting; rather yawn-provoking.

w Jan Fortune, *novel* Rebecca Yancey Williams d Frank Borzage ph Charles Lawton Jnr m David Snell

Frank Morgan, Spring Byington, Kathryn Grayson, Elizabeth Patterson, Louise Beavers

Vanity Fair
US 1932 78m bw

The story of Becky Sharp is told in modern dress. A poorly made independent venture which rapidly dropped from sight. Myrna Loy, Conway Tearle, Barbara Kent, Walter Byron, Anthony Bushell. Written by F. Hugh Herbert from the novel by W. M. Thackeray; directed by Chester M. Franklin; for Hoffman / Allied.
'Poor photography, tepid direction, poor dialogue.'—*Variety*

The Vanquished
US 1953 84m Technicolor

After the Civil War, a returning Confederate officer finds corruption in his home town. Uninspiring semi-western. John Payne, Jan Sterling, Colleen Gray, Lyle Bettger, Willard Parker, Roy Gordon. Written by Winston Miller, Frank Moss and Lewis R. Foster, from a novel by Karl Brown; directed by Edward Ludwig; for Pine-Thomas / Paramount.

Variety**
Germany 1925 104m (24 fps) bw
  silent
UFA
aka: *Vaudeville*

An ageing acrobat seduces a young girl and later kills another man who is interested in her.
Crude, vivid backstage story, inventively presented to overcome the dullness and tawdriness of the plot.

w E. A. Dupont, Leo Birinsky, *novel* Frederick Hollander d E. A. Dupont ph Karl Freund

Emil Jannings, Lya de Putti, Maly Delschaft, Warwick Ward

'A continually roving lens seizes the best angle for every detail, expression and scene.'—*Leon Moussinac*

'The enduring power of the movie is not in its far from original story but in the restless, subjective camera and the fast editing which make it an almost voluptuous experience.'—*Pauline Kael, 70s*

Variety Girl
US 1947 83m bw
Paramount (Daniel Dare)

Of all the young hopefuls arriving in Hollywood, one girl becomes a star.
The slightest of excuses for a tour of the Paramount studios, with all the contract stars doing bits. It doesn't add up to much.

w Edmund Hartmann, Frank Tashlin, Monte Brice, Robert Welch d George Marshall ph Lionel Lindon, Stuart Thompson md Joseph J. Lilley, Troy Saunders

Mary Hatcher, Olga San Juan, De Forrest Kelley, Glenn Tryon; and Bob Hope, Bing Crosby, Gary Cooper, Ray Milland, Alan Ladd, Barbara Stanwyck, Paulette Goddard, Dorothy Lamour, Veronica Lake, Sonny Tufts, Joan Caulfield, William Holden, Lizabeth Scott, Burt Lancaster, Gail Russell, Diana Lynn, Sterling Hayden, Robert Preston, William Bendix, Barry Fitzgerald, Billy de Wolfe, George Pal Puppetoons, Cecil B. de Mille, Mitchell Leisen, George Marshall, Spike Jones and his City Slickers, etc.

Variety Jubilee
GB 1942 92m bw

Two generations in the life of a music hall. Naïve romance with fascinating appearances by some famous names of variety. Lesley Brook, Ellis Irving, Reginald Purdell, George Robey, Charles Coborn, Ella Retford, Wilson Keppel and Betty, The Ganjou Brothers and Juanita, Slim Rhyder, Betty Warren as Florrie Forde; Marie Lloyd Jnr as Marie Lloyd; Tom Finglass as Eugene Stratton; John Rorke as Gus Elen. Written by Kathleen Butler; directed by Maclean Rogers; for Butcher's.

Varsity Show
US 1937 120m bw
Warner (Louis F. Edelman)

Collegians stage a revue.
Mild musical.

w Warren Duff, Richard Macaulay, Jerry Wald, Sig Herzig d William Keighley ph Sol Polito, George Barnes ch Busby Berkeley songs Richard Whiting, Johnny Mercer

Dick Powell, Priscilla Lane, Rosemary Lane, Fred Waring and his Pennsylvanians, Buck and Bubbles, Johnny 'Scat' Davis, Ted Healy, Walter Catlett

'A rah-rah musical entertainment made to order for early autumn business when college boys start pegging out the pigskin.'—*Variety*

Vault of Horror*
GB 1973 86m Eastmancolor
Metromedia / Amicus (Milton Subotsky)

Five men trapped in the basement of a skyscraper tell of their recurring dreams.
All-star horror omnibus, plainly but well staged.

w Milton Subotsky, *stories* William Gaines d Roy Ward Baker ph Denys Coop m Douglas Gamley

Daniel Massey, Anna Massey, Terry-Thomas, Glynis Johns, Curt Jurgens, Dawn Addams, Michael Craig, Edward Judd, Tom Baker, Denholm Elliott

The Velvet Touch*
US 1948 97m bw
RKO / Independent Artists (Frederick Brisson)

A famous actress murders her producer and is struck by conscience but allows a detective to find his own way to the truth.
Solid murder melodrama with an excellent theatrical atmosphere.

w Leo Rosten d John Gage ph Joseph Walker m Leigh Harline

Rosalind Russell, Leo Genn, Sidney Greenstreet, Claire Trevor, Leon Ames, Frank McHugh

Vendetta
US 1950 84m bw
RKO / Howard Hughes

The daughter of an esteemed Corsican family takes vengeance on her father's enemies.
Outmoded ethnic melodrama with nothing to recommend it.

w W. R. Burnett, *novel* Columba by Prosper Mérimée d Mel Ferrer ph Franz Planer, Al Gilks m Roy Webb md Constantin Bakaleinikoff

Faith Domergue, George Dolenz, Donald Buka, Hilary Brooke, Nigel Bruce, Joseph Calleia, Hugo Haas

The Venetian Affair
US 1966 92m Metrocolor Panavision
MGM / Jerry Thorpe

A reporter investigates the death in Venice of an American diplomat.
Uninteresting and complicated spy thriller with pleasant locations.

w E. Jack Neuman, *novel* Helen MacInnes d Jerry Thorpe ph Milton Krasner, Enzo Serafin m Lalo Schifrin

Robert Vaughn, Karl Boehm, Elke Sommer, Ed Asner, Boris Karloff, Felicia Farr, Roger C. Carmel, Luciana Paluzzi, Joe de Santis

Venetian Bird*
GB 1952 95m bw
Rank / British Film Makers (Betty E. Box)
US title: *The Assassin*

A private detective goes to Venice to reward a wartime partisan, who turns out to have become a notorious criminal.
Standard action fare with a nod to *The Third Man* but not much excitement or sense of place.

w Victor Canning, from his novel d Ralph Thomas ph Ernest Steward m Nino Rota

Richard Todd, Eva Bartok, John Gregson, George Coulouris, Margot Grahame, Walter Rilla, Sidney James

Vengeance
GB / Germany 1962 83m bw
CCC / Raymond Stross
aka: *The Brain*

After a fatal accident, the brain of a tycoon is

kept alive and persuades a doctor to find his murderer.

Twisty remake of *Donovan's Brain* (qv), not too badly done.

w Robert Stewart, Philip Mackie *d* Freddie Francis *ph* Bob Hulke *m* Ken Jones

Anne Heywood, Peter Van Eyck, Cecil Parker, Bernard Lee, Maxine Audley, Jeremy Spenser, Miles Malleson

The Vengeance of Fu Manchu
GB 1967 92m Eastmancolor
Anglo Amalgamated / Harry Alan Towers

The Yellow Peril plans a crime syndicate to counter Interpol, and creates a double for Nayland Smith . . .

Limp addition to a series which started well, but was subsequently robbed of period flavour.

w Harry Alan Towers, *novels* Sax Rohmer *d* Jeremy Summers *ph* John Von Kotze *m* Malcolm Lockyer

Christopher Lee, Douglas Wilmer, Tony Ferrer, Tsai Chin, Howard Marion Crawford, Wolfgang Kieling

The Vengeance of She
GB 1967 101m Technicolor
Hammer (Aida Young)

A girl is possessed by the spirit of long-dead Queen Ayesha.

Grotesquely unpersuasive reincarnation melodrama, a long long way from its inspiration.

w Peter O'Donnell *d* Cliff Owen *ph* Wolfgang Suschitzky *m* Mario Nascimbene

John Richardson, Olinka Berova, Edward Judd, Colin Blakely, Derek Godfrey, Noel Willman, André Morell, Jill Melford

Vengeance Valley
US 1951 82m Technicolor
MGM (Nicholas Nayfack)

A western rancher keeps his foster-brother's misdeeds from their father.

Well-made character western, a little short on action.

w Irving Ravetch, *novel* Luke Short *d* Richard Thorpe *ph* George Folsey *m* Rudolph G. Kopp

Burt Lancaster, Robert Walker, Ray Collins, Joanne Dru, Sally Forrest, John Ireland, Carleton Carpenter, Ted de Corsia

Venom
GB 1981 92m Technicolor
Aribage / Morison (Martin Bregman)

A kidnap plan goes awry when a deadly snake is let loose in a besieged house.

Hoary melodrama which veers between dullness, artificial suspense and unpleasant detail.

w Robert Carrington, *novel* Alan Scholefield *d* Piers Haggard *ph* Gilbert Taylor *m* Michael Kamen

Sterling Hayden, Klaus Kinski, Oliver Reed, Sarah Miles, Cornelia Sharpe, Nicol Williamson, Susan George

'Woefully archaic in its British B-picture reliance on very cheap thrills, and without any self-parodic saving grace.'—*Time Out*

● *Video: Thorn EMI*

Vera Cruz**
US 1953 94m Technicolor Superscope
UA / Hecht-Lancaster (James Hill)

Adventurers in 1860 Mexico become involved in a plot against Emperor Maximilian.

Terse, lively western melodrama with unusual locations and comedy and suspense touches. Great outdoor entertainment.

w Roland Kibbee, James R. Webb, Borden Chase *d* Robert Aldrich *ph* Ernest Laszlo *m* Hugo Friedhofer

Gary Cooper, Burt Lancaster, Denise Darcel, Cesar Romero, George Macready, Sarita Montiel, Ernest Borgnine, Morris Ankrum, Charles Bronson

The Verdict*
US 1946 86m bw
Warner (William Jacobs)

A retired Scotland Yard inspector continues to work on a case which vexes him.

Victorian murder mystery with very unconvincing Hollywood sets and curious casting, but rather nicely detailed.

w Peter Milne, *novel* The Big Bow Mystery by Israel Zangwill *d* Don Siegel *ph* Ernest Haller *m* Frederick Hollander

Sidney Greenstreet, Peter Lorre, Joan Lorring, George Cousouris, Rosalind Ivan, Paul Cavanagh, Arthur Shields

Verdict*
France / Italy 1974 97m Eastmancolor
Concordia / CCC (Carlo Ponti)

A gangster's widow kidnaps the judge who is trying her son for rape and murder.

Tortuous but watchable melodrama with star performances and the director's usual eagerness to exploit legal morality.

w Andre Cayatte, Henri Coupon, *novel* Henri Coupon *d* Andre Cayatte *ph* Jean Badal *m* Louiguy

Sophia Loren, Jean Gabin, Henri Garcin, Julien Bertheau

'Not exciting enough to qualify as a thriller nor penetrating enough to make you support Gallic penal reform.'—*Michael Billington, Illustrated London News*

The Verdict*
US 1982 128m Technicolor
TCF / Zanuck-Brown (Richard D. Zanuck, David Brown)

An ageing and failed attorney is unexpectedly handed a case of medical malpractice and successfully sues a hospital.

Complex and interesting but rather sombrely handled exposé of legal and medical ethics.

w David Mamet, *novel* Barry Reed *d* Sidney Lumet *ph* Andrzej Bartkowiak *m* Johnny Mandel *pd* Edward Pisoni

Paul Newman, *James Mason*, Charlotte Rampling, Jack Warden, Milo O'Shea, Lindsay Crouse, Edward Binns, Wesley Addy

AAN: best picture; Paul Newman; James Mason; Sidney Lumet; screenplay (adaptation)

● *Video: CBS / Fox*

Veronika Voss**
West Germany 1982 104m bw
Maura / Tango / Rialto / Trio / Maran (Thomas Schühly)

In the fifties, a distraught star of the previous decade flees from her own image, but finds that her psychiatrist is her own worst enemy. Fascinatingly convoluted puzzle play with enough to say for a year of late-night discussions; but the bleached-out black and white photography is an unnecessary strain.

w Peter Märthesheimer, Pea Fröhlich, Rainer Werner Fassbinder *d* Rainer Werner Fassbinder *ph* Xaver Schwarzenberger *m* Peer Raben

Rosel Zech, Hilmar Thate, Annemarie Düringer, Doris Schade, Cornelia Froboess

'A dazzling parable of all cinema, of the penalties of living out one another's fantasies.'—*Sight and Sound*

Vertigo**
US 1958 128m Technicolor
Vistavision
(Paramount) Alfred Hitchcock

A detective with a fear of heights is drawn into complex plot in which a girl he loves pparently falls to her death. Then he meets er double . . .

Double identity thriller which doesn't really hang together but has many sequences in Hitchcock's best style despite central miscasting.

w Alec Coppel, Samuel Taylor, *novel* D'entre les Morts by Pierre Boileau, Thomas Narcejac *d* Alfred Hitchcock *ph* Robert Burks *m* Bernard Herrmann

James Stewart, Kim Novak, Barbara Bel Geddes, Tom Helmore, Henry Jones

The Very Edge
GB 1962 89m bw Cinevision
British Lion / Garrick / Raymond Stross

An obsessive young man menaces a mother-to-be.

Rather unpleasant suspenser, adequately presented.

w E. J. Howard *d* Cyril Frankel *ph* Bob Huke *m* David Lee

Anne Heywood, Richard Todd, Jack Hedley, Jeremy Brett, Nicole Maurey, Barbara Mullen, Maurice Denham, William Lucas

Very Important Person**
GB 1961 98m bw
Rank / Independent Artists (Julian Wintle,
   Leslie Parkyn)
US title: *A Coming-Out Party*

A senior British scientist is caught by the Nazis
and has to be rescued.
Very satisfactory British comedy with a few
suspense scenes; POW fare with a difference.

w Jack Davies *d* Ken Annakin *ph* Ernest
Steward *m* Reg Owen

James Robertson Justice, Stanley Baxter, Leslie
Phillips, Eric Sykes, Richard Wattis, Colin
Gordon

A Very Special Favor*
US 1965 105m Technicolor
Universal / Lankershim (Robert Arthur)

A Frenchman with a spinster daughter asks an
American lawyer to 'initiate' her.
Tasteless, smirking comedy with several funny
scenes, glossily photographed in the lap of
luxury and interesting in its early use of
homosexuality as a comedy subject.

w Nate Monaster, Stanley Shapiro *d* Michael
Gordon *ph* Leo Tover *m* Vic Mizzy

Rock Hudson, Charles Boyer, Leslie Caron,
Nita Talbot, Dick Shawn, *Walter Slezak*, Larry
Storch

The Very Thought of You
US 1944 99m bw
Warner (Jerry Wald)

Problems of a wartime marriage.
Tepid romantic potboiler.

w Alvah Bessie, Delmer Daves *d* Delmer
Daves *ph* Bert Glennon *m* Franz Waxman

Dennis Morgan, Eleanor Parker, Dane Clark,
Faye Emerson, Beulah Bondi, Henry Travers,
William Prince, Andrea King

Vessel of Wrath**
GB 1938 93m bw
Mayflower (Erich Pommer)
US title: *The Beachcomber*

In the Dutch East Indies, the missionary's
spinster sister falls for a drunken
beachcomber.
First-rate character comedy, remade as *The
Beachcomber* (qv).

w Bartlett Cormack, B. Van Thal, *story* W.
Somerset Maugham *d* Erich Pommer
ph Jules Kruger *m* Richard Addinsell

Charles Laughton, Elsa Lanchester, Robert
Newton, Tyrone Guthrie, Dolly Mollinger,
Eliot Makeham
   'The moment this film starts you recognize
the master touch.'—*Variety*

The Vicar of Bray
GB 1937 68m bw

The ex-tutor of Charles I persuades him to
pardon a traitor. Mild historical fable with
song; in its way quite refreshing. Stanley
Holloway, Hugh Miller, Margaret Vyner,
Felix Aylmer, Esmond Knight, Garry Marsh.
Written by H. Fowler Mear; directed by
Henry Edwards; for Twickenham.

The Vice Squad*
US 1931 78m bw

Stool pigeons account for many arrests of
supposed prostitutes. Rather draggy exposé of
police methods, allegedly torn from the
headlines. Kay Francis, Paul Lukas, Judith
Wood, William B. Davidson, Rockcliffe
Fellowes, Esther Howard. Written by Oliver
H. P. Garrett; directed by John Cromwell; for
Paramount. 'Should draw adult attention in
the large cities.'—*Variety*

Vice Squad
US 1953 88m bw
UA / Jules Levy, Arthur Gardner
GB title: *The Girl in Room 17*

A police captain tracks down two bank
robbers who have killed a cop.
A day in the life of a police captain, quite
watchable but scarcely engrossing.

w Lawrence Roman, *novel* Harness Bull by
Leslie T. White *d* Arnold Laven *ph* Joseph
C. Biroc *m* Herschel Burke Gilbert

Edward G. Robinson, Paulette Goddard, K.
T. Stevens, Porter Hall, Adam Williams,
Edward Binns, Lee Van Cleef

Vice Versa*
GB 1947 111m bw
Rank / Two Cities (Peter Ustinov, George H.
   Brown)

A magic stone enables an unhappy Victorian
boy to change places with his pompous father.
Funny moments can't disguise the fact that this
overlong comedy is a bit of a fizzle, its talented
creator not being a film-maker. A pity, as
British films have so rarely entered the realms
of fancy.

w Peter Ustinov, *novel* F. Anstey *d* Peter
Ustinov

Roger Livesey, Kay Walsh, Anthony Newley,
James Robertson Justice, David Hutcheson,
Petula Clark, Joan Young
   'A repository of English oddities.'—*John
Russell Taylor*

The Vicious Circle*
GB 1957 84m bw
Romulus (Peter Rogers)
US title: *The Circle*

An actress is found dead in Dr Latimer's flat
and the weapon turns up in the boot of his
car . . .
Entertaining whodunnit from a TV serial.

w Francis Durbridge, from his serial The Brass
Candlestick *d* Gerald Thomas *ph* Otto
Heller *m* Stanley Black

John Mills, Derek Farr, Noelle Middleton,
Roland Culver, Wilfrid Hyde White, Mervyn
Johns, René Ray, Lionel Jeffries, Lisa Daniely

Vicki*
US 1953 85m bw
TCF (Leonard Goldstein)

A girl model is murdered, and her sister
proves that her boy friend is innocent, despite
the efforts of a brutal detective.

Very competent if uninspired remake of *I
Wake Up Screaming* (qv).

w Dwight Taylor *d* Harry Horner *ph* Milton
Krasner *m* Leigh Harline

Jeanne Crain, Jean Peters, Richard Boone,
Elliott Reid, Casey Adams, Alex D'Arcy, Carl
Betz, Aaron Spelling

Victim***
GB 1961 100m bw
Rank / Allied Film Makers / Parkway
   (Michael Relph)

A barrister with homosexual inclinations
tracks down a blackmailer despite the risk to
his own reputation.
A plea for a change in the law is very smartly
wrapped up as a murder mystery which allows
all aspects to be aired, and the London
locations are vivid.

w Janet Green, John McCormick *d* Basil
Dearden *ph* Otto Heller *m* Philip Green

Dirk Bogarde, Sylvia Syms, John Barrie,
Norman Bird, Peter McEnery, Anthony
Nicholls, Dennis Price, *Charles Lloyd Pack*,
Derren Nesbitt, John Cairney, Hilton
Edwards, Peter Copley, Donald Churchill,
Nigel Stock
   'Ingenious, moralistic, and moderately
amusing.'—*Pauline Kael, 70s*
● *Video: Rank*

Victor / Victoria*
GB 1982 134m Technicolor
   Panavision
MGM / Peerford / Ladbroke
   Entertainments / Blake Edwards

In 1934 Paris, a girl singer becomes successful
when she poses as a female impersonator, but
it causes complications in her love life.
The story was previously filmed more
innocuously as a Jessie Matthews vehicle, *First
a Girl*; Edwards makes it a sexually harping,
grotesque low comedy, but there are
pleasurable moments.

wd Blake Edwards, from the German film of
1933 Viktor und Viktoria *wd* Rheinhold
Schunzel *ph* Dick Bush *m* Henry Mancini
pd Rodger Maus

Julie Andrews, James Garner, *Robert Preston*,
Lesley Anne Warren, Alex Karras, John
Rhys-Davies, Graham Stark
   'An audience pleaser in the worst sense.'—
New Yorker
   'Edwards' idea of European sophistication
and Gallic naughtiness is seen throughout to
be depressingly crude, parochial and second-
hand, based on old American farces and
reprises of his own Clouseau routines.'—
Sunday Times

AA: original song score (Henry Mancini,
Leslie Bricusse)
AAN: Julie Andrews; Robert Preston; Lesley
Ann Warren; screenplay (adaptation);
costume design; art direction
● *Video: MGM / UA*

VERY IMPORTANT PERSON. Leslie Phillips is never downhearted, and James Robertson Justice might just have an escape plan in mind.

Victoria the Great*
GB 1937 112m bw (Technicolor sequence)
British Lion / Imperator / Herbert Wilcox
Episodes in the life of Queen Victoria.
A decent film with all the British virtues, and a milestone in the cinema of its time. Script and performances are excellent; production sometimes falters a little.
w Robert Vansittart, Miles Malleson, plays Victoria Regina by Laurence Housman
d Herbert Wilcox ph F. A. Young, William V. Skall m Anthony Collins
Anna Neagle, Anton Walbrook, H. B. Warner, Walter Rilla, Mary Morris, C. V. France, Charles Carson, Felix Aylmer, Derrick de Marney

'The effect of the final colour reel is to make the picture look like something enamelled on pottery and labelled "A Present from Blackpool".'—James Agate

The Victors*
GB 1963 175m bw Panavision
Columbia / Open Road (Carl Foreman)
World War II adventures of an American infantry platoon.
Patchy compendium with moral too heavily stressed but plenty of impressive scenes and performances along the way. The mixture of realism and irony, though, doesn't really mix.
w Carl Foreman, novel The Human Kind by Alexander Baron d Carl Foreman
ph Christopher Challis m Sol Kaplan

George Peppard, George Hamilton, Albert Finney, Melina Mercouri, Eli Wallach, Vince Edwards, Rosanna Schiaffino, James Mitchum, Jeanne Moreau, Elke Sommer, Senta Berger, Peter Fonda, Michael Callan
'Doggerel epic.'—John Coleman
'War has revealed Mr Foreman as a pompous bore.'—John Simon
'Having made a point through an image it continually feels the need to state it all over again by way of dialogue.'—Penelope Houston

Victory*
US 1940 77m bw
Paramount (Anthony Veiller)
A Dutch East Indies recluse rescues a girl and is menaced by three villains who think he is wealthy.

Curious, ineffective but occasionally compelling attempt to translate the untranslatable to the screen.

w John L. Balderston, *novel* Joseph Conrad *d* John Cromwell *ph* Leo Tover *m* Frederick Hollander

Fredric March, Betty Field, *Cedric Hardwicke*, Sig Rumann, Margaret Wycherly, Jerome Cowan, Fritz Feld, Rafaela Ottiano

'There is achieved a combination of amateur theatricals and earnest emptiness of motive and motion that will throw a blanket of reminiscent affection around this solemn, unusual and exotic buffoonery.'—*Otis Ferguson*

'A mood of impending doom and horror more than makes up for its slow and deliberate action . . . a fine and penetrating motion picture melodrama.'—*New York World Telegram*

'This is an unusual film at almost every level, yet it's unusual and disturbing, too.'—*Pauline Kael, 70s*

'Not a film of flamboyant hues . . . but it has quality, weight, and above all, compelling drama.'—*Philadelphia Record*

† The story was previously filmed in 1919 by Maurice Tourneur (with Jack Holt) and in 1930 by William Wellman (with Richard Arlen)

Victory

US 1981 117m Metrocolor Panavision
Lorimar / Victory Company / Tom Stern (Freddie Fields)

alternative and GB release title: *Escape to Victory*

A German POW camp in 1943 houses many international football stars. A Nazi officer sees propaganda in a game against a German side, but the allies make it an opportunity for escape.
Flabby and unconvincing POW story with agreeably old-fashioned values sacrificed to trendy casting and a silly ending.

w Evan Jones, Yabo Yablonsky *d* John Huston *ph* Gerry Fisher *m* Bill Conti *pd* J. Dennis Washington

Sylvester Stallone, Michael Caine, Pele, Bobby Moore, Max Von Sydow, George Mikell, Daniel Massey

'Even readers of the *Boy's Own Paper* might have blenched . . . ludicrous beyond belief.'—*Tom Milne, MFB*

Victory through Air Power***

US 1943 65m Technicolor
Walt Disney

The history of aviation and the theories of Major Alexander de Seversky.
What was thought by many to be propaganda was in fact a demonstration of Disney's own fascination with the theories of a controversial figure. The cartoon segments are put together with the studio's accustomed brilliance.

w various *d* H. C. Potter (live action), various *m* Edward J. Plumb, Paul J. Smith, Oliver J. Wallace

AAN: Edward J. Plumb, Paul J. Smith, Oliver J. Wallace

Videodrome

Canada 1982 89m colour

A videodrome TV channel induced pornographic hallucinations in the viewer. Dangerous when it is not risible, this thoroughly tawdry concept is made worse by being slickly done. James Woods, Sonja Smits, Deborah Harry, Peter Dvorsky. Written and directed by David Cronenberg; for Filmplan International. 'Almost as incoherent as it is speculative.'—*Sight and Sound*

The View from Pompey's Head*

US 1955 97m Eastmancolor
                    Cinemascope
TCF (Philip Dunne)
GB title: *Secret Interlude*

A New York lawyer returns on a case to the small town of his youth, and falls in love again with his old sweetheart.
Routine Marquand-type novelette, long on atmosphere and short on plot.

wd Philip Dunne, *novel* Hamilton Basso *ph* Joe MacDonald *m* Elmer Bernstein

Richard Egan, Dana Wynter, Cameron Mitchell, Sidney Blackmer, Marjorie Rambeau

A View from the Bridge

France 1961 117m bw
Transcontinental (Paul Graetz)
original title: *Vu du Pont*

A longshoreman on the New York waterfront has passionate feelings for his wife's niece, and these erupt when she announces her engagement.
Solemn, self-examining melodrama, poorly adapted from the stage.

w Norman Rosten, *play* Arthur Miller *d* Sidney Lumet *ph* Michel Kelber *m* Maurice Leroux

Raf Vallone, Maureen Stapleton, Carol Lawrence, Jean Sorel, Raymond Péllégrin, Morris Carnovsky, Harvey Lembeck, Vincent Gardenia

† The film was shot in several languages.

Vigil in the Night

US 1940 96m bw
RKO (George Stevens)

Two nurses are attracted to the same doctor; one dies during an epidemic.
Dull, downbeat romantic melodrama with a miscast lead.

w Fred Guiol, P. J. Wolfson, Rowland Leigh, *novel* A. J. Cronin *d* George Stevens *ph* Robert de Grasse *m* Alfred Newman

Carole Lombard, Anne Shirley, Brian Aherne, Julien Mitchell, Robert Coote, Peter Cushing, Ethel Griffies

The Viking Queen

GB 1967 91m Technicolor
Warner / Hammer (John Temple-Smith)

During the first century AD, the queen of the Iceni tries to keep peace with the occupying Romans but has trouble with hot-headed Druids.
Stuff and nonsense from the Dark Ages; light should not have been shed upon it.

w Clarke Reynolds *d* Don Chaffey *ph* Stephen Dade *m* Gary Hughes

Don Murray, Carita, Donald Houston, Andrew Keir, Patrick Troughton, Adrienne Corri, Niall MacGinnis, Wilfrid Lawson, Nicola Pagett

The Vikings***

US 1958 116m Technirama
UA / KD Productions (Jerry Bresler)

Two Viking half-brothers quarrel over the throne of Northumbria.
Slightly unpleasant and brutal but extremely well-staged and good-looking epic in which you can almost feel the harsh climate. Fine colour, strong performances, natural settings, vivid action, and all production values as they should be.

w Calder Willingham, *novel* The Viking by Edison Marshall *d* Richard Fleischer *ph* Jack Cardiff *m* Mario Nascimbene credit titles United Productions of America narrator Orson Welles

Kirk Douglas, Tony Curtis, Ernest Borgnine, Janet Leigh, Alexander Knox, Frank Thring, James Donald, Maxine Audley, Eileen Way

Villa Rides!

US 1968 125m Technicolor
                    Panavision
Paramount (Ted Richmond)

1912 Mexico: an American pilot who has been gun-running for the rebels is pressed into more active service.
Bang-bang actioner which pauses too often for reflection and local colour.

w Robert Towne, Sam Peckinpah *d* Buzz Kulik *ph* Jack Hildyard *m* Maurice Jarre *ad* Ted Howarth

Yul Brynner, Robert Mitchum, Charles Bronson, Grazia Bucetta, Herbert Lom, Alexander Knox, Fernando Rey, Jill Ireland

Village of Daughters

GB 1961 86m bw
MGM (George H. Brown)

An unemployed commercial traveller in an Italian village finds himself choosing a bride for a successful emigré.
Voluble, gesticulating minor comedy.

w David Pursall, Jack Seddon *d* George Pollock *ph* Geoffrey Faithfull *m* Ron Goodwin

Eric Sykes, Warren Mitchell, Scilla Gabel, Carol White, Grégoire Aslan, John Le Mesurier

Village of the Damned**

GB 1960 78m bw
MGM (Ronald Kinnoch)

Children born simultaneously in an English village prove to be super-intelligent and deadly beings from another planet.
Modestly made but absorbing and logical science fiction, cleanly presented.

w *Stirling Silliphant, Wolf Rilla, Geoffrey Barclay, novel* The Midwich Cuckoos by *John Wyndham d Wolf Rilla ph Geoffrey Faithfull m* Ron Goodwin

George Sanders, Barbara Shelley, Michael Gwynn, Martin Stephens, Laurence Naismith
† Sequel: *Children of the Damned* (qv).

A Village Tale*
US 1935 79m bw
RKO (David Hempstead)

Envy leads to a clash between two rural landowners.
Unusual but very interesting attempt by Hollywood to film with integrity an old-fashioned country novel. Very dated, but pleasant to watch.

w *Allan Scott, novel* Phil Strong *d John Cromwell ph* Nicholas Musuraca *m* Alberto Columbo

Randoph Scott, Robert Barrat, Kay Johnson, Arthur Hohl, Janet Beecher, Edward Ellis, Donald Meek, Dorothy Burgess, Andy Clyde, Guinn Williams
'Depressing story without marquee strength. Restricted in appeal.'—*Variety*

Villain
GB 1971 98m Technicolor Panavision
EMI / Kastner / Ladd / Kanter

The come-uppance of a cowardly, sadistic, homosexual East End gang boss with a mother fixation.
Very unpleasant and unentertaining British low life shocker, plainly inspired by *White Heat*.

w *Dick Clement, Ian La Frenais, novel* The Burden of Proof by James Barlow *d* Michael Tuchner *ph* Christopher Challis *m* Jonathan Hodge

Richard Burton, Ian MacShane, Nigel Davenport, Joss Ackland, Cathleen Nesbitt, Donald Sinden, T. P. McKenna, Fiona Lewis
● *Video: Thorn EMI*

The Villain
US 1979 89m Metrocolor
Columbia / Rastar (Paul Maslansky, Mort Engelberg)
GB title: *Cactus Jack*

An incompetent outlaw rides from one disaster to another.
No doubt amusing in conception, this attempt to put the cartoon character Wile E. Coyote into human form lamentably misfires, six minutes being an ideal length for that kind of comedy.

w *Robert G. Kane d* Hal Needham *ph* Bobby Byrne *m* Bill Justis

Kirk Douglas, Arnold Schwarzenegger, Ann-Margret, Paul Lynde, Ruth Buzzi, Jack Elam, Strother Martin
'Timing is entirely absent from this limp, laughless fiasco, as is any evidence of imagination . . . desperation is the keynote.'—*Paul Taylor, MFB*

The Villain Still Pursued Her*
US 1940 66m bw
(RKO) Harold B. Franklin

An innocent family suffers at the hands of a villainous landlord.
Clumsy burlesque of old time melodrama, interesting that it was done at all and with this cast.

w *Elbert Franklin d* Edward Cline *ph* Lucien Ballard *m* Frank Tours

Buster Keaton, Alan Mowbray, Anita Louise, Hugh Herbert, Joyce Compton, Margaret Hamilton, Billy Gilbert

The Vintage
US 1957 92m Metrocolor
Cinemascope
MGM (Edwin H. Knopf)

Two fugitives from justice cause trouble when they become grape pickers.
Steamy drama with an unconvincing French setting; a Hollywood aberration.

w *Michael Blankfort, novel* Ursula Keir *d* Jeffrey Hayden *ph* Joseph Ruttenberg *m* David Raksin

Mel Ferrer, John Kerr, Michèle Morgan, Pier Angeli, Theodore Bikel, Leif Erickson

The Violent Enemy
GB 1968 98m Eastmancolor
Trio / Group W. (Wilfrid Eades)

An IRA explosives expert escapes from a British jail but quarrels with his leaders.
Dullish political melodrama needlessly rubbing salt in old wounds.

w *Edmund Ward, novel* A Candle for the Dead by Hugh Marlowe *d* Don Sharp *ph* Alan Hume *m* John Scott

Tom Bell, Ed Begley, Susan Hampshire, Noel Purcell, Michael Standing

The Violent Men*
US 1955 96m Technicolor
Cinemascope
Columbia (Lewis J. Rachmil)
GB title: *Rough Company*

A crippled cattle baron drives small landowners from his valley, while his wife has an affair with his younger brother.
So much snarling goes on that this seems like a gangster film in fancy dress, but it does hold the attention.

w *Harry Kleiner, novel* Donald Hamilton *d* Rudolph Maté *ph* Burnett Guffey, W. Howard Greene *m* Max Steiner

Edward G. Robinson, Barbara Stanwyck, Glenn Ford, Brian Keith, Dianne Foster, May Wynn, Warner Anderson, Basil Ruysdael

The Violent Ones*
US 1967 90m Eastmancolor
Madison / Harold Goldman

In a small Mexican town, three American hobos are interrogated after the rape and murder of a local girl.
Rather well shot murder mystery with emphasis on character, leading to a desert chase climax.

w *Doug Wilson, Charles Davis d* Fernando Lamas *ph* Fleet Southcott *m* Martin Skiles

Fernando Lamas, Aldo Ray, David Carradine, Tommy Sands

Violent Playground
GB 1958 108m bw
Rank (Michael Relph)

A junior liaison officer in the Liverpool slums falls in love with the sister of a fire-raiser.
'Realistic' melodrama sabotaged by an entirely schematic and predictable plot; enervatingly dull until the siege climax.

w *James Kennaway d* Basil Dearden *ph* Reg Wyer *m* Philip Green

Stanley Baker, Anne Heywood, David McCallum, Peter Cushing, John Slater, Clifford Evans

'The bank robbers that caught a town with its morals down!'
Violent Saturday*
US 1955 90m De Luxe Cinemascope
TCF (Buddy Adler)

Crooks move quietly into a small town with the intention of robbing the bank.
Interesting little melodrama which the wide screen robs of its proper tension. Adequate presentation and performance.

w *Sidney Boehm d* Richard Fleischer *ph* Charles G. Clarke *m* Hugo Friedhofer

Richard Egan, Victor Mature, Stephen McNally, Sylvia Sidney, Virginia Leith, Tommy Noonan, Lee Marvin, Margaret Hayes, J. Carrol Naish, Ernest Borgnine

Violette Nozière*
France / Canada 1977 122m
Eastmancolor
Filmel / Cinevideo (Roger Morand)

In 1933 Paris, an eighteen-year-old girl leads a double life, gets syphilis, poisons her parents and is convicted of murder.
Oddly erratic but interesting recapitulation of a famous French murder case, not quite typical of its director.

w *Odile Barski, Herve Bromberger, Frederic Grendel d* Claude Chabrol *ph* Jean Rabier *m* Pierre Jansen *pd* Jacques Brizzio

Isabelle Huppert, Jean Carmier, Stephane Audran, Bernadette Lafont

The VIPs**
GB 1963 119m Metrocolor Panavision
MGM (Anatole de Grunwald)

Passengers at London Airport are delayed by fog and spend the night at a hotel.
Multi-story compendium cunningly designed to exploit the real-life Burton–Taylor romance. In itself, competent rather than stimulating.

w *Terence Rattigan d* Anthony Asquith *ph* Jack Hildyard *m* Miklos Rozsa

Richard Burton, Elizabeth Taylor, Maggie Smith, Rod Taylor, *Margaret Rutherford*, Louis Jourdan, Elsa Martinelli, Orson Welles, Linda Christian, Dennis Price, Richard

Wattis, David Frost, Robert Coote, Joan Benham, Michael Hordern, Lance Percival, Martin Miller

'If Mr Rattigan's Aunt Edna still goes to the pictures she should like his latest offering, especially if she has a good lunch first.'— *Brenda Davies*

AA: Margaret Rutherford

The Virgin and the Gypsy*
GB 1970 95m colour
Kenwood / Dimitri de Grunwald (Kenneth Harper)

A Midlands clergyman's daughter falls in love with a gypsy fortune teller.
Slow, sensitive, stylish picturization of a Lawrence novella, with generally good performances.

w Alan Plater, story D. H. Lawrence d Christopher Miles ph Robert Huke m Patrick Gowers pd Terence Knight

Joanna Shimkus, Franco Nero, Honor Blackman, Michael Burns, Maurice Denham, Fay Compton, Kay Walsh, Norman Bird

● *Video: VCL*

Virgin Island
GB 1958 94m Eastmancolor
British Lion / Countryman (Leon Clore, Graham Tharp)

A young couple set up house on a tiny Caribbean island.
Pleasant comedy slowed down by lack of plot and too much conversation.

w Philip Rush, Pat Jackson, book Our Virgin Island by Robb White d Pat Jackson ph Freddie Francis m Clifton Parker

Virginia Maskell, John Cassavetes, Sidney Poitier, Isabel Dean, Colin Gordon

'Twentieth Century Fox spectacularly spreads before you the violent age and velvet cape of Sir Walter Raleigh!'

The Virgin Queen*
US 1955 92m De Luxe Cinemascope
TCF (Charles Brackett)

The relationship of Queen Elizabeth I and Sir Walter Raleigh.
Unhistorical charade, quite pleasantly made and worth noting for its star performance.

w Harry Brown, Mindret Lord d Henry Koster ph Charles G. Clarke m Franz Waxman

Bette Davis, Richard Todd, Joan Collins, Herbert Marshall, Jay Robinson, Dan O'Herlihy, Robert Douglas, Romney Brent

The Virgin Soldiers**
GB 1969 96m Technicolor
Columbia / Carl Foreman (Leslie Gilliat, Ned Sherrin)

Serio-comic adventures of recruits in the British army in 1960 Singapore.
Autobiographical fragments, mostly from below the belt, sharply observed and often very funny.

w John Hopkins, novel Leslie Thomas d John Dexter ph Ken Higgins m Peter Greenwell

Hywel Bennett, Nigel Patrick, *Lynn Redgrave*, Nigel Davenport, *Rachel Kempson*, Michael Gwynn, Tsai Chin

'A kind of monstrous mating of *Private's Progress* and *The Family Way*, with bits of *The Long and the Short and the Tall* thrown in for good measure.'—*David Pirie*

† Sequel 1977: *Stand Up Virgin Soldiers*.

● *Video: RCA / Columbia*

The Virgin Spring*
Sweden 1959 87m bw
Svensk Filmindustri (Allan Ekelund)
original title: *Jungfrukällan*

When her murderers are killed, a spring bubbles up from the spot where a young maiden met her death.
Stark and rather lovely filming of a medieval legend, with heavy symbolism and a strong pictorial sense.

w Ulla Isaakson d Ingmar Bergman ph Sven Nykvist m Erik Nordgren

Max Von Sydow, Brigitta Valberg, Gunnel Lindblom, Brigitta Pettersson

AA: best foreign film

● *Video: Longman*

Virginia City*
US 1940 121m bw
Warner (Robert Fellows)

A dance hall girl is really a southern spy helping a rebel colonel to steal a gold shipment from her Yankee boy friend.
Lumpy western in Warner's best budget but worst manner: the stars look unhappy and the plot progresses in fits and starts.

w Robert Buckner d Michael Curtiz ph Sol Polito m Max Steiner

Errol Flynn, Randolph Scott, Miriam Hopkins, Humphrey Bogart, Frank McHugh, Alan Hale, Guinn Williams, John Litel, Moroni Olsen, Russell Hicks, Douglass Dumbrille

The Virginian*
US 1929 95m bw
Paramount (Louis D. Lighton)

A stalwart ranch foreman has to see his best friend hanged for rustling, and defeats the local bad man.
Standard western with famous clichés, e.g. 'Smile when you say that . . .'

w Edward E. Paramore Jnr, Howard Estabrook, novel Owen Wister d Victor Fleming ph J. Roy Hunt

Gary Cooper, Walter Huston, Richard Arlen, Mary Brian, Chester Conklin, Eugene Pallette

The Virginian
US 1946 90m Technicolor
Paramount (Paul Jones)

Forgettable remake of the above.

w Frances Goodrich, Albert Hackett d Stuart Gilmore ph Harry Hallenberger m Daniele Amfitheatrof

Joel McCrea, Brian Donlevy, Sonny Tufts, Barbara Britton, William Frawley, Henry O'Neill, Fay Bainter

Viridiana**
Spain / Mexico 1961 91m bw
Uninci / Films 59 / Gustavo Alatriste (Munoz Suay)

A novice about to take her vows is corrupted by her wicked uncle and installs a load of beggars in his house.
Often hilarious surrealist melodrama packed with shades of meaning, most of them sacrilegious. A fascinating film to watch.

w Luis Bunuel, Julio Alajandro d Luis Bunuel ph José F. Agayo

Silvia Pinal, Francisco Rabal, Fernando Rey
'One of the cinema's few major philosophical works.'—*Robert Vas*

Virtue
US 1932 68m bw

A woman of the streets is regenerated through marriage. Routine matinée programmer.
Carole Lombard, Pat O'Brien, Mayo Methot, Jack La Rue, Ward Bond. Written by Robert Riskin from a story by Ethel Hill; directed by Eddie Buzzell; for Columbia. 'A lot of plot is squeezed into the running time . . . the picture will be liked.'—*Variety*

The Virtuous Bigamist see Four Steps in the Clouds

The Virtuous Sin
US 1930 81m bw
Paramount
GB title: *Cast Iron*

A girl tries to help her student husband when war takes him away from bacteriology.
Stilted romantic drama.

w Martin Brown, Louise Long, novel Lajos Zilahy d George Cukor, Louis Gasnier ph David Abel

Walter Huston, Kay Francis, Kenneth MacKenna, Paul Cavanagh
'Average programme flicker . . . cast names all from legit . . . nor is there much excuse for the picture running 80 minutes when 70 would have been better.'—*Variety*

The Visit
US 1964 100m bw Cinemascope
TCF / Deutschefox / Cinecittà / Dear Film / Films du Siècle / PECF (Julien Derode, Anthony Quinn)

A millionairess offers a fortune to her home town, providing someone will kill her ex-lover.
A realistic production ill befits an essentially theatrical play, and all the effort goes for nothing.

w Ben Barzman, play Friedrich Durrenmatt d Bernhard Wicki ph Armando Nannuzzi m Hans-Martin Majewski

Ingrid Bergman, Anthony Quinn, Paolo Stoppa, Hans-Christian Blech, Valentina Cortesa, Irina Demick, Claude Dauphin, Eduardo Ciannelli

Visit to a Chief's Son
US 1974   92m   De Luxe   Panavision
UA / Robert Halmi

An American anthropologist and his son hope
to film the rituals of an African tribe.
Minor adventure film with a happy resolution,
based on a photomontage by the producer, a
Life photographer.

w Albert Ruben   d Lamont Johnson
ph Ernest Day   m Francis Lai

Robert Mulligan, Johnny Sekka, John Philip
Hodgdon

Visit to a Small Planet
US 1959   101m   bw
Paramount / Wallis–Hazen

A young man from outer space takes a look at
Earth and falls in love.
A satirical play disastrously adapted for the
moronic comedy of an unsuitable star.

w Edmund Beloin, Henry Garson, *play* Gore
Vidal   d Norman Taurog   ph Loyal Griggs
m Leigh Harline

Jerry Lewis, Joan Blackman, Earl Holliman,
Fred Clark, John Williams, Jerome Cowan,
Gavin Gordon, Lee Patrick

Les Visiteurs du Soir*
France 1942   110m   bw
André Paulvé
aka: *The Devil's Envoys*

The devil sends messengers to earth to corrupt
two lovers, but he fails: even though he turns
them to stone, their hearts still beat.
Made during the Occupation, this stately
medieval fable was intended to be significant:
the devil was Hitler, and the heartbeat that of
France. Perhaps because it is so conscious of
hidden meanings, it moves rather stiffly but is
often beautiful to behold.

w Jacques Prévert, Pierre Laroche   d Marcel
Carné   ph Roger Hubert   m Joseph Kosma,
Maurice Thiriet   ad Alexandre Trauner,
Georges Wakhevitch

Arletty, *Jules Berry*, Marie Déa, Alain Cuny,
Fernand Ledoux, Marcel Herrand
'There are wonderful images, but the movie
is heavy on the allegorical and becomes rather
slow and stylized.'—*Pauline Kael, 70s*

Visiting Hours
Canada 1981   105m   colour   Panavision
Filmplan International (Claude Héroux)

A homicidal maniac is at large in a hospital.
Tedious shocker wasting a reliable idea.

w Brian Taggert   d Jean Claude Lord
ph René Verzier   m Jonathan Goldsmith

Michael Ironside, Lee Grant, Linda Purl,
William Shatner, Lenore Zann, Harvey Atkin

I Vitelloni
Italy / France 1953   109m   bw
Peg / Cité (Lorenzo Pegoraro)
aka: *Spivs*

In a small Italian resort, aimless young people
get into various kinds of trouble.
Interesting in its realistic detail, this sharply

observed slice of life is long enough for its
basic purposelessness to become apparent.

w Federico Fellini, Ennio Flaiano, Tullio
Pinelli   d Federico Fellini   ph Otello Martelli,
Tasatti, Carlini   m Nino Rota

Franco Fabrizi, Franco Interlenghi, Eleonora
Ruffo, Alberto Sordi

AAN: script

Viva Knievel
US 1977   104m   Technicolor
Panavision

Evel Knievel becomes involved with drug
smugglers. Abysmal attempt to turn a
stuntman into an actor; a most ramshackle
vehicle. Evel Knievel, Gene Kelly, Lauren
Hutton, Leslie Nielsen, Red Buttons,
Cameron Mitchell, Marjoe Gortner. Written
by Antonio Santillan and Norman Katkov;
directed by Gordon Douglas; for Warner. 'A
paste-and-scissors B picture of quite
breathtaking inanity.'—*Financial Times*.

Viva Las Vegas
US 1964   85m   Metrocolor
MGM (Jack Cummins, George Sidney)
GB title: *Love in Las Vegas*

A sports car racer has fun in the gambling city.
Tolerable star musical.

w Sally Benson   d George Sidney   ph Joseph
Biroc   md George Stoll

Elvis Presley, Ann-Margret, Cesare Danova,
William Demarest, Nicky Blair, Jack Carter

Viva Maria!
France / Italy 1965   120m
Eastmancolor   Panavision
Novelles Editions / Artistes Associés / Vides
(Oscar Dancigers, Louis Malle)

An Irish anarchist girl arrives in Central
America and joins a group of strolling players.
All show and no substance, this is a colour
supplement of a film, neither fish, flesh nor
good red herring.

w Louis Malle, Jean-Claude Carrière   d Louis
Malle   ph Henri Decaë   m Georges Delerue
ad Bernard Evein

Jeanne Moreau, Brigitte Bardot, George
Hamilton, Paulette Dubost, Claudio Brook

'1001 nights of glorious romantic
adventure!'

Viva Max
US 1969   93m   Eastmancolor
Commonwealth United / Mark Carliner

A Mexican general marches his troops into
Texas and seizes the Alamo.
Flat comedy with mildly amusing passages but
too much noise, bluster and sentiment.

w Elliott Baker, *novel* James Lehrer   d Jerry
Paris   ph Jack Richards   m Hugo Montenegro

Peter Ustinov, *John Astin*, Pamela Tiffin,
Jonathan Winters, Keenan Wynn, Henry
Morgan, Alice Ghostley

Viva Villa*
US 1934   110m   bw
MGM (David O. Selznick)

The career of a Mexican rebel.

Gutsy action drama with some smoothing over
of fact in the name of entertainment. A big,
highly competent production of its year.

w Ben Hecht   d Jack Conway   ph James Wong
Howe, Charles G. Clarke   m Herbert Stothart

Wallace Beery, Fay Wray, Leo Carrillo,
Donald Cook, Stuart Erwin, George E. Stone,
Joseph Schildkraut, Henry B. Walthall,
Katherine de Mille
'Glorified western . . . strong b.o. fodder,
handicapped a bit perhaps by its abnormal
masculine appeal.'—*Variety*
'A strange poem of violence.'—*John Baxter,
1968*
'A glorified horse opera . . . the spectator's
excitement is incited by the purely physical
impact of the furious riding and war
sequences, by the frequent sadism, and by the
lively musical score.'—*Irving Lerner*

AAN: best picture; script

Viva Zapata**
US 1952   113m   bw
TCF (Darryl F. Zanuck)

A Mexican revolutionary is finally betrayed by
a friend.
Moody, good-looking star vehicle taking a
romanticized but glum view of history.

w John Steinbeck   d Elia Kazan   ph Joe
MacDonald   m Alex North   md Alfred
Newman

Marlon Brando, Jean Peters, Joseph
Wiseman, Anthony Quinn, Arnold Moss,
Margo, *Frank Silvera*

AA: Anthony Quinn
AAN: John Steinbeck; Alex North; Marlon
Brando

Vivacious Lady*
US 1938   90m   bw
RKO (George Stevens)

A nightclub singer marries a botany professor
and has trouble with his parents.
Pleasant romantic comedy for two popular
stars.

w P. J. Wolfson, Ernest Pagano   d George
Stevens   ph Robert de Grasse   m Roy Webb

Ginger Rogers, James Stewart, Charles
Coburn, Beulah Bondi, James Ellison,
Frances Mercer, Franklin Pangborn, Grady
Sutton, Jack Carson

AAN: Robert de Grasse

Vogues of 1938*
US 1937   108m   Technicolor
Walter Wanger
reissue title: *All This and Glamour Too*

Rival fashion houses compete at the Seven
Arts Ball.
A fashion show with threads of plot,
interesting for clothes and cast, all working
hard.

w Bella and Samuel Spewack   d Irving
Cummings   ph Ray Rennahan   m Victor
Young   md Boris Morros   ch Seymour Felix

Joan Bennett, Walter Baxter, Helen Vinson, Mischa Auer, Alan Mowbray, Jerome Cowan, Alma Kruger, Marjorie Gateson, Penny Singleton, Hedda Hopper

AAN: song 'That Old Feeling' (*m* Sammy Fain, *ly* Lew Brown)

The Voice in the Mirror
US 1958 102m bw Cinemascope

A reformed alcoholic thinks back on his past life. Glum case history of no particular point or persuasiveness. Richard Egan, Julie London, Walter Matthau, Arthur O'Connell, Troy Donahue, Mae Clarke, Ann Doran. Written by Larry Marcus; directed by Harry Keller; for Universal-International.

A Voice in the Wind
US 1944 85m bw

Two refugees from the Nazis meet again and die on a remote island. Pretentious romantic claptrap, fascinating only for a few of the impressionist effects it contrives on the lowest of budgets. Francis Lederer, Sigrid Gurie, J. Carrol Naish. Written by Frederick Torberg; directed by *Arthur Ripley*; for Arthur Ripley. 'Like a mid-thirties French melodrama drenched in the Rembrandt-and-molasses manner of German films of the early to middle twenties. Even within those terms it is much less good than it might be, solemn, unimaginative, thinly detailed; but it is also richly nostalgic if you have any feeling for bad period art.'—*James Agee.*

The Voice of Bugle Ann°
US 1936 70m bw
MGM (John Considine Jnr)

When a dog is killed its embittered owner seeks revenge.
Old-fashioned country tale, rather heavy-going but emotionally strong.

w Harvey Gates, Samuel Hoffenstein, *novel* Mackinlay Kantor *d* Richard Thorpe *ph* Ernest Haller

Lionel Barrymore, Maureen O'Sullivan, Eric Linden, Dudley Digges, Spring Byington, Charley Grapewin
'A very fine movie indeed.'—*Pare Lorentz*

The Voice of Merrill
GB 1952 84m bw
Tempean (Robert Baker, Monty Berman)
US title: *Murder Will Out*

Three men are suspected of murder but one becomes a potential victim.
Complicated murder thriller which intrigues but hardly satisfies.

wd John Gilling *ph* Monty Berman *m* Frank Cordell

Valerie Hobson, James Robertson Justice, Edward Underdown, Henry Kendall, Garry Marsh, Sam Kydd

The Voice of the Turtle°°
US 1948 103m bw
Warner (Charles Hoffman)
aka: *One for the Book*

A girl shares her apartment with a soldier on leave.

A three-character play is smoothly filmed, slightly broadened, and burnished till its pale wit glows nicely.

w John Van Druten, from his play *d* Irving Rapper *ph* Sol Polito *m* Max Steiner

Eleanor Parker, Ronald Reagan, Eve Arden, Wayne Morris, Kent Smith

Voices
GB 1973 91m Technicolor
(Hemdale) Warden (Robert Enders)

A young couple in an old country house are haunted by the voice of their dead son.
Twisty little ghost story which would have been more effective at one third of its length.

w George Kirgo, Robert Enders, *play* Richard Lortz *d* Kevin Billington *ph* Geoffrey Unsworth *m* Richard Rodney Bennett

Gayle Hunnicutt, David Hemmings

● *Video: VCL*

Voltaire°
US 1933 72m bw
Warner (Ray Griffith)

The life and times of the 18th-century French wit.
One of the better Arliss charades, because the film is as stagey as his performance.

w Paul Green, Maude T. Howell, *novel* George Gibbs, E. Laurence Dudley *d* John Adolfi *ph* Tony Gaudio

George Arliss, Doris Kenyon, Margaret Lindsay, Reginald Owen, Alan Mowbray, David Torrence, Douglass Dumbrille, Theodore Newton
'Sumptuously staged and photographed . . . sufficiently modern story to get interest.'—*Variety*

Von Richthofen and Brown
US 1971 97m De Luxe
UA / Roger Corman (Gene Corman)
GB title: *The Red Baron*

During World War I, a Canadian pilot takes on Germany's air ace.
The airplanes are nice, but the film is grounded by plot and dialogue.

w John and Joyce Corrington *d* Roger Corman *ph* Michael Reed *m* Hugo Friedhofer

John Phillip Law, Don Stroud, Barry Primus, Karen Huston, Corin Redgrave, Hurd Hatfield

Von Ryan's Express°°
US 1965 117m De Luxe Cinemascope
TCF (Saul David)

In an Italian POW camp during World War II, an unpopular American captain leads English prisoners in a train escape.
Exhilarating action thriller with slow spots atoned for by nail-biting finale, though the downbeat curtain mars the general effect.

w Wendell Mayes, Joseph Landon, *novel* Davis Westheimer *d* Mark Robson *ph* William H. Daniels, Harold Lipstein *m* Jerry Goldsmith

Frank Sinatra, Trevor Howard, Sergio Fantoni, Edward Mulhare, Brad Dexter, John Leyton, Wolfgang Preiss, James Brolin, Adolfo Celi, Rafaela Cara

● *Video: CBS / Fox*

Voyage of the Damned°
GB 1976 155m Eastmancolor
ITC / Associated General (Robert Fryer)

In 1939, a ship leaves Hamburg for Cuba with Jewish refugees; but Cuba won't take them.
High-minded, expensive, but poorly devised rehash of *Ship of Fools*, with too many stars in cameos and not enough central plot.

w Steve Shagan, David Butler, *book* Gordon Thomas, Max Morgan-Witts *d* Stuart Rosenberg *ph* Billy Williams *m* Lalo Schifrin

Faye Dunaway, Max Von Sydow, Oskar Werner, Malcolm McDowell, James Mason, Orson Welles, Katharine Ross, Ben Gazzara, Lee Grant, Sam Wanamaker, Julie Harris, Helmut Griem, Luther Adler, Wendy Hiller, Nehemiah Persoff, Maria Schell, Fernando Rey, Donald Houston, Jose Ferrer, Denholm Elliott, Janet Suzman
'Not a single moment carries any conviction.'—*New Yorker*
'The movie stays surprisingly distanced and impersonal, like a panning shot that moves too quickly for all the details to register.'—*Charles Champlin, Los Angeles Times*
'With a story that is true (or thereabouts), tragic in its detail and implications, and about which it is impossible to take a neutral attitude, you feel an absolute bounder unless you give it the thumbs up.'—*Barry Took, Punch*

AAN: script; Lalo Schifrin; Lee Grant

● *Video: Precision*

Voyage to the Bottom of the Sea°
US 1961 105m De Luxe Cinemascope
TCF / Windsor (Irwin Allen)

USN Admiral Nelson takes scientists in his futuristic atomic submarine to explode a belt of radiation.
Childish but sometimes entertaining science fiction which spawned a long-running TV series.

w Irwin Allen, Charles Bennett *d* Irwin Allen *ph* Winton Hoch, John Lamb *m* Paul Sawtell, Bert Shefter *ad* J. M. Smith, Herman A. Blumenthal

Walter Pidgeon, Robert Sterling, Joan Fontaine, Peter Lorre, Barbara Eden, Michael Ansara, Henry Daniell, Regis Toomey, Frankie Avalon

● *Video: CBS / Fox*

The Vulture
GB 1967 92m bw

A family curse transforms a scientist into a giant vulture. Incredible nonsense—incredible that anyone should try to get away with it. Fun for those who like to watch actors in trouble. Robert Hutton, Akim Tamiroff, Broderick Crawford, Diane Clare. Written and directed by Lawrence Huntington; for Lawrence Huntington Productions.

W

W
US 1973 95m De Luxe
Bing Crosby Productions (Mel Ferrer)

A young wife is threatened by her psychotic
first husband.
Tedious rehash of several frightened lady
themes, all rather sick.

w Gerald di Pego, James Kelly d Richard
Quine ph Gerry Hirschfeld m Johnny
Mandell

Twiggy, Michael Witney, Eugene Roche, Dirk
Benedict, John Vernon

The W Plan*
GB 1930 105m bw
BIP / Wardour (Victor Saville)

A British spy helps destroy Germany's secret
tunnels.
Slightly fantasticated spy / war action which
was a big popular success at the time.

w Victor Saville, Miles Malleson, Frank
Launder, novel Graham Seton d Victor
Saville ph F. A. Young, Werner Brandes

Brian Aherne, Madeleine Carroll, Gordon
Harker, Gibb McLaughlin, George Merritt,
Mary Jerrold

'One of the best pictures yet from England,
but unconvincing b.o. for the US. Lacks
punch.'—Variety
'Fast, spectacular action, fine acting and
notably realistic war scenes.'—NFT, 1971

'On screen he played the child-hating, dog-
hating, acid-tongued old swindler. It was
no act!'

W. C. Fields and Me
US 1976 112m Technicolor
Universal (Jay Weston)

The rise to Hollywood fame of alcoholic
comedian W. C. Fields.
Untruthful and rather boring biopic, with
minor compensations.

w Bob Merrill, book Carlotta Monti d Arthur
Hiller ph David M. Walsh m Henry Mancini
pd Robert Boyle

Rod Steiger, Valerie Perrine, John Marley,
Jack Cassidy (as John Barrymore), Paul
Stewart (as Ziegfeld), Billy Barty, Bernadette
Peters

'Steiger's impersonation largely keeps pace
with the overriding vulgarity of the
enterprise.'—Sight and Sound
'A stupid and pointless slander.'—Judith
Crist
'Just the sort of memorial Fields might have
wished for Baby Leroy.'—Les Keyser,
Hollywood in the Seventies

WW and the Dixie Dancekings
US 1975 94m TVC
TCF (Stanley S. Canter)

In a southern state in the 1950s, a crook uses a
travelling band as an alibi and stays to
promote them.
Combination of American Graffiti and Easy
Rider, either tiresome or tolerable according
to one's mood. Very flashy, anyway.

w Thomas Rickman d John G. Avildsen
ph Jim Crabe m Dave Grusin

Burt Reynolds, Art Carney, Conny Van
Dyke, Jerry Reed, Ned Beatty

Wabash Avenue*
US 1950 92m Technicolor
TCF (William Perlberg)

During the Chicago World's Fair of 1892, a
shimmy dancer is pursued by two men.
Bright rehash of Coney Island (qv), with solid
tunes and performances.

w Harry Tugend, Charles Lederer d Henry
Koster ph Arthur E. Arling md Lionel
Newman

Betty Grable, Victor Mature, Phil Harris,
Reginald Gardiner, Margaret Hamilton,
James Barton, Barry Kelley

AAN: song 'Wilhelmina' (m Josef Myrow,
ly Mack Gordon)

The Wackiest Ship in the Army
US 1960 99m Technicolor
Cinemascope
Columbia / Fred Kohlmar

In the South Pacific during World War II a
decrepit sailing ship with an inexperienced
crew manages to confuse Japanese patrols and
land a scout behind enemy lines.
Slapstick war comedy with fragments of
action; effect rather muddled.

wd Richard Murphy, story Herbert Carlson
ph Charles Lawton m George Duning

Jack Lemmon, Ricky Nelson, John Lund,
Chips Rafferty, Tom Tully, Joby Baker,
Warren Berlinger, Richard Anderson

Waco
US 1966 85m Technicolor

A gunfighter is hired to straighten out a
corrupt town. Routine western programmer
with familiar faces in cameo parts. Howard
Keel, Jane Russell, Wendell Corey, Brian
Donlevy, John Smith, Gene Evans, DeForest
Kelley, Terry Moore, John Agar, Richard
Arlen, Robert Lowery, Willard Parker, Fuzzy

Knight. Written by Steve Fisher, from the
novel Emporia by Harry Sanford and Max
Lamb; directed by R. G. Springsteen; for
A. C. Lyles / Paramount.

The Wages of Fear***
France / Italy 1953 140m bw
Filmsonor / CICC / Vera
original title: Le Salaire de la Peur

The manager of a Central American oilfield
offers big money to drivers who will take
nitro-glycerine into the jungle to put out an oil
well fire.
After too extended an introduction to the less
than admirable characters, this fascinating film
resolves itself into a suspense shocker with one
craftily managed bad moment after another.

wd Henri-Georges Clouzot, novel Georges
Arnaud ph Armand Thirard m Georges
Auric

Yves Montand, Folco Lulli, Peter Van Eyck,
Charles Vanel, Vera Clouzot, William Tubbs

'As skilful as, in its preoccupation with
violence and its unrelieved pessimism, it is
unlikeable.'—Penelope Houston, Sight and
Sound
'It has some claim to be the greatest
suspense thriller of all time; it is the suspense
not of mystery but of Damocles' sword.'—
Basil Wright, 1972
† See Sorcerer, a lamentable remake.

Wagonmaster**
US 1950 86m bw
RKO / Argosy (John Ford, Merian C.
Cooper)

Adventures of a Mormon wagon train
journeying towards Utah in 1879.
Low-key Ford western, essentially a collection
of incidents, fondly and enjoyably presented.

w Frank Nugent, Patrick Ford d John Ford
ph Bert Glennon m Richard Hageman

Ben Johnson, Joanne Dru, Harry Carey Jnr,
Ward Bond, Charles Kemper, Alan Mowbray,
Jane Darwell, Russell Simpson

'The feel of the period, the poetry of space
and of endeavour, is splendidly
communicated.'—Lindsay Anderson
'What emerges at the end is nothing less
than a view of life itself, the view of a
poet.'—Patrick Gibbs, 1965
● Video: Kingston

The Wagons Roll at Night
US 1941 83m bw
Warner (Harlan Thompson)

The sweetheart of a circus owner makes a pass
at the new young lion-tamer.

Dull remake of *Kid Galahad* (qv), whose plot was borrowed from *Tiger Shark* (qv). Warners were good at this kind of retreading, but gradually poor quality began to show.

w Fred Niblo Jnr, Barry Trivers *d* Ray Enright *ph* Sid Hickox *m* Heinz Roemheld

Humphrey Bogart, Sylvia Sidney, Eddie Albert, Joan Leslie, Sig Rumann, Cliff Clark, Frank Wilcox

Waikiki Wedding*
US 1937   89m   bw
Paramount (Arthur Hornblow Jnr)

A press agent in Hawaii promotes a Pineapple Queen contest.
Light-hearted, empty-headed musical very typical of this studio . . . except that this one is quite good.

w Frank Butler, Walter de Leon, Don Hartman, Francis Martin *d* Frank Tuttle *ph* Karl Struss *m* Leo Shukin *md* Boris Morros

Bing Crosby, Shirley Ross, Bob Burns, Martha Raye, George Barbier, Leif Erickson, Grady Sutton, Granville Bates, Anthony Quinn
   'Shouldn't have any trouble getting by . . . it's saccharine celluloid, sugar-coated.'—*Variety*

AA: song 'Sweet Leilani' (*m / ly* Harry Owens)

Wait til the Sun Shines, Nellie*
US 1952   108m   Technicolor
TCF (George Jessel)

The life of a small-town barber, from marriage through tragedy to retirement.
Amiable, leisurely family drama with pleasant settings; small beer, but oddly compulsive.

w Allan Scott, *novel* Ferdinand Reyher *d* Henry King *ph* Leon Shamroy *m* Alfred Newman

David Wayne, Jean Peters, Hugh Marlowe, Albert Dekker, Alan Hale Jnr, Helene Stanley

Wait until Dark**
US 1967   108m   Technicolor
Warner Seven Arts (Mel Ferrer)

A photographer unwittingly smuggles a drug-filled doll into New York, and his blind wife, alone in their flat, is terrorized by murderous crooks in search of it.
Sharp suspenser with shock moments, from a successful play; in this case the claustrophobic atmosphere helps, though a lack of light relief makes itself felt.

w Robert and Jane Howard-Carrington, *play* Frederick Knott *d* Terence Young *ph* Charles Lang *m* Henry Mancini *ad* George Jenkins

Audrey Hepburn, Alan Arkin, Richard Crenna, Efrem Zimbalist Jnr, Jack Weston

AAN: Audrey Hepburn

'It thrills the women!'
'To the last gun—to the last plane—to the last man!'

Wake Island*
US 1942   78m   bw
Paramount (Joseph Sistrom)

During World War II, marines fight to hold an American base on a small Pacific island.
Terse, violent flagwaver, well done within its limits.

w W. R. Burnett, Frank Butler *d* John Farrow *ph* Theodor Sparkuhl, William C. Mellor *m* David Buttolph

Brian Donlevy, Macdonald Carey, Robert Preston, William Bendix, Albert Dekker, Walter Abel, Mikhail Rasumny, Rod Cameron, Barbara Britton
   'Hollywood's first intelligent, honest and completely successful attempt to dramatize the deeds of an American force on a fighting front.'—*Newsweek*

AAN: best picture; script; John Farrow; William Bendix

Wake Me When It's Over
US 1960   126m   De Luxe   Cinemascope
TCF / Mervyn Le Roy

Soldiers holding a Pacific island build a de luxe hotel from surplus war material.
Aptly-titled army farce on the lines of *The Teahouse of the August Moon* but constructed from inferior material. Yawningly tedious.

w Richard Breen, *novel* Howard Singer *d* Mervyn Le Roy *ph* Leon Shamroy *m* Cyril Mockridge

Ernie Kovacs, Dick Shawn, Jack Warden, Margo Moore, Nobu McCarthy, Don Knotts, Robert Emhardt

Wake of the Red Witch**
US 1948   106m   bw
Republic (Edmund Grainger)

The owner and captain of a ship settle their differences to seek treasure on an East Indian island.
Rattling good action yarn told in flashback, with adequate production and performances.

w Harry Brown, Kenneth Gamet, *novel* Garland Roark *d* Edward Ludwig *ph* Reggie Lanning *m* Nathan Scott

John Wayne, *Luther Adler*, Gail Russell, Gig Young, Adele Mara, Eduard Franz, Grant Withers, Henry Daniell, Paul Fix, Dennis Hoey

Wake Up and Dream
US 1946   92m   Technicolor
TCF (Walter Morosco)

A little girl is determined to find her brother who is missing in action in World War II.
Ambitious but unappealing whimsy which descends into sentimentality; either way it bewildered audiences and critics.

w Elick Moll, *novel* The Enchanted Voyage by Robert Nathan *d* Lloyd Bacon *ph* Harry Jackson *m* Cyril Mockridge *md* Emil Newman

June Haver, John Payne, Connie Marshall, Charlotte Greenwood, John Ireland, Clem Bevans, Lee Patrick

Wake Up and Live*
US 1937   91m   bw
TCF (Kenneth MacGowan)

Success and failure in the radio world as a commentator and a bandleader fight a verbal duel in public.
Fast-moving spoof in which something is always happening, and usually something funny.

w Harry Tugend, Jack Yellen, *book* Dorothea Brande *d* Sidney Lanfield *ph* Edward Cronjager *m* Louis Silvers *songs* Mack Gordon, Harry Revel

Walter Winchell, Ben Bernie and his band, Alice Faye, Jack Haley, Patsy Kelly, Ned Sparks, Grace Bradley, Walter Catlett, Joan Davis, Douglas Fowley, Miles Mander, Etienne Girardot
   'Thoroughly satisfying film entertainment.'—*Variety*

Walk a Crooked Mile
US 1948   91m   bw
Columbia (Edward Small)

British and American agents investigate the leakage of atomic secrets.
Moderate semi-documentary spy thriller.

w George Bruce *d* Gordon Douglas *ph* George Robinson *m* Paul Sawtell

Louis Hayward, Dennis O'Keefe, Louise Allbritton, Carl Esmond, Raymond Burr, Onslow Stevens

Walk a Crooked Path
GB 1969   88m   Eastmancolor
Hanover (John Brason)

A housemaster at a boys' school is accused of homosexuality.
Po-faced melodrama in a minor key; reasonably effective but not exciting.

w Barry Perowne *d* John Brason *ph* John Taylor *m* Leslie Bridgewater

Tenniel Evans, Faith Brook, Christopher Coll, Patricia Haines, Pat Endersby, Margery Mason, Peter Copley

Walk, Don't Run*
US 1966   114m   Technicolor
Panavision
Columbia / Granley (Sol C. Siegel)

In Tokyo during the Olympics accommodation is hard to find, and two men move in with a girl.
Witless reprise of *The More the Merrier*, notable only for the Tokyo backgrounds and for Cary Grant's farewell appearance.

w Sol Saks *d* Charles Walters *ph* Harry Stradling *m* Quincy Jones

Cary Grant, Samantha Eggar, Jim Hutton, *John Standing*, Miiko Taka
   'Too long as are most comedies today, it seems to take its title far too literally; but there are several very funny sequences, a jaunty score, and the unflawed elegance of Mr Grant.'—*Arthur Knight*

Walk East on Beacon*
US 1952 98m bw
Columbia (Louis de Rochemont)
GB title: *The Crime of the Century*

The FBI exposes communist spies in the US.
Fast-moving semi-documentary spy thriller
modelled on the same producer's *The House
on 92nd Street.*

w Leo Rosten *d* Alfred Werker *ph* Joseph
Brun *m* Louis Applebaum

George Murphy, Finlay Currie, Virginia
Gilmore, Karel Stepanek, Louisa Horton

'There weren't supposed to be any more
  surprises in their lives. And then they
  met each other!'

A Walk in the Spring Rain
US 1969 98m Technicolor Panavision
Columbia / Pingee (Stirling Silliphant)

A college lecturer's wife, on holiday in the
mountains, falls in love with a local man.
Romance for the middle-aged, nicely done if
lacking in surprise.

w Stirling Silliphant, *novel* Rachel Maddox
d Guy Green *ph* Charles B. Lang *m* Elmer
Bernstein

Ingrid Bergman, Anthony Quinn, Fritz
Weaver, Katherine Crawford

'Not one line or scene is believably written
or acted and the direction is so lazy it appears
to have been mailed in during the postal
strike.'—*Richard Roud*

A Walk in the Sun***
US 1946 117m bw
Lewis Milestone Productions

The exploits of a single army patrol during the
Salerno landings of 1943, on one vital
morning.
Vivid war film in a minor key, superbly
disciplined and keenly acted.

w Robert Rossen, *novel* Harry Brown *d* Lewis
Milestone *ph* Russell Harlan *m* Fredric
Efrem Rich

Dana Andrews, Richard Conte, Sterling
Holloway, John Ireland, George Tyne,
Herbert Rudley, Richard Benedict, Norman
Lloyd, Lloyd Bridges, Huntz Hall

'Concerned with the individual rather than
the battlefield, the film is finely perceptive,
exciting, and very moving.'—*Penelope
Houston*

'A swiftly overpowering piece of work.'—
Bosley Crowther

'A notable war film, if not the most notable
war film to come from America.'—*Richard
Winnington*

'After nearly two hours one is sorry when it
ends.'—*Richard Mallett, Punch*

Walk like a Dragon
US 1960 95m bw
Paramount / James Clavell

In 1870 San Francisco, a cowboy sets free a
Chinese slave girl but incurs racial intolerance
when he takes her home.
Curious 'liberated' western which gets itself in
a muddle and doesn't come off at all.

w James Clavell, Dan Mainwaring *d* James
Clavell *ph* Loyal Griggs *m* Paul Dunlap

Jack Lord, James Shigeta, Nobu McCarthy,
Mel Tormé, Josephine Hutchinson, Rodolfo
Acosta

Walk on the Wild Side
US 1962 114m bw
Columbia / Famous Artists (Charles K.
  Feldman)

In the thirties, a penniless farmer finds the girl
he once loved working in a New Orleans
brothel.
A brilliant title sequence heralds the dreariest
and most verbose of self-conscious
melodramas, quite missing the sensational
effect promised by the advertising.

w John Fante, Edmund Morris, *novel* Nelson
Algren *d* Edward Dmytryk *ph* Joe
MacDonald *m* Elmer Bernstein *credits* Saul
Bass

Jane Fonda, Capucine, Barbara Stanwyck,
Laurence Harvey, Anne Baxter, Richard Rust

'Since the film prides itself in calling a spade
a spade, it is surprising to find all concerned
reacting to their material as though they were
up to their waists in a quagmire.'—*MFB*

'A side of life you never expected to see on
the screen!'—*publicity*

AAN: title song (*m* Elmer Bernstein, *ly* Mack
David)

Walk Softly Stranger
US 1950 81m bw
RKO (Robert Sparks)

A crook on the run falls for a crippled girl,
who promises to wait for him.
Dismal love-conquers-all melodrama.

w Frank Fenton *d* Robert Stevenson
ph Harry J. Wild *m* Frederick Hollander

Alida Valli, Joseph Cotten, Spring Byington,
Paul Stewart, Jack Paar, Jeff Donnell, John
McIntire

Walk the Proud Land
US 1956 88m Technicolor
  Cinemascope
U-I (Aaron Rosenberg)

An Indian agent persuades the army to use
less violent methods.
Fair standard western with a thoughtful and
sympathetic attitude.

w Gil Doud, Jack Sher *d* Jesse Hibbs
ph Harold Lipstein *m* Joseph Gershenson

Audie Murphy, Anne Bancroft, Pat Crowley,
Robert Warwick, Charles Drake, Tommy
Rall, Jay Silverheels

Walkabout*
Australia 1970 100m Eastmancolor
Max L. Raab / Si Litvinoff

A man kills himself in the desert and his small
children trek among the aborigines to safety.
Eerily effective contrast of city with native life,
a director's and photographer's experimental
success.

w Edward Bond, *novel* James Vance Marshall
d / ph Nicolas Roeg *m* John Barry

Jenny Agutter, Lucien John, David Gimpell

The Walking Dead*
US 1936 66m bw
Warner (Louis F. Edelman)

A man is revived after electrocution and takes
revenge on his enemies.
Dour but well mounted horror thriller in a
shadowy style very typical of its director.

w Ewart Adamson, Peter Milne, Robert
Adams, Lillie Hayward *d* Michael Curtiz
ph Hal Mohr

Boris Karloff, Edmund Gwenn, Marguerite
Churchill, Ricardo Cortez, Barton MacLane,
Warren Hull, Henry O'Neill

'Weak story and haphazardly interpolated
assortment of scientific abadaba prevent
Karloff from making much of a shocker out of
this one.'—*Variety*

Walking My Baby Back Home*
US 1953 95m Technicolor
U-I (Ted Richmond)

Ex-army musicians hit on a combination of
symphonic and dixieland jazz.
The lightest of light musicals, this highly
polished offering remains mildly pleasing
though thinly written throughout.

w Don McGuire, Oscar Brodney *d* Lloyd
Bacon *ph* Irving Glassberg *md* Joseph
Gershenson

Donald O'Connor, Janet Leigh, Buddy
Hackett, Lori Nelson, Scat Man Crothers,
Kathleen Lockhart, George Cleveland, John
Hubbard

The Walking Stick*
GB 1970 101m Metrocolor Panavision
MGM / Winkast (Alan Ladd Jnr)

A repressed girl polio victim falls reluctantly in
love with a painter who involves her in his
criminal schemes.
Slow moving character romance which has its
heart in the right place but too often promises
suspense which never comes, and is made in a
chintzy cigarette commercial style.

w George Bluestone, *novel* Winston Graham
d Eric Till *ph* Arthur Ibbetson *m* Stanley
Myers

David Hemmings, Samantha Eggar, Phyllis
Calvert, Ferdy Mayne, Emlyn Williams,
Francesca Annis, Dudley Sutton

Walking Tall*
US 1973 125m De Luxe
Bing Crosby Productions (Mort Briskin)

A Tennessee farmer-sheriff meets violence
with violence and becomes a local hero.
True story of an American vigilante, made
with modest competence; its great commercial
success may have been due to the support of
the righteous, or of those who revel in
violence.

w Mort Briskin *d* Phil Karlson *ph* Jack
Marta *m* Walter Scharf

Joe Don Baker, Elizabeth Hartman, Gene
Evans, Noah Beery Jnr

'A terrifying image of Nixon's silent
majority at work.'—*Gareth Jones*

'It generates a primitive, atavistic sort of power: it awakens more apprehension and dredges up more complicated and contradictory emotions than one anticipates.'—*Gary Arnold*
† Sequel 1976: *Part Two Walking Tall*. (GB title: *Legend of the Lawman*.) 1977: *Walking Tall: Final Chapter*

Wall of Noise
US 1963   112m   bw
Warner (Joseph Landon)

A racehorse trainer falls for the boss's wife.
Complex but predictable melodrama of the old school, adequately presented and performed.
w Joseph Landon, *novel* Daniel Michael Stein d Richard Wilson ph Lucien Ballard m William Lava

Suzanne Pleshette, Ty Hardin, Dorothy Provine, Ralph Meeker, Simon Oakland, Murray Matheson, Robert F. Simon

Wallflower
US 1948   77m   bw

Two sisters chase the same man; the less aggressive gets him. So-so comedy on familiar lines. Joyce Reynolds, Janis Paige, Robert Hutton, Edward Arnold, Jerome Cowan, Barbara Brown. Written by Phoebe and Henry Ephron, from the play by Reginald Denham and Mary Orr; directed by Frederick de Cordova; for Warner.

The Walls of Jericho
US 1948   106m   bw
TCF (Lamar Trotti)

An influential small-town newspaperman is undermined by his vindictive wife.
Filmed novel of standard competence but minimum interest, ending in a courtroom scene.
w Lamar Trotti, *novel* Paul Wellman d John M. Stahl ph Arthur Miller m Cyril Mockridge

Cornel Wilde, Linda Darnell, Anne Baxter, Kirk Douglas, Ann Dvorak, Marjorie Rambeau, Henry Hull, Colleen Townsend

The Waltz King
US 1963   95m   Technicolor
Walt Disney (Peter V. Herald)

The life of young Johann Strauss in 1850s Vienna.
Medium-budget international family musical, tolerably well done.
w Maurice Tombragel d Steve Previn ph Gunther Anders md Helmuth Froschauer

Kerwin Mathews, Brian Aherne, Senta Berger, Peter Kraus, Fritz Eckhardt

The Waltz of the Toreadors
GB 1962   105m   Technicolor
Rank / Wintle–Parkyn (Peter de Sarigny)

A lecherous retired general finds his past creeping up on him and loses his young mistress to his son.

Lukewarm adaptation of a semi-classic comedy, disastrously translated to English settings and characters.
w Wolf Mankowitz, *play* Jean Anouilh d John Guillermin ph John Wilcox m Richard Addinsell pd Wilfrid Shingleton

Peter Sellers, Margaret Leighton, Dany Robin, John Fraser, Cyril Cusack, Prunella Scales

Waltz Time
GB 1933   82m   bw

Things are not what they seem to be at a Viennese masked ball. Pleasant but slight musical comedy vaguely derived from *Die Fledermaus*. Evelyn Laye, Fritz Schultz, Gina Malo, Jay Laurier, Frank Titterton. Written by A. P. Herbert; directed by William Thiele; for Gaumont.

Waltz Time
GB 1945   100m   bw

At a Viennese ball, an Empress poses as her masked friend to win a philandering count.
Rather plodding operetta which also has an unattributed allegiance to *Die Fledermaus*.
Carol Raye, Peter Graves, Patricia Medina, Thorley Walters, Richard Tauber, Harry Welchman, George Robey, Anne Ziegler, Webster Booth. Written by Montgomery Tully, Jack Whittingham, Henry C. James and Karl Rossier; directed by Paul Stein; for British National.

Waltzes from Vienna
GB 1933   80m   bw
GFD / Gaumont (Tom Arnold)
US title: *Strauss's Great Waltz*

A romance of the Strausses.
There is very little music and very little Hitchcock in this extremely mild romantic comedy.
w Alma Reville, Guy Bolton, *play* Guy Bolton d Alfred Hitchcock ph Glen MacWilliams

Jessie Matthews, Esmond Knight, Frank Vosper, Fay Compton, Edmund Gwenn, Robert Hale, Hindle Edgar
'I hate this sort of thing. Melodrama is the only thing I can do.'—*Alfred Hitchcock*

The Wanderers
US 1979   117m   Technicolor

In 1963, teenage street gangs fight in the Bronx. A bad boys' *American Graffiti*, all violence and unpleasantness. Ken Wahl, John Friedrich, Karen Allen, Tonie Kalem, Linda Manz. Written by Rose and Philip Kaufman, from the novel by Richard Price; directed by Philip Kaufman; for PSO / Polyc.

The Wandering Jew
GB 1933   111m   bw
Gaumont / Twickenham (Julius Hagen)

A Jew is condemned to live forever, but dies in the Spanish Inquisition.
Ambitious fantasy which comes off pretty well for those in the mood, but was a curious choice for a British studio at the time.

w H. Fowler Mear, *play* E. Temple Thurston d Maurice Elvey

Conrad Veidt, Marie Ney, Basil Gill, Anne Grey, Dennis Hoey, John Stuart, Peggy Ashcroft, Francis L. Sullivan, Felix Ayler, Abraham Sofaer
'A beautiful production, a historic triumph—and most likely a commercial error.'—*Variety*

Wanted for Murder*
GB 1946   103m   bw
Marcel Hellman

A man, obsessed with the fact that his father was the public hangman, becomes a murderer himself.
Curiously stagey melodrama with intermittent use of London backgrounds; an interesting curiosity.
w Emeric Pressburger, Rodney Ackland, Maurice Cowan d Lawrence Huntington ph Max Greene m Mischa Spoliansky

Eric Portman, Dulcie Gray, Derek Farr, Roland Culver, Stanley Holloway, Barbara Everest, Bonar Colleano, Kathleen Harrison
'A pleasant and unpretentious thriller of the second or third grade.'—*James Agee*

The War against Mrs Hadley*
US 1942   86m   bw
MGM (Irving Asher)

A Washington matron tries to ignore the war and preserve her social life.
Efficient little propaganda piece with a middle-aged heroine.
w George Oppenheimer d Harold S. Bucquet ph Karl Freund m David Snell

Fay Bainter, Edward Arnold, Richard Ney, Jean Rogers, Sara Allgood, Spring Byington, Van Johnson, Isobel Elsom, Halliwell Hobbes, Miles Mander, Frances Rafferty, Connie Gilchrist
'If this film is, as some have labelled it, the American *Mrs Miniver*, then some of us must have grave illusions about our own (or the English) way of life.'—*Bosley Crowther*
AAN: George Oppenheimer

War and Peace**
US / Italy 1956   208m   Technicolor Vistavision
Carlo Ponti / Dino de Laurentiis

A Russian family's adventures at the time of Napoleon's invasion.
Despite miscasting and heavy dubbing, the pictorial parts of this précis of a gargantuan novel are powerful and exciting enough; the human side drags a little.
w Bridget Boland, Robert Westerby, King Vidor, Mario Camerini, Ennio de Concini, Ivo Perelli, *novel* Leo Tolstoy d King Vidor, (battle scenes) *Mario Soldati* ph Jack Cardiff, (battle scenes) *Aldo Tonti* m Nino Rota ad Mario Chiari

Audrey Hepburn, Henry Fonda, Mel Ferrer, *Herbert Lom*, John Mills, Oscar Homolka, Wilfrid Lawson, Vittorio Gassman, Anita Ekberg, Helmut Dantine, Milly Vitale, Barry Jones

'The film has no more warmth than pictures in an art gallery.'—*Philip T. Hartung*
AAN: King Vidor; Jack Cardiff

War and Peace•••
USSR 1967   507m   Sovcolor   'Scope
   70mm
Mosfilm

An immensely long Russian version with some of the most magnificently spectacular battle scenes ever filmed. A treat for the eyes throughout, and perhaps less taxing than reading the novel, which it follows punctiliously.

w Sergei Bondarchuk, Vasili Solovyov
d Sergei Bondarchuk *ph* Anatoli Petritsky
m Vyacheslav Ovchinnikov

Lyudmila Savelyeva, Sergei Bondarchuk, Vyacheslav Tikhonov
† The film was five years in production and cost between 50 and 70 million dollars.

AA: best foreign film

The War between Men and Women
US 1972   105m   Technicolor
   Panavision
National General / Jalem / Llenroc / 4D
   (Danny Arnold)

A half-blind cartoonist marries a divorcee and is troubled by her ex-husband.
Semi-serious comedy vaguely based on Thurber, but not so that you'd notice, apart from the blind hero; generally neither funny nor affecting.

w Mel Shavelson, Danny Arnold, based on the writings of James Thurber *d* Melville Shavelson *ph* Charles F. Wheeler *m* Marvin Hamlisch *pd* Stan Jolley

Jack Lemmon, Barbara Harris, Jason Robards Jnr, Herb Edelman, Lisa Gerritsen

War Games•
US 1983   113m   Metrocolor
MGM-UA / Sherwood (Leonard Goldberg, Harold Schneider)

A teenager unwittingly taps his home computer into the Pentagon and pretends to be Russia on the point of launching missiles.
Mildly intriguing science fantasy which becomes uncomfortable and finally boring because of the excess of jargon and flashing lights.

w Lawrence Lasker, Walter F. Parkes *d* John Badham *ph* William A. Fraker *m* Arthur B. Rubenstein *pd* Angelo P. Graham

Matthew Broderick, Dabney Coleman, John Wood, Ally Sheedy, Barry Corbin, Kent Williams
'All the film's adventure and suspense is inevitably at odds with its ostensible sentiments . . . [but] the result has a kind of seamless efficiency.'—*Steve Jenkins, MFB*
AAN: screenplay, cinematography

War Hunt
US 1961   83m   bw
TD Enterprises (Terry Sanders)

Korea 1953: a kill-crazy private is befriended by a war orphan but finally has to be shot.

Vaguely commendable but not very expert indictment of the realities of war.

w Stanford Whitmore *d* Denis Sanders
ph Ted McCord *m* Bud Shank

John Saxon, Robert Redford, Sidney Pollack, Charles Aidman, Tommy Matsuda

The War Lord••
US 1965   121m   Technicolor
   Panavision
Universal / Court (Walter Seltzer)

An officer of the Duke of Normandy has trouble with Druids and the law of *droit de seigneur*.
Complex medieval melodrama with an air of fantasy about it; generally likeably strange, but the production should have been more stylized and fanciful.

w John Collier, Millard Kaufman, *play* The Lovers by Leslie Stevens *d* Franklin Schaffner *ph* Russell Metty *m* Jerome Moross *ad* Alexander Golitzen, Henry Bumstead

Charlton Heston, Richard Boone, Rosemary Forsyth, Maurice Evans, Guy Stockwell, Niall MacGinnis, Henry Wilcoxon, James Farentino

The War Lover
GB 1962   105m   bw
Columbia / Arthur Hornblow Jnr

In 1943, a Flying Fortress commander based in East Anglia has the wrong ideas about women and war.
Solemn character drama punctuated by aerial battles.

w Howard Koch, *novel* John Hersey *d* Philip Leacock *ph* Bob Huke *m* Richard Addinsell

Steve McQueen, Shirley Anne Field, Robert Wagner, Gary Cockrell, Michael Crawford

War Nurse
US 1930   79m   bw

Problems of a nurse behind the lines in World War I. Ambitious but unsuccessful attempt to do another *Big Parade*; a lack of style and story kills it. Robert Montgomery, Anita Page, June Walker, Robert Ames, Zasu Pitts, Marie Prevost, Helen Jerome Eddy, Hedda Hopper. Written by Becky Gardner, Joe Farnham, from an anonymous autobiography, directed by Edgar Selwyn; for MGM. 'Won't get anywhere in the major houses; too filled with audible suffering to class as entertainment.'—*Variety*

War of the Wildcats
US 1943   102m   bw
Republic (Robert North)
aka: *In Old Oklahoma*

A lady writer causes friction between an oil operator and a cowboy.
Action potboiler which once passed an hour and three-quarters quite painlessly.

w Ethel Hill, Eleanore Griffith, Thomson Burtis *d* Albert S. Rogell *ph* Jack Marta *m* Walter Scharf

John Wayne, Martha Scott, Albert Dekker, George 'Gabby' Hayes, Marjorie Rambeau, Dale Evans, Grant Withers, Sidney Blackmer

The War of the Worlds•
US 1952   85m   Technicolor
Paramount / George Pal

Terrifying aliens invade Earth via the American midwest.
Spectacular battle scenes are the mainstay of this violent fantasy, which goes to pieces once the cardboard characters open their mouths.

w Barre Lyndon, *novel* H. G. Wells *d* Byron Haskin *ph* George Barnes *ad* Hal Pereira, Albert Nozaki *m* Leith Stevens

Gene Barry, Ann Robinson, Les Tremayne, Bob Cornthwaite, Sandra Giglio
● *Video: CIC*

The War Wagon••
US 1967   99m   Technicolor   Panavision
Universal / Batjac (Marvin Schwartz)

Two cowboys and an Indian plan to ambush the gold wagon of a crooked mining contractor.
Exhilarating but simply-plotted action western with strong comedy elements and a cast of old reliables.

w Clair Huffaker, from his novel Badman *d* Burt Kennedy *ph* William H. Clothier *m* Dmitri Tiomkin

John Wayne, Kirk Douglas, Howard Keel, Robert Walker, Keenan Wynn, Bruce Cabot, Gene Evans, Bruce Dern
'It all works splendidly.'—*MFB*

The Ware Case•
GB 1938   79m   bw
Ealing / Capad (S. C. Balcon)

A nobleman is suspected of murdering his wife's rich brother.
Courtroom melodrama twice filmed as a silent; stagey but reasonably compelling in its way.

w Robert Stevenson, Roland Pertwee, E. V. H. Emmett, *play* G. P. Bancroft *d* Robert Stevenson *ph* Ronald Neame *m* Ernest Irving

Clive Brook, Jane Baxter, Barry K. Barnes, C. V. France, Francis L. Sullivan, Frank Cellier, Edward Rigby, Peter Bull, Athene Seyler, Ernest Thesiger
† Previous versions had been made in 1917 (with Matheson Lang) and 1930 (with Stewart Rome).

Warlock•
US 1959   123m   De Luxe   Cinemascope
TCF (Edward Dmytryk)

The cowardly citizens of a small western town hire a gunman as their unofficial marshal.
Overlong, talkative and somewhat pretentious star western with good sequences.

w Robert Alan Aurthur, *novel* Oakley Hall *d* Edward Dmytryk *ph* Joe MacDonald *m* Leigh Harline

Henry Fonda, Richard Widmark, Anthony Quinn, Dorothy Malone, Dolores Michaels, Wallace Ford, Tom Drake, Richard Arlen, Regis Toomey, Don Beddoe, De Forrest Kelley

Warlords of Atlantis
GB 1978 96m Technicolor
EMI / John Dark, Kevin Connor

Victorian sea scientists discover a lost land under the Mediterranean.
Predictable compote of monsters and unwearable costumes, without a trace of wit in the script. For infants only.

w Brian Hayles d Kevin Connor ph Alan Hume m Mike Vickers pd Elliot Scott

Doug McClure, Peter Gilmore, Shane Rimmer, Lea Brodie, Michael Gothard

A Warm December
GB / US 1972 101m Technicolor
First Artists / Verdon (Melville Tucker)

A widowed American doctor in London falls for a mysterious African girl who turns out to be the dying niece of a diplomat.
Weird mishmash of Love Story, Brief Encounter and Dark Victory, getting the worst of all worlds.

w Lawrence Roman d Sidney Poitier ph Paul Beeson m Coleridge-Taylor Parkinson

Sidney Poitier, Esther Anderson, George Baker, Johnny Sekka, Earl Cameron

● Video: Guild

Warn London
GB 1934 74m bw

A London policeman who is the double of a well-known burglar replaces him and infiltrates an international gang. Exuberant minor thriller which made a good novelty booking at the time. Edmund Gwenn, John Loder, Leonora Corbett, D. A. Clarke-Smith. Written by Charles Bennett, Billie Bristow, from the novel by Denison Clift; directed by T. Hayes Hunter; for British Lion.

Warn That Man
GB 1943 82m bw

German spies pose as an English nobleman and his staff but are routed by an unexpected guest. On the stage this must have been an effective comedy-thriller, but the film is stymied by stiff handling. Gordon Harker, Raymond Lovell, Jean Kent, Finlay Currie, Philip Friend, Frederick Cooper. Written by Vernon Sylvaine, Lawrence Huntington, from the play by Vernon Sylvaine; directed by Lawrence Huntington; for ABPC. 'Slick drama, mounting success, and spectacular military enterprise.'—The Cinema

'What's a little bullet between friends?'
Warning Shot°
US 1966 100m Technicolor
Paramount / Bob Banner (Buzz Kulik)

While looking for a psychopathic killer, a cop shoots dead a man who draws a gun on him. But the dead man's gun cannot be found, and the officer is suspended . . .
Watchable mystery decked out with guest stars; possibly intended as a TV movie.

w Mann Rubin, novel 711—Officer Needs Help by Whit Masterson d Buzz Kulik ph Joseph Biroc m Jerry Goldsmith

David Janssen, Lillian Gish, Ed Begley, Keenan Wynn, Sam Wanamaker, Eleanor Parker, Stefanie Powers, Walter Pidgeon, George Sanders, George Grizzard, Steve Allen, Carroll O'Connor, Joan Collins

Warning to Wantons
GB 1948 104m bw

A nobleman takes in a flirtatious girl and finds she causes trouble for him and his family. Interminable comedy-drama made even duller by the Independent Frame production method, which cut costs but restricted movement. Harold Warrender, Anne Vernon, David Tomlinson, Sonia Holm, Marie Burke, Judy Kelly. Written by Donald B. Wilson and James Laver, from the novel by Mary Mitchell; directed by Donald B. Wilson; for Aquila / GFD.

Warpath
US 1951 93m Technicolor
Paramount (Nat Holt)

An ex-army captain tracks down the outlaws who murdered his girl.
Goodish standard western.

w Frank Gruber d Byron Haskin ph Ray Rennahan m Paul Sawtell

Edmond O'Brien, Dean Jagger, Forrest Tucker, Harry Carey Jnr, Wallace Ford, Polly Bergen

'These are the armies of the night . . .'
The Warriors
US 1979 94m Movielab
Paramount (Laurence Gordon)

A New York street gang runs into trouble when making a cross-city journey.
A sick exploitation movie about urban violence, poorly made into the bargain.

w David Shaber, Walter Hill, novel Sol Yurick d Walter Hill ph Andrew Laszlo m Barry de Vorzon

Michael Beck, James Remar, Thomas Waites, Dorsey Wright, Brian Tyler, David Harris

● Video: CIC

The Warrior's Husband
US 1933 75m bw

The Greeks break into Amazonia and conquer the women, provoking a worm to turn. A weird attempt by Hollywood to film a whimsical comedy which belonged only on Broadway, where the Greeks no doubt have a word for it. Elissa Landi, Marjorie Rambeau, Ernest Truex, David Manners, Helen Ware, Maude Eburne. Written by Sonya Levien from the play by Julian Thompson; directed by Walter Lang; for Jesse L. Lasky / Fox. 'Novel farce will need astute exploitation aid.'—Variety

Washington Masquerade
US 1932 92m bw

A high-minded senator is corrupted by a worthless girl. Solid star melodrama. Lionel

Barrymore, Karen Morley, Nils Asther, C. Henry Gordon, William Collier Snr. Written by John Meehan and Samuel Blythe, from the play The Claw by Henri Bernstein; directed by Charles Brabin; for MGM. (GB title: Mad Masquerade.)

Washington Merry-go-round°
US 1932 75m bw

A crusading young congressman attacks the crooks in the government. Naive comedy-drama with a miscast star. Lee Tracy, Constance Cummings, Alan Dinehart, Walter Connolly, Clarence Muse, Arthur Vinton. Written by Jo Swerling from an original by Maxwell Anderson; directed by James Cruze; for Columbia. 'Lots of flagwaving and political timeliness the chief appeal.'—Variety

Washington Story
US 1952 82m bw
MGM (Dore Schary)
GB title: Target for Scandal

A lady reporter goes to Washington to expose corruption, but falls for an honest congressman.
Standard flagwaver which takes itself a shade too seriously.

wd Robert Pirosh ph John Alton m Conrad Salinger

Van Johnson, Patricia Neal, Louis Calhern, Sidney Blackmer, Philip Ober, Patricia Collinge, Elizabeth Patterson, Moroni Olsen

Watch on the Rhine°°
US 1943 114m bw
Warner (Hal B. Wallis)

A German refugee and his family are pursued by Nazi agents in Washington.
Talky play doesn't make much of a film, though the talk is good talk and the performances outstanding; but it made a prestige point or two for Hollywood.

w Dashiell Hammett, play Lillian Hellman d Herman Shumlin ph Merritt Gerstad, Hal Mohr m Max Steiner

Paul Lukas, Bette Davis, Lucile Watson, George Coulouris, Donald Woods, Geraldine Fitzgerald, Beulah Bondi, Henry Daniell

AA: Paul Lukas
AAN: best picture; script; Lucile Watson

Watch the Birdie
US 1950 71m bw
MGM (Harry Ruskin)

A photographer meets a rich girl and saves her from a crook.
Unhappy remake of Buster Keaton's The Cameraman, enlivened by a chase finale, but not helped by the star playing three members of the same family.

w Ivan Tors, Devery Freeman, Harry Ruskin d Jack Donohue ph Paul C. Vogel m George Stoll

Red Skelton, Arlene Dahl, Ann Miller, Leon Ames, Pamela Britton, Richard Rober

The Watcher in the Woods
US 1980 / 82   100m or 83m   Technicolor
Walt Disney (Tom Leetch)

The teenage daughter of an American composer has strange and apparently supernatural experiences in the British countryside.
Unsatisfactory attempt by the Disney people to aim at a wider audience than is expected of them. The mixture of cuteness, menace and the supernatural simply doesn't gell, and the film was much re-edited between its two appearances.

w Brian Clemens, Harry Spaulding, Rosemary Anne Sisson, *novel* Florence Engel Randall *d* John Hough (and Vincent McEveety) *ph* Alan Hume *m* Stanley Myers

Bette Davis, Carroll Baker, David McCallum, Lynn-Holly Johnson, Kyle Richards, Ian Bannen, Richard Pasco

The Watchmaker of St Paul*
France 1973   105m   Eastmancolor
Lira (Raymond Danon)
original title: *L'Horloger de St Paul*

A watchmaker's tranquil life is shattered when he learns that his son is wanted for murder.
Solid character drama with careful writing and acting.

w Jean Aurenche, Pierre Bost, Bertrand Tavernier, *novel* L'Horloger D'Everton by Georges Simenon *d* Bertrand Tavernier *ph* Pierre William Glenn *m* Philippe Sarde

Philippe Noiret, Jean Rochefort, Sylvain Rougerie, Christine Pascal

The Water Babies
GB / Poland 1978   92m   colour
Ariadne / Studio Miniatur Filmowych (Peter Shaw)

An 1850 chimney sweep evades his pursuers by jumping into a pool, where he becomes involved in an underwater adventure.
The live action bookends are strangely subdued, the animated middle totally characterless and seeming to bear little relation to the rest. A considerable disappointment.

w Michael Robson, *novel* Charles Kingsley *d* Lionel Jeffries *ph* Ted Scaife *m* Phil Coulter

James Mason, Billie Whitelaw, Bernard Cribbins, Joan Greenwood, David Tomlinson, Tommy Pender

● Video: Thorn EMI

Water Birds see The Living Desert

The Water Gypsies
GB 1932   80m   bw

Adventures of two girls who live on a Thames barge. Rather naive and ordinary version of a successful book which many years later emerged as a stage musical; the film production has a stagey look throughout. Ann Todd, Sari Maritza, Richard Bird, Frances

Doble, Ian Hunter, Anthony Ireland. Written by Basil Dean, Miles Malleson, Alma Reville, John Paddy Carstairs from the novel by A. P. Herbert; directed by Maurice Elvey; for ATP. 'Should do business in the best type of places.'—*Variety*

'The desires and loneliness of seafaring men and their women!'

Waterfront
GB 1950   80m   bw
GFD / Conqueror
US title: *Waterfront Women*

A drunken ship's fireman comes back to Liverpool after many years and causes trouble.
Unintentionally funny melodrama which gives the actors a lot of trouble.

w John Brophy, Paul Soskin, *novel* John Brophy *d* Michael Anderson *ph* Harry Waxman *md* Muir Mathieson

Robert Newton, Richard Burton, Kathleen Harrison, Susan Shaw, Avis Scott, Kenneth Griffith

Waterhole Three
US 1967   100m   Techniscope
Paramount

Sheriff, crooks and a gambler seek buried loot.
Rather irritatingly immoral western with a hero who defines rape as assault with a friendly weapon; in between it tries hard for the ballad style.

w Joseph Steck, Robert R. Young *d* William Graham *ph* Robert Burks *m* Dave Grusin

James Coburn, Carroll O'Connor, Margaret Blye, Claude Akins, Joan Blondell, Timothy Carey

'The men, the battle, the glory the world will remember forever!'

Waterloo*
Italy / USSR 1970   132m   Technicolor Panavision
Columbia / DDL / Mosfilm (Dino de Laurentiis)

Historical events leading up to the 1815 battle. The battle forms the last hour of this historical charade, and looks both exciting and splendid, though confusion is not avoided. The rest is a mixed blessing.

w H. A. L. Craig, Sergei Bondarchuk *d* Sergei Bondarchuk *ph* Armando Nannuzzi *m* Nino Rota *pd* Mario Garbuglia

Rod Steiger, Christopher Plummer, Orson Welles, Jack Hawkins, Virginia McKenna, Dan O'Herlihy, Rupert Davies, Ian Ogilvy, Michael Wilding

Waterloo Bridge*
US 1931   72m   bw
Universal (Carl Laemmle Jnr)

An army officer marries a ballerina; when he is reported missing his family ignore her and she sinks into prostitution.
One for the ladies, who lapped it up.

w Tom Reed, Benn W. Levy, *play* Robert E. Sherwood *d* James Whale *ph* Arthur Edeson

Mae Clarke, Kent Douglass, Doris Lloyd, Ethel Griffies, Enid Bennett, Frederick Kerr, Bette Davis

'Just fair programme fodder, and it ought to be better. Not helped by an uninspiring sad ending.'—*Variety*

Waterloo Bridge**
US 1940   103m   bw
MGM (Sidney Franklin)

Lush, all-stops-out remake of the above; for yet another version see *Gaby*.

w S. N. Behrman, Hans Rameau, George Froeschel *d* Mervyn Le Roy *ph* Joseph Ruttenberg *m* Herbert Stothart

Vivien Leigh, Robert Taylor, Lucile Watson, Virginia Field, Maria Ouspenskaya, C. Aubrey Smith, Steffi Duna

'The director uses candlelight and rain more effectively than he does the actors.'—*New Yorker, 1977*

AAN: Joseph Ruttenberg; Herbert Stothart

The Waterloo Bridge Handicap*
GB 1978   21m   colour

Commuters enjoy a daily race across Westminster Bridge. Amusing trifle, well shot and edited. Leonard Rossiter, Lynda Bellingham, John Quentin, Gordon Laye. Written and directed by *Ross Cramer*; edited by *Sean Barton*; for Fetter / Paramount.

Waterloo Road*
GB 1944   76m   bw
GFD / Gainsborough (Edward Black)

A soldier whose wife is enamoured of a petty crook absents himself to settle matters.
What at the time seemed cheerful realism now seems chronically forced, but amusing moments can still be found.

w Sidney Gilliat, *story* Val Valentine *d* Sidney Gilliat *ph* Jack Cox *md* Louis Levy

John Mills, Stewart Granger, Joy Shelton, Alastair Sim, Beatrice Varley, Alison Leggatt, Jean Kent

'The harsh rattle of trains over a viaduct, the clamour of the street market, the wailing of sirens and the crash of bombs are the accompaniment of this wartime love story.'—*Richard Winnington*

'Unpretentious, credible, continuously entertaining and just the right length.'—*Richard Mallett, Punch*

Watermelon Man
US 1970   100m   Technicolor
Columbia / Johanna (John B. Bennett)

A bigoted insurance salesman wakes up one morning to find he has turned into a black man.
Spasmodically funny racial comedy, compromised by the impossibility of a black man playing white even with heavy make-up.

w Herman Raucher *d* Melvin Van Peebles *ph* W. Wallace Kelley *m* Melvin Van Peebles

Godfrey Cambridge, Estelle Parsons, Howard Caine, Mantan Moreland

Waters of Time°
GB 1951 37m bw

A poetic impression of the Port of London, from the mouth of the Thames to Kingston. Notably stylish documentary, made to coincide with the Festival of Britain. Written, directed and edited by *Basil Wright* and *Bill Launder*; for the Port of London Authority.

Watership Down
GB 1978 92m Technicolor
Nepenthe (Martin Rosen)

A colony of rabbits seek a new home following a vision of the destruction of their warren. A brilliantly written if somewhat pretentious parable becomes a rather flatly made cartoon in which it is difficult to distinguish one rabbit from another; the whole thing becomes a bit doomladen for family audiences, while adults will presumably prefer to re-read the novel.

wd Martin Rosen, *novel* Richard Adams *animation* d Tony Guy *m* Angela Morley

voices: John Hurt, Richard Briers, Ralph Richardson, Zero Mostel, Roy Kinnear, Denholm Elliott, John Bennett, Simon Cadell

● *Video: Thorn EMI*

Watusi
US 1959 85m Technicolor
MGM (Al Zimbalist)

Harry Quartermain retraces his father's footsteps to King Solomon's Mines. Skilful re-use of *King Solomon's Mines* footage; acceptable Boys' Own Paper stuff.

w James Clavell *d* Kurt Neumann *ph* Harold E. Wellman

George Montgomery, Taina Elg, David Farrar, Rex Ingram, Dan Seymour

Waxworks°
Germany 1924 62m approx (24 fps) bw silent
Neptun-Film
original title: *Das Wachsfigurenkabinett*

A young poet in a fairground waxwork museum concocts stories about Haroun al Raschid, Ivan the Terrible and Jack the Ripper.
The form later became familiar in such horror films as *Torture Garden* and *Tales from the Crypt*, but here the emphasis is not on horror but on grotesquerie, and indeed the idea is somewhat more entertaining than the rather plodding execution.

w Henrik Galeen *d* Paul Leni *ph* Helmar Lerski *ad* Paul Leni, Ernst Stern, Alfred Junge

William Dieterle, Emil Jannings, Conrad Veidt, Werner Krauss

The Way Ahead°°°
GB 1944 115m bw
GFD / Two Cities (John Sutro, Norman Walker)
US title: *Immortal Battalion*

Adventures of a platoon of raw recruits during World War II.

Memorable semi-documentary originally intended as a training film; the warm humour of the early scenes, however, never leads quite naturally into the final action and tragedy.

w Eric Ambler, Peter Ustinov *d* Carol Reed *ph* Guy Green *m* William Alwyn

David Niven, Stanley Holloway, Raymond Huntley, *William Hartnell*, James Donald, John Laurie, Leslie Dwyer, Hugh Burden, Jimmy Hanley, Renée Asherson, Penelope Dudley Ward, Reginald Tate, Leo Genn, Mary Jerrold, Peter Ustinov

Way Back Home
US 1932 81m bw

Problems of a Maine preacher.
Unintentionally hilarious farrago of dark deeds in a small town, from a radio serial.
Phillips Lord, Bette Davis, Effie Palmer, Bennett Kilpack, Frank Albertson, Mrs Phillips Lord. Written by Jane Murfin; directed by William A. Seiter; for RKO.

Way Down East°°
US 1920 110m approx (24 fps) bw with
       colour sequence silent
D. W. Griffith

A country girl is seduced; her baby dies; her shame is revealed; but a kindly farmer rescues her from drowning and marries her.
Old-fashioned tearjerker impeccably mounted and very typical of its director in its sentimental mood. The ice floe sequence is famous for its excitement and realism.

w Anthony Paul Kelly, Joseph R. Grismer, D. W. Griffith, *play* Lottie Blair Parker *d* D. W. Griffith *ph* Billy Bitzer, Henrik Sortov

Lillian Gish, Richard Barthelmess, Lowell Sherman, Creighton Hale

   'Griffith took a creaking, dated stage melodrama and turned it into a melodramatic epic.'—*Pauline Kael, 70s*

Way Down East
US 1935 85m bw
TCF (Winfield Sheehan)

Tedious and unwise remake.

w Howard Estabrook, William Hurlbut *d* Henry King

Rochelle Hudson, Henry Fonda, Slim Summerville, Edward Trevor, Margaret Hamilton, Andy Devine, Spring Byington, Russell Simpson, Sara Haden

Way for a Sailor
US 1930 83m bw
MGM

Adventures of a tough seafarer and a pet seal.
Thin vehicle for a declining star whose talkie voice was at odds with his image.

w Laurence Stallings, W. L. River, *novel* Albert Richard Wetjen *d* Sam Wood *ph* Percy Hilburn

John Gilbert, Wallace Beery, Leila Hyams, Jim Tully, Polly Moran, Doris Lloyd
   'It throws John Gilbert for a loss, and it's not his fault. His voice is okay.'—*Variety*

Way of a Gaucho
US 1952 91m Technicolor
TCF (Philip Dunne)

An Argentine gaucho joins the militia and fights Indians.
Mildly interesting western-in-disguise.

w Philip Dunne, *novel* Herbert Childs *d* Jacques Tourneur *ph* Harry Jackson *m* Sol Kaplan

Rory Calhoun, Gene Tierney, Richard Boone, Hugh Marlowe, Everett Sloane, Enrique Chaico

The Way of All Flesh°
US 1928 94m (24 fps) bw silent
Paramount

A respectable man leaves his wife, goes to the dogs, and is too ashamed to come back.
Star character drama, most watchable now when it goes over the top.

d Victor Fleming

Emil Jannings

AA: Emil Jannings
AAN: best picture
† Remade 1940 with Akim Tamiroff.

Way Out West°°°°
US 1937 66m bw
Hal Roach (Stan Laurel)

Laurel and Hardy come to Brushwood Gulch to deliver the deed to a gold mine.
Seven reels of perfect joy, with the comedians at their very best in brilliantly-timed routines, plus two song numbers as a bonus.

w Jack Jevne, Charles Rogers, James Parrott, Felix Adler *d* James Horne *ph* Art Lloyd, Walter Lundin *m* Marvin Hatley

Stan Laurel, Oliver Hardy, James Finlayson, Sharon Lynne, Rosina Lawrence
   'Thin returns indicated . . . for added feature on duallers.'—*Variety*
   'Not only one of their most perfect films, it ranks with the best screen comedy anywhere.'—*David Robinson, 1962*
   'The film is leisurely in the best sense; you adjust to a different rhythm and come out feeling relaxed as if you'd had a vacation.'—*New Yorker, 1980*

AAN: Marvin Hatley

'Of course he's naughty! But that's the way you love him best!'

The Way to Love
US 1933 80m bw
Paramount (Benjamin Glazer)

A would-be Paris tourist guide works as a pavement hawker and helps a showgirl evade her knife-thrower partner.
Thin star vehicle with a few pleasant moments.

w Gene Fowler, Benjamin Glazer *d* Norman Taurog *ph* Charles Lang *m / ly* Ralph Rainger, Leo Robin

Maurice Chevalier, Edward Everett Horton, Ann Dvorak, Arthur Pierson, Minna Gombell, Blanche Frederici, Douglass Dumbrille, John Miljan
   'The poorest of the Chevaliers but poor entertainment which will get by on the strength of the star.'—*Variety*

The Way to the Gold
US 1957 94m bw Cinemascope
TCF (David Weisbart)

An ex-convict seeks hidden loot but is pursued
by competitors.
Gloomy, self-pitying melodrama.

w Wendell Mayes, novel Wilber Steele
d Robert D. Webb ph Leo Tover m Lionel
Newman

Jeffrey Hunter, Sheree North, Barry Sullivan,
Walter Brennan, Ruth Donnelly, Neville
Brand

The Way to the Stars****
GB 1945 109m bw
Two Cities (Anatole de Grunwald)
US title: Johnny in the Clouds

World War II as seen by the guests at a small
hotel near an airfield.
Generally delightful comedy drama suffused
with tragic atmosphere but with very few flying
shots, one of the few films which instantly
bring back the atmosphere of the war in
Britain for anyone who was involved.

w Terence Rattigan, Anatole de Grunwald
poem John Pudney d Anthony Asquith
ph Derrick Williams m Nicholas Brodszky

John Mills, Rosamund John, Michael
Redgrave, Douglass Montgomery, Basil
Radford, Stanley Holloway, Joyce Carey,
Renée Asherson, Felix Aylmer, Bonar
Colleano, Trevor Howard, Jean Simmons

'Not for a long time have I seen a film so
satisfying, so memorable, or so successful in
evoking the precise mood and atmosphere of
the recent past.'—Richard Mallett, Punch

'Humour, humanity, and not a sign of
mawkishness . . . a classic opening sequence,
with the camera wandering through an
abandoned air base, peering in at each detail
in the nissen huts, the sleeping quarters, the
canteens, noting all the time a procession of
objects each of which will have its own special
significance in the action of the film.'—Basil
Wright, 1972

Way Way Out
US 1966 105m De Luxe Cinemascope
TCF / Coldwater / Jerry Lewis (Malcolm
Stuart)

In 1994 a weather expert on the moon has
woman trouble.
Dismal sex farce with an unusual backdrop;
painful to sit through.

w William Bowers, Laslo Vadnay d Gordon
Douglas ph William H. Clothier m Lalo
Schifrin

Jerry Lewis, Connie Stevens, Robert Morley,
Dick Shawn, Anita Ekberg, Dennis Weaver,
Howard Morris, Brian Keith

'Everything seemed so important then—
     even love!'

The Way We Were**
US 1973 118m Eastmancolor
Panavision
Columbia / Rastar (Ray Stark)

The romance and marriage of an upper-crust
young novelist and a Jewish bluestocking girl,
from college to Hollywood in the thirties,
forties and fifties.
Instant nostalgia for Americans, some fun and
a lot of boredom for everybody is provided by
this very patchy star vehicle which makes a
particular mess of the McCarthy witch hunt
sequence but has undeniable moments of
vitality.

w Arthur Laurents, from his novel d Sydney
Pollack ph Harry Stradling Jnr m Marvin
Hamlisch

Barbra Streisand, Robert Redford, Patrick
O'Neal, Viveca Lindfors, Bradford Dillman,
Lois Chiles, Allyn Ann McLerie, Herb
Edelman, Murray Hamilton

'Not one moment of the picture is anything
but garbage under the gravy of false
honesty.'—Stanley Kauffmann

'A real curate's egg of a movie, composed of
so many disparate parts as to put you in mind
of Leacock's knight, who got on his horse and
rode off furiously in all directions.'—Benny
Green, Punch

AA: Marvin Hamlisch; title song (m Marvin
Hamlisch, ly Alan and Marilyn Bergman)
AAN: Harry Stradling Jnr; Barbra Streisand

The Way West*
US 1967 122m De Luxe Panavision
UA / Harold Hecht

Hazards of a wagon train between Missouri
and Oregon in 1843.
Semi-spectacular western which looks good
but falls apart dramatically, especially in its
insistence on a sub-plot about a most unlikely
nymphet.

w Ben Maddow, Mitch Lindemann, novel A.
B. Guthrie Jnr d Andrew V. McLaglen
ph William H. Clothier m Bronislau Kaper

Kirk Douglas, Robert Mitchum, Richard
Widmark, Lola Albright, Michael Witney,
Sally Field, Stubby Kaye, Jack Elam

'A jerk's idea of an epic; big stars, big
landscapes, bad jokes, folksy-heroic music to
plug up the holes, and messy hang-ups.'—
Pauline Kael

The Wayward Bus
US 1957 89m bw Cinemascope
TCF (Charles Brackett)

A landslide strands an assortment of bus
passengers in a lonely farmhouse . . .
. . . but not the old dark house, unfortunately:
this lot does nothing but talk, and the plot
never really forms.

w Ivan Moffat, novel John Steinbeck d Victor
Vicas ph Charles G. Clarke m Leigh Harline

Dan Dailey, Jayne Mansfield, Joan Collins,
Rick Jason, Dolores Michaels, Larry Keating,
Betty Lou Keim

We Are Not Alone*
US 1939 112m bw
Warner (Henry Blanke)

A man having an innocent affair is accused of
murdering his wife.
Gloomy, well-acted drama with a rather
uneasy English setting.
w James Hilton, Milton Krims, novel James
Hilton d Edmund Goulding ph Tony
Gaudio m Max Steiner

Paul Muni, Jane Bryan, Flora Robson,
Raymond Severn, Una O'Connor, Henry
Daniell, Montagu Love, James Stephenson,
Cecil Kellaway

'It has dignity and warmth and is genuinely
moving . . . handsomely produced, skilfully
directed, and eloquently played.'—Variety

We Dive at Dawn
GB 1943 98m bw
GFD / Gainsborough (Edward Black)

World War II adventures of a British
submarine disabled in the Baltic.
Fairly routine war suspenser.

w J. P. Williams, Val Valentine, Frank
Launder d Anthony Asquith ph Jack Cox

John Mills, Eric Portman, Reginald Purdell,
Niall MacGinnis, Joan Hopkins, Josephine
Wilson, Jack Watling

● Video: Rank

We Faw Down
US 1928 20m bw silent

Stan and Ollie have an evening out, but their
lies to their wives become apparent. Moderate
star comedy, later elaborated in Sons of the
Desert. Laurel and Hardy, Bess Flowers,
Vivien Oakland. Written by H. M. Walker;
directed by Leo McCarey; for Hal Roach.

We Have Our Moments
US 1937 63m bw

Gangsters hide their loot in the trunk of a
schoolteacher going to Europe on a vacation.
Rather slackly handled comedy with amusing
bits. James Dunn, Sally Eilers, Mischa Auer,
David Niven, Warren Hymer, Marjorie
Gateson, Thurston Hall. Written by Bruce
Manning, Charles Grayson, David Belden,
Frederick Stephani; directed by Alfred
Werker; for Edmund Grainger / Universal.
'As the number two feature on doubles it will
manage to get by.'—Variety

We Joined the Navy
GB 1962 105m Eastmancolor
Cinemascope
Dial / Daniel M. Angel

A carefree naval commander and three cadets
get involved in the affairs of a small
Mediterranean country.
Desperate naval farce which sinks from script
malnutrition in reel two.

w Arthur Dales, novel John Winton
d Wendy Toye ph Otto Heller m Ron
Grainer

Kenneth More, Lloyd Nolan, Mischa Auer,
Joan O'Brien, Jeremy Lloyd, Dinsdale
Landen, Derek Fowlds

We Live Again*
US 1934 85m bw
Samuel Goldwyn

A Russian prince is brought up in the country

WAY OUT WEST.   They all want the deed: Oliver Hardy, Sharon Lynne, James Finlayson.

and falls in love with a servant girl whose life later takes a downward path.
Beautifully made but dramatically uninteresting version of a Russian classic.

w Preston Sturges, Maxwell Anderson, Leonard Praskins, *novel* Resurrection by Leo Tolstoy *d* Rouben Mamoulian *ph* Gregg Toland *m* Alfred Newman

Fredric March, Anna Sten, Jane Baxter, C. Aubrey Smith, Ethel Griffies, Jessie Ralph, Sam Jaffe

'It's a class picture basically. That limits its mass b.o. appeal.'—*Variety*

We of the Never Never*

Australia 1982   134m   Eastmancolor
   Technovision
Adams Packer / Film Corporation of
   Western Australia / GTC (Greg Tepper)

Around 1900, a city girl marries the owner of an isolated cattle station.
Longwinded but attractively photographed recollections of another time and another place. Not really very memorable despite a plethora of incident.

w Peter Schreck, *book* Mrs Aeneas Gunn *d* Igor Auzins *ph* Gary Hansen *m* Peter Best

Angela Punch McGregor, Arthur Dignam, Tony Barry, Tommy Lewis

'Tasteful period re-creation, choked-back emotionalism, a *Men of Two Worlds* attempt at assuaging colonial guilt, and the kind of tidily suffering heroine Deborah Kerr used to play.'—*Kim Newman, MFB*

We Were Dancing

US 1942   93m   bw
MGM (Robert Z. Leonard, Orville Dull)

A Polish princess elopes from her engagement party with a gigolo.
Leaden romantic comedy produced in high style.

w Claudine West, Hans Rameau, George Froeschel, partly based on the play Tonight at 8.30 by Noel Coward *d* Robert Z. Leonard *ph* Robert Planck *m* Bronislau Kaper

WAY OUT WEST.   Stan simply can't imagine why Ollie keeps falling into water.

Norma Shearer, Melvyn Douglas, Gail
Patrick, Lee Bowman, *Marjorie Main,*
Reginald Owen, Alan Mowbray, Florence
Bates, Sig Rumann, Dennis Hoey, Heather
Thatcher, Connie Gilchrist

We Were Strangers[*]
US 1949 105m bw
Columbia / Horizon (Sam Spiegel)
Cuban rebels in the thirties plan to assassinate
a politician and have to build a tunnel through
a cemetery.
Well-made but very downbeat adventure
story, too cheerless to be exciting.

w Peter Viertel, John Huston, *novel* Rough
Sketch by Robert Sylvester *d* John Huston
ph Russell Metty *m* Georges Antheil

John Garfield, Jennifer Jones, Pedro
Armendariz, Gilbert Roland, Wally Cassell,
Ramon Novarro, David Bond, Jose Perez
'There is so much about this film I cannot
swallow—the implausibilities of detail, the
convention of broken accents, the literary
conversaziones, the naïve doctrines of
revolution . . . [but] it continues to haunt the
mind and has therefore had its say.'—*Richard
Winnington*

We Who Are about to Die
US 1937 82m bw
Life on Death Row. Modest prison
melodrama with a lot of opportunity for
character actors to display hysteria. Preston
Foster, Ann Dvorak, John Beal, Ray Mayer,
Gordon Jones, Russel Hopton, J. Carrol

Naish, Willie Fung, Paul Hurst, Frank Jenks,
Barnett Parker, John Wray, John Carroll.
Written by John Twist, David Lamson;
directed by Christy Cabanne; for RKO. 'An
action drama of considerable tension that
should please the general run of fans with
plenty of special charm for the kids and the
menfolk.'—*Variety*

The Weak and the Wicked
GB 1953 88m bw
ABPC / Marble Arch (Victor Skutezky)
Flashbacks show how various women came to
find themselves in prison.
Predictable portmanteau drama with stalwart
performances.

w J. Lee Thompson, Anne Burnaby, *book* Who Lie in Gaol by Joan Henry *d* J. Lee Thompson *ph* Gilbert Taylor *m* Leighton Lucas

Glynis Johns, John Gregson, Diana Dors, Jane Hylton, Sidney James, Olive Sloane, Eliot Makeham, A. E. Matthews, Athene Seyler, Sybil Thorndike, Anthony Nicholls, Joan Haythorne

The Weaker Sex

GB 1948 84m bw

Day-to-day problems of a well-to-do war widow. Mild suburban comedy which sparkled more on stage, with such curtain lines as: 'Quick, the fishmonger's got fish!' Ursula Jeans, Cecil Parker, Joan Hopkins, Derek Bond, Lana Morris, Thora Hird, John Stone. Written by Esther McCracken and Paul Soskin, from the play *No Medals* by Esther McCracken; directed by Roy Baker; for Paul Soskin / Two Cities.

The Weapon

GB 1956 81m bw Superscope 235 Penclean (Frank Bevis)

A boy finds a loaded revolver on a bomb site and mistakenly thinks he has killed someone with it.
Standard suspenser with a cast worthy of something more interesting.

w Fred Freiburger *d* Val Guest *ph* Reg Wyer *m* James Stevens

Lizabeth Scott, Steve Cochran, George Cole, Herbert Marshall, Nicole Maurey, Jon Whiteley, Laurence Naismith

The Web*

US 1947 87m bw
U-I

A financier hires a young lawyer as his bodyguard and lures him into committing murder.
Modestly well staged and glossy thriller.

w William Bowers, Bertram Millhauser *d* Michael Gordon *ph* Irving Glassberg *m* Hans Salter

Edmond O'Brien, Vincent Price, Ella Raines, William Bendix

The Webster Boy

GB 1961 83m bw
Emmet Dalton
US title: *Middle of Nowhere*

A teenager suffers at the hands of a sadistic schoolmaster.
Curious, totally unbelievable melodrama.

w Ted Allen *d* Don Chaffey *ph* Gerald Gibbs *m* Wilfrid Joseph

Richard O'Sullivan, John Cassavetes, David Farrar, Elizabeth Sellars, Niall MacGinnis

A Wedding*

US 1978 125m De Luxe
TCF / Lion's Gate (Thommy Thompson, Robert Altman)

Two families converge for a fashionable wedding, but the day is beset by calamities.

Wide-ranging satirical comedy which despite excellent moments goes on far too long, is rather too black, and is sabotaged by the director's *penchant* for having fourteen people talking at the same time. An exhausting experience.

w John Considine, Patricia Resnick, Allan Nicholls, Robert Altman *d* Robert Altman *ph* Charles Rosher *md* Tom Walls

Carol Burnett, Paul Dooley, Amy Stryker, Mia Farrow, Peggy Ann Garner, Lillian Gish, Nina Van Pallandt, Vittorio Gassman, Howard Duff, Desi Arnaz Jnr, Dina Merrill, Geraldine Chaplin, Viveca Lindfors, Lauren Hutton, John Cromwell

● *Video: CBS / Fox*

The Wedding March**

US 1928 196m approx (24 fps) bw silent
Paramount / Celebrity

A Habsburg prince loves a poor girl but is forced to marry a crippled princess, who dies; he is then murdered by the poor girl's enraged defender.
A marathon dose of Stroheim's favourite subject, sex, with some violence and a few fetishes thrown in. Full of fascinating touches, but desperately overlong, it was originally released in two parts, but failed to draw.

w Harry Carr, Erich Von Stroheim *d* Erich Von Stroheim *ph* Hal Mohr, Ben Reynolds *ad* Erich Von Stroheim, Richard Day

Erich Von Stroheim, Fay Wray, Zasu Pitts, Matthew Betz, Maude George, Cesare Gravina, George Fawcett
'A pitilessly authentic portrait of decadent Imperialist Austria.'—*Georges Sadoul*
'The slowness, heaviness, mindlessness of this temple of unnaturalness through which man passes as through a forest of clichés defied description.'—*John Simon, 1967*
† In 1975 there was published a pictorial record, *The Complete Wedding March*, by Herman G. Weinberg.

The Wedding Night*

US 1935 83m bw
Samuel Goldwyn

A Connecticut author causes tragedy when he takes an interest in the local Polish immigrant farmers and especially in the daughter of one of them.
Interesting and unusual but slightly tediously told drama.

w Edith Fitzgerald *d* King Vidor *ph* Gregg Toland *m* Alfred Newman

Gary Cooper, Anna Sten, Sig Rumann, Helen Vinson, Ralph Bellamy, Esther Dale
'Fine artistic film, possibly too artistic.'—*Variety*
'Convincing and curiously powerful.'—*New York Herald Tribune*

'He gave her something to remember him by!'

Wedding Present*

US 1936 81m bw
Paramount (B. P. Schulberg)

A pair of crack newspaper reporters take their jobs and themselves lightly.

Whimsical star comedy with some funny scenes.

w Joseph Anthony, *story* Paul Gallico *d* Richard Wallace *ph* Leon Shamroy

Cary Grant, Joan Bennett, George Bancroft, Conrad Nagel, Gene Lockhart, William Demarest, Edward Brophy
'Grant and Bennett try hard, but the combination of story, direction and whatnot is pretty much against them.'—*Variety*

Wedding Rehearsal

GB 1932 84m bw
Ideal / Alexander Korda

A Guards officer foils his grandmother's plans to get him married by finding suitors for all the young ladies offered.
Frail comedy with unsure technique.

w Lajos Biro, Arthur Wimperis *d* Alexander Korda *ph* L. Rowson *m* Kurt Schroeder

Roland Young, George Grossmith, John Loder, Lady Tree, Wendy Barrie, Maurice Evans, Joan Gardner, Merle Oberon, Kate Cutler, Edmund Breon

Wee Willie Winkie**

US 1937 99m bw
TCF (Gene Markey)

A small girl becomes the mascot of a British regiment in India.
Vaguely based on a Kipling tale, this was the most expensive Temple vehicle and a first-rate family action picture with sentimental asides.

w Ernest Pascal, Julien Josephson, *story* Rudyard Kipling *d* John Ford *ph* Arthur Miller *m* Alfred Newman

Shirley Temple, Victor McLaglen, C. Aubrey Smith, June Lang, Michael Whalen, Cesar Romero, Constance Collier, Gavin Muir
'Will add another clean-up to her cycle, but those knees are losing their contour . . . a pretentiously produced melodrama which launches the leading feminine box office star into a distinctly new phase of her career and story material.'—*Variety*

Weekend at the Waldorf*

US 1945 130m bw
MGM (Arthur Hornblow Jnr)

Four stories about guests at New York's largest hotel.
Disguised version of *Grand Hotel*, with the same stories twisted; the talent at hand, however, is serviceable rather than inspiring.

w Sam and Bella Spewack *d* Robert Z. Leonard *ph* Robert Planck *md* Johnny Green

Ginger Rogers, Walter Pidgeon, Van Johnson, Lana Turner, Robert Benchley, Edward Arnold, Constance Collier, Leon Ames, Warner Anderson, Phyllis Thaxter, Keenan Wynn, Porter Hall, Samuel S. Hinds, George Zucco, Xavier Cugat

Weekend in Havana

US 1941 80m Technicolor
TCF (William Le Baron)

A shopgirl in Havana falls for a shipping executive.

.·"You wanted a big wedding, baby, and I'm handing you a riot"!

Miss *Big Brown Eyes* would rather race to a fire than trip to the altar and Cary is the lad who tuned the fire-gongs to the Wedding March.

Adolph Zukor presents

JOAN BENNETT and CARY GRANT
in
"Wedding Present"

with **GEORGE BANCROFT**
CONRAD NAGEL • GENE LOCKHART
Directed by Richard Wallace • Based on the Story by Paul Gallico
a B. P. SCHULBERG Production • A Paramount Picture

WEDDING PRESENT.   A forgotten comedy which rang the box office bell in 1936.

Routine Fox musical showcasing familiar talents: adequate wartime escapist fare.
w Karl Tunberg, Darrell Ware d Walter Lang ph Ernest Palmer md Alfred Newman
Alice Faye, John Payne, Carmen Miranda, Cesar Romero, Cobina Wright Jnr, George Barbier, Sheldon Leonard, Leonid Kinskey

Weekend Marriage
US 1932 64m bw
A wife wants to remain independent. Comedy drama with nothing new to say about a familiar subject. Loretta Young, Norman Foster, George Brent, Aline MacMahon, Vivienne Osborne. Written by Sheridan Gibney from the novel Part-Time Wives by Faith Baldwin; directed by Thornton Freeland; for First National. 'Unimportant rewrite on familiar theme minus necessary key strength.'—*Variety*

Weekend with Father
US 1951 83m bw
U-I (Ted Richmond)
A widow and a widower fall in love when taking their respective children to a summer camp.
Mechanical comedy of upsets and embarrassments.
w Joseph Hoffman d Douglas Sirk
ph Clifford Stine m Frank Skinner
Van Heflin, Patricia Neal, Gigi Perreau, Virginia Field, Richard Denning

Weird Woman
US 1944 64m bw
A professor brings home from the South Seas a wife who seems to bring murder in her wake. Stiff and stilted thriller from an interesting original; one of the disappointing *Inner Sanctum* series. Lon Chaney, Evelyn Ankers, Anne Gwynne, Ralph Morgan, Elizabeth Risdon. Written by Brenda Weisberg, from the novel *Conjure Wife* by Fritz Leiber; directed by Reginald Le Borg; for Universal.

Welcome Danger*
US 1929 110m bw
Harold Lloyd
The meek son of a police chief gets involved in a tong war.
Moderate early talkie comedy showing the star in some trouble with pace and dialogue.
w Clyde Bruckman, Lex Neal, Felix Adler, Paul Gerard Smith d Clyde Bruckman
ph Walter Lundin, Henry Kohler
Harold Lloyd, Barbara Kent, Noah Young, Charles Middleton

Welcome Home Soldier Boys
US 1972 92m De Luxe
Four war veterans go home and start a wave of violence. Clumsily brutal anti-war tract which merely repels. Joe Don Baker, Paul Koslo, Alan Vint, Billy Green Bush. Written by Guerdon Trueblood; directed by Richard Crompton; for TCF.

Welcome Mr Washington
GB 1944 90m bw

A US sergeant in an English village falls for a local lady. Mild plea for harmony between allies; rather embarrassing to watch even at the time. Barbara Mullen, Donald Stewart, Peggy Cummins, Graham Moffatt, Martita Hunt. Written by Jack Whittingham, from a novel by Noel Streatfeild; directed by Leslie Hiscott; for British National / Shaftesbury.

Welcome Stranger
US 1947 107m bw
Paramount (Sol C. Siegel)

A genial young doctor fills in for a crusty old one on vacation in a small town.
Formula sentimental comedy, one of several reuniting the stars of *Going My Way*.

w Arthur Sheekman d Elliott Nugent ph Lionel Lindon m Robert Emmett Dolan

Bing Crosby, Barry Fitzgerald, Joan Caulfield, Wanda Hendrix, Frank Faylen, Elizabeth Patterson, Robert Shayne, Percy Kilbride

Welcome to Arrow Beach
US 1973 99m colour
Brut (Jack Cushingham)

A photographer living in a California beach community has become a cannibal after his experiences in the Korean War.
Abysmal horror movie with insufficient plot.

w Wallace C. Bennett, Jack Gross Jnr d Laurence Harvey ph Gerald Perry Finnerman m Tony Camillo

Laurence Harvey, Joanna Pettet, Stuart Whitman, John Ireland, Meg Foster

Welcome to Hard Times*
US 1967 103m Metrocolor
MGM / Max E. Youngstein, David Carr
GB title: *Killer on a Horse*

A small western town arms itself against a mysterious bandit.
Curiously likeable, almost symbolic suspense western which has a good start and middle but not much idea how to end.

wd Burt Kennedy, novel E. L. Doctorow ph Harry Stradling Jnr m Harry Sukman

Henry Fonda, Janice Rule, Keenan Wynn, Janis Paige, John Anderson, Warren Oates, Fay Spain, Edgar Buchanan, Aldo Ray, Lon Chaney Jnr, Elisha Cook Jnr

Welcome to LA*
US 1976 106m De Luxe
Lion's Gate / Robert Altman

A young composer in Los Angeles has a varied sex life.
Fragmentary, vaguely mystical, momentarily interesting, frequently confusing slice of life as seen through misty glasses.

wd Alan Rudolph ph Dave Myers m Richard Baskin

Keith Carradine, Sally Kellerman, Geraldine Chaplin, Harvey Keitel, Lauren Hutton, Viveca Lindfors, Sissy Spacek, Denver Pyle

'The supposedly free-form, improvisational dynamics of an Altman movie have here become a strictly choreographed ballet.'— *Richard Combs, MFB*

Welcome to the Club
GB 1970 88m bw
Welcome (Sam Lomberg)

Hiroshima 1945; an American Quaker sergeant upsets military protocol.
Pale satirical comedy shot in Copenhagen.

w Clement Biddle Wood, from his novel d Walter Shenson ph Mikael Salomon m Ken Thomas

Brian Foley, Jack Warden, Lee Meredith, Andy Jarrett

The Well*
US 1951 85m bw
Cardinal / Harry M. Popkin (Clarence Greene, Leo Popkin)

A black child falls down a well, and the town unites to save her.
Forceful high-pitched melodrama, cut to a do-gooder pattern which became very familiar.

w Russel Rouse, Clarence Greene d Leo Popkin, Russel Rouse ph Ernest Laszlo m Dmitri Tiomkin

Richard Rober, Henry Morgan, Barry Kelley, Christine Larson

AAN: script

The Well Groomed Bride*
US 1946 75m bw
Paramount (Fred Kohlmar)

A naval officer searches San Francisco for a magnum of champagne with which to launch a ship.
Thin but cheerful star comedy.

w Claude Binyon, Robert Russell d Sidney Lanfield ph John F. Seitz m Roy Webb

Ray Milland, Olivia de Havilland, Sonny Tufts, James Gleason, Constance Dowling, Percy Kilbride, Jean Heather

We'll Meet Again
GB 1942 84m bw

A girl singer suffers while her boy friend loves another. Unassuming star vehicle for the Forces' Sweetheart. Vera Lynn, Geraldo, Patricia Roc, Ronald Ward, Donald Gray, Frederick Leister. Written by James Seymour and Howard Thomas; directed by Phil Brandon; for Columbia.

'Paramount's thundering romance of the winning of the west!'

Wells Fargo*
US 1937 115m bw
Paramount (Frank Lloyd)

How the express delivery service was built up.
Large-scale, entertaining western with overmuch emphasis on domestic issues.

w Paul Schofield, Gerald Geraghty, John Boland, story Stuart N. Lake d Frank Lloyd ph Theodor Sparkuhl m Victor Young

Joel McCrea, Bob Burns, Frances Dee, Lloyd Nolan, Henry O'Neill, Mary Nash, Ralph Morgan, John Mack Brown, Porter Hall, Clarence Kolb

'Big b.o. right across the playdate board.'— *Variety*

Went the Day Well?**
GB 1942 92m bw
Ealing (S. C. Balcon)
US title: *Forty-eight Hours*

Villagers resist when German paratroopers invade an English village and the squire proves to be a quisling.
Could-it-happen melodrama which made excellent wartime propaganda; generally well staged.

w Angus MacPhail, John Dighton, Diana Morgan, story Graham Greene d Alberto Cavalcanti ph Willie Cooper m William Walton

Leslie Banks, Elizabeth Allen, Frank Lawton, Basil Sydney, Valerie Taylor, Mervyn Johns, Edward Rigby, Marie Lohr, C. V. France, David Farrar

We're Going to Be Rich
US 1938 80m bw

In the South African goldfields in 1880, a singer leaves her worthless husband for a publican. First American attempt to take over Our Gracie; it didn't work, but the damage was done. Gracie Fields, Victor McLaglen, Brian Donlevy, Coral Browne, Gus McNaughton. Written by Monty Banks, Rohama Siegel and Sam Hellman; directed by Monty Banks; for TCF. 'Will do well in England. In the States, will slide into the duals.'—*Variety*

We're in the Money
US 1935 65m bw

Adventures of female process servers working for a dizzy lawyer. Minor comedy using up contract artistes. Joan Blondell, Glenda Farrell, Hugh Herbert, Ross Alexander, Hobart Cavanaugh. Written by F. Hugh Herbert, Brown Holmes, Erwin Gelsey, George Bilson; directed by Ray Enright; for Warners. 'Only those exhibitors whose clients get hysterial on short notice will profit from it.'—*Variety*

We're No Angels*
US 1954 106m Technicolor
Vistavision
Paramount (Pat Duggan)

Three escaped Devil's Island convicts help a downtrodden storekeeper and his family to outwit a scheming relative.
Whimsical, overstretched period comedy suffering from miscasting but with some pleasantries along the way.

w Ranald MacDougall, play La Cuisine des Anges by Albert Husson d Michael Curtiz ph Loyal Griggs m Frederick Hollander

Humphrey Bogart, Peter Ustinov, Aldo Ray, Joan Bennett, Basil Rathbone, Leo G. Carroll, John Smith

'It's a circus! Something doing every minute!'

We're Not Dressing°
US 1934 77m bw
Paramount (Benjamin Glazer)

A spoiled heiress shipwrecked on a Pacific island is tamed by an easy-going sailor.
Pleasant, madly dated, light-hearted variation on a much-filmed play, resolving itself into a series of comic turns.

w Horace Jackson, Francis Martin, George Marion Jnr, *play* The Admirable Crichton by J. M. Barrie d Norman Taurog ph Charles Lang *songs* Harry Revel, Mack Gordon

Bing Crosby, Carole Lombard, George Burns, Gracie Allen, Leon Errol, Ethel Merman, Jay Henry, Ray Milland
'Tiptop audience appeal musical.'—*Variety*

We're Not Married°
US 1952 85m bw
TCF (Nunnally Johnson)

Six couples find that they were never legally married.
Amiable, smartly-played compendium of sketches on a familiar theme.

w Nunnally Johnson d Edmund Goulding ph Leo Tover m Cyril Mockridge

Ginger Rogers, Fred Allen, Victor Moore, Paul Douglas, Eve Arden, Marilyn Monroe, David Wayne, Louis Calhern, Zsa Zsa Gabor, Mitzi Gaynor, Eddie Bracken, James Gleason, Jane Darwell

We're on the Jury
US 1937 71m bw

Disagreements break out in the jury room after a murder trial. More comedy than drama, a modest remake of *Ladies of the Jury* (qv). Helen Broderick, Victor Moore, Philip Huston, Louise Latimer, Robert McWade. Written by Franklin Coen from the play by John Frederick Ballard; directed by Ben Holmes; for RKO. 'Good secondary b.o. value.'—*Variety*

We're Only Human
US 1936 67m bw

A police sergeant loses a convicted prisoner and catches him again. Routine bang-bang melodrama with unconvincing dialogue. Preston Foster, Jane Wyatt, James Gleason, Arthur Hohl, Jane Darwell, Christian Rub, Moroni Olson, Mischa Auer. Written by Rian James from a story by Thomas Walsh; directed by James Flood; for Edward Kaufman / RKO. 'Nothing which will raise it above double-feature standards.'—*Variety*

The Werewolf
US 1956 80m bw
Columbia / Clover (Sam Katzman)

In a small mountain town, a victim of radiation exposure periodically becomes a werewolf and is hounded down.
Absurd and tedious thriller which wastes an interesting background.

w Robert E. Kent, James B. Gordon d Fred F. Sears ph Edwin Linden m Mischa Bakaleinikoff

Steven Ritch, Don McGowan, Joyce Holden

Werewolf of London°
US 1935 75m bw
Universal (Stanley Bergerman)

Werewolves fight for a rare Tibetan flower with curative properties.
Patchy horror film which lurches from excellent suspense scenes to tedious chunks of superfluous dialogue. In many ways a milestone in the history of its kind.

w Robert Harris d Stuart Walker ph Charles Stumar m Karl Hajos

Henry Hull, Warner Oland, Valerie Hobson, Spring Byington, Lester Matthews, Zeffie Tilbury, Ethel Griffies
'Horror attempt that doesn't horrify sufficiently. Requires a build-up and may disappoint.'—*Variety*

West Eleven
GB 1963 93m bw
(ABP) Daniel M. Angel (Vivian Cox)

A young London drifter is offered £10,000 to commit murder.
Dingy but not very convincing 'realist' melodrama with a jazzy style which induces weariness.

w Keith Waterhouse, Willis Hall, *novel* The Furnished Room by Laura del Rivo d Michael Winner ph Otto Heller m Stanley Black, Acker Bilk

Alfred Lynch, Eric Portman, Kathleen Harrison, Diana Dors, Kathleen Breck, Freda Jackson, Finlay Currie, Harold Lang

West of Broadway
US 1932 68m bw

A millionaire gets married while drunk and regrets it the next day. Unappetizing light drama which did no good to anyone concerned with it. John Gilbert, El Brendel, Lois Moran, Madge Evans, Ralph Bellamy, Frank Conroy, Hedda Hopper. Written by Gene Markey, J. K. McGuinness, Ralph Graves, Bess Meredyth; directed by Harry Beaumont; for MGM. 'Rates neighbourhood and grind spotting only.'—*Variety*

West of Shanghai
US 1937 64m bw

Fugitives in the Far East are saved by the self-sacrifice of a Chinese war lord. Unpersuasive melodrama remade from *The Bad Man* (1930), heavily depending on a star performance. Boris Karloff, Beverly Roberts, Ricardo Cortez, Gordon Oliver, Vladimir Sokoloff. Written by Crane Wilbur; directed by John Farrow; for Warner.
† First released as *Warlord*.

West of the Pecos
US 1934 70m bw

In Texas after the Civil War a girl masquerades as a boy in order to get things done. Moderate western. Richard Dix, Martha Sleeper, Samuel S. Hinds, Fred Kohler, Louise Beavers, Willie Best ('Sleep 'n Eat'). Written by Milton Krims, John Twist, from the novel by Zane Grey; directed by Phil Rosen; for RKO. 'Superior entertainment of the horse opera type.'—*Variety*

West of Zanzibar
US 1928 70m at 24 fps bw silent

A paralysed magician turned ivory trader settles an old score. Corny star vehicle remade in 1932 as *Kongo*, with Walter Huston. Lon Chaney, Lionel Barrymore, Jacqueline Gadsden, Mary Nolan. Written by Waldemar Young and Elliott Clawson; directed by Tod Browning; for MGM.

West of Zanzibar
GB 1954 94m Technicolor
Ealing (Leslie Norman)

Native tribesmen move towards Mombasa and are drawn into ivory smuggling.
Fairly feeble follow-up to *Where No Vultures Fly*; quite good to look at but clearly not an original.

w Max Catto, Jack Whittingham d Harry Watt ph Paul Beeson m Alan Rawsthorne

Anthony Steel, Sheila Sim, William Simons, Orlando Martins, Martin Benson, Edric Connor, Howard Marion Crawford

West Point of the Air
US 1935 90m bw
MGM (Monta Bell)

The army sergeant father of an air cadet has great hopes for him.
Routine sentimental flagwaver.

w James J. McGuinness, John Monk Saunders, Frank Wead, Arthur J. Beckhard d Richard Rosson ph Clyde de Vinna, Charles A. Marshall, Elmer Dyer

Wallace Beery, Robert Young, Maureen O'Sullivan, Lewis Stone, James Gleason, Rosalind Russell, Russell Hardie, Henry Wadsworth, Robert Taylor
'Trite story holds it down to just moderate entertainment rating.'—*Variety*

West Point Story°
US 1950 107m bw
Warner (Louis F. Edelman)
GB title: *Fine and Dandy*

A Broadway producer stages a show at the military academy.
Thin and rather tedious musical saved by its irrepressible star.

w John Monks Jnr, Charles Hoffman, Irving Wallace d Roy del Ruth ph Sid Hickox md Ray Heindorf *songs* Sammy Cahn, Jule Styne

James Cagney, Virginia Mayo, Doris Day, Gordon Macrae, Gene Nelson, Alan Hale Jnr, Roland Winters, Jerome Cowan

AAN: Ray Heindorf

West Side Story***
US 1961 155m Technicolor
Panavision 70
(UA) Mirisch / Seven Arts (Robert Wise)

The Romeo and Juliet story in a New York dockland setting.

The essentially theatrical conception of this entertainment is nullified by determinedly realistic settings which make much of it seem rather silly, but production values are fine and the song numbers electrifying.

w Ernest Lehman, play Arthur Laurents, after Shakespeare d Robert Wise, Jerome Robbins ph Daniel L. Fapp m Leonard Bernstein ly Stephen Sondheim pd Boris Leven

Natalie Wood (sung by Marni Nixon), Richard Beymer (sung by Jimmy Bryant), Russ Tamblyn, Rita Moreno, George Chakiris

AA: best picture; Robert Wise, Jerome Robbins; Daniel L. Fapp; Rita Moreno; George Chakiris

AAN: Ernest Lehman; musical direction (Saul Chaplin, Johnny Green, Sid Ramin, Irwin Kostal)

● Video: Intervision

Westbound
US 1959 69m Warnercolor

A stagecoach manager is entrusted with Californian gold, which attracts assorted villains. Stalwart star western which served its purpose. Randolph Scott, Virginia Mayo, Karen Steele, Andrew Duggan, Michael Pate. Written by Berne Giler; directed by Budd Boetticher; for Warner.

Western Approaches***
GB 1944 83m Technicolor
Crown Film Unit
US title: The Raider

Torpedoed merchantmen in the Atlantic are used by a U-boat as a decoy.

A fictional story is played to great documentary effect by men of the allied navies. One of the outstanding 'factual' films of the war years.

wd Pat Jackson ph Jack Cardiff m Clifton Parker

Western Union**
US 1941 94m Technicolor
TCF (Harry Joe Brown)

Politicians and crooks hamper the laying of cross country cables.

First rate western with familiar excitements.

w Robert Carson, novel Zane Grey d Fritz Lang ph Edward Cronjager m David Buttolph

Randolph Scott, Robert Young, Dean Jagger, Virginia Gilmore, Slim Summerville, John Carradine, Chill Wills, Barton MacLane

'It is impossible to know what clichés the director may have prevented, but it is enough and too much to see those he left in.'—Otis Ferguson

'Two women helped him overthrow the most ruthless power in the west!'
The Westerner**
US 1940 99m bw
Samuel Goldwyn

Judge Roy Bean comes to grief through his love for Lily Langtry.

Moody melodramatic western with comedy touches; generally entertaining, the villain more so than the hero.

w Jo Swerling, Niven Busch, story Stuart N. Lake d William Wyler ph Gregg Toland m Dmitri Tiomkin

Gary Cooper, Walter Brennan, Doris Davenport, Fred Stone, Paul Hurst, Chill Wills, Charles Halton, Forrest Tucker, Dana Andrews, Lilian Bond, Tom Tyler

AA: Walter Brennan
AAN: Stuart N. Lake

Westward Ho the Wagons
US 1956 85m Technicolor
Cinemascope
Walt Disney (Bill Walsh)

A wagon train defends itself against Indians. Slow and simple-minded family western.

w Tom Blackburn d William Beaudine ph Charles Boyle m George Bruns

Fess Parker, Kathleen Crowley, Jeff York, David Stollery, Sebastian Cabot, George Reeves

Westward Passage
US 1932 73m bw
RKO (David O. Selznick)

A wealthy girl weds a poor novelist but wants the rich full life for their children.

Dogged romantic drama with only the casting of interest.

w Bradley and Humphrey King, novel Margaret Ayer Barnes d Robert Milton ph Lucien Andriot m Max Steiner

Ann Harding, Laurence Olivier, Zasu Pitts, Irving Pichel, Juliette Compton, Florence Roberts

'Slow, prone to be dull, and hardly warm weather theatre inducement.'—Variety

Westward the Women*
US 1951 118m bw
MGM (Dore Schary)

In the 1850s an Indian scout leads 150 Chicago women to meet husbands in California. Good-looking episodic western, apparently intended mainly to amuse but seldom rising to the occasion.

w Charles Schnee d William Wellman ph William Mellor m Jeff Alexander

Robert Taylor, Denise Darcel, John McIntire, Marilyn Erskine, Hope Emerson, Lenore Lonergan, Julie Bishop

'Where nothing can possibly go wrongg . . .'
Westworld**
US 1973 89m Metrocolor Panavision
MGM (Paul N. Lazarus III)

In a millionaire holiday resort which recreates the past, a western badman robot goes berserk

and relentlessly attacks two visitors. Unusual and amusing but under-produced melodrama with slipshod story development and continuity, atoned for by memorable moments and underlying excitement.

wd Michael Crichton ph Gene Polito m Fred Karlin ad Herman Blumenthal

Yul Brynner, Richard Benjamin, James Brolin, Norman Bartold, Alan Oppenheimer

● Video: MGM / UA

The Wet Parade*
US 1932 122m bw
MGM (Hunt Stromberg)

A politician points to the corruption caused by prohibition.

Sociologically interesting melodrama.

w John Lee Mahin, novel Upton Sinclair d Victor Fleming ph George Barnes

Walter Huston, Myrna Loy, Neil Hamilton, Lewis Stone, Jimmy Durante, Wallace Ford, Dorothy Jordan, John Miljan, Robert Young

'Final impression strongly anti-liquor, but outside of reaction that may bring, picture hasn't much chance. What it lacks as entertainment isn't covered by propaganda possibilities.'—Variety

AAN: best picture

We've Never Been Licked
US 1943 103m bw

A young American raised in Japan finds himself on the wrong side after Pearl Harbor. Shoddy flagwaver, low on talent and inspiration. Richard Quine, Anne Gwynne, Noah Beery Jnr, Harry Davenport, Martha O'Driscoll, William Frawley, Robert Mitchum. Written by Norman Reilly Raine and Nick Grinde; directed by John Rawlins; for Walter Wanger / Universal. (GB title: Texas to Tokyo.)

'He had a price on his head . . . she had a price on her heart!'
Wharf Angel
US 1934 65m bw

To quote Variety, prostie goes softie for sailor with murder rap hanging over his head. Dim little fogbound melodrama. Victor McLaglen, Dorothy Dell, Preston Foster, Alison Skipworth. Written by Sam Hoffenstein, Frank Partos, Steve Avery, Frederick Schlick; directed by William Cameron Menzies and George Somnes; for Paramount. 'Poor stuff for de luxe audiences: old-fashioned, drab, lacking in box office draw.'—Variety

What a Carve Up
GB 1961 88m bw

A madman fakes his own death in order to murder his relatives. Spooky house farce, allegedly a remake of The Ghoul but bearing little resemblance to it. Sid James, Kenneth Connor, Shirley Eaton, Dennis Price, Donald Pleasence, Michael Gough, Valerie Taylor. Written by Ray Cooney, Tony Hilton, from the novel The Ghoul by Frank King; directed by Pat Jackson; for Baker-Berman (New World).

BARBARY COAST!

Where the tides of human passions roll up strange wrecks of life and love . . . . a haven for crushed derelicts . . .

such as Toy, who knew men but never heard of love!

TURK...at home in any port!

COMO...a price on his head!

MOTHER BRIGHT ...her purple past made history!

"Wharf Angel"

A Paramount Picture with

VICTOR McLAGLEN
DOROTHY DELL
PRESTON FOSTER
ALISON SKIPWORTH

WHARF ANGEL. Victor McLaglen, a veteran of John Ford westerns of the forties, had been an undoubted star for twenty years and more.

What a Life
US 1939 75m bw

Henry Aldrich has difficulties in high school.
First of the domestic comedy series (see under
Henry) which became more farcical and had a
different cast; this episode closely followed the
Broadway success. Jackie Cooper, Betty Field,
John Howard, Janice Logan, Lionel Stander,
Hedda Hopper, Dorothy Stickney. Written by
Charles Brackett and Billy Wilder from the
play by Clifford Goldsmith; directed by
Theodore Reed; for Paramount. 'A fine
comedy drama, excellent for family trade.'—
Variety

What a Way to Go°
US 1963 111m De Luxe Cinemascope
TCF / APJAC / Orchard (Arthur P. Jacobs)

An immensely rich girl tells her psychiatrist
how all her husbands proved not only
successful but accident-prone.
Wild, mainly agreeable, star-and-gag-laden
black comedy which starts on too high a note
and fails to sustain.

w Betty Comden, Adolph Green d J. Lee-
Thompson ph Leon Shamroy md Nelson
Riddle ly Comden and Green songs Jule
Styne

Shirley Maclaine, Bob Cummings, Dick Van
Dyke, Robert Mitchum, Gene Kelly, Dean
Martin, Paul Newman, Reginald Gardiner,
Margaret Dumont

What a Woman
US 1943 90m bw

An author's agent gets into romantic
escapades with her writers. Ho-hum romantic
comedy, quickly forgotten. Rosalind Russell,
Brian Aherne, Willard Parker, Ann Savage,
Alan Dinehart. Written by Therese Lewis and
Barry Trivers; directed by Irving Cummings;
for Columbia. (Aka: *The Beautiful Cheat*.)

'Off to grandmother's house they go,
For love in the attic and death down
    below!'
What Became of Jack and Jill?
GB 1971 90m De Luxe
Palomar / Amicus (Milton Subotsky)

A young man tries to hasten his grandmother's
death but she has the last laugh.
Feeble suspenser with a dim ending.

w Roger Marshall, *novel* The Ruthless Ones
by Laurence Moody d Bill Bain ph Gerry
Turpin m Carl Davis

Vanessa Howard, Paul Nicholas, Mona
Washbourne, Peter Copley, Peter Jeffrey

What Changed Charley Farthing
GB 1975 101m Eastmancolor
Patina–Hidalgo (Tristam Cones)

A philandering sailor has adventures in Cuba.
Weirdly ineffective comedy actioner which
never gets started and should never have been
thought of.

w David Pursall, Jack Seddon, *novel* Mark
Hebdon d Sidney Hayers ph Graham Edgar
m Angela Arteaga

Doug McClure, Lionel Jeffries, Warren
Mitchell, Hayley Mills, Dilys Hamlett,
Fernando Sancho

What Did You Do in the War, Daddy?
US 1966 115m De Luxe Panavision
UA / Mirisch / Geoffrey (Owen Crump,
Blake Edwards)

In 1943, an Italian town surrenders readily to
the Americans providing its wine festival and
football match can take place.
Silly war comedy with insufficient jokes for its
wearisome length. The performances are
bright enough.

w William Peter Blatty d Blake Edwards
ph Philip Lathrop m Henry Mancini

James Coburn, Dick Shawn, Sergio Fantoni,
Giovanni Ralli, Aldo Ray, Harry Morgan,
Carroll O'Connor, Leon Askin

What Every Woman Knows°
US 1934 90m bw

A quiet little wife encourages her husband into
parliament. Adequate version of the
sentimental play, very pleasantly acted. *Helen
Hayes*, *Brian Aherne*, Madge Evans, Lucile
Watson, Dudley Digges, Henry Stephenson,
Donald Crisp, David Torrence. Written by
Monckton Hoffe, John Meehan, James Kevin
McGuinness, from the play by J. M. Barrie;
directed by Gregory La Cava; for MGM.
'Cinch b.o., a swell woman's picture.'—
Variety

What, No Beer?
US 1933 65m bw

A barber rushes to be first on the market with
beer after its legalization, but finds himself
premature and at odds with gangsters. Topical
farce ending in a slapstick mêlée. Buster
Keaton, Jimmy Durante, Rosco Ates, Phyllis
Barry, John Miljan, Henry Armetta. Written
by Carey Wilson, Jack Cluett, Robert E.
Hopkins; directed by Edward Sedgwick; for
MGM. 'A commercial little laugh picture.'—
Variety

What Price Glory?°
US 1952 111m Technicolor
TCF (Sol. C. Siegel)

In 1917 France Captain Flagg and Sergeant
Quirt spar for the same girl.
Stagey remake of the celebrated silent film and
play; watchable if not exactly inspired.

w Phoebe and Henry Ephron, *play* Maxwell
Anderson, Lawrence Stallings d John Ford
ph Joe MacDonald m Alfred Newman

James Cagney, Dan Dailey, Corinne Calvet,
William Demarest, Robert Wagner, Marisa
Pavan, James Gleason

'A heart-touching drama of the world, the
flesh and the movies!'
What Price Hollywood?°
US 1932 87m bw
RKO (Pandro S. Berman)

A waitress becomes a film star with the help of
a drunken director who later commits suicide.
Fairly trenchant early study of the mores of
the film city, later revamped as *A Star Is Born*.

w Jane Murfin, Ben Markson, Gene Fowler,
Rowland Brown, *story* Adela Rogers St John
d George Cukor ph Charles Rosher m Max
Steiner *montage* Slavko Vorkapitch

Constance Bennett, Lowell Sherman, Neil
Hamilton, Gregory Ratoff, Brooks Bendict,
Louise Beavers, Eddie Anderson
'Many of the scenes are like sketches for the
later versions, but this film has its own
interest, especially because of its glimpses into
the studio life of the time.'—*New Yorker*, 1977
AAN: Adela Rogers St John

Whatever Happened to Aunt Alice?°
US 1969 101m Metrocolor
Associates and Aldrich / Palomar

A genteel widow murders her housekeepers
for their private incomes.
Ladylike shocker with some black humour and
good performances.

w Theodore Apstein, *novel* The Forbidden
Garden by Ursula Curtiss d Lee H. Katzin
ph Joseph Biroc m Gerald Fried

Geraldine Page, Ruth Gordon, Rosemary
Forsyth, Robert Fuller, Mildred Dunnock

● Video: Rank

'Sister, sister, oh so fair, why is there blood
all over your hair?'
Whatever Happened to Baby Jane?°
US 1962 132m bw
Warner Seven Arts / Associates and Aldrich
(Robert Aldrich)

In middle age, a demented ex-child star lives
in an old Hollywood mansion with her invalid
sister, and tension leads to murder.
Famous for marking the first time Hollywood's
ageing first ladies stooped to horror, and
followed by *Hush Hush Sweet Charlotte* and
the other *Whatevers*, this dreary looking
melodrama only occasionally grabs the
attention and has enough plot for about half
its length. The performances, however, are
striking.

w Lukas Heller, *novel* Henry Farrell
d Robert Aldrich ph Ernest Haller m Frank
de Vol

Bette Davis, Joan Crawford, Victor Buono,
Anna Lee
'It goes on and on, in a light much dimmer
than necessary, and the climax, when it
belatedly arrives, is a bungled, languid
mingling of pursuers and pursued . . .'—*New
Yorker*
AAN: Ernest Haller; Bette Davis; Victor
Buono
● Video: Warner

What's Good for the Goose
GB 1969 104m Eastmancolor
Tigon (Tony Tenser, Norman Wisdom)

An assistant bank manager falls for a girl
hitch-hiker and tries to recover his youth.
Embarrassing attempt to build a sexy vehicle
for a star whose sentimental mugging always
appealed mainly to children.

w Norman Wisdom d Menaham Golan
ph William Brayne m Reg Tilsley

Norman Wisdom, Sally Geeson, Sally
Bazeley, Derek Francis, Terence Alexander

What's New Pussycat?

US / France 1965 108m Technicolor
UA / Famous Artists (Charles K. Feldman)

A fashion editor is distracted by beautiful
girls.
Zany sex comedy with many more misses than
hits, a product of the wildly swinging sixties
when it was thought that a big budget and
stars making fools of themselves would
automatically ensure a success.

w Woody Allen d Clive Donner ph Jean
Badal m Burt Bacharach

Peter O'Toole, Peter Sellers, Woody Allen,
Ursula Andress, Romy Schneider, Capucine,
Paula Prentiss

'Unfortunately for all concerned, to make
something enjoyably dirty a lot of taste is
required.'—John Simon

AAN: title song (m Burt Bacharach, ly Hal
David)

● Video: Warner

What's So Bad About Feeling Good?

US 1965 94m Technicolor
Universal (George Seaton)

A 'happy virus' is carried into New York by a
toucan, and affects the lives of various people.
Flimsy pretext for a comedy, further
hampered by a less than sparkling script. The
actors have their moments.

w George Seaton, Robert Pirosh d George
Seaton ph Ernesto Caparros m Frank de Vol

George Peppard, Mary Tyler Moore, Dom De
Luise, John McMartin, Susan St James, Don
Stroud, Charles Lane

What's the Matter with Helen?*

US 1971 101m De Luxe
Filmways / Raymax (George Edwards,
James C. Pratt)

In 1934 Hollywood, two women run a dancing
school for child stars; one of them is a killer.
More Baby Jane melodramatics, quite lively
and with interesting period detail.

w Henry Farrell d Curtis Harrington
ph Lucien Ballard m David Raksin
pd Eugene Lourié

Debbie Reynolds, Shelley Winters, Micheal
MacLiammoir, Dennis Weaver, Agnes
Moorehead

'A cast of seasoned troupers cannot quite
alter the impression that they are all working
to revive a stiff.'—Bruce Williamson

What's Up, Doc?**

US 1972 94m Technicolor
Warner / Saticoy (Peter Bogdanovich)

In San Francisco, an absent-minded young
musicologist is troubled by the attentions of a
dotty girl who gets him involved with crooks
and a series of accidents.

Madcap comedy, a pastiche of several thirties
originals. Spectacular slapstick and willing
players are somewhat let down by exhausted
patches and a tame final reel.

w Buck Henry, David Newman, Robert
Benton d Peter Bogdanovich ph Laszlo
Kovacs m Artie Butler pd Polly Platt

Barbra Streisand, Ryan O'Neal, Kenneth
Mars, Austin Pendleton, Madeleine Kahn,
Mabel Albertson, Sorrell Booke

'A comedy made by a man who has seen a
lot of movies, knows all the mechanics, and
has absolutely no sense of humour. Seeing it is
like shaking hands with a joker holding a joy
buzzer: the effect is both presumptuous and
unpleasant.'—Jay Cocks

'It's all rather like a 19th-century imitation
of Elizabethan blank verse drama.'—Stanley
Kauffmann

'It freely borrows from the best screen
comedy down the ages but has no discernible
style of its own.'—Michael Billington,
Illustrated London News

● Video: Warner

The Wheeler Dealers

US 1963 106m Metrocolor Panavision
MGM / Filmways (Martin Ransohoff)
GB title: Separate Beds

A Texas tycoon with a flair for the stock
market sets Wall Street agog by manipulating
a mysterious and non-existent new product.
Fun for financiers, but barely worth following
for the rest. A slick, loud, hollow show.

w G. J. W. Goodman, Ira Wallach d Arthur
Hiller ph Charles Lang Jnr m Frank de Vol

James Garner, Lee Remick, Phil Harris, Chill
Wills, Jim Backus, Louis Nye, John Astin

When a Man Loves

US 1927 83m at 24 fps bw silent with
synchronized music

A hero escapes from a prison ship and gives
his all for love of a worthless woman. Freely
adapted version of Manon Lescaut, successful
because of the real-life romance of the stars.
John Barrymore, Dolores Costello, Warner
Oland, Stuart Holmes, Holmes Herbert.
Written by Bess Meredyth; directed by Alan
Crosland; for Warner

When a Stranger Calls

US 1979 97m colour

A policeman determinedly chases a baby-
murdering maniac. Middling screamer
extended from a short, The Sitter; a passive
midsection separates a suspenseful start and
finish. Charles Durning, Tony Beckley, Carol
Kane, Colleen Dewhurst, Rachel Roberts.
Written by Steve Feke and Fred Walton;
directed by Fred Walton; for Melvin Simon /
UA.

When Comedy Was King***

US 1959 84m bw
Robert Youngson Productions

Valuable compilation of silent comedy
sequences, with the high print quality and
poor commentary to be expected from this

source. Extracts include Buster Keaton in
Cops, Laurel and Hardy in Big Business, and a
Fatty Arbuckle comedy.

ed Robert Youngson

When Dinosaurs Ruled the Earth

GB 1969 100m Technicolor
Hammer (Aida Young)

In prehistoric times, a girl is swept out to sea
by a cyclone and adopted by a dinosaur.
Sequel to One Million Years BC, all very silly
but tolerably well done.

wd Val Guest ph Dick Bush m Mario
Nascimbene sp Jim Danforth

Victoria Vetri, Patrick Allen, Robin Hawdon,
Patrick Holt, Imogen Hassall

When Eight Bells Toll*

GB 1971 94m Eastmancolor
Panavision
Winkast (Elliott Kastner)

A naval secret service agent investigates the
pirating of gold bullion ships off the Scottish
coast.
Acceptable kill-happy thriller: humourless
James Bondery graced by splendid Scottish
landscapes.

w Alistair MacLean, from his novel d Etienne
Perier ph Arthur Ibbetson m Wally Stott

Anthony Hopkins, Robert Morley, Corin
Redgrave, Jack Hawkins, Ferdy Mayne,
Derek Bond, Nathalie Delon

When I Grow Up*

US 1951 90m bw
Horizon (S. P. Eagle)

A boy about to run away changes his mind
after reading his grandfather's diaries.
Pleasant, sentimental family film with an
unusual approach.

wd Michael Kanin ph Ernest Laszlo
m Jerome Moross

Bobby Driscoll, Robert Preston, Charley
Grapewin, Martha Scott, Ralph Dumke

When in Rome

US 1952 78m bw
MGM (Clarence Brown)

A gangster in Rome steals a priest's clothes
and is accepted in his place.
Typically American religious comedy, nicely
made but straying somewhat over the top
when the gangster reforms and becomes a
monk.

w Charles Schnee, Dorothy Kingsley, Robert
Buckner d Clarence Brown ph William
Daniels m Carmen Dragon

Van Johnson, Paul Douglas, Joseph Calleia,
Carlo Rizzo, Tudor Owen, Aldo Silvani,
Dono Nardi

When Knights Were Bold

GB 1929 80m at 24 fps bw silent

An incompetent heir dreams that he lives in
medieval times. Naïve romp which pleased at
the time. Nelson Keys, Miriam Seeger, Eric
Bransby Williams. Written by Tim Whelan

and Herbert Wilcox, from a play by Charles Marlow; directed by Tim Whelan; for Herbert Wilcox. (Remade in 1936 with Jack Buchanan, Fay Wray and Garry Marsh; for Max Schach.)

When Ladies Meet*
US 1933 73m bw
MGM

A successful lady novelist falls in love with her married publisher.
Smartish comedy of manners which still has a sting.
w John Meehan, Leon Gordon, *play* Rachel Crothers d Harry Beaumont ph Ray June
Ann Harding, Robert Montgomery, *Myrna Loy, Alice Brady*, Frank Morgan, Margaret Burton, Luis Alberni
'Nice production. Well-spaced comedy helps, and picture should be an outstander.'—*Variety*

When Ladies Meet
US 1941 108m bw
MGM (Robert Z. Leonard, Orville O. Dull)

Over-produced and very talkative remake of the above.
w S. K. Lauren, Anita Loos d Robert Z. Leonard ph Robert Planck m Bronislau Kaper
Joan Crawford, Robert Taylor, Greer Garson, Spring Byington, Herbert Marshall, Rafael Strom, Olaf Hytten

When Love Is Young
US 1937 75m bw

A Broadway stage star returns to her home town in hopes of marrying her old beau, but he is found wanting. Very moderate comedy to fill a programme. Virginia Bruce, Kent Taylor, Walter Brennan, Greta Meyer, Christian Rub, Sterling Holloway, Nydia Westman. Written by Eve Greene, Joseph Fields, from the story Class Prophecy by Eleanore Griffin; directed by Hal Mohr; for Robert Presnell / Universal. 'Will provide average filmgoers with averagely good amusement.'—*Variety*

When My Baby Smiles at Me
US 1948 98m Technicolor
TCF (George Jessel)

A vaudevillian goes on the skids but is saved by his wife.
Routine musical handling of a dreary drama previously filmed as *Dance of Life* (1929) and *Swing High Swing Low* (qv).
w Lamar Trotti, *play* Burlesque by George Manker Walters, Arthur Hopkins d Walter Lang ph Harry Jackson md Alfred Newman
Betty Grable, Dan Dailey, Jack Oakie, June Havoc, Richard Arlen, James Gleason, Jean Wallace
AAN: Alfred Newman; Dan Dailey

When Strangers Marry*
US 1944 67m bw
Monogram
aka: *Betrayed*

A young bride in New York discovers that she may have married a murderer.

Much-praised second feature: a bit stodgy now, but still entertaining.
w Philip Yordan, Dennis Cooper d William Castle ph Ira Morgan m Dmitri Tiomkin
Dean Jagger, Kim Hunter, Robert Mitchum, Neil Hamilton, Lou Lubin, Milt Kibbee, Dewey Robinson
'The obviousness of the low budget is completely overcome by the solid craftsmanship of the direction, script, music, editing and performances.'—*Don Miller*
'Taking it as a whole I have seldom for years now seen one hour so energetically and sensibly used in a film.'—*James Agee*

When the Bough Breaks
GB 1947 81m bw
GFD / Gainsborough (Betty Box)

The bewildered wife of a bigamist allows her child to be adopted and then regrets it.
Peg's Paper stuff in the then-accepted Gainsborough tradition.
w Peter Rogers d Lawrence Huntington ph Bryan Langley m Clifton Parker
Patricia Roc, Rosamund John, Bill Owen, Patrick Holt, Brenda Bruce, Leslie Dwyer, Jane Hylton

When the Daltons Rode*
US 1940 80m bw
Universal

Adventures of the Dalton Gang.
Good standard western with whitewashed bad men for heroes.
w Harold Shumate, Stuart Anthony, Lester Cole d George Marshall ph Hal Mohr m Frank Skinner
Randolph Scott, Kay Francis, Brian Donlevy, Andy Devine, George Bancroft, Stuart Erwin

When the Legends Die*
US 1972 105m De Luxe
Sagoponack (Stuart Millar)

A young Indian boy, frustrated by life on the reservations, is helped by an old rodeo rider who becomes his guardian.
Dour modern western; rather stylishly done and an eloquent plea for freedom, but dramatically uncompelling.
w Robert Dozier, *novel* Hal Borland d Stuart Millar ph Richard Kline m Glenn Paxton
Richard Widmark, Frederic Forrest, Luana Anders, Vito Scotti

When Time Ran Out
US 1980 109m Technicolor
Panavision
Warner / Irwin Allen

Inhabitants of a South Sea island are threatened by a volcano.
Incredibly inept disaster movie, with all clichés on hand in the characters of some downcast actors.
w Carl Foreman, Stirling Silliphant, *novel* The Day the World Ended by Max Morgan Witts and Gordon Thomas d James Goldstone ph Fred J. Koenekamp m Lalo Schifrin

Paul Newman, Jacqueline Bisset, William Holden, Edward Albert, Burgess Meredith, Valentina Cortesa, Red Buttons, Alex Carras, Ernest Borgnine, James Franciscus
'Disaster movies don't come any more disastrous than this.'—*Tom Milne, MFB*

When Tomorrow Comes**
US 1939 82m bw
Universal (John M. Stahl)

A waitress falls for a concert pianist with a mad wife.
Fascinating star romantic drama, a successful follow-up to *Love Affair*; full of clichés, but impeccably set and acted. The stuff that Hollywood dreams were made of.
w Dwight Taylor, *story* James M. Cain d John M. Stahl ph John Mescall m Charles Previn
Charles Boyer, Irene Dunne, Barbara O'Neil, Nydia Westman, Onslow Stevens
'A persuasive love story . . . a director's achievement.'—*Variety*
† The same story was remade twice in 1956, as *Serenade* and *Interlude*, and in 1968 as *Interlude* (all qv).

When We Are Married*
GB 1942 98m bw
British National (John Baxter)

In 1890s Yorkshire, three couples celebrating their silver wedding are told they were never legally married.
A very funny play smartly filmed with a superb cast of character actors.
w Austin Melford, Barbara K. Emery, *play* J. B. Priestley d Lance Comfort
Raymond Huntley, Marian Spencer, Lloyd Pearson, Olga Lindo, Ernest Butcher, Ethel Coleridge, Sydney Howard, Barry Morse, Lesley Brook, Marjorie Rhodes, Charles Victor, Cyril Smith, George Carney

When Willie Comes Marching Home*
US 1949 82m bw
TCF (Fred Kohlmar)

During World War II, events suddenly transform a small-town air training instructor into a war hero.
Awkwardly paced comedy which could have been much funnier but does amuse in fits and starts.
w Mary Loos, Richard Sale d John Ford ph Leo Tover m Alfred Newman
Dan Dailey, Colleen Townshend, Corinne Calvet, William Demarest, Evelyn Varden, James Lydon, Mae Marsh, Lloyd Corrigan
AAN: original story (Sy Gomberg)

When Worlds Collide
US 1951 82m Technicolor
Paramount (George Pal)

Another planet is found to be rushing inevitably towards earth, but before the collision a few people escape in a space ship.
Stolid science fiction with a spectacular but not marvellous climax following seventy minutes of inept talk.

w Sidney Boehm, *novel* Philip Wylie, Edwin Balmer *d* Rudolph Maté *ph* John Seitz, W. Howard Greene *m* Leith Stevens

Richard Derr, Barbara Rush, Larry Keating, Peter Hanson, John Hoyt

AAN: John Seitz, W. Howard Greene

When You're in Love*
US 1937 110m bw
Columbia (Everett Riskin)
GB title: *For You Alone*

A European opera singer takes on a husband in order to get into the United States.
Pleasing musical star vehicle with comedy touches.

wd Robert Riskin *ph* Joseph Walker *md* Alfred Newman

Grace Moore, Cary Grant, Aline MacMahon, Henry Stephenson, Thomas Mitchell, Catherine Doucet, Luis Alberni, Emma Dunn
'Nice musical with fair quota of giggles . . . should do nice biz.'—*Variety*

Where Angels Go, Trouble Follows
US 1968 95m Eastmancolor
Columbia / William Frye

Nuns from a convent school take pupils to a California youth rally, and learn a thing or two.
Peripatetic comedy, rather frantically assembled; a sequel to *The Trouble with Angels*.

w Blanche Hanalis *d* James Neilson *ph* Sam Leavitt *m* Lalo Schifrin

Rosalind Russell, Stella Stevens, Binnie Barnes, Mary Wickes, Milton Berle, Arthur Godfrey, Robert Taylor, Van Johnson, Susan St James

Where Danger Lives
US 1950 84m bw
RKO (Irving Cummings Jnr)

A doctor falls in love with a murderous patient and is drawn into her schemes.
Standard *film noir* of its time, competent enough in its depressing way.

w Charles Bennett *d* John Farrow *ph* Nicholas Musuraca *m* Roy Webb

Faith Domergue, Robert Mitchum, Claude Rains, Maureen O'Sullivan, Charles Kemper

Where Do We Go from Here?*
US 1945 77m Technicolor
TCF (William Perlberg)

A writer stumbles on a genie who takes him through periods of American history, including a voyage with Christopher Columbus.
Well-staged and rather funny charade with at least one memorable song.

w Morrie Ryskind *d* Gregory Ratoff *ph* Leon Shamroy *songs* Kurt Weill, Ira Gershwin

Fred MacMurray, June Haver, Joan Leslie, Gene Sheldon, Anthony Quinn, Carlos Ramirez, Fortunio Bonanova, Alan Mowbray, Herman Bing, Otto Preminger
'Nine parts heavy facetiousness to one part very good fun.'—*James Agee*

'Don't tell your doctor about this film—it could give him ideas!'

Where Does it Hurt?
US 1971 88m colour
Josef Shaftel (Rod Amateau, William Schwarz)

Adventures of a profiteering hospital administrator.
Dislikeable, plodding smut in the form of black comedy.

wd Rod Amateau, *novel* The Operator by Budd Robinson, Rod Amateau *ph* Brick Marquard *m* Keith Allison

Peter Sellers, Jo Ann Pflug, Rick Lenz, Eve Druce
● *Video: VCL*

Where Eagles Dare**
GB 1969 155m Metrocolor
Panavision 70
MGM / Winkast (Elliott Kastner)

During World War II, seven British paratroopers land in the Bavarian Alps to rescue a high-ranking officer from an impregnable castle.
Archetypal schoolboy adventure, rather unattractively photographed but containing a sufficient variety of excitements.

w Alistair MacLean, from his novel *d* Brian G. Hutton *ph* Arthur Ibbetson, H. A. R. Thompson *m* Ron Goodwin

Richard Burton, Clint Eastwood, Mary Ure, Patrick Wymark, Michael Hordern, Donald Houston, Peter Barkworth, Robert Beatty
● *Video: MGM / UA*

Where It's At
US 1969 106m De Luxe
UA / Frank Ross

The owner of a Las Vegas gambling hotel tries to make his son take an interest in the business.
Flaccid comedy drama which belies its credits.

wd Garson Kanin *ph* Burnett Guffey *m* Benny Olsen

David Janssen, Rosemary Forsyth, Robert Drivas, Brenda Vaccaro

Where Love Has Gone*
US 1964 114m Techniscope
Paramount / Embassy (Joseph E. Levine)

A middle-aged man is appalled to hear that his teenage daughter has killed her mother's lover.
Squalid, glossy pulp fiction lightly based on the Lana Turner case, distinguished only by the game performances of its leading ladies.

w John Michael Hayes, *novel* Harold Robbins *d* Edward Dmytryk *ph* Joe MacDonald *m* Walter Scharf

Susan Hayward, Bette Davis, Mike Connors, Joey Heatherton, Jane Greer, George Macready
'A typical Robbins pastiche of newspaper clippings liberally shellacked with sentiment and glued with sex.'—*Newsweek*

AAN: title song (*m* James Van Heusen, *ly* Sammy Cahn)

Where No Vultures Fly*
GB 1951 107m Technicolor
Ealing (Leslie Norman)
US title: *Ivory Hunter*

Adventures of an East African game warden.
Pleasantly improving family film, nicely shot on location; a sequel, *West of Zanzibar*, was less impressive.

w W. P. Lipscomb, Ralph Smart, Leslie Norman *d* Harry Watt *ph* Geoffrey Unsworth *m* Alan Rawsthorne

Anthony Steele, Dinah Sheridan, Harold Warrender, Meredith Edwards
'These expeditionary films are really journalistic jobs. You get sent out to a country by the studio, stay as long as you can without getting fired, and a story generally crops up.'—*Harry Watt*

Where Sinners Meet
US 1934 68m bw

A millionaire eccentric kidnaps eloping couples to find out whether they are making a mistake. Stagebound whimsy saddled with an absurd American title. Diana Wynyard, Clive Brook, Billie Burke, Reginald Owen, Alan Mowbray, Gilbert Emery, Phyllis Barry. Written by H. W. Hanemann from the play The Dover Road by A. A. Milne; directed by J. Walter Ruben; for RKO. 'Despite fine performances and good production, very dubious.'—*Variety*. (GB title: *The Dover Road*.)

Where the Boys Are
US 1960 99m Metrocolor
Cinemascope
MGM / Euterpe (Joe Pasternak)

Four college girls spend the Easter vacation near a Florida military post in search of conquests.
Mindless, frothy youth musical, quite smoothly done.

w George Wells, *novel* Glendon Swarthout *d* Henry Levin *ph* Robert Bronner *m* George Stoll

George Hamilton, Dolores Hart, Paula Prentiss, Jim Hutton, Yvette Mimieux, Connie Francis, Frank Gorshin, Chill Wills, Barbara Nichols

Where the Boys Are
US 1984 94m colour

The 1960 musical becomes a teenage sex movie; neither version has much to do with the original novel. Lisa Hartman, Lorna Luft, Wendy Schaal, Lynn-Holly Johnson, Russel Todd, Howard McGillin. Written by Stu Krieger, Jeff Burkhart; directed by Hy Averback; for ITC. 'A travesty . . . insufferably coy.'—*Tom Milne, MFB*

Where the Buffalo Roam
US 1980 99m Technicolor

Adventures of a mad attorney and an eccentric journalist. Way out black comedy, for connoisseurs only. Peter Boyle, Bill Murray, Bruno Kirby, René Auberjonois, R. G. Armstrong. Written by John Kaye; directed by Art Linson; for Blue Dolphin / Universal.

Where the Hot Wind Blows
France / Italy 1958   125m   bw
MGM / Cité Films / Groupe des Quatre /
   Titanus (Jacques Bar)
original French title: *La Loi (The Law)*

In an Adriatic port, a voluptuous young girl is
pursued by the aged local squire, a racketeer,
her brother-in-law and a young agriculturist.
Guess who wins her.
Hoary melodrama with the emphasis on
virility and illicit passion. Long and tiresome,
it failed to justify the pretensions with which it
announced itself at the time.

w Jules Dassin, Diego Fabbri, *novel* Roger
Vailland *d* Jules Dassin *ph* Otello Martelli
m Roman Vlad

Gina Lollobrigida, Yves Montand, Marcello
Mastroianni, Pierre Brasseur, Melina
Mercouri, Paolo Stoppa
† An English version was generally available.

Where the Sidewalk Ends
US 1950   95m   bw
TCF (Otto Preminger)

A tough policeman accidentally kills a suspect
and tries to implicate a gang leader.
Gloomy *policier* with curious moral values.

w Rex Connor (Ben Hecht), *novel* William L.
Stuart *d* Otto Preminger *ph* Joseph La
Shelle *m* Cyril Mockridge

Dana Andrews, Gene Tierney, Gary Merrill,
Bert Freed, Tom Tully, Karl Malden, Ruth
Donnelly, Craig Stevens, Robert Simon

Where the Spies Are
GB 1965   113m   Metrocolor   Panavision
MGM / Val Guest

A country doctor is bribed to become a spy by
the promise of a car he greatly covets.
Patchy spy adventure which never settles into
a comfortable style but provides occasional
entertainment along its bumpy way.

w Wolf Mankowitz, Val Guest, *novel*
Passport to Oblivion by James Leasor
d Val Guest *ph* Arthur Grant *m* Mario
Nascimbene

David Niven, Françoise Dorleac, Nigel
Davenport, John Le Mesurier, Ronald Radd,
Cyril Cusack, Eric Pohlmann

Where There's a Will*
GB 1936   81m   bw
Gainsborough (Edward Black, Sidney
   Gilliat)

A seedy education expert sponges on his rich
relations but redeems himself by rounding up
gangsters at a Christmas party.
Rather slapdash star comedy with very good
scenes along the way.

w Will Hay, Robert Edmunds, Ralph Spence
d William Beaudine *ph* Charles Van Enger
md Louis Levy

Will Hay, Hartley Power, Gibb McLaughlin,
Graham Moffatt, Norma Varden, Gina Malo

'If you laugh yourself sick at this picture—
   sue Bob Hope!'

Where There's Life
US 1947   75m   bw
Paramount (Paul Jones)

A timid New Yorker turns out to be heir to
the throne of a Ruritanian country, and is
harassed by spies of both sides.
Mild star comedy with slow patches.

w Allen Boretz, Melville Shavelson *d* Sidney
Lanfield *ph* Charles Lang Jnr *m* Irwin
Talbot

Bob Hope, Signe Hasso, William Bendix,
George Coulouris

Where Were You When the Lights Went Out?*
US 1968   94m   Metrocolor   Panavision
MGM (Everett Freeman, Martin Melcher)

New York's famous electrical blackout in 1965
has its effect on the life of a musical comedy
star.
Cheerful sex farce with intriguing beginnings;
the later confinement to one set is just a bit
harmful.

w Everett Freeman, Karl Tunberg, *play*
Claude Magnier *d* Hy Averback
ph Ellsworth Fredericks *m* Dave Grusin

Doris Day, Terry-Thomas, Patrick O'Neal,
Robert Morse, Lola Albright, Jim Backus,
Ben Blue

Where's Charley?*
GB 1952   97m   Technicolor
Warner

An Oxford undergraduate impersonates the
rich aunt of his best friend.
Slow and rather stately musical version of the
famous farce *Charley's Aunt*, unsatisfactorily
shot on a mixture of poor sets and sunlit
Oxford locations; worth cherishing for the
ebullient performance of its over-age star.

w John Monks Jnr, *play* Brandon Thomas (via
stage musical, *book* George Abbott *m* Frank
Loesser) *d* David Butler *ph* Erwin Hillier
ch Michael Kidd

Ray Bolger, Robert Shackleton, Mary
Germaine, Allyn McLerie, Margaretta Scott,
Horace Cooper

Where's Jack?*
GB 1968   119m   Eastmancolor
Paramount / Oakhurst (Stanley Baker)

In 18th-century London Jack Sheppard
becomes a romantic highwayman at the behest
of underworld leader Jonathan Wild.
Deliberately unromantic, squalid and 'realistic'
period piece which takes no hold on the fancy
despite the considerable care which was
obviously taken in all departments.

w Rafe and David Newhouse *d* James
Clavell *ph* John Wilcox *m* Elmer Bernstein
pd Cedric Dawe

Tommy Steele, Stanley Baker, Fiona Lewis,
Alan Badel, Dudley Foster, Sue Lloyd, Noel
Purcell

Where's Poppa?*
US 1970   82m   De Luxe
Jerry Tokovsky / Martin Worth

A Jewish lawyer's aged mother constantly
harms his love life, and he considers various
means of getting rid of her.
Much-censored black comedy which might
have been funnier in a complete form. Even
so, it has its moments.

w Robert Klane, from his novel *d* Carl
Reiner *ph* Jack Priestly *m* Jack Elliott

George Segal, Ruth Gordon, Trish Van
Devere, Ron Leibman

Where's That Fire?*
GB 1939   73m   bw
TCF (Edward Black)

An incompetent village fire brigade
accidentally saves the crown jewels from
thieves.
Routine but not despicable star comedy, long
thought lost; flat patches are well separated by
hilarious sequences.

w Marriott Edgar, Val Guest, J. O. C. Orton
d Marcel Varnel *ph* Arthur Crabtree

Will Hay, Moore Marriott, Graham Moffatt,
Peter Gawthorne, Eric Clavering, Charles
Hawtrey

W.H.I.F.F.S.
US 1975   92m   Technicolor   Panavision
Brut (C. O. Erickson)
GB title: *C.A.S.H.*

An impotent army veteran finds that a
criminal career, helped by stolen army gas,
helps his sex life.
Over-the-top comedy with vaguely anti-war
and anti-pollution leanings.

w Malcolm Marmorstein *d* Ted Post
ph David M. Walsh *m* John Cameron

Elliott Gould, Eddie Albert, Harry Guardino,
Godfrey Cambridge, Jennifer O'Neill
† Rather typical of the film was its ambiguous
catch line: 'The biggest bang in history!'

AAN: song, 'Now That We're in Love'

While I Live
GB 1947   85m   bw
Edward Dryhurst
Reissue title: *The Dream of Olwen.*

A Cornishwoman believes an amnesiac girl to
be the reincarnation of her dead sister.
Silly melodrama which achieved phenomenal
popularity, despite poor production, because
of its haunting theme tune *The Dream of
Olwen* by Charles Williams.

w John Harlow, Doreen Montgomery, *play*
This Same Garden by Robert Bell *d* John
Harlow *ph* F. A. Young *m* Charles Williams

Tom Walls, Sonia Dresdel, Carol Raye,
Clifford Evans, Patricia Burke, John Warwick,
Edward Lexy

While the City Sleeps
US 1956   100m   bw   Superscope
RKO (Bert Friedlob)

Three chief executives of a newspaper empire
are pitted against each other in a search for a
murder scoop.

Star-packed but leaden-paced news bureau melodrama; a major disappointment considering the talent.

w Casey Robinson, *novel* The Bloody Spur by Charles Einstein d Fritz Lang ph Ernest Laszlo m Herschel Burke Gilbert

Dana Andrews, George Sanders, Ida Lupino, Sally Forrest, Thomas Mitchell, Rhonda Fleming, Vincent Price, Howard Duff, James Craig, Robert Warwick, John Barrymore Jnr

● *Video: Kingston*

While the Patient Slept
US 1935 65m bw

A nurse hired to look after a stricken millionaire finds herself in the middle of a murder case. Announced as the first of a series of Clue Club Mysteries, this was derived from a source similar to, or possibly the same as, *Miss Pinkerton* (qv). It sufficed. Aline MacMahon, Guy Kibbee, Lyle Talbot, Patricia Ellis, Allen Jenkins, Gene Solow, Brown Holmes, Robert Barrat, Hobart Cavanaugh. Written by Robert N. Lee from a novel by Mignon G. Eberhart; directed by Ray Enright; for First National. 'Seems probable that it will please wherever mysteries are liked.'—*Variety*

While the Sun Shines
GB 1946 81m bw
ABPC / Anatole de Grunwald

An American soldier and a young Frenchman seek to woo Lady Elizabeth away from her intended.
Mild wartime comedy, rather stagey and considerably undercast.

w Terence Rattigan, from his play d Anthony Asquith ph Jack Hildyard

Brenda Bruce, Ronald Howard, Bonar Colleano, Ronald Squire, Barbara White, Margaret Rutherford, Miles Malleson, Joyce Grenfell

The Whip Hand
US 1951 82m bw
RKO (Lewis J. Rachmil)

A fisherman finds himself unwelcome in a lonely town run by ex-Nazi, now communist, bacteriologists.
Preposterous, pretentious anti-communist low-budgeter, mildly enjoyable for its sheer gall.

w George Bricker, Frank L. Moss d / pd William Cameron Menzies ph Nicholas Musuraca m Paul Sawtell

Elliott Reid, Carla Balenda, Edgar Barrier, Raymond Burr

Whiplash
US 1948 90m bw
Warner (William Jacobs)

A painter becomes a prizefighter.
Hokey, unpersuasive romantic melodrama.

w Maurice Geraghty, Harriet Frank Jnr d Lewis Seiler ph Peverell Marley m Franz Waxman

Dane Clark, Alexis Smith, Zachary Scott, Eve Arden, Jeffrey Lynn, S. Z. Sakall, Alan Hale, Douglas Kennedy

Whipsaw*
US 1935 88m bw
MGM (Harry Rapf)

A G-man infiltrates a gang by wooing its girl member.
Fairly snappy romantic drama which further established both its stars.

w Howard Emmett Rogers d Sam Wood ph James Wong Howe m William Axt

Spencer Tracy, Myrna Loy, Harvey Stephens, Clay Clements, William Harrigan
'Should do okay biz . . . romance and sex angles mingling with the light touch of sophistication so popular nowadays carries events along at a speedy pace that is unabated until the fadeout.'—*Variety*

Whirlpool
US 1934 69m bw

A convict is released and makes contact with the daughter who never knew him. Heavily plotted melodrama with an unhappy ending; technically quite proficient. Jack Holt, Jean Arthur, Allen Jenkins, Donald Cook, Lila Lee, John Miljan, Ward Bond. Written by Dorothy Howell, Ethel Hill, Howard Emmett Rogers; directed by Roy William Neill; for Columbia. 'One of the most surefire father and daughter stories ever screened, with heart interest running high throughout . . . well above fair in entertainment appeal.'—*Variety*

Whirlpool*
US 1950 98m bw
TCF (Otto Preminger)

A girl is accused of a murder committed by her hypnotist, who has willed himself out of a hospital bed.
Silly murder melodrama; glossy production makes it entertaining.

w Lester Barstow, Andrew Solt, *novel* Guy Endore d Otto Preminger ph Arthur Miller m David Raksin

Gene Tierney, *Jose Ferrer,* Richard Conte, Charles Bickford, Barbara O'Neil, Eduard Franz, Fortunio Bonanova
'It is sometimes difficult to discover from Miss Tierney's playing whether she is or is not under hypnosis.'—*MFB*

† Lester Barstow=Ben Hecht.

Whirlpool
GB 1959 95m Eastmancolor
Rank (George Pitcher)

A killer escapes in Cologne; his girl friend separates from him and gets a lift down the Rhine in a barge; the trip reforms her and she betrays her lover.
Modestly attractive travelogue with the burden of a very boring melodrama.

w Lawrence P. Bachmann d Lewis Allen ph Geoffrey Unsworth m Ron Goodwin

Juliette Greco, O. W. Fischer, William Sylvester, Marius Goring, Muriel Pavlow

Whisky Galore****
GB 1948 82m bw
Ealing (Monja Danischewsky)
US title: *Tight Little Island*

During World War II, a ship full of whisky is wrecked on a small Hebridean island, and the local customs and excise man has his hands full.
Marvellously detailed, fast-moving, well-played and attractively photographed comedy which firmly established the richest Ealing vein.

w Compton Mackenzie, Angus Macphail, *novel* Compton Mackenzie d Alexander Mackendrick ph Gerald Gibbs m Ernest Irving

Basil Radford, Joan Greenwood, Jean Cadell, Gordon Jackson, James Robertson Justice, Wylie Watson, John Gregson, Morland Graham, Duncan Macrae, Catherine Lacey, Bruce Seton, Henry Mollinson, Compton Mackenzie, A. E. Matthews
'Brilliantly witty and fantastic, but wholly plausible.'—*Sunday Chronicle*

● *Video: Thorn EMI*

The Whisperers
GB 1966 106m bw
UA / Seven Pines (Michael S. Laughlin, Ronald Shedlo)

An old lady hears voices and is put upon by her son, her wandering husband, and various others.
Interesting but cold and finally unsatisfactory character melodrama; even the acting, though in a sense admirable, is too genteel.

w Bryan Forbes, *novel* Robert Nicolson d Bryan Forbes ph Gerry Turpin m John Barry

Edith Evans, Eric Portman, Avis Bunnage, Nanette Newman, Gerald Sim, Ronald Fraser

AAN: Edith Evans

'The epic spectacle of America's most flaming era!'
Whispering Smith
US 1948 88m Technicolor
Paramount (Mel Epstein)

A government agent investigating robberies finds his friend is implicated.
Fairly entertaining detective western.

w Frank Butler, Karl Lamb, *novel* Frank H. Spearman d Leslie Fenton ph Ray Rennahan m Adolph Deutsch

Alan Ladd, Robert Preston, Brenda Marshall, Donald Crisp, William Demarest, Fay Holden, Murvyn Vye, Frank Faylen

Whispering Smith Hits London
GB 1951 82m bw
Exclusive / Hammer (Anthony Hinds)

An American detective in London investigates the case of a suicide which may be murder.
Tolerable programmer of its time: competence without inspiration.

w John Gilling d Francis Searle ph Walter Harvey m Frank Spencer

Richard Carlson, Greta Gynt, Herbert Lom,
Rona Anderson, Alan Wheatley, Dora Bryan,
Reginald Beckwith

The Whistle at Eaton Falls*
US 1951 96m bw
Columbia (Louis de Rochemont)
GB title: *Richer than the Earth*

The story of a strike at a small-town plastics
factory.
Reasonably absorbing semi-documentary with
a final 'solution' which rather evades the
issues.

w Lemist Esler, Virginia Shaler d Robert
Siodmak ph Joseph Brun m Louis
Applebaum

Lloyd Bridges, Dorothy Gish, Carleton
Carpenter, Murray Hamilton, James
Westerfield, Lenore Lonergan

Whistle Down the Wind*
GB 1961 99m bw
Rank / Allied Film Makers / Beaver (Richard
  Attenborough)

Three north country children think a murderer
on the run is Jesus Christ.
Charming allegorical study of childhood
innocence, extremely well made, amusing, and
avoiding sentimentality.

w *Keith Waterhouse, Willis Hall, novel* Mary
Hayley Bell d *Bryan Forbes ph* Arthur
Ibbetson m Malcolm Arnold

Hayley Mills, Bernard Lee, Alan Bates,
Norman Bird, Elsie Wagstaff, Alan Barnes
● *Video: Rank*

Whistle Stop
US 1946 84m bw
United Artists / Nero

A city girl returns to her small-town home and
finds herself torn between a night club
proprietor and an indolent charmer.
Would-be *film noir,* miscast and rather glum
when it isn't unintentionally funny.

w Philip Yordan, *novel* Maritta M. Wolff
d Leonide Moguy ph Russell Metty
m Dmitri Tiomkin

George Raft, Ava Gardner, Tom Conway,
Victor McLaglen

The Whistler
Originally a radio series of suspense stories
introduced by someone whistling the theme
tune, this was turned into a fairly workmanlike
series of second features quite unrelated to
each other except for the leading actor,
Richard Dix, who alternated as hero and
villain, and William Castle, who directed or
produced most of them.
1944: THE WHISTLER, THE MARK OF
THE WHISTLER
1945: THE POWER OF THE WHISTLER
1946: THE VOICE OF THE WHISTLER
1947: MYSTERIOUS INTRUDER, THE
SECRET OF THE WHISTLER, THE 12th
HOUR
1948: THE RETURN OF THE WHISTLER

Whistling in the Dark*
US 1941 77m bw
MGM (George Haight)

A radio detective is kidnapped by a criminal
who wants him to devise a perfect murder
which will then be pinned on him.
Scatty comedy-thriller which, though it now
seems slow to start, was popular enough to
warrant two sequels (*Whistling in Brooklyn,
Whistling in Dixie*).

w Robert McGonigle, Harry Clark, Albert
Mannheimer, *play* Laurence Gross, Edward
Childs Carpenter d S. Sylvan Simon
ph Sidney Wagner m Bronislau Kaper

Red Skelton, Conrad Veidt, Ann Rutherford,
Virginia Grey, Eve Arden, Rags Ragland,
Don Douglas, Lloyd Corrigan
† The play was previously filmed in 1933 with
Ernest Truex, and this version is now shown
on TV as *Scared.*

The White Angel*
US 1936 91m bw
Warner (Henry Blanke)

The life of Florence Nightingale.
Starchy biopic; the Victorian atmosphere is
never quite caught.

w Mordaunt Shairp, Michael Jacoby
d William Dieterle ph Tony Gaudio

Kay Francis, Ian Hunter, Donald Woods,
Nigel Bruce, Donald Crisp, Henry O'Neill,
Billy Mauch, Halliwell Hobbes

White Banners*
US 1938 88m bw
Warner (Henry Blanke)

A social worker tries to solve the problems of
a troubled family among whom is her own son,
a fact unknown to him.
Moderate middle-class drama.

w Lenore Coffee, Cameron Rogers, Abem
Finkel, *novel* Lloyd C. Douglas d Edmund
Goulding ph Charles Rosher m Max Steiner

Fay Bainter, Claude Rains, Jackie Cooper,
Bonita Granville, Henry O'Neill, James
Stephenson, Kay Johnson
  'Emotional drama, okay for the family trade
. . . there is something fine and tender about
it.'—*Variety*
AAN: Fay Bainter

The White Buffalo
US 1977 97m Technicolor
Dino de Laurentiis (Pancho Kohner)

Wild Bill Hickok and Chief Crazy Horse join
forces to kill a marauding white buffalo.
Ridiculous symbolic western, not helped by
the very artificial looking beast of the title.

w Richard Sale, from his novel d J. Lee
Thompson ph Paul Lohmann m John Barry

Charles Bronson, Jack Warden, Will
Sampson, Kim Novak, Clint Walker, Stuart
Whitman, John Carradine, Slim Pickens, Cara
Williams, Douglas Fowley
  'The dried husk of a *Moby Dick* allegory
seems to be rattling around here amidst all the
other dead wood.'—*Jonathan Rosenbaum,
MFB*

● *Video: Guild*

White Cargo*
US 1942 90m bw
MGM (Victor Saville)

White rubber planters are driven mad with
desire for a scheming native girl.
Antediluvian melodrama previously filmed in
1930. Good for laughing at, and the star
looked great as Tondelayo.

w Leon Gordon, from his play and *novel*
Hell's Playground by Vera Simonton
d Richard Thorpe m Bronislau Kaper

Hedy Lamarr, Walter Pidgeon, Richard
Carlson, Frank Morgan, Bramwell Fletcher,
Richard Ainley, Reginald Owen
† There was also a British version in 1929
(silent) with Leslie Faber and Gypsy Rhouma;
and a few months later it emerged with added
dialogue.

White Christmas*
US 1954 120m Technicolor
  Vistavision
Paramount (Robert Emmett Dolan)

Two entertainers boost the popularity of a
winter resort run by an old army buddy.
Humdrum musical lifted only by its stars; a
revamp of *Holiday Inn,* which was much
better.

w Norman Krasna, Norman Panama, Melvin
Frank d Michael Curtiz ph Loyal Griggs
songs Irving Berlin

Bing Crosby, Danny Kaye, Rosemary
Clooney, Vera-Ellen, Dean Jagger, Mary
Wickes, Sig Rumann, Grady Sutton
AAN: 'Count Your Blessings Instead of
Sheep'

The White Cliffs of Dover*
US 1944 126m bw
MGM (Sidney Franklin)

An American girl who marries into the British
aristocracy loses a husband in World War I
and a son in World War II.
Tearful flagwaver with some entertaining
scenes in the first half and the general sense of
an all-stops-out production.

w Claudine West, Jan Lustig, George
Froeschel, *poem* Alice Duer Miller
d Clarence Brown ph George Folsey
m Herbert Stothart

Irene Dunne, Alan Marshal, Frank Morgan,
May Whitty, Roddy McDowall, C. Aubrey
Smith, Gladys Cooper, Peter Lawford, Van
Johnson
  'A long, earnest, well-intentioned, over-
emotionalized cliché.'—*Richard Mallett,
Punch*
  'This sterling silver picture . . . is such a
tribute to English gentility as only an
American studio would dare to make.'—*New
York Times*
  'Sentimental patriotism . . . a truly
monstrous cultural artifact.'—*Pauline Kael,
70s*
AAN: George Folsey

White Corridors*
GB 1951 102m bw
GFD / Vic (Joseph Janni, John Croydon)

Life in a small Midlands hospital.
Competent multi-drama which found a big
audience.

w Jan Read, Pat Jackson, *novel* Yeoman's
Hospital by Helen Ashton *d* Pat Jackson
ph C. Pennington-Richards

James Donald, Googie Withers, Godfrey
Tearle, Petula Clark, Jack Watling, Moira
Lister, Barry Jones, Megs Jenkins, Basil
Radford
'This quality of professionalism is
comparatively rare in British films.'—*Gavin
Lambert*

White Cradle Inn
GB 1947 83m bw
British Lion / Peak Films
US title: *High Fury*

A Swiss hotel owner adopts a refugee boy and
is menaced by her ne'er-do-well husband, who
finally sacrifices himself for the boy.
Unimpressive little drama which wastes its
cast, but provides beautiful scenery.

w Harold French, Lesley Storm *d* Harold
French *ph* Deric Williams

Madeleine Carroll, Michael Rennie, Ian
Hunter, Anne Marie Blanc, Michael McKeag

The White Dawn
US 1976 110m Movielab
Paramount / American Film Properties
(Martin Ransohoff)

In 1900, survivors from a whaling ship are
cared for by Eskimos, who turn on them when
nature proves unkind.
Unpleasant fable with lots of bitter weather
and subtitled Eskimos. Scarcely an
entertainment, and its message is mumbled.

w James Houston, Tom Rickman *d* Philip
Kaufman *ph* Michael Chapman *m* Henry
Mancini

Warren Oates, Timothy Bottoms, Lou
Gossett, Eskimo cast

White Dog
US 1982 90m Metrocolor
Paramount / Edgar J. Scherick

A dog is trained to attack blacks only.
Oddball thriller with racist overtones; not a
happy thought.

w Samuel Fuller, Curtis Hanson, *book*
Romain Gary *d* Samuel Fuller *ph* Bruce
Surtees *m* Ennio Morricone

Kristy McNichol, Paul Winfield, Burl Ives,
Jameson Parker, Lynne Moody, Marshall
Thompson

White Feather*
US 1955 100m Technicolor
Cinemascope
TCF / Panoramic (Robert L. Jacks)

A cavalry colonel tries to hold back gold
prospectors until the Cheyenne have moved
on to their new reservations.

Old-fashioned cowboys and (sympathetic)
Indians, very efficiently done.

w Delmer Daves, Leo Townsend *d* Robert
Webb *ph* Lucien Ballard *m* Hugo Friedhofer

Robert Wagner, John Lund, Jeffrey Hunter,
Debra Paget, Eduard Franz, Noah Beery Jnr,
Hugh O'Brian, Virginia Leith, Emile Meyer

'Pick up the pieces, folks, Jimmy's in action
again!'

White Heat***
US 1949 114m bw
Warner (Louis F. Edelman)

A violent, mother-fixated gangster gets his
comeuppance when a government agent is
infiltrated into his gang.
This searing melodrama reintroduced the old
Cagney and then some: spellbinding suspense
sequences complemented his vivid and
hypnotic portrayal.

w Ivan Goff, Ben Roberts, *story* Virginia
Kellogg *d Raoul Walsh ph* Sid Hickox
m Max Steiner

James Cagney, Edmond O'Brien, *Margaret
Wycherly*, Virginia Mayo, Steve Cochran,
John Archer
'The most gruesome aggregation of
brutalities ever presented under the guise of
entertainment.'—*Cue*
'In the hurtling tabloid traditions of the
gangster movies of the thirties, but its matter-
of-fact violence is a new post-war style.'—
Time
'A wild and exciting picture of mayhem and
madness.'—*Life*

AAN: Virginia Kellogg

● *Video: Warner*

The White Hell of Pitz Palu*
Germany 1929 approx 90m bw

Mountaineers have a difficult ascent of Pitz
Palu. Classic semi-documentary, noted for its
pictorial compositions more than its dramatic
qualities. Written and directed by G. W. Pabst
and Dr Arnold Fank; for UFA. 'An
astonishing and, to me, wildly terrifying
film.'—*James Agate.*

White Lightning
US 1973 101m De Luxe
United Artists / Levy–Gardner–Laven

A convict escapes to wreak vengeance on the
corrupt sheriff who had killed his brother.
Heavy-going southern melodrama which
comes to life only during its occasional fits of
violence. *Gator* was a kind of sequel.

w William Norton *d* Joseph Sargent
ph Edward Rosson *m* Charles Bernstein

Burt Reynolds, Jennifer Billingsley, Ned
Beatty, Matt Clark, Bo Hopkins, Louise
Latham, Diane Ladd

The White Parade
US 1934 80m bw

Incidents at the nurses' training school of a
midwestern hospital. Smooth but very
predictable semi-documentary. Loretta
Young, John Boles, Dorothy Wilson, Muriel

Kirkland, Sara Haden, Astrid Allwyn, Jane
Darwell, Frank Conroy. Written by Sonya
Levien, Ernest Pascal, from the novel by Rian
James; directed by Irving Cummings; for Jesse
L. Lasky / Fox. 'Sympathetic comedy drama
with strong *femme* draw value.'—*Variety*

White Savage
US 1943 75m Technicolor
Universal (George Waggner)
GB title: *White Captive*

The queen of a beautiful South Sea island has
trouble with shark hunters and crooks after
her mineral deposits.
Self-admitted hokum strung loosely and
colourfully around its star: big box office in the
middle of the war.

w Richard Brooks *d* Arthur Lubin *ph* Lester
White, William Snyder *m* Frank Skinner

Maria Montez, Jon Hall, Sabu, Thomas
Gomez, Sidney Toler, Paul Guilfoyle, Turhan
Bey, Don Terry
'It may be that these semi-burlesques were
more fun to make than to watch.'—*Pauline
Kael, 70s*

White Shadows in the South Seas*
US 1927 88m (sound version) bw
MGM

An alcoholic doctor in Tahiti finds happiness
with a native girl until he is killed by white
colonials.
Rather boring melodrama illuminated by
superb photography.

w Ray Doyle, Jack Cunningham, *book*
Frederick J. O'Brien *d* W. S. Van Dyke
(and Robert Flaherty) *ph* Clyde de Vinna and
others (including Flaherty)

Monte Blue, Raquel Torres

AA: Clyde de Vinna

The White Sister
US 1933 110m bw
MGM (Hunt Stromberg)

When her lover is reported killed in the war,
an Italian noblewoman takes the veil . . . but
he comes back.
Tiresome romantic drama from another age, a
big prestige production of its time.

w Donald Ogden Stewart, *novel* F. Marion
Crawford, Walter Hackett *d* Victor Fleming
ph William Daniels *m* Herbert Stothart

Helen Hayes, Clark Gable, Lewis Stone,
Louise Closser Hale, May Robson, Edward
Arnold
'An eloquent yoking of marquee names . . .
certain money maker for general release.'—
Variety

White Tie and Tails
US 1946 81m bw

A butler left in charge of the house gets ideas
above his station. Modest comedy which lacks
the required high style. Dan Duryea, Ella
Raines, William Bendix, Richard Gaines,
Clarence Kolb, Frank Jenks. Written by
Bertram Millhauser, from the novel *The
Victoria Docks at Eight* by Rufus King and
Charles Leakon; directed by Charles Barton;
for Universal.

The White Tower
US 1950 98m Technicolor
RKO (Sid Rogell)

Various people have personal reasons for climbing an Alpine mountain.
Pretentiously symbolic melodrama with some good action sequences and curiously stilted performances.

w Paul Jarrico, *novel* James Ramsay Ullman d Ted Tetzlaff *ph* Ray Rennahan *m* Roy Webb

Glenn Ford, Claude Rains, Alida Valli, Oscar Homolka, Cedric Hardwicke, Lloyd Bridges, June Clayworth

'The main interest is a curiosity as to who will fall over which precipice when.'— *Penelope Houston*
● *Video: Kingston*

The White Unicorn
GB 1947 97m bw
GFD / John Corfield (Harold Huth)
US title: *Bad Sister*

In a home for delinquent girls, the worst offender exchanges reminiscences with the warden.
Peg's Paper melodrama in complex flashback form.

w Robert Westerby, A. R. Rawlinson, Moie Charles, *novel* Flora Sandstrom d Bernard Knowles *ph* Reg Wyer *m* Bretton Byrd

Margaret Lockwood, Joan Greenwood, Ian Hunter, Dennis Price, Guy Middleton, Catherine Lacey, Mabel Constanduros, Paul Dupuis

White Witch Doctor
US 1953 96m Technicolor
TCF (Otto Lang)

A nurse in the Congo converts a gold-seeking adventurer.
Stale hokum in which the animals are the most interesting feature.

w Ivan Goff, Ben Roberts, *novel* Louise A. Stinetorf d Henry Hathaway *ph* Leon Shamroy *m* Bernard Herrmann

Susan Hayward, Robert Mitchum, Walter Slezak, Timothy Carey

'Alone among outcasts who hadn't seen a white woman in ten years!'

White Woman
US 1933 68m bw
Paramount

A cockney overseer in the Malaysian jungle takes back a cabaret singer as his bride.
Risible melodrama with an obvious outcome.

w Norman Reilly Raine, Frank Butler d Stuart Walker *ph* Harry Fischbeck

Charles Laughton, Carole Lombard, Kent Taylor, Charles Bickford, Percy Kilbride, Charles Middleton, James Bell

'Bromidic South Sea stuff . . . seems best for dual bills.'— *Variety*
† Remade as *Island of Lost Men*.

White Zombie**
US 1932 74m bw
American Securities Corporation (Edward Halperin)

Haitian zombies work a sugar mill for a white schemer.
Genuinely eerie horror film with a slow, stagey, out-of-this world quality coupled with an interesting sense of composition.

w Garnett Weston d Victor Halperin *ph* Arthur Martinelli *md* Abe Meyer

Bela Lugosi, Madge Bellamy, John Harron, Joseph Cawthorn

'Fine work of Lugosi is backed by good cast and bizarre staging . . . not quite up to Broadway.'— *Variety*
'A Gothic fairy tale filled with dreamlike imagery, traditional symbols, echoes of Romanticism, and (probably unintentional) psychosexual overtones.'— *Carlos Clarens*
'For those absolutely dedicated to gothic silliness.'— *New Yorker, 1977*

Who?
GB 1974 93m Eastmancolor
British Lion / Hemisphere / Maclean

An American scientist is captured by the Russians after a car crash and returned six months later as a somewhat suspect android.
So-what mixture of character drama and James Bondery; aiming clearly at no particular audience, it failed to get a release.

w John Gould, *novel* Algis Budrys d Jack Gold *ph* Petrus Schloemp *m* John Cameron

Elliott Gould, Trevor Howard, Joseph Bova, Ed Grover, James Noble, Lyndon Brook

Who Dares Wins
GB 1982 125m colour
Rank / Richmond Light Horse / Euan Lloyd (Raymond Menmuir)

An SAS captain infiltrates a ruthless anti-nuclear group which finally holds the American Secretary of State to ransom.
Crude exploitation of the SAS's successful relief of the Iranian Embassy. The entertainment is thick ear at best, and some of the dialogue and performances have to be seen to be believed.

w Reginald Rose d Ian Sharp *ph* Phil Meheux *m* Roy Budd, Jerry and Marc Donahue *pd* Syd Cain

Lewis Collins, Judy Davis, Ingrid Pitt, Richard Widmark, Edward Woodward, Robert Webber, Kenneth Griffith, Norman Rodway

'It should manage to offend anybody—punk, pacifist or policeman—inclined to take seriously the subject of global security.'— *Philip Strick, MFB*
'Cinematically antiquated and with hawkish politics poking unappealingly through the thin cloak of fiction.'— *Sight and Sound*
● *Video: Rank*

Who Done It?
US 1942 77m bw
Universal (Alex Gottlieb)

Soda jerks in a New York radio station catch a murderer.

So-so comedy thriller, fatally lacking atmosphere (and good jokes).

w Stanley Roberts, Edmund Joseph, John Grant d Erle C. Kenton *ph* Charles Van Enger *m* Frank Skinner

Bud Abbott, Lou Costello, William Gargan, Louise Allbritton, Patric Knowles, Don Porter, Jerome Cowan, William Bendix, Mary Wickes, Thomas Gomez

Who Done It?
GB 1956 85m bw
Ealing (Michael Relph, Basil Dearden)

An ice-rink sweeper sets up as a private eye and captures a ring of spies.
Lively but disappointing film debut for a star comic whose screen personality proved too bland.

w T. E. B. Clarke d Basil Dearden *ph* Otto Heller *m* Philip Green

Benny Hill, Belinda Lee, David Kossoff, Garry Marsh, Ernest Thesiger, Thorley Walters

Who Goes There?
GB 1952 85m bw
British Lion / London Films (Anthony Kimmins)
US title: *The Passionate Sentry*

In a Grace and Favour house near St James' Palace, a guardsman is involved in a trail of romantic intrigue.
Very British romantic farce, dully and quickly filmed from a West End success.

w John Dighton, from his play d Anthony Kimmins *ph* John Wilcox, Ted Scaife *m* Muir Mathieson

Peggy Cummins, Valerie Hobson, George Cole, Nigel Patrick, A. E. Matthews, Anthony Bushell

Who Is Harry Kellerman and Why Is He Saying These Terrible Things About Me?
US 1971 108m De Luxe
Cinema Center (Ulu Grosbard, Herb Gardner)

A New York composer is persecuted by a mysterious figure which turns out to be himself.
Wild, shapeless, satirical psycho-comedy-melodrama. Not very good.

w Herb Gardner d Ulu Grosbard *ph* Victor Kemper *pd* Harry Horner

Dustin Hoffman, Barbara Harris, Jack Warden, David Burns, Gabriel Dell, Dom De Luise

AAN: Barbara Harris

Who Is Killing the Great Chefs of Europe?*
US 1978 112m Metrocolor
Warner / Aldrich / Lorimar (Merv Adelson, Lee Rich, William Aldrich)
GB title: *Too Many Chefs*

A fast food entrepreneur in London finds himself at the centre of a series of grisly murders.

Unusual and lighthearted black comedy against the background of international gastronomy.

w Peter Stone, novel Nan and Ivan Lyons d Ted Kotcheff ph John Alcott m Henry Mancini

George Segal, Jacqueline Bisset, *Robert Morley*, Jean-Pierre Cassel, Philippe Noiret, Jean Rochefort, Madge Ryan

Who Killed Mary What's Her Name?
US 1971 90m De Luxe
Cannon (George Manasse)

An ex-boxer determines to solve the murder of a prostitute.
Old-fashioned whodunnit with something to say grafted on every five minutes: an unsatisfactory mix.

w John O'Toole d Ernest Pintoff ph Greg Sandor m Gary McFarland

Red Buttons, Alice Playten, Sylvia Miles, Sam Waterston

'The hand that rocks the cradle has no flesh on it!'

Who Slew Auntie Roo?
GB 1972 91m Movielab
AIP / Hemdale (John Pellatt)
US title: Whoever Slew Auntie Roo?

A madwoman menaces two orphan children.
Pointless and slenderly plotted adaptation of *Hansel and Gretel*, crude in all departments.

w Robert Blees, Jimmy Sangster d Curtis Harrington ph Desmond Dickinson m Ken Jones

Shelley Winters, Ralph Richardson, Mark Lester, Lionel Jeffries, Chloe Franks, Hugh Griffith, Rosalie Crutchley, Pat Heywood
'Not content with being a delicate fantasy of childish nightmare, it tries to add a totally inappropriate seasoning of Grand Guignol.'—Tom Milne

Who Was That Lady?°
US 1960 115m bw
Columbia / Ansark / George Sidney (Norman Krasna)

A professor seen kissing a student persuades a friend to tell his wife that they are both FBI agents on duty. Foreign spies believe them . . .
Agreeably wacky comedy with a strained and prolonged middle section leading to a totally zany climax.

w Norman Krasna, from his play d George Sidney ph Harry Stradling m André Previn

Tony Curtis, Dean Martin, Janet Leigh, James Whitmore, John McIntire, Barbara Nichols, Larry Keating

The Whole Town's Talking°
US 1935 86m bw
Columbia (Lester Cowan)
GB title: Passport to Fame

A gangster finds it convenient occasionally to pose as his double, a meek little clerk.
Pleasingly neat comedy, well staged and acted.

w Jo Swerling, Robert Riskin, novel W. R. Burnett d John Ford ph Joseph August

Edward G. Robinson, Jean Arthur, Arthur Hohl, Wallace Ford, Arthur Byron, Donald Meek, Edward Brophy, Etienne Girardot
'Wow comedy-melodrama . . . swell entertainment.'—Variety
'A lively and satisfactory combination of farce and melodrama.'—Richard Watts Jnr

The Whole Truth°
GB 1958 84m bw
Columbia / Romulus (Jack Clayton)

A jealous husband poses as a detective in order to murder his wife and incriminate a film producer.
A filmed play, but quite a solidly carpentered murder thriller with a couple of neat twists.

w Jonathan Latimer, play Philip Mackie d John Guillermin ph Wilkie Cooper m Mischa Spoliansky

Stewart Granger, George Sanders, Donna Reed, Gianna Maria Canale

Who'll Stop the Rain?
US 1978 125m colour
UA / Gabriel Katzka, Herb Jaffe
GB title: Dog Soldiers

A Vietnam veteran takes to smuggling heroin into the US, but gets his wife and friend involved with gangsters.
Heavy-going, downbeat character drama with action sequences; well enough done, but the kind of movie that does nothing for anybody.

w Judith Roscoe, book Dog Soldiers by Robert Stone d Karel Reisz ph Richard H. Kline m Laurence Rosenthal

Nick Nolte, Tuesday Weld, Michael Moriarty, Anthony Zerbe, Richard Masur, David Opatoshu, Roy Sharkey, Gail Strickland
'Just another ambition-downer, a wasted effort to make something meaningful out of wasted lives.'—Richard Schickel, Time
● Video: Warner

Wholly Moses
US 1980 109m Metrocolor Panavision

A shepherd hears God talking to Moses, and thinks he himself has been ordained to set his people free. Inept and tasteless biblical spoof which must set back by about ten years the reputations of all connected with it. Dudley Moore, James Coco, Paul Sand, Jack Gilford, Dom DeLuise, John Houseman, Madeleine Kahn. Written by Guy Thomas; directed by Gary Weis; for David Begelman / Columbia.
'Deadly dullness of both writing and execution render pointless any attempt to single out blame for misfire, which leaves many talented performers flailing about in desperate attempts to generate laughs.'—Variety.

Whoopee°
US 1930 94m Technicolor
Samuel Goldwyn, Florenz Ziegfeld

A timid young man is catapulted into various adventures.
Early sound musical from a popular Broadway show, later remade as Up in Arms (qv).

w William Conselman, musical play William Anthony McGuire, play The Nervous Wreck

by Owen Davis d Thornton Freeland ph Lee Garmes, Ray Rennahan, Gregg Toland ch Busby Berkeley songs Walter Donaldson, Gus Kahn

Eddie Cantor, Eleanor Hunt, Paul Gregory, Jack Rutherford, Ethel Shutta
'Dandiest of screen musicals and okay dough-getter.'—Variety

'You are cordially invited to George and Martha's for an evening of fun and games!'
Who's Afraid of Virginia Woolf?°°°
US 1966 129m bw
Warner (Ernest Lehman)

A college professor and his wife have an all-night shouting match and embarrass their guests.
As a film of a play, fair to middling; as a milestone in cinematic permissiveness, very important; as an entertainment, sensational for those in the mood.

w Ernest Lehman, play Edward Albee d Mike Nichols ph Haskell Wexler m Alex North

Richard Burton, Elizabeth Taylor, George Segal, Sandy Dennis
'A magnificent triumph of determined audacity.'—Bosley Crowther
'One of the most scathingly honest American films ever made.'—Stanley Kauffmann

AA: Haskell Wexler; Elizabeth Taylor; Sandy Dennis
AAN: best picture; Ernest Lehman; Mike Nichols; Alex North; Richard Burton; George Segal

● Video: Warner

Who's Been Sleeping in My Bed?
US 1963 103m Technicolor Panavision
Paramount / Amro (Jack Rose)

A TV matinee idol finds he is a sex symbol also in his private life.
Coy bedroom farce with no real action but a smattering of jokes.

w Jack Rose d Daniel Mann ph Joseph Ruttenberg m George Duning

Dean Martin, Elizabeth Montgomery, Martin Balsam, Jill St John, Richard Conte, Carol Burnett, Louis Nye, Yoko Tani, Elizabeth Fraser

'The most riotous bedtime story ever!'
Who's Got the Action?
US 1962 93m Technicolor Panavision
Paramount / Amro (Jack Rose)

A bored wife and her law partner husband have remarkable success betting on horses.
Badly cast and rather slow comedy with flashes of wit.

w Jack Rose, novel Four Horse Players Are Missing by Alexander Rose d Daniel Mann ph Joseph Ruttenberg m George Duning

Dean Martin, Lana Turner, Eddie Albert, Walter Matthau, Nita Talbot, Margo, Paul Ford, John McGiver

Who's Minding the Mint?*
US 1967 97m Technicolor
Columbia / Norman Maurer

An employee of the US mint and his friends find a means of printing bills at night. Smartly-made action comedy with good performances.

w R. S. Allen, Harvey Bullock d Howard Morris ph Joseph Biroc m Lalo Schifrin

Jim Hutton, Dorothy Provine, Milton Berle, Joey Bishop, Bob Denver, Walter Brennan, Victor Buono, Jack Gilford

Who's Minding the Store?*
US 1963 90m Technicolor
Paramount / York / Jerry Lewis (Paul Jones)

An accident-prone young man gets a job in a department store.
Better-than-average star comedy, slapstick being allowed precedence over sentimentality.

w Frank Tashlin, Harry Tugend d Frank Tashlin ph W. Wallace Kelley m Joseph J. Lilley

Jerry Lewis, Jill St John, Agnes Moorehead, John McGiver, Ray Walston, Nancy Kulp

Whose Life Is It Anyway?
US 1981 118m Metrocolor
MGM / Martin C. Schute, Ray Cooney (Lawrence P. Bachmann)

Totally paralysed after a car crash, a young sculptor lies in hospital wanting to die.
Ill-advised film of a very static play which was a freak success on account of various very good leading performances. It makes a very uneasy movie.

w Brian Clark, Reginald Rose, play Brian Clark d John Badham ph Mario Tosi m Arthur B. Rubenstein

Richard Dreyfuss, John Cassavetes, Christine Lahti, Bob Balaban, Kenneth McMillan
● Video: MGM / UA

Why Shoot the Teacher?
Canada 1976 99m colour
WSTT / Fraser Films (Lawrence Hertzog)

In 1935 a school teacher finds a chilly reception when he settles in a Saskatchewan village.
Unsatisfactory but occasionally quite entertaining comedy-drama which hovers around the Cold Comfort Farm mark.

w James Defilice, novel Max Braithwaite d Silvio Narizzano ph Marc Champion m Ricky Hyslop

Bud Cort, Samantha Eggar, Chris Wiggins, Gary Reineke

Why We Fight****
US War Office 1942–5 (Frank Capra) bw

A series of feature-length compilations for primary showing to the armed forces, these were superbly vigorous documentaries which later fascinated the public at large. Editing, music and diagrams were all used to punch home the message. Individual titles were:

'Prelude to War' (53m) w Eric Knight, Anthony Veiller d Frank Capra
'The Nazis Strike' (42m) w as above d as above
'Divide and Conquer' (58m) w Anthony Veiller, Robert Heller d Frank Capra, Anatole Litvak
'The Battle of Britain' (54m) wd Anthony Veiller
'The Battle of Russia' (80m) w Anthony Veiller, Robert Heller, Anatole Litvak, d Anatole Litvak
'The Battle of China' (60m) w Eric Knight, Anthony Veiller d Frank Capra, Anatole Litvak
'War Comes to America' (70m) w Anthony Veiller d Anatole Litvak

All had editing by William Hornbeck, music by Dmitri Tiomkin and commentary by Walter Huston.

Why Worry?*
US 1923 60m approx (24 fps) bw silent Hal Roach - Harold Lloyd

A hypochondriac is cured when he gets mixed up in a South American revolution.
Moderate star comedy with highlights well spaced out.

d Sam Taylor, Fred Newmeyer

Harold Lloyd, Jobyna Ralston, Leo White

Wicked
US 1931 57m bw

A woman is innocently sent to prison and when she comes out sets about finding the child she had to sign away. Woman's picture, packed with predictable incident. Elissa Landi, Victor McLaglen, Theodore Von Eltz, Alan Dinehart, Una Merkel, Oscar Apfel, Irene Rich. Written by anonymous hands; directed by Allan Dwan; for Fox. 'Old-fashioned tearjerker now too old to jerk tears or grosses.'—Variety

'If every woman has her price . . . there's a reason!'

Wicked as They Come
GB 1956 94m bw
Columbia / Film Locations (Maxwell Setton)
US title: Portrait in Smoke

A beauty contest winner from the slums makes money and luxury her goal.
Busy melodrama which interests without edifying.

wd Ken Hughes co-w Robert Westerby, Sigmund Miller ph Basil Emmott m Malcolm Arnold

Arlene Dahl, Herbert Marshall, Phil Carey, Michael Goodliffe, David Kossoff, Sidney James, Ralph Truman, Faith Brook

The Wicked Lady*
GB 1945 104m bw
GFD / Gainsborough (R. J. Minney)

In the days of Charles II, Lady Skelton befriends a highwayman and takes to crime.
The most commercially successful of the Gainsborough costume charades because of its atmosphere of gloomy sin. Dramatically turgid and surprisingly poorly acted and directed, but with good period detail. It had to be reshot for America because of the ladies' décolletage.

wd Leslie Arliss, novel The Life and Death of the Wicked Lady Skelton by Magdalen King-Hall ph Jack Cox m Hans May md Louis Levy

Margaret Lockwood, James Mason, Griffith Jones, Patricia Roc, Michael Rennie, Enid Stamp-Taylor, Felix Aylmer, Martita Hunt, David Horne
  'A mixture of hot passion and cold suet pudding.'—Manchester Guardian
  'Rather dull and juvenile in its determination to be daring.'—Richard Mallett, Punch

The Wicked Lady
GB 1983 99m colour

A remake with colour, sex and violence. Pictorially quite attractive, but that's about all. Faye Dunaway, Alan Bates, John Gielgud, Denholm Elliott, Prunella Scales, Oliver Tobias, Glynis Barber, Joan Hickson. Written by Leslie Arliss, Michael Winner; directed by Michael Winner; photographed by Jack Cardiff; for Cannon. 'The images look as cheap as expensive greetings cards.'—Sunday Times
● Video: Guild

A Wicked Woman
US 1934 71m bw
MGM (Harry Rapf)

A woman kills her drunken husband to protect her children, later confesses and is exonerated. The tail end of the mother love saga, better made than most.

w Florence Ryerson, Zelda Sears, novel Anne Austin d Charles Brabin ph Lester White

Mady Christians, Charles Bickford, Betty Furness, William Henry, Jackie Searle, Robert Taylor, Paul Harvey

The Wicker Man*
GB 1973 86m Eastmancolor
British Lion (Peter Snell)

A policeman flies to a remote Scottish isle to investigate the death of a child, and finds himself in the hands of diabolists.
Old-fashioned but remarkably well made scare story, with effective shock moments.

w Anthony Shaffer d Robin Hardy ph Harry Waxman m Paul Giovanni ad Seamus Flannery

Edward Woodward, Britt Ekland, Christopher Lee, Ingrid Pitt, Diane Cilento
  'An encouraging achievement for those who had begun to despair of the British cinema.'—David McGillivray
● Video: Thorn EMI

Wide Open Faces
US 1938 67m bw

Public enemies congregate in a wayside inn where missing loot is supposedly buried.

Moderately amusing slapstick farce. Joe E. Brown, Jane Wyman, Alison Skipworth, Lyda Roberti, Alan Baxter, Lucien Littlefield, Sidney Toler, Berton Churchill. Written by Earle Snell, Clarence Marks, Joe Bigelow, Richard Flournoy; directed by Kurt Neumann; for David L. Loew (Columbia). 'On the corny side, strictly for dual bills.'—*Variety*

The Widow from Chicago
US 1930   63m   bw

A woman mixes with a gang to avenge her brother's murder. Bottom-of-the-barrel gangster drama, presented with little flair. Alice White, Edward G. Robinson, Neil Hamilton, Frank Baxter, E. H. Calvert. Written by Earl Baldwin; directed by Edward Cline; for First National. 'Barely makes programme grade . . . will have to struggle to break even.'—*Variety*

Widow from Monte Carlo
US 1935   60m   bw

The theft of an indiscreet letter causes much embarrassment in an English country house. Society comedy-drama with curious farcical asides: not an obvious success. Warren William, Dolores del Rio, Louise Fazenda, Colin Clive, Herbert Mundin, Warren Hymer. Written by F. Hugh Herbert, Charles Belden, from the play by Ian Hunter and A. E. W. Mason; directed by Arthur G. Collins; for Warners. 'Behind the eight ball where big-time dates are concerned.'—*Variety*

Wife, Doctor and Nurse*
US 1937   84m   bw
TCF (Raymond Griffith)

A romantic triangle as the title suggests. Agreeable fluff with a mildly surprising end (for 1937) suggesting a *ménage à trois*.

w Kathryn Scola, Darrell Ware, Lamar Trotti d Walter Lang ph Edward Cronjager m Arthur Lange

Loretta Young, Warner Baxter, Virginia Bruce, Jane Darwell, Sidney Blackmer, Maurice Cass, Minna Gombell, Elisha Cook Jnr, Lon Chaney Jnr
 'A smart comedy that will please all.'— *Variety*

Wife, Husband and Friend*
US 1939   80m   bw
TCF (Nunnally Johnson)

A man sabotages his wife's efforts to become a professional singer.
Modestly agreeable romantic comedy later remade as *Everybody Does It* (qv).

w Nunnally Johnson, *story* James M. Cain d Gregory Ratoff ph Ernest Palmer m David Buttolph

Loretta Young, Warner Baxter, Binnie Barnes, Cesar Romero, George Barbier, J. Edward Bromberg, Eugene Pallette, Helen Westley
 'Diverting farce comedy with appeal pointed to class audiences.'—*Variety*

The Wife of General Ling
GB 1937   72m   bw

In China, a merchant's white wife unmasks him as a criminal. Stilted melodrama. Griffith Jones, Inkijinoff, Adrianne Renn, Alan Napier, Anthony Eustrel, Hugh McDermott, Gibson Gowland. Written by Akos Tolnay, Reginald Long, Peter Cheyney, Dorothy Hope; directed by Ladislas Vajda; for John Stafford / Premier. 'Hardly up to West End level.'—*Variety*

The Wife Takes a Flyer
US 1942   86m   bw
Columbia (B. P. Schulberg)
GB title: *A Yank in Dutch*

A Dutchwoman whose husband is in the asylum takes in a fugitive USAF pilot in his place although a Nazi officer is billeted on the household.
Downright peculiar World War II comedy which at the time seemed the height of bad taste—and no laughs.

w Gina Kaus, Jay Dratler d Richard Wallace ph Franz Planer m Werner Heyman

Joan Bennett, Franchot Tone, Allyn Joslyn, Cecil Cunningham, Lloyd Corrigan, Georgia Caine
 'Kicks in the pants, belching, and exaggerated face-making are lifted from burlesque to decorate this feeble attempt.'— *New York Post*

Wife versus Secretary*
US 1936   88m   bw
MGM (Hunt Stromberg)

A publisher's wife starts to believe rumours about his attention to his secretary.
Practised star comedy drama which provided thoroughly satisfactory entertainment of a kind the cinema seems to have forgotten.

w Norman Krasna, Alice Duer Miller, John Lee Mahin, *novel* Faith Baldwin d Clarence Brown ph Ray June m Herbert Stothart, Edward Ward

Clark Gable, Myrna Loy, Jean Harlow, May Robson, George Barbier, James Stewart, Hobart Cavanaugh
 'A real box office picture for the sticks and the stems.'—*Variety*
 'See this picture if you enjoy the spectacle of three clever stars shining for all they are worth.'—*Film Weekly*

The Wilby Conspiracy*
GB 1975   105m   De Luxe
UA / Optimus / Baum–Dantine (Stanley Sopel)

A British mining engineer is persuaded to help a black revolutionary in his flight from Cape Town to Johannesburg.
Reasonably exciting political chase thriller with a sufficiency of twists and action sequences; philosophy is present but secondary.

w Rod Amateau, Harold Nebenzal, *novel* Peter Driscoll d Ralph Nelson ph John Coquillon m Stanley Myers

Sidney Poitier, Michael Caine, Nicol Williamson, Prunella Gee, Saeed Jaffrey, Persis Khambatta

The Wild Affair*
GB 1965   87m   bw
Seven Arts (Richard Patterson)

An office Christmas party nearly turns into an orgy.
Curious little comedy drama which plays almost like the Road to Ruin and has an attractive but miscast leading lady. Interesting elements.

wd John Krish, *novel* The Last Hours of Sandra Lee by William Sansom ph Arthur Ibbetson m Martin Slavin

Nancy Kwan, Terry-Thomas, Jimmy Logan, Bud Flanagan, Betty Marsden, Gladys Morgan, Paul Whitsun-Jones, Donald Churchill, Victor Spinetti

The Wild and the Innocent
US 1959   85m   Eastmancolor
     Cinemascope

A trapper is torn between a mountain girl and a city tart. Oddly old-fashioned western, like *The Gold Rush* without laughs. Audie Murphy, Joanne Dru, Gilbert Roland, Sandra Dee, Jim Backus, Peter Breck. Written by Sy Gomberg and Jack Sher; directed by Jack Sher; for Universal-International.

The Wild and the Willing
GB 1962   112m   bw
Rank / Box–Thomas (Betty E. Box)
US title: *Young and Willing*

A troublesome student at a provincial university seduces the wife of his professor. Watchable sex melodrama with an interesting background on which no one seems to have quite enough grip; 'realism' is simply there to be exploited.

w Nicholas Phipps, Mordecai Richler, *play* The Tinker by Laurence Dobie, Robert Sloman d Ralph Thomas ph Ernest Steward m Norrie Paramor

Virginia Maskell, Paul Rogers, Ian McShane, Samantha Eggar, John Hurt, Catherine Woodville, John Standing, Jeremy Brett

Wild and Wonderful
US 1963   88m   Eastmancolor
U-I / Harold Hecht

A French film star poodle makes friends with an American gambler.
Amiable zany comedy in a set-bound Gay Paree.

w Larry Markes, Michael Morris, Waldo Salt d Michael Anderson ph Joseph La Shelle m Morton Stevens

Tony Curtis, Christine Kaufmann, Larry Storch, Marty Ingels, Jacques Aubuchon, Jules Munshin

Wild and Woolly
US 1937   90m   bw

During a small-town frontier celebration an attempt to rob the bank is thwarted. Pleasant family western with music. Jane Withers,

Walter Brennan, Pauline Moore, Alfalfa Switzer, Jack Searl, Berton Churchill, Lon Chaney Jnr. Written by Lynn Root, Frank Fenton; directed by Alfred Werker; for John Stone / Fox. 'Whatever its companion feature happens to be, this is the one the audience talks about on the way home.'—*Variety*

The Wild Angels*
US 1966 85m Pathecolor Panavision
AIP (Roger Corman)

A Californian motorcycle gang is run on semi-religious, ritualistic, Nazi lines.
Much-banned melodrama, cheaply made but vigorously handled and of some interest on social and historical levels.

w Charles B. Griffith *d* Roger Corman
ph Richard Moore *m* Mike Curb

Peter Fonda, Nancy Sinatra, Bruce Dern, Michael J. Pollard

Wild Bill Hickok Rides
US 1941 81m bw

Wild Bill helps a homesteader keep his land.
Oddly cast, rather naïve little western.
Constance Bennett, Bruce Cabot, Warren William, Ward Bond, Howard da Silva.
Written by Charles Grayson, Paul Gerard Smith and Raymond Schrock; directed by Ray Enright; for Warner.

The Wild Blue Yonder
US 1952 98m bw
Republic (Herbert J. Yates)
GB title: *Thunder Across the Pacific*

Incidents in the lives of bomber pilots in the Pacific during World War II.
Routine action flagwaver.

w Richard Tregaskis *d* Allan Dwan
ph Reggie Lanning *m* Victor Young

Wendell Corey, Vera Hruba Ralston, Forrest Tucker, Phil Harris, Walter Brennan, Ruth Donnelly

Wild Boys of the Road*
US 1933 88m bw
Warner (Robert Presnell)
GB title: *Dangerous Days*

Boys of poor families take to the road in gangs.
Vivid social melodrama of its day, now rather overstated.

w Earl Baldwin *d* William Wellman
ph Arthur Todd

Frankie Darro, Rochelle Hudson, Edwin Philips, Arthur Hohl
'A depressing evening in the theatre, one which the general fan public will gladly avoid.'—*Variety*

Wild Brian Kent
US 1936 57m bw

An amiable western con man helps a town to rid itself of a villain. Mild comedy drama.
Ralph Bellamy, Mae Clarke, Helen Lowell, Stanley Andrews, Lew Kelly. Written by Earle Snell, Don Swift, from the novel The Recreation of Brian Kent by Harold Bell Wright; directed by Howard Bretherton; for Sol Lesser / TCF. 'Little to commend it.'—*Variety*

'Nine men who came too late and stayed too long!'
'The land had changed. They hadn't. The earth had changed. They couldn't!'

The Wild Bunch***
US 1969 145m Technicolor
Panavision 70
Warner Seven Arts / Phil Feldman

In 1914, Texas bandits are ambushed by an old enemy and die bloodily in defence of one of their number against a ruthless Mexican revolutionary.
Arguably the director's best film, and one which set a fashion for blood-spurting violence in westerns. Undeniably stylish, thoughtful, and in places very exciting.

w Walon Green, Sam Peckinpah *d* Sam Peckinpah *ph* Lucien Ballard *m* Jerry Fielding *ad* Edward Carrere

William Holden, Ernest Borgnine, Robert Ryan, Edmond O'Brien, Warren Oates, Jaime Sanchez, Ben Johnson, Strother Martin, L. Q. Jones, Albert Dekker
'A western that enlarged the form aesthetically, thematically, demonically.'—*Stanley Kauffmann, 1972*
'We watch endless violence to assure us that violence is not good.'—*Judith Crist, 1976*
'The bloody deaths are voluptuous, frightening, beautiful. Pouring new wine into the bottle of the western, Peckinpah explodes the bottle; his story is too simple for this imagist epic.'—*Pauline Kael, New Yorker*
'One of the most moving elegies for a vanished age ever created within the genre.'—*Time Out, 1984*

AAN: script; Jerry Fielding
● *Video: Warner*

The Wild Country
US 1970 100m Technicolor
Walt Disney (Ron Miller)

In the late 1880s a farmer buys a dilapidated Wyoming ranch and falls foul of a local rancher who controls the water supply.
Predictable family western in the familiar Disney style.

w Calvin Clements Jnr, Paul Savage, *novel* Little Britches by Ralph Moody *d* Robert Totten *ph* Frank Phillips *m* Robert Bronner

Steve Forrest, Vera Miles, Jack Elam, Ronny Howard, Morgan Woodward

'The best ******* mercenaries in the business!'
The Wild Geese
GB 1978 134m Eastmancolor
Rank / Richmond (Euan Lloyd)

Adventures of four British mercenaries in a central African state.
All-star blood and guts with a few breezy touches in the script.

w Reginald Rose, *novel* Daniel Carney
d Andrew V. McLaglen *ph* Jack Hildyard
m Roy Budd

Roger Moore, Richard Burton, Richard Harris, Hardy Kruger, Stewart Granger, Jack Watson, Frank Finlay, Kenneth Griffith, Barry Foster, Jeff Corey, Ronald Fraser, Percy Herbert, Patrick Allen, Jane Hylton
● *Video: Rank*

Wild Geese Calling
US 1941 77m bw
TCF (Harry Joe Brown)

A young adventurer in Oregon weds the girl friend of a conniving gambler.
Minor semi-western which never really finds a style.

w Horace McCoy, *novel* Stewart Edward White *d* John Brahm *ph* Lucien Ballard *m* Alfred Newman

Joan Bennett, Henry Fonda, Warren William, Ona Munson, Barton MacLane, Russell Simpson, Iris Adrian

Wild Harvest
US 1947 92m bw
Paramount (Robert Fellows)

A romantic triangle develops among wheat harvesters on the western plains.
Standard star hokum.

w John Monks Jnr *d* Tay Garnett *ph* John F. Seitz *m* Hugo Friedhofer

Alan Ladd, Dorothy Lamour, Robert Preston, Lloyd Nolan, Dick Erdman, Allen Jenkins, Will Wright

Wild in the Country
US 1961 114m De Luxe Cinemascope
TCF / Company of Artists (Jerry Wald)

A rebellious hillbilly is involved with three women.
Weird confection designed to show the star in all his facets.

w Clifford Odets, *novel* The Lost Country by J. R. Salamanca *d* Philip Dunne *ph* William C. Mellor *m* Kenyon Hopkins

Elvis Presley, Hope Lange, Tuesday Weld, Millie Perkins, John Ireland, Gary Lockwood
'One can't help feeling he was better off prior to this misguided bid for class.'—*MFB*

Wild in the Sky
US 1971 83m colour
AIP / Bald Eagle (William T. Naud, Dick Gautier)

Three young offenders skyjack a B52 jet bomber.
Black comedy melodrama, uncontrolled but with some engaging absurdities.

w William T. Naud, Dick Gautier *d* William T. Naud *ph* Thomas E. Spalding *m* Jerry Styner

Brandon de Wilde, Keenan Wynn, Dick Gautier, Tim O'Connor, James Daly, Robert Lansing

Wild in the Streets*
US 1968 97m Perfectcolor
AIP (Jack Cash)

In the imminent future, a pop singer becomes president and launches a campaign for teenage emancipation.

Satirical melodrama with a profusion of wild gags, some of which hit the target.

w Robert Thom d Barry Shear ph Richard Moore m Les Baxter

Shelley Winters, Chris Jones, Diane Varsi, Hal Holbrook, Millie Perkins

'Blatant, insensitive, crummy-looking . . . enjoyable at a pop, comic-strip level.'—*New Yorker*, 1977

Wild Is the Wind

US 1957 114m bw Vistavision
Paramount / Hal B. Wallis

A widowed Italian sheep rancher in Nevada marries his wife's sister from Italy, but she falls for his adopted son.
Intense Cold Comfort Farm melodrama with a strong similarity to *They Knew What They Wanted*; the strain shows, and the performances are tiresomely noisy.

w Arnold Schulman d George Cukor ph Charles Lang Jnr m Dmitri Tiomkin

Anna Magnani, Anthony Quinn, Tony Franciosa, Dolores Hart, Joseph Calleia

AAN: title song (m Dmitri Tiomkin, ly Ned Washington); Anna Magnani; Anthony Quinn

The Wild Man of Borneo

US 1941 78m bw
MGM

An unsuccessful braggart comes to live with his daughter in a Manhattan boarding house.
Mildly likeable though very predictable sentimental comedy from an old Broadway warhorse.

w Waldo Scott, John McClain, play Herman J. Mankiewicz, Marc Connelly d Robert B. Sinclair ph Oliver T. Marsh m David Snell

Frank Morgan, Mary Howard, Dan Dailey, Billie Burke, Donald Meek, Bonita Granville, Marjorie Main, Connie Gilchrist, Walter Catlett, Andrew Tombes, Phil Silvers, Joe Yule

The Wild North

US 1951 97m Anscocolor
MGM (Stephen Ames)

A mountie gets his man but needs his help getting back to base.
Standard adventure story with avalanche and wolf attacks.

w Frank Fenton d Andrew Marton
ph Robert Surtees m Bronislau Kaper

Stewart Granger, Wendell Corey, Cyd Charisse

'That streetcar man has a new desire!'

The Wild One**

US 1954 79m bw
Columbia / Stanley Kramer

Hoodlum motorcyclists terrorize a small town.
Brooding, compulsive, well-made little melodrama which was much banned because there was no retribution. As a narrative it does somewhat lack dramatic point.

w John Paxton, story The Cyclists' Raid by Frank Rooney d Laslo Benedek ph Hal Mohr m Leith Stevens

Marlon Brando, Lee Marvin, Mary Murphy, Robert Keith, Jay C. Flippen

'A picture that tries to grasp an idea, even though the reach falls short.'—*New York Times*

† 'What are you rebelling against?' 'What've you got?'—sample dialogue.

†† Sharpness of photography was achieved by the Garutso lens.

The Wild Party

US 1956 81m bw
UA / Security (Sidney Harmon)

An ex-football player and some Los Angeles layabouts plot a kidnap.
Unpleasant melodrama laced with sex, violence and loud music.

w John McPartland d Harry Horner ph Sam Leavitt m Buddy Bregman

Anthony Quinn, Carol Ohmart, Jay Robinson, Arthur Franz, Nehemiah Persoff, Kathryn Grant, Paul Stewart

The Wild Party

US 1974 91m Movielab
AIP / Edgar Lansbury, Joseph Beruh (Ismail Merchant)

In 1929, a silent film comedian on the skids throws a party to show his latest movie.
Evocative of its period but virtually confined to a single set which becomes boring, this collection of unlikely events and tedious people has only obvious points to make and its final descent into tragedy is not compelling.

w Walter Marks, poem Joseph Moncure March d James Ivory ph Walter Lassally m Larry Rosenthal

James Coco, Raquel Welch, Perry King, Tiffany Bolling, Royal Dano, David Dukes, Dena Dietrich

'Seems to promise a pointillist precision about its characters and milieu which it never quite delivers.'—*Jonathan Rosenbaum*

Wild River*

US 1960 115m De Luxe Cinemascope
TCF (Elia Kazan)

In 1933 a Tennessee Valley Authority inspector incurs the wrath of a local matriarch who will not leave her valley even though it is to be flooded.
Interesting liberal-minded sociological drama marred by an added love story, as the similar *Last Days of Dolwyn* was marred by melodrama. Well made but somehow unmemorable.

w Paul Osborn, novels Borden Deal, William Bradford Huie d Elia Kazan ph Ellsworth Fredericks m Kenyon Hopkins

Montgomery Clift, Jo Van Fleet, Lee Remick, Albert Salmi, Jay C. Flippen, James Westerfield, Bruce Dern

Wild Rovers

US 1971 132m Metrocolor
Panavision 70
MGM / Geoffrey (Blake Edwards, Ken Wales)

A middle-aged cowboy, depressed with the state of his life, joins with a younger man to become a bank robber.
Fashionable, derivative, quite unsuccessful western tragi-comedy mixing in shades of every director from Ford to Peckinpah.

wd Blake Edwards ph Philip Lathrop m Jerry Goldsmith

William Holden, Ryan O'Neal, Karl Malden, Lynn Carlin, Tom Skerritt, Joe Don Baker, Rachel Roberts, Leora Dana, Moses Gunn

'An existentialist western which will not do much for existentialism, the western, or the box office.'—*Charles Champlin, Los Angeles Times*

Wild Strawberries***

Sweden 1957 93m bw
Svensk Filmindustri (Allan Ekelund)
original title: *Smultronstället*

An elderly professor has a nightmare and thinks back over his long life.
A beautifully paced and acted, but somewhat obscure piece of probing symbolism.

wd Ingmar Bergman ph Gunnar Fischer m Erik Nordgren

Victor Sjostrom, Ingrid Thulin, Gunnar Bjornstrand, Bibi Andersson, Naima Wifstrand, Jullan Kindahl

'The work of a man obsessed by cruelty, especially spiritual cruelty, trying to find some resolution.'—*Kenneth Cavander, MFB*

AAN: script

● *Video: Longman*

The Wildcats of St Trinian's

GB 1980 91m Technicolor
Wildcat (E. M. Smedley-Aston)

The awful schoolgirls get unionized, and kidnap an Arab's daughter to gain attention. Crude and belated tailpiece to a series which was never very satisfactory. (See *The Belles of . . . , Blue Murder at . . . , The Pure Hell of . . . , The Great St Trinian's Train Robbery.*)

wd Frank Launder ph Ernest Steward m James Kenelm Clarke

Sheila Hancock, Michael Hordern, Joe Melia, Thorley Walters, Rodney Bewes, Maureen Lipman, Ambrosine Philpotts

Will Any Gentleman?

GB 1953 84m Technicolor

A meek bank clerk is hypnotized and becomes a ladies' man. Efficient comedy from a stage success. George Cole, Veronica Hurst, Jon Pertwee, Heather Thatcher, James Hayter, William Hartnell, Diana Decker, Joan Sims, Alan Badel. Written by Vernon Sylvaine, from his play; directed by Michael Anderson; for ABPC.

'Will heats up slow, but when he gets there, he's hell with the hide off!'

Will Penny*

US 1967 109m Technicolor
Paramount / Fred Engel / Walter Seltzer / Tom Gries

A middle-aged cowpuncher falls foul of a family of maniacal cut-throats.

Realistically spare, laconic, uncomforting western with a curiously melodramatic set of villains.

wd Tom Gries *ph* Lucien Ballard *m* David Raksin

Charlton Heston, Joan Hackett, Donald Pleasence, Lee Majors, Bruce Dern, Anthony Zerbe, Clifton James, Ben Johnson

Will Success Spoil Rock Hunter?
US 1957 95m Eastmancolor
Cinemascope
TCF (Frank Tashlin)
GB title: *Oh! For a Man!*

A timid advertising executive is touted for a publicity stunt as the world's greatest lover.
A too-wild satire on TV commercials: less frenzied direction and gag-writing would have prised more humour from the situations.

w Frank Tashlin, *play* George Axelrod
d Frank Tashlin *ph* Joe MacDonald *m* Cyril Mockridge

Jayne Mansfield, Tony Randall, Betsy Drake, Joan Blondell, John Williams, Henry Jones, Mickey Hargitay

'The one film you should not see alone! Where your nightmare ends, *Willard* begins!'
Willard°
US 1971 95m De Luxe
Cinerama / Bing Crosby (Mort Briskin)

A shy, withdrawn young man breeds and trains rats to kill his enemies.
Modest, rather unusual suspenser which builds well after a slow start; only horrifying to people who can't stand rats. A sequel, *Ben* (qv), later appeared.

w Gilbert Ralston, *novel* Ratman's Notebooks by Stephen Gilbert *d* Daniel Mann
ph Robert B. Hauser *m* Alex North *rat trainer* Moe de Sesso

Bruce Davison, Elsa Lanchester, Ernest Borgnine, Sondra Locke, Michael Dante, J. Pat O'Malley

Willie and Phil
US 1980 116m De Luxe
TCF (Paul Mazursky, Tony Ray)

Two men and a woman enjoy a variable *ménage à trois* throughout the seventies.
Curious attempt at an American *Jules et Jim*; not badly done if you have to do it, but why do it?

wd Paul Mazursky *ph* Sven Nykvist *m* Claude Bolling

Michael Ontkean, Margot Kidder, Ray Sharkey

'Truffaut's film existed both in the real world and in a world of the imagination. Mazursky's has no imagination and doesn't even touch a passable form of reality.'—*Sunday Times*

● *Video: CBS / Fox*

Willy Wonka and the Chocolate Factory°
US 1971 100m Technicolor
David Wolper

A boy wins a tour of the local chocolate factory and finds himself in the power of a magician.
Semi-satiric Grimms Fairy Tale pastiche which looks good but never seems quite happy with itself.

w Roald Dahl, from his novel *d* Mel Stuart *ph* Arthur Ibbetson *songs* Leslie Bricusse, Anthony Newley *md* Walter Scharf
ad Harper Goff

Gene Wilder, Jack Albertson, Peter Ostrum, Roy Kinnear, Aubrey Woods

AAN: Walter Scharf

Wilson°°°
US 1944 154m Technicolor
TCF (Darryl F. Zanuck)

The rise and fall of an American president.
Admirably careful biopic which raises no particular excitement but entertains and instructs on various levels.

w Lamar Trotti *d* Henry King *ph* Leon Shamroy *m* Alfred Newman *ad* James Basevi, Wiard Ihnen

Alexander Knox, Charles Coburn, Cedric Hardwicke, Geraldine Fitzgerald, Thomas Mitchell, Ruth Nelson, William Eythe, Vincent Price, Mary Anderson, Ruth Ford, Sidney Blackmer, Stanley Ridges, Eddie Foy Jnr, Charles Halton, Thurston Hall, J. M. Kerrigan, Francis X. Bushman

'Not without tedium, but worth seeing as an enormous expensive curiosity.'—*Richard Mallett, Punch*
'Rich with the sense of movement and multitude.'—*Daily Sketch*

AA: Lamar Trotti; Leon Shamroy
AAN: best picture; Henry King; Alfred Newman; Alexander Knox

Winchester 73°°
US 1950 92m bw
U-I (Aaron Rosenberg)

Long-time enemies settle an old grudge.
Entertaining, popular, hard-riding, hard-shooting western of the old school.

w Robert L. Richards, Borden Chase, *story* Stuart N. Lake *d* Anthony Mann *ph* William Daniels *m* Frank Skinner *md* Joseph Gershenson

James Stewart, Shelley Winters, Dan Duryea, Stephen McNally, Millard Mitchell, Charles Drake, John McIntire, Will Geer, Jay C. Flippen, Rock Hudson, Tony Curtis, John Alexander, Steve Brodie

The Wind°°°
US 1927 75m (sound version 1928) bw
MGM

A sheltered Virginia girl goes to live on the rough and windy Texas prairie, marries a man she doesn't love and kills a would-be rapist.
Heavy melodrama with a strong visual sense.

w Frances Marion, *novel* Dorothy Scarborough *d* Victor Sjostrom *ph* John Arnold

Lillian Gish, Lars Hanson, Montagu Love, Dorothy Cummings

'So penetrating is the atmosphere that one can almost feel the wind itself and taste the endless dust.'—*Georges Sadoul*
'Unrelieved by the ghost of a smile . . . but its relentlessness is gripping . . . a fine and dignified achievement.'—*Pictureplay*

Wind across the Everglades
US 1958 93m Technicolor
(Warner) Schulberg Productions (Stuart Schulberg)

Florida 1900: a young schoolteacher tracks down those responsible for hunting rare birds for their feathers, and becomes a game warden.
Dull, meandering adventure story with a purpose, relying heavily on violence and eccentric characters.

w Budd Schulberg *d* Nicholas Ray *ph* Joseph Brun

Christopher Plummer, Burl Ives, Gypsy Rose Lee, Emmett Kelly, George Voskovec, Tony Galento, Mackinlay Kantor

The Wind and the Lion
US 1975 119m Metrocolor Panavision
Columbia / MGM (Herb Jaffe, Phil Rawlins)

In 1904 Tangier, an American widow and her children are kidnapped by a Riffian chief, and the eyes of the world are focused on the incident.
Basing itself very lightly on an actual event, this adventure story is both confused as a narrative and unexciting as an action piece: the camera stops too often to look at sunsets, the plot stops too often for philosophizing, and there are too many underexplained characters and incidents fitting into the international jigsaw.

wd John Milius *ph* Billy Williams *m* Jerry Goldsmith

Sean Connery, Candice Bergen, Brian Keith, John Huston, Geoffrey Lewis, Steve Kanaly, Vladek Sheybal

'When the actors begin to talk (which they do incessantly) the flat-footed dialogue and the amateurish acting take one back to the low-budget buffoonery of Maria Montez and Turhan Bey.'—*Pauline Kael, New Yorker*

AAN: Jerry Goldsmith

The Wind Cannot Read
GB 1958 115m Eastmancolor
Rank (Betty E. Box)

In India and Burma during World War II, a flying officer falls in love with a Japanese language instructor suffering from a brain disease.
Or, love is a many-splendoured dark victory. Old-fashioned romance for addicts, well enough produced.

w Richard Mason, from his novel *d* Ralph Thomas *ph* Ernest Steward *m* Angelo Lavagnino

Dirk Bogarde, Yoko Tani, Ronald Lewis,
John Fraser, Anthony Bushell, Michael
Medwin

Windbag the Sailor
GB 1936 85m bw
Gainsborough (Edward Black)

An incompetent seaman is washed away on an
old ketch and lands on a South Sea isle.
Rather uninventive star comedy with
inevitable pleasing moments.

w Marriott Edgar, Stafford Dickens, Will
Hay d William Beaudine ph Jack Cox
md Louis Levy

Will Hay, Moore Marriott, Graham Moffatt,
Norma Varden

Windom's Way*
GB 1957 108m Technicolor
Rank (John Bryan)

A doctor on a Far Eastern island tries to quell
a native uprising.
Tolerably well intentioned action melodrama,
topical because of Malaya; dramatically rather
sober and predictable.

w Jill Craigie, novel James Ramsay Ullman
d Ronald Neame ph Christopher Challis
m James Bernard

Peter Finch, Mary Ure, Natasha Parry, Robert
Flemyng, Michael Hordern

The Window***
US 1949 73m bw
RKO

A New York slum boy is always telling tall
tales, so no one believes him when he actually
witnesses a murder . . . except the murderer.
Classic little second feature, entertaining and
suspenseful; unfortunately it had few
successful imitators.

w Mel Dinelli d Ted Tetzlaff ph William
Steiner m Roy Webb

Bobby Driscoll, Barbara Hale, Arthur
Kennedy, Paul Stewart, Ruth Roman
'Logical, well-shaped, cohesive, admirably
acted, beautifully photographed and cut to a
nicety.'—Richard Winnington

A Window in London
GB 1939 77m bw

A crime passionel is witnessed from a passing
train. Modest Anglo-Saxon remake of the
French film Metropolitan. Michael Redgrave,
Sally Gray, Paul Lukas, Hartley Power,
Patricia Roc. Written by Ian Dalrymple and
Brigid Cooper; directed by Herbert Mason;
for G and S / GFD. (US title: Lady in
Distress.)

Wing and a Prayer*
US 1944 97m bw
TCF (William Becker, William Morosco)

Life aboard an aircraft carrier.
Standard action flagwaver.

w Jerome Cady d Henry Hathaway ph Glen
MacWilliams m Hugo Friedhofer

Don Ameche, Cedric Hardwicke, Dana
Andrews, Charles Bickford, Richard Jaeckel,
Henry Morgan

AAN: Jerome Cady

WILL SUCCESS SPOIL ROCK HUNTER?   Tony Randall gives Jayne Mansfield a whirl.

The Winged Serpent*
US 1982 92m colour
Samuel Z. Arkoff / Larry Cohen
aka: Q, The Winged Serpent

A monstrous bird of prey terrorizes New
York.
Old-fashioned monster movie with a few twists
including religious allegory and a touch of
political satire.

wd Larry Cohen ph Fred Murphy m Robert
Ragland sp Randy Cook, David Allen, Peter
Kuran

Michael Moriarty, David Carradine, Candy
Clark, Richard Roundtree

Winged Victory**
US 1944 130m bw
TCF (Darryl F. Zanuck)

During World War II, pilots are inducted,
trained and sent on dangerous missions.
Solid, competent, best-foot-forward flagwaver
of the highest inspirational intention.

w Moss Hart, from his play d George Cukor
ph Glen MacWilliams m David Rose

Lon McCallister, Jeanne Crain, Edmond
O'Brien, Jane Ball, Mark Daniels, Don
Taylor, Lee J. Cobb, Judy Holliday, Peter
Lind Hayes, Alan Baxter, Red Buttons, Barry
Nelson, Gary Merrill, Karl Malden, Martin
Ritt, Jo-Carroll Dennison
'I suppose it is all right, but I don't enjoy
having anyone tell me, so cheerfully and
energetically, that the Air Force personnel is
without exception composed of boy scouts old
enough to shave.'—James Agee

'There is no question that Mr Hart captured
much of the gallantry and pathos of youth
rushing towards dangerous adventures with
surface enthusiasm and inner dread.'—Bosley
Crowther, New York Times

Wings*
US 1927 136m (24 fps) bw silent
Paramount (B. P. Schulberg)

Two young men join the Air Service during
World War I, and one eventually shoots down
the other by accident.
An epic of early aviation, still stirring in its
action sequences.

w Hope Loring, Harry D. Lighton d William
Wellman ph Harry Perry

Clara Bow, Charles Buddy Rogers, Richard
Arlen, Gary Cooper, Jobyna Ralston, El
Brendel
'Air battles are photographed from every
conceivable angle, producing many bold
cinematic effects . . . so much in fact happens
in the air that it is impossible to take it all
in.'—National Board of Review

AA: best picture; best engineering effects
(Roy Pomeroy)

Wings for the Eagle
US 1942 85m bw
Warner (Robert Lord)

Aircraft workers do their bit during World
War II.
Home Front propaganda, well enough
produced.

THE WINDOW. A simple but effective retelling of the story about the boy who cried wolf.

w Byron Morgan, Harrison Orkow d Lloyd
Bacon ph Tony Gaudio m Frederick
Hollander

Ann Sheridan, Dennis Morgan, Jack Carson,
George Tobias, Don Defore

Wings in the Dark*
US 1935 75m bw
Paramount (Arthur Hornblow Jnr)

Embittered after being blinded in an accident,
a research flier finally leaps into action when
his stranded girl friend needs help.
Satisfactory romantic melodrama.

w Jack Kirkland, Frank Partos d James
Flood ph William C. Mellor

Cary Grant, Myrna Loy, Roscoe Karns,
Hobart Cavanaugh, Dean Jagger, Bert
Hanlon, Samuel S. Hinds.

'Unconvincing and improbable story, but
handled so deftly that it may nose through to
moderate grosses.'—Variety

The Wings of Eagles*
US 1957 110m Metrocolor
Cinemascope
MGM (Charles Schnee)

A navy flier breaks his neck in an accident and
on recovery becomes a Hollywood writer.
Sentimental biopic of Frank 'Spig' Wead, a
routine, easy-going assignment for its director
(who is caricatured by Ward Bond as John
Dodge).

w Frank Fenton, William Wister Haines
d John Ford ph Paul C. Vogel m Jeff
Alexander

John Wayne, Maureen O'Hara, Ward Bond,
Dan Dailey, Ken Curtis, Edmund Lowe,
Kenneth Tobey, Sig Rumann, Henry O'Neill

Wings of the Hawk
US 1953 81m Technicolor 3-D
U-I (Aaron Rosenberg)

Mexico 1911: a gold miner falls into the hands
of revolutionaries.
Routine bang-bang, rather sloppily produced.

w James E. Moser d Budd Boetticher
ph Clifford Stine m Frank Skinner

Van Heflin, Julie Adams, George Dolenz,
Pedro Gonzales-Gonzales, Rodolfo Acosta,
Antonio Moreno, Abbe Lane

Wings of the Morning*
GB 1937 89m Technicolor
TCF (Robert T. Kane)

In 1899, a gypsy princess marries an Irish
nobleman; in 1937, romance again blooms
between their descendants.
Britain's first Technicolor film was great to
look at and quite charming, though slight; its
major attractions being horse races, songs
from John McCormack, and a heroine dressed
for plot purposes as a boy.

w Tom Geraghty, story Donn Byrne d Harold
Schuster ph Ray Rennahan, Jack Cardiff
m Arthur Benjamin

Henry Fonda, Annabella, Stewart Rome, John
McCormack, Leslie Banks, Irene Vanbrugh,
Harry Tate, Edward Underdown, Helen Haye

'A wholesome, refreshing and altogether
likeable little romance.'—Frank S. Nugent

Wings of the Navy
US 1938 89m bw
Warner (Lou Edelman)

The loves and careers of navy pilots.
Competent animated recruiting poster.

w Michael Fessier d Lloyd Bacon ph Arthur
Edeson, Elmer Dyer

George Brent, Olivia de Havilland, John
Payne, Frank McHugh, John Litel, Victor
Jory, Henry O'Neill, John Ridgely

'A convincer to mould public opinion and
support in favour of current government plans
for wide expansion of American air defence
forces.'—Variety

Wings over Honolulu
US 1937 78m bw

A young naval airman is posted to Hawaii and
followed by his bride. Lightweight flagwaver,
all smiles at the end. Ray Milland, Wendy
Barrie, William Gargan, Kent Taylor, Polly
Knowles, Samuel S. Hinds. Written by Isabel
Dawn, Boyce DeGaw, Mildred Cram;
directed by H. C. Potter; for Universal.

Winner Take All*
US 1932 76m bw

A prizefighter rises to fame and helps a sick
girl and her child. Slightly-plotted comedy-
drama allowing its star full rein. James
Cagney, Marian Nixon, Guy Kibbee, Clarence
Muse, Virginia Bruce, Dickie Moore. Written
by Wilson Mizner, Robert Lord, Gerald
Beaumont; directed by Roy del Ruth; for
Warners. 'Enjoyable prizefight talker:
sprightly gags and bits bolster conventional
story.'—Variety

Winning*
US 1969 123m Technicolor
Panavision 70
Universal / Newman–Foreman (John
Foreman)

A racing driver's professional problems strain
his relationship with his wife.
Cliché track melodrama with pretensions, well
but needlessly made.

w Howard Rodman d James Goldstone
ph Richard Moore m Dave Grusin

Paul Newman, Joanne Woodward, Richard
Thomas, Robert Wagner, David Sheiner, Clu
Gulager

The Winning of Barbara Worth*
US 1926 97m (24 fps) bw silent
Samuel Goldwyn

Desert engineers vie for the daughter of a
landowner.
Forgettable action romance, a big hit in its day
because of the climactic flood sequence, which
still thrills.

w Frances Marion, novel Harold Bell Wright
d Henry King ph George Barnes m Ted
Henkel

Ronald Colman, Vilma Banky, Charles Lane,
Gary Cooper, Paul McAllister

The Winning Team
US 1952 98m bw
Warner (Bryan Foy)

A telephone linesman becomes a great
baseball player despite trouble with his vision
after an accident.
Standard biopic of Grover Cleveland
Alexander; all very pleasant but no surprises.

w Ted Sherdeman, Seeleg Lester, Merwin
Gerard d Lewis Seiler ph Sid Hickox
m David Buttolph

Doris Day, Ronald Reagan, Frank Lovejoy,
Eve Miller, James Millican, Russ Tamblyn

The Winslow Boy***
GB 1948 117m bw
British Lion / London Films (Anatole de
Grunwald)

A naval cadet is expelled for stealing a postal
order; his father spends all he had on proving
his innocence.
Highly enjoyable middle-class British
entertainment based on an actual case;
performances and period settings are alike
excellent, though the film is a trifle overlong.

w Terence Rattigan, Anatole de Grunwald,
play Terence Rattigan d Anthony Asquith
ph Frederick Young m William Alwyn

Robert Donat, Cedric Hardwicke, Margaret
Leighton, Frank Lawton, Jack Watling, Basil
Radford, Kathleen Harrison, Francis L.
Sullivan, Marie Lohr, Neil North, Wilfrid
Hyde White, Ernest Thesiger

'Only a clod could see this film without
excitement, laughter and some slight moisture
about the eyes.'—Daily Telegraph

● Video: Thorn EMI

Winter Carnival
US 1939 89m bw
(UA) Walter Wanger

College romances over a holiday weekend.
Nondescript romantic comedy.

w Lester Cole, Budd Schulberg d Charles
Riesner ph Merrit Gerstad m Werner
Janssen

Ann Sheridan, Richard Carlson, Helen
Parrish, Virginia Gilmore, Robert Walker

'Slick production of an undistinguished yarn
about the annual Dartmouth winter sports.'—
Variety

Winter Light*
Sweden 1962 80m bw
Svensk Filmindustri (Allan Ekelund)
original title: Nattvardsgasterna

A widowed village pastor loses his vocation.
In a sense almost parody Bergman; in another,
one of his clearest statements of despair. The
middle section of a pessimistic trilogy which
also included Through a Glass Darkly and The
Silence.

wd Ingmar Bergman *ph* Sven Nykvist
m none

Max Von Sydow, Ingrid Thulin, Gunnar
Bjornstrand, Gunnel Lindblom

'The film-maker's mastery alone does not
guarantee a great film. *Winter Light* is scarcely
even a good one.'—*John Simon, 1967*

Winter Meeting
US 1948 104m bw
Warner (Henry Blanke)

A repressed spinster falls for a naval hero
intent on becoming a priest.
Dreary talk marathon which did its star's
career no good at all.

w Catherine Turney, *novel* Ethel Vance
d Bretaigne Windust *ph* Ernest Haller
m Max Steiner

Bette Davis, James Davis, Janis Paige, John
Hoyt, Florence Bates, Walter Baldwin

Winter of Our Dreams*
Australia 1981 90m Eastmancolor
Vega Films (Richard Mason)

A bookseller investigates the suicide of an old
girl friend, and becomes involved with an
unhappy prostitute.
Intriguing character drama with a tendency to
haunt the mind, though its effectiveness
depends largely on its acting.

wd John Duigan *ph* Tom Cowan *m* Sharyn
Calcraft

Judy Davis, Bryan Brown, Cathy Downes,
Baz Luhrmann

● Video: Polygram

'Like a thunderbolt of naked light it struck
  Broadway—now it tears at your heart on
  the screen!'

Winterset**
US 1936 78m bw
RKO

On the New York waterfront, a drifter
determines to avenge his father's death.
Very dated poetic melodrama, here given a
talky, artificial production which at the time
impressed many critics but is now fairly
difficult to endure.

w Anthony Veiller, *play* Maxwell Anderson
d Alfred Santell *ph* Peverell Marley
md Nathaniel Shilkret

Burgess Meredith, Eduardo Ciannelli, Margo,
Paul Guilfoyle, John Carradine, Edward Ellis,
Stanley Ridges, Maurice Moscovitch, Myron
McCormick, Mischa Auer

'Not big box office . . . in certain locales
they may even wonder what it's all about.'—
Variety

'Still in a grand manner that just won't do
on the screen . . . but there are fine moments
in the performances, and there's something
childishly touching in the florid dramatic
effects.'—*New Yorker, 1978*

AAN: Nathaniel Shilkret

Wintertime
US 1943 82m bw
TCF (William Le Baron)

A Norwegian skating star comes to Canada

where her uncle's winter resort is on its
uppers.
The last of the star's Fox musicals is pure
routine.

w Edward Moran, Jack Jevne, Lynn Starling
d John Brahm *ph* Glen MacWilliams
m Alfred Newman *md* Charles Henderson

Sonja Henie, Jack Oakie, Cesar Romero, S.
Z. Sakall, Carole Landis, Cornel Wilde,
Woody Herman and his Band

Wise Girl
US 1937 70m bw

A rich girl goes bohemian in Greenwich
village. Pretty absurd romantic comedy which
strains the patience. Miriam Hopkins, Ray
Milland, Walter Abel, Henry Stephenson,
Alec Craig, Guinn Williams, Margaret
Dumont. Written by Allan Scott, Charles
Norman; directed by Leigh Jason; for Edward
Kaufman / RKO. 'Slow-moving narrative,
considerable silliness, lack of convincing
plot.'—*Variety*

The Wiser Sex
US 1932 72m bw

A society girl goes undercover to save her
public prosecutor boy friend from smears.
Unattractive comedy-melodrama which never
seems to get going. Claudette Colbert, Melvyn
Douglas, Lilyan Tashman, William Boyd,
Ross Alexander, Douglass Dumbrille. Written
by Harry Hervey, Caroline Franke from the
play Her Confessions by Clyde Fitch; directed
by Berthold Viertel; for Paramount. 'Story a
handicap: picture suffers accordingly.'—
Variety

The Wistful Widow of Wagon Gap*
US 1947 78m bw
U-I (Robert Arthur)

In old Montana, an accident-prone wayfarer
accidentally kills a man and has to look after
his family.
Tame and disappointing comedy vehicle.

w D. D. Beauchamp, William Bowers
d Charles T. Barton, Robert Lees, Frederic I.
Rinaldo, John Grant *ph* Charles Van Enger
m Walter Shumann

Bud Abbott, Lou Costello, Marjorie Main,
Audrey Young, George Cleveland

Witchcraft*
GB 1964 79m bw
TCF / Lippert (Robert Lippert, Jack Parsons)

A family of witches take revenge on their
longtime enemies.
Spasmodically arresting horror film spoiled by
too complex a plot line and some variable
acting.

w Harry Spaulding *d* Don Sharp *ph* Arthur
Lavis *m* Carlo Martelli

Jack Hedley, Lon Chaney Jnr, Marie Ney, Jill
Dixon, David Weston

'Unpretentious and uncommonly
gripping.'—*MFB*

Witchcraft through the Ages**
Sweden 1922 83m approx (24 fps) bw
  silent
Svensk Filmindustri
original title: *Haxan*

A 'documentary' investigation of the history of
witchcraft, with acted examples.
Fascinating reconstruction of ancient rituals,
still maintaining its power to frighten.

wd Benjamin Christensen *ph* Johan
Ankarstjerne

Oscar Stribolt, Clara Pontoppidan, Karen
Winther

The Witches
GB 1966 90m Technicolor
Hammer (Anthony Nelson Keys)
US title: *The Devil's Own*

A schoolmistress finds witchcraft in an English
village.
Chintzy horror with predictable development
and risible climax.

w Nigel Kneale, *novel* The Devil's Own by
Peter Curtis *d* Cyril Frankel *ph* Arthur
Grant *m* Richard Rodney Bennett

Joan Fontaine, Kay Walsh, Alec McCowen,
Gwen Ffrangcon Davies, Ingrid Brett, John
Collin, Michèle Dotrice, Leonard Rossiter,
Martin Stephens, Carmel McSharry

The Witches of Salem*
France / East Germany 1957 143m bw
Borderie / CICC / DEFA / Pathé (Raymond
  Borderie)
original title: *Les Sorcieres de Salem*

In 1692 Massachusetts, jealousies lead to
accusations of witchcraft and multiple trials
and executions.
An account of a horrifying historical fact
which was also intended to reflect on the
McCarthy witch hunts of the fifties; but the
film, despite splendid acting, is too literal and
slow-moving.

w Jean-Paul Sartre, *play* The Crucible by
Arthur Miller *d* Raymond Rouleau
ph Claude Renoir *m* Georges Auric

Simone Signoret, Yves Montand, Mylène
Demongeot, Jean Debucourt

'Keep the children home! And if you're
  squeamish, stay home with them!'

Witchfinder General*
GB 1968 87m Eastmancolor
Tigon (Arnold Miller)
US title: *The Conqueror Worm*

In 1645 a villainous lawyer finds it profitable to
travel the country instigating witch hunts.
Savage, stylish minor horror melodrama with a
growing reputation as the best work of its
young director. Not for the squeamish despite
its pleasing countryside photography.

w Michael Reeves, Tom Baker, *novel* Ronald
Bassett *d* Michael Reeves *ph* John Coquillon
m Paul Ferris, Jim Morahan

Vincent Price, Rupert Davies, Ian Ogilvy,
Patrick Wymark, Hilary Dwyer

● Video: Hokushin

'He made a murderer of the boy who was to marry his own daughter!'

The Witching Hour
US 1934   65m   bw

A gambler hypnotizes a young man into taking the blame for a murder. Stalwart melodrama, reasonably well done. John Halliday, Guy Standing, Judith Allen, Tom Brown, William Frawley. Written by Anthony Veiller, Salisbury Field, from the play by Augustus Thomas; directed by Henry Hathaway; for Bayard Veiller / Paramount. NB: There was a previous (silent) version in 1921.

With a Song in My Heart*
US 1952   117m   Technicolor
TCF (Lamar Trotti)

Singer Jane Froman is crippled in a plane crash but finally makes a comeback. Romanticized showbiz biopic with the singer providing voice only. Adequate production and plenty of familiar tunes made this a successful mass appeal sob story.

w Lamar Trotti d Walter Lang ph Leon Shamroy md Alfred Newman

Susan Hayward, David Wayne, Rory Calhoun, Thelma Ritter, Una Merkel, Robert Wagner, Helen Westcott

AA: Alfred Newman
AAN: Susan Hayward; Thelma Ritter

With Six You Get Egg Roll
US 1968   99m   De Luxe   Panavision
Cinema Center / Arwin (Martin Melcher)

A widow with three sons marries a widower with one daughter.
Quite a bright and inventive family comedy.

w Gwen Bagni, Paul Dubov d Howard Morris ph Ellsworth Fredericks, Harry Stradling Jnr m Robert Mersey

Doris Day, Brian Keith, Pat Carroll, Barbara Hershey

Within the Law
US 1939   66m   bw

A girl wrongly convicted studies law in prison and later takes her revenge on the real culprit. Reasonably interesting melodrama, filmed several times previously: in 1912, 1917, 1923 and in 1932 as *Paid*. Ruth Hussey, Tom Neal, Paul Kelly, William Gargan, Paul Cavanagh, Samuel S. Hinds, Rita Johnson, Sidney Blackmer. Written by Charles Lederer, Edith Fitzgerald, from the play by Bayard Veiller; directed by Gustav Machaty; for MGM. 'Certain of appeal where cops and robbers click.'—*Variety*

Without a Trace
US 1983   120m   De Luxe
TCF (Stanley R. Jaffe)

A mother solves the mystery of her missing child.
Fairly interesting modern melodrama with emphasis on character rather than the somewhat arbitrarily resolved plot.

w Beth Gutcheon, from her novel Still Missing d Stanley R. Jaffe ph John Bailey m Jack Nitsche pd Paul Sylbert

Kate Nelligan, Judd Hirsch, David Dukes, Stockard Channing, Jacqueline Brookes, Keith McDermott, Kathleen Widdoes
'Dignified understatement is the keynote.'—*Tom Milne, MFB*

Without Love*
US 1945   111m   bw
MGM (Lawrence Weingarten)

The housing shortage in wartime Washington causes a widow to allow a scientist to move in with her, quite platonically.
Altered version of a popular play; rather long-drawn-out and disappointing considering the talent on hand.

w Donald Ogden Stewart, *play* Philip Barry d Harold S. Bucquet ph Karl Freund m Bronislau Kaper

Spencer Tracy, Katharine Hepburn, Lucille Ball, Keenan Wynn, Carl Esmond, Patricia Morison, Felix Bressart, Gloria Grahame
'One of those glossy conversation pieces that MGM does up so handsomely.'—*Rose Pelswick*

Without Reservations
US 1946   101m   bw
RKO / Jesse L. Lasky

A famous woman writer heads for Hollywood by train and meets a marine who seems ideal for her male lead.
Would-be zany romantic comedy à la *It Happened One Night*; doesn't quite come off.

w Andrew Solt d Mervyn Le Roy ph Milton Krasner m Roy Webb

Claudette Colbert, John Wayne, Don Defore, Phil Brown, Frank Puglia

Without Warning
US 1952   70m   bw
UA / Allart

A sex maniac murders a succession of blondes. Semi-documentary, low-budget police thriller with all elements adequate for their purpose.

w Bill Raynor d Arnold Laven ph Joseph Biroc m Herschel Burke Gilbert

Adam Williams, Edward Binns, Meg Randall

The Witness Chair
US 1936   64m   bw

A secretary accidentally kills her nasty employer and almost allows an associate to take the blame. Stiff, old-fashioned melodrama which served its purpose. Ann Harding, Walter Abel, Douglass Dumbrille, Frances Sage, Moroni Olsen, Margaret Hamilton. Written by Rian James and Gertrude Purcell, from the story by Rita Weiman; directed by George Nicholls Jnr; for RKO.

Witness for the Prosecution***
US 1957   114m   bw
UA / Theme / Edward Small (Arthur Hornblow Jnr)

A convalescent QC takes on a murder defence and finds himself in a web of trickery.

Thoroughly likeable though relentlessly over-expanded movie version of a clever stage thriller. Some miscasting and artificiality is condoned by smart dialogue and handling, one celebrated performance, and a handful of surprises.

w Billy Wilder, Harry Kurnitz, *play* Agatha Christie d Billy Wilder ph Russell Harlan m Matty Melneck

Charles Laughton, Tyrone Power, Marlene Dietrich, John Williams, Henry Daniell, Elsa Lanchester, Norma Varden, Una O'Connor, Ian Wolfe

AAN: best picture; Billy Wilder; Charles Laughton; Elsa Lanchester

Witness to Murder*
US 1954   81m   bw
UA / Chester Erskine

A lonely woman sees a strangling in the flat across the street; the police don't believe her but the murderer does.
Predictable but quite effective screamer with a nick-of-time dénouement.

w Chester Erskine d Roy Rowland ph John Alton m Herschel Burke Gilbert

Barbara Stanwyck, George Sanders, Gary Merrill, Jesse White, Harry Shannon, Claire Carleton

Wives and Lovers
US 1963   103m   bw
(Paramount) Hal B. Wallis

A successful author moves his family into Connecticut, where sex rears its ugly head. Would-be sophisticated comedy with insufficient bubbles.

w Edward Anhalt, *play* The First Wife by Jay Presson Allen d John Rich ph Lucien Ballard m Lyn Murray

Van Johnson, Janet Leigh, Ray Walston, Shelley Winters, Martha Hyer, Jeremy Slate

Wives under Suspicion
US 1938   68m   bw

A district attorney involved in a love-triangle murder discovers a similar situation developing in his own life. Flat remake of the same director's *The Kiss Before the Mirror*; of little interest. Warren William, Gail Patrick, Ralph Morgan, William Lundigan, Constance Moore. Written by Myles Connelly; directed by James Whale; for Universal.

The Wiz*
US 1978   134m   Technicolor
Universal / Motown (Robert Cohen)

A black version of *The Wizard of Oz*, set in New York.
Glossy version of the Broadway musical hit; it offers some rewards, but on the whole the first is the best.

w Joel Schumacher, from play with ly / m by Charlie Smith, book by William Brown d Sidney Lumet ph Oswald Morris pd Tony Walton m Quincy Jones md Quincy Jones songs Charlie Smales

Diana Ross, Michael Jackson, Nipsey Russell, Ted Ross, Lena Horne, Richard Pryor, Mabel King, Theresa Merritt

AAN: Oswald Morris; Quincy Jones

● *Video: CIC*

The Wizard of Oz*
US 1939 102m Technicolor
MGM (Mervyn Le Roy)

Unhappy Dorothy runs away from home, has adventures in a fantasy land, but finally decides that happiness was in her own back yard all the time.

Classic fairy tale given vigorous straightforward treatment, made memorable by performances, art direction and hummable tunes.

w Noel Langley, Florence Ryerson, Edgar Allan Wolfe, *book* Frank L. Baum *d* Victor Fleming *ph* Harold Rosson *songs* E. Y. Harburg, Harold Arlen *md* Herbert Stothart *ad* Cedric Gibbons, William A. Horning

Judy Garland, Frank Morgan, Ray Bolger, Jack Haley, Bert Lahr, Margaret Hamilton, Billie Burke, Charley Grapewin, Clara Blandick

SCARECROW (Ray Bolger):
'I could while away the hours
Conversin' with the flowers,
Consultin' with the rain.
And perhaps I'd deserve you
And be even worthy erv you
If I only had a brain . . .'

COWARDLY LION (Bert Lahr):
'Oh, it's sad to be admittin'
I'm as vicious as a kitten
Widout de vim and voive;
I could show off my prowess,
Be a lion, not a mowess,
If I only had de noive.'

GLINDA, the good witch (Billie Burke):
'Close your eyes and tap your heels together three times. And think to yourself, there's no place like home.'

DOROTHY (Judy Garland): 'If I ever go looking for my heart's desire again, I won't look any further than my own back yard, because if it isn't there, I never really lost it to begin with.'

DOROTHY, LION, SCARECROW, TIN-MAN:
'We're off to see the Wizard,
The wonderful Wizard of Oz.
We hear he is a whiz of a wiz,
If ever a wiz there was.
If ever a wever a wiz there was,
The Wizard of Oz is one because,
Because of the wonderful things he does . . .'

'There's an audience for it wherever there's a projection machine and a screen.'—*Variety*

'I don't see why children shouldn't like it, but for adults there isn't very much except Bert Lahr.'—*Richard Mallett, Punch*

'As for the light touch of fantasy, it weighs like a pound of fruitcake soaking wet.'—*Otis Ferguson*

† Ray Bolger was originally cast as the tin man but swapped roles with Buddy Ebsen who was to have been the scarecrow. Ebsen then got

THE WIZARD OF OZ. A line-up of famous characters: Ray Bolger, Frank Morgan, Bert Lahr, Jack Haley, Judy Garland . . . and Toto.

sick from the metal paint and was replaced by Jack Haley. Edna May Oliver was originally cast as the wicked witch. For Dorothy MGM wanted Shirley Temple, but Twentieth Century Fox wouldn't loan her.

†† The sepia scenes at beginning and end were directed by King Vidor.

AA: song 'Over the Rainbow'; Herbert Stothart

AAN: best picture

● *Video: MGM / UA*

Wolf Larsen
US 1958 83m bw
AA (Lindsley Parsons)

Serviceable remake of *The Sea Wolf* (qv) without the Nietzschean overtones.

w Jack de Witt, Turnley Walker *d* Harmon Jones *ph* Floyd Crosby *m* Paul Dunlap

Barry Sullivan, Peter Graves, Thayer David, Gita Hall

'His hideous howl a dirge of death!'
The Wolf Man*
US 1940 70m bw
Universal (George Waggner)

The son of an English squire comes home, is bitten by a gypsy werewolf, and becomes one himself.

Dazzlingly cast, moderately well staged, but dramatically very disappointing horror piece which established a new Universal monster who later met Frankenstein, Abbott and Costello, and several other eccentrics.

w Curt Siodmak *d* George Waggner *ph* Joseph Valentine *m* Hans Salter, Frank Skinner *md* Charles Previn

Lon Chaney Jnr, Claude Rains, Warren William, Ralph Bellamy, Bela Lugosi, *Maria Ouspenskaya*, Patric Knowles, Evelyn Ankers, Fay Helm

MALEVA (Maria Ouspenskaya):
'Even the man who is pure in heart
And says his prayers by night
May become a wolf when the wolf bane blooms
And the moon is pure and bright . . .'

BEAST OF THE SEVEN SEAS!

In every roaring port they knew the "Wolf" and his savage crew...and what befell his human prey!

BARRY SULLIVAN   PETER GRAVES

Based on JACK LONDON'S lustiest story!

WOLF LARSEN

with GITA HALL

Produced by LINDSLEY PARSONS • Directed by HARMON JONES • Screenplay by JACK DeWITT and TURNLEY WALKER

WOLF LARSEN.   It looks like an epic but in fact it's a cheap reworking of a very familiar story originally called *The Sea Wolf*.

'It will tear the scream from your throat!'

Wolfen
US 1981 115m Technicolor
Panavision
Warner / Orion (Rupert Hitzig)

Mutilation murders in New York turn out to be the work of savage beasts descended from Indian hunters who went underground in despair at the future of mankind.

Nuthatch horror movie with a message, though providing little of either commodity. Clearly a waste of money.

w David Eyre, Michael Wadleigh, *novel* Whitley Strieber *d* Michael Wadleigh *ph* Gerry Fisher, Fred Abeles *m* James Horner *pd* Paul Sylbert

Albert Finney, Diane Venora, Edward James Olmos, Gregory Hines, Tom Noonan

'A thriller so slow, complicated and frankly rather dull that one's sympathy is all on the side of the predators.'—*Daily Mail*

● *Video: Warner*

Woman Accused*
US 1933 73m bw
Paramount

A woman kills her ex-lover in a struggle and goes on the run.

Intriguing rigmarole written as a magazine serial by ten well-known authors contributing a chapter each. The result confirms the method.

w Bayard Veiller, *serial* Rupert Hughes, Vicki Baum, Zane Grey, Vina Delmar, Irvin S. Cobb, Gertrude Atherton, J. P. McEvoy, Ursula Parrott, Polan Banks, Sophie Kerr *d* Paul Sloane *m* Karl Struss

Nancy Carroll, Cary Grant, John Halliday, Irving Pichel, Louis Calhern, Jack La Rue, John Lodge

'It may convince producers and exhibitors that new writing talent should be encouraged . . . business possibilities anything but bright on so-so cast names.'—*Variety*

A Woman Alone
GB 1936 78m bw

In nineteenth-century Russia, a captain falls for a peasant girl. Uninteresting melodrama with stilted actors. Anna Sten, Henry Wilcoxon, Viola Keats, John Garrick, Rimilly Lunge. Written by Leo Lania and Warren Chetham Strode, from a novel by Fedor Ozep; directed by Eugene Frenke; for Garrett-Klement. (US title: *Two Who Dared*.)

Woman Chases Man
US 1937 71m bw
Samuel Goldwyn

A lady architect persuades a millionaire to help his land developer father.

Thin, lame comedy which constantly amazes by its lack of success.

w Joseph Anthony, Mannie Seff, David Hertz, *story* Lynn Root, Frank Fenton *d* John G. Blystone *ph* Gregg Toland *m* Alfred Newman

Miriam Hopkins, Joel McCrea, Charles Winninger, Erik Rhodes, Broderick Crawford, Leona Maricle, Ella Logan, Charles Halton

'Laughs stopped at the Music Hall when the action on the screen became so insanely illogical, and dull, that the amazed disappointment of the house expressed itself in chilly silence.'—*Variety*

'A pleasant warm weather fabrication—lightweight, attractively tailored and not meant to withstand the rigours of wear or the chill blasts of the critics.'—*Frank S. Nugent*

† The unhappy production began as a vehicle for Miss Hopkins. Writers who worked on it include Ben Hecht, Sam and Bella Spewack, and Dorothy Parker. Directors involved were Edward Ludwig, William Wyler and Gregory La Cava.

A Woman Commands
US 1932 85m bw

A cabaret entertainer rejects her lover for a king, but regains him when the king is murdered. Romantic melodrama of the silent school, quite unrevivable. Pola Negri, Basil Rathbone, Roland Young, H. B. Warner, Anthony Bushell, Reginald Owen. Written by Thilde Forster; directed by Paul Stein; for RKO Pathe.

The Woman from Monte Carlo
US 1931 68m bw

The wife of a naval officer is suspected of adultery. Stiff marital melodrama based on a silent film *The Night Watch*; it worked no wonders for its German star. Lil Dagover, Walter Huston, Warren William, Robert Warwick, John Wray. Written by Harvey Thew; directed by Michael Curtiz; for Warner. 'Looks a light draw at best.'—*Variety*

Woman Hater
GB 1948 105m bw
GFD / Two Cities (William Sistrom)

An English nobleman tries to disprove a film star's statement that she hates men and loves solitude.

Incredibly slight material is interminably stretched out, well beyond an excellent cast's ability to help.

w Robert Westerby, Nicholas Phipps *d* Terence Young *ph* André Thomas *m* Lambert Williamson

Stewart Granger, Edwige Feuillère, Ronald Squire, Mary Jerrold, Jeanne de Casalis

The Woman I Love*
US 1937 85m bw
RKO (Albert Lewis)
GB title: *The Woman Between*

In World War I France, a pilot loves his superior officer's wife.

Well-made romantic action melodrama from a well-praised original.

w Mary Borden, French film *L'Equipage* and novel of same name by Joseph Kessel *d* Anatole Litvak *ph* Charles Rosher *m* Arthur Honegger, Maurice Thiriet

Paul Muni, Miriam Hopkins, Louis Hayward, Colin Clive, Minor Watson, Elizabeth Risdon, Paul Guilfoyle, Mady Christians

'Needs all the marquee help it can get . . . spotty business indicated.'—*Variety*

Woman in a Dressing Gown*
GB 1957 94m bw
Godwin / Willis / J. Lee-Thompson

After twenty years of marriage, a wife's slatternly ways alienate her once devoted husband, and he asks for a divorce.

Classic British TV play adequately filmed but now rather dated and irritating.

w Ted Willis, from his play *d* J. Lee-Thompson *ph* Gilbert Taylor *m* Louis Levy

Yvonne Mitchell, Anthony Quayle, Sylvia Syms, Andrew Ray, Carole Lesley

Woman in Hiding
US 1949 92m bw
U-I (Michael Kraike)

After escaping her husband's attempts to murder her, a woman goes into hiding while evidence is being accumulated against him. Modest suspenser with too many near escapes and not much else.

w Oscar Saul *d* Michael Gordon *ph* William Daniels *m* Frank Skinner

Ida Lupino, Howard Duff, Stephen McNally, John Litel, Taylor Holmes, Irving Bacon, Peggy Dow, Joe Besser, Don Beddoe

'The detail is full of things interesting and amusing at the time and pleasant to remember afterwards.'—*Richard Mallett, Punch*

The Woman in Question*
GB 1949 88m bw
GFD / Javelin (Teddy Baird)
US title: *Five Angles on Murder*

Police investigating a woman's death build up several different impressions of her.

Multi-flashback melodrama which somehow doesn't quite come off despite all round.

w John Cresswell *d* Anthony Asquith *ph* Desmond Dickinson *m* John Wooldridge

Jean Kent, Dirk Bogarde, Susan Shaw, John McCallum, Hermione Baddeley, Charles Victor, Duncan Macrae, Lana Morris, Vida Hope

The Woman in Red
US 1935 68m bw

A professional horsewoman marries into society and is ill received. Stiff class melodrama partly redeemed by its star. Barbara Stanwyck, Genevieve Tobin, John Eldredge, Gene Raymond, Philip Reed. Written by Mary McCall Jnr and Peter Milne, from the novel *North Shore* by Wallace Irwin; directed by Robert Florey; for Warner.

The Woman in Red*
US 1984 86m De Luxe
Orion (Victor Drai)

A middle-aged married man has fantasies of infidelity.

Moderately successful transfer to America of a French comedy success.

w,d Gene Wilder, from the film *Un Eléphant Ça Trompe Enormement* by Jean-Loup Dabadie, Yves Robert *ph* Fred Schuler *m* John Morris *pd* David L. Snyder *ed* Christopher Greenbury

Gene Wilder, Charles Grodin, Joseph Bologna, Judith Ivey, Gilda Radner

The Woman in Room 13
US 1932 58m bw

The wife of an innocent convict tricks the real culprit into a confession. Stagey melodrama which just about fills an hour. Elissa Landi, Ralph Bellamy, Neil Hamilton, Myrna Loy, Gilbert Roland. Written by Guy Bolton from the play by Sam Shipman, Max Marcin and Percival Wilde; directed by Henry King; for Fox. 'Just another factory-made release.'—*Variety*

Woman in the Dark
US 1935 68m bw

A man convicted of manslaughter gets himself on his release into another awkward situation. Moderate semi-crime melodrama. Fay Wray, Melvyn Douglas, Ralph Bellamy, Roscoe Ates. Written by Sada Cowan from a story by Dashiell Hammett; directed by Phil Rosen; for Select / RKO. 'Marquee weakness only thing that may keep it out of single-feature houses . . . murder mystery fare of sufficient relish to keep 'em from leaving the table.'—*Variety*

The Woman in the Hall
GB 1947 93m bw
GFD / IP / Wessex (Ian Dalrymple)

A well-intentioned woman takes to begging and becomes a bad influence on her daughter. Finger-wagging novelette makes an unrewarding film.

w G. B. Stern, Ian Dalrymple, Jack Lee *novel* G. B. Stern *d* Jack Lee *ph* C. Pennington-Richards and H. E. Fowle *m* Temple Abady

Ursula Jeans, Cecil Parker, Jean Simmons, Jill Raymond, Edward Underdown, Joan Miller

The Woman in the Moon*
Germany 1929 125m (24 fps) bw silent

Two scientists are forced to journey to the moon by criminals anxious to mine its gold deposits. Heavy-handed fantasy which is not among its director's best work. Willy Fritsch, Gerda Maurus, Gusti Stark-Gatettenbaur. Written by Thea Von Harbou; directed by Fritz Lang; for UFA. 'Half of it could be removed; as it is, it winds ponderously on.'—*Variety*. (Original title: *Frau im Mond*.)

'It was the look in her eyes that did it. How could he resist? How could he know it meant murder?'

The Woman in the Window***
US 1944 95m bw
International (Nunnally Johnson)

A grass widow professor befriends a girl who gets him involved with murder.

A refreshingly intelligent little thriller which was criticized at the time for a cop-out ending; this can now be seen as a decorative extra to a story which had already ended satisfactorily. Good middlebrow entertainment.

w Nunnally Johnson, *novel* Once Off Guard by J. H. Wallis *d* Fritz Lang *ph* Milton Krasner *m* Arthur Lang, Hugo Friedhofer

Edward G. Robinson, Joan Bennett, *Raymond Massey, Dan Duryea*, Edmund Breon, Thomas Jackson, Dorothy Peterson, Arthur Loft
'A perfect example of its kind, and a very good kind too.'—*James Shelley Hamilton*
'The accumulation of tiny details enlarged as though under a district attorney's magnifying glass gives reality a fantastic and anguishing appearance.'—*Jacques Bourgeois*
'In its rather artificial, club library style an effective and well made piece, absorbing, diverting and full of often painful suspense.'—*Richard Mallett, Punch*

AAN: Arthur Lang, Hugo Friedhofer

'Born in shame—living in mystery—what is her sinister secret?'

The Woman in White*
US 1948 109m bw
Warner (Henry Blanke)

The new tutor of a strange household finds himself among eccentrics, villains and ill-used ladies.
A Victorian thriller which is long on atmosphere but not so hot on suspense or plot development. The cast helps a lot.

w Stephen Morehouse Avery, *novel* Wilkie Collins *d* Peter Godfrey *ph* Carl Guthrie *m* Max Steiner

Gig Young, Eleanor Parker, *Sidney Greenstreet*, Alexis Smith, Agnes Moorehead, John Emery, *John Abbott*, Curt Bois
'The Wilkie Collins novel is given the studious, stolid treatment ordinarily reserved for the ritual assassination of a great classic. This is not intended as a recommendation.'—*James Agee*
'Greenstreet and others move through the murky passages of the story like visitors in some massive Gothic museum, and they move, on the whole, with stately discretion, and do not scribble on the objects or show anything but the greatest veneration for them.'—*C. A. Lejeune*

The Woman Next Door
France 1981 106m Fujicolor
Les Films du Carrosse / TF1

An engineer is embarrassed when an old flame, now married, comes to live next door; their love rekindles but ends in tragedy. Rather uninteresting melodrama with a failure to communicate its apparent personal importance for the director.

w François Truffaut, Suzanne Schiffman, Jean Aurel *d* François Truffaut *ph* William Lubtchansky *m* Georges Delerue

Gérard Depardieu, Fanny Ardant, Henri Garcin, Michele Baumgarner

Woman Obsessed
US 1959 102m De Luxe Cinemascope TCF (Sidney Boehm)

In the Canadian Rockies, a pioneer woman's small son does not take to his new stepfather. Antediluvian pulp fiction with quicksand and a forest fire for highlights. Shades of D. W. Griffith, and badly done into the bargain.

w Sidney Boehm, *novel* John Mantley *d* Henry Hathaway *ph* William C. Mellor *m* Hugo Friedhofer

Susan Hayward, Stephen Boyd, Dennis Holmes, Theodore Bikel, Barbara Nichols, Ken Scott, Arthur Franz

A Woman of Affairs
US 1928 90m (24 fps) bw silent MGM

A wild rich girl goes from man to man and finally kills herself in a car crash. Romantic star tosh from a fashionable novel of the time.

w Bess Meredyth, *novel* The Green Hat by Michael Arlen *d* Clarence Brown *ph* William Daniels

Greta Garbo, Lewis Stone, John Gilbert, John Mack Brown, Douglas Fairbanks Jnr, Hobart Bosworth

A Woman of Distinction
US 1950 85m bw
Columbia (Buddy Adler)

The lady dean of a New England school falls for a British astronomer. Pratfall farce for ageing stars. No go.

w Charles Hoffman *d* Edward Buzzell *ph* Joseph Walker *m* Werner Heymann *md* Morris Stoloff

Rosalind Russell, Ray Milland, Edmund Gwenn, Janis Carter, Mary Jane Saunders, Francis Lederer, Jerome Courtland

A Woman of Paris**
US 1923 85m (24 fps) bw silent (music track added 1976)
Charles Chaplin

A country girl goes to the city, becomes a demi-mondaine, and inadvertently causes the death of the one man she loves. Remarkably simply-handled 'road to ruin' melodrama; its subtleties of treatment make it still very watchable for those so inclined.

wd Charles Chaplin *m* Rollie Totheroh, Jack Wilson

Edna Purviance, Adolphe Menjou, Carl Miller, Lydia Knott
'A thoroughly workmanlike entertainment and a candidate for honours and dollars entirely independent of the drawing power built up by Chaplin in other fields.'—*Variety*
'After five minutes of watching the sparkling new print, the spell begins to work. Chaplin is neatly turning the clichés inside out, like a glove.'—*Alan Brien, Sunday Times, 1980*
'Mr Chaplin as writer and director has not done anything radical or anything esoteric; he has merely used his intelligence to the highest degree, an act which for many years has ceased to be expected of motion picture people.'—*Robert E. Sherwood*

'The plot is desperately simple, but played with a control, a complete absence of histrionic vehemence, rare in the early twenties.'—*Dilys Powell, Punch, 1980*

† Chaplin appeared unbilled as a railway porter. The film was not a commercial success and he withdrew it for fifty years.

Woman of Straw*

GB 1964 114m Eastmancolor
UA / Novus (Michael Relph)

A rich old man's nurse conspires with his nephew in a murder plot.
Rather half-hearted but good-looking star melodrama which ventures into Hitchcock territory.

w Robert Muller, Stanley Mann, Michael Relph, *novel* Catherine Arley *d* Basil Dearden *ph* Otto Heller *m* Muir Mathieson *pd* Ken Adam

Gina Lollobrigida, Sean Connery, *Ralph Richardson*, Johnny Sekka, Laurence Hardy, Alexander Knox

Woman of the Dunes*

Japan 1964 127m bw
Teshigahara (Kiichi Ichikawa)
original title: *Suna no Onna*

An entomologist on a deserted beach finds an attractive young widow living in a shack at the bottom of a huge sand pit, spends the night with her, can't escape, and finally doesn't want to.
Unique sex melodrama, all shifting sand and picturesque angles, with a clear meaning; but far too long.

w Kobo Abe *d* Hiroshi Teshigahara *ph* Hiroshi Segawa

Eiji Okada, Kyoko Kishoda
'Teasingly opaque, broodingly erotic.'— *MFB*

AAN: Hiroshi Teshigahara

Woman of the North Country

US 1952 90m Trucolor
Republic (Joseph Kane)

Minnesota 1890: rivalry over an iron ore mine erupts between a young engineer and an ambitious woman.
Standard western.

w Norman Reilly Raine *d* Joseph Kane *ph* Jack Marta *m* R. Dale Butts

Ruth Hussey, Rod Cameron, John Agar, Gale Storm, Jim Davis, J. Carrol Naish

Woman of the River*

Italy / France 1955 95m Technicolor
Ponti de Laurentiis / Films du Centaure

A peasant girl has nothing but trouble after falling for a handsome smuggler.
Lively melodrama whose primary purpose was to demonstrate the physical charms of its new star. It succeeded well enough in the *Bitter Rice* tradition.

w Basilio Franchina, Giorgio Bassani, Pier Paolo Pasolini, Florestano Vancini, Antonio Antoviti, Mario Soldati, *story* Alberto

Moravia, Ennio Flainio *d* Mario Soldati *ph* Otello Martelli *m* Angelo Lavangini, Armando Trovaioli

Sophia Loren, Gerard Oury, Rik Battaglia, Lise Bourdin

Woman of the Year***

US 1942 114m bw
MGM (Joseph L. Mankiewicz)

A sports columnist marries a lady politician; they have nothing in common but love.
Simple, effective, mildly sophisticated comedy which allows two splendid stars, in harness for the first time, to do their thing to the general benefit.

w Ring Lardner Jnr, Michael Kanin *d* George Stevens *ph* Joseph Ruttenberg *m* Franz Waxman

Spencer Tracy, Katharine Hepburn, Fay Bainter, Reginald Owen, William Bendix, Dan Tobin, Minor Watson, Roscoe Karns
'Between them they have enough charm to keep any ball rolling.'—*William Whitebait*

AA: script
AAN: Katharine Hepburn

The Woman on Pier 13

US 1949 73m bw
RKO (Jack J. Gross)
aka: *I Married a Communist*

A shipping executive is blackmailed by communists, who know of a youthful crime, into helping them spy.
Laboured witch-hunt melodrama.

w Charles Grayson, Robert Hardy Andrews *d* Robert Stevenson *ph* Nicholas Musuraca *m* Leigh Harline

Laraine Day, Robert Ryan, John Agar, Thomas Gomez, Janis Carter, Richard Rober, William Talman

The Woman on the Beach

US 1947 71m bw
RKO (Jack J. Gross)

A mentally ailing coastguard meets a *femme fatale* and comes between her and her sadistic husband.
Nuthouse melodrama which neither convinces nor compels for a moment.

w Frank Davis, Jean Renoir, *novel* None So Blind by Mitchell Wilson *d* Jean Renoir *ph* Leo Tover, Harry Wild *m* Hanns Eisler

Joan Bennett, Robert Ryan, Charles Bickford, Nan Leslie, Walter Sande
'One may have to strain to see it as more than an over-aestheticized, interesting failure.'—*Pauline Kael, 70s*

Woman on the Run

US 1950 77m bw
Universal-International / Fidelity (Howard Welsch)

A man runs away after witnessing a murder; his wife is menaced by the killer.
Slightly unusual thriller which alas fails to thrill.

w Norman Foster, Alan Campbell *d* Norman Foster *ph* Hal Mohr *m* Emil Newman

Ann Sheridan, Dennis O'Keefe, Robert Keith, Ross Elliott

A Woman Rebels*

US 1936 88m bw
RKO (Pandro S. Berman)

A Victorian miss fights for women's rights and has an illegitimate baby.
Interesting, half-forgotten star drama.

w Anthony Veiller, Ernest Vajda, *novel* Portrait of a Rebel by Netta Syrett *d* Mark Sandrich *ph* Robert de Grasse *m* Roy Webb *ad* Van Nest Polglase

Katharine Hepburn, Herbert Marshall, Elizabeth Allan, Donald Crisp, Doris Dudley, David Manners, Van Heflin, Lucile Watson, Eily Malyon
'Delving into the fascinating ugliness of Victorian England, RKO Radio have found material that is picturesque, humorous and tragic.'—*Frank Nugent, New York Times*

The Woman They Almost Lynched

US 1952 90m bw

An innocent girl out west is blamed for a crime wave and almost executed as a spy.
Incredible, random-plotted western with a few entertaining moments. Joan Leslie, Audrey Totter, John Lund, Brian Donlevy, Ben Cooper. Written by Steve Fisher, from a story by Michael Fessier; directed by Allan Dwan; for Republic.

Woman Times Seven

US / France 1967 99m De Luxe
TCF / Embassy (Arthur Cohn)

Seven sketches, in each of which a woman behaves typically of her sex.
Humourless after-dinner entertainment.

w Cesare Zavattini *d* Vittorio de Sica *ph* Christian Matras *m* Riz Ortolani

Shirley Maclaine, Peter Sellers, Rossano Brazzi, Vittorio Gassman, Lex Barker, Elsa Martinelli, Robert Morley, Adrienne Corri, Patrick Wymark, Alan Arkin, Michael Caine, Anita Ekberg, Philippe Noiret

Woman to Woman

GB 1923 83m at 24 fps bw silent

A shell-shocked officer marries into Society and later adopts his son by a French ballerina.
Far-fetched melodrama in what later became the *Random Harvest* style; a great box-office hit of its time. Betty Compson, Clive Brook, Josephine Earle, Marie Ault. Written by Alfred Hitchcock, from the play by Michael Morton; directed by Graham Cutts; for Balcon, Freedman and Saville. (Victor Saville directed a sound remake in 1929, with Betty Compson and George Barraud; and in 1946 Maclean Rogers had another shot with Adele Dixon and Douglass Montgomery.)

A Woman under the Influence*

US 1974 146m colour
Faces International (Sam Shaw)

A white collar worker's marriage goes sour.
Insanely long case history in close up, with all parties constantly on the brink of hysteria.
Often sharply observed, but hard to sit through.

wd John Cassavetes ph Mitch Breit m Bo
Harwood

Peter Falk, Gena Rowlands

AAN: John Cassavetes (as director); Gena
Rowlands

The Woman with No Name
GB 1950   83m   bw

An amnesiac wife finds herself threatened
from all sides. Hoary melodrama with some
unintentional laughs. Phyllis Calvert, Edward
Underdown, Helen Cherry, Richard Burton,
Anthony Nicholls, James Hayter, Betty Ann
Davies. Written by Ladislas Vajda and Guy
Morgan, from the novel *Happy Now I Go* by
Theresa Charles; directed by Ladislas Vajda
and George More O'Ferrall; for IFP / ABP.
(US title: *Her Panelled Door*.)

The Woman's Angle
GB 1952   86m   bw
ABP / Leslie Arliss / Bow Belles (Walter
Mycroft)

In a divorce court three flashbacks tell of the
life of a composer.
Damp little formula drama for matinee
audiences, refashioned from a successful silent
film.
wd Leslie Arliss, *novel* Three Cups of Coffee
by Ruth Feiner ph Erwin Hillier m Robert
Gill; the Mansell Concerto by Kenneth Leslie
Smith

Edward Underdown, Cathy O'Donnell, Lois
Maxwell, Claude Farrell, Peter Reynolds,
Marjorie Fielding

'Whatever I am, men made me!'
A Woman's Face**
US 1941   105m   bw
MGM (Victor Saville)

A scarred and embittered woman turns to
crime but jibs at murder.
Curious, unexpected but very entertaining
melodrama with a courtroom frame, Swedish
settings, an excellent cast and some bravura
sequences.
w Donald Ogden Stewart, *play* Il Était une
Fois by Francis de Croisset d George Cukor
ph Robert Planck m Bronislau Kaper

Joan Crawford, Melvyn Douglas, *Conrad
Veidt*, Osa Massen, Reginald Owen, Albert
Basserman, Marjorie Main, Donald Meek,
Connie Gilchrist

† Also involved in the script were Elliott Paul
and Christopher Isherwood.

A Woman's Secret
US 1949   85m   bw
RKO (Herman J. Mankiewicz)

An ex-singer grooms a girl as her successor but
lives to regret it.
Downright peculiar little *film noir* by the
co-author of *Citizen Kane* (though not so that
you'd notice).
w Herman J. Mankiewicz, *novel* Mortgage on
Life by Vicki Baum d Nicholas Ray
ph George Diskant m Frederick Hollander
md Constantin Bakaleinikoff

Maureen O'Hara, Gloria Grahame, Melvyn
Douglas, Bill Williams, Victor Jory, Mary
Phillips

A Woman's Vengeance*
US 1948   96m   bw
U-I

A man is convicted for the murder of his
invalid wife, actually committed by a jealous
woman in love with him but later spurned.
Interesting but very stagey melodrama from
one of its author's more commercial ventures.
w Aldous Huxley, from his story and play The
Gioconda Smile d Zoltan Korda ph Russell
Metty m Miklos Rozsa

Charles Boyer, Jessica Tandy, Ann Blyth,
Cedric Hardwicke, Mildred Natwick

'A rather literary movie, but most movies
aren't even that; much less are they real
movies.'—*James Agee*

'It's a great big wonderful woman's world
because men are in it!'
Woman's World**
US 1954   94m   Technicolor
Cinemascope
TCF (Charles Brackett)

Three top salesmen and their wives are
summoned to New York by the boss, who
seeks to choose a new general manager.
Amusing, superficial pattern comedy-drama
for an all-star cast, backed by all-round
technical competence.
w Claude Binyon, Mary Loos, Richard Sale
d Jean Negulesco ph Joe MacDonald m Cyril
Mockridge

Clifton Webb, Lauren Bacall, Van Heflin, June
Allyson, Fred MacMurray, Arlene Dahl,
Cornel Wilde, Elliott Reid, Margalo Gillmore

Wombling Free
GB 1977   96m   Eastmancolor
Rank / Ian Shand

The furry creatures who live under
Wimbledon Common at last make contact
with humans.
Disastrous attempt to film a popular TV series
for children. The series came in five-minute
chunks; this elephantine transcription leaves
several talents high and dry.
wd Lionel Jeffries, from characters created by
Elizabeth Beresford ph Alan Hume m Mike
Batt

David Tomlinson, Frances de la Tour, Bonnie
Langford, Bernard Spear

'A fiasco. If you really must take your kids,
it would be less of a pain to go shopping at the
same time.'—*Derek Malcolm, Guardian*

'135 women with men on their minds!'
The Women***
US 1939   132m   bw (Technicolor
sequence)
MGM (Hunt Stromberg)

A New York socialite gets a divorce but later
thinks better of it.
Bitchy comedy drama distinguished by an
all-girl cast ('135 women with men on their

minds'). An over-generous slice of real
theatre, skilfully adapted, with rich sets,
plenty of laughs, and some memorable scenes
between the fighting ladies.
w Anita Loos, Jane Murfin, play Clare
Boothe d George Cukor ph Oliver T. Marsh,
Joseph Ruttenberg m Edward Ward, David
Snell

Norma Shearer, Joan Crawford, *Rosalind
Russell*, Mary Boland, Paulette Goddard, Joan
Fontaine, Lucile Watson, Phyllis Povah,
Virginia Weidler, Ruth Hussey, Margaret
Dumont, Marjorie Main, Hedda Hopper

'Smash hit of solid proportions for extended
runs and heavy profits . . . a strong woman
entry but still has plenty of spicy lines and
situations for the men.'—*Variety*

'A mordant, mature description of the social
decay of one corner of the American middle
class.'—*Time*

'So marvellous that we believe every
Hollywood studio should make at least one
thoroughly nasty picture a year.'—*New York
Times*

'Whether you go or not depends on whether
you can stand Miss Shearer with tears flowing
steadily in all directions at once, and such an
endless damn back fence of cats.'—*Otis
Ferguson*

Women Are Like That
US 1938   78m   bw

A separated couple meet again years later and
find each other changed. Witless elaboration
of a good idea: far too slow and talky. Kay
Francis, Pat O'Brien, Ralph Forbes, Melville
Cooper, Thurston Hall, Grant Mitchell.
Written by Horace Jackson, Albert Z. Carr;
directed by Stanley Logan; for Warners.
'Terribly tiresome, slow and talky.'—*Variety*

Women in Love***
GB 1969   130m   De Luxe
UA / Brandywine (Larry Kramer)

Two girls have their first sexual encounters in
the Midlands during the twenties.
Satisfactory rendering of a celebrated novel,
with excellent period detail atoning for rather
irritating characters. The nude wrestling scene
was a famous first.
w Larry Kramer, *novel* D. H. Lawrence
d Ken Russell ph Billy Williams m Georges
Delerue

Glenda Jackson, Jennie Linden, Alan Bates,
Oliver Reed, Michael Gough, Alan Webb

'They should take all the pretentious
dialogue off the soundtrack and call it Women
in Heat.'—*Rex Reed*

'Two-thirds success, one-third ambitious
failure.'—*Michael Billington, Illustrated
London News*

AA: Glenda Jackson
AAN: Larry Kramer; Ken Russell; Billy
Williams

Women in the Wind
US 1939   63m   bw

Conflict arises between contestants in the
Women's Air Derby. Formula multi-character

picture, only moderately watchable. Kay Francis, William Gargan, Victor Jory, Maxie Rosenbloom, Eddie Foy Jnr, Eve Arden. Written by Lee Katz, Albert DeMond, from the novel by Francis Walton; directed by John Farrow; for Mark Hellinger / Warners. 'Good programmer for duals and cinch for action spots.'—*Variety*

Women of All Nations
US 1931 72m bw
Fox

Flagg and Quirt, back in the Marines, have amorous adventures in Sweden, Nicaragua and Egypt.
Routine fun and games with the heroes of *What Price Glory*.
w Barry Connors *d* Raoul Walsh *ph* Lucien Andriot *m* Reginald H. Bassett

Edmund Lowe, Victor McLaglen, Greta Nissen, El Brendel, Fifi D'Orsay, Bela Lugosi, Humphrey Bogart

Women of Glamour
US 1937 65m bw

A man is loved by a society flower and a gold-digger, and chooses the latter. Minor woman's picture. Melvyn Douglas, Virginia Bruce, Reginald Denny, Leona Maricle, Pert Kelton. Written by Lynn Starling, Mary McCall Jnr, from a story by Milton Herbert Gropper; directed by Gordon Wiles; for Columbia. 'Featherweight triangle headed for the dual round-up.'—*Variety*

Women of Twilight
GB 1952 89m bw
Romulus (Daniel M. Angel)

Unmarried mothers are victimized by a professional baby farmer.
Sordid, claustrophobic and ham-handed version of an exploitation play designed to provide another monstrous part for its star.
w Anatole de Grunwald, *novel* Sylvia Rayman *d* Gordon Parry *ph* Jack Asher *m* Alan Gray

Freda Jackson, René Ray, Lois Maxwell, Joan Dowling, Dora Bryan, Vida Hope, Mary Germaine, Laurence Harvey

Won Ton Ton, the Dog Who Saved Hollywood
US 1976 92m colour
Paramount / David V. Picker, Arnold Schulman, Michael Winner

In twenties Hollywood, a lost Alsatian dog becomes a movie star but later suffers some ups and downs before being reunited with his mistress.
Scatty, unlikeable comedy with too frantic a pace, apparently in desperation at the dearth of funny lines and situations. The sixty 'guest stars' barely get a look in; the director seems to think (erroneously) that their appearance makes some kind of point even though they have nothing to do. Altogether, an embarrassment.
w Arnold Schulman, Cy Howard *d* Michael Winner *ph* Richard H. Kline *m* Neal Hefti

Madeleine Kahn, Art Carney, Bruce Dern, Ron Leibman; and Dennis Morgan, William Demarest, Virginia Mayo, Rory Calhoun, Henry Wilcoxon, Ricardo Montalban, Jackie Coogan, Johnny Weissmuller, Aldo Ray, Ethel Merman, Joan Blondell, Yvonne de Carlo, Andy Devine, Broderick Crawford, Richard Arlen, Jack La Rue, Dorothy Lamour, Phil Silvers, Gloria de Haven, Stepin Fetchit, Rudy Vallee, George Jessel, Ann Miller, Janet Blair, the Ritz Brothers, Victor Mature, Fernando Lamas, Cyd Charisse, Huntz Hall, Edgar Bergen, Peter Lawford, Regis Toomey, Alice Faye, Milton Berle, John Carradine, Walter Pidgeon, etc.
'The film tries to conceal its deficiencies in comic ideas and comic skill by doing everything at the pace of a clockwork toy with a too-tight spring.'—*Dave Robinson, Times*

Wonder Bar**
US 1934 84m bw
Warner (Robert Lord)

Love and hate backstage at a Paris night club.
Curious musical drama with an interesting cast and fairly stunning numbers.
w Earl Baldwin, *play* Geza Herczeg, Karl Farkas, Robert Katscher *d* Lloyd Bacon *ph* Sol Polito *ch* Busby Berkeley *songs* Harry Warren, Al Dubin *ad* Jack Okey

Al Jolson, Kay Francis, Dolores del Rio, Ricardo Cortez, Dick Powell, Guy Kibbee, Ruth Donnelly, Hugh Herbert, Louise Fazenda, Fifi D'Orsay
'Romance, flash, dash, colour, songs, star-studded talent, and almost every known requisite to ensure sturdy attention and attendance.'—*Variety*

Wonder Man***
US 1945 97m Technicolor
Samuel Goldwyn

A mild-mannered student is persuaded by the ghost of his dead twin to avenge his murder.
Smooth, successful mixture of *Topper*, a nightclub musical, a gangster drama and the star's own brand of fooling; this is possibly his best vehicle.
w Don Hartman, Melville Shavelson, Philip Rapp, *story* Arthur Sheekman *d* Bruce Humberstone *ph* Victor Milner, William Snyder *md* Louis Forbes, Ray Heindorf *sp* John Fulton

Danny Kaye, Vera-Ellen, Virginia Mayo, Steve Cochran, S. Z. Sakall, Allen Jenkins, Ed Brophy, Donald Woods, Otto Kruger, Richard Lane, Natalie Schaefer
AAN: Louis Forbes, Ray Heindorf; song 'So in Love' (*m* David Rose, *ly* Leo Robin)

The Wonderful Country
US 1959 96m Technicolor
UA / DRM (Chester Erskine)

A wandering gunman is offered a job by the Texas Rangers.
Complexly plotted western offering a range of familiar exploits.

w Robert Ardrey, *novel* Tom Lea *d* Robert Parrish *ph* Floyd Crosby, Alex Phillips *m* Alex North

Robert Mitchum, Julie London, Pedro Armendariz, Gary Merrill, Jack Oakie, Albert Dekker, Charles McGraw, John Banner, Jay Novello

Wonderful Life*
GB 1964 113m Techniscope
EMI / Elstree Distributors / Ivy (Kenneth Harper)

Four entertainers on a luxury liner are hired by a film crew in Africa.
Slight but zestful youth musical with highly illogical detail; the highlight is a ten-minute spoof history of the movies.
w Peter Myers, Ronald Cass *d* Sidney J. Furie *ph* Ken Higgins *pd* Stanley Dorfman

Cliff Richard, Walter Slezak, Susan Hampshire, Melvyn Hayes, Richard O'Sullivan, Una Stubbs, Derek Bond, Gerald Harper, the Shadows

The Wonderful World of the Brothers Grimm*
US 1962 134m Technicolor Cinerama
MGM / Cinerama / George Pal

An account of the lives of the German fairy tale writers is supplemented by three of their stories, *The Dancing Princess*, *The Cobbler and the Elves* and *The Singing Bone*.
Saccharine, heavy-handed pantomime with insufficient comedy, menace or spectacle.
w David P. Harmon, Charles Beaumont, William Roberts *d* Henry Levin, George Pal *ph* Paul C. Vogel *m* Leigh Harline *songs* Bob Merrill *ad* George W. Davis, Edward Carfagno

Laurence Harvey, Karl Boehm, Claire Bloom, Barbara Eden, Walter Slezak, Oscar Homolka, *Martita Hunt*, Russ Tamblyn, Yvette Mimieux, *Jim Backus*, Beulah Bondi, Terry-Thomas, Buddy Hackett, Otto Kruger
AAN: Paul C. Vogel; Leigh Harline

The Wonders of Aladdin
Italy 1961 92m Technicolor Cinemascope
Embassy / Lux

With the help of a genie, Aladdin defeats a usurper and wins the princess's hand.
Flat and disappointing pantomime with virtually no charm.
w Luther Davis *d* Henry Levin, Mario Bava *ph* Tonino Delli Colli *m* Angelo Lavagnino

Donald O'Connor, Vittorio de Sica, Aldo Fabrizi, Michèle Mercier

The Wooden Horse**
GB 1950 101m bw
British Lion / Wessex / London Films (Ian Dalrymple)

During World War II, British prisoners escape from Stalag Luft III by tunnelling under a vaulting horse.
Standard, solid POW drama with predictable but exciting and occasionally moving developments.

w Eric Williams, from his novel d Jack Lee
ph C. Pennington-Richards m Clifton Parker

Leo Genn, David Tomlinson, Anthony Steele.
David Greene, Michael Goodliffe, Bryan
Forbes, Jacques Brunius

● *Video: Thorn EMI*

Words and Music••
US 1948 121m Technicolor
MGM *(Arthur Freed)*

The songwriting collaboration of Richard
Rodgers and Lorenz Hart.
Musical biopic which packs in a lot of good
numbers and manages a script which is neither
too offensive nor too prominent.

w Fred Finklehoffe d Norman Taurog
ph Charles Rosher, Harry Stradling
md Lennie Hayton ch Robert Alton, Gene
Kelly

Tom Drake, Mickey Rooney, Perry Como,
Mel Tormé, Betty Garrett, *June Allyson,* Lena
Horne, Ann Sothern, Allyn McLerie, *Gene
Kelly,* Vera-Ellen, Cyd Charisse, Janet Leigh,
Marshall Thompson

Work is a Four-Letter Word
GB 1968 93m Technicolor
Universal / Cavalcade (Thomas Clyde)

A power station attendant is interested only in
growing mushrooms, which have a chaotic
effect on his private life.
Weakly futuristic industrial fantasy which the
author would probably claim to be about lack
of communication. Bored audiences might
have a similar view.

w Jeremy Brooks, *play* Eh? by Henry
Livings d Peter Hall ph Gilbert Taylor
m Guy Woolfenden

David Warner, Cilla Black, Elizabeth Spriggs,
Zia Mohyeddin, Joe Gladwin

The Working Man
US 1933 78m bw

A wealthy shoe manufacturer hands over his
business, goes on holiday, and finds himself
helping his bitterest rival. Palatable star
parable. George Arliss, Bette Davis,
Theodore Newton, J. Farrell MacDonald.
Written by Maude T. Howell and Charles
Kenyon, from the novel by Edgar Franklin;
directed by John Adolfi; for Warner.

The World According to Garp•
US 1982 136m Technicolor
Warner / Pan Arts (George Roy Hill, Robert
  L. Crawford)

A young man grows up with a determination
to become a writer.
Unlikely and uneasy film version of a
somewhat cerebral novel; any drama there
might have been in the original got lost in the
transition, but at least the intention is to be
applauded.

w Steve Tesich, *novel* John Irving d George
Roy Hill ph Miroslav Ondricek md David
Shire pd Henry Bumstead ed Stephen A.
Rotter

Robin Williams, Mary Beth Hurt, Glenn
Close, John Lithgow, Hume Cronyn, Jessica
Tandy, Swoosie Kurtz
  'Rather like watching a puppy chasing its
own tail: engaging, touching, but pointless.'—
Margaret Hinxman, Daily Mail

AAN: John Lithgow; Glenn Close (supporting
actor)

The World Changes•
US 1933 91m bw
Warner (Robert Lord)

A simple farmer becomes a powerful
executive, and success goes to his head.
Adequate moral drama of its time, well staged
and acted.

w Edward Chodorov d Mervyn Le Roy
ph Tony Gaudio

Paul Muni, Aline MacMahon, Mary Astor,
Donald Cook, Patricia Ellis, Jean Muir,
Margaret Lindsay, Guy Kibbee, Alan
Dinehart
  'It won't appeal to the hotsy-totsy type of
fan, but the parents will bring the youngsters,
which should sort of balance things.'—*Variety*

The World in His Arms•
US 1952 104m Technicolor
Universal (Aaron Rosenberg)

In old San Francisco, a seal-poaching sea
captain meets a Russian countess.
Romantic melodrama with plushy period
backgrounds and a fair measure of action,
climaxing in a boat race.

w Borden Chase d Raoul Walsh ph Russell
Metty m Frank Skinner

Gregory Peck, Ann Blyth, Anthony Quinn,
John McIntire, Andrea King, Carl Esmond,
Eugenie Leontovich

World in My Corner•
US 1955 85m bw
U-I (Aaron Rosenberg)

A penniless would-be prizefighter becomes the
protégé of a millionaire and wins his daughter
but not the crucial fight.
Well-done minor melodrama.

w Jack Sher d Jesse Hibbs ph Maury
Gertsman m Joseph Gershenson

Audie Murphy, Barbara Rush, Jeff Morrow,
John McIntire, Tommy Rall, Howard St John

The World Is Full of Married Men
GB 1979 106m Eastmancolor
New Realm / Married Men Productions
  (Adrienne Fancey)

The wife of an advertising executive tries to
pay him out in kind for his infidelity.
Tedious jet-setting morality play which shows
in great detail all the vices it wags a finger at.

w Jackie Collins, from her novel d Robert
Young ph Ray Parslow m Frank Musker,
Dominic Bugatti

Carroll Baker, Anthony Franciosa, Sherrie
Cronn, Paul Nicholas, Gareth Hunt, Georgina
Hale, Anthony Steel

The World Moves On•
US 1934 104m bw
Fox (Winfield Sheehan)

The saga of a Louisiana family up to World
War I.
Careful, good-looking general entertainment.

w Reginald C. Berkeley d John Ford
ph George Schneiderman m Max Steiner

Madeleine Carroll, Franchot Tone, Reginald
Denny, Stepin Fetchit, Lumsden Hare, Louise
Dresser, Sig Rumann
  'Pacifistic picture inviting endorsement from
all bodies. Big on production and cast with six
minutes of superb war stuff.'—*Variety*

The World of Henry Orient••
US 1964 106m De Luxe Panavision
UA / Pan Arts (Jerome Hellman)

Two rich 14-year-old New York girls build
fantasies around a concert pianist.
Charming, immaculately mounted,
refreshingly unusual but overlong comedy.

w Nora and Nunnally Johnson, novel Nora
Johnson d George Roy Hill ph Boris
Kaufman, Arthur J. Ornitz m Elmer
Bernstein pd James Sullivan

Tippy Walker, Merri Spaeth, Peter Sellers,
Angela Lansbury, Paula Prentiss, Phyllis
Thaxter, Tom Bosley, Bibi Osterwald

The World of Suzie Wong
GB 1960 129m Technicolor
Paramount / Ray Stark (Hugh Perceval)

A Hong Kong prostitute falls in love with the
artist for whom she poses.
Dull, set-bound romantic melodrama without
much gusto.

w John Patrick, play Paul Osborn d Richard
Quine ph Geoffrey Unsworth m George
Duning

William Holden, *Nancy Kwan,* Sylvia Syms,
Michael Wilding, Laurence Naismith, Jackie
Chan
  'Maybe one day it will all make the grade as
a musical.'—*MFB*

The World Owes Me a Living
GB 1944 91m bw

A man gets his memory back and recalls his
air force career. Pointless flagwaving farrago.
David Farrar, Judy Campbell, Sonia Dresdel,
Jack Livesey, John Laurie, Wylie Watson.
Written by Vernon Sewell and Erwin Reiner,
from the novel by John Llewellyn Rhys;
directed by Vernon Sewell; for British
National.

World Premiere•
US 1940 70m bw
Paramount

A zany film producer thinks up some wild
publicity schemes for his new film and
accidentally traps some Nazi spies.
Occasionally amusing farce mainly notable for
its star.

w Earl Felton d Ted Tetzlaff ph Daniel Fapp

John Barrymore, Ricardo Cortez, Frances Farmer, Sig Rumann, Fritz Feld, Eugene Pallette, Luis Alberni, Virginia Dale, Don Castle

The World Ten Times Over
GB 1963 93m bw
Cyclops (Michael Luke)
US title: *Pussycat Alley*

Two semi-prostitutes try to improve their lot.
Dreary, derivative low-life drama with flashy technique.
wd Wolf Rilla *ph* Larry Pizer *m* Edwin Astley

Sylvia Syms, June Ritchie, Edward Judd, William Hartnell, Francis de Wolff

The World, the Flesh and the Devil°
US 1959 95m bw Cinemascope
MGM / Sol C. Siegel / Harbel

Trapped for five days in a mine cave-in, a man struggles to the surface to find a dead world devastated by atomic war; but still alive are the elements of an eternal triangle . . .
Enterprising but rather disappointing fantasy which tends to become merely glum and rather self-consciously carries a panic button message.
wd Ranald MacDougall *ph* Harold J. Marzorati *m* Miklos Rozsa *ad* William A. Horning, Paul Groesse

Harry Belafonte, Inger Stevens, Mel Ferrer

World without End
US 1956 80m Technicolor Cinemascope
AA (Richard Heermance)

A space ship breaks the time barrier and returns to earth in 2508, to find that intelligent humans have been driven underground by mutants.
Reasonably lively sci-fi with horror elements, and a plot borrowed from H. G. Wells.
wd Edward Bernds *ph* Ellsworth Fredericks *m* Leith Stevens

Hugh Marlowe, Nancy Gates, Rod Taylor

The World's Greatest Athlete
US 1973 92m Technicolor
Walt Disney (Bill Walsh)

An American sports coach on an African holiday finds a young Tarzan with amazing powers.
Simple-minded comedy with lame tomfoolery and trickwork.
w Gerald Gardiner, Dee Caruso *d* Robert Scheerer *ph* Frank Phillips *m* Marvin Hamlisch

Tim Conway, Jan-Michael Vincent, John Amos, Roscoe Lee Browne

The World's Greatest Lover
US 1977 89m De Luxe
TCF (Gene Wilder)

In the twenties, a rival studio starts a search for a man to surpass Valentino.
Imitative slapstick extravaganza in which anything goes but hardly anything pleases.

wd Gene Wilder *ph* Gerald Hirschfeld *m* John Morris

Gene Wilder, Carol Kane, Dom DeLuise, Fritz Feld
'Infantile humour for young, slow kids who want everything pounded at them.'—*Pauline Kael, New Yorker*
† The film carries a credit to Federico Fellini, 'for encouragement at the right time'.

Worm's Eye View
GB 1951 77m bw
ABFD / Byron (Henry Halsted)

Incidents in the lives of a group of RAF billetees.
Plotless comedy from a highly successful stage romp; plainly made and empty-headed but not disagreeable.
w R. F. Delderfield, from his play *d* Jack Raymond *ph* James Wilson *m* Tony Lowry, Tony Fones

Ronald Shiner, Garry Marsh, Diana Dors, Eric Davis, John Blythe

The Worst Woman in Paris
US 1933 75m bw

An American girl unfairly gets a bad reputation in Paris and on her way home becomes a heroine in Kansas. Silly, pointless story on which good production values are wasted. Benita Hume, Adolphe Menjou, Harvey Stephens, Helen Chandler, Margaret Seddon. Written by Marion Dix, Monta Bell, Martin Brown; directed by Monta Bell; for Jesse L. Lasky / Fox. 'Does not give promise of scoring in any placement.'—*Variety*

The Wrath of God
US 1972 111m Metrocolor Panavision
MGM / Rainbow / Cineman (William S. Gilmore Jnr)

During a twenties Central American revolution, a bootlegger joins forces with a defrocked priest.
Noisy, violent adventure yarn which works up to a gory climax but does not take itself too seriously.
wd Ralph Nelson, *novel* James Graham *ph* Alex Phillips Jnr *m* Lalo Schifrin

Robert Mitchum, Frank Langella, Rita Hayworth, Victor Buono, John Colicos

The Wreck of the Mary Deare°
US 1959 108m Metrocolor Cinemascope
MGM / Blaustein–Baroda (David Blaustein)

An insurance fraud comes to light when a salvage boat is rescued from high seas.
Curious, star-studded amalgam of seafaring action and courtroom melodrama, originally intended for Hitchcock.
w Eric Ambler, *novel* Hammond Innes *d* Michael Anderson *ph* Joseph Ruttenberg, F. A. Young *m* George Duning

Charlton Heston, Gary Cooper, Michael Redgrave, Emlyn Williams, Cecil Parker, Alexander Knox, Virginia McKenna, Richard Harris

The Wrecking Crew
US 1968 104m Technicolor
Columbia / Meadway / Claude (Irving Allen)

Special agent Matt Helm recovers bullion stolen from a Danish train.
Camped-up spy buffoonery with the usual nubile ladies and a production which seeks to be flashy but succeeds only in being tatty.
w William McGivern, *novel* Donald Hamilton *d* Phil Karlson *ph* Sam Leavitt *m* Hugo Montenegro

Dean Martin, Elke Sommer, Sharon Tate, Nancy Kwan, Nigel Green, Tina Louise

'The story of a family's ugly secret and the stark moment that thrust their private lives into public view!'
Written on the Wind°°
US 1956 99m Technicolor
U-I (Albert Zugsmith)

A secretary marries her oil tycoon boss and finds herself the steadying force in a very rocky family.
The sheerest Hollywood moonshine: high-flying melodramatic hokum which moves fast enough to be very entertaining.
w George Zuckerman, *novel* Robert Wilder *d* Douglas Sirk *ph* Russell Metty *m* Frank Skinner

Lauren Bacall, *Robert Stack, Dorothy Malone*, Rock Hudson, Robert Keith, Grant Williams
AA: Dorothy Malone
AAN: title song (*m* Victor Young, *ly* Sammy Cahn); Robert Stack

Wrong Again
US 1929 20m bw silent

A horse instead of a painting is delivered to a rich man's house. Pleasing but not very inventive star comedy. Laurel and Hardy, Del Henderson. Written by Lewis R. Foster, Leo McCarey and H. M. Walker; directed by Leo McCarey; for Hal Roach.

The Wrong Arm of the Law°
GB 1962 94m bw
Romulus / Robert Verlaise (Aubrey Baring, E. M. Smedley Aston)

London gangsters plan retaliation against Australian interlopers, and offer Scotland Yard a temporary truce.
Forgettable but pretty funny crook comedy in the British vein, with pacy script and excellent comedy timing.
w John Warren, Len Heath *d* Cliff Owen *ph* Ernest Steward *m* Richard Rodney Bennett

Peter Sellers, Lionel Jeffries, Bernard Cribbins, Davy Kaye, Nanette Newman, Bill Kerr, John Le Mesurier

The Wrong Box°
GB 1966 110m Technicolor
Columbia / Salamander (Bryan Forbes)

Two elderly Victorian brothers are the last survivors of a tontine (an involved form of lottery) and try to murder each other.
Well-intentioned and star-studded black farce

in which the excellent period trappings and stray jokes completely overwhelm the plot.

w Larry Gelbart, Burt Shevelove, *novel* Robert Louis Stevenson, Lloyd Osbourne *d* Bryan Forbes *ph* Gerry Turpin *m* John Barry *ad* Ray Simm

Ralph Richardson, John Mills, Michael Caine, *Wilfrid Lawson*, Nanette Newman, Peter Cook, Dudley Moore, Peter Sellers, Tony Hancock, Thorley Walters, Cicely Courtneidge, Irene Handl, John Le Mesurier, Gerald Sim, Norman Bird, Tutte Lemkow

'A slapdash affair in which anything goes, irrespective of whether or not it fits.'—*Tom Milne*

Wrong Is Right
US 1982   117m   Metrocolor
Columbia / Richard Brooks
GB title: *The Man with the Deadly Lens*

An international TV commentator discovers that the world is being manipulated by the CIA.
Wild satiric melodrama which takes potshots at everything and usually misses.

wd Richard Brooks, *novel* The Deadly Angels by Charles McCarry *ph* Fred J. Koenekamp *m* Artie Kane *pd* Edward Carfagno *ed* George Grenville

Sean Connery, George Grizzard, Katharine Ross, Robert Conrad, G. D. Spradlin, John Saxon, Henry Silva, Leslie Nielsen, Robert Webber, Rosalind Cash, Hardy Kruger, Dean Stockwell, Ron Moody

'Intended as a sharply cynical overview of the current political scene, it emerges as a drearily murky thriller.'—*Sight and Sound*

The Wrong Man*
US 1957   105m   bw
Warner (Herbert Coleman)

A New York musician is mistaken by police for an armed bandit, and both witnesses and circumstances prevent the truth from emerging.
True but downbeat story from the headlines, filmed with remarkably little persuasion; not its director's *métier* despite evidence of his usual thoroughness.

w Maxwell Anderson, Angus MacPhail *d* Alfred Hitchcock *ph* Robert Burks *m* Bernard Herrmann

Henry Fonda, Vera Miles, Anthony Quayle, Harold J. Stone, Esther Minciotti

● *Video: Warner*

WUSA*
US 1970   117m   Technicolor
Panavision
Paramount / Mirror / Coleytown / Stuart Rosenberg (Paul Newman, John Foreman)

A penniless wanderer causes chaos when he becomes the announcer for a right-wing radio station.
A farcical melodrama for the intelligentsia, and for the most part a thoroughgoing bore. The last part offers a compensation or two.

w Robert Stone, from his novel Hall of Mirrors *d* Stuart Rosenberg *ph* Richard Moore *m* Lalo Schifrin

Paul Newman, Joanne Woodward, Laurence Harvey, Anthony Perkins, Pat Hingle, Cloris Leachman, Don Gordon, Robert Quarry, Bruce Cabot, Moses Gunn, Wayne Rogers

'The most significant film I've ever made and the best.'—*Paul Newman*

'Torn with desire . . . twisted with hate!'
Wuthering Heights****
US 1939   104m   bw
Samuel Goldwyn

The daughter of an unhappy middle-class Yorkshire family falls passionately in love with a gypsy who has been brought up with her. Despite American script and settings, this wildly romantic film makes a pretty fair stab at capturing the power of at least the first half of a classic Victorian novel, and in all respects it's a superb Hollywood production of its day and a typical one, complete with ghostly finale and a first-rate cast.

w Ben Hecht, Charles MacArthur, *novel* Emily Brontë *d* William Wyler *ph* Gregg Toland *m* Alfred Newman

Laurence Olivier, Merle Oberon, David Niven, Hugh Williams, Flora Robson, Geraldine Fitzgerald, Donald Crisp, Leo G. Carroll, Cecil Kellaway, *Miles Mander*

CATHY (Merle Oberon): 'I don't think I belong in heaven, Ellen. I dreamt once I was there. I dreamt I went to heaven and that heaven didn't seem to be my home and I broke my heart with weeping to come back to earth and the angels were so angry they flung me out in the middle of the heath on top of Wuthering Heights and I woke up sobbing with joy.'

HEATHCLIFF (Laurence Olivier): 'What do they know of heaven or hell, Cathy, who know nothing of life? Oh, they're praying for you, Cathy. I'll pray one prayer with them. I'll repeat till my tongue stiffens: Catherine Earnshaw, may you not rest while I live on. I killed you. Haunt me, then! Haunt your murderer! I know that ghosts have wandered on the earth. Be with me always—take any form—drive me mad! Only do not leave me in this dark alone where I cannot find you. I cannot live without my life! I cannot die without my soul . . .'

'Sombre dramatic tragedy, productionally fine, but with limited appeal.'—*Variety*

'Unquestionably one of the most distinguished pictures of the year.'—*Frank S. Nugent, New York Times*
'A pattern of constant forward motion, with overtones maintained throughout the rise of interest and suspense.'—*Otis Ferguson*
'A strong and sombre film, poetically written as the novel not always was, sinister and wild as it was meant to be, far more compact dramatically than Miss Brontë had made it.'—*Richard Mallett, Punch*

AA: Gregg Toland
AAN: best picture; script; William Wyler; Alfred Newman; Laurence Olivier; Geraldine Fitzgerald

'The power, the passion, the terror!'
Wuthering Heights*
GB 1970   105m   Movielab
AIP (John Pellatt)

Somewhat rewritten and overkeen to find a 1970 mood and interpretation for what can only be a period piece, this disappointing version marks a Z-film company's first determined effort to enter the big-time.

w Patrick Tilley *d* Robert Fuest *ph* John Coquillon *m* Michel Legrand

Anna Calder-Marshall, Timothy Dalton, Harry Andrews, Pamela Brown, Judy Cornwell, James Cossins, Rosalie Crutchley, Julian Glover, Hugh Griffith, Ian Ogilvy, Aubrey Woods

● *Video: Guild*

Wyoming
US 1940   88m   bw

A Missouri badman is persuaded to try an honest life. Well-liked minor western responsible for the first teaming of its inelegant stars. Wallace Beery, Marjorie Main, Leo Carrillo, Ann Rutherford, Joseph Calleia, Lee Bowman, Henry Travers. Written by Jack Jevne and Hugo Butler; directed by Richard Thorpe; for MGM. (GB title: *Bad Man of Wyoming*.)

Wyoming
US 1947   84m   bw

Early settlers in the west meet trouble from government squatters. Minor western for undemanding audiences. Bill Elliott, Vera Ralston, John Carroll, George 'Gabby' Hayes, Albert Dekker. Written by Lawrence Hazard and Gerald Geraghty; directed by Joe Kane; for Republic.

X—The Man with X-Ray Eyes
US 1963 80m Pathecolor
 'Spectarama'
AIP (Roger Corman)
GB title: *The Man with the X-Ray Eyes*

A scientist gives himself X-ray vision and goes mad.

Interesting but rather unpleasant horror story with moments of cleverness but a general air of disappointment.

w Robert Dillon, Ray Russell *d Roger Corman ph* Floyd Crosby *m* Les Baxter

Ray Milland, Diana Van Der Vlis, Harold J. Stone, John Hoyt, Don Rickles, John Dierkes

 'When the dialogue suggests that Xavier is being driven insane by strange and satanic visions, what one actually sees is rather a comedown.'—*MFB*

 'Concise, confident, and not an ounce overweight.'—*NFT, 1967*

X the Unknown*
GB 1956 81m bw
Hammer (Anthony Hinds)

A mysterious force feeds on radiation from a research station on a Scottish moor, and becomes a seeping mass.

Minor sci-fi horror with a monster like liquid lino, rushed into release to cash in on *The Quatermass Experiment*.

w Jimmy Sangster *d* Leslie Norman *ph* Gerald Gibbs *m* James Bernard

Dean Jagger, Edward Chapman, Leo McKern, William Lucas, John Harvey, Peter Hammond, Michael Ripper, Anthony Newley

Xanadu
US 1980 93m Technicolor
Universal / Lawrence Gordon

The muse Terpsichore comes to earth and becomes involved in the opening of a roller-derby disco.

Misguided attempt at a clean nostalgic musical, apparently conceived in a nightmare after somebody saw *Down to Earth* on the late show.

w Richard Christian Danus, Marc Reid Rubel *d* Robert Greenwald *ph* Victor J. Kemper *m* Barry de Vorzon *songs* Jeff Lynne, John Farrar *pd* John W. Corso

Olivia Newton-John, Gene Kelly, Michael Beck

 'Truly a stupendously bad film whose only salvage is the music.'—*Variety*

 'A forties musical submerged by contemporary tat.'—*Guardian*

† Gene Kelly uses the same character name, Danny McGuire, as he did in *Cover Girl*.

● *Video: CIC*

The Yakuza
US 1975 112m Technicolor
Panavision
Warner (Sydney Pollack, Michael
Hamilburg)

Japanese gangsters kidnap the daughter of a
Los Angeles shipping magnate.
Violent thriller roughly exploiting an ancient
Japanese genre.

w Paul Schrader, Robert Towne d Sydney
Pollack ph Okazaki Kozo, Duke Callaghan
m Dave Grusin

Robert Mitchum, Takakura Ken, Brian Keith,
Kishi Keilo, Okada Eiji
 'No more than a curious footnote to the
western exploitation of oriental action
movies.'—Tony Rayns

Yangtse Incident*
GB 1957 113m bw
British Lion / Wilcox/Neagle (Herbert
Wilcox)
US title: Battle Hell; aka: Escape of the
Amethyst

In 1949 a British frigate is shelled and held
captive by communist shore batteries in the
Yangtse.
Stalwart but not very exciting British war
heroics.

w Eric Ambler, book Franklin Gollings
d Michael Anderson ph Gordon Dines
m Leighton Lucas

Richard Todd, William Hartnell, Akim
Tamiroff, Donald Houston, Keye Luke,
Sophie Stewart, Robert Urquhart, James
Kenney, Barry Foster

A Yank at Eton
US 1942 88m bw
MGM (John Considine Jnr)

A rich, wild American boy is sent to Eton to
cool down.
Tame, tasteless imitation of A Yank at Oxford
with younger participants.

w George Oppenheimer, Lionel Houser,
Thomas Phipps d Norman Taurog ph Karl
Freund, Charles Lawton m Bromisla Kaper

Mickey Rooney, Freddie Bartholemew, Ian
Hunter, Edmund Gwenn, Alan Mowbray,
Tina Thayer, Marta Linden, Alan Napier,
Terry Kilburn

A Yank at Oxford**
GB 1938 105m bw
MGM (Michael Balcon)

A cocky young American student comes to
Oxford and meets all kinds of trouble.
A huge pre-war success which now seems
naïve, this was the first big Anglo-American
production from a team which went on to
make The Citadel and Goodbye Mr Chips
before war stymied them.

w Malcolm Stuart Boylan, Walter Ferris,
George Oppenheimer, Leon Gordon, Roland
Pertwee, John Monk Saunders, Sidney Gilliat,
Michael Hogan d Jack Conway ph Harold
Rosson Edward Ward

Robert Taylor, Vivien Leigh, Maureen
O'Sullivan, Lionel Barrymore, Robert Coote,
Edmund Gwenn, C. V. France, Griffith Jones,
Morton Selten
 'A draw picture for Taylor at a critical
moment in his meteoric bid for fame.'—
Variety
† A total of 31 writers are alleged to have
worked without credit.

A Yank in the RAF*
US 1941 98m bw
TCF (Lou Edelman)

An American chorine stranded in London falls
for the titular gentleman.
Silly but entertaining wartime flagwaver.

w Karl Tunberg, Darrell Ware, story Melville
Crossman (Zanuck) d Henry King ph Leon
Shamroy m Alfred Newman

Tyrone Power, Betty Grable, John Sutton,
Reginald Gardiner, Donald Stuart, Morton
Lowry, Richard Fraser, Bruce Lester

A Yank on the Burma Road
US 1942 66m bw
MGM (Samuel Marx)
GB title: China Caravan

A tough truck driver in the Far East abandons
profit for heroism when he hears of Pearl
Harbor.
Crass action flagwaver.

w George Kahn, Hugo Butler, David Lang
d George B. Seitz ph Lester White

Barry Nelson, Laraine Day, Stuart Crawford,
Keye Luke, Sen Yung
 'Glib humbug, playing tiddleywinks with
high stakes.'—Theodore Strauss

Yankee Doodle Dandy***
US 1942 126m bw
Warner (Hal B. Wallis, William Cagney)

The life story of dancing vaudevillian George
M. Cohan.
Outstanding showbiz biopic, with unassuming
but effective production, deft patriotic
backdrops and a marvellous, strutting,
magnetic star performance.

w Robert Buckner, Edmund Joseph
d Michael Curtiz ph James Wong Howe
m Heinz Roemheld md Heinz Roemheld,
Ray Heindorf songs George M. Cohan

James Cagney, Joan Leslie, Walter Huston,
Rosemary de Camp, Richard Whorf, George
Tobias, Jeanne Cagney, Irene Manning, S. Z.
Sakall, George Barbier, Frances Langford,
Walter Catlett, Eddie Foy Jnr

COHAN (James Cagney) at end of vaudeville
act: 'My mother thanks you. My father thanks
you. My sister thanks you. And I thank you.'

COHAN: 'Where else in the world could a
plain guy like me sit down and talk things over
with the head man?'

ROOSEVELT (Captain Jack Young): 'Well
now, you know, Mr Cohan, that's as good a
description of America as I've ever heard.'

AA: music direction; James Cagney
AAN: best picture; original story (Robert
Buckner); Michael Curtiz; Walter Huston
● Video: MGM

Yankee Pasha
US 1954 84m Technicolor

An American adventurer in nineteenth-
century Marseilles saves his girl friend from
pirates. Studio-bound hokum for double-
featuring. Jeff Chandler, Rhonda Fleming,
Mamie Van Doren, Lee J. Cobb, Bart
Roberts, Hal March. Written by Joseph
Hoffman, from the novel by Edison Marshall;
directed by Joseph Pevney; for Universal-
International.

Yanks**
GB 1979 141m Technicolor
United Artists / Joe Janni-Lester Persky /
CIP

Romances of American GIs billeted on a
Lancashire town during World War II.
Not an entirely promising subject, this
overlong piece maintains its interest by sheer
skill of dramaturgy and cinematic narrative.

w Colin Welland, Walter Bernstein d John Schlesinger ph Dick Bush m Richard Rodney Bennett pd Brian Morris

Vanessa Redgrave, Richard Gere, William Devane, Lisa Eichhorn, Rachel Roberts, Chick Vennera

The Year of Living Dangerously*
Australia 1982 114m Eastmancolor
MGM / McElroy and McElroy / Peter Weir

A young Australian journalist takes his first international assignment in Indonesia.
Freshly observed but ultimately pointless political parable which undoubtedly means more to its maker than it will to audiences.

w David Williamson, Peter Weir, C. J. Koch, novel C. J. Koch d Peter Weir ph Russell Boyd m Maurice Jarre ed Bill Anderson

Mel Gibson, Sigourney Weaver, Linda Hunt, Michael Murphy, Bill Kerr, Noel Ferrier
AA: Linda Hunt

● Video: MGM / UA

'They tamed a tropic wilderness!'
The Yearling**
US 1946 134m Technicolor
MGM (Sidney Franklin)

The son of an old-time country farmer is attached to a stray deer.
Excellent family film for four-handkerchief patrons.

w Paul Osborn, novel Marjorie Kinnan Rawlings d Clarence Brown ph Charles Rosher, Leonard Smith m Herbert Stothart

Gregory Peck, Jane Wyman, Claude Jarman Jnr, Chill Wills, Clem Bevans, Margaret Wycherly, Henry Travers, Forrest Tucker
AA: Charles Rosher, Leonard Smith (and Arthur Arling)
AAN: best picture; Clarence Brown; Gregory Peck; Jane Wyman

The Years Between
GB 1946 100m bw
GFD / Sydney Box

An MP returns after being presumed dead in the war and finds his wife has been elected in his place.
Stilted variation on the Enoch Arden theme; plot and performances alike unpersuasive.

w Muriel and Sydney Box, play Daphne du Maurier d Compton Bennett ph Reg Wyer

Michael Redgrave, Valerie Hobson, Flora Robson, Felix Aylmer, James McKechnie, Dulcie Gray, Edward Rigby

The Yellow Balloon
GB 1952 80m bw
ABP (Victor Skuzetsky)

A small boy who thinks he has killed his friend is terrorized by a murderer.
Tense but not especially rewarding suspenser, clearly borrowed from The Window.

w Anne Burnaby, J. Lee-Thompson d J. Lee-Thompson ph Gilbert Taylor m Philip Green

Kenneth More, William Sylvester, Kathleen Ryan, Andrew Ray, Bernard Lee, Veronica Hurst

The Yellow Cab Man
US 1950 84m bw
MGM (Richard Goldstone)

A taxi-driving inventor is pursued by crooks after his secret formula.
Moderate star comedy.

w Devery Freeman, Albert Beich d Jack Donohue ph Harry Stradling m Scott Bradley

Red Skelton, Gloria de Haven, Walter Slezak, Edward Arnold, James Gleason, Paul Harvey, Jay C. Flippen

Yellow Canary*
GB 1943 98m bw
RKO / Imperator (Herbert Wilcox)

A socialite suspected of being a Nazi sympathizer is really a British spy.
Mild wartime melodrama chiefly notable for allotting an apparently unsympathetic part to the beloved Miss Neagle.

w De Witt Bodeen, Miles Malleson, story Pamela Bower d Herbert Wilcox ph Max Greene

Anna Neagle, Richard Greene, Nova Pilbeam, Lucie Mannheim, Cyril Fletcher, Albert Lieven, Margaret Rutherford, Marjorie Fielding

Yellow Canary
US 1963 93m bw Cinemascope
TCF / Cooga Mooga (Maury Dexter)

The baby son of a singing idol is kidnapped.
Rather dreary suspenser with too much dialogue.

w Rod Serling, novel Easy Come Easy Go by Whit Masterson d Buzz Kulik ph Floyd Crosby m Kenyon Hopkins

Pat Boone, Barbara Eden, Steve Forrest, Jack Klugman, Jesse White, John Banner, Jeff Corey

Yellow Dog
GB 1973 101m Eastmancolor
Scotia–Barber / Akari (Terence Donovan)

A Japanese agent in London keeps watch on a mysterious scientist.
Incoherent spy thriller with a few hybrid oddities.

w Shinobu Hashimoto d Terence Donovan ph David Watkin m Ron Grainer

Jiro Tamiya, Robert Hardy, Carolyn Seymour, Joseph O'Conor

Yellow Jack*
US 1938 83m bw
MGM (Jack Cummings)

In 1899 Cuba a marine offers himself as a guinea pig to combat yellow fever.
Solid, unsurprising, period medical melodrama with conventional romantic sidelights.

w Edward Chodorov, play Sidney Howard, Paul de Kruif d George B. Seitz ph Lester White m William Axt

Robert Montgomery, Virginia Bruce, Lewis Stone, Andy Devine, Henry Hull, Charles Coburn, Buddy Ebsen, Henry O'Neill, Janet Beecher
'Okay for single billing, but no wow.'—Variety

The Yellow Rolls Royce*
GB 1964 122m Metrocolor Panavision
MGM (Anatole de Grunwald)

Three stories about the owners of an expensive car; an aristocrat, a gangster, and a wandering millionairess.
Lukewarm all-star concoction lacking either good stories or a connecting thread.

w Terence Rattigan d Anthony Asquith ph Jack Hildyard m Riz Ortolani pd Vincent Korda

Rex Harrison, Jeanne Moreau, Edmund Purdom, Moira Lister, Roland Culver, Shirley Maclaine, George C. Scott, Alain Delon, Art Carney, Ingrid Bergman, Omar Sharif, Joyce Grenfell
'Tame, bloodless, smothered in elegance and the worst kind of discreetly daring good taste.'—Peter John Dyer

Yellow Sands
GB 1938 68m bw

A Cornish family sets to bickering over a will.
Reliable comedy from a popular stage original. Marie Tempest, Wilfrid Lawson, Belle Chrystall, Robert Newton, Patrick Barr, Edward Rigby. Written by Michael Barringer and Rodney Ackland, from the play by Eden and Adelaide Phillpotts; directed by Herbert Brenon; for ABPC.

'It was a moment for being a woman . . . for only a woman's revenge could keep her alive—now!'
Yellow Sky**
US 1948 98m bw
TCF (Lamar Trotti)

Outlaws on the run take over a desert ghost town.
Gleaming, stylish western melodrama which benefits from its unusual and confined setting.

w Lamar Trotti, story W. R. Burnett d William Wellman ph Joe MacDonald m Alfred Newman

Gregory Peck, Anne Baxter, Richard Widmark, Robert Arthur, John Russell, Henry Morgan, James Barton

Yellow Submarine*
GB 1968 87m De Luxe
King Features / Apple (Al Brodax)

The happy kingdom of Pepperland is attacked by the Blue Meanies.
Way-out cartoon fantasia influenced by Beatlemania and the swinging sixties; hard to watch for non-addicts.

w Lee Minoff, Al Brodax, Jack Mendelsohn, Erich Segal d George Duning m John Lennon, Paul McCartney

The Yellow Ticket*
US 1931 76m bw
Fox
GB title: The Yellow Passport

In Russia during the pogroms, a Jewish girl pretends to be a prostitute in order to get a travel permit to see her dying father.
Curious anti-Russian melodrama deriving its plot from La Tosca.

w *Jules Furthman, Guy Bolton, play* Michael
Morton *d* Raoul Walsh *ph* James Wong
Howe

Elissa Landi, Laurence Olivier, Lionel
Barrymore, Walter Byron, Sarah Padden,
Mischa Auer, Boris Karloff

Yellowbeard

US 1983   96m   De Luxe
Orion / Seagoat (Carter de Haven Jnr)

Farcical adventures of a 17th-century pirate
captain.

A spoofy saga in deliberately bad taste, this
ragbag of old gags and new unpleasantness
sank rapidly to the bottom of the box office
barrel.

w Graham Chapman, Peter Cook, Bernard
McKenna *d* Mel Damski *ph* Gerry Fisher
m John Morris *pd* Joseph R. Jennings

Graham Chapman, Peter Boyle, Cheech and
Chong, Peter Cook, Marty Feldman, Michael
Hordern, Eric Idle, Madeline Kahn, James
Mason, John Cleese, Kenneth Mars, Spike
Milligan, Susannah York, Beryl Reid, Ferdy
Mayne, Peter Bull.

'The atrocious script and haphazard
direction elicit generally embarrassing
performances from all concerned.'—*Kim
Newman, MFB*

Yellowstone Kelly

US 1959   91m   Technicolor
Warner

A fur trapper prevents war between Indians
and whites.

Standard western with routine excitements
and a cast of TV faces.

w Burt Kennedy *d* Gordon Douglas *ph* Carl
Guthrie *m* Howard Jackson

Clint Walker, Edd Byrnes, John Russell, Ray
Danton, Claude Akins

Yentl*

GB 1983   133m   Technicolor
MGM–UA / Barwood / Ladbroke (Barbra
Streisand, Rusty Lemorande)

Many years ago in Poland, a Jewish girl tries
to get on in the world by dressing as a boy.

A personal and some would say megalomaniac
extravagance by its producer-director-writer-
star, who before embarking should have
learned the value of brevity. Nevertheless
there is about the enterprise a certain heavy
style which may appeal strongly to Jews while
precluding the interest and understanding of
others.

w Jack Rosenthal, Barbra Streisand,
story Isaac Bashevis Singer *d* Barbra
Streisand *ph* David Watkin *m* Michel
Legrand *pd* Roy Walker *ed* Terry Rawlings

Barbra Streisand, Mandy Patinkin, Amy
Irving, Nehemiah Persoff, Steven Hill, David
de Keyser, Bernard Spear

AAN: Amy Irving; song score; song 'Papa,
Can You Hear Me?'; art director

Yes, Giorgio*

US 1982   110m   Metrocolor
MGM–UA / Peter Fetterman

A top international tenor falls for the lady
throat specialist who cures his ailment.

Nostalgic musical romance, fine in its way but
out of key with the modern film business. A
treat for television viewers.

w Norman Steinberg, *novel* Anne Piper
d Franklin J. Schaffner *ph* Fred J.
Koenekamp *m* John Williams *pd* William D.
Creber

Luciano Pavarotti, Kathryn Harrold, Eddie
Albert, Paola Borboni

AAN: original song, 'If We Were In Love' by
John Williams, Alan and Marilyn Bergman

● *Video: MGM / UA*

Yes, Madam

GB 1938   77m   bw

Heirs to a fortune are obliged to act as
servants for three months. Agreeable minor
comedy. Bobby Howes, Diana Churchill, Billy
Milton, Fred Emney, Bertha Belmore, Wylie
Watson, Vera Pearce. Written by Clifford
Grey, Bert Lee and William Freshman, from
the novel by K. R. G. Browne; directed by
Norman Lee; for ABPC. (Previously filmed in
1933 with Frank Pettingell and Kay
Hammond.)

Yes Mr Brown*

GB 1933   90m   bw

A businessman's secretary pretends to be his
wife after the latter has walked out on him.

One of its star's most fondly remembered
musical farces, a thin thing but his own.
Jack Buchanan, Elsie Randolph,
Hartley Power, Clifford Heatherley, Vera
Pearce. Written by Douglas Furber from the
play Business with America by Paul Frank,
Ludwig Hershfield; directed by Herbert
Wilcox, Jack Buchanan; for Herbert Wilcox /
British and Dominions.

Yes My Darling Daughter

US 1939   86m   bw
Warner (Ben Glazer)

Lovers elope and are pursued by her family.
Mildly amusing domestic comedy.

w Casey Robinson, *play* Mark Reed
d William Keighley *ph* Charles Rosher

Priscilla Lane, Jeffrey Lynn, Roland Young,
Fay Bainter, May Robson, Genevieve Tobin,
Ian Hunter

Yes Sir, That's My Baby

US 1949   82m   Technicolor
U–I (Leonard Goldstein)

Ex-service undergraduates and their wives
have trouble settling down to studies.
Witless and exhausting college comedy.

w Oscar Brodney *d* George Sherman
ph Irving Glassberg *m* Walter Scharf

Donald O'Connor, Gloria de Haven, Charles
Coburn, Barbara Brown, Joshua Shelley

Yesterday, Today and Tomorrow

Italy / France 1963   119m   Techniscope
CCC / Concordia / Joseph E. Levin (Carlo
Ponti)

Three stories of naughty ladies.

A relentlessly boring compendium with
everybody shouting at once.

w Eduardo de Filippp, Cesare Zavattini,
others *d* Vittorio de Sica *ph* Giuseppe
Rotunno *m* Armando Trovajoli

Marcello Mastroianni, Sophia Loren

'A sad intimation of the sort of rainy day the
Italian cinema is currently having.'—*MFB*

AA: best foreign film

Yesterday's Enemy

GB 1959   95m   bw   Megascope
Columbia / Hammer (T. S. Lyndon-Haynes)

In 1942 Burma, a British unit violently takes
over a village and finds an unsolved puzzle.

Would-be ironic war suspenser, economically
made but quite effective in putting its message
across.

w Peter R. Newman, from his TV play *d* Val
Guest *ph* Arthur Grant *m* none

Stanley Baker, Guy Rolfe, Leo McKern,
Philip Ahn, Gordon Jackson, David Oxley,
Richard Pasco, Russell Waters, Bryan Forbes,
David Lodge, Percy Herbert

Yesterday's Hero

GB 1979   95m   colour
Columbia / CinemaSeven (Elliott Kastner)

A successful footballer goes to the bad but
redeems himself.

Totally uninteresting sporting version of the
Road to Ruin.

w Jackie Collins *d* Neil Leifer *ph* Brian
West *md* Stanley Myers *pd* Keith Wilson

Ian McShane, Suzanne Somers, Adam Faith,
Paul Nicholas, Sam Kydd

Yield to the Night*

GB 1956   99m   bw
ABP (Kenneth Harper)
US title: *Blonde Sinner*

A condemned murderess relives the events
which led to her arrest.

Gloomy prison melodrama vaguely based on
the Ruth Ellis case and making an emotional
plea against capital punishment.

w John Cresswell, Joan Henry, *novel* Joan
Henry *d* J. Lee-Thompson *ph* Gilbert
Taylor *m* Ray Martin

Diana Dors, Yvonne Mitchell, Michael Craig,
Marie Ney, Athene Seyler, Geoffrey Keen

Yol**

Switzerland 1982   114m   Fujicolor
Güney / Cactus / Maran / Antenne 2 / Swiss
Television

Five convicts are released on a week's leave,
and their various circumstances lead them to
tragedy.

Rewarding if heavy-going Turkish saga which
exhausts the spectator almost as much as its
long-suffering characters. It feels and looks
like an epic.

w Yilmaz Güney *d* Serif Gören *ph* Erdogan Engin *m* Sebastian Argol

Tarik Akan, Halil Ergün, Necmettin Cobanoglu, Serif Sezer

Yolanda and the Thief*
US 1945 108m Technicolor
MGM (Arthur Freed)

A con man poses as the guardian angel of a naïve heiress.

Laboured musical fantasy with arty Mexican settings; not a success in any way, but with a few effective moments.

w Irving Brecher, *story* Ludwig Bemelmans, Jacques Théry *d* Vincente Minnelli *ph* Charles Rosher *m* Lennie Hayton *songs* Harry Warren, Arthur Freed

Fred Astaire, Lucille Bremer, Frank Morgan, Leon Ames, Mildred Natwick
  'The most extreme of the big musical mistakes.'—*New Yorker, 1979*

'Every time she says I love you, she breaks the law!'
You and Me
US 1938 90m bw
Paramount (Fritz Lang)

A department store owner employs ex-convicts, one of whom has not quite reformed. Curious comedy drama which never has a hope of coming off.

w Virginia Van Upp, *story* Norman Krasna *d* Fritz Lang *ph* Charles Lang Jnr *m* Kurt Weill

Sylvia Sidney, George Raft, Harry Carey, Barton MacLane, Warren Hymer, Roscoe Karns, George E. Stone, Adrian Morris
  'Lang's individual touch is visible everywhere . . . but for the ordinary George Raft fan it will not only be unappreciated, it will be actually confusing.'—*National Board of Review*

You Belong to Me
US 1934 67m bw

An alcoholic vaudeville comic plays father to an orphan. Muddled backstage melodrama which would be enjoyed by fans of the star.
Lee Tracy, Helen Mack, Helen Morgan, Lynne Overman, David Holt. Written by Walter DeLeon, Elizabeth Alexander; directed by Alfred Werker; for Louis D. Lighton / Paramount. 'Should gain attention in the nabe spots.'—*Variety*

You Belong to Me*
US 1941 94m bw
Columbia (Wesley Ruggles)
GB title: *Good Morning, Doctor*

A playboy becomes jealous of the male patients of his doctor wife.
Mild comedy for two stars who are well capable of keeping it afloat.

w Claude Binyon, Dalton Trumbo *d* Wesley Ruggles *ph* Joseph Walker *m* Frederick Hollander

Barbara Stanwyck, Henry Fonda, Edgar Buchanan, Roger Clark, Ruth Donnelly, Melville Cooper, Maude Eburne

You Came Along
US 1945 103m bw
Paramount (Hal B. Wallis)

A girl from the treasury department falls in love with one of three GIs she takes on a war bond tour, but he dies of leukemia.
Weird mishmash of farce and sentimentality; quite watchable in its way, but an odd showcase for a new female star.

w Robert Smith, Ayn Rand *d* John Farrow *ph* Daniel L. Fapp *m* Victor Young

Lizabeth Scott, Robert Cummings, Don Defore, Charles Drake, Julie Bishop, Kim Hunter, Rhys Williams, Franklin Pangborn, Minor Watson

You Can't Buy Everything*
US 1934 72m bw

A woman obsessed by her mounting bank balance almost ruins the lives of her family. Unusual and rather well-acted period melodrama with a pleasing cast. *May Robson*, Jean Parker, Lewis Stone, Mary Forbes, Reginald Mason. Written by Dudley Nichols, Lamar Trotti; directed by Charles F. Reisner; for MGM.

You Can't Cheat an Honest Man*
US 1939 79m bw
Universal (Lester Cowan)

Trials and tribulations of a circus owner. Flat, desultory and generally disappointing comedy vehicle for an irresistible star combination.

w George Marion Jnr, Richard Mack, Everett Freeman, *story* Charles Bogle (W. C. Fields) *d* George Marshall *ph* Milton Krasner *m* Charles Previn

W. C. Fields, Edgar Bergen (with Charlie McCarthy and Mortimer Snerd), Constance Moore, Mary Forbes, Thurston Hall, Charles Coleman, Edward Brophy
  'Fairly amusing but lacks sustained overall interest.'—*Variety*

You Can't Get Away with Murder
US 1939 78m bw
Warner (Sam Bischoff)

A juvenile delinquent teams up with a gangster and takes a prison rap for him. Standard post-Dead End crime melodrama with no surprises.

w Robert Buckner, Don Ryan, Kenneth Gamet, *play* Chalked Out by Lewis Lawes, Jonathan Finn *d* Lewis Seiler *ph* Sol Polito *m* Heinz Roemheld

Humphrey Bogart, Billy Halop, Gale Page, John Litel, Henry Travers, Harvey Stephens, Harold Huber
  'Strictly a filler for the duals . . . ponderous and slow moving.'—*Variety*

You Can't Have Everything*
US 1937 99m bw
TCF (Lawrence Schwab)

A failed play is turned into a musical. Lively backstage comedy with good moments.

w Harry Tugend, Jack Yellen, Karl Tunberg *d* Norman Taurog *ph* Lucien Andriot

md David Buttolph *songs* Mack Gordon, Harry Revel

Alice Faye, *the Ritz Brothers,* Don Ameche, Charles Winninger, Gypsy Rose Lee, Tony Martin, Arthur Treacher, Louis Prima, Tip Tap and Toe, Wally Vernon
  'An expert piecing together of story, melody, blackouts, night club specialties and production numbers.'—*Variety*

You Can't Have Everything
US 1970 90m Eastmancolor
Koala (Lou Brandt)
aka: *Cactus in the Snow*

An 18-year-old virgin GI is about to leave for Vietnam when he picks up a girl and spends a happy but platonic twenty-four hours.
An agreeably understated little love story for those absorbed by teenage sex problems.

wd Martin Zweibach *ph* David M. Walsh *m* Joe Parnello

Richard Thomas, Mary Layne, Lucille Benson, Oscar Beregi

You Can't Run Away from It
US 1956 96m Technicolor
  Cinemascope
Columbia (Dick Powell)

An heiress runs away from a marriage arranged by her father, and falls for an amiable reporter.
Flat remake of *It Happened One Night,* with practically no comic sense or talent.

w Claude Binyon, Robert Riskin *d* Dick Powell *ph* Charles Lawton Jnr *m* George Duning *md* Morris Stoloff

June Allyson, Jack Lemmon, Charles Bickford, Jim Backus, Stubby Kaye, Paul Gilbert, Allyn Joslyn

You Can't Take It with You**
US 1938 127m bw
Columbia (Frank Capra)

The daughter of a highly eccentric New York family falls for a rich man's son.
A hilarious, warm and witty play is largely changed into a tirade against big business, but the Capra expertise is here in good measure and the stars all pull their weight.

w Robert Riskin, *play* George S. Kaufman, Moss Hart *d* Frank Capra *ph* Joseph Walker *m* Dmitri Tiomkin

Jean Arthur, Lionel Barrymore, James Stewart, Edward Arnold, Spring Byington, Mischa Auer, Ann Miller, Samuel S. Hinds, Donald Meek, H. B. Warner, Halliwell Hobbes, Mary Forbes, Dub Taylor, Lillian Yarbo, Eddie Anderson, *Harry Davenport*
  GRANDPA VANDERHOF (Lionel Barrymore) offering a prayer: 'Well, sir, here we are again. We had a little trouble, but that's not your fault. You spread the milk of human kindness, and if some of it gets curdled, that's our look-out. Anyway, things have turned out fine. Alice is going to marry Tony. The Kirbys are going to live with us for a while. And everybody on the block is happy. We've all got our health—and as far as anything else is concerned, we'll leave it up to you. Thank you.'

'The comedy is wholly American, wholesome, homespun, human, appealing, and touching in turn.'—*Variety*

'Shangri-La in a frame house.'—*Otis Ferguson*

AA: best picture; Frank Capra

AAN: Robert Riskin; Joseph Walker; Spring Byington

'It's bedlam in Islam!'
You Can't Win 'em All
GB 1970 99m Technicolor Panavision
Columbia / SRO (Gene Corman)

In 1922, two rival American mercenaries have adventures in the Mediterranean.
Hectic, overplotted comedy actioner.

w Leo V. Gordon *d* Peter Collinson *ph* Ken Higgins *m* Bert Kaempfert

Tony Curtis, Charles Bronson, Michèle Mercier, Grégoire Aslan, Patrick Magee

You for Me
US 1952 71m bw
MGM (Henry Berman)

A millionaire patient is courted by a needy hospital and falls for a popular nurse.
Cheerful but thin little programme-filler.

w William Roberts *d* Don Weis *ph* Paul Vogel *m* Alberto Columbo

Peter Lawford, Jane Greer, Gig Young, Paula Corday, Elaine Stewart

You Gotta Stay Happy
US 1948 100m bw
Universal (Karl Tunberg)

A runaway heiress joins cargo pilots on a transcontinental hop with some very queer passengers.
Ho-hum imitation of a Capra comedy; the effort shows.

w Karl Tunberg, *story* Robert Carson *d* H. C. Potter *ph* Russell Metty *m* Daniele Amfitheatrof

Joan Fontaine, James Stewart, Eddie Albert, Roland Young, Willard Parker, Percy Kilbride, Porter Hall, Paul Cavanagh, Halliwell Hobbes

You Live and Learn
GB 1937 80m bw

American night-club dancers are stranded in Paris and helped by a nitwit Englishman who turns out to be not what he seems. Rather flat comedy which gets flatter as it goes along.
Glenda Farrell, Claude Hulbert, Glen Alyn, John Carol, James Stephenson, George Galleon. Written by Brock Williams and Tom Phipps from a story by Norma Petterson; directed by Arthur Woods; for Warners.

You Made Me Love You
GB 1934 69m bw

A temperamental heiress is tamed by an amorous songwriter. Flimsy comedy with amusing moments. Thelma Todd, Stanley Lupino, John Loder, James Carew, Gerald Rawlinson. Written by Frank Launder from a story by Stanley Lupino; directed by Monty Banks; for British International.

You Must Be Joking*
GB 1965 100m bw
Columbia / Ameran (Charles H. Schneer)

Assorted army personnel vie in an extended initiative test.
Slam-bang location comedy with more hits than misses: cheerful entertainment.

w Alan Hackney *d* Michael Winner *ph* Geoffrey Unsworth *m* Laurie Johnson

Terry-Thomas, Lionel Jeffries, Michael Callan, Gabriella Licudi, *Denholm Elliott,* Lee Montague, Bernard Cribbins, Wilfrid Hyde White, James Robertson Justice, Richard Wattis, James Villiers

You Never Can Tell*
US 1951 78m bw
U-I (Leonard Goldstein)
GB title: *You Never Know*

An Alsatian dog is murdered and is sent back from heaven in the guise of a private detective to expose his killer.
Self-confidently outrageous comedy fantasy in the wake of *Here Comes Mr Jordan;* not badly done if you accept the premise.

w Lou Breslow, David Chandler *d* Lou Breslow *ph* Maury Gertsman *m* Hans Salter

Dick Powell, Peggy Dow, Charles Drake, Joyce Holden, Albert Sharpe, Sara Taft

You Only Live Once**
US 1937 85m bw
Walter Wanger

A petty crook framed for murder breaks out of prison and tries to escape to Canada with his wife.
Gloomy melodrama partly based on Bonnie and Clyde and incorporating a plea for justice; very well made and acted.

w Graham Baker, *story* Gene Towne *d* Fritz Lang *ph* Leon Shamroy *m* Alfred Newman

Sylvia Sidney, Henry Fonda, Barton MacLane, Jean Dixon, William Gargan, Jerome Cowan, Chic Sale, Margaret Hamilton, Warren Hymer

'Crack blend of spectacular drama and romance . . . good direction, strong scripting and an arresting production.'—*Variety*

'Again and again in this film we find what can only be described as camera style, the use of the pictorial image to narrate with the maximum of emotional impact.'—*Dilys Powell*

You Only Live Twice**
GB 1967 117m Technicolor Panavision
UA / Eon (Harry Saltzman, Albert R. Broccoli)

James Bond goes to Japan.
The Bond saga at its most expensive and expansive, full of local colour and in-jokes, with an enormously impressive set for the climactic action.

w Roald Dahl, *novel* Ian Fleming *d* Lewis Gilbert *ph* Freddie Young, Bob Huke *m* John Barry *pd* Ken Adam

Sean Connery, Tetsuro Tamba, Akiko Wakabayashi, Mie Hama, Karin Dor, Bernard Lee, Lois Maxwell, Desmond Llewellyn, *Charles Gray, Donald Pleasence*

● Video: Warner

You Said a Mouthful
US 1932 75m bw

The inventor of an unsinkable bathing suit is mistaken for a champion swimmer. Tepid star comedy. Joe E. Brown, Ginger Rogers, Sheila Terry, Guinn Williams, Oscar Apfel. Written by Robert Lord and Bolton Mallory; directed by Lloyd Bacon; for Warner.

You Were Meant for Me
US 1948 92m bw
TCF (Fred Kohlmar)

A small-town girl marries a bandleader.
Mildly pleasing, muted, musical romance, with good twenties atmosphere.

w Elick Moll, Valentine Davies *d* Lloyd Bacon *ph* Victor Milner *md* Lionel Newman *songs* various

Jeanne Crain, Dan Dailey, Oscar Levant, Barbara Lawrence, Selena Royle, Percy Kilbride, Herbert Anderson

You Were Never Lovelier*
US 1942 97m bw
Columbia (Louis F. Edelman)

An Argentinian hotel tycoon tries to interest his daughter in marriage by creating a mysterious admirer.
Pleasing musical, a follow up for the stars of *You'll Never Get Rich.*

w Michael Fessier, Ernest Pagano, Delmer Daves *d* William A. Seiter *ph* Ted Tetzlaff *songs* Jerome Kern, Johnny Mercer *m* Leigh Harline

Fred Astaire, Rita Hayworth, Adolphe Menjou, Leslie Brooks, Adele Mara, Isobel Elsom, Gus Schilling, Xavier Cugat and his Orchestra, Larry Parks

AAN: Leigh Harline; song 'Dearly Beloved'

You Will Remember
GB 1940 86m bw

The life of the late Victorian songwriter Leslie Stuart. Pleasant, rather surprising, minor British biopic. Robert Morley, Emlyn Williams, Dorothy Hyson, Tom E. Finglass, Nicholas Phipps, Allan Jeayes. Written by Lydia Hayward; directed by Jack Raymond; for Jack Raymond Productions.

You'll Find Out*
US 1940 97m bw
RKO (David Butler)

Kay Kyser's band is hired to play for a 21st birthday party at a gloomy mansion; they help save the life of the girl concerned.
Cheerful if slow-starting spooky house send-up with a splendid trio of villains.

w James V. Kern, David Butler *d* David Butler *ph* Frank Redman *m* Roy Webb *songs* James McHugh, Johnny Mercer

YOU CAN'T GET AWAY WITH MURDER.   Humphrey Bogart tells Billy Halop and Harold Huber who's boss.

Kay Kyser, Boris Karloff, Peter Lorre, Bela Lugosi, Dennis O'Keefe, Ginny Simms, Helen Parrish, Alma Kruger, Ish Kabibble

AAN: song, 'I'd Know You Anywhere'

You'll Like My Mother
US 1972 92m Technicolor
Universal / Bing Crosby Productions (Mort Briskin)

Pregnant widow visits neurotic mother-in-law in a snowbound mansion.
Predictable frightened lady shocker aiming somewhere between *Psycho* and *Fanatic*; of strictly routine interest.

w Jo Heims, *novel* Naomi Hintze *d* Lamont Johnson *ph* Jack Marta *m* Gil Melle

Rosemary Murphy, Patty Duke, Richard Thomas, Sian Barbara Allen

You'll Never Get Rich*
US 1941 88m bw
Columbia (Sam Bischoff)

A Broadway dance director helps his philandering producer by taking a romantically-inclined showgirl off his hands.
Smart comedy-musical which set its female lead as a top star.

w Michael Fessier, Ernest Pagano *d* Sidney Lanfield *ph* Philip Tannura *ch* Robert Alton *songs* Cole Porter *m* Morris Stoloff

Fred Astaire, Rita Hayworth, Robert Benchley, John Hubbard, Osa Massen, Frieda Inescort, Guinn Williams, Donald MacBride

AAN: Morris Stoloff; song 'Since I Kissed My Baby Goodbye'

Young America
US 1932 74m bw
GB title: *We Humans*

Two young boys get into trouble with the law.
Dog-eared domestic flagwaver.

w William Conselman, *play* John Frederick Ballard *d* Frank Borzage *ph* George Schneiderman

Spencer Tracy, Doris Kenyon, Tommy Conlon, Ralph Bellamy, Beryl Mercer, Sarah Padden

'Hokey propaganda for juvenile courts. Not for smart houses and doubtful elsewhere unless there is a preponderance of mothers.'— *Variety*

Young and Innocent***
GB 1937 80m bw
GFD / Gainsborough (Edward Black)
US title: *A Girl Was Young*

A girl goes on the run with her boy friend when he is suspected of murder.

Pleasant, unassuming chase melodrama with a rather weak cast but plenty of its director's touches.

w Charles Bennett, Alma Reville, *novel* A Shilling for Candles by Josephine Tey
d Alfred Hitchcock *ph* Bernard Knowles *m* Louis Levy

Nova Pilbeam, Derrick de Marney, Mary Clare, Edward Rigby, Basil Radford, George Curzon, Percy Marmont, John Longden

● *Video: Rank*

Young and Willing
US 1942 83m bw
UA (made by Paramount) (Edward H. Griffith)

Impecunious actors in a New York boarding house hit on a great play.
Very mild, innocuous comedy which passed quickly from the public memory.

w Virginia Van Upp, *play* Francis Swann *d* Edward H. Griffith *ph* Leo Tover *m* Victor Young

William Holden, Susan Hayward, Eddie Bracken, Robert Benchley, Martha O'Driscoll, Barbara Britton, James Brown, Mabel Paige

Young as you Feel*
US 1931 78m bw

In order to reform his family a father pretends to be as irresponsible as they are. Medium star vehicle. Will Rogers, Fifi D'Orsay, Lucien Littlefield, Donald Dillaway. Written by Edwin Burke from the play Father and the Boys by George Ade; directed by Frank Borzage; for Fox. 'Looks fair b.o. due to star.'—*Variety*

Young at Heart**
US 1954 117m Warnercolor
(Warner) Arwin (Henry Blanke)

The daughters of a small-town music teacher have romantic problems.
Softened, musicalized remake of *Four Daughters* (qv), an old-fashioned treat with roses round the door and a high standard of proficiency in all departments.

w Julius J. Epstein, Lenore Coffee, *novel* Fannie Hurst *d* Gordon Douglas *ph* Ted McCord *md* Ray Heindorff

Doris Day, Frank Sinatra, Ethel Barrymore, Gig Young, Dorothy Malone, Robert Keith, Elizabeth Fraser, Alan Hale Jnr

● *Video: BBC*

Young Bess*
US 1953 112m Technicolor
MGM (Sidney Franklin)

The early years of Elizabeth I and her romance with Tom Seymour.
Historical fiction, wildly unreliable as to fact and dramatically not very rewarding. The character actors have the best of it.

w Arthur Wimperis, Jan Lustig, *novel* Margaret Irwin *d* George Sidney *ph* Charles Rosher *m* Miklos Rozsa

YOU CAN'T TAKE IT WITH YOU.   Everybody finds the way to happiness: Lionel Barrymore, James Stewart, Jean Arthur, Edward Arnold.

Jean Simmons, Stewart Granger, Charles Laughton (as Henry VIII), Kay Walsh, Deborah Kerr, Guy Rolfe, Kathleen Byron, Cecil Kellaway, Robert Arthur, Leo G. Carroll, Elaine Stewart, Dawn Addams, Rex Thompson

Young Billy Young
US 1969   89m   De Luxe
UA / Talbot–Youngstein (Max Youngstein)

A young western gunman is helped out of scrapes by a mysterious stranger bent on revenge.
Good-looking but rather ineffective western which throws away good production values.

wd Burt Kennedy,   *novel* Who Rides with Wyatt by Will Henry   *ph* Harry Stradling Jnr   *m* Shelly Manne

Robert Mitchum, Angie Dickinson, Robert Walker Jnr, David Carradine, John Anderson, Paul Fix

Young Cassidy*
GB 1964   110m   Technicolor
MGM / Sextant (Robert D. Graff, Robert Emmett Ginna)

A romantic view of the early Dublin life of writer Sean O'Casey.
Ambling, unconvincing but generally interesting picture of a past time.

w John Whiting, from the writings of Sean O'Casey   *d* Jack Cardiff, John Ford   *ph* Ted Scaife   *m* Sean O'Riada

Rod Taylor, Maggie Smith, Edith Evans, Flora Robson, Michael Redgrave, Julie Christie, Jack MacGowran, Sian Phillips, T. P. McKenna

Young Dillinger
US 1964   102m   bw
Alfred Zimbalist

An embittered young convict becomes Public Enemy Number One.
Fantasized, forgettable biopic with violent moments.

w Arthur Hoerl, Don Zimbalist   *d* Terry Morse   *ph* Stanley Cortez   *m* Shorty Rogers

Nick Adams, John Ashley, Robert Conrad, Mary Ann Mobley, Victor Buono, John Hoyt, Reed Hadley

The Young Doctors*
US 1961   102m   bw
UA / Drexel / Stuart Millar / Laurence Turman

Old Dr Pearson resents his modern young assistant and almost causes a tragedy.
Routine medical melo of the Kildare / Gillespie kind, given a Grade A production and cast.

w Joseph Hayes,   *novel* The Final Diagnosis by Arthur Hailey   *d* Phil Karlson   *ph* Arthur J. Ornitz   *m* Elmer Bernstein

Fredric March, Ben Gazzara, Dick Clark, Eddie Albert, Ina Balin, Aline MacMahon, Edward Andrews, Arthur Hill, George Segal, Rosemary Murphy

Young Doctors in Love
US 1982   95m   Metrocolor
TCF / ABC (Jerry Bruckheimer)

Goings-on in a modern hospital.
Spoof soap opera in the wake of *Airplane* but seeming more like a flat edition of *Carry On*.

w Michael Elias, Rich Eustis   *d* Garry Marshall   *ph* Don Peterman   *m* Maurice Jarre

Michael McKean, Sean Young, Harry Dean Stanton, Patrick MacNee, Hector Elizondo, Dabney Coleman

Young Eagles*
US 1930   71m   bw
Paramount

The adventures of American aviators in World War I.
Spirited early sound actioner.

w William McNutt, Grover Jones   *d* William Wellman   *ph* Archie Stout

Charles Rogers, Jean Arthur, Paul Lukas, Stuart Erwin, Virginia Bruce, James Finlayson
   'Pint-sized version of *Wings*. Comedy and production almost square silly plot.'—*Variety*

Young Frankenstein**
US 1974   108m   bw
TCF / Gruskoff / Venture / Jouer / Crossbow (Michael Gruskoff)

Young Frederick Frankenstein, a brain surgeon, goes back to Transylvania and pores over his grandfather's notebooks.
The most successful of Mel Brooks' parodies, Mad Magazine style; the gleamingly reminiscent photography is the best of it, the script being far from consistently funny, but there are splendid moments.

w Gene Wilder, Mel Brooks   *d* Mel Brooks   *ph* Gerald Hirschfeld   *m* John Morris   *ad* Dale Hennesy

Gene Wilder, Marty Feldman, Madeleine Kahn, *Peter Boyle,* Cloris Leachman, Kenneth Mars, Gene Hackman, Richard Haydn

AAN: script

● *Video: CBS / Fox*

Young Giants
US 1983   97m   De Luxe   Panavision

A San Diego priest helps a boys' home by re-organizing a football team so that an old priest can die happy. Shades of *Going My Way*, but somewhat ineptly done, with a guest appearance from Pele as *deus ex machina*.
Peter Fox, John Huston, Lisa Wills, F. William Parker, Severn Darden. Written by Tom Moyer, Terrill Tannen, Mike Lammers; directed by Terrill Tannen; for Entertainment Enterprises. 'At least it has the courage of its throwback convictions.'—*Kim Newman, MFB*

The Young Girls of Rochefort
France 1967 126m Eastmancolor
Franscope
Parc Film / Madeleine / Seven Arts (Mag
Bodard, Gilbert de Goldschmidt)
original title: *Les Demoiselles de Rochefort*

Two country girls join a travelling dancing
troupe, and find love on the day of the fair.
Flat, empty tribute to the Hollywood musical,
which never inspires despite the presence of
one of its greatest stars.

wd Jacques Demy *ph* Ghislain Cloquet
m Michel Legrand

Catherine Deneuve, François Dorléac,
George Chakiris, Gene Kelly, Danielle
Darrieux, Grover Dale, Michel Piccoli

AAN: Michel Legrand

The Young in Heart***
US 1938 91m bw
David O. Selznick

A family of charming confidence tricksters
move in on a rich old lady but she brings out
the best in them.
Delightful, roguish romantic comedy, perfectly
cast and pacily handled.

w Paul Osborn, Charles Bennett, *novel* The
Gay Banditti by I. A. R. Wylie *d* Richard
Wallace *ph* Leon Shamroy *m* Franz Waxman
*Douglas Fairbanks Jnr, Janet Gaynor, Roland
Young, Billie Burke, Minnie Dupree,* Paulette
Goddard, Richard Carlson, Henry Stephenson

'Sentimental drama, vastly touching and
entertaining . . . has everything to ensure box
office success.'—*Variety*
'It comes as a gentle breeze in the hurricane
of hurly burly comedies that have hurtled
across the screen of late.'—*Motion Picture
Herald*
AAN: Leon Shamroy; Franz Waxman

The Young Land
US 1957 89m Technicolor
(Columbia) C. V. Whitney (Patrick Ford)

A young sheriff arrests a gunman and after the
trial has to save him from lynching.
Rather stiff attempt at a youth western.

w Norman Shannon Hall *d* Ted Tetzlaff
ph Winton C. Hoch, Henry Sharp
Dan O'Herlihy, Patrick Wayne, Yvonne
Craig, Dennis Hopper

AAN: song 'Strange Are the Ways of Love'
(*m* Dmitri Tiomkin, *ly* Ned Washington)

The Young Lions**
US 1958 167m bw Cinemascope
TCF (Al Lichtman)

World War II adventures of two Americans
and a German skiing instructor.
Three strands are loosely interwoven into a
would-be modern epic; the result is well
mounted and generally absorbing but uneven
and decidedly overlong.

w Edward Anhalt, *novel* Irwin Shaw
d Edward Dmytryk *ph* Joe MacDonald
m Hugo Friedhofer

Marlon Brando, Montgomery Clift, Dean
Martin, Hope Lange, Barbara Rush, May
Britt, Maximilian Schell, Lee Van Cleef
'Episodic and overproduced, like a wartime
Grand Hotel.'—*Pauline Kael, 70s*
AAN: Joe MacDonald; Hugo Friedhofer
● *Video: CBS / Fox*

The Young Lovers*
GB 1954 96m bw
GFD / Group Films (Anthony Havelock-
Allan)
US title: *Chance Meeting*

A US Embassy man in London falls in love
with the daughter of an Iron Curtain minister.
Romeo and Juliet, cold war style, quite nicely
put together with a thriller climax.

w Robin Estridge, *story* George Tabori
d Anthony Asquith *ph* Jack Asher
m Tchaikovsky

Odile Versois, David Knight, David Kossoff,
Joseph Tomelty, Paul Carpenter, Theodore
Bikel, Jill Adams

'Put down your trumpet, jazz man—I'm in
the mood for love!'
Young Man with a Horn*
US 1950 112m bw
Warner (Jerry Wald)
GB title: *Young Man of Music*

The professional and romantic tribulations of a
trumpet player.
Overwrought character melodrama based on
the life of Bix Beiderbecke; quite absorbing
though occasionally risible.

w Carl Foreman, Edmund H. North, *novel*
Dorothy Baker *d* Michael Curtiz *ph* Ted
McCord *m* Ray Heindorf
Kirk Douglas, Lauren Bacall, Doris Day,
Hoagy Carmichael, Juano Hernandez, Jerome
Cowan, Mary Beth Hughes, Nestor Paiva

Young Man with Ideas*
US 1952 84m bw
MGM (Gottfried Reinhardt, William H.
Wright)

A small-town lawyer tries to better himself in
Los Angeles.
Modestly likeable comedy which doesn't add
up to much.

w Arthur Sheekman *d* Mitchell Leisen
ph Joseph Ruttenberg *m* David Rose
Glenn Ford, Ruth Roman, Nina Foch, Denise
Darcel, Donna Corcoran, Mary Wickes,
Sheldon Leonard

Young Man's Fancy
GB 1939 77m bw

A young Victorian lord avoids an unsuitable
match by eloping to Paris. Rather pallid
romantic comedy with likeable period detail.
Griffith Jones, Anna Lee, Seymour Hicks,
Billy Bennett, Edward Rigby, Francis L.
Sullivan. Written by Roland Pertwee, Rodney
Ackland and E. V. H. Emmett; directed by
Robert Stevenson; for Ealing.

Young Mr Lincoln***
US 1939 100m bw
TCF (Kenneth MacGowan)

Abraham Lincoln as a young country lawyer
stops a lynching and proves a young man
innocent of murder.
Splendid performances and period atmosphere
are rather nipped in the bud by second-feature
courtroom twists, but this is a marvellous
old-fashioned entertainment with its heart in
the right place.

w Lamar Trotti *d* John Ford *ph* Bert
Glennon *w* Alfred Newman
Henry Fonda, Alice Brady, Marjorie Weaver,
Arleen Whelan, Eddie Collins, Richard
Cromwell, Donald Meek, Eddie Quillan,
Spencer Charters

'A dignified saga of early Lincolniana, paced
rather slowly . . . lack of romance interest is
one of the prime factors which deter the film
from interpreting itself into big box office.'—
Variety
'Its simple good faith and understanding are
an expression of the country's best life that
says as much as forty epics.'—*Otis Ferguson*
'Period details are lovingly sketched in—a
log splitting contest, a tug of war, a tar barrel
rolling match . . .'—*Charles Higham*
'Its source is a womb of popular and
national spirit. This could account for its unity,
its artistry, its genuine beauty.'—*Sergei
Eisenstein*
'A film which indisputably has the right to
be called Americana.'—*New York Times*
'In spite of the excitements of a murder, a
near-lynching and a crackerjack trial, it
remains a character study.'—*New York Sun*
'One of John Ford's most memorable
films.'—*Pauline Kael, 70s*
AAN: Lamar Trotti

The Young Mr Pitt*
GB 1942 118m bw
TCF (Edward Black)

Britain's youngest prime minister quells the
threat of invasion by Napoleon.
Shapeless and overlong but generally diverting
historical pastiche timed as wartime
propaganda against Hitler.

w Frank Launder, Sidney Gilliat *d* Carol
Reed *ph* Frederick A. Young *m* Charles
Williams *ad* Vetchinsky
Robert Donat, Robert Morley, Phyllis Calvert,
John Mills, Raymond Lovell, Max Adrian,
Felix Aylmer, Albert Lieven

The Young Ones*
GB 1961 108m Technicolor
Cinemascope
ABP (Kenneth Harper)
US title: *Wonderful to be Young*

The son of a tycoon starts a youth club and
puts on a musical to raise funds.
A shopworn idea is the springboard for a
brave try in a field where Britain was
presumed to have failed; despite the
enthusiasm with which it was greeted at the
time, it has dated badly.

w Peter Myers, Ronald Cass *d* Sidney J. Furie *ph* Douglas Slocombe *m* Stanley Black

Cliff Richard, Robert Morley, Carole Grey, Richard O'Sullivan, Melvyn Hayes, Gerald Harper, Robertson Hare

● Video: Thorn EMI

Young People
US 1940 78m bw
TCF (Harry Joe Brown)

Vaudevillians retire to give their daughter a proper upbringing, but find that showbiz is in her blood.
Pleasant but unremarkable comedy-drama with music, marking the end of its star's association with the studio.

w Edwin Blum, Don Ettlinger *d* Allan Dwan *ph* Edward Cronjager *md* Alfred Newman

Shirley Temple, Jack Oakie, Charlotte Greenwood, Arleen Whelan, George Montgomery, Kathleen Howard, Mae Marsh

The Young Philadelphians°
US 1959 136m bw
Warner (producer not credited)
GB title: *The City Jungle*

A forceful young lawyer pushes his way to the top of the snobbish Philadelphia heap despite threats to expose his illegitimacy.
Novel on film, gleamingly done and acted with assurance.

w James Gunn, *novel* The Philadelphian by Richard Powell *d* Vincent Sherman *ph* Harry Stradling *m* Ernest Gold

Paul Newman, Barbara Rush, Alexis Smith, Brian Keith, Billie Burke, John Williams, Otto Kruger, Diane Brewster, Robert Vaughn, Paul Picerni, Robert Douglas

AAN: Harry Stradling; Robert Vaughn

The Young Savages°
US 1961 103m bw
UA / Contemporary (Pat Duggan)

An assistant DA prosecutes three hoodlums for murder but begins to feel that one is not guilty.
Tough, realistic melodrama of the New York slums, with roughhouse climaxes and a political conscience.

w Edward Anhalt, J. P. Miller, *novel* A Matter of Conviction by Evan Hunter *d* John Frankenheimer *ph* Lionel Lindon *m* David Amram

Burt Lancaster, Shelley Winters, John David Chandler, Dina Merrill, Edward Andrews, Telly Savalas

The Young Stranger°
US 1957 84m bw
RKO (Stuart Millar)

The 16-year-old son of a film executive gets into trouble with the police.
Reasonably stimulating film of a TV play about the kind of causeless rebel who quickly became a cliché.

w Robert Dozier *d* John Frankenheimer *ph* Robert Planck *m* Leonard Rosenman

James MacArthur, Kim Hunter, James Daly, James Gregory, Whit Bissell

Young Tom Edison°
US 1940 82m bw
MGM (John Considine Jnr)

First of a two-parter (see *Edison the Man*) tracing Edison's first experiments.
Reasonably factual and absorbing junior biopic.

w Bradbury Foote, Dore Schary, Hugo Butler *d* Norman Taurog *ph* Sidney Wagner *m* Edward Ward

Mickey Rooney, Eugene Pallette, George Bancroft, Fay Bainter, Virginia Weidler, Victor Kilian, Lloyd Corrigan
'A picture for all of the people in all of the places.'—*Motion Picture Herald*

Young Warriors
US 1983 103m colour

After the sister of one of them dies after being raped, high-school graduates set themselves up as vigilantes. Dangerous rubbish. Ernest Borgnine, Richard Roundtree, Lynda Day George, James Van Patten, Anne Lockhart, Tom Reilly, Dick Shawn. Written by Lawrence D. Foldes, Russell W. Colgin; directed by Lawrence D. Foldes; for Cannon.
'A lurid mishmash.'—*Jo Imeson, MFB*

The Young Widow
US 1946 100m bw
UA / Hunt Stromberg

The widow of a World War II flier returns to the Virginia farm where they had spent happy hours.
Glum sudser with talent all at sea.

w Richard Macaulay, Margaret Buell Wilder, *novel* Clarissa Fairchild Cushman *d* Edwin L. Marin *ph* Lee Garmes *m* Carmen Dragon *pd* Nicolai Remisoff

Jane Russell, Louis Hayward, Faith Domergue, Marie Wilson, Kent Taylor, Penny Singleton, Connie Gilchrist, Cora Witherspoon

Young Winston°°
GB 1972 157m Eastmancolor
Panavision
Columbia / Open Road / Hugh French (Carl Foreman)

The adventurous life of Winston Churchill up to his becoming an MP.
Generally engaging if lumpy film which switches too frequently from action to family drama to politics to character study and is not helped by irritating directorial tricks.

w Carl Foreman, *book* My Early Life by Winston Churchill *d* Richard Attenborough *ph* Gerry Turpin *m* Alfred Ralston *pd* Don Ashton, Geoffrey Drake

Simon Ward, Robert Shaw, Anne Bancroft, Jack Hawkins, Ian Holm, *Anthony Hopkins*, John Mills, Patrick Magee, Edward Woodward

AAN: Carl Foreman

Young Wives' Tale
GB 1951 79m bw

A playwright and his slaphappy wife share a house with a super-efficient couple. Very mild but palatable comedy set 'at the wrong end of

St John's Wood'. Joan Greenwood, Nigel Patrick, Derek Farr, Guy Middleton, Athene Seyler, Helen Cherry, Audrey Hepburn, Irene Handl. Written by Anne Burnaby, from the play by Ronald Jeans; directed by Henry Cass; for ABPC.

Young Woodley
GB 1929 79m bw

A schoolboy falls in love with his teacher's wife. Modest early talkie version of a play thought mildly shocking at the time. Madeleine Carroll, Frank Lawton, Sam Livesey, Gerald Rawlinson, Billy Milton. Written by John Van Druten and Victor Kendall, from the play by John Van Druten; directed by Thomas Bentley; for BIP. (A silent version made earlier in the same year, with Marjorie Hume and Robin Irvine, was never released.)

Youngblood Hawke
US 1964 137m bw
Warner (Delmer Daves)

A Kentucky truck driver becomes a successful novelist and is spoiled by New York success.
Absurdly archetypal soap opera from a bestseller, spilling over with every imaginable cliché; some of its excesses are glossily entertaining.

w Delmer Daves, *novel* Herman Wouk *d* Delmer Daves *ph* Charles Lawton *m* Max Steiner

James Franciscus, Genevieve Page, Suzanne Pleshette, Eva Gabor, *Mary Astor*, Lee Bowman, Edward Andrews, John Emery, Don Porter

The Youngest Profession
US 1943 82m bw
MGM (B. F. Ziedman)

Teenage autograph hounds cause trouble at the MGM studio.
Innocuous comedy with guest stars.

w George Oppenheimer, Charles Lederer, Leonard Spiegelgass, *book* Lillian Day *d* Edward Buzzell *ph* Charles Lawton *m* David Snell

Virginia Weidler, Jean Porter, Edward Arnold, John Carroll, Agnes Moorehead, Greer Garson, William Powell, Lana Turner, Walter Pidgeon, Robert Taylor

Your Witness°
GB 1950 100m bw
Warner / Coronado (Joan Harrison)
US title: *Eye Witness*

An American lawyer comes to an English village to defend a war buddy on a murder charge.
Interesting but ineffective blend of comedy and courtroom procedure intended to contrast English and American ways.

w Hugo Butler, Ian Hunter, William Douglas Home *d* Robert Montgomery *ph* Gerald Gibbs *m* Malcolm Arnold

Robert Montgomery, Leslie Banks, Patricia Cutts, Felix Aylmer, Andrew Cruickshank, Harcourt Williams, Jenny Laird, Michael Ripper

You're a Big Boy Now*
US 1967 96m Eastmancolor
Warner Seven Arts (William Fadiman)

A young assistant librarian discovers girls.
Freewheeling semi-surrealist comedy with
exhilarating moments and the inevitable
letdowns associated with this kind of campy
high style.

wd Francis Ford Coppola, novel David
Benedictus ph Andy Laszlo m Bob Prince

Peter Kastner, Elizabeth Hartman, Geraldine
Page, Julie Harris, Rip Torn, Tony Bill,
Karen Black, Michael Dunn

AAN: Geraldine Page

You're a Sweetheart
US 1937 96m bw
Universal (B. G. De Sylva)

A Broadway star suffers from her press agent's
bright ideas.
Muffed musical with all concerned ill at ease
with below par material.

w Monte Brice, Charles Grayson d David
Butler ph George Robinson md Charles
Previn songs various

Alice Faye, George Murphy, Ken Murray,
William Gargan, Frances Hunt, Frank Jenks,
Andy Devine, Charles Winninger, Donald
Meek

'Just what the doctor ordered for the
holiday first runs . . . enough entertainers for
two shows.'—Variety

You're Darn Tootin'***
US 1929 20m bw silent

Two musicians get into trouble at work, in
their digs and in the street. Star comedy which
though early in their teaming shows Stan and
Ollie at their best in a salt shaker routine and
in a surreal pants-ripping contest. Laurel and
Hardy, Agnes Steele. Written by H. M.
Walker; directed by Edgar Kennedy; for Hal
Roach.

You're in the Army Now**
US 1941 79m bw
Warner (Ben Stoloff)

Two incompetent vacuum cleaner salesmen
accidentally join the army.
An excellent vehicle for two star comedians
who have often suffered from poor material,
with a silent-comedy-style climax involving a
house on wheels.

w Paul Gerard Smith, George Beatty d Lewis
Seiler ph James Van Trees

*Jimmy Durante, Phil Silvers, Donald
MacBride*, Jane Wyman, Regis Toomey

You're in the Navy Now*
US 1951 93m bw
TCF (Fred Kohlmar)
aka: *USS Teakettle*

Trouble results when the navy instals steam
turbines in an experimental patrol craft.
Amusing service comedy with good script
touches and capable performances.

w Richard Murphy d Henry Hathaway
ph Joe MacDonald m Cyril Mockridge

Gary Cooper, Millard Mitchell, Jane Greer,
Eddie Albert, John McIntire, Ray Collins,
Harry Von Zell, Jack Webb, Richard Erdman

You're My Everything*
US 1949 94m Technicolor
TCF (Lamar Trotti)

A Boston socialite marries a hoofer and
becomes a movie star.
Pleasant twenties comedy with good period
detail and lively performances.

w Lamar Trotti, Will Hays Jnr d Walter
Lang ph Arthur E. Arling m Alfred
Newman

Anne Baxter, Dan Dailey, Anne Revere,
Stanley Ridges, Shari Robinson, Henry
O'Neill, Selena Royle, Alan Mowbray, Buster
Keaton

You're Never Too Young
US 1955 103m Technicolor
Vistavision
Paramount / Hal B. Wallis (Paul Jones)

An apprentice barber on the run from a
murderer poses as a 12-year-old child to travel
half fare.
Unattractive revamping of *The Major and the
Minor* (qv), with the star team trying too
obviously to make bricks with inferior straw.

w Sidney Sheldon d Norman Taurog
ph Daniel L. Fapp m Arthur Schwarz

Dean Martin, Jerry Lewis, Diana Lynn, Nina
Foch, Raymond Burr, Veda Ann Borg

You're Only Young Once see The Hardy
Family

You're Only Young Twice
GB 1952 81m bw
Group Three (Terry Bishop)

The puritanical head of a Scottish university is
laid low by circumstance and his own folly.
Misfire eccentric comedy which deserves
marks for trying but fails to amuse.

w Reginald Beckwith, Lindsay Galloway,
Terry Bishop, play What Say They by James
Bridie d Terry Gilbert ph Jo Jago

Duncan Macrae, Charles Hawtrey, Joseph
Tomelty, Patrick Barr, Diane Hart, Robert
Urquhart

You're Telling Me*
US 1934 66m bw
Paramount

A small-town inventor meets a princess and
makes the social grade.
Meaninglessly-titled star vehicle which is often
defiantly unamusing but does include the
famous golf routine.

w Walter de Leon, Paul M. Jones d Erle C.
Kenton ph Alfred Gilks m Arthur Johnston

W. C. Fields, Larry 'Buster' Crabbe, Joan
Marsh, Adrienne Ames, Louise Carter

'The kind of comedy that Chaplin used to
do in two reels, but stretched out like
Carnera's suspenders to run an even six.'—
Variety

Yours Mine and Ours*
US 1968 111m Technicolor
UA / Desilu / Walden (Robert F. Blumofe)

A widower with nine children marries a widow
with eight, and they settle in an old San
Francisco house.
Generally appealing comedy, based on fact
and well suited to its stars.

w Mel Shavelson, Mort Lachman d Mel
Shavelson ph Charles Wheeler m Fred
Karlin

Lucille Ball, Henry Fonda, Van Johnson

Youth Takes a Fling
US 1938 77m bw

A reluctant truck driver is chased by a
department store salesgirl. Mildy scatty
comedy which failed to ring the bell. Joel
McCrea, Andrea Leeds, Frank Jenks,
Dorothea Kent, Isabel Jeans, Virginia Grey,
Grant Mitchell, Willie Best. Written by Myles
Connelly; directed by Archie Mayo; for Joe
Pasternak / Universal. 'Good standard
entertainment with many light and diverting
passages.'—*Variety*

Z•••
France / Algeria 1968   125m
   Eastmancolor
Reggane / ONCIC / Jacques Pérrin

A leading opposition MP is murdered at a
rally. The police are anxious to establish the
event as an accident, but the examining
magistrate proves otherwise.
An exciting police suspense drama which also
recalls events under the Greek colonels and
was therefore highly fashionable for a while
both as entertainment and as a political *roman
à clef*.

w Costa-Gavras, Jorge Semprun, *novel* Vassili
Vassilikos *d* Costa-Gavras *ph* Raoul
Coutard *m* Mikis Theodorakis

Jean-Louis Trintignant, Jacques Pérrin, Yves
Montand, François Périer, Irene Papas,
Charles Denner

AAN: best picture; direction

 'It will blow your mind!'
Zabriskie Point
US 1969   112m   Metrocolor   Panavision
MGM / Carlo Ponti

A rebellious Los Angeles student steals a
private airplane, meets an aimless girl, and
finds a revelation in Death Valley . . .
Highly self-indulgent and unattractive fantasy
about escape from the crudities of our over-
civilized world. An expensive failure and an
awful warning of what happens if you give an
arty director carte blanche.

wd Michelangelo Antonioni *ph* Alfio Contini
m pop songs

Mark Frechette, Daria Halprin, Rod Taylor,
Paul Fix

 'Not even a good tourist's notebook . . .
from the choice of Death Valley as a symbol
of American civilization to the inclusion of gag
signs on bar-room walls to the shots of garish
billboards, this film sticks to the surface,
stranded.'—*Stanley Kauffman*

 'A huge, jerry-built, crumbling ruin of a
movie.'—*Pauline Kael, New Yorker*

 'A small, sad shambles of a film that has
obviously been salvaged from a larger
shambles. Bad enough to give anti-
Americanism a bad name.'—*Joseph
Morgenstern, Newsweek*

Zandy's Bride
US 1974   116m   Technicolor
   Panavision
Warner (Harry Matofsky)

Life for a frontier family.
Dour semi-western.

w Marc Norman, *novel* The Stranger by
Lillian Bos Ross *d* Joan Troell *ph* Jordan
Cronenweth *m* Fred Karlin

Gene Hackman, Liv Ullmann, Eileen
Heckart, Harry Dean Stanton, Joe Santos,
Frank Cady

Zapped!
US 1982   98m   CFI

A high-school boffin discovers his own
telekinetic powers, by which he is able to tear
everyone's clothes off at the senior prom. Mild
adolescent smut, half-way between *Porky's*
and the unbearable Disney comedies of the
sixties. Scott Baio, Willie Aames, Robert
Mandan, Scatman Crothers. Written by Bruce
Rubin, Robert J. Rosenthal; directed by
Robert J. Rosenthal; for Thunder Associates.

Zarak•
GB 1956   99m   Technicolor
   Cinemascope
Columbia / Warwick (Phil C. Samuel)

An Afghan outlaw finally saves a British
officer at the cost of his own life.
Box-office actioner, shot in Morocco with a
weird cast and the help of old movie clips.

w Richard Maibaum *d* Terence Young *2nd
unit* Yakima Canutt *ph* John Wilcox, Ted
Moore, Cyril Knowles *m* William Alwyn
ad John Box

Victor Mature, Michael Wilding, Anita
Ekberg, Bonar Colleano, Finlay Currie,
Bernard Miles, Eunice Gayson, Peter Illing,
Frederick Valk, André Morell

Zardoz
GB 1973   105m   De Luxe   Panavision
TCF / John Boorman

Life in 2293, when the earth has become
wasteland and a mass of Brutals are ruled by a
few Exterminators who have both memory
and intelligence.
Pompous, boring fantasy for the so-called
intelligentsia.

wd John Boorman *ph* Geoffrey Unsworth
m David Munrow *pd* Anthony Pratt

Sean Connery, Charlotte Rampling, John
Alderton

 'A glittering cultural trash pile . . the most
gloriously fatuous movie since *The Oscar*.'—
New Yorker

● *Video: CBS / Fox*

Zaza
US 1938   83m   bw
Paramount (Albert Lewin)

A 1904 French chanteuse is in love with a
married aristocrat.
Rather flat period romantic drama with
interesting credits.

w Zoe Atkins, *play* Pierre Berton, Charles
Simon *d* George Cukor *ph* Charles Lang
songs Frank Loesser, Frederick Hollander

Claudette Colbert, Herbert Marshall, Bert
Lahr, Constance Collier, Helen Westley,
Genevieve Tobin, Walter Catlett, Rex
O'Malley

 'Fine production with hefty woman-
appeal.'—*Variety*
† The original David Belasco stage production
made Mrs Leslie Carter famous. Silent film
versions starred Pauline Frederick in 1915 and
Gloria Swanson in 1923.

Zazie dans le Métro••
France 1960   88m   Eastmancolor
Nouvelles Editions (Irène Leriche)

A naughty little girl has a day in Paris and
causes chaos.
Inventive little comedy which almost turns into
a French *Hellzapoppin*, with everybody
chasing or fighting everybody else.

wd Louis Malle, *novel* Raymond Queneau
ph Henri Raichi

Catherine Demongeot, Philippe Noiret,
Vittorio Caprioli

Zebra in the Kitchen
US 1965   93m   Metrocolor
MGM / Ivan Tors

A young boy tries to improve the lot of zoo
animals.
Pleasing family film.

w Art Arthur *d* Ivan Tors *ph* Lamar Boren

Jay North, Martin Milner, Andy Devine,
Joyce Meadows, Jim Davis

Zee and Co.•
GB 1971   109m   colour
Columbia / Zee Films (Kastner–Ladd–
   Kanter)
US title: *X, Y and Zee*

A successful architect battles with his
termagant wife and seeks an affair.
Overwritten but entertaining sexual
melodrama about an absolute bitch. The flow
of bad language was new at the time.

w Edna O'Brien *d* Brian G. Hutton *ph* Billy Williams *m* Stanley Myers *ad* Peter Mullins

Elizabeth Taylor, Michael Caine, Susannah York, Margaret Leighton, John Standing

'Miss Taylor is rapidly turning into a latterday Marie Dressler.'—*Tom Milne*

'A slice-of-jet-set-life nightmare far beyond the dreams of the piggiest male chauvinist . . . the distinction of this film is that its characters are repulsive, its style vulgar, its situations beyond belief and its dialogue moronic.'—*Judith Crist*

Zelig**

US 1983   79m (including about 5m of credits)   bw

Orion / Rollins-Joffe (Robert Greenhut)

A parody documentary tracing a chameleon-like nonentity who contrives to have been associated with all the major events of the twentieth century.

The central idea is more elusive than appealing, and the mid-section of psychiatric consultation is downright dull, but considerable amusement derives from the technical trickery which puts Woody Allen in pictorial association with Hitler, Roosevelt and Eugene O'Neill. In all, an after-dinner treat for the intellectuals.

w,d Woody Allen *ph* Gordon Willis *m* Dick Hyman *pd* Mel Bourne

Woody Allen, Mia Farrow

'We can all admire the brilliance and economy with which it is made. But is it funny enough? I take leave to doubt it.'—*Derek Malcolm, Guardian*

AAN: cinematography; costume design

Zenobia

US 1939   83m   bw

Hal Roach

GB title: *Elephants Never Forget*

A small-town doctor finds himself looking after a performing elephant.

Very mild small-town comedy made during a break-up in the Laurel and Hardy contract.

w Corey Ford, Arnold Belgard, Walter De Leon *d* Gordon Douglas *ph* Karl Struss *m* Marvin Hatley

Oliver Hardy, Harry Langdon, Jean Parker

Zeppelin*

GB 1971   97m   Technicolor   Panavision

Warner / Getty and Fromkess (Owen Crump)

In 1915, the British need to steal secrets from the zeppelin works at Friedrichshafen. Undistinguished but entertaining period actioner with adequate spectacle but wooden performances.

w Arthur Rowe, Donald Churchill *d* Etienne Périer *ph* Alan Hume *m* Roy Budd *sp* Wally Veevers

Michael York, Elke Sommer, Peter Carsten, Marius Goring, Anton Diffring, Andrew Keir, Rupert Davies

Zéro de Conduite**

France 1933   45m approx   bw

Gaumont / Franco Film / Aubert

Boys return from the holiday to a nasty little boarding school, where the headmaster is an unpleasant dwarf and all the staff are hateful. A revolution breaks out . . .

A clear forerunner of *If* . . . and one of the most famous of surrealist films, though it pales beside Bunuel and is chiefly valuable for being funny.

w Jean Vigo *ph* Boris Kaufman *m* Maurice Jaubert

Jean Dasté, Louis Lefébvre, Gilbert Pruchon, le nain Delphin

'One of the most influential films ever made.'—*New Yorker, 1978*

Zero Hour!

US 1957   83m   bw

(Paramount) Bartlett / Champion (John Champion)

Half the passengers and all the crew of a jet plane are stricken with food poisoning and a shell-shocked ex-fighter pilot has to land the plane.

Adequate air melodrama with a premise which later served for *Terror in the Sky* (TV) and *Airport 75*.

w Arthur Hailey, John Champion, Hall Bartlett, *teleplay* Flight into Danger by Arthur Hailey *d* Hall Bartlett *ph* John F. Warren *m* Ted Dale

Dana Andrews, Linda Darnell, Sterling Hayden, Elroy Hirsch, Jerry Paris

Zero Population Growth

US 1971   96m   Eastmancolor

Sagittarius (Thomas F. Madigan)

In the 21st century there is a death penalty for having children, but a young couple defy the authorities.

Good sci-fi quickly develops into sticky sentimentality.

w Max Ehrlich, Frank de Felita *d* Michael Campus *ph* Michael Reed *m* Jonathan Hodge *pd* Tony Masters

Oliver Reed, Geraldine Chaplin, Diane Cilento, Don Gordon, Bill Nagy, Aubrey Woods

Ziegfeld Follies**

US 1944 (released 1946)   110m   Technicolor

MGM (Arthur Freed)

In heaven, Florenz Ziegfeld dreams up one last spectacular revue.

A rather airless all-star entertainment in which the comedy suffers from the lack of an audience but some of the production numbers are magnificently stylish.

w various *d* Vincente Minnelli *ph* George Folsey, Charles Rosher *m* various *ad* Cedric Gibbons, Merrill Pye, Jack Martin Smith

Fred Astaire, Lucille Ball, Bunin's Puppets, William Powell, Jimmy Durante, Edward Arnold, *Fannie Brice*, Lena Horne, Lucille Bremer, Esther Williams, Judy Garland, *Red Skelton*, *Gene Kelly*, James Melton, Hume Cronyn, Victor Moore, Marion Bell

'Between opening and closing is packed a prodigious amount of material, some of which is frankly not deserving of the lavish treatment accorded it.'—*Film Daily*

'The fastidious are advised to head for the lobby while Kathryn Grayson sings 'There's Beauty Everywhere' against magenta foam skies.'—*Pauline Kael, 70s*

Ziegfeld Girl*

US 1941   131m   bw

MGM (Pandro S. Berman)

The professional and romantic problems of Ziegfeld chorus girls.

Adequate big-budget drama with music.

w Marguerite Roberts, Sonya Levien *d* Robert Z. Leonard *ph* Ray June *m* Herbert Stothart *ch* Busby Berkeley *songs* various

James Stewart, Judy Garland, Hedy Lamarr, Lana Turner, Tony Martin, Jackie Cooper, Ian Hunter, *Charles Winninger*, Al Shean, Edward Everett Horton, Philip Dorn, Paul Kelly, Eve Arden, Dan Dailey, Fay Holden, Felix Bressart

'Heaping portions of show life in the opulent days of Flo Ziegfeld, the man who wanted bigger and better staircases.'—*C. A. Lejeune*

Zigzag*

US 1970   104m   Metrocolor   Panavision

MGM / Freeman–Enders

GB title: *False Witness*

A dying man frames himself for an unsolved murder so that the reward money, claimed under another name, will go to his wife. Complex thriller which sustains itself pretty well most of the way, but lacks humour and character.

w John T. Kelley *d* Richard A. Colla *ph* James A. Crabe *m* Oliver Nelson

George Kennedy, Anne Jackson, Eli Wallach, Steve Ihnat, William Marshall, Joe Maross

The Zombies of Mora Tau

US 1957   71m   bw

A diver plans to salvage a subterranean West African treasure; but it is guarded by zombies. Modest addition to the walking dead cycle. Gregg Palmer, Allison Hayes, Autumn Russell, Morris Ankrum. Written by Raymond T. Marcus; directed by Edward Cahn; for Sam Katzman / Columbia. (GB title: *The Dead That Walk*.)

Zoo in Budapest*

US 1933   83m   bw

Fox (Jesse Lasky)

An orphan waif runs away to live with a zookeeper.

Curious little romance remembered for its luminescent photography.

w Dan Totheroh, Louise Long, Rowland V. Lee *d* Rowland V. Lee *ph* Lee Garmes

Loretta Young, Gene Raymond, O. P. Heggie, Wally Albright, Paul Fix

'Appeal for all classes . . . a subject of great photographic and pictorial beauty.'—*Variety*

'Richly composed impressionistic images, assisted by highly imaginative use of sound and background music, create a poem that Murnau himself would have envied.'—*NFT, 1971*

Zorba the Greek°°
GB 1964   142m   bw
TCF / Rockley / Cacoyannis

A young English writer in Crete is befriended by a huge gregarious Greek who comes to dominate his life.
A mainly enjoyable character study of a larger-than-life character, this film made famous by its music does not really hang together dramatically and has several melodramatic excrescences.

wd Michael Cacoyannis, *novel* Nikos Kazantzakis *ph* Walter Lassally *m* Mikis Theodorakis

Anthony Quinn, Alan Bates, Lila Kedrova, Irene Papas
  'For all its immense length, the film never gets down to a clear statement of its theme, or comes within measuring distance of its vast pretensions.'—*Brenda Davies*

AA: Walter Lassally; Lila Kedrova
AAN: best picture; Michael Cacoyannis (as writer and director); Anthony Quinn

'Zany! Zexy! Zensational!'
Zorro the Gay Blade
US 1981   93m   De Luxe
Melvin Simon (George Hamilton, C. O. Erickson)

Zorro, the masked avenger, not only pretends to be a fop but is one. Luckily he has a twin brother.
Abysmal attempt to do for Zorro what *Love at First Bite* did for Dracula.

w Hal Dresner *d* Peter Medak *ph* John A. Alonzo *m* Max Steiner themes

George Hamilton, Lauren Hutton, Brenda Vaccaro, Ron Leibman, James Booth

Zotz!
US 1962   87m   bw
Columbia / William Castle

A professor finds a rare coin with occult powers.
Footling farce patterned after *The Absent-Minded Professor*. Poor, to say the least.

w Ray Russell, *novel* Walter Karig *d* William Castle *ph* Gordon Avil *m* Bernard Green

Tom Poston, Fred Clark, Jim Backus, Cecil Kellaway, Margaret Dumont

Zulu°
GB 1964   135m   Technirama
Paramount / Diamond (Stanley Baker, Cyril Endfield)

In 1879 British soldiers stand fast against the Zulus at Rorke's Drift.

Standard period heroics, well presented and acted.

w John Prebble, Cy Endfield *d* Cy Endfield *ph* Stephen Dade *m* John Barry

Stanley Baker, Jack Hawkins, *Michael Caine*, Ulla Jacobsson, James Booth, Nigel Green, Ivor Emmanuel, Paul Daneman

Zulu Dawn
US / Netherlands 1979   117m   Technicolor   Panavision
Samarkand / Zulu Dawn NV (Barrie Saint Clair)

In 1878, 1,300 British troops are massacred at Ulundi.
Confusing historical action adventure, very similar to *Zulu* but failing in its cross-cut attempt to show both sides.

w Cy Enfield, Anthony Storey *d* Douglas Hickox *ph* Ousama Rawi *m* Elmer Bernstein *pd* John Rosewarne

Burt Lancaster, Denholm Elliott, Peter O'Toole, John Mills, Simon Ward, Nigel Davenport, Michael Jayston, Ronald Lacey, Freddie Jones, Christopher Cazenove, Ronald Pickup, Anna Calder-Marshall

● *Video: Intervision*

TOP TENS

Everybody plays the game of selecting his or her ten favourite films, but the results can be interesting only when a historical perspective is attempted. The British Film Institute has now organized four polls of international critics, in 1952, 1962, 1972 and 1982, and the findings are given below, together with the number of votes cast for each film. It does seem that even critics are unable to make absolute judgements, and that some of the earlier selections at least were merely fashionable.

1952
Bicycle Thieves 25
City Lights 19
The Gold Rush 19
The Battleship Potemkin 16
Louisiana Story 12
Intolerance 12
Greed 11
Le Jour Se Lève 11
The Passion of Joan of Arc 11
Brief Encounter 10
Le Million 10
La Règle du Jeu 10

1962
Citizen Kane 22
L'Avventura 20
La Règle du jeu 19
Greed 17
Ugetsu Monogatari 17
The Battleship Potemkin 16
Bicycle Thieves 16
Ivan the Terrible 16
La Terra Trema 14
L'Atalante 13

1972
Citizen Kane 32
La Règle du Jeu 28
The Battleship Potemkin 16
Eight and a Half 15
L'Avventura 15
Persona 12
The Passion of Joan of Arc 11
The General 10
The Magnificent Ambersons 10
Ugetsu Monogatari 9
Wild Strawberries 9

1982
Citizen Kane 45
La Règle du Jeu 31
Seven Samurai 15
Singin' in the Rain 15
Eight and a Half 14
The Battleship Potemkin 13
L'Avventura 12
The Magnificent Ambersons 12
Vertigo 12
The General 11
The Searchers 11

Thus the only films to appear in all four lists are *The Battleship Potemkin* and *La Règle du Jeu*; and some titles, such as *Louisiana Story*, *La Terra Trema* and *Vertigo* (unseen for many years) are momentary aberrations.

I suppose it is only fair for the compiler to produce his own list. Out of many hundreds of favourites, I suppose the following have come to be the films I can watch and rewatch very frequently with most pleasure and renewed application:

Citizen Kane
Trouble in Paradise
The Bride of Frankenstein
Le Million
A Matter of Life and Death
Lost Horizon (1937)
Sons of the Desert
The Philadelphia Story
The Maltese Falcon
The Lady Vanishes

The trouble is that even looking at the list makes me feel guilty about the ones I have had to leave out: *The 39 Steps* (1935), *Oh Mr Porter*, *Gaslight* (1940), *Singin' in the Rain, To Be or Not to Be* (1942), *Dr Jekyll and Mr Hyde* (1931), *Orphée, Les Enfants du Paradis, The Old Dark House, Way Out West, All That Money Can Buy, Casablanca, The General, Miracle in Milan, The Magnificent Ambersons . . .*

A WORD ON SHAPE

It is a matter of some perplexity to me that film-makers, who presumably care about their art, persist in packaging it in a shape which will be available at the time of cinema release to only a small fraction of the film's primary audience, and probably to nobody at all in the future. Whether mass audiences from now on see a film on video, cable, satellite or free television, they will watch it through a set which can present it in an aspect ratio of 4 units across to 3 units down, or 1.33 to 1, which was the standard ratio in cinemas until 1952 and subsequently became known as the 'academy' shape. It is still the shape of the individual frame on the celluloid. The process of televising actually trims a bit off the edge all round, as can be seen from occasional missing letters on titles, but let's not quibble about that.

The purpose of CinemaScope, announced with a flourish of trumpets in 1953, was to show that the movies were bigger than television. This purpose it accomplished, more or less, by producing a picture shape of 2.35 to 1, or more than seven units across to three units down; and all it needed was a new screen and a new lens in the projector (unlike the nine-days wonder of 3-D which involved the installation of expensive equipment). The 35mm film strip and its 4 × 3 image shape were retained, but the action was photographed through a prismatic or anamorphic lens which squeezed up the image on the film so that all the people looked tall and narrow; a corresponding lens in the projector then opened up the image sideways to its new screen shape.

During the fight for CinemaScope licences, which were granted sparingly at first by the copyright holder, in the hope of putting up their value and therefore their price, rivals devised a simpler method of achieving 'wide screen' which was quickly adapted by all producers and exhibitors because it required no licence, cost even less than CinemaScope, and looked different from television. No prismatic lenses were involved: the top and bottom strips of the old 4 × 3 shape were simply not used, and the middle strip was put through a magnifying lens in the cinema, giving a screen shape which varied between 1.66 to 1 and 1.85 to 1. (VistaVision added to this a deep-focus process, claiming that the central strip of film could even be projected at 2 to 1: the drawback was that all the action had to be gathered into this strip, so that VistaVision films, when projected on television, look very distant and lacking in close-ups.) Sometimes the picture area not required was left in the frame (which makes such films easily transmittable on TV); more often than not it was masked, which causes black bands at top and bottom of the TV screen.

Alas, any films made before 1952, including all one's carefully-composed favourites, when put through the new aperture plates, also had their tops and bottoms cut off, thus robbing audiences of actors' heads and dancers' feet in a quite alarming way; but there was nothing to be done because cinema managers (a) didn't care about ruining the composition of old films, and (b) couldn't afford to have screen masking which moved up and down as well as sideways (to accommodate CinemaScope).

A confused period followed. The simple 'wide screen' was referred to mainly as such, but sometimes as Metroscope or some other trade name aimed to confuse. CinemaScope was, according to studio, varied as Megascope, Warnerscope, Camerascope, Tohoscope, Superscope, Hammerscope, Techniscope and Franscope. There followed also some super wide screen systems such as Todd AO, Camera 65, Cinerama 70, which were shot on 70mm for extra clarity when projected on giant screens, then reduced to 35mm

(Continued on p. 1115)

A What you see on television

◯ Portion of frame as scanned on TV

▓ Area projected on cinema 'wide screen' (standard from 1953). This can vary, according to screen shape at particular cinemas, between 1.66 to 1 and 1.85 to 1.

☆ These areas may or may not be required for cinema projection but are extra to director's intent. Television likes them to be filled with action, but they are often masked in order to guide cinema projectionists.

'Academy' frame (standard until 1953)

'Academy' frame

CinemaScope image

CinemaScope image

B What you see at the cinema

▓ Cinema 'wide screen' (may vary between 1.66:1 and 1.85:1)

▓ Dotted areas above and below, though part of film frame, are not required for wide-screen projection but are visible on TV.

◄ ► Masking can move sideways to give CinemaScope shape

CinemaScope for general release. All these anamorphic systems (which eventually came down to one, Panavision*) give trouble on television for an obvious reason. Only half the picture can be accommodated at any one time, and the transmission controller, unless the work has been done in the lab, must continually pan and scan in search of the optimum framing for the particular scene. (The alternative, used in most European countries, is to 'strip' the complete CinemaScope image across the centre band of the screen, but this results in a very small, though well defined, picture.) Since most fifties and sixties films were shot in poor colour and dim lighting, the wise television buyer avoids them when he can, for they can never look satisfactory on the small screen. How would you like the Mona Lisa if you could see her only from forehead to chin, or with one ear missing? The ultimate buffoonery came when MGM made a so-called CinemaScope version of *Gone with the Wind* by taking the middle strip of each 1.33 to 1 frame and blowing it up to giant screen proportions. The ugly out-of-focus mess which resulted can be imagined: yet MGM subsequently proposed to sell this version to television companies, who would have had to pan and scan it, thus achieving at any one time the transmission of no more than one third of the original image!

More and more producers have come to rely on a high-priced television sale as part of the process of paying off overheads. Yet never is television able to transmit a post-1953 film in the version originally intended. Cable and satellite channels may transmit the sex, violence and bad language which are prohibited from 'free' television, but they can never overcome the shape problem. With so few real cinemas capable of projecting in the original ratio such monster films as *Star Wars* and *Superman* and *Raiders of the Lost Ark*, don't the likes of Spielberg and Lucas care that their work will be seen as they intended it by only a tiny fraction of its eventual audience? What's wrong with four by three anyway? It did no harm to *Gone with the Wind* or *Citizen Kane* or *The Grapes of Wrath* or *Les Enfants du Paradis*. (Imagine if you can, a CinemaScope version of Laurel and Hardy or Buster Keaton or Lubitsch's *Trouble in Paradise*.) As Fritz Lang said, CinemaScope is a fine shape if you want to show a snake or a funeral. Or, one might generously add, somebody lying down or a row of Indians silhouetted on a hilltop. But for shots of people talking in groups of up to three it never has made sense. And if you work it out, groups of up to three are what motion pictures are all about.

---

* Watch out, by the way, for the confusing credit Photographed with Panavision Equipment. This is not the same as Photographed in Panavision and involves no anamorphic process.

The Decline and Fall of the Movie

It is only fair that the author of a book which categorizes fifty years of films should give some account of his own prejudices. I have spent more than forty years seeing, talking about and writing about films, so my affection for the medium in its 'golden age' can hardly be doubted. Even then, however, the worthwhile movies were the tip of the iceberg: probably eighty per cent of what was produced was ghastly rubbish, which is why this book deals with ten thousand movies, not all of them good, out of a total output of four times that number. The best kind of film buff loves the movie business for what it can be at its best, not for its journeyman 'B' features, its crackpot experiments, its cheapjack exploitation screamies or those relentlessly boring bottom-of-the-bill fillers.

Jonathan Swift said in 1725: 'I hate and detest that animal called man, although I heartily love John, Peter, Thomas and so forth.' This book encapsulates my Johns, my Peters and my Thomases; this essay complains bitterly that they have lately been so few in number, and attempts, admittedly by some slight use of exaggeration, to throw light on a confused and unhappy segment of cinema history.

When Sam Peckinpah made *Straw Dogs* from a novel called *The Siege of Trencher's Farm* he thought it unnecessary to explain to his audience the significance of his new title which, his publicists informed us on request, was taken from an old Chinese proverb. And when Stanley Kubrick made *A Clockwork Orange* he did not bother to retain the section of the Anthony Burgess novel which explained why it was so called. These almost identical incidents exemplify the kind of arrogance which besets film-makers in the seventies. Steeped in the history of Hollywood's golden age, they have no idea what made it work so well, and as soon as they become successful they begin to despise their audiences and are concerned only to over-spend enormous budgets while putting across some garbled self-satisfying message which is usually anti-establishment, anti-law-and-order and anti-entertainment.

In this they are assisted by such long-haired publications as *Sight and Sound* and a variety of earnest critics who bend over backwards to see 'significance' where none exists and to ascribe all the film's virtues and faults to the director, or in the current jargon the *auteur*. (Would any theatrical critic dream of judging a play solely on the director's contribution, or a literary critic of reviewing a book solely on the basis of its layout on the printed page?) If cinema, which is the creation of so many people, can be an art at all, it must be a folk art which appeals to innocent and sophisticate alike, and can be easily appreciated by both. This happy state of affairs was reached thirty-five years ago by unpretentious and slick productions of the studio system such as *The Maltese Falcon* and *Stagecoach*, which used every camera trick in the book without blinding the audience to the characters and the plot. Nowadays one has to fight one's way through the thick showy surface in order to get to a story which all too often is not worth following.

One problem is that modern films are largely made by people with no sense of humour, people who do not realize that they must please the mass audience if the industry in which they work is to survive. Old-time screenwriters such as Ben Hecht, Dudley Nichols and Lamar Trotti would no doubt be viewed by these young men as cynical hacks, but at least they took pains to please their audience with all the expertise at their command, and they still expressed their own views in a vein of sardonic humour which ran through most of the scripts of the thirties and forties and was there to please and satisfy the minority of film-goers who sought it out.

The absurd pretensions of some modern film-makers certainly cause amusement wherever sensible people congregate, but the advocates of sanity are in no position to have the last word. The present set-up of the film industry encourages wilder and wickeder sensations, from homicidal sharks to diabolical babies, as these are the only subjects which lure large audiences. The successes, however, are all one-offs: no one is much interested in sequels, preferring to wait for horrors of some other variety. The result is that only one film in twenty or thirty makes a profit, but the custodians of the cash have no option but to go on investing in the hope that the occasional fluke will make a fortune, which will then be quickly dissipated by a string of failures. Universal's phenomenally successful *Jaws*, for instance, was immediately followed by such commercial duds as *Gable and Lombard*, *W. C. Fields and Me*, *The Great Waldo Pepper* and *The Hindenberg*, and the studio is still looking for another hit. The sad fact is that no policy can be devised because the people in charge of the money have no idea what is likely to appeal, and they are forced to put their faith in reputedly brilliant directors who have no idea either but are quite prepared to spend large sums of other people's money in flying their own flimsy kites. The flimsiness is sometimes astonishing. The director of an abysmal 1976 comedy called *Harry and Walter go to New York* announced to the press, as a selling point, that it was 'Laurel and Hardy with real people.' Had he inquired of his mass audience, he would surely have been told that Stan and Ollie had more reality in their little fingers than was to be found in the entire crew of *Harry and Walter go to New York*, whether before or behind the camera.

One should of course add that many films these days are not supposed to make money. The adage which used to run 'you're only as good as your last picture' has been changed to 'you're only as big as your last budget', and it is no trick to get a big budget when many films are conceived by industrialists as tax losses: all you have to do is get in the news by holding outlandish views or even making pornography, and Hollywood these days opens its doors to you because at least you must have learnt how to point a camera or arrest public attention. The ones to suffer are the audiences, who have foisted upon them material which they have every right to expect to be professional, and which all too often is not, just the result of untalented exhibitionists spending someone else's money in whatever way happens to divert them most. Even if there is a profit, their habit is to take the money and run, not to invest it in better production facilities as used to happen in the good old days.

Work is thus produced for a small group of jet-setters; meanwhile that patient paying audience discovers that not only the films but the standards of physical cinema comfort are far worse than they were thirty years ago; since then the cost of admission has risen at a phenomenal rate, the average cost in Britain now being twenty times more than in 1956. What other commodity has risen in price to this extent? Television is infinitely cheaper and can be viewed in the comfort of one's own home: no wonder so many people prefer it.

So the movie industry hastens on its way to perdition and catastrophe, a fate which surely cannot be delayed more than another few years, and for which simple-minded greed, lack of foresight and a large measure of incompetence are chiefly responsible. Those of us who are old enough and who still care about the movies sigh frequently for the halcyon days when Harry Cohn and

Louis B. Mayer sat in their front offices, for their intellectual limitations were far less harmful and sometimes far more stimulating to the medium than the excesses of the present incumbents, who seldom stay long enough to make their presences felt and certainly not long enough for any sense of continuity to develop. There is for instance no continuity of employment, which makes the unions tougher and tougher to deal with in an industry which was always volatile in its labour relations: every film is a fresh project for which cast and crew have to be accumulated, and the way things are there is no bank of trained talent to fall back on. As Billy Wilder said, you spend eighty per cent of your time making deals and twenty per cent making pictures. The old moguls had enough common sense and business acumen to keep the system working so that costs were comparatively low and one could afford the occasional interesting failure to please the intellectuals.

How did the movie world go so wrong? You can trace it to the restlessness after World War II, when the regular audience declined and television was a coming threat and the bosses knew that new trends had to be found but no one knew what they might be in a glum and depressed world. When actors began to want a say in production and seemed willing to risk their own money, the bosses were delighted to share the possible losses; instead they found themselves being eased out and their profits halved, their studios no longer vast employment centres with a constant production line but simply enclosed space and facilities which could be rented out to the highest bidder.

The old moguls were getting older and couldn't fight the developing situation, the new young ones were businessmen who often backed the wrong horse because they didn't understand the industry. Meanwhile the old showmen had one last irrelevant fling. If television was the enemy, they reasoned, then give the paying public what television cannot provide. Technology now allowed films to be shot on real locations, which was splendid but had two handicaps. First, the units were away from central control for a long time, and the costs were phenomenal; second, the magic was lost, for the real Paris was by no means so romantic or mysterious as Paramount's backlot which had served as Paris for so many years, nor could the lighting of it be so carefully controlled. The new realistic films were slower, because the travel costs had to be justified and travelogue largely took the place of drama. (Did anyone complain about the lack of shots of San Francisco in *The Maltese Falcon*?)

The other way to combat television was to change the shape and effect of the entertainment screen. 3-D was tried, but audiences hated wearing polaroid glasses in order to get a three-dimensional image which producers largely utilized by hurling knives, tennis balls, spiders and even grubby redskins into the audience's lap: this was fairground stuff. Cinemascope was then seized upon by Hollywood: twice as wide as the ordinary image and capable of the most spectacular effects. There is no record that the paying audience ever especially liked Cinemascope, or could even remember whether or not a film was in the process, but once the expensive equipment was installed in theatres there was no turning back. Unfortunately the technique involved a reversion in many cinematic effects to the days of D. W. Griffith. The compression of the wide image on to the film and its subsequent expansion in the projector made the photography grainy, especially in black and white, which was henceforth virtually abandoned. (At about the same time a transference to safety stock lost us the glamorous luminescent 'Feel' which had been possible with nitrate and which can still be seen in old prints.) The new shape was impossible to compose for; as Fritz Lang said, it was fine for funerals, but what painter through the ages had ever selected it unless to cut up into a triptych? Editing was cut to a minimum because on an image so large each cut made the audience jump. Instead, and cheaper, the camera stayed still while the cast roved around the empty spaces in front of it, and there was an absurd number of shots in which the leading actors reclined so as better to fit the frame. Close-ups and subtle nuances were forgotten: no longer did the camera direct you to the drama, you had to look around and find it yourself. It is rather astonishing that directors with an eye to their reputations still persist in using the scope format, for after initial release the future of any film these days is on television, and no scope film, will satisfactorily adapt to the TV screen.

In many cinemas Cinemascope was even a fraud, for it had to be on a screen smaller in area than the old image, which was now being referred to sneeringly as 'postage stamp'. This happened when the old screen had already occupied all the width allowed by the cinema's structure: to get the CinemaScope shape, if you could not go any wider, height had to be sacrificed, and audiences wondered why suddenly they were looking at a ribbon of picture across the middle of the space which the fine old screen had occupied.

Cinemascope was patented by Fox, so the other companies all hastened to produce their own variations: Warnerscope, Metroscope, Techniscope, Superscope, Megascope, Camerascope, Panavision, each with its own cheap colour process. Projectionists all over the world were confused by these new names, and seldom knew whether they were projecting a film as they were supposed to. The results were often truly appalling, with lack of focus, too much brightness and wrong screen masking among the most common faults. Paramount's Vistavision, a non-anamorphic process, used the full frame ratio but was intended for projection at anything between 1.33:1 and 2:1, so that the essential action had to take place in a strip along the centre of the picture; consequently, to see a Vistavision print on a 1.33:1 screen was painful indeed, as all the action seemed to take place in the middle distance with great areas of unused space at the top and bottom of the image, and composition, which any painter knows to be all-important, was no longer possible. By the mid-fifties, however, 1.33:1 was no longer generally available, as 'wide screen' had become *de rigueur* even for non-anamorphic films: these cut off the top and bottom of the frame and magnified the rest. This meant that revivals were impossible unless one was prepared to suffer dancers without feet and actors without heads!

The result of all this technical uncertainty was that by the mid-fifties movies were in danger of becoming mere expensive sideshows, uninteresting to anyone of sensitivity. At the same time, an element of sophistication crept away from the popular arts: whereas in the thirties and forties smooth and educated idols had been set up for general approbation, the fifties and sixties showed an alarming tendency not merely to make heroes of 'people like us' but to rub our noses firmly in the gutter by devising stories whose leading characters had few redeeming features. Censorship had been absurdly tight and must obviously relax, but it was unwise and unexpected that the floodgates should open as they did, to admit movies which would previously have been considered anti-social rubbish. It was right, for instance, for Otto Preminger to fight the idiocies of the Production Code with his *The Moon Is Blue* and *The Man with the Golden Arm*, but it was a pity he won his battle with a leaden piece of schoolboy smut and an absurdly melodramatic updating of The Road to Ruin. Such films simply made one yearn to go back to the days of *Trouble in Paradise* and *The*

Palm Beach Story, or for the true social concern expressed in the considered, powerful and moving masterpieces of Frank Capra, John Ford, or the early Chaplin.

The talents which had made Hollywood great were certainly nearing retirement by now, but it was perhaps unwise as well as churlish for the new wave to pension them off quite as hurriedly as they did, because there was no comparable talent to take their place. Great art directors like Anton Grot and Hans Dreier, great cameramen like Arthur Miller and James Wong Howe, great directors like Michael Curtiz and William Dieterle were either tossed aside or forced to work on material totally unsuited to their talents and not at all comparable to the films which had made their names. The results were big-budget disasters such as *The Egyptian* and *Omar Khayyam*; meanwhile the young directors were copying low-budget television techniques which for every *Marty* produced a dozen flatly realistic bores.

By the early sixties Hollywood had decided on a new image, but it had lost its old loyalties – the golden age audiences as well as the talents were getting older – and had to appeal deliberately to the 'emancipated' young generation. This meant a virtual abolition of censorship, and from the release of *Who's Afraid of Virginia Woolf?* in 1966 to that of *The Texas Chainsaw Massacre* and *The Devil in Miss Jones* ten years later is but a short step. The film is no longer an art, or even a craft: after a brief 'swinging' period it became an exploitation industry designed to take quick money from suckers, led by maverick Ken Russells rather than conscientious Irving Thalbergs, to plaudits from irresponsible critics whenever some totally untalented new director 'does his thing'. There is no justification except box office for films like *The Exorcist* or *Mandingo*, none except self-indulgence for a $12 million coffee-table film like *Barry Lyndon*, while the popularity even in sophisticated circles of shoddy pornography like *Deep Throat* and *Death Weekend* should stand as an awful warning to the leaders of our society that a vivid young art form has overreached itself and is well and truly on the verge of disaster. It is all very well to say in defence of such films that large numbers of people flock to see them: so they did once to bear-baiting and public executions and witch hunts, but the human race long ago prided itself on having passed that stage.

The movies will be lucky if, in their search for sensationalism, they do not check themselves out altogether. Audiences have dwindled rapidly and are still dwindling; so is the number of cinemas. The lush old two-thousand seaters have turned into supermarkets, and instead each city has its ineptly-run boxes of mini-cinemas, the effect of which is rather like sitting in cheaply decorated funeral parlours and paying through the nose for the privilege. The family outing to the cinema is a thing of the past: few families can afford it or can find a suitable film, except once or twice a year when the Disney organization stirs itself; and *their* standards are by no means as high as they were, as a comparison of *Robin Hood* with *Bambi* or *Pinocchio* will immediately show. (The fact that such an uninventive computerized cartoon as *Robin Hood* can do well at the box office is an instance of how starved the public is for the older, gentler forms of entertainment.)

Another problem besetting the cinema in the sixties was its adoption by verbose and pompous critics who were determined to turn it into serious art. True art is the work of one man, or at least his personal vision: each film is the work of several hundred people. Of these, admittedly the director has the most control, but to assign to him the role of *auteur* and to ignore the contribution of producer, writer, photographer, composer and editor is arrant nonsense, except possibly in the cases of such as Hitchcock and Kubrick who do control almost every aspect of their output. The new cinema journalism simply encouraged the worst motives of the new breed of film-maker, who came to know that whatever idiocy he perpetrated would be staunchly defended, researched and psychoanalysed by one of these mercenaries in search of a cause. If a character spat on the pavement this would be taken as his final shedding of his working-class upbringing; if he went to bed with a girl it would symbolize his treachery to his own beliefs and his giving in to the snares of Mammon. Listen to a modern critic in the British Film Institute's *Monthly Film Bulletin*, once a terse and reliable guide to film trends, on *Alice Doesn't Live Here Any More*: 'What Scorsese has done, however, is to rescue an American cliché from the bland, flat but much more portentous naturalism of such as *Harry and Tonto* and restore it to an emotional and intellectual complexity through his particular brand of baroque realism.' Or on Rafelson's *Stay Hungry*: 'What distinguishes him from other film-makers of the "head" generation is both the poetic sureness of his fragmentary, allusive style, and the elliptical observation which prevents his social themes from being spiked too easily on the cultural antitheses of that bygone era.' Spare us.

Some of the elements missing from modern cinema are to be found in television, certainly in the UK with its brilliant documentaries, sharp comedies, serious art programmes and single plays; Americans are less lucky except on their public broadcasting system. But television is a private enjoyment, and one inevitably misses the sense of comradeship, of sharing a pleasure, that the cinema used to fulfil. Who having experienced them can forget the feeling of a full house being pleasurably chilled by *The Cat and the Canary*, or rolling in the aisles at Laurel and Hardy, or hoping against hope that Colman will find his *Lost Horizon*? What modern films can produce the sheer entertainment value and unforgettable, vivid scenes of such as *The Philadelphia Story*, *Stagecoach*, *Rebecca*, *Camille*, *Casablanca*, *Citizen Kane*, *Singin' in the Rain*, *A Night at the Opera*, *The Lady Vanishes*, and *The Third Man*? These were all intelligent films, all made for the despised mass audience, and they all made money because they were produced with impeccable professionalism and star talent, and because to these qualities they added heart and good humour. Where is the good humour in *Jaws*? Where is the heart in *The Exorcist*? These are rides on fairground ghost trains: one pays for the thrill, but one comes out more depressed than uplifted.

Of course there are some genuine talents at work in films today. One respects the likes of Jack Nicholson and Ellen Burstyn and Al Pacino and Glenda Jackson, but they are all depressingly committed to their own self-expression and to the depiction of mankind with warts and all, not to pleasing, stimulating or improving the public. They need control; but where are the likes of Lubitsch to control them? Of Sturges? Of Ben Hecht? Of James Whale? Of Donald Ogden Stewart? Of S. J. Perelman? Of Robert Benchley and Dorothy Parker? The films produced by Altman and Scorsese and Ashby are doubtless stimulating in their violent, abrasive way but they are not the whole of life. David Lean and John Schlesinger and Arthur Penn are meticulous craftsmen, but they are driven by commerce into the excesses of *Ryan's Daughter* and *Marathon Man* and *The Missouri Breaks*. In the acting league, where are our up-and-coming replacements for David Niven, Cary Grant, Melvyn Douglas, Katharine Hepburn, Ronald Colman? When again will it be the turn of grace and elegance? When indeed will actors want to work? Marlon Brando, Elizabeth Taylor and their like prefer to demand an impossibly high fee, and if they do not get it to sit comfortably at home on the proceeds of their previous hits.

Hollywood at its best – and for Hollywood also read Ealing and Tobis Klangfilm and Svenske Filmindustri – was the purveyor of an expensive and elegant craft which at times touched art, though seldom throughout a whole film. Reality was seldom sought, but why should it be? Real life is not dramatic anyway: even *Taxi Driver* is a heightening, a selection, an emphasis. So are all the great realist films from *The Battleship Potemkin* to *The Grapes of Wrath*. And so are the great works of Beethoven, of Rembrandt, of Michelangelo. Film stands to life as poetry to prose, and its comments were at their most apt and stylish when movies were confined to the sound stage and the backlot. Freedom from that confinement has not made them any better: it has only made them diffuse and patchy and overlong, and colour has made things worse because it apes reality whereas black and white conjured up its own mood and its own comment. Today's screens are too large for the eye to take in. Sound tracks are so 'realistic' as to be incoherent. Big budgets are wasted on movies which would have been ten times as effective if a little imagination had been used or required. Kaleidoscopic effects dazzle the eye and befuddle the brain; immensely long precredits sequences make one think the film is nearly over before it actually starts; characterization flies out the window because sex and violence must be fitted in somehow. Plot doesn't matter; since swinging London was invented every film has become a 'happening': which is another way of saying that anything goes and lack of professionalism cannot be criticized.

All right, this essay is a deliberate hatchet job by a disappointed fan who has turned devil's advocate. Some of the new films clearly have virtues which the old ones didn't possess: one is grateful for *The Graduate* and *Charlie Bubbles* and *Cabaret* and *One Flew over the Cuckoo's Nest*, which for various reasons could never have been made in the old Hollywood. But if my thesis were not largely true, how would one explain the enormous popularity of old movies on television, or the recent deluge of books about them? Why, out of more than sixty films on British television over the Christmas of 1976, were *White Heat* (1948), *A Night at the Opera* (1935) and *Yankee Doodle Dandy* (1942) the most discussed and appreciated? Nostalgia is only a trendy word to describe something which people have at last learned to appreciate because it has been taken away from them. No one in his right mind would be nostalgic for PRC second features or for much of the pure assembly line product which inevitably poured out of the studios when they were working at full pitch. And one must progress. But surely not to the wasteful ineptitude which confronts us at the cinema these days. Not to *Lucky Lady*, *Mother Jugs and Speed*, *At Long Last Love* or *Harry and Walter go to New York*. Must modern audiences really put up with inane or violent rubbish and appear to enjoy it simply because they are supposed not to know any better? We may not be able to get the golden age back, but we can cry for it. If 'they' fail to respond we can at least appreciate the best of it, and learn from that best. This book, I hope, may help a few people to do that.

Postscript

The preceding essay was written seven years ago, but it seems to have dated in very few respects save that the prophesied decline has been a longer and more complex business than any of us imagined, the advent of such new outlets as cable and video having put back the evil day. Certainly the old pleasures of a family visit to the cinema are experienced now by almost nobody, partly because admission prices continue to skyrocket and partly because the films themselves are totally unsuitable. Thirty years ago, more than half the films on release had 'U' certificates, with a mere handful of titles labelled 'Adults Only'. Now the boot is on the other foot: the vast majority of movies are for people aged fifteen and over, and when very occasionally a 'U' film happens along, it does no business because the potential audience thinks it must be bland beyond belief.

During the same period the number of British cinemas has dwindled to a twentieth of what it was, and few indeed of those remaining make a healthy profit. This decline is more marked in Britain than anywhere else in the world, but it is scarcely surprising in a period when the cost of a reasonable seat has risen from 10 or 15p to a suburban average of £2.70 and a West End top of £4.70; this to sit in boxlike tripled or quadrupled cinemas which are uncomfortable and badly run, often with poor sound and picture quality, while the audience endures tedious advertisements and extended intervals in place of the brisk supporting programmes which some of us still remember. In some other parts of the world, probably those with more isolated communities and a less varied and attractive television service, it appears that there is still a sufficiently considerable cinema audience, though it stays more or less within the age range of 16 to 24, which producers interpret as meaning that films have to be filled with sex, violence and gutter language. This is by no means to libel all persons between 16 and 24 years old, but it does seem that those who would prefer something less excessive are prepared to patronize the cinema only in its less commercially viable art forms.

Producers with little sense of history have proved more than willing to go on spending other people's money in increasingly large amounts, and it has become clear that the best this process is likely to throw up is a couple of prestige pictures a year plus half a dozen blockbuster adventures at the level of the old newspaper comic strips. This is perhaps the most astonishing development of all. Adults thirty years ago might possibly have enjoyed *E.T.*, as they enjoyed *The Wizard of Oz*, but can you imagine them willingly sitting through *Star Wars*, *Ghostbusters* or *Gremlins*? I am not denying that when one is in the mood for something very easy these films can provide a modicum of simple enjoyment, but by and large they are hokum entertainments by and for the untrained mind, and I think one should feel just a little ashamed of submitting to them at a time when a once-great art is providing nothing more stimulating.

One way or another, the end of the cinema has been staved off for another indefinite while. British Film Year is unlikely to have much influence one way or the other. Critics and audience will continue to grit their teeth through expensive flops like *Heaven's Gate*, *Give My Regards to Broad Street* and *Dune* for the sake of the occasional product of a superior mind: *Gandhi* or *Chariots of Fire* or *A Passage to India*. How long a glamour industry can go on surviving by the skin of its teeth is obviously unsafe to predict, but in the end it is the exhibitors who will call the tune. Now beset by a greater-than-ever emphasis on home entertainment, with even the newest attractions almost simultaneously available on video, they must surely continue to close their empty halls at an even greater rate than has been recently evident; and without cinemas in which films can be seen there will eventually be no way in which producers can get their money back on big-budget enterprises. That may not be entirely a bad thing, for perhaps before too long we may see a return to wit, charm and expertise in place of the mounting excesses of the last quarter-century.

L.H.
January 1985